BOOKS
IN PRINT®

1995-96

This edition of
BOOKS IN PRINT 1995-96
was prepared by the R.R. Bowker's
Database Publishing Group in
collaboration with the Publication Systems Department

Database Publishing Group
Leigh Yuster-Freeman, Vice President, Production - Bibliographies

Editorial
Beverley Lamar, Senior Managing Editor
Doret Dixon, Senior Editor
Edward Han, Ila Joseph, George Krubski, Assistant Editors
Dorothy Perry-Gilchrist, Coordinator
Kathleen A. Keiderling, Associate Editor, Enhancements

Subject Guide
Judy Salk, Executive Editor
Angela Barrett and Kate Magrath, Senior Associate Editors
Mark D. MacDonald and Joseph V. Tondi, Assistant Editors

Quality Control
Raymond Padilla, Senior Editor
Daniel Dickholtz, Senior Associate Editor

Production
Doreen Gravesande, Production Director
Myriam Nunez, Managing Editor
Barbara Holton and Frank McDermott, Senior Editors
Megan Roxberry and John D. Smith, Senior Associate Editors
Clarice D. Isaacs, Assistant Editor

Electronic Data Transfer Group
Frank Accurso, Senior Managing Editor
Mary Craig Daley, Managing Editor
William Zavorskas, Senior Associate Editor

**Publishers Authority Data
&
International Standard Book Number Agency**
Don Riseborough, Senior Managing Editor
William D. McCahery and Lynn Ann Sahner, Senior Editors
Diana Fumando, Coordinator
Janet Weiss, Assistant Editor

Data Collection & Processing Group
Bonnie Walton, Manager
Cheryl Patrick and Rhonda McKendrick, Coordinators
Leslie Fisher and Cynthia Werry, Assistant Coordinators

Editorial Systems Group
John Roney, Vice President, Information Systems
Gary Aiello, Director, Bibliographical and Advertising Systems
Mark Heinzelman and John Nesselt, Project Leaders

Computer Operations Group
Nick Wikowski, Director, Network/Computer Operations
Max Kobrinsky, Manager
Jack Murphy, Supervisor

Robert H. Doran, Jr., Publisher

BOOKS IN PRINT®

1995-96

VOLUME 5

TITLES ◆ A-D

R.R. BOWKER

A Reed Reference Publishing Company
New Providence, New Jersey

Published by R.R. Bowker
A Reed Reference Publishing Company
121 Chanlon Rd., New Providence, New Jersey 07974

Andrew W. Meyer, Chief Operating Officer
Peter E. Simon, Vice President, Business Development and Database Publishing
Stanley Walker, Senior Vice President, Corporate Marketing
Edward J. Roycroft, Senior Vice President, Sales

R.R. Bowker has used its best efforts in collecting and
preparing material for inclusion in Books in Print 1994-95, but
does not warrant that the information herein is complete or
accurate, and does not assume, and hereby disclaims, any liability to
any persons for any loss or damage caused by errors or omissions in
Books In Print 1995-96, whether such errors or omissions result
from negligence, accident or any other cause.

International Standard Book Numbers: Set 0-8352-3644-7
Vol. 1 0-8352-3645-5, Vol. 2 0-8352-3646-3
Vol. 3 0-8352-3647-1, Vol. 4 0-8352-3648-X
Vol. 5 0-8352-3649-8, Vol. 6 0-8352-3650-1
Vol. 7 0-8352-3651-X, Vol. 8 0-8352-3652-8
OP-OSI 0-8352-3653-6
Vol. 9 0-8352-3654-4
International Standard Serial Number 0068-0214
Library of Congress Catalog Card Number 4-12648

Printed and bound in the United States of America

ISBN 0-8352-3644-7

9 780835 236447

FOREWORD

For forty-seven years, *Books in Print* has served the library and book trade communities as *the* definitive bibliographic resource. This latest edition—fully updated, and featuring over 142,000 new titles—provides unparalleled coverage of the full range of books currently published or distributed in the United States.

Books in Print was first published in 1948. Since then it's grown from a one-volume work that covered 85,000 titles from 357 publishers to today's multivolume authoritative resource encompassing some 1.6 million titles produced by over 46,000 publishing houses. This growth reflects both the dramatic expansion of the publishing industry and Bowker's commitment to making *Books in Print* the most authoritative and comprehensive reference of its kind.

In keeping with this commitment, we continue to expand and improve **BowkerPower,** a state-of-the-art electronic data interchange and processing system, that houses the *Books in Print* database. **BowkerPower** offers improved communication with publishers, new information control and acquisition methods, additional bibliographic elements, customized output, and multiple delivery formats. Bowker's position as the ISBN Agency for the United States and our **BowkerPower** system equals dramatic information flow and control, and an unprecedented level of authority and accuracy for the entire *Books in Print Family of Resources.*

Subject Guide to Books in Print—Provides quick access by subject to all the non-fiction titles covered in *Books in Print*. The 1995-96 *Subject Guide* classifies more than 1,155,640 non-fiction titles under more than 74,500 Library of Congress subject headings.

Books in Print Supplement—This three-volume, mid-year supplement brings you up-to-date on all titles released after publication of *Books in Print*. We anticipate that the 1995-96 edition will feature almost 75,000 new titles, 400,000 revised entries, and 100,000 OP/OSI titles.

Forthcoming Books—A versatile collection development and acquisitions tool that lets you anticipate demand; lists some 170,000 soon-to-be published books with annotations annually.

Keeping *Books in Print* up-to-date is a massive undertaking — there are over 4,500 new publishers included this year alone, plus the 142,124 just-published titles,

and revisions to another 330,000 entries. Gathering and collating all this information is but a part of the job — users need the information in readily accessible, easy-to-use formats.

Besides the hardcopy version of *Books in Print, Subject Guide to Books in Print, Books in Print Supplement,* and *Forthcoming Books,* our database is available on our monthly CD-ROMs (Books in Print Plus, Books in Print with Book Reviews Plus, Ingram — Books in Print Plus, Ingram — Books in Print with Book Reviews Plus, Bowker/Whitaker Global Books in Print, Books in Print Plus — Canadian edition, and Books in Print With Book Reviews Plus — Canadian edition), thru online services Knight Ridder Information Inc. (Dialog), OVID, OCLC, and on library OPAC systems. Our database is also available via tape leasing and is currently used by book wholesalers and distributors, major universities, and document delivery services for purchasing, inventory control, and reference needs.

A SPECIAL NOTE TO OUR BOOKS IN PRINT USERS: Beginning with this year's 1995-96 edition, the out-of-print titles will not be available as a separate volume, but will be available, without charge, on Reed Reference Publishing's *World Wide Web Site.* Discussion with our customers has convinced us that the out-of-print and out-of-stock data will be used more frequently in this electronic form. Please visit our Web Site at *http://www.reedref.com* for op and osi titles going back to 1989, including 152,538 new OP and OSI entries. Out-of-print titles are also available on the *Books Out of Print Plus* CD-ROM and many online services.

Our objective at R.R. Bowker is to find new ways to enable library and book trade professionals to do their job with greater ease and efficiency. We feel the accuracy and convenience *Books in Print 1995-96* offers in its many available formats, demonstrates our commitment to this ideal. We are dedicated to maintaining *Books in Print* as the definitive bibliographic reference.

We sincerely hope you feel this 1995-96 Edition meets your needs, and I welcome your comments and suggestions.

Leigh C. Yuster-Freeman
and Staff

BOWKERPOWER™

R.R. Bowker proudly introduces **BowkerPower**™, a bold new electronic data interchange and processing system that is certain to make a major impact on the book industry.

Developed with the needs of both publishers and subscribers in mind, **BowkerPower** enhances traditional methods of data acquisition, validation, and distribution. Its many features include:

• **The ability to receive and enter the thousands of titles published each year via various electronic formats.**
BowkerPower is on duty 24-hours a day, ready to capture bibliographic data as soon as it is sent via a dedicated line, modem, magnetic tape, cartridge, diskette, or the Internet. With virtually no delay, this data is transferred into the system and made available to our subscribers. The speed, accuracy, and convenience of this system is second to none.

• **The capability to immediately update a publisher's title file**.
With **BowkerPower**, publishers will be able to submit corrections to their title files as soon as these changes occur. Subscribers can now consult *Books in Print* with even greater confidence, knowing that **BowkerPower** assures them of the most up-to-date ordering information at all times.

BowkerPower stands ready to assist you in making current and accurate title information available to our many subscribing bookstores and libraries. For more information, visit our Web site at http:/www.ReedRef.com. Publishers interested in taking full advantage of **BowkerPower** should call our **BowkerPower Hotline** at **908-771-8700**.

DATABASES and PUBLICATIONS
of the
Database Publishing Group

BIP DATABASE

R.R. Bowker is committed to providing the most complete and current bibliographic information to valued subscribers. For this reason, thousands of entries in this directory have been added and updated by electronic data transfer. This is a service which allows participating publishers to submit information from their own current databases on magnetic tape or diskette, for assimilation into the BOOKS IN PRINT database. Such a process assures our publishers that their information is current and accurate. It also allows our subscribers to consult our directory and place their orders with confidence.

Publishers interested in taking advantage of electronic data transfer are invited to call the Electronic Data Transfer Group at 908-771-8700 for further details.

Books in Print was produced from the BIP Database of R.R. Bowker. This database is used to produce a complete, complementary line of bibliographic publications that gives booksellers, librarians, publishers, and all other book, CD-ROM, on-line, and microfiche users access to the latest bibliographic and ordering information. Following is a description of this database and its publications.

The bibliographic database was begun in 1948 primarily as a listing of titles included in Bowker's *Publishers' Trade List Annual (PTLA)*. The computerization of this database during the late nineteen-sixties using the Bibliographic Information Publication System (BIPS) made it possible for Bowker to expand the amount of information included in the bibliographic entries and to increase the number of essential tools of the trade we produced.

During the early nineteen-seventies, the database was greatly expanded to include information from additional publishers whose titles were not included in *PTLA*. Since that time, the database has been composed of and compiled from information received on an on-going basis directly from publishers. To that end, in 1995, **BowkerPower**, a new Electronic Data Interchange system of data acquisition, validation, and delivery was introduced by R.R. Bowker in order to continue this company's commitment to provide subscribers with the most current and complete bibliographic information available. **BowkerPower** allows participating publishers to input data instantly via dedicated phone line, modem, magnetic tape, or PC diskette, for use in the BOOKS IN PRINT database. On a continuing basis, or prior to each publication from the database, publishers are asked to review and correct their entries, providing current price, availability, and ordering information. They are also asked to update their list with recently published and forthcoming titles.

The database includes scholarly, popular, adult, juvenile, reprint, and all other types of books covering all subjects, provided they are published or exclusively distributed in the United States and are available to the trade or to the general public for single or multiple copy purchase. All editions and bindings are included: hardcover, paperbound, library binding, perfect binding, boards, spiral binding, text editions, teachers' editions, and workbooks.

Bibles—including Standard Christian versions, the Bhagavad Gita, Koran, Torah, and other sacred works—are excluded, although commentaries, histories and versions other than the standard English are extensively covered. Free books not included with a title offered for sale; unbound material, pamphlets and booklets; periodicals and serials; puzzles, cartoons, cut-outs and coloring books that are not in a children's text; calendars and appointment books; maps not appearing in a book; microfilms and audiovisual material not accompanying a book; books available only to members of an organization; subscription-only titles; books sold only to schools; and music manuscripts, sheet music, song books and librettos are all ineligible for listing in *Books in Print*. Foreign publications are listed only when bibliographic information is submitted by a United States distributor who has sole rights to distribute such titles in the United States.

Bibliographic entries contain the following information when available: author, co-author, editor, co-editor, translator, co-translator, title, original title, number of volumes, volume number, edition, whether or not reprinted, Library of Congress catalog card number, subject information, series information, language if other than English, whether or not illustrated, page numbers, grade range, date of publication, type of binding if other than cloth over boards, price, ISBN, imprint, publisher, and distributor, if other than the publisher.

In addition to the various publications described below, the full BIP database is available for use through CD-ROM, microfiche and online services. The latter two media also include two years of out-of-print information.

Other databases of the Database Publishing Group include: Textbook Database, Publishers' Authority Database, the American Book Publishing Record Database, Bowker's Serials Bibliography Database, Bowker's Audio/Video Databases, and Bowker's Software Database.

The Database Publishing Group's other publications include: *American Book Publishing Record; American Book Publishing Record Cumulative, 1876-1849; American Book Publishing Record Cumulative, 1950-1977; American Book Publishing Record Cumulative; 1980-1984; Art Books, 1950-1979; Art Books, 1980-1984; Health Science Books, 1876-1982; Law Books, 1876-1981; Words on Cassette; Bowker's Complete Video Directory; Performing Arts Books, 1876-1981; Pure and Applied Science Books, 1876-1982; Ulrich's International Periodicals Directory; Weekly Record;* and the *Software Encyclopedia.*

DESCRIPTION OF PUBLICATIONS

Books in Print®

An annual publication listing all in-print and forth-coming titles from more than 46,000 publishers.
Indexes: *Author/Title/OP-OSI Titles & Authors/Key to Publishers' & Distributors' Abbreviations/Name Index/ Publishers' & Distributors' Toll-Free Number/Wholesalers & Distributors Index/Geographic Index to Wholesalers & Distributors/New Publishers/Inactive & Out of Business Publishers*

Subject Guide to Books in Print®

A companion volume to *Books in Print*, this annual lists all in-print and forthcoming titles except fiction, literature, poetry, and drama by one author, under more than 74,000 Library of Congress (LC) subject headings.
Indexes: *Subject/Key to Publishers' & Distributors' Abbreviations/Subject Thesaurus of Bowker's on-line databases.*

Books in Print® Supplement

An annual publication which updates *Books in Print* by listing all entries which have changes or additions to price, date of publication, ISBN, LC card number, or availability. Expands *Books in Print* by listing backlist titles new to the database and titles published since January or forthcoming through July. Expands *Subject Guide To Books In Print* by listing all new and forthcoming titles under LC subject headings.
Indexes: *Author/Title/Subject/Key to Publishers' & Distributors' Abbreviations*

Forthcoming Books

A bi-monthly publication that lists and subject classifies books which will be published within a five month cycle while also cumulating updated information about books published in the U.S.A. since the previous summer. Asterisks indicate titles new to the database since the last issue. Also included are publisher-paid enhanced entries.
Indexes: *Subject/Author/Title New Publishers & Distributors/Key to Publishers' & Distributors' Abbreviations*

Books in Series

A publication listing in-print *and* out-of-print titles in popular, scholarly, and professional series.
Indexes: *Series Heading/Series/Author/ Title/Subject Index to Series/ Directory of Publishers' & Distributors' Abbreviations*

Paperbound Books in Print®

A semi-annual publication listing all in-print and forthcoming paper trade and paper text editions. Entries are listed under approximately 470 subject headings:
Indexes: *Author/Title/Subject/Key to Publishers' & Distributors' Abbreviations*

Children's Books in Print®

An annual publication listing all books written for children. Grade or reading levels, where available, are indicated.
Indexes: *Author/Title/Illustrator Awards/Key to Publishers' & Distributors' Abbreviations*

Subject Guide To Children's Books In Print®

A companion to *Children's Books In Print* this annual lists fiction and non-fiction titles under appropriate Sears or LC subject headings.
Indexes: *Subject/Key to Publishers' & Distributors' Abbreviations*

Medical And Health Care Books And Serials In Print

An annual subject selection of entries on medicine, psychiatry, dentistry, nursing, and allied areas of the health field *and* a selection of the same subject areas from the Bowker International Serials Database.
Indexes: *Book Section: Subject/Author/Title/ Key to Publishers' & Distributors' Abbreviations Serial Section: Subject/Title*

The Complete Directory Of Large Print Books And Serials

An Annual publication listing all books which are produced in 14 point or larger type and intended for the visually handicapped. This volume is printed in 9 point type.
Indexes: *Subject/Textbook/Title/Author/Serials Key to Publishers' & Distributors' Abbreviations*

OTHER DATABASES

AUDIO/VIDEO DATABASE

PUBLICATIONS:

Words on Cassette

An annual bibliography of Spoken Word Audio Cassettes covering subjects from well known books to radio shows. Bibliographic information includes Title, Author(s), Reader(s)-Performer(s), Release Date, No. of Cassettes, Running Time, Order Numbers, ISBNs, Producer-Distributor and a brief annotation.
Indexes: *Title/Author/Reader-Performer/Subject/ Producer/Distributor*

Bowker's Complete Video Directory

A 3 volume annual bibliography with video titles ranging from Feature Films to Children's Video, How-to tapes to Documentaries, Sports to Travel.
Indexes: *Title, Genre or Subject, Cast/Director, Series, Closed-Captioned, Laser, 8mm, Spanish language, International Standards, Manufacturers/Distributors, Awards, Services & Suppliers.*

MICROCOMPUTER SOFTWARE DATABASE

PUBLICATIONS:

Software Encyclopedia

An annual 2-volume publication listing over 16,000 software products for microcomputers. Full versions of each entry are given in the Title Index. Information includes Title, Version, Author(s), Compatibility, Memory Required, Customer Support, other Requirements, Price; ISBN order No., and a brief description. Abridged entries are given in the System Compatability/Applications Index, which covers 14 computer systems and some 650 applications. A Publisher/Title Index is also included:
Indexes: *Title/System Compatibility— Applications/Publisher-Title*

TEXTBOOK DATABASE

The Textbook Database was separated from the BIP Database and expanded beyond the BIPS scope in 1973. Included are book and non-book materials for kindergarten through the first year of college as well as pedagogical material available and related to the educational world but not marketed to nor always available to the trade. The database includes all editions and bindings (hardcover, paperbound boards, spiral binding, reprints) as well as kits, maps, audio-visual materials and other teaching aids. Bibliographic entries contain the same elements as on the BIPS Database.

PUBLICATIONS:

El-Hi Textbooks And Serials in Print

An annual publication listing in-print and forthcoming titles. Entries are classified by subject and are listed in the appropriate category either by title or under their series name. Title and Author Indexes contain page references to the Main Subject Index.
Indexes: *Subject/Title/Author/Series/Serials Key to Publishers' & Distributors' Abbreviations*

PUBLISHERS' AUTHORITY DATABASE

PUBLICATIONS:

Publishers, Distributors & Wholesalers of the U.S., 1995-96.

Publishers, Distributors and Wholesalers of the United States

The main (Name) index of this publication contains the full company name with editorial and ordering addresses for some publishers currently listed in Bowker's Publisher Authority Database and active in the United States. In addition, an ISBN index supplies the ISBN prefixes, a Key to Abbreviations Index supplies the publishers' abbreviations used in *Books In Print* and a Wholesalers & Distributors Index supplies the full name and addresses for United States wholesalers and distribution. This directory is a useful companion tool to users of *Books In Print* as it increases the number of people who can use it simultaneously, and to librarians, booksellers, and others who need a comprehensive and up-to-date directory of U.S. publishing companies.
Indexes: *Name Index/Imprints, Subsidiaries & Divisions/Key to Abbreviations Index/ Publishers' & Distributors' Toll-Free & Fax Numbers/Wholesalers & Distributors Index/Geographic Index to Publishers, Distributors & Wholesalers/ ISBN Prefixes/Publishers By Fields of Activity/Inactive & Out of Business Publishers.*

THE BOWKER INTERNATIONAL SERIALS DATABASE

This database contains up-to-date information on 146,768 active serial titles published by approximately 77,986 serial publishers and corporate authors around the world and is maintained by the Bowker Serials Bibliography Department.

PUBLICATIONS:

Ulrich's International Periodicals Directory (annual); **Ulrich's Update** (3 times a year). This database is also available online and in microfiche and CD-ROM formats.

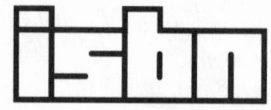

INTERNATIONAL STANDARD BOOK NUMBER

The 1995-96 BOOKS IN PRINT is the sixteenth edition where each title or edition of a title is listed with an ISBN. All publishers were notified and requested to submit a valid ISBN for their titles.

During the past decade, the majority of the publishers complied with the requirements of the standard and implemented the ISBN. At present, approximately 97% of all new titles and all new editions are submitted for listing with a valid ISBN.

To fulfill the responsibility of accomplishing total book numbering, the ISBN Agency allocated the ISBN prefixes 0-317, 0-318, 0-614, 0-615, 0-685 and 0-686 to number the titles in the BOOKS IN PRINT database without an ISBN. Titles not having an ISBN at the closing date of this publication were assigned an ISBN with one of these prefixes by the International Standard Book Numbering Agency.

Titles numbered within the prefixes 0-317, 0-318, 0-614, 0-615, 0-685 and 0-686 are:

—Publishers who did not assign ISBNs to their titles.

—Distributors with titles published and imported from countries not in the ISBN system, or not receiving the ISBN from the originating publisher.

—Errors from transposition and transcription which occurred in transmitting the ISBN to the BOOKS IN PRINT database.

All the ISBNs listed in BOOKS IN PRINT are validated by using the check digit control, and only valid ISBNs are listed in the database.

All publishers participating in the ISBN system having titles numbered within the prefixes 0-317, 0-318, 0-614, 0-615, 0-685 and 0-686 will receive a computer printout, requesting them to submit the correct ISBN.

Publishers not participating in the ISBN system may request from the ISBN Agency the assignment of an ISBN Publisher Prefix, and start numbering their titles.

The Book Industry System Advisory Committee (BISAC) has developed a standard format for data transmission, and many companies are already accepting orders transmitted on magnetic tape using the ISBN.

BISAC has also developed several other formats, also using the ISBN, including the title status format from which it is possible to update bibliographic information by magnetic tape exchange. BOOKS IN PRINT has been participating in such an exchange with many publishers, and welcomes inquiries from prospective participants.

The ISBN Agency and the Database Publishing Group of R.R. Bowker wish to express their appreciation to all publishers who collaborated in making the ISBN system the standard of the publishing industry.

SAN, an acronym of Standard Address Number, is a unique identification code for each address of each organization in or served by the book industry.

SANs are assigned to publishers, distributors, wholesalers, associations, software producers and manufacturers in the U.S.

The SAN itself merely defines an address. It becomes functional only in its application to activities such as purchasing, invoicing, billing, shipping, receiving, paying, crediting and refunding.

For additional information related to the ISBN total numbering, please contact Emery Koltay, Director of the ISBN/SAN Agency c/o R.R. Bowker.

How to Use
BOOKS IN PRINT
1995-96

This 48th annual edition of *Books In Print* was produced from records stored on magnetic tape, edited by computer programs, and set in type by computer-controlled photocomposition. This edition, in nine volumes, lists 1,156,916 available titles and an additional 152,538 titles declared Out-of-Print or Out-of-Stock indefinitely since July 1994 — a total of 1,309,454 titles from 46,007 United States publishers. Volumes 1-4 constitute an alphabetically-arranged author index. Volumes 5-8 constitute an alphabetically-arranged title index. Volume 9 contains information about all the publishers whose titles are listed in the first eight volumes of *Books In Print*. Seven indexes are included. *Symbols & Abbreviations* is a listing of the active publishers in *Books In Print*, arranged alphabetically by the abbreviations of the publishers' or distributors' names used in each bibliographic entry. The *Name Index* contains the same information as the *Symbols & Abbreviations*. Entries are arranged by full company name, and includes address(es), ISBN Prefix(es), SAN, toll-free telephone number(s), ordering/distribution address(es) & telephone number(s) & imprints with their name abbreviations. *The Publishers' & Distributors' Toll-Free Index* is arranged by full company name, and lists ISBN Prefix(es), city, state, zip code and toll-free telephone number(s). If a publisher's distributor has a toll-free telephone number, that number is provided, along with the distributor's name in parentheses. Multiple distributors are provided. *Wholesalers & Distributors* are arranged alphabetically by company name, and contains full address and ordering information, SAN(s), and, where applicable, ISBN prefix(es) and toll-free telephone numbers. The *Geographic Index to Wholesalers & Distributors* lists the companies found in Wholesalers & Distributors alphabetically by company name within each state. Puerto Rico, Guam, and the U.S. Virgin Islands are

also included. City name appears in parentheses following company name. The *New Publishers* Index is arranged alphabetically by the abbreviation used in the bibliographic entries in *Books In Print*. This index lists publishers added to R.R. Bowker's Publisher Authority Database since the last edition of *Books In Print*. Following the abbreviation, the full company name is given. For complete address and ordering information, refer either to the *Symbols & Abbreviations,* or to the *Name Index. The Inactive & Out-of-Business Publishers Index* is arranged alphabetically by the company name abbreviation, and lists companies that have either gone out of business, or have moved without leaving a forwarding address. R.R. Bowker has used its best efforts to collect and prepare this index. The assistance of the users of *Books In Print* is solicited to aid us to trace these companies. If the users of *Books In Print* know the current addresses for any of these companies, please write to R.R. Bowker, 121 Chanlon Road, New Providence, NJ 07974, Attention: Publishers' Authority Database.

ALPHABETICAL ARRANGEMENT
OF AUTHOR AND TITLE INDEXES

Within each index entries are filed alphabetically by word, with the following exceptions:

Initial articles of titles in English, French, German, Italian and Spanish are deleted from the title index.

M', Mc and Mac are filed as if they were *Mac* and are interfiled with other names beginning with Mac; for example, Macan, MacAnally, Macardle, McAree, McArthur, Macarthur, M'Aulay, Macaulay, McAuley. Within a specific name grouping *Mc* and *Mac* are interfiled according to the given name of author; for example,

Macdonald, Agnes; McDonald, Alexander; MacDonald, Anne L.; McDonald, Austin F; MacDonald, Betty. Compound names are listed under the first part of the name, and cross-references appear under the last part of the name.

Entries beginning with initial letters (whether authors' given names, or titles) are filed first, e.g., Smith, H.C., comes before Smith, Harold A.; B E A M A Directory comes before Baal, Babylon.

Numerals, including year dates, are written out in most cases and are filed alphabetically.

> Seven Years in Tibet
> Seventeen
> Seventeen famous operas
> Seventeen-Fifteen to the present
> Seventeen party book
> Seventeen reader
> Seventeenth century

U.S., UN, Dr., Mr., and St. are filed as though they were spelled out. In the author index, however, "Dr. Seuss" files as "Dr. Seuss" rather than "Doctor Seuss" or "Seuss."

SPECIAL NOTE ON HOW TO FIND AN AUTHOR'S COMPLETE LISTING

In sorting author listings by computer it is not possible to group the entire listing for an author together unless a standard spelling and format for each name is used. The information in *Books In Print* comes directly from publishers or from their catalogs. Where publishers do not submit an author's name in consistent form, his listings in the author index may be divided into several groups.

Variant forms of an author's first and middle names may not be adjacent in the filing sequence, as in: Aiken, Conrad and Aiken, Conrad P. or Jung, C.G. or Jung, Carl G. For most surnames, variant forms of entry will fall close together but for the most common surnames (Smith, Brown, etc.) it is suggested you check specifically for all variant forms of first and middle names.

Foreign names which may or may not be given with a prefix will not be adjacent in the filing sequence, such as Balzac and de Balzac and Goethe or von Goethe. German names with umlauts may appear in two alphabets because of the varying treatment of the umlauted vowel; Müller, F. Max or Mueller, F. Max. Acronyms for names of corporate authors may appear in two or more groups of listings if one form is presented with no space between initials— UNESCO, and another with spaces, U N E S C O.

You will find cross-references to the variant forms of an author's name wherever we anticipated that his listings might not be filed together. To the extent practicable, we hope in future editions to reduce the number of variant forms of author's names in *Books In Print*.

INFORMATION INCLUDED IN AUTHOR AND TITLE ENTRIES

Entries include the following bibliographic information, when available: author, co-author, editor, co-editor, translator, co-translator, title, number of volumes, edition, Library of Congress number, series information, page numbers, language if other than English, whether or not illustrated, grade range, year of publication, type of binding if other than cloth over boards, price. International Standard Book Number, publisher's order number, imprint and publisher. When an entry includes the prices for both the hardcover and paperback editions, the publication date within the entry refers to the hardcover binding; however, when the paperback binding is the only one included in the entry, the publication date is the paperback publication date. (Information on the International Standard Book Numbering System developing in the United States and other English-speaking countries is available from R.R. Bowker.)

Entries marked with an asterisk indicate titles never before appearing in *Books In Print*.

GENERAL EDITORIAL POLICIES

In order to insure that the essential information in these listings is uniform, complete, and easy to find, the following editorial policies have been maintained:

When two authors or editors are responsible for a book, full bibliographic information is included in the author entry for the author or editor named first, and a cross-reference directs the user from the second author or editor to the primary entry, e.g., Wilson, Robert E., jt. auth. See Fensch, E. A. If more than two authors or editors are responsible for a certain publication, only the name of the first is given followed by *et al*.

Titles of single volumes as part of a set are given if the volumes are sold singly. Some series are also listed in the Title Index.

The Bible, the Book of Common Prayer, catechisms, hymnals and books of this type cannot always be recorded with full description. Since incomplete information is misleading, the user of this book is directed to the appropriate publisher's trade lists.

Every effort is made by most publishers to submit their material with consideration for its accuracy throughout the life of this edition of *Books In Print*. Most publishers anticipate price changes, list forthcoming books even if publication dates and prices are not set, and for the most part try not to list books that may shortly become unavailable. In spite of these efforts, a certain amount of unanticipated change in price will occur and a certain number of titles in this edition will become unavailable before the new edition of *Books In Print* is published. *The Books In Print Supplement* 1995-96 to be published in March 1996 will reflect any changes which have occurred in the interim. All prices are subject to change without notice.

Most prices are list prices. Lack of uniformity in publishers' data prohibits indicating trade discounts. An "a" follows some of the trade edition prices and indicates that a specially priced library edition is available; "t" indicates a tentative price; "g" a guaranteed binding on a juvenile title; and "x" a short discount—20%, or less. Short discount information is generally supplied by publishers to Bowker for each publication. However, all publishers do not uniformly supply this information and Bowker can only transmit this information when it is provided. PLB indicates a publishers' library binding. YA indicates that a title may be used for young adults. An "i" following the price indicates an invoice price. Specific policies for such titles should be obtained from the individual publishers.

Publishers' and distributors' names, in most instances, are abbreviated. A key to these abbreviations will be found in the *Key to Publishers' and Distributors' Abbreviations,* the first index of Volume 9. Entries in this key are arranged alphabetically by the abbreviations used in the bibliographic entries. A complete listing is provided, which contains: abbreviation used, company name, editorial address(es), ordering address(es), telephone number(s), toll-free telephone number(s), imprints, ISBN prefix(es), Standard Address Number(s) (SAN), and business affiliation.

For example:

Crown Pub Group (*Crown Publishing Group, 0-517*), Affil. of Random Hse. Inc., 201 E. 50th St., New York, NY 10022 (SAN 200-2639) Tel 212-751-2600; Toll-free: 800-726-0600 (Customer Service only). Imprints: C Potter Pubs (Potter, Clarkson Publishers); Harmony (Harmony Books); Bell Tower (Bell Tower); Crown (Crown); Living Language (Living Language); Orion Bks (Orion Books); Ebury Pr Stationery (Ebury Press Stationery); Panache (Panache Press)

If a bibliographic entry contains a "Pub. by" note after the ISBN, the title should not be ordered from the publisher, but from the company whose abbreviation appears at the end of the entry. For example, the title below should be ordered from Coronet Bks.

Kronholm, Tryggve & Riad, Eva, eds. On the Dignity of Man: Oriental & Classical Studies in Honour of Frithiof Rundgren, 524p. (orig.). 1986. text ed. 47.50x (ISBN 91-227-00839-X, Pub. by Almqvist & Wiksell). Coronet Bks.

The SAN (Standard Address Number) is a unique identification code for each address of each organization in or served by the book industry.

A dagger (†) preceding an entry, and the note 'CIP' following an entry indicate that the publisher participates in the 'Cataloguing in Publication' program. This information was provided by The Library of Congress. For complete information about this program, please write to the CIP offices of the Library of Congress, Washington, DC 20540.

Entries appearing in bold print indicate that the publisher is also listed in Publishers' Trade List Annual 1995.

TYPES OF PUBLICATIONS NOT FULLY REPRESENTED IN *Books In Print*

This edition of *Books In Print* indexes the listings of some 46,000 publishers — a total of 1,309,454 titles, including 152,538 titles declared out-of-print or out-of-stock indefinitely since July 1994. Certain classes of publications are, however, not represented in *Books In Print.* These include some professional law book publications, subscription reference sets and book club editions.

Current information was obtained from all publishers in the BIP Database. These publishers include regular contributors to Bowker's Advance Book Information

system and less active publishers who responded to our request for *Books In Print* information. Publishers were asked to correct and update computer listings of the *Books In Print* master file. If this was not possible we obtained the latest edition of the publisher's catalogue or trade order list. Every effort by correspondence, telephone and personal contact with publishers was made to get up-to-date, complete information on the in-print titles published and distributed in the United States for inclusion in *Books In Print.*

These criteria of inclusion were followed: Books must be available to the trade; this excludes books available only to members of a particular organization, subscription-only titles, or those sold only to schools. Books must be available for single copy purchase. No attempt was made to include things other than books, such as periodicals, puzzles, calendars, microfilms, or audio-visual materials (unless accompanied by a text). Free material not included with a book for sale and material available only in quantities are also omitted.

Imported books must have a sole U.S. distributor. Distributors of Spanish language books published outside the U.S. have informed us that sole rights to these titles are not available. These books, therefore, are not listed in *Books In Print* but are fully covered in *Libros En Venta* and supplements to *Libros En Venta.* Some U.S. distributors of these books are listed in the Wholesalers & Distributors Index in Volume 10. Distributors of books imported from France and Germany often do not have sole rights to these titles. These books listed in *Books In Print* as available from *one* distributor may also be available from other distributors of French or German books. For distributors of French or German titles, refer to the *American Book Trade Directory, 41st edition,* also published by R.R. Bowker.

OTHER BIBLIOGRAPHIC PUBLICATIONS TO SUPPLEMENT Books *In Print*

Although *Books In Print* looks ahead, it cannot, of course, contain information that was unknown to the publishers when they submitted data in July. Next March, *Books In Print Supplement* will be published, giving price changes, titles which have gone out-of-print and new books published or announced in the 6 months following the publication of *Books In Print.* This volume is arranged by author, title and subject.

A Bowker tool for keeping up with new titles is *Forthcoming Books,* a separate, bimonthly publication which provides subject-author-title indexes to all books due to appear in the forthcoming 5 month period and a culmination of all books that have appeared since the previous July.

Paperbound Books In Print includes all published and forthcoming paper trade and paper text editions published or exclusively distributed in the U.S. Beginning in 1978 a service of two complete editions published in the Spring and Fall replaced the old service of one base volume and two supplements. The complete service includes both the Spring and Fall volumes. The Spring edition will be published in March and the Fall in September.

A complete description of other publications from the BIPS Database is included in preceding pages.

Publishers Weekly, especially its forecasts, is another way of keeping up with later information about new books. The special announcement issues (Fall, Spring) are available separately.

All forecasts are, of course, necessarily incomplete, and to some extent inaccurate or unfulfilled. A record of the new books as actually published is therefore available in a Dewey subject classification, as well as an author and title index in the monthly American Book Publishing Record. This publication also provides full cataloguing information.

El-Hi Textbooks In Print is more comprehensive than *Books In Print* when it comes to textbooks for elementary and secondary schools. *Bowker's Law Books and Serials in Print*, an annual Bowker publication started in 1982, provides comprehensive coverage of law books.

Out-of-print books may be sought through the columns of the *AB Bookman's Weekly,* Box AB, Clifton, New Jersey 07015.

LIST OF ABBREVIATIONS

a (after price)	specially priced library edition available
abr.	abridged
adapt.	adapted
aft.	afterword
Amer.	American
anno.	annotated by
annot.	annotation(s)
ans.	answer(s)
app.	appendix
Apple II	Apple II disk
approx.	approximately
ARA	Arabic
assn.	association
audio	analog audio cassette
auth.	author
bd.	bound
bdg.	binding
bds.	boards
bibl(s).	bibliography(ies)
bk(s).	book(s)
bklet(s).	booklet(s)
boxed	boxed set, slipcase, or caseboard
Bro.	Brother
C	college audience level
CAT	Catalan
CHI	Chinese
co.	company
comm.	commission, committee
comment.	commentaries
comp.	compiled
cond.	condensed
contrib.	contributed
corp.	corporation
CRO	Croatian
CZE	Czech
DAN	Danish
dept.	department
des.	designed
diag(s).	diagram(s)
digital audio	digital audio cassette
dir.	director
disk	software disk or diskette
dist.	distributed
Div.	Division
doz.	dozen
DUT	Dutch
ea.	each
ed.	edited, edition, editor
eds.	editions, editors
educ.	education
elem.	elementary
ency.	encyclopedia
ENG	English
enl.	enlarged
epil.	epilogue
exp.	expurgated
expr.	experiments
fac.	facsimile
fasc.	fascicule
fict.	fiction
fig(s).	figure(s)

FIN	Finnish
flmstrp.	filmstrip
footn.	footnotes
for.	foreign
FRE	French
frwd.	foreword
g (after price)	guaranteed juvenile binding
gen.	general
GER	German
GRE	Greek
gr.	grade(s)
hdbk.	handbook
HEB	Hebrew
HUN	Hungarian
i	invoice price (see publisher for specific pricing policies)
Illus.	illustrated, illustration(s), illustrator(s)
in prep.	in preparation
incl.	includes, including
info.	information
inst.	institute
intro.	introduction
ISBN	International Standard Book Number
ITA	Italian
i.t.a.	initial teaching alphabet
J	junvenile audience level
JPN	Japanese
Jr.	Junior
jt. auth.	joint author
jt. ed.	joint editor
k	kindergarten audience level
KOR	Korean
lab.	laboratory
lang(s).	language(s)
LAT	Latin
LC	Library of Congress
lea.	leather
lib.	library
lit.	literature, literary
lp	record, album, long playing
ltd. ed.	limited edition
mac hd	144M, Mac
mac ld	800K, Mac
mass mkt.	mass market paperbound
math.	mathematics
mic. film	microfilm
mic. form	microform
mod.	modern
mor.	morocco
MS(S)	manuscript(s)
natl.	national
net	net price (see publisher for specific pricing policies)
NOR	Norwegian
no(s).	number(s)
o.p.	out of print
orig.	original text, not a reprint (paperback)
o.s.i.	out of stock indefinitely
p.	pages
pap.	paper

per.	perfect binding
PER	Persian (Modern)
photos	photographer, photographs
PLB	publisher's library binding
POL	Polish
pop. ed.	popular edition
POR	Portuguese
prep.	preparation
probs.	problems
prog. bk.	programmed book
ps	preschool audience level
pseud.	pseudonym
pt(s).	part(s)
pub.	published, publisher, publishing
pubn.	publication
ref(s).	reference(s)
reprod(s).	reproduction(s)
ret.	retold by
rev.	revised
rpm.	revolution per minute (phono records)
RUS	Russian
SAN	Standard Address Number
S&L	Signed and Limited
SER	Serbian
scp	single copy Direct to Consumer Price
sec.	section
sel.	selected
ser.	series
Soc.	Society
sols.	solutions
s.p.	school price
SPA	Spanish
Sr. (after given name)	Senior
Sr. (before given name)	Sister
St.	Saint
subs.	subsidiary
subsc.	subscription
suppl.	supplement
SWE	Swedish
t	after price, tentative price
tech.	technical
text ed.	text edition
tr.	translated, translation, translator
trans.	transparencies
univ.	university
vdisk	videodisc
VHS	video, VHS format
vol(s).	volume(s)
wkbk.	workbook
x (after price)	short discount (20% or less)
YA	young adult audience level
yrbk.	yearbook
3.5 hd	1.44M, 35 disk, DOS
3.5 ld	720, 35 Disk, DOS
5.25 hd	1.2M, 525 Disk, DOS
5.25 ld	360K, 525 Disk, DOS

ANNOTATED ENTRIES

To help you make informed decisions concerning acquisitions and title recommendations, this edition of *Books In Print* includes Publisher Provided Annotations on thousands of the latest titles. Knowing what these books are about as soon as you find them in these pages gives you a valuable advantage in evaluating specific selections.

Publishers who want to highlight any of their titles in this manner should contact Bowker Advertising Sales at 1-908-464-6800, ext. 6749 for more information.

This service will grow with future editions of *Books In Print,* and we know you will find it useful. Please send us your comments—not only regarding this new feature—but also concerning any other improvements you'd liked to see included in *Books In Print.*

A

BOOKS IN PRINT®
1995-96

Volume 5
TITLES
A-D

A

*A. Alan Lindsay. 150p. 1996. pap. 7.95 (*0-7610-0466-1*) NW Pub.

A - D at the Peter Joseph Gallery. Ed. by Peter T. Joseph & Elisabeth Cunnick. (Illus.). (Orig.). 1992. pap. text ed. 15.00 (*1-881658-00-7*) P J Gallery.

A - O. Elizabeth Willis. 32p. 1991. pap. 4.00 (*1-879645-02-5*) Garlic MA.

A-A-America! & Stone. rev. ed. Edward Bond. (Methuen Modern Plays Ser.). 115p. 1982. pap. 8.95 (*0-413-48320-7*, A0001, Pub. by Methuen UK) Heinemann.

A. A. E. Disderi & the Carte de Viste Portrait Photograph. Elizabeth A. McCauley. LC 84-17281. (Publications in the History of Art: No. 31). (Illus.). 262p. 1985. text ed. 42.50 (*0-300-03169-6*) Yale U Pr.

***A. A. Milne: Creator of Winnie the Pooh.** Jill Wheeler. Ed. by Rosemary Wallner. (Young at Heart Ser.). 1992. pap. 4.95 (*1-56239-373-1*) Abdo & Dghtrs.

A. A. Milne: Creator of Winnie the Pooh. Jill Wheeler. Ed. by Rosemary Wallner. LC 92-16570. (Young at Heart Ser.). (J). (gr. 4). 1992. lib. bdg. 13.99 (*1-56239-114-3*) Abdo & Dghtrs.

***A. A. Milne (Author of Winnie-the-Pooh)** Carol Greene. LC 95-10108. (Rookie Biography Ser.). (J). 1995. write for info. (*0-516-04270-X*) Childrens.

A. A. Seagull. Susan E. McCloud. (J). pap. 4.95 (*0-88494-721-1*) Bookcraft Inc.

A. Alekhine: Agony of a Chess Genius. Pablo Moran. Ed. by Frank X. Mur & Dale A. Brandreth. LC 89-42737. 328p. 1989. lib. bdg. 38.50x (*0-89950-440-X*) McFarland & Co.

A. Alekhine vs E. D. Bogolijubow: World's Chess Championship, 1934. Ed. by Fred Reinfeld & Reuben Fine. pap. 4.95 (*0-486-21813-9*) Dover.

A-Alkanolamines see Encyclopedia of Chemical Technology

A an Av Es. Alan Davies. 28p. (Orig.). 1981. pap. 5.50 (*0-937013-04-8*) Potes Poets.

A & P Technician Oral & Practical Test Guide. Steve DeVries. LC 93-5671. (Illus.). 113p. 1993. pap. text ed. 9.95 (*0-89100-428-9*, EA-428) IAP.

A & P Technician Powerplant. 2nd ed. IAP, Inc Staff. LC 92-3012. (Illus.). 444p. 1992. pap. text ed. 24.95 (*0-89100-396-7*, EA-ITP-P2); 9.95 (*0-89100-401-7*, EA-ITP-PW2) IAP.

A & P Technician Powerplant Instructor Guide. IAP, Inc. Staff. LC 93-2624. (Illus.). 57p. 1993. pap. text ed. 12.95 (*0-89100-430-0*, EA-ITP-PI2) IAP.

A & P Technician Powerplant Study Guide. IAP, Inc. Staff. LC 92-44736. (Illus.). 336p. 1992. pap. text ed. 9.95 (*0-89100-372-X*, EA-ITP-PSG2) IAP.

A. Aubrey Bodine, Baltimore Pictorialist, 1906-1970. Kathleen M. Ewing. LC 85-45042. (Illus.). 104p. 1985. 34.95 (*0-8018-3151-2*) Johns Hopkins.

A-B Alphabook. Karen Sevaly. Ed. by Richard Sevaly et al. (Illus.). 128p. (Orig.). 1993. pap. text ed. 10.95 (*0-943263-21-2*, TF1801) Teachers Friend Pubns.

A B C. Nicola Smee. (J). (gr. k up). 1993. 7.00 (*0-00-195465-2*) Collins SF.

A B C. Illus. by Tony Tallarico. (Tiny Bks.). 28p. (J). (ps-1). 1988. bds. 2.95 (*0-448-48817-5*, Tuffy) Putnam Pub Group.

A, B, C, Bunny. Pamela Kennedy. (CottonTale Book Ser.). (Illus.). 12p. (J). (ps-00). 1990. bds. 4.99 (*0-929608-69-0*) Focus Family.

A-B-C Christmas. Amy Houts. (Little Deer Bks.). (Illus.). 28p. (J). (ps-00). 1993. 5.49 (*0-7847-0063-X*, 24-03843) Standard Pub.

A, B, C, D, Tummy, Toes, Hands, Knees. B. G. Hennessy. (Illus.). 32p. (J). (ps-1). 1991. pap. 4.99 (*0-14-050739-6*, Puffin) Puffin Bks.

A, B, C, D, Tummy, Toes, Hands, Knees. B. G. Hennessy. (Illus.). 32p. (J). (ps-1). 1989. pap. 13.95 (*0-670-81703-1*) Viking Child Bks.

A. B. C. de Babar. Illus. by Jean De Brunhoff. LC 94-5913. (J). (gr. 3 up). 1995. 12.00 (*0-679-86842-9*) Random Bks Yng Read.

A B C for Book-Collectors. rev. ed. John Carter. (Higher Education Ser.). (Illus.). 1952. 22.50 (*0-394-41403-9*) Knopf.

A. B. C. Manual For Law Enforcement Personnel, N. Y. S. 55p. 1994. pap. 4.95 (*0-930137-65-5*) Looseleaf Law.

A. B. C. Murders. Agatha Christie. (Hercule Poirot Mystery Ser.). 192p. 1991. pap. text ed. 4.99 (*0-425-13024-X*) Berkley Pub.

A. B. C. Murders. Agatha Christie. (Agatha Christie Ser.). 256p. 1985. 12.95 (*0-396-08698-5*, Putnam) Putnam Pub Group.

A. B. C. Murders. large type ed. Agatha Christie. (Popular Author Ser.). 344p. 1988. lib. bdg. 16.95 (*0-8161-4459-1*) G K Hall.

A. B. C. of Fashionable Animals. Ed. by Welleran Poltarnees et al. (Illus.). 64p. (J). 1991. 12.95 (*0-88138-122-5*, Green Tiger S&S) S&S Childrens.

A B C of Stock Speculation. Samuel A. Nelson. LC 89-60256. 232p. 1989. reprint ed. 45.00 (*1-55888-805-5*) Omnigraphics Inc.

A, B, C of the Biosphere. Max Finch. (Imagine a Biosphere Ser.). 32p. 1993. 14.95 (*1-882428-11-0*) Biosphere Pr.

A, B, C of the Biosphere. Max Finch. (Imagine a Biosphere Ser.). 32p. (J). 1993. pap. 7.95 (*1-882428-03-X*) Biosphere Pr.

A-B-C of Truth. Brown Landone. 98p. 1926. reprint ed. spiral bd. 4.40 (*0-7873-1108-1*) Mokelumne.

A-B-C One-Two-Three Craft Book: Make a Cloth Book of Exciting Learning Toys. Phyllis Fiarotta & Noel Fiarotta. LC 93-40989. (Illus.). 128p. 1994. 19.95 (*0-8069-0671-5*) Sterling.

A-B-C, 1-2-3: A Teacher - Parent Resource for Teaching Beginning Concepts. rev. ed. Sue Goldsmith. Ed. by Jan Keeling. (Illus.). 80p. (Orig.). (ps-2). 1993. pap. text ed. 7.95 (*0-86530-024-0*, IP-240) Incentive Pubns.

A B Cedar: An Alphabet of Trees. George-Ella Lyon. LC 88-22797. (Illus.). 32p. (J). (ps-1). 1989. 14.95 (*0-531-05795-X*); lib. bdg. 14.99 (*0-531-08395-0*) Orchard Bks Watts.

***A-B Counseling Workshop.** Project Adventure Staff. 144p. 1995. pap. text ed., spiral bd. 4.39 (*0-614-06048-6*) Kendall-Hunt.

A. B. Frost: American Sportsman's Artist. 2nd ed. Henry W. Lanier. (Fifty Greatest Bks.). (Illus.). 170p. 1990. reprint ed. 39.95 (*1-56416-003-3*) Derrydale Pr.

A. B. Frost Book. Henry M. Reed. (Illus.). 176p. 1993. 49.95 (*0-941711-13-7*) Wyrick & Co.

A. B. Jackson: Retrospective Exhibition. Thomas W. Styron. LC 81-70107. (Illus.). 63p. 1981. pap. 6.00 (*0-940744-35-X*) Chrysler Museum.

A B Seas. Laurie Kimpton-Lorence. (Illus.). 158p. (Orig.). 1986. pap. 10.95 (*0-945265-06-9*) Accord Comm.

A, B, See! Tana Hoban. LC 81-6890. (Illus.). 32p. (J). (gr. k-3). 1982. lib. bdg. 14.93 (*0-688-00833-X*) Greenwillow.

A. Berlese: Complete Acarological Works, 5 vols., Set. Ed. by L. Van Der Hammen. (Illus.). 1977. lib. bdg. 263.00 (*90-6193-582-2*) Kluwer Ac.

A. Bertram Chandler: Master Navigator of Space. 2nd ed. Gordon Benson, Jr. & Phil Stephensen-Payne. (Galactic Central Bibliographies Ser.: No. 3). ix, 43p. (C). 1990. lib. bdg. 17.00x (*0-8095-4702-3*) Borgo Pr.

***A-Boat: Six Oceanographic Cruises in the World's Biggest Ketch.** C. Dana Densmore. (Illus.). 195p. (Orig.). 1995. pap. 17.00 (*0-9645207-0-2*) C D Densmore.

A. Bogdanov: Essays in Tektology. A. Bogdanov. Tr. by George Gorelik. (Systems Inquiry Ser.). 280p. (Orig.). (C). 1980. pap. text ed. 16.95x (*0-914105-06-X*) Intersystems Pubns.

A-Bomb Radiation Effects Digest. Ed. by Itsuzo Shigematsu. 1994. pap. text ed. 30.00 (*3-7186-5463-6*, Harwood Acad Pubs) Gordon & Breach.

A Bord de l'Etoile Matutine. Pierre M. Orlan. (FRE.). 1983. pap. 10.95 (*0-7859-4188-6*) Fr & Eur.

A. Bronson Alcott: His Life & Philosophy, 2 Vols, Set. Franklin B. Sanborn & William T. Harris. LC 65-23481. 1893. 35.00 (*0-8196-0161-6*) Biblo.

A. Bronson Alcott's Life & Philosophy, 2 vols., Set. Franklin B. Sanborn. 1972. 200.00 (*0-87968-571-9*) Gordon Pr.

***A Bug C.** Edna Romero. (Illus.). 48p. (J). (ps-3). 1993. pap. 10.95 (*1-880812-07-X*) S Ink WA.

A-C Carrier Control Systems. Keith A. Ivey. LC 64-23843. 363p. 1964. reprint ed. pap. 103.50 (*0-8357-5000-0*, 2007399) Bks Demand.

***A. C. Circuits.** Stan Fulton. (C). 1995. 17.60 (*1-56870-163-2*) RonJon Pub.

A. C. Generators: Design & Application. Robert L. Ames. (Electronic & Electrical Engineering Research Ser.). 1990. text ed. 185.00 (*0-471-92589-6*) Wiley.

A. C. Gilbert's Heritage. Ed. by Donald J. Heimburger. LC 83-80571. (Illus.). 164p. 1983. 24.95 (*0-685-06952-4*); pap. 15.95 (*0-911581-01-4*) Heimburger Hse Pub.

***A. C. Green.** rev. ed. J. C. Webster. LC 95-13334. (Today's Heroes Ser.). Orig. Title: Victory. (J). 1995. write for info. (*0-310-20207-8*) Zondervan.

A. C. Machines: Electromagnetics & Design. Brian Chalmers & Alan Williamson. (Electronic & Electrical Engineering Research Ser.). 1991. text ed. 98.00 (*0-471-93003-2*) Wiley.

A-C Plus Plus Primer. Stanley B. Lippman. (Illus.). 448p. (C). 1989. pap. text ed. 23.96 (*0-201-16487-6*) Addison-Wesley.

A. C. Roessler Photo Cachet Catalogue. Barry Newton. Ed. by Michael Mellone. (Illus.). 1977. pap. 15.00 (*0-89794-002-4*) FDC Pub.

A. C. Roessler's Standard Historical Souvenir Airmail Catalog. A. C. Roessler. Ed. by Michael Mellone. (Illus.). 1978. pap. 4.50 (*0-89794-007-5*) FDC Pub.

A. C. T. I. Lynn Blymire et al. (J). (gr. k-4). 1981. pap. 3.00 (*0-931992-40-0*) Penns Valley.

A-Choo. Elayne Reiss & Rita Freidman. (Illus.). (J). (gr. k-1). 1990. 12.50 (*0-89796-864-6*) New Dimens Educ.

A-Choo Confusion. Elayne Weimann & Rita Friedman. (Fables from the Letter People Ser.). (Illus.). 30p. (J). (ps-1). 1988. lib. bdg. 12.95 (*0-89796-000-9*) New Dimens Educ.

***A-Counting We Will Go.** Rozanne J. Williams. (Emergent Readers Ser.). 16p. (J). (gr. k-2). 1995. 2.49 (*0-916119-93-9*) Creat Teach Pr.

***A. D.** Saab Lofton. 320p. (Orig.). 1995. pap. 12.00 (*0-9622937-8-4*) III Pub.

***A. D. A Memoir.** Kate Millett. 256p. 1995. 23.00 (*0-393-03524-7*) Norton.

***A. D. A. M. Student Atlas of Anatomy.** Illus. by A. D. A. M. Software Inc. Staff. LC 95-11593. 1995. write for info. (*0-683-00042-X*) Williams & Wilkins.

***A. D. D. from A to Z: A Comprehensive Guide to Attention Deficit Disorder.** William N. Bender & Phillip J. McLaughlin. 76p. 1994. teacher ed 195.00 (*1-57035-016-7*, 60KIT) Sopris.

***A. D. Hope.** Darling. Date not set. 22.95 (*0-8057-7049-6*, Twayne) Macmillan.

A. D. Hope. Kevin Hart. (Australian Writers Ser.). 144p. 1993. pap. 15.95 (*0-19-553268-6*) OUP.

A. D. Hope: Questions of Poetic Strength. Walter Tonetto. 1993. text ed. 27.95 (*81-85218-74-9*, Pub. by Prestige II) Advent Bks Div.

A. D. L. Handbook on Israel: Pocket Size Resource Guide. Intro. by Samuel W. Lewis. (Illus.). 170p. 1985. 9.95 (*0-88464-057-4*) ADL.

***A. D. Momigliano: Studies on Modern Scholarship.** G. W. Bowerstock & T. J. Cornell. 1994. pap. 17.00 (*0-520-08545-0*) U CA Pr.

A. D. 1991: The Genesis of Holocaust. Henry R. Hall. (Prophetic Ser.). 375p. (Orig.). 1985. pap. 4.95 (*0-930351-01-0*) Spirit Prophecy.

A. D. S. Collections - Actuality & Possibility see Washington Words

A. D. Sakharov: Collected Scientific Works. Sakharov. 200p. 1982. 65.00 (*0-8247-1714-7*) Dekker.

A. D. 2000. Alvarado M. Fuller. LC 71-154441. (Utopian Literature Ser.). (Illus.). 1976. reprint ed. 33.95 (*0-405-03524-1*) Ayer.

A. D. 2000: The Computer & the Millennium. Charles W. Curry, Jr. 29p. 1994. pap. text ed. 10.95 (*0-9640456-0-5*) CC Communs.

A. D. 2100. John W. Andrews. LC 71-82113. (Illus.). 1969. 25.95 (*0-8283-1033-5*) Branden Pub Co.

A. D. 1250: Ancient Peoples of the Southwest. Lawrence W. Cheek. LC 93-910480. (Illus.). 175p. 1994. 49.95 (*0-916179-45-1*) Ariz Hwy.

A Dios por el Atomo. Samuel Vila. (SPA.). 2.95 (*84-7228-013-6*, 220002, Pub. by Edit Clie SP) TSELF.

A Donde Va la Tierra? Where Is Planet Earth Going? Albalat I. Gil. (SPA.). 4.25 (*84-7645-437-6*, 223541, Pub. by Edit Clie SP) TSELF.

***A. E. Houseman Revisited.** Terence A. Hoagwood. LC 95-2015. (English Authors Ser.: Vol. 514). 1995. write for info. (*0-8057-7026-7*, Twayne) Macmillan.

A. E. Housman. Keith Jebb. 1992. pap. 15.95 (*1-85411-050-0*) Dufour.

A. E. Housman. Keith Jebb. Ed. by John P. Ward. (Border Lines Ser.). (Illus.). 147p. 1992. 35.00 (*1-85411-049-7*, Pub. by Seren Bks UK); pap. 15.95 (*0-685-59675-3*, Pub. by Seren Bks UK) Dufour.

A. E. Housman. Andrew Gow. LC 72-699. (English Literature Ser.: No. 33). 1972. reprint ed. lib. bdg. 75.00 (*0-8383-1423-6*) M S G Haskell Hse.

A. E. Housman: A Collection of Critical Essays. Ed. by Christopher Ricks. (Twentieth Century Views Ser.). 1968. 12.95 (*0-13-395913-9*, Spectrum Bks); pap. 1.95 (*0-13-395905-8*, STC83, Spectrum Bks) P-H.

A. E. Housman: The Critical Heritage. Ed. by Philip Gardner. (Critical Heritage Ser.). 700p. 1993. 150.00 (*0-415-03298-9*, A7404) Routledge.

***A. Edward Maumenee, M. D. The Wilmer Ophthalmological Institute at the Johns Hopkins University & the Stanford Medical School.** A. Edward Maumenee. (Ophthalmology Oral History Ser.). (Illus.). xxx, 267p. 1994. pap. 45.00 (*1-56055-068-6*) FAAO.

***A-F.** (ANY SERIES TITLE). Date not set. 1.00 (*0-615-00273-0*) Plenum.

A. F. B. T. R. Cookbook. 2nd ed. Fundraising Committee. Ed. by Olivia Schultz. reprint ed. 7.50 (*0-686-39886-6*) Am Brain Tumor.

***A for Antarctica.** Jonathan Chester. LC 94-43606. (Illus.). 32p. (J). (gr. k up). 1995. 12.95 (*1-883672-24-4*) Tricycle Pr.

***A4 Murder.** large type ed. P. A. Foxall. (Linford Mystery Library). 320p. 1995. pap. 14.95 (*0-7089-7645-X*, Linford) Ulverscroft.

An Asterisk (*) at the beginning of an entry indicates that the title is appearing in BIP for the first time.

A

A. G. A. Gas Measurement Manual, Pts. 12-13. rev. ed. American Gas Association Transmission Measurement Committee. 100p. 1978. pap. 7.00 (0-318-12579-X, XQO278) Am Gas Assn.

A. G. A. Plastic Pipe Manual for Gas Service. 71p. 1977. pap. 5.00 (0-318-12580-3, XR0877) Am Gas Assn.

A. G. Russell's Knife Trader's Guide. A. G. Russell & Goldie Russell. Ed. by Angus Laidlaw. 160p. (Orig.). 1991. pap. 10.00 (0-943997-25-9) P Wahl.

A. G. Science of Regeneration: Sex Enlightenment. 161p. 1968. reprint ed. spiral bd. 8.25 (0-7873-0010-1) Mokelumne.

A. G. Spalding & the Rise of Baseball: The Promise of American Sport. Peter Levine. 1986. pap. 10.95 (0-19-504220-4) OUP.

A. Gellii Noctes Atticae: Recognovit Brevique Adnotatione Critica Instruxit Tomus II: Libri XI-XX. Aulus Gellius. Ed. by P. K. Marshall. (Oxford Classical Texts Ser.). 336p. 1990. 42.50 (0-19-814652-3); 45.00 (0-19-814651-5) OUP.

A. H. A. Low-Salt Cookbook. A. H. A. Staff. 1992. pap. 15.00 (0-8129-2045-7, Times Bks) Random.

A. H. Fox: The Finest Gun in the World. deluxe limited ed. Michael McIntosh. LC 92-74003. (Illus.). 408p. 1994. 95.00 (0-924357-25-8, 21100-B) Countrysport Pr.

A. H. Fox: The Finest Gun in the World. enl. rev. ed. Michael McIntosh. LC 92-74003. (Illus.). 408p. 1994. 49.00 (0-924357-24-X, 21100-A) Countrysport Pr.

A. Haar Memorial Conference, 2 vols. Ed. by J. Szabados & K. Tandori. (Colloquia Mathematica Societatis Janos Bolyai Ser.: No. 49). 1018p. 1987. 187.25 (0-444-70095-1, North Holland) Elsevier.

A History's Anthropology: The Death of William Gooch see Death of William Gooch: A History's Anthropology

A. Hyatt Mayor: Selected Writings & a Bibliography. Intro. by Polly Cone. (Illus.). 200p. 1983. 7.95 (0-87099-332-1) Metro Mus Art.

***A. I. A. Guide to Boston.** Michael Southworth & Susan Southworth. (Voyager Book Ser.). (Illus.). 544p. 1992. pap. 19.95 (1-56440-035-2) Globe Pequot.

A. I. D. S. A Bibliography. Robert D. Reed. 1986. pap. 11.00 (0-88247-757-9) R & E Pubs.

A. I. D. S. A Study. Loretta Kurban. 1991. pap. 8.00 (0-938863-23-1) Libra Press Chi.

A. I. D. S. Everything You Must Know about Acquired Immune Defiency Syndrome - the Killer Epidemic of the 80s. Janet Baker. LC 83-62309. (Illus.). 128p. 1983. 8.95 (0-88247-700-5) R & E Pubs.

A. I. D. S. How & Where to Find Facts & Do Research. Robert D. Reed. 1986. pap. 5.00 (0-88247-758-7) R & E Pubs.

A. I. D. S. Index of Modern Medical & Scientific Reviews Compiling 7000 References. American Health Research Institute Staff. Ed. by Alphonse R. Abell. LC 88-47537. 159p. 1990. 44.50 (0-88164-778-0); pap. 39.50 (0-88164-779-9) ABBE Pubs Assn.

A. I. D. S. Your Child & the School. Robert D. Reed & Danek Kaus. 1986. pap. 5.00 (0-88247-756-0) R & E Pubs.

A. I. D. S. Vol. I of XII: Index of Modern Authors & Scientific Reviews for Inclusions in Current Research, Pt. I of XII. American Health Research Institute Staff. LC 90-56331. 200p. 1991. 44.50 (1-55914-222-7); pap. 39.50 (1-55914-223-5) ABBE Pubs Assn.

A. I. D. S. Vol. III of XII: Index of Modern Authors & Scientific Reviews for Inclusions in Current Research, Pt. III of XII. American Health Research Institute Staff. LC 90-56331. 200p. 1991. 44.50 (1-55914-272-3); pap. 39.50 (1-55914-273-1) ABBE Pubs Assn.

A. I. D. S. Vol. IV of XII: Index of Modern Authors & Scientific Reviews for Inclusions in Current Research, Pt. IV of XII. American Health Research Institute Staff. LC 90-56331. 200p. 1991. 44.50 (1-55914-274-X); pap. 39.50 (1-55914-275-8) ABBE Pubs Assn.

A. I. D. S. Vol. IX of XII: Index of Modern Authors & Scientific Reviews for Inclusions in Current Research. American Health Research Institute Staff. LC 90-56331. 160p. 1991. 44.50 (1-55914-356-8); pap. 39.50 (1-55914-357-6) ABBE Pubs Assn.

A. I. D. S. Vol V of XII: Index of Modern Authors & Scientific Reviews for Inclusions in Current Research, Pt. V of XII. American Health Research Institute Staff. LC 90-56331. 200p. 1991. 44.50 (1-55914-298-7); pap. 39.50 (1-55914-299-5) ABBE Pubs Assn.

A. I. D. S. Vol. VI of XII: Index of Modern Authors & Scientific Reviews for Inclusions in Current Research, Pt. VI of XII. American Health Research Institute Staff. LC 90-56331. 200p. 1991. 44.50 (1-55914-300-2); pap. 39.50 (1-55914-301-0) ABBE Pubs Assn.

A. I. D. S. Vol. VII of XII: Index of Modern Authors & Scientific Reviews for Inclusions in Current Research. American Health Research Institute Staff. LC 90-56331. 160p. 1991. 44.50 (1-55914-324-X); pap. 39.50 (1-55914-325-8) ABBE Pubs Assn.

A. I. D. S. Vol. VIII of XII: Index of Modern Authors & Scientific Reviews for Inclusions in Current Research. American Health Research Institute Staff. LC 90-56331. 160p. 1991. 44.50 (1-55914-326-6); pap. 39.50 (1-55914-327-4) ABBE Pubs Assn.

A. I. D. S. Vol. X of XII: Index of Modern Authors & Scientific Reviews for Inclusions in Current Research. American Health Research Institute Staff. LC 90-56331. 160p. 1991. 44.50 (1-55914-388-6); pap. 39.50 (1-55914-389-4) ABBE Pubs Assn.

A. I. D. S. Vol. XI of XII: Index of Modern Authors & Scientific Reviews for Inclusions in Current Research, Part XI of XII. American Health Research Institute Staff. LC 90-56331. 200p. 1991. 44.50 (1-55914-444-0); pap. 39.50 (1-55914-445-9) ABBE Pubs Assn.

A. I. D. S. Vol. XII of XII: Index of Modern Authors & Scientific Reviews for Inclusions in Current Research, Part XII of XII. American Health Research Institute Staff. LC 90-56331. 200p. 1991. 44.50 (1-55914-456-4); pap. 39.50 (1-55914-457-2) ABBE Pubs Assn.

A. I. D. S. - Occurrence & Transmission: Medical Subject Analysis with Reference Bibliography. Martin D. Raber. LC 85-48178. 150p. 1986. 39.50 (0-88164-490-0); pap. 34.50 (0-88164-491-9) ABBE Pubs Assn.

A. I. D. S. & Its Therapy: Index of Modern Information. Scott E. Nyland. LC 90-182. 143p. 1990. 39.50 (1-55914-136-0); pap. 29.50 (1-55914-137-9) ABBE Pubs Assn.

A. I. S. I. Practical Guide to Census Bloopers. Ronald V. Jackson. 1990. 10.00 (0-89593-839-1) Accelerated Index.

A Is for Addiction. Cheryl S. Johnson & Richard L. Johnson. (Living Skills Ser.). 100p. 1993. teacher ed 4.95 (1-884245-13-7); student ed 2.95 (1-884245-14-5); pap. text ed. 4.95 (1-884245-12-9) Life Choices.

A Is for Adult: An Alphabet Book for Grown-Ups. Warren Hanson. 1993. pap. 5.95 (0-931674-24-7) Waldman Hse Pr.

A Is for Aesthetic: Essays on Creative & Aesthetic Education. Peter Abbs. 225p. 1989. 70.00 (1-85000-424-2, Falmer Pr); pap. 33.00 (1-85000-425-0, Falmer Pr) Taylor & Francis.

A Is for Africa. Ifeoma Onyefulu. LC 92-39964. (Illus.). 32p. (J). (ps-3). 1993. 14.99 (0-525-65147-0, Cobblehill Bks) Dutton Child Bks.

A Is for Africa: Looking at Africa Through the Alphabet. Ife Nii-owoo. LC 90-81575. (Young Reader's Ser.). (Illus.). 32p. (J). (ps-00). 1992. 12.95 (0-86543-182-5); pap. 5.95 (0-86543-183-3) Africa World.

A Is for Alibi. Sue Grafton. 224p. 1987. mass mkt. 5.99 (0-553-27991-2) Bantam.

A Is for Alibi. Sue Grafton. 288p. 1982. 21.95 (0-8050-1334-2) H Holt & Co.

A Is for Alibi. large type ed. Sue Grafton. 354p. 1991. pap. 15.95 (0-8161-5144-X) G K Hall.

A Is for Alibi. Sue Grafton. 1994. reprint ed. lib. bdg. 29.95 (1-56849-284-7) Buccaneer Bks.

A Is for All. Marian Winters. 1968. pap. 4.75 (0-8222-0000-7) Dramatists Play.

A Is for Alligator. Hallie Love. (Special Studies). (Illus.). 64p. (J). (gr. 1 up). 1993. 15.95 (1-879244-02-0) Windom Bks.

A Is for Aloha. Stephanie Feeney. LC 85-50569. (Illus.). 64p. (J). (ps-3). 1985. 8.95 (0-8248-0722-7) UH Pr.

A Is for Always. Lisa Jackson. 1994. mass mkt. 3.50 (0-373-09914-2, 1-09914-2) Harlequin Bks.

A Is for Angry: An Animal & Adjective Alphabet. Sandra Boynton. LC 83-40038. 48p. (J). (ps-00). 1987. pap. 5.95 (0-89480-507-X, 1507) Workman Pub.

A Is for Animals. David Pelham. (J). (ps). 1991. boxed 15.95 (0-671-72495-9, S&S Bks Young Read) S&S Childrens.

A Is for Animals. Gayle Shirley. (Illus.). 56p. (J). (ps-3). 1991. pap. 8.95 (1-56044-025-2) Falcon Pr MT.

A Is for Annabelle. Tasha Tudor. LC 60-15911. (Illus.). 64p. (J). (ps-1). 1988. reprint ed. pap. 5.95 (0-02-688534-4, Aladdin Paperbacks) S&S Childrens.

A Is for Apple. Sue Schildge. Ed. by Vernon Taylor. (Illus.). 140p. 1994. pap. 9.95 (1-878816-02-0) Schildge Pub.

A Is for Apple. Elizabeth Shaver. (Illus.). 36p. 1986. pap. 2.50 (0-317-56368-8) Shaker Her Soc.

A Is for Art. Ed. by Marjorie Moon. (Illus.). (Orig.). (J). (ps-2). 1988. pap. 10.95 (0-317-91187-2) M Moon.

A Is for Art, an Alphabetical Tour of the Milwaukee Art Museum. Marjorie N. Moon. 1988. pap. 10.95 (0-9620834-0-2) M Moon.

***A Is for Astronaut: My First Lift-the-Flap ABC.** Sian Tucker. (Illus.). (J). (ps). 1995. 11.95 (0-671-51086-X, Litl Simon S&S) S&S Childrens.

A Is for Ox. Barry Sanders. 288p. 1994. 23.00 (0-679-41711-7) Pantheon.

A. J. Cook. Paul Davies. (Lives of the Left Ser.). 224p. 1988. text ed. 45.00 (0-7190-2160-X, Pub. by Manchester Univ Pr UK) St Martin.

***A. J. Foyt.** Josh Wilker. LC 95-8237. (Race Car Legends Ser.). (J). 1996. write for info. (0-7910-3178-0); pap. write for info. (0-7910-3179-9) Chelsea Hse.

A. J. Gordon: Su Vida y Su Obra: Life & Work of A. J. Gordon. Ernesto B. Gordon. (SPA.). 6.95 (84-7645-282-9, 223336, Pub. by Edit Clie SP) TSELF.

A. J. Lindstrom. O. N. Olson. LC 58-2906. (Augustana Historical Society Publication Ser.: Vol. 16). 47p. 1957. pap. 3.00 (0-910184-16-X) Augustana.

A. J. M. Smith: An Annotated Bibliography. Anne Burke. 103p. (C). 1983. pap. text ed. 9.00 (0-920763-66-9, Pub. by ECW Press CN) Genl Dist Srvs.

A. J. M. Smith & His Works. Michael Darling. (Illus.). 56p. (C). 1990. pap. text ed. 9.95 (1-55022-026-8, Pub. by ECW Press CN) Genl Dist Srvs.

***A. J. Munnings.** Stanley Booth. (Illus.). 50p. Date not set. pap. 25.00 (0-85667-325-0) Scala Books.

A. J. Muste: Pacifist & Prophet. Jo Ann Robinson. Ed. by Eleanore P. Mather. LC 81-80219. 31p. 1981. pap. 3.00 (0-87574-235-1) Pendle Hill.

A. J. P. Taylor: The Traitor Within the Gates. Robert Cole. LC 93-13506. 1993. text ed. 39.95 (0-312-10066-3) St Martin.

A. J. Tomlinson. Lillie Duggar. 1964. 15.95 (0-934942-00-5) White Wing Pub.

A. James Manchin: A Biography of Controversy. Greg Icenhower. Ed. by Bob Teets. (Illus.). 224p. 1990. 16.95 (0-929915-03-8) Headline Bks.

A. J.'s Mom Gets a New Job. Lawrence Balter. (Stepping Stone Stories Ser.). (Illus.). 40p. (J). (gr. 3-7). 1990. 5.95 (0-8120-6151-9) Barron.

A. K. A. Bob Perelman. 1984. per. 9.00 (0-935724-18-4) Figures.

A K A Ducks. R. Tow, Jr. LC 93-70247. 214p. 1993. 20.00 (0-9627936-1-2) Bk Elan.

A. K. A. Katherine Walden. Ellen Feldman. 1990. mass mkt. 4.50 (0-440-10219-7) Dell.

A. K. A. Narc. Ray Brown & Raymond Angus. 256p. (Orig.). 1991. mass mkt. 4.95 (0-671-69261-5) PB.

***A. K. A. Ruby Brooklyn.** Maria Rand. (Illus.). 390p. (Orig.). 1994. pap. 13.95 (0-9642457-3-6) Goddesses We Aint.

A-K (German-English) Part II, Vol. 1 see Langenscheidt New Muret-Sanders Encyclopedic Dictionary

***A. K.'s Fly Box.** A. K. Best. (Illus.). 224p. 1996. 35.00 (1-55821-362-7) Lyons & Burford.

A. L. Williams Replacement Empire. Joseph M. Belth. LC 86-27715. 64p. (Orig.). 1987. pap. 10.00 (0-941173-00-3) Insur Forum.

A la Aspen. Catherine G. Crabtree. (Illus.). 190p. (Orig.). 1978. pap. 12.95 (0-937070-00-9) Crabtree.

A la Aspen: Restaurant Recipes. rev. ed. Catherine G. Crabtree. Date not set. pap. 12.95 (0-937070-05-X) Crabtree.

A la Carte. Lou Greenstein. LC 92-27132. 1992. 34.95 (0-86636-184-7) PBC Intl Inc.

A la Carte: A Tour of Dining History. Lou Greenstein. 1994. pap. 24.95 (0-86636-240-1) PBC Intl Inc.

A la Carte Enterprises: Office Manual. M. J. Ruey. 1976. text ed. 12.75 (0-07-054266-X) McGraw.

A la Decouverte de la France. M. Bonneau & E. Bonneau. (C). 1981. 30.00 (0-7175-0904-4, Pub. by S Thornes Pubs UK) St Mut.

A la Decouverte de Paris. K. Heurlin. (C). 1983. 30.00 (0-7175-1006-9, Pub. by S Thornes Pubs UK) St Mut.

A la Francaise: Correct French for English Speakers. Marie G. Geno & Barbara M. Schegerin. Ed. by Alton O. Roberts. (UVM Curriculum Ser.). 353p. (C). 1987. pap. text ed. 15.95 (0-318-24034-3, U0974) Hatier Pub.

***A la Gloire de l'Image et Art Poetique Con Quince Litografias de Zao Wou-Ki.** deluxe limited ed. Roger Caillois. (Ediciones Especiales y de Bibliofilo Ser.). (Illus.). 128p. (FRE.). 1993. 7,500.00 (84-343-0241-1) Elliots Bks.

A la Ingerencia Extrana la Virtud Domestica: Biografia de Manuel Marquez Sterling. Carlos Marquez-Sterling. LC 86-81071. (Coleccion Cuba y Sus Jueces Ser.). (Illus.). 267p. (Orig.). (SPA.). 1986. pap. 12.00 (0-89729-425-4) Ediciones.

A la Mode: Women's Fashions in French Art, 1850-1900. Maura Feeney. (Illus.). 35p. 1982. pap. 2.00 (0-931102-13-8) S & F Clark Art.

A la New Orleans: Restaurant Recipes. Michael Grady. (Orig.). 1980. pap. 12.95 (0-937070-02-5) Crabtree.

***A la Ofensiva.** Eduardo De Acha. LC 94-72068. (Coleccion Cuba y Sus Jueces). 82p. (Orig.). (SPA.). 1994. pap. 9.95 (0-89729-746-6) Ediciones.

A la Page: Culture et Litterature. Elisabeth Marlow & Veronique Morrison. 320p. (C). 1985. pap. text ed. 22.75 (0-03-063244-7) HB Coll Pubs.

A la Page - Grammaire. 4th ed. Elisabeth Marlow & Veronique Morrison. 240p. (C). 1985. pap. text ed. 26.75 (0-03-063246-3) HB Coll Pubs.

A la Premiere Personne: Voix Intimes. Ronni L. Gordon & David M. Stillman. 224p. (FRE.). (C). 1990. pap. text ed. 18.75 (0-03-028764-2) HB Coll Pubs.

A la Recherche de la Memoire: Le Patrimoine Culturel Actes du Colloque Organise par la Section des Bibliotheques d'Art de l'IFLA, Paris, 16-19 Aout 1989. Ed. by Huguette Rouit & Jean-Marcel Humbert. (IFLA Publication Ser.: Vol. 62). 330p. 1992. lib. bdg. 65.00 (3-598-21790-0) K G Saur.

A la Recherche de la Topologie Perdue. Lucien Guillou & Alexis Marin. (Progress in Mathematics Ser.: Vol. 62). 272p. 1986. 49.50 (0-8176-3329-4) Birkhauser.

***A la Recherche des Mots: French Edition of the Word-Finding Program.** Daniel J. Carlson. Ed. by Chantal Desmarais. Tr. by Lise Archambault. 137p. (FRE.). 1993. pap. text ed. 64.00 (0-9609464-9-7) Imaginart Pr.

A la Recherche du Temps Perdu, 4 vols., Vol. 1. Marcel Proust. Ed. by Jacques Tadie. 1987. lib. bdg. 145.00 (0-7859-3879-6) Fr & Eur.

A la Recherche du Temps Perdu, Vol. 1. deluxe ed. Marcel Proust. (Pleiade Ser.). 400p. (FRE.). 1969. 89.95 (2-07-011126-1) Schoenhof.

A la Recherche du Temps Perdu, Vol. 2. Marcel Proust. Ed. by Jean-Yves Tadie. (FRE.). 1988. lib. bdg. 145.00 (0-7859-3882-6) Fr & Eur.

A la Recherche du Temps Perdu, Vol. 2. deluxe ed. Marcel Proust. (Pleiade Ser.). 376p. (FRE.). 1969. 89.95 (2-07-011136-9) Schoenhof.

A la Recherche du Temps Perdu, Vol. 3. Marcel Proust. Ed. by Jean-Yves Tadie. (FRE.). 1988. lib. bdg. 150.00 (0-7859-3884-2) Fr & Eur.

A la Recherche du Temps Perdu, Vol. 3. deluxe ed. Marcel Proust. (Pleiade Ser.). 488p. (FRE.). 1969. 89.95 (2-07-011143-1) Schoenhof.

A la Recherche du Temps Perdu, Vol. 4. Marcel Proust. Ed. by Jean-Yves Tadie. (FRE.). 1989. lib. bdg. 155.00 (0-7859-3886-9) Fr & Eur.

A la Recherche du Temps Perdu, Vol. 4. deluxe ed. Marcel Proust. (Pleiade Ser.). 504p. (FRE.). 1989. 89.95 (2-07-011164-4) Schoenhof.

A la Recherche du Temps Perdu see Oeuvres

***A la Rencontre de Philippe.** Gilberte Furstenberg. 1993. student ed 295.00 (0-300-05695-8); teacher ed 35.00 (0-300-05650-8); 15.00 (0-300-05693-1); vdisk 185.00 (0-300-05691-5) Yale U Pr.

A la Rencontre des Mots: Methode d'Analyse et d'Acquisition du Vocabulaire. Jacques Bourgeacq. 274p. (Orig.). (C). 1993. pap. text ed. 27.50 (0-8191-9116-7) U Pr of Amer.

A la Rose. Kay Cameron. 84p. 1988. pap. 4.95 (1-879945-02-9) Katydid Pubns.

A la San Francisco: Restaurant Recipes. Catherine G. Crabtree. (Illus.). 240p. (Orig.). 1980. pap. 12.95 (0-937070-01-7) Crabtree.

A la Seattle: Restaurant Recipes. (Orig.). 1987. pap. 12.95 (0-937070-08-4) Crabtree.

***A La Sombra del Roble: La Empresa Privada Familiar y Su Continuidad. Ernesto Poza-Valle. (Illus.). 168p. (SPA.). 1995. 25.00 (0-9645105-9-6) Ed Univ Para.**
A LA SOMBRA DEL ROBLE: LA EMPRESA PRIVADA FAMILIAR Y SU CONTINUIDAD is "must reading for Spanish-speaking entrepreneurs & family business owners in the US, Latin America, & Spain" So says ROGER NAGER, EXECUTIVE DIRECTOR, ARTHUR ANDERSEN CENTER FOR FAMILY BUSINESS. Did you know that between 70 & 88% of these businesses will not survive into the next generation? Not because of government regulation or global competition. But because of the managerial practices established by the founding entrepreneur. About 50% of these firms were founded after WWII, so the majority will face succession in the next decade. How can business owners prevent becoming one of the statistics? "Turn to someone who has lived through many successions both in the US & Latin America", says DR. LEON DANCO, AUTHOR, BEYOND SURVIVAL. The competitive advantages of family-owned businesses are: emphasis on niches, quality, speed to market, agility given changing competitive dynamics & stock concentration. A LA SOMBRA DEL ROBLE gives practical advice on achieving competitive advantage, developing a growth strategy, assembling a board of directors, starting a family council & keeping family harmony. CONTACT EDITORIAL UNIVERSITARIA, 37300 JACKSON RD., CHAGRIN FALLS, OH, 44022, TEL/FAX (216) 247- 6353. ***Publisher Provided Annotation.***

A la Texas: Restaurant Recipes. Catherine G. Crabtree. 1986. spiral bd. 14.95 (0-937070-04-1) Crabtree.

A l'Ami Qui Ne M'A Pas Sauve la Vie. Herve Guibert. (Folio Ser.: No. 2366). (FRE.). pap. 9.95 (2-07-038503-5) Schoenhof.

A las Fuentes del Cristianismo: To the Fountain of Christianity. Samuel Vila. (SPA.). 1994. 5.95 (84-399-5767-X, 220418, Pub. by Edit Clie SP) TSELF.

A las Orillas del Rio Kwai. Ernest Gordon. Orig. Title: Miracle on the River Kwai. 320p. (SPA.). 1986. 6.95 (0-8297-0553-8) Life Pubs Intl.

A l'Ecoute de . . . Publicites Radio France. H. Jay Siskin. 1989. teacher ed 9.95 (0-934034-12-5); student ed, digital audio 12.95 (0-934034-11-7); audio 9.95 (0-934034-10-9) Olivia & Hill.

A-Level Chemistry. E. N. Ramsden. 784p. (C). 1988. pap. 95.00 (0-85950-154-X, Pub. by S Thornes Pubs UK) St Mut.

A-Level Law. 2nd ed. A. M. Dugdale et al. 664p. 1992. pap. 26.00 (0-406-00267-3, UK) Butterworth Legal Pubs.

A-Level Physics. R. Muncaster. (C). 1989. text ed. 140.00 (0-7487-0050-1, Pub. by S Thornes Pubs UK) St Mut.

***A-Level Physics.** Roger Muncaster. 960p. (C). 1994. pap. 57.00x (0-7478-1584-4, Pub. by S Thornes Pubs UK) St Mut.

A. Lincoln: His Last Twenty Four Hours. W. Emerson Reck. LC 85-43587. 240p. 1987. lib. bdg. 23.95x (0-89950-216-4) McFarland & Co.

A. Lincoln: His Last Twenty-Four Hours. W. Emerson Reck. (Illus.). 256p. (C). 1994. reprint ed. pap. 14.95 (1-57003-008-1) U of SC Pr.

A l'Ombre de Rimbaud. Alexandre L. Amprimoz. (Stanford French & Italian Studies: Vol. 43). 86p. (Orig.). (FRE.). 1986. pap. 46.50 (0-915838-58-3) Anma Libri.

A l'Ombre des Jeunes Filles en Fleurs. Marcel Proust. 492p. (FRE.). 1992. pap. 24.95 (0-7859-1639-3, 2070724913) Fr & Eur.

A l'Ombre des Jeunes Filles en Fleurs. Marcel Proust. (Folio Ser.: No. 1946). 568p. (FRE.). 1988. pap. 12.95 (2-07-038051-3, 1428) Schoenhof.

A l'Ombre des Jeunes Filles en Fleurs, Vol. 9. Marcel Proust. 1965. 12.95 (0-685-74005-6, F52240) Fr & Eur.

A l'Ombre des Jeunes Filles en Fleurs, Bk. 2: A la Recherche du Temps Perdu. Marcel Proust. (FRE.). 1972. pap. 13.95 (0-8288-3758-9, F119540) Fr & Eur.

A los Que Dios Ha Juntado En Matrimonio. David R. Mace. 96p. 1986. reprint ed. pap. 3.50 (0-311-40036-1, Edit Mundo) Casa Bautista.

An Asterisk (*) at the beginning of an entry indicates that the title is appearing in BIP for the first time.

A

An Asterisk (*) at the beginning of an entry indicates that the title is appearing in BIP for the first time.

3

A

***A-Z of Applied Quality for Clinical Managers in Hospitals.** Ed. by D. Barnett & N. Kemp. 176p. 1994. 38.25 (*1-56593-376-1*, 0671) Singular Publishing.

***A-Z of Applied Quality for Clinical Managers in Hospitals.** Chris Code & Dave J. Muller. 400p. 1995. pap. 75.00 (*1-56593-139-4*, 1150) Singular Publishing.

A-Z of Astronomy. Patrick Moore. (Illus.). (Orig.). 1987. pap. 13.50 (*0-393-30505-8*) Norton.

A-Z of Cars of the 1920s. (Illus.). 224p. 1994. 39.95 (*1-870979-48-6*, Pub. by Bay View Bks UK) Motorbooks Intl.

***A-Z of Cars of the 1920s.** Nick Baldwin. 1994. 39.95 (*1-870979-53-2*, Pub. by Bay View Bks UK) Motorbooks Intl.

A-Z of Cars of the 1930s. Michael Sedgewick & Mark Gillies. (Illus.). 216p. 1993. pap. 19.95 (*1-870979-38-9*, Pub. by Bay View Bks UK) Motorbooks Intl.

A-Z of Cars of the 1970s. Graham Robson. (Illus.). 216p. 1993. pap. 19.95 (*1-870979-40-0*) Motorbooks Intl.

A-Z of Cars of the 1980s. Martin Lewis. (Illus.). 160p. 1994. 32.95 (*1-870979-54-0*, Pub. by Bay View Bks UK) Motorbooks Intl.

***A-Z of Child Development.** Richard Woolfson. 1995. pap. 12.95 (*0-285-63163-2*) Atrium Pubs.

A-Z of Collectors' Terms. Therle Hughes. 1993. 5.98 (*1-55521-819-9*) Bk Sales Inc.

A-Z of Companion Planting. Pamela Allardice. (Illus.). 208p. (Orig.). 1993. pap. 18.00 (*0-207-17424-5*, Pub. by Angus & Robertson AT) HarpC.

A-Z of Counselling Theory & Practice. William Stewart. LC 92-23363. 1992. write for info. (*1-56593-055-X*) Singular Publishing.

A-Z of Cut Flowers: Fresh & Dried. Gilly Love. (Illus.). 192p. 1994. 22.95 (*0-670-85226-0*, Viking) Viking Penguin.

A-Z of Deciduous Trees & Shrubs. Reader's Digest Editors. LC 94-13100. (Successful Gardening Ser.). (Illus.). 176p. 1994. 18.98 (*0-89577-615-4*) RD Assn.

A-Z of European Brands, 1990. Ed. by Euromonitor Staff. 375p. 1991. 150.00 (*0-86338-465-X*, Pub. by Europa Pubns UK) Omnigraphics Inc.

***A-Z of Evergreen Trees & Shrubs.** Reader's Digest Editors. LC 94-47610. (Successful Gardening Ser.). (Illus.). 176p. 1995. 18.98 (*0-89577-698-7*) RD Assn.

***A-Z of Film, Television & Video Terms.** Alex Bushby. 128p. 1994. 16.95 (*0-948905-89-1*) Chapman & Hall.

A-Z of Horse Diseases & Health Problems: Signs-Diagnoses-Causes-Treatment. Tim Hawcroft. Ed. by Sean Frawley. 312p. 1990. 22.50 (*0-87605-884-5*) Howell Bk.

A-Z of House Plants. Carole Johnson-Barker & Kristo Pienaar. (Illus.). 128p. (C). 1989. 135.00 (*1-85368-061-3*, Pub. by New Holland Pubs UK) St Mut.

A-Z of Microwave Cooking. Mary Klinzman & Shirley Guy. 240p. (C). 1988. 110.00 (*1-85368-011-7*, Pub. by New Holland Pubs UK) St Mut.

***A-Z of Natural Therapies.** Judy Jacka. 333p. (Orig.). 1995. pap. 14.95 (*0-85091-293-8*, Pub. by Lothian Pub AT) Seven Hills Bk.

A-Z of Nuclear Jargon. Jonathon Green. 224p. 1986. text ed. 37.50 (*0-7102-0641-0*, 06410, RKP) Routledge.

A-Z of Offshore Oil & Gas: An Illustrated International Glossary & Reference Guide to the Offshore Oil & Gas Industries & Their Technology. 2nd ed. Harry Whitehead. LC 82-84656. 438p. 1983. reprint ed. pap. 124.90 (*0-8357-2652-5*, 2040184) Bks Demand.

A-Z of Opera. Mary Hamilton. 224p. 1990. 22.95 (*0-8160-2340-9*) Facts on File.

A-Z of Perennials. Reader's Digest Editors. LC 93-26149. (Successful Gardening Ser.). (Illus.). 176p. 1993. 18.98 (*0-89577-554-9*) RD Assn.

A-Z of Practical Advice for Women after Breast Cancer Surgery. 5th ed. Maria Hussain & E. Mayer-Spitzweck. (Illus.). 121p. (Orig.). 1993. pap. text ed. 17.50 (*3-88603-473-9*, Pub. by W Zuckschwerdt GW) Scholium Intl.

A-Z of Psychic Secrets. Paul Summers. Ed. by Thorguard Templar. 105p. (Orig.). 1993. 25.00 (*1-883147-85-9*) Intern Guild ASRS.

A-Z of Sailing Terms. abr. ed. Ed. by Ian Dear & Peter Kemp. (Oxford Paperback Reference Ser.). (Illus.). 224p. 1992. pap. 11.95 (*0-19-286147-6*) OUP.

A-Z of Sewing Machine. Maxine Henry. (Illus.). 128p. 1994. pap. 19.95 (*0-7134-7324-X*, Pub. by Batsford UK) Trafalgar.

A-Z of Ships Badges, 1919-1989, Vol. 1. Maritime Books Staff. (C). 1986. text ed. 100.00 (*0-685-38766-6*, Pub. by Maritime Bks UK) St Mut.

A-Z of Ships Badges, 1919-1989, Vol. 2. Maritime Books Staff. (C). 1986. text ed. 100.00 (*1-870842-02-2*, Pub. by Maritime Bks UK) St Mut.

A-Z of Sports Cars since 1945. Mike Lawrence. (Illus.). 256p. 1991. 39.95 (*1-870979-23-0*) Motorbooks Intl.

A-Z of the Middle East. Alain Gresh & Dominique Vidal. Tr. by Bob Cumming. LC 90-12983. 288p. (C). 1990. pap. 15.00 (*0-86232-881-0*, Pub. by Zed Books UK) Humanities.

A-Z of U. K. Brands. Euromonitor Staff. (C). 1990. 300.00 (*0-86338-324-6*, Pub. by Euromonitor Pubns UK) Gale.

A-Z of U. K. Marketing Data. Euromonitor Staff. (C). 1990. 300.00 (*0-86338-191-X*, Pub. by Euromonitor Pubns UK) Gale.

A-Z of U. K. Marketing Data 1985. 256p. 1985. 180.00 (*0-903706-83-0*, Pub. by Euromonitor Pubns UK) St Mut.

A-Z of Video & Audio - Visual Jargon. Suzan St. Maur. 192p. 1986. pap. 32.50 (*0-7102-0640-2*, 06402, RKP) Routledge.

A-Z of Woman's Sexuality. Ada P. Kahn & Linda H. Holt. (Illus.). 272p. 1990. 24.95 (*0-8160-1996-7*) Facts on File.

A-Z of Women's Health. 2nd ed. Derek Llewellyn-Jones. (Oxford Paperback Reference Ser.). (Illus.). 272p. 1990. pap. 14.95 (*0-19-286112-3*) OUP.

A-Z of Works Ralley Cars. Graham Robson. (Illus.). 176p. 1994. 32.95 (*1-870979-42-7*, Pub. by Bay View Bks UK) Motorbooks Intl.

***A-Z Reference Book of Childhood Conditions.** Patricia Gilbert. 160p. (Orig.). (C). 1995. pap. text ed. 44.75 (*1-56593-332-X*, 0662) Singular Publishing.

A Zenei Iras - Olvasas Modszertana see Musical Reading & Writing: Teacher's Manual

***A-3 Skywarrior in Action.** Jim Sullivan. (Aircraft in Action Ser.). (Illus.). 50p. 1995. pap. 8.95 (*0-89747-328-0*) Squad Sig Pubns.

***A-6 Intruder in Action.** Joe Michaels. (Aircraft in Action Ser.). (Illus.). 50p. Date not set. pap. 8.95 (*0-89747-302-7*) Squad Sig Pubns.

***A-10 "Mini" in Action.** Ken Neubeck. (Mini in Action Ser.). (Illus.). 50p. 1995. pap. 5.95 (*0-89747-335-3*) Squad Sig Pubns.

A-10 Thunderbolt. Bill Sweetman. (Combat Aircraft Ser.). 1992. 9.99 (*0-517-06738-2*) Random Hse Value.

A-10 Warthog. Dana Bell. Ed. by Terry Spohn. LC 93-1019. (Detail & Scale Ser.: Vol. 19). (Illus.). 72p. 1993. reprint ed. pap. 11.95 (*0-89024-171-6*) Kalmbach.

A-10 Warthog, Vol. 19. (Detail & Scale Ser.). (Illus.). 72p. 10.95 (*0-8306-8030-6*, 25030) TAB Bks.

A-10 Warthog in Action. (Aircraft in Action Ser.). (Illus.). 50p. 1984. pap. 8.95 (*0-89747-122-9*, 1049) Squad Sig Pubns.

A-10 Warthog (The Tank Killer) in Detail & Scale. Dana Bell. Ed. by Ernest J. Gentle. (Detail & Scale Ser.: Vol. 19). (Illus.). 72p. (Orig.). pap. 8.95 (*0-8168-5030-5*, 25030, TAB-Aero) TAB Bks.

***A-20 Havoc in Action.** Jim Mesko. (Aircraft in Action Ser.). (Illus.). 50p. 1994. pap. 8.95 (*0-89747-317-5*) Squad Sig Pubns.

A-26 Invader in Action. Jim Mesko. (Aircraft in Action Ser.). (Illus.). 50p. 1993. pap. 8.95 (*0-89747-296-9*, 1134) Squad Sig Pubns.

A-37 - T-37 Dragonfly in Action. Terry Love. (Aircraft in Action Ser.). (Illus.). 50p. 1991. pap. 8.95 (*0-89747-239-X*, 1114) Squad Sig Pubns.

***A-6 Walk Around.** Lou Drendel. (Walk Around Ser.). (Illus.). 80p. 1994. pap. 14.95 (*0-89747-327-2*) Squad Sig Pubns.

A-7 Corsair II Pt. I. William G. Holder. (Colors & Markings Ser.). (Illus.). 1990. pap. 10.95 (*0-8306-3452-5*) TAB Bks.

A-7 Corsair II Pt. III: USAF & Ang Versions Colors & Markings. Bert Kinzey. (Colors & Markings Ser.: Vol. 19). 1991. pap. 12.95 (*0-8306-2151-2*) TAB Bks.

A-7 Corsair II in Action. Al Adcock. (Aircraft in Action Ser.). (Illus.). 50p. 1991. pap. 8.95 (*0-89747-272-1*, 1120) Squad Sig Pubns.

AA: The Way It Began. Bill Pittman. LC 87-73390. 252p. (Orig.). 1988. pap. 8.95 (*0-934125-08-2*) Glen Abbey Bks.

***AA - Ordnance Survey Leisure Guide: Cotswolds.** 1992. pap. text ed. 15.95 (*1-55650-515-9*) Hunter NJ.

***AA - Ordnance Survey Leisure Guide: Lake District.** 1992. pap. text ed. 15.95 (*1-55650-519-1*) Hunter NJ.

***AA - Ordnance Survey Leisure Guide: Scottish Highlands.** Automobile Staff. 1992. pap. text ed. 15.95 (*1-55650-518-3*) Hunter NJ.

Aa-Choo! Wendy Orr. (Illus.). 32p. (J). (ps-3). 1992. lib. bdg. 14.95 (*1-55037-209-2*, Pub. by Annick CN); pap. 4.95 (*1-55037-208-4*, Pub. by Annick CN) Firefly Bks Ltd.

AA Complete Book of London. Automobile Association of England Staff. 192p. 1992. 32.95 (*0-393-03369-4*) Norton.

AA Country Walks in Britain. Automobile Association of England Staff. 256p. 1992. 46.95 (*0-393-03064-4*) Norton.

AA en Prisiones: De Preso a Preso. Alcoholics Anonymous World Services, Inc., Staff. Orig. Title: AA in Prison: Inmate to Inmate. 136p. (SPA.). 1991. pap. 2.95 (*0-916856-46-1*) AAWS.

AA Grapevine Index. 333p. (Orig.). 1992. 40.00 (*0-933685-21-1*) A A Grapevine.

AA in Prison: Inmate to Inmate see AA en Prisiones: De Preso a Preso

A.A. Llega a Su Mayor Edad. 338p. (SPA.). 1975. pap. 3.15 (*0-916856-10-0*) AAWS.

AA Today. (Illus.). 111p. reprint ed. pap. 5.00 (*0-933685-15-7*) A A Grapevine.

AA Town Walks in Britain. (AA Ser.). (Illus.). 136p. (Orig.). 1991. pap. 16.95 (*1-55650-490-X*) Hunter NJ.

***AA Truck Supplement to Restorer's Model a Shop Manual.** Jim Schild. (Illus.). 96p. (Orig.). 1993. pap. 12.95 (*0-9624958-5-9*) Natl Archery.

AA-1025: The Memoirs of an Anti-Apostle. Marie Carre. LC 91-75254. 135p. 1991. reprint ed. pap. 4.00 (*0-89555-449-6*) TAN Bks Pubs.

***AAA: The Complete Guide to the Finest Hotels & Restaurants.** AAA Staff. 1995. pap. 17.95 (*1-56251-144-0*) AAA.

AAA All-in-One Guides. 1989. 12.95 (*0-685-25922-6*, Collier S&S) S&S Trade.

AAA Autotest, 1991. 1991. write for info. (*0-916748-64-2*, Collier S&S) S&S Trade.

AAA Autotest, 1994. American Automobile Association Staff. 1993. pap. 12.95 (*1-56251-091-6*) AAA.

AAA Autotest, 1995: The Autmotive Answer Book. American Automobile Association Staff. 1995. pap. 12.95 (*1-56251-136-X*) AAA.

AAA Bed & Breakfast: Britain 1992. American Automobile Association Staff. 472p. 1992. pap. 14.95 (*1-56251-021-5*) AAA.

AAA Bed & Breakfast Britain, 1994. American Automobile Association Staff. 1994. pap. 14.95 (*1-56251-094-0*) AAA.

AAA Bed & Breakfast Britain, 1995. American Automobile Association Staff. 1995. pap. 14.95 (*1-56251-140-8*) AAA.

AAA Britain for Free, 1992. American Automobile Assn. Staff. 161p. 1992. pap. 12.95 (*1-56251-000-2*) AAA.

AAA Britain Road Atlas, 1993. American Automobile Association Staff. (Illus.). 92p. 1993. pap. 18.95 (*1-56251-065-7*) AAA.

AAA Britain Road Atlas, 1995. American Automobile Assocation Staff. 1995. pap. 18.95 (*1-56251-137-8*) AAA.

AAA Car Buyer's Handbook! James A. Boerger. 1990. write for info. (*0-916748-66-9*, Collier S&S) S&S Trade.

AAA Caribbean Travelbook, 1995. American Automobile Association Staff. 1994. pap. 7.95 (*1-56251-143-2*) AAA.

AAA Europe Road Atlas, 1993. American Automobile Association Staff. (Illus.). 128p. 1993. pap. 18.95 (*1-56251-067-3*) AAA.

AAA Europe Road Atlas, 1995. American Automobile Association Staff. 1995. pap. 18.95 (*1-56251-139-4*) AAA.

AAA Europe Travelbook, 1994. American Automobile Association Staff. 1994. pap. 9.95 (*1-56251-087-8*) AAA.

AAA Europe Travelbook, 1995. American Automobile Association Staff. 1994. pap. 9.95 (*1-56251-142-4*) AAA.

AAA France Road Atlas, 1993. American Automobile Association Staff. 1993. pap. 18.95 (*1-56251-066-5*) AAA.

AAA France Road Atlas, 1995. American Automobile Association Staff. 1995. pap. 18.95 (*1-56251-138-6*) AAA.

AAA Guide to National Parks. American Autobomile Association Staff. LC 92-27001. 336p. 1994. pap. 15.00 (*0-02-062049-7*, Collier S&S) S&S Trade.

AAA Guide to North America's Theme Parks. (Illus.). 240p. 1991. pap. 10.95 (*0-02-030250-9*, Collier S&S) S&S Trade.

AAA Mexico Travelbook 1994. American Automobile Association Staff. 1993. pap. 9.95 (*1-56251-088-6*) AAA.

AAA Mexico Travelbook, 1995. American Automobile Association Staff. 1994. pap. 11.95 (*1-56251-141-6*) AAA.

AAA-Ninety-One: Proceedings of the Ninth National Conference on Artificial Intelligence, 2 vols., Set. Ed. by American Assoc. for Artificial Intelligence Staff. (AAAI Press Ser.). (Illus.). 900p. 1991. pap. 75.00 (*0-262-51059-6*) MIT Pr.

AAA North American Road Atlas. 1989. write for info. (*0-318-65176-9*) Macmillan.

***AAA North American Road Atlas 1995.** AAA Staff. 1994. pap. 7.95 (*1-56251-131-9*) AAA.

AAA Photo Journey to New York City. American Automobile Assn. Staff. (Illus.). 96p. 1992. pap. 12.95 (*1-56251-012-6*) AAA.

AAA Photo Journey to Orlando & Central Florida. American Automobile Assn. Staff. (Illus.). 96p. 1992. pap. 12.95 (*1-56251-013-4*) AAA.

AAA Photo Journey to San Francisco. American Automobile Assn. Staff. (Illus.). 96p. 1992. pap. 12.95 (*1-56251-014-2*) AAA.

AAA Photo Journey to Washington, D.C. American Automobile Assn. Staff. (Illus.). 96p. 1992. pap. 12.95 (*1-56251-011-8*) AAA.

AAA Pocket Atlas: Germany & Benelux. American Automobile Association Staff. (Illus.). 1994. pap. 9.95 (*1-56251-035-5*) AAA.

AAA Pocket Atlas: Italy, Austria & Switzerland. American Automobile Association Staff. (Illus.). 1994. pap. 9.95 (*1-56251-033-9*) AAA.

AAA Pocket Atlas: Spain & Portugal. American Automobile Association Staff. (Illus.). 1994. pap. 9.95 (*1-56251-034-7*) AAA.

AAA Pocket Atlas, 1992: Britain. American Automobile Association Staff. (Illus.). 96p. 1992. pap. 9.95 (*1-56251-003-7*) AAA.

AAA Pocket Atlas, 1992: France. American Automobile Association Staff. (Illus.). 96p. 1992. pap. 9.95 (*1-56251-004-5*) AAA.

AAA Pocket Atlas, 1992: London. American Automobile Association Staff. (Illus.). 96p. 1992. pap. 9.95 (*1-56251-005-3*) AAA.

AAA Road Atlas, 1988. American Automobile Association Staff. 1987. pap. 5.95 (*0-317-66546-4*) Random.

AAA Road Atlas, 1995: United States, Canada Mexico. American Automobile Association Staff. 1994. pap. 7.95 (*1-56251-128-9*) AAA.

AAA Travel Activity Book: The Official AAA Fun Book for Kids. (Illus.). 144p. (J). (gr. k-6). 1990. 4.95 (*0-02-689512-9*, Collier S&S) S&S Trade.

AAA Travel Activity Book: The Official AAA Fun Book for Kids. Tom Koken et al. (Illus.). 144p. (J). 1990. pap. 4.95 (*1-56288-071-3*) Checkerboard.

AAA Travel Guide to Europe. American Automobile Association Staff. 568p. 1987. pap. 8.95 (*0-317-63131-4*) Random.

***AAA-USAC National Midget Auto Racing Hall of Fame.** Ed Watson. (Illus.). 160p. (Orig.). 1995. pap. 20.00 (*0-9627653-4-1*) Witness Prods.

***AAAI - 94: Proceedings of the Twelfth National Conference on Artificial Intelligence.** American Association for Arti. Staff. 1994. pap. 85.00x (*0-262-51078-2*) MIT Pr.

AAAI 92 Proceedings of the Tenth National Conference on AI. Ed. by AAAI Press Staff. (Illus.). 1000p. 1992. pap. 75.00 (*0-262-51063-4*) MIT Pr.

AAAI 93: Proceedings of the Eleventh National Conference on Artificial Intelligence. Ed. by AAAI Press Staff. (Illus.). 1000p. 1993. pap. 75.00 (*0-262-51071-5*) MIT Pr.

AAAS Handbook, 93-94: Officers Organization Activities. 1993. pap. 10.95 (*0-87168-542-6*) AAAS.

AAAS Report XVII: Research & Development FY 1993. Intersociety Working Group Staff. 340p. 1992. 16.95 (*0-87168-441-1*, 92-10S) AAAS.

AAAS Science & Technology Policy Yearbook 1991. Meredith et al. 432p. 1991. 19.95 (*0-87168-427-6*, 91-34S) AAAS.

AAAS Science & Technology Policy Yearbook, 1992. Ed. by Stephen D. Nelson et al. 400p. 1993. pap. 19.95 (*0-87168-503-5*, 92-24S) AAAS.

AAAS Science & Technology Policy Yearbook, 1993. Ed. by Albert H. Teich. 414p. 1994. pap. 19.95 (*0-87168-534-5*) AAAS.

AAAS Science Book List for Children: A Selected & Annotated List of Science & Mathematics Books for Children in Elementary Schools, & for Children's Collections in Public Libraries. 3rd ed. Hilary J. Deason. LC 75-169601. (AAAS Miscellaneous Publication Ser.: No. 72-1). 267p. reprint ed. pap. 76.10 (*0-7837-0057-1*, 2040304) Bks Demand.

AAAS Science Book List Supplement. Ed. by Kathryn Wolff & Jill Storey. LC 78-6540. (AAAS Publication Ser.: No. 78-5). 475p. reprint ed. pap. 135.40 (*0-7837-0058-X*, 2040305) Bks Demand.

AACE Recommended Practices & Standards. 1991. ring bd. 185.00 (*0-317-04230-0*) AACE Intl.

AACJC Membership Directory, 1992. Lela Sellis. Ed. by Jim Mahoney. 1992. 44.00 (*0-87117-242-9*) Am Assn Comm Coll.

AACJC Statistical Yearbook. Lela Sellis. Ed. by Jim Mahoney. 1992. 44.00 (*0-87117-243-7*) Am Assn Comm Coll.

AACJC Statistical Yearbook, 1991. Ed. by Jim Mahoney & Lela Sallis. 1991. 38.50 (*0-87117-233-X*, 1321) Am Assn Comm Coll.

AACN Financial Management. Bertram. 303p. 1991. 30.95 (*0-8016-6537-X*) Mosby Yr Bk.

AACN Managing the Environment. Spicer. 208p. 1990. pap. 28.95 (*0-8016-6536-1*) Mosby Yr Bk.

AACN Personnel Management. Cardin. 248p. 1989. pap. 27.95 (*0-8016-6538-8*) Mosby Yr Bk.

AACN Procedure Manual for Critical Care. 3rd ed. American Association for Critical Care Nurses Staff. Ed. by Rochelle L. Boggs & Maribeth Wooldridge-King. (Illus.). 976p. 1993. pap. text ed. 55.50 (*0-7216-3073-1*) Saunders.

AACN Tissue & Organ Transplantation: Implications for Professional Nursing Practitioners. Smith. (Illus.). 368p. 1990. 44.95 (*0-8016-5526-9*) Mosby Yr Bk.

AACN's Clinical Reference for Critical-Care Nursing. Kinney et al. 1792p. 1988. 69.95 (*0-07-034721-2*) Mosby Yr Bk.

AACN's Clinical Reference for Critical Care Nursing. 3rd ed. Ed. by Marguerite Rodgera Kinney et al. LC 92-48549. 1993. 75.00 (*0-8016-6452-7*) Mosby Yr Bk.

AACN's Reference for Critical Care Nursing. Marguerite R. Kinney et al. (Illus.). 1981. text ed. 69.95 (*0-07-001133-8*) McGraw.

AACP Roster of Faculty & Professional Staff in Colleges of Pharmacy: Annual. 100.00 (*0-937526-00-2*) AACP Alexandria.

AACR, DDC, MARC & Friends: The Role of CIG in Bibliographic Control. Ed. by Byford et al. 130p. 1993. 55.00 (*1-85604-023-2*, LAP0232, Pub. by Lib Assn Pub UK) UNIPUB.

AACRAO Member Guide, 1992-93. American Association of Collegiate Registrars & Admissions Officers Staff. Ed. by Henrianne Wakefield. 300p. (Orig.). 1992. pap. text ed. 50.00 (*0-929851-13-7*) Am Assn Coll Registrars.

***AACRAO Strategic Enrollment Management Casebook.** American Association of Collegiate Registrars & Admissions Officers Staff. Ed. by Michael G. Dolence. LC 95-13756. 1995. write for info. (*0-929851-38-2*) Am Assn Coll Registrars.

AACRAO Survey of Grading Policies in Member Institutions: A Report. American Association of Collegiate Registrars & Admissions Officers Staff. 44p. 1971. reprint ed. pap. 25.00 (*0-8357-5002-7*, 2024078) Bks Demand.

AACR2 & Serials: The American View. Ed. by Neal L. Edgar. LC 83-8404. (Cataloging & Classification Quarterly Ser.: Vol. 3, Nos. 2 & 3). 154p. 1983. text ed. 49.95 (*0-86656-233-8*) Haworth Pr.

AACR2 Goes Public. Art Libraries Society of North America Staff. (Occasional Papers: No. 1). 64p. (Orig.). 1982. pap. 5.00 (*0-942740-00-9*) Art Libs Soc.

***AACTE Briefing Book, 1993.** 1994. 12.00 (*0-89333-118-X*) AACTE.

AADE Reference Manual for Evaluation of Diabetes Education Programs. American Association of Diabetes Educators Staff. 26p. 1982. pap. text ed. 4.00 (*0-686-39261-2*) Am Assn Diabetes Ed.

AAECC-10: Applied Algebra, Algebraic Algorithms, & Error-Correcting Codes - 10th International Symposium, San Juan de Puerto Rico, Puerto Rico, May 10-14, 1993 - Proceedings. Ed. by Gerard Cohen et al. LC 93-15375. (Lecture Notes in Computer Science Ser.: Vol. 673). 1993. 54.00 (*0-387-56686-4*) Spr-Verlag.

AAECC-5. Ed. by L. Huguet. (Lecture Notes in Computer Science Ser.: Vol. 356). vi, 419p. 1989. pap. 47.00 (*0-387-51082-6*, 3091) Spr-Verlag.

An Asterisk (*) at the beginning of an entry indicates that the title is appearing in BIP for the first time.

AAECC-6. Ed. by Teo Mora. (Lecture Notes in Computer Science Ser.: Vol. 357). ix, 481p. 1989. pap. 51.00 (0-387-51083-4, 3092) Spr-Verlag.

AAF-CIF Track & Field Coaches Manual. Amateur Athletic Foundation Staff. (Illus.). 223p. (C). 1994. pap. 34.95 (0-685-72202-3) Amateur Ath LA.

AAHA Directory of Members, 1995. rev. ed. American Association of Homes for the Aging Staff. LC 78-641009. 214p. (Orig.). 1986. pap. text ed. 50.00 (0-943774-31-4) Am Assn Homes.

AAI Policy Kit. 437p. 1991. 9.00 (0-686-95947-7) Alliance Am Insurers.

***A'aisa's Gifts: A Study of Magic & the Self.** Michele Stephen. LC 94-24807. 1995. 50.00 (0-520-08761-5); pap. 20.00 (0-520-08829-8) U CA Pr.

AALL Annual Meetings: An Annotated Index of the Recordings. Frank G. Houdek & Susan D. Goldner. LC 89-10120. (American Association of Law Libraries Publications Ser.: No. 32). 250p. 1989. ring bd. 37.50 (0-8377-0133-3) Rothman.

AALL Reference Book: A Compendium of Facts, Figures & Historical Information about the American Association of Law Libraries. Comp. by Frank G. Houdek. LC 94-18865. 1994. 55.00 (0-89941-893-7, 308160) W S Hein.

AALS Directory of Law Teachers. 1250p. 1994. pap. 200.00 (0-318-13403-9) Assn Am Law Schls.

***Aama in America: A Pilgrimage of the Heart.** Broughton Coburn. 1995. 22.95 (0-385-47417-2, Anchor NY) Doubleday.

***AAMI: Biological Evaluation of Medical Devices, 1995 Edition.** AAMI Staff. (Standards & Recommended Practices Ser.). (Illus.). 216p. (Orig.). 1995. pap. 165.00 (1-57020-032-7, BIOT2-177) Assn Adv Med Instrn.

***AAMI: Breakthrough Management: A New Model for Hospital Technical Services.** AAMI Staff. (Illus.). 46p. (Orig.). 1995. pap. 118.00 (1-57020-037-8, BRE-177) Assn Adv Med Instrn.

***AAMI: Designing, Testing & Labeling Reusable Medical Devices for Reprocessing in Health Care Facilities.** AAMI Staff. (Illus.). 53p. (Orig.). 1995. pap. 62.00 (1-57020-029-7, TIR12-177) Assn Adv Med Instrn.

***AAMI: Dry Heat (Heated Air) Sterilizers.** AAMI Staff. (Illus.). 20p. (Orig.). 1995. pap. 51.00 (1-57020-031-9, ST50-177) Assn Adv Med Instrn.

***AAMI: First Use Hemodialyzers.** AAMI Staff. (Illus.). 18p. (Orig.). 1995. pap. 51.00 (1-57020-038-6, RD16-177) Assn Adv Med Instrn.

***AAMI: Hemodializer Blood Tubing.** AAMI Staff. (Illus.). 10p. (Orig.). 1995. pap. 51.00 (1-57020-027-0, RD17) Assn Adv Med Instrn.

***AAMI: Sterilization of Health Care Products - Requirements for Validation & Routine Control-Radiation Sterilization.** AAMI Staff. (Illus.). 48p. (Orig.). 1995. pap. 62.00 (1-57020-033-5, ST1137-177) Assn Adv Med Instrn.

***AAMI: Sterilization Pt. 1: Good Hospital Practices 1995 Edition.** AAMI Staff. (Standards & Recommended Practices Ser.). (Illus.). 442p. (Orig.). 1995. pap. 235.00 (1-57020-034-3, STBK5-1-177) Assn Adv Med Instrn.

***AAMI: Sterilization Pt. 2: Hospital & Industrual Process Control, 1995 Edition.** AAMI Staff. (Standards & Recommended Practices Ser.). (Illus.). 434p. (Orig.). 1995. pap. 235.00 (1-57020-035-1) Assn Adv Med Instrn.

***AAMI: 30th Annual Meeting Proceedings.** AAMI Staff. (Illus.). (Orig.). 1995. pap. 40.00 (1-57020-036-X, AMP95-177) Assn Adv Med Instrn.

***AAMI Standards & Recommended Practices-Biomedical Equipment, Supplemental Vol. 25: BEBK45.** AAMI Staff. (AAMI Standards & Recommended Practices Ser.). (Illus.). 912p. (Orig.). 1994. pap. 200.00 (1-57020-026-2) Assn Adv Med Instrn.

AAMI Standards & Recommended Practices-Sterilization Vol. 15: STBK45. suppl. ed. AAMI Staff. (AAMI Standards & Recommended Practices Ser.). (Illus.). 1060p. (Orig.). 1994. pap. 200.00 (1-57020-018-1) Assn Adv Med Instrn.

AAMI Standards & Recommended Practices, Vol. 1: Sterilization. (Illus.). 712p. 1992. pap. text ed. 250.00 (0-910275-01-7, STBK4-113) Assn Adv Med Instrn.

AAMI Standards & Recommended Practices, Vol. 2: Biomedical Equipment. (Illus.). 860p. pap. text ed. 250.00 (0-910275-00-9, BZBK4-113) Assn Adv Med Instrn.

AAMI Standards & Recommended Practices, Vol. 3: Dialysis. 1993. 150.00 (1-57020-005-X, DSBK3-113) Assn Adv Med Instrn.

AAMI Sterilization-Related Terms & Definitions. 20.00 (0-685-65433-8, STGL-113) Assn Adv Med Instrn.

***AAMI 29th Annual Meeting & Exposition Proceedings: AMP94.** AAMI Staff. 112p. (Orig.). 1994. pap. 75.00 (1-57020-014-9) Assn Adv Med Instrn.

***AAMT Book of Style for Medical Transcription.** Claudia Tessier. 519p. (Orig.). (C). 1994. pap. text ed. 79.00 (0-935229-22-1) Am Assoc Med.

A&P: A Study in Price-Cost Behavior & Public Policy. Morris A. Adelman. LC 59-14733. (Economic Studies: No. 113). (Illus.). 551p. 1959. 35.00x (0-674-00050-1) HUP.

A&P Coloring Workbook. 4th ed. Elaine N. Marieb. (C). 1994. pap. text ed. 20.50 (0-8053-4171-4) Benjamin-Cummings.

A&P Coloring Workbook: A Complete Study Guide. 3rd ed. Elaine N. Marieb. 350p. (C). 1991. write for info. (0-318-69059-4) Addison-Wesley.

A&P Histology Mini Reference. Templin. 16p. 1989. write for info. (0-8016-6163-3) Mosby Yr Bk.

A&P Lecture Notes I. Moques Bizenueh & Robert Keck. 112p. (C). 1994. spiral bd. 15.95 (0-8403-9421-7) Kendall-Hunt.

A&P Lecture Notes II. Moques Bizuneh & Katie Elias. 112p. (C). 1994. spiral bd. 11.96 (0-8403-9517-5) Kendall-Hunt.

A&P Mechanics Airframe Handbook AC 65-15A: Airframe Handbook. FAA Staff. (Mechanic Ser.). (Illus.). (C). 1988. reprint ed. pap. text ed. 18.95 (1-56027-023-3, ASA-AC65-15A) Av Suppl & Acad.

A&P Mechanic's Certification Guide. 4th ed. Federal Aviation Administration Staff. LC 91-15117. (Aviation Maintenance Training Course Ser.). 64p. (C). 1976. pap. 5.00 (0-89100-082-8, EA-AC65-2D) IAP.

A&P Mechanics General Handbook AC 65-9A: General Handbook. rev. ed. FAA-DOT Staff. (Mechanic Ser.). (Illus.). 549p. (C). 1976. reprint ed. pap. text ed. 19.95 (1-56027-064-0, ASA-AC65-9A) Av Suppl & Acad.

A&P Mechanics Powerplant Handbook AC 65-12A: Powerplant Handbook. FAA Staff. (Mechanic Ser.). (Illus.). (C). 1988. reprint ed. pap. text ed. 15.95 (1-56027-024-1, ASA-AC65-12A) Av Suppl & Acad.

A&P Technician: Airframe. IAP, Inc. Staff. LC 92-46752. (Illus.). 348p. 1992. student ed, pap. text ed. 9.95 (0-89100-373-8, EA-ITP-ASG2) IAP.

A&P Technician: Airframe. IAP, Inc. Staff. LC 92-46752. (Illus.). 86p. 1993. teacher ed, pap. text ed. 12.95 (0-89100-431-9, EA-ITP-AI2) IAP.

A&P Technician: Airframe. 2nd ed. IAP, Inc Staff. LC 92-3011. (Illus.). 124p. 1992. student ed 9.95 (0-89100-402-5, EA-ITP-AW2); pap. text ed. 25.95 (0-89100-395-9, EA-ITP-A2) IAP.

A&P Technician: General. IAP, Inc. Staff & David L. Jones. LC 93-2616. (Illus.). 66p. 1993. teacher ed, pap. text ed. 12.95 (0-89100-427-0, EA-ITP-GI2) IAP.

A&P Technician: General. 2nd ed. IAP, Inc. Staff. LC 92-46753. (Illus.). 237p. 1992. student ed, pap. text ed. 9.95 (0-89100-371-1, EA-ITP-GSG2) IAP.

A&P Technician: General. 2nd ed. IAP, Inc. Staff. LC 91-48117. (Illus.). 204p. 1992. student ed 9.95 (0-89100-400-9, EA-ITP-GW2); pap. text ed. 23.95 (0-89100-391-6, EA-ITP-G2) IAP.

***Aani & the Tree Huggers.** Jeannine Atkins. LC 95-2036. (Illus.). 32p. (J). (gr. k-4). 1995. 14.95 (1-880000-24-5) Lee & Low Bks.

***AAOA Homestudy Course in Otolaryngic Allergy.** 2nd ed. Jacquelynne Corey. 416p. 1995. student ed, pap. text ed. 135.00 (1-887064-01-X) J M Ryan.

AAOG XCI - AGS, Vol. 3. Trans. 1985. pap. 70.00 (0-8016-5080-1) Mosby Yr Bk.

AAOS Guide to the Ethical Practice of Orthopaedic Surgery. 66p. 1992. 25.00 (0-89203-066-6) Amer Acad Ortho Surg.

AAOS Instructional Course Lectures, No. XXXVI. Ed. by Paul P. Griffin. LC 43-17054. (Illus.). 527p. 1987. text ed. 65.00 (0-89203-019-4) Amer Acad Ortho Surg.

AAOS Instructional Course Lectures, No. XLI. Ed. by Robert E. Eilert. (Illus.). 600p. 1992. 110.00 (0-89203-057-7) Amer Acad Ortho Surg.

AAOS Instructional Course Lectures, XXXVIII. Ed. by Joseph S. Barr, Jr. LC 43-17054. (Illus.). 502p. 1989. 75.00 (0-89203-028-3) Amer Acad Ortho Surg.

***AAOS Instructional Course Lectures Vol. 43.** Ed. by Michael F. Schafer. (Illus.). 644p. 1994. 110.00 (0-89203-102-6) Amer Acad Ortho Surg.

***AAOS Instructional Course Lectures Vol. 44.** Ed. by Douglas Jackson. (Illus.). 1995. 110.00 (0-89203-115-8) Amer Acad Ortho Surg.

AAOS Instructional Course Lectures, XL, Index Vols. XXVI-XL, Index Vols. XXVI-XL. Ed. by Hugh S. Tullos. LC 43-17054. (Illus.). 368p. 1991. 75.00 (0-89203-043-7) Amer Acad Ortho Surg.

AAOS Instructional Course Lectures, XXXVII. Ed. by Frank H. Bassett, III. LC 43-17054. (Illus.). 299p. 1988. 65.00 (0-89203-022-4) Amer Acad Ortho Surg.

AAOS Instructional Course Lectures, 1990, Vol. 39. Ed. by Walter B. Greene et al. LC 43-17054. (Illus.). 600p. 1990. 75.00 (0-89203-032-1) Amer Acad Ortho Surg.

Aap It! A Microwave Cookbook Just for Kids. Tamar Petersell. (J). (gr. 4-7). 1993. 12.95 (0-943706-13-0) Pitspopany.

AAPT Apparatus Competition. Ed. by AAPT Apparatus Committee Staff. (Occasional Publications). (Illus.). 224p. (Orig.). 1984. pap. text ed. 18.00 (0-917853-10-5, OP21) Am Assn Physics.

***Aardvarks.** Don Rothaus. (Nature Bks.). (Illus.). 32p. (J). (gr. 2-6). 1995. lib. bdg. 22.79 (1-56766-181-5) Childs World.

Aardvarks, Disembark! Ann Jonas. LC 89-27225. (Illus.). 40p. (J). (ps up). 1990. 14.95 (0-688-07206-2); lib. bdg. 14.88 (0-688-07207-0) Greenwillow.

Aardvarks, Disembark! Ann Jonas. (Illus.). 40p. (J). (ps-3). 1994. pap. 4.99 (0-14-055309-6) Puffin Bks.

Aardvarks to Zebras: A Menagerie of Facts, Fiction & Fantasy about the Wonderful World of Animals. Melissa S. Tulin. LC 94-17474. 1994. 14.95 (0-8065-1548-1, Citadel Pr) Carol Pub Group.

Aaron & Gayla's Alphabet Book. Eloise Greenfield. (Illus.). 20p. (J). 1992. 9.95 (0-86316-208-8) Writers & Readers.

Aaron & Gayla's Alphabet Book. Eloise Greenfield. (J). (ps). 1994. pap. 6.95 (0-86316-213-4) Writers & Readers.

Aaron & Gayla's Counting Book. Eloise Greenfield. (Illus.). 20p. (J). 1992. 9.95 (0-86316-209-6) Writers & Readers.

Aaron & Gayla's Counting Book. Eloise Greenfield. (J). (ps). 1993. pap. 6.95 (0-86316-214-2) Writers & Readers.

Aaron Burr: A Biography. Nathan Schachner. LC 83-45794. (Illus.). reprint ed. 57.50 (0-404-20227-6) AMS Pr.

Aaron Burr: A Biography Compiled from Rare, & in Many Cases Unpublished, Sources, 2 vols., Set. Samuel H. Wandell. (BCL1 - U. S. History Ser.). 1991. reprint ed. lib. bdg. 150.00 (0-7812-6124-4) Rprt Serv.

Aaron Burr: Controversial Politician of Early America. Jerome Mushkat. Ed. by D. Steve Rahmas & Gerald Kurland. (Outstanding Personalities Ser.: No. 71). 32p. (YA). (gr. 7-12). 1974. lib. bdg. 4.95 (0-87157-571-X) SamHar Pr.

Aaron Burr & the American Literary Imagination. Charles J. Nolan, Jr. LC 79-8291. (Contributions in American Studies: No. 45). 210p. 1980. text ed. 55.00 (0-313-21256-2, NAB/, Greenwood Pr) Greenwood.

Aaron Burr Conspiracy. Walter F. McCaleb. Bd. with New Light on Aaron Burr. 476p. 1966. reprint ed. 20.00 (0-87266-021-4) Argosy.

***Aaron Burr the Proud Pretender.** Alexander. Date not set. write for info. (0-8371-7128-8) Greenwood.

***Aaron Copland.** Mike Venezia. LC 94-36344. (Getting to Know the World's Greatest Composers Ser.). (Illus.). 32p. (J). (ps-4). 1995. lib. bdg. 12.90 (0-516-04538-5) Childrens.

Aaron Copland. Arthur V. Berger. (Music Reprint Ser.). 120p. 1990. reprint ed. lib. bdg. 25.00 (0-306-76266-8) Da Capo.

Aaron Copland: A Bio-Bibliography. Joann Skowronski. LC 84-22417. (Bio-Bibliographies in Music Ser.: No. 2). x, 273p. 1985. text ed. 45.00 (0-313-24091-4, SKC/, Greenwood Pr) Greenwood.

***Aaron Douglas: Art, Race, & the Harlem Renaissance.** Amy Kirschke. (Illus.). 256p. 1995. text ed. 45.00 (0-87805-775-7); pap. 19.95 (0-87805-800-1) U Pr of Miss.

Aaron Goes to the Shelter: A Story about Abuse, Placement & Protective Services. Phyllis Nasta. 29p. (ENG & SPA.). (J). (gr. k-6). 1994. pap. 6.95 (1-880702-00-2) Whole Child.

Aaron Goes to the Shelter: A Story & Workbook Guide about Abuse, Placement & Protective Services. Phyllis Nasta. (Illus.). 37p. (Orig.). (J). (gr. k-6). 1992. pap. text ed. 5.95 (1-880702-01-0) Whole Child.

Aaron Hill: Poet, Dramatist, Projector. Dorothy Brewster. LC 13-21690. reprint ed. 32.50 (0-404-01076-8) AMS Pr.

Aaron Johnson: Faithful Steward. Alan P. Johnson. (Illus.). 652p. 1991. 29.00 (0-9631599-0-9) A P Johnson.

Aaron Ladner Lindsley: Founder of Alaska Missions. (Shorey Historical Ser.). 9p. reprint ed. pap. 2.25 (0-8466-0050-1, S50) Shorey.

Aaron T. Beck. Marjorie Weishaar. (Key Figures in Counselling & Psychotherapy Ser.). (Illus.). 160p. (C). 1993. text ed. 44.00 (0-8039-8564-9); pap. text ed. 18.95 (0-8039-8565-7) Sage.

Aaron, the High Priest. Zev Paamoni. (Shulsinger Biblical Ser.). (Illus.). (J). (gr. 5-10). 1970. 3.00 (0-914080-27-X) Shulsinger Sales.

Aaron Thy Brother. Conor Farrington. (Irish Play Ser.). 1975. pap. 1.95 (0-912262-38-9) Proscenium.

***Aaron Tippin: Lookin' Back at Myself.** Ed. by Jeannette DeLisa. 44p. (Orig.). (YA). 1995. pap. text ed. 14.95 (0-89724-568-7) Warner Brothers.

Aaron to Zuverink: Baseball Players of the Fifties. Richard Marazzi & Len Fiorito. 552p. 1984. mass mkt. 4.50 (0-380-68445-4, 68445) Avon.

***Aaronic Foundational Ministries.** Ed. by Paul M. Edwards. 125p. (Orig.). 1995. pap. text ed. write for info. (0-8309-0718-1) Herald Hse.

Aaronic Priesthood & You. Vaughn J. Featherstone. LC 87-15731. 99p. (YA). (gr. 8-12). 1993. reprint ed. pap. 8.95 (0-87579-755-5) Deseret Bk.

Aaron's Code: Meta-Art, Artificial Intelligence & the Work of Harold Cohen. Pamela McCorduck. LC 90-36940. (Illus.). 224p. (C). 1995. text ed. write for info. (0-7167-2173-2) W H Freeman.

Aaron's Rod. D. H. Lawrence. Ed. by Mara Kalnins. (Cambridge Edition of the Works of D. H. Lawrence). 400p. 1988. 94.95 (0-521-25250-4); pap. 32.95 (0-521-27246-7) Cambridge U Pr.

Aaron's Rod. large type ed. D. H. Lawrence. (Classics Ser.). 480p. 1982. 23.95 (0-7089-8068-6, Charnwood) Ulverscroft.

Aaron's Shirt. Deborah Gould. LC 88-10414. (Illus.). 32p. (J). (ps-2). 1989. lib. bdg. 13.95 (0-02-736351-1, Bradbury S&S) S&S Childrens.

***Aaron's Solution.** James Pritchett. Ed. by Sharon Daniels et al. 140p. (Orig.). 1994. pap. 8.95 (0-9643232-0-6) Pandamonium.

AARP Pharmacy Service Prescription Drug Handbook. rev. ed. AARP Staff. (Illus.). 960p. 1992. pap. 18.00 (0-685-52541-4, Harper Ref) HarpC.

AARP Prescription Drug Handbook. Tub. 1992. pap. 17.95 (0-06-263501-8) HarpC.

Aarvy Aardvark Finds Hope: A Read-Aloud Story for People of All Ages. Donna O'Toole. (Illus.). 80p. (Orig.). (J). (ps up). 1989. audio 10.95 (0-685-20985-7, Mntn Rainbow) Rainbow NC.

Aarvy Aardvark Finds Hope: A Read-Aloud Story for People of All Ages. Donna O'Toole. (Illus.). 80p. (Orig.). (J). (ps up). 1989. teacher ed 6.95 (1-878321-26-9, Mntn Rainbow); pap. 11.95 (1-878321-25-0, Mntn Rainbow) Rainbow NC.

AAS - AIAA Astrodynamics Conference 1991. Ed. by Bernard Kaufman et al. LC 57-43769. (Advances in the Astronautical Sciences Ser.: Vol. 76, Pts. I, II & III). (Illus.). 2590p. 1992. lib. bdg. 390.00 (0-87703-347-1, Pub. by Am Astro Soc) Univelt Inc.

AAS - AIAA Astrodynamics Conference 1991, Vol. 63, AAS. Ed. by Bernard Kaufman et al. LC 57-43769. (Advances in the Astronautical Sciences Ser.: Vol. 76, Pts. I, II & III). (Illus.). 2590p. 1992. Vol. 63 AAS. fiche 75.00 (0-87703-348-X, Pub. by Am Astro Soc) Univelt Inc.

AAS - AIAA Spaceflight Mechanics Meeting. Ed. by Robert G. Melton et al. LC 57-43769. (Advances in the Astronautical Sciences Ser.: Vol. 82 I & II). (Illus.). 1993. lib. bdg. 240.00 (0-87703-368-4, Pub. by Am Astro Soc); fiche 15.00 (0-87703-369-2, Pub. by Am Astro Soc) Univelt Inc.

AAS - AIAA Spaceflight Mechanics 1992. Ed. by Roger E. Diehl et al. LC 57-43769. (Advances in the Astronautical Sciences Ser.: Vol. 79, Pts. I & II). (Illus.). 1312p. 1992. lib. bdg. 240.00 (0-87703-358-7, Pub. by Am Astro Soc) Univelt Inc.

AAS - AIAA Spaceflight Mechanics 1992, Vol. 65, AAS. Ed. by Roger E. Diehl et al. LC 57-43769. (Advances in the Astronautical Sciences Ser.: Vol. 79, Pts. I & II). (Illus.). 1312p. 1992. Vol. 65 AAS. fiche 40.00 (0-87703-359-5, Pub. by Am Astro Soc) Univelt Inc.

AAS-AIAA Astrodynamics Conference, 1987. Ed. by John K. Soldner et al. (Advances in the Astronautical Sciences Ser.: Vol. 65, Pts. I & II). (Illus.). 1774p. 1988. lib. bdg. 180.00 (0-87703-285-8); pap. text ed. 150.00 (0-87703-286-6) Am Astronaut.

AAS-AIAA Astrodynamics Conference, 1989. Ed. by Catherine L. Thornton et al. LC 57-43769. (Advances in the Astronautical Sciences Ser.: Vol. 71, Pts. 1-2). (Illus.). 1472p. 1990. lib. bdg. 200.00 (0-87703-317-X, Pub. by Am Astro Soc); pap. text ed. 170.00 (0-87703-318-8, Pub. by Am Astro Soc) Univelt Inc.

AAS Index: Numerical-Chronological-Author, 1954-1978. Ed. by H. Jacobs. lib. bdg. 40.00 (0-87703-102-9, Pub. by Am Astro Soc); pap. 30.00 (0-87703-103-7, Pub. by Am Astro Soc) Univelt Inc.

AASA-AIA Exhibition of School Architecture 1990. American Association of School Administrators Staff. 82p. (Orig.). 1990. pap. 15.00 (0-87652-154-5, 021-00292) Am Assn Sch Admin.

Aasaa Di Vaar: A Part of Sikh Scriptures. Ujagar S. Bawa. (Books on Sikhism Ser.). 184p. (YA). (gr. 8-12). 1993. 12.50 (0-942245-08-3) Wash Sikh Ctr.

AASHTO Bridge Maintenance Manual. 9.00 (0-686-20951-6, BM-2) AASHTO.

***AASHTO LRFD Bridge Design Specifications - SI.** (Bridges Ser.). 1116p. (C). 1994. pap. text ed. 54.50 (1-56051-074-9) AASHTO.

***AASHTO LRFD Bridge Design Specifications - U. S.** (Bridges Ser.). 1116p. (C). 1994. pap. text ed. 54.50 (1-56051-073-0) AASHTO.

AASHTO Maintenance Manual. 1987. 15.00 (0-686-20952-4, MM-2) AASHTO.

***AASHTO Provisional Standards.** (Materials Ser.). 588p. (C). 1995. pap. text ed. 68.75 (1-56051-033-1) AASHTO.

AASHTO 1914-1989: Moving America into the Future. AASHTO Staff. (Reference Bks.). (Illus.). 288p. (Orig.). (C). 1989. pap. text ed. 25.00 (1-56051-007-2) AASHTO.

AAUP Directory, 1988-89: Annual Directory of Information Concerning University Press Publishing in U. S. LC 54-43046. 144p. (Orig.). 1988. pap. 11.95 (0-945103-01-8) Assn Am Univ.

AAUP Directory, 1991-1992. AAUP Staff. 1991. pap. 14.95 (0-945103-05-0) U Ch Pr.

AAUW Report: How Schools Shortchange Girls. 128p. 1992. 16.95 (0-8106-2501-6) NEA.

AAVP-7A1 LVTP-7A1 & Variance. Ed Gilbert & Allen Swan. (Illus.). 46p. (Orig.). 1988. pap. 6.95 (0-945808-00-3) Full Detail.

AAVSO Supernova Search Manual. Robert O. Evans. 280p. (Orig.). 1993. pap. 50.00 (1-878174-11-8) Am Assn Var Star.

Ab Initio Calculation of the Structures & Properties of Molecules. Clifford E. Dykstra. 276p. 1988. 107.75 (0-444-43013-X) Elsevier.

Ab Initio Determination of Molecular Properties. A. Hinchliffe. (Illus.). 176p. 1987. 105.00 (0-85274-523-0) IOP Pub.

Ab Initio Methods in Quantum Chemistry, Pt. 1. Ed. by K. P. Lawley. LC 86-9168. (Advances in Chemical Physics Ser.: No. 67). (Illus.). 566p. 1987. reprint ed. pap. 161.40 (0-8357-4619-4, 2037551) Bks Demand.

Ab Initio Molecular Orbital Theory. Warren J. Hehre et al. LC 84-19524. 548p. 1986. text ed. 120.00 (0-471-81241-2) Wiley.

Ab Initio Variational Calculations of Molecular Vibrational-Rotational Spectra. D. Searles & E. Von Nagy-Felsobuki. LC 93-38673. (Lecture Notes in Chemistry Ser.: Vol. 61). 1994. 39.00 (0-387-57465-4) Spr-Verlag.

Ab Urbe Condita, 5 vols. Incl. Vol. 1. Books 1-5. 2nd ed. Ed. by R. M. Ogilvie et al. 1974. 35.00 (0-19-814661-2); Vol. 2. Books 6-10. Ed. by R. S. Conway et al. 1920. 34.50 (0-19-814621-3); Vol. 3. Books 21-25. Ed. by R. S. Conway & S. K. Johnson. 1929. 32.50 (0-19-814622-1); Vol. 4. Books 26-30. Ed. by R. S. Conway & S. K. Johnson. 1934. 39.00 (0-19-814623-X); Vol. 5. Books 31-35. Ed. by Alexander H. McDonald. 1965. 35.00 (0-19-814646-9); (Oxford Classical Texts Ser.). write for info. (0-318-54801-1) OUP.

Ab Urbe Condita, Bk. 6. Livy. Ed. by Christina S. Kraus. (Cambridge Greek & Latin Classics Ser.). 368p. (C). 1995. 64.95 (0-521-41002-9); pap. 22.95 (0-521-42238-8) Cambridge U Pr.

Ab Urbe Condita Construction in Greek, a Study of the Classification of the Participle. Frank P. Jones. (LD Ser.: Vol. 28). 1939. pap. 16.00 (0-527-00774-9) Periodicals Srv.

ABA: A Birthday Book. Linda Franklin. (Keepbooks Ser.). 128p. 1990. reprint ed. 16.00 (0-685-30141-9) Country Diary.

ABA Address Book. Linda Franklin. 128p. 1990. reprint ed. write for info. (0-318-66588-3) Country Diary.

An Asterisk (*) at the beginning of an entry indicates that the title is appearing in BIP for the first time.

***Aba Bayefsky in Kensington Market.** Aba Bayefsky. (Illus.). 128p. 1995. lib. bdg. 43.00 (*0-8095-4884-4*) Borgo Pr.

ABA-BNA Lawyers' Manual on Professional Conduct: Bibliography. ABA, Center for Professional Responsibility Staff. 517p. 1984. pap. 35.00 (*0-87179-485-3*) BNA.

***ABA Book Buyer's Handbook, 1994-1995.** Ed. by Linda M. Miller et al. 846p. 1994. pap. write for info. (*1-879556-14-6*) ABA.

***ABA Book Buyer's Returns Handbook, 1994 to 1995.** Ed. by Linda M. Miller et al. 342p. 1994. 50.00 (*1-879556-15-4*) ABA.

ABA Checklist: Birds of the Continental United States & Canada. 4th ed. Checklist Committee of the American Birding Assoc. Staff. LC 90-84826. 92p. 1990. pap. 10.00 (*1-878788-25-6*); disk 10.00 (*1-878788-26-4*) Amer Birding Assn.

ABA Children's Bookselling Resource Handbook. 2nd rev. ed. Ed. by Rosemary Hawkins & Elizabeth Szabla. 150p. 1993. pap. 13.95 (*1-879556-02-2*) ABA.

ABA Commission on Taxpayer Compliance Report & Recommendations. 73p. 1987. pap. write for info. (*0-318-66179-9*, 547-0271-01) Amer Bar Assn.

ABA Criminal & Juvenile Justice Policies: A Road Map for State Legislators & Policymakers. 84p. 1986. pap. 10.00 (*0-685-29685-7*, 509-0025-01) Amer Bar Assn.

ABA Criminal Justice Mental Health Standards. 530p. 1989. pap. 15.00 (*0-89707-450-5*, 509-0041-001) Amer Bar Assn.

ABA Grand Jury Policy & Model Act 1977-82. 2nd ed. 40p. 1982. pap. 10.00 (*0-685-18982-1*, 509-0013-01) Amer Bar Assn.

***ABA Guide to Home Ownership: The Complete & Easy Guide to All the Law Every Home Owner Should Know.** ABA Staff. 1995. pap. 12.00 (*0-8129-2535-1*, Times Bks) Random.

***ABA Guide to Wills & Estates: Everything You Need to Know about Wills, Trusts, Estates, & Taxes.** ABA Staff. 1995. pap. 12.00 (*0-8129-2536-X*, Times Bks) Random.

ABA Lawyering Skills: Course Materials, Client Instructions. 150p. 1982. ring bd. 15.00 (*0-685-42956-3*, 341-0003) Amer Bar Assn.

ABA Lawyering Skills: Course Materials, Participants' Copy, Group A. 200p. 1982. ring bd. 15.00 (*0-685-42958-X*, 341-0004) Amer Bar Assn.

ABA Lawyering Skills: Course Materials, Participants' Copy, Group B. 200p. 1982. ring bd. 15.00 (*0-318-36488-3*, 341-0005) Amer Bar Assn.

ABA Lawyering Skills: Instructor's Manual. 230p. 1982. ring bd. 70.00 (*0-685-11081-8*, 341-0002) Amer Bar Assn.

ABA Lending Made Easy. 200p. 1990. spiral bd. 69.00 (*0-89982-346-7*, 169800); spiral bd. 49.00 (*0-685-63183-4*, 169800) Am Bankers.

ABA Model Procurement Code for State & Local Governments. 97p. 1979. pap. 9.95 (*0-89707-227-8*, 539-0056) Amer Bar Assn.

ABA Model Procurement Code for State & Local Governments Recommended Regulations. 315p. 1981. pap. 22.95 (*0-89707-228-6*, 539-0057) Amer Bar Assn.

ABA Policies & Procedures Handbook. 308p. 1992. pap. write for info. (*0-318-66090-3*, 149-0017) Amer Bar Assn.

ABA Policy Recommendations on Youth Alcohol & Drug Problems. 124p. 1986. pap. 6.00 (*0-685-19037-4*, 517-0008-01) Amer Bar Assn.

***ABA Sales & Use Tax Desk Book, 1993-94 Edition.** American Bar Association, Section of Taxation Staff. Ed. by D. Michael Young & John T. Piper. 1994. 240.00 (*1-57073-096-2*) ABA Prof Educ Pubns.

ABA Sales & Use Tax Deskbook. 780p. 1993. pap. 240.00 (*0-89707-655-9*, 547-0406) Amer Bar Assn.

ABA Source Book: Marketing & Merchandising Guide. 1988. ring bd. 25.00 (*1-879556-03-0*) ABA.

ABA Standards for Criminal Justice, 4 vols., Set. 2nd ed. American Bar Association Staff. LC 79-91936. 1980. ring bd. 325.00 (*0-316-03709-5*) Little.

ABA Standards for Criminal Justice: Prosecution Function & Defense Function. 3rd ed. LC 93-17567. 248p. 1993. write for info. (*0-89707-850-0*, 509-0055, ABA Crim Just) Amer Bar Assn.

***Abaco: The History of an Out Island & Its Cays.** 2nd ed. Steve Dodge. (Illus.). 200p. 1995. pap. text ed. 19.50 (*0-932265-34-0*) White Sound.

***Abacos: Island Jewels of the Bahamas.** Gordon Smith et al. 1994. pap. 7.00 (*0-9642152-0-9*) Parliament Hse.

Abacus. Mary Karr. LC 86-32442. (Wesleyan New Poets Ser.). 62p. 1987. 12.95 (*0-8195-2134-5*, Wesleyan Univ Pr) U Pr of New Eng.

Abacus: A Brief History of the World's First Computing System & How to Use It. Jesse Dilson. (Illus.). 144p. 1995. pap. 12.95 (*0-312-10409-X*) St Martin.

***Abacus: Its History & Its Applications.** Frances R. Metallo. (Hi Map Ser.: No. 17). 60p. Date not set. pap. text ed. 11.99 (*0-614-05309-9*, HM 5617) COMAP Inc.

Abacus & the Rose see Science & Human Values

Abacus & the Sword: The Japanese Penetration of Korea, 1859-1910. Peter Duus. LC 94-6118. (Twentieth-Century Japan Ser.: Vol. 4). 1995. 45.00x (*0-520-08614-7*) U CA Pr.

Abacus Arithmetic. Welton J. Crook. LC 58-7709. (Illus.). 1958. pap. 2.95 (*0-87015-078-2*) Pacific Bks.

Abacus Made Easy. 2nd large type ed. M. Davidow. 110p. (J). (gr. 2-12). 1975. 10.28 (*0-317-01865-5*, 4-00100-00) Am Printing Hse.

Abadeha: The Philippine Cinderella. Myrna J. De La Paz. (Illus.). 28p. (J). (gr. k-7). 1991. 13.95 (*0-9629255-0-0*) Pacific Queen.

Abagar of Philip Stanislavov: Rome 1651. Bozhidar Raikov. 54p. 1979. 193.00 (*0-569-08620-5*, Pub. by Collets UK) Pro-Am Music.

Abahn. Marguerite Duras. Incl. Sabana. (*0-318-51918-6*); David. (*0-318-51919-4*); 12.95 (*0-8288-6077-7*, F99720) Fr & Eur.

Abair: Pocket Gaelic-English-Gaelic Dictionary. J. MacDonald & R. Renton. 1990. pap. 19.95 (*0-8288-3376-1*, F132981) Fr & Eur.

Abalienations & Forty-Nine Others. Michael T. Kelly. (Illus.). 69p. (Orig.). 1988. write for info. (*0-318-63688-3*) Michael Kelly.

Abalone Book. Peter C. Howorth. LC 78-13204. (Illus.). 80p. 1978. pap. 7.95 (*0-87961-077-8*) Naturegraph.

Abalone Farming. Ric Fallu. (Illus.). 192p. 1991. 59.95 (*0-85238-171-9*) Blackwell Sci.

Abalone, Gross & Fine Structure. Gerrit Bevelander. (Illus.). 1988. pap. 18.00 (*0-940168-05-7*) Boxwood.

Abalone Heart. Barbara Meyn. Ed. by Tom Trusky. LC 88-71465. (Ahsahta Press Modern & Contemporary Poets of the West Ser.). 75p. (Orig.). 1988. pap. 6.95 (*0-916272-37-0*) Ahsahta Pr.

***Abalos & Herreros.** Zaera. 1994. pap. text ed. 28.95 (*84-252-1598-6*, Pub. by Gustavo Gili SP) Rizzoli Intl.

Abandon Hope: The Way to Fulfillment. 2nd ed. Justin F. Stone. 129p. 1989. pap. 9.95 (*0-9620812-2-1*) Good Karma.

Abandon Ship! An Overboard Collection. Chip Dunham. (Illus.). 128p. (Orig.). 1992. pap. 8.95 (*0-8362-1895-7*) Andrews & McMeel.

Abandoned. Paul Gallico. 256p. 1991. pap. text ed. 12.95 (*1-55882-097-3*, Lib Crime Classics) Intl Polygonics.

Abandoned. Jeri Massi. (Light Line Ser.). 136p. (Orig.). (J). (gr. 5-8). 1989. pap. 5.95 (*0-89084-467-4*) Bob Jones Univ Pr.

Abandoned. Vickie York. (Intrigue Ser.). 1993. mass mkt. 2.99 (*0-373-22231-9*, 1-22231-4) Harlequin Bks.

Abandoned: A Nostalgic Look at Rural America. William D. Adams. (Illus.). 112p. 1986. text ed. 29.95 (*0-914641-06-9*) TX Gardener Pr.

Abandoned: The Betrayal of the American Middle Class since World War II. William J. Quirk & R. Randall Bridwell. 468p. 1992. 21.95 (*0-8191-8459-4*) Madison Bks UPA.

Abandoned: The Betrayal of the American Middle Class since World War II. William J. Quirk & R. Randall Bridwell. 468p. 1993. pap. 16.95 (*1-56833-022-7*) Madison Bks UPA.

Abandoned Baobab: The Autobiography of a Senegalese Woman. Ken Bugul. Tr. by Marjolijn De Jager. LC 91-25424. 160p. 1991. 18.95 (*1-55652-113-8*); pap. 9.95 (*1-55652-114-6*) L Hill Bks.

Abandoned by Lincoln: A Military Biography of General John Pope. Wallace Schutz & Walter Trenerry. 272p. 1990. 32.50 (*0-252-01675-0*) U of Ill Pr.

Abandoned Car of Lost Lake. annuals Richard Fretwell & Jill Hathaway. (Barret Mystery Ser.: No. 2). 206p. (gr. 3-8). 1985. 8.95 (*0-912241-02-0*) Hathaway Hse.

***Abandoned Child.** Marie Morgart. Ed. by Deanna Hammond. 130p. (Orig.). Date not set. pap. text ed. 9.95 (*1-882185-26-9*) Crnrstone Pub.

Abandoned Child Within: On Losing & Regaining Self-Worth. Kathrin Asper. Tr. by Sharon E. Rooks. LC 93-321. (Psychology Ser.). (Illus.). 336p. 1993. 29.95 (*0-88064-203-3*); pap. 16.95 (*0-88064-204-1*) Fromm Intl Pub.

Abandoned Children: Foundlings & Child Welfare in Nineteenth-Century France. Rachel G. Fuchs. LC 83-425. (Modern European History Ser.). 357p. (C). 1984. 64.50 (*0-87395-748-2*); pap. 21.95 (*0-87395-750-4*) State U NY Pr.

Abandoned Country. Thomas Rabbitt. LC 87-71454. (Poetry Ser.). 1988. 16.95 (*0-88748-062-4*); pap. 9.95 (*0-88748-063-2*) Carnegie-Mellon.

Abandoned Farm & Connie's Mistake. Mary J. Holmes. (Notable American Authors Ser.). 1992. reprint ed. lib. bdg. 75.00 (*0-7812-3153-1*) Rprt Serv.

Abandoned House. Susan Fawcett. 24p. 1988. 3.00 (*0-943710-01-4*) Silver App Pr.

Abandoned in Alaska; Or, Frank Reade Jr.'s Thrilling Search for a Lost Gold Claim with His New Electric Wagon. Luis Senarens. Bd. with For Six Weeks Buried in a Deep Sea Cave; Or Frank Reade, Jr.'s Great Submarine Search. (Frank Reade Library: Vol. 7). 1985. 91.00 (*0-8240-3546-1*) Garland.

***Abandoned in the Wasteland: Children, Television, & the First Amendment.** Newton Minow & Craig Lamay. 224p. 1995. 20.00 (*0-8090-2311-3*) Hill & Wang.

Abandoned Latitudes. John Thomas et al. LC 83-60078. (Invisible City Ser.). (Illus.). 96p. (Orig.). 1983. pap. 6.00 (*0-88031-062-6*) Invisible-Red Hill.

Abandoned Middle: The Ethics & Politics of Abortion in America. Hal Miller. 80p. (Orig.). (C). 1988. pap. text ed. 5.50 (*0-317-01537-0*) Penumbra Press.

Abandoned Middle: The Ethics & Politics of Abortion in America. Hal Miller. LC 88-90864. 92p. (Orig.). (C). 1988. pap. text ed. 7.95 (*0-929645-00-6*) Penumbra MA.

Abandoned Money Book: How to Get Your Share of Billions of Dollars of Unclaimed Money. Richard S. Johnson. LC 92-11564. 150p. (Orig.). 1992. pap. 9.95 (*1-877639-08-7*, MIE Pub) Military Information.

Abandoned Muses: The Orphan Muses see New French-Language Plays

Abandoned Narcotic: Kava & Cultural Instability in Melanesia. Ron Brunton. (Cambridge Studies in Social & Cultural Anthropology: No. 69). (Illus.). (C). 1990. 49.95 (*0-521-37375-1*) Cambridge U Pr.

***Abandoned Ones: The Imprisonment & Uprising of the Mariel Boat People.** Mark S. Hamm. 224p. 1995. 28.95 (*1-55553-230-6*) NE U Pr.

Abandoned Prayers. Gregg Olsen. 1990. mass mkt. 4.95 (*0-445-21076-1*) Warner Bks.

***Abandoned Rake.** Emily Hendrickson. (Regency Romance Ser.). 224p. (Orig.). 1995. mass mkt. 3.99 (*0-451-18269-3*, Sig) NAL-Dutton.

Abandoned Seas: Reversing the Decline of the Oceans. Peter Weber. 70p. (Orig.). 1993. pap. 5.00 (*1-878071-16-5*) Worldwatch Inst.

Abandoned to Their Fate: Social Policy & Practice Toward Severely Retarded People in America, 1820-1920. Philip M. Ferguson. LC 93-21887. (Health, Society, & Policy Ser.). 232p. 1993. 34.95 (*1-56639-154-7*) Temple U Pr.

Abandoned Women & Poetic Tradition. Catherine R. Stimpson. (Women in Culture & Society Ser.). 328p. 1988. lib. bdg. 47.00 (*0-226-48452-1*); pap. text ed. 16.95 (*0-226-48454-8*) U Ch Pr.

Abandoning Method: Sociological Studies in Methodology. Derek L. Phillips. LC 72-13598. (Jossey-Bass Behavioral Science Ser.). 218p. 1973. reprint ed. pap. 62.20 (*0-8357-5003-5*, 2027765) Bks Demand.

Abandoning the Victims: The U.N. Advisory Service Program in Guatemala. Lawyers Committee for Human Rights Staff. 101p. 1990. lib. bdg. 8.00 (*0-934143-31-5*); pap. text ed. 10.00 (*0-685-37748-2*) Lawyers Comm Human.

***Abandonings: Photographs of Other Tail County, Minnesota.** Maxwell MacKenzie. (Illus.). 64p. 1995. 22.95 (*1-880216-34-5*) Elliott & Clark.

Abandonment of City Manager Government by South Dakota Municipalities. Eugene W. Kimmel. 1966. 5.00 (*1-55614-017-7*) U of SD Gov Res Bur.

Abandonment of Delinquent Behavior: Promoting the Turnaround. Ed. by Richard L. Jenkins & Waln K. Brown. LC 88-1135. 238p. 1988. text ed. 55.00 (*0-275-92928-0*, C2928, Praeger Pubs) Greenwood.

Abandonment of Settlements & Regions: Ethnoarchaeological & Archaeological Approaches. Ed. by Catherine M. Cameron & Steve A. Tomka. (New Directions in Archaeology Ser.). (Illus.). 216p. (C). 1993. 54.95 (*0-521-43333-9*) Cambridge U Pr.

Abandonment of the Jews. David S. Wyman. LC 84-42711. 480p. 1986. pap. 16.00 (*0-394-74077-7*) Pantheon.

Abandonment to Divine Providence. Jean-Pierre De Caussade. 1993. mass mkt. 9.00 (*0-385-46871-7*) Doubleday.

Abarbenel Al Hatorah, 3 Vols, Set. Don I. Abarbenel. (HEB.). 45.00 (*0-87559-078-0*) Shalom.

Abarth King of Small Cars. Alfred S. Cosentino. 344p. 1986. 27.95 (*0-929991-11-7*) A S Cosentino Bks.

Abarth Owners International, No. 001-88. Alfred S. Cosentino. 108p. 1988. 12.95 (*0-929991-12-5*) A S Cosentino Bks.

Abarth Owners International, No. 002-88. Alfred S. Cosentino. 110p. 1988. 12.95 (*0-929991-13-3*) A S Cosentino Bks.

Abarth Owners International, No. 003-89. Alfred S. Cosentino. 110p. 1989. 12.95 (*0-929991-14-1*) A S Cosentino Bks.

Abarth Owners International, No. 004-89. Alfred S. Cosentino. 112p. 1989. 12.95 (*0-929991-15-X*) A S Cosentino Bks.

Abascisic Acid: Physiology & Biochemistry. Ed. by W. J. Davies & H. G. Jones. (Environmental Plant Biology Ser.). 280p. 1991. 125.00 (*1-872748-65-1*, Pub. by Bios Scientific UK) Coronet Bks.

Abasement of the Northmores see Author of Beltraffio

***Abastenia St. Leger Eberle.** James T. Demitrion. LC 80-66884. (Illus.). 59p. 1980. pap. 8.00 (*0-614-06996-3*) Edmundson.

Abastos de Alimentos Para el Hogar. Luis Berrios-Ortiz. LC 82-2773. (Illus.). ix, 119p. (Orig.). (C). 1982. pap. 5.00 (*0-8477-2778-5*) U of PR Pr.

Abate Juan Andres, Literary Historian & Defender of Spanish & Medieval Hispano-Arab Learning, Literature & Culture, 1740-1917. Guido Mazzeo. 228p. 1965. 5.00 (*0-318-22340-6*) Hispanic Inst.

Abating Treatment with Critically Ill Patients: Ethical & Legal Limits to the Medical Prolongation of Life. Robert F. Weir. (Illus.). 472p. 1989. 37.50 (*0-19-504528-9*) OUP.

Abba. Evelyn Underhill. LC 82-80476. (Treasures from the Spiritual Classics Ser.). 64p. 1982. reprint ed. pap. 2.95 (*0-8192-1313-6*) Morehouse Pub.

Abba: Father of All Who Will Listen. Matt Sluys & Ruth A. Sluys. 112p. (Orig.). 1994. pap. 7.95 (*1-883928-07-9*) Longwood.

Abba: Guides to Wholeness & Holiness East & West. Ed. by John R. Sommerfeldt. (Cistercian Studies: No. 38). 1982. 22.95 (*0-87907-838-3*) Cistercian Pubns.

Abba: How God Parents Us. David Mains & Karen Mains. LC 88-37312. 160p. (Orig.). 1989. pap. 7.99 (*0-87788-002-6*) Shaw Pubs.

Abba! Father! Gerald O'Mahony. (C). 1988. 39.00 (*0-85439-194-0*, Pub. by St Paul Pubns UK) St Mut.

Abba Father: The Lord's Pattern for Prayer. R. Kent Hughes. LC 85-72920. 128p. 1986. pap. 5.99 (*0-89107-377-9*) Crossway Bks.

Abba, Father! We Long to See Your Face: Theological Insights into the First Person of God-Trinity. Jean Galot. Tr. by Angeline Bouchard. LC 92-13014. 248p. 1992. pap. 12.95 (*0-8189-0645-6*) Alba.

ABBA Gold. John Tobler. LC 94-17528. (Illus.). 1994. pap. 13.95 (*0-312-11227-0*) St Martin.

Abba Hillel Silver: A Profile in American Judaism. Marc L. Raphael. LC 89-7581. 282p. 1989. 49.50 (*0-8419-1059-6*) Holmes & Meier.

Abba, Padre: Abba, Father. Jose M. Martinez. (SPA.). 9.95 (*84-7645-383-3*, 223533, Pub. by Edit Clie SP) TSELF.

ABBA's Child. Brennan Manning. LC 94-14008. 192p. (Orig.). 1994. pap. 10.00 (*0-89109-826-7*) NavPress.

Abbas Effendi: His Life & Teachings see Master in Akka: Including Recollections of the Greatest Holy Leaf

Abbas Pasha Manuscript: And the Horses & Horsemen of Arabia & Egypt During the Time of Abbas Pasha, 1800-1860. Ed. by Judith Forbis. Tr. by Gulsun Sherif. (Illus.). 730p. 1993. 180.00 (*0-9625644-2-7*) Ansata Pubns.

Abbasid Belles Lettres. Ed. by Julia Ashtiany. (Cambridge History of Arabic Literature Ser.). (Illus.). (C). 1990. 110.00 (*0-521-24016-6*) Cambridge U Pr.

Abbasid Tradition: Qur'ans of the 8th to 10th Centuries. Francois Deroche. (Nassar D. Khalili Collection of Islamic Art: Vol. I). (Illus.). 192p. 1992. 275.00 (*0-19-727600-8*) OUP.

Abbaye de Theleme. 2nd ed. Francois Rabelais. 40p. (FRE.). 1949. pap. 14.95 (*0-7859-5376-0*, F31160) Fr & Eur.

Abbayes et Prieures de l'Ancienne France, 10 vols. Andre Beaunier & Jean M. Besse. lxviii, 2963p. reprint ed. write for info. (*0-318-71318-7*, Pub. by Georg Olms GW) Lubrecht & Cramer.

Abbe C. Georges Bataille. (Folio Ser.: No. 106). (FRE.). 1972. pap. 9.95 (*2-07-036106-3*) Schoenhof.

Abbe C. Georges Bataille. (FRE.). 1972. pap. 11.95 (*0-7859-1697-0*, 2070361063) Fr & Eur.

Abbe C. Georges Bataille. Tr. by Philip A. Facey. LC 82-17704. 160p. 1983. 13.95 (*0-7145-2709-2*) M Boyars Pubs.

Abbe C. Georges Bataille. Tr. by Philip A. Facey. 158p. 1994. reprint ed. pap. 11.95 (*0-7145-2848-X*) M Boyars Pubs.

Abbe Gregoire, 1787-1831: The Odyssey of an Egalitarian. Ruth F. Necheles. LC 75-105987. 333p. (C). 1971. text ed. 55.00 (*0-8371-3312-2*, NAG/&, Greenwood Pr) Greenwood.

Abbe Mouret's Transgression. Emile Zola. (Pocket Classic Ser.). 1993. pap. 6.00 (*0-7509-0280-9*) A Sutton Pub.

Abbe Prevost & English Literature. George R. Havens. (Elliott Monographs: Vol. 9). 1921. pap. 15.00 (*0-527-02613-1*) Periodicals Srv.

Abbe Prevost & English Literature. George R. Havens. LC 65-15884. (Studies in Comparative Literature: No. 35). 1969. reprint ed. lib. bdg. 75.00 (*0-8383-0568-7*) M S G Haskell Hse.

Abbe Tigrane. Ferdinand Fabre. Tr. & Intro. by Robert Liddell. LC 88-70562. 182p. 1988. 25.00 (*0-7206-0693-4*, Pub. by P Owen Ltd UK) Dufour.

Abbess: A Romance, Set. William H. Ireland. LC 73-22764. (Gothic Novels II Ser.). 905p. 1979. reprint ed. 96.95 (*0-405-06015-7*) Ayer.

***Abbess of Crewe: A Modern Morality Tale.** Muriel Spark. LC 95-1628. (New Directions Bibelot Ser.). 116p. 1995. pap. 6.00 (*0-8112-1296-3*, 805) New Directions.

Abbess of Port Royal, & Other French Studies. Maria E. MacKaye. 1977. 12.95 (*0-8369-7228-7*, 8027) Ayer.

Abbess Thaisia of Leushino: An Autobiography of a Spiritual Daughter of St. John of Kronstadt. Thaisia. Ed. by St. Herman of Alaska Brotherhood Staff. Tr. by Alexander Cheremetieff et al. LC 89-64025. (Modern Matericon Ser.). (Illus.). 344p. (Orig.). 1990. pap. 15.00 (*0-938635-42-5*) St Herman AK.

Abbesse de Castro eu Autres Chroniques Italiennes. Stendhal, pseud. (FRE.). 1984. pap. 12.95 (*0-7859-3114-7*) Fr & Eur.

Abbeville County: Southern Life-Styles Lost in Time. Lester W. Ferguson. LC 93-27946. 1993. 25.00 (*0-87152-475-9*) Reprint.

Abbey Collection of Colour-Plate Books in Aquatint & Lithography, 1770-1860: A Bibliographical Catalogue, 4 vols., Set. (Illus.). 1816p. 1991. reprint ed. 600.00 (*1-55660-134-4*) A Wofsy Fine Arts.

Abbey Cookbook: Inspired Recipes from the Great Atlanta Restaurant. Hans Bertram. LC 81-20225. (Illus.). 224p. 1982. pap. 10.95 (*0-916782-26-3*) Harvard Common Pr.

Abbey, Ireland's National Theatre, 1904-1979. Hugh Hunt. LC 79-53497. (Illus.). 1979. text ed. 46.50 (*0-231-04906-4*) Col U Pr.

Abbey of St. Asaph: A Novel. Isabella Kelly. Ed. by Devendra P. Varma. LC 77-2041. (Gothic Novels III Ser.). 1977. lib. bdg. 87.95 (*0-405-10140-6*) Ayer.

Abbey of St. Germain des Pres in the Seventeenth Century. Maarten Ultee. LC 81-2265. (Illus.). 224p. (C). 1981. text ed. 35.00x (*0-300-02562-9*) Yale U Pr.

Abbey of Theleme see Famous Utopias of the Renaissance

Abbey Psalter: The Book of Psalms Used by the Trappist Monks of Genesee Abbey. John Abbot & Eudes Bamberger. LC 81-80871. 368p. 1981. 29.95 (*0-8091-0316-8*) Paulist Pr.

Abbey Theatre: Interviews & Recollections. Ed. by E. H. Mikhail. LC 86-3407. 220p. 1986. 59.00 (*0-389-20616-4*, N8174) B&N Imports.

Abbey Theatre, Cradle of Genius. Fay Gerard. LC 83-45759. reprint ed. 24.50 (*0-404-20097-4*) AMS Pr.

Abbey Theatre Series of Plays: A Bibliography. Frances-Jane French. 1970. 15.95 (*0-85105-149-9*) Dufour.

Abbeys & Priories of Wales. Rod N. Cooper. (Illus.). 100p. (C). 1992. 59.00 (*0-7154-0712-0*, Pub. by C Davies Pubs) St Mut.

Abbey's Road. Edward Abbey. 224p. 1991. pap. 11.00 (*0-452-26564-9*, Plume) NAL-Dutton.

Abbey's Road: Take the Other. Edward Abbey. 1979. pap. 8.95 (*0-525-48233-4*, Dutton) NAL-Dutton.

Abbie an' Slats, Vol. 1. Al Capp & Raeburn Van Buren. Ed. by Herb Galewitz. (U. S. Classics Ser.). (Illus.). 80p. (Orig.). 1983. pap. 5.95 (*0-912277-14-9*) K Pierce Inc.

Abbie an' Slats, Vol. 2. Al Capp et al. Ed. by Herb Galewitz. (U. S. Classics Ser.). (Illus.). 80p. (Orig.). 1984. pap. 5.95 (*0-912277-24-6*) K Pierce Inc.

Abbie Hoffman: American Rebel. Marty Jezer. LC 92-7766. (Illus.). 325p. 1992. 22.95 (*0-8135-1850-4*) Rutgers U Pr.

An Asterisk (*) at the beginning of an entry indicates that the title is appearing in BIP for the first time.

Abbie Hoffman: American Rebel. Marty Jezer. LC 92-7766. (Illus.). 345p. 1993. pap. 14.95 (*0-8135-2017-7*) Rutgers U Pr.

Abbie in Love. Barbara Corcoran. 192p. 1981. pap. 1.95 (*0-345-29734-2*) Ballantine.

Abbot: A Genealogical Register of the Descendants of George Abbot, of Andover; George Abbot, of Rowley; Thomas Abbot, of Andover; Arthur Abbot of Ipswich; Robt. Abbot of Branford, Ct., & George Abbot of Norwalk, Ct. Abiel Abbot & Ephraim Abbot. 217p. 1988. reprint ed. lib. bdg. 40.50 (*0-8328-0082-1*); reprint ed. pap. 32.50 (*0-8328-0083-X*) Higginson Bk Co.

Abbot Aelred Carlyle, Caldey Island, & the Anglo-Catholic Revival in England. Rene Kollar. LC 93-46216. (AUS VII: Vol. 177). 384p. (C). 1995. text ed. 57.95 (*0-8204-2469-2*) P Lang Pubs.

Abbot & the Dwarf: Tales of Wisdom from the Desert. Derek Webster. 120p. (C). 1990. 39.00 (*0-85439-416-8*, Pub. by St Paul Pubns UK) St Mut.

Abbot in Monastic Tradition. Pierre Salmon. Tr. by Claire Lavoie. LC 78-158955. (Cistercian Studies: No. 14). 148p. 1972. 9.95 (*0-87907-814-6*) Cistercian Pubns.

Abbot of Montserrat: Or, the Pool of Blood. William C. Green. LC 77-2038. (Gothic Novels III Ser.). 1977. reprint ed. lib. bdg. 51.95 (*0-405-10137-6*) Ayer.

Abbot of Stockbridge. Philip McCutchan. 192p. 1992. 23.95 (*0-340-51340-3*, Pub. by H & S UK) Trafalgar.

Abbot Suger & Saint Denis. Ed. by Paula L. Gerson. (Illus.). 320p. 1988. 35.00 (*0-8109-1517-0*) Abrams.

Abbot Suger & Saint Denis. Ed. by Paula L. Gerson. (Illus.). 320p. 1986. 35.00 (*0-87099-408-5*, Abrams) Metro Mus Art.

Abbott Almanac. LC 87-73125. 1988. write for info. (*0-87502-227-8*) Benjamin Co.

Abbott & Costello: The Classic Comics. Intro. by Tom Mason & S. A. Bennett. LC 89-32810. (Illus.). 138p. 1989. pap. 9.95 (*0-944735-17-7*) Malibu Graphics.

Abbott & Costello Meet Frankenstein: The Original Shooting Script. Gregory W. Mank. Ed. by Philip J. Riley. LC 89-63447. (Universal Filmscript Series: Classic Comedy Films: Vol. 1). (Illus.). 168p. (Orig.). 1990. pap. 19.95 (*1-882127-10-2*) Magicimage Filmbooks.

Abbott Labs: What's Not in the Annual Report. Market Intelligence Staff. 321p. (Orig.). 1992. 995.00 (*1-56753-378-7*) Frost & Sullivan.

Abbott Lawrence Lowell: 1856-1943. Henry A. Yeomans & Walter P. Metzger. LC 76-55181. (Academic Profession Ser.). (Illus.). 1977. reprint ed. lib. bdg. 48.95 (*0-405-10009-4*) Ayer.

Abbreviated Dictionary of Synonyms: Diccionario Abreviado de Sinonimos. Fernando Corripio. 478p. 1980. pap. 17.95 (*0-8288-2038-4*, S50157) Fr & Eur.

Abbreviated Italian-Spanish, Spanish-Italian Dictionary: Diccionario Abreviado Italiano-Espanol-Italiano. Vox Staff. 735p. (ITA & SPA.). 1980. 39.95 (*0-8288-0379-X*, S31760) Fr & Eur.

Abbreviated Military Dictionary. deluxe ed. 334p. (PER & RUS.). 1954. 9.95 (*0-8288-6870-0*, M-9106) Fr & Eur.

Abbreviated Russian-Korean Dictionary. Touloup. 648p. (KOR & RUS.). 9.95 (*0-8288-6078-5*, M9055) Fr & Eur.

Abbreviated Russian-Persian Technical Dictionary. G. Geuunshvili. 477p. (PER & RUS.). 1974. 35.00 (*0-8288-5972-8*, M9053) Fr & Eur.

Abbreviated Turkish-Russian Dictionary of New Words. H. G. Antelava. 95p. (RUS & TUR.). 1978. pap. 19.95 (*0-8288-4859-9*, M9054) Fr & Eur.

Abbreviation of the Introduction to Astrology: Together with the Medieval Latin Translation of Adelard of Bath. Ed. by Charles Burnett et al. Tr. by Keiji Yamamoto et al. LC 94-2489. (Islamic Philosophy, Theology & Science, Studies & Texts Ser.: Vol. 15). 1994. 57.25 (*90-04-09997-2*) E J Brill.

Abbreviation of Titles of Publications. (National Information Standards Ser.). 1985. 12.00 (*0-88738-996-1*, Z39.5) Transaction Pubs.

Abbreviation of Writing by Character. Edmond Willis. LC 77-7442. (English Experience Ser.: No. 899). 1977. reprint ed. lib. bdg. 20.00 (*90-221-0899-6*) Walter J Johnson.

Abbreviations Dictionary. 7th ed. R. DeSola. 966p. 1991. 135.00 (*0-8288-0001-4*, M8229) Fr & Eur.

Abbreviations Dictionary. 8th ed. Ralph DeSola. 1992. 74. 95 (*0-8493-4247-3*, PE1693) CRC Pr.

Abbreviations Dictionary. 9th ed. karen Kerchelich & Dean Stahl. LC 94-20525. 1,376p. 1994. 79.95 (*0-8493-8944-5*, 8944) CRC Pr.

Abbreviations Guide to French Forms in Justice & Administration. 2nd ed. G. Leistner. 101p. (ENG, FRE & GER.). 1975. 49.95 (*0-8288-5785-7*) Fr & Eur.

Abbreviations in Greek: Inscriptions, Papyri, Manuscripts & Early Printed Books. Al. N. Oikonomides. 214p. (Orig.). 1986. 25.00 (*0-89005-049-X*) Ares.

Abbreviations of Names of Serials. 33p. Date not set. write for info. (*0-8218-0000-0*, ABBR) Am Math.

Abbreviations of Nuclear Power Plant Engineering. G. H. Freyberger. 280p. (ENG & GER.). 1979. 75.00 (*0-8288-4717-7*, M7288) Fr & Eur.

Abby. Jeannette Caines. LC 73-5480. (Illus.). 32p. (J). (ps-3). 1973. lib. bdg. 13.89 (*0-06-020922-4*) HarpC Child Bks.

Abby. Jeannette Caines. LC 73-5480. (Trophy Picture Bk.). (Illus.). 32p. (J). (ps-3). 1984. pap. 4.95 (*0-06-443049-9*, Trophy) HarpC Child Bks.

***Abby.** Garrett Christopher. Ed. by J. Friedland & R. Kessler. (Novel-Ties Ser.). (J). (gr. k-1). 1994. student ed, pap. text ed. 14.95 (*1-56982-080-5*) Lrn Links.

***Abby: Summer Vacation.** Sheila Duncan. Ed. by M. L. Jones. (Abby Ser.). 85p. (Orig.). 1995. pap. 6.95 (*1-882270-32-0*) Old Rugged Cross.

Abby Aldrich Rockefeller: The Woman in the Family. Bernice Kert. LC 93-12169. 1993. 35.00 (*0-394-56975-X*) Random.

Abby Aldrich Rockefeller Folk Art Center Address Book. M. McNeil. (Museum Gift Bks.). (Illus.). 160p. 1984. 14. 95 (*0-939456-10-9*) Galison.

Abby, My Love. Hadley Irwin. LC 84-24571. 168p. (YA). (gr. 7 up). 1985. text ed. 13.95 (*0-689-50323-7*, McElderry) S&S Childrens.

Abby Smith & Her Cows: With a Report of the Law Case Decided Contrary to Law. Julia E. Smith. LC 72-2622. (American Women Ser.: Images & Realities). 98p. 1974. reprint ed. 16.95 (*0-405-04478-X*) Ayer.

Abby Williams Hill & the Lure of the West. Ronald Fields. LC 88-38520. (Illus.). 120p. 1990. text ed. 35.00 (*0-295-97026-X*) U of Wash Pr.

Abby Williams Hill & the Lure of the West. Ronald Fields. LC 88-38520. (Illus.). 120p. 1989. 29.95 (*0-917048-63-6*) Wash St Hist Soc.

***Abby's Wish.** Liza St. John. LC 94-40436. (Publish-a-Book). (Illus.). (J). 1995. write for info. (*0-8114-7272-8*) Raintree Steck-V.

ABC. (Little Bitty Ser.). (Illus.). 20p. (Orig.). (J). (ps). 1991. bds. 2.50 (*0-8120-6266-3*) Barron.

ABC. (Snapshot Concept Board Bks.). (Illus.). 24p. (Orig.). (J). (ps). 1994. bds. 2.95 (*1-56458-533-6*) Dorling Kindersley.

ABC. (Orig.). 5.00 (*0-686-23328-X*) Rochester Folk Art.

***ABC.** (Show Baby Ser.). 12p. (J). 1994. bds. 2.98 (*0-86112-826-5*) Brimax Bks.

***ABC.** (Show Me Ser.). 12p. (J). 1994. bds. 2.98 (*0-86112-993-8*) Brimax Bks.

***ABC.** (Learning Together Ser.). 32p. (J). 1994. 2.98 (*1-85854-120-4*) Brimax Bks.

***ABC.** (Teddy Bears Ser.). 32p. (J). 1994. 3.98 (*0-86112-814-1*) Brimax Bks.

ABC. Jan Pienkowski. (Illus.). (J). (ps). 1989. 2.95 (*0-671-68133-8*, Litl Simon S&S) S&S Childrens.

ABC. Richard Scarry. (ITA.). 1976. 19.95 (*0-686-16892-5*) Intl Lang.

ABC. Cyndy Szekeres. LC 82-839989. (Golden Sturdy Bks.). (Illus.). 22p. (J). (ps up). 1983. write for info. (*0-307-12120-8*, 12120, Golden Bks) Western Pub.

ABC. William Wegman. (Illus.). 64p. (J). (ps-2). 1994. 17.95 (*1-56282-696-4*); lib. bdg. 17.89 (*1-56282-699-9*) Hyprn Child.

ABC: Alphabetization of the Popular Mind. Ivan Illich & Barry Sanders. 1989. pap. 8.76 (*0-679-72192-4*, Vin) Random.

ABC: Board Games. Lillian Lieberman. (Illus.). 64p. (J). (ps-2). 1991. pap. 7.95 (*1-878279-31-9*) Monday Morning Bks.

ABC: Box Games. Lillian Lieberman. (Illus.). 64p. 1991. pap. 7.95 (*1-878279-30-0*) Monday Morning Bks.

ABC: Costume & Textiles from the Los Angeles County Museum of Art. (Illus.). 32p. (J). (gr. 2 up). 1988. 12.95 (*0-8109-1877-3*) Abrams.

ABC: Folder Games. Lillian Lieberman. (Illus.). 64p. 1991. pap. 7.95 (*1-878279-29-7*) Monday Morning Bks.

ABC: International Constructivist Architecture, 1922-1939. Sima Ingberman. LC 93-36771. (Illus.). 195p. 1994. 42. 50 (*0-262-09031-7*) MIT Pr.

ABC: Musical Instruments from the Metropolitan Museum of Art. (ABC Ser.). (Illus.). 32p. (J). (gr. 2 up). 1988. 12.95 (*0-8109-1878-1*) Abrams.

ABC: National Museum of American History. Florence C. Mayers. (ABC Ser.). (Illus.). 32p. (J). 1989. 12.95 (*0-8109-1875-7*) Abrams.

ABC: Teaching Human Rights. 56p. 1990. 3.00 (*92-1-100430-6*, 90.I.5) UN.

ABC: The Wild West Buffalo Bill Historical Center, Cody, Wyoming. Florence C. Mayers. LC 90-440. (Illus.). 32p. (J). 1990. 12.95 (*0-8109-1903-6*) Abrams.

ABC - Aunt Sally & Sacred Cow. Clement Semmler. 246p. 1981. 29.95 (*0-522-84216-X*) Intl Spec Bk.

ABC - Sign with Me. Susan P. Shroyer & Joan G. Kimmel. (Sign with Me Ser.). 32p. (Orig.). (J). (ps-2). 1987. pap. 4.95 (*0-939849-00-3*) Sugar Sign Pr.

ABC (Active Basic Communication), Program 1. Pace International Research, Inc. Staff. (ABC Video Ser.). (Illus.). 157p. 1984. text ed. 8.95 (*0-89209-215-7*); pap. text ed. 4.25 (*0-89209-326-9*); audio 4.00 (*0-89209-327-7*); vhs 115.00 (*0-89209-178-9*) Pace Intl Res.

ABC (Active Basic Communication), Program 10. Pace International Research, Inc. Staff. (ABC Video Ser.). (Illus.). 171p. 1984. text ed. 8.95 (*0-89209-224-6*); pap. text ed. 4.25 (*0-89209-344-7*); audio 4.00 (*0-89209-345-5*); vhs 115.00 (*0-89209-187-8*) Pace Intl Res.

ABC (Active Basic Communication), Program 11. Pace International Research, Inc. Staff. (ABC Video Ser.). (Illus.). 151p. 1984. text ed. 8.95 (*0-89209-225-4*); pap. text ed. 4.25 (*0-89209-346-3*); audio 4.00 (*0-89209-347-1*); vhs 115.00 (*0-89209-188-6*) Pace Intl Res.

ABC (Active Basic Communication), Program 12. Pace International Research, Inc. Staff. (ABC Video Ser.). (Illus.). 173p. 1984. text ed. 8.95 (*0-89209-226-2*); pap. text ed. 4.25 (*0-89209-348-X*); audio 4.00 (*0-89209-349-8*); vhs 115.00 (*0-89209-189-4*) Pace Intl Res.

ABC (Active Basic Communication), Program 13. Pace International Research, Inc. Staff. (ABC Video Ser.). (Illus.). 153p. 1984. text ed. 8.95 (*0-89209-227-0*); pap. text ed. 4.25 (*0-89209-375-7*); audio 4.00 (*0-89209-376-5*); vhs 115.00 (*0-89209-190-8*) Pace Intl Res.

ABC (Active Basic Communication), Program 14. Pace International Research, Inc. Staff. (ABC Video Ser.). (Illus.). 153p. 1984. text ed. 8.95 (*0-89209-228-9*); pap. text ed. 4.25 (*0-89209-377-3*); audio 4.00 (*0-89209-378-1*); vhs 115.00 (*0-89209-191-6*) Pace Intl Res.

ABC (Active Basic Communication), Program 15. Pace International Research, Inc. Staff. (ABC Video Ser.). (Illus.). 177p. 1984. text ed. 8.95 (*0-89209-229-7*); pap. text ed. 4.25 (*0-89209-379-X*); audio 4.00 (*0-89209-380-3*); vhs 115.00 (*0-89209-192-4*) Pace Intl Res.

ABC (Active Basic Communication), Program 16. Pace International Research, Inc. Staff. (ABC Video Ser.). (Illus.). 145p. 1984. text ed. 8.95 (*0-89209-230-0*); pap. text ed. 4.25 (*0-89209-381-1*); audio 4.00 (*0-89209-382-X*); vhs 115.00 (*0-89209-193-2*) Pace Intl Res.

ABC (Active Basic Communication), Program 2. Pace International Research, Inc. Staff. (ABC Video Ser.). (Illus.). 177p. 1984. text ed. 8.95 (*0-89209-216-5*); pap. text ed. 4.25 (*0-89209-328-5*); audio 4.00 (*0-89209-329-3*); vhs 115.00 (*0-89209-179-7*) Pace Intl Res.

ABC (Active Basic Communication), Program 3. Pace International Research, Inc. Staff. (ABC Video Ser.). (Illus.). 149p. 1984. text ed. 8.95 (*0-89209-217-3*); pap. text ed. 4.25 (*0-89209-330-7*); audio 4.00 (*0-89209-331-5*); vhs 115.00 (*0-89209-180-0*) Pace Intl Res.

ABC (Active Basic Communication), Program 4. Pace International Research, Inc. Staff. (ABC Video Ser.). (Illus.). 167p. 1984. text ed. 8.95 (*0-89209-218-1*); pap. text ed. 4.25 (*0-89209-332-3*); audio 4.00 (*0-89209-333-1*); vhs 115.00 (*0-89209-181-9*) Pace Intl Res.

ABC (Active Basic Communication), Program 5. Pace International Research, Inc. Staff. (ABC Video Ser.). (Illus.). 147p. 1984. text ed. 8.95 (*0-89209-219-X*); pap. text ed. 4.25 (*0-89209-334-X*); audio 4.00 (*0-89209-335-8*); vhs 115.00 (*0-89209-182-7*) Pace Intl Res.

ABC (Active Basic Communication), Program 6. Pace International Research, Inc. Staff. (ABC Video Ser.). (Illus.). 167p. 1984. text ed. 8.95 (*0-89209-220-3*); pap. text ed. 4.25 (*0-89209-336-6*); audio 4.00 (*0-89209-337-4*); vhs 115.00 (*0-89209-183-5*) Pace Intl Res.

ABC (Active Basic Communication), Program 7. (ABC Video Ser.). (Illus.). 133p. 1984. text ed. 8.95 (*0-89209-221-1*); pap. text ed. 4.25 (*0-89209-338-2*); audio 4.00 (*0-89209-339-0*); vhs 115.00 (*0-89209-184-3*) Pace Intl Res.

ABC (Active Basic Communication), Program 8. Pace International Research, Inc. Staff. (ABC Video Ser.). (Illus.). 195p. 1984. text ed. 8.95 (*0-89209-222-X*); pap. text ed. 4.25 (*0-89209-340-4*); audio 4.00 (*0-89209-341-2*); vhs 115.00 (*0-89209-185-1*) Pace Intl Res.

ABC (Active Basic Communication), Program 9. Pace International Research, Inc. Staff. (ABC Video Ser.). (Illus.). 157p. 1984. text ed. 8.95 (*0-89209-223-8*); pap. text ed. 4.25 (*0-89209-342-0*); audio 4.00 (*0-89209-343-9*); vhs 115.00 (*0-89209-186-X*) Pace Intl Res.

ABC Alphabet Book, No. 1. Jane Ho. 29p. (J). (ps). Date not set. 20.00 (*0-9619126-0-X*) J H Childs Bks.

ABC (America Before Columbus) Joseph Robinette. 40p. (J). (gr. k-8). 1984. pap. 4.00 (*0-88680-212-1*) I E Clark.

***ABC & T for Teddy.** Lois Becker & Mark Stratton. Ed. by Mary Becker et al. (Teddy Ruxpin Tell Me Again Ser.). (Illus.). 24p. (J). 1995. audio, pap. 11.95 (*0-934323-82-8*) Alchemy Comms.

ABC & XYZ of Bee Culture: An Encyclopedia of Beekeeping. 40th rev. ed. Ed. by Roger Morse & Kim Flottum. (Illus.). 528p. 1990. 25.00 (*0-936028-01-7*) A I Root.

ABC & You. (Toddler Books Ser.: No. 905-5). (J). (ps-00). 1990. boxed 3.95 (*0-7214-5274-4*) Ladybird Bks.

ABC Astronomie. Weigert & Zimmerman. 480p. (GER.). 1974. 35.00 (*0-8288-5973-6*, M7289) Fr & Eur.

ABC Basic Chart Reading. Lynne Palmer. 76p. 1974. 10.00 (*0-86690-136-1*, P1363-014) Am Fed Astrologers.

ABC Bestiary. Deborah Blackwell. 1989. 15.00 (*0-374-30005-4*) FS&G.

ABC Bestiary. Alfred Van Loen. Ed. by Stanley H. Barkan. (Review Art & Poetry Ser.: No. 1). 64p. 1989. 20.00 (*0-89304-352-4*); 15.00 (*0-89304-356-7*); pap. 10.00 (*0-89304-353-2*); 300.00 (*0-89304-354-0*); 35.00 (*0-89304-355-9*); write for info. (*0-318-65305-2*) Cross-Cultrl NY.

ABC Bestiary. deluxe limited ed. Alfred Van Loen. Ed. by Stanley H. Barkan. (Review Art & Poetry Ser.: No. 1). 64p. 1989. 100.00 (*0-89304-350-8*); 50.00 (*0-89304-351-6*); pap. 50.00 (*0-89304-357-5*) Cross-Cultrl NY.

ABC Bible & Holiday Stories. Daisy P. Aronoff. (Illus.). 58p. (J). (ps-7). 1992. reprint ed. pap. 15.95 (*1-878612-28-X*) Sunflower Co.

ABC Block Book. Jean Hirashima. (Chunky Shape Bks.). (Illus.). 22p. (J). (ps). 1994. 3.25 (*0-679-83712-4*) Random Bks Yng Read.

ABC Book of Early Americana. Eric Sloane. LC 89-24603. (Illus.). 64p. (J). 1990. 16.95 (*0-8050-1294-X*) H Holt & Co.

ABC Book of Feelings. Marlys Boddy. (Illus.). 32p. (J). (ps-3). 1991. 8.99 (*0-570-04190-2*, 56-1649) Concordia.

ABC Book of God's Creatures. Mary M. Landis. (Jewel Bks.). 1993. pap. 2.15 (*0-317-05265-9*) Rod & Staff.

***ABC Books & Activities: From Pre-School to High School.** Cathie H. Cooper. LC 95-9728. (School Library Media Ser.: No. 5). 1995. write for info. (*0-8108-3013-2*) Scarecrow.

ABC Books of the Pennsylvania Germans: Bd. with Abraham Harley Cassel, Nineteenth Century Pennsylvania-German American Book Collector; & Marriages Performed at the Evangelical Lutheran Church...1748-1767, Vol. VII. Walter Klinefelter et al. LC 68-4243. 1973. 15.00 (*0-911122-29-X*) Penn German Soc.

ABC Bunny. Wanda Gag. LC 33-27359. (Illus.). (J). (gr. k-2). 1978. 14.95 (*0-698-20000-4*, Sandcastle Bks); pap. 6.95 (*0-698-20683-5*, Sandcastle Bks) Putnam Pub Group.

***ABC Career Book for Boys: El Libro de Carreros Para Ninos.** Linda Stockdale. Tr. by Bottom Line Communications Staff. (Children at Work Ser.). (Illus.). 32p. (J). (gr. 1-4). 1995. pap. 9.95 (*0-9622514-6-1*) Columbia San Fran.

***ABC Career Book for Girls: El Libro de Carreras para Ninas.** 2nd ed. Linda Stockdale. Tr. by Bottom Line Communications Staff. LC 91-73132. (Children at Work Ser.). (Illus.). 32p. (J). (gr. 1-4). 1995. pap. 9.95 (*0-9622514-5-3*) Columbia San Fran.

***ABC Career Book for Girls: El Libro de Carreras para Ninas.** 3rd ed. Linda Stockdale. Tr. by Bottom-Line Communications Staff. LC 91-73132. (Children at Work Ser.). (Illus.). 32p. (SPA.). (J). (gr. 1-4). 1995. pap. text ed. 9.95 (*1-884830-00-5*) Columbia San Fran.

ABC Career Book for Girls: Introducing the Career Pals. Peggy Turner & Linda S. Brewer. Ed. by Myrlys Hollis. (Illus.). 32p. (J). (gr. 1-4). 1992. pap. 6.95 (*0-9622514-2-9*) Columbia San Fran.

ABC Chart Erection. Palmer. 224p. 1971. 11.00 (*0-86690-137-X*, P1364-014) Am Fed Astrologers.

ABC Christmas Book. (Illus.). 20p. (J). (ps-5). 1986. pap. 4.00 (*0-914510-16-9*) Evergreen.

***ABC Circus.** Illus. by Judy Shimono. 48p. (J). (ps-k). 1995. teacher ed 6.95 (*0-614-06861-4*, WPH 1404) Totline Bks.

ABC Circus: The Great Big Circus Unit with Alphabet Cards. Jean Warren. Ed. by Gayle Bittinger. LC 90-71744. (ABC Ser.). (Illus.). (Orig.). 1991. pap. text ed. 6.95 (*0-911019-42-1*) Warren Pub Hse.

ABC-CLIO Literary Companion to the Encyclopedia of Allegory. David A. Leeming. 250p. 1996. lib. bdg. 65. 00 (*0-87436-781-6*) ABC-CLIO.

ABC-CLIO Online. Susan K. Kinnell. 1992. lib. bdg. 49.00 (*0-87436-611-9*) ABC-CLIO.

ABC Clip & Copy. Sharon Rybak. 208p. (J). (ps-2). 1991. 14.95 (*0-86653-586-1*, GA1301) Good Apple.

ABC Coloring Book. Richard Hefter. (J). 1978. pap. 2.50 (*0-486-22969-6*) Dover.

ABC Colouring Book. (Illus.). (J). (ps-6). pap. 2.95 (*0-565-00834-X*, Pub. by Natural Hist Mus UK) Parkwest Pubns.

ABC Come Play with Me. Bank Street College of Education Editors. (Bunny Bks.). (Illus.). 64p. (J). (ps-00). 1985. 3.95 (*0-8120-3617-4*) Barron.

ABC Come See Wyoming. Maria C. Kidner. (Illus.). 56p. (Orig.). (J). (gr. k-3). 1990. pap. 4.95 (*0-9625920-0-5*) Rainbow Rhapsody.

ABC Come See Wyoming. rev. ed. Maria C. Kidner. (Illus.). 56p. (Orig.). (J). (gr. k-3). 1990. reprint ed. pap. 4.95 (*0-9625920-1-3*) Rainbow Rhapsody.

ABC Crafts & Cooking. Lynn Ransford et al. (Illus.). 64p. (J). (ps-2). 1987. student ed 7.95 (*1-55734-090-0*) Tchr Create Mat.

ABC de AutoCad 12. Date not set. pap. text ed. 24.95 (*968-6346-64-3*, Pub. by Ventura Ediciones MX) Computer & Tech.

***ABC de Babar.** Jean De Brunhoff. 46p. (J). 1978. 24.95 (*0-7859-8776-2*) Fr & Eur.

ABC de dBase IV 1.5. Yazmin J. Parra. 358p. 1992. pap. text ed. 24.95 (*968-6346-59-7*, Pub. by Ventura Ediciones MX) Computer & Tech.

***ABC de Esperanto.** Ionel Onet. 15p. 1994. pap. 1.00 (*1-882251-08-3*) Eldonejo Bero.

ABC de MC Word. Alan Neibauer. 373p. 1992. pap. text ed. 22.95 (*968-6346-21-X*, Pub. by Ventura Ediciones MX) Computer & Tech.

ABC de Puerto Rico. De Matos Freyre. 1966. 8.95 (*0-87751-005-9*) E Torres & Sons.

ABC de Quattro Pro 4 para el DOS. Alan Simpson & Douglas Wolf. 311p. 1992. pap. text ed. 24.95 (*968-6346-42-2*, Pub. by Ventura Ediciones MX) Computer & Tech.

ABC de WordPerfect 5.1. Alan R. Neibauer. 306p. 1991. pap. text ed. 24.95 (*968-6346-24-4*, Pub. by Ventura Ediciones MX) Computer & Tech.

ABC de WordPerfect 5.1 para Windows. Alan R. Neibauer. 312p. 1993. pap. text ed. 24.95 (*968-6346-51-1*, Pub. by Ventura Ediciones MX) Computer & Tech.

ABC de 123 para Windows. Robert Cowart. 350p. 1993. pap. text ed. 24.95 (*968-6346-61-9*, Pub. by Ventura Ediciones MX) Computer & Tech.

ABC de 123 Version 2.4 para DOS. Chris Gilbert & Laurie Williams. 328p. 1992. pap. text ed. 24.95 (*968-6346-65-1*, Pub. by Ventura Ediciones MX) Computer & Tech.

ABC del AutoCad Version 11. Alan Miller. 348p. 1992. pap. text ed. 25.95 (*968-6346-35-X*, Pub. by Ventura Ediciones MX) Computer & Tech.

ABC del DOS 4. Alan R. Miller. 270p. 1991. pap. text ed. 22.95 (*968-6346-09-0*, Pub. by Ventura Ediciones MX) Computer & Tech.

ABC del DOS 5. Alan R. Miller. 264p. 1992. pap. text ed. 22.95 (*968-6346-33-3*, Pub. by Ventura Ediciones MX) Computer & Tech.

A

An Asterisk (*) at the beginning of an entry indicates that the title is appearing in BIP for the first time. 7

A

ABC del MS Word para Windows. Alan Neibauer. 415p. 1992. pap. text ed. 24.95 (968-6346-57-0, Pub. by Ventura Ediciones MX) Computer & Tech.

ABC del Novell Netware. Hector G. Tejera. 244p. 1991. pap. text ed. 25.95 (968-6346-23-6, Pub. by Ventura Ediciones MX) Computer & Tech.

ABC del 123 Version 3. Judd Robbins. 261p. 1993. pap. text ed. 24.95 (968-6346-75-9, Pub. by Ventura Ediciones MX) Computer & Tech.

ABC der Optik. Muetze. 960p. (GER.). 1991. 95.00 (0-8288-6079-3, M-7290) Fr & Eur.

ABC des Buchhandels. W. Stoeckle. 135p. (GER.). 1975. pap. 55.00 (0-8288-5786-5, M7291) Fr & Eur.

ABC Dictionary I: Arabic & English. Librairie du Liban Staff. (ARA & ENG.). (J). (ps-4). 1983. 6.00 (0-86685-336-7) Intl Bk Ctr.

ABC Dictionary I: Arabic & French. Librairie du Liban Staff. (ARA & FRE.). (J). (ps-4). 1983. 6.00 (0-86685-310-3) Intl Bk Ctr.

ABC Dictionary I: Arabic & German. Librairie du Liban Staff. (ARA & GER.). (J). (ps-4). 1983. 6.00 (0-86685-309-X) Intl Bk Ctr.

ABC Dictionary Tamhidi: Arabic & French. Librairie du Liban Staff. (ARA & FRE.). (J). (ps-4). 1983. 6.00 (0-86685-315-4) Intl Bk Ctr.

ABC Dictionary Tamhidi: Arabic & German. Librairie du Liban Staff. (ARA & GER.). (J). (ps-4). 1983. 6.00 (0-86685-313-8) Intl Bk Ctr.

ABC Dictionary Tamhidi: Arabic & Italian. Librairie du Liban Staff. (ARA & ITA.). (J). (ps-4). 1983. 6.00 (0-86685-316-2) Intl Bk Ctr.

ABC Dinosaurs: And Other Prehistoric Creatures. Illus. by Jan Pienkowski. 10p. (J). (ps-00). 1993. 18.99 (0-525-67468-3, Lodestar Bks) Dutton Child Bks.

ABC; Egyptian Art from the Brooklyn Museum. Florence C. Mayers. (ABC Ser.). (Illus.). 32p. 1988. 12.95 (0-8109-0888-3) Abrams.

ABC Et-Cetera: The Life & Times of the Roman Alphabet. Alexander Humez & Nicholas Humez. LC 85-70148. 256p. 1987. pap. 14.95 (0-87923-664-7) Godine.

ABC Excel 4 para Windows. Alan R. Neibauer. 292p. 1993. pap. text ed. 24.95 (968-6346-58-9, Pub. by Ventura Ediciones MX) Computer & Tech.

ABC Exhibit. Leonard E. Fisher. LC 90-6639. (Illus.). 32p. (J). (ps up). 1991. text ed. 15.95 (0-02-735251-X, Mac Bks Young Read) S&S Childrens.

*ABC Farm. Illus. by Judy Shimono. 48p. (J). (ps-k). 1995. teacher ed 6.95 (0-614-06859-2, WPH 1402) Totline Bks.

ABC Farm: The Great Big Farm Unit with Alphabet Cards. Jean Warren. Ed. by Gayle Bittinger. LC 90-71742. (ABC Ser.). (Illus.). 48p. (Orig.). 1991. pap. text ed. 6.95 (0-911019-40-5) Warren Pub Hse.

ABC Feelings: A Coloring - Learning Book. rev. ed. Alexandra Delis-Abrams. Ed. by Joan Follendore. (Illus.). 64p. (J). (gr. 3-8). 1991. reprint ed. pap. text ed. 7.95 (1-879889-00-5) Adage Pubns.

*ABC for Book Collectors. 7th ed. John Carter. Ed. & Rev. by Nicolas Barker. LC 94-29934. 224p. 1995. 25.00 (1-884718-05-1) Oak Knoll.

ABC for Christmas. Dick Jacobson & Bob Naujoks. 55p. (Orig.). pap. 4.95 (0-941988-04-X) K Q Assocs.

ABC Guide to the Federal Court of Australia. Matthew Smith. xvii, 230p. 1986. pap. 40.00 (0-455-20686-4, Pub. by Law Bk Co) W W Gaunt.

ABC Hawaii: A Reference Guide - Everything to Know about the Islands. Randy Mita. 208p. 1994. pap. 14.95 (0-935180-84-2) Mutual Pub HI.

*ABC Herbal: A Simplified Guide to Natural Health Care for Children. Steven H. Horne. 82p. (Orig.). 1994. pap. text ed. 7.95 (1-885653-04-2) W W Whitman.

ABC House. McKenzie. (J). 1994. 14.95 (0-8050-1946-4) H Holt & Co.

ABC I: Arabic Italian Dictionary. Librairie du Liban Staff. (J). (ps-4). 1983. 6.00 (0-86685-308-1) Intl Bk Ctr.

ABC I Can Be. Zoe Gorham. (J). (ps-3). 1993. pap. 3.95 (0-85953-129-5) Childs Play.

*ABC I Can Be. Verna Wilkins. (I Can Be Ser.). (Illus.). 24p. (J). 1995. lib. bdg. 12.95 (1-56674-118-1) Forest Hse.

*ABC in the Woods. National Geographic Staff. (Little Learners' Library). (J). (ps). 1994. 4.50 (0-7922-1832-9) Natl Geog.

ABC Islamic Reader. M. A. Qazi. (J). pap. 3.50 (0-935782-07-9) Kazi Pubns.

ABC Limericks. Jonathon J. Thompson, Jr. (Illus.). 40p. (J). (gr. 3-6). 1992. 3.95 (0-933479-04-2) Thompson.

ABC Manager's Primer: Straight Talk on Activity Based Costing. Gary Cokins. 1993. pap. 15.00 (0-86641-220-4) Inst Mgmt Account.

ABC Mazes. Waneta B. Bullock & Ganelle Loveless. (Ann Arbor Educational Ser.). (Illus.). 56p. (J). (gr. k-1). 1979. pap. 8.00 (0-87879-713-0, Ann Arbor Div) Acad Therapy.

ABC Memory Book: In Stages, One, Two & Three. rev. ed. N. A. Woychuk. (Illus.). 59p. (Orig.). 1978. pap. 8.95 (1-880960-09-5) Script Memory Fl.

ABC Museum of Fine Arts, Boston. Florence C. Mayers. (Illus.). 32p. 1986. 12.95 (0-8109-1847-1) Abrams.

ABC Museum of Modern Art, New York. Florence C. Mayers. (ABC Ser.). (Illus.). 32p. 1986. 12.95 (0-8109-1849-8) Abrams.

ABC Mystery. Doug Cushman. LC 92-9621. (Illus.). 32p. (J). (ps-2). 1993. 14.95 (0-06-021226-8); lib. bdg. 14.89 (0-06-021227-6) HarpC Child Bks.

ABC National Air & Space Museum. Florence C. Mayers. (ABC Ser.). (Illus.). 32p. 1987. 12.95 (0-8109-1859-5) Abrams.

ABC of Acid-Base Chemistry: The Elements of Physiological Blood-Gas Chemistry for Medical Students & Physicians. rev. ed. Horace W. Davenport. LC 79-88230. 1974. pap. text ed. 10.00 (0-226-13703-1) U Ch Pr.

ABC of AIDS. 3rd rev. ed. Ed. by Michael W. Adler. (Illus.). 86p. 1993. pap. 25.00 (0-7279-0761-1, BMJ Pubng Grp) Amer Coll Phys.

ABC of Alcohol. Ed. by Alex Paton. (Illus.). 35p. 1982. pap. 16.00 (0-7279-0192-3, Pub. by British Med Jrnl UK) Amer Coll Phys.

ABC of Alcohol. 3rd ed. Alex Paton. 48p. 1994. pap. text ed. 17.00 (0-7279-0812-X, BMJ Pubng Grp) Amer Coll Phys.

ABC of Anarchism. Alexander Berkman. (Orig.). 1984. lib. bdg. 89.95 (0-87700-649-0) Revisionist Pr.

ABC of Anarchism. 3rd ed. Alexander Berkman & Peter Newell. 86p. (Orig.). 1980. pap. 5.00 (0-317-00634-7) Left Bank.

ABC of Antenatal Care. Geoffrey Chamberlain. (Illus.). 84p. 1992. pap. text ed. 25.00 (0-7279-0313-6, Pub. by British Med Jrnl UK) Amer Coll Phys.

ABC of Asthma. 2nd ed. John Rees & John Price. (Illus.). 34p. 1985. pap. 16.00 (0-7279-0226-1, Pub. by Brit Med Assn UK) Amer Coll Phys.

ABC of Avalanche Safety. 2nd ed. E. R. LaChapelle. LC 85-21393. (Illus.). 112p. 1985. pap. 6.95 (0-89886-103-9) Mountaineers.

ABC of BASIC: An Introduction to Programming for Librarians. Eric J. Hunter. LC 82-246082. (Illus.). 120p. 1982. reprint ed. pap. 34.20 (0-7837-5291-1, 2045045) Bks Demand.

ABC of Breaking & Schooling Horses. Josephine Knowles. 196p. 1990. 70.00 (0-85131-559-3, Pub. by J A Allen & Co UK) St Mut.

ABC of Child Abuse. 2nd ed. Ed. by Roy Meadow. (Illus.). 75p. 1989. pap. text ed. 27.00 (0-7279-0764-6, BMJ Pubng Grp) Amer Coll Phys.

A.B.C. of Child Abuse Work. Jean G. Moore. LC 85-9738. 105p. 1985. pap. 19.95 (0-566-00860-2) Ashgate Pub Co.

ABC of Child Protection Work. 2nd ed. Jean Moore. 120p. 1992. pap. 16.95 (1-85742-027-6, Pub. by Ashgate UK) Ashgate Pub Co.

A.B.C. of Chinese Painting, Bk. 1. Ning Yeh. 134p. 1992. pap. write for info. (0-9618307-1-9) Ning & Ling Yeh.

ABC of Clinical Genetics. Helen M. Kingston. (Illus.). 62p. 1989. pap. 28.00 (0-7279-0263-6, Pub. by Brit Med Assn UK) Amer Coll Phys.

ABC of Color. W. E. B. Du Bois. 216p. (Orig.). 1989. pap. 4.95 (0-7178-0391-0) Intl Pubs Co.

ABC of Colorectal Diseases. Ed. by D. J. Jones & M. H. Irving. (Illus.). 103p. 1993. pap. 28.00 (0-7279-0755-7, BMJ Pubng Grp) Amer Coll Phys.

ABC of Communism. rev. ed. Nikolai Bukharin & Evgeny Preobrazhensky. (Ann Arbor Paperbacks Ser.). 432p. 1988. text ed. 44.50x (0-472-09112-3, Ann Arbor Bks) U of Mich Pr.

ABC of (D) GW. Gwyn Williams. 232p. 1985. 45.00 (0-85088-854-9, Pub. by Collets) St Mut.

ABC of Dermatology. Paul K. Buxton. (Illus.). 98p. 1988. pap. text ed. 28.00 (0-7279-0758-1, BMJ Pubng Grp) Amer Coll Phys.

ABC of Diabetes. 3rd ed. Peter J. Watkins. (Illus.). 56p. 1988. pap. text ed. 18.00 (0-7279-0763-8, BMJ Pubng Grp) Amer Coll Phys.

ABC of Ecology. 2nd ed. Frances Wosmek. LC 82-70224. (Illus.). 60p. (ENG, FRE & SPA.). (J). (ps-3). 1990. pap. 3.50 (0-943864-00-3) Davenport.

*ABC of Evidence. 4th ed. R. Bartley & C. Brahe. 846p. 1988. boxed 64.00 (0-908508-03-4, Austral) Butterworth Legal Pubs.

ABC of Eyes. A. R. Elkington & P. T. Khaw. (Illus.). 55p. 1988. pap. 27.00 (0-7279-0240-7, Pub. by Brit Med Assn UK) Amer Coll Phys.

*ABC of Fashionable Animals. Edens. (J). Date not set. 12.95 (0-671-75201-4, S&S Bks Young Read) S&S Childrens.

ABC of Healthy Travel. 4th ed. Eric Walker. Ed. by Glyn Williams & Fiona Raeside. (Illus.). 49p. 1993. pap. text ed. 16.00 (0-7279-0762-X, BMJ Pubng Grp) Amer Coll Phys.

*ABC of Hieroglyphs - Ancient Egyptian Writing. Jaromir Malek. (Illus.). 48p. 1995. pap. 8.95 (1-85444-052-7, 0527, Pub. by Ashmolean Mus UK) A Schwartz & Co.

ABC of Hindi, Panjabi, Urdu. Harinder J. Dhillon. 164p. (Orig.). (HIN, PAN & URD.). 1988. student ed 16.00 (0-9617188-6-2) H J Dhillon.

ABC of Hypertension. (Illus.). 52p. 1987. pap. 18.00 (0-7279-0193-1, Pub. by Brit Med Assn UK) Amer Coll Phys.

ABC of Imagery. Akhter Ahsen. LC 87-71955. 128p. 1987. pap. 9.95 (0-913412-33-3) Brandon Hse.

ABC of Influence: Ezra Pound & the Remaking of American Poetic Tradition. Christopher Beach. LC 91-3972. (C). 1992. 35.00 (0-520-07527-7) U CA Pr.

ABC of Lettering. 5th ed. J. I. Biegeleisen. LC 86-11881. (Illus.). 255p. 1986. reprint ed. 21.95 (0-911380-72-8) ST Pubns.

ABC of Major Trauma. Ed. by David Skinner & Peter Driscoll. Tr. by Richard Earlam. (Illus.). 117p. 1991. pap. text ed. 28.00 (0-7279-0291-1, Pub. by British Med Jrnl UK) Amer Coll Phys.

ABC of Monitoring Drug Therapy. J. K. Aronson et al. 48p. 1993. pap. text ed. 16.00 (0-7279-0791-3, BMJ Pubng Grp) Amer Coll Phys.

ABC of Music. Imogen Holst. (Oxford Paperback Reference Ser.). 208p. 1963. reprint ed. pap. 10.95 (0-19-317103-1) OUP.

ABC of Nutrition. 2nd ed. Ed. by A. Stewart Truswell. (Illus.). 106p. 1992. pap. 18.00 (0-7279-0315-2, Pub. by British Med Jrnl UK) Amer Coll Phys.

ABC of One to Seven. 3rd ed. H. B. Valman. 152p. 1993. pap. text ed. 17.00 (0-7279-0768-9, BMJ Pubng Grp) Amer Coll Phys.

ABC of Otolaryngology. Harold Ludman. (Illus.). 58p. 1993. pap. text ed. 18.00 (0-7279-0765-4, BMJ Pubng Grp) Amer Coll Phys.

ABC of Poisoning. John Henry & Glyn Volans. (Illus.). 76p. 1985. pap. 19.00 (0-7279-0142-7, Pub. by Brit Med Assn UK) Amer Coll Phys.

ABC of Poultry Raising: A Complete Guide for the Beginner or Expert. J. H. Florea. (Illus.). 18.25 (0-8446-5186-9) Peter Smith.

ABC of Poultry Raising: A Complete Guide for the Beginner or Expert. 3rd ed. J. H. Florea. LC 75-8092. 256p. 1977. reprint ed. pap. 4.95 (0-486-23201-8) Dover.

ABC of Psychology. 1,982th ed. Ed. by Leonard Kristal. LC 82-1524. (Illus.). 253p. 1982. reprint ed. pap. 72.20 (0-8357-5598-3, 2035237) Bks Demand.

ABC of Reading. Ezra Pound. LC 60-30304. 1960. pap. 9.95 (0-8112-0151-1, NDP89) New Directions.

ABC of Resuscitation. 2nd ed. T. R. Evans. (Illus.). 72p. 1990. pap. text ed. 19.00 (0-7279-0260-1, Pub. by British Med Jrnl UK) Amer Coll Phys.

ABC of Revolution. Robert L. Merriam. (Illus.). 52p. (Orig.). 1976. pap. 1.75 (0-686-32502-8) R L Merriam.

ABC of Sexually Transmitted Diseases. 2nd ed. Ed. by Michael W. Adler. (Illus.). 71p. 1990. pap. 28.00 (0-7279-0261-X, Pub. by Brit Med Assn UK) Amer Coll Phys.

ABC of Sleep Disorders. Colin M. Chapiro. 104p. 1993. pap. text ed. 28.00 (0-7279-0794-8, BMJ Pubng Grp) Amer Coll Phys.

ABC of Spinal Cord Injury. 2nd ed. Ed. by David Grundy & Andrew Swain. (Illus.). 61p. 1986. pap. text ed. 18.00 (0-7279-0760-3, BMJ Pubng Grp) Amer Coll Phys.

ABC of Stage Lighting. Francis Reed. (Illus.). 144p. (C). 1992. pap. text ed. 16.95 (0-89676-119-3) Drama Bk.

ABC of Stock Speculation. S. A. Nelson. LC 63-22761. 1964. reprint ed. 16.00 (0-87034-054-9) Fraser Pub Co.

ABC of the Foreign Exchanges. George Clare. Ed. by Mira Wilkins. LC 78-3905. (International Finance Ser.). (Illus.). 1979. reprint ed. lib. bdg. 19.95 (0-405-11210-6) Ayer.

ABC of the NRA. Charles L. Dearing et al. (Brookings Institution Reprint Ser.). reprint ed. lib. bdg. 28.00 (0-697-00154-7) Irvington.

ABC of the Welsh Revolution. Derrick Hearne. 288p. 1989. 25.00 (0-86243-015-1, Pub. by Y Lolfa UK) St Mut.

ABC of Transfusion. 2nd ed. Marcela Contreras. (Illus.). 66p. 1990. pap. text ed. 28.00 (0-7279-0754-9, BMJ Pubng Grp) Amer Coll Phys.

ABC of Vascular Diseases. Ed. by John H. Wolfe et al. (Illus.). 79p. 1992. pap. text ed. 28.00 (0-7279-0259-8, Pub. by British Med Jrnl UK) Amer Coll Phys.

ABC of VAT: And Customs & Excise Terms. Gavin MaFarlane. 250p. (C). 1991. 34.00 (1-85431-163-8, Pub. by Blackstone Pr UK) W W Gaunt.

ABC of Witchcraft. Doreen Valiente. (Illus.). 416p. 1984. reprint ed. pap. 11.95 (0-919345-77-8) Phoenix WA.

ABC of Writing. Emma Tennant. 183p. (Orig.). 1993. pap. 8.95 (0-571-16966-X) Faber & Faber.

ABC of Yoga. rev. ed. Kareen Zebroff. (Illus.). 150p. 1988. pap. 14.95 (0-88976-049-7) Gordon Soules Bk.

ABC Papers. Frances Clark. 32p. (gr. k-6). 1947. pap. text ed. 5.95 (0-87487-198-0) Summy-Birchard.

ABC para Ninos - for Children: A Spanish-English ABC Coloring Book. Barbara Ezratty. (Illus.). 32p. (Orig.). (J). (ps-3). 1994. pap. 3.95 (0-942929-08-X) Omni Arts.

ABC Picture Dictionary: English to Arabic. Librairie du Liban Staff. 1991. 4.95 (0-86685-460-6) Intl Bk Ctr.

ABC Presidents: Conversations & Correspondence with the Presidents of Argentina, Brazil, & Chile. Robert J. Alexander. LC 92-3676. 336p. 1992. text ed. 47.95 (0-275-94110-8, C4110, Praeger Pubs) Greenwood.

ABC Programmer's Handbook. Geurts et al. 150p. 1990. pap. text ed. 26.80 (0-13-000027-2) P-H.

ABC Punch-Out Stencils. Carol B. Grafton. (Illus.). (J). (gr. k-3). 1993. pap. 3.95 (0-486-27662-7) Dover.

ABC Rhymes for Young Muslims. Leila Kishta. Ed. by Hamid Quinlan. LC 83-70183. (Illus.). 32p. (J). (gr. 1-6). 1983. pap. 3.00 (0-89259-044-0) Am Trust Pubns.

ABC Sillies. Jan Portugal. LC 83-10291. (Living on This Planet Ser.). (Illus.). 56p. (Orig.). (J). (ps-1). 1983. pap. 3.00 (0-937148-13-X) Wild Horses.

*ABC Space. Illus. by Judy Shimono. 48p. (J). (ps-k). 1995. teacher ed 6.95 (0-614-06858-4, WPH 1401) Totline Bks.

ABC Space: The Great Big Space Unit with Alphabet Cards. Jean Warren. Ed. by Gayle Bittinger. LC 90-71741. (ABC Ser.). (Illus.). 48p. (Orig.). 1991. pap. text ed. 6.95 (0-911019-39-1) Warren Pub Hse.

*ABC Talking Book Adventures. Stephen McTaggart & Debra McTaggart. (Talking Book Adventures Ser.). (Illus.). 12p. (J). 1995. text ed. 19.95 (0-9627001-2-6) Futech Educ Prods.

ABC Tamhidi Arabic-Spanish Dictionary. Librairie du Liban Staff. (ARA & SPA.). (J). (ps-4). 1983. 6.00 (0-86685-312-X) Intl Bk Ctr.

ABC: the Alef-Bet Book: The Israel Museum, Jerusalem. Florence C. Mayers. LC 88-27501. (ABC Ser.). (Illus.). 32p. (J). (gr. k up). 1989. 12.95 (0-8109-1885-4) Abrams.

ABC Video Series - Videocassette 1 Business. ABC Distribution Co. Staff. 176p. Date not set. write for info. (0-13-007089-0) P-H.

*ABC Zoo. Illus. by Judy Shimono. 48p. (J). (ps-k). 1995. teacher ed 6.95 (0-614-06860-6, WPH 1403) Totline Bks.

ABC Zoo: The Great Big Zoo Unit with Alphabet Cards. Jean Warren. Ed. by Gayle Bittinger. LC 90-71743. (ABC Ser.). (Illus.). 48p. (Orig.). 1991. pap. text ed. 6.95 (0-911019-41-3) Warren Pub Hse.

ABCDEFGHIJKLMNOPQRSTUVWXYZ. James Krusoe. (Tadbks.). (Illus.). 32p. 1984. pap. 10.00 (0-89807-107-0) Illuminati.

ABCDEFGHIJKLMNOPQRSTUVWXYZ. Illus. by Robert Tallon. LC 76-86987. 64p. (ENG & SPA.). (J). (gr. k-2). 1969. lib. bdg. 15.95 (0-87460-131-2) Lion Bks.

ABCDEFGHIJKLMNOPQRSTUVWXYZ. deluxe limited ed. James Krusoe. (Tadbks.). (Illus.). 32p. 1984. 20.00 (0-89807-108-9) Illuminati.

ABCDEFGHIJKLMNOPQRSTUVWXYZ in English & French. Beatrice Rich. LC 81-20838. (Illus.). 64p. (J). (gr. k-2). 1983. lib. bdg. 15.95 (0-87460-353-6) Lion Bks.

ABCDrive! A Car Trip Alphabet. Naomi Howland. LC 93-11530. (J). (ps-1). 1994. 13.95 (0-395-66414-4, Clarion Bks) HM.

Abcedario Pittorico. Pellegrino A. Orlandi. (Documents of Art & Architectural History Ser.: Vol. 6). (Illus.). 447p. (ITA.). 1981. reprint ed. lib. bdg. 50.00 (0-89371-106-3) Broude Intl Edns.

ABCL: An Object-Oriented Concurrent System. Ed. by Akinori Yonezawa. (Computer Systems Ser.). (Illus.). 325p. 1990. 45.00x (0-262-24029-7) MIT Pr.

ABCs. (Let's Have Fun Spanish-English Coloring & Activity Bks.). (Illus.). 32p. (J). (ps-1). 1992. pap. 2.95 (1-56144-104-X, Honey Bear Bks) Modern Pub NYC.

ABCs. Gabriele. (J). 1985. pap. 1.95 (0-911211-65-9) Penny Lane Pubns.

ABCs. Bob Reese. LC 92-12188. (School Days Ser.). (Illus.). 24p. (J). (ps-2). 1992. lib. bdg. 9.75 (0-516-05577-1) Childrens.

ABCs African Art Coloring Book. Jay Monteith. (Illus.). 32p. (J). (ps-3). 1992. pap. text ed. 6.95 (0-9627366-3-5) Arts & Comns NY.

ABCs & All Their Tricks. Margaret M. Bishop. 1986. 22.95 (0-88062-149-4) Mott Media.

ABCs & Nine Twelves of Porsche Engines: Porsche Engines & the Future of the Human Race. rev. ed. Harry C. Pellow. (Illus.). 700p. 1981. per. 29.95 (0-941210-04-9) HCP Res.

ABCs Beginning Sounds. Shirley Ross. (Rainbow Skill Builders Ser.: Level 1). 80p. (Orig.). (J). (ps). 1985. pap. 2.95 (0-8431-2506-3) Price Stern.

*ABC's for Book Lovers. deluxe limited ed. Linda J. Sandlin. 52p. 1992. 135.00 (1-886015-02-3) Sandlins Bks.

ABCs for Christian Writers. Irene B. Harrell. 1990. pap. 1.00 (0-915541-73-4) Star Bks Inc.

*ABC's for Godly Living. Gordon Lindsay, pseud. 1992. 8.95 (0-89985-283-1) Christ for the Nations.

ABCs for King's Kids. Harold Hill & Irene B. Harrell. LC 84-63097. 1985. pap. 2.95 (0-88270-587-3) Bridge Pub.

ABCs for Teachers: A Devotional for Christian Educators. Billie M. Jeffries. (Illus.). 64p. (Orig.). 1991. pap. text ed. write for info. (0-9635533-0-5) B Jeffries.

ABCs for the Child With-in. Nancy Northrop. (Illus.). 30p. 1993. pap. 5.95 (0-9627894-2-9) LNR Pubns.

ABCs for Young LDS. rev. ed. Marilynne T. Linford. 1991. pap. 5.95 (0-88494-794-7) Bookcraft Inc.

ABCs from the Book of Life. Teresa R. Turner. 32p. (J). (gr. k-2). 1991. pap. 3.95 (0-9633509-3-5) T R Turner.

ABCs in Arabic. (Ladybird Stories Ser.). (Illus.). (J). (ps-3). 1987. 3.95 (0-86685-180-1) Intl Bk Ctr.

ABCs Lessons of Love: Sermon on the Mount for Children. Francine M. O'Connor. (Illus.). 48p. (J). (gr. 6-8). 1991. pap. text ed. 4.95 (0-89243-345-0) Liguori Pubns.

ABCs of a Really Good Speech: For Managers, Ministers, & Most of the Rest of Us Who Are Less Than Confident Speakers. Page E. Moyer. LC 89-82274. (Illus.). 120p. (Orig.). 1990. pap. 12.95 (0-9625294-0-0) Circle NY.

ABCs of Acting: (The Art, Business & Craft) Jeremy Whelan. Ed. by Tom Wiecks. LC 89-91818. (Illus.). 160p. (Orig.). 1990. pap. 10.95 (0-935566-26-0) Grey Heron.

ABCs of Advising Student Activities. Jan Kurtz. 76p. (Orig.). 1988. pap. text ed. 9.00 (0-88210-203-6) Natl Assn Principals.

ABCs of Aerobics. Shaun Pendleton & Belinorlec. 112p. 1993. pap. 12.95 (0-8403-8608-7) Kendall-Hunt.

ABCs of Agency Evaluation, Acquisition & Merger. Rose McCullough. 1991. 18.00 (0-942326-37-7, 30181) Rough Notes.

ABCs of an Author-Illustrator Visit. Sharron L. McElmeel. (Professional Growth Ser.). 100p. 1994. 29.95 (0-938865-33-1) Linworth Pub.

ABCs of Angels. Donna S. Gates. 1992. mass mkt. 6.00 (0-345-38227-7) Ballantine.

ABC's of Antihypertensive Therapy. Franz Messerli. 288p. 1994. write for info. (1-881063-03-8) Raven.

ABCs of Arbitrage: Tax Rules for Investment of Bond Proceeds by Municipalities. Frederic L. Ballard, Jr. 406p. 1992. pap. 69.95 (0-89707-755-5, 533-0045) Amer Bar Assn.

ABCs of Art. National Gallery of Art of London Staff. (Illus.). 32p. (J). 1994. 7.95 (0-87663-631-8) Universe.

ABCs of Art: Wall Frieze. National Gallery of Art Staff. (J). (ps-3). 1994. pap. 6.50 (1-55550-912-6) Universe.

ABCs of Assurance. John H. Gerstner. 114p. (Orig.). 1991. pap. 7.95 (1-877611-39-5) Soli Deo Gloria.

ABCs of Astrology & Astronomy. Bernice P. Grebner. 227p. (Orig.). 1993. pap. 12.95 (0-9626273-2-1) Grebner Bks Pub.

ABCs of Audio-Visual Equipment & the School Projectionist Manual. 2nd ed. Philip Mannino. pap. 4.00 (0-911328-01-7) Sch Proj Club.

ABCs of AutoCAD Release 12. Alan R. Miller. LC 92-61600. 316p. 1992. pap. 22.95 (0-7821-1038-X) Sybex.

An Asterisk (*) at the beginning of an entry indicates that the title is appearing in BIP for the first time.

An Asterisk (*) at the beginning of an entry indicates that the title is appearing in BIP for the first time.

9

A

A

ABCs of Sports Medicine. Ed. by James H. McMaster. LC 80-20636. 400p. 1982. lib. bdg. 35.00 (*0-88275-890-X*) Krieger.

ABCs of Starting a Business. Valerie White. 1990. pap. 3.50 (*0-9626622-0-8*) Publicity Plus.

ABCs of Starting a Private School. Bonnie Schreiter. LC 81-86220. 125p. 1982. pap. 17.95 (*0-88247-665-3*) R & E Pubs.

ABCs of State & Local Government in America. Edo Quiko. LC 81-51458. (Illus.). 70p. 1982. 9.95 (*0-88247-602-5*) R & E Pubs.

ABCs of Stress: A Submarine Psychologist's Perspective. Benjamin B. Weybrew. LC 92-11956. 240p. 1992. text ed. 55.00 (*0-275-94233-3*, C4233, Praeger Pubs) Greenwood.

ABCs of Stress Management: Taking Control of Your Life. Ivor L. Livingston. Ed. by James B. Van Treese. (Illus.). 212p. 1990. pap. 7.95 (*1-880416-58-1*) NW Pub.

***ABCs of Success: How to Get the Most Life Has to Offer.. .You Deserve It.** John F. Sabol. 90p. (Orig.). 1994. pap. text ed. write for info. (*1-885591-11-X*) Morris Pubng.

ABCs of Swimming. Michael H. Jones. 128p. (C). 1990. pap. text ed. 11.95 (*0-8403-6070-3*) Kendall-Hunt.

ABCs of Taxes: A Poor Man's Primer. Eulalia Cain. 1978. pap. 7.75 (*0-89420-051-8*, 481000); audio 22.75 (*0-89420-197-2*, 481004) Natl Book.

ABCs of Texas Wildflowers. Glenna Grimmer. Ed. by M Roberts. (Illus.). 64p. (J). (gr. 2-5). 1982. 9.95 (*0-89015-358-2*) Sunbelt Media.

ABCs of the Bible. Reader's Digest Editors. LC 90-45962. (Illus.). 336p. 1991. 32.00 (*0-89577-375-9*, Random) RD Assn.

ABCs of the Earthworm Business. Ruth Myers. (Orig.). 1969. pap. 5.00 (*0-9600102-2-X*) Shields.

***ABCs of the Frontier.** Brian Wyant & Eric Wyant. (Illus.). 128p. 1995. pap. 16.50 (*1-883788-03-X*) Event Horzn.

ABC's of the Human Body. Reader's Digest Editors. LC 85-14470. (Illus.). 336p. 1987. 28.00 (*0-89577-220-5*, Random) RD Assn.

ABCs of the Human Mind. Reader's Digest Editors. LC 89-36711. (Illus.). 336p. 1990. 28.00 (*0-89577-345-7*, Random) RD Assn.

ABCs of the Mass...for Children. Francine M. O'Connor. (Illus.). 32p. (Orig.). (J). (ps-4). 1988. pap. 3.95 (*0-89243-291-8*) Liguori Pubns.

ABCs of the Old Testament...for Children. Francine M. O'Connor. (Illus.). 32p. (J). (gr. 1-5). 1989. pap. 3.95 (*0-89243-310-8*) Liguori Pubns.

ABCs of the Open Classroom. Lesley Gingell. LC 72-12723. (Illus.). 288p. 1973. 19.95 (*0-88280-004-3*) ETC Pubns.

ABCs of the Prophetical Scriptures. George H. Clement. pap. 3.99 (*0-87377-008-0*) GAM Pubns.

ABCs of the Rosary. Francine M. O'Connor & Kathryn Boswell. (Illus.). 32p. (J). (gr. 1-4). 1984. pap. 3.95 (*0-89243-221-7*) Liguori Pubns.

ABCs of the Sacraments...for Children. Francine M. O'Connor. (Illus.). 32p. (J). (gr. k-3). 1989. pap. 3.95 (*0-89243-298-5*) Liguori Pubns.

ABCs of the Soviet-American Nuclear Arms Race. Ray Perkins, Jr. LC 90-36499. 272p. (C). 1991. pap. 25.95 (*0-534-14526-4*) Intl Thomson.

ABCs of the Ten Commandments. Francine M. O'Connor & Kathryn Boswell. (Illus.). 32p. (Orig.). (J). (gr. 1-4). 1980. pap. 3.95 (*0-89243-125-3*) Liguori Pubns.

ABCs of Thinking with Caldecott Books. Intro. by Edythe Bernhardt & Nancy Polette. (Illus.). 124p. (J). (gr. 1-4). 1988. pap. 12.95 (*0-913839-70-1*) Bk Lures.

ABCs of Thoroughbred Handicapping. James Quinn. Ed. by Randy Ladenheim. LC 88-10025. (Illus.). 416p. 1988. 22.95 (*0-688-06550-3*) Morrow.

ABC's of Triangle, Square, Circle: The Bauhaus & Design Theory. Ed. by Ellen Lupton & J. Abbott Miller. (Illus.). 64p. (Orig.). 1991. pap. 21.95 (*1-878271-42-3*) Princeton Arch.

ABCs of Typography: A Practical Guide to the Art & Science of Typography. rev. ed. Sandra B. Ernest-Moriarty. LC 77-80333. 188p. (C). 1984. text ed. 15.75 (*0-88108-010-1*); pap. 12.95 (*0-88108-011-X*) Art Dir.

ABCs of Uniforms & Outfits. Barbara Williams. LC 90-72115. 44p. 1991. pap. 3.95 (*1-55523-420-8*) Winston-Derek.

ABCs of VBS. rev. ed. Eleanor Daniel. Ed. by Karen Brewer. (Illus.). 128p. 1994. pap. text ed. 5.99 (*0-7847-0008-7*, 18-03216) Standard Pub.

ABCs of What a Girl Can Be. Vivian S. Epstin. (Illus.). 32p. (J). (ps-3). 1980. 5.95 (*0-9601002-2-9*) V S Epstein.

ABCs of What Is Black. Vivian R. Saccone. LC 92-84105. (Illus.). 44p. (J). (ps-3). 1994. pap. 5.95 (*1-55523-583-2*) Winston-Derek.

***ABC's of What Is Kwanzaa.** Vivian R. Saccone. LC 95-60992. (Illus.). 44p. (J). (gr. k-4). 1995. pap. 9.95 (*1-55523-750-9*) Winston-Derek.

ABCs of Windows 3.1. Alan R. Neibauer. LC 91-67907. 306p. (C). 1992. pap. 19.95 (*0-89588-839-4*) Sybex.

ABCs of Winning. Ronald M. Sahara. 94p. 1988. student ed 3.49 (*0-318-37378-5*) Bk Power IL.

ABCs of Winning. 2nd ed. Ronald M. Sahara. 192p. 1988. text ed. 18.95 (*0-910807-00-0*) Bk Power IL.

ABCs of Word 6 for Windows: Version X. Alan R. Neibauer. LC 93-86869. 292p. 1993. 19.99 (*0-7821-1415-6*) Sybex.

ABCs of WordPerfect 5.1 for DOS. Alan R. Neibauer. LC 89-63762. 352p. 1989. 19.95 (*0-89588-672-3*) Sybex.

ABCs of WordPerfect 6 for DOS. Alan R. Neibauer. LC 93-84822. 309p. 1993. pap. 19.95 (*0-7821-1177-7*) Sybex.

ABCs of WordPerfect 6 for Windows. Alan R. Neibauer. LC 93-86064. 310p. 1993. 19.99 (*0-7821-1384-2*) Sybex.

ABCs of Worship: A Concise Dictionary. Donald W. Stake. 129p. (Orig.). 1992. pap. 9.99 (*0-664-25246-X*) Westminster John Knox.

ABCs of 1-2-3 Release 2.4 for DOS. Chris Gilbert & Laurie Williams. LC 92-61128. 325p. 1992. 19.95 (*0-7821-1131-9*) Sybex.

***ABC's Operations Management Software.** Steve Zimmerman. 100p. 1994. disk, pap. write for info. (*0-256-14295-5*); disk, pap. write for info. (*0-256-14296-3*) Irwin.

ABCs the American Indian Way. Richard Red Hawk. (Illus.). 55p. (Orig.). (J). (ps-8). 1988. pap. 6.95 (*0-940113-15-5*) Sierra Oaks Pub.

***ABC's to Better Hearing.** John G. Clark. (Illus.). 87p. 1992. pap. text ed. 9.95 (*0-9632001-0-0*) Hearcare.

Abd al-Qadir & the Algerians: Resistance to the French & Internal Consolidation. Raphael Danziger. LC 76-18061. 1977. 49.50 (*0-8419-0236-4*, Africana) Holmes & Meier.

Abdallatif's Eines Arabischen Arztes, Denkwurdigkeiten Egyptens. Abdallatif. xii, 348p. reprint ed. write for info. (*0-318-71477-9*, Pub. by Georg Olms GW) Lubrecht & Cramer.

***Abdi & the Elephants.** Mary W. Gehman. (Illus.). 104p. (Orig.). (J). (gr. 6-8). 1995. pap. 5.95 (*0-8361-3699-3*) Herald Pr.

Abdicating Democratic Authority: Human Rights in Peru. Americas Watch Staff. 162p. 1984. 8.00 (*0-938579-17-7*, Fund Free Exp) Hum Rts Watch.

Abdication. Edmund Candler. LC 92-63034. 280p. 1993. reprint ed. pap. 13.95 (*0-9627987-4-6*) Turtle Point Pr.

Abdication of Emperor Nicholas II of Russia. Nicolas de Basily. 200p. 1984. 25.00 (*0-940670-26-7*) Kingston Pr.

Abdication of Responsibility: The Commonwealth & Human Rights. Ed. by Human Rights Watch Staff. 82p. (Orig.). 1991. pap. 7.00 (*1-56432-047-2*) Hum Rts Watch.

ABDO Frame Rule. Association of British Disp. Opticians Staff. (C). 1989. 40.00 (*0-89771-749-X*, Pub. by Assn Brit Dispen Opticians UK) St Mut.

Abdomen see Jamieson's Illustrations of Regional Anatomy

Abdominal C.T. For Resident & Clinician. Richard A. Sorgen & Robert D. Russo, Jr. 192p. 1982. 39.50 (*0-87527-289-4*) Green.

Abdominal Disease in Equine Practice. (Compendium Collection). 1994. pap. text ed. 43.00 (*1-884254-15-2*) Vet Lrn Syst.

Abdominal Injuries, 2 vols., Vols. 10 & 10A. Jules R. Kalisch & Harold Williams. (Courtroom Medicine Ser.). 1974. Updates. ring bd. write for info. (*0-8205-1253-2*) Bender.

Abdominal Magnetic Resonance Imaging. Ros. 576p. 1992. 99.00 (*0-8016-6310-5*) Mosby Yr Bk.

***Abdominal Pain: Guide to Rapid Diagnosis.** Nyhus et al. (C). 1994. pap. text ed. 19.95 (*0-8385-0068-4*) Appleton & Lange.

Abdominal Plain Film. Stephen R. Baker. (Illus.). 431p. 1990. boxed 115.00 (*0-8385-7896-9*, A7896-2) Appleton & Lange.

Abdominal Sonography. Mordecai Koenigsberg & Janet Hoffman-Tretin. (Illus.). 144p. 1991. Extracted from Atlas of Radiologic Imaging. 65.00 (*1-56375-006-6*, GM0195) Mosby Yr Bk.

Abdominal Sonography. Eric E. Sauerbrei et al. 304p. 1992. 93.50 (*0-88167-917-8*) Raven.

Abdominal Stomas: Indications, Operative Techniques, & Patient Care. Jerome S. Abrams. LC 84-3670. 207p. reprint ed. pap. 59.00 (*0-8357-7868-1*, 2036285) Bks Demand.

Abdominal Trauma: Surgical & Radiologic Diagnosis. H. M. Delaney & R. Jason. (Illus.). 224p. 1981. 106.00 (*0-387-90502-2*) Spr-Verlag.

Abdominal Trauma: With Additional Chapters from Urogenital Trauma, Vol. II. 2nd ed. Ed. by F. William Blaidsell & Donald D. Trunkey. LC 92-49807. (Trauma Management Ser.: Vol. 1-2). 1992. 79.00 (*0-86577-453-6*); write for info. (*3-13-598902-X*) Thieme Med Pubs.

Abdominal Ultrasound. Carol A. Mittelstaedt. LC 86-17143. (Illus.). 734p. reprint ed. pap. 180.00 (*0-7837-6264-X*, 2045976) Bks Demand.

Abdominal Wall Hernias. Madden. 368p. 1989. text ed. 125.00 (*0-7216-1288-1*) Saunders.

Abdominal Wound Infections. Murray J. Casey et al. 181p. (C). 1993. pap. text ed. write for info. (*1-880906-00-7*) IDI Pubns.

Abdominal Wound Infections. Muuay Casey et al. (Illus.). 137p. (C). 1993. text ed. 29.95 (*1-880906-01-5*) IDI Pubns.

Abdominelle Ultraschalldiagnostik. Aufbau- und Abschlusskurs: Begleittext zu den Ultraschallkursen & der Medizinischen Poliklinik der Universitat Munchen. Ed. by W. G. Zoller et al. (Journal: Bildgebung-Imaging: Vol. 56, Suppl. 2 (1989)). (Illus.). 84p. 1989. pap. 30.50 (*3-8055-5013-8*) S Karger.

Abducted! Mary J. Kelso. (Lynne Garrett Adventure Ser.: No. 2). (Illus.). 144p. (Orig.). (YA). (gr. 6 up). 1987. pap. 6.95 (*0-9621406-0-0*) MarKel Pr.

Abducted. Hilda Stahl. (Amber Ainslie Detective Ser.). 137p. (Orig.). 1989. pap. 5.99 (*0-934998-35-3*) Bethel Pub.

Abducted! The Story of the Intruders Continues... Debbie Jordan & Kathy Mitchell. 288p. 1994. 21.00 (*0-7867-0129-3*) Carroll & Graf.

Abduction. Mette Newth. Tr. by Tiina Nunnally & Steve Murray. (YA). (gr. 7 up). 1989. 14.95 (*0-374-30008-9*) FS&G.

Abduction. Mette Newth. (YA). 1993. pap. 3.95 (*0-374-40009-1*) FS&G.

***Abduction: Human Encounters with Aliens.** John E. Mack. 1995. mass mkt. 6.99 (*0-345-39300-7*) Ballantine.

Abduction: Human Encounters with Aliens. John E. Mack. LC 93-38116. (Illus.). 352p. 1994. text ed. 22.00 (*0-684-19539-9*, Scribners) S&S Trade.

***Abduction: Human Encounters with Aliens.** large type ed. John E. Mack. 1994. pap. 21.95 (*1-56895-082-9*) Wheeler Pub.

Abduction in Chinatown: A Crying Freeman Graphic Novel. Kazuo Koike. (Illus.). 272p. 1993. pap. 15.95 (*0-929279-96-4*) Viz Commns Inc.

Abduction of the Wizard. K. Bulychev. 124p. (C). 1987. 45.00 (*0-317-92424-9*, Pub. by Collets UK) Pro-Am Music.

Abduction...Dawn. 64p. 1992. per. 10.00 (*0-87431-177-2*, 40053) West End Games.

***Abductions: Stop Them Now.** Karyn K. Mitchell. (Illus.). 96p. (Orig.). 1995. per., pap. text ed. 9.95 (*0-9640822-3-3*) Mind Rivers.

Abductive Inference: Computation, Philosophy, Technology. John R. Josephson & Susan G. Josephson. (Illus.). 365p. (C). 1994. 49.95 (*0-521-43461-0*) Cambridge U Pr.

Abductive Inference Models for Diagnostic Problem Solving. Y. Peng & J. A. Reggia. Ed. by D. W. Loveland et al. (Symbolic Computation - Artificial Intelligence Ser.). (Illus.). xii, 284p. 1990. 44.00 (*0-387-97343-5*) Spr-Verlag.

Abdul & the Designer Tennis Shoes. William McDaniels. (YA). 1990. pap. 6.95 (*0-913543-15-2*) African Am Imag.

Abdu'l-Baha: The Centre of the Covenant of Baha'u'llah. rev. ed. H. M. Balyuzi. (Illus.). 576p. 1971. reprint ed. pap. 16.25 (*0-85398-043-8*, 331-037) G Ronald Pub.

Abdu'l-Baha in America: Mahmud's Diary. Mahmud-i Zarqani. Date not set. 22.50 (*0-933770-61-8*) Kalimat.

Abdu'l-Baha, the Master. George Townshend. 1987. 9.50 (*0-85398-253-8*) G Ronald Pub.

Abdul Ghaffar Khan: The Frontier Gandhi. S. R. Bakshi. (C). 1992. 34.00 (*0-685-61703-3*, Pub. by Anmol II) S Asia.

Abdullah Ansari of Herat (1006-1089 C.E.) An Early Sufi Master. A. G. Farhadi. (Curzon Sufi Ser.: No. 1). 228p. (C). 1995. pap. 18.50 (*0-7007-0313-6*) Humanities.

Abdullah the Fisherman. Bauer. Date not set. 12.95 (*1-55774-023-2*) Modan-Adama Bks.

Abe Ajay. Lee Hall. LC 89-16596. (Illus.). 176p. 1990. text ed. 50.00 (*0-295-96841-9*); pap. 24.95 (*0-295-96973-3*) U of Wash Pr.

Abe & Malka's One Hundred Guitar Accompaniment Patterns. Abe Mandelblatt & Malka Mandelblatt. (Illus.). 200p. 1974. pap. 17.95 (*0-8256-2812-1*, AM41369) Music Sales.

Abe Fortas: A Biography. Laura Kalman. (Illus.). 544p. (C). 1990. 37.00 (*0-300-04669-3*) Yale U Pr.

Abe Fortas: A Biography. Laura Kalman. (Illus.). 512p. (C). 1992. reprint ed. pap. 20.00 (*0-300-05258-8*) Yale U Pr.

Abe Haas, Portrait of a Proud Businessman. (Illus.). 22p. 1979. reprint ed. pap. 1.00 (*0-318-03052-7*) Magnes Mus.

Abe Kosoff Remembers. Abe Kosoff. (Illus.). 1981. lib. bdg. 40.00 (*0-915262-45-2*); pap. 19.50 (*0-686-64443-3*) S J Durst.

Abe Lincoln: Log Cabin to White House. Sterling North. LC 87-4654. (Landmark Bks.: No. 61). (Illus.). 160p. (J). (gr. 5-9). 1987. pap. 4.99 (*0-394-89179-1*) Random Bks Yng Read.

Abe Lincoln: The Young Years. Keith Brandt. LC 81-23172. (Illus.). 48p. (J). (gr. 4-6). 1982. lib. bdg. 10.79 (*0-89375-750-0*); pap. text ed. 3.50 (*0-89375-751-9*) Troll Assocs.

***Abe Lincoln & the Colonel.** (Teddy Ser.). (J). (gr. 1-2). 1992. pap. text ed. 2.95 (*0-9636154-1-6*) Teddy & Frnds.

Abe Lincoln Grows Up. Carl Sandburg. LC 74-17180. (Illus.). 222p. (YA). (gr. 7 up). 1940. reprint ed. 19.95 (*0-15-201037-8*, HB Juv Bks) HarBrace.

Abe Lincoln Grows Up. Carl Sandburg. LC 74-17180. (Illus.). 222p. (YA). (gr. 7 up). 1975. reprint ed. pap. 5.95 (*0-15-602615-5*, HB Juv Bks) HarBrace.

Abe Lincoln in Illinois. Robert E. Sherwood. 1939. pap. 4.75 (*0-8222-0001-5*) Dramatists Play.

Abe Lincoln in Song & Story. Ailene S. Goodman. LC 88-753827. (J). (gr. 4-12). 1989. 11.98 (*0-9620704-0-8*) A S Goodman.

***Abe Lincoln Laughing: Humorous Anecdotes from Original Sources by & about Abraham Lincoln.** Ed. by P. M. Zall. LC 94-45374. 206p. (C). 1995. pap. 14.00x (*0-87049-889-4*) U of Tenn Pr.

Abe Lincoln's Hat. Martha Brenner. LC 93-31867. (Step into Reading Bks.). (Illus.). 48p. (Orig.). (J). (gr. k-2). 1994. pap. 3.99 (*0-679-84977-7*) Random Bks Yng Read.

Abe Lincoln's Hat. Martha Brenner. LC 93-31867. (Step into Reading Bks.). (Illus.). 48p. (Orig.). (J). (gr. k-2). 1994. lib. bdg. 9.99 (*0-679-94977-1*) Random Bks Yng Read.

Abe Martin of Brown Counnty, Indiana. Frank M. Hubbard. LC 83-46024. (Illus.). reprint ed. 22.50 (*0-404-19935-6*) AMS Pr.

ABE Staff Training. Hy Hoffman & Jules Pagano. 58p. 1971. 4.00 (*0-88379-007-6*) A A A C E.

Abear for Parents & Children. David W. Andrews & Lawrence H. Soberman. LC 92-72527. (Illus.). 160p. (Orig.). 1992. pap. 15.95 (*0-9635074-0-0*) Family Support.

Abecedario de Pulpa y Papel. David Saltman. Tr. by Rose Bechtel. 52p. (SPA.). 1990. 15.00 (*0-89852-508-X*, 0101R110S) TAPPI.

Abecedarium. Cobun Britton. 1990. pap. 8.95 (*0-86316-001-8*) Writers & Readers.

Abecedary. Goffredo Parise. Tr. by James Marcus. LC 90-60881. 147p. 1990. pap. 10.95 (*0-910395-61-6*) Marlboro Pr.

Abecedary. Goffredo Parise. Tr. by James Marcus. LC 90-60881. 147p. 1990. 17.95 (*0-910395-60-8*) Marlboro Pr.

Abeille. Jean Goguel. (Methodique Ser.). 1336p. (FRE.). 1971. 95.00 (*0-7859-1210-X*, 207010642X) Fr & Eur.

Abel & Bela. Robert Pinget. Tr. by Barbara Wright. LC 87-42246. 48p. 1987. 4.00 (*0-87376-052-2*) Red Dust.

Abel Being Dead, Yet Speaketh. John Norton. LC 78-8184. 1978. reprint ed. 50.00 (*0-8201-1310-7*) Schol Facsimiles.

Abel Gance: A Politics of Spectacle. Norman King. (Illus.). 260p. 1984. 37.50 (*0-85170-135-3*, Pub. by British Film Inst UK); pap. 15.95 (*0-85170-136-1*, Pub. by British Film Inst UK) Ind U Pr.

Abel Integral Equations: Analysis & Applications. R. Gorenflo & S. Vessella. (Lecture Notes in Mathematics Ser.: Vol. 1461). vii, 215p. 1991. pap. 33.00 (*0-387-53668-X*) Spr-Verlag.

Abel Parker Upshur: Conservative Virginian 1790-1844. Claude H. Hall. LC 64-63005. (Illus.). 1964. 7.50 (*0-87020-038-0*) State Hist Soc Wis.

Abel Sanchez. 2nd ed. Miguel De Unamuno. 176p. (SPA.). 1991. pap. 8.95 (*0-7859-5011-7*) Fr & Eur.

Abel Sanchez & Other Stories. Miguel De Unamuno. Tr. by Anthony Kerrigan. 267p. 1956. pap. 9.95 (*0-89526-923-6*) Regnery Pub.

Abel Sanchez. Una Historia de Pasion. Miguel Unamuno. Ed. by Isabel Criado. (Nueva Austral Ser.: Vol. 102). (SPA.). 1991. pap. text ed. 14.95 (*84-239-1902-1*) Elliots Bks.

Abelard & Heloise: Their Lives, Their Love, Their Letters. Donald E. Ericson. LC 89-82393. 166p. (Orig.). 1990. pap. 10.95 (*0-9617271-1-X*) Bennett-Edwards.

Abelard & the Origin & Early History of the Universities. Gabriel Compayre. 1967. 10.00 (*0-403-00009-2*) Scholarly.

Abelard & the Origin & Early History of the Universities. Gabriel Compayre. LC 75-90094. (BCL Ser.: II). 1969. reprint ed. 11.50 (*0-404-01639-1*) AMS Pr.

Abeles Symposium: Fatigue of Concrete. American Concrete Institute Staff. LC 73-92588. (American Concrete Institute Publication Ser.: SP-41). (Illus.). 358p. reprint ed. pap. 102.10 (*0-8357-5004-3*, 2013340) Bks Demand.

Abelian Coverings of the Complex Projective Plane Branched along Configurations of Real Lines. Eriko Hironaka. LC 93-24886. (Memoirs Ser.: Vol. 502). 85p. 1993. pap. 28.00 (*0-8218-2564-X*) Am Math.

***Abelian Functions: Abel's Theorem & the Allied Theory of Theta Functions.** H. F. Baker. (Cambridge Mathematical Library). 700p. (C). 1995. pap. write for info. (*0-521-49877-5*) Cambridge U Pr.

Abelian Functions & Modular Functions of Several Variables see Topics in Complex Function Theory

Abelian Group Theory. Fuchs et al. LC 89-163. (CONM Ser.: Vol. 87). 289p. 1989. pap. text ed. 43.00 (*0-8218-5068-7*, CONM-87) Am Math.

Abelian Group Theory. Ed. by R. Goebel et al. (Lecture Notes in Mathematics Ser.: Vol. 1006). 771p. 1983. 62.30 (*0-387-12335-0*) Spr-Verlag.

Abelian Group Theory: Proceedings of the Third Oberwolfach Conference on Abelian Group August 11-17, 1985. Ed. by R. Gobel & E. A. Walker. x, 548p. 1987. text ed. 117.00 (*2-88124-166-2*) Gordon & Breach.

Abelian Group Theory & Related Topics: Conference on Abelian Groups, August 1-7, 1993, Oberwolfach, Germany. Ed. by Rudiger Gobel et al. LC 94-25813. (Contemporary Mathematics Ser.: Vol. 171). 1994. write for info. (*0-8218-5178-0*) Am Math.

Abelian Groups. 3rd ed. L. Fuchs & I. N. Sneddon. LC 59-15029. (International Series of Monographs on Pure & Applied Mathematics). 1960. 152.00 (*0-08-009206-3*, Pub. by Pergamon Repr UK) Franklin.

Abelian Groups: Proceedings of the 1991 Curacao Conference. Ed. by Laszlo Fuchs & Rudiger Gobel. LC 93-18116. (Lecture Notes in Pure & Applied Mathematics Ser.: Vol. 146). 280p. 1993. Alk. paper. 110.00 (*0-8247-8901-6*) Dekker.

Abelian Groups & Modules. A. P. Misina & L. A. Skornjakov. LC 76-22560. (Translations Ser.: No. 2, Vol. 107). 160p. 1976. 50.00 (*0-8218-3057-0*, TRANS 2-107) Am Math.

Abelian Groups & Noncommutative Rings: A Collection of Papers in Memory of Robert B. Warfield, Jr. Ed. by L. Fuchs et al. LC 92-13697. (Contemporary Mathematics Ser.: Vol. 130). 394p. 1992. 49.00 (*0-8218-5142-X*, CONM-130) Am Math.

Abelian Subalgebras of Von Neumann Algebras. Donald Bures. LC 52-42839. (Memoirs Ser.: No. 1/110). 127p. 1971. pap. text ed. 16.00 (*0-8218-1810-4*, MEMO 1/110) Am Math.

Abelian Varieties. Serge A. Lang. 260p. 1983. reprint ed. pap. 29.80 (*0-387-90875-7*) Spr-Verlag.

***Abelian Varieties: Proceedings of the International Conference, Held in Egloffstein (Germany), October 3-8, 1993.** Ed. by Wolfgang Barth et al. LC 94-47103. 352p. (C). 1995. lib. bdg. 128.95 (*3-11-014411-5*) De Gruyter.

Abeline Ambush. Jon Sharpe. (Trailsman Ser.: No. 144). 176p. (Orig.). 1993. pap. 3.50 (*0-451-17756-8*, Sig) NAL-Dutton.

Abell Family in America: Robert Abell of Rehobeth, MA: His English Ancestry & Immigrants; Abell Families in England. H. A. Abell & L. P. Abell. (Illus.). 339p. 1992. reprint ed. lib. bdg. 61.00 (*0-8328-2606-5*); reprint ed. pap. 51.00 (*0-8328-2607-3*) Higginson Bk Co.

***Abell's Exploration of the Universe.** 7th ed. George O. Abell et al. (C). 1995. text ed. 54.25 (*0-03-001034-9*) SCP.

Abel's Daughter. Intro. by Nancy A. Walker. LC 92-36458. (Rachel Maddux Ser.: No. 5). 200p. (C). 1993. 28.95 (*0-87049-781-2*) U of Tenn Pr.

An Asterisk (*) at the beginning of an entry indicates that the title is appearing in BIP for the first time.

Abel's Grin. Harry Weldon. 28p. (Orig.). 1971. ring bd. 1.00 (*0-685-30027-7*) Cottonwood KS.

Abel's Island. William Steig. LC 75-35916. (Sunburst Ser.). (Illus.). 128p. (J). (gr. 1 up). 1976. 15.00 (*0-374-30010-0*) FS&G.

Abel's Island. William Steig. LC 75-35916. (Sunburst Ser.). (Illus.). 128p. (J). (gr. 1 up). 1985. pap. 4.95 (*0-374-40016-4*, Sunburst Bks) FS&G.

Abemama - An Atoll: Latitude Zero Degrees Twenty-Four Minutes North, Longitude One Hundred Seventy-Three Degrees Fifty-Two Minutes East. Charles J. Flora. LC 94-96118. (Illus.). 249p. (Orig.). 1994. pap. 33.00 (*0-9631036-2-8*) Jero Enter. Describes possible origins & prehistory of a small central Pacific atoll & provides insights into environmental circumstances of today. More than 100 photographs of scenes, organisms, places & people. 20 tables of data about tides, temperatures, salinites, dissolved oxygen, nutrients, species of coral, fish & more. Written for anyone interested in the natural history of atolls. Order from JERO, Box 95, Everson, WA 98247. ***Publisher Provided Annotation.***

Abena & the Rock: A Story from Ghana. Ed. by Gill McLean. LC 93-12122. (BBC TV Science Challenge Ser.). (Illus.). (J). 1993. 7.95 (*1-870516-08-7*) Childs Play.

Abenaki. Colin G. Calloway. (Indians of North America Ser.). (Illus.). 112p. (J). (gr. 5 up). 1989. lib. bdg. 17.95 (*1-55546-687-7*) Chelsea Hse.

Abenaki. Colin G. Calloway. 1994. pap. 7.95 (*0-7910-0351-5*) Chelsea Hse.

Abenaki Captive. Muriel L. Dubois. LC 92-23994. 1993. pap. write for info. (*0-87614-601-9*, Carolrhoda) Lerner Group.

Abenaki Captive. Muriel L. Dubois. LC 92-23994. (J). (gr. 4-7). 1993. 19.95 (*0-87614-753-8*, Carolrhoda) Lerner Group.

Abend Debugging for COBOL Programmers. Bernard H. Boar. LC 75-42457. 333p. reprint ed. pap. 95.00 (*0-7837-3429-8*, 2057750) Bks Demand.

Abendliche Hauser. rev. ed. Edward H. Von Keyserling. Ed. by Theodore B. Hewitt. (Illus.). (GER.). 1961. pap. text ed. 5.95 (*0-89197-000-2*) Irvington.

Abeng. Michelle Cliff. 180p. 1990. pap. 8.95 (*0-525-48569-4*, Dutton) NAL-Dutton.

***Abeng.** Michelle Cliff. 224p. 1995. pap. 10.95 (*0-452-27483-4*, Plume) NAL-Dutton.

Abeng. Michelle Cliff. 1992. reprint ed. pap. 10.95 (*0-14-015314-4*, Penguin Bks) Viking Penguin.

Abenteur in Deutschland. Ursula Meyer & Alice Wolfson. (Illus.). (J). (gr. 9-12). 1976. pap. text ed. 4.75 (*0-88345-276-6*, 18485) Prentice ESL.

Abercrombie, the Abercrombies of Baltimore: Genealogical & Biographical Sketch of the Family of David Abercrombie Who Settled in Baltimore, MD in 1848. R. T. Abercrombie. 35p. 1993. reprint ed. pap. 7.00 (*0-8328-3636-2*) Higginson Bk Co.

Abercrombie's Aunt & Other Stories. large type ed. Jan Webster. (General Fiction Ser.). 256p. 1992. 21.95 (*0-7089-2760-2*) Ulverscroft.

***Aberdeen: An Illustrated Architectural Guide.** W. A. Brogden. (Illus.). 152p. (C). 1986. pap. 35.00x (*1-873190-26-3*, Pub. by Rutland Pr UK) St Mut.

Aberdeen - Final Edition. Bob Crampsey. 200p. (C). 1990. pap. text ed. 60.00 (*1-870978-30-7*) St Mut.

Aberdeen & the Enlightenment: Proceedings of a Conference Held at the University of Aberdeen. Jennifer E. Carter & Joan Pittock. (Illus.). 272p. 1987. pap. text ed. 30.00 (*0-08-034524-7*, Pub. by Aberdeen U Pr) Macmillan.

Aberdeen in the Nineteenth Century: The Making of the Modern City. John S. Smith & David Stevenson. (Illus.). 110p. 1988. pap. 9.95 (*0-08-036575-2*, Pub. by Aberdeen U Pr) Macmillan.

Aberdeen University & the Education of Women, 1860-1920: Bajanellas & Semilinas. Lindy Moore. (Quincentennial Studies in the History of the University of Aberdeen). (Illus.). 192p. 1991. pap. text ed. 17.90 (*0-08-040918-0*, Pub. by Aberdeen U Pr) Macmillan.

Aberdeen University 1945-1981: Regional Roles & National Needs. Ed. by John D. Hargreaves & Angela Forbes. (Quincentennial Studies in the History of the University of Aberdeen). 152p. 1989. pap. 17.75 (*0-08-037971-0*, Pub. by Aberdeen U Pr) Macmillan.

Aberdeenshire to Africa: Northeast Scots & British Overseas Expansion. J. Hargreaves. (Illus.). 1982. text ed. 20.00 (*0-08-025764-X*, Pergamon Pr); pap. text ed. 11.00 (*0-08-028459-0*, Pergamon Pr) Elsevier.

Abergavenny Nine Hundred: A Pictorial Celebration. Albert Lyons. (C). 1989. 70.00 (*1-870402-55-3*, Pub. by D Brown & Sons Ltd UK) St Mut.

Aberration & Optical Design Theory. G. G. Slyusarev. (Illus.). 674p. 1984. 226.00 (*0-85274-357-2*) IOP Pub.

Aberration of Starlight. Gilbert Sorrentino. LC 92-29480. 213p. 1993. teacher ed write for info. (*1-56478-052-X*) Dalkey Arch.

Aberration of Starlight. Gilbert Sorrentino. LC 92-29480. 213p. 1993. reprint ed. pap. 9.95 (*1-56478-028-7*) Dalkey Arch.

Aberration Theory Made Simple. Ed. by Virendra N. Mahajan. (Tutorial Texts Ser.: Vol. TT 6). 157p. 1991. 38.00 (*0-8194-0536-1*) SPIE.

Aberrations of Mourning: Writing on German Crypts. Laurence A. Rickels. LC 87-18958. 418p. 1988. 39.95 (*0-8143-1826-6*) Wayne St U Pr.

Aberrations of Optical Systems. W. T. Welford. (Optics & Optoelectronics Ser.). (Illus.). 294p. 1986. 85.00 (*0-85274-564-8*) IOP Pub.

Abert & Kaibab. Bob Reese. (Grand Canyon Ser.). (Illus.). (J). (gr. k-6). 1987. 7.95 (*0-89868-226-6*); pap. 2.95 (*0-89868-227-4*); pap. 20.00 (*0-685-50872-2*) ARO Pub.

***Abe's Story: A Holocaust Memoir.** Abram Korn. 208p. 1995. 17.50 (*1-56352-206-3*) Longstreet Pr Inc.

Abeunt Studia in Mores: A Festschrift for Helga Doblin on Philosophies of Education, & Personal Learning in the Humanities & Moral Sciences. Sarah A. Merrill et al. 364p. (C). 1990. text ed. 38.00 (*0-8204-1224-4*) P Lang Pubs.

ABF Commentaries on Model Debenture Indenture Provisions 1965, Model Debenture Indenture Provisions All Registered Issues 1967, & Certain Negotiable Provisions. LC 79-127110. xvii, 589p. 1986. reprint ed. lib. bdg. 115.00 (*0-89941-512-1*, 304480) W S Hein.

Abhaengigkeit der Schwermetallaufnahme hoeherer Pilze von der Substratzusammensetzung und von Standortsfaktoren. Gudrun Dietl. (Bibliotheca Mycologica Ser.: Vol. 110). (Illus.). 178p. (GER.). 1987. 45.50 (*3-443-59011-X*) Lubrecht & Cramer.

Abhandlungen der Fries'schen Schule, 2 vols. in 1. 371p. 1964. reprint ed. write for info. (*0-318-70645-8*, Pub. by Georg Olms GW) Lubrecht & Cramer.

Abhandlungen zum Strafrecht zur Rechtsphilosophie. Hans Welzel. viii, 366p. (GER.). (C). 1975. 134.60 (*3-11-004792-6*) De Gruyter.

Abhandlungen Zur Arabischen Philologie, Pts. I & II. Ignaz Goldziher. 524p. 1982. reprint ed. write for info. (*3-487-07218-1*, Pub. by Georg Olms GW) Lubrecht & Cramer.

Abhandlungen zur Erinnerung an Hirsch Perez Chajes. V. Aptowitzer et al. LC 07-7163. (Jewish Philosophy, Mysticism & History of Ideas Ser.). 1980. reprint ed. lib. bdg. 66.95 (*0-405-12237-3*) Ayer.

Abhandlungen Zur Geschichte Des Ausgehenden Romertums. Johannes Sundwall. LC 75-7344. (Roman History Ser.). (GER.). 1975. reprint ed. 26.95 (*0-405-07065-9*) Ayer.

Abhandlungen Zur Romischen Religion. Alfred Domaszewski. 240p. 1977. reprint ed. write for info. (*3-487-06448-0*, Pub. by Georg Olms GW) Lubrecht & Cramer.

Abhandlungen Zur Romischen Religion. Alfred Von Domaszewski. LC 75-10633. (Ancient Religion & Mythology Ser.). (Illus.). (GER.). 1976. reprint ed. 23.95 (*0-405-07008-X*) Ayer.

Abhath Nadwat Is'ham al Fikr al Islami fi al Iqtisad al Mu'asir: Proceedings of the Conference on the Contribution of Islamic Thought in Contemporary Economics. 2nd ed. Nadwat I. Mu'asir & Jad A. Al Haqq. (Silsilat Islamiyat al Ma'rifah: No. 11). 754p. 1993. 25.00 (*1-56564-149-3*); pap. 15.00 (*1-56564-155-8*) IIIT VA.

***ABHB Annual Bibliography of the History of the Printed Book & Libraries Vol. 23.** Ed. by Dept. of Spec. Coll. of Koninklijke Bibliotheek Staff. 482p. (C). 1995. lib. bdg. 198.00 (*0-7923-3249-0*) Kluwer Ac.

ABHB: Annual Bibliography of the History of the Printed Books & Libraries, Vol. 20: Publications of 1989 & Additions from the Preceding Years. Ed. by Department of Special Collections Staff. 436p. (C). 1991. lib. bdg. 184.00 (*0-7923-1362-3*) Kluwer Ac.

ABHB: Annual Bibliography of the History of the Printed Books & Libraries, Vol. 21: Publications of 1990 & Additions from the Preceding Years. Ed. by International Federation of Library Associations & Institutions. (Annual Bibliography Ser.). 512p. (C). 1992. lib. bdg. 184.50 (*0-7923-1899-4*) Kluwer Ac.

ABHB Annual Bibliography of the History of the Printed Books & Libraries, Vol. 22: Publications of 1991 & Additions from the Preceding Years. Ed. by International Federation of Library Associations & Institutions, Department of Special Collections of Koninklijke Bibliotheek Staff. (ABHB Ser.). 448p. (C). 1993. lib. bdg. 162.00 (*0-7923-2373-4*) Kluwer Ac.

Abhidharmakosabhasyam, 4 vols., Set. Louis De la Vallee Poussin. Tr. by Leo M. Pruden. LC 87-71231. 1600p. (C). 1990. text ed. 300.00 (*0-89581-913-9*, Asian Human Pr) Jain Pub Co.

Abhijnana-Sakuntala. Kalidasa. Tr. by M. B. Emeneau. LC 76-23457. 115p. 1977. reprint ed. text ed. 35.00 (*0-8371-9009-6*, EMAS, Greenwood Pr) Greenwood.

Abhijnanasakuntalam of Kalidasa. Ed. by M. R. Kale. (C). 1994. reprint ed. text ed. 12.50x (*81-208-0283-7*, Pub. by Motilal Banarsidass II) S Asia.

Abhimanyu. K. P. Balaji. 216p. 1978. pap. 3.95 (*0-86131-000-4*, Pub. by Orient Longman Ltd II) Apt Bks.

Abhimanyu. K. P. Balaji. 1978. 3.75 (*0-8364-0226-X*); pap. 2.00 (*0-8364-0227-8*) S Asia.

Abhinavagupta. G. T. Deshpande. (C). 1992. pap. 5.00 (*0-8364-2824-2*, Pub. by Sahitya Akademi II) S Asia.

Abhinavagupta on Indian Aesthetics. Y. S. Walimbe. 1980. 9.50 (*0-8364-0624-9*, Pub. by Ajanta II) S Asia.

Abhorrence of Love: Studies in Rituals & Mystic Aspects in Catullus' Poem of Attis. Britt-Mari Nasstrom. (Uppsala Women's Studies, Women in Religion: No. 3). 98p. (Orig.). 1989. pap. 29.50x (*91-554-2492-9*, Pub. by Almqv & Wiksell SW) Coronet Bks.

Abhorrences. Edward Dorn. LC 90-34816. 178p. (Orig.). 1990. 20.00 (*0-87685-801-9*); pap. 12.50 (*0-87685-800-0*) Black Sparrow.

Abhorrences, signed ed. deluxe ed. Edward Dorn. LC 90-34816. 178p. (Orig.). 1990. 30.00 (*0-87685-802-7*) Black Sparrow.

Abiah Darby 1716-1794: Wife of Abraham Darby Second of Coalbrookdale. Rachel Labouchere. (C). 1989. 36.00 (*1-85072-018-5*, Pub. by W Sessions UK); 21.00 (*1-85072-017-7*, Pub. by W Sessions UK) St Mut.

Abide in Christ. Andrew Murray. 1992. pap. 3.97 (*1-55748-298-5*) Barbour & Co.

Abide in Christ. Andrew Murray. 1992. pap. 4.95 (*0-87508-370-6*) Chr Lit.

Abide in Christ. Andrew Murray. (Kregel Large Print Inspirational Classics Ser.). 283p. 9.99 (*0-8254-5314-3*) Kregel.

Abide in Christ. Andrew Murray. 208p. 1980. pap. 3.99 (*0-88368-091-2*) Whitaker Hse.

Abide in Christ. Andrew Murray. 1992. pap. 5.99 (*0-7208-0752-2*) Zondervan.

Abide in Christ. Andrew Murray. (Christian Library). 1985. reprint ed. text ed. 7.99 (*0-916441-10-5*) Barbour & Co.

***Abide in Love.** Ernesto Cardenal. Tr. by Dinah Livingstone. 160p. (Orig.). 1995. pap. 12.95 (*1-57075-011-4*) Orbis Bks.

Abide in Me: A Pocket Guide to Daily Scriptural Prayer. David E. Rosage. 229p. (Orig.). 1985. pap. text ed. 5.99 (*0-89283-243-6*, Vine Bks) Servant.

Abide, Joshua & Other Stories. 2nd ed. Edith L. Tiempo. 115p. 1993. pap. 7.50 (*971-10-0521-2*, Pub. by New Day Pub PH) Cellar.

Abide the Dark Dawn. Susan E. McCloud. LC 91-76003. 251p. 1991. 6.95 (*1-56236-302-6*) Aspen Bks.

***Abiding Appalachia: Where Mountain & Atom Meet.** Marilou Awiakta. LC 94-35462. 1994. write for info. (*0-916078-38-8*) Iris Pr.

Abiding Appalachia: Where Mountain & Atom Meet. Marilou B. Awiakta. LC 78-12970. (Illus.). 94p. 1978. pap. 8.95 (*0-918518-15-6*) Iris Pr.

Abiding Astonishment: Psalms, Modernity, & the Making of History. Walter Brueggemann. (Literary Currents in Biblical Interpretation Ser.). 96p. (Orig.). 1991. pap. 8.99 (*0-664-25134-X*) Westminster John Knox.

***Abiding in Christ.** Reginald Hollis. 95p. 1994. pap. 8.00 (*0-9642201-0-5*) Anselm Pr.

Abiding in Christ. J. Mummert. 1991. 6.95 (*0-937032-79-4*) Light&Life Pub Co MN.

Abiding in Christ's Love. Stephen D. Eyre & Jacalyn Eyre. (Spiritual Encounter Guides Ser.). 64p. (Orig.). 1994. pap. 4.99 (*0-8308-1183-4*, 1183) InterVarsity.

Abiding in the Vine. Hildy Chandler & Michael Chandler. 250p. 1993. pap. 10.99 (*0-9635424-4-3*) Gatehse Minist.

Abiding Like John. N. A. Woychuk. 36p. (Orig.). 1987. pap. 1.50 (*1-880960-05-2*) Script Memory Fl.

***Abiding Love.** Melody Morgan. 400p. (Orig.). 1995. mass mkt. 4.99 (*0-8439-3825-0*) Dorchester Pub Co.

Abiding Study Guide. Coyle. 1982. pap. 3.99 (*0-87123-411-4*) Bethany Hse.

Abiding Word, Set. Ed. by Theodore Laetsch. 1974. pap. 49.95 (*0-570-07203-4*, 12HH2612) Concordia.

Abie the Agent: An Original Compilation, First Collection of the Complete First Year of the Daily Strip, 1914-15. Harry Hershfield. Ed. by Bill Blackbeard. LC 76-53045. (Classic American Comic Strips Ser.). (Illus.). 1977. 18.00 (*0-88355-645-6*); pap. 10.00 (*0-88355-644-8*) Hyperion Conn.

***Abie to Yutan, Nebraska's Pictorial History.** Jerry A. Jacobitz. (Illus.). 336p. 1994. text ed. 44.95 (*0-9647403-0-3*) J A Jacobitz.

Abie's Irish Rose. Anne Nichols. LC 74-29510. (Modern Jewish Experience Ser.). 1975. reprint ed. 30.95 (*0-405-06736-4*) Ayer.

Abiezer Coppe: Selected Writings. Abiezer Coppe. (Orig.). 1987. pap. 12.50 (*0-948518-25-1*) Left Bank.

Abigail. Joan Druett. LC 87-26562. (Illus.). 416p. 1988. 19.95 (*0-394-56535-5*) Random.

***Abigail.** Patti L. Kinzie. Ed. by Cherie M. Davis. (Mormon Girl Ser.). (Illus.). 95p. (Orig.). (J). (gr. 3-7). 1995. pap. text ed. 5.95 (*1-886046-41-7*) Dovetail Pr.

Abigail. Ruth M. Stephenson. (Illus.). 32p. (Orig.). (J). (ps-5). 1988. pap. 7.95 (*0-945705-00-X*) Young Life Pub.

Abigail. large type ed. Lois Henderson. (Large Print Inspirational Ser.). 351p. 1988. pap. 8.95 (*0-8027-2622-4*) Walker & Co.

Abigail Adams. Akers. 1980. 15.95 (*0-316-02041-9*) Little.

Abigail Adams. Angela Osborne. (American Women of Achievement Ser.). (Illus.). 112p. (YA). (gr. 5 up). 1989. 17.95 (*1-55546-635-4*); pap. 9.95 (*0-7910-0405-8*) Chelsea Hse.

Abigail Adams. Ruth Waldrop. LC 88-6137. (First Ladies Ser.). (Illus.). 109p. (J). (gr. 3 up). 1988. lib. bdg. 10.95 (*0-9616894-2-0*); pap. 6.95 (*0-9616894-1-2*) RuSK Inc.

Abigail Adams. Janet Whitney. LC 77-100190. 357p. 1970. reprint ed. text ed. 59.75 (*0-8371-3435-8*, WHAA, Greenwood Pr) Greenwood.

Abigail Adams: A Biography. Phyllis L. Levin. 1988. pap. 10.95 (*0-345-35473-7*, Ballantine Trade) Ballantine.

Abigail Adams: A Life of Letters, Loyalties & Love. Natalie S. Bober. LC 94-19259. 192p. (J). 1995. text ed. 15.95 (*0-689-31760-3*, Atheneum Bks Young) S&S Childrens.

Abigail Adams: Adviser to a President. Dennis B. Fradin. LC 88-31331. (Colonial Profiles Ser.). (Illus.). 48p. (J). (gr. 3-6). 1989. lib. bdg. 14.95 (*0-89490-228-8*) Enslow Pubs.

Abigail Adams: An American Woman. Charles W. Akers. LC 79-2241. (Library of American Biography). (C). 1987. 16.00 (*0-673-39318-6*) HarpCollege.

***Abigail Adams: An American Woman.** Charles W. Akers. (Library of American Biography). 208p. 1995. reprint ed. pap. 15.95 (*1-886746-19-2*) Talman Pub.

Abigail Adams: Dear Partner. Helen Stone-Peterson. (Discovery Biographies Ser.). (Illus.). 80p. (J). (gr. 2-6). 1991. reprint ed. lib. bdg. 12.95 (*0-7910-1402-9*) Chelsea Hse.

Abigail Adams: First Lady of Faith & Courage. Evelyn Witter. LC 76-2416. (Sower Ser.). (Illus.). (J). (gr. 3-6). 1976. pap. 6.95 (*0-915134-94-2*) Mott Media.

Abigail Adams: Girl of Colonial Days. Jean B. Wagoner. LC 92-345. (Childhood of Famous Americans Ser.). (Illus.). 192p. (J). (gr. 7 up). 1992. pap. 3.95 (*0-689-71657-5*, Aladdin Paperbacks) S&S Childrens.

Abigail Adams & the American Revolution: A Personal History. Rosemary S. Keller. 1981. 41.95 (*0-405-14091-6*) Ayer.

Abigail & Mistletoe. Karen R. Smith. (Special Edition Ser.). 1994. mass mkt. 3.50 (*0-373-09930-4*, 1-09930-8) Silhouette.

Abigail Challenges the Telephone Company. Robert L. Merriam. (Illus.). 8p. (Orig.). (J). (ps-6). 1972. pap. 1.50 (*0-686-32483-8*) R L Merriam.

***Abigail's Drum.** John Minahan. (Illus.). 64p. (J). (gr. 2-5). 1995. lib. bdg. 14.95 (*0-945912-51-X*) Pippin Pr.

Abigail's New Home. Dorothy L. Taylor. LC 82-238196. (Valley View Farm Tales Ser.). (Illus.). 20p. (J). (gr. k-3). 7.50 (*0-9610640-0-5*) D L Taylor.

Abijah Bigelow, Revolutionary Soldier. Ellen D. Haddock. (Illus.). 33p. (Orig.). 1976. pap. 1.50 (*0-935549-02-1*) MI City Hist.

Abilene: The Key City. Juanita D. Jachry. LC 86-7818. (Illus.). 128p. 1986. 22.95 (*0-89781-150-X*) Preferred Mktg.

Abilene: The Sharpshooter. Ladd. (Gunsmoke Western Ser.). 12.95 (*0-86220-930-7*, C0722, Gunsmoke) Chivers N Amer.

Abilene Bk. V: The Half-Breed. Ladd. (Gunsmoke Western Ser.). 12.95x (*0-86220-935-8*, C0723, Gunsmoke) Chivers N Amer.

***Abilene Gamble.** Margaret Conlin. 304p. (Orig.). 1995. pap. text ed. 5.50 (*0-515-11685-8*) Jove Pubns.

Abilene Paradox & Other Meditations on Management. Jerry Harvey. LC 88-45176. 160p. 1988. text ed. 22.95 (*0-669-19179-5*) Free Pr.

***Abilene Paradox & Other Parables about Management.** Harvey. 1995. pap. 12.00 (*0-02-874019-X*) Free Pr.

Abilities, Motivation, & Methodology: The Minnesota Symposium on Learning & Individual Differences. Ed. by R. Kanfer et al. 536p. (C). 1989. text ed. 99.95 (*0-8058-0495-1*); pap. 45.00 (*0-8058-0496-X*) L Erlbaum Assocs.

Abilities of Gifted Children. Edwina Pendarvis et al. 496p. (C). 1989. Casebound. text ed. write for info. (*0-13-002072-9*) P-H.

Abilities of Man, Their Nature & Measurement. Charles E. Spearman. LC 73-121291. reprint ed. 49.50 (*0-404-06174-5*) AMS Pr.

Ability Development from Age Zero. Shinichi Suzuki. Orig. Title: Saino Kaihatsu Wa Zero-Sai Kara. 96p. (Orig.). 1969. pap. text ed. 12.95 (*0-87487-580-3*) Summy-Birchard.

***Ability Forum Fourth Annual Conference Proceedings, Set, Vol. 1 & 2.** Ed. by Joyce J. Barker. (Agility Forum Conference Proceedings Ser.). 1053p. (Orig.). 1995. pap. 75.00 (*1-885166-04-4*) Agile Manufact.

Ability Grouping & Cooperative Learning. rev. ed. Ed. by CTY Center for Talented Youth Staff. 135p. 1994. pap. 13.00 (*1-881622-12-6*) JHU Ctr Talent Youth.

***Ability Grouping & Tracking: Current Issues & Concerns.** Patricia Brown & Paul D. Goren. Ed. by Karen Glass. 42p. (Orig.). 1993. pap. text ed. 15.00 (*1-55877-213-8*) Natl Governor.

Ability of High School Pupils to Select Essential Data in Solving Problems. Benjamin W. Daily. LC 73-176704. (Columbia University. Teachers College. Contributions to Education Ser.: No. 190). reprint ed. 37.50 (*0-404-55190-4*) AMS Pr.

Ability to Challenge DNA Evidence. (Research Synthesis Report Ser.: No. 9). 60p. 1993. pap. 15.00 (*0-11-341062-X*, HM1062X, Pub. by HMSO UK) UNIPUB.

Ability to Love. Allan Fromme. 1977. pap. 7.00 (*0-87980-000-3*) Wilshire.

Ability to Mourn: Disillusionment & the Social Origins of Psychoanalysis. Peter Homans. LC 88-4656. 404p. 1989. 34.95 (*0-226-35111-4*) U Ch Pr.

Ability to Name Cats: Teaching Children to Write Poetry. Sandy Brownjohn. 90p. 1989. pap. text ed. 9.95 (*0-340-50339-4*, Pub. by Hodder & Stoughton Ltd UK) Lubrecht & Cramer.

Ability to Risk: Reading Skills for Beginning Students of ESL. Leslie J. Noone. (Illus.). 200p. (C). 1985. pap. text ed. 15.75 (*0-13-000357-3*) P-H.

Abimes du Coeur. Catherine Rihoit. (FRE.). 1984. pap. 13.95 (*0-7859-4206-8*) Fr & Eur.

Abinadi. Sherrie Johnson. 1994. pap. 4.95 (*0-87579-858-6*) Deseret Bk.

Abingdon Abbey: Chronicon Monasterii de Abingdon, 2 vols., Set. Ed. by Joseph Stevenson. (Rolls Ser.: No. 2). 1972. reprint ed. pap. 90.00 (*0-8115-1001-8*) Periodicals Srv.

Abingdon Abbey: Chronicon Monasterii de Abingdon, 2 vols., Vol. 1. Ed. by Joseph Stevenson. (Rolls Ser.: No. 2). 1972. reprint ed. write for info. (*0-8115-1002-6*) Periodicals Srv.

Abingdon Abbey: Chronicon Monasterii de Abingdon, 2 vols., Vol. 2. Ed. by Joseph Stevenson. 1972. reprint ed. Vol.2. write for info. (*0-318-58896-X*) Periodicals Srv.

Abingdon Christmas Drama Collection for Children. John Bates & Nina Bates. 40p. (Orig.). 1993. pap. 5.25 (*0-687-07774-5*) Abingdon.

A

***Abingdon Clergy Income Tax Guide 1995 for 1994 Returns.** Deloitte & Touche. 96p. (Orig.). 1994. pap. 9.95 (*0-687-01095-0*) Abingdon.

***Abingdon Clergy Income Tax Guide 1996 for 1995 Returns.** Deloitte & Touche Staff. 96p. (Orig.). 1995. pap. 9.95 (*0-687-00987-1*) Abingdon.

Abingdon Easter Drama & Program Collection. Barbara Rowland & Curt McCormack. 40p. (Orig.). 1993. pap. 5.25 (*0-687-11478-0*) Abingdon.

***Abingdon Guide to Funding Ministry.** Ed. by Donald W. Joiner & Norma Wimberley. 144p. (Orig.). 1995. pap. 16.95 (*0-687-00477-2*) Abingdon.

Abingdon Preacher's Manual: 1995 Edition. Comp. by Michael Duduit. 448p. (Orig.). 1994. 19.95 (*0-687-00571-X*) Abingdon.

***Abingdon Preaching Annual, 1996 Edition.** Ed. & Comp. by Michael Duduit. 448p. 1995. 19.95 (*0-687-00121-8*) Abingdon.

***Abingdons Bible Handbook for Young Readers.** Deverell. 1995. (*0-687-00809-3*) Abingdon.

***Abingdon's Christmas Drama Collection.** Georgianna Summers. 48p. (Orig.). 1995. pap. 5.25 (*0-687-00575-2*) Abingdon.

Abingdon's Christmas Pageants & Plays. Evelyn Minshull. 64p. 1990. pap. 5.25 (*0-687-00425-X*) Abingdon.

***Abingdon's Easter Drama Collection.** 48p. (Orig.). 1995. pap. 5.25 (*0-687-00813-1*) Abingdon.

Abingdon's Mother's Day Recitations. Evelyn Minshull. 56p. 1989. pap. 4.75 (*0-687-00486-1*) Abingdon.

Abingdon's Speeches & Recitations for Young Children. 64p. (Orig.). 1994. pap. 5.95 (*0-687-08676-0*) Abingdon.

Abinger Harvest. E. M. Forster. LC 36-10167. 363p. 1901. pap. 10.00 (*0-15-602610-4*, Harvest Bks) HarBrace.

ABIOS for IBM PS-2 Computers & Compatibles: The Complete Guide to ROM-Based System Software for OS-2. Phoenix Technologies Staff. 1989. pap. 26.95 (*0-201-51805-8*) Addison-Wesley.

***Abitare Annual 9.** Abitare Magazine Staff. (Illus.). 304p. 1994. 52.50 (*0-8230-6372-0*) Watsn-Guptill.

Abithana Kosha: The Tamil Classical Dictionary. M. Phillay. (ENG & TAM.). 1985. 29.95 (*0-8288-1723-5*, M14481) Fr & Eur.

Abiyoyo. Pete Seeger. LC 93-25730. (Illus.). 48p. (J). (ps up). 1994. reprint ed. pap. 4.95 (*0-689-71810-1*, Aladdin Paperbacks) S&S Childrens.

Abiyoyo: Based on a South African Lullaby & Folk Story. Pete Seeger. LC 85-15341. (Illus.). 48p. (J). (ps-4). 1986. text ed. 15.95 (*0-02-781490-4*, Mac Bks Young Read) S&S Childrens.

Abject Art: Repulsion & Desire in American Art. Jack Ben-Levi et al. (Illus.). 80p. (Orig.). 1993. pap. 12.95 (*0-87427-090-1*) Whitney Mus.

Abjection, Melancholia & Love. Ed. by John Fletcher & Andrew Benjamin. 224p. 1990. 55.00 (*0-415-04155-4*, A3784); pap. 14.95 (*0-415-04190-2*, A3788) Routledge.

Abkhasians: The Long-Living People of the Caucasus. Sula Benet. LC 73-21655. (Case Studies in Cultural Anthropology). (C). 1974. pap. text ed. 13.50 (*0-03-088040-8*) HB Coll Pubs.

Abkhaz. B. G. Hewitt. (Descriptive Grammars Ser.). 292p. 1979. pap. 72.50 (*0-7099-3743-1*, Pub. by Croom Helm UK) Routledge Chapman & Hall.

Abkurzungen der Informationsverarbeitung: German-English-French-Spanish-Italian. Friedrich Von Ammon. 203p. 1985. 250.00 (*0-7859-6947-0*, M15301) Fr & Eur.

***Abkurzungen in der Technik: Kleines Lexikon.** Fachbuch Verlag Staff. 371p. (GER.). 1991. 49.95 (*0-7859-8317-1*, 3343007315) Fr & Eur.

Ablation in Cardiac Arrhythmias. Ed. by Melvin M. Scheinman & Guy Fontaine. (Illus.). 520p. 1987. 75.00 (*0-87993-274-0*) Futura Pub.

Ablative Plastics: Papers. Ed. by Gaetano F. D'Alelio & John A. Parker. LC 76-143687. (Illus.). 504p. reprint ed. pap. 143.70 (*0-8357-5005-1*, 2055032) Bks Demand.

Ablaut & Ambiguity: Phonology of a Moroccan Arabic Dialect. Jeffrey Heath. LC 86-30050. (Linguistics Ser.). 366p. 1987. 89.50 (*0-88706-511-2*); pap. 29.95 (*0-88706-512-0*) State U NY Pr.

Ablaut in the Modern Dialects of the South of England. W. A. Badham. (English Dialects Society Publications Ser.: No. 63). 1972. reprint ed. pap. 15.00 (*0-8115-0483-2*) Periodicals Srv.

Ablaze: The Story of Chernobyl. Piers P. Read. LC 92-56840. 416p. 1993. 25.00 (*0-679-40819-3*) Random.

Ablaze for God. Wesley L. Duewel. 1989. pap. 14.99 (*0-310-36181-8*) Zondervan.

Ablaze for His Honor & Glory. Dolores Kuhn & Leonard Alpers. (Illus.). 113p. (Orig.). 1985. pap. 8.95 (*0-9614422-0-4*) Myrtle Tree Pubns.

Ablaze with Light & Life. Lou Stoumen. (Illus.). 224p. 1992. 34.95 (*0-89087-671-1*); pap. 24.95 (*0-89087-670-3*) Celestial Arts.

Able, Active & Aggressive: History of the O'Connell Family of Massachusetts. Lenahan O'Connell & James W. Ryan. (Illus.). 327p. 1994. 35.00 (*0-9641376-0-7*) Elizabeth-James.

Able & Equal: A Gentle Path to Peace. Denton L. Roberts. 162p. 1987. 15.95 (*0-9613559-0-5*); pap. 9.95 (*0-9613559-9-9*) Human Esteem Pub.

Able Gardener: Overcoming Barriers of Age & Physical Limitations. Kathleen Yeomans. LC 91-58925. (Illus.). 192p. 1993. 27.95 (*0-88266-790-4*, Garden Way Pub); pap. 16.95 (*0-88266-789-0*, Garden Way Pub) Storey Comm Inc.

Able Gate. large type ed. Douglas Hirt. LC 92-45879. 1993. 15.95 (*1-56054-675-1*) Thorndike Pr.

Able McLaughlins. Margaret Wilson. 1991. lib. bdg. 21.95 (*1-56849-054-2*) Buccaneer Bks.

Able McLaughlins. Margaret Wilson. LC 23-13896. 264p. 1994. reprint ed. 18.95x (*0-87797-250-8*) Cherokee.

Able Scientists-Disabled Persons: Careers in the Sciences. S. Phyllis Stearner. LC 84-60396. (Illus.). 80p. 1984. pap. 12.95 (*0-916555-00-8*) J R Assocs.

Able Seaman. Jack Rudman. (Career Examination Ser.: C-1). 1994. pap. 29.95 (*0-8373-0001-0*) Nat Learn.

Able Seaman & Lifeboatman: Revised Edition "G", Bk. 1. Richard Block et al. 658p. (Orig.). 1991. pap. text ed. 68.00 (*1-879778-00-9*, BK-105-01) Marine Educ.

Able Seaman & Lifeboatman: Revised Edition "G", Bk. 2. Richard Block et al. 502p. (Orig.). 1991. pap. text ed. 52.00 (*1-879778-01-7*, BK-105-02) Marine Educ.

Able Seaman RNVR. H. J. Messer. (C). 1989. 49.00 (*0-86303-475-6*) St Mut.

Able to the Uttermost. C. H. Spurgeon. 240p. 1985. reprint ed. pap. 8.95 (*1-56186-216-9*) Pilgrim Pubns.

Ables Creek Site: A Protohistoric Cemetery in Southeast Arkansas. H. Edwin Jackson. LC 92-13729. (Arkansas Archeological Survey Research Ser.: No. 42). (Illus.). 1992. 12.00 (*1-56349-072-2*) AR Archaeol.

Ables to Zoldak, Vol. II. Ed. by Bill Borst. 96p. 1990. pap. 6.95 (*0-9612260-5-6*) Krank Pr.

Ables to Zoldak, Vol. III. Ed. by Bill Borst. 108p. 1991. pap. 7.95 (*0-9612260-6-4*) Krank Pr.

Ables to Zoldak: From Ables Through Gutteridge, Vol. 1. St. Louis Browns Fan Club Staff. Ed. by Bill Borst. 1988. 6.95 (*0-685-44818-5*) Krank Pr.

***Ablodesafui.** Afrikadzata Deku (Afrikan Culture Institute) Staff. LC 91-72670. (Ewe Poetry Ser.). 90p. 1995. write for info. (*1-56454-014-6*) Cont Afrikan.

ABM Treaty: To Defend or Not to Defend. Ed. by Walther Stutzle et al. (SIPRI Strategic Issue Papers). 232p. 1987. 55.00 (*0-19-829123-X*); pap. 21.50 (*0-19-829119-1*) OUP.

ABMS Compendium of Certified Medical Specialists, 1988-89, 7 vols., Set. 2nd ed. LC 86-656198. 10000p. 1988. lib. bdg. 240.00 (*0-934277-12-5*) Am Bd Med Spec.

ABMS Non-Ferrous Metal Data Publication. American Bureau of Metal Statistics, Inc. Staff. 1989. write for info. (*0-910064-23-7*) Am Bur Metal.

ABMS Non-Ferrous Metal Data Publication. Incl. 1974 YearbookLC 21-15719. 1975. 70.00 (*0-910064-08-3*); 1975 YearbookLC 21-15719. 1976. 70.00 (*0-910064-09-1*); LC 21-15719. write for info. (*0-318-50458-8*) Am Bur Metal.

Abnakis & Their History. Eugene Vetromile. LC 76-43884. 1977. reprint ed. 32.50 (*0-404-15741-6*) AMS Pr.

Abner Cook: Master Builder on the Texas Frontier. Kenneth Hafertepe. (Illus.). 240p. 1991. 29.95 (*0-87611-102-9*); pap. 16.95 (*0-87611-101-0*) Tex St Hist Assn.

Abner Cook: Master Builder on the Texas Frontier. limited ed. Kenneth Hafertepe. (Illus.). 240p. 1991. boxed 75.00 (*0-87611-103-7*) Tex St Hist Assn.

Abner Doubleday, Young Baseball Pioneer. Montrew Dunham. LC 93-45400. (J). 1995. pap. 3.95 (*0-689-71788-1*, Aladdin Paperbacks) S&S Childrens.

Abnormal Aging: The Psychology of Senile & Presenile. Edgar Miller. LC 76-28175. 176p. 1992. reprint ed. pap. 50.20 (*0-8357-5006-X*, 2022408) Bks Demand.

Abnormal Cells: New Products & Risk. Ed. by H. E. Hopps & J. C. Petricciani. 120p. 1985. 40.00 (*0-931767-01-6*) Soc In Vitro Biol.

Abnormal Fetal Growth. Ed. by M. Y. Divon. 432p. 1991. 64.00 (*0-444-01572-8*) Elsevier.

Abnormal Formation Pressures. Walter H. Fertl. (Developments in Petroleum Science Ser.: Vol. 2). 382p. 1976. 69.25 (*0-444-41328-6*) Elsevier.

Abnormal Hypnotic Phenomena, a Survey of Nineteenth-Century Cases, Vol. 1: France. Eric J. Dingwell. LC 68-85483. 344p. reprint ed. pap. 98.10 (*0-8357-5008-6*, 2003094) Bks Demand.

Abnormal Hypnotic Phenomena, a Survey of Nineteenth-Century Cases, Vol. 2: Belgium & the Netherlands, Germany, & Scandinavia. G. Zorab et al. Ed. by Eric J. Dingwell. LC 68-85483. 272p. reprint ed. pap. 77.60 (*0-8357-5010-8*, 2003094) Bks Demand.

Abnormal Hypnotic Phenomena, a Survey of Nineteenth-Century Cases, Vol. 3: Russia & Poland, Italy, Spain, Portugal & Latin America. Ludmilla Zielinski et al. LC 68-85483. 228p. reprint ed. pap. 65.00 (*0-8357-5009-4*, 2003094) Bks Demand.

Abnormal Hypnotic Phenomena, a Survey of Nineteenth-Century Cases, Vol. 4: The United States of America, Great Britain. Allan Angoff & Eric J. Dingwall. LC 68-85483. 190p. reprint ed. pap. 54.20 (*0-8357-5007-8*, 2003094) Bks Demand.

Abnormal Load on Power Systems: Report on the Symposium on Transient, Fluctuating & Distorting Loads & Their Effects on Power Systems & Communications, 25th & 26th February. Ed. by J. E. Robinson. LC 65-63212. (Institution of Electrical Engineers Conference Report Ser.: No. 8). 192p. reprint ed. pap. 54.80 (*0-8357-5011-6*, 2050830) Bks Demand.

Abnormal Loads. ICHCA Staff. 128p. (C). 1984. 110.00 (*0-906297-44-3*, Pub. by ICHCA UK) St Mut.

Abnormal Morphology of Bovine Spermatozoa. A. D. Barth & R. J. Oko. LC 89-1770. (Illus.). 294p. (C). 1989. text ed. 57.95 (*0-8138-0112-5*) Iowa St U Pr.

Abnormal Offenders, Delinquency, & the Criminal Justice System. Ed. by John Gunn & David P. Farrington. LC 81-14657. (Wiley Series on Current Research in Forensic Psychiatry & Psychology: No. 1). (Illus.). 394p. reprint ed. pap. 112.30 (*0-8357-3107-3*, 2039363) Bks Demand.

Abnormal Postural Reflex Activity Caused by Brain Lesions. 3rd ed. Berta Bobath. 128p. 1985. pap. text ed. 29.95 (*0-7506-0469-7*) Buttrwrth-Heinemann.

***Abnormal Pressure While Drilling.** Jean-Paul Mouchet & Alan Mitchell. (Illus.). 264p. (C). 1989. pap. text ed. 32.00 (*2-901026-28-1*) Technip.

Abnormal Psychology. Timothy W. Costello & Joseph T. Costello. LC 90-56016. (College Outline Ser.). 304p. (Orig.). (C). 1992. pap. 13.00 (*0-06-467121-6*, Harper Ref) HarpC.

***Abnormal Psychology.** Frank Costin. 1976. 9.00 (*0-256-01480-9*) Irwin Prof Pubng.

Abnormal Psychology. Joseph J. Mehr. 578p. (C). 1983. text ed. 50.75 (*0-03-056631-2*) HB Coll Pubs.

***Abnormal Psychology.** Thomas F. Oltmanns & Robert E. Emery. LC 94-35274. 704p. 1994. text ed. write for info. (*0-13-007295-8*) P-H.

Abnormal Psychology. Richard S. Perrotto & Culkin. (C). 1992. 46.50 (*0-673-46413-X*) HarpCollege.

Abnormal Psychology. Richard S. Perrotto & Culkin. (C). 1993. student ed 17.00 (*0-673-46772-4*) HarpCollege.

Abnormal Psychology. David L. Rosenhan & Martin E. Seligman. (C). 1989. Casebook & study guide. student ed, pap. text ed. 17.95 (*0-393-95698-9*); Test item file. pap. text ed. write for info. (*0-393-95702-0*) Norton.

Abnormal Psychology. Jack Rudman. (ACT Proficiency Examination Program Ser.: PEP-53). 1994. pap. 23.95 (*0-8373-5903-1*) Nat Learn.

***Abnormal Psychology.** Jack Rudman. (ACT Proficiency Examination Program Ser.: PEP-53). 1994. 39.95 (*0-8373-5928-7*) Nat Learn.

***Abnormal Psychology.** 2nd ed. Brown & Benchmark Staff. (C). 1995. vdisk write for info. (*0-697-24266-8*) Brown & Benchmark.

Abnormal Psychology. 2nd ed. Comer. 816p. (C). 1994. text ed. write for info. (*0-7167-2494-4*) McGraw.

Abnormal Psychology. 2nd ed. Robert G. Meyer & Paul G. Salmon. 580p. (C). 1988. pap. text ed. 55.00 (*0-685-18688-1*, H11778); Instr's. manual. teacher ed, pap. text ed. 70.00 (*0-205-11177-7*, H11786) Allyn.

Abnormal Psychology. 2nd ed. Spencer A. Rathus et al. LC 93-13056. 1993. text ed. write for info. (*0-13-044918-0*) P-H Gen Ref & Trav.

Abnormal Psychology. 2nd ed. David L. Rosenhan & Martin E. Seligman. (C). 1989. Instr's. manual. teacher ed, pap. text ed. write for info. (*0-393-95700-4*); disk write for info. (*0-318-63776-6*) Norton.

***Abnormal Psychology.** 3rd ed. David L. Rosenhan et al. LC 94-41703. (C). 1995. student ed, pap. text ed. 17.95x (*0-393-96658-5*) Norton.

***Abnormal Psychology.** 3rd ed. David L. Rosenhan & Martin E. Seligman. LC 94-27953. (C). 1995. text ed. 61.95 (*0-393-96644-5*) Norton.

***Abnormal Psychology.** 3rd ed. David L. Rosenhan & Martin E. Seligman. LC 94-27953. (C). Date not set. teacher ed, pap. text ed. write for info. (*0-393-96659-3*) Norton.

Abnormal Psychology. 5th ed. Gerald C. Davison & John M. Neale. 1989. Net. text ed. write for info. (*0-471-52112-4*) Wiley.

***Abnormal Psychology.** 6th ed. Gerald C. Davison et al. 1993. pap. text ed. write for info. (*0-471-01275-0*) Wiley.

Abnormal Psychology. 6th ed. Gerald C. Davison & John M. Neale. 816p. 1993. Net. text ed. write for info. (*0-471-55771-4*) Wiley.

***Abnormal Psychology.** 6th ed. Gerald C. Davison & Jill M. Hooley. 1993. text ed. write for info. (*0-471-00999-7*) Wiley.

Abnormal Psychology. 6th ed. Irwin G. Sarason & Barbara R. Sarason. 640p. (C). 1988. Casebound. text ed. write for info. (*0-13-003765-6*) P-H.

Abnormal Psychology, Set. Gerald C. Davison & John M. Neale. 1989. Study guide set, 1989. student ed write for info. (*0-471-52111-6*) Wiley.

***Abnormal Psychology: An Integrated Approach.** David H. Barlow & Mark Durand. LC 94-35287. 812p. 1995. text ed. 58.95 (*0-534-20358-2*) Brooks-Cole.

Abnormal Psychology: Current Perspectives. 5th ed. Richard R. Bootzin & Joan R. Acocella. 672p. 1988. student ed 10.50 (*0-685-18206-1*) McGraw.

Abnormal Psychology: Current Perspectives. 6th ed. Richard R. Bootzin et al. LC 92-49206. 1993. Set. text ed. write for info. (*0-07-911168-8*) McGraw.

Abnormal Psychology: Current Perspectives. 6th ed. Richard R. Bootzin et al. LC 92-49206. 1993. write for info. (*0-07-006536-5*) McGraw.

***Abnormal Psychology: Current Perspectives.** 7th rev. ed. Lauren B. Alloy et al. LC 95-16246. 1995. write for info. (*0-07-006615-9*) McGraw.

Abnormal Psychology: Experiences, Origins, & Interventions. 2nd ed. Michael J. Goldstein et al. (C). 1987. text ed. 47.00 (*0-673-39507-3*) HarpCollege.

Abnormal Psychology: Its Experience & Behavior. Peter McKellar. 352p. 1989. 49.95 (*0-415-02812-4*, A3869); pap. 14.95 (*0-415-03132-X*, A3873) Routledge.

Abnormal Psychology: Patterns, Issues, Interventions. Frank Costin & Juris G. Draguns. 752p. 1989. text ed. write for info. (*0-471-51682-1*); Net. text ed. write for info. (*0-471-60610-3*); Net. text ed. write for info. (*0-471-51683-X*); Net. text ed. write for info. (*0-471-51684-8*); pap. text ed. 18.95 (*0-471-62146-3*, NET) Wiley.

***Abnormal Psychology: The Human Experience of Psychological Disorders Updated with DSM-III.** Richard P. Halgin & Susan K. Whitbourne. (C). 1993. text ed. write for info. (*0-697-27666-X*); student ed, pap. write for info. (*0-697-27669-4*); boxed write for info. (*0-697-27665-1*) Brown & Benchmark.

***Abnormal Psychology: The Human Experience of Psychological Disorders with DSM-IV.** Richard P. Halgin & Susan K. Whitbourne. 540p. (C). 1994. boxed write for info. (*0-697-27385-7*) Brown & Benchmark.

***Abnormal Psychology: The Human Experience of Psychological Disorders with DSM-IV.** Richard P. Halgin & Susan K. Whitbourne. 311p. (C). 1994. student ed, pap. write for info. (*0-697-27388-1*) Brown & Benchmark.

Abnormal Psychology: The Problem of Maladaptive Behavior. 7th ed. Irwin G. Sarason & Barbara R. Sarason. 688p. (C). 1992. text ed. write for info. (*0-13-007022-X*) P-H.

***Abnormal Psychology: Update with DSM-IV.** 2nd ed. Holmes. (C). 1994. text ed. 46.75 (*0-673-99635-2*) HarpCollege.

***Abnormal Psychology: Update with DSM-IV.** 2nd ed. Lutz. (C). 1994. student ed, text ed. 14.00 (*0-673-46910-7*) HarpCollege.

***Abnormal Psychology: With Student Study Guide & Case Studies in Abnormal Psychology.** 6th ed. Gerald C. Davison & John M. Neale. 1994. text ed. write for info. (*0-471-10656-9*) Wiley.

***Abnormal Psychology: With 3rd Edition Case Studies, Set.** 6th ed. Gerald C. Davison & Thomas F. Oltmanns. 1993. text ed. write for info. (*0-471-01000-6*) Wiley.

Abnormal Psychology - Instructor's Manual. Comer. (C). 1995. pap. text ed. write for info. (*0-7167-2299-2*) W H Freeman.

Abnormal Psychology, a Perspectives Approach. 4th ed. James D. Smrtic. 298p. 1990. pap. text ed. 16.95 (*0-89529-460-5*) Avery Pub.

Abnormal Psychology & Modern Life. 8th ed. Robert C. Carson et al. (C). 1987. text ed. 41.50 (*0-673-18932-5*) HarpCollege.

Abnormal Psychology & Modern Life. 9th ed. Carson & James N. Butcher. (C). 1991. 22.50 (*0-673-46649-3*) HarpCollege.

Abnormal Psychology & Modern Life. 9th ed. Robert S. Carson & James N. Butcher. LC 91-20863. (C). 1991. 10.00 (*0-673-46617-5*, Harper Ref) HarpC.

***Abnormal Psychology & Modern Life: New Update with DSM-IV.** 9th ed. Carson & Butcher. (C). 1994. text ed. 47.00 (*0-673-99634-4*) HarpCollege.

Abnormal Psychology & Modern Life: Study Guide. Carson & James N. Butcher. (C). 1987. pap. text ed. 13.50 (*0-673-18933-3*) HarpCollege.

***Abnormal Psychology & Study Guide Set.** 6th ed. Gerald C. Davison & John M. Neale. 1994. text ed. write for info. (*0-471-10655-0*) Wiley.

Abnormal States of Brain & Mind. Allan J. Hobson. (Readings from the Encyclopedia of Neuroscience Ser.). 135p. 1988. 32.50 (*0-8176-3397-9*) Birkhauser.

***Abnormal Subsurface Pressure.** Ed. by George B. Vockroth. (AAPG Reprint Ser.: No. 11). (Illus.). 205p. 1974. pap. 6.00 (*0-89181-536-8*) AAPG.

Abnormalities of Intestinal Motility. M. E. Zenilman. (Medical Intelligence Unit Ser.). 100p. 1992. 89.95 (*1-879702-16-9*) R G Landes.

Abnormalities of Personality: Within & Beyond the Realm of Treatment. Michael H. Stone. 350p. 1993. 50.00 (*0-393-70127-1*) Norton.

Abnormalities of Respiration During Sleep: Diagnosis, Pathophysiology Treatment. Ed. by Eugene C. Fletcher. 224p. 1986. text ed. 64.00 (*0-8089-1812-5*, 791281, Grune) Saunders.

Abnormality & Normality: The Mothering of Thalidomide Children. Ethel Roskies. LC 70-37757. (Illus.). 365p. 1972. 44.95 (*0-8014-0691-9*) Cornell U Pr.

Abnormally Happy: A Gay Dictionary. Richard Summerbell. (Illus.). 68p. (Orig.). Date not set. pap. 4.95 (*0-919573-41-X*, Pub. by New Star Bks CN) InBook.

Abo Addresses & Other Recent Essays on Judaism in Time & Eternity. Jacob Neusner. LC 93-39349. (USF Studies in the History of Judaism). 232p. 1994. 77.95 (*1-55540-933-4*, 240022) Scholars Pr GA.

Abo Allah, Teacher, Healer. Walter C. Lanyon. 77p. 1975. spiral bd. 4.40 (*0-7873-0533-2*) Mokelumne.

Abo-Khatwa's English-Arabic Encyclopedia of Biology & Biochemistry. Ahmed N. Abo-Khatwa. (Illus.). 1900p. (ARA & ENG.). (C). 1991. 36.00 (*0-9629071-0-3*) A N Abou-Khatwa.

Aboard the USS Florida: 1863-65. William F. Keeler. Ed. by Robert W. Daly. LC 79-6112. (Navies & Men Ser.). 1980. reprint ed. lib. bdg. 25.95 (*0-405-13041-4*) Ayer.

Abodah Zarah, 2 vols. (ENG & HEB.). 30.00 (*0-910218-77-3*) Bennet Pub.

Abode of Illusions: The Garden of Chang Ta-Ch'ien. Richard E. Strassberg. (Illus.). 47p. 1983. pap. 24.00 (*0-685-66766-9*) Pacific Asia.

Abode of Love. Audrey Menen. 176p. 1990. mass mkt. 6.95 (*0-14-012346-6*, Penguin Bks) Viking Penguin.

Abode of Snow. Andrew Wilson. 1979. 70.00 (*0-7855-0306-4*, Pub. by Ratna Pustak Bhandar) St Mut.

Abode of Snow. Ed. by Andrew Wilson. (Illus.). (C). 1979. 100.00 (*0-89771-099-1*, Pub. by Ratna Pustak Bhandar) St Mut.

Abode of Snow. Kenneth Mason. (Illus.). 384p. 1987. reprint ed. 22.95 (*0-89886-142-X*) Mountaineers.

Abode of Snow: Observation on a Journey from Chinese Tibet to the Indian Caucasus Through the Upper Valleys of the Himalayas. Andrew Wilson. LC 93-1052. (Exotic Travel Ser.: No. 1). 480p. 1993. reprint ed. pap. 12.95 (*1-55921-100-8*) Moyer Bell.

Abolishing Death: A Salvation Myth of Russian Twentieth-Century Literature. Irene Masing-Delic. LC 92-13992. 376p. (C). 1992. 42.50 (*0-8047-1935-7*) Stanford U Pr.

Abolishing Lawyer Tyranny. Jane Doe. 200p. (Orig.). (C). 1993. pap. 19.95 (*1-884094-02-3*) Ft Dearborn.

Abolishing the Diplock Courts. S. C. Greer & A. White. (C). 1988. 40.00 (*0-900137-27-4*, Pub. by NCCL UK) St Mut.

Abolishing the War System. Marcus G. Raskin. 1992. lib. bdg. 30.00 (*0-9623718-9-0*); pap. 14.00 (*0-9623718-8-2*) Aletheia Pr.

Abolition. Jonathan Schell. 224p. 1986. pap. 3.95 (*0-380-69912-5*) Avon.

Abolition a Sedition. Calvin Colton. LC 72-1054. reprint ed. 32.50 (*0-404-00017-7*) AMS Pr.

An Asterisk (*) at the beginning of an entry indicates that the title is appearing in BIP for the first time.

An Asterisk (*) at the beginning of an entry indicates that the title is appearing in BIP for the first time.

13

A

Abortion: Understanding Differences. Ed. by Sidney Callahan & Daniel Callahan. LC 84-9965. (Hastings Center Series in Ethics). 360p. 1984. 54.50 (*0-306-41640-9*, Plenum Pr) Plenum.

***Abortion: Understanding the Controversy.** JoAnn B. Guernsey. (Illus.). (YA). (gr. 6 up). 1994. 17.50 (*0-8225-2605-0*, Lerner Publctns) Lerner Group.

Abortion: Yes or No? John L. Grady. LC 79-53228. 32p. 1968. reprint ed. pap. 1.50 (*0-89555-117-9*) TAN Bks Pubs.

Abortion - the American Holocaust. Kent Kelly. LC 81-65240. (Illus.). 149p. (Orig.). 1981. pap. 2.95 (*0-9604138-1-2*) Calvary Pr.

Abortion & American Politics. Barbara H. Craig & David M. O'Brien. LC 92-41395. (Illus.). 400p. (Orig.). (C). 1993. 30.00 (*0-934540-88-8*); pap. text ed. 24.95x (*0-934540-89-6*) Chatham Hse Pubs.

Abortion & Dialogue: Pro-Choice, Pro-Life, & American Law. Ruth Colker. LC 91-46603. 208p. 1992. 29.95 (*0-253-31393-7*); pap. 12.95 (*0-253-20738-X*, MB-738) Ind U Pr.

Abortion & Divorce in Western Law. Mary A. Glendon. 224p. 1989. pap. 17.95 (*0-674-00161-3*) HUP.

Abortion & Family Planning Bibliography for 1988. LC 72-78877. Orig. Title: Abortion Bibliography. xxii, 190p. 1990. 35.00 (*0-87875-407-5*) Whitston Pub.

Abortion & Family Planning Bibliography for 1987. LC 72-78877. Orig. Title: Abortion Bibliography. xxii, 198p. 1990. 30.00 (*0-87875-404-0*) Whitston Pub.

Abortion & Family Planning Bibliography for 1989-1990. 500p. 1992. 55.00 (*0-87875-420-2*) Whitston Pub.

Abortion & Family Planning Bibliography for 1991. LC 72-78877. 263p. 1993. 35.00 (*0-87875-440-7*) Whitston Pub.

Abortion & Family Planning Bibliography, 1992. LC 73-78877. 190p. 1994. write for info. (*0-87875-454-7*) Whitston Pub.

Abortion & Healing: A Cry to Be Whole. 2nd ed. Michael T. Mannion. LC 86-60382. (Illus.). 96p. (Orig.). 1986. pap. 5.95 (*0-934134-35-9*) Sheed & Ward MO.

***Abortion & Options Counseling: A Comprehensive Reference.** rev. ed. Anne Baker. LC 95-75149. (Illus.). 59p. 1995. pap. write for info. (*0-9644777-0-X*) Hope Clinic for Women.

Abortion & RU-486 (Mifepristone) Index of New Information & Research Bible. Karl J. Cominsky. 150p. 1994. 44.50 (*0-7883-0216-7*); pap. 39.50 (*0-7883-0217-5*) ABBE Pubs Assn.

Abortion & Slavery: History Repeats. J. C. Willke. 1984. pap. 3.50 (*0-685-08782-4*) Hayes.

Abortion & Social Justice. Ed. by Thomas W. Hilgers et al. LC 72-6690. (Illus.). 328p. 1980. reprint ed. 12.95 (*0-937930-05-9*); reprint ed. pap. 7.95 (*0-937930-00-8*) Sun Life.

Abortion & the Christian. John J. Davis. LC 84-6890. 128p. 1984. pap. 4.99 (*0-87552-221-1*) Presby & Reformed.

Abortion & the Constitution: Reversing Roe v. Wade Through the Courts. Ed. by Paige C. Cunningham et al. LC 87-287. 320p. (Orig.). 1987. pap. 12.95 (*0-87840-447-3*) Georgetown U Pr.

Abortion & the Politics of Motherhood. Kristin Luker. LC 83-47849. (California Series on Social Choice & Political Economy: Vol. 3). 350p. (C). 1984. pap. 30.00 (*0-520-04314-6*); pap. 14.00 (*0-520-05597-7*) U CA Pr.

Abortion & the Ransom of the Sacred. Damian Fedoryka & Rene H. Gracida. viii, 64p. (Orig.). 1991. pap. 4.95 (*0-931888-40-9*) Christendom Pr.

Abortion & the Status of the Fetus. William B. Bondeson et al. 1983. lib. bdg. 73.00 (*90-277-1493-2*) Kluwer Ac.

Abortion & Woman's Choice: The State, Sexuality & Reproductive Freedom. rev. ed. Rosalind P. Petchesky. (Northeastern Series in Feminist Theory). 412p. 1990. pap. text ed. 14.95 (*1-55553-075-3*) NE U Pr.

***Abortion at Work: Ideology & Practice in a Feminist Clinic.** Wendy Simonds. 280p. (C). 1996. text ed. 48.00 (*0-8135-2244-7*); pap. text ed. 16.95 (*0-8135-2245-5*) Rutgers U Pr.

Abortion: Beyond Personal Choice: Looking at Life. Center for Learning Network. (Molly Kelly Ser.). 12p. (YA). (gr. 9-12). 1992. pap. text ed. 0.80 (*1-56077-222-0*) Ctr Learning.

Abortion Bibliography see Abortion & Family Planning Bibliography for 1988

Abortion Bibliography see Abortion & Family Planning Bibliography for 1987

Abortion Bibliography for 1970. LC 72-78877. 120p. 1972. 7.50 (*0-87875-024-X*) Whitston Pub.

Abortion Bibliography for 1971. LC 72-78877. 125p. 1973. 11.00 (*0-87875-030-4*) Whitston Pub.

Abortion Bibliography for 1972. LC 72-78877. xx, 223p. 1973. 11.00 (*0-87875-044-4*) Whitston Pub.

Abortion Bibliography for 1973. LC 72-78877. xxiii, 237p. 1974. 11.00 (*0-87875-056-8*) Whitston Pub.

Abortion Bibliography for 1974. LC 72-78877. 1975. 15.00 (*0-87875-079-7*) Whitston Pub.

Abortion Bibliography for 1976. LC 72-78877. 1978. 17.00 (*0-87875-126-2*) Whitston Pub.

Abortion Bibliography for 1977. LC 72-78877. 306p. 1979. 19.50 (*0-87875-148-3*) Whitston Pub.

Abortion Bibliography for 1979. LC 72-78877. 535p. (C). 1982. 38.50 (*0-87875-225-0*) Whitston Pub.

Abortion Bibliography for 1980. 400p. 1982. 38.50 (*0-87875-260-9*) Whitston Pub.

Abortion Bibliography for 1981. LC 72-78877. 405p. 1984. 38.50 (*0-87875-278-1*) Whitston Pub.

Abortion Bibliography for 1982, Vol. 13. LC 72-78877. 400p. 1985. 38.50 (*0-87875-290-0*) Whitston Pub.

Abortion Bibliography for 1983. LC 72-78877. xxix, 360p. 1986. 40.00 (*0-87875-294-3*) Whitston Pub.

Abortion Bibliography for 1984. LC 72-78877. xxviii, 386p. 1986. 40.00 (*0-87875-329-X*) Whitston Pub.

Abortion Bibliography for 1985. LC 72-78877. xxvi, 271p. 1988. 30.00 (*0-87875-359-1*) Whitston Pub.

Abortion Bibliography for 1986. LC 72-78877. 285p. 1989. 35.00 (*0-87875-369-9*) Whitston Pub.

Abortion, Birth Control, & Surrogate Parenting: An Islamic Perspective. Abul F. Ebrahim. 103p. (Orig.). 1989. pap. 12.00 (*0-89259-081-5*) Am Trust Pubns.

Abortion, Choice, & Contemporary Fiction: The Armageddon of the Maternal Instinct. Judith Wilt. 200p. 1990. 19.95 (*0-226-90158-0*) U Ch Pr.

Abortion Controversy. (Current Controversies Ser.). 240p. 1995. lib. bdg. 19.95 (*1-56510-229-0*, 2290); pap. text ed. 11.55 (*1-56510-228-2*, 2282) Greenhaven.

Abortion Controversy. Carol A. Emmens. 128p. (YA). 1987. lib. bdg. 5.95 (*0-671-64209-X*, Julian Messner); lib. bdg. 12.98 (*0-671-62284-6*, Julian Messner) Silver Burdett Pr.

Abortion Controversy. rev. ed. Carol A. Emmens. LC 86-28532. 144p. (YA). (gr. 7 up). 1991. lib. bdg. 13.98 (*0-671-74539-5*, Julian Messner); pap. 6.95 (*0-671-74967-6*, Julian Messner) Silver Burdett Pr.

Abortion Controversy: A Documentary History. Ed. by Eva R. Rubin. LC 93-25068. (Primary Documents in American History & Contemporary Issues Ser.: Vol. 1). 312p. 1994. text ed. 45.00 (*0-313-28476-8*, RAY/, Greenwood Pr) Greenwood.

Abortion Controversy: An Anthology. Francis Beckwith & Louis Pojman. (Philosophy Ser.). 300p. (C). 1994. pap. text ed. 27.50 (*0-86720-956-9*) Jones & Bartlett.

Abortion Debate. Claudia M. Caruana. LC 92-22417. (Headliners Ser.). (Illus.). 64p. (YA). (gr. 5-8). 1992. lib. bdg. 15.90 (*1-56294-311-1*) Millbrook Pr.

Abortion Debate in the United States & Canada: A Source Book. Maureen Muldoon. LC 91-3658. 256p. 1991. 34.00 (*0-8240-5260-9*, SS648) Garland.

Abortion Decisions of the Supreme Court, 1973 Through 1989: A Comprehensive Review with Historical Commentary. Dan Drucker. LC 89-43620. 220p. 1990. lib. bdg. 32.50x (*0-89950-459-0*) McFarland & Co.

Abortion Decisions of the United States Supreme Court: The 1970's. Ed. by Maureen Harrison & Steve Gilbert. (Abortion Decisions Ser.). 238p. (Orig.). 1993. pap. 15.95 (*0-9628014-4-5*) Excellent Bks.

Abortion Decisions of the United States Supreme Court: The 1980's. Ed. by Maureen Harrison & Steve Gilbert. (Abortion Decisions Ser.). 269p. (Orig.). 1993. pap. 15.95 (*0-9628014-5-3*) Excellent Bks.

Abortion Decisions of the United States Supreme Court: The 1990's. Ed. by Maureen Harrison & Steve Gilbert. (Abortion Decisions Ser.). 298p. (Orig.). 1993. pap. 15.95 (*0-9628014-6-1*) Excellent Bks.

***Abortion Dilemma: Personal Views on a Public Issue.** Miriam Claire. 290p. 1995. 24.95 (*0-306-45080-1*, Plenum Pr) Plenum.

Abortion Dispute & the American System. Gilbert Y. Steiner. LC 82-45978. 103p. 1983. pap. 8.95 (*0-8157-8125-3*) Brookings.

Abortion, Doctors & the Law: Some Aspects of the Legal Regulation of Abortion in England from 1863 to 1982. John L. Keown. (Cambridge History of Medicine Ser.). (Illus.). 220p. 1988. 64.95 (*0-521-34574-X*) Cambridge U Pr.

Abortion Eve. Lyvely & Farmer. (On Abortion Ser.). (Illus.). 1973. 1.25 (*0-918440-01-7*) Nanny Goat.

Abortion Factbook, 1992: Readings, Trends & State & Local Data to 1988. Ed. by Stanley K. Henshaw & Jennifer Van Vort. LC 87-73492. 212p. 1992. pap. 30.00 (*0-939253-07-0*) Guttmacher Inst.

Abortion Handbook: History, Clinical Practice & Psychology of Abortion. 2nd ed. Arthur F. Ide. LC 87-21388. (Woman in History Ser.: vol. 76). (Illus.). xiv, 153p. (Orig.). 1987. pap. 10.00 (*0-934659-07-9*) Liberal Pr.

Abortion Handbook: The History, Legal Practice & Psychology of Abortion. 3rd ed. Arthur F. Ide. LC 88-13390. (Illus.). xviii, 178p. 1988. pap. 10.00 (*0-934659-08-7*) Liberal Pr.

Abortion Holocaust: Today's Final Solution. William Brennan. LC 82-83960. (Illus.). 230p. (Orig.). 1983. pap. 6.95 (*0-911439-01-3*) Landmark Pr.

Abortion in a Changing World, 2 vols., 1. Ed. by Robert E. Hall. LC 70-99219. reprint ed. pap. 99.50 (*0-8357-5015-9*, 2006871) Bks Demand.

Abortion in a Changing World, 2 vols., 2. Ed. by Robert E. Hall. LC 70-99219. 228p. reprint ed. pap. 65.00 (*0-8357-5016-7*) Bks Demand.

Abortion in America: The Origins & Evolution of National Policy, 1800-1900. James C. Mohr. (Illus.). 1979. reprint ed. pap. 10.95 (*0-19-502616-0*) OUP.

Abortion in Debate: Church of Scotland Board of Social Responsibility. Saint Andrew Press Staff. 160p. (C). 1988. pap. text ed. 40.00 (*0-685-40455-2*) St Mut.

Abortion in England, 1900-1967. Barbara Brookes. 256p. 1988. lib. bdg. 55.00 (*0-7099-5046-2*, A1773) Routledge Chapman & Hall.

Abortion in Nineteenth Century America. LC 73-20643. (Sex, Marriage & Society Ser.). 234p. 1976. reprint ed. 23.95 (*0-405-05791-1*) Ayer.

Abortion, in Perspective. Donald DeMarco. 1982. pap. 5.95 (*0-910728-07-0*) Hayes.

Abortion in the Church. Maxwell E. Latham, Jr. LC 89-85219. (Illus.). 216p. (Orig.). 1990. pap. 6.95 (*1-878153-00-5*) Light The World.

Abortion in the New Europe: A Comparative Handbook. Ed. by Bill Rolston & Anna Eggert. LC 93-44510. 344p. 1994. text ed. 75.00 (*0-313-28723-6*, Greenwood Pr) Greenwood.

Abortion in the Seventies: Proceedings of the Western Regional Conference on Abortion. Ed. by Warren M. Hern & Bonnie Andrikopoulos. (Illus.). 313p. (Orig.). 1977. pap. 5.00 (*0-9601326-1-9*) Natl Abort Fed.

Abortion in the United States: A Compilation of State Legislation, 1992 Supplement. Ed. by Howard A. Hood. LC 90-86246. 294p. 1993. 65.00 (*0-89941-753-1*, 307050) W S Hein.

Abortion Is a Blessing. Anne N. Gaylor. LC 75-24775. 140p. 1976. 7.95 (*0-88437-006-2*) Psych Dimensions.

Abortion Is a Woman's Right. Pat Grogan et al. 44p. 1989. reprint ed. 3.00 (*0-87348-485-1*) Pathfinder NY.

Abortion Is Not a Sin: A New-Age Look at an Age-Old Problem. K. B. Welton. 288p. 1988. pap. 9.95 (*0-944361-00-5*) Pandit Pr.

Abortion Laws: A Survey of Current World Legislation. (International Digest of Health Legislation Ser: Vol. 21, No. 3). 78p. 1970. reprint ed. pap. 4.80 (*92-4-169213-8*, 5) World Health.

Abortion, Medicine & the Law. 4th rev. ed. Ed. by J. Douglas Butler & David F. Walbert. (Illus.). 816p. 1992. lib. bdg. 65.00 (*0-8160-2535-5*) Facts on File.

Abortion, Medicine, & the Law. Ed. by J. Douglas Butler & David F. Walbert. LC 85-16137. 811p. reprint ed. pap. 180.00 (*0-7837-2676-7*, 2043047) Bks Demand.

Abortion: My Story, God's Grace: Christian Women Tell Their Stories. Ed. by Anne Eggebroten. LC 94-3062. 238p. 1994. lib. bdg. 19.95 (*0-932727-70-0*, N Paradigm Bks); pap. 12.95 (*0-932727-69-7*, N Paradigm Bks) Hope Pub Hse.

Abortion Papers Ireland: Ireland. Ailbhe Smyth. 208p. (Orig.). 1992. pap. 23.99 (*1-85594-045-0*, Pub. by Attic IE) InBook.

Abortion, Person As Thing. G. Curtsinger. 1988. pap. 3.00 (*0-941179-37-0*) Latitudes Pr.

Abortion Policy: An Evaluation of the Consequences for Maternal & Infant Health. Jerome S. Legge, Jr. LC 84-16356. 182p. 1985. 64.50 (*0-87395-958-2*); pap. 21.95 (*0-87395-959-0*) State U NY Pr.

Abortion Politics. Janine Brodie et al. 224p. 1992. pap. 21.00 (*0-19-540866-7*) OUP.

Abortion Politics: Mutiny in the Ranks of the Right. Michelle McKeegan. 320p. 1992. text ed. 24.95 (*0-02-920533-6*) Free Pr.

Abortion Politics: The Hawaii Experience. Patricia G. Steinhoff & Milton Diamond. LC 77-3655. 266p. 1977. pap. text ed. 6.95 (*0-8248-0498-8*) UH Pr.

Abortion, Politics, & the Courts: Roe vs. Wade & Its Aftermath. Eva R. Rubin. LC 86-22847. (Contributions in American Studies: No. 89). 264p. 1987. text ed. 55.00 (*0-313-25614-4*, RBA/, Greenwood Pr) Greenwood.

Abortion Politics in American States. Ed. by Mary C. Segers & Timothy A. Byrnes. 300p. 1994. text ed. 55.00 (*1-56324-449-7*); pap. text ed. 19.95 (*1-56324-450-0*) M E Sharpe.

***Abortion Politics in the Federal Courts: Right vs. Right.** Barbara M. Yarnold. LC 95-6944. 176p. 1995. text ed. 49.95 (*0-275-95291-6*, Praeger Pubs) Greenwood.

***Abortion Politics in the U. S. & Canada.** Raymond Tatalovich. (Comparative Politics Ser.). (Illus.). 256p. 1995. 55.00 (*1-56324-417-9*); pap. text ed. 21.95 (*1-56324-418-7*) M E Sharpe.

Abortion Politics in the United States & Canada: Studies in Public Opinion. Ed. by Ted G. Jelen & Marthe A. Chandler. LC 93-43074. 232p. 1994. text ed. 55.00 (*0-275-94561-8*, Praeger Pubs) Greenwood.

Abortion Practice. Warren M. Hern. (Illus.). 368p. 1990. reprint ed. pap. text ed. 34.95 (*0-685-34694-3*) Alpenglo Graphics.

Abortion Practice. Warren M. Hern. (Illus.). 368p. 1990. reprint ed. write for info. (*0-9625728-0-2*) Alpenglo Graphics. Originally published by JB Lippincott in 1984, this book has become the standard text in the abortion field. Reviews: "...a thorough & comprehensive textbook on abortion service provision...should be part of the library of all abortion practitioners & all those interested in the impact of unwanted pregnancy on women's physical & mental health...;" "...the first comprehensive work offering a clear & concise treatise on one of the most frequently performed procedures in the United States today...this book will serve as the yardstick by which all other information on abortion must be measured;" "...an excellent addition to the library of anyone providing medical services to women in the reproductive age group." Amici curiae brief of the National Abortion Federation & Planned Parenthood Federation of America in Webster v. Reproductive Health Services: "...the authoritative medical treatise on abortion practice." ABORTION PRACTICE is written in a clear, non-technical style in order to be useful for not only health professionals but social scientists, lawyers, public officials, & interested citizens. The author, a public health physician & epidemiologist, is Director of the Boulder Abortion Clinic. ***Publisher Provided Annotation.***

Abortion Practice in Britain & the United States. Colin Francome. 224p. 1986. pap. text ed. 16.95 (*0-04-179004-9*) Routledge Chapman & Hall.

Abortion Privacy Doctrine, A Compendium & Critique of Federal Abortion Cases, 1980. Lynn D. Wardle. LC 80-80930. xv, 337p. 1980. lib. bdg. 40.00 (*0-89941-059-6*, 301860) W S Hein.

Abortion Pro & Con: (Debater's Manual) Richard Anderson. 1977. pap. 3.00 (*0-686-31357-7*) Right to Life.

Abortion Question. Hyman Rodman et al. 250p. 1990. pap. text ed. 15.50 (*0-231-05333-9*) Col U Pr.

Abortion Questions & Answers. 1991. lib. bdg. 75.00 (*0-8490-4231-3*) Gordon Pr.

***Abortion Rates in the United States: The Influence of Opinion & Policy.** Matthew E. Wetstein. (SUNY Series in Health Care Politics & Policy). 160p. (C). 1996. text ed. 49.50x (*0-7914-2847-8*); pap. text ed. 16.95x (*0-7914-2848-6*) State U NY Pr.

Abortion Regimes. Kerry A. Petersen. (Medico-Legal Issues Ser.). 201p. 1993. 59.95 (*1-85521-159-9*, Pub. by Dartmth Pub UK) Ashgate Pub Co.

Abortion Revolution. Allen Quist. 1980. 4.95 (*0-8100-0115-2*, 12N1721) Northwest Pub.

Abortion Rights As Religious Freedom. Peter S. Wenz. (Ethics & Action Ser.). (C). 1991. 49.95 (*0-87722-857-4*); pap. 22.95 (*0-87722-858-2*) Temple U Pr.

Abortion Rites: A Social History of Abortion in America. Marvin N. Olasky. LC 92-12118. 320p. (Orig.). 1992. pap. 13.99 (*0-89107-687-5*) Crossway Bks.

***Abortion Rites: A Social History of Abortion in America.** Marvin Olasky. 336p. 1995. reprint ed. pap. 14.95 (*0-89526-723-3*) Regnery Pub.

Abortion Services Handbook. Warren M. Hern. 112p. (Orig.). 1978. pap. text ed. 5.00 (*0-917634-04-7*) Creative Infomatics.

Abortion Statistics. (Office of Population Censuses & Surveys Reference Series AB: No. 18, 1991). 81p. 1993. pap. 17.00 (*0-11-691546-3*, HM15463, Pub. by HMSO UK) UNIPUB.

Abortion Stories: Fiction on Fire. Ed. by Rick Lawler. LC 92-61240. 248p. (Orig.). 1992. pap. 11.00 (*0-9624394-1-X*) MinRef Pr.

Abortion, the Bible & the Christian. Donald P. Shoemaker. 1976. 4.00 (*0-910728-15-1*); pap. 1.25 (*0-910728-08-9*) Hayes.

Abortion Then & Now: Creative Responses to Restricted Access. Ed. by National Women's Health Network Staff. 110p. (Orig.). 1992. pap. 12.95 (*0-939522-00-4*) Nat Womens Hlth Netwk.

Abortion to Zoophilia: A Sourcebook of Sexual Facts. Anne Mandetta & Patricia Gustaveson. LC 75-31909. (Illus.). 1975. pap. text ed. 3.00 (*0-89055-114-6*) Carolina Pop Ctr.

Abortion Without Apology: Radical History for the 1990s. Ninia Baehr. 72p. (Orig.). (C). 1990. pap. 6.00 (*0-89608-384-5*) South End Pr.

Abortionist: A Woman Against the Law. Rickie Solinger. LC 94-15206. 1995. text ed. 24.95 (*0-02-929865-2*) Macmillan.

Abortive Revolution: China under Nationalist Rule, 1927-1937. Lloyd E. Eastman. (East Asian Monographs: No. 153). 398p. 1990. pap. 18.00 (*0-674-00176-1*) HUP.

Aborto: Derecho Fundamental de la Mujer. Pat Grogan et al. (Illus.). 46p. 1988. reprint ed. 3.50 (*0-87348-486-X*) Pathfinder NY.

***Aborto: Una Guia para Tomar Decisiones Eticas.** 2nd ed. Majorie R. Maguire & Daniel Maguire. Ed. by Caridad Inda & Sara Newberry. Tr. by Elena Alvarez & Mary Rivera. 19p. (Orig.). (SPA.). 1987. pap. 3.00 (*0-915365-25-1*) Cath Free Choice.

Aborto (Abortion) El una Mirada Racional-Tema Emocional (A Rational Look-Emotional Issue) R. C. Sproul. (SPA.). 1993. 6.99 (*1-56063-441-3*, 498541) Editorial Unilit.

***ABOS Marine Bluebook, 1995.** Intertec Publishing Staff. 1994. 149.95 (*0-87288-574-7*, ABOS46) Intertec Pub.

Abounding in Mercy - Mother Austin Carroll. Mary H. Muldrey. (Illus.). 452p. (Orig.). 1988. 23.50 (*0-944784-00-3*); pap. 9.00 (*0-944784-01-1*) Habersham.

About a Loving God. Joe Barone. 1991. pap. 7.50 (*1-55673-355-0*, 9154) CSS OH.

About AIDS. LC 93-34109. (For Your Information Ser.). 1993. 5.95 (*1-56420-019-1*); audio 16.00 (*1-56420-020-5*) New Readers.

About Alcohol & Other Drugs. LC 93-34102. (For Your Information Ser.). 1993. 5.95 (*1-56420-015-9*); audio 16.00 (*1-56420-016-7*) New Readers.

About Alcoholism: A Common Sense Perspective. Donald A. Staccia. Ed. by Kathryn R. Anderson. (Illus.). 176p. (Orig.). 1986. pap. 6.95 (*0-9616402-1-9*) Acosep Corp.

About Angels. Lily Cavell. (Illus.). 1986. spiral bd. 7.95 (*1-885038-00-3*) Uriel Press.

About Ballet Class. Ed. by Sharon S. Sanchez. (Illus.). 32p. (Orig.). (J). (ps up). 1990. pap. 5.95 (*0-9626651-0-X*) Dance Data.

About Ballet Performance. Sharon S. Sanchez. (Illus.). 32p. (J). (ps up). 1990. pap. 5.95 (*0-9626651-1-8*) Dance Data.

About Bats: A Chiropteran Biology Symposium. Ed. by Bob H. Slaughter & Dan W. Walton. LC 71-138650. (Fondren Science Ser.: No. 11). 347p. reprint ed. pap. 98.90 (*0-8357-8779-6*, 2033427) Bks Demand.

About Beauty: A Thomistic Interpretation. Armand A. Maurer. LC 83-70939. 141p. (Orig.). 1983. pap. text ed. 6.95 (*0-9605456-1-1*, 85-06065) U of St Thomas.

About Behaviorism. B. F. Skinner. 1976. pap. 9.00 (*0-394-71618-3*, Vin) Random.

An Asterisk (*) at the beginning of an entry indicates that the title is appearing in BIP for the first time.

An Asterisk (*) at the beginning of an entry indicates that the title is appearing in BIP for the first time.

15

A

Above & Beyond. Phil Eisenberg. 40p. (Orig.). 1991. pap. 6.00 (*1-879533-05-7*) Poetic Page.

Above & Beyond. Jay Strack. 1994. pap. 9.99 (*0-8499-3827-9*) Word Inc.

***Above & Beyond.** Jay Strack. 1994. 12.99 (*0-8499-1164-8*) Word Inc.

Above & Beyond Parsley: Food for the Senses. Jr. League of Kansas City, MO, Inc. Staff. (Illus.). 296p. 1992. 26.95 (*0-9607076-2-X*) Jr League KC.

Above Below - One Michigan...Two States of Mind. Curt G. Knoblock. LC 84-72798. (Illus.). 1984. pap. 8.95 (*0-932212-40-9*) Avery Color.

Above Carmel, Monterey & the Big Sur. Robert Cameron & Harold Gilliam. LC 94-94170. 96p. 1994. pap. 14.50 (*0-918684-44-7*) Cameron & Co.

Above Chicago. Robert Cameron. LC 92-93090. 160p. 1992. 29.50 (*0-918684-27-7*) Cameron & Co.

***Above Ground: Stories about Life & Death by New Southern Writers.** Ed. by Thomas Conner, Jr. & Robert E. Skinner. (Occasional Publications Ser.: No. 1). (Illus.). 200p. (Orig.). 1993. pap. 11.95 (*1-883275-00-8*) Xavier Rev.

Above Ground Steel Storage Tank Handbook. Digrado. 1995. text ed. 69.95 (*0-442-01845-2*) Van Nos Reinhold.

Above Hawaii. Robert Cameron. LC 77-88840. 160p. 1977. 29.50 (*0-918684-02-1*) Cameron & Co.

Above Life's Turmoil. James Allen. 163p. 1993. pap. 15.00 (*0-89540-203-3*, SB-203) Sun Pub.

Above London. Robert Cameron & Alistair Cooke. LC 80-80944. 160p. 1980. 29.50 (*0-918684-10-2*) Cameron & Co.

Above Los Angeles. Robert W. Cameron. LC 90-81499. 160p. 1990. 29.50 (*0-918684-48-X*) Cameron & Co.

Above Mackinac. Robert Cameron & Phil Porter. LC 94-94165. 96p. 1994. pap. 14.50 (*0-918684-38-2*) Cameron & Co.

Above New York. Robert W. Cameron et al. LC 87-73037. 160p. 1988. 29.50 (*0-918684-42-0*) Cameron & Co.

Above Paris. Robert Cameron & Pierre Salinger. LC 84-71415. 160p. 1984. 29.50 (*0-918684-19-6*) Cameron & Co.

***Above Reproach: A Guide for Wolf Hybrid Owners.** Dorothy Prendergrast et al. (Illus.). 200p. (Orig.). 1995. pap. 23.00 (*0-9623640-1-0*) Rudelhaus Enter.

Above San Diego. Robert W. Cameron. 1990. 29.50 (*0-918684-24-2*) Cameron & Co.

Above San Francisco. Herb Caen & Robert Cameron. LC 86-71483. 160p. 1986. 29.50 (*0-918684-28-5*) Cameron & Co.

Above Seattle. Robert Cameron & Emmett Watson. LC 94-94006. 160p. 1994. 29.50 (*0-918684-41-2*) Cameron & Co.

Above Suspicion. Helen MacInnes. LC 54-928. 1954. 24.95 (*0-15-102707-2*) HarBrace.

Above Suspicion. Joe Sharkey. 1993. 23.00 (*0-671-79644-5*) S&S Trade.

***Above Suspicion Vol. 1.** Joe Sharkey. 1994. pap. 4.99 (*0-312-95394-1*) St Martin.

Above the Bottom Line: An Introduction to Business Ethics. Robert C. Solomon & Kristine R. Hanson. 434p. (C). 1983. text ed. 33.25 (*0-15-500390-9*) HB Coll Pubs.

Above the Bottom Line: An Introduction to Business Ethics. 2nd ed. Robert C. Solomon. LC 93-77629. 528p. 1994. pap. 33.75 (*0-15-501051-4*) HarBrace.

Above the Bottom Line: Stories & Advice on Integrity. Hanoch Teller. 416p. (YA). (gr. 8 up). 1988. write for info. (*0-9614772-5-3*) NYC Pub Co.

Above the Bottomline. Hanoch Teller. 1988. 16.95 (*0-685-24648-5*) Feldheim.

Above the Ceiling. Tom Henry. (Illus.). 196p. (Orig.). 1992. pap. text ed. 12.00 (*0-945495-28-5*) T Henrys CECB.

Above the Clouds. Elizabeth Ashby & Ernest Clevenger, Jr. 196p. 1979. 12.00 (*0-88428-046-2*); pap. 8.50 (*0-88428-047-0*) Parchment Pr.

Above the Clouds. Jonathan Bach. LC 92-26185. 1993. 20.00 (*0-688-11760-0*) Morrow.

***Above the Clouds: Status Culture of the Modern Japanese Nobility.** Takie S. Lebra. 1992. pap. 16.00 (*0-520-07602-8*) U CA Pr.

Above the Clouds: Status Culture of the Modern Japanese Nobility. Takie S. Lebra. (C). 1992. 45.00 (*0-520-07600-1*) U CA Pr.

Above the First Position. Markwood Holmes & Russell Webber. (Illus.). 55p. 1955. pap. 9.25 (*0-8258-0176-1*, 0-3807) Fischer Inc NY.

Above the Forest: A Study of Andamanese Ethnoanemology, Cosmology, & the Power of Ritual. Vishvajit Pandya. 356p. 1993. 24.00 (*0-19-562971-X*) OUP.

Above the Land. Julie Agoos. LC 86-26675. 96p. 1987. 16.00 (*0-300-03861-5*) Yale U Pr.

Above the Law. Doreen O. Malek. (Desire Ser.). 1994. mass mkt. 2.99 (*0-373-05869-1*, 1-05869-2) Silhouette.

Above the Law. Robert Robin. 1992. 20.00 (*0-671-74425-9*) PB.

Above the Law. Robert Robin. Ed. by Jane Rosenman. 384p. 1993. reprint ed. mass mkt. 5.50 (*0-671-74424-0*, Pocket Star Bks) PB.

***Above the Law: Covering Congress under Federal Employment Laws.** Thomas W. Reed & Bradley J. Cameron. 113p. 1994. 25.00 (*0-916559-53-X*, 2051-MO-4035) EPF.

Above the Law: Police & the Excessive Use of Force. Jerome H. Skolnick. 1994. pap. 12.95 (*0-02-929153-4*) Free Pr.

Above the Law: Police Use of Excessive Force & What to Do about It. Jerome Skolnick & James Fyfe. 264p. 1993. text ed. 27.95 (*0-02-929312-X*) Free Pr.

Above the Law: The Hidden Career of John Volz, U.S.A. R. E. Payne. 281p. 1995. pap. 1,795.00 (*1-885308-00-0*) Sr Polit Action.

Above the Lines: The Aces of the German Air Service, Naval Air Service & Flanders Marine Corps, 1914-1918. Norman L. Franks et al. (Illus.). 320p. 1994. 49.95 (*0-948817-73-9*, Pub. by Grub St Pubns UK) Seven Hills Bk.

Above the Lower Sky. Tom Deitz. LC 94-17819. 1994. 23.00 (*0-688-13716-4*, AvoNova) Avon.

Above the Mountains. Michael Gebert. LC 89-36785. 1993. pap. 13.95 (*0-87949-306-2*) Ashley Bks.

Above the Noise of the Crowd. John Forney. LC 86-71493. (Illus.). 214p. 1986. 14.95 (*0-932919-03-0*) Albright & Co.

Above the River. James Wright. 432p. 1992. pap. 15.00 (*0-374-52282-0*, Noonday) FS&G.

Above the Thunder. Ted Findlay. 1987. pap. 10.95 (*0-89334-031-6*) Humanics Ltd.

***Above the Tree Line.** Kathy Mangan. LC 94-70462. (Poetry Ser.). 64p. 1995. pap. 11.95 (*0-88748-191-4*) Carnegie-Mellon.

Above the Treeline. Dick Gallup. (Orig.). 1976. 3.00 (*0-929844-08-4*) Big Sky Bolinas.

***Above the Trenches: A Complete Record of the Fighter Aces & Units of the British Empire Air Forces, 1915-1920.** 2nd ed. Christopher Shores et al. (Illus.). 368p. 1995. 55.00 (*1-898697-21-3*, Pub. by Grub St Pubns UK) Seven Hills Bk.

Above Timberline: A Rocky Mountain Journal. Dwight Smith. Ed. by Alan Anderson, Jr. LC 90-39736. 250p. (Orig.). 1990. reprint ed. pap. 16.95 (*0-87108-799-5*) Pruett.

Above Top Secret: The Worldwide UFO Cover-Up. Timothy Good. LC 89-10230. 1989. pap. 14.00 (*0-688-09202-0*, Quill) Morrow.

Above Washington. Robert Cameron. LC 79-89078. 160p. 1979. 29.50 (*0-918684-08-0*) Cameron & Co.

Above Yosemite. Robert W. Cameron & Harold Gilliam. LC 83-90192. 1983. 29.50 (*0-918684-20-X*) Cameron & Co.

Aboveground Storage Tank Management: A Practical Guide. 220p. 1990. pap. text ed. 59.00 (*0-86587-202-3*) Gov Insts.

Aboveground Storage Tanks. Richard K. Miller & Marcia Rupnow. (Survey on Technology & Markets Ser.: No. 215). 50p. 1994. pap. text ed. 200.00 (*1-55865-246-9*) Future Tech Surveys.

Aboveground Storage Tanks. Philip E. Myers. 1995. text ed. 80.00 (*0-07-044272-X*) McGraw.

Aboveground Storage Tanks: A State-of-the-Art Review, Vol. 1. A. R. Ciuffreda et al. (Illus.). 384p. (Orig.). 1991. 65.00 (*1-877914-27-4*) NACE Intl.

Aboveground Storage Tanks - Current Issues Vol. 2: Design, Operations, Maintenance, Inspection, & the Environment. Ed. by P. A. Collins et al. (Illus.). 448p. 1992. pap. text ed. 113.00 (*1-877914-37-1*) NACE Intl.

Aboveground Tank State Regulatory Guide. CEEM Information Services Staff. 483p. 1992. pap. 195.00 (*1-883337-00-3*) Ctr Energy Envir.

ABR Handbook: Auditory Brainstem Response. 2nd ed. Michael E. Glasscock et al. (Illus.). 150p. 1987. text ed. 43.00 (*0-86577-202-9*) Thieme Med Pubs.

Abra-Ca-Dazzle: Easy Magic Tricks. Ray Broekel & Laurence B. White, Jr. Ed. by Ann Fay. LC 81-11578. (Albert Whitman Idea Bks.). (Illus.). 48p. (J). (gr. 3 up). 1982. lib. bdg. 11.95 (*0-8075-0121-2*) A Whitman.

Abra Cadaver. Johnny Hart & B. Parker. 1983. pap. 1.95 (*0-449-12459-2*) Fawcett.

Abra Cadaver. John Mattera. 1982. 2.50 (*0-87129-202-5*, A28) Dramatic Pub.

Abra la Puerta a Otro Idioma-Ingles. Victoria M. Tewell. (Illus.). 30p. (Orig.). 1987. pap. 4.50 (*0-934329-10-9*) Baggiani-Tewell.

Abrabanel on Pirke Avot. Isaac Abrabanel. Tr. & Intro. by Abraham Chill. 503p. 1991. 29.95 (*0-87203-135-7*) Hermon.

Abracadabra. Stephen Ajay. 1977. per. 2.50 (*0-912284-88-9*) New Rivers Pr.

Abracadabra. Stephen Gresham. 384p. 1988. pap. 3.95 (*0-8217-2350-2*) Zebra.

Abracadabra. Amy Jones. Ed. by Nancy R. Thatch. LC 93-13421. (Books for Students by Students Ser.). (Illus.). 29p. (J). (gr. 3-5). 1993. lib. bdg. 14.95 (*0-933849-46-X*) Landmark Edns.

Abracadabra. Endel Markowitz. (Illus.). write for info. (*0-318-56833-0*) Haymark.

Abracadabra. Eric Priestley. Ed. by C. Natale Peditto. LC 94-12721. (Open Mouth Poetry Ser.). 118p. (Orig.). 1994. pap. 9.95 (*1-884773-02-8*) Heat Press.

Abracadabra to Zigzag. Nancy Lecourt. (Illus.). (J). (ps-3). 1991. 13.95 (*0-688-09481-3*); lib. bdg. 13.88 (*0-688-09482-1*) Lothrop.

Abracadabra to Zigzag: An Alphabet Book. Nancy Lecourt. LC 92-12503. (Illus.). 32p. (J). (ps-3). 1992. pap. 4.99 (*0-14-054470-4*) Puffin Bks.

***Abracadaver.** Peter Lovesey. 224p. 1994. 16.95 (*0-7451-8645-9*, Black Dagger) Chivers N Amer.

Abracadaver. large type ed. Ralph McInerny. (Nightingale Ser.). 1990. pap. 12.95 (*0-8161-4904-6*) G K Hall.

Abradizil. Andrew Gibson. (Illus.). 164p. (J). (gr. 3-7). 1992. pap. 4.95 (*0-571-16508-7*) Faber & Faber.

Abraham. (Little Fish Books about Bible People). (J). 1991. 0.79 (*0-8307-1416-2*, 5608900) Regal.

Abraham. Susan L. Lingo & Melissa C. Downey. (Graded Activity - Resource Bks.). (Illus.). 32p. (J). (ps-7). 1992. student ed 3.99 (*0-87403-915-0*, 23-02525) Standard Pub.

Abraham. F. B. Meyer. 1993. pap. 5.95 (*0-87508-340-4*) Chr Lit.

Abraham. F. B. Meyer. (SPA.). 5.50 (*84-7228-678-9*, 220001, Pub. by Edit Clie SP) TSELF.

Abraham. James Poole. 16p. 1994. pap. 2.00 (*1-880573-16-4*) Grace WI.

***Abraham.** Ed. by Jennifer Wilger. (Bible Big Bks.). (Illus.). 8p. (J). 1995. pap. 14.99 (*1-55945-437-7*) Group Pub.

Abraham. Gordon Stowell. Tr. by S. D. Lerin. (Libros Pescaditos Sobre Personajes Biblicos Ser.). (Illus.). 24p. (J). (gr. 1). 1981. reprint ed. pap. 0.75 (*0-311-38511-7*, Edit Mundo) Casa Bautista.

***Abraham: A Sign of Hope for Jews, Christians and Muslims, Vol. 1.** Karl-Josef Kuschel. 320p. 1995. 29.95 (*0-8264-0808-7*) Continuum.

Abraham: Cuaderno del Alumno. Marten Woudstra. (SPA.). 1985. 1.20 (*1-55955-052-X*) CITE MI.

Abraham: Manual del Maestro. rev. ed. Galen Meyer. (SPA.). 1985. 3.00 (*1-55955-053-8*) CITE MI.

***Abraham: Trusting the God Who Calls.** Galen Meyer. (Revelation Ser.). 1995. teacher ed 5.50 (*1-56212-088-3*) CRC Pubns.

***Abraham - The Man & the Symbol: A Jungian Interpretation of the Biblical Story.** Gustav Dreifuss & Judith Riemer. 120p. (Orig.). 1995. pap. 14.95 (*0-933029-94-2*) Chiron Pubns.

Abraham & All the Families of the Earth: A Commentary on the Book of Genesis 12-50. J. Gerald Janzen. LC 93-13846. (International Theological Commentary Ser.). 230p. (Orig.). 1993. pap. 17.99 (*0-8028-0148-X*) Eerdmans.

Abraham & Isaac. Illus. by Gavin Rowe. LC 84-18076. (People of the Bible Ser.). 32p. (J). (gr. k-4). 1985. 14.95 (*0-8172-1994-3*) Raintree Steck-V.

Abraham & Sarah. Susan Crowder. (Illus.). 14p. (Orig.). 1987. pap. 1.50 (*0-912927-23-2*, X023) St John Kronstadt.

***Abraham & Sarah: The Long Journey.** Roberta K. Dorr. 512p. 1995. 19.99 (*0-345-40090-9*, Moorings) Ballantine.

Abraham & Sarah's Great Adventure. Patricia Duncan. 1992. pap. 3.95 (*1-55673-477-8*, 7927) CSS OH.

Abraham Baldwin: Patriot, Educator, & Founding Father. E. Merton Coulter. LC 87-10486. 304p. 1987. 24.95 (*0-918339-06-5*) Vandamere.

Abraham Bisno, Union Pioneer: An Autobiographical Account of Bisno's Early Life & the Beginnings of Unionism in the Women's Garment Industry. Abraham Bisno. LC 67-20752. 262p. reprint ed. pap. 74.70 (*0-8357-5018-3*, 2023719) Bks Demand.

***Abraham Cahan.** Marovitz. 1995. text ed. 26.95 (*0-8057-3993-9*) Macmillan.

Abraham Clark & the Quest for Equality in the Revolutionary Era, 1774 - 1794. Ruth Bogin. LC 81-65872. 219p. 1982. 30.00 (*0-8386-3100-2*) Fairleigh Dickinson.

Abraham Connection: A Jew, Christian & Muslim in Dialogue. Ed. by Benjamin J. Hubbard & George Grose. LC 94-71253. (Church & the World Ser.: Vol. VI). 264p. (Orig.). 1994. pap. 19.95 (*0-940121-18-2*, P210, Cross Roads Bks) Cross Cultural Pubns.

Abraham Cowley. James G. Taaffe. LC 70-120525. (English Authors Ser.). 1972. lib. bdg. 15.95 (*0-8057-1124-4*) Irvington.

Abraham Cowley Essays, Plays & Sundry Verses. Abraham Cowley. reprint ed. lib. bdg. 79.00 (*0-7812-0102-0*) Rprt Serv.

Abraham Divided: An LDS Perspective on the Middle East. Daniel C. Peterson. LC 91-76006. 377p. (Orig.). 1992. pap. 12.95 (*1-56236-203-8*) Aspen Bks.

Abraham Esau's War: A Black South African War in the Cape, 1899-1902. Bill Nasson. (African Studies: No. 68). (Illus.). 272p. (C). 1991. 64.95 (*0-521-38512-1*) Cambridge U Pr.

Abraham, Faith under Seige. Lester Sumrall. 66p. (Orig.). 1985. pap. 1.95 (*0-937580-86-4*) LeSEA Pub Co.

Abraham Fornander: A Biography. Eleanor H. Davis. LC 78-31368. (Illus.). 336p. 1979. 13.95 (*0-8248-0459-7*) UH Pr.

Abraham Fraunce, Symbolicae Philosophiae Liber. Ed. by John Manning. Tr. by Estelle Haan. LC 89-45845. (Studies in the Emblem: No. 7). 1991. 63.00 (*0-404-63707-8*) AMS Pr.

Abraham, Friend of God. Penny Frank. (Story Bible Ser.: No. 4). (J). (ps-3). 1984. 3.99 (*0-85648-729-5*) Lion USA.

Abraham, Friend of God. Gordon Lindsay. (Old Testament Ser.: Vol. 4). 1964. 1.95 (*0-89985-126-6*) Christ for the Nations.

Abraham Fund Directory of Institutions & Organizations Fostering Coexistence Between Jews & Arabs in Israel. Abraham Fund Staff. Ed. by Anita Weiner et al. 720p. (Orig.). (C). 1991. pap. 75.00 (*0-9629529-0-7*) Abraham Fund.

Abraham Galante: A Biography. Albert E. Kalderon. (Illus.). 124p. 1983. 10.00 (*0-87203-111-X*) Hermon.

Abraham Geiger & Liberal Judaism: The Challenge of the Nineteenth Century. Tr. by Ernst J. Schlochauer. 305p. 1981. reprint ed. pap. 9.95 (*0-87820-800-3*) Hebrew Union Coll Pr.

Abraham Heschel's Idea of Revelation. Lawrence Perlman. LC 89-6191. 171p. 1989. 46.95 (*1-55540-350-6*, 14 01 71) Scholars Pr GA.

Abraham Ibn Esra Als Grammatiker: Ein Beitrag zur Geschichte der Hebraischen Sprachwissenschaft. Wilhelm Bacher. Ed. by Steven Katz. LC 79-7125. (Jewish Philosophy, Mysticism & History of Ideas Ser.). 1980. reprint ed. lib. bdg. 18.95 (*0-405-12239-X*) Ayer.

Abraham, Isaac, Jacob & Zev. Jerry Marcus. LC 81-70363. 225p. 1982. 13.95 (*0-941394-00-X*) Brittany Pubns.

Abraham Isaac Kook: The Lights of Penitence, Lights of Holiness, the Moral Principles. Essays, Letters & Poems. Tr. by Ben Zion Bokser. LC 78-70465. (Classics of Western Spirituality Ser.). 448p. 1978. pap. 19.95 (*0-8091-2159-X*) Paulist Pr.

Abraham Joshua Heschel. Byron L. Sherwin. 53p. (Orig.). (C). 1979. pap. 3.95 (*0-935982-39-6*, BLS-03) Spertus Coll.

Abraham Joshua Heschel: Exploring His Life & Thought. John C. Merkle. 184p. 1985. text ed. 19.95 (*0-02-920970-6*) Macmillan.

Abraham Kuenen (1828-1891) His Major Contributions to the Study of the Old Testament. Ed. by P. B. Dirksen & A. Van der Kooij. LC 92-40325. 1993. 51.50 (*90-04-09732-5*) E J Brill.

Abraham Lincoln. (YA). 1992. 4.99 (*0-517-06996-2*) Random Hse Value.

Abraham Lincoln. (Great Americans Ser.). (Illus.). 24p. (J). (gr. 2-5). 1987. pap. 2.50 (*0-671-62982-4*, Litl Simon S&S) S&S Childrens.

Abraham Lincoln. (Illus.). (J). (gr. 2-5). 1991. 8.95 (*0-8167-2568-3*) Troll Assocs.

Abraham Lincoln. Rae Bains. LC 84-2581. (Illus.). 32p. (J). (gr. 3-6). 1985. lib. bdg. 9.49 (*0-8167-0146-6*); pap. text ed. 2.95 (*0-8167-0147-4*) Troll Assocs.

Abraham Lincoln. Joanne Barkan. Ed. by Bonnie Brook. (Let's Celebrate Ser.). (Illus.). 32p. (J). (gr. k-2). 1990. 4.95 (*0-671-69113-9*); lib. bdg. 6.95 (*0-671-69107-4*) Silver Pr.

Abraham Lincoln. Roger Bruns. (World Leaders - Past & Present Ser.). (Illus.). 112p. (YA). (gr. 5 up). 1986. lib. bdg. 17.95 (*0-87754-597-9*); pap. 9.95 (*0-7910-0649-2*) Chelsea Hse.

Abraham Lincoln. David R. Collins. LC 76-2456. (Sower Ser.). (Illus.). (J). (gr. 3-6). 1976. pap. 6.95 (*0-915134-93-4*) Mott Media.

Abraham Lincoln. Ingri D'Aulaire. (J). (ps-3). 1987. mass mkt. 10.00 (*0-440-40690-0*) Dell.

Abraham Lincoln. Lee Morgan & Pietro Cattaneo. (What Made Them Great Ser.). (Illus.). 104p. (J). (gr. 5-8). 1990. lib. bdg. 12.95 (*0-382-09973-7*) Silver Burdett Pr.

Abraham Lincoln. Kathie B. Smith. LC 86-28060. (Great Americans Ser.). (Illus.). 24p. (J). (gr. 4-6). 1987. lib. bdg. 5.99 (*0-685-18829-9*, Julian Messner) Silver Burdett Pr.

Abraham Lincoln. Anna Sproule. LC 91-50540. (People Who Made a Difference Ser.). (Illus.). 68p. (J), (gr. 3-4). 1992. lib. bdg. 21.26 (*0-8368-0620-4*) Gareth Stevens Inc.

Abraham Lincoln. Godfrey R. Charnwood. LC 83-45730. reprint ed. 49.50 (*0-404-20056-7*) AMS Pr.

Abraham Lincoln, 2 Vols, Set. John T. Morse, Jr. LC 73-128958. (American Statesmen Ser.: Nos. 25, 26). reprint ed. 95.00 (*0-404-50892-8*) AMS Pr.

Abraham Lincoln: A Biography. Benjamin P. Thomas. LC 68-7853. 1979. reprint ed. 18.00 (*0-394-60468-7*, Modern Lib) Random.

Abraham Lincoln: A Documentary Portrait Through His Speeches & Writings. Ed. & Intro. by Don E. Fehrenbacher. LC 76-53865. 288p. 1964. 24.50 (*0-8047-0942-4*); pap. 9.95 (*0-8047-0946-7*) Stanford U Pr.

Abraham Lincoln: A History (with John G. Nicolay) John M. Hay. (Notable American Authors Ser.). 1992. reprint ed. lib. bdg. 75.00 (*0-7812-3056-X*) Rprt Serv.

Abraham Lincoln: A New Portrait. Ed. by Henry B. Kranz. LC 72-279. (Essay Index Reprint Ser.). 1977. reprint ed. 18.95 (*0-8369-2798-2*) Ayer.

Abraham Lincoln: A Press Portrait. Ed. by Herbert Mitgang. LC 88-33072. 552p. 1989. reprint ed. pap. 17.95 (*0-8203-1137-5*) U of Ga Pr.

Abraham Lincoln: A Spiritual Biography. large type ed. Elton Trueblood. (Large Print Inspirational Ser.). 256p. 1986. pap. 14.95 (*0-8027-2550-3*) Walker & Co.

Abraham Lincoln: Apostle of Freedom. Garry De Young. 22p. (Orig.). 1983. pap. 5.00 (*0-936128-04-6*) De Young Pr.

***Abraham Lincoln: Autobiographical Narrative.** Abraham Lincoln. (American Autobiography Ser.). 77p. 1995. reprint ed. lib. bdg. 69.00 (*0-7812-8578-X*) Rprt Serv.

Abraham Lincoln: Citizen of New Salem. Paul Horgan. (Illus.). 90p. 1961. write for info. (*0-686-74487-X*) Macmillan.

Abraham Lincoln: For the People. Anne Colver. (Discovery Biographies Ser.). (Illus.). 80p. (J). (gr. 2-6). 1992. reprint ed. lib. bdg. 12.95 (*0-7910-1414-2*) Chelsea Hse.

***Abraham Lincoln: From Skeptic to Prophet.** Wayne C. Temple. (Illus.). 352p. Date not set. write for info. (*1-878044-19-2*) Mayhaven Pub.

Abraham Lincoln: His Speeches & Writings. Roy P. Basler. (Quality Paperbacks Ser.). (Illus.). 888p. 1990. reprint ed. pap. 17.95 (*0-306-80404-2*) Da Capo.

Abraham Lincoln: His Speeches & Writings. Abraham Lincoln. Ed. by Roy P. Basler. LC 46-11909. 1968. reprint ed. 73.00 (*0-527-57100-8*) Periodicals Srv.

Abraham Lincoln: His Speeches & Writings. Abraham Lincoln. (History - United States Ser.). 843p. 1993. reprint ed. lib. bdg. 199.00 (*0-7812-4898-1*) Rprt Serv.

Abraham Lincoln: Leader of a Nation in Crisis. Anna Sproule. LC 90-10374. (People Who Have Helped the World Ser.). (Illus.). 68p. (J). (gr. 5-6). 1992. lib. bdg. 21.26 (*0-8368-0216-0*) Gareth Stevens Inc.

Abraham Lincoln: Mini-Play, 2 pts., Pt. 1. (U. S. History Ser.). (J). (gr. 5 up). 1978. 6.50 (*0-89550-317-4*) Stevens & Shea.

Abraham Lincoln: Mini-Play, 2 pts., Pt. 2. (U. S. History Ser.). (J). (gr. 5 up). 1978. 6.50 (*0-89550-325-5*) Stevens & Shea.

Abraham Lincoln: President of a Divided Country. Carol Greene. LC 89-33845. (Rookie Biographies Ser.). (Illus.). 48p. (J). (gr. k-3). 1989. lib. bdg. 12.90 (*0-516-04206-8*); pap. 4.95 (*0-516-44206-6*) Childrens.

Abraham Lincoln: Sixteenth President of the United States. Rebecca Stefoff. Ed. by Richard G. Young. LC 88-28488. (Presidents of the United States Ser.). (Illus.). (J). (gr. 5-9). 1989. lib. bdg. 17.26 (*0-944483-14-3*) Garrett Ed Corp.

An Asterisk (*) at the beginning of an entry indicates that the title is appearing in BIP for the first time.

Abraham Lincoln: Sources & Style of Leadership. Ed. by Frank J. Williams et al. LC 94-12321. (Contributions in American History Ser.: No. 159). 208p. 1994. text ed. 55.00 (0-313-29359-7, Greenwood Pr) Greenwood.

Abraham Lincoln: The Complete Politician. William L. Huganir. (Illus.). 402p. 1992. text ed. 17.95 (0-9635518-0-9) W L Huganir.

Abraham Lincoln: The Freedom President. Susan Sloate. (Great Lives Ser.). (Illus.). 128p. 1989. pap. 3.95 (0-449-90375-3, Columbine) Fawcett.

Abraham Lincoln: The Great Emancipator. Augusta Stevenson. (Childhood of Famous Americans Ser.). (Illus.). 192p. (J). (gr. 2-6). 1986. reprint ed. pap. 3.95 (0-02-042030-7, Aladdin Paperbacks) S&S Childrens.

Abraham Lincoln: The Man & His Faith. G. Frederick Owen. 232p. 1981. pap. 9.99 (0-8423-0000-7) Tyndale.

Abraham Lincoln: The Man Behind the Myths. Stephen B. Oates. 240p. 1994. reprint ed. pap. 12.00 (0-06-092472-1, PL) HarpC.

Abraham Lincoln: The Prairie Years, Vol. II. Carl Sandburg. (Illus.). 1939. 40.00 (0-15-100777-2) HarBrace.

Abraham Lincoln: The Prairie Years & the War Years. Carl Sandburg. 1993. 12.98 (0-88365-832-1) Galahad Bks.

Abraham Lincoln: The Prairie Years & The War Years, 1 vol. Carl Sandburg. LC 54-9720. 762p. 1954. 49.95 (0-15-100638-5) HarBrace.

Abraham Lincoln: The Prairie Years & the War Years. Carl Sandburg. LC 74-8388. (Illus.). 762p. 1974. reprint ed. pap. 19.95 (0-15-602611-2, Harvest Bks) HarBrace.

Abraham Lincoln: The Prairie Years & the War Years, Set. Carl Sandburg. (History - United States Ser.). 1992. reprint ed. lib. bdg. 150.00 (0-7812-6171-6) Rprt Serv.

Abraham Lincoln: To Preserve the Union. Russell Shorto. (History of the Civil War Ser.). (Illus.). 160p. (J). (gr. 5 up). 1990. lib. bdg. 12.95 (0-382-09937-0); pap. 7.95 (0-382-24046-4) Silver Burdett Pr.

Abraham Lincoln: Unforgettable American. Mabel Kunkel. LC 76-1368. (Illus.). 448p. 1976. 20.00 (0-935680-27-6) Kentucke Imprints.

Abraham Lincoln: Word for Word. Ed. by Maureen Harrison & Steve Gilbert. 409p. (Orig.). 1994. pap. 19.95 (1-880780-06-2) Excellent Bks.

Abraham Lincoln - Franklin D. Roosevelt. Naunerle C. Farr. (Pendulum Illustrated Biography Ser.). (Illus.). (J). (gr. 4-12). 1979. student ed 1.25 (0-88301-378-9); pap. text ed. 2.95 (0-88301-354-1) Pendulum Pr.

Abraham Lincoln: A Man for All the People: A Ballad. Myra C. Livingston. LC 93-2731. (Illus.). 32p. (J). (ps-3). 1993. lib. bdg. 15.95 (0-8234-1049-8) Holiday.

Abraham Lincoln & American Political Religion. Glen E. Thurow. LC 76-12596. 133p. 1976. 49.50 (0-87395-334-7) State U NY Pr.

Abraham Lincoln & His Family - Paper Dolls. Tom Tierney. (J). 1989. pap. 3.95 (0-486-26024-0) Dover.

Abraham Lincoln & His Mailbag: Two Documents. Edward D. Neill. Ed. by Theodore C. Blegen. LC 64-23313. (Publications of the Minnesota Historical Society). 60p. reprint ed. pap. 25.00 (0-8357-3316-5, 2039540) Bks Demand.

Abraham Lincoln & Reconstruction: The Louisiana Experiment. Peyton McCrary. LC 78-51181. 1978. 69.50 (0-691-04660-3) Princeton U Pr.

Abraham Lincoln & Reconstruction: The Louisiana Experiment. Peyton McCrary. LC 78-51181. 441p. reprint ed. pap. 125.70 (0-7837-1404-1, 2041758) Bks Demand.

Abraham Lincoln & the American Political Tradition. Ed. by John L. Thomas. LC 85-20973. 176p. 1986. lib. bdg. 25.00 (0-87023-512-5) U of Mass Pr.

Abraham Lincoln & the Downfall of American Slavery. Noah Brooks. LC 73-14436. (Heroes of the Nations Ser.). reprint ed. 49.50 (0-404-58254-0) AMS Pr.

Abraham Lincoln & the End of Slavery. Russell Shorto. (Gateway Civil Rights Ser.). (Illus.). 32p. (J). (gr. 2-4). 1991. lib. bdg. 13.40 (1-878841-12-2); pap. 4.95 (1-878841-36-X) Millbrook Pr.

Abraham Lincoln & the Quakers. Daniel Bassuk. LC 87-60763. (Orig.). 1987. pap. 3.00 (0-87574-273-4) Pendle Hill.

Abraham Lincoln & the Rothschilds. 1991. lib. bdg. 79.95 (0-8490-4421-9) Gordon Pr.

Abraham Lincoln & the Second American Revolution. James M. McPherson. 192p. 1991. 20.00 (0-19-505542-X) OUP.

Abraham Lincoln & the Second American Revolution. James M. McPherson. (Illus.). 192p. 1992. pap. 9.95 (0-19-507606-0) OUP.

Abraham Lincoln & the Union. Oscar Handlin & Lilian Handlin. (Library of American Biography). (C). 1987. pap. text ed. 16.00 (0-673-39340-2) HarpCollege.

***Abraham Lincoln & the Union.** Oscar Handlin & Lilian Handlin. (Library of American Biography). 192p. 1995. reprint ed. pap. 15.95 (1-886746-21-4) Talman Pub.

Abraham Lincoln & the Union: Chronicle of the Embattled North. Nathaniel W. Stephenson. (History - United States Ser.). 272p. 1992. reprint ed. lib. bdg. 79.00 (0-7812-6167-8) Rprt Serv.

Abraham Lincoln & the United States. Kenneth C. Wheare. (History - United States Ser.). 286p. 1993. reprint ed. lib. bdg. 79.00 (0-7812-4822-1) Rprt Serv.

Abraham Lincoln & the Washington Territory. H. D. Smiley. 39p. 1988. pap. 4.95 (0-87770-432-5) Ye Galleon.

Abraham Lincoln & the Western Territories. Ralph McGinnis & Calvin Smith. 1993. text ed. 28.95 (0-8304-1247-6); pap. text ed. 18.95 (0-8304-1375-8) Nelson-Hall.

Abraham Lincoln, by Some Men Who Knew Him. Ed. & Frwd. by Paul M. Angle. LC 78-90601. (Essay Index Reprint Ser.). 1980. 23.95 (0-8369-1242-X) Ayer.

***Abraham Lincoln: Contemporary: An American Legacy.** Ed. by Frank J. Williams & William D. Pederson. (Illus.). 224p. 1995. 29.95 (1-882810-01-5, 108) Savas Woodbury.

Abraham Lincoln Encyclopedia. Mark E. Neely, Jr. (Quality Paperbacks Ser.). (Illus.). 368p. 1984. pap. 18.95 (0-306-80209-0) Da Capo.

Abraham Lincoln Fact Book & Teacher's Guide. 64p. 1983. pap. 4.95 (0-915992-07-8) Eastern Acorn.

***Abraham Lincoln Illustrated Envelopes & Letter Paper.** James W. Milgram. (Illus.). 272p. 1984. 21.95 (0-9614018-0-X) Northbrook Pub.

Abraham Lincoln of the Sea: The Life of Andrew Furuseth. Arnold Berwick. LC 92-64186. (Illus.). 176p. 1993. 19.95 (0-9633611-0-4) Odin Pr CA.

Abraham Lincoln (President's Biographies) Jim Hargrove. (Encyclopedia of Presidents Ser.). (Illus.). 100p. (J). (gr. 4-7). 1988. 14.40 (0-516-01359-9) Childrens.

Abraham Lincoln, Public Speaker. Waldo W. Braden. LC 88-6793. viii, 119p. (C). 1993. pap. 8.95 (0-8071-1852-4) La State U Pr.

Abraham Lincoln, the Backwoods Boy. Horatio Alger, Jr. (Works of Horatio Alger Jr.). 1989. reprint ed. 75.00 (0-7812-3550-2) Rprt Serv.

Abraham Lincoln the Orator: Penetrating the Lincoln Legend. Lois J. Einhorn. LC 91-46971. (Great American Orators: Critical Studies, Speeches & Sources: No. 16). 248p. 1992. text ed. 47.95 (0-313-26168-7, ELN, Greenwood Pr) Greenwood.

***Abraham Lincoln, the War Years Vol. 1.** Carl Sandburg. 1939. 40.00 (0-15-101604-6) HarBrace.

Abraham Lincoln, 1809-1858, 2 vols., Set. Albert J. Beveridge. (History - United States Ser.). 1992. reprint ed. lib. bdg. 150.00 (0-7812-6169-4) Rprt Serv.

Abraham Lincoln's Ancestry: German or English? M. D. Learned's Investigatory History, with an Appendix on Daniel Boone. Don H. Tolzmann. (Illus.). 164p. (Orig.). 1993. pap. text ed. 20.00 (1-55613-754-0) Heritage Bk.

***Abraham Lincoln's Autobiography.** Abraham Lincoln. (American Autobiography Ser.). 45p. 1995. reprint ed. lib. bdg. 69.00 (0-7812-8579-8) Rprt Serv.

Abraham Lincoln's Flag: We Won't Give up a Star. Howard Miller. (Illus.). 26p. (J). (gr. 4-6). 1990. pap. text ed. 4.95 (0-939631-19-9) Thomas Publications.

Abraham Lincoln's Social & Political Thought. R. D. Rucker. 1991. 15.95 (0-533-09579-4) Vantage.

Abraham "Oregon" Smith: Pioneer, Folk Hero, & Tale-Teller (Doctoral Dissertation, Wesleyan University, 1949. William H. Jansen. Ed. by Richard M. Dorson. LC 77-70602. (International Folklore Ser.). 1977. reprint ed. lib. bdg. 33.95 (0-405-10101-5) Ayer.

***Abraham Robinson: The Creation of Non-Standard Analysis: Personal & Mathematical Odyssey.** Joseph W. Dauben. LC 94-32715. 1995. 49.50 (0-691-03745-0) Princeton U Pr.

Abraham, Sarah & the Promised Son. Robert Mitchell. (Arch Bks.: No. 21). 1984. pap. 1.99 (0-317-00725-4, 59-1284) Concordia.

Abraham, Sarah, & the Promised Son: Genesis 17, 18: 1-15, 21: 1-7. Arch Books Staff. (J). 1993. pap. 1.99 (0-570-06183-0) Concordia.

Abraham Stone: Country Mouse, City Rat. Joe Kubert. (Illus.). 48p. 1991. pap. 9.95 (1-56398-009-6) Malibu Graphics.

Abraham Stone: Country Mouse, City Rat. deluxe limited ed. Joe Kubert. (Illus.). 48p. 1991. 34.95 (1-56398-010-X) Malibu Graphics.

Abraham-Su Vida y Sus Tiempos: The Life & Times of Abraham. William J. Deane. (SPA.). 6.95 (84-7645-167-9, 223209, Pub. by Edit Clie SP) TSELF.

Abraham the Initiator on Spirit, Will & Ego. Judi Sutherland & Larry Sutherland. (Illus.). 288p. (Orig.). (C). 1989. pap. text ed. 17.95 (0-685-30788-3) Additive Creations.

Abraham: The Lord Will Provide: A Bible Study Commentary. Edward G. Dobson. LC 92-31854. 224p. 1993. 12.99 (0-8007-1668-X) Revell.

Abraham y Jose el Patriarca: Personas Importantes de la Biblia. Tomas De La Fuente. (Illus.). 76p. (SPA.). 1982. pap. 2.50 (0-940048-03-5) Austin Bilingual Lang Ed.

***Abraham Zabludovsky: Architect, 1979-1993.** 312p. 1995. pap. write for info. (0-614-06566-6) Princeton Arch.

Abrahamic Covenant. Hawtin. LC 87-73131. 156p. 1988. pap. 5.00 (0-934666-26-1) Artisan Sales.

Abraham's Great Discovery. Bernard M. Zlotowitz & Dina Maiben. LC 91-60474. (Illus.). 32p. (J). (gr. k-4). 1991. boxed 11.95 (0-911389-04-0) NightinGale Res.

Abram Talked with God. (Little Learner Ser.). 24p. (J). (gr. 2-5). 1985. 5.95 (0-570-08950-6, 56-1541) Concordia.

***Abram Tertz & the Poetics of Crime.** Catharine T. Nepomnyashchy. LC 94-40946. (Studies of the Harriman Institute). 1995. write for info. (0-300-06210-9) Yale U Pr.

Abramos la Biblia. G. M. Lear. Orig. Title: Let's Open the Bible. 200p. (SPA.). 1989. pap. 4.99 (0-8254-1438-5) Kregel.

Abrams. R. P. Hunnicutt. 1990. 60.00 (0-89141-388-X) Presidio Pr.

Abrams Story. Henry L. Reimers. 60p. 1977. 7.50 (0-87770-181-4) Ye Galleon.

Abramtsevo: Historical, Artistic & Literary. Ed. by Collet's Holdings, Ltd. Staff. 258p. 1981. 75.00 (0-317-39467-3, Pub. by Collets UK) St Mut.

Abrasion-Resistant & Low Friction Lining Materials. 1991. 210.00 (0-9510103-2-8) St Mut.

Abrasive Ages. William G. Pinkstone. LC 74-23797. (Illus.). 136p. 1975. 10.00 (0-915010-01-1) Sutter House.

Abrasive Materials. (Metals & Minerals Ser.). 1994. lib. bdg. 250.95 (0-8490-5682-9) Gordon Pr.

Abrasive Materials: Garnet, Silica Stone, Diamonds, Staurolite, Emery, Tripoli. (Metals & Minerals Ser.). 1993. lib. bdg. 255.95 (0-8490-8951-4) Gordon Pr.

Abrasives. L. Coes. LC 78-153451. (Applied Mineralogy Ser.: Vol. 1). (Illus.). 1971. 47.00 (0-387-80968-6) Spr-Verlag.

Abravanel. Lowell M. Durham. LC 89-37172. (Illus.). 227p. reprint ed. pap. 64.70 (0-7837-6868-0, 2046698) Bks Demand.

Abraxas. Jacques Audiberti. 289p. (FRE.). 1977. pap. 16.95 (0-7859-2751-4, 2070297756) Fr & Eur.

Abraxas. Arlene Zekowski. LC 64-21951. (Illus.). 1964. pap. 20.00 (0-913844-07-1) Am Canadian.

Abreactions. Marcus Rome. 144p. (Orig.). 1989. pap. 15.00 (0-913559-13-X) Birch Brook Pr.

Abreactions. deluxe limited ed. Marcus Rome. 144p. (Orig.). 1989. 35.00 (0-913559-12-1) Birch Brook Pr.

Abrege de la Vie des Peintres. Roger De Piles. 540p. 1969. reprint ed. write for info. (0-318-71389-6, Pub. by Georg Olms GW) Lubrecht & Cramer.

Abrege de la Vie des Peintres. Roger D. Piles. 540p. 1969. reprint ed. write for info. (0-318-71940-1, Pub. by Georg Olms GW) Lubrecht & Cramer.

Abri. rev. ed. Edith Schaeffer. LC 91-47977. 256p. 1992. reprint ed. pap. 10.99 (0-89107-668-9) Crossway Bks.

Abridged Biography & Genealogy MI, Vol. 1. 2nd ed. 1994. write for info. (0-8103-6879-X); 432.00 (0-8103-6878-1) Gale.

Abridged Biography & Genealogy MI, Vol. 2. 2nd ed. 1994. write for info. (0-8103-6880-3) Gale.

Abridged Biography & Genealogy MI, Vol. 3. 2nd ed. 1994. write for info. (0-8103-6881-1) Gale.

Abridged Dewey Decimal Classification & Relative Index. 12th rev. ed. Melvil Dewey. LC 90-31428. 857p. 1990. 88.00 (0-910608-42-3) Forest Pr.

Abridged Economics Glossary. Isaac Paenson. (ENG, FRE, RUS & SPA.). 1983. write for info. (0-8288-0152-5, M 15495) Fr & Eur.

Abridged Field Guide to the Maine Writer. Ed. by George Benington. 36p. (Orig.). 1984. pap. 2.95 (0-913341-04-5) Coyote Love.

Abridged Greek-English Lexicon. Ed. by Henry G. Liddell & Robert Scott. (ENG & GRE.). 1935. 29.95 (0-19-910207-4) OUP.

Abridged History of Greek Literature. Alfred Croiset & Maurice Croiset. Tr. by G. F. Heffelbower. LC 78-131510. reprint ed. 42.50 (0-404-01857-2) AMS Pr.

Abridged Readers' Guide to Periodical Literature, Vols. 17-60: 1960-1994. 1993. 100.00 (0-685-73470-6) Wilson.

Abridged Typicon. Ed. by Feodor S. Kovalchuk. 248p. (C). 1985. 14.95 (1-878997-14-9) St Tikhons Pr.

Abridgement: The Secret Doctrine. Katherine Hillard & Helena P. Blavatsky. 584p. 1968. reprint ed. spiral bd. 16.50 (0-7873-0409-3) Mokelumne.

Abridgement of All Sea-Lawes. William Welwood. LC 72-6039. (English Experience Ser.: No. 565). 88p. 1973. reprint ed. 25.00 (90-221-0565-2) Walter J Johnson.

Abridgement of Mental Philosophy. Thomas Upham. LC 79-10925. (History of Psychology Ser.). 1979. reprint ed. lib. bdg. 75.00 (0-8201-1331-X) Schol Facsimiles.

***Abridgement of New Zealand Case Law, 18 vols., Set.** H. Jenner Wily. Date not set. write for info. (0-409-60000-8, NZ) Butterworth Legal Pubs.

Abridgement of the Debates of Congress, 16 Vols, Set. Ed. by Thomas H. Benton. reprint ed. lib. bdg. 2,880.00 (0-404-00770-8) AMS Pr.

Abridgement of the Indian Affairs Contained in Four Folio Volumes: Transacted in the Colony of New York from the Year 1687 to 1751. Peter Wraxall. Ed. by Charles H. Macillwain. LC 67-27998. 1972. reprint ed. 26.95 (0-405-09104-4) Ayer.

Abridgement of the Secret Doctrine. Helena P. Blavatsky. Ed. by Elizabeth Preston & Christmas Humphreys. 1968. pap. 8.95 (0-8356-0009-2, Quest) Theos Pub Hse.

Abriss der Geschichte Israels und Judas: Lieder der Hudhailiten. Julius Wellhausen. (Skizzen und Vorarbeiten Ser.: 1 Heft). iv, 175p. (ARA & GER.). 1985. 123.10 (3-11-009765-6) De Gruyter.

Abriss der Kartographie Brandenburgs 1771-1821. Wolfgang Scharfe. (Illus.). xii, 357p. (C). 1972. 104.60 (3-11-003898-6) De Gruyter.

Abriss Des Romischen Staatsrechts. Theodor Mommsen. Ed. by J. P. Mayer. LC 78-67369. (European Political Thought Ser.). (GER.). 1980. reprint ed. lib. bdg. 30.95 (0-405-11721-3) Ayer.

Abriss Einer Funktionellen Semantik. Gabor O. Nagy. (Janua Linguarum, Series Minor: No. 137). 1973. 61.55 (90-279-2519-4) Mouton.

Abroad: British Literary Traveling Between the Wars. Paul Fussell, Jr. (Illus.). 1980. 25.00 (0-19-502767-1) OUP.

Abroad: British Literary Traveling Between the Wars. Paul Fussell, Jr. (Illus.). 1982. pap. 10.95 (0-19-503068-0) OUP.

Abroad & Beyond: Patterns in American Overseas Education. Craufurd D. Goodwin & Michael Nacht. 175p. 1988. pap. 12.95 (0-521-35742-X) Cambridge U Pr.

Abruestungsatlas. Chancen und Risiken Des Amerikanischen Truppenabzugs Aus Der BRD. B. Luber. (Anstoesse Zur Friedensarbeit Ser.). 98p. (GER.). 1990. pap. 17.50 (3-487-09377-4, Pub. by Georg Olms GW) Lubrecht & Cramer.

Abrupt Climatic Change - Evidence & Implications. Ed. by W. H. Berger & L. D. Labeyrie. (C). 1987. lib. bdg. 107.00 (90-277-2604-3) Kluwer Ac.

Abrustung & Konventionelle Stabilitat in Europa. Erwin Muller & Gotz Neuneck. 203p. 1990. pap. 36.00 (3-7890-1974-7, Pub. by Nomos Verlags GW) Intl Bk Import.

ABS - TCS & Brake Technology Developments: SAE International Congress & Exposition 1994, 15 papers. (Special Publications). 1994. pap. 45.00 (1-56091-470-X, SP-1018) Soc Auto Engineers.

ABS - Traction Control & Advanced Brake Systems. 132p. 1992. pap. 45.00 (1-56091-231-6, SP-914) Soc Auto Engineers.

ABS-TCS & Brake Technology: Eighteen Papers. 1993. 59.00 (1-56091-338-X, SP-953) Soc Auto Engineers.

ABS Traction Control. 1988. 29.00 (0-89883-671-9, SP744) Soc Auto Engineers.

ABS Traction Control & Brake Components. 1990. 59.00 (1-56091-024-0, SP815) Soc Auto Engineers.

Absalom, Absalom. William Faulkner. 1966. pap. text ed. write for info. (0-07-553657-9); pap. text ed. 4.50 (0-685-04217-0) McGraw.

Absalom, Absalom. William Faulkner. (C). 1966. pap. write for info. (0-318-54357-5, T78) Random.

Absalom, Absalom! William Faulkner. LC 91-26767. (William Faulkner Annotations to Novels Ser.). 192p. 1991. 15.00 (0-8240-4235-2) Garland.

Absalom, Absalom! William Faulkner. LC 90-50211. (Vintage International Ser.). 336p. 1991. pap. 9.95 (0-679-73218-7, Vin) Random.

Absalom, Absalom! William Faulkner. 1993. 15.50 (0-679-60072-8, Modern Lib) Random.

Absalom, Absalom! rev. ed. William Faulkner. Ed. by Noel Polk. LC 86-6488. 320p. 1986. 25.00 (0-394-55634-8) Random.

Absalom, Absalom! The Questioning of Fictions. Robert D. Parker. (Twayne's Masterwork Studies: No. 76). 184p. (C). 1991. text ed. 21.95 (0-8057-8071-8, Twayne); pap. 12.95 (0-8057-8116-1, Twayne) Macmillan.

Absalom, Absalom! Notes. James Roberts. 1982. pap. 3.75 (0-8220-0110-1) Cliffs.

Absaraka: Home of the Crows. Margaret I. Carrington. LC 83-6951. (Illus.). iv, 284p. 1983. reprint ed. 30.00 (0-8032-1423-5); reprint ed. pap. 8.95 (0-8032-6315-5) U of Nebr Pr.

Absaroka Ambush. William W. Johnstone. 288p. 1993. mass mkt. 3.99 (1-55817-689-6, Pinnacle NY) Windsor NY.

Absatzwege der Baumwollindustrie in den 80er Jahren. Rudolf Wittgen. (Schriften zur Textilindustrie Ser.: Vo. 28). xiv, 308p. (GER.). 1982. 54.60 (3-8204-5821-2) P Lang Pubs.

Abschatzung fur Differentialoperationen. I. W. Gelman & W. G. Mazja. 192p. (GER.). 1980. text ed. 65.00 (0-8176-1275-0) Birkhauser.

Abscisic Acid. Ed. by Frederick T. Addicott. LC 81-23406. 624p. 1983. text ed. 115.00 (0-275-90932-8, C0932, Praeger Pubs) Greenwood.

Abscission. Frederick T. Addicott. LC 81-4065. (Illus.). 376p. 1982. 65.00 (0-520-04288-3) U CA Pr.

***A...B...Sea.** Bobbie Kalman. (Crabapple Ser.). (Illus.). 32p. (J). (ps-3). 1995. lib. bdg. 15.95 (0-86505-625-0); pap. 5.95 (0-86505-725-7) Crabtree Pub Co.

Absence. Jean-Denis Bredin. 192p. (FRE.). 1988. pap. 10.95 (0-7859-2235-0, 207037937X) Fr & Eur.

Absence. Peter Handke. Tr. by Ralph Manheim. 1990. 18.95 (0-374-10022-5) FS&G.

Absence & Lateness: How to Reduce It, How to Control It. Louise Pitone. 1987. pap. 24.95 (1-55645-515-1) Busn Legal Reports.

Absence from Felicity: The Story of Helen Schucman & Her Scribing of A Course in Miracles. Kenneth Wapnick. LC 91-8916. 540p. (Orig.). 1991. pap. 16.00 (0-933291-08-6) Foun Miracles.

Absence Makes the Heart. Lynne Tillman. 1991. pap. 12.95 (1-85242-176-2) Serpents Tail.

Absence of a Cello. Ira Wallach. 1964. pap. 4.75 (0-8222-0003-1) Dramatists Play.

Absence of Angels. William Penn. LC 93-27526. 274p. 1994. 24.00 (1-877946-42-7) Permanent Pr.

***Absence of Angels: A Novel.** W. S. Penn. LC 94-34607. (American Indian Literature & Critical Studies: Vol. 14). 272p. 1995. pap. 13.95 (0-8061-2714-7) U of Okla Pr.

Absence of Decision: Foreign Students in American Colleges & Universities: A Report on Policy Formation & the Lack Thereof. Craufurd D. Goodwin & Michael Nacht. LC 83-192775. (IIE Research Reports: No. 1). 61p. reprint ed. pap. 25.00 (0-8357-5019-1, 2027775) Bks Demand.

***Absence of Light.** Lindsey. 1995. mass mkt. (0-553-56941-4) Bantam.

Absence of Light. David L. Lindsey. 1994. 23.00 (0-385-42311-X) Doubleday.

Absence of Myth: Writings on Surrealism. Georges Bataille. Ed. & Tr. by Michael Richardson. LC 94-964. 1994. 27.95 (0-86091-419-4) Routledge Chapman & Hall.

Absence of the Dead Is Their Way of Appearing. Mary W. Trautmann. LC 83-62665. (Orig.). (C). 1984. pap. 8.95 (0-939416-04-2) Cleis Pr.

Absence of the Father & the Dance of Zygotes. Mary E. McAnally. Ed. by Jim Dochniak. (U. S. A. Poetry Chapbook Ser.: No. 1). 20p. (C). 1982. pap. 1.95 (0-937724-00-9) Shadow Pr.

Absence of War. David Hare. 96p. (Orig.). 1994. pap. 9.95 (0-571-17071-4) Faber & Faber.

Absences. Denis Jean. 57p. (Orig.). 1984. pap. 10.00 (0-932662-50-1) St Andrews NC.

Absences. James Tate. LC 88-63522. (Classic Contemporaries Ser.). 1990. pap. 10.95 (0-88748-091-8) Carnegie-Mellon.

Absent Are Always in the Wrong - For Jack Kerouac. Joy Walsh. (Illus.). 75p. 1986. pap. 25.00 (0-934953-25-2) Water Row Pr.

Absent at the Creation. Bradley Seidman. LC 83-90254. 1984. 10.95 (0-87212-175-5) Libra.

A

An Asterisk (*) at the beginning of an entry indicates that the title is appearing in BIP for the first time. 17

A

Absent Authority: Issues in Contemporary Indian English Criticism. John O. Perry. 1993. text ed. 45.00 (*81-207-1506-3*, Pub. by Sterling Pubs II) Apt Bks.

Absent Body. Drew Leder. 224p. 1990. lib. bdg. 34.95 (*0-226-46999-9*); pap. text ed. 14.95 (*0-226-47000-8*) U Ch Pr.

Absent Father: Virginia Woolf & Walter Pater. Perry Meisel. LC 79-19289. 1980. text ed. 37.00 (*0-300-02401-0*) Yale U Pr.

Absent Father & Public Policy in the Program of Aid to Dependent Children. Maurine McKeany. LC 60-64080. (University of California Publications in Social Welfare: Vol. 1). 140p. reprint ed. pap. 39.90 (*0-8357-5020-5*, 2021396) Bks Demand.

*__Absent Father in Modern Drama, 54.__ Paul Rosefeldt. LC 94-28595. (American University Studies: Series III, Vol. 54). 176p. (C). 1995. text ed. 38.95 (*0-8204-2629-6*) P Lang Pubs.

Absent Fathers, Lost Sons: The Search for Masculine Identity. Guy Corneau. Tr. by Larry Shouldice. LC 90-53373. (C. G. Jung Foundation Bks.). 208p. (Orig.). 1991. pap. 11.00 (*0-87773-603-0*) Shambhala Pubns.

Absent Fountain. Paul Murray. 72p. (C). 1991. 24.00 (*0-948268-99-9*, Pub. by Dedalus Pr IE); pap. 15.00 (*0-948268-98-0*, Pub. by Dedalus Pr IE) St Mut.

Absent Friends. Frederick Busch. 1989. 18.95 (*0-394-57426-5*) Knopf.

Absent Friends. Frederick Busch. LC 91-13846. 288p. 1991. reprint ed. pap. 11.95 (*0-8112-1175-4*, NDP721) New Directions.

Absent from School: The Story of a Truancy Centre. Bob Grunsell. (Chameleon Education Ser.). Orig. Title: Born to Be Invisible. 128p. (Orig.). 1981. pap. 4.95 (*0-906495-42-3*) Writers & Readers.

Absent from the Majority: Working Class Women in America. Nancy Seifer. (Illus.). 96p. 1973. pap. 2.25 (*0-87495-016-3*) Am Jewish Comm.

Absent in the Spring. large type ed. Mary Westmacott. 1978. 21.95 (*0-7089-0115-8*) Ulverscroft.

Absent Love: A Chronicle. Rosa Montero. Tr. by Cristina De la Torre & Diana Glad. LC 90-28657. xxiv, 188p. 1991. 30.00 (*0-8032-3141-5*); pap. 9.95 (*0-8032-8176-5*) U of Nebr Pr.

Absent Marx: Class Analysis & Liberal History in Twentieth-Century America. Ian R. Tyrrell. LC 85-17709. (Contributions in American History Ser.: No. 115). 288p. 1986. text ed. 55.00 (*0-313-24876-1*, TYA/, Greenwood Pr) Greenwood.

*__Absent-Minded Imperialism: Britain & the Expansion of Empire in Nineteenth-Century Brazil.__ Peter Riviere. 224p. 1995. text ed. 59.50 (*1-85043-913-3*) St Martin.

Absent-Minded Toad. Javier Rondon. Tr. by Kathryn Corbett. LC 94-14407. (Illus.). 32p. (J). (ps-1). 1994. 9.95 (*0-916291-53-7*) Kane-Miller Bk.

*__Absent Mothers & Orphaned Fathers: Narcissism & Abjection in Lessing's Aesthetic & Dramatic Production.__ Susan E. Gustafson. (Kritik: German Literary Theory & Cultural Studies). 316p. 1994. text ed. 36.95x (*0-8143-2503-3*) Wayne St U Pr.

Absent One: Mourning Ritual, Tragedy & the Performance of Ambivalence. Susan L. Cole. LC 84-43063. 179p. 1985. 28.50 (*0-271-00391-X*) Pa St U Pr.

Absent One: Mourning Ritual, Tragedy, & the Performance of Ambivalence. Susan L. Cole. 192p. 1991. pap. 14.95 (*0-271-00785-0*) Pa St U Pr.

Absent Shakespeare. Mark J. Mirsky. LC 92-55118. (C). 1994. write for info. (*0-8386-3511-3*) Fairleigh Dickinson.

Absent Traveller: Prakrit Love Poetry from the Gashasaptasati of Satavahanan Hala. Arvind K. Mehrotra. 1991. 10.00 (*0-86311-253-6*, Pub. by Ravi Dayal II) S Asia.

Absent Traveller: Prakrit Love Poetry from the Gathasaptasati of Satavahana Hala. Ed. by A. K. Mehrotra. xii, 92p. 1991. 15.95 (*0-685-50305-4*) Apt Bks.

Absent Voice: Narrative Comprehension in the Theater. Stanton B. Garner, Jr. LC 88-28727. 240p. 1989. 22.50 (*0-252-01607-6*) U of Ill Pr.

*__Absent Without Leave: Two Novellas.__ Heinrich Boll. Tr. by Leila Vennewitz. LC 95-12350. (European Classics Ser.). 1995. write for info. (*0-8101-1231-0*); pap. text ed. write for info. (*0-8101-1209-4*) Northwestern U Pr.

Absentee. Maria Edgeworth. Ed. by W. J. McCormack & Kim Walker. (World's Classics Ser.). 368p. 1988. pap. 9.95 (*0-19-281682-9*) OUP.

Absentee American: Repatriates' Perspectives on America. Carolyn D. Smith. 130p. 1994. pap. 12.95 (*0-9639260-0-4*) Aletheia.

Absentee American: Repatriates' Perspectives on America & Its Place in the Contemporary World. Carolyn D. Smith. LC 91-15500. 144p. 1991. text ed. 45.00 (*0-275-93655-4*, C3655, Praeger Pubs) Greenwood.

Absentee Entrepreneurship & the Dynamics of the Motor Vehicle Industry in Argentina. Maria B. Nofal. LC 87-15159. 288p. 1989. text ed. 75.00 (*0-275-92607-9*, C2607, Praeger Pubs) Greenwood.

Absentee Landowning & Exploitation in West Virginia, 1760-1920. Barbara Rasmussen. LC 94-5096. 224p. 1994. lib. bdg. 29.95x (*0-8131-1880-8*) U Pr of Ky.

Absentee Ownership & Business Enterprise in Recent Times: The Case of America. Thorstein B. Veblen. LC 63-23516. (Reprints of Economic Classics Ser.). v, 445p. 1964. reprint ed. 45.00 (*0-678-00048-4*) Kelley.

Absenteeism: New Approaches to Understanding, Measuring, & Managing Employee Absence. Paul S. Goodman et al. LC 84-47985. (Joint Publication in the Jossey-Bass Management Series & the Jossey-Bass Social & Behavioral Science Ser.). 460p. reprint ed. pap. 131.10 (*0-7837-2506-X*, 2042665) Bks Demand.

Absenteeism & Turnover of Hospital Employee. James L. Price & Charles W. Mueller. LC 85-23779. (Monographs in Organizational Behavior & Industrial Relations: Vol. 5). 282p. 1986. 73.25 (*0-89232-441-4*) Jai Pr.

Absenteeism Checklist. Gene L. Dent. (Practical Management Ser.). 20p. (Orig.). 1990. pap. text ed. 4.00 (*1-878403-02-8*) Martin-Dennison Pr.

Absenteeism in the Workplace. James H. Ballagh et al. 256p. 1987. 35.00 (*0-318-33179-9*, 5288) Commerce.

Absenteeism, Work Loss & Illness Behavior: Medical Analysis Index with Reference Bibliography. Clayton R. Mellows. LC 85-47855. 150p. 1987. 39.50 (*0-88164-384-X*); pap. 34.50 (*0-88164-385-8*) ABBE Pubs Assn.

Absinthe: History in a Bottle. Barnaby Conrad, III. LC 88-12669. (Illus.). 160p. (Orig.). 1988. 29.95 (*0-87701-566-X*) Chronicle Bks.

Absinthe: The Green Goddess. Aleister Crowley. (Orig.). 1994. pap. 5.95 (*1-55818-270-5*) Holmes Pub.

Absinthe - The Cocaine of the Nineteenth Century: A History of the Hallucinogenic Drug & Its Effect on Artists & Writers in Europe & the United States. Doris Lanier. (Illus.). 192p. 1995. lib. bdg. 29.95 (*0-89950-989-4*) McFarland & Co.

Absolom Daak: Dalek Killer. Steve Moore et al. 96p. 1990. 8.95 (*1-85400-113-2*) Marvel Entmnt.

Absolute Age Determination: Physical & Chemical Dating Methods & Their Application. M. A. Geyh & H. Schleicher. (Illus.). 500p. 1990. pap. 69.00 (*0-387-51276-4*) Spr-Verlag.

Absolute Analysis. F. Nevanlinna & R. Nevanlinna. Tr. by P. Emig. LC 73-75652. (Grundlehren der Mathematischen Wissenschaften Ser.: Vol. 102). (Illus.). 280p. 1973. 72.00 (*0-387-05917-2*) Spr-Verlag.

Absolute & die Wirklichkeit in Schellings Philosophie: Mit der Erstedition einer Handschrift aus dem Berliner Schelling-Nachlass. Barbara Loer. LC 73-93164. (Quellen & Studien zur Philosophie: Vol. 7). (Illus.). viii, 288p. (C). 1974. 134.65 (*3-11-004329-7*) De Gruyter.

Absolute at Large. Karel Capek. LC 73-13248. (Classics of Science Fiction Ser.). 257p. 1989. reprint ed. 28.00 (*0-88355-104-7*) Hyperion Conn.

Absolute Barbeque. Kansas City Barbeque Inner Circle Staff. Ed. by Bill Venable et al. (Illus.). 176p. (Orig.). 1993. pap. 9.95 (*1-882907-04-3*) Old Market.

Absolute Beginner's Cookbook: Or, How Long Do I Cook a Three-Minute Egg? Jackie Eddy & Eleanor Clark. (Illus.). 235p. 1990. spiral bd. 12.95 (*1-55958-008-9*) Prima Pub.

*__Absolute Beginner's Cookbook 2, or, Which Way Do I Fold Eggwhites?__ Jackie Eddy & Eleanor Clark. LC 94-36553. 1995. write for info. (*1-55958-663-X*) Prima Pub.

Absolute Beginner's Guide to Access. Greg Perry. 336p. 1993. 16.95 (*0-672-30366-3*) Sams.

Absolute Beginner's Guide to Memory Management. Michael L. Miller. 300p. 1993. disk, pap. 16.95 (*0-672-30282-9*) Sams.

*__Absolute Beginners Guide to Multimedia.__ Ron Wodaski. 1994. cd-rom, pap. 29.99 (*0-672-30524-0*) Sams.

Absolute Beginners Guide to Networking. Mark Gibbbs. 400p. 1993. pap. 19.95 (*0-672-30326-4*) Sams.

*__Absolute Beginner's Guide to Networking.__ 2nd ed. Mark Gibbs. 388p. 1994. 22.00 (*0-672-30553-4*) Sams.

Absolute Beginners Guide to Programming. Greg Perry. 400p. 1993. pap. 19.95 (*0-672-30269-1*) Sams.

Absolute Beginner's Guide to UNIX. Sams Development Group Staff. 1994. pap. 19.95 (*0-672-30460-0*) Sams.

*__Absolute Beginner's Guide to Virtual Reality.__ Ron Wodaski. (Illus.). 350p. (Orig.). 1995. pap. text ed. 29.99 (*0-672-30701-4*) Sams.

Absolute Beginner's Guide to Windows. Michael Hyde. 300p. 1993. 16.95 (*0-672-30359-0*) Sams.

Absolute Beneath the Relative & Other Essays. Stanley L. Jaki. LC 88-20771. 244p. (Orig.). (C). 1989. lib. bdg. 47.00 (*0-8191-7182-4*) U Pr of Amer.

Absolute Chronology of the Aegean Early Bronze Age: Archaeology, Radiocarbon & History. S. W. Manning. (Monographs in Mediterranean Archaeology). (Illus.). 235p. 1992. 30.00 (*1-85075-336-9*, Pub. by Sheffield Acad UK) CUP Services.

Absolute Comic. Edith Kern. LC 80-10478. 229p. reprint ed. pap. 65.30 (*0-8357-3440-4*, 2039697) Bks Demand.

Absolute Computer File Security. John J. Williams. Ed. by Laurie Williams. (Illus.). 52p. (Orig.). 1990. pap. 29.00 (*0-934274-10-X*) Consumertronics.

Absolute Differential Calculus: Calculus of Tensors. Tullio Levi-Civita. Ed. by Enrico Persico. Tr. by Marjorie Long. LC 76-27497. (Illus.). 480p. 1977. reprint ed. pap. text ed. 9.95 (*0-486-63401-9*) Dover.

*__Absolute Empowerment: Mastering Psychophysics.__ Frank Fracasso. (Illus.). 168p. (C). 1991. 14.95 (*0-9630034-0-2*) FMS.

Absolute Form: Modalitat, Individualitat, und das Prinzip der Philosophie nach Kant und Hegel. Thomas S. Hoffman. vii, 358p. (GER.). (C). 1991. lib. bdg. 129.25 (*3-11-012875-6*) De Gruyter.

*__Absolute Happiness: The Way to a Life of Complete Fulfillment.__ Michael D. Rowland. Ed. by Jill Kramer. 256p. 1995. pap. 12.95 (*1-56170-219-6*) Hay House.

Absolute Last Chance Diet Book. John Kolness. 1991. pap. 5.95 (*0-918259-37-1*) CCC Pubns.

Absolute or Relative Motion? A Study from a Machian Point of View of the Discovery & the Structure of Dynamical Theories - the Discovery of Dynamics, pt. 1. J. B. Barbour. 600p. 1989. 110.00 (*0-521-32467-X*) Cambridge U Pr.

Absolute Power. deluxe limited ed. Ray Russell. 256p. 1992. 49.00 (*0-940776-27-8*) Maclay Assoc.

Absolute Power: Nonexistence-Existence. Joseph Abbott, Jr. LC 85-91153. (Illus.). (Orig.). 1985. pap. 26.50 (*0-9615351-0-5*) Directions Unltd.

Absolute Proof. Paul Kuttner. LC 84-1794. 445p. 1984. 15.95 (*0-911025-05-7*) Dawnwood Pr.

Absolute Prosperity: Growth for All Nations. J. Ray Estefania. (Victory Ser.: No. 2). (Illus.). 1989. 19.95 (*0-945542-02-X*) Park & Park Pub.

Absolute Radiometry: Electrically Calibrated Thermal Detectors of Optical Radiation. Ed. by F. Hengstberger. 266p. 1989. text ed. 104.00 (*0-12-340810-5*) Acad Pr.

Absolute Rulers. Michael Pollard. Ed. by Rebecca Stefoff. LC 91-33297. (Pioneers in History Ser.). (Illus.). 48p. (J). (gr. 5-8). 1992. lib. bdg. 19.93 (*1-56074-034-5*) Garrett Ed Corp.

Absolute Stability of Nonlinear Control Systems. Liao Xiao-xin. LC 92-31009. (Mathematics & Its Applications Chinese Ser.: Vol. 5). 1993. lib. bdg. 82.00 (*0-7923-1988-5*) Kluwer Ac.

Absolute Summability of Fourier Series & Orthogonal Series. Y. Okuyama. (Lecture Notes in Mathematics Ser.: Vol. 1067). vi, 118p. 1984. pap. 28.10 (*0-387-13355-0*) Spr-Verlag.

Absolute Surrender. Andrew Murray. 7.99 (*0-916441-04-0*, Christian Lib) Barbour & Co.

Absolute Surrender. Andrew Murray. pap. 4.50 (*0-8024-0560-6*) Moody.

Absolute Surrender. Andrew Murray. 128p. 1981. pap. 3.99 (*0-88368-093-9*) Whitaker Hse.

*__Absolute Truths.__ Howatch. pap. write for info. (*0-449-22392-2*) Fawcett.

Absolute Truths. Susan Howatch. 1995. 25.00 (*0-679-41206-9*) McKay.

*__Absolute Truths: A Novel.__ large type ed. Susan Howatch. LC 94-46952. 967p. 1995. 25.95 (*0-7838-1219-1*) Hall.

Absolute Unlawfulness of the Stage Entertainment Fully Demonstrated. William Law. Bd. with Stage Defended. John Dennis & William Law. LC 75-170493.; Law Outlaw'd: A Short Reply to Mr. Law's Long Declamation Against the Stage. William Law. LC 75-170493. LC 75-170493. (English Stage Ser.: Vol. 49). 1973. Set lib. bdg. 64.00 (*0-8240-0632-1*) Garland.

Absolute Value of Human Action in the Theology of Juan Luis Segundo. Frances Stefano. 330p. (C). 1992. lib. bdg. 52.00 (*0-8191-8511-6*) U Pr of Amer.

Absolute Zhirinovsky: A Transparent View of the Distinguished Russian Statesman. Graham Frazer & George Lancelle. LC 94-19514. 1994. 7.95 (*0-14-024339-9*, Penguin Bks) Viking Penguin.

Absolutely! You Can Create Positive Life Changes. Charlene Shea. 136p. (Orig.). 1991. pap. text ed. 12.95 (*0-9629269-0-6*) Diversity Pubs.

Absolutely Delicious. Linda Allard. LC 93-33244. 1994. 24.00 (*0-679-43305-8*) Random.

Absolutely Every (Almost) Bed & Breakfast in California: Monterey to San Diego. Intro. by Toni Knapp. (Rocky Mountain Ser.). 300p. (Orig.). 1993. pap. 14.95 (*1-882092-10-4*) Travis Ilse.

Absolutely Every Bed & Breakfast in Arizona (Almost) Toni Knapp. LC 91-21736. (Rocky Mountain Ser.). 176p. (Orig.). 1992. pap. 10.95 (*1-882092-06-6*) Travis Ilse.

Absolutely Every Bed & Breakfast in Arizona (Almost) 2nd ed. Ed. by Toni Knapp. (Rocky Mountain Ser.). 240p. (Orig.). 1994. pap. 15.95 (*1-882092-12-0*) Travis Ilse.

Absolutely Every Bed & Breakfast in Colorado (Almost) 2nd ed. Toni Knapp. LC 92-8158. (Rocky Mountain Ser.). 304p. 1992. pap. 12.95 (*1-882092-08-2*) Travis Ilse.

Absolutely Every Bed & Breakfast in Colorado (Almost) 3rd ed. Ed. by Toni Knapp. (Rocky Mountain Ser.). 300p. 1994. pap. 16.95 (*1-882092-11-2*) Travis Ilse.

*__Absolutely Every Bed & Breakfast in Illinois (Almost)__ Ed. by Toni Knapp. (Mississippi River Ser.). 300p. 1995. pap. text ed. 15.95 (*1-882092-14-7*) Travis Ilse.

Absolutely Every Bed & Breakfast in New Mexico (Almost) Toni Knapp. LC 91-23714. (Rocky Mountain Ser.). 174p. (Orig.). 1992. pap. 10.95 (*1-882092-07-4*) Travis Ilse.

Absolutely Every Bed & Breakfast in Northern California (Almost) Ed. by Toni Knapp. (Rocky Mountain Ser.). 320p. (Orig.). 1995. pap. 16.95 (*1-882092-13-9*) Travis Ilse.

Absolutely Every Bed & Breakfast in Texas (Almost) Ed. by Toni Knapp. (Rocky Mountain Ser.). 350p. (Orig.). 1992. pap. 14.95 (*1-882092-09-0*) Travis Ilse.

*__Absolutely Every Bed & Breakfast in Texas (Almost)__ 2nd ed. Ed. by Toni Knapp. (Rocky Mountain Ser.). 350p. 1995. pap. 18.95 (*1-882092-15-5*) Travis Ilse.

*__Absolutely Fabulous.__ Jennifer Saunders. Ed. by Amy Einhorn. 192p. (Orig.). 1995. pap. 12.00 (*0-671-52714-2*) PB.

Absolutely Free! A Biblical Reply to Lordship Salvation. Zane C. Hodges. 238p. 1989. pap. 9.95 (*0-685-74794-8*) Redencion Viva.

Absolutely Free: Fun Stuff by Mail for the Entire Family. Dawn Hardy. 1994. pap. 9.95 (*1-55958-500-5*) Prima Pub.

Absolutely Mad Inventions. A. E. Brown & H. A. Jeffcott, Jr. Orig. Title: Beware of Imitations. (Illus.). 1970. reprint ed. pap. 2.95 (*0-486-22596-8*) Dover.

*__Absolutely Nothing to Get Alarmed About: The Complete Charles Wright.__ Charles Wright. 400p. 1994. lib. bdg. 33.00 (*0-8095-9143-X*) Borgo Pr.

Absolutely Perfect Summer. Jeffrey A. Nesbit. 211p. (Orig.). (YA). (gr. 9-12). 1990. pap. 6.99 (*0-87788-005-0*) Shaw Pubs.

Absolutely, Positively Perfect Book of Basic Gardening. O. Leander & Candy Tuft. LC 94-19210. (Illus.). 1994. pap. write for info. (*0-89865-903-5*) Donning Co.

Absolutely Shira. Libby Lazewnik. 190p. (J). (gr. 6-9). 1993. 12.95 (*1-56871-032-1*) Targum Pr.

*__Absolutely Summing Operators.__ Joe Diestel et al. (Studies in Advanced Mathematics: No. 43). 500p. (C). Date not set. 59.95 (*0-521-43168-9*) Cambridge U Pr.

Absolutely True Story of My Visit to Yellowstone with the Terrible Rupes. Willo D. Roberts. LC 94-14436. (J). (gr. 3-7). 1994. text ed. 14.95 (*0-689-31939-8*, Mac Bks Young Read) S&S Childrens.

Absolutely Unforgettable Parties: Great Ideas for Party People. Janet Litherland. Ed. by Arthur Zapel. LC 89-13519. (Illus.). 192p. (Orig.). 1990. pap. 9.95 (*0-916260-63-1*, B135) Meriwether Pub.

*__Absolutely Vegetarian.__ Lorine Tadej. 172p. 1994. 8.95 (*0-945383-92-4*) Teach Servs.

Absolutely Worst Fart Book. H. Kavet. 96p. 1992. pap. 5.95 (*0-88032-416-3*) Ivory Tower Pub.

Absolutes in Moral Theology? Ed. by Charles E. Curran. LC 75-3988. 320p. 1976. reprint ed. text ed. 59.75 (*0-8371-7450-3*, CUMT, Greenwood Pr) Greenwood.

Absolution. Olaf Olafsson. 272p. 1994. 20.00 (*0-679-42891-7*) Pantheon.

Absolutism & Its Consequentialist Critics. Ed. by Joram Haber. 210p. (C). 1993. lib. bdg. 52.00 (*0-8476-7839-3*); pap. text ed. 19.95 (*0-8476-7840-7*) Rowman.

Absolutism & Its Discontents: State & Society in Seventeenth Century France & England. Michael S. Kimmel. 256p. 1987. 39.95x (*0-88738-180-4*) Transaction Pubs.

Absolutism & Relativism in Philosophy & Politics. Hans Kelsen. (Reprint Series in Social Sciences). (C). 1993. reprint ed. pap. text ed. 1.00 (*0-8290-3728-4*, P-149) Irvington.

Absolutism & Ruling Class: The Formation of the Russian Political Order, 1700-1825. John P. LeDonne. 400p. 1991. 55.00 (*0-19-506805-X*) OUP.

Absolutism & Society in Seventeenth-Century France: State Power & Provincial Aristocracy in Languedoc. William Beik. LC 84-9561. (Cambridge Studies in Early Modern History). (Illus.). 375p. 1989. pap. 21.95 (*0-521-36782-4*) Cambridge U Pr.

Absolutism & the Eighteenth-Century Origins of Compulsory Schooling in Prussia & Austria. James Van Horn Melton. (Illus.). 1988. 59.95 (*0-521-34668-1*) Cambridge U Pr.

Absolutism in Seventeenth-Century Europe. Ed. by John Miller. LC 90-36375. 256p. 1991. text ed. 49.95 (*0-312-04930-7*) St Martin.

Absorb the Colors. Ed. by Beverly Voldseth & Karen H. Wee. (Illus.). 108p. (Orig.). (C). 1984. pap. text ed. 6.95 (*0-9614314-0-7*) Heywood Pubs.

Absorbed Specific Energy & or Strain Energy Density Criterion. G. Sih et al. 1982. lib. bdg. 140.00 (*90-247-2598-4*) Kluwer Ac.

Absorbency: Textile Science & Technology, Vol. 7. Ed. by P. K. Chatterjee. 334p. 1985. 125.75 (*0-444-42377-X*) Elsevier.

Absorbent Mind. 1990. write for info. (*81-900106-3-8*, Pub. by Kalakshetra Pubns II) N Montessori.

*__Absorbent Mind.__ Maria Montessori. LC 95-18404. 1995. pap. write for info. (*0-8050-4156-7*, Owl) H Holt & Co.

Absorbent Mind. Maria Montessori. 1993. reprint ed. lib. bdg. 25.95x (*1-56849-212-X*) Buccaneer Bks.

Absorbent Polymer Technology. Ed. by L. Brannon-Peppas & R. S. Harland. (Studies in Polymer Science: No. 8). 278p. 1990. 120.00 (*0-444-88654-0*) Elsevier.

Absorption: Fundamentals & Applications. Roman Zarzycki et al. LC 92-46597. 1993. pap. text ed. 76.00 (*0-08-040262-3*, Pergamon Pr); text ed. 175.00 (*0-08-040263-1*, Pergamon Pr) Elsevier.

Absorption & Scattering of Light by Small Particles. Craig F. Bohren & Donald R. Huffman. 530p. 1983. text ed. 134.00 (*0-471-05772-X*) Wiley.

Absorption & Theatricality: Painting & Beholder in the Age of Diderot. Michael Fried. (Illus.). xviii, 250p. 1988. pap. text ed. 14.95 (*0-226-26213-8*) U Ch Pr.

Absorption & Utilization of Amino Acids, 3 Vols., Vol. I. Ed. by Mendel Friedman. 272p. 1989. 191.00 (*0-8493-6006-4*, QP561) CRC Pr.

Absorption & Utilization of Amino Acids, 3 Vols., Vol. II. Ed. by Mendel Friedman. 304p. 1989. 204.00 (*0-8493-6007-2*, QP566) CRC Pr.

Absorption & Utilization of Amino Acids, 3 Vols., Vol. III. Ed. by Mendel Friedman. 304p. 1989. 204.00 (*0-8493-6008-0*, QP561) CRC Pr.

*__Absorption Chillers & Heat Pumps.__ Keith E. Herold & Reinhard Radermacher. 256p. 1995. 74.95 (*0-8493-9427-9*, 9427) CRC Pr.

Absorption Cooling Process: A Critical Literature Review. R. T. Ellington et al. (Research Bulletin Ser.: No. 14). iv, 43p. 1957. 5.00 (*0-317-56826-4*) Inst Gas Tech.

Absorption from Solution at the Solid Liquid Interface. Ed. by Geoffrey D. Parfitt & Colin H. Rochester. 1983. text ed. 180.00 (*0-12-544980-1*) Acad Pr.

*__Absorption of Light by Surface Water.__ J. H. Hakvoort. (Studies in Integrated Water Management: No. 2). 160p. (Orig.). 1994. pap. 52.50x (*90-407-1023-6*, Pub. by Delft U Pr NE) Coronet Bks.

*__Absorption of Orally Administered Enzymes.__ Ed. by M. L. Gardner & K. J. Steffens. (Illus.). 104p. 1995. pap. 28.00 (*3-540-58747-0*) Spr-Verlag.

Absorption Spectra & Chemical Bonding in Complexes. C. K. Jorgensen. LC 61-12437. 1962. 148.00 (*0-08-009627-1*, Pub. by Pergamon Repr UK) Franklin.

Absorption Spectra in the Infrared Region, 2 vols., 1. Ed. by L. Lang et al. LC 75-647671. reprint ed. pap. 80.00 (*0-8357-5021-3*, 2025747) Bks Demand.

Absorption Spectra in the Infrared Region, 2 vols., 2. Ed. by L. Lang et al. LC 75-647671. 319p. reprint ed. pap. 91.00 (*0-8357-5022-1*) Bks Demand.

Absorption Spectra in the Ultraviolet & Visible Region, Vol. XXIV. L. Lang. 420p. 1982. 295.00 (*0-569-08738-4*, Pub. by Collets UK) Pro-Am Music.

An Asterisk (*) at the beginning of an entry indicates that the title is appearing in BIP for the first time.

Absorption Spectroscopy in Mineralogy: First European Meeting, Academia Nazionale del Lincei, Palazzo Corsini, Rome, Italy, 4-7 Oct., 1989. Ed. by A. Mottana & F. Barragato. 294p. 1990. 89.75 (*0-444-88799-7*) Elsevier.

Absorption, Surface Area & Porosity. 2nd ed. S. J. Gregg & K. S. Sing. 1982. text ed. 126.00 (*0-12-300956-1*) Acad Pr.

***Absorptive Capacity of Kuwait.** Ragaei E. Mallakh & Jacob K. Atta. LC 81-2020. (Illus.). 204p. 1981. 20.00 (*0-669-04541-1*) Intl Res Ctr Energy.

***Abstainer Pill.** Porter B. Williamson. 400p. (Orig.). 1995. pap. 9.95 (*0-918356-00-8*) MSC Inc.

***Abstainer Pill.** Porter B. Williamson. LC 94-94053. 400p. (Orig.). 1995. pap. 18.95 (*0-918356-09-1*) MSC Inc.

Abstinence. Lanford Wilson. 1989. pap. 2.75 (*0-8222-0004-X*) Dramatists Play.

***Abstinence.** Dale Zevin. (Comprehensive Health for Middle Grades Ser.). (J). (gr. 6-9). 1996. 24.00 (*1-56071-463-8*, H565) ETR Assocs.

***Abstinence: Health Facts.** Netha L. Thacker & Kathleen R. Miner. LC 94-44827. 1995. write for info. (*1-56071-576-6*) ETR Assocs.

***Abstinence: Members of Overeaters Anonymous Share Their Experience, Strength, & Hope.** Overeaters Anonymous, Inc. Staff. LC 94-67576. 1994. pap. 6.99 (*0-9609898-7-0*) Overeaters Anym.

Abstinence in Action: Food Planning for Compulsive Eaters. Barbara McFarland & Ann M. Erb. 140p. 1989. pap. 16.95 (*0-89486-538-2*, 5045A) Hazelden.

Abstinence in Islam. Al-Ghazali. Tr. by Caesar E. Farah. (Islamic Studies Ser.: No. 1). 1992. 25.00 (*0-88297-050-X*); pap. 12.00 (*0-88297-048-8*) Bibliotheca.

Abstinence Makes the Heart Grow Fonder. Carole Marsh. (Smart Sex Stuff Ser.). (J). (gr. 2-12). 1994. 24.95 (*1-55609-273-3*); pap. 14.95 (*1-55609-208-3*) Gallopade Pub Group.

***Abstinent Cooking for Food Addicts.** 1995. 14.00 (*0-9638074-3-9*) Food Addicts.

Abstract: Thermoplastic Polyesters. 210p. 1992. 2,750.00 (*0-89336-884-9*, P-131) BCC.

Abstract Algebra. Crown et al. (Pure & Applied Mathematics Ser.: Vol. 99). 416p. 1986. 125.00 (*0-8247-7456-6*) Dekker.

Abstract Algebra. Richard Foote & David Dummit. 656p. (C). 1990. text ed. write for info. (*0-13-004771-6*) P-H.

Abstract Algebra. J. C. Kelly. (Mathematics & Its Applications Ser.). 1991. pap. 29.95 (*0-13-005000-8*, 540702) P-H.

Abstract Algebra. J. C. Kelly. 200p. 1995. text ed. 50.00 (*0-13-004987-5*) P-H.

Abstract Algebra. Dennis Kletzing. 624p. (C). 1991. text ed. 56.00 (*0-15-500391-7*) SCP.

Abstract Algebra. 2nd ed. Israel N. Herstein. 300p. (C). 1990. text ed. write for info. (*0-02-353822-8*) Macmillan.

Abstract Algebra: A First Course. Dan Saracino. LC 79-18692. (Illus.). 1980. text ed. write for info. (*0-201-07391-9*) Addison-Wesley.

Abstract Algebra: A First Course. rev. ed. Dan Saracino. (Illus.). 233p. (C). 1992. reprint ed. text ed. 32.95 (*0-88133-665-3*) Waveland Pr.

Abstract Algebra: A First Look. Joseph E. Kuczkowski & Judith L. Gersting. LC 76-14663. (Pure & Applied Mathematics Ser.: No. 38). (Illus.). 335p. 1977. pap. 95.50 (*0-7837-0964-1*, 2041269) Bks Demand.

Abstract Algebra: A First Undergraduate Course. 5th ed. Abraham P. Hillman & Gerald L. Alexanderson. LC 93-16675. 1994. text ed. 63.95 (*0-534-19128-2*) PWS Pubs.

Abstract Algebra: An Introduction. Thomas W. Hungerford. 512p. (C). 1990. text ed. 59.00 (*0-03-030558-6*) SCP.

Abstract Algebra: Theory & Applications. Thomas W. Judson. LC 93-17126. 1994. text ed. 63.95 (*0-534-93684-9*) PWS Pubs.

Abstract Algebra & Famous Impossibilities. rev. ed. A. Jones et al. (Universitext Tracts in Mathematics Ser.). (Illus.). x, 187p. 1993. pap. 29.95 (*0-387-97661-2*) Spr-Verlag.

Abstract Algebra & Solution by Radicals. John E. Maxfield & Margaret W. Maxfield. (Illus.). 224p. 1992. reprint ed. pap. 7.95 (*0-486-67121-6*) Dover.

Abstract Algebra with Applications. Norman J. Bloch. (Illus.). 448p. (C). 1986. text ed. write for info. (*0-13-000985-7*) P-H.

Abstract Algebra with Applications, 1. Karlheinz Spindler. LC 93-32090. 776p. 1994. 79.75 (*0-8247-9144-4*) Dekker.

Abstract Algebra with Applications, 2. Karlheinz Spindler. LC 93-32090. 552p. 1994. 79.75 (*0-8247-9159-2*) Dekker.

Abstract & Concrete Categories. Strecker et al. 1990. text ed. 97.95 (*0-471-60922-6*) Wiley.

Abstract & Surrealist Art in America. Sidney Janis. LC 70-91375. (Contemporary Art Ser.). (Illus.). 1970. reprint ed. 21.95 (*0-405-00729-9*) Ayer.

Abstract Art. Anna Moszynska. LC 89-51347. (World of Art Ser.). (Illus.). 1990. pap. 14.95 (*0-500-20237-0*) Thames Hudson.

Abstract Art: A Cultural History. Hilton Kramer. 175p. 1994. 22.95 (*0-02-918700-1*) Free Pr.

Abstract Automata. P. H. Starke. 1972. 43.75 (*0-444-10349-X*, North Holland); pap. 28.25 (*0-444-10354-6*, North Holland) Elsevier.

Abstract Blues. Rayfield Waller. LC 88-70737. (YA). (gr. 12 up). 1988. pap. 5.00 (*0-940713-01-2*) Broadside Pr.

Abstract Currents in Ecuadorian Art. annuals Jacqueline Barnitz. (Illus.). 48p. 1977. pap. text ed. 3.00 (*0-89192-235-0*, Ctr Inter-Am Rel) Interbk Inc.

Abstract Data Types: Their Specification, Representation, & Use. Peter D. Thomas et al. (Oxford Applied Mathematics & Computing Science Ser.). (Illus.). 268p. 1988. 75.00 (*0-19-859663-4*) OUP.

Abstract Data Types: Their Specification, Representation, & Use. Peter D. Thomas et al. (Oxford Applied Mathematics & Computing Science Ser.). (Illus.). 268p. 1988. pap. 27.95 (*0-19-859668-5*) OUP.

Abstract Data Types & Ada. Richard Mitchell. 400p. 1992. pap. text ed. 47.00 (*0-13-006099-2*) P-H.

Abstract Data Types & Algorithms. 2nd ed. Manoochehr Azmoodeh. Ed. by F. H. Sumner. (Computer Science Ser.). (Illus.). 400p. (C). 1990. text ed. 80.00 (*0-333-51209-X*, Pub. by Macmill Educ UK); pap. text ed. 42.50 (*0-333-51210-3*, Pub. by Macmill Educ UK) Scholium Intl.

Abstract Data Types & Modula-2. Richard Mitchell. 400p. 1991. pap. text ed. 47.00 (*0-13-006081-X*) P-H.

Abstract Data Types in Standard ML. Rachel Harrison. 250p. (Orig.). 1993. pap. text ed. 54.95 (*0-471-93844-0*) Wiley.

Abstract Design & How to Create It. Amor Fenn. (Illus.). 224p. 1993. reprint ed. pap. text ed. 6.95 (*0-486-27673-2*) Dover.

Abstract Design in American Quilts: A Biography of an Exhibition. Jonathan Holstein. (Illus.). 230p. 1992. pap. 39.95 (*1-880584-00-X*) Kent Qult.

Abstract Design in American Quilts: A Biography of an Exhibition. limited ed. Jonathan Holstein. (Illus.). 230p. 1992. 100.00 (*1-880584-01-8*) Kent Qult.

Abstract Entities. Roger Teichmann. 208p. 1992. text ed. 55.00 (*0-312-06824-7*) St Martin.

Abstract Evolution Equations, Periodic Problems & Applications. Daniel Daners & Pablo K. Medina. (Pitman Research Notes in Mathematics Ser.). 249p. (Orig.). 1993. pap. text ed. 59.95 (*0-470-22081-3*) Halsted Pr.

Abstract Expressionism. David Anfam. LC 89-50635. (World of Art Ser.). (Illus.). 1990. pap. 14.95 (*0-500-20243-5*) Thames Hudson.

Abstract Expressionism: A Critical Record. Ed. by David Shapiro & Cecile Shapiro. (Illus.). 416p. (C). 1990. pap. 24.95 (*0-521-36733-6*) Cambridge U Pr.

Abstract Expressionism: A Critical Record. Ed. by David Shapiro & Cecile Shapiro. (Illus.). 416p. (C). 1990. 64.95 (*0-521-36493-0*) Cambridge U Pr.

Abstract Expressionism: Creators & Critics. Ed. by Clifford Ross. (Illus.). 288p. 1991. 49.50 (*0-8109-1908-7*) Abrams.

Abstract Expressionism: The Critical Developments. Michael Auping. (Illus.). 304p. 1987. 49.50 (*0-8109-1866-8*) Abrams.

Abstract Expressionism: Works on Paper: Selections from the Metropolitan Museum of Art. Lisa M. Messinger. LC 92-33802. (Illus.). 176p. 1993. 45.00 (*0-685-62556-7*); 45.00 (*0-8109-6424-4*) Abrams.

Abstract Expressionism - A Tribute to Harold Rosenberg: Paintings & Drawings from Chicago Collections. Harold Rosenberg. LC 79-67698. (Illus.). 48p. (Orig.). 1979. pap. 4.00 (*0-935573-06-2*) D & A Smart Museum.

Abstract Expressionism & the Modern Experience. Stephen Polcari. (Illus.). 400p. (C). 1991. 69.95 (*0-521-40453-3*) Cambridge U Pr.

Abstract Expressionism & the Modern Experience. Stephen Polcari. (Illus.). 432p. (C). 1993. pap. 29.95 (*0-521-44826-3*) Cambridge U Pr.

Abstract Expressionist Painting In America. William C. Seitz. LC 82-18734. (Ailsa Mellon Bruce Studies in American Art). (Illus.). 514p. 1983. text ed. 60.00 (*0-674-00215-6*) HUP.

Abstract Functioning in the Blind. Edmund J. Rubin. LC 64-2911. (American Foundation for the Blind Research Ser.: No. 11). 64p. reprint ed. pap. 25.00 (*0-7837-0128-4*, 2040411) Bks Demand.

Abstract Harmonic Analysis, Vol. 1. 2nd ed. E. Hewitt & K. A. Ross. (Grundlehren der Mathematischen Wissenschaften Ser.: Band 115). ix, 519p. 1987. 79.00 (*0-317-61426-6*) Spr-Verlag.

***Abstract Harmonic Analysis: Structure & Analysis for Compact Groups. Analysis on Locally Compact Abelian Groups, 152.** 2nd ed. E. Hewitt & K. A. Ross. Ed. by M. Berger et al. 771p. 1994. reprint ed. pap. text ed. 59.00 (*0-387-58318-1*) Spr-Verlag.

***Abstract Harmonic Analysis Vol. 2: Structure & Analysis for Compact Groups, Analysis on Locally Compact Abelian Groups.** E. Hewitt & K. A. Ross. LC 63-12898. (Grundlehren der Mathematischen Wissenschaften Ser.: Vol. 152). 1988. 89.00 (*0-387-04832-4*) Spr-Verlag.

Abstract Harmonic Analysis Vol. I: Structure of Topological Groups, Integration Theory, Group Representations. 2nd ed. E. Hewitt & K. A. Ross. (Comprehensive Studies in Mathematics: Vol. 115). ix, 519p. 1994. pap. 59.00 (*0-387-94190-8*) Spr-Verlag.

Abstract Homotopy & Simple Homotopy Theory. K. H. Kamps & T. Porter. 300p. 1995. text ed. 59.00 (*981-02-1602-5*) World Scientific Pub.

Abstract Labour: A Critique. Jean-Marie Vincent. Tr. by Jim Cohen. LC 91-16454. 192p. 1991. text ed. 49.95 (*0-312-06717-8*) St Martin.

Abstract Lie Algebras. David J. Winter. 1972. text ed. 30.00 (*0-262-23051-8*) MIT Pr.

Abstract Linear Algebra. M. L. Curtis & J. Hempel. (Universitext Ser.). 184p. 1990. pap. text ed. 29.00 (*0-387-97263-3*) Spr-Verlag.

Abstract Machine Models for Highly Parallel Computers. Ed. by J. R. Davy & P. M. Dew. 352p. 1995. 53.00 (*0-19-853796-4*) OUP.

Abstract Measurement Theory. Louis Narens. 400p. 1985. 45.00 (*0-262-14037-3*) MIT Pr.

Abstract Objects. Edward N. Zalta. 1983. lib. bdg. 89.00 (*90-277-1474-6*) Kluwer Ac.

***Abstract of Augusta County, Virginia Death Registers, 1853-1896.** Margaret C. Reese. viii, 236p. 1983. pap. 12.50x (*0-935931-55-4*) Borgo Pr.

Abstract of Augusta County, Virginia Death Registers, 1853-1896. Margaret C. Reese. viii, 236p. (C). 1983. reprint ed. lib. bdg. 31.00x (*0-8095-8210-4*) Borgo Pr.

Abstract of Four Lectures on Buddhist Literature in China. Samuel Beal. LC 78-72376. reprint ed. 26.00 (*0-404-17226-1*) AMS Pr.

***Abstract of Graves of Revolutionary Patriots, 4 Vol. Set.** Patricia L. Hatcher. 990p. 1988. 100.00 (*0-944065-04-X*) Pioneer Heritage.

Abstract of Graves of Revolutionary Patriots, Vol. 1, A-D. Patricia L. Hatcher. LC 87-61590. 276p. 1987. 25.00 (*0-944065-00-7*); pap. 23.00 (*0-944065-05-8*) Pioneer Heritage.

Abstract of Graves of Revolutionary Patriots, Vol. 2, E-K. Patricia L. Hatcher. LC 87-61590. 242p. 1987. 25.00 (*0-944065-01-5*); pap. 23.00 (*0-944065-06-6*) Pioneer Heritage.

Abstract of Graves of Revolutionary Patriots, Vol. 3, L-R. Patricia L. Hatcher. LC 87-61590. 240p. 1988. 25.00 (*0-944065-02-3*); pap. 23.00 (*0-944065-07-4*) Pioneer Heritage.

Abstract of Graves of Revolutionary Patriots, Vol. 4, S-Z. Patricia L. Hatcher. LC 87-61590. 232p. 1988. 25.00 (*0-944065-03-1*); pap. 23.00 (*0-944065-08-2*) Pioneer Heritage.

Abstract of Land Grant Surveys of Augusta & Rockingham Counties, Virginia, 1761-1791. Peter C. Kaylor. 150p. 1991. reprint ed. 18.50 (*0-685-60463-2*, 3140) Clearfield Co.

Abstract of North Carolina Wills: Compiled from Original & Recorded Wills in the Office of the Secretary of State. J. Bryan Grimes. 536p. 1985. reprint ed. 37.50 (*0-89308-575-8*, NC 31) Southern Hist Pr.

Abstract of Probate Records, Washington County, Ohio: Wills, Estates & Guardianships (1789-1855) Bernice Graham & Elizabeth S. Cottle. 154p. 1993. reprint ed. pap. 16.00 (*0-685-65709-4*, 9084) Clearfield Co.

Abstract of Reports of the Immigration Commission, with Conclusions & Recommendations & Views of the Minority: A Study of the Reports of the Immigration Commission, 1907-1910; 2 vols., Vol. 1 & 2. William P. Dillingham & William S. Bennet. 70.50 (*0-317-28306-5*, 19705) Ayer.

Abstract of the Answers & Returns: The Census Report for 1801, Set, Vols. 1-2. Great Britain, Census Office Staff. LC 79-366591. 1968. reprint ed. lib. bdg. 150.00x (*0-678-05225-5*) Kelley.

Abstract of the Eleventh Census, 1890. U. S. Census Office Staff. LC 75-22855. (America in Two Centuries Ser.). 1976. reprint ed. 23.95 (*0-405-07722-X*) Ayer.

Abstract of the Evidence Delivered Before a Select Committee of the House of Commons, in the Years 1790 & 1791, on the Part of the Petitioners for the Abolition of the Slave Trade. LC 79-83940. (Black Heritage Library Collection). 1977. 15.95 (*0-8369-8502-8*) Ayer.

Abstract of the Fourteenth Census of the United States, 1920. U. S. Bureau of the Census Staff. LC 75-22859. (America in Two Centuries Ser.). 1976. reprint ed. 104.95 (*0-405-07725-4*) Ayer.

Abstract of the Original Titles of Record in the General Land Office of Texas. 200p. 1964. reprint ed. 45.00 (*0-685-13268-4*, PA1-38-7526) Jenkins.

Abstract of the Returns of the Fifth Census, 1830. U. S. Census Office Staff. LC 75-22849. (America in Two Centuries Ser.). 1976. reprint ed. 13.95 (*0-405-07717-3*) Ayer.

Abstract of the Twelfth Census of the United States, 1900. 3rd ed. U. S. Bureau of the Census Staff. LC 75-22856. (America in Two Centuries Ser.). 1976. reprint ed. 39.95 (*0-405-07723-8*) Ayer.

Abstract of Wills Catham County, Georgia, 1773-1817. Mable F. LeFar & Caroline P. Wilson. 160p. 1985. 7.50 (*0-915156-06-7*, SP 6) Natl Genealogical.

Abstract Options. Frances Colpitt & Phyllis Plous. (Illus.). 68p. 1989. 18.00 (*0-942006-17-8*) U of CA Art.

Abstract Options. Phyllis Plous & Frances Colpitt. (Illus.). 68p. 1989. pap. 14.95 (*0-295-96874-5*) U of Wash Pr.

Abstract Painting: Its Origin & Meaning. Adrian Heath. 1953. 7.95 (*0-85458-828-0*) Transatl Arts.

Abstract Painting & Sculpture in America. Andrew C. Ritchie. LC 70-86432. (Museum of Modern Art Publications in Reprint). (Illus.). 1969. reprint ed. 24.95 (*0-405-01544-5*) Ayer.

Abstract Painting & Sculpture in America 1927-1944. Ed. by John R. Lane & Susan C. Larsen. LC 83-3850. (Illus.). 256p. 1983. pap. text ed. 24.95 (*0-88039-006-9*) Mus Art Carnegie.

***Abstract Reasoning.** Jack Rudman. (Career Examination Ser.: CS-26). 1994. pap. 23.95 (*0-8373-6726-3*) Nat Learn.

Abstract Relations. Thomas E. Connors. LC 79-50423. (Illus.). 128p. (C). 1980. pap. 12.50 (*0-913204-12-9*) December Pr.

Abstract Ribbons. Rita S. Spalding. 64p. (Orig.). 1992. 9.95 (*0-9633941-0-X*) R S Spalding.

Abstract Sculpture in America, 1930-70. P. Andrew Spahr. (Illus.). 72p. (Orig.). (C). 1991. pap. text ed. 15.00 (*0-917418-91-3*) Am Fed Arts.

Abstract Set Theory. Thoralf A. Skolem. (Mathematical Lectures Ser.: No. 8). (Orig.). 1962. pap. 5.95 (*0-268-00000-X*) U of Notre Dame Pr.

Abstract Society. Edward C. Ellenbrook. (Illus.). 64p. (Orig.). 1985. pap. 3.25 (*0-941634-02-7*) In Valley Wichitas.

Abstract Spaces & Approximation. Ed. by Paul L. Butzer & B. Szokefalvi-Nagy. (International Series of Numerical Mathematics: No. 10). 423p. 1980. 84.00 (*0-8176-0194-5*) Birkhauser.

Abstract Systems Theory. M. D. Mesarovic & Y. Takahara. (Lecture Notes in Control & Information Sciences Ser.: Vol. 116). viii, 439p. 1989. pap. 70.00 (*0-387-50529-6*) Spr-Verlag.

***Abstract Thought & Profound Quotations: With Some of Thomas's Wonderous Thoughts.** Thomas K. DuGan. Ed. by Jack Housely. (Illus.). 104p. (Orig.). (YA). (gr. 10). 1995. pap. 10.00 (*1-878342-11-8*) Bentworth Pr.

Abstract, 1988-89. Ed. by Robert McCarter. (Illus.). 120p. (Orig.). (C). 1989. pap. write for info. (*0-9623829-0-6*) CUGSA.

Abstract, 1989-90. Ed. by Robert McCarter. (Illus.). 136p. (Orig.). 1990. pap. write for info. (*0-9623829-1-4*) CUGSA.

Abstract, 1990-91. Ed. by Robert McCarter. (Illus.). 128p. (Orig.). (C). 1991. pap. 19.95 (*0-9623829-2-2*) CUGSA.

Abstract 1991-92. Ed. by Thomas Hanrahan. (Abstract Ser.). (Illus.). (Orig.). (C). 1992. pap. 19.95 (*0-9623829-4-9*) CUGSA.

Abstract 1992-93. Ed. by Thomas Hanrahan. (Illus.). (Orig.). (C). 1993. pap. 19.95 (*0-9623829-7-3*) CUGSA.

***Abstract 93-94.** Ed. by Thomas Hanrahan. (Abstract Ser.). (Illus.). 144p. (Orig.). (C). 1994. pap. 20.95 (*1-883584-02-7*) CUGSA.

***Abstract 94-5.** Ed. by Tom Hanrahan. (Abstract Ser.). (Illus.). 144p. (Orig.). (C). 1995. pap. 19.95 (*1-883584-05-1*) CUGSA.

Abstracting & Indexing: Research Subject Analysis Index with Reference Bibliography. American Health Research Institute Staff. LC 85-47873. 150p. 1987. 39.50 (*0-88164-418-8*); pap. 34.50 (*0-88164-419-6*) ABBE Pubs Assn.

Abstracting & Indexing Services Directory. Ed. by John Schmittroth, Jr. 176p. 1982. pap. 200.00 (*0-8103-1649-8*) Gale.

Abstracting & Indexing Services in Perspective: Miles Conrad Memorial Lectures 1969-1983. Ed. by M. Lynne Neufeld et al. LC 82-84484. viii, 305p. 1983. text ed. 27.50 (*0-87815-043-9*) Info Resources.

Abstracting Concepts & Methods. Harold Borko & Charles L. Bernier. (Library & Information Science Ser.). 250p. 1975. text ed. 53.00 (*0-12-118650-4*) Acad Pr.

Abstracting, Information Retrieval, & the Humanities. Helen R. Tibbo. (Providing Access to Historical Literature Publications in Librarianship: No. 48). 276p. 1993. 35.00 (*0-685-72677-0*) Assn Coll & Res Libs.

Abstracting, Information Retrieval, & the Humanities: Providing Access to Historical Literature. Ed. by Helen R. Tibbo. LC 93-1049. (Publications in Librarianship: No. 48). 288p. (Orig.). 1993. pap. text ed. 35.00 (*0-8389-3430-7*) ALA.

Abstracting Scientific & Technical Literature. Robert Maizell et al. LC 78-9756. 316p. 1979. reprint ed. 29.50 (*0-88275-703-2*) Krieger.

Abstraction & Aging: A Social Psychological Analysis. J. S. Lee. (Recent Research in Psychology Ser.). (Illus.). 136p. 1990. pap. 48.00 (*0-387-97433-4*) Spr-Verlag.

Abstraction & Concept Formation: An Interpretative Investigation into a Group of Psychological Frames of Reference. Anatol Pikas. Tr. by Neil Tomkinson. LC 66-3915. 177p. reprint ed. pap. 50.50 (*0-8357-5023-X*, 2002973) Bks Demand.

Abstraction & Empathy. Wilhelm Worringer. Tr. by Michael Bullock. 144p. 1963. text ed. 26.00 (*0-8236-0020-3*) Intl Univs Pr.

Abstraction, Creation, Art Non-Figuratif, No. 1-5. LC 68-9226. (Contemporary Art Ser.). (Illus.). (FRE.). 1968. reprint ed. 60.95 (*0-405-00711-6*) Ayer.

Abstraction, Geometry, Painting: Selected Geometric Abstract Painting in America Since 1945. Ed. by Michael Auping. (Illus.). 240p. 1989. 49.50 (*0-8109-1027-6*) Abrams.

Abstraction in Art & Nature: A Program of Study for Artists, Teachers, & Students. Nathan C. Hale. LC 92-41717. (Illus.). 288p. 1993. reprint ed. pap. 14.95 (*0-486-27482-9*) Dover.

Abstraction in Avant-Garde Films. Maureen C. Turim. LC 84-28100. (Studies in Cinema: No. 32). (Illus.). 173p. reprint ed. pap. 49.40 (*0-8357-1629-5*, 2070487) Bks Demand.

Abstraction in Science & Morals. Stephen Korner. LC 70-130715. (Arthur Stanley Eddington Memorial Lectures: 24). 40p. reprint ed. pap. 25.00 (*0-8357-5024-8*, 2051380) Bks Demand.

Abstraction Mechanisms & Language Design. Paul N. Hilfinger. (Association for Computing Machinery Distinguished Dissertation Ser.). (Illus.). 160p. 1983. 32.50 (*0-262-08134-2*) MIT Pr.

Abstraction, Relation, & Induction: Three Essays in the History of Thought. Julius R. Weinberg. 168p. 1965. 17.50 (*0-299-03540-9*) U of Wis Pr.

Abstractions & Programming in Turbo Pascal. Dale O. Shaffer & David C. Platt. LC 93-43619. 1994. pap. text ed. 45.25 (*0-03-096363-X*) SCP.

Abstracts. Judy Miller. (Illus.). 92p. (Orig.). 1988. pap. 11.96 (*0-912833-11-4*) J Miller Pubns.

Abstracts: Proceedings of the European Anatomical Congress, 4th. European Anatomical Congress, Staff. (Acta Anatomica Ser.: Vol. 99, No. 3). 1977. 73.00 (*3-8055-2776-4*) S Karger.

Abstracts: Proceedings of the International Congress of Logopedics & Phoniatrics, 17th, Copenhagen, 1977. International Congress of Logopedics & Phoniatrics Staff. Ed. by E. Loebell et al. (Journal: Vol. 28, No. 4-5). 1977. 40.00 (*3-8055-2755-1*) S Karger.

An Asterisk (*) at the beginning of an entry indicates that the title is appearing in BIP for the first time.

19

A

Abstracts: Proceedings of the International Congress on Cardiac Rehabilitation, 1st, Hamburg, Sept. 12-14, 1977. International Congress on Cardiac Rehabilitation Staff. Ed. by K. Koenig. (Journal: Vol. 62, No. 2). 1977. 24.00 (*3-8055-2774-8*) S Karger.

Abstracts: Proceedings of the International Symposium on Bio-Telemetry, 4th, Garmisch-Partenkirchen, May, 1978. International Symposium on Bio-Telelemetry Staff. Ed. by H. P. Kimmich. (Biotelemetry & Patient Monitoring Journal: Vol. 5, No. 1). 1978. pap. 28.00 (*3-8055-2911-2*) S Karger.

Abstracts: Proceedings of the International Symposium on Inborn Errors of Metabolism in Man, Tel Aviv, 1977. International Symposium on Inborn Errors of Metabolism in Man Staff. Ed. by O. Sperling. (Journal: Vol. 27, No. 3). 1977. 29.75 (*3-8055-2710-1*) S Karger.

Abstracts: Proceedings of the Seventh International Congress of Pharmacology, Paris 1978. IUPHAR Staff. Ed. by J. R. Boissier et al. LC 78-40891. 1978. 416.00 (*0-08-023768-1*, Pub. by Pergamon Repr UK) Franklin.

Abstracts: Willbook IA, 1815-1836, Tyler County, West Virginia. Mary D. Atkinson. LC 80-67523. 220p. 1980. pap. text ed. 15.00 (*0-937436-03-8*) Atkinson.

Abstracts - Lectures Presented at IFDC Training Program: Plant Nutrient Management for Sustainable Agriculture: Muscle Shoals, Alabama, U. S. A., September 14-25, 1992 Abstracts. LC 93-20753. (Special Publications: No. SP-19). 37p. 1993. pap. text ed. 4.00 (*0-88090-104-7*) Intl Fertilizer.

Abstracts - Sixth International Conference on Cyclic Nucleotides, Calcium, & Protein Phosphorylation, Bethesda, Maryland. Ed. by Robert S. Adelstein et al. (Advances in Second Messenger & Phosphoprotein Research Ser.: Vol. 21A). 112p. 1988. pap. text ed. 54.50 (*0-88167-430-3*) Raven.

***Abstracts & Extracts of the Legislative Acts & Resolutions of the State of Ohio: 1803-1821.** Mary Bowman. 1994. 29.95 (*0-935057-77-3*) OH Genealogical.

Abstracts & Indexes in Science & Technology: A Descriptive Guide. 2nd ed. Dolores B. Owen. LC 84-10902. 252p. 1984. 22.50 (*0-8108-1712-8*) Scarecrow.

Abstracts & Recursion Theory. Montague. (Studies in Logic). write for info. (*0-444-86159-9*, North Holland) Elsevier.

Abstracts from the Asia-Pacific Clinical Symposium (CarboMedics) Ed. by Silent Partners, Inc. Staff. 38p. (Orig.). 1992. pap. write for info. (*1-878353-25-X*) Silent Partners.

Abstracts from the Engine of Liberty & Uniontown Advertiser, 1813-1815. Ed. by Joe Getty. 84p. (Orig.). 1993. pap. 11.99 (*0-685-65891-0*) Hist Soc Carroll.

Abstracts from the "Port Tobacco Times" & "Charles County Advertiser", Vol. 2: 1855-1869. Comp. by Roberta J. Wearmouth. (Illus.). 222p. (Orig.). 1992. pap. 18.00 (*1-55613-524-6*) Heritage Bk.

Abstracts from the Port Tobacco Times & Charles County Advertiser, 1844-1854, Vol. 1. Roberta J. Wearmouth. (Illus.). 226p. (Orig.). 1990. pap. 20.00 (*1-55613-353-7*) Heritage Bk.

Abstracts from the Port Tobacco Times & Charles County Advertiser, 1870-1875, Vol. 3. Roberta J. Wearmouth. 254p. (Orig.). 1993. pap. text ed. 21.00 (*1-55613-878-4*) Heritage Bk.

Abstracts from the Sixth Hungarian Conference on Biomedical Engineering & 2nd Imeko Conference on Measurement in Clinical Medicine, Balatonfured, 18-20 September, 1984. 313p. 1984. 405.00 (*0-317-89599-0*, Pub. by Collets UK) Pro-Am Music.

Abstracts from the 1982 Symposium on Leisure Research: Held in Conjunction with the 1982 NRPA Congress for Recreation & Parks, Louisville, Kentucky, October 1982. Symposium on Leisure Research Staff. 156p. reprint ed. pap. 44.50 (*0-7837-1543-9*, 2041828) Bks Demand.

Abstracts from the 1983 Symposium on Leisure Research: Held in Conjunction with the 1983 NRPA Congress for Recreation & Parks, Kansas City, Missouri, October 1983. Symposium on Leisure Research Staff. 143p. reprint ed. pap. 40.80 (*0-7837-1542-0*, 2041827) Bks Demand.

***Abstracts from the 1993 ASHA Conference on Cochlear Implants: The State-of-the-Art.** Ed. by Maureen Thompson. 35p. 1994. pap. text ed. 24.00 (*0-910329-77-X*, 0111849) Am Speech Lang Hearing.

Abstracts of Bristol County, Massachusetts Probate Records, 1687-1745. H. L. Rounds. 392p. 1993. reprint ed. pap. 30.00 (*0-685-65682-9*, 5020) Clearfield Co.

Abstracts of Bristol County, Massachusetts Probate Records, 1745-1762. H. L. Rounds. 365p. 1988. 30.00 (*0-8063-1226-2*, 5022) Genealog Pub.

Abstracts of CISW Grants: Completed Projects & Works in Progress. Ed. by Lillian Bridwell-Bowles & Paul Prior. (Monograph Ser.: Vol. 4). 42p. (Orig.). 1992. pap. 3.50 (*1-881221-03-2*) U Minn Ctr Interdis.

Abstracts of CISW Grants: Completed Projects & Works in Progress 1989-93. 2nd ed. Ed. by Lillian Bridwell-Bowles & Mark Olson. (Monograph Ser.: Vol. 4). 62p. Date not set. 5.50 (*1-881221-09-1*) U Minn Ctr Interdis.

Abstracts of Death Records for Johnson County, Tennessee, 1908 to 1941. Eddie M. Nikazy. 482p. (Orig.). 1992. pap. 33.00 (*1-55613-665-X*) Heritage Bk.

Abstracts of Deed Books One & Two: Henry County, Virginia, Feb. 1776-July 1784. Lela C. Adams. 188p. 1983. reprint ed. pap. 20.00 (*0-89308-358-5*, VA 43) Southern Hist Pr.

Abstracts of Deed Books Three & Four: Henry County, Virginia, Aug. 1784-June 1792. 136p. 1984. reprint ed. pap. 18.50 (*0-89308-359-3*, VA 44) Southern Hist Pr.

Abstracts of Deeds, 1830-1838: Deed Book A, Washington County, AR. Lois N. Miller. 166p. 1990. 31.50 (*1-878193-14-7*); pap. 25.00 (*1-878193-15-5*) L N Miller Geog Pubns.

Abstracts of Development Studies, 1988. Ed. by Jack Hopkins & Michael Parrish. 100p. (Orig.). (C). 1989. pap. text ed. 10.00 (*0-9617990-1-3*) Ars Biblio.

Abstracts of Duplin County, North Carolina, Deeds, 1784-1813, Vol. 1. Eleanor S. Draughon. 256p. 1986. reprint ed. pap. 27.50 (*0-89308-598-7*, NC 33) Southern Hist Pr.

Abstracts of Early Deeds of Edgecomb County, North Carolina 1759-1772. Comp. by Joseph W. Watson. LC 93-8587. 1993. 32.50 (*0-87152-472-4*) Reprint.

***Abstracts of Early Deeds of Edgecombe County, North Carolina, 1772-1788 Vol. II.** Joseph W. Watson. 372p. 1995. 32.50 (*0-87152-486-4*) Reprint.

Abstracts of Fauquier County, Virginia: Wills, Inventories, & Accounts, 1759-1800. John K. Gott. 348p. 1994. reprint ed. pap. 28.00 (*0-685-75087-6*, 2290) Clearfield Co.

Abstracts of Gloucestershire Inquisitions Post Mortem, Pt. I, Nos. 1-11: Charles I, 1625-1636 see Index to Wills Proved & Administrations Granted in the Court of the Archdeacon of Berkshire: 1508-1652

Abstracts of Inquisitiones Post Mortem for Gloucestershire Returned into the Court of Chancery During the Plantagenet Period, Pt. IV: 20 Henry III to 29 Edward I, 1236-1300. Ed. by Sidney J. Madge. (British Record Society Index Library Ser.: Vol. 30). 1972. reprint ed. pap. 19.00 (*0-8115-1475-7*) Periodicals Srv.

Abstracts of Inquisitiones Post Mortem for Gloucestershire Returned into the Court of Chancery During the Plantagenet Period, Pt. V: 30 Edward I to 32 Edward III, 1302-1358. Ed. by Edward A. Fry. (British Record Society Index Library Ser.: Vol. 40). 1972. reprint ed. pap. 30.00 (*0-8115-1485-4*) Periodicals Srv.

Abstracts of Inquisitiones Post Mortem for Gloucestershire Returned into the Court of Chancery During the Plantagenet Period, Pt. VI: 33 Edward III to 14 Henry IV, 1359-1413. British Record Society Staff. (Index Library: Vol. 47). 1972. reprint ed. pap. 19.00 (*0-8115-1492-7*) Periodicals Srv.

Abstracts of Inquisitiones Post Mortem for Gloucestershire Returned into the Court of Chancery During the Stuart Period, Pt. III: Miscellaneous Series, 13-18 Charles I, 1637-1642. Ed. by W. P. Phillimore & George S. Fry. (British Record Society Index Library Ser.: Vol. 13). 1972. reprint ed. pap. 19.00 (*0-8115-1458-7*) Periodicals Srv.

Abstracts of Inquisitiones Post Mortem for Gloucestershire Returned into thr Court of Chancery During the Stuart Period, Pt. III: Miscellaneous Series, 1-8 Charles I, 1625-1632. Ed. by Edward A. Fry. (British Record Society Index Library Ser.: Vol. 21). 1972. pap. 19.00 (*0-8115-1466-8*) Periodicals Srv.

Abstracts of Inquisitiones Post Mortem for the City of London Returned into the Court of Chancery During the Tudor Period, Pt. II: 4-9, Elizabeth, 1561-1577. Ed. by Sidney J. Madge. (British Record Society Index Library Ser.: Vol. 26). 1972. reprint ed. pap. 19.00 (*0-8115-1471-4*) Periodicals Srv.

Abstracts of Inquisitiones Post Mortem for the City of London Returned into the Court of Chancery During the Tudor Period, Pt. III: 19-45 Elizabeth, 1577-1603. Ed. by Edward A. Fry. (British Record Society Index Library Ser.: Vol. 36). 1972. reprint ed. pap. 30.00 (*0-8115-1481-1*) Periodicals Srv.

Abstracts of Inquisitiones Post Mortem for Wiltshire Returned into the Court of Chancery During the Plantagenet Period: 21 Edward II to 51 Edward III, 1327-1377. British Record Society Staff. (Index Library: Vol. 48). 1972. reprint ed. pap. 30.00 (*0-8115-1493-5*) Periodicals Srv.

Abstracts of Inquisitiones Post Mortem for Wiltshire Returned into the Court of Chancery During the Plantagenet Period: 27 Henry III to 20 Edward II, 1242-1326. Ed. by Edward A. Fry. (British Record Society Index Library Ser.: Vol. 37). 1972. reprint ed. pap. 44.00 (*0-8115-1482-X*) Periodicals Srv.

Abstracts of Inquisitiones Post Mortem for Wiltshire Returned into the Court of Chancery During the Stuart Period: 9-12 Charles I, 1633-38. Ed. by Edward A. Fry & G. S. Fry. (British Record Society Index Library Ser.: Vol. 23). 1972. reprint ed. pap. 44.00 (*0-8115-1468-4*) Periodicals Srv.

Abstracts of Inquisitiones Post Mortem Relating to the City of London Returned into the Court of Chancery During the Tudor Period, Pt. I: Henry VII to 3 Elizabeth, 1485-1561. Ed. by George S. Fry. (British Record Society Index Library Ser.: Vol. 15). 1972. reprint ed. pap. 19.00 (*0-8115-1460-9*) Periodicals Srv.

Abstracts of Land Entries: Gates, Chowan, Perquimans, Pasquotank, Camden, & Currituck Cos, NC. A. B. Pruitt. (Illus.). 198p. (Orig.). (YA). (gr. 12). 1992. pap. 18.75 (*0-944992-44-7*) ABP Abstracts.

***Abstracts of Letters of Resignations of Militia Officers in North Carolina 1779-1840.** Timothy Kearney. 144p. 1995. 20.00 (*0-614-04972-5*) N C Genealogical.

Abstracts of Lincoln Co, NC, Deeds (1786-1793) Books 3, 4, & 16. A. B. Pruitt. (Illus.). 159p. (Orig.). 1988. pap. 14.50 (*0-944992-12-9*) ABP Abstracts.

Abstracts of Marriages & Deaths & Other Articles of Interest in the Newspapers of Frederick & Montgomery Counties, Maryland, 1831-1840. L. Tilden Moore. vi, 431p. 1991. pap. 26.50 (*1-55613-478-9*) Heritage Bk.

Abstracts of Nottinghamshire Marriage Licences, Vol. 1: Archdeaconry Court, 1577-1700; Peculiar of Southwell, 1588-1754. Ed. by Thomas M. Blagg & Arthur Wadsworth. (British Record Society Index Library Ser.: Vol. 58). 1972. reprint ed. pap. 52.00 (*0-8115-1503-6*) Periodicals Srv.

Abstracts of Nottinghamshire Marriage Licences, Vol. 2: Archdeaconry Court, 1701-1753; Peculiar of Southwell, 1755-1853. (British Record Society Index Library Ser.: Vol. 60). 1972. reprint ed. pap. 56.00 (*0-8115-1505-2*) Periodicals Srv.

Abstracts of Obituaries in the Western Christian Advocate, 1834-1850. Comp. by Margaret R. Waters et al. 438p. 1988. 25.00 (*0-87195-009-X*) Ind Hist Soc.

Abstracts of Old Ninety-Six & Abbeville District, S. C. Wills & Bonds. 2nd ed. Pauline Young. 797p. 1977. reprint ed. 40.00 (*0-89308-036-5*) Southern Hist Pr.

Abstracts of Order Book No. "0," Patrick County, Virginia, 1791-August 1800. Lela C. Adams. 130p. 1984. pap. 20.00 (*0-89308-427-1*) Southern Hist Pr.

Abstracts of Orphans Court Minutes: Mobile County Alabama, 1813-1837. Clinton P. King & Meriem A. Barlow. LC 87-71364. 239p. 1987. 22.50 (*0-943609-00-3*) AL Ancestors.

Abstracts of Papers Presented in Scientific Sections see International Congress of History of Science, University of California, Berkeley, 1985

Abstracts of Papers Presented in Symposia see International Congress of History of Science, University of California, Berkeley, 1985

Abstracts of Pittsylvania County, Virginia, Wills 1767-1820. Lela C. Adams. 408p. 1985. 37.50 (*0-89308-581-2*) Southern Hist Pr.

Abstracts of Research, '89. 1989. 10.00 (*0-88314-413-1*) AAHPERD.

Abstracts of Sales of Confiscated Land & Property in North Carolina. A. B. Pruitt. (Illus.). 249p. (Orig.). (YA). (gr. 12). 1990. pap. 23.00 (*0-944992-26-9*) ABP Abstracts.

Abstracts of Some Greenville, South Carolina, Records Concerning Black People, Free & Slave, 1791-1861, Vol. 1. Anne K. McCuen. LC 89-24121. 240p. 1991. 25.00 (*0-87152-440-6*) Reprint.

Abstracts of Studies in Business Communication: 1900 through 1970. Jane F. White & Patty G. Campbell. 280p. (Orig.). 1982. pap. 10.98 (*0-931874-11-4*) Assn Busn Comm.

Abstracts of Technical Papers: Annual Conference-Dallas, 61st. Water Pollution Control Federation Staff. 1988. pap. 20.00 (*0-318-40174-6*) Water Environ.

Abstracts of Technical Papers: 63rd Annual Conference, Washington, D. C. Water Pollution Control Federation Staff. 275p. 1990. pap. 25.00 (*0-943244-99-4*) Water Environ.

Abstracts of Technical Studies in Art & Archeology, 1943-1952. Comp. by Rutherford J. Gettens & Bertha M. Usilton. (Occasional Papers Ser.: Vol. 2, No. 2). 1955. pap. 6.00 (*0-934686-04-1*) Freer.

Abstracts of Tennessee Death Records for Carter County, 1908-1925. Eddie M. Nikazy. 485p. 1993. pap. text ed. 32.50 (*1-55613-738-9*) Heritage Bk.

Abstracts of the Annual Meeting of the Association for Asian Studies. Ed. by Carol Kelingos. xx, 198p. (Orig.). 1992. pap. 5.00 (*0-924304-10-3*) Assn Asian Studies.

Abstracts of the Annual Meeting of the Association for Asian Studies, 1993. Ed. by Carol Kelingos. xx, 200p. (Orig.). (C). 1993. pap. 5.00 (*0-924304-11-1*) Assn Asian Studies.

Abstracts of the Collected Works of C. G. Jung. Ed. by Carrie L. Rothgeb. 136p. 1993. pap. 19.95 (*1-85575-035-X*, Pub. by Karnac Bks UK) Brunner-Mazel.

Abstracts of the Early Deeds of Granville County, North Carolina, 1746-1765. Ed. by Joseph W. Watson. LC 93-8586. 1993. 32.50 (*0-87152-473-2*) Reprint.

***Abstracts of the Eighth International Conference on Geochronology, Cosmochronology & Isotope Geology.** Ed. by M. A. Lanphere et al. (Illus.). 384p. (Orig.). (C). 1994. pap. text ed. 75.00x (*0-7881-1349-6*) Diane Pub.

***Abstracts of the Eighth International Symposium on Purine & Pyrimidine Metabolism.** 88p. (C). 1994. per. 25.00 (*0-9641293-0-2*) IN U Conf.

Abstracts of the European Nutrition Conference, 2nd, Munich, 1976. European Nutrition Conference Staff. Ed. by N. Zoellner et al. (Journal: Vol. 20, No. 3). 1976. 29.75 (*3-8055-2441-2*) S Karger.

Abstracts of the International Association of Logopedics & Phoniatrics 18th Congress, Washington, D.C. August, 1980. International Association of Logopedics & Phoniatrics Staff. Ed. by E. Loebell. (Journal: Folia Phoniatrica: Vol. 32, No. 3). 110p. 1980. 26.50 (*3-8055-1249-X*) S Karger.

Abstracts of the International Conference on Gastrointestinal Cancer, Tel Aviv, Israel, November 1977. International Conference on Gastrointestinal Cancer Staff. Ed. by P. Rozen. (Journal: Vol. 16, No. 3). 1977. pap. 17.00 (*3-8055-2843-4*) S Karger.

Abstracts of the International Conference on Renal Transport of Organic Substances Held in Innsbruck, July, 1980. Ed. by S. Silbernagel. (Journal: Renal Physiology & Biochemistry: Vol. 2, No. 3). (Illus.). 66p. 1980. pap. 22.50 (*3-8055-1641-X*) S Karger.

Abstracts of the Minutes of the Court of Pleas & Quarter Sessions, Rowan Co., N.C., 1753-1762. Jo W. Linn. 177p. 1978. 30.00 (*0-918470-02-1*) J W Linn.

Abstracts of the Minutes of the Court of Pleas & Quarter Sessions, Rowan Co., N.C., 1763-1774. Jo W. Linn. 208p. 1979. 30.00 (*0-918470-03-X*) J W Linn.

Abstracts of the Minutes of the Court of Pleas & Quarter Sessions, Rowan County, N.C., 1775-1789. Jo W. Linn. LC 81-84591. 250p. 1982. 35.00 (*0-918470-13-7*) J W Linn.

Abstracts of the Probate Records of Strafford County, N.H. 1771-1799. 2nd ed. Helen F. Evans. xv, 237p. (Orig.). 1983. 35.00 (*0-917890-37-X*) Heritage Bk.

Abstracts of the Second International Congress on Child Abuse & Neglect. International Congress on Child Abuse & Neglect, 2nd, London 1978. Ed. by A. White Franklin. LC 78-41195. 1979. pap. 130.00 (*0-08-023438-0*, Pub. by Pergamon Repr UK) Franklin.

Abstracts of the Sixteenth International Conference on the Physics of Electronic & Atomic Collisions: Abstracts of Contributed Papers from the XVI International ICPEAC held in New York, NY, July 26-August 1, 1989. Ed. by A. Dalgarno et al. (Illus.). 968p. 1989. pap. 70.00 (*0-88318-631-4*) Am Inst Physics.

Abstracts of the Sixth European Bioenergetics Conference August 26-31, 1990, the Netherlands. K. Van Dam. 1990. 51.50 (*0-444-81385-3*) Elsevier.

Abstracts of the Standard Edition of the Complete Psychological Works of Sigmund Freud. Ed. by Carrie L. Rothgeb. LC 73-2144. 770p. (C). 1973. text ed. 75.00x (*0-8236-0030-0*) Intl Univs Pr.

Abstracts of the Standard Edition of the Complete Psychological Works of Sigmund Freud. Ed. by Carrie L. Rothgeb. LC 73-17649. 320p. 1993. pap. 35.00 (*1-56821-140-6*) Aronson.

Abstracts of the Standard Edition of the Complete Works of Sigmund Freud. Ed. by Carrie L. Rothgeb. 315p. 1987. 35.00 (*0-87668-135-6*) Aronson.

Abstracts of the Twelfth CINP Congress, Gothenberg, Sweden, 22-26 June, 1980. 400p. 1980. 164.00 (*0-08-026383-6*, Pub. by Pergamon Repr UK) Franklin.

Abstracts of the Twenty-Seventh Conference. Ed. by A. Reyes Schramm. 108p. 1983. 7.00 (*0-318-17462-6*) Intl Coun Trad.

Abstracts of the Washington County Reporter 1808-1814. Comp. by Bonnie Malmat. 323p. 1990. pap. text ed. 19.95 (*1-55856-041-6*) Closson Pr.

***Abstracts of the Wills & Administrations of Northampton County, VA 1632-1802.** James H. Marshall. 736p. 1994. 59.50 (*0-89725-163-6*, 1446) Picton Pr.

***Abstracts of the Wills & Estate Records of Granville County, North Carolina, 1808-1833 Vol. II.** Zae H. Gwynn. Ed. by Joseph W. Watson. 344p. 1995. 32.50 (*0-87152-485-6*) Reprint.

Abstracts of the Wills & Estates Records of Rowan County, N.C., 1753-1805 & Tax Lists of 1759-1778. Jo W. Linn. 216p. 1980. 30.00 (*0-918470-04-8*) J W Linn.

Abstracts of the 1994 Annual Meeting of the Association for Asian Studies. Ed. by Carol Kelingos. xxx, 200p. Date not set. pap. 7.00 (*0-924304-18-9*) Assn Asian Studies.

Abstracts of Theses & Dissertations in Adult Education, Syracuse University. Comp. by A. Charters. 1979. 4.50 (*0-686-65496-X*, MSS 11) Syracuse U Cont Ed.

***Abstracts of Vital Records from Raleigh, NC Newspapers 1820-1829.** Comp. by Lori S. Neal. 791p. 1995. 50.00 (*0-614-04973-3*) N C Genealogical.

***Abstracts of Washington County PA Willbooks (1776-1841), Set, Bks. 1-5.** Bob Closson & Mary Closson. 769p. 1995. text ed. 39.95 (*1-55856-196-X*) Closson Pr.

Abstracts of Wills, Administrations, & Marriages of Fauquier County, Virginia, 1759-1800. Junie E. King. LC 78-51004. 101p. 1986. reprint ed. pap. 7.50 (*0-8063-0801-X*) Genealog Pub.

Abstracts of Wills & Estates, Barbour County, Ala., 1852-1856, Vol. 3. Helen S. Foley. 122p. 1976. pap. 12.50 (*0-89308-183-3*) Southern Hist Pr.

Abstracts of Wills & Other Records, Currituck & Dare Counties, North Carolina, 1663-1850. Gordon C. Jones. 156p. 1991. reprint ed. pap. 17.50 (*0-685-60420-9*, 3085) Clearfield Co.

Abstracts of Wills, Inventories & Accounts, Patrick County, Virginia, 1791-1823. Lela C. Adams. 110p. 1972. pap. 17.50 (*0-89308-356-9*, VA 42) Southern Hist Pr.

Abstracts of Wills of Cumberland Country, Virginia Will Book 1 & 2, 1749-1782. Katherine Reynolds. 104p. 1984. 17.50 (*0-89308-430-1*) Southern Hist Pr.

Abstracts of Wills on File in the Surrogate's Office, City of New York, 1665-1801: Collections, New York Historical Society, 1892-1908, 17 vols. write for info. (*0-318-56190-5*) NY Hist Soc.

Abstracts of Wills on File in the Surrogate's Office, City of New York, 1665-1801: Collections, New York Historical Society, 1892-1908, 17 vols., Set. 8.00 (*0-685-73867-1*) NY Hist Soc.

Abstracts of Wills Recorded in Orange County, North Carolina, 1752-1800 & 1800-1850, 2 vols. in 1. Ruth H. Shields. 450p. 1991. reprint ed. 27.50 (*0-685-60424-1*, 1350) Clearfield Co.

Abstracts on Crime & Juvenile Delinquency: Cumulative Index 1968-1984. 382p. 1986. lib. bdg. 295.00 (*0-89941-465-6*, 109510); Edition 1983-1984. lib. bdg. 155.00 (*0-685-55835-5*) W S Hein.

Abstracts on Sustainable Agriculture. Comp. by Jurgen Carls. viii, 372p. (C). 1990. pap. 17.50 (*3-528-02060-1*, Pub. by Vieweg & Sohn GW) Ballen Bkslr.

Abstracts on Sustainable Agriculture, Vol. 4: 1991. Ed. by Jurgen Carls. viii, 487p. 1992. pap. 25.00 (*3-528-02065-2*, Pub. by Vieweg & Sohn GW) Ballen Bkslr.

Abstracts, References, & Key Words of Publications Relating to the Cotton Leafworm, Alabama Argillacea, Vol. 10. Say, Thomas, Foundation Staff et al. LC 85-70066. 136p. 1985. 25.00 (*0-938522-25-6*) Entomol Soc.

Abstracts, Sixth World Congress of the International Rehabilitation Medicine Association, Madrid, 17-22 June, 1990. Ed. by R. J. Parreno. (International Congress Ser.: No. 927). 348p. 1990. 80.00 (*0-444-81132-X*, Excerpta Medica) Elsevier.

An Asterisk (*) at the beginning of an entry indicates that the title is appearing in BIP for the first time.

An Asterisk (*) at the beginning of an entry indicates that the title is appearing in BIP for the first time.

21

A

AC Electronics. Heathkit-Zenith Educational Systems Staff. (Spectrum Fundamentals of Electronics Ser.). (Illus.). 280p. 1983. 19.95 (*0-13-002121-0*); pap. 12.95 (*0-13-002113-X*) P-H.

AC Electronics. rev. ed. Heath Company Staff. (Fundamental Electronics Ser.). (Illus.). 545p. 1982. ring bd. 54.95 (*0-87119-064-8*, EE-3102A) Heathkit-Zenith Ed.

AC Loss & Macroscopic Theory of Superconductors. W. J. Carr, Jr. xii, 158p. 1983. text ed. 156.00 (*0-677-05700-8*) Gordon & Breach.

A.C. Motor Design: Rotating Magnetic Fields in a Changing Environment. H. C. DeJong. 185p. 1988. 67.00 (*0-89116-741-2*) Hemisp Pub.

AC Motors for High Performance Applications: Analysis & Control. Yamamura. (Electrical Engineering & Electronics Ser.: Vol. 30). 232p. 1986. 99.75 (*0-8247-7492-2*) Dekker.

AC Power Conditioners: Designs & Applications. James W. Clark. 208p. 1989. text ed. 61.00 (*0-12-175460-X*) Acad Pr.

AC Power Systems Handbook. Jerry Whitaker. (Illus.). 400p. 1991. 55.00 (*0-8493-7412-X*, QA) CRC Pr.

AC 1 Fundamentals. Buck Engineering Staff. Ed. by Buck Engineering Tech. Writers. (F. A. C. E. T. Ser.: Vol. 3). (Illus.). 60p. 1988. teacher ed, pap. text ed. 11.00 (*0-86657-013-6*); ring bd. 13.00 (*0-86657-012-8*) Buck Eng Co.

AC 2 Fundamentals. Buck Engineering Staff. Ed. by Buck Engineering Tech. Writers. (F. A. C. E. T. Ser.: Vol. 4). (Illus.). 56p. 1988. teacher ed, pap. text ed. 11.00 (*0-86657-015-2*); ring bd. 12.00 (*0-86657-014-4*) Buck Eng Co.

ACA Legal Series, Vol. 1: Preparing for Court Appearances. Theodore P. Remley, Jr. 64p. (C). 1991. pap. text ed. 12.95 (*1-55620-077-3*) Am Coun Assn.

ACA Legal Series, Vol. 2: Documentation in Counseling Records. Robert W. Mitchell. Ed. by Theodore P. Remley, Jr. 75p. (C). 1992. pap. text ed. 12.95 (*1-55620-084-6*) Am Coun Assn.

ACA Legal Series, Vol. 3: Law & Management of a Counseling Agency or Private Practice. Ronald K. Bullis. Ed. by Theodore P. Remley, Jr. LC 92-20722. (C). 1992. pap. text ed. 12.95 (*1-55620-101-X*) Am Coun Assn.

ACA Legal Series, Vol. 4: Counseling Minor Clients. Mark M. Salo & Stephen Shumate. Ed. by Theodore P. Remley, Jr. 75p. (C). 1993. pap. text ed. 12.95 (*1-55620-103-6*, 72304) Am Coun Assn.

ACA Legal Series, Vol. 5: The Counselor As Expert Witness. William J. Weikel & Paula R. Hughes. Ed. by Theodore P. Remley, Jr. 75p. (C). 1993. pap. text ed. 12.95 (*1-55620-106-0*, 72305) Am Coun Assn.

ACA Legal Series, Vol. 6: Confidentiality & Privileged Communication. Gibbs L. Arthur, Jr. & Carl D. Swanson. Ed. by Theodore P. Remley, Jr. 75p. (C). 1993. pap. text ed. 12.95 (*1-55620-105-2*, 72306) Am Coun Assn.

Acacia. Claude Simon. Tr. by Richard Howard. LC 90-52554. 304p. 1991. 23.50 (*0-394-58771-5*) Pantheon.

Acacia Auriculiformis. K. Pinyopusarerk. 154p. (Orig.). 1990. pap. 10.00 (*0-933595-41-7*) Winrock Intl.

***Acacia Mangium: Growing & Utilization.** 280p. (Orig.). (C). 1993. pap. text ed. 19.95x (*0-933595-82-4*) Winrock Intl.

Acacia Terrace. Barbara K. Wilson. (J). 1990. 13.95 (*0-590-42885-3*) Scholastic Inc.

Acacias: Hungarians of the Mississippi Valley. Leslie Konnyu. LC 76-6789. (Illus.). 1976. pap. text ed. 8.50 (*0-685-68332-X*) Hungarian Rev.

***Acacias for Rural, Industrial & Environmental Development.** 258p. (Orig.). (C). 1993. pap. text ed. 27.50x (*0-933595-83-2*) Winrock Intl.

Acacias of South East Australia. Terry Tame. (Illus.). 240p. 1993. 34.95 (*0-86417-475-6*, Pub. by Kangaroo Pr AT) Seven Hills Bk.

ACAD: Airman's Civil Aviation Dictionary. Frank Beau Artuso. (Illus.). 234p. (Orig.). (C). 1992. pap. text ed. 13.95 (*0-9634854-4-X*) Acad Pubns.

Academe. Paul Groves. LC 88-83233. 72p. (Orig.). 1988. pap. 12.95 (*0-907476-98-8*, Pub. by Poetry Wales Pr UK) Dufour.

Academia & the Luster of Capital. Sande Cohen. LC 92-35102. 210p. (C). 1993. text ed. 39.95 (*0-8166-2230-2*); pap. text ed. 16.95 (*0-8166-2231-0*) U of Minn Pr.

Academia in Transition: Mid-Career Change or Early Retirement. Carl V. Patton. (Illus.). 230p. 1984. reprint ed. lib. bdg. 47.50 (*0-8191-4100-3*) U Pr of Amer.

Academia Revisited. 194p. 1993. 16.95 (*0-912598-58-1*) Florham.

Academia's Golden Age: Universities in Massachusetts, 1945-1970. Richard M. Freeland. 568p. 1992. 60.00 (*0-19-505464-4*) OUP.

Academic Acceleration of Gifted Children. Ed. by Thomas W. Southern & Eric D. Jones. (Education & Psychology of the Gifted Ser.: No. 4). 272p. (C). 1991. text ed. 44.95 (*0-8077-3069-6*); pap. text ed. 21.95 (*0-8077-3068-8*) Tchrs Coll.

***Academic Achievement of White, Black, & Hispanic Students in Teacher Education Programs.** 1993. 25.00 (*0-89333-094-9*) AACTE.

Academic Adaptations: Higher Education Prepares for the 1980s & 1990s. Verne A. Stadtman. LC 80-8000. (Carnegie Council Ser.). 234p. reprint ed. pap. 66.70 (*0-8357-4961-4*, 2037893) Bks Demand.

Academic Administration: Planning, Budgeting, & Decision Making with Multiple Objectives. Sang M. Lee & James C. Van Horn. LC 81-24061. (Illus.). 266p. reprint ed. pap. 75.90 (*0-8357-4102-8*, 2036868) Bks Demand.

Academic Administrator Grid. Robert R. Blake et al. LC 80-8908. (Jossey-Bass Series in Higher Education). (Illus.). 443p. reprint ed. pap. 126.30 (*0-8357-4806-5*, 2037743) Bks Demand.

Academic Advising: An Annotated Bibliography. Comp. by Virginia N. Gordon. LC 94-2865. (Bibliographies & Indexes in Education Ser.: No. 14). 184p. 1994. text ed. 55.00 (*0-313-28843-7*, Greenwood Pr) Greenwood.

***Academic Advising: Organizing & Delivering Services for Student Success.** Ed. by Margaret C. King. LC 85-644753. (New Directions for Community Colleges Ser.: No. 82). 118p. (Orig.). 1993. pap. 16.95 (*1-55542-687-5*) Jossey-Bass.

Academic Advising for Student Success: A System of Shared Responsibility. Susan H. Frost. Ed. & Frwd. by Jonathan D. Fife. LC 91-66412. (ASHE-ERIC Higher Education Report Ser.: No. 3). 97p. 1991. pap. 17.00 (*1-878380-06-0*) GWU Schl E&HD.

Academic Alert: Strategies for Success in the Two Year Schools, Preliminary Edition. Carol R. Davenport. 144p. (C). 1991. pap. text ed. 14.95 (*0-8403-6748-1*) Kendall-Hunt.

Academic Alternatives: Exploration & Decision Making. 2nd ed. Virginia Gordon & Susan Sears. 112p. 1989. spiral bd. 20.95 (*0-8403-5358-8*) Kendall-Hunt.

***Academic Alternatives: Exploration & Decision Making.** 3rd ed. Virginia N. Gordon & Susan J. Sears. 1994. per. 16.00 (*0-89787-818-3*) Gorsuch Scarisbrick.

***Academic American Encyclopedia.** LC 94-42537. 1995. write for info. (*0-7172-2059-1*) Grolier Inc.

Academic American Encylcopedia, 21 vols., Set. LC 93-8360. 1994. write for info. (*0-7172-2053-2*) Grolier Inc.

Academic & Developmental Learning Disabilities. Samuel A. Kirk & James C. Chalfant. LC 83-82702. 337p. (C). 1984. text ed. 36.95 (*0-89108-124-0*) Love Pub Co.

Academic & Entrepreneurial Research: The Consequences of Diversity in Federal Evaluation Studies. Ilene N. Bernstein & Howard E. Freeman. LC 74-83208. 108p. 1975. text ed. 25.00 (*0-87154-109-2*) Russell Sage.

Academic & Scientific Traditions in China, Japan, & the West. Shigeru Nakayama & Jerry Dusenberry. 251p. 1984. 37.50 (*0-86008-339-X*, Pub. by U of Tokyo JA) Col U Pr.

***Academic & Special Libraries in the U.K. & Republic of Ireland 1994 Labels.** 272p. 1994. 160.00 (*0-85365-959-1*, LAP9591, Pub. by Lib Assn Pub UK) UNIPUB.

Academic & Workplace Sexual Harassment: A Resource Manual. Michele A. Paludi & Richard B. Barickman. LC 90-24364. (Psychology of Women Ser.). 235p. 1991. 59.50 (*0-7914-0829-9*); pap. 19.95 (*0-7914-0830-2*) State U NY Pr.

Academic Apprenticeship. Ellsworth Barnard. (Illus.). viii, 268p. 1985. 10.00 (*0-9605458-2-4*) Dinosaur.

Academic Capitalism & Literary Value. Harold Fromm. LC 90-22246. 304p. 1991. 35.00 (*0-8203-1350-5*); pap. 16.00 (*0-8203-1399-8*) U of Ga Pr.

Academic Careers of Experimental Computer Scientists. National Research Council, Commission on PHysical Sciences, Mathematics, & Applications Staff & Committee on Academic Careers for Experimental Computer Scientists Staff. 152p. (Orig.). (C). 1993. pap. text ed. 27.00 (*0-309-04931-8*) Natl Acad Pr.

Academic Chairperson's Handbook. John W. Creswell et al. LC 90-30548. xiv, 128p. 1990. 20.00 (*0-8032-1450-2*) U of Nebr Pr.

Academic Commodore 64. Richard Mowe & Ron Mummaw. LC 84-9978. 1984. pap. 16.95 (*0-8359-0017-7*, Reston) P-H.

Academic Community: Discourse or Discord? Ed. by Ronald Barnett. (Higher Education Policy Ser.: No. 20). 250p. 1993. 58.00 (*1-85302-534-8*, Pub. by J Kingsley Pubs UK) Taylor & Francis.

***Academic Competitions for Gifted Students: A Resource Book for Teachers & Parents.** Mark K. Tallent-Runnels & Ann C. Candler-Lotven. 272p. 1995. 53.95 (*0-8039-6155-3*); pap. 24.95 (*0-8039-6156-1*) Corwin Pr.

Academic Component of Priestly Formation: Average Superiority Will Do Faithful & Critical Reason in Theology. J. Dougherty & J. McDermott. (Analecta Ser.: No. II). 26p. (C). 1988. pap. 3.50 (*0-910919-05-4*) Mariel Pubns.

Academic Computers in Service. Charles J. Mosmann. LC 72-13602. (Jossey-Bass Higher Education Ser.). 202p. reprint ed. pap. 57.60 (*0-8357-5027-2*, 2025665) Bks Demand.

Academic Computing Guide. Matt Finley. 43p. (C). 1993. student ed 1.90 (*1-56870-075-X*) RonJon Pub.

Academic Crisis of the Community College. Dennis McGrath & Martin B. Spear. LC 90-34599. (SUNY Series, Literacy, Culture, & Learning: Theory & Practice). 195p. 1991. 59.50 (*0-7914-0562-1*); pap. 19.95x (*0-7914-0563-X*) State U NY Pr.

Academic Culture & Faculty Development. Mervin Freedman. LC 79-84482. 1979. pap. 11.95 (*0-917430-02-6*) Montaigne.

Academic Dean: Dove, Dragon, & Diplomat. 2nd ed. Allan Tucker & Robert A. Bryan. (ACE-Oryx Series on Higher Education). 320p. 1991. text ed. 29.95 (*0-02-932695-8*, ACE-Oryx) Oryx Pr.

Academic Discourse & Critical Consciousness. Patricia Bizzell. LC 92-11967. (Series in Composition, Literacy, & Culture). 304p. (C). 1993. 49.95 (*0-8229-3730-1*); pap. text ed. 19.95 (*0-8229-5485-0*) U of Pittsburgh Pr.

***Academic Distinctions: Theory & Methodology in the Sociology of School Knowledge.** James G. Ladwig. 192p. 1995. 55.00x (*0-415-91187-7*, B7167, Routledge NY); pap. 17.95 (*0-415-91188-5*, B7171, Routledge NY) Routledge.

Academic Effectiveness. USNA (SPEAKS) Staff. 64p. 1992. spiral bd. 3.72 (*0-8403-7946-3*) Kendall-Hunt.

Academic Effectiveness. USNA (Taylor) Staff. 80p. 1994. per. 5.61 (*0-8403-9458-6*) Kendall-Hunt.

Academic Employment & Retrenchment: Judicial Review & Administrative Action. Robert M. Hendrickson & Barbara A. Lee. Ed. & Frwd. by Jonathan D. Fife. LC 84-153995. (ASHE-ERIC Higher Education Report Ser.: No. 8, 1983). 133p. (Orig.). 1983. pap. 7.50 (*0-913317-07-1*) GWU Schl E&HD.

Academic Entrepreneurs: Developing University-Industry Relations. Rikard Stankiewicz. LC 85-22227. 200p. 1986. text ed. 39.95 (*0-312-00200-9*) St Martin.

Academic Environment: A Handbook for Evaluating Faculty Employment Opportunities. Karl W. Lanks. LC 90-81847. 138p. (Orig.). (C). 1990. pap. text ed. 12.95 (*0-9626658-0-0*) Faculty Brooklyn.

Academic Ethic. Edward Shils. LC 84-6. 112p. 1984. pap. text ed. 7.95 (*0-226-75332-8*) U Ch Pr.

Academic Ethic. Edward Shils. LC 84-6. 112p. 1984. lib. bdg. 12.00 (*0-226-75330-1*) U Ch Pr.

Academic Excellence Versus Public Service: The Development of Adult Higher Education in California. Kathleen Rockhill. 320p. 1983. 34.95 (*0-87855-491-2*) Transaction Pubs.

***Academic Focus Japan.** Ed. by Gretchen Shinoda. 560p. (Orig.). 1994. pap. text ed. 45.00 (*0-614-03251-2*) Natl Planning.

Academic Freedom. Ed. & Intro. by Haig Bosmajian. (First Amendment in the Classroom Ser.: No. 4). 175p. 1988. text ed. 35.00 (*1-55570-004-7*) Neal-Schuman.

Academic Freedom. Lynne V. Cheney. 30p. 1992. pap. text ed. 3.00 (*1-878802-13-5*) J M Ashbrook Ctr Pub Affairs.

Academic Freedom. Conrad Russell. LC 92-30810. 128p. 1993. 49.95 (*0-415-03714-X*, B0289); pap. 14.95 (*0-415-03715-8*, B0409) Routledge.

Academic Freedom. Ed. by Malcolm Tight. 1988. 85.00 (*0-335-09531-3*, Open Univ Pr) Taylor & Francis.

Academic Freedom: A Selected Bibliography Commemorating the Symposium on Academic Freedom. David Burch. 23p. (Orig.). 1987. pap. 10.00 (*0-935630-21-X*) U of Tex Tarlton Law Lib.

Academic Freedom: An Essay in Definition. Russell Kirk. LC 77-3073. 210p. 1977. reprint ed. text ed. 55.00 (*0-8371-9566-7*, KIAF, Greenwood Pr) Greenwood.

Academic Freedom & Catholic Higher Education. James J. Annarelli. LC 86-27152. (Contributions to the Study of Education Ser.: No. 21). 257p. 1987. text ed. 55.00 (*0-313-25425-7*, ANA/, Greenwood Pr) Greenwood.

Academic Freedom & Human Rights Abuses in Africa. Africa Watch Staff. LC 90-86085. 120p. 1991. pap. write for info. (*0-929692-77-2*, Africa Watch) Hum Rts Watch.

Academic Freedom & the Adult Student in Catholic Higher Education. John A. Vigilanti. 200p. (C). 1992. 24.50 (*0-89464-714-8*) Krieger.

Academic Freedom & the Japanese Imperial University, 1868-1939. Byron K. Marshall. (C). 1992. 40.00 (*0-520-07821-7*) U CA Pr.

***Academic Freedom in American Higher Education: Rights, Responsibilities & Limitations.** Robert K. Poch. Ed. & Frwd. by Jonathan D. Fife. (ASHE-ERIC Higher Education Report Ser.: No. 4). 85p. (Orig.). 1994. pap. 18.00x (*1-878380-25-7*) GWU Schl E&HD.

Academic Freedom in Our Time. Robert M. MacIver. LC 67-18441. 329p. 1967. reprint ed. 60.00 (*0-87752-065-8*) Gordian.

Academic Freedom in the Age of the University. Walter P. Metzger. LC 61-2328. 232p. 1961. pap. text ed. 16.00 (*0-231-08512-5*) Col U Pr.

Academic Freedom, No. 2: A Human Rights Report. World University Service Staff. Ed. by John Daniel et al. 192p. (C). 1993. text ed. 49.95 (*1-85649-219-2*, Pub. by Zed Books UK) Humanities.

***Academic Freedom Three: Education & Human Rights.** Ed. by John Daniel et al. (World University Service Series on Academic Freedom). 256p. (C). 1994. text ed. 59.95 (*1-85649-301-6*, Pub. by Zed Books UK) Humanities.

***Academic Freedom Three: Education & Human Rights.** Ed. by John Daniel et al. (World University Service Series on Academic Freedom). 256p. (C). 1994. pap. 25.00 (*1-85649-302-4*, Pub. by Zed Books UK) Humanities.

Academic Freedom under Israeli Military Occupation: Report of WUS-ICJ Mission of Enquiry into Higher Education in the West Bank & Gaza. Adam Roberts et al. 87p. reprint ed. pap. 25.00 (*0-8357-5028-0*, 2027734) Bks Demand.

Academic Freedom, 1990: A Human Rights Report. World University Service Staff. Ed. by Laksiri Fernando et al. 208p. (C). 1990. text ed. 49.95 (*0-86232-972-8*, Pub. by Zed Books UK); pap. 17.50 (*0-86232-973-6*, Pub. by Zed Books UK) Humanities.

***Academic Freedom 4: Education & Human Rights.** Ed. by Frederiek De Vlaming. 256p. 1996. pap. 25.00 (*1-85649-378-4*, Pub. by Zed Books UK) Humanities.

***Academic Freedom 4: Education & Human Rights.** Ed. by Frederiek De Vlaming. 256p. (C). 1996. text ed. 69.95 (*1-85649-377-6*, Pub. by Zed Books UK) Humanities.

Academic Fundamentals for Power Plant Operations, 2 vols., 1. General Physics Corporation Staff. 468p. reprint ed. pap. 121.70 (*0-8357-5029-9*, 2032609) Bks Demand.

Academic Fundamentals for Power Plant Operations, 2 vols., 2. General Physics Corporation Staff. 468p. reprint ed. pap. 93.00 (*0-8357-5030-2*) Bks Demand.

Academic Fundamentals for Power Plant Operations, 2 vols., Set. (Illus.). 786p. 1979. ring bd. 169.50 (*0-87683-060-2*) GP Pub.

Academic Gamesmanship: Student-Oriented Change in Higher Education. Alexander W. Astin. LC 76-12520. (Illus.). 224p. 1976. text ed. 49.95 (*0-275-90243-9*, C0243, Praeger Pubs) Greenwood.

***Academic Health Center & Health Care Reform: Proceedings of the Duke Private Sector Conference, 1994.** Private Sector Conference. Ed. by Ralph Snyderman et al. LC 95-7174. 1995. pap. write for info. (*0-7817-0326-3*) Raven.

***Academic Health Centers in the Managed Care Environment.** Ed. by David Korn et al. 250p. 1995. pap. 20.00 (*1-879694-10-7*) AAH Ctrs.

Academic Heraldy in America. Kevin Sheard. (Illus.). 1962. 8.95 (*0-918616-06-9*) Northern Mich.

Academic Heritage: The Transmission of Excellence-Cardiology at the Ohio State University. Charles F. Wooley. LC 92-14923. (Illus.). 320p. 1993. 50.00 (*0-87993-533-2*) Futura Pub.

Academic Impact of Foreign Graduate Students: Perceptions of Faculty. Y. G-M. Lulat. LC 94-6859. 205p. 1995. lib. bdg. 39.90 (*0-944265-13-8*, Cerebrum Bks) Librosmondiale.

***Academic Impact of Foreign Graduate Students: Perceptions of Faculty.** Y. G-M. Lulat. 205p. 1995. pap. text ed. 29.90 (*0-944265-16-2*, Cerebrum Bks) Librosmondiale.

***Academic Initiatives in Total Quality for Higher Education.** Harry V. Roberts. 1995. 45.00 (*0-87389-326-3*) ASQC Qual Pr.

Academic Instruction in Early Childhood: Challenge or Pressure? Ed. by Leslie Rescorla et al. LC 85-644581. (New Directions for Child Development Ser.: No. CD). 1991. 17.95 (*1-55542-769-3*) Jossey-Bass.

Academic Integrity & Student Development: Legal Issues & Policy Considerations. William L. Kibler et al. LC 87-27667. 110p. 1994. pap. 16.95 (*0-912557-08-7*) Coll Admin Pubns.

Academic Intrapreneur: Strategy, Innovation, & Management in Higher Education. Baron Perlman et al. LC 88-6609. 224p. 1988. text ed. 49.95 (*0-275-92951-5*, C2951, Praeger Pubs) Greenwood.

Academic Janus: The Private College & Its Faculty. Reece McGee. LC 70-149913. (Jossey-Bass Higher Education Ser.). 288p. reprint ed. 82.10 (*0-8357-9293-5*, 2013819) Bks Demand.

Academic Job Digest: International Supplement. Allison-Garrett. Ed. by W. E. Garrett. 60p. (Orig.). 1990. pap. text ed. 29.99 (*1-878235-02-8*) Taylor Pub MI.

Academic Job Digest: Tired of the Corp World? Allison-Garrett. 91p. (Orig.). 1990. pap. 29.99 (*1-878235-10-9*) Taylor Pub MI.

Academic Job Search Handbook. Mary M. Heiberger & Julia M. Vick. LC 91-42531. (Illus.). 192p. (Orig.). (C). 1992. pap. text ed. 13.95 (*0-8122-1375-0*) U of Pa Pr.

Academic Labor: Markets & Careers. Ed. by David Breneman & Ted Youn. (Stanford Series on Education & Public Policy). 250p. 1988. 65.00 (*1-85000-414-5*, Falmer Pr); pap. 28.00 (*1-85000-415-3*, Falmer Pr) Taylor & Francis.

Academic Leadership in Community Colleges. Ed. by Alan T. Seagren et al. LC 93-31026. 1994. 15.00 (*0-8032-4242-5*) U of Nebr Pr.

Academic Librarians & Cataloging Networks: Visibility, Quality Control, & Professional Status. Ruth Hafter. LC 85-24761. (Contributions in Librarianship & Information Science Ser.: No. 57). 162p. 1986. text ed. 45.00 (*0-313-24821-4*, HLB) Greenwood.

Academic Librarianship: Past, Present, & Future - A Festschrift for David Kaser upon His 65th Birthday. Ed. by John V. Richardson, Jr. & Jinnie Y. Davis. 175p. 1989. lib. bdg. 32.50 (*0-87287-669-1*) Libs Unl.

Academic Librarianship: Yesterday, Today, & Tomorrow. Ed. by Robert Stueart. LC 81-18866. 284p. 1982. 39.95 (*0-918212-52-9*) Neal-Schuman.

Academic Librarianship in a Transformational Age: Program, Politics, & Personnel. Allen B. Veaner Associates Staff. (Professional Librarian Ser.). 440p. 1989. text ed. 40.00 (*0-8161-1866-3*, Hall Reference); pap. 28.50 (*0-8161-1875-2*, Hall Reference) Macmillan.

***Academic Libraries.** 1995. lib. bdg. 252.95 (*0-8490-6764-2*) Gordon Pr.

Academic Libraries: Research Perspectives. Ed. by Mary J. Lynch. LC 90-32120. (ACRL Publications in Librarianship: No. 47). 279p. reprint ed. pap. 79.60 (*0-7837-5906-1*, 2045704) Bks Demand.

Academic Libraries: The Changing Knowledge Centers of Colleges & Universities. Barbara B. Moran. Ed. by Jonathan D. Fife. LC 85-61910. (ASHE-ERIC Higher Education Report Ser.: No. 8, 1984). 97p. (Orig.). 1985. pap. 7.50 (*0-913317-17-9*) GWU Schl E&HD.

Academic Libraries: The Dimensions of Their Effectiveness. Joseph McDonald & Basney Micikas. LC 93-14464. (New Directions in Information Management Ser.). 208p. 1994. text ed. 49.95 (*0-313-27269-7*, Greenwood Pr) Greenwood.

***Academic Libraries: Their Rationale & Role in American Higher Education.** Gerard B. McCabe & Ruth J. Person. LC 94-40319. (Contributions in Librarianship & Information Science Ser.: Vol. 84). 248p. 1995. text ed. 55.00 (*0-313-28597-7*, Greenwood Pr) Greenwood.

Academic Libraries Achieving Excellence in Higher Education: Proceedings of the Sixth National Conference of the Association of College & Research Libraries. Ed. by Thomas Kirk. 522p. 1992. 49.95 (*0-685-72690-8*); 44.95 (*0-685-72691-6*) Assn Coll & Res Libs.

***Academic Libraries & Training.** Ed. by Maryruth P. Glogowski. LC 94-37215. (Foundations in Library & Information Science Ser.: Vol. 29). 1994. write for info. (*1-55938-598-7*) Jai Pr.

***Academic Libraries As High-Tech Gateways: A Guide to Design & Space Decisions.** Richard J. Bazillion & Connie Braun. LC 95-14035. (Illus.). 225p. (Orig.). 1995. pap. text ed. 40.00 (*0-8389-0656-7*) ALA.

An Asterisk (*) at the beginning of an entry indicates that the title is appearing in BIP for the first time.

An Asterisk (*) at the beginning of an entry indicates that the title is appearing in BIP for the first time.

23

***Academic's Handbook.** 2nd ed. Ed. by A. Leigh DeNeef & Craufurd D. Goodwin. LC 95-16775. 1995. pap. write for info. (0-8223-1673-0) Duke.

***Academic's Handbook.** 2nd ed. Ed. by Leigh DeNeef & Crafurd D. Goodwin. LC 95-16775. 1995. write for info. (0-8223-1661-7) Duke.

Academics in Court: The Consequences of Faculty Discrimination Litigation. George R. LaNoue & Barbara A. Lee. LC 87-5047. 1987. text ed. 42.50 (0-472-10086-6); pap. text ed. 19.95 (0-472-08070-9) U of Mich Pr.

***Academics Staff Appraisal.** Jacqui Abbott & Alan Lonsdale. 141p. 1992. pap. 48.00 (0-7300-1516-5, Pub. by Deakin Univ AT) St Mut.

Academie de Droit International Recueil Des Cours, Collected Courses of the Hague Academy of International Law, 1980, Vol. I, Tome 166. 448p. (C). 1981. lib. bdg. 117.00 (90-286-2731-6) Kluwer Ac.

Academie du Vin Wine Course. 2nd rev. ed. Steven Spurrier & Michel Dovaz. 224p. 1991. text ed. 23.00 (0-02-613261-3) Macmillan.

Academie Imperiale de Musique: Histoire Litteraire, Musicale, Politique et Galant de Ce Theatre, de 1645 a 1855, 2 vols. Francois H. Blaze. LC 80-2258. 1981. reprint ed. 95.00 (0-404-18804-4) AMS Pr.

Academie Royal des Sciences (1666-1683) John M. Hirscfield. LC 80-2092. (Development of Science Ser.). (Illus.). 1981. lib. bdg. 23.95 (0-405-13857-1) Ayer.

Academie Royale de Musique au 18e Siecle, 2 vols., Set. Emile Campardon. LC 73-141152. (Music Ser.). 1971. reprint ed. lib. bdg. 110.00 (0-306-70090-5) Da Capo.

Academies of Art, Past & Present. Nikolaus Pevsner. LC 78-87379. (Illus.). 332p. 1973. reprint ed. lib. bdg. 49.50 (0-306-71603-8) Da Capo.

***Academikit Study Organizer.** Irene Kleiman & Carol Shulman. 118p. (C). 1992. teacher ed 14.95 (0-9638804-1-1); student ed 12.95 (0-9638804-3-8); ring bd. 26.95 (0-9638804-0-3) Dynamic Lrning.

Academy & Community: A Study of the Jewish Identity & Involvement of Professors. Albert G. Crawford & Rela G. Monson. LC 80-68432. 40p. 1980. pap. 2.00 (0-685-00263-2) Am Jewish Comm.

Academy & Community: The Foundation of the French Historical Profession. William R. Keylor. LC 74-81867. 352p. (C). 1975. 34.95 (0-674-00255-5) HUP.

Academy & Traditions of Jewish Learning. Ed. by Jacob Neusner. LC 92-36348. (Judaism in Cold War America, 1945-1990 Ser.: Vol. 9). 344p. 1993. 56.00 (0-8153-0081-6) Garland.

Academy Award Winners. Ronal Bergan et al. 352p. 1994. 19.98 (0-8317-0410-1) Smithmark.

***Academy Awards: A Celebration in Song.** 376p. (Orig.). 1994. pap. 26.95 (0-89724-270-X, XW1522) Warner Brothers.

Academy Awards Handbook. John Harkness. 256p. 1994. mass mkt. 4.50 (1-55817-887-2, Pinnacle NY) Windsor NY.

***Academy Awards Handbook.** John Harkness. 336p. 1995. pap. 4.99 (0-8217-0105-3) Zebra.

***Academy Awards Handbook.** John Harkness. 1995. pap. 4.99 (0-7860-0105-4, Pinnacle NY) Windsor NY.

Academy Awards Index: The Complete Categorical & Chronological Record. Comp. by Richard Shale. LC 92-40226. 816p. 1993. text ed. 75.00 (0-313-27738-9, SYK, Greenwood Pr) Greenwood.

Academy Days: A History of Greenwich Academy from 1826 to 1986. Nanette B. Burrows et al. LC 87-23585. (Illus.). 144p. 1987. 30.00 (0-685-19378-0) Phoenix Pub.

Academy in Crisis: The Political Economy of Higher Education. Ed. by John W. Sommer. LC 94-9271. 250p. 1994. 34.95 (1-56000-182-8) Transaction Pubs.

***Academy in Crisis: The Political Economy of Higher Education.** Ed. by John W. Sommer. 1994. pap. 19.95 (1-56000-801-6) Transaction Pubs.

***Academy Mystery Novellas Vol. I: Women Sleuths.** 232p. pap. 8.00 (0-89733-157-5) Academy Chi Pubs.

***Academy Mystery Novellas Vol. II: Police Procedurals.** 232p. 1985. pap. 8.00 (0-89733-158-3) Academy Chi Pubs.

Academy Mystery Novellas Vol. III: Locked Room Puzzles. Ed. by Martin H. Greenberg & Bill Pronzini. 225p. 1986. pap. 8.00 (0-89733-225-3) Academy Chi Pubs.

Academy Mystery Novellas Vol. IV: Great British Detectives. Ed. by Martin H. Greenberg & Edward D. Hoch. 220p. 1987. pap. 8.00 (0-89733-266-0) Academy Chi Pubs.

Academy Mystery Novellas Vol. V: Women Write Murder. Ed. by Martin H. Greenberg & Edward D. Hoch. 224p. 1987. pap. 8.00 (0-89733-267-9) Academy Chi Pubs.

Academy of Arts. Collets Staff. 224p. 1982. 18.00 (0-317-57200-8, Pub. by Collets UK) St Mut.

Academy of Europe: Rome in the Eighteenth Century. Frederick Den Broeder. 168p. 1973. 7.50 (0-918386-11-X) W Benton Mus.

Academy of Higher Laughing. Zeth, pseud. Ed. by James B. Van Treese. 220p. 1994. pap. 7.95 (1-56901-157-5) NW Pub.

Academy of Love. large type ed. Clare F. Holmes. LC 93-14402. 1993. pap. 14.95 (0-8161-5841-X) Hall.

Academy of Management 1981: Proceedings. Ed. by Kae H. Chung. 1981. 12.00 (0-915350-20-3) Acad of Mgmt.

Academy of Management 1982: Proceedings. Ed. by Kae H. Chung. 12.00 (0-686-97952-4) Acad of Mgmt.

Academy of One. Martin Grayson. 88p. 1984. 12.95 (0-915639-00-9) Cos Cob Pr.

Academy Papers. American Academy of Arts & Letters Staff. LC 70-117749. (Essay Index Reprint Ser.). 1977. 21.95 (0-8369-1641-7) Ayer.

Academy System of the State of New York. George F. Miller. LC 76-89205. (American Education: Its Men, Institutions & Ideas, Ser., No. 1). 1977. reprint ed. 18.95 (0-405-01443-0) Ayer.

Acadia: The Geography of Early Nova Scotia to 1760. Andrew H. Clark. LC 68-9829. (Illus.). 470p. reprint ed. pap. 134.00 (0-8357-6000-6, 2034275) Bks Demand.

Acadia: The Story Behind the Scenery. Robert Rothe. LC 78-78121. (Illus.). 48p. 1979. pap. 6.95 (0-916122-57-3) KC Pubns.

***Acadia Activities Guide.** 10p. 1993. 6.95 (0-915992-57-4) Eastern Acorn.

Acadia National Park: Maine's Intimate Parkland. Alan Nyiri. (Illus.). 80p. 1986. pap. 12.95 (0-89272-219-3) Down East.

***Acadia National Park: Wildlife Watcher's Guide.** Ruth G. Grierson. (Wildlife Watchers). (Illus.). 96p. (Orig.). 1995. pap. write for info. (1-55971-455-7) NorthWord.

Acadia National Park & Mount Desert Island. Paul Granat. 1991. 9.99 (0-517-62363-3) Random Hse Value.

Acadia National Park Coloring Book. (Illus.). 24p. (J). (ps-6). 1991. pap. 3.00 (0-934745-20-X) Acadia Pub Co.

Acadia National Park, ME. rev. ed. Ed. by Trails Illustrated Staff. (Illus.). 1994. Folded Topographical Map. 8.99 (0-925873-95-0) Trails Illustrated.

Acadia National Park Postbox Collection: A Book to Keep & 15 Different Cards to Send. (Postbox Ser.). 1994. boxed 10.95 (0-8118-0318-X) Chronicle Bks.

Acadia Seacoast: A Guidebook for Appreciation. Lynn Haaland. Ed. by Louise Mills & Mercy Johnson. (Illus.). 32p. (Orig.). (J). (gr. k up). 1984. pap. 3.00 (0-915189-01-1) Oceanus.

Acadia Trolls: Laura's Story of the Balance Rock on Mount Desert Island. Anita Bjorndahl. Ed. by Mercy Johnson. LC 86-2564. (Illus.). 32p. (Orig.). 1986. lib. bdg. 17.77 (0-915189-02-X); pap. 9.95 (0-915189-03-8) Oceanus.

***Acadian-Cajun Genealogy: Step by Step.** Timothy Hebert. 146p. (Orig.). 1994. pap. 10.00 (0-940984-87-3) U of SW LA Ctr LA Studies.

Acadian Descendants, Vol. I. Janet B. Jehn. LC 73-153975. (Illus.). 177p. (Orig.). 1972. pap. 13.95 (0-939444-01-1) Acadian Genealogy.

Acadian Descendants, Vol. II. Janet B. Jehn. LC 73-153975. 505p. (Orig.). 1975. pap. 21.95 (0-939444-02-X) Acadian Genealogy.

Acadian Descendants, Vol. III. Janet B. Jehn. LC 73-153975. 267p. (Orig.). 1979. pap. 14.50 (0-939444-03-8) Acadian Genealogy.

Acadian Descendants, Vol. IV. Janet B. Jehn. LC 73-153975. (Illus.). 497p. (Orig.). 1980. pap. 23.00 (0-939444-00-3) Acadian Genealogy.

Acadian Descendants, Vol. VI. Janet B. Jehn. LC 73-153975. (Illus.). 200p. (Orig.). 1982. pap. 15.95 (0-939444-06-2) Acadian Genealogy.

Acadian Descendants, Vol. VII. Janet B. Jehn. LC 73-153975. 439p. (Orig.). 1987. pap. 22.95 (0-939444-10-0) Acadian Genealogy.

***Acadian Descendants Vol. IX.** Janet B. Jehn. LC 73-153975. 229p. (Orig.). 1994. pap. 24.95 (0-939444-12-7) Acadian Genealogy.

Acadian Descendants Vol. VIII: Genealogy of Gabrielle Forest & Pierre Brasseaux. Janet B. Jehn & Clarence J. D'Entremont. LC 73-53975. 288p. (Orig.). 1991. pap. 21.95 (0-939444-11-9) Acadian Genealogy.

Acadian Descendants, Vol. V: A Tree of Forests. Janet B. Jehn. LC 73-153975. (Illus.). 260p. (Orig.). 1984. pap. 21.95 (0-939444-05-4) Acadian Genealogy.

Acadian Exiles in the Colonies. Janet B. Jehn. LC 73-153975. (Illus.). 366p. 1977. pap. 23.00 (0-939444-04-6) Acadian Genealogy.

Acadian General: Alfred Mouton & the Civil War. William Arceneaux. (U. S. L. History Ser.). 220p. 1981. 15.00 (0-940984-00-8) U of SW LA Ctr LA Studies.

Acadian Hard Times: The Farm Security Administration in Maine's St. John Valley, 1940-1943. C. Stewart Doty. LC 90-23304. (Illus.). xiii, 186p. 1991. pap. 24.95 (0-89101-071-8) U Maine Pr.

***Acadian Miracle.** D. LeBlanc. 1966. 13.95 (0-614-06315-9) Claitors.

Acadian Miracle. J. Dudley LeBlanc. 1966. write for info. (0-685-27202-8) Claitors.

Acadian Orogeny: Recent Studies in New England, Maritime Canada, & the Autochthonous Foreland. Ed. by D. C. Roy & J. W. Skehan. (Special Paper Ser.: No. 275). 1993. pap. 42.50 (0-8137-2275-6) Geol Soc.

Acadian Pedigree. J. C. Fruge. 1972. 10.00 (0-87511-596-9) Claitors.

Acadian to Cajun: Transformation of a People, 1803-1877. Carl A. Brasseaux. LC 92-17759. (Illus.). 304p. 1992. 42.50 (0-87805-582-7); pap. 17.95 (0-87805-583-5) U Pr of Miss.

Acadiana Flora: Native & Naturalized Woody Plants of South-Central Louisiana. William D. Reese & Garrie Landry. (Illus.). 126p. 1992. 15.00 (0-940984-77-6) U of SW LA Ctr LA Studies.

Acadiana Profile's Cajun Cooking, Pt. 1. Ed. by Trent Angers & Sue McDonough. (Illus.). 240p. 1988. spiral bd. 10.00 (0-939524-02-3) Angers Pub.

Acadiana Profile's Cajun Cooking, Pt. 2. Ed. by Trent Angers. 192p. 1989. spiral bd. 10.00 (0-939524-01-5) Angers Pub.

Acadiana Profile's Cajun Cooking, Pt. 1: From the Kitchens of South Louisiana. Ed. by Trent Angers. (Illus.). 240p. 1991. pap. 11.95 (0-925417-03-3) Acadian Hse Pub.

Acadiana Profile's Cajun Cooking, Pt. 2: By the People of the Cajun Country. Ed. by Trent Angers. 193p. 1991. pap. 9.95 (0-925417-05-X) Acadian Hse Pub.

Acadiana Unlimited. Marilyn Hudson. 1969. 4.95 (0-87511-061-4) Claitors.

Acadia's Biking Guide. Tom St. Germain. (Illus.). 64p. (Orig.). 1993. pap. 4.95 (0-9629997-2-5) Parkman Pubns.

Acali Experiment: Six Women & Five Men on a Raft Across the Atlantic. Santiago Genoves. LC 79-51447. (Illus.). 1979. write for info. (0-8129-0855-4, Times Bks) Random.

Acambaro: Frontier Settlement on the Tarascan-Aztec Border. Shirley Gorenstein. (Publications in Anthropology: No. 32). (Illus.). 303p. 1985. pap. 13.75 (0-935462-23-6) Vanderbilt Pubns.

Acambaro-Archaeology's Astounding Scandal: The Conspiracy Against Julsrud's Incredible Discovery. John H. Tierney. LC 83-70806. (Illus.). 160p. (Orig.). 1983. pap. 9.95 (0-912361-00-X) Trine Bks.

Acanthaster & the Coral Reef: a Theoretical Perspective: Proceedings of a Workshop Held at the Australian Institute of Marine Science, Townsville, August 6-7, 1988. R. Bradbury. (Lecture Notes in Biomathematics Ser.: Vol. 88). vi, 339p. 1991. pap. 44.00 (0-387-53501-2) Spr-Verlag.

Acanthaster Planci: Major Management Problem of Coral Reefs. Ed. by Birkeland. 1990. 205.00 (0-8493-6599-6, QL384) CRC Pr.

Acanthodii. Robert Denison. Ed. by O. Kuhn & H. P. Schultze. (Handbook of Paleoichthyology: Vol. 5). (Illus.). 62p. 1979. text ed. 65.00 (3-437-30291-4) Lubrecht & Cramer.

Acaoohkiwina & Acimowina: Traditional Narratives of the Rock Cree Indians. Robert A. Brightman. (Canadian Museum of Civlization Mercury Series-Canadian Ethnology Service: No. 113). xii, 228p. 1990. pap. 19.95 (0-660-10786-4) U Ch Pr.

Acappella. Margherita Faulkner. 32p. 1983. pap. 5.00 (0-913719-69-2) High-Coo Pr.

Acapulco Rampage. Don Pendleton. (Executioner Ser.: No. 26). 1989. pap. 3.50 (1-55817-284-X, Pinnacle NY) Windsor NY.

Acapulco to San Juan: Another Maritime Pictorial. (Illus.). 1988. pap. 11.95 (0-9607530-3-6) Seacoast CA.

Acarbose: Proceedings of the International Symposium on Acarbose Effects on Carbohydrate & Fat Metabolism, First, Montreux, October 8-10, 1981. Ed. by W. Creutzfeldt. (International Congress Ser.: No. 594). 588p. 1982. 114.00 (0-444-90283-X, I-278-82, Excerpta Medica) Elsevier.

Acarbose for the Treatment of Diabetes Mellitus. Ed. by W. Creutzfeldt. (Illus.). 210p. 1989. 58.00 (0-387-19145-3) Spr-Verlag.

Acarology: Proceedings of the International Congress, 4th. E. Piffl. 752p. 1979. 243.00 (0-317-89576-1, Pub. by Collets UK) Pro-Am Music.

Acari: Reproduction, Development & Life History Strategies. Ed. by Reinhart Schuster & Paul W. Murphy. (Illus.). 454p. 1991. 155.00 (0-412-36070-5, A5227) Chapman & Hall.

Acarine Biocontrol Agents: An Illustrated Key & Manual. Uri Gerson & Robert L. Smiley. (Illus.). 160p. 1990. 92.50 (0-412-36060-8, A4459) Chapman & Hall.

Acarology: Mites & Human Welfare. Tyler A. Woolley. LC 87-13701. 484p. 1988. text ed. 89.95 (0-471-04168-8) Wiley.

Acarology Six, 2 vols., Set. D. A. Griffiths & C. E. Bowman. LC 79-17386. (Acarology Ser.). 1984. text ed. 295.00 (0-470-27412-3) P-H.

Acarology Six, 2 vols., Vol. 2. D. A. Griffiths & C. E. Bowman. LC 79-17386. (Acarology Ser.). 700p. 1984. text ed. 149.00 (0-470-27411-5) P-H.

Acarya: Sankara of Kaladi, a Story. I. S. Madugula. 143p. (C). 1991. reprint ed. text ed. 16.00 (81-208-0009-5, Pub. by Motilal Banarsidass II) S Asia.

Acastos. Iris Murdoch. 144p. 1988. mass mkt. 5.95 (0-14-008696-X, Penguin Bks) Viking Penguin.

Acathist Hymn to the Name of Jesus. deluxe ed. Joseph Raya. Ed. by Jose de Vinck. 40p. 1989. reprint ed. 5.75 (0-911726-46-2, CODE NJB) Alleluia Pr.

Acatos Ceramics & Glass International Auction Records 1991. (Illus.). 980p. 1992. 135.00 (0-9627767-4-2) Archer Fields.

***ACC Basketball.** Peter C. Bjarkman. (Illus.). 256p. (Orig.). 1995. pap. 14.95 (0-614-06062-1) Masters Pr IN.

ACC Basketball: An Illustrated History. Ron Morris et al. 304p. 1988. 39.95 (0-9609548-9-9) Village Sports.

ACC Basketball Stat Book. John C. Prouty et al. 362p. 1993. pap. 11.95 (0-9640369-0-8) Willow Oak.

***Accardo: The Genuine Godfather.** William F. Roemer, Jr. (Illus.). 368p. 1995. 23.95 (1-55611-467-2) D I Fine.

Accelerated Aging: Photochemical & Thermal Aspects. Robert L. Feller. (Research in Conservation Ser.: No. 4). (Illus.). 296p. 1994. pap. 30.00 (0-89236-125-5) J P Getty Trust.

Accelerated Amortization. David A. Thomas. LC 58-62909. (Michigan Business Studies: Vol. 13, No. 4). 112p. reprint ed. pap. 32.00 (0-8357-5033-7, 2022078) Bks Demand.

Accelerated & Outdoor Durability Testing of Organic Materials, No. 1202. Ed. by Warren D. Ketola & Douglas Grossman. LC 94-15430. (Special Technical Publication: No. 1202). (Illus.). 280p. 1994. 63.00 (0-8031-1863-5, 0401202014) ASTM.

Accelerated Basic Exam Series. Anthony Schools Corp. Staff. (Real Estate License Course Ser.). 106p. (Orig.). 1994. pap. text ed. 18.00 (0-941833-46-1) Anthony Schools.

Accelerated Convergence Treatment of R-N Lattice Sums & Modulated Phases in the BaSiO-CaSiO System of ABX KSO-Related Structures: A Special Issue of the Journal Crystallography Reviews. D. E. Williams et al. 64p. 1989. text ed. 46.00 (2-88124-708-3) Gordon & Breach.

Accelerated Cooling of Steel: Proceedings of a Symposium. Ed. by P. D. Southwick. LC 86-8533. (Illus.). 618p. reprint ed. pap. 176.20 (0-8357-5034-5, 2032589) Bks Demand.

Accelerated Depreciation in the United States, 1954-1960. Norman B. Ture. (Fiscal Studies Ser.: No. 9). 258p. 1967. 67.10 (0-87014-457-X) Natl Bur Econ Res.

Accelerated Dragons. John Donaldson & Jeremy Silman. 1993. pap. 19.95 (1-85744-011-0, Maxwell Macmillan) Macmillan.

Accelerated Learning. Colin Rose & Diana Rose. (Illus.). 240p. (Orig.). (C). 1985. pap. text ed. 9.95 (0-905553-12-8, Pub. by Accel Lrn Sys UK) Acclrtd Learn.

Accelerated Learning. Colin Rose. (Orig.). 1987. pap. 11.95 (0-440-50044-3, Dell Trade Pbks) Dell.

Accelerated Learning: French. Michele Bate & Arthur Miller. Ed. by Diana Rose. (Illus.). 391p. (Orig.). 1986. student ed, pap. 199.00 (0-905553-23-3, Pub. by Accel Lrn Sys UK) Acclrtd Learn.

Accelerated Learning: German. Lisa Schlotmann et al. Ed. by Diana Rose. (Illus.). 227p. (Orig.). 1986. student ed, pap. 199.00 (0-905553-21-7, Pub. by Accel Lrn Sys UK) Acclrtd Learn.

Accelerated Learning: How You Learn Determines What You Learn. Roger G. Swartz. (Illus.). 247p. 1991. pap. 7.95 (0-929240-38-3) Essential Med Info Syst Inc.

Accelerated Learning: Italian. Gigi Gatti-Doyle & Terry Doyle. Ed. by Diana Rose. (Illus.). 244p. (Orig.). 1991. student ed, pap. 199.00 (0-905553-24-1, Pub. by Accel Lrn Sys UK) Acclrtd Learn.

Accelerated Learning: Spanish. Juan Kattan-Ibarra & Dennis Stockton. Ed. by Diana Rose. (Illus.). 256p. (Orig.). 1986. student ed, pap. 199.00 (0-905553-22-5, Pub. by Accel Lrn Sys UK) Acclrtd Learn.

Accelerated Life Testing & Experts' Opinions in Reliability: Proceedings of the Enrico Fermi Internat. School of Physics, Course CII, 28 July-1 Aug., 1986. Ed. by Carlo A. Clarotti & Dennis V. Lindley. (Enrico Fermi International Summer School of Physics Ser.: Vol. 102). 236p. 1988. 82.00 (0-444-87101-2, North Holland) Elsevier.

***Accelerated Performance-Based Tests for Asphalt-Aggregate Mixes & Their Use in Mix Design & Analysis Systems.** (SHRP Ser.: A-417). (Illus.). 158p. (Orig.). (C). 1994. pap. text ed. 10.00 (0-309-05823-6) Natl Res Coun.

Accelerated Processing of Meat: Proceedings of a Workshop on Accelerated Processing in the Slaughter House, Istituto Sperimentale per la Zootecnia, Monterotondo, Rome, Itlay, 29-31 October, 1985. Ed. by A. C. Romita et al. 292p. 1987. 63.00 (1-85166-156-5, Pub. by Elsevier Applied Sci UK) Elsevier.

***Accelerated Schools in Action: Lessons from the Field.** Christine Finnan et al. (Illus.). 304p. 1995. 49.95 (0-8039-6242-8); pap. 24.95 (0-8039-6243-6) Corwin Pr.

Accelerated Schools Resource Guide. Wendy S. Hopfenberg et al. LC 93-15387. (Education-Higher Education Ser.). 393p. 1993. 39.95 (1-55542-545-3) Jossey-Bass.

***Accelerated SSADM.** HMSO Staff. 86p. 1994. pap. 60.00 (0-11-330603-2, HM06032, Pub. by HMSO UK) UNIPUB.

Accelerated Strength Testing. American Concrete Institute Staff. LC 78-58275. (ACI Publication Ser.: No. SP-56). (Illus.). 327p. 1978. reprint ed. pap. 93.20 (0-7837-5221-0, 2044952) Bks Demand.

Accelerated Systems Development. Susan Folkes & Susan Stubanvoll. LC 92-13319. 375p. 1992. pap. text ed. 52.00 (0-13-006073-9) P-H.

Accelerated Testing: Statistical Models, Test Plans & Data Analysis. Wayne Nelson. (Series in Probability & Mathematics). 601p. 1990. text ed. 110.00 (0-471-52277-5) Wiley.

Accelerating Food Production in Sub-Saharan Africa. Ed. by John W. Mellor et al. LC 86-10684. 448p. 1987. text ed. 39.50 (0-8018-3390-6) Johns Hopkins.

Accelerating Innovation. Marvin L. Patterson. LC 92-34006. 1993. text ed. 29.95 (0-442-01378-7) Van Nos Reinhold.

Accelerating Learning: The Use of Suggestion in the Classroom. Allyn Prichard & Jean Taylor. 144p. 1980. pap. text ed. 10.00 (0-87879-249-X) Acad Therapy.

***Accelerating Literacy: A Handbook to Assist Educators in Creating Balanced Literacy Instruction.** Rena M. Walker. 220p. 1995. teacher ed, pap. 32.95 (1-887035-00-1) Walker Ent.

***Accelerating Literacy: Lesson Planner.** Rena M. Walker. 140p. 1995. 6.95 (0-614-07207-7) Walker Ent.

***Accelerating the Educational Advancement of Minorities: A Nation-Building & Region-Building Imperative for America's Third Century.** L. Scott Miller. LC 94-31669. 1995. write for info. (0-300-05793-8) Yale U Pr.

Accelerator: The Theory-Fingerboard Connection. Howard Roberts et al. (Howard Roberts Guitar Manuals Ser.). 207p. (Orig.). 1980. pap. 16.95 (0-89915-014-4) Playback Mus Pub.

Accelerator Instrumentation. Ed. by Edward R. Beadle & Vincent J. Castillo. LC 90-55838. (Conference Proceeding Ser.: No. 212). 232p. 1990. lib. bdg. 80.00 (0-88318-645-4) Am Inst Physics.

Accelerator Instrumentation. Ed. by Elliott S. McCrory. LC 91-55347. (AIP Conference Proceedings Ser., Subseries: Particle & Fields: No. 229, 44). 304p. 1991. lib. bdg. 85.00 (0-88318-832-5) Am Inst Physics.

Accelerator Instrumentation: Second Annual Workshop. Ed. by Elliot S. McCrory. 220p. 1991. 75.00 (0-685-60542-6) Am Inst Physics.

Accelerator Instrumentation: Third Annual Workshop. Ed. by W. Barry et al. (Conference Proceeding Ser.: No. 252). 304p. 1992. 90.00 (0-88318-934-8) Am Inst Physics.

An Asterisk (*) at the beginning of an entry indicates that the title is appearing in BIP for the first time.

Accelerator Instrumentations: Fourth Annual Workshop. Stover Hinkson. (AIP Conference Proceedings Ser.: No. 281, Particles & Fields Series 52). (Illus.). 368p. 1993. text ed. 125.00 (1-56396-190-3, AIP Pr) Am Inst Physics.

Accelerator Mass Spectrometry. T. S. Liu & K. Li. Ed. by C. E. Chen et al. (Beijing Inst of Modern Phys Ser.: Vol. 4). 350p. 1992. text ed. 94.00 (981-02-0493-0) World Scientific Pub.

Accelerator Mass Spectrometry. Tuniz. 1995. write for info. (0-8493-4538-3) CRC Pr.

*Accelerator Physics at the Superconducting Super Collider. Ed. by Yiton T. Yan et al. (Conference Proceedings Ser.: No. 326). (Illus.). 696p. (C). 1995. text ed. 125.00 (0-614-02557-5, AIP Pr) Am Inst Physics.

Accendi la Fiamma del Mio Cuore, 2 vols., Vol. I. Gurumayi Chidvilasananda. Ed. by Swami Kripananda. 250p. 1989. 25.00 (0-911307-12-5) SYDA Found.

Accendi la Fiamma del Mio Cuore, 2 vols., Vol. II. Gurumayi Chidvilasananda. Ed. by Swami Kripananda. 246p. 1989. 25.00 (0-911307-13-3) SYDA Found.

Accent African: Traditional & Contemporary Hairstyles for the Black Woman. 3rd ed. Carla Brown & Valerie Thomas-Osborne. 72p. 1991. pap. 8.95 (0-9629827-0-9) Cult Express.

Accent & Syllable Structure in Passamaquoddy. Philip S. LeSourd. LC 92-36574. (Outstanding Dissertations in Linguistics Ser.). 496p. 1992. 105.00 (0-8153-0213-4) Garland.

Accent Anthology: Selections from Accent, a Quarterly of New Literature, 1940-1945. Ed. by Kerker Quinn & Charles Shattuck. LC 70-156601. (Essay Index Reprint Ser.). 1977. reprint ed. 38.95 (0-8369-2302-2) Ayer.

*Accent English: Arabic Speakers. 144p. audio 89.50 (0-685-76698-5) Audio-Forum.

*Accent English: Chinese Speakers. 144p. audio 89.50 (0-685-76699-3, SEN150) Audio-Forum.

*Accent English: French Speakers. 144p. audio 89.95 (0-685-76700-0) Audio-Forum.

*Accent English: Greek Speakers. 144p. audio 89.50 (0-685-76701-9) Audio-Forum.

Accent English: Sounds of American Speech for Arabic Speakers. Harold Stearns. (Accent English Ser.). (Illus.). 144p. 1990. spiral bd., pap. 79.50 (0-924799-03-X) Am Articulat.

Accent English: Sounds of American Speech for Chinese Speakers. Harold Stearns. (Illus.). 136p. 1988. spiral bd., pap. 79.50 (0-924799-04-8) Am Articulat.

Accent English: Sounds of American Speech for French Speakers. Harold Stearns. (Illus.). 136p. 1988. spiral bd., pap. 79.50 (0-924799-06-4) Am Articulat.

Accent English: Sounds of American Speech for Greek Speakers. Harold Stearns. (Illus.). 144p. 1993. spiral bd., pap. 79.50 (0-924799-12-9) Am Articulat.

Accent English: Sounds of American Speech for Indonesian Speakers. Harold Stearns. (Illus.). 1988. spiral bd., pap. 79.50 (0-924799-07-2) Am Articulat.

Accent English: Sounds of American Speech for Japanese Speakers. Harold Stearns. (Illus.). 136p. 1988. spiral bd., pap. 79.50 (0-924799-01-3) Am Articulat.

Accent English: Sounds of American Speech for Korean Speakers. Harold Stearns. (Illus.). 136p. 1988. spiral bd., pap. 79.50 (0-924799-05-6) Am Articulat.

Accent English: Sounds of American Speech for Russian Speakers. Harold Stearns. (Illus.). 136p. 1989. spiral bd., pap. 79.50 (0-924799-09-9) Am Articulat.

Accent English: Sounds of American Speech for Spanish Speakers. Harold Stearns. (Illus.). 136p. 1990. spiral bd., pap. 79.50 (0-924799-00-5) Am Articulat.

Accent English: Sounds of American Speech for Tagalog Speakers. Harold Stearns. (Illus.). 136p. 1989. spiral bd., pap. 79.50 (0-924799-10-2) Am Articulat.

Accent English: Sounds of American Speech for Thai Speakers. Harold Stearns. 136p. 1989. spiral bd., pap. 79.50 (0-924799-08-0) Am Articulat.

Accent English: Sounds of American Speech for Vietnamese Speakers. Harold Stearns. (Illus.). 136p. 1988. spiral bd., pap. 79.50 (0-924799-02-1) Am Articulat.

*Accent Method of Voice Therapy. M. Nasser Kotby. (Illus.). 96p. (Orig.). (C). 1995. pap. text ed. 39.95 (1-56593-090-8, 0395) Singular Publishing.

*Accent Modification: Materials & Activities. Harold T. Edwards & Kathy Strattman. (Illus.). 128p. (C). 1995. spiral bd. 32.95 (1-56593-452-0, 1070) Singular Publishing.

*Accent Modification Instructor's Manual & Audiotape. Harold T. Edwards & Kathy Strattman. 128p. (C). 1995. audio, pap. text ed. 37.50 (1-56593-453-9, 1072) Singular Publishing.

Accent on Delos. Ella B. Pettee. 168p. 1994. pap. 10.95 (0-8059-3527-4) Dorrance.

Accent on Form: An Anticipation of the Science of Tomorrow. Lancelot L. Whyte. LC 72-10702. 198p. 1973. reprint ed. text ed. 35.00 (0-8371-6622-5, WHAF, Greenwood Pr) Greenwood.

Accent on Learning. Kathryn P. Cross. LC 75-24003. (Jossey-Bass Series in Higher Education). 311p. reprint ed. pap. 88.70 (0-7837-6510-X, 2045622) Bks Demand.

Accent on Living Buyer's Guide. Ed. by Betty Garee. 145p. Date not set. pap. 12.00 (0-915708-35-3) Cheever Pub.

Accent on Living Reprint Series, No. 1. Ed. by Raymond C. Cheever. 26p. 1975. pap. text ed. 1.95 (0-915708-01-9) Cheever Pub.

Accent on Murder: A Captain Heimrich Mystery. large type ed. Richard Lockridge & Frances Lockridge. LC 93-13220. 1993. 17.95 (1-56054-301-9) Thorndike Pr.

Accent on ORFF: An Introductory Approach. Konnie Saliba. 144p. (C). 1990. pap. text ed. 38.00 (0-13-005208-6) P-H.

Accent on Rhythm: Music Activities for the Aged. 3rd rev. ed. Donna Douglass. (MMB Horizon Ser.: No. 1). 88p. 1985. pap. 16.00 (0-918812-47-X, ST 015) MMB Music.

Accent on Youth: Piano Solos of Favorite Songs & Hymns. Vicky L. Hammond & Jerry Smith. 24p. (Orig.). (YA). 1989. pap. 6.95 (0-9624262-7-X) Hammond Dalby Music.

*Accent Reduction International. Shellie R. Bader. 167p. 1995. pap. write for info. (0-9646666-0-X) Clear Speech.

Accent U. S. A. & Ameri-Speak, 2 bks., Bk. 1. Jane Y. Goodman. (Sound Approach to Standard American Dialect Ser.: Bks. 1 & 2). 66p. 1991. audio, pap. text ed. 79.95 (0-9632323-0-4) J Y Goodman.

Accent U. S. A. & Ameri-Speak, 2 bks., Bk. 2. Jane Y. Goodman. (Sound Approach to Standard American Dialect Ser.: Bks. 1 & 2). 71p. 1991. audio, pap. text ed. 79.95 (0-9632323-1-2) J Y Goodman.

Accent U. S. A. & Ameri-Speak, 2 bks., Set. Jane Y. Goodman. (Sound Approach to Standard American Dialect Ser.: Bks. 1 & 2). 1991. audio, pap. text ed. 159. 90 (0-685-54727-2) J Y Goodman.

Accents - to Write This Child. Claus Wittmaack. 104p. 1990. pap. 12.95 (0-921254-19-9, Pub. by Penumbra Pr CN) U of Toronto Pr.

Accents & Ascendings. Bob Stanish. 144p. (J). (gr. 3-8). 1990. 12.95 (0-86653-566-7, GA1155) Good Apple.

Accents of England & British Isles. John C. Wells. 1982. pap. 22.95 (0-521-28540-2) Cambridge U Pr.

Accents of English: An Introduction. John C. Wells. 1982. pap. 24.95 (0-521-29719-2) Cambridge U Pr.

Accents of God: A Treasury of the World's Sacred Scriptures. M. K. Rohani. (Illus.). 96p. 1992. 12.95 (1-85168-023-3) Onewrld Pubns.

*Accents on Accessories. 144p. 1995. 24.95 (0-8487-1452-0) Oxmoor Hse.

Accents on Opera: A Series of Brief Essays Stressing Known & Little Known Facts & Facets of a Familiar Art. Boris Goldovsky & Mary E. Peltz. LC 77-156651. (Essay Index Reprint Ser.). 1977. reprint ed. 27.95 (0-8369-2398-7) Ayer.

Accentual Change & Language Contact: Comparative Survey & a Case Study of Early Northern Europe. Joe Salmons. LC 91-17262. (Illus.). 256p. 1992. 32.50 (0-8047-1659-5) Stanford U Pr.

Accentual Patterns of the Slavic Languages. Edward Stankiewicz. LC 91-37379. 450p. (C). 1993. 49.50 (0-8047-2029-0) Stanford U Pr.

Accentuation of Nominal Compounds in Lithuanian. Frederic T. Wood. (LD Ser.: No. 7). 1930. pap. 16.00 (0-527-00753-6) Periodicals Srv.

Accept Me As I Am: Best Books of Juvenile Nonfiction on Impairments & Disabilities. Joan B. Friedberg et al. (Serving Special Needs Ser.). 363p. 1985. 36.00 (0-8352-1974-7) Bowker.

Accept No Limitations: A Black Woman Encounters Corporate America. Marjorie L. Kimbrough. LC 90-47400. 144p. 1991. 13.95 (0-687-00694-5) Abingdon.

Accept Responsibility Module, Connections: School & Work Transitions - Work Skills-Work Maturity Skills. National Center for Research in Vocational Education Staff. 1987. write for info. (0-318-67156-5, SP100CB12) Ctr Educ Trng Employ.

Accept This Gift: Selections from a Course in Miracles. Ed. by Frances Vaughan & Roger Walsh. 112p. 1992. pap. 7.95 (0-87477-721-6) J P Tarcher.

Accept This Offering: The Eucharist As Sacrifice Today. Kenneth Stevenson. 88p. 1989. pap. 5.95 (0-8146-1823-5) Liturgical Pr.

Accept Yourself with Love & Confidence. John M. Scott. LC 90-62654. 128p. (Orig.). 1991. pap. 5.95 (0-87973-449-3, 449) Our Sunday Visitor.

Acceptability in Language. Sidney Greenbaum. (Contributions to the Sociology of Langauge Ser.: No. 17). 1977. 24.65 (90-279-7623-6) Mouton.

Acceptability of Cell Substrates for Production of Biologicals. (Technical Report Ser.: No. 747). 29p. 1987. pap. 3.00 (92-4-120747-7) World Health.

Acceptable Arrangement. Jeanne Savery. 203p. 1993. 19.95 (0-8027-1254-1) Walker & Co.

Acceptable Entertainment. Paul Laster & Renee Riccardo. LC 88-80322. 1988. pap. 14.00 (0-916365-25-5) Ind Curators.

Acceptable Evidence: Science & Values in Risk Management. Ed. by Deborah G. Mayo & Rachelle D. Hollander. (Environmental Ethics & Science Policy Ser.). (Illus.). 304p. 1991. 49.95 (0-19-506372-4) OUP.

Acceptable Evidence: Science & Values in Risk Management. Ed. by Deborah G. Mayo et al. (Environmental Ethics & Science Policy Ser.). (Illus.). 304p. 1994. reprint ed. pap. 19.95 (0-19-508929-4) OUP.

Acceptable Loss. Kregg P. Jorgenson. 1991. mass mkt. 4.99 (0-8041-0792-0) Ivy Books.

Acceptable Losses. Irwin Shaw. 320p. 1983. mass mkt. 4.95 (0-380-64162-3) Avon.

Acceptable Losses. large type ed. Irwin Shaw. 400p. 1984. 23.95 (0-7089-8191-7, Charnwood) Ulverscroft.

Acceptable Risk. Robin Cook. 432p. 1995. 23.95 (0-399-13971-0) Putnam Pub Group.

Acceptable Risk. Baruch Fischhoff et al. LC 81-9957. 208p. 1984. pap. 18.95 (0-521-27892-9) Cambridge U Pr.

*Acceptable Risk. large type ed. Robin Cook. LC 95-3699. (Large Print Book Ser.). 1995. 26.95 (1-56895-173-6) Wheeler Pub.

Acceptable Risk? Making Decisions in a Toxic Environment. Lee Clarke. 1989. 35.00 (0-520-06303-1) U CA Pr.

Acceptable Risk? Making Decisions in a Toxic Environment. Lee Clarke. 242p. 1991. reprint ed. pap. 14.00 (0-520-07657-5) U CA Pr.

Acceptable Sacrifice. John Bunyan. pap. 6.99 (0-87377-016-1) GAM Pubns.

Acceptable Sludge Disposal Techniques. 1978. 25.00 (0-944989-10-1, 030078) Hazardous Mat Control.

Acceptable Time. Madeleine L'Engle. (YA). (gr. 7 up). 1989. 18.00 (0-374-30027-5) FS&G.

Acceptable Time. Madeleine L'Engle. 1990. reprint ed. mass mkt. 3.99 (0-440-20814-9, LFL) Dell.

Acceptance. Vincent P. Collins. pap. 12.50 (0-87029-072-X) Abbey.

*Acceptance & Change: Content & Context in Psychotherapy. Ed. by Steven C. Hayes et al. (Illus.). 272p. (C). 1994. pap. text ed. 34.95 (1-878978-19-5) Context Pr.

*Acceptance & Change: Content & Context in Psychotherapy. Ed. by Steven C. Hayes et al. (Illus.). 272p. (C). 1994. text ed. 46.95 (1-878978-20-9) Context Pr.

Acceptance: Establishing the Covenant see Torah Anthology: Meam Lo'ez

Acceptance Sampling in Quality Control. Schilling. (Statistics: Textbooks & Monographs: Vol. 42). 1982. 85. 00 (0-8247-1347-8) Dekker.

Acceptance Testing of Radiological Imaging Equipment: Proceedings of the Symposium Held on October 1-2, 1981. Ed. by Pei-Jan P. Lin et al. (American Association of Physicists in Medicine Symposium Ser.: No. 1). 310p. 1982. 40.00 (0-88318-400-1) Am Inst Physics.

Acceptance Therapy. Lisa Engelhardt. LC 92-71076. (Illus.). 76p. 1991. pap. 3.95 (0-87029-245-5) Abbey.

Accepted Dental Therapeutics. 39th ed. American Dental Association, Council on Dental Therapeutics Staff. (C). 1982. 15.00 (0-934510-10-5) Am Dental.

*Accepting & Peaceful. Ellen Larson. Ed. by Debbie Bible. (Value Builders Ser.). (J). 1995. 7.95 (0-7814-5093-4, 10074) Cook.

Accepting Criticism. (Pocket Power Ser.). 16p. (Orig.). 1986. pap. 1.00 (0-89486-367-3, 5336B) Hazelden.

Accepting Criticism - Role Playing. Barbara L. McCombs & Linda Brannan. (Skills for Job Success Ser.). (Illus.). 52p. (Orig.). 1990. pap. 39.95 (1-56119-055-1) Educ Pr MD.

Accepting Each Other: Individuality & Intimacy in Your Loving Relationship. Michael L. Emmons & Robert E. Alberti. LC 91-22918. 240p. (Orig.). 1991. pap. 9.95 (0-915166-77-1) Impact Pubs CA.

Accepting Others: Beyond Barriers & Stereotypes. Mike Nappa. (Active Bible Curriculum Ser.). (Illus.). 48p. 1992. pap. 9.99 (1-55945-126-2) Group Pub.

Accepting Ourselves: A Moment to Reflect. Hazelden Foundation Staff. 1990. pap. 15.00 (0-06-255367-4) Harper SF.

Accepting Ourselves: A Moment to Reflect. Hazelden Staff. 1990. pap. 11.70 (0-685-46034-7, Hazelden SF) Harper SF.

Accepting Powerlessness. Judi Hollis. 32p. 1983. pap. 2.00 (0-89486-214-6, 1221B) Hazelden.

Accepting the Readiness Idea. Linda D. Pass. 40p. (Orig.). 1992. pap. text ed. 6.00 (0-935493-84-0) Programs Educ.

Accepting the Universe. John Burroughs. Ed. by George W. Lugg. LC 86-31430. 224p. 1987. 15.50 (0-935834-58-3) Rainbow Books.

Accepting Your Power to Heal: The Personal Practice of Therapeutic Touch. Dolores Krieger. LC 92-42936. (Illus.). 224p. (Orig.). 1993. pap. 10.95 (1-879181-04-5) Bear & Co.

Accepting Yourself: Liking Yourself All of the Time. Dale R. Olen. (Illus.). 64p. (Orig.). 1992. pap. 5.95 (1-56583-005-9) Life Skills WI.

Access: A Developer's Guide. Michael T. Gilbert. 1993. disk, pap. text ed. 39.95 (1-55851-335-3) M&T Bks.

Access: From the Ground Up. Martin S. Matthews. (Illus.). 400p. (Orig.). 1993. pap. 19.95 (1-55958-303-7) Prima Pub.

Access: Fundamentals of Literacy & Communication. Steven J. Molinsky & Bill Bliss. 128p. (C). 1990. pap. text ed. 10.25 (0-13-004235-8) P-H.

Access: The Pick Enquiry Language. M. Bull. (Illus.). 350p. 1991. pap. 49.95 (0-442-31319-5) Chapman & Hall.

Access - The Parent Guide. LinguiSystems Staff. 1993. 11. 95 (1-55999-395-2) LinguiSystems.

Access, Allocations & Nominations: The Role of Housing Associations. HMSO Staff. 118p. 1992. pap. 18.00 (0-11-752725-4, HM27254, Pub. by HMSO UK) UNIPUB.

Access America: An Atlas of the National Parks for Visitors with Disabilities. Peter Shea et al. LC 87-72038. (Illus.). 464p. (Orig.). 1988. 89.95 (0-944187-00-5) N Cartographic.

Access & Delivery in Continuing Education & Training. B. Bridge & S. Salt. (C). 1992. 50.00 (1-85041-066-6, Pub. by Univ Nottingham UK) St Mut.

Access & Excellence. John E. Roueche & George Baker, III. 1986. 27.50 (0-87117-162-7) Am Assn Comm Coll.

Access & Institutional Change. Oliver Fulton. 160p. 1989. 85.00 (0-335-09234-9, Open Univ Pr) Taylor & Francis.

Access Asia: Guide to Specialists & Their Current Research. Ed. by Diane Lu & Michael Zung. 100p. 1991. pap. text ed. 50.00 (0-9631625-0-0) Nat Bur Asian.

Access Basic Cookbook. Chris St. Valentine. LC 93-15953. 1993. pap. 34.95 (0-201-62636-5) Addison-Wesley.

*Access Basic Example Book. John Craig. (Example Ser.). 1995. disk, pap. 24.95 (1-55622-472-9) Wordware Pub.

*Access Compliance: ADA California Checklist. Dorothy L. Grant et al. 303p. 1994. student ed 149.95 (0-9633709-4-4) ACR Grp.

*Access Denied: A Plan to Misdirect & Misinform Our People. Ricardo Scott. (Reggae Livity - Ras Cardo Ser.). (Illus.). 100p. (Orig.). Date not set. pap. text ed. write for info. (1-883427-24-X) Crnerstone GA.

Access Disputes in Child-Care. Spencer Millham et al. (Illus.). viii, 118p. 1989. 48.95 (0-566-05820-0, Pub. by Gower UK); pap. text ed. 28.95 (0-566-07087-1, Pub. by Gower UK) Ashgate Pub Co.

*Access, Distribution & Equity of Services in Two Texas Home Health Care Programs. Cecilia Garza. 1995. 12. 95 (0-8062-5160-3) Carlton.

Access EPA: Clearinghouses & Hotlines. 95p. (Orig.). (C). 1994. pap. text ed. 19.95 (0-7881-0719-4) Diane Pub.

Access EPA: Library & Information Services. 110p. (Orig.). (C). 1994. pap. text ed. 19.95 (0-7881-0722-4) Diane Pub.

Access EPA: Major EPA Dockets. 105p. (Orig.). (C). 1994. pap. text ed. 19.95 (0-7881-0718-6) Diane Pub.

Access EPA: Major EPA Environmental Databases. 86p. (Orig.). (C). 1994. pap. text ed. 19.95 (0-7881-0720-8) Diane Pub.

Access EPA: Public Information Tools. 105p. (Orig.). (C). 1994. pap. text ed. 19.95 (0-7881-0717-8) Diane Pub.

Access EPA: Records Management Programs. 92p. (Orig.). (C). 1994. pap. text ed. 19.95 (0-7881-0721-6) Diane Pub.

Access EPA: State Environmental Libraries. 85p. (Orig.). (C). 1994. pap. text ed. 19.95 (0-7881-0723-2) Diane Pub.

Access EPA: The Consolidated Volume. 205p. (Orig.). (C). 1994. pap. text ed. 39.95 (0-7881-0716-X) Diane Pub.

Access Fashion Four. Ed. by John Venekamp. 1992. pap. 20.00 (0-9629574-3-7) Access Mktng.

Access Fashion Three. Ed. by John Venekamp. 1991. pap. 20.00 (0-9629574-2-9) Access Mktng.

Access Fashion Two. Ed. by John Venekamp. (Orig.). 1991. pap. 20.00 (0-9629574-1-0) Access Mktng.

Access for All. Schaeffer & Eliott Sclar. 1980. text ed. 44.00 (0-231-05164-6); pap. text ed. 17.50 (0-231-05165-4) Col U Pr.

Access for Smart Beginners. Brady Computer Books Development Group Staff. 1994. pap. 35.00 (1-56686-156-X) Brady Compu Bks.

Access for Windows by Example. Suzie W. Jones & Webster & Associates Staff. 526p. (Orig.). 1993. Incl. disk. pap. 29.95 (1-86398-003-2) Prima Pub.

Access for Windows Hot Tips. Roger Jennings. (Hot Tips Ser.). (Illus.). 224p. (Orig.). 1993. pap. 12.99 (1-56529-234-0) Que.

Access for Windows Power Programming. Persobke & Liozbanski. 1993. pap. 45.00 (1-56529-194-8) Que.

Access for Windows Quick Reference. Lisa Monito. (Quick Reference Ser.). (Illus.). 192p. (Orig.). 1993. pap. 9.95 (1-56529-233-2) Que.

Access for Windows Quickstart. 1994. pap. 21.95 (1-56529-681-8) Que.

Access for Windows SureSteps. Que Development Group Staff. (Illus.). 350p. (Orig.). 1993. pap. 24.95 (1-56529-534-X) Que.

*Access Guide to Ethnic Conflicts in Europe & the Former Soviet Union. Ed. by Bruce Seymore, II. 182p. 1994. pap. 19.95 (1-878597-08-6) Access Sec Info Serv.

*Access Guide to International Affairs Internships in the Washington, D. C., Area. Ed. by Bruce Seymore, II & Susan D. Krutt. 133p. 1994. pap. 17.95 (1-878597-09-4) Access Sec Info Serv.

Access Guide to MoMA. 1988. 9.95 (0-13-599887-5) P-H.

ACCESS Guide to the Persian Gulf Crisis. Ed. by Bruce Seymore, II & Stephen Young. (Persian Gulf Guide Ser.). 61p. 1991. pap. text ed. 7.50 (1-878597-01-9) Access Sec Info Serv.

*Access Hawaii. 6th ed. 192p. Date not set. 18.50 (0-06-277142-6, Harper Ref) HarpC.

Access in Paris: A Guide fo Those Who Have Problems Getting Around. Gordon Couch. 1994. pap. 11.95 (1-870948-62-9, Pub. by Quiller Pr UK) St Mut.

Access Information: Research in Business. 3rd ed. Bobbie J. Pollard et al. 292p. 1993. per. 26.95 (0-8403-8943-4) Kendall-Hunt.

Access Information: Research in Social Sciences & Humanities. Kristin McDonough & Eleanor Langstaff. 300p. 1991. pap. text ed. 25.95 (0-8403-6739-2) Kendall-Hunt.

Access Insider. Margaret L. Young. LC 93-28663. 532p. 1993. pap. text ed. 26.95 (0-471-30430-1) Wiley.

Access Issues Working Group Papers. 91p. 1993. 20.00 (0-317-05189-X) NARUC.

Access List to the Open University Literary Trust. Mary C. Rodgers. 50p. (Orig.). 1993. pap. 7.00 (0-89848-273-9) Open Univ Am.

Access Mechanisms & Data Structure Support in Data Base Management Systems. Robert M. Curtice. LC 76-372283. (QED Monograph Series. Data Base Management: No. 1). 66p. reprint ed. pap. 25.00 (0-8357-5035-3, 2032005) Bks Demand.

Access Method Systems Guide. Kevin Duggan. LC 86-64009. (Illus.). 176p. 1987. spiral bd. 25.00 (0-9613848-1-6) MARIS.

Access Mexico: Emerging Market Handbook & Directory. R Pardo-Maurer & Judith Rodriguez. (Emerging Market Access Ser.). (Illus.). 650p. 1992. 239.00 (1-881765-00-8) Cambridge Data & Dev.

Access Nippon, 1992: How to Succeed in Japan. 4th ed. Ed. by Akira Kadokura. (Illus.). 534p. (Orig.). 1991. pap. 29.95 (1-878753-09-6) Ref Press.

Access Nippon, 1993: How to Succeed in Japan. 5th ed. Ed. by Akira Kadokura. 424p. 1992. pap. 34.95 (1-878753-13-4) Ref Press.

Access Nippon, 1994: How to Succeed in Japan. 6th ed. Ed. by Hiroko Asami. 400p. (Orig.). 1994. pap. 34.95 (1-878753-42-8) Ref Press.

*Access, Ownership & Resource Sharing. Ed. by Sul H. Lee. LC 95-4208. 1995. write for info. (1-56024-727-4) Haworth Pr.

An Asterisk (*) at the beginning of an entry indicates that the title is appearing in BIP for the first time. 25

A

Access Points to the Law Library: Card Catalog Interpretation. Elizabeth W. Matthews. LC 82-80900. vi, 66p. 1982. lib. bdg. 30.00 (*0-89941-156-8*, 302290) W S Hein.

Access Policy & Procedures & the Law in U.S. Higher Education. Larry G. Simon et al. (Access to Higher Education Ser.: No. 6). 124p. 1978. pap. 6.00 (*0-89192-215-6*) Interbk Inc.

Access Power Programming. 2nd ed. Que Development Staff. 1994. Incl. diskette. pap. 49.90 (*1-56529-763-6*) Que.

ACCESS Program: Adolescent Curriculum for Communication & Effective Social Skills. Hill M. Walker et al. (Walker Social Skills Curriculum Ser.). (Orig.). 1987. student ed 9.00 (*0-89079-154-6*, 0367); student ed 39.00 (*0-89079-153-8*, 0366); 49.00 (*0-685-67559-9*) PRO-ED.

Access Programming by Example. Greg Perry. (By Example Ser.). (Illus.). 608p. (Orig.). 1993. pap. 27.95 (*1-56529-305-3*) Que.

Access Programming by Example. 2nd ed. Greg Perry. (Orig.). 1994. pap. 27.95 (*1-56529-659-1*) Que.

Access Programming for Dummies. Robert Krumm. 1994. pap. 19.95 (*1-56884-091-8*) IDG Bks.

Access Security Screening: Challenges & Solutions. Ed. by Theofolus P. Tsacoumis. LC 92-14646. (STP Ser.: Vol. 1127). (Illus.). 90p. 1992. text ed. 50.00 (*0-8031-1472-9*, 04-011270-47) ASTM.

Access Services: A Handbook. Ann C. Paietta. LC 90-53601. 220p. 1991. lib. bdg. 24.95x (*0-89950-599-6*) McFarland & Co.

Access Services: The Convergence of Reference & Technical Services. Ed. by Gillian M. McCombs. LC 91-35637. (Reference Librarian Ser.). 190p. 1991. lib. bdg. 39.95 (*1-56024-170-5*) Haworth Pr.

Access Services in Libraries: New Solutions for Collection Management. Frwd. by Gregg Sapp. LC 92-34445. (Collection Management Ser.: Vol. 17, Nos. 1/2). (Illus.). 240p. 1993. 49.95 (*1-56024-417-8*) Haworth Pr.

Access Surgery. G. Kootstra & P. J. Jorning. 350p. 1982. text ed. 60.00 (*0-85200-453-2*) Kluwer Ac.

***Access the Best of the Internet.** 1995. pap. write for info. (*0-7821-1677-9*) Sybex.

***Access the Internet!** Peal. 1995. 19.99 (*0-7821-1721-X*) Sybex.

Access the Internet. David Peal. LC 94-66406. 240p. 1994. pap. 19.99 (*0-7821-1529-2*) Sybex.

***Access the Internet.** David Peal. 1995. 19.99 (*0-7821-1744-9*) Sybex.

***Access Theater.** Rod Lathim & Cynthia Wisehart. 1996. write for info. (*0-614-05603-9*) WRS Group.

Access Through Innovation: New Colleges for New Students. James W. Hall. (ACE-Oryx Series on Higher Education). 208p. 1991. 29.95 (*0-02-897177-9*, ACE-Oryx) Oryx Pr.

Access to Agreement: A Consumer Study of Mediation in Family Disputes. Gwynn Davies & Marion Roberts. 256p. 1988. 85.00 (*0-335-09840-1*, Open Univ Pr); pap. 32.00 (*0-335-09830-4*, Open Univ Pr) Taylor & Francis.

***Access to Air Travel for People with Reduced Mobility.** 132p. (Orig.). 1995. pap. 30.00x (*92-821-1200-4*) OECD.

Access to Art: A Museum Directory for Blind & Visually Impaired People. Ed. by Irma Shore & Beatrice Jacinto. LC 88-34393. 144p. 1989. audio 19.95 (*0-89128-161-4*) Am Foun Blind.

Access to Art: A Museum Directory for Blind & Visually Impaired People. braille ed. Ed. by Irma Shore & Beatrice Jacinto. LC 88-34393. 144p. 1989. 19.95 (*0-89128-160-6*) Am Foun Blind.

Access to Art: A Museum Directory for Blind & Visually Impaired People. large type ed. Ed. by Irma Shore & Beatrice Jacinto. LC 88-34393. 144p. 1989. 19.95 (*0-89128-156-8*) Am Foun Blind.

Access to Basic Infrastructure by the Urban Poor. Aurelio Menendez. (Economic Development Institute Policy Seminar Report Ser.: No. 28). 96p. 1991. 7.95 (*0-8213-1815-2*, 11815) World Bank.

Access to Cardiac Kidney Transplantation. Joel D. Kallich et al. LC 93-8688. 1993. write for info. (*0-8330-1408-0*, MR-202-HCFA) Rand Corp.

Access to Communication: Developing the Basics of Communication with People with Severe Learning Difficulties Through Intensive Interaction. Melanie Nind & David Hewett. 244p. 1994. pap. 34.00 (*1-85346-206-3*, Pub. by D Fulton UK) Taylor & Francis.

Access to Education for the Disabled: A Guide to Compliance with Section 504 of the Rehabilitation Act of 1973. Salome M. Heyward. LC 92-54090. 336p. 1992. pap. 38.50 (*0-89950-732-8*) McFarland & Co.

Access to Electronic Journals in Libraries: Policy Issues & Case Studies. Dennis Benamati & Dave Tyckoson. (Supplement to Computers in Libraries Ser.: No. 65). 200p. 1994. pap. 39.50 (*0-88736-874-3*) Learned Info.

Access to Energy: Two Thousand & After. Melvin A. Conant. LC 79-15015. (Essays for the Third Century Ser.). 144p. 1979. 16.00 (*0-8131-0401-7*) U Pr of Ky.

Access to Government Documents: Papers Presented to a Session of the American Historical Association, December, 1972. Ed. by Forrest C. Pogue. 53p. 1974. 17.95 (*0-89126-008-0*) MA-AH Pub.

Access to Health. Rebecca J. Donatelle et al. (Illus.). 608p. (C). 1988. pap. text ed. write for info. (*0-13-001025-1*) P-H.

Access to Health. 3rd ed. Rebecca J. Donatelle & Lorraine G. Davis. LC 93-31892. 1993. pap. text ed. write for info. (*0-13-078551-2*) P-H.

Access to Health, Brief. 2nd ed. Rebecca J. Donatelle & Lorraine G. Davis. 464p. 1993. pap. text ed. write for info. (*0-13-007782-8*) P-H.

Access to Health Care. Center for Health Economics Research Staff. (Key Indicators for Policy Ser.). (Illus.). 96p. (Orig.). 1993. pap. write for info. (*0-942054-09-1*) R W Johnson Found.

Access to Health Care: States Respond to Growing Crisis. (Illus.). 94p. (Orig.). (C). 1993. pap. text ed. 35.00 (*1-56806-327-X*) Diane Pub.

Access to Health Care in America. Institute of Medicine, Committee on Monitoring Access to Health Care Staff. 300p. (C). 1993. text ed. 34.95 (*0-309-04742-0*) Natl Acad Pr.

Access to Higher Education: Two Perspectives. A Comparative Study of the Federal Republic of Germany & the United States of America. James A. Perkins. 84p. 1978. pap. 2.50 (*0-89192-219-9*) Interbk Inc.

Access to Information: Materials, Technologies, & Services for Print-Impaired Readers. Tom McNulty & Dawn M. Suvino. 161p. 1993. pap. 28.00 (*0-8389-7641-7*) ALA.

Access to Inner Worlds: The Story of Brad Absetz. Colin Wilson. LC 87-26875. 192p. 1990. pap. 8.95 (*0-89087-501-4*) Celestial Arts.

***Access to Juvenile Records for the Purchase of Firearms.** 54p. (Orig.). (C). 1994. pap. text ed. 35.00x (*0-7881-1063-2*) Diane Pub.

Access to Legal Education & the Legal Professions. Ed. by R. Dhavan et al. 1989. U.K. pap. 76.00 (*0-406-70065-6*) Butterworth Legal Pubs.

Access to Library Resources Through Technology & Preservation: Proceedings of the 1988 U.S. - U.S.S.R. Seminar, July 5-8, 1988, Washington, DC. Ed. by Robert P. Doyle. LC 89-6618. (Illus.). 165p. 1994. reprint ed. pap. 47.10 (*0-7837-5949-5*, 2045748) Bks Demand.

Access to Literature: A Chair for My Mother. LinguiSystems Staff. 1993. student ed 16.95 (*1-55999-363-4*) LinguiSystems.

Access to Literature: A Wrinkle in Time. LinguiSystems Staff. 1993. student ed 16.95 (*1-55999-384-7*) LinguiSystems.

Access to Literature: Julie of the Wolves. LinguiSystems Staff. 1993. student ed 16.95 (*1-55999-381-2*) LinguiSystems.

Access to Literature: Maniac Magee. LinguiSystems Staff. 1993. student ed 16.95 (*1-55999-387-1*) LinguiSystems.

Access to Literature: Mr. Popper's Penguins. LinguiSystems Staff. 1993. student ed 16.95 (*1-55999-369-3*) LinguiSystems.

Access to Literature: Shiloh. LinguiSystems Staff. 1993. student ed 16.95 (*1-55999-378-2*) LinguiSystems.

Access to Literature: Summer of the Swans. LinguiSystems Staff. 1993. student ed 16.95 (*1-55999-375-8*) LinguiSystems.

Access to Literature: The Boxcar Children. LinguiSystems Staff. 1993. student ed 16.95 (*1-55999-360-X*) LinguiSystems.

Access to Literature: The Mixed-Up Files of Mrs. Basil E. Frankweiler. LinguiSystems Staff. 1993. student ed 16.95 (*1-55999-372-3*) LinguiSystems.

Access to Literature: The Mouse & the Motorcycle. LinguiSystems Staff. 1993. student ed 16.95 (*1-55999-366-9*) LinguiSystems.

Access to Mass Transit for Blind & Visually Impaired Travelers. Ed. by Mark M. Uslan et al. LC 89-18332. 192p. 1990. 25.95 (*0-89128-166-5*) Am Foun Blind.

Access to Media: A Guide to Integrating & Computerizing Catalogs. Sheila S. Intner. LC 84-1035. 301p. (Orig.). 1985. pap. 39.95 (*0-918212-88-X*) Neal-Schuman.

Access to Official Information in New Zealand. Ian Eagles. 420p. 1992. 125.00 (*0-19-558185-7*) OUP.

Access to Prenatal Care: Key to Preventing Low Birthweight. American Nurses Association Staff. (Illus.). 93p. (Orig.). (C). 1987. pap. 5.00 (*1-55810-067-9*, MCH-16) Am Nurses Pub.

***Access to Primary Health Care for Children with HIV: A Guide for Pediatricians, Family Physicians & Nurse Practitioners.** Robert H. Parrott & Mary Rathlev. 1993. pap. 9.95 (*0-9634295-1-5*) Childs Hosp.

Access to Reading & Language Arts - 2 Grade Set. LinguiSystems Staff. 1993. student ed 77.70 (*1-55999-269-7*) LinguiSystems.

Access to Reading & Language Arts - 2 Literary Concepts: Student Book. LinguiSystems Staff. 1993. student ed 14.95 (*1-55999-273-5*) LinguiSystems.

Access to Reading & Language Arts - 2 Study Skills: Study Book. LinguiSystems Staff. 1993. student ed 14.95 (*1-55999-307-3*) LinguiSystems.

Access to Reading & Language Arts - 2 Vocabulary: Student Book. LinguiSystems Staff. 1993. student ed 14.95 (*1-55999-267-0*) LinguiSystems.

Access to Reading & Language Arts - 2 Word Analysis: Student Book. LinguiSystems Staff. 1993. student ed 14.95 (*1-55999-270-0*) LinguiSystems.

Access to Reading & Language Arts - 2 Writing: Teachers Guide & Student Book. LinguiSystems Staff. 1993. student ed 14.95 (*1-55999-310-3*) LinguiSystems.

Access to Reading & Language Arts - 3 Grade Set. LinguiSystems Staff. 1993. student ed 77.70 (*1-55999-277-8*) LinguiSystems.

Access to Reading & Language Arts - 3 Literary Concepts: Teachers Guide & Student Book. LinguiSystems Staff. 1993. student ed 14.95 (*1-55999-322-7*) LinguiSystems.

Access to Reading & Language Arts - 3 Reading & Listening Comprehension: Teachers Guide & Student Book. LinguiSystems Staff. 1993. student ed 14.95 (*1-55999-303-0*) LinguiSystems.

Access to Reading & Language Arts - 3 Study Skills: Teachers Guide & Student Book. LinguiSystems Staff. 1993. student ed 14.95 (*1-55999-275-1*) LinguiSystems.

Access to Reading & Language Arts - 3 Vocabulary: Teachers Guide & Student Book. LinguiSystems Staff. 1993. student ed 14.95 (*1-55999-316-2*) LinguiSystems.

Access to Reading & Language Arts - 3 Word Analysis: Teachers Guide & Student Book. LinguiSystems Staff. 1993. student ed 14.95 (*1-55999-319-7*) LinguiSystems.

Access to Reading & Language Arts - 3 Writing: Teachers Guide & Student Book. LinguiSystems Staff. 1993. student ed 14.95 (*1-55999-278-6*) LinguiSystems.

Access to Reading & Language Arts - 4 Grade Set. LinguiSystems Staff. 1993. student ed 77.70 (*1-55999-283-2*) LinguiSystems.

Access to Reading & Language Arts - 4 Literary Concepts: Teachers Guide & Student Book. LinguiSystems Staff. 1993. student ed 14.95 (*1-55999-287-5*) LinguiSystems.

Access to Reading & Language Arts - 4 Reading & Listening Comprehension: Teachers Guide & Student Book. LinguiSystems Staff. 1993. student ed 14.95 (*1-55999-296-4*) LinguiSystems.

Access to Reading & Language Arts - 4 Study Skills: Teachers Guide & Student Book. LinguiSystems Staff. 1993. student ed 14.95 (*1-55999-290-5*) LinguiSystems.

Access to Reading & Language Arts - 4 Vocabulary: Teachers Guide & Student Book. LinguiSystems Staff. 1993. student ed 14.95 (*1-55999-281-6*) LinguiSystems.

Access to Reading & Language Arts - 4 Word Analysis: Teachers Guide & Student Book. LinguiSystems Staff. 1993. student ed 14.95 (*1-55999-284-0*) LinguiSystems.

Access to Reading & Language Arts - 4 Writing: Teachers Guide & Student Book. LinguiSystems Staff. 1993. student ed 14.95 (*1-55999-293-X*) LinguiSystems.

Access to Reading & Language Arts - 5 Grade Set. LinguiSystems Staff. 1993. student ed 77.70 (*1-55999-326-X*) LinguiSystems.

Access to Reading & Language Arts - 5 Literary Concepts: Teachers Guide & Student Book. LinguiSystems Staff. 1993. student ed 14.95 (*1-55999-330-8*) LinguiSystems.

Access to Reading & Language Arts - 5 Reading & Listening Comprehension: Teachers Guide & Student Book. LinguiSystems Staff. 1993. student ed 14.95 (*1-55999-339-1*) LinguiSystems.

Access to Reading & Language Arts - 5 Study Skills: Teachers Guide & Student Book. LinguiSystems Staff. 1993. student ed 14.95 (*1-55999-333-2*) LinguiSystems.

Access to Reading & Language Arts - 5 Vocabulary: Teachers Guide & Student Book. LinguiSystems Staff. 1993. student ed 14.95 (*1-55999-299-9*) LinguiSystems.

Access to Reading & Language Arts - 5 Word Analysis: Teachers Guide & Student Book. LinguiSystems Staff. 1993. student ed 14.95 (*1-55999-327-8*) LinguiSystems.

Access to Reading & Language Arts - 5 Writing: Teachers Guide & Student Book. LinguiSystems Staff. 1993. student ed 14.95 (*1-55999-336-7*) LinguiSystems.

Access to Reading & Language Arts - 6 Grade Set. LinguiSystems Staff. 1993. student ed 77.70 (*1-55999-344-8*) LinguiSystems.

Access to Reading & Language Arts - 6 Literary Concepts: Teachers Guide & Student Book. LinguiSystems Staff. 1993. student ed 14.95 (*1-55999-348-0*) LinguiSystems.

Access to Reading & Language Arts - 6 Reading & Listening Comprehension: Teachers Guide & Student Book. LinguiSystems Staff. 1993. student ed 14.95 (*1-55999-357-X*) LinguiSystems.

Access to Reading & Language Arts - 6 Study Skills: Teachers Guide & Student Book. LinguiSystems Staff. 1993. student ed 14.95 (*1-55999-351-0*) LinguiSystems.

Access to Reading & Language Arts - 6 Vocabulary: Teachers Guide & Student Book. LinguiSystems Staff. 1993. student ed 14.95 (*1-55999-342-1*) LinguiSystems.

Access to Reading & Language Arts - 6 Word Analysis: Teachers Guide & Student Book. LinguiSystems Staff. 1993. student ed 14.95 (*1-55999-345-6*) LinguiSystems.

Access to Reading & Language Arts - 6 Writing: Teachers Guide & Student Book. LinguiSystems Staff. 1993. student ed 14.95 (*1-55999-354-5*) LinguiSystems.

Access to Resources in the Eighties: Proceedings of the First International Conference of Slavic Librarians & Information Specialists. Ed. by Marianna T. Choldin. LC 82-60216. (Russica Bibliography Ser.: No. 2). (Orig.). 1982. pap. 12.00 (*0-686-97604-5*) Russica Pubs.

Access to Scholarly Information: Issues & Strategies. Ed. by Sul H. Lee. LC 85-60595. (Library Management Ser.: No. 9). 1985. 30.00 (*0-87650-189-7*) Pierian.

Access to Taxis. OECD Staff. 224p. (Orig.). 1992. pap. 27.00 (*92-821-1166-0*) OECD.

Access to the American Mind: The Damaging Impact of the New Mass Media. Martin H. Seiden. 280p. 1990. 18.95 (*0-944007-71-6*) Sure Sellers.

Access to the Past: Museum Programs & Handicapped Visitors. Alice P. Kenney. LC 80-24106. 131p. 1980. pap. 6.95 (*0-910050-45-7*) AASLH.

Access to the World: A Travel Guide for the Handicapped. Louise Weiss. LC 82-12108. 239p. reprint ed. pap. 68.20 (*0-7837-5336-5*, 2045076) Bks Demand.

Access to U.S. Government Information: Guide to Executive & Legislative Authors & Authority. Comp. by Jerold Zwirn. LC 89-27373. (Bibliographies & Indexes in Law & Political Science Ser.: No. 12). 176p. 1989. text ed. 49.95 (*0-313-26851-7*, ZGA, Quorum Bks) Greenwood.

Access to Western Esotericism. Antoine Faivre. LC 94-2064. (SUNY Series in Western Esoteric Traditions). 369p. 1994. 59.50 (*0-7914-2177-5*); pap. 19.95 (*0-7914-2178-3*) State U NY Pr.

Access to Writing: A Process Approach. Betty J. Anderson. 240p. (C). 1991. spiral bd. 27.95 (*0-8403-7084-9*) Kendall-Hunt.

***Access Travel U. S. A. A Directory for People with Disabilities.** Candida H. Cremona. 176p. (Orig.). 1994. pap. text ed. 19.95 (*0-9642279-0-8*) Creat Hosp Concepts.

Access vs. Assets: A Comprehensive Guide to Resource Sharing for Academic Librarians. Barbara B. Higginbotham & Sally Bowdoin. LC 93-16601. (Frontiers of Access Ser.: No. 1). 470p. 1993. lib. bdg. 60.00 (*0-8389-0607-9*) ALA.

Access Workshop: Tools & Techniques for Rapid Application Developments. Robert Krumm. 1993. pap. 44.95 (*1-56686-040-7*) Brady Compu Bks.

Access Yosemite National Park: An Atlas & Guide for Visitors with Disabilities. (Illus.). 32p. (Orig.). 1988. pap. 7.95 (*0-944187-02-1*) N Cartographic.

***Access Your Brain's Joy Center: A Natural Alternative to Using Alcohol, Nicotine, Drugs or Overeating to Cope with Life's Pressures & Challenges.** Pete A. Sanders, Jr. 90p. 1994. digital audio 29.95 (*0-9641911-0-5*) Free Soul.

Access, 1991-92: A Resource Guide to Legal Automation. 148p. 1994. pap. 34.95 (*0-89707-951-5*, 511-0327) Amer Bar Assn.

Access 2 Developers Guide. 2nd ed. Roger Jennings. 1994. disk, pap. 44.95 (*0-672-30453-8*) Sams.

Access 2 for Dummies. Scott Palmer. 1994. pap. 19.95 (*1-56884-090-X*) IDG Bks.

***Access 2 for Windows Quickstart Corporate Edition.** Ricardo Birmele. 1994. pap. 29.99 (*1-56529-729-6*) Que.

Access 2 Unleashed. Edward Jones. 1994. disk, pap. 34.95 (*0-672-30494-5*) Sams.

***Access 2.0 Advanced.** 100p. 1994. 29.95 (*1-57533-031-8*) Comput Confidence.

Access 2.0 from the Ground Up. Martin Matthews. 1994. pap. 19.95 (*1-55958-511-0*) Prima Pub.

***Access 2.0 Introduction.** 150p. 1994. 29.95 (*1-57533-030-X*) Comput Confidence.

Access 2.0 VisiRef. Que Development Group Staff. 1994. pap. 12.99 (*1-56529-863-2*) Que.

AccessAsia: A Guide to Specialists & Current Research. 1, 992th ed. Ed. by Diane Lu & Michael Zung. 180p. 1992. 75.00 (*0-9631625-1-9*) Nat Bur Asian.

AccessAsia: A Guide to Specialists & Current Research. 2nd ed. Ed. by Kimbrely Wilhelm. 422p. 1993. pap. 75.00 (*0-9631625-2-7*) Nat Bur Asian.

AccessAsia: A Guide to Specialists & Current Research 1994. 3rd ed. Ed. by William B. Abnett et al. 462p. 1994. pap. 75.00 (*0-9631625-3-5*) Nat Bur Asian.

***AccessAsia: A Guide to Specialists & Current Research (1995)** 4th ed. Ed. by Richard J. Ellings et al. 566p. 1995. 75.00 (*0-9631625-4-3*) Nat Bur Asian.

Accessibility & Utilization: Geographical Perspectives on Health Care Delivery. Alunt Joseph & David Phillips. 220p. (C). 1984. pap. 90.00 (*0-06-318276-9*, Pub. by P Chapman Pub UK) St Mut.

Accessibility Checklist: An Evaluation System for Buildings & Outdoor Settings. 2nd ed. Ed. by Susan Goltsman et al. (Illus.). 168p. (Orig.). 1993. pap. 29.95 (*0-944661-26-2*) MIG Comns.

Accessibility Checklist: An Evaluation System for Buildings & Outdoor Settings. 2nd ed. Ed. by Susan M. Goltsman et al. 52p. (Orig.). 1993. pap. 20.00 (*0-944661-27-0*) MIG Comns.

Accessibility of Resources for Educators of Adults. A. Charters. (MS Ser.: No. 9). 1977. 3.50 (*0-686-63885-9*, MSS 9) Syracuse U Cont Ed.

Accessible Art: A Layman's Look at Seattle's Public Art. Ed. by Corinne Murray. LC 90-82681. (Illus.). (Orig.). 1990. pap. text ed. 12.95 (*0-9626878-0-4*, 72920) At Your Fingertips.

Accessible Building Design: A Disabled Users Guide to an Accessible Building. (Illus.). 52p. (Orig.). (C). 1993. pap. text ed. 24.95 (*1-56806-537-X*) Diane Pub.

***Accessible Building Product Guide.** John P. S. Salmen et al. 1995. pap. text ed. 59.95 (*0-471-10947-9*) Wiley.

Accessible Categories: The Foundations of Categorical Model Theory. Makkai & Pare. LC 89-18125. (CONM Ser.: Vol. 104). 176p. 1991. reprint ed. pap. 34.00 (*0-8218-5111-X*, CONM-104) Am Math.

Accessible Design Handbook: The ADA Troubleshooter Guide & Workbook. Cash-Callagan & Company, Inc. Staff. 100p. 1991. ring bd. 129.95 (*0-9633145-0-5*) Cash-Callahan.

Accessible Gardening for People with Physical Disabilities: A Guide to Methods, Tools, & Plants. Janeen R. Adil. (Illus.). 324p. (C). 1994. pap. 16.95 (*0-933149-56-5*) Woodbine House.

Accessible Home of Your Own. Ed. by Raymond C. Cheever & Betty Garee. LC 90-80563. (Illus.). 52p. reprint ed. pap. 4.50 (*0-915708-29-9*) Cheever Pub.

Accessible Housing Design File. Barrier Free Environments, Inc. Staff. (Illus.). 320p. 1991. pap. 49.95 (*0-442-00775-2*) Van Nos Reinhold.

Accessible Landscapes: Designing for Inclusion. Philip S. Evans & Brian Donnelly. 64p. 1993. pap. text ed. 14.95 (*0-9641244-0-8*) SF St Univ.

Accessible Museum: Model Programs of Accessibility for Persons with Disabilities & Older People. LC 92-29831. 1992. write for info. (*0-931201-16-0*) Am Assn Mus.

***Accessible School: Universal Design for Educational Environments.** Laurel B. Bar & Judith D. Galluzzo. (Illus.). 224p. (Orig.). 1995. pap. text ed. 39.95 (*0-944661-20-3*) MIG Comns.

Accessing Antiquity: The Computerization of Classical Studies. Ed. by Jon Solomon. 185p. 1993. 35.00 (*0-8165-1390-2*) U of Ariz Pr.

Accessing C: Tips from the Experts. 2nd ed. Ed. by Strawberry Software Staff. (Illus.). 320p. 1989. pap. 39.95 (*0-442-20662-3*) Van Nos Reinhold.

***Accessing Community Resources Vol. 13: Discharge Planning.** Ed. by William H. Burke. (HDI Professional Series on Head Injury Rehabilitation). 67p. Date not set. pap. 8.00 (*1-882855-20-5*) HDI Pubs.

An Asterisk (*) at the beginning of an entry indicates that the title is appearing in BIP for the first time.

Accessing English Literary Periodicals: A Guide to the Microfilm Collection with Title, Subject, Editor, & Reel Number Indexes. Ed. by Grace Puravs et al. LC 81-16124. 1981. 30.00 (0-8357-0231-6) Univ Microfilms.

***Accessing Federal Adoption Subsidies after Legalization.** Tim O'Hanlon. (Orig.). 1995. pap. text ed. 14.95 (0-87868-569-3) Child Welfare.

Accessing Human Services: International Perspectives. Ed. by Risha W. Levinson & Karen S. Haynes. LC 84-16012. (Social Science Delivery Systems Ser.: No. 7). 320p. reprint ed. pap. 91.20 (0-8357-4820-0, 2037757) Bks Demand.

Accessing Noun-Phrase Antecedents. Mira Ariel. (Croom Helm Linguistic Ser.). 272p. 1990. 85.00 (0-415-00306-7, A3941) Routledge.

Accessing Private Industry Council Funding. Michael Howe. 43p. (Orig.). (C). 1987. spiral bd. 9.95 (0-942071-07-7) M Wright & Assocs.

***Accessing the Economic Bulletin Board.** 1995. lib. bdg. 255.95 (0-8490-7430-4) Gordon Pr.

Accessing the Global Network: Weaving Technology & Trade in the Pacific. Ed. by Dan J. Wedemeyer & Mark D. Lofstrom. (PTC '91 Proceedings Ser.). 915p. 1991. pap. text ed. 45.00 (1-880672-02-2) Pac Telecom.

Accession of Henry II in England: Royal Government Restored, 1149-1159. Emilie Amt. LC 93-27942. 320p. 1993. text ed. 63.00 (0-85115-348-8, Boydell Pr) Boydell & Brewer.

Accessions to Repositories & Reports Added to the National Register of Archives. 71p. 1992. pap. 30.00 (0-11-440229-9, HM02299, Pub. by HMSO UK) UNIPUB.

Accessions to Repositories & Reports Added to the National Register of Archives 1989. 71p. 1990. pap. 16.00 (0-11-440241-8, HM2418) UNIPUB.

Accessions to Repositories & Reports Added to the National Register of Archives 1990. 71p. 1991. pap. 18.00 (0-11-440228-0, HM2280) UNIPUB.

Accessories. (Looking Good Ser.). (Illus.). (J). (gr. 5 up). 1987. lib. bdg. 15.94 (0-86625-281-9) Rourke Corp.

Accessories after the Fact: The Warren Commission, the Authorities & the Report. Sylvia Meagher. 1992. pap. 15.00 (0-679-74315-4, Vin) Random.

Accessories for the Light Microscope, Vol. 16. Robert B. McLaughlin. LC 74-79374. (Illus.). 1975. 30.00 (0-904962-00-8) Microscope Pubns.

Accessory Apartments in Single-Family Housing. Martin Gellen. LC 85-149. 219p. 1985. text ed. 3.00x (0-88285-105-5) Ctr Urban Pol Res.

Accessory Cells in HIV & Other Retroviral Infections. Ed. by P. Racz et al. (Illus.). viii, 212p. 1991. 158.50 (3-8055-5323-4) S Karger.

Accessory Mascots: The Automotive Accents of Yesteryear. 1910-1940. Dan Smith. (Illus.). 136p. 1990. pap. 19.95 (0-9623873-0-4) Auto Quarterly.

Accident. Carol Carrick. LC 76-3532. (Illus.). 32p. (J). (ps-3). 1981. pap. 5.95 (0-89919-041-3, Clarion Bks) HM.

Accident. Diane Hoh. (J). 1991. pap. 3.25 (0-590-44330-5) Scholastic Inc.

Accident. David Plante. 160p. 1991. 18.95 (0-395-56925-7) HM.

Accident. Danielle Steel. 1994. 23.95 (0-385-30602-4); 200.00 (0-385-31215-6); 28.95 (0-385-31116-8) Delacorte.

***Accident.** Danielle Steel. 1995. mass mkt. 6.99 (0-440-21754-7) Dell.

Accident. Todd Strasser. (J). (gr. k up). 1990. pap. 3.50 (0-440-20635-9, LFL) Dell.

Accident. Elie Wiesel. Tr. by Anne Borchardt. 120p. 1991. pap. 8.00 (0-374-52311-8, Noonday) FS&G.

Accident. Nicholas Mosley. LC 85-72479. 195p. 1985. reprint ed. 20.00 (0-916583-10-4); reprint ed. pap. 9.95 (0-916583-11-2) Dalkey Arch.

Accident: A Day's News. Christa Wolf. Tr. by Heike Schwarzbauer & Rick Takvarian. 122p. 1989. 15.95 (0-374-10046-2) FS&G.

Accident: A Day's News. Christa Wolf. Tr. by Heike Schwarzbauer & Rick Takvorian. 1991. pap. 7.95 (0-374-52254-5, Noonday) FS&G.

Accident & Emergency: Diagnosis & Management. 2nd ed. Anthony F. Brown. 408p. 1992. 39.95 (0-7506-0858-7) Buttrwrth-Heinemann.

***Accident & Emergency Data & Drug Guide.** Morris & Kinder. 1995. pap. write for info. (0-7506-2035-8, Focal) Buttrwrth-Heinemann.

Accident & Emergency Handbook. 5th ed. David H. Wilson & Michael Flowers. LC 85-4169. 256p. 1985. pap. text ed. 39.95 (0-407-00328-2) Buttrwrth-Heinemann.

Accident & Emergency Management. Louis Theodore et al. 1989. text ed. 99.95 (0-471-61911-6) Wiley.

Accident & Emergency Management: Problems & Solutions. Ed. by Ryan Dupont et al. 187p. (Orig.). (C). 1991. student ed, pap. 49.50 (1-56081-094-7) VCH Pubs.

Accident & Emergency Medicine. David G. Ferguson & David I. Fodden. LC 92-49913. (Colour Guide Ser.). 1993. 19.95 (0-443-04512-7) Churchill.

Accident & Emergency Medicine. G. S. Laing. 225p. 1988. pap. 29.50 (0-387-19508-4) Spr-Verlag.

Accident & Emergency Nursing. 2nd ed. Mike Walsh. 312p. 1990. pap. text ed. 45.00 (0-7506-0630-4) Buttrwrth-Heinemann.

Accident Facts, 1984. National Safety Council Staff. 97p. pap. 27.70 (0-8357-5037-X, 2025010) Bks Demand.

Accident Facts, 1985. National Safety Council Staff. 98p. pap. 28.00 (0-8357-5036-1, 2026711) Bks Demand.

Accident Facts, 1987. National Safety Council Staff. (Illus.). 109p. reprint ed. pap. 31.10 (0-8357-5038-8, 2033113) Bks Demand.

Accident Facts, 1988. National Safety Council Staff. (Illus.). 107p. reprint ed. pap. 30.50 (0-8357-6875-9, 2035573) Bks Demand.

Accident Facts, 1989. National Safety Council Staff. (Illus.). 107p. reprint ed. pap. 30.50 (0-7837-1098-4, 2041630) Bks Demand.

Accident Facts, 1990. National Safety Council Staff. 112p. reprint ed. pap. 32.00 (0-7837-6436-7, 2046436) Bks Demand.

Accident Facts, 1991. National Safety Council Staff. LC 91-60648. 112p. reprint ed. pap. 32.00 (0-7837-6437-5, 2046437) Bks Demand.

***Accident Facts, 1992.** National Safety Council Staff. LC 91-60648. (Illus.). 112p. Date not set. reprint ed. pap. 32.00 (0-7837-9215-8, 2049965) Bks Demand.

Accident Facts, 1993. LC 91-60648. 112p. 1993. pap. 19.95 (0-87912-172-6, 02173-0000) Natl Safety Coun.

Accident Investigation: A New Approach. 44p. 1983. 13.95 (0-87912-037-1, 15646-0000) Natl Safety Coun.

Accident Investigation for Supervisors. Ted Ferry. 55p. 1988. pap. 20.00 (0-939874-80-6) ASSE.

Accident Investigator's Handbook. F. Stephenson. 1992. text ed. write for info. (0-442-01284-5) Van Nos Reinhold.

Accident Kids. Boyer. LC 73-93019. (Safety Ser.). (Illus.). 32p. (J). (gr. 2-5). 1974. lib. bdg. 9.95 (0-87783-119-X) Oddo.

Accident Kids. deluxe ed. Boyer. LC 73-93019. (Safety Ser.). (Illus.). 32p. (J). (gr. 2-5). 1974. pap. 3.94 (0-87783-120-3) Oddo.

Accident of Birth: A Chronicle of My Times, 1926-1990. Robert F. McKellar. LC 93-60913. (Illus.). 508p. 1994. pap. 11.95 (1-55523-654-5) Winston-Derek.

Accident Prevention: A Worker's Education Manual. 2nd rev. ed. ix, 175p. 1986. 14.00 (92-2-103392-9) Intl Labour Office.

Accident Prevention & Injury Control: Medical & Behavioral Subject Analysis & Research Index with Bibliography. Peter J. Kasnevitch. LC 83-71645. 147p. 1984. 39.50 (0-88164-030-1); pap. 34.50 (0-88164-031-X) ABBE Pubs Assn.

Accident Prevention & Investigation. Ramsey. 1995. text ed. 69.95 (0-442-01839-8) Van Nos Reinhold.

***Accident Prevention & OSHA Compliance.** Patrick A. Michaud. LC 94-44946. 320p. 1995. 65.00 (1-56670-150-3, L1150) Lewis Pubs.

Accident Prevention for Hotels, Motels, & Restaurants. Robert L. Kohr. LC 90-49783. 340p. 1991. text ed. 49.95 (0-442-23955-6) Van Nos Reinhold.

Accident Prevention Manual for Business & Industry, Vol. I: Administrations & Programs. 10th ed. LC 91-66437. (Occupational Safety & Health Ser.). 563p. 1992. 99.95 (0-87912-155-6, 12144-000) Natl Safety Coun.

Accident Prevention Manual for Business & Industry, Vol. II: Engineering & Technology. 10th ed. LC 91-66437. (Occupational Safety & Health Ser.). 792p. 1992. 99.95 (0-87912-156-4, 12146-000) Natl Safety Coun.

Accident Prevention Manual for Industrial Operations, 2 vols. National Safety Council Staff. Ed. by Frank E. McElroy. LC 80-81376. pap. write for info. (0-8357-5043-4, 2032042) Bks Demand.

Accident Prevention Manual for Industrial Operations. 7th ed. National Safety Council Staff. LC 74-79025. 1533p. reprint ed. pap. 180.00 (0-8357-5039-6, 2020315) Bks Demand.

Accident Prevention Manual for Industrial Operations. National Safety Council Staff. 544p. reprint ed. pap. 155.10 (0-8357-5040-X, 2029208) Bks Demand.

Accident Prevention Manual for Industrial Operations, Vol. 1, Administration & Programs. National Safety Council Staff. Ed. by Frank E. McElroy. LC 80-81376. 768p. pap. 180.00 (0-8357-5044-2) Bks Demand.

Accident Prevention Manual for Industrial Operations, Vol. 2, Engineering & Technology. National Safety Council Staff. Ed. by Frank E. McElroy. LC 80-81376. pap. 160.00 (0-685-73966-X) Bks Demand.

Accident Prevention Manual for Industrial Operations, Vols. 1 & 2. 9th ed. National Safety Council Staff. LC 86-63578. (Occupational Safety & Health Ser.). (Illus.). 541p. reprint ed. Vol. 1, Administration & Programs, 541p. pap. 154.20 (0-7837-3071-3, 2042632) Bks Demand.

Accident Prevention Manual for Industrial Operations, Vols. 1 & 2. National Safety Council Staff. LC 86-63578. (Occupational Safety & Health Ser.). (Illus.). 512p. reprint ed. Vol. 2, Engineering & Technology, 512p. pap. 146.00 (0-7837-3072-1, 2042632) Bks Demand.

Accident Prevention Manual for Training Programs. Ed. by Merle E. Strong. LC 74-83068. 500p. reprint ed. pap. 142.50 (0-8357-5045-0, 2011585) Bks Demand.

Accident Prevention Manual, Vol. 3: Environmental Management. 600p. 1994. 99.95 (0-87912-170-X, 12156-0000) Natl Safety Coun.

Accident Prone. large type ed. John Penn. (Mystery Ser.). 1990. 21.95 (0-7089-2159-0) Ulverscroft.

Accident Prone Man. Franz K. Baskett. LC 93-18469. 80p. (Orig.). 1994. pap. 12.95 (0-914061-40-2) Orchises Pr.

Accident Proneness: Research Occurrence Causation & Prevention of Road Accidents. L. Shaw & H. Sichel. LC 73-105137. (International Series of Monographs in Experimental Social Psychology: Vol. 11). 1971. 200.00 (0-08-006916-9, Pub. by Pergamon Repr UK) Franklin.

***Accident Reconstruction.** James C. Collins. (Illus.). 308p. 1979. pap. 29.95 (0-398-06069-X) C C Thomas.

Accident Reconstruction. fac. ed. James C. Collins. (Illus.). 308p. 1979. 49.95x (0-398-03907-0) C C Thomas.

Accident Reconstruction: Automobiles, Tractor-Semitrailers, Motorcycles & Pedestrians. 1987. 75.00 (0-89883-454-6, P193) Soc Auto Engineers.

Accident Reconstruction: Human, Vehicle, & Environmental Factors. 1990. 69.00 (1-56091-023-2, SP814) Soc Auto Engineers.

Accident Reconstruction: Technology & Animation. 1991. 69.00 (1-56091-117-4, SP-853) Soc Auto Engineers.

Accident Reconstruction: Technology & Animation II. 136p. 1992. pap. 49.00 (1-56091-224-3, SP-907) Soc Auto Engineers.

Accident Reconstruction: Technology & Animation III, Twenty-seven Papers. 1993. 82.00 (1-56091-331-2, SP-946) Soc Auto Engineers.

***Accident Reconstruction: Technology & Animation V-1995 International Congress & Exposition Meeting.** 1995. pap. 86.00 (1-56091-633-8, SP1083) Soc Auto Engineers.

Accident Reconstruction Technologies: Pedestrians & Motorcycles in Automotive Collisions. 1990. 99.00 (1-56091-010-0, PT35) Soc Auto Engineers.

Accident Reconstruction: Technology & Animation IV: SAE International Congress & Exposition 1994, 29 papers. (Special Publications). 1994. pap. 86.00 (1-56091-482-3, SP-1030) Soc Auto Engineers.

Accident Sequence Modeling: Human Actions, System Response , Intelligent Decision Support. Ed. by G. E. Apostolakis et al. 480p. 1988. 147.75 (1-85166-210-3) Elsevier.

Accident That Changed My Life. Randy Gaboriault. Ed. by Ruth Barenbaum & Barry Lane. (Opening Doors Ser.: No. 1). (Illus.). 32p. (Orig.). 1989. pap. 3.95 (1-877829-05-6) Opening Doors.

Accidental. Linda Cooney. (Sunset High Ser.: No. 8). 1986. pap. 2.50 (0-449-13123-8) Fawcett.

Accidental Archaeologist: Memoirs of Jesse D. Jennings. Frwd. by Jesse D. Jennings & C. Melvin Aikens. LC 94-9300. (Illus.). 240p. 1994. text ed. 29.95 (0-87480-452-3) U of Utah Pr.

***Accidental Bond: The Power of Sibling Relationships.** Susan Merrell. LC 94-48375. 1995. 23.00 (0-8129-2211-5, Times Bks) Random.

***Accidental Bride.** Jackie Merritt. (Desire Ser.). 1995. pap. 3.25 (0-373-05914-0, 1-05914-6) Silhouette.

Accidental Bride. Sheila Rabe. 224p. 1994. mass mkt. 3.99 (0-8217-4597-2) Zebra.

Accidental Bridegroom. Ann Major. 1994. mass mkt. 2.99 (0-373-05889-6, 1-05889-0) Harlequin Bks.

Accidental Century. Harrington. 1985. pap. 12.95 (0-02-548200-9) Macmillan.

Accidental Dad. Anne Peters. (Silhouette Romance Ser.). 1993. pap. 2.75 (0-373-08946-5, 5-08946-1) Silhouette.

Accidental Editor. Gloria Campbell & Molly Gerhard. (Illus.). 82p. (Orig.). Date not set. pap. text ed. write for info. (0-9631679-1-X) GR Comm Col Edu TC.

Accidental Empires: How the Boys of Silicon Valley Make Their Millions, Battle Foreign Competition & Still Can't Get a Date. Robert X. Cringely. 320p. 1992. 19.18 (0-201-57032-7) Addison-Wesley.

Accidental Empires: How the Boys of Silicon Valley Make Their Millions, Battle Foreign Competition & Still Can't Get a Date. Robert X. Cringely. 1993. pap. 12.00 (0-88730-621-7) Harper Busn.

Accidental Explorers: Surprises & Side Trips in the History of Discovery. Rebecca Stefoff. (Extraordinary Explorers Ser.). (Illus.). 152p. (J). 1993. lib. bdg. 22.00 (0-19-507685-0) OUP.

Accidental Family. Fyodor Dostoyevsky. Tr. by Richard Freeborn. (World's Classics Ser.). 630p. 1994. pap. 10.95 (0-19-282836-3) OUP.

Accidental Grace: Poems by Luke. Joseph A. Brown. Ed. by Charles H. Rowell. (Callaloo Poetry Ser.). 58p. 1986. pap. 7.50 (0-912759-08-9) U Pr of Va.

Accidental Grandeur: A Defense of Narrative Vagueness in Ancient Epic Literature. John R. Harris. (Classical Studies). 207p. (C). 1989. text ed. 34.50 (0-8204-0739-9) P Lang Pubs.

Accidental Hostess: Florida's Guide to Coping with Constant Company. 2nd ed. Moni Arnowitz et al. (Illus.). 156p. (Orig.). 1991. pap. 9.95 (0-9627414-1-8) Accidental Hostess.

Accidental Injury: Biomechanics & Prevention. Ed. by Alan Nahum & John Melvin. LC 92-2381. 1993. 110.00 (0-387-97881-X) Spr-Verlag.

***Accidental Journey: A Cambridge Internee's Memoir of World War II.** Mark Lynton. 352p. 1995. 23.95 (0-87951-577-5) Overlook Pr.

Accidental Man. Iris Murdoch. 448p. 1988. pap. 11.00 (0-14-003611-3, Penguin Bks) Viking Penguin.

Accidental Missionaries: How a Vacation Turned into a Vocation. Wallace Ohrt. LC 90-48587. 190p. (Orig.). 1990. pap. 9.99 (0-8308-1741-7, 1741) InterVarsity.

Accidental or Incendiary. fac. ed. Richard D. Fitch & Edward A. Porter. (Illus.). 224p. 1975. 37.95x (0-398-00582-6) C C Thomas.

Accidental Princess. Margaret St. George. (American Romance Ser.). 1994. mass mkt. 3.50 (0-373-16518-8, 1-16518-2) Harlequin Bks.

Accidental Proletariat: Workers, Politics, & Crisis in Gorbachev's Russia. Walter D. Connor. (Illus.). 382p. 1991. text ed. 45.00 (0-691-07787-8) Princeton U Pr.

Accidental Releases of Air Toxics: Prevention, Control & Mitigation. Daniel S. Davis et al. LC 89-8858. (Pollution Technology Review Ser.: No. 170). (Illus.). 649p. 1990. 86.00 (0-8155-1210-4) Noyes.

Accidental Romance. Elizabeth Mansfield. 208p. 1994. pap. text ed. 3.99 (0-515-11481-2) Jove Pubns.

Accidental Shootings: Many Deaths & Injuries Caused by Firearms Could Be Prevented. (Illus.). 52p. (Orig.). (C). 1993. pap. text ed. 25.00 (1-56806-553-1) Diane Pub.

Accidental Tourist. Anne Tyler. LC 85-40161. 368p. 1985. 25.00 (0-394-54689-X) Knopf.

Accidental Tourist. Anne Tyler. 1986. mass mkt. 6.99 (0-425-09291-7) Berkley Pub.

***Accidental Witch.** Anne Mazer. LC 94-44284. (Illus.). 128p. (J). (gr. 3-7). 1995. 13.95 (0-7868-0088-7); lib. bdg. 13.89 (0-7868-2073-X) Hyprn Child.

Accidental Zucchini: An Unexpected Alphabet. Max Grover. LC 93-2488. (J). 1993. 13.95 (0-15-277695-8, Browndeer Pr) HarBrace.

Accidentally on Purpose. Michael York. Ed. by Julie Rubenstein. (Illus.). 528p. 1993. reprint ed. mass mkt. 5.99 (0-671-79591-0) PB.

***Accidentally Yours...** Gerda Feldmann. (Illus.). 340p. (Orig.). 1995. pap. write for info. (0-9646408-0-5) G Feldmann.

Accidents: 1950-1962. (Epidemiological & Vital Statistics Report Ser: Vol. 18, No. 3). (ENG & FRE.). 1965. pap. 2.80 (0-686-09165-5) World Health.

Accidents & Emergencies. Ed. by Charles B. Clayman. LC 91-45392. (American Medical Association Home Medical Library). (Illus.). 144p. 1992. 16.98 (0-89577-423-2) RD Assn.

Accidents & Emergencies. 6th rev. ed. Ed. by R. H. Hardy & John Bache. LC 93-47418. (Oxford Medical Publications). (Illus.). 512p. (C). 1994. 29.95 (0-19-262434-2) OUP.

Accidents & Emergencies in Children. R. J. Morton. (Oxford Handbooks in Emergency Medicine Ser.). 1992. pap. 32.50 (0-19-261929-2) OUP.

Accidents & Emergencies in Children. R. J. Morton & B. M. Phillips. (Oxford Handbooks in Emergency Medicine Ser.: No. 2). (Illus.). 208p. 1992. 55.00 (0-19-262222-6) OUP.

Accidents & Hard Work: Stories from My Life. Andrew Tromblay. (Stories We Tell Ser.). 51p. 1993. pap. 4.00 (1-884983-04-9) Homegrown Bks.

Accidents, Compensation & the Law. P. S. Atiyah. (C). 1987. 190.00 (0-685-33806-1, Pub. by Witherby & Co UK) St Mut.

Accidents, Compensation & the Law. V. P. Srivastava. (C). 1973. 45.00 (0-685-39767-X) St Mut.

Accidents, Compensation & the Law. V. P. Srivastava. 577p. 1978. 130.00 (0-317-57730-1) St Mut.

Accidents in Children & Young People. (Statistics Quarterly Ser.: Vol. 39, No. 3). 1986. pap. 12.60 (0-318-23395-9) World Health.

Accidents in North American Mountaineering, 1989. Ed. by John E. Williamson. 95p. 1989. pap. 7.00 (0-930410-40-8) Amer Alpine Club.

Accidents in North American Mountaineering 1990. Ed. by John E. Williamson. 80p. 1990. pap. 7.00 (0-685-60644-9) Amer Alpine Club.

Accidents in North American Mountaineering 1991. Ed. by John E. Williamson. 76p. 1991. pap. 7.00 (0-930410-47-5) Amer Alpine Club.

Accidents in North American Mountaineering 1992. Ed. by John E. Williamson. 80p. 1992. pap. 7.00 (0-930410-52-1) Amer Alpine Club.

Accidents in North American Mountaineering, 1993. Ed. by Jed Williamson. 88p. 1993. pap. 7.50 (0-930410-56-4) Amer Alpine Club.

Accidents in Occupations & Industry: Medical Subject Analysis & Research Index with Bibliography. Mary B. Schneply. LC 83-71646. 152p. 1983. 39.50 (0-88164-012-3); pap. 34.50 (0-88164-013-1) ABBE Pubs Assn.

Accidents in the Year 2000. Ed. by R. M. Labre. (C). 1989. lib. bdg. 45.00 (0-685-44900-9); pap. text ed. 60.00 (0-7923-0475-6) Kluwer Ac.

Accidents of All Types & Forms: Medical Analysis Index with Research Bibliography. American Health Research Institute Staff. LC 85-47574. 150p. 1987. 39.50 (0-88164-322-X); pap. 34.50 (0-88164-323-8) ABBE Pubs Assn.

Accidents of Influence: Writing As a Woman & a Jew in America. Norma Rosen. LC 91-29320. (Modern Jewish Literature & Culture Ser.). 210p. (C). 1992. 57.50 (0-7914-1091-9); pap. 18.95 (0-7914-1092-7) State U NY Pr.

Accidents Will Happen: A Small Town Guide to Planning for Hazardous Materials Response. National Association of Towns & Townships Staff. (Illus.). 64p. (Orig.). 1990. pap. 10.00 (0-925532-03-7) Natl Assn Town & Twps.

Accion Democratica: Evolution of a Modern Political Party in Venezuela. John D. Martz. 1965. 69.50x (0-691-07500-X) Princeton U Pr.

***Accion Democratica: Evolution of a Modern Political Party in Venezuela.** John D. Martz. LC 65-17147. Date not set. reprint ed. pap. 130.30 (0-7837-9383-9, 2060127) Bks Demand.

Accius - Lexicon Accianum. Ed. by Antonius De Rosalia. (Alpha-Omega, Reihe A Ser.: Bd. LIII). xxiv, 204p. 1982. write for info. (3-487-07261-0, Pub. by Georg Olms GW) Lubrecht & Cramer.

Acclimatization: A Sensory & Conceptual Approach to Ecological Involvement. Steve VanMatre. LC 89-39497. 132p. 1972. 10.95 (0-87603-022-3) Am Camping.

***Accomack County: Virginia Publick Claims.** Janice L. Abercrombie & Richard Slatten. (Virginia Publick Claims Ser.). ix, 6p. 1991. pap. 5.00x (0-8095-8501-4) Borgo Pr.

Accomack County: Virginia Publick Claims. Janice L. Abercrombie & Richard Slatten. (Virginia Publick Claims Ser.). ix, 6p. (C). 1991. reprint ed. lib. bdg. 15.00x (0-8095-8300-3) Borgo Pr.

Accomack County, Virginia, Census, 1850. Patricia Scherzinger. iv, 128p. (Orig.). 1988. pap. text ed. 16.50 (1-55613-096-1) Heritage Bk.

Accomack County, Virginia Certificates & Rights 1663-1709, & Tithables 1663-1695. Stratton Nottingham. vi, 230p. (Orig.). 1993. pap. 17.00 (1-55613-741-9) Heritage Bk.

Accomack County, Virginia Eighteen Sixty Census. E. Crowson & Susan Hite. 225p. (Orig.). 1987. pap. 25.00 (1-55613-081-3) Heritage Bk.

A

An Asterisk (*) at the beginning of an entry indicates that the title is appearing in BIP for the first time.

Accomack (Virginia) Land Causes, 1728-1825. Stratton Nottingham. 178p. 1990. reprint ed. pap. 17.50 (*1-55613-280-8*) Heritage Bk.

Accommodating an HIV Infected Client. (Mart Ser.: Bk. 4). 32p. 1994. 5.00 (*1-885565-04-6*) Mart.

Accommodating Disability. Marsha Saxton. 1987. pap. 2.00 (*0-913937-23-1*) Rational Isl.

Accommodating Protest: Working Women, the New Veiling, & Change in Cairo. Arlene MacLeod. 240p. (C). 1993. text ed. 32.00 (*0-231-07280-5*); pap. 14.00 (*0-231-07281-3*) Col U Pr.

Accommodation: The Politics of Race in an American City. Jim Schutze. 200p. 1987. pap. 14.95 (*0-317-56606-7*, Citadel Pr) Carol Pub Group.

Accommodation & Accessibility: Implementing the ADA on a Local Level. 20p. 1992. 12.95 (*0-89128-240-8*) Am Foun Blind.

Accommodation & Cleaning Services, Vol. 2. Ed. by Stanley Thornes. (C). 1989. 80.00 (*0-09-151001-5*, Pub. by S Thornes Pubs UK) St Mut.

Accommodation & Cleaning Services, Vol. 1: Operations, Vol. 1. David Allen. (Illus.). 328p. (Orig.). 1983. pap. 37.50 (*0-7487-0290-3*, Pub. by Stanley Thornes UK) Trans-Atl Phila.

Accommodation & Cleaning Services, Vol. 2: Management. David Allen. (Illus.). 128p. (Orig.). 1983. pap. 29.50 (*0-7487-0331-4*, Pub. by Stanley Thornes UK) Trans-Atl Phila.

Accommodation & Refraction of the Eye. F. C. Donders. LC 78-27045. (Classics in Ophthalmology Ser.). 656p. 1979. reprint ed. lib. bdg. 49.50 (*0-88275-839-X*) Krieger.

Accommodation & Resistance: The French Left, Indochina & the Cold War, 1944-1954. Edward Rice-Maximin. LC 86-4624. (Contributions to the Study of World History Ser.: No. 2). 186p. 1986. text ed. 45.00 (*0-313-25355-2*, RMX/, Greenwood Pr) Greenwood.

Accommodation & Social Cohesion in the Urban Environment. P. Burton et al. 113p. 1990. pap. 17.00 (*92-826-0020-3*, SY-56-89-287-EN-C) UNIPUB.

Accommodation Management. Christine Jones & J. Valerie Jowett. (Illus.). 320p. 1993. pap. 34.95 (*0-7134-6937-4*, Pub. by Batsford UK) Trafalgar.

Accommodation of Trucks on the Highway: Safety in Design. Ed. by Bob L. Smith & John M. Mason, Jr. (Symposium Proceedings Ser.). 200p. 1988. 22.00 (*0-87262-644-X*) Am Soc Civil Eng.

Accommodation of Utility Plant Within the Rights-of-Way of Urban Streets & Highways. (ASCE Manual & Report on Engineering Practice Ser.: No. 14). 214p. 1974. pap. 18.00 (*0-87262-207-X*) Am Soc Civil Eng.

Accommodation of Utility Plant Within the Rights-of-Way of Urban Streets & Highways: Manual of Improved Practice. Kendell E. Bert et al. 102p. (Orig.). 1974. pap. text ed. 25.00 (*0-917084-24-1*) Am Public Works.

Accommodation of Utility Plant Within the Rights-of-Way of Urban Streets & Highways: State-of-the-Art. (Special Report Ser.: No. 44). (Illus.). 160p. 1974. 18.00 (*0-917084-06-3*) Am Public Works.

Accommodation Process in Industry. Melvin J. Vincent. LC 30-22559. vi, 112p. 1982. reprint ed. lib. bdg. 25.00x (*0-89370-700-7*) Borgo Pr.

Accommodation Register. (C). 1987. 45.00 (*0-317-89878-7*, Pub. by Birmingham Midland Soc UK) St Mut.

Accommodation Without Assimilation: Sikh Immigrants in an American High School. Margaret Gibson. LC 87-47861. (Anthropology of Contemporary Issues Ser.). 272p. 1988. 39.95 (*0-8014-2122-5*); pap. 14.95 (*0-8014-9503-2*) Cornell U Pr.

Accomodation. Schutze. 1987. 14.95 (*0-8065-1046-3*, Citadel Pr) Carol Pub Group.

Accomodation Operations see Front Office Operations

Accompaniment Guitar: A Beginner's Guide to Song Accompaniment for Individual or Classroom Use. Jack Buckingham. (Illus.). 80p. (J). 1979. pap. 7.00 (*0-8258-0003-X*, 05065) Fischer Inc NY.

Accompaniment on Theorbo & Harpsichord: Denis Delair's Treatise of 1690. Denis Delair. Tr. by Charlotte Mattax. LC 90-49917. (Publications of the Early Music Institute). (Illus.). 176p. (Orig.). 1991. pap. 14.95 (*0-253-28592-5*) Ind U Pr.

***Accompaniments to Murder.** Barbara R. Priest. 145p. (Orig.). Date not set. pap. 7.95 (*0-7610-0360-6*) NW Pub.

Accompaninge the Players: Essays Celebrating Thomas Middleton, 1581-1980. Ed. by Kenneth Friedenreich. LC 81-69121. (Studies in the Renaissance: No. 8). 1983. 39.50 (*0-404-62278-X*) AMS Pr.

Accompanying Alice. large type ed. Terese Ramin. (Silhouette Special Edition Ser.). 1993. 17.95 (*0-373-58837-2*, Silhouette Lrg Print); pap. 16.95 (*0-373-58929-8*, Silhouette Lrg Print) Chivers N Amer.

Accompanying Basics. Joyce Grill. (Illus.). 56p. 1987. pap. text ed. 5.95 (*0-8497-9316-5*, WP154) Kjos.

Accompanying Teacher's Aid: A Handbook of Tests, Suggestions, Answers for South Carolina Living (3rd grade Social Studies text. 1987. pap. 5.00 (*0-915114-06-2*) Lewis-Sloan.

Accompanying the Violin. Katherine D. Johnson. LC 84-81153. (Illus.). 80p. 1984. pap. text ed. 9.95 (*0-8497-5160-8*, WP85); audio 8.95 (*0-685-08849-9*, CWP85) Kjos.

Accomplir l'Homme: Lettres Inedites 1926-1952. Pierre Teilhard De Chardin. 1992. 15.95 (*0-8288-6080-7*, F128030) Fr & Eur.

Accomplished Senator in 1568 A.D. Laurence G. Gozliski. LC 92-53234. 1992. write for info. (*1-881284-05-0*) Am Inst Polish.

Accomplishing the Accomplished: The Vedas As a Source of Valid Knowledge in Sankara. Anantanand Rambachan. LC 91-10279. (Society for Asian & Comparative Philosophy Monographs: No. 10). 182p. (C). 1991. pap. text ed. 15.00 (*0-8248-1358-8*) UH Pr.

Accomplishment Ratio: A Treatment of the Inherited Determinants of Disparity in School Product. Raymond H. Franzen. LC 71-176784. (Columbia University. Teachers College. Contributions to Education Ser.: No. 125). reprint ed. 37.50 (*0-404-55125-4*) AMS Pr.

Accomplishments & Impacts of Reservoirs. Ed. by Gordon G. Green & Earl E. Eiker. 239p. 1983. pap. 27.00 (*0-87262-382-3*) Am Soc Civil Eng.

Accompt Rekenynge & Confession of the Faith of Huldrik Zwinglius. Ulrich Zwingli. Tr. by Thomas Cotsforde. LC 79-84148. (English Experience Ser.: No. 964). Orig. Title: Swinglische Bekenntuis. 156p. 1979. reprint ed. lib. bdg. 25.00 (*90-221-0964-X*) Walter J Johnson.

Accord & the Australian Labour Movement. Gwyn Singleton. 1990. pap. 24.95 (*0-522-84421-9*) Intl Spec Bk.

***Accordian Breathing & Dance.** Ruth L. Schwartz. (Pitt Poetry Ser.). 80p. (C). 1995. 24.95x (*0-8229-3898-7*); pap. 10.95 (*0-8229-5571-7*) U of Pittsburgh Pr.

According to Custom. Eamon Kelly. 1986. pap. 7.95 (*0-85342-739-9*) Dufour.

According to Doyle. Doyle Brunson. (Illus.). (Orig.). 1984. pap. text ed. 6.95 (*0-89746-003-0*) Gambling Times.

According to Hakluyt: Tales of Adventure & Exploration. Delbert Young. 197p. 1973. 5.95 (*0-7720-0587-7*, Pub. by Stoddart Pubng CN) Genl Dist Srvs.

According to Her Contours. Nancy Boutilier. LC 92-27428. 233p. (Orig.). (C). 1992. 25.00 (*0-87685-885-X*); pap. 12.50 (*0-87685-884-1*) Black Sparrow.

According to Her Contours, signed ed. deluxe ed. Nancy Boutilier. LC 92-27428. 233p. (Orig.). (C). 1992. 30.00 (*0-87685-886-8*) Black Sparrow.

According to Hoyle. Albert H. Morehead. 1976. 21.95 (*0-8488-0348-5*) Amereon Ltd.

According to Hoyle. rev. ed. Ed. by Richard L. Frey. 1985. mass mkt. 5.99 (*0-449-21112-6*, Crest) Fawcett.

***According to Jake & the Kid.** W. O. Mitchell. 1995. pap. 9.95 (*0-7710-6071-8*, Pub. by McClelland & Stewart CN) Firefly Bks Ltd.

According to Luke. Frank L. Cox. 1941. pap. 2.75 (*0-88027-030-6*) Firm Foun Pub.

According to Mark. Penelope Lively. 1989. pap. 10.00 (*0-06-097199-1*, PL) HarpC.

According to Paul: Studies in the Theology of the Apostle. Joseph A. Fitzmyer. LC 93-20453. 176p. 1993. pap. 12.95 (*0-8091-3390-3*) Paulist Pr.

***According to Promise.** Gordon J. Keddie. 1992. pap. 11.99 (*0-85234-295-0*, Pub. by Evangel Pr UK) Presby & Reformed.

According to Promise. C. H. Spurgeon. 1979. pap. 3.95 (*1-56186-340-8*) Pilgrim Pubns.

According to St. John. William Babula. 1989. 14.95 (*0-8184-0491-4*) Carol Pub Group.

According to the Evidence. Henry Cecil. 160p. (Orig.). 1988. pap. 5.95 (*0-89733-295-4*) Academy Chi Pubs.

According to the Pattern. Grace L. Hill. 1976. reprint ed. lib. bdg. 21.95 (*0-89190-016-0*, Rivercity Pr) Amereon Ltd.

According to the Pattern. Grace L. Hill. 1990. reprint ed. lib. bdg. 19.95 (*0-89968-518-8*) Buccaneer Bks.

According to the Power That Worketh in Me. Josephine Gross. 1991. 12.95 (*0-533-09347-3*) Vantage.

***According to the Word of God: Personal Prayers & Confessions.** Barbara J. Beeler. (Illus.). 100p. (Orig.). 1994. pap. text ed. 10.00 (*0-9643586-0-3*) REED IT.

According to White Eyes. Willis C. Brenton. LC 86-17414. 1988. pap. 13.95 (*0-87949-256-2*) Ashley Bks.

Accordion Car-Tunes. Carl Herman. 16p. 1993. 3.95 (*1-877673-16-1*) Cottonwood Pr.

***Accordion Man: The Legendary Dick Contino.** Bob Bove. 176p. 1994. write for info. (*0-942407-29-6*) Father & Son.

Accordion Music from Around the World. Frank Zucco. 1993. 5.95 (*1-56222-562-6*, 94834) Mel Bay.

Accordion Music from the British Isles. Frank Zucco. 1993. 5.95 (*1-56222-320-8*, 94684) Mel Bay.

Accosting the Golden Spire. Iris W. Collett. LC 88-82327. 1988. pap. text ed. 9.95 (*0-913878-43-X*) T Horton & Dghts.

Account: Alvar Nunez Cabeza de Vaca's Relacion. Ed. by Jose Fernandez & Martin Favata. Tr. by Martin Favata. LC 92-45113. 180p. (Orig.). 1993. pap. 10.00 (*1-55885-060-0*) Arte Publico.

Account & History of the Tazewell Family. Littleton W. Tazewell. Ed. by Anne E. Tazewell Bradford. LC 91-77877. (Illus.). 136p. (Orig.). 1993. pap. 15.00 (*1-878515-97-7*) W S Dawson.

Account Book for the Borough of Swansea, Wales 1640-1660: A Study in Local Administration During the Civil War & Interregnum. Michael Price. LC 90-5645. (Welsh Studies: Vol. 1). (Illus.). 340p. 1990. lib. bdg. 99.95 (*0-88946-480-4*) E Mellen.

Account Book of a Kentish Estate, 1616-1704. Ed. by E. C. Lodge. (British Academy, London, Records of the Social & Economic History of England & Wales Ser.: Vol. 6). 1972. reprint ed. pap. 75.00 (*0-8115-1246-0*) Periodicals Srv.

Account Book of Conrad Weiser: Berks County, Pennsylvania, 1746-1760. Ed. by Larry M. Neff & Frederick S. Weiser. LC 81-84666. (Sources & Documents Ser.: No. 6). (Illus.). 1981. 15.00 (*0-911122-43-5*) Penn German Soc.

Account Book of Francis Jackson: Treasurer of the Vigilance Committee of Boston. 83p. 1974. 3.00 (*0-317-33890-0*) Bostonian Soc.

Account Books of Benjamin Mildmay, Earl Fitzwater. A. C. Edwards. 224p. 1984. 30.00 (*0-317-43665-1*, Pub. by Regency Press) St Mut.

Account Books of Jonathan Swift. Paul V. Thompson & Dorothy J. Thompson. LC 83-1298. 496p. 1984. 70.00 (*0-87413-240-1*) U Delaware Pr.

Account Clerk. Jack Rudman. (Career Examination Ser.: C-2). 1994. pap. 19.95 (*0-8373-0002-9*) Nat Learn.

Account Clerk-Stenographer. Jack Rudman. (Career Examination Ser.: C-3220). 1994. pap. 19.95 (*0-8373-3220-6*) Nat Learn.

Account Clerk-Typist. Jack Rudman. (Career Examination Ser.: C-3221). 1994. pap. 19.95 (*0-8373-3221-4*) Nat Learn.

Account for Your Own Success: Everything You Need to Manage Your Own Business & Personal Finances. Dan Meyer. (Illus.). 176p. 1993. pap. 16.95 (*0-932150-04-7*) MCS.

Account of Afro-American in Southeast Kansas, 1884-1984. Marguerite M. Marshall et al. (Illus.). 106p. 1986. pap. 12.95 (*0-89745-091-4*) Sunflower U Pr.

Account of an Embassy to the Court of the Teshoo Lama in Tibet. Samuel Turner. (C). 1991. reprint ed. 38.00 (*81-206-0687-6*, Pub. by Asian Educ Servs II) S Asia.

Account of Arnold's Campaign Against Quebec. John J. Henry. LC 67-29019. (Eyewitness Accounts of the American Revolution Ser., No. 1). 1971. reprint ed. 16.95 (*0-405-01113-X*) Ayer.

Account of Fungus Exsiccati Containing Material from the Americas. J. A. Stevenson. 1971. 120.00 (*3-7682-5436-4*) Lubrecht & Cramer.

Account of Jamaica, & Its Inhabitants. John Stewart. LC 70-157377. (Black Heritage Library Collection). 1977. 22.95 (*0-8369-8815-9*) Ayer.

***Account of Koonawur in the Himalaya.** Alexander Gerard. Ed. by George Lloyd. (C). 1993. reprint ed. 38.00x (*81-7387-000-4*, Pub. by Indus Pub II) S Asia.

Account of Louisiana. Thomas Jefferson. 40p. 1985. pap. 3.95 (*0-87770-378-7*) Ye Galleon.

Account of Pedestrian Journeys in the Russian Possessions of America, 1842-1844. Lavrentii A. Zagoskin. (West Coast Studies: No. 5). 256p. Date not set. lib. bdg. write for info. (*0-89370-834-8*); pap. write for info. (*0-89370-934-4*) Borgo Pr.

Account of Sir Isaac Newton's Philosophical Discoveries. Ed. by Colin Maclaurin. (Anglistica & Americana Ser.: No. 87). (Illus.). 440p. 1971. reprint ed. 83.20 (*3-487-04002-6*, Pub. by Georg Olms GW) Lubrecht & Cramer.

Account of Some of the Descendants of Capt. Thomas Brattle. E. D. Harris. (Illus.). 90p. 1990. reprint ed. lib. bdg. 26.00 (*0-8328-1444-X*); reprint ed. pap. 18.00 (*0-8328-1445-8*) Higginson Bk Co.

Account of Some of the Descendants of John Russell, Who Came to Boston, 1635; Together with Some Sketches of the Allied Families of Wadsworth, Tuttle, & Beresford. G. W. Russell. Ed. by E. S. Welles. (Illus.). 318p. 1989. reprint ed. lib. bdg. 57.50 (*0-8328-1040-1*); reprint ed. pap. 47.50 (*0-8328-1041-X*) Higginson Bk Co.

Account of Some of the Early Settlers of West Dunstable, Monson & Hollis, New Hampshire. Charles S. Spaulding. 251p. 1988. reprint ed. lib. bdg. 37.50 (*0-8328-0080-5*, NH0027) Higginson Bk Co.

***Account of Sufi Mysticism: With a Glossary of Their Symbolic Terms.** Ed. by H. Wiberforce-Clarke. 1994. pap. 5.95 (*1-55818-300-0*, Near Eastern) Holmes Pub.

Account of the Black Charaibs in the Island of St. Vincents. William Young. 128p. 1971. reprint ed. 30.00 (*0-7146-1955-8*, Pub. by F Cass Pubs UK) Intl Spec Bk.

Account of the British Settlement of Aden in Arabia. F. M. Hunter. 232p. 1968. reprint ed. 35.00 (*0-7146-1986-8*, BHA-01986, Pub. by F Cass Pubs UK) Intl Spec Bk.

Account of the Descendants of John Bridge, Cambridge, 1632. William F. Bridge. (Illus.). 122p. 1988. reprint ed. lib. bdg. 32.00 (*0-8328-0316-2*); reprint ed. pap. 22.00 (*0-8328-0317-0*) Higginson Bk Co.

Account of the Destruction of the Jesuits. Jean D'Alembert. 1973. 59.95 (*0-87968-575-1*) Gordon Pr.

Account of the Discoveries of the Portuguese in the Interior of Angola & Mozambique. Thomas E. Bowdich. LC 74-15013. reprint ed. 52.50 (*0-404-12008-3*) AMS Pr.

Account of the District of Purnea in 1809-1810. 60.00 (*0-8364-1922-7*, Pub. by Usha II) S Asia.

Account of the District of Shahbad in 1812-1813. Francis Buchanan. 1986. reprint ed. 44.00 (*0-8364-1923-5*, Pub. by Usha II) S Asia.

Account of the Districts of Bihar & Patna in 1811-1812, 2 vols. Francis Buchanan. 1986. reprint ed. 75.00 (*0-8364-1924-3*, Pub. by Usha II) S Asia.

***Account of the East-Indies 1688-1723 Vol. 2: Being the Observations & Remarks of Captain Alexander Hamilton, 2 vols., Set.** Alexander Hamilton. (C). 1995. reprint ed. 68.00x (*81-206-1012-1*, Pub. by Asian Educ Servs II) S Asia.

Account of the Empire of Morocco & the Districts of Suse & Tafilelt. James G. Jackson. (Illus.). 328p. 1968. reprint ed. 47.50 (*0-7146-1820-9*, Pub. by F Cass Pubs UK) Intl Spec Bk.

Account of the English Dramatick Poets. Gerard Langbaine. (Anglistica & Americana Ser.: No. 9). 556p. 1968. reprint ed. 89.70 (*0-685-66488-0*, 05102000, Pub. by Georg Olms GW) Lubrecht & Cramer.

Account of the English Dramatick Poets. Gerard Langbaine. No. 9. 556p. 1968. reprint ed. write for info. (*0-318-71924-X*, Pub. by Georg Olms GW) Lubrecht & Cramer.

Account of the English Dramatick Poets, 1691, 2 vols., Set. Gerard Langbaine. LC 92-22686. (Augustan Reprints Ser.: No. 5 (1971)). 1992. 75.00 (*0-404-70105-1*) AMS Pr.

Account of the European Settlements in America, 2 Vols. in 1. Edmund E. Burke. LC 77-141082. (Research Library of Colonial Americana). 1972. reprint ed. 58.95 (*0-405-03277-3*) Ayer.

Account of the European Settlements in America, 6 pts. in 2 vols., 1. Edmund Burke. reprint ed. write for info. (*0-404-01238-8*) AMS Pr.

Account of the European Settlements in America, 6 pts. in 2 vols., 2. Edmund Burke. reprint ed. write for info. (*0-404-01239-6*) AMS Pr.

Account of the European Settlements in America, 6 pts. in 2 vols., Set. Edmund Burke. reprint ed. 30.00 (*0-404-01237-X*) AMS Pr.

Account of the First Discovery, & Natural History of Florida: A Facsimile Reproduction of the 1763 Edition with an Introduction & Index by Robert L. Gold. William Roberts. LC 76-1971. 189p. reprint ed. pap. 53.90 (*0-7837-0598-0*, 2040946) Bks Demand.

Account of the Foxglove & Its Medical Uses 1785-1985. J. K. Aronson. (Illus.). 350p. 1986. 45.00 (*0-19-261501-7*) OUP.

Account of the Genus Sedum As Found in Cultivation. R. L. Praeger. (Illus.). 1967. pap. 27.60 (*3-7682-0446-4*) Lubrecht & Cramer.

Account of the George-Hewitt Mayoralty Campaign in the Municipal Election of 1886. Louis F. Post. LC 75-341. (Radical Tradition in America Ser.). 202p. 1975. reprint ed. 19.25 (*0-88355-244-2*) Hyperion Conn.

Account of the Gold Coast of Africa. Henry Meredith. (Illus.). 264p. 1967. 35.00 (*0-7146-1039-9*, Pub. by F Cass Pubs UK) Intl Spec Bk.

Account of the Growth of Deism in England. William Stephens. LC 92-22970. (Augustan Reprints Ser.: No. 261 (1990)). reprint ed. 12.00 (*0-404-70261-9*) AMS Pr.

Account of the Kingdom of Nepal. Kirkpatrick. (Illus.). 408p. 1986. reprint ed. 26.00 (*0-8364-1750-X*, Pub. by Manohar II) S Asia.

Account of the Life & Character of Christopher Ludwick: Baker-General of the Army of the U. S. During the Revolutionary War. Benjamin Rush. 1972. reprint ed. 19.50 (*0-8422-8133-9*) Irvington.

Account of the Life & Writings of Hugh Blair. John Hill. LC 78-67524. (Scottish Enlightenment Ser.). reprint ed. 27.50 (*0-404-17213-X*) AMS Pr.

Account of the Life & Writings of John Home, Esq. Henry MacKenzie. LC 78-67532. reprint ed. 27.50 (*0-404-17196-6*) AMS Pr.

Account of the Liverpool & Manchester Railway. Henry Booth. (Illus.). 104p. 1969. reprint ed. 30.00 (*0-7146-1433-5*, Pub. by F Cass Pubs UK) Intl Spec Bk.

Account of the Mammals & Birds of the Lower Colorado Valley, with Especial Reference to the Distributional Problems Presented. Joseph Grinnell. Ed. by Keir B. Sterling. LC 77-81116. (Biologists & Their World Ser.). (Illus.). 1978. reprint ed. lib. bdg. 24.95 (*0-405-10708-0*) Ayer.

Account of the Musical Performances in Westminster Abbey. Charles Burney. LC 78-31784. (Music Reprint Ser.). 1979. reprint ed. 39.50 (*0-306-79524-8*) Da Capo.

Account of the Mutiny on HMS Bounty. large type ed. William Bligh. Ed. by Robert Bowman. 213p. 1990. 9.97 (*1-85089-405-1*, Pub. by ISIS UK) Transaction Pubs.

Account of the Natives of the Tonga Islands in the South Pacific Ocean, 2 vols., Set. William Mariner. LC 75-35204. reprint ed. 124.50 (*0-404-14290-7*) AMS Pr.

Account of the Nuttall Ornithological Club 1873 to 1919. Charles Foster Batchelder. (Memoirs Ser.: Vol. 8). (Illus.). 109p. 1937. 2.50 (*1-877973-07-6*) Nuttall Ornith.

Account of the Only Known Manuscript of Shakespeare's Plays. James O. Halliwell-Phillipps. LC 73-144627. reprint ed. 31.50 (*0-404-03049-1*) AMS Pr.

Account of the Origin & Early Prosecution of the Indian War in Oregon. Charles S. Drew. 48p. 1973. reprint ed. 7.50 (*0-87770-046-X*) Ye Galleon.

Account of the People Called Shakers. Thomas Brown. LC 77-17584. reprint ed. 49.50 (*0-404-08459-1*) AMS Pr.

Account of the Plague Which Raged at Moscow, 1771. Charles De Mertens. 1977. reprint ed. 19.00 (*0-89250-007-7*) Orient Res Partners.

Account of the Principal Lazarettos in Europe. 2nd ed. John Howard. 1973. reprint ed. write for info. (*0-318-62183-5*) Patterson Smith.

Account of the Principal Lazarettos in Europe see Prisons & Lazarettos

Account of the Principalities of Wallachia & Moldavia: With Various Political Observations Relating to Them. William Wilkinson. LC 76-135837. (Eastern Europe Collection Ser.). 1971. reprint ed. 19.95 (*0-405-02779-6*) Ayer.

Account of the Proceedings on the Trial of Susan B. Anthony on the Charge of Illegal Voting at the Presidential Election in Nov. 1872. Susan B. Anthony. LC 74-3923. (Women in America Ser.). 220p. 1976. reprint ed. 21.95 (*0-405-06072-6*) Ayer.

Account of the Red River in Louisiana. Thomas Freeman & Peter Custis. 75p. 1985. reprint ed. 14.95 (*0-87770-328-0*) Ye Galleon.

Account of the Remarkable Occurrences in the Life & Travels of Col. James Smith. James Smith. 190p. 1993. reprint ed. lib. bdg. 25.00 (*0-8328-2994-3*) Higginson Bk Co.

Account of the Sandwich Islands: The Hawaiian Journal of John B. Whitman, 1813-1815. Ed. by John D. Holt. (Illus.). 1979. 4.95 (*0-914916-49-1*) Ku Paa.

Account of the Slave Trade on the Coast of Africa. Alexander Falconbridge. LC 77-168002. reprint ed. 31.50 (*0-404-00255-2*) AMS Pr.

An Asterisk (*) at the beginning of an entry indicates that the title is appearing in BIP for the first time.

An Asterisk (*) at the beginning of an entry indicates that the title is appearing in BIP for the first time.

29

A

Accounting: An Introduction, Pt. I. Nanci Lee & Jane Kelley. 960p. (C). 1988. student ed, pap. text ed. 18.50 (*0-15-500439-5*) Dryden Pr.

Accounting: An Introduction, Pt. I. Nanci Lee & Jane Kelley. 960p. (C). 1989. student ed 7.00 (*0-15-500449-2*) Dryden Pr.

Accounting: An Introduction, Pt. II. Nanci Lee & Jane Kelley. 960p. (C). 1989. write for info. (*0-318-67134-4*) Dryden Pr.

Accounting: An Introduction, Pts. I & II. Nanci Lee & Jane Kelley. 960p. (C). 1989. trans. write for info. (*0-318-67135-2*) Dryden Pr.

Accounting: Auditing. Jack Rudman. (ACT Proficiency Examination Program Ser.: PEP-14). 1994. pap. 23.95 (*0-8373-5514-1*) Nat Learn.

Accounting: Basic Principles. 5th ed. Horace R. Brock et al. LC 84-12578. 432p. 1985. text ed. 21.95 (*0-07-008262-6*) McGraw.

Accounting: Cost Accounting & Analysis. Jack Rudman. (ACT Proficiency Examination Program Ser.: PEP-12). 1994. pap. 23.95 (*0-8373-5512-5*) Nat Learn.

Accounting: Its Principles & Problems. Henry R. Hatfield. LC 78-12596. 1971. reprint ed. text ed. 25.00 (*0-914348-02-7*) Scholars Bk.

Accounting: Principles & Applications. 6th ed. Horace R. Brock et al. (Illus.). 1168p. (C). 1990. text ed. 22.25 (*0-07-008738-5*); Study guide & working papers. student ed write for info. (*0-07-008741-5*); Comprehensive test. 0.90 (*0-07-008754-7*); Course management & solutions manual. write for info. (*0-07-008744-X*); Comprehensive tests. 0.90 (*0-07-008755-5*); Spreadsheet applications, IBM. write for info. (*0-07-839307-8*) McGraw.

Accounting: Principles & Applications. 6th ed. Horace R. Brock et al. 1990. College Course. text ed. write for info. (*0-07-008288-X*) McGraw.

Accounting: Principles & Applications, Pt. 1. 5th ed. Horace R. Brock et al. LC 84-12592. 1024p. 1986. text ed. 37.95 (*0-07-008260-X*) McGraw.

Accounting: Principles & Applications, Pt. 1. 6th ed. Horace R. Brock et al. (Illus.). 1168p. (C). 1990. text ed. 39.95 (*0-07-008736-9*) McGraw.

Accounting: Principles & Applications, Pt. 2. 5th ed. Horace R. Brock et al. 456p. 1986. pap. text ed. 20.95 (*0-07-008284-7*) McGraw.

Accounting: Principles & Applications, Pt. 2. 6th ed. Horace R. Brock et al. (Illus.). 1168p. (C). 1990. text ed. 21.25 (*0-07-008739-3*) McGraw.

Accounting: Principles & Applications, Pt. 3. 6th ed. Horace R. Brock et al. (Illus.). 1168p. (C). 1990. text ed. 21.25 (*0-07-008740-7*) McGraw.

Accounting: Systems & Procedures. 5th ed. David H. Weaver et al. 640p. 1988. pap. text ed. 23.20 (*0-07-069356-0*) McGraw.

Accounting: Systems & Procedures, 3 pts., Set. 4th ed. David H. Weaver et al. 608p. 1982. text ed. 24.60 (*0-07-069320-X*) McGraw.

Accounting: Systems & Procedures, Advanced Course. David H. Weaver et al. 1982. text ed. 23.32 (*0-07-068931-8*) McGraw.

Accounting: Systems & Procedures, Pt. 1 - Elements of Financial Records. 4th ed. David H. Weaver et al. 256p. 1982. text ed. 10.56 (*0-07-069321-8*) McGraw.

Accounting: Systems & Procedures, Pt. 2 - Accounting Subsystems. 4th ed. David H. Weaver et al. LC 81-12335. 224p. 1982. text ed. 10.56 (*0-07-069322-6*) McGraw.

Accounting: Systems & Procedures, Pt. 3 - Special Accounting Systems & Procedures. 4th ed. David H. Weaver et al. LC 81-12335. 192p. 1982. text ed. 10.56 (*0-07-069323-4*) McGraw.

Accounting: Text & Cases. 8th ed. Robert N. Anthony & James S. Reece. 1056p. (C). 1988. text ed. 69.95 (*0-256-03570-9*) Irwin.

Accounting: The Basis for Business Decisions. Walter B. Meigs & Robert F. Meigs. (Illus.). 1136p. (C). 1985. Demo disk, TSR 80. disk write for info. (*0-07-041617-6*); Demo disk, Apple II+. Apple II write for info. (*0-07-041616-8*) McGraw.

Accounting: The Basis for Business Decisions. 8th ed. Robert F. Meigs & Walter B. Meigs. 1990. 43.95 (*0-685-54081-2*); CYMA General Ledger Pkg. (3 1/2" version). pap. text ed. 18.63 (*0-07-835516-8*) McGraw.

Accounting: The Basis for Business Decisions. 9th ed. Robert F. Meigs. 1992. text ed. write for info. (*0-07-041385-1*); Acctg. worksheets, Group A problems, Chapters 1-15. write for info. (*0-07-043066-7*); Acctg. worksheets, Group B problems, Chapters 1-15. write for info. (*0-07-043068-3*) McGraw.

Accounting: The Basis for Business Decisions. 9th ed. Robert F. Meigs. 1992. Acctg. worksheets, Group A problems, Chapters 14-26. write for info. (*0-07-043067-5*); Acctg. worksheets, Group B problems, Chapters 14-26. write for info. (*0-07-043069-1*) McGraw.

Accounting: The Basis for Business Decisions. 9th ed. Robert F. Meigs. 1993. Acctg. cycle application, Facts-by-FAX. pap. text ed. write for info. (*0-07-043071-3*); Acctg. cycle application, Color Copy Co. pap. text ed. write for info. (*0-07-043072-1*) McGraw.

Accounting: The Basis for Business Decisions. 9th ed. Robert F. Meigs. 1993. Study guide. student ed, pap. text ed. write for info. (*0-07-043063-2*) McGraw.

Accounting: The Basis for Business Decisions. 9th ed. Robert F. Meigs. 1993. Acctg. cycle application, Next Dimension; Acctg. cycle application, Echo Paint Co. (0-07-043098-5). pap. text ed. write for info. (*0-07-043092-6*) McGraw.

Accounting: The Basis for Business Decisions, Seventh Edition. Visual Classroom Displays. 7th ed. Walter B. Meigs & Robert F. Meigs. 1988. pap. text ed. write for info. (*0-07-074326-6*) McGraw.

Accounting: The Language of Business. 9th ed. Roman L. Weil et al. 1994. pap. text ed. 12.95 (*0-913878-51-0*) T Horton & Dghts.

Accounting: The Lighter Side, 1989 Edition. Edward N. Coffman & Daniel L. Jensen. 1990. pap. text ed. write for info. (*0-07-011562-1*) McGraw.

Accounting: The Lighter Side, 1990 Edition. Edward N. Coffman. 1990. pap. text ed. write for info. (*0-07-011576-1*) McGraw.

Accounting: 1993 Edition. 2nd ed. Charles T. Horngren & Harrison. 1992. text ed. write for info. (*0-13-061334-7*) P-H.

Accounting - A Social Institution: A Unified Theory for the Measurement of the Profit & Non-Profit Sectors. Julius Cherny et al. LC 91-25524. 224p. 1992. text ed. 55.00 (*0-89930-690-X*, HPJ, Quorum Bks) Greenwood.

Accounting: A Library of Quantifications: (Theory Formulation Problems in Accounting) Stanley C. Salvary. LC 85-24543. (McQueen Accounting Monograph Ser.: Vol. 1). xii, 65p. (Orig.). (C). 1985. pap. 10.00 (*0-935951-00-8*) U AR Acc Dept.

Accounting Analysis of the Efficiency of Public Enterprises. Ivan Turk. (ICPE Monograph: No. 19). 92p. 1985. pap. 10.00 (*92-9038-918-4*, Pub. by Intl Ctr Pub Ent XV) Kumarian Pr.

Accounting & Accountability in Public Administration. Ed. by Richard E. Brown. (PAR Classics Ser.: No. VII). 200p. 1988. 17.95 (*0-936678-11-9*) Am Soc Pub Admin.

Accounting & Auditing Careers. (Career Examination Ser.: C-3428). 1994. pap. 23.95 (*0-8373-3428-4*) Nat Learn.

Accounting & Auditing Clerk. Jack Rudman. (Career Examination Ser.: C-5). 1994. pap. 19.95 (*0-8373-0005-3*) Nat Learn.

Accounting & Auditing Disclosure Manual. Allan B. Afterman & Rowan H. Jones. 1993. pap. 120.00 (*0-685-69593-X*, AADM) Warren Gorham & Lamont.

Accounting & Auditing Disclosure Manual. Allan B. Afterman & Rowan H. Jones. 1994. pap. 125.00 (*0-685-69594-8*) Warren Gorham & Lamont.

Accounting & Auditing for Employee Benefit Plans, No. 2254. 2nd ed. Paul Rosenfield. 624p. 1987. boxed 142.00 (*0-88712-793-2*) Warren Gorham & Lamont.

Accounting & Auditing for Employee Benefit Plans, No. 2254. 2nd suppl. ed. Paul Rosenfield. 624p. 1991. Supplemented annually, write for info. 68.00 (*0-7913-1038-8*) Warren Gorham & Lamont.

***Accounting & Auditing for Nonprofit.** 600p. (C). 1994. 295.00 (*0-7605-0650-7*) Rector Pr.

Accounting & Auditing in a New Environment: A Guide to Personal Survival Skills & Professional Growth. Albert J. Harnois. LC 94-16784. 224p. 1994. 24.95 (*0-8144-0250-X*) AMACOM.

***Accounting & Auditing of Small Businesses.** rev. ed. Joe G. Bushong. LC 94-32962. (Studies in Entrepreneurship Ser.). (Illus.). 144p. 1995. 45.00 (*0-8153-1935-5*) Garland.

Accounting & Auditing Research: A Practical Guide. 3rd ed. Thomas R. Weinrich & Alan Reinstein. (C). 1992. text ed. 25.95 (*0-538-81510-8*, AJ97CA) S-W Pub.

Accounting & Auditing Update Handbook 1989. Douglas R. Carmichael et al. 461p. reprint ed. pap. 131.40 (*0-8357-4114-1*, 2036894) Bks Demand.

***Accounting & Auditing Update Handbook, 1991.** fac. ed. Douglas R. Carmichael et al. LC 89-643780. 488p. 1990. pap. 139.10 (*0-7837-8238-1*, 2049002) Bks Demand.

Accounting & Auditing Update Service. Allan B. Afterman. 240.00 (*0-685-69592-1*, AAUS) Warren Gorham & Lamont.

Accounting & Budgeting in Public & Nonprofit Organizations: A Manager's Guide. C. William Garner. LC 91-8376. (Public Administration - Nonprofit Sector Ser.). 272p. 1991. 36.95 (*1-55542-336-1*) Jossey-Bass.

Accounting & Business Fluctuations. Delmas D. Ray. LC 60-6718. 196p. reprint ed. pap. 55.90 (*0-7837-4925-2*, 2044591) Bks Demand.

Accounting & Business Practice, Sr. H. S. Jack Rudman. (Teachers License Examination Ser.: T-1). 1994. pap. 23.95 (*0-8373-8001-4*) Nat Learn.

Accounting & Control in the Foreign Exchange Market. 2nd ed. Ian J. Martin. 336p. 1993. boxed 130.00 (*0-406-01362-4*, UK) Butterworth Legal Pubs.

***Accounting & Cost Controls for Sawmill Manufacturers.** Jerry G. King. 116p. 1988. pap. text ed. 19.50 (*0-933179-02-2*) Bus Account Pubns.

Accounting & Federal Regulation. James P. Bedingfield. (Illus.). 336p. 1981. pap. text ed. 32.00 (*0-8359-0051-7*, Reston) P-H.

***Accounting & Finance: CEBS Study Manual - Course VI.** Ed. by Wharton School Staff. (Illus.). 1994. student ed 65.00 (*0-89154-483-6*) Intl Found Employ.

***Accounting & Finance Developer's Guide with Visual BASIC.** Jack Purdum. 1995. disk, pap. 39.99 (*0-672-30616-6*) Sams.

Accounting & Finance for CPCU Eight. rev. ed. R. Robert Rackley. (CPCU Ser.). 1985. 155.00 (*0-88171-104-7*) Insurance Achiev.

***Accounting & Finance for Lawyers in a Nutshell.** Charles H. Meyer. (Nutshell Ser.). 407p. 1994. pap. text ed. 17.00 (*0-314-04763-8*) West Pub.

Accounting & Finance for Non-Specialists. Peter Atrill & Eddie McLaney. LC 94-13289. 1994. 37.90 (*0-13-309865-6*) P-H Intl.

***Accounting & Finance in China.** Ed. by John Blake & Simon Gao. LC 94-39780. 320p. 1995. 89.95x (*0-415-11812-3*, C0476) Routledge.

Accounting & Finance in Mass Transit. Philip C. Cheng. LC 80-70920. (Illus.). 336p. 1982. text ed. 73.25 (*0-86598-035-7*) Rowman.

Accounting & Financial Disclosure: A Guide to Basic Concepts. Stanley Siegel. LC 83-12505. 259p. (C). 1993. reprint ed. pap. text ed. 18.50 (*0-314-74733-8*) West Pub.

Accounting & Financial Globalization. Ed. by Joshua Ronen. LC 90-26406. 184p. 1991. text ed. 55.00 (*0-89930-618-7*, RAF/, Quorum Bks) Greenwood.

***Accounting & Financial Management.** Ed. by Jill Muehrcke. (Leadership Ser.). 115p. 1993. spiral bd. 20.00 (*0-614-07095-3*) Soc Nonprofit Org.

Accounting & Financial Management for Builders, Remodelers, & Developers. 3rd ed. Emma Shinn. Ed. by Doris M. Tennyson. (Illus.). 1993. 25.00 (*0-86718-386-1*) Home Builder.

Accounting & Financial Reporting by State & Local Governments: An Experiment. American Institute of Certified Public Accountants Staff. LC 81-186653. 65p. reprint ed. pap. 25.00 (*0-8357-6419-2*, 2035786) Bks Demand.

Accounting & Financial Reporting for Governmental & Nonprofit Organizations: Basic Concepts. Robert W. Ingram et al. 1991. pap. text ed. write for info. (*0-07-031714-3*) McGraw.

Accounting & Industrial Relations: Some Historical Evidence on Their Interaction. Philip D. Bougen. Ed. by Richard P. Brief. (Foundations of Accounting Ser.: No. 3). 333p. 1988. 15.00 (*0-8240-6115-2*) Garland.

Accounting & Information Systems. 3rd ed. Joseph W. Wilkinson. 1296p. 1991. Net. text ed. write for info. (*0-471-61561-7*) Wiley.

Accounting & Information Systems. 4th ed. John Page & Paul Hooper. 864p. (C). 1992. text ed. write for info. (*0-13-006040-2*) P-H.

Accounting & Information Systems: Study Guide. 3rd ed. Joseph W. Wilkinson. 328p. 1991. Net. pap. text ed. write for info. (*0-471-53614-8*) Wiley.

Accounting & Information Systems Canadian CEBS Course VI Study Manual. 2nd ed. Dalhousie University Staff. 505p. 1992. student ed, pap. 55.00 (*0-89154-444-5*) Intl Found Employ.

Accounting & Information Theory, Vol. 2. Baruch Lev. (Studies in Accounting Research). 84p. 1969. 12.00 (*0-86539-014-2*) Am Accounting.

Accounting & Its Legal Implications: A Guide for Managers, Business Owners, & Entrepreneurs. David W. Tate. 210p. 1994. 35.00 (*1-55623-761-8*) Irwin Prof Pubng.

Accounting & Law in a Nutshell. E. McGruder Faris. LC 83-23509. (Nutshell Ser.). 377p. 1990. reprint ed. pap. text ed. 15.50 (*0-314-79453-0*) West Pub.

Accounting & Management: Field Study Perspectives. William J. Bruns, Jr. & Robert S. Kaplan. 1988. text ed. 35.00 (*0-07-103216-9*) McGraw.

Accounting & Record System for the Retail Pharmacy. Medical Economics Company Staff. 1977. pap. 49.95 (*0-87489-990-7*) Med Economics.

Accounting & Recordkeeping for the Self-Employed. Jack Fox. LC 94-16687. 1994. text ed. 36.95 (*0-471-03216-6*); pap. text ed. 16.95 (*0-471-03217-4*) Wiley.

Accounting & Reporting. Nathan M. Bisk. (CPA Comprehensive Exam Review Ser.). 1994. pap. 31.95 (*0-88128-639-7*) Totaltape.

***Accounting & Reporting: Campbell Williams CPA Review.** H. James Williams & Carole C. Williams. (C). 1994. 35.00 (*0-9635927-2-6*) C Williams Pub.

***Accounting & Reporting Pt. I.** (CPA Review Ser.: Vol. III). 304p. 1995. pap. 19.95 (*0-538-84717-4*) S-W Pub.

***Accounting & Reporting Pt. II.** (CPA Review Ser.: Vol. III). 304p. 1995. pap. 20.95 (*0-538-84718-2*) S-W Pub.

Accounting & Reporting for Nonprofit Organizations. John P. Listro. 280p. 1992. per. 24.95 (*0-8403-8067-4*) Kendall-Hunt.

Accounting & Reporting Standards for Corporate Financial Statements & Preceding Statements & Supplements. American Accounting Association Staff. 64p. 1957. 2.00 (*0-86539-006-1*) Am Accounting.

***Accounting & Science: Natural Inquiry & Commercial Reason.** Ed. by Michael Power. (Environmental Chemistry Ser.). 285p. (C). Date not set. write for info. (*0-521-55325-3*) Cambridge U Pr.

***Accounting & Science: Natural Inquiry & Commercial Reason.** Ed. by Michael Power. 285p. (C). 1995. pap. write for info. (*0-521-55699-6*) Cambridge U Pr.

Accounting & Tax Aspects for Computer Software Manufactures. Robert W. McGee. LC 87-15140. 176p. 1987. text ed. 55.00 (*0-275-92273-1*, C2273, Praeger Pubs) Greenwood.

Accounting & Tax Highlights. Allan B. Afterman & George Roe. 230.00 (*0-685-69595-6*, ATH) Warren Gorham & Lamont.

***Accounting & Taxation.** Walter F. O'Connor. (Business Library). 320p. 1990. pap. 16.95 (*0-8120-4154-2*) Barron.

***Accounting & Taxes for Magicians.** Robert A. Steiner. 87p. (Orig.). 1995. pap. 20.00 (*0-9623473-2-9*) Wide-Awake Bks.

Accounting & the Enterprise: A Social Analysis. T. Colwyn Jones. LC 94-17769. 256p. 1995. 55.00x (*0-415-07207-7*, B3426); pap. 22.95 (*0-415-07208-5*, B3430) Routledge.

Accounting & the Law. 4th ed. Thompson et al. 1978. text ed. 29.00 (*0-88277-433-6*) Foundation Pr.

Accounting & the Law, Problem Material to Accompany Cases & Materials On. George C. Thompson et al. 190p. 1990. reprint ed. pap. text ed. 7.95 (*0-88277-452-2*) Foundation Pr.

Accounting Applications for Spreadsheets. Paul Rosen & Marvin Brother. 104p. 1988. 15.50 (*0-936862-37-8*, AC/SP); teacher ed 10.00 (*0-936862-44-0*, AS-TM); trans. 175.00 (*0-936862-42-4*, AS-TOR); disk 65.00 (*0-936862-71-8*, SAD-1, SAD-3) DDC Pub.

Accounting Applications for Spreadsheets Solutions Booklet. Marvin Brother & Paul Rosen. 54p. 1988. pap. text ed. (*1-56243-007-6*, AC/SP-SOL) DDC Pub.

Accounting Applications for the Microcomputer. S. S. Hamilton. (Microcomputer Software Program Ser.). 1983. text ed. 13.25 (*0-07-025736-1*) McGraw.

Accounting As a Variable in Mergers. Russell D. Langer. Ed. by Richard P. Brief. LC 77-87303. (Development of Contemporary Accounting Thought Ser.). 1978. lib. bdg. 26.95 (*0-405-10942-3*) Ayer.

Accounting As Social & Institutional Practice. Ed. by Anthony G. Hopwood & Peter Miller. LC 93-45992. (Cambridge Studies in Management: No. 24). (Illus.). 332p. (C). 1994. 59.95 (*0-521-39092-3*); pap. 19.95 (*0-521-46965-1*) Cambridge U Pr.

Accounting Assistant. Jack Rudman. (Career Examination Ser.: C-1071). 1994. pap. 23.95 (*0-8373-1071-7*) Nat Learn.

Accounting Bibliography: Historical Approach. Walter Hausdorfer. LC 85-72685. 1987. 31.60 (*0-9602956-5-8*) Bay Books.

Accounting, Budgeting & Finance: A Reference for Managers. Charles J. Woelfel. LC 89-77450. 512p. 1990. 59.95 (*0-8144-5988-9*) AMACOM.

Accounting Business Software Directory for OS-2 Computers. ICP Staff & Larry A. Welke. Ed. by Sheila Cunningham & Marilyn Law. 1990. pap. 24.95 (*0-88094-180-4*) Intl Computer.

Accounting by Agricultural Producers & Agricultural Cooperatives. American Institute of Certified Public Accountants Staff. 81p. reprint ed. pap. 25.00 (*0-8357-5064-7*, 2023960) Bks Demand.

Accounting Certification, Educational, & Reciprocity Requirements: An International Guide. Jack R. Fay. LC 92-9807. 320p. 1992. text ed. 69.50 (*0-89930-640-3*, FIG, Quorum Bks) Greenwood.

Accounting Concept of Revenue. George J. Staubus. Ed. by Richard P. Brief. (Dimensions of Accounting Theory & Practice Ser.). 1980. 17.95 (*0-405-13497-5*) Ayer.

***Accounting Concepts.** 8th ed. (C). 1994. pap. 19.95 (*0-256-15177-6*) Irwin Prof Pubng.

***Accounting Concepts & Applications.** 5th rev. ed. K. Fred Skousen et al. LC 95-10761. Orig. Title: Accounting Principles & Applications. 1996. text ed. 62.95 (*0-538-84294-6*) S-W Pub.

Accounting Control & Organization Behavior. 1987. 39.95 (*0-434-91480-0*) Buttrwrth-Heinemann.

Accounting Control Systems: A Technical, Social, & Behavioral Integration. 2nd ed. Intro. by Jan Bell. LC 90-25172. 420p. (C). 1991. text ed. 29.95 (*1-55876-020-2*) Wiener Pubs Inc.

Accounting Controls & the Soviet Economic Reforms of 1966. Bertrand Horwitz. (Studies in Accounting Research: Vol. 4). 74p. 1970. 12.00 (*0-86539-016-9*) Am Accounting.

Accounting, Costing & Cost Estimation: Welsh Industry, 1700-1830. Haydn Jones. ix, 285p. 1985. 45.00 (*0-7083-0882-1*, Pub. by U of Wales UK) Bks Intl VA.

Accounting Curricula for East-West Joint Ventures. 92p. 10.00 (*92-1-104329-8*, E.90.II.A.2) UN.

Accounting Cycle. Jay Jacquet & William L. Miller, Jr. Ed. by Michael G. Crisp. LC 91-77127. (Fifty-Minute Ser.). 100p. (Orig.). 1992. pap. 9.95 (*1-56052-146-5*) Crisp Pubns.

Accounting Desk Book. 8th ed. Douglas L. Blensly & Tom M. Plank. LC 84-21102. 542p. 1984. text ed. 59.50 (*0-87624-011-2*, Inst Busn Plan) P-H.

Accounting Desk Book. 9th ed. Douglas L. Blensly & Tom M. Plank. 780p. 1989. text ed. 69.95 (*0-13-003559-9*) P-H.

Accounting Dictionary: Diccionario de Contabilidad. 4th ed. Jose M. Martin. 270p. (SPA.). 1982. 29.95 (*0-8288-1289-6*, S50180) Fr & Eur.

Accounting Education for the Twenty-First Century: The Global Challenge. Ed. by Jane O. Burns & Belverd E. Needles. LC 94-9175. 1994. text ed. 145.00 (*0-08-042405-8*, Pergamon Pr) Elsevier.

Accounting Education in Economic Development Management. A. J. Enthoven. 1981. 89.75 (*0-444-86195-5*) Elsevier.

***Accounting Equation.** W. M. Renwick. 1991. pap. 21.00 (*0-409-49283-3*, Austral) Butterworth Legal Pubs.

***Accounting Essentials.** 200p. (Orig.). 1995. pap. 135.00 (*0-7605-1477-1*) Rector Pr.

***Accounting Essentials.** 330p. (Orig.). (ACE & RUS.). 1995. pap. 125.00 (*0-7605-1476-3*) Rector Pr.

Accounting Essentials. 2nd ed. Neal Margolis & N. Paul Harmon. LC 85-12332. 319p. 1985. pap. text ed. 14.95 (*0-471-82721-5*) Wiley.

***Accounting Essentials: An Introduction for Non-Accounting Majors.** B. Popoff. 161p. 1991. pap. 36.00 (*0-409-30484-0*, Austral); pap. 36.00 (*0-614-05474-5*, Austral) Butterworth Legal Pubs.

Accounting Ethics: A Practical Guide for Professionals. Philip G. Cottell, Jr. & Terry M. Perlin. LC 89-24368. 192p. 1990. text ed. 49.95 (*0-89930-401-X*, CTF/, Quorum Bks) Greenwood.

Accounting, Evaluation & Economic Behavior. Raymond J. Chambers. LC 66-13944. 1975. reprint ed. text ed. 20.00 (*0-914348-15-9*) Scholars Bk.

Accounting Executive. Jack Rudman. (Career Examination Ser.: C-1072). 1994. pap. 34.95 (*0-8373-1072-5*) Nat Learn.

***Accounting, Financial Facts Or Phantasmagoria? Professorial Lecture.** P. W. Wolnizer. 1991. pap. 21.00 (*0-7300-1450-9*, Pub. by Deakin Univ AT) St Mut.

Accounting for a Simplified Firm Owning Depreciable Assets: Seventeen Essays & a Synthesis Based on a Common Case. Ed. by Robert R. Sterling & Arthur L. Thomas. LC 79-18604. 1979. text ed. 20.00 (*0-914348-27-2*) Scholars Bk.

An Asterisk (*) at the beginning of an entry indicates that the title is appearing in BIP for the first time.

Accounting for Advertising Assets. Dale L. Flesher. 1979. pap. 4.50 (*0-938004-01-8*) U MS Bus Econ.

Accounting for Aggression: Perspectives on Aggression & Violence. Gerda Siann. 260p. 1985. pap. text ed. 19.95 (*0-04-301188-8*) Routledge Chapman & Hall.

Accounting for Anyone. Wayne S. Boutell. (Illus.). 240p. 1982. pap. 25.95 (*0-13-001602-0*) P-H.

Accounting for Banks. James M. Koltveit. LC 82-61894. 1982. Looseleaf updates available. write for info. (*0-8205-1023-8*) Bender.

Accounting for Business. P. Atrill et al. 320p. 1991. pap. 32.95 (*0-7506-0044-6*) Buttrwrth-Heinemann.

Accounting for Business Combinations. Caroline Strobel. 1991. pap. 59.95 (*1-55840-452-X*) Exec Ent Pubns.

***Accounting for Business Combinations & Restructurings.** Ed. by Caroline Strobel. 1994. pap. text ed. 59.95 (*0-471-11242-9*) Wiley.

Accounting for Changing Prices: Replacement Cost & General Price Level Adjustments. James A. Largay & John Livingston. LC 76-7491. (Wiley Hamilton Publication). 317p. reprint ed. pap. 90.40 (*0-8357-5065-5*, 2025177) Bks Demand.

Accounting for Corporate Reputation. Ahmed Riahi-Belkaoui & Ellen L. Pavlik. LC 92-8401. 272p. 1992. text ed. 59.95 (*0-89930-717-5*, BKK, Quorum Bks) Greenwood.

Accounting for Corporate Retained Earnings. David Green, Jr. Ed. by Richard P. Brief. LC 80-1496. (Dimensions of Accounting Theory & Practice Ser.). 1980. lib. bdg. 17.95 (*0-405-13490-8*) Ayer.

Accounting for Costs As Fixed & Variable. Maryanne M. Mowen. 75p. 10.95 (*0-86641-117-8*, 85180) Inst Mgmt Account.

Accounting for Data Processing Costs. Robert W. McGee. LC 87-24933. 208p. 1988. text ed. 55.00 (*0-89930-214-9*, MGA/, Quorum Bks) Greenwood.

Accounting for Decision Making & Control. Jerold L. Zimmerman. LC 93-46068. 672p. (C). 1994. text ed. 68.95 (*0-256-12854-5*) Irwin Prof Pubng.

***Accounting for Effective Decision Making: A Manager's Guide to Corporate, Financial & Cost Reporting.** Martin Mellman et al. LC 94-3720. 650p. (C). 1994. text ed. 50.00 (*1-55623-066-4*) Irwin Prof Pubng.

Accounting for Employee Capital Accumulation Plans. American Institute of Certified Public Accountants Staff. (Issues Paper Ser.). 207p. reprint ed. pap. 59.00 (*0-7837-0276-0*, 2040589) Bks Demand.

Accounting for Equipment Leases: A Complete Guide. Sudhir P. Amembal & Shawn Halladay. (Illus.). 500p. 1991. 115.00 (*0-945988-03-6*) Amembal & Halladay.

Accounting for Fixed Assets. Raymond H. Peterson. (Wiley Institute of Management Accountants Professional Book Ser.). 224p. 1994. text ed. 60.00 (*0-471-53703-9*) Wiley.

Accounting for Fundamentalisms: The Dynamic Character of Movements. Ed. by Martin E. Marty & R. Scott Appleby. LC 93-36621. (Fundamentalism Project Ser.: Vol. 4). (C). 1994. 47.50 (*0-226-50885-4*) U Ch Pr.

Accounting for Government Contracts: Cost Accounting Standards. Lane K. Anderson. 1981. Looseleaf updates avail. write for info. (*0-8205-1024-6*) Bender.

Accounting for Government Contracts: Federal Acquisition Regulation. Lane K. Anderson. 1985. Looseleaf updates avail. write for info. (*0-8205-1183-8*) Bender.

Accounting for Governmental & Non-profit Entities. 8th ed. Hay. 832p. (C). 1988. text ed. 70.95 (*0-256-06581-0*) Irwin.

Accounting for Governmental & Nonprofit Entities. 9th ed. Leon E. Hay & Earl R. Wilson. 832p. (C). 1991. text ed. 70.95 (*0-256-08313-4*, 01-0488-09) Irwin.

Accounting for Governmental & Nonprofit Entities. 10th ed. Leon E. Hay & Earl R. Wilson. LC 93-43984. (Series in Undergraduate Accounting). (Illus.). 808p. (C). 1994. text ed. 70.95 (*0-256-13216-X*) Irwin.

Accounting for Hospitality, Tourism & Leisure. Gareth Owen. 352p. (Orig.). 1994. pap. 49.50 (*0-273-60263-2*, Pub. by Pitman Pub Ltd UK) Trans-Atl Phila.

Accounting for Human Assets. Roger H. Hermanson. 78p. 1986. pap. 19.95 (*0-88406-193-0*, RM99) GA St U Busn Pr.

Accounting for Income Taxes. Robert W. McGee. 250p. 12.95 (*0-86641-102-X*, 84155) Inst Mgmt Account.

Accounting for Income Taxes: A Review of Alternatives. D. R. Beresford et al. LC 83-81594. (Financial Accounting Standards Board Research Report Ser.). (Illus.). 156p. (Orig.). 1983. pap. 6.00 (*0-910065-18-7*) Finan Acct Found.

Accounting for Income Taxes: Analysis & Commentary. Price Waterhouse Staff et al. 1990. 39.50 (*0-7913-0115-X*) Warren Gorham & Lamont.

Accounting for Installment Lending Activities of Finance Companies. American Institute of Certified Public Accountants Staff. (Issues Paper Ser.). 91p. reprint ed. pap. 26.00 (*0-7837-0274-4*, 2040583) Bks Demand.

Accounting for Lawyers. Charles Meyer & W. Douglas Kilbourn, Jr. 1994. student ed 30.00 (*1-55917-002-6*, 4318); audio 135.00 (*1-55917-000-X*) Natl Prac Inst.

Accounting for Lawyers, Materials on. David R. Herwitz. LC 80-18163. (University Casebook Ser.). 612p. 1991. reprint ed. text ed. 29.50 (*0-88277-014-4*) Foundation Pr.

Accounting for Lawyers, 1990. (Corporate Law & Practice Course Handbook, 1985-86 Ser.). 368p. 1990. 17.50 (*0-685-69371-6*) PLI.

Accounting for Lawyers, 1992. 479p. 1992. pap. 70.00 (*0-685-69370-8*) PLI.

Accounting for Lawyers 1993. (Corporate Law & Practice Course Handbook, 1985-86 Ser.: Vol. 821). 539p. 1993. 70.00 (*0-685-69719-3*, B4-7038) PLI.

***Accounting for Liabilities.** fac. ed. Leonard Lorensen. LC 91-41025. (Accounting Research Monograph: No. 4). 189p. 1992. pap. 53.90 (*0-7837-8235-7*, 2047999) Bks Demand.

Accounting for Losses on Sovereign Debt: Implications for New Lending. Jack M. Guttentag & Richard Herring. LC 88-34742. (Essays in International Finance Ser.: No. 172). 1989. pap. text ed. 8.00 (*0-88165-079-X*) Princeton U Int Finan Econ.

Accounting for Management Control. Clive R. Emmanuel et al. 464p. 1990. pap. 35.00 (*0-412-37480-3*, A4814) Chapman & Hall.

***Accounting for Managers.** Graham Mott. 160p. (Orig.). 1994. pap. text ed. 25.95 (*0-7494-1216-X*, Pub. by Kogan Page UK) Nichols Pub.

Accounting for Managers. Roger Oldcorn. LC 92-39190. 1993. 12.95 (*0-415-00230-3*, Routledge NY) Routledge.

Accounting for Managers. James Willimson et al. LC 82-71152. 613p. (C). 1982. text ed. 79.95 (*0-931920-38-8*); student ed 16.95 (*0-685-53911-3*) Dame Pubns.

Accounting for Managers: Text & Cases. William J. Bruns, Jr. LC 93-8521. (C). 1994. pap. 60.95 (*0-538-83310-6*, AS65AA) S-W Pub.

Accounting for Managers & Investors. 2nd ed. Michael H. Granof et al. 102p. (C). 1992. text ed. write for info. (*0-13-007923-5*) P-H.

Accounting for Marketing. Richard M. Wilson. (Advanced Management Accounting & Finance Ser.). (Illus.). 100p. 1996. pap. write for info. (*0-12-757845-5*) Acad Pr.

Accounting for Marketing & Business. K. Kotas. (C). 1989. 135.00 (*0-09-172968-8*, Pub. by S Thornes Pubs UK) St Mut.

Accounting for Multinational Enterprises. Dhia D. Alhashim & James W. Robertson. LC 77-13732. (Key Issues Lecture Ser.). 1978. pap. write for info. (*0-672-97183-6*) Macmillan.

***Accounting for Murder: A John Putnam Thatcher Mystery.** Emma Lathen. 192p. 1995. pap. 7.00 (*1-57283-000-X*) S&S Trade.

Accounting for Non-Accountants. 2nd rev. ed. John N. Myer. 1979. 14.95 (*0-8015-0026-5*, 01451-440, Dutton) NAL-Dutton.

***Accounting for Non-Accounting Students.** 3rd ed. J. R. Dyson. 480p. (Orig.). 1993. pap. 42.50x (*0-273-60435-X*, Pub. by Pitman Pub Ltd UK) Trans-Atl Phila.

Accounting for Nonprofit Organizations. John P. Listro. 136p. 1983. per. 19.95 (*0-8403-2912-1*) Kendall-Hunt.

Accounting for Overseas Operations. C. A. Westwick. 150p. 1986. text ed. 85.00 (*0-566-02586-8*, Pub. by Gower UK) Ashgate Pub Co.

Accounting for Public Utilities. Robert L. Hahne & Gregory E. Aliff. 1983. Looseleaf updates available. write for info. (*0-8205-1016-5*) Bender.

Accounting for Relationships: Explanation, Representation & Knowledge. Ed. by Rosalie Burnett et al. (Illus.). 480p. 1988. text ed. 75.00 (*0-416-41410-9*) Routledge Chapman & Hall.

Accounting for Research & Development. J. Batty. 236p. 1988. text ed. 79.95 (*0-566-02714-3*, Pub. by Gower UK) Ashgate Pub Co.

Accounting for Slower Economic Growth: The United States in the 1970s. Edward F. Denison. LC 79-20341. 212p. 1979. 35.95 (*0-8157-1802-0*); pap. 15.95 (*0-8157-1801-2*) Brookings.

Accounting for Social Responsibility: A Historical Perspective. Stanley X. Lewis & Robert I. Glover. 95p. (C). 1986. pap. text ed. 19.50 (*0-933179-00-6*) Bus Account Pubns.

Accounting for Software Costs. Robert W. McGee. 200p. 12.95 (*0-86641-104-6*, 84153) Inst Mgmt Account.

Accounting for Software Used Internally. Management Accounting Practices Committee. (Issues Paper). 24p. 5.00 (*0-86641-122-4*, 85178) Inst Mgmt Account.

Accounting for State Industrial & Commercial Enterprises in a Developing Country. M. H. Perera. Ed. by Richard P. Brief. LC 80-1516. (Dimensions of Accounting Theory & Practice Ser.). 1980. lib. bdg. 35.95 (*0-405-13495-9*) Ayer.

Accounting for Stock Options. Daniel L. Sweeney. LC 60-63312. (Michigan Business Studies: Vol. 14, No. 5). 236p. reprint ed. pap. 67.30 (*0-8357-5067-1*, 2022079) Bks Demand.

Accounting for Success: A History of Price Waterhouse in America, 1890-1990. David G. Allen & Kathleen McDermott. LC 92-15492. 400p. 1993. 35.00 (*0-87584-328-X*) Harvard Busn.

Accounting for Success: A History of Price Waterhouse in America, 1890-1990. David G. Allen & Kathleen McDermott. 1993. text ed. 35.00 (*0-07-103390-4*) McGraw.

Accounting for the Environment: Green Accounting. Rob Gray et al. LC 93-6808. 368p. 1994. text ed. 39.95 (*1-55876-075-X*, Pub. by P Chapman UK); pap. 24.95 (*1-55876-076-8*, Pub. by P Chapman UK) Wiener Pubs Inc.

Accounting for the Money That Grows on & Is Spent on Trees: Seminar Proceedings, May 14 & 15, 1981. Ed. by William R. Sizemore. 99p. reprint ed. pap. 28.30 (*0-7837-6039-6*, 2045852) Bks Demand.

Accounting for the New Business: How to Do Your Own Accounting Simply, Easily & Accurately. Christopher R. Malburg. LC 94-8710. (Business Advisors Ser.). 1994. 29.95 (*1-55850-350-1*); pap. 10.95 (*1-55850-349-8*) Adams Pubng.

Accounting for the Translation of Foreign Currencies: The Effects of Statement 52 on Equity Analysts. Paul A. Griffin & Richard P. Castanias. LC 86-81640. (Financial Accounting Standards Board Research Report Ser.). 112p. 1987. pap. 21.00 (*0-910065-22-5*) Finan Acct Found.

Accounting for Transsexualism & Transhomosexuality. Bryan Tully. 300p. 1992. text ed. 65.00 (*1-871177-08-1*, Pub. by Whiting & Birch UK) Paul & Co Pubs.

Accounting for Transsexualism & Transhomosexuality. Brian Tully. 300p. 1993. reprint ed. pap. 27.50 (*1-871177-04-9*, Pub. by Whiting & Birch UK) Paul & Co Pubs.

Accounting for United States Economic Growth: 1929-1969. Edward F. Denison. LC 74-278. 355p. 1974. pap. 18.95 (*0-8157-1803-9*) Brookings.

Accounting for Value As Well As Original Cost: A Solution to the Appreciation Problem, 2 vols. in one. Harry G. Baldwin & William B. Holz. Ed. by Richard P. Brief. LC 77-87263. (Development of Contemporary Accounting Thought Ser.). 1978. reprint ed. lib. bdg. 24.95 (*0-405-10892-3*) Ayer.

Accounting for Your Art: A Low-Maintenance Bookkeeping System for Entertainment Artists. Julie Kraft. 314p. 1994. Wkbk. student ed 16.95 (*0-9641705-0-7*) J Kraft.

Accounting Fundamentals. 2nd ed. Paul. 1991. pap. 64.95 (*0-409-10012-9*) Buttrwrth-Heinemann.

Accounting Fundamentals. 5th ed. Frank Hoffman et al. LC 93-7989. 1993. pap. 27.00 (*0-02-802474-5*); Incl. software. pap. 32.00 (*0-02-802475-3*) Glencoe.

Accounting Fundamentals: A Gregg Text-Kit for Adult Education. 3rd ed. Frank Hoffman & Esther Flashner. 1980. text ed. 33.20 (*0-07-029208-6*) McGraw.

Accounting Fundamentals: A Gregg Text-Kit in Continuing-Adult Education. 4th ed. Frank Hoffman et al. 256p. 1987. text ed. 31.95 (*0-07-029210-8*) McGraw.

Accounting Fundamentals: A Self-Instructional Approach. 2nd ed. Stephen A. Moscove. 1981. teacher ed write for info. (*0-8359-0062-2*, Reston) P-H.

Accounting Fundamentals: Study Guide-Working Papers. P. Charlene Schick et al. (Illus.). 342p. 1987. pap. text ed. write for info. (*0-13-002270-5*) P-H.

Accounting Fundamentals: Yorston, Smyth & Brown. 9th ed. E. Bryan Smyth & W. John Kenley. vii, 823p. 1991. pap. 45.00 (*0-455-21013-6*, Pub. by Law Bk Co); student ed 59.00 (*0-455-21044-6*, Pub. by Law Bk Co) W W Gaunt.

Accounting Fundamentals for Non-Accountants. 2nd ed. Stephen A. Moscove. (Illus.). 320p. 1984. 25.95 (*0-8359-0036-3*, Reston) P-H.

Accounting Fundamentals for Nonfinancial Executives. Allen Sweeny. LC 77-1064. 1977. pap. text ed. 6.95 (*0-07-062583-2*) McGraw.

Accounting Fundamentals Text-Kit. 2nd ed. N. Fritz & Frank Hoffman. 1971. 32.75 (*0-07-022498-6*) McGraw.

Accounting Guide for Common Interest Realty Associations: An Analysis of the AICPA Guidelines. Ed. by Gary A. Porter. (C). 1991. pap. 12.95 (*0-941301-18-4*) CAI.

Accounting Guide for Government Contracts. 10th ed. Paul M. Trueger. 1212p. 1991. 95.00 (*0-685-59627-3*, 4937) Commerce.

Accounting Handbook. Joel G. Siegel & Jae K. Shim. 832p. 1990. 29.95 (*0-8120-6176-4*) Barron.

***Accounting Handbook.** 2nd ed. Joel G. Siegel & Jae K. Shim. LC 94-44568. 1995. write for info. (*0-8120-6449-6*) Barron.

Accounting Handbook for Solicitors. B. F. Jacomb et al. vii, 150p. 1986. pap. 39.50 (*0-455-20656-2*, Pub. by Law Bk Co) W W Gaunt.

Accounting History: Some British Contributions. Ed. by R. H. Parker & B. S. Yamey. 672p. 1994. 72.00 (*0-19-828886-7*) OUP.

Accounting I. Jack Rudman. (Regents External Degree Ser.: REDP-1). 1994. pap. 23.95 (*0-8373-5601-6*) Nat Learn.

***Accounting I: Introductory, Intermediate & Advanced Courses; Financial Accounting; Auditing.** Comp. by Richard Schwindt. (Business Administration Reading Lists and Course Outlines Ser.: 1). (Illus.). 222p. (Orig.). (C). 1995. pap. text ed. 25.00 (*0-88024-161-6*) Eno River Pr.

Accounting II. Jack Rudman. (Regents External Degree Ser.: REDP-2). 1994. pap. 23.95 (*0-8373-5602-4*) Nat Learn.

***Accounting II: Managerial Accounting, Financial Statement Analysis & Tax.** Comp. by Richard Schwindt. (Business Administration Reading Lists and Course Outlines Ser.: 2). (Illus.). 222p. (Orig.). (C). 1995. pap. text ed. 25.00 (*0-88024-162-4*) Eno River Pr.

Accounting III. Jack Rudman. (Regents External Degree Ser.: REDP-3). 1994. pap. 23.95 (*0-8373-5603-2*) Nat Learn.

Accounting Imformation Systems & Business Organizations. 4th ed. Barry E. Cushing & Marshall B. Romney. LC 86-17301. (Illus.). 775p. (C). 1987. text ed. write for info. (*0-201-10317-6*) Addison-Wesley.

Accounting in a Business Context. (Business in Context Ser.). (Illus.). 320p. 1991. pap. 38.00 (*0-412-37510-9*, A5040) Chapman & Hall.

Accounting in Australia: Historical Essays. Ed. by Robert H. Parker. (Accounting History & Thought Ser.). 500p. 1990. reprint ed. 50.00 (*0-8240-3324-8*) Garland.

Accounting in Business. 6th ed. R. J. Bull et al. 550p. 1990. U.K. pap. 34.00 (*0-406-50056-8*, UK) Butterworth Legal Pubs.

Accounting in Developing Countries: A Framework for Standard Setting. Felix E. Amenkhienan. LC 85-20892. (Research for Business Decisions Ser.: No. 82). (Illus.). 113p. reprint ed. pap. 32.30 (*0-8357-1717-8*, 2070356) Bks Demand.

Accounting in Eighteenth Century Scotland. M. J. Mepham. Ed. by Richard P. Brief. (Foundations of Accounting Ser.: No. 11). 666p. 1988. 25.00 (*0-8240-6117-9*) Garland.

Accounting in Life & Health Insurance Companies. Judy B. Rich et al. LC 86-83715. (FLMI Insurance Education Program Ser.). 1987. student ed, pap. text ed. 10.00 (*0-915322-86-2*) LOMA.

Accounting in Life & Health Insurance Companies. Paul J. Zucconi et al. LC 86-83715. (FLMI Insurance Education Program Ser.). 1987. text ed. 36.00 (*0-915322-85-4*) LOMA.

Accounting in Perspective. Ed. by Robert R. Sterling & William F. Bentz. LC 78-26732. 1979. text ed. 20.00 (*0-914348-25-6*) Scholars Bk.

Accounting in Socialist Countries. Ed. by D. T. Bailey. (International Accounting Ser.). 224p. 1988. lib. bdg. 75.00 (*0-415-00429-2*, A1458) Routledge.

Accounting in the Business Environment. John Watts. 416p. (Orig.). 1993. pap. 57.50x (*0-273-60111-3*, Pub. by Pitman Pub Ltd UK) Trans-Atl Phila.

Accounting in the Developing Countries. Ahmed Riahi-Belkaoui. LC 93-50070. 232p. 1994. text ed. 65.00 (*0-89930-821-X*, Quorum Bks) Greenwood.

Accounting in the Dual Economy. Janice M. Belkaoui & Ahmed R. Belkaoui. LC 91-17. 176p. 1991. text ed. 55.00 (*0-89930-615-2*, BKB/, Quorum Bks) Greenwood.

Accounting in the Hotel & Catering Industry. 4th ed. Peter Harris & Peter Hazzard. 224p. 1987. pap. 36.50 (*0-7487-1057-4*, Pub. by Stanley Thornes UK) Trans-Atl Phila.

Accounting in the Soviet Union. Ehiel Ash & Robert Strittmatter. LC 90-24129. 208p. 1992. text ed. 59.95 (*0-275-93069-6*, C3069, Praeger Pubs) Greenwood.

Accounting in Theory & Practice. George Lisle. LC 75-18475. (History of Accounting Ser.). (Illus.). 1979. reprint ed. 34.95 (*0-405-07557-X*) Ayer.

***Accounting in Transition: The Implications of Political & Economic Reform in Central Europe.** Ed. by Neil Garrod & Stuart McLeay. LC 94-46314. 1995. write for info. (*0-415-08349-4*) Routledge.

Accounting Information Disclosure & Collective Bargaining. Bernard Foley & Keith Maunders. LC 78-31148. 210p. 1981. 45.00 (*0-8419-0481-2*) Holmes & Meier.

Accounting Information Sources. Rosemary Demarest. LC 70-120908. (Management Information Guide Ser.: No. 18). 424p. 1971. 68.00 (*0-8103-0818-5*) Gale.

***Accounting Information Systems.** James A. Hall. LC 94-34796. 900p. 1995. text ed. 65.75 (*0-314-04468-X*) West Pub.

Accounting Information Systems. James O. Hicks, Jr. & Wayne E. Leininger. (Illus.). 748p. (C). 1986. Instr's. manual. teacher ed, pap. text ed. write for info. (*0-314-98611-1*) West Pub.

Accounting Information Systems. Richard Lindhe & Steven D. Grossman. LC 80-67524. 380p. (C). 1980. text ed. 69.95 (*0-931920-23-X*) Dame Pubns.

Accounting Information Systems. 2nd ed. Ulric J. Gelinas, Jr. et al. LC 92-33640. 1993. text ed. 64.95 (*0-538-82486-7*) S-W Pub.

Accounting Information Systems. 2nd ed. James O. Hicks, Jr. & Wayne E. Leininger. (Illus.). 748p. (C). 1986. text ed. 63.75 (*0-314-85246-8*) West Pub.

Accounting Information Systems. 2nd ed. Edward L. Summers. (C). 1991. write for info. (*0-395-43347-9*) HM Soft Schl Col Div.

Accounting Information Systems. 3rd ed. James L. Boockholdt. 896p. (C). 1992. text ed. 69.95 (*0-256-10841-2*) Irwin.

***Accounting Information Systems.** 3rd ed. Ulric J. Gellinas, Jr. & Allan E. Oram. LC 95-8764. 1996. pap. 57.95 (*0-538-85197-X*) S-W Pub.

Accounting Information Systems. 3rd ed. John F. Nash & Cynthia D. Heagy. LC 92-32937. 1993. text ed. 58.95 (*0-538-82484-0*) S-W Pub.

Accounting Information Systems. 4th ed. Cecily K. Bodnar & William S. Hopwood. (C). 5.25 hd write for info. (*0-318-68770-4*); 3.5 hd write for info. (*0-318-68771-2*) P-H.

***Accounting Information Systems.** 6th ed. George H. Bodnar & William S. Hopwood. LC 94-34852. 1994. text ed. write for info. (*0-13-322356-6*) P-H.

Accounting Information Systems: A Book of Readings. James R. Davis & Barry E. Cushing. LC 78-74681. pap. write for info. (*0-201-01099-2*) Addison-Wesley.

Accounting Information Systems: A Comprehensive Approach. 6th ed. Barry E. Cushing & Marshall B. Rommey. LC 93-6598. (C). 1994. text ed. 62.50 (*0-201-58025-X*) Addison-Wesley.

Accounting Information Systems: A Comprehensive Survey of Accounting Systems in Organizations. 5th ed. Barry E. Cushing & Marshall D. Romney. (Illus.). 900p. (C). 1989. text ed. write for info. (*0-318-64908-X*) Addison-Wesley.

Accounting Information Systems: A Cycle Approach. 2nd ed. Leonard A. Robinson et al. 656p. (C). 1986. text ed. 37.95 (*0-06-045515-2*) HarpCollege.

Accounting Information Systems: A Cycle Approach. 3rd ed. James R. Davis et al. 760p. 1990. Net. text ed. write for info. (*0-471-61560-9*) Wiley.

Accounting Information Systems: Concepts & Practice for Effective Decisions. 4th ed. Stephen A. Moscove et al. 774p. 1990. Net. teacher ed write for info. (*0-471-51626-0*); Net. text ed. write for info. (*0-471-50449-1*) Wiley.

Accounting Information Systems: Essential Concepts & Applications. 2nd ed. Joseph W. Wilkinson. 976p. 1993. Net. text ed. write for info. (*0-471-57573-9*) Wiley.

***Accounting Information Systems: Essential Concepts & Applications Second Edition on Lotus 1-2-3 & Database Software Applied to Ais Cases Set.** Joseph Wilkinson et al. 1993. pap. text ed. write for info. (*0-471-00101-5*) Wiley.

***Accounting Information Systems: Essential Concepts & Applications Second Edition on Lotus 1-2-3 & Database Software Applied to Ais Cases Set.** Joseph Wilkinson et al. 1993. pap. text ed. write for info. (*0-471-00104-X*) Wiley.

A

An Asterisk (*) at the beginning of an entry indicates that the title is appearing in BIP for the first time. 31

Accounting Information Systems: Theory & Practice. 2nd ed. Robert A. Leitch & Roscoe K. Davis. 768p. (C). 1992. text ed. write for info. (0-13-006032-1) P-H.

Accounting Information Systems: Transaction Processing & Controls. 2nd ed. David H. Li & James L. Boockholdt. 824p. (C). 1990. text ed. 69.95 (0-256-03575-X) Irwin.

***Accounting Information Systems: Transaction Processing & Controls.** 4th ed. J. L. Boockholdt. LC 95-12099. (Undergraduate Accounting Ser.). 864p. (C). 1995. text ed. 69.95 (0-256-16680-3) Irwin.

***Accounting Information Systems, International.** 3rd ed. James Boockholdt. (C). 1994. student ed, text ed. 35.50 (0-256-11415-3) Irwin.

***Accounting, Information Technology & Business Solutions.** 2nd rev. ed. Anita S. Hollander et al. LC 95-1861. Orig. Title: Event-Driven Business Solutions. 5440p. (C). 1995. 57.95 (0-256-10566-9) Irwin.

Accounting Issues & Credit Evaluation. Ed. by Joan Behr. (Special Collection from the Journal of Commercial Bank Lending). 128p. (Orig.). 1992. pap. 37.00 (0-936742-88-7, 36047) Robt Morris Assocs.

Accounting Issues for Lawyers, Teaching Materials. 4th ed. Ted J. Fiflis. (American Casebook Ser.). 706p. 1991. text ed. 49.00 (0-314-86280-3) West Pub.

Accounting Literature in the United States Before Mitchell & Jones (1796) Contributions by Four English Writers, Through American Editions, & Two Pioneer Local Authors. Ed. by Terry K. Sheldahl & Richard P. Brief. LC 88-38984. (Foundations of Accounting Ser.: No. 16). 510p. 1989. 25.00 (0-8240-6131-4) Garland.

Accounting Literature Index. 2nd ed. Jean L. Heck. 1992. pap. text ed. write for info. (0-00-702784-2) McGraw.

Accounting Literature Index. 3rd ed. Jean L. Heck. 1993. pap. text ed. write for info. (0-07-027788-5) McGraw.

Accounting Machine Operator. Jack Rudman. (Career Examination Ser.: C-1073). 1994. pap. 23.95 (0-8373-1073-3) Nat Learn.

Accounting Made Simple. rev. ed. Joseph P. Simini. (Made Simple Ser.). (Illus.). 192p. 1988. pap. 12.00 (0-385-23280-2) Doubleday.

Accounting, Management Control & Business Organisation: An Institutional Perspective. W. B. Seal. 228p. 1993. 59.95 (1-85628-503-0, Pub. by Avebury Pub UK) Ashgate Pub Co.

Accounting Method. C. Rufus Rorem. LC 82-48382. (Accountancy in Transition Ser.). 613p. 1982. lib. bdg. 20.00 (0-8240-5327-3) Garland.

Accounting Method for Radiation Doses to Long Lived Natural Radionuclides, No. EUR12509. A. D. Karpf. 49p. 1990. pap. 6.00 (92-826-1065-9, CD-NA-12509-EN-C) UNIPUB.

Accounting Mission. Frank S. Bray. LC 73-84525. 1973. reprint ed. text ed. 20.00 (0-914348-01-9) Scholars Bk.

Accounting Model. 2nd ed. C. Torben Thomsen. (Illus.). 151p. (C). 1991. pap. 14.95 (1-879024-00-4) BIP CA.

Accounting on Your IBM PC. Michael Scorgie & Anne Magnus. 224p. (C). 1984. pap. 21.95 (0-8359-0025-8, Reston) P-H.

Accounting Policy Formulation: The Role of Corporate Management. Lauren Kelly-Newton. (A-W Paperback Series in Accounting). 1980. pap. write for info. (0-201-05291-1) Addison-Wesley.

Accounting Practice: Selected Questions & Unofficial Answers Indexed to Content Specification Outline. American Institute of Certified Public Accountants Staff. Ed. by James D. Blum & David S. Dexter. LC 84-160638. 267p. reprint ed. pap. 76.10 (0-8357-5068-X, 2025093) Bks Demand.

***Accounting Practices & Procedures Manual for Life Insurance Companies.** 156p. (C). 1994. ring bd. 150.00 (0-89382-298-1) Nat Assn Insu Comm.

***Accounting Practices & Procedures Manual for Property - Casualty Insurers.** 158p. (C). 1994. ring bd. 150.00 (0-89382-297-3) Nat Assn Insu Comm.

Accounting Practices for Hotels, Motels, & Restaurants. Paul R. Dittmer. LC 79-142507. 1971. write for info. (0-672-96063-X); text ed. write for info. (0-672-96062-1) Macmillan.

Accounting Practices for Savings Institutions. Institute of Financial Education Staff. 1988. pap. 39.95 (0-912857-48-X) Inst Finan Educ.

Accounting Practices in the Petroleum Industry. Robert H. Irving & Verden R. Draper. LC 58-12430. 255p. reprint ed. pap. 72.70 (0-8357-5069-8, 2013054) Bks Demand.

Accounting Primer. Elwin W. Midgett. 1968. pap. 3.50 (0-451-62500-5, Ment) NAL-Dutton.

Accounting Principles. Michael A. Diamond et al. (C). 1994. text ed. write for info. (0-538-81676-7, AB68AA) S-W Pub.

Accounting Principles. Jack E. Kiger et al. (C). 1984. text ed. 34.95 (0-394-34318-2); Student Mastery Guide, Vol. 1. write for info. (0-394-33763-8); Student Mastery Guide, Vol. 2. write for info. (0-394-33764-6); Working Papers, Vol. 1. write for info. (0-394-33878-2); Practice Set: Accounting Cycle. write for info. (0-394-33762-X); Practice Set: Corporation. write for info. (0-394-33761-1); Computer Practice Set for Apple. write for info. (0-394-33886-3); C. write for info. (0-394-33885-5) Random.

Accounting Principles. Jack E. Kiger et al. (C). 1987. text ed. 28.00 (0-394-35482-6); A/C cycle practice set. 9.95 (0-394-36593-3); Corporation practice set. 9.95 (0-394-36596-8) Random.

Accounting Principles. 4th ed. Jack L. Smith et al. LC 92-15751. 1992. Small business application with forms, Acme Auto Parts. pap. text ed. write for info. (0-07-043073-X) McGraw.

Accounting Principles. 4th ed. Jack L. Smith et al. LC 92-15751. 1992. Financial statement analysis case, Premium Foods Corporation. pap. text ed. write for info. (0-07-043074-8) McGraw.

Accounting Principles. 4th ed. Jack L. Smith et al. LC 92-15751. 1992. Blank forms for problems & cases. write for info. (0-07-043070-5) McGraw.

Accounting Principles. 4th ed. Jack L. Smith et al. LC 92-15751. 1993. text ed. write for info. (0-07-059183-0); Instr's manual to Critical Thinking Guide. teacher ed, pap. text ed. write for info. (0-07-043090-X) McGraw.

Accounting Principles. 4th ed. Jack L. Smith et al. LC 92-15751. 1993. VHS case videotapes. vhs write for info. (0-07-043089-6) McGraw.

Accounting Principles. 4th ed. Lanny M. Solomon et al. Ed. by Horan. LC 92-26316. 1200p. (C). 1993. text ed. 65.75 (0-314-01191-9) West Pub.

Accounting Principles. 5th ed. Roger H. Hermanson et al. 1386p. (C). 1991. text ed. 63.95 (0-256-08916-7) Irwin.

Accounting Principles. 7th ed. Robert N. Anthony & James S. Reece. LC 94-19478. 704p. (C). 1994. text ed. 68.95 (0-256-12401-9) Irwin.

Accounting Principles. 16th ed. Philip E. Fess. (C). 1989. text ed. write for info. (0-538-80600-1, AB70QA) S-W Pub.

Accounting Principles. 17th ed. Philip E. Fess & Carl S. Warren. LC 92-31633. 1993. text ed. 61.95 (0-538-81850-6) S-W Pub.

Accounting Principles, 1. 4th ed. Roger H. Hermanson et al. (C). 1989. 20.95 (0-256-07425-9) Irwin.

Accounting Principles, 2. 4th ed. Roger H. Hermanson et al. (C). 1989. student ed 20.95 (0-256-07422-4) Irwin.

Accounting Principles, I. Jack E. Kiger et al. (C). 1987. 16.95 (0-685-17556-1) Random.

Accounting Principles: Acme Auto Parts, A Computerized Small Business Application with Forms, IBM 5.25 Disk. 4th ed. Educational Computer Systems. 1993. pap. text ed. write for info. (0-07-831882-3) McGraw.

***Accounting Principles: Business Papers Practice Set & Working Papers, Vol. 1.** 3rd ed. Jerry J. Weygandt et al. 1993. text ed. write for info. (0-471-00818-4) Wiley.

***Accounting Principles: With General Ledger Software & Working Papers-Chapters 2-6.** 3rd ed. Jerry Weygandt et al. 1994. text ed. write for info. (0-471-10712-3) Wiley.

Accounting Principles: With Working Papers & Lotus Problems. 2nd ed. Jerry J. Weygandt et al. 1990. Net. pap. text ed. write for info. (0-471-53130-8) Wiley.

Accounting Principles: With Working Papers & Lotus Problems. 3rd ed. Jerry J. Weygandt & Donald E. Kieso. Ed. by Walter G. Kell. 1312p. (C). 1993. text ed. write for info. (0-471-57064-8) Wiley.

***Accounting Principles: With Working Papers & Lotus Problems, Set.** Jerry J. Weygandt et al. 1993. text ed., disk write for info. (0-471-01491-5) Wiley.

***Accounting Principles: With Working Papers-Vol. 1, Business Papers Practice Set & General Ledger.** 3rd ed. Jerry J. Weygandt et al. 1994. text ed., disk write for info. (0-471-11367-0) Wiley.

***Accounting Principles Vol. 1: With Working Papers, General Ledger, & Lotus 3.5 Problems, Set.** 3rd ed. Jerry J. Weygandt et al. 1994. student ed, text ed. write for info. (0-471-11698-X) Wiley.

Accounting Principles see Accounting

Accounting Principles & Applications. 4th ed. Skouseu et al. LC 92-24772. 1993. text ed. 64.95 (0-538-81163-3) S-W Pub.

Accounting Principles & Applications see Accounting Concepts & Applications

Accounting Principles & Practice. S. Hall. 148.00 (0-08-010332-4, Pub. by Pergamon Repr UK) Franklin.

Accounting Principles & Practices. 4th ed. L. Paden Neeley & Frank Imke. 1072p. (C). 1990. text ed. write for info. (0-318-68084-X, AV63DA) S-W Pub.

Accounting Principles & Practices. 5th ed. L. Paden Neeley. LC 94-19432. 1995. pap. 48.95 (0-538-83194-4) S-W Pub.

Accounting Principles & Wiley College Hills: Business Papers Version Set. 2nd ed. Jerry J. Weygandt et al. 1990. Net. text ed. write for info. (0-471-54039-0) Wiley.

Accounting Principles for Savings Institutions. Institute of Financial Education Staff. 1987. pap. 34.95 (0-912857-43-9) Inst Finan Educ.

Accounting Principles for the Autonomous Corporate Entity. Henry P. Hill. LC 86-25587. (Illus.). 156p. 1987. text ed. 55.00 (0-89930-212-2, HLC/, Quorum Bks) Greenwood.

***Accounting Principles: Study Guide Vol. 2: With Lotus 3.5 & General Ledger Software.** 3rd ed. Jerry J. Weygandt et al. 1994. text ed. write for info. (0-471-03893-8) Wiley.

Accounting Principles-Working Papers: Group A, Chapters 12-24. 2nd ed. Ronald J. Thacker. pap. write for info. (0-13-002824-X) P-H.

Accounting Principles-Working Papers: Group B, Chapters 12-24. 2nd ed. Ronald J. Thacker. 1979. pap. write for info. (0-13-002840-1) P-H.

***Accounting Problem Solver.** Research & Education Association Staff. 1000p. 1995. text ed. 23.95 (0-89891-973-8) Res & Educ.

Accounting Profession. John W. Buckley & Marlene H. Buckley. LC 74-8880. (Melville Series on Management, Accounting, & Information Systems). (Illus.). 231p. reprint ed. pap. 65.90 (0-8357-5070-1, 2015174) Bks Demand.

Accounting Profession in Canada. Fuller J. Landau & Mann J. Landau. (Professional Accounting in Foreign Countries Ser.). 75p. reprint ed. pap. 25.00 (0-7837-0278-7, 2040599) Bks Demand.

Accounting Profession in France. BEFEC Mulguin & Associates Staff & Seidman & Seidman Staff. Ed. by Susan Sgromo & Steven Moliterno. (Professional Accounting in Foreign Countries Ser.). 135p. (Orig.). 1988. pap. text ed. 30.00 (0-87051-005-3) Am Inst CPA.

Accounting Profession in Hong Kong. American Institute of Certified Public Accountants Staff. Ed. by Susan Sgromo & Steven Moliterno. (Professional Accounting in Foreign Countries Ser.). 104p. 1988. pap. text ed. 30.00 (0-87051-004-5) Am Inst CPA.

Accounting Profession in Japan. American Institute of Certified Public Accountants Staff. (Professional Accounting in Foreign Countries Ser.). 87p. reprint ed. pap. 25.00 (0-7837-3035-7, 2042893) Bks Demand.

Accounting Profession in Mexico. AICPA Staff. (Professional Accounting in Foreign Countries Ser.). 88p. (Orig.). 1988. pap. text ed. 30.00 (0-87051-056-8) Am Inst CPA.

Accounting Profession in the Netherlands. American Institute of Certified Public Accountants Staff. (Professional Accounting in Foreign Countries Ser.). 96p. reprint ed. pap. 27.40 (0-7837-1055-0, 2041535) Bks Demand.

Accounting Profession in the Philippines. American Institute of Certified Public Accountants Staff. (Professional Accounting in Foreign Countries Ser.). 64p. 1989. 30.00 (0-87051-058-4) Am Inst CPA.

Accounting Profession in Washington State: A Century of Progress. W.S.C.P.A. Staff. 208p. 1989. boxed, per. 23.00 (0-8403-5603-X) Kendall-Hunt.

Accounting Queries. Harold C. Edey. LC 82-82487. (Accountancy in Transition Ser.). 296p. 1982. lib. bdg. 20.00 (0-8240-5335-4) Garland.

Accounting Reform in Central & Eastern Europe. OECD Staff. 160p. (Orig.). 1992. pap. 28.00 (92-64-13609-6) OECD.

Accounting Research & Accounting Practice: European Perspectives. A. Hopwood. 1994. 53.33 (0-13-004789-9) P-H.

Accounting Research Directory: Database of Accounting Literature. 3rd ed. Lawrence D. Brown et al. LC 93-21572. 1994. 69.95 (1-55876-068-7) Wiener Pubs Inc.

Accounting Research Methods: Do the Facts Speak for Themselves? Wanda A. Wallace. 105p. (C). 1991. text ed. 49.95 (0-256-10047-0, 01-3454-01) Irwin.

Accounting Responses to Changing Prices: Experimentation with Four Models, by Task Force on Conceptual Framework for Accounting & Reporting, AICPA. American Institute of Certified Public Accountants. 237p. reprint ed. 67.60 (0-8357-5071-X, 2027574) Bks Demand.

Accounting, Self-Instruction Manual. Selma H. Lamkin. (Orig.). (C). 20.00 (0-686-32949-X) Nikmal Pub.

Accounting Services for Your Small Business: A Guide for Evaluating Company Performance, Obtaining Financing, Selling Your Business. Raymond J. Lipay. LC 82-13647. 270p. reprint ed. pap. 77.00 (0-7837-3512-X, 2057845) Bks Demand.

Accounting Services, the International Economy, & Third World Development. David L. McKee & Don E. Garner. LC 92-16548. 176p. 1992. text ed. 47.95 (0-275-94115-9, C4115, Praeger Pubs) Greenwood.

Accounting Simplified: An Introductory Text. Gayle A. Stelter & Ambrose S. Kodet. 1981. write for info. (0-672-97177-1); write for info. (0-672-97180-1); write for info. (0-672-97179-8) Macmillan.

Accounting Software & the Microcomputer: A Practical Guide to Evaluation & Implementation. Winsten. 356p. 1990. pap. text ed. 95.00 (0-471-85312-7) Wiley.

Accounting Software Directory for IBM & Compatible DOS Computers. ICP Staff & Larry A. Welke. Ed. by Sheila Cunningham & Marilyn Law. 1990. pap. 19.95 (0-88094-173-1) Intl Computer.

Accounting Standards. 4th ed. John Blake. 320p. 1993. pap. 42.50 (0-273-60102-4, Pub. by Pitman Pub Ltd UK) Trans-Atl Phila.

***Accounting Standards.** 5th ed. John Blake. 320p. 1995. pap. 52.50 (0-273-61417-7) Trans-Atl Phila.

***Accounting Standards: Current Text As of June 1, 1993, Vol. 1.** Financial Accounting Standards Board Staff. 1340p. 1993. pap. 180.00 (0-7837-8480-5, 2049285) Bks Demand.

***Accounting Standards: Current Text As of June 1, 1993, Vol. 2.** Financial Accounting Standards Board Staff. 1074p. 1993. pap. 180.00 (0-7837-8481-3, 2049285) Bks Demand.

Accounting Standards: Original Pronouncements, July 1973-June 1986. Financial Accounting Standards Board. Incl. Original Pronouncements Through June 1973. 1986. 14.95 (0-07-020946-4); Statements of Financial Accounting Concepts 1-6. 1986. 10.95 (0-07-020943-X); Current Text, General Standards. 1986. 19.95 (0-07-020948-0); 1986. 19.95 (0-07-020944-8) McGraw.

Accounting Standards Complexity. Jean D. Martin & Robert C. Elmore. 80p. 1994. 15.00 (0-910586-99-3) Finan Exec.

Accounting Standards Setting in the Member States. EC Staff. 56p. 1993. pap. 10.00 (92-826-5784-1, C1-78-93-516-EN-C, Pub. by Europ Com) UNIPUB.

Accounting Structured in APL, Vol. 6. Yuji Ijiri. LC 83-73175. (Studies in Accounting Education). 151p. 1984. 12.00 (0-86539-047-9) Am Accounting.

Accounting Student Perceptions of Business & Professional Ethics. James H. Sellers & Edward E. Milam. 50p. (Orig.). 1981. pap. 4.50 (0-938004-00-X) U MS Bus Econ.

Accounting Students & Abstract Reasoning. George E. Shute. 71p. 1979. 12.00 (0-86539-011-8) Am Accounting.

Accounting Study Supplement. Western Michigan University, Department of Accounting Staff. (C). 1993. student ed 12.00 (1-881592-23-5) Hayden-McNeil.

Accounting System for Private Carriers. 1970. 2.50 (0-686-31453-0) Private Carrier.

Accounting Systems & Practice in Europe. 3rd ed. K. M. Oldham. 335p. 1987. text ed. 89.95 (0-566-02612-0) Ashgate Pub Co.

Accounting Systems for Law Offices. William J. Burke & Carl W. Bradbury. 1978. Looseleaf updates available. write for info. (0-8205-1014-9) Bender.

Accounting Systems of U. S. Government Agencies. Thomas Canada. 1983. 22.00 (0-87771-013-9) Grad School.

Accounting Systems Specialist. (Career Examination Ser.: C-1070). 1994. pap. 39.95 (0-8373-1070-9) Nat Learn.

Accounting Technician (U.S.P.S.) Jack Rudman. (Career Examination Ser.: C-2252). 1994. pap. 27.95 (0-8373-2252-9) Nat Learn.

Accounting Terms & Book-Keeping Procedures Explained. Diane Houghton & Ralph G. Wallace. 278p. (Orig.). 1980. pap. text ed. 25.95 (0-566-00393-7) Ashgate Pub Co.

***Accounting, Text & Cases.** 9th rev. ed. Robert N. Anthony et al. LC 94-21933. 1072p. (C). 1994. text ed. 69.95 (0-256-12372-1) Irwin.

Accounting: The Basis for Business Decisions: Problem Supplement II Solutions Manual. Brenda M. Mallouk. (C). 1990. pap. text ed. write for info. (0-07-551001-4, Pub. by McGraw-H Ryerson CN) McGraw.

***Accounting the Business Environment.** 2nd ed. John Watts. 640p. 1995. pap. 73.50 (0-273-61560-2) Trans-Atl Phila.

Accounting the Easy Way. 2nd ed. Peter J. Eisen. (Easy Way Ser.). 384p. 1989. pap. 9.95 (0-8120-4187-9) Barron.

***Accounting the Easy Way.** 3rd ed. Peter J. Eisen. LC 95-14303. 1995. write for info. (0-8120-9409-3) Barron.

Accounting Theory. 2nd ed. Vernon Kam. LC 08-922715. 1990. Net. text ed. write for info. (0-471-50704-0) Wiley.

Accounting Theory. 3rd ed. Ahmed R. Belkaoui. 106p. (C). 1992. student ed 4.75 (0-03-097205-1) Dryden Pr.

Accounting Theory. 5th ed. Eldon Hendriksen & Michael Van Breda. 734p. (C). 1991. text ed. 69.95 (0-256-08146-8, 01-0230-05) Irwin.

Accounting Theory: A Conceptual & Institutional Approach. 3rd ed. H. Wolk. 600p. (C). 1992. text ed. 62.95 (0-538-82158-2, AT60CA) S-W Pub.

Accounting Theory: An Outline of Its Structure with a New Introduction by the Author. Harry Norris. Ed. by Richard P. Brief. LC 80-1512. (Dimensions of Accounting Theory & Practice Ser.). 1980. reprint ed. lib. bdg. 17.95 (0-405-13537-8) Ayer.

***Accounting Theory: Integrating Behaviour & Measurement.** Sven-Erik Johansson & Lars Ostman. 385p. 1995. pap. 62.50 (0-273-60512-7) Trans-Atl Phila.

Accounting Theory: Selected Questions & Unofficial Answers Indexed to Content Specification Outline. American Institute of Certified Public Accountants Staff. Ed. by James D. Blum & Charles A. Rhuda. LC 84-160551. 111p. reprint ed. pap. 31.70 (0-8357-5072-8, 2025094) Bks Demand.

Accounting Theory: Text & Readings. 4th ed. Richard G. Schroeder et al. 1991. Net. text ed. write for info. (0-471-52769-6) Wiley.

***Accounting Theory: Text & Readings.** 5th ed. Richard G. Schroeder et al. LC 94-3616. 1994. text ed. write for info. (0-471-30532-4) Wiley.

***Accounting Theory & GAAP: Interpretation & Application 1994.** 2nd ed. Patrick Delaney. 1994. text ed. write for info. (0-471-04317-6) Wiley.

Accounting Theory & Policy: A Reader. 2nd ed. Robert Bloom & Pieter T. Elgers. 660p. (C). 1987. pap. text ed. 34.00 (0-15-500478-6) Dryden Pr.

Accounting Theory & Policy Making. 1985. 31.95 (0-434-91914-4) Buttrwrth-Heinemann.

Accounting Theory & Practice. 5th ed. M. W. Glautier & Brian Underdown. 736p. (Orig.). 1994. pap. 67.50 (0-273-60472-4, Pub. by Pitman Pub Ltd UK) Trans-Atl Phila.

***Accounting Theory Text & Readings: GAAP Interpretation & Application 1994.** 4th ed. Richard G. Schroeder et al. text ed. write for info. (0-471-05778-9) Wiley.

***Accounting Thesaurus: Accounting Through 500 Years.** R. J. Chambers. 1100p. 1995. 110.00 (0-08-042573-9, Pergamon Pr) Elsevier.

Accounting Thought & Education: Six English Pioneers. J. Kitchen & R. H. Parker. LC 83-49507. (Accounting History & the Development Ser.). 126p. 1984. lib. bdg. 15.00 (0-8240-6331-7) Garland.

Accounting Today: Principles & Applications. Mark F. Asman et al. (Illus.). 920p. (C). 1986. text ed. 65.75 (0-314-69644-X); Transparency masters. student ed, text ed. write for info. (0-314-97113-0); Instr's. resource manual. pap. text ed. write for info. (0-314-96587-4); Study guide. student ed, pap. text ed. 21.75 (0-314-96588-2) West Pub.

Accounting Trainee. Jack Rudman. (Career Examination Ser.: C-6). 1994. pap. 23.95 (0-8373-0006-1) Nat Learn.

***Accounting Trends & Techniques: 46th Annual Cumulative Survey of the Accounting Aspects of the Annual Reports of 600 Industrial & Merchandising Corporations to Which Are Added Excerpts...the Reports Analyzed Are Those with Fiscal Years Ended Not Later Than February 2, 1992.** 46th ed. American Institute of Certified Public Accountants Staff. Ed. by Jack Shohet & Richard Rikert. LC 48-2517. 536p. 1992. pap. 152.80 (0-7837-8534-8, 2049347) Bks Demand.

An Asterisk (*) at the beginning of an entry indicates that the title is appearing in BIP for the first time.

***Accounting Trends & Techniques: 47th Annual Cumulative Survey of the Accounting Aspects of the Annual Reports of 600 Industrial & Merchandising Corporations to Which Are Added Excerpts...the Reports Analyzed Are Those with Fiscal Years Ended Not Later Than January 31, 1993.** 47th ed. American Institute of Certified Public Accountants Staff. Ed. by Jack Shohet & Richard Rikert. LC 48-2517. 600p. 1993. pap. 171.00 (*0-7837-8535-6*, 2049348) Bks Demand.

Accounting with Lotus 1-2-3. Wendy M. Greenfield. 176p. 1989. pap. 27.95 (*0-13-003583-1*) P-H.

Accounting with Microcomputer. Lewis M. Elia & Joseph A. Fall. 1986. 6.50 (*0-87350-605-7*); Apple II 45.00 (*0-87350-787-8*); 42.50 (*0-87350-788-6*) Milady Pub.

Accounting with New Views: Educational Version. Robert H. Phillips, Jr. 264p. (Orig.). (C). 1989. pap. text ed. 39.95 (*0-8162-6739-1*) Holden-Day.

Accounting with Symphony. Wendy M. Greenfield. (Illus.). 197p. 1986. 29.95 (*0-13-001660-8*); disk, pap. 39.95 (*0-685-17143-4*) P-H.

Accounting, 1993 Edition: Chapters 1-19. 2nd ed. Horngren. 1993. text ed. 35.00 (*0-13-077935-0*) P-H.

Accounting's Changing Role in Social Conflict. Cheryl R. Lehman. LC 91-47864. (Critical Accounting Research Ser.). 186p. (C). 1995. 39.95 (*1-55876-030-X*) Wiener Pubs Inc.

***Accounting's Changing Role in Social Conflict.** Cheryl R. Lehman. LC 91-47864. (Critical Accounting Research Ser.). 186p. (C). 1995. pap. text ed. 24.95x (*1-55876-101-2*) Wiener Pubs Inc.

Accounts. Ed. by M. A. Nardone. 150p. (C). 1990. 60.00 (*0-685-52525-2*, Pub. by HLT Pubns UK) St Mut.

Accounts: Their Construction & Interpretation for Business Men & Students of Affairs. William M. Cole. LC 75-18462. (History of Accounting Ser.). 1976. 36.95 (*0-405-07546-4*) Ayer.

Accounts, Accounting & Accountability: Essays in Memory of Peter Bird. Ed. by G. MacDonald & Brian Rutherford. 240p. 1990. 57.50 (*0-412-02781-X*, A4461, Chap & Hall NY) Chapman & Hall.

Accounts & Audit of Insurance Brokers & FIMBRA Mem. Clark Whitehill. 290p. 1994. pap. write for info. (*0-406-02266-6*, UK) Butterworth Legal Pubs.

***Accounts & Audit of Leases.** Roger Chadder. 1995. boxed write for info. (*0-406-02013-2*, UK) Butterworth Legal Pubs.

Accounts & Audit of Property Companies. Simon Bevan & Peter Chidgey. 1994. pap. write for info. (*0-406-01648-8*, U.K.) Butterworth Legal Pubs.

Accounts & Papers Relating to Mary Queen of Scots. Ed. by Allan J. Crosby & John Bruce. (Camden Society, London. Publications, First Ser.: No. 93). reprint ed. 37.50 (*0-404-50193-1*) AMS Pr.

Accounts Demystified: How to Understand & Use Company Accounts. Anthony Rice. 192p. (Orig.). 1993. pap. 45.00x (*0-273-60154-7*, Pub. by Pitman Pubng UK) St Mut.

Accounts, Designs & Roses. Arlene J. Nelson. (Teachings of the Master, Sinat Schirah "Suggestions for Learning" Ser.). 240p. (Orig.). 1988. pap. 12.95 (*0-685-26083-6*, TXU 307-298) Loveline Prodns.

***Accounts, Excuses & Apologies.** William L. Benoit. 1995. pap. 14.95 (*0-7914-2186-4*) State U NY Pr.

Accounts Investigator. Jack Rudman. (Career Examination Ser.: C-1862). 1994. pap. 27.95 (*0-8373-1862-9*) Nat Learn.

Account's Legal Reponsibility. Saul Levy. Ed. by Richard P. Brief. LC 80-1509. (Dimensions of Accounting Theory & Practice Ser.). 1980. reprint ed. lib. bdg. 31.95 (*0-405-13534-3*) Ayer.

Accounts of European Science, Technology, & Medicine Written by American Travelers Abroad, 1735-1860: In the Collections of the American Philosophical Society. Darwin H. Stapleton. LC 85-71739. (American Philosophical Society Library Publication Ser.: No. 9). 56p. reprint ed. pap. 25.00 (*0-8357-3412-9*, 2039669) Bks Demand.

Accounts of Nations. Z. Kenessey. LC 94-75424. 251p. 1994. 82.00 (*90-5199-156-8*) IOS Press.

Accounts of Religious Revivals in Many Parts of the United States from 1815 to 1818: Collected from Numerous Publications & Letters from Persons of Piety & Correct Information. Joshua Bradley. (Revival Library). 300p. (C). 1980. reprint ed. lib. bdg. 15.00 (*0-940033-13-5*) R O Roberts.

Accounts of Religious Revivals in Many Parts of the United States from 1815-1818. Joshua Bradley. 300p. 1980. 15.00 (*0-939464-35-7*) Labyrinth Pr.

Accounts of Shipwrecks & Other Disasters. William Allen. (Works of William Allen). 1989. reprint ed. lib. bdg. 79.00 (*0-7812-1767-9*) Rprt Serv.

Accounts of the Apparition of Mrs. Veal (1705-1766) Daniel Defoe et al. LC 92-22890. (Augustan Reprints Ser.: No. 115 (1965)). reprint ed. 12.00 (*0-404-70115-9*, BF1473) AMS Pr.

Accounts of the Great Chamberlains of Scotland, 3 Vols, Set. Ed. by Thomas Thomson. 1845. 250.00 (*0-404-52810-4*) AMS Pr.

Accounts of the Gypsies of India. Ed. by David MacRitchie. LC 75-3461. (Illus.). reprint ed. 24.00 (*0-404-16893-0*) AMS Pr.

Accounts of the Northern Ireland Housing Executive for Year Ended 31 March 90... HMSO Staff. (Command Paper Ser.: No. 1453). 60p. 1991. pap. 25.00 (*0-10-114532-2*, HM2435) UNIPUB.

Accounts of the Second, Third, & Twelfth Annual Gatherings of the Bailey-Bayley Family Association. 123p. 1988. reprint ed. lib. bdg. 28.75 (*0-8328-0158-5*); reprint ed. pap. 18.75 (*0-8328-0159-3*) Higginson Bk Co.

Accounts Overdue: Natural Resource Depreciation in Costa Rica. large type ed. Tropical Science Center Staff. 110p. 1991. Large format. pap. 14.95 (*0-915825-66-X*, CRRAP) World Resources Inst.

Accounts Payable Practice Set. Fred C. Archer, Jr. et al. 1969. text ed. 12.96 (*0-07-002196-1*) McGraw.

Accounts Payable Solutions Using Lotus. J. N. Howell. 40p. 1989. pap. 25.00 (*0-932223-09-5*) Churchill PC.

Accounts Receivable, Financial Arrangements & Collections, Vol 1: A Complete How-to Manual for the Doctor & Staff. Robert D. Westerman. 436p. 1993. 295.00 (*0-9629983-1-1*) R Westerman.

Accounts Receivable Financing. Raymond J. Saulnier & Neil H. Jacoby. (Financial Research Program III: Studies in Business Financing: No. 3). 172p. 1943. reprint ed. 45.50 (*0-87014-131-7*); reprint ed. mic. film 22.80 (*0-685-61236-8*) Natl Bur Econ Res.

Accounts Receivable Information System. Credit Research Foundation Staff. 12p. 1974. 40.00 (*0-939050-02-1*) Credit Res NYS.

***Accounts Receivable Management for the Medical Practice.** J. Dennis Mock. (Orig.). 1995. pap. 39.95 (*0-07-600714-6*) Hlthcare Mgmt Grp.

Accounts Receivable Practice Set. Fred C. Archer et al. 1970. text ed. 12.96 (*0-07-002195-3*) McGraw.

Accounts Rendered by Papal Collectors in England, 1317-1378. William E. Lunt. LC 67-19647. (American Philosophical Society, Memoirs Ser.: Vol. 70). 633p. reprint ed. pap. 180.00 (*0-8357-5073-6*, 2019712) Bks Demand.

Acoustic Emission Nondestructive Evaluation of Yankee Dryers. Claudio Allevato & David Williams. Ed. by W. G. Corboy. LC 92-23971. 1992. write for info. (*0-89852-301-X*, 0101R208) TAPPI.

Accoutability in Namibia: Human Rights & the Transition to Democracy. Ed. by Human Rights Watch Staff. 134p. (Orig.). 1992. pap. 10.00 (*1-56432-077-4*) Hum Rts Watch.

Accoutrements of Ozone & Other Running Stories. Brian Soneda. LC 89-50556. (Illus.). 134p. (Orig.). 1989. pap. 8.95 (*0-9623142-2-6*) Tenth Teardrop.

Accoutrements of the Army of the United States. Ed. by Jacques N. Jacobsen. 1989. 4.00 (*0-913150-89-4*) Pioneer Pr.

ACCP SEEK Critical Care Medicine: Assessment in Critical Care & Pulmonology: Self-Education & Evaluation of Knowledge, 2 bks., Set. J. G. Weg et al. Ed. by American College Testing Staff. (ACCP-SEEK Annual Self-Assessment Ser.). (Illus.). 250p. 1992. pap. text ed. 200.00 (*0-916609-01-4*) Am Chest Phys.

***ACCP SEEK Critical Care Medicine: Assessment in Critical Care & Pulmonology: Self-Education & Evaluation of Knowledge, 2 Vols., Set.** J. G. Weg et al. Ed. by American College of Chest Physicians Staff. (ACCP SEEK Annual Self-Assessment Ser.). (Illus.). 171p. 1994. pap. text ed. 150.00 (*0-916609-05-7*) Am Chest Phys.

***ACCP SEEK Critical Care Medicine: Assessment in Critical Care & Pulmonology: Self-Education & Evaluation of Knowledge, 2 vols., Set.** J. G. Weg et al. Ed. by American College of Chest Physicians Staff. (ACCP SEEK Annual Self-Assessment Ser.). (Illus.). 110p. 1994. pap. 150.00 (*0-916609-03-0*) Am Chest Phys.

ACCP SEEK Pulmonary Medicine, 1994-95, 2 vols., Set. rev. ed. John G. Weg et al. (Illus.). 1993. write for info. (*0-916609-02-2*) Am Chest Phys.

***Accreditation: Protecting the Professional or the Consumer?** Ellie Scrivens. LC 94-44778. (State of Health Ser.). 1995. 79.00 (*0-335-19492-3*, Open Univ Pr); pap. write for info. (*0-335-19491-5*, Open Univ Pr) Taylor & Francis.

Accreditation - Approval Manual for Dietetic Education Programs. 2nd ed. American Dietetic Association Staff. LC 87-71110. 132p. (Orig.). 1991. pap. 28.45 (*0-88091-031-3*) Am Dietetic Assn.

Accreditation Criteria & Procedures of the National Academy of Early Childhood Programs. LC 84-62064. 59p. 1984. pap. text ed. 7.00 (*0-912674-91-1*, NAEYC #920) Natl Assn Child Ed.

Accreditation Handbook. 90p. ring bd. 35.00 (*0-685-65743-4*, E-1) Am Phys Therapy Assn.

Accreditation Handbook for Ambulatory Health Care: 1989-90 Edition. rev. ed. Ed. by Ronald S. Moen. 73p. 1989. pap. 30.00 (*0-685-18876-0*) Accredit Assn Ambulatory.

Accreditation Handbook for Ambulatory Health Care 1992-93. rev. ed. 67p. 1991. pap. 40.00 (*0-932915-05-1*) Accredit Assn Ambulatory.

Accreditation Manual for Hospitals: 1989 Edition. 370p. 1988. pap. 60.00 (*0-86688-170-0*) Joint Comm Hlthcare.

Accreditation Manual for Hospitals: 1990 Edition. 275p. 1988. pap. 90.00 (*0-86688-207-3*) Joint Comm Hlthcare.

Accreditation Manual for Long Term Care Facilities, 1980 Edition. Joint Commission on Accreditation of Hospitals. 86p. 1979. 12.50 (*0-685-43370-6*, LTC-202) Joint Comm Hlthcare.

Accreditation of Historically & Predominantly Black Colleges & Universities. Ed. by Wilma J. Roscoe. LC 88-39408. (Illus.). 68p. (Orig.). (C). 1989. lib. bdg. 25.00 (*0-8191-7288-X*, NAEOHE) U Pr of Amer.

Accreditation of Teacher Education: The Story of CATE 1984-1989. Gordon MacIntyre. 224p. 1991. 65.00 (*1-85000-980-5*, Falmer Pr); pap. 31.00 (*1-85000-981-3*, Falmer Pr) Taylor & Francis.

***Accreditation of the Two-Year College.** Ed. by Carolyn Prager. LC 85-644753. (New Directions for Community Colleges Ser.: No. 83). 110p. (Orig.). 1993. pap. 16.95 (*1-55542-718-9*) Jossey-Bass.

Accreditation Practices for Inspections, Tests, & Laboratories. Ed. by Harvey E. Schock, Jr. LC 89-38230. (Special Technical Publication Ser.: No. 1057). (Illus.). 155p. 1989. text ed. 25.00 (*0-8031-1279-3*, 04-010570-32) ASTM.

Accreditation Requirements Manual. 5th rev. ed. Ed. by Francis S. Jones. 235p. (C). 1994. pap. text ed. 35.00 (*1-56395-035-9*) Am Assn Blood.

Accredited Institutions of Postsecondary Education. Ed. by Sherry S. Harris. 483p. 25.00 (*0-318-13850-6*) Coun Postsecondary Accredit.

Accredited Institutions of Postsecondary Education: 1987-88 Edition. 1989. text ed. 39.95 (*0-02-900963-4*, 2008) Macmillan.

Accredited Institutions of Postsecondary Education, 1985-1986. rev. ed. Sherry S. Harris. 418p. (Orig.). 1986. pap. text ed. 22.50 (*0-02-913970-8*) Macmillan.

Accredited Institutions of Postsecondary Education, 1988-89: Programs - Candidates. Sherry S. Harris. (Ace-Macmillan Series on Higher Education). 508p. 1988. 22.50 (*0-02-900634-1*) Macmillan.

Accredited Institutions of Postsecondary Education, 1993-94. Ed. by William A. Wade. LC 93-32154. 720p. 1994. pap. 39.95 (*0-89774-915-4*) Oryx Pr.

Accredited Management Organization Profile: 1990 Edition. rev. ed. Institute of Real Estate Management Staff. Ed. by Nancye J. Kirk. 22p. 1991. pap. text ed. 24.95 (*0-944298-58-3*) Inst Real Estate.

Accredited Management Organization Profile: 1994 Edition. rev. ed. IREM Research Department Staff. 22p. 1994. pap. 29.95 (*0-685-71657-0*, 834) Inst Real Estate.

Accredited Residential Manager Profile: 1990 Edition. rev. ed. Institute of Real Estate Management Staff. 22p. 1990. pap. text ed. 24.95 (*0-944298-55-9*) Inst Real Estate.

Accrediting Occupational Training Programs. Roland V. Stoodley, Jr. 79p. 1983. 6.50 (*0-318-22012-1*, IN251) Ctr Educ Trng Employ.

Accrediting Standards & Guidelines: A Current Profile. Dorothy G. Petersen. 168p. 1979. 8.25 (*0-318-13851-4*) Coun Postsecondary Accredit.

Accreditors. H. R. Kells. 64p. 1983. 3.30 (*0-318-17062-0*) Coun Postsecondary Accredit.

Accreted Terranes of the North Cascades Range, Washington. Ed. by Tabor. (IGC Field Trip Guidebooks Ser.). 72p. 1989. 21.00 (*0-87590-612-5*, T307) Am Geophysical.

Accretion. A. Treves et al. Ed. by M. Abranowitz. 372p. (C). 1989. text ed. 53.00 (*981-02-0077-3*) World Scientific Pub.

Accretion Disks & Magnetic Fields in Astrophysics. Ed. by G. Belvedere. (C). 1989. lib. bdg. 112.50 (*0-7923-0295-8*) Kluwer Ac.

Accretion Disks in Compact Stellar Systems. J. C. Wheeler. (Advanced Series in Astrophysics & Cosmology). 432p. 1993. text ed. 109.00 (*981-02-1273-9*) World Scientific Pub.

Accretion Power in Astrophysics. 2nd ed. Juhan Frank et al. (Cambridge Astrophysics Ser.: No. 21). (Illus.). 320p. (C). 1992. 79.95 (*0-521-40306-5*); pap. 39.95 (*0-521-40863-6*) Cambridge U Pr.

Accretion-Powered Compact Binaries. Ed. by Christopher W. Mauche. (Illus.). 496p. (C). 1990. 69.95 (*0-521-40212-3*) Cambridge U Pr.

Accretion Tectonics in the Circum-Pacific Regions. Ed. by Mitsuo Hashimoto & S. Uyeda. 1983. lib. bdg. 177.00 (*90-277-1561-0*) Kluwer Ac.

Accrual Accounting in Developing Countries. 62p. 8.50 (*92-1-123047-0*, E.84.11.H.2) UN.

ACCSAP - Adult Clinical Cardiology Self Assessment Program. American College of Cardiology Staff. Ed. by Richard P. Lewis. LC 93-70707. (Illus.). 300p. 1993. text ed. 395.00 (*1-882764-01-3*) Am Coll Cardiology.

***ACCU-Data User's Guide 4.1.** ACCU-Weather, Inc. Staff. 304p. 1995. pap. text ed., ring bd. 7.75 (*0-7872-1078-1*) Kendall-Hunt.

Acculturation & Personality among the Wisconsin Chippewa. Victor Barnouw. LC 76-43646. (AAA Memoir Ser.: No. 72). reprint ed. 39.50 (*0-404-15481-6*) AMS Pr.

Acculturation of Anti-Culture: A Study of Trillings Beyond Culture. Kamalini Dravid. 64p. 1989. text ed. 8.95 (*81-7045-034-9*, Pub. by Associated Pub Hse II) Advent Bks Div.

Acculturation of the Italo-Americans in Norristown, Pennsylvania: 1900-1950. Francis A. Ianni. LC 91-2690. (Immigrant Communities & Ethnic Minorities in the U. S. & Canada Ser.: No. 79). 1991. 52.50 (*0-404-19489-3*) AMS Pr.

Acculturation of the Lithuanians of Chester, Pennsylvania. Peter P. Jonitis. LC 83-45357. (Immigrant Communities & Ethnic Minorities in the U. S. & Canada Ser.: No. 12). 1986. 76.50 (*0-404-19410-9*) AMS Pr.

***Accumulated Index of Jewish Bibliographical Periodicals.** R. Dan. 276p. (C). 1979. 78.00x (*963-05-1047-2*, Pub. by Akad Kiado HU) St Mut.

***Accumulating Cats.** Mary L. Stahl. (Illus.). 56p. Date not set. write for info. (*1-886075-09-3*) Grass Rt Ent.

Accumulation & Development: The Logic of Industrial Civilization. Celso Furtado. LC 83-40058. 225p. 1983. text ed. 45.00 (*0-312-00239-4*) St Martin.

Accumulation & Power: An Economic History of the United States. Richard B. Du Boff. LC 88-39542. 252p. (C). 1989. pap. text ed. 20.95 (*0-87332-559-1*) M E Sharpe.

***Accumulation, Exchange & Development: Essays on the Indian Economy.** Krishna Bharadwaj. 400p. 1994. 42.00 (*0-8039-9176-2*) Sage.

Accumulation of Capital. 3rd ed. Joan Robinson. LC 85-12465. xvi, 440p. 1986. reprint ed. lib. bdg. 45.00 (*0-87991-266-9*); reprint ed. pap. 22.95 (*0-87991-260-X*) Porcupine Pr.

Accumulation of Capital - An Anti-Critique & Imperialism & the Accumulation of Capital. Rosa Luxemburg & Nikolai I. Bukharin. Tr. by Rudolf Wichmann. LC 72-81768. 299p. reprint ed. pap. 85.30 (*0-8357-6001-4*, 2034339) Bks Demand.

Accumulation of Organic Carbon in Marine Sediments. R. Stein. (Lecture Notes in Earth Sciences Ser.: Vol. 34). 217p. 1991. pap. 39.00 (*0-387-53813-5*) Spr-Verlag.

Accumulation on a World Scale: A Critique of the Theory of Underdevelopment, 2 vols., 2. Samir Amin. Tr. by Brian Pearce. LC 72-92028. 314p. reprint ed. pap. 89.50 (*0-8357-6003-0*, 2034354) Bks Demand.

Accumulation on a World Scale: A Critique of the Theory of Underdevelopment, 2 vols., Vol. 1. Samir Amin. Tr. by Brian Pearce. LC 72-92028. 365p. reprint ed. pap. 104.10 (*0-8357-6002-2*, 2034354) Bks Demand.

***Accupril (Quinapril) Review of Preclinical & Clinical Data.** LC 91-75285. (Illus.). 189p. 1991. text ed. 28.95 (*0-924428-04-X*) Phys Sci Pub.

Accuracy in Molecular Processes: Its Control & Relevance to Living Systems. B. L. Kirkwood et al. (Illus.). 450p. 1986. text ed. 105.00 (*0-412-26940-6*, 9772) Chapman & Hall.

Accuracy in Rhythm. Richard Ely. 46p. 1981. pap. 9.95 (*0-938170-03-1*) Wimbledon Music.

Accuracy in X-Ray Intensity Measurements. Ed. by S. C. Abrahams. (Transactions of the American Crystallographic Association Ser.: Vol. 1). 112p. 1965. pap. 25.00 (*0-686-60372-9*) Polycrystal Bk Serv.

Accuracy Inspection of NC-Machine Tools: Double Ball Bar Method. Y. Kakino et al. Ed. by Johannes Heidenhain. LC 93-37467. 200p. (C). 1993. text ed. write for info. (*1-56990-160-0*) Hanser-Gardner.

Accuracy of Classical Images. Elmont King. 1994. 34.95 (*0-913412-83-X*) Brandon Hse.

Accuracy of Element Abundances from Stellar Atmospheres. Ed. by R. Wehrse. (Lecture Notes in Physics Ser.: Vol. 356). vi, 109p. 1990. 42.00 (*0-387-52365-0*) Spr-Verlag.

Accuracy of Machine Tools. Ed. by D. N. Reshetov & V. T. Portman. 304p. 1988. 68.00 (*0-7918-0004-0*, 800040) ASME Pr.

Accuracy of Spatial Databases. Ed. by Michael F. Goodchild. 350p. 1989. 90.00 (*0-85066-847-6*) Taylor & Francis.

Accuracy of Telephone Reference-Information Services in Academic Libraries: Two Studies. Marcia J. Myers & Jassim M. Jirjees. LC 82-10785. 282p. 1983. 25.00 (*0-8108-1584-2*) Scarecrow.

Accuracy of Voluntary Movement see On Inhibition

Accurate Business Forecasting. Harvard Business Review Staff. (Financial Manager Ser.). 101p. 1991. pap. 19.95 (*0-87584-291-7*) Harvard Busn.

Accurate Business Forecasting. Harvard Business School Press Staff. 1991. 19.95 (*0-07-103351-3*) McGraw.

Accurate English: A Complete Course in Pronunciation. Rebecca M. Dauer. 256p. 1992. pap. text ed. 18.25 (*0-13-007253-2*) P-H.

Accurate Molecular Structures: Their Determination & Importance. Ed. by Aldo Domenicano & Istvan Hargittai. (International Union of Crystallography Monographs on Crystallography: No. 1). (Illus.). 600p. 1992. 125.00 (*0-19-855556-3*) OUP.

***Accurate Muscle Testing for Foods & Supplements Plus Balancing Meridians.** Elizabeth Barhydt & Hamilton Barhydt. (Illus.). 64p. 1992. pap. 10.00 (*0-9605346-3-6*) Loving Life.

Accurate Numerical Algorithms. Ed. by C. Ullrich & J. Wolff Von Gudenberg. (Research Reports ESPRIT: Vol. 1). ix, 234p. 1989. pap. 29.00 (*0-387-51477-5*, 3388) Spr-Verlag.

Accurate Perspective Simplified. Howard J. Ashley. LC 73-89328. (Illus.). 224p. (C). 1974. text ed. 16.00 (*0-914214-01-2*) Abak Pr.

Accurate Price Guide for Miniature Lamps I & II. Ruth E. Smith & Helen A. Feltner. LC 88-62163. 48p. 1988. pap. 10.00 (*0-88740-142-2*) Schiffer.

Accurate Scientific Computations. Ed. by W. L. Miranker & R. A. Toupin. (Lecture Notes in Computer Science Ser.: Vol. 235). xiii, 205p. 1986. pap. 33.00 (*0-387-16798-6*) Spr-Verlag.

Accurate Single-Crystal Diffractometry, New Orleans, 1990. (American Crystallographic Association Lecture Notes Ser.: No. 11). 1991. pap. 15.00 (*0-685-51616-4*) Polycrystal Bk Serv.

Accurate World Horoscopes. Doris C. Doane. 353p. 1984. 30.00 (*0-86690-241-4*, D2351-014) Am Fed Astrologers.

Accursed Share, Vol. 1. Georges Bataille. Tr. by Robert Hurley. LC 87-34072. 197p. 1988. 24.95 (*0-942299-10-8*); pap. 12.95 (*0-942299-11-6*) Zone Bks.

Accursed Share, Vols. II & III. Georges Bataille. Tr. by Robert Hurley. LC 87-34072. 460p. 1992. 32.95 (*0-942299-20-5*); pap. 18.95 (*0-942299-21-3*) Zone Bks.

Accursed Wives. Bruce Baston. (Illus.). 28p. (Orig.). 1994. pap. 3.50 (*0-9626708-7-1*) Talisman IN.

***Accusations of Child Sexual Abuse.** Hollida Wakefield & Ralph Underwager. 530p. 1988. pap. 49.95 (*0-398-06476-8*) C C Thomas.

Accusations of Child Sexual Abuse. Hollida Wakefield & Ralph Underwager. 530p. (C). 1988. text ed. 93.95x (*0-398-05423-1*) C C Thomas.

Accused - R. Craig Smith: The Spy Left Out in the Cold. Norman R. Hamilton. LC 87-80150. 288p. 1987. 16.98 (*0-89290-290-3*) Horizon Utah.

Accused Nurse. large type ed. Jane Converse. 1990. 21.95 (*0-7089-2293-7*) Ulverscroft.

An Asterisk (*) at the beginning of an entry indicates that the title is appearing in BIP for the first time. 33

A

Accused, the Accusers. Socialist Publishing Society Staff. LC 74-89715. (American Labor, from Conspiracy to Collective Bargaining Ser., No. 1). 188p. 1971. reprint ed. 13.95 (0-405-02149-6) Ayer.

Accutech Pneumatic Fracturing Extraction & Hot Gas Injection, Phase One: Applications Analysis Report. (Illus.). 53p. (Orig.). (C). 1994. pap. text ed. 45.00 (0-7881-0773-9) Diane Pub.

Ace. Mark Dunster. 26p. (Orig.). 1985. pap. 4.00 (0-89642-126-0) Linden Pubs.

Ace! A Marine Night-Fighter Pilot in World War II. R. Bruce Porter & Eric Hammel. (Illus.). 300p. 1985. 25.00 (0-935553-01-0) Pacifica Pr.

Ace: A Marine Night-Fighter Pilot in World War II. R. Bruce Porter & Eric Hammel. 304p. 1987. mass mkt. 4.99 (0-515-09159-6) Jove Pubns.

Ace: The Very Important Pig. Dick King-Smith. LC 90-1447. (Illus.). 144p. (J). (gr. 2-7). 1990. 13.00 (0-517-57832-8); lib. bdg. 13.99 (0-517-57833-6) Crown Bks Yng Read.

Ace: The Very Important Pig. braille ed. Deborah King-Smith. 112p. (J). 1990. vinyl bd. 8.96 (1-56956-178-8, BR8565) W A T Braille.

***ACE & the Vascular Wall - from Genotype to Therapy: Journal: Cardiology 1995, Vol. 86, Suppl. 1.** Ed. by Detlev Ganten et al. (Journal Ser.: Vol. 86, Suppl. 1, 1995). (Illus.). iv, 46p. 1995. pap. 21.75 (3-8055-6154-7) S Karger.

Ace Any Test. 2nd ed. Ron Fry. (How to Study Ser.). 128p. (C). 1994. pap. 6.95 (1-56414-079-2) Career Pr Inc.

Ace! Autobiography of a Fighter Pilot World War II. Melvyn Paisley & Vicki Paisley. 350p. 1992. 22.95 (0-8283-1943-X) Branden Pub Co.

Ace Factor. Michael Spick. 256p. 1989. mass mkt. 4.95 (0-380-70825-6) Avon.

Ace Factor. Michael Spick. (Illus.). 184p. 1988. 26.95 (0-87021-002-5) Naval Inst Pr.

Ace Fugue Shroud Method. Jerry Irvine & Korey Kline. (Advanced Information Report Ser.: No. 4). 8p. 1984. 1.50 (0-912468-02-5, AIR-4) CA Rocketry.

Ace in the Hole. Zeke Masters. (Faro Blake Ser.: No. 8). 176p. 1983. pap. 2.25 (0-671-46485-X) PB.

***Ace in the Hole - Yukon Ride.** Gene Curry. (Saddler Double Edition Ser.). 352p. 1995. mass mkt. 4.99 (0-8439-3750-5) Dorchester Pub Co.

ACE-Inhibition: State of the Art. Ed. by H. R. Brunner. (Journal: Cardiology: Vol. 76, Suppl. 2, 1989). (Illus.). iv, 68p. 1989. pap. 24.00 (3-8055-5062-6) S Karger.

Ace Inhibitors: Central Actions. John M. Starr & Lawrence J. Whalley. LC 93-35781. 272p. 1994. 75.00 (0-7817-0072-8) Raven.

***Ace Inhibitors: Current Use & Future Prospects.** Ed. by Michael Schachter. 1995. 89.00 (1-85317-121-2) Scovill Paterson.

ACE Inhibitors at the Kidney. Ed. by K. Arakawa et al. (Journal: Nephron: Vol. 54, Supl. 1, 1990). (Illus.). iv, 100p. 1990. pap. 40.00 (3-8055-5180-0) S Karger.

Ace of Diamonds. Bruce Thorstad. Ed. by Doug Grad. 256p. (Orig.). 1994. mass mkt. 3.99 (0-671-88583-9) PB.

Ace of Freedoms: Thomas Merton's Christ. George Kilcourse. LC 92-53741. 1993. text ed. 34.95 (0-268-00636-9) U of Notre Dame Pr.

Ace of Freedoms: Thomas Merton's Christ. George Kilcourse. (C). 1994. pap. text ed. 14.95 (0-268-00637-7) U of Notre Dame Pr.

Ace of Hearts: The Westerns of Zane Grey. Arthur G. Kimball. LC 93-7024. 278p. (C). 1993. 27.50 (0-87565-121-6) Tex Christian.

Ace of Spades. large type ed. Dell Shannon. 1992. 18.95 (0-7451-8385-9, Atlantic Lrg Print); pap. 16.95 (0-7927-1151-3, Atlantic Lrg Print) Chivers N Amer.

Ace of Spies. Don Von Elsner. LC 84-223761. 127p. 1982. pap. 5.95 (0-939460-22-X) Devyn Pr.

Ace of the Piney Woods. Maurice W. Thomas. LC 89-52118. (Illus.). 258p. 1991. pap. 7.95 (1-55523-307-4) Winston-Derek.

Ace Profile: Colonel Rex T. Barber. William Hess. (American Fighter Pilot Ser.: Vol. I, No. 2). 32p. 1993. pap. write for info. (1-883393-01-9) Mustang Int.

Ace Profile: General Charles E. Yeager. William Hess. (American Fighter Pilot Ser.: Vol. I, No. 1). 32p. 1993. pap. write for info. (1-883393-00-0) Mustang Int.

Ace Reid: Cowpoke. John R. Erickson. (Illus.). 190p. 1984. 15.95 (0-916941-00-0) Maverick Bks.

Ace Science-Fiction Double Books. Roger Robinson. 16p. (C). 1990. reprint ed. lib. bdg. 15.00x (0-8095-4604-3) Borgo Pr.

ACE Teams. Andrew Leigh & Michael Maynard. 280p. 1993. 49.50 (0-7506-0664-9) Buttrwrth-Heinemann.

ACE Teams: Creating Star Performance in Business. Andrew Leigh & Michael Maynard. 280p. 1994. pap. 15.95 (0-7506-1883-3) Buttrwrth-Heinemann.

ACE the Technical Interview: How to Get Your Next Job in the Computer Industry. Michael Rothstein. LC 93-20953. 420p. 1993. pap. text ed. 19.95 (0-07-054030-6) McGraw.

ACE Two (Advanced Communications Exercises) Word Finding Insight & Reasoning Visual Perception. Kathryn J. Tomlin. 1993. student ed, spiral bd. 31.95 (1-55999-396-0) LinguiSystems.

***Ace Ventura: Pet Detective.** Cerasini. 1995. pap. 3.99 (0-679-87496-8) Random.

***Ace Ventura, Pet Detective.** Jack Bernstein et al. LC 95-3832. (Pictureback Ser.). (J). 1995. 2.99 (0-679-87604-9) Random.

***Ace Ventura 2.** Cerasini. 1995. pap. 3.99 (0-679-87497-6) Random.

***Ace Ventura 2: Movie Storybook.** Korman. 1995. pap. 7.99 (0-679-87625-1) Random.

ACE 1: The Original ACE (Advanced Communication Exercises) rev. ed. Kathryn J. Tomlin. (Cognitive Rehabilitation Ser.: Pt. 2). 1986. student ed, spiral bd. 31.95 (1-55999-000-7) LinguiSystems.

ACEC International Engineering Directory. 129p. 1989. 50.00 (0-686-48334-0) Am Consul Eng.

ACEC Membership Directory, 1990-91. American Consulting Engineers Council Staff. 550p. 1988. 140.00 (0-318-41580-1) Am Consul Eng.

Aceita de Arbol de Te Australiano (Australian Tea Tree Oil Handbook) 101 Maneras de Usar el Aceite de Arbol Dete. Cynthia B. Olsen. Ed. by Chris Gerlach. Tr. by Kathleen B. Isberg. (Illus.). 48p. (Orig.). (SPA.). 1991. pap. 3.50 (0-9628882-2-2) Kali Pr.

Aceldama: Aleister Crowley's First Book. Aleister Crowley. 1993. reprint ed. pap. 5.95 (1-55818-249-7) Holmes Pub.

Aceleradores de Particulas. (Serie de Fisica: No. 7). (SPA.). 1982. pap. 3.50 (0-8270-1539-9) OAS.

***Acentric Labyrinth.** Mendoza. 1995. text ed. 26.95 (1-85230-640-8) Element MA.

Acerbic Amusings. Werner Low. (WEP Poetry Ser.: No. 1). 1978. pap. 1.00 (0-917976-03-7, White Ewe Pr) Thunder Baas Pr.

Acerca de "Centesimus Annus" Real Academia de Ciencias Morales y Politicas Staff. (Nueva Austral Ser.: Vol. 245). (SPA.). 1991. pap. text ed. 24.95x (84-239-7245-3) Elliots Bks.

Acerca de Ortega. Julian Marias. (Nueva Austral Ser.: Vol. 214). (SPA.). 1991. pap. text ed. 24.95 (84-239-7214-3) Elliots Bks.

Acerca de Su Declaracion: 95 Preguntas y Respuestas. (Illus.). 28p. (SPA.). 1993. pap. text ed. 1.80 (0-88450-521-9, 6100) Lawyers & Judges.

***Acercamiento a la Literatura Afrocubana.** Armando Gonzalez-Perez. LC 94-70691. (Coleccion Ebano y Canela). 224p. (Orig.). (SPA.). 1994. pap. 19.00 (0-89729-717-2) Ediciones.

Acercando las Personas a Jesus. Jonah Moyo & Grace Holland. (SPA.). 1980. 8.50 (1-55955-054-6) CITE MI.

Acerquemonos Al Senor: Let Us Draw Nigh. Andrew Murray. (SPA.). 3.25 (84-7228-890-0, 220011, Pub. by Edit Clie SP) TSELF.

Aces. George McCauley. 78p. (Orig.). 1991. pap. 8.95 (0-9622889-2-6) Something More.

Aces: A Novel of World War II. Robert Denny. 1991. 18.95 (1-55611-225-4) D I Fine.

ACES - Advocacy, Counseling & Entitlement Services Manual. Ed. by Ellen Bach. LC 92-198905. 300p. (Orig.). 1990. 40.00 (0-88156-111-8) Comm Serv Soc NY.

***Aces Against Germany.** Hammel. (Illus.). (J). 1995. mass mkt. 5.50 (0-671-52907-2) PB.

Aces Against Germany. Eric Hammel. LC 93-6548. (American Aces Speak Ser.: Vol. 2). 1993. 24.95 (0-89141-441-X) Presidio Pr.

Aces Against Japan, Vol. 1: The American Aces Speak. Eric Hammel. 1992. 24.95 (0-89141-440-1) Presidio Pr.

Aces & Airplanes of WW One. Bellerophon Staff. (J). (gr. 1-9). 1992. pap. 3.95 (0-88388-037-7) Bellerophon Bks.

Aces & Wingmen II, Vol. I. Danny Morris. Ed. by Thomas A. Frisque. (Illus.). 256p. (C). 1989. lib. bdg. 39.95 (0-9623080-1-3) Aviation Usk.

***Ace's Guide to Star Reach & Master of Orion.** Shay Addams. (Illus.). 256p. (Orig.). 1995. pap. 18.95 (1-57280-044-5) IFTW Bks.

Aces High. Bernard Fitzimmons. 1988. 19.99 (0-517-66576-X) Random Hse Value.

Aces High: A Tribute to the Highest Scoring Fighter Pilots of the British & Commonwealth Air Forces in WWII. Christopher Shores & Clive Williams. (Illus.). 663p. 1994. 69.95 (1-898697-00-0, Pub. by Grub St Pubns UK) Seven Hills Bk.

***ACES Manual: A Guide to Government Benefit Programs for Individuals & Families in New York City.** Ed. by Ellen Bach. 300p. 1995. 50.00 (0-88156-166-5) Comm Serv Soc NY.

***Aces of the Deep: Official Player Guide.** Shay Addams. (Illus.). 256p. (Orig.). 1995. pap. 18.95 (1-57280-005-4) IFTW Bks.

Aces of the Eighth. Gene Stafford. (Aircraft Specials Ser.). (Illus.). 64p. 1973. pap. 9.95 (0-89747-055-9, 6001) Squad Sig Pubns.

Aces of the Mound. (Baseball's Best Ser.). (Illus.). 24p. (J). (gr. 1 up). 1991. pap. 3.95 (0-671-73635-3, Litl Simon S&S) S&S Childrens.

Aces of the SW Pacific. Gene Stafford. (Aircraft Specials Ser.). (Illus.). 64p. 1977. pap. 9.95 (0-89747-063-X, 6011) Squad Sig Pubns.

Aces over Europe Official Strategy Guide. Tom Basham. 1994. pap. 19.95 (1-55958-520-X) Prima Pub.

Aces Scientific. Bobby Goldman. LC 80-123418. 169p. 1978. pap. 9.95 (0-939460-03-3) Devyn Pr.

Aces Wild. E. Jefferson Clay. Bd. with Badge for Brazos. 1980. Set pap. 2.25 (0-505-51470-2) Dorchester Pub Co.

Aces Wilde. large type ed. Ben Bridges. (Dales Western Ser.). 218p. 1993. pap. 16.95 (1-85389-407-9, Dales) Ulverscroft.

Acesulfame-K. Ed. by D. P. Mayer & F. H. Kemper. (Food Science & Technology Ser.: Vol. 47). 256p. 1991. 115.00 (0-8247-8530-4) Dekker.

Acetabular Dysplasia-Skeletal Dysplasias in Childhood. Ed. by U. H. Weil. (Progress in Orthopedic Surgery Ser.: Vol.2). (Illus.). 1978. 37.00 (0-387-08400-2) Spr-Verlag.

Acetaminophen: Index of New Information with Authors & Subjects. rev. ed. Am Health Res Inst Staff. 1994. 44.50 (0-7883-0158-6); pap. 39.50 (0-7883-0159-4) ABBE Pubs Assn.

Acetaria: A Discourse of Sallets. deluxe ed. John Evelyn. LC 85-12630. (Illus.). 148p. 1986. bds. 200.00 (0-933841-01-9) Still Point TX.

Acetelyne-Based Chemicals from Coal & Other Natural Resources. Robert J. Tedeschi. (Chemical Industries Ser.: Vol. 6). (Illus.). 232p. 1982. 135.00 (0-8247-1358-3) Dekker.

Acetic Acid & Its Derivatives. V. Agreda & J. Zoeller. (Chemical Industries Ser.: Vol. 49). 456p. 1993. 180.00 (0-8247-8792-7) Dekker.

Acetogenesis. Ed. by Harold L. Drake. LC 93-43138. 1994. 80.00 (0-412-03211-2, Chap & Hall NY) Chapman & Hall.

***Acetonitrile.** Ed. by World Health Organization Staff. (Environmental Health Criteria Ser.). 110p. 1993. pap. 18.00 (92-4-157154-3) World Health.

Acetylator Genes & Drug Response. Wendell W. Weber. 270p. 1987. 55.00 (0-19-503932-7) OUP.

Acetylcholine: An Approach to the Molecular Mechanism of Action. M. J. Michelson & E. V. Ziemel. LC 73-11271. 252p. 1973. 110.00 (0-08-017159-1, Pub. by Pergamon Repr UK) Franklin.

Acetylene--Index of New Information & Medical Research Bible. Kathryn P. Schumburg. 150p. 1994. 44.50 (0-7883-0084-9); pap. 39.50 (0-7883-0085-7) ABBE Pubs Assn.

Acetylene Cylinder Charging Plants. (Fifty Ser.). 1989. pap. 16.75 (0-685-58090-3, 51A) Natl Fire Prot.

ACFA Parade of Royalty. (Illus.). 200p. 1994. (0-318-62026-X) Am Cat Fanciers.

***Achaemenid History Vol. 1: Sources, Structures & Synthesis.** Ed. by Heleen Sancisi-Weerdenburg. xiv, 196p. 1987. pap. text ed. 49.50 (90-6258-401-2, Pub. by Netherlands Inst NE) Eisenbrauns.

***Achaemenid History Vol. 2: The Greek Sources.** Ed. by Heleen Sancisi-Weerdenburg & Amelie Kuhrt. xiii, 175p. 1988. pap. text ed. 46.50 (90-6258-402-0, Pub. by Netherlands Inst NE) Eisenbrauns.

***Achaemenid History Vol. 3: Method & Theory.** Ed. by Amelie Kuhrt & Heleen Sancisi-Weerdenburg. xv, 228p. 1988. pap. text ed. 55.25 (90-6258-403-9, Pub. by Netherlands Inst NE) Eisenbrauns.

***Achaemenid History Vol. 4: Centre & Periphery.** Ed. by Heleen Sancisi-Weerdenburg & Amelie Kuhrt. xv, 274p. 1990. text ed. 74.25 (90-6258-404-7, Pub. by Netherlands Inst NE) Eisenbrauns.

***Achaemenid History Vol. 5: The Roots of the European Tradition.** Ed. by Heleen Sancisi-Weerdenburg & Jan W. Drijvers. xii, 170p. 1990. text ed. 61.00 (90-6258-405-5, Pub. by Netherlands Inst NE) Eisenbrauns.

***Achaemenid History Vol. 6: Asia Minor & Egypt: Old Cultures in a New Empire.** Ed. by Heleen Sancisi-Weerdenburg & Amelie Kuhrt. xviii, 367p. 1991. text ed. 81.25 (90-6258-406-3, Pub. by Netherlands Inst NE) Eisenbrauns.

***Achaemenid History Vol. 7: Through Travellers' Eyes.** Ed. by Heleen Sancisi-Weerdenburg & Jan W. Drijvers. xi, 223p. 1991. text ed. 62.75 (90-6258-407-1, Pub. by Netherlands Inst NE) Eisenbrauns.

***Achaemenid History Vol. 8: Continuity & Change.** Ed. by Heleen Sancisi-Weerdenburg et al. Date not set. text ed. write for info. (0-614-04008-6, Pub. by Netherlands Inst NE) Eisenbrauns.

Achaemenid Imperial Administration in Syria-Palestine & the Missions of Ezra & Nehemiah. Kenneth G. Hoglund. LC 92-26311. (Society of Biblical Literature Dissertation Ser.). 274p. 1992. 44.95 (1-55540-456-1, 062125); pap. 29.95 (1-55540-457-X) Scholars Pr GA.

***Achaemenid Sculpture.** Ann Farkas. xiii, 138p. 1974. pap. text ed. 72.50 (0-614-03993-2, Pub. by Netherlands Inst NE) Eisenbrauns.

Acharnians: The Comedies of Aristophanes. Aristophanes. Ed. by Sommerstein. (Classical Texts Ser.: Vol. 1). 1980. 49.95 (0-85668-167-9, Pub. by Aris & Phillips UK); pap. 24.95 (0-85668-172-5, Pub. by Aris & Phillips UK) David Brown.

Acharnians of Aristophanes. Aristophanes. Ed. by W. R. Connor. LC 78-18610. (Greek Text & Commentaries Ser.). (ENG & GRE.). 1979. reprint ed. lib. bdg. 30.95 (0-405-11450-8) Ayer.

Acharnians of Aristophanes. Ed. by Richard T. Elliott. xliii, 241p. 1982. reprint ed. 44.20 (3-487-07178-9, Pub. by Georg Olms GW) Lubrecht & Cramer.

Acharya Shankara. Swami Apurvananda. 362p. 1985. pap. 7.95 (0-87481-529-0, Pub. by Ramakrishna Math II) Vedanta Pr.

Ache for a Child. Debra Bridwell. 180p. (Orig.). 1994. pap. 9.99 (1-56476-248-3, Victor Books) SP Pubns.

***Ache Life History: The Ecology & Demography of a Foraging People.** Kim Hill & A. Magdalena Hurtado. (Foundations of Human Behavior Ser.). 504p. 1995. text ed. write for info. (0-202-02037-1); lib. bdg. write for info. (0-202-02036-3) Aldine de Gruyter.

Ache, Presencia Africana Tradiciones Goruba-Lucumi en la Narrative Cubana: Tradiciones Yoruba-Lucumi en la Narrativa Cubana. Julia C. Hewitt. (American University Studies: Romance Languages & Literature: Ser. II, Vol. 66). 317p. 1988. text ed. 44.50 (0-8204-0573-6) P Lang Pubs.

Achebe or Soyinka? A Re-Interpretation & a Study in Contrasts. Kole Omotoso. (New Perspectives on African Literature Ser.: No. 3). 240p. 1995. lib. bdg. 70.00 (0-905450-38-8, Pub. by H Zell Pubs UK) Bowker-Saur.

Achebe's World: The Historical & Cultural Context of Chinua Achebe's Novels. Robert M. Wren. LC 79-3101. (Illus.). 221p. (Orig.). 1980. 22.00 (0-89410-005-X); pap. 12.00 (0-89410-006-8) Three Continents.

Achehnese, Vol. I. Christian Snouck Hurgronje. Tr. by A. W. O'Sullivan. LC 76-44736. (Monographs in Anthropology). (Illus.). 472p. (C). 1984. reprint ed. 145.00 (0-404-15820-X) AMS Pr.

Achehnese, Vol. II. Christian Snouck Hurgronje. Tr. by A. W. O'Sullivan. (Illus.). 392p. (C). 1984. reprint ed. write for info. (0-318-57958-8) AMS Pr.

Acheson Country: A Memoir. David C. Acheson. LC 92-40856. 1993. 23.00 (0-393-03530-1) Norton.

ACHIEV-Blue (Activities for Children Involving Everyday Vocabulary) Rosemary Huisingh et al. (J). (ps-5). 1989. 198.70 (1-55999-002-3) LinguiSystems.

ACHIEV-Blue Books (Activities for Children Involving Everyday Vocabulary) Rosemary Huisingh et al. (J). (ps-5). 1986. student ed, spiral bd. 49.95 (1-55999-004-X) LinguiSystems.

ACHIEV-Blue Lesson Plans: Activities for Children Involving Everyday Vocabulary. LinguiSystems Staff. 1990. student ed, spiral bd. 27.95 (1-55999-098-8) LinguiSystems.

ACHIEV for Phonology: A Beginning Activity-Based Program for Phonological Remediation, 2 vols. Kellie S. Martin et al. (Illus.). (Orig.). (ps-2). 1990. Activities book, 260p.; Storybook 1, 193p.; Storybook 2, 200p. student ed, spiral bd. 49.95 (1-55999-118-6) LinguiSystems.

ACHIEV-Red (Activities for Children Involving Everyday Vocabulary) Package. Linda Zachman et al. (J). (ps-5). 1989. 198.70 (1-55999-001-5) LinguiSystems.

ACHIEV-Red Books (Activities for Children Involving Everyday Vocabulary) Linda Zachman et al. (J). (ps-5). 1985. student ed, spiral bd. 49.95 (1-55999-005-8) LinguiSystems.

ACHIEV-Red Lesson Plans: Activities for Children Involving Everyday Vocabulary. LinguiSystems Staff. 1990. student ed, spiral bd. 27.95 (1-55999-099-6) LinguiSystems.

ACHIEV-Red Sing-a-Longs Manual (Activities for Children Involving Everyday Vocabulary - Home & Family Vocabulary) LinguiSystems Staff. (J). (ps-3). 1989. 27.95 (1-55999-006-6) LinguiSystems.

Achievable Carburizing Specifications. Roy F. Kern. (Fall Technical Meeting Papers 88FTM1). (Illus.). 9p. 1988. pap. text ed. 30.00 (1-55589-506-9) AGMA.

Achieve Language Land - Blue Instruction Manual. Linda Zachman et al. 1988. teacher ed 34.95 (1-55999-092-9) LinguiSystems.

Achieve Language Land - Red Instruction Manual. Linda Zachman et al. 1988. teacher ed 34.95 (1-55999-093-7) LinguiSystems.

Achieve Total Quality. David Hutchins. 1991. pap. 19.95 (0-13-006057-7) P-H.

Achieve Your Dreams. Kathleen F. Russell & Larry C. Wall. 160p. (Orig.). 1994. pap. 5.95 (0-9635176-3-5) Walrus Prods.

Achieve Your Goals: Create Your Best Future. F. Tim Holt. LC 91-74153. (Illus.). 128p. (Orig.). 1992. pap. 5.95 (0-9630552-5-9) Info Pub.

Achievement & Addiction: A Guide to the Treatment of Professionals. Edgar P. Nace. 272p. 1995. 32.95 (0-87630-753-5) Brunner-Mazel.

***Achievement & Assurance of Safety: Proceedings of the Third Safety-Critical Systems Symposium, Brighton, UK, 7-9 February, 1995.** Ed. by Felix Redmill & Tom Anderson. LC 94-46761. 1995. pap. 69.00 (3-540-19922-5) Spr-Verlag.

Achievement & Motivation: A Social-Developmental Perspective. Ed. by Ann K. Boggiano & Thane S. Pittman. (Illus.). 250p. (C). 1993. 44.95 (0-521-32220-0) Cambridge U Pr.

Achievement & Task Motivation. Ed. by J. H. Van Den Bercken et al. vi, 276p. (Orig.). 1986. 25.00 (90-265-0739-9, Pub. by Swets Pub Serv NE) Taylor & Francis.

Achievement-Based Curriculum Development in Physical Education. Janet A. Wessel & Luke Kelly. LC 85-12854. 347p. reprint ed. pap. 98.90 (0-7837-2754-2, 2043134) Bks Demand.

Achievement Factors: Candid Interviews with Some of the Most Successful People of Our Time. B. Eugene Griessman. LC 90-53190. 310p. 1993. pap. 14.95 (0-89384-228-1) Pfeiffer & Co.

Achievement, Happiness, Popularity & Success: A Self-Esteem Book for Young People. Bettie B. Youngs & Brian S. Tracy. Ed. by Cathy Baldwin. LC 88-90808. 169p. (Orig.). (YA). (gr. 5-12). 1989. pap. 12.95 (0-929354-00-1) Phoenix Educ Found.

Achievement in American Society. Ed. by Bernard C. Rosen et al. 640p. (C). 1969. text ed. 18.50 (0-87073-000-2) Schenkman Bks Inc.

Achievement in the First Two Years of School: Patterns & Processes. Karl L. Alexander & Doris R. Entwisle. (Monographs of the Society for Research in Child Development: No. 217 53.1). 160p. 1988. pap. text ed. 9.75 (0-226-01356-1) U Ch Pr.

Achievement Motivation in Perspective. Heinz Heckhausen et al. Tr. by Margaret Woodruff & Robert Wicklund. 1985. text ed. 91.00 (0-12-336160-5) Acad Pr.

Achievement Motive. David C. McClelland. LC 75-34465. (Illus.). Date not set. 42.50 (0-8290-1167-6) Irvington.

Achievement of American Sport Literature: A Critical Appraisal. Ed. by Wiley L. Umphlett. LC 89-46419. 216p. 1991. 38.50 (0-8386-3400-1) Fairleigh Dickinson.

***Achievement of Brian Friel.** Ed. by Alan Peacock. 267p. (C). 1994. lib. bdg. 67.50 (0-86140-349-5, Pub. by C Smythe Ltd UK) B&N Imports.

Achievement of Christina Rossetti. Ed. by David A. Kent. LC 87-47548. 402p. (C). 1988. 47.50 (0-8014-1937-9); pap. 17.95 (0-8014-9677-2) Cornell U Pr.

Achievement of Cormac McCarthy. Vereen Bell. LC 88-5906. (Southern Literary Studies). xiii, 141p. 1988. text ed. 27.50 (0-8071-1408-1) La State U Pr.

An Asterisk (*) at the beginning of an entry indicates that the title is appearing in BIP for the first time.

An Asterisk (*) at the beginning of an entry indicates that the title is appearing in BIP for the first time.

35

A

Achieving the Aim. Mikhael M. Botvinnik. LC 80-40437. (Russian Chess Ser.). (Illus.). 226p. 1981. 21.95 (0-08-024120-4, Pergamon Pr) Elsevier.

Achieving the Competitive Edge Through Integrated Technology Management. Gerard H. Gaynor. (Engineering & Technology Management Ser.). 320p. 1991. text ed. 50.00 (0-07-023444-2) McGraw.

Achieving the Complete School: Strategies for Effective Mainstreaming. Douglas Biklen et al. (Special Education Ser.). 224p. (C). 1985. pap. text ed. 18.95 (0-8077-2772-5) Tchrs Coll.

***Achieving the Dream: How Communities & Schools Can Improve Education for Immigrant Students.** 95p. (Orig.). 1993. pap. 10.00 (1-880002-05-1) Natl Coal Advocates.

Achieving Total Quality: Integrating Business Strategy & Customer Needs. Wayne H. Brunetti. LC 93-7276. 256p. 1993. text ed. 24.95 (0-527-91724-9) Qual Resc.

Achieving Total Quality Management: A Program for Action. Michel Perigord. LC 90-48163. (Illus.). 392p. 1991. 50.00x (0-915299-60-7) Prod Press.

***Achieving TQM on Projects: The Journey of Continuous Improvement.** Russell W. Darnall. LC 94-24743. (Perspective Ser.). 120p. 1994. 30.00 (1-880410-35-4); pap. 25.00 (1-880410-36-2) Proj Mgmt Inst.

***Achieving Trustee Involvement in Fundraising.** Ed. by Timothy L. Seiler & Kay S. Grace. (New Directions for Philanthropic Fundraising Ser.: No. 4). 117p. (Orig.). 1994. pap. 19.95 (0-7879-9970-9) Jossey-Bass.

***Achieving World Class Manufacturing Through Process Control.** Shunta. (Illus.). 220p. (C). 1994. text ed. 52.00 (0-13-309030-2) P-H.

***Achieving World Class Standards: The Challenge for Educating Teachers.** Ed. by Barbara Lieb. 53p. (Orig.). (C). 1994. pap. text ed. 35.00 (0-7881-1387-9) Diane Pub.

***Achieving Your NVQ.** IPM Staff. (Assessment of NVQs & SVQs Ser.: No. 9). (C). 1994. 62.25x (0-08-042153-9, Pub. by IPM Hse UK) St Mut.

Achieving Your Potential in Christ. A. Coniaris. 1993. pap. 9.95 (0-937032-93-X) Light&Life Pub Co MN.

Achille Bocchi & the Emblem Book As Symbolic Form. Elizabeth S. Watson. LC 92-20390. (Illus.). 256p. (C). 1994. 75.00 (0-521-40057-0) Cambridge U Pr.

Achilleion: A Neolithic Settlement in Thessaly, Greece, 6400-5600 B.C. Marija Gimbutas et al. LC 89-7527. (Monumenta Archaeologica Ser.: No. 14). (Illus.). 388p. 1989. text ed. 35.00 (0-917956-65-6) UCLA Arch.

***Achilles.** Ed. by Harold Bloom. (Major Literary Characters Ser.). 224p. Date not set. 29.95 (0-7910-0913-0) Chelsea Hse.

Achilles: Paradigms of the War Hero from Homer to the Middle Ages. Katherine C. King. (Illus.). 355p. (C). 1987. 50.00 (0-520-05571-3) U CA Pr.

Achilles: Paradigms of the War Hero from Homer to the Middle Ages. Katherine C. King. (Illus.). 355p. 1991. pap. 16.00 (0-520-07407-6) U CA Pr.

Achilles & Company. Ned Conquest. LC 88-192272. 185p. 1988. 22.50 (0-9627485-0-1) Apollonian Pr.

Achilles' Choice. Larry Niven & Steven Barnes. 1992. mass mkt. 4.99 (0-8125-1083-6) Tor Bks.

Achilles Heel Reader: Men, Sexual Politics & Socialism. Ed. by Victor J. Seidler. (Male Orders Ser.). (Illus.). 246p. 1991. 49.95 (0-415-06350-7, A5892); pap. 15.95 (0-415-06351-5, A5896) Routledge.

Achilles in Vietnam: Traumatic Stress & the Undoing of Character. Jonathan Shay. Ed. by Lee Goerner. 288p. 1994. text ed. 20.00 (0-689-12182-2, Atheneum S&S) S&S Trade.

Achilles Syndrome. P. Clarkson. 1994. pap. 13.95 (1-85230-499-5) Element MA.

Achim von Arnim's Novellensammlung 1812: Balance & Meditation. Thomas P. Bonfiglio. (Studies in Modern German Literature: Vol. 14). 233p. 1988. text ed. 31.95 (0-8204-0480-2) P Lang Pubs.

***Aching Heart: Dealing with Pain.** Slightly Off Center Writers Group Staff. (Orig.). 1995. pap. 9.95 (1-56721-128-3) Twnty-Fifth Cent Pr.

Aching Hearth: Family Violence in Life & Literature. Ed. by S. M. Deats & L. T. Lenker. LC 91-6279. (Illus.). 286p. 1991. 24.95 (0-306-43761-9, Plenum Insight) Plenum.

Achitophel, or the Picture of a Wicked Politician. Nathanael Carpenter. LC 79-84094. (English Experience Ser.: No. 914). 76p. 1979. reprint ed. lib. bdg. 20.00 (90-221-0914-3) Walter J Johnson.

Achnantes, eine Monographie der Gattung: Mit Definitio der Gattung Cocconeis und Nachtraegen zu den Naviculaceae. H. Lange-Bertalot & K. Krammer. (Bibliotheca Diatomologica Ser.: Vol. 18). (Illus.). 392p. (GER.). 1989. lib. bdg. 152.00 (3-443-57009-7, Pub. by Cramer GW) Lubrecht & Cramer.

Achromatic Microscope. Richard Beck. (History of Microscopy Ser.). 272p. 1987. reprint ed. 55.20 (0-940095-06-8) Sci Heritage Ltd.

***Achtung-Panzer! The Development of Armoured Forces, Their Tactics & Operational Potential.** Heinz Guderian. (Illus.). 208p. 1995. pap. 14.95 (1-85409-282-0, Pub. by Arms & Armour UK) Sterling.

ACI Detailing Manual. 1988. 106.95 (0-686-70073-2, SP-66) ACI.

***ACI Detailing Manual.** 244p. 1994. spiral bd. 106.95 (0-614-02520-6, SP66(94)) ACI.

ACI Manual of Concrete Practice, 5 pts. Incl. Pt. 1. 1994. 118.50 (0-686-70198-4); Pt. 2. 1994. 118.50 (0-686-70199-2); Pt. 3. 1994. 118.50 (0-686-70200-X); Pt. 4. 1994. 118.50 (0-686-70201-8); Pt. 5. 1995. 118.50 (0-686-70202-6); 1994. Set cd-rom write for info. (0-318-50395-6) ACI.

ACI Manual of Concrete Practice, 5 pts., Set. Incl. Pt. 1. 1994. 118.50 (0-686-70198-4); Pt. 2. 1994. 118.50 (0-686-70199-2); Pt. 3. 1994. 118.50 (0-686-70200-X); Pt. 4. 1994. 118.50 (0-686-70201-8); Pt. 5. 1995. 118.50 (0-686-70202-6); 1994. 592.50 (0-685-00107-5) ACI.

ACI Ten Year Index: 1959-1968. 256p. 1970. 37.75 (0-685-85156-7, I-68) ACI.

ACI Ten Year Index: 1969-1978. 200p. 42.75 (0-317-32072-6, 1-78) ACI.

***Acid.** Edward Falco. LC 95-16887. (C). 1996. text ed. 25.00 (0-268-00646-6); pap. text ed. 14.95 (0-268-00647-4) U of Notre Dame Pr.

Acid & Alkaline. 5th rev. ed. Herman Aihara. Ed. by Stan Hodson. 121p. 1986. pap. 5.95 (0-918860-44-X) G Ohsawa.

Acid & Bases: A Guide to Understanding Acid-Base Disorders. Jerome Lowenstein. (Illus.). 168p. 1993. 35.00 (0-19-507572-2); pap. 14.95 (0-19-507573-0) OUP.

Acid & Sour Gas Treating Processes. Ed. by Stephen A. Newman. LC 84-25339. 820p. 1985. 47.00 (0-87201-839-3) Gulf Pub.

Acid-Base. Horacio J. Adrogue & Donald E. Wesson. LC 94-18243. (Basics of Medicine Ser.). 224p. 1994. pap. 24.95 (0-86542-428-4) Blackwell Sci.

Acid-Base. Horacio J. Adrogue & Donald E. Wesson. LC 91-75540. (A & W Basics in Medicine Ser.). 204p. (C). 1991. text ed. 29.95 (0-9630670-0-1) Libra & Gemini.

Acid-Base. Jordan J. Cohen & Jerome P. Kassirer. 1982. 77.00 (0-316-15011-8) Little.

Acid-Base & Blood Gas Regulation: For Medical Students Before & after Graduation. Giles F. Filley. LC 74-135681. 223p. reprint ed. pap. 63.60 (0-8357-5076-0, 2056510) Bks Demand.

Acid-Base & Electrolyte Disorders. Horacio Adrogue. (Contemporary Management in Critical Care Ser.: Vol. 1, No. 2). (Illus.). 240p. 1991. text ed. 34.95 (0-443-08829-2) Churchill.

Acid-Base Balance. Alan Y. Cohen. (Illus.). 127p. 1990. pap. text ed. 16.95 (0-910271-01-7) Critical Care Pr.

Acid Base Balance: A Manual for Clinicians. 2nd ed. Jorge A. Quintero. LC 77-81798. 152p. 1981. 12.50 (0-87527-148-0) Green.

Acid-Base Catalysis. Ed. by K. Tanabe et al. LC 89-14763. 532p. 1989. lib. bdg. 170.00 (0-89573-891-0) VCH Pubs.

***Acid-Base Catalysis II: Proceedings of the International Symposium on Acid-Base Catalysis II, Sapporo, Japan, December 2-4, 1993.** Ed. by H. Hattori et al. (Studies in Surface Science & Catalysis: Vol. 90). 584p. 1994. 328.50 (0-444-98655-3) Elsevier.

Acid-Base Disorders. Heinz Valtin & John Gennari. 316p. 1986. 31.95 (0-316-89559-8) Little.

Acid-Base Equilibria. E. King & E. Guggenheim. LC 64-21219. (International Encyclopedia of Physical Chemistry & Chemical Physics Ser.: No. 4). 1965. 149.00 (0-08-010848-2, Pub. by Pergamon Repr UK) Franklin.

Acid Base Equilibria: Equilibrium Properties of Electrolyte Solutions. E. King & R. Robinson. LC 64-21219. (International Encyclopedia of Physical Chemistry & Chemical Physics Ser.: Vol. 4: TP15). 1965. 148.00 (0-08-018986-5, Pub. by Pergamon Repr UK) Franklin.

Acid-Base Physiology: A Direct Approach. James L. Gamble, Jr. 144p. 1982. text ed. 35.00 (0-8018-2629-2) Johns Hopkins.

Acid-Base Reaction Cements: Their Biomedical & Industrial Applications. Alan D. Wilson & John W. Nicholson. (Chemistry of Solid State Materials Ser.: No. 2). (Illus.). 350p. (C). 1993. 99.95 (0-521-37222-4) Cambridge U Pr.

Acid-Base Regulation & Body Temperature. Ed. by Herman Rahn & Omar Prakash. (Developments in Critical Care, Medicine, & Anesthesiology Ser.). 1985. lib. bdg. 101.50 (0-89838-708-6) Kluwer Ac.

Acid-Base Regulation in Animals. Ed. by N. Heisler. 440p. 1986. 206.25 (0-444-80696-2) Elsevier.

***Acid Bath.** Nancy Herndon. 272p. (Orig.). 1995. pap. text ed. 4.99 (0-425-14551-4, Prime Crime) Berkley Pub.

Acid Deposition. Ed. by S. Beilke & A. J. Elshout. 1983. lib. bdg. 70.00 (90-277-1588-2) Kluwer Ac.

Acid Deposition: Atmospheric Processes in Eastern North America. National Research Council Staff. LC 83-61851. (Review of Current Scientific Understanding Ser.). 391p. reprint ed. pap. 111.50 (0-7837-5038-2, 2044714) Bks Demand.

Acid Deposition: Causes & Effects. University of Florida Staff. LC 83-82073. (Illus.). 316p. 1983. pap. text ed. 42.00 (0-86587-060-8) Gov Insts.

Acid Deposition: Long-Term Trends. National Research Council. 520p. (Orig.). 1986. pap. 34.95 (0-309-03647-X) Natl Acad Pr.

Acid Deposition: Origins, Impacts & Abatement Strategies. Ed. by J. W. Longhurst. (Illus.). 364p. 1991. 218.00 (0-387-53741-4) Spr-Verlag.

Acid Deposition & Acidification of Soils & Waters. J. O. Reuss & D. W. Johnson. (Ecological Studies: Vol. 59). (Illus.). viii, 119p. 1986. 60.00 (0-387-96290-5) Spr-Verlag.

Acid Deposition & Vehicle Emissions: European Environmental Pressures on Britain. Peter G. Brackley. (Joint Energy Programme Ser.: No. 22). 137p. 1987. text ed. 52.95 (0-566-05125-7, Pub. by Dartmth Pub UK) Ashgate Pub Co.

Acid Deposition at High Elevation Sites. Ed. by M. H. Unsworth & D. Fowler. (C). 1988. lib. bdg. 222.00 (90-277-2835-6) Kluwer Ac.

Acid Digestion Process for Radioactive Waste. Ed. by L. Cecille & R. Simon. LC 83-10792. (Radioactive Waste Management Ser.: Vol. 11). (Illus.). x, 108p. 1983. text ed. 91.00 (3-7186-0174-5) Gordon & Breach.

Acid Dreams: The CIA, LSD, & the Sixties Rebellion. Martin Lee & Bruce Shlain. 384p. (Orig.). 1987. pap. 13.95 (0-8021-3062-3) Grove-Atltic.

***Acid Fingers.** Christopher A. Fitts. (Illus.). 128p. 1995. 16.00 (0-9635689-9-X); pap. 10.00 (0-9635689-0-6) Storm Grove.

***Acid House: Stories.** Irvine Welsh. LC 94-36703. 304p. 1995. pap. 11.00 (0-393-31280-1, Norton Paperbks) Norton.

***Acid-Peptic Disorders of the Upper Gastrointestinal Tract.** Harris R. Clearfield. 1995. write for info. (1-884065-04-X) Assocs in Med.

***Acid-Peptic Disorders of the Upper Gastrointestinal Tract: Diagnosis & Management.** Harris R. Clearfield. LC 94-75975. 1995. write for info. (1-884065-03-1) Assocs in Med.

***Acid Politics: Environmental & Energy Policies in Britain & Germany.** Christiansen Boehmer & Jim Skea. LC 09-48870. 1994. text ed. 44.95 (0-471-94485-8) Wiley.

Acid Politics: Environmental & Energy Policies in Britain & Germany. S. Boehmer-Christiansen & J. Skea. 256p. 1992. text ed. 41.95 (1-85293-116-7, Pub. by Pinter Pubs Ltd UK) CRC Pr.

Acid Precipitation: A Bibliography. DOE Technical Information Center Staff. 734p. 1983. pap. 30.00 (0-87079-500-7, DOE/TIC-3399); fiche 9.00 (0-87079-501-5, DOE/TIC-3399) DOE.

Acid Precipitation Series, 7 vols., Set. Ed. by John I. Teasley. 1984. 365.00 (0-250-40565-2) Buttrwrth-Heinemann.

Acid Rain. John D. Baines. LC 89-21656. (Conserving Our World Ser.). (Illus.). 48p. (J). (gr. 4-9). 1990. lib. bdg. 22.13 (0-8114-2385-9); pap. 5.95 (0-8114-3450-8) Raintree Steck-V.

Acid Rain. Ed. by Charles G. Gunnerson & Beatrice E. Willard. 174p. 1979. pap. 19.00 (0-87262-202-9) Am Soc Civil Eng.

Acid Rain. Colin Hocking et al. Ed. by Lincoln Bergman & Kay Fairwell. (Great Explorations in Math & Science (GEMS) Ser.). (Illus.). 168p. (YA). (gr. 6-10). 1990. pap. 15.00 (0-912511-74-5) Lawrence Science.

Acid Rain. Eileen Lucas. LC 91-3879. (Saving Planet Earth Ser.). 128p. (J). (gr. 4-8). 1991. lib. bdg. 20.55 (0-516-05503-8) Childrens.

Acid Rain. Christina G. Miller & Louise A. Berry. LC 86-8605. (Illus.). 128p. (YA). (gr. 7 up). 1986. lib. bdg. 12.98 (0-671-60177-6, Julian Messner) Silver Burdett Pr.

***Acid Rain.** J. M. Patten. LC 94-24207. (Eye on the Environment Ser.). (J). 1995. write for info. (1-55916-099-3) Rourke Bk Co.

Acid Rain. Gail Stewart. LC 90-5854. (Overview Ser.). (Illus.). 112p. (J). (gr. 5-8). 1990. lib. bdg. 16.95 (1-56006-111-1) Lucent Bks.

Acid Rain. Mary Turck. LC 90-35495. (Earth Alert Ser.). (Illus.). 48p. (J). (gr. 6). 1990. text ed., lib. bdg. 12.95 (0-89686-547-9, Crstwood Hse) Silver Burdett Pr.

Acid Rain. Peter Tyson. (Earth at Risk Ser.). (Illus.). 128p. (YA). (gr. 5 up). 1992. lib. bdg. 19.95 (0-7910-1577-7) Chelsea Hse.

Acid Rain: A Bibliography of Canadian Federal & Provincial Government Documents. Albert H. Joy. LC 90-21522. 264p. 1990. text ed. 59.95 (0-313-28052-5, JBC/, Greenwood Pr) Greenwood.

Acid Rain: A Bibliography of Research Annotated for Easy Access. G. Harry Stopp, Jr. LC 85-10858. 192p. 1985. 20.00 (0-8108-1822-1) Scarecrow.

Acid Rain: A Source Guide. 1991. lib. bdg. 250.00 (0-8490-4896-6) Gordon Pr.

***Acid Rain: A Student's First Sourcebook.** Jack L. Durham. (Illus.). 59p. (Orig.). (C). 1994. pap. text ed. 20.00x (0-7881-1492-1) Diane Pub.

Acid Rain: An Issue in Canadian-American Relations. John E. Carroll. LC 82-82205. (Canadian-American Committee Ser.). 98p. (Orig.). (C). 1982. pap. 6.00 (0-89068-064-7) Natl Planning.

Acid Rain: Current Situation & Remedies. Ed. by J. Rose. LC 94-1936. (Environmental Topics Ser.: Vol. 4, No. 1945-5294). 1993. text ed. 95.00 (2-88124-850-0) Gordon & Breach.

Acid Rain: Economic Assessment. Ed. by Paulette Mandelbaum. LC 85-17021. (Environmental Science Research Ser.: Vol. 33). 302p. 1985. 75.00 (0-306-42102-X, Plenum Pr) Plenum.

Acid Rain: Engineering Solutions, Regulatory Aspects-The Second International Conference. Ed. by Robert G. Schwieger & Thomas C. Elliott. LC 66-52994. (Illus.). 563p. 1986. 130.00 (0-89116-458-8) Hemisp Pub.

Acid Rain: How Serious & What to Do. Ed. by David Hafemeister. (Occasional Publications). (Illus.). 56p. (Orig.). (C). 1986. pap. text ed. 10.00 (0-917853-15-6, OP55) Am Assn Physics.

Acid Rain: Locating the Author's Main Idea. Robert Anderson. LC 93-14018. (Opposing Viewpoints Juniors Ser.). (Illus.). 32p. (J). (gr. 4-7). 1994. lib. bdg. 11.95 (1-56510-089-1) Greenhaven.

Acid Rain: Reign of Controversy. Archie M. Kahan. LC 86-7688. (Illus.). 238p. 1986. 14.95 (1-55591-003-3) Fulcrum Pub.

Acid Rain: Rhetoric & Reality. Chris C. Park. LC 87-20398. 1989. pap. 25.00 (0-416-92200-7) Routledge Chapman & Hall.

Acid Rain: Rhetoric & Reality. Chris C. Park. (Illus.). 272p. 1990. pap. 25.00 (0-685-26313-4) Routledge Chapman & Hall.

***Acid Rain: The Controversy.** Arnold Krochmal & Connie Krochmal. 99p. (YA). (gr. 7-12). 1995. pap. write for info. (1-57515-054-9) PPI Pubng.

Acid Rain: The View from the States. Acid Rain Information Clearinghouse Staff. 181p. 1988. pap. text ed. 58.00 (0-86587-754-8) Gov Insts.

Acid Rain - Fisheries. American Fisheries Society Northeastern Division Staff. Ed. by R. E. Johnson. LC 82-74271. 357p. 1982. text ed. 26.50 (0-913235-26-1) Am Fisheries Soc.

Acid Rain & Acid Waters. 2nd ed. Gwyneth Howells. 1995. text ed. 50.00 (0-13-336751-7) P-H.

Acid Rain & Emissions Trading: Implementing a Market Approach to Pollution Control. Roger K. Raufer & Stephen L. Feldman. 176p. (C). 1988. 45.50 (0-8476-7555-6) Rowman.

Acid Rain & Friendly Neighbors: The Policy Dispute Between Canada & the United States. rev. ed. Hilliard Roderick. Ed. by Jurgen Schmandt. LC 88-25605. (Duke Press Policy Studies). (Illus.). 340p. (C). 1989. lib. bdg. 48.00 (0-8223-0870-3) Duke.

Acid Rain Controversy. James L. Regens & Robert W. Rycroft. LC 87-35769. (Series in Policy & Institutional Studies). (Illus.). 246p. (Orig.). 1988. pap. 19.95x (0-8229-5404-4) U of Pittsburgh Pr.

Acid Rain Curriculum. Harriett Stubbs et al. (Illus.). (J). (gr. 4-8). 1985. teacher ed 19.95 (0-935577-00-9) Acid Rain Found.

Acid Rain Curriculum: Grades 6-12. E. Hessler. Ed. by H. S. Stubbs. (Life, Earth, Physical & Environmental Sciences, Social Studies, Biology, Chemistry Ser.). (Illus.). (YA). (gr. 6-12). 1986. 59.95 (0-935577-03-3) Acid Rain Found.

Acid Rain Debate: Science & Special Interests in Policy Formation. Bruce A. Forster. LC 92-47434. (Natural Resources & Environmental Policy Ser.). 168p. (C). 1993. text ed. 32.95 (0-8138-1684-X) Iowa St U Pr.

Acid Rain Hazard. LC 91-50340. (Environment Alert! Ser.). (Illus.). 32p. (J). (gr. 3-8). 1993. lib. bdg. 17.27 (0-8368-0697-2) Gareth Stevens Inc.

Acid Rain in Canada: A Selected Bibliography. John J. Miletich. LC 83-15159. (CPL Bibliographies Ser.: No. 124). 1983. 6.00 (0-86602-124-8) CPL Biblios.

Acid Rain in Minnesota: Teachers' Resource Guide. Edward W. Hessler & Harriett S. Stubbs. 40p. (Orig.). 1984. 10.00 (0-935577-14-9) Acid Rain Found.

Acid Rain in Minnesota '89. rev. ed. Margorie Borchard. (Illus.). 24p. 1989. 8.95 (0-935577-15-7) Acid Rain Found.

Acid Rain Reader. Harriett S. Stubbs et al. (Illus.). 20p. (J). (gr. 4-8). 1989. 5.95 (0-935577-12-2) Acid Rain Found.

Acid Rain Reader. Harriett S. Stubbs et al. (Illus.). 20p. (J). (gr. 4-8). 1989. pap. 2.50 (0-685-17881-1) Acid Rain Found.

Acid Rain Report: General. 37p. 1990. 17.00 (0-317-02706-9) NARUC.

***Acid Rain Research: Do We Have Enough Answers? Proceedings of a Speciality Conference, 's-Hertogenbosch, the Netherlands, 10-12 October 1994.** Ed. by G. J. Heij & J. W. Erisman. (Studies in Environmental Science: Vol. 64). 504p. 1995. 170.50 (0-444-82038-8) Elsevier.

Acid Rain Resource Directory. Ed. by Harriett S. Stubbs & Acid Rain Foundation, Inc. Staff. 1986. 10.00 (0-935577-04-1) Acid Rain Found.

Acid Rain Science Projects. Edward W. Hessler & Harriett S. Stubbs. 20p. (J). (gr. 5-12). 1987. 9.95 (0-935577-09-2) Acid Rain Found.

Acid Rain Sourcebook. Ed. by Robert G. Schwieger & Thomas C. Elliot. (Illus.). 296p. 1984. text ed. 45.00 (0-07-055738-1) McGraw.

Acid Rain 1986: A Handbook for States & Provinces; Research-Information-Policy: Proceedings of a Wingspread Conference, September 23-25, 1986. Ed. by Harriett S. Stubbs. (Orig.). 1986. 59.00 (0-935577-07-6) Acid Rain Found.

Acid-Related Diseases: Improving the Treatment Options - Journal: Digestion, Vol. 51, Suppl. 1, 1992. Ed. by J. Dent & N. D. Yeomans. (Illus.). vi, 126p. 1992. pap. 37.75 (3-8055-5685-3) S Karger.

***Acid Related Disorders: Mystery to Mechanism: Mechanism to Management.** George Sachs et al. (Illus.). 122p. 1995. write for info. (0-9639943-0-1) QSR Medical.

Acid Rock. Warren Murphy. (Destroyer Ser.: No. 13). 1989. pap. 3.50 (1-55817-195-9, Pinnacle NY) Windsor NY.

Acid Soil & Acid Rain. 2nd ed. Ivan R. Kennedy. (Research Studies in Botany & Related Applied Fields). 260p. 1992. text ed. 119.95 (0-471-93404-6) Wiley.

***Acid Stained Steel.** Rollie Judge. 260p. 1995. pap. 8.95 (0-7610-0022-4) NW Pub.

Acid Stress & Aquatic Microbial Interactions. Ed. by Salem S. Rao. 192p. 1989. 156.00 (0-8493-5168-5, QR105) CRC Pr.

Acid Sulfate Weathering. Ed. by J. A. Kittrick et al. (Special Publication Ser.). 234p. 1982. 12.50 (0-89118-770-7) Soil Sci Soc Am.

Acid Sulphate Soil: A Baseline for Research & Development. Ed. by D. Dent. (C). 1991. text ed. 460.00 (0-89771-593-4, Pub. by Intl Bk Distr II) St Mut.

Acid Sulphate Soils. H. Dost. (C). 1991. text ed. 395.00 (0-89771-599-3, Pub. by Intl Bk Distr II) St Mut.

Acid Toxicity & Aquatic Animals. Ed. by R. Morris et al. (Society for Experimental Biology Seminar Ser.: No. 34). 300p. 1989. 79.95 (0-521-33435-7) Cambridge U Pr.

Acidic Deposition: State of Science & Technology, 8 vols., Set. (Acid Rain Ser.). 1994. lib. bdg. 9,575.95 (0-8490-5625-X) Gordon Pr.

Acidic Deposition & Aquatic Ecosystems: Regional Case Studies. Ed. by D. F. Charles. (Illus.). 688p. 1991. 108.00 (0-387-97316-8) Spr-Verlag.

Acidic Deposition & Forests. (Resource Policy Ser.). 56p. (Orig.). 1984. pap. 4.50 (0-939970-25-2, SAF 84-14) Soc Am Foresters.

Acidic Depostion & Forest Soils. D. Binkley et al. (Ecological Studies: Vol. 72). (Illus.). 150p. 1990. 60.00 (0-387-96889-X) Spr-Verlag.

An Asterisk (*) at the beginning of an entry indicates that the title is appearing in BIP for the first time.

Acidic Emissions Control Technology & Costs. T. E. Emmel et al. LC 89-8712. (Pollution Technology Review Ser.: No. 168). (Illus.). 155p. 1990. 39.00 (*0-8155-1208-2*) Noyes.

Acidic Precipitation. Ed. by D. C. Adriano & A. H. Johnson. (Advances in Environmental Science Ser.: Vol. 2). (Illus.). 435p. 1989. 239.00 (*0-387-97000-2*, 2837) Spr-Verlag.

Acidic Precipitation. Ed. by A. H. Bresser & W. Salomons. (Advances in Environmental Science Ser.: Vol. 5). (Illus.). 352p. 1990. 179.00 (*0-387-97111-4*, 3198) Spr-Verlag.

Acidic Precipitation. Ed. by S. E. Lindberg et al. (Advances in Environmental Science Ser.: Vol. 3). (Illus.). xiv, 332p. 1989. 129.00 (*0-685-31289-5*, 2993) Spr-Verlag.

Acidic Precipitation. Ed. by Hans C. Martin. 1987. lib. bdg. 411.50 (*1-55608-021-2*) Kluwer Ac.

Acidic Precipitation. Ed. by S. A. Norton et al. (Advances in Environmental Science Ser.: Vol. 4). (Illus.). xiv, 293p. 1989. 169.00 (*0-387-97026-6*, 2939) Spr-Verlag.

Acidic Precipitation: Case Studies. Ed. by D. C. Adriano & M. Havas. (Advances in Environmental Science Ser.: Vol. 1). (Illus.). 312p. 1989. 149.00 (*0-387-96929-2*, 2468) Spr-Verlag.

Acidification & Its Policy Implications: Proceedings of an International Conference, Amsterdam, May 5-9, 1986. Ed. by T. Schneider. (Studies in Environmental Science: No. 30). 514p. 1986. 154.00 (*0-444-42725-2*) Elsevier.

Acidification in Finland. Ed. by P. Kauppi et al. (Illus.). 1200p. 1990. 96.00 (*0-387-52213-1*) Spr-Verlag.

Acidification in Tropical Countries: (SCOPE 36) Ed. by Henning Rodhe & R. Herrera. LC 88-5667. 405p. 1988. text ed. 350.00 (*0-471-91870-9*) Wiley.

Acidification of Freshwater Ecosystems: Implications for the Future: Report of the Dahlem Workshop on Acidification of Freshwater Ecosystems Held in Berlin, September 27-October 2, 1992. Ed. by C. E. Steinberg & R. F. Wright. LC 93-28725. (Environmental Sciences Research Report: Dahlem Workshop Reports: No. 14). 1994. text ed. 115.00 (*0-471-94206-5*) Wiley.

Acidification of Organic Waters in Kejimkujik National Park, Nova Scotia: Proceedings of a Symposium on the Acidification of Organic Waters in Kejimkujik National Park, Nova Scotia, Canada, Held in Wolfville, Nova Scotia, October 25-27, 1988. Ed. by Joseph J. Kerekes. (C). 1990. lib. bdg. 204.50 (*0-7923-0618-X*) Kluwer Ac.

Acidification Research in the Netherlands: Final Report of the Dutch Priority Programme on Acidification. Ed. by G. J. Heij & T. Schneider. (Studies in Environmental Science: Vol. 46). 772p. 1991. 215.50 (*0-444-88831-4*) Elsevier.

***Acidity & Basicity of Solids: Theory, Assessment & Utility: Proceedings of the NATO Advanced Study Institute, La Colle sur Loup (Nice), France, June 13-25, 1993.** Ed. by Jacques Fraissard & Leonidas Petrakis. LC 94-31448. (NATO Advanced Science Institutes Series C: Vol. 444). 500p. (C). 1994. lib. bdg. 183.00 (*0-7923-3110-9*) Kluwer Ac.

Acidity & the Properties of Major Industrial Acids. Ian M. Campbell. (Illus.). 256p. 1992. 65.00 (*0-412-40330-7*, A7321) Chapman & Hall.

Acidizing Fundamentals. Bert B. Williams et al. 132p. 1979. 27.50 (*0-89520-205-0*, 30406) Soc Petrol Engineers.

Acidosis--Index of New Information & Medical Research Bible. Timmy R. Laforre. 150p. 1994. 44.50 (*0-7883-0086-5*); pap. 39.50 (*0-7883-0087-3*) ABBE Pubs Assn.

***Acids & Bases.** J. M. Patten. LC 95-6213. (Let's Wonder About Science Ser.). (J). 1995. write for info. (*1-55916-128-0*) Rourke Bk Co.

Acing College: A Professor's Guide to Beating the System. Joshua Halberstam. 192p. (Orig.). 1991. pap. 9.00 (*0-14-013998-2*, Penguin Bks) Viking Penguin.

Acing the New SAT: Scholastic Assessment Test. Marcia Lawrence & Charles Piemonte. LC 94-14769. 400p. 1994. pap. 12.95 (*0-452-27233-5*, Plume) NAL-Dutton.

Acis & Galatea, Vol. 3. George F. Handel. Bd. with Allegro Ed Il Pensieroso (6) (Collected Works (Group 2)). 1971. Set text ed. 62.10 (*0-576-28356-8*, Pub. by Gregg Intl Pubs UK) Gregg Intl.

Acke - Prostredi - Action - Environment - Tomas Ruller: Documentations of Performances by the Czech Artist, 1984-89. (Illus.). 26p. 1993. pap. 14.00 (*80-85233-02-9*) Feldman Fine Arts.

Ackerley: The Life of J. R. Ackerley. Peter Parker. 1989. 27.95 (*0-374-10050-0*) FS&G.

Ackerley: The Life of J. R. Ackerley. Peter Parker. (Illus.). 288p. 1991. pap. 15.00 (*0-374-52279-0*, Noonday) FS&G.

Ackerman & Del Regato's Cancer: Diagnosis, Treatment, & Prognosis. 6th ed. Juan A. Del Regato & Harlan J. Spjut. (Illus.). 1984. 115.00 (*0-8016-1251-9*) Mosby Yr Bk.

***Ackerman Charles Heidsieck Guide to the Best Hotels & Restaurants in Great Britain & Ireland - 1995.** rev. ed. Ed. by Roy Ackerman. (Illus.). 558p. 1995. pap. 18.95 (*0-9522458-2-5*, Pub. by Leading Guides UK) Seven Hills Bk.

Ackermann's Costume Plates: Women's Fashions in England, 1818-1828. Rudolph Ackermann. Ed. by Stella Blum. (Illus.). 1978. pap. 6.95 (*0-486-23690-0*) Dover.

Ackerman's Surgical Pathology. 7th ed. Rosai. (Illus.). 2112p. 1988. text ed. 230.00 (*0-8016-4176-4*) Mosby Yr Bk.

Ackerman's Surgical Pathology. 8th ed. Juan Rosai. 2300p. 1994. 259.00 (*0-8016-7004-7*) Mosby Yr Bk.

Acknowledge the Wonder. Frances Wosmek. (Illus.). 158p. (Orig.). 1988. pap. 6.95 (*0-8356-0628-7*, Quest) Theos Pub Hse.

***Acknowledging Consumption.** Ed. by Daniel Miller. LC 94-37293. (Material Cultures Ser.). (Illus.). 304p. 1995. 65.00x (*0-415-10688-5*, C0226); pap. 19.95 (*0-415-10689-3*, C0227) Routledge.

Ackoff's Fables: Irreverant Reflections on Business & Bureaucracy. Russell L. Ackoff. 1991. text ed. 22.95 (*0-471-53194-4*) Wiley.

Ack's Hacks. Al Ackerman. 16p. (Orig.). 1984. pap. 2.50 (*0-935350-11-X*) Luna Bisonte.

***ACL Deficient Knee.** Ed. by Edward M. Woitys. 148p. 1994. 30.00 (*0-89203-118-2*) Amer Acad Ortho Surg.

ACL Teaching Kit: An Instructor's Resource. Grauer-Cavallaro. 1989. 89.00 (*0-8016-0174-6*) Mosby Yr Bk.

ACLS: Certification Preparation & a Comprehensive Review. 3rd ed. Grauer & Cavallaro. 758p. 1993. 45.00 (*0-8016-7453-0*) Mosby Yr Bk.

ACLS: Mega Code Review - Study Guide. Grauer & Cavallaro. 288p. 1988. 25.95 (*0-8016-2937-3*) Mosby Yr Bk.

ACLS: Mega Code Review-Study Guide. 2nd ed. Grauer & Cavallaro. 380p. 1993. 25.95 (*0-8016-1980-7*) Mosby Yr Bk.

ACLS: Quick Review Study Guide. Barbara Aehlert. 1993. pap. 12.50 (*0-8151-0007-8*) Mosby Yr Bk.

ACLS Certification Preparation, Vol. 1. 3rd ed. Ken Grauer & Cavallaro. 288p. 1993. pap. 19.95 (*0-8016-7069-1*) Mosby Yr Bk.

ACLS Certification Preparation & a Comprehensive Review, Vol. 2. 3rd ed. Ken Grauer. 685p. 1993. pap. 34.95 (*0-8016-7070-5*) Mosby Yr Bk.

***ACLS Senarois-Core Concepts for Case-Based Learning.** Cummins. 1995. pap. text ed. (*0-8151-1517-2*) Mosby Yr Bk.

ACLS Survey of Scholars: Final Report of Views on Publications, Computers, & Libraries. Herbert C. Morton & Anne J. Price. (Illus.). 148p. (Orig.). (C). 1989. pap. text ed. 23.00 (*0-8191-7261-8*) Am Coun Lrnd Soc.

***ALCU Helped Put My Family Together Again"** ACLU Staff. 12p. (Orig.). 1988. pap. write for info. (*0-914031-11-2*) Amer Civil Lib.

***ACM - Multimedia Conference Proceedings, 1994.** ACM - Multimedia Staff. (C). 1994. pap. text ed. 69.95 (*0-201-60974-6*) Addison-Wesley.

ACM Conference on Object-Oriented Programming Systems, Languages & Applications - OOPSLA 87. (Sigplan Notices Ser.: Vol. 22, No. 12). (Illus.). 508p. 1987. pap. text ed. 40.00 (*0-89791-247-0*, 548871) Assn Compu Machinery.

ACM Conference on Object-Oriented Programming Systems, Languages & Applications - OOPSLA 88. (Sigplan Notices Ser.: Vol. 23, No. 11). (Illus.). 404p. 1988. pap. text ed. 32.00 (*0-685-29565-6*, 548881) Assn Compu Machinery.

ACM Conference on Personal & Small Computers. (SIGPC Notes: Vol. 6, No. 2). (Illus.). 267p. 1983. pap. text ed. 24.00 (*0-89791-123-7*, 609830) Assn Compu Machinery.

ACM Conference on Programming Language, Design & Implementation. (Sigplan Notices Ser.: Vol. 23, No. 7). (Illus.). 339p. 1988. pap. text ed. 29.00 (*0-89791-269-1*, 548880) Assn Compu Machinery.

ACM SIGART: International Symposium on Methodologies for Intelligent Systems. LC 55-2861. (Illus.). 464p. 1986. pap. text ed. 37.00 (*0-89791-206-3*) Assn Compu Machinery.

ACM Sigart International Conference on Artificial Intelligence & Law. 257p. 1987. pap. text ed. 23.00 (*0-89791-230-6*, 604870) Assn Compu Machinery.

ACM SIGBDP-SIGCPR Conference on the Rising Tide of Expert Systems in Business. 235p. 1987. pap. text ed. 22.00 (*0-89791-222-5*, 472871) Assn Compu Machinery.

ACM SIGCPR International Conference on Management of Information Systems Personnel. 217p. 1988. pap. text ed. 22.00 (*0-89791-262-4*, 443880) Assn Compu Machinery.

ACM Siggraph '91 Conference. ACM Press Staff. (C). 1991. pap. text ed. 50.50 (*0-201-56291-X*) Addison-Wesley.

ACM Sigmetrics & Performance, 1989: International Conference on Measurement & Modeling of Computer Systems, Held May 23-26, 1989 in Berkeley, California. (Illus.). 254p. 1989. pap. text ed. 16.00 (*0-89791-315-9*, 488890) Assn Compu Machinery.

ACM SIGOIS Conference on Office Information Systems, No. 2. (SIGOIS Newsletter Ser.: Vol. 5, Nos. 1-2). (Illus.). 228p. 1984. pap. text ed. 22.00 (*0-685-32252-1*) Assn Compu Machinery.

ACM Sigplan Symposium on Parallel Programming Experience with Applications, Languages & Systems. (Sigplan Notices Ser.: Vol. 23, No. 9). (Illus.). 246p. 1988. pap. text ed. 22.00 (*0-89791-276-4*, 551880) Assn Compu Machinery.

ACM SIGSMALL - PC Symposium on Small Systems: 1990 SIGSMALL - PC on Small Systems, Held in Arlington, VA, March 28-30, 1990. Ed. by Hal Berghel et al. (Illus.). ix, 304p. 1990. pap. text ed. 23.00 (*0-89791-347-7*, 609900) Assn Compu Machinery.

ACM SIGSMALL - PC Symposium on Small Systems, 1985. (Illus.). 260p. 1985. pap. text ed. 24.00 (*0-89791-154-7*, 609850) Assn Compu Machinery.

ACM Sigsoft 1989: Third Symposium on Software Testing, Analysis, & Verification (TAV3), Held December 13-15, 1989, Key West, Florida. 230p. 1989. pap. text ed. 20.00 (*0-89791-342-6*, 594892) Assn Compu Machinery.

ACM Symposium on Computational Geometry. (Illus.). 325p. 1985. pap. text ed. 28.00 (*0-89791-163-6*, 429850) Assn Compu Machinery.

ACM Symposium on LISP & Functional Programming, 1982. (Illus.). 264p. 1982. pap. text ed. 29.00 (*0-89791-082-6*) Assn Compu Machinery.

ACM Symposium on LISP & Functional Programming, 1984. (Illus.). 364p. 1984. pap. text ed. 31.00 (*0-89791-142-3*) Assn Compu Machinery.

ACM Symposium on LISP & Functional Programming, 1986. (Illus.). 371p. 1986. pap. text ed. 31.00 (*0-89791-200-4*) Assn Compu Machinery.

ACM Turing Award Lectures. Ed. by Robert Ashenhurst. (ACM Press Anthology Ser.). (C). 1987. text ed. 34.95 (*0-317-59560-1*) Addison-Wesley.

ACM Turing Award Lectures: The First Twenty Years, 1966-1985. (C). 1987. text ed. 39.75 (*0-201-07794-9*) Addison-Wesley.

ACM Turing Award Lectures: The First Twenty Years: 1966-1985. ACM Staff. (ACM Press Anthology Ser.). (Illus.). 504p. (C). 1991. pap. text ed. 24.75 (*0-201-54885-2*) Addison-Wesley.

Acmaeidae: Invertebrates of the San Francisco Bay Estuary System, Vol. 2. David R. Lindberg. Ed. by Welton L. Lee. (Illus.). 1981. text ed. 12.50 (*0-910286-72-8*) Boxwood.

***ACME Directory of Members, 1994-95.** Association of Management Consulting Firms Staff. 70p. (C). 1994. 50.00 (*0-614-00303-2*) ACME.

ACME Survey of Key Management Information. LC 87-83741. 265p. 1987. 100.00 (*0-318-33225-6*) ACME.

ACME Survey of Key Management Information. LC 88-71918. 298p. 1988. 425.00 (*0-318-41421-X*) ACME.

ACME Theatre Very Great Poets Series, Vol. II. ACME Theatre Staff. 1987. 5.00 (*0-932526-14-4*) Nexus Pr.

***ACME 1994 Survey of European Key Management Information.** Association of Management Consulting Firms Staff. (Illus.). 60p. (C). 1994. 295.00 (*0-614-00304-0*) ACME.

***ACME 1994 Survey of European Key Management Information.** Association of Management Consulting Firms Staff. (Illus.). 60p. (C). 1994. lib. bdg. 75.00 (*0-614-00305-9*) ACME.

***ACME 1994 Survey of United States Key Management Information.** Association of Management Consulting Firms Staff. (Illus.). 138p. (C). 1994. 495.00 (*0-614-00306-7*) ACME.

***ACME 1994 Survey of United States Key Management Information.** Association of Management Consulting Firms Staff. (Illus.). 138p. (C). 1994. lib. bdg. 125.00 (*0-614-00307-5*) ACME.

Acmeist Movement in Russian Poetry: Culture & the Word. Justin Doherty. (Modern Languages & Literature Monographs). 400p. 1995. 60.00 (*0-19-815888-2*) OUP.

ACMR China's Top One Hundred Thousand Companies, 1994. All China Marketing Research Staff. 4000p. (Orig.). 1994. pap. 290.00 (*0-9641047-6-8*) China Commun.

Acne. Cunliff. 1989. 84.95 (*0-8151-2075-3*, Yr Bk Med Pubs) Mosby Yr Bk.

Acne & Rosacea. 2nd rev. ed. Gerd Plewig & Albert M. Kligman. LC 92-49778. 1992. 198.00 (*0-387-52277-8*) Spr-Verlag.

Acne? Try Nature's Remedy. Stephen T. Machutta, Sr. LC 88-92625. 90p. (Orig.). (YA). (gr. 3-11). 1991. pap. 9.95 (*0-9621489-0-3*) New Begin Life.

ACOG Guide to Planning for Pregnancy, Birth, & Beyond see Planning for Pregnancy, Birth, & Beyond

ACOL: The Complete System. Eric Crowhurst. 1992. 20.00 (*1-85744-506-6*, Maxwell Macmillan) Macmillan.

Acol Bridge Made Easy. Ron Klinger. 96p. 1987. pap. 7.95 (*0-575-03931-0*, Pub. by V Gollancz UK) Trafalgar.

Acol the Swiss Way. Ernst Jacobi & Stanley Hartland. 1993. pap. 14.95 (*0-533-10257-X*) Vantage.

Acolyte Handbook. Ralph R. Van Loon. LC 86-46430. 64p. 1987. pap. 5.00 (*0-8006-2059-3*, 1-2059, Fortress Pr) Augsburg Fortress.

Acoma. H. L. James. LC 88-61474. (Illus.). 96p. 1988. pap. 14.95 (*0-88740-133-3*) Schiffer.

Acoma. Peter Neill. LC 77-92932. 1978. pap. 3.95 (*0-918172-03-9*) Leetes Isl.

Acoma. Tryntje V. Seymour. (Illus.). 295.00 (*0-915998-05-X*) Lime Rock Pr.

Acoma: Pueblo in the Sky. rev. ed. Ward A. Minge. LC 91-20689. (Illus.). 262p. 1991. reprint ed. pap. 24.95 (*0-8263-1301-9*) U of NM Pr.

Acoma & Laguna Pottery. Rick Dillingham & Melinda Elliott. Ed. by Joan K. O'Donnell. (Illus.). 256p. 1992. pap. 24.95 (*0-933452-32-2*, U of Wash Pr) Schol Am Res.

Acoma Culture Province: An Archeological Concept. Reynold Ruppe. LC 90-21599. (Evolution of North American Indians Ser.: Vol. 21). 320p. 1991. reprint ed. 20.00 (*0-8240-6110-1*) Garland.

Acomodando la Discapacidad. Marsha Saxton. (SPA.). 1993. pap. 2.00 (*0-913937-72-X*) Rational Isl.

Acompaname. Michael Milne. 448p. 1991. pap. text ed. 34.95 (*0-8403-6857-7*) Kendall-Hunt.

Aconcagua: A Climbing Guide. R. J. Secor. (Illus.). 144p. 1994. pap. 15.95 (*0-89886-406-2*) Mountaineers.

Aconcagua - The Stone Sentinel: Perspectives of an Expedition. Thomas E. Taplin. LC 92-75052. (Illus.). 236p. 1992. 29.95 (*0-9634807-1-5*); pap. 17.95 (*0-9634807-2-3*) E Ely.

Aconites of India: A Monograph by Otto Stapf, with A Sketch of the Life of Francis Hamilton (Once Buchanan), Vol X, Pt. 2. Royal Botanic Garden, Calcutta Staff. (Illus.). lxxv, 197p. 50.00 (*0-88065-014-1*, Messers Today & Tomorrow) Scholarly Pubns.

Acontecimientos del Fin (Finding Events) M. Ramos. (SPA.). Date not set. 1.79 (*1-56063-120-1*, 498143) Editorial Unilit.

Acontecimientos del Principio (Beginning Events: How It All Began) M. Ramos. (SPA.). 1.79 (*1-56063-318-2*, 498157) Editorial Unilit.

Acops Yearbook 1986-1987. Advisory Committee on Pollution of the Sea, London, UK. 120p. 1987. 35.00 (*0-317-66305-4*, Pergamon Pr) Elsevier.

Acorn Alone. Michael McClure. Ed. by Jon Robertson. LC 94-6638. (Illus.). (J). 1994. 14.95 (*0-87604-326-0*) ARE Pr.

Acorn Eaters. Els Pelgrom. Tr. by Johanna H. Prins & Johanna W. Prins. LC 93-34210. (J). (gr. 4 up). 1994. 16.00 (*0-374-30029-1*) FS&G.

Acorn Guide to Door County, Wisconsin. Kristin Visser. 1994. pap. 9.95 (*1-879483-17-3*) Prairie Oak Pr.

***Acorn Guide to Milwaukee.** Joan Strasbaugh. LC 95-4059. 1995. pap. 9.95 (*1-879483-25-4*) Prairie Oak Pr.

Acorn Guide to Northwest Illinois. Don Davenport. LC 93-27179. 148p. 1994. pap. 9.95 (*1-879483-14-9*) Prairie Oak Pr.

Acorn Pancakes, Dandelion Salad & 38 Other Wild Recipes. Jean C. George. LC 93-42490. Orig. Title: The Wild, Wild Cookbook. (Illus.). 64p. (J). 1995. reprint ed. 14.95 (*0-06-021549-6*); reprint ed. lib. bdg. 14.89 (*0-06-021550-X*) HarpC Child Bks.

***Acorn People.** Michael Golden. Ed. by J. Friedland & R. Kessler. (Novel-Ties Ser.). (YA). 1992. student ed, pap. text ed. 15.95 (*0-88122-713-7*) Lrn Links.

Acorn People. Ron Jones. (YA). 1990. mass mkt. 3.99 (*0-553-27385-X*) Bantam.

Acorn Plan. Tim McLaurin. 1989. pap. 9.95 (*0-393-30616-X*) Norton.

Acorn to Oak Tree. Oliver S. Owen. LC 94-6302. (J). 1994. lib. bdg. 14.96 (*1-56239-289-1*) Abdo & Dghtrs.

***Acorn Tree & Other Folktales.** Ed. by Anne F. Rockwell. LC 94-29277. (Illus.). 40p. (J). (gr. 4 up). 1995. 16.00 (*0-688-10746-X*); lib. bdg. 15.93 (*0-688-13723-7*) Greenwillow.

***Acorn Winter.** Elizabeth Webster. 1994. lib. bdg. 20.00 (*0-7278-4643-4*) Severn Hse.

Acoustic Analysis of Speech. Ray D. Kent & Charles Read. (Illus.). 248p. (Orig.). (C). 1992. pap. text ed. 34.95 (*1-879105-43-8*) Singular Publishing.

***Acoustic Analysis Speech.** Kent. 1992. 39.95 (*1-56593-364-8*, 0227) Singular Publishing.

Acoustic & Elastic Wave Scattering Using Boundary Elements. J. Jeferson Do Rego Silva. LC 94-70419. (Topics in Engineering Ser.: Vol. 18). 148p. 1994. 69.00 (*1-56252-217-5*) Computational Mech MA.

Acoustic & Electrical Methods in Triboengineering. Ed. by V. A. Belyi. (Illus.). xiv, 256p. 1988. 60.00 (*0-89864-041-5*) Allerton Pr.

Acoustic & Vibration Sensors & Test Equipment: Opening of Under-Penetrated Global Markets. Market Intelligence Staff. 276p. (Orig.). 1992. 1,695.00 (*1-56753-054-0*) Frost & Sullivan.

Acoustic Behaviour of Insects: An Evolutionary Perspective. Winston J. Bailey. (Illus.). 250p. 1990. 87.50 (*0-412-31980-2*, A5001) Chapman & Hall.

Acoustic Blues Guitar: Intermediate Level. Kenny Sulton. (Illus.). 52p. (Orig.). 1993. pap. text ed. 15.95 (*0-931759-73-0*) Centerstream Pub.

Acoustic Bubble. Timothy G. Leighton. (Illus.). 640p. 1994. text ed. 150.00 (*0-12-441920-8*) Acad Pr.

Acoustic Charge Transport: Device Technology & Applications. Robert L. Miller et al. LC 92-10502. (Microwave Ser.). 606p. 1992. text ed. 85.00 (*0-89006-520-9*) Artech Hse.

Acoustic Communication. Barry Truax. Ed. by Melvin J. Voigt. LC 84-20372. (Communication & Information Science Ser.). 256p. 1985. 45.00 (*0-89391-263-8*); pap. 24.50 (*0-89391-307-3*) Ablex Pub.

Acoustic Communication in Birds: Vol. 1: Sounds Production, Perception & Design Features of Sounds. Ed. by Donald Kroodsma et al. (Communication & Behavior Ser.). 318p. 1983. text ed. 59.95 (*0-12-426801-3*) Acad Pr.

Acoustic Communication in Birds: Vol. 2: Song Learning & Its Consequences. Ed. by Donald Kroodsma et al. (Communication & Behavior Ser.). 318p. 1983. text ed. 59.95 (*0-12-426802-1*) Acad Pr.

Acoustic Cues for Constituent Structure: A Series of Experiments on the Nature of Spoken Sentence Structures. Robert J. Scholes. (Janua Linguarum, Ser. Minor: No. 121). 80p. 1971. pap. text ed. 16.95 (*90-279-1855-4*) Mouton.

Acoustic Design. Duncan Templeton. (Illus.). 152p. 1987. text ed. 49.95 (*0-85139-018-8*) Buttrwrth-Heinemann.

Acoustic Design, Vol. 1. Michael Rettinger. 288p. 1977. 41.95 (*0-317-99711-4*) Peninsula CA.

Acoustic Emission. Ed. by J. Eisenblaetter. (Illus.). 320p. 1988. 76.00 (*3-88355-131-7*) IR Pubns.

Acoustic Emission. Ed. by James R. Matthews. LC 82-20928. (Nondestructive Testing Monographs & Tracts: Vol. 2). (Illus.). viii, 167p. 1983. text ed. 105.00 (*0-677-16490-4*) Gordon & Breach.

Acoustic Emission. Ed. by R. W. Nichols. (Illus.). 121p. 1976. 63.00 (*0-85334-681-X*, Pub. by Elsevier Applied Sci UK) Elsevier.

***Acoustic Emission.** fac. ed. R. V. Williams. LC 80-141934. (Illus.). 132p. 1980. reprint ed. pap. 37.70 (*0-7837-7990-9*, 2047746) Bks Demand.

Acoustic Emission: Current Practice & Future Directions, STP, 1077. W. Sachse et al. LC 90-25872. (Special Technical Publication Ser.). (Illus.). 450p. 1991. text ed. 62.00 (*0-8031-1389-7*, 04-010770-22) ASTM.

Acoustic Emission: Techniques & Applications. Jack C. Spanner. 288p. 1974. 34.75 (*0-318-21496-2*, 752) Am Soc Nondestructive.

Acoustic Emission - STP 505. 337p. 1972. 22.50 (*0-8031-0116-3*, 04-505000-22) ASTM.

Acoustic Emission-Microseismic Activity in Geologic Structures & Materials. H. R. Hardy & F. W. Leighton. (Rock & Soil Mechanics Ser.: Vol. 8). 680p. 1984. 50.00 (*0-87849-046-9*, Pub. by Trans Tech GW) LPS Dist Ctr.

A

An Asterisk (*) at the beginning of an entry indicates that the title is appearing in BIP for the first time. 37

A

Acoustic Emission Monitoring of Pressurized Systems - STP 697. 228p. 1979. 26.50 (0-8031-0271-2, 04-697000-22) ASTM.

Acoustic Emission Nondestructive Evaluation of Yankee Dryers. Claudio Allevato & David Williams. Ed. by W. G. Corboy. LC 92-23971. reprint ed. pap. 97.20 (0-7837-3205-8, 2043201) Bks Demand.

Acoustic Emission Testing of Aerial Devices & Associated Equipment Used in the Utility Industries. Ed. by Allen H. Bingham et al. LC 92-19624. (Special Technical Publication Ser.: No. 1139). (Illus.). 90p. 1992. text ed. 21.00 (0-8031-1433-8, 04-011390-21) ASTM.

Acoustic Emissions in Geotechnical Engineering Practice - STP 750. Ed. by Drnevich & Gray. 218p. 1981. 25.00 (0-8031-0788-9, 04-750000-38) ASTM.

Acoustic Fields & Waves in Solids, 2 vols., Set. 2nd rev. ed. Bertram A. Auld. 1990. 109.00 (0-89464-490-4) Krieger.

Acoustic Fields & Waves in Solids, 2 vols., Vol. I. rev. ed. Bertram A. Auld. 446p. 1990. 61.50 (0-89874-782-1) Krieger.

Acoustic Fields & Waves in Solids, 2 vols., Vol. II. rev. ed. Bertram A. Auld. 432p. 1990. 60.50 (0-89874-783-X) Krieger.

Acoustic Guitar: Adjustment, Care, Maintenance, & Repair, Vol. I. Don E. Teeter. LC 74-5962. (Illus.). 250p. 1980. 42.95 (0-8061-1219-0) U of Okla Pr.

Acoustic Guitar: Adjustment, Care, Maintenance, & Repair, Vol. II. Don E. Teeter. LC 79-5962. (Illus.). 202p. 1980. 42.95 (0-8061-1607-2) U of Okla Pr.

Acoustic Guitar Answer Book. Sharon Isbin. (Illus.). 64p. (Orig.). 1994. pap. text ed. write for info. (0-9626081-6-5) String Letter.

Acoustic Guitar Guide: Everything You Need to Know to Buy & Maintain a New or Used Guitar. Larry Sandberg. LC 90-28593. (Illus.). 260p. 1991. pap. 14.95 (1-55652-104-9) A cappella Bks.

Acoustic Guitar of Martin Simpson. Martin Simpson. Ed. by Mark Hanson. 80p. (Orig.). (C). 1994. pap. 17.95 (0-936799-11-0) Accent Music.

Acoustic Guitars & Other Fretted Instruments: A Photographic History. George Gruhn & Walter Carter. (Illus.). 320p. 1993. 49.95 (0-87930-240-2) Miller Freeman.

Acoustic Insulation of Pipes, Valves & Flanges. EEMUA Staff. 1982. 110.00 (0-85931-088-4, Pub. by EEMUA UK) St Mut.

Acoustic JamTrax for Guitar. Mark Hanson. (Illus.). 1993. pap. 11.95 (0-8256-1352-3) Music Sales.

Acoustic Microscopy. Andrew Briggs. (Monographs on the Physics & Chemistry of Materials: No. 46). 300p. 1992. 95.00 (0-19-851377-1) OUP.

Acoustic Mirror: The Female Voice in Psychoanalysis & Cinema. Kaja Silverman. LC 87-45834. (Theories of Representation & Difference Ser.). 268p. 1988. 39.95 (0-253-30284-6); pap. 12.95 (0-253-20474-7, MB-474) Ind U Pr.

Acoustic Neuroma: Proceedings of the First International Conference on Acoustic Neuroma. Ed. by M. Tos & J. Thomsen. LC 92-23671. (Illus.). 1002p. 1992. 244.00 (90-6299-085-1) Kugler Pubns.

Acoustic Phonetics: A Course of Basis Readings. Ed. by Dennis B. Fry. LC 76-16916. (Illus.). 501p. reprint ed. pap. 142.80 (0-8357-5077-9, 2030595) Bks Demand.

Acoustic Properties of Wakes see Physics of Sound in the Sea

***Acoustic Radiation & Wave Propagation: 1994 International Mechanical Engineering Congress & Exposition, Chicago, Illinois - November 6-11, 1994.** (Noice Control & Acoustics Ser.: Vol. 17). 172p. 1994. 74.00 (0-7918-1429-7, G00924) ASME.

Acoustic Reflex: Scientific Aspects & Clinical Applications. Shlomo Silman. LC 83-22318. 1984. text ed. 91.00 (0-12-643450-6) Acad Pr.

Acoustic Resonance Scattering: Proceedings of a Symposium. Ed. by Herbert Uberall. LC 91-23329. 341p. 1992. text ed. 130.00 (2-88124-513-7) Gordon & Breach.

***Acoustic Rock Jam Trax for Guitar.** Contrib by Mark Hanson. 1994. 11.95 (0-8256-1380-9, AM91305) Music Sales.

Acoustic Sense of Animals. William C. Stebbins. (Illus.). 192p. (C). 1983. 29.95 (0-674-00326-8) HUP.

Acoustic Sensing & Probing: Fourth Course of the International School on Physical Acoustics. Adriano Alippi. 204p. 1992. text ed. 121.00 (981-02-0912-6) World Scientific Pub.

Acoustic Signal Processing for Ocean Exploration: Proceedings of the NATO Advanced Study Institute on Acoustic Signal Processing for Ocean Exploration, Funchal, Madeira, Portugal, July 26-August 7, 1992. Ed. by Josee M. Moura & Isabel M. Lourtie. LC 92-43800. (NATO Advanced Study Institutes Series C, Mathematical & Physical Sciences: No. 388). 1993. lib. bdg. 250.00 (0-7923-2133-2) Kluwer Ac.

Acoustic Systems in Biology. Neville H. Fletcher. 352p. 1992. 65.00 (0-19-506940-4) OUP.

Acoustic Theory of Speech Production. rev. ed. Gunnar Fant. (D A C S R Ser.: No. 2). 1970. text ed. 54.70 (90-279-1600-4) Mouton.

Acoustic, Thermal Wave & Optical Characterization of Materials: Proc. of Symp. C., European-Materials Research Society Spring Conf., Strasbourg, France, 30 May-2 June, 1989. Ed. by G. M. Crean et al. 370p. 1990. reprint ed. 107.75 (0-444-88552-8, North Holland) Elsevier.

Acoustic Trauma & Cochlear Microcirculation see Nystagmus As a Resultant in Accordance with the Theoretical Principals of the Physical Mechanisms of the Normal Human Labyrinths

Acoustic Wave Sensors: Theory, Design, & Physico-Chemical Applications. David S. Ballantine. 1993. pap. 54.95 (0-12-077460-7) Acad Pr.

Acoustic Waves in Boreholes. Ed. by Frederick Paillet & C. H. Cheng. (Illus.). 176p. 1991. 98.95 (0-8493-8890-2, TN871) CRC Pr.

Acoustical & Environmental Robustness in Automatic Speech Recognition. Alejandro Acero. LC 92-31211. (International Series in Engineering & Computer Science, VLSI, Computer Architecture, & Digital Screen Processing). (C). 1992. lib. bdg. 69.50 (0-7923-9284-1) Kluwer Ac.

Acoustical Design of Concert Halls & Theatres. V. L. Jordan. (Illus.). xiv, 225p. 1980. 74.00 (0-85334-853-7, Pub. by Elsevier Applied Sci UK) Elsevier.

Acoustical Design of Music Education Facilities. Ed. by Edward R. McCue & Richard H. Talaske. LC 90-83693. 236p. 1990. pap. 20.00 (0-88318-810-4) Am Inst Physics.

Acoustical Designing in Architecture. V. O. Knudsen & C. M. Harris. LC 80-67079. 408p. 1980. pap. 20.00 (0-88318-267-X); pap. 17.50 (0-317-01120-0) Acoustical Soc Am.

Acoustical Foundations of Music. 2nd ed. John Backus. LC 68-54957. (Illus.). (C). 1977. text ed. 29.95 (0-393-09096-5) Norton.

Acoustical Imaging, No. 20. Ed. by Yu Wei & Benli Gu. (Illus.). 791p. 1994. 149.50 (0-306-44585-9, Plenum Pr) Plenum.

Acoustical Imaging, Vol. 15. Ed. by Hugh W. Jones. LC 69-12533. 704p. 1987. 110.00 (0-306-42565-3, Plenum Pr) Plenum.

Acoustical Imaging, Vol. 16. Ed. by L. W. Kessler. LC 69-12533. (Illus.). 670p. 1988. 125.00 (0-306-43011-8, Plenum Pr) Plenum.

Acoustical Imaging, Vol. 17. Ed. by H. Shimizu et al. (Illus.). 784p. 1989. 155.00 (0-306-43150-5, Plenum Pr) Plenum.

Acoustical Imaging, Vol. 18. Ed. by H. Lee & G. Wade. (Illus.). 536p. 1991. 125.00 (0-306-43900-X, Plenum Pr) Plenum.

Acoustical Imaging, Vol. 19. Ed. by H. Ermert & H. P. Harjes. (Illus.). 964p. (C). 1992. 165.00 (0-306-44198-5, Plenum Pr) Plenum.

Acoustical Measurements. rev. ed. Leo L. Beranek. LC 88-82582. 841p. 1988. 35.00 (0-88318-590-3) Acoustical Soc Am.

Acoustical Oceanography: Principles & Applications. Clarence S. Clay & Herman Medwin. LC 77-1133. (Ocean Engineering Ser.). 544p. 1977. text ed. 99.95 (0-471-16041-5) Wiley.

Acoustical Properties of Precast Concrete. (PCI Journal Reprints Ser.). 22p. 1978. pap. 5.00 (0-686-39936-6, JR-198) P-PCI.

Acoustical Studies of Mandarin Vowels & Tones. John M. Howie. LC 74-19529. (Princeton-Cambridge Studies in Chinese Linguistics: Vol. 6). 302p. reprint ed. pap. 86.10 (0-8357-5078-7, 2024578) Bks Demand.

Acoustics. Leo L. Beranek. LC 86-70671. 492p. 1986. pap. 20.00 (0-88318-494-X) Acoustical Soc Am.

***Acoustics.** Clarence A. Powell. 1966. pap. 6.00 (0-615-00360-5) Atlantis Edns.

Acoustics. William W. Seto. (Schaum Outline Ser.). 1970. pap. text ed. 12.95 (0-07-056328-4) McGraw.

Acoustics: An Introduction to Its Physical Principles & Applications. Allan D. Pierce. LC 89-80362. 678p. 1989. pap. 30.00 (0-88318-612-8) Acoustical Soc Am.

Acoustics & Electroacoustics. Mario Rossi. Tr. by Patrick R. Roe. LC 88-2176. (Illus.). 768p. reprint ed. pap. 180.00 (0-7837-4620-2, 2044341) Bks Demand.

***Acoustics & Noise Control for Architects & Builders.** Irvine. 1996. write for info. (0-89464-922-1) Krieger.

Acoustics & Performance of Music. Jurgen Meyer. Tr. by John Bowsher & Sibylle Westphal. (Illus.). 240p. 100.26 (0-933224-28-1) Bold Strummer Ltd.

Acoustics & Sound Systems in Schools. Frederick S. Berg. LC 93-16561. (Illus.). 267p. (Orig.). (C). 1993. pap. text ed. 44.95x (1-56593-079-7) Singular Publishing.

Acoustics & the Built Environment. Anita Lawrence. 242p. 1989. 77.50 (1-85166-308-8) Elsevier.

Acoustics Dictionary. W. Reichardt. 109p. (DUT, ENG, FRE & GER.). 1983. 95.00 (0-8288-0056-1, M6245) Fr & Eur.

Acoustics, Elasticity & Thermodynamics of Porous Media: Twenty-One Papers. M. A. Biot. Ed. by Ivan Tolstoy. 272p. 1991. 25.00 (1-56396-014-1) Am Inst Physics.

Acoustics for Liturgy. E. A. Sovik. Ed. by David Philippart. (Meeting House Essays: Architecture & Art for Liturgy Ser.). (Illus.). 64p. (Orig.). 1992. pap. 6.00 (0-929650-53-0) Liturgy Tr Pubns.

Acoustics for You. James H. Prout & Gordon R. Bienvenue. LC 88-7699. 276p. (C). 1990. lib. bdg. 29.50 (0-89464-328-2) Krieger.

Acoustics in the Built Environment: Advice for the Design Team. Ed. by Duncan Templeton et al. LC 92-39206. 1993. 85.00 (0-7506-0538-3, Butterwrth Archit) Buttrwrth-Heinemann.

Acoustics of American English Speech: A Dynamic Approach. J. P. Olive et al. LC 92-44839. 408p. 1993. 59.00 (0-387-97984-0) Spr-Verlag.

Acoustics of Auditoriums in Public Buildings. Leonid I. Makrinenko. Ed. by J. S. Bradley. Tr. by R. S. Rattner. LC 94-16573. 1994. write for info. (1-56396-360-4) Am Inst Physics.

Acoustics of Crime: The New Science of Forensic Phonetics. H. Hollien. (Applied Psycholinguistics & Communication Disorders Ser.). (Illus.). 380p. 1990. 54.50 (0-306-43467-9, Plenum Pr) Plenum.

Acoustics of Ducts & Mufflers. M. L. Munjal. 328p. 1987. text ed. 115.00 (0-471-84738-0) Wiley.

Acoustics of Layered Media I. L. M. Brekhovskikh & O. A. Godin. (Wave Phenomena Ser.: Vol. 5). (Illus.). 255p. 1990. 83.00 (0-387-51038-9, 2834) Spr-Verlag.

Acoustics of Layered Media II: Point Source & Bounded Beams. L. M. Brekhovskikh & O. A. Godin. Ed. by L. B. Felsen et al. (Wave Phenomena Ser.: Vol. 10). (Illus.). 408p. 1992. text ed. 89.00 (0-387-52646-3) Spr-Verlag.

Acoustics of Music. Wilmer T. Bartholomew. LC 79-17650. (Illus.). 242p. 1980. reprint ed. text ed. 38.50 (0-313-22087-5, BAAC, Greenwood Pr) Greenwood.

Acoustics of Music. Wilmer T. Bartholomew. (Music Book Index Ser.). 242p. 1992. reprint ed. lib. bdg. 79.00 (0-7812-9513-0) Rprt Serv.

Acoustics of Porous Media. Thierry Bourbie et al. 352p. 1987. 99.00 (0-87201-025-2) Gulf Pub.

***Acoustics of Porous Media.** Thierry Bourbie et al. (Illus.). 352p. (C). 1986. text ed. 137.00 (2-7108-0516-2) Technip.

Acoustics of Solids. A. I. Beltzer. ix, 237p. 1988. 77.00 (0-387-18888-6) Spr-Verlag.

Acoustics of Wood. Voichita Bucur. 1994. write for info. (0-8493-4801-3) CRC Pr.

Acoustics of Worship Spaces. Ed. by David Lubman & Ewart A. Wetherill. LC 85-70273. 91p. 1985. 20.00 (0-88318-466-4) Acoustical Soc Am.

Acousto-Optic Devices: Principles, Design & Applications. Jeiping Xu & Robert Stroud. (Pure & Applied Optics Ser.: No. 1349). 672p. 1992. text ed. 105.00 (0-471-61638-9) Wiley.

Acousto-Optic, Electro-Optic, & Magneto-Optic Devices & Applications. Ed. by Lucero. 186p. 1987. 43.00 (0-89252-788-9, 753) SPIE.

Acousto-Optic Signal Processing: Fundamentals & Applications. Pankaj K. Das & Casimer De Cusatis. (Acoustics Library). 425p. 1991. text ed. 79.00 (0-89006-464-4) Artech Hse.

Acousto-Optic Signal Processing: Theory & Implementation. Ed. by Norman J. Berg & John N. Lee. (Optical Engineering Ser.: Vol. 2). (Illus.). 504p. 1983. 140.00 (0-8247-1667-1) Dekker.

Acousto-optical Devices & Their Applications. L. N. Magdich & V. Y. Molchanov. 176p. 1989. text ed. 135.00 (2-88124-677-X) Gordon & Breach.

Acousto-Optics. Korpel. (Optical Engineering Ser.: Vol. 16). 288p. 1988. 125.00 (0-8247-7891-X) Dekker.

Acousto-Optics. J. Sapriel. Tr. by Simon Francis & Barbara Kelly. LC 78-16173. 142p. reprint ed. pap. 40.50 (0-8357-5079-5, 2030382) Bks Demand.

Acousto-Optics & Acoustic Microscopy. Ed. by S. M. Gracewski & T. Kundu. (AMD Ser.: Vol. 140). 204p. 1992. 52.50 (0-7918-1075-5, G00719) ASME.

Acousto-Ultrasonics: Theory & Application. Ed. by J. C. Duke, Jr. LC 88-23507. (Illus.). 364p. 1988. 95.00 (0-306-43013-4, Plenum Pr) Plenum.

Acoustoelectronics 'Ninety-One: Proceedings of the 5th Conference. L. Spassov et al. 184p. 1992. text ed. 67.00 (981-02-0919-3) World Scientific Pub.

Acoustooptical Phenomena in Liquid Crystals. O. A. Kapustina & N. N. Andreev. (Molecular Crystals & Liquid Crystals Ser.). 164p. 1984. pap. text ed. 135.00 (0-677-06605-8) Gordon & Breach.

ACP-EEC Convention of LOME: Third Convention, Compilation of Texts, January 1, 1990-31 December 1990, Vol. 15. 332p. 1992. pap. 19.00 (92-824-0941-4, BX-72-91-932-EN-C, Pub. by Europ Com) UNIPUB.

***ACP-EEC Convention of Lome (3rd Convention) Compilation of Texts 1 January 1991-31 December 1991, Vol. 16.** European Communities Staff. 431p. 1994. pap. 25.00 (92-824-1081-1, BX76-92-310ENC, Pub. by Europ Com) UNIPUB.

ACPA in Today's Intellectual World: Proceedings, 1983, Vol. 57. Ed. by Marc F. Griesbach et al. LC 82-73233. 250p. 1984. pap. 20.00 (0-918090-17-2) Am Cath Philo.

Acquaintance & Date Rape: An Annotated Bibliography. Sally K. Ward et al. LC 94-21870. (Bibliographies & Indexes in Women's Studies Ser.: Vol. 21). 232p. 1994. text ed. 55.00 (0-313-29149-7, Greenwood Pr) Greenwood.

Acquaintance Rape: The Hidden Crime. Ed. by Andrea Parrot & Laurie Bechhofer. (Personality Processes Ser.). 401p. 1991. text ed. 52.50 (0-471-51023-8) Wiley.

Acquaintance Rape & Sexual Assault Prevention Training Manual. 5th ed. Andrea Parrot. 1991. 19.95 (1-55691-076-2, 762) Learning Pubns.

Acquainted with Grief. C. Gadda. LC 69-12804. 244p. 1985. pap. 8.95 (0-8076-1115-8) Braziller.

Acquainted with the Night. Sollace Hotze. 256p. (J). (gr. 7 up). 1992. 13.95 (0-395-61576-3, Clarion Bks) HM.

Acquainted with the Night. large type ed. Sollace Hotze. LC 93-18333. 298p. 1993. lib. bdg. 15.95 (1-56054-690-5) Thorndike Pr.

ACQUIRE: Answer - Comprehend - Question - Interpret - Reason - Express. Linda B. Collins & Sandra S. Chadwell. 160p. 1990. pap. text ed. 34.95 (0-937857-14-9, 1572) Speech Bin.

Acquired Aphasia. 2nd ed. Ed. by Martha T. Sarno. 600p. 1991. text ed. 59.95 (0-12-619321-5) Acad Pr.

Acquired Aphasia in Children. Ed. by Isabel P. Martins et al. 328p. 1991. lib. bdg. 112.50 (0-7923-1315-1) Kluwer Ac.

Acquired Apraxia of Speech in Aphasic Adults. Ed. by Paula S. Square-Storer. (Brain Damage Behaviour & Cognition Ser.). 312p. 1991. 59.95 (0-86377-183-1); pap. 36.00 (0-86377-184-X) L Erlbaum Assocs.

Acquired Colour Vision Deficiencies: Proceedings of the International Research Group on Colour Vision Deficiencies Symposium, 1st, Ghent, Belgium, 1971. International Research Group on Colour Vision Deficiencies Staff. Ed. by G. Verriest. (Modern Problems in Ophthalmology Ser.: Vol. 11). (Illus.). 1972. 59.25 (3-8055-1303-8) S Karger.

Acquired Hearing Loss: Psychological & Psychosocial Implications. Alan J. Thomas. 1985. text ed. 102.00 (0-12-687920-6) Acad Pr.

Acquired Immune Deficiency Syndrome. Ed. by Irving J. Selikoff et al. LC 85-2965. (Annals Ser.: Vol. 437). 622p. 1984. lib. bdg. 140.00 (0-89766-268-7); pap. 140.00 (0-89766-269-5) NY Acad Sci.

Acquired Immune Deficiency Syndrome. Ed. by D. B. Weiner. (Journal: Pathobiology: Vol. 60, No. 4, 1992). (Illus.). 80p. 1992. pap. 33.75 (3-8055-5633-0) S Karger.

Acquired Immune Deficiency Syndrome: Biological, Medical, Social, & Legal Issues. Gerald J. Stine. LC 92-19795. 496p. (C). 1992. text ed. 48.00 (0-13-019811-0) P-H.

***Acquired Immune Deficiency Syndrome: Biological, Medical, Social, & Legal Issues.** 2nd ed. Gerald J. Stine. LC 95-2430. 1995. text ed. write for info. (0-13-356890-3) P-H.

Acquired Immune Deficiency Syndrome: Manual for Professional Health Care Providers. Elise John et al. LC 86-9669. (Illus.). 66p. 1986. student ed 19.95 (0-937825-00-X) Cabashon Pub.

Acquired Immune Deficiency Syndrome: Reprint from Pathobiology, Vol. 60, No. 4, 1992. Ed. by D. B. Weiner. (Illus.). 80p. 1992. 33.75 (3-8055-5680-2) S Karger.

Acquired Immune Deficiency Syndrome (AIDS) & Chemical Dependency. 1990. lib. bdg. 250.00 (0-87700-894-9) Revisionist Pr.

Acquired Immune Hemolytic Anemias. Lawrence D. Petz & George Garratty. LC 79-19235. 478p. reprint ed. pap. 136.30 (0-7837-3156-6, 2042829) Bks Demand.

Acquired Immunity Deficiency Syndrome (AIDS) A Source Guide. 1991. lib. bdg. 75.00 (0-8490-4888-5) Gordon Pr.

Acquired Immunodeficiency Syndrome. Ed. by Eva Klein. (Progress in Allergy Ser.: Vol. 37). (Illus.). x, 398p. 1986. 220.00 (3-8055-4156-2) S Karger.

Acquired Immunodeficiency Syndrome: Current Issues & Scientific Studies. Ed. by Pascal J. Imperato. (Illus.). 134p. 1989. 45.00 (0-306-43188-2, Plenum Med Bk) Plenum.

Acquired Immunodeficiency Syndrome: Legal & Regulatory Policy. William J. Curran & Lawrence O. Gostin. (Special Studies on AIDS). 400p. 1988. text ed. 45.00 (1-55572-008-0) Univ Pub Group.

Acquired Immunodeficiency Syndrome (AIDS) Advances in Host Defense Mechanisms, Vol. 5. Ed. by John I. Gallin & Anthony S. Fauci. 190p. 1985. text ed. 72.00 (0-88167-077-4) Raven.

Acquired Neurogenic Disorders. Thomas P. Marquardt. (Illus.). 208p. 1982. text ed. write for info. (0-13-003814-8) P-H.

Acquired Neurological Speech-Language Disorders in Childhood. Ed. by Bruce E. Murdoch. (Brain Damage, Behavior & Cognition Ser.). 360p. 1990. 79.95 (0-86377-190-4); pap. 39.95 (0-86377-191-2) L Erlbaum Assocs.

Acquired of the Angels: The Lives & Works of Master Guitar Makers John D'Angelico & James L. D'Aquisto. Paul W. Schmidt. LC 90-22399. (Illus.). 109p. 1991. 29.50 (0-8108-2346-2) Scarecrow.

Acquired Resistance of Micro-Organisms to Chemotherapeutic Drugs. Ed. by H. Schoenfeld et al. (Antibiotics & Chemotherapy Ser.: Vol. 20). (Illus.). 1976. 111.25 (3-8055-2198-7) S Karger.

Acquired Taste: The French Origins of Modern Cooking. T. Sarah Peterson. (Illus.). 280p. 1994. 24.95 (0-8014-3053-4) Cornell U Pr.

Acquired Tastes. Peter Mayle. 1993. pap. 9.95 (0-553-37183-5) Bantam.

Acquired Tastes. large type ed. Peter Mayle. 300p. 1992. reprint ed. lib. bdg. 20.95 (1-56054-543-7) Thorndike Pr.

Acquiring a Fortune: Financial Novice to Millionaire. Howard L. Balsley & James J. Conway. LC 91-11856. 128p. 1991. lib. bdg. 13.95 (0-931541-18-2) Mancorp Pub.

***Acquiring Companies & Business in Europe.** Ed. by Nigel Carrington & Beatrix P. De Araujo. 1994. pap. text ed. 40.00 (0-471-95051-3) Wiley.

Acquiring Culture: Cross-Cultural Studies in Child Development. Ed. by Gustav Johoda & Ioan M. Lewis. 288p. 1988. lib. bdg. 79.95 (0-7099-4335-0, Pub. by Croom Helm UK) Routledge Chapman & Hall.

Acquiring Defense Systems. 1994. lib. bdg. 350.00 (0-8490-8411-3) Gordon Pr.

Acquiring Knowledge of the Ideas: A Study of Plato's Methods in the Phaedo, the Symposium & the Central Books of the Republic. Ludwig C. Chen. (Palingenesia Ser.: No. XXXV). 248p. (Orig.). 1992. pap. 77.50x (3-515-05862-1) Coronet Bks.

Acquiring Language in a Conversational Context: Behavioral Development. C. J. Howe. LC 81-66381. (Series of Monographs). 1981. text ed. 88.00 (0-12-356920-6) Acad Pr.

Acquiring Major Systems Contracts: Bidding Methods & Winning Strategies. Marshall H. Kaplan. LC 88-5496. 288p. 1988. text ed. 64.95 (0-471-85247-3) Wiley.

Acquiring Optimal Health. Gary P. Todd. 128p. (Orig.). 1994. pap. 8.95 (1-878901-92-3) Hampton Roads Pub Co.

Acquiring or Selling the Privately Held Company, 1992. 883p. 1992. pap. 70.00 (0-685-69372-4) PLI.

Acquiring Or Selling the Privately Held Company 1993. (Corporate Law & Practice Course Handbook, 1985-86 Ser.: Vol. 812). 936p. 1993. 70.00 (0-685-69718-5, B4-7034) PLI.

An Asterisk (*) at the beginning of an entry indicates that the title is appearing in BIP for the first time.

Acquiring Parks & Recreation Facilities Through Mandatory Dedication: A Comprehensive Guide. Ronald A. Kaiser & James D. Mertes. LC 86-50112. (New Directions in Leisure Ser.). 150p. 1986. 29.95 (0-910251-13-4) Venture Pub PA.

Acquiring Skills: Market Failures, Their Symptoms & Policy Responses. Ed. by Alison Booth & Dennis J. Snower. (Illus.). 300p. (C). 1994. write for info. (0-521-47205-9) Cambridge U Pr.

Acquiring the Future: America's Survival & Success in the Global Economy. Joseph E. Pattison. 350p. 1989. text ed. 30.00 (1-55623-184-9) Irwin Prof Pubng.

Acquiring Water for Energy: Institutional Aspects. Ed. by Gary Weatherford et al. LC 81-69876. 1982. 26.00 (0-918334-42-X) WRP.

Acquisition, Adaptation, & the Development of Technologies: Japan's Experience & Its Lessons. Ed. by Ryoshin Minami et al. LC 94-12855. (Studies in Modern Japanese Enconomy). 1994. write for info. (0-312-12241-1) St Martin.

Acquisition & Development Directory, 1989-1990. 3rd ed. Ed. by Sylvia Schneble. 410p. 1989. 125.00 (0-942283-03-1) Omniartists Mgmt.

Acquisition & Performance of Cognitive Skills. Ann M. Colley et al. 330p. 1989. text ed. 143.00 (0-471-91461-4) Wiley.

Acquisition & Pioneering of Old Oregon & In the Beginning. Clarence Bagley. 181p. 1983. reprint ed. 12.95 (0-87770-280-2) Ye Galleon.

Acquisition & Protection of Ownership. D. Carey Miller. 408p. 1986. 24.00 (0-7021-1777-3, Pub. by Juta SA); pap. 20.00 (0-7021-2366-8, Pub. by Juta SA) W W Gaunt.

Acquisition & Use of Geotechnical Information. (National Cooperative Highway Research Program Report Ser.: No. 33). 40p. 1976. 4.00 (0-309-02427-7) Transport Res Bd.

Acquisition & Utilization of Aquatic Habitat Inventory Information. Ed. by Neil B. Armantrout. 376p. 1982. pap. 22.50 (0-913235-19-9) Am Fisheries Soc.

Acquisition Behavior of U. S. Manufacturing Firms, 1946-1965. H. Igor Ansoff et al. LC 79-163771. (Illus.). 160p. reprint ed. pap. 45.60 (0-7837-6193-7, 2045915) Bks Demand.

Acquisition Decision. Woods Gordon. 102p. 16.95 (0-86641-110-0, 84162) Inst Mgmt Account.

Acquisition List Pamphlet File. rev. ed. Alexander N. Charters & Edward Goodman. (E. S. Bird Library). 1983. 8.00 (0-87060-073-7, MSS 13) Syracuse U Cont Ed.

Acquisition Mating Dance & Other Essays on Negotiating. James C. Freund. 226p. 1987. 55.00 (0-13-003807-5) Aspen Law.

Acquisition of American Sign Language. Ed. by Newport & Meier. (Crosslinguistic Study of Language Acquisition Ser.). 80p. 1990. pap. 14.95 (0-89859-849-4) L Erlbaum Assocs.

Acquisition of Aspect & Modality: The Case of Past Reference in Turkish. Ayhan Aksu-Koc. (Cambridge Studies in Linguistics). 350p. 1988. 59.95 (0-521-33119-6) Cambridge U Pr.

Acquisition of Defense Systems. Ed. by J. S. Przemieniecki. LC 93-27833. (Education Ser.). 358p. 1993. 61.95 (1-56347-069-1) AIAA.

***Acquisition of Discourse Proficiency: A Study of the Ability of German School Students to Produce Written Texts in English as a Foreign Language.** Alasdair N. Archibald. 1994. pap. 52.95 (3-631-47831-3) P Lang Pubs.

Acquisition of Egyptian Arabic As a Native Language. Margaret K. Omar. 1973. pap. text ed. 58.75 (90-279-2468-6) Mouton.

Acquisition of Foreign Materials for U. S. Libraries. 2nd ed. Ed. by Theodore Samore. LC 82-5963. 230p. 1982. text ed. 22.50 (0-8108-1560-5) Scarecrow.

Acquisition of Gender. A. E. Mills. (Language & Communication Ser.: Vol. 20). (Illus.). 180p. 1986. 71.00 (0-387-16740-4) Spr-Verlag.

Acquisition of German: The Crosslinguistic Study of Language Acquisition. Ed. by Anne Mills. (Crosslinguistic Study of Language Acquisition Ser.). 136p. 1986. pap. 14.95 (0-89859-841-9) L Erlbaum Assocs.

Acquisition of Hebrew. Ed. by Berman & Slobin. (Crosslinguistic Study of Language Acquisition Ser.). 144p. 1986. pap. 17.50 (0-89859-842-7) L Erlbaum Assocs.

Acquisition of Imported Technology for Industrial Development: Problems of Strategy & Management in the Arab Region. 299p. 1990. 35.00 (92-1-128112-1, 90.II.L.3) UN.

Acquisition of Irish: A Case Study. Maire Owens. (Multilingual Matters Ser.: No. 72). 300p. 1992. 99.00 (1-85359-114-9, Pub. by Multilingual Matters UK); pap. 39.95 (1-85359-113-0, Pub. by Multilingual Matters UK) Taylor & Francis.

Acquisition of Japanese. Ed. by Clancy & Slobin. (Crosslinguistic Study of Language Acquisition Ser.). 176p. 1986. pap. 24.50 (0-89859-843-5) L Erlbaum Assocs.

Acquisition of Kaluli. Schieffelin. (Crosslinguistic Study of Language Acquisition Ser.). 96p. 1986. pap. 14.95 (0-89859-844-3) L Erlbaum Assocs.

Acquisition of Language. Helen S. Cairns. Ed. by Harvey Halpern. LC 86-423. (PRO-ED Studies in Communicative Disorders). (Illus.). 56p. (Orig.). 1986. pap. text ed. 9.00 (0-89079-088-4, 1378) PRO-ED.

Acquisition of Literacy: Ethnographic Perspectives. Bambi Schieffelin & Perry Gilmore. Ed. by Roy O. Freedle. LC 86-1037. (Advances in Discourse Processes Ser.: Vol. 21). 296p. 1986. text ed. 75.00 (0-89391-206-9); pap. 39.50 (0-89391-379-0) Ablex Pub.

Acquisition of Marine Surveying Technologies. 260p. 1986. 25.00 (92-1-104194-5, 86.II.A.18) UN.

Acquisition of Marine Surveying Technologies. 176p. 1988. pap. 16.50 (92-1-104303-4, E.88.II.A.19) UN.

Acquisition of Mauritian Creole. Dany Adone. LC 94-547. (Language Acquisition & Language Disorders (LALD) Ser.: No. 9). xi, 167p. 1994. lib. bdg. 40.00 (1-55619-246-0) Benjamins North Am.

Acquisition of Modal Auxiliaries in the Language of Children. Diana Major. (Janua Linguarum, Series Minor: No. 195). 1974. pap. text ed. 49.25 (90-279-2664-6) Mouton.

Acquisition of Narratives: Learning to Use Language. Michael Bamberg. (New Babylon Studies in the Social Sciences: No. 49). 245p. (C). 1988. text ed. 113.10 (0-89925-285-0) Mouton.

Acquisition of Phonology: A Case Study. Neilson V. Smith. LC 72-95409. 282p. reprint ed. pap. 80.40 (0-8357-5080-9, 2026353) Bks Demand.

Acquisition of Polish. Smoczynska. (Crosslinguistic Study of Language Acquisition Ser.). 120p. 1986. pap. 14.95 (0-89859-845-1) L Erlbaum Assocs.

Acquisition of Reading in Dutch: A State of the Art. Ed. by Pieter Reitsma & Ludo Verhoeven. (Studies on Language Acquisition). 160p. (Orig.). (C). 1989. pap. 46.15 (90-6765-490-6) Mouton.

Acquisition of Reading Skills: Cognitive Constraints & Cognitive Universals. Ed. by Barbara R. Foorman & Alexander W. Siegel. 188p. (C). 1986. text ed. 36.00 (0-89859-642-4) L Erlbaum Assocs.

Acquisition of Romance, with Special Reference to French. Ed. by Clark & Slobin. (Crosslinguistic Study of Language Acquisition Ser.). 120p. 1986. pap. 17.50 (0-89859-846-X) L Erlbaum Assocs.

Acquisition of Skill see Mental Measurements of the Blind

Acquisition of Strategic Knowledge. Thomas R. Gruber. (Perspectives in Artificial Intelligence Ser.: Vol. 4). 311p. 1989. text ed. 68.00 (0-12-304754-4) Acad Pr.

Acquisition of Symbolic Skills. Ed. by Don Rogers & John A. Sloboda. LC 83-9464. (NATO Conference Series III, Human Factors: Vol. 22). 636p. 1983. 115.00 (0-306-41368-X, Plenum Pr) Plenum.

Acquisition of Syntax in Bilingual Children. Carolyn Kessler. LC 72-76735. (Illus.). 121p. reprint ed. pap. 34.50 (0-7837-6330-1, 2046043) Bks Demand.

Acquisition of the Consumer Role by Adolescents. George P. Moschis. LC 78-10344. (Research Monograph: No. 82). 139p. 1978. pap. 20.00 (0-88406-124-8) GA St U Busn Pr.

Acquisition of the Holy Spirit in Ancient Russia. Ivan M. Kontzevitch. Ed. by St. Herman of Alaska Brotherhood Staff. Tr. by Olga Koshansky. LC 88-63597. (Acquisition of the Holy Spirit in Russia Ser.). (Illus.). 368p. (Orig.). (C). 1989. pap. 20.00 (0-938635-26-3) St Herman AK.

***Acquisition of the Lexicon.** Ed. by Lila Gleitman & Barbara Landau. LC 94-28973. (Lingua Special Issue Ser.). 1994. pap. 39.95x (0-262-57109-9, Bradford Bks) MIT Pr.

Acquisition of Turkish. Ed. by Aksu-Koc & Slobin. (Crosslinguistic Study of Language Acquisition Ser.). 64p. 1986. pap. 14.95 (0-89859-848-6) L Erlbaum Assocs.

Acquisition of Two Languages from Birth: A Case Study. Annick De Houwer. (Cambridge Studies in Linguistics: Supplementary Volumes). (Illus.). 272p. (C). 1990. 74.95 (0-521-36652-6) Cambridge U Pr.

Acquisition of Typewriting Skills. 2nd ed. Leonard J. West. 448p. 1983. text ed. write for info. (0-672-98444-X) Macmillan.

Acquisition of Verb Placement: Functional Categories & V2 Phenomena in Language Acquisition. Ed. by Jurgen M. Meisel. LC 92-23956. (Studies in Theoretical Psycholinguistics: Vol. 16). 464p. (C). 1992. lib. bdg. 147.00 (0-7923-1906-0) Kluwer Ac.

Acquisition of Written Language: Response & Revision. Sarah W. Freedman. Ed. by Marcia Farr. LC 85-13427. (Writing Research Ser.: Vol. 3). 312p. (C). 1985. text ed. 55.00 (0-89391-227-1); pap. 29.50 (0-89391-324-3) Ablex Pub.

Acquisition Priorities: Aspects of Postwar Painting in Europe. Thomas M. Messer. LC 83-60337. (Illus.). 104p. (Orig.). 1983. pap. 12.95 (0-89207-041-2) S R Guggenheim.

Acquisition Search Programs. Jerold L. Freier. LC 80-26356. 32p. 1981. pap. 3.95 (0-87576-094-5) Pilot Bks.

Acquisition Strategy for Petroleum Marketeers. John E. Wargin. 105p. 15.00 (0-685-65570-9) Petro Mktg Ed Found.

Acquisition, Tracking, & Pointing, No. II. Ed. by Kimbrell. 1988. 45.00 (0-89252-922-9, 887) SPIE.

Acquisition, Tracking, & Pointing III. Ed. by Sankaran Gowrinathan. 387p. 1989. 53.00 (0-8194-0147-1, VOL. 1111) SPIE.

Acquisition, Tracking, & Pointing IV. Ed. by Sankaran Gowrinathan. 1990. 53.00 (0-8194-0355-5, VOL. 1304) SPIE.

Acquisition, Tracking, & Pointing V, Vol. 1482. M. K. Masten & L. A. Stockum. 1991. 70.00 (0-8194-0591-4) SPIE.

Acquisitions, Vol. 4. Ed. by James E. Rush. LC 83-9584. (Library Systems Evaluation Guides Ser.). (Illus.). 253p. 1984. ring bd. 59.50 (0-912803-04-5) Rush Assoc.

Acquisitions: How to Create a Winning Advertising Program for Your Company. Sharon L. Blanding. (Entrepreneur's Guide Ser.). 200p. 1991. pap. 24.95 (1-55738-202-6) Probus Pub Co.

Acquisitions: The First Decade. Duncan Robinson et al. LC 86-51189. (Illus.). 40p. (Orig.). 1986. pap. 5.95 (0-930606-54-X) Yale Ctr Brit Art.

Acquisitions: Where, What, & How - A Guide to Orientation & Procedures for Students in Librarianship, Librarians, & Academic Faculty. Theodore Grieder. LC 77-84762. (Contributions in Librarianship & Information Science Ser.: No. 22). 277p. 1978. text ed. 59.95 (0-8371-9890-9, GAL/) Greenwood.

Acquisitions & Development Directory, 1989-89. 2nd ed. Ed. by Sylvie Schneble. 460p. (Orig.). 1988. pap. 125.00 (0-942283-02-3) Omniartists Mgmt.

Acquisitions & Mergers. George D. McCarthy. LC 63-15017. 361p. reprint ed. pap. 102.90 (0-8357-5081-7, 2016632) Bks Demand.

Acquisitions & Mergers: Accounting, Financial & Strategic Issues. Cedric Holt & Martin Reynolds. 304p. 1993. 55.00 (0-415-00430-6, A2502) Routledge.

Acquisitions & Mergers: Negotiated & Contested Transactions, 4 vols., Set. Simon M. Lorne. LC 85-4103. (Securities Law Ser.). 1985. ring bd. 445.00 (0-87632-462-6) Clark Boardman Callaghan.

Acquisitions & Mergers in a Troubled Environment 1991, 2 vols., Set. (Corporate Law & Practice Ser.). 1548p. 1992. pap. text ed. 17.50 (0-685-56879-2, B4-6981) PLI.

Acquisitions & Mergers 1989, 2 vols., Set. LC 80-83002. (Corporate Law & Practice Course Handbook, 1985-86 Ser.). 1545p. 1989. 30.00 (0-685-69373-2) PLI.

Acquisitions Budget. LC 89-33790. (Acquisitions Librarian Ser.: No. 2). 246p. 1989. text ed. 49.95 (0-86656-930-8) Haworth Pr.

Acquisitions, Budgets & Material Costs: Issues & Approaches. Sul H. Lee. LC 87-29867. (Journal of Library Administration & Supplement: No. 2). (Illus.). 165p. 1988. 39.95 (0-86656-690-2) Haworth Pr.

Acquisitions-Circulation Interface. Ed. by Sharon M. Edge. 104p. 1981. pap. 13.00 (0-08-026761-0, Pergamon Pr) Elsevier.

Acquisitions, Collection Development & Collection Use. David F. Kohl. LC 85-6023. (Handbook for Library Management Ser.). 409p. 1985. lib. bdg. 49.00 (0-87436-433-7) ABC-CLIO.

Acquisitions in a Deleveraging Environment. (Corporate Law & Practice Course Handbook, 1985-86 Ser.: Vol. 787). 249p. 1992. 70.00 (0-685-65491-5, B4-7011) PLI.

Acquisitions Manual. Sumner N. Levine. 1989. 64.95 (0-13-405929-8) P-H.

Acquisitions Manual: A Guide to Negotiating & Evaluating Business Acquisitions. Ed. by Sumner N. Levine. 1989. 64.95 (0-317-03936-9) NY Inst Finance.

Acquisitions Manual: Manual de Adquisiciones - Manual de Aquisicoes. William Ilgen & Deborah Jakubs. (Bibliography & Reference Ser.: No. 21). 95p. 1988. pap. 20.00 (0-917617-18-5) SALALM.

Acquisitions, Mergers, Sales, Buyouts & Takeovers: A Handbook with Forms. Charles A. Scharf et al. LC 85-6566. 452p. 1985. text ed. 59.95 (0-13-003120-8) P-H.

Acquisitions, Mergers, Sales, Buyouts & Takeovers: A Handbook with Forms. Charles A. Scharf et al. 520p. 1991. 93.27 (0-13-005596-4, 130601) P-H.

Acquisitions 1973-1980. Robert A. Sobieszek et al. LC 81-81748. (Illus.). 64p. (Orig.). 1981. pap. 10.00 (0-935398-02-3) G Eastman Hse.

Acquisitions of Mathematics Concepts & Processes. Ed. by Richard Lesh & Marsha Landau. LC 83-2845. (Developmental Psychology Ser.). 1983. text ed. 79.00 (0-12-444220-X) Acad Pr.

Acquisitions under the Hart-Scott-Rodino Antitrust Improvements Act, 2 vols., Set. rev. ed. Stephen M. Axinn et al. 1100p. 1988. ring bd. 140.00 (0-317-05392-2, 00550) NY Law Pub.

Acquisitions Yearbook, 1991. Edward E. Shea. 1991. 65.00 (0-13-005265-5) P-H.

Acquisitions Yearbook, 1992. Edward E. Shea. 1992. 65.00 (0-13-007311-3, Busn) P-H.

Acquist. Elizabeth Sewell. LC 82-83593. viii, 81p. 1984. 12.95 (0-89386-006-9); pap. 9.95 (0-89386-007-7) Acorn NC.

Acquittal of God: A Theology for Vietnam Veterans. Uwe Siemon-Netto. LC 89-35816. 108p. (Orig.). 1990. pap. 9.95 (0-8298-0833-7) Pilgrim OH.

Acre of England. L. J. Manners. 160p. 1980. pap. 35.00 (0-905418-06-9, Pub. by Gresham Bks UK) St Mut.

***Acre of Light: Living with Cancer.** Mark Nepo. 1994. pap. 9.95 (0-87886-138-6) Greenfld Rev Lit.

Acres & Heirlooms: The Survival of Britain's Historic. Madeleine Beard. 256p. 1989. 25.00 (0-415-03264-4, A2094) Routledge.

***Acres & Pains.** S. J. Perelman. LC 94-24655. (Illus.). 128p. 1995. pap. 12.95 (1-55821-359-7) Lyons & Burford.

Acres for Cents: Delinquent Tax Auctions in Frontier Iowa. Robert P. Swierenga. LC 75-23868. (Contributions in American History Ser.: No. 46). 263p. 1976. text ed. 59.95 (0-8371-8167-4, SWA/, Greenwood Pr) Greenwood.

Acres of Diamonds. R. Conwell. 1987. 7.95 (0-933062-23-0) R H Sommer.

Acres of Diamonds. Russell Conwell. 1993. pap. 1.49 (1-55748-421-X) Barbour & Co.

Acres of Diamonds. Russell H. Conwell. 1982. pap. 3.99 (0-515-09028-X) Jove Pubns.

Acres of Diamonds: All Good Things Are Possible, Right Where You Are, & Now! Russell H. Conwell. Ed. by Bianca Leonardo. 160p. (YA). (gr. 8-12). 1993. reprint ed. pap. text ed. 10.95 (0-930852-25-7) Tree Life Pubns.

Acres of Diamonds see Treasury of Christian Classics

Acres of Flint: Sarah Orne Jewett & Her Contemporaries. rev. ed. Perry D. Westbrook. LC 80-20501. 204p. 1981. 25.00 (0-8108-1357-2) Scarecrow.

Acres U. S. A. Primer. Charles Walters. LC 79-50540. 449p. 1982. 20.00 (0-911311-37-8) Halcyon Hse.

***Acret's Construction Industry Guide to Mechanic Liens, Stop Notices & Payment Bonds, 1994.** James Acret. LC 94-27203. (Construction Law Ser.). 1994. write for info. (0-07-172649-7) Shepards-McGraw.

Acrisolemos Nuestro Idioma. Fermin Velasco. 192p. (SPA.). 1989. reprint ed. pap. 9.95 (0-89729-503-X) Ediciones.

ACRL - Historically Black Colleges & Universities Library Statistics, 1988-89. Comp. by Robert E. Molyneux. 101p. 1991. 35.95 (0-8389-7547-X); 25.95 (0-685-59355-X) Assn Coll & Res Libs.

ACRL University Library Statistics, 1987-88. Comp. by Robert E. Molyneux. 79p. 1989. 49.95 (0-8389-7288-8); 29.95 (0-685-58538-7) Assn Coll & Res Libs.

ACRL University Library Statistics, 1988-1989. Comp. by Denise Bedford. 79p. 1990. 29.95 (0-685-58665-0); pap. text ed. 49.95 (0-8389-7446-5) Assn Coll & Res Libs.

ACRL University Library Statistics, 1990-91. University of Illinois-Urbana, Library Research Center Graduate School of Library & Information Science. 80p. (Orig.). (C). 1992. pap. text ed. 69.95 (0-8389-7587-9); pap. text ed. 39.95 (0-685-59356-8) Assn Coll & Res Libs.

***Acrobat.** Ivan Bulloch & Diane James. (I Want to Be Ser.). (Illus.). 32p. (J). (gr. 1-3). 1995. 13.95 (1-56847-363-X) Thomson Lrning.

***Acrobat Quick Tour: Understand & Create Electronic Documents.** Barrie Sosinsky & Elisabeth Parker. 150p. 1995. 14.00 (1-56604-255-0) Ventana Pr.

Acrobatics Book. Jack Wiley. LC 78-58043. (Illus.). 208p. 1979. pap. 6.95 (0-89037-141-5) Anderson World.

Acrobatics of the Heart. Roy Flanders. (Orig.). pap. write for info. (0-934219-06-0) Great Point Pr.

Acrobats & Line. Israel Horovitz. 1971. pap. 4.75 (0-8222-0006-6) Dramatists Play.

***Acrobats of the Gods.** Blackmer. 1995. pap. 15.00 (0-919123-38-4) Atrium Pubs.

Acrobats of the Soul: Comedy & Virtuosity in Contemporary American Theatre. Ron Jenkins. LC 88-12394. (Illus.). 192p. 1988. pap. 15.95 (0-930452-72-0) Theatre Comm.

Acrochaetiaceae (Rhodophyta) An Annotated Bibliography. D. J. Garbary. (Bibliotheca Phycologica Ser.: Vol. 77). 266p. 1987. pap. 71.50 (3-443-60004-2) Lubrecht & Cramer.

Acromegaly. Ed. by G. M. Besser. (Journal: Hormone Research: Vol. 33, Suppl. 1, 1990). (Illus.). vi, 36p. 1990. pap. 17.75 (3-8055-5207-6) S Karger.

Acromegaly: A Century of Scientific & Clinical Progress. Ed. by R. J. Robbins & Schlomo Melmed. LC 87-13016. (Serono Symposia U. S. A. Ser.). (Illus.). 302p. 1987. 75.00 (0-306-42618-8, Plenum Pr) Plenum.

Acronym Book: Acronyms in Aerospace & Defense. 2nd ed. Comp. by Fernando B. Morinigo. 210p. 1992. 39.95 (0-930403-63-0) AIAA.

Acronym Soup: A Stirring Guide to Our Newest Word Form. Gilda Feldman & Phil Feldman. LC 93-34440. 1994. 20.00 (0-688-12160-8) Morrow.

Acronymal Dictionary: Medical Edition. Robert L. Schattner. Ed. by Allen S. Schattner. 200p. (C). 1988. 23.00 (0-945889-00-3); pap. 16.00 (0-945889-01-1) Omnimed Inc.

Acronyms & Abbreviations Covering the United Nations System & Other International Organizations. 406p. 1981. pap. 26.00 (92-1-002021-9, MULT.81.I.26) UN.

Acronyms & Abbreviations Covering the United Nations System & Other International Organizations. United Nations Staff. (Terminology Bulletin Ser.: No. 311). 36p. 1981. 49.95 (0-8288-7361-5, 9210020219) Fr & Eur.

Acronyms & Abbreviations in Government Contracting. Ed. by Joan N. Phillips. LC 93-27383. 1993. 20.00 (0-935165-24-X) GWU Gov Contracts.

Acronyms & Abbreviations in Molecular Spectroscopy. D. A. Wendisch. (Illus.). 344p. 1990. 79.00 (0-387-51348-5, 3194) Spr-Verlag.

Acronyms & Abbreviations of Computer Technology & Telecommunications. Comp. by David Tavaglione. LC 92-23505. 304p. 1992. 49.75 (0-8247-8747-1) Dekker.

Acronyms Commonly Used in Mexico. Ed. by Patricia A. Sullivan & Maria Telles-McGeagh. 29p. (Orig.). (C). 1990. pap. text ed. 5.25 (0-937795-09-7) Border Res Inst.

Acronyms Initialisms & Abbreviations Dictionary, 3 pts. 19th ed. Jennifer Mossman. 1994. write for info. (0-318-68502-7) Gale.

Acronyms Initialisms & Abbreviations Dictionary, Pt. 1, A-F. 18th ed. Jennifer Mossman. 1993. write for info. (0-8103-8204-0) Gale.

Acronyms Initialisms & Abbreviations Dictionary, Pt. 2, G-O. 18th ed. Jennifer Mossman. 1993. write for info. (0-8103-8205-9) Gale.

Acronyms Initialisms & Abbreviations Dictionary, Pt. 3, P-Z. 18th ed. Jennifer Mossman. 1993. write for info. (0-8103-8206-7) Gale.

Acronyms Initialisms & Abbreviations Dictionary, Vol. 1. 18th ed. Jennifer Mossman. 1993. 245.00 (0-8103-8203-2) Gale.

Acronyms Initialisms & Abbreviations Dictionary, Vol. 1. 19th ed. Jennifer Mossman. 1994. 245.00 (0-8103-5566-3, 030045) Gale.

***Acronyms, Initialisms, & Abbreviations Dictionary, 3 Vols., Vol. 1.** 20th ed. Ed. by Mary R. Bonk. (Acronyms, Initialisms, & Abbreviations Directory Ser.). 1995. 285.00 (0-8103-5627-9) Gale.

***Acronyms of Light: Letting Inner Guidance Help Teach.** Linda Claire. (Good News about You! Ser.). 79p. 1987. pap. 4.99 (0-9644324-0-4) Clarity Prods.

Acropolis. 2nd ed. Gerhart Rodenwalt. LC 58-6859. (Illus.). 167p. reprint ed. pap. 47.60 (0-8357-5082-5, 2016258) Bks Demand.

Acropolis see Greek Museums

An Asterisk (*) at the beginning of an entry indicates that the title is appearing in BIP for the first time.

A

Acropolis of Athens As Described by Pausanias. O. Jahn & A. Michaelis. 143p. 35.00 (0-89005-047-3) Ares.

Acropolois Restoration. Richard Economakis. 220p. 1994. 69.00 (1-85490-344-6, Academy Edits) St Martin.

Across. Peter Handke. Tr. by Ralph Manheim. 1986. 14.95 (0-374-10054-3) FS&G.

Across a Distance of Knives. Rocco Lo Bosco. Ed. by Chuck Taylor. (Orig.). 1982. pap. 4.95 (0-941720-08-X) Slough Pr TX.

Across a Rebel Sea. Cheryl Biggs. 416p. 1993. mass mkt. 4.50 (0-8217-4385-6) Zebra.

Across a Starlit Sea. Rebecca Brandewyne. 1991. reprint ed. 19.95 (0-7278-4075-4) Severn Hse.

Across Africa & Arabia. (Trade & Travel Routes Ser.). (Illus.). 128p. (YA). 1990. 17.95 (0-8160-1878-2) Facts on File.

***Across America: Second-Grade Curriculum.** Donna R. Fisher & Christine J. Dillon. (Illus.). 645p. 1994. ring bd. 50.00 (0-913717-57-6) Hewitt Res Fnd.

Across America on an Emigrant Train. Jim Murphy. LC 92-38650. 160p. (J). 1993. 16.95 (0-395-63390-7, Clarion Bks) HM.

***Across America Reader: A Second-Grade Reader.** Donna R. Fisher & Christine J. Dillon. (Illus.). 275p. 1994. pap. 9.95 (0-913717-58-4, 1992) Hewitt Res Fnd.

***Across America Student Workbook: Second-Grade Curriculum.** Donna R. Fisher & Christine J. Dillon. (Illus.). 339p. 1994. ring bd. 30.00 (0-913717-59-2, 2010) Hewitt Res Fnd.

Across Arctic America, Narrative of the Fifth Thule Expedition. Knud J. Rasmussen. LC 68-55213. 388p. 1970. reprint ed. text ed. 35.00 (0-8371-1489-6, RAAA, Greenwood Pr) Greenwood.

Across Arizona in 1883. Ed. by William R. Jones. (Illus.). 16p. 1977. reprint ed. pap. 3.95 (0-89646-011-8) Vistabooks.

Across Asia by Land. (Trade & Travel Routes Ser.). (Illus.). 128p. (YA). 1990. 17.95 (0-8160-1874-X) Facts on File.

Across Asia's Snows & Deserts. deluxe limited ed. W. Morden. (Illus.). 413p. 1993. boxed 100.00 (1-57157-006-3) Safari Pr.

Across Atlanta: A Resident's Guide. 2nd rev. ed. Jane Schneider & Marge McDonald. 162p. 1994. pap. 9.95 (1-56145-088-X) Peachtree Pubs.

Across Australia, 2 vols, Set. Baldwin Spencer & F. J. Gillen. LC 73-12482. reprint ed. 155.00 (0-404-11227-7) AMS Pr.

Across China. Peter Jenkins. 384p. 1988. mass mkt. 5.95 (0-449-21456-7, Crest) Fawcett.

***Across Continents & Cultures: The Art & Life of Henry Ossawa Tanner.** Dewey F. Mosby. LC 95-4078. (Illus.). 128p. 1995. pap. 25.00 (0-942614-24-0) Nelson-Atkins.

Across Cultures. Matthew Uzukwu. LC 93-90510. 230p. 1993. pap. 9.00 (0-9637326-2-5) Feli Pub.

Across Cultures: A Reader for Writers. Sheena Gillespie & Robert Singleton. 450p. 1990. pap. text ed. 21.00 (0-205-13065-8, H3065) Allyn.

Across Cultures: A Reader for Writers. 2nd ed. Sheena Gillespie & Robert Singleton. LC 92-21758. 1992. pap. text ed. write for info. (0-205-14577-9) Allyn.

***Across Cultures: A Reader for Writers.** 3rd ed. Sel. by Sheena Gillespie & Robert Singleton. LC 95-3626. 1995. pap. text ed. write for info. (0-205-17398-5) Allyn.

Across Cultures: The Spectrum of Women's Lives. Ed. by Emily K. Abel & M. L. Pearson. (Studies in Gender & Culture: Vol. 4). iv, 156p. 1989. pap. text ed. 18.00 (0-677-22050-2) Gordon & Breach.

Across Cultures: Universal Themes in Literature. William Smalzer & Phyllis L. Lim. LC 93-27952. 1994. pap. 19.95 (0-8384-3986-1) Heinle & Heinle.

Across Five Aprils. Irene Hunt. 100p. 1986. pap. 3.99 (0-425-10241-6, Berkley-Pacer) Berkley Pub.

***Across Five Aprils.** Irene Hunt. LC 92-46736. 212p. (J). (gr. 4 up). 1993. pap. 5.45 (0-8136-7202-3) Silver Pr.

Across Five Aprils. Irene Hunt. LC 92-46736. 212p. (J). (gr. 4 up). 1993. 10.95 (0-382-24367-6); lib. bdg. 12.95 (0-382-24358-7) Silver Pr.

Across Five Aprils: A Study Guide. Sandi Witt. (Novel-Ties Ser.). (YA). (gr. 9-12). 1990. pap. text ed. 15.95 (0-88122-394-8) Lrn Links.

Across Forever. Janice Bennett. 416p. 1994. pap. 4.50 (0-7860-0013-9, Pinnacle NY) Windsor NY.

Across My Path. LaSalle Pickett. LC 74-128287. (Essay Index Reprint Ser.). 1977. 19.95 (0-8369-1841-X) Ayer.

Across New Guinea from the Fly to the Sepik. Ivan F. Champion. LC 75-32804. (Illus.). 1976. reprint ed. 41.50 (0-404-14108-0) AMS Pr.

Across Oka. Robert Holman. (Methuen New Theatrescripts Ser.). 71p. (Orig.). (C). 1988. pap. 8.95 (0-413-19360-8, A0338, Pub. by Methuen UK) Heinemann.

Across Our Wide Missouri, 2 vols., Vol. 1. Bob Priddy. 1982. pap. 20.00 (0-8309-0331-3) Ind Pr MO.

Across Our Wide Missouri, 2 vols., Vol. 2. Bob Priddy. 1984. pap. 20.00 (0-8309-0397-6) Ind Pr MO.

Across Our Wide Missouri Vol. III: More Stories. Bob Priddy. 1994. pap. text ed. 20.00 (0-8309-0657-6) Herald Hse.

Across Realtime. Vernor Vinge. 1991. mass mkt. 5.99 (0-671-72098-8) Baen Bks.

Across Siberia: On the Great Post-Road. Charles Wenyon. LC 74-115595. (Russia Observed Ser.). (Illus.). 1971. reprint ed. 18.95 (0-405-03138-6) Ayer.

Across Spoon River. Edgar L. Masters. (Prairie State Bks.). pap. 14.95 (0-252-06051-2) U of Ill Pr.

Across Spoon River: An Autobiography. Edgar L. Masters. (American Biography Ser.). 426p. 1991. reprint ed. lib. bdg. 89.00 (0-7812-8276-4) Rprt Serv.

Across State Lines: Applying the Conflict of Laws to Your Practice. 221p. 1989. pap. 39.95 (0-89707-408-4, 515-0093-01) Amer Bar Assn.

Across Sussex with Belloc: In the Footsteps of the Four Men. Bob Copper. (Illus.). 160p. 1994. 30.00 (0-7509-0603-0) A Sutton Pub.

Across the Acheron. Monique Wittig. Tr. by David Le Vay & Margaret Crosland. LC 87-71417. 119p. 1987. 27.00 (0-7206-0664-0, Pub. by P Owen Ltd UK) Dufour.

Across the Appalachians: Washington, D.C. to Lake Michigan. P. P. Karan & Wilford A. Bladen. LC 92-10536. (Touring North America Ser.). (Illus.). 150p. 1992. 25.00 (0-8135-1878-4); pap. 9.95 (0-8135-1879-2) Rutgers U Pr.

Across the Atlantic & Beyond: The Migration of German & Swiss Immigrants to America. Charles R. Haller. (Illus.). xii, 324p. (Orig.). 1993. pap. 32.00 (1-55613-697-8) Heritage Bk.

Across the Black Waters. Mulk R. Anand. (Orient Paperbacks Ser.). 322p. 1980. pap. 5.95 (0-86578-081-1) Ind-US Inc.

***Across the Blue Line.** Barry Levenson. 1995. 17.95 (1-882146-46-8) A D G Prods.

Across the Blue Mountains. Emma C. Clark. LC 93-12118. (J). 1993. 14.95 (0-15-201220-6) HarBrace.

***Across the Board: Bulletin Boards, Activities, & Awards to Reinforce Basic Content Skills.** Lynn Brisson. Ed. & Intro. by Leslie Britt. (Illus.). 80p. (Orig.). (J). (gr. 1-3). 1995. pap. text ed. 8.95 (0-86530-312-6, 1P312-6) Incentive Pubns.

Across the Border: Rural Development in Mexico & Recent Migration to the United States. Harry E. Cross & James A. Sandos. LC 81-6276. 198p. 1981. pap. 13.95 (0-87772-280-3) UCB IGS.

Across the Border: The True Story of the Satanic Cult Killings in Matamoros, Mexico. Gary Provost. 256p. 1989. mass mkt. 4.50 (0-671-69319-0) PB.

Across the Boundaries of Race & Class: An Exploration of Work & Family among Black Female Domestic Servants. Bonnie T. Dill. LC 93-6019. 176p. 1993. 45.00 (0-8153-1542-2) Garland.

Across the Bridge. Mavis Gallant. 198p. 1994. pap. 10.95 (0-7867-0143-9) Carroll & Graf.

Across the Bridge. Cleta M. Long. (Illus.). 101p. 1990. pap. 9.95 (0-9619468-2-2) McClain.

Across the Bridge: Nine Short Stories. Mavis Gallant. LC 92-27270. 1993. 19.00 (0-679-42213-7) Random.

***Across the Bridge: Stories.** braille ed. Mavis Gallant. 346p. 1994. vinyl bd. 27.68 (1-56956-528-7, BR9512) W A T Braille.

Across the Channel. John Rea. LC 85-62783. (Illus.). 80p. 1986. pap. write for info. (0-918702-07-0) Eilean Ban Pub.

***Across the Columbia Plain: Railroad Expansion on the Interior Northwest, 1885-1893.** Peter J. Lewty. LC 94-39630. (Illus.). 286p. (Orig.). 1995. 35.00 (0-87422-115-3); pap. 25.00 (0-87422-114-5) Wash St U Pr.

Across the Continent: A Summer's Journey to the Rocky Mountains, the Mormons, & the Pacific States with Speaker Colfax. Samuel Bowles. (American Biography Ser.). 438p. 1991. reprint ed. lib. bdg. 89.00 (0-7812-8032-X) Rprt Serv.

Across the Continent in a Caravan & the Reminiscences of Captain Aram. James T. Watson & Joseph Aram. 21p. 1988. pap. 4.95 (0-87770-439-2) Ye Galleon.

Across the Creek: Faulkner Family Stories. Jim Faulkner. LC 86-5629. (Illus.). 110p. 1986. 16.95 (0-87805-302-6) U Pr of Miss.

Across the Curriculum. Hilary Radnor. LC 93-42673. (Education Matters Ser.). 176p. 1994. 60.00 (0-304-32832-4) Cassell.

Across-the-Curriculum Guide, Diggy Armadillo Goes to Fort Worth Stock Show & Rodeo, Bk. 1: 140 Creative Activites. Ann Pugh. 60p. (Orig.). 1992. 10.00 (1-879465-01-9) Diggy & Assocs.

Across-the-Curriculum Guide, Diggy Armadillo Goes to Fort Worth Stock Show & Rodeo, Bk. 1: 140 Creative Activites. Ann Pugh. 60p. (Orig.). (J). (gr. k-5). 1992. Eng. & Spa. audio 6.00 (0-685-60626-0) Diggy & Assocs.

Across the Everglades. Hugh Willoughby. (Illus.). 192p. 1992. pap. 9.95 (0-912451-46-7) Florida Classics.

Across the Everglades: A Play for the Screen. Budd Schulberg. LC 58-12429. 126p. 1958. 16.95 (0-910278-68-7) Boulevard.

Across the Face of France: Liberation & Recovery, 1944-63. James A. Huston. LC 83-21724. (Illus.). 270p. 1984. reprint ed. pap. text ed. 23.00 (0-8191-2747-7) U Pr of Amer.

Across the Frontiers. Werner Heisenberg. Tr. by Peter Heath. LC 90-14214. x, 230p. 1990. 35.00 (0-918024-80-3); pap. text ed. 16.00 (0-918024-81-1) Ox Bow.

Across the Frontiers: Ireland in the 1990s. Ed. by Richard Kearney. 280p. 1989. 40.00 (0-86327-209-6, Pub. by Wolfhound Pr IE); pap. 18.95 (0-86327-210-X, Pub. by Wolfhound Pr IE) Dufour.

Across the Gap: From War to Peace. Maxine T. Lechene. 1994. 9.95 (0-8062-4864-5) Carlton.

Across the Generations: Old People & Young Volunteers. Adrian Webb & Christine Farrell. 1975. 30.00 (0-317-05781-2, Pub. by Natl Inst Soc Work) St Mut.

***Across the Generations: Selecting & Using Intergenerational Resources.** Helen F. James. 120p. 1995. pap. text ed. 14.00 (0-917846-52-4, 95629) Highsmith Pr.

Across the Grain. Jean Ferris. 212p. (YA). 1990. 15.00 (0-374-30030-5) FS&G.

Across the Grain. Jean Ferris. (J). (ps-3). 1993. pap. 3.95 (0-374-40057-1) FS&G.

Across the Great Divide: The Band & America. Barney Hoskyns. (Illus.). 448p. 1994. pap. 14.95 (0-7868-8027-9) Hyperion.

Across the Great River. Irene B. Hernandez. LC 89-289. 120p. (Orig.). 1991. pap. 9.50 (0-934770-96-4) Arte Publico.

Across the Layers: Poems Old & New. Albert Goldbarth. LC 92-38270. 232p. 1993. 35.00 (0-8203-1547-8); pap. 16.95 (0-8203-1548-6) U of Ga Pr.

Across the Milky Way; Or, Frank Reade, Jr.'s Great Astronomical Trip with His Air-Ship "The Shooting Star" Luis Senarens. Bd. with Sinking Star; Or, Frank Reade, Jr.'s Trip into Space with His New Air-Ship "Saturn" (Frank Reade Library: Vol. 10). 1986. 85.00 (0-8240-3549-6) Garland.

Across the Narrow Sea. Sam H. Bell. 304p. 1987. 21.00 (0-85640-377-6, Pub. by Blackstaff Pr IE); pap. 11.95 (0-85640-378-4, Pub. by Blackstaff Pr IE) Dufour.

Across the Narrow Seas. large type ed. James Pattinson. (General Ser.). 1993. 20.95 (0-7089-2811-0) Ulverscroft.

***Across the Oceans: Studies from East to West in Honor of Richard K. Seymour.** Ed. by Irmengard Rauch & Cornelia N. Moore. LC 95-14377. 208p. (C). 1995. pap. text ed. 25.00x (0-8248-1693-5) UH Pr.

Across the Olympic Mountains: The Press Expedition, 1889-90. Robert L. Wood. (Illus.). 240p. 1988. reprint ed. pap. 12.95 (0-89886-219-1) Mountaineers.

Across the Onion: A History of East Montpelier, Vermont 1781-1981. Ellen C. Hill & Marilyn S. Blackwell. (Illus.). 370p. 1983. 25.00 (0-9612222-0-4) E Montpelier Hist Soc.

Across the Pacific: An Inner History of American-East Asian Relations. rev. ed. Akira Iriye. 448p. 1992. 45.00 (1-879176-08-4); pap. 19.95 (1-879176-07-6) Imprint Pubns.

Across the Pacific: Contemporary Korean & Korean American Art. Young C. Lee et al. Tr. by Su G. Kim & Myung Y. Kang. (Illus.). 102p. (Orig.). (C). 1993. pap. text ed. 26.00 (0-9604514-4-7) Queens Mus.

Across the Plains: An 1862 Journey from Omaha to Oregon. William Smedley. LC 93-49833. (Illus.). 96p. (Orig.). 1994. pap. 9.95 (1-55566-123-8) Johnson Bks.

Across the Plains & over the Divide. Randall H. Hewitt. (Illus.). 1964. reprint ed. 20.00 (0-87266-015-X) Argosy.

Across the Plains by Prairie Schooner. Fred Lockley. (Shorey Historical Ser.). 23p. pap. 3.75 (0-8466-0190-7, S190) Shorey.

***Across the Plains in the Donner Party.** Ed. by Karen Zeinert. (Illus.). 140p. (YA). (gr. 6 up). 1995. lib. bdg. write for info. (0-208-02404-2) Shoe String.

Across the Plains in the Donner Party: 1846-47. Virginia R. Murphy. Ed. by William R. Jones. (Illus.). 64p. 1980. pap. 6.95 (0-89646-063-0) Vistabooks.

Across the Plains in 1853. Dillis B. Ward. (Shorey Historical Ser.). 55p. 1983. reprint ed. pap. 4.95 (0-8466-0061-7, S61) Shorey.

Across the Plains in 1864 with Additional Paymaster Samuel C. Staples. Darlis A. Miller. 96p. 1980. pap. text ed. 20.00 (0-89126-098-6) MA-AH Pub.

Across the Pond. Michael McCormick. 1993. 10.95 (0-533-10579-X) Vantage.

Across the Pond: A Day on the Links. Michael T. Schaefer. (Illus.). 72p. (C). 1993. 29.95 (0-9638607-0-4) Shepherds Cottage.

***Across the Reef: The Marine Assault of Tarawa.** Joseph H. Alexander. (Illus.). 53p. (Orig.). (C). 1994. pap. text ed. 24.95x (0-7881-1187-6) Diane Pub.

***Across the Rhine Vol. 1: The Official Strategy Guide.** James M. Day. 1994. pap. 19.95 (1-55958-615-X) Prima Pub.

Across the Rio to Freedom. Rosalie Schwartz. (Southwestern Studies: No. 44). 1975. 10.00 (0-87404-102-3) Tex Western.

Across the River: Politics & Education in the City. Joseph Viteritti. LC 83-12714. 366p. 1983. 34.95 (0-8419-0883-4); pap. 17.50 (0-8419-0884-2) Holmes & Meier.

Across the River & into the Trees. Ernest Hemingway. LC 75-100353. 320p. 1977. text ed. 40.00 (0-684-15313-0, Scribners); pap. 9.95 (0-684-71795-6, SL 202, Scribners) S&S Trade.

Across the River & into the Trees. Ernest Hemingway. 320p. 1985. pap. 5.95 (0-684-18496-6, Scribners) S&S Trade.

Across the River & into the Trees. Ernest Hemingway. 320p. 1988. pap. 7.00 (0-02-051920-6, Collier S&S) S&S Trade.

Across the Rockies to the Columbia. John K. Townsend. LC 86-14639. (Illus.). 278p. reprint ed. pap. 79.30 (0-7837-4643-1, 2044367) Bks Demand.

Across the Running Tide. Michael J. Cohen. (Illus.). 1979. pap. 10.00 (0-89166-010-0) Cobblesmith.

Across the San Juan Mountains. T. A. Rickard. Ed. by Jack L. Benham. (Illus.). 178p. (Orig.). 1980. reprint ed. pap. 8.95 (0-941026-03-5) Bear Creek Pub.

Across the Savannas to Mecca: The Overland Pilgrimage Route from West Africa. J. S. Birks. (Illus.). 161p. 1978. 35.00 (0-7146-6005-1, Pub. by F Cass Pubs UK) Intl Spec Bk.

Across the Sea of Suns. Gregory Benford. 368p. 1994. mass mkt. 5.99 (0-553-28211-5, Bantam Classics) Bantam.

Across the Sea of Suns. Gregory Benford. LC 83-17851. 400p. 1984. 25.00 (0-671-44668-1) Ultramarine Pub.

Across the Shining Mountains: The Odyssey Nathaniel Wyeth. Christian McCord. LC 86-7238. (Frontier Library). 450p. 1987. 18.95 (0-915463-31-8) Green Hill.

Across the Smiling Meadow. Bess S. Aldrich. 20.95 (0-8488-0068-0, Amereon Hse) Amereon Ltd.

Across the Spirituality Pole. Jeanne E. Martinelli. 32p. (Orig.). 1989. pap. text ed. 5.00 (0-685-29005-0) J E Martinelli.

***Across the Straits.** Kyffin Williams. 223p. 1993. 48.00 (0-86383-994-0, Pub. by Gomer Pr UK) St Mut.

Across the Stream. Mirra Ginsburg. LC 81-20306. (Illus.). 24p. (J). (ps-1). 1982. 15.95 (0-688-01204-3); lib. bdg. 15.88 (0-688-01206-X) Greenwillow.

Across the Stream. Mirra Ginsburg. LC 81-20306. (Illus.). 24p. (J). (ps up). 1991. reprint ed. pap. 3.95 (0-688-10477-0, Mulberry) Morrow.

Across the Street. Georges Simenon. 1992. 18.95 (0-15-103266-1) HarBrace.

***Across the Street: Self-Help Graphics & Chicano Art in Los Angeles.** Bolton Colburn. LC 94-46424. 1995. write for info. (0-940872-21-8) Laguna Beach.

Across the Sub-Arctics of Canada: A Journey of 3200 Miles by Canoe & Snowshoe Through the Hudson Bay Region. 3rd enl. rev. ed. James W. Tyrrell. LC 74-5886. (Illus.). reprint ed. 49.50 (0-404-11695-7) AMS Pr.

Across the Thlassa Mey. Dennis McCarthy. 1991. mass mkt. 4.95 (0-345-35310-2, Del Rey) Ballantine.

Across the Tundra. Marjorie Vandervelde. (Indian Culture Ser.). (J). (gr. 4-12). 1972. 4.95 (0-89992-053-5) Coun India Ed.

Across the Unknown. Stewart E. White. 336p. 1987. reprint ed. pap. 9.95 (0-89804-150-3) Ariel GA.

***Across the Valley.** Janice B. Williams. 250p. 1996. pap. 8.95 (0-7610-0519-6) NW Pub.

Across the Water, Unit 1. (Networks Ser.). (J). (gr. 1). 1991. 7.45 (0-88106-701-6) Charlesbridge Pub.

Across the Water Activity Book, Unit 1. (Networks Ser.). (J). (gr. 1). 1991. 3.90 (0-88106-703-2) Charlesbridge Pub.

Across the West: Human Population Movement & the Expansion of the Numa. Ed. by David Madsen & David Rhode. 256p. (C). 1994. text ed. 50.00 (0-87480-465-5) U of Utah Pr.

Across the Wheatgrass: A Collection of Hearthside Stories about Uncommon People, Wildlife, Days Afield, & Things, Times & Places of Some Centennial Years. H. Ted Upgren, Jr. LC 88-50045. (Illus.). 211p. (Orig.). (YA). (gr. 8-12). 1988. 18.95 (0-9620122-0-3); pap. 12.95 (0-9620122-1-1) Windfeather Pr.

***Across the Wide Atlantic - 14th Annual Conference.** Ed. by Jane Hedlin. 1994. 8.00 (0-913233-28-5) AFRA.

***Across the Wide Dark Sea: The Mayflower Journey.** Jean Van Leeuwen. LC 91-16926. (Illus.). 32p. (J). (gr. 1-4). 1995. 15.99 (0-8037-1166-2); lib. bdg. 15.89 (0-8037-1167-0) Dial Bks Young.

Across the Wide Missouri. Bernard A. De Voto. (American Heritage Library). (Illus.). 480p. 1980. pap. 12.95 (0-395-08374-5, 25, SenEd) HM.

Across the Wide Missouri. Bernard A. De Voto. LC 83-45742. (Illus.). reprint ed. 94.50 (0-404-20079-6) AMS Pr.

Across the Wide Missouri: The Diary of a Journey from Virginia to Missouri in 1819 & Back Again in 1822, with a Description of the City of Cincinnati. James B. Campbell. Ed. by Mary W. Burgess. LC 84-268. (Stokvis Studies in Historical Chronology & Thought: No. 4). 139p. (Orig.). 1990. lib. bdg. 27.00x (0-89370-169-6); pap. 17.00x (0-89370-269-2) Borgo Pr.

Across the Wild River. Bill Gutman. (J). (gr. 4-7). 1993. mass mkt. 3.50 (0-06-106159-X, Harp PBks) HarpC.

Across the Wire: Life & Hard Times on the Mexican Border. Luis A. Urrea. LC 92-12680. 1993. mass mkt. 9.00 (0-385-42530-9, Anchor NY) Doubleday.

Across the Wounded Galaxies: Interviews with Contemporary American Science Fiction Writers. Ed. by Larry McCaffery. (Illus.). 280p. 1990. 29.95 (0-252-01692-0) U of Ill Pr.

Across the Wounded Galaxies: Interviews with Contemporary American Science Fiction Writers. Ed. by Larry McCaffery. (Illus.). 300p. 1991. pap. 12.95 (0-252-06140-3) U of Ill Pr.

***Across the Years.** Ed. by Dorothy Prendergast. (Illus.). 1995. pap. write for info. (0-614-04961-X) Rudelhaus Enter.

Across the Years. large type ed. Helga Moray. 320p. 1988. 15.95 (0-7089-1917-0) Ulverscroft.

Across the Zodiac, 2 vols. in 1. Percy Greg. LC 73-13271. (Classics of Science Fiction Ser.). 602p. 1974. reprint ed. 30.25 (0-88355-125-X); reprint ed. pap. 10.00 (0-88355-154-3) Hyperion Conn.

Across Time. Nina Beaumont. (Historical Ser.). 1994. mass mkt. 3.99 (0-373-28803-4, 1-28803-4) Harlequin Bks.

Across Time & Death. Jenny Cockell. 1994. pap. 10.00 (0-671-88986-9, Fireside) S&S Trade.

Across Time's Fence. Florence R. Masten. 1978. pap. 2.00 (0-911183-07-8) Rockland County Hist.

Acrostic Summarized Bible. Barry Huddleston. LC 78-2329. (Orig.). 1991. pap. 6.99 (0-8010-4351-4) Baker Bk.

Acrostics. Maralene Wesner & Miles Wesner. 100p. (Orig.). 1991. pap. 4.95 (0-936715-29-4) Diversity Okla.

Acrylamide. (Environmental Health Criteria Ser.: No. 49). 121p. 1985. pap. 7.20 (92-4-154189-X) World Health.

Acrylic Art Is Fun, No. III. Brenda Harris. 72p. (Orig.). 1989. pap. 14.95 (0-943295-12-2) Graphics Plus FL.

Acrylic Art Is Fun, Vol. II. Brenda Harris. Ed. by Judy B. McCaffrey. 72p. (Orig.). 1987. pap. text ed. 14.95 (0-943295-01-7) Graphics Plus FL.

Acrylic Art Is Fun, No. II: Thirteen New Paintings in Four Stages & Full Color. Brenda Harris. (Illus.). 72p. 1988. pap. 14.95 (0-943295-07-6) Graphics Plus FL.

Acrylic Cement in Orthopaedic Surgery. John Charnley. LC 73-153779. 139p. reprint ed. pap. 39.70 (0-8357-3378-5, 2039624) Bks Demand.

***Acrylic Fiber Technology & Applications.** Masson. 629p. 1995. 175.00 (0-8247-8977-6) Dekker.

Acrylic Painter's Pocket Palette. Ian Sidaway. 64p. 1994. 16.95 (0-89134-581-7) North Light Bks.

Acrylic Painter's Reference Book. Susan A. Bentley. (Illus.). 112p. 1989. pap. 9.95 (0-941284-65-4) J Shaw Studio.

An Asterisk (*) at the beginning of an entry indicates that the title is appearing in BIP for the first time.

A

An Asterisk (*) at the beginning of an entry indicates that the title is appearing in BIP for the first time.

41

A

Actes du Proces de Paul de Samosate: Etude sur la Christologie du IIIe au IVe Siecle. (Paradosis; Etudes de Litterature et de Theologie Ancienne, 6.) Henri De Riedmatten. LC 82-45822. (Orthodoxies & Heresies in the Early Church Ser.). 1989. reprint ed. 24.50 (*0-404-62392-1*) AMS Pr.

Actes sans Paroles II see Comedies et Actes Divers

ACTH & LPH in Health & Disease. Ed. by T. B. Van Wimersma Greidanus & L. H. Rees. (Frontiers of Hormone Research Ser.: Vol. 8). (Illus.). x, 210p. 1981. 105.75 (*3-8055-1977-X*) S Karger.

ACTH & Related Peptides: Structure, Regulation, & Action, Vol. 297. (Annals Ser.). 664p. 1977. 60.00 (*0-89072-043-6*) NY Acad Sci.

ACTH, Cushing's Syndrome, & Other Hypercortisolemic States. Dieter K. Ludecke et al. (Progress in Endocrine Research & Therapy Ser.: Vol. 5). 352p. 1990. 110.50 (*0-88167-718-3*) Raven.

***Actin: Biophysics, Biochemistry & Cell Biology.** Ed. by James E. Estes & Paul J. Higgins. LC 94-26868. (Advances in Experimental Medicine & Biology Ser.: Vol. 358). 236p. 1994. 79.50 (*0-306-44810-6*) Plenum.

Acting. John Harrop. (Theatre Concepts Ser.). 128p. 1992. 39.95 (*0-415-05961-5*, A6927); pap. 12.95 (*0-415-05962-3*, A6931) Routledge.

Acting. Ruth Rawson. LC 68-21664. (Theatre Student Ser.). (Illus.). (YA). (gr. 7 up). 1970. lib. bdg. 14.95 (*0-8239-0151-3*) Rosen Group.

Acting: A Drama Studio Source Book. John Miles-Brown. 110p. 1987. pap. 14.95 (*0-7206-0632-2*, Pub. by P Owen Ltd UK) Dufour.

***Acting: A Handbook.** Cole. 1995. write for info. (*0-517-88477-1*) Random Hse Value.

Acting: A Handbook of the Stanislavski Method. Toby Cole. 1955. pap. 8.95 (*0-517-05035-8*, Crown) Crown Pub Group.

Acting: In Person & In Style. 4th ed. Jerry L. Crawford. 528p. (C). 1991. pap. write for info. (*0-697-10718-3*) Brown & Benchmark.

Acting: Its Theory & Practice. Lane Crauford. LC 75-84510. 1972. 23.95 (*0-405-08400-5*, Pub. by Blom Pubns UK) Ayer.

Acting: Onstage & Off. Robert Barton. (Illus.). 320p. (C). 1989. teacher ed write for info. (*0-318-64062-7*); text ed. 29.50 (*0-03-009904-8*) HB Coll Pubs.

Acting: Onstage & Off. 2nd ed. Robert Barton. (Illus.). 320p. (C). 1992. pap. text ed. write for info. (*0-318-69241-4*) HB Coll Pubs.

Acting: Practice, Preparation, Performance. Itkn. (C). 1994. text ed. 25.00 (*0-673-46350-8*) HarpCollege.

***Acting: Preparation, Practice & Performance.** Itkin. 1994. pap. text ed. (*0-8230-4950-7*) Watsn-Guptill.

Acting: The Creative Process. 3rd ed. Hardie Albright & Arnita Albright. 393p. (C). 1980. pap. 31.95 (*0-534-00744-9*) Intl Thomson.

Acting: The First Six Lessons. Richard Boleslavsky. 1949. 15.95 (*0-87830-000-7*, Theatre Arts Bks) Routledge Chapman & Hall.

***Acting Alone.** Tom Bradley. 274p. 1994. 19.95 (*1-56313-444-6*); pap. 12.95 (*1-56313-723-2*) BrownTrout Pubs Inc.

Acting & Action in Shakespearean Tragedy. Michael Goldman. LC 84-17745. 164p. 1985. text ed. 32.50x (*0-691-06630-2*) Princeton U Pr.

Acting & Directing. 3rd ed. Russell J. Grandstaff. 88p. 1990. pap. 10.95 (*0-8442-5132-1*, Natl Textbk) NTC Pub Grp.

Acting & Reflecting. Ed. by Wilfried Sieg. (C). 1989. lib. bdg. 91.50 (*0-7923-0512-4*) Kluwer Ac.

Acting & Stage Movement: A Complete Handbook for Amateurs & Professionals. Edwin C. White et al. LC 85-60573. (Illus.). 193p. (YA). (gr. 11-12). 1985. reprint ed. pap. text ed. 9.95 (*0-916260-30-5*, B187) Meriwether Pub.

Acting & Theater. C. Evans. (Illus.). 64p. (J). (gr. 6 up). 1992. lib. bdg. 13.96 (*0-88110-505-8*, Usborne); pap. 7.95 (*0-7460-0699-3*, Usborne) EDC.

Acting & Thinking: The Political Thought of Hannah Arendt. Leah Bradshaw. 1989. 45.00 (*0-8020-2625-7*) U of Toronto Pr.

Acting As a Business: Strategies for Success. Brian O'Neil. LC 93-9183. 1993. pap. 13.95 (*0-435-08623-5*, 08623) Heinemann.

Acting As a Way of Salvation: A Study of Raganuga Bhakti Sadhana. David L. Haberman. (Illus.). 232p. 1988. 45.00 (*0-19-505321-4*) OUP.

Acting As Reading: The Place of the Reading Process in the Actor's Work. David Cole. LC 92-1640. (Theater: Theory - Text - Performance Ser.). 278p. (C). 1992. text ed. 39.50 (*0-472-10302-4*) U of Mich Pr.

Acting Between the Lines: The Field Day Theatre Company & Irish Cultural Politics, 1980-84. Marilynn J. Richtarik. (English Monographs). 320p. 1995. 55.00 (*0-19-818247-3*) OUP.

Acting for Film & TV. Leslie Abbott. (Illus.). 200p. 1993. pap. text ed. 16.95 (*0-89863-165-3*) Star Pub CA.

Acting for Real: Drama Therapy Process, Technique, & Performance. Renee Emunah. LC 93-44042. 336p. 1994. 49.95 (*0-87630-747-0*); pap. 24.95 (*0-87630-730-6*) Brunner-Mazel.

***Acting for the Camera.** Tony Barr. 320p. 1994. lib. bdg. 29.00 (*0-8095-9148-0*) Borgo Pr.

Acting for the Camera. Tony Barr. 1986. pap. 12.00 (*0-06-097034-0*, PL) HarpC.

Acting from the Ultimate Consciousness. Eric Morris. 1992. pap. 11.95 (*0-9629709-1-3*) Ermor Enter.

Acting Funny: Comic Theory & Practice in Shakespeare's Plays. Ed. by Frances Teague. LC 92-55090. Date not set. write for info. (*0-8386-3524-5*) Fairleigh Dickinson.

Acting Games: Improvisations & Exercises. Marsh Cassady. Ed. by Theodore O. Zapel. LC 93-37322. (Illus.). (Orig.). 1993. pap. 12.95 (*0-916260-92-5*, B168) Meriwether Pub.

Acting Gay: Male Homosexuality in Modern Drama. John C. Clum. (Illus.). 300p. 1992. 29.95 (*0-231-07510-3*) Col U Pr.

Acting Gay: Male Homosexuality in Modern Drama. John M. Clum. LC 93-38337. (Between Men - Between Women Ser.). (C). 1994. pap. write for info. (*0-231-07511-1*) Col U Pr.

Acting God. Lee Lozowick. LC 80-85142. 64p. 1980. pap. 3.95 (*0-934252-05-X*) Hohm Pr.

Acting-In: Practical Applications of Psychodramatic Methods. 2nd ed. Adam Blatner. LC 88-19960. 192p. (C). 1989. pap. 23.95 (*0-8261-1401-6*) Springer Pub.

Acting in Atlanta: An Introductory Guide to the Atlanta & Regional Film & Television Market. 3rd ed. Nan McElroy. 95p. 1994. pap. 16.95 (*1-885436-21-1*) Twoworkingactors.

Acting in Atlanta: An Introductory Guide to the Atlanta Film & Television Market. 2nd ed. Nan McElroy. 80p. 1994. pap. 15.95 (*1-885436-20-3*) Twoworkingactors.

Acting in Atlanta Directory, Jan. 1994. Nan McElroy. 1994. pap. 10.95 (*1-885436-50-5*) Twoworkingactors.

***Acting in Chicago: H-T Break into Film, TV & Theatre.** Belinda Bremner. 120p. 1994. pap. 10.95 (*1-56850-038-6*) Chicago Plays.

Acting in Commercials: A Guide to Auditioning & Performing on Camera. Joan See. (Illus.). 160p. 1993. pap. 16.95 (*0-8230-8325-X*, Back Stage Bks) Watsn-Guptill.

Acting in Faith: A Study Guide on the Philippines. James E. Palm & Eunice B. Poethig. 48p. (Orig.). 1989. pap. 4.95 (*0-377-00193-7*) Friendship Pr.

Acting in Film: An Actor's Take on Movie Making. Michael Caine. Ed. by Maria Aitken. (Acting Series & BBC Master Class). (Illus.). 160p. (Orig.). 1989. 14.95 (*0-936839-86-4*) Applause Theatre Bk Pubs.

Acting in Film: An Actor's Take on Movie Making. Michael Caine. Ed. by Maria Aitken. (Acting Series & BBC Master Class). (Illus.). 160p. (Orig.). 1989. vhs 49.95 (*1-55783-034-7*) Applause Theatre Bk Pubs.

Acting in Film: An Actor's Take on Movie Making. Michael Caine. Ed. by Maria Aitken. (Acting Ser.). (Illus.). 160p. (Orig.). 1992. pap. 8.95 (*1-55783-124-6*) Applause Theatre Bk Pubs.

Acting in Industrials: The Business of Acting for Business. William P. Steele. LC 94-7635. 175p. 1994. pap. 15.95 (*0-435-08640-5*) Heinemann.

Acting in Opera. George E. Shea. LC 79-28364. (Music Reprint Ser.). (Illus.). 1980. reprint ed. lib. bdg. 22.50 (*0-306-76004-5*) Da Capo.

Acting in Person & in Style. 5th ed. Jerry L. Crawford et al. 384p. (C). 1994. pap. text ed. write for info. (*0-697-20133-3*) Brown & Benchmark.

Acting in Restoration Comedy. Simon Callow. Ed. by Maria Aitken. (Acting Series & BBC Master Class). (Illus.). 128p. (Orig.). 1992. text ed. 14.95 (*1-55783-119-X*) Applause Theatre Bk Pubs.

Acting in Restoration Comedy. Simon Callow. Ed. by Maria Aitken. (Acting Series & BBC Master Class). (Illus.). 128p. (Orig.). 1992. vhs 79.95 (*1-55783-035-5*) Applause Theatre Bk Pubs.

***Acting in Shakespeare.** Robert Cohen. LC 90-36912. 230p. (C). 1991. text ed. 37.95 (*0-87484-951-9*) Mayfield Pub.

***Acting in Television Commercials for Fun & Profit.** expanded ed. Squire Fridell. 1995. pap. 15.00 (*0-517-88437-2*, Crown) Crown Pub Group.

Acting in Television Commercials for Fun & Profit--Expanded & Updated. Squire Fridell. (Illus.). 208p. 1987. pap. 12.95 (*0-517-56424-6*, Harmony) Crown Pub Group.

Acting in the Cinema. James Naremore. 316p. 1988. pap. 14.00 (*0-520-07194-8*) U CA Pr.

Acting in the Cinema. James Naremore. (C). 1988. 35.00 (*0-520-06228-0*) U CA Pr.

Acting in the Million Dollar Minute: The Art & Business of Performing in TV Commercials. Tom Logan. LC 84-12048. (Illus.). 175p. (Orig.). 1984. pap. 7.95 (*0-89461-041-4*) Broadcasting Pubns.

Acting Is Believing: A Basic Method. 5th ed. Charles J. McGaw & Gary Blake. 272p. (C). 1986. text ed. 34.75 (*0-03-007169-0*) HB Coll Pubs.

Acting Is Believing: A Basic Method. 6th ed. Charles McGaw & Larry D. Clark. 288p. (C). 1992. text ed. 36.00 (*0-03-055334-2*) HB Coll Pubs.

Acting Is Everything: An Actor's Guidebook for a Successful Career in Los Angeles. 7th ed. Judy Kerr. LC 91-61808. 400p. 1994. pap. 14.95 (*0-9629496-1-2*) Sept Pub.

Acting It Out: 74 Short Plays for Starting Discussions with Teenagers. Joan Sturkie & Marsh Cassidy. LC 90-35353. 358p. (Orig.). (C). 1991. pap. 22.00 (*0-89390-178-4*) Resource Pubns.

Acting It Out Junior. Joan Sturkie & Marsh Cassidy. LC 92-29698. 252p. (J). 1993. pap. text ed. 16.00 (*0-89390-240-3*) Resource Pubns.

Acting Lesson. Willard Simms. 1967. pap. 2.75 (*0-8222-0007-4*) Dramatists Play.

Acting Lessons for Teachers: Using Performance Skills in the Classroom. Robert T. Tauber & Cathy S. Mester. LC 94-13736. 192p. 1994. text ed. 55.00 (*0-275-94823-4*, Praeger Pubs); pap. text ed. 16.95 (*0-275-94824-2*, Praeger Pubs) Greenwood.

Acting Like a Pro: Who's Who, What's What, & the Way Things Really Work in the Theatre. Mary McTigue. (Illus.). 288p. (Orig.). 1992. pap. 14.95 (*1-55870-223-7*) Betterway Bks.

Acting Male: Masculinities in the Films of James Stewart, Jack Nicholson, & Clint Eastwood. Dennis Bingham. LC 93-37678. (Illus.). 280p. (C). 1994. text ed. 45.00 (*0-8135-2073-8*); pap. 15.95 (*0-8135-2074-6*) Rutgers U Pr.

Acting Million Dollar. 1987. pap. 7.95 (*0-89461-091-0*) Broadcasting Pubns.

Acting Natural: Monologs, Dialogs, & Playlets for Teens. Peg Kehret. Ed. by Arthur L. Zapel. LC 91-43552. (Orig.). (YA). (gr. 9-12). 1992. pap. text ed. 10.95 (*0-916260-84-4*, B133) Meriwether Pub.

Acting Naturally: Mark Twain in the Culture of Performance. Randall Knoper. LC 94-14467. 1995. 35.00 (*0-520-08619-8*) U CA Pr.

Acting on Ethics in City Planning. Elizabeth Howe. LC 93-28828. 408p. (C). 1994. text ed. 29.95 (*0-88285-147-0*) Ctr Urban Pol Res.

Acting on Faith: Worship Plays from the Covenant Players, Vol. 1. Charles M. Tanner. 64p. (Orig.). 1994. pap. 17.95 (*0-687-09752-5*) Abingdon.

Acting on Information Received. large type ed. Glyn Hardwicke. 1990. 21.95 (*0-7089-2191-4*) Ulverscroft.

Acting on Principle: An Essay on Kantian Ethics. Onora Nell. LC 74-20647. 167p. reprint ed. pap. 47.60 (*0-8357-5083-3*, 2022725) Bks Demand.

Acting on Principles: A Thomistic Perspective in Making Moral Decisions. Janko Zager. 254p. (Orig.). 1983. pap. text ed. 24.00 (*0-8191-3690-5*) U Pr of Amer.

Acting on Your Faith: Congregations Making a Difference: A Guide to Success in Service & Social Action. Victor N. Claman et al. (Illus.). 194p. (Orig.). 1994. pap. 25.00 (*0-9639701-0-0*) Insights MA.

Acting One. 2nd ed. Robert Cohen. 219p. (C). 1992. 32.95 (*1-55934-119-X*) Mayfield Pub.

Acting Our Age. P. Sellars. Date not set. pap. 9.95 (*0-06-092233-8*) HarpC.

Acting Out. 2nd ed. Ed. by Lawrence E. Abt & Stuart L. Weissman. LC 76-53942. 336p. 1976. reprint ed. 40.00 (*0-87668-287-5*) Aronson.

Acting Out: Feminist Performances. Ed. by Lynda Hart & Peggy Phelan. LC 93-16280. 350p. (C). 1993. text ed. 49.50 (*0-472-09479-3*); pap. text ed. 18.95 (*0-472-06479-7*) U of Mich Pr.

Acting-Out Elderly: Issues for Helping Professionals. Ed. by Miriam K. Aronson et al. LC 82-23430. (Advanced Models & Practice in Aged Care Ser.: No. 1). 132p. 1983. text ed. 39.95 (*0-917724-76-3*) Haworth Pr.

Acting Out Faith. Gordon C. Bennett. LC 86-6141. 160p. (Orig.). 1986. pap. 10.99 (*0-8272-0016-1*) Chalice Pr.

***Acting Out Jesus' Parables.** Stephen Parolini. Ed. by Lois Keffer & Joani Schultz. (Projects with a Purpose for Youth Ministry Ser.). 38p. 1994. pap. 9.99 (*1-55945-147-5*) Group Pub.

***Acting Out Participant Examples in the Classroom.** Stanton E. Wortham. LC 94-35673. (Pragmatics & Beyond, New Ser.: No. 30). xiii, 177p. 1994. lib. bdg. 49.00x (*1-55619-299-1*) Benjamins North Am.

Acting Out the Miracles & Parables: 52 Five-Minute Plays for Education & Worship. Kathleen Glavich. LC 88-50330. (Illus.). (Orig.). (J). (gr. 4-6). 1988. pap. 12.95 (*0-89622-363-9*) Twenty-Third.

Acting Person. Karol Wojtyla. Tr. by Andrzej Potocki. (Analecta Husserliana Ser.: No. 10). 1979. lib. bdg. 87.50 (*90-277-0969-6*); lib. bdg. 50.00 (*90-277-0985-8*) Kluwer Ac.

Acting, Playing, Singing Religion for Children. Elizabeth Huntley. LC 86-17476. 1989. 22.95 (*0-87949-273-2*) Ashley Bks.

Acting Power. Robert Cohen. LC 77-89918. 266p. (C). 1978. text ed. 35.95 (*0-87484-408-8*) Mayfield Pub.

Acting President: Ronald Reagan & the Supporting Players Who Helped Him Create the Illusion That Held America Spellbound. Bob Schieffer & Gary P. Gates. 416p. 1990. pap. 9.95 (*0-685-46352-4*, Dutton) NAL-Dutton.

Acting Primer: A Course in Making Choices. Lynda Belt. LC 92-62050. 48p. 1993. pap. 14.95 (*0-9620799-4-4*) Thespis Prodns.

Acting Primer: Student Handbook. Lynda Belt. LC 92-62050. 60p. 1993. pap. 5.95 (*0-9620799-9-5*) Thespis Prodns.

Acting Problems. Judith Berke. 32p. 1993. pap. 6.00 (*1-878851-02-0*) Silverfish Rev Pr.

Acting Professionally: Raw Facts about Careers in Acting. 3rd ed. Robert S. Cohen. 1982. pap. 7.95 (*0-06-463453-1*, EH 570) HarpC.

Acting Professionally: Raw Facts about Careers in Acting. 4th ed. Robert Cohen. 168p. (C). 1990. pap. text ed. 13.95 (*0-87484-940-3*) Mayfield Pub.

Acting (Re)Considered: Theories & Practices. Ed. by Phillip B. Zarrilli. LC 93-48186. (Worlds of Performance Ser.). (Illus.). 320p. 1994. 65.00x (*0-415-09858-0*, B3135, Routledge NY) Routledge.

***Acting (Re)Considered: Theories & Practices.** Ed. by Phillip B. Zarrilli. LC 93-48186. (Worlds of Performance Ser.). (Illus.). 1994. pap. 18.95x (*0-415-09859-9*, B3139) Routledge.

Acting Shakespeare. John Gielgud & John Miller. 192p. 1992. text ed. 20.00 (*0-684-19511-9*, Scribners) S&S Trade.

Acting Shakespeare. Bertram Joseph. LC 77-79132. (Illus.). 1969. reprint ed. 11.95 (*0-87830-522-X*, Theatre Arts Bks) Routledge Chapman & Hall.

Acting Skills. Hugh Morrison. (Illus.). 150p. 1992. pap. text ed. 13.95 (*0-87830-034-1*, A9672, Theatre Arts Bks) Routledge Chapman & Hall.

Acting Solo: The Art of One-Man Shows. Jordan R. Young. LC 89-8363. (Illus.). 216p. 1989. 21.95 (*0-940410-84-2*, Moonstone Pr); pap. 11.95 (*0-940410-85-0*, Moonstone Pr) Past Times.

Acting Step by Step. Marsh Cassidy. LC 88-8500. (Illus.). 186p. (C). 1990. pap. text ed. 10.00 (*0-89390-120-2*) Resource Pubns.

Acting Through Exercises: A Synthesis of Classical & Contemporary Approaches. John Gronbeck-Tedesco. 277p. (C). 1992. pap. text ed. 31.95 (*0-87484-947-0*) Mayfield Pub.

Acting Truths & Fictions. Lawrence Parke. (Orig.). 1995. write for info. (*0-318-70265-7*) Acting World Bks.

***Acting Truths & Fictions.** Lawrence Parke. LC 95-75729. 448p. (Orig.). 1995. pap. 22.50 (*0-9615288-7-7*) Acting World Bks.

Acting under Uncertainty: Multidisciplinary Conceptions. George M. Von Furstenberg. (C). 1990. lib. bdg. 93.00 (*0-7923-9063-6*) Kluwer Ac.

Acting Up! Doug Smee. (YA). 1990. 8.50 (*0-8341-9076-1*, MP-661) Lillenas.

Acting Up! An Innovative Approach to Creative Drama for Older Adults. Marcie Telander et al. 186p. 1982. 16.95 (*0-88020-108-8*, A58) Dramatic Pub.

Acting up Again! Thirteen Scripture Sketches for Youth. Doug Smee. 1993. 8.50 (*0-685-72870-6*, MP-679) Lillenas.

Acting with Both Sides of Your Brain: Perspectives on the Creative Process. Ramon Delgado. 288p. (C). 1986. text ed. 33.25 (*0-03-000104-8*) HB Coll Pubs.

***Acting with Shakespeare: The Comedies.** Janet Suzman. (Acting Ser.). (Illus.). 128p. (Orig.). Date not set. pap. 12.95 (*1-55783-215-3*) Applause Theatre Bk Pubs.

Acting with Style. 2nd ed. John Harrop & Sabin Epstein. 352p. (C). 1989. Casebound. text ed. write for info. (*0-13-003591-2*) P-H.

***Acting with Style: High Comedy.** Maria Aitken. (Illus.). 128p. (Orig.). 1995. pap. 12.95 (*1-55783-214-5*) Applause Theatre Bk Pubs.

***Acting with the Movie Stars.** Don Brenon. (Illus.). (Orig.). 1995. pap. 19.95 (*0-9642102-0-7*, TXU624991) D Bar T.

Acting Without Agony: An Alternative to the Method. 2nd ed. Don Richardson. LC 93-24467. 1993. pap. text ed. 32.00 (*0-205-15165-5*) Allyn.

Acting Women: Images of Women in Theatre. Lesley Ferris. 192p. 1989. 45.00 (*0-8147-2598-8*) NYU Pr.

Actinide-Lanthanide Separations: Proceedings of the International Symposium. Ed. by G. R. Choppin et al. 400p. 1985. 78.00 (*9971-978-68-7*) World Scientific Pub.

Actinide Processing: Methods & Materials. Ed. by Brajendra Mishra & William A. Averill. LC 94-75038. 394p. 1994. 140.00 (*0-87339-265-5*) Minerals Metals.

Actinide Recovery from Waste & Low Grade Sources. James D. Navratil & W. W. Schulz. (Radioactive Waste Management Ser.: Vol. 6). xiv, 386p. 1982. text ed. 190.00 (*3-7186-0105-2*) Gordon & Breach.

Actinides: Chemistry & Physical Properties. Ed. by L. Manes. (Structure & Bonding Ser.: Vol. 59-60). (Illus.). 250p. 1985. 106.00 (*0-387-13752-1*) Spr-Verlag.

Actinides in Intermediate Level Liquid Waste: Removal by Oxalic Acid..., No. EUR 13250. H. Bokelund et al. 60p. 1991. pap. 9.00 (*92-826-2234-7*, CD-NA-13250-EN-C, Pub. by Europ Com) UNIPUB.

Actinides in Perspective: Proceedings of the Conference Held at Pacific Grove, CA, Sept. 10-15, 1981. Ed. by N. M. Edelstein. (Illus.). 620p. 1982. 248.00 (*0-08-029193-7*, Pub. by Pergamon Repr UK) Franklin.

Actinides, Master Index, Vol. 4 see Comprehensive Inorganic Chemistry

Actinometry & Atmospheric Optics. Ed. by V. K. Pyldmaa. 392p. 1971. text ed. 96.50 (*0-7065-1125-5*, Pub. by Keter Pub IS) Coronet Bks.

Actinometry, Atmospheric Optics, Ozonometry. Ed. by G. P. Gushchin. 208p. 1974. text ed. 55.00 (*0-7065-1443-2*, Pub. by Keter Pub IS) Coronet Bks.

Actinomycete Taxonomy: Special Publ. No. 6. Ed. by A. Dietz & W. D. Thayer. 380p. 1980. 30.00 (*0-318-16572-4*) Society Indust Microb.

Actinomycete Taxonomy: Special Publ. No. 6. Ed. by A. Dietz & W. D. Thayer. 380p. 1980. 25.00 (*0-318-16573-2*) Soc Indus Microbio.

Actinomycetes in Biotechnology. Ed. by Michael Goodfellow et al. 501p. 1988. text ed. 139.00 (*0-12-289673-4*) Acad Pr.

Actinomycosis of the Thorax. George E. Farrell. (Illus.). 104p. 1981. 22.50 (*0-87527-205-3*) Green.

Action. Donald G. Brown. LC 68-132946. 164p. reprint ed. pap. 46.80 (*0-8357-5084-1*, 2014146) Bks Demand.

Action: Essay on a Critique of Life & a Science of Practice. Maurice Blondel. Tr. by Oliva Blanchette. LC 83-401133. 448p. 1984. text ed. 36.95 (*0-268-00605-9*) U of Notre Dame Pr.

Action Advertiser Marketplace Recipes, 1981-87, Vol. 1: A Collection from Our Readers. Crystal S. Carew. 300p. (Orig.). 1988. pap. text ed. 7.95 (*0-9620986-0-4*) Action Advertising Inc.

Action Against Oil Pollution. ITOPE Staff et al. 1981. 60.00 (*0-317-61140-2*, Pub. by Witherby & Co UK) St Mut.

Action Against Unemployment see Development of the Co-Operative Movement in Asia

Action Agenda for Managing the Nation's Floodplains: A Review of Floodplain Management in the United States, an Assessment Report. (Special Publications: No. 25). 22p. 1992. 4.00 (*0-685-62422-6*) Natural Hazards.

***Action Agenda to Redesign State Government.** Ed. by Gerry Feinstein. 96p. (Orig.). 1993. pap. text ed. 22.50 (*1-55877-219-7*) Natl Governor.

Action Alphabet. Marty Neumeier & Byron Glaser. LC 84-25322. (Illus.). 56p. (J). (ps-1). 1985. 14.00 (*0-688-05703-9*); lib. bdg. 13.93 (*0-688-05704-7*) Greenwillow.

***Action Alphabet.** Shelley Rotner. LC 94-32212. 1995. 14.95 (*0-689-80086-X*, Mac Bks Young Read) S&S Childrens.

An Asterisk (*) at the beginning of an entry indicates that the title is appearing in BIP for the first time.

A

Action Amiga: Computer Graphics Animation & Video Production Manual. John W. Oakes. LC 88-26158. (Illus.). 140p. (Orig.). (C). 1989. pap. text ed. 19.50 (*0-8191-7209-X*) U Pr of Amer.

Action & Adventure. J. Steffens & J. Carr. (Enrichment & Gifted Ser.). (J). (gr. 7-12). 1983. 9.95 (*0-88160-101-2*, LW 1007) Learning Wks.

Action & Agency: Fourth Roundtable on Law & Semiotics. Roberta Kevelson. LC 91-7179. (Semiotics & the Human Sciences Ser.: Vol. 2). 448p. (C). 1991. text ed. 62.95 (*0-8204-1520-0*) P Lang Pubs.

Action & Conviction in Early Modern Europe: Essays in Memory of E. H. Harbison. Ed. by Theodore K. Rabb & Jerrold E. Seigel. LC 68-27407. 487p. reprint ed. pap. 138.80 (*0-8357-3388-2*, 2039644) Bks Demand.

Action & Existence: Anarchism for Business Administration. Pierre Guillet de Monthoux. LC 82-1892. 310p. reprint ed. pap. 88.40 (*0-8357-5085-X*, 2030749) Bks Demand.

Action & Image: Dramatic Structure in Cinema. Roy Armes. LC 93-10963. 1994. text ed. 69.95 (*0-7190-3554-6*, Pub. by Manchester Univ Pr UK); text ed. 19.95 (*0-7190-3555-4*, Pub. by Manchester Univ Pr UK) St Martin.

Action & Insight. Paul L. Wachtel. LC 86-22828. 400p. 1987. lib. bdg. 45.00 (*0-89862-685-4*) Guilford Pr.

Action & Interpretation. Christopher Hookway. Ed. by P. Pettit. LC 77-7875. 178p. 1978. 44.95 (*0-521-21740-7*) Cambridge U Pr.

Action & Its Environment: Toward a New Synthesis. Jeffrey C. Alexander. 352p. 1990. text ed. 47.00 (*0-231-06208-7*); pap. text ed. 19.50 (*0-231-06209-5*) Col U Pr.

Action & Knowledge: Breaking the Monopoly with Participatory Action-Research. Ed. by Orlando Fals-Borda & Muhammad A. Rahman. LC 90-24300. 190p. (Orig.). 1991. pap. 16.50 (*0-945257-31-7*) Apex Pr.

Action & Other Stories. Charles E. Montague. LC 70-134971. (Short Story Index Reprint Ser.). 1977. 19.95 (*0-8369-3702-3*) Ayer.

Action & Persuasion: Dramatic Performance in Eighteenth-Century France. Angelica Goodden. (Illus.). 224p. 1986. 49.95 (*0-19-815836-X*) OUP.

Action & Reaction: Proceedings of a Symposium to Commemorate the Tercentenary of Newton's Principia. Ed. by Paul Theerman & Adele F. Seeff. LC 91-50589. (Illus.). 328p. (C). 1993. 39.50 (*0-87413-446-3*) U Delaware Pr.

Action & Reaction in World Politics: International Systems in Perspective. Richard N. Rosecrance. LC 77-2329. 314p. 1977. reprint ed. text ed. 35.00 (*0-8371-9548-9*, ROAR, Greenwood Pr) Greenwood.

Action & Reflection in Teacher Education. Ed. by Gareth R. Harvard & Phil Hodkinson. LC 94-9903. 336p. 1994. pap. 24.50 (*1-56750-058-7*) Ablex Pub.

***Action & Reflection in Teacher Education.** Ed. by Gareth R. Harvard & Phil Hodkinson. LC 94-9903. (Illus.). 336p. 1994. 47.50 (*0-89391-897-0*) Ablex Pub.

Action & Value in Criminal Law. Ed. by Stephen Shute et al. LC 93-28961. 328p. (C). 1994. 55.00 (*0-19-825806-2*, Clarendon Pr) OUP.

***Action Arcade Adventures.** Diana Gruber. 1994. pap. 39.95 (*1-883577-06-3*) Coriolis Grp.

Action Art: A Bibliography of Artists' Performances from Futurism to Fluxus & Beyond. Comp. by John Gray. LC 92-46415. (Art Reference Collection Ser.: No. 16). 360p. 1993. text ed. 79.50 (*0-313-28916-6*, GR8916, Greenwood Pr) Greenwood.

Action at Aquila. Hervey Allen. 1993. reprint ed. lib. bdg. 89.00 (*0-7812-5420-5*) Rprt Serv.

Action at the Bitterroot. large type ed. Paul E. Lehman. LC 92-37076. 1993. 19.95 (*0-7927-1447-4*, Curley Lrg Print); pap. 17.95 (*0-7927-1446-6*, Curley Lrg Print) Chivers N Amer.

***Action at the Galudoghson Dec. 14, 1742: Col. James Patton, Capt. John McDowell & the 1st Battle with the Indians in the Valley of Virginia.** Lyman C. Draper. Ed. & Intro. by Jared C. Lobdell. 44p. (Orig.). 1995. pap. text ed. 13.00 (*0-7884-0192-0*) Heritage Bk.

Action at the Grassroots: Fighting Poverty & Environmental Decline. Alan B. Durning. (Orig.). (C). 1989. pap. 5.00 (*0-916468-89-5*) Worldwatch Inst.

***Action Before Westport.** Howard N. Monnett. Ed. & Intro. by John H. Monnett. (Illus.). 240p. (Orig.). 1995. reprint ed. pap. 19.95 (*0-614-06699-9*) Univ Pr Colo.

Action Biology - Advanced Placement. Mary P. Davis. (Illus.). 540p. (YA). (gr. 11-12). 1988. pap. text ed. 21.33 (*0-931054-18-4*) Clark Pub.

Action Biology - for the First Year. Mary P. Davis. (Illus.). 494p. (YA). (gr. 10). 1988. pap. text ed. 21.33 (*0-931054-19-2*) Clark Pub.

Action Book of Sports. Highlights for Children Staff. (Illus.). 32p. (J). (gr. 3-8). 1988. pap. 2.95 (*0-87534-229-9*) Highlights.

Action by Night. Ernest Haycox. 1991. pap. 3.50 (*1-55817-504-0*, Pinnacle NY) Windsor NY.

Action by Night. large type ed. Ernest Haycox. LC 93-32208. 1994. 19.95 (*0-7929-1876-2*, Roundup Lrg Print Westerns); 19.95 (*0-7927-1876-3*, Roundup Lrg Print Westerns); pap. 17.95 (*0-7929-1875-4*, Roundup Lrg Print Westerns); pap. 17.95 (*0-7927-1875-5*, Roundup Lrg Print Westerns) Chivers N Amer.

Action Careers: Employment in the High-Risk Job Market. Ragnar Benson. 360p. reprint ed. pap. 9.95 (*0-8065-1079-X*, Citadel Pr) Carol Pub Group.

Action Centered Leadership. John Adair. 186p. 1979. text ed. 49.95 (*0-566-02143-9*) Ashgate Pub Co.

Action Control. Ed. by Julius Kuhl & J. Beckmann. (Social Psychology Ser.). 320p. 1985. 70.00 (*0-387-13445-X*) Spr-Verlag.

Action Counseling for Behavior Change. 2nd ed. Richard Dustin & Rickey George. LC 77-8686. 241p. 1977. 10.50 (*0-910328-20-X*) Sulzburger & Graham Pub.

Action, Decision, & Intention. Ed. by Robert Audi. 1986. lib. bdg. 50.00 (*90-277-2274-9*) Kluwer Ac.

Action Diagrams: Clearly Structured Specifications, Programs & Procedures. 2nd ed. James Martin & Carma L. McClure. 176p. 1988. pap. text ed. 30.00 (*0-13-004268-4*) P-H.

***Action Directe: Ultra-Left Terrorism in France, 1979-1987.** Michael Y. Dartnell. LC 94-34936. 1995. 32.50 (*0-7146-4566-4*, Pub. by F Cass Pubs UK) Intl Spec Bk.

Action Does It. Tom Johnson. LC 85-11000. 80p. (Orig.). 1985. pap. text ed. 5.95 (*0-941992-06-3*) Los Arboles Pub.

Action English Pictures. Maxine Frauman-Prickel. (Illus.). 120p. (YA). (gr. 7 up). 1985. pap. text ed. 19.95 (*0-13-009077-8*) Alemany Pr.

Action et Reactions. Rudyard Kipling. (FRE.). 1979. pap. 10.95 (*0-7859-2420-5*, 2070371298) Fr & Eur.

Action Family Handbook: Twil Aug. Weber. (J). (gr. 3). 1985. 2.80 (*0-02-658350-X*) Macmillan.

Action Figure! The Life & Times of Doonesbury's Uncle Duke. G. B. Trudeau. (Illus.). 224p. (Orig.). 1992. pap. 19.95 (*0-8362-1702-0*) Andrews & McMeel.

Action Figures. Robert S. Young. LC 92-7697. (Collectibles Ser.). (Illus.). 64p. (YA). (gr. 5 up). 1992. text ed., lib. bdg. 13.95 (*0-87518-516-9*, Dillon Silver Burdett) Silver Burdett Pr.

Action for Educational Equity: A Guide for Parents & Members of Community Groups. James Crowfoot et al. 184p. (Orig.). 1982. pap. text ed. 9.00 (*0-917754-19-0*) Inst Responsive.

Action for Mental Health. Joint Commission on Mental Illness & Health. Ed. by Gerald N. Grob. LC 78-22569. (Historical Issues in Mental Health Ser.). 1980. reprint ed. lib. bdg. 30.95 (*0-405-11922-4*) Ayer.

Action for the Defense. Kathie Wei & Ron Andersen. 248p. 1980. pap. 6.95 (*0-87643-038-8*) Barclay Bridge.

***Action Fractions.** Rachel McAnallen & Ellen Frye. (Ms. Math Presents Ser.). 40p. (YA). 1993. 6.00 (*1-886915-02-4*) Koplow Games.

Action Fractions with Hexadrons & Pattern Blocks. Rachel McAnallen & Ellen Frye. (Ms. Math Presents Ser.). 40p. (J). (gr. 2 up). 1995. 20.00 (*1-886915-00-8*) Koplow Games. ACTION FRACTIONS demonstrates a concrete approach to fractions. It is written for children ages seven & up as well as for teachers & parents of those children. The book offers you some tools for learning fractions - a pretend gold mine & a bag of gold! Using pattern blocks & dice, you'll add & subtract fractions by adding & subtracting pieces of gold. Math is a language that should be spoken & an art that should be seen & touched. ACTION FRACTIONS encourages learners to speak fractionese, to visualize fractions & to feel fractions. Publisher: Koplow Games, Box 965, Hull, MA 02045. 671-482-4011.** ***Publisher Provided Annotation.

***Action Fractions with Hexahedron.** Rachel McAnallen & Ellen Frye. (Ms. Math Presents Ser.). 40p. (YA). 1993. 8.50 (*1-886915-01-6*) Koplow Games.

Action Francaise: Royalism & Reaction in Twentieth-Century France. Eugen Weber. LC 62-15267. xiv, 594p. 1962. 62.50 (*0-8047-0134-2*) Stanford U Pr.

Action Francaise & Revolutionary Syndicalism. Paul Mazgaj. LC 79-4229. 293p. reprint ed. pap. 83.60 (*0-8357-4422-1*, 2037242) Bks Demand.

Action Group Case Studies Manual. Granary Pr Ltd Staff. 60p. (C). 1986. 80.00 (*0-86236-023-4*, Pub. by Granary UK) St Mut.

Action Guide for Effective Discipline in the Home & School. Margaret K. Cater. LC 91-77889. 390p. (Orig.). 1992. pap. text ed. 23.95 (*1-55959-027-0*) Accel Devel.

Action Guide for Emergency Service Personnel. Rescue Training Association Staff. 656p. 1985. pap. text ed. 39.00 (*0-89303-301-4*) P-H.

Action Guide to Government Grants, Loans, & Giveaways. George Chelekis. LC 92-38818. 512p. (Orig.). 1993. pap. 24.95 (*0-399-51792-8*, Perigree Bks) Berkley Pub.

Action Guide to School Improvement. Susan Loucks-Horsley & Leslie F. Hergert. LC 85-70038. 82p. 1985. pap. text ed. 5.00 (*0-87120-130-5*, 611-85360) Assn Supervision.

Action Guide to Sure-Sale Real Estate Listings. Chester H. McCall, Sr. 1979. 49.50 (*0-13-003111-9*) Exec Reports.

Action in Affirmation: Towards an Unambiguous Profession of Nursing. Jerome P. Lysaught. (Illus.). 224p. 1980. text ed. 28.95 (*0-07-039271-4*) McGraw.

Action in Africa: The Experience of People Involved in Government, Business & Aid. Ed. by Douglas Rimmer. LC 93-38558. 192p. 1994. pap. 19.95 (*0-435-08098-9*) Heinemann.

Action in Aquatics: CNCA Eighteenth National Aquatic Conference: Phoenix, AZ, Del Webb's Towne House, November 22-26, 1974. Council for National Cooperation in Aquatics Staff. Ed. by Bernard E. Empleton. LC 77-358552. (Illus.). 238p. reprint ed. pap. 67.90 (*0-8357-3833-7*, 2036558) Bks Demand.

Action in Awareness. Jean Klein. (Illus.). (Orig.). Date not set. pap. write for info. (*1-877769-20-7*) Third Millennium.

Action in Elementary Social Studies. David W. Van Cleaf. 384p. (C). 1990. text ed. 55.00 (*0-13-013210-1*) P-H.

Action in Late Ming Thought: The Reorientation of Lu K'un & Other Scholar Officials. Joanna F. Handlin. LC 82-2762. 270p. 1983. 47.50 (*0-520-04380-4*) U CA Pr.

Action in Social Context: Perspectives on Early Development. Ed. by J. J. Lockman & N. L. Hazen. (Perspectives in Developmental Psychology Ser.). (Illus.). 326p. 1989. 54.50 (*0-306-43139-4*, Plenum Pr) Plenum.

Action in Teacher Education: Tenth Year Anniversary Issue. Judith Christensen. Ed. by John Sikula. 1988. 12.50 (*0-685-41073-0*) Assn Tchr Ed.

Action in Waiting. Karl Barth. Bd. with Joy in the Lord. LC 75-90295. LC 75-90295. 80p. 1969. Set pap. 3.50 (*0-87486-203-5*) Plough.

Action in Waiting. 2nd ed. Karl Barth & Christoph Blumhardt. LC 79-485. 80p. 1979. pap. 5.50 (*0-87486-223-X*) Plough.

Action Information Message, Set. Joseph S. Renzulli. 1981. pap. 24.95 (*0-936386-27-4*) Creative Learning.

Action, Intention, & Reason. Robert Audi. 362p. 1994. 43.50x (*0-8014-2866-1*); pap. 18.95 (*0-8014-8105-8*) Cornell U Pr.

Action into Nature: An Essay on the Meaning of Technology. Barry Cooper. LC 90-50975. (Loyola Lecture Series in Political Analysis). (C). 1991. text ed. 34.95 (*0-268-00629-6*) U of Notre Dame Pr.

Action Is Eloquence: Shakespeare's Language of Gesture. David M. Bevington. LC 84-673. 241p. reprint ed. pap. 68.70 (*0-7837-1510-2*, 2041787) Bks Demand.

Action Kit for Music Education. 1991. 37.50 (*0-685-53389-1*, 2330) Music Ed Natl.

Action, Knowledge & Reality: Studies in Honor of Wilfrid Sellars. Hector-Neri Castaneda. LC 74-8419. 374p. (C). 1975. text ed. write for info. (*0-672-61213-5*, Bobbs) Macmillan.

Action Learning: A Practitioners Guide. Ed. by Ian McGill & Liz Beaty. 180p. 1992. pap. 48.00 (*0-7494-0580-5*, Pub. by Kogan Page Educ UK) Taylor & Francis.

Action Learning in Practice. 2nd ed. Mike Pedler. 384p. 1991. text ed. 69.95 (*0-566-02859-X*, Pub. by Gower UK) Ashgate Pub Co.

Action Letters for Small Business Owners. Wilbur Cross. 240p. 1991. text ed. 65.00 (*0-471-52812-9*) Wiley.

***Action Man: The Gold Medal Doll for Boys.** Frances Baird. (Illus.). 144p. (Orig.). Date not set. pap. 24.95 (*1-872727-36-0*, Pub. by New Cavendish UK) Pincushion Pr.

Action Management: The Essentials. Ed. by Derek Torrington & Jane Weightman. 210p. (C). 1991. 110.00 (*0-85292-473-9*, Pub. by IPM Hse UK) St Mut.

Action Now! A Citizen's Guide to Better Communities. Richard W. Poston. LC 76-949. 270p. 1976. 11.85 (*0-8093-0760-X*); pap. 7.95 (*0-8093-0763-4*) S Ill U Pr.

Action of Ben Johnson's Poetry. Sara J. Van den Berg. LC 86-40217. 224p. 1987. 37.50 (*0-87413-308-4*) U Delaware Pr.

Action of Human Resources & Poverty on One Another: What We Have Yet to Learn. Jere R. Behrman. (Living Standards Measurement Study Working Paper Ser.: No. 74). 168p. 1990. 10.95 (*0-8213-1689-3*, 11689) World Bank.

Action of Ionizing Radiation on Ion-Exchange Materials. E. V. Egorov & P. D. Novikov. 262p. 1967. text ed. 65.60 (*0-7065-0591-3*, Pub. by Keter Pub IS) Coronet Bks.

Action of Natural Selection on Man. Alfred R. Wallace. reprint ed. write for info. (*0-318-62221-1*) AMS Pr.

Action of Neuroleptic Drugs. 2nd ed. M. Haase & P. Janssen. xxi, 344p. 1985. 153.50 (*0-444-80434-X*) Elsevier.

Action on AIDS: National Policies in Comparative Perspective. Ed. by Barbara A. Misztal & David Moss. LC 89-26034. (Contributions in Medical Studies: No. 28). 280p. 1990. text ed. 59.95 (*0-313-26369-8*, MZA/, Greenwood Pr) Greenwood.

Action on Akaisha Outstation. Terry K. Amthor. 32p. (YA). (gr. 10-12). 1985. 6.00 (*0-915795-46-9*, 9101) Iron Crown Ent Inc.

Action on the First Tee: How to Cash in on Your Favorite Sport. Doug Sanders & Russ Pate. LC 87-1927. 160p. 1987. pap. 8.95 (*0-87833-551-X*) Taylor Pub.

Action-Oriented Decisions in Ambulatory Medicine. Clement J. McDonald. LC 80-20451. (Illus.). 394p. reprint ed. pap. 112.30 (*0-8357-5086-8*, 2033003) Bks Demand.

Action Pack. Chana Sharfstein. (Illus.). 69p. (Orig.). 1987. teacher ed 13.95 (*0-916177-26-2*); 6.95 (*0-916177-27-0*); 5.95 (*0-916177-28-9*) Am Eng Pubns.

Action Pack, Set. Chana Sharfstein. (Illus.). (Orig.). 1987. 19.95 (*0-916177-29-7*) Am Eng Pubns.

Action Packet on Jumping Rope: Individual Rope Skills. Jerry D. Poppen. LC 82-72160. 62p. (Orig.). 1989. pap. text ed. 6.50 (*0-9608868-3-4*) Action Prods.

Action Packet on Physical Fitness Activities. Jerry D. Poppen. LC 82-72160. 64p. (Orig.). 1989. pap. text ed. 6.50 (*0-9608868-2-6*) Action Prods.

Action Planning & Responsive Design: Issues of Housing, Building, Planning & Development in the Third World. Ed. by Steven Groak. 350p. 1984. pap. 74.00 (*0-08-031310-8*, Pergamon Pr) Elsevier.

Action Plans: Eighty Student-Centered Language Activities. Marion MacDonald & Sue Rogers-Gordon. 1984. pap. 19.95 (*0-8384-2712-X*, Newbury) Heinle & Heinle.

Action Plans: The New Woman's Survival Guide. Linda H. Allen. (Illus.). 190p. (Orig.). 1987. pap. 6.95 (*0-87491-876-6*) Acropolis.

Action Plant. Paul Simons. (Illus.). 288p. 1992. 27.95 (*0-631-13899-4*) Blackwell Pubs.

Action Profiling. Pamela Ramsden & Joan Zacharias. 386p. 1993. 88.95 (*0-566-02727-5*, Pub. by Gower UK) Ashgate Pub Co.

Action Program to Confront the Coming Economic Crisis. 2nd ed. Ed. by Doug Jenness. 34p. 1989. 3.00 (*0-87348-528-9*) Pathfinder NY.

Action Refinement in Process Algebras. Luca Aceto. (Distinguished Dissertations in Computer Science Ser.: No. 3). 288p. (C). 1992. 59.95 (*0-521-43111-5*) Cambridge U Pr.

***Action Replay - a Media Memoir.** David P. Jones. 199p. 1993. pap. 30.00 (*1-85902-016-X*, Pub. by Gomer Pr UK) St Mut.

Action Research: A Qualitative Approach to Educational Studies. Frank A. Stone. 22p. 1981. 2.50 (*0-685-10005-7*) I N Thut World Educ Ctr.

Action Research: A Short Modern History. Robin McTaggart. 134p. (C). 1991. pap. 68.00 (*0-7300-1217-4*, EED402, Pub. by Deakin Univ AT) St Mut.

Action Research & Organizational Development. J. Barton Cunningham. LC 92-1744. 288p. 1993. text ed. 55.00 (*0-275-94265-1*, C4265, Praeger Pubs) Greenwood.

Action Research Designs for Training & Development, 5 vols. 672p. pap. (*0-318-62032-4*, NTDSP) Am Soc Train & Devel.

Action Research for Change & Development. Zuber-Skerritt. 234p. 1991. text ed. 68.95 (*1-85628-140-X*, Pub. by Avebury Pub UK) Ashgate Pub Co.

Action Research for Educational Change. John Elliott. (Developing Teachers & Teaching Ser.). 192p. 1991. 85.00 (*0-335-09690-5*, Open Univ Pr); pap. 32.00 (*0-335-09689-1*, Open Univ Pr) Taylor & Francis.

***Action Research for Health & Social Care: A Guide to Practice.** Elizabeth Hart & Meg Bond. LC 94-34021. 1995. 75.00 (*0-335-19263-7*, Open Univ Pr); pap. 24.95 (*0-335-19262-9*, Open Univ Pr) Taylor & Francis.

Action Research in Higher Education: Examples & Reflection. Ortrun Zuber-Skerritt. 128p. 1992. pap. 29.95 (*0-7494-0741-7*, Pub. by Kogan Page Educ UK) Taylor & Francis.

Action Research in the Secondary School. R. P. Gregory. 224p. (C). 1988. lib. bdg. 45.00 (*0-415-00122-6*, A2395) Routledge.

Action Research Planner. Ed. by Deakin University Press Staff. 154p. (C). 1988. pap. 47.00x (*0-7300-0521-6*, ECT432, Pub. by Deakin Univ AT) St Mut.

Action Research Reader. Ed. by Deakin University Press Staff. 430p. (C). 1988. 59.00 (*0-7300-0564-X*, Pub. by Deakin Univ AT) St Mut.

Action Research, Special Needs & School Development. Ed. by Gordon H. Bell et al. 204p. 1994. pap. 32.00 (*1-85346-274-8*, Pub. by D Fulton UK) Taylor & Francis.

Action Rhymes. Ed. by Pie Corbett. LC 92-26445. (Nursery Library). (Illus.). 32p. (J). (ps-00). 1993. pap. 4.95 (*1-85697-900-8*, Kingfisher LKC) LKC.

Action Rhymes & Rhythms. Louise Kohr. (Illus.). 64p. 1990. pap. 3.99 (*0-87403-626-7*, 14-03200) Standard Pub.

***Action Robots: A Pop-Up Book Showing How They Work.** Tim Reeve. LC 95-2543. (Illus.). (J). 1995. 16.95 (*0-8037-1843-8*) Dial Bks Young.

Action Science: Concepts, Methods, & Skills for Research & Intervention. Chris Argyris et al. LC 85-45051. (Social & Behavioral Science Ser.). 500p. 1985. 39.95x (*0-87589-665-0*) Jossey-Bass.

Action Semantics. Peter D. Mosses. (Tracts in Theoretical Computer Science Ser.: No. 26). 400p. (C). 1992. 54.95 (*0-521-40347-2*) Cambridge U Pr.

Action Series & Sequels: A Bibliography of Espionage, Vigilante & Soldier-of-Fortune Novels. Bernard A. Drew. LC 88-11007. 336p. 1988. lib. bdg. 54.00 (*0-8240-8396-2*) Garland.

Action Skateboarding. Jan Andrejtschitsch et al. LC 91-40328. (Illus.). 128p. (YA). (gr. 10-12). 1992. 16.95 (*0-8069-8500-3*) Sterling.

Action Skateboarding. Jan Andrejtschitsch et al. (Illus.). 128p. (YA). (gr. 10-12). 1993. pap. 10.95 (*0-8069-8501-1*) Sterling.

Action Sociology & Dynamics of Rural Development. Ed. by R. K. Gupta & S. P. Srivastva. (C). 1989. 49.00 (*81-202-0250-3*, Pub. by Ajanta II) S Asia.

Action Songs for Children. Date not set. 7.95 (*1-56222-285-6*, 94692) Mel Bay.

Action Speaks Louder: A Handbook of Structured Group Techniques. 5th ed. A. Jane Remocker & Elizabeth T. Storch. (Illus.). 190p. (Orig.). 1992. pap. text ed. 39.95 (*0-443-04364-7*) Churchill.

Action, Symbolism & Order: The Existential Dimensions of Politics in Modern Citizenship. Robert J. Pranger. LC 68-20548. 1968. 17.50 (*0-8265-1115-5*) Vanderbilt U Pr.

Action Theater: The Improvisation of Presence. Ruth Zaporah. (Illus.). 250p. (Orig.). (C). 1995. pap. 20.00 (*1-55643-186-4*) North Atlantic.

Action Theory. Ed. by John A. Meacham. (Journal: Human Development: Vol. 27, No. 3-4). (Illus.). 112p. 1984. 31.25 (*3-8055-3895-2*) S Karger.

Action Theory: Proceedings. Ed. by Myles Brand. LC 76-6882. (Synthese Library: No. 97). 1976. lib. bdg. 112.50 (*90-277-0671-9*) Kluwer Ac.

Action Theory & Social Science. Igmar Porn. (Synthese Library: No. 120). 1977. lib. bdg. 56.50 (*90-277-0846-0*) Kluwer Ac.

Action Theory & the Human Condition. Talcott Parsons. LC 77-94084. 1978. text ed. 22.95 (*0-02-923990-7*) Free Pr.

Action Theory for Public Administration. Michael M. Harmon. LC 93-74290. 204p. (C). 1994. reprint ed. text ed. 36.95 (*0-9639874-1-0*) Chatelaine.

An Asterisk (*) at the beginning of an entry indicates that the title is appearing in BIP for the first time. 43

A

Action Therapy & Adlerian Theory: Selected Papers. Walter E. O'Connell. LC 75-16932. 253p. (Orig.). 1975. pap. text ed. 8.00 (0-918560-06-3) Adler Sch Prof Psy.

Action to the Word: Structure & Style in Shakespearean Tragedy. David Young. 248p. (C). 1990. text ed. 25.00 (0-300-04534-4) Yale U Pr.

Action Tools for Successful Management. Margaret M. Gootnick. 192p. 1989. pap. text ed. 17.95 (0-8403-5455-X) Kendall-Hunt.

***Action Trucks - Fire Engine.** David Hawcock. (J). (ps-2). 1995. 3.95 (0-8050-3376-9) H Holt & Co.

***Action Trucks - Four-Wheel Drive.** David Hawcock. (J). (ps-2). 1995. 3.95 (0-8050-3378-5) H Holt & Co.

***Action Trucks - Transit Mixer.** David Hawcock. (J). (ps-2). 1995. 3.95 (0-8050-3377-7) H Holt & Co.

Action 2000: Praying Scripture in a Contemporary Way, Cycle C. Mark Link. (Mark Link, S. J., Library). 416p. 1994. pap. 8.95 (0-7829-0362-2, 22047) Tabor Pub.

***Actionable Misrepresentation.** 3rd ed. 1973. boxed 165.00 (0-406-38190-9, U.K.) Butterworth Legal Pubs.

Actionable Non-Disclosure. 2nd ed. Spencer et al. 1990. 363.00 (0-406-38180-1, U.K.) Butterworth Legal Pubs.

Actions. Illus. by Tedd Arnold. (Nursery Rhyme Concept Bks.). 16p. (J). (ps). 1992. pap. 3.95 (0-671-77824-2, Litl Simon S&S) S&S Childrens.

***Actions & Interactions of GABA & Benzodiazepines: A Biological Council Symposium.** Ed. by N. G. Bowery. LC 83-42617. (Illus.). reprint ed. pap. 89.00 (0-7837-9573-4, 2060322) Bks Demand.

Actions & Other Events: The Unifier-Multiplier Controversy. Karl Pfeifer. (American University Studies: Philosophy: Ser. V). 210p. (C). 1989. text ed. 24.95 (0-8204-1044-6) P Lang Pubs.

Actions & Structure: Research Methods & Social Theory. Ed. by Nigel G. Fielding. 208p. (C). 1988. text ed. 39.95 (0-8039-8147-3) Sage.

Actions & Uses of Ophthalmic Drugs. 3rd ed. P. H. Davies et al. (Illus.). 248p. 1989. text ed. 90.00 (0-407-00799-7) Buttrwrth-Heinemann.

Actions for Health, No. 2. Mary S. Garzino. LC 92-18740. (Contemporary Health Ser.). (Illus.). 1992. write for info. (1-56071-096-9) ETR Assocs.

Actions for Health: Grade 3. LC 92-8719. (Contemporary Health Ser.). 1992. write for info. (1-56071-097-7) ETR Assocs.

Actions for Health, Grade 1. Mary S. Garzino. LC 92-461. (Contemporary Health Ser.). 1992. write for info. (1-56071-095-0) ETR Assocs.

Actions of Discrete Amenable Groups on von Neumann Alegbras. Adrian Ocneanu. (Lecture Notes in Mathematics Ser.: Vol. 1138). v, 115p. 1985. pap. 46.20 (0-387-15663-1) Spr-Verlag.

Actions of Finite Groups on the Hyperfinite Type II (Subscript 1) Factor. Vaughan Jones. LC 80-22560. (Memoirs Ser.: No. 28/237). 70p. 1980. pap. 16.00 (0-8218-2237-3, MEMO 28/237) Am Math.

Actions of Linearly Reductive Groups on Affine Pi-Algebras. Vonessen. LC 89-15148. (MEMO Ser.: Vol. 81/414). 106p. 1989. pap. 19.00 (0-8218-2477-5, MEMO 81/414) Am Math.

Actions of Prolactin on Molecular Processes. Ed. by James A. Rillema. 256p. 1987. 198.00 (0-8493-5376-9, QP572) CRC Pr.

Actions of the Low Countries. Roger Williams. Ed. by D. W. Davies. (Documents Ser.). 1978. 16.50 (0-918016-40-1) Folger Bks.

Actions of the Low Countries. Roger Williams. LC 72-25705. (English Experience Ser.: No. 280). 134p. 1970. reprint ed. 35.00 (90-221-0280-7) Walter J Johnson.

Actions Speak Louder Than Verbs. Herb Miller. LC 88-22642. 128p. 1989. pap. 6.95 (0-687-00712-7) Abingdon.

Actions, Styles, & Symbols in Kinetic Family Drawings (KFD) An Interpretative Manual. R. C. Burns & S. H. Kaufman. LC 70-186854. 320p. 1972. pap. 22.95 (0-87630-228-2) Brunner-Mazel.

Actis & Deidis of the Illustere & Vailyeand Campioun Schir William Wallace, Knicht of Ellerslie. Henry The Minstrel. LC 71-144585. reprint ed. 74.50 (0-404-08557-1) AMS Pr.

***Actium & Augustus: The Politics & Emotions of Civil War.** Robert A. Gurval. LC 95-1844. 1995. 37.50 (0-472-10590-6) U of Mich Pr.

Activated Barrier Crossing: Applications in Physics, Chemistry & Biology. G. R. Fleming & P. Hanggi. 336p. 1993. text ed. 95.00 (981-02-1372-7) World Scientific Pub.

Activated Carbon: Surface Chemistry & Adsorption from Solution. James S. Mattson & Harry B. Mark, Jr. LC 74-138502. (Illus.). 247p. reprint ed. pap. 70.40 (0-8357-6004-9, 2034548) Bks Demand.

***Activated Carbon Applications in the Food & Pharmaceutical Industries.** Glenn Roy. LC 94-61026. 200p. 1994. text ed. 65.00 (1-56676-198-0) Technomic.

Activated Carbon for Water Treatment. 2nd ed. Heinrich Sontheimer et al. 722p. 1988. 94.00 (3-922671-20-9, 90523) Am Water Wks Assn.

Activated Carbon Technology. S. Peters. (General Engineering Ser.). 1991. text ed. write for info. (0-442-00810-4) Van Nos Reinhold.

Activated Charcoal: Antidotal & Other Medical Uses. Cooney. (Drugs & the Pharmaceutical Sciences Ser.: Vol. 9). 176p. 1980. 99.75 (0-8247-6913-9) Dekker.

***Activated Charcoal in Medical Applications.** David O. Cooney. LC 94-40860. 1995. write for info. (0-8247-9300-5) Dekker.

Activated Church. Karl A. Barden. 182p. (Orig.). 1992. pap. 7.99 (1-56043-067-2) Destiny Image.

Activated Metals in Organic Synthesis. P. Cintas & Navin Sullivan. 1993. 49.95 (0-8493-7863-X, QD262) CRC Pr.

Activated Partial Thromboplastin Time Test (APTT) Proposed Guideline, Vol. 2. National Committee for Clinical Laboratory Standards. 1982. 40.00 (1-56238-056-7, H29-P) Natl Comm Clin Lab Stds.

Activated Prothrombin Complex Concentrates: Managing Hemophilia With Factor VIII Inhibitor. Ed. by G. Mariani. LC 81-23358. 256p. 1982. text ed. 65.00 (0-275-91373-2, C1373, Praeger Pubs) Greenwood.

Activated Sludge. Activated Sludge Task Force Staff. LC 87-50920. (Manual of Practice, Operations & Maintenance Ser.: No. 9). 182p. 1987. pap. 33.50 (0-943244-97-8, MOM9PA) Water Environ.

Activated Sludge: A Comparison of Oxygen & Air Systems. 118p. 1983. pap. 15.00 (0-87262-362-9) Am Soc Civil Eng.

Activated Sludge: Theory & Practice. N. F. Gray. (Illus.). 288p. 1990. 80.00 (0-19-856341-8) OUP.

***Activated Sludge Bulking & Foaming Control.** Jiri Wanner. LC 94-60912. 338p. 1994. text ed. 75.00 (1-56676-121-2) Technomic.

Activated Sludge Microbiology. Water Pollution Control Federation Staff. 80p. 1989. pap. text ed. 24.00 (0-685-28313-5) Water Environ.

***Activated Sludge Operations for Pulp & Papermills.** Paul H. Klopping et al. 208p. 1995. pap. text ed. 40.00 (1-883615-20-8) Callan & Brooks.

Activated Sludge Operators' Guide. Ronald G. Schuyler. 1995. write for info. (0-87371-640-X) Lewis Pubs.

Activated Sludge Plant Operation & Management 1995. Gasser. Date not set. write for info. (0-87371-920-4) Lewis Pubs.

Activated Sludge Process Design & Control, Vol. 1: Theory & Practice. Ed. by W. Wesley Eckenfelder & Peter Grau. LC 92-53517. (Water Quality Management Library). 280p. 1992. text ed. 75.00 (0-87762-889-0) Technomic.

Activated Sludge Processes: Theory & Practice. Ganczarczyk. (Pollution Engineering & Technology Ser.: Vol. 23). 280p. 1983. 125.00 (0-8247-1758-9) Dekker.

***Activated Sludge Treatment of Industrial Wastewater.** W. W. Eckenfelder & Jack L. Musterman. LC 95-60698. 300p. 1995. text ed. 85.00 (1-56676-302-9) Technomic.

Activating Leadership in the Small Church: (Clergy & Laity Working Together) Steve Burt. Ed. by Douglas A. Walrath. 144p. 1988. pap. 11.00 (0-8170-1099-8) Judson.

Activating the Passive Church: Diagnosis & Treatment. Lyle E. Schaller. LC 81-3460. 160p. (Orig.). 1981. pap. 10.95 (0-687-00716-X) Abingdon.

Activating Theory: Lesbian, Gay, Bisexual Politics. Ed. by Joseph Bristow & Angie Wilson. 256p. (C). 1993. pap. 19.95 (0-85315-790-1, Pub. by Lawrence & Wishart UK) Humanities.

Activation Analysis, I. Ed. by Zeev B. Alfassi. 496p. 1990. 144.00 (0-8493-4583-9, QD606) CRC Pr.

Activation Analysis, II. Ed. by Zeev B. Alfassi. 496p. 1990. 144.00 (0-8493-4584-7, QD606) CRC Pr.

***Activation Analysis in Environmental Protection.** Ed. by V. M. Nazarov & M. V. Frontasieva. (Illus.). 520p. (C). 1995. pap. text ed. 60.00 (0-911767-90-8) Hadronic Pr Inc.

Activation & Desensitization of Transducing Pathways. Ed. by T. M. Konijn et al. (NATO ASI Series H: Cell Biology: Vol. 44). (Illus.). xi, 320p. 1990. 122.00 (0-387-50382-X) Spr-Verlag.

Activation & Recovery of Associations. Fred Schwartz & Richard O. Rouse. (Psychological Issues Monograph: No. 9, Vol. 3, No. 1). 140p. (Orig.). 1962. text ed. 26.00 (0-8236-0040-8) Intl Univs Pr.

Activation de l'Energie. Pierre T. De Chardin. 428p. 1963. 24.95 (0-8288-7425-5) Fr & Eur.

Activation de l'Energie. Pierre Teilhard De Chardin. (FRE.). 1955. pap. 29.95 (0-7859-1243-6, 2020028646) Fr & Eur.

Activation, Deactivation, & Poisoning of Catalysts. John B. Butt & Eugene E. Petersen. 495p. 1988. text ed. 138.00 (0-12-147695-2) Acad Pr.

Activation of Alkanes. Hill. 1989. text ed. 89.95 (0-471-60016-4) Wiley.

Activation of Dioxygen & Homogenous Catalytic Oxidation. Derek H. Barton et al. (Illus.). 498p. (C). 1993. 125.00 (0-306-44591-3, Plenum Pr) Plenum.

Activation of DNA Replication in Eukaryotes. D. L. Dobbs. (Molecular Biology Intelligence Unit Ser.). write for info. (1-57059-114-8) R G Landes.

Activation of Energy. Pierre Teilhard De Chardin. Tr. by Rene Hague. LC 75-142104. (Helen & Kurt Wolff Bk.). 416p. 1972. reprint ed. pap. 6.95 (0-15-602860-3, Harvest Bks) HarBrace.

Activation of Grignard Reagents by Transition Metal Compounds. H. Felkin & G. Swierczewski. 1976. pap. 15.50 (0-08-020465-1, Pergamon Pr) Elsevier.

Activation of Hormone & Growth Factor Receptors Molecular Mechanisms & Consequences: Proceedings of the NATO Advanced Research Workshop on "Molecular Mechanisms & Consequences of Activaton of Hormone & Growth Factor Receptors" Held in Nafplion, Greece, September 25-30, 1988. Ed. by Michael N. Alexis & Constantin E. Sekeris. (C). 1989. lib. bdg. 134.00 (0-7923-0573-6) Kluwer Ac.

Activation of Saturated Hydrocarbons by Transition Metal Complexes. A. E. Shilov. LC 84-6817. 1984. lib. bdg. 39.00 (0-318-00433-X) Kluwer Ac.

Activation Spectrometry in Chemical Analysis. Susan J. Parry. (Chemical Analysis: a Series of Monographs on Analytical Chemistry & Its Applications: No. 1075). 264p. 1991. text ed. 99.95 (0-471-63844-7) Wiley.

Activation to Acquisition: Functional Aspects of the Basal Forebrain Cholinergic System. R. T. Richardson. (Illus.). 392p. 1991. 98.00 (0-8176-3467-3) Spr-Verlag.

***Activators: Activity Structures to Engage Student's Thinking Before Instruction.** Jon Saphier & Mary A. Haley. 43p. (Orig.). (J). 1993. student ed, pap. text ed. 12.95 (1-886822-04-2) Res Better Teach.

Activators & Inhibitors of Complement. Ed. by R. B. Sim. LC 92-14814. (C). 1992. lib. bdg. 148.00 (0-7923-1819-6) Kluwer Ac.

Active Acting: Exercises & Improvisations Leading to Performances. Leslie Abbott. 192p. (C). 1987. pap. text ed. 15.95 (0-89863-114-9) Star Pub CA.

Active & Adaptive Optical Components. M. A. Ealey. 1992. 77.00 (0-8194-0671-6, 1543) SPIE.

Active & Adaptive Optical Systems. M. A. Ealey. 1992. 70.00 (0-8194-0670-8, 1542) SPIE.

Active & Experiential Learning. Patrick Whitaker. Ed. by Peter Lang & Ron Best. (Studies in Pastoral Care, Personal & Social Education). 176p. Date not set. text ed. 70.00 (0-304-32783-2); pap. text ed. 24.95 (0-304-32782-4) Cassell.

Active & Passive Analog Filter Design: An Introduction. Lawrence P. Huelsman. LC 92-40111. (Series in Electrical & Computer Engineering). 1993. text ed. write for info. (0-07-030860-8) McGraw.

***Active & Passive Control of Mechanical Vibration: 1994 International Mechanical Engineering Congress & Exposition, Chicago, Illinois - November 6-11, 1994.** (PVP Ser.: Vol. 289). 80p. 1994. 40.00 (0-7918-1387-8, G00882) ASME.

Active & Passive Pressure Tables. J. Kerisel & E. Absi. 234p. (C). 1990. text ed. 85.00 (90-6191-886-3, Pub. by A A Balkema NE) Ashgate Pub Co.

Active & Reasonable Efforts to Preserve Families: A Guide for Delivering Services in Compliance with the Indian Child Welfare Act of 1978 (PL 95-608 & the Adoption Assistance & Child Welfare Act of 1980 (PL 92-272) Robert J. Hunner et al. 290p. (C). 1986. student ed 40.00 (0-943321-00-X) NW Res Assocs.

Active Assessment for Active Science: A Guide for Elementary School Teachers. George E. Hein & Sabra Price. LC 94-20529. 155p. 1994. pap. text ed. 18.00 (0-435-08361-9) Heinemann.

Active Asset Allocation: Gaining Advantage in a Highly Efficient Stock Market. Walter R. Good et al. 304p. 1993. text ed. 44.95 (0-07-023730-1) McGraw.

Active Asset Allocation: State-of-the-Art Portfolio Policies, Strategies & Tactics. rev. ed. Ed. by Robert D. Arnott & Frank J. Fabozzi. (Institutional Investor Publication Ser.). 430p. 1992. 65.00 (1-55738-237-9) Probus Pub Co.

***Active Bank Risk Management: Enhancing Investment & Credit Portfolio Performance.** Globecon Group Ltd. Staff. 275p. 1995. 60.00 (1-55738-758-3) Probus Pub Co.

Active Birth: The New Approach to Giving Birth Naturally. rev. ed. Janet Balaskas. Ed. by Linda Ziedrich. LC 91-32334. (Illus.). 224p. 1992. 19.95 (1-55832-037-7); pap. 12.95 (1-55832-038-5) Harvard Common Pr.

Active Catholic. Gabriel Palau. LC 84-50405. 224p. 1984. reprint ed. pap. 6.00 (0-89555-238-8) TAN Bks Pubs.

***Active Citizenship & the Governing of Schools.** Rosemary Deem et al. LC 95-5848. 1995. write for info. (0-335-19184-3, Open Univ Pr); pap. write for info. (0-335-19183-5, Open Univ Pr) Taylor & Francis.

***Active Citizenship Today: A Handbook for High School Teachers.** Close Up Foundation, Constitutional Rights Foundation. LC 94-36898. 1994. write for info. (0-932765-59-9) Close Up Fnd.

***Active Citizenship Today: A Handbook for Middle School Teachers: A Joint Project of Close Up Foundation & Constitutional Rights Foundation.** Lois Berkowitz & David Zack. Ed. by Marshall Croddy & Mary Jane Turner. LC 94-37639. 1994. write for info. (0-932765-60-2) Close Up Fnd.

***Active Citizenship Today Field Guide.** Charles Degelman et al. (J). 1994. write for info. (0-932765-58-0) Close Up Fnd.

Active Close Binaries. Ed. by Cafer Ibanoglu. (C). 1990. lib. bdg. 259.50 (0-7923-0907-3) Kluwer Ac.

Active Communities: Healthy Families. Gay M. Gross. 100p. (Orig.). 1987. pap. 20.00 (0-932622-11-9) Ctr Public Rep.

Active Community: Towards a Political-Territorial Framework for Rural Development in Asia. (Working Papers Ser.: No. 79-2). 69p. 1981. pap. 5.00 (0-686-75152-3, CRD001) UNIPUB.

Active Composing & Thinking: Teacher's Manual (Act II) Mark Aulls. 192p. 1988. ring bd. 33.90 (0-8403-4312-4) Kendall-Hunt.

Active Composing & Thinking: Teacher's Manual (Act III) Mark Aulls. 160p. 1988. ring bd. 33.90 (0-8403-4315-9) Kendall-Hunt.

Active Composing & Thinking: Writer's Notebook (Act II) Mark Aulls & William Holt. 192p. 1988. per. 7.90 (0-8403-4311-6) Kendall-Hunt.

Active Composing & Thinking: Writer's Notebook (Act III) Mark Aulls & William Holt. 208p. (C). 1988. per. 7.90 (0-8403-4314-0) Kendall-Hunt.

Active Composing & Thinking (Act II) Mark Aulls & William Holt. 272p. 1988. boxed 21.90 (0-8403-4310-8) Kendall-Hunt.

Active Composing & Thinking (Act III) Mark Aulls & William Holt. 272p. 1988. boxed 21.90 (0-8403-4313-2) Kendall-Hunt.

Active Computer-Vision by Cooperative Focus & Stereo. E. P. Krotkov. (Perception Engineering Ser.). (Illus.). xii, 160p. 1989. 65.00 (0-387-97103-3, 3177) Spr-Verlag.

Active Control of Noise & Vibration - 1992. Ed. by C. J. Radcliffe et al. (DSC Ser.: Vol. 38). 372p. 1992. 65.00 (0-7918-2093-9, G00737) ASME.

Active Control of Sound. P. A. Nelson & S. J. Elliott. 436p. 1993. pap. text ed. 49.95 (0-12-515426-7) Acad Pr.

***Active Control of Vibration & Noise: 1994 International Mechanical Engineering Congress & Exposition, Chicago, Illinois - November 6-11, 1994.** (Design Engineering Ser.: Vol. 75). 548p. 1994. 120.00 (0-7918-1402-5, G00897) ASME.

Active Eating: Never Be Afraid to Eat Again. Arthur A. Hawkins, II. 77p. 1992. pap. 8.00 (0-685-55151-2); pap. text ed. 8.00 (1-881297-07-1) Info Res Lab.

Active English: Pronunciation & Speech. A. Bens. 1977. pap. text ed. write for info. (0-13-003392-8) P-H.

Active English: Understand, Practice, Communicate, Bk. 1. Pat Porter & Allen W. Sharp. 224p. 1977. pap. text ed. 13.75 (0-13-003400-2) P-H.

Active English: Understand, Practice, Communicate, Bk. 2. Pat Porter & Allen W. Sharp. (Illus.). 272p. 1977. pap. text ed. 13.75 (0-13-003418-5) P-H.

Active Experiments: Proceedings of Symposium 1 of the COSPAR 26 Plenary Meeting Held in Toulouse, France, 30 June - 11 July 1986. G. Haerendel & M. Mendillo. (Advances in Space Research Ser.: No. 8). (Illus.). 298p. 1988. pap. 56.00 (0-08-036863-8, Pergamon Pr) Elsevier.

Active Experiments - Critical Ionization Velocity. Ed. by N. Brenning & M. Mendillo. (Advances in Space Research Ser.: No. 10). (Illus.). 182p. 1989. pap. 105.00 (0-08-040164-3, Pergamon Pr) Elsevier.

***Active Experiments in Space Plasmas.** Ed. by M. T. Rietveld. (Advances in Space Research (RJ) Ser.: Vol. 15). 156p. 1995. pap. 94.00 (0-08-042620-4) Elsevier.

Active Experiments in Space Plasmas. Ed. by C. T. Russell. (Advances in Space Research Ser.: Vol. 1, No. 2). (Illus.). 468p. 1981. pap. 72.00 (0-08-027158-8, Pergamon Pr) Elsevier.

Active Eye. Michael Mills & William Schiff. 150p. 1989. student ed, pap. 10.00 (1-56321-031-2); vhs write for info. (1-56321-034-7); disk 99.00 (1-56321-030-4) L Erlbaum Assocs.

Active Eye, Set. Michael Mills & William Schiff. 150p. 1989. pap. 750.00 (1-56321-033-9); pap. 99.00 (1-56321-032-0) L Erlbaum Assocs.

***Active Filing for Paper Records.** Ann Bennick. 43p. 1989. pap. 44.00 (0-614-07284-0, A4523); sl. 76.00 (0-614-07283-2, A4524) Assn Recs Mgrs & Admin.

Active Filing for Paper Records, Set. Ann Bennick. 43p. 1989. sl., pap. 111.00 (0-933887-30-2, A4522) Assn Recs Mgrs & Admin.

Active-Filter Cookbook. Donald E. Lancaster. LC 74-33839. (Illus.). 1975. pap. 24.95 (0-672-21168-8) Sams.

Active Filter Design. Allan Waters. 1991. text ed. 30.00 (0-07-068453-7) McGraw.

Active Filter Design. Arthur B. Williams. LC 75-4288. (Modern Frontiers in Applied Science Ser.). (Illus.). 203p. reprint ed. pap. 57.90 (0-8357-5087-6, 2030132) Bks Demand.

Active Filter Design Handbook: For Use with Programmable Pocket Calculators & Minicomputers. George S. Moschytz & P. Horn. LC 80-40845. (Illus.). 324p. reprint ed. pap. 92.40 (0-7837-6732-3, 2046360) Bks Demand.

Active Filters. Heath Company Staff. (Electronics Technology Ser.). (Illus.). 304p. (C). 1979. teacher ed 9.95 (0-87119-030-3) Heathkit-Zenith Ed.

Active Filters. rev. ed. Heath Company Staff. (Electronics Technology Ser.). (Illus.). 304p. (C). 1979. reprint ed. pap. text ed. 18.95 (0-87119-029-X); reprint ed. ring bd. 39.95 (0-87119-031-1) Heathkit-Zenith Ed.

Active Footsteps. Caroline N. Churchill. Ed. by Annette K. Baxter. LC 79-8781. (Signal Lives Ser.). (Illus.). 1980. reprint ed. lib. bdg. 30.95 (0-405-12830-4) Ayer.

Active Galactic Nuclei. Ed. by H. R. Miller & P. J. Witta. (Lecture Notes in Physics Ser.: Vol. 307). xi, 438p. 1988. 53.00 (0-387-19492-4) Spr-Verlag.

Active Galactic Nuclei. Ed. by Donald E. Osterbrock & Joseph S. Miller. (C). 1989. lib. bdg. 175.50 (0-7923-0256-7); pap. text ed. 77.50 (0-7923-0257-5) Kluwer Ac.

Active Galactic Nuclei: Saas-Fee Advanced Course 20, Lecture Notes 1990, Swiss Society for Astrophysics & Astronomy. R. D. Blandford et al. (Illus.). 308p. 1991. 49.50 (0-387-53285-4) Spr-Verlag.

Active Galactic Nucleii. Ian Robson. 350p. 1994. text ed. 110.95 (0-13-005463-1) P-H.

Active Games for Children with Movement Problems. Ed. by Alan Brown. 256p. (C). 1987. 45.00 (0-317-93191-1, Pub. by P Chapman Pub UK) St Mut.

Active Games for Children with Movement Problems. Alan Brown. 256p. (C). 1989. pap. text ed. 18.95 (0-8077-2996-5) Tchrs Coll.

***Active Hearing.** Ed. by A. Flock et al. LC 94-41161. (Wenner Grenn International Ser.: Vol. 65). 1995. 125.00 (0-08-042514-3, Pergamon Pr) Elsevier.

***Active History in Key Stages 3 & 4.** Alan Farmer & Peter Knight. 160p. 1995. pap. 24.95 (1-85346-305-1, Pub. by D Fulton UK) Taylor & Francis.

Active Infrared Systems & Technology. Ed. by Roper. 138p. 1987. 36.00 (0-89252-841-9, 806) SPIE.

Active Instrument for Propaganda: The American Public Library During World War I. Wayne A. Wiegand. LC 88-38489. 205p. 1989. text ed. 45.00 (0-313-26702-2, WGV/, Greenwood Pr) Greenwood.

***Active Interview, Vol. 37.** James A. Holstein & Jabur F. Gubrium. (Qualitative Research Methods Ser.). 96p. 1995. pap. 9.50 (0-8039-5895-1) Sage.

***Active Interview, Vol. 37.** James A. Holstein & Jabur F. Gubrium. LC 95-5766. (Qualitative Research Methods Ser.: No. 37). 96p. 1995. 21.50 (0-8039-5894-3) Sage.

Active Japanese. 2nd ed. Mieko S. Han. 225p. (Orig.). (C). 1988. pap. text ed. 19.50 (0-685-30425-6) Inst Inter Studies Pr.

44

An Asterisk (*) at the beginning of an entry indicates that the title is appearing in BIP for the first time.

***Active Japanese.** 2nd ed. Mieko S. Han. 225p. (Orig.). (C). 1988. pap. text ed. 21.00 (*1-878463-01-2*) Inst Inter Studies Pr.

Active Lavas: Monitoring & Modelling. Ed. by Christopher J. Kilburn & Giuseppe Luongo. 352p. 1993. 125.00 (*1-85728-007-5*, Pub. by UCL Pr UK) Taylor & Francis.

Active Learner. Michael Shermis & Susan Moke. Ed. by Carl B. Smith. (Successful Learner Ser.). (Illus.). 160p. (Orig.). 1996. pap. 9.95 (*0-9628556-9-3*) Grayson Bernard Pubs.

***Active Learner.** 2nd rev. ed. Sallie Brown & Douglas Miller. 295p. (C). 1996. pap. text ed. write for info. (*0-935732-60-8*) Roxbury Pub Co.

Active Learner: Successful Study Strategies. Sallie A. Brown & Douglas E. Miller. (Illus.). 320p. 1992. pap. text ed. write for info. (*0-935732-36-5*) Roxbury Pub Co.

Active Learning: A Parent's Guide to Helping Your Teen Make the Grade in School. Peter D. Lenn. LC 92-34814. 224p. 1993. pap. 10.00 (*0-14-017653-5*, Penguin Bks) Viking Penguin.

Active Learning: A Study Skills Workbook. Rory Donnelly. (Illus.). 320p. (C). 1990. pap. text ed. 17.50 (*0-03-005982-8*) HB Coll Pubs.

Active Learning: Creating Excitement in the Classroom. Ed. by Charles C. Bonwell & James A. Eison. LC 91-65608. (ASHE-ERIC Higher Education Report Ser.: No. 1). 98p. 1991. pap. 17.00 (*1-878380-08-7*) GWU Schl E&HD.

Active Learning: Rappin' & Rhymin' Rosella R. Wallace. LC 90-91394. (Orig.). 1991. pap. 9.95 (*0-9627707-8-7*) Upbeat Pub.

***Active Learning for Children with Disabilities.** P. Bailey et al. Ed. by Lois Fowkes. (Active Learning Ser.). (Illus.). 160p. (Orig.). (J). (ps). 1995. teacher ed, pap. 21.20 (*0-201-49402-7*) Altrntv Pub Grp.

Active Learning for Infants. Debby Cryer. 1987. text ed. 23.25 (*0-201-21334-6*) Addison-Wesley.

Active Learning for Ones. Debby Cryer. 1987. text ed. 23.25 (*0-201-21335-4*) Addison-Wesley.

Active Learning for Threes. Debby Cryer. 1988. text ed. 23.25 (*0-201-21337-0*) Addison-Wesley.

Active Learning for Twos. Debby Cryer. 1988. text ed. 23.25 (*0-201-21336-2*) Addison-Wesley.

Active Learning for Young Children. Lynn Molyneux. (Illus.). 228p. 1989. 19.95 (*0-685-29143-X*) Trellis Bks Inc.

Active Learning in a Family Day Care Setting: Preschool. Susan McCartney. (Illus.). 184p. (Orig.). 1991. pap. 9.95 (*0-673-46401-6*) GdYrBks.

Active Learning in Social Studies: Promoting Cognitive & Social Growth. Roberta Woolever & Kathryn P. Scott. (C). 1988. text ed. 42.50 (*0-673-39756-4*) HarpCollege.

Active Life: A Spirituality of Work, Creativity, & Caring. Parker J. Palmer. LC 89-45932. 160p. 1992. pap. 5.00 (*0-06-066459-2*) Harper SF.

Active Life: Wisdom for Work, Creativity, & Caring. Parker J. Palmer. LC 91-55088. 160p. 1991. reprint ed. pap. 11.00 (*0-06-066458-4*) Harper SF.

Active Life & Contemplative Life: A Study of the Concepts from Plato to the Present. M. Elizabeth Mason. Ed. by George E. Ganss. 1961. pap. 10.00 (*0-87462-418-5*) Marquette.

Active Listening: Building Skills for Understanding. Marc Helgesen & Steve Brown. (C). 1994. teacher ed, pap. 12.95 (*0-521-39885-1*) Cambridge U Pr.

Active Listening: Building Skills for Understanding (Student's Book) Marc Helgesen & Steve Brown. 1993. pap. 11.95 (*0-521-39882-7*) Cambridge U Pr.

***Active Listening: Introducing Skills for Understanding.** Marc Helgesen & Steven Brown. (Illus.). 80p. (C). 1995. pap. write for info. (*0-521-39881-9*); teacher ed, pap. write for info. (*0-521-39884-3*); pap. write for info. (*0-521-39887-8*) Cambridge U Pr.

Active Listening Program (ALP) Carrie Van der Laan. (Illus.). 113p. (Orig.). (YA). (gr. 5-12). 1986. Incl. manual, 36 3x5 cards, 50 4x6 cards, carrying tote. 39.00 (*0-930599-02-0*) Thinking Pubns.

***Active Living: The Miracle Medicine for a Long & Healthy Life.** Gordon W. Stewart. LC 94-41353. (Illus.). 144p. (Orig.). 1994. pap. write for info. (*0-87322-678-X*, PSTE0678) Human Kinetics.

***Active Management: Structured Training Activities & Exercises.** Clifford Johnson. 300p. 1995. ring bd. 95.00 (*0-87425-986-X*) Human Res Dev Pr.

Active Margin Basins. Ed. by Kevin T. Biddle. (AAPG Memoir Ser.: No. 52). (Illus.). 324p. 1991. 60.00 (*0-89181-330-6*) AAPG.

***Active Margins & Marginal Basins of the Western Pacific.** Ed. by Brian Taylor & James Natland. LC 95-9944. (Geophysical Monographs: Vol. 88). 1995. write for info. (*0-87590-045-3*) Am Geophysical.

Active Materials & Adaptive Structures: Proceedings of the ADPA-AIAA-ASME-SPIE Conference, Held in Alexandria, Virginia, 4-8 November 1991. G. Knowles. (Illus.). 940p. 1992. 212.00 (*0-7503-0191-0*) IOP Pub.

Active Math: Mathematics Activities for the Primary Years. Barbara Berman & Fredda J. Friederwitzer. 120p. (C). 1991. teacher ed 50.00 (*1-880744-04-X*) Educ Support.

Active Measures. Janet Morris & David Drake. 1985. pap. 3.95 (*0-317-18176-9*) S&S Trade.

Active Measures, Quiet War & Two Socialist Revolutions. Lawrence B. Sulc. Ed. by Hale, Nathan, Institute Staff. 46p. (Orig.). 1985. pap. 10.00 (*0-935067-05-1*) Nathan Hale Inst.

Active Meditation. Robert R. Leichtman & Carl Japikse. 1990. pap. 19.95 (*0-89804-041-8*) Ariel GA.

Active Network Analysis: Advanced Series in Electrical & Computer Engineering, Vol. 2. W. K. Chen. 660p. (C). 1991. text ed. 106.00 (*9971-5-0912-1*); pap. text ed. 61.00 (*9971-5-0913-X*) World Scientific Pub.

Active Network Analysis - Problems & Solution. W. K. Chen. (Electrical & Computer Engineering Ser.). 1993. text ed. 28.00 (*981-02-1404-9*) World Scientific Pub.

Active Network Analysis - Problems & Solutions. W. K. Chen. (Electrical & Computer Engineering Ser.). 308p. 1993. pap. text ed. 36.00 (*981-02-1336-0*) World Scientific Pub.

Active Network Design with Signal Filtering Applications. Claude S. Lindquist. LC 76-14238. 1977. 49.95 (*0-917144-01-5*) Steward & Sons.

Active Network Design with Signal Filtering Applications: Solutions Manual. Claude S. Lindquist. 1978. 19.95 (*0-917144-02-3*) Steward & Sons.

Active Noise Control. Richard K. Miller & Terri C. Walker. LC 88-81665. (Survey on Technology & Markets Ser.: No. 74). 50p. 1989. pap. text ed. 200.00 (*1-55865-073-3*) Future Tech Surveys.

Active Noise Control. M. O. Tokhi & R. R. Leitch. (Oxford Engineering Science Ser.: No. 29). (Illus.). 224p. 1992. 70.00 (*0-19-856243-8*) OUP.

***Active Noise Suppression: Fundamentals & Technologies.** G. Rosenhouse. 200p. 1995. 85.00 (*1-56252-297-3*) Computational Mech MA.

Active Non-Violence: A Way of Personal Peace. Gerard A. Vanderhaar. LC 89-85348. 144p. (Orig.). 1990. pap. 7.95 (*0-89622-392-2*) Twenty-Third.

***Active Nonviolence: A Way of Life, a Strategy for Change.** Ed. by Richard Deats et al. (Illus.). 62p. 1991. 6.00 (*0-911810-78-1*, Fellwship Pubns) Fellowship of Recon.

Active Oxygen. Ed. by Christopher S. Foote et al. LC 94-20876. (Structure Energetics & Reactivity in Chemistry Ser.: Vol. 2). Date not set. write for info. (*0-412-03441-7*) Chapman & Hall.

Active Oxygens, Lipid Peroxides & Antioxidants. Ed. by Kunio Yagi. LC 93-5735. 1993. 84.50 (*0-8493-7769-2*, RB170) CRC Pr.

Active Parenting: A Trainer's Manual. Shelley E. Leavitt. 150p. (Orig.). 1982. pap. 6.95 (*0-938510-02-9*, 81-001) Boys Town Pr.

Active Parenting: Teaching Courage, Cooperation & Responsibility. Michael Popkin. 1987. pap. 12.00 (*0-06-254061-0*, PL) HarpC.

Active Parenting Family Guide: Tobacco, Alcohol & Other Drugs. Ed. by Nancy Ballance. (Illus.). 32p. (Orig.). 1993. pap. text ed. 2.50 (*1-880283-05-0*) Active Parenting.

***Active Parenting of Teens: Leader's Guide.** Michael H. Popkin. (Illus.). 148p. 1990. ring bd. 25.95 (*0-9618020-2-2*) Active Parenting.

***Active Parenting of Teens: Parent's Guide.** Michael H. Popkin. (Illus.). 192p. (Orig.). 1990. pap. text ed. 13.95 (*0-9618020-3-0*) Active Parenting.

***Active Parenting of Teens: The Basics, Parent's Guide.** Michael H. Popkin. (Illus.). 144p. (Orig.). 1994. pap. text ed. 13.95 (*1-880283-10-7*) Active Parenting.

Active Parenting Today: The Basics: A Guide for Parents of 2 to 12 Year Olds. Michael H. Popkin. (Illus.). 112p. (Orig.). 1993. pap. 13.95 (*1-880283-06-9*) Active Parenting.

Active Parenting Today Leader's Guide: For Parents of 2-12 Year Olds. Michael H. Popkin. 168p. 1993. spiral bd. 24.95 (*1-880283-04-2*) Active Parenting.

Active Parenting Today Parent's Guide: For Parents of 2-12 Year Olds. Michael H. Popkin. 168p. 1993. pap. 13.95 (*1-880283-03-4*) Active Parenting.

Active Participation at Mass: What It Is & How to Attain It. Anthony B. Buono. LC 93-41295. 1994. pap. 5.95 (*0-8189-0682-0*) Alba.

Active Perception. Ed. by Yiannis Aloimonos. (Computer Vision Ser.). 304p. 1993. text ed. 59.95 (*0-8058-1290-3*) L Erlbaum Assocs.

Active Perception & Robot Vision. Ed. by Arun K. Sood & Harry Wechsler. LC 92-38509. 1993. 198.00 (*0-387-55047-X*) Spr-Verlag.

***Active Portfolio Management: Quantitative Theory & Applications.** Richard C. Grinold. 1994. 65.00 (*1-55738-824-5*) Probus Pub Co.

Active Psychotherapy. Harold Greenwald. LC 84-45026. 384p. 1984. reprint ed. 40.00 (*0-87668-663-3*) Aronson.

***Active Questioning: Questioning Still Makes the Difference.** Nancy L. Johnson. (Illus.). 112p. 1995. pap. 11.95 (*1-880505-13-4*) Pieces of Lrning.

Active Radar Electronic Countermeasures. E. J. Chrzanowski. 246p. 1990. 75.00 (*0-89006-290-0*) Artech Hse.

Active RC Filter Design. M. Herpy & J. C. Berka. (Studies in Electrical & Electronic Engineering: No. 18). 320p. 1986. 97.50 (*0-444-99558-7*) Elsevier.

Active Reader: An Introductory Reading-Communication Text for Students of ESL-EFL. Christine P. Cassanve & Diane Williams. (Illus.). 176p. (C). 1987. pap. text ed. 16.50 (*0-13-003740-0*) P-H.

Active Reader: Composing in Reading & Writing. Anne R. Gere & Jeffrey Carroll. 544p. (C). 1990. pap. text ed. 19.50 (*0-03-014132-X*); pap. text ed. 28.50 (*0-03-014133-8*) HB Coll Pubs.

Active Reader for Writers. Sandra Panman & Richard Panman. 288p. (Orig.). 1991. pap. text ed. 12.95 (*0-912813-16-4*) Active Lrn.

Active Reading for ESL Learners. Julia I. Bhasin et al. 112p. (C). 1993. per. 14.95 (*0-8403-8946-9*) Kendall-Hunt.

Active Reading in the Arts & Sciences. 2nd ed. Shirley Quinn & Susan F. Irvings. 500p. 1990. pap. text ed. write for info. (*0-205-13062-3*, H3062-0) Allyn.

Active Real Estate Lenders. 150p. 1995. 35.00 (*0-685-55407-4*) B Klein Pubns.

Active Repertoire for Black. Drazen Marovic. 184p. 1992. pap. 16.95 (*0-8050-2320-8*, Pub. by Batsford Chess UK) H Holt & Co.

Active Retirement Guide. Nancy Tuft. (C). 1992. 80.00 (*0-86242-119-5*, Pub. by Age Concern Eng UK) St Mut.

Active Review of French: Selected Patterns, Vocabulary, & Pronunciation Problems for Speakers of English. Robert L. Politzer & Michie P. Hagiwara. LC 63-15633. 264p. reprint ed. pap. 75.30 (*0-8357-5088-4*, 2055978) Bks Demand.

Active Robot Vision: Camera Heads, Model Based Navigation & Reactive Control. H. Christensen et al. 200p. 1993. text ed. 67.00 (*981-02-1321-2*) World Scientific Pub.

Active Service. Stephen Crane. (Works of Stephen Crane Ser.). 1990. reprint ed. lib. bdg. 79.00 (*0-7812-2432-2*) Rprt Serv.

Active Shareholder: Exercising Your Rights, Increasing Your Profits, & Minimizing Your Risks. William F. Mahoney. 289p. 1993. text ed. 21.95 (*0-471-57100-8*) Wiley.

Active Solar Collectors & Their Applications. Ari Rabl. LC 84-14861. (Illus.). 517p. 1985. text ed. 59.00 (*0-19-503546-1*) OUP.

Active Solar Heating Systems Design Manual. 500p. 1988. 76.00 (*0-910110-54-9*) Am Heat Ref & Air Eng.

Active Solar Heating Systems Installation Manual. Ed. by M. Geshwiler. (C). 1991. pap. 45.00 (*0-910110-78-6*) Am Heat Ref & Air Eng.

Active Solar Systems. Ed. by George Lof. (Illus.). 825p. 1992. 80.00x (*0-262-12167-0*) MIT Pr.

Active Sound Absorption. Claude J. Mazzola. LC 92-93587. (Illus.). 113p. (Orig.). (C). 1993. pap. text ed. 49.50 (*0-9636316-0-8*) NAMLAK.

Active Spirituality. Charles R. Swindoll. LC 94-8584. 1994. write for info. (*0-8499-1169-9*) Word Pub.

Active Spirituality: A Guide for Seekers & Ministers. Kent I. Groff. LC 93-73157. 228p. (Orig.). 1993. pap. 12.95 (*1-56699-117-X*, AL146) Alban Inst.

Active Structural Control: Theory & Practice. T. T. Soong. 1990. 69.95 (*0-582-01782-3*, Drumbeat) Longman.

Active Talk: The Effective Use of Discussion in Learning. Morry Van Ments. LC 90-63783. 160p. 1991. text ed. 39.95 (*0-312-06087-4*) St Martin.

Active Teaching Leader's Guide: Enhancing Discipline, Self-Esteem & Student Performance. Michael H. Popkin. (Illus.). 176p. (J). (gr. k-6). 1994. spiral bd. 39.95 (*1-880283-07-7*) Active Parenting.

Active Teaching Teacher's Handbook: Enhancing Discipline, Self-Esteem & Student Performance. Michael H. Popkin. (Illus.). 191p. (Orig.). 1994. pap. 14.95 (*1-880283-08-5*) Active Parenting.

***Active Techniques & Group Psychotherapy.** Ted Saretsky. LC 77-87149. 294p. 1995. pap. text ed. 35.00 (*1-56821-398-0*) Aronson.

***Active Tectonics.** Edward A. Keller & Nicholas Pinter. (Illus.). 304p. 1994. pap. write for info. (*0-02-363261-5*, Merrill Pub Co) Macmillan.

Active Tectonics: Impact on Society. National Research Council. 280p. 1986. text ed. 29.95 (*0-309-03638-0*) Natl Acad Pr.

Active Telescope Systems. Ed. by F. Roddier. 568p. 1989. 77.00 (*0-8194-0150-1*, VOL. 1114) SPIE.

Active Touch-The Mechanism of Recognition of Objects by Manipulation: A Multidisciplinary Approach. Ed. by G. Gordon. 1978. 123.00 (*0-08-022647-7*, Pub. by Pergamon Repr UK) Franklin.

Active Training: A Handbook of Techniques, Designs, Case Examples & Tips. Mel Silberman. 240p. 1990. text ed. 42.95 (*0-669-24262-4*) Free Pr.

***Active Travel Resource Guide: 1995 Edition.** Ed. by Daniel Browdy. 672p. (Orig.). 1994. pap. 19.95 (*0-9643658-0-4*) Ultimate Vent.

Active Twenty-Four Hours. Alan Davies. 100p. (Orig.). 1984. pap. 5.00 (*0-937804-11-8*) Segue NYC.

Active Vision. Andrew Blake & Alan Yuille. (Artificial Intelligence Ser.). (Illus.). 171p. 1992. 52.50 (*0-262-02351-2*) MIT Pr.

Active Voice: A Writing Program Across the Curriculum. James Moffett. LC 81-6156. 160p. (Orig.). (C). 1981. pap. text ed. 14.00 (*0-86709-001-4*) Boynton Cook Pubs.

Active Voice: A Writing Program Across the Curriculum. 2nd ed. James Moffett. 203p. (Orig.). 1992. pap. text ed. 17.00 (*0-86709-289-0*, 0289) Boynton Cook Pubs.

***Active Voices: Women in Jewish Culture.** Ed. by Maurie Sacks. LC 94-30759. 1995. write for info. (*0-252-02154-1*); pap. text ed. write for info. (*0-252-06453-4*) U of Ill Pr.

Active Voices, I: A Writer's Reader. James Moffett et al. 265p. (J). (gr. 4-6). 1987. teacher ed 1.75 (*0-86709-184-3*) Boynton Cook Pubs.

Active Voices, I: A Writer's Reader. James Moffett et al. 265p. (J). (gr. 4-6). 1987. text ed. 16.50 (*0-86709-091-X*) Boynton Cook Pubs.

Active Voices, II: A Writer's Reader. James Moffett & Phyllis Tashlik. 317p. (J). (gr. 7-9). 1987. teacher ed 1.75 (*0-86709-182-7*) Boynton Cook Pubs.

Active Voices, II: A Writer's Reader. James Moffett & Phyllis Tashlik. 317p. (YA). (gr. 7-9). 1987. pap. text ed. 16.50 (*0-86709-111-8*) Boynton Cook Pubs.

Active Voices, III: A Writer's Reader. James Moffett et al. 414p. (YA). (gr. 10-12). 1987. pap. text ed. 17.50 (*0-86709-113-4*) Boynton Cook Pubs.

Active Voices, III: A Writer's Reader. James Moffett et al. 414p. (YA). (gr. 10-12). 1987. teacher ed 1.75 (*0-86709-180-0*) Boynton Cook Pubs.

Active Voices IV. James Moffett et al. LC 85-27996. 344p. (Orig.). (C). 1985. pap. text ed. 18.50 (*0-86709-115-0*) Boynton Cook Pubs.

Active Voices IV. James Moffett et al. LC 85-27996. 344p. (Orig.). (C). 1986. teacher ed 1.75 (*0-86709-179-7*) Boynton Cook Pubs.

***Actively Run Your I. R. A. for Your Best Interest.** John V. Kamin. 14p. 1988. pap. 7.00 (*0-911353-12-7*) Forecaster Pub.

Actively Seeking Nutrition. Richard Duquet. 27p. 1978. pap. 2.00 (*0-934332-20-7*) LEpervier Pr.

***Actively Seeking Work? The Politics of Unemployment & Welfare Policy in the United States & Great Britain.** Desmond King. 344p. 1995. pap. text ed. 17.95 (*0-226-43622-5*) U Ch Pr.

***Actively Seeking Work? The Politics of Unemployment & Welfare Policy in the United States & Great Britain.** Desmond King. 344p. 1995. lib. bdg. 50.00 (*0-226-43621-7*) U Ch Pr.

Actividad Optica, Dispersion Rotatoria Optica y Dicroismo Circular en Quimica Organica. 2nd ed. OAS, General Secretariat, Department of Scientific & Technological Affairs Staff. (Serie de Quimica: Monografia No. 11). 70p. (SPA.). (C). 1981. pap. 3.50 (*0-8270-1418-X*) OAS.

Actividades de Ciencia para Poner en Secuencia. Joy Evans & Jo E. Moore. Tr. by Jan Mayer et al. (Illus.). 32p. (SPA.). (J). (ps-1). 1990. pap. text ed. 4.95 (*1-55799-188-X*) Evan-Moor Corp.

Actividades Diarias Despues de Tu Reemplazo Total de Rodilla. Janet V. Platt et al. Tr. by Dyhalma Irizarry. (Illus.). (C). 1993. pap. text ed. write for info. (*1-56900-005-0*) Am Occup Therapy.

Actividades Dinamicas para el Aprendizaje. LeRoy Ford. Tr. by Raimundo J. Ericson. 118p. (SPA.). 1987. pap. 4.50 (*0-311-11046-0*) Casa Bautista.

Actividades Educativas para Preescolares. Priscila M. Patacsil. 172p. (J). (ps). 1988. pap. 6.25 (*0-311-11049-5*) Casa Bautista.

Actividades Navidenas: Christmas Activities. (Games for Children Ser.). 32p. (J). 1987. pap. 1.50 (*0-311-26613-4*) Casa Bautista.

Actividades y Asignaciones: Cuaderno del Estudiante. Hank Resnik et al. Ed. by Juan Callejas et al. Tr. by Marta B. Luobriel et al. (Destrezas para la Adolescencia Ser.). (Illus.). (Orig.). (SPA.). (YA). (gr. 6-8). 1991. student ed 4.85 (*1-56095-022-6*) Quest Intl.

Activism in American Librarianship, 1962-1973. Mary Lee Bundy. Ed. by Frederick J. Stielow. LC 87-236. (Contributions in Librarianship & Information Science Ser.: No. 58). 224p. 1987. text ed. 55.00 (*0-313-24602-5*, BUA/) Greenwood.

Activism Replaces Isolationism: U. S. Public Attitudes 1940-1975. H. S. Foster. LC 83-81284. 420p. 1983. 14.95 (*0-9611128-1-6*) Foxhall Pr.

Activism That Makes Sense: Congregations & Community Organization. Gregory F. Pierce. LC 83-82016. 148p. (Orig.). 1984. reprint ed. pap. 8.95 (*0-914070-53-3*, 111) ACTA Pubns.

***Activist Parent's Guide to Learning Disabilities.** Smith. 1996. 22.00 (*0-02-874051-3*) Free Pr.

Activist Unionism: The Institutional Economics of Solomon Barkin. Donald R. Stabile. LC 93-23795. (Studies in Institutional Economics Ser.). 304p. 1993. text ed. 57.95 (*1-56324-292-3*); pap. text ed. 23.95 (*1-56324-293-1*) M E Sharpe.

Activites de Formation a la Vitamine a pour la Sante et le Developpement Communautaires. Helen Keller International Staff. LC 93-395669. (Illus.). 72p. (Orig.). (FRE.). 1993. 10.00 (*0-915173-27-1*) Helen Keller Intl.

Activities Aide. Jack Rudman. (Career Examination Ser.: C-3101). 1994. pap. 19.95 (*0-8373-3101-3*) Nat Learn.

Activities Almanac: The Best of School Library Media Activities Monthly 1984-1989. Montgomery Walker. (School Library Media Activities Monthly). 225p. 1990. pap. text ed. 24.95 (*0-87436-569-4*) ABC-CLIO.

Activities & Action in Groupwork. Ed. by Ruth Middleman. LC 83-309. (Social Work with Groups Ser.: Vol. 6, No. 1). 105p. 1983. text ed. 29.95 (*0-86656-228-1*) Haworth Pr.

Activities & Assignments: Student Workbook. Hank Resnik. Ed. by Linda Barr. (Skills for Adolescence Ser.). (Illus.). 178p. (YA). (gr. 6-8). 1988. student ed 4.85 (*0-933419-26-0*) Quest Intl.

Activities & Games. rev. ed. Lucy C. LeGros. (Illus.). 75p. (Orig.). (J). (gr. k-2). 1989. pap. 7.95 (*0-318-41419-8*) Creat Res NC.

Activities & Investigations in Economics. Elmer Clawson. (YA). 1993. teacher ed, pap. 12.95 (*0-201-49006-4*) Addison-Wesley.

Activities & Investigations in Economics. 2nd ed. Elmer Clawson. (YA). 1994. pap. text ed. 9.95 (*0-201-49005-6*) Addison-Wesley.

Activities & Quizzes for the Long-Term Care Nursing Assistant Training Manual. Martha H. Jackson & Judi R. Van Vleet. 192p. 1992. pap. text ed. 14.00 (*1-878812-08-4*) Hlth Prof Pr.

Activities & the "Well Elderly" Ed. by Phyllis M. Foster. LC 83-4326. (Activities, Adaptation & Aging Ser.: Vol. 3, No. 2). 120p. 1983. text ed. 29.95 (*0-86656-230-3*) Haworth Pr.

Activities Director. Jack Rudman. (Career Examination Ser.: C-2949). 1994. pap. 29.95 (*0-8373-2949-3*) Nat Learn.

Activities for Active Learning & Teaching: Selections from the "Mathematics Teacher" Ed. by Christian R. Hirsch & Robert A. Laing. LC 93-23027. (Illus.). 244p. (Orig.). 1993. pap. 11.00 (*0-87353-363-1*) NCTM.

***Activities for Adolescents in Therapy: A Handbook of Facilitating Guidelines & Planning Ideas for Group Therapy with Troubled Adolescents.** Susan T. Dennison. (Illus.). 236p. 1988. pap. 29.95 (*0-398-06089-4*) C C Thomas.

Activities for Adolescents in Therapy: A Handbook of Facilitating Guidelines & Planning Ideas for Group Therapy with Troubled Adolescents. Susan T. Dennison. (Illus.). 236p. (C). 1988. text ed. 46.95x (*0-398-05409-6*) C C Thomas.

An Asterisk (*) at the beginning of an entry indicates that the title is appearing in BIP for the first time.

A

***Activities for All Seasons.** Karen Finch. (Illus.). 96p. (Orig.). (J). (gr. k-5). 1994. 7.95 (*1-885476-06-X*) Finch Fmly Games.

Activities for an Interactive Classroom. Ed. by Jeff Golub. 143p. 1994. pap. 16.95 (*0-8141-0046-5*) NCTE.

Activities for Before & After School. Mardi Gork & David Pratt. (Illus.). 96p. (Orig.). 1991. pap. text ed. 8.95 (*0-86530-211-1*, IP 193-2) Incentive Pubns.

Activities for Children in Therapy: A Guide for Planning & Facilitating Therapy with Troubled Children. Susan T. Dennison & Connie K. Glassman. (Illus.). 304p. (C). 1987. spiral bd. 46.95 (*0-398-05294-8*) C C Thomas.

Activities for Cooperative Learning. Marzella Brown. (Illus.). 48p. (J). (gr. 2-5). 1990. student ed 6.95 (*1-55734-109-5*) Tchr Create Mat.

***Activities for Diversity Training.** Jonamay Lambert & Selma Myers. 1994. ring bd. 139.95 (*0-87425-980-0*) Human Res Dev Pr.

***Activities for Empowerment.** Donna Berry et al. 1994. ring bd. 139.95 (*0-87425-964-9*) Human Res Dev Pr.

Activities for Individualized Career Exploration & Planning. rev. ed. David Winefordner. 48p. (YA). (gr. 9-12). 1993. 24.95 (*1-56191-196-8*) Meridian Educ.

Activities for Integrating the Language Arts. Carol Jenkins & John Savage. (Illus.). 224p. 1983. text ed. 29.00 (*0-13-003699-4*) P-H.

Activities for Junior High School & Middle School Mathematics: Readings from the "Arithmetic Teacher" & the "Mathematics Teacher" Ed. by Loren L. Henry. LC 81-14024. (Illus.). 218p. 1981. pap. 12.00 (*0-87353-188-4*) NCTM.

***Activities for Little Learners, Vol. 1.** Karen Finch. (Illus.). 96p. (Orig.). (J). (gr. 1). 1994. teacher ed 7.95 (*1-885476-01-9*) Finch Fmly Games.

***Activities for Little Learners, Vol. 1.** Karen Finch. (Illus.). 96p. (Orig.). (J). (ps-k). 1994. teacher ed 7.95 (*1-885476-00-0*) Finch Fmly Games.

Activities for Parent Groups. rev. ed. Gary Wilson. (Illus.). 160p. 1995. pap. 16.95 (*0-89334-165-7*) Humanics Ltd.

***Activities for Problem Solving.** Beryl Badger & Ian Chaston. 248p. 1991. text ed. 169.95 (*1-85904-042-X*, Pub. by Gower UK) Ashgate Pub Co.

***Activities for Public Sector Training.** Mary Griffiths. 1995. pap. 76.95 (*0-566-07651-9*, Pub. by Gower UK) Ashgate Pub Co.

Activities for Rainy Days & Sundays. Sharon Herington. 70p. 1982. pap. 4.95 (*0-8341-0786-4*) Beacon Hill.

Activities for Reflect-It Hinged Mirror. Carol Desoe. (Illus.). 72p. (J). (gr. 4-8). 1994. pap. text ed. 8.95 (*0-938587-73-0*) Cuisenaire.

Activities for School-Age Child Care. rev. ed. Barbara Blakeley et al. LC 89-60449. (Illus.). 92p. 1989. pap. text ed. 6.00 (*0-935989-26-9*, NAEYC#214) Natl Assn Child Ed.

Activities for Succeeding in the World of Work. Grady Kimbrell & Ben S. Vineyard. 1981. pap. 8.88 (*0-02-669590-1*) Glencoe.

Activities for Teacher Training. Elaine M. Ward. 1991. pap. 7.95 (*1-877871-33-8*, 4150) Ed Ministries.

Activities for Teaching K-6 Math-Science Concepts. Walter A. Farmer & Margaret A. Farrell. (Classroom Activities Ser.). (Illus.). 42p. (Orig.). (C). 1989. pap. 7.50 (*0-912047-07-0*) Sch Sci Math.

Activities for Teaching Russian & Soviet Studies in the High School. Ed. by Robert Cole & Janet Vaillant. (Illus.). (Orig.). 1993. pap. 21.95 (*0-89994-328-4*) Soc Sci Ed.

Activities for Teaching Using the Whole Language Approach. Sam E. Brown & Rebecca S. Everett. (Illus.). 132p. (C). 1990. spiral bd. 29.95x (*0-398-05691-9*) C C Thomas.

Activities for the Abacus: A Hands on Approach to Arithmetic. 2nd ed. Joan A. Cotter. (Illus.). 152p. 1988. pap. 18.00 (*0-9609636-4-2*) Activities Learning.

Activities for the Advancement of Women: Equality, Development & Peace. 69p. 1986. 10.50 (*92-1-130107-6*, E.85.IV.11) UN.

Activities for the Aged & Infirm: A Handbook for the Untrained Worker. Toni Merrill. (Illus.). 392p. 1979. 57.95 (*0-398-01294-6*) C C Thomas.

***Activities for the Aged & Infirm: A Handbook for the Untrained Worker.** Toni Merrill. (Illus.). 392p. 1979. pap. 33.95 (*0-398-06287-0*) C C Thomas.

Activities for the Career Discovery Encyclopedia. Hopke et al. 36p. (Orig.). (J). (gr. 5-6). 1991. pap. 14.95 (*1-56191-188-7*) Meridian Educ.

Activities for the Career Discovery Encyclopedia. Hopke et al. 36p. (Orig.). (J). (gr. 7-8). 1991. pap. 14.95 (*1-56191-189-5*) Meridian Educ.

Activities for the Changing Earth System. 292p. 1993. student ed 10.00 (*1-883756-00-6*) Ohio St U Res.

Activities for the Children's Dictionary of Occupations. Barbara Parramore & Bill Hopke. (Illus.). 20p. (J). (gr. 3-4). 1992. student ed 12.95 (*1-56191-191-7*) Meridian Educ.

Activities for the Children's Dictionary of Occupations. Barbara Parramore & Bill Hopke. (Illus.). 20p. (J). (gr. 5-6). 1992. student ed 12.95 (*1-56191-192-5*) Meridian Educ.

Activities for the Elderly, Vol. 1: A Guide to Quality Programming. Sandra D. Parker et al. (Activities Ser.). 171p. 1993. reprint ed. pap. 30.00 (*1-882883-00-4*) Idyll Arbor.

Activities for the Elderly, Vol. 2: A Guide to Working with Residents with Significant Physical & Cognitive Disabilities. Sandra Parker & Carol Will. (Activities Ser.). 170p. 1993. pap. 30.00 (*1-882883-01-2*) Idyll Arbor.

Activities for the Mind: Memories, Dreams, & Thoughts Revisited. Jim Brennan. (Illus.). 253p. 1991. 39.95 (*0-929442-09-1*) Publicare Pr.

Activities for the New Physical Education: A Resource Book for the Middle School Teacher. Means et al. 240p. 1988. pap. text ed. 16.95 (*0-88725-097-1*) Hunter Textbks.

Activities for the Study of Gifted-Talented Persons. Joyce Juntune. 39p. 1984. pap. 6.75 (*0-912773-05-7*) One Hund Twenty Creat.

Activities for the Young Scientist. 1984. 10.00 (*0-939418-80-0*) Ferguson-Florissant.

Activities for Trainers: Fifty Useful Designs. Cyril R. Mill. LC 80-50465. 226p. 1980. pap. 34.95 (*0-88390-159-5*) Pfeiffer & Co.

***Activities for Training Farmworkers on Pesticide Safety: Trainer's Guide.** Association of Farmworker Opportunity Programs Staff. 53p. 1994. pap. text ed. write for info. (*1-886567-03-4*) Assn Farmwrker.

Activities for Transportation Technology Systems. Everett Sheets & Alan R. De Old. LC 92-1728. 120p. 1993. pap. text ed. 12.95 (*0-8273-5609-9*) Delmar.

Activities for Two Year Olds. 1982. 8.00 (*0-939418-42-8*) Ferguson-Florissant.

Activities from the "Mathematics Teacher" Ed. by Evan Maletsky & Christian Hirsch. LC 81-4028. (Illus.). 140p. (J). (gr. 7 up). 1981. pap. 10.00 (*0-87353-173-6*) NCTM.

Activities Handbook for Teachers of Young Children, 5 Vols. 5th ed. Doreen J. Croft. (C). 1989. pap. 43.56 (*0-395-43207-3*) HM.

Activities Handbook for the Teaching of Psychology, Vol. 1. rev. ed. Ed. by Ludy T. Benjamin, Jr. & Kathleen D. Lowman. LC 81-1648. 254p. (Orig.). 1981. pap. 20.00 (*0-912704-34-9*) Am Psychol.

Activities Handbook for the Teaching of Psychology, Vol. 3. Ed. by Vivian P. Makosky et al. (Illus.). 384p. (C). 1990. 25.00 (*1-55798-081-0*) Am Psychol.

***Activities Handbook, Teaching a Psychology of People Vol. 1: Resources for Gender & Sociocultural Awareness.** 7th ed. American Psychological Association Staff. 244p. (C). 1994. write for info. (*0-697-27870-0*) Brown & Benchmark.

***Activities Handbook, Teaching a Psychology of People Vol. 2: Resources for Gender & Sociocultural Awareness.** 7th ed. American Psychological Association Staff. 345p. (C). 1994. write for info. (*0-697-27871-9*) Brown & Benchmark.

Activities in Action: Proceedings of the National Association of Activity Professionals 1990 Conference. Phyllis M. Foster. (Activities, Adaptation & Aging Ser.: Vol. 15 No. 4). (Illus.). 111p. 1991. text ed. 29.95 (*1-56024-132-2*) Haworth Pr.

***Activities in Astronomy.** Darrel Hoff et al. 224p. (C). 1995. pap. text ed. 23.95 (*0-7872-0614-8*) Kendall-Hunt.

Activities in Astronomy. 3rd ed. Darrel Hoff et al. 192p. (C). 1994. pap. text ed., spiral bd. 20.95 (*0-8403-6825-9*) Kendall-Hunt.

Activities in Professional Communication. 2nd ed. Mary H. Brown & Cathy Floyd. 192p. 1993. spiral bd. 19.95 (*0-8403-8813-6*) Kendall-Hunt.

Activities in Self Instructional Texts. Fred Lockwood. (Illus.). 160p. (C). 1992. pap. text ed. 29.95 (*0-89397-379-3*) Nichols Pub.

Activities in the Earth Sciences. Helen Challand. LC 82-9444. (Science Activities Ser.). (Illus.). (YA). (gr. 5 up). 1982. lib. bdg. 14.33 (*0-516-00506-5*) Childrens.

Activities in the Life Sciences. Helen Challand. LC 82-9442. (Science Activities Ser.). (Illus.). (YA). (gr. 5 up). 1982. lib. bdg. 14.33 (*0-516-00507-3*) Childrens.

Activities in the Physical Sciences. Helen J. Challand. LC 83-26224. (Science Activities Ser.). (Illus.). 96p. (YA). (gr. 5 up). 1984. lib. bdg. 14.33 (*0-516-00504-9*) Childrens.

Activities Integrating Oral Communication Skills for Students Grades K-8. Ed. by Arlie V. Daniel. 338p. (Orig.). (C). 1992. pap. text ed. 32.00 (*0-944811-12-4*) Speech Commun Assn.

Activities Manual: First Year German. John LaLande et al. 176p. (GER.). (C). 1985. pap. text ed. write for info. (*0-07-554344-3*) McGraw.

Activities Nineteen Forty-Four to Forty-Six: The Transition to Peace see Collected Writings

Activities Nineteen Forty-One to Nineteen Forty-Six: Shaping the Postwar World: Bretton Woods & Reparations see Collected Writings

Activities Nineteen Forty to Forty-Three: External War Finance see Collected Writings

Activities Nineteen Forty to Nineteen Forty-Four: Shaping the Postwar World: The Clearing Union see Collected Writings

Activities Nineteen Forty to Nineteen Forty-Six: Shaping the Postwar World: Employment & Commodities see Collected Writings

Activities, Nineteen Fourteen to Nineteen Nineteen: The Treasury & Versailles see Collected Writings

Activities: Nineteen Six to Nineteen Fourteen: India & Cambridge see Collected Writings

Activities Nineteen Thirty-Nine to Forty-Five: Internal War Finance see Collected Writings

Activities Nineteen Thirty-One to Thirty Nine: World Crises & Policies in Britain & America see Collected Writings

Activities Nineteen Twenty-Nine to Thirty-One: Rethinking Employment & Unemployment Policies see Collected Writings

Activities Nineteen Twenty to Twenty-Two: Treaty Revision & Reconstruction see Collected Writings

Activities Nineteen Twenty-Two to Thirty-Two: The End of Reparations see Collected Writings

Activities Nineteen Twenty-Two to Twenty-Nine: The Return to Gold & Industrial Policy see Collected Writings

Activities of Daily Living Curriculum for Handicapped Adults. Magic Valley Rehabilitation Services, Inc. Staff. Ed. by Jeffery C. Crumrime & Chuck Tiller. 800p. 1981. reprint ed. pap. 35.00 (*0-916671-06-2*) Material Dev.

Activities of Jacob Hamblin in the Region of the Colorado see Mormon Towns in the Region of the Colorado

Activities of the Elementary School Principal for the Improvement of Instruction: The Kind of Supervisory Program Which a City Superintendent of Schools Should Set up for His Elementary School Principals. William P. Dyer. LC 70-176738. (Columbia University. Teachers College. Contributions to Education Ser.: No. 274). reprint ed. 37.50 (*0-404-55274-9*) AMS Pr.

Activities of the Holy Spirit. Edmund J. Fortman. LC 84-13786. 199p. 1984. 5.95 (*0-8199-0881-9*, Frncscn Herld) Franciscan Pr.

Activities of the OECD. 118p. (Orig.). 1993. pap. text ed. write for info. (*0-318-32996-4*, ECD140) OECD.

Activities of Transnationals Corporations in South Africa & Namibia & the Responsibilities of Home Countries with Respect to Their Operations in This Area. 59p. 1986. 7.00 (*92-1-104171-6*, E.85.II.A.16) UN.

Activities, Readings, & Skills for Teacher Support Specialists. Mims & Carr. 240p. (C). 1991. pap. text ed. 26.95 (*0-8403-6995-6*) Kendall-Hunt.

Activities Specialist. Jack Rudman. (Career Examination Ser.: C-1074). 1994. pap. 23.95 (*0-8373-1074-1*) Nat Learn.

Activities That Build Young Women, Vol. 1. Cindy Perry. 48p. (YA). 1993. pap. 6.98 (*0-88290-456-6*) Horizon Utah.

Activities That Build Young Women, Vol. 2. Cindy Parry. 48p. (YA). 1993. pap. 6.98 (*0-88290-457-4*) Horizon Utah.

Activities That Inspire Young Women, Vol. 1. Cindy Parry. 48p. 1994. 6.98 (*0-88290-489-2*, 2063) Horizon Utah.

***Activities That Inspire Young Women, Vol. 2.** Cindy Parry. 48p. (YA). 1994. pap. 6.98 (*0-88290-490-6*, 2064) Horizon Utah.

Activities Therapy. Anne C. Mosey. LC 73-79286. 205p. 1973. 28.00 (*0-911216-41-3*) Raven.

Activities with Developmentally Disabled Elderly & Older Adults. Ed. by M. Jean Keller. LC 90-5310. (Activities, Adaptation & Aging Ser.). (Illus.). 154p. 1990. text ed. 39.95 (*1-56024-092-X*) Haworth Pr.

Activities with Myths. 2nd ed. Nancy Karl. (Illus.). 48p. 1991. pap. 5.95 (*1-879287-00-5*) Bk Lures.

Activities with Plants of Southwest. Kino Learning Center Staff. 1981. pap. 9.99 (*0-685-34592-0*) Trillium Pr.

Activity Accounting: An Activity-Based Costing Approach. Wiley National Association of Accountants Staff & James A. Brimson. 1991. text ed. 65.00 (*0-471-53985-6*) Wiley.

***Activity Analysis: A Primer.** Haru Hirama. 106p. (C). 1992. pap. text ed. 22.95 (*0-935273-05-0*) Chess Pub.

Activity Analysis Handbook. 2nd ed. Nancy K. Lamport et al. LC 92-60370. (Illus.). 150p. (Orig.). (C). 1993. student ed 26.00 (*1-55642-215-6*) SLACK Inc.

Activity Analysis of Production & Allocation: Proceedings of a Conference. Tjalling C. Koopmans. Ed. by Armen Alchian et al. (Cowles Commission for Research in Economics, Monograph Ser.: No. 13). 419p. reprint ed. pap. 119.50 (*0-8357-8007-4*, 2033787) Bks Demand.

Activity & Aging. John R. Kelly. (Focus Editions Ser.: Vol. 161). (Illus.). 320p. (C). 1993. text ed. 49.95 (*0-8039-5273-2*); pap. text ed. 24.95 (*0-8039-5274-0*) Sage.

Activity & Understanding: Structure of Action & Orientated Linguistics. V. S. Fain & L. I. Rubanov. 250p. 1995. text ed. 53.00 (*981-02-1837-0*) World Scientific Pub.

Activity & Volunteer Service Policies & Procedures. 3rd ed. Pamela Sander. (Illus.). 160p. (C). 1991. ring bd. 36.95 (*1-877735-10-8*, 112) M&H Pub Co TX.

Activity Assemblies for Christian Collective Worship 5-11. Elizabeth Peirce. 224p. 1991. pap. 28.00 (*1-85000-729-2*, Falmer Pr) Taylor & Francis.

Activity Assemblies for Multi-Racial Schools 5-11. Liz Peirce. 160p. 1992. pap. 27.00 (*0-7507-0049-1*, Falmer Pr) Taylor & Francis.

***Activity-Based Approach to Early Intervention.** Diane Bricker et al. (Orig.). 1994. vhs 39.00 (*1-55766-186-3*) P H Brookes.

Activity-Based Approach to Early Intervention. Diane Bricker & Julian J. Cripe. 240p. (Orig.). (C). 1994. reprint ed. 55.00 (*1-55766-087-5*, BRI) P H Brookes.

***Activity-Based Cost Management: A Breakthrough New Approach to Seeking Out All the Costs.** 1995. 55.00 (*0-8144-0251-8*) AMACOM.

Activity Based Costing. Michael Oguin. 1991. 69.95 (*0-13-853318-0*, Busn) P-H.

Activity Based Costing: The Key to World Class Performance. Peter L. Grieco, Jr. & Mel Pilachauski. 500p. 1993. 26.95 (*0-945456-10-7*) PT Pubns.

***Activity Based Costing: The Key to World Class Performance.** Peter L. Grieco, Jr. & Mel Pilachauski. 500p. 1994. pap. 18.00 (*0-945456-15-8*) PT Pubns.

***Activity Based Costing & Performance.** Douglas W. Webster & Karen B. Burk. (Illus.). 141p. 1994. 39.95 (*0-922255-00-8*) American Management Systems Inc.

***Activity Based Costing & Performance.** Douglas W. Webster & Karen B. Burk. (Illus.). 141p. 1994. pap. 34.95 (*0-922255-01-6*) American Management Systems Inc.

Activity-Based Costing for Marketing & Manufacturing. Ronald J. Lewis. LC 92-31710. 248p. 1993. text ed. 59.95 (*0-89930-801-5*, LYB, Quorum Bks) Greenwood.

Activity-Based Costing for Small & Mid-Sized Businesses: An Implementation Guide. Douglas T. Hicks. 1992. text ed. 68.00 (*0-471-57287-X*) Wiley.

Activity Based Costing Handbook. Frank Collins. 1991. pap. 59.95 (*1-55840-671-9*) Exec Ent Pubns.

***Activity-Based Costing in Financial Institutions.** Julie Mabberley. 240p. 1993. 141.00 (*0-273-03921-0*, Pub. by Pitman Pubng UK) St Mut.

***Activity Based Early Intervention: Strategies for Families, Caregivers, & Interventionists.** D. Dean Richey. 288p. 1995. 32.95 (*0-8273-6700-7*) Delmar.

***Activity-Based Intervention & an Activity-Based Approach to Early Intervention.** Bricker et al. 1994. vhs 55.00 (*0-614-03674-7*) P H Brookes.

***Activity-Based Management: Arthur Andersen's Lessons from the ABM Battlefield.** R. Steven Player & David E. Keys. 224p. 1995. 24.95 (*1-57101-054-8*) MasterMedia Ltd.

Activity-Based Management for Service Organizations, Government Entities, & Nonprofits. James Brimson & John Antos. LC 93-36445. 1994. text ed. 65.00 (*0-471-01351-X*) Wiley.

***Activity-Based Management in Action.** Ed. by Patrick L. Romano & Claire Barth. (Illus.). 160p. 1994. pap. 35.00 (*0-86641-227-1*, 94289) Inst Mgmt Account.

***Activity-Based Models for Cost Management Systems.** Ronald J. Lewis. LC 94-37876. 296p. 1995. text ed. 59.95 (*0-89930-965-8*, Quorum Bks) Greenwood.

Activity Book. (Crayola Creativity Ser.). (Illus.). 260p. 1988. 75.00 (*0-86696-211-5*) Binney & Smith.

Activity Books. Highlights for Children Staff. (Illus.). 32p. (J). (gr. 1-6). 1989. pap. 2.95 (*0-87534-381-3*); pap. 2.95 (*0-87534-382-1*); pap. 2.95 (*0-87534-383-X*); pap. 2.95 (*0-87534-384-8*); pap. 2.95 (*0-87534-385-6*) Highlights.

Activity Books. Highlights for Children Staff. (Illus.). 32p. (J). (gr. 1-6). 1989. pap. 2.95 (*0-87534-386-4*); pap. 2.95 (*0-87534-387-2*); pap. 2.95 (*0-87534-388-0*); pap. 2.95 (*0-87534-389-9*); pap. 2.95 (*0-87534-390-2*) Highlights.

Activity Books. Highlights for Children Staff. (Illus.). 32p. 1991. pap. 2.95 (*0-87534-328-7*) Highlights.

Activity Care Plans for Long Term Care Facilities: If You Didn't Write It Down, It Wasn't Done! rev. ed. Pamela Sander. 212p. (C). 1993. pap. text ed. 21.95 (*1-877735-05-1*, 106) M&H Pub Co TX.

***Activity Centers.** Marilyn LaPenta & Joan Bielitz. Ed. by Susan Evento. (Macmillan Early Skills Program - Conversion Ser.). 64p. (J). (ps-2). Date not set. pap. text ed. 9.95 (*1-56784-507-X*) Newbridge Comms.

***Activity Coefficients at Infinite Dilution.** J. Gmehling et al. Ed. by Gerhard Kreysa. (Dechema Chemistry Data Ser.: Vol. 9, Pts. 3 & 4). (Illus.). 975p. 1994. lib. bdg. 450.00x (*3-926959-49-5*, Pub. by Dechema GW) Scholium Intl.

Activity Coefficients at Infinite Dilution, Vol. 9, Parts 1 & 2, 2 vols., Set. J. Gmehling et al. (Dechema Chemistry Data Ser.). 950p. 1986. text ed. 361.00 (*3-921567-79-3*, Pub. by Dechema GW) Scholium Intl.

Activity Coefficients in Electrolyte Solutions. 2nd ed. Kenneth S. Pitzer. (Illus.). 536p. 1991. 236.00 (*0-8493-5415-3*, QD565) CRC Pr.

Activity Costing for Engineers. John Innes et al. LC 94-6085. (Engineering Management Ser.: Vol. 1). 1994. write for info. (*0-86380-160-9*) Wiley.

***Activity Costing for Engineers.** John Innes et al. (Engineering Management Ser.: Vol. 1). 154p. 1994. text ed. 79.95 (*0-471-94439-4*) Wiley.

Activity Director's "Bag of Tricks" rev. ed. Dennis Goodwin. 94p. 1986. reprint ed. pap. 7.95 (*0-936885-00-9*) Activity Factory.

***Activity Experiments & Programming Within Long-Term Care.** Ted Tedrick & Elaine R. Green. LC 95-60643. 252p. (C). 1995. text ed. 32.95 (*0-910251-74-6*, AEX77) Venture Pub PA.

Activity Fun: Activities for Ages 3-8. Joy Deich. 80p. 1991. teacher ed, pap. 12.95 (*0-9629698-8-5*) Aaron Lake Pub.

Activity Gourmet. Peggy Powers. LC 91-66393. (Illus.). 135p. (Orig.). 1991. spiral bd. 15.95 (*0-910251-51-7*) Venture Pub PA.

Activity, Health & Fitness in Old Age. Jean Macheath. LC 83-40128. 224p. 1984. text ed. 45.00 (*0-312-00390-0*) St Martin.

***Activity Holidays 95.** National Tourist Board Staff. (Illus.). 144p. (Orig.). 1995. pap. 8.95 (*0-7117-0805-3*, Pub. by Jarrold Pub UK) Seven Hills Bk.

***Activity Ideas for the Budget Minded.** Debra Cassistre. LC 94-70600. 120p. 1994. pap. 10.95 (*0-943873-15-0*) Elder Bks.

Activity in Cool Star Envelopes. Ed. by O. Havnes et al. (C). 1988. lib. bdg. 117.50 (*90-277-2706-6*) Kluwer Ac.

Activity in Red-Dwarf Stars. Ed. by Patrick B. Byrne & Marcello Rodono. 1983. lib. bdg. 183.00 (*90-277-1601-3*) Kluwer Ac.

Activity Manual for an Atlas of Virginia. Virginia Geographic Alliance Staff. 112p. 1991. spiral bd. 16.95 (*0-8403-6940-9*) Kendall-Hunt.

***Activity Math: Using Manipulatives in the Classroom Grades K Through 3.** Anne Bloomer. (J). (gr. k-3). 1992. pap. 32.00 (*0-201-45505-6*) Addison-Wesley.

***Activity Math: Using Manipulatives in the Classroom Grades 4 Through 6.** Anne Bloomer. (J). (gr. 4-6). 1992. 32.00 (*0-201-45506-4*) Addison-Wesley.

Activity Measurement in Psychology & Medicine. W. W. Tryon. (Applied Clinical Psychology Ser.). (Illus.). 270p. 1991. 42.50 (*0-306-43786-4*, Plenum Pr) Plenum.

Activity Mind-Set Guide, Set. Gene Galleli. 1977. Sold only as a set of 5. 1.95 (*0-914634-53-4*, 7722) DOK Pubs.

Activity of Politics & Related Essays. Wendell J. Coats, Jr. LC 88-42861. 176p. 1989. 32.50 (*0-941664-95-3*) Susquehanna U Pr.

Activity of Young Children During Sleep: An Objective Study, Vol. 18. Chester R. Garvey. LC 39-28089. (Illus.). x, 102p. 1970. reprint ed. text ed. 45.00 (*0-8371-8073-2*, CWGY, Greenwood Pr) Greenwood.

Activity-Oriented Classrooms. Milly Cowles & Jerry Aldridge. 80p. 1992. 8.95 (*0-8106-0352-7*) NEA.

An Asterisk (*) at the beginning of an entry indicates that the title is appearing in BIP for the first time.

A

An Asterisk (*) at the beginning of an entry indicates that the title is appearing in BIP for the first time.

47

Acts & Resolutions of the General Council of the Choctaw Nation, Passed at Its Regular Session, 1902 & Extra Session, 1902. LC 73-88771. (Constitutions & Laws of the American Indian Tribes Ser. 2: Vol. 17). 1973. reprint ed. lib. bdg. 9.00 (0-8420-1711-9) Scholarly Res Inc.

Acts & Resolutions of the General Council of the Choctaw Nation, Passed at Its Regular Session, 1904. Bd. with Acts & Resolutions of the General Council of the Choctaw Nation, Passed at Its Extraordinary & Regular Sessions, 1905. LC 75-3693. LC 75-3693. (Constitutions & Laws of the American Indian Tribes Ser. 2: Vol. 26). 1975. reprint ed. 14.00 (0-8420-1884-0) Scholarly Res Inc.

Acts & Resolutions of the General Council of the Choctaw Nation, Passed at Its Extraordinary & Regular Sessions, 1905 see Acts & Resolutions of the General Council of the Choctaw Nation, Passed at Its Regular Session, 1904

Acts & Resolutions of the National Council of the Muskogee Nation of 1893. LC 75-3696. (Constitutions & Laws of the American Indian Tribes Ser. 2: Vol. 29). 1975. reprint ed. 11.00 (0-8420-1887-5) Scholarly Res Inc.

Acts & Resolutions of the National Council of the Muskogee Nation of 1893 & 1899, Inclusive. LC 75-3697. (Constitutions & Laws of the American Indian Tribes Ser. 2: Vol. 30). 1975. reprint ed. 12.00 (0-8420-1888-3) Scholarly Res Inc.

Acts & Romans. Albert Barnes. 1885. 32.99 (0-8010-0844-1) Baker Bk.

***Acts & Romans.** (Quick Studies). (Illus.). (YA). (gr. 9-12). Date not set. 16.95 (0-7814-0026-0, 78469) Cook.

Acts, Catholic Epistles & Revelation. William Kelly. (Introductory Lecture Ser.). 580p. 7.95 (0-88172-096-8) Believers Bkshelf.

Acts for Our Times: A Study of the Acts of the Apostles. Charles Yrigoyen, Jr. (Abingdon's Lay Bible Studies). 112p. (Orig.). 1992. pap. 6.95 (0-687-00771-2) Abingdon.

Acts in Action, Vol. 1. Gordon Lindsay. (Book of Acts Ser.). 1979. pap. 1.95 (0-89985-962-3) Christ for the Nations.

Acts in Prayer. E. W. Price. LC 74-15278. 1974. pap. 0.99 (0-8054-9209-7) Broadman.

Acts (New International Version) large type ed. write for info. (0-318-68639-2, 5020) LBW.

Acts of Abuse: Sex Offenders & the Criminal Justice System. Adam Sampson. LC 93-17215. 1994. write for info. (0-415-07372-3); pap. write for info. (0-415-07373-1) Routledge.

Acts of Andrew in the Country of the Cannibals: Translations from the Greek, Latin, & Old English. Robert Boenig. LC 90-19952. (Library of Medieval Literature: Vol. 70B). 176p. 1991. 22.00 (0-8240-7088-7) Garland.

Acts of Apostles: Building Faith Communities. Leonard Doohan. LC 93-47959. (Scripture for Worship & Education Ser.). 240p. 1994. 14.95 (0-89390-292-6) Resource Pubns.

Acts of Apostles: Leader's Guide. Leonard Doohan. (Scripture for Worship & Education Ser.). 48p. (Orig.). 1994. teacher ed 6.95 (0-89390-300-0) Resource Pubns.

Acts of Attention: The Poems of D. H. Lawrence. 2nd ed. Sandra M. Gilbert. LC 89-11265. 396p. (C). 1990. pap. 16.95 (0-8093-1599-8) S Ill U Pr.

Acts of Betrayal. John Trenhaile. 1992. mass mkt. 5.99 (0-06-109983-X, Harp PBks) HarpC.

Acts of Compassion: Caring for Others & Helping Ourselves. Robert Wuthnow. 263p. 1991. text ed. 35.00 (0-691-07390-2) Princeton U Pr.

Acts of Compassion: Caring for Others & Helping Ourselves. Robert Wuthnow. 346p. 1993. pap. text ed. 14.95 (0-691-02493-6) Princeton U Pr.

Acts of Contrition. John Cooney. 368p. 1991. 20.00 (0-517-57677-5, Crown) Crown Pub Group.

Acts of Contrition. John Cooney. 1994. mass mkt. 5.99 (0-671-78316-5) PB.

Acts of Courage. Mary K. Donev & Stef Donev. (Hayes Adventure Ser.). (Illus.). 48p. (J). (gr. 5-9). 1985. pap. 5.95 (0-88625-091-9) Durkin Hayes Pub.

Acts of David II, 1329-71. Ed. by Bruce Webster. 550p. 1982. 60.00 (0-85224-395-2, Pub. by Edinburgh U Pr UK) Col U Pr.

Acts of Discovery: Visions of America in the Lewis & Clark Journals. Albert Furtwangler. LC 92-29916. 280p. 1993. 29.95 (0-252-02002-2) U of Ill Pr.

Acts of Faith. Erich Segal. 1993. mass mkt. 6.99 (0-553-56070-0) Bantam.

Acts of Faith. Iyanla Vanzant. 1993. pap. 9.00 (0-671-86416-5, Fireside) S&S Trade.

Acts of Faith. Rajiva Wijesinha. 181p. 1986. pap. 9.00 (81-7013-032-8, Pub. by Navrang) S Asia.

Acts of Faith. large type ed. Erich Segal. 1992. pap. 27.50 (0-385-42343-8) BDD LT Grp.

Acts of Faith. Hans Koning. LC 87-26338. 182p. 1993. reprint ed. 8.95 (0-942986-18-0) LongRiver Bks.

***Acts of Faith: A Memoir.** Faith A. McFadden. 274p. (Orig.). 1994. pap. 14.95 (0-89870-527-4) Ignatius Pr.

***Acts of Faith: Stories.** Ed. by Jane Mead & Reid Sherline. 180p. 1995. 18.95 (0-943221-25-0) Timken Pubs.

***Acts of Fiction: Resistance & Resolution from Sade to Baudelaire.** Scott Carpenter. LC 94-42527. (Illus.). 192p. 1995. 35.00 (0-271-01450-4) Pa St U Pr.

Acts of God: The Old Farmer's Almanac Unpredictable Guide to Weather & Natural Disasters. Ed. by Benjamin A. Watson. LC 92-42605. 1993. 20.00 (0-679-73794-4) Random.

Acts of God & Acts of Man: Recent Trends in Natural Disasters & Major Industrial Accidents. (Illus.). 65p. (Orig.). (C). 1993. pap. text ed. 35.00 (1-56806-371-7) Diane Pub.

Acts of God & the People, 1620-1730. Peter L. Rumsey. LC 86-19292. (Studies in Religion: No. 2). 181p. reprint ed. pap. 51.60 (0-8357-1761-5, 2070521) Bks Demand.

Acts of Hope: Creating Authority in Literature, Law & Politics. James B. White. (Illus.). 368p. 1994. 45.00 (0-685-72674-6); pap. 16.95 (0-685-72675-4) U Ch Pr.

Acts of Hope: Creating Authority in Literature, Law, & Politics. James B. White. LC 94-8877. 1994. 27.50 (0-226-89510-6) U Ch Pr.

***Acts of Hope: Creating Authority in Literature, Law & Politics.** James B. White. xvi, 322p. 1995. pap. 15.95x (0-226-89511-4) U Ch Pr.

Acts of Implication: Suggestion & Covert Meaning in the Works of Dryden, Swift, Pope & Austen. Irvin Ehrenpreis. (Beckman Lectures). 150p. 1981. 45.00 (0-520-04047-3) U CA Pr.

Acts of Inclusion: Studies Bearing on an Elementary Theory of Romanticism. Michael Cooke. LC 78-21909. (Illus.). 1979. 37.00 (0-300-02303-0) Yale U Pr.

Acts of Interpretation: The Text in Its Context. Ed. by Mary J. Carruthers & Elizabeth D. Kirk. LC 82-13148. 385p. 1982. 27.95 (0-937664-60-X) Pilgrim Bks OK.

Acts of Kindness: How to Join the Kindness Revolution. Hanoch McCarty & Melodee McCarty. 200p. (Orig.). 1994. pap. 10.00 (1-55874-295-6, 2956) Health Comm.

Acts of King Arthur & His Noble Knights. John Steinback. 1993. pap. 17.00 (0-374-52378-9, Noonday) FS&G.

Acts of Knowledge: Pope's Later Poems. Fredric V. Bogel. LC 78-75194. 248p. 1981. 35.00 (0-8387-2380-2) Bucknell U Pr.

Acts of Life. Tom T. Hall. LC 86-6998. 136p. 1986. 16.95 (0-938626-70-1); pap. 9.95 (0-938626-71-X) U of Ark Pr.

***Acts of Light: Emily Dickinson, Small ed.** Emily Dickinson et al. (Illus.). 168p. 1995. 18.95 (0-8212-2175-2) Bulfinch Pr.

Acts of Literature. Jacques Derrida. Ed. by Derek Attridge. 432p. 1991. 49.95 (0-415-90056-5, A2410, Routledge NY); pap. 16.95 (0-415-90057-3, A2414, Routledge NY) Routledge.

Acts of Love. Maureen Daly. LC 86-1863. 176p. (J). (gr. 7 up). 1986. pap. 12.95 (0-590-33873-0) Scholastic Inc.

Acts of Love. Maureen Daly. 192p. (YA). (gr. 7 up). 1987. pap. 2.75 (0-590-43631-7) Scholastic Inc.

Acts of Love. Deana James. 448p. 1992. mass mkt. 5.99 (0-8217-3985-9) Zebra.

***Acts of Love.** Roberta Latow. 400p. (Orig.). 1995. mass mkt. 5.50 (0-380-77415-1) Avon.

Acts of Love. Emily Listfield. 320p. 1994. 21.95 (0-670-85278-3, Viking) Viking Penguin.

***Acts of Love.** Emily Listfield. 384p. 1995. pap. 10.95 (0-14-023281-8, Penguin Bks) Viking Penguin.

Acts of Love. James McKinley. LC 87-708. 160p. 1987. 17.95 (0-932576-47-8); pap. 8.95 (0-932576-67-2) Breitenbush Bks.

Acts of Meaning. Jerome Bruner. LC 90-40485. 179p. 1990. text ed. 25.00 (0-674-00360-8) HUP.

Acts of Meaning. Jerome Bruner. (Jerusalem Lectures). 208p. 1992. pap. text ed. 10.95 (0-674-00361-6) HUP.

Acts of Mercy. Bill Pronzini & Barry N. Malzberg. 256p. 1985. reprint ed. pap. 2.95 (0-8439-2219-2) Dorchester Pub Co.

Acts of Mind: Conversations with Contemporary Poets. Richard Jackson. LC 82-4767. xi, 240p. 1983. pap. 16.50 (0-8173-0228-X) U of Ala Pr.

Acts of Murder. Jonathan Goodman. LC 92-37555. 1993. pap. 8.95 (0-8184-0570-8, L Stuart) Carol Pub Group.

Acts of Naming: The Family Plot in Fiction. Michael Ragussis. 256p. 1987. 42.00 (0-19-504070-8) OUP.

Acts of Our Being: A Reflection on Agency & Responsibility. Edward Pols. LC 81-16319. 248p. 1982. lib. bdg. 30.00x (0-87023-354-8) U of Mass Pr.

Acts of Parliament. Gavin Souter. (Illus.). 658p. 1988. 24.95 (0-522-84367-0) Intl Spec Bk.

Acts of Parliament Concerning Wales, 1714-1901. T. I. Jones. (History & Law Ser.: No. 17). 343p. 1959. 28.50 (0-7083-0101-0, Pub. by U of Wales UK) Bks Intl VA.

Acts of Passion. Deana James. 1992. mass mkt. 5.99 (0-8217-3713-9) Zebra.

Acts of Piety in the Early Church. Ed. by Everett Ferguson. LC 92-41588. (Studies in Early Christianity: Vol. 17). 392p. 1993. 62.00 (0-8153-1077-3) Garland.

Acts of Recovery: Essays on Culture & Politics. Jeffrey Hart. LC 89-40230. 256p. 1989. text ed. 30.00 (0-87451-504-1) U Pr of New Eng.

Acts of Regeneration: Allegory & Archetype in the Works of Norman Mailer. Robert J. Begiebing. LC 80-50416. 223p. reprint ed. pap. 63.60 (0-7837-2361-X, AU00426) Bks Demand.

Acts of Robert I, 1306-29. Ed. by A. A. Duncan. (Regesta Regum Scottorum Ser.: No. 5). 500p. 1987. 99.00 (0-85224-543-2, Pub. by Edinburgh U Pr UK) Col U Pr.

***Acts of Service: Spontaneity, Commitment, Tradition in the Nonscripted Theatre.** Jonathan Fox. LC 94-90366. 290p. (Orig.). 1994. pap. 23.00 (0-9642350-0-5) Tusitala.

Acts of Submission. Joie Cook. 28p. (Orig.). 1990. pap. 4.00 (0-916397-04-1) Manic D Pr.

Acts of Subversion. Liz McManus. 236p. (Orig.). 1991. pap. 12.95 (1-85371-124-1, Pub. by Poolbeg Pr IE) Dufour.

Acts of Supremacy: The British Empire & the Stage, 1790-1930. J. S. Bratton et al. LC 90-29087. (Studies in Imperialism). 240p. 1991. text ed. 59.95 (0-7190-2583-4, Pub. by Manchester Univ Pr UK) St Martin.

Acts of Teaching: How to Teach Writing. Joyce A. Carroll & Edward E. Wilson. (Illus.). 350p. 1993. pap. text ed. 30.00 (1-56308-039-7) Teacher Ideas Pr.

Acts of the Anti-Slavery Apostles. Parker Pillsbury. LC 76-82212. (Anti-Slavery Crusade in America Ser.). 1970. reprint ed. 43.95 (0-405-00651-9) Ayer.

Acts of the Anti-Slavery Apostles. Parker Pillsbury. LC 70-92758. 503p. 1969. reprint ed. text ed. 59.75 (0-8371-2183-3, PIA&, Negro U Pr) Greenwood.

Acts of the Apostles. William Barclay. 1993. pap. 22.00 (0-7152-0276-6) St Mut.

Acts of the Apostles. Charles W. Carter & Ralph Earle. pap. 10.99 (0-88019-050-7) Schmul Pub Co.

Acts of the Apostles. Ed. by E. Galbiati. (Illus.). 450p. 1988. pap. 4.50 (0-317-67454-4, SC0010) Pauline Bks.

Acts of the Apostles. Ed. by E. Galbiati-Mimep. (Illus.). (C). 1988. 39.00 (0-85439-098-7, Pub. by St Paul Pubns UK) St Mut.

Acts of the Apostles. Marshall I. Howard. (Old Testament Guides Ser.). (C). 1992. pap. 9.95 (1-85075-372-5, Pub. by Sheffield Acad UK) CUP Services.

Acts of the Apostles. Luke Johnson. (Sacra Pagina Ser.: No. 5). 600p. (Orig.). 1992. pap. text ed. 29.95 (0-8146-5807-5, M Glazier) Liturgical Pr.

Acts of the Apostles. I. Howard Marshall. (Tyndale New Testament Commentaries Ser.). (Orig.). 1980. pap. 9.99 (0-8028-1423-9) Eerdmans.

Acts of the Apostles. G. Campbell Morgan. 560p. 1924. 21.99 (0-8007-0000-7) Revell.

Acts of the Apostles. John W. Packer. (Cambridge Bible Commentary on the New English Bible, New Testament Ser.). (Orig.). (C). 1966. pap. 19.95 (0-521-09383-X) Cambridge U Pr.

Acts of the Apostles. Charles Ryrie. (Everyman's Bible Commentary Ser.). (C). 1967. pap. 7.99 (0-8024-2044-3) Moody.

Acts of the Apostles. Lester Sumrall. 114p. (C). 1986. pap. text ed. 10.00 (0-937580-92-9) LeSEA Pub Co.

Acts of the Apostles. Thomas Walker. LC 84-7854. 626p. 1984. 22.99 (0-8254-4020-3) Kregel.

Acts of the Apostles. Ellen G. White. 633p. 1911. 12.95 (0-8163-0033-X, 01092-6); pap. 9.50 (0-8163-0034-8, 01093-4) Pacific Pr Pub Assn.

Acts of the Apostles. rev. ed. William Neil. Ed. by Matthew Black. (New Century Bible Commentary Ser.). 272p. 1981. pap. 14.99 (0-8028-1904-4) Eerdmans.

Acts of the Apostles, 2 vols. in 1. J. A. Alexander. (Banner of Truth Geneva Series Commentaries). 498p. 1991. reprint ed. 34.95 (0-85151-309-3) Banner of Truth.

Acts of the Apostles, Pt. 1. Anthony L. Ash. LC 79-632639. 175p. 1984. 12.95 (0-915547-24-4) Abilene Christ U.

Acts of the Apostles, Pt. 2. Richard Oster. LC 79-63269. 180p. 1984. 12.95 (0-915547-25-2) Abilene Christ U.

Acts of the Apostles: Introduction, Translation & Commentary. French L. Arrington. 368p. 1988. 16.95 (0-913573-73-6) Hendrickson MA.

Acts of the Apostles: Life in Action. Roy L. Laurin. LC 85-8158. 408p. 1985. pap. 12.99 (0-8254-3127-1) Kregel.

Acts of the Apostles: Missionary Message of the New Testament. F. Townley Lord. 119p. 1946. 4.50 (0-87921-003-6) Attic Pr.

***Acts of the Apostles: When the Church Connects to Ultimate Power.** E. G. White. (Bible Study Companion Set Ser.: Vol. 4). 382p. (Orig.). (C). 1993. pap. 7.95 (1-883012-53-8) Remnant Pubns.

Acts of the Apostles see Daily Study Bible: New Testament

Acts of the Apostles - New Testament, No. 5. William S. Kurz & Robert J. Karris. LC 82-20872. (Collegeville Bible Commentary Ser.). (Illus.). 112p. (C). 1983. pap. 3.95 (0-8146-1305-5) Liturgical Pr.

Acts of the Apostles & the Letters of St. Paul. E. Ridley Lewis. (London Divinity Ser.). 160p. 1964. reprint ed. 6.50 (0-227-67519-3) Attic Pr.

Acts of the Apostles (Everyman's Bible Commentary) see Hechos de los Apostoles (Comentario Biblico Portavoz)

Acts of the Apostles, Pt. 1 see New Testament for Spiritual Reading

Acts of the Apostles, Pt. 2 see New Testament for Spiritual Reading

Acts of the Apostles, Vol. 1 see Calvin's New Testament Commentaries

Acts of the Apostles, Vol. 2 see Calvin's New Testament Commentaries

Acts of the Australian Parliament, 73 vols., Set. Australian Government Staff. 336.00 (0-409-48716-3) Butterworth Legal Pubs.

Acts of the Christian Martyrs. pap. 6.95 (0-89981-002-0) Eastern Orthodox.

Acts of the Holy Spirit. write for info. (1-56441-023-4) M Hickey Min.

Acts of the Holy Spirit. A. T. Pierson. 127p. 1980. pap. 3.99 (0-87509-274-8) Chr Pubns.

Acts of the Martyrdom of St. Eudoxia. Tr. by J. A. Fastre. 1992. pap. 3.95 (0-89981-131-0) Eastern Orthodox.

Acts of the Pagan Martyrs. Ed. by W. R. Connor. LC 78-18588. (Greek Texts & Commentaries Ser.). 1979. reprint ed. lib. bdg. 27.95 (0-405-11430-3) Ayer.

Acts of the Tapestry Symposium. Ed. by Anna Bennett. LC 77-91645. (Illus.). 1979. pap. 15.00 (0-88401-031-7) Fine Arts Mus.

Acts of Theft. Arthur A. Cohen. (Phoenix Fiction Ser.). viii, 312p. 1987. pap. 9.95 (0-226-11250-0) U Ch Pr.

Acts of Union: Selected Poems 1974-1989. Nigel Jenkins. 144p. (C). 1990. pap. 21.00x (0-86383-529-5, Pub. by Gomer Pr UK) St Mut.

Acts of War. Richard Holmes. 1989. pap. 14.95 (0-02-914851-0) Free Pr.

Acts of War: The Behavior of Men in Battle. Richard Holmes. 420p. 1986. 27.95 (0-02-915020-5) Free Pr.

Acts of Will: The Life & Work of Otto Rank. E. James Lieberman. LC 84-21121. (Illus.). 485p. 1985. text ed. 32.95 (0-02-919020-7) Free Pr.

Acts of Will: The Life & Work of Otto Rank. 2nd ed. E. James Lieberman. LC 93-28227. (Illus.). 536p. 1993. reprint ed. pap. 18.95 (0-87023-871-X) U of Mass Pr.

Acts of Worship: Seven Stories. Yukio Mishima. 196p. (C). 1989. 17.95 (0-87011-937-0) Kodansha.

Acts of Worship: Seven Stories. Yukio Mishima. Tr. & Intro. by John Bester. 224p. 1995. reprint ed. pap. 9.00 (0-87011-824-2) Kodansha.

***Acts One-Fourteen Vol. 1.** C. K. Barrett. (International Critical Commentary Ser.). 720p. 1994. text ed. 64.95 (0-567-09653-X, Pub. by T & T Clark UK) Bks Intl VA.

Acts Story. G. Raymond Carlson. LC 78-57178. (Radiant Life Ser.). 128p. (Orig.). 1978. teacher ed 4.50 (0-88243-184-6, 32-0184); pap. 2.95 (0-88243-913-8, 02-0913) Gospel Pub.

Acts to Second Corinthians: Acts to Philemon see Numerical Bible

Acts Two: Thirty-Eight. Bob L. Ross. 1976. pap. 2.95 (1-56186-503-6) Pilgrim Pubns.

Acts Without Words, I & II, Mimes see Krapp's Last Tape & Other Dramatic Pieces

Acts Word Puzzles. John H. Tiner. (Illus.). 48p. (J). 1986. pap. 2.95 (1-56794-040-4, C2300) Star Bible.

Acts: Working Together in Christ's Mission see Hechos: Colaborando en la Mision de Cristo

Acts 1-12. John MacArthur, Jr. (MacArthur New Testament Commentary Ser.). 1994. 19.99 (0-8024-0759-5) Moody.

Acts 1-12: God Moves in the Early Church. rev. ed. Chuck Christensen & Winnie Christensen. (Fisherman Bible Studyguide Ser.). 68p. 1979. 4.99 (0-87788-007-7) Shaw Pubs.

Acts 1-9. Verlyn Verbrugge. (Five on One Intensive Bible Studies). 91p. (Orig.). (C). 1989. teacher ed 9.95 (0-930265-63-7); student ed, pap. text ed. 5.25 (0-930265-58-0) CRC Pubns.

Acts 10-18. Verlyn Verbrugge. (Five on One Intensive Bible Studies). 91p. (Orig.). (C). 1989. teacher ed 9.95 (0-930265-64-5); student ed, pap. text ed. 5.25 (0-930265-59-9) CRC Pubns.

Acts 19-28. Verlyn Vebrugge. (Five on One Intensive Bible Studies). 95p. (Orig.). (C). 1989. teacher ed 9.95 (0-930265-65-3); student ed, pap. text ed. 5.25 (0-930265-60-2) CRC Pubns.

Actual & Potential Use of Laboratory Schools in State Normal Schools & Teachers Colleges. Edward I. Williams. (Columbia University. Teachers College. Contributions to Education Ser.: No. 846). reprint ed. 37.50 (0-404-55846-1) AMS Pr.

***Actual Experience of a CEO: How to Make Continuous Improvement in Manufacturing Succeed for Your Company.** Hank McHale. 1995. 24.00 (0-87389-329-8) ASQC Qual Pr.

Actual Malice: Twenty-Five Years after Times vs. Sullivan. W. Wat Hopkins. LC 88-32475. 226p. 1989. text ed. 55.00 (0-275-93246-X, C3246, Praeger Pubs) Greenwood.

Actual Minds, Possible Words. Jerome Bruner. LC 85-27297. 215p. 1987. pap. text ed. 12.00 (0-674-00366-7) HUP.

Actual Minds, Possible Worlds. Jerome Bruner. (Jerusalem Lectures). 192p. 1990. 29.95 (0-674-00365-9) HUP.

Actual Problems in Paediatric Surgery. Tibor Verebely. 332p. 1983. 182.00 (0-569-08764-3, Pub. by Collets UK) Pro-Am Music.

Actual Standing in EPH Gestosis: Proceedings of the Meeting of the Society for the Study of Pathophysiology of Pregnancy-Organization Gestosis, 16th, Aachen, 15-18 June, 1984. Ed. by C. Goecke. (International Congress Ser.: No. 657). 504p. 1985. 156.00 (0-444-80656-3, Excerpta Medica) Elsevier.

Actual Trends in Thyroid Physiopathology. Ed. by T. Lemarchand-Beraud & L. Vanhaelst. (Journal: Hormone Research: Vol. 26, No. 1-4, 1987). ii, 230p. 1987. 155.25 (3-8055-4582-7) S Karger.

Actual Type - Determining Who You Really Are. Terence Duniho. 32p. 1993. pap. text ed. 5.95 (1-878287-32-X, BDAA) Type & Temperament.

Actualidad del Quijote y Otros Ensayos. Ismael Reyes-Garcia. LC 83-21679. (UPREX, Ensayo Ser.: No. 66). 121p. (Orig.). (SPA.). 1984. pap. 3.00 (0-8477-0066-6) U of PR Pr.

Actualist Anthology. Ed. by Morty Sklar & Darrell Gray. LC 77-81513. (Contemporary Anthology Ser.: No. 1). (Illus.). 144p. (C). 1977. 10.00 (0-930370-03-1); pap. 5.00 (0-930370-02-3) Spirit That Moves.

Actuality & Provisionality: Eternity & Election in the Theology of Karl Barth. John E. Colwell. LC 92-5142. (Rutherford Studies in Contemporary Theology). 470p. 1992. reprint ed. 109.95 (0-7734-1639-0) E Mellen.

Actuality of Walter Benjamin. Ed. by Laura Marcus & Linda Nead. (New Formations Ser.: No. 20). 176p. (C). 1993. pap. 19.95 (0-85315-761-8, Pub. by Lawrence & Wishart UK) Humanities.

Actualization & Interpretation in the Old Testament. Joseph W. Groves. LC 86-13926. (Society of Biblical Literature Dissertation Ser.). 255p. 1987. pap. 14.95 (0-89130-966-7) Scholars Pr GA.

Actualizations: You Don't Have to Rehearse to Be Yourself. Stewart Emery. Ed. by Neal Rogin. 237p. (C). 1980. reprint ed. 18.95 (0-8290-0222-7); reprint ed. pap. 6.95 (0-8290-0965-5) Irvington.

Actualizing Therapy: Foundations for a Scientific Ethic. Everett L. Shostrom. Ed. by Lila Knapp & Robert R. Knapp. LC 75-17255. 1976. text ed. 16.00 (0-912736-14-3) EDITS Pubs.

An Asterisk (*) at the beginning of an entry indicates that the title is appearing in BIP for the first time.

Actually, I Used to Be a Princess. Unada. 32p. (J). (gr. k-3). pap. 2.99 (0-87406-659-X) Willowisp Pr.

Actuarial Clerk. Jack Rudman. (Career Examination Ser.: C-2417). 1994. pap. 23.95 (0-8373-2417-3) Nat Learn.

Actuarial Fundamentals for Multiemployer Plans. 2nd ed. Daniel F. McGinn. Ed. by Mary J. Brzezinski. LC 92-72176. 187p. (Orig.). 1992. pap. 39.00 (0-89154-439-9) Intl Found Employ.

Actuarial Issues in the Fee-for-Service Prepaid Medical Group. 2nd ed. Harry L. Sutton, Jr. & Allen J. Sorbo. (Going Prepaid Ser.). (Orig.). (C). 1993. pap. 31.00 (0-933948-33-6, 3296) Ctr Res Ambulatory.

Actuarial Mathematics. Newton L. Bowers, Jr. et al. LC 86-61747. 650p. 1986. text ed. 65.00 (0-938959-10-7) Soc Actuaries.

Actuarial Mathematics. Ed. by H. Panjer. LC 86-3306. (Proceedings of Symposia in Applied Mathematics Ser.: Vol. 35). 127p. 1990. reprint ed. pap. 29.00 (0-8218-0096-5, PSAPM-35) Am Math.

Actuarial Practice of Life Assurance. H. F. Fisher & J. Young. (C). 1965. 90.00 (0-685-33805-3, Pub. by Witherby & Co UK) St Mut.

Actuarial Projections for the Old-Age, Survivors & Disability Insurance Program of Social Security in the United States of America. George H. Andrews & John A. Beekman. LC 87-1101. (Illus.). 188p. 1987. text ed. 25.00 (0-9623118-1-2) Acturarial Education.

Actuarial Refunds Table. Financial Publishing Co. Staff. 200p. 1984. pap. 15.00 (0-87600-840-6) Finan Pub.

Actuarial Values Alpha Volume: Remainder, Income & Annuity Factors for One-Life, Two-Lives & Term Certains; Interest Rates from 2.2 Percent to 26.0 Percent. (Internal Revenue Service Publications: No. 1457). 803p. 1989. pap. 32.00 (0-16-004708-0, S/N 048-004-02287-7) USGPO.

Actuarial Values, Beta Volume: Unitrust Remainder Factors for One Life, Two Lives & Term Certain; Adjusted Payout Rates from 2.2 Percent to 26.0 Percent. (Internal Revenue Service Publications: No. 1458). 527p. 1989. per. 29.00 (0-16-004709-9, S/N 048-004-02288-5) USGPO.

Actuarial Values, Gamma Volume: Tables for Computation of Depreciation Adjustment Factors, Interest Rates from 2.2 Percent to 26.0 Percent, for Income Tax Purposes Only. (Internal Revenue Service Publications: No. 1459). 124p. 1989. per. 6.00 (0-16-004710-2, S/N 048-004-02289-3) USGPO.

Actuaries, 1989: The Ivanhoe Guide. Witherby's Editorial Staff. (C). 1989. 60.00 (0-685-33804-5, Pub. by Witherby & Co UK) St Mut.

Actuary. Jack Rudman. (Career Examination Ser.: C-7). 1994. pap. 39.95 (0-8373-0007-X) Nat Learn.

Actuary in Practice, Tolley's. Chris Long. (C). 1989. 150.00 (0-685-33803-7, Pub. by Witherby & Co UK) St Mut.

Actuellement. D. Barnes. (C). 1990. student ed 80.00 (0-7487-0126-5, Pub. by S Thornes Pubs UK); teacher ed 175.00 (0-7487-0127-3, Pub. by S Thornes Pubs UK); audio 88.00 (0-685-38650-3, Pub. by S Thornes Pubs UK) St Mut.

Actuelles: Ecrits Politiques. Albert Camus. (FRE.). 1977. pap. 10.95 (0-7859-2847-2) Fr & Eur.

***Acu-Impulsor Therapy: Treatment with Piezoelectric Impulses.** Peter Mandel. Tr. by Christopher Baker & Judith Harrison. (Illus.). 190p. 1988. text ed. 59.00 (3-925806-11-3) Medicina Bio.

ACU-Yoga: Self Help Techniques to Relieve Tension. Michael Gach & Carolyn Marco. (Illus.). (Orig.). 1981. pap. 15.00 (0-87040-489-X) Japan Pubns USA.

ACUAR AALTO Guide. Michael Trencher. (Illus.). 228p. (Orig.). 1995. pap. 19.95 (0-910413-55-X) Princeton Arch.

Acuara Ochun de Caracoles Verdes: Poemas de un Caiman Presente: (Canto a mi Habana) Jose Sanchez-Boudy. LC 87-81614. (Coleccion Espejo de Paciencia Ser.). 46p. (Orig.). (SPA.). 1987. pap. 5.00 (0-89729-449-1) Ediciones.

Acuario: Astro-Numerogia. Michael J. Kurban. Tr. by Loretta H. Kurban. LC 86-91277. (Illus.). (Orig.). (SPA.). 1992. pap. 8.00 (0-938863-55-X) Libra Press Chi.

Acuenergy. Patti Lloyd. 208p. 1982. 12.95 (0-89557-060-2) Woodland UT.

Acumen: Educational Version 2.0, 3.5. Acumen International Staff. (C). 1991. pap. text ed. write for info. (0-13-005786-X) P-H.

***Acumen's Threshold.** Philip H. Franck. 240p. 1995. pap. 8.95 (1-56901-743-3) NW Pub.

Acumoxa Therapy: Reference & Study Guide. Paul Zmiewski. Ed. by Richard Felt. 208p. (Orig.). 1989. pap. 19.95 (0-912111-22-4) Paradigm Publns.

Acumoxa Therapy, Vol. 2: Treatment of Disease. Paul Zmiewski & Richard Feit. 160p. (Orig.). (C). 1990. pap. 17.95 (0-912111-27-5) Paradigm Publns.

Acupinch Cramp Relief...in Seconds. Milton F. Allen. (Illus.). 64p. 1981. pap. 1.95 (0-9607456-0-2) Acupinch.

***Acupressure.** Eliana Harvey & Mary J. Oatley. (Headway Lifeguides Ser.). (Illus.). 128p. 1995. pap. 13.95 (0-340-61106-5, Pub. by Hodder & Stoughton Ltd UK) Trafalgar.

Acupressure for Athletes. 2nd rev. ed. David J. Nickel. LC 86-12097. (Illus.). 176p. 1987. pap. 10.95 (0-8050-0128-X, Owl) H Holt & Co.

Acupressure for Common Ailments: A Gaia Original. Chris Jarmey & John Tindall. (Illus.). 96p. (Orig.). 1991. pap. 11.95 (0-671-73135-1, Fireside) S&S Trade.

Acupressure for Everybody: Gentle, Effective Techniques for Healing & Relaxing. Cathryn Bauer. 160p. (Orig.). 1991. pap. 11.95 (0-8050-1579-5, Owl) H Holt & Co.

Acupressure for Health. Jacqueline Young. (Illus.). 144p. 1994. pap. 12.00 (0-7225-2702-0) Thorsons SF.

Acupressure for the Boater: Alternative Emergency Medical Procedures. Michael Friedman. Ed. by Liz Jacobsen. (Illus.). 43p. (Orig.). 1983. pap. 4.95 (0-912561-01-7) Counsel & Stress.

Acupressure for the Boater & Backpacker. Michael Friedman. (Illus.). 43p. (Orig.). 1989. pap. 16.95 (0-912561-09-2) Counsel & Stress.

***Acupressure for the Soul.** Nancy Fallon. 150p. (Orig.). 1993. pap. 11.95 (0-929385-49-7) Light Tech Comns Servs.

Acupressure for Women. Cathryn Bauer. LC 87-5440. (Well-Woman Ser.). 1987. pap. 8.95 (0-89594-232-1) Crossing Pr.

Acupressure for Your Beauty & Health: Magic at the Tips of Your Fingers. Andrew Kim. (Illus.). 32p. (Orig.). 1988. pap. 3.95 (0-317-92302-1) Kims Pub.

Acupressure Handbook. M. Blate. 216p. 1977. pap. 9.95 (0-8050-0146-8) H Holt & Co.

Acupressure Techniques. Julian Kenyon. (Illus.). 128p. 1987. pap. 10.95 (0-89281-280-X, Heal Arts VT) Inner Tradit.

Acupressure Warmup: A System of Athletic Preparation & Injury Prevention. Marc Coseo. Ed. by Robert L. Felt. (Illus.). 144p. (Orig.). 1992. pap. 16.95 (0-912111-34-8) Paradigm Publns.

Acupressure Way of Health: Jin Shin Do. Iona M. Teeguarden. (Illus.). (Orig.). 1978. pap. 14.00 (0-87040-421-0) Japan Pubns USA.

Acupressure's Potent Points: A Guide to Self-Care for Common Ailments. Michael R. Gach. 1990. 15.95 (0-553-34970-8) Bantam.

Acupuncture. Michael Nightingale. (Alternataive Health Ser.). (Illus.). 128p. (Orig.). 1994. pap. 12.95 (0-8048-3004-5) C E Tuttle.

Acupuncture. G. Stux. 360p. 1987. 96.00 (0-387-17331-5) Spr-Verlag.

Acupuncture. rev. ed. Felix Mann. (Illus.). 192p. 1973. pap. 8.00 (0-394-71727-9, Vin) Random.

Acupuncture. 2nd ed. Felix Mann. LC 92-20085. 1992. pap. 22.50 (0-7506-0700-9) Buttrwrth-Heinemann.

Acupuncture: A Comprehensive Text. Shanghai College of Traditional Medicine Staff. Ed. by John O'Connor & Dan Bensky. Tr. by Dan Bensky. LC 81-65416. (Illus.). 741p. 1981. 65.00 (0-939616-00-9) Eastland.

Acupuncture: A Source Guide. 1991. lib. bdg. 250.00 (0-8490-4884-2) Gordon Pr.

Acupuncture: A Viable Medical Alternative. Marie Cargill. LC 94-12069. 200p. 1994. pap. text ed. 12.95 (0-275-94881-1, Praeger Pubs) Greenwood.

Acupuncture: An International Bibliography. Billy K. Tam & Mariam S. Tam. LC 73-5772. 137p. 1973. 20.00 (0-8108-0625-8) Scarecrow.

Acupuncture: How It Works, How It Cures. Peter Firebrace & Sandra Hill. 1994. 19.95 (0-87983-639-3) Keats.

Acupuncture: Is It for You? J. R. Worsley. (Illus.). 128p. 1991. pap. 11.95 (1-85230-047-7) Element MA.

Acupuncture - Art & Science: Index of Modern Authors & Subjects with Guide for Rapid Research. Stanley X. Garrett. LC 90-56288. 160p. 1991. 44.50 (1-55914-384-3); pap. 39.50 (1-55914-385-1) ABBE Pubs Assn.

Acupuncture Anesthesia. First Hospital, Shanghai, People's Republic of China et al. (Illus.). 1975. 30.00 (0-916524-00-0) US Direct Serv.

***Acupuncture, Art & Science: Index of Modern Authors & Subjects with Guide for Rapid Research.** Stanley X. Garrett. LC 94-35175. 1994. pap. text ed. write for info. (0-7883-0359-7) ABBE Pubs Assn.

***Acupuncture, Art & Science: Index of Modern Authors & Subjects with Guide for Rapid Research.** Stanley X. Garrett. LC 94-35175. 1994. write for info. (0-7883-0358-9) ABBE Pubs Assn.

Acupuncture Case Histories from China. Ed. by Jirui Chen & Nissi Wang. (Illus.). 300p. 1988. text ed. 35.00 (0-939616-07-6) Eastland.

Acupuncture Certification Examination Review Book of Questions & Answers. Ralph A. Dale. 87p. 1985. student ed, spiral bd. 25.00 (1-877589-03-9) Dialectic Pubns.

Acupuncture Comprehensive Prescription Index, Vol. II. Ralph A. Dale. (Illus.). 550p. 1991. 125.00 (1-877589-05-5) Dialectic Pubns.

Acupuncture Directory. (Orig.). 1974. pap. 2.50 (0-914322-00-1) Chans Corp.

Acupuncture, Electropuncture Anaesthesia. Pedro Chan. pap. 2.95 (0-87505-149-9) Borden.

Acupuncture Energetics. Mark Seem. (Illus.). 144p. (Orig.). (C). 1987. pap. 14.95 (0-89281-435-7) Inner Tradit.

Acupuncture Energetics: Classification & Treatment of Disease in Traditional Chinese Medicine. Nguyen Van Nghi. Tr. by Mark D. Seem. (Illus.). 1000p. (Orig.). 1983. 75.00 (0-910263-00-0) Raiko.

Acupuncture for Animals. Sheldon Altman. 300p. 25.00 (0-317-31551-X) Chans Corp.

Acupuncture for the Practitioner. Luc De Schepper. LC 85-90075. (Medical Sciences, General Medicine Ser.). (Illus.). 328p. (Orig.). 1985. 39.95 (0-9614734-0-1) LDS Pubns.

Acupuncture Imaging: A Guide for Practitioners & Their Patients. Mark Seem. (Illus.). 96p. 1991. 16.95 (0-89281-375-X) Inner Tradit.

***Acupuncture in Clinical Practice.** N. Ellis. 336p. 1994. 37.99 (1-56593-179-3, 0494) Singular Publishing.

Acupuncture in Gynaecology & Obstetrics. Royston Low. 1990. 14.95 (0-7225-2108-1) Thorsons SF.

Acupuncture in Holistic Practice: Selected Journal Articles, 1975-1993, Vol. V. Ralph A. Dale. (Illus.). 1984. 125.00 (1-877589-08-X) Dialectic Pubns.

Acupuncture in Practice. Luc De Schepper. (Illus.). 350p. (Orig.). (C). 1994. pap. 39.95 (0-942501-03-9) Full of Life.

Acupuncture in the Treatment of Children. rev. ed. Julian Scott. LC 91-71899. (Illus.). 275p. (C). 1991. text ed. 45.00 (0-939616-13-0) Eastland.

Acupuncture Is & Is Not. Pedro Chan. (Illus.). 1974. pap. 0.95 (0-914322-01-X) Chans Corp.

Acupuncture Made Easy. Tr. by Poul Hwang et al. (Illus.). 100p. 1975. text ed. 9.50 (0-685-01030-9); pap. text ed. 6.95 (0-685-01031-7) Chans Corp.

Acupuncture Manual & Comprehensive Five Element Index, Vol. I. Ralph A. Dale. (Illus.). 1984. 125.00 (1-877589-04-7) Dialectic Pubns.

Acupuncture, Meridian Theory & Acupuncture Points. Li Ding. Tr. by You Benlin & Wang Zhaorong. (Illus.). 414p. (C). 1992. reprint ed. text ed. 60.00 (0-8351-2143-7) China Bks.

Acupuncture Patterns & Practice. Li Xuemei & Zhao Jingyi. LC 92-85309. (Illus.). 205p. 1993. text ed. 35.00 (0-939616-16-5) Eastland.

***Acupuncture Point Combinations: The Key to Clinical Success.** Jeremy Ross. LC 94-43497. 1995. write for info. (0-443-05006-6) Churchill.

Acupuncture Points: Images & Functions. Arnie Lade. LC 88-82703. 363p. (C). 1989. text ed. 29.50 (0-939616-08-4) Eastland.

Acupuncture Points & Meridians in the Dog. Luc A. Janssens. 1984. 60.00 (0-317-44766-1) Intl Vet Acup.

Acupuncture, the Ancient Chinese Art of Healing. Felix Mann. (Illus.). 19.50 (0-8446-4583-4) Peter Smith.

Acupuncture Treatment. Shin Hak Pang. LC 73-92157. (Illus.). 1973. 6.95 (0-914524-00-3) Dong Nam P & C.

Acupuncture Treatment of Pain: Safe & Effective Methods for Using Acupuncture in Pain Relief. Leon Chaitow. 192p. (Orig.). 1990. pap. text ed. 19.95 (0-89281-383-0) Inner Tradit.

Acupuncture with Your Fingers: An 18-Point Healing System. rev. ed. Ralph A. Dale. (Illus.). 55p. 1992. pap. 6.75 (1-877589-01-2) Dialectic Pubns.

Acupuncture with Your Fingers: An 18-Point Healing System. 6th rev. ed. Ralph A. Dale. (Illus.). 55p. 1992. 12.00 (1-877589-00-4) Dialectic Pubns.

Acupuncture Without Needles. J. V. Cerney. 1986. 6.95 (0-13-003848-2) P-H.

Acupuncturist's Business Management Guide, Vol. 4: Patient Communication, Public Relations & Marketing. Cynthia F. Bestani & Peter G. Fernandez. 1990. 39.75 (0-944876-21-8) Focus Practice.

Acupuncturist's Front Office Procedure: The Training & Reference Manual. Cynthia F. Bestani & Peter G. Fernandez. (Acupuncturist's Business Management Guide Ser.: Vol. II). 1988. 38.50 (0-944876-19-6) Focus Practice.

Acupuntura con Sus Dedos: Un Sistema Curativo de Dieciocho Puntos. rev. ed. Ralph A. Dale. Tr. by Ronald Lorenzana. (Illus.). 55p. (Orig.). (SPA.). 1993. pap. 6.75 (1-877589-02-0) Dialectic Pubns.

Acura, 1986-93. Ed. by Chilton Staff. 880p. 1994. pap. 21.95 (0-8019-8426-2) Chilton.

Acute Abdominal Syndromes: Their Diagnosis & Treatment According to Combined Chinese-Western Medicine. Alan Marcus. LC 91-77707. 161p. (Orig.). 1991. pap. text ed. 16.95 (0-936185-31-7) Blue Poppy.

Acute Alcoholic Intoxication: A Critical Review. Henry W. Newman. x, 207p. 1941. 29.50 (0-8047-0995-5) Stanford U Pr.

***Acute Alcoholic Intoxication: A Critical Review.** fac. ed. Henry W. Newman. LC 41-28278. 111p. 1941. reprint ed. pap. 30.00 (0-7837-7919-4, 2047675) Bks Demand.

Acute & Chronic Renal Failure. M. Boulton-Jones. (Topics in Renal Disease Ser.). 116p. 1981. lib. bdg. 23.00 (0-85200-420-6) Kluwer Ac.

Acute & Secretory Otitis Media. Ed. by J. Sade. LC 86-20940. (Illus.). 574p. 1986. lib. bdg. 140.00 (90-6299-023-1, Pub. by Kugler NE) Kugler Pubns.

Acute & Sub-Acute Toxicology. Vernon K. Brown. (Illus.). (C). 1992. pap. 22.95 (0-521-42757-6) Cambridge U Pr.

Acute Aneurysm Surgery. K. Sano et al. (Illus.). 300p. 1987. 147.00 (0-387-81987-8) Spr-Verlag.

***Acute Cardiac Care: Community & Hospital Management of Myocardial Infarction.** Kevin Jennings. (Illus.). 226p. 1994. pap. 35.00 (0-19-263006-7) OUP.

Acute Care: Based on the Proceedings of the Sixth International Symposium on Critical Care Medicine, Rio De Janeiro, 1977. Ed. by B. M. Tavares. (Anaesthesiologie & Intensivmedizin Ser.: Vol. 116). (Illus.). 1979. pap. 61.00 (0-387-09210-2) Spr-Verlag.

***Acute Care (Alternative Site) Makers.** 155p. (Orig.). 1995. pap. 1,295.00 (0-7605-2296-0) Rector Pr.

Acute Care Hospital Challenge: Product Line Management, Matrix Management or Functional Management...Its Implications for the Future of Addication Treatment. Ronald J. Hunsicker. LC 92-80717. 70p. (C). 1992. pap. text ed. write for info. (0-9632545-0-2) The Terraces.

Acute Care Nursing in the Home: A Holistic Approach. Malloy & Hartshorn. (Illus.). 606p. 1988. text ed. 36.50 (0-397-54661-0) Lippincott.

***Acute Catabolic State.** A. Revhaug. 320p. 1995. 128.00 (3-540-58445-5) Spr-Verlag.

***Acute Catabolic State.** Ed. by A. Revhaug. LC 95-10442. (Update Intensive Care & Emergency Medicine Ser.: Vol. 21). 1995. write for info. (0-387-58445-5) Spr-Verlag.

Acute Cervical Spinal Column & Cord Injury. David A. Herz & Janice E. Looman. Ed. by Oliver D. Grin & Dorothy L. Bouwman. (Patient Education Ser.). (Illus.). 22p. (Orig.). 1990. pap. text ed. 3.00 (0-929689-38-0) Ludann Co.

Acute Childhood Leukemia. Ed. by C Pochedly. (Modern Problems in Pediatrics Ser.: Vol. 16). (Illus.). viii, 214p. 1975. 75.25 (3-8055-2065-4) S Karger.

Acute Cocaine Intoxication: Current Methods of Treatment. 1994. lib. bdg. 256.95 (0-8490-9040-7) Gordon Pr.

Acute Continuous Renal Replacement Therapy. Ed. by Emil P. Paganini. (Developments in Nephrology Ser.). (C). 1986. lib. bdg. 80.50 (0-89838-793-0) Kluwer Ac.

Acute Coronary Care in the Thrombolytic Era. Califf. 790p. 1988. 72.00 (0-8151-1416-8, Yr Bk Med Pubs) Mosby Yr Bk.

Acute Coronary Care in the Thrombolytic Era. 2nd ed. Califf. 528p. 1993. 78.00 (0-8016-6753-4) Mosby Yr Bk.

Acute Coronary Care, 1986. Ed. by Robert M. Califf & Galen S. Wagner. 1985. lib. bdg. 88.50 (0-89838-762-0) Kluwer Ac.

Acute Coronary Care, 1987. Ed. by Robert M. Califf & Galen S. Wagner. 1986. lib. bdg. 118.50 (0-89838-842-2) Kluwer Ac.

Acute Diarrhea in Childhood. Ciba Foundation Staff. LC 76-13875. (Ciba Foundation Symposium: New Ser.: 42). 385p. reprint ed. pap. 109.80 (0-8357-5089-2, 2022170) Bks Demand.

Acute Diseases, Pts. I-II: Their Uniform Treatment by Natural Methods: Mental, Emotional & Psychic Disorders. H. Lindlahr. 54p. 1973. spiral bd. 5.50 (0-7873-0562-6) Mokelumne.

Acute Disorders of the Abdomen: Diagnosis & Treatment. V. Sreenivas. (Illus.). 150p. 1980. pap. 41.00 (0-387-90483-2) Spr-Verlag.

Acute Enteric Infections in Children: New Prospects for Treatment & Prevention. T. Holme et al. 550p. 1982. 207.75 (0-444-80328-9) Elsevier.

Acute Geriatric Medicine. M. D. Lye. LC 85-12727. (Modern Geriatric Medicine Ser.). 1985. lib. bdg. 78.00 (0-85200-801-5) Kluwer Ac.

***Acute Government: The Devil's Curse.** Macey Casebeer. 72p. 1995. pap. 19.95 (0-9645546-4-X) Calgold Pubns.

Acute Grief: Counseling the Bereaved. Ed. by Otto S. Margolis. LC 80-21020. (Foundation of Thanatology Ser.). 320p. 1981. text ed. 52.00 (0-231-04586-7) Col U Pr.

Acute Grief: Loss of an Adult Child. Otto S. Margolis. LC 87-18315. 208p. 1988. text ed. 55.00 (0-275-91304-X, C1304, Praeger Pubs) Greenwood.

Acute Head Injury. Ruth Garner. Ed. by Jo Campling. (Therapy in Practice Ser.: No. 13). 152p. 1990. pap. 23.00 (0-412-32420-2, A4419) Chapman & Hall.

Acute Heart Failure. Ed. by J. L. Vincent & C. Perret. (Update in Intensive Care & Emergency Medicine Ser.: Vol. 6). (Illus.). 430p. 1988. pap. 95.00 (0-387-19169-0) Spr-Verlag.

Acute Heart Failure in Intensive Care: A New Approach. Ed. by P. Foex & I. A. Davidson. (Journal: Cardiology: Vol. 77, Suppl. 3, 1990). (Illus.). iv, 68p. 1990. pap. 21.00 (3-8055-5255-6) S Karger.

Acute Hemorrhagic Conjunctivitis: Etiology, Epidemiology & Clinical Manifestations. Ed. by K. Ishii et al. (Illus.). xiv, 438p. 1989. 256.00 (3-8055-4997-0) S Karger.

Acute Leukemia: Approach to Diagnosis. Harold Schumacher. LC 89-24618. (Illus.). 312p. 1990. 78.00 (0-89640-170-7) Igaku-Shoin.

Acute Leukemias: Biologic, Diagnostic & Therapeutic Determinants. Stass. (Hematology Ser.: Vol. 6). 496p. 1987. 170.00 (0-8247-7766-2) Dekker.

Acute Leukemias - Pharmacokinetics: Pharmacokinetics & Management of Relapsed & Refractory Disease. Ed. by W. Hiddemann et al. (Illus.). 816p. 1992. pap. 198.00 (0-387-53949-2) Spr-Verlag.

Acute Leukemias 4: Prognostic Factors & Treatment Strategies. T. Buchner et al. LC 93-27989. (Haematology & Blood Transfusion Ser.: No. 36). 1993. 225.00 (0-387-56951-0) Spr-Verlag.

***Acute Low Back Problems in Adults.** 1995. lib. bdg. 251.95 (0-8490-6846-0) Gordon Pr.

Acute Medical Problems in the Post-Operative Patient. Ed. by George A. Porter. (Illus.). 224p. 1987. pap. 32.00 (0-443-08428-9) Churchill.

Acute Medicine: A Practical Guide. Ed. by D. Sprigings & J. B. Chambers. (Illus.). 416p. 1990. pap. 34.95 (0-632-02169-1, Blackwell Sci) Mosby Yr Bk.

***Acute Medicine: A Practical Guide to the Management of Medical Emergencies.** 2nd ed. David Springings et al. LC 94-3731. 1995. write for info. (0-632-03652-4) Blackwell Sci.

***Acute Medicine Algorithms.** Mervyn Singer & Andrew R. Webb. (Illus.). 184p. 1995. 57.50 (0-19-262460-1); pap. 29.95 (0-19-262459-8) OUP.

Acute Myocardial Infarction. Ed. by B. J. Gersh & S. H. Rahimtoola. (Current Topics in Cardiology Ser.: Vol. 1). 500p. 1990. 89.00 (0-444-01545-0) Elsevier.

Acute Myocardial Infarction. Ed. by David McCall. (Contemporary Management in Internal Medicine Ser.: Vol. 2, No. 2). (Illus.). 213p. 1992. text ed. 36.00 (0-443-08838-1) Churchill.

Acute Myocardial Infarction. Ed. by Carl J. Pepine. LC 70-6558. (Cardiovascular Clinics Ser.: Vol. 20, No. 1). (Illus.). 329p. (C). 1989. text ed. 75.00 (0-8036-6858-9) Davis Co.

Acute Myocardial Infarction: Emerging Concepts of Pathogenesis & Treatment. Ed. by Robert H. Cox. LC 88-27576. 218p. 1989. text ed. 69.50 (0-275-92438-6, C2438, Praeger Pubs) Greenwood.

Acute Myocardial Infarction: Setting Priorities for Effectiveness Research. Institute of Medicine Staff. 72p. (C). 1991. pap. text ed. 15.00 (0-309-04380-8) Natl Acad Pr.

An Asterisk (*) at the beginning of an entry indicates that the title is appearing in BIP for the first time. 49

A

Acute Myocardial Infarction (Heart Attack) Robert C. Davidson & Denise Busman. Ed. by Oliver D. Grin & Dorothy L. Bouwman. (Patient Education Ser.). (Illus.). 30p. (Orig.). 1992. pap. text ed. 3.00 (0-929689-47-X) Ludann Co.

Acute Neuroscience Nursing: Concepts & Care. Jane Lundgren. 400p. (C). 1986. 52.50 (0-86720-355-2) Jones & Bartlett.

Acute Non-Traumatic Intracranial Bleedings. B. P. Jensen et al. (Advances in Neurosurgery Ser.: Vol. 11). (Illus.). 430p. 1983. pap. 86.00 (0-387-12538-8) Spr-Verlag.

Acute Obstetrics: A Practical Guide. Martha C. Heppard. 325p. 1991. pap. 27.95 (0-8016-2147-X) Mosby Yr Bk.

Acute Pain: Mechanisms & Management. Ed. by Raymond S. Sinatra et al. LC 92-8611. 1992. 77.00 (0-8016-4677-4) Mosby Yr Bk.

Acute Pain Management. Ed. by Michael J. Cousins & Garry D. Phillips. (Clinics in Critical Care Medicine Ser.: Vol. 8). (Illus.). 300p. 1986. pap. 58.00 (0-443-08336-3) Churchill.

Acute Pain Management. Ed. by Michael J. Cousins & Garry D. Phillips. LC 85-22382. (Clinics in Critical Care Medicine Ser.). (Illus.). 318p. reprint ed. pap. 90.70 (0-7837-6822-2, 2046654) Bks Demand.

***Acute Pain Management: Operative or Medical Procedure & Trauma.** 1995. lib. bdg. 252.95 (0-8490-6802-9) Gordon Pr.

Acute Pain Management: Operative or Medical Procedures & Trauma. 1994. lib. bdg. 260.00 (0-8490-9032-6) Gordon Pr.

***Acute Pain Management: Operative or Medical Procedures & Trauma.** 1995. lib. bdg. 255.95 (0-8490-7575-0) Gordon Pr.

Acute Pain Management in Infants, Children & Adolescents: Operative & Medical Procedures. 1994. lib. bdg. 250.00 (0-8490-8541-1) Gordon Pr.

Acute Pancreatitis. AACN Staff. (Critical Care Nurse Educational Publication Ser.). 48p. 1993. 24.00 (0-8403-8673-7) Kendall-Hunt.

Acute Pancreatitis. Glazer. 1988. text ed. 121.00 (0-7020-1248-3) Saunders.

Acute Pancreatitis: Diagnosis & Therapy. Ed. by Edward L. Bradley, III. LC 93-24917. 320p. 1994. 131.50 (0-7817-0091-4) Raven.

Acute Paranoia. 80p. 10.00 (0-87431-034-2, 80105) West End Games.

Acute Peripheral Vascular Surgery. enl. rev. ed. M. Staudacher. LC 85-17328. (Illus.). 170p. 1985. 74.00 (0-387-81874-X) Spr-Verlag.

Acute Phase of Ischemic Heart Disease & Myocardial Infarction. A. J. Adgey. 1982. lib. bdg. 107.50 (90-247-2675-1) Kluwer Ac.

Acute Phase Proteins: Molecular Biology, Biochemistry, & Clinical Applications. Ed. by Andrzej Mackiewicz et al. 1993. 250.00 (0-8493-6913-4, RB131) CRC Pr.

Acute Phase Proteins in the Acute Phase Response. Ed. by M. B. Pepys. (Argenteuil Symposia Ser.). (Illus.). xviii, 210p. 1989. 96.00 (0-387-19582-3, 3483) Spr-Verlag.

Acute-Phase Response to Injury & Infection: The Roles of Interleukin One & Other Mediators. Ed. by A. H. Gordon et al. (Research Monographs in Cell & Tissue Physiology: Vol. 10). 1985. 165.25 (0-444-80648-2) Elsevier.

Acute Poisoning: Diagnosis & Management. 2nd ed. A. T. Proudfoot. 253p. 1993. pap. 45.00 (0-7506-1445-5) Buttrwrth-Heinemann.

Acute Problems in Resuscitation & Hypothermia: Proceedings of a Symposium on the Application of Deep Hypothermia in Terminal States, Sept. 15-19, 1964. Vladimir A. Negovskii. Tr. by Basil Haigh. LC 65-20214. 98p. reprint ed. pap. 28.00 (0-8357-5090-6, 2020667) Bks Demand.

Acute Psychiatric Care: An Occupational Therapy Guide to Exercises in Daily Living Skills. Patricia L. Simmons & Linda Mullins. LC 80-54633. 166p. 1981. pap. 25.00 (1-55642-210-5) SLACK Inc.

Acute Pulmonary Insufficiency: The Role of Haemostatic, Fibrinolytic & Related Mechanisms. Ed. by Tom Saldeen. (Illus.). viii, 147p. 1985. pap. 75.40 (3-11-010567-5) De Gruyter.

Acute Rejection of Liver Grafts. Ed. by G. Gubernatis. LC 93-15552. (Medical Intelligence Unit Ser.). 1993. 89.95 (1-879702-64-9) R G Landes.

Acute Renal Disorders & Renal Emergencies. Ed. by Jose Strauss. (Developments in Nephrology Ser.). 1984. lib. bdg. 88.50 (0-89838-663-2) Kluwer Ac.

Acute Renal Failure. Ed. by Vittorio E. Andreucci. 1984. lib. bdg. 178.00 (0-89838-627-6) Kluwer Ac.

Acute Renal Failure. Barry M. Brenner & J. Michael Lazarus. (Illus.). 837p. 1983. text ed. 155.00 (0-7216-1964-9) Saunders.

Acute Renal Failure. Ed. by D. Seybold & U. Gessler. (Illus.). viii, 268p. 1982. pap. 33.00 (3-8055-3579-1) S Karger.

Acute Renal Failure. 2nd ed. Ed. by Barry M. Brenner & J. Michael Lazarus. LC 87-22425. (Illus.). 967p. reprint ed. pap. 180.00 (0-7837-6260-7, 2045972) Bks Demand.

Acute Renal Failure. 3rd ed. J. Michael Lazarus & Barry M. Brenner. (Illus.). 632p. 1993. text ed. 119.95 (0-443-08792-X) Churchill.

Acute Renal Failure. Ed. by Barry M. Brenner & Jay H. Stein. LC 80-21863. (Contemporary Issues in Nephrology Ser.: No. 6). (Illus.). 308p. reprint ed. pap. 87.80 (0-8357-6575-X, 2035961) Bks Demand.

Acute Renal Failure: Clinical & Experimental. Ed. by Alberto Amerio et al. LC 87-7714. (Advances in Experimental Medicine & Biology Ser.: Vol. 212). 212p. 1987. 85.00 (0-306-42556-4, Plenum Pr) Plenum.

Acute Renal Failure: Correlations Between Morphology & Function. Ed. by Kim Solez & Andrew Whelton. LC 83-18818. (Kidney Disease Ser.: No. 4). (Illus.). 507p. reprint ed. pap. 144.50 (0-7837-0799-1, 2041113) Bks Demand.

Acute Renal Failure: Diagnosis & Treatment. 2nd ed. Ed. by Kim Solez & Lorraine C. Racusen. 536p. 1991. 150.00 (0-8247-8225-9) Dekker.

***Acute Renal Failure in the Critically Ill.** Ed. by R. Bellomo & C. Ronco. LC 94-42307. (Update in Intensive Care & Emergency Medicine Ser.: Vol. 20). 1995. 125.00 (3-540-58401-3) Spr-Verlag.

Acute Renal Insufficiency Made Ridiculously Simple. Carlos Rotellar. (Illus.). 56p. (Orig.). 1992. pap. text ed. 9.95 (0-940780-09-7) MedMaster.

Acute Respiratory Failure. Ed. by Roger C. Bone et al. (Illus.). 473p. 1987. 73.00 (0-443-08366-5) Churchill.

Acute Respiratory Infections: Laboratory Manual of Bacteriological Procedures. (Western Pacific Education in Action Ser.: No. 1). 152p. 1986. 12.00 (92-9061-131-6) World Health.

Acute Respiratory Infections in South-East Asia. (SEARO Technical Publications: No. 8). 58p. 1986. pap. 1.80 (92-9022-147-X) World Health.

Acute Revascularization of the Infarcted Heart. Reves. 112p. 1987. text ed. 41.95 (0-8089-1870-2, Grune) Saunders.

Acute Rheumatic & Immunological Disease: Management of the Critically Ill Patient. Mandell. 640p. 1994. 195.00 (0-8247-9125-8) Dekker.

Acute Stroke. Vladimir Hachinski & John W. Norris. LC 85-6880. (Contemporary Neurology Ser.: No. 27). (Illus.). 286p. 1985. 50.00 (0-8036-4502-3) Davis Co.

Acute Toxicities of Organic Chemicals to Fathead Minnows (Pimephales promelas) Ed. by N. J. Chinoy. (Advances in Agricultural Biotechnology Ser.). 1984. lib. bdg. 106.50 (90-247-2908-4) Kluwer Ac.

Acute Toxicities of Organic Chemicals to Fathead Minnows (Pimephales promelas)., Vol. 2. Ed. by D. L. Geiger et al. (Toxicity of Organic Chemicals Ser.). (Illus.). 326p. (Orig.). 1985. pap. 75.00 (0-9614968-1-9) Ctr Lake Superior.

Acute Toxicities of Organic Chemicals to Fathead Minnows (Pimephales promelas), Vol. 1. Ed. by L. T. Brooke et al. LC 85-116909. (Toxicity of Organic Chemicals Ser.). (Illus.). 414p. (Orig.). 1984. pap. 75.00 (0-9614968-0-0) Ctr Lake Superior.

Acute Toxicities of Organic Chemicals to Fathead Minnows (Pimephales promelas), Vol. 3. Ed. by D. L. Geiger et al. (Toxicity of Organic Chemicals Ser.). (Illus.). 328p. (Orig.). 1986. pap. 75.00 (0-9614968-2-7) Ctr Lake Superior.

Acute Toxicities of Organic Chemicals to Fathead Minnows (Pimephales promelas), Vol. 4. Ed. by D. L. Geiger et al. (Toxicity of Organic Chemicals Ser.). (Illus.). 355p. (Orig.). 1988. pap. 75.00 (0-9614968-3-5) Ctr Lake Superior.

Acute Toxicities of Organic Chemicals to Fathead Minnows (Pimephales promelas), Vol. 5. Ed. by D. L. Geiger et al. (Toxicity of Organic Chemicals Ser.). (Illus.). 311p. (Orig.). 1990. pap. 75.00 (0-9614968-5-1) Ctr Lake Superior.

Acute Toxicity in Theory & Practice: With Special Reference to the Toxicology of Pesticides. Vernon K. Brown. LC 79-42905. (Monographs in Toxicology: Environmental & Safety Aspects). (Illus.). 169p. reprint ed. pap. 48.20 (0-8357-5091-4, 2030406) Bks Demand.

Acute Toxicity Testing. Ed. by Alan M. Goldberg. (Alternative Methods in Toxicology Ser.: Vol. 2). 292p. 1984. text ed. 185.00 (0-913113-03-4) M Liebert.

Acute Toxicology Testing: Perspectives & Horizons. Shayne C. Gad & Christopher P. Chengelis. (Illus.). 525p. 1989. text ed. 62.50 (0-936923-06-7) Telford Pr.

Acute Virus Infections of Poultry. Ed. by J. B. McFerran & M. S. McNulty. (Current Topics in Veterinary Medicine & Animal Science Ser.). 1986. lib. bdg. 115.50 (0-89838-809-0) Kluwer Ac.

Acutely Traumatized Small Animal Patient. Timothy H. Brasmer. (Major Problems in Veterinary Medicine Ser.: Vol. 2). (Illus.). 192p. 1984. text ed. 58.50 (0-7216-1917-7) Saunders.

ACWA: Administrative Careers with America. Eve P. Steinberg. 224p. 1991. pap. 13.00 (0-13-005984-6, Arco Test) P-H Gen Ref & Trav.

ACWA: Administrative Careers with America. 2nd ed. Eve P. Steinberg. LC 93-45503. 1994. pap. 13.00 (0-671-88573-1, Arco Test) P-H Gen Ref & Trav.

ACWA Test. Ed. by Federal Jobs Digest Staff. 200p. (Orig.). 1995. pap. 19.95 (0-914327-53-4) Breakthrgh NY.

Acyclic Dithiocarboxylic Acid Esters: Reactions & Syntheses. Shinzi Kato & Masaru Ishida. Ed. by A. Senning. (Sulfur Report Ser.: Vol. 8, Pt. 4). 170p. 1988. pap. text ed. 175.00 (3-7186-4859-8) Gordon & Breach.

Acyclic Organonitrogen Stereodynamics. Ed. by Joseph B. Lambert & Yoshito Takeuchi. (Methods in Stereochemical Analysis Ser.). 304p. 1991. text ed. 125.00 (1-56081-555-8) VCH Pubs.

Acyclische Kohlenwasserstoffe, Hydroxy-Verbindungen und Oxo-Verbindungen. Beilstein Institute for Literature of Organic Chemistry Staff. (Beilsteins Handbuch der Organischen Chemie Ser., 4th Ed., 4th Suppl.: Vol. 1, Pt. 6). 569p. 1975. 613.00 (0-387-07221-7) Spr-Verlag.

Acyclische Verbindungen. LC 22-79. (Beilsteins Handbuch der Organischen Chemie Ser., 4th Ed., 4th Suppl.: Bund 2, Teil 3). 1976. 1,213.00 (0-387-07756-1) Spr-Verlag.

Acyclische Verbindungen. Beilstein Institute for Literature of Organic Chemistry Staff. Ed. by H. G. Boit. LC 72-95756. (Beilsteins Handbuch der Organischen Chemie Ser., 4th Ed., 4th Suppl.: Vol. 2, Pt. 1). 692p. 1975. 704.00 (0-387-07311-6) Spr-Verlag.

Acyclovir Therapy for Herpes Virus Infections. Baker. 344p. 1990. 135.00 (0-8247-8091-4) Dekker.

Acyclovir Uses & Research: Index of Modern Information. Clarence M. Kupferman. LC 88-47852. 150p. 1988. 39.50 (0-88164-952-X); pap. 34.50 (0-88164-953-8) ABBE Pubs Assn.

Ad Abba. David C. Wood. LC 87-90173. (Illus.). 200p. (Orig.). 1988. pap. 9.95 (0-9616862-1-9) XyloPub Ltd.

Ad Absurdum: A Hans Weigel Anthology. Tr. by Katharina M. Wilson & Robert Harrison. LC 87-70746. (Studies in German Literature, Linguistics & Culture: Vol. 37). (Illus.). 157p. 1987. 29.00 (0-938100-58-0) Camden Hse.

Ad Demonicum et Panegyricus. Isocrates. Ed. by W. R. Connor & John E. Sandys. LC 78-18604. (Greek Texts & Commentaries Ser.). (Illus.). (ENG & GRE.). 1979. reprint ed. lib. bdg. 27.95 (0-405-11444-3) Ayer.

Ad Feminam. Ed. by Alice Bach. xiv, 242p. (Orig.). 1989. pap. 15.00 (0-9624564-0-3) Union Seminary.

Ad Game: Playing to Win. Edward J. McGee & G. Robert Cox. 160p. 1990. pap. 15.95 (0-13-004490-3) P-H.

***Ad Hoc Monadnock: A Literary Anthology.** Marie L. St. Onge. 250p. Date not set. 15.00 (0-9645002-0-5) Monadnock Writers.

Ad Infinitum. Michael Klauke. Ed. by John H. Goodwin. LC 87-83374. (Illus.). 58p. (Orig.). 1988. pap. write for info. (0-915427-09-5); Artist's book. 15.00 (0-317-65935-9) Spirit Sq Ctr.

Ad Infinitum: A Fiction. Richard Kostelanetz. 1973. pap. 10.00 (0-932360-62-9) Archae Edns.

Ad Infinitum - the Ghost in Turing's Machine: Taking God Out of Mathematics & Putting the Body Back In: An Essay in Corporeal Semiotics. Brian Rotman. LC 92-26420. 224p. 1993. 39.50 (0-8047-2127-0); pap. 12.95 (0-8047-2128-9) Stanford U Pr.

Ad Kit Four. Larry Notman. 5.00 (0-686-84765-2) Newspaper Serv.

Ad Kit Three. Larry Notman. (Illus.). 1979. pap. 5.00 (0-918488-08-7) Newspaper Serv.

Ad Konings's Book of Cichlids & All the Other Fishes of Lake Malawi. Ad Konings. (Illus.). 495p. 1990. 99.95 (0-86622-527-7, TS157) TFH Pubns.

Ad Lib: Flying the B-24 Liberator in World War II. William Carigan. (Illus.). 96p. 1993. reprint ed. pap. 17.00 (0-89745-099-X) Sunflower U Pr.

Ad-Libbing Poems, 1978-1986. Tom Miles. LC 87-71905. 50p. (Orig.). 1987. pap. 3.75 (0-938711-01-6) Tecolote Pubns.

Ad Litteram: Authoritative Texts & Their Medieval Readers. Ed. by Mark D. Jordan & Kent Emery, Jr. LC 91-50563. (Conferences in Medieval Studies: Vol. 3). (C). 1992. text ed. 39.95 (0-268-00632-6) U of Notre Dame Pr.

Ad Lucilium Epistulae Morales, 2 Vols, Vol. 1, Bks. 1-13. Lucius Annaeus Seneca. (Oxford Classical Texts Ser.). 1965. Vol. 1. Bks. 1-13. 24.95 (0-19-814644-2) OUP.

Ad Lucilium Epistulae Morales, 2 Vols, Vol. 2, Bks. 14-20. Lucius Annaeus Seneca. (Oxford Classical Texts Ser.). 1965. Vol. 2. Bks. 14-20. 24.95 (0-19-814649-3) OUP.

Ad M. Brutum Orator. M. Tullius Cicero. xcix, 257p. 1973. reprint ed. lib. bdg. 57.20 (3-487-04591-5, Pub. by Georg Olms GW) Lubrecht & Cramer.

Ad Men & Women: A Biographical Dictionary of Advertising. Ed. by Edd Applegate. LC 93-28040. 424p. 1994. text ed. 75.00 (0-313-27801-6, Greenwood Pr) Greenwood.

A.D. Momigliano: Studies on Modern Scholarship. Arnaldo Momigliano. Ed. by G. W. Bowersock & T. J. Cornell. Tr. by T. J. Cornell. LC 93-42827. 1994. 40.00 (0-520-07001-1); pap. 17.00 (0-520-85450-0) U CA Pr.

Ad Organum Faciendum et Item de Organo. Ed. by Jay S. Huff. (Musical Theorists in Translation Ser.: Vol. 8). 1969. lib. bdg. 27.00 (0-912024-28-3) Inst Mediaeval Mus.

Ad Police. Toshimichi Suzuki. (Illus.). 144p. (Orig.). 1994. pap. 14.95 (1-56931-005-X) Viz Commns Inc.

Ad Polyporaceae I. Amauroderma & Ganoderma. E. J. Corner. (Nova Hedwigia Beiheft Ser.: No. 75). (Illus.). 182p. 1983. text ed. 52.00 (3-7682-5475-5) Lubrecht & Cramer.

Ad Polyporaceae 7: The Xanthochroic Polypores. E. J. Corner. (Nova Hedwigia Beiheft Ser.: No. 101). (Illus.). 175p. 1991. lib. bdg. 105.00 (3-443-51023-X, Pub. by Cramer-Borntraeger GW) Lubrecht & Cramer.

Ad Polyporaceas 4: The Genera Daedalea, Flabellonhora, Etc. E. J. Corner. (Nova Hedwigia Beiheft Ser.: No. 86). (Illus.). 274p. 1987. lib. bdg. 125.00 (3-443-51008-6) Lubrecht & Cramer.

Ad Polyporaceas 4: The Genus Trametes. E. J. Corner. (Nova Hedwigia Ser.: No. 97). (Illus.). 197p. 1989. text ed. 130.00 (3-443-51019-1, Pub. by Cramer-Borntraeger GW) Lubrecht & Cramer.

Ad Polyporaceas 5: The Genera Albatrellus, Boletopsis, Etc. E. J. Corner. (Nova Hedwigia Ser.: No. 96). (Illus.). 218p. 1989. text ed. 85.00 (3-443-51018-3, Pub. by Cramer GW) Lubrecht & Cramer.

Ad Polyporaceas 2 & 3. E. J. Corner. (Illus.). 222p. 1984. lib. bdg. 80.00 (3-7682-5478-X) Lubrecht & Cramer.

Ad Reinhardt. Yve-Alain Bois. LC 90-50800. (Illus.). 144p. 1991. 45.00 (0-8478-1336-3) Rizzoli Intl.

***Ad Reinhardt.** Inboden. 1987. (0-500-09170-6) Thames Hudson.

Ad Reinhart, Joseph Kosuth, Felix Gonzalez-Torres: Symptoms of Interference, Conditions of Possibility. Ed. by Joseph Kosuth. (Art & Design Ser.: No. 34). (Illus.). 120p. (Orig.). 1994. pap. 26.95 (1-85490-217-2, Academy Edits) St Martin.

Ad Sales: Interviews with Twenty-Three Top Magazine Executives. Jim Mann. Ed. by Theodus Carroll. 1987. 59.95 (0-918110-15-7) Hanson Pub Grp.

Ad Serenissmum Jacobum Quintum Strena. James Fifth King Of Scotland. LC 74-26227. (English Experience Ser.: No. 127). 8p. 1969. reprint ed. 10.00 (90-221-0127-4) Walter J Johnson.

Ad Valorem Appraisers: The New Professionals. LC 72-76987. (ASA Monograph Ser.: No. 6). 1975. 5.00 (0-937828-15-7) Am Soc Appraisers.

Ad Valorem Assessment of Telecommunications Property: A Bibliography, Directory & Resource Guide. Ed. by Robert M. Clatanoff. (CPL Bibliographies Ser.: No. 83). 32p. 1982. 8.00 (0-86602-083-7) Coun Plan Librarians.

ADA. Ruth Shimer. Ed. by Robert Shimer. (Illus.). 220p. 1989. pap. text ed. 12.00 (0-685-30433-7) Amigo Projects.

ADA: A Development Approach. Fintan Culwin. 616p. 1992. pap. text ed. 48.00 (0-13-489147-3) P-H.

Ada: A Life & Legacy. Dorothy Stein. (History of Computing Ser.). (Illus.). 368p. 1985. pap. 12.95 (0-262-69116-7) MIT Pr.

Ada: A Programme for Jenny. Ruth H. Shimer. (Illus.). 225p. (Orig.). 1991. pap. 15.00 (0-9625192-0-0) Amigo Projects.

ADA: A Programmer's Guide with Microcomputer Examples. James Stanley et al. write for info. (0-318-59578-8) Addison-Wesley.

***ADA: An Advanced Introduction.** Narain Gehani. LC 94-35124. 1994. write for info. (0-929306-15-5) Silicon Pr.

ADA: An Introduction. 2nd ed. Henry Ledgard. (Illus.). 135p. 1987. pap. text ed. 30.00 (0-387-90814-5) Spr-Verlag.

ADA: Applications & Administration. 2nd ed. Philip Johnson. 224p. 1990. text ed. 43.00 (0-07-032627-4, 23040) McGraw.

ADA: Art & Science of Computing. Walter J. Savitch. Ed. by John Thompson. (C). 1992. pap. text ed. 46.25 (0-8053-7070-6) Benjamin-Cummings.

ADA: As a Second Language. Norman Cohen. 1986. pap. text ed. write for info. (0-07-011589-3) McGraw.

ADA: Concurrent Programming. 2nd ed. Narain Gehani. 230p. 1991. 30.95 (0-929306-08-2) Silicon Pr.

Ada: Langauge & Methodology. David A. Watt et al. (Illus.). 560p. 1987. pap. text ed. 55.00 (0-13-004078-9) P-H.

ADA: Problem Solving & Program Design. Michael B. Feldman & Elliot B. Koffman. LC 92-20775. (Illus.). 704p. (C). 1992. pap. text ed. 46.25 (0-201-50006-X) Addison-Wesley.

ADA: Problem Solving & Program Design. Michael B. Feldman & Elliot B. Koffman. LC 92-20775. (C). 1993. pap. text ed. 43.25 (0-201-52279-9) Addison-Wesley.

ADA: Ten Steps to Compliance. Ed. by Karen Henry. 328p. (Orig.). (C). 1993. pap. text ed. 40.00 (1-878630-52-0) CA Chamber Commerce.

***ADA: Ten Steps to Compliance.** Karen Henry. 400p. 1995. pap. 75.00 (0-614-06734-0) Amer CC Pubs.

ADA: Towards Maturity. Ed. by L. Collingbourne. (Studies in Computer & Communications Systems: Vol. 6). 250p. 1993. 75.00 (90-5199-142-8, Pub. by IOS Pr NE) IOS Press.

ADA Action Guide for State & Local Governments. Adaptive Environments Center Staff. LC 93-6960. (Disability Law Practice Ser.). 170p. 1993. 32.90 (0-934753-88-1) LRP Pubns.

***ADA & Vertical Transportation.** Edward A. Donoghue. (Illus.). 144p. (Orig.). 1993. pap. text ed. 45.00 (1-886536-05-8) Elevator Wrld.

Ada Byron Lovelace: The Lady & the Computer. Mary Dodson Wade. LC 94-12678. (People in Focus Ser.). (J). 1994. text ed. 13.95 (0-87518-598-3, Dillon Silver Burdett) Silver Burdett Pr.

ADA Challenge, Nineteen Eighty-Eight: Strategies Risk & Payoffs. John Keller. 190p. 1988. pap. 174.00 (0-935453-22-9) Pasha Pubns.

Ada-Chowtal on Sitar (Anthology of Poorav Baj) S. Bandyopadhyaya. (C). 1990. 10.00 (81-7018-595-5, Pub. by BR Pub II) S Asia.

ADA Compliance Guidebook: A Checklist for Your Building. 79p. (Orig.). 1991. pap. 50.00 (0-943130-01-8) Build Own & Man.

ADA Compliance Guidebook: A Checklist for Your Building. Building Owners & Managers Assn. Staff. 1991. pap. text ed. 50.00 (0-943130-00-X) Build Own & Man.

ADA Compliance Guidelines: California Access Code. Dorothy L. Grant et al. 416p. 1993. vinyl bd. 59.95 (0-9633709-6-0) ACR Grp.

ADA Compliance Manual for Employers. Jonathan L. Alder & Maureen F. Moore. 432p. 1994. ring bd. 89.50 (0-409-25691-9) Michie Butterworth.

ADA Compliance Manual for Employers. suppl. ed. Jonathan L. Alder & Maureen F. Moore. 1994. ring bd. 39.00 (0-685-74455-8) Butterworth Legal Pubs.

ADA Compliance Manual for Higher Education: A Guide to Title I. Robert L. Duston et al. 242p. 1992. 90.00 (1-878240-20-X) Coll & U Personnel.

ADA Compliance Pricing Guide: Costs for the Seventy-Five Most Needes ADA Compliance Projects. R. S. Means Co., Inc., Adaptive Environments Center Staff. Ed. by Mary Greene & Phillip Waier. (Illus.). 200p. 1994. 69.95 (0-87629-351-8) R S Means.

***ADA Cost Catalog for Access Modifications: Adaptive Environments.** LC 94-76290. 222p. 1994. pap. 35.00 (0-934753-68-7) LRP Pubns.

ADA Essential Function Identification: A Definitive Application of Title I. Roger A. Thrush. (Illus.). 125p. (Orig.). 1993. pap. write for info. (0-9638200-0-1) AccessAbility.

An Asterisk (*) at the beginning of an entry indicates that the title is appearing in BIP for the first time.

ADA-Europe '93: Proceedings of the 12th Ada-Europe International Conference, "Ada Sans Frontieres", Paris, France, June 14-18, 1993. Ed. by M. Gauthier. (Lecture Notes in Computer Science Ser.: Vol. 688). viii, 353p. 1993. pap. 54.00 (*0-387-56802-6*) Spr-Verlag.

Ada: Experiences & Prospects: Proceedings of the Ada-Europe International Conference, Dublin, 1990. Ed. by Barry Lynch. (Ada Companion Ser.). (Illus.). 300p. (C). 1990. 74.95 (*0-521-39522-4*) Cambridge U Pr.

ADA for Experienced Programmers. A. Nico Habermann & Dewayne E. Perry. LC 82-20757. (Computer Science Ser.). (Illus.). 496p. (C). 1983. pap. text ed. 37.75 (*0-201-11481-X*) Addison-Wesley.

ADA from the Beginning. Jan Skansholm. (Illus.). 640p. (C). 1988. pap. text ed. 38.75 (*0-201-17522-3*) Addison-Wesley.

ADA from the Beginning. 2nd ed. Jan Skansholm. Tr. by Shirley Booth. LC 93-49729. (C). 1994. pap. text ed. 39.75 (*0-201-62448-6*) Addison-Wesley.

ADA Generic Library. David R. Musser. 1989. 49.00 (*0-387-97133-5*, 3398) Spr-Verlag.

ADA Handbook. Ed. by Maureen Harrison & Steve Gilbert. (Landmark Laws Ser.). 252p. (Orig.). 1992. pap. 15.95 (*1-880780-00-3*) Excellent Bks.

ADA Handbook: A Guide to the Americans with Disability Act. Linthicum et al. 176p. (C). 1992. pap. text ed. 17.95 (*0-8403-7882-3*) Kendall-Hunt.

ADA Handbook: Employment & Construction Issues Affecting Your Business. Martha R. Williams & Marcia L. Russell. LC 92-36286. 192p. 1993. pap. 29.95 (*0-7931-0595-1*, 1520-02, Real Estate Ed) Dearborn Finan.

ADA Impact: Key Questions & Answers about the American with Disabilities Act. Ed. by D. J. Scherer. 16p. 1992. pap. 3.75 (*0-918734-42-8*) Reymont.

ADA in Action: With Practical Programming Examples. Do-While Jones. 1989. text ed., disk 65.00 (*0-471-50747-4*) Wiley.

***Ada in Europe: Proceedings of the First International Eurospace-Ada Symposium, Copenhagen, Denmark, September 26-30, 1994.** Ed. by Marcel Toussaint. LC 94-45545. (Lecture Notes in Computer Science: Vol. 887). 1994. pap. write for info. (*0-387-58822-1*); pap. write for info. (*3-540-58822-1*) Spr-Verlag.

ADA in Practice: Books on Professional Computing Series. C. N. Ausnit et al. (Illus.). xv, 195p. 1985. pap. 44.00 (*0-387-96182-8*) Spr-Verlag.

Ada in Transition. Ed. by W. J. Taylor. (Studies in Computer & Communications Systems: Vol. 4). 212p. 1993. pap. 72.00 (*90-5199-113-4*, Pub. by IOS Pr NE) IOS Press.

Ada, la Desordenada - Libro Grande: Messey Bessey-Big Book. Patricia McKissack & Fredrick McKissack. (Rookie Reader Big Bks.). 32p. (J). (ps-2). 1988. lib. bdg. 22.95 (*0-516-59508-3*) Childrens.

Ada, la Desordenada (Messy Bessey) Patricia McKissack & Fredrick McKissack. LC 87-15079. (Rookie Readers - Spanish Ser.). (Illus.). 32p. (SPA.). (J). (ps-2). 1988. lib. bdg. 10.35 (*0-516-32083-1*); pap. 2.95 (*0-516-52083-0*) Childrens.

Ada Language Reference Manual. Intro. by David A. Fisher. 336p. (C). 1986. pap. text ed. 12.95 (*0-9618252-0-0*) Gensoft Corp.

ADA Language Vocabulary: A French-English Terminology. 105p. (Orig.). (ENG & FRE.). (C). 1994. pap. text ed. 43.95 (*0-7881-0415-2*) Diane Pub.

ADA Mandate for Social Change. Ed. by Paul Wehman. 320p. (C). 1993. pap. text ed. 32.00 (*1-55766-117-0*) P H Brookes.

ADA: Moving Towards Two Thousand: 11th ADA-Europe International Conference, Zandvoort, the Netherlands, June 1-5, 1992 Proceedings. Ed. by J. Van Katwijk et al. LC 92-16606. (Lecture Notes in Computer Science Ser.: Vol. 603). viii, 324p. 1992. pap. 48.00 (*0-387-55585-4*) Spr-Verlag.

ADA News & Regulations: For the Private Sector. Patricia A. Morrissey. 350p. 1993. 350.00 (*1-880955-01-6*) Legi-Slate.

Ada, or Ardor. Vladimir Nabokov. 1989. pap. 10.95 (*0-685-26529-3*, Vin) Random.

ADA or Ardor. Vladimir Nabokov. LC 89-40107. (Vintage International Ser.). 608p. 1990. pap. 16.00 (*0-679-72522-9*, Vin) Random.

ADA Policy & Law: Selected Actions Brought under the ADA & Related State Statutes. Buraff Publications Staff. (Orig.). Date not set. write for info. (*1-882594-04-5*) Buraff Pubns.

Ada Potato. Judith Caseley. LC 87-19738. (Illus.). 24p. (J). (ps up). 1989. 11.95 (*0-688-07742-0*); lib. bdg. 11.88 (*0-688-07743-9*) Greenwillow.

***ADA Problem Solving & Program.** 2nd ed. Michael Feldman. (C). 1993. pap. 47.50 (*0-201-53364-2*) Addison-Wesley.

ADA Programmer's Guide with Microcomputer Examples. James Stanley. 1985. pap. 21.95 (*0-201-16416-7*) Addison-Wesley.

ADA Programmer's Handbook. Dean W. Gonzalez. (C). 1991. pap. text ed. 18.25 (*0-8053-2529-8*) Benjamin-Cummings.

ADA Programmer's Handbook & Language Reference Manual. Dean W. Gonzalez. (C). 1991. pap. text ed. 26.95 (*0-8053-2528-X*) Benjamin-Cummings.

***ADA "Questions & Answers" Pamphlet: 1992.** 1992. pap. 5.00x (*0-614-06148-2*, 2033-PP-4040) EPF.

ADA Reference Manual. 320p. 1988. 30.95 (*0-9615336-6-8*) Silicon Pr.

Ada Rehan. 2nd enl. rev. ed. William Winter. LC 74-82852. (Illus.). 1972. 23.95 (*0-405-09085-4*) Ayer.

ADA Resource Directory: A Guide to Accessibility in Hawaii. Bruce M. Clark. 108p. 1994. pap. 26.95 (*0-9641990-0-9*) Access Planning.

Ada Software Repository & the DDN. Richard Conn. 160p. (Orig.). 1986. pap. 16.95 (*0-918432-78-2*) Baseline Bks.

ADA Software Tools Interfaces. Ed. by P. J. Wallis. (Lecture Notes in Computer Science Ser.: Vol. 180). iii, 164p. 1984. pap. 27.00 (*0-387-13878-1*) Spr-Verlag.

ADA Source Book: What You Need to Know about the Americans with Disabilities Act: A Guide for Small & Medium Size Business. Michael J. Landini, Jr. 70p. 1991. 9.95 (*0-88713-624-9*) Nat Alliance.

ADA: the Choice for Ninety Two: ADA-Europe International Conference Athens, Greece, May 13-17, 1991 Proceedings. D. Christodoulakis. Ed. by G. Goos & J. Hartmanis. (Lecture Notes in Computer Science Ser.: Vol. 499). vi, 411p. 1991. pap. 41.00 (*0-387-54092-X*) Spr-Verlag.

Ada; the Design Choice: Proceedings of the Ada-Europe International Conference, Madrid 1989. A. Alvarez. (Ada Companion Ser.). (Illus.). 350p. (C). 1989. 64.95 (*0-521-38130-4*) Cambridge U Pr.

Ada, The Enchantress of Numbers: The Letters of Lord Byron's Daughter & Her Description of the First Computer. Betty A. Toole. (Illus.). 456p. 1992. 29.95 (*0-912647-09-4*) Strawberry.

ADA Title III - Compliance Made practical. 40p. 1992. pap. 24.95 (*0-685-71673-2*, 736) Inst Real Estate.

ADA Title Three: Compliance Made Practical. Institute of Real Estate Management Staff. (Illus.). 44p. 1992. pap. text ed. 24.95 (*0-944298-76-1*) Inst Real Estate.

***ADA Training Manual: (Trainer's Guide, Visual Aids)** 1992. 950.00 (*0-614-06168-7*, 2036-TM-4045) EPF.

ADA Training Manual for Managers & Supervisors: A Guide to Americans with Disabilities Act Compliance. 56p. 1992. pap. 12.50 (*0-685-67113-5*, 4729) Commerce.

Ada Yearbook, 1992. Ed. by F. Long. 336p. 1992. 69.95 (*0-442-31581-3*) Chapman & Hall.

ADA Yearbook 1993. Ed. by C. Loftus. LC 92-63411. (Studies in Computer & Communications Systems: Vol. 5). 450p. 1993. 94.00 (*90-5199-124-X*, Pub. by IOS Pr NE) IOS Press.

ADA Yearbook, 1994. C. Loftus. LC 94-75423. (Studies in Computer & Communications Ser.). 460p. 1994. 94.00 (*90-5199-155-X*) IOS Press.

***ADA Yearbook 1995.** Ratcliffe. LC 95-75768. 1995. 82.00 (*90-5199-218-1*) IOS Press.

Adab al Ikhtilaf fi al Islam (Ethics of Disagreement in Islam) 5th ed. Taha Jabir al'Alwani. LC 91-38927. (Silsilat Qadaya al Fikr al Islami Ser.: No. 2). 168p. (Orig.). (ARA.). (C). 1987. pap. text ed. 5.00 (*0-912463-08-2*) IIIT VA.

Adae Murimuth Continuatio Chronicarum: Robertus de Avesbury de Gestis Mirabilibus Regis Edwardi Tertii. Ed. by Edward M. Thompson. (Rolls Ser.: No. 93). 1972. reprint ed. 80.00 (*0-8115-1170-7*) Periodicals Srv.

Adages, No. II:1 to II vi 100. Desiderius Erasmus. Tr. & Anno. by Roger Mynors. (Collected Works of Erasmus: No. 33). 456p. 1991. 100.00 (*0-8020-5954-6*) U of Toronto Pr.

Adages, No. I vi 1 to I x 100. Desiderius Erasmus. Ed. & Tr. by Roger Mynors. (Collected Works of Erasmus: No. 32). 412p. 1987. 80.00 (*0-8020-2412-2*) U of Toronto Pr.

Adages: Collected Works of Erasmus II VII 1 to III III 100. Desiderius Erasmus. Tr. by R. A. Mynors. (Collected Works of Erasmus: No. 34). 512p. 1992. 85.00 (*0-8020-2831-4*) U of Toronto Pr.

Adages (One to Five Hundred) Erasmus. Tr. by Margaret M. Phillips & R. A. Mynors. (Collected Works of Erasmus: Vol. 31). 1982. 75.00 (*0-8020-2373-8*) U of Toronto Pr.

***Adaguide: The WriteTechnique.** (Guide to Software Package Ser.). 63p. 1994. disk, ring bd. 99.00 (*1-878205-70-6*) GR Press.

Adair County Kentucky 1810-1840: Censuses. Rowena Lawson. iv, 69p. (Orig.). 1986. pap. 10.50 (*0-917890-84-1*) Heritage Bk.

Adair History & Genealogy. James B. Adair. (Illus.). 330p. 1991. reprint ed. lib. bdg. 61.50 (*0-8328-1801-1*); reprint ed. pap. 51.50 (*0-8328-1802-X*) Higginson Bk Co.

Adair History & Genealogy. James B. Adair. (Illus.). 408p. 1990. reprint ed. 37.50 (*0-89308-086-1*, FH 1) Southern Hist Pr.

Adalaide Eden. Paul Slazinski. 54p. (Orig.). 1991. pap. 6.12 (*0-685-48267-7*) Dayspring Pr.

Adalat: A Comprehensive Review. Ed. by P. R. Lichtlen & A. Reale. (Illus.). 248p. 1991. 51.00 (*0-387-54033-4*) Spr-Verlag.

Adalbert Stifter & the Idyll: A Study of Witiko. Barbara S. Stone. LC 89-12989. (American University Studies: Germanic Languages & Literature: Ser. I, Vol. 80). 243p. 1990. text ed. 40.50 (*0-8204-0515-9*) P Lang Pubs.

Adalberto Libera. Ed. by Francesco Garofalo & Luca Veresani. LC 91-19759. (Illus.). 208p. (Orig.). 1992. 24.95 (*1-878271-14-8*) Princeton Arch.

Adaline Kent Award Exhibition, 1991 - Mildred Howard: Ten Little Children Standing in a Line (One Got Shot, & Then There Were Nine) Amalia Mesa-Bains & Judith Bettelheim. (Illus.). 1991. pap. 5.00 (*0-930495-10-1*) San Fran Art Inst.

Adaline Kent Award, 1994: Armando Rascon: Occupied Aztlan. Norma Alarcon. Tr. by Inma Guiu. LC 94-65445. (Illus.). 42p. (Orig.). (ENG & SPA.). 1994. pap. 5.00 (*0-930495-23-3*) San Fran Art Inst.

Adam. Brian Bassett. (Illus.). 128p. (Orig.). 1989. pap. 8.95 (*0-8362-1841-8*) Andrews & McMeel.

Adam & Andrea Learn & Grow: Understanding Church Words from a Kid's Viewpoint. Sheri Martens. (Illus.). 80p. (J). (ps-5). 1989. pap. 7.95 (*0-919797-81-4*) Kindred Prods.

Adam & Eve. (Bible Story Ser.: No. S846-12). (J). (ps-2). 1989. boxed 3.95 (*0-7214-5259-0*) Ladybird Bks.

Adam & Eve. 1991. pap. 4.95 (*1-878320-93-9*) Masquerade.

Adam & Eve. Penny Frank. (Story Bible Ser.: No. 2). (J). (ps-3). 1988. 3.99 (*0-85648-727-9*) Lion USA.

Adam & Eve. Penny Frank. LC 92-29470. (Children's Story Bible Ser.). (Illus.). (J). 1992. 6.95 (*0-7459-2609-6*) Lion USA.

***Adam & Eve.** Penny Frank. (Illus.). (J). 1992. pap. 1.99 (*0-7459-1747-X*) Lion USA.

Adam & Eve. Gordon Lindsay. (Old Testament Ser.: Vol. 2). 1964. 1.95 (*0-89985-124-X*) Christ for the Nations.

Adam & Eve. Illus. by Jim Russell. LC 82-23060. (People of the Bible Ser.). 32p. (J). (gr. k-4). 1983. 14.65 (*0-8172-1981-1*) Raintree Steck-V.

Adam & Eve. Elise Title. (Temptation Ser.). 1992. mass mkt. 2.99 (*0-373-25512-8*, 1-25512-4) Harlequin Bks.

Adam & Eve. Marcus Van Heller. 196p. 1985. pap. 3.95 (*0-88184-185-4*) Carroll & Graf.

Adam & Eve: The Bible Story. Warwick Hutton. LC 86-27690. (Illus.). 32p. (J). 1987. text ed., lib. bdg. 14.95 (*0-689-50433-0*, McElderry) S&S Childrens.

Adam & Eve & Five Other Stories. Peter Enns & Glen Forsberg. (Stories that Live Ser.: Bk. 1). (Illus.). 24p. (J). (ps-5). 1985. audio 4.95 (*0-936215-01-1*) STL Intl.

Adam & Eve & Pinch Me. A. E. Coppard. 1976. 21.95 (*0-8488-0971-8*) Amereon Ltd.

Adam & Eve & Pinch-Me. Julie Johnston. LC 93-21023. (YA). (gr. 7 up). 1994. 15.95 (*0-316-46990-4*) Little.

***Adam & Eve & Pinch-Me.** Julie Johnston. 192p. (YA). (gr. 7 up). 1995. pap. 3.99 (*0-14-037588-0*) Puffin Bks.

Adam & Eve & Pinch Me: Tales. Alfred E. Coppard. LC 70-106274. (Short Story Index Reprint Ser.). 1977. 21.95 (*0-8369-3451-2*) Ayer.

Adam & Eve Bad Advice Rag. Al Blair. 4p. 1990. pap. 3.95 (*0-930366-24-7*) Northcountry Pub.

Adam & Eve-olution. Ken Brown. (Illus.). 104p. (Orig.). 1989. pap. 4.95 (*0-941104-45-1*) Real Comet.

Adam & Eve Sindrome. Roy Masters. LC 85-80750. 266p. 1985. pap. text ed. 12.95 (*0-933900-11-2*) Foun Human Under.

Adam & Eve Story: The History of Cataclysms. Chan Thomas. 232p. (Orig.). 1993. 17.95 (*1-884600-02-6*); pap. 12.95 (*1-884600-01-8*) Bengal Tiger. This is the Book of the Century! At LAST someone - this time a basic research scientist - has come forth with proof of cataclysms, which are worldwide supersonic inundations such as Noah's flood. They were discovered by great men such as Andre DeLuc, Baron Georges Cuvier & Guy de Dolomieu, & have remained unsolved mysteries ever since. Now the author takes you through thrilling solutions of finding the process of catclysms, their timetable, & the derivation of trigger, a 20-year search. Truly, CATACLYSMS LEAVE NO ONE UNTOUCHED! He describes the next cataclysm in awesome detail plus the deterioration of civilization & the escalation of crime before the next cataclysm. It just so happens that the author's scientific prediction of the next cataclysm agrees with clairvoyants Nostradamus', Cayce's, & Scallion's predictions. Never before have facts been presented in such a spine-tingling, inspiring fashion; & never have so many secrets been unlocked in one book. This is the most stirring subject, written in the most intriguing, engrossing, & exciting style ever. You will remember this exceptional book for years! Available from: Bengal Tiger Press, Drawer 1212, South Chatham, MA 02659; Tel: 800-431-4590; FAX: 508-432-0697. ***Publisher Provided Annotation.***

***Adam & Eve Story: The History of Cataclysms.** 2nd ed. Chan Thomas. 243p. (Orig.). 1995. 17.95 (*1-884600-06-9*); pap. 12.95 (*1-884600-07-7*) Bengal Tiger.

Adam & Evolution. Maris Ross & David S. Jeans. 256p. 1974. 25.00 (*0-8464-1289-6*) Beekman Pubs.

Adam & His Family. Robert Baden. (Arch Bks.). (Illus.). 24p. (J). (gr. k-4). 1986. pap. 1.99 (*0-570-06198-9*, 59-1421) Concordia.

Adam & His Kin: The Lost History of Their Lives & Times. Ruth Beechick. (Illus.). 176p. (Orig.). 1990. pap. 8.95 (*0-940319-07-1*) Arrow Press.

Adam & His Work: A Bibliography of Sources by & about Paul Goodman (Nineteen Eleven to Nineteen Seventy-Two) Tom Nicely. LC 79-11662. (Author Bibliographies Ser.: No. 42). 362p. 1979. 32.50 (*0-8108-1219-3*) Scarecrow.

Adam & the Kabbalistic Tree. Z'ev Ben Shimon Halevi. 332p. 1974. pap. 15.00 (*0-87728-263-3*) Weiser.

Adam & the Magic Marble: A Magical Adventure. Adam Buehrens & Carol Buehrens. LC 90-23906. (Illus.). 108p. (Orig.). (J). (gr. k-10). 1991. pap. 6.95 (*1-878267-30-2*) Hope Pr CA.

Adam & the Train. Heinrich Boll. Tr. by Leila Vennewitz. Bd. with Train. LC 71-127920. LC 71-127920. 288p. 1974. reprint ed. Set pap. text ed. 7.95 (*0-07-006409-1*) McGraw.

Adam Bede. George Eliot. 1976. 29.95 (*0-8488-0481-3*) Amereon Ltd.

Adam Bede. George Eliot. 1992. pap. 20.00 (*0-679-40991-2*) McKay.

Adam Bede. George Eliot. Ed. by John Paterson. LC 68-5227. (J). (gr. 9 up). 1968. pap. 9.96 (*0-395-05204-1*, RivEd) HM.

Adam Bede. George Eliot. 1961. pap. 5.95 (*0-451-52527-2*, Sig Classics); pap. write for info. (*0-451-52256-7*, Sig Classics) NAL-Dutton.

Adam Bede. George Eliot. (English Library). 1980. mass mkt. 6.95 (*0-14-043121-7*, Penguin Classics) Viking Penguin.

Adam Bede. George Eliot. 466p. 1977. reprint ed. lib. bdg. 27.95 (*0-89966-265-X*) Buccaneer Bks.

Adam Bede. George Eliot. 1992. reprint ed. lib. bdg. 27.95 (*0-89968-276-6*, Lghtyr Pr) Buccaneer Bks.

Adam Bomb: Achieving Peace in the Battle of the Sexes. Marlene Caroselli. 200p. 1993. pap. 11.95 (*0-922411-04-2*) CPD CA.

Adam Book see Emily & Adam

Adam by Adam see Adam on Adam: The Autobiography of Adam Clayton Powell, Jr.

Adam Cast Forth. Charles M. Doughty. LC 75-41078. reprint ed. 31.50 (*0-404-14535-3*) AMS Pr.

Adam Christology As the Exegetical & Theological Substructure of Second Corinthians 4 7-5 21. C. Marvin Pate. 184p. (C). 1991. lib. bdg. 47.50 (*0-8191-8188-9*) U Pr of Amer.

Adam Clayton Powell: Portrait of a Marching Black. James Haskins. LC 91-78317. 1992. 35.00 (*0-86543-339-9*); pap. 12.95 (*0-86543-340-2*) Africa World.

Adam Clayton Powell, Jr. Robert Jakoubek. (Black Americans of Achievement Ser.). (Illus.). 112p. (J). 1988. lib. bdg. 17.95 (*1-55546-606-0*); pap. 9.95 (*0-7910-0213-6*) Chelsea Hse.

Adam Clayton Powell, Jr. Al-Imam Obaba. (Great Nubian Quiz Bks.). (Illus.). 43p. (Orig.). (YA). 1989. pap. 3.95 (*0-916157-06-7*) African Islam Miss Pubns.

Adam Clayton Powell, Jr. A Black Power Political Educator. E. Curtis Alexander. LC 81-69171. (African American Educator Ser.: Vol. II). (Illus.). 174p. (Orig.). 1983. pap. 9.95 (*0-938818-03-1*) ECA Assoc.

Adam Clayton Powell, Jr. The Political Biography of an American Dilemma. Charles V. Hamilton. (Illus.). 448p. 1991. 24.95 (*0-689-12062-1*, Atheneum S&S) S&S Trade.

Adam Clayton Powell, Jr. The Political Biography of an American Dilemma. Charles V. Hamilton. (Illus.). 576p. 1992. pap. 15.00 (*0-02-003471-7*, Collier S&S) S&S Trade.

***Adam Clayton Powell Jr. & the Harlem Renaissance.** E. Curtis Alexander. 1987. 3.95 (*0-938818-14-7*) ECA Assoc.

Adam Clayton Powell, Jr. Speaks Out. E. Curtis Alexander. 84p. 1990. pap. 8.95 (*0-938818-23-6*) ECA Assoc.

Adam Danced: The Cross & the Seven Deadly Sins. George W. Rutler. 64p. (Orig.). 1989. pap. 6.95 (*0-931888-34-4*) Christendom Pr.

Adam Davy's Five Dreams about Edward 2nd. F. J. Furnivall. Incl. Life of St. Alexius. 1972. (*0-318-54011-8*); Solomon's Book of Wisdom. 1972. (*0-318-54012-6*); St. Jeremies Fifteen Tokens Before Doomsday. 1972. (*0-318-54013-4*); Lamentation of Souls. 1972. (*0-318-54014-2*); (EETS, OS Ser.: No. 69). 1972. reprint ed. 25.00 (*0-527-00068-X*) Periodicals Srv.

Adam de Saint-Victor, les Proses Texte et Musique see Melanges de Musicologie Critique

Adam de Wodeham: Tractatus de Indivisibilibus. Ed. by Rega Wood. (C). 1988. lib. bdg. 172.00 (*90-277-2424-5*) Kluwer Ac.

Adam, Enoch & Noah. Norman L. Heap. 1992. 16.00 (*0-945905-01-7*) Family Hstory Pubns.

Adam, Eve & the Serpent. Elaine Pagels. LC 87-43227. 224p. 1988. 17.95 (*0-394-52140-4*) Random.

Adam, Eve & the Serpent. Elaine Pagels. 1989. pap. 9.00 (*0-679-72232-7*, Vin) Random.

Adam Homo. Frederik Paludan-Muller. Tr. by Stephen Klass. LC 81-58568. (Illus.). 543p. (Orig.). (C). 1981. pap. 26.95 (*0-936726-02-4*) Twickenham Pr.

Adam I Eva: Adam & Eve. Roman Gershgorin. (Illus.). 184p. (Orig.). (RUS.). 1992. pap. 3.00 (*1-881910-05-9*) Adventure NY.

Adam Kok's Griquas: A Study in the Development of Stratification in South Africa. Robert Ross. LC 75-43368. (African Studies Ser.: 21). 208p. reprint ed. pap. 59.30 (*0-8357-5092-2*, 2024526) Bks Demand.

Adam Lowe, No. 76. Kyoichi Tsuzuki. (Art Random Ser.). (Illus.). 48p. 1992. 32.95 (*4-7636-8578-3*, Pub. by Kyoto Shoin JA) Bks Nippan.

Adam Mickiewicz: The National Poet of Poland. Monica M. Gardner. LC 74-135807. (Eastern Europe Collection Ser.). 1971. reprint ed. 21.95 (*0-405-02749-4*) Ayer.

Adam Mickiewicz, Poet of Poland: A Symposium. Ed. by Manfred Kridl. LC 75-90540. 292p. 1970. reprint ed. text ed. 59.75 (*0-8371-2783-1*, KRAM, Greenwood Pr) Greenwood.

Adam Mouse's Book of Poems. Lilian Moore. LC 91-42223. (Illus.). 64p. (J). (ps-5). 1992. text ed., lib. bdg. 12.95 (*0-689-31765-4*, Atheneum Bks Young) S&S Childrens.

Adam, "New Born & Perfect" The Renaissance Promise of Eternity. Giancarlo Maiorino. LC 86-46144. (Illus.). 172p. (C). 1987. 22.50 (*0-253-30405-9*) Ind U Pr.

Adam, Noah, Abraham. 1992. pap. 2.29 (*0-7814-0037-6*, Chariot Bks) Chariot Family.

A

Adam of Eynsham: Magna Vita S. Hugonsi, Episcopi Lincolniensis. Ed. by James F. Dimcock. (Rolls Ser.: No. 37). 1972. reprint ed. 45.00 (*0-8115-1089-1*) Periodicals Srv.

Adam of Ife: Black Women in Praise of Black Men. Intro. by Naomi L. Madgett. LC 91-61410. (Illus.). 235p. (Orig.). 1992. pap. 15.00 (*0-916418-80-4*) Lotus.

Adam of the Road. Elizabeth J. Gray. (Illus.). 320p. (J). (gr. 4-8). 1942. pap. 16.99 (*0-670-10435-3*) Viking Child Bks.

***Adam of the Road.** braille ed. Elizabeth J. Gray. 300p. 1993. text ed. 24.00 (*1-56956-490-6*, BR9192) W A T Braille.

Adam of the Road. Elizabeth J. Gray. (Illus.). (J). (gr. 3-7). 1987. reprint ed. pap. 4.99 (*0-14-032464-X*, Puffin) Puffin Bks.

Adam on Adam: The Autobiography of Adam Clayton Powell, Jr. Adam C. Powell, Jr. LC 94-20247. Orig. Title: Adam by Adam. 1994. reprint ed. 12.95 (*0-8065-1538-4*, Citadel Pr) Carol Pub Group.

Adam or Ape: A Sourcebook of Discoveries about Early Man. Ed. by L. S. Leakey et al. 450p. 1982. 24.95 (*0-87073-700-7*); pap. text ed. 16.95 (*0-87073-701-5*) Schenkman Bks Inc.

Adam Principle: Genes, Genitals, Hormones & Gender - Selected Readings in Sexology. John Money. (New Concepts in Human Sexuality Ser.). 364p. (C). 1993. 39.95 (*0-87975-804-X*) Prometheus Bks.

Adam Project. William Woolfolk. 1984. pap. 2.95 (*0-449-12658-7*) Fawcett.

***Adam Raccoon & Bully Garumph.** Glen Keane. (Parables for Kids Ser.). (Illus.). 32p. (J). (gr. 1-3). 1995. 10.99 (*1-55513-367-3*) Chariot Family.

Adam Raccoon & the Circusmaster. Glen Keane. LC 86-26889. (J). (ps-2). 1987. 6.99 (*1-55513-090-9*, Chariot Bks) Chariot Family.

Adam Raccoon & the Flying Machine. Glen Keane. LC 88-17006. (Parables for Kids Ser.). (Illus.). 48p. (J). (ps-2). 1989. 6.99 (*1-55513-287-1*, Chariot Bks) Chariot Family.

Adam Raccoon & the Mighty Giant. Glen Keane. Ed. by Julie Smith. LC 89-31229. (Parables for Kids). (Illus.). 48p. (J). (gr. 1-3). 1991. 7.99 (*1-55513-362-2*, Chariot Bks) Chariot Family.

Adam Raccoon & the Race to Victory Mountain. Glen Keane. Ed. by Julie Smith. LC 92-6998. (Parables for Kids Ser.). (Illus.). 48p. (J). (gr. 1-3). Date not set. 7.99 (*1-55513-363-0*, Chariot Bks) Chariot Family.

Adam Raccoon at Forever Falls. Glen Keane. LC 86-24318. (Parables for Kids Ser.). (J). (ps-2). 1987. 6.99 (*1-55513-087-9*, Chariot Bks) Chariot Family.

Adam Raccoon in Lost Woods. Glen Keane. LC 86-30951. (Parables for Kids Ser.). (J). (ps-2). 1987. 6.99 (*1-55513-088-7*, Chariot Bks) Chariot Family.

Adam Rener, Collected Works. Ed. by Robert Parker. (Gesamtausgaben - Collected Works Ser.: Vol. II, Pt. 2). 160p. 1975. lib. bdg. 7.00 (*0-912024-43-7*) Inst Mediaeval Mus.

Adam Smith. R. H. Campbell & Andrew S. Skinner. LC 82-3308. 231p. 1982. 32.50 (*0-312-00423-0*) St Martin.

Adam Smith. R. H. Campbell & Andrew S. Skinner. 231p. 1985. pap. 13.95 (*0-312-00424-9*) St Martin.

Adam Smith. Francis Hirst. 1971. 59.95 (*0-87968-576-X*) Gordon Pr.

Adam Smith: Critical Assessments. Ed. by John C. Wood. LC 93-28216. 1994. write for info. (*0-415-08731-7*, Routledge NY) Routledge.

Adam Smith: Desire, History, & Value. Michael J. Shapiro. (Modernity & Political Thought Ser.: Vol. 4). 176p. (C). 1993. text ed. 39.95 (*0-8039-4584-1*); pap. text ed. 17.95 (*0-8039-4585-X*) Sage.

Adam Smith: International Perspectives. Hiroshi Mizuta & Chuhei Sugiyama. LC 92-25575. 1993. text ed. 75.00 (*0-312-08937-6*) St Martin.

Adam Smith: The Man & His Works. E. G. West. LC 76-9436. 1977. reprint ed. 10.00 (*0-913966-06-1*) Liberty Fund.

Adam Smith & His Legacy for Modern Capitalism. Patricia H. Werhane. (Illus.). 240p. 1991. 37.50 (*0-19-506828-9*) OUP.

Adam Smith & Modern Economics. Edwin G. West. 256p. 1990. text ed. 67.95 (*1-85278-313-3*, Pub. by E Elgar Pub UK) Ashgate Pub Co.

Adam Smith & Modern Economics. Edwin G. West. 212p. 1993. pap. 22.95 (*1-85278-744-9*, Pub. by E Elgar Pub UK) Ashgate Pub Co.

Adam Smith & Modern Political Economy: Bicentennial Essays on the Wealth of Nations. Ed. by Gerald P. O'Driscoll, Jr. LC 78-10181. 197p. reprint ed. pap. 56.20 (*0-8357-6757-4*, 2035414) Bks Demand.

Adam Smith & the Philosophy of Law & Economics. Ed. by Robin P. Malloy & Jerry Evensky. LC 94-9710. (Law & Philosophy Library: Vol. 20). 240p. (C). 1994. lib. bdg. 88.50 (*0-7923-2796-9*) Kluwer Ac.

Adam Smith & the Wealth of Nations: 1776-1976 Bicentennial. Ed. by Fred R. Glahe. LC 77-91609. (Illus.). 182p. reprint ed. pap. 51.90 (*0-8357-5505-3*, 2035120) Bks Demand.

Adam Smith as Student & Professor: With Unpublished Documents. William R. Scott. LC 65-26379. (Reprints of Economic Classics Ser.). 1965. reprint ed. 45.00 (*0-678-00130-8*) Kelley.

Adam Smith Goes to Moscow: A Dialogue on Radical Reform. Walter Adams & James W. Brick. LC 93-16275. 176p. 1993. text ed. 29.95 (*0-691-03283-1*) Princeton U Pr.

***Adam Smith Goes to Moscow: A Dialogue on Radical Reform.** Walter Adams. 1994. pap. 12.95 (*0-691-00053-0*) Princeton U Pr.

Adam Smith in His Time & Ours: Designing the Decent Society. Jerry Z. Muller. 180p. 1992. text ed. 24.95 (*0-02-922234-6*) Free Pr.

***Adam Smith in His Time & Ours: Designing the Decent Society.** Jerry Z. Muller. LC 95-13210. 1995. write for info. (*0-691-00161-8*) Princeton U Pr.

Adam Smith, Malthus & Marx. Terence Byres. Ed. by Malcolm Yapp et al. (World History Ser.). (Illus.). 32p. (YA). (gr. 6-11). 1980. reprint ed. pap. text ed. 4.35 (*0-89908-021-9*) Greenhaven.

Adam Smith Meets "Greedy Gus" A Review of the "Wealth of Nations" Then & Now. J. Edmund Clarke. 1992. 13.95 (*0-533-09547-6*) Vantage.

Adam Smith Reviewed. Ed. by Peter Jones & Andrew S. Skinner. 240p. 1992. text ed. 55.00 (*0-7486-0346-8*, Pub. by Edinburgh U Pr UK) Col U Pr.

Adam Smith, 1776-1926: Lectures to Commemorate the Sesquicentennial of the Publication of "The Wealth of Nations" John M. Clark et al. LC 88-32065. (Reprints of Economic Classics Ser.). 1989. reprint ed. 35.00 (*0-678-00138-3*) Kelley.

Adam Smith The Wealth of Nations: New Interdisciplinary Essays. Ed. by Stephen Copley & Kathryn Sutherland. LC 94-16671. (Texts in Culture Ser.). 1995. text ed. write for info. (*0-7190-3942-8*, Pub. by Manchester Univ Pr UK); text ed. write for info. (*0-7190-3943-6*, Pub. by Manchester Univ Pr UK) St Martin.

Adam Smith, 1723-1790, 2 vols., Set. Mark Blaug. (Pioneers in Economics Ser.: No. 12). 592p. 1991. text ed. 172.95 (*1-85278-474-1*, Pub. by E Elgar Pub UK) Ashgate Pub Co.

Adam Smith's an Inquiry into the Nature & Causes of the Wealth of Nations: A Concordance. Ed. by Fred R. Glahe. LC 92-31799. 1992. write for info. (*0-8476-7797-4*) Rowman.

Adam Smith's Discourse: Canonicity, Commerce, & Conscience. Vivienne Brown. LC 93-24462. 1994. write for info. (*0-415-08160-2*, Routledge NY); write for info. (*0-415-09593-X*, Routledge NY) Routledge.

Adam Smith's Economics: Its Place in the Development of Economic Thought. Maurice Brown. 208p. 1988. lib. bdg. 60.00 (*0-7099-5079-9*) Routledge Chapman & Hall.

Adam Smith's Legacy: His Place in the Development of Modern Economics. Ed. by Michael Fry. LC 91-25698. (Illus.). 240p. 1992. 35.00 (*0-415-06164-4*, A5483) Routledge.

***Adam Smith's System of Liberty, Wealth, & Virtue: The Moral & Political Foundations of the Wealth of Nations.** Athol Fitzgibbons. (Illus.). 224p. 1995. 39.95 (*0-19-828923-5*) OUP.

Adam Smith's Theory of Value & Distribution. Rory O'Donnell. LC 89-70271. 250p. 1990. text ed. 49.95 (*0-312-04508-5*) St Martin.

Adam Steinfeld's Stupid Bar Tricks. Adam Steinfeld & Bret McCormick. 96p. 1993. pap. text ed. 5.95 (*0-939639-02-5*) Now Thats Funny.

Adam Straight & the Mysterious Neighbor. Kersten Hamilton. Ed. by LoraBeth Norton. LC 91-3373. (Adam Straight Ser.). 96p. (J). (gr. 4-6). Date not set. pap. 4.99 (*1-55513-385-1*, Chariot Bks) Chariot Family.

Adam Straight to the Rescue. Kersten Hamilton. Ed. by LoraBeth Norton. LC 91-14949. (Adam Straight Ser.). 96p. (J). (gr. 4-6). Date not set. pap. 4.99 (*1-55513-386-X*, Chariot Bks) Chariot Family.

***Adam Style.** Steven Parissien. (Illus.). 240p. 1995. pap. 35.00 (*0-7148-3453-X*, Pub. by Phaidon Press UK) Chronicle Bks.

Adam Style. Steven Parissien. (Illus.). 240p. 1992. 60.00 (*0-89133-197-2*) Preservation Pr.

Adam, the Altaic Ring & "The Children of the Sun" James R. Granger, Jr. LC 87-51202. (Illus.). 200p. (Orig.). 1988. pap. 12.95 (*0-945023-00-6*) Uraeus Pub.

Adam, the Baby, & the Man from Mars. Irwin Edman. LC 68-24850. (Essay Index Reprint Ser.). 1977. reprint ed. 23.95 (*0-8369-0404-4*) Ayer.

***Adam Then & Now.** Vicki L Thompson. (Superromance Ser.). 1995. pap. 3.75 (*0-373-70637-5*, 1-70637-3) Harlequin Bks.

Adam Was an Ape. Anthony A. Aiya. LC 85-90505. 120p. (Orig.). 1986. pap. text ed. 8.00 (*0-936869-00-3*) Meseraule Prnting.

Adam Zigzag. Barbara Barrie. LC 93-8735. (J). 1994. 14.95 (*0-385-31172-9*) Delacorte.

Adamant: Cowinner of the 1988 Iowa Poetry Prize. Mary Ruefle. LC 88-38575. (Iowa Poetry Prize Ser.). 87p. 1989. text ed. 17.95 (*0-87745-235-0*); pap. 10.95 (*0-87745-236-9*) U of Iowa Pr.

Adamantane: The Chemistry of Diamond Molecules. Raymond C. Fort. LC 75-2746. (Studies in Organic Chemistry: No. 5). (Illus.). 412p. reprint ed. pap. 117.50 (*0-7837-0836-X*, 2041150) Bks Demand.

Adamantine Gate or Those Double Doors of Heaven. Elmer Blakey. 1993. 12.95 (*0-533-10222-7*) Vantage.

Adamantine Sherlock Holmes: The Adventures in Tibet & India. Hapi. 144p. 1974. pap. 5.95 (*0-916926-00-1*) Kanthaka.

Adamantios Korais: A Study in Greek Nationalism. Stephen G. Chaconas. LC 68-58555. (Columbia University. Studies in the Social Sciences: No. 490). reprint ed. 22.50 (*0-404-51490-1*) AMS Pr.

***Adamco Lodge - We Call It the Cabin: Ancient Neighbor to the Pecos Wilderness.** Charles W. Adams. 1995. 11.95 (*0-614-05600-4*) Vantage.

Adamov: Plays, Vol. I Contains Parody, Invasion, All Against All, Professor Taranne, Vol. 1. Arthur Adamov. Tr. by Peter Meyer et al. 200p. (Orig.). 1996. pap. 13.95 (*0-7145-4164-8*) Riverrun NY.

***Adams: History of the Adams Family of North Staffordshire with Numerous Pedigree Charts & Notes on Allied Families.** Percy W. Adams. (Illus.). 480p. 1994. reprint ed. lib. bdg. 82.00 (*0-8328-4283-4*); reprint ed. pap. 72.00 (*0-8328-4284-2*) Higginson Bk Co.

Adams: The Manufacturing of Flaked Stone Tools at a Paleoindian Site in Western Kentucky. Thomas N. Sanders. LC 90-39707. (Illus.). 160p. (Orig.). 1990. pap. 15.95 (*0-9615462-4-7*) Persimmon NY.

Adams & Jefferson: A Revolutionary Dialogue. Merrill D. Peterson. LC 76-1145. (Illus.). 1978. pap. 10.95 (*0-19-502355-2*) OUP.

Adam's Apple. Jean Gralley. 1981. 2.50 (*0-87129-369-2*, A27) Dramatic Pub.

Adam's Apple: The Struggle Against Ourselves to Know, Vol. 161. Dante Cantrill. LC 93-47399. (American University Studies: Philosophy: Ser. V, Vol. 161). 237p. (C). 1994. text ed. 41.95 (*0-8204-2440-4*) P Lang Pubs.

Adams-Cobb, Vol. I. Ed. by William C. Davis. (Confederate General Ser.). (Illus.). 288p. 1991. 29.95 (*0-918678-63-3*) Natl Hist Soc.

Adams County, 2 vols., Set. Dorothy W. Creigh. Incl. Story of Adams County. LC 73-176266. 1972. 25.00 (*0-934858-00-4*); People. LC 73-176266. 1971. 10.00 (*0-934858-01-2*); LC 73-176266. (Illus.). 32.50 (*0-934858-02-0*) Adams County.

Adams County Court Facility Study. Fred Russillo & Chang-Ming Yeh. 50p. 1991. 3.00 (*0-685-55337-X*, WRO132) Natl Ctr St Courts.

***Adams County, Ohio Deeds, 1797-1806.** T.L.C. Genealogy Staff. 165p. (Orig.). 1990. spiral bd., pap. 12.00 (*1-886633-34-7*) TLC Genealogy.

***Adams County, Ohio Deeds, 1806-1812.** T.L.C. Genealogy Staff. LC 90-71768. 198p. (Orig.). 1990. spiral bd., pap. 14.00 (*1-886633-35-5*) TLC Genealogy.

Adams County Pioneer Memoirs. Gladys M. Sutherland. 100p. 1983. 12.00 (*0-87770-304-3*) Ye Galleon.

***Adams Cover Letter Almanac.** Ed. by Adams Publishing Staff. (Almanacs Ser.). 768p. (Orig.). 1995. pap. 10.95 (*1-55850-497-4*) Adams Pubng.

Adams Dagbok see Adam's Diary

Adam's Diary. Joseph G. Caruso. (Illus.). 26p. (Orig.). (J). (gr. k up). 1989. pap. 4.00 (*0-88680-313-6*); 15.00 (*0-88680-314-4*) I E Clark.

Adam's Diary. Knut Faldbakken. Tr. by Sverre Lyngstad. LC 87-5870. (Modern Scandinavian Literature in Translation Ser.). Orig. Title: Adams Dagbok. x, 246p. 1988. pap. 12.95 (*0-8032-6866-1*) U of Nebr Pr.

Adam's Diary. Mark Twain. (Illus.). 96p. 1984. pap. 6.95 (*0-932458-27-0*) Star Rover.

Adam's Diary. Samuel L. Clemens. (Works of Samuel Clemens). 1989. reprint ed. lib. bdg. 79.00 (*0-7812-0328-7*) Rprt Serv.

Adams Dictionary of American History, 8 vols., Set. rev. ed. LC 76-6735. 1977. text ed. 695.00 (*0-684-13856-5*, Scribners) S&S Trade.

Adam's Eden. Daisy L. Cook. LC 89-36802. 1993. pap. 14.95 (*0-87949-303-8*) Ashley Bks.

Adam's Eden. Faith Baldwin. 202p. reprint ed. lib. bdg. 17.95 (*0-88411-630-1*, Aeonian Pr) Amereon Ltd.

***Adam's Fall.** Sandra Brown. 1994. mass mkt. 4.99 (*0-553-56768-3*) Bantam.

Adam's Fall. large type ed. Sandra Brown. LC 94-6748. 1994. 23.95 (*1-56895-068-3*) Wheeler Pub.

Adams Family. James T. Adams. LC 73-21487. (Illus.). 364p. 1974. reprint ed. text ed. 35.00 (*0-8371-6427-3*, ADAF, Greenwood Pr) Greenwood.

***Adam's Family Bk. 1: Adam, Abram, Sarah & Other Bibles Heroes.** Jill Briscoe & Stuart Briscoe. LC 94-36790. (Illus.). 1994. write for info. (*0-8010-1087-X*) Baker Bk.

Adams Family Correspondence, 4 vols. Adams Family. Incl. Vols. 1 & 2. Dec. 1761-May 1776 & June 1776-Mar. 1778. LC 63-14964. 984p. 1963. Set. 90.00 (*0-674-00400-0*); Set. Volume 3, Apr. 1778-Sep. 1780; Volume 4. Oct. 1780-Sept. 1782. LC 63-14964. 979p. 1973. 90.00 (*0-674-00405-1*); LC 63-14964. (Adams Papers: No. 2). (Illus.). write for info. (*0-318-52993-9*) HUP.

Adams Family Correspondence, Vols. 5 & 6: October 1782-December 1785, Vol. 5. Ed. by Richard A. Ryerson et al. (Adams Papers Ser.: No. 2). (Illus.). 960p. 1992. text ed. 112.00 (*0-674-00406-X*) HUP.

Adams Federalists. Manning J. Dauer. LC 68-17645. (Illus.). 320p. reprint ed. pap. 91.20 (*0-8357-5093-0*, 2025807) Bks Demand.

Adams' Heart Disease in Infants, Children & Adolescents, 2 vols., Set. 5th ed. George C. Emmanouilides et al. (Illus.). 2016p. 1994. 294.00 (*0-683-02999-1*) Williams & Wilkins.

Adam's Island. William Marshall. (I Love to Read Collection). (Illus.). (J). (gr. 3-8). 1992. lib. bdg. 12.79 (*0-89565-889-5*) Childs World.

Adams-Jefferson Letters: The Complete Correspondence Between Thomas Jefferson & Abigail & John Adams. Ed. by Lester J. Cappon. LC 88-14258. (Institute of Early American History & Culture Ser.). iii, 638p. (C). 1988. reprint ed. 45.00 (*0-8078-1807-0*); reprint ed. pap. 19.95 (*0-8078-4230-3*) U of NC Pr.

***Adams Jobs Almanac, 1995.** Adams Editors Staff. 1994. pap. 15.00 (*1-55850-422-2*) Adams Pubng.

Adams' Lameness in Horses. 4th ed. Ed. by Ted S. Stashak. LC 85-5787. (Illus.). 906p. 1987. text ed. 99.50 (*0-8121-0980-5*) Williams & Wilkins.

Adams Middle School Principal Monroe City Schools Simulation Entire Simulation Package. Gerald R. Rasmussen. (Illus.). (Orig.). (C). 1986. audio, pap. text ed. 185.00 (*0-922971-49-8*, AMS 116) Univ Council Educ Admin.

Adams Middle School Principalship Adams Middle School Background Materials Monroe City Simulation Faculty Handbook. Gerald R. Rasmussen. (Orig.). (C). 1986. pap. text ed. 5.50 (*0-922971-38-2*, AMS 103) Univ Council Educ Admin.

Adams Middle School Principalship Monroe City School Simulation Secondary School Principal In-Basket IV. J. Arthur Howard et al. (Illus.). 75p. (Orig.). (C). 1983. pap. text ed. 8.25 (*0-922971-95-1*, AD-E4) Univ Council Educ Admin.

Adams Middle School Principalship Monroe City School Simulation Secondary School Principalship In-Basket I. Ward Sybouts. (Illus.). 44p. (Orig.). (C). 1983. pap. text ed. 5.15 (*0-922971-92-7*, AD-E1) Univ Council Educ Admin.

Adams Middle School Principalship Monroe City Schools Simulation License Fee. (C). 1986. pap. text ed. 100.00 (*0-922971-50-1*, AMS 120) Univ Council Educ Admin.

Adams Middle School Superintendency Monroe City School Simulation Assistant Superintendent for Business Services Background Information. Thelbert Drake & Wilbur Venerable. 70p. (Orig.). (C). 1983. pap. text ed. 8.25 (*0-922971-88-9*, ADD) Univ Council Educ Admin.

Adams Middle School Superintendency Monroe City School Simulation Assistant Superintendent for Business Services In-Basket II. Thelbert Drake & Wilbur Venerable. (Illus.). 51p. (Orig.). (C). 1983. pap. text ed. 6.40 (*0-922971-90-0*, AD-D2) Univ Council Educ Admin.

Adams Middle School Superintendency Monroe City School Simulation Assistant Superintendent for Instruction In-Basket II. Rutgers University Graduate Students et al. 58p. (Orig.). (C). 1983. pap. text ed. 8.25 (*0-922971-87-0*, AD-C2) Univ Council Educ Admin.

Adams Middle School Superintendency Monroe City School Simulation Assistant Superintendent of Instruction Background Information. Rutgers University Graduate Students et al. 50p. (Orig.). (C). 1983. pap. text ed. 8.25 (*0-922971-85-4*, AD-C) Univ Council Educ Admin.

Adams National Historic Site: A Family's Legacy to America. Wilhelmina S. Harris. (Illus.). 64p. 1990. reprint ed. pap. 6.50 (*0-915992-48-5*) Eastern Acorn.

***Adam's Progress: A Picaresque Tale.** Donald K. Frank. LC 91-67760. 128p. (Orig.). 1994. pap. 9.00 (*1-56002-133-0*) Aegina Pr.

Adams Resume Almanac. Ed. by Adams Editors Staff. LC 94-8685. 1994. pap. 10.95 (*1-55850-358-7*) Adams Pubng.

Adam's Righting Revolution: One Child's Literary Development from Infancy Through Grade One. Judith A. Schickedanz. LC 89-49688. (Illus.). 155p. 1990. pap. text ed. 18.00 (*0-435-08511-5*, 08511) Heinemann.

Adam's Soul: The Collected Tales of Howard Schwartz. Howard Schwartz. LC 92-20735. 320p. 1992. 30.00 (*0-87668-315-4*) Aronson.

Adam's Story. Ulmer. LC 59-1292. (Arch Bks.). 24p. (Orig.). (J). (gr. k-4). 1985. pap. 1.99 (*0-570-06191-1*) Concordia.

Adams Suburban District Simulation: Entire Simulation Package. Gerald R. Rasmussen. (Illus.). (Orig.). (C). 1986. audio, pap. text ed. 230.00 (*1-55996-140-6*) Univ Council Educ Admin.

Adams Suburban District Simulation: License Fee. (C). 1986. pap. text ed. 100.00 (*1-55996-141-4*) Univ Council Educ Admin.

Adam's Table. 2nd rev. ed. Reggi Burnett. LC 93-61037. (Illus.). 96p. (Orig.). 1994. 8.95 (*0-945383-59-2*) Teach Servs.

Adam's Task: Calling Animals by Name. Vicki Hearne. 1986. 17.95 (*0-394-54214-2*) Knopf.

Adam's Task: Calling Animals by Name. Vicki Hearne. LC 94-14717. 1994. pap. 12.00 (*0-06-097634-9*, PL) HarpC.

***Adams the Pilot: The Life & Times of Captain William Adams: 1564-1620.** William Corr. 256p. (C). 1995. text ed. 49.95 (*1-873410-44-1*, Pub. by Japan Library) Humanities.

***Adam's Vow: (Bundles of Joy)** Karen R. Smith. (Sil Romance Ser.). 1995. mass mkt. 2.99 (*0-373-19075-1*, 1-19075-0) Silhouette.

Adams vs. Texas. Randall Adams. 1992. mass mkt. 5.99 (*0-312-92778-9*) St Martin.

Adam's War. Sonia Levitin. LC 93-13833. (J). 1994. 13.99 (*0-8037-1506-4*); lib. bdg. 13.89 (*0-8037-1507-2*) Dial Bks Young.

Adams Women: Abigail & Louisa Adams, Their Sisters & Daughters. Paul C. Nagel. (Illus.). 320p. 1987. 30.00 (*0-19-503874-6*) OUP.

Adams Women: Abigail & Louisa Adams, Their Sisters & Daughters. Paul C. Nagel. (Illus.). 324p. 1989. reprint ed. pap. 10.95 (*0-19-505920-4*) OUP.

Adan Se Despide. Enrique Macin. Ed. by Dos Pasos. (Palabra Nueva Ser.). (Orig.). (SPA.). 1988. pap. 12.00 (*0-9615403-3-8*) Dos Pasos Ed.

Adanson: The Bicentennial of Michel Adanson's "Familles des Plantes", 2 vols., 1. Ed. by G. H. Lawrence. (Illus.). 392p. 1964. 19.00 (*0-913196-23-1*); pap. 17.00 (*0-913196-25-8*) Hunt Inst Botanical.

Adanson: The Bicentennial of Michel Adanson's "Familles des Plantes", 2 vols., 2. Ed. by G. H. Lawrence. (Illus.). 243p. 1964. 15.00 (*0-913196-24-X*); pap. 13.00 (*0-913196-26-6*) Hunt Inst Botanical.

ADAPSO Sales & Use Tax Survey. rev. ed. Ronald J. Palenski. write for info. (*0-318-62080-4*) ITAA.

Adaptability: The Significance of Variability from Molecule to Ecosystem. Ed. by Michael Conrad. LC 82-24558. 408p. 1983. 89.50 (*0-306-41223-3*, Plenum Pr) Plenum.

Adaptability among the Elementary Schools of an American City. George W. Ebey. LC 71-176741. (Columbia University. Teachers College. Contributions to Education Ser.: No. 817). reprint ed. 37.50 (*0-404-55817-8*) AMS Pr.

An Asterisk (*) at the beginning of an entry indicates that the title is appearing in BIP for the first time.

An Asterisk (*) at the beginning of an entry indicates that the title is appearing in BIP for the first time.

53

A

A

Adaptive Intelligent Systems: Proceedings of the Third BANKAI Workshop, Brussels, Belgium, 12-14 October 1992. BANKAI Workshop Staff. LC 93-9382. 250p. 1993. 137.50 (*0-444-89838-7*) Elsevier.

Adaptive Knowing. James K. Feibleman. 1977. pap. text ed. 65.50 (*90-247-1890-2*) Kluwer Ac.

Adaptive Language Disorders of Young Adults with Learning Disabilities. Carol Weller et al. LC 92-16006. (Illus.). 237p. (Orig.). (C). 1992. pap. text ed. 34.95 (*1-879105-82-9*) Singular Publishing.

Adaptive Learning Environments: Foundations & Frontiers. Ed. by Marlene Jones et al. LC 92-10285. (NATO ASI Series. Series F, Computer & Systems Sciences. Special Programme AET: Vol. 85). viii, 408p. 1992. 103.00 (*0-387-55459-9*) Spr-Verlag.

Adaptive Markov Control Processes. O. Hernandez-Lerma. (Applied Mathematical Sciences Ser.: Vol. 79). (Illus.). xiv, 148p. 1989. 44.00 (*0-387-96966-7*) Spr-Verlag.

Adaptive Mechanisms in Gaze Control. Ed. by Alain Berthoz & G. M. Jones. (Reviews of Oculomotor Research Ser.: No. 1). 1985. 180.50 (*0-444-80483-8*) Elsevier.

***Adaptive Methods - Algorithms, Theory & Applications: Proceedings of the Ninth GAMM-Seminar Kiel, January 22-24, 1993.** Ed. by Wolfgang Hackbusch & Gabriel Wittum. (Notes on Numerical Fluid Mechanics Ser.: Vol. 46). viii, 272p. 1994. 77.00 (*3-528-07646-1*) Ballen Bkslr.

Adaptive Methods for Control System Design. Ed. by Madan M. Gupta. LC 86-10562. 488p. 1986. 69.95 (*0-87942-207-6*, PC01651) Inst Electrical.

Adaptive Methods for Partial Differential Equations. Joseph Flaherty et al. LC 89-21597. (Proceedings in Applied Mathematics Ser.: No. 39). xi, 265p. 1989. pap. 33.50 (*0-89871-242-4*) Soc Indus-Appl Math.

Adaptive Methods in Underwater Acoustics. Heinz G. Urban. 800p. 1985. 69.95 (*90-277-1982-9*) Peninsula CA.

Adaptive, Multilevel, & Hierarchical Computational Strategies. Ed. by A. K. Norr. (AMD Ser.: Vol. 157). 157p. 1992. 72.50 (*0-7918-1134-4*, G00778) ASME.

Adaptive Neural Network. Y. Burnod. 1991. pap. 53.33 (*0-13-019464-6*) P-H.

Adaptive Optics & Optical Structures. Ed. by R. K. Tyson & J. Schulte in den Baumen. 1990. 62.00 (*0-8194-0318-0*, VOL. 1271) SPIE.

Adaptive Optics for Astronomy: Proceedings of the NATO Advanced Study Institute on Adaptive Optics for Astronomy Cargese, Corse, France, June 29-July 9, 1993. Ed. by Danielle M. Alloin & Jean-Marie Mariotti. LC 94-4222. (NATO Advanced Study Institutes Series C, Mathematical & Physical Sciences: Vol. 423). 356p. 1994. lib. bdg. 127.00 (*0-7923-2748-9*) Kluwer Ac.

Adaptive Optics for Large Telescopes. LC 92-80635. (Technical Digest Series, 1992: Vol. 19). 250p. (Orig.). 1992. Postconference. pap. 75.00 (*1-55752-250-2*); Conference. pap. 48.00 (*1-55752-249-9*) Optical Soc.

Adaptive Optimal Control: The Thinking Man's G.P.C. Robert P. Bithmead et al. 244p. 1990. boxed 66.67 (*0-13-013277-2*) P-H.

Adaptive Parsing: Self-Extending Natural Language Interfaces. Jill F. Lehman. (C). 1991. lib. bdg. 69.50 (*0-7923-9183-7*) Kluwer Ac.

Adaptive Pattern Recognition & Neural Networks. Yoh-Han Pao. (Illus.). 288p. (C). 1989. text ed. 43.25 (*0-201-12584-6*) Addison-Wesley.

Adaptive Physiology to Stressful Environments. Ed. by S. Samueloff & Mohamed K. Yousef. 224p. 1987. 129.00 (*0-8493-6458-2*, QP82, CRC Reprint) Franklin.

Adaptive Play for Special Needs Children: Strategies to Enhance Communication & Learning. Caroline R. Musselwhite. LC 90-52761. (Illus.). 249p. (C). 1986. pap. text ed. 27.00 (*0-89079-303-4*, 1751) PRO-ED.

Adaptive Processes in Visual & Oculomotor System. Ed. by E. L. Keller & D. S Zee. 1986. 88.00 (*0-08-032012-0*, Pergamon Pr) Elsevier.

Adaptive Protection of the Heart: Protecting Against Stress & Ischemic Damage. Felix Z. Meerson. (Illus.). 320p. 1990. 121.00 (*0-8493-5150-2*, QP114) CRC Pr.

Adaptive Radar Detection & Estimation. Simon Haykin & Allan Steinhardt. (Series in Remote Sensing). 1992. text ed. 108.00 (*0-471-54468-X*) Wiley.

Adaptive Reasoning for Real-World Problems: A Schema-Based Approach. Roy Turner. 272p. 1994. text ed. 49.95 (*0-8058-1298-9*) L Erlbaum Assocs.

Adaptive Response of Native Amazonians. Ed. by Raymond B. Hames & William T. Vickers. LC 82-18399. (Studies in Anthropology). 1983. text ed. 75.00 (*0-12-321250-2*) Acad Pr.

Adaptive Reuse. Ed. by Richard L. Austin. (Illus.). 128p. 1987. text ed. 29.95 (*0-317-58455-3*) Van Nos Reinhold.

Adaptive Seascape: The Mechanism of Evolution. David J. Merrell. LC 93-29841. 1994. 34.95 (*0-8166-2348-1*) U of Minn Pr.

Adaptive Signal Processing. S. T. Alexander. (Texts & Monographs in Computer Science). (Illus.). 185p. 1986. 54.00 (*0-387-96380-4*) Spr-Verlag.

Adaptive Signal Processing. Ed. by L. D. Davisson & G. Longo. (CISM International Centre for Mechanical Sciences Ser.: No. 324). (Illus.). x, 203p. 1992. pap. 45.00 (*0-387-82333-6*) Spr-Verlag.

Adaptive Signal Processing. S. Haykin. 1992. 70.00 (*0-8194-0693-7*, 1565) SPIE.

Adaptive Signal Processing. Leon H. Sibul. LC 87-2812. 352p. 1987. 49.95 (*0-87942-224-6*, PCO2147) Inst Electrical.

Adaptive Signal Processing. Bernard Widrow & Samuel D. Stearns. (Illus.). 528p. (C). 1985. text ed. 80.00 (*0-13-004029-0*) P-H.

Adaptive Signal Processing Algorithms: Stability & Performance. Victor Solo & Xuan Kong. LC 93-38907. 1994. text ed. 73.00 (*0-13-501263-5*) P-H.

Adaptive Signal Processing for Radar. Ramon Nitzberg. (Radar Library). 424p. 1992. text ed. 88.00 (*0-89006-586-1*) Artech Hse.

Adaptive Statistical Procedures & Related Topics. Ed. by John Van Ryzin. LC 86-83371. (IMS Lecture Notes - Monograph Ser.: Vol. 8). x, 476p. (C). 1987. pap. 40.00 (*0-940600-09-9*) Inst Math.

Adaptive Strategies & Population Ecology of Northern Grouse. Ed. by Arthur T. Bergerud & Michael W. Gratson. LC 86-19248. (Illus.). 832p. 1988. text ed. 59.95 (*0-8166-1469-5*) U of Minn Pr.

Adaptive Strategies & Population Ecology of Northern Grouse, Vol. I, Population Studies. Ed. by Arthur T. Bergerud & Michael W. Gratson. LC 86-19248. (Illus.). 420p. 1988. pap. text ed. 24.95 (*0-8166-1470-9*) U of Minn Pr.

Adaptive Strategies & Population Ecology of Northern Grouse, Vol. II, Theory & Synthesis. Ed. by Arthur T. Bergerud & Michael W. Gratson. LC 86-19248. (Illus.). 396p. 1988. pap. text ed. 24.95 (*0-8166-1471-7*) U of Minn Pr.

***Adaptive Structures & Composite Materials: Analysis & Application: 1994 International Mechanical Engineering Congress & Exposition, Chicago, Illinois - November 6-11, 1994.** (AD - MD Ser.: Vol. 45, Vol. 54). 416p. 1994. 100.00 (*0-7918-1458-0*, G00953) ASME.

Adaptive Structures & Material Systems. Ed. by G. P. Carman & E. Garcia. LC 93-73594. (AD Ser.: Vol. 35). 463p. 1994. pap. 85.00 (*0-7918-1041-0*) ASME.

Adaptive System Identification & Signal Processing Algorithms. Ed. by Nicholas Kalouptsidis & Sergios Theodoridis. LC 92-40993. (International Series in Acoustics, Speech, & Signal Processing). 450p. 1993. text ed. 65.00 (*0-13-006545-5*) P-H.

Adaptive Systems in Control & Signal Processing 1983: Proceedings of the IFAC Symposium, San Francisco, California, June 1983. IFAC Symposium Staff & Ioan D. Landau. (IFAC Proceedings Ser.). 420p. 1984. 163.00 (*0-08-030565-2*, Pub. by Pergamon Repr UK) Franklin.

Adaptive Systems in Control & Signal Processing, 1989. Ed. by M. A. Johnson et al. LC 90-6796. (IFAC Proceedings Ser.: No. 9001). 620p. 1990. 285.00 (*0-08-035727-X*, Pergamon Pr) Elsevier.

***Adaptive Systems in Control & Signal Processing, 1992: Selected Papers from the Fourth IFAC Symposium, Grenoble, France, 1-3 July 1992.** Ed. by L. Dugard et al. 1995. pap. 91.00 (*0-08-042596-8*, Pergamon Pr) Elsevier.

Adaptive Systems with Reduced Models. Petros A. Ioannou & Peter V. Kokotovic. (Lecture Notes in Control & Information Sciences Ser.: Vol. 47). 164p. 1983. pap. 20.00 (*0-387-12150-1*) Spr-Verlag.

Adaptive Technologies for Learning & Work Environments. Joseph J. Lazzaro. LC 92-46993. (Illus.). 250p. 1993. pap. 35.00 (*0-8389-0615-X*) ALA.

Adaptive Technology for Special Human Needs. Arlene Brett & Eugene F. Provenzo, Jr. LC 94-17216. (SUNY Series in Computers in Education). 140p. 1995. text ed. 44.50 (*0-7914-2307-7*); pap. 14.95x (*0-7914-2308-5*) State U NY Pr.

Adaptive Use: Development Economics, Process, & Profiles. W. Paul O'Mara et al. LC 78-56054. (Illus.). 246p. (C). 1978. 43.95 (*0-87420-582-4*, A08) Urban Land.

Adaptive User Interfaces. Ed. by Dermont Browne et al. (Computers & People Ser.). (Illus.). 227p. 1990. text ed. 50.00 (*0-12-137755-5*) Acad Pr.

Adaptive User Interfaces: Principles & Practice. Ed. by Matthias Schneider-Hufschmidt et al. LC 93-8442. (Human Factors in Information Technology Ser.: Vol. 10). 1993. 108.75 (*0-444-81545-7*, North Holland) Elsevier.

Adaptive User Support: Ergonomic Design of Manually & Automatically Adaptable Software. Ed. by Reinhard Oppermann. (Computers, Cognition, & Work Ser.). 272p. 1994. text ed. 49.95 (*0-8058-1655-0*) L Erlbaum Assocs.

***Adaptors & Innovators.** Ed. by Michael Kirton. 256p. 1994. pap. 22.95 (*0-415-11662-7*, B4509) Routledge.

Adaptors & Innovators: Styles of Creativity & Problem-Solving. Ed. by Michael J. Kirton. 304p. 1989. 65.00 (*0-415-02424-2*) Routledge.

ADA's Effect on the Landlord - Tenant Relationship Special Report. Mark A. Senn et al. (Real Estate Practice Library). 128p. 1993. pap. text ed. 75.00 (*0-471-59861-5*) Wiley.

Adastra Reader: The Collected Chapbooks. Ed. by Gary Metras. LC 87-70119. (Illus.). 248p. (Orig.). 1987. pap. 10.00 (*0-938566-32-6*) Adastra Pr.

Adat & Dinas: Balinese Communities in the Indonesian State. Carol Warren. LC 92-35881. (South-East Asian Social Science Monographs). (Illus.). 400p. 1993. 55.00 (*0-19-588609-7*) OUP.

Adat Law in Indonesia. Barend Ter Haar. Ed. by E. Adamson Hoebel & A. Arthur Schiller. LC 77-86985. 1977. reprint ed. 26.50 (*0-404-16725-X*) AMS Pr.

Adbashing: Surviving the Attacks on Advertising. Jack Myers. 325p. (Orig.). (C). 1993. pap. text ed. 17.95 (*0-9635864-0-8*) Amer Media Coun.

ADC '94: Proceedings of the Australasian Database Conference. R. Sacks-Davis. 400p. 1993. text ed. 108.00 (*981-3049-00-6*) World Scientific Pub.

***ADCHEM '94 - Advanced Control of Chemical Processes: Proceedings of the IFAC Symposium, Kyoto, Japan, 25-27 May, 1994.** International Federation of Automatic Control, Triennial World Congress, 7th, Helsinki, Finland, June 1978. Ed. by D. Bonvin. LC 94-43037. 558p. 1994. pap. 91.00 (*0-08-042229-2*, Pergamon Pr) Elsevier.

ADD: Helping Your Child. Warren Umansky & Barbara S. Smalley. 224p. (Orig.). 1994. pap. 10.99 (*0-446-67013-8*) Warner Bks.

***Add - A Lifetime Challenge.** Mary J. Johnson. 132p. (Orig.). 1994. pap. text ed. 14.95 (*1-885988-02-8*) Add Resources.

Add a Little Spice. Bethany Campbell. (Romance Ser.). 1993. pap. 2.89 (*0-373-03260-9*, 1-03260-6) Harlequin Bks.

ADD & the College Student: A Guide for High School & College Students with Attention Deficit Disorder. Ed. by Patricia O. Quinn. LC 93-36668. 128p. 1994. pap. 13.95 (*0-945354-58-4*) Magination Pr.

ADD Hyperactivity Handbook for Schools: Effective Strategies for Identifying & Teaching ADD Students in Elementary & Secondary Schools. Harvey C. Parker. (Illus.). 330p. (Orig.). 1992. pap. 27.00 (*0-9621629-2-2*) Spec Pr FL.

ADD Hyperactivity Workbook for Parents, Teachers & Kids. Harvey C. Parker. (Illus.). 108p. (Orig.). 1988. 12.95 (*0-685-23302-2*) Spec Pr FL.

Add It Up! (Sesame Street Ser.: No. 13). (J). 1989. pap. 1.49 (*0-553-18396-6*) Bantam.

***Add Justice to Your Shopping List: A Guide for Reshaping Food Buying Habits.** Marilyn Voran. LC 85-81539. (Illus.). reprint ed. pap. 25.00 (*0-7837-9055-4*, 2049806) Bks Demand.

Add Life to Your Years: How to Make Each Day Count. Hillel E. Silverman. LC 92-5702. 1992. write for info. (*0-88125-423-1*) Ktav.

Add-On Monthly Payment Tables. Financial Publishing Co. Staff. 256p. 1984. pap. 9.00 (*0-87600-893-7*) Finan Pub.

Add Spice to Your Travels. Bill MacRobbie. (Illus.). 196p. 1980. pap. 4.95 (*0-9605244-0-1*) B Sales.

Add Value to Your Service: The Key to Success. Ed. by Carol Surprenant. LC 87-31919. (Proceedings Ser.). (Illus.). 214p. (Orig.). 1988. pap. text ed. 27.00 (*0-87757-190-2*) Am Mktg.

Addams Chronicles. 1993. mass mkt. 5.99 (*0-06-109249-5*, Harp PBks) HarpC.

Addams Chronicles: Everything You Ever Wanted to Know about the Addams Family. Stephen Cox. (Illus.). 160p. 1991. reprint ed. lib. bdg. 27.00x (*0-8095-9135-9*) Borgo Pr.

Addams Family. 32p. (J). 1991. pap. 2.50 (*0-590-45539-7*) Scholastic Inc.

Addams Family in "Sir Pugsley" Adapt. by Conrad Kash. (Sound Story Books-Deluxe Editions Ser.). (Illus.). 24p. (J). (ps-4). 1993. 20.00 (*0-307-74031-5*, 64031, Golden Pr) Western Pub.

Addams Family Revealed. James Van Hise. 1991. pap. 14.95 (*1-55698-300-X*) Movie Pubs Servs.

Addams Family Values. Ann Hodgman. Ed. by Ruth Ashby. 112p. (Orig.). (J). 1993. mass mkt. 3.99 (*0-671-88001-2*, Minstrel Bks) PB.

Addams Family Values. Todd Strasser. Ed. by Rebecca Todd. 208p. (Orig.). 1993. mass mkt. 4.99 (*0-671-88036-5*) PB.

***Addbook One: Experiments in Digital & Analog Electronics.** Howard V. Malmstadt et al. (Addbook Ser.: Bk. 1). 1977. pap. text ed. 17.00 (*0-89704-019-8*) E&L Instru.

Added Dimension: The Art of Mind of Flannery O'Connor. 2nd ed. Melvin J. Friedman. LC 66-11070. xviii, 263p. 1977. pap. 20.00 (*0-8232-0711-0*) Fordham.

Added Upon. Nephi Anderson. 7.95 (*0-88494-487-5*) Bookcraft Inc.

Added Value Negotiating: The Breakthrough Method for Building Balanced Deals. Karl Albrecht & Steve Albrecht. LC 92-43739. 205p. 1993. text ed. 25.00 (*1-55623-967-X*) Irwin Prof Pubng.

Added Value of Geographical Information Systems in Public & Environmental Health. Ed. by Marion J. De Lepper. (GeoJournal Library). 370p. (C). 1995. lib. bdg. 139.50 (*0-7923-1887-0*) Kluwer Ac.

Addenda Section 1993: A Supplement to Webster's Third New International Dictionary. Merriam-Webster Staff. 1993. pap. 5.00 (*0-87779-100-7*) Merriam-Webster Inc.

Addenda und Corrigenda Zu der Von Berthold Litzmann Erarbeiteten Ausgabe. Ed. by Michael Struck. 230p. Date not set. write for info. (*0-318-71948-7*, Pub. by Georg Olms GW) Lubrecht & Cramer.

Addendum: ADA Exchanges, Nutrients, Calories, Cholest, Sodium. 16p. 1988. write for info. (*0-318-63122-9*) K-D Enter.

***Addendum to Modern Dance Fundamentals.** Odette Blum. 84p. 1991. spiral bd. 14.95 (*0-87127-195-8*) Princeton Bk Co.

Addendum to the Boating Accident Investigation Text. Kirsten et al. 78p. (C). 1993. pap. text ed. 5.00 (*1-55989-467-9*) Underwrtrs Labs.

Addendum to the Proceedings on Object-Oriented Programming Systems, Languages & Applications - OOPSLA 87. (Sigplan Notices Ser.: Vol. 23, No. 5). (Illus.). 143p. 1987. pap. text ed. 16.00 (*0-89791-266-7*, 548872) Assn Compu Machinery.

Adder. Peter Stafford. 1989. pap. 25.00 (*0-85263-879-5*, Pub. by Shire UK) St Mut.

Adders 'N Keyes: One Month in the Life of a Sole Proprietorship. 2nd ed. Brenda M. Mallouk. (C). 1991. pap. text ed. write for info. (*0-07-551221-1*, Pub. by McGraw-H Ryerson CN) McGraw.

Addict. Jerome McDonough. (Illus.). 47p. (Orig.). (YA). (gr. 7-12). 1985. pap. 3.50 (*0-88680-241-5*) I E Clark.

Addict Aftercare: Recovery Training & Self-Help. 1986. lib. bdg. 79.95 (*0-8490-3502-3*) Gordon Pr.

Addict to Yearning: Inspirational Philosophy & Religion. Merle Lighton. 1952. 5.00 (*0-910892-00-8*, 910892) Lighton Pubns.

Addicted. Joan Morrone. LC 85-82145. 125p. (Orig.). 1986. pap. 6.00 (*0-9616771-0-4*) J & R Pub.

***Addicted? A Guide to Understanding Addiction.** Tom O'Connell. LC 90-91803. 210p. (Orig.). 1990. pap. text ed. 19.00 (*0-9620318-0-1*) Sanctuary Comns.

Addicted, in Their Own Words: Kids Talking about Drugs. Joel Engel. 1990. pap. 3.95 (*0-8125-9446-0*) Tor Bks.

***Addicted to Crime.** Hodge & McMurran. Date not set. text ed. 39.95 (*0-471-95079-3*) Wiley.

Addicted to Love: Facts about Sexual Addictions. rev. ed. 1994. pap. 0.25 (*0-89230-223-2*) Do It Now.

Addicted to "Love" Recovery from Unhealthy Dependencies in Romance. Stephen Arterburn. 288p. 1992. pap. 12.99 (*0-89283-802-7*, Vine Bks) Servant.

***Addicted to "Love" Understanding Dependencies of the Heart: Romance, Relationships, & Sex.** Stephen Arterburn. 307p. 1995. pap. 10.99 (*0-89283-930-9*, Vine Bks) Servant.

Addicted to Mediocrity. Franky Schaeffer. LC 80-85325. (Illus.). 128p. 1981. pap. 6.99 (*0-89107-214-4*); pap. 6.99 (*0-89107-353-1*) Crossway Bks.

Addicted to Recovery: Exposing the False Gospel of Psychotherapy: Escaping the Trap of Victim Mentality. Gary Almy et al. LC 94-11489. (Psychiatry & Religion Ser.). 1994. 11.99 (*1-56507-185-9*) Harvest Hse.

***Addicted to Romance: The Life & Adventures of Elinor Glyn.** Joan Hardwick. (Illus.). 320p. 1995. 40.00 (*0-233-98866-1*, Pub. by A Deutsch UK) Trafalgar.

Addicted to Sail. Norris D. Hoyt. (Illus.). 220p. 1987. 19.95 (*0-393-03316-3*) Norton.

Addicted to Suicide: A Woman Struggling to Live. Mary Savage. 144p. 1979. pap. text ed. 14.95 (*0-87073-907-7*) Schenkman Bks Inc.

Addicted to Symphonies. Lenore H. Hughes. (Illus.). 43p. (Orig.). 1985. pap. 3.00 (*0-9604772-2-5*) Hughes Pub.

Addicted to the Addict: From Codependency to Recovery. Kenneth G. Reiners. LC 87-50843. 64p. (Orig.). (YA). (gr. 9-12). 1987. pap. 5.50 (*0-934104-06-9*) Woodland.

Addicted to War: Why the U. S. Government Can't Kick Militarism. Joel Andreas. (Illus.). 64p. (Orig.). 1992. lib. bdg. 19.95 (*0-86571-242-5*); pap. 7.95 (*0-86571-243-3*) New Soc Pubs.

Addiction. Walter E. Kloss. Ed. by Richard W. Coffen. 96p. 1987. pap. 5.95 (*0-8280-0390-4*) Review & Herald.

Addiction. rev. ed. Gilda Berger. LC 92-17093. 144p. (YA). (gr. 9-12). 1992. lib. bdg. 14.77 (*0-531-11144-X*) Watts.

Addiction: Distinguishing Between Fact & Opinion. Bradley Steffens. LC 93-29058. (Opposing Viewpoints Juniors Ser.). (Illus.). 32p. (J). (gr. 4-7). 1994. lib. bdg. 11.95 (*1-56510-094-8*) Greenhaven.

Addiction: From Biology to Drug Policy. Avram Goldstein. LC 93-14243. (C). 1995. text ed. 22.95 (*0-7167-2384-0*) W H Freeman.

Addiction: Processes of Change. Ed. by Griffith Edwards & Malcolm Lader. (Society for the Study of Addiciton Monograph Ser.: No. 3). (Illus.). 256p. 1995. 98.00 (*0-19-262433-4*) OUP.

Addiction: The High-Low Trap. Irving Cohen. 1995. pap. 12.95 (*0-929173-10-4*) Health Press.

***Addiction & Co-Dependency: HP 605.** Eberhart. 49p. (C). 1989. student ed write for info. (*0-933195-60-5*) Allied Hlth Pubns.

***Addiction & Family Systems.** Ed. by Anne M. Christner. 1994. 49.95 (*1-884937-07-1*) Manisses Communs.

Addiction & Grace: Love & Spirituality in the Healing of Addictions. Gerald G. May. LC 88-45147. (Illus.). 208p. 1991. reprint ed. pap. 11.00 (*0-06-065537-2*) Harper SF.

***Addiction & Recovery of Gay & Lesbian Persons.** Ed. by Robert J. Kus. 1994. pap. 9.95 (*1-56023-055-X*) Haworth Pr.

***Addiction & Recovery of Gay & Lesbian Persons.** Ed. by Robert J. Kus. 97p. 1994. 29.95 (*1-56024-668-5*) Haworth Pr.

Addiction & Responsibility: An Inquiry into the Addictive Mind. Francis F. Seeburger. LC 93-25168. 200p. 1993. 19.95 (*0-8245-1365-7*) Crossroad NY.

***Addiction & Responsibility: An Inquiry into the Addictive Mind.** Francis F. Seeburger. 224p. 1995. pap. 14.95 (*0-8245-1501-3*) Crossroad NY.

***Addiction & Sigmund Freud: Freud's Psychology Applied to Addiction.** Dan Rivers. 350p. (Orig.). 1995. pap. 29.95 (*0-9644355-2-7*) Mercie Pub.

Addiction & the Vulnerable Self: Modified Dynamic Group Therapy for Substance Abusers. Edward J. Khantzian et al. LC 90-3821. 176p. 1990. lib. bdg. 24.95 (*0-89862-172-0*) Guilford Pr.

Addiction, Change & Choice: The New View of Alcholism. Vincent Fox. 256p. (Orig.). 1994. pap. 14.95 (*0-9613289-7-5*) See Sharp Pr.

Addiction Counselor. Jack Rudman. (Career Examination Ser.: C-2150). 1994. pap. 29.95 (*0-8373-2150-6*) Nat Learn.

Addiction in America Series, 55 bks. Ed. by Gerald N. Grob et al. 1981. write for info. (*0-318-50781-1*) Ayer.

Addiction in Human Development: Developmental Perspectives on Addiction & Recovery. Jacqueline Wallen. LC 91-32981. 170p. 1993. pap. 14.95 (*1-56024-247-7*) Haworth Pr.

Addiction in Human Development: Developmental Perspectives on Addiction & Recovery. Jacqueline Wallen. LC 91-32981. (Illus.). 176p. 1993. lib. bdg. 39.95 (*1-56024-246-9*) Haworth Pr.

An Asterisk (*) at the beginning of an entry indicates that the title is appearing in BIP for the first time.

Addiction in the Nursing Profession: Approaches to Intervention & Recovery. Ed. by Mary Haack & Tonda Hughes. LC 88-24961. 288p. 1989. 32.95 (*0-8261-6150-2*) Springer Pub.

Addiction Potential of Abused Drugs & Drug Classes. Carlton K. Erickson et al. LC 90-4639. (Advances in Alcohol & Substance Abuse Ser.: Vol. 9, Nos. 1 & 2). 201p. 1990. text ed. 39.95 (*0-86656-975-8*) Haworth Pr.

Addiction Process: Effective Social Work Approaches. Ed. by Edith M. Freeman. 304p. (Orig.). (C). 1992. pap. text ed. 33.95 (*0-8013-0377-X*, 78158) Longman.

Addiction Reform in the Progressive Age: Scientific & Social Responses to Drug Dependence in the United States 1870 to 1930. Arnold Jaffe. Ed. by Gerald N. Grob. LC 80-1269. (Addiction in America Ser.). (Illus.). 1981. lib. bdg. 35.95 (*0-405-13556-4*) Ayer.

Addiction Specialist. Jack Rudman. (Career Examination Ser.: C-1075). 1994. pap. 29.95 (*0-8373-1075-X*) Nat Learn.

Addiction to Love. Susan Peadbody. 1994. pap. 9.95 (*0-89087-715-7*) Celestial Arts.

Addiction to Love. rev. ed. Susan Peabody. (Illus.). 132p. (Orig.). 1994. pap. 9.95 (*0-89815-715-3*) Ten Speed Pr.

***Addiction to Perfection.** Woodman. 1995. pap. 18.00 (*0-919123-11-2*) Atrium Pubs.

Addictionary: A Primer of Recovery Terms & Concepts, from Abstincence to Withdrawal. Jan R. Wilson & Judith A. Wilson. LC 92-19070. 1992. pap. 25.00 (*0-671-79380-2*) Hazelden.

Addictions. Walter Gabrielson & Edward Wortz. 60p. 1991. pap. write for info. (*1-880658-00-3*) San Barb CAF.

Addictions: Concepts & Strategies for Treatment. Ed. by Judith A. Lewis. LC 94-9159. 393p. 1994. 49.00 (*0-8342-0563-7*) Aspen Pub.

Addictions: Multidisciplinary Perspectives & Treatments. Ed. by Harvey B. Milkman & Howard J. Shaffer. LC 84-47871. 224p. 1984. text ed. 37.95 (*0-669-08739-4*) Free Pr.

Addictions: Personal Influences & Scientific Movement. Griffith Edwards. 384p. (C). 1990. 44.95 (*0-88738-343-2*) Transaction Pubs.

Addictions & Psychological Dysfunctions in Nursing: The Profession's Response to the Problem. American Nurses Association Staff. 61p. (Orig.). (C). 1984. pap. 8.00 (*1-55810-068-7*, PMH-6) Am Nurses Pub.

Addictions Counseling: A Practical Guide to Counseling People with Chemical & Other Addictions. Dianne Doyle Pita. 144p. 1992. 17.95 (*0-8245-1349-5*) Crossroad NY.

Addictions Counseling: A Practical Guide to Counseling People with Chemical & Other Addictions. Dianne D. Pita. 144p. 1994. pap. 18.95 (*0-8245-1386-X*) Crossroad NY.

Addictions Curriculum for Nurses & Other Helping Professionals, Vol. 1: The Undergraduate Level. Ed. by Elizabeth M. Burns et al. LC 93-18559. (Teaching of Nursing Ser.: Vol. 14). 288p. 1993. 46.95 (*0-8261-8190-2*) Springer Pub.

Addictions Curriculum for Nurses & Other Helping Professionals, Vol. 2: The Graduate Level - Advanced Knowledge & Practice. Ed. by Elizabeth M. Burns et al. LC 93-18559. (Teaching of Nursing Ser.: Vol. 15). 392p. 1993. pap. 49.95 (*0-8261-8191-0*) Springer Pub.

Addictions Handbook. Alvin Silverstein et al. LC 90-14093. (Issues in Focus Ser.). 192p. (J). (gr. 6 up). 1991. lib. bdg. 18.95 (*0-89490-205-9*) Enslow Pubs.

Addictions Treatment for Older Adults: Evaluation of an Innovative Client-Centered Approach. Kathryn Graham et al. LC 93-29334. (Illus.). 245p. 1994. lib. bdg. 39.95 (*1-56024-856-4*); pap. 17.95 (*1-56024-857-2*) Haworth Pr.

***Addictive Behavior.** Edward T. Welch & Gary S. Shogren. LC 94-45529. (Strategic Pastoral Counseling Resources Ser.). 176p. 1995. 16.99 (*0-8010-9737-1*) Baker Bk.

Addictive Behaviors. Ed. by Howard Shaffer. LC 83-18619. (Advances in Alcohol & Substance Abuse Ser.: Vol. 3, Nos. 1 & 2). 172p. 1984. text ed. 39.95 (*0-86656-243-5*) Haworth Pr.

Addictive Behaviors: Prevention & Early Intervention. T. Loberg. 240p. 1989. 48.50 (*90-265-0934-0*, Pub. by Swets Pub Serv NE) Taylor & Francis.

Addictive Behaviors Across the Life Span: Prevention, Treatment, & Policy Issues. John S. Baer et al. (Illus.). 330p. (C). 1993. text ed. 52.00 (*0-8039-5078-0*); pap. text ed. 25.00 (*0-8039-5079-9*) Sage.

Addictive Behaviors in Women. Ed. by Ronald R. Watson. LC 93-48458. (Drug & Alcohol Abuse Reviews Ser.: Vol. 5). (Illus.). 532p. 1994. text ed. 69.50 (*0-89603-257-4*) Humana.

***Addictive Behaviour: Cue Exposure Theory & Practice.** Ed. by D. Colin Drummond et al. LC 94-23956. (Series in Clinical Psychology). 1995. text ed. 49.95 (*0-471-94454-8*) Wiley.

Addictive Disorders. E. Fleming. (SPA.). 1993. 45.45 (*84-8086-066-9*) Mosby Yr Bk.

Addictive Disorders in Arctic Climates: Theory, Research & Practice at the Novosibirsk Institute. Bernard Segal & Caesar Korolenko. LC 90-4611. (Drugs & Society Ser.: Vol. 4, Nos. 3-4). 125p. 1990. text ed. 29.95 (*1-56024-036-9*) Haworth Pr.

Addictive Disorders Update: Alcoholism, Drug Abuse, Gambling. S. Yolles. Ed. by Pasquale Carone et al. LC 81-6880. (Problems of Industrial Psychiatric Medicine Ser.: Vol. 7). 192p. 1982. 35.95 (*0-89885-034-7*) Human Sci Pr.

Addictive Organization: Why We Overwork, Cover up, Pick up the Pieces, Please the Boss, & Perpetuate Sick Organizations. Anne W. Schaef & Diane Fassel. LC 87-45720. 240p. 1990. pap. 11.00 (*0-06-254874-3*) Harper SF.

Addictive Personality. W. Miles Cox. (Encyclopedia of Psychoactive Drugs - Compact Paperback Library). (Illus.). 32p. (YA). (gr. 5 up). 1991. pap. 4.49 (*0-7910-0006-0*) Chelsea Hse.

Addictive Personality. W. Miles Cox. (Encyclopedia of Psychoactive Drugs Ser.: No. 1). (Illus.). (YA). (gr. 5 up). 1992. lib. bdg. 19.95 (*0-685-52233-4*) Chelsea Hse.

Addictive Personality: Roots, Rituals, & Recovery. Craig Nakken. 125p. (Orig.). 1989. pap. 9.00 (*0-89486-489-0*, 5149A) Hazelden.

Addictive Personality: Understanding Compulsion in Our Lives. Craig Nakken. LC 88-45140. 128p. (Orig.). 1988. pap. 10.00 (*0-06-255488-3*) Harper SF.

Addictive Relationships: Reclaiming Your Boundaries. Joy Miller. (Orig.). 1989. pap. 7.95 (*1-55874-003-1*) Health Comm.

Addictive Relationships: Why Love Goes Wrong in Recovery. Terrence T. Gorski. 31p. (Orig.). 1993. pap. text ed. 3.00 (*0-8309-0636-3*) Herald Hse.

Addictive States (Association for Research in Nervous & Mental Disease (ARNMD)), Vol. 70. Association for Research in Nervous & Mental Disease (ARNMD) Staff. Ed. by Charles P. O'Brien & Jerome H. Jaffe. 304p. 1992. 110.50 (*0-88167-855-4*) Raven.

Addictive Thinking: Understanding Self-Deception. 1990. pap. 10.00 (*0-06-255397-6*, Hazelden SF) Harper SF.

Addictive Thinking: Why Do We Lie to Ourselves? Why Do Others Believe Us? Abraham J. Twerski. 124p. (Orig.). 1990. pap. 8.95 (*0-89486-612-5*, 5088A) Hazelden.

Addicts & Families in Recovery. Cynthia Orange. 20p. (Orig.). 1986. pap. 1.55 (*0-89486-403-3*, 5215B) Hazelden.

Addicts Who Survived: An Oral History of Narcotic Use in America, 1923-1965. David T. Courtwright et al. LC 88-20583. (Illus.). 416p. 1989. 29.95 (*0-87049-587-9*) U of Tenn Pr.

Addie Across the Prairie. Laurie Lawlor. LC 85-15548. (Illus.). 128p. (J). (gr. 3-6). 1986. 11.95 (*0-8075-0165-4*) A Whitman.

Addie Across the Prairie. Laurie Lawlor. Ed. by Patricia MacDonald. (Illus.). 128p. (J). 1991. reprint ed. mass mkt. 3.99 (*0-671-70147-9*, Minstrel Bks) PB.

***Addie & the Movie Mystery.** Leanne Lucas. (Addie McCormick Adventures Ser.: Bk. 8). (J). 1995. mass mkt. 3.99 (*1-56507-348-7*) Harvest Hse.

***Addie Fay & Old Yellow Streak.** Betty J. Saarinen. 230p. Date not set. pap. 8.95 (*0-7610-0404-1*) NW Pub.

Addie McCormick & the Chicago Surprise. Leanne Lucas. (Addie McCormick Adventure Ser.: Bk. 4). (J). 1993. mass mkt. 3.99 (*1-56507-082-8*) Harvest Hse.

Addie McCormick & the Computer Pirate. Leanne C. Lucas. LC 93-32203. (Addie McCormick Adventure Ser.: Bk. 6). (Orig.). (J). (gr. 5 up). 1994. mass mkt. 3.99 (*1-56507-165-4*) Harvest Hse.

Addie McCormick & the Mystery of the Missing Scrapbook. Leanne Lucas. LC 92-10569. (Addie McCormick Adventure Ser.: Bk. 2). 1992. mass mkt. 3.99 (*1-56507-063-1*) Harvest Hse.

Addie McCormick & the Mystery of the Skeleton Key. Leanne Lucas. (Addie McCormick Adventure Ser.: Bk. 5). (J). (gr. 4-7). 1993. mass mkt. 3.99 (*1-56507-147-6*) Harvest Hse.

Addie McCormick & the Secret of the Scarlet Box. Leanne Lucas. 1994. mass mkt. 3.99 (*1-56507-230-8*) Harvest Hse.

Addie McCormick & the Stolen Statue. Leanne Lucas. (Addie McCormick Adventure Ser.: Bk. 3). (YA). (gr. 4 up). 1993. mass mkt. 3.99 (*1-56507-080-1*) Harvest Hse.

Addie McCormick & the Stranger in the Attic. Leanne Lucas. LC 92-2234. (Addie McCormick Adventure Ser.: Bk. 1). 1992. mass mkt. 3.99 (*1-56507-052-6*) Harvest Hse.

Addie Meets Max. Joan Robins. LC 84-48329. (Early I Can Read Bk.). (Illus.). 32p. (J). (ps-3). 1985. lib. bdg. 14.89 (*0-06-025064-X*) HarpC Child Bks.

Addie Runs Away. Joan Robins. LC 88-24350. (Trophy Early I Can Read Bk.). (Illus.). 32p. (J). (ps-2). 1991. pap. 3.50 (*0-06-444147-4*, Trophy) HarpC Child Bks.

Addie's Bad Day. Joan Robins. LC 92-13101. (I Can Read Bk.). (Illus.). 32p. (J). (ps-2). 1993. 14.00 (*0-06-021297-7*); lib. bdg. 14.89 (*0-06-021298-5*) HarpC Child Bks.

***Addie's Bad Day.** Joan Robins. LC 92-13101. (Trophy I Can Read Book). (Illus.). (J). (ps-3). 1994. pap. 3.50 (*0-06-444183-0*, Trophy) HarpC Child Bks.

Addie's Dakota Winter. Laurie Lawlor. Ed. by Kathy Tucker. Tr. by Toby Gowing. LC 89-5564. (Illus.). 160p. (J). (gr. 2-6). 1989. lib. bdg. 11.95 (*0-8075-0171-9*) A Whitman.

Addie's Dakota Winter. Laurie Lawlor. Ed. by Patricia MacDonald. 160p. (J). 1991. reprint ed. pap. 2.99 (*0-671-70148-7*, Minstrel Bks) PB.

***Addie's Lament.** DeLoras Scott. (Historical Ser.). 1995. mass mkt. 4.50 (*0-373-28877-8*, 1-28877-8) Harlequin Bks.

Addie's Long Summer. Laurie Lawlor. Ed. by Kathleen Tucker. LC 91-34877. (Illus.). 176p. (J). (gr. 3-6). 1992. lib. bdg. 11.95 (*0-8075-0167-0*) A Whitman.

***Addie's Long Summer.** Laurie Lawlor. (Illus.). (J). (gr. 3-6). 1995. reprint ed. pap. 3.50 (*0-671-52607-3*, Minstrel Bks) PB.

Addimu: Offerings to the Orichas. Oba Ecun. Ed. by O Baecun Books, Inc. Staff. LC 91-90227. 198p. (Orig.). (C). 1992. pap. text ed. 22.00 (*0-926603-07-8*) Obaecun Bks.

Addimu: Ofrendas a Los Orichas. Cecilio Prez. LC 88-82519. (Illus.). 201p. (SPA.). (C). 1988. pap. 24.95 (*0-918901-51-0*) Obaecun Bks.

Adding & Subtracting see Key to Fractions Series

Adding & Subtraction Puzzles. R. Gee & K. Bryant-Mole. (Math Skills Ser.). (Illus.). 32p. (J). (gr. 2-6). 1993. pap. 4.95 (*0-7460-1074-5*) EDC.

Adding Dust Collector Fines to Asphalt Paving Mixtures. (National Cooperative Highway Research Program Report Ser.: No. 252). 90p. 1982. 8.40 (*0-309-03422-1*) Transport Res Bd.

Adding Eye Appeal to Foods. Bruce H. Axler. 1974. pap. 3.70 (*0-672-96115-6*, Bobbs) Macmillan.

Adding Fiber to Your Diet. rev. ed. Marion J. Franz. 16p. 1988. pap. 3.95 (*0-937721-07-7*) Chronimed.

Adding Life to Years: Organized Geriatrics Services in Great Britain & Implications for the United States. William H. Barker. LC 86-46279. (Johns Hopkins Series in Contemporary Medicine & Public Health). 272p. 1987. text ed. 38.00 (*0-8018-3455-4*) Johns Hopkins.

Adding Logic to Fire Prevention Systems. John A. Campbell. 1982. 4.65 (*0-686-37669-2*, TR 82-5) Society Fire Protect.

Adding Machine: Collected Essays. William S. Burroughs. 201p. 1986. 16.95 (*0-8050-0000-3*) Seaver Bks.

Adding Machine: Selected Essays. William J. Burroughs. LC 92-46690. 216p. (C). 1993. reprint ed. pap. 11.95 (*1-55970-210-9*) Arcade Pub Inc.

Adding On. (Home Repair & Improvement Ser.). (Illus.). 136p. 1979. 14.60 (*0-8094-2414-2*); lib. bdg. 20.60 (*0-8094-2415-0*) Time-Life.

***Adding On.** Editors of Time-Life Books. LC 95-18960. (Home Repair & Improvement Ser.: Vol. 9). (Illus.). 128p. 1995. write for info. (*0-7835-3870-7*) Time-Life.

Adding On: How to Design & Build the Perfect Addition for Your Home. Rodale's Home Improvement Books Staff & Ken Burton. (Illus.). 384p. 1994. 27.95 (*0-87596-605-5*) Rodale Pr Inc.

Adding Space Without Adding On. Creative Homeowner Press Staff. 1992. pap. 9.95 (*0-696-02479-9*) Meredith Bks.

Adding Space Without Adding On. Herb Hughes. Ed. by Shirley Horowitz. LC 81-67295. (Illus.). 160p. (Orig.). 1980. pap. 9.95 (*0-932944-60-4*) Creative Homeowner.

Adding Structure to BASIC with Comal 80. Max A. Bramer. 288p. 1987. write for info. (*0-201-14632-0*) Addison-Wesley.

Adding up the Sums No. 2: Comparative Information for Schools. 52p. 1993. pap. 15.00 (*0-11-886111-5*, HM61115, Pub. by HMSO UK) UNIPUB.

Adding Value: A Systematic Guide to Business-Driven Management & Leadership. Gerard Egan. LC 93-2936. (Management Ser.). 225p. 1993. 29.95 (*1-55542-542-9*) Jossey-Bass.

Addio; Madretta, & Other Plays. Stark Young. LC 76-40396. (One-Act Plays in Reprint Ser.). 1976. reprint ed. 16.50 (*0-8486-2011-9*) Roth Pub Inc.

Addison. William J. Courthope. Ed. by John Morley. LC 68-58375. (English Men of Letters Ser.). reprint ed. lib. bdg. 41.50 (*0-404-51707-2*) AMS Pr.

Addison: The Freeholder. Joseph Addison. Ed. by James Leheny. 1980. 85.00 (*0-19-812494-5*) OUP.

Addison & Steele: The Critical Heritage. Edward Bloom & Lillian Bloom. (Critical Heritage Ser.). 1980. 65.00 (*0-7100-0375-7*, 03757, RKP) Routledge.

Addison & Steele Are Dead: The English Department, Its Canon, & the Professionalization of Literary Criticism. Brian McCrea. LC 88-40600. 280p. 1990. 40.00 (*0-87413-366-1*) U Delaware Pr.

Addison House. Clare McNally. 304p. (Orig.). 1988. mass mkt. 4.50 (*0-380-75587-4*) Avon.

Addison Hutton: Quaker Architect Eighteen Thirty-Four to Nineteen Sixteen. Elizabeth B. Yarnall. (Illus.). 112p. 1974. 30.00 (*0-87982-013-6*) Art Alliance.

***Addison Mizner, Architect of Dreams & Realities, 1872-1933.** Christina Orr-Cahall. 64p. 1977. 16.95 (*0-615-00347-8*) Norton Gal Art.

Addison N. Scurlock: Historic Photographs. (Illus.). 1976. 2.25 (*0-686-20544-8*) Corcoran.

Addison-Wesley: The First Fifty years, 1942-1992. Addison-Wesley Publishing Company. LC 93-24799. 1993. write for info. (*0-201-56700-8*) Addison-Wesley.

Addison-Wesley Kids Activity Book, No. 1. M. Walker. (Illus.). 48p. 1989. student ed 2.95 (*0-201-52123-7*) Addison-Wesley.

Addison Wesley Manual of Nursing Practice. Delores F. Saxton et al. 1983. text ed. 27.96 (*0-201-07145-2*, Health Sci) Addison-Wesley.

Addison-Wesley Manual of Pediatric Nursing Procedures. Kathleen M. Speer & Carolyn L. Swann. LC 92-49339. (C). 1993. text ed. 32.25 (*0-8053-7645-3*) Benjamin-Cummings.

Addison-Wesley Photo Atlas of Nursing Procedures. Pamela L. Swearingen. LC 84-6305. (Illus.). 1984. text ed. 22.36 (*0-201-07868-6*, Health Sci); pap. 35.00 (*0-685-08676-3*) Addison-Wesley.

Addison-Wesley Photo Atlas of Nursing Procedures. Pamela L. Swearingen. 1984. pap. text ed. 20.76 (*0-201-12941-8*) Addison-Wesley.

Addison-Wesley's Nursing Examination. 2nd ed. Sally L. Lagerquist. 1982. pap. 26.50 (*0-201-14190-6*, Health Sci) Addison-Wesley.

Addison-Wesley's Nursing Examination Review. 3rd ed. Sally L. Lagerquist. 1987. pap. 23.75 (*0-201-14497-2*) Addison-Wesley.

Addison Wesley's Nursing Examination Review. 4th ed. Sally L. Lagerquist. 752p. (C). 1991. pap. text ed. 32.25 (*0-8053-4002-5*) Addison-Wesley.

Addison Wesley's Photo Atlas of Nursing Procedures. 2nd ed. Pamela L. Swearingen. 688p. (C). 1991. pap. text ed. 48.50 (*0-201-13239-7*) Addison-Wesley.

Addisonian Tradition in France: Passion & Objectivity in Social Observation. Ralph A. Nablow. LC 89-45404. (Illus.). 280p. 1990. 42.50 (*0-8386-3379-X*) Fairleigh Dickinson.

Addition. Karen Hilderbrand & Kim Thompson. (Rap with the Facts Ser.). (Illus.). 48p. (J). (gr. 3). 1991. student ed 6.99 (*0-9632249-2-1*) Twin Sisters.

Addition. Schaffer, Frank, Publications Staff. (Help Your Child Learn Ser.). (Illus.). 24p. (J). (gr. 1-3). 1978. student ed 3.98 (*0-86734-007-X*, FS-3008) Schaffer Pubns.

Addition. Emery Silliman & Liz Jonson. Ed. by Judith E. Nayer. (Learn Today for Tomorrow Ser.). (Illus.). 32p. (J). (gr. k-1). 1991. student ed 1.95 (*1-878624-57-1*) McClanahan Bk.

***Addition.** David L. Stienecker. (Discovering Math Ser.). 32p. (J). (gr. 3-5). 1995. lib. bdg. write for info. (*0-7614-0593-3*, Benchmark NY) Marshall Cavendish.

Addition. Kim M. Thompson & Karen M. Hilderbrand. (Rap with the Facts Ser.). (Illus.). 24p. (J). (gr. 1-4). 1993. student ed, audio 9.98 (*1-882331-20-6*, TWIN 402) Twin Sisters.

***Addition: Basic Facts.** Bob DeWeese. (Math at Home Ser.). (Illus.). 44p. 1994. teacher ed, pap. text ed. 2.95 (*1-55799-310-6*, EMC 603) Evan-Moor Corp.

Addition: No Regrouping. H. S. Lawrence. (Puzzles & Practice Ser.). (Illus.). 30p. (Orig.). (ENG & SPA.). (J). (gr. 1-6). 1992. student ed, pap. 3.95 (*0-931993-49-0*, GP-049) Garlic Pr OR.

Addition & Elimination Reactions of Aliphatic Compounds see Comprehensive Chemical Kinetics

Addition & Subtraction: No Regrouping. H. S. Lawrence. (Puzzles & Practice Ser.). (Illus.). 30p. (Orig.). (ENG & SPA.). (J). (gr. 1-6). 1992. student ed, pap. 3.95 (*0-931993-51-2*, GP-051) Garlic Pr OR.

***Addition & Subtraction No. 2.** Little Golden Books Staff. (J). Date not set. pap. 3.59 (*0-307-03654-5*) Western Pub.

***Addition & Subtraction Country.** Brad Caudle & Richard Caudle. (Illus.). (J). (gr. 1 up). 1995. audio 9.95 (*1-878489-33-X*, RL933) Rock & Learn Educ Prod.

***Addition & Subtraction Rock.** Brad Caudle & Richard Caudle. (J). (gr. 1 up). 1993. audio, pap. 9.95 (*1-878489-06-2*) Rock & Learn Educ Prod.

Addition Annie. David Gisler. LC 91-17654. (Rookie Reader Ser.). (Illus.). 32p. (J). (ps-2). 1991. lib. bdg. 10.35 (*0-516-02007-2*); pap. 2.95 (*0-516-42007-0*) Childrens.

***Addition Facts in Five Minutes a Day.** Susan C. Anthony. (Math Facts in Five Minutes a Day Ser.). 88p. (Orig.). (J). (gr. 1-3). 1995. teacher ed, spiral bd. 11.95 (*1-879478-05-6*, 056) Instr Res Co.

***Addition Rap.** Brad Caudle & Richard Caudle. (J). (gr. 1 up). 1992. audio, pap. 9.95 (*1-878489-09-7*) Rock & Learn Educ Prod.

Addition Skills. Francis Fennell. (Rainbow Skill Builders Ser.: Level 3). 80p. (Orig.). (J). (ps-3). 1984. pap. 2.95 (*0-8431-2503-9*) Price Stern.

Addition Theorems: The Addition Theorems of Group Theory & Number Theory. Henry B. Mann. LC 76-16766. 124p. 1976. reprint ed. text ed. 15.50 (*0-88275-418-1*) Krieger.

Addition Wipe-off Book. (Mathematics Wipe-off Bks.). 24p. (Orig.). (J). (gr. 1 up). 1988. pap. 1.95 (*0-590-42012-7*) Scholastic Inc.

Addition Wrap-ups: Individual Sets. Marion W. Stuart. Date not set. text ed. write for info. (*0-943343-01-1*) Lrn Wrap-Ups.

Additional Adventures of Messrs. Box & Cox: A Continuation of the Dramatic History of Box & Cox. W. S. Gilbert. Ed. by Ralph MacPhail, Jr. Bd. with Penelope Anne. LC 75-304933. LC 75-304933. (Illus.). 74p. 1974. Set pap. 10.00 (*0-9601580-0-6*) Parenthesis Pr.

Additional Book-Keeping Exercises. P. Newton. (C). 1989. 40.00 (*0-85950-841-2*, Pub. by S Thornes Pubs UK) St Mut.

***Additional Insured Book.** 2nd ed. Donald S. Malecki & Jack P. Gibson. 286p. 1994. pap. 49.98 (*1-886813-02-7*) Intl Risk Mgt.

Additional Letters of John Stuart Mill. Ed. by Michael L. Filipiuk & John M. Robson. 1991. 110.00 (*0-8020-2768-7*) U of Toronto Pr.

***Additional Problems to Organic Chemistry.** Marye A. Fox & James K. Whitesell. (Chemistry Ser.). 32p. Date not set. pap. 10.00 (*0-86720-912-7*) Jones & Bartlett.

Additional Protocol, 1990: Shipping, No. 4. (Miscellaneous Treaty Ser.: No. 7). 16p. 1990. pap. 5.00 (*0-10-109872-3*, HM8723) UNIPUB.

Additional Reasons for Our Immediately Emancipating Spanish America. William Burke. LC 73-128426. reprint ed. 12.50 (*0-404-01240-X*) AMS Pr.

Additional Short Syllables in Ovid. Margaret W. Herr. (LD Ser.: No. 35). 1937. pap. 16.00 (*0-527-00771-4*) Periodicals Srv.

***Additional Studies of the Arts, Crafts & Customs of the Guiana Indians, with Special Reference to Those Southern British Guiana.** Ed. by Walter E. Roth. (Bureau of American Ethnology Bulletins Ser.). 110p. 1995. lib. bdg. 79.00 (*0-7812-4091-3*) Rprt Serv.

Additions & Corrections to Vermont Imprints. McCorison. 1985. 3.50 (*0-912296-72-0*, Am Antiquarian) Am Antiquarian.

Additions & Corrections to Vermont Imprints, 1778-1820, 1. Comp. by Marcus A. McCorison. (Orig.). 1968. pap. 5.00 (*0-912296-35-6*, Am Antiquarian) Am Antiquarian.

Additions & Corrections to Vermont Imprints, 1778-1820, 2. Comp. by Marcus A. McCorison. (Orig.). 1968. pap. 3.00 (*0-912296-36-4*, Am Antiquarian) Am Antiquarian.

Additions Aux Dictionnaires Arabes. Edmond Fagnan. ix, 194p. reprint ed. write for info. (*0-318-71507-4*, Pub. by Georg Olms GW) Lubrecht & Cramer.

Additions Aux Dictionnaires Arabes (Arabic-French) E. Fagnan. 194p. (ARA & FRE.). 1969. 25.00 (*0-86685-107-0*) Intl Bk Ctr.

A

An Asterisk (*) at the beginning of an entry indicates that the title is appearing in BIP for the first time.

A

Additions to the Family Eulepethidae Chamberlin (Polychaeta: Aphroditacea) Marian H. Pettibone. LC 86-600055. (Smithsonian Contributions to Zoology Ser.: No. 441). 55p. reprint ed. pap. 25.00 (0-8357-5097-3, 2029361) Bks Demand.

Additive & Cancellative Interacting Particle Systems. D. Griffeath. (Lecture Notes in Mathematics Ser.: Vol. 724). 1979. pap. 13.00 (3-540-09508-X) Spr-Verlag.

Additive Migration from Plastics into Food. T. R. Crompton. 1979. 106.00 (0-08-022465-2, Pub. by Pergamon Repr UK) Franklin.

Additive Number Theory of Polynomials over a Finite Field. Gove W. Effinger & David R. Hayes. (Oxford Mathematical Monographs). 176p. 1991. 45.00 (0-19-853583-X) OUP.

Additive Subgroups of Topological Vector Spaces. W. Banaszczyk. (Lecture Notes in Mathematics Ser.: Vol. 1466). vii, 178p. 1991. pap. 27.00 (0-387-53917-4) Spr-Verlag.

Additive Theory of Prime Numbers. Lo-Keng Hua. Tr. by N. H. Ng. LC 65-23103. (Translations of Mathematical Monographs: Vol. 13). 190p. 1965. 42.00 (0-8218-1563-6, MMONO-13) Am Math.

Additives. Rhoda Nottridge. LC 92-33083. (J). 1993. pap. 5.95 (0-87614-609-4, Carolrhoda) Lerner Group.

Additives Book. rev. ed. Beatrice T. Hunter. LC 79-93436. 144p. 1980. pap. 2.25 (0-87983-223-1) Keats.

Additives for Plastics. 150.00 (0-317-57787-5) T-C Pubns CA.

Additives for Plastics. J. Stepek & H. Daoust. (Polymers, Properties & Applications Ser.: Vol. 5). (Illus.). 243p. 1983. 160.00 (0-387-90753-X) Spr-Verlag.

Additives Guide. Christopher C. Hughes. LC 87-2122. 156p. reprint ed. pap. 44.50 (0-7837-4515-X, 2044294) Bks Demand.

Additives to Blood Collection Devices - Herapin: Tentative Standard, Vol. 8. rev. ed. National Committee for Clinical Laboratory Standards. 1988. 40.00 (1-56238-053-2, H24-T) Natl Comm Clin Lab Stds.

Address. Harriot Curtis. (Works of Harriot Curtis Ser.). 1990. reprint ed. lib. bdg. 79.00 (0-685-27800-X) Rprt Serv.

Address & Telephone Book. (Illus.). 144p. 1995. 9.98 (0-8317-0189-7) Smithmark.

Address Before the Senior Class in Divinity College, Cambridge. Ralph Waldo Emerson. (Notable American Authors Ser.). 1992. reprint ed. lib. bdg. 75.00 (0-7812-2805-0) Rprt Serv.

Address Book. (Illus.). 128p. 1993. 9.95 (0-943972-24-8) Homestead WY.

***Address Book.** (Janet Bolton Ser.). (Illus.). 128p. 1995. 9.95 (0-8069-3969-9) Sterling.

Address Book. Linda C. Franklin. (Old Fashioned Keepbook Ser.). (Illus.). 128p. 1981. 16.00 (0-934504-07-5) Michel Pub Co.

Address Book: Direct Access to over 3,500 Celebrities, Corporate Execs, & Other VIPs. Michael Levine. LC 92-31749. 288p. 1993. pap. 9.95 (0-399-51793-6, Perigree Bks) Berkley Pub.

***Address Book No. 7: How to Reach Anyone Who Is Anyone.** Michael Levine. LC 94-33188. 288p. (Orig.). 1995. pap. 11.00 (0-399-52149-6, Perigree Bks) Berkley Pub.

***Address Book for Germanic Genealogy.** 5th ed. Ernest Thode. 174p. 1994. pap. 24.95 (0-614-03833-2, 5757) Genealog Pub.

Address Book of Some Assemblies of Christians. 1993. pap. 6.95 (0-937396-93-1) Walterick Pubs.

Address in Time. Elizabeth Bartlett. LC 78-75102. 1979. 13.95 (0-8023-1271-3) Dufour.

Address of the Eye: A Phenomenology of Film Experience. Vivian Sobchack. (Illus.). 376p. 1992. text ed. 55.00 (0-691-03195-9); pap. text ed. 19.95 (0-691-00874-4) Princeton U Pr.

Address on the Truth, Dignity, Power & Beauty of the Principles of Peace, & on the Unchristian Character & Influence of War & the Warrior. Thomas S. Grimke. LC 72-137542. (Peace Movement in America Ser.). 56p. 1972. reprint ed. lib. bdg. 17.95 (0-89198-070-9) Ozer.

Address to the Board of Governors by Lewis T. Preston: The Remarks of the President of the World Bank Group at the 1992 Annual Meetings, September 22, Washington, D. C. 12p. write for info. (0-8213-2284-2, 12284); write for info. (0-8213-2285-0, 12285); write for info. (0-8213-2287-7, 12287); write for info. (0-8213-2286-9, 12286) World Bank.

Address to the Congress of the United States on Restrictions upon Foreign Commerce. Charles B. Brown. (Works of Charles Brockden Brown). 1989. reprint ed. lib. bdg. 79.00 (0-7812-2075-0) Rprt Serv.

Address to the Congress of the United States on the British Treaty. Charles B. Brown. (Works of Charles Brockden Brown). 1989. reprint ed. lib. bdg. 79.00 (0-7812-2074-2) Rprt Serv.

Address to the Government of the United States on the Cession of Louisiana. Charles B. Brown. (Works of Charles Brockden Brown). 1989. reprint ed. lib. bdg. 79.00 (0-7812-2071-8) Rprt Serv.

Address to the Inhabitants of the British Settlements, on the Slavery of the Negroes in America. 2nd ed. Benjamin Rush. (Anti-Slavery Crusade in America Ser.). 92p. 1980. reprint ed. 11.95 (0-405-00656-X) Ayer.

Address to the Irish People. Percy Bysshe Shelley. Ed. by Thomas J. Wise. LC 74-30290. (Shelley Society, Second Ser.: No. 6). reprint ed. 20.00 (0-404-11508-X) AMS Pr.

Address to the Negroes of the State of New York. Jupiter Hammon. 1976. 59.95 (0-87968-577-8) Gordon Pr.

Address to the People of the South. John C. Calhoun. (Works of John Calswell Calhoun Ser.). 1990. reprint ed. lib. bdg. 79.00 (0-7812-2238-9) Rprt Serv.

***Address Unknown.** Kressmann Taylor. 64p. 1995. 12.99 (1-884910-17-3) Story Pr Ohio.

Address Unknown: The Homeless in America. James D. Wright. (Social Institutions & Social Change Ser.). 192p. (Orig.). (C). 1989. lib. bdg. 41.95 (0-202-30364-0); pap. text ed. 20.95 (0-202-30365-9) Aldine de Gruyter.

***Address Unknown: The Human Face of Homelessness.** Christopher B. Gerboth et al. 88p. 1995. pap. 7.95 (0-9643560-0-7) CO Endowment.

***Addresses.** Illus. by Anne Geddes. (Anne Geddes Line Ser.). 89p. Date not set. 12.95 (1-55912-000-2) CEDCO Pub.

Addresses. John M. Hay. (Notable American Authors Ser.). 1992. reprint ed. lib. bdg. 75.00 (0-7812-3058-6) Rprt Serv.

Addresses & Public Papers of James Baxter Hunt, Jr., Governor of North Carolina, Vol. One Vol. 1, 1977-1981. Ed. by Memory F. Mitchell. (Illus.). xxxii, 881p. 1982. 3.00 (0-86526-178-4) NC Archives.

Addresses & Public Papers of James Grubbs Martin, Governor of North Carolina, 1985-1989 Vol. 1, 1985-1989, Vol. 1. Ed. by Jan-Michael Poff. (Illus.). 1089p. 1992. 3.00 (0-86526-250-0) NC Archives.

Addresses & Reprints. Moncure D. Conway. (Works of Moncure Daniel Conway Ser.). 1990. reprint ed. lib. bdg. 79.00 (0-7812-2347-4) Rprt Serv.

Addresses at the Funeral of Henry George. Ed. by Edmund Yardley. 1982. lib. bdg. 150.00 (0-8490-3223-7) Gordon Pr.

Addresses by Worthy Matron & Worthy Patron. Elizabeth McBride. 44p. 1983. pap. 3.50 (0-88053-359-5, S 306) Macoy Pub.

Addresses Delivered at the Semi-Centennial Celebration of the Dedication of the First Unitarian Church, South Natick (Massachusetts) November 20, 1878. Horatio Alger, Sr. & J. P. Sheaf, Jr. (Illus.). 41p. 1977. reprint ed. pap. 6.00 (0-686-35760-4) G K Westgard.

***Addresses for Women's Day.** Aurelia R. Downey. 53p. (YA). (gr. 9-12). 1978. pap. 3.00 (0-9641602-0-X) A R Downey.

Addresses of John Hay. John Hay. LC 77-121477. (Essay Index Reprint Ser.). 1977. 23.95 (0-8369-1755-3) Ayer.

Addresses on Government & Citizenship. Elihu Root. LC 70-86779. (Essay Index Reprint Ser.). 1977. 29.95 (0-8369-1190-3) Ayer.

Addresses on International Subjects. Elihu Root. LC 74-86780. (Essay Index Reprint Ser.). 1977. 26.95 (0-8369-1191-1) Ayer.

Addresses on War. Charles Sumner. Bd. with Letters to Charles Sumner on His Oration on the True Grandeur of Nations. LC 74-147699. LC 74-147699. (Library of War & Peace; Proposals for Peace: a History). 1972. Set lib. bdg. 46.00 (0-8240-0226-1) Garland.

Addresses to the German Nation. Fichte J. Gottlieb. Ed. by R. F. Jones & G. H. Turnbull. LC 78-12431. 269p. 1979. reprint ed. text ed. 59.75 (0-313-21207-4, FIAG, Greenwood Pr) Greenwood.

***Addresses to Young Men.** John A. James. 496p. (J). (gr. 5-12). 1995. reprint ed. 29.95 (1-877611-97-2) Soli Deo Gloria.

Addresses upon the American Road, 1933-1938. Herbert C. Hoover. 1977. 18.95 (0-8369-7251-1, 8050) Ayer.

Addressing Frank Kermode: Essays in Criticism & Interpretation. Ed. by Margaret Tudeau-Clayton & Martin Warner. 232p. 1991. 29.95 (0-252-01816-8) U of Ill Pr.

Addressing Machine Operator. Jack Rudman. (Career Examination Ser.: C-1892). 1994. pap. 19.95 (0-8373-1892-0) Nat Learn.

Addressing Machine Supervisor. Jack Rudman. (Career Examination Ser.: C-1893). 1994. pap. 23.95 (0-8373-1893-9) Nat Learn.

Addressing Malnutrition in Africa: Low-Cost Possibilities for Government Agencies & Donors. F. James Levinson. (Social Dimensions of Adjustment in Sub-Saharan Africa Working Paper Ser.: No. 13). 44p. 1991. 6.95 (0-8213-1897-7, 11897) World Bank.

Addressing Overseas Business Letters: A Secretary's Handbook. Derek Allen. 96p. 1992. pap. 9.95 (0-572-01421-X, Pub. by W Foulsham UK) Trans-Atl Phila.

Addressing Sexual Harassment in the Workplace: Trainer's Package. Pfeiffer & Co Staff. LC 92-93295. 134p. 1992. ring bd. 99.95 (0-88390-320-2) Pfeiffer & Co.

Addressing Societal Needs of the 1980's Through Civil Engineering Research. Workshop Proceedings Staff. LC 82-70765. 335p. 1982. pap. 39.00 (0-87262-300-9) Am Soc Civil Eng.

Addressing the Needs of Returning Women. Ed. by Linda H. Lewis. LC 85-644750. (New Directions for Continuing Education Ser.: No. ACE 39). 1988. 16.95 (1-55542-880-0) Jossey-Bass.

***Addressing the Problems of Youth At-Risk: Approaches That Work.** Ed. by Jack W. Miller. 237p. (Orig.). 1994. pap. 10.00 (0-9640143-0-0) GSU Coll Educ.

Addressing Turkish Genocide Apologists, April 6 - June 16, 1989, Vol. V: On UNIX (R) UseNet World Wide Computer Network. Intro. by David Davidian. 480p. (Orig.). 1989. pap. text ed. write for info. (0-318-65522-5) SDP Armenia.

Addressing Turkish Genocide Apologists, February 4 - June 3, 1988, Vol. I: On UNIX (R) UseNet World Wide Computer Network. Intro. by David Davidian. 411p. (Orig.). 1989. pap. text ed. write for info. (0-318-65518-7) SDP Armenia.

Addressing Turkish Genocide Apologists, June 3 - August 17, 1988, Vol. II: On UNIX (R) UseNet World Wide Computer Network. Intro. by David Davidian. 304p. (Orig.). 1989. pap. text ed. write for info. (0-318-65519-5) SDP Armenia.

Addressing Turkish Genocide Apologists, November 23 - December 23, 1988: On UNIX (R) UseNet World Wide Computer Network, Vol. IV. Intro. by David Davidian. 179p. (Orig.). 1989. pap. text ed. write for info. (0-318-65521-7) SDP Armenia.

Addressing Turkish Genocide Apologists, October 11 - November 21, 1988, Vol. III: On UNIX (R) UseNet World Wide Computer Network. Intro. by David Davidian. 326p. (Orig.). 1989. pap. text ed. write for info. (0-318-65520-9) SDP Armenia.

Addressing Vocational Training & Retraining Through Educational Technology: Policy Alternatives. Dennis R. Herschback. 62p. 1984. 5.75 (0-318-22014-8, IN276) Ctr Educ Trng Employ.

Addressograph Machine Operator. Jack Rudman. (Career Examination Ser.: C-1076). 1994. pap. 19.95 (0-8373-1076-8) Nat Learn.

***Addy, 6 vols., Set.** Porter. 1994. 74.95 (1-56247-088-4) Pleasant Co.

***ADDY Book: The Annual of the American Advertising Federation.** Rotovison S. A. Staff. (Illus.). 592p. 1995. 65.00 (0-8230-6436-0) Watsn-Guptill.

Addy Learns a Lesson. Connie Porter. (American Girls Collection Ser.). (Illus.). 70p. (Orig.). (J). (gr. 2-5). 1993. lib. bdg. 12.95 (1-56247-078-7); pap. 5.95 (1-56247-077-9) Pleasant Co.

Addy Paper Doll. Pleasant Company Staff. (American Girls Collection). 24p. (Orig.). (J). (gr. 2-5). 1994. pap. 5.95 (1-56247-126-0) Pleasant Co.

Addy Save the Day. Connie Porter. (American Girls Collection Ser.). (Illus.). 72p. (J). (gr. 2-5). 1994. lib. bdg. 12.95 (1-56247-084-1); pap. 5.95 (1-56247-083-3) Pleasant Co.

Addy Starr. Ruth R. Langan. 352p. 1992. 19.00 (0-7278-4370-2) Severn Hse.

***Addy Starr.** Ruth R. Langan. 368p. 1994. mass mkt. 4.99 (0-505-51989-5, Love Spell) Dorchester Pub Co.

Addy's Boxed Set. Connie Porter. (American Girl Collection). 460p. (J). (gr. 2-5). Date not set. lib. bdg. 74.95 (0-685-75412-X); boxed, pap. 34.95 (1-56247-087-6) Pleasant Co.

Addy's Cookbook. Pleasant Company Staff. (American Girls Collection Ser.). 48p. (Orig.). (J). (gr. 2-5). 1994. pap. 5.95 (1-56247-123-6) Pleasant Co.

Addy's Craft Book. Pleasant Company Staff. (American Girls Collection). 48p. (Orig.). (J). (gr. 2-5). 1994. pap. 5.95 (1-56247-124-4) Pleasant Co.

Addy's Surprise: A Christmas Story. Connie Porter. LC 93-5162. (American Girls Collection Ser.). (Illus.). (J). 1993. 12.95 (1-56247-080-9); pap. 5.95 (1-56247-079-5) Pleasant Co.

Addy's Theater Kit. Pleasant Company Staff. (American Girls Collection). 48p. (Orig.). (J). (gr. 2-5). 1994. pap. 5.95 (1-56247-125-2) Pleasant Co.

Adel der Russischen Ostseeprovinzen: Estland, Kurland, Livland, Oesel, 2 vols. in one. J. Siebmacher. (Illus.). 800p. (GER.). 1990. reprint ed. 440.00 (0-317-03837-0) Szwede Slavic.

Adel von Galizien, Lodomerien U. der Bukowina. F. H. Rosenfeld & J. Bojnicic. 275p. (GER & POL.). 1990. reprint ed. 195.00 (0-317-03845-1) Szwede Slavic.

Adel von Kroatien und Slavonien. J. Bojnicic. 258p. (CRO & GER.). 1990. reprint ed. 150.00 (0-317-03844-3) Szwede Slavic.

Adela Cathcart. George MacDonald. (George MacDonald Original Works: Series IV). 462p. 1994. reprint ed. 18.00 (1-881084-23-X) Johannesen.

Adela, the Octoroon. H. L. Hosmer. LC 71-39091. (Black Heritage Library Collection). 1977. reprint ed. 24.95 (0-8369-9029-3) Ayer.

Adelaide Alsop Robineau: Glory in Porcelain. Ed. by Peg Weiss. LC 81-9107. (Illus.). 251p. 1981. pap. 24.95 (0-8156-0171-9) Syracuse U Pr.

Adelaide, Daly & Moyle Rivers see Survey of Tidal River Systems in the Northern Territory & Their Crocodile Populations: Monographs

Adelaide (Sartario) see Italian Opera Librettos, Vol. I, 1640-1770

Adelante. Eduardo Neale-Silva & Robert L. Nicholas. (C). 1985. student ed, audio 220.00 (0-07-554511-X) McGraw.

Adelante. 2nd ed. Eduardo Neale-Silva & Robert L. Nicholas. LC 80-21015. (C). 1981. text ed. 24.50 (0-394-33282-2) Random.

Adelante. 3rd ed. Eduardo Neale-Silva & Robert L. Nicholas. (C). 1985. text ed. write for info. (0-07-554508-X) McGraw.

Adelante. 3rd ed. Eduardo Neale-Silva & Robert L. Nicholas. (C). 1985. student ed, pap. text ed. 13.03 (0-07-554509-8) McGraw.

Adelante Por el Camino Del Congreso Constituyente. Marxist-Leninist Party, USA Staff. Ed. by National Executive Committee of the MLP, USA. (Illus.). 52p. (Orig.). (SPA.). 1981. pap. 1.00 (0-86714-012-7) Marxist-Leninist.

Adelardo Lopez de Ayala. Edward V. Coughlin. LC 77-5670. (Twayne's World Authors Ser.). 152p. (C). 1977. 17.95 (0-8057-6303-1) Irvington.

Adelasia Ed Aleramo & Excerpts from Other Operas. Giovanni S. Mayr. LC 90-754562. (Italian Opera Ser., 1810-1840). 368p. 1991. text ed. 119.00 (0-8240-6560-3) Garland.

Adelbert Ames, 1835-1933: Broken Oaths & Reconstruction in Mississippi. Blanche A. Ames. (Illus.). 1964. 25.00 (0-87266-000-1) Argosy.

Adele & the Beast. Jacques Tardi. Tr. by Elisabeth Bell. (Adventures of Adele Blanc-Sec Ser.). 48p. 1990. pap. 9.95 (0-918348-85-4) NBM.

***Adele Hugo: La Miserable.** Dow. 1993. per. 14.95 (0-86492-168-3, Pub. by Goose Ln Edits CN) InBook.

Adele ou la Marguerite Suivi de la Valse des Toreadors. Jean Anouilh. 256p. (FRE.). 1987. pap. 10.95 (0-7859-1880-9, 2070370577) Fr & Eur.

Adele, Ou la Marquerite. Jean Anouilh. (FRE.). 1970. pap. 10.95 (0-8288-9012-9, F81812) Fr & Eur.

Adele Wiseman: An Annotated Bibliography. Ruth Panofsky. 150p. (C). 1992. text ed. 30.00 (1-55022-103-5, Pub. by ECW Press CN) Genl Dist Srvs.

Adelfas. La Lola Se Va a los Puertos. Manuel Y. Machado. Ed. by Damaso Chicharro Chamorro. (Nueva Austral Ser.: Vol. 271). (SPA.). 1993. pap. text ed. 34.95x (84-239-7271-2) Elliots Bks.

***Adelhelm Abbey.** Nicholas P. Newlin. 1995. 19.95 (0-533-11426-8) Vantage.

Adelina Patti: Queen of Hearts. John F. Cone. LC 92-39331. (Opera Biography Ser.: No. 3). (Illus.). 524p. 1993. 39.95 (0-931340-60-8, Amadeus Pr) Timber.

***Adeline Mowbray.** Amelia Opie. LC 94-44529. (Revolution & the Age of Romanticism, 1789-1834, Ser.). 1995. 85.00 (1-85477-188-4, Pub. by Woodstock Bks UK) Cassell.

***Adeline Street.** Carol L. Williams. LC 94-20292. (J). 1995. 14.95 (0-385-31075-7) Delacorte.

Adelma Goes Herbing. Margaret S. Messing. LC 93-94108. (Illus.). 64p. (Orig.). (J). 1994. pap. 6.00 (1-56002-383-X, Univ Edtns) Aegina Pr.

Adelphi Calendar Project, 1806-1850: Sans Pareil Theatre 1806-1819 - Adelphi Theatre 1819-1850. Ed. by Alfred L. Nelson et al. LC 89-11968. (London Stage 1800-1900 Ser.: No. 1). 248p. 1990. 195.00 (0-313-25882-1, DUG/, Greenwood Pr) Greenwood.

Adelphi Library, 8 vols., Set. Alford et al. 1984. text ed. 150.00 (0-312-00438-9) St Martin.

Adelphi Papers, 1994. 1994. 17.00 (0-685-75351-4) Macmillan.

Adelphi Theatre Calendar: The Adelphi Calendar Project 1806-1900 - the Adelphi Theatre 1850-1900, Pt. II. Ed. by Alfred L. Nelson et al. LC 89-11968. (London Stage, 1800-1900 - a Documentary Record & Calendar of Performances Ser.). 296p. 1993. 225.00 (0-313-28882-8, GR8882) Greenwood.

Adelphoe. Terence. Ed. by R. H. Martin. LC 75-36173. (Cambridge Greek & Latin Classics Ser.). 250p. 1976. pap. 21.95 (0-521-29001-5) Cambridge U Pr.

Adelphoe see Brothers

Adelson: Two Rolls No Coffee. Illus. by Jim Adelson. 234p. 1990. 10.95 (0-911007-17-2) Prairie Hse.

Aden, Arabie. Paul Nizan. Tr. by Joan Pinkham. 159p. 1987. pap. text ed. 12.00 (0-231-06357-1) Col U Pr.

Adena People. William S. Webb & Charles E. Snow. LC 75-10598. (Illus.). 390p. 1974. reprint ed. 41.00x (0-87049-159-8); reprint ed. pap. 18.95 (0-87049-568-2) U of Tenn Pr.

***Adenauer: From the German Empire to the Federal Republic, 1876-1952.** Hans-Peter Schwarz. 1000p. 1995. 49.95 (1-57181-870-7) Berghahn Bks.

Adenauer to Kohl: The Development of the German Chancellorship. Heidrun Abromeit et al. Ed. by Stephen Padgett. LC 94-2059. 1994. 35.00 (0-87840-556-9) Georgetown U Pr.

Adenine Nucleotides in Cellular Energy Transfer & Signal Transduction. Ed. by S. Papa et al. LC 92-17729. (Molecular & Cell Biology Updates Ser.). ix, 476p. 1992. 116.00 (0-8176-2673-5, Pub. by Birkhauser Vlg SZ) Birkhauser.

Adenocarcinoma & Other Poems. Colin Ross. (C). 1989. 60.00 (0-907839-38-X, Pub. by Brynmill Pr Ltd UK) St Mut.

Adenomatous Polyps of the Colon. R. Lev. (Illus.). 160p. 1989. 87.00 (0-387-96985-3, 2730) Spr-Verlag.

***Adenosine & Adenine Nucleotides: From Molecular Biology to Integrative Physiology.** International Symposium on Adenosine & Adenine Nucleotides Staff. Ed. by Luiz Belardinelli et al. LC 94-40345. 576p. (C). 1995. lib. bdg. 275.00 (0-7923-3190-7) Kluwer Ac.

Adenosine & Adenine Nucleotides: Physiology & Pharmacology. Ed. by David M. Paton. 350p. 1988. 125.00 (0-85066-416-0) Taylor & Francis.

Adenosine & Adenine Nucleotides as Regulators of Cellular Function. John W. Phillis. (Illus.). 408p. 1991. 236.00 (0-8493-6928-2, QP625) CRC Pr.

Adenosine & Adenosine Receptors. Ed. by Michael Williams. LC 90-4000. (Receptors Ser.). (Illus.). 1990. 89.50 (0-89603-163-2) Humana.

Adenosine Deaminase in Disorders of Purine Metabolism & in Immune Deficiency. George L. Tritsch. (Annals Ser.: Vol. 451). 345p. 1985. text ed. 80.00 (0-89766-296-2); pap. text ed. 80.00 (0-89766-297-0) NY Acad Sci.

Adenosine in the Nervous System. Ed. by Trevor W. Stone. (Neuroscience Perspectives Ser.). (Illus.). 278p. 1991. text ed. 69.95 (0-12-672640-X) Acad Pr.

Adenovirus DNA. Ed. by Walter Doerfler. (Developments in Molecular Virology Ser.). 1985. lib. bdg. 129.00 (0-89838-758-2) Kluwer Ac.

Adenoviruses. Ed. by Harold S. Ginsberg. LC 84-8264. (Viruses Ser.). 622p. 1984. 125.00 (0-306-41592-5, Plenum Pr) Plenum.

Adept. Katherine Kurtz. 1991. mass mkt. 5.50 (0-441-00343-5) Ace Bks.

Adept, Bk. I. Katherine Kurtz & Deborah Harris. 336p. 1992. reprint ed. 20.00 (0-7278-4378-8) Severn Hse.

***Adept: Dagger Magic, No. 4.** Katherine Kurtz & Deborah T. Harrid. LC 94-22436. (The Adept Ser.). 384p. 1995. 19.95 (0-441-00149-1) Ace Bks.

Adept: The Lodge of the Lynx. Kathrine Kurtz & Deborah T. Harris. 1992. mass mkt. 5.50 (0-441-00344-3) Ace Bks.

Adept No. 3: The Templar Treasure. Katherine Kurtz. 320p. (Orig.). 1993. mass mkt. 4.99 (0-441-00345-1) Ace Bks.

An Asterisk (*) at the beginning of an entry indicates that the title is appearing in BIP for the first time.

Adepts, Masters & MAHATMAS. Harold W. Percival. LC 92-82024. (Illus.). 184p. (Orig.). 1993. reprint ed. pap. 14.95 (*0-911650-11-3*, 113) Word Foun.

***Adept's Way.** FASA Staff. (Earthdawn Ser.). 1995. pap. 18.00 (*1-55560-260-6*) FASA Corp.

Adequacy of Sample Size in Health Studies. Stanley Lemeshow et al. 1989. text ed. 64.95 (*0-471-92517-9*) Wiley.

Adequate Response: The War Poetry of Wilfred Owen & Siegfried Sassoon. Arthur E. Lane. LC 74-39905. 191p. reprint ed. pap. 54.50 (*0-7837-3795-5*, 2043615) Bks Demand.

Adequately Considered: An American Perspective on Louis Janssens' Personalist Morals. Dolores L. Christie. (Louvain Theological & Pastoral Monographs). 200p. (Orig.). 1990. pap. 24.99 (*0-8028-0564-7*) Eerdmans.

Adesso! Danesi. 1992. text ed. 50.95 (*0-8384-1986-0*) Heinle & Heinle.

Adesso! Danesi. 1992. student ed, pap. 29.95 (*0-8384-1987-9*) Heinle & Heinle.

ADF: Automatic Direction Finding Computer Instruction Manual. A. Tuell Moore & H. M. Gibson. (ENG & SPA.). 1984. teacher ed 3.50 (*0-317-91368-9*) MAG Mfg.

ADF: Automatic Direction Finding Computer Instruction Manual. rev. ed. A. Tuell Moore & H. M. Gibson. (ENG & SPA.). 1984. reprint ed. 5.85 (*0-317-91367-0*); reprint ed. 3.95 (*0-317-91369-7*) MAG Mfg.

ADFL Bulletin. 64p. 15.00 (*0-317-01160-X*); teacher ed 30.00 (*0-317-03280-1*) Assn Dept Lang.

Adhan over Anatolia. M. Kazi. pap. 7.95 (*0-87141-054-0*) Am Trust Pubns.

ADHD - Hyperactivity: A Consumer's Guide for Parents & Teachers. Michael Gordon. 178p. (Orig.). 1990. pap. 14.95 (*0-9627701-0-8*) GSI Pubns.

***ADHD & Teens: A Parent's Guide to Making It Through the Tough Years.** Colleen Alexander-Roberts. 208p. 1995. pap. 12.95 (*0-87833-899-3*) Taylor Pub.

ADHD in the Schools: Assessment & Intervention Strategies. George J. DuPaul & Gary Stoner. LC 93-46055. (School Practitioner Ser.). 269p. 1994. lib. bdg. 25.00 (*0-89862-245-X*, 2245) Guilford Pubns.

ADHD Parenting Handbook: Practical Advice for Parents from Parents. Colleen Alexander-Roberts. 176p. 1994. pap. 10.95 (*0-87833-862-4*) Taylor Pub.

Adhering to Medical Regimens: Pilot Experiments in Patient Education & Social Support. Robert D. Caplan et al. LC 76-620035. 284p. 1976. pap. 14.00 (*0-87944-207-7*) Inst Soc Res.

Adhering to Medical Regimens: Pilot Experiments in Patient Education & Social Support. Robert D. Caplan. LC 76-620035. (Illus.). 296p. reprint ed. pap. 84.40 (*0-7837-5281-4*, 2045019) Bks Demand.

Adhesion, 1. Ed. by K. W. Allen. 1981. 84.75 (*0-85334-735-2*, Pub. by Elsevier Applied Sci UK) Elsevier.

Adhesion, 2. Ed. by K. W. Allen. 1981. 66.75 (*0-85334-743-3*, Pub. by Elsevier Applied Sci UK) Elsevier.

Adhesion, 3. Ed. by K. W. Allen. 1981. 74.00 (*0-85334-808-1*, Pub. by Elsevier Applied Sci UK) Elsevier.

Adhesion, 4. Ed. by K. W. Allen. 1981. 74.00 (*0-85334-861-8*, Pub. by Elsevier Applied Sci UK) Elsevier.

Adhesion, 5. Ed. by K. W. Allen. 1981. 74.00 (*0-85334-929-0*, Pub. by Elsevier Applied Sci UK) Elsevier.

Adhesion, Vol. 6. Ed. by K. W. Allen. (Illus.). x, 210p. 1983. 97.25 (*0-85334-106-0*, Pub. by Elsevier Applied Sci UK) Elsevier.

Adhesion, Vol. 7. Ed. by K. W. Allen. (Illus.). 271p. 1983. 97.25 (*0-85334-195-8*, Pub. by Elsevier Applied Sci UK) Elsevier.

Adhesion, Vol. 8. Ed. by K. W. Allen. (Illus.). 220p. 1984. 97.25 (*0-85334-252-0*, I-518-83, Pub. by Elsevier Applied Sci UK) Elsevier.

Adhesion: Fundamentals & Practice. United Kingdom, Ministry of Technology Staff. 322p. 1971. text ed. 241.00 (*0-677-61430-6*) Gordon & Breach.

Adhesion: Papers from the Annual Conference on Adhesion & Adhesives, 22nd, City University, London, U. K., Vol. 9. Ed. by K. W. Allen. 198p. 1985. 84.75 (*0-85334-328-4*, Pub. by Elsevier Applied Sci UK) Elsevier.

Adhesion & Adhesives: Science & Technology. A. J. Kinloch. 500p. 1987. text ed. 85.00 (*0-412-27440-X*) Chapman & Hall.

Adhesion & Adsorption of Polymers, 2 vols., Set. Ed. by L. H. Lee. Incl. Pt. A. LC 80-262. 504p. 1980. 89.50 (*0-306-40427-3*); Pt. B. LC 80-262. 456p. 1980. 89.50 (*0-306-40428-1*); LC 80-262. (Polymer Science & Technology Ser.: Vols. 12A & B). 1980. 145.00 (*0-685-04067-4*, Plenum Pr) Plenum.

Adhesion & Bonding in Composites. Yosomiya et al. 376p. 1990. 125.00 (*0-8247-8149-X*) Dekker.

Adhesion & Friction. Ed. by M. Grunze & H. J. Kreuzer. (Surface Sciences Ser.: Vol. 17). (Illus.). vii, 129p. 1989. 56.00 (*0-387-51526-7*, 3397) Spr-Verlag.

Adhesion & Microorganism Pathogenicity. Ciba Foundation Staff. LC 81-19829. (Ciba Foundation Symposium: New Ser.: No. 80). (Illus.). 356p. reprint ed. pap. 101.50 (*0-8357-8780-X*, 2033610) Bks Demand.

Adhesion & the Formulation of Adhesives. 2nd ed. W. C. Wake. (Illus.). 326p. 1982. 84.75 (*0-85334-134-6*, Pub. by Elsevier Applied Sci UK) Elsevier.

Adhesion Aspects of Polymeric Coatings. Ed. by K. L. Mittal. LC 82-24870. 670p. 1983. 145.00 (*0-306-41250-0*, Plenum Pr) Plenum.

Adhesion in Leukocyte Homing & Differentiation. Ed. by D. Dunon et al. (Current Topics in Microbiology & Immunology Ser.: Vol. 184). (Illus.). 260p. 1993. write for info. (*3-540-56756-9*) Spr-Verlag.

Adhesion in Leukocyte Homing & Differentiation. D. Dunon et al. (Current Topics in Microbiology & Immunology Ser.: Vol. 184). 230p. 1993. 119.00 (*0-387-56756-9*) Spr-Verlag.

Adhesion in Solids. Ed. by D. M. Mattox et al. (Symposium Proceedings Ser.: Vol. 119). 1988. text ed. 42.00 (*0-931837-89-8*) Materials Res.

Adhesion International: Proceedings of the 10th Annual Meeting of the Adhesion Society Inc., Williamsburg, Virginia, U. S. A. Louis H. Sharpe. xvi, 776p. 1988. text ed. 114.00 (*0-677-21930-X*) Gordon & Breach.

***Adhesion Measurement of Films & Coatings.** Ed. by K. L. MIttal. 444p. 1994. 147.50 (*90-6764-182-0*, Pub. by VSP NE) Coronet Bks.

Adhesion Measurement of Thin Films, Thick Films & Bulk Coatings - STP 640. Ed. by K. L. Mittal. 410p. 1978. 39.25 (*0-8031-0272-0*, 04-640000-25) ASTM.

Adhesion Molecules. Ed. by Craig D. Wegner. (Handbook of Immunopharmacology Ser.). (Illus.). 384p. 1994. text ed. 67.50 (*0-12-741440-1*) Acad Pr.

***Adhesion Molecules & Cell Signaling: Biology & Clinical Applications.** Ed. by Peter c. Weber. LC 95-178. (Topics in Molecular Medicine Ser.: Vol. 1). 1995. write for info. (*0-7817-0323-9*) Raven.

Adhesion Molecules FactsBook. Ed. by Rod Pigott & Christine Power. (Facts Book Ser.). (Illus.). 200p. 1993. pap. text ed. 42.00 (*0-12-555180-0*) Acad Pr.

Adhesion of Dust & Powder. 2nd ed. Anatolii D. Zimon. Tr. by Robert K. Johnston. LC 80-16154. 450p. 1982. 95.00 (*0-306-10962-X*, Consultants) Plenum.

Adhesion of Dust & Powder. Anatolii D. Zimon. LC 69-12547. 436p. reprint ed. pap. 124.30 (*0-8357-5098-1*, 2056109) Bks Demand.

Adhesion of Polymeric Coatings to Copper. University of Cambridge Staff. 143p. 1968. 21.45 (*0-317-34495-1*, 64) Intl Copper.

***Adhesion Receptors as Therapeutic Agents.** Michael A. Horton. 336p. 1995. 189.95 (*0-8493-7655-6*) CRC Pr.

Adhesion Science & Technology. Lieng-Huang Lee. Incl. Pt. A. LC 75-35744. 470p. 1975. (*0-306-36493-X*); Pt. B. LC 75-35744. 456p. 1975. (*0-306-36494-8*); LC 75-35744. (Polymer Science & Technology Ser.: Vols. 9A & 9B). 1975. write for info. (*0-318-55304-X*, Plenum Pr) Plenum.

Adhesion Science Review 1987. Ed. by Hal F. Brinson et al. (Illus.). 328p. 1988. 40.00 (*0-9619517-1-0*) VA Tech Ctr Adhesion Sci.

Adhesion to Microorganisms to Surfaces. Ed. by D. C. Ellwood et al. (Special Publications of the Society for General Microbiology). 1979. text ed. 105.00 (*0-12-236650-6*) Acad Pr.

Adhesion 10. Ed. by K. W. Allen. 200p. 1986. 86.50 (*0-85334-418-3*, Pub. by Elsevier Applied Sci UK) Elsevier.

Adhesion 11. Ed. by K. W. Allen. 193p. 1987. 81.00 (*1-85166-079-8*, Pub. by Elsevier Applied Sci UK) Elsevier.

Adhesion 12: Prceedings of the 25th Annual Conference on Adhesion & Adhesives, the City University, London, 31st March-1st April 1987. Ed. by K. W. Allen. 266p. 1988. 88.25 (*1-85166-193-X*) Elsevier.

Adhesion 13: Proceedings of the 26th Annual Conference Held at the City University, London, UK. K. W. Allen. 294p. 1989. 93.75 (*1-85166-331-2*) Elsevier.

Adhesion 14: Twenty-Seventh Annual Conference on Adhesion & Adhesives, The City University, London, U. K. Ed. by K. W. Allen. 276p. 1990. 90.00 (*1-85166-482-3*) Elsevier.

Adhesion 15: Proceedings of the 28th Annual Conference on Adhesion & Adhesives Held at the City University of London. Ed. by K. W. Allen. 240p. 1991. 100.00 (*1-85166-584-6*) Elsevier.

Adhesive Bonding. Ed. by L. H. Lee. (Illus.). 510p. 1991. 115.00 (*0-306-43471-7*, Plenum Pr) Plenum.

Adhesive Bonding of Aluminum Alloys. Thrall & Shannon. LC 85-10445. (Materials Engineering Ser.: Vol. 1). 520p. 1985. 155.00 (*0-8247-7405-1*) Dekker.

Adhesive Bonding of Composites Materials, 1970-Jan. 1988. 210p. 85.00 (*0-686-48264-6*, LS102) T-C Pubns CA.

Adhesive Development for the Installation of Copper Plumbing. 88p. 1983. write for info. (*0-318-60087-0*, 350) Intl Copper.

Adhesive Strength in Fibre-Polymer Systems. J. A. Gorbatkina. Tr. by A. A. Beknasarov. LC 92-33965. (Ellis Horwood Series in Polymer Science & Technology). 1992. 115.00 (*0-13-005455-0*, Tavistock-E Horwood) Routledge Chapman & Hall.

Adhesively Bonded Joints: Testing, Analysis & Design, STP 981. Ed. by W. S. Johnson. LC 88-6912. (Special Technical Publication (STP) Ser.). (Illus.). 320p. 1988. text ed. 49.00 (*0-8031-0993-8*, 04-981000-25) ASTM.

Adhesives: Adherends, Adhesion. Nicholas J. De Lollis. LC 79-13871. 352p. 1980. lib. bdg. 37.50 (*0-88275-981-7*) Krieger.

Adhesives & Adhesive Bonding: Theoretical & Practical Aspects. George Epstein. 121p. 1984. 55.00 (*0-938648-16-0*) T-C Pubns CA.

Adhesives & Sealants. David Lammas. (Workshop Practice Ser.: No. 21). (Illus.). 144p. (Orig.). 1991. pap. 26.50 (*0-85486-048-7*, Pub. by Argus Books UK) Trans-Atl Phila.

Adhesives & Sealants, Vol. 3. EMH Staff. (Engineered Materials Handbook Ser.: Vol. 3). 893p. 1990. 147.00 (*0-87170-281-9*, 6012U) ASM.

***Adhesives & Sealants Market.** 400p. (Orig.). 1994. pap. 1,395.00 (*1-57205-904-4*) Rector Pr.

Adhesives Desk-Top Data Bank. International Plastics Selector, Inc. Staff. 150.00 (*0-686-48215-8*, 0301) T-C Pubns CA.

Adhesives for Industry. Ed. by George Epstein & Frances D. Tabrisky. (Illus.). 293p. 1980. 38.00 (*0-685-68821-6*) T-C Pubns CA.

Adhesives for Industry: Proceedings of a Special Conference, June 1980, Los Angeles, California. (Illus.). 293p. 40.00 (*0-938648-04-7*, 0103) T-C Pubns CA.

Adhesives for Packaging. Business Communications Co., Inc. Staff. 221p. 1987. pap. 1,950.00 (*0-89336-611-0*, GA-061) BCC.

Adhesives for the Composite Wood Panel Industry. G. S. Koch et al. LC 86-33300. (Illus.). 144p. 1987. 36.00 (*0-8155-1115-9*) Noyes.

Adhesives from Renewable Resources. Ed. by Richard W. Hemingway et al. LC 88-39293. (ACS Symposium Ser.: No. 385). 525p. 1989. 99.95 (*0-8412-1562-6*) Am Chemical.

Adhesives in Civil Engineering. G. C. Mays & A. R. Hutchinson. (Illus.). 342p. (C). 1992. 120.00 (*0-521-32677-X*) Cambridge U Pr.

Adhesives in Engineering Design. W. A. Lees. 156p. (C). 1984. text ed. 110.00 (*0-85072-150-4*) St Mut.

Adhesives in Manufacturing. Schneberger. (Manufacturing Engineering & Materials Processing Ser.: Vol. 11). 704p. 1983. 199.00 (*0-8247-1894-1*) Dekker.

Adhesives in Modern Manufacturing. Douglas F. Weyher. Ed. by E. J. Bruno. LC 79-93212. (Manufacturing Data Ser.). 198p. reprint ed. pap. 56.50 (*0-8357-5099-X*, 2016000) Bks Demand.

Adhesives Properties, Preparation, & Applications, 1982-May 1987. 235p. 85.00 (*0-686-48262-X*, LS101) T-C Pubns CA.

Adhesives Redbook: Adhesives Age Directory. Adhesive Age Magazine Staff. 55.00 (*0-686-48218-2*, 0501) T-C Pubns CA.

Adhesives, Sealants, & Coatings for Space & Harsh Environments. Ed. by L. H. Lee. LC 88-21002. (Polymer Science & Technology Ser.: Vol. 37). (Illus.). 550p. 1988. 125.00 (*0-306-42989-6*, Plenum Pr) Plenum.

Adhesives, Sealants & Coatings for the Electronics Industry. 2nd ed. Ernest W. Flick. LC 91-44715. 1002p. 1992. 135.00 (*0-8155-1295-3*) Noyes.

Adhesives Technology Handbook. Arthur H. Landrock. LC 85-15329. (Illus.). 444p. 1986. 64.00 (*0-8155-1040-3*) Noyes.

Adhesives Used on Building Materials, 1970-April 1987. 200p. pap. 85.00 (*0-686-48269-7*, LS104) T-C Pubns CA.

Adhesivs-Structural: Formulations & Applications. 200p. 1985. pap. 85.00 (*0-686-48265-4*, LS103) T-C Pubns CA.

Adhocracy. Robert H. Waterman, Jr. 128p. 1993. pap. 8.95 (*0-393-31084-1*) Norton.

Adhocracy: The Power to Change. Robert H. Waterman, Jr. LC 92-1750. 128p. 1992. 15.95 (*0-393-03414-3*) Norton.

Adhyatma Ramayana. Valmiki. Tr. by Tapasyananda. 376p. 1987. 9.95 (*0-87481-535-5*, Pub. by Ramakrishna Math II) Vedanta Pr.

Adhyatma Ramayana. Brahmandapurana Puranas. Tr. by Lala B. Nath. LC 73-3828. (Sacred Books of the Hindus: Extra Vol. 1). reprint ed. 25.00 (*0-404-57846-2*) AMS Pr.

***Adi Da Upanishad.** Adi Da. 350p. Date not set. pap. 32.00 (*1-57097-013-0*) Dawn Horse Pr.

Adiabatic Engine: Past, Present & Future Developements. 1984. 29.00 (*0-89883-116-4*, PT28) Soc Auto Engineers.

Adiabatic Engines & Systems. 1987. 19.00 (*0-89883-971-8*, SP700) Soc Auto Engineers.

Adiabatic Representation in Quantum Theory: Rigorous Results & Applications. B. L. Markovski & S. I. Vinitsky. 400p. 1995. text ed. 86.00 (*981-02-0847-2*) World Scientific Pub.

Adiabatic Shear Localization: Occurrence, Theories & Applications. Y. Bai & B. Dodd. (Illus.). 300p. 1992. 155.00 (*0-08-041266-1*, Pergamon Pr) Elsevier.

Adiabatic Waves in Liquid-Vapor Systems. G. E. Meier & P. A. Thompson. (International Union of Theoretical & Applied Mechanics Symposia Ser.). (Illus.). 456p. 1990. 96.00 (*0-387-50203-3*) Spr-Verlag.

Adibuddha. Kanai L. Hazra. (C). 1986. 24.00 (*81-7018-302-2*, Pub. by BR Pub II) S Asia.

ADIcycle: IBM Framework for Application. Stephen L. Montgomery. (Illus.). 250p. 1991. text ed. 49.95 (*0-442-30825-6*) Van Nos Reinhold.

Adieu a l'Adolescence: Poeme. Francois Mauriac. 19.95 (*0-8288-6081-5*, F112530) Fr & Eur.

Adieu au Sud. Maurice Denuziere. 653p. (FRE.). 1989. pap. 11.95 (*0-7859-2092-7*, 2070380408) Fr & Eur.

Adieu aux Armes. Ernest Hemingway. (FRE.). 1982. pap. 11.95 (*0-7859-2627-5*, 207036027X) Fr & Eur.

Adieu du Chasseur. William Humphrey. 462p. (FRE.). 1979. pap. 11.95 (*0-7859-2413-2*, 2070370917) Fr & Eur.

Adieu Gary Cooper. Romain Gary. (FRE.). 1991. pap. 10.95 (*0-7859-2929-0*) Fr & Eur.

Adieu Gary Cooper: La Comedie Americaine, Tome 2. Romain Gary. (Folio Ser.: No. 2328). (FRE.). 1991. pap. 8.95 (*2-07-038452-7*) Schoenhof.

Adieu la Vie, Adieu l'Amour (Demian Il Fera Nuit) Horace McCoy. 306p. (FRE.). 1987. pap. 11.95 (*0-7859-4513-X*, 207037887X) Fr & Eur.

Adieu l'Ami. Sebastien Japrisot. 154p. (FRE.). 1986. pap. 10.95 (*0-7859-2521-X*, 2070377776) Fr & Eur.

Adieu, Ma Jolie. Raymond Chandler. 301p. (FRE.). 1988. pap. 11.95 (*0-7859-2102-8*, 2070380792) Fr & Eur.

Adieux. Francois-Regis Bastide. 320p. (FRE.). 1980. pap. 11.95 (*0-7859-1923-6*, 2070372219) Fr & Eur.

Adikia in Platons "Politeia" Interpretationen zu den Burchen VIII & IX. D. Hellwig. 179p. (Orig.). (GER.). 1980. pap. 35.00 (*90-6032-190-1*, Pub. by B R Gruener NE) Benjamins North Am.

Adios a la Ansiedad. William Backus. (SPA.). Date not set. pap. 8.99 (*0-88113-138-5*) Edit Betania.

Adios a la Paz. Daniel Habana. LC 85-80698. (Coleccion Caniqui Ser.). 195p. (Orig.). (SPA.). 1986. pap. 9.95 (*0-89729-378-9*) Ediciones.

Adios al Falso Documento de Identidad: Farewell to the Fake I. D. Peter Gillquist. (SPA.). 3.95 (*84-7228-432-8*, 220010, Pub. by Edit Clie SP) TSELF.

***Adios, Anna: Friends & Amigos.** Giff. 1995. pap. 3.50 (*0-440-41070-3*) Dell.

Adios, Bandido! E. Jefferson Clay. Bd. with Desparados on the Loose. 1980. Set pap. 2.25 (*0-505-51459-1*) Dorchester Pub Co.

Adios, Berry. Chaya Shinhav. Tr. by C. C. Writer & Lisa C. Nielsen. (Hippy Ser.). (Illus.). 24p. (Orig.). (SPA.). (J). (ps). 1992. pap. text ed. 3.00 (*1-56134-154-1*) Dushkin Pub.

Adios Columbus. Vistas Latinas Staff. Ed. by Miriam Hernandez. LC 92-43211. (Illus.). 1993. 8.00 (*0-933699-28-X*) Hillwood Art Galry.

Adios Falcon. Wenceslao S. Deliz. LC 85-1116. (Ninos y Letras Ser.). 15p. (SPA.). (J). (ps-3). 1985. pap. 2.00 (*0-8477-3530-3*) U of PR Pr.

***Adios! Hola!** Barbara S. Hazen. (J). (ps-3). 1994. 14.95 (*0-689-31952-5*, Atheneum S&S) S&S Trade.

Adios, Hollywood: My Story, by Dick, Dog of Oaxaca. Told to Rose L. Goldenberg. 176p. 1994. 18.95 (*0-312-10455-3*, Pub. by Thomas Dunne Bks) St Martin.

Adios, Mr. Moxley: Thirteen Stories. Josephine Jacobsen. 157p. 1986. 17.95 (*0-916253-02-3*); pap. 10.95 (*0-916253-01-5*) Bk Serv Assocs.

Adios Mundo Cruel: Good Bye World. Leslie Miller. (SPA.). 4.25 (*84-7228-629-0*, 220004, Pub. by Edit Clie SP) TSELF.

Adios Pequeno - Bye Bye, Baby. Janet Ahlberg & Allan Ahlberg. Tr. by Maria Puncel. (Illus.). 28p. (SPA.). (J). (gr. k-1). 1990. write for info. (*84-372-6613-0*) Santillana.

Adios to Tears: The Memoirs of a Japanese-Peruvian Internee in U. S. Concentration Camps. Seiichi Higashide. 256p. (Orig.). 1993. pap. 19.00 (*0-9640816-0-1*) E & E Kudo.

Adipocyte & Obesity: Cellular & Molecular Mechanisms. Ed. by Aubie Angel et al. 328p. 1983. text ed. 83.00 (*0-89004-946-7*) Raven.

Adipose Child. Ed. by Zvi Laron. (Pediatric & Adolescent Endocrinology Ser.: Vol.1). 250p. 1976. 71.25 (*3-8055-2343-2*) S Karger.

Adipose Tissue. Ed. by L. Robert. (Frontiers of Matrix Biology Ser.: Vol. 2). (Illus.). 200p. 1976. 73.00 (*3-8055-2223-1*) S Karger.

Adipose Tissue & Reproduction. Ed. by Rose E. Frisch. (Progress in Reproductive Biology & Medicine Ser.: Vol. 14). (Illus.). x, 142p. 1990. 111.25 (*3-8055-5066-9*) S Karger.

Adipose Tissue in Childhood. F. P. Bonnet. 192p. 1981. 119.00 (*0-8493-5771-3*, QP88, CRC Reprint) Franklin.

Adirondack Album, Vol. I. Barney Fowler. (Illus.). 200p. (Orig.). 1974. pap. 11.95 (*0-9605556-1-7*) Outdoor Assocs.

Adirondack Album, Vol. 2. Barney Fowler. (Illus.). 200p. (Orig.). 1980. pap. 11.95 (*0-685-03753-3*) Outdoor Assocs.

Adirondack Album, Vol. 3. Barney Fowler. (Illus.). 192p. (Orig.). 1982. pap. 11.95 (*0-685-05687-2*) Outdoor Assocs.

Adirondack Album I. 1983. 11.95 (*0-317-03659-9*, North Country) Outdoor Assocs.

Adirondack Album II. Barney Fowler. (Illus.). 200p. 1983. 11.95 (*0-9605556-0-9*, North Country) Outdoor Assocs.

Adirondack Album III. Barney Fowler. (Illus.). 200p. 1983. pap. 11.95 (*0-9605556-2-5*, North Country) Outdoor Assocs.

***Adirondack Alphabet Book.** Sheri Amsel. (Illus.). 32p. (J). 1994. pap. 7.50 (*0-925168-33-5*) North Country.

Adirondack Archive: The Trail to Windover. Elisabeth Hudnut Clarkson. LC 93-8211. 260p. 1993. 30.00 (*0-925168-17-3*) North Country.

Adirondack Bibliography. Ed. by Dorothy A. Plum. 1958. 10.00 (*0-910020-28-0*) Adirondack Mus.

Adirondack Bibliography: Supplement 1956-65. Ed. by Dorothy A. Plum. 1973. 10.00 (*0-910020-29-9*, Adirondack Mus) Syracuse U Pr.

Adirondack Book: A Complete Guide. Elizabeth Folwell. (Illus.). 1992. pap. 16.95 (*0-936399-30-9*) Berkshire Hse.

Adirondack Books 1966-1992: An Annotated Bibliography with a Partial Listing of Book-Length Materials of the Year 1993. Douglas B. Welch. LC 94-7689. 160p. 1994. 27.50 (*0-925168-27-0*) North Country.

Adirondack Bridgebuilder from Charleston: Life & Times of Robert Cogdell Gilchrist. Rosemary M. Pelkey. LC 93-6165. 1993. pap. 15.00 (*0-925168-23-8*) North Country.

Adirondack Cabin Country. Paul Schaefer. (Illus.). 216p. (Orig.). Date not set. pap. 17.95 (*0-8156-0275-8*) Syracuse U Pr.

Adirondack Campsites. W. D. Mulholland. 42p. 1993. reprint ed. lib. bdg. 69.00 (*0-7812-5258-X*) Rprt Serv.

Adirondack Canoe Routes. William Howard. 33p. 1993. reprint ed. lib. bdg. 69.00 (*0-7812-5257-1*) Rprt Serv.

Adirondack Canoe Waters: North Flow. 3rd rev. ed. Paul Jamieson & Donald Morris. LC 87-33378. (Illus.). 368p. 1991. pap. 15.95 (*0-935272-43-7*) ADK Mtn Club.

Adirondack Canoe Waters: South & West Flow. 2nd rev. ed. Alec Proskine. LC 88-34398. (Canoe Guide Ser.: Vol. 2). 176p. 1994. reprint ed. pap. 12.95 (*0-935272-50-X*) ADK Mtn Club.

A

An Asterisk (*) at the beginning of an entry indicates that the title is appearing in BIP for the first time.

Adirondack Chair. Ed. by Workbench Magazine Staff. (Workbench Plans Ser.). (Illus.). 15p. Date not set. 12.95 (*0-86675-073-8*) KC Pub.

Adirondack Country. William C. White. LC 67-22222. (Illus.). 1967. 19.95 (*0-394-41855-7*) Knopf.

Adirondack Country. William C. White. LC 67-22222. (New York State Bks.). (Illus.). 368p. 1985. pap. 12.95 (*0-8156-0193-X*) Syracuse U Pr.

Adirondack Cross-Country Skiing: A Guide to 70 Trails. Dennis Conroy & Shirley Matzke. (Illus.). 284p. (Orig.). 1992. pap. 16.00 (*0-88150-249-9*, Backcountry) Countryman.

Adirondack Faces. Photos by Mathias Oppersdorff. LC 90-28862. (Illus.). 136p. 1991. 34.95 (*0-8156-0260-X*) Syracuse U Pr.

Adirondack Fishing in the 1930s: A Lost Paradise. Vincent Engels. (Illus.). 164p. (C). 1994. pap. 13.95 (*0-8156-0291-X*) Syracuse U Pr.

Adirondack Forest & Stream: An Outdoorsman's Reader. Donald Wharton. (Illus.). 131p. (Orig.). 1992. pap. 13.95 (*0-9641548-0-3*) Pine Mtn Pr.

Adirondack Furniture: And the Rustic Tradition. Graig Gilborn. (Illus.). 352p. 1987. 65.00 (*0-8109-1844-7*) Abrams.

Adirondack Golf Courses: Past & Present. 2nd ed. J. Peter Martin. (Illus.). 112p. 1987. reprint ed. pap. text ed. 14.95 (*0-685-48039-9*) Adirondack Golf.

***Adirondack Golf Courses Past & Present.** J. Peter Martin. 112p. (Orig.). 1987. pap. text ed. 14.95 (*0-9618820-0-X*) Adirondack Golf.

Adirondack Golf Courses...Past & Present. J. Peter Martin. (Illus.). 112p. (Orig.). 1987. pap. 14.95 (*0-685-19312-8*) Adirondack Golf.

Adirondack Guide-Boat. Kenneth Durant & Helen Durant. (Illus.). xvii, 250p. 1980. pap. 19.95 (*0-87742-125-0*) Adirondack Mus.

Adirondack Guide-Boat. Kenneth Durant & Helen Durant. LC 80-80778. (Illus.). 250p. 1981. pap. 19.95 (*0-685-32902-X*) Cornell U Pr.

Adirondack Mammals. D. Andrew Saunders. (Illus.). 216p. (Orig.). 1989. pap. 13.95 (*0-8156-8115-1*) Syracuse U Pr.

***Adirondack Mountain Club Canoe Guide to the Central Hudson & Delaware Watersheds.** Ed. by Mark Freeman. (Illus.). 200p. 1995. pap. 16.95 (*0-935272-78-X*) ADK Mtn Club.

Adirondack Mountain Club Canoe Guide to Western & Central New York State. Ed. by Mark Freeman. LC 93-25704. (Canoe Guide Ser.: Vol. 3). (Illus.). 256p. 1994. pap. 16.95 (*0-935272-59-3*) ADK Mtn Club.
Detailed route descriptions of 80 of the best paddle trips in western & central New York State, for white water & flat water enthusiasts alike. Includes launch sites, scenery & points of interest, difficulty levels, special cautions, paddling distances, & campsites & takeouts. Described in the ADIRONDACK MOUNTAIN CLUB CANOE GUIDE TO WESTERN & CENTRAL NEW YORK STATE are the waters of Lake Erie, Lake Ontario, & Finger Lake drainages, & in the Allegheny River watershed & part of the Susquehanna River watershed. Refers to International Scale of River Difficulty for classifying white water. This guide is the third in a series of guides to the canoeable waters of New York State. The project had its genesis in Paul Jamieson's ADIRONDACK CANOE WATERS: NORTH FLOW, first published by the Adirondack Mountain Club in 1975 & today regarded as a classic. To order, call: 1-800-395-8080 (M-F, 9am-4pm EST; within US), or write: ADK, RR 3, Box 3055, Lake George, NY 12845-9522. Mail orders add $4 shipping & handling. NYS residents add sales tax. ***Publisher Provided Annotation.***

Adirondack Mountains - A Section of Deep Proterozoic Crust. Ed. by Whitney. (IGC Field Trip Guidebooks Ser.). 72p. 1989. 21.00 (*0-87590-592-7*, T164) Am Geophysical.

Adirondack Park: A Political History. Frank Graham, Jr. LC 78-54900. (Illus.). 346p. 1984. pap. 16.95 (*0-8156-0192-1*) Syracuse U Pr.

***Adirondack Park Mountain Bike Preliminary Trail & Route Listing.** Adirondack North Country Assoc., Staff & Adirondack Mountain Club Staff. LC 95-12981. (Illus.). 280p. 1994. pap. 14.95 (*0-935272-77-1*) ADK Mtn Club.

***Adirondack Passage.** Christine Jerome. 1995. pap. 12.00 (*0-06-092582-5*, PL) HarpC.

Adirondack Passage: The Cruise of the Canoe Sairy Gamp. Christine Jerome. 224p. 1994. 20.00 (*0-06-016435-2*, HarpT) HarpC.

Adirondack Pilgrimage. Paul Jamieson. LC 86-20685. (Illus.). 248p. 1986. pap. 15.95 (*0-935272-39-9*) ADK Mtn Club.

Adirondack Portfolio. Jack Wikoff. LC 83-2280. 229p. 1983. pap. 7.95 (*0-940170-09-4*) Station Hill Pr.

Adirondack Portfolio, 2 vols. in 1. Jack Wikoff. Bd. with Penelope 472p. 1983. 20.00 (*0-685-06509-X*) Open Bk Pubns.

Adirondack Portraits: A Piece of Time. Jeanne R. Foster. Ed. by Noel Riedinger-Johnson. (New York State Bks.). (Illus.). 216p. (Orig.). 1986. text ed. 39.95x (*0-8156-2377-1*); pap. 17.95 (*0-8156-0205-7*) Syracuse U Pr.

Adirondack Princess. Doris E. Schulyer. 140p. (Orig.). 1982. pap. text ed. 8.00 (*0-914821-00-8*) Worden Pr.

***Adirondack Princess.** Doris E. Schuyler. 137p. (Orig.). 1982. pap. 12.00 (*0-9628208-2-2*) Canal Side Pubs.

Adirondack Princess, Bk. II. Doris E. Schuyler. 182p. (Orig.). 1990. pap. text ed. 10.00 (*0-9628208-0-6*) Canal Side Pubs.

Adirondack Railroads, Real & Phantom. Harold K. Hochschild. (Illus.). 20p. 1962. pap. 5.95 (*0-8156-8020-1*, Adirondack Mus) Syracuse U Pr.

Adirondack Railroads, Real & Phantom. rev. ed. Harold K. Hochschild. (Township Thirty-Four Ser.). (Illus.). 1982. reprint ed. 5.95 (*0-910020-06-X*) Adirondack Mus.

Adirondack Reader. 2nd ed. Ed. by Paul Jamieson. LC 82-20625. 544p. (C). 1983. 29.50 (*0-935272-21-6*); pap. 18.50 (*0-935272-22-4*) ADK Mtn Club.

Adirondack Rebellion. Anthony N. D'Elia. (Illus.). 1979. text ed. 10.00 (*0-686-25749-9*) Onchiota Bks.

Adirondack Regiment, One Hundred Eighteenth NY Volunteers. Cunningham. 1976. 23.00 (*0-8488-0244-6*) Amereon Ltd.

Adirondack Resort. rev. ed. Harold K. Hochschild. (Township Thirty-Four Ser.). (Illus.). 1988. reprint ed. 7.95 (*0-910020-07-8*) Adirondack Mus.

Adirondack Resort in the Nineteenth Century: Blue Mountain Lake, 1870-1900, Stagecoaches & Luxury Hotels. Harold K. Hochschild. (Illus.). 1962. pap. 7.95 (*0-8156-8021-X*, Adirondack Mus) Syracuse U Pr.

Adirondack Sampler: Day Hikes for All Seasons. 3rd ed. Bruce Wadsworth. LC 91-36397. 128p. 1992. pap. 10.95 (*0-935272-60-7*) ADK Mtn Club.

***Adirondack Sampler II: Backpacking Trips for All Seasons.** 2nd ed. Bruce Wadsworth. LC 95-11687. (Illus.). 128p. 1995. pap. 10.95 (*0-935272-75-5*) ADK Mtn Club.

Adirondack Spruce, A Study of the Forest in Ne-Ha-Sa-Ne Park. Gifford Pinchot. LC 77-125756. (American Environmental Studies). 1974. reprint ed. 17.95 (*0-405-02682-X*) Ayer.

Adirondack Steamboats on Raquette & Blue Mountain Lakes. Harold K. Hochschild. (Illus.). 33p. 1962. pap. 4.95 (*0-8156-8025-2*) Adirondack Mus.

Adirondack Stories. Philander Deming. 1972. reprint ed. 36.50 (*0-8422-8038-3*) Irvington.

Adirondack Tragedy: The Gillette Murder Case of 1906. Joseph W. Brownell & Patricia Wawrzaszek. LC 86-3121. (Illus.). 216p. (Orig.). 1986. pap. 9.95 (*0-932334-45-8*, NY73056) Hrt of the Lakes.

Adirondack Upland Flora: An Ecological Perspective. Michael Kudish. Ed. by Madge G. Heller. (Illus.). 320p. 1992. 45.00 (*0-918517-16-8*) Chauncy Pr.

Adirondack Voices: Woodsmen & Woods Lore. Robert D. Bethke. LC 94-21332. (Illus.). 160p. 1994. reprint ed. pap. 14.95 (*0-8156-0287-1*) Syracuse U Pr.

Adirondack Wilderness: A Story of Man & Nature. Jane E. Keller. (Illus.). 264p. 1980. pap. 16.95 (*0-8156-0150-6*) Syracuse U Pr.

Adirondack Wildguide: A Natural History of the Adirondack Park. Michael G. DiNunzio. (Illus.). 160p. 1984. 20.95 (*0-9613403-0-4*); pap. 14.95 (*0-9613403-1-2*) ADK Mtn Club.

Adirondacks. Nathan Farb. (Illus.). 184p. pap. 29.95 (*0-8478-0584-0*) Rizzoli Intl.

Adirondacks: A Special World. William M. Healy. (Illus.). 128p. 1986. 27.50 (*0-932052-41-X*) North Country.

Adirondacks: Forever Wild. George Wuerthner. (New York Geographic Ser.: No. 1). (Illus.). 104p. (Orig.). 1988. pap. 15.95 (*0-938314-44-0*) Am Wrld Geog.

Adirontreks: Places & People in the Adirondacks. John Vesty. LC 90-82523. (Illus.). 268p. (Orig.). (YA). (gr. 8). 1991. pap. 19.95 (*0-9626876-0-X*) J Vesty Co.

ADIS: Address Data Interchange Specification. Ed. by Norman W. Scharpf. 94p. 1986. 120.00 (*0-933505-04-3*); pap. 72.00 (*0-685-25397-X*) Graph Comm Assn.

Aditi & Other Deities in the Veda. M. P. Pandit. 1979. 6.95 (*0-941524-01-9*) Lotus Light.

Adivais of Bangladesh. Lewis B. Sckolnick. (Civil Rights Reporter Ser.). (Illus.). 60p. (Orig.). (C). 1994. pap. 45.00 (*1-57205-114-0*) Rector Pr.

Adivinanza a Traves de Five Hundred Anos de Cultura Hispana: Antologia Historica. Jorge A. Santana. 440p. 1992. pap. 19.50 (*1-881781-00-3*) Spanish Press.

Adivino. Rene De Goscinny & M. Uderzo. (Illus.). (SPA.). (J). 19.95 (*0-8288-6082-3*, S26630) Fr & Eur.

Adjacent Kingdom: Collected Last Poems. Thomas Blackburn. Ed. by Jean MacVean. LC 88-61443. 94p. (Orig.). 1988. pap. 15.95 (*0-7206-0707-8*, Pub. by P Owen Ltd UK) Dufour.

Adjectival Category: Criteria for Differentiation & Identification. Ed. by D. N. Shankara Bhat. LC 94-11533. (Studies in Language Companion Series: Vol. 24). 1994. 65.00 (*1-55619-376-9*) Benjamins North Am.

Adjective Generation Technique (AGT) Research & Applications. Bem P. Allen & Charles R. Potkay. 500p. 1984. text ed. 49.50 (*0-8290-0718-0*) Irvington.

Adjectives & Adverbs. Barbara Gregorich. (Horizons II Ser.). (Illus.). 24p. (J). (gr. 3-4). 1980. student ed 3.50 (*0-89403-596-7*) EDC.

Adjectives & Nominalizations. Zeno Vendler. 1968. pap. text ed. 34.65 (*90-279-0083-3*) Mouton.

Adjectives & Other Words. Ernest Weekley. LC 70-111872. (Essay Index Reprint Ser.). 1977. 20.95 (*0-8369-1635-2*) Ayer.

Adjectives de Celine: Introduction et Glossaire A-C. (Adjectives de Celine). 271p. (Orig.). (FRE.). (C). 1992. pap. 24.00 (*1-884868-03-7*) Montparnasse.

Adjectives from Proper Names see Doughty's English

Adjectives Will Cost Extra. Garry B. Trudeau. (Illus.). 1987. pap. 2.95 (*0-449-21567-9*) Fawcett.

***Adjoint Equations & Analysis of Complex Systems.** Guri I. Marchuk. LC 94-22318. (Mathematics & Its Applications Ser.: 295). 480p. (C). 1995. lib. bdg. 218.00 (*0-7923-3013-7*) Kluwer Ac.

Adjoint of a Semigroup of Linear Operators. Jan Van Neerven. LC 92-37396. 1992. 39.00 (*0-387-56260-5*) Spr-Verlag.

Adjudicating Constitutional Issues. Chester J. Antieau. LC 85-3056. 441p. 1985. lib. bdg. 40.00 (*0-379-20844-X*) Oceana.

Adjudication of Criminal Justice, Problems & References. Ronald L. Carlson. (American Casebook Ser.). 130p. 1986. pap. text ed. 16.00 (*0-314-25371-8*) West Pub.

Adjudication Officers' Guide, 10 vols., Set. Incl. Vol. 1. Adjudication. 1988. ring bd. 35.00 (*0-11-761401-7*, HM3271, Pub. by HMSO UK); Vol. 2. Subjects Common to All Benefits. 1988. ring bd. 50.00 (*0-11-761402-5*, HM3272, Pub. by HMSO UK); Vol. 3. Income Support, Social Fund, Maternity & Funeral Expenses. 1988. ring bd. 75.00 (*0-11-761403-3*, HM3273, Pub. by HMSO UK); Vol. 4. Family Credit. 1988. ring bd. 35.00 (*0-11-761404-1*, HM3274, Pub. by HMSO UK); Vol. 5. Child Benefit, Child Benefit Increase: Guardian's Allowance. 1988. ring bd. 30.00 (*0-11-761405-X*, HM3275, Pub. by HMSO UK); Vol. 6. Subjects Common to Benefits Other Than Income-Related & Child Benefit. 1988. ring bd. 45.00 (*0-11-761406-8*, HM3276, Pub. by HMSO UK); Vol. 7. Benefits for Incapacity, Invalidity, Severe Disablement & Maternity. 1988. ring bd. 40.00 (*0-11-761407-6*, HM3277, Pub. by HMSO UK); Vol. 8. Industrial Injuries Benefits. 1988. ring bd. 50.00 (*0-11-761408-4*, HM3278, Pub. by HMSO UK); Vol. 9. Widow's Benefits: Retirement Pension. 1988. ring bd. 30.00 (*0-11-761409-2*, HM3279, Pub. by HMSO UK); Vol. 10. Unemployment Benefit. 1988. ring bd. 50.00 (*0-11-761410-6*, HM3280, Pub. by HMSO UK); 1988. Complete Pkg., Vols. 1-10. Set ring bd. 360.00 (*0-685-58259-0*, HM3281) UNIPUB.

Adjudicator. Jack Rudman. (Career Examination Ser.: C-1087). 1994. pap. 39.95 (*0-8373-1087-3*) Nat Learn.

Adjunct Study Guide. Danny G. Langdon. LC 77-25457. (Instructional Design Library). (Illus.). 100p. 1978. 23.95 (*0-87778-105-2*) Educ Tech Pubns.

***Adjunction Theory of Complex Projective Varieties Vol. 16.** Mauro C. Beltrametti & Andrew J. Sommese. (De Gruyter Expositions in Mathematics). 419p. (C). 1995. lib. bdg. 89.95 (*3-11-014355-0*) De Gruyter.

Adjunctive Medical Therapy of Acromegalic Patients. J. W. Nortier. (Clinical Research Ser.: No. 2). x, 91p. (Orig.). (C). 1984. pap. text ed. 23.10 (*3-11-013365-2*) Mouton.

Adjunctive Therapy: 1985 Edition. Frank T. Langilotti. (Illus.). 152p. 1985. 30.00 (*0-938470-03-5*) NY Chiro Coll.

Adjuncts to Cancer Surgery. Steven G. Economou et al. LC 90-6034. (Illus.). 703p. 1991. text ed. 137.50 (*0-8121-1327-6*) Williams & Wilkins.

Adjust or Self-Destruct see Ajustarse o Autodestruirse

Adjustable Rate Mortgages. 2nd ed. Jack P. Friedman & Jack C. Harris. 304p. 1993. pap. 6.95 (*0-8120-1529-0*) Barron.

Adjustable Rate Mortgages & Mortgage Backed Securities: The Complete Reference Guide for Originators, Issuers, & Investors. Jess Lederman. 500p. 1991. text ed. 95.00 (*1-55623-232-2*) Irwin Prof Pubng.

Adjustable Speed AC Drive Systems. Ed. by Bimal K. Bose. LC 80-27789. 460p. 1981. pap. 49.95 (*0-87942-145-2*, PP01412) Inst Electrical.

***Adjusted Lives: Stories of Structural Adjustments.** F. Odun Balogun. LC 95-6644. 1995. write for info. (*0-86543-486-7*); pap. write for info. (*0-86543-487-5*) Africa World.

Adjusted to Death. Jacqueline Girdner. 1991. pap. 3.99 (*1-55773-453-4*, Charter Bks) Diamond.

Adjuster. Gerald Libonati. LC 94-71378. 292p. 1995. pap. 10.95 (*0-9640965-0-1*) Avant G Bks.

Adjusting Educational Policies: Conserving Resources While Raising School Quality. Ed. by Bruce Fuller & Aklil Habrte. (Discussion Paper Ser.: No. 132). 62p. 1992. 6.95 (*0-8213-1932-9*, 11932) World Bank.

Adjusting for Terms of Financing: A Bibliography. Robert M. Clatanoff. (Bibliographic Ser.). 8p. 1982. pap. 5.00 (*0-88329-115-0*) IAAO.

***Adjusting Foundations.** John Hejduk. Ed. by Kim Shkapich. (Illus.). 224p. (Orig.). 1995. pap. 35.00 (*1-885254-06-7*) Monacelli Pr.

Adjusting Investigation. Barry Zalma. 1992. 39.50 (*1-56461-112-4*, 46210) Rough Notes.

Adjusting Liab Fraud. Barry Zalma. 1992. 39.50 (*1-56461-114-0*, 46230) Rough Notes.

Adjusting Liability Claims: The New CGL, Cumis & the Tort of Bad Faith. Barry Zalma. 1992. 39.50 (*1-56461-113-2*, 46220) Rough Notes.

Adjusting Liability Claims - Basics. Barry Zalma. 1992. 39.50 (*1-56461-111-6*, 46200) Rough Notes.

Adjusting Privatization: Case Studies from Developing Countries. Christopher S. Adam et al. 400p. (C). 1993. pap. 29.95 (*0-435-08084-9*, 08084) Heinemann.

Adjusting Property Claims: Advanced Topics. Barry Zalma. Date not set. write for info. (*1-56461-132-9*) Rough Notes.

Adjusting Property Claims: Fraud. Barry Zalma. Date not set. 39.50 (*1-56461-181-7*) Rough Notes.

Adjusting Property Claims: Regulatory, Legal & Bad Faith Issues. Barry Zalma. Date not set. write for info. (*1-56461-130-2*) Rough Notes.

Adjusting Property Claims: The Basics. Barry Zalma. Date not set. write for info. (*1-56461-129-9*) Rough Notes.

Adjusting the Balance: Federal Policy & Victim Services. Steven R. Smith & Susan Freinkel. LC 87-15027. (Contributions in Political Science Ser.). 225p. 1988. text ed. 49.95 (*0-313-25305-6*, SHL/, Greenwood Pr) Greenwood.

Adjusting to a New Boss. Barbara L. McCombs & Linda Brannan. (Skills for Job Success Ser.). (Illus.). 32p. (Orig.). 1990. student ed, pap. 4.95 (*1-56119-025-X*) Educ Pr MD.

Adjusting to a New Boss. Barbara L. McCombs & Linda Brannan. (Skills for Job Success Ser.). (Illus.). 32p. (Orig.). (YA). (gr. 7-12). 1990. teacher ed 1.95 (*1-56119-026-8*); disk 39.95 (*1-56119-113-2*) Educ Pr MD.

Adjusting to a New Boss, Set. Barbara L. McCombs & Linda Brannan. (Skills for Job Success Ser.). (Illus.). 32p. (Orig.). (YA). (gr. 7-12). 1990. 44.95 (*1-56119-071-3*) Educ Pr MD.

Adjusting to Policy Failure in African Economies. Ed. by David E. Sahn. LC 93-29987. (Food Systems & Agrarian Change Ser.). (Illus.). 440p. 1994. 49.95 (*0-8014-2906-4*); pap. 19.95 (*0-8014-8136-8*) Cornell U Pr.

Adjusting to Reality: Beyond "State vs. Market" in Economic Development. Robert Klitgaard. 303p. 1991. pap. 11.95 (*1-55815-157-5*); 2.00 (*1-55815-186-9*) ICS Pr.

Adjusting to Reality: Philosophical & Psychological Ideas in the Post-Civil War Novels of Ramon J. Sender. Anthony M. Trippet. 1987. 63.00 (*0-7293-0251-2*, Pub. by Tamesis Bks Ltd UK) Boydell & Brewer.

Adjusting to Regulatory, Pricing & Marketing Realities: Proceedings of the Institute of Public Utilities Annual Conference, 14th, Williamsburg, VA, 1982. Michigan State University, Institute of Public Utilities, Staff. LC 83-62894. (MSU Public Utilities Papers). 781p. reprint ed. pap. 180.00 (*0-8357-5100-7*, 2029405) Bks Demand.

Adjusting to Scarcity: Proceedings of the American Academy of Political & Social Science, 79th. American Academy of Political & Social Science Staff. Ed. by Richard D. Lambert & Marvin E. Wolfgang. LC 74-29624. (Annals Ser.: No. 420). 250p. 1975. pap. 18.00 (*0-87761-191-2*) Am Acad Pol Soc Sci.

Adjusting to Success: Balance of Payments Policy in the East Asian NICs. rev. ed. Bela Balassa & John Williamson. LC 90-4373. (Policy Analyses in International Economics Ser.: No. 17). 158p. reprint ed. pap. 45.10 (*0-7837-4221-5*, 2043910) Bks Demand.

Adjusting to the Light. Miller Williams. 64p. 1992. text ed. 18.95 (*0-8262-0851-7*); pap. 9.95 (*0-8262-0852-5*) U of Mo Pr.

Adjusting to Volatile Energy Prices. Philip K. Verleger, Jr. 262p. 1993. pap. 16.00 (*0-88132-069-2*) Inst Intl Eco.

Adjustment. Scribner Staff. 1984. write for info. (*0-684-99999-4*, Scribners) S&S Trade.

Adjustment: Applying Psychology in a Complex World. Robert S. Feldman. (C). 1989. text ed. write for info. (*0-07-020406-3*) McGraw.

Adjustment: The Psychology of Change. William R. Miller et al. 608p. (C). 1990. Casebound. text ed. write for info. (*0-13-004342-7*) P-H.

Adjustment & Assimilation of Slovenian Refugees. Giles E. Gobetz. Ed. by Francesco Cordasco. LC 80-860. (American Ethnic Groups Ser.). 1981. lib. bdg. 24.95 (*0-405-13423-1*) Ayer.

Adjustment & Competence: Concepts & Applications. Tony Grasha & Daniel Kirschenbaum. LC 85-22702. (Illus.). 511p. (C). 1986. text ed. 54.75 (*0-314-93183-X*); Instr's. manual. teacher ed, pap. text ed. write for info. (*0-314-96629-3*); Study guide. student ed, pap. text ed. 20.00 (*0-314-96630-7*) West Pub.

Adjustment & Economic Performance in Industrialized Countries: A Synthesis. Geoffrey Renshaw. (Employment, Adjustment & Industrialization Ser.: No. 8). xiii, 110p. (Orig.). 1986. 32.00 (*92-2-105509-4*); pap. 24.00 (*92-2-105510-8*) Intl Labour Office.

Adjustment & Equity in Chile. Patricio Meller. 102p. (Orig.). 1992. pap. 31.00 (*92-64-13619-3*) OECD.

An Asterisk (*) at the beginning of an entry indicates that the title is appearing in BIP for the first time.

Adjustment & Equity in Cote D'Ivoire. OECD Staff. 172p. (Orig.). 1992. pap. 31.00 (*92-64-13654-1*) OECD.

Adjustment & Equity in Developing Countries: A New Approach. OECD Staff. 112p. (Orig.). 1992. pap. 31.00 (*92-64-13664-9*) OECD.

Adjustment & Equity in Ecuador. OECD Staff. 174p. (Orig.). 1991. pap. 31.00 (*92-64-13539-1*) OECD.

Adjustment & Equity in Ghana. OECD Staff. 164p. (Orig.). 1992. pap. 31.00 (*92-64-13757-2*) OECD.

Adjustment & Equity in Indonesia. Erik Thorbecke. 264p. (Orig.). 1992. pap. 31.00 (*92-64-13651-7*) OECD.

Adjustment & Equity in Malaysia. David Demery & Lionel Demery. (Adjustment & Equity in Developing Countries Ser.). 102p. (Orig.). 1992. pap. text ed. 31.00 (*92-64-13601-0*, 41-91-20-1) OECD.

Adjustment & Equity in Morocco. Christian Morrison. (Adjustment & Equity in Developing Countries Ser.). 150p. (Orig.). 1991. pap. text ed. 31.00 (*92-64-13589-8*, 41-91-21-1) OECD.

Adjustment & Financing in the Developing World: The Role of the International Monetary Fund. Ed. by Tony Killick. LC 82-9213. (Illus.). xviii, 232p. 1982. 12.00 (*0-939934-18-3*); pap. 8.00 (*0-939934-19-1*) Intl Monetary.

Adjustment & Financing in the Developing World: The Role of the International Monetary Fund. Ed. by Tony Killick. LC 82-9213. 250p. reprint ed. pap. 71.30 (*0-8357-5101-5*, 2020604) Bks Demand.

Adjustment & Growth: The Challenges of Life. 5th ed. Spencer A. Rathus & Jeffrey S. Nevid. Ed. by Eve Howard. (Illus.). 600p. (C). 1992. text ed. 42.75 (*0-03-074418-0*) HB Coll Pubs.

Adjustment & Growth in a Changing World. 4th ed. Vince Napoli et al. Ed. by Marshall. 514p. (C). 1992. pap. text ed. 48.00 (*0-314-93372-7*) West Pub.

***Adjustment & Growth in a Changing World.** 5th ed. Vince Napoli et al. LC 94-32602. 575p. 1995. text ed. write for info. (*0-314-04557-0*) West Pub.

Adjustment & Personal Growth: Seven Pathways. 2nd ed. Frank J. Bruno. LC 82-8520. 466p. 1983. Net. text ed. write for info. (*0-471-09296-7*) Wiley.

***Adjustment & Poverty: Options & Choices.** Frances Stewart. LC 94-46809. (Priorities for Development Economics Ser.). 1995. write for info. (*0-415-09134-9*); pap. write for info. (*0-415-12436-0*) Routledge.

Adjustment & Technology: The Case of Rice. OECD Staff. 160p. (Orig.). 1993. pap. 24.00 (*92-64-13942-7*) OECD.

Adjustment Computation, Practical Least Squares for Surveyors. 3rd ed. Paul R. Wolf. (Illus.). 284p. 1987. reprint ed. pap. 35.00 (*0-910845-26-3*, 464) Landmark Ent.

Adjustment, Conditionality, & International Financing. Ed. by Joaquin Muns. xi, 214p. 1985. reprint ed. English. pap. 10.00 (*0-939934-28-0*); reprint ed. Span. pap. 10.00 (*0-939934-29-9*) Intl Monetary.

Adjustment Crisis in the Third World. Ed. by Richard E. Feinberg & Valerina Kallab. (U. S. Third World Policy Perspectives Ser.). 200p. (C). 1984. 32.95 (*0-88738-040-9*); pap. 17.95 (*0-87855-988-4*) Transaction Pubs.

***Adjustment Disorders & Brief Treatment.** Daniel J. Araoz & Marie A. Carrese. 228p. 1995. text ed. write for info. (*0-87630-790-X*) Brunner-Mazel.

Adjustment in Africa: Lessons from Country Case Studies. Ed. by Rashid Faruqee & Ishrat Husain. LC 94-9664. (Regional & Sectoral Study Ser.). 448p. 1994. 26.95 (*0-8213-2787-9*, 12787) World Bank.

Adjustment in Africa: Reform, Results, & the Road Ahead. LC 93-47887. (Policy Research Report Ser.). 304p. (C). 1994. pap. text ed. 19.95 (*0-19-520994-X*) World Bank.

***Adjustment in Africa: Reforms, Results, & the Road Ahead.** World Bank Staff. (World Bank Policy Research Report Ser.). 304p. (FRE.). 1994. write for info. (*0-8213-2530-2*, 12530) World Bank.

***Adjustment in Africa: Summary.** World Bank Staff. 24p. 1994. write for info. (*0-8213-2795-X*, 12795) World Bank.

***Adjustment in Africa: Summary.** World Bank Staff. 24p. (FRE.). 1994. write for info. (*0-8213-2796-8*, 12796) World Bank.

Adjustment in Intercultural Marriage. Ed. by Wen-Shing Tseng et al. 144p. reprint ed. pap. 41.10 (*0-8357-6005-7*, 2034644) Bks Demand.

Adjustment in Oil-Importing Developing Countries: A Comparative Economic Analysis. Pradeep K. Mitra. LC 92-36214. (Illus.). 375p. (C). 1994. 54.95 (*0-521-44316-4*) Cambridge U Pr.

Adjustment in the Urban System: The Tasman Bridge Collapse & Its Effects on Metropolitan Hobart. Lee & L. J. Wood. (Progress in Planning Ser.: Vol. 15, Pt. 2). 85p. 1981. pap. 16.25 (*0-08-026810-2*) Elsevier.

Adjustment Inventory. Hugh M. Bell. write for info. (*0-8047-1061-9*) Stanford U Pr.

Adjustment Lending & Mobilization of Private & Public Resources for Growth. LC 92-31341. (Policy & Research Ser.: No. 22). 109p. 1992. 7.95 (*0-8213-2208-7*, 12208) World Bank.

Adjustment Lending Policies for Sustainable Growth. Country Economics Department Staff. (Policy & Research Ser.: No. 14). 130p. 1990. 9.95 (*0-8213-1674-5*, 11674) World Bank.

Adjustment Lending Revisited: Policies to Restore Growth. Ed. by Vittorio Corbo et al. 196p. 1992. 17.95 (*0-8213-2061-0*, 12061) World Bank.

Adjustment of Property Losses. P. I. Thomas & P. B. Reed. (C). 1977. 355.00 (*0-685-33802-9*, Pub. by Witherby & Co UK) St Mut.

Adjustment of Property Losses. 4th ed. Paul I. Thomas & Prentiss B. Reed, Sr. (Illus.). 1977. text ed. 44.95 (*0-07-064215-X*) McGraw.

Adjustment of Public Liability Claims. A. J. Cleary. (C). 1983. 160.00 (*0-685-33801-0*, Pub. by Witherby & Co UK) St Mut.

Adjustment of Schizophrenics in the Community. G. Serban. LC 79-9404. (Illus.). 338p. 1980. text ed. 40.00 (*0-88331-106-2*) Luce.

Adjustment of School Organization to Various Population Groups. Robert A. McDonald. LC 70-177021. (Columbia University. Teachers College. Contributions to Education Ser.: No. 75). reprint ed. 22.50 (*0-404-55075-4*) AMS Pr.

Adjustment or Delinking? The African Experience. Ed. by Azzam Mahjoub. Tr. by A. M. Berrett. LC 89-9027. (UNU Studies in African Political Economy). (Illus.). 272p. (C). 1990. text ed. 55.00 (*0-86232-842-X*, Pub. by Zed Books UK); pap. 17.50 (*0-86232-843-8*, Pub. by Zed Books UK) Humanities.

Adjustment Policies & Development Strategies in the Arab World. Ed. by Said El-Naggar. LC 87-21377. ix, 201p. (ARA & ENG.). 1987. pap. 12.00 (*0-939934-96-5*) Intl Monetary.

Adjustment Policies & Development Strategies in the Arab World: Papers Presented at a Seminar Held in Abu Dhabi, United Arab Emirates, February 16-18, 1987. Ed. by Said El-Naggar. LC 87-21377. 210p. reprint ed. pap. 59.90 (*0-8357-5102-3*, 2030989) Bks Demand.

Adjustment Policies in Development Planning Socio-Economic Development in Sri Lanka. Efraim Gutkind. 369p. 1988. text ed. 85.95 (*0-566-05613-5*, Pub. by Avebury Pub UK) Ashgate Pub Co.

Adjustment Processes for Exchange Economies & Noncooperative Games. Antoon Van den Elzen. LC 93-36418. (Lecture Notes in Economics & Mathematical Systems Ser.: Vol. 402). 1993. 41.00 (*0-387-57310-0*) Spr-Verlag.

***Adjustment Processes in Russian Defence Enterprises Within the Framewoork of Conversion & Transition.** Pfaffenberger. Ed. by Opitz. (Studies on Conversion Research). (C). 1995. pap. text ed. 93.00 (*3-8258-2028-9*) Westview.

Adjustment Programs in Africa: The Recent Experience. Justin B. Zulu & Saleh M. Nsouli. (Occasional Paper Ser.: No. 34). 37p. 1985. pap. 7.50 (*1-55775-056-4*) Intl Monetary.

Adjustment, Structural Change & Economic Efficiency: Aspects of Monetary Cooperation in Eastern Europe. Jozef M. Van Brabant. (Cambridge Russian, Soviet & Post-Soviet Studies: No. 58). (Illus.). 544p. 1987. 79.95 (*0-521-33455-1*) Cambridge U Pr.

Adjustment to Adult Hearing Loss. Ed. by Harold Orlans. (Illus.). 204p. (C). 1991. reprint ed. pap. text ed. 29.95 (*1-879105-47-0*, A056) Singular Publishing.

Adjustment with Growth in Latin America. Alberto Eguren. (EDI Policy Seminar Report Ser.: No. 22). 24p. 1990. 6.95 (*0-8213-1433-5*, 11433) World Bank.

Adjustments: The Making of a Chiropractor. Terry Cox & Terry Cox-Joseph. 1993. 9.95 (*1-878901-54-0*) Hampton Roads Pub Co.

Adjustments for Tax Purposes in Highly Inflationary Economics, Vol. 9. Ed. by IFA Staff. 1985. lib. bdg. 56.00 (*90-6544-216-2*) Kluwer Ac.

Adjuvant Nutrition in Cancer Treatment. Ed. by Patrick Quillin. (Illus.). 400p. (C). 1993. write for info. (*0-9638263-0-1*) Cancer Treatment.

Adjuvant Therapy for Colon & Rectum Cancer. 1991. lib. bdg. 250.00 (*0-8490-4222-4*) Gordon Pr.

Adjuvant Therapy of Breast Cancer. Ed. by I. Craig Henderson & William L. McGuire. (Cancer Treatment & Research Ser.). 480p. (C). 1992. lib. bdg. 177.00 (*0-7923-1656-8*) Kluwer Ac.

Adjuvant Therapy of Breast Cancer IV. Ed. by H. J. Senn et al. LC 92-49032. (Recent Results in Cancer Research Ser.: Vol. 127). 1993. 145.00 (*0-387-55304-5*) Spr-Verlag.

Adjuvant Therapy of Cancer, No. VI. 6th ed. Charles G. Salmon. (Illus.). 672p. 1990. text ed. 73.50 (*0-7216-3630-6*) Saunders.

Adjuvant Therapy of Cancer 5. 5th ed. Charles G. Salmon. 1987. text ed. 70.50 (*0-8089-1880-X*, Grune) Saunders.

Adjuvant Therapy of Cancer 7. Charles G. Salmon. 1993. 69.50 (*0-397-51341-0*) Lippincott.

Adjuvant Therapy of Primary Breast Cancer. Ed. by H. J. Senn et al. (Recent Results in Cancer Research Ser.: Vol. 115). (Illus.). 304p. 1989. 119.00 (*0-387-18810-X*, 2887) Spr-Verlag.

Adjuvants & Agrochemicals, 2 vols., Vol. I. Ed. by Paul N. Chow et al. 240p. 1989. 191.00 (*0-8493-6532-5*, S587) CRC Pr.

Adjuvants & Agrochemicals, 2 vols., Vol. II. Ed. by Paul N. Chow et al. 256p. 1989. 191.00 (*0-8493-6533-3*, S587) CRC Pr.

Adjuvants for Agrochemicals. Foy. 1992. 288.00 (*0-8493-6317-9*, S587) CRC Pr.

Adkins Life Skills Program: Career Development Series. 2nd ed. Winthrop R. Adkins. Ed. by Donald D. Davis. (Ten Unit Multi-Media Counseling - Learning Curriculum Ser.). 1985. write for info. (*1-56223-000-X*) Inst Life Coping Skills.

Adkins Life Skills Program: Career Development Series, Unit 1: Exploring Who I Am & Where I Want to Go. 2nd ed. Winthrop R. Adkins. Ed. by Donald D. Davis. (Ten Unit Multi-Media Counseling - Learning Curriculum Ser.). 1985. write for info. (*1-56223-001-8*); student ed write for info. (*1-56223-011-5*) Inst Life Coping Skills.

Adkins Life Skills Program: Career Development Series, Unit 10: Keeping a Job: Strategies That Help. 2nd ed. Winthrop R. Adkins. Ed. by Donald D. Davis. (Ten Unit Multi-Media Counseling - Learning Curriculum Ser.). 1985. write for info. (*1-56223-010-7*); student ed write for info. (*1-56223-020-4*) Inst Life Coping Skills.

Adkins Life Skills Program: Career Development Series, Unit 2: Exploring the World of Work. 2nd ed. Winthrop R. Adkins. Ed. by Donald D. Davis. (Ten Unit Multi-Media Counseling - Learning Curriculum Ser.). 1985. write for info. (*1-56223-002-6*); student ed write for info. (*1-56223-012-3*) Inst Life Coping Skills.

Adkins Life Skills Program: Career Development Series, Unit 3: Making Good Career Decisions. 2nd ed. Winthrop R. Adkins. Ed. by Donald D. Davis. (Ten Unit Multi-Media Counseling - Learning Curriculum Ser.). 1985. write for info. (*1-56223-003-4*); student ed write for info. (*1-56223-013-1*) Inst Life Coping Skills.

Adkins Life Skills Program: Career Development Series, Unit 4: Finding Job Information & Contacting Employers. 2nd ed. Winthrop R. Adkins. Ed. by Donald D. Davis. (Ten Unit Multi-Media Counseling - Learning Curriculum Ser.). 1985. write for info. (*1-56223-004-2*); student ed write for info. (*1-56223-014-X*) Inst Life Coping Skills.

Adkins Life Skills Program: Career Development Series, Unit 5: Using Employment Agencies & Personal Contacts. 2nd ed. Winthrop R. Adkins. Ed. by Donald D. Davis. (Ten Unit Multi-Media Counseling - Learning Curriculum Ser.). 1985. write for info. (*1-56223-005-0*); student ed write for info. (*1-56223-015-8*) Inst Life Coping Skills.

Adkins Life Skills Program: Career Development Series, Unit 6: Planning & Handling Time Effectively. 2nd ed. Winthrop R. Adkins. Ed. by Donald D. Davis. (Ten Unit Multi-Media Counseling - Learning Curriculum Ser.). 1985. write for info. (*1-56223-006-9*); student ed write for info. (*1-56223-016-6*) Inst Life Coping Skills.

Adkins Life Skills Program: Career Development Series, Unit 7: Developing a Career Plan. 2nd ed. Winthrop R. Adkins. Ed. by Donald D. Davis. (Ten Unit Multi-Media Counseling - Learning Curriculum Ser.). 1985. write for info. (*1-56223-007-7*); student ed write for info. (*1-56223-017-4*) Inst Life Coping Skills.

Adkins Life Skills Program: Career Development Series, Unit 8: Presenting Myself on Paper: Application Forms & Resumes. 2nd ed. Winthrop R. Adkins. Ed. by Donald D. Davis. (Ten Unit Multi-Media Counseling - Learning Curriculum Ser.). 1985. write for info. (*1-56223-008-5*); student ed write for info. (*1-56223-018-2*) Inst Life Coping Skills.

Adkins Life Skills Program: Career Development Series, Unit 9: Developing Effective Interviewing Skills. 2nd ed. Winthrop R. Adkins. Ed. by Donald D. Davis. (Ten Unit Multi-Media Counseling - Learning Curriculum Ser.). 1985. write for info. (*1-56223-009-3*); student ed write for info. (*1-56223-019-0*) Inst Life Coping Skills.

Adkins Site: A Paleo-Indian Habitation & Associated Stone Structure. Richard M. Gramley. LC 87-32822. 119p. (C). 1988. pap. 17.50 (*0-9615462-2-0*) Ctr Study First Am.

ADLA 2. 1986. 40.00 (*0-317-39891-1*) Art Dir Club.

Adlai Stevenson & American Politics: The Odyssey of a Cold War Liberal. Jeff Broadwater. LC 93-43000. (Twayne's Twentieth-Century American Biography Ser.). 304p. 1994. text ed. 27.95 (*0-8057-7798-9*, Twayne); pap. 14.95 (*0-8057-7799-7*, Twayne) Macmillan.

Adlai Stevenson Memorial Lecture Series: The First Twenty-Five Years, 1966-1991. Ed. by John K. Boaz. 212p. (C). 1994. lib. bdg. 52.00 (*0-8191-9628-2*); pap. text ed. 22.00 (*0-8191-9629-0*) U Pr of Amer.

Adler Special Manuscript Collection from the Library of the Jewish Theological Seminary: An Index to the Microfilm Collection. University Microfilms International Staff. LC 81-2980. 1981. pap. 15.00 (*0-8357-0221-9*) Univ Microfilms.

Adlerian Counseling: A Practical Approach for a New Decade. 3rd ed. T. J. Sweeney. LC 88-82676. 508p. (C). 1989. 30.95 (*0-915202-84-0*) Accel Devel.

Adlerian Counseling & Psychotherapy. 2nd ed. Don C. Dinkmeyer et al. 368p. (C). 1987. pap. write for info. (*0-675-20614-6*, Merrill Pub Co) Macmillan.

Adlerian Lexicon: Fifty-Nine Terms Associated with the Individual Psychology of Alfred Alder. Jane Griffith & Robert L. Powers. LC 84-11100. 73p. (Orig.). 1984. pap. text ed. 10.00 (*0-918287-00-6*) AIAS.

***Adler's Philosophical Dictionary: 125 Key Terms for the Philosopher's Lexicon.** Mortimer J. Adler. 1995. 20.00 (*0-684-80360-7*, Scribners) S&S Trade.

Adler's Physiology of the Eye. Hart. (SPA.). 1993. 160.90 (*84-8086-070-7*) Mosby Yr Bk.

Adler's Physiology of the Eye: Clinical Application. 9th ed. Ed. by William M. Hart, Jr. LC 92-12791. 888p. 1992. 84.00 (*0-8016-2107-0*) Mosby Yr Bk.

Adman: Morris Hite's Methods for Winning the Ad Game. Russ Pate. (Illus.). 225p. 1988. 24.95 (*0-935014-12-8*) E-Heart Pr.

Admetus. Emma Lazarus. LC 77-104508. reprint ed. lib. bdg. 36.00 (*0-8398-1152-7*) Irvington.

Administered Politics: Elite Political Culture in Sweden. Thomas J. Anton. 1980. lib. bdg. 58.00 (*0-89838-025-1*) Kluwer Ac.

Administered Prices: A Compendium on Public Policy. U. S. Senate Subcommittee on Anti-Trust & Monopoly. LC 75-39278. (Getting & Spending: the Consumer's Dilemma Ser.). (Illus.). 1976. reprint ed. 29.95 (*0-405-08053-0*) Ayer.

Administered Protection in America. Alan A. Rugman & Andrew Anderson. 208p. 1987. lib. bdg. 45.00 (*0-7099-4286-9*, Pub. by Croom Helm UK) Routledge Chapman & Hall.

Administering & Supervising Occupational Education. Curtis Finch & Robert McGough. (Illus.). 302p. (C). 1991. reprint ed. pap. text ed. 19.95 (*0-88133-640-8*) Waveland Pr.

Administering Christian Education. Robert K. Bower. LC 64-22018. 1964. pap. 10.99 (*0-8028-1559-6*) Eerdmans.

Administering College & University Housing: A Legal Perspective. rev. ed. Ed. by Donald D. Gehring. LC 92-17050. 120p. 1994. pap. 18.95 (*0-912557-13-3*) Coll Admin Pubns.

Administering Danger in the Workplace: The Law & Politics of Occupational Health & Safety Regulation in Ontario, 1850-1914. Eric Tucker. 320p. 1990. 45.00 (*0-8020-5855-8*); pap. 19.95 (*0-8020-6765-4*) U of Toronto Pr.

A

***Administering Grants, Contracts & Funds: Evaluating & Improving Your Grants System.** David G. Bauer. LC 94-38180. (American Council on Education Series on Higher Education). 233p. 1994. 36.95 (*0-89774-832-8*) Oryx Pr.

Administering Human Resources: A Behavioral Approach to Educational Administration. Ed. by Francis M. Trusty. LC 71-146311. (Orig.). 1971. 32.50 (*0-8211-1903-6*); text ed. 31.00 (*0-685-03188-8*) McCutchan.

Administering Management Development Institutions in Africa. Kami Rwegasira. 1988. text ed. 68.95 (*0-566-05501-5*, Pub. by Avebury Pub UK) Ashgate Pub Co.

Administering Medications. Phyllis T. Bayt. (Health Occupations Ser.). 1982. write for info. (*0-672-61538-X*); pap. write for info. (*0-672-61522-3*) Macmillan.

Administering Medications. Phyllis T. Bayt. 1982. pap. 23.75 (*0-02-685190-3*) Macmillan.

Administering Medications: A Competency-Based Program for Health Occupations. 3rd ed. Phyllis T. Bayt. LC 93-16412. 1993. text ed. write for info. (*0-02-800886-3*); Inst's. manual. teacher ed write for info. (*0-02-800887-1*) Glencoe.

Administering Nursing Service. 2nd ed. Marie DiVincenti. 350p. 1977. 20.50 (*0-316-18651-1*) Little.

Administering Oregon Estates, 1991. rev. ed. Ed. by Jim Perry. write for info. (*0-318-61743-9*) OR Bar CLE.

Administering Pension Plans. Bernard Forseter & Daniel Sussman. 260p. write for info. (*0-318-59766-7*) Fed Pubns Inc.

Administering Preschool Programs in Public Schools: Practitioner's Handbook. Patricia S. Miller & James O. McDowelle. LC 92-20133. (Illus.). 298p. (Orig.). (C). 1992. pap. text ed. 34.95x (*1-879105-78-0*) Singular Publishing.

Administering Programs for Young Children. Ed. by Janet F. Brown. LC 84-61999. 216p. 1984. pap. text ed. 7.00 (*0-912674-90-3*, NAEYC #307) Natl Assn Child Ed.

Administering Public Policy. Ed. by H. George Frederickson & Charles Wise. (C). 1976. pap. 12.00 (*0-918592-16-X*) Pol Studies.

***Administering Successful Programs for Adults.** Galbraith. 1995. lib. bdg. write for info. (*0-89464-886-1*) Krieger.

Administering Targeted Social Programs in Latin America: From Platitudes to Practice. Margaret E. Grosh. LC 93-40676. 184p. 1994. write for info. (*0-8213-2620-1*) World Bank.

Administering Technical Functions in the Food Industry. Samuel A. Matz. (Illus.). 300p. 1995. text ed. 69.00 (*0-942849-12-4*) Pan Tech Intl.

Administering the Community College Learning Resources Program. Wanda K. Johnston. LC 93-23546. 304p. 1994. text ed. 38.50 (*0-8161-1952-X*); pap. 24.50 (*0-8161-1953-8*) G K Hall.

Administering the Company Accounting Function. 2nd ed. Jerome V. Bennett. LC 80-25947. 375p. 1981. text ed. 59.95 (*0-13-004804-6*) P-H.

Administering the School Library Media Center. 3rd ed. Betty J. Morris et al. 567p. 1992. 45.00 (*0-8352-3092-9*) Bowker.

Administering the Taylor Law: Public Employee Relations in New York. Ronald Donovan. (Cornell Studies in Industrial & Labor Relations: No. 23). 264p. 1990. 32.00 (*0-87546-163-8*); pap. 14.95 (*0-87546-164-6*) ILR Pr.

Administracao Da Divida De Paises Latino-Americanos: Aspectos Legais E Regulamentares. Ralph Reisner et al. 1991. write for info. (*0-940602-05-9*) IADB.

Administracion De la Deuda De los Paises Latinoamericanos: Aspectos Juridicos y Reglamentarios. Ed. by Ralph Reisner et al. 1991. write for info. (*0-940602-50-4*) IADB.

Administracion De una Revolucion: La Reforma Del Poder Ejecutivo En Puerto Rico Bajo el Gobernador Tugwell, 1941-1946. Charles T. Goodsell. 216p. 1978. pap. 4.50 (*0-8477-2207-4*) U of PR Pr.

Administracion del Control de Perdidas. 250p. 30.00 (*0-318-17999-7*) Inter-Am Safety.

Administracion En Extension. W. H. Morgan. pap. 3.10 (*0-8477-2209-0*) U of PR Pr.

Administracion Financiera: Para Gerentes y Directivos de Cooperativas de Ahorro. WCCU (World Council of Credit Unions, Inc.) Staff. 208p. (C). 1990. pap. text ed. 24.95 (*0-8403-6296-X*) Kendall-Hunt.

Administracion (Management) Un Enfoque Biblico (A Biblical Approach) Myron Rush. (SPA.). 1992. 4.99 (*1-56063-357-3*, 490215) Editorial Unilit.

Administrating Education: International Challenge. Ed. by Meredydd G. Hughes. (Illus.). 319p. (C). 1975. pap. 45.00 (*0-485-12026-7*, Pub. by Athlone Pr UK) Humanities.

Administration - Supervision. 1991. pap. 10.00 (*0-910553-31-9*) Ken-Bks.

Administration & Economic Development in India. Ralph J. Braibanti et al. Ed. by Joseph J. Spengler. LC 63-9006. (Duke University, Commonwealth-Studies Center, Publication Ser.: No. 18). 320p. reprint ed. pap. 91.20 (*0-8357-5103-1*, 2023369) Bks Demand.

Administration & Finance Report. Ed. by Susan McCormick. (ASTC Science Center Survey Report Ser.). (Illus.). 78p. 1989. pap. 15.00 (*0-685-29593-1*) AST Ctrs.

An Asterisk (*) at the beginning of an entry indicates that the title is appearing in BIP for the first time. 59

Administration & Leadership in Student Affairs: Actualizing Student Development in Higher Education. 2nd ed. T. K. Miller & R. B. Winston. LC 90-81438. 864p. (Orig.). (C). 1991. 36.95 (*1-55959-022-X*) Accel Devel.

Administration & Management of Criminal Justice Organizations: A Book of Readings. 2nd rev. ed. Stan Stojkovic et al. 538p. (Orig.). (C). 1993. pap. text ed. 21.95 (*0-88133-764-1*) Waveland Pr.

***Administration & Managment of Programs for Young Children.** Cynthia Shoemaker. LC 94-3610. 1995. write for info. (*0-02-410041-2*) Merrill.

Administration & Operation of the College Union, No. 1. 3rd ed. Marlis Miller & Denise Galey. 108p. 1988. pap. 60.00 (*0-317-93265-9*) Assn Coll Unions Intl.

Administration & Policy-Making in Education. rev. ed. John Walton. LC 69-13193. 240p. reprint ed. pap. 68.40 (*0-8357-5104-X*, 2023115) Bks Demand.

Administration & Supervision. 4th ed. Harry W. Koch. 1984. 8.00 (*0-913164-42-9*) Ken-Bks.

Administration & Supervision. 5th ed. Harry W. Koch. 1984. 8.00 (*0-910553-04-1*) Ken-Bks.

Administration & Supervision for Safety in Sports. Ed. by Joseph Borozne et al. LC 78-107560. (Sports Safety Monographs: No. 1). 67p. reprint ed. pap. 25.00 (*0-8357-5105-8*, 2026607) Bks Demand.

Administration & Supervision in Business Education. 253p. 1978. 9.00 (*0-933964-16-1*) Natl Busn Ed Assoc.

Administration & Supervision in Laboratory Medicine. 2nd ed. Snyder & Senhauser. (Illus.). 525p. 1989. text ed. 51.50 (*0-397-50857-3*) Lippincott.

Administration & Supervision of Music. 2nd rev. ed. Robert L. Cowden & Robert H. Klotman. (Illus.). 328p. 1991. reprint ed. text ed. 45.00 (*0-02-871211-0*) Schirmer Bks.

Administration & Supervision of Reading Programs. Ed. by Shelley Wepner et al. 296p. 1988. text ed. 38.95 (*0-8077-2929-9*); pap. text ed. 19.95 (*0-8077-2928-0*) Tchrs Coll.

***Administration & Supervision of Reading Programs.** 2nd ed. Ed. by Shelley Wepner et al. (Language & Literacy Ser.). 304p. (C). 1995. pap. text ed. 21.95x (*0-8077-3414-4*) Tchrs Coll.

***Administration & Supervision of Reading Programs.** 2nd ed. Ed. by Shelley Wepner et al. (Language & Literacy Ser.). 304p. (C). 1995. text ed. 44.00x (*0-8077-3415-2*) Tchrs Coll.

Administration & Supervision of the Reading - Writing Program. Marguerite C. Radencich. 1994. 39.95 (*0-205-15217-1*, Longwood Div) Allyn.

Administration As a Profession. Ed. by Jonathan D. Fife & Lester F. Goodchild. LC 84-644752. (New Directions for Higher Education Ser.: No. HE 76). 1991. 16.95 (*1-55542-772-3*) Jossey-Bass.

Administration Committee. 53p. 1994. 5.00 (*0-317-01632-6*) NARUC.

Administration Education in Transition. Vocino & Heimovics. (Annals of Public Administration Ser.: Vol. 2). 160p. 1982. 75.00 (*0-8247-1674-4*) Dekker.

Administration for Development in Nigeria: Introduction & Readings. Ed. by Paul Collins. 337p. (Orig.). 1980. pap. text ed. 21.95x (*978-2308-00-5*) Transaction Pubs.

Administration for Developmental Disabilities: FY 85 Annual Report. U. S. Department of Health & Human Services Editorial Staff. 70p. 1986. write for info. (*0-318-61571-1*) US HHS.

Administration in Business. 3rd ed. Josephine Shaw. (Illus.). 352p. 1986. pap. text ed. 23.00 (*0-273-02584-8*) Trans-Atl Phila.

Administration in Zambia. William Tordoff. LC 80-52300. 326p. (C). 1981. 37.50 (*0-299-08570-8*) U of Wis Pr.

Administration Needs for Educational Reform in Guidance & Counseling. John L. Banks. LC 93-3924. 125p. 1993. 54.95 (*1-880921-31-6*); pap. 34.95 (*1-880921-29-4*) Austin & Winfield.

Administration of a Public Health Agency: A Case Study of the New York City Department of Health. Pascal J. Imperato. 226p. 1983. 35.95 (*0-89885-122-X*) Human Sci Pr.

Administration of Adult Education. Ed. by Coolie Verner & Thurman White. 1965. 3.50 (*0-88379-029-7*) A A A C E.

Administration of Aesthetics: Censorship, Political Criticism, & the Public Sphere. Ed. by Richard Burt. LC 94-3881. 1994. text ed. 49.95 (*0-8166-2365-1*); pap. text ed. 21.95 (*0-8166-2367-8*) U of Minn Pr.

Administration of American Telecommunications Policy: An Original Anthology, 2 vols., Set. Ed. by John M. Kittross & Christopher H. Sterling. LC 80-481. (Historical Studies in Telecommunications). 1980. lib. bdg. 80.95 (*0-405-13191-7*) Ayer.

Administration of American Telecommunications Policy, Vol. 1. John M. Kittross. 40.95 (*0-405-13234-4*) Ayer.

Administration of American Telecommunications Policy, Vol. 2. John M. Kittross. 40.95 (*0-405-13235-2*) Ayer.

***Administration of an Early Childhood Education Center: ECE 121 Course.** California College for Health Sciences Staff. 300p. (C). 1992. ring bd. write for info. (*0-614-07433-9*) Allied Hlth Pubns.

Administration of Archives. J. H. Hodson. LC 72-163642. 224p. 1972. 98.00 (*0-08-016676-8*, Pub. by Pergamon Repr UK) Franklin.

Administration of British Foreign Relations. Donald G. Bishop. LC 74-3761. 410p. 1974. reprint ed. text ed. 75.00 (*0-8371-7461-9*, BIBF, Greenwood Pr) Greenwood.

Administration of Continuing Education: A Guide for Administrators. Ed. by Nathan C. Shaw. LC 74-81993. 1969. reprint ed. pap. 2.45 (*0-686-00782-4*, 758-01060) A A A C E.

Administration of Court Reporting in the State Courts. National Center for State Courts Staff. 48p. 1973. 2.88 (*0-685-15840-3*, MAB-001) Natl Ctr St Courts.

Administration of Criminal Justice in England & Wales. C. Shoolbred & H. Williams. LC 66-16882. 1966. 72.00 (*0-08-011780-5*, Pub. by Pergamon Repr UK) Franklin.

Administration of Criminal Justice, 1949-1956: A Selected Bibliography. Dorothy C. Tompkins. LC 77-108219. (Criminology, Law Enforcement, & Social Problems Ser.: No. 102). 1970. reprint ed. 30.00 (*0-87585-102-9*) Patterson Smith.

Administration of Deceased Estates. 2nd ed. L. A. Kernick. 287p. 1989. pap. 50.00 (*0-7021-2309-9*, Pub. by Juta SA) W W Gaunt.

Administration of Egypt in the Old Kingdom: The Highest Offices & Their Holders. Nigel Strudwick. 380p. 1985. 82.50 (*0-7103-0107-3*, Pub. by Kegan Paul Intl UK) Routledge Chapman & Hall.

Administration of Environmental Health Programmes: A Systems View. M. Schaefer. (Public Health Papers: No. 59). 1974. pap. 4.80 (*92-4-130059-0*) World Health.

Administration of Federal Work Relief. A. W. MacMahon et al. LC 73-167845. (FDR & the Era of the New Deal Ser.). 408p. 1971. reprint ed. lib. bdg. 49.50 (*0-306-70326-2*) Da Capo.

Administration of Government Contracts. 2nd ed. John Cibinic, Jr. & Ralph C. Nash, Jr. 1184p. 1985. 55.00 (*0-935165-16-9*); pap. 35.00 (*0-935165-17-7*) GWU Gov Contracts.

***Administration of Government Contracts.** 3rd ed. John Cibinic, Jr. & Ralph C. Nash, Jr. LC 94-39185. 1994. boxed, pap. write for info. (*0-935165-32-0*) GWU Gov Contracts.

Administration of Health Service. Charles M. Montacute. (C). 1987. pap. 120.00 (*0-685-28612-6*) St Mut.

Administration of High School Athletics. 7th ed. Irvin A. Keller & Charles E. Forsythe. (Illus.). 416p. 1983. text ed. 68.00 (*0-13-005728-2*) P-H.

Administration of Home Economics in City Schools: A Study of Present & Desired Practices in the Organization of the Home Economics Program. Annie I. Dyer. LC 76-176737. (Columbia University. Teachers College. Contributions to Education Ser.: No. 318). reprint ed. 37.50 (*0-404-55318-4*) AMS Pr.

Administration of Imperialism: Joseph Chamberlain at the Colonial Office. LC 72-89874. (Duke University, Commonwealth-Studies Center, Publication Ser.: No. 37). 106p. reprint ed. pap. 30.30 (*0-8357-5106-6*, 2023416) Bks Demand.

Administration of India: (Eighteen Fifty-Eight to Nineteen Twenty-Four. S. A. Hussain. 323p. 1985. 44.95 (*0-318-37292-4*) Asia Bk Corp.

Administration of Injustice: Military Accountability in Guatemala. Washington Office on Latin America Staff. 80p. (Orig.). (C). 1989. pap. text ed. 7.00 (*0-929513-12-6*) WOLA.

Administration of Insurance. Neil Crockford. (C). 1987. 250.00 (*0-685-33800-2*, Pub. by Witherby & Co UK) St Mut.

Administration of Intensive English Language Programs. Ed. by Ralph P. Barrett. 109p. 1982. 12.00 (*0-912207-25-6*) NAFSA Washington.

Administration of Iowa: A Study in Centralization. Harold M. Bowman. LC 70-82248. (Columbia University. Studies in the Social Sciences: No. 46). reprint ed. 20.00 (*0-404-51046-9*) AMS Pr.

Administration of Islam in Indonesia. Deliar Noer. (Monograph Ser.: No. 58). 1978. pap. 4.50 (*0-87763-002-X*) Cornell Mod Indo.

***Administration of Justice.** Mackay. (1993 Hamlyn Lecture Ser.). 1994. 28.00 (*0-421-52250-X*); text ed. 12.00 (*0-421-52260-7*) W W Gaunt.

Administration of Justice. 5th ed. Paul B. Weston & Kenneth M. Wells. (Illus.). 336p. (C). 1987. text ed. write for info. (*0-13-006412-2*) P-H.

Administration of Justice: Law Enforcement, Courts, & Corrections. John A. Humphrey & Michael Milakovich. LC 80-17467. 293p. 1981. pap. 24.95 (*0-87705-449-5*) Human Sci Pr.

Administration of Justice from Homer to Aristotle, 2 vols, Set. Robert J. Bonner & Gertrude S. Smith. LC 70-101917. (BCL Ser.: I). reprint ed. 79.50 (*0-404-00650-7*) AMS Pr.

Administration of Justice in Drunk Driving Cases. Joseph W. Little. LC 75-11643. (University of Florida Monographs: Social Sciences: No. 53). (Illus.). 238p. reprint ed. pap. 67.90 (*0-7837-4956-2*, 2044622) Bks Demand.

Administration of Justice in the United States. Ed. by Robert M. Folgelson. LC 73-3813. (Criminal Justice in America Ser.). 1974. reprint ed. 20.95 (*0-405-06136-6*) Ayer.

Administration of Maintenance & Operations in California School Districts: A Handbook for School Administrators & Governing Boards. California Department of Education Staff. 96p. 1986. pap. 6.75 (*0-8011-0272-3*) Calif Education.

Administration of Merit-Type Teachers' Salary Schedules. Lloyd P. Young. LC 79-177610. (Columbia University. Teachers College. Contributions to Education Ser.: No. 552). reprint ed. 37.50 (*0-404-55552-7*) AMS Pr.

Administration of Normandy Under Saint Louis. Joseph R. Strayer. (Mediaeval Academy of America Publications: Vol. 13). 1932. 35.00 (*0-527-01686-1*) Periodicals Srv.

Administration of Normandy Under Saint Louis. Joseph R. Strayer. LC 72-171362. reprint ed. 34.50 (*0-404-06297-0*) AMS Pr.

Administration of Physical Education & Sport Programs. 3rd ed. Lawrence E. Horine. 320p. (C). 1995. boxed write for info. (*0-697-15244-8*) Brown & Benchmark.

Administration of Police Training in India. K. M. Mathur. (C). 1987. 58.50 (*81-212-0100-4*, Pub. by Gian Publng Hse II) S Asia.

Administration of Primary Education under Montford Reforms & Its Impact on West Bengal. Biswa R. Purkait. LC 84-902647. 1985. 14.50 (*0-8364-1273-7*, Pub. by Mukhopadhyaya II) S Asia.

Administration of Public Airports. 3rd ed. Laurence E. Gesell. LC 91-76708. (Illus.). 512p. (Orig.). (C). 1992. text ed. 38.00 (*0-9606874-7-5*) Coast Aire.

Administration of Public Education: A Sourcebook for the Leadership & Management of Educational Institutions. 4th ed. Stephen V. Knezevich. 592p. (C). 1990. text ed. 58.00 (*0-06-043737-5*) HarpCollege.

***Administration of Public Safety in Higher Education.** David Nichols. (Illus.). 264p. 1987. pap. 33.95 (*0-398-06306-0*) C C Thomas.

Administration of Public Safety in Higher Education. David Nichols. (Illus.). 264p. 1987. 55.95x (*0-398-05330-8*) C C Thomas.

Administration of Public Solid Waste. F. T. Lancaster. 178p. 1992. spiral bd. 35.00 (*0-918334-79-9*) WRP.

Administration of Research, Development, & Implementation Activities in Highway Agencies. (National Cooperative Highway Research Program Report Ser.: No. 113). 49p. 1984. 8.00 (*0-309-03869-3*) Transport Res Bd.

Administration of Rural Production in an Early Mesopotamian Town. Henry T. Wright. LC 74-629199. (University of Michigan, Museum of Anthropology, Anthropological Papers: No. 38). 176p. reprint ed. pap. 50.20 (*0-8357-5107-4*, 2022613) Bks Demand.

Administration of Schools for Young Children. 3rd ed. Phyllis Click. (Early Childhood Education Ser.). 244p. 1989. teacher ed 10.00 (*0-8273-3658-6*); pap. text ed. 24.50 (*0-8273-3657-8*) Delmar.

***Administration of Schools for Young Children.** 4th ed. Phyllis M. Click & Donald W. Click. LC 95-4185. 1995. write for info. (*0-8273-5876-8*) Delmar.

Administration of Social Welfare: A Survey of National Organizational Arrangements. 53p. 1985. 7.00 (*92-1-130096-7*, E.85.IV.1) UN.

Administration of State Capital Improvement Programs: Nine Selected Profiles. J. David Stewart & Dan Y. Buehler. Ed. by Michael C. Robinson. (Special Report Ser.: No. 45). (Illus.). 1979. pap. text ed. 18.00 (*0-917084-29-2*) Am Public Works.

Administration of Student Personnel Services in Teacher-Training Institutions of the United States. Marion E. Townsend. LC 70-177699. (Columbia University. Teachers College. Contributions to Education Ser.: No. 536). reprint ed. 37.50 (*0-404-55536-5*) AMS Pr.

Administration of Technical-Vocational Education: Principles & Methods. Dhirendra Verma. 1990. text ed. 27.95 (*81-207-1267-6*, Pub. by Sterling Pubs II) Apt Bks.

Administration of the Changing Secondary School. Glen F. Ovard. 1966. text ed. write for info. (*0-685-14568-9*) Macmillan.

Administration of the Colonies. Thomas Pownall. LC 79-146155. (Era of the American Revolution Ser.). 1971. reprint ed. lib. bdg. 49.50 (*0-306-70123-5*) Da Capo.

Administration of the Colonies: 1668. Thomas Pownall. LC 93-36377. 1993. 75.00 (*0-8201-1487-1*) Schol Facsimiles.

Administration of the Human Services: A Practical Workbook for Managers. Art Knighton & Nancy Heidelman. 196p. (C). 1983. pap. text ed. 22.95 (*0-472-08036-9*) U of Mich Pr.

Administration of the Illyrian Provinces of the French Empire, 1809-1813. Frank J. Bundy. Ed. by William H. McNeill & David H. Pinkney. (Modern European History Ser.). 696p. 1987. lib. bdg. 20.00 (*0-8240-8032-7*) Garland.

Administration of the Massachusetts Courts. National Center for State Courts Staff. 62p. 1974. 3.72 (*0-685-15090-9*, MAB-002) Natl Ctr St Courts.

Administration of the Moghul Empire. Ishtiaq H. Quereshi. 1990. reprint ed. 11.50 (*81-85418-00-4*, Pub. by Low Price II) S Asia.

Administration of the Public Library. Alice Gertzog & Edwin Beckerman. LC 94-9880. 601p. 1994. 59.50 (*0-8108-2857-X*) Scarecrow.

Administration of the Punjab: A Study in British Policy, 1875-1905. Kamla Sethi. 1990. 42.50 (*81-85199-39-6*, Pub. by Renaiss Publng Hse II) S Asia.

Administration of the Small Public Library. 3rd ed. Darlene E. Weingand. LC 91-42064. 213p. (C). 1992. text ed. 27.00 (*0-8389-0583-8*) ALA.

Administration of the Sultanate of Delhi. 5th ed. I. Qureshi. 1971. 28.50 (*0-317-89899-X*) Coronet Bks.

Administration of Trusts in Florida. Florida Bar Staff. LC 80-70874. 336p. 1981. boxed 35.00 (*0-910373-36-1*, 207) FL Bar Legal Ed.

Administration of United States Foreign Policy. Richard A. Johnson. LC 76-162689. 433p. reprint ed. pap. 123.50 (*0-8357-7748-0*, 2036105) Bks Demand.

Administration of Vocational Education. R. C. Wenrich et al. (Illus.). 234p. 1988. pap. 30.96 (*0-8269-4051-X*) Am Technical.

Administration of Wills, Trusts, & Estates. Gordon W. Brown. 90p. 1993. teacher ed 15.00 (*0-8273-5054-6*); text ed. 42.95 (*0-8273-5053-8*) Delmar.

Administration, Personnel, Buildings & Equipment. David F. Kohl. LC 85-6023. (Handbooks for Library Management Ser.). 304p. 1984. lib. bdg. 49.00 (*0-87436-431-0*) ABC-CLIO.

Administration Software Education Solutions Guide. 1989. 23.00 (*1-879075-00-8*) List Srvcs.

Administrations in the Archdeaconry of Northhampton, 1677-1710: Extracted by Henry I. Longden see Scotland's Border Country

Administration's 1985 Tax Proposals: AEI Legislative Analysis, 99th Congress, No. 53. American Enterprise Institute for Public Policy Research Staff. LC 85-167620. 117p. 1985. 6.00 (*0-8447-0268-4*) Am Enterprise.

Administrative Accountant. Jack Rudman. (Career Examination Ser.: C-1078). 1994. 39.95 (*0-8373-1078-4*) Nat Learn.

Administrative Action: The Techniques of Organization & Management. 2nd ed. William H. Newman. 1963. text ed. 48.00 (*0-13-007195-1*) P-H.

Administrative Agencies of the U. S. A. Their Decisions & Authority. Dalmas H. Nelson. LC 63-13433. (Wayne State University Studies: No. 15: Political Science). 352p. reprint ed. pap. 100.40 (*0-8357-5108-2*, 2027652) Bks Demand.

Administrative Aide. Jack Rudman. (Career Examination Ser.: C-8). 1994. pap. 23.95 (*0-8373-0008-8*) Nat Learn.

Administrative Analysis for Local Government: Practical Application of Selected Techniques. David N. Ammons. 176p. 1991. pap. 21.95 (*0-89854-145-X*) U of GA Inst Govt.

Administrative Analysis of the King County (WA) District Courts. National Center for State Courts Staff. 179p. 1975. 10.74 (*0-685-15091-7*, MAB-003) Natl Ctr St Courts.

Administrative Analyst. Jack Rudman. (Career Examination Ser.: C-2144). 1994. pap. 34.95 (*0-8373-2144-1*) Nat Learn.

Administrative & Compliance Costs of Taxation. International Fiscal Association Staff. (Cahiers de Droit Fiscal International Ser.). 650p. 1989. 103.00 (*90-6544-414-9*) Kluwer Law Tax Pubs.

***Administrative & Compliance Costs of Taxation.** Cedric Sandford et al. 307p. (C). 1989. 175.00x (*0-9515157-0-5*, Pub. by Fiscal Pubns UK) St Mut.

Administrative & Financial Laws for Local Government in North Carolina. 1,991th ed. Comp. by Frayda S. Bluestein. 932p. 1992. 65.00 (*1-56011-210-7*, ADMN) Institute Government.

Administrative & Management Theory. Ed. by John B. Miner. (History of Management Thought Ser.). 456p. 1995. 112.95 (*1-85521-475-X*, Pub. by Dartmth Pub UK) Ashgate Pub Co.

Administrative Appeals Tribunal & Policy Review. Jennifer M. Sharpe. xxvi, 232p. 1986. 49.50 (*0-455-20680-5*, Pub. by Law Bk Co) W W Gaunt.

Administrative Appeals Unit Reporter. Ed. by Allen E. Kaye. 150p. 1992. lib. bdg. 289.00 (*1-878677-40-3*) Amer Immi Law Assn.

Administrative Appraisal of the NLRB. 3rd ed. Edward B. Miller. LC 80-85253. (Labor Relations & Public Policy Ser.: No.16). 169p. 1981. pap. 15.00 (*0-89546-029-7*) U PA Wharton Ctr Human Resc.

Administrative Argument. Christopher Hood & Michael Jackson. 221p. 1991. text ed. 55.95 (*1-85521-023-1*, Pub. by Dartmth Pub UK) Ashgate Pub Co.

Administrative Aspects of Education for Librarianship: A Symposium. Ed. by Mary B. Cassata & Herman L. Totten. LC 75-15726. 425p. 1975. 25.00 (*0-8108-0829-3*) Scarecrow.

Administrative Assessor. Jack Rudman. (Career Examination Ser.: C-2596). 1994. pap. 29.95 (*0-8373-2596-X*) Nat Learn.

Administrative Assistant. Jack Rudman. (Career Examination Ser.: C-9). 1994. pap. 23.95 (*0-8373-0009-6*) Nat Learn.

Administrative Assistant I. Jack Rudman. (Career Examination Ser.: C-1848). 1994. pap. 27.95 (*0-8373-1848-3*) Nat Learn.

Administrative Assistant II. Jack Rudman. (Career Examination Ser.: C-1849). 1991. pap. 24.00 (*0-8373-1849-1*) Nat Learn.

***Administrative Assistant's & Secretary's Handbook.** J. Stroman & K. Wilson. Ed. by Susan H. O'Keefe. 320p. 1995. 21.95 (*0-8144-0273-9*) AMACOM.

Administrative Associate. Jack Rudman. (Career Examination Ser.: C-67). 1994. pap. 27.95 (*0-8373-0067-3*) Nat Learn.

Administrative Attorney. Jack Rudman. (Career Examination Ser.: C-2597). 1994. pap. 39.95 (*0-8373-2597-8*) Nat Learn.

Administrative Auditor of Accounts. Jack Rudman. (Career Examination Ser.: C-2598). 1994. pap. 39.95 (*0-8373-2598-6*) Nat Learn.

Administrative Behavior. 3rd ed. Herbert A. Simon. LC 75-18009. 1976. 29.95 (*0-02-928970-X*); pap. 14.95 (*0-02-929000-7*) Free Pr.

Administrative Behavior of Federal Bureau Chiefs. Herbert Kaufman. LC 81-10128. 220p. 1981. 31.95 (*0-8157-4844-2*); pap. 12.95 (*0-8157-4843-4*) Brookings.

Administrative Bureau During the Old Regime: The Bureau of Commerce & Its Relations to French Industry from May 1781 to November 1783. Harold T. Parker. LC 92-50634. 160p. 1993. Alk. paper. 29.50 (*0-87413-467-6*) U Delaware Pr.

Administrative Business Promotion Coordinator. Jack Rudman. (Career Examination Ser.: C-2599). 1994. pap. 39.95 (*0-8373-2599-4*) Nat Learn.

***Administrative Career: A Casebook on Entry, Equity, & Endurance.** Catherine Marshall & Katherine L. Kasten. (Illus.). 160p. 1994. 38.00 (*0-8039-6088-3*); pap. 18.00 (*0-8039-6089-1*) Corwin Pr.

Administrative Careers & the Marketplace. Ed. by Kathryn M. Moore & Susan B. Twombly. LC 85-644752. (New Directions for Higher Education Ser.: No. HE 72). 1990. 16.95 (*1-55542-808-8*) Jossey-Bass.

Administrative Careers Examination. Jack Rudman. (Career Examination Ser.: C-69). 1994. pap. 23.95 (*0-8373-0069-X*) Nat Learn.

Administrative Careers with America. (Career Examination Ser.: C-50). 1994. 23.95 (*0-8373-3550-7*) Nat Learn.

Administrative Claim Examiner. Jack Rudman. (Career Examination Ser.: C-2600). 1994. pap. 27.95 (*0-8373-2600-1*) Nat Learn.

An Asterisk (*) at the beginning of an entry indicates that the title is appearing in BIP for the first time.

An Asterisk (*) at the beginning of an entry indicates that the title is appearing in BIP for the first time.

61

A

Administrative Office Management: An Introduction. 5th ed. Zane K. Quible. 624p. (C). 1991. pap. text ed. write for info. (*0-13-005935-8*) P-H.

Administrative Office Management Systems. 2nd ed. Eleanor H. Tedesco & Robert B. Mitchell. LC 83-1269. (C). 1987. text ed. 38.95 (*0-471-01201-7*); Decision Manual. pap. text ed. 16.50 (*0-471-01200-9*) P-H.

Administrative Office Services. Larry R. Fiber. 1985. teacher ed write for info. (*0-8359-9126-1*, Reston); text ed. 21.95 (*0-8359-9125-3*, Reston) P-H.

Administrative Officer. Jack Rudman. (Career Examination Ser.: C-1079). 1994. pap. 29.95 (*0-8373-1079-2*) Nat Learn.

Administrative Officer I. Jack Rudman. (Career Examination Ser.: C-1850). 1994. pap. 29.95 (*0-8373-1850-5*) Nat Learn.

Administrative Officer II. Jack Rudman. (Career Examination Ser.: C-1852). 1994. pap. 34.95 (*0-8373-1852-1*) Nat Learn.

Administrative Parent: A Study of the Assumption of Parental Rights. M. R. Adcock & O. Rowlands. (C). 1989. 60.00 (*0-903534-47-9*, Pub. by Brit Ag for Adopt & Fost UK) St Mut.

Administrative Park & Recreation Manager. Jack Rudman. (Career Examination Ser.: C-2606). 1994. pap. 34.95 (*0-8373-2606-0*) Nat Learn.

Administrative Partitioning of Costa Rica: Politics & Planners. Marilyn A. Dorn. (Research Papers Ser.: No. 222). (Illus.). 140p. 1989. pap. 12.00 (*0-89065-126-4*) U Chicago Comm Geo.

Administrative Personnel Examiner. Jack Rudman. (Career Examination Ser.: C-70). 1994. pap. 39.95 (*0-8373-0070-3*) Nat Learn.

Administrative Personnel Review: Eleventh Judicial Circuit, Dade County, Florida, Final Report. National Center for State Courts Staff. 66p. 1986. 4.00 (*0-685-15198-0*, SERO-017) Natl Ctr St Courts.

Administrative Planning. Floyd Waterman. 62p. (Orig.). 1982. pap. 7.00 (*1-55719-088-7*) U NE CPAR.

***Administrative Plant Manager.** (Career Examination Ser.: Series 1). Date not set. pap. 39.95 (*0-8373-3627-9*) Nat Learn.

Administrative Policies & Procedures for Home Health Care. 2nd ed. Judith M. Bulau. LC 91-22035. 548p. 1991. ring bd. 160.00 (*0-8342-0241-7*) Aspen Pub.

Administrative Politics in British Government. Andrew I. Gray & W. I. Jenkins. LC 85-3264. 256p. 1985. text ed. 39.95 (*0-312-00461-3*) St Martin.

Administrative Power in the Individual Massachusetts Courts. National Center for State Courts Staff. 125p. 1975. 7.50 (*0-685-15094-1*, NERO-005) Natl Ctr St Courts.

Administrative Presidency. Richard P. Nathan. LC 82-21712. 180p. (C). 1983. pap. write for info. (*0-02-386210-6*) Macmillan.

Administrative Presidency Revisited: Public Lands, the BLM, & the Reagan Revolution. Robert F. Durant. LC 91-14098. (Environmental Public Policy & the Presidency: Contemporary Issues Ser.). 401p. 1992. 59.50 (*0-7914-0959-7*); pap. 19.95 (*0-7914-0960-0*) State U NY Pr.

Administrative Problems in Pakistan. Ed. by Guthrie S. Birkhead. LC 66-25174. 239p. reprint ed. pap. 68.20 (*0-8357-5110-4*, 2027398) Bks Demand.

Administrative Procedures: A Practical Manual. JoAnne J. Trow. 1982. 13.50 (*0-317-42935-3*) Natl Assn Women.

Administrative Procedures for Changing Curriculum Patterns for Selected State Teachers Colleges. Herman L. Offner. LC 76-177131. (Columbia University. Teachers College. Contributions to Education Ser.: No. 898). reprint ed. 37.50 (*0-404-55898-4*) AMS Pr.

Administrative Procedures for Conducting Recreational Sports Tournaments, from Archery to Wrestling. 2nd ed. Francis M. Rokosz & Howard H. Taylor. LC 93-33148. (Illus.). 418p. (C). 1994. spiral bd. 71.95 (*0-398-05895-4*) C C Thomas.

Administrative Procedures for Small Institutions. National Association of College & University Business Officers Staff. Ed. by Lanora Welzenbach. 254p. 1985. 26.00 (*0-915164-28-0*) NACUBO.

Administrative Procedures in the Electronic Office. Rosanne B. Sanders. 464p. (C). 1990. text ed. write for info. (*0-13-019472-7*) P-H.

Administrative Process. Robert H. Roy. 248p. 1958. 36.50x (*0-8018-0566-X*); pap. 13.95x (*0-8018-0567-8*) Johns Hopkins.

Administrative Process. 4th ed. Glen O. Robinson & Ernest Gellhorn. Ed. by Harold H. Bruff. (American Casebook Ser.). 800p. 1993. text ed. 45.50 (*0-314-02377-1*) West Pub.

Administrative Process, Second Annual Review of (1990) 222p. 1990. pap. text ed. 35.00 (*1-56986-020-3*) Federal Bar.

Administrative Process, the First Annual Review. 50p. 1989. pap. text ed. 10.00 (*1-56986-019-X*) Federal Bar.

***Administrative Process, 1995 Supplement to The.** Glen O. Robinson et al. (American Casebook Ser.). 53p. (C). 1995. pap. text ed. 7.00 (*0-314-06720-5*) West Pub.

Administrative Project Coordinator. Jack Rudman. (Career Examination Ser.: C-1080). 1994. pap. 29.95 (*0-8373-1080-6*) Nat Learn.

Administrative Psychiatry. William A. Bryan. LC 58-14143. 1958. reprint ed. 46.00 (*0-8154-0034-9*) Cooper Sq.

Administrative Public Information Specialist. Jack Rudman. (Career Examination Ser.: C-2607). 1994. pap. 27.95 (*0-8373-2607-9*) Nat Learn.

Administrative Reform Comes of Age. Gerald E. Caiden. (Studies in Organization: No. 28). xii, 347p. (C). 1991. lib. bdg. 46.95 (*3-11-012895-0*); pap. 26.95 (*3-11-012645-1*) De Gruyter.

Administrative Reform in Nepal. Madhab P. Poudyal. 1989. 42.50 (*81-85135-41-X*, Pub. by Natl Bk Org II) S Asia.

Administrative Reforms in a Developing Society. Ed. by M. Kistaiah. 132p. 1990. text ed. 19.95 (*81-207-1111-4*, Pub. by Sterling Pubs II) Apt Bks.

Administrative Reforms of Frederick William First of Prussia. Reinhold A. Dorwart. LC 70-138221. (C). 1971. reprint ed. text ed. 65.00 (*0-8371-5578-9*, DOAR, Greenwood Pr) Greenwood.

Administrative Regulation: A Study in Representation of Interests. rev. ed. Avery Leiserson. LC 74-12761. 292p. 1975. reprint ed. lib. bdg. 22.50 (*0-8371-7744-8*, LEAR, Greenwood Pr) Greenwood.

Administrative Responsiveness in India. Pardeep Sahni. (C). 1992. 19.00 (*81-7304-008-7*, Pub. by Manohar II) S Asia.

***Administrative Review.** Ed. by Edmund N. Smith. (C). Date not set. pap. 35.00 (*1-56395-028-6*) Am Assn Blood.

Administrative Role of Chief Justices & Supreme Courts. National Center for State Courts Staff. 48p. 1979. pap. write for info. (*0-89656-038-4*, R-046) Natl Ctr St Courts.

Administrative Rulemaking: Politics & Processes, No. 122. William F. West. LC 84-12825. (Contributions in Political Science Ser.). ix, 217p. 1985. text ed. 49.95 (*0-313-24157-0*, WAR/, Greenwood Pr) Greenwood.

Administrative Science & Politics in the U. S. S. R. & the U. S.: Soviet Responses to American Management Techniques. James C. Thompson & Richard Vidmer. (Illus.). 224p. (C). 1983. text ed. 39.95 (*0-03-059633-5*, Bergin & Garvey) Greenwood.

Administrative Science in the Soviet Union & the United States. James C. Thompson & Richard Vidmer. LC 82-12977. 224p. 1983. text ed. 49.95 (*0-275-91089-X*, C1089, Praeger Pubs) Greenwood.

Administrative Science Quarterly: Cumulative Index Volumes 1-30, 1956-1985. Ed. by Johnson Graduate School of Management, Cornell University Staff. 1989. 125.00 (*0-89232-731-6*) Jai Pr.

Administrative Secrecy in Developed Countries. Ed. by Donald C. Rowat. LC 78-16376. (International Institute of Administrative Sciences Ser.). 1979. text ed. 52.00 (*0-231-04596-4*) Col U Pr.

Administrative Secretary. Jack Rudman. (Career Examination Ser.: C-1081). 1994. pap. 27.95 (*0-8373-1081-4*) Nat Learn.

Administrative Secretary. 2nd ed. R. I. Anderson et al. 1976. text ed. 36.95 (*0-07-001747-6*) McGraw.

Administrative Service Officer. Jack Rudman. (Career Examination Ser.: C-10). 1994. pap. 29.95 (*0-8373-0010-X*) Nat Learn.

Administrative Services Clerk. Jack Rudman. (Career Examination Ser.: C-2869). 1994. pap. 27.95 (*0-8373-2869-1*) Nat Learn.

Administrative Services Manager. Jack Rudman. (Career Examination Ser.: C-2712). 1994. pap. 34.95 (*0-8373-2712-1*) Nat Learn.

Administrative Space Analyst. Jack Rudman. (Career Exam Ser.: No. C-3517). 1994. 39.95 (*0-8373-3517-5*) Nat Learn.

Administrative Staff Analyst. Jack Rudman. (Career Examination Ser.: C-1553). 1994. pap. 34.95 (*0-8373-1553-0*) Nat Learn.

Administrative Staffing Implications of Court System Unification in North Dakota: Technical Assistance Report. National Center for State Courts Staff. 151p. 1981. 9.06 (*0-685-15200-6*, NCRO-016) Natl Ctr St Courts.

Administrative State. 2nd ed. Dwight Waldo. LC 83-18393. 222p. (C). 1984. 29.50 (*0-8419-0880-X*); pap. 15.95 (*0-8419-0886-9*) Holmes & Meier.

Administrative Structure of the New York State Court System. National Center for State Courts Staff. 133p. 1980. 7.98 (*0-685-15095-X*, NERO-092) Natl Ctr St Courts.

Administrative Structures for Environmental Management in the E.C. 189p. 1993. pap. 16.00 (*92-826-5152-5*, CR-77-92-134-EN, Pub. by Europ Com) UNIPUB.

Administrative Superintendent of Buildings & Grounds. Jack Rudman. (Career Examination Ser.: C-1707). 1994. pap. 29.95 (*0-8373-1707-X*) Nat Learn.

Administrative Superintendent of Highway Operations. Jack Rudman. (Career Examination Ser.: C-2608). 1994. pap. 39.95 (*0-8373-2608-7*) Nat Learn.

Administrative Supervisor of Building Maintenance. Jack Rudman. (Career Examination Ser.). 1994. 34.95 (*0-8373-3617-1*, C-3617) Nat Learn.

Administrative Systems Abroad. Ed. by Krishna K. Tummala. LC 82-16130. (Illus.). 386p. (C). 1983. lib. bdg. 60.50 (*0-8191-2734-5*) U Pr of Amer.

Administrative Team Contracts. American Association of School Administrators Staff & National School Boards Association. (Administrative Team Career Development Ser.: Bk. 5). 3.50 (*0-87652-004-2*, 021-00855) Am Assn Sch Admin.

Administrative Theories & Politics: An Inquiry into the Structure & Processes of Modern Government. Peter Self. LC 72-98025. (Canadian University Paperbooks Ser.: No. 148). 308p. reprint ed. pap. 87.80 (*0-8357-4168-0*, 2036942) Bks Demand.

Administrative Theories of Hamilton & Jefferson. 2nd ed. Lynton K. Caldwell. LC 87-28535. 265p. (C). 1987. 35.00 (*0-8419-1049-9*); pap. 19.50 (*0-8419-1050-2*) Holmes & Meier.

Administrative Theory in Transition. Dan Griffiths. 134p. (C). 1985. 45.00 (*0-7300-0341-8*, Pub. by Deakin Univ AT) St Mut.

Administrative Thinkers. Ed. by D. Ravindra Prasad et al. 300p. 1989. text ed. 35.00 (*81-207-0954-3*, Pub. by Sterling Pubs II) Apt Bks.

Administrative Trainee. Jack Rudman. (Career Examination Ser.: C-1082). 1994. pap. 23.95 (*0-8373-1082-2*) Nat Learn.

Administrative Transformation in Central & Eastern Europe: Towards Public Sector Reform in Post-Communist Societies. Ed. by Joachim J. Hesse. LC 93-27364. 256p. 1993. 29.95 (*0-631-19056-2*) Blackwell Pubs.

Administrative Tribunal Law & Procedure. K. P. Chakravarti. (C). 1989. 138.00 (*0-685-36558-1*) St Mut.

Administrative Tribunals Act. Eastern Book Co. Staff. (C). 1987. 65.00 (*0-685-22638-7*) St Mut.

Administrative Tribunals Act, 1985: With Rules & Noti. 2nd ed. K. N. Goyal. (C). 1990. 250.00 (*0-685-39527-8*) St Mut.

Administrative Tribunals Cases. (C). 1989. 684.00 (*0-89771-697-3*) St Mut.

Administrative Tribunals Cases, 2 vols., Set. Eastern Book Co. Staff. (C). 1987. 115.00 (*0-685-25172-1*) St Mut.

Administrative Tribunals Cases, Jan. to April 1991, Vol. 15. E. B. C. Staff. (C). 1991. text ed. 200.00 (*0-89771-463-6*) St Mut.

Administrative Tribunals Cases, Sept. to Dec. 1990, Vol. 14. E. B. C. Staff. (C). 1991. text ed. 180.00 (*0-89771-462-8*) St Mut.

Administrative Tribunals Cases, 1986 to 1988, 8 vols., Set. Eastern Book Co. Staff. (C). 1989. 1,280.00 (*0-685-27893-X*) St Mut.

***Administrative Tribunals Handbook.** 76p. 1988. pap. 36.00 (*0-409-70227-7*, NZ) Butterworth Legal Pubs.

Administrative Unification of the Maine State Courts: Full Report. National Center for State Courts Staff. 204p. 1975. pap. write for info. (*0-89656-000-7*, R-020) Natl Ctr St Courts.

Administrative Warfare. Terence F. Moore. 114p. 1992. pap. 9.95 (*0-9633518-5-0*) Ivory Grp.

Administrator. Jack Rudman. (Career Examination Ser.: C-1077). 1994. pap. 29.95 (*0-8373-1077-6*) Nat Learn.

Administrator Competency Study. Robert E. Norton & Lois G. Harrington. 114p. 1987. 10.50 (*0-318-35277-X*, RD 268) Ctr Educ Trng Employ.

Administrator Employment Contracts. C. Kay Freeman. Ed. by Dennis Barnhardt. (Strategic Agreements Ser.: Vol. III). 220p. 1989. pap. 95.00 (*0-933948-17-4*) Med Group Mgmt.

Administrator I. Jack Rudman. (Career Examination Ser.: C-1769). 1994. pap. 29.95 (*0-8373-1769-X*) Nat Learn.

Administrator II. Jack Rudman. (Career Examination Ser.: C-1691). 1994. pap. 34.95 (*0-8373-1691-X*) Nat Learn.

Administrator III. Jack Rudman. (Career Examination Ser.: C-2175). 1994. pap. 39.95 (*0-8373-2175-1*) Nat Learn.

Administrator IV. Jack Rudman. (Career Examination Ser.: C-2176). 1994. pap. 39.95 (*0-8373-2176-X*) Nat Learn.

Administrator, Student, Teacher in Community College. Charles A. Heidenreich. 1974. pap. 3.00 (*0-685-41767-0*) Heidenreich.

Administrators at Risk: Tools & Technologies for Securing Your Future. Jamieson McKenzie. 170p. 1993. 19.95 (*1-879639-27-0*) Natl Educ Serv.

***Administrator's Complete School Discipline Guide: Creating an Environment Where All Kids Can Learn.** Robert D. Ramsey. LC 94-31881. 1994. pap. (*0-13-079401-5*) P-H.

Administrator's Guide. 2nd ed. DeRoche. 1987. text ed. 39.95 (*0-205-10512-2*, H05127) Allyn.

Administrator's Guide - Self Esteem. Shaun Hains. Ed. by Diane Parker. LC 92-50910. 60p. 1993. spiral bd. 7.95 (*0-88247-970-9*) R & E Pubs.

Administrator's Guide to Curriculum Mapping. Donald F. Weinstein. LC 85-19281. 149p. 1986. text ed. 29.95 (*0-13-008608-8*, Busn) P-H.

Administrator's Guide to Library Building Maintenance. Dianne Lueder & Sally Webb. LC 92-5566. 290p. (C). 1992. pap. text ed. 45.00 (*0-8389-3409-9*) ALA.

Administrator's Guide to Microcomputer Resources. Gale Zahniser et al. 99p. 1983. 9.50 (*0-318-22015-6*, RD239B) Ctr Educ Trng Employ.

Administrator's Guide to New Programs for Faculty Management & Evaluation. Rita S. Dunn & Kenneth J. Dunn. 1976. text ed. 24.95 (*0-13-008623-1*, Parker Publishing Co) P-H.

Administrator's Guide to Personal Productivity: With the Time Management Checklist. 256p. 1993. 29.95 (*1-883001-01-3*) Eye On Educ.

***Administrator's Guide to School-Community Relations.** George E. Pawlas. LC 94-25310. (Illus.). 300p. 1995. 39.95x (*1-883001-13-7*) Eye On Educ.

Administrator's Guide to Whole Language. Gail Heald-Taylor. 196p. (Orig.). (C). 1989. pap. text ed. 16.95 (*0-913461-97-0*) R Owen Pubs.

***Administrator's Guide to X.400 Addressing.** Mizumori. (Communications Ser.). 1995. (*0-442-02060-0*) Van Nos Reinhold.

Administrator's Handbook for Child Care Education. John W. Lorton & Bertha L. Walley. LC 86-15204. 160p. 1987. pap. 12.95 (*0-89334-094-4*) Humanics Ltd.

Administrator's Handbook for Community Health & Home Care Services. Anne S. Smith. 514p. 1988. 175.00 (*0-88737-400-X*, 21-2220) Natl League Nurse.

Administrator's Handbook for Improving Faculty Morale. Phi Delta Kappa Commission on Teacher-Faculty Morale et al. LC 85-61680. 70p. 1985. pap. 7.00 (*0-87367-795-1*) Phi Delta Kappa.

Administrator's Manual for Plastics Education. Robert S. Krolick. LC 78-8937. 1978. pap. write for info. (*0-672-97186-0*) Macmillan.

Administrator's Policy Handbook for Preschool Mainstreaming. Barbara J. Smith & Deborah F. Rose. 205p. 1993. pap. text ed. 39.95 (*0-685-70638-9*) Brookline Bks.

Administrators Solving the Problems of Practice: Decision-Making Concepts, Cases, & Consequences. Wayne K. Hoy & C. John Tarter. LC 93-48156. 1994. pap. text ed. 20.25 (*0-205-15594-4*) Allyn.

Adminstrative Law & Practice, Vol. 1. Charles H. Koch, Jr. 603p. 1985. Vol.1 603. text ed. 125.00 (*0-314-88026-7*) West Pub.

Adminstrative Law & Practice, Vol. 2. Charles H. Koch, Jr. 498p. 1985. write for info. (*0-318-58378-X*) West Pub.

Adminstrative Rulemaking. James T. O'Reilly. 480p. 1983. text ed. 95.00 (*0-07-047738-8*) Shepards-McGraw.

Admirable Crichton etc. see Works of J. M. Barrie

Admirable Woman. Arthur A. Cohen. LC 82-49342. 240p. 1988. pap. 10.95 (*0-87923-705-8*) Godine.

Admiral: The Memoirs of Albert Gleaves, Admiral, USN. LC 85-8419. (Illus.). 286p. (Orig.). 1985. pap. 12.95 (*0-932727-02-6*) Hope Pub Hse.

Admiral & His Lady Columbus & Filipa of Portugal. Maria De Freitas Treen. (Illus.). 1989. 17.95 (*0-8315-0191-X*) Speller.

Admiral & the Deck Boy: One Boy's Journey with Christopher Columbus. Genevieve A. O'Connor. LC 91-17978. (Illus.). 168p. (J). (gr. 10 up). 1991. 12.95 (*1-55870-218-0*) Shoe Tree Pr.

Admiral Arleigh Burke: A Biography. E. B. Potter. 1990. 24.95 (*0-394-58424-4*) Random.

Admiral De Grasse & American Independence. Charles L. Lewis. LC 79-6113. (Navies & Men Ser.). (Illus.). 1980. reprint ed. lib. bdg. 44.95 (*0-405-13042-2*) Ayer.

Admiral Farragut. Alfred T. Mahan. LC 68-26360. (American Biography Ser.: No. 32). 1969. reprint ed. lib. bdg. 75.00 (*0-8383-0268-8*) M S G Haskell Hse.

Admiral Farragut. Alfred T. Mahan. (History - United States Ser.). 333p. 1992. reprint ed. lib. bdg. 89.00 (*0-7812-6177-5*) Rprt Serv.

Admiral Farragut. Alfred T. Mahan. LC 74-108509. 1970. reprint ed. 14.00 (*0-403-00217-6*) Scholarly.

Admiral Halsey's Story. William Halsey & J. Bryan. (Politics & Strategy of World War II Ser.). 1976. reprint ed. lib. bdg. 37.50 (*0-306-70770-5*) Da Capo.

***Admiral Halsey's Story.** William Halsey. (American Autobiography Ser.). 310p. 1995. reprint ed. lib. bdg. 89.00 (*0-7812-8546-1*) Rprt Serv.

Admiral Halsey's Story. William F. Halsey & Joseph Bryan. reprint ed. 21.95 (*0-89201-093-2*) Zenger Pub.

Admiral Harold R. Stark: Architect of Victory, 1939-1945. B. Mitchell Simpson, III. Ed. by William N. Still, Jr. (Studies in Maritime History). 338p. 1989. 24.95 (*0-87249-596-5*) U of SC Pr.

Admiral Hornblower in the West Indies. C. S. Forester. 1989. pap. 12.95 (*0-316-28941-8*) Little.

Admiral Hornblower in the West Indies see Indomitable Hornblower

Admiral Issue of Canada. George C. Marler. (Illus.). 566p. 1982. 35.00 (*0-933580-08-8*) Am Philatelic Society.

Admiral John H. Towers: The Struggle for Naval Air Supremacy. Clark G. Reynolds. LC 91-14694. 576p. 1991. 39.95 (*0-87021-031-9*) Naval Inst Pr.

Admiral of the Amazon: John Randolph Tucker, His Confederate Colleagues & Peru. David P. Werlich. (Illus.). 500p. 1990. 35.00 (*0-8139-1270-9*) U Pr of Va.

Admiral of the Hills: Biography of Chester W. Nimitz. Frank A. Driskill & Dede Casad. (Illus.). 312p. 1983. pap. 14.95 (*0-89015-364-7*) Sunbelt Media.

Admiral of the Mosquitoes: Columbus & America in Light & Dark Verse. Mollee Kruger. LC 89-92764. (Illus.). 100p. (Orig.). 1991. pap. 9.95 (*0-913184-00-4*) Maryben Bks.

Admiral of the New Empire: The Life & Career of George Dewey. Ronald Spector. Ed. by William N. Still, Jr. (Classics in Maritime History Ser.). 240p. 1988. reprint ed. 29.95 (*0-87249-559-0*); reprint ed. pap. 14.95 (*0-87249-568-X*) U of SC Pr.

Admiral of the Ocean Sea: A Life of Christopher Columbus. abr. ed. Samuel E. Morison. (Illus.). 704p. 1991. pap. 24.95 (*0-316-58478-9*) Little.

Admiral Satan: The Life & Campaigns of Suffren, Scourge of the Royal Navy. Roderick Cavaliero. 224p. 1994. text ed. 49.50 (*1-85043-686-X*, Pub. by I B Tauris UK) St Martin.

Admiral Seymour's Expedition & Taku Forts, 1900. Ed. by Colin Narbeth. 88p. (C). 1987. 60.00 (*0-902633-69-4*, Pub. by Picton UK) St Mut.

Admiral William A. Moffett, Architect of Naval Aviation. William F. Trimble. LC 93-7962. (History of Aviation Ser.). (Illus.). 400p. 1993. 29.95 (*1-56098-320-5*) Smithsonian.

Admiral William Shepherd Benson, First Chief of Naval Operations. Mary Klachko & David F. Trask. LC 87-1530. (Illus.). 268p. 1987. 35.00 (*0-87021-035-1*) Naval Inst Pr.

Admirals & Empires: The United States Navy & the Caribbean, 1898-1945. Donald A. Yerxa. LC 90-29162. (Illus.). 202p. 1991. text ed. 39.95 (*0-87249-750-X*) U of SC Pr.

Admirals, Generals, & American Foreign Policy, 1898-1914. Richard D. Challener. LC 72-732. 443p. 1973. pap. 126.30 (*0-7837-0556-5*, 2040900) Bks Demand.

Admirals of the Caribbean. Francis R. Hart. LC 77-165640. (Select Bibliographies Reprint Ser.). 1977. reprint ed. 34.95 (*0-8369-5949-3*) Ayer.

Admirals of the New Steel Navy. Ed. by James C. Bradford. LC 89-13517. 416p. 1990. 42.95 (*0-87021-003-3*) Naval Inst Pr.

Admiral's Wolfpack. Jean Noli. (World-at-War Ser.). 1982. pap. 2.50 (*0-89083-630-2*) Zebra.

Admiralties: Operations of the First Cavalry Division (February 29-May 18, 1944) (Armed Forces in Action Ser.). (Illus.). 161p. reprint ed. per. 5.50 (*0-16-002003-4*, S/N 008-029-00202-7) USGPO.

An Asterisk (*) at the beginning of an entry indicates that the title is appearing in BIP for the first time.

Admiralty. N. A. Rodger. 216p. (C). 1988. 120.00 (0-900963-94-8, Pub. by T Dalton UK) St Mut.

Admiralty. 2nd ed. Gilmore & Black. 1975. text ed. 36.00 (0-88277-409-3) Foundation Pr.

Admiralty: Adaptable to Courses Utilizing Healy & Sharpe's Casebook on Admiralty. Casenotes Publishing Co., Inc. Staff. Ed. by Norman S. Goldenberg et al. (Legal Briefs Ser.). 1986. pap. write for info. (0-87457-005-0, 1290) Casenotes Pub.

Admiralty: Adaptable to Courses Utilizing Lucas' Casebook on Admiralty. Casenotes Publishing Co., Inc. Staff. Ed. by Norman S. Goldenberg et al. (Legal Briefs Ser.). 1983. pap. write for info. (0-87457-006-9, 1291) Casenotes Pub.

Admiralty: Cases & Materials On. 3rd ed. Jo D. Lucas. (University Casebook Ser.). 1146p. 1986. text ed. 41.95 (0-88277-352-6) Foundation Pr.

Admiralty: Island in Contention. LC 72-92087. (Alaska Geographic Ser.: Vol. 1, No. 3). (Illus.). 1973. pap. 7.50 (0-88240-022-3) Alaska Geog Soc.

Admiralty: Jurisdiction, Law, & Practice. M. M. Cohen. xxxvii, 505p. 1993. reprint ed. 52.50 (0-8377-2023-0) Rothman.

Admiralty & Commercial Court Forms: Forms & Precedents. 2nd ed. David Steel & Luke Parsons. (British Shipping Laws Ser.). 350p. 1993. 192.00 (0-421-46140-3, Pub. by Sweet & Maxwl) W W Gaunt.

Admiralty & Maritime Law. Thomas J. Schoenbaum. LC 87-10503. (Hornbook Ser.). 692p. 1993. student ed, text ed. 33.50 (0-314-42108-4) West Pub.

***Admiralty & Maritime Law.** 2nd ed. Thomas J. Schoenbaum. LC 87-10503. (Hornbook Ser.). 1071p. (C). 1994. text ed. 44.00 (0-314-03722-5) West Pub.

Admiralty & Maritime Law. Thomas J. Schoenbaum. LC 87-10503. (Hornbook Ser.). 900p. 1989. reprint ed. text ed. write for info. (0-314-44096-8) West Pub.

Admiralty & Maritime Law, Vol. 1. 2nd ed. Thomas J. Schoenbaum. LC 87-10503. (Practitioner Treatise Ser.). 1042p. 1994. text ed. write for info. (0-314-02710-6) West Pub.

Admiralty & Maritime Law, Vol. 2. 2nd ed. Thomas J. Schoenbaum. LC 87-10503. 1042p. 1994. text ed. write for info. (0-318-72514-2) West Pub.

Admiralty & Maritime Law, 1992: Pocket Part. Thomas J. Schoenbaum. (Hornbook Ser.). 185p. (C). 1992. pap. text ed. 17.50 (0-314-01069-6) West Pub.

Admiralty, Cases, & Materials. Nicholoas J. Healy & David J. Sharpe. LC 85-29367. (American Casebook Ser.). 876p. 1992. reprint ed. text ed. 49.00 (0-314-98021-0) West Pub.

Admiralty in a Nutshell. 2nd ed. Frank L. Maraist. (Nutshell Ser.). 379p. (C). 1992. reprint ed. pap. text ed. 17.50 (0-314-64765-1) West Pub.

Admiralty Island: Fortress of the Bears. L. J. Campbell & Penny Rennick. (Alaska Geographic Ser.: Vol. 18, No. 3). (Illus.). 96p. (Orig.). 1991. pap. 17.95 (0-88240-198-X) Alaska Geog Soc.

Admiralty Jurisdiction & Practice in South Africa. D. J. Shaw. 291p. 1987. write for info. (0-7021-1816-8, Pub. by Juta SA) W W Gaunt.

Admiralty Jurisdiction in America. Theodore M. Etting. vii, 107p. 1986. reprint ed. lib. bdg. 20.00 (0-8377-0547-9) Rothman.

Admiralty, 1991 Statute: Rule & Case Supplement for Use with Cases & Materials On. 3rd ed. Jo D. Lucas. (University Casebook Ser.). 408p. (C). 1991. pap. text ed. 14.00 (0-88277-940-0) Foundation Pr.

Admirations. Lex Runciman. LC 88-31219. 72p. 1989. 15.95 (0-89924-062-3); pap. 8.50 (0-89924-061-5) Lynx Hse.

Admirer. Debra Franklin. (Scream Ser.: No. 7). 224p. 1994. pap. 3.50 (0-8217-4482-8) Zebra.

***Admissibility of Human Rights Petitions: The Case Law of the European Commission of Human Rights & the Human Rights Committee.** Tom Zwart. LC 94-33490. (International Studies in Human Rights: Vol. 36). 1994. lib. bdg. 112.00 (0-7923-3146-X) Kluwer Ac.

Admissible Dual of GL(N) Via Compact Open Subgroups. Colin J. Bushnell & Philip C. Kutzko. LC 92-33614. (Annals of Mathematics Studies: No. 129). 313p. (C). 1993. text ed. 65.00 (0-691-03256-4); pap. text ed. 24.95 (0-691-02114-7) Princeton U Pr.

Admissible Sets & Structures: An Approach to Definability Theory. K. J. Barwise. (Perspectives in Mathematical Logic Ser.). (Illus.). 400p. 1976. 59.00 (0-387-07451-1) Spr-Verlag.

Admissible Solutions of Hyperbolic Conservation Laws. Tai-Ping Liu. LC 80-28506. (Memoirs Ser.: No. 30/240). 78p. 1981. pap. 16.00 (0-8218-2240-3, MEMO 30/240) Am Math.

Admission & Academic Placement of Students from Bahrain, Oman, Qatar, United Arab Emirates, Yemen Arab Republic. Ed. by J Kent Johnson. (Illus.). 114p. (Orig.). 1984. pap. text ed. 20.00 (0-912207-06-X, Pier Pubns) NAFSA Washington.

Admission & Placement of Students from Bangladesh, India, Pakistan, Sri Lanka. Ed. by Leo J. Sweeney & Valerie Woolston. 384p. 1986. 25.00 (0-912207-30-2, Pier Pubns) NAFSA Washington.

Admission & Placement of Students from Canada. Ed. by James S. Frey. 630p. (Orig.). 1989. pap. 30.00 (0-685-51169-3, Pier Pubns) NAFSA Washington.

Admission & Placement of Students from Central America. Ed. by Caroline Aldrich-Langen & Kathleen Sellew. 237p. 1987. 25.00 (0-912207-31-0, Pier Pubns) NAFSA Washington.

Admission & Placement of Students from Poland. Josef Silny. Ed. by Edward Devlin. LC 92-17605. 1992. write for info. (0-910054-98-3) Am Assn Coll Registrars.

Admission & Placement of Students from the Czech & Slovak Federal Republic. Josef Silny et al. LC 92-18301. 1992. write for info. (0-910054-99-1) Am Assn Coll Registrars.

Admission & Placement of Students from the Republic of Hungary. Karlene N. Dickey & Desmond Bevis. (PIER Reports (Projects in International Education Research Workshop Reports)). (Illus.). 128p. (Orig.). 1990. pap. 15.00 (0-929851-03-X) Am Assn Coll Registrars.

Admission & Placement of Students from Yugoslavia. Ed. by Karlene Dickey & Desmond Bevis. 102p. (Orig.). 1990. pap. text ed. 30.00 (0-685-59088-7, Pier Pubns) NAFSA Washington.

Admission & Placement of Students from Yugoslavia. Karlene N. Dickey & Desmond Bevis. (PIER Reports (Projects in International Education Research Workshop Reports)). (Illus.). 112p. (Orig.). 1990. pap. 15.00 (0-929851-04-8) Am Assn Coll Registrars.

***Admission Decisions.** abr. ed. National Issues Staff. (Abridged Ser.). 76p. 1994. 49.50 (0-7872-0501-X) Kendall-Hunt.

Admission Decisions: Should Immigration Be Restricted? NIF Staff. 32p. 1994. 2.95 (0-8403-9446-2) Kendall-Hunt.

***Admission Decisions: Should Immigration be Restricted?** abr. ed. 32p. 1994. 2.95 (0-8403-9447-0) Kendall-Hunt.

Admission Decisions Manual. Ed. by Ellen H. Taliaferro. 269p. 1987. 45.00 (0-87189-873-X) Aspen Pub.

***Admission of Guilt, Restraining Orders, Opposition to Release, & In-Court Statements of CIA Officer Aldrich Hazen Ames.** Hayden B. Peake. Ed. by Elizabeth Bancroft. (Nightmover Case Ser.: Vol. 3). 1994. 24.95 (1-878292-13-7) Natl Intel Bk Ctr.

Admission of Kansas: A Speech. William H. Seward. (Shorey Historical Ser.). 16p. reprint ed. pap. 2.75 (0-8466-0056-0, S56) Shorey.

Admission of the 31st State by the 31st Congress: An Annotated Bibliography of Congressional Speeches upon the Admission of California. Robert G. Cowan. LC 85-21272. 139p. 1985. reprint ed. lib. bdg. 27.00x (0-89370-865-8) Borgo Pr.

Admission Test Passbook Series. Jack Rudman. 1994. pap. write for info. (0-8373-5000-X) Nat Learn.

Admission to College by Certificate. Joseph L. Henderson. LC 72-176858. (Columbia University. Teachers College. Contributions to Education Ser.: No. 50). reprint ed. 37.50 (0-404-55050-9) AMS Pr.

Admission to Higher Education in the United States: A German Critique. Ulrich Teichler. (Access to Higher Education Ser.). 146p. 1978. pap. text ed. 5.00 (0-89192-218-0) Interbk Inc.

Admission to Medical Education in Ten Countries. Ed. by Barbara B. Burn. (Access to Higher Education Ser.). 1978. pap. 6.00 (0-89192-214-8) Interbk Inc.

***Admission to the New York State Bar: A Compendium of Statutes & Rules.** Daniel C. Brennan. LC 92-61677. 87p. 1992. ring bd. 35.00 (0-942954-56-4) NYS Bar.

Admissions, Academic Records, & Registrar Services. Ed. by C. James Quann et al. LC 79-88109. (Jossey-Bass Series in Higher Education). (Illus.). 509p. reprint ed. pap. 145.10 (0-8357-4918-5, 2037848) Bks Demand.

Admissions Guide to Selective Business Schools. Matthew May. 1990. pap. 16.95 (0-8442-8556-0, VGM Career Bks) NTC Pub Grp.

Admissions Guide to Selective Business Schools. Matthew May. 192p. 1991. 29.95 (0-8442-8550-1, Passport Bks) NTC Pub Grp.

Admissions Officer. Jack Rudman. (Career Examination Ser.: C-1083). 1994. pap. 23.95 (0-8373-1083-0) Nat Learn.

Admissions Professions: A Guide for Staff Development & Program Management. Claire Swann & Ron Ancrum. 128p. 1991. pap. text ed. 20.00 (0-929851-08-0) Am Assn Coll Registrars.

Admit the Act & Win the Criminal Case. David C. Cohen. 1980. 74.50 (0-13-008656-8) Exec Reports.

Admit to Murder. large type ed. Margaret Yorke. LC 92-41072. 1993. 19.95 (0-7927-1530-6, Eagle Lrg Print); pap. write for info. (0-7927-1529-2, Eagle Lrg Print) Chivers N Amer.

Admitting Clerk. Jack Rudman. (Career Examination Ser.: C-71). 1994. pap. 23.95 (0-8373-0071-1) Nat Learn.

Admitting Department Policy & Procedure Guideline Manual. Barbara Jenings. 1990. 55.00 (1-879575-03-5) Acad Med Sys.

Admitting the Holocaust: Collected Essays. Lawrence L. Langer. LC 94-13368. 202p. 1995. 23.00 (0-19-509357-7) OUP.

Admonitions of an Egyptian Sage from a Hieratic Papyrus in Leiden. Alan H. Gardiner. 116p. 1990. reprint ed. 63.70 (3-487-02129-3, Pub. by Georg Olms GW) Lubrecht & Cramer.

Admonitions of St. Francis of Assisi. 22p. 1987. 0.99 (0-8199-0914-9, Frncscn Herld) Franciscan Pr.

Admonitions of St. Francis of Assisi. Lothar Hardick et al. Tr. by David Smith. 399p. 1983. 15.00 (0-8199-0869-X, Frncscn Herld) Franciscan Pr.

ADNON see Norwegian-English Administrative Dictionary

***Ado-Toys.** Frederikle Huygen. 80p. 1995. pap. 22.50 (90-6918-132-0) Dist Art Pubs.

Adobe: Build It Yourself. 2nd rev. ed. Paul G. McHenry, Jr. LC 85-8432. (Illus.). 158p. 1985. pap. 22.95 (0-8165-0948-4) U of Ariz Pr.

Adobe: Building & Living with Earth. Orlando Romero & David Larkin. LC 94-11692. (Illus.). 1994. 50.00 (0-395-56693-2) HM.

Adobe: Homes & Interiors in Taos, Santa Fe & the Southwest. rev. ed. Laurel Seth & Sandra Seth. (Illus.). 280p. 1990. 47.50 (0-942655-00-1) Archit CT.

Adobe Abodes. Lenore H. Hughes. LC 84-82473. (Illus.). 223p. (Orig.). 1986. pap. 10.95 (0-9604772-0-9) Hughes Pub.

Adobe Acrobat Handbook: Digital Publishing in the Post-Gutenberg Era. W. David Schwaderer. 282p. 1993. disk, pap. 19.95 (0-672-30393-0) Sams.

***Adobe Alternative: How to Pour Adobe.** Stan Ferris. Ed. & Illus. by Cris Coffey. 28p. (Orig.). 1994. 9.00 (1-882400-11-9) Featherweed.

Adobe & Rammed Earth Buildings: Design & Construction. Paul G. McHenry, Jr. LC 89-5053. (Illus.). 217p. 1989. reprint ed. pap. 24.95 (0-8165-1124-1) U of Ariz Pr.

***Adobe Angels: The Ghosts of Albuquerque, Vol. I, No. 2.** Antonio R. Garcez. (Illus.). 114p. (Orig.). 1994. pap. 12.00 (0-9634029-2-7) Red Rabbit Pr.

***Adobe Angels: The Ghosts of Santa Fe.** Antonio R. Garcez. 1992. pap. 12.00 (0-9634029-0-0) Red Rabbit Pr.

Adobe Anthology. Ed. by Claudia Lunstroth. 78p. 1993. pap. 5.00 (0-9639737-0-3) Adobe Bkstore.

***Adobe Anthology Vol. 2.** Ed. by Claudia Lunstroth. (Illus.). 84p. (Orig.). 1994. pap. 7.50 (0-9639737-1-1) Adobe Bkstore.

Adobe Architecture. 2nd ed. Ed. by Myrtle Stedman & Wilfred Stedman. LC 87-10024. (Illus.). 48p. 1987. pap. 6.95 (0-86534-111-7) Sunstone Pr.

Adobe Book. John F. O'Connor. LC 72-95653. (Illus.). 160p. 1973. lib. bdg. 29.95 (0-941270-06-8); pap. 15.95 (0-941270-19-X) Ancient City Pr.

Adobe Days. Sarah B. Smith. LC 87-5936. (Illus.). xxviii, 154p. 1987. reprint ed. pap. 6.95 (0-8032-9178-7) U of Nebr Pr.

***Adobe Doorways.** Mary J. Fry. 64p. 1995. per. 9.95 (1-883852-01-3) Sage Pr OK.

Adobe Doorways. Dorothy L. Pillsbury. LC 52-11521. 208p. 1983. reprint ed. 16.95 (0-89016-076-7); reprint ed. pap. 8.95 (0-89016-070-8) Lightning Tree.

Adobe Empire. large type ed. Lauran Paine. LC 93-13365. 1993. 18.95 (0-7927-1701-5, Roundup Lrg Print Westerns); pap. 16.95 (0-7927-1700-7, Roundup Lrg Print Westerns) Chivers N Amer.

Adobe Illustrator: A Visual Guide to the Macintosh. Linnea Dayton. 1994. pap. 28.95 (0-201-40723-X) Addison-Wesley.

***Adobe Illustrator for the Mac Designers Guide.** Cynthia S. Williams. LC 94-68476. 310p. 1994. pap. 26.99 (0-7821-1304-4) Sybex.

Adobe Illustrator for Windows. Adobe Systems Staff et al. LC 93-73014. (Classroom in a Book Ser.). (Illus.). 320p. (Orig.). 1994. pap. text ed. 44.95 (1-56830-053-0) Adobe Calif.

Adobe Illustrator Macintosh. Adobe Systems Staff et al. LC 93-73010. (Classroom in a Book Ser.). (Illus.). 320p. (Orig.). 1994. pap. text ed. 44.95 (1-56830-056-5) Adobe Calif.

***Adobe Illustrator Paths & Curves.** Kenneth Batelman. LC 95-14989. 1995. pap. text ed. 24.95 (0-471-12027-8) Wiley.

Adobe Illustrator 3.0 Complete. Sharyn Venit. 1991. pap. 24.95 (0-201-57756-9) Addison-Wesley.

Adobe Illustrator 3.0 Official Handbook. Tony Bove. 1991. pap. 24.95 (0-679-79069-1) Random.

Adobe Illustrator 3.2 Designer's Guide. David A. Holzgang. LC 92-61124. 358p. 1992. 24.95 (0-7821-1002-9) Sybex.

Adobe Illustrator 5.0. 4th ed. Tony Bove. 1993. pap. 27.00 (0-679-79163-9) Random.

Adobe Illustrator 5.0 Complete. 3rd ed. Sharyn Venit. 1994. pap. 32.95 (0-201-62720-5) Addison-Wesley.

Adobe Joe: Wit, Wisdom & Commentary. Peter Eichstaedt. (Illus.). 96p. (Orig.). 1987. pap. 7.95 (0-685-26589-7) Apache Canyon Pr.

***Adobe Kingdom No. 1: New Mexico 1598 - 1958 As Experienced by the Families Lucero De Gadsy y Baca.** Donald L. Lucero. Ed. by Charlene G. Simmo & Mary O. Vera. (Illus.). 275p. (Orig.). 1995. pap. text ed. write for info. (0-9628974-3-4) El Escrito.

Adobe Notes. Kate Chapman & Dorothy Stewart. (Illus.). 44p. 1977. 4.50 (0-941270-10-6) Ancient City Pr.

Adobe Palace. Joyce Brandon. 1993. mass mkt. 5.99 (0-345-36096-6) Ballantine.

Adobe Photoshop for Macintosh. Adobe Systems Staff et al. Tr. by Impress Group Staff & Prentice Hall Staff. LC 93-78060. (Classroom in a Book Ser.). (Illus.). 320p. (Orig.). 1994. pap. text ed. 44.95 (1-56830-055-7); pap. text ed. 44.95 (4-8443-5412-4); pap. text ed. 44.95 (2-910565-00-9) Adobe Calif.

Adobe Photoshop for Macintosh: Classroom in a Book. 2nd ed. Adobe Press Staff et al. (Classroom in a Book Ser.). (Illus.). Date not set. pap. 49.95 (1-56830-118-9) Hayden.

***Adobe Photoshop for Windows.** Adobe Systems Staff & Prentice-Hall Muncher Staff. LC 93-73013. (Classroom in a Book Ser.). (Illus.). 320p. (Orig.). 1993. pap. text ed. 44.95 (1-56830-054-9) Adobe Calif.

Adobe Photoshop for Windows: Classroom in a Book. 2nd ed. Adobe Press Staff et al. (Classroom in a Book Ser.). (Illus.). 1994. pap. 49.95 (1-56830-120-0) Hayden.

Adobe Photoshop Handbook. David Biedney. 1995. pap. 32.00 (0-679-75325-7) Random.

Adobe Photoshop Now! New Riders Publishing Staff. 300p. 1994. pap. 35.00 (1-56205-200-4) New Riders Pub.

Adobe Premier for Macintosh: Classroom in a Book. 2nd ed. Adobe Press Staff et al. LC 93-78059. (Classroom in a Book Ser.). (Illus.). 256p. 1994. pap. 49.95 (1-56830-119-7) Hayden.

***Adobe Premiere for Windows: Classroom in a Book.** Adobe Press Staff. (Illus.). 272p. (Orig.). 1995. pap. 50.00 (1-56830-172-3) Alpha Bks IN.

Adobe Premiere MacIntosh. Adobe Systems Staff. Tr. by Impress Group Staff & Prentice Hall Staff. LC 93-73013. (Classroom in a Book Ser.). (Illus.). 320p. (Orig.). (GER.). 1993. pap. text ed. 44.95 (3-930436-01-9) Adobe Calif.

Adobe Premiere MacIntosh. Adobe Systems Staff. Tr. by Impress Group Staff & Prentice Hall Staff. LC 93-78059. (Classroom in a Book Ser.). (Illus.). 320p. (Orig.). 1994. pap. text ed. 44.95 (1-56830-052-2); pap. text ed. 44.95 (4-8443-5413-2) Adobe Calif.

Adobe Remodeling & Fireplaces. Myrtle Stedman. LC 86-5744. (Illus.). 48p. (Orig.). 1986. pap. 6.95 (0-86534-086-2) Sunstone Pr.

Adobe Type 1 Font Format. Adobe Systems Incorporated Staff. 1990. pap. 16.95 (0-201-57044-0) Addison-Wesley.

Adobe Type 1 Font Format. 2nd ed. Adobe Systems Incorporated Staff. 1995. pap. 16.95 (0-201-60854-5) Addison-Wesley.

Adobe Whitewater Club of New Mexico's Handbook of River Safety & Rescue. Charles Hammersley. (AWC Ser.). (Illus.). 29p. (Orig.). 1985. pap. 3.95 (0-910467-03-X) Heritage Assocs.

Adobes of Twentynine Palms. Pat Rimmington. LC 88-51614. (Illus.). 144p. (Orig.). 1988. pap. 12.00 (0-9617961-3-8) Desert Moon Pr.

Adogmatic State: A Conception. Apostolos N. Depastas. 1989. 11.95 (0-533-08051-7) Vantage.

***Adolescence.** Louise Kaplan. 1995. pap. 14.00 (0-684-80062-4, Touchstone Bks) S&S Trade.

Adolescence. Rebecca Stefoff. (Life Cycle Ser.). (Illus.). 104p. (YA). (gr. 6-12). 1990. 18.95 (0-7910-0033-8) Chelsea Hse.

Adolescence. Nicholas Tucker. LC 90-21868. (Human Development Ser.). (Illus.). 64p. (J). (gr. 5-9). 1991. lib. bdg. 11.95 (0-8114-7805-X) Raintree Steck-V.

Adolescence. 2nd ed. W. Eastwood Atwater. (Illus.). 432p. (C). 1988. pap. text ed. write for info. (0-13-008699-1) P-H.

Adolescence. 2nd ed. Robert E. Grinder. LC 77-7239. (Illus.). 628p. reprint ed. pap. 179.00 (0-8357-5111-2, 2020341) Bks Demand.

Adolescence. 2nd ed. Laurence Steinberg. 480p. (C). 1989. text ed. 34.95 (0-394-38623-X) Knopf.

Adolescence. 3rd ed. Eastwood Atwater. 464p. (C). 1991. text ed. write for info. (0-13-007469-1) P-H.

Adolescence. 3rd ed. Laurence Steinberg. LC 92-15734. 1992. text ed. write for info. (0-07-061218-8) McGraw.

Adolescence: A Contemporary View. Linda Nielson. 700p. (C). 1986. text ed. 42.75 (0-03-070493-6) HB Coll Pubs.

Adolescence: A Contemporary View. 2nd ed. Linda Nielsen. (Illus.). 760p. (C). 1991. text ed. 42.75 (0-03-032853-5) HB Coll Pubs.

***Adolescence: A Developmental Transition.** 2nd ed. Douglas C. Kimmel & Irving B. Weiner. LC 94-28382. 1994. text ed. write for info. (0-471-58264-6) Wiley.

Adolescence: A Developmental View. Rhoda Cummings. (Illus.). 704p. (Orig.). (C). Date not set. pap. text ed. write for info. (0-15-500284-8) HB Coll Pubs.

Adolescence: A Social Psychological Analysis. 4th ed. Hans Sebald. 368p. (C). 1991. text ed. write for info. (0-13-006008-9) P-H.

***Adolescence: A Time of Change.** William S. Meyers. 20p. 1995. 2.95 (1-56456-091-0) W Gladden Found.

Adolescence: An Anthropological Inquiry. Alice Schlegel & Herbert Barry, III. 250p. 1991. text ed. 29.95 (0-02-927895-3) Free Pr.

Adolescence: An Ethological Perspective. R. C. Savin-Williams. (Illus.). 260p. 1986. 76.00 (0-387-96369-3) Spr-Verlag.

***Adolescence: An Introduction.** John W. Santrock. 688p. (C). 1995. student ed write for info. (0-697-15066-6); boxed write for info. (0-697-15032-1) Brown & Benchmark.

Adolescence: An Introduction. 4th ed. John W. Santrock. 688p. (C). 1990. write for info. (0-318-66914-5) Brown & Benchmark.

Adolescence: An Introduction. 5th ed. John W. Santrock. 656p. (C). 1993. pap. text ed. write for info. (0-697-12753-2); student ed write for info. (0-697-12755-9) Brown & Benchmark.

***Adolescence: An Introduction.** 6th ed. John W. Santrock. 688p. (C). 1995. pap. text ed. write for info. (0-697-15033-X) Brown & Benchmark.

Adolescence: Continuity, Change & Diversity. Nancy J. Cobb. 678p. (C). 1992. teacher ed write for info. (1-55934-148-3); pap. text ed. 42.95 (0-87484-888-1); trans. write for info. (0-318-68874-3); disk write for info. (0-318-68876-X); write for info. (0-318-68875-1) Mayfield Pub.

***Adolescence: Continuity, Change, & Diversity.** Nancy J. Cobb. LC 94-29682. 674p. (C). 1994. pap. text ed. 44.95 (1-55934-392-3) Mayfield Pub.

***Adolescence: Guiding Youth Through the Perilous Ordeal.** Miller Newton. 224p. (C). 1995. 27.00 (0-393-70194-8) Norton.

Adolescence: Its Social Psychology. Charlotte M. Fleming. 1969. reprint ed. pap. text ed. 24.95 (0-8236-8004-5, 020060) Intl Univs Pr.

***Adolescence: Psychotherapy & the Emergent Self.** Mark McConville. LC 95-16964. (Social & Behavioral Sciences). 1995. 32.95 (0-7879-0124-5) Jossey-Bass.

Adolescence: The Survival Guide for Parents & Teenagers. Elizabeth Fenwick & Tony Smith. LC 93-15780. (Illus.). 1994. 19.95 (1-56458-330-9) Dorling Kindersley.

Adolescence: The Transitional Years. J. R. Hopkins. 494p. (C). 1983. text ed. 42.75 (0-15-500790-4, HOP) HB Coll Pubs.

Adolescence: Theories, Research, Applications. Larry C. Jensen. (Illus.). 573p. (C). 1985. text ed. 52.00 (0-314-85251-4); Instr's. manual. teacher ed, pap. text ed. write for info. (0-314-87100-4) West Pub.

An Asterisk (*) at the beginning of an entry indicates that the title is appearing in BIP for the first time.

A

Adolescence, Adolescents. 2nd large type ed. Barbara S. Fuhrmann. (C). 1990. text ed. 41.50 (0-673-52018-8) HarpCollege.

Adolescence & Character Disturbance. James B. McCarthy. LC 94-16770. 218p. (Orig.). (C). reprint ed. lib. bdg. 48.50 (0-8191-9582-0); reprint ed. pap. text ed. 24.50 (0-8191-9583-9) U Pr of Amer.

Adolescence & Culture. Aaron H. Esman. Ed. by Arnold M. Cooper & Steven Marcus. (Psychoanalysis & Culture Ser.). 118p. (C). 1990. text ed. 25.00 (0-231-06972-3); pap. 9.95 (0-231-06973-1) Col U Pr.

Adolescence & Death. Charles A. Corr & Joan McNeil. LC 85-31713. 304p. 1986. 33.95 (0-8261-4930-8) Springer Pub.

***Adolescence & Delinquency: The Collective Management of Reputation.** Nicholas Emier & Stephen Reicher. (Social Psychology & Society Ser.). 240p. (C). 1995. write for info. (0-631-13802-1); pap. write for info. (0-631-16823-0) Blackwell Pubs.

***Adolescence & Developmental Breakdown: A Psychoanalytic View.** Moses Laufer & M. Egle Laufer. 224p. 1995. pap. 30.95 (1-85575-108-9) Brunner-Mazel.

Adolescence & Poverty: Challenge for the 1990s. Ed. by Peter Edelman & Joyce Ladner. 200p. 1991. 45.00 (0-944237-31-2); pap. 16.50 (0-944237-32-0) Ctr National Policy.

Adolescence & Puberty. Ed. by John Bancroft & June Machover Reinisch. (Kinsey Institute Ser.: No. 3). (Illus.). 320p. 1990. 39.95 (0-19-505336-2) OUP.

Adolescence & Self-Esteem. Patricia Wellingham-Jones. (Illus.). 54p. (Orig.). 1984. pap. 10.00 (0-939221-01-2) Wellingham-Jones.

Adolescence & Work: Influences of Social Structure, Labor Markets & Culture. David Stern & Dorothy Eichorn. (Walsh Osipow Voc Psych Ser.). 392p. (C). 1989. text ed. 79.95 (0-89859-964-4) L Erlbaum Assocs.

Adolescence & Youth. 4th ed. Conger. (C). 1990. text ed. 57.00 (0-06-041343-3) HarpCollege.

Adolescence & Youth: Study Guide. 4th ed. Conger. (C). 1991. 19.50 (0-06-044579-3) HarpCollege.

Adolescence & Youth in Early Modern England. Ilana K. Ben-Amos. LC 93-38314. 320p. 1994. 32.50 (0-300-05597-8) Yale U Pr.

Adolescence, Careers, & Cultures. Ed. by Wim Meeus et al. LC 92-45751. (Prevention & Intervention in Childhood & Adolescence Ser.: No. 13). x, 428p. (C). 1993. lib. bdg. 98.95 (3-11-013679-1) De Gruyter.

Adolescence, Discipline & Waldorf Education. Eugene Schwartz. 1991. 12.95 (0-945803-11-7) R Steiner Col Pubns.

Adolescence in a Moroccan Town. Susan S. Davis & Douglas A. Davis. LC 88-16897. (Adolescents in a Changing World Ser.). 288p. (C). 1989. text ed. 42.00 (0-8135-1368-5) Rutgers U Pr.

Adolescence in Context: The Interplay of Family, School, Peers, & Work in Adjustment. Ed. by Rainer K. Silbereisen & Eberhand Todt. LC 93-3850. 1993. 79.00 (0-387-94060-X) Spr-Verlag.

Adolescence in the Life Cycle: Psychological Change & the Social Context. Ed. by S. E. Dragastin & G. H. Elder, Jr. LC 74-22002. 336p. reprint ed. 95.80 (0-8357-9146-7, 2050705) Bks Demand.

Adolescence in the 1990s: Risk & Opportunity. Ed. by Ruby Takanishi. LC 93-36058. (Special Issues for the Teachers College Record Ser.). 240p. (C). 1993. pap. text ed. 17.95 (0-8077-3330-X) Tchrs Coll.

Adolescence Is Not an Illness. Bruce Narramore. LC 91-23784. 224p. 1991. pap. 8.99 (0-8007-5416-6) Revell.

Adolescence-Its Psychology & Its Relation to Physiology, Anthropology, Sociology, Sex, Crime, Religion & Education, 2 vols., 1. Stanley G. Hall. LC 79-89183. (American Education: Its Men, Institutions & Ideas, Ser.). 1975. reprint ed. 42.95 (0-405-01422-8) Ayer.

Adolescence-Its Psychology & Its Relation to Physiology, Anthropology, Sociology, Sex, Crime, Religion & Education, 2 vols., 2. Stanley G. Hall. LC 79-89183. (American Education: Its Men, Institutions & Ideas, Ser.). 1975. reprint ed. 38.95 (0-405-01423-6) Ayer.

Adolescence-Its Psychology & Its Relation to Physiology, Anthropology, Sociology, Sex, Crime, Religion & Education, 2 vols., Set. Stanley G. Hall. LC 79-89183. (American Education: Its Men, Institutions & Ideas, Ser.). 1970. reprint ed. 71.95 (0-405-01421-X) Ayer.

Adolescence, Its Social Psychology: With an Introduction to Recent Findings from the Fields of Anthropology, Physiology, Medicine, Psychometrics & Sociometry. Charlotte M. Fleming. LC 49-900. 270p. reprint ed. pap. 77.00 (0-8357-5112-0, 2010710) Bks Demand.

Adolescence of Zhenya Luvers. Boris Pasternak. pap. 1.25 (0-8065-0306-8, Citadel Pr) Carol Pub Group.

Adolescence to Adulthood: Change & Stability in the Lives of Young Men. Jerald G. Bachman. LC 78-109016. (Youth in Transition Ser.: No. 6). 350p. reprint ed. pap. 99.80 (0-7837-5241-5, 2044975) Bks Demand.

Adolescent. Fyodor Dostoyevsky. Tr. by Andrew R. MacAndrew. 608p. 1981. reprint ed. pap. 16.95 (0-393-00995-5) Norton.

Adolescent: Development, Relationships & Culture. 6th ed. F. Philip Rice. 650p. 1989. text ed. 45.00 (0-205-12310-4, H23104) Allyn.

Adolescent: Development, Relationships, & Culture. 7th ed. F. Philip Rice. LC 92-37109. 1992. text ed. write for info. (0-205-14125-0) Allyn.

***Adolescent: Development, Relationships & Culture.** 8th ed. F. Philip Rice. 1995. text ed. 55.00 (0-205-18444-8, H84445) Allyn.

Adolescent see Understanding the Pupil

Adolescent Abortion: Psychological & Legal Issues. Ed. by Gary B. Melton. LC 85-31812. (Children & the Law Ser.). xiii, 152p. 1986. 25.00 (0-8032-3094-X) U of Nebr Pr.

Adolescent Abuse & Neglect: A Comprehensive Treatment Approach. Kasumi K. Hirayama. 1982. teacher ed 5.00 (0-89695-016-6); trans. 25.00 (0-89695-018-2); vhs 175.00 (0-89695-019-0); 3.00 (0-89695-017-4) U Tenn CSW.

Adolescent Abuse & Neglect: A Comprehensive Treatment Approach, Set. Kasumi K. Hirayama. 1982. write for info. (0-89695-015-8) U Tenn CSW.

Adolescent Aggression: A Study of the Influence of Child-Training Practices & Family Inter-Relationships. Albert Bandura & Richard H. Walters. LC 59-12125. 489p. reprint ed. 139.40 (0-8357-9518-7, 2012404) Bks Demand.

Adolescent & Adult Psychoeducational Profile, Vol. IV. Gary B. Mesibov et al. LC 78-13415. (Individualized Assessment & Treatment for Autistic & Developmentally Disabled Children Ser.). (Illus.). 150p. (Orig.). 1987. pap. 49.00 (0-89079-152-X, 1425) PRO-ED.

Adolescent & Adult Psychoeducational Profile: A Comprehensive Evaluation of the Autistic & Developmentally Disabled. Eric Schopler et al. pap. write for info. (0-8290-1792-5) Irvington.

Adolescent & AIDS: Generation in Jeopardy: Epidemiology, Prevention & Policy. Ralph J. DiClemente. 312p. (C). 1992. text ed. 45.00 (0-8039-4181-1); pap. text ed. 21.50 (0-8039-4182-X) Sage.

Adolescent & His Environment. Ed. by H. Thomae & T. Endo. (Contributions to Human Development Ser.: Vol. 1). (Illus.). 109p. 1974. 35.25 (3-8055-1651-7) S Karger.

Adolescent & His World. Irene M. Josselyn. LC 52-2279. 126p. reprint ed. pap. 36.00 (0-8357-5113-9, 2030822) Bks Demand.

Adolescent & Mood Disturbance. Harvey Golombek & Barry D. Garfinkel. LC 82-13044. xvi, 285p. 1983. text ed. 40.00x (0-8236-0085-8) Intl Univs Pr.

Adolescent & Young Adult Fact Book. Children's Defense Fund Staff. 164p. (Orig.). 1991. pap. 12.95 (0-938008-83-8) Childrens Defense.

Adolescent Anger Control. Feindler. (Practitioner Guidebook Ser.). (C). 1986. pap. 25.95 (0-205-14324-5, H4324, Longwood Div) Allyn.

Adolescent Art Therapy. Debra G. Linesch. LC 87-21866. 256p. 1988. 29.95 (0-87630-486-2) Brunner-Mazel.

Adolescent As Decision-Maker: Applications to Development & Education. Ed. by Judith Worell & Fred Danner. (Educational Psychology Ser.). 320p. 1989. text ed. 73.00 (0-12-764052-5) Acad Pr.

Adolescent Assertiveness & Social Skills Training: A Clinical Handbook. Ed. by Iris E. Fodor. LC 92-20357. 296p. 1992. 39.95 (0-8261-7490-6) Springer Pub.

Adolescent Behavior: Medical Subject Analysis with Research Bibliography. Uriel Rottlevy. LC 84-45645. 150p. 1987. 39.50 (0-88164-240-1); pap. 34.50 (0-88164-241-X) ABBE Pubs Assn.

Adolescent Behavior & Society: A Book of Readings. 4th ed. Rolf E. Muuss. 1990. pap. text ed. write for info. (0-07-044164-2) McGraw.

Adolescent Behavior Therapy Handbook. Eva Feindler & Grace Kalfus. LC 90-9448. (Behavior Therapy & Behavioral Medicine Ser.: Vol. 22). 480p. 1990. 48.95 (0-8261-6400-5) Springer Pub.

Adolescent Blues. Jose Carmona. 64p. 1992. 12.95 (0-8403-7881-5) Kendall-Hunt.

Adolescent Boys in High School: A Psychological Study of Coping & Adaptation. Ed. by James G. Kelly. LC 78-21652. 285p. reprint ed. pap. 81.30 (0-7837-0159-4, 2040456) Bks Demand.

Adolescent Criminal: An Examination of Today's Juvenile Offender. R. Barri Flowers. LC 89-13429. 256p. 1990. lib. bdg. 28.50x (0-89950-479-5) McFarland & Co.

Adolescent Crisis: Family Counseling Approaches. Eva Leveton. LC 84-10502. 304p. 1984. 28.95 (0-8261-4500-0) Springer Pub.

Adolescent d'Autrefois. Francois Mauriac. 10.95 (0-8288-6083-1, F113000) Fr & Eur.

Adolescent Development. John S. Dacey & Maureen E. Kenny. 560p. 1994. pap. text ed. write for info. (0-697-14442-9); Study guide. student ed, pap. text ed. write for info. (0-697-20997-0) Brown & Benchmark.

Adolescent Development: An Ecological Perspective. James Garbarino. (C). 1985. write for info. (0-675-20301-5, Merrill Pub Co) Macmillan.

***Adolescent Development: Early Through Late Adolescence.** David E. Balk. LC 94-25195. 590p. 1995. pap. 44.95 (0-534-20040-0) Brooks-Cole.

Adolescent Development & Behavior. 2nd ed. Jerome B. Dusek. 1991. pap. text ed. 29.00 (0-13-009119-7, 670107) P-H.

Adolescent Development in School Science. Ed. by Philip Adey. 400p. 1989. 70.00 (1-85000-428-5, Falmer Pr); pap. 38.00 (1-85000-429-3, Falmer Pr) Taylor & Francis.

Adolescent Development in the Family. Ed. by Harold D. Grotevant & Catherine R. Cooper. LC 83-82344. (New Directions for Child Development Ser.: No. CD 22). 1983. pap. 17.95 (0-87589-934-X) Jossey-Bass.

Adolescent Development, Psychopathology, & Treatment. H. Spencer Bloch. 278p. 1995. text ed. 50.00 (0-8236-0065-3) Intl Univs Pr.

Adolescent Dilemma: International Perspectives on Family Planning - Rights of Minors. Ed. by Hyman Rodman & Jan Trost. LC 86-608. 272p. 1986. text ed. 49.95 (0-275-92080-1, C2080, Praeger Pubs) Greenwood.

Adolescent Drinking & Disorder. Niall Coggans et al. Ed. by Bill Gillham. (Facts About...Ser.). 96p. 1995. 55.00 (0-304-32664-X); pap. 17.95 (0-304-32666-6) Cassell.

Adolescent Drinking & Family Life. Geoff Lowe et al. LC 93-19119. 1993. text ed. 38.00 (3-7186-5413-X); pap. text ed. 22.00 (3-7186-5414-8) Gordon & Breach.

Adolescent Drug Abuse. Niall Coggans & John Davies. (Facts About Ser.). 96p. 1991. text ed. 45.00 (0-304-32274-1); pap. text ed. 13.95 (0-304-32280-6) Cassell.

Adolescent Drug Use Prevention: Common Features of Promising Community Programs. (Illus.). 81p. (Orig.). (C). 1994. pap. text ed. 35.00 (0-7881-0269-9) Diane Pub.

Adolescent, Etc. Fyodor Dostoyevsky. (FRE.). 1956. 89.95 (0-8288-3435-0, F90470) Fr & Eur.

Adolescent Fatherhood. Ed. by Arthur B. Elster & Michael E. Lamb. 224p. (C). 1986. text ed. 39.95 (0-89859-540-1) L Erlbaum Assocs.

Adolescent Fertility in Kenya. Benjamin Gyepi-Garbrah. (Adolescent Fertility in Sub-Sahara Africa Ser.: Vol. 4). 62p. (Orig.). 1985. write for info. (0-933853-03-3) Pathfinder Fund.

Adolescent Fertility in Liberia. Benjamin Gyepi-Garbrah. (Adolescent Fertility in Sub-Sahara Africa Ser.: Vol. 2). 55p. (Orig.). 1985. write for info. (0-933853-01-7) Pathfinder Fund.

Adolescent Fertility in Nigeria. Benjamin Gyepi-Garbrah. (Adolescent Fertility in Sub-Sahara Africa Ser.: Vol. 3). 69p. (Orig.). 1985. write for info. (0-933853-02-5) Pathfinder Fund.

Adolescent Fertility in Sierra Leone. Benjamin Gyepi-Garbrah. (Adolescent Fertility in Sub-Sahara Africa Ser.: Vol. 5). 1985. write for info. (0-7338-5364-1) Pathfinder Fund.

Adolescent Fertility in Sub-Sahara Africa: An Overview. Benjamin Gyepi-Garbrah. (Adolescent Fertility in Sub-Sahara Africa Ser.: Vol. 1). 51p. (Orig.). 1985. write for info. (0-933853-00-9) Pathfinder Fund.

Adolescent Girls in the Juvenile Justice System. National Council of Jewish Women Staff. (Illus.). 89p. 1984. pap. text ed. 4.50 (0-941840-18-2) NCJW.

Adolescent Group Psychotherapy. Ed. by Fern J. Azima & Lewis H. Richmond. (American Group Psychotherapy Association Monographs: No. 4). 260p. 1989. 32.50 (0-8236-2255-X, BN#00082) Intl Univs Pr.

Adolescent Group Therapy: A Social Competency Model. George R. Holmes et al. LC 91-2693. 176p. 1991. text ed. 45.00 (0-275-94024-1, C4024, Praeger Pubs) Greenwood.

Adolescent Growth & Motor Performance: A Longitudinal Study of Belgian Boys. Gaston P. Beunen et al. LC 87-31864. (HKP Sport Science Monograph Ser.). (Illus.). 112p. (Orig.). 1988. pap. 22.00x (0-87322-160-5, BBEU0160) Human Kinetics.

Adolescent Gynecology: A Guide for Clinicians. Ed. by Alfred M. Bongiovanni. LC 82-22396. 276p. 1983. 55.00 (0-306-41203-9, Plenum Med Bk) Plenum.

***Adolescent Health: Abstracts of Active Projects FY 1994.** National Center for Education in Maternal & Child Health Staff. 350p. 1994. pap. text ed. write for info. (1-57285-004-3) Nat Ctr Educ.

***Adolescent Health: Reassessing the Passage to Adulthood.** Judith Senderowitz. LC 94-48163. (Discussion Paper Ser.: No. 272). 64p. 1995. 7.95 (0-8213-3157-4, 13157) World Bank.

Adolescent Health Care: A Practical Guide. rev. ed. Lawrence S. Neinstein. (Illus.). 1112p. 1991. pap. 59.00 (0-683-06373-1) Williams & Wilkins.

Adolescent Health Care: A Practical Guide. 2nd rev. ed. Lawrence S. Neinstein. (Illus.). 1112p. 1991. 59.00 (0-683-06374-X) Williams & Wilkins.

***Adolescent Health Legislation: State Action 1992-1994.** Melissa Hough-Savage. 36p. 1994. 10.00 (1-55516-610-5, 6132) Natl Conf State Legis.

***Adolescent Health Problems: Behavioral Perspectives.** Ed. by Jan L. Wallander & Lawrence J. Siegel. LC 95-10042. 1995. lib. bdg. 30.00 (0-89862-113-5) Guilford Pr.

Adolescent Healthcare: Use, Costs & Problems of Access, Vol. 2. (In Adolescent Profile Ser.). 22.00 (0-89970-413-1, OP018091) AMA.

Adolescent Identity Formation. Gerald R. Adams et al. (Advances in Adolescent Development Ser.: Vol. 4). (Illus.). 320p. 1992. 52.00 (0-8039-4617-1); pap. 24.00 (0-8039-4618-X) Sage.

Adolescent in Group & Family Therapy. 2nd ed. Ed. by Max Sugar. LC 86-16157. xx, 296p. (C). 1986. pap. text ed. 13.95 (0-226-77964-5) U Ch Pr.

Adolescent in the American Novel since 1960. Mary Jean DeMarr & Jane S. Bakerman. 363p. 1986. 35.00 (0-8044-3067-5, F Ungar Bks) Continuum.

Adolescent in the Family. Patricia Noller & Victor Callan. (Adolescence & Society Ser.). 350p. 1991. 72.50 (0-415-01089-6, A4928); pap. 16.95 (0-415-01090-X, A4932) Routledge.

Adolescent in the Family: A Study of Personality Development in the Home Environment. White House Conference on Child Health & Protection Staff. LC 79-169401. (Family in America Ser.). 478p. 1979. reprint ed. 28.95 (0-405-03878-X) Ayer.

Adolescent Language Disorders: A Video Inservice for Educators, 8 bks., Set. Vicki A. Reed & Marcia Miles. 251p. (C). 1989. 450.00 (0-930599-54-3) Thinking Pubns.

Adolescent Life Experiences. 3rd ed. Gerald R. Adams et al. LC 93-14517. 1994. text ed. 47.95 (0-534-16236-3) Brooks-Cole.

Adolescent Lifeworld: Theoretical & Empirical Orientations in Socialization Processes of Dutch Youth. F. J. Van der Linden. 256p. 1991. pap. 36.00 (90-265-1151-5, Pub. by Swets Pub Serv NE) Taylor & Francis.

Adolescent Literacy: What Works & Why. 2nd ed. Judith Davidson & David Koppenhaver. LC 92-13812. (Reference Library of Social Science: Vol. 828). 352p. 1993. 55.00 (0-8153-0877-9); pap. 18.95 (0-8153-0920-1) Garland.

Adolescent Literature As a Complement to the Classics. Ed. by Joan F. Kaywell. (Illus.). 272p. (Orig.). (YA). (gr. 7-12). 1992. pap. text ed. 27.95 (0-926842-23-4) CG Pubs Inc.

***Adolescent Literature As a Complement to the Classics, Vol. 2.** Ed. by Joan F. Kaywell. (Illus.). 296p. (Orig.). (YA). (gr. 7-12). 1994. pap. text ed. 27.95 (0-926842-43-9) CG Pubs Inc.

***Adolescent Medicine.** Ronald Shenker. LC 93-45850. (Monographs in Clinical Pediatrics: Vol. 7). 1994. text ed. 65.00 (3-7186-5509-8) Gordon & Breach.

Adolescent Medicine. 2nd ed. Adele D. Hofmann & Donald E. Greydanus. 631p. 1989. boxed 90.00 (0-8385-0075-7, A0075-0) Appleton & Lange.

Adolescent Medicine: A Practical Guide. Strasburg. 1991. 56.00 (0-316-81872-0) Little.

Adolescent Medicine: Topics, Vol. 2. Ed. by Ralph I. Lopez. LC 76-17896. (Illus.). 232p. 1980. text ed. 45.00 (0-88331-107-0) Luce.

Adolescent Medicine - Psychiatry - Dermatology - Endocrine & Metabolism - Office Pediatrics. S. J. Emans et al. (Current Opinion in Pediatrics, 1993 Ser.). (Illus.). 128p. (Orig.). 1993. pap. text ed. 34.95 (1-85922-016-9) Current Science.

***Adolescent Medicine Psychiatry Dermatology.** Ed. by Anders. Tr. by Hansen & Schachner. (Current Opinion in Pediatrics Ser.). (Illus.). 510p. (Orig.). 1994. pap. text ed. 34.95 (1-85922-639-6) Current Science.

***Adolescent Molester.** William Breer. (Illus.). 240p. 1987. pap. 29.95 (0-398-06028-2) C C Thomas.

Adolescent Molester. William Breer. (Illus.). 240p. (C). 1987. 48.95x (0-398-05351-0) C C Thomas.

Adolescent Mothers in Later Life. Frank F. Furstenberg, Jr. et al. LC 87-709. (Human Development in Cultural & Historical Contexts Ser.). 224p. 1987. 44.95 (0-521-33417-9) Cambridge U Pr.

Adolescent Mothers in Later Life. Frank F. Furstenberg, Jr. et al. (Human Development in Cultural & Historical Contexts Ser.). (Illus.). 204p. (C). 1989. pap. 18.95 (0-521-37968-7) Cambridge U Pr.

Adolescent Nutrition. Ed. by Myron Winick. LC 81-19748. (Current Concepts in Nutrition Ser.: No. 11). 196p. reprint ed. pap. 55.90 (0-7837-3482-4, 2057815) Bks Demand.

***Adolescent Nutrition: Assessment & Management.** Ed. by Vaughn I. Rickert. LC 95-7376. (Series in Clinical Nutrition). 1995. write for info. (0-412-05661-5) Chapman & Hall.

Adolescent Obstetrics & Gynecology. A. Karen Kreutner & Dorothy Reycroft-Hollingsworth. (Illus.). 1978. 66.50 (0-8151-5200-0, Yr Bk Med Pubs) Mosby Yr Bk.

Adolescent Obstetrics & Gynecology. Ed. by A. K. Kreutner & Dorothy R. Hollingsworth. LC 77-95229. (Illus.). 675p. reprint ed. pap. 180.00 (0-685-33216-0, 2056917) Bks Demand.

Adolescent-Parental Separation. Michael Bloom. LC 79-13928. 1980. text ed. 24.95 (0-89876-035-6) Gardner Pr.

Adolescent Parenthood. Ed. by Max Sugar. LC 82-21610. 237p. 1984. text ed. 29.95 (0-88331-108-9) Luce.

Adolescent Passage: Developmental Issues. Peter Blos. LC 78-61245. 538p. (Orig.). 1979. 70.00 (0-8236-0095-5) Intl Univs Pr.

Adolescent Peer Pressure: Theory, Corelates, & Program Implications for Drug Abuse Prevention. 1986. lib. bdg. 250.00 (0-8490-3503-1) Gordon Pr.

Adolescent Period: A Graphic Atlas. F. K. Shuttleworth. (SRCD Ser.: Vol. 14, No. 1). 1949. 21.00 (0-527-01547-4) Periodicals Srv.

Adolescent Personality & Behavior: MMPI Patterns of Normal, Delinquent, Dropout, & Other Outcomes. Starke R. Hathaway & Elio D. Monachesi. LC 63-23057. 207p. reprint ed. pap. 59.00 (0-8357-3331-9, 2039556) Bks Demand.

***Adolescent Portraits: Identity, Relationships, Challenges.** 2nd ed. Andrew Garrod. LC 94-34869. 1994. pap. text ed. write for info. (0-205-15823-4) Allyn.

Adolescent Pregnancy & Parenthood: An Annotated Guide. Ann Creighton-Zollar. LC 89-25506. (Reference Books on Family Issues). 268p. 1990. 42.00 (0-8240-4295-6) Garland.

Adolescent Pregnancy & Prenatal Care. Karen Poirier-Brode. Ed. by J. J. Head. LC 84-71144. (Carolina Biology Readers Ser.: No. 148). (Illus.). 16p. (Orig.). (YA). (gr. 10 up). 1987. pap. text ed. 2.75 (0-89278-348-6, 45-9748) Carolina Biological.

Adolescent Pregnancy in an Urban Environment: Issues, Programs, & Evaluation. Janet B. Hardy & Laurie S. Zabin. (Illus.). 492p. (Orig.). (C). 1991. lib. bdg. 74.00 (0-87766-519-2); pap. text ed. 43.50 (0-87766-520-6) Urban Inst.

Adolescent Pregnancy Prevention: A Guidebook for Communities. Claire D. Brindis. (Illus.). 280p. (Orig.). 1991. pap. 24.50 (1-879552-00-0) Stanford CRDP.

Adolescent Pregnancy: The Challenge: A Framework for Prevention & Parenting. (Illus.). 150p. (Orig.). (C). 1993. pap. text ed. 34.95 (0-7881-0083-1) Diane Pub.

Adolescent Prejudice. Charles Y. Glock et al. 260p. reprint ed. text ed. 26.95 (0-8290-2350-X); reprint ed. pap. text ed. 8.95 (0-8290-0281-2) Irvington.

Adolescent Problem Behaviors: Issues & Research. Ed. by Robert D. Ketterlinus & Michael E. Lamb. 240p. 1994. text ed. 49.95 (0-8058-1156-7); pap. 24.95 (0-8058-1157-5) L Erlbaum Assocs.

Adolescent Psychiatric Nursing. Hogarth. (Illus.). 320p. 1990. pap. 27.95 (0-8016-3229-3) Mosby Yr Bk.

Adolescent Psychiatry, Vol. 7. Ed. by Sherman C. Feinstein & Peter L. Giovacchini. LC 70-147017. 1979. lib. bdg. 27.50 (0-226-24052-5) U Ch Pr.

Adolescent Psychiatry, Vol. 8. Sherman C. Feinstein & Peter L. Giovacchini. LC 70-147017. 544p. 1981. lib. bdg. 27.50 (0-226-24053-3) U Ch Pr.

An Asterisk (*) at the beginning of an entry indicates that the title is appearing in BIP for the first time.

Adolescent Psychiatry, Vol. 9. Ed. by Sherman C. Feinstein & Peter L. Giovacchini. LC 70-147017. 5841p. 1982. lib. bdg. 32.95 (*0-226-24054-1*) U Ch Pr.

Adolescent Psychiatry, Vol. 10. Ed. by Sherman C. Feinstein et al. LC 70-147017. 624p. 1983. lib. bdg. 32. 95 (*0-226-24056-8*) U Ch Pr.

Adolescent Psychiatry, Vol. 11. Ed. by Max Sugar. LC 70-147017. 300p. (C). 1984. lib. bdg. 24.95 (*0-226-77962-9*) U Ch Pr.

Adolescent Psychiatry, Vol. 12. Ed. by Sherman C. Feinstein et al. LC 70-147017. 570p. (C). 1985. lib. bdg. 32.50 (*0-226-24058-4*) U Ch Pr.

Adolescent Psychiatry, Vol. 14. Ed. by Sherman C. Feinstein. 648p. (C). 1987. lib. bdg. 37.50 (*0-226-24060-6*) U Ch Pr.

Adolescent Psychiatry, Vol. 15. Ed. by Sherman C. Feinstein & Aaron H. Esman. 600p. 1988. lib. bdg. 40.00 (*0-226-24061-4*) U Ch Pr.

Adolescent Psychiatry, Vol. 17. Ed. by Sherman C. Feinstein. 600p. 1990. lib. bdg. 40.00 (*0-226-24063-0*) U Ch Pr.

Adolescent Psychiatry, Vol. 19. Ed. by Sherman C. Feinstein & Richard C. Marohn. 592p. 1993. lib. bdg. 44.95 (*0-226-24065-7*) U Ch Pr.

***Adolescent Psychiatry, Vol. 21.** Ed. by Richard C. Marohn. 1996. write for info. (*0-88163-195-7*) Analytic Pr.

***Adolescent Psychiatry, Vol. 22.** Ed. by Richard C. Marohn. 1997. write for info. (*0-88163-196-5*) Analytic Pr.

***Adolescent Psychiatry, Vol. 23.** Ed. by Richard C. Marohn. 1998. write for info. (*0-88163-197-3*) Analytic Pr.

***Adolescent Psychiatry, Vol. 24.** Ed. by Richard C. Marohn. 1999. write for info. (*0-88163-198-1*) Analytic Pr.

***Adolescent Psychiatry Vol. 20: The Annals of the American Society for Adolescent Psychiatry.** Ed. by Richard C. Marohn. 552p. 1995. 45.00 (*0-88163-194-9*) Analytic Pr.

Adolescent Psychiatry, Vol. 13: Developmental & Clinical Studies. Ed. by Sherman C. Feinstein. LC 70-147017. xii, 592p. (C). 1986. lib. bdg. 35.00 (*0-226-24059-2*) U Ch Pr.

Adolescent Psychiatry, Vol. 16: Developmental & Clinical Studies. Ed. by Sherman C. Feinstein. LC 70-147017. 600p. 1989. lib. bdg. 40.00 (*0-226-24062-2*) U Ch Pr.

Adolescent Psychiatry, Vol. 18: Developmental & Clinical Studies. Ed. by Sherman C. Feinstein. 586p. 1992. lib. bdg. 42.95 (*0-226-24064-9*) U Ch Pr.

Adolescent Psychiatry, Vol. 6: Developmental & Clinical Studies. Ed. by Sherman C. Feinstein & Peter L. Giovacchini. (Adolescent Psychiatry Ser.). 1979. lib. bdg. 27.50 (*0-226-24051-7*) U Ch Pr.

***Adolescent Psychology: A Developmental View.** 3rd ed. Norman A. Sprinthall. LC 94-25518. 1995. pap. text ed. write for info. (*0-07-060544-0*) McGraw.

Adolescent Psychology: A Developmental View. 2nd ed. Norman A. Sprinthall. 1990. 47.50 (*0-394-37516-5*) Random.

Adolescent Psychology: Medical Analysis Index with Research Bibliography. Sylvia S. Gelstein. LC 85-47575. 150p. 1987. 39.50 (*0-88164-324-6*); pap. 34.50 (*0-88164-325-4*) ABBE Pubs Assn.

Adolescent Psychotherapy. Ed. by Marcia Slomowitz. LC 90-871. (Clinical Practice Ser.: No. 16). 200p. 1991. text ed. 31.00 (*0-88048-181-1*) Am Psychiatric.

Adolescent Radioactive Black Belt Hamsters: America the Beautiful. Chin & Parsonovich. (Illus.). 1990. 29.95 (*0-913035-42-4*); pap. 9.95 (*0-913035-43-2*) Eclipse Bks.

Adolescent Relapse Prevention Workbook: A Guide to Staying Off Drugs & Alcohol. Dennis Daley & Charles Sproule. 1991. 11.50 (*1-55691-077-0*) Learning Pubns.

Adolescent Relations with Mothers, Fathers, & Friends. James Youniss & Jacqueline Smollar. LC 84-28067. viii, 202p. 1987. reprint ed. pap. text ed. 9.95 (*0-226-96488-4*) U Ch Pr.

Adolescent Reproductive Behavior. 178p. 1988. 22.00 (*92-1-151173-9*, E. 88. XIII.8) UN.

Adolescent Reproductive Behaviour, Vol. II: Evidence from Developing Countries. 139p. 17.50 (*92-1-151184-4*, E. 89.XIII.10) UN.

Adolescent Reproductive Health. Smith & Mumford. LC 83-20492. 1985. text ed. 31.95 (*0-89876-096-8*) Gardner Pr.

***Adolescent Rights: Are Young People Equal Under the Law?** Keith Greenberg. (Issues of Our Times Ser.). (Illus.). 64p. (J). (gr. 5-8). 1995. lib. bdg. 15.98 (*0-8050-3877-9*) TFC Bks NY.

Adolescent Risk Taking. Ed. by Nancy J. Bell & Robert W. Bell. (Illus.). 192p. 1992. text ed. 46.00 (*0-8039-5064-0*); pap. text ed. 21.95 (*0-8039-5065-9*) Sage.

***Adolescent Rorschach Responses: Developmental Trends from 10 to 16 Years.** 2nd rev. ed. Louise B. Ames et al. LC 94-49579. (Master Work Ser.). (Illus.). 1995. pap. 35.00 (*1-56821-466-9*) Aronson.

Adolescent Runaways Causes & Consequences. Mark D. Janus et al. LC 86-45037. 176p. 1987. pap. 14.95 (*0-669-15280-3*) Free Pr.

Adolescent Self. David B. Wexler. 1991. 22.95 (*0-393-70114-X*) Norton.

Adolescent Self-Disclosure: Its Facilitation Through Themes, Therapeutic Techniques & Interview Conditions. Marlene C. Mills. LC 84-47529. (American University Studies: Psychology: Ser. VIII, Vol. 3). 198p. (C). 1985. text ed. 23.50 (*0-8204-0115-3*) P Lang Pubs.

Adolescent Separation Anxiety, Set. Henry G. Hansburg. 60p. (Orig.). 1980. pap. 50.00 (*0-89874-293-5*) Krieger.

Adolescent Sex & Love Addicts. Eric Griffin-Shelley. LC 94-1149. 184p. 1994. text ed. 49.95 (*0-275-94681-9*, Praeger Pubs) Greenwood.

Adolescent Sex Roles & Social Change. Lloyd B. Lueptow. LC 83-7842. (Illus.). 352p. 1984. text ed. 52.00 (*0-231-05712-1*) Col U Pr.

Adolescent Sexual Behavior & Childbearing. Laurie S. Zabin & Sarah C. Hayward. (Developmental Clinical Psychology & Psychiatry Ser.: Vol. 26). (Illus.). 140p. (C). 1993. text ed. 37.00 (*0-8039-4258-3*); pap. text ed. 16.95 (*0-8039-4259-1*) Sage.

Adolescent Sexualities: Overviews & Principles of Intervention. Ed. by Paula Allen-Meares & David Shore. LC 86-228200. (Journal of Social Work & Human Sexuality: Vol. 5, No. 1). 114p. 1986. text ed. 32.95 (*0-86656-569-8*) Haworth Pr.

Adolescent Sexuality. Ed. by Thomas P. Gullotta et al. (Advances in Adolescent Development Ser.: Vol. 5). (Illus.). 248p. (C). 1992. 52.00 (*0-8039-4772-0*); pap. 24. 00 (*0-8039-4773-9*) Sage.

***Adolescent Sexuality.** Jules H. Masserman & Victor M. Uribe. 118p. 1989. pap. 16.95 (*0-398-06270-6*) C C Thomas.

Adolescent Sexuality. Jules H. Masserman & Victor M. Uribe. 118p. (C). 1989. text ed. 31.95x (*0-398-05629-3*) C C Thomas.

***Adolescent Sexuality: A Comprehensive Peer-Parent Curriculum.** Lois A. Wodarski & John S. Wodarski. LC 95-7434. 168p. (C). 1995. text ed. 43.95x (*0-398-06516-0*); pap. text ed. 29.95x (*0-398-06517-9*) C C Thomas.

Adolescent Sexuality: New Challenges for Social Work. Ed. by Paula Allen-Meares & Constance H. Shapiro. LC 89-1668. (Journal of Social Work & Human Sexuality: Vol. 8, No. 1). (Illus.). 178p. 1989. text ed. 39.95 (*0-86656-901-4*) Haworth Pr.

Adolescent Sexuality & Gynecology. Donald E. Greydanus et al. LC 89-12765. 326p. reprint ed. pap. 93.00 (*0-7837-2712-7*, 2043091) Bks Demand.

Adolescent Sexuality & Pregnancy. Patricia Voydanoff & Brenda W. Donnelly. (Family Studies Text Ser.: Vol. 12). (Illus.). 136p. (C). 1990. text ed. 37.00 (*0-8039-3385-1*); pap. text ed. 16.95 (*0-8039-3386-X*) Sage.

Adolescent Sexuality & Teenage Pregnancy: A Selected, Annotated Bibliography with Summary Forewords. Ed. by Karen R. Stewart. 1976. pap. 2.00 (*0-89055-117-0*) Carolina Pop Ctr.

Adolescent Sexuality in Social Context. Susan M. Moore & Doreen A. Rosenthal. LC 93-9869. (Adolescence & Society Ser.). 272p. 1993. 59.95 (*0-415-07527-0*, B0890); pap. 17.95 (*0-415-07528-9*, B0894) Routledge.

Adolescent Social Behavior & Health. Ed. by Charles E. Irwin, Jr. LC 85-644581. (New Directions for Child Development Ser.: No. CD 37). 1987. 17.95 (*1-55542-939-4*) Jossey-Bass.

Adolescent Socialization in Cross-Cultural Perspective. Ed. by Irving Tallman et al. (Monograph). 1983. text ed. 51. 00 (*0-12-683180-7*) Acad Pr.

Adolescent Society: The Social Life of the Teenager & Its Impact on Education. James S. Coleman et al. LC 81-1737. (Illus.). xvi, 368p. 1981. reprint ed. text ed. 65.00 (*0-313-22934-1*, COADS, Greenwood Pr) Greenwood.

Adolescent Spine. Ed. by N. A. Keim. (Illus.). 254p. 1981. 88.00 (*0-387-90612-6*) Spr-Verlag.

Adolescent Spirituality: Pastoral Ministry for High School & College Youth. Charles M. Shelton. 1989. pap. 11.95 (*0-8245-0917-X*) Crossroad NY.

Adolescent Spirituality: Pastoral Ministry for High School & College Youth. rev. ed. Charles M. Shelton. 366p. 1983. 12.75 (*0-8294-0422-8*) Loyola Univ Pr.

Adolescent Storm & Stress: An Evaluation of the Mead-Freeman Controversy. James E. Cote. (Research Monographs in Adolescence). 200p. 1994. text ed. 49.95 (*0-8058-1506-6*) L Erlbaum Assocs.

Adolescent Stress: Causes & Consequences. Ed. by Mary E. Colten & Susan Gore. (Social Institutions & Social Change Ser.). 344p. 1991. lib. bdg. 47.95 (*0-202-30420-5*); pap. text ed. 22.95 (*0-202-30421-3*) Aldine de Gruyter.

***Adolescent Struggle for Selfhood & Identity.** John J. Mitchell. 218p. (Orig.). (C). 1992. pap. text ed. 18.95x (*1-55059-050-2*) Temeron Bks.

Adolescent Subcultures & Delinquency. Herman Schwendinger & Julia S. Schwendinger. LC 84-26329. 544p. 1985. text ed. 85.00 (*0-275-90161-0*, C0161, Praeger Pubs); pap. text ed. 24.95 (*0-275-91656-1*, B1656, Praeger Pubs) Greenwood.

Adolescent Substance Abuse: A Comprehensive Guide to Theory & Practice. Y. Kaminer. (Critical Issues in Psychiatry Ser.). (Illus.). 256p. (C). 1994. 37.50 (*0-306-44692-8*) Plenum.

Adolescent Substance Abuse: A Guide to Prevention & Treatment. Ed. by Mark Singer & Richard E. Isralowitz. LC 83-13015. (Child & Youth Services Ser.: Vol. 6, Nos. 1 & 2). 123p. 1983. text ed. 29.95 (*0-86656-185-4*) Haworth Pr.

***Adolescent Substance Abuse: An Empirical-Based Health Paradigm.** John S. Wodarski & Marvin D. Feit. LC 94-29995. (Illus.). 220p. 1995. lib. bdg. 29.95 (*1-56024-879-3*) Haworth Pr.

***Adolescent Substance Abuse: Asesssment, Treatment, & Prevention.** Oscar G. Bukstein. LC 94-40264. (Series on Personality Processes). 1995. text ed. 39.95 (*0-471-55080-9*) Wiley.

Adolescent Substance Abuse: Etiology, Treatment & Prevention. Gary W. Lawson & Ann W. Lawson. LC 92-11363. 576p. 1992. pap. 41.00 (*0-8342-0254-9*) Aspen Pub.

Adolescent Suicidal Behavior. David K. Curran. LC 87-8650. 208p. (C). 1987. text ed. 55.00 (*0-89116-618-1*); pap. text ed. 25.00 (*0-89116-781-1*) Hemisp Pub.

Adolescent Suicidal Behavior: A Family Systems Model. Roma J. Heillig. LC 83-3594. (Research in Clinical Psychology Ser.: No. 7). 169p. reprint ed. pap. 48.20 (*0-8357-1390-3*, 2070391) Bks Demand.

Adolescent Suicide. Andre Haim. LC 73-9250. 310p. 1975. text ed. 42.50 (*0-8236-0090-4*) Intl Univs Pr.

Adolescent Suicide: A School-Based Approach to Assessment & Intervention. William G. Kirk. LC 93-84471. 192p. (Orig.). 1993. pap. text ed. 14.95 (*0-87822-336-3*, 4672) Res Press.

Adolescent Suicide: Assessment & Intervention. Alan L. Berman & David A. Jobes. 283p. (Orig.). 1991. pap. text ed. 17.50 (*1-55798-114-0*); boxed 35.00 (*1-55798-107-8*) Am Psychol.

Adolescent Suicide: Identification & Intervention. 40p. (Orig.). 1987. pap. text ed. 3.95 (*0-9613416-5-3*) Comm Intervention.

Adolescent Suicide: Recognition, Treatment & Prevention. Ed. by Gordon Northrup & Barry Garfinkel. LC 89-19773. (Residential Treatment for Children & Youth Ser.: Vol. 7, No. 1). (Illus.). 116p. 1990. text ed. 29.95 (*0-86656-949-9*) Haworth Pr.

Adolescent Suicide: With a New Preface. Jerry Jacobs. 1980. 26.50 (*0-8290-0113-1*); pap. text ed. 12.95 (*0-8290-0114-X*) Irvington.

Adolescent Through Fiction: A Psychological Approach. Norman Kiell. LC 59-6716. 521p. 1965. text ed. 62.50 (*0-8236-0080-7*); pap. text ed. 24.95 (*0-8236-8006-1*, 20080) Intl Univs Pr.

Adolescente de Voluntad Firme. J. Dobson. (SPA.). Date not set. 1.79 (*0-685-74901-0*, 497418) Editorial Unilit.

Adolescentes Como Padres - La Jornada de tu Embarazo y el Nacimiento de tu Bebe: Como Cuidar de ti Misma y de tu Recien Nacido si Eres una Adolescente Embarazada. Jeanne W. Lindsay & Jean Brunelli. Tr. by Argentina Palacios. LC 92-43626. (Illus.). 24p. (SPA.). 1993. teacher ed 2.50 (*0-930934-72-5*); student ed 2.50 (*0-930934-71-7*); pap. text ed. 9.95 (*0-930934-69-5*) Morning Glory.

Adolescents. 2nd ed. Gary M. Ingersoll. 448p. (C). 1989. Casebound. boxed write for info. (*0-13-008665-7*) P-H.

Adolescents: Theoretical & Helping Perspectives. Inger P. Davis. LC 84-20175. 1985. lib. bdg. 60.50 (*0-89838-165-7*) Kluwer Ac.

***Adolescents, Alcohol & Drugs: A Practical Guide for Those Who Work with Young People.** Judith H. Jaynes & Cheryl A. Rugg. 210p. 1988. pap. 24.95 (*0-398-06180-7*) C C Thomas.

Adolescents, Alcohol & Drugs: A Practical Guide for Those Who Work with Young People. Judith H. Jaynes & Cheryl A. Rugg. 210p. (C). 1988. text ed. 39.95x (*0-398-05393-6*) C C Thomas.

***Adolescents & ADD: Gaining the Advantage.** Quinn. 128p. 1995. pap. 12.95 (*0-945354-70-3*) Brunner-Mazel.

Adolescents & AIDS: Stopping the Time Bomb. (State Legislative Reports: Vol. 15, No. 12). 11p. 1990. 5.00 (*1-55516-268-1*, 7302-1512) Natl Conf State Legis.

Adolescents & Moral Development. Robert Coles. write for info. (*0-318-65156-4*) Addison-Wesley.

Adolescents & Schools: Improving the Fit. Adria Steinberg. (HEL Reprint Ser.: No. 1). 96p. 1993. pap. 15.00 (*1-883433-00-2*) Harv Educ Letter.

***Adolescents & the HIV-AIDS Epidemic: Stemming the Tide.** Susan S. Messina. 41p. 1993. 15.00 (*1-55516-646-6*, 6646) Natl Conf State Legis.

***Adolescents & the Media: Medical & Psychological Impact.** Victor C. Strasburger. LC 94-45245. (Developmental Clinical Psychology & Psychiatry Ser.: Vol. 33). 144p. 1995. text ed. 37.00 (*0-8039-5499-9*); pap. text ed. 16.95 (*0-8039-5500-6*) Sage.

***Adolescents & Their Families.** George H. Orvin. 224p. 1995. boxed 21.95 (*0-88048-651-1*, 8651) Am Psychiatric.

Adolescents & Their Families: An Introduction to Assessment & Intervention. Mark Worden. LC 91-7909. (Illus.). 224p. 1991. lib. bdg. 39.95 (*1-56024-101-2*); pap. 14.95 (*1-56024-102-0*) Haworth Pr.

Adolescents & Their Families: Paths of Ego Development. Stuart T. Hauser et al. 285p. 1991. text ed. 32.95 (*0-02-914260-1*) Free Pr.

Adolescents & Their Music: If It's Too Loud, You're Too Old. Ed. by Jonathon S. Epstein. LC 93-33839. (New Directions in Sociology; Reference Library of Social Science: Vol. 804). 434p. 1994. 55.00 (*0-8153-0614-8*, SS804) Garland.

Adolescents at Risk: A Guide to Fiction & Nonfiction for Young Adults, Parents, & Professionals. Joan F. Kaywell. LC 93-20834. 288p. 1993. text ed. 45.00 (*0-313-29039-3*) Greenwood.

Adolescents at Risk: Prevalence & Prevention. Joy G. Dryfoos. (Illus.). 288p. 1991. reprint ed. pap. 14.95 (*0-19-507268-5*) OUP.

Adolescents, Family, & Friends: Social Support after Parents Divorce or Remarriage. Kandi Stinson. LC 90-7800. 184p. 1991. text ed. 49.95 (*0-275-93465-9*, C3465, Praeger Pubs) Greenwood.

***Adolescents Grow in Groups: Experiences in Adolescent Group Psychotherapy.** Ed. by Irving H. Berkovitz. LC 94-41040. 268p. 1995. pap. 30.00 (*1-56821-442-1*) Aronson.

***Adolescents in Fiji.** Willie Dari et al. 1994. pap. 15.00 (*0-9606272-2-7*) Macduff Pr.

Adolescents in Foster Families. Ed. by Jane Aldgate et al. LC 89-2359. 192p. (Orig.). (C). 1989. pap. 26.95 (*0-925065-05-6*) Lyceum IL.

Adolescents in School. Claude E. Buxton. LC 72-91290. 190p. reprint ed. pap. 54.20 (*0-8357-5114-7*, 2021986) Bks Demand.

Adolescents in School & Society. Gary M. Ingersoll. 480p. (C). 1982. teacher ed 2.00 (*0-669-02326-4*); text ed. 25. 50 (*0-669-02325-6*) Heath.

Adolescents in Wartime. Ed. by James H. Bossard & Eleanor S. Boll. LC 74-1668. (Children & Youth Ser.). 180p. 1974. reprint ed. 20.95 (*0-405-05947-7*) Ayer.

Adolescents, Literature & Work with Youth. Ed. by Pamela J. Weiner & Ruth M. Stein. LC 84-29001. (Child & Youth Services Ser.: Vol. 7, Nos. 1 & 2). 137p. 1985. text ed. 39.95 (*0-86656-120-X*) Haworth Pr.

Adolescents out of Step: Their Treatment in a Psychiatric Hospital. Peter G. Beckett. LC 65-13538. (Lafayette Clinic Monographs in Psychiatry: No. 2). 191p. reprint ed. pap. 54.50 (*0-8357-5115-5*, 2027653) Bks Demand.

Adolescents, Sex & Contraception. Ed. by D. Byrne & W. A. Fisher. 336p. 1983. 59.95 (*0-89859-217-8*) L Erlbaum Assocs.

Adolescents Worlds: Drug Use & Athletic Activity. M. F. Stuck. LC 90-34288. 184p. 1990. text ed. 49.95 (*0-275-93647-3*, C3647, Praeger Pubs) Greenwood.

Adoleszentenpsychosen. M. H. Friedrich. (Bibliotheca Psychiatrica Ser.: No. 163). (Illus.). xii, 144p. 1983. pap. 55.25 (*3-8055-3640-2*) S Karger.

Adolf Galland: A Pilot's Life in War & Peace. Anton Weiler & Werner Held. 150p. 1986. pap. 14.95 (*0-912173-08-4*) Champlin Museum.

Adolf Glassbrenner: His Development from "Jungdeutscher" to "Vormaerzler" Heinz Bulmahn. (German Language & Literature Monographs: No. 6). x, 159p. 1978. 39.00x (*90-272-0966-9*, GLLM 6) Benjamins North Am.

Adolf Hiremy-Hirschl: The Beauty of Decline. Edward A. Maser & Gert Schiff. Ed. by Sue Taylor. LC 84-60648. (Illus.). 32p. (Orig.). 1984. pap. 8.00 (*0-9613449-0-3*) R Ramsay Gallery.

***Adolf Hitler.** Eleanor H. Ayer. LC 95-1277. (Importance Of Ser.). (J). 1995. 16.95 (*1-56006-072-7*) Lucent Bks.

Adolf Hitler. Eileen Heyes. LC 93-31269. (YA). (gr. 7 up). 1994. lib. bdg. 16.90 (*1-56294-343-X*) Millbrook Pr.

Adolf Hitler. Bob Italia. Ed. by Rosemary Wallner. LC 90-82613. (World War Two Leaders Ser.). (Illus.). 32p. (J). (gr. 4). 1990. lib. bdg. 11.96 (*0-939179-79-2*) Abdo & Dghtrs.

Adolf Hitler. John Toland. 688p. 1986. pap. 12.95 (*0-345-33848-0*); mass mkt. 5.95 (*0-345-34317-4*) Ballantine.

Adolf Hitler. John Toland. 1035p. 1992. pap. 18.95 (*0-385-42053-6*, Anchor NY) Doubleday.

Adolf Hitler. Dennis Wepman. (World Leaders - Past & Present Ser.). (Illus.). 112p. (YA). (gr. 5 up). 1985. lib. bdg. 17.95 (*0-87754-578-2*); pap. 9.95 (*0-7910-0575-5*) Chelsea Hse.

Adolf Hitler: A Psychological Interpretation of His Views on Architecture, Art & Music. Sherree O. Zalampas. LC 89-83365. 171p. (C). 1990. lib. bdg. 34.95 (*0-87972-487-0*); pap. 16.95 (*0-87972-488-9*) Bowling Green Univ.

Adolf Hitler: His Family, Childhood, & Youth. Bradley F. Smith. LC 66-25727. (Publication Ser.: No. 62). 1967. pap. 6.95 (*0-8179-1622-9*) Hoover Inst Pr.

Adolf Hitler: Pictures of the Life of the Fuehrer. Zigaretten Bildendienst. (Illus.). 134p. 1979. 30.00 (*0-910667-04-7*) Northstar Bks.

Adolf Hitler & the Third Reich in American Magazines, 1923-1939. Michael Zalampas. LC 89-61742. 266p. (C). 1989. lib. bdg. 35.95 (*0-87972-461-7*); pap. 18.95 (*0-87972-462-5*) Bowling Green Univ.

Adolf Loos. Panayotis Tournikiotis. LC 94-21141. (Illus.). 196p. 1994. 24.95 (*1-878271-80-6*) Princeton Arch.

***Adolf Loos: Theory & Works.** Aldo Rossi & Benedetto Gravagnuolo. (Illus.). 228p. Date not set. pap. 39.95 (*0-948835-16-8*) Dist Art Pubs.

Adolf von Harnack: Liberal Theology at Its Height. H. Martin Rumscheidt. 336p. 1991. pap. 14.00 (*0-8006-3406-3*) Augsburg Fortress.

***Adolph Gottlieb: A Retrospective.** Lawrence Alloway & Mary D. MacNaughton. (Illus.). 176p. 1995. 50.00 (*1-55595-124-4*); pap. 35.00 (*1-55595-125-2*) Hudson Hills.

Adolph Lewisohn Collection of Modern French Paintings & Sculptures. LC 68-9241. (Contemporary Art Ser.). (Illus.). 1968. reprint ed. 30.95 (*0-405-00723-X*) Ayer.

Adolph Menzel: The Graphic Work. rev. ed. Elfried Bock. (Illus.). 576p. (ENG & GER.). 1991. reprint ed. 150.00 (*1-55660-124-7*) A Wofsy Fine Arts.

***Adolph Menzel: Works in Harvard Collections.** Annette Schlagenhauff. (Illus.). 36p. 1995. pap. 7.50 (*0-916724-78-6*, 4786) Harvard Art Mus.

Adolph Rupp: Kentucky's Basketball Baron. Russell Rice. (Illus.). 250p. 1994. 22.95 (*0-915611-98-8*) Sagamore Pub.

Adolphe. Benjamin Constant. (FRE.). 1973. pap. 10.95 (*0-685-73250-9*, F59309) Fr & Eur.

Adolphe. Benjamin Constant. 282p. (FRE.). 1988. pap. 11. 95 (*0-7859-2190-7*, 2253045888) Fr & Eur.

Adolphe. Benjamin Constant. Tr. by Leonard W. Tancock. (Classics Ser.). 1980. mass mkt. 8.95 (*0-14-044134-4*, Penguin Classics) Viking Penguin.

Adolphe: Anecdote Trouvee Dans les Papiers D'un Inconnu. Benjamin Constant. Ed. by C. P. Courtney. (French Texts Ser.). 224p. (FRE.). 1989. pap. text ed. 14.95 (*0-631-16205-4*, Pub. by Duckworth UK) Focus Info Gr.

Adolphe Appia: Artist & Visionary of the Modern Theatre. Richard C. Beacham. LC 94-133. (Contemporary Theatre Studies: Vol. 6). 1994. 67.00 (*3-7186-5507-1*); pap. 30.00 (*3-7186-5508-X*) Gordon & Breach.

Adolphe Appia: Prophet of the Modern Theater: A Profile. Walther R. Volbach. LC 68-27547. (Illus.). 260p. reprint ed. pap. 74.10 (*0-8357-5116-3*, 2029785) Bks Demand.

Adolphe Appia: Texts on Theatre. Tr. & Comment by Richard C. Beacham. LC 92-28283. (Illus.). 256p. 1993. 49.95 (*0-415-06823-1*, B0356) Routledge.

A

An Asterisk (*) at the beginning of an entry indicates that the title is appearing in BIP for the first time. 65

Adolphe; le Cahier Rouge; Cecile. Benjamin Constant. (Folio Ser.: No. 514). (FRE.). pap. 9.95 (2-07-036514-X) Schoenhof.
Adolphe Quetelet As Statistician. Frank H. Hankins. LC 74-76680. (Columbia University. Studies in the Social Sciences: No. 84). reprint ed. 14.50 (0-404-51084-1) AMS Pr.
Adonais. Percy Bysshe Shelley. Ed. by Thomas J. Wise. LC 74-30284. (Shelley Society, Second Ser.: No. 1). 1886. reprint ed. 20.00 (0-404-11503-9) AMS Pr.
Adonais. Percy Bysshe Shelley. LC 92-36905. 38p. 1992. reprint ed. 40.00 (1-85477-113-2, Pub. by Woodstock Bks UK) Cassell.
Adoniram Judson. Faith C. Bailey. (Golden Oldies Ser.). 128p. Date not set. pap. 4.99 (0-8024-0287-9) Moody.
Adonis Garcia: A Picaresque Novel. Luis Zapata. Tr. by E. A. Lacey. 208p. (Orig.). 1981. lib. bdg. 25.00 (0-917342-79-8) Gay Sunshine.
Adopted & Loved Forever. Annetta E. Dellinger. (Illus.). (J). (ps-2). 1987. 5.99 (0-570-04167-8, 56-1624) Concordia.
Adopted Break Silence. Jean Paton. (Adoption Ser.). 1954. pap. 8.00 (0-318-36159-0) Orphan Voyage.
Adopted by the Eagles. Paul Goble. LC 93-24247. (Illus.). 40p. (J). (ps up). 1994. text ed. 15.95 (0-02-736575-1, Bradbury S&S) S&S Childrens.
Adopted Child: Family Life with Double Parenthood. Christa Hoffman-Riem. 276p. 1989. 39.95 (0-88738-241-X) Transaction Pubs.
Adopted Child Comes of Age. Lois Rayner. 1980. 40.00 (0-317-05782-0, Pub. by Natl Inst Soc Work) St Mut.
Adopted Child Comes of Age. Lois Raynor. LC 79-41348. (London. National Institute for Social Work Training. National Institute Social Services Library: No. 36). 176p. reprint ed. pap. 50.20 (0-8357-5117-1, 2023180) Bks Demand.
Adopted Children. rev. ed. Jan De Hartog. 268p. 1987. pap. text ed. 13.95 (0-915361-65-5) Modan-Adama Bks.
Adopted Children at Home & School: The Integration after Eight Years of 116 Thai Children in the Dutch Society. R. A. Hoksbergen et al. 106p. 1987. pap. 15.50 (90-265-0845-X, Pub. by Swets Pub Serv NE) Taylor & Francis.
Adopted from Asia: How It Feels to Grow up in America. Frances M. Koh. LC 93-72354. 96p. (J). (gr. 5 up). 1993. 15.95 (0-9606090-6-7) EastWest Pr.
Adopted Like Me. Jeffrey R. LaCure. 24p. (J). (ps-2). 1993. pap. 9.95 (0-9635717-0-2) Adoption Advocate.
Adopted One. Sara B. Stein. (Open Family Ser.). (Illus.). (J). (gr. k-6). 1979. 12.95 (0-8027-6346-4); pap. 8.95 (0-8027-7224-2) Walker & Co.
Adopted Son of Salem. Polly S. Buck. 1971. 10.95 (0-87233-020-6) Bauhan.
Adopted Woman. Katrina Maxtone-Graham. 1982. write for info. (0-318-56975-2) Eleventh Hour.
Adopted Woman. Katrina Maxtone-Graham. LC 82-71563. 1983. 21.95 (0-943362-00-8) Remi Bks.
Adopting a Child. O'Neil & Brown. (Changing Behavior Through Understanding Ser.). 20p. (Orig.). 1991. pap. text ed. 2.95 (1-56456-046-5) W Gladden Found.
Adopting a Child: A Guide for People Interested in Adoption. P. Chennells & C. Hammond. (C). 1989. 39.00 (0-903534-91-6, Pub. by Brit Ag for Adopt & Fost UK) St Mut.
Adopting a Child Independently in the State of Florida. Mary A. Scherer. (Orig.). 1993. pap. 5.95 (1-881962-03-2) Adopt Adv Pr.
Adopting a Stream: A Northwest Handbook. Steve Yates. 126p. 1989. pap. 14.95 (0-295-96796-X) U of Wash Pr.
Adopting after Infertility. Patricia Irwin Johnston. LC 92-21825. 320p. 1995. pap. 14.00 (0-944934-10-2) Perspect Indiana.
Adopting Cats & Kittens: A Care & Training Guide. Connie Jankowski. LC 92-29844. (Illus.). 128p. 1993. pap. 8.00 (0-87605-736-9) Howell Bk.
Adopting Conservation on the Farm: An International Perspective of the Socioeconomics of Soil & Water Conservation. Ed. by Ted L. Napier et al. 530p. 1994. pap. text ed. 40.00 (0-935734-31-7) Soil & Water Conserv.
Adopting in America: How to Adopt Within One Year. Randall B. Hicks. 344p. (Orig.). 1993. pap. 13.95 (0-9631638-9-2) Wordslinger.
***Adopting in America: How to Adopt Within One Year.** Randall B. Hicks. LC 95-61149. 344p. (Orig.). 1995. pap. 14.95 (0-9631638-0-9) Wordslinger.
***Adopting in California: How to Adopt Within One Year.** rev. ed. Randall B. Hicks. LC 95-61157. 144p. 1995. pap. 9.95 (0-9631638-1-7) Wordslinger.
Adopting in California: How to Find a Child. Randall Hicks. 1992. pap. 9.95 (0-9631638-6-8) Wordslinger.
***Adopting Lasting Treasure.** Jackie Johnson. 176p. (Orig.). 1994. pap. 6.95 (0-89228-020-4) Impact Christian.
Adopting New Medical Technology Vol. IV, Vol. 4. Institute of Medicine, Committee on Technological Innovation in Medicine Staff. Ed. by Annetine C. Gelijns & Holly V. Dawkins. (Medical Innovation at the Crossroads Ser.). 240p. (Orig.). (C). 1994. pap. text ed. 27.00 (0-309-05035-9) Natl Acad Pr.
Adopting Older Children. Alfred Kadushin. LC 71-125918. 245p. 1970. text ed. 39.50 (0-231-03322-2) Col U Pr.
Adopting or Fostering a Sexually Abused Child. Catherine Macaskill. 176p. 1992. pap. 34.95 (0-7134-6760-6, Pub. by Batsford UK) Trafalgar.
Adopting the Older Child. Claudia L. Jewett. LC 77-26973. 1978. pap. 9.95 (0-916782-09-3) Harvard Common Pr.
Adopting the Racing Greyhound. Cynthia A. Branigan. LC 92-9627. 160p. 1992. 13.00 (0-87605-190-5) Howell Bk.
Adopting Your Child: Options, Answers, & Actions. Nancy T. Reynolds. (Reference Ser.). 1993. pap. 12.95 (0-88908-295-2) Self-Counsel Pr.
Adoption. Gerri Glotzbach. (Family Ser.). (Illus.). 64p. (YA). (gr. 7 up). 1990. lib. bdg. 17.27 (0-86593-078-3); lib. bdg. 12.95 (0-685-36294-9) Rourke Corp.
Adoption. Gail B. Stewart. LC 89-1525. (Facts About Ser.). (Illus.). 48p. (J). (gr. 5-6). 1989. text ed., lib. bdg. 12.95 (0-89686-443-X, Crstwood Hse) Silver Burdett Pr.
Adoption. 2nd ed. Kelly A. Sifferman. (Layman's Law Guides Ser.). 128p. 1994. pap. 8.95 (1-56414-082-2) Career Pr Inc.
Adoption: A Guide for Those Who Want to Adopt. Robert Souaid et al. 25p. (Orig.). 1982. pap. 2.00 (0-686-37425-8) Coun NY Law.
Adoption: A Handful of Hope. enl. rev. ed. Suzanne Arms. LC 88-13861. (Illus.). 320p. 1989. pap. 14.95 (0-89087-551-0) Celestial Arts.
Adoption: A Second Chance. Barbara Tizard. LC 77-84940. 1978. pap. 22.95 (0-02-932610-9) Free Pr.
Adoption: An Annotated Bibliography, Vol. 10. Lois R. Melina. LC 86-31964. (Reference Books on Family Issues: Vol. 10). 314p. 1987. lib. bdg. 42.00 (0-8240-8942-1, SS374) Garland.
Adoption: Essays in Social Policy, Law, & Sociology. Ed. by Philip Bean. 336p. 1984. 47.50 (0-422-78410-9, NO. 9152, Pub. by Tavistock UK) Routledge Chapman & Hall.
Adoption: International Perspectives. Ed. by Euthymia D. Hibbs. 342p. 1991. 45.00 (0-8236-0096-3) Intl Univs Pr.
Adoption: Opposing Viewpoints. (Opposing Viewpoints Ser.). (Illus.). 312p. 1995. lib. bdg. 19.95 (1-56510-213-4, 2134); pap. text ed. 11.55 (1-56510-212-6, 2126) Greenhaven.
Adoption: Parenthood Without Pregnancy. Charlene Canape. 320p. 1988. mass mkt. 4.95 (0-380-70505-2) Avon.
Adoption: The Facts, Feelings & Issues of a Double Heritage. rev. ed. Jeanne DuPrau. Ed. by Jane Steltenpohl. 128p. (YA). (gr. 7 up). 1990. lib. bdg. 12.98 (0-671-69328-X, Julian Messner); lib. bdg. 5.95 (0-671-69329-8, Julian Messner) Silver Burdett Pr.
Adoption: The Law & Practice. Nasreen Pearce. 544p. (C). 1991. 120.00 (1-85190-104-3, Pub. by Tolley Pubng UK) St Mut.
Adoption & Amendment of Constitutions in Europe & America. Charles Borgeaud. Tr. by Charles D. Hazen. xxi, 353p. 1989. reprint ed. lib. bdg. 37.50 (0-8377-1950-X) Rothman.
Adoption & Diffusion of Imported Technology: The Case of Korea. W. H. Park & J. L. Enos. 224p. 1985. 55.00 (0-7099-2030-X, Pub. by Croom Helm UK) Routledge Chapman & Hall.
***Adoption & Diffusion of the European Currency Unit: An Empirical Study among European Companies.** Yvonne M. Van Everdingen. (Tinbergen Institute Research Ser.: No. 95). 300p. 1995. pap. 26.50 (90-5170-330-9, Pub. by Thesis Pubs NE) IBD Ltd.
Adoption & Disclosure: A Review of the Law. Madelyn DeWoody. 1993. 12.95 (0-87868-577-4) Child Welfare.
Adoption & Disruption: Rates, Risks, & Responses. Richard P. Barth & Marianne Berry. (Modern Applications of Social Work Ser.). 264p. 1988. lib. bdg. 48.95 (0-202-36049-0); pap. text ed. 24.95 (0-202-36054-7) Aldine de Gruyter.
Adoption & Foster Care. Kathlyn Gay. LC 89-36476. (Issues in Focus Ser.). (Illus.). 128p. (J). (gr. 6 up). 1990. lib. bdg. 17.95 (0-89490-239-3) Enslow Pubs.
Adoption & the Family System: Strategies for Treatment. Miriam Reitz & Kenneth W. Watson. LC 91-44266. 340p. 1992. lib. bdg. 30.00 (0-89862-797-4) Guilford Pr.
Adoption As Sons of God: An Exegetical Investigation into the Background in the Pauline Corpus. James M. Scott. (WissUNT Neuen Testament Ser.: No. 2-48). 368p. (Orig.). 1992. pap. 64.50 (3-16-145895-8, Pub. by J C B Mohr GW) Coronet Bks.
Adoption Assistance: Joining the Family of Employee Benefits. (National Report on Work & Family Special Report Ser.: No. 4). 32p. 1988. 35.00 (0-87179-994-4) BNA.
Adoption Awareness: A Guide for Teachers, Counselors, Nurses, & Caring Others. Jeanne W. Lindsay & Catherine P. Monserrat. LC 88-34540. (Illus.). 288p. (Orig.). 1989. 15.95 (0-930934-33-4); pap. 9.95 (0-930934-32-6) Morning Glory.
Adoption Bibliography & Multi-Ethnic Sourcebook. LC 76-16225. (Illus.). 1977. 7.50 (0-918416-02-7) Open Door Soc.
Adoption Choices: A Guidebook to National & International Adoption Resources. E. Paul. 1991. pap. 24.95 (0-8103-9403-0) Visible Ink Pr.
Adoption Controversies. Karen Liptak. LC 93-19810. (Changing Family Ser.). (Illus.). 160p. 1993. lib. bdg. 14.49 (0-531-13032-0) Watts.
Adoption Crisis: The Truth Behind Adoption & Foster Care. Carole A. McKelvey & JoEllen Stevens. (Illus.). 420p. 1994. 22.95 (1-55591-172-2) Fulcrum Pub.
Adoption Directory. 2nd ed. E. Paul. 1995. 65.00 (0-8103-7495-1) Gale.
Adoption Encounter: Hurt, Transition, Healing. Mary J. Rillera. 171p. (Orig.). 1991. pap. 15.95 (0-941770-05-2) Pure CA.
Adoption Experiences. Steven L. Nickman. LC 85-8957. (Teen Survival Library). 192p. (J). (gr. 7 up). 1985. lib. bdg. 14.98 (0-671-50817-2, Julian Messner) Silver Burdett Pr.
Adoption Factbook, 1989: United States Data, Issues, Regulations & Resources. rev. ed. 300p. 1989. pap. 39.95 (0-9615820-1-4) Natl Adoption.
Adoption for Troubled Children: Prevention & Repair of Adoptive Failures Through Residential Treatment. Ed. by Douglas Powers. LC 83-26424. (Residential Group Care & Treatment Ser.: Vol. 2, Nos. 1-2). 201p. 1984. text ed. 39.95 (0-86656-245-1) Haworth Pr.
***Adoption Handbook.** 250p. (Orig.). 1995. pap. 65.00 (0-7605-1472-0) Rector Pr.
Adoption, Identity & Social Policy: The Search for Distant Relatives. Erica Haimes & Noel Timms. 114p. 1985. text ed. 59.95 (0-566-00888-2) Ashgate Pub Co.
Adoption in America: Coming of Age. Hal Aigner. LC 86-60829. 216p. 1986. pap. 8.95 (0-937572-02-0) Paradigm Pr.
Adoption in America Coming of Age. rev. ed. Hal Aigner. LC 92-14585. 240p. 1992. pap. 9.95 (0-937572-04-7) Paradigm Pr.
Adoption in Eastern Oceania. Ed. by Vern Carroll. LC 77-89650. (Association for Social Anthropology in Oceania Monographs: No. 1). (Illus.). 436p. reprint ed. pap. 124.30 (0-8357-6006-5, 2034635) Bks Demand.
Adoption in Old Babylonian Nippur & the Archive of Mannum-mesu-lissur. Elizabeth C. Stone & David I. Owen. LC 91-346. (Mesopotamian Civilizations Ser.: Vol. 3). x, 149p. 1991. text ed. 36.50 (0-931464-53-6) Eisenbrauns.
Adoption in the Nineteen Eighties: PHS 90-1250. No. 181. write for info. (0-318-69628-2) Natl Ctr Health Stats.
Adoption in the Two Jurisdictions of Ireland: A Comparative Study. Kerry O'Halloran. 256p. 1994. 59.95 (1-85628-904-4, Pub. by Avebury Pub UK) Ashgate Pub Co.
Adoption in Worldwide Perspective. Ed. by R. A. Hoksbergen. 200p. 1986. 20.00 (90-265-0738-0, Pub. by Swets Pub Serv NE) Taylor & Francis.
Adoption Information Improvement Feasibility Study: Final Report. 101p. 1986. 6.00 (0-685-18266-5, NCSC-051) Natl Ctr St Courts.
Adoption Is for Always. Linda W. Girard. Ed. by Abby Levine. LC 86-15843. (Albert Whitman Concept Bks.). (Illus.). 32p. (J). (gr. 1-5). 1986. lib. bdg. 11.95 (0-8075-0185-9); pap. 4.95 (0-8075-0187-5) A Whitman.
Adoption Law & Practice, 2 vols. Joan Holinger. 1988. write for info. (0-8205-1375-X) Bender.
***Adoption Law & Practice.** D. C. Manooja. (C). 1993. 32.00x (81-7100-581-0, Pub. by Deep) S Asia.
***Adoption Law in Ireland.** 1992. boxed 92.00 (1-85475-110-7, IE) Butterworth Legal Pubs.
Adoption Life Cycle: The Children & Their Families Through the Years. Elinor B. Rosenberg. LC 92-9031. 250p. 1992. text ed. 24.95 (0-02-927055-3) Free Pr.
Adoption Literature for Children & Young Adults: An Annotated Bibliography. Susan G. Miles. LC 91-31854. (Bibliographies & Indexes in Sociology Ser.: No. 21). 232p. 1991. text ed. 45.00 (0-313-27606-4, MBK/, Greenwood Pr) Greenwood.
Adoption of Agricultural Practices for the Development of Heritable Resistance to Pests & Pathogens in Forest Crops. Gibson J. Burley & M. R. Speight. 1980. 60.00 (0-85074-057-6) St Mut.
Adoption of Children with Special Needs: Issues in Law & Policy. 250p. 1985. pap. 15.00 (0-685-18983-X, 549-0019-01) Amer Bar Assn.
***Adoption of Hybrid Maize in Zambia: Effects on Gender Roles, Food Consumption, & Nutrition.** Shubh K. Kumar. LC 94-48103. (Research Reports: Vol. 100). 1994. write for info. (0-89629-103-0) Intl Food Policy.
Adoption of the Fourteenth Amendment. Horace E. Flack. 1908. 11.75 (0-8446-1182-4) Peter Smith.
Adoption of the Fourteenth Amendment. Horace E. Flack. LC 78-64271. (Johns Hopkins University. Studies in the Social Sciences. Thirtieth Ser. 1912: 26). reprint ed. 11.50 (0-404-61373-X) AMS Pr.
***Adoption Option: A Practical Handbook for Prospective Adoptive Parents.** Kalynn George. 126p. 1990. pap. 16.95 (0-398-06147-5) C C Thomas.
Adoption Option: A Practical Handbook for Prospective Adoptive Parents. Kalynn George. 126p. (C). 1990. text ed. 31.95x (0-398-05701-X) C C Thomas.
Adoption Papers. Jackie Kay. 64p. (Orig.). 1991. pap. 14.95 (1-85224-156-X, Pub. by Bloodaxe Bks UK) Dufour.
***Adoption, Paternity & Other Florida Family Practice.** 3rd ed. Florida Bar Legal Education Staff. LC 94-72554. 404p. 1994. disk, ring bd. 85.00 (0-945979-60-6, 212) FL Bar Legal Ed.
Adoption Practice & Procedure. Nasreen Pearce. 133p. 1984. 90.00 (0-906840-79-1, Pub. by Fourmat Pub UK) St Mut.
Adoption Project. A. Brodzinsky. 1992. 22.00 (0-385-41402-1) Doubleday.
Adoption, Race, & Identity: From Infancy Through Adolescence. Rita J. Simon. LC 91-23869. 240p. 1992. text ed. 49.95 (0-275-93748-8, C3748, Praeger Pubs) Greenwood.
***Adoption Reader: Birth Mothers, Adoptive Mothers & Adopted Daughters Tell Their Stories.** Ed. by Susan Wadia-Ells. 288p. (Orig.). 1995. pap. text ed. 14.95 (1-878067-65-6) Seal Pr Feminist.
Adoption Reality: A Paradox. Ginni D. Snodgrass. Tr. by I. R. Jacobsen. 92p. (Orig.). 1990. pap. 5.95 (0-9620410-2-5) GS Enterprise.
Adoption Recommendations of the Curriculum Development & Supplemental Materials Commission to the State Board of Education, 1988: California Basic Instructional Materials in English-Language Arts. California Department of Education Staff. 64p. 1988. pap. 3.50 (0-8011-0795-4) Calif Education.
Adoption Recommendations of the Curriculum Development & Supplemental Materials Commission to the State Board of Education, 1989: California Basic Instructional Materials in Bilingual Language Arts & Visual & Performing Arts-Visual Arts & Music. California Department of Education Staff. 88p. 1989. pap. 3.50 (0-8011-0838-1) Calif Education.
Adoption Recommendations of the Curriculum Development & Supplemental Materials Commission to the State Board of Education, 1990: California Basic Instructional Materials in History-Social Science. California Department of Education Staff. 88p. 1990. pap. 5.00 (0-8011-0913-2) Calif Education.
Adoption Recommendations of the Curriculum Development & Supplemental Materials Commission to the State Board of Education, 1991: California Basic Instructional Materials in English As a Second Language & Foreign Language. California Department of Education Staff. 58p. 1991. pap. 5.50 (0-8011-1013-0) Calif Education.
Adoption Recommendations of the Curriculum Development & Supplemental Materials Commission to the State Board of Education, 1992: California Basic Instructional Materials in Science. California Department of Education Staff. 60p. 1992. pap. 5.50 (0-8011-1063-7) Calif Education.
***Adoption Recommendations of the Curriculum Development & Supplemental Materials Commission to the State Board of Education, 1993: California Basic Instructional Materials in History-Social Science.** California Department of Education Staff. 58p. 1993. pap. 5.50 (0-8011-1103-X) Calif Education.
***Adoption Recommendations of the Curriculum Development & Supplemental Materials Commission to the State Board of Education, 1994: California Basic Instructional Materials in Science, Follow-up.** California Department of Education Staff. 16p. 1994. pap. 5.50 (0-8011-1151-X) Calif Education.
Adoption Resource Book. rev. ed. Lois Gilman. 367p. (Orig.). 1991. reprint ed. lib. bdg. 29.00x (0-8095-9114-6) Borgo Pr.
Adoption Resource Book. 3rd enl. ed. Lois Gilman. LC 91-36432. 400p. (Orig.). 1992. pap. 13.00 (0-06-273043-6, HarpT) HarpC.
Adoption Resource Guide. Julia L. Posner. 1990. pap. 29.95 (0-87868-370-4) Child Welfare.
Adoption Resources for Mental Health Professionals. Ed. by Pamela V. Grabe. 400p. 1989. pap. 24.95 (0-88738-793-4) Transaction Pubs.
Adoption Reunions: A Book for Adoptees, Birthparents & Adoptive Families. Michelle McColm. 175p. (Orig.). 1993. pap. 15.95 (0-929005-41-4, Pub. by Second Story Pr CN) InBook.
Adoption Searchbook: Techniques for Tracing People. Mary J. Rillera. 15.95 (0-941770-02-8) Triadoption Lib.
Adoption Searchbook: Techniques for Tracing People. 3rd rev. ed. Mary J. Rillera. 210p. 1991. reprint ed. pap. 18.95 (0-910143-00-5) Pure CA.
Adoption Searcher's Handbook: A Guidebook for Adoptees, Birth Parents & Others Involved in the Adoption Search. Norma Tillman. (Illus.). 110p. (Orig.). (C). 1994. pap. text ed. 39.95 (0-7881-0513-2) Diane Pub.
***Adoption, Social Work & Social Theory: Making the Connections.** Tim O'Shaughnessy. 287p. 1994. 59.95 (1-85628-883-8, Pub. by Avebury Pub UK) Ashgate Pub Co.
Adoption Stories for Young Children. Randall B. Hicks. 48p. (Orig.). 1994. pap. 8.95 (0-9631638-3-3) Wordslinger.
***Adoption Stories for Young Children.** Randall B. Hicks. LC 95-61150. (Illus.). 56p. (Orig.). (J). (ps-2). 1995. pap. 8.95 (0-9631638-2-5) Wordslinger.
Adoption Story. Marguerite Ryan. 240p. reprint ed. pap. 3.95 (0-8439-3048-9) Dorchester Pub Co.
Adoption Triangle. Julia Tugendadt. 160p. Date not set. 29.95 (0-7475-1010-5, Pub. by Bloomsbury Pub Ltd UK) Trafalgar.
Adoption Triangle: Sealed or Opened Records: How they affect adoptees, Birthparents & Adoptive Parents. 2nd ed. Arthur D. Sorosky et al. LC 89-85839. 236p. 1989. pap. 9.95 (0-931722-59-4) Corona Pub.
Adoption Triangle Training Pack. British Agencies for Adoption & Fostering Editors. (C). 1989. 500.00 (0-903534-90-8, Pub. by Brit Ag for Adopt & Fost UK) St Mut.
Adoption Without Fear. Ed. by James L. Gritter. LC 88-72307. (Illus.). 176p. (Orig.). 1989. pap. 8.95 (0-931722-71-3) Corona Pub.
Adoption Yes...But. enl. rev. ed. Ginni D. Snodgrass. Ed. by J. Douglas Watson. 92p. 1990. pap. 5.95 (0-9620410-1-7) GS Enterprise.
Adoptions & Name Changes, Minnesota Territory & State, 1855-1881. Stina B. Green. LC 94-17225. 1994. pap. 8.00 (0-915709-15-5) Pk Geneal Bk.
Adoptions & the Sexually Abused Child. Joan McNamara & Bernard McNamara. 1990. write for info. (0-939561-06-9) Univ South ME.
Adoptive Cellular Immunotherapy of Cancer. Stevenson. (Immunology Ser.: Vol. 48). 264p. 1989. 125.00 (0-8247-8111-2) Dekker.
Adoptive Family: The Healing Resource for the Sexually Abused Child. 1990. pap. 14.95 (0-87868-360-7) Child Welfare.
Adoptive Kinship: A Modern Institution in Need of Reform. rev. ed. H. David Kirk. LC 83-670044. 200p. (Orig.). 1985. reprint ed. pap. 15.95 (0-914539-01-9) Ben-Simon.
Adoptive Masonry. Thomas Lowe. 6.00 (0-685-19462-0) Powner.
Adoptive Parent Study: A Report of Survey of Parents Raising Adopted Minority, Older, & Handicapped Children. Lawrence L. Shornack. 1976. 1.25 (0-918416-01-9) Open Door Soc.
Adoptive Rite. Robert Macoy. 8.50 (0-685-19463-9) Powner.
Adoptive Rite. rev. ed. Robert Macoy. 303p. 1994. reprint ed. text ed. 9.00 (0-88053-300-5, S 073) Macoy Pub.
Adora. Bertrice Small. 440p. 1985. mass mkt. 5.95 (0-345-33506-6) Ballantine.

An Asterisk (*) at the beginning of an entry indicates that the title is appearing in BIP for the first time.

An Asterisk (*) at the beginning of an entry indicates that the title is appearing in BIP for the first time.

67

A

Adsorption Processes for Water Treatment. Samuel D. Faust & Osman M. Aly. (Illus.). 480p. 1986. text ed. 89. 95 (*0-409-90000-1*) Buttrwrth-Heinemann.

Adsorption Processes on Semiconductor & Dielectric Surfaces I. V. F. Kiselev & O. V. Krylov. (Chemical Physics Ser.: Vol. 32). (Illus.). 295p. 1985. 83.00 (*0-387-12416-0*) Spr-Verlag.

Adsorption Techniques in Drinking Water Treatment, Vol. 3. Ed. by Paul V. Roberts et al. (Journal of Environmental Pathology, Toxicology & Oncology Ser.: Vol. 7, No. 7/8, 1987). 438p. 43.50 (*0-685-34725-7*) Chem-Orbital.

Adsorption Technology: A Step-by-Step Approach to Process Evaluation & Application. Frank Slejko. (Chemical Industries Ser.: Vol. 19). 240p. 1985. 125.00 (*0-8247-7285-7*) Dekker.

Adsorption Technology for Air & Water Pollution Control. Kenneth E. Noll. (Illus.). 420p. 1991. 85.00 (*0-87371-340-0*, TD883) Lewis Pubs.

ADSP 2100 Family User's Manual. Analog Devices, Inc. Staff. 448p. 1992. pap. text ed. 32.00 (*0-13-006958-2*) P-H.

***ADSP-21000 Family Application Handbook Vol. 1.** Analog Devices, Inc. Staff Computer Products Div. Staff. (Analog Devices Technical Reference Bks.). (Illus.). 344p. (Orig.). 1994. pap. 22.00 (*0-916550-14-1*) Analog Devices.

ADSTRAT: A Decision Support System for Advertising Strategy. Hubert Gatignon. 160p. (C). 1990. Incl. 5 1/4 disk. pap. text ed. 32.50 (*0-89426-180-0*); Incl. 3 1/2 disk. pap. text ed. 32.50 (*0-89426-181-9*); Instr. manual. teacher ed, pap. text ed. 32.50 (*0-89426-191-6*) Boyd & Fraser.

Adulescentia: The Ecologues of Mantuan. Baptista Mantuanus. Ed. by James J. Wilhelm. Tr. by Lee Piepho. LC 89-16967. (World Literature in Translation Ser.: Vol. 14). 206p. 1989. 52.00 (*0-8240-3309-4*) Garland.

Adult - Pediatric Guide. 5th ed. Emergidose. 1991. 24.95 (*0-8016-1473-2*); ring bd. 39.95 (*0-8016-1478-3*) Mosby Yr Bk.

Adult Abnormal Psychology. Edgar Miller & Peter J. Cooper. (Illus.). 400p. 1988. text ed. 89.00 (*0-443-03513-X*) Churchill.

***Adult Add.** Thomas A. Whiteman et al. 160p. 1995. pap. 12.00 (*0-89109-906-9*, NavPr) NavPress.

Adult Age Differences in Memory. Alison M. Mackenzie. (C). 1991. 35.00 (*1-85041-037-2*, Pub. by Univ Nottingham UK) St Mut.

Adult Analysis & Childhood Sexual Abuse. Ed. by Howard B. Levine. 232p. 1990. text ed. 29.95 (*0-88163-083-7*) Analytic Pr.

Adult & Continuing Education: Theory & Practice. 2nd ed. Peter Jarvis. LC 94-8487. 304p. 1994. pap. 22.95 (*0-415-10242-1*, B3959) Routledge.

Adult & Continuing Education Collections: A Descriptive List of Manuscript Holdings in Syracuse University Libraries. Comp. by A. Charters. 1977. 5.00 (*0-686-50189-6*, MSS 16) Syracuse U Cont Ed.

Adult & Continuing Education in Australia: Issues & Practices. Ed. by Mark Tennant. 208p. 1991. 67.50 (*0-415-04675-0*, A4538) Routledge.

Adult & Immature Tabanidae (Diptera) of California. Woodrow S. Middlekauff & Robert S. Lane. LC 78-66042. (Bulletin of the California Insect Survey Ser.: No. 22). (Illus.). 105p. reprint ed. pap. 30.00 (*0-8357-5119-8*, 2032897) Bks Demand.

Adult & Pediatric Urology. 2nd ed. Jay Gillenwater. 1990. 269.00 (*0-8151-3545-9*) Mosby Yr Bk.

Adult APL Survey (APL-A) 39.95 (*0-8373-6989-4*, ATS-60B); 23.95 (*0-8373-6964-9*, ATS-60B) Nat Learn.

Adult Art Psychotherapy: Issues & Applications. Ed. by Helen B. Landgarten & Darcy Lubbers. LC 90-15103. (Illus.). 224p. 1991. 27.95 (*0-87630-593-1*) Brunner-Mazel.

Adult BBS Guidebook. Billy Wildhack. 128p. 1993. pap. 10. 00 (*0-9636091-9-X*) Keyhole Pubns.

Adult Behavior Therapy Casebook. Ed. by Cynthia G. Last & Michel Herson. LC 93-6252. 1994p. 1993. 59.50 (*0-306-44451-8*) Plenum.

Adult Biliteracy in the United States: A Response to Linguistic & Cultural Diversity. Ed. by David Spener. LC 93-45622. (Language in Education Ser.). 237p. (Orig.). 1994. pap. text ed. 20.50 (*0-937354-83-X*) Delta Systems.

Adult Body Image. Kate Bennett. (C). 1991. 35.00 (*1-85041-035-6*, Pub. by Univ Nottingham UK) St Mut.

Adult Cardiac Surgery. R. M. Bojar. (Illus.). 1992. 100.00 (*0-86542-140-4*) Blackwell Sci.

Adult Care Monitoring. Levine & Fromm. 500p. 1994. 69. 00 (*0-8016-6962-6*) Mosby Yr Bk.

***Adult Career Development: Concepts, Issues, & Practices.** H. Daniel Lea & Zandy B. Leibowitz. 1992. pap. text ed. 36.00 (*1-55620-095-1*) Am Coun Assn.

Adult Career Guidance, Options: Expanding Educational Services for Adults. National Center for Research in Vocational Education Staff. 1987. 12.95 (*0-317-03853-2*, SP500FA) Ctr Educ Trng Employ.

Adult Catechesis in the Christian Community: Some Principles & Guidelines. 27p. (Orig.). 1990. pap. 4.00 (*1-55833-059-3*) Natl Cath Educ.

Adult Catechesis in the Christian Community: Some Principles & Guidelines. United States Catholic Conference Staff. Ed. by Jack McBride. 60p. (C). 1992. student ed, pap. text ed. 3.95 (*1-55586-520-8*) US Catholic.

Adult-Child Conversation: Studies in Structure & Process. Ed. by Peter French & Margaret MacLure. 1981. text ed. 39.95 (*0-312-00515-6*) St Martin.

Adult Child Guide to What's "Normal" John Friel. 1990. pap. 9.95 (*1-55874-090-2*) Health Comm.

Adult-Child Interaction & the Promise of Language Acquisition. Jean A. Rondal. 240p. 1985. text ed. 55.00 (*0-275-90157-2*, C0157, Praeger Pubs) Greenwood.

Adult-Child Relations. Rudolf Dreikurs. 1972. reprint ed. pap. 6.00 (*0-918560-13-6*) Adler Sch Prof Psy.

Adult-Child Research & Experience: Personal & Professional Legacies of a Dysfunctional, Co-Dependent Family. Robert E. Haskell. Ed. by Glenn R. Caddy. LC 92-21896. (Developments in Clinical Psychology Ser.). 272p. (C). 1992. text ed. 55.00 (*0-89391-755-9*); pap. text ed. 27.50 (*1-56750-077-3*) Ablex Pub.

Adult Children: The Secrets of Dysfunctional Families. John Friel & Linda Friel. 1988. pap. 8.95 (*0-932194-53-2*) Health Comm.

Adult Children, Adult Choices: Outgrowing Codependency. Mary Ramey. LC 92-12728. 168p. (Orig.). 1992. pap. 10.95 (*1-55612-406-6*, LL1406) Sheed & Ward MO.

Adult Children & Aging Parents. Jane E. Myers. 216p. 1989. 19.95 (*0-8403-5448-7*) Am Coun Assn.

Adult Children & the Almighty. Melinda Fish. LC 90-25777. 1991. pap. 8.99 (*0-8007-9178-9*) Chosen Bks.

Adult Children of Abusive Parents: A Healing Program for Those Who Have Been Physically, Sexually, or Emotionally Abused. Steven Farmer. 288p. 1990. pap. 10.00 (*0-345-36388-4*, Ballantine Trade) Ballantine.

Adult Children of Alcoholics. Phyllis Tainey. LC 88-24398. (Workshop Models for Family Life Education Ser.). 110p. (Orig.). 1988. pap. 15.95 (*0-87304-222-0*) Families Intl.

Adult Children of Alcoholics. Janet G. Woititz. 1990. pap. 8.95 (*1-55874-112-7*) Health Comm.

Adult Children of Alcoholics. large type ed. Janet G. Woititz. (General Ser.). 231p. 1991. text ed. 16.95 (*0-8161-5053-2*, Large Print Bks) Hall.

Adult Children of Alcoholics: A Workbook for Healing. Patty McConnell. 150p. (Orig.). 1986. pap. 11.95 (*0-86683-526-1*) Harper SF.

Adult Children of Alcoholics: Ministers & the Ministries. Rachel Callahan. 1990. pap. 9.95 (*0-8091-3120-X*) Paulist Pr.

Adult Children of Alcoholics Syndrome. Wayne Kritsberg. 176p. (Orig.). 1988. mass mkt. 5.50 (*0-553-27279-9*) Bantam.

***Adult Children of Fairly Functional Parents: A Nest of My Own in the Family Tree.** Becky Freeman & Ruthie Arnold. 1994. write for info. (*0-8054-6155-8*) Broadman.

Adult Children of Jewish Parents: The Last Recovery Program You'll Ever Need. Anna Sequoia. 1993. pap. 10.00 (*0-517-88116-0*, Crown) Crown Pub Group.

Adult Children of Legal or Emotional Divorce: Healing Your Long-Term Hurt. Jim Conway. LC 90-43614. 272p. 1992. 10.99 (*0-8308-1381-0*, 1381, Saltshaker Bk) InterVarsity.

Adult Children of Normal Parents. Jennifer Berman. Ed. by Eric Tobias. (Illus.). 80p. (Orig.). 1994. pap. 8.00 (*0-671-86489-0*) PB.

Adult Children Raising Children: Sparing Your Child from Co-dependency Without Being Perfect Yourself. Randy C. Rolfe. 160p. 1989. 8.95 (*1-55874-055-4*) Health Comm.

Adult Children Who Won't Grow Up: How to Finally Cut the Cord That Binds You. Larry Stockman & Cynthia S. Graves. 237p. 1990. reprint ed. pap. 9.95 (*1-55958-043-7*) Prima Pub.

Adult Christ at Christmas. Raymond E. Brown. 50p. 1978. pap. 3.95 (*0-8146-0997-X*) Liturgical Pr.

Adult Civic Education. Frwd. by David L. Boggs & William D. Dowling. 152p. (C). 1991. text ed. 34.95 (*0-398-05724-9*) C C Thomas.

***Adult Civic Education.** David L. Boggs. 152p. 1991. pap. 19.95 (*0-398-06024-X*) C C Thomas.

Adult Clinical Problems: A Cognitive-Behavioural Approach. Ed. by Wendy Dryden & Robert Rentoul. (Illus.). 384p. 1991. 82.50 (*0-415-01136-1*, A5403); pap. 25.00 (*0-415-01137-X*, A5407) Routledge.

Adult Cognition: An Experimental Psychology of Human Aging. Timothy A. Salthouse. (Cognitive Development Ser.). (Illus.). 253p. 1982. 63.00 (*0-387-90728-9*) Spr-Verlag.

Adult Cognitive Development: Methods & Models. Robert A. Mines. LC 85-16969. 192p. 1985. text ed. 37.50 (*0-275-90012-6*, C0012, Praeger Pubs) Greenwood.

***Adult Comedy Action Drama.** Richard Prince. 1995. 60.00 (*1-881616-36-3*, Pub. by Scalo Pubs) Dist Art Pubs.

Adult Comics: An Introduction. Roger Sabin. LC 92-6670. (New Accents Ser.). (Illus.). 256p. 1993. 49.95 (*0-415-04418-9*, A4429); pap. 15.95 (*0-415-04419-7*, A7894) Routledge.

Adult Commitment: An Ethics of Trust. Elizabeth Willems. 214p. (C). 1990. lib. bdg. 39.00 (*0-8191-7709-1*) U Pr of Amer.

Adult Congenital Heart Disease. Ed. by William C. Roberts. LC 86-11565. (Illus.). 752p. 1987. text ed. 85. 00 (*0-8036-7420-1*) Davis Co.

***Adult Connect the Dots.** H. Kavet. 96p. 1994. pap. 5.95 (*0-88032-458-9*) Ivory Tower Pub.

Adult Day Care: A Practical Guide. Carole L. O'Brien. LC 81-16212. (Nursing-Health Science Ser.). 400p. (C). 1982. 40.00 (*0-8185-0506-0*) Jones & Bartlett.

Adult Day Care: A Practical Guidebook & Manual. Intro. by Lenore A. Tate. LC 88-2773. (Activities, Adaptation & Aging Ser.: Vol. 11, No. 2). (Illus.). 144p. 1988. text ed. 29.95 (*0-86656-711-9*) Haworth Pr.

Adult Day Care: A Program of Services for the Functionally Impaired. Ruth Von Behren. 44p. 1988. pap. text ed. 6.00 (*0-910883-43-2*) Natl Coun Aging.

Adult Day Care: An Annotated Bibliography. Ed. by Betty Shepherd & Kathleen Howley. 141p. 1987. pap. text ed. 7.95 (*0-910883-53-X*) Natl Coun Aging.

Adult Day Care: Findings from a National Survey. William G. Weissert et al. LC 89-43486. (Series in Contemporary Medicine & Public Health). 136p. 1990. text ed. 37.50x (*0-8018-4001-5*); 3.5 hd 39.00 (*0-8018-4007-4*); 5.25 hd 39.00 (*0-8018-4014-7*) Johns Hopkins.

Adult Day Care: The Relationship of Formal & Informal Systems of Day Care. Patricia M. Kirwin. LC 91-28351. (Studies on Elderly in America). 256p. 1991. 62. 00 (*0-8153-0512-5*) Garland.

Adult Day Care for Alzheimer's Patients: Impact on Family Caregivers. Rosalie A. Guttman. LC 91-28434. (Studies on Elderly in America). 176p. 1991. 47.00 (*0-8153-0524-9*) Garland.

Adult Day Care in America: Summary of a National Survey. Ruth Von Behren. 34p. (Orig.). 1986. pap. 5.95 (*0-910883-29-7*, 2020) Natl Coun Aging.

Adult Development. S. Krause. 1985. write for info. (*0-275-90002-9*, C0002, Praeger Pubs) Greenwood.

Adult Development. Linda Smolak. 560p. (C). 1992. text ed. write for info. (*0-13-009044-1*) P-H.

Adult Development. 2nd ed. Susan K. Whitbourne. LC 86-4893. 432p. 1986. text ed. 42.95 (*0-275-92106-9*, C2106, Praeger Pubs) Greenwood.

Adult Development: A New Dimension in Psychodynamic Theory & Practice. Calvin A. Colarusso & Robert A. Nemiroff. LC 80-20250. (Critical Issues in Psychiatry Ser.). 320p. 1981. 42.50 (*0-306-40619-5*, Plenum Pr) Plenum.

Adult Development: An Overview of Recent Research. P. Allman. (C). 1988. text ed. 32.00 (*0-685-22144-X*, Pub. by Univ Nottingham UK) St Mut.

Adult Development: An Overview of Recent Research. Paula Allman. (C). 1986. reprint ed. 35.00 (*0-902031-46-5*, Pub. by Univ Nottingham UK) St Mut.

Adult Development: Implications for Adult Education. Sharan B. Merriam. 39p. 1984. 4.75 (*0-318-22018-0*, IN282) Ctr Educ Trng Employ.

Adult Development: Implications for Staff Development. Judy-Arin Krupp. (Illus.). 160p. (Orig.). 1981. pap. text ed. 13.00 (*0-9613245-1-1*) Adult Dev Learn.

Adult Development & Aging. Bert Hayslip, Jr. 640p. (C). 1990. text ed. 38.25 (*0-06-045012-6*) HarpCollege.

Adult Development & Aging. David F. Hultsch & Francine Deutsch. (Illus.). 448p. 1981. text ed. write for info. (*0-07-031156-0*); pap. text ed. write for info. (*0-07-031157-9*) McGraw.

Adult Development & Aging. F. Philip Rice. 411p. 1985. teacher ed write for info. (*0-318-61421-9*) Allyn.

Adult Development & Aging. 2nd ed. John C. Cavanaugh. LC 92-2316. (C). 1993. text ed. 53.95 (*0-534-17250-4*) Brooks-Cole.

Adult Development & Aging. 2nd ed. Bert Hayslip, Jr. & Paul E. Panek. LC 91-31643. (C). 1992. 59.50 (*0-06-500244-X*) HarpCollege.

Adult Development & Aging. 2nd ed. Marion Perlmutter & Elizabeth Hall. 608p. (C). 1992. Net. text ed. write for info. (*0-471-51846-8*) Wiley.

Adult Development & Aging. 2nd ed. John M. Rybash et al. 672p. (C). 1991. pap. write for info. (*0-697-03312-0*) Brown & Benchmark.

Adult Development & Aging. 3rd ed. John M. Rybash et al. 624p. (C). 1994. pap. text ed. write for info. (*0-697-10503-2*) Brown & Benchmark.

Adult Development & Aging. 3rd ed. K. Warner Schaie & Willis. (C). 1991. text ed. 59.50 (*0-673-52011-0*) HarpCollege.

Adult Development & Aging: Myths & Emerging Realities. 2nd ed. Richard Schulz & Robert B. Ewen. 528p. (C). 1993. text ed. write for info. (*0-02-407781-X*) Macmillan.

Adult Development & Learning: A Handbook on Individual Growth & Competence in the Adult Years. Alan B. Knox. LC 76-50719. (Higher Education Ser.). 700p. 1977. 55.00x (*0-87589-319-8*) Jossey-Bass.

Adult Development of C. G. Jung. John-Raphael Staude. 144p. 1981. 17.95 (*0-7100-0749-3*, 07493, RKP) Routledge.

Adult Development of Career Army Officers. Jeffrey A. McNally. LC 91-8028. 296p. 1991. text ed. 65.00 (*0-275-93698-8*, C3698, Praeger Pubs) Greenwood.

Adult Development, Vol. 2: Models & Methods in the Study of Adolescent & Adult Thought, Vol. 2. Ed. by Michael L. Commons et al. LC 88-27425. 296p. 1990. text ed. 59.95 (*0-275-92755-5*, C2755, Praeger Pubs) Greenwood.

Adult Domestic Violence: Constitutional, Legislative & Equitable Issues. Ann M. Boylan & Nadine Taub. (Illus.). 430p. (Orig.). 1981. 5.00 (*0-941077-12-8*, 31, 841) NCLS Inc.

***Adult Dyslexic: Assessment, Counseling & Training.** David McLoughlin et al. 150p. 1994. text ed. 34.95 (*1-56593-241-2*, 0561) Singular Publishing.

Adult Echocardiography: A Handbook for Technicians. Mary C. Bishop. LC 84-62545. (Illus.). 120p. (Orig.). 1985. pap. 14.95 (*0-931028-60-4*) Precept Pr.

***Adult Education.** A. S. Seetharamu & M. D. Usha. (Illus.). vii, 500p. 1994. 42.00x (*81-7024-589-3*, Pub. by Ashish Pub Hse II) Nataraj Bks.

Adult Education. Michael Stephens. Ed. by C. E. Wragg. (Education Matters Ser.). 144p. 1990. text ed. 50.00 (*0-304-31949-X*); pap. text ed. 17.95 (*0-304-31955-4*) Cassell.

Adult Education. 2nd rev. ed. C. L. Kundu. 225p. 1986. text ed. 22.50 (*81-207-0079-1*, Pub. by Sterling Pubs II) Apt Bks.

Adult Education: Evolution & Achievements in a Developing Field of Study. John M. Peters et al. LC 91-13977. (Higher & Adult Education Ser.). 525p. 1991. 42.00 (*1-55542-381-7*) Jossey-Bass.

Adult Education: Foundations of Practice. Gordon G. Darkenwald & Sharan B. Merriam. 260p. (C). 1990. 52. 00 (*0-690-01541-0*) HarpCollege.

Adult Education: International Perspectives from China. Ed. by Chris Duke. 272p. 1986. 37.50 (*0-7099-4509-4*, Pub. by Croom Helm UK) Routledge Chapman & Hall.

***Adult Education: Understanding Feminist Methodologies.** Ed. by Shirley Walters & Linzi Manicom. 256p. (C). 1996. text ed. 59.95 (*1-85649-349-0*, Pub. by Zed Books UK); pap. 22.50 (*1-85649-350-4*, Pub. by Zed Books UK) Humanities.

Adult Education - A Comparative Study. Robert Peers. (C). 1972. 45.00 (*0-7100-7410-7*, Pub. by Univ Nottingham UK) St Mut.

Adult Education Activity of Selected International Organizations. Alexander N. Charters. 1971. 5.00 (*0-87060-076-1*, WPT 4) Syracuse U Cont Ed.

Adult Education & Cultural Development. David Jones. (International Perspectives on Adult & Continuing Education Ser.). 224p. (C). 1988. lib. bdg. 49.50 (*0-415-00553-1*) Routledge.

Adult Education & Phenomenological Research. Sherman M. Stanage. LC 86-32204. 436p. (C). 1987. lib. bdg. 39. 50 (*0-89874-907-7*) Krieger.

Adult Education & Political Systems. W. E. Styler. 171p. (C). 1984. 60.00x (*1-85041-000-3*, Pub. by Univ Nottingham UK) St Mut.

Adult Education & Social Policy. Colin Griffin. Ed. by Peter Jarvis. (International Perspectives on Adult & Continuing Education Ser.). 256p. 1987. 39.95 (*0-7099-3812-8*, Pub. by Croom Helm UK) Routledge Chapman & Hall.

Adult Education & Socialist Pedagogy: Radical Forum on Adult Education. Frank Youngman. 288p. 1986. 57.50 (*0-7099-2911-0*, Pub. by Croom Helm UK) Routledge Chapman & Hall.

Adult Education & the Arts. D. J. Jones & A. F. Chadwick. (C). 1981. 35.00 (*0-902031-54-6*, Pub. by Univ Nottingham UK); text ed. 60.00 (*0-685-44257-8*, Pub. by Univ Nottingham UK) St Mut.

Adult Education & the Challenges of the 1990's. Ed. by Walter Leirman & Jindra Kulich. 224p. 1987. lib. bdg. 47.50 (*0-7099-4169-2*, Pub. by Croom Helm UK) Routledge Chapman & Hall.

Adult Education & the State. Peter Jarvis. LC 92-37660. 192p. 1993. 52.50 (*0-415-06532-1*, A7710, Routledge NY) Routledge.

Adult Education & the Voluntary Associations in France. W. S. Toynbee. 44p. (C). 1985. 60.00 (*0-317-94043-0*, Pub. by Univ Nottingham UK) St Mut.

Adult Education & the Voluntary Associations in France. Ed. by W. S. Toynbee. (C). 1985. 35.00 (*1-85041-009-7*, Pub. by Univ Nottingham UK) St Mut.

Adult Education & the Working Class: Education for the Missing Millions. Ed. by Richard Taylor & Kevin Ward. (Radical Forum on Adult Education Ser.). 224p. 1986. 35.00 (*0-7099-2461-5*, Pub. by Croom Helm UK) Routledge Chapman & Hall.

Adult Education & Theological Interpretations. Ed. by Peter Jarvis & Nicholas Walters. 360p. (Orig.). (C). 1992. 47.50 (*0-89464-587-0*) Krieger.

Adult Education & Training in Industrialized Countries. Richard E. Peterson et al. LC 81-84672. 512p. 1981. text ed. 47.95 (*0-275-90701-5*, C0701, Praeger Pubs) Greenwood.

Adult Education & Worldview Construction. Leon McKenzie. 160p. (C). 1991. lib. bdg. 19.50 (*0-89464-488-2*) Krieger.

Adult Education as Theory, Practice & Research: The Captive Triangle. Robin Usher & Ian Bryant. 224p. 1989. pap. 35.00 (*0-415-02359-9*, A3273) Routledge.

Adult Education As Vocation. Michael Collins. 256p. 1991. text ed. 39.95 (*0-415-00554-X*, A2478) Routledge.

Adult Education, Community Development & Older People: Releasing the Resource. Christopher Pilley. (Council of Europe Ser.). 70p. 1990. text ed. 50.00 (*0-304-32263-6*); pap. text ed. 14.95 (*0-304-32271-7*) Cassell.

Adult Education, Community Development & the Working Class. T. Lovett. 176p. (C). 1982. text ed. 60.00 (*0-685-44259-4*, Pub. by Univ Nottingham UK) St Mut.

Adult Education, Community Development & the Working Class. Ed. by Tom Lovett. (C). 1982. 35.00 (*0-902031-84-8*, Pub. by Univ Nottingham UK) St Mut.

Adult Education for Community Development. Edwin Hamilton. LC 91-40321. (Contributions to the Study of Education Ser.: No. 55). 184p. 1992. text ed. 47.95 (*0-313-27612-9*, HAX, Greenwood Pr) Greenwood.

Adult Education for Social Change. T. V. Rao & Anil Bhatt. 1980. 15.00 (*0-685-04704-0*, Pub. by Manohar II) S Asia.

Adult Education in a Multicultural Society. Ed. by Beverly B. Cassara. 288p. 1990. 45.00 (*0-415-03644-5*, A4323) Routledge.

Adult Education in Church & Synagogue. Huey B. Long. LC 73-13292. (Occasional Papers: No. 37). 1973. pap. 2.50 (*0-87060-061-3*, OCP 37) Syracuse U Cont Ed.

Adult Education in Developing Countries. 2nd ed. Edwin Townsend-Coles. 1977. 92.00 (*0-08-021293-X*, Pub. by Pergamon Repr UK) Franklin.

Adult Education in the American Experience: From the Colonial Period to the Present. Harold W. Stubblefield & Patrick Keane. (Higher & Adult Education Ser.). 384p. 1994. 38.95 (*0-7879-0025-7*) Jossey-Bass.

Adult Education in the Parish: A Practical Handbook. Kathy D. Rucker. 92p. 1990. 4.95 (*0-86716-125-6*) St Anthony Mess Pr.

Adult Education in the United States: Its Scope, Nature & Future Direction. David Harman. 1985. 2.75 (*0-318-20328-6*, OC105) Ctr Educ Trng Employ.

An Asterisk (*) at the beginning of an entry indicates that the title is appearing in BIP for the first time.

An Asterisk (*) at the beginning of an entry indicates that the title is appearing in BIP for the first time.

69

A

Adult Years: Mastering the Art of Self-Renewal. Frederic M. Hudson. LC 91-9922. (Social & Behavioral Science - Higher & Adult Education Ser.). 304p. 1991. 31.95 (*1-55542-365-5*) Jossey-Bass.

Adultera. Theodor Fontane. Tr. by Lynn R. Eliason. (American University Studies: Ser. I, Vol. 90). 200p. (C). 1990. text ed. 41.95 (*0-8204-1285-6*) P Lang Pubs.

Adulteration of Fruit Juice Beverages. Nagy et al. (Food Science & Technology Ser.: Vol. 30). 568p. 1988. 189.00 (*0-8247-7912-6*) Dekker.

Adulteress. Richard Westbrook. 64p. 1975. 13.95 (*0-88289-073-5*) Pelican.

Adulteress's Child: Authorship & Desire in the Nineteenth-Century Novel. Naomi Segal. LC 92-28893. 264p. 1993. 29.95 (*0-7456-0509-5*) Blackwell Pubs.

***Adultery & Divorce in Calvin's Geneva.** Robert M. Kingdon. LC 94-13197. (Harvard Historical Studies: No. 118). 224p. 1995. text ed. 29.95 (*0-674-00520-1*, KINADU); pap. text ed. 14.95 (*0-674-00521-X*, KINADX) HUP.

Adultery & Other Choices. Andre Dubus. LC 77-78392. 192p. 1978. pap. 10.95 (*0-87923-284-6*) Godine.

Adultery & Other Private Matters: Your Right to Personal Freedom in Marriage. Lonny Myers & Hunter Leggitt. LC 75-4701. (Illus.). 221p. 1975. 26.95 (*0-911012-51-6*) Nelson-Hall.

Adultery in the Novel: Contract & Transgression. Tony Tanner. LC 79-4948. 400p. (C). 1981. pap. 16.95 (*0-8018-2471-0*) Johns Hopkins.

Adultery in the United States: Close Encounters of the Sixth (or Seventh) Kind. Philip E. Lampe. LC 87-9641. 224p. 1988. 29.95 (*0-87975-375-7*) Prometheus Bks.

Adultery, the Forgivable Sin: Healing the Inherited Patterns of Betrayal in Your Family. Bonnie Eaker-Weil & Ruth Winter. LC 92-39180. 1993. 17.95 (*1-55972-185-5*, Birch Ln Pr) Carol Pub Group.

***Adultery, the Forgivable Sin: Healing the Inherited Patterns of Betrayal in Your Family.** Bonnie E. Weil. 1994. pap. 12.95 (*0-8038-9364-7*) Hastings.

Adulthood. Ed. by Erik H. Erikson. (C). 1978. pap. text ed. 11.95 (*0-393-09086-8*) Norton.

Adulthood. Elizabeth Sinclair-House & Alison Muir. LC 90-28921. (Human Development Ser.). (Illus.). 48p. (J). (gr. 5-9). 1991. lib. bdg. 11.95 (*0-8114-7806-8*) Raintree Steck-V.

Adulthood & Aging. Robert Till & James Lugo. 259p. (C). 1993. pap. text ed. 37.75 (*1-56226-145-2*) CT Pub.

Adulthood & Aging: An Interdisciplinary Development View. 3rd ed. Douglas C. Kimmel. LC 08-938339. 1989. Net. text ed. write for info. (*0-471-63580-4*) Wiley.

Adulthood Rites. Octavia E. Butler. 288p. 1989. mass mkt. 5.50 (*0-445-20903-8*) Warner Bks.

Adultodontics: You Are Just the Right Age for Braces. Joan Bendl. (Illus.). 50p. (Orig.). 1987. lib. bdg. 4.95 (*0-935343-05-9*) Peartree.

Adults & Children in the Roman Empire. Thomas Wiedemann. LC 88-51383. 256p. (C). 1989. text ed. 32.00 (*0-300-04380-5*) Yale U Pr.

Adults As Learners. Jack Mottweiler. (Christian Education Ministries Ser.). 95p. (Orig.). 1984. pap. 3.95 (*0-89367-098-7*) Light & Life.

Adults As Learners: Increasing Participation & Facilitating Learning. K. Patricia Cross. LC 80-26985. (Classics Ser.). 332p. 1992. reprint ed. pap. 22.95 (*1-55542-445-7*) Jossey-Bass.

Adults As Learners: Increasing Participation & Facilitating Learning. Kathryn P. Cross. LC 80-26985. (Jossey-Bass Series in Higher Education). 328p. reprint ed. pap. 93.50 (*0-7837-2507-8*, 2042666) Bks Demand.

Adult's Guide to Style. Anthony F. Gregorc. 80p. 1995. reprint ed. pap. 14.95 (*0-934481-01-6*) Gregorc Assocs.

Adults in College: A Survival Guide. Wanda Schindley. 272p. (Orig.). 1992. pap. 14.95 (*0-912011-42-4*) Dallas Pub MPTX.

***Adults in Higher Education: International Perspectives on Access & Participation.** Ed. by Pat Davies. LC 95-1109. 250p. 1995. 49.50 (*1-85302-286-1*, Pub. by J Kingsley Pubs UK) Taylor & Francis.

Adults in Higher Education - Policies & Practice in Great Britain & North America: Reports Prepared for the Centre for Educational Development & Innovation of the Organization for Economic Cooperation & Development (OECD) Ed. by Hans G. Schutze et al. 181p. (Orig.). 1987. pap. text ed. 50.00x (*91-22-00837-3*, Pub. by Almqv & Wiksell SW) Coronet Bks.

Adults in the Colleges of Further Education. E. S. Marks & K. T. Elsdon. (C). 1991. 45.00 (*1-85041-042-9*, Pub. by Univ Nottingham UK) St Mut.

Adults Learning. Jennifer Rogers. 256p. 1977. pap. 16.00 (*0-335-00044-4*, Open Univ Pr) Taylor & Francis.

Adults Learning. 3rd ed. Jenny Rogers. 256p. 1989. pap. 22.00 (*0-335-09215-2*, Open Univ Pr) Taylor & Francis.

Adults Learning for Development. Alan Rogers. 256p. 1992. text ed. 60.00 (*0-304-32523-6*); pap. text ed. 19.95 (*0-304-32420-5*) Cassell.

Adults Learning Projects: A Fresh Approach to Theory & Practice in Adult Learning. Allen M. Tough. (Research in Education Ser.: No. 1). 211p. reprint ed. pap. 60.20 (*0-8357-5121-X*, 2029355) Bks Demand.

Adults Molested As Children: A Survivor's Guide for Women & Men. Euan Bear & Peter T. Dimock. (Safer Society Ser.: No. 4). 67p. 1988. pap. 12.95 (*1-884444-03-2*) Safer Soc.

Adults of the Subfamily Tanypodinae (Pelopiinae) in North America (Diptera: Chironomidae) Selwyn S. Roback. (Monograph: No. 17). (Illus.). 410p. (Orig.). 1971. pap. 8.00 (*0-910006-25-3*) Acad Nat Sci Phila.

Adults with Learning Difficulties: Curriculum, Choice & Empowerment: A Handbook of Good Practice. Jeannie Sutcliffe. 144p. 1990. pap. 24.00 (*0-335-09609-3*, Open Univ Pr) Taylor & Francis.

Adults with Learning Disabilities: An Overview for the Adult Educator. Jovita M. Ross-Gordon. 1989. 7.00 (*0-317-03009-4*, IN337) Ctr Educ Trng Employ.

Advaita Siddhih: Sections on Mithyatva. Madhusudana Saraswati. Tr. by Karuna Bhattacharya. (C). 1992. 15.00 (*81-85636-00-1*, Pub. by Motilal Banarsidass II) S Asia.

Advaita Vedanta: A Philosophical Reconstruction. Eliot Deutsch. LC 69-19282. (C). 1969. pap. text ed. 6.50 (*0-8248-0271-3*, Eastwest Ctr Pr) UH Pr.

***Advaita Vedanta of Brahma-Siddhi.** Allen W. Thrasher. (C). 1993. text ed. 16.00 (*81-208-0982-3*, Pub. by Motilal Banarsidass II) S Asia.

Advaitic Theism of the Bhagavata Purana. Danial P. Sheridan. 229p. 1986. 14.00 (*81-208-0179-2*, Pub. by Motilal Banarsidass II) S Asia.

Advance: Painting, Graphic Art, Sculpture. Laima Reihmane. (C). 1987. 135.00 (*0-685-22615-8*, Pub. by Collets UK) Pro-Am Music.

Advance Acoustics. D. P. Roychaudhury. 1985. 82.00 (*0-317-38746-4*, Current Dist) St Mut.

Advance & Retreat. John B. Hood. (Illus.). 376p. 1993. reprint ed. pap. 14.95 (*0-306-80534-0*) Da Capo.

Advance & Retreat: Personal Experiences in the U. S. & Confederate States Armies. John B. Hood. Ed. by Richard N. Current. LC 59-13547. (Indiana University Civil War Centennial Ser.). (Illus.). 1968. reprint ed. 33.00 (*0-527-42200-2*) Periodicals Srv.

Advance & Retreat in Representative Self-Government, 1840-1900: Select Documents on the Constitutional History of the British Empire & Commonwealth. Ed. by Frederick Madden & David Fieldhouse. LC 84-21213. (Documents in Imperial History Ser.: Vol. 5, No. 5). 848p. 1991. text ed. 135.00 (*0-313-27757-5*, MNT/, Greenwood Pr) Greenwood.

Advance & Retreat to Saratoga, 2 vols. in 1. Clarence Bennett. LC 72-8741. (American Revolutionary Ser.). (Illus.). 1979. reprint ed. lib. bdg. 29.00 (*0-8398-0186-6*) Irvington.

Advance Australian Painting. Auckland City Art Gallery Staff. (Illus.). 106p. 1991. pap. 24.95 (*0-86463-164-2*) U of Wash Pr.

Advance Bibliography of Law & Related Fields. 1984. 560.00 (*0-686-89490-1*) Rothman.

Advance Course Hardware Retailing. NRHA Staff. 640p. 1992. 49.00 (*0-8403-7658-8*) Kendall-Hunt.

***Advance Data from Vital & Health Statistics, Nos. 71-80.** National Center for Health Statistics Staff. LC 94-1867. (Series Reports: Series 16, No. 8). 118p. Date not set. 8.00 (*0-614-02913-9*, 017-022-01239-1) Natl Ctr Health Stats.

***Advance Data from Vital & Health Statistics, Nos. 81-90.** National Center for Health Statistics Staff. LC 94-1868. (Series Reports: Series 16, No. 9). 99p. Date not set. 7.50 (*0-614-02914-7*, 017-022-01240-5) Natl Ctr Health Stats.

***Advance Data from Vital & Health Statistics, Nos. 91-100.** National Center for Health Statistics Staff. LC 94-1869. (Series Reports: Series 16, No. 10). 87p. Date not set. 6.00 (*0-614-02915-5*, 017-022-01245-6) Natl Ctr Health Stats.

***Advance Data from Vital & Health Statistics, Nos. 101-110.** National Center for Health Statistics Staff. LC 94-1870. (Series Reports: Series 16, No. 11). 93p. Date not set. 6.00 (*0-614-02916-3*, 94PB-135928) Natl Ctr Health Stats.

***Advance Data from Vital & Health Statistics, Nos. 111-120.** National Center for Health Statistics Staff. LC 94-1871. (Series Reports: Series 16, No. 12). 105p. Date not set. 7.50 (*0-614-02917-1*, PB94-142874) Natl Ctr Health Stats.

***Advance Data from Vital & Health Statistics, Nos. 121-130.** National Center for Health Statistics Staff. LC 94-1872. (Series Reports: Series 16, No. 13). 98p. Date not set. 7.00 (*0-614-02918-X*, PB94-139748) Natl Ctr Health Stats.

Advance Data from Vital & Health Statistics, Nos. 21-30: PHS 90-1862. (Vital & Health Statistics Ser. 16: Compilations of Advance Data from Vital & Health Statistics: No. 3). 90p. 4.75 (*0-685-61587-1*, 017-022-01108-5) Natl Ctr Health Stats.

Advance Data from Vital & Health Statistics, Nos. 31-40: PHS 90-1863. (Vital & Health Statistics Ser. 16: Compilations of Advance Data from Vital & Health Statistics: No. 4). 96p. 4.75 (*0-685-61586-3*, 017-022-01115-8) Natl Ctr Health Stats.

Advance Directives & the Pursuit of Death with Dignity. Norman L. Cantor. LC 92-46072. (Medical Ethics Ser.). 1993. 24.95 (*0-253-31304-X*) Ind U Pr.

Advance Directives in Medicine. Ed. by Chris Hackler et al. LC 89-3562. 202p. 1989. text ed. 55.00 (*0-275-93233-8*, C3233, Praeger Pubs) Greenwood.

Advance Economics of Development & Planning. O. S. Shrivastava. 878p. 1985. 29.95 (*0-318-37330-0*) Asia Bk Corp.

Advance Educational Technologies for Mathematics & Science. Ed. by David L. Ferguson. LC 93-19193. (NATO ASI Series F: Computer & Systems Sciences, Special Programme AET: Vol. 107). 1993. 179.00 (*0-387-56531-0*) Spr-Verlag.

Advance Family Law Seminar for Advocates of the Poor Manual, I. 1988. 48.50 (*0-685-30172-9*, 44,360A) NCLS Inc.

Advance Family Law Seminar for Advocates of the Poor Manual, II. 1988. 40.00 (*0-685-30173-7*, 44,360B) NCLS Inc.

Advance Force-Pearl Harbor. Burl Burlingame. (Illus.). 480p. (Orig.). 1993. pap. 22.00 (*0-9629227-1-4*) Pacific Mono.

Advance from Broadway. Norris Houghton. (Select Bibliographies Reprint Ser.). 1977. 28.95 (*0-8369-5653-2*) Ayer.

Advance in Fishery Biology: Biology, Exploitation, Rearing, & Propagation of Coregonid Fishes. Proceedings of the Symposium on Coregonid Fishes, Thonon, France, Oct. 1984. Ed. by K. Dabrowski & A. Champigneulle. (Advances in Limnology Heft Ser.: No. 22). (Illus.). 386p. 1986. pap. 102.00 (*3-510-47020-6*) Lubrecht & Cramer.

Advance in Offshore Oil & Gas Pipeline Technology. Ed. by R. F. De La Mare. LC 84-82620. (Illus.). 380p. 1985. 74.00 (*0-87201-035-X*) Gulf Pub.

Advance in Stereotactic & Functional Neurosurgery: Proceedings of the Sixth Meeting of the European Society for Stereotatic & Functional Neurisurgery, Rome 1983. Ed. by J. Gybels et al. (Acta Neurochirugica - Supplementum Ser.: No. 33). (Illus.). 600p. 1984. pap. 184.00 (*0-387-81773-5*) Spr-Verlag.

Advance Locator for Capitol Hill, 1963: With Biographical Material on Members. Ed. by C. B. Brownson. LC 59-13987. 196p. 1963. pap. 2.50 (*0-685-58881-5*) Staff Direct.

Advance Locator for Capitol Hill, 1964: With Biographical Material on Members. 2nd ed. Ed. by C. B. Brownson. LC 59-13987. 196p. 1964. pap. 2.50 (*0-87289-005-8*) Staff Direct.

Advance Locator for Capitol Hill, 1965: With Biographical Material on Members. 3rd ed. Ed. by C. B. Brownson. LC 59-13987. 196p. 1965. pap. 2.50 (*0-87289-007-4*) Staff Direct.

Advance Locator for Capitol Hill, 1966: With Biographical Material on Members. 4th ed. Ed. by C. B. Brownson. LC 59-13987. 196p. 1966. pap. 1.50 (*0-87289-009-0*) Staff Direct.

Advance Locator for Capitol Hill, 1967: With Biographical Material on Members. 5th ed. Ed. by C. B. Brownson. LC 59-13987. 196p. 1967. pap. 2.00 (*0-87289-012-0*) Staff Direct.

Advance Locator for Capitol Hill, 1968: With Biographical Material on Members. 6th ed. Ed. by C. B. Brownson. LC 59-13987. 196p. 1968. pap. 2.50 (*0-87289-014-7*) Staff Direct.

Advance Locator for Capitol Hill, 1969: With Biographical Material on Members. 7th ed. Ed. by C. B. Brownson. LC 59-13987. 196p. 1969. pap. 2.50 (*0-87289-017-1*) Staff Direct.

Advance Locator for Capitol Hill, 1970: With Biographical Material on Members. 8th ed. Ed. by C. B. Brownson. LC 59-13987. 193p. 1970. pap. 2.50 (*0-87289-019-8*) Staff Direct.

Advance Locator for Capitol Hill, 1971: With Biographical Material on Members. 9th ed. Ed. by C. B. Brownson. LC 59-13987. 196p. 1971. pap. 3.50 (*0-87289-022-8*) Staff Direct.

Advance Locator for Capitol Hill, 1972: With Biographical Material on Members. 10th ed. Ed. by C. B. Brownson. LC 59-13987. 196p. 1972. pap. 3.50 (*0-87289-024-4*) Staff Direct.

Advance Locator for Capitol Hill, 1973: With Biographical Material on Members. 11th ed. Ed. by C. B. Brownson. LC 59-13987. 200p. 1973. pap. 3.50 (*0-87289-027-9*) Staff Direct.

Advance Materials Revolution & the Japanese System of Innovation. Helena M. Lastres. LC 94-16019. 1994. text ed. 65.00 (*0-312-12055-9*) St Martin.

Advance Medical Directives. Alan D. Lieberson. LC 92-82793. 1992. 145.00 (*0-685-59919-1*) Clark Boardman Callaghan.

Advance MS-DOS Batch File Programming. Dan Gookin. 1991. 24.95 (*0-8306-6681-8*) TAB Bks.

Advance Notice Provisions in Plant Closing Legislation. Ronald G. Ehrenberg & George H. Jakubson. LC 88-39749. 101p. 1988. pap. text ed. 10.00 (*0-88099-070-8*) W E Upjohn.

Advance of African Capital: The Growth of Nigerian Private Enterprise. Tom Forrest. LC 94-12171. 1994. text ed. 47.50 (*0-8139-1562-7*) U Pr of Va.

Advance of American Nursing. 2nd ed. Philip A. Kalisch & Beatrice J. Kalisch. (Illus.). 851p. (C). 1986. text ed. 34.50 (*0-673-39392-5*) Lippincott.

Advance of the American Short Story. Edward J. O'Brien. LC 74-145217. 314p. 1972. reprint ed. 29.00 (*0-403-01134-5*) Scholarly.

Advance of the English Novel. William L. Phelps. LC 74-145233. 1971. reprint ed. 24.00 (*0-403-01149-3*) Scholarly.

Advance of the English Novel. William L. Phelps. (BCL1-PR English Literature Ser.). 334p. 1992. reprint ed. lib. bdg. 89.00 (*0-7812-7114-2*) Rprt Serv.

Advance on Chaos: The Sanctifying Imagination of Wallace Stevens. David M. La Guardia. LC 83-40012. 210p. 1983. text ed. 25.00 (*0-87451-269-7*) U Pr of New Eng.

Advance Patternmaking. 1983. reprint ed. pap. 8.95 (*0-917914-09-0*) Lindsay Pubns.

Advance Placement Exam in U.S. Government & Politics. Joan U. Levy. 1994. pap. 15.00 (*0-671-84780-5*, Arco Test) P-H Gen Ref & Trav.

Advance Plan. S. Mikielle Chatman. (Series XII Book Group). 90p. 1992. pap. 8.00 (*1-881146-04-9*) Fat Chance.

Advance Printing of Paper Summaries: IS&T's Annual Conference, 44th, May 12-17, 1991, The Radisson Hotel, St. Paul, MN. Society for Imaging Science & Technology Staff. 636p. reprint ed. pap. 180.00 (*0-7837-0993-5*, 2041299) Bks Demand.

Advance Report of Final Divorce Statistics, 1988: PHS 91-1120, Vol. 39. No. 12, Supp. 2. 1991. write for info. (*0-318-69610-X*) Natl Ctr Health Stats.

Advance Report of Final Marriage Statistics, 1988, Vol. 40, No. 4 Supp. PHS 91-1120. 1991. write for info. (*0-318-69616-9*) Natl Ctr Health Stats.

***Advance Report of Final Natality Statistics, 1992 Vol. 43, No. 5.** suppl. ed. National Center for Health Statistics Staff. (Monthly Vital Statistics Report Ser.). 88p. Date not set. write for info. (*0-614-02948-1*) Natl Ctr Health Stats.

***Advance Report of Maternal & Infant Health Data from the Birth Certificate, 1991 Vol. 42, No. 11.** suppl. ed. National Center for Health Statistics Staff. (Monthly Vital Statistics Report Ser.). 32p. Date not set. write for info. (*0-614-02946-5*) Natl Ctr Health Stats.

Advance, Retreat: Selected Short Stories. Richard Rive. 131p. 1989. 19.95 (*0-312-03689-2*) St Martin.

Advance, Retreat: Selected Short Stories. Richard Rive. (Illus.). 128p. 1990. pap. 10.95 (*0-312-04772-X*) St Martin.

Advance Text of Resolutions & Decisions Adopted by General Assembly at Its 41st Session. 591p. 1987. 40.00 (*92-1-100306-7*, E.87.I.2) UN.

Advance Text of Resolutions & Decisions Adopted by the General Assembly: 43rd Session. 649p. 1989. 40.00 (*92-1-100406-3*, E.89.I.3) UN.

Advance Text of Resolutions & Decisions Adopted by the General Assembly at Its Forty-Fifth Session. 734p. 1990. 60.00 (*92-1-100451-9*) UN.

Advance Text of Resolutions & Decisions Adopted by the General Assembly during Its 44th Session, 1989. 669p. 45.00 (*92-1-100429-2*, E.90.I.4) UN.

Advance to Barbarism: The Development of Total Warfare from Sarajevo to Hiroshima. Frederick J. Veale. 363p. (C). 1993. reprint ed. pap. text ed. 11.00 (*0-939484-45-5*, 0989) Inst Hist Rev.

Advance to Revolution, Seventeen Sixty to Seventeen Seventy-Five. Murray N. Rothbard. LC 76-18978. (Conceived in Liberty Ser.: Vol. III). 373p. (C). 1988. reprint ed. pap. text ed. 13.95 (*0-317-90517-1*) Independent Inst.

***Advanced A-D & D-A Conversion Techniques & Their Applications: Proceedings of the Second International Conference, Held at Robinson College, Cambridge, U. K., 1994.** Second International Conference Staff. (Conference Publications: No. 393). 185p. 1994. pap. 76.00 (*0-85296-617-2*) IEEE Comp Soc.

Advanced Abacus: Theory & Practice. Takashi Kojima. LC 62-15064. 160p. 1991. reprint ed. pap. 8.95 (*0-8048-0003-0*) C E Tuttle.

Advanced Abnormal Child Psychology. Ed. by Michel Hersen & Robert T. Ammerman. 464p. 1995. text ed. 99.95 (*0-8058-1203-2*); pap. 45.00 (*0-8058-1204-0*) L Erlbaum Assocs.

Advanced Abnormal Psychology. Ed. by M. Hersen & Vincent B. Van Hasselt. 1994. 45.00 (*0-306-44547-6*, Plenum Pr) Plenum.

***Advanced AC Circuits.** Tom Adamson. Ed. by Kelly Gorham. 29p. 1994. student ed write for info. (*0-8064-0326-8*, E23) Bergwall.

Advanced Accelerator Concepts. Ed. by Chan Joshi. LC 89-45914. (AIP Conference Proceedings Ser.: No. 193). 496p. 1989. lib. bdg. 70.00 (*0-88318-393-5*) Am Inst Physics.

Advanced Accelerator Concepts. Ed. by J. S. Wurtele. (AIP Conference Proceedings Ser.: No. 279). (Illus.). 1000p. 1993. text ed. 125.00 (*1-56396-191-1*, AIP Pr) Am Inst Physics.

Advanced Accelerator Concepts: Proceedings from the International Symposium on Advanced Accelerator Concepts Held in Madison, Wisconsin, August 1986. Ed. by Fredrick E. Mills. (AIP Conference Proceedings Ser.: No. 156). 610p. 1987. 75.00 (*0-685-58860-2*) Am Inst Physics.

Advanced Accountancy. S. K. Paul. (C). 1989. 125.00 (*0-685-50343-7*, Current Dist) St Mut.

Advanced Accounting. Andrew A. Haried. 832p. 1991. teacher ed 50.00 (*0-471-53339-4*) Wiley.

Advanced Accounting. Jack Rudman. 1994. 39.95 (*0-8373-5563-X*, PEP-13) Nat Learn.

Advanced Accounting. 2nd ed. Calvin Engler & Leopold A. Bernstein. 967p. (C). 1989. text ed. 69.95 (*0-256-03571-7*) Irwin.

Advanced Accounting. 2nd ed. Daniel L. Jensen. 1988. text ed. write for info. (*0-07-555463-1*) McGraw.

***Advanced Accounting.** 3rd ed. Calvin Engler et al. LC 94-37805. (Series in Undergraduate Accounting). 1200p. (C). 1994. text ed. 69.95 (*0-256-08853-5*) Irwin.

Advanced Accounting. 3rd ed. Joe B. Hoyle. 1087p. (C). 1990. text ed. 65.95 (*0-256-08318-5*, 01-1685-03) Irwin.

Advanced Accounting. 3rd ed. Daniel L. Jensen. 1994. text ed. write for info. (*0-07-032667-3*) McGraw.

Advanced Accounting. 3rd rev. ed. Daniel L. Jensen. LC 93-21688. 1994. text ed. write for info. (*0-07-074322-3*) McGraw.

Advanced Accounting. 4th ed. Paul M. Fischer et al. (C). 1989. text ed. write for info. (*0-538-80872-1*, AD90DAZ) S-W Pub.

Advanced Accounting. 4th ed. Joe B. Hoyle. LC 93-13312. 1184p. (C). 1993. text ed. 69.95 (*0-256-12407-8*) Irwin.

Advanced Accounting. 5th ed. Floyd A. Beams. 1056p. 1991. text ed. 75.00 (*0-13-010489-2*) P-H.

Advanced Accounting. 5th ed. Paul M. Fischer et al. LC 92-13754. 1993. write for info. (*0-538-82251-1*) S-W Pub.

Advanced Accounting. 5th ed. Charles H. Griffin et al. (C). 1985. student ed 22.95 (*0-256-02966-0*) Irwin.

Advanced Accounting. 5th ed. Andrew A. Haried et al. 1991. disk 20.00 (*0-471-54509-0*); disk 20.00 (*0-471-54508-2*); disk write for info. (*0-471-54503-1*); disk 20.00 (*0-471-54502-3*); write for info. (*0-471-53333-5*); Net. write for info. (*0-471-53336-X*); write for info. (*0-471-53337-8*) Wiley.

***Advanced Accounting.** 6th ed. Paul M. Fischer & William J. Taylor. LC 94-28895. 1200p. 1995. text ed. 64.95 (*0-538-84126-5*) S-W Pub.

An Asterisk (*) at the beginning of an entry indicates that the title is appearing in BIP for the first time.

Advanced Accounting. 6th ed. Charles H. Griffin et al. 1213p. (C). 1990. text ed. 65.95 (0-256-06962-X, 01-0225-06) Irwin.

***Advanced Accounting.** 6th ed. Charles H. Griffin et al. (C). 1990. student ed, text ed. 23.95 (0-256-06963-8) Irwin.

Advanced Accounting. 6th ed. Andrew A. Haried et al. LC 93-46004. 1994. text ed. write for info. (0-471-58888-1) Wiley.

Advanced Accounting. 7th ed. James R. Boatsman et al. LC 93-10648. 1136p. (C). 1993. text ed. 69.95 (0-256-10819-6) Irwin.

***Advanced Accounting.** 7th ed. Ula Motekat. 359p. (C). 1993. student ed, text ed. 24.95 (0-256-12045-5) Irwin.

Advanced Accounting: Appendix on the Law Relating to Accounts by J. E. G. Dep Montmorency. Lawrence R. Dicksee. LC 75-18464. (History of Accounting Ser.). (Illus.). 1979. reprint ed. 31.95 (0-405-07547-2) Ayer.

Advanced Accounting: Concepts & Practice. 4th ed. Arnold J. Pahler & Joseph E. Mori. 1310p. (C). 1990. text ed. 61.75 (0-15-501204-5) Dryden Pr.

Advanced Accounting: Concepts & Practice. 5th ed. Arnold J. Pahler & Joseph E. Mori. LC 93-71908. 1325p. (C). 1993. text ed. 68.00 (0-03-098697-4) Dryden Pr.

Advanced Accounting: Concepts & Practice. 5th ed. Arnold J. Pahler & Joseph E. Mori. LC 93-71908. 1325p. (C). 1994. 207.50 (0-03-006818-5); 207.50 (0-03-006817-7) Dryden Pr.

***Advanced Accounting: GAAP Interpretation & Application 1994.** 5th ed. Patrick R. Delaney et al. text ed. write for info. (0-471-06244-8) Wiley.

***Advanced Accounting: Interpretation & Application, 1994.** 6th ed. Andrew A. Haried & Patrick R. Delaney. text ed. write for info. (0-471-02468-6) Wiley.

Advanced Accounting: Syllabus. W. R. Singleton & E. R. Johansson. 1977. pap. text ed. 13.85 (0-89420-016-X, 352050); audio 250.85 (0-89420-124-7, 352000) Natl Book.

Advanced Accounting: Yorston, Smyth & Brown. 10th ed. E. Bryan Smyth et al. vii, 799p. 1988. teacher ed 28.00 (0-455-20911-1, Pub. by Law Bk Co); pap. 61.00 (0-455-20799-2, Pub. by Law Bk Co) W W Gaunt.

Advanced Accounting: Concepts & Practice: Instructor's Resource Manual & Testbook to Accompany. 5th ed. Arnold J. Pahler & Joseph E. Mori. 500p. (C). 1994. pap. text ed. 41.75 (0-03-003589-9) Dryden Pr.

Advanced Accounting Examinations. 3rd ed. Harry W. Koch. 1988. 8.00 (0-910553-18-1) Ken-Bks.

Advanced Accounting Practice U. K. Howard. 1985. pap. 44.95 (0-85258-241-2) Chapman & Hall.

***Advanced Accounting Working Papers.** 2nd ed. Calvin Engler. 528p. (C). 1989. text ed. 24.95 (0-256-08088-7) Irwin.

***Advanced Accounting Working Papers.** 6th ed. Charles H. Griffin et al. (C). 1991. text ed. 22.95 (0-256-09179-X) Irwin.

***Advanced Adaptive Control.** H. Wang et al. LC 95-11906. 256p. 1995. text ed. 96.00 (0-08-042020-6, Pergamon Pr) Elsevier.

***Advanced Addition.** (Tai Mathematics Ser.). (J). 1995. 5.25 (0-88106-153-0, M001) Charlesbridge Pub.

***Advanced Addition: Carrying.** Bob DeWeese. (Math at Home Ser.). (Illus.). 44p. 1994. teacher ed, pap. text ed. 2.95 (1-55799-311-4, EMC 604) Evan-Moor Corp.

***Advanced Adobe Photoshop for Macintosh.** Adobe Press Staff. (Illus.). (Orig.). Date not set. pap. 49.95 (0-614-06066-4) Hayden.

Advanced Adobe Photoshop for Windows. Adobe Press Staff et al. (Seminar in a Book Ser.). (Illus.). 208p. (Orig.). 1994. pap. 49.95 (1-56830-116-2) Hayden.

Advanced Aerial Devices Reported During the Korean War. Richard F. Haines. 85p. (Orig.). 1990. pap. 9.95 (0-9618082-1-7) LDA Pr CA.

Advanced Aerohemodynamics. 1984. 17.95 (0-930835-04-2) Med Res Assocs.

Advanced Aerospace Hydraulic Systems & Components. 100p. 1991. pap. 25.00 (1-56091-179-4, SP-885) Soc Auto Engineers.

Advanced Aerospace Materials. Horst Buhl. LC 92-30704. x, 373p. 1992. 125.00 (3-540-55888-8); 125.00 (0-387-55888-8) Spr-Verlag.

Advanced Affirmative Civil Enforcement Conference. 38p. (Orig.). 1993. 15.00 (1-56986-230-3) Federal Bar.

Advanced Airbreathing Propulsion. Y. M. Timnat. (Orbit Ser.). (C). 1995. lib. bdg. write for info. (0-89464-049-6) Krieger.

Advanced Airbrush Book. Cecil Misstear et al. (Illus.). 160p. 1984. text ed. 44.95 (0-442-28424-1) Van Nos Reinhold.

Advanced Aircraft Systems. David A. Lombardo. (Practical Flying Ser.). 1993. text ed. 30.00 (0-07-038602-1); pap. text ed. 18.95 (0-07-038603-X) McGraw.

Advanced Aircraft Systems: Understanding Your Airplane. David A. Lombardo. (Illus.). 304p. 1993. text ed. 29.95 (0-8306-3997-7, 4170); pap. text ed. 18.95 (0-8306-3998-5, 4170) TAB Bks.

Advanced Algebra. Thomas J. McHale & Paul T. Witzke. (Milwaukee Area Technical College Mathematics Ser.). 1972. pap. text ed. 32.76 (0-201-04633-4) Addison-Wesley.

Advanced Algebraic Techniques see Series in Mathematics Modules

Advanced Algorithms & Architectures for Signal Processing, No. II. Ed. by Luk. 255p. 1987. 51.00 (0-89252-861-3, 826) SPIE.

Advanced Algorithms & Architectures for Signal Processing III. Ed. by F. T. Luk. 1988. 59.00 (0-8194-0010-6, 975) SPIE.

Advanced Algorithms & Architectures for Signal Processing IV. Ed. by Franklin T. Luk. 508p. 1989. 70.00 (0-8194-0188-9, VOL. 1152) SPIE.

Advanced Algorithms & Architectures for Speech Understanding. Ed. by G. Pirani et al. (Research Reports ESPRIT, Project 26 SIP: Vol. 1). xiv, 274p. 1990. pap. 35.00 (0-387-53402-4) Spr-Verlag.

***Advanced Algorithms for Neural Networks: A C++ Sourcebook.** Timothy Masters. LC 94-43390. 1995. disk, pap. 44.95 (0-471-10588-0) Wiley.

Advanced Alloys in the Soviet Aviation Industry: Enhancing Fatigue Strength of Mi-26 Helicopter Components. Valery Weinstein. Ed. by Rebecca Krafft. 112p. (Orig.). 1986. pap. text ed. 75.00 (1-55831-056-8) Delphic Associates.

Advanced Alternative Fuels Technology. (International Fuels & Lubricants Meeting & Exposition, 1993 Ser.). pap. 56.00 (1-56091-434-3, SP-995) Soc Auto Engineers.

Advanced Aluminum & Titanium Structures: Presented at the Winter Annual Meeting of the American Society of Mechanical Engineers, Washington, D.C., November 15-20, 1981. American Society of Mechanical Engineers Staff. Ed. by J. W. Goodman. LC 81-69003. (AD Ser.: No. 02). (Illus.). 49p. reprint ed. pap. 25.00 (0-8357-2905-2, 2039142) Bks Demand.

Advanced Amateur Astronomy. Gerald North. 1991. text ed. 50.00 (0-7486-0253-4, Pub. by Edinburgh U Pr UK) Col U Pr.

Advanced Analysis: Steel Frames Theory. Chen. 1993. 95.00 (0-8493-8281-5) CRC Pr.

Advanced Analysis & Design of Plated Structures. V. Kristek & M. Skaloud. (Developments in Civil Engineering Ser.: No. 32). 336p. 1991. 128.75 (0-444-98765-7) Elsevier.

Advanced Analytic Number Theory, Pt. One: Ramification Theoretic Methods. Carlos J. Moreno. LC 82-22620. (Contemporary Mathematics Ser.: No. 5). 190p. 1983. pap. 27.00 (0-8218-5015-6, CONM-15) Am Math.

Advanced Anarchist Arsenal. David Harber. (Illus.). 144p. 1991. pap. 15.00 (0-87364-634-7) Paladin Pr.

Advanced & Duplicate Bridge Student Text. Shirley Silverman. 1976. pap. 2.95 (0-87643-021-3) Barclay Bridge.

Advanced & Professional Typewriting. 2nd ed. Molly Sedgwick. 168p. (Orig.). 1985. pap. text ed. 22.95 (0-273-01933-3, Pub. by Pitman Pub Ltd UK) Trans-Atl Phila.

Advanced Anecdotes in American English. Leslie A. Hill. (Anecdotes in American English Ser.). (Illus.). (Orig.). 1981. pap. text ed. 5.75 (0-19-502603-9) OUP.

Advanced Anecdotes in American English. Leslie A. Hill. (Anecdotes in American English Ser.). (Illus.). (Orig.). 1981. audio 17.50 (0-19-502830-9) OUP.

Advanced Animation & Rendering Techniques. Alan Watt. (C). 1992. text ed. 45.25 (0-201-54412-1) Addison-Wesley.

Advanced ANSI COBOL with Structured Programming: For VS COBOL IITM & Microsoft - Micro Focus COBOL. 2nd ed. Gary D. Brown. 528p. 1992. pap. text ed. 44.95 (0-471-54786-7) Wiley.

Advanced Anti-Trust Workshop: Twenty-Second Annual. (Corporate Law & Practice Course Handbook, 1985-86 Ser.). 375p. 1992. pap. 70.00 (0-685-69374-0) PLI.

Advanced Appleworks. David Bolocan. 256p. 1986. pap. 16.95 (0-8306-0148-1, 2648P) TAB Bks.

Advanced Appleworks. 2nd ed. David Bolocan & Tim Tow. 1988. pap. text ed. 17.95 (0-07-157419-0) McGraw.

Advanced AppleWorks. 2nd ed. David Bolocan & Tim Tow. (Illus.). 260p. 1988. pap. 17.95 (0-8306-9348-3, 3048) TAB Bks.

Advanced Applications Using WordPerfect 5.0, Lotus 1-2-3 & dBASE IV: Cases & Solutions. Fritz H. Grupe. 688p. (C). 1991. spiral bd. write for info. (0-697-11902-5) Bus & Educ Tech.

Advanced Applications Using WordPerfect 5.1 - Lotus 1-2-3 Version 2.2 - dBASE IV. Fritz H. Grupe. 732p. (C). 1992. spiral bd. write for info. (0-697-13500-4) Bus & Educ Tech.

Advanced Applications WordPerfect 5.1: Cases & Solutions. Fritz H. Grupe. 248p. (C). 1992. spiral bd. write for info. (0-697-13498-9) Bus & Educ Tech.

Advanced Appraisal Methods. Henry S. Harrison. (Orig.). 1994. pap. text ed. 29.95 (0-927054-18-3) H Sq Co.

Advanced Arabic Composition & Conversation. Raji M. Rammuny. 1980. 16.95 (0-86685-410-X); student ed 16.95 (0-86685-411-8) Intl Bk Ctr.

Advanced Arabic I. 1991. student ed 8.00 (0-87415-219-4, 87) OSU Foreign Lang.

Advanced Arabic II. 1991. student ed 8.00 (0-87415-221-6, 88) OSU Foreign Lang.

Advanced Arc Welding. Richard Hunter. (Series 908). (Orig.). 1984. 8.00 (0-8064-0383-7, 908); audio 399.99 (0-8064-0384-5) Bergwall.

***Advanced Archer: How to Stay Calm at the Center.** Thomas Whitney & Vishnu Karmakar. 128p. (Orig.). 1992. teacher ed, pap. 12.95 (1-881234-00-2) Ctr Vision.

Advanced Arrhythmias. Louise A. Smith. (Orig.). 1987. pap. write for info. (0-932491-80-4) Res Appl Inc.

Advanced Arrhythmias: A Practice Workbook. Smith & Fish. 1986. 24.00 (0-8016-5201-4) Mosby Yr Bk.

Advanced Arthritis Study Guide. Competence Assurance Systems Staff. 1986. pap. text ed. 235.00 (0-89147-068-9) CAS.

Advanced Assembler Language & MVS Interfaces for Systems & Applications Programmers. Carmine Cannatello. 1991. pap. text ed. 43.50 (0-471-50435-1) Wiley.

Advanced Assembly Language. Allen L. Wyatt, Sr. (Illus.). (Orig.). 1992. pap. 39.95 (1-56529-037-2) Que.

Advanced Atlas of Histology. W. H. Freeman & Brian Bracegirdle. (Heinemann Biology Atlases Ser.). 1976. text ed. 25.00 (0-435-60317-5, 60317) Heinemann.

Advanced Audio Production Techniques. Tyree S. Ford. (Illus.). 160p. 1993. pap. 24.95 (0-240-80082-6, Focal) Buttrwrth-Heinemann.

Advanced Auditing: Fundamentals of EDP & Statistical Audit Technology. Miklos Vasarhelyi & W. Thomas Lin. 640p. (C). 1988. text ed. 63.50 (0-201-05328-4) Addison-Wesley.

Advanced Autocad Release 12. 3rd ed. Robert M. Thomas. LC 92-63118. 485p. 1993. pap. 29.95 (0-7821-1187-4) Sybex.

Advanced Automotive Technologies 1993. Ed. by M. Ahmadian. LC 89-46295. 419p. Date not set. pap. 75.00 (0-7918-1046-1) ASME.

Advanced Backgammon, Vol. 1: Positional Play. Bill Robertie. 288p. 1993. pap. 30.00 (1-880604-02-7) Gammon Pr.

Advanced Backgammon, Vol. 2: Technical Play. Bill Robertie. 288p. 1993. pap. 30.00 (1-880604-03-5) Gammon Pr.

Advanced Backstabbing & Mudslinging Techniques. George Hayduke. 192p. 1991. pap. 7.95 (0-8184-0560-0, L Stuart) Carol Pub Group.

Advanced Bacterial Genetics. Ed. by R. Davis et al. LC 80-25695. 254p. (Orig.). 1980. student ed 38.00 (0-87969-130-1) Cold Spring Harbor.

Advanced Balisong Manual. Jeff Imada. (Orig.). 1989. pap. 11.95 (0-938676-07-5) Know Now Pub.

Advanced Balisong Manual. Jeff Imada. (Illus.). 128p. (Orig.). 1986. pap. 11.95 (0-318-42473-8, 5192) Unique Pubns.

***Advanced Balisong Manual.** Jeff Imada. (Orig.). 1991. pap. 9.95 (0-86568-117-1) Unique Pubns.

Advanced B&W Darkroom Book. Bob Nadler. LC 79-9934. (Illus.). 80p. 1979. pap. 8.95 (0-933596-00-6) F-Twenty-Two.

Advanced Banking in the UK. Euromonitor Staff. 126p. (C). 1987. 705.00 (0-86338-209-6, Pub. by Euromonitor Pubns UK) Gale.

Advanced Bankruptcy Workshop, 2 vols., Set. (Commercial Law & Practice Ser.). 1168p. 1992. pap. text ed. 80.00 (0-685-56863-6, A4-4359) PLI.

Advanced Bankruptcy Workshop: Case Studies in Handling Chapter 11 Problems, Set. (Commercial Law & Practice Ser.). 1739p. 1990. 30.00 (0-685-48524-2, A4-4325) PLI.

Advanced Bankruptcy Workshop 1993. (Commercial Law & Practice Course Handbook Ser.: Vols. 649 & 650). 1086p. 1993. 70.00 (0-685-69700-2, A4-4408) PLI.

Advanced BASIC: A Modular Approach. Eileen Schoaff. (Illus.). 431p. 1986. text ed. 41.00 (0-314-98072-5) West Pub.

Advanced Basic & Beyond for the IBM PC: Revised & Enlarged. 2nd ed. Larry J. Goldstein. 450p. (C). 1987. 19.95 (0-13-010307-1) P-H.

Advanced BASIC Meta-Analysis: Version 1.10. Brian Mullen. 184p. (C). 1989. text ed. 29.95 (0-8058-0502-8) L Erlbaum Assocs.

Advanced BASIC Meta-Analysis, 1989. B. Mullen. 29.95 (0-685-48947-7); 3.5 ld 79.95 (1-56321-036-3); 5.25 ld 79.95 (1-56321-035-5) LEA S&AM.

***Advanced Bass Fishing.** Dick Sternberg. LC 94-36044. (Hunting & Fishing Library). 128p. 1995. 19.95 (0-86573-041-5) Cy De Cosse.

***Advanced Bass Techniques.** Rich Zaleski. LC 92-85328. (Complete Angler's Library). 250p. 1993. write for info. (0-914697-51-X) N Amer Outdoor Grp.

Advanced Batch File Programming. 3rd ed. Dan Gookin. 528p. 1991. pap. 29.95 (0-8306-2532-1, Windcrest) TAB Bks.

Advanced Beadwork. Ruth F. Poris. (Illus.). 152p. (Orig.). 1990. per. 14.99 (0-9616422-0-3) Golden Hands Pr.

Advanced Beam Dynamics Workshop on Effects of Errors in Accelerators, Their Diagnosis & Correction: AIP Conference Proceedings, No. 255. Ed. by Alex Chao. LC 92-52842. (AIP Conference Proceedings Ser.). (Illus.). 440p. 1992. 95.00 (1-56396-006-0) Am Inst Physics.

Advanced Biochemical Engineering. Ed. by Henry R. Bungay, III & Georges Belfort. LC 86-15834. 304p. 1987. text ed. 77.95 (0-471-81279-X) Wiley.

Advanced Biology: A Course Manual. Anthony V. DeFina. (Illus.). 434p. (Orig.). 1984. teacher ed 27.50 (0-916209-06-7); student ed, pap. 25.00 (0-916209-02-4) Owlet Pubns.

***Advanced Black & White Photography.** Eastman. 1995. pap. text ed. 14.95 (0-87985-005-1) Saunders Photo.

***Advanced Black-&-White Photography.** rev. ed. Hubert Birnbaum et al. (Illus.). 104p. (C). Date not set. pap. text ed. write for info. (0-87985-760-9, Kodak) Saunders Photo.

Advanced Blowout & Well Control. Robert D. Grace. 336p. 1994. 65.00 (0-88415-260-X) Gulf Pub.

Advanced Book Program - Mathematica Journal. 1990. pap. 74.75 (0-201-59931-7); pap. 14.95 (0-201-59901-5) Addison-Wesley.

Advanced Book Program - Mathematica Journal. 2nd ed. 1990. pap. 74.75 (0-201-59932-5); pap. 14.95 (0-201-59902-3) Addison-Wesley.

Advanced Boundary Element Methods. Ed. by T. A. Cruse. (Illus.). 510p. 1988. 99.00 (0-387-17454-0) Spr-Verlag.

Advanced Bowhunting Guide. Roger Maynard. (Illus.). 224p. (Orig.). 1984. pap. 14.95 (0-88317-115-5) Stoeger Pub Co.

Advanced Building Control Systems & Devices. Business Communications Co., Inc. Staff. 158p. 1990. 1,950.00 (0-89336-743-5, G089R) BCC.

Advanced Bulgarian 1. Lyubomira P. Gribble & Charles E. Gribble. (Illus.). 218p. (Orig.). (BUL.). (C). 1987. student ed, pap. text ed. 11.00 (0-87415-111-2, 47) OSU Foreign Lang.

Advanced Bulgarian 1. Lyubomira P. Gribble & Charles E. Gribble. (Illus.). 172p. (Orig.). (BUL.). (C). 1987. teacher ed, pap. 9.00 (0-87415-112-0, 47A); audio 5.00 (0-87415-113-9, 47B) OSU Foreign Lang.

Advanced Bulgarian 2. Lyubomira P. Gribble & Charles E. Gribble. (Illus.). 190p. (Orig.). (BUL.). (C). 1987. student ed, pap. text ed. 10.00 (0-87415-114-7, 48); audio 5.00 (0-87415-116-3, 48B) OSU Foreign Lang.

Advanced Bulgarian 2. Lyubomira P. Gribble & Charles E. Gribble. (Illus.). 168p. (Orig.). (BUL.). (C). 1987. teacher ed, pap. 10.00 (0-87415-115-5, 48A) OSU Foreign Lang.

Advanced Business Arabic. Raji Rammuny. 1994. 22.95x (0-86685-416-9) Intl Bk Ctr.

Advanced Business Communication. 2nd ed. John M. Penrose, Jr. et al. LC 92-28661. 430p. 1993. text ed. 58.95 (0-534-93259-2) Intl Thomson.

Advanced Business Contacts. Nick Brieger & Jeremy Comfort. LC 93-30935. 1993. 11.50 (0-13-010422-1) P-H Intl.

Advanced C. Peter Hipson. (Illus.). (Orig.). 1992. pap. 39.95 (0-672-30168-7) Sams.

Advanced C: Tips & Techniques. Paul Anderson & Gail Anderson. 456p. 1988. pap. 29.95 (0-672-48417-X) Sams.

Advanced C Plus Plus. Namir C. Shammas. 1992. disk, pap. 39.95 (0-672-30158-X) Sams.

Advanced C Plus Plus Book. M. T. Skinner. LC 92-31598. (Orig.). 1992. 40.00 (0-13-088493-6) P-H.

Advanced C Plus Plus Book. M. T. Skinner. 300p. (Orig.). 1992. 29.95 (0-929306-10-4) Silicon Pr.

Advanced C Plus Plus Programming Styles & Idioms. James O. Coplien. (Illus.). 368p. (C). 1992. pap. text ed. 39.75 (0-201-54855-0) Addison-Wesley.

Advanced C Programmer's Guide to OS-2. Augie Hansen & Vaughn Vernon. 500p. 1990. pap. 26.95 (0-201-52328-0) Addison-Wesley.

Advanced C Programming. Waite Group Staff. 288p. 1985. pap. 21.95 (0-317-37790-6) S&S Trade.

Advanced C Programming: Practical Solutions to Advanced Programming Problems. Peter Norton Computing Group Staff & Steven Qualline. 1991. disk, pap. 39.95 (0-13-663170-3); pap. 29.95 (0-13-663188-6) Brady Compu Bks.

Advanced C Programming for Displays: Character Displays, Windows, & Keyboards for Unix & MS-DOS. Marc J. Rochkind. (Illus.). 272p. 1987. 35.95 (0-13-010240-7) P-H.

Advanced C Programming on the IBM PC. Herbert Mayer. (Orig.). 1991. 24.95 (0-8306-8694-0); 24.95 (0-8306-8695-9) TAB Bks.

Advanced C Programming on the IBM PC. Herbert G. Mayer. (Illus.). 400p. (Orig.). 1989. 33.95 (0-8306-9163-4, Windcrest) TAB Bks.

Advanced C Structured Programming: Data Structure Design & Implementation in C. John W. Ogilvie. 432p. 1990. pap. text ed. 26.95 (0-471-51943-X); write for info. (0-471-53580-X) Wiley.

Advanced Calculus. Paul C. DuChateau. (College Outline Ser.). 256p. (Orig.). 1992. pap. 13.00 (0-06-467139-9, Harper Ref) HarpC.

Advanced Calculus. Murray R. Spiegel. (Orig.). 1963. pap. text ed. 14.95 (0-07-060229-8) McGraw.

Advanced Calculus. David V. Widder. 1989. pap. 10.95 (0-486-66103-2) Dover.

Advanced Calculus. 3rd ed. R. Creighton Buck. LC 77-2859. (McGraw-Hill International Series in Pure & Applied Mathematics). (Illus.). 1978. text ed. write for info. (0-07-008728-8) McGraw.

Advanced Calculus. 3rd ed. Wilfred Kaplan. 721p. (C). 1984. text ed. 48.76 (0-201-11680-4, Adv Bk Prog) Addison-Wesley.

Advanced Calculus. 3rd ed. Angus E. Taylor & W. Robert Mann. LC 81-16141. 732p. (C). 1983. Net. text ed. write for info. (0-471-02566-6) Wiley.

Advanced Calculus. 4th ed. Wilfred Kaplan. (Illus.). 746p. (C). 1991. text ed. 72.25 (0-201-57888-3) Addison-Wesley.

Advanced Calculus: A Course Arranged with Special Reference to the Needs of Students of Applied Mathematics. Frederick S. Woods. 407p. reprint ed. pap. 116.00 (0-8357-5122-8, 2000161) Bks Demand.

***Advanced Calculus: A Course in Mathematical Analysis.** Patrick M. Fitzpatrick. LC 94-41176. 1996. text ed. 74.95 (0-534-92612-6) PWS Pubs.

Advanced Calculus: A Differential Forms Approach. 3rd ed. Harold M. Edwards. LC 93-20657. (Illus.). 528p. 1995. 49.50 (0-8176-3707-9) Birkhauser.

Advanced Calculus: An Introduction to Analysis. 3rd ed. Watson Fulks. LC 78-5268. 731p. 1978. Net. text ed. write for info. (0-471-02195-4) Wiley.

Advanced Calculus: An Introduction to Modern Analysis. Ed. by Voxman & Goetschel. (Pure & Applied Mathematics Ser.: Vol. 63). 696p. 1981. 160.00 (0-8247-6949-X) Dekker.

Advanced Calculus & Its Applications. John C. Amazigo & Lester A. Rubenfeld. LC 80-283. 407p. 1980. Net. text ed. write for info. (0-471-04934-4) Wiley.

Advanced Calculus & Vector FIE Field Theory. K. Urwin. LC 65-25340. 1966. 121.00 (0-08-010761-3, Pub. by Pergamon Repr UK) Franklin.

Advanced Calculus for Applications. 2nd ed. Francis B. Hildebrand. (Illus.). 816p. 1976. text ed. write for info. (0-13-011189-9) P-H.

Advanced Calculus for Users. A. Robert. 366p. 1989. 59.00 (0-444-87324-4, North Holland) Elsevier.

***Advanced Calculus of Several Variables.** unabridged ed. C. H. Edwards, Jr. (Illus.). 480p. 1995. pap. text ed. 13.95 (0-486-68336-2) Dover.

An Asterisk (*) at the beginning of an entry indicates that the title is appearing in BIP for the first time.

Advanced Calculus Problem Solver. rev. ed. Research & Education Association Staff. LC 81-52799. (Illus.). 1056p. 1994. pap. text ed. 29.95 (*0-87891-533-8*) Res & Educ.

Advanced Calculus with Applications in Statistics. Andre I. Khuri. LC 92-45033. (Probability & Mathematical Statistics: Applied Probability & Statistics Section Ser.). 466p. 1993. text ed. 59.95 (*0-471-53459-5*) Wiley.

Advanced Calligraphy. Katherine Jeffares. 1979. pap. 7.00 (*0-87980-372-X*) Wilshire.

Advanced Card & Identification Technology Sourcebook, 1994. Ed. by Ben Miller. 192p. (Orig.). 1993. pap. 125.00 (*1-878413-02-3*) Warfel & Miller.

Advanced Cardiac Life Support. James Paturas & Andrew Weinberg. (Emergency Care Ser.). (C). 1995. pap. text ed. 29.95 (*0-86720-819-8*) Jones & Bartlett.

Advanced Cardiac Life Support: Certification Preparation & Review. Bruce R. Shade et al. (Illus.). 640p. 1985. pap. text ed. 26.95 (*0-89303-272-7*) P-H.

Advanced Cardiac Life Support: Certification Preparation & Review. 2nd ed. Bruce R. Shade & Joann Grif Alspach. (Illus.). 400p. 1988. pap. text ed. 27.95 (*0-317-62369-9*) P-H.

Advanced Cardiac Life Support: The Practical Approach. Advanced Life Support Group, Hope Hospital Staff. LC 92-49023. 1993. write for info. (*0-412-48390-4*) Chapman & Hall.

Advanced Cardiac Life Support Algorithms & Drugs: A Handbook for Adult & Pediatric Providers, 1993. Subcommittee on Advanced Cardiac Life Support Staff. (Illus.). 54p. (Orig.). 1993. pap. text ed. write for info. (*0-87493-625-X*) Am Heart.

Advanced Career Strategies: Corporate Smarts for Women on the Way Up. Marilyn Machlowitz. 220p. 1984. 15.95 (*0-943066-04-2*) CareerTrack Pubns.

Advanced Cartooning. B. Kliban. (Illus.). 160p. 1993. pap. 7.95 (*0-8362-1710-1*) Andrews & McMeel.

Advanced Case Management: New Strategies for the Nineties. Norma R. Raiff & Barbara R. Shore. (Human Services Guides Ser.: Vol. 66). (Illus.). 180p. (C). 1993. text ed. 39.95 (*0-8039-5308-9*); pap. text ed. 17.95 (*0-8039-3872-1*) Sage.

Advanced Cementitious Systems: Mechanisms & Properties. Ed. by F. P. Glasser et al. (Symposium Proceedings Ser.: Vol. 245). 1992. text ed. 69.00 (*1-55899-139-5*) Materials Res.

Advanced Cements & Chemically Bonded Ceramics: Materials Research Society International Symposium Proceedings-IMAM, No. 13. Ed. by M. Daimon et al. 266p. 1989. text ed. 65.00 (*1-55899-042-9*) Materials Res.

Advanced Ceramic Manual, Technical Data for the Studio Potter. John W. Conrad. 278p. (Orig.). (C). 1988. pap. 29.90 (*0-935921-05-2*) Falcon Co.

Advanced Ceramic Powders for Structural Components, Coatings & Electronics Applications. Business Communications Co., Inc. Staff. 206p. 1990. 2,650.00 (*0-89336-730-3*, GB-102) BCC.

***Advanced Ceramic Tools for Machining Application-I.** Ed. by Xing Sheng Shi & It- Meng Low. (Key Engineering Materials Ser.: Vol. 96). (Illus.). 272p. (C). 1994. 92.00 (*0-87849-684-X*, Inform) LPS Dist Ctr.

Advanced Ceramics. Business Communications Co., Inc. Staff. 132p. 1985. 1,750.00 (*0-89336-255-7*, GB-058R) BCC.

Advanced Ceramics. Ed. by C. Ganguly et al. 580p. 1991. text ed. 168.00 (*0-87849-547-9*, Pub. by Trans Tech GW) LPS Dist Ctr.

Advanced Ceramics. Ed. by Shinroku Saito. (Illus.). 288p. 1988. 90.00 (*0-19-856335-3*) OUP.

Advanced Ceramics: Based on the Proc. of the Lecture Meeting, Held at the Nagatsuta Campus, Tokyo Institute of Technology, 4-5 Sept. 1986, Vol. II. Ed. by S. Somiya. 226p. 1989. 77.50 (*1-85166-214-6*) Elsevier.

Advanced Ceramics Three: Proceedings of an Invited Lecture Meeting to Mark the Retirement of Professor S. Somiya from the Tokyo Institute of Technology, Held in Tokyo, Japan, 27 May 1988. Ed. by S. Somiya. 254p. 1990. 130.00 (*1-85166-485-8*) Elsevier.

Advanced Cha Cha Breaks. (Ballroom Dance Ser.). 1985. lib. bdg. 76.00 (*0-87700-755-1*) Revisionist Pr.

Advanced Cha-Cha Breaks. (Ballroom Dance Ser.). 1986. lib. bdg. 250.00 (*0-8490-3393-4*) Gordon Pr.

Advanced Chapter Eleven Bankruptcy Practice, 2 vols. suppl. ed. Thomas J. Salerno. (Bankruptcy Practice Library). 1376p. 1991. 70.00 (*0-471-55411-1*) Wiley.

Advanced Chapter Eleven Bankruptcy Practice, 2 vols. suppl. ed. Thomas J. Salerno. (Bankruptcy Practice Library). 840p. 1993. ring bd. write for info. (*0-471-58377-4*) Wiley.

Advanced Chapter Eleven Bankruptcy Practice, 2 vols., Vol. 2. Thomas J. Salerno. (Bankruptcy Practice Library). 1222p. 1993. Set. 270.00 (*0-471-55294-1*) Wiley.

Advanced Chapter Eleven Bankruptcy Practice, 1992 Supplement, 2 vols., Set. Thomas J. Salerno. 1392p. 1992. ring bd. 95.00 (*0-471-57040-0*) Wiley.

Advanced Chemical Methods for Soil & Clay Minerals Research. Ed. by J. W. Stucki & L. Banwart. 488p. 1980. lib. bdg. 58.00 (*0-686-29003-8*) Kluwer Ac.

Advanced Chemical Rocket Propulsion. Ed. by M. Timnat. (Combustion Treatise Ser.). 286p. 1987. text ed. 109.00 (*0-12-691355-2*) Acad Pr.

Advanced Chess. L. Watts & C. Varley. (Usborne Guides Ser.). (Illus.). 32p. (J). (gr. 5 up). 1991. lib. bdg. 12.96 (*0-88110-503-1*, Usborne); pap. 6.95 (*0-7460-0617-9*, Usborne) EDC.

Advanced Chinese Reader. Ed. by Tien-yi Li & Richard F. Chang. 442p. (Orig.). (CHI & ENG.). 1992. pap. text ed. 47.50 (*962-201-533-6*, Pub. by Chinese Univ HK) Coronet Bks.

Advanced Chord Progressions. William L. Fowler. LC 84-71709. (Guitar Ser.: Bk. 4). (Illus.). 84p. 1985. pap. text ed. 10.00 (*0-943894-07-7*) Fowler Music.

Advanced Chord Voicings, Bk. 3. William L. Fowler. LC 84-71709. (Illus.). 76p. 1984. pap. text ed. 10.00 (*0-943894-06-9*) Fowler Music.

Advanced Christian Training. Jean Gibson. (Orig.). 1986. pap. 9.00 (*0-937396-04-4*) Walterick Pubs.

Advanced CICS Design Techniques, Concepts & Guidelines. 2nd ed. Joseph E. Summerville. (Illus.). 320p. 1987. pap. 42.95 (*0-442-28213-3*) Van Nos Reinhold.

Advanced Circuit Analysis. Paul E. Bennett. 685p. (C). 1992. text ed. write for info. (*0-318-69070-5*) SCP.

Advanced Circuit Analysis with the HP-42S. Robert Boyd. (Illus.). (Orig.). (C). 1988. pap. text ed. 9.95 (*0-685-54319-6*, 2063S) EduCALC Pubns.

Advanced Claim Drafting & Amendment Writing Workshop. (Patents, Copyrights, Trademarks, & Literary Property Ser.). 492p. 1991. pap. text ed. 65.00 (*0-685-56908-X*, G4-3876) PLI.

Advanced Claim Drafting & Amendment Writing Workshop 1992. (Patents, Copyrights, Trademarks, & Literary Property Ser.: Vol. 353). 488p. 1992. 70.00 (*0-685-65516-4*, G4-3889) PLI.

***Advanced Class: FCC License Preparation (Valid 7/1/95 to 6/30/99)** 2nd ed. Gordon West. Ed. by Gerald Luecke & David A. Wolf. (FCC License Preparation Ser.). (Illus.). 208p. (YA). 1995. pap. 11.95 (*0-945053-13-4*) Master Pubng.

Advanced Class Radio Amateur FCC Test Manual. Martin Schwartz. LC 84-73020. (Illus.). 128p. 1995. pap. 9.95 (*0-912146-23-0*, 26-01) Ameco.

Advanced Classical & Quantum Dynamics: From Classical Paths to Path Integrals. W. Dittrich & M. Reuter. 368p. 1992. pap. text ed. 39.00 (*0-387-51992-0*) Spr-Verlag.

Advanced Classical Thermodynamics. George Emanuel. (Education Ser.). 250p. 1987. 49.95 (*0-930403-28-2*) AIAA.

Advanced Cleaning Product Formulations, Vol. 2. Ernest W. Flick. LC 89-30274. 394p. 1994. 64.00 (*0-8155-1346-1*) Noyes.

Advanced Cleaning Product Formulations: Household, Industrial, Automotive. Ernest W. Flick. LC 89-30274. 372p. 1989. 56.00 (*0-8155-1186-8*) Noyes.

Advanced Clipper dBASE. Gary Beam. 1991. 29.95 (*0-8306-6652-4*) TAB Bks.

Advanced Clipper dBASE Compiler Applications. Gary Beam. (Illus.). 304p. 1988. pap. 17.95 (*0-317-67260-6*, 3007) TAB Bks.

Advanced CMOS Logic Data Book. Texas Instruments Engineering Staff. 300p. 1988. 13.75 (*0-685-62485-4*, SCAD001B) Tex Instr Inc.

Advanced CMOS Logic Designer's Handbook. Texas Instruments Engineering Staff. 296p. 1988. 11.95 (*0-685-62484-6*, SCAA001B) Tex Instr Inc.

Advanced Coatings Technology. Pref. by Sandy Labana. (Illus.). 256p. 1991. 85.00 (*1-56378-001-1*) ESD.

Advanced COBOL Techniques: A Lab Manual. Floyd C. Schwartz. 160p. (C). 1984. spiral bd. 17.95 (*0-8403-3326-9*) Kendall-Hunt.

Advanced Combat Ju-Jutsu: Entrance to Secrets. D'Arcy Rahming. LC 92-61754. (Illus.). (Orig.). 1993. pap. 24.95 (*0-9627898-3-6*) Mdrn Bu-Jutsu.

Advanced Combat Shotgun: The Stressfire Concept. Massad F. Ayoob. 1982. 9.95 (*0-936279-11-7*) Police Bkshelf.

Advanced Combustion Methods. Felix J. Weinberg. 1986. text ed. 138.00 (*0-12-742340-0*) Acad Pr.

Advanced Commodity Spread Trading. Harold Goldberg. 1985. 65.00 (*0-930233-07-7*) Windsor.

Advanced Commodity Trading Techniques. J. D. Hamon. 1981. 65.00 (*0-930233-06-9*) Windsor.

Advanced Communication Skills Handbook. Pref. by James J. Messina. (Professional Handbook Ser.). 61p. (Orig.). 1982. pap. text ed. 10.00 (*0-931975-12-3*) Advanced Dev Sys.

***Advanced Compiling for High Performance Architectures.** Ken Kennedy & John R. Allen. 1995. 58.95 (*1-55860-286-0*) Morgan Kaufmann.

***Advanced Components for Electric & Hybrid Electric Vehicles.** 1995. lib. bdg. 260.75 (*0-8490-7438-X*) Gordon Pr.

***Advanced Components for Electric & Hybrid Electric Vehicles: Workshop Proceedings.** (Illus.). 217p. (Orig.). (C). 1995. pap. text ed. 50.00 (*0-7881-1621-5*) Diane Pub.

Advanced Components for Electric & Hybrid Vehicles: Workshop Proceedings (1993) Ed. by K. L. Stricklett. (Illus.). 217p. 1994. lib. bdg. 135.00 (*0-89934-238-8*, BT926); pap. 75.00x (*0-89934-237-X*, BT026) Busn Tech Info Serv.

Advanced Composite Materials. 350p. 1988. pap. 1,495.00 (*0-941285-23-5*) FIND-SVP.

Advanced Composite Materials. Louis A. Pilato & Michael J. Michno. LC 94-10694. 1994. write for info. (*3-540-57563-4*); 79.00 (*0-387-57563-4*) Spr-Verlag.

Advanced Composite Materials - Environmental Effects - STP 658. Ed. by J. R. Vinson. 295p. 1978. 26.00 (*0-8031-0274-7*, 04-658000-33) ASTM.

Advanced Composite Materials & Structures: Fully Refereed Papers at an International Conference, Taipei, Taiwan, May 1986. Ed. by G. C. Sih & S. E. Hsu. 809p. 1987. lib. bdg. 210.00 (*90-6764-083-2*, Pub. by VSP NE) Coronet Bks.

Advanced Composite Materials Index 1975-84. Ed. by N. Balasubramanian. LC 86-51396. 190p. 1987. pap. 19.50 (*0-87762-511-5*) Technomic.

Advanced Composite Materials Products & Manufacturers. Ed. by D. J. De Renzo. LC 88-4227. (Illus.). 1091p. 1988. 98.00 (*0-8155-1155-8*) Noyes.

Advanced Composite Mold Making. John J. Morena. LC 92-42441. 446p. (C). 1994. reprint ed. lib. bdg. 67.50 (*0-89464-825-X*) Krieger.

Advanced Composite Technologies. 766p. 1993. 89.00 (*1-56378-014-3*) ASM.

Advanced Composites. C. Foreman. (Illus.). 189p. 1990. pap. text ed. 22.95 (*0-89100-358-4*, EA-358) IAP.

Advanced Composites. Ed. by I. K. Partridge. 446p. 1990. 122.50 (*1-85166-387-8*) Elsevier.

Advanced Composites: Design, Materials & Processing Technologies. 372p. 1993. 110.00 (*0-87170-451-X*, 6321NR) ASM.

Advanced Composites - Special Topics. Ed. by George Epstein & William Bandaruk. (Illus.). 403p. 1979. 56.00 (*0-938648-05-5*) T-C Pubns CA.

Advanced Composites Materials in Civil Engineering Structures. Ed. by Srinivasa L. Iyer & Rajan Sen. LC 90-26044. 443p. 1991. pap. text ed. 40.00 (*0-87262-797-7*) Am Soc Civil Eng.

Advanced Composites Special Topics. 2nd rev. ed. 415p. 1989. 56.00 (*0-686-48240-9*, 0102) T-C Pubns CA.

***Advanced Composites Technologies: Proceedings of the 9th Annual ASM/ESD Conference November 8-11 1993.** 766p. 1993. 85.00 (*0-87170-516-8*, 6269U) ASM Intl.

Advanced Composites Technology. rev. ed. Ed. by George Epstein. (Illus.). 279p. 1989. reprint ed. 42.00 (*0-938648-06-3*, 0104) T-C Pubns CA.

***Advanced Composites X - 1994: Proceedings of the 10th Annual ASM/ESD Advanced Composites Conference & Exposition.** 1994. 105.00 (*0-87170-542-7*, 6454U) ASM Intl.

Advanced Composites 93: International Conference on Advanced Composite Materials. T. Chandra & A. K. Dhingra. LC 93-79341. 1433p. 1993. 164.00 (*0-87339-251-5*) Minerals Metals.

Advanced Composition. 2nd ed. Hans P. Guth. (American English Today Ser.). 1980. text ed. 12.04 (*0-07-025013-8*) McGraw.

Advanced Computational Methods for Material Modeling. Ed. by D. J. Benson & R. A. Asaro. LC 93-73602. (PVP Ser., Vol. 268; AMD Ser.: Vol. 180). 243p. Date not set. pap. 65.00 (*0-7918-1251-0*) ASME.

Advanced Computational Methods in Heat Transfer, Vol. 1. Ed. by C. A. Brebbia et al. LC 90-82732. (Heat Transfer Ser.). 439p. 1990. 107.00 (*0-945824-68-8*) Computational Mech MA.

Advanced Computational Methods in Heat Transfer, Vol. 3. Ed. by C. A. Brebbia et al. LC 90-82732. (Heat Transfer Ser.). 542p. 1990. 131.00 (*0-945824-70-X*) Computational Mech MA.

Advanced Computational Methods in Heat Transfer: Proceedings of the First International Conference on Advanced Computational Methods in Heat Transfer, July 17-19, 1990, Portsmouth, UK, 3 vols., Set. L. C. s A. Wrobel et al. Ed. by Carlos A. Brebbia. (Illus.). ix, 1358p. 1990. 345.00 (*0-387-52879-2*) Spr-Verlag.

Advanced Computational Methods in Heat Transfer: Proceedings of the Second International Conference on Advanced Computational Methods in Heat Transfer (Heat Transfer 92) Held in Milan, Italy, July 7-10, 1992, 2 vols., Set. Ed. by L. C. Wrobel & A. J. Nowak. LC 92-70433. (Heat Transfer Ser.: Vol. 2). 1992. 520.00 (*1-56252-101-2*) Computational Mech MA.

Advanced Computational Methods in Heat Transfer III: Proceedings of the Third International Conference. Ed. by L. C. Wrobel et al. LC 94-72460. (Heat Transfer Ser.: Vol. 3). 608p. 1994. text ed. 147.00 (*1-56252-189-6*) Computational Mech MA.

Advanced Computational Methods in Heat Transfer: Proceedings of the Second International Conference (Heat Transfer '92), Held in Milan, Italy, July 7-10, 1992: Conduction, Radiation & Phase Change, Vol. 1. Ed. by L. C. Wrobel & A. J. Nowak. LC 92-70433. (Heat Transfer Ser.: Vol. 2). 806p. 1992. 275.00 (*1-56252-125-X*) Computational Mech MA.

Advanced Computational Methods in Heat Transfer: Proceedings of the Second International Conference (Heat Transfer '92), Held in Milan, Italy, July 7-10, 1992: Natural-Forced Convention & Combustion Simulation, Vol. 2. Ed. by L. C. Wrobel & A. J. Nowak. LC 92-70433. (Heat Transfer Ser.: Vol. 2). 720p. 1992. 245.00 (*1-56252-126-8*) Computational Mech MA.

Advanced Computational Methods in Heat Transfer, Vol. 1: Heat Conduction, Convection, Radiation: Proceedings of the First International Conference on Advanced Computational Methods in Heat Transfer, July 17-19, 1990, Portsmouth, UK. L. C. Wrobel et al. (Illus.). ix, 429p. 1990. 122.00 (*0-387-52877-6*) Spr-Verlag.

Advanced Computational Methods in Heat Transfer, Vol. 2: Natural & Forced Convection: Proceedings of the First International Conference on Advanced Computational Methods in Heat Transfer, July 17-19, 1990, Portsmouth, UK. L. C. Wrobel et al. Ed. by Carlos A. Brebbia. (Illus.). ix, 397p. 1990. 115.00 (*0-387-52878-4*) Spr-Verlag.

Advanced Computational Methods in Heat Transfer, Vol. 3: Phase Change & Combustion Simulation: Proceedings of the First International Conference on Advanced Computational Methods in Heat Transfer, July 17-19, 1990, Portsmouth, UK. L. C. Wrobel et al. Ed. by Carlos A. Brebbia. (Illus.). ix, 532p. 1990. 341.00 (*0-387-52874-1*) Spr-Verlag.

Advanced Computations & Trials for Car Radiators. Gruppo Professionale Staff. 62p. 1968. 9.30 (*0-317-34496-X*, 124) Intl Copper.

Advanced Computations in Materials Processing. Ed. by V. Prasad & R. V. Arimilli. (HTD Ser.: Vol. 241). 92p. 1993. 35.00 (*0-7918-1154-9*, G00798) ASME.

***Advanced Computer Applications 1994: Proceedings of the Pressure Vessels & Piping Conference, Minneapolis, MN, 1994.** Ed. by P. Langsten. LC 94-71262. (PVP Ser.: Vol. 274). 147p. 1994. pap. 50.00 (*0-7918-1197-2*) ASME.

Advanced Computer Architecture. Dharma P. Agrawal. LC 86-80958. 383p. 1986. pap. 9.95 (*0-8186-0667-3*, 667) IEEE Comp Soc.

Advanced Computer Architecture: Parallelism, Scalability, Programmability. Kai Hwang. LC 92-44944. (Computer Science; Computer Organization & Architecture; Electrical Ser.). 1993. text ed. write for info. (*0-07-031622-8*) McGraw.

***Advanced Computer-Assisted Techniques in Drug Discovery.** Ed. by Han Van De Waterbeemd. LC 94-39495. (Methods & Principles in Medicine Chemistry Ser.: Vol. 3). 1994. 100.00 (*3-527-29248-9*) VCH Pubs.

Advanced Computer R&D in the U. S. S. R. Valery Bykhovsky. 109p. (Orig.). 1989. teacher ed 75.00 (*1-55831-092-4*) Delphic Associates.

Advanced Computing Concepts & Techniques in Control Engineering. Ed. by M. J. Denham & A. J. Laub. (NATO Asi Series F: Vol. 47). (Illus.). vi, 518p. 1988. 113.00 (*0-387-50037-5*) Spr-Verlag.

***Advanced Concepts for Geriatric Nursing Assistants.** Carolyn A. MacDonald. LC 94-61648. (Illus.). 224p. 1994. pap. 28.95 (*0-910251-71-1*, ACG73) Venture Pub PA.

Advanced Concepts in Alcoholism: Proceedings of the Symposium on Alcoholism from the International Congress on Applied Psychology, Edinburgh, July 1982. H. G. Tittmar. LC 83-22155. 172p. 1984. 43.00 (*0-08-030777-9*, Pergamon Pr) Elsevier.

Advanced Concepts in Arrhythmias. 2nd ed. Marriott & Conover. (Illus.). 432p. 1989. text ed. 39.95 (*0-8016-3239-0*) Mosby Yr Bk.

Advanced Concepts in Operating Systems. Mukesh Singhai. 1993. text ed. write for info. (*0-07-057572-X*) McGraw.

Advanced Consequence Modelling. G. Melhem. (Chemical Engineering Ser.). 1991. text ed. write for info. (*0-442-00755-8*) Van Nos Reinhold.

Advanced Construction Techniques. Jerry Irvine. (Advanced Information Report Ser.: No. 10). 48p. 1984. 4.95 (*0-912468-22-X*, AIR-10) CA Rocketry.

Advanced Contemplation - The Peace Within You: The Notebooks of Paul Brunton, Vol. 15. Paul Brunton. Ed. by Timothy Smith. (Illus.). 352p. 1988. 29.95 (*0-943914-42-6*); pap. 16.95 (*0-943914-43-4*) Larson Pubns.

Advanced Continuous Simulation Language (ACSL) Reference Manual. 10th ed. Mitchell & Gauthier Associates (MGA) Inc., Staff. 384p. 1991. pap. 15.00 (*0-925649-00-7*) Mitchell & Gauthier.

Advanced Control in Computer Integrated Manufacturing. Ed. by Henry M. Morris et al. (Proceedings of the 13th. Annual Advanced Control Conference). 200p. 1987. 30.00 (*0-931682-23-1*) Purdue U Pubns.

Advanced Control Issues for Robot Manipulators. Ed. by N. Sadegh & F. L. Lewis. (DSC Ser.: Vol. 39). 48p. 1992. 25.00 (*0-7918-1097-6*, G00741) ASME.

Advanced Control of Chemical Processes (ADCHEM '91) Selected Papers from the IFAC Symposium, Toulouse, France, 14-16 October 1991. Ed. by K. Najim & E. Dufour. LC 92-2270. (IFAC Symposia Ser.: Vol. 1992, No. 8). 1992. 130.00 (*0-08-041267-X*, Pergamon Pr) Elsevier.

Advanced Control Systems Design. Bernard Friedland. 544p. 1993. boxed 54.00 (*0-13-014010-4*) P-H.

Advanced Controlled Delivery Technology. 206p. 1991. 2,150.00 (*0-89336-855-5*, C-010U) BCC.

Advanced Controlled Delivery Technology, No. C-010X. 245p. 1994. 2,650.00 (*1-56965-008-X*) BCC.

Advanced Conversational Chinese. Teng Ssu Yu. LC 65-12042. 309p. reprint ed. pap. 88.10 (*0-8357-5123-6*, 2020169) Bks Demand.

***Advanced Conversational English. Peter Petrovich. 230p. 1995. pap. text ed. 25.00 (*0-9647271-4-5*) P Petrovich. ADVANCED CONVERSATIONAL ENGLISH by Peter Petrovich is designed to review what students at the intermediate level have already learned & to add to their knowledge of the language at the advanced level. It consists of twenty-four lessons presented in a dialogue form each divided into five sections. Every dialogue has an introduction to the scenario of the dialogue letting the student know beforehand the mood of the conversation. Each lesson has lexical, idiomatic, vocabulary & grammatical ties to the material presented in this book. ADVANCED CONVERSATIONAL ENGLISH also contains a list of 142 irregular verbs - all illustrated by an example sentence, 600 most important idioms, 1500 antonyms (500 verbs, 500 nouns, 500 adjectives) which are absolutely necessary for students of the English language. The answer key at the end of the book will help those students who use this book for self-instruction. ADVANCED CONVERSATIONAL ENGLISH offers an effective approach**

An Asterisk (*) at the beginning of an entry indicates that the title is appearing in BIP for the first time.

to the often complicated task of mastering advanced conversational skills in a foreign language. By the end of this course, students will learn advanced grammatical structures, enable themselves to correctly interpret & use many idiomatic expressions, greatly increase vocabulary skills, & effortlessly express themselves like native speakers. The author has written 5 books & is accomplished in 4 languages. Paper (52, 000 words on 230 pages) Price $25. Satisfaction guaranteed. To order ADVANCED CONVERSATIONAL ENGLISH contact Peter Petrovich, 13032 Blodgett Ave., Downey, CA 90242. 310-869-8238. ***Publisher Provided Annotation.***

Advanced Converters & Near Breeders: Proceedings of the Wingspread Conference, Racine, Wisconsin, 1975. Ed. by P. J. Howe. 1975. 76.00 (*0-08-020523-2*, Pub. by Pergamon Repr UK) Franklin.

Advanced Cooperative Learning: Playing with Elements. Miguel Kagan & Spencer Kagan. (Illus.). 104p. 1993. pap. text ed. 20.00 (*1-879097-16-8*) Kagan Cooperative.

Advanced Cost Accounting: Processing, Developing & Analyzing Financial & Cost Data for Management. Jae K. Shim. Ed. by Norman Henteleff. (Illus.). 600p. (Orig.). (C). 1994. pap. 75.00 (*1-882312-09-0*) Delta Pub CA.

Advanced Cost Accounting - Problems & Solutions. S. P. Arora & T. S. Soni. 864p. 1990. 85.00 (*81-209-0010-3*, Pub. by Pitambar Pub II) St Mut.

Advanced Cost & Management Accountancy. M. Mukherji & R. Roychowdhury. (C). 1989. 135.00 (*0-89771-437-7*, Current Dist) St Mut.

Advanced Country Fiddle. Marylin Bos. 38p. (Orig.). 1989. pap. text ed. 7.95 (*0-931759-38-2*) Centerstream Pub.

***Advanced Course Hardware Retail.** National Retail Hardware Association Staff. 640p. 1995. 15.40 (*0-7872-0487-0*) Kendall-Hunt.

Advanced Course in Personal Magnetism. Theron Q. Dumont. 281p. 1972. reprint ed. 12.00 (*0-911662-46-4*) Yoga.

Advanced Course in Practical Physics. C. Chattopadhyay. (C). 1989. 70.00 (*0-89771-404-0*, Current Dist) St Mut.

Advanced Course in Yogi Philosophy. Yogi Ramacharaka. 12.00 (*0-911662-02-2*) Yoga.

Advanced Creative Ojo Book. Diane Thomas. LC 75-44655. 1976. pap. 2.95 (*0-918126-01-0*) Hunter Ariz.

***Advanced Criminal Procedure, Cases, Comments & Questions.** 8th ed. Yale Kamisar & Wayne R. LaFave. Ed. by Jerold H. Israel. (American Casebook Ser.). 959p. (C). 1994. pap. text ed. 40.00 (*0-314-05725-0*) West Pub.

Advanced Critical Care Nursing: A Case Study Approach. Kathryn T. Von Rueden & Connie A. Walleck. 368p. 1989. 55.00 (*0-8342-0044-9*) Aspen Pub.

Advanced Cross Country Riding: How to Succeed in Horse Trials. Jane Holderness-Roddam. (Illus.). 176p. 1994. 29.95 (*0-7063-7164-X*, Pub. by Ward Lock UK) Sterling.

***Advanced Cryogenics.** Ed. by Colin A. Bailey. 1971. pap. 65.00 (*0-306-30458-9*) Da Capo.

Advanced Crystal Therapeutics. Ojela Frank. Ed. by Dorian Caruso & Eugene Frank. (Illus.). 235p. (Orig.). (C). 1988. pap. 12.95 (*0-9619010-1-2*) Holistic Hlth.

***Advanced Cycle Trading: Cutting-Edge Techniques for Profitting from Market Tops & Bottoms.** Al Gietzen. 250p. 1995. 29.95 (*1-55738-888-1*) Probus Pub Co.

Advanced Czech 1. Charles E. Townsend & Tanya McAuley. 97p. (Orig.). (CZE.). (C). 1986. teacher ed, pap. 7.00 (*0-87415-118-X*, 49A); student ed, pap. text ed. 8.50 (*0-87415-117-1*, 49) OSU Foreign Lang.

Advanced Czech 1, 4 cass., Set. Charles E. Townsend & Tanya McAuley. (Orig.). (CZE.). (C). 1986. audio 20.00 (*0-87415-119-8*, 49B) OSU Foreign Lang.

Advanced Czech 2. Charles E. Townsend & Tanya McAuley. 118p. (Orig.). (CZE.). (C). 1986. teacher ed, pap. 8.00 (*0-87415-121-X*, 50A); student ed, pap. text ed. 10.00 (*0-87415-120-1*, 50) OSU Foreign Lang.

Advanced Czech 2, 3 cass., Set. Charles E. Townsend & Tanya McAuley. (Orig.). (CZE.). (C). 1986. audio 15.00 (*0-87415-122-8*, 50B) OSU Foreign Lang.

Advanced Dam Engineering for Design, Construction & Rehabilitation. Robert B. Jansen. (Illus.). 832p. 1988. text ed. 119.95 (*0-442-24397-9*) Chapman & Hall.

Advanced Data Analysis with Systat. Kris Kirby. 1993. text ed. 44.95 (*0-442-30860-4*) Van Nos Reinhold.

Advanced Database Systems. Ed. by Nabil R. Adam & Bharat K. Bhargava. LC 93-43688. (Lecture Notes in Computer Science Ser.). (Illus.). xv, 452p. 1993. 65.00 (*0-387-57507-3*) Spr-Verlag.

Advanced Database Systems: Tenth British National Conference on Databases, BNCDD 10, Aberdeen, Scotland, July 6-8, 1992 Proceedings, Vol. 618. Ed. by M. D. Gray et al. LC 92-18582. x, 260p. 1992. pap. 47.00 (*0-387-55693-1*) Spr-Verlag.

Advanced Day Planner User's Guide. Hyrum W. Smith. (Illus.). 176p. 1987. 12.95 (*0-939817-01-2*, 5519) Franklin Inc.

Advanced dBASE III Application. R. Baker. 1991. 24.95 (*0-8306-6625-7*) TAB Bks.

Advanced dBASE III Applications. Richard H. Baker. (Illus.). 448p. (Orig.). 1985. 28.95 (*0-8306-0418-9*, 2618); pap. 21.95 (*0-8306-0318-2*, 2618) TAB Bks.

Advanced dBASE IV for Windows. Fritz H. Grupe. 208p. 1997. spiral bd. write for info. (*0-697-17135-3*) Bus & Educ Tech.

Advanced dBASE IV Programming. Cary N. Prague & James E. Hammitt. 1989. pap. 22.95 (*0-8306-9376-9*, 3076P) TAB Bks.

Advanced dBASE IV Programming. Philip J. Pratt & Mary Z. Last. LC 92-35336. 554p. 1992. pap. 39.25 (*0-87835-958-3*) Boyd & Fraser.

Advanced Debate. 4th ed. Ed. by David A. Thomas & John P. Hart. 592p. 1993. teacher ed 10.60 (*0-8442-5254-9*, Natl Textbk); text ed. 26.60 (*0-8442-5252-2*, Natl Textbk) NTC Pub Grp.

Advanced Deer Hunter's Bible. John Weiss. LC 93-8180. 1993. pap. 12.00 (*0-385-42351-9*) Doubleday.

***Advanced Demolition Legion: The ADL in Action.** Gyeorgos C. Hatonn. (Phoenix Journals). 222p. 1994. pap. 6.00 (*1-56935-035-3*) Phoenix Source.

Advanced Dermatologic Diagnosis. Walter P. Shelley & E. Dorinda Shelley. (Illus.). 1315p. 1992. text ed. 225.00 (*0-7216-3433-8*) Saunders.

Advanced Dermatology Study Guide. Competence Assurance Systems Staff. 1980. pap. text ed. 235.00 (*0-89147-062-X*) CAS.

Advanced Design in Nursing Research. Pamela J. Brink & Marilynn J. Wood. 336p. (C). 1989. text ed. 46.00 (*0-8039-2742-8*) Sage.

Advanced Design of Ventilation Systems for Contaminant Control. H. D. Goodfellow. (Chemical Engineering Monographs: No. 23). 746p. 1985. 218.00 (*0-444-42546-2*) Elsevier.

Advanced Design Problems: To Accompany Engineering Drawing & Designs. 2nd ed. Cecil H. Jensen & D. Viosinet. 1981. pap. text ed. 16.95 (*0-07-032522-7*) McGraw.

Advanced Design Processes: Rule Generated Architecture. David Watson. 166p. (C). 1990. pap. 96.00 (*0-7300-0730-8*, ARC485, Pub. by Deakin Univ AT) St Mut.

Advanced Diemaking. D. Eugene Ostergaard. (Diemaking Ser.). 166p. 43.95 (*0-07-046093-0*) McGraw.

Advanced Diemaking: Instructor's Guide. National Tooling & Machining Association Staff. xxxx, 21p. 1981. pap. 5.95 (*0-910399-35-2*, 5004) Natl Tool & Mach.

Advanced Digital Audio. Kenneth C. Pohlmann. (Illus.). 500p. (Orig.). 1991. pap. 39.95 (*0-672-22768-1*) Sams.

Advanced Digital Electronics. 2nd rev. ed. Dean L. Smith. (Illus.). 260p. (Orig.). 1984. pap. text ed. 30.00 (*0-918699-00-2*) D L Smith.

Advanced Digital Logic Concepts. Joan Cormier et al. (Illus.). 136p. (Orig.). 1983. pap. text ed. 10.00 (*0-86657-002-0*) Buck Eng Co.

Advanced Digital Signal Processing: Theory & Applications. Glenn Zelniker & Fred J. Taylor. LC 93-20903. (Electrical Engineering & Electronics Ser.: Vol. 86). 688p. 1994. 165.00 (*0-8247-9145-2*) Dekker.

Advanced Dim-Mak. Erle Montaigue. (Illus.). 328p. 1994. pap. 35.00 (*0-87364-779-3*) Paladin Pr.

Advanced Diving Technology & Techniques. 3rd ed. NAUI Staff. (Illus.). 298p. 1992. pap. 29.95 (*0-916974-54-5*, 097) NAUI.

***Advanced Division.** (Tai Mathematics Ser.). (J). 1995. 5.25 (*0-88106-159-X*, M007) Charlesbridge Pub.

***Advanced Division: Long Division.** Bob DeWeese. (Math at Home Ser.). (Illus.). 44p. 1994. teacher ed, pap. text ed. 2.95 (*1-55799-317-3*, EMC 610) Evan-Moor Corp.

Advanced Domestic Ticketing & Tours. Jean Ford-Woodcock. 1987. 14.00 (*0-911563-03-2*) Brdgwtr Pub Co.

Advanced DOS 5.0 & Windows 3.1. Fritz H. Grupe. 184p. (C). 1994. spiral bd. write for info. (*0-697-17136-1*) Brown & Benchmark.

Advanced Dredging Techniques, Vol. 2, Pt. 1: Finding & Recovering Paystreaks. Dave McCracken. (Illus.). 176p. (Orig.). (C). 1983. pap. 7.95 (*0-685-75274-7*) New Era CA.

Advanced Dredging Techniques, Vol. 2, Pt. 2: Succeeding at a Gold Dredging Venture. Dave McCracken. (Illus.). 164p. (Orig.). (C). 1983. pap. 7.95 (*0-685-75273-9*) New Era CA.

Advanced Driver Training Services. ADTS Staff. 112p. 1991. pap. text ed. 9.95 (*0-8403-7124-1*) Kendall-Hunt.

Advanced Dungeons & Dragons: Castle Guide. 1990. 15.00 (*0-88038-837-4*) TSR Inc.

Advanced Dungeons & Dragons: Castles, Set. 1990. boxed 24.95 (*0-88038-883-8*) TSR Inc.

Advanced Dungeons & Dragons: Complete Fighter Manual. 2nd ed. Aaron Allston. 1989. pap. 15.00 (*0-88038-779-3*) TSR Inc.

Advanced Dungeons & Dragons: Complete Priest Manual. 1990. 15.00 (*0-88038-818-8*) TSR Inc.

Advanced Dungeons & Dragons: Complete Thief Manual. 2nd ed. Douglas Niles. 1990. pap. 10.95 (*0-88038-780-7*) TSR Inc.

Advanced Dungeons & Dragons: Complete Wizard Manual. 1990. pap. 15.00 (*0-88038-838-2*) TSR Inc.

Advanced Dungeons & Dragons: Dungeon Master's Guide. 2nd ed. Cook. 192p. 1989. pap. 18.00 (*0-88038-729-7*) TSR Inc.

Advanced Dungeons & Dragons: Forgotten Realms, Adventure Book. Jeff Grubb. 1990. 20.00 (*0-88038-828-5*) TSR Inc.

Advanced Dungeons & Dragons: Lankhmar, City of Adventure. Douglas Niles. 1985. pap. 12.00 (*0-88038-247-3*) TSR Inc.

Advanced Dungeons & Dragons: Legends & Lore Reprints. 2nd ed. 1990. 20.00 (*0-88038-844-7*) TSR Inc.

Advanced Dungeons & Dragons Dragonlance Adventures. Tracy Hickman & Margaret Weis. 1987. 15.00 (*0-88038-452-2*) TSR Inc.

Advanced Dungeons & Dragons, Vol. 4: Monstrous Compedium: Dragonlance Appendix. 1990. 20.00 (*0-88038-822-6*) TSR Inc.

Advanced Dungeons & Dragons, Vol. 5: Monstrous Compendium. 1990. 9.95 (*0-88038-836-6*) TSR Inc.

Advanced Dungeons & Dragons, Vol. 6: Monstrous Compendium: Kara-tur Appendix. 1990. 9.95 (*0-88038-851-X*) TSR Inc.

Advanced Dungeons & Dragons, Vol. 7: Monstrous Compendium. 1990. 9.95 (*0-88038-871-4*) TSR Inc.

Advanced Dynamic Kicks. George Chung & Cynthia Rothrock. Ed. by Mike Lee. LC 86-60095. 128p. (Orig.). 1986. pap. 12.95 (*0-89750-129-2*, 444) Ohara Pubns.

Advanced Dynamics. Andrew W. Marris & Charles E. Stoneking. LC 76-8007. 318p. 1976. reprint ed. 25.50 (*0-88275-403-3*) Krieger.

Advanced Dynamics of Marine Structures. J. P. Hooft. LC 82-2716. (Ocean Engineering, a Wiley Ser.). (Illus.). 360p. reprint ed. pap. 103.50 (*0-8357-7936-X*, 2057009) Bks Demand.

Advanced Econometric Methods. T. B. Fomby et al. (Illus.). 600p. 1984. 65.50 (*0-387-90908-7*) Spr-Verlag.

Advanced Econometric Methods. T. B. Fomby et al. (Illus.). xix, 624p. 1992. pap. 45.00 (*0-387-96868-7*) Spr-Verlag.

Advanced Econometrics. Takeshi Amemiya. (Illus.). 576p. 1995. 49.95 (*0-674-00560-0*) HUP.

Advanced Econometrics: A Bridge to the Literature. Edward Greenberg & Charles E. Webster, Jr. 358p. (C). 1991. reprint ed. lib. bdg. 66.50 (*0-89464-556-0*) Krieger.

Advanced Economic Theory. 8th enl. rev. ed. M. L. Jhingan. 1992. pap. 25.00 (*81-220-0137-8*, Pub. by Konark Pubs Pvt Ltd II) Advent Bks Div.

Advanced Economic Theory. 8th rev. ed. M. L. Jhingan. 980p. 1990. text ed. 45.00 (*81-220-0010-X*, Pub. by Konark Pubs Pvt Ltd II) Advent Bks Div.

Advanced Educational Technology in Technology Education. Ed. by A. Gordon et al. (NATO ASI Series F: Computer & Systems Sciences, Special Programme AET: Vol. 109). viii, 253p. 1993. 69.00 (*0-387-56554-X*) Spr-Verlag.

Advanced Electric Circuits. A. M. Brookes. 1966. 87.00 (*0-08-011610-8*, Pub. by Pergamon Repr UK) Franklin.

***Advanced Electricity.** Glenn Sutherland. 99p. (C). 1994. 16.51 (*1-56870-152-7*) RonJon Pub.

Advanced Electrocardiography. Stanley Anderson et al. (Biophysical Measurement Ser.). (Illus.). 120p. (Orig.). (C). 1992. 28.00 (*0-9627449-4-8*) SpaceLabs.

***Advanced Electromagnetism: Foundations, Theory & Applications.** Terence W. Barrett & Dale M. Grimes. 650p. 1995. text ed. 124.00 (*981-02-2095-2*) World Scientific Pub.

Advanced Electronic Communications Systems. 3rd ed. Wayne Tomasi. LC 93-5579. 1993. text ed. 70.00 (*0-13-219999-8*) P-H.

Advanced Electronic Packaging Materials: Materials Research Society Symposium Proceedings, Vol. 167. Ed. by A. Barfknecht et al. 1990. text ed. 42.00 (*1-55899-055-0*) Materials Res.

Advanced Electronic Packaging Systems Technology Through 2000. 137p. 1992. 2,650.00 (*0-89336-913-6*, GB-156) BCC.

***Advanced Electronic Projects for Your Home & Automobile.** Stephen Kamichik. Date not set. 18.95 (*0-7906-1065-5*) H W Sams.

Advanced Electronic Tune Up. Peter Novellino. 1984. student ed 6.00 (*0-8064-0179-6*, 464); audio 219.00 (*0-8064-0180-X*) Bergwall.

Advanced Elocution: Designed As a Practical Treatise for Teachers & Students. J. W. Shoemaker. LC 79-50849. (Granger Poetry Library). 1979. reprint ed. 28.75 (*0-89609-169-4*) Roth Pub Inc.

Advanced Emergency Care: For Paramedic Practice. Shirley Jones et al. (Illus.). 928p. 1991. 46.00 (*0-397-51259-7*); pap. 38.50 (*0-397-54592-4*) Lippincott.

Advanced Emission Control Technologies. (International Fuels & Lubricants Meeting & Exposition, 1993 Ser.). pap. 53.00 (*1-56091-436-X*, SP-997) Soc Auto Engineers.

Advanced Emission Controls for Power Plants. OECD Staff. 236p. (Orig.). 1993. pap. 40.00 (*92-64-03865-5*) OECD.

***Advanced Endoscopic Sinus Surgery.** James A. Stankiewicz. LC 94-23525. 1994. write for info. (*0-8151-7944-8*) Mosby Yr Bk.

Advanced Engine Demonstration Project. Robert Liden. 1987. pap. 4.95 (*0-685-24742-2*) Research Analysts.

Advanced Engineered Pesticides. Kim. 440p. 1993. 165.00 (*0-8247-8990-3*) Dekker.

Advanced Engineering Analysis. J. N. Reddy & M. L. Rasmussen. 504p. (C). 1990. reprint ed. 59.50 (*0-89464-498-X*) Krieger.

Advanced Engineering Dynamics. Jerry H. Ginsberg. 432p. (C). 1990. text ed. 56.75 (*0-06-042308-0*) HarpCollege.

***Advanced Engineering Dynamics.** 2nd ed. Jerry H. Ginsberg. LC 94-44728. (Illus.). 550p. (C). 1995. write for info. (*0-521-47021-8*) Cambridge U Pr.

Advanced Engineering Economics. Chan S. Park & Gunther Sharp-Bette. 740p. 1990. Net. text ed. write for info. (*0-471-79989-0*) Wiley.

Advanced Engineering Mathematics. Michael D. Greenberg. (Illus.). 960p. (C). 1988. pap. text ed. write for info. (*0-13-010505-8*) P-H.

Advanced Engineering Mathematics. Stanley I. Grossman & Williams Derrick. 1089p. (C). 1990. text ed. 84.00 (*0-06-042534-2*) HarpCollege.

Advanced Engineering Mathematics. Ladis D. Kovach. LC 81-14936. (Mathematics Ser.). (Illus.). 1000p. (C). 1982. text ed. 40.76 (*0-201-10340-0*) Addison-Wesley.

Advanced Engineering Mathematics. Dennis G. Zill & Michael R. Cullen. 1200p. 1992. text ed. 79.95 (*0-534-92800-5*) PWS Pubs.

Advanced Engineering Mathematics. 2nd ed. A. C. Bajpal. 1990. pap. text ed. 59.95 (*0-471-92595-0*) Wiley.

Advanced Engineering Mathematics. 2nd ed. Ladis D. Kovach et al. (Illus.). 800p. (C). 1991. text ed. write for info. (*0-201-54707-4*) Addison-Wesley.

Advanced Engineering Mathematics. 3rd ed. Peter V. O'Neil. 1460p. (C). 1991. text ed. 79.95 (*0-534-13584-6*) PWS Pubs.

***Advanced Engineering Mathematics.** 4th ed. Peter V. O'Neil. LC 94-35425. 1248p. 1995. text ed. 79.95 (*0-534-94320-9*) PWS Pubs.

Advanced Engineering Mathematics. 5th ed. Clarence R. Wylie & Louis C. Barrett. (Illus.). 1120p. 1982. text ed. write for info. (*0-07-072188-2*) McGraw.

***Advanced Engineering Mathematics.** 6th ed. C. Ray Wylie. 1995. text ed. 76.75 (*0-07-072206-4*) McGraw.

Advanced Engineering Mathematics. 7th ed. Erwin Kreyszig. 1992. Net. text ed. write for info. (*0-471-55380-8*) Wiley.

***Advanced Engineering Mathmatics & Maple Manual.** 7th ed. Erwin Kreyszig. 1994. text ed. write for info. (*0-471-04664-7*) Wiley.

Advanced Engineering Thermodynamics. Adrian Bejan. LC 88-5509. 704p. 1988. text ed. 89.95 (*0-471-83043-7*) Wiley.

Advanced Engineering Thermodynamics. 2nd ed. Rowland S. Benson. 1977. 147.00 (*0-08-020719-7*, Pub. by Pergamon Repr UK) Franklin.

Advanced English - Chinese Pinyin Dictionary. 736p. (CHI & ENG.). 1993. reprint ed. pap. 14.95 (*0-89346-316-7*) Heian Intl.

Advanced English Grammar, with Exercises. George L. Kittredge & Frank E. Farley. LC 75-171545. reprint ed. 45.00 (*0-404-03731-3*) AMS Pr.

Advanced EPR: Applications in Biology & Biochemistry. Ed. by A. J. Hoff. 918p. 1989. 261.75 (*0-444-88050-X*) Elsevier.

***Advanced Esoteric Dowsing Bk. 2: For the Dowser Interested in Spiritual Science.** (Illus.). 70p. (Orig.). 1994. pap. text ed. 6.95 (*1-885186-96-7*) Amber Pr OK.

***Advanced Esoteric Dowsing Bk. 3: For the Dowser Interested in Spiritual Science.** (Illus.). 154p. (Orig.). 1994. pap. text ed. 14.95 (*1-885186-42-8*) Amber Pr OK.

***Advanced Esoteric Dowsing Bk. I: For the Dowser Interested in Spiritual Science.** (Illus.). 43p. (Orig.). 1994. pap. text ed. 4.95 (*1-885186-61-4*) Amber Pr OK.

Advanced Essay Writing in Russian. G. Scanlan. 73p. (C). 1986. 43.00 (*0-317-92392-7*, Pub. by Collets UK) Pro-Am Music.

Advanced Evoked Potentials. Ed. by Hans Luders. (Topics in Neurosurgery Ser.). (C). 1989. lib. bdg. 104.00 (*0-89838-963-1*) Kluwer Ac.

Advanced Excel. David Bolocan. (Illus.). 224p. 1986. 26.95 (*0-8306-0368-9*, 2668H) TAB Bks.

Advanced Exercises in Microeconomics. Paul Champsaur & Jean-Claude Milleron. Tr. by John P. Bonin & Helene Bonin. (Illus.). 288p. 1983. 45.00 (*0-674-00525-2*) HUP.

Advanced Experimental Techniques in the Mechanics of Materials. Philip H. Francis & Ulric S. Lindholm. x, 452p. 1973. text ed. 320.00 (*0-677-12570-4*) Gordon & Breach.

Advanced Experimental Techniques in Turbomachinery. Ed. & Intro. by David Japikse. LC 86-70542. (Illus.). 272p. (Orig.). (C). 1986. pap. text ed. 49.50 (*0-933283-01-6*) Concepts ETI.

Advanced Explosive Kicks. Chong Lee. LC 78-61152. (Specialties Ser.). (Illus.). 1978. pap. 14.95 (*0-89750-060-1*, 133) Ohara Pubns.

Advanced Fashion Sketchbook. Bina Abling. (Illus.). 144p. (C). 1990. text ed. 27.00 (*0-87005-679-4*) Fairchild.

Advanced Fiber Communications Technologies. L. G. Kazovsky. 1992. 53.00 (*0-8194-0710-0*, 1579) SPIE.

Advanced Fibers & Composites. Francis S. Galasso. xvi, 178p. 1989. text ed. 114.00 (*2-88124-320-7*) Gordon & Breach.

Advanced Fibers & Composites for Elevated Temperatures: Proceedings of a Symposium Sponsored by the Metallurgical Society of AIME & the American Society for Metals Joint Composite Materials Committee at the 108th AIME Annual Meeting, New Orleans, Louisiana, February 20-21, 1979. Metallurgical Society of AIME Staff. Ed. by I. Ahmad & B. R. Noton. LC 80-82650. (Metallurgical Society of AIME Conference Proceedings Ser.). 260p. reprint ed. pap. 74.10 (*0-8357-5124-4*, 2025899) Bks Demand.

Advanced Fiddling. Craig Duncan. 1993. 9.95 (*0-87166-487-9*, 93971); disk, vhs 18.95 (*0-87166-489-5*, 93971); audio 9.98 (*0-87166-488-7*, 93971) Mel Bay.

Advanced Field Theory. Hiroom Umezawa. LC 92-40005. 1993. write for info. (*1-56396-081-8*) Am Inst Physics.

Advanced Financial Accounting. Richard E. Baker et al. 1989. Acctg. worksheets. pap. text ed. write for info. (*0-07-003368-4*) McGraw.

Advanced Financial Accounting. Taylor. 1991. 39.95 (*0-7506-0018-7*) Buttrwrth-Heinemann.

Advanced Financial Accounting. 2nd ed. Richard Baker et al. 1993. Acctg. worksheets. pap. write for info. (*0-07-003364-1*) McGraw.

Advanced Financial Accounting. 2nd ed. Richard E. Baker. 1993. text ed. write for info. (*0-07-003447-8*) McGraw.

Advanced Financial Accounting. 2nd ed. Ronald J. Huefner. 985p. (C). 1986. text ed. 57.25 (*0-15-501847-7*); 6.40 (*0-15-501850-7*) HB Coll Pubs.

Advanced Financial Accounting. 2nd ed. Peter Taylor & Brian Underdown. 320p. 1993. pap. write for info. (*0-7506-1307-6*) Buttrwrth-Heinemann.

Advanced Financial Accounting. 3rd ed. Ronald J. Huefner & James A. Largay, III. 1200p. (C). 1991. text ed. 60.00 (*0-15-501800-0*) Dryden Pr.

A

An Asterisk (*) at the beginning of an entry indicates that the title is appearing in BIP for the first time. 73

Advanced Financial Accounting. 4th ed. R. W. Lewis & D. Pendrill. 640p. (Orig.). 1994. pap. 62.50 (*0-273-60500-3*, Pub. by Pitman Pub Ltd UK) Trans-Atl Phila.

Advanced Fingerprint Technology. Ed. by H. C. Lee & R. E. Gaensslen. (Series in Forensic & Police Science). (Illus.). 401p. 1991. 44.95 (*0-444-01579-5*, CRC Reprint) Franklin.

Advanced First Aid. Susan Landers. (C). 1993. student ed 14.00 (*1-881592-00-6*) Hayden-McNeil.

Advanced First Aid Afloat. 4th ed. Peter F. Eastman. (Illus.). 224p. 1995. pap. 14.95 (*0-87033-465-4*) Cornell Maritime.

Advanced Fitness Assessment & Exercise Prescription. 2nd ed. Vivian H. Heyward. LC 90-20806. (Illus.). 368p. (C). 1991. text ed. 38.00x (*0-87322-314-4*, BHEY0314) Human Kinetics.

Advanced Fixed-Income Portfolio Management: The State of the Art. Gifford Fong & Frank J. Fabozzi. 1994. 65.00 (*1-55738-568-8*) Probus Pub Co.

***Advanced Fixture Design for FMS.** Ed. by A. Y. Nee et al. (Advanced Manufacturing Ser.). 1994. 89.00 (*0-387-19908-X*) Spr-Verlag.

Advanced Flight Control System Design. Chin-Fang Lin. 440p. 1993. text ed. 84.00 (*0-13-006305-3*) P-H.

Advanced Floral Design. Redbook Florist Services Educational Advisory Committee. LC 92-80132. (Encycloflora Ser.). (Illus.). 326p. (Orig.). 1992. pap. text ed. 34.95 (*1-56963-024-0*) Redbk Florist.

Advanced Fluid Catalytic Cracking Technology. Ed. by Kang C. Chuang et al. LC 92-37374. (AIChE Symposium Ser.: No. 291, Vol. 88, 1992). 144p. 1992. 75.00 (*0-8169-0578-9*) Am Inst Chem Eng.

Advanced Fly Fishing for Steelhead. Deke Meyer. (Illus.). 160p. (Orig.). 1992. 34.95 (*1-878175-11-4*); pap. 24.95 (*1-878175-10-6*) F Amato Pubns.

Advanced Fly Fishing Techniques: Secrets of an Avid Fisherman. Lefty Kreh. 1992. 25.00 (*0-385-29941-9*) Delacorte.

Advanced Fly Fishing Techniques: Secrets of an Avid Fisherman. Lefty Kreh. 1994. pap. 15.95 (*0-385-30835-3*, Delta) Dell.

Advanced Food Service. John Fuller. 240p. (Orig.). 1992. pap. 48.50 (*0-7487-1107-4*, Pub. by Stanley Thornes UK) Trans-Atl Phila.

Advanced Formulations in the Boundary Element Method. Ed. by M. H. Aliabadi & C. A. Brebbia. LC 92-75033. (Computational Engineering Ser.). 304p. 1993. 144.00 (*1-56252-111-X*) Computational Mech MA.

***Advanced FORTRAN Programming for Windows.** Templeman. Date not set. pap. text ed. 39.95 (*0-471-95685-6*) Wiley.

***Advanced Fractions.** (Tai Mathematics Ser.). (J). 1995. 5.25 (*0-88106-162-X*, M010) Charlesbridge Pub.

Advanced Fracture Mechanics. Melvin F. Kanninen & Carl H. Popelar. (Oxford Engineering Science Ser.). (Illus.). 1985. 59.00 (*0-19-503532-1*) OUP.

Advanced Framework User's Guide. Adam B. Green. write for info. (*0-318-59633-4*) S&S Trade.

Advanced Framing: Techniques, Troubleshooting, & Structural Design. Journal of Light Construction Staff. Ed. by Steven Bliss. LC 92-90097. (Illus.). 281p. 1992. pap. 24.95 (*0-9632268-0-0*) Builderburg Grp.

Advanced French for Exceptional Cats. Henri De La Barbe. 1992. 11.50 (*0-679-41764-8*, Villard Bks) Random.

Advanced Freshwater Fishing Strategies. Dick Sternberg. LC 94-12933. 1994. 24.95 (*0-86573-045-8*) Cy De Cosse.

***Advanced Fuel Injection Systems.** Peter A. Bilotta. Ed. by Kelly Gorham. 17p. 1994. student ed write for info. (*0-8064-0272-5*, A44) Bergwall.

Advanced Fusing Techniques Glass Fusing Book Two. Boyce Lundstrom. Ed. by Kathleen Lundstrom. LC 83-50657. 144p. (Orig.). 1989. pap. 40.00 (*0-9612282-1-0*) Vitreous Pubns.

Advanced Gasification: Methanol Production from Wood-Results of the EEC Pilot Programme. Ed. by A. A. Beenackers & W. Van Swaay. 1986. lib. bdg. 85.50 (*90-277-2212-9*) Kluwer Ac.

Advanced General Relativity. John Stewart. (Monographs on Mathematical Physics). (Illus.). 236p. (C). 1993. pap. 27.95 (*0-521-44946-4*) Cambridge U Pr.

Advanced Generalist Practice: With an International Perspective. Maria O'Neil McMahon. LC 93-39940. 1993. text ed. write for info. (*0-13-120635-4*) P-H.

Advanced Geometric Modelling for Engineering Applications. Ed. by F. L. Krause & H. Jansen. 458p. 1990. 113.00 (*0-444-88830-6*, North Holland) Elsevier.

Advanced Glasses. Business Communications Co., Inc. Staff. 174p. 1986. pap. 1,950.00 (*0-89336-498-3*, GB-094) BCC.

***Advanced, Glasses & Ceramics Materials, Processing New Development Application.** 1995. 27.50 (*0-614-03501-5*, GB094R) BCC.

***Advanced, Glasses & Ceramics Materials, Processing New Development Applications.** 1995. 27.50 (*0-614-03469-8*, GB094R) BCC.

Advanced Golf. DeDe Owens & Linda K. Bunker. LC 92-5940. (Illus.). 176p. 1992. pap. 15.95 (*0-88011-464-9*, POWE0464) Human Kinetics.

***Advanced Grace Disciple Course.** Lee C. Turner. 168p. 1994. pap. 11.95 (*0-9645054-1-X*) Grace Disc.

Advanced Grammar Book. Steer & Carlisi. 1991. pap. 20.95 (*0-8384-2666-2*) Heinle & Heinle.

Advanced Grammar for ESL. Helen H. Schmidt. 1995. pap. text ed. 16.00 (*0-13-096942-7*) P-H.

Advanced Graphics on the VGA, XGA, TIGA Cards Using Borland C Plus Plus. Ian O. Angell. 1992. pap. text ed. 36.95 (*0-470-21833-9*) Halsted Pr.

Advanced Graphics Programming Using C - C Plus Plus. Loren Heiny. LC 93-14717. 432p. 1993. pap. text ed. 34.95 (*0-471-57159-8*) Wiley.

Advanced Graphics Workbook. 50p. 1990. 50.00 (*0-685-48642-7*) Indus Fabrics.

Advanced Greek Unseens. Cook & Marchant. Ed. by Anthony Bowen. 1980. 14.95 (*0-906515-47-5*, Pub. by Brstl Class Pr UK) Focus Info Gr.

Advanced Group Leadership. Jeffrey A. Kottler. LC 93-15942. 1994. text ed. 44.95 (*0-534-21150-X*) Brooks-Cole.

Advanced Guard see SAFRA Papers

Advanced Guide to Enochian Magick: A Complete Manual of Angelic Magick. Gerald J. Schueler. LC 87-45243. (High Magick Ser.). (Illus.). 448p. (Orig.). 1987. pap. 12.95 (*0-87542-711-1*) Llewellyn Pubns.

Advanced Guide to Radio Control Sport Flying. Douglas R. Pratt. (Illus.). 128p. 1988. pap. 9.95 (*0-8306-9360-2*, 3060P) TAB Bks.

Advanced Guided Vehicles: Aspects of the Oxford AGV Project. S. Cameron & P. Probert. (Robotics & Automated Systems Ser.). 200p. 1994. text ed. 48.00 (*981-02-1393-X*, World Scientific Pub) World Scientific Pub.

Advanced Guitar. Harry A. Taussig. 128p. 1981. pap. 14.95 (*0-8256-0163-0*) Music Sales.

Advanced Guitar Case Chord Book. Askold Buk. (Illus.). 68p. 1992. pap. 4.95 (*0-8256-1243-8*, AM80227) Music Sales.

Advanced Guitar Case Scale Book. Darryl Winston. (Illus.). 48p. 1993. pap. 4.95 (*0-8256-1370-1*) Music Sales.

Advanced Gundog Training: Practical Fieldwork & Competition. Martin Deeley. (Illus.). 176p. 1994. 34.95 (*1-85223-771-6*, Pub. by Crowood Pr UK) Trafalgar.

Advanced Harmony. 3rd ed. Robert W. Ottman. (Illus.). 416p. 1984. pap. text ed. 57.33 (*0-13-011370-0*) P-H.

Advanced Harmony, Theory & Practice. 4th ed. Robert W. Ottman. 384p. 1992. pap. text ed. 52.00 (*0-13-006016-X*) P-H.

Advanced Health Physics Library, 8 vols., Set. (Illus.). 1300p. 1983. 595.00 (*0-87683-692-9*) GP Pub.

Advanced Heat Conduction. Yovanovich. 1989. write for info. (*0-89116-323-9*) CRC Pr.

Advanced High Technology Machining Systems. Business Communications Co., Inc. Staff. (Illus.). 150p. 1986. pap. 1,750.00 (*0-89336-476-2*, GB-087) BCC.

Advanced Home Schooling Workshop Notes. Gregg Harris. 54p. 1992. student ed 10.00 (*0-923463-79-8*) Noble Pub Assocs.

Advanced Home Wiring. Cy DeCosse Incorporated Staff. LC 91-37337. (Black & Decker Home Improvement Library). 128p. 1992. 14.95 (*0-86573-718-5*); pap. 12.95 (*0-86573-719-3*) Cy De Cosse.

Advanced Houses Program Technical Requirements. (Illus.). 49p. (Orig.). (C). 1993. pap. text ed. 30.00 (*1-56806-628-7*) Diane Pub.

Advanced Hungarian 1. Martha Pereszlenyi-Pinter. (Illus.). 111p. (Orig.). (HUN.). (C). 1987. teacher ed, pap. 8.00 (*0-87415-124-4*, 51A); student ed, pap. text ed. 19.00 (*0-87415-123-6*, 51); audio 5.00 (*0-87415-125-2*, 51B) OSU Foreign Lang.

Advanced Hungarian 2. Julianna N. Ludanyi. (Illus.). 123p. (Orig.). (HUN.). (C). 1988. teacher ed, pap. 8.00 (*0-87415-127-9*, 52A); student ed, pap. text ed. 16.00 (*0-87415-126-0*, 52); audio 5.00 (*0-87415-128-7*, 52B) OSU Foreign Lang.

Advanced Hustle. Earl Atkinson. (Ballroom Dance Ser.). 1986. lib. bdg. 250.00 (*0-8490-3623-2*) Gordon Pr.

Advanced IBM BASIC Faster & Better, Vol. I. Lewis Rosenfelder. (IBM Information Ser.). (Illus.). 396p. (Orig.). 1985. pap. 19.95 (*0-932679-01-3*); disk 29.95 (*0-685-43124-X*) Blue Cat.

Advanced III-V Compound Semiconductor Growth, Processing & Devices. Ed. by S. J. Pearton et al. (Symposium Proceedings Ser.: Vol. 240). 1992. text ed. 66.00 (*1-55899-134-4*) Materials Res.

Advanced Imaging Techniques. Thomas H. Newton & D. Gordon Potts. (Modern Neuroradiology Ser.: Vol. 2). 348p. 1983. 83.50 (*0-685-38980-4*, CL0002) Raven.

Advanced Immunoassays in Rheumatology. Teodorescu. 1994. 169.95 (*0-8493-5974-0*, RC934) CRC Pr.

Advanced Immunochemistry. 2nd ed. Ed. by Eugene D. Day. 716p. 1990. pap. text ed. 110.00 (*0-471-56768-X*) Wiley.

Advanced Immunology. 2nd ed. D. K. Male et al. (Illus.). 304p. 1991. 69.95 (*0-397-44771-X*); pap. 45.00 (*0-397-44586-5*, GM0051) Mosby Yr Bk.

Advanced in Oilseed Research, Vol. 1: Rapeseeds & Mustard. D. M. Kumar. (C). 1992. text ed. 225.00 (*81-7233-046-4*, Pub. by Scientific Pubs II) St Mut.

Advanced Indoor Exercise. Benyo Press Staff. (Runner's World Ser.). 1982. pap. 9.95 (*0-02-499460-X*) Macmillan.

Advanced Indoor Exercise. Provost. (Runner's World Ser.). 1981. pap. 16.95 (*0-02-499470-7*) Macmillan.

Advanced Indoor Exercises. 9.95 (*0-685-17514-6*) Anderson World.

Advanced Industrial Development: Restructuring, Relocation & Renewal. Donald A. Hicks. LC 85-13876. (Lincoln Institute of Land Policy Book Ser.). 343p. reprint ed. pap. 97.80 (*0-7837-5750-6*, 2045412) Bks Demand.

Advanced Industrial Economics. Stephen Martin. LC 92-25471. 1993. pap. 34.95 (*0-631-17852-X*) Blackwell Pubs.

Advanced Industrial Hygiene. T. Lee. 1990. text ed. write for info. (*0-442-23532-1*) Van Nos Reinhold.

Advanced Information Processing: Proceedings of a Joint Symposium Information Processing & Software Systems Design Automation USSR Academy of Sciences, Siemens AG, FRG Moscow, June 5-6, 1990. Ed. by Heinz Schwartzel & I. Mizin. 416p. 1993. pap. 39.00 (*0-387-52683-8*) Spr-Verlag.

Advanced Information Processing Applications. Carolou Skeans & Ann Hern. (C). 1984. teacher ed write for info. (*0-8359-0076-2*, Reston); pap. text ed. write for info. (*0-8359-0069-X*, Reston) P-H.

Advanced Information Processing in Automatic Control (AIPAC'89) Selected Papers from the IFAC-IMACS-IFORS Symposium, Nancy, France, 3-5 July 1989. Ed. by R. Husson. (IFAC Proceedings Ser.: IFPS 9005). 570p. 1990. 265.00 (*0-08-037034-9*, Pergamon Pr) Elsevier.

Advanced Information Processing Techniques for LAN & MAN Management. Ed. by J. P. Claude. LC 93-34574. (IFIP Transactions C: Communication Systems Ser.: Vol. C-17). 1993. write for info. (*0-444-81634-8*, North Holland) Elsevier.

Advanced Information Systems Engineering: Proceedings of the Fourth International Conference, CAiSE 1992, Manchester, U. K., May 12-15, 1992. Ed. by Peri Loucopoulos et al. LC 92-16718. (Lecture Notes in Computer Science Ser.: Vol. 593). xi, 650p. 1992. pap. 85.00 (*0-387-55481-5*) Spr-Verlag.

Advanced Information Systems Engineering: Proceedings of the Second Nordic Conference CAiSE '90, Stockholm, Sweden, May 8-10, 1990. Ed. by B. Steinholtz et al. (Lecture Notes in Computer Science Ser.: Vol. 436). x, 392p. 1990. pap. 41.80 (*0-387-52625-0*) Spr-Verlag.

Advanced Information Systems Engineering: Proceedings of the Third Nordic Conference CAiSE '91, Trondheim, Norway, May 13-15, 1991. R. Andersen et al. Ed. by G. Goos & J. Hartmanis. (Lecture Notes in Computer Science Ser.: Vol. 498). vi, 579p. 1991. pap. 52.00 (*0-387-54059-8*) Spr-Verlag.

Advanced Information Systems Engineering: Proceedings of the 5th International Conference, CAiSE '93, Paris, France, June 8-11, 1993. Ed. by C. Rolland et al. (Lecture Notes in Computer Science Ser.: Vol. 685). v, 648p. 1993. pap. 92.00 (*0-387-56777-1*) Spr-Verlag.

***Advanced Information Systems Engineering: 6th International Conference, CAISE '94, Utrech, the Netherlands, June 6-10, 1994.** G. Wijers & S. Brinkkemper. (Lecture Notes in Computer Science: 811). 420p. 1994. 54.00 (*0-387-58113-8*) Spr-Verlag.

Advanced Information Systems for Lawyers. V. Mital & L. Johnson. 304p. 1992. 54.95 (*0-442-31591-0*) Chapman & Hall.

Advanced Information Technologies for Industrial Material Systems. Ed. by Shimon Y. Nof & C. L. Moodie. (NATO Asi Series F: Vol. 53). x, 710p. 1989. 133.00 (*0-387-50905-4*) Spr-Verlag.

Advanced Information Technology in the New Industrial Society: The Kingston Seminars. Ed. by Arthur Cotterell. (Illus.). 128p. 1988. pap. 18.95 (*0-19-853290-3*) OUP.

Advanced Informix 4GL Programming. Art Taylor. 384p. 1994. pap. text ed. 42.00 (*0-13-301318-9*) P-H.

Advanced Infrared Detectors & Systems: Related Conference Proceedings. (IEE Conference Publications: No. 263). 1986. 55.00 (*0-85296-332-7*, IC263) Inst Elect Eng.

Advanced Inorganic Chemistry. 5th ed. F. Albert Cotton & Geoffrey Wilkinson. LC 87-20728. 1455p. 1988. text ed. 69.95 (*0-471-84997-9*) Wiley.

Advanced Installation Guide for Hydronic Heating Systems. 2nd ed. 60p. (C). 1973. 10.50 (*0-942711-02-5*, 250) Hydronics Inst.

Advanced Instrumental Methods of Chemical Analysis. Jaroslav Churacek. 734p. 1993. text ed. write for info. (*0-13-913195-7*) P-H.

***Advanced Instrumentation & Computer I-O Design: A Model-Based Approach.** Garrett. 1994. pap. 39.95 (*0-7803-1053-5*) Inst Electrical.

Advanced Instrumentation & Computer I-O Design: Real-Time System Computer Interface Engineering. Patrick H. Garrett. LC 93-39730. (Illus.). 304p. 1994. text ed. 39.95 (*0-7803-1060-8*) Inst Electrical.

Advanced Intel Microprocessors: 80286, 80386, & 80486. Barry B. Brey. LC 92-11880. 768p. (C). 1993. write for info. (*0-02-314245-6*) Macmillan.

Advanced Interactive Video Design. Nicholas V. Iuppa & Karl Anderson. (Illus.). 150p. 1988. 45.00 (*0-86729-170-2*) Knowledge Indus.

Advanced Interest Rate & Currency Swaps: State-of-the-Art Products, Strategies & Risk Management Applications. Ed. by Ravi E. Dattatreya & Kensuke Hotta. 450p. 1993. 65.00 (*1-55738-444-4*) Probus Pub Co.

Advanced Interpretation of Clinical Laboratory Data. Ed. by Camille Heusghem et al. (Clinical & Biochemical Analysis Ser.: Vol. 13). (Illus.). 448p. 1982. 155.00 (*0-8247-1744-9*) Dekker.

***Advanced Interviewing Techniques.** Brian Jud. Ed. by Charles Lipka. 16p. (Orig.). (C). 1995. student ed, pap. 1.45 (*1-880218-18-6*) Mktg Dir Inc.

Advanced Intraoperative Technologies in Neurosurgery. Ed. by V. A. Fasano. (Illus.). 330p. 1986. 89.00 (*0-387-81880-4*) Spr-Verlag.

***Advanced Introduction: ANSI C Edition.** 2nd ed. Narain Gehani. LC 94-26969. 1994. pap. write for info. (*0-929306-17-1*) Silicon Pr.

Advanced Investigative Techniques for Obtaining Information & Conducting Interviews. U. S. Government Staff. Ed. by Ralph D. Thomas. 100p. 1990. pap. text ed. 19.95 (*0-918487-37-4*) Thomas Pubns TX.

Advanced Investigative Techniques for Private Financial Records. R. A. Nossen. (Orig.). 1986. lib. bdg. 79.95 (*0-8490-3602-X*) Gordon Pr.

Advanced Japanese Conversation. Hamako Chaplin & Samuel Martin. 1976. 9.95 (*0-88710-000-7*); audio write for info. (*0-88710-127-5*) Yale Far Eastern Pubns.

***Advanced Karate-Do: Concepts, Techniques, & Training Methods.** Elmar T. Schmeisser. (Illus.). 214p. (Orig.). 1994. pap. 16.50 (*0-911921-16-8*) Focus Pubns MO.

Advanced Lake Fly-Fishing: The Skillful Tuber. Robert Alley. (Illus.). 120p. (Orig.). 1991. 29.95 (*0-936608-98-6*); pap. 14.95 (*0-936608-97-8*) F Amato Pubns.

Advanced Land Descriptions: Manual of Instruction for Preparing Land Descriptions. Paul Cuomo & Roy Minnick. (Illus.). 181p. 1993. 55.00 (*0-910845-53-0*) Landmark Ent.

Advanced Laser Concepts & Applications, Vol. 1501. S. Singer. 1991. 58.00 (*0-8194-0610-4*) SPIE.

Advanced Latin Hustle. (Ballroom Dance Ser.). 1986. lib. bdg. 250.00 (*0-8490-3392-6*) Gordon Pr.

Advanced Latin Hustle. (Ballroom Dance Ser.). 1985. lib. bdg. 67.95 (*0-87700-754-3*) Revisionist Pr.

Advanced Latin Unseens: Drawn from the Collection of Cook & Merchant. Ed. by Anthony Bowen. 100p. 1980. 13.95 (*0-906515-54-8*, Pub. by Brstl Class Pr UK) Focus Info Gr.

Advanced Law Firm Mismanagement. Arnold B. Kanter. LC 92-33557. (Illus.). 224p. (Orig.). 1993. pap. 12.95 (*0-945774-20-6*, PS3561.A477A65) Catbird Pr.

Advanced Lectures in Quantitative Economics II. Ed. by Aart J. De Zeeuw. (Illus.). 272p. 1993. pap. text ed. 39.95 (*0-12-214685-9*) Acad Pr.

Advanced Level see Competency Tests for Basic Reading Skills

Advanced Level see Durrell Listening-Reading Series: Form DE

Advanced Level see Durrell Listening-Reading Series: Form EF

Advanced Level Accounting. H. Randall. 464p. (C). 1990. 50.00 (*1-870941-36-5*) St Mut.

Advanced Level Chinese Literature, 2 vols., I. Ed. by P. H. Ho & P. L. Chan. (C). 1992. pap. text ed. 24.00 (*962-209-311-6*, Pub. by Hong Kong U Pr HK) St Mut.

Advanced Level Chinese Literature, 2 vols., II. Ed. by P. H. Ho & P. L. Chan. (C). 1992. pap. text ed. 24.00 (*962-209-312-4*, Pub. by Hong Kong U Pr HK) St Mut.

Advanced Level Chinese Literature Commentary, 1. Ed. by P. L. Chan & K. K. Chan. (C). 1993. pap. text ed. 21.00 (*962-209-313-2*, Pub. by Hong Kong U Pr HK) St Mut.

Advanced Level Chinese Literature Commentary, 2. Ed. by P. L. Chan & K. K. Chan. (C). 1993. pap. text ed. 21.00 (*962-209-314-0*, Pub. by Hong Kong U Pr HK) St Mut.

Advanced Level Essay Writing: German. Eileen Holly & Anne Sansome. 1989. pap. text ed. 11.88 (*0-582-35604-0*, 78048) Longman.

Advanced Lie-Detection Techniques. R. D. Thomas. (Law Enforcement Ser.). 1986. lib. bdg. 150.00 (*0-8490-3717-4*) Gordon Pr.

Advanced Lie-Detection Techniques. Ralph D. Thomas. 65p. 1986. pap. text ed. 10.00 (*0-317-30221-3*) Thomas Pubns TX.

Advanced Life Support Skills. Allison et al. 320p. 1993. pap. 31.95 (*0-8016-7426-3*) Mosby Yr Bk.

Advanced Light Microscopy: Specialized Methods, Vol. 2. M. Pluta. 484p. 1989. 166.75 (*0-444-98918-8*) Elsevier.

Advanced Light Microscopy, Vol. 1: Principles & Basic Properties. M. Pluta. 460p. 1988. 146.25 (*0-444-98939-0*) Elsevier.

Advanced Light Microscopy, Vol. 3: Measuring Techniques. M. Pluta. 718p. 1993. 242.75 (*0-444-98819-X*, North Holland) Elsevier.

Advanced Lighting Guidelines. 2nd ed. California Energy Commission Staff. (Illus.). 200p. (Orig.). (C). 1993. pap. text ed. 45.00 (*0-941375-67-6*) Diane Pub.

Advanced Lindy. (Ballroom Dance Ser.: No. 2). 1985. lib. bdg. 75.00 (*0-87700-778-0*) Revisionist Pr.

Advanced Lindy, No. 2. (Ballroom Dance Ser.). 1986. lib. bdg. 250.00 (*0-8490-3286-5*) Gordon Pr.

Advanced Lindy & Jitterbug. (Ballroom Dance Ser.). 1986. lib. bdg. 250.00 (*0-8490-3287-3*) Gordon Pr.

Advanced Lindy & Jitterbug. (Ballroom Dance Ser.). 1985. lib. bdg. 68.00 (*0-87700-779-9*) Revisionist Pr.

***Advanced Linear Algebra.** Jimmie Gilbert & Linda Gilbert. (Illus.). 405p. (C). 1995. text ed. 39.95 (*0-12-282970-0*) Acad Pr.

Advanced Linear Algebra. Steven Roman. LC 92-11860. (Graduate Texts in Mathematics Ser.: Vol. 135). (Illus.). xii, 363p. 1992. 49.90 (*0-387-97837-2*) Spr-Verlag.

Advanced Linear Models: Theory & Applications. Song-Gui Wang & Shein-Chung Chow. LC 93-37224. (Statistics: Vol. 141). 552p. 1994. 165.00 (*0-8247-9169-X*) Dekker.

Advanced Listening Comprehension. Patricia Dunkel & Frank Pialorsi. 232p. (C). 1982. pap. 20.95 (*0-8384-2963-7*, Newbury) Heinle & Heinle.

Advanced Lock Picking. Steven M. Hampton. (Illus.). 56p. 1989. pap. 10.00 (*0-87364-515-4*) Paladin Pr.

Advanced Logic & Bus Interface Logic Data Book. Texas Instruments Engineering Staff. 1086p. 1991. 15.95 (*0-685-62488-9*, SCYD001) Tex Instr Inc.

Advanced Logic for Applications. Richard E. Grandy. (Synthese Library: No. 110). 1977. lib. bdg. 65.50 (*90-277-0781-2*) Kluwer Ac.

Advanced Logic for Applications. Richard E. Grandy. (Pallas Paperbacks Ser.: No. 13). 1979. pap. text ed. 36.50 (*90-277-1034-1*) Kluwer Ac.

Advanced Logic Programming for Language Processing. Patrick Saint-Dizier. (Illus.). 300p. 1994. text ed. 59.95 (*0-12-614860-0*) Acad Pr.

Advanced Logic Programming Language, Vol. 1: Prolog-2 User Guide. Tony Dodd. 400p. (C). 1990. text ed. 39.95 (*0-89391-670-6*) Ablex Pub.

Advanced Logic Programming Language, Vol. 2: Prolog-2 Encyclopedia. Tony Dodd. 400p. (C). 1990. text ed. 39.95 (*0-89391-669-2*) Ablex Pub.

An Asterisk (*) at the beginning of an entry indicates that the title is appearing in BIP for the first time.

Advanced Logistics & Road Freight Transport. OECD Staff. 184p. (Orig.). 1992. pap. 64.00 (*92-64-13730-0*) OECD.

***Advanced Logo: Language for Learning.** Michael Friendly. 1988. disk 89.95 (*1-56321-120-3*); disk, pap. 49.95 (*1-56321-150-5*); disk 29.95 (*1-56321-149-1*) L Erlbaum Assocs.

Advanced Logo: Language for Learning. Michael Friendly. 676p. 1988. 99.95 (*0-89859-933-4*); pap. 39.95 (*0-8058-0074-3*); Apple II 29.95 (*1-56321-055-X*) L Erlbaum Assocs.

Advanced Lotus 1-2-3, Version 2.4. Anna L. Slepecky. LC 93-24434. (Glencoe Seminar Ser.). 1993. teacher ed write for info. (*0-02-801079-5*); student ed write for info. (*0-02-801078-7*) Glencoe.

Advanced Low-Power Schottky-Advanced Schottky Data Book. Texas Instruments Engineering Staff. LC 82-74481. 992p. 1983. pap. 14.95 (*0-89512-113-1*, SDAD0011) Tex Instr Inc.

Advanced Machine Design in Fortran. D. K. Sinha & T. R. Hsu. 1988. 70.00 (*0-685-24871-2*, 98-1-B); disk 70.00 (*0-685-24872-0*, 98-1-IMSD); disk 48.00 (*0-685-24873-9*, 98-1-IUCSD) Kern Intl.

Advanced Machine Tool Technology & Manufacturing Processes. C. Thomas Olivo. Ed. by H. G. Putnam. LC 89-64000. (Illus.). 608p. (C). 1991. 39.95 (*0-938561-04-9*); teacher ed 15.95 (*0-938561-06-5*); student ed 9.95 (*0-938561-05-7*) C T Olivo.

Advanced Machine Work. R. H. Smith. 1984. reprint ed. pap. 25.95 (*0-917914-23-6*) Lindsay Pubns.

Advanced Machining. Graham T. Smith. (Illus.). 320p. 1989. 115.00 (*0-387-50650-0*) Spr-Verlag.

Advanced Machining for Quality & Productivity: Proc. 2nd Int'l Conf. on the Behaviorial Materials in Machining. Proceedings of the 2nd Int'l Conference on the Behavior of Materials in Machining Staff. 176p. 1991. pap. 80.00 (*0-901716-24-3*, Pub. by Inst Materials UK) Ashgate Pub Co.

Advanced Macroeconomics: Beyond IS-LM. Derek Leslie. LC 92-38140. 1993. 17.95 (*0-07-707724-5*) McGraw.

Advanced Magical Arts. R. J. Stewart. 1989. pap. 13.95 (*1-85230-045-0*) Element MA.

Advanced Magick Quest Course, Bk. 4: Milanthros. Igos Research. 107p. 25.00 (*1-57179-037-3*) Intern Guild ASRS.

Advanced Management - Parking Lots: A Self Study Approach. International Council of Shopping Centers Staff. (Illus.). student ed, audio 59.95 (*0-913598-32-1*, 606); 29.95 (*0-685-08319-5*) Intl Coun Shop.

Advanced Management - Roofs: A Self Study Approach. International Council of Shopping Centers Staff. (Illus.). 1983. student ed, audio 59.95 (*0-913598-31-3*, 600); 29.95 (*0-685-08318-7*) Intl Coun Shop.

Advanced Management Accounting. 2nd ed. Hirsch. (C). 1994. text ed. 64.95 (*0-538-82535-9*) S-W Pub.

Advanced Management Accounting. 2nd ed. Robert S. Kaplan & Anthony A. Atkinson. 704p. (C). 1989. text ed. write for info. (*0-13-011560-6*) P-H.

Advanced Manufacturing Strategy & Management. D. K. MacBeth. 180p. 1989. 79.00 (*0-387-51113-X*) Spr-Verlag.

Advanced Manufacturing Systems. Ed. by R. D. Eanes. 850p. 1987. 153.00 (*0-387-17253-X*) Spr-Verlag.

Advanced Manufacturing Systems Exposition & Conference: Proceedings of the Conference Session, April 18-21, 1988, McCormick Place North, Chicago, IL. Advanced Manufacturing Systems Exposition & Conference (1988: Chicago, IL) Staff. 923p. reprint ed. pap. 180.00 (*0-8357-5127-9*, 2032912) Bks Demand.

Advanced Manufacturing Systems Exposition & Conference: Proceedings of the Conference Sessions, December 15-17, 1987, Anaheim Convention Center, Anaheim, CA. Advanced Manufacturing Systems Exposition & Conference (1987: Anaheim, CA) Staff. 470p. reprint ed. pap. 134.00 (*0-8357-5126-0*, 2032910) Bks Demand.

Advanced Manufacturing Systems Exposition & Conference: Proceedings of the Conference Sessions, McCormick Place, Chicago, IL, June 24-26, 1986, Including 2nd International Conference on Simulation in Manufacturing: 4th International Conference on Automated Guided Vehicle Systems. Advanced Manufacturing Systems Exposition & Conference Staff (1986, Chicago, Il). 855p. reprint ed. pap. 180.00 (*0-8357-5125-2*, 2029368) Bks Demand.

Advanced Manufacturing Technology. T. H. Allegri. 1989. text ed. 44.50 (*0-07-156542-6*) McGraw.

Advanced Manufacturing Technology. Theodore H. Allegri, Sr. (Illus.). 496p. 1989. 44.50 (*0-8306-2746-4*, NO. 2746, TAB/TPR) TAB Bks.

Advanced Manufacturing Technology Management. Mike Harrison. 176p. (Orig.). 1990. pap. 38.50 (*0-273-03196-1*, Pub. by Pitman Pub Ltd UK) Trans-Atl Phila.

Advanced Marketing Strategy: Phenomena, Analysis & Decisions. Glen Urban. 1990. text ed. 70.00 (*0-13-851940-4*) P-H.

Advanced Masonry. (Home Repair & Improvement Ser.). (Illus.). 136p. 1982. 14.60 (*0-8094-3466-0*); lib. bdg. 20.60 (*0-8094-3467-9*) Time-Life.

Advanced Masonry Skills. 2nd ed. Richard T. Kreh, Sr. LC 82-70523. (Illus.). 455p. 1983. pap. text ed. 29.95 (*0-8273-2148-1*) Delmar.

Advanced Mass Spectrometry: Applications in Organic & Analytical Chemistry. U. P. Schlunegger. LC 80-40512. (Illus.). 150p. 1980. 71.00 (*0-08-023842-4*, Pub. by Pergamon Repr UK) Franklin.

***Advanced Master Handgunning: Secrets & Surefire Techniques to Make You a Winner.** Charles Stephens. (Illus.). 72p. 1994. pap. 10.00 (*0-87364-787-4*) Paladin Pr.

***Advanced Material: Affordable Processes: 23rd International SAMPE Technical Conference, Concord Resort Hotel, Kiamesha Lake, NY, October 21-24, 1991.** International SAMPE Technical Conference Staff. Ed. by Robert L. Carri et al. (International SAMPE Technical Conference Ser.: No. 23). (Illus.). reprint ed. pap. 180.00 (*0-7837-9627-7*, 2060381) Bks Demand.

***Advanced Materials: "Fifty Years of Progress in Materials Science & Technology" October 17-20, 1994.** (International Technical Conference Proceeding Ser.: Vol. 26). 1994. 75.00 (*0-938994-71-9*) SAMPE.

Advanced Materials: Expanding the Horizons, October 26-28, 1993. (International Technical Conference Proceedings Ser.: Vol. 25). 1993. 55.00 (*0-938994-68-9*) SAMPE.

Advanced Materials: Performance Through Technology Insertion, May 10-13, 1993. (International Symposium & Exhibition Proceedings Ser.: Vol. 38). 1993. 50.00 (*0-938994-67-0*) SAMPE.

***Advanced Materials: Performance Through Technology Insertion: 35th International SAMPE Symposium & Exhibition, Anaheim, Convention Center, Anaheim, CA, May 10-13, 1993, Bk. 1.** International SAMPE Symposium & Exhibition Staff. Ed. by Vince Bailey et al. (Science of Advanced Materials & Process Enginnering Ser.: No. 38). (Illus.). 1131p. reprint ed. pap. 180.00 (*0-7837-9621-8*, 2060377) Bks Demand.

***Advanced Materials: Performance Through Technology Insertion: 35th International SAMPE Symposium & Exhibition, Anaheim, Convention Center, Anaheim, CA, May 10-13, 1993, Bk. 2.** International SAMPE Symposium & Exhibition Staff. Ed. by Vince Bailey et al. (Science of Advanced Materials & Process Enginnering Ser.: No. 38). (Illus.). 1101p. reprint ed. pap. 180.00 (*0-7837-9622-6*, 2060377) Bks Demand.

Advanced Materials: Policies & Technological Challenges. OECD Staff. 188p. (Orig.). 1990. pap. 40.00 (*92-64-13255-4*) OECD.

Advanced Materials: The Big Payoff, 21st International SAMPE Technical Conference, Inns at the Park, Atlantic City, New Jersey, September 25-28, 1989. International SAMPE Technical Conference Staff et al. Ed. by Wegman et al. LC 89-216450. (International SAMPE Technical Conference Ser.: No. 21). 1104p. reprint ed. pap. 180.00 (*0-7837-1294-4*, 2041435) Bks Demand.

***Advanced Materials: The Challenge for the Next Decade: 35th International SAMPE Symposium & Exhibition, Anaheim, Convention Center, Anaheim, CA, April 2-5, 1990, Bk. 1.** International SAMPE Symposium & Exhibition Staff. Ed. by Gerry Janicki et al. (Science of Advanced Materials & Process Enginnering Ser.: No. 35). (Illus.). 1239p. reprint ed. pap. 180.00 (*0-7837-9619-6*, 2060376) Bks Demand.

***Advanced Materials: The Challenge for the Next Decade: 35th International SAMPE Symposium & Exhibition, Anaheim, Convention Center, Anaheim, CA, April 2-5, 1990, Bk. 2.** International SAMPE Symposium & Exhibition Staff. Ed. by Gerry Janicki et al. (Science of Advanced Materials & Process Enginnering Ser.: No. 35). (Illus.). 1231p. reprint ed. pap. 180.00 (*0-7837-9620-X*, 2060376) Bks Demand.

Advanced Materials - Affordable Processes. (International Technical Conference Proceedings Ser.: Vol. 23). 1235p. 1991. 40.00 (*0-938994-62-X*) SAMPE.

Advanced Materials - Application of Mineral & Metallurgical Processing Principles. Intro. by V. I. Lakshmanan. LC 89-63668. (Illus.). 248p. (Orig.). 1990. pap. 58.50 (*0-87335-089-8*) SMM&E Inc.

Advanced Materials & Coatings for Combustion Turbines. 265p. 1993. 63.00 (*0-87170-487-0*) ASM.

Advanced Materials & Processes, Vols. 1 & 2: Proceedings of the 1st European Conference on Advanced Materials & Processes EUROMAT '89, Set. Ed. by H. E. Exner & V. Schumacher. (Illus.). 1481p. 1990. lib. bdg. 278.00 (*3-88355-167-8*, Pub. by DGM Metallurgy Info GW) IR Pubns.

Advanced Materials & Processing: The Fiscal Year 1994 Federal Program. 56p. (Orig.). (C). 1993. pap. text ed. 40.00 (*0-7881-0071-8*) Diane Pub.

Advanced Materials & Processing: The Fiscal Year 1993 Program: The Federal Program in Materials Science & Technology. (Illus.). 211p. (Orig.). (C). 1993. pap. text ed. 60.00 (*1-56806-078-5*) Diane Pub.

Advanced Materials Development in the Soviet Shipbuilding Industry. Yaacov Epshtein. Ed. by Patra McSharry. (Illus.). 118p. (Orig.). 1989. pap. 75.00 (*1-55831-114-9*) Delphic Associates.

***Advanced Materials: Expanding the Horizons: 25th International SAMPE Technical Conference, Adam's Mark Hotel, Philadelphia, PA, October 26-28, 1993.** International SAMPE Technical Conference Staff. Ed. by Ronald Trabocco & Ted Lynch. (International SAMPE Technical Conference Ser.: No. 25). (Illus.). reprint ed. pap. 180.00 (*0-7837-9629-3*, 2060383) Bks Demand.

Advanced Materials for Air Frames, No. GB-122. Business Communications Co., Inc. Staff. 338p. 1990. 2,950.00 (*0-89336-703-6*) BCC.

Advanced Materials for Severe Service Applications: Proceedings of a Japan-U. S. Joint Seminar, Tokyo, Japan, May 19-23, 1986. Ed. by K. Iida & A. J. McEvily. 420p. 1987. 119.00 (*1-85166-096-8*, Pub. by Elsevier Applied Sci UK) Elsevier.

Advanced Materials in Future Transportation Design. 1988. 19.00 (*0-89883-681-6*, SP754) Soc Auto Engineers.

Advanced Materials in Sports Equipment. K. Easterling. (Illus.). 192p. 1992. pap. 34.50 (*0-412-40120-7*, A9469) Chapman & Hall.

***Advanced Materials: Looking Ahead to the 21st Century: 22th International SAMPE Technical Conference, Boston Park Plaza Hotel, Boston, MA, November 6-8, 1990.** International SAMPE Technical Conference Staff. Ed. by Leon D. Michelove et al. LC 91-150454. (International SAMPE Technical Conference Ser.: No. 22). (Illus.). reprint ed. pap. 180.00 (*0-7837-9630-7*, 2060384) Bks Demand.

Advanced Materials Markets: Meeting Their Promise in the 1990s. 327p. 1992. spiral bd., vinyl bd. 1,275.00 (*0-914993-99-2*) Tech Insights.

***Advanced Materials: Meeting the Economic Challenge: 24th International SAMPE Technical Conference, Westin Harbour Castle Hotel, Toronto, Canada, October 20-22, 1992.** International SAMPE Technical Conference Staff. Ed. by T. S. Reinhart et al. (International SAMPE Technical Conference Ser.: No. 24). (Illus.). reprint ed. pap. 180.00 (*0-7837-9631-5*, 2060385) Bks Demand.

Advanced Materials Technology '87: International SAMPE Symposium & Exhibition, 32nd, Anaheim Convention Center, Anaheim, California, April 6-9, 1987. International SAMPE Symposium & Exhibition Staff. Ed. by Ralph Carson et al. (Science of Advanced Materials & Process Enginnering Ser.: No. 32). 1625p. reprint ed. pap. 180.00 (*0-7837-1284-7*, 2041425) Bks Demand.

***Advanced Materials '93 Part 1.** Ed. by S. Somiya et al. 1936p. 1995. 703.00 (*0-444-81996-7*) Elsevier.

Advanced Math for Astrological Students. J. Allen Jones. LC 85-73310. 80p. 1986. 9.00 (*0-86690-311-9*, J1234-014) Am Fed Astrologers.

Advanced Math for Engineers & Scientists. Paul C. DuChateau. LC 91-58267. (Outline Ser.). 352p. (Orig.). (C). 1992. pap. 13.00 (*0-06-467151-8*, Harper Ref) HarpC.

Advanced Mathematical Analysis. R. Beals. LC 73-6884. (Graduate Texts in Mathematics Ser.: Vol. 12). 288p. (C). 1988. 39.95 (*0-387-90065-9*) Spr-Verlag.

Advanced Mathematical Methods. A. Ostaszewski. (London School of Economics Mathematics Ser.). (Illus.). 400p. (C). 1991. 125.00 (*0-521-24788-8*); pap. 42.95 (*0-521-28964-5*) Cambridge U Pr.

Advanced Mathematical Methods for Engineering & Science Students. G. Stephenson & P. M. Radmore. (Illus.). 240p. (C). 1990. 64.95 (*0-521-36312-8*); pap. 24.95 (*0-521-36860-X*) Cambridge U Pr.

Advanced Mathematical Methods for Scientists & Engineers. Carl M. Bender & Steven A. Orszag. (International Series in Pure & Applied Mathematics). (Illus.). 1978. text ed. write for info. (*0-07-004452-X*) McGraw.

Advanced Mathematical Tools in Metrology: Proceedings of the International Workshop. P. Ciarlini et al. (Series on Advances in Mathematics). 288p. 1994. text ed. 86.00 (*981-02-1758-7*) World Scientific Pub.

Advanced Mathematics: An Incremental Development. John Saxon. (YA). (gr. 10-12). 1989. text ed. 36.00 (*0-939798-37-9*); teacher ed 36.00 (*0-939798-38-7*); teacher ed 17.00 (*0-939798-57-3*); teacher ed 39.00 (*0-939798-39-5*); teacher ed, disk write for info. (*1-56577-011-0*) Saxon Pubs OK.

Advanced Mathematics: An Introductory Course. Richard Brown & David Robbins. (gr. 11-12). 1980. text ed. 54.04 (*0-395-29335-9*) HM.

Advanced Mathematics: An Introductory Course. Richard Brown & David Robbins. (gr. 11-12). 1981. Instr's. guide & solutions manual. teacher ed, pap. 31.08 (*0-395-29336-7*) HM.

***Advanced Mathematics & Mechanics Applications Using MATLAB.** Howard B. Wilson, Jr. & Louis H. Turcotte. 432p. 1994. 59.95 (*0-8493-2482-3*, 2482) CRC Pr.

Advanced Mathematics for Avionics Technicians. Frank Harris. LC 92-24393. (Avionics Technician Training Course Ser.). 119p. (Orig.). 1980. pap. text ed. 8.95 (*0-89100-122-0*, EA-MAT) IAP.

Advanced Mathematics for Economists: Static & Dynamic Optimization. Peter J. Lambert. 224p. 1985. pap. 32.95 (*0-631-14139-1*) Blackwell Pubs.

Advanced Mathematics for Engineers. Kaplan. 929p. reprint ed. 60.00 (*1-878907-53-0*) TechBooks.

Advanced Mathematics for Engineers & Scientists. Murray R. Spiegel. (Schaum Outline Ser.). 1970. pap. text ed. 13.95 (*0-07-060216-6*) McGraw.

Advanced Mathematics for Science: A Sequel to Mathematics for Science. William L. Ferrar. 1969. pap. 5.00 (*0-19-853144-3*) OUP.

Advanced Mathematics for Technical Students. A. Geary. 582p. reprint ed. pap. 165.90 (*0-8357-5128-7*, 2010171) Bks Demand.

Advanced Mechanics of Materials. Robert D. Cook & Warren C. Young. LC 84-7841. 560p. (C). 1985. text ed. write for info. (*0-02-324620-0*) Macmillan.

Advanced Mechanics of Materials. 5th ed. Arthur P. Boresi et al. 816p. 1993. text ed. write for info. (*0-471-55157-0*) Wiley.

***Advanced Medical Applications of Shape Memory Alloy Implants.** Yuri N. Zhuk. (Illus.). 56p. (C). Date not set. text ed. 345.00 (*1-886974-11-X*) First Med Pub.

Advanced Medical Life Support: Adult Medical-Cardiac Emergencies. Rothenberg. 224p. 1987. pap. text ed. 29.95 (*0-8016-4284-1*) Mosby Yr Bk.

Advanced Medical Radiation Dosimetry. K. N. Rajan. 522p. 1992. pap. 20.00 (*0-87692-706-1*) Med Physics Pub.

Advanced Medicine: Topics in Therapeutics, No. 1. A. M. Breckenridge. (Pitman Medical Conference Reports). (Illus.). 200p. 1975. pap. 42.00 (*0-8464-0114-2*) Beekman Pubs.

Advanced Medicine: Topics in Therapeutics, No. 2. (Pitman Medical Conference Reports). (Orig.). 1975. pap. 42.00 (*0-8464-0113-4*) Beekman Pubs.

Advanced Medicine: Topics in Therapeutics, No. 3. A. M. Breckenridge. (Pitman Medical Conference Reports). (Illus.). 1976. pap. 42.00 (*0-8464-0115-0*) Beekman Pubs.

Advanced Medicine: Topics in Therapeutics, No. 4. A. M. Breckenridge. (Pitman Medical Conference Reports). (Illus.). 1977. pap. 42.00 (*0-8464-0116-9*) Beekman Pubs.

Advanced Medicine, Eleven: Proceedings of the 11th Annual Symposium on Advanced Medicine 1975. Ed. by A. F. Lant. (Illus.). 450p. (Orig.). 1975. pap. text ed. 42.00 (*0-8464-0112-6*) Beekman Pubs.

Advanced Medicine Twelve: Proceedings of the 12th Annual Symposium of Advanced Medicine, 1976. Ed. by D. K. Peters. (Illus.). 1976. pap. 42.00 (*0-8464-0117-7*) Beekman Pubs.

Advanced Medicine Twenty-two. David R. Triger. 1986. pap. text ed. 58.95 (*0-7020-1171-1*, Bailliere-Tindall) Saunders.

Advanced Metallization & Processing for Semiconductor Devices & Circuits, No. Two. Ed. by A. Katz et al. (Materials Research Society Symposium Proceedings Ser.: Vol. 260). 1992. text ed. 66.00 (*1-55899-155-7*) Materials Res.

Advanced Metallization for Devices & Circuits - Science, Technology, & Manufacturability, No. Three: Materials Research Society Symposium Proceedings, Vol. 337. Ed. by S. P. Murarka et al. 1994. text ed. 57.00 (*1-55899-237-5*) Materials Res.

Advanced Metallization for ULSI Application, 1992. Ed. by T. S. Cale & F. S. Pintchovski. (Conference Proceedings Ser.: Vol. V-8). 1993. text ed. 65.00 (*1-55899-192-1*) Materials Res.

Advanced Metallization for ULSI Applications. Ed. by V. V. Rana et al. (Materials Research Society Conference Proceedings Ser.: Vol. VLSI-7). 577p. 1992. text ed. 62.00 (*1-55899-152-2*) Materials Res.

Advanced Metallization for ULSI Applications in 1993: Proceedings of the Conference held October 5-7, 1993, San Diego, California, USA., & October 26-27, 1993, Tokyo, Japan. Ed. by David P. Favreau et al. (Conference Proceedings Ser.: Vol. 1048-0854). 1994. text ed. 67.00 (*1-55899-235-9*) Materials Res.

***Advanced Metallization for ULSI Applications in 1994: Proceedings of the Conference Held October 4-6, 1994, Austin, Texas.** Ed. by Roc Blumenthal & Guido Janssen. LC 95-4971. (MRS Conference Proceedings Ser.: Vol. 10). 563p. 1995. 72.00 (*1-55899-279-0*, V10N) Materials Res.

Advanced Metallizations in Microelectronics: Symposium Proceedings Ser., Vol. 181. Ed. by A. Katz et al. 1990. text ed. 46.00 (*1-55899-070-4*) Materials Res.

Advanced Methodologies in Coal Characterization. Ed. by H. Charvosset & B. Nickel-Pepin-Donat. (Coal Science & Technology Ser.: No. 15). 442p. 1990. 182.00 (*0-444-88695-8*) Elsevier.

Advanced Methods for Satellite & Deep Space Communications: Proceedings of an International Seminar Organized by Deutsche Forschungsanstalt fur Luft- und Raumfahrt, Bonn, Germany, September 1992. Ed. by J. Hagenauer. LC 92-26473. (Lecture Notes in Control & Information Sciences Ser.: Vol. 182). vii, 210p. 1992. pap. 55.00 (*0-387-55851-9*) Spr-Verlag.

Advanced Methods in Adaptive Control for Industrial Application. Ed. by K. Warwick et al. (Lecture Notes in Control & Information Sciences Ser.: Vol. 158). (Illus.). 341p. 1991. pap. 51.00 (*0-387-53835-6*) Spr-Verlag.

Advanced Methods in Neural Computing. Philip D. Wasserman. LC 93-12320. 1993. text ed. 39.95 (*0-442-00461-3*) Van Nos Reinhold.

Advanced Methods in Plant Breeding & Biotechnology. Ed. by David R. Murray. (Biotechnology in Agriculture Ser.: No. 4). 365p. 1991. 95.00 (*0-85198-706-0*) CAB Intl.

Advanced Methods in Protein Microsequence Analysis. Ed. by B. Wittmann-Liebold et al. 455p. 1987. 196.00 (*0-387-16997-0*) Spr-Verlag.

Advanced Methods in Psychobiology. Ed. by Joseph N. Hingtgen et al. LC 87-3949. 320p. (C). 1987. text ed. 34.00 (*0-88937-011-7*) Hogrefe & Huber Pubs.

Advanced Methods in Reliability Testing, Volume 2. Dimitri Kececioglu. 1994. text ed. 48.00 (*0-13-300633-6*) P-H.

Advanced Methods of Machining. J. A. McGeough. 300p. 1988. text ed. 52.50 (*0-412-31970-5*) Chapman & Hall.

Advanced Methods of Marketing Research. Ed. by Richard P. Bagozzi. 384p. (Orig.). (C). 1994. pap. 39.95 (*1-55786-549-3*) Blackwell Pubs.

Advanced Methods of Pharmacokinetic & Pharmacodynamic Systems Analysis. Ed. by D. Z. D'Argenio. (Illus.). 220p. 1991. 75.00 (*0-306-44028-8*, Plenum Pr) Plenum.

***Advanced Methods of Pharmacokinetic & Pharmacodynamic Systems Analysis Vol. 2: Proceedings of a Meeting Held in Los Angeles, California, May 21-22, 1993.** Ed. by David Z. D'Argenio. 220p. 1995. 75.00 (*0-306-45018-6*, Plenum Pr) Plenum.

Advanced Methods of Physiological System Modeling, Vol. I. Intro. by Vasilis Z. Marmarelis. (Illus.). 344p. (C). 1987. reprint ed. text ed. 35.00 (*0-941639-01-0*) USC Biomedical.

Advanced Methods of Physiological System Modeling, Vol. 2. Ed. by V. Z. Marmarelis. (Illus.). 310p. 1989. 79.50 (*0-306-43259-5*, Plenum Pr) Plenum.

***Advanced Methods of Physiological System Modeling, Vol. 3.** Ed. by V. Z. Marmarelis. (Illus.). 270p. 1994. 85.00 (*0-306-44819-X*, Plenum Pr) Plenum.

A

An Asterisk (*) at the beginning of an entry indicates that the title is appearing in BIP for the first time. 75

A

Advanced Microcomputer Applications. Robert T. Grauer. 1992. pap. text ed. write for info. (*0-07-024159-7*) McGraw.

Advanced Microcomputer Applications. Terry D. Lundgren & Norman A. Garrett. 800p. (C). 1994. pap. write for info. (*0-02-372681-4*) Macmillan.

Advanced Micropipette Techniques for Cell Physiology. Kenneth T. Brown & Dale G. Flaming. LC 85-29481. (IBRO Handbook Series: Methods in the Neurosciences). 296p. 1987. text ed. 140.00 (*0-471-90952-1*, Wiley-Interscience) Wiley.

Advanced Microprocessor Architectures. Luigi Ciminiera & Adriano Valenzano. 400p. (C). 1988. text ed. 43.25 (*0-201-14550-2*) Addison-Wesley.

Advanced Microprocessor Interfacing. Andrew M. Veronis. (C). 1984. text ed. 35.00 (*0-8359-0056-8*, Reston) P-H.

Advanced Microprocessors. Ed. by A. Gupta & H. D. Toong. LC 83-6092. 368p. 1983. 59.95 (*0-87942-167-3*, PC01602) Inst Electrical.

Advanced Microprocessors. Heath Company Staff. (Illus.). 1192p. 1983. 99.95 (*0-87119-042-7*, EE-8088); pap. text ed. 24.95 (*0-87119-043-5*, EE-8088); 9.95 (*0-87119-045-1*); 11.95 (*0-87119-044-3*) Heathkit-Zenith Ed.

Advanced Microprocessors. Daniel Tabak. 528p. 1991. text ed. 50.00 (*0-07-062807-6*) McGraw.

***Advanced Microprocessors.** 2nd ed. Daniel Tabak. LC 94-27979. 1994. 60.00 (*0-07-062843-2*) McGraw.

Advanced Microprocessors & High-Level Language Computer Architecture. V. M. Milutinovic. LC 85-80875. 597p. 1986. pap. 9.95 (*0-8186-0623-1*, 623) IEEE Comp Soc.

Advanced Microprocessors, II. Amar Gupta. LC 87-3234. 344p. 1987. 49.95 (*0-87942-231-9*, PCO2170) Inst Electrical.

Advanced Microsoft Access. John Viescas. 1994. disk, pap. 39.95 (*1-55615-594-8*) Microsoft.

Advanced Midi User's Guide see Murphy's Law Midi Book

Advanced Military Cryptography. rev. ed. William F. Friedman. LC 76-53120. 116p. 1976. reprint ed. lib. bdg. 24.30 (*0-89412-077-8*); reprint ed. pap. 14.80 (*0-89412-011-5*) Aegean Park Pr.

Advanced Mineralogy, Vol. 2. Ed. by Arnold S. Marfunin. LC 94-13315. 1995. 133.00 (*0-387-57255-4*) Spr-Verlag.

Advanced Model Railroads. Dave Lowery. LC 93-70585. (Illus.). 80p. 1993. 12.98 (*1-56138-223-X*) Courage Bks.

Advanced Modelling for CAD - CAM Systems. Ed. by H. Grabowski et al. (Research Reports ESPRIT, Project 322, CAD Interfaces: Vol. 7). vi, 113p. 1991. pap. 20.00 (*0-387-53943-3*) Spr-Verlag.

Advanced Models: Manufacturing Systems Management. Brandimarte. 1995. write for info. (*0-8493-8332-3*, CRC Reprint) Franklin.

***Advanced Models for Manufacturing Systems Management.** Agostino Villa & Paolo Brandimarte. 250p. 1995. 59.95 (*0-614-05289-0*, 8332) CRC Pr.

Advanced Models of Cognition for Medical Training & Practice. Ed. by D. A. Evans & V. I. Patel. (NATO ASI Series F Computer & Systems Sciences, Special Programme AET: Vol. 97). (Illus.). xi, 372p. 1992. 124.00 (*0-387-55884-5*) Spr-Verlag.

Advanced Modern Engineering Mathematics. Glyn James & David Burley. LC 93-42297. (C). 1993. pap. text ed. 36.75 (*0-201-56519-6*) Addison-Wesley.

Advanced Modula 2 Programming for the IBM PC, XT & AT. David W. Carroll. 300p. 1987. 39.00 (*0-444-01206-0*) Elsevier.

Advanced Molecular Genetics. K. N. Timmis. Ed. by A. Puhler. (Illus.). 320p. 1986. 129.00 (*0-387-12740-2*) Spr-Verlag.

Advanced Money: Planning Investments on Your Computer. Charles Seiter & Steven Nichols. 160p. 1985. pap. write for info. (*0-201-06598-3*) Addison-Wesley.

***Advanced Monte Carlo Computer Programs for Radiation Transport.** 484p. (Orig.). 1995. pap. 93.00 (*92-64-14376-9*, Pub. by Econ & Coop Dev FR) OECD.

Advanced Montessori Method, Vol. I. 1990. write for info. (*81-900106-6-2*, Pub. by Kalakshetra Pubns II) N Montessori.

Advanced Montessori Method, Vol. II. 1990. write for info. (*81-900106-7-0*, Pub. by Kalakshetra Pubns II) N Montessori.

Advanced Moroccan Arabic. Ernest T. Abdel-Massih. LC 74-161877. 244p. (C). 1974. pap. text ed. 20.00 (*0-932098-08-8*) UM Ctr MENAS.

Advanced MOS Devices. Dieter K. Schroder. LC 85-28585. (Modular Series in Solid State Devices). (Illus.). 208p. (C). 1987. pap. text ed. 46.25 (*0-201-16506-6*) Addison-Wesley.

***Advanced Mountain Biking.** Derek Purdy. (Illus.). 160p. 1995. pap. 17.95 (*1-85688-046-X*) Lyons & Burford.

Advanced MS-DOS: Batch File Programming. 2nd ed. Dan Gookin. (Illus.). 504p. 1991. pap. 24.95 (*0-8306-7745-3*, Windcrest) TAB Bks.

Advanced MS-DOS Batch File. Dan Gookin. 1991. 24.95 (*0-8306-7678-3*) TAB Bks.

Advanced MS-DOS Batch File. 2nd ed. Dan Gookin. 1991. 24.95 (*0-8306-1662-4*); 24.95 (*0-8306-1677-2*) TAB Bks.

Advanced MS-DOS Batch File Programming. 3rd ed. Dan Gookin. (Orig.). 1991. pap. text ed. 29.95 (*0-07-023931-2*) McGraw.

***Advanced Multi-Microprocessor Bus Architectures.** Ed. by Janusz Zalewski. LC 94-77620. 472p. 1994. pap. text ed. 44.00 (*0-8186-6327-8*, BP06327) IEEE Comp Soc.

Advanced Multibody System Dynamics: Simulation & Software Tools. Ed. by W. O. Schiehlen. 488p. (C). 1993. lib. bdg. 115.00 (*0-685-66363-9*) Kluwer Ac.

Advanced Multibody System Dynamics: Simulation & Software Tools: International Symposium, Stuttgart, Germany, 22-24 March 1993. Ed. by W. O. Schiehlen. LC 93-3084. (Solid Mechanics & Its Applications Ser.: Vol. 20). 1993. lib. bdg. 115.00 (*0-7923-2192-8*) Kluwer Ac.

***Advanced Multimedia Programming.** Steve Rimmer. 1994. pap. 39.95 (*0-07-911898-4*, Windcrest) TAB Bks.

***Advanced Multiplication.** (Tai Mathematics Ser.). (J). 1995. 5.25 (*0-88106-157-3*, M005) Charlesbridge Pub.

***Advanced Multiplication: Two-Four Digit.** Bob DeWeese. (Math at Home Ser.). (Illus.). 44p. 1994. teacher ed, pap. text ed. 2.95 (*1-55799-315-7*, EMC 608) Evan-Moor Corp.

Advanced Multiplication & Division. Martha Palmer. Ed. by Joan Hoffman. (I Know It! Bks.). (Illus.). 32p. (J). (gr. 5-6). 1980. student ed 1.99 (*0-938256-36-X*) Sch Zone Pub Co.

Advanced Music Reading. William Thomson. LC 69-11974. 245p. (Orig.). (C). 1986. reprint ed. pap. text ed. 18.25 (*0-940459-02-7*) Everett Bks.

Advanced Muzzle Loader's Guide. Toby Bridges. 256p. 1985. pap. 14.95 (*0-88317-126-0*) Stoeger Pub Co.

Advanced MVS JCL Examples: Using MVS ESA on the Job. James G. Janossy. 1994. pap. text ed. 44.95 (*0-471-30990-7*) Wiley.

Advanced Nacherzahlungen. K. S. Whitton. 1969. 4.10 (*0-08-013065-8*, Pergamon Pr) Elsevier.

***Advanced Natural Study Guide.** Ed. by Dennis Hamilton. 1995. 65.00 (*1-878960-20-2*) WH&O Intl.

Advanced Neural Computers. Ed. by Rolf Eckmiller. 500p. 1990. 66.75 (*0-444-88400-9*, North Holland) Elsevier.

Advanced Newsgathering. Bryce T. McIntyre. LC 90-38842. 304p. 1991. text ed. 65.00 (*0-275-93521-3*, C3521, Praeger Pubs); pap. text ed. 17.95 (*0-275-93522-1*, B3522, Praeger Pubs) Greenwood.

Advanced Ninety-Minute Resume: For Resume Revisers. Peggy Schmidt. LC 91-45722. 128p. 1992. pap. 7.95 (*1-56079-151-9*) Petersons Guides.

Advanced Novel Separations. BCC Staff. 76p. 1989. 1,750.00 (*0-89336-604-8*, C107) BCC.

Advanced Novel Separations, No. C-107R. 196p. 1994. 2,450.00 (*1-56965-011-X*) BCC.

Advanced Nuclear Energy Systems: Papers Presented at 1976 ASME-ANS International Conference on Advanced Nuclear Energy Systems, Pittsburgh, Pennsylvania, March 14-17, 1976. ASME-ANS International Conference on Advanced Nuclear Energy Systems Staff. LC 76-48469. 655p. reprint ed. pap. 180.00 (*0-8357-8689-7*, 2033637) Bks Demand.

***Advanced Nuclear Reactors & U. S. Energy Security in the 1990's.** Ed. by James Scaminaci, 3rd. (Illus.). 71p. (Orig.). 1989. pap. text ed. write for info. (*0-943057-10-8*) US Global Strat.

Advanced Nugget Hunting with the Fisher Gold Bug Metal Detector. Pieter Heydelaar & David Johnson. (Nugget Hunting Ser.). 44p. 1988. 4.00 (*1-883170-02-8*) FRL.

Advanced Number Theory. Harvey Cohn. (Illus.). 1980. reprint ed. pap. 6.95 (*0-486-64023-X*) Dover.

Advanced Nunchaku. Fumio Demura & Dan Ivan. Ed. by Gilbert Johnson & Geraldine Adachi. LC 76-40816. (Weapons Ser.). (Illus.). 1976. pap. text ed. 9.95 (*0-89750-021-0*, 126, Wehman) Ohara Pubns.

Advanced Nursing & Health Care Research. McLaughlin. (Illus.). 512p. 1990. text ed. 58.50 (*0-7216-3098-7*) Saunders.

Advanced Nutrition: Macronutrients. Carolyn D. Berdanier. LC 94-11519. (Modern Nutrition). (Illus.). 336p. 1994. 75.00 (*0-8493-8500-8*, 8500) CRC Pr.

***Advanced Nutrition & Human Metabolism.** 2nd ed. Jim Groff & Sareen Gropper. LC 94-24711. 550p. 1995. text ed. 68.50 (*0-314-04467-1*) West Pub.

Advanced Obedience - Easier Than You Think. Joel M. McMains. (Illus.). 256p. 1993. 25.95 (*0-87605-522-6*) Howell Bk.

Advanced Obstetrics & Gynecology Study Guide. Competence Assurance Systems Staff. 1980. pap. text ed. 235.00 (*0-89147-111-1*) CAS.

***Advanced Oil Heat: A Guide.** Petroleum Marketers Association of America Staff. 272p. 1994. per., pap. text ed. 12.81 (*0-7872-0395-5*) Kendall-Hunt.

***Advanced Openstep Programming: Portable Distributed Objects Client-Server Distributed Computing.** Craighill. Date not set. 49.95 (*0-471-30859-5*) Wiley.

Advanced Operator Training. (Illus.). 200p. 1984. ring bd. 95.00 (*0-87683-695-3*) GP Pub.

Advanced Ophthalmic Diagnostics & Therapeutics. Ed. by Susan C. Benes. LC 87-43111. (Ophthalmic Technical Skills Ser.: Vol. II). 208p. 1991. pap. text ed. 40.00 (*1-55642-030-7*) SLACK Inc.

Advanced Optical Detectors & Detector Materials. Business Communications Co., Inc. Staff. 240p. 1988. 2,250.00 (*0-89336-634-X*, GB-103B) BCC.

Advanced Optical Instrumentation for Remote Sensing of the Earth's Surface from Space. Ed. by G. Duchossois et al. 154p. 1989. 42.00 (*0-8194-0165-X*, VOL. 1129) SPIE.

Advanced Optical Manufacturing & Testing, Vol. 1333. L. R. Baker et al. 1990. 70.00 (*0-8194-0394-6*) SPIE.

Advanced Optical Manufacturing & Testing Two. V. J. Doherty. 1992. 62.00 (*0-8194-0659-7*, 1531) SPIE.

Advanced Optical Material - Update, No. GB-103R. Business Communications Co., Inc. Staff. 235p. 1990. 2,950.00 (*0-89336-786-9*) BCC.

Advanced Optical Thin Films, No. GB-141. Business Communications Co., Inc. Staff. 330p. 1991. 2,950.00 (*0-89336-811-3*) BCC.

Advanced Options Trading: The Analysis & Evaluation of Trading Strategies Hedging Tactics. Robert T. Daigler. 1993. 55.00 (*1-55738-552-1*) Probus Pub Co.

Advanced Optoelectronic Technology. Ed. by Ostrowsky & Puech. 1987. 45.00 (*0-89252-899-0*, 864) SPIE.

Advanced Ordinary Differential Equations. K. O. Friedrichs. 216p. 1965. text ed. 130.00 (*0-677-00960-7*); pap. text ed. 62.00 (*0-677-00965-8*) Gordon & Breach.

Advanced Ordinary Differential Equations. 2nd ed. A. G. Kartsatos. 290p. (C). 1993. text ed. 39.50 (*0-931541-35-2*) Mancorp Pub.

Advanced Organic Chemistry, Pt. A - Structure & Mechanisms. Francis A. Carey. LC 76-54956. reprint ed. pap. 152.30 (*0-8357-5129-5*, 2024720) Bks Demand.

Advanced Organic Chemistry, Pt. B - Reactions & Synthesis. abr. ed. Francis A. Carey. LC 76-54956. 547p. pap. 155.90 (*0-8357-5130-9*) Bks Demand.

Advanced Organic Chemistry: Part B: Reactions & Synthesis. 3rd ed. Frank A. Carey & R. J. Sundberg. LC 90-6851. (Illus.). 830p. 1990. 69.50 (*0-306-43456-3*, Plenum Pr); pap. 34.50 (*0-306-43457-1*, Plenum Pr) Plenum.

Advanced Organic Chemistry: Pt. A: Structure & Mechanisms. 3rd ed. Frank A. Carey & R. J. Sundberg. LC 90-6851. (Illus.). 832p. 1990. 69.50 (*0-306-43440-7*, Plenum Pr) Plenum.

Advanced Organic Chemistry: Reactions, Mechanisms, & Structures. 4th ed. Jerry March. 1495p. 1992. text ed. 59.95 (*0-471-60180-2*) Wiley.

***Advanced Organic Chemistry of Nucleic Acids.** Z. Shabarova & A. Bogdanov. LC 94-22848. 1994. write for info. (*1-56081-719-4*) VCH Pubs.

Advanced Organic Chemistry, Pt. A: Structure & Mechanisms. 3rd ed. Frank A. Carey & R. J. Sundberg. LC 90-6851. (Illus.). 832p. 1990. pap. 32.50 (*0-306-43447-4*, Plenum Pr) Plenum.

Advanced Organic Solid State Materials: Materials Research Society Symposium Proceedings, Vol. 173. Ed. by L. Y. Chiang et al. 1990. text ed. 47.00 (*1-55899-061-5*) Materials Res.

Advanced OS-2 Presentation Manager Programming. Thomas E. Burge & Joseph Celi, Jr. LC 93-7135. 1993. pap. text ed. 34.95 (*0-471-59198-X*) Wiley.

Advanced OS-2 Programming: The Microsoft Guide to the OS-2 Kernel for Assembly Language & C Programmers. Ray Duncan. LC 88-21103. (OS-2 Programmer's Library). 800p. 1989. pap. 24.95 (*1-55615-045-8*) Microsoft.

Advanced Osseointegration Surgery: Maxillfacial Applications. Philip Worthington & P. I. Branemark. LC 91-40446. (Illus.). 1992. text ed. 140.00 (*0-86715-242-7*) Quint Pub Co.

Advanced Oxidation Processes. Rice. 1995. write for info. (*0-87371-203-X*) Lewis Pubs.

Advanced Oxidation Processes for Control of Off-Gas Emissions from VOC Stripping. 108p. 1989. pap. 17.50 (*0-89867-482-4*, 90556) Am Water Wks Assn.

Advanced Oxyacetlene Flame Cutting. Robert O'Con & Richard Carr. (Series 910). (Orig.). 1985. 8.00 (*0-8064-0387-X*); audio 459.00 (*0-8064-0388-8*) Bergwall.

Advanced Paediatric Life Support. 288p. 1993. pap. text ed. 38.00 (*0-7279-0792-1*, BMJ Pubng Grp) Amer Coll Phys.

Advanced Pagemaker 4.0 for Windows. Craig Danuloff & William Sanders. (Illus.). 250p. (Orig.). 1991. pap. 27.95 (*1-55958-070-4*) Prima Pub.

Advanced Paramedic. Adams. 1991. write for info. (*0-8151-0067-1*, Yr Bk Med Pubs) Mosby Yr Bk.

Advanced Pattern Book: For Pine Needle Raffia Basketry. rev. ed. Jeannie McFarland. (Illus.). 64p. (C). 1993. reprint ed. pap. 11.00 (*0-9618828-1-6*) Baskets & Bullets.

Advanced Peer Counseling in Youth Groups. Joan Sturkie & Siang-Yang Tan. 160p. 1993. pap. 15.99 (*0-310-37301-8*) Zondervan.

Advanced Peer Counseling Training Curriculum. Michael Donnelly et al. 1989. student ed 3.50 (*1-56117-006-2*); English wkbk. teacher ed 75.00 (*1-56117-030-5*) Telesis CA.

Advanced Photography. James L. Pomeroy. LC 89-92366. (Illus.). 140p. 1991. pap. text ed. 22.95 (*0-9625017-2-7*) Palms & Rhodes Pub.

Advanced Photography. 5th ed. Michael Langford. (Illus.). 320p. 1989. pap. 25.00 (*0-240-51088-7*, Focal) Buttrwrth-Heinemann.

Advanced Photon & Particle Techniques for the Characterization of Defects in Solids, Vol. 41. Ed. by J. B. Roberto et al. LC 85-5061. (Materials Research Society Symposium Proceedings Ser.). 1985. text ed. 43.00 (*0-931837-06-5*) Materials Res.

Advanced Photoshop - Macintosh. Adobe Systems Staff et al. (Seminar in a Book Ser.). (Illus.). 208p. (Orig.). 1994. pap. text ed. 49.95 (*1-56830-117-0*) Adobe Calif.

Advanced PICK Programming. William K. Meyer. (Illus.). 320p. 1989. 29.95 (*0-8306-2999-8*) TAB Bks.

Advanced Picture Chords for Guitar. Russ Shipton. (Illus.). 1980. pap. 6.95 (*0-86001-690-0*, AM25040) Music Sales.

***Advanced Pilot's Flight Manual: Including FAA Written Test Questions (Airplanes) Plus Answers & Explanations & Practical (Flight) Test.** 6th ed. William K. Kershner. LC 94-29137. 1995. pap. 27.95 (*0-8138-1303-4*) Iowa St U Pr.

Advanced Pipework. 1989. 90.00 (*0-685-05795-X*) St Mut.

***Advanced Piston Shooting: How to Stay Calm at the Center.** Vishnu Karmakar & Thomas Whitney. 192p. (Orig.). 1995. teacher ed, pap. write for info. (*1-881234-01-0*) Ctr Vision.

Advanced Placement Chemistry Student Handbook. David P. Licata. (YA). (gr. 10-12). 1993. pap. text ed. 12.95 (*0-9636095-0-5*) Licatas Edutype.

Advanced Placement Course Description Booklets for May 1994, 16 bks., Set. 1994. 80.00 (*0-685-70060-7*, 201644) College Bd.

Advanced Placement English: Theory, Politics & Pedagogy. Ed. by Elizabeth Metzger & Evelyn Ashton-Jones. 205p. (Orig.). 1989. pap. text ed. 18.50 (*0-86709-246-7*) Boynton Cook Pubs.

Advanced Placement Examination in Biology. rev. ed. Research & Education Association Staff. LC 88-90702. (Illus.). 592p. 1994. pap. text ed. 15.95 (*0-87891-652-0*) Res & Educ.

Advanced Placement Examination in Calculus AB. rev. ed. Research & Education Association Staff. (Illus.). 416p. 1994. pap. text ed. 15.95 (*0-87891-646-6*) Res & Educ.

Advanced Placement Examination in Calculus BC. rev. ed. Research & Education Association Staff. (Illus.). 368p. 1994. pap. text ed. 15.95 (*0-87891-647-4*) Res & Educ.

Advanced Placement Examination in Chemistry. rev. ed. Research & Education Association Staff. (Illus.). 528p. 1994. pap. text ed. 16.95 (*0-87891-648-2*) Res & Educ.

Advanced Placement Examination in Computer Science. rev. ed. Research & Education Association Staff. (Illus.). 384p. 1994. pap. text ed. 14.95 (*0-87891-882-5*) Res & Educ.

Advanced Placement Examination in Computer Science. 2nd ed. Elayne Schulman et al. (Arco Academic Test Preparation Ser.). 1988. pap. 12.95 (*0-13-038688-X*, Arco Test) P-H Gen Ref & Trav.

Advanced Placement Examination in European History. 2nd ed. Joan U. Levy et al. LC 92-34477. 1993. 14.00 (*0-671-84777-5*, Arco Test) P-H Gen Ref & Trav.

Advanced Placement Examination in Physics. rev. ed. Research & Education Association Staff. (Illus.). 1994. pap. text ed. 16.95 (*0-87891-881-7*) Res & Educ.

Advanced Placement Examination in Psychology. rev. ed. Research & Education Association Staff. (Illus.). 336p. 1994. pap. text ed. 15.95 (*0-87891-883-3*) Res & Educ.

Advanced Placement Physics by Satellite: Laboratory Manual. Shull & Randall. 208p. (C). 1991. spiral bd. 9.95 (*0-8403-6981-6*) Kendall-Hunt.

Advanced Plant Physiology. Ed. by Malcolm B. Wilkins. 514p. 1988. pap. text ed. 48.95 (*0-685-26818-7*) Wiley.

Advanced Polish 1. Jerzy R. Krzyzanowski. (OSU Foreign Language Publications: No. 9). (Illus.). 357p. (Orig.). (POL.). (C). 1984. teacher ed, pap. 8.00 (*0-87415-005-1*, 9A); student ed, pap. text ed. 18.00 (*0-87415-004-3*) OSU Foreign Lang.

Advanced Polish 1, 8 cass., Set. Jerzy R. Krzyzanowski. (OSU Foreign Language Publications: No. 9). (Illus.). (Orig.). (POL.). (C). 1984. audio 40.00 (*0-87415-006-X*, 9B) OSU Foreign Lang.

Advanced Polish 2. Jerzy R. Krzyzanowski. (OSU Foreign Language Publications: No. 10). (Illus.). 122p. (POL.). (C). 1984. teacher ed, pap. 8.00 (*0-87415-008-6*, 10A); student ed, pap. text ed. 18.00 (*0-87415-007-8*) OSU Foreign Lang.

Advanced Polish 2, 5 cass., Set. Jerzy R. Krzyzanowski. (OSU Foreign Language Publications: No. 10). (POL.). (C). 1984. audio 25.00 (*0-87415-009-4*, 10B) OSU Foreign Lang.

Advanced Polymer Composite: Principles & Applications. Bor Z. Jang. 1994. 103.00 (*0-87170-491-9*) ASM.

Advanced Polymer Composites. Business Communications Co., Inc. Staff. 346p. 1988. 2,650.00 (*0-89336-675-7*, P0-23N) BCC.

Advanced Polymer Composites for Structural Applications: SPE-APC '88 Technical Conference, November 14-17, 1988. Society of Plastics Engineers Staff. 554p. reprint ed. pap. 157.90 (*0-8357-3620-2*, 2036321) Bks Demand.

Advanced Pool Player's Handbook. James R. Lawson. Ed. by Bill Thompson. 124p. (Orig.). 1994. pap. 18.95 (*0-945071-91-4*) Lawco.

Advanced Power Cable Technology: Basic Concepts & Testing, Vol. I. Toshikatsu Tanaka & Allan Greenwood. 232p. 1983. 144.00 (*0-8493-5165-0*, TK3351, CRC Reprint) Franklin.

Advanced Power Cable Technology: Present & Future, Vol. II. Toshikatsu Tanaka & Allan Greenwood. 288p. 1983. 156.00 (*0-8493-5166-9*, TK3351, CRC Reprint) Franklin.

Advanced Power Sources for Space Missions. 156p. 1989. pap. text ed. 23.50 (*0-309-03999-1*) Natl Acad Pr.

Advanced Power Systems Analysis & Dynamics. 2nd ed. L. P. Singh. (C). 1987. pap. 11.50 (*0-85226-733-9*, Pub. by Wiley Eastern II) S Asia.

***Advanced PowerBuilder 4.0 Techniques.** Darius D. Deyhimi et al. 1995. pap. text ed. 44.95 (*0-471-04989-1*) Wiley.

Advanced Powerplant Concepts: SAE International Congress & Exposition 1994, 13 papers. (Special Publications). 1994. pap. 35.00 (*1-56091-490-4*, SP-1038) Soc Auto Engineers.

***Advanced Practical Cookery.** Ceserani et al. 1995. text ed. 34.95 (*0-470-24960-9*) Wiley.

Advanced Practice Book for the Degrees of Reading Power Test, No. I. Barbara Dershowitz. 121p. 1990. student ed 5.25 (*1-56078-019-3*) Comp Pr.

Advanced Practice for the TOEFL. Michael A. Pyle. (Cliffs Test Preparation Guides Ser.). 259p. (Orig.). 1992. pap. text ed. 19.95 (*0-8220-2007-6*) Cliffs.

***Advanced Practice Nursing.** Ed. by Mariah Snyder & Michaelene Mirr. (Illus.). 280p. 1995. write for info. (*0-8261-8850-8*) Springer Pub.

Advanced Practitioner: Current Practice Issues. 3rd ed. Joellen B. Hawkins & Janice A. Thibodeau. LC 93-60215. 208p. (Orig.). 1993. pap. text ed. 15.00 (*0-913292-38-9*) Tiresias Pr.

***Advanced Practitioner: Current Practice Issues.** 4th ed. Joellen B. Hawkins & Janice A. Thibodeau. (Orig.). 1996. pap. text ed. write for info. (*0-913292-31-1*) Tiresias Pr.

***Advanced Practitioner Exam Review for Respiratory Care: Guidelines for Success.** Wojciechowski. 486p. 1994. pap. text ed. 37.95 (*0-8273-7270-1*) Delmar.

An Asterisk (*) at the beginning of an entry indicates that the title is appearing in BIP for the first time.

An Asterisk (*) at the beginning of an entry indicates that the title is appearing in BIP for the first time.

77

Advanced Short Baton Techniques: Modern Methods Made Easy. fac. ed. George M. Pekar & Timothy N. Oettmeier. (Illus.). 112p. (C). 1984. spiral bd. 21.95 (0-398-04897-5) C C Thomas.

Advanced Sightsinging & Ear Training: Strategies & Applications. Bruce Benward. 192p. (C). 1989. spiral bd. write for info. (0-697-03868-8) Brown & Benchmark.

Advanced Sign Language Vocabulary: A Resource Text for Educators, Interpreters, Parents & Sign Language Instructors. Janet R. Coleman & Elizabeth E. Wolf. (Illus.). 202p. (C). 1991. pap. text ed. 43.95 (0-398-05722-2) C C Thomas.

Advanced Signal Processing. Ed. by D. J. Creasey et al. 340p. 1985. boxed 99.00 (0-86341-037-5, TE013) Inst Elect Eng.

Advanced Signal Processing Algorithms, Architectures, & Implementations, Vol. 1348. F. T. Luk. 1990. 77.00 (0-8194-0409-8) SPIE.

Advanced Signal Processing Algorithms, Architectures, & Implementations Two. F. T. Luk. 1992. 70.00 (0-8194-0694-5, 1566) SPIE.

Advanced Silicon & Semiconducting Silicon Alloy-Based Materials & Devices. Ed. by Johan F. Nijs. (Illus.). 488p. 1994. 160.00 (0-7503-0299-2) IOP Pub.

Advanced Simulation in Biomedicine. Ed. by D. P. Moller. (Advances in Simulation Ser.: Vol. 3). (Illus.). xi, 203p. 1989. pap. 49.00 (0-387-97184-X) Spr-Verlag.

Advanced Skiing. Marty Hurn. (Adventure Sports Ser.). (Illus.). 128p. (Orig.). 1990. pap. 15.95 (0-8117-3027-1) Stackpole.

Advanced Skills & Knowledge of Cost Engineering, Vol. 1. Ed. by Donald F. McDonald, Jr. 102p. 1989. pap. 32.50 (0-930284-39-9) AACE Intl.

Advanced Skills in Emergency Care: A Text for the Intermediate EMT. Alexander M. Butman et al. 1982. 18.50 (0-940432-01-3, Emergency Training) Educ Direction.

Advanced Skip Trace Techniques. rev. ed. Ralph D. Thomas. 68p. 1990. pap. 19.95 (0-918487-43-9) Thomas Pubns TX.

Advanced SNA Networking: A Guide to Using VTAM-NCP. Jay Ranade & George Sackett. (Ranade Ser.). (Illus.). 256p. 1991. text ed. 48.00 (0-07-051143-8) McGraw.

***Advanced Social Psychology.** Abraham Tesser. LC 94-30982. 1994. text ed. write for info. (0-07-063392-4) McGraw.

***Advanced Software Applications in Japan.** Edward A. Feigenbaum et al. LC 94-23430. (Advanced Computing & Telecommunications Ser.). (Illus.). 653p. 1995. 86.00 (0-8155-1360-7) Noyes.

Advanced Software Design Techniques. Robert J. Rader. (Illus.). 172p. 1979. text ed. 19.95 (0-89433-046-2) Petrocelli.

Advanced Software Design Techniques. TAB Books Staff. 1979. text ed. 19.95 (0-07-156012-2) McGraw.

Advanced Soil Mechanics. Braja M. Das. 511p. 1983. pap. 59.50 (0-89116-980-6) Hemisp Pub.

Advanced Solid State Chemistry: Proceedings of the 2nd International Symposium, Pardubice, Czechoslovakia, 26-30, June, 1989. Ed. by M. Frumar et al. (Materials Science Monographs: No. 60). 460p. 1990. 136.00 (0-444-98786-X) Elsevier.

Advanced Solid-State Lasers. LC 89-61983. (Proceedings Ser.: Vol. 6). 300p. 1990. lib. bdg. 82.00 (1-55752-120-4) Optical Soc.

Advanced Solid State Lasers. LC 90-63014. (Proceedings Ser.: Vol. 10). 350p. 1991. lib. bdg. 82.00 (1-55752-179-4) Optical Soc.

Advanced Solid State Lasers. LC 92-80500. (Proceedings Ser.: Vol. 13). 350p. 1992. text ed. 82.00 (1-55752-224-3) Optical Soc.

Advanced Solid State Lasers. LC 92-62711. (Proceedings Ser.: Vol. 15). 300p. 1993. text ed. 82.00 (1-55752-276-6) Optical Soc.

Advanced Solid State Lasers. LC 93-87354. (Proceedings Ser.: Vol. 20). 350p. 1994. text ed. 82.00 (1-55752-323-1) Optical Soc.

Advanced Space Experiments. Ed. by O. L. Tiffany et al. (Advances in the Astronautical Sciences Ser.: Vol. 25). (Illus.). 1969. 40.00 (0-87703-028-6, Pub. by Am Astro Soc) Univelt Inc.

Advanced Spanish Course. K. L. Mason. 1967. 11.40 (0-08-012272-8, Pergamon Pr); pap. text ed. 9.80 (0-08-012271-X, Pergamon Pr) Elsevier.

Advanced Spanish Course. 2nd ed. Timms & Pulgar. 1971. pap. text ed. 16.24 (0-582-36480-9, 72430) Longman.

Advanced Spatial Statistics. Daniel A. Griffith. (C). 1988. lib. bdg. 133.00 (90-247-3627-7) Kluwer Ac.

Advanced Spectural Analysis, Vol. III. Ed. by Simon Haykin. 1995. text ed. 70.00 (0-13-061540-4) P-H.

***Advanced Speech Applications: European Research on Speech Technology.** S. Pfleger & J. P. Lefevre. (Project Group Speech Technology Ser.: Vol. 1). 320p. 1994. pap. 50.00 (0-387-58142-1) Spr-Verlag.

Advanced Speed Practice for Machine Shorthand. (C). reprint ed. pap. 10.95 (0-685-31746-3); reprint ed. pap. text ed. 8.95 (0-685-31747-1) Stenograph Corp.

Advanced Sport Diver: Workbook. 2nd ed. Clinchy. 35p. 1992. pap. 4.95 (0-8016-9032-3) Mosby Yr Bk.

Advanced Spreadsheet Modeling with Lotus 1-2-3. Jackson. LC 88-5598. 230p. 1988. pap. 59.50 (0-471-91989-6) Wiley.

Advanced Squad Leader: WWII Tactical Warfare. Donald J. Greenwood. (Illus.). 200p. (YA). (gr. 9 up). 1989. 45.00 (0-911605-50-9) Avalon Hill.

Advanced Stamp Collecting: A Serious Collector's Guide to the Collection & Study of Postage Stamps & Related Materials. Barry Krause. (Illus.). 160p. (Orig.). 1990. pap. 9.95 (1-55870-159-1) Betterway Bks.

Advanced Standard Arabic: Through Authentic Tests & Audiovisual Materials, Pt. 2. Raji Rammuny. 116p. 1994. pap. text ed. 19.95 (0-472-08262-0) U of Mich Pr.

Advanced Standard Arabic: Through Authentic Texts & Audiovisual Materials, Pt. 1. Raji Rammuny. 326p. 1994. pap. text ed. 24.95 (0-472-08261-2) U of Mich Pr.

Advanced Statistical Mechanics. R. K. Pathria. (International Series on Natural Philsophy). 1972. text ed. 76.00 (0-08-016747-0, Pergamon Pr) Elsevier.

Advanced Statistical Mechanics. R.K. Pathria. (International Series on Parallel Computation: No. 45). 1972. pap. text ed. 50.00 (0-08-018994-6, Pergamon Pr) Elsevier.

Advanced Strategies in Financial Risk Management. Ed. by Robert J. Schwartz & Clifford W. Smith, Jr. LC 92-47036. 1993. 65.00 (0-13-068883-5) P-H.

Advanced Strength & Applied Elasticity. Ansel C. Ugural & S. K. Fenster. LC 74-27388. (C). 1975. 50.00 (0-444-00160-3); teacher ed write for info. (0-318-51815-5) P-H.

Advanced Strength & Applied Elasticity. 3rd ed. A. C. Ugural & S. K. Fenster. LC 93-38077. 592p. 1994. text ed. 68.00 (0-13-137589-X) P-H Gen Ref & Trav.

Advanced Strength & Applied Elasticity: The SI Version. Ansel C. Ugural & S. K. Fenster. 424p. 1981. 41.25 (0-444-00428-9) P-H.

Advanced Strength & Applied Stress Analysis. Richard G. Budynas. (Illus.). (C). 1977. text ed. write for info. (0-07-008828-4) McGraw.

Advanced Strength of Materials. J. P. Den Hartog. ix, 379p. 1987. reprint ed. pap. text ed. 9.95 (0-486-65407-9) Dover.

Advanced Structural Analysis of Microcomputers. R. Hussein. (Illus.). 287p. 1990. text ed. 49.95 (0-925760-11-0) SciTech Pubs.

Advanced Structural & Functional Materials: Proceedings of an International Seminar Organized by Deutsche Forschungsanstalt fur Luft & Raumfahrt, DLR, Koln, June 1991. Ed. by W. Bunk. (Illus.). vi, 219p. 1991. 69.00 (0-387-53783-X) Spr-Verlag.

Advanced Structural Ceramics. Business Communications Co., Inc. Staff. 355p. 1987. pap. 2,950.00 (0-89336-635-8, GB-107) BCC.

Advanced Structural Dynamics. J. M. Donea. (Illus.). 470p. 1980. 120.75 (0-85334-859-6, Pub. by Elsevier Applied Sci UK) Elsevier.

***Advanced Structural Equation Modeling Techniques.** Ed. by George A. Marcoulides & Randall E. Schumacker. 300p. 1996. text ed. 45.00 (0-8058-1819-7) L Erlbaum Assocs.

Advanced Structural Materials: Proceedings of the International '90 Conference, Beijing, PR China, 18-22 June, 1990. Ed. by Y. Han. (Chinese Materials Research Society Symposia Ser.: No. 2). 868p. 1991. 271.00 (0-444-89008-4, North Holland) Elsevier.

Advanced Structural Materials: Proceedings of the International '90 Conference, Beijing, PR China, 18-22 June, 1990, Set. Ed. by Y. Han. (Chinese Materials Research Society Symposia Ser.: No. 2). 868p. 1991. 728.50 (0-444-89016-5, North Holland) Elsevier.

Advanced Structured BASIC. Richard Carney. 337p. (C). 1988. pap. text ed. 36.00 (0-15-501234-7) Dryden Pr.

Advanced Structured BASIC Using MicroSoft's BASIC & QuickBASIC. Lloyd C. Onyett. 345p. (C). 1988. pap. text ed. 25.00 (0-669-15442-3); Instr.'s guide. teacher ed 2.00 (0-669-15441-5) Heath.

Advanced Structured COBOL. Edward J. Coburn. 705p. (C). 1988. pap. text ed. 43.00 (0-15-501873-6) Dryden Pr.

Advanced Structured COBOL. Edward J. Coburn. 705p. (C). 1988. teacher ed, pap. text ed. 10.75 (0-15-501874-4); disk 38.25 (0-15-501875-2) Dryden Pr.

Advanced Structured COBOL. 2nd ed. Gerard A. Paquette et al. 608p. (C). 1991. student ed write for info. (0-697-07773-X); pap. write for info. (0-697-07771-3) Bus & Educ Tech.

Advanced Structured COBOL. 3rd ed. Khan & Martin. (C). 1993. pap. 40.95 (0-87835-950-8, BF9508) S-W Pub.

Advanced Structured COBOL: Batch, On-Line & Data-Base Concepts. Tyler Welburn. LC 82-73737. (Illus.). 654p. (Orig.). (C). 1983. pap. text ed. 51.95 (0-87484-558-0, 558) Mayfield Pub.

Advanced Studies in Pure Mathematics, Vol. 18, Pt. A: Recent Topics in Differential & Analytic Geometry. Ed. by K. Aomoto et al. 443p. 1991. text ed. 138.00 (0-12-001018-6) Acad Pr.

Advanced Studies in Pure Mathematics, Vol. 18, Pt. B: Kahler Metrics & Moduli Spaces. Ed. by K. Aomoto et al. 457p. 1991. text ed. 138.00 (0-12-001011-9) Acad Pr.

Advanced Study in the History of Medieval India, Vol. 1. 2nd rev. ed. J. L. Mehta. 376p. 1987. text ed. 37.50 (81-207-0573-4, Pub. by Sterling Pubs II) Apt Bks.

***Advanced Subtraction.** (Tai Mathematics Ser.). (J). 1995. 5.25 (0-88106-154-9, M002) Charlesbridge Pub.

***Advanced Subtraction: Borrowing.** Bob DeWeese. (Math at Home Ser.). (Illus.). 44p. 1994. teacher ed, pap. text ed. 2.95 (1-55799-313-0, EMC 606) Evan-Moor Corp.

Advanced Supervisory Practices. Ed. by John Matzer, Jr. LC 92-15124. (Municipal Management Ser.). 1992. pap. 29.95 (0-87326-087-2) Intl City-Cnty Mgt.

Advanced Surface Coatings: A Handbook of Surface Engineering. Ed. by D. S. Rickerby & A. Matthews. 320p. 1991. 145.00 (0-412-02541-8, A4219, Blackie & Son-Chapman NY) Routledge Chapman & Hall.

Advanced Surface Processes for Optoelectronics. Ed. by T. Venkatesan et al. (Symposium Proceedings Ser.: Vol. 126). 1988. text ed. 44.00 (0-931837-96-0) Materials Res.

Advanced Surface Treatment Systems. Business Communications Co., Inc. Staff. (Illus.). 250p. 1986. pap. 1,950.00 (0-89336-497-5, GB-090) BCC.

Advanced Swaps & Derivative Financial Products. Daniel P. Cunningham. 266p. 1991. pap. text ed. 17.50 (0-685-49924-3, B4-6973) PLI.

Advanced Swimming: Steps to Success. David G. Thomas. LC 90-31279. (Activity Ser.). (Illus.). 168p. (Orig.). 1990. pap. text ed. 15.95 (0-88011-389-8, PTH00389) Human Kinetics.

Advanced Synergetics. H. Haken. (Synergetics Ser.: Vol. 20). (Illus.). 160p. 1993. 69.00 (0-387-12162-5) Spr-Verlag.

Advanced Synthesis of Engineered Structural Materials. 228p. 1993. 98.00 (0-87170-466-8) ASM.

Advanced System Development - Feasibility Techniques. J. Daniel Couger et al. LC 82-2818. 522p. reprint ed. pap. 148.80 (0-7837-2371-7, 2040057) Bks Demand.

***Advanced System Modelling & Simulation with Block Diagram Languages.** Nicholas M. Karayanakis. 364p. 1995. 69.95 (0-8493-9479-1, 9479) CRC Pr.

Advanced Systematic Golf see Better Golf: The Systematic Way

Advanced Systems Development Management. John de S. Coutinho. LC 83-24815. 452p. (C). 1984. reprint ed. lib. bdg. 46.50 (0-89874-727-9) Krieger.

Advanced Tactile Sensing for Robotics. H. R. Nicholls. (Series in Robotics & Automated Systems: No. 5). 250p. 1992. text ed. 81.00 (981-02-0870-7) World Scientific Pub.

Advanced Tango. (Ballroom Dance Ser.). 1986. lib. bdg. 250.00 (0-8490-3285-7) Gordon Pr.

Advanced Tango. (Ballroom Dance Ser.). 1985. lib. bdg. 250.00 (0-87700-777-2) Revisionist Pr.

Advanced Technical Ceramics. Ed. by Shigeyuki Somiya. 353p. 1989. pap. write for info. (0-12-654631-2) Acad Pr.

Advanced Techniques for Characterizing Microstructures. Ed. by F. W. Wiffen & J. A. Spitznagel. LC 82-81288. (Technology of Metallurgy Ser.). (Illus.). 534p. reprint ed. pap. 152.20 (0-8357-5132-5, 2052265) Bks Demand.

Advanced Techniques for Clay Mineral Analysis. Ed. by J. J. Fripiat. (Developments in Sedimentology Ser.: Vol. 34). 236p. 1982. 82.00 (0-444-42002-9) Elsevier.

Advanced Techniques for in Situ Studies of Zooplankton Abundance Distribution & Behavior. W. Gary Sprules et al. (Advances in Limnology Ser.: No. 36). (Illus.). 140p. 1992. pap. 60.75 (3-510-47037-0, Pub. by E Schweizerbartsche GW) Lubrecht & Cramer.

Advanced Techniques for Integrated Circuit Processing, Vol. 1392. J. Bondur & T. R. Turner. 1991. 86.00 (0-8194-0461-6) SPIE.

Advanced Techniques for Microstructural Characterization. Ed. by T. R. Anantharaman & R. Krishnan. 400p. 1988. text ed. 85.00 (0-87849-563-0, Pub. by Trans Tech GW) LPS Dist Ctr.

Advanced Techniques for Radiotherapy. Ed. by Marco Castiglioni & Argeo A. Benco. LC 92-49636. (Eurocourses: Advanced Scientific Techniques Ser.: Vol. 2). 144p. (C). 1992. lib. bdg. 62.50 (0-7923-1588-X) Kluwer Ac.

Advanced Techniques for Surface Engineering. Ed. by W. Gissler & H. A. Jehn. LC 92-33610. (Eurocourses: Mechanical & Materials Science Ser.: Vol. 1). 1992. lib. bdg. 135.00 (0-7923-2006-9) Kluwer Ac.

Advanced Techniques in Biological Electron Microscopy 3. Ed. by J. K. Koehler. (Illus.). 305p. 1986. 99.00 (0-387-16400-6) Spr-Verlag.

Advanced Techniques in Chromosome Research. Ed. by Kenneth W. Adolph. 472p. 1991. 175.00 (0-8247-8430-8) Dekker.

Advanced Techniques in Data Communications. 2nd rev. ed. Ralph Glasgal. LC 76-1794. 160p. reprint ed. pap. 45.60 (0-8357-5133-3, 2025051) Bks Demand.

Advanced Techniques in Neuro-Linguistic Programming. Phill Boas & Jane Brooks. (Skill Builder Ser.). 144p. 1986. pap. 10.00 (0-943920-08-6) Metamorphous Pr.

Advanced Techniques in Skin Surgery. Bennett. Date not set. pap. 70.00 (0-8016-0599-7) Mosby Yr Bk.

Advanced Techniques in the Optimum Design of Structures. Ed. by S. Hernandez. LC 92-75030. (Topics in Engineering Ser.: Vol. 12). 214p. 1993. 97.00 (1-56252-134-9) Computational Mech MA.

Advanced Techniques in the Practice of Operations Research. H. J. Greenberg et al. (Publications in Operations Research Ser.: Vol. 4). 470p. 1982. 81.75 (0-444-00750-4, North Holland) Elsevier.

Advanced Techniques of Population Analysis. Shivalingappa S. Halli & K. V. Rao. (Demographic Methods & Population Analysis Ser.). (Illus.). 230p. 1992. 29.50 (0-306-43997-2, Plenum Pr) Plenum.

Advanced Techniques of Riding: The Official Instruction Handbook of The German National Equestrian Federation. German National Equestrian Federation Staff. Tr. by Gisela Holstein. (Illus.). 160p. 1987. 19.95 (0-939481-03-0) Half Halt Pr.

Advanced Technobiology. Ed. by B. Rybak. 712p. 1979. lib. bdg. 120.50 (90-286-0299-2) Kluwer Ac.

Advanced Technolgoies: ASCE Third International Conference, July 25-28. Ed. by Christ T. Hendrickson & Kumares C. Sinha. LC 93-5096. (Rise into the Future Ser.: Vol. 2). 257p. 1993. 76.00 (0-87262-916-3); write for info. (0-87262-972-4) Am Soc Civil Eng.

Advanced Technologies: Architecture, Planning, Civil Engineering. Ed. by M. R. Beheshti & K. Zreik. 1993. write for info. (0-444-81566-X) Elsevier.

Advanced Technologies: Improving Industrial Efficiency. Ed. by F. William Payne. LC 84-48433. 300p. 1985. 39.95 (0-88173-001-7) Fairmont Pr.

Advanced Technologies: Pros & Cons. Candy F. Drew. (Illus.). 160p. 1993. pap. text ed. 30.00 (1-883355-15-X) Odelle Pubns.

Advanced Technologies Applied to Training Design. Ed. by Robert J. Seidel & Paul R. Chatelier. LC 92-26766. (Defense Research Ser.: Vol. 4). 1992. 115.00 (0-306-44308-2, Plenum Pr) Plenum.

***Advanced Technologies for Air Traffic Flow Management: Proceedings of an International Seminar Organized by Deutsche Forschungsanstalt fur Luft- und Raumfahrt (DLR), Bonn, Germany, April 1994.** Ed. by H. Winter & H. G. NuBer. (Lecture Notes in Control & Information Sciences: Vol. 198). 224p. 1994. pap. 56.00 (0-387-19895-4) Spr-Verlag.

Advanced Technologies for Communicating with Motorists: A Synthesis of Human Factors & Traffic Management Issues. Kevin N. Balke & Gerald L. Ullman. 54p. (Orig.). (C). 1994. pap. text ed. 35.00 (0-7881-0189-7) Diane Pub.

Advanced Technologies for Electric Demand-Side Management, 3 vols., Set. Organisation for Economic Cooperation & Development Staff. (Orig.). 1991. pap. 118.00 (92-64-13563-4) OECD.

Advanced Technologies in Failure Prevention: Proceedings of the 43rd Meeting of the Mechanical Failures Prevention Group. Ed. by T. Robert Shives. (Illus.). 275p. (C). 1991. 54.95 (0-521-41226-9) Cambridge U Pr.

Advanced Technologies in Research, Diagnosis & Treatment of AIDS & in Oncology. Ed. by G. Giraldo et al. (Antibiotics & Chemotherapy Ser.: Vol. 46). (Illus.). viii, 70p. 1994. 52.00 (3-8055-5970-4) S Karger.

Advanced Technology. Ed. by Philip H. Abelson & Mary Dorfman. LC 80-67368. (AAAS Publication Ser.: No. 80-8). 167p. 1980. pap. 47.60 (0-7837-0068-7, 2040315) Bks Demand.

Advanced-Technology Core Curriculum Guide. Daniel M. Hull & Carolyn A. Prescott. 212p. 1985. pap. 28.00 (1-55502-015-1) CORD Commns.

Advanced Technology Databook. A. Fletcher. 250p. 1995. 630.00 (1-85617-192-2, Pub. by Elsevier Applied Sci UK) Elsevier.

Advanced Technology for Command & Control Systems Engineering. Ed. by Stephen J. Andriole. LC 90-19757. 1990. 29.95 (0-916159-22-1) AFCEA Intl Pr.

***Advanced Technology for Design & Fabrication of Composite Materials & Structures: Applications to the Automotive, Marine, Aerospace & Construction Industry.** Ed. by G. C. Sih et al. LC 94-46549. 460p. (C). 1995. lib. bdg. 218.00 (0-7923-3303-9) Kluwer Ac.

***Advanced Technology for Product & Process Integration: 1995 International Congress & Exposition Meeting.** 1995. pap. 56.00 (1-56091-629-X, SP1079) Soc Auto Engineers.

Advanced Technology for Road Transport: IVHS & ATT. Ed. by Ian Catling. LC 93-38272. 1993. 81.00 (0-89006-613-2) Artech Hse.

Advanced Technology in Critical Care Nursing. John M. Clochesy. 203p. 1988. 50.00 (0-8342-0023-6) Aspen Pub.

Advanced Technology in Design & Visual Arts. I. Kerlow. 1993. text ed. write for info. (0-442-01305-1) Van Nos Reinhold.

Advanced Technology in Education. Royal Van Horn. 286p. (C). 1991. pap. 34.95 (0-534-14124-2) Intl Thomson.

Advanced Technology in Satellite Communication Antennas: Electrical & Mechanical Design. Ed. by Takashi Kitsuregawa. (Artech House Antenna Library). 415p. 1990. 59.00 (0-89006-387-7) Artech Hse.

Advanced Technology in Water Management. Ed. by K. F. Roberts. 257p. 1991. text ed. 76.00 (0-7277-1638-7, Pub. by T Telford UK) Am Soc Civil Eng.

Advanced Technology of Plasticity, 1987, 2 Vols., Vol. 1 & 2. Ed. by Arbetisgemeinschaft Umformtechnik & Forschungsgesellschaft Umformtechnik. 1200p. 1987. pap. text ed. 161.00 (0-387-17915-1) Spr-Verlag.

Advanced Technology Optical Telescopes IV. Ed. by L. Barr. 1990. 117.00 (0-8194-0280-X, VOL. 1236) SPIE.

Advanced Technology's Impact on Compressor Design & Development. 1989. 12.00 (0-89883-791-X, SP800) Soc Auto Engineers.

Advanced Telematics in Road Transport: Proceedings of the DRIVE Conference, Brussels, Belgium, 4-6 Feb., 1991, 2 vols., Set. Ed. by Commission of the European Communities, Directorate-General Telecommunications, Information Industries & Innovation Staff. 1542p. 1991. 257.00 (0-444-89043-2) Elsevier.

Advanced Telescope Making Techniques, Vol. 1: Optics. Ed. by Allan Mackintosh. LC 86-18935. (Illus.). 320p. 1986. pap. text ed. 19.95 (0-943396-11-5) Willmann-Bell.

Advanced Telescope Making Techniques, Vol. 2: Mechanical. Ed. by Allan Mackintosh. LC 86-18935. (Illus.). 320p. 1986. pap. text ed. 19.95 (0-943396-12-3) Willmann-Bell.

***Advanced Teleservices & High-Speed Commnication Architectures: Proceedings of the Second International Workshop, IWACA '94, Heidelberg, Germany, September 26-28, 1994.** Ed. by Ralf Steinmetz & IWACA Staff. LC 94-32622. (Lecture Notes in Computer Science: Vol. 868). 1994. write for info. (0-387-58494-3) Spr-Verlag.

Advanced Television & Electronic Imaging for Film & Video. Ed. by Joyce R. Hurwitz. 1993. pap. 25.00 (0-940690-21-7) Soc Motion Pic & TV Engrs.

***Advanced Television Studio Production Manual.** Thomas A. Young & Kathryn E. Young. (Illus.). 38p. (Orig.). (C). 1995. pap. text ed. 20.00 (0-9647170-1-8) Young Media.

Advanced Tennis. 4th ed. Chester W. Murphy. 136p. (C). 1988. pap. write for info. (0-697-07274-6) Brown & Benchmark.

Advanced Test Anxiety Research, Vol. 6. A. R. Schwarzer et al. 1989. 48.00 (90-265-0964-2, Pub. by Swets Pub Serv NE) Taylor & Francis.

An Asterisk (*) at the beginning of an entry indicates that the title is appearing in BIP for the first time.

Advanced Theories of Hypoid Gears. X. C. Wang & S. K. Ghosh. LC 93-49575. (Studies in Applied Mechanics: No. 36). 241p. 1994. 185.75 (*0-444-81705-0*) Elsevier.

Advanced Theory of Deep Geomagnetic Sounding. M. N. Berdichevsky & M. S. Zhdanov. (Methods in Geochemistry & Geophysics Ser.: Vol. 19). 400p. 1984. 148.75 (*0-444-42189-0*) Elsevier.

Advanced Theory of Language As Choice & Chance. G. Herdan. (Communications & Cybernetics Ser.: Vol. 4). (Illus.). 1966. 61.00 (*0-387-03584-2*) Spr-Verlag.

Advanced Theory of Statistics: Classical Inference & Relationship, Vol. 2. 5th ed. Maurice Kendall et al. (Charles Griffin Book Ser.). (Illus.). 640p. 1991. 95.00 (*0-19-520909-5*) OUP.

Advanced Theory of Vibrations: Nonlinear Vibration, One-Dimensional Machine Members & Structures. J. S. Rao. LC 92-14502. 1992. text ed. 54.95 (*0-470-21861-4*) Halsted Pr.

***Advanced Therapeutic Endoscopy.** Ed. by Jamie S. Barkin & Cesar A. O'Phelan. LC 90-8645. (Illus.). 383p. 1990. pap. 109.20 (*0-7837-8355-8*, 2049145) Bks Demand.

Advanced Therapeutic Endoscopy. 2nd ed. Jamie Barkin & Cesar A. O'Phelan. 434p. 1995. 139.00 (*0-7817-0155-4*) Raven.

Advanced Thermodynamics for Engineers. Kenneth Wark. LC 94-13915. (Series in Mechanical Engineering). 1994. text ed. write for info. (*0-07-068292-5*) McGraw.

Advanced Thermoplastic Composites: Characterization & Processing. Hans-Henning Kausch. 376p. (C). 1992. text ed. 94.50 (*1-56990-046-9*) Hanser-Gardner.

Advanced Thin-Layer Chromatography. Michael Lederer. 1971. 21.50 (*0-317-17781-8*) Elsevier.

***Advanced Thoracoscopic Procedures.** Michael J. Mack. 1995. 135.00 (*0-942219-79-1*) Quality Med Pub.

Advanced Tomographic Imaging Methods for the Analysis of Materials: Materials Research Society Symposium Proceedings, Vol. 217. Ed. by J. L. Ackerman & W. A. Ellingson. 1991. text ed. 58.00 (*1-55899-109-3*) Materials Res.

Advanced Tonfa. Tadashi Yamashita. Ed. by Mike Lee. LC 87-63018. (Weapons Ser.). 256p. 1987. pap. 16.95 (*0-89750-117-9*, 456) Ohara Pubns.

Advanced Topics in Artificial Intelligence. Ed. by R. T. Nossum. (Lecture Notes in Artificial Intelligence Ser.: Vol. 345). vii, 233p. 1989. pap. 34.00 (*0-387-50676-4*) Spr-Verlag.

Advanced Topics in Artificial Intelligence: Proceedings of the International Summer School, Prague, Czechoslavakia, July 6-17, 1992. Ed. by V. Marik et al. LC 92-17999. (Lecture Notes in Artificial Intelligence Ser.: Vol. 617). ix, 484p. 1992. pap. 67.00 (*0-387-55681-8*) Spr-Verlag.

***Advanced Topics in Dataflow Computing & Multithreading.** Ed. by Lubomir Bic et al. LC 94-25601. 1994. write for info. (*0-8186-6541-6*); pap. write for info. (*0-8186-6540-8*) IEEE Comp Soc.

***Advanced Topics in Dataflow Computing & Multithreading (2-95)** Ed. by Lubomir Bic et al. 412p. 1995. text ed. 54.00 (*0-8186-6542-4*, BP06542) IEEE Comp Soc.

Advanced Topics in DB2. Blaine Lucyk. (Illus.). 400p. (C). 1993. text ed. 47.50 (*0-201-57652-X*) Addison-Wesley.

Advanced Topics in Digital Signal Processing. John G. Proakis et al. (Illus.). 624p. (C). 1992. text ed. write for info. (*0-02-396841-9*) Macmillan.

Advanced Topics in Materials Science & Engineering. Ed. by J. L. Moran-Lopez & Juan M. Sanchez. LC 93-12843. 1993. 95.00 (*0-306-44487-9*, Plenum Pr) Plenum.

Advanced Topics in Shannon Sampling & Interpolation Theory. Ed. by Robert J. Marks, II & J. B. Thomas. LC 92-25590. (Texts in Electrical Engineering Ser.). (Illus.). 376p. 1992. 69.00 (*0-387-97906-9*) Spr-Verlag.

Advanced Topics in Signal Processing. Joe S. Lim & Alan V. Oppenheim. (Illus.). 512p. 1987. text ed. 77.00 (*0-13-013129-6*) P-H.

Advanced Topics in Turbomachinery Technology. Ed. & Intro. by David Japikse. LC 86-70543. (Illus.). 472p. (Orig.). (C). 1986. pap. text ed. 59.50 (*0-933283-02-4*) Concepts ETI.

Advanced Topics in UNIX. Ronald J. Leach. LC 94-10834. 1994. disk, pap. 49.95 (*0-471-03685-4*); pap. text ed. 34.95 (*0-471-03663-3*) Wiley.

Advanced Topics in Wet & Chemistry Short Course, 1991: Clairon Hotel, Cincinnati, OH, October 30-November 1. Technical Association of the Pulp & Paper Industry Staff. (TAPPI Notes Ser.). (Illus.). 108p. reprint ed. pap. 29.20 (*0-7837-1645-1*, 2041939) Bks Demand.

Advanced Topics of Law & Information Technology. Ed. by G. P. Vandenberghe & Y. Poullet. 272p. 1989. pap. 90.00 (*90-6544-391-6*) Kluwer Law Tax Pubs.

Advanced Torts: Cases & Materials. Peter B. Kutner & Osborne M. Reynolds, Jr. LC 89-62032. 772p. 1990. lib. bdg. 50.00 (*0-89089-375-6*) Carolina Acad Pr.

Advanced Torts: Cases & Materials. suppl. ed. Peter B. Kutner & Osborne M. Reynolds, Jr. 772p. 1993. write for info. (*0-318-66634-0*) Carolina Acad Pr.

Advanced Training for dBASE IV Ver. 2. Jacqueline Jonas. 80p. (Orig.). 1989. pap. text ed. 195.00 (*0-917792-66-1*); audio, disk write for info. (*0-318-64968-3*) OneOnOne Comp Trng.

Advanced Training for Lotus 1-2-3, Rel. 3.0 & 3.1. B. Alan August. Ed. by Charles Wolf. 72p. (Orig.). 1990. audio, disk 195.00 (*0-917792-82-3*) OneOnOne Comp Trng.

Advanced Training for Lotus 1-2-3 Release 2.X. B. Alan August. Ed. by Gayle Jensen. 85p. (Orig.). 1990. audio, disk write for info. (*0-318-65580-2*) OneOnOne Comp Trng.

Advanced Training for Lotus 1-2-3 Release 2.X. B. Alan August. Ed. by Gayle Jensen. 85p. (Orig.). 1990. pap. text ed. 195.00 (*0-917792-74-2*) OneOnOne Comp Trng.

***Advanced Training for Microsoft Excel 5 for Windows.** B. Alan August. Ed. by Janice Rinehart. 1995. pap. text ed. 195.00 (*1-56562-063-1*) OneOnOne Comp Trng.

***Advanced Training for Microsoft Word 6 for Windows.** Linda K. Schwartz. Ed. by Deborah Paulsen. 1995. pap. text ed. 195.00 (*1-56562-066-6*) OneOnOne Comp Trng.

Advanced Training for Paradox: Managing Data. Jacqueline Jonas. Ed. by Karen E. Hannum. 50p. (Orig.). 1992. Incl. disk & 2 cass. pap. text ed. 95.00 (*1-56562-006-2*) OneOnOne Comp Trng.

Advanced Training for Paradox: Personal Programmer. Jacqueline Jonas. Ed. by Karen E. Hannum. 50p. (Orig.). 1992. audio, disk 95.00 (*1-56562-007-0*) OneOnOne Comp Trng.

Advanced Training for Quattro Pro for Windows: Graphs & Charts. 50p. (Orig.). 1992. audio, disk 85.00 (*1-56562-030-5*) OneOnOne Comp Trng.

Advanced Training for Quattro Pro 3 & 4: Formulas & Functions. B. Alan August. Ed. by Karen E. Hannum. 65p. (Orig.). 1992. audio, disk 85.00 (*0-917792-90-4*) OneOnOne Comp Trng.

Advanced Training for Quattro Pro 3 & 4 Macros. B. Alan August. Ed. by Karen E. Hannum. 65p. (Orig.). 1991. audio, disk 85.00 (*0-917792-89-0*) OneOnOne Comp Trng.

***Advanced Training for the Dressage Horse: Medium to Grand Prix Level.** Tricia Gardiner. (Illus.). 176p. 1995. 29.95 (*0-7063-7147-X*, Pub. by Ward Lock UK) Sterling.

Advanced Training for WordPerfect for Windows: Long Documents. Sally Hargrave. Ed. by Christine Reid. 50p. (Orig.). 1993. audio, disk 95.00 (*1-56562-015-1*) OneOnOne Comp Trng.

Advanced Training for WordPerfect for Windows: Macros & Merges. Sally Hargrave. 50p. (Orig.). 1992. audio, disk 95.00 (*1-56562-012-7*) OneOnOne Comp Trng.

Advanced Training for WordPerfect 5. Sally Hargrave. 80p. (Orig.). 1989. pap. text ed. 145.00 (*0-917792-68-8*); audio, disk write for info. (*0-318-64960-8*) OneOnOne Comp Trng.

Advanced Training for WordPerfect 5.1. Sally Hargrave. Ed. by Kathy M. Berkemeyer. (Illus.). 98p. (Orig.). (C). 1990. audio, disk 125.00 (*0-917792-78-5*) OneOnOne Comp Trng.

***Advanced Training for WordPerfect 6.1 for Windows.** Kimi Nance. Ed. by Natalie B. Young. 1995. pap. text ed. 195.00 (*1-56562-065-8*) OneOnOne Comp Trng.

Advanced Training in French Pronunciation. Pierre Delattre. 1949. pap. 3.95 (*0-910408-03-3*); lp 8.25 (*0-910408-04-1*) Coll Store.

Advanced Transport & Spatial System Models: Applications to Korea. T. J. Kim. (Illus.). xx, 255p. 1990. 45.00 (*0-387-97277-3*) Spr-Verlag.

Advanced Transportation Control Systems: Millimeter Wave, Microwave, & Optical. 1992. 2,450.00 (*0-89336-948-9*, GB-162) BCC.

***Advanced Trauma Life Support Course.** American College of Surgeons Staff. (Illus.). (Orig.). 1994. student ed write for info. (*1-880696-06-1*) Am Coll Surgeons.

***Advanced Trauma Life Support Course.** American College of Surgeons Staff. (Illus.). (Orig.). (SPA.). 1994. student ed write for info. (*1-880696-05-3*) Am Coll Surgeons.

***Advanced Treasure Hunting with the Fisher Quick Silver Series Metal Detectors.** Andy Sabisch. 1995. write for info. (*1-883170-05-2*) FRL.

Advanced Treatise on Herbology. E. E. Shook. 1991. lib. bdg. 250.00 (*0-87700-993-7*) Revisionist Pr.

Advanced Treatise on Herbology. Edward E. Shook. 240p. 1993. reprint ed. spiral bd. 33.00 (*0-7873-0789-0*) Mokelumne.

Advanced Treatise on Physical Chemistry, 4 vols. James R. Partington. Incl. Vol. 1. Fundamental Principles-The Properties of Gases. LC 49-50157. 985p. pap. 180.00 (*0-8357-5134-1*); Vol. 2. Properties of Liquid. LC 49-50157. 492p. pap. 140.30 (*0-8357-5135-X*); Vol. 3. Properties of Solids. LC 49-50157. 699p. pap. 180.00 (*0-8357-5136-8*); Vol. 5. Molecular Spectra & Structure Dielectrics & Dipole Moments. LC 49-50157. 575p. pap. 163.90 (*0-8357-5137-6*); LC 49-50157. reprint ed. Set pap. write for info. (*0-318-58067-5*, 2005890) Bks Demand.

Advanced Treatment Technologies for Removal & Disposal of Micropollutants: Proceedings of an IAWPRC Seminar held in Antwerp, Belgium, 24-25 September 1984. Ed. by A. Van Haute. LC 82-645900. (Illus.). 86p. 1986. pap. 52.00 (*0-08-034148-9*, Pub. by PPL UK) Elsevier.

Advanced Triaxial Testing of Soil & Rock, STP 977. Ed. by Robert T. Donaghe et al. LC 88-19070. (Special Technical Publication (STP) Ser.). (Illus.). 900p. 1988. text ed. 120.00 (*0-8031-0983-0*, 04-977000-38) ASTM.

Advanced Trigonometry. abr. ed. Kenneth S. Miller & J. B. Walsh. LC 76-7918. 116p. (C). 1977. 13.00 (*0-88275-391-6*) Krieger.

Advanced Truck Suspensions. 1989. 19.00 (*0-89883-793-6*, SP802) Soc Auto Engineers.

Advanced Turbo C Programmers Guide. Donna M. Mosich et al. 339p. 1988. pap. text ed. 21.95 (*0-471-63742-4*) Wiley.

Advanced Turbo C Programming. Keith Weiskamp. 559p. 1988. text ed. 72.00 (*0-12-742689-2*); pap. text ed. 45.00 (*0-12-742690-6*) Acad Pr.

***Advanced Turkish I No. 108: OSU Foreign Language Publications.** Muge Galin. Ed. by Otterbein College Dept. Foreign Languages Staff. (Turkish Individualized Instruction Ser.). (Illus.). 242p. (Orig.). (TUR.). (C). 1994. student ed, pap. 13.00 (*0-87415-253-4*) OSU Foreign Lang.

***Advanced Turkish I No. 108A: OSU Foreign Language Publications.** Muge Galin. Ed. by Otterbein College Dept. Foreign Languages Staff. (Turkish Individualized Instruction Ser.). (Illus.). 171p. (Orig.). (TUR.). (C). 1994. teacher ed, pap. 9.00 (*0-87415-254-2*) OSU Foreign Lang.

Advanced Two-Stroke Engines: Fourteen Papers. 1993. 45.00 (*1-56091-327-4*, SP-942) Soc Auto Engineers.

Advanced Typing Skills. T. J. Foster. (C). 1986. 60.00 (*0-85950-161-2*, Pub. by S Thornes Pubs UK) St Mut.

Advanced Ukrainian 1. Assya Humesky & Kateryna Dowbenko. (Illus.). 118p. (Orig.). (UKR.). (C). 1987. teacher ed, pap. 8.00 (*0-87415-136-8*, 55A); student ed, pap. text ed. 27.00 (*0-87415-135-X*, 55) OSU Foreign Lang.

Advanced Ukrainian 1, 2 cass., Set. Assya Humesky & Kateryna Dowbenko. (Orig.). (UKR.). (C). 1987. audio 10.00 (*0-87415-137-6*, 55B) OSU Foreign Lang.

Advanced Ukrainian 2. Assya Humesky & Kateryna Dowbenko. (Illus.). 131p. (Orig.). (UKR.). (C). 1987. teacher ed, pap. 9.00 (*0-87415-139-2*, 56A); student ed, pap. text ed. 32.00 (*0-87415-138-4*, 56) OSU Foreign Lang.

Advanced Ukrainian 2, 2 cass., Set. Assya Humesky & Kateryna Dowbenko. (Orig.). (UKR.). (C). 1987. audio 10.00 (*0-87415-140-6*, 56B) OSU Foreign Lang.

Advanced Ultrasonic Testing Systems: A State-of-the-Art Survey. H. S. Silvus. 76p. 1976. 42.50 (*0-318-21479-2*, 330) Am Soc Nondestructive.

Advanced UNIX Programming. Marc J. Rochkind. 265p. 1985. pap. 35.95 (*0-13-011800-1*) P-H.

Advanced Use of Advanced Medical Technology with the Elderly. Ed. by Freddie Homburger. LC 94-1496. 296p. (C). 1994. text ed. 44.95 (*0-8261-8410-3*) Springer Pub.

Advanced User's Guide to Novell DOS 7. Brian Underdahl. LC 93-35631. 1994. pap. text ed. 22.95 (*0-471-01629-2*) Wiley.

Advanced Value of Gold (1862) see Inquiry into the Nature of Value & of Capital

Advanced VersaCAD. James A. Suderman. 352p. 1991. teacher ed 8.00 (*0-8273-3537-7*); pap. text ed. 39.95 (*0-8273-3536-9*) Delmar.

Advanced Visual BASIC. Norton, Peter, Computing Group Staff & Steven Holzner. LC 92-5690. (Illus.). (Orig.). 1992. pap. 39.95 (*1-56686-000-8*) Brady Compu Bks.

Advanced Visual Basic: A Developer's Guide. Mark S. Burgess. 1993. disk, pap. 39.95 (*0-201-60828-6*) Addison-Wesley.

Advanced Visual Interfaces (AVI '92) Proceedings of the International Workshop. T. Catarci et al. (Computer Science Ser.). 436p. 1992. text ed. 116.00 (*981-02-1123-6*) World Scientific Pub.

Advanced Volleyball Everyone. Kathy Davis. 203p. 1991. pap. text ed. 12.95 (*0-88725-167-6*) Hunter Textbks.

Advanced VSE System Programming Techniques. Leo J. Langevin. LC 90-8529. 224p. 1990. 34.95 (*0-89435-365-9*) Wiley.

Advanced VSE Systems Programming Techniques. Leo J. Langevin. 203p. 1993. text ed. 42.95 (*0-471-58029-5*) Wiley.

***Advanced Walleye Strategies.** Mark Romanack. LC 92-62042. (Complete Angler's Library). 250p. 1993. write for info. (*0-914697-52-8*) N Amer Outdoor Grp.

Advanced Waste Treatment. 2nd ed. Kenneth D. Kerri. (Illus.). 571p. (C). 1993. pap. text ed. 20.00 (*1-884701-03-5*) CA St U Ofc Water.

Advanced Wastewater Treatment & Reclamation. Ed. by J. Kurbiel. (Water Science & Technology Ser.). Orig. Title: Water Science & Technology, Vol. 24, No. 7. (Illus.). 294p. 1991. pap. 100.00 (*0-08-040779-X*, Pergamon Pr) Elsevier.

Advanced Water-Cooled Reactor Technologies: Rationale, State of Progress & Outlook - Report by an Expert Group. OECD, Nuclear Energy Agency Staff. 103p. (Orig.). 1989. pap. 28.00 (*92-64-13302-X*) OECD.

Advanced Water Treatment Technology: Quality, Reuse & Tertiary Treatment Markets, No. GB-055R. 284p. 1993. 1,950.00 (*0-89336-880-6*) BCC.

Advanced Weapons Training. (Illus.). 270p. 1988. 18.00 (*0-939235-01-3*) Spec Trning Unit.

Advanced Weight Control Techniques for Nurses: Behavior Modification. Elizabeth Somer & Ralph LaForge. LC 94-60360. 232p. (Orig.). (C). 1993. pap. text ed. 49.95 (*1-878025-50-3*) Western Schls.

Advanced Whitetail Details. Deer & Deer Hunting Magazine Staff. LC 92-74792. 24p. 1993. pap. 14.95 (*0-87341-229-X*) Krause Pubns.

Advanced Wild Turkey Hunting & World Records. Dave Harbour. LC 83-14684. (Illus.). 264p. 1983. 19.95 (*0-8329-0286-1*, Winchester Pr) New Win Pub.

Advanced Windows NT. Jeffrey Richter. 1993. pap. 39.95 (*1-55615-567-0*) Microsoft.

Advanced Windows Programming. Martin Heller. 1992. 72.90 (*0-471-55172-4*); pap. text ed. 32.95 (*0-471-54711-5*); disk 39.95 (*0-471-55171-6*) Wiley.

***Advanced Windows Programming: The Developer's Guide to the Win32 API for Windows NT & Windows 95.** Jeffrey Richter. 1995. cd-rom, pap. 44.95 (*1-55615-677-4*) Microsoft.

Advanced Windows Programming in Smalltalk. Dan Shafer & W. Scott Herndon. 1992. pap. write for info. (*1-881513-04-1*) Reader Netwk.

Advanced Windsurfing. John Conway. (Adventure Sports Ser.). 1989. pap. 15.95 (*0-8117-2303-8*) Stackpole.

Advanced Wing Chun. William Cheung. Ed. by Mike Lee. LC 87-43325. (Illus.). 256p. (Orig.). 1988. pap. 19.95 (*0-89750-118-7*, 457) Ohara Pubns.

Advanced Win32 Programmming. Martin Heller. LC 93-550. 400p. 1993. Includes disk. 44.95 (*0-471-59245-5*) Wiley.

Advanced Wiring. rev. ed. Time-Life Books Editors. (Home Repair & Improvement Ser.). (Illus.). 128p. 1989. write for info. (*0-8094-7366-6*); text ed. write for info. (*0-8094-7368-2*); lib. bdg. write for info. (*0-8094-7367-4*) Time-Life.

Advanced Wood Adhesives Technology. Antonio Pizzi. LC 94-21042. 304p. 1994. 115.00 (*0-8247-9266-1*) Dekker.

Advanced Woodwork & Furniture Making. John L. Feirer & Gilbert R. Hutchings. 1978. teacher ed 4.64 (*0-02-662150-9*); text ed. 18.60 (*0-02-662080-4*); student ed 7.32 (*0-02-662120-7*); 20.00 (*0-02-662070-7*) Bennett IL.

Advanced Woodwork & Furniture Making. rev. ed. John L. Feirer & Gilbert R. Hutchings. (gr. 9-12). 1982. text ed. 26.40 (*0-02-662110-X*) Bennett IL.

Advanced Woodworking. (Home Repair & Improvement Ser.). (Illus.). 136p. 1984. 14.60 (*0-8094-3478-4*); lib. bdg. 21.93 (*0-8094-3479-2*) Time-Life.

Advanced Word Processing Applications: Job-Based Tasks. Lloyd Brooks. 1992. student ed 11.95 (*1-56118-382-2*); teacher ed 8.00 (*1-56118-383-0*); 3.5 hd 69.00 (*1-56118-385-7*); 5.25 hd 69.00 (*1-56118-384-9*) Paradigm MN.

Advanced WordPerfect Express: A Complete Easy-to-Use Book/Disk Tutorial, PC Edition. Philip Casella. LC 92-26756. 288p. 1992. disk, pap. 40.00 (*1-55623-921-1*) Irwin Prof Pubng.

Advanced WordPerfect for Windows. Jane Troop & Dale Craig. LC 93-19269. 1993. write for info. (*0-938661-62-0*) Franklin Beedle.

Advanced WordPerfect Made Perfectly Easy Using Version 5.1. Sharon A. Fisher-Larson. LC 92-35234. 1993. write for info. (*0-02-801228-3*) Glencoe.

Advanced Wordperfect 5.1, Set. Gonzalez. 1991. write for info. (*0-07-909586-0*); write for info. (*0-07-909585-2*) McGraw.

Advanced WordPerfect 6.0: Desktop Publishing. Nita H. Rutkosky. 384p. Date not set. text ed. 31.00 (*1-56118-712-7*) Paradigm MN.

Advanced WordPerfect 6.0 for DOS. O'Donnell et al. 1994. pap. text ed. write for info. (*0-07-070413-9*) McGraw.

Advanced WordPerfect 6.0 with Desktop Publishing. Jane Troop & Dale Craig. LC 93-33485. 1993. write for info. (*0-938661-71-X*) Franklin Beedle.

Advanced Wreck-Diving Guide. Gary Gentile. LC 87-47997. (Illus.). 144p. (Orig.). 1988. pap. 12.95 (*0-87033-380-1*) Cornell Maritime.

Advanced X-Ray-EUV Radiation Sources & Applications, Vol. 1345. J. P. Knauer & G. K. Shenoy. 1990. 62.00 (*0-8194-0406-3*) SPIE.

Advanced X Windows Application Programming. 2nd ed. Kevin Reichard. 1994. Incl. CD-ROM. pap. 34.95 (*1-55851-344-2*) M&T Bks.

***Advanced X Windows Applications Programming.** Kevin Reichard & Eric F. Johnson. LC 94-34030. 1994. 44.95 (*1-55828-344-7*) M&T Bks.

Advanced Yang Style Tai Chi Chuan, Vol. 1. 4th ed. Jwing-Ming Yang. (Illus.). 288p. 1986. pap. 18.95 (*0-940871-02-5*, B007) YMAA Pubn.

Advanced Yang Style Tai Chi Chuan, Vol. 2. 3rd ed. Jwing-Ming Yang. (Illus.). 254p. 1986. pap. 18.95 (*0-940871-03-3*, B008) YMAA Pubn.

Advanced Yang Style Tai Chi Chuan, Vol. 1: Tai Chi Theory & Tai Chi Jing. 4th ed. Yang Jwing-Ming. (Illus.). 288p. 1986. 24.95 (*0-940871-16-5*, B007HC) YMAA Pubn.

Advanced Yang Style Tai Chi Chuan, Vol. 2: Martial Applications. 3rd ed. Yang Jwing-Ming. (Illus.). 254p. 1986. 24.95 (*0-940871-14-9*, B008HC) YMAA Pubn.

Advanced Years. Elizabeth Sinclair-House & Alison Muir. LC 90-28922. (Human Development Ser.). (Illus.). 64p. (J). (gr. 5-9). 1991. lib. bdg. 11.95 (*0-8114-7807-6*) Raintree Steck-V.

***Advanced Zeolite Science & Applications.** Ed. by J. C. Jansen et al. LC 94-22193. (Studies in Surface Science & Catalysis: Vol. 85). 1994. 243.00 (*0-444-82001-9*) Elsevier.

Advancees in Speech Signal Processing. Ed. by Sadaoki Furui. (Electrical Engineering & Electronics Ser.: Vol. 76). 896p. 1991. 215.00 (*0-8247-8540-1*) Dekker.

Advancement of Crops & Monitoring of Environment: Symposium Held at Indore. Ed. by G. P. Verma et al. (Progress in Ecology Ser.: Vol. IX). (Illus.). 425p. 1988. 35.00 (*1-55528-013-7*, Pub. by Today & Tomorrows P & P II) Scholarly Pubns.

***Advancement of Intelligent Production: Proceedings of the 7th International Conference on Production-Precision Engineering, & 4th International Conference on High Technology, Chiba, Japan, September 15-17, 1994.** Seventh International Conference on Production-Precision Engineering Staff & Fourth International Conference on High Technology Staff. Ed. by E. Usui. 848p. 1994. text ed. 245.50 (*0-444-81901-0*) Elsevier.

Advancement of Learning. Reginald Hill. 1987. pap. 4.50 (*0-451-14656-5*, Sig) NAL-Dutton.

Advancement of Learning. Francis Bacon. (Books of the Monarchs of England). 624p. (C). 1989. reprint ed. 330.00 (*1-85297-012-X*, Pub. by Archival Facs UK) St Mut.

***Advancement of Learning: With a Brief Memoir of the Author.** Francis Bacon. 170p. 1994. pap. 16.95 (*1-56459-436-X*) Kessinger Pub.

Advancement of Science: Science Without Legend, Objectivity Without Illusions. Philip Kitcher. LC 92-19532. 432p. 1993. 45.00 (*0-19-504628-5*) OUP.

***Advancement of Science: Science Without Legend, Objectivity Without Illusions.** Philip Kitcher. (Illus.). 432p. 1995. pap. 18.95 (*0-19-509653-3*) OUP.

Advancement of Science & Its Burdens: The Jefferson Lecture & Other Essays. Gerald J. Holton. (Illus.). 368p. 1986. pap. 18.95 (*0-521-27243-2*) Cambridge U Pr.

An Asterisk (*) at the beginning of an entry indicates that the title is appearing in BIP for the first time.

Advancement of Veterinary Science, Vol. 1: Veterinary Medicine Beyond 2000. A. R. Michell. (Advancement of Veterinary Science Ser.: Vol. 1). 240p. 1993. 66.50 (*0-85198-759-1*) CAB Intl.

Advancement of Veterinary Science, Vol. 2: Veterinary Education: the Future. A. R. Michell. (Advancement of Veterinary Science Ser.: Vol. 2). 240p. 1993. 66.50 (*0-85198-760-5*) CAB Intl.

Advancement of Veterinary Science, Vol. 3: History of the Healing Professions. A. R. Michell. (Advancement of Veterinary Science Ser.: Vol. 3). 140p. 1993. 47.50 (*0-85198-761-3*) CAB Intl.

Advancement of Veterinary Science, Vol. 4: Veterinary Science - Growth Points & Comparative Medicine. Ed. by A. R. Michell. 225p. 1993. text ed. 66.50 (*0-85198-762-1*) CAB Intl.

Advancement Through Service: A History of the Frontiers International. Frederick Johnson & Leonard Bethel. 156p. (C). 1991. lib. bdg. 46.00 (*0-8191-8298-2*) U Pr of Amer.

***Advancements in ABS - TCS & Brake Technology: 1995 International Congress & Exposition Meeting.** 1995. pap. 38.00 (*1-56091-625-7*, SP1075) Soc Auto Engineers.

Advancements in Aerodynamics, Fluid Mechanics, & Hydraulics. Ed. by R. E. Arndt et al. 1026p. 1986. 88.00 (*0-87262-539-7*) Am Soc Civil Eng.

Advancements in Electric & Hybrid Electric Vehicle Technology: SAE International Congress & Exposition 1994, 15 papers. (Special Publications). 1994. pap. 49.00 (*1-56091-475-0*, SP-1023) Soc Auto Engineers.

***Advancements in Engine Management & Driveline Controls: 1995 International Congress & Exposition Meeting.** 1995. pap. 36.00 (*1-56091-636-2*, SP1086) Soc Auto Engineers.

***Advancements in Synthesis & Processes: 3rd International SAMPE Metals & Metals Processing Conference, Westin Harbour Castle Hotel, Toronto, Canada, October 20-22, 1992.** International SAMPE Metals & Metals Processing Conference Staff. Ed. by F. H. Froes et al. (International SAMPE Metals & Metals Processing Conference Staff: No. 3). (Illus.). reprint ed. pap. 180.00 (*0-7837-9639-0*, 2060429) Bks Demand.

Advances. Mary Joseph. 1983. 14.95 (*0-02-559890-2*) Macmillan.

Advances & Applications of Quantitative Texture Analysis. Ed. by H. J. Bunge & C. Esling. 316p. 1991. lib. bdg. 83.00 (*3-88355-164-3*, Pub. by DGM Metallurgy Info GW) IR Pubns.

Advances & Innovations in the Bond & Mortgage Markets. Ed. by Frank J. Fabozzi. 450p. 1989. 65.00 (*1-55738-016-3*) Probus Pub Co.

Advances & Technical Standards in Neurosurgery, Vol. 1. Ed. by H. Krayenbuhl et al. LC 74-10499. (Illus.). 220p. 1978. 81.00 (*0-387-81218-0*) Spr-Verlag.

Advances & Technical Standards in Neurosurgery, Vol. 2. Ed. by H. Krayenbuhl. LC 74-10499. (Illus.). 217p. 1975. 86.00 (*0-387-81293-8*) Spr-Verlag.

Advances & Technical Standards in Neurosurgery, Vol. 3. Ed. by H. Krayenbuhl. LC 74-10499. (Illus.). 1976. 73.00 (*0-387-81381-0*) Spr-Verlag.

Advances & Technical Standards in Neurosurgery, Vol. 4. N. A. Lassan. LC 74-10499. 1977. 73.00 (*0-387-81423-X*) Spr-Verlag.

Advances & Technical Standards in Neurosurgery, Vol. 5. Ed. by H. Krayenbuehl et al. LC 74-10499. (Illus.). 1978. 102.00 (*0-387-81441-8*) Spr-Verlag.

Advances & Technical Standards in Neurosurgery, Vol. 6. H. Krayenbuehl et al. LC 74-10499. (Illus.). 1979. 86.00 (*0-387-81518-X*) Spr-Verlag.

Advances & Technical Standards in Neurosurgery, Vol. 7. Ed. by H. Krayenbuehl et al. (Illus.). 217p. 1980. 102.00 (*0-387-81592-9*) Spr-Verlag.

Advances & Technical Standards in Neurosurgery, Vol. 8. Ed. by H. Krayenbuehl et al. (Illus.). 328p. 1981. 115.00 (*0-387-81665-8*) Spr-Verlag.

Advances & Technical Standards in Neurosurgery, Vol. 10. Ed. by H. Krayenbuhl et al. (Illus.). 250p. 1984. 102.00 (*0-387-81750-6*) Spr-Verlag.

Advances & Technical Standards in Neurosurgery, Vol. 11. Ed. by L. Symon et al. (Illus.). 260p. 1985. 102.00 (*0-387-81806-5*) Spr-Verlag.

Advances & Technical Standards in Neurosurgery, Vol. 12. Ed. by L. Symon. (Illus.). 200p. 1986. 88.00 (*0-387-81877-4*) Spr-Verlag.

Advances & Technical Standards in Neurosurgery, Vol. 13. Ed. by L. Symon. (Illus.). 200p. 1986. 86.00 (*0-387-81885-5*) Spr-Verlag.

Advances & Technical Standards in Neurosurgery, Vol. 14. Ed. by L. Symon et al. (Illus.). 240p. 1987. 113.00 (*0-387-81930-4*) Spr-Verlag.

Advances & Technical Standards in Neurosurgery, Vol. 15. Ed. by L. Symon et al. (Illus.). 200p. 1988. 106.00 (*0-387-82013-2*) Spr-Verlag.

Advances & Technical Standards in Neurosurgery, Vol. 16. Ed. by L. Symon et al. (Illus.). 200p. 1989. 111.00 (*0-387-82060-4*) Spr-Verlag.

Advances & Technical Standards in Neurosurgery, Vol. 17. Ed. by L. Symon et al. (Illus.). 276p. 1990. 127.00 (*0-387-82117-1*, 3829) Spr-Verlag.

Advances & Technical Standards in Neurosurgery, Vol. 18. Ed. by L. Symon et al. (Illus.). xv, 209p. 1991. 124.00 (*0-387-82243-7*) Spr-Verlag.

Advances & Technical Standards in Neurosurgery, Vol. 19. Ed. by L. Symon et al. (Illus.). 248p. 1992. 129.00 (*0-387-82287-9*) Spr-Verlag.

Advances & Technical Standards in Neurosurgery, Vol. 20. Ed. by L. Symon et al. (Illus.). 320p. 1993. 160.00 (*0-387-82383-2*) Spr-Verlag.

***Advances & Technical Standards in Neurosurgery, Vol. 21.** Ed. by L. Symon et al. 300p. 1994. 149.00 (*0-387-82482-0*) Spr-Verlag.

Advances & Technical Standards in Neurosurgery, Vol.9. Ed. by H. Krayenbuehl et al. (Illus.). 177p. 1983. 81.00 (*0-387-81718-2*) Spr-Verlag.

Advances & Trends in Structural & Solid Mechanics: Proceedings of the Symposium, Washington D.C., October 4-7, 1982. Ed. by A. K. Noor & J. M. Housner. 587p. 1983. 180.00 (*0-08-029990-3*, Pergamon Pr) Elsevier.

Advances & Utilization of Chromatography: Proceedings of the International Symposium, 4th, Bratislava, 1973. J. Janak et al. 1974. reprint ed. 89.50 (*0-317-17782-6*) Elsevier.

Advances Cientificos Mas Notables Del Siglo XX (Tomo II) Ed. by Maria E. Alvarez del Real. (Illus.). 320p. (Orig.). (SPA.). 1991. pap. 5.95 (*1-56259-003-0*) Editorial Amer.

***Advances Computational & Design Techniques in Applied Electromagnetic Systems: Proceedings of the International ISEM Symposium Held in Seoul, Korea, 22-24 June, 1994.** International ISEM Symposium on Advanced Computational & Design Techniques in Applied Electromagnetic Systems Staff. Ed. by Song-yop Hahn. LC 94-43934. (Studies in Applied Electromagnetics in Materials: Vol. 6). 1994. 267.75 (*0-444-82139-2*) Elsevier.

Advances Educational Psychology for Educators, Researchers, & Policymakers. Michael Pressley & Christine McCormick. LC 93-49883. 722p. (C). 1995. 45.00 (*0-673-46914-X*) HarpCollege.

Advances in Accelerator Physics & Technologies. H. Schopper. (Advanced Series on Directions in High Energy Physics). 600p. 1993. text ed. 121.00 (*981-02-0957-6*) World Scientific Pub.

Advances in Accounting, Vol. 1. Ed. by Bill N. Schwartz et al. 1984. 73.25 (*0-89232-397-3*) Jai Pr.

Advances in Accounting, Vol. 2. Bill N. Schwartz. 1985. 73.25 (*0-89232-514-3*) Jai Pr.

Advances in Accounting, Vol. 3. Ed. by Bill N. Schwartz. 358p. 1986. 73.25 (*0-89232-655-7*) Jai Pr.

Advances in Accounting, Vol. 4. Ed. by Bill N. Schwartz. 328p. 1987. 73.25 (*0-89232-685-9*) Jai Pr.

Advances in Accounting, Vol. 5. Ed. by Bill N. Schwartz et al. 1987. 73.25 (*0-89232-788-X*) Jai Pr.

Advances in Accounting, Vol. 6. Ed. by Bill N. Schwartz. 1988. 73.25 (*0-89232-892-4*) Jai Pr.

Advances in Accounting, Vol. 7. Ed. by Bill N. Schwartz et al. 256p. 1989. 73.25 (*0-89232-960-2*) Jai Pr.

Advances in Accounting, Vol. 8. Ed. by Bill N. Schwartz et al. 330p. 1990. 73.25 (*1-55938-067-5*) Jai Pr.

Advances in Accounting, Vol. 9. Ed. by Bill N. Schwartz et al. 1991. 73.25 (*1-55938-255-4*) Jai Pr.

Advances in Accounting: Supplement 1. Ed. by Jagdish S. Gangolly et al. 231p. 1989. 73.25 (*1-55938-047-0*) Jai Pr.

Advances in Accounting Information Systems, Vol. 1. Ed. by Gary Grudnitski & Steven G. Sutton. 1991. 73.25 (*1-55938-575-8*) Jai Pr.

***Advances in Acoustic Microscopy, Vol. 1.** Ed. by G. Andrew Briggs. 320p. 1995. 79.50 (*0-306-44798-3*, Plenum Pr) Plenum.

***Advances In Acoustic Technology.** J.M. Hernandez. (European Community-Aeronautics Research Ser.). Date not set. text ed. 74.95 (*0-471-95149-8*) Wiley.

Advances in Adaptive Control. Ed. by Kumpati S. Narendra et al. LC 91-16922. (Illus.). 424p. (C). 1991. text ed. 69.95 (*0-87942-278-5*, PC0272-5) Inst Electrical.

Advances in Adhesives: Application, Materials, & Safety. Ed. by D. Brewis & J. Comyn. 306p. 1983. 66.00 (*0-938648-32-2*) T-C Pubns CA.

Advances in Adolescent Mental Health, Vol. 4: Contraception, Pregnancy & Parenting. Ed. by Arlene R. Stiffman & Ronald A. Feldman. 300p. 1990. 88.00 (*1-85302-088-5*, Pub. by J Kingsley Pubs UK) Taylor & Francis.

Advances in Adult T-Cell Leukemia & HTLV-I Research. Ed. by Kiyoshi Takatsuki et al. (Gann Monograph on Cancer Research Ser.: No. 39). 1992. 83.95 (*0-8493-7746-3*, RC643) CRC Pr.

Advances in Aerobiology. Ed. by R. Leuschner & G. Boehm. (BioSeries-EXS: No. 51). 300p. 1987. 85.00 (*0-8176-1803-1*) Birkhauser.

Advances in Aeronautical Sciences: Proceedings of the 1st International Congress on Aeronautical Science, Madrid, September, 1958. T. Von Karman & A. Ballantyne. Vol. 2. 1959. write for info. (*0-318-69650-9*, Pub. by Pergamon Repr UK) Franklin.

Advances in Aerosol Physics, 7 vols. Ed. by V. A. Fedoseev. 1221p. 1972. text ed. 370.00 (*0-7065-1122-0*, Pub. by Keter Pub IS) Coronet Bks.

Advances in Aerospace Structures & Materials, 1982: Presented at the Winter Annual Meeting of the American Society of Mechanical Engineers, Phoenix, AZ, November 14-19, 1982. American Society of Mechanical Engineers Staff. Ed. by Robert M. Laurenson & Umur Yuceoglu. LC 81-69004. (AD Ser.: No. 03). (Illus.). 146p. reprint ed. pap. 41.70 (*0-8357-2904-4*, 2039141) Bks Demand.

Advances in Aerospace Structures, Materials, & Dynamics: A Symposium on Composites. U. Yuceoglu et al. 1983. pap. text ed. 40.00 (*0-317-02538-4*, H00272) ASME.

Advances in Age Pigments Research, Vol. 64. Totaro E. Aloj et al. (Advances in the Biosciences Ser.). (Illus.). 430p. 1987. 94.00 (*0-08-035721-0*, Pergamon Pr) Elsevier.

***Advances in Agile Manufacturing: Integrating Technology, Organization & People.** P. T. Kidd & W. Karowski. LC 94-77316. (Advances in Design & Manufacturing Ser.: Vol. 4). 715p. 1994. 130.00 (*90-5199-176-2*) IOS Press.

Advances in Agriculture: A User Friendly Guide to the Latest Technology. Dan Burrus & Patti Thomsen. 73p. (Orig.). 1991. pap. 9.95 (*1-880136-53-8*) Intl Mgmt Pubns.

Advances in Agronomy, Vol. 35. Ed. by Nyle C. Brady. (Serial Publication Ser.). 1982. text ed. 151.00 (*0-12-000735-5*) Acad Pr.

Advances in Agronomy, Vol. 36. Ed. by Nyle C. Brady. (Serial Publication Ser.). 1983. text ed. 151.00 (*0-12-000736-3*) Acad Pr.

Advances in Agronomy, Vol. 37. Ed. by Nyle C. Brady. (Serial Publication Ser.). 1984. text ed. 140.00 (*0-12-000737-1*) Acad Pr.

Advances in Agronomy, Vol. 38. Ed. by Nyle C. Brady. (Illus.). 375p. 1986. text ed. 140.00 (*0-12-000738-X*) Acad Pr.

Advances in Agronomy, Vol. 39. Ed. by Nyle C. Brady. (Serial Publication Ser.). 308p. 1986. text ed. 140.00 (*0-12-000739-8*) Acad Pr.

Advances in Agronomy, Vol. 40. Ed. by Nyle C. Brady. (Serial Publication Ser.). 300p. 1986. text ed. 140.00 (*0-12-000740-1*) Acad Pr.

Advances in Agronomy, Vol. 41. Ed. by Nyle C. Brady. (Serial Publication Ser.). 456p. 1987. text ed. 140.00 (*0-12-000741-X*) Acad Pr.

Advances in Agronomy, Vol. 42. Ed. by Nyle C. Brady. (Serial Publication Ser.). 400p. 1989. text ed. 109.00 (*0-12-000742-8*) Acad Pr.

Advances in Agronomy, Vol. 43. Ed. by Nyle C. Brady. (Serial Publication Ser.). 373p. 1990. text ed. 104.00 (*0-12-000743-6*) Acad Pr.

Advances in Agronomy, Vol. 44. Ed. by Nyle C. Brady. 294p. 1990. text ed. 94.00 (*0-12-000744-4*) Acad Pr.

Advances in Agronomy, Vol. 45. Ed. by Nyle C. Brady. (Illus.). 378p. 1991. text ed. 83.00 (*0-12-000745-2*) Acad Pr.

Advances in Agronomy, Vol. 46. Ed. by Donald L. Sparks. (Illus.). 309p. 1991. text ed. 83.00 (*0-12-000746-0*) Acad Pr.

Advances in Agronomy, Vol. 47. Ed. by Donald L. Sparks. (Illus.). 403p. 1992. text ed. 89.00 (*0-12-000747-9*) Acad Pr.

Advances in Agronomy, Vol. 48. Ed. by Donald L. Sparks. (Illus.). 313p. 1992. text ed. 69.00 (*0-12-000748-7*) Acad Pr.

Advances in Agronomy, Vol. 49. Ed. by Donald L. Sparks. (Illus.). 315p. 1993. text ed. 79.95 (*0-12-000749-5*) Acad Pr.

Advances in Agronomy, Vol. 50. Ed. by Donald L. Sparks. (Illus.). 277p. 1993. text ed. 79.95 (*0-12-000750-9*) Acad Pr.

Advances in Agronomy, Vol. 51. Ed. by Donald L. Sparks. (Illus.). 290p. 1993. text ed. 70.00 (*0-12-000751-7*) Acad Pr.

Advances in Agronomy, Vol. 52. Ed. by Donald L. Sparks. (Illus.). 281p. 1994. text ed. 79.95 (*0-12-000752-5*) Acad Pr.

Advances in Agronomy, Vol. 53. Ed. by Donald L. Sparks. (Illus.). 193p. 1994. text ed. 69.95 (*0-12-000753-3*) Acad Pr.

***Advances in Agronomy, Vol. 55.** Ed. by Donald L. Sparks. (Illus.). 415p. 1995. boxed write for info. (*0-12-000755-X*) Acad Pr.

Advances in Agronomy, Vols. 1-24. Ed. by A. G. Norman. Incl. Vol. 13. 1961. 75.00 (*0-12-000713-4*); write for info. (*0-318-50155-4*) Acad Pr.

***Advances in Agronomy Vol. 54, Vol. 54.** Ed. by Donald L. Sparks. (Illus.). 358p. 1995. boxed 89.00 (*0-614-05259-9*) Acad Pr.

Advances in Air Sampling. American Conference of Governmental Industrial Hygienists Staff. (Illus.). 409p. 1988. 69.95 (*0-87371-115-7*, RA576) Lewis Pubs.

Advances in Allergology & Applied Immunology: Proceedings of the International Congress of Allergology, 10th, Jerusalem, Israel, Nov., 1979. International Congress of Allergology Staff. Ed. by A. Oehling et al. (Illus.). 680p. 1980. 330.00 (*0-08-025519-1*, Pub. by Pergamon Repr UK) Franklin.

Advances in Allergology & Clinical Immunology. Ed. by P. Godard et al. (Illus.). 700p. 1992. pap. 120.00 (*1-85070-396-5*) Prthnon Pub.

Advances in Altered States of Consciousness & Human Potentialities, Vol. 1. Ed. by Theodore X. Barber et al. LC 76-42132. 700p. 1980. 69.95 (*0-88437-002-X*) Psych Dimensions.

Advances in American Medicine: Essays at the Bicentennial, Vols. 1 & 2. Ed. by John Z. Bowers & Elizabeth F. Purcell. LC 76-3162. reprint ed. write for info. (*0-8357-5138-4*, 2026692); reprint ed. pap. 116.80 (*0-685-73817-5*) Bks Demand.

Advances in Ammonia Metabolism & Hepatic Encephalopathy: Proceedings of the 6th International Symposium, Vaalsbroek Castle, the Netherlands, 27-29 April, 1987. Ed. by P. B. Soeters et al. (Intenational Congress Ser.: No. 761). 608p. 1988. 192.50 (*0-444-80957-0*, Excerpta Medica) Elsevier.

Advances in Analysis & Detection of Explosives: Proceedings of the 4th International Symposium, September 7-10, 1992, Jerusalem, Israel. Ed. by Jehuda Yinon. LC 92-46546. 1993. lib. bdg. 217.00 (*0-7923-2138-3*) Kluwer Ac.

Advances in Analysis of Structural Masonry. Ed. by Subhash C. Anand. 164p. 1986. 21.00 (*0-87262-553-2*) Am Soc Civil Eng.

***Advances in Analysis, Probability, & Mathematical Physics: Contributions of Nonstandard Analysis.** Ed. by Sergio A. Albeverio et al. LC 94-35635. (Mathematics & Its Applications Ser.: Vol. 314). 1994. lib. bdg. 115.00 (*0-7923-3191-5*) Kluwer Ac.

Advances in Analytical Geochemistry, Vol. 1. Ed. by Marvin W. Rowe & Marian Hyman. 1992. 97.50 (*1-55938-332-1*) Jai Pr.

***Advances in Analytical Methods in Modeling of Aerodynamic Flows.** Ed. by J. D. Walker et al. LC 94-27716. (Illus.). 214p. 1994. pap. text ed. 49.95 (*1-56347-093-4*, 93-4(890)) AIAA.

Advances in Analytical Toxicology, Vol. II. R. Baselt. 1989. 54.95 (*0-8151-0522-3*, Yr Bk Med Pubs) Mosby Yr Bk.

Advances in Andean Archaeology. Ed. by David L. Browman. (World Anthropology Ser.). (Illus.). xvi, 580p. 1978. 66.15 (*90-279-7550-7*) Mouton.

Advances in Anesthesia, Vol. 2. Ed. by Robert K. Stoelting. LC 84-644411. 471p. reprint ed. pap. 134.30 (*0-8357-5139-2*, 2029733) Bks Demand.

Advances in Anesthesia, Vol. 4. Advances in Anesthesia Staff. LC 84-644411. 393p. reprint ed. pap. 102.20 (*0-8357-6296-3*, 2034261) Bks Demand.

Advances in Anesthesia, Vol. 8. Stoelting. 1991. 59.95 (*0-8151-8261-9*, Yr Bk Med Pubs) Mosby Yr Bk.

Advances in Anesthesia, Vol. 9. Stoelting. 327p. 1991. 59.95 (*0-8151-8262-7*) Mosby Yr Bk.

Advances in Anesthesia, Vol. 10. Stoelting. 323p. 1992. 59.95 (*0-8151-8275-9*) Mosby Yr Bk.

Advances in Anesthesia, Vol. 11. Carol L. Lake. 350p. 1993. 59.95 (*0-8151-8276-7*, Yr Bk Med Pubs) Mosby Yr Bk.

Advances in Anesthesia, Vol. 12. Carol L. Lake. 350p. 1994. 59.95 (*0-8151-8277-5*, Yr Bk Med Pubs) Mosby Yr Bk.

Advances in Anesthesia, Vol. 13. Carol L. Lake. 350p. 1995. 59.95 (*0-8151-8278-3*, Yr Bk Med Pubs) Mosby Yr Bk.

Advances in Anesthesia, Vol. 14. Carol L. Lake. 350p. 1996. write for info. (*0-8151-5277-9*, Yr Bk Med Pubs) Mosby Yr Bk.

Advances in Anesthesia, Vol. 15. Carol L. Lake. 350p. 1997. write for info. (*0-8151-5278-7*, Yr Bk Med Pubs) Mosby Yr Bk.

Advances in Animal & Comparative Physiology: Proceedings of the 28th International Congress of Physiological Sciences, Budapest, 1980. G. Pethes & V. L. Frenyo. LC 80-41894. (Advances in Physiological Sciences Ser.: Vol. 20). (Illus.). 400p. 1981. 182.00 (*0-08-027341-6*, Pub. by Pergamon Repr UK) Franklin.

Advances in Animal Cell Biology. R. E. Spier et al. (Illus.). 600p. 1989. text ed. 175.00 (*0-407-01499-3*) Buttrwrth-Heinemann.

Advances in Animal Cell Technology: Cell Engineering, Evaluation & Exploitation. Ed. by R. G. Spier & W. B. Hennessen. (Developments in Biological Standardization Ser.: Vol. 66). (Illus.). xii, 586p. 1987. pap. 200.00 (*3-8055-4556-8*) S Karger.

Advances in Animal Welfare Science 1984. Michael A. Fox. Ed. by Linda D. Mickley. 1985. lib. bdg. 97.50 (*0-89838-699-3*) Kluwer Ac.

Advances in Animal Welfare Science 1985. Ed. by M. W. Fox & Linda D. Mickley. 1986. lib. bdg. 109.00 (*0-89838-776-0*) Kluwer Ac.

Advances in Animal Welfare Science 1986-87. Ed. by M. W. Fox & Linda D. Mickley. (C). 1987. lib. bdg. 128.00 (*0-89838-889-9*) Kluwer Ac.

Advances in Anti-Rheumatic Therapy. Rainsford. 1994. write for info. (*0-8493-4937-0*) CRC Pr.

Advances in Antineoplastic Agent Design, Vol. 1. Ed. by Wayne K. Anderson. 1992. 90.25 (*1-55938-154-X*) Jai Pr.

Advances in Antiviral Agent Design, Vol. 1. Ed. by Erik De Clercq. 1991. 90.25 (*1-55938-155-8*) Jai Pr.

Advances in Applied Biology, Vol. 5. Ed. by Tom H. Coaker. LC 76-1065. (Serial Publication Ser.). 1980. text ed. 174.00 (*0-12-040905-4*) Acad Pr.

Advances in Applied Biology, Vol. 6. Ed. by Tom H. Coaker. LC 76-1065. (Serial Publication Ser.). 332p. 1981. text ed. 174.00 (*0-12-040906-2*) Acad Pr.

Advances in Applied Biology, Vol. 7. Ed. by Tom H. Coaker. (Serial Publication Ser.). 1983. text ed. 174.00 (*0-12-040907-0*) Acad Pr.

Advances in Applied Biology, Vol. 8 & 9. Ed. by Tom H. Coaker. (Serial Publication Ser.). 1983. text ed. 174.00 (*0-12-040908-9*) Acad Pr.

Advances in Applied Biology, Vol. 10. Ed. by Tom H. Coaker. (Serial Publication Ser.). 1984. text ed. 174.00 (*0-12-040910-0*) Acad Pr.

Advances in Applied Business Strategy, Vol. 1. Ed. by Robert B. Lamb. 1984. 73.25 (*0-89232-402-3*) Jai Pr.

Advances in Applied Business Strategy, Vol. 2. Ed. by Robert B. Lamb. 1991. 73.25 (*0-89232-576-3*) Jai Pr.

Advances in Applied Developmental Psychology, Vol. 1. Ed. by Irving E. Sigel. (Advances in Applied Developmental Psychology Ser.). 224p. 1985. text ed. 59.50 (*0-89391-090-2*) Ablex Pub.

***Advances in Applied Developmental Psychology Coming Home to Preschool: The Sociocultural Context of Early Education.** Irving E. Sigel et al. 432p. (Orig.). 1993. 65.00 (*0-89391-875-X*) Ablex Pub.

***Advances in Applied Developmental Psychology Vol. 10: Sibling Relationships: Their Causes & Consequences.** Rand D. Conger et al. Ed. by Gene H. Brody. (Advances in Applied Developmental Psychology Ser.). 1995. write for info. (*1-56750-180-X*); pap. write for info. (*1-56750-181-8*) Ablex Pub.

Advances in Applied Lipid Research, Vol. 1. Ed. by Fred B. Padley. 1991. 90.25 (*1-55938-317-8*) Jai Pr.

Advances in Applied Mathematics & Mechanics in China, Vol. 2. Chien Weizang. (International Academic Publishers Ser.). (Illus.). 350p. 1990. 86.00 (*0-08-036975-8*, Pergamon Pr) Elsevier.

An Asterisk (*) at the beginning of an entry indicates that the title is appearing in BIP for the first time.

An Asterisk (*) at the beginning of an entry indicates that the title is appearing in BIP for the first time.

81

A

Advances in Biochemical Engineering-Biotechology: Bioprocesses & Applied Enzymology, Vol. 42. Ed. by A. Fiechter & J. Reiser. (Illus.). 232p. 1990. 118.00 (0-387-52793-1) Spr-Verlag.

Advances in Biochemistry & Biology of Membranes, Vol. 1. Ed. by Alan M. Tartakoff. 1991. 90.25 (1-55938-344-5) Jai Pr.

Advances in Bioclimatology, Vol. 1. R. L. Desjardins et al. Ed. by G. Stanhill et al. (Illus.). x, 157p. 1992. 89.00 (0-387-53843-7) Spr-Verlag.

Advances in Bioclimatology: Vol. 3. Ed. by G. Stanhill et al. (Illus.). 1994. 116.00 (0-387-56381-4) Spr-Verlag.

Advances in Bioclimatology, Vol. 2: The Bioclimatology of Frost - Its Occurrence, Impact & Protection. J. D. Kalma et al. Ed. by G. Stanhill et al. (Illus.). 160p. 1992. 89.00 (0-387-53855-0) Spr-Verlag.

***Advances in Bioengineering: 1994 International Mechanical Engineering Congress & Exposition, Chicago, Illinois - November 6-11, 1994.** (BED Ser.: Vol. 28). 480p. 1994. 110.00 (0-7918-1430-0, G00925) ASME.

Advances in Bioengineering, 1976: Presented at the Winter Meeting of the American Society of Mechanical Engineers, New York, N. Y., Dec. 5-10, 1976. American Society of Mechanical Engineers Staff. Ed. by Charles R. Smith. (Illus.). 48p. reprint ed. pap. 25.00 (0-8357-5141-4, 2016867) Bks Demand.

Advances in Bioengineering, 1979: Papers Presented at the Winter Annual Meeting of the American Society of Mechanical Engineers, New York, New York, December 2-7, 1979. American Society of Mechanical Engineers Staff. Ed. by Michael K. Wells. LC 74-81161. (Illus.). 197p. reprint ed. pap. 56.20 (0-8357-2857-9, 2039092) Bks Demand.

Advances in Bioengineering, 1981: Presented at the Winter Annual Meeting of the American Society of Mechanical Engineers, Washington, D.C., November 15-20, 1981. American Society of Mechanical Engineers Staff. Ed. by David C. Viano. LC 74-81161. (Illus.). 240p. reprint ed. pap. 68.40 (0-8357-2826-9, 2039062) Bks Demand.

Advances in Bioengineering, 1982: Presented at the Winter Annual Meeting of the American Society of Mechanical Engineers, Phoenix, Arizona, November 14-19, 1982. American Society of Mechanical Engineers Staff. Ed. by Lawrence Thibault. LC 74-81161. (Illus.). 186p. reprint ed. pap. 53.10 (0-8357-2816-1, 2039055) Bks Demand.

Advances in Bioengineering, 1983: Presented at the Winter Annual Meeting of the American Society of Mechanical Engineers, Boston, MA, November 13-18, 1983. American Society of Mechanical Engineers Staff. Ed. by Donald L. Bartel. LC 74-81161. 162p. reprint ed. pap. 46.20 (0-8357-8690-0, 2033655) Bks Demand.

Advances in Bioengineering 1993. Ed. by J. M. Tarbell. LC 74-81161. (BED Ser.: Vol. 26). 658p. Date not set. pap. 90.00 (0-7918-1031-3) ASME.

Advances in Bioheat & Mass Transfer 1993. Ed. by R. B. Roemer. LC 93-73599. (HTD Ser.: Vol. 268). 145p. Date not set. pap. 47.50 (0-7918-1047-X) ASME.

Advances in Biological & Medical Physics, 17 vols. Incl. Vol. 6. Ed. by Cornelius A. Tobias et al. 1959. (0-12-005206-7); Vol. 7. Ed. by John H. Lawrence & J. G. Hamilton. 1960. (0-12-005207-5); Vol. 8. Ed. by John H. Lawrence & J. G. Hamilton. 1963. (0-12-005208-3); Vol. 9. Ed. by John H. Lawrence et al. 1964. (0-12-005209-1); Vol. 10. Ed. by John H. Lawrence & J. G. Hamilton. 1965. (0-12-005210-5); Vol. 11. Ed. by John H. Lawrence & J. G. Hamilton. 1967. (0-12-005211-3); Vol. 12. Ed. by John H. Lawrence & J. G. Hamilton. 1968. (0-12-005212-1); Vol. 13. Ed. by John H. Lawrence & J. G. Hamilton. 1971. (0-12-005213-X); Vol. 14. Ed. by John H. Lawrence & J. G. Hamilton. 1973. (0-12-005214-8); Vol. 15. Ed. by John H. Lawrence & J. G. Hamilton. 1974. (0-12-005215-6); Vol. 16. Ed. by John H. Lawrence & J. G. Hamilton. 1978. 85.00 (0-12-005216-4); write for info. (0-318-50161-9) Acad Pr.

Advances in Biological Heat & Mass Transfer - 1992. Ed. by J. J. McGrath. (HTD Ser.: Vol. 231). 152p. 1992. 45.00 (0-7918-1111-5, G00755) ASME.

Advances in Biological Treatment of Lignocellulosic Materials: Proceedings of a Workshop, Lisbon, Portugal, 25-27 Oct. 1989. Ed. by M. P. Coughlan & M. T. Collaco. 360p. 1990. 104.50 (1-85166-542-0) Elsevier.

Advances in Biological Waste Treatment: Proceedings of Third Conference of Biological Waste Treatment, Manhattan, April 1960. W. Wesley Eckenfelder & J. McCabe. LC 61-10913. 1963. 180.00 (0-08-010769-9, Pub. by Pergamon Repr UK) Franklin.

Advances in Biology of Skin, Vols. 3 & 4. W. Montagna et al. Incl. Vol. 4. Sebaceous Glands. 1963. 116.00 (0-08-009945-9); write for info. (0-318-55120-9, Pub. by Pergamon Repr UK) Franklin.

Advances in Biomagnetic Separation. Ed. by Mathias Uhlen & Erik Hornes. (Illus.). 200p. 1994. pap. text ed. 19.00 (1-881299-01-5) Eaton Pub Co.

Advances in Biomagnetism. Ed. by Samuel J. Williamson et al. (Illus.). 790p. 1989. pap. 145.00 (0-306-43483-0, Plenum Pr) Plenum.

Advances in Biomaterials I. Ed. by Stuart Lee. LC 86-72347. 292p. 1987. 29.00 (0-87762-504-2) Technomic.

Advances in Biomedical Alcohol Research: Proceedings of the Fifth ISBRA-RSA Congress, Toronto, Canada, 17-22 June 1990. Ed. by Harold Kalant et al. 530p. 1991. 125.00 (0-08-040828-1, Pergamon Pr) Elsevier.

Advances in Biomedical Engineering, 2 pts., Pt. 1. Ed. by David O. Cooney. LC 80-10862. (Biomedical Engineering & Instrumentation Ser.: No. 6). (Illus.). 358p. reprint ed. pap. 96.70 (0-7837-0844-0, 2041157) Bks Demand.

Advances in Biomedical Engineering, 2 pts., Pt. 2. Ed. by David O. Cooney. LC 80-10862. (Biomedical Engineering & Instrumentation Ser.: No. 6). (Illus.). 366p. reprint ed. pap. 104.40 (0-7837-0845-9) Bks Demand.

Advances in Biomedical Engineering: Results of the 4th EC Medical & Health Research Programme (1987-1991) Ed. by J. E. Beneken & V. Thevin. LC 92-75336. (Studies in Health Technology & Informatics: Vol. 7). 374p. 1993. 130.00 (90-5199-119-3, Pub. by IOS Pr NE) IOS Press.

Advances in Biomedical Imaging, Vol. 1. Ed. by Dov Jaron & Oleh Tretiak. 1991. 90.25 (1-55938-345-3) Jai Pr.

Advances in Biomedical Measurement. Ed. by Ewart R. Carson et al. LC 88-12533. (Illus.). 512p. 1988. 125.00 (0-306-42923-3, Plenum Pr) Plenum.

Advances in Biomedical Polymers. Ed. by Charles G. Gebelein. LC 86-25415. (Polymer Science & Technology Ser.: Vol. 35). 416p. 1987. 89.50 (0-306-42467-3, Plenum Pr) Plenum.

Advances in Biomolecular Simulations. Ed. by Richard Lavery et al. LC 91-58106. (Conference Proceeding Ser.: No. 239). (Illus.). 392p. 1992. lib. bdg. 85.00 (0-88318-940-2) Am Inst Physics.

Advances in Biophysical Chemistry, Vol. 1. Ed. by C. Allen Bush. 247p. 1990. 90.25 (1-55938-159-0) Jai Pr.

Advances in Biophysical Chemistry, Vol. 2. Ed. by C. Allen Bush. 1991. 90.25 (1-55938-318-6) Jai Pr.

***Advances in Bioprocess Engineering.** Ed. by E. Galindo & O. T. Ramirez. LC 94-30302. 541p. (C). 1994. lib. bdg. 260.00 (0-7923-3072-2) Kluwer Ac.

Advances in Biosensors, Vol. 1. Ed. by A. P. Turner. 296p. 1991. 90.25 (1-55938-240-6) Jai Pr.

Advances in Biosensors, Vol. 2. Ed. by A. P. Turner. 296p. 1992. 90.25 (1-55938-270-8) Jai Pr.

Advances in Biotechnology & Bioengineering, Vol. 1. Ed. by D. A. Wase. 1992. 90.25 (1-55938-346-1) Jai Pr.

Advances in Body Composition Assessment. Timothy G. Lohman. LC 92-1476. (Current Issues in Exercise Science Ser.: Monograph No. 3). (Illus.). 160p. 1992. pap. 19.00x (0-87322-327-6, BLOH0327) Human Kinetics.

Advances in Bond Analysis & Portfolio Strategies. Frank J. Fabozzi. 300p. 1987. 65.00 (0-917253-62-0) Probus Pub Co.

Advances in Bone Marrow Purging & Processing: Proceedings of the Fourth International Symposium on Advances in Bone Marrow Purging & Processing Research. Ed. by Adrian P. Gee et al. LC 94-20805. (Progress in Clinical & Biological Research Ser.: Vol. 389). 1994. text ed. 175.00 (0-471-01453-2, Wiley-Liss) Wiley.

Advances in Bone Marrow Purging & Processing: Proceedings of the Third International Symposium on Bone Marrow Purging & Processing, Held in San Diego, California, October 1991. Diana A. Worthington-White et al. Ed. by Adrian P. Gee & Samuel Gross. LC 92-18106. (Progress in Clincial & Biological Research Ser.: Vol. 377). 600p. 1992. text ed. 194.00 (0-471-58844-X, Wiley-Liss) Wiley.

Advances in Boron & the Boranes: A Volume in Honor of Anton B. Burg. Ed. by Joel F. Liebman et al. LC 87-21705. (Molecular Structure & Energetics Ser.). 547p. 1988. lib. bdg. 95.00 (0-89573-272-6) VCH Pubs.

Advances in Botanical Research, Vol. 5. Ed. by R. D. Preston & W. H. Woolhouse. (Serial Publication Ser.). 1978. text ed. 174.00 (0-12-005905-3) Acad Pr.

Advances in Botanical Research, Vol. 7. Ed. by Harold W. Woolhouse. LC 62-21144. (Serial Publication Ser.). 1980. text ed. 174.00 (0-12-005907-X) Acad Pr.

Advances in Botanical Research, Vol. 8 & 9. Ed. by Harold W. Woolhouse. (Serial Publication Ser.). 1981. text ed. 174.00 (0-12-005908-8) Acad Pr.

Advances in Botanical Research, Vol. 8 & 9. Ed. by Harold W. Woolhouse. (Serial Publication Ser.). 1982. text ed. 174.00 (0-12-005909-6) Acad Pr.

Advances in Botanical Research, Vol. 10. Ed. by Harold W. Woolhouse. (Serial Publication Ser.). 320p. 1983. text ed. 174.00 (0-12-005910-X) Acad Pr.

Advances in Botanical Research, Vol. 11. Ed. by J. A. Callow & Harold W. Woolhouse. (Serial Publication Ser.). 1985. text ed. 140.00 (0-12-005911-8) Acad Pr.

Advances in Botanical Research, Vol. 12. Ed. by J. A. Callow. (Serial Publication Ser.). 304p. 1986. text ed. 140.00 (0-12-005912-6) Acad Pr.

Advances in Botanical Research, Vol. 13. Ed. by R. A. Preston. (Serial Publication Ser.). 224p. 1987. text ed. 107.00 (0-12-005913-4) Acad Pr.

Advances in Botanical Research, Vol. 14. Ed. by J. A. Callow. (Serial Publication Ser.). 198p. 1988. text ed. 105.00 (0-12-005914-2) Acad Pr.

Advances in Botanical Research, Vol. 15. Ed. by J. A. Callow. (Serial Publication Ser.). 211p. 1989. text ed. 105.00 (0-12-005915-0) Acad Pr.

Advances in Botanical Research, Vol. 16. Ed. by J. A. Callow. (Serial Publication Ser.). 273p. 1989. text ed. 116.00 (0-12-005916-9) Acad Pr.

Advances in Botanical Research, Vol. 17. Ed. by J. A. Callow. (Serial Publication Ser.). 303p. 1990. text ed. 132.00 (0-12-005917-7) Acad Pr.

Advances in Botanical Research, Vol. 18. Ed. by J. A. Callow. (Illus.). 327p. 1991. text ed. 83.00 (0-12-005918-5) Acad Pr.

Advances in Botanical Research, Vol. 19. Ed. by J. A. Callow. (Illus.). 344p. 1993. text ed. 98.00 (0-12-005919-3) Acad Pr.

Advances in Botanical Research, Vol. 20. Ed. by J. Callow. (Illus.). 256p. 1994. text ed. 82.50 (0-12-005920-7) Acad Pr.

Advances in Botanical Research, Vols. 1-3. Incl. Vol. 3. 1970. 65.00 (0-12-005903-7); (Serial Publication Ser.). write for info. (0-318-50162-7) Acad Pr.

***Advances in Botanical Research Incorporating Advances in Plant Pathology, Vol. 21.** Ed. by J. A. Callow et al. (Illus.). 250p. 1995. boxed write for info. (0-12-005921-5) Acad Pr.

Advances in Boundary Element Methods for Fracture Mechanics. Ed. by M. H. Aliabadi & C. A. Brebbia. LC 92-70559. (Computational Engineering Ser.). 304p. 1993. 166.00 (0-945824-85-8) Computational Mech MA.

Advances in Boundary Element Techniques. Ed. by James H. Kane et al. LC 92-31541. (Computational Mechanics Ser.). 1993. 145.00 (0-387-55921-3) Spr-Verlag.

***Advances in Boundary Elements, 3 vols.** Ed. by C. A. Brebbia & J. J. Connor. Incl. Vol. 1. Computations & Fundamentals. LC 89-61999. 294p. 1989. 107.00 (0-945824-10-6); Vol. 2. Field & Field Flow Solutions. LC 89-61999. 494p. 1989. 107.00 (0-945824-11-4); Vol. 3. Stress Analysis. abr. ed. LC 89-61999. 460p. 1989. 107.00 (0-945824-12-2); LC 89-61999. (BEM Ser.: Vol. 11). 265.00 (1-85312-027-8) Computational Mech MA.

Advances in Brain Resuscitation. Ed. by H. Takeshita et al. (Illus.). 344p. 1991. 129.00 (0-387-70067-6) Spr-Verlag.

Advances in Breast Cancer Detection. Ed. by S. Brunner et al. (Recent Results in Cancer Research Ser.: Vol. 119). 208p. 1990. 90.00 (0-387-52089-9) Spr-Verlag.

Advances in Brucellosis Research. Ed. by L. Garry Adams. (Illus.). 542p. 1990. 10.00x (0-89096-447-5) Tex A&M Univ Pr.

Advances in Bryology: Publication of the International Association of Bryologists. Ed. by Norton G. Miller. (Bryophyte Ultrastructure Ser.: Vol. 3). 281p. 1989. text ed. 80.00 (3-443-52001-4, Pub. by Gebrueder Borntraeger GW) Lubrecht & Cramer.

Advances in Bryology: 1984, Vol. 2. Ed. by W. Schultze-Motel. (Illus.). 224p. 1985. lib. bdg. 56.00 (0-685-42851-6) Lubrecht & Cramer.

Advances in Bryology, Vol. 4: Bryophyte Systematics. Ed. by N. G. Miller. (Illus.). 264p. 1991. pap. 112.00 (3-443-52002-2, Pub. by Cramer-Borntraeger GW) Lubrecht & Cramer.

Advances in Business Financial Management. Philip L. Cooley. 480p. (C). 1990. pap. text ed. 34.00 (0-03-009943-9) Dryden Pr.

Advances in Business Marketing, Vol. 1. Ed. by Arch G. Woodside. 280p. 1986. 73.25 (0-89232-579-8) Jai Pr.

Advances in Business Marketing, Vol. 2. Arch G. Woodside. 1987. 73.25 (0-89232-820-7) Jai Pr.

Advances in Business Marketing, Vol. 3. Ed. by Arch G. Woodside. 1988. 73.25 (0-89232-914-9) Jai Pr.

Advances in CAD-CAM: Proceedings of the International IFIP-IFAC Conference on Programming Research & Operations Logistics in Advanced Manufacturing Technology, PROLOMAT 82, 5th, Leningrad, U. S. S. R., May 16-18, 1982. Ed. by T. M. Ellis & O. I. Semenkov. xviii, 720p. 1983. 92.50 (0-444-86549-7, I-35-83, North Holland) Elsevier.

Advances in CAD-CAM Workstations: Case Studies. Ed. by Peter C. Wang. 1986. lib. bdg. 77.50 (0-89838-206-8) Kluwer Ac.

Advances in Cancer Chemotherapy, Vol. 1: 1979. Ed. by Andre Rosowsky. LC 79-643464. (Illus.). 309p. reprint ed. pap. 88.10 (0-7837-0796-7, 2041110) Bks Demand.

***Advances in Cancer Research.** Ed. by George F. Woude & George Klein. (Illus.). 326p. 1995. boxed write for info. (0-12-006667-X) Acad Pr.

Advances in Cancer Research, Vol. 46. Ed. by George Klein & Sidney Weinhouse. (Serial Publication Ser.). 288p. 1986. text ed. 106.00 (0-12-006646-7) Acad Pr.

Advances in Cancer Research, Vol. 47. Ed. by George Klein & Sidney Weinhouse. (Serial Publication Ser.). 360p. 1986. text ed. 106.00 (0-12-006647-5) Acad Pr.

Advances in Cancer Research, Vol. 48. Ed. by George Klein & Sidney Weinhouse. (Serial Publication Ser.). 373p. 1987. text ed. 106.00 (0-12-006648-3) Acad Pr.

Advances in Cancer Research, Vol. 49. Ed. by George Klein & Sidney Weinhouse. (Serial Publication Ser.). 417p. 1987. text ed. 126.00 (0-12-006649-1) Acad Pr.

Advances in Cancer Research, Vol. 50. Ed. by George Klein & Sidney Weinhouse. (Serial Publication Ser.). 329p. 1988. text ed. 92.00 (0-12-006650-5) Acad Pr.

Advances in Cancer Research, Vol. 51. Ed. by George Klein & Sidney Weinhouse. (Serial Publication Ser.). 437p. 1988. text ed. 127.00 (0-12-006651-3) Acad Pr.

Advances in Cancer Research, Vol. 52. Ed. by George F. Vande Woude & George Klein. (Serial Publication Ser.). 450p. 1989. text ed. 104.00 (0-12-006652-1) Acad Pr.

Advances in Cancer Research, Vol. 53. Ed. by George F. Van de Woude & George Klein. (Serial Publication Ser.). 339p. 1989. text ed. 96.00 (0-12-006653-X) Acad Pr.

Advances in Cancer Research, Vol. 54. Ed. by George F. Vande Woude & George Klein. (Serial Publication Ser.). 341p. 1990. text ed. 92.00 (0-12-006654-8) Acad Pr.

Advances in Cancer Research, Vol. 55. Ed. by George F. Vande Woude & George Klein. (Serial Publication Ser.). 325p. 1990. text ed. 92.00 (0-12-006655-6) Acad Pr.

Advances in Cancer Research, Vol. 56. Ed. by George F. Woude & George Klein. 372p. 1991. text ed. 87.00 (0-12-006656-4) Acad Pr.

Advances in Cancer Research, Vol. 57. Ed. by George F. Vande Woude & George Klein. (Illus.). 484p. 1991. text ed. 94.00 (0-12-006657-2) Acad Pr.

Advances in Cancer Research, Vol. 58. Ed. by George F. Vande Woude & George Klein. (Illus.). 224p. 1992. text ed. 69.95 (0-12-006658-0) Acad Pr.

Advances in Cancer Research, Vol. 59. Ed. by George F. Vande Woude & George Klein. (Illus.). 341p. 1992. text ed. 75.00 (0-12-006659-9) Acad Pr.

Advances in Cancer Research, Vol. 60. Ed. by George F. Vande Woude & George Klein. (Illus.). 312p. 1992. text ed. 70.00 (0-12-006660-2) Acad Pr.

Advances in Cancer Research, Vol. 61. Ed. by George F. Vande Woude & George Klein. (Illus.). 246p. 1993. text ed. 75.00 (0-12-006661-0) Acad Pr.

Advances in Cancer Research, Vol. 62. Ed. by George F. Vande Woude & George Klein. (Illus.). 503p. 1993. text ed. 69.00 (0-12-006662-9) Acad Pr.

Advances in Cancer Research, Vol. 63. Ed. by George F. Vandewoude & George Klein. (Illus.). 357p. 1994. text ed. 79.00 (0-12-006663-7) Acad Pr.

Advances in Cancer Research, Vol. 64. Ed. by George F. Vande Woude & George Klein. (Illus.). 305p. 1994. text ed. 75.00 (0-12-006664-5) Acad Pr.

Advances in Cancer Research, Vol. 65. Ed. by George F. Vande Woude & George Klein. (Illus.). 235p. 1994. text ed. 69.00 (0-12-006665-3) Acad Pr.

Advances in Cancer Research, Vols. 1-18. Ed. by Jesse P. Greenstein & Alexander Haddow. Incl. Vol. 9. 1965. 80.00 (0-12-006609-2); Vol. 11. 1969. 80.00 (0-12-006611-4); Vol. 16. 1972. 75.00 (0-12-006616-5); (Serial Publication Ser.). write for info. (0-318-50164-3) Acad Pr.

Advances in Cancer Research, Vols. 19-23, & 25. Incl. Vol. 21. 1975. 80.00 (0-12-006621-1); (Serial Publication Ser.). write for info. (0-318-50163-5) Acad Pr.

***Advances in Cancer Research Vol. 66, Vol. 66.** Ed. by George F. Vande Woude & George Klein. (Illus.). 355p. 1995. boxed 79.00 (0-12-006666-1) Acad Pr.

Advances in Carbanion Chemistry, Vol. 1. Ed. by Victor A. Snieckus. 1991. 90.25 (0-89232-859-2) Jai Pr.

Advances in Carbocation Chemistry, Vol. 1. Ed. by Xavier Creary. 1989. 90.25 (0-89232-860-6) Jai Pr.

Advances in Carbocation Chemistry, Vol. 2. Ed. by Xavier Creary. 1991. 90.25 (0-89232-952-1) Jai Pr.

Advances in Carbohydrate Analysis, Vol. 1. Ed. by Charles A. White. 1991. 90.25 (0-685-74350-0) Jai Pr.

Advances in Carbohydrate Analysis, Vol. 2. Ed. by Charles A. White. 1992. 90.25 (1-55938-266-X) Jai Pr.

Advances in Carbohydrate Chemistry, Vols. 1-29. Incl. Vol. 5. Ed. by C. S. Hudson et al. 1950. (0-12-007205-X); Vol. 7. Ed. by C. S. Hudson et al. 1952. (0-12-007207-6); Vol. 8. Ed. by C. S. Hudson et al. 1953. (0-12-007208-4); Vol. 13. Ed. by Ward Pigman & Melville L. Wolfrom. 1958. (0-12-007213-0); Vol. 15. Ed. by Ward Pigman & Melville L. Wolfrom. 1961. (0-12-007215-7); Vol. 19. Ed. by Ward Pigman & Melville L. Wolfrom. 1964. (0-12-007219-X); Vol. 32. 1976. 90.00 (0-12-007232-7); write for info. (0-318-50165-1) Acad Pr.

Advances in Carbohydrate Chemistry, Vols. 20-24. Incl. Vol. 5. Ed. by C. S. Hudson et al. 1950. (0-12-007205-X); Vol. 7. Ed. by C. S. Hudson et al. 1952. (0-12-007207-6); Vol. 8. Ed. by C. S. Hudson et al. 1953. (0-12-007208-4); Vol. 13. Ed. by Ward Pigman & Melville L. Wolfrom. 1958. (0-12-007213-0); Vol. 15. Ed. by Ward Pigman & Melville L. Wolfrom. 1961. (0-12-007215-7); Vol. 19. Ed. by Ward Pigman & Melville L. Wolfrom. 1964. (0-12-007219-X); Vol. 32. 1976. 90.00 (0-12-007232-7); write for info. (0-318-50166-X) Acad Pr.

Advances in Carbohydrate Chemistry, Vols. 30-32. Incl. Vol. 5. Ed. by C. S. Hudson et al. 1950. (0-12-007205-X); Vol. 7. Ed. by C. S. Hudson et al. 1952. (0-12-007207-6); Vol. 8. Ed. by C. S. Hudson et al. 1953. (0-12-007208-4); Vol. 13. Ed. by Ward Pigman & Melville L. Wolfrom. 1958. (0-12-007213-0); Vol. 15. Ed. by Ward Pigman & Melville L. Wolfrom. 1961. (0-12-007215-7); Vol. 19. Ed. by Ward Pigman & Melville L. Wolfrom. 1964. (0-12-007219-X); Vol. 32. 1976. 90.00 (0-12-007232-7); write for info. (0-318-50167-8) Acad Pr.

Advances in Carbohydrate Chemistry & Biochemistry, Vol. 40. Ed. by R. Stuart Tipson & Derek Horton. (Serial Publication Ser.). 402p. 1982. text ed. 163.00 (0-12-007240-8) Acad Pr.

Advances in Carbohydrate Chemistry & Biochemistry, Vol. 41. Ed. by R. Stuart Tipson & Derek Horton. (Serial Publication Ser.). 1983. text ed. 151.00 (0-12-007241-6) Acad Pr.

Advances in Carbohydrate Chemistry & Biochemistry, Vol. 42. Ed. by Ward Pigman & Melville L. Wolfrom. (Serial Publication Ser.). 1984. text ed. 139.00 (0-12-007242-4) Acad Pr.

Advances in Carbohydrate Chemistry & Biochemistry, Vol. 44. Ed. by R. Stuart Tipson & Derek Horton. (Serial Publication Ser.). 438p. 1987. text ed. 128.00 (0-12-007244-0) Acad Pr.

Advances in Carbohydrate Chemistry & Biochemistry, Vol. 45. Ed. by R. Stuart Tipson & Derek Horton. (Serial Publication Ser.). 326p. 1987. text ed. 128.00 (0-12-007245-9) Acad Pr.

Advances in Carbohydrate Chemistry & Biochemistry, Vol. 46. Ed. by R. Stuart Tipson & Derek Horton. (Serial Publication Ser.). 344p. 1988. text ed. 115.00 (0-12-007246-7) Acad Pr.

Advances in Carbohydrate Chemistry & Biochemistry, Vol. 47. Ed. by R. Stuart Tipson & Derek Horton. (Serial Publication Ser.). 432p. 1989. text ed. 120.00 (0-12-007247-5) Acad Pr.

Advances in Carbohydrate Chemistry & Biochemistry, Vol. 48. Ed. by R. Stuart Tipson & Derek Horton. 423p. 1990. text ed. 116.00 (0-12-007248-3) Acad Pr.

Advances in Carbohydrate Chemistry & Biochemistry, Vol. 49. Ed. by Derek Horton. 286p. 1991. text ed. 88.00 (0-12-007249-1) Acad Pr.

Advances in Carbohydrate Chemistry & Biochemistry, Vol. 50. Ed. by Derek Horton. (Illus.). 390p. 1994. text ed. 95.00 (0-12-007250-5) Acad Pr.

An Asterisk (*) at the beginning of an entry indicates that the title is appearing in BIP for the first time.

A

A

Advances in Chromatography, Vol. 32. Ed. by J. Calvin Giddings et al. 296p. 1991. 165.00 (*0-8247-8563-0*) Dekker.
Advances in Chromatography, Vol. 34. Ed. by Brown & Grushka. 456p. 1994. 165.00 (*0-8247-9087-1*) Dekker.
***Advances in Chromatography, Vol. 35.** Ed. by Brown & Gruska. 448p. 1995. 165.00 (*0-8247-9361-7*) Dekker.
Advances in Chromatography, Vol. 30: Selectivity & Retention in Chromatography. J. C. Giddings et al. 280p. 1989. 165.00 (*0-8247-8155-4*) Dekker.
Advances in Chromatography, 1970. A. Zlatkis. 442p. 1970. text ed. 239.00 (*0-677-65390-5*) Gordon & Breach.
Advances in Chromatography, 1971. A. Zlatkis. 286p. 1971. text ed. 180.00 (*0-677-65380-8*) Gordon & Breach.
Advances in Chromosome & Cell Genetics. Ed. by A. K. Sharma & Archana Sharma. LC 85-5496. viii, 312p. 1985. text ed. 162.00 (*2-88124-038-0*) Gordon & Breach.
Advances in Chromotography, Vol. 28. J. C. Giddings et al. 392p. 1989. 165.00 (*0-8247-7878-2*) Dekker.
Advances in Civil Engineering Through Engineering Mechanics: Proceedings of the American Society of Civil Engineers Conference, North Carolina State Univ., May 1977. Ed. by American Society of Civil Engineers Staff. 634p. 1977. pap. 40.00 (*0-87262-087-5*) Am Soc Civil Eng.
Advances in Cladistics: Proceedings of the Second Meeting of the Willi Hennig Society, Vol. 2. Ed. by Norman I. Platnick & Vicki A. Funk. 288p. 1983. text ed. 55.00 (*0-231-05646-X*) Col U Pr.
Advances in Classical Trajectory Methods, Vol. 1. Ed. by William Hase. 1991. 90.25 (*1-55938-162-0*) Jai Pr.
***Advances in Classification Research Vol. 3.** Ed. by Raya Fidel et al. 216p. 1993. pap. 39.50 (*0-938734-79-2*) Learned Info.
Advances in Classification Research, Vol. 1: Proceedings of the 1st ASIS SIG - CR Classification Research Workshop. Ed. by Susanne M. Humphrey & Barbara H. Kwasnik. 1991. 39.50 (*0-938734-53-9*) Learned Info.
Advances in Classification Research, Vol. 2: Proceedings of the 2nd ASIS Sig-CR Classification Research Workshop. Ed. by Barbara H. Kwasnik & Raya Fidel. 227p. 1992. pap. 39.50 (*0-938734-57-9*) Learned Info.
***Advances in Clinical Andrology.** Ed. by Christopher L. Barratt & I. D. Cooke. (C). 1988. lib. bdg. 63.00 (*0-7462-0034-X*) Kluwer Ac.
Advances in Clinical Chemistry, Vol. 23. Ed. by A. L. Latner & M. K. Schwartz. (Serial Publication Ser.). 1983. text ed. 149.00 (*0-12-010323-0*) Acad Pr.
Advances in Clinical Chemistry, Vol. 25. Ed. by Herbert E. Speigel. (Serial Publication Ser.). 1986. text ed. 116.00 (*0-12-010325-7*) Acad Pr.
Advances in Clinical Chemistry, Vol. 26. Ed. by Herbert E. Speigel. (Serial Publication Ser.). 376p. 1987. text ed. 106.00 (*0-12-010326-5*) Acad Pr.
Advances in Clinical Chemistry, Vol. 27. Ed. by Herbert E. Spiegel. (Serial Publication Ser.). 400p. 1989. text ed. 126.00 (*0-12-010327-3*) Acad Pr.
Advances in Clinical Chemistry, Vol. 28. Ed. by Herbert E. Spiegel. 251p. 1990. text ed. 92.00 (*0-12-010328-1*) Acad Pr.
Advances in Clinical Chemistry, Vol. 29. Ed. by Herbert E. Spiegel. (Illus.). 290p. 1992. text ed. 79.95 (*0-12-010329-X*) Acad Pr.
Advances in Clinical Chemistry, Vol. 30. Ed. by Herbert E. Spiegel. (Illus.). 389p. 1993. text ed. 89.00 (*0-12-010330-3*) Acad Pr.
***Advances in Clinical Chemistry, Vol. 31.** Ed. by Herbert E. Spiegel. (Illus.). 283p. 1994. boxed 85.00 (*0-12-010331-1*) Acad Pr.
Advances in Clinical Chemistry, Vol. 31. Ed. by Herbert E. Spiegel. (Illus.). 283p. 1994. boxed 85.00 (*0-12-010221-8*) Acad Pr.
Advances in Clinical Chemistry, Vols. 1-15. Ed. by Harry Sobotka & C. P. Stewart. Incl. Vol. 1. 1958. 74.50 (*0-12-010301-X*); Vol. 15. 1972. 75.00 (*0-12-010315-X*); (Serial Publication Ser.). write for info. (*0-318-50171-6*) Acad Pr.
Advances in Clinical Child Psychology, Vol. 3. Ed. by Benjamin B. Lahey & Alan E. Kazdin. LC 77-643411. (Illus.). 494p. 1980. 45.00 (*0-306-40374-9*, Plenum Pr) Plenum.
Advances in Clinical Child Psychology, Vol. 4. Ed. by Benjamin B. Lahey & Alan E. Kazdin. LC 77-643411. 380p. 1981. 65.00 (*0-306-40705-1*, Plenum Pr) Plenum.
Advances in Clinical Child Psychology, Vol. 5. Ed. by Benjamin B. Lahey & Alan E. Kazdin. LC 77-643411. 392p. 1982. 65.00 (*0-306-41043-5*, Plenum Pr) Plenum.
Advances in Clinical Child Psychology, Vol. 6. Ed. by Benjamin B. Lahey & Alan E. Kazdin. LC 77-643411. 344p. 1983. 65.00 (*0-306-41330-2*, Plenum Pr) Plenum.
Advances in Clinical Child Psychology, Vol. 7. Ed. by Benjamin B. Lahey & Alan E. Kazdin. LC 77-643411. 368p. 1984. 65.00 (*0-306-41659-X*, Plenum Pr) Plenum.
Advances in Clinical Child Psychology, Vol. 8. Ed. by Benjamin B. Lahey & Alan E. Kazdin. LC 77-643411. 344p. 1985. 65.00 (*0-306-41963-7*, Plenum Pr) Plenum.
Advances in Clinical Child Psychology, Vol. 9. Ed. by Benjamin B. Lahey & Alan E. Kazdin. LC 77-643411. 420p. 1986. 65.00 (*0-306-42241-7*, Plenum Pr) Plenum.
Advances in Clinical Child Psychology, Vol. 10. Ed. by Benjamin B. Lahey & Alan E. Kazdin. LC 77-643411. 378p. 1987. 65.00 (*0-306-42536-X*, Plenum Pr) Plenum.
Advances in Clinical Child Psychology, Vol. 11. Ed. by Benjamin B. Lahey & Alan E. Kazdin. LC 77-643411. (Illus.). 414p. 1988. 69.50 (*0-306-42892-X*, Plenum Pr) Plenum.
Advances in Clinical Child Psychology, Vol. 12. Ed. by Benjamin B. Lahey & Alan E. Kazdin. (Illus.). 275p. 1989. 69.50 (*0-306-43271-4*, Plenum Pr) Plenum.
Advances in Clinical Child Psychology, Vol. 13. Ed. by Benjamin B. Lahey & Alan E. Kazdin. LC 77-643411. (Illus.). 426p. 1990. 69.50 (*0-306-43479-2*, Plenum Pr) Plenum.
Advances in Clinical Child Psychology, Vol. 14. Ed. by Benjamin B. Lahey & Alan E. Kazdin. (Illus.). 346p. 1991. 69.50 (*0-306-43957-3*, Plenum Pr) Plenum.
Advances in Clinical Child Psychology, Vol. 15. Ed. by Thomas H. Ollendick & Ronald J. Prinz. (Illus.). 365p. (C). 1993. 69.50 (*0-306-44273-6*, Plenum Pr) Plenum.
Advances in Clinical Child Psychology, Vol. 16. Ed. by Thomas H. Ollendick & Ronald J. Prinz. 1994. 69.50 (*0-306-44552-2*, Plenum Pr) Plenum.
***Advances in Clinical Child Psychology, Vol. 17.** Ed. by Thomas H. Ollendick & Ronald J. Prinz. LC 77-643411. 406p. 1995. 79.50 (*0-306-44799-1*) Plenum.
Advances in Clinical Child Psychology, Vols. 1 & 2. Incl. Vol. 2. LC 77-643411. 308p. 1979. (*0-306-40105-3*); LC 77-643411. (Illus.). 65.00 (*0-685-04069-0*, Plenum Pr) Plenum.
Advances in Clinical Neuropsychology, Vol. 1. Ed. by Gerald Goldstein. LC 84-645578. 198p. 1984. 65.00 (*0-306-41502-X*, Plenum Pr) Plenum.
Advances in Clinical Neuropsychology, Vol. 2. Ed. by Ralph E. Tarter & Gerald Goldstein. LC 84-645578. 248p. 1984. 65.00 (*0-306-41722-7*, Plenum Pr) Plenum.
Advances in Clinical Neuropsychology, Vol. 3. Ed. by Gerald Goldstein & Ralph E. Tarter. LC 84-645578. 436p. 1986. 65.00 (*0-306-42290-5*, Plenum Pr) Plenum.
Advances in Clinical Rehabilitation, Vol. 1. Ed. by Myron Eisenberg & Roy Grzesiak. (Series on Clinical Rehabilitation). 368p. 1987. 36.95 (*0-8261-5060-8*) Springer Pub.
Advances in Clinical Rehabilitation, Vol. 2. Ed. by Myron G. Eisenberg & Roy Grzesiak. (Series on Clinical Rehabilitation). 288p. 1988. 34.95 (*0-8261-5061-6*) Springer Pub.
Advances in Clinical Rehabilitation, Vol. 3. Ed. by M. G. Eisenberg & Roy C. Grzesiak. 336p. 1990. 48.95 (*0-8261-5062-4*) Springer Pub.
Advances in Clinical Social Work Practice. Ed. by Carel B. Germain. LC 85-9208. 266p. 1985. pap. text ed. 20.95 (*0-87101-130-1*) Natl Assn Soc Wkrs.
Advances in Clinical Social Work Research. Ed. by Lynn Videka-Sherman & William J. Reid. LC 90-38698. 440p. 1990. 31.95 (*0-87101-186-7*) Natl Assn Soc Wkrs.
Advances in CNS Drug-Receptor Interactions, Vol. 1. Ed. by Joseph G. Cannon. 1991. 90.25 (*1-55938-163-9*) Jai Pr.
Advances in Coal & Mineral Processing Using Flotation. Ed. by R. R. Klimpel. LC 89-63388. (Illus.). 384p. 1989. pap. 60.00 (*0-87335-087-1*) SMM&E Inc.
***Advances in Coal & Mineral Processing Using Flotation: Proceedings of an Engineering Foundation Conference, Palm Coast, Florida, December 3-8, 1989.** fac. ed. Ed. by Subhash Chander et al. LC 89-63388. (Illus.). 384p. 1989. reprint ed. pap. 109.50 (*0-7837-7854-6*, 2047613) Bks Demand.
Advances in Coal Spectroscopy. Ed. by H. L. Meuzelaar. (Modern Analytical Chemistry Ser.). (Illus.). 408p. 1991. 89.50 (*0-306-43796-1*, Plenum Pr) Plenum.
Advances in Coal Utilization Technology III, Symposium, May 14-18, 1979. (Synthetic Fuels Ser.). 784p. 1979. 60.00 (*0-910091-06-4*) Inst Gas Tech.
Advances in Coal Utilization Technology IV: April 20-24, 1981. 968p. 1981. 75.00 (*0-910091-05-6*) Inst Gas Tech.
Advances in Coastal & Ocean Engineering, Vol. 1. L. F. L. Philip. 300p. 1995. text ed. 86.00 (*981-02-1824-9*) World Scientific Pub.
Advances in Coconut Research & Development: Proceedings of the International Symposium on Coconut Research & Development. M. K. Nair. 780p. (C). 1993. text ed. 118.00 (*1-881570-27-4*) Intl Sci Pub.
Advances in Cognition, Education, & Deafness. Ed. by David S. Martin. LC 91-10693. (Illus.). 457p. 1991. 34.95 (*0-930323-79-3*) Gallaudet Univ Pr.
Advances in Cognitive-Behavioral Research & Therapy, Vol. 1. Ed. by Philip C. Kendall. (Serial Publication Ser.). 321p. 1982. text ed. 116.00 (*0-12-010601-9*) Acad Pr.
Advances in Cognitive-Behavioral Research & Therapy, Vol. 2. Ed. by Philip C. Kendall. (Serial Publication Ser.). 1983. text ed. 116.00 (*0-12-010602-7*) Acad Pr.
Advances in Cognitive-Behavioral Research & Therapy, Vol. 3. Ed. by Philip C. Kendall. (Serial Publication Ser.). 1984. text ed. 116.00 (*0-12-010603-5*) Acad Pr.
Advances in Cognitive-Behavioral Research & Therapy, Vol. 4. Ed. by Philip C. Kendall. 1985. text ed. 119.00 (*0-12-010604-3*) Acad Pr.
Advances in Cognitive-Behavioral Research & Therapy, Vol. 5. Ed. by Philip C. Kendall. (Serial Publication Ser.). 285p. 1986. text ed. 126.00 (*0-12-010605-1*) Acad Pr.
Advances in Cold Rolling Technology. 1985. text ed. 30.00 (*0-904357-79-1*, Pub. by Inst Materials UK) Ashgate Pub Co.
Advances in Colloid Structures: Preparation, Characterization, & Applications. Ed. by Johan Sjoblom et al. (Progress in Colloid & Polymer Science Ser.: Vol. 88). 148p. 1992. 87.00 (*0-387-91409-9*) Spr-Verlag.
Advances in Color Vision. LC 91-68079. (Technical Digest Series, 1992: Vol. 4). 200p. (Orig.). 1992. Postconference. pap. 66.00 (*1-55752-220-0*); Conference. pap. 43.00 (*1-55752-219-7*) Optical Soc.
Advances in Combustion Toxicology, Vol. 1. Ed. by Gordon E. Hartzell. 322p. 1988. 55.00 (*0-87762-590-5*) Technomic.
Advances in Combustion Toxicology, Vol. 2. Ed. by Gordon E. Hartzell. 308p. 1988. 55.00 (*0-87762-591-3*) Technomic.
Advances in Combustion Toxicology, Vol. 3. Ed. by Gordon E. Hartzell. 1991. 75.00 (*0-87762-886-6*) Technomic.
Advances in Communication Systems, 4 vols. 1975. lib. bdg. 95.00 (*0-12-010974-3*) Acad Pr.
Advances in Communication Systems, 4 vols, Vol. 1. 1965. 80.00 (*0-12-010901-8*) Acad Pr.
Advances in Communication Systems, 4 vols, Vol. 2. 1966. 80.00 (*0-12-010902-6*) Acad Pr.
Advances in Communication Systems, 4 vols, Vol. 3. 1968. 80.00 (*0-12-010903-4*) Acad Pr.
Advances in Communications & Signal Processing. Ed. by W. A. Porter & S. C. Kak. (Illus.). 384p. 1989. pap. 63.00 (*0-387-51424-4*, 3308) Spr-Verlag.
Advances in Comparative & Environmental Physiology, Vol. 2. Ed. by R. Gilles et al. (Illus.). 300p. 1988. pap. text ed. 96.00 (*0-387-18829-0*) Spr-Verlag.
Advances in Comparative & Environmental Physiology, Vol. 5. (Illus.). 240p. 1989. 97.00 (*0-387-50825-2*, 2701) Spr-Verlag.
Advances in Comparative & Environmental Physiology, Vol. 7. Ed. by R. Gilles et al. (Illus.). 240p. 1991. 96.00 (*0-387-52896-2*) Spr-Verlag.
Advances in Comparative & Environmental Physiology, Vol. 8. Ed. by R. Gilles et al. (Illus.). 152p. 1991. 65.00 (*0-387-52897-0*) Spr-Verlag.
Advances in Comparative & Environmental Physiology, Vol. 15. Ed. by R. Gilles et al. (Illus.). 147p. 1993. 145.00 (*0-387-55489-0*) Spr-Verlag.
Advances in Comparative & Environmental Physiology: Volume & Osmolality Control in Animal Cells, Vol. 9. Ed. by R. Gilles et al. (Illus.). 260p. 1991. 129.00 (*0-387-53356-7*) Spr-Verlag.
Advances in Comparative & Environmental Physiology Vol. 20. Ed. by R. Gilles et al. (Illus.). viii, 320p. 1994. 199.00 (*0-387-57357-7*) Spr-Verlag.
Advances in Comparative & Environmental Physiology, Vol. 11: Mechanics of Animal Locomotion. Ed. by R. McNeill Alexander et al. (Illus.). 288p. 1992. 119.00 (*0-387-54119-5*) Spr-Verlag.
Advances in Comparative & Environmental Physiology, Vol. 12: Muscle Contraction & Cell Motility: Molecular & Cellular Aspects. Ed. by R. Gilles et al. (Illus.). 270p. (C). 1992. 129.00 (*0-387-54542-5*) Spr-Verlag.
Advances in Comparative & Environmental Physiology, Vol. 13: Blood & Tissue Oxygen Carriers. Ed. by R. Gilles et al. (Illus.). 430p. 1993. 249.00 (*0-387-53657-4*) Spr-Verlag.
Advances in Comparative & Environmental Physiology, Vol. 14: Interaction of Cell Volume & Cell Function. Ed. by R. Gilles et al. (Illus.). 324p. 1993. 234.00 (*0-387-54854-8*) Spr-Verlag.
Advances in Competitive Intelligence. Ed. by John E. Prescott. 228p. (Orig.). 1989. pap. 24.95 (*0-9621241-0-9*) SCIP.
Advances in Composite Materials. Ed. by G. Piatti. (Illus.). 405p. 1978. 128.00 (*0-85334-770-0*, Pub. by Elsevier Applied Sci UK) Elsevier.
Advances in Composite Materials: Proceedings of the Third International Conference on Composite Materials, Paris, France, 26-29 August, 1980, 2 vols., Set. Ed. by A. R. Bunsell et al. LC 80-40997. 2000p. 1980. 373.00 (*0-08-026717-3*, Pub. by Pergamon Repr UK) Franklin.
Advances in Composite Tribology. Ed. by Klaus Friedrich. LC 93-10612. (Composite Materials Ser.: Vol. 8). 1993. Alk. paper. write for info. (*0-444-89079-3*) Elsevier.
Advances in Computational Complexity Theory. Jin-Yi Cai. LC 93-25900. (DIMACS Series in Discrete Mathematics & Theoretical Computer Science: No. 13). 232p. 1993. 84.00 (*0-8218-6597-8*) Am Math.
Advances in Computational Mathematics. H. P. Dikshit & C. A. Micchelli. (Series on Approximations & Decomposition). 336p. 1994. text ed. 95.00 (*981-02-1633-5*) World Scientific Pub.
***Advances in Computational Methods in Fluid Dynamics.** Ed. by K. N. Ghia. (Fluid Engineering Division Conference Ser.: Vol. 196). 421p. 1994. pap. 62.50 (*0-7918-1378-9*) ASME.
Advances in Computer-Aided Bearing Design: Presented at ASME-ASLE Lubrication Conference, October 5-7, 1982, Washington, D.C. ASME-ASLE Lubrication Conference Staff. Ed. by C. M. Chang & F. E. Kennedy. LC 82-72978. (Illus.). 156p. reprint ed. pap. 44.50 (*0-8357-2828-5*, 2039064) Bks Demand.
***Advances in Computer-Aided Engineering.** Ed. by Delft University Staff. 286p. (Orig.). 1994. pap. 67.50x (*90-407-1017-1*, Pub. by Delft U Pr NE) Coronet Bks.
***Advances in Computer-Aided Engineering (CAE) of Polymer Processing: 1994 International Mechanical Engineering Congress & Exposition, Chicago, Illinois - November 6-11, 1994.** (MD - HTD Ser.: Vol. 49, Vol. 283). 384p. 1994. 100.00 (*0-7918-1390-8*, G00885) ASME.
Advances in Computer Aided Engineering Design, Vol. 2. Ed. by Ibrahim N. Hajj. 1988. 73.25 (*0-89232-457-0*) Jai Pr.
Advances in Computer-Aided Engineering Design: Computer-Aided Design of VLSI Circuits & Systems, Vol. 1. Ed. by Alberto Sangiovanni-Vincentelli. 1985. 73.25 (*0-89232-400-7*) Jai Pr.
Advances in Computer & Image Processing, Vol. 1. Ed. by Thomas S. Huang. 350p. 1983. 73.25 (*0-89232-280-2*) Jai Pr.
Advances in Computer Architecture. Glenford J. Myers. LC 77-19001. (Illus.). 329p. 1978. pap. 94.70 (*0-7837-3529-4*, 2057865) Bks Demand.
Advances in Computer Architecture. 2nd ed. Glenford J. Myers. LC 81-11374. 545p. 1982. text ed. 139.00 (*0-471-07878-6*) Wiley.
Advances in Computer-Assisted Learning: Selected Proceedings from the CAL 85 Symposium. P. R. Smith. 260p. 1986. 106.00 (*0-08-031813-4*, Pub. by PPL UK) Franklin.
Advances in Computer-Based Human Assessment. Ed. by Peter L. Dann. (C). 1991. lib. bdg. 133.00 (*0-7923-1071-3*) Kluwer Ac.
Advances in Computer Chess, No. 5. Ed. by D. F. Beal. 322p. 1989. 51.50 (*0-444-87159-4*, North Holland) Elsevier.
Advances in Computer Chess: Proceedings of the International Conference, Brunel University, U. K., 1984, No. 4. Ed. by D. F. Beal. (Chess Ser.). (Illus.). 200p. 1986. 39.95 (*0-08-029763-3*, P115, D135, Pub. by PPL UK) Elsevier.
Advances in Computer Chess II. Malcolm R. Clarke. 142p. 1980. 16.00 (*0-85224-377-4*, Pub. by Edinburgh U Pr UK) Col U Pr.
Advances in Computer Chess in 3 Parts: Proceedings of the International Conference on Advances in Computer Chess, London, UK, April, 1981. International Conference on Advances in Computer Chess Staff. Ed. by Malcolm R. Clarke. LC 78-309646. (Chess Ser.). 182p. 1982. 84.00 (*0-08-026898-6*, Pergamon Pr) Elsevier.
Advances in Computer Chess, No. 6. D. F. Beal. (Artificial Intelligence Ser.). 200p. 1991. 47.00 (*0-13-006537-4*, 220501) P-H.
Advances in Computer Communications. Wesley W. Chu. LC 74-77722. (Modern Frontiers in Applied Science Ser.). 505p. reprint ed. pap. 144.00 (*0-8357-5150-3*, 2056082) Bks Demand.
Advances in Computer Graphics Hardware, No. 4. Ed. by R. L. Grimsdale & W. Strafler. (Eurographic Seminars Ser.). (Illus.). viii, 284p. 1991. 98.00 (*0-387-53473-3*) Spr-Verlag.
Advances in Computer Graphics Hardware 1. Ed. by W. Strasser. (Eurographic Seminars Ser.). (Illus.). x, 147p. 1987. 59.00 (*0-387-18222-5*) Spr-Verlag.
Advances in Computer Graphics Hardware 2. Ed. by A. A. Kuijk & W. Strasser. (Eurographic Seminars Ser.). (Illus.). viii, 258p. 1988. 99.00 (*0-387-50109-6*) Spr-Verlag.
Advances in Computer Graphics Hardware 3. Ed. by A. A. Kuijk. (Eurographic Seminars Ser.). (Illus.). viii, 216p. 1991. 79.00 (*0-387-53488-1*) Spr-Verlag.
Advances in Computer Graphics Hardware 5: Rendereing, Ray Tracing & Visualization Systems. Ed. by R. L. Grimsdale et al. (Eurographic Seminars Ser.). 196p. 1992. 69.00 (*0-387-54291-4*) Spr-Verlag.
Advances in Computer Graphics 1. Ed. by G. Enderle et al. (Eurographic Seminars Ser.). x, 514p. 1986. 100.00 (*0-387-13804-8*) Spr-Verlag.
Advances in Computer Graphics 2. Ed. by F. R. Hopgood et al. (Eurographic Seminars, Tutorials & Perspectives in Computer Graphics Ser.). (Illus.). 196p. 1986. 69.00 (*0-387-16910-5*) Spr-Verlag.
Advances in Computer Graphics 3. Ed. by M. M. De Ruitter. (Eurographic Seminars Ser.). (Illus.). vii, 323p. 1988. 89.00 (*0-387-18788-X*) Spr-Verlag.
Advances in Computer Graphics 5. Ed. by W. Purgathofer & J. Schonhut. (Eurographic Seminars Ser.). (Illus.). viii, 221p. 1989. 89.00 (*0-387-51420-1*, 3290) Spr-Verlag.
Advances in Computer Graphics 6. Ed. by Gladys Garcia & I. Herman. (Eurographic Seminars Ser.). 460p. 1991. 117.00 (*0-387-53455-5*) Spr-Verlag.
Advances in Computer Methodology for Management, Vol. 1. Ed. by Roman V. Tuason. 1988. 73.25 (*0-89232-458-9*) Jai Pr.
Advances in Computer Methods for Systematic Biology: Artificial Intelligence, Databases, Computer Vision. Ed. by Renaud Fortuner. LC 92-24949. 584p. 1993. text ed. 65.00 (*0-8018-4492-4*) Johns Hopkins.
Advances in Computer Programming Management, Vol. 1. Ed. by Thomas A. Rullo. LC 81-640183. (Heyden Advances Library in EDP Management). 254p. reprint ed. pap. 72.40 (*0-8357-5151-1*, 2032691) Bks Demand.
Advances in Computer Security Management, Vol. 1. Ed. by Thomas A. Rullo. LC 81-641060. (Heyden Advances Library in EDP Management). 263p. reprint ed. pap. 75.00 (*0-8357-5152-X*, 2032688) Bks Demand.
Advances in Computer Security Management, Vol. 2. Marvin M. Wofsey. (Wiley-Heyden Advances in EDP Management Library). 268p. 1983. text ed. 82.50 (*0-471-26234-X*, Pub. by Wiley Heyden) Wiley.
Advances in Computer System Security, Vol. I. Ed. by Rein Turn. LC 81-65989. (Artech House Telecommunications Library). (Illus.). 413p. (Orig.). reprint ed. pap. 117.80 (*0-8357-5584-3*, 2035215) Bks Demand.
Advances in Computer System Security, Vol. 2. Ed. by Rein Turn. LC 81-65989. (Artech House Telecommunications Library). 360p. (Orig.). reprint ed. pap. 102.60 (*0-7837-2364-4*, 2035215) Bks Demand.
Advances in Computer System Security, Vol. III. Ed. by Rein Turn. (Telecommunications Applications Library). 376p. (Orig.). 1988. text ed. 29.00 (*0-89006-315-X*) Artech Hse.
Advances in Computer Systems Analysis, Vol. 1. Ed. by Len Troncale. 1988. 73.25 (*0-89232-872-X*) Jai Pr.

An Asterisk (*) at the beginning of an entry indicates that the title is appearing in BIP for the first time.

A

***Advances in Cyclic Nucleotide Research: Third International Conference on Cyclic Nucleotides New Orleans, LA, USA, July 17-22, 1977, Vol. 9.** fac. ed. Ed. by William J. George & Louis J. Ignarro. LC 71-181305. (Illus.). 831p. Date not set. pap. 180.00 (*0-7837-7238-6*, 2047062) Bks Demand.

***Advances in Cyclic Nucleotide Research Vol. 3.** fac. ed. Ed. by Paul Greengard & G. Alan Robison. LC 71-181305. (Illus.). 416p. Date not set. pap. 118.60 (*0-7837-7242-4*, 2047062) Bks Demand.

***Advances in Cyclic Nucleotide Research Vol. 4.** fac. ed. Ed. by Paul Greengard & G. Alan Robison. LC 71-181305. (Illus.). 500p. Date not set. pap. 142.50 (*0-7837-7241-6*, 2047062) Bks Demand.

***Advances in Cyclic Nucleotide Research Vol. 6.** Ed. by Paul Greengard & G. Alan Robison. LC 71-181305. (Illus.). 368p. Date not set. pap. 104.90 (*0-7837-7239-4*, 2047062) Bks Demand.

***Advances in Cyclic Nucleotide Research Vol. 13.** Ed. by Paul Greengard & G. Alan Robison. LC 71-181305. (Illus.). 352p. Date not set. pap. 100.40 (*0-7837-7235-1*, 2047062) Bks Demand.

Advances in Cycloaddition, Vol. 1. Ed. by Dennis P. Curran. 208p. 1988. 90.25 (*0-89232-861-4*) Jai Pr.

Advances in Cycloaddition, Vol. 1. Ed. by Charles A. White. 1991. 90.25 (*1-55938-265-1*) Jai Pr.

Advances in Cycloaddition, Vol. 2. Ed. by Dennis P. Curran. 220p. 1990. 90.25 (*0-89232-951-3*) Jai Pr.

Advances in Cycloaddition, Vol. 3. Ed. by Dennis P. Curran. 1991. 90.25 (*1-55938-319-4*) Jai Pr.

Advances in Data Base Management, Vol. 1. Ed. by Thomas A. Rullo. LC 81-640184. (Heyden Advances Library in EDP Management). 223p. reprint ed. pap. 63.60 (*0-8357-5154-6*, 2032687) Bks Demand.

Advances in Data Base Theory, Vol. 1. Ed. by Herve Gallaire et al. LC 81-116229. 440p. 1981. 89.50 (*0-306-40629-2*, Plenum Pr) Plenum.

Advances in Data Base Theory, Vol. 2. Ed. by Herve Gallaire et al. LC 81-116229. 432p. 1984. 89.50 (*0-306-41636-0*, Plenum Pr) Plenum.

Advances in Data Communications Management, Vol. 1. Ed. by Thomas A. Rullo. LC 81-641056. (Heyden Advances Library in EDP Management). 261p. reprint ed. pap. 74.40 (*0-8357-5155-4*, 2032690) Bks Demand.

Advances in Data Processing Management, Vol. 1. Ed. by Thomas A. Rullo. LC 81-640185. (Heyden Advances Library in EDP Management). (Illus.). 218p. reprint ed. pap. 62.20 (*0-8357-5156-2*, 2032686) Bks Demand.

Advances in Database Research: Proceedings of the 4th Australian Database Conference. M. E. Orlowska & M. P. Papazoglou. 388p. 1993. text ed. 116.00 (*981-02-1331-X*) World Scientific Pub.

***Advances in Database Systems.** Ed. by J. Paredaens & L. Tenenbaum. (CISM International Centre for Mechanical Sciences Ser.: Vol. 347). 377p. 1994. pap. 85.00 (*3-211-82614-9*) Spr-Verlag.

Advances in Database Technology - EDBT 1990. Ed. by Francois Bancilhon et al. (Lecture Notes in Computer Science Ser.: Vol. 416). ix, 452p. 1990. pap. 45.10 (*0-387-52291-3*) Spr-Verlag.

Advances in Database Technology - EDBT '88. Ed. by J. William Schmidt et al. (Lecture Notes in Computer Science Ser.: Vol. 303). x, 620p. 1988. pap. 62.00 (*0-387-19074-0*) Spr-Verlag.

Advances in Database Technology - EDBT '92. Ed. by A. Pirotte et al. (Lecture Notes in Computer Science Ser.: Vol. 580). 551p. 1992. pap. 73.00 (*0-387-55270-7*) Spr-Verlag.

Advances in Database Technology - EDBT '94: Proceedings of the Fourth International Conference on Extending Database Technology, Cambridge, UK, March 28-31, 1994. Ed. by Matthias Jarke et al. LC 94-889. (Lecture Notes in Computer Science Ser.: Vol. 779). xi, 406p. 1994. pap. text ed. 54.00 (*0-387-57818-8*) Spr-Verlag.

Advances in Databases: Proceedings of the 11th British National Conference on Databases, BNCOD 11. Keele, UK, July 7-9, 1993. Ed. by M. F. Worboys & A. F. Grundy. (Lecture Notes in Computer Science Ser.: Vol. 696). x, 276p. 1993. pap. 44.00 (*0-387-56921-9*) Spr-Verlag.

Advances in Decision Research: Edited Proceedings of the 11th Conference on Subjective Probability, Utility & Decision Making, Cambridge, UK, Aug. 23-27, 1987. Ed. by Lee R. Beach et al. 330p. 1989. 100.00 (*0-444-87148-9*, North Holland) Elsevier.

Advances in Dental Anthropology. Ed. by Larsen Kelley. 1991. text ed. 149.95 (*0-471-56839-2*) Wiley.

Advances in Dermatology, Vol. 5. Callen. 320p. 1989. 59.95 (*0-8151-1418-4*, Yr Bk Med Pubs) Mosby Yr Bk.

Advances in Dermatology, Vol. 6. Peter W. Callen. 368p. 1990. 59.95 (*0-8151-1419-2*, Yr Bk Med Pubs) Mosby Yr Bk.

Advances in Dermatology, Vol. 7. Callen. 363p. 1991. 59.95 (*0-8151-1390-0*) Mosby Yr Bk.

Advances in Dermatology, Vol. 8. Callen. 385p. 1992. 59.95 (*0-8151-1391-9*) Mosby Yr Bk.

Advances in Dermatology, Vol. 9. Callen. 350p. 1993. 59.95 (*0-8151-1392-7*, Yr Bk Med Pubs) Mosby Yr Bk.

Advances in Dermatology, Vol. 10. Callen. 350p. 1994. 59.95 (*0-8151-1393-5*, Yr Bk Med Pubs) Mosby Yr Bk.

Advances in Dermatology, Vol. 11. Callen. 350p. 1995. 59.95 (*0-8151-1394-3*, Yr Bk Med Pubs) Mosby Yr Bk.

Advances in Dermatology, Vol. 12. Callen. 270p. 1996. 59.95 (*0-8151-1395-1*, Yr Bk Med Pubs) Mosby Yr Bk.

Advances in Descriptive Psychology, Vol. 1. Ed. by Keith Davis. 389p. 1981. 40.00 (*0-89232-179-2*) Descriptive Psych Pr.

Advances in Descriptive Psychology, Vol. 1. Ed. by Keith E. Davis. 370p. 70.00 (*0-9625661-7-9*) Descriptive Psych Pr.

Advances in Descriptive Psychology, Vol. 2. Ed. by Keith E. Davis. 289p. 1982. 70.00 (*0-9625661-6-0*) Descriptive Psych Pr.

Advances in Descriptive Psychology, Vol. 2. Ed. by Keith E. Davis & Thomas O. Mitchell. 289p. 1982. 40.00 (*0-89232-225-X*) Descriptive Psych Pr.

Advances in Descriptive Psychology, Vol. 3. Ed. by Keith E. Davis & Raymond M. Bergner. 311p. 70.00 (*0-9625661-5-2*) Descriptive Psych Pr.

Advances in Descriptive Psychology, Vol. 3. Ed. by Keith E. Davis & Thomas O. Mitchell. 311p. 1983. 40.00 (*0-89232-293-4*) Descriptive Psych Pr.

Advances in Descriptive Psychology, Vol. 4. Ed. by Keith E. Davis & Thomas O. Mitchell. 314p. 1985. 70.00 (*0-9625661-4-4*) Descriptive Psych Pr.

Advances in Descriptive Psychology, Vol. 4. Ed. by Keith E. Davis & Thomas O. Mitchell. 310p. 1985. 40.00 (*0-89232-358-2*) Descriptive Psych Pr.

Advances in Descriptive Psychology, Vol. 5. Ed. by A. O. Putman & K. E. Davis. 320p. 1990. 70.00 (*0-685-68006-1*) Descriptive Psych Pr.

Advances in Descriptive Psychology, Vol. 5. Anthony O. Putnam. Ed. by Keith E. Davis. 320p. 1990. 70.00 (*0-9625661-0-1*) Descriptive Psych Pr.

Advances in Descriptive Psychology, Vol. VI: Clinical Topics: Adolescent-Family Problems, Bulimia, Chronic Mental Illness, & Mania. Ed. by Mary K. Roberts & Raymond M. Bergner. 316p. (C). 1991. 70.00 (*0-9625661-1-X*) Descriptive Psych Pr.

Advances in Desert & Arid Land Technology & Development. Ed. by A. Bishay & W. G. McGinnies. (Advances in Desert & Arid Land Technology & Development Ser.: Vol. 1). 630p. 1979. text ed. 267.00 (*3-7186-0002-1*) Gordon & Breach.

Advances in Design Automation - 1993, 2 vols., Set. Ed. by B. J. Gilmore et al. 1993. 200.00 (*0-685-70656-7*) ASME.

Advances in Design Automation - 1993, Vol. 1. Ed. by B. J. Gilmore et al. (DE Ser.: Vol. 65-1). 788p. 1993. 120.00 (*0-7918-1181-6*, G0826A) ASME.

Advances in Design Automation - 1993, Vol. 2. Ed. by B. J. Gilmore et al. (DE Ser.: Vol. 65-2). 628p. 1993. 95.00 (*0-685-70655-9*, G0826B) ASME.

***Advances in Design Automation 1994: Proceedings of the Design Automation Conference, Minneapolis, MN, 2 vols.** Design Automation Conference Staff. 1220p. 1994. pap. 200.00 (*0-7918-1283-9*) ASME.

Advances in Design Optimization. Ed. by Hojjat Adeli. LC 93-32183. 1994. write for info. (*0-419-16960-1*, E & FN Spon) Routledge Chapman & Hall.

Advances in Detailed Reaction Mechanisms. Vol. 1: Radical, Single Electron Transfers & Concerted Reactions. Ed. by James M. Coxon. 1991. 90.25 (*1-55938-164-7*) Jai Pr.

Advances in Development & Behavioral Pediatrics, Vol. 10. Ed. by Mark L. Wolraich. 270p. 1992. 99.00 (*1-85302-150-4*, Pub. by J Kingsley Pubs UK) Taylor & Francis.

Advances in Developmental & Behavioral Pediatrics, Vol. 9. Ed. by Mark L. Wolraich & Donald K. Routh. 300p. 1990. 88.00 (*1-85302-071-0*, Pub. by J Kingsley Pubs UK) Taylor & Francis.

Advances in Developmental Biochemistry, Vol. 1. Ed. by Paul Wassarman. 1991. 90.25 (*1-55938-347-X*) Jai Pr.

Advances in Developmental Biology, Vol. 1. Ed. by Paul Wassarman. 1991. 90.25 (*1-55938-348-8*) Jai Pr.

Advances in Developmental Disorders, Vol. 1. Rowland P. Barrett et al. 1987. 73.25 (*0-89232-841-X*) Jai Pr.

Advances in Developmental Disorders, Vol. 2. Ed. by Rowland P. Barrett & Johnny L. Matson. 320p. 1993. 95.00 (*1-85302-093-1*, Pub. by J Kingsley Pubs UK) Taylor & Francis.

Advances in Developmental Psychology, Vol. 1. Ed. by Michael E. Lamb & Ann L. Brown. (Advances in Developmental Psychology Ser.). 256p. 1981. text ed. 49.95 (*0-89859-103-1*) L Erlbaum Assocs.

Advances in Developmental Psychology, Vol. 2. Ed. by Michael E. Lamb & Ann L. Brown. 224p. (C). 1982. text ed. 49.95 (*0-89859-244-5*) L Erlbaum Assocs.

Advances in Developmental Psychology, Vol. 3. Ed. by Michael E. Lamb et al. 312p. (C). 1984. text ed. 59.95 (*0-89859-366-2*) L Erlbaum Assocs.

Advances in Developmental Psychology, Vol. 4. Ed. by Michael E. Lamb et al. 376p. 1986. 79.95 (*0-89859-675-0*) L Erlbaum Assocs.

Advances in Diabetes Epidemiology: Proceedings of the International Symposium on the Advances in Diabetes Epidemiology, Abbaye de Fontevraud, France, 3-7 May 1982. Ed. by E. Eschwege. (INSERM Symposium Ser.: No. 22). 408p. 1983. 134.00 (*0-444-80453-6*) Elsevier.

Advances in Diagnostic Visual Optics. Ed. by C. M. Breinin & I. M. Siegel. (Optical Sciences Ser.: Vol. 41). (Illus.). 280p. 1983. 57.00 (*0-387-13079-9*) Spr-Verlag.

Advances in Diesel Particulate Control. 1990. 69.00 (*1-56091-025-9*, SP816) Soc Auto Engineers.

Advances in Differential & Integral Equations. Ed. by John A. Nohel. (Miscellaneous Bks.: No. 10). xvi, 207p. 1969. 21.50 (*0-89871-037-5*) Soc Indus-Appl Math.

Advances in Differential Geometry & Topology. F. Tricerri. 192p. 1990. text ed. 61.00 (*981-02-0494-9*); pap. text ed. 33.00 (*981-02-0495-7*) World Scientific Pub.

***Advances in Discourse Processes Vol. 37: Pragmatics, Discourse & Text: Some Systemically Inspired Approaches.** Ed. by Erich H. Steiner & Robert Veltman. 256p. 1988. 55.00 (*0-89391-546-7*) Ablex Pub.

Advances in Disease. Ed. by Kerry F. Harris. (Vector Research Ser.: Vol. 5). (Illus.). 315p. 1988. 149.00 (*0-387-96738-9*) Spr-Verlag.

Advances in Disease Vector Research, Vol. 6. Ed. by Kerry F. Harris. (Illus.). xviii, 363p. 1989. 169.00 (*0-387-97080-0*, 3108) Spr-Verlag.

Advances in Disease Vector Research, Vol. 7. Ed. by K. F. Harris. (Illus.). 296p. 1990. 129.00 (*0-387-97335-4*) Spr-Verlag.

Advances in Disease Vector Research, Vol. 8. Ed. by K. F. Harris. (Illus.). xvii, 209p. 1991. 129.00 (*0-387-97478-4*) Spr-Verlag.

Advances in Disease Vector Research, Vol. 9. Ed. by K. F. Harris. (Illus.). 368p. 1992. 218.00 (*0-387-97791-0*) Spr-Verlag.

Advances in Disease Vector Research, Vol. 10. Ed. by K. F. Harris. (Illus.). 304p. 1993. 198.00 (*0-387-94073-1*) Spr-Verlag.

Advances in Distributed & Parallel Processing, 1. Ed. by Harry W. Tyrer. LC 93-48551. 392p. 1994. 75.00 (*0-89391-579-3*) Ablex Pub.

Advances in Distributed & Parallel Processing, 2. Ed. by Harry W. Tyrer. LC 93-48551. 312p. 1994. 75.00 (*0-89391-880-6*) Ablex Pub.

***Advances in Distributed Hydrology: Selected Papers from International Workshop by ISMES.** Ed. by R. Rosso et al. 1994. 55.00 (*0-918334-81-0*) WRP.

Advances in Distributed Processing Management, Vol. 1. Ed. by Thomas A. Rullo. (Wiley-Heyden Advances in EDP Management Library). 200p. 1980. text ed. 76.95 (*0-471-25997-7*, Pub. by Wiley Heyden) Wiley.

Advances in Distributed Processing Management, Vol. 1. Ed. by Thomas A. Rullo. LC 81-641059. (Heyden Advances Library in EDP Management). 217p. reprint ed. pap. 61.90 (*0-8357-5157-0*, 2032689) Bks Demand.

***Advances in Distributed Sensor Integration: Theory & Application.** S. S. Iyengar et al. LC 95-3383. 1995. text ed. 65.00 (*0-13-360033-5*) P-H.

Advances in Distributed System Reliability. Suresh Rai & Dharma P. Agrawal. LC 89-45997. 347p. 1990. 9.95 (*0-8186-8907-2*, 1907) IEEE Comp Soc.

Advances in Distribution Channel Research, Vol. 1. Ed. by Gary L. Frazier. 1988. 73.25 (*0-89232-821-5*) Jai Pr.

Advances in DNA Sequence Specific Agents, Vol. 1, Pt. A: Methods Used to Evaluate Sequence Specificity of DNA Reactive Compounds. Ed. by Laurence H. Hurley. 1991. 90.25 (*1-55938-165-5*) Jai Pr.

Advances in DNA Sequence Specific Agents, Vol. 1, Pt. B: Sequence Specificity of Drugs That Interact with DNA in the Minor Groove. Ed. by Laurence H. Hurley. 1991. 90.25 (*1-55938-166-3*) Jai Pr.

Advances in Dopamine Research: Proceedings Satellite Symposium 8th International Congress Pharm, Okayam 7-81. M. Kohsaka & T. Shohmori. LC 82-492. (Advances in the Biosciences Ser.: Vol. 37). 1982. 148.00 (*0-08-027391-2*, Pub. by Pergamon Repr UK) Franklin.

Advances in Down Syndrome. Ed. by Valentine Dmitriev & Patricia Oelwein. LC 88-4617. 324p. 1988. pap. 31.00 (*0-87562-092-2*, 3666) PRO-ED.

Advances in Drug Delivery Systems. Ed. by J. M. Anderson & S. W. Kim. (Controlled Release Ser.: No. 1). 412p. 1986. 179.50 (*0-444-42594-2*) Elsevier.

Advances in Drug Delivery Systems: Proceedings of the 3rd International Symposium, Salt Lake City, UT, Feb. 24-27, 1987, Vol. 3. Ed. by J. M. Anderson & S. W. Kim. 396p. 1988. 148.75 (*0-444-42927-1*) Elsevier.

Advances in Drug Delivery Systems, No. 4: Proceedings of the 4th International Symposium,Salt Lake City, UT, February 21-24, 1989. Ed. by J. M. Anderson et al. 370p. 1990. 177.00 (*0-444-88225-1*) Elsevier.

Advances in Drug Delivery Systems, No. 5: Proceedings of the Fifth International Symposium on Recent Advances in Drug Delivery Systems, Salt Lake City, UT, U. S. A., February 25-28, 1991. Ed. by James M. Anderson et al. LC 92-9992. 1992. write for info. (*0-444-88664-8*) Elsevier.

***Advances in Drug Delivery Systems 6: Proceedings of the Sixth International Symposium on Recent Advances in Drug Delivery Systems, Salt Lake City, UT, U. S. A., 21-24 February 1993.** Sixth International Symposium on Recent Advances in Drug Delivery Systems Staff. Ed. by J. M. Anderson et al. 350p. 1994. text ed. 200.00 (*0-444-82027-2*) Elsevier.

Advances in Drug Research, Vol. 9. Ed. by N. J. Harper et al. (Serial Publication Ser.). 1975. text ed. 168.00 (*0-12-013309-1*) Acad Pr.

Advances in Drug Research, Vol. 13. Ed. by N. J. Harper & A. B. Simmonds. (Serial Publication Ser.). 1984. text ed. 168.00 (*0-12-013313-X*) Acad Pr.

Advances in Drug Research, Vol. 14. Ed. by N. J. Harper et al. (Serial Publication Ser.). 1985. text ed. 168.00 (*0-12-013314-8*) Acad Pr.

Advances in Drug Research, Vol. 16. Ed. by Bernard Testa. (Serial Publication Ser.). 614p. 1988. text ed. 168.00 (*0-12-013316-4*) Acad Pr.

Advances in Drug Research, Vol. 17. Ed. by Bernard Testa. (Serial Publication Ser.). 479p. 1988. text ed. 139.00 (*0-12-013317-2*) Acad Pr.

Advances in Drug Research, Vol. 18. Ed. by Bernard Testa. (Serial Publication Ser.). 549p. 1989. text ed. 157.00 (*0-12-013318-0*) Acad Pr.

Advances in Drug Research, Vol. 19. Ed. by Bernard Testa. (Serial Publication Ser.). 581p. 1990. text ed. 176.00 (*0-12-013319-9*) Acad Pr.

Advances in Drug Research, Vol. 20. Ed. by Bernard Testa. (Illus.). 319p. 1991. text ed. 117.00 (*0-12-013320-2*) Acad Pr.

Advances in Drug Research, Vol. 21. Ed. by Bernard Testa. (Illus.). 299p. 1991. text ed. 127.00 (*0-12-013321-0*) Acad Pr.

Advances in Drug Research, Vol. 22. Ed. by Bernard Testa. (Illus.). 205p. 1992. text ed. 75.00 (*0-12-013322-9*) Acad Pr.

Advances in Drug Research, Vol. 23. Ed. by Bernard Testa. (Illus.). 233p. 1992. text ed. 92.00 (*0-12-013323-7*) Acad Pr.

Advances in Drug Research, Vol. 24. Ed. by Bernard Testa. (Illus.). 288p. 1993. text ed. 85.00 (*0-12-013324-5*) Acad Pr.

Advances in Drug Research, Vol. 25. Ed. by Bernard Testa & Urs Meyer. (Illus.). 288p. 1994. text ed. 75.00 (*0-12-013325-3*) Acad Pr.

***Advances in Drug Research, Vol. 26.** Ed. by Bernard Testa. (Illus.). 272p. 1995. boxed 75.00 (*0-12-013326-1*) Acad Pr.

Advances in Drug Research, Vols. 1-3 & 5-7. Ed. by N. J. Harper & A. B. Simmonds. Incl. Vol. 1. 1964. 47.00 (*0-12-013301-6*); Vol. 3. 1966. 60.00 (*0-12-013303-2*); Vol. 6. 1972. 60.00 (*0-12-013306-7*); write for info. (*0-318-50175-9*) Acad Pr.

Advances in Drug Therapy of Gastroesophageal Reflux Disease. Ed. by C. Scarpignato. (Frontiers of Gastrointestinal Research Ser.: Vol. 20). (Illus.). xii, 372p. 1992. 238.50 (*3-8055-5360-9*) S Karger.

Advances in Drying, Vol. 1. A. S. Mujumdar. 1980. 55.00 (*0-07-043975-3*) McGraw.

Advances in Drying, Vol. 3. Ed. by Arun S. Mujumdar. LC 80-10432. (Advances in Drying Ser.). (Illus.). 361p. 1984. text ed. 93.00 (*0-89116-297-6*) Hemisp Pub.

Advances in Drying, Vol. 4. Arun S. Mujumdar. 421p. 1987. 136.00 (*0-89116-408-1*) Hemisp Pub.

Advances in Drying, Vol. 5. Ed. by Arun S. Mujumdar. 350p. 1991. 87.50 (*0-685-40759-4*) Hemisp Pub.

Advances in Drying, Vol. 5. Ed. by Arun S. Mujumdar. 375p. 1992. 99.50 (*0-89116-109-0*) Hemisp Pub.

Advances in Dynamic Games & Applications. Ed. by Tamer Basar & Alain Haurie. LC 94-937. (Annals of the International Society of Dynamic Games Ser.: Vol. 1). 418p. 1994. 79.50 (*0-8176-3691-9*) Birkhauser.

Advances in Dynamic Systems & Stability: Lectures Given at the Symposium in Atlanta, Georgia, December 1991, on the Occasion of the 65th Birthday of Bruno A. Boley. Ed. by D. E. Beskos & F. Ziegler. LC 92-15846. (Acta Mechanica, Supplementum Ser.: No. 3). (Illus.). 210p. 1992. write for info. (*3-211-82368-9*); pap. 173.00 (*0-387-82368-9*) Spr-Verlag.

Advances in Dynamical Systems & Quantum Physics. S. Albeverio et al. 400p. 1995. text ed. 128.00 (*981-02-1821-4*) World Scientific Pub.

Advances in Early Education & Day Care, Vol. 1. Ed. by Sally Kilmer. 225p. 1980. lib. bdg. 73.25 (*0-89232-127-X*) Jai Pr.

Advances in Early Education & Day Care, Vol. 2. Ed. by Sally Kilmer. 300p. 1981. 73.25 (*0-89232-149-0*) Jai Pr.

Advances in Early Education & Day Care, Vol. 3. Ed. by Sally J. Kilmer. 1983. 73.25 (*0-89232-206-3*) Jai Pr.

Advances in Early Education & Day Care, Vol. 4. Ed. by Sally J. Kilmer. 1986. 73.25 (*0-89232-454-6*) Jai Pr.

Advances in Early Education & Day Care, Vol. 5. Ed. by Sally J. Kilmer. 1988. 73.25 (*0-89232-811-8*) Jai Pr.

Advances in Echo Imaging Using Contrast Enhancement. Ed. by N. C. Nanda. LC 92-46545. 408p. (C). 1993. lib. bdg. 122.00 (*0-7923-2137-5*) Kluwer Ac.

Advances in Ecological Research, Vol. 7. Ed. by J. B. Cragg. (Serial Publication Ser.). 1971. text ed. 167.00 (*0-12-013907-3*) Acad Pr.

Advances in Ecological Research, Vol. 12. Ed. by J. B. Cragg. (Serial Publication Ser.). 1982. text ed. 127.00 (*0-12-013912-X*) Acad Pr.

Advances in Ecological Research, Vol. 13. Ed. by A. MacFadyen & E. David Ford. (Serial Publication Ser.). 1983. text ed. 127.00 (*0-12-013913-8*) Acad Pr.

Advances in Ecological Research, Vol. 14. Ed. by J. B. Cragg. (Serial Publication Ser.). 1984. text ed. 127.00 (*0-12-013914-6*) Acad Pr.

Advances in Ecological Research, Vol. 15. Ed. by A. Macfayden & E. D. Ford. (Serial Publication Ser.). 448p. 1986. text ed. 127.00 (*0-12-013915-4*) Acad Pr.

Advances in Ecological Research, Vol. 16. Ed. by A. Macfayden & E. D. Ford. (Serial Publication Ser.). 300p. 1987. text ed. 108.00 (*0-12-013916-2*) Acad Pr.

Advances in Ecological Research, Vol. 18. Ed. by Michael Begon et al. (Serial Publication Ser.). 330p. 1988. text ed. 107.00 (*0-12-013918-9*) Acad Pr.

Advances in Ecological Research, Vol. 19. Ed. by Michael Begon et al. (Serial Publication Ser.). 357p. 1989. text ed. 99.00 (*0-12-013919-7*) Acad Pr.

Advances in Ecological Research, Vol. 20. Ed. by Michael Begon et al. 281p. 1990. text ed. 99.00 (*0-12-013920-0*) Acad Pr.

Advances in Ecological Research, Vol. 21. Ed. by Michael Begon et al. (Illus.). 403p. 1991. text ed. 105.00 (*0-12-013921-9*) Acad Pr.

Advances in Ecological Research, Vol. 23. Ed. by Michael Begon & Alastair H. Fitter. (Illus.). 355p. 1992. text ed. 99.00 (*0-12-013923-5*) Acad Pr.

Advances in Ecological Research, Vol. 24. Ed. by Michael Begon & Alastair H. Fitter. (Illus.). 424p. 1993. text ed. 95.00 (*0-12-013924-3*) Acad Pr.

Advances in Ecological Research, Vol. 25. Ed. by Michael Begon & Alastair H. Fitter. (Illus.). 320p. 1994. text ed. 90.00 (*0-12-013925-1*) Acad Pr.

***Advances in Ecological Research, Vol. 26.** Ed. by M. Begon & A. H. Fitter. (Illus.). 367p. 1995. text ed. write for info. (*0-12-013926-X*) Acad Pr.

Advances in Econometrics, Vol. 1. Ed. by R. L. Basmann & George F. Rhodes. (Orig.). 1982. lib. bdg. 73.25 (*0-89232-138-5*) Jai Pr.

Advances in Econometrics, Vol. 6. Ed. by George F. Rhodes, Jr. 1987. 73.25 (*0-89232-795-2*) Jai Pr.

Advances in Econometrics: Exact Distribution Analysis in Linear Simultaneous Equation Models, Vol. 2. Ed. by R. L. Basmann & George F. Rhodes, Jr. 315p. 1983. 73.25 (*0-89232-183-0*) Jai Pr.

An Asterisk (*) at the beginning of an entry indicates that the title is appearing in BIP for the first time.

An Asterisk (*) at the beginning of an entry indicates that the title is appearing in BIP for the first time.

Advances in Environmental Science & Engineering, Vol. 1. James R. Pfafflin & Edward N. Ziegler. 292p. 1979. text ed. 207.00 (*0-677-16070-4*) Gordon & Breach.

Advances in Environmental Science & Engineering, Vol. 2. James R. Pfafflin & Edward N. Ziegler. 228p. 1979. text ed. 207.00 (*0-677-14810-0*) Gordon & Breach.

Advances in Environmental Science & Engineering, Vol. 3. James R. Pfafflin & Edward N. Ziegler. 240p. 1980. text ed. 239.00 (*0-677-15760-6*) Gordon & Breach.

Advances in Environmental Science & Engineering, Vol. 4. Ed. by James R. Pfafflin & Edward N. Ziegler. 188p. 1981. text ed. 215.00 (*0-677-16250-2*) Gordon & Breach.

Advances in Environmental Science & Engineering, Vol. 5. Ed. by James R. Pfafflin & Edward N. Ziegler. 220p. 1986. text ed. 206.00 (*2-88124-184-0*) Gordon & Breach.

Advances in Environmental Science & Technology, Vol. 5. Ed. by James Pitts, Jr. & Robert L. Metcalf. LC 74-644364. 382p. 1975. 39.50 (*0-471-69088-0*) Wiley.

Advances in Environmental Sensors & Monitoring: Technologies & Opportunities to Meet Changing Government Regulations. 311p. 1991. spiral bd., vinyl bd. 1,030.00 (*0-914993-83-6*) Tech Insights.

*__Advances in Enzyme Regulation.__ Weber. (Advances in Enzyme Regulation Ser.: No. 35). 1995. text ed. write for info. (*0-08-042639-5*, Pergamon Pr) Elsevier.

Advances in Enzyme Regulation. Ed. by George Weber. Incl. Vol. 1. LC 63-19609. 1964. 175.00 (*0-08-010298-0*); Vol. 2. LC 63-19609. 1964. 130.00 (*0-08-010768-0*); Vol. 6. LC 63-19609. 1968. 130.00 (*0-08-012836-X*); Vol. 7. LC 63-19609. 1969. 130.00 (*0-08-006396-9*); Vol. 8. LC 63-19609. 1970. 130.00 (*0-08-016116-2*); Vol. 9. LC 63-19609. 1971. 130.00 (*0-08-016775-6*); Vol. 10. LC 63-19609. 1972. 130.00 (*0-08-016955-4*); Vol. 11. Index to Vols. 1-10. LC 63-19609. 1975. 79.00 (*0-08-017149-4*); Vol. 12. LC 63-19609. 1974. 130.00 (*0-08-018004-3*); Vol. 13. LC 63-19609. 1975. 130.00 (*0-08-018238-0*); Vol. 14. LC 63-19609. 1976. 130.00 (*0-08-020238-1*); Vol. 15. LC 63-19609. 1977. 130.00 (*0-08-021507-6*); Vol. 16. LC 63-19609. 1978. 190.00 (*0-08-022646-9*); Vol. 18. LC 63-19609. (Illus.). 440p. 1980. 155.00 (*0-08-025915-4*); LC 63-19609. write for info. (*0-318-55122-5*, Pergamon Pr) Elsevier.

Advances in Enzyme Regulation, Vol. 19. Ed. by George Weber. 1981. 155.00 (*0-08-027393-9*, Pergamon Pr) Elsevier.

Advances in Enzyme Regulation: Proceeding of the Twenty-Eighth Symposium on Regulation of Enzyme Activity & Synthesis in Normal & Neoplastic Tissues Held at Indiana University School of Medicine, Indianapolis, Indiana, 2-3 October 1988, Vol. 28. Ed. by George Weber. (Advances in Enzyme Regulation Ser.: Vol. 28). (Illus.). 442p. 1989. 285.00 (*0-08-037370-4*, Pub. by PPL UK) Elsevier.

Advances in Enzyme Regulation: Proceedings of the Symposium Regulation of Enzyme Activity & Synthesis in Normal & Neoplastic Tissues, 22nd, Held at Indiana University School of Medicine, Indianapolis, U. S. A., 3-4 October 1983, Vol. 22. Ed. by George Weber. LC 63-19609. (Illus.). 600p. 1984. 190.00 (*0-08-031498-8*, Pergamon Pr) Elsevier.

Advances in Enzyme Regulation: Proceedings of the Thirtieth Symposium on Regulation of Enzyme Activity & Synthesis in Normal & Neoplastic Tissues Held at Indiana University School of Medicine, Indianapolis, Indiana, 2-3 October 1989. Ed. by George Weber. (Advances in Enzyme Regulation Ser.: No. 30). (Illus.). 472p. 1990. 385.00 (*0-08-040172-4*, Pergamon Pr) Elsevier.

Advances in Enzyme Regulation: Proceedings of the Thirty First Symposium on Regulation of Enzyme Activity & Synthesis in Normal & Neoplastic Tissues, Indianapolis, Indiana, 1-2 October 1990, Vol. 31. Ed. by George Weber. (Advances in Enzyme Regulation Ser.: No. 94). (Illus.). 496p. 1991. 455.00 (*0-08-041142-8*, Pergamon Pr) Elsevier.

Advances in Enzyme Regulation: Proceedings of the 17th Symposium on Regulation of Enzyme Activity & Synthesis in Normal & Neoplastic Tissues, Indiana University School of Medicine, Indianapolis, 2-3 October 1978, Vol. 17. Ed. by George Weber. (Illus.). 1979. 155.00 (*0-08-024424-6*, Pergamon Pr) Elsevier.

Advances in Enzyme Regulation: Proceedings of the 20th Symposium on Regulation of Activity & Synthesis in Normal & Neoplastic Tissues Held at Indiana University School of Medicine, Indianapolis, October 5-6, 1981, Vol. 20. Ed. by George Weber. LC 63-19609. (Illus.). 420p. 1982. 145.00 (*0-08-028898-7*, Pergamon Pr) Elsevier.

Advances in Enzyme Regulation: Proceedings of the 21st Symposium on Regulation of Activity & Synthesis in Normal & Neoplastic Tissues, held at Indiana University School of Medicine, Indianapolis, October 4-5, 1982, Vol. 21. George Weber. LC 63-19609. (Illus.). 448p. 1983. 165.00 (*0-08-030430-3*, Pergamon Pr) Elsevier.

Advances In Enzyme Regulation: Proceedings of the 23rd Symposium on Regulation of the Enzyme Activity & Synthesis in Normal & Neoplastic Tissues, Held at Indiana University School of Medicine, Indianapolis, October 1-2, 1984, Vol. 23. Ed. by George Weber. LC 63-19609. (Illus.). 482p. 1985. 200.00 (*0-08-032727-3*, Pub. by PPL UK) Elsevier.

Advances in Enzyme Regulation: Proceedings of the 25th Symposium on Regulation of Enzyme Activity & Synthesis in Normal & Neoplastic Held at Indiana University School of Medicine, Indianapolis, September-October, 1985. Ed. by George Weber. (Illus.). 550p. 1986. 225.00 (*0-08-034153-5*, Pub. by PPL UK) Elsevier.

Advances in Enzyme Regulation: Proceedings of the 26th Symposium on Regulation of Enzyme Activity & Synthesis Held at Indiana University School of Medicine, Indianapolis, September 1986. Ed. by George Weber. LC 63-19609. (Advances in Enzyme Regulation Ser.: No. 26). (Illus.). 450p. 1987. 225.00 (*0-08-035576-5*, Pergamon Pr) Elsevier.

Advances in Enzyme Regulation: Proceedings of the 34th Symposium on Regulation of Enzyme Activity & Synthesis in Normal & Neoplastic Tissues Held at Indiana University School of Medicine, Indianapolis, IN, 4-5 October, 1993, Vol. 34. Ed. by George Weber. (Illus.). 454p. 1994. 545.00 (*0-08-042482-1*) Elsevier.

Advances in Enzyme Regulation, Vol. 3: Proceedings of Third Symposium on Enzyme Regulation Activity, Indianapolis, October 1964. George Weber & C. Weber. LC 63-190609. 1965. 196.00 (*0-08-010998-5*, Pub. by Pergamon Repr UK) Franklin.

Advances in Enzyme Regulation, Vol. 4: Proceedings of the 4th Symposium Regulation Enzyme Activity & Synthesis Indiana School of Medicine, Oct. 1965. George Weber & C. Weber. LC 63-19609. 1966. 156.00 (*0-08-011575-6*, Pub. by Pergamon Repr UK) Franklin.

Advances in Enzyme Regulation, Vol. 5: Proceedings of the 5th Symposium on Regulating Enzyme Activity, Indianapolis, Oct. 1966. George Weber & C. Weber. LC 63-19609. 1967. 195.00 (*0-08-012365-1*, Pub. by Pergamon Repr UK) Franklin.

Advances in Enzyme Regulation 33. Ed. by George Weber & Catherine E. Weber. 404p. 1993. 475.00 (*0-08-042193-8*, Pergamon Pr) Elsevier.

Advances in Enzymic Hydrolysis of Cellulose & Related Materials: Proceedings of the Symposium of the American Chemical Society Army Research, March, 1962. E. Reese. LC 62-22051. 1963. 126.00 (*0-08-009947-5*, Pub. by Pergamon Repr UK) Franklin.

Advances in Enzymology: And Related Areas of Molecular Biology, 6 vols., Vol. 60. Ed. by Alton Meister. 417p. 1992. text ed. 98.00 (*0-471-81282-X*) Wiley.

Advances in Enzymology: And Related Areas of Molecular Biology, 6 vols., Vol. 61. Ed. by Alton Meister. 557p. 1992. text ed. 98.00 (*0-471-81830-5*) Wiley.

Advances in Enzymology: And Related Areas of Molecular Biology, 6 vols., Vol. 62. Ed. by Alton Meister. 455p. 1992. text ed. 98.00 (*0-471-61770-9*) Wiley.

Advances in Enzymology: And Related Areas of Molecular Biology, 6 vols., Vol. 63. Ed. by Alton Meister. 551p. 1990. text ed. 119.95 (*0-471-50984-1*) Wiley.

Advances in Enzymology: And Related Areas of Molecular Biology, 6 vols., Vol. 64. Ed. by Alton Meister. 494p. 1991. text ed. 119.95 (*0-471-50949-3*) Wiley.

Advances in Enzymology: And Related Areas of Molecular Biology, 6 vols., Vol. 65. Ed. by Alton Meister. 448p. 1992. text ed. 119.95 (*0-471-52760-2*) Wiley.

*__Advances in Enzymology & Other Related Areas of Molecular Biology, Vol. 70.__ Meister. Date not set. text ed. write for info. (*0-471-04097-5*) Wiley.

Advances in Enzymology & Related Areas of Molecular Biology, Vol. 66. Ed. by Alton Meister. 334p. 1993. text ed. 135.00 (*0-471-55769-2*) Wiley.

Advances in Enzymology & Related Areas of Molecular Biology, Vol. 67. Alton Meister. 528p. 1993. text ed. 119.95 (*0-471-58279-4*) Wiley.

Advances in Enzymology & Related Areas of Molecular Biology, Vol. 68. Ed. by Alton Meister. 237p. 1994. text ed. 129.95 (*0-471-31071-9*) Wiley.

*__Advances in Enzymology & Related Areas of Molecular Biology, Vol. 69.__ Ed. by Alton Meister. 1994. text ed. 136.95 (*0-471-01767-1*) Wiley.

*__Advances in Enzymology & Related Areas of Molecular Biology Vol. 71.__ Ed. by Meister. Date not set. pap. text ed. write for info. (*0-471-12648-9*) Wiley.

Advances in Epileptology: The Fourteenth Epilepsy International Symposium. Epilepsy International Symposium Staff. Ed. by Maurice Parsonage et al. LC 82-42785. (Advances in Epileptology Ser.). (Illus.). 344p. reprint ed. pap. 98.10 (*0-7837-7093-6*, 2046918) Bks Demand.

*__Advances in Epileptology: The Thirteenth Epilepsy International Symposium.__ fac. ed. Epilepsy International Symposium Staff. Ed. by Haruo Akimoto et al. LC 81-40860. (Advances in Epileptology Ser.). (Illus.). 559p. 1994. pap. 159.40 (*0-7837-7308-0*, 2047064) Bks Demand.

*__Advances in Epileptology: The Twelfth Epilepsy International Symposium.__ fac. ed. Epilepsy International Symposium Staff. Ed. by Mogens Dam et al. LC 81-40860. (Advances in Epileptology Ser.). (Illus.). 715p. 1994. pap. 180.00 (*0-7837-7307-2*, 2047063) Bks Demand.

*__Advances in Epileptology: The XIth Epilepsy International Symposium.__ fac. ed. Epilepsy International Symposium Staff. Ed. by Raffaele Canger et al. LC 80-5055. (Illus.). 510p. Date not set. pap. 145.40 (*0-7837-7255-6*, 2047050) Bks Demand.

Advances in Epileptology: The 15th Epilepsy International Symposium. Ed. by Roger J. Porter et al. (Advances in Epileptology Ser.). 710p. 1984. text ed. 175.50 (*0-89004-561-5*) Raven.

Advances in Epileptology: The 16th Epilepsy International Symposium. Ed. by Peter Wolf et al. (Illus.). 816p. 1987. 239.00 (*0-88167-222-X*) Raven.

Advances in Epitaxy & Endotaxy: Part A - Eutectics & Eutectiods & Part B - Growth of Monocrystalline Layers, 2 vols., Set. H. G. Schneider et al. 500p. 1990. 159.00 (*0-444-98871-8*, MSM 53) Elsevier.

Advances in Ergometry. Ed. by N. Bachl et al. (Illus.). 544p. 1991. pap. 65.00 (*0-387-53684-1*) Spr-Verlag.

Advances in Ergonomics: Human Factors I. Ed. by Anil Mital. 368p. 1984. 95.00 (*0-444-87659-6*, North Holland) Elsevier.

Advances in Essential Oil Industry. Ed. by L. D. Kapoor. 284p. 1977. 10.00 (*0-88065-142-3*, Messers Today & Tomorrow) Scholarly Pubns.

Advances in European Geothermal Research. Ed. by Albert S. Strub & P. Ungemach. 1096p. 1980. lib. bdg. 126.50 (*90-277-1138-0*) Kluwer Ac.

Advances in European Solar Radiation Climatology. J. K. Page. (C). 1986. 100.00 (*0-685-33086-9*, Pub. by Interntl Solar Energy Soc UK) St Mut.

Advances in Evapotranspiration. LC 85-73413. 453p. 1985. pap. 37.00 (*0-916150-75-5*, P1485) Am Soc Ag Eng.

Advances in Exercise Adherence. Ed. by Rod K. Dishman. LC 93-47608. (Illus.). 416p. 1994. text ed. 39.00x (*0-87322-664-X*, BDIS0664) Human Kinetics.

Advances in Exercise Physiology: Proceedings of the International Symposium of Physiology, New Delhi-Patiala, Oct., 1974. International Symposium of Physiology Staff. Ed. by E. Jokl et al. (Medicine & Sport Science Ser.: Vol. 9). 160p. 1976. 76.00 (*3-8055-2291-6*) S Karger.

Advances in Experiential Social Processes. Ed. by Cary L. Cooper & Clayton P. Alderfer. LC 77-22060. 235p. reprint ed. pap. 67.00 (*0-8357-5162-7*, 2030373) Bks Demand.

Advances in Experiential Social Processes, Vol. 2. Ed. by Clayton P. Alderfer & Cary L. Cooper. LC 77-22060. (Illus.). 341p. reprint ed. pap. 97.20 (*0-8357-5163-5*, 2030433) Bks Demand.

Advances in Experimental Clinical Psychology. Henry E. Adams & William K. Boardman. 230p. 1971. 99.00 (*0-08-016399-8*, Pub. by Pergamon Repr UK) Franklin.

Advances in Experimental Mechanics & Biomimetics. Ed. by W. F. Jones & J. M. Whitney. (AD Series, Vol. 29: AMD Ser.: Vol. 146). 132p. 1992. 45.00 (*0-7918-1096-8*, G00740) ASME.

Advances in Experimental Social Psychology, Vol. 12. Ed. by Leonard Berkowitz. (Serial Publication Ser.). 1979. text ed. 116.00 (*0-12-015212-6*) Acad Pr.

Advances in Experimental Social Psychology, Vol. 13. Ed. by Leonard Berkowitz. (Serial Publication Ser.). 1980. text ed. 116.00 (*0-12-015213-4*) Acad Pr.

Advances in Experimental Social Psychology, Vol. 14. Ed. by Leonard Berkowitz. (Serial Publication Ser.). 1981. text ed. 116.00 (*0-12-015214-2*) Acad Pr.

Advances in Experimental Social Psychology, Vol. 15. Ed. by Leonard Berkowitz. (Serial Publication Ser.). 270p. 1982. text ed. 116.00 (*0-12-015215-0*) Acad Pr.

Advances in Experimental Social Psychology, Vol. 16. Ed. by Leonard Berkowitz. (Serial Publication Ser.). 1984. text ed. 116.00 (*0-12-015216-9*) Acad Pr.

Advances in Experimental Social Psychology, Vol. 17. Ed. by Leonard Berkowitz. (Serial Publication Ser.). 1984. text ed. 116.00 (*0-12-015217-7*) Acad Pr.

Advances in Experimental Social Psychology, Vol. 18. Ed. by Leonard Berkowitz. LC 64-23452. (Serial Publication Ser.). 1984. text ed. 116.00 (*0-12-015218-5*) Acad Pr.

Advances in Experimental Social Psychology, Vol. 20. Ed. by Leonard Berkowitz. (Serial Publication Ser.). 351p. 1987. text ed. 99.00 (*0-12-015220-7*) Acad Pr.

Advances in Experimental Social Psychology, Vol. 22. Ed. by Leonard Berkowitz. (Serial Publication Ser.). 364p. 1989. text ed. 91.00 (*0-12-015222-3*) Acad Pr.

Advances in Experimental Social Psychology, Vol. 23. Ed. by Mark P. Zanna. (Serial Publication Ser.). 350p. 1990. 73.00 (*0-12-015223-1*) Acad Pr.

Advances in Experimental Social Psychology, Vol. 24. Ed. by Mark P. Zanna. (Illus.). 359p. 1991. text ed. 66.00 (*0-12-015224-X*) Acad Pr.

Advances in Experimental Social Psychology, Vol. 25. Ed. by Mark P. Zanna. (Illus.). 397p. 1992. text ed. 65.00 (*0-12-015225-8*) Acad Pr.

Advances in Experimental Social Psychology, Vol. 26. Ed. by Mark P. Zanna. (Illus.). 433p. 1993. text ed. 65.00 (*0-12-015226-6*) Acad Pr.

Advances in Experimental Social Psychology, Vols. 2-8 & 10-11. Incl. Vol. 3. LC 64-23452. 1967. text ed. 127.00 (*0-12-015203-7*); Vol. 5. LC 64-23452. 1971. text ed. 127.00 (*0-12-015205-3*); Vol. 6. LC 64-23452. 1972. text ed. 127.00 (*0-12-015206-1*); Vol. 7. LC 64-23452. 1974. text ed. 127.00 (*0-12-015207-X*); Vol. 8. LC 64-23452. 1975. text ed. 127.00 (*0-12-015208-8*); Vol. 10. LC 64-23452. 1977. text ed. 127.00 (*0-12-015210-X*); Vol. 11. LC 64-23452. 1978. text ed. 127.00 (*0-12-015211-8*); LC 64-23452. (Serial Publication Ser.). write for info. (*0-318-50181-3*) Acad Pr.

Advances in Experimental Social Psychology: Social Psychological Studies of the Self: Perspectives & Programs, Vol. 21. Ed. by Leonard Berkowitz. 361p. 1988. text ed. 99.00 (*0-12-015221-5*) Acad Pr.

*__Advances in Experimental Social Psychology Vol. 27, Vol. 27.__ Mark P. Zanna. (Illus.). 317p. 1995. boxed 59.95 (*0-12-015227-4*) Acad Pr.

Advances in Factories of the Future, CIM & Robotics. Ed. by Michel Costaftis & Francois Vernadat. LC 93-16288. (Manufacturing Research & Technology Ser.: Vol. 16). 1993. write for info. (*0-444-89856-5*) Elsevier.

Advances in Family Intervention, Vol. 5: Assessment & Therapy. Ed. by John P. Vincent. 250p. 1991. 85.00 (*1-85302-073-7*, Pub. by J Kingsley Pubs UK) Taylor & Francis.

Advances in Family Psychiatry, Vol. 1. Ed. by John G. Howells. LC 78-13895. 559p. 1980. text ed. 50.00 (*0-8236-0097-1*) Intl Univs Pr.

Advances in Family Psychiatry, Vol. 2. Ed. by John G. Howells. LC 78-13895. 565p. 1980. text ed. 50.00 (*0-8236-0101-3*) Intl Univs Pr.

Advances in Fatigue Lifetime Predictive Techniques. Ed. by M. R. Mitchell & R. W. Landgraf. LC 91-36055. (Special Technical Publication Ser.: No. 1122). (Illus.). 500p. 1992. text ed. 104.00 (*0-8031-1423-0*, 04-011220-30) ASTM.

Advances in Fatigue Lifetime Predictive Technique, Vol. 2: STP 1211. Ed. by M. R. Mitchell & R. Landgraf. (Special Technical Publication Ser.). (Illus.). 1993. text ed. 71.00 (*0-685-70545-5*, 04-012110-30) ASTM.

Advances in Fatigue Science & Technology. Ed. by C. Moura Branco & L. Guerra Rosa. (C). 1989. lib. bdg. 281.50 (*0-7923-0105-6*) Kluwer Ac.

Advances in Feature-Based Manufacturing. Ed. by Jami J. Shah et al. LC 94-44. (Manufacturing Research & Technology Ser.: Vol. 20). 1994. write for info. (*0-444-81600-3*) Elsevier.

Advances in Ferrites: Proceedings of the Fifth International Conference on Ferrites, January 10-13, 1989, Bombay, India, 2 vols., Set. Ed. by C. M. Srivastava & M. J. Patni. (Illus.). 1224p. (C). 1989. 88.50x (*81-204-0437-8*) S Asia.

Advances in Fetal Physiology: Reviews in Honor of G. C. Liggins. Ed. by P. D. Gluckman et al. LC 89-23124. (Research in Perinatal Medicine Ser.: No. VIII). (Illus.). 1989. 102.50 (*0-916859-41-X*) Perinatology.

Advances in Fiber Composite Materials. Ed. by Takehito Fukuda et al. LC 94-2214. (Current Japanese Materials Research Ser.: Vol. 12). 1994. write for info. (*0-444-81793-X*) Elsevier.

Advances in Fiber Optics Communications. Henry F. Taylor. LC 88-8193. (Artech House Telecommunications Library). 367p. reprint ed. pap. 104.60 (*0-7837-3021-7*, 2042919) Bks Demand.

Advances in Fibre Science. Ed. by Samir Mukhopadhyay. 218p. 1993. 395.00 (*1-870812-37-9*, Pub. by Textile Institue UK) St Mut.

Advances in Field Theory. Ed. by Susan A. Wheelan. 344p. (C). 1990. text ed. 44.00 (*0-8039-3979-5*) Sage.

Advances in Filtering & Optimal Stochastic Control: Proceedings; Cocoyoc, Mexico 1982. Ed. by Wendall H. Fleming & L. G. Gorostiza. (Lecture Notes in Control & Information Sciences Ser.: Vol. 42). 392p. 1982. pap. 33.00 (*0-387-11936-1*) Spr-Verlag.

Advances in Financial Planning & Forecasting, Vol. 1. Ed. by Cheng F. Lee. 1985. 73.25 (*0-89232-355-8*) Jai Pr.

Advances in Financial Planning & Forecasting, Vol. 2. Ed. by Cheng F. Lee. 1987. 73.25 (*0-89232-624-7*) Jai Pr.

Advances in Financial Planning & Forecasting, Vol. 3. Ed. by Cheng F. Lee. 1987. 73.25 (*0-89232-651-4*) Jai Pr.

Advances in Financial Planning & Forecasting, Supplement 1: Taiwan's Foreign Exchange, Exports & Financial Analysis. Ed. by Cheng-Few Lee & Sheng-Cheng Hu. 276p. 1989. 68.50 (*1-55938-049-7*) Jai Pr.

Advances in Financial Planning & Forecasting, Vol. 4: International Dimensions. Ed. by Cheng-Few Lee & Raj Aggarwal. 1990. 65.50 (*1-55938-001-2*) Jai Pr.

Advances in Fingerprint Technology. Lee. 1991. 50.00 (*0-685-66704-9*, HV6074) CRC Pr.

Advances in Fingerprint Technology. Ed. by Henry C. Lee & R. E. Gaesslen. LC 93-46614. (CRC Series in Forensic & Police Science). 1994. write for info. (*0-8493-9513-5*) CRC Pr.

Advances in Finishing: Furniture & Flat Panels. 73p. 1984. 20.00 (*0-935018-03-4*); 12.00 (*0-317-17416-9*) Forest Prod.

*__Advances in Finite Element Analysis in Fluid Dynamics: 1994 International Mechanical Engineering Congress & Exposition, Chicago, Illinois - November 6-11, 1994.__ (FED Ser.: Vol. 200). 88p. 1994. 44.00 (*0-7918-1413-0*, G00908) ASME.

Advances in Finite Element Analysis in Fluid Dynamics - 1992. Ed. by M. N. Dhaubhadel et al. (FED Ser.: Vol. 137). 124p. 1992. 37.50 (*0-7918-1066-6*, G00710) ASME.

Advances in Finite Element Analysis in Fluid Dynamics, 1993. Ed. by M. N. Dhaubhadel et al. LC 93-73724. 125p. 1993. pap. text ed. 40.00 (*0-7918-1015-1*) ASME.

Advances in Finite Geometries & Designs: Proceedings of the Third Isle of Thorns Conference, 1990. Ed. by J. W. Hirschfeld et al. 440p. 1991. 69.00 (*0-19-853592-9*) OUP.

Advances in Fisheries Technology & Biotechnology for Increased Profitability. Ed. by Michael N. Voigt & J. Richard Botta. LC 90-70987. 580p. 1990. 49.00 (*0-87762-785-1*) Technomic.

Advances in Fluid Dynamics. W. F. Ballhaus & M. Yousuff Hussaini. (Illus.). x, 315p. 1989. 61.00 (*0-387-97163-7*, 3533) Spr-Verlag.

Advances in Fluid Mechanics Measurement. Ed. by M. Gad-El-Hak. (Lecture Notes in Engineering Ser.: Vol. 45). (Illus.). viii, 610p. 1989. pap. 103.00 (*0-387-51136-9*, 2943) Spr-Verlag.

Advances in Fluid Structure Interaction Dynamics. Ed. by F. J. Moody & Y. W. Shin. (PVP Ser.: Vol. 75). 184p. 1983. text ed. 17.00 (*0-317-02546-5*, H00261); pap. text ed. 34.00 (*0-317-02547-3*) ASME.

Advances in Fluidics: Proceedings of the Fluidics Symposium, Chicago, 1967. Fluidics Symposium Staff. Ed. by Forbes T. Brown. LC 67-23027. (Illus.). 466p. reprint ed. pap. 132.90 (*0-8357-5164-3*, 2013308) Bks Demand.

Advances in Fluidization Engineering. Ed. by Lang Shih Fan. LC 90-837. (AIChE Symposium Ser.: Vol. 86, No. 276). 136p. 1990. pap. 52.00 (*0-8169-0488-X*) Am Inst Chem Eng.

88

An Asterisk (*) at the beginning of an entry indicates that the title is appearing in BIP for the first time.

Advances in Fluidized Systems. Ed. by Alan W. Weimer. LC 91-8282. (Symposium Ser.: Vol. 87, No. 281). 148p. (Orig.). 1991. pap. 75.00 (*0-8169-0544-4*, S281) Am Inst Chem Eng.

Advances in Foam Aging: A Topic in Energy Conservation, Vol. 1. Ed. by D. A. Brandreth. (Illus.). 226p. (Orig.). 1986. 38.00 (*0-939433-01-X*) Caissa Edit.

Advances in Food & Nutrition Research, Vol. 33. Ed. by John E. Kinsella. (Serial Publication Ser.). 458p. 1989. text ed. 114.00 (*0-12-016433-7*) Acad Pr.

Advances in Food & Nutrition Research, Vol. 34. Ed. by John E. Kinsella. (Serial Publication Ser.). 463p. 1990. text ed. 108.00 (*0-12-016434-5*) Acad Pr.

Advances in Food & Nutrition Research, Vol. 35. Ed. by John E. Kinsella. (Illus.). 378p. 1991. text ed. 94.00 (*0-12-016435-3*) Acad Pr.

Advances in Food & Nutrition Research, Vol. 36. Ed. by John E. Kinsella. (Illus.). 361p. 1992. text ed. 85.00 (*0-12-016436-1*) Acad Pr.

Advances in Food & Nutrition Research, Vol. 37. Ed. by John E. Kinsella. (Illus.). 437p. 1993. text ed. 89.00 (*0-12-016437-X*) Acad Pr.

Advances in Food Emulsions & Foams. Ed. by E. Dickinson & G. Stainsby. 386p. 1988. 93.75 (*1-85166-200-6*) Elsevier.

Advances in Food Engineering Operations. Singh. 1992. 139.95 (*0-8493-7902-4*, QP) CRC Pr.

Advances in Food Research, Vol. 28. Ed. by C. O. Chichester. (Serial Publication Ser.). 403p. 1982. text ed. 132.00 (*0-12-016428-0*) Acad Pr.

Advances in Food Research, Vol. 29. Ed. by E. M. Mrak & George F. Stewart. (Serial Publication Ser.). 1984. text ed. 114.00 (*0-12-016429-9*) Acad Pr.

Advances in Food Research, Vol. 30. Ed. by C. O. Chichester et al. (Serial Publication Ser.). 408p. 1986. text ed. 114.00 (*0-12-016430-2*) Acad Pr.

Advances in Food Research, Vol. 31. Ed. by C. O. Chichester et al. (Serial Publication Ser.). 509p. 1988. text ed. 119.00 (*0-12-016431-0*) Acad Pr.

Advances in Food Research, Vol. 32. Ed. by C. O. Chichester & B. S. Schweigert. (Serial Publication Ser.). 513p. 1988. text ed. 105.00 (*0-12-016432-9*) Acad Pr.

Advances in Food Research, Vols. 1-24. George F. Stewart et al. Ed. by G. F. Stewart. Incl. Vol. 12. 1964. (*0-12-016412-4*); Vol. 15. 1967. 70.00 (*0-12-016415-9*); Vol. 18. 1970. 70.00 (*0-12-016418-3*); Vol. 22. 1976. 70. 00 (*0-12-016422-1*); Vol. 22. 1976. (*0-12-016487-6*); (Serial Publication Ser.). write for info. (*0-318-50182-1*) Acad Pr.

Advances in Food Science, Vol. 1. Ed. by Brian M. McKenna. 1991. 90.25 (*1-55938-354-2*) Jai Pr.

***Advances in Forensic Haemogenetics.** Ed. by W. Bar & Zurich. 5. 677p. 1994. pap. 82.00 (*0-387-57643-6*) Spr-Verlag.

Advances in Forensic Haemogenetics, No. 2. Ed. by W. R. Mayr. 670p. 1988. pap. 87.60 (*0-387-18765-0*) Spr-Verlag.

Advances in Forensic Haemogenetics 4: 14th Congress of the International Society of Forensic Haemogenetics (Internationale Gesellschaft fur Forensische Hamogenetik e.V.) Mainz, September 18-21, 1991. Ed. by C. Rittner & P. M. Schneider. (Illus.). 480p. 1992. pap. 68.00 (*0-387-55194-8*) Spr-Verlag.

Advances in Forensic Psychology & Psychiatry, Vol. 1. Robert W. Rieber. (Advances in Forensic Psych & Psychiatry Ser.). 200p. 1984. text ed. 55.00 (*0-89391-191-7*) Ablex Pub.

Advances in Forensic Psychology & Psychiatry, Vol. 2. Robert W. Rieber. (Advances in Forensic Psych. & Psychiatry Ser.). 224p. 1987. text ed. 55.00 (*0-89391-291-3*) Ablex Pub.

Advances in Forensic Science, Vol. 4. Lee. 1990. 69.95 (*0-8151-5393-7*, Yr Bk Med Pubs) Mosby Yr Bk.

Advances in Forestry Research in India. International Book Dist. Staff. 400p. 1987. 360.00 (*0-685-54021-9*, Pub. by Intl Bk Distr II) St Mut.

Advances in Forestry Research in India, Vols. 1-6. Ram Parkash. 265p. 1990. 148.00 (*0-685-49623-6*, Pub. by Intl Bk Distr II) St Mut.

Advances in Forestry Research in India, Vols. 1-8. Ram Prakash. 265p. (C). 1988. text ed. 295.00 (*0-685-74393-4*, Pub. by Intl Bk Distr II) St Mut.

Advances in Forestry Research in India, Vols. 1-10. Ram Parkash. 265p. 1993. 198.00 (*81-7089-901-X*, Pub. by Intl Bk Distr II) St Mut.

Advances in Fracture Research: Proceedings of the 5th International Conference on Fracture, 1981, Cannes, France, 6 vols., Set. D. Francois. LC 80-41879. (International Series of Monographs on the Strength & Fracture of Materials & Structures). 3000p. 1982. 80.00 (*0-08-025428-4*, Pub. by Pergamon Repr UK) Franklin.

***Advances in Fracture Resistance & Structural Integrity: Selected Papers from the Eighth International Conference on Fractures (ICF8), Kyiv, Ukraine, 8-14 June 1993.** Ed. by V. V. Panasyuk. LC 94-34031. (International Series on the Strength & Fracture of Materials & Structure). 1994. 210.00 (*0-08-042256-X*, Pergamon Pr) Elsevier.

Advances in Free Radical Chemistry, Vol. 1. Ed. by Dennis D. Tanner. 1990. 90.25 (*0-89232-862-2*) Jai Pr.

Advances in Free Radical Chemistry, Vol. 2. Ed. by Dennis D. Tanner. 1991. 90.25 (*1-55938-321-6*) Jai Pr.

Advances in Free-Radical Chemistry, Vol. 6. Ed. by Gareth H. Williams. LC 65-27404. (Illus.). 333p. reprint ed. pap. 95.00 (*0-8357-8782-6*, 2033352) Bks Demand.

Advances in Fruit Breeding see Fruit Breeding, Vol. 1, Temperate Fruits

Advances in Fruit Breeding see Fruit Breeding, Vol. 2, Nuts

Advances in Fruit Breeding see Fruit Breeding, Vol. 3, Subtropical & Tropical Fruits

Advances in Fuel Management: Proceedings in Pinehurst, NC March 2-5, 1986. 633p. 1986. 66.00 (*0-89448-123-1*, 700109) Am Nuclear Soc.

***Advances in Fundamental Physics: Proceedings of Conference Held in Olympia Greece, Sept. 1993.** Ed. by Michele Barone & Franco Selleri. (Illus.). xii, 474p. (C). Date not set. pap. text ed. 85.00 (*0-911767-72-X*) Hadronic Pr Inc.

Advances in Fusion & Processing of Glass. Ed. by Arun K. Varshneya et al. LC 92-42211. (Ceramic Transactions Ser.: Vol. 29). 663p. 1993. 69.00 (*0-944904-56-4*) Am Ceramic.

Advances in Futures & Options Research, 2 vol. set, Vol. 1. Ed. by Frank J. Fabozzi. 1986. 115.00 (*0-89232-667-0*) Jai Pr.

Advances in Futures & Options Research, Vol. 1, 2 Pts. Ed. by Frank J. Fabozzi. 1986. 73.25 (*0-89232-665-4*); 73.25 (*0-89232-666-2*) Jai Pr.

Advances in Futures & Options Research, Vol. 2. Ed. by Frank J. Fabozzi. 1987. 73.25 (*0-89232-829-0*) Jai Pr.

Advances in Futures & Options Research, Vol. 3. Ed. by Frank J. Fabozzi. 408p. 1989. 65.50 (*0-89232-926-2*) Jai Pr.

Advances in Futures & Options Research, Vol. 4. Ed. by Frank J. Fabozzi. 1991. 65.50 (*1-55938-060-8*) Jai Pr.

Advances in Fuzzy Sets, Possibility Theory, & Applications. Ed. by Paul P. Wang. LC 83-11077. 434p. 1983. 105.00 (*0-306-41390-6*, Plenum Pr) Plenum.

***Advances in Fuzzy Theory & Technology, Vol. II.** Ed. by Paul P. Wang. (Illus.). 384p. 1994. lib. bdg. 69.00 (*0-9643456-1-7*) P P Wang.

Advances in Gas Phase Ion Chemistry, Vol. 1. Ed. by Nigel Adams & Lucia M. Babcock. 1992. 90.25 (*1-55938-331-3*) Jai Pr.

Advances in Gastrointestinal Radiology, Vol. 1. Herlinger. 197p. 1991. 69.95 (*0-8151-4300-1*) Mosby Yr Bk.

Advances in Gastrointestinal Radiology, Vol. 2. Herlinger. 250p. 1992. 79.95 (*0-8151-4301-X*) Mosby Yr Bk.

Advances in Gender & Communication Research. Ed. by Lawrence B. Nadler et al. LC 87-13350. 428p. (Orig.). 1987. pap. text ed. 34.00 (*0-8191-6478-X*) U Pr of Amer.

Advances in Gene Technology, Vol. 1. Ed. by Peter J. Greenaway. 274p. 1990. 90.25 (*1-55938-204-X*) Jai Pr.

Advances in Gene Technology, Vol. 2. Ed. by Peter J. Greenaway. 1991. 90.25 (*1-55938-268-6*) Jai Pr.

Advances in Gene Technology: Human Genetic Disorders, Proceedings of the 16th Miami Winter Symposium. Julius Schultz & William J. Whelan. Ed. by Walter A. Scott et al. (International Council of Scientific Unions Short Reports: No. 1). (Illus.). 300p. 1984. 59.95 (*0-521-26749-8*) Cambridge U Pr.

Advances in Gene Technology: Molecular Biology of the Endocrine System: Proceedings of the 18th Miami Winter Symposium. D. Puett et al. (ICSU Short Reports: No. 4). 402p. 1986. 69.95 (*0-521-32658-3*) Cambridge U Pr.

Advances in Gene Technology: The Molecular Basis of Immune Diseases, Vol. 10. Ed. by J. Streilein et al. (ICSU Short Series Reports: Vol. 10). (Illus.). 276p. 1990. pap. 50.00 (*0-19-963184-0*, IRL Pr) OUP.

Advances in Gene Technology: Molecular Neurobiology & Neuropharmacology: Molecular Neurobiology & Neuropharmacology, Vol. 9. R. L. Rotundo et al. Ed. by F. Ahmad et al. (ICSU Short Series Reports: Vol. 9). (Illus.). 180p. 1989. pap. 50.00 (*1-85221-205-5*, IRL Pr) OUP.

Advances in Genetic Programming. Ed. by Kenneth L. Kinnear, Jr. (Bradford Series in Complex Adaptive Systems). (Illus.). 360p. 1994. 47.50 (*0-262-11188-8*) MIT Pr.

Advances in Genetics, Vol. 22. Ed. by M. Demerec. (Serial Publication Ser.). 1984. text ed. 121.00 (*0-12-017622-X*) Acad Pr.

Advances in Genetics, Vol. 25. Ed. by E. W. Caspari & John G. Scandelios. 319p. 1988. text ed. 92.00 (*0-12-017625-4*) Acad Pr.

Advances in Genetics, Vol. 26. Ed. by John G. Scandalios. (Serial Publication Ser.). 202p. 1989. text ed. 80.00 (*0-12-017626-2*) Acad Pr.

Advances in Genetics, Vol. 29. Ed. by John G. Scandalios & Theodore R. Wright. (Illus.). 367p. 1991. text ed. 83.00 (*0-12-017629-7*) Acad Pr.

Advances in Genetics, Vol. 30. Ed. by John G. Scandalios & Theodore R. Wright. (Illus.). 377p. 1992. text ed. 65.00 (*0-12-017630-0*) Acad Pr.

Advances in Genetics, Vol. 31. Ed. by Jeffrey C. Hall & Jay C. Dunlap. 291p. 1994. text ed. 59.00 (*0-12-017631-9*) Acad Pr.

Advances in Genetics, Vols. 1-18. Alexander Sokoloff. Ed. by M. Demerec. Incl. Suppl. 1. Genetics of Tribolium & Related Species. 1966. 55.00 (*0-12-017661-0*); write for info. (*0-318-50184-8*) Acad Pr.

Advances in Gegetics: Genetic Regulatory Hierarchies in Development, Vol. 27. Ed. by Theodore R. Wright & John G. Scandalios. 468p. 1990. text ed. 97.00 (*0-12-017627-0*) Acad Pr.

Advances in Genetics: Genomic Responses to Environmental Stress, Vol. 28. Ed. by John G. Scandalios & Theordore R. Wright. 308p. 1990. text ed. 77.00 (*0-12-017628-9*) Acad Pr.

Advances in Genetics: Molecular Genetics of Development, Vol. 24. Ed. by John G. Scandalios & E. W. Caspari. 529p. 1987. text ed. 121.00 (*0-12-017624-6*) Acad Pr.

Advances in Genetics: Serial Publication, Vol. 23. Ed. by M. Demerac. 1985. text ed. 121.00 (*0-12-017623-8*) Acad Pr.

Advances in Genetics Information: A Guide for State Policy Makers. 200p. 1993. pap. write for info. (*0-87292-975-2*, C-048-92) Coun State Govts.

Advances in Genome Biology, Vol. 1: Unfolding the Genome. Ed. by Ram S. Verma. 1991. 90.25 (*1-55938-349-6*) Jai Pr.

Advances in Geodesy. Ed. by E. W. Grafarend & R. H. Rapp. (Reprint Volumes Ser.). 1984. 23.00 (*0-87590-235-9*) Am Geophysical.

Advances in Geophysical Data Processing, Vol. 3. Ed. by Marwaan Simaan. 1988. 73.25 (*0-89232-620-4*) Jai Pr.

Advances in Geophysical Data Processing: Two Dimensional Transforms, Vol. 2. Marwaan Simaan. 320p. 1985. 73.25 (*0-89232-463-5*) Jai Pr.

Advances in Geophysical Data Processing: Vertical Seismic Profiles, Vol. 1. Ed. by Marwaan Simaan. 1984. 73.25 (*0-89232-401-5*) Jai Pr.

Advances in Geophysical Research, Vol. 1. Institute of Geophysics, Beijing, China Staff. (International Academic Publishers Ser.). 352p. 1990. 94.00 (*0-08-036927-8*, Pergamon Pr) Elsevier.

Advances in Geophysics, Vol. 25. Ed. by Barry Saltzman. (Serial Publication Ser.). 1983. text ed. 142.00 (*0-12-018825-2*) Acad Pr.

Advances in Geophysics, Vol. 26. Ed. by H. E. Landsberg. (Serial Publication Ser.). 1984. text ed. 142.00 (*0-12-018826-0*) Acad Pr.

Advances in Geophysics, Vol. 30. Ed. by Barry Saltzman. (Serial Publication Ser.). 248p. 1988. text ed. 112.00 (*0-12-018830-9*) Acad Pr.

Advances in Geophysics, Vol. 31. Ed. by Barry Saltzman. (Serial Publication Ser.). 290p. 1989. text ed. 116.00 (*0-12-018831-7*) Acad Pr.

Advances in Geophysics, Vol. 32. Ed. by Barry Saltzman & Renata Dmowska. 352p. 1990. text ed. 116.00 (*0-12-018832-5*) Acad Pr.

Advances in Geophysics, Vol. 33. Ed. by Renata Dmowski & Barry Saltzman. (Illus.). 321p. 1991. text ed. 105.00 (*0-12-018833-3*) Acad Pr.

Advances in Geophysics, Vol. 34. Ed. by Renata Dmowska & Barry Saltzman. (Illus.). 265p. 1993. text ed. 95.00 (*0-12-018834-1*) Acad Pr.

Advances in Geophysics, Vol. 36. Ed. by Renata Dmowska & Barry Saltzman. (Illus.). 217p. 1994. text ed. 89.00 (*0-12-018836-8*) Acad Pr.

Advances in Geophysics, Vols. 1-17. Ed. by H. E. Landsberg. Incl. Vol. 12. 1967. (*0-12-018812-0*); write for info. (*0-318-50185-6*) Acad Pr.

Advances in Geophysics: Issues in Atmospheric & Oceanic Modeling , Weather Dynamics, Vol. 28. (Serial Publication Ser.: Pt. B). 1985. pap. 41.50 (*0-12-000004-0*) Acad Pr.

Advances in Geophysics Vol. 29: Anonalous Atmospheric Flows & Blocking. Ed. by Barry Saltzman et al. (Serial Publication Ser.). 1986. text ed. 142.00 (*0-12-018829-5*) Acad Pr.

Advances in Geophysics Vol. 35: Seismological Structure of Slabs. Ed. by Renata Dmowska & Barry Saltzman. (Illus.). 185p. 1994. text ed. 85.00 (*0-12-018835-X*) Acad Pr.

Advances in Geophysics, Pt. A: Issues in Atmospheric & Oceanic Modeling: Climate Dynamics, Vol. 28. (Serial Publication Ser.). 1985. text ed. 156.00 (*0-12-018828-7*) Acad Pr.

Advances in Geophysics, Pt. B: Issues in Atmospheric & Oceanic Modeling, Part B: Weather Dynamics, Vol. 28. (Serial Publication Ser.). 1985. text ed. 125.00 (*0-12-018849-X*) Acad Pr.

Advances in Geophysics, Supplement 2: Principles & Applications of Microearthquake Networks. W. H. Lee & S. W. Steward. LC 80-70588. 1981. text ed. 96.00 (*0-12-018862-7*) Acad Pr.

Advances in Geotechnical Engineering. LC 92-40597. (Research Record Ser.: Vol. 1369). 1992. 24.00 (*0-309-05410-9*) Transport Res Bd.

***Advances in GIS Research: Proceedings of the Sixth International Symposium on Spatial Data Handling.** International Symposium on Spatial Data Handling Staff. Ed. by Thomas C. Waugh & Richard G. Healey. LC 94-44438. 1995. write for info. (*0-7484-0315-9*) Taylor & Francis.

Advances in GLIM & Statistical Modelling: Proceedings of the GLIM92 Conference & the 7th International Workshop on Statistical Modelling Munich, 13-17 July 1992. Ed. by Ludwig Fahrmeir et al. LC 92-17534. (Lecture Notes in Statistics Ser.: Vol. 78). x, 225p. 1992. pap. 36.00 (*0-387-97873-9*) Spr-Verlag.

Advances in Glucuronide Conjugation. Ed. by Matern Siegfried et al. 1985. lib. bdg. 160.50 (*0-85200-901-1*) Kluwer Ac.

Advances in Glycobiology, Vol. 1. Ed. by Thomas E. Rademacher. 1991. 90.25 (*1-55938-350-X*) Jai Pr.

***Advances in Gold & Silver Processing: Proceedings of the Symposium at GOLDTech 4, Reno, NV, September 10-12, 1990.** Symposium at GOLDTech Staff. Ed. by Maurice C. Fuerstenau & James L. Hendrix. LC 90-62222. (Illus.). reprint ed. pap. 86.40 (*0-7837-9173-9*, 2049872) Bks Demand.

Advances in Graph Theory. Ed. by Bela Bollobas. (Annals of Discrete Mathematics Ser.: Vol. 3). 296p. 1978. 70.25 (*0-444-85075-9*, North Holland) Elsevier.

Advances in Grid Generation. Ed. by K. Ghia & U. Ghia. (FED Ser.: Vol. 5). 219p. 1983. pap. text ed. 40.00 (*0-317-02550-3*, G00222) ASME.

Advances in Groundwater Hydrology. Ed. by Zubair A. Saleem. LC 77-92093. 341p. reprint ed. pap. 97.20 (*0-8357-5165-1*, 2017812) Bks Demand.

Advances in Group Processes, Vol. 1. Edward J. Lawler. 73. 25 (*0-89232-369-8*) Jai Pr.

Advances in Group Processes, Vol. 2. Ed. by Edward J. Lawler. 1985. 73.25 (*0-89232-524-0*) Jai Pr.

Advances in Group Processes, Vol. 3. Ed. by Edward J. Lawler. 1986. 73.25 (*0-89232-572-0*) Jai Pr.

Advances in Group Processes, Vol. 4. Barry Markovsky. Ed. by Edward J. Lawler et al. 1987. 73.25 (*0-89232-733-2*) Jai Pr.

Advances in Group Processes, Vol. 5. Ed. by Edward J. Lawler. 1988. 73.25 (*0-89232-893-2*) Jai Pr.

Advances in Group Psychotherapy: Integrating Research & Practice. Ed. by Robert R. Dies & K. Roy MacKenzie. LC 83-206. (American Group Psychotherapy Association Monographs). xvii, 226p. 1985. text ed. 30. 00 (*0-8236-0107-2*, 00107) Intl Univs Pr.

Advances in Group Work Research. Ed. by Aaron M. Brower & Sheldon D. Rose. LC 89-77595. (Journal of Social Service Research: Vol. 13, No. 2). 124p. 1990. text ed. 29.95 (*0-86656-983-9*) Haworth Pr.

Advances in Gynaecological Pathology. Ed. by D. Lowe & H. Fox. (Illus.). 384p. 1992. text ed. 110.00 (*0-443-04377-9*) Churchill.

Advances in Gynecological Endocrinology, 2 vols., Set. Ed. by A. R. Genazzani et al. (Illus.). 1989. 110.00 (*1-85070-208-X*) Prthnon Pub.

Advances in Gynecology & Obstetrics Series, 6 vols., Set. Ed. by B. Belfort et al. (Illus.). 1989. 425.00 (*1-85070-238-1*) Prthnon Pub.

Advances in Health Economics & Health Services Research, Vol. 2. Ed. by Richard M. Scheffler. 300p. 1981. 73.25 (*0-89232-100-8*) Jai Pr.

Advances in Health Economics & Health Services Research, Vol. 3. Ed. by Richard M. Scheffler. 1982. 73.25 (*0-89232-222-5*) Jai Pr.

Advances in Health Economics & Health Services Research, Vol. 4. Ed. by Richard M. Scheffler & Luois F. Rossiter. 1984. 73.25 (*0-89232-260-8*) Jai Pr.

Advances in Health Economics & Health Services Research, Vol. 5. Richard Scheffler. 73.25 (*0-89232-487-2*) Jai Pr.

Advances in Health Economics & Health Services Research, Vol. 8. Ed. by Richard M. Scheffler & Louis F. Rossiter. 1988. 73.25 (*0-89232-735-9*) Jai Pr.

Advances in Health Economics & Health Services Research: An Annual Compilation of Research, Vol. I. Ed. by Richard M. Scheffler. 1979. lib. bdg. 73.25 (*0-89232-042-7*) Jai Pr.

Advances in Health Economics & Health Services Research: Mergers in Health Care - The Performance of Multi-Institutional Organizations, Vol. 7. Ed. by Richard M. Scheffler & Louis F. Rossiter. 300p. 1986. 73.25 (*0-89232-573-9*); write for info. (*0-317-58925-3*) Jai Pr.

Advances in Health Economics & Health Services Research, Vol. 6: Biased Selection in Health Care Market. Ed. by Richard M. Scheffler. 1986. 73.25 (*0-89232-519-4*) Jai Pr.

Advances in Health Economics & Health Services Research, Vol. 9: Private Sector Involvement In Health Care: Implications for Access, Cost, & Quality. Ed. by Richard M. Scheffler & Louis F. Rossiter. 1989. 73.25 (*0-89232-937-8*) Jai Pr.

Advances in Health Education: Current Research 1988-1993, Vols. 1-4. Ed. by James H. Humphrey. LC 86-47857. 1988. 37.50 (*0-404-63550-4*) AMS Pr.

Advances in Health Education & Promotion, Vol. 3. Ed. by William B. Ward & Frances M. Lewis. 300p. 1991. 88.00 (*1-85302-074-5*, Pub. by J Kingsley Pubs UK) Taylor & Francis.

Advances in Health Risk Assessment for Systemic Toxicants & Chemical Mixtures. Ed. by Jerry F. Stara & Linda S. Erdreich. LC 85-63294. (Illus.). 364p. 1986. 65.00 (*0-911131-90-6*) Princeton Sci Pubs.

***Advances in Heat & Mass Transfer in Biological Systems: 1994 International Mechanical Engineering Congress & Exposition, Chicago, Illinois - November 6-11, 1994.** (HTD Ser.: Vol. 288). 168p. 1994. 68.00 (*0-7918-1406-8*, G00901) ASME.

Advances in Heat Transfer. (Engineering Systems Design & Analysis Ser.: Vol. 1). 208p. 1994. pap. 45.00 (*0-7918-1280-4*, H0912A) ASME.

Advances in Heat Transfer, Vol. 16. Ed. by Thomas F. Irvine, Jr. & James P. Hartnett. (Serial Publication Ser.). 1984. text ed. 160.00 (*0-12-020016-3*) Acad Pr.

Advances in Heat Transfer, Vol. 18. Ed. by James P. Hartnett & Thomas F. Irvine, Jr. (Serial Publication Ser.). 1987. text ed. 160.00 (*0-12-020018-X*) Acad Pr.

Advances in Heat Transfer, Vol. 19. Ed. by James P. Hartnett & Thomas F. Irvine, Jr. (Serial Publication Ser.). 316p. 1989. text ed. 158.00 (*0-12-020019-8*) Acad Pr.

Advances in Heat Transfer, Vol. 20. Ed. by James P. Hartnett & Thomas F. Irvine, Jr. (Serial Publication Ser.). 402p. 1990. text ed. 160.00 (*0-12-020020-1*) Acad Pr.

Advances in Heat Transfer, Vol. 21. Ed. by James P. Hartnett & Thomas F. Irvine, Jr. (Illus.). 355p. 1991. text ed. 138.00 (*0-12-020021-X*) Acad Pr.

Advances in Heat Transfer, Vol. 23. Ed. by James P. Hartnett et al. (Illus.). 471p. 1993. text ed. 125.00 (*0-12-020023-6*) Acad Pr.

Advances in Heat Transfer, Vol. 24. Ed. by James P. Hartnett et al. (Illus.). 325p. 1994. text ed. 110.00 (*0-12-020024-4*) Acad Pr.

Advances in Heat Transfer, Vol. 25. Ed. by James P. Hartnett et al. (Illus.). 433p. 1994. text ed. 129.00 (*0-12-020025-2*) Acad Pr.

Advances in Heat Transfer, Vols. 1-14. Incl. Vol. 11. 1975. (*0-12-020075-9*); (Serial Publication Ser.). write for info. (*0-318-50186-4*) Acad Pr.

Advances in Heat Transfer: Bioengineering Heat Transfer, Vol. 22. Young I. Cho. (Illus.). 443p. 1992. text ed. 130. 00 (*0-12-020022-8*) Acad Pr.

***Advances in Heat Transfer Vol. 26, Vol. 26.** Ed. by James P. Hartnett et al. (Illus.). 335p. 1995. boxed 119.00 (*0-12-020026-0*) Acad Pr.

A

An Asterisk (*) at the beginning of an entry indicates that the title is appearing in BIP for the first time. 89

***Advances in Heat Transfer Vol. 27: Radiative Heat Transfer by the Monte Carlo Method.** Wen-Jei Yang et al. Ed. by James P. Hartnett et al. (Illus.). 216p. 1995. boxed write for info. (*0-12-020027-9*) Acad Pr.

Advances in Helio & Asteroseismology. Ed. by Jorgen Christensen-Dalsgaard & Soren Frandsen. (C). 1987. lib. bdg. 169.50 (*90-277-2614-0*); pap. text ed. 69.50 (*90-277-2615-9*) Kluwer Ac.

Advances in Hematological Methods: The Blood Count. Van Assendelft & J. M. England. 272p. 1982. 144.00 (*0-8493-6596-1*, RB45, CRC Reprint) Franklin.

Advances in Hepatic Encephalopathy & Metabolic Nitrogen Exchange. Capocaccia. 1995. write for info. (*0-8493-8964-X*) CRC Pr.

Advances in Hepatic Enecephalopathy & Urea Cycle Diseases. Ed. by G. Kleinberger et al. (Illus.). xii, 770p. 1985. pap. 127.25 (*3-8055-3995-9*) S Karger.

Advances in Heterocyclic Chemistry. Ed. by Alan R. Katrikzky. (Serial Publication Ser.). write for info. (*0-318-50187-2*) Acad Pr.

Advances in Heterocyclic Chemistry, Vol. 30. Ed. by Alan R. Katritzky. (Serial Publication Ser.). 1982. text ed. 169.00 (*0-12-020630-7*) Acad Pr.

Advances in Heterocyclic Chemistry, Vol. 31. Alan R. Katritzky. (Serial Publication Ser.). 1982. text ed. 169.00 (*0-12-020631-5*) Acad Pr.

Advances in Heterocyclic Chemistry, Vol. 32. Ed. by Alan R. Katritzky. (Serial Publication Ser.). 396p. 1982. text ed. 169.00 (*0-12-020632-3*) Acad Pr.

Advances in Heterocyclic Chemistry, Vol. 33. Ed. by Alan R. Katritzky. (Serial Publication Ser.). 1983. text ed. 169.00 (*0-12-020633-1*) Acad Pr.

Advances in Heterocyclic Chemistry, Vol. 34. Ed. by Alan R. Katritzky. (Serial Publication Ser.). 1983. text ed. 175.00 (*0-12-020634-X*) Acad Pr.

Advances in Heterocyclic Chemistry, Vol. 35. Alan R. Katritzky. (Serial Publication Ser.). 1984. text ed. 175.00 (*0-12-020635-8*) Acad Pr.

Advances in Heterocyclic Chemistry, Vol. 36. Ed. by Alan R. Katritzky. (Serial Publication Ser.). 1984. text ed. 187.00 (*0-12-020636-6*) Acad Pr.

Advances in Heterocyclic Chemistry, Vol. 37. Ed. by Alan R. Katritzky. (Serial Publication Ser.). 1984. text ed. 176.00 (*0-12-020637-4*) Acad Pr.

Advances in Heterocyclic Chemistry, Vol. 39. Ed. by Alan R. Katritzky. (Serial Publication Ser.). 1986. text ed. 175.00 (*0-12-020639-0*) Acad Pr.

Advances in Heterocyclic Chemistry, Vol. 40. Ed. by Alan R. Katritzky. (Serial Publication Ser.). 320p. 1986. text ed. 152.00 (*0-12-020640-4*) Acad Pr.

Advances in Heterocyclic Chemistry, Vol. 41. Alan R. Katritzky. (Serial Publication Ser.). 376p. 1987. text ed. 140.00 (*0-12-020641-2*) Acad Pr.

Advances in Heterocyclic Chemistry, Vol. 42. Ed. by Alan R. Katritzky. (Serial Publication Ser.). 410p. 1987. text ed. 152.00 (*0-12-020642-0*) Acad Pr.

Advances in Heterocyclic Chemistry, Vol. 43. A. G. Sykes. (Serial Publication Ser.). 353p. 1988. text ed. 152.00 (*0-12-020643-9*) Acad Pr.

Advances in Heterocyclic Chemistry, Vol. 44. Alan R. Katritzky. (Serial Publication Ser.). 379p. 1988. text ed. 128.00 (*0-12-020644-7*) Acad Pr.

Advances in Heterocyclic Chemistry, Vol. 45. Ed. by Alan R. Katritzky. (Serial Publication Ser.). 349p. 1989. text ed. 138.00 (*0-12-020645-5*) Acad Pr.

Advances in Heterocyclic Chemistry, Vol. 46. Ed. by Alan R. Katritzky. (Serial Publication Ser.). 320p. 1989. text ed. 130.00 (*0-12-020646-3*) Acad Pr.

Advances in Heterocyclic Chemistry, Vol. 48. Ed. by Alan R. Katritzky. (Serial Publication Ser.). 393p. 1990. text ed. 127.00 (*0-12-020648-X*) Acad Pr.

Advances in Heterocyclic Chemistry, Vol. 49. Ed. by Alan R. Katritzky. (Serial Publication Ser.). 474p. 1990. 125. 00 (*0-12-020649-8*) Acad Pr.

Advances in Heterocyclic Chemistry, Vol. 50. Ed. by Alan R. Katritzky. (Serial Publication Ser.). 320p. 1990. text ed. 127.00 (*0-12-020650-1*) Acad Pr.

Advances in Heterocyclic Chemistry, Vol. 51. Ed. by Alan R. Katritzky. 301p. 1990. text ed. 126.00 (*0-12-020751-6*) Acad Pr.

Advances in Heterocyclic Chemistry, Vol. 53. Ed. by Alan R. Katritzky. (Illus.). 429p. 1992. text ed. 99.00 (*0-12-020753-2*) Acad Pr.

Advances in Heterocyclic Chemistry, Vol. 54. Ed. by Alan R. Katritzky. (Illus.). 452p. 1992. text ed. 105.00 (*0-12-020754-0*) Acad Pr.

Advances in Heterocyclic Chemistry, Vol. 55. Ed. by Alan R. Katritzky. (Illus.). 358p. 1992. text ed. 105.00 (*0-12-020755-9*) Acad Pr.

Advances in Heterocyclic Chemistry, Vol. 56. Ed. by Alan R. Katritzky. (Illus.). 428p. 1993. text ed. 105.00 (*0-12-020756-7*) Acad Pr.

Advances in Heterocyclic Chemistry, Vol. 57. Ed. by Alan R. Katritzky. (Illus.). 411p. 1993. text ed. 110.00 (*0-12-020757-5*) Acad Pr.

Advances in Heterocyclic Chemistry, Vol. 58. Ed. by Alan R. Katritzky. (Illus.). 345p. 1993. text ed. 99.00 (*0-12-020758-3*) Acad Pr.

Advances in Heterocyclic Chemistry, Vol. 59. Ed. by Alan R. Katritzky. (Illus.). 369p. 1994. text ed. 105.00 (*0-12-020759-1*) Acad Pr.

Advances in Heterocyclic Chemistry, Vol. 60. Ed. by Alan R. Katritzky. 462p. 1994. text ed. 99.00 (*0-12-020760-5*) Acad Pr.

Advances in Heterocyclic Chemistry, Vol. 61. Ed. by Alan R. Katritzky. (Illus.). 328p. 1994. 99.00 (*0-12-020761-3*) Acad Pr.

Advances in Heterocyclic Chemistry, Vol. 61. Ed. by Alan R. Katritzky. (Illus.). 400p. 1994. write for info. (*0-318-72515-0*) Acad Pr.

***Advances in Heterocyclic Chemistry, Vol. 63.** Ed. by Alan R. Katritzky. (Illus.). 408p. 1995. boxed write for info. (*0-12-020763-X*) Acad Pr.

Advances in Heterocyclic Chemistry, Vols. 1-16. Ed. by Alan R. Katritzky. Incl. Vol. 3. 1964. 89.00 (*0-12-020603-X*); Vol. 14. 1972. 89.00 (*0-12-020614-5*); (Serial Publication Ser.). write for info. (*0-318-50188-0*) Acad Pr.

Advances in Heterocyclic Chemistry: Aminomethylenemalonates & Their Use in Heterocyclic Synthesis, Vol. 52. Ed. by Alan R. Katritzky et al. (Illus.). 304p. 1991. text ed. 109.00 (*0-12-020752-4*) Acad Pr.

Advances in Heterocyclic Chemistry: Electrophilic Substitution of Heterocycles; Quantitative Aspects, Vol. 47. Ed. by Alan R. Katritzky & Roger Taylor. 467p. 1990. text ed. 164.00 (*0-12-020647-1*) Acad Pr.

***Advances in Heterocyclic Chemistry Vol. 62, Vol. 62.** Ed. by Alan R. Katritzky. (Illus.). 388p. 1995. boxed 99.00 (*0-12-020762-1*) Acad Pr.

Advances in Heterocyclic Chemistry Supplement, No. 2. Ed. by Alan R. Katritzky & A. J. Boulton. 432p. 1982. text ed. 158.00 (*0-12-020652-8*) Acad Pr.

Advances in Heterocyclic Natural Product Synthesis, Vol. 1. Ed. by William H. Pearson. 193p. 1991. 90.25 (*1-55938-169-8*) Jai Pr.

Advances in Heterocyclic Natural Product Synthesis, Vol. 2. Ed. by William H. Pearson. 1992. 90.25 (*1-55938-333-X*) Jai Pr.

Advances in High-Tc Superconductors. Ed. by J. J. Pouch et al. (Materials Science Forum Ser.: Vol.137-139). (Illus.). 802p. (C). 1993. text ed. 210.00 (*0-87849-667-X*, Pub. by Trans Tech SZ) LPS Dist Ctr.

Advances in High Temperature Superconductivity. D. Andreone et al. 364p. 1993. text ed. 121.00 (*981-02-1297-6*) World Scientific Pub.

Advances in Himalayan Ecology. G. S. Rajwar. (Recent Researches in Ecology, Environment & Pollution Ser.: Vol. 6). (Illus.). 360p. 1991. 59.00 (*1-55528-241-5*, Messers Today & Tomorrow) Scholarly Pubns.

Advances in Histamine Research: Proceedings of a Satellite Symposium to the 8th International Congress of Pharmacology, July 26-27, 1981, Okayama, Japan. Ed. by B. Uvnas & K. Tasaka. (Illus.). 260p. 1982. 81.00 (*0-08-028006-4*, H130, Pergamon Pr) Elsevier.

Advances in Holography, 3 vols., Vol. 1. Ed. by Nabil H. Farhat. LC 75-647639. (Illus.). 184p. reprint ed. pap. 49. 70 (*0-7837-0721-5*, 2041047) Bks Demand.

Advances in Holography, 3 vols., Vol. 2. Ed. by Nabil H. Farhat. LC 75-647639. (Illus.). 205p. reprint ed. pap. 58. 50 (*0-7837-0722-3*) Bks Demand.

Advances in Holography, 3 vols., Vol. 3. Ed. by Nabil H. Farhat. LC 75-647639. (Illus.). 263p. reprint ed. pap. 75. 00 (*0-7837-0723-1*) Bks Demand.

Advances in Holomorphy. Ed. by J. A. Barroso. (Mathematics Studies: Vol. 34). 766p. 1979. 107.75 (*0-444-85265-4*, North Holland) Elsevier.

Advances in Homotopy Theory: Papers in Honour of I. M. James, Cortona 1988. Ed. by B. Steer & W. Sutherland. (London Mathematical Society Lecture Note Ser.: No. 139). (C). 1990. pap. 37.95 (*0-521-37907-5*) Cambridge U Pr.

Advances in Hopf Algebras. Ed. by Jeffrey Bergen & Susan Montgomery. LC 94-804. (Lecture Notes in Pure & Applied Mathematics Ser.: Vol. 158). 344p. 1994. pap. text ed. 135.00 (*0-8247-9065-0*) Dekker.

***Advances in Hot Deformation Textures & Microstructures: Proceedings of a Symposium Sponsored by TMS & ASM International Pittsburgh, PA.** Ed. by John J. Jonas. LC 94-75874. 592p. 1994. 146.00 (*0-87339-225-6*) Minerals Metals.

Advances in Human - Computer Interaction, Vol. 2. H. Rex Hartson & Deborah Hix. 384p. 1988. text ed. 75.00 (*0-89391-428-2*) Ablex Pub.

Advances in Human-Computer Interaction, Vol. 1. H. Rex Hartson. Ed. by Ben Shneiderman. (Human-Computer Interaction Ser.). 300p. (C). 1985. text ed. 75.00 (*0-89391-244-1*) Ablex Pub.

Advances in Human-Computer Interaction, Vol. 3. H. Rex Hartson & Deborah Hix. 224p. (C). 1992. text ed. 75.00 (*0-89391-751-6*) Ablex Pub.

Advances in Human Computer Interaction, Vol. 4. H. Rex Hartson & Deborah Hix. 292p. 1993. 69.50 (*0-89391-934-9*) Ablex Pub.

Advances in Human Factors in Nuclear Power Systems: Proceedings in Knoxville, TN April 21-24, 1986. 525p. 60.00 (*0-89448-125-8*, 700111) Am Nuclear Soc.

Advances in Human Factors Research on Man - Computer Interactions: Nuclear & Beyond Topical Meeting, Nashville, TN, June 10-14, 1990. 425p. 1990. 90.00 (*0-89448-152-5*, 700146) Am Nuclear Soc.

Advances in Human Genetics, Vol. 2. Ed. by Harry Harris. LC 77-84583. 330p. reprint ed. pap. 94.10 (*0-8357-5166-X*, 2055786) Bks Demand.

Advances in Human Genetics, Vol. 11. Ed. by Harry Harris & Kurt Hirschhorn. LC 77-84583. 404p. 1981. 75.00 (*0-306-40688-8*, Plenum Pr) Plenum.

Advances in Human Genetics, Vol. 12. Ed. by Harry Harris & Kurt Hirschhorn. LC 77-84583. 488p. 1982. 75.00 (*0-306-40949-6*, Plenum Pr) Plenum.

Advances in Human Genetics, Vol. 13. Ed. by Harry Harris & Kurt Hirschhorn. LC 77-84583. 332p. 1983. 75.00 (*0-306-41431-7*, Plenum Pr) Plenum.

Advances in Human Genetics, Vol. 14. Ed. by Harry Harris & Kurt Hirschhorn. LC 77-84583. 414p. 1985. 75.00 (*0-306-41752-9*, Plenum Pr) Plenum.

Advances in Human Genetics, Vol. 15. Ed. by Harry Harris & Kurt Hirschhorn. LC 77-84583. 318p. 1986. 75.00 (*0-306-42155-0*, Plenum Pr) Plenum.

Advances in Human Genetics, Vol. 16. Ed. by Harry Harris & Kurt Hirschhorn. LC 77-84583. 502p. 1987. 75.00 (*0-306-42330-8*, Plenum Pr) Plenum.

Advances in Human Genetics, Vol. 17. Ed. by Harry Harris & Kurt Hirschhorn. LC 77-84583. (Illus.). 230p. 1988. 75.00 (*0-306-42856-3*, Plenum Pr) Plenum.

Advances in Human Genetics, Vol. 18. Ed. by Harry Harris & Kurt Hirschhorn. (Illus.). 406p. 1989. 75.00 (*0-306-43130-0*, Plenum Pr) Plenum.

Advances in Human Genetics, Vol. 19. Ed. by Harry Harris & Kurt Hirschhorn. (Illus.). 358p. 1989. 75.00 (*0-306-43298-6*, Plenum Pr) Plenum.

Advances in Human Genetics, Vol. 20. Ed. by Harry Harris & Kurt Hirschhorn. (Illus.). 115p. 1991. 75.00 (*0-306-43998-0*, Plenum Pr) Plenum.

Advances in Human Genetics, Vol. 21. Ed. by Harry Harris & Kurt Hirschhorn. (Illus.). 144p. (C). 1993. 89.50 (*0-306-44292-2*, Plenum Pr) Plenum.

***Advances in Human Genetics, Vol. 22.** Ed. by H. Harris & K. Hirschhorn. (Illus.). 255p. (C). 1995. 75.00 (*0-306-44845-9*, Plenum Pr) Plenum.

Advances in Human Genetics, Vols. 1-10. Incl. Vol. 9. LC 77-84583. 394p. 1979. 59.50 (*0-306-40219-X*, Plenum Pr); Vol. 10. LC 77-84583. 412p. 1980. 59.50 (*0-306-40386-2*, Plenum Pr); LC 77-84583. (Illus.). write for info. (*0-318-55305-8*, Plenum Pr) Plenum.

Advances in Human Nutrition, Vol. 2. Ed. by Edward J. Calabrese & George H. Scherr. LC 81-82478. 300p. 35. 00 (*0-930376-35-8*) Chem-Orbital.

Advances in Human Nutrition, Vol. 3. Ed. by John J. Kabara & George H. Scherr. LC 81-83797. 286p. 23.50 (*0-930376-39-0*) Chem-Orbital.

***Advances in Human Reproduction: Proceedings of the 8th World Congress on Human Reproduction Jointly with the 4th World Conference on Fallopian Tube in Health & Disease, Bali, Indonesia, April 1993.** Ed. by F. A. Moeloek et al. LC 94-21471. (International Congress, Symposium, & Seminar Ser.). 1994. 88.00 (*1-85070-521-6*) Prthnon Pub.

Advances in Humor & Psychotherapy. Ed. by William F. Fry, Jr. & Waleed A. Salameh. LC 93-17202. 332p. 1993. 38.70 (*0-943158-78-8*, AHPBP, Prof Resc Pr) Pro Resource.

Advances in Hydroscience, Vols. 1-12. Chow Ven Te. Incl. Vol. 3. 1967. 87.50 (*0-12-021803-8*); Vol. 10. 1975. lib. bdg. 120.00 (*0-12-021874-7*); Vol. 11. 1978. lib. bdg. 120.00 (*0-12-021876-3*); Vol. 12. 1981. lib. bdg. 95.00 (*0-12-021878-X*); (Serial Publication Ser.). write for info. (*0-318-50189-9*) Acad Pr.

Advances in Hypersonics II, 3 vols., Set. Ed. by J. J. Bertin et al. LC 92-26882. 1993. 299.00 (*0-8176-3664-1*) Birkhauser.

Advances in Hypersonics II, Vol. 1. Ed. by J. J. Bertin et al. LC 92-26882. x, 437p. 1992. 129.00 (*0-8176-3639-0*) Birkhauser.

Advances in Hypersonics II, Vol. 2. Ed. by J. J. Bertin et al. LC 92-26882. x, 270p. 1992. 129.00 (*0-8176-3663-3*) Birkhauser.

Advances in Hypersonics II, Vol. 3. Ed. by J. J. Bertin et al. LC 92-26882. x, 427p. 1992. 129.00 (*0-8176-3672-2*) Birkhauser.

Advances in Hypertension. Kotchen. 448p. 1993. 65.00 (*0-397-51332-1*) Lippincott.

Advances in Hypertension 1992. Kotchen & Frohlich. (Illus.). 448p. 1991. text ed. 49.50 (*0-397-51131-0*) Lippincott.

Advances in Hypervelocity Techniques: Prodeedings of the Second Symposium on Hypervelocity Techniques, Sponsored by University of Denver, Denver Research Institute, 20 & 21 March, 1962. Denver Research Institute Hypervelocity Symposium Staff. Ed. by Arthur M. Krill. LC 62-3095. 807p. reprint ed. 180.00 (*0-8357-5167-8*, 2019386) Bks Demand.

Advances in Ice Technology: Proceedings of the Third International Conference on Ice Technology (ITC 92) Held in Cambridge, Massachusetts, August 11-13, 1992. Ed. by T. K. Murthy. LC 92-81588. (ITC Ser.: Vol. 3). 376p. 1992. 159.00 (*1-56252-104-7*) Computational Mech MA.

Advances in Image Analysis. Ed. by Y. Mahdavieh & R. C. Gonzalez. LC 92-25969. 1992. 92.00 (*0-8194-1046-2*); pap. 77.00 (*0-8194-1047-0*) SPIE.

Advances in Image Compression & Automatic Target Recognition. Ed. by Andrew G. Tescher. 267p. 1989. 53.00 (*0-8194-0135-8*, VOL. 1099) SPIE.

Advances in Image Processing. Tescher. Ed. by Oosterlinck. 409p. 1987. 64.00 (*0-89252-839-7*, 804) SPIE.

Advances in Imaging & Electron Physics, Vol. 90. Ed. by Peter W. Hawkes et al. (Illus.). 441p. 1994. text ed. 99. 00 (*0-12-014732-7*) Acad Pr.

***Advances in Imaging & Electron Physics Vol. 91, Vol. 91.** Ed. by Peter W. Hawkes et al. (Illus.). 297p. 1995. boxed 99.00 (*0-12-014733-5*) Acad Pr.

***Advances in Imaging & Electron Physics Vol. 92, Vol. 92.** Ed. by Peter W. Hawkes et al. (Illus.). 219p. 1995. boxed 85.00 (*0-12-014734-3*) Acad Pr.

***Advances in Imaging & Electron Physics Vol. 93, Vol. 93.** Ed. by Peter W. Hawkes et al. (Illus.). 338p. 1995. boxed 99.00 (*0-12-014735-1*) Acad Pr.

Advances in Immunity & Cancer Therapy, Vol. 1. (Illus.). 220p. 1985. 85.00 (*0-387-96083-X*) Spr-Verlag.

Advances in Immunity & Cancer Therapy, Vol. 2. P. K. Ray. (Illus.). 305p. 1986. 91.00 (*0-387-96258-1*) Spr-Verlag.

Advances in Immunoassay, Vol. 1. Ed. by Catherine M. Sturgeon. 1991. 90.25 (*1-55938-322-4*) Jai Pr.

Advances in Immunohistochemistry. De Lellis. 1984. 87.00 (*0-89352-215-5*) Mosby Yr Bk.

Advances in Immunohistochemistry. Ed. by Ronald A. DeLellis. (Illus.). 508p. 1988. text ed. 105.00 (*0-88167-394-3*) Raven.

Advances in Immunology, Vol. 34. Ed. by Frank J. Dixon & Henry G. Kunkel. (Serial Publication Ser.). 1983. text ed. 120.00 (*0-12-022434-8*) Acad Pr.

Advances in Immunology, Vol. 35. Frank J. Dixon. (Serial Publication Ser.). 1984. text ed. 120.00 (*0-12-022435-6*) Acad Pr.

Advances in Immunology, Vol. 36. Ed. by Frank J. Dixon. (Serial Publication Ser.). 1984. text ed. 120.00 (*0-12-022436-4*) Acad Pr.

Advances in Immunology, Vol. 37. Ed. by Frank J. Dixon. (Serial Publication Ser.). 1985. text ed. 120.00 (*0-12-022437-2*) Acad Pr.

Advances in Immunology, Vol. 38. Ed. by Frank J. Dixon. (Serial Publication Ser.). 424p. 1986. text ed. 120.00 (*0-12-022438-0*) Acad Pr.

Advances in Immunology, Vol. 39. Ed. by Frank J. Dixon. (Serial Publication Ser.). 323p. 1986. text ed. 120.00 (*0-12-022439-9*) Acad Pr.

Advances in Immunology, Vol. 40. Ed. by Frank J. Dixon et al. (Serial Publication Ser.). 456p. 1987. text ed. 108.00 (*0-12-022440-2*) Acad Pr.

Advances in Immunology, Vol. 41. Ed. by Frank J. Dixon. (Serial Publication Ser.). 476p. 1987. text ed. 96.00 (*0-12-022441-0*) Acad Pr.

Advances in Immunology, Vol. 42. Ed. by Frank J. Dixon. (Serial Publication Ser.). 344p. 1988. text ed. 96.00 (*0-12-022442-9*) Acad Pr.

Advances in Immunology, Vol. 43. Frank J. Dixon. (Serial Publication Ser.). 328p. 1988. text ed. 96.00 (*0-12-022443-7*) Acad Pr.

Advances in Immunology, Vol. 44. Ed. by Frank J. Dixon. (Serial Publication Ser.). 401p. 1989. text ed. 104.00 (*0-12-022444-5*) Acad Pr.

Advances in Immunology, Vol. 45. Ed. by Frank J. Dixon. (Serial Publication Ser.). 459p. 1989. text ed. 106.00 (*0-12-022445-3*) Acad Pr.

Advances in Immunology, Vol. 46. Ed. by Frank J. Dixon. (Serial Publication Ser.). 355p. 1989. text ed. 92.00 (*0-12-022446-1*) Acad Pr.

Advances in Immunology, Vol. 47. Ed. by Frank J. Dixon. (Serial Publication Ser.). 460p. 1989. text ed. 104.00 (*0-12-022447-X*) Acad Pr.

Advances in Immunology, Vol. 48. Ed. by Frank J. Dixon. (Serial Publication Ser.). 380p. 1990. text ed. 92.00 (*0-12-022448-8*) Acad Pr.

Advances in Immunology, Vol. 49. Ed. by Frank J. Dixon. (Illus.). 439p. 1991. text ed. 83.00 (*0-12-022449-6*) Acad Pr.

Advances in Immunology, Vol. 50. Ed. by Frank J. Dixon. (Illus.). 343p. 1991. text ed. 77.00 (*0-12-022450-X*) Acad Pr.

Advances in Immunology, Vol. 51. Ed. by Frank J. Dixon. (Illus.). 397p. 1992. text ed. 75.00 (*0-12-022451-8*) Acad Pr.

Advances in Immunology, Vol. 52. Ed. by Frank J. Dixon. (Illus.). 496p. 1992. text ed. 80.00 (*0-12-022452-6*) Acad Pr.

Advances in Immunology, Vol. 53. Ed. by Frank J. Dixon. (Illus.). 342p. 1993. text ed. 75.00 (*0-12-022453-4*) Acad Pr.

Advances in Immunology, Vol. 54. Ed. by Frank J. Dixon. (Illus.). 443p. 1993. text ed. 89.00 (*0-12-022454-2*) Acad Pr.

Advances in Immunology, Vol. 55. Ed. by Frank J. Dixon. (Illus.). 456p. 1993. text ed. 85.00 (*0-12-022455-0*) Acad Pr.

Advances in Immunology, Vol. 56. Ed. by Frank J. Dixon. 501p. 1994. text ed. 89.00 (*0-12-022456-9*) Acad Pr.

***Advances in Immunology, Vol. 57.** Ed. by Frank J. Dixon. (Illus.). 391p. 1994. boxed 80.00 (*0-12-022457-7*) Acad Pr.

***Advances in Immunology, Vol. 59.** Ed. by Frank J. Dixon. (Illus.). 416p. 1995. boxed write for info. (*0-12-022459-3*) Acad Pr.

***Advances in Immunology, Vol. 60.** Ed. by Frank J. Dixon. (Illus.). 420p. 1995. boxed write for info. (*0-12-022460-7*) Acad Pr.

Advances in Immunology, Vols. 1-29. Incl. Vol. 1. Ed. by William H. Taliaferro & J. H. Humphrey. LC 61-17057. 1961. 75.00 (*0-12-022401-1*); Vol. 3. Ed. by F. J. Dixon, Jr. et al. LC 61-17057. 1963. 70.00 (*0-12-022403-8*); Vol. 12. Ed. by William H. Taliaferro & J. H. Humphrey. LC 61-17057. 1970. 70.00 (*0-12-022412-7*); LC 61-17057. 1980. 57.00 (*0-686-66773-5*); Incl. Vol. 1. 75.00 (*0-12-022401-1*); Vol. 3. 70.00 (*0-12-022403-8*); Vol. 12. 70.00 (*0-12-022412-7*); Set text ed. 142.00 (*0-12-022430-5*) Acad Pr.

***Advances in Immunology Vol. 58, Vol. 58.** Ed. by Frank J. Dixon. (Illus.). 472p. 1995. boxed 85.00 (*0-12-022458-5*) Acad Pr.

Advances in Immunopharmacology: Proceedings of the First International Conference on Immunopharmacology, 29 July-1 August 1980, Brighton. John W. Hadden et al. LC 80-42270. (Illus.). 538p. 1981. 219.00 (*0-08-026384-4*, Pub. by Pergamon Repr UK) Franklin.

Advances in Immunopharmacology 3: Proceedings of the Third International Conference on Immunopharmacology, Florence, Italy, 6-9 May 1985. Ed. by L. Chedid et al. LC 85-29870. 504p. 1986. 214. 00 (*0-08-032008-2*, Pub. by Pergamon Repr UK) Franklin.

Advances in Industrial & Labor Relations, Vol. 1. Ed. by David B. Lipsky & Joel M. Douglas. 1983. 73.25 (*0-89232-250-0*) Jai Pr.

Advances in Industrial & Labor Relations, Vol. 2. Ed. by David B. Lipsky. 1985. 73.25 (*0-89232-444-9*) Jai Pr.

Advances in Industrial & Labor Relations, Vol. 3. Ed. by David B. Lipsky. 1986. 73.25 (*0-89232-642-5*) Jai Pr.

An Asterisk (*) at the beginning of an entry indicates that the title is appearing in BIP for the first time.

An Asterisk (*) at the beginning of an entry indicates that the title is appearing in BIP for the first time.

91

A

Advances in Investment Analysis & Portfolio Management, Vol. 1. Ed. by Dean F. Reilly. 73.25 (*0-89232-354-X*) Jai Pr.

Advances in Investment Analysis & Portfolio Management, Vol. 1. Ed. by Son-Nan Chen & Cheng-Few Lee. 1991. 73.25 (*1-55938-135-3*) Jai Pr.

Advances in Irrigation, Vol. 1. Ed. by Daniel J. Hillel. (Serial Publication Ser.). 302p. 1982. text ed. 104.00 (*0-12-024301-6*) Acad Pr.

Advances in Irrigation, Vol. 2. Ed. by Daniel J. Hillel. (Serial Publication Ser.). 1983. text ed. 104.00 (*0-12-024302-4*) Acad Pr.

Advances in Irrigation & Drainage: Surviving External Pressures. Ed. by John Borelli et al. LC 83-71586. 568p. 1983. pap. 48.00 (*0-87262-370-X*) Am Soc Civil Eng.

Advances in Irrigation Engineering, Vol. 4. Ed. by Daniel J. Hillel. 372p. 1987. text ed. 146.00 (*0-12-024304-0*) Acad Pr.

Advances in ISDN & Broadband ISDN. William Stallings. LC 92-4188. 272p. 1992. text ed. 45.00 (*0-8186-2797-2*, 2797) IEEE Comp Soc.

Advances in Joining Newer Structural Materials: Proceedings of the International Conference Held in Montreal, Canada, 23-25 July 1990, under the Auspices of the International Institute of Welding. Ed. by IIW Staff. LC 90-34528. (Illus.). 320p. 1990. 170.00 (*0-08-040736-6*, Pergamon Pr) Elsevier.

Advances in Kinetic Theory: Selected Papers. B. Perthame. (Series on Advances in Mathematics). 200p. 1994. text ed. 61.00 (*981-02-1671-8*) World Scientific Pub.

Advances in Kinetic Theory & Continuum Mechanics: Proceedings of a Symposium Held in Honor of Professor Henri Cabannes at the University Pierre et Marie Curie, Paris, France, on 6 July 1990. Ed. by R. Gatignol & Soubbaramayer. (Illus.). xi, 309p. 1991. 69.00 (*0-387-53945-X*) Spr-Verlag.

Advances in Laboratory Automation: Robotics, 1985. Ed. by Gerald L. Hawk & Janet R. Strimaitis. (Illus.). 540p. 1986. 55.00 (*0-931565-01-4*) Zymark Corp.

Advances in Laboratory Automation: Robotics, 1986. Ed. by Gerald L. Hawk & Janet R. Strimaitis. (Illus.). 640p. 1987. 55.00 (*0-931565-02-2*) Zymark Corp.

Advances in Laboratory Automation - Robotics 1988. Ed. by Janet R. Strimaitis & Gerald L. Hawk. (Illus.). 567p. 1989. 65.00 (*0-931565-04-9*) Zymark Corp.

Advances in Laboratory Automation-Robotics, 1984. Ed. by Gerald L. Hawk & Janet R. Strimaitis. (Illus.). 360p. 1984. 45.00 (*0-931565-00-6*) Zymark Corp.

Advances in Languages & Compilers for Parallel Processing. Ed. by Alexander Nicolau et al. (Pitman Ser.). (Illus.). 480p. 1991. pap. 40.00 (*0-262-64028-7*) MIT Pr.

Advances in Large Scale Systems: Theory & Applications, Vol. 1. Ed. by Jose B. Cruz, Jr. 1984. 73.25 (*0-89232-252-7*) Jai Pr.

Advances in Laser Medicine II: Safety & Laser Tissue Interaction. Ed. by H. P. Berlien et al. 540p. 1989. 92.00 (*0-685-38667-8*, VOL. 1143) SPIE.

Advances in Laser Science, II. Ed. by Marshall Lapp et al. LC 87-71962. (Conference Proceeding Ser.: No. 160). 768p. 1987. lib. bdg. 85.00 (*0-88318-360-9*) Am Inst Physics.

Advances in Laser Science IV: Optical Science & Engineering Series 10. Ed. by James L. Gole et al. LC 89-85595. (AIP Conference Proceedings Ser.: No. 191). 808p. 1989. lib. bdg. 85.00 (*0-88318-391-9*) Am Inst Physics.

Advances in Laser-Science 1. Ed. by William C. Stwalley & Marshall Lapp. LC 86-71536. (AIP Conference Proceedings Ser.: No. 146). 800p. 1986. lib. bdg. 85.00 (*0-88318-345-5*) Am Inst Physics.

Advances in Laser Spectroscopy, Vol. 2. Ed. by Bruce A. Garetz & John R. Lombardi. 261p. 1983. text ed. 350.00 (*0-471-26281-1*) Wiley.

***Advances in Laser Spectroscopy Vol. 2.** fac. ed. Ed. by Bruce A. Garetz & John R. Lombardi. (Illus.). 271p. 1994. pap. 77.30 (*0-7837-7666-7*, 2047419) Bks Demand.

Advances in Lattice Gauge Theories: Proceedings of the Conference on Advances in Lattice Gauge Theories, Tallahassee, Florida, April 10-13, 1985. Ed. by D. W. Duke. 460p. 1985. 100.00 (*9971-5-0030-2*) World Scientific Pub.

Advances in Lead-Acid Batteries: Proceedings of the Symposium. Symposium on Advances in Lead-Acid Batteries Staff. Ed. by Kathryn R. Bullock & D. Pavlov. LC 84-73405. (Electrochemical Society Proceedings Ser.: No. 84-14). (Illus.). 546p. reprint ed. pap. 155.70 (*0-7837-4425-0*, 2052485) Bks Demand.

Advances in Learning & Behavioral Disabilities, Supplement 1. Ed. by Kenneth D. Gadow. 1986. Suppl. 1: Methodological Issues in Human Psychopharmacology. 73.25 (*0-89232-643-3*) Jai Pr.

Advances in Learning & Behavioral Disabilities, Vol. 1. Ed. by Kenneth D. Gadow & Irv. Bialer. 450p. 1981. 73.25 (*0-89232-209-8*) Jai Pr.

Advances in Learning & Behavioral Disabilities, Vol. 3. K. Gadow. 1985. 73.25 (*0-89232-333-7*) Jai Pr.

Advances in Learning & Behavioral Disabilities, Vol. 4. Ed. by Kenneth D. Gadow. 360p. 1985. 73.25 (*0-89232-532-1*) Jai Pr.

Advances in Learning & Behavioral Disabilities, Vol. 6. Ed. by Kenneth D. Gadow. 1988. 73.25 (*0-89232-799-5*) Jai Pr.

Advances in Lectin Research, Vol. 1. Ed. by H. Franz. 200p. 1988. 69.00 (*0-387-17972-0*) Spr-Verlag.

Advances in Lectin Research, Vol. 3. Ed. by H. Franz. (Illus.). 152p. 1990. 64.00 (*0-387-51240-3*, 3191) Spr-Verlag.

Advances in Lectin Research, Vol. 4. Ed. by H. Franz. (Illus.). 128p. 1991. 128.00 (*0-387-52940-3*) Spr-Verlag.

Advances in Legume Science: Proceedings of the International Legume Conference, Held at Kew 1978, Vol. 1. Ed. by R. J. Summerfield & A. H. Bunting. 667p. 1980. pap. text ed. 45.00 (*0-85521-223-3*, Pub. by Royal Botanic Garden UK) Lubrecht & Cramer.

Advances in Librarianship, Vol. 14. Ed. by Wesley Simonton. (Serial Publication Ser.). 320p. 1986. text ed. 75.00 (*0-12-024614-7*) Acad Pr.

Advances in Librarianship, Vol. 16. Ed. by Irene P. Godden. (Illus.). 229p. 1992. text ed. 60.00 (*0-12-024616-3*) Acad Pr.

Advances in Librarianship, Vol. 17. Ed. by Irene P. Godden. 288p. 1993. text ed. 59.95 (*0-12-024617-1*) Acad Pr.

Advances in Librarianship, Vol. 18. Ed. by Irene P. Godden. (Illus.). 242p. 1994. text ed. 59.95 (*0-12-024618-X*) Acad Pr.

Advances in Librarianship, Vols. 1-8. Incl. Vol. 7. LC 79-88675. 1977. 65.00 (*0-685-00040-0*); LC 79-88675. (Serial Publication Ser.). write for info. (*0-318-50193-7*) Acad Pr.

Advances in Library Administration & Organization, Vol. 2. Ed. by Gerard B. McCabe & Bernard Kreissman. 373p. 1983. 73.25 (*0-89232-214-4*) Jai Pr.

Advances in Library Administration & Organization, Vol. 3. G. McCabe et al. 320p. 1984. 73.25 (*0-89232-386-8*) Jai Pr.

Advances in Library Administration & Organization, Vol. 4. Ed. by Gerard B. McCabe & Bernard Kreissman. 233p. 1985. 73.25 (*0-89232-566-6*) Jai Pr.

Advances in Library Administration & Organization, Vol. 5. Gerard B. McCabe. 307p. 1986. 73.25 (*0-89232-674-3*) Jai Pr.

Advances in Library Administration & Organization, Vol. 6. Ed. by Gerard B. McCabe & Bernard Kreissman. 1987. lib. bdg. 73.25 (*0-89232-724-3*) Jai Pr.

Advances in Library Administration & Organization, Vol. 7. Ed. by Gerard B. McCabe & Bernard Kreissman. 1988. 73.25 (*0-89232-817-7*) Jai Pr.

Advances in Library Administration & Organization: A Research Annual. Ed. by Gerard B. McCabe & Bernard Kreissman. 302p. 1989. 73.25 (*0-89232-967-X*) Jai Pr.

Advances in Library & Information Science, Vol. 3. Ed. by C. D. Sharma & D. C. Ojha. (C). 1992. text ed. 150.00 (*81-7233-023-5*, Pub. by Scientific Pubs II) St Mut.

Advances in Library Automation & Networking, Vol. 1. Ed. by Joe A. Hewitt. 1987. 73.25 (*0-89232-385-X*) Jai Pr.

Advances in Library Automation & Networking, Vol. 2. Ed. by Joe A. Hewitt. 1987. lib. bdg. 73.25 (*0-89232-673-5*) Jai Pr.

Advances in Library Resource Sharing, Vol. 1. Ed. by Jennifer Cargill & Diane Graves. 250p. 1990. lib. bdg. 55.00 (*0-88736-490-X*) Mecklermedia.

Advances in Life Prediction Methods. Ed. by D. A. Woodford & J. R. Whitehead. 382p. 1983. pap. text ed. 60.00 (*0-317-03524-X*, H00255) ASME.

***Advances in Linear Logic.** Ed. by Jean-Yves Girard et al. (London Mathematical Society Lecture Note Ser.: No. 222). (Illus.). 384p. (C). 1995. pap. write for info. (*0-521-55961-8*) Cambridge U Pr.

Advances in Lipid Methodology - One. Ed. by William W. Christie. (Oily Press Lipid Library: Vol. 2). (Illus.). 370p. 1992. 58.00 (*0-9514171-1-8*, Pub. by Oily Pr UK) Matreya.

Advances in Lipid Methodology II. Ed. by William W. Christie. (Illus.). 335p. (C). 1993. 62.00 (*0-9514171-3-4*, Pub. by Oily Pr UK) Matreya.

Advances in Lipid Research, Vol. 21. Ed. by David Kritchevsky & Rodolfo Paoletti. (Serial Publication Ser.). 1985. text ed. 139.00 (*0-12-024921-9*) Acad Pr.

Advances in Lipid Research, Vol. 22. Ed. by Rodolfo Paoletti & David Kritchevsky. (Serial Publication Ser.). 199p. 1988. text ed. 85.00 (*0-12-024922-7*) Acad Pr.

Advances in Lipid Research, Vol. 23. Ed. by Rodolfo Paoletti & David Kritchevsky. (Serial Publication Ser.). 305p. 1989. text ed. 104.00 (*0-12-024923-5*) Acad Pr.

Advances in Lipid Research, Vol. 24: Skin Lipids. Ed. by Richard Havel et al. (Illus.). 355p. 1991. text ed. 98.00 (*0-12-024924-3*) Acad Pr.

Advances in Lipid Research, Vol. 25: Sphingolipids: Functions & Breakdowns, Pt. A. Ed. by Richard Havel et al. (Illus.). 339p. 1993. text ed. 85.00 (*0-12-024925-1*) Acad Pr.

Advances in Lipid Research, Vol. 26: Regulation & Function of Sphingolipid Metabolism, Pt. B. Ed. by Robert M. Bell et al. (Illus.). 384p. 1993. text ed. 85.00 (*0-12-024926-X*) Acad Pr.

***Advances in Liquid Chromatography.** T. Hanai & H. Hatano. 300p. 1995. text ed. 91.00 (*981-02-1906-7*) World Scientific Pub.

Advances in Liquid Crystal Research & Applications: Proceedings of the Third Liquid Crystal Conference of the Socialist Countries, Budapest, 27-31 August 1979. Ed. by L. Bata. 1000p. 1981. 535.00 (*0-08-026191-4*, Pub. by Pergamon Repr UK) Franklin.

Advances in Liquid Crystals, Vol. 5. Ed. by Glenn H. Brown. 1983. text ed. 158.00 (*0-12-025005-5*) Acad Pr.

Advances in Liquid Crystals, Vol. 6. Ed. by Glenn H. Brown. (Serial Publication Ser.). 1983. text ed. 158.00 (*0-12-025006-3*) Acad Pr.

Advances in Liquid Crystals, Vols. 1-3. Ed. by Glenn H. Brown. Incl. Vol. 1. LC 74-17973. 1975. lib. bdg. 95.00 (*0-12-025074-8*); Vol. 2. LC 74-17973. 1976. lib. bdg. 100.00 (*0-12-025076-4*); Vol. 3. LC 74-17973. 1978. lib. bdg. 90.00 (*0-12-025078-0*); LC 74-17973. (Serial Publication Ser.). write for info. (*0-318-50195-3*) Acad Pr.

Advances in Local & Metropolitan Area Networks. William Stallings. LC 93-35716. 500p. 1993. text ed. 60.00 (*0-8186-5042-7*, 5042) IEEE Comp Soc.

Advances in Local Area Networks. Karl Kummerle et al. LC 87-420. 616p. 1987. 49.95 (*0-87942-217-3*, PCO2105) Inst Electrical.

Advances in Localized Corrosion. (Illus.). 474p. 1990. 10.00 (*1-877914-13-4*) NACE Intl.

Advances in Logic Programming & Automated Reasoning, Vol. 1. Ralph W. Wilkerson. 420p. 1991. text ed. 75.00 (*0-89391-683-8*) Ablex Pub.

***Advances in Logic Programming & Automated Reasoning Vol. 2.** Chilukuri D. Moham et al. 240p. 1995. 55.00 (*0-89391-841-5*) Ablex Pub.

***Advances in Logic Programming Theory.** Ed. by Giorgio Levi. (International Schools for Computer Scientists Ser.). 268p. 1995. text ed. 72.00 (*0-19-853853-7*) OUP.

Advances in Long-Term Care, Vol. I. Ed. by Paul R. Katz et al. 288p. 1991. text ed. 44.95 (*0-8261-6830-2*) Springer Pub.

Advances in Long-Term Care, Vol. II. Ed. by Paul R. Katz et al. 288p. 1992. 47.95 (*0-8261-6831-0*) Springer Pub.

Advances in Low-Temperature Biology, Vol. 1. Ed. by Peter L. Steponkus. 1991. 90.25 (*1-55938-351-8*) Jai Pr.

Advances in Low-Temperature Plasma Chemistry, Technology, Applications, Vol. 1. Ed. by Herman V. Boenig. LC 84-51635. 377p. 1984. 24.50 (*0-87762-373-2*) Technomic.

Advances in Low-Temperature Plasma Chemistry, Technology, Applications, Vol. 2. Ed. by Herman V. Boenig. LC 85-650565. 290p. 1988. 24.50 (*0-87762-541-7*) Technomic.

Advances in Low-Temperature Plasma Chemistry, Technology, Applications, Vol. 3. Ed. by Herman V. Boenig. LC 85-650565. 274p. 1991. 24.50 (*0-87762-746-0*) Technomic.

Advances in Low-Temperature Plasma Chemistry, Technology, Applications, Vol. 4. Ed. by Herman V. Boenig. 1991. 24.50 (*0-87762-779-7*) Technomic.

Advances in Luminesince Spectroscopy - STP 863. Ed. by L. J. Cline Love & Delyle Eastwood. LC 84-71320. (Illus.). 129p. 1985. pap. text ed. 26.00 (*0-8031-0412-X*, 04-863000-39) ASTM.

Advances in Machine Tool Design & Research. S. A. Tobias & F. Koenigsberger. write for info. (*0-318-57471-3*, Pergamon Pr) Elsevier.

Advances in Machine Tool Design & Research: Proceedings Fourth International Machine Tool Design & Research Conference, Manchester College, September 1963. S. A. Tobias & F. Koenigsberger. LC 63-19240. 1964. 204.00 (*0-08-010757-5*, Pub. by Pergamon Repr UK) Franklin.

Advances in Machine Tool Design & Research: Proceedings of Fifth International Machine Tool Design & Research Conference, University of Birmingham, Sept. 1964. S. A. Tobias & F. Koenigsberger. LC 63-19240. 1965. 245.00 (*0-08-010996-9*, Pub. by Pergamon Repr UK) Franklin.

Advances in Machine Tool Design & Research: Proceedings of the 3rd International MTDR Conference, University of Birmingham, September, 1962. S. A. Tobias & F. Koenigsberger. LC 63-19240. 1963. 204.00 (*0-08-010295-6*, Pub. by Pergamon Repr UK) Franklin.

Advances in Machine Tool Design & Research: Proceedings of the 6th International MTDR Conference, Manchester College, Sept. 1965. S. A. Tobias & F. Koenigsberger. LC 66-18691. 1966. 325.00 (*0-08-011430-X*, Pub. by Pergamon Repr UK) Franklin.

Advances in Machine Tool Design & Research 1966: Proceedings of the 7th International Mtdr Conference, University of Birmingham, Sept. 1966. S. A. Tobias & F. Koenigsberger. LC 66-17931. 1967. 292.00 (*0-08-012047-4*, Pub. by Pergamon Repr UK) Franklin.

Advances in Machine Tool Design & Research 1968: Proceedings 9th International MTDR Conference University of Birmingham, 9-68, Pts. 1 & 2. S. A. Tobias & F. Koenigsberger. LC 74-79867. 1969. 552.00 (*0-08-013369-X*, Pub. by Pergamon Repr UK) Franklin.

Advances in Machine Tool Design & Research, 1969: Proceedings 10th International MTDR Conference Univ Manchester 9-69. S. A. Tobias & F. Koenigsberger. LC 63-19240. 1970. 306.00 (*0-08-015661-4*, Pub. by Pergamon Repr UK) Franklin.

Advances in Machine Tool Design & Research 1970: Proceedings 11th International MTDR Conference University Birmingham 9-70, Set. S. A. Tobias & F. Koenigsberger. LC 63-19240. 1971. 496.00 (*0-08-016559-1*, Pub. by Pergamon Repr UK) Franklin.

Advances in Machine Vision. Ed. by J. L. Sanz. (Perception Engineering Ser.). (Illus.). 380p. 1988. 96.00 (*0-387-96822-9*) Spr-Verlag.

Advances in Machine Vision: Strategies & Applications. Ed. by Colin Archibald & Emil Petriu. LC 92-19672. (Series in Computer Science: Vol. 32). 450p. 1992. text ed. 81.00 (*981-02-0976-2*) World Scientific Pub.

Advances in Macromolecular Carbohydrate Research, Vol. 1. Ed. by Robert J. Sturgeon. 1991. 90.25 (*1-55938-323-2*) Jai Pr.

Advances in Magnesium Alloys & Composites. Ed. by H. Paris & W. H. Hunt. LC 88-60116. (Illus.). 152p. 1989. 65.00 (*0-87339-038-5*, 324) Minerals Metals.

Advances in Magnesium Alloys & Composites: Proceedings of a Symposium Sponsored by the International Magnesium Association & the Non-Ferrous Metals Committee, Held at the Annual Meeting of the Minerals, Metals, & Materials Society in Phoenix, Arizona, January 26, 1988. fac. ed. Minerals, Metals, & Materials Society Staff. Ed. by Henry G. Paris & W. H. Hunt. LC 88-60116. (Illus.). 153p. pap. 43.70 (*0-7837-6966-0*, 2052523) Bks Demand.

Advances in Magnetic & Optical Resonance, Vol. 15. Ed. by Warren S. Warren. 267p. 1990. text ed. 116.00 (*0-12-025515-4*) Acad Pr.

Advances in Magnetic & Optical Resonance, Vol. 16. Ed. by Warren S. Warren. (Illus.). 277p. 1991. text ed. 95.00 (*0-12-025516-2*) Acad Pr.

Advances in Magnetic & Optical Resonance, Vol. 17. Ed. by Warren S. Warren. (Illus.). 165p. 1992. text ed. 75.00 (*0-12-025517-0*) Acad Pr.

Advances in Magnetic & Optical Resonance, Vol. 18. Ed. by Warren S. Warren. (Illus.). 185p. 1994. text ed. 95.00 (*0-12-025518-9*) Acad Pr.

Advances in Magnetic Resonance, Vol. 10. Ed. by John S. Waugh. 196p. 1983. text ed. 134.00 (*0-12-025510-3*) Acad Pr.

Advances in Magnetic Resonance, Vol. 11. Ed. by John S. Waugh. 1983. text ed. 134.00 (*0-12-025511-1*) Acad Pr.

Advances in Magnetic Resonance, Vol. 12. Ed. by John S. Waugh. 438p. 1988. text ed. 134.00 (*0-12-025512-X*) Acad Pr.

Advances in Magnetic Resonance, Vol. 13. Ed. by Warren S. Warren. 277p. 1989. text ed. 114.00 (*0-12-025513-8*) Acad Pr.

Advances in Magnetic Resonance, Vol. 14. Ed. by Warren S. Warren. 296p. 1990. text ed. 109.00 (*0-12-025514-6*) Acad Pr.

Advances in Magnetic Resonance Imaging, Vol. 1. Ed. by Ephraim Feig. 272p. (C). 1989. text ed. 55.00 (*0-89391-445-2*) Ablex Pub.

Advances in Magnetic Resonance, Supplement 2: NMR Imaging in Biomedicine. John S. Waugh et al. 1982. text ed. 134.00 (*0-12-025562-6*) Acad Pr.

Advances in Magnetohydrodynamics: Proceedings of Colloquium Department of Fuel Technology & Chemical Engineering. I. McGrath & R. Sidall. LC 62-22054. 1963. 68.00 (*0-08-009815-0*, Pub. by Pergamon Repr UK) Franklin.

Advances in Magnetospheric Physics with GEOS-1 & ISEE. Ed. by K. Knott et al. 1979. lib. bdg. 68.50 (*0-686-25183-0*) Kluwer Ac.

Advances in Man-Machine Systems Research, Vol. 1. Ed. by William B. Rouse. 1984. 73.25 (*0-89232-404-X*) Jai Pr.

Advances in Man-Machine Systems Research, Vol. 2. Ed. by William B. Rouse. 1985. 73.25 (*0-89232-466-X*) Jai Pr.

Advances in Man-Machine Systems Research, Vol. 3. Ed. by William B. Rouse. 1987. 73.25 (*0-89232-659-X*) Jai Pr.

Advances in Man-Machine Systems Research, Vol. 4. Ed. by William B. Rouse. 1988. 73.25 (*0-89232-753-7*) Jai Pr.

Advances in Management & Conservation of Soil Fauna. G. K. Veeresh et al. (C). 1991. 50.00 (*81-204-0598-6*, Pub. by Oxford IBH II) S Asia.

Advances in Management Education. Ed. by John E. Beck & Charles Cox. LC 80-40117. (Illus.). 370p. reprint ed. pap. 105.50 (*0-8357-5169-4*, 2033048) Bks Demand.

Advances in Manufacturing: Proceedings of the International Conference Held in Singapore, 9-11 October 1984. IFS Staff. 300p. 1985. 128.25 (*0-444-87625-1*, North Holland) Elsevier.

***Advances in Manufacturing Eight: Proceedings of the 10th National Conference on Manufacturing Research.** Ed. by Keith Case & Steven T. Newman. 699p. 1994. pap. 99.00x (*0-7484-0254-3*, Pub. by Tay Francis Ltd UK) Taylor & Francis.

***Advances in Manufacturing Systems: Design, Modeling & Analysis.** Ed. by R. S. Sodhi et al. LC 94-34765. (Manufacturing Research & Technology Ser.: Vol. 22). 1994. write for info. (*0-444-81971-1*) Elsevier.

Advances in Manufacturing Systems - Research & Development. J. Peklenik. 196p. 1971. 86.00 (*0-08-016497-8*, Pub. by Pergamon Repr UK) Franklin.

Advances in Manufacturing Systems Integration & Processes: Fifteenth Conference on Production Research & Technology. Ed. by David A. Dornfeld. LC 88-63275. (Illus.). 649p. 1989. pap. text ed. 60.00 (*0-87263-344-6*) SME.

Advances in Marine Biology, Vol. 16. Ed. by F. S. Russell. (Serial Publication Ser.). 1979. text ed. 209.00 (*0-12-026116-2*) Acad Pr.

Advances in Marine Biology, Vol. 19. Ed. by J. H. Blaxter et al. (Serial Publication Ser.). 1982. text ed. 187.00 (*0-12-026119-7*) Acad Pr.

Advances in Marine Biology, Vol. 20. Ed. by J. H. Blaxter et al. (Serial Publication Ser.). 1982. text ed. 187.00 (*0-12-026120-0*) Acad Pr.

Advances in Marine Biology, Vol. 21. F. S. Russell. (Serial Publication Ser.). 1984. text ed. 150.00 (*0-12-026121-9*) Acad Pr.

Advances in Marine Biology, Vol. 22. Ed. by J. H. Blaxter. (Serial Publication Ser.). 1985. text ed. 150.00 (*0-12-026122-7*) Acad Pr.

Advances in Marine Biology, Vol. 23. Ed. by J. H. Blaxter. (Serial Publication Ser.). 1987. text ed. 150.00 (*0-12-026123-5*) Acad Pr.

Advances in Marine Biology, Vol. 24. Ed. by J. H. Blaxter & Alan J. Southward. (Serial Publication Ser.). 473p. 1988. text ed. 150.00 (*0-12-026124-3*) Acad Pr.

Advances in Marine Biology, Vol. 25. Ed. by J. H. Blaxter & Alan J. Southward. 274p. 1989. text ed. 92.00 (*0-12-026125-1*) Acad Pr.

Advances in Marine Biology, Vol. 26. Ed. by J. H. Blaxter et al. 314p. 1990. text ed. 109.00 (*0-12-026126-X*) Acad Pr.

Advances in Marine Biology, Vol. 28. Ed. by J. H. Blaxter & Alan J. Southward. (Illus.). 452p. 1992. text ed. 118.00 (*0-12-026128-6*) Acad Pr.

Advances in Marine Biology, Vol. 29. Ed. by J. H. Blaxter & Alan J. Southward. (Illus.). 352p. 1993. text ed. 99.95 (*0-12-026129-4*) Acad Pr.

An Asterisk (*) at the beginning of an entry indicates that the title is appearing in BIP for the first time.

An Asterisk (*) at the beginning of an entry indicates that the title is appearing in BIP for the first time.

93

Advances in Molecular & Cellular Immunology, Vol. 1. Ed. by B. Singh. 1991. 90.25 (1-55938-353-4) Jai Pr.

***Advances in Molecular Bioinformatics.** S. Schulze-Kremer. LC 94-77312. (Frontiers in Artificial Intelligence Ser.: Vol. 22). 259p. 1994. pap. 79.00 (90-5199-172-X) IOS Press.

Advances in Molecular Biology & Targeted Treatment for AIDS. Ed. by A. Kumar. (GWUMC Department of Biochemistry Annual Spring Symposia Ser.). (Illus.). 352p. 1991. 95.00 (0-306-43901-8, Plenum Pr) Plenum.

Advances in Molecular Electronic Structure Theory, Vol. 2. Ed. by Thom H. Dunning, Jr. 1991. 90.25 (0-89232-957-2) Jai Pr.

Advances in Molecular Electronic Structure Theory, Vol. 1: Calculation & Characterization of Molecular Potential Energy Surfaces. Ed. by Thom H. Dunning, Jr. 275p. 1990. 90.25 (0-89232-956-4) Jai Pr.

Advances in Molecular Genetics of Plant-Microbe Interactions, Vol. 2. Ed. by Eugene W. Nester & Desh P. Verma. LC 92-35081. (Current Plant Science & Biotechnology in Agriculture Ser.). 640p. (C). 1992. lib. bdg. 137.50 (0-7923-2045-X) Kluwer Ac.

Advances in Molecular Modeling, Vol. 3. Ed. by Dennis Liotta. 1992. 90.25 (1-55938-326-7) Jai Pr.

***Advances in Molecular Plant Nematology.** Ed. by F. Lamberti et al. (NATO ASI Series A, Life Sciences: 268). (C). 1994. 95.00 (0-306-44822-X, Plenum Pr) Plenum.

Advances in Molecular Vibrations & Collision Dynamics, Vol. 1, Pt. A. Ed. by Joel M. Bowman. 1991. 90.25 (1-55938-294-5) Jai Pr.

Advances in Molecular Vibrations & Collision Dynamics, Vol. 1, Pt. B. Ed. by Joel M. Bowman. 1991. 90.25 (1-55938-295-3) Jai Pr.

Advances in Molten Salt Chemistry, 4 vols. Ed. by J. Braunstein et al. Incl. Vol. 4. LC 78-131884. 456p. 1981. 105.00 (0-306-40833-3); LC 78-131884. write for info. (0-318-55306-6, Plenum Pr) Plenum.

Advances in Molten Salt Chemistry, Vol. 5. Ed. by Gleb Mamantov & C. B. Mamantov. 290p. 1983. 115.50 (0-444-42238-2) Elsevier.

Advances in Molten Salt Chemistry, Vol. 6. Ed. by Gleb Mamantov et al. 362p. 1987. 159.00 (0-444-42822-4) Elsevier.

Advances in Morphogenesis, 10 vols. Incl. Vol. 1. Ed. by M. Abercrombie & J. Brachet. 1961. (0-12-028601-7); Vol. 2. Ed. by M. Abercrombie & J. Brachet. 1963. (0-12-028602-5); Vol. 3. Ed. by M. Abercrombie & J. Brachet. 1964. (0-12-028603-3); Vol. 4. Ed. by M. Abercrombie & J. Brachet. 1965. (0-12-028604-1); Vol. 5. Ed. by M. Abercrombie & J. Brachet. 1966. (0-12-028605-X); Vol. 6. Ed. by M. Abercrombie & J. Brachet. 1967. (0-12-028606-8); Vol. 7. Ed. by T. J. King et al. 1968. (0-12-028607-6); Vol. 8. Ed. by T. J. King et al. 1970. (0-12-028608-4); Vol. 9. Ed. by T. J. King et al. 1971. (0-12-028609-2); Vol. 10. Ed. by M. Abercrombie & J. Brachet. 1973. (0-12-028610-6); write for info. (0-318-50204-6) Acad Pr.

Advances in Mossbauer Spectroscopy: Applications to Research in Physics, Chemistry & Biology. Ed. by B. V. Thosar & P. K. Iyengar. (Studies in Physical & Theoretical Chemistry: Vol. 25). 924p. 1983. 287.25 (0-444-42186-6) Elsevier.

Advances in Motivation & Achievement, Vol. 6. Ed. by Martin L. Maehr. 1989. 73.25 (0-89232-889-4) Jai Pr.

Advances in Motivation & Achievement: Motivation & Adulthood, Vol. 4. Ed. by Martin L. Maehr. 1986. 73.25 (0-89232-544-5) Jai Pr.

Advances in Motivation & Achievement: The Effects of School Desegregation on Motivation & Achievement, Vol. 1. Ed. by Martin L. Maehr. 1984. 73.25 (0-89232-290-X) Jai Pr.

Advances in Motivation & Achievement: Women in Science, Vol. 2. Ed. by Martin L. Maehr. 1984. 73.25 (0-89232-288-8) Jai Pr.

Advances in Motor Development Research, 4 vols. Ed. by Jane E. Clark & James H. Humphrey. LC 86-47829. (Illus.). 1993. 37.50 (0-404-63450-8) AMS Pr.

Advances in Mucosal Immunology. Ed. by T. C. MacDonald et al. (C). 1990. lib. bdg. 276.00 (0-7462-0113-3) Kluwer Ac.

***Advances in Mucosal Immunology Pts. A & B: Proceedings of the Seventh International Congress of Mucosal Immunology, Held in Prague, Czechoslovakia, August 16-21, 1992.** Ed. by Jiri Mestecky et al. (Advances in Experimental Medicine & Biology Ser.: Vol. 371). 1520p. 1995. 245.00 (0-306-45012-7) Plenum.

Advances in Multiaxial Fatigue STP 1191. Ed. by David L. McDowell & Rod Ellis. LC 93-11048. (Special Technical Publication Ser.). (Illus.). 465p. 1993. text ed. 108.00 (0-8031-1862-7, 04-011910-30) ASTM.

Advances in Multidimensional Luminescence, Vol. 1. Ed. by Isiah M. Warner & Linda B. McGowan. 205p. 1990. 90.25 (1-55938-172-8) Jai Pr.

Advances in Multidimensional Luminescence, Vol. 2. Ed. by Isiah M. Warner & Linda B. McGowan. 1992. 90.25 (1-55938-327-5) Jai Pr.

Advances in Multiphase Flow & Related Problems. Ed. & Intro. by George Papanicolaou. LC 87-60050. (Proceedings in Applied Mathematics Ser.: No. 26). (Illus.). x, 295p. 1987. text ed. 29.50 (0-89871-212-2) Soc Indus-Appl Math.

Advances in Multiphoton Processes & Spectroscopy, Vol. 7. Ed. by S. H. Lin. 320p. (C). 1991. text ed. 98.00 (981-02-0718-2) World Scientific Pub.

Advances in Multiphoton Processes & Spectroscopy, Vol. 8. S. H. Lin et al. 408p. 1993. text ed. 91.00 (981-02-1543-6) World Scientific Pub.

Advances in Multiplexing in Automobiles. 1990. 49.00 (1-56091-015-1, SP806) Soc Auto Engineers.

Advances in Multivariate Statistical Analysis. A. K. Gupta. (C). 1987. lib. bdg. 133.00 (90-277-2531-4) Kluwer Ac.

Advances in Mutagenesis Research, Vol. 2. Ed. by G. Obe. (Illus.). 384p. 1991. 128.00 (0-387-52428-2) Spr-Verlag.

Advances in Mutagenesis Research, Vol. 3. Ed. by G. Obe et al. (Illus.). ix, 197p. 1991. 149.00 (0-387-53359-1) Spr-Verlag.

Advances in Mutagenesis Research, Vol. 4. Ed. by G. Obe et al. (Illus.). x, 241p. 1993. 169.00 (0-387-55411-4) Spr-Verlag.

Advances in Mutagenesis Research, Vol. 5. Ed. by G. Obe et al. (Illus.). 240p. 1994. 179.00 (0-387-56641-4) Spr-Verlag.

***Advances in Myrmecology.** Ed. by James C. Trager. LC 87-15078. (Illus.). 551p. 1988. pap. text ed. 103.00 (90-04-08475-4) E J Brill.

Advances in Natural Language Generation. Michael Zock & Gerard Sabah. Ed. by Robin P. Fawcett. LC 88-17820. (Communication in Artificial Intelligence Ser.: Vol. 1). 240p. (C). 1988. text ed. 45.00 (0-89391-527-0) Ablex Pub.

Advances in Natural Language Generation. Michael Zock & Gerard Sabah. Ed. by Robin P. Fawcett. (Communication in Artificial Intelligence Ser.: Vol. 2). 240p. (C). 1988. text ed. 45.00 (0-89391-537-8) Ablex Pub.

Advances in Natural Product Chemistry. Ed. by Atta-ur Rahman. LC 92-23126. 1992. text ed. 140.00 (3-7186-5319-2) Gordon & Breach.

Advances in Nd: YAG Laser Surgery. Ed. by S. N. Joffe & Y. Oguro. (Illus.). 465p. 1987. 180.00 (0-387-96506-8) Spr-Verlag.

Advances in Near IR Measurements, Vol. 1. Ed. by Gabor Patonay. 1991. 90.25 (1-55938-173-6) Jai Pr.

Advances in Nemertean Biology: Proceedings of the Third International Meeting on Menertean Biology, Y Coleg Normal, Bangor, North Wales, August 10-15, 1991. Ed. by R. Gibson et al. LC 93-6201. (Developments in Hydrobiology Ser.: Vol. 89). 1993. lib. bdg. 172.00 (0-7923-2482-X) Kluwer Ac.

Advances in Neonatal Screening: Proceedings of the Sixth International Symposium, Austin, TX, November 16-19, 1986, & the Fifth National Symposium, Austin, TX, November 20, 1986. Ed. by B. L. Therrell, Jr. (International Congress Ser.: No. 741). 592p. 1987. 177.00 (0-444-80906-6) Elsevier.

Advances in Nephrology, Vol. 16. Grunfeld. 1986. 69.95 (0-8151-3585-8, Yr Bk Med Pubs) Mosby Yr Bk.

Advances in Nephrology, Vol. 20. Jean-Pierre Grunfeld. 352p. 1991. 69.95 (0-8151-3589-0, Yr Bk Med Pubs) Mosby Yr Bk.

Advances in Nephrology, Vol. 21. Jean-Pierre Grunfeld. 411p. 1991. 69.95 (0-8151-3590-4, Yr Bk Med Pubs) Mosby Yr Bk.

Advances in Nephrology, Vol. 22. Grunfeld. 449p. 1992. 69.95 (0-8151-3591-2) Mosby Yr Bk.

Advances in Nephrology, Vol. 23. Grunfeld. 350p. 1993. 69.95 (0-8151-3592-0, Yr Bk Med Pubs) Mosby Yr Bk.

Advances in Nephrology, Vol. 24. Grunfeld. 350p. 1994. 69.95 (0-8151-3593-9, Yr Bk Med Pubs) Mosby Yr Bk.

Advances in Nephrology, Vol. 25. Grunfeld. 350p. 1995. 69.95 (0-8151-3594-7, Yr Bk Med Pubs) Mosby Yr Bk.

Advances in Nephrology, Vol. 26. Grunfeld. 350p. 1996. 69.95 (0-8151-3595-5, Yr Bk Med Pubs) Mosby Yr Bk.

Advances in Nephrology: Proceedings of the International Congress, 6th, Florence, June, 1975. Ed. by S. Giovannetti & V. Bonomini. (Illus.). 800p. 1976. 143.25 (3-8055-2287-8) S Karger.

Advances in Nephrology & Dialysis. Ed. by G. Colasanti. (Contributions to Nephrology Ser.: Vol. 77). (Illus.). vi, 202p. 1990. 143.25 (3-8055-5064-2) S Karger.

Advances in Nephrology & Dialysis. Ed. by G. D'Amico & G. Colasanti. (Contributions to Nephrology Ser.: Vol. 45). (Illus.). x, 214p. 1985. 104.00 (3-8055-3963-0) S Karger.

Advances in Nephrology from the Necker Hospital, Vol. 12 - 1983. Advances in Nephrology from the Necker Hospital Staff. LC 73-154325. (Illus.). 374p. reprint ed. pap. 106.60 (0-8357-7673-5, 2057001) Bks Demand.

Advances in Nephrology from the Necker Hospital, Vol. 13 - 1984. Advances in Nephrology from the Necker Hospital Staff. LC 73-154325. (Illus.). 408p. reprint ed. pap. 116.30 (0-8357-7674-3, 2057002) Bks Demand.

Advances in Nephrology from the Necker Hospital, Vol. 14 - 1985. Advances in Nephrology from the Necker Hospital Staff. LC 73-154325. (Illus.). 544p. reprint ed. pap. 155.10 (0-8357-7675-1, 2057003) Bks Demand.

Advances in Neural & Behavior Development, Vol. 4. Vivien A. Casagrande. Ed. by Paul Shinkman. 256p. (C). 1993. text ed. 55.00 (0-89391-823-7) Ablex Pub.

Advances in Neural & Behavioral Development, Vol. 1. Ed. by Richard Aslin. (Advances in Neural & Behavioral Development Ser.). 296p. 1985. text ed. 65.00 (0-89391-223-9) Ablex Pub.

Advances in Neural & Behavioral Development, Vol. 2. Ed. by Richard N. Aslin. (Advances in Neural & Behavioral Development Ser.). 256p. 1986. text ed. 65.00 (0-89391-370-7) Ablex Pub.

Advances in Neural & Behavioral Development, Vol. 3. Ed. by Paul Shinkman. (Advances in Neural & Behavioral Development Ser.). 288p. 1988. text ed. 65.00 (0-89391-346-4) Ablex Pub.

Advances in Neural Information Processing Systems, Vol. 1. Ed. by David Touretzky. 800p. (C). 1989. text ed. 49.95 (1-55860-015-9) Morgan Kaufmann.

Advances in Neural Information Processing Systems, Vol. 2. Ed. by David Touretzky. 1990. 49.95 (1-55860-100-7) Morgan Kaufmann.

Advances in Neural Information Processing Systems, Vol. 3. Ed. by Richard P. Lippmann et al. 1130p. 1991. 49.95 (1-55860-184-8) Morgan Kaufmann.

Advances in Neural Information Processing Systems, Vol. 4. Ed. by John E. Moody et al. 1993. text ed. 54.95 (1-55860-222-4) Morgan Kaufmann.

Advances in Neural Information Processing Systems, Vol. 5. Ed. by Jack D. Cowan & C. Lee Giles. 1050p. (C). 1993. 54.95 (1-55860-274-7) Morgan Kaufmann.

Advances in Neural Information Processing Systems, Vol. 6. Ed. by Jack D. Cowan et al. 1200p. 1994. text ed. 54.95 (1-55860-322-0) Morgan Kaufmann.

Advances in Neural Science, Vol. 1. Ed. by Sudarshan Malhotra. 1992. 90.25 (1-55938-356-9) Jai Pr.

Advances in Neuro-Oncology. Ed. by Paul L. Kornblith & Michael D. Walker. (Illus.). 576p. 1988. 75.00 (0-87993-275-9) Futura Pub.

Advances in Neurobehavioral Toxicology: Applications in Environmental & Occupational Health. Ed. by Barry L. Johnson et al. (Illus.). 1990. 99.95 (0-87371-374-5, RA1224) Lewis Pubs.

Advances in Neuroblastoma Research, No. 3. Ed. by Audrey E. Evans et al. LC 09-13148. (Progress in Clinical & Biological Research Ser.). 1991. text ed. 198.00 (0-471-56085-5) Wiley.

Advances in Neuroblastoma Research: Proceedings of the Sixth Symposium on Advances in Neuroblastoma Research, Held in Philadelphia, Pennsylvania, May 13-15, 1993. Ed. by Audrey E. Evans et al. LC 93-48803. (Progress in Clinical & Biological Research Ser.: No. 385). 1994. text ed. 164.95 (0-471-01454-0, Wiley-Liss) Wiley.

Advances in Neurochemistry, Vol. 4. Bernard W. Agranoff & M. H. Aprison. 242p. (C). 1982. 59.50 (0-306-40678-0, Plenum Pr) Plenum.

Advances in Neuroendocrine Physiology. Ed. by K. B. Ruf & G. Tolis. (Frontiers of Hormone Research Ser.: Vol. 10). (Illus.). vi, 142p. 1982. 78.50 (3-8055-2949-X) S Karger.

Advances in Neuroendocrinology. Andrew V. Nalbandov. LC 63-7252. 537p. reprint ed. pap. 153.10 (0-8357-5174-0, 2022260) Bks Demand.

Advances in Neurology. Ed. by J. S. Chopra et al. (International Congress Ser.: No. 883). 1990. 160.00 (0-444-81116-8, Excerpta Medica) Elsevier.

Advances in Neuroscience & Schizophrenia. Ed. by A. Hussain Tuma et al. (Journal of Neural Transmission Ser.: Suppl. 36). 160p. 1992. pap. 73.00 (0-387-82347-6) Spr-Verlag.

Advances in Neurosurgery: Intracerebral Hemorrhages Hydrocephalus Malresorptivus Peripheral Nerves, Vol. 21. Ed. by R. Lorenz et al. (Illus.). 360p. 1993. pap. 79.00 (0-387-56304-0) Spr-Verlag.

Advances in Neurotoxicology: Proceedings of the International Congress on Neurotoxicology, Varese, 27-30 September 1979. Luigi Manzo. LC 80-40319. (Illus.). 404p. 1980. 174.00 (0-08-024953-1, Pub. by Pergamon Repr UK) Franklin.

Advances in Neutron Capture Theory. Ed. by R. F. Barth et al. (Illus.). 756p. (C). 1993. 169.50 (0-306-44567-0, Plenum Pr) Plenum.

Advances in New Crops: Proceeding of the First National Symposium New Crops: Research, Development, Economics. Ed. by Jules Janick. LC 89-28075. (Illus.). 576p. 1990. 65.00 (0-88192-166-1) Timber.

Advances in Nitrate Therapy. Adam Schneeweiss. (Illus.). 170p. 1988. 52.20 (0-387-18655-7) Spr-Verlag.

Advances in Nitrate Therapy. 2nd enl. rev. ed. Adam Schneeweiss & M. Weiss. 232p. 1990. 59.00 (0-387-52798-2) Spr-Verlag.

Advances in Nitrogen Cycling in Agricultural Ecosystems. Ed. by J. R. Wilson. 451p. (Orig.). 1988. pap. text ed. 60.00 (0-85198-603-X) CAB Intl.

Advances in Nitrogen Cycling in Agricultural Ecosystems: Proceedings of the Symposium...Held in Australia 1987. Ed. by J. R. Wilson. 451p. 1988. pap. text ed. 62.50 (0-685-33285-3, Pub. by CAB Commonwlth Agr UK) Lubrecht & Cramer.

Advances in Nitrogen Hetercycles, Vol. 1. Ed. by Frank W. Fowler. 1992. 90.25 (0-89232-864-9) Jai Pr.

Advances in Non-Destructive Examination for Structural Integrity: Proceedings of the International Seminar on Non-Destructive Examination in Relation to Structural Integrity, 2nd, Paris, Aug. 24-25, 1981. Ed. by R. W. Nichols. (Illus.). 447p. 1983. 142.25 (0-85334-158-3, I-459-82, Pub. by Elsevier Applied Sci UK) Elsevier.

Advances in Non-Linear Spectroscopy. Ed. by R. J. Clark & R. E. Hester. (Advances in Spectroscopy Ser.). 363p. 1988. text ed. 492.00 (0-471-91652-8) Wiley.

Advances in Non-Verbal Communication: Sociocultural, Clinical, Esthetic & Literary Perspectives. Ed. by Fernando Poyatos. LC 92-599. xxiv, 412p. 1992. 118.00 (1-55619-121-9); pap. 29.95 (1-55619-491-9) Benjamins North Am.

Advances in Noninvasive Cardiology. Ed. by J. Meyer et al. (Developments in Cardiovascular Medicine Ser.). 1983. lib. bdg. 94.00 (0-89838-576-8) Kluwer Ac.

Advances in Nonlinear Acoustics. H. Hobaek. 716p. 1993. text ed. 128.00 (981-02-1477-4) World Scientific Pub.

Advances in Nonlinear Dynamics & Control: A Report from Russia. Ed. by Alexander B. Kurzhanski. LC 93-39908. (Progress in Systems & Control Theory Ser.: Vol. 17). 1993. 94.50 (0-8176-3736-2) Birkhauser.

Advances in Nonlinear Dynamics & Stochastic Processes: Proceedings of the meeting on Nonlinear Dynamics Arcetri, Florence, January 7-8 1985. Ed. by R. Livi & A. Politi. 232p. 1985. 41.00 (9971-5-0018-3) World Scientific Pub.

Advances in Nonlinear Parameter Optimization. R. Schmidt. (Lecture Notes in Control & Information Sciences Ser.: Vol. 37). 159p. 1982. pap. 20.00 (0-387-11396-7) Spr-Verlag.

Advances in Nonlinear Polymers & Inorganic Crystals, Liquid Crystals, & Laser Media. Ed. by Musikant. 1987. 45.00 (0-89252-859-1, 824) SPIE.

Advances in Nonprofit Marketing, Vol. 1. Ed. by Russell W. Belk. 1985. 73.25 (0-89232-254-3) Jai Pr.

Advances in Nonprofit Marketing, Vol. 2. Ed. by Russell W. Belk. 1987. 73.25 (0-89232-622-0); write for info. (0-317-58927-X) Jai Pr.

Advances in Nonprofit Marketing, Vol. 3. Ed. by Russell W. Belk. 1988. 73.25 (0-89232-825-8) Jai Pr.

Advances in Nonradiative Processes in Solids. Ed. by Baldassare Di Bartolo. (NATO ASI Series B, Physics: Vol. 249). (Illus.). 630p. 1991. 145.00 (0-306-43838-0, Plenum Pr) Plenum.

Advances in Nuclear Dynamics. Ed. by W. Bauer. 300p. (C). 1991. text ed. 89.00 (981-02-0696-8) World Scientific Pub.

Advances in Nuclear Dynamics: Proceedings of the Tenth Winter Workshop on Nuclear Dynamics. W. Bauer et al. 332p. 1994. text ed. 86.00 (981-02-1802-8) World Scientific Pub.

Advances in Nuclear Dynamics: Proceedings of the 8th Winter Workshop on Nuclear Dynamics. W. Bauer & B. Back. 300p. 1992. text ed. 95.00 (981-02-1036-1) World Scientific Pub.

Advances in Nuclear Dynamics: Proceedings of the 9th Winter Workshop Nuclear Dynamics. B. B. Back et al. 328p. 1993. text ed. 114.00 (981-02-1565-7) World Scientific Pub.

Advances in Nuclear Engineering Computations & Radiation Shielding Topical Meeting, Santa Fe, NM, April 9-13, 1989. 930p. 1989. 110.00 (0-89448-148-7, 700144) Am Nuclear Soc.

Advances in Nuclear Physics, Vol. 12. Ed. by J. W. Negele & Erich Vogt. LC 67-29001. 272p. 1981. 79.50 (0-306-40708-6, Plenum Pr) Plenum.

Advances in Nuclear Physics, Vol. 13. Ed. by J. W. Negele & Erich Vogt. LC 67-29001. 334p. 1984. 89.50 (0-306-41313-2, Plenum Pr) Plenum.

Advances in Nuclear Physics, Vol. 14. Ed. by J. W. Negele & Erich Vogt. LC 67-29001. 302p. 1984. 89.50 (0-306-41524-0, Plenum Pr) Plenum.

Advances in Nuclear Physics, Vol. 15. Ed. by J. W. Negele & Erich Vogt. LC 67-29001. 232p. 1985. 89.50 (0-306-41864-9, Plenum Pr) Plenum.

Advances in Nuclear Physics, Vol. 16. Ed. by J. W. Negele & Erich Vogt. LC 67-29001. 342p. 1985. 89.50 (0-306-41997-1, Plenum Pr) Plenum.

Advances in Nuclear Physics, Vol. 17. Ed. by J. W. Negele & Erich Vogt. LC 67-29001. 386p. 1986. 89.50 (0-306-42333-2, Plenum Pr) Plenum.

Advances in Nuclear Physics, Vol. 18. Ed. by J. W. Negele & Erich Vogt. LC 67-29001. 474p. 1988. 95.00 (0-306-42700-1, Plenum Pr) Plenum.

Advances in Nuclear Physics, Vol. 19. Ed. by J. W. Negele & Erich Vogt. (Illus.). 396p. 1989. 95.00 (0-306-43046-0, Plenum Pr) Plenum.

Advances in Nuclear Physics, Vol. 20. Ed. by J. W. Negele & Erich Vogt. (Illus.). 390p. 1991. 95.00 (0-306-43861-5, Plenum Pr) Plenum.

Advances in Nuclear Physics, Vol. 21. Ed. by J. W. Negele & Erich Vogt. 1994. 95.00 (0-306-44548-4, Plenum Pr) Plenum.

Advances in Nuclear Quadrupole Resonance, 4 vols., 2. Ed. by J. A. Smith. LC 77-367974. (Illus.). 284p. reprint ed. pap. 81.00 (0-8357-8788-5, 2033354) Bks Demand.

Advances in Nuclear Quadrupole Resonance, 4 vols., 3. Ed. by J. A. Smith. LC 77-367974. (Illus.). 259p. reprint ed. pap. 73.90 (0-8357-8789-3, 2033354) Bks Demand.

Advances in Nuclear Quadrupole Resonance, 4 vols., 4. Ed. by J. A. Smith. LC 77-367974. (Illus.). 283p. reprint ed. pap. 80.70 (0-8357-8790-7, 2033354) Bks Demand.

Advances in Nuclear Quadrupole Resonance, 4 vols., Vol. 1. Ed. by J. A. Smith. LC 77-367974. (Illus.). 452p. reprint ed. pap. 128.90 (0-8357-8787-7, 2033354) Bks Demand.

Advances in Nuclear Quadrupole Resonance, Vol. 5. Ed. by J. A. Smith. LC 77-367974. (Illus.). 194p. reprint ed. pap. 55.30 (0-8357-2803-X, 2033354) Bks Demand.

Advances in Nuclear Science & Technology, Vol. 21. Ed. by Jeffery D. Lewins & Martin Becker. LC 62-13039. (Illus.). 308p. 1990. 85.00 (0-306-43614-0, Plenum Pr) Plenum.

Advances in Nuclear Science & Technology, Vol. 22. Jeffery D. Lewins. Ed. by Martin Becker. (Illus.). 242p. 1992. 85.00 (0-306-44094-6, Plenum Pr) Plenum.

Advances in Nuclear Science & Technology, Vols. 1-9. Incl. Vol. 1. Ed. by E. J. Henley et al. 1962. (0-12-029301-3); Vol. 2. Ed. by E. J. Henley et al. 1964. (0-12-029302-1); Vol. 4. Ed. by E. J. Henley et al. 1968. (0-12-029304-8); Vol. 5. Ed. by E. J. Henley et al. 1969. (0-12-029305-6); Vol. 6. Ed. by E. J. Henley et al. 1972. (0-12-029306-4); Vol. 7. Ed. by E. J. Henley et al. 1973. (0-12-029307-2); Vol. 9. Ed. by E. J. Henley et al. 1976. (0-12-029309-9); write for info. (0-318-50205-4) Acad Pr.

Advances in Nuclear Science & Technology, Vol. 13. Ed. by Jeffery D. Lewins & Martin Becker. LC 62-13039. 480p. 1981. 110.00 (0-306-40637-3, Plenum Pr) Plenum.

Advances in Nuclear Science & Technology, Vol. 14: Sensitivity & Uncertainty Analysis of Reactor Performance Paramaters. Ed. by Jeffery D. Lewins & Martin Becker. LC 82-3654. 388p. 1982. 95.00 (0-306-40994-1, Plenum Pr) Plenum.

Advances in Nuclear Science & Technology, Vol. 16. Ed. by Jeffery D. Lewins & Martin Becker. LC 62-13039. 596p. 1983. 135.00 (0-306-41486-4, Plenum Pr) Plenum.

Advances in Nuclear Science & Technology, Vol. 17: Simulators for Nuclear Power. Ed. by Jeffery D. Lewins & Martin Becker. LC 85-31170. 244p. 1986. 75.00 (0-306-42234-4, Plenum Pr) Plenum.

An Asterisk (*) at the beginning of an entry indicates that the title is appearing in BIP for the first time.

Advances in Nuclear Science & Technology, Vol. 18. Ed. by Jeffery D. Lewins & Martin Becker. LC 62-13059. 434p. 1987. 105.00 (0-306-42289-1, Plenum Pr) Plenum.

Advances in Nuclear Science & Technology, Vol. 19: Festschrift in Honor of Eugene Wigner. Ed. by Jeffery D. Lewins & Martin Becker. LC 62-13039. 508p. 1987. 120.00 (0-306-42543-2, Plenum Pr) Plenum.

Advances in Nuclear Science & Technology, Vol. 20. Ed. by Jeffery D. Lewins & Martin Becker. (Illus.). 242p. 1988. 85.00 (0-306-43082-7, Plenum Pr) Plenum.

Advances in Nuclear Science & Technology, Vol.15. Ed. by Jeffery D. Lewins & Martin Becker. LC 62-13039. 418p. 1983. 105.00 (0-306-41392-2, Plenum Pr) Plenum.

Advances in Number Theory: The Proceedings of the Third Conference of the Canadian Number Theory Association, August 18-24, 1991, the Queen's University at Kingston. Ed. by Fernando Q. Gouvea & Noriko Yui. LC 92-42788. 560p. 1993. 75.00 (0-19-853668-2) OUP.

Advances in Numerical Analysis: Large-Scale Matrix Problems & the Numerical Solution of Partial Differential Equations, Vol. 3. Ed. by John Gilbert & Donald Kershaw. LC 93-43305. (Illus.). 224p. 1994. 45.00 (0-19-853463-9, Clarendon Pr) OUP.

Advances in Numerical Analysis: Nonlinear Partial Differential Equations & Dynamical Systems, Vol. 1. Ed. by Will Light. (Illus.). 224p. 1991. 52.00 (0-19-853438-8) OUP.

Advances in Numerical Analysis: Wavelets, Subdivision Algorithms, & Radial Basis Functions, Vol. 2. Ed. by Will Light. 224p. 1992. 49.95 (0-19-853439-6) OUP.

***Advances in Numerical Methods & Applications: Proceedings of the 3rd International Conference.** I. T. Dimov et al. 440p. 1994. text ed. 109.00 (981-02-1926-1) World Scientific Pub.

Advances in Numerical Partial Differential Equations & Optimization: Proceedings of the Fifth Mexico-United States Workshop. Ed. by S. Gomez et al. LC 91-658. (Proceedings in Applied Mathematics Ser.: No. 47). xii, 365p. 1991. pap. 47.50 (0-89871-269-6) Soc Indus-Appl Math.

Advances in Numerical Simulation Techniques for Penetration & Perforation of Solids. Ed. by E. P. Chen & V. K. Luk. LC 93-73261. 201p. Date not set. pap. 55.00 (0-7918-1025-9) ASME.

Advances in Nutrition & Cancer. Ed. by V. Zappia et al. LC 93-49575. (Advances in Experimental Medicine & Biology Ser.: Vol. 348). 1994. 65.00 (0-306-44670-7, Plenum Pr) Plenum.

Advances in Nutrition & Top Sport. Ed. by F. Brouns. (Medicine & Sport Science Ser.: Vol. 32). (Illus.). viii, 222p. 1991. 178.50 (3-8055-5376-5) S Karger.

Advances in Nutritional Research, Vol. 4. Ed. by H. H. Draper. LC 78-64045. 358p. 1982. 75.00 (0-306-40786-8, Plenum Pr) Plenum.

Advances in Nutritional Research, Vol. 5. Ed. by H. H. Draper. LC 78-64045. 272p. 1983. 75.00 (0-306-41095-8, Plenum Pr) Plenum.

Advances in Nutritional Research, Vol. 6. Ed. by H. H. Draper. LC 78-64045. 352p. 1984. 75.00 (0-306-41811-8, Plenum Pr) Plenum.

Advances in Nutritional Research, Vol. 7. Ed. by H. H. Draper. LC 78-64045. 290p. 1986. 75.00 (0-306-42213-1, Plenum Pr) Plenum.

Advances in Nutritional Research, Vol. 8. Ed. by H. H. Draper. LC 78-640645. (Illus.). 161p. 1990. 55.00 (0-306-43512-8, Plenum Pr) Plenum.

Advances in Nutritional Research, Vols. 1-3. Incl. Vol. 1. LC 78-640645. 362p. 1977. 59.50 (0-306-34321-5); Vol. 2. LC 78-640645. 264p. 1979. 59.50 (0-306-40213-0); Vol. 3. LC 78-640645. 378p. 1980. 59.50 (0-306-40415-X); LC 78-640645. (Illus.). write for info. (0-318-55307-4, Plenum Pr) Plenum.

***Advances in Nutritional Research Vol. 9: Nutrition & Osteoporosis.** Ed. by Harold H. Draper. 330p. 1995. 79.50 (0-306-44893-9, Plenum Pr) Plenum.

Advances in Nutritional Surveillance: The Cornell Nutritional Surveillance Program, 1981-1987. Katherine Tucker et al. (Monograph Ser.). (C). 1989. pap. text ed. 12.00 (1-56401-002-3) Cornell Food.

Advances in Object-Oriented Database Systems. Ed. by K. R. Dittrich. (Lecture Notes in Computer Science Ser.: Vol. 334). vii, 373p. 1989. pap. 42.00 (0-387-50345-5, 2310) Spr-Verlag.

***Advances in Object-Oriented Databased Systems, Vol. 130.** A. Dogac et al. (Computer & Systems Sciences Ser.). 515p. 1994. 79.00 (0-387-57825-0) Spr-Verlag.

Advances in Object-Oriented Graphics I. Ed. by E. Blake & P. Wisskirchen. (Eurographic Seminars Ser.). (Illus.). viii, 218p. 1991. 98.00 (0-387-53480-6) Spr-Verlag.

Advances in Object Oriented Software Engineering. Dino Mandrioli. 1992. text ed. 64.00 (0-13-006578-1) P-H.

Advances in Obsidian Glass Studies: Archaeological & Geochemical Perspectives. Ed. by R. E. Taylor. LC 76-43192. (Illus.). 360p. 1977. 32.00 (0-8155-5050-2, NP) Noyes.

***Advances in Occupant Protection Technologies for the Mid-Nineties: 1995 International Congress & Exposition Meeting.** 1995. pap. 86.00 (1-56091-627-3, SP1077) Soc Auto Engineers.

***Advances in Ocular Immunology & Immunopathology of the Eye: Proceedings of the Sixth International Symposium on the Immunology & Immunopathology of the Eye, Bethesda, U. S. A.** Ed. by Robert B. Nussenblatt et al. LC 94-35302. (International Congress Ser.). 479p. 1995. 370.00 (0-444-81742-5) Elsevier.

***Advances in Onboard System Technologies.** Ed. by Core A. Del. (European Community-Aeronautics Research Ser.). Date not set. text ed. 56.95 (0-471-95148-X) Wiley.

Advances in Oncology. M. Ghione et al. 288p. 1988. text ed. 123.00 (3-7186-0464-7) Gordon & Breach.

Advances in Operations Research: Proceedings of the European Congress on Operation Research, 2nd, Stockholm, Sweden, November 29, 1977. Ed. by M. Roubens. 1977. 97.50 (0-7204-0718-4, North Holland) Elsevier.

***Advances in Operations Research in the Oil & Gas Industry: Proceedings of the Workshop Held at HEC - Montreal, June 13 & 14, 1991.** Ed. by M. Breton & G. Zaccour. 1991. pap. text ed. 73.00 (2-7108-0610-X) Technip.

Advances in Ophthalmology, Vol. 26. Ed. by M. J. Roper-Hall et al. 1972. 107.25 (3-8055-1354-2) S Karger.

Advances in Ophthalmology, Vol. 29. Ed. by E. B. Streiff et al. 200p. 1975. 86.50 (3-8055-1709-2) S Karger.

Advances in Ophthalmology, Vol. 32. Ed. by E. B. Streiff et al. (Illus.). 250p. 1976. 102.50 (3-8055-2222-3) S Karger.

Advances in Ophthalmology, Vol. 34. Ed. by E. B. Streiff et al. 1977. 103.25 (3-8055-2406-4) S Karger.

Advances in Ophthalmology, Vol. 35. Ed. by M. J. Roper-Hall et al. (Illus.). (GER.). 1978. 105.75 (3-8055-2657-1) S Karger.

Advances in Ophthalmology, Vol. 39. Ed. by M. J. Roper-Hall et al. (Illus.). 1979. 150.50 (3-8055-3030-7) S Karger.

Advances in Ophthalmology, Vol. 40. Ed. by M. J. Roper-Hall et al. (Illus.). 1979. 125.75 (3-8055-3031-5) S Karger.

Advances in Ophthalmology, Vol. 41. Ed. by E. B. Streiff. (Illus.). xvii, 216p. 1980. 128.00 (3-8055-0375-X) S Karger.

Advances in Ophthalmology, Vol. 42. Ed. by E. B. Streiff. (Illus.). 164p. 1981. 78.50 (3-8055-1025-X) S Karger.

Advances in Optical & Electron Microscopy, Vol. 3. Ed. by V. E. Cosslett & R. Barer. (Serial Publication Ser.). 1969. text ed. 184.00 (0-12-029903-8) Acad Pr.

Advances in Optical & Electron Microscopy, Vol. 4. Ed. by V. E. Cosslett & R. Barer. (Serial Publication Ser.). 1971. text ed. 184.00 (0-12-029904-6) Acad Pr.

Advances in Optical & Electron Microscopy, Vol. 7. Ed. by V. E. Cosslett & R. Barer. (Serial Publication Ser.). 1979. text ed. 184.00 (0-12-029907-0) Acad Pr.

Advances in Optical & Electron Microscopy, Vol. 9. V. E. Cosslett & R. Barer. LC 62-25134. (Serial Publication Ser.). 1985. text ed. 157.00 (0-12-029909-7) Acad Pr.

Advances in Optical & Electron Microscopy, Vol. 10. Ed. by R. Barer & V. E. Coslett. (Serial Publication Ser.). 280p. 1987. text ed. 157.00 (0-12-029910-0) Acad Pr.

Advances in Optical & Electron Microscopy, Vol. 11. Ed. by Tom Mulvey & Colin Sheppard. (Serial Publication Ser.). 220p. 1989. text ed. 97.00 (0-12-029911-9) Acad Pr.

Advances in Optical & Electron Microscopy, Vol. 12. Ed. by Tom Mulvey & Colin Sheppard. 363p. 1991. text ed. 116.00 (0-12-029912-7) Acad Pr.

Advances in Optical & Electron Microscopy, Vol. 13. Ed. by Tom Mulvey & Colin Sheppard. (Illus.). 320p. 1994. text ed. 99.00 (0-12-029913-5) Acad Pr.

Advances in Optical & Electron Microscopy, Vol. 14. Ed. by Tom Mulvey & Colin Sheppard. (Illus.). 320p. 1994. text ed. 99.00 (0-12-029914-3) Acad Pr.

Advances in Optical Fabrication & Metrology Including Large Optics. Ed. by J. B. Arnold & R. E. Parks. 1989. 65.00 (0-8194-0001-7, 966) SPIE.

Advances in Optical-Fiber Communications, Vol. 1. Ed. by Tingye Li. 1985. text ed. 105.00 (0-12-447301-6) Acad Pr.

Advances in Optical Fibre Sensors. (Press Monograph Ser.). 1992. write for info. (0-8194-0801-8, PM07HC); pap. write for info. (0-8194-0802-6, PM07) SPIE.

Advances in Optical Imaging. LC 94-65349. (Proceedings Ser.: Vol. 21). 300p. 1994. text ed. 75.00 (1-55752-337-1) Optical Soc.

Advances in Optical Information Processing, No. III. Ed. by Pape. 1988. 51.00 (0-89252-971-7, 936) SPIE.

Advances in Optical Information Processing IV. Ed. by D. R. Pape. 1990. 70.00 (0-8194-0347-4, VOL. 1296) SPIE.

Advances in Optical Structure Systems. Ed. by J. Breakwell et al. 1990. 70.00 (0-8194-0354-7, VOL. 1303) SPIE.

Advances in Optimization: Proceedings of the 6th French-German Colloquium on Optimization, Held at Lambrecht, FRG, June 2-8, 1991. Ed. by W. Oettli & D. Pallaschke. LC 92-5741. (Lecture Notes in Economics & Mathematical Systems Ser.: Vol. 382). 1992. write for info. (3-540-55446-7) Spr-Verlag.

Advances in Optimization: Proceedings of the 6th French-German Colloquium on Optimization, Held at Lambrecht, FRG, June 2-8, 1991. Ed. by W. Oettli et al. (Lecture Notes in Economics & Mathematical Systems Ser.: Vol. 382). (Illus.). x, 527p. 1992. pap. 78.00 (0-387-55446-7) Spr-Verlag.

Advances in Optimization & Approximation. Ed. by Ding-Zhu Du & Jie Sun. LC 94-9739. (Nonconvex Optimization & Its Applications Ser.: Vol. 1). 404p. (C). 1994. lib. bdg. 141.50 (0-7923-2785-3) Kluwer Ac.

Advances in Optimization & Control. Ed. by H. A. Eiselt & G. Pederzoli. (Lecture Notes in Economics & Mathematical Systems Ser.: Vol. 302). viii, 372p. 1988. pap. 50.20 (0-387-18962-9) Spr-Verlag.

Advances in Optimization & Numerical Analysis: Proceedings of the Sixth Workshop on Optimization & Numerical Analysis, Oaxaca, Mexico. Ed. by Susana Gomez & Jean-Pierre Hennart. LC 93-45679. (Mathematics & Its Applications Ser.). 280p. (C). 1994. lib. bdg. 99.00 (0-7923-2673-3) Kluwer Ac.

***Advances in Optotronics & Avionics Technologies.** Ed. by Garcia. Date not set. text ed. 59.95 (0-471-95362-8) Wiley.

Advances in Oral Radiology. Allan B. Reiskin. LC 79-21095. (Postgraduate Dental Handbook Ser.: No. 12). (Illus.). 328p. reprint ed. pap. 93.50 (0-8357-7600-X, 2056922) Bks Demand.

Advances in Order Restricted Statistical Inference. Ed. by R. L. Dykstra et al. (Lecture Notes in Statistics Ser.: Vol. 37). (Illus.). viii, 295p. 1986. pap. 54.00 (0-387-96419-3) Spr-Verlag.

Advances in Organic Coatings, Vol. 5. Patsis Parfitt. 384p. 1983. 190.00 (0-8247-1905-0) Dekker.

Advances in Organic Coatings, Vol. 6. Patsis Parfitt. LC 83-10379. 544p. 1983. 190.00 (0-8247-7044-7) Dekker.

Advances in Organic Coatings Science & Technology, Vol. 10: Proceedings of the Conference, 12th. Ed. by Angelos V. Patsis. LC 86-643074. 220p. 1988. 49.00 (0-87762-563-8) Technomic.

Advances in Organic Coatings Science & Technology, Vol. 11: Proceedings of the 13th Conference. Ed. by A. V. Patsis. LC 89-50154. 265p. 1989. 49.00 (0-87762-603-0) Technomic.

Advances in Organic Coatings Science & Technology, Vol. 9: Proceedings of the Eleventh Conference. Ed. by Angelos V. Patsis. 215p. 1987. 49.00 (0-87762-525-5) Technomic.

Advances in Organic Geochemistry: Proceedings of the International Meeting, Milan, 1962. U. Colombo & G. D. Hobson. LC 63-18138. (Earth Science Ser.: Vol. 15). 1964. 218.00 (0-08-010272-7, Pub. by Pergamon Repr UK) Franklin.

Advances in Organic Geochemistry, 1964: Proceedings of the International Mtg Rueil-Malmaison, 1964. G. D. Hobson & M. Louis. LC 65-28549. (International Series of Monographs on Earth Sciences: Vol. 24). 1966. 140.00 (0-08-011577-2, Pub. by Pergamon Repr UK) Franklin.

Advances in Organic Geochemistry, 1964-1966: Proceedings. Ed. by G. D. Hobson. 1970. 244.00 (0-08-012758-4, Pub. by Pergamon Repr UK) Franklin.

Advances in Organic Geochemistry, 1968: Proceedings. P. A. Schenck. (C). 1969. 92.00 (0-08-006628-3, Pub. by Pergamon Repr UK) Franklin.

Advances in Organic Geochemistry, 1971. H. R. Von Gaertner & H. Wehner. 1972. 299.00 (0-08-017598-8, Pub. by Pergamon Repr UK) Franklin.

Advances in Organic Geochemistry 1979: Proceedings of the 9th International Meeting on Organic Geochemistry Held at Newcastle-Upon-Tyne, England, Sept. 1979. Ed. by A G. Douglas & J. R. Maxwell. LC 80-41078. (International Series on Earth Sciences: Vol. 36). (Illus.). 750p. 1980. 328.00 (0-08-024017-8, Pub. by Pergamon Repr UK) Franklin.

Advances in Organic Geochemistry, 1981: Proceedings of the 10th International Meeting on Organic Geochemistry, University of Bergen, Norway, 14-18 September 1981. International Meeting on Organic Geochemistry Staff. Ed. by Malvin Bjoroy et al. LC 82-17563. (Illus.). 902p. reprint ed. pap. 180.00 (0-8357-3074-3, 2039331) Bks Demand.

Advances in Organic Geochemistry 1983. Ed. by P. A. Schenck et al. 944p. 1985. 160.00 (0-317-66811-0, Pergamon Pr) Elsevier.

Advances in Organic Geochemistry, 1987: Organic Geochemistry in Petroleum Exploration & Analytical Geochemistry: Proceedings of the 13th International Meeting on Organic Geochemistry, Venice, September 21-25, 1987, Pts. 1 & 2. Ed. by L. Mattavelli & L. Novelli. (Organic Geochemistry Ser.: No. 13). (Illus.). 1199p. 1989. 310.00 (0-08-037236-8, Pergamon Pr) Elsevier.

Advances in Organic Synthesis: Theory & Application, Vol. 1. Ed. by Tomas Hudlicky. 1988. 73.25 (0-89232-865-7) Jai Pr.

Advances in Organization Development, Vol. 1. Ed. by Fred Massarik. LC 89-17852. 384p. 1990. text ed. 69.50 (0-89391-242-5) Ablex Pub.

Advances in Organization Development, Vol. 2. Fred Massarik. (Advances in Organization Development Ser.). 176p. (C). 1992. text ed. 65.00 (0-89391-809-1) Ablex Pub.

***Advances in Organization Development Vol. 3.** Barry Rosenblatt et al. 200p. 1995. write for info. (1-56750-102-8) Ablex Pub.

Advances in Organized Media, Vol. 1. Ed. by Janos H. Fendler. 1991. 90.25 (1-55938-174-4) Jai Pr.

Advances in Organobromine Chemistry I. Ed. by J. R. Desmurs & B. Gerard. (Industrial Chemistry Library: Vol. 3). 300p. 1991. 151.50 (0-444-89274-5) Elsevier.

***Advances in Organobromine Chemistry II: Proceedings of ORGABROM '93, Held in Jerusalem, June 28 - July 2, 1993.** Ed. by Jean-Roger Desmurs et al. LC 94-39317. (Industrial Chemistry Library: Vol. 7). 428p. 1994. 254.25 (0-444-82105-8) Elsevier.

Advances in Organometallic & Inorganic Polymer Science. Ed. by Charles E. Carraher, Jr. et al. LC 82-5074. (Illus.). 465p. reprint ed. pap. 132.60 (0-7837-0945-5, 2041249) Bks Demand.

Advances in Organometallic Chemistry, Vol. 22. Ed. by F. Gordon Stone & Robert West. (Serial Publication Ser.). 1983. text ed. 148.00 (0-12-031122-4) Acad Pr.

Advances in Organometallic Chemistry, Vol. 23. Ed. by F. Gordon Stone & Robert West. (Serial Publication Ser.). 1984. text ed. 148.00 (0-12-031123-2) Acad Pr.

Advances in Organometallic Chemistry, Vol. 25. F. Gordon Stone & Robert West. (Serial Publication Ser.). 1986. text ed. 148.00 (0-12-031125-9) Acad Pr.

Advances in Organometallic Chemistry, Vol. 26. Ed. by F. Gordon Stone & Robert West. (Serial Publication Ser.). 375p. 1986. text ed. 152.00 (0-12-031126-7) Acad Pr.

Advances in Organometallic Chemistry, Vol. 27. Ed. by F. Gordon Stone & Robert West. (Serial Publication Ser.). 385p. 1987. text ed. 136.00 (0-12-031127-5) Acad Pr.

Advances in Organometallic Chemistry, Vol. 28. F. Gordon Stone & Robert West. (Serial Publication Ser.). 471p. 1988. text ed. 143.00 (0-12-031128-3) Acad Pr.

Advances in Organometallic Chemistry, Vol. 29. F. Gordon Stone & Robert West. (Serial Publication Ser.). 369p. 1989. text ed. 138.00 (0-12-031129-1) Acad Pr.

Advances in Organometallic Chemistry, Vol. 30. Ed. by F. Gordon Stone & Robert West. (Serial Publication Ser.). 319p. 1990. text ed. 109.00 (0-12-031130-5) Acad Pr.

Advances in Organometallic Chemistry, Vol. 31. Ed. by F. Gordon Stone & Robert West. 407p. 1990. text ed. 132.00 (0-12-031131-3) Acad Pr.

Advances in Organometallic Chemistry, Vol. 32. Ed. by F. Gordon Stone & Robert West. (Illus.). 408p. 1991. text ed. 127.00 (0-12-031132-1) Acad Pr.

Advances in Organometallic Chemistry, Vol. 33. Ed. by F. Gordon Stone & Robert West. (Illus.). 408p. 1991. text ed. 138.00 (0-12-031133-X) Acad Pr.

Advances in Organometallic Chemistry, Vol. 34. Ed. by F. Gordon Stone & Robert West. (Illus.). 340p. 1992. text ed. 105.00 (0-12-031134-8) Acad Pr.

Advances in Organometallic Chemistry, Vol. 35. Ed. by F. Gordon Stone & Robert West. (Illus.). 306p. 1993. text ed. 105.00 (0-12-031135-6) Acad Pr.

Advances in Organometallic Chemistry, Vol. 36. Ed. by F. Gordon Stone & Robert West. (Illus.). 372p. 1994. text ed. 105.00 (0-12-031136-4) Acad Pr.

Advances in Organometallic Chemistry, Vol. 37. Ed. by F. Gordon Stone & Robert West. (Illus.). 334p. 1995. boxed 105.00 (0-12-031137-2) Acad Pr.

Advances in Organometallic Chemistry, Vols. 1-17. Ed. by F. Gordon Stone & Robert West. Incl. Vol. 1. 1964. 80.00 (0-12-031101-1); Vol. 10. 1972. 90.00 (0-12-031110-0); Vol. 14. 1976. lib. bdg. 110.00 (0-12-031173-9); Vol. 16. 1977. lib. bdg. 100.00 (0-12-031177-1); Vol. 17. 1979. lib. bdg. 100.00 (0-12-031179-8); (Serial Publication Ser.). write for info. (0-318-50206-2) Acad Pr.

Advances in Oto-Rhino-Laryngology, Vol. 41 & 42, Set. Ed. by E. Pirodda & O. Pompeiano. (Illus.). xiv, 556p. 1988. 251.25 (3-8055-4911-3) S Karger.

Advances in Otolaryngology, Vol. 4. Myers. 206p. 1990. 69.95 (0-8151-6262-6, Yr Bk Med Pubs) Mosby Yr Bk.

Advances in Otolaryngology: Head & Neck, Vol. 3. Myers. 368p. 1989. 69.95 (0-8151-6261-8, Yr Bk Med Pubs) Mosby Yr Bk.

Advances in Otolaryngology: Head & Neck Surgery. Myers et al. 320p. 1995. 69.95 (0-8151-6267-7, Yr Bk Med Pubs) Mosby Yr Bk.

Advances in Otolaryngology: Head & Neck Surgery, Vol. 5. Myers. 215p. 1991. 69.95 (0-8151-6263-4) Mosby Yr Bk.

Advances in Otolaryngology: Head & Neck Surgery, Vol. 6. Myers et al. 290p. 1992. 69.95 (0-8151-6264-2) Mosby Yr Bk.

Advances in Otolaryngology - Head & Neck Surgery. Myers et al. 320p. 1993. 69.95 (0-8151-6265-0, Yr Bk Med Pubs) Mosby Yr Bk.

Advances in Otolaryngology - Head & Neck Surgery. Myers et al. 320p. 1994. 69.95 (0-8151-6266-9, Yr Bk Med Pubs) Mosby Yr Bk.

Advances in Otolaryngology - Head & Neck Surgery. Myers et al. 320p. 1996. 69.95 (0-8151-6268-5, Yr Bk Med Pubs) Mosby Yr Bk.

Advances in Oxygenated Processes, Vol. 1. Ed. by Alfons L. Baumstark. 1988. 73.25 (0-89232-866-5) Jai Pr.

Advances in Oxygenated Processes, Vol. 2. Ed. by Alfons L. Baumstark. 236p. 1990. 90.25 (0-89232-950-5) Jai Pr.

Advances in Oxygenated Processes, Vol. 3. Ed. by Alfons L. Baumstark. 1991. 90.25 (1-55938-328-3) Jai Pr.

Advances in Pain Therapy I. Ed. by J. Chrubasik et al. 1992. write for info. (0-318-69521-9) Spr-Verlag.

Advances in Pain Therapy II. J. Chrubasik et al. (Illus.). 230p. 1993. pap. write for info. (3-540-56917-0) Spr-Verlag.

Advances in Pain Therapy One. Ed. by J. Chrubasik et al. (Illus.). 96p. 1992. pap. 40.00 (0-387-55536-6) Spr-Verlag.

Advances in Paleozoic Botany. Ed. by M. Streel et al. 1972. reprint ed. 33.50 (0-444-41080-5) Elsevier.

Advances in Palynology. P. K. Nair. 500p. (C). 1981. text ed. 400.00 (0-89771-603-5, Pub. by Intl Bk Distr II) St Mut.

Advances in Parallel Algorithms. I. Dimov & O. Tonev. LC 93-81158. 212p. 1994. pap. 77.00 (90-5199-151-7) IOS Press.

Advances in Parallel Algorithms. Ed. by Lydia Kronsjo & Dean Shumsheruddin. LC 92-16740. 481p. 1992. text ed. 81.95 (0-470-21907-6) Halsted Pr.

Advances in Parallel & Distributed Simulation. Ed. by Vijay Madisetti et al. (Simulation Ser.: Vol. 23, No. 1). 250p. 1991. 60.00 (0-911801-78-2, SS23-1) Soc Computer Sim.

Advances in Parallel & Distributed Systems, IEEE Workshop On (APADS '93) LC 93-79937. 184p. 1993. pap. text ed. 50.00 (0-8186-5250-6, 5250) IEEE Comp Soc.

Advances in Parapsychological Research, No. 7. Ed. by Stanley Krippner. LC 77-9518. 294p. 1994. lib. bdg. 55.00 (0-89950-902-9) McFarland & Co.

Advances in Parapsychological Research, Vol. 3. Ed. by Stanley Krippner. LC 77-9518. 352p. 1982. 59.50 (0-306-40944-5, Plenum Pr) Plenum.

Advances in Parapsychological Research, Vol. 1: Psychokinesis. Ed. by Stanley Krippner. LC 77-9518. 246p. 1977. 59.50 (0-306-32501-2, Plenum Pr) Plenum.

Advances in Parapsychological Research, Vol. 2: Extrasensory Perception. Ed. by Stanley Krippner. LC 77-9518. 318p. 1978. 59.50 (0-306-40082-0, Plenum Pr) Plenum.

An Asterisk (*) at the beginning of an entry indicates that the title is appearing in BIP for the first time. 95

Advances in Parapsychological Research 6. Ed. by Stanley Krippner. LC 77-9518. 319p. 1990. lib. bdg. 55.00 (0-89950-495-7) McFarland & Co.

Advances in Parasitic Hymenoptera Research. Ed. by Virendra K. Gupta. (Illus.). viii, 546p. 1988. reprint ed. 69.95 (0-916846-50-4) Assoc Pubs FL.

Advances in Parasitology, Vol. 18. Ed. by W. H. Lumsden et al. (Serial Publication Ser.). 1980. text ed. 187.00 (0-12-031718-4) Acad Pr.

Advances in Parasitology, Vol. 19. Ed. by W. H. Lumsden et al. (Serial Publication Ser.). 224p. 1982. text ed. 187.00 (0-12-031719-2) Acad Pr.

Advances in Parasitology, Vol. 20. Ed. by W. H. Lumsden et al. (Serial Publication Ser.). 1982. text ed. 187.00 (0-12-031720-6) Acad Pr.

Advances in Parasitology, Vol. 21. (Serial Publication Ser.). 336p. 1982. text ed. 158.00 (0-12-031721-4) Acad Pr.

Advances in Parasitology, Vol. 22. (Serial Publication Ser.). 416p. 1983. text ed. 158.00 (0-12-031722-2) Acad Pr.

Advances in Parasitology, Vol. 24. Ed. by John R. Baker. (Serial Publication Ser.). 1985. text ed. 158.00 (0-12-031724-9) Acad Pr.

Advances in Parasitology, Vol. 25. Ed. by John R. Baker & Ralph Muller. (Serial Publication Ser.). 352p. 1986. text ed. 127.00 (0-12-031725-7) Acad Pr.

Advances in Parasitology, Vol. 26. Ed. by John R. Baker & Ralph Muller. (Serial Publication Ser.). 300p. 1987. text ed. 108.00 (0-12-031726-5) Acad Pr.

Advances in Parasitology, Vol. 27. Ed. by John R. Baker & Ralph Muller. (Serial Publication Ser.). 263p. 1988. text ed. 107.00 (0-12-031727-3) Acad Pr.

Advances in Parasitology, Vol. 28. Ed. by John R. Baker & Ralph Muller. (Serial Publication Ser.). 300p. 1989. text ed. 107.00 (0-12-031728-1) Acad Pr.

Advances in Parasitology, Vol. 29. Ed. by John R. Baker & Ralph Muller. (Serial Publication Ser.). 326p. 1990. text ed. 99.00 (0-12-031729-X) Acad Pr.

Advances in Parasitology, Vol. 30. Ed. by John R. Baker & Ralph Muller. (Illus.). 261p. 1991. text ed. 85.00 (0-12-031730-3) Acad Pr.

Advances in Parasitology, Vol. 31. Ed. by John R. Baker & Ralph Muller. (Illus.). 464p. 1992. text ed. 105.00 (0-12-031731-1) Acad Pr.

Advances in Parasitology, Vol. 32. Ed. by John R. Baker & Ralph Muller. (Illus.). 480p. 1993. text ed. 95.00 (0-12-031732-X) Acad Pr.

Advances in Parasitology, Vol. 33. Ed. by John R. Baker & J. R. Muller. (Illus.). 299p. 1994. text ed. 79.00 (0-12-031733-8) Acad Pr.

Advances in Parasitology, Vol. 34. Ed. by J. R. Baker et al. (Illus.). 299p. 1994. text ed. 69.00 (0-12-031734-6) Acad Pr.

Advances in Parasitology, Vol. 35. Ed. by J. R. Baker et al. (Illus.). 387p. 1995. boxed 85.00 (0-12-031735-4) Acad Pr.

***Advances in Parasitology, Vol. 36.** Ed. by J. R. Baker et al. (Illus.). 424p. 1995. text ed. write for info. (0-12-031736-2) Acad Pr.

Advances in Parasitology, Vols. 1 & 4-15. Incl. Vol. 4. 1967. 70.00 (0-12-031704-4); Vol. 5. 1968. 55.00 (0-12-031705-2); Vol. 6. 1969. 75.00 (0-12-031706-0); Vol. 7. 1969. 75.00 (0-12-031707-9); Vol. 8. 1970. 60.00 (0-12-031708-7); Vol. 10. 1972. 70.00 (0-12-031710-9); Vol. 11. 1974. 98.00 (0-12-031711-7); Vol. 12. 1974. 85.00 (0-12-031712-5); Vol. 14. 1976. 80.00 (0-12-031714-1); write for info. (0-318-50207-0) Acad Pr.

Advances in Particulate Materials. Animesh Bose. 448p. 1995. write for info. (0-7506-9156-5) Buttrwrth-Heinemann.

Advances in Pathology, Vol. 2. Fenoglio. 280p. 1989. 54.95 (0-8151-6834-9, Yr Bk Med Pubs) Mosby Yr Bk.

Advances in Pathology, Vol. 3. Weinstein. 336p. 1990. 59.95 (0-8151-9167-7, Yr Bk Med Pubs) Mosby Yr Bk.

Advances in Pathology, Vol. 4. Fenoglio. 253p. 1991. 59.95 (0-8151-3396-0) Mosby Yr Bk.

Advances in Pathology, Vol. 5. Weinstein. 457p. 1992. 64.95 (0-8151-3397-9) Mosby Yr Bk.

Advances in Pathology (Anatomic & Clinical) Laboratory Medicine: Proceedings of the Triennial World Congress of the World Association of Societies of Pathology, 11th, Jerusalem, Israel, Sept. 20-25, 1981, 1. World Association of Societies of Pathology Staff & E. Levy. LC 82-11202. (Illus.). 542p. 1982. 226.00 (0-08-028878-2, Pub. by Pergamon Repr UK) Franklin.

Advances in Pathology (Anatomic & Clinical) Laboratory Medicine: Proceedings of the Triennial World Congress of the World Association of Societies of Pathology, 11th, Jerusalem, Israel, Sept. 20-25, 1981, 2. World Association of Societies of Pathology Staff & E. Levy. LC 82-11202. (Illus.). 542p. 1982. 241.00 (0-08-028879-0, Pub. by Pergamon Repr UK) Franklin.

Advances in Pathology (Anatomic & Clinical) Laboratory Medicine: Proceedings of the Triennial World Congress of the World Association of Societies of Pathology, 11th, Jerusalem, Israel, Sept. 20-25, 1981, Set. World Association of Societies of Pathology Staff & E. Levy. LC 82-11202. (Illus.). 542p. 1982. 467.00 (0-08-029777-3, Pub. by Pergamon Repr UK) Franklin.

Advances in Pathology & Laboratory Medicine. Fenoglio. 250p. 1993. 59.95 (0-8151-3393-6, Yr Bk Med Pubs) Mosby Yr Bk.

Advances in Pathology & Laboratory Medicine. Weinstein. 250p. 1994. 59.95 (0-8151-3394-4, Yr Bk Med Pubs) Mosby Yr Bk.

Advances in Pathology & Laboratory Medicine. Weinstein. 250p. 1995. 59.95 (0-8151-3398-7, Yr Bk Med Pubs) Mosby Yr Bk.

Advances in Pathology & Laboratory Medicine. Weinstein. 250p. 1996. 59.95 (0-8151-3399-5, Yr Bk Med Pubs) Mosby Yr Bk.

Advances in Pattern Recognition & Applications. F. Casacuberta & A. Senfeliv. 276p. 1994. text ed. 86.00 (981-02-1872-9) World Scientific Pub.

Advances in Pattern Recognition Systems Using Neural Network. I. Guyon & P. S. Wang. (World Scientific Machine Perception & Artificial Intelligence Ser.). 250p. 1994. text ed. 89.00 (981-02-1444-8) World Scientific Pub.

Advances in Pediatric Infectious Diseases. Aronoff. 241p. 1993. 59.95 (0-8151-0311-5, Yr Bk Med Pubs) Mosby Yr Bk.

Advances in Pediatric Infectious Diseases. Aronoff. 241p. 1994. 59.95 (0-8151-0313-1, Yr Bk Med Pubs) Mosby Yr Bk.

Advances in Pediatric Infectious Diseases. Aronoff. 241p. 1995. 59.95 (0-8151-0314-X, Yr Bk Med Pubs) Mosby Yr Bk.

Advances in Pediatric Infectious Diseases, Vol. 5. Aronoff. 264p. 1990. 54.95 (0-8151-0307-7, Yr Bk Med Pubs) Mosby Yr Bk.

Advances in Pediatric Infectious Diseases, Vol. 6. Aronoff. 216p. 1991. 54.95 (0-8151-0308-5, Yr Bk Med Pubs) Mosby Yr Bk.

Advances in Pediatric Infectious Diseases, Vol. 7. Aronoff. 209p. 1991. 54.95 (0-8151-0309-3) Mosby Yr Bk.

Advances in Pediatric Infectious Diseases, Vol. 8. Aronoff. 214p. 1992. 59.95 (0-8151-0310-7) Mosby Yr Bk.

Advances in Pediatric Sport Sciences: Biological Issues, Vol. 1. Ed. by Richard A. Boileau. (Advances in Pediatric Sport Sciences Ser.). 224p. 1984. text ed. 40.00 (0-931250-71-4, BBOI0071) Human Kinetics.

Advances in Pediatric Sport Sciences, Vol. 2: Behavioral Issues. Ed. by Daniel Gould & Maureen R. Weiss. LC 85-644893. (Illus.). 272p. (C). 1987. text ed. 40.00 (0-87322-089-7, BGOU0089) Human Kinetics.

Advances in Pediatric Sport Sciences, Vol. 3: Biological Issues, Vol. 3. Ed. by Oded Bar-Or. LC 85-644893. (Advances in Pediatric Sport Sciences Ser.). (Illus.). 264p. 1989. text ed. 40.00 (0-87322-204-0, BBAR0204) Human Kinetics.

Advances in Pediatrics. Barness. 424p. 1991. 59.95 (0-8151-0516-9) Mosby Yr Bk.

Advances in Pediatrics, Vol. 23. Barness. 1976. 59.95 (0-8151-0495-2) Mosby Yr Bk.

Advances in Pediatrics, Vol. 28. Lewis A. Barness. 1981. 54.50 (0-8151-0500-2) Mosby Yr Bk.

Advances in Pediatrics, Vol. 29. Ed. by Lewis A. Barness. 1982. 54.50 (0-8151-0501-0) Mosby Yr Bk.

Advances in Pediatrics, Vol. 31 - 1984. Advances in Pediatrics Staff. LC 42-22236. 516p. reprint ed. pap. 147.10 (0-8357-7672-7, 2057000) Bks Demand.

Advances in Pediatrics, Vol. 36. Lewis A. Barness. 512p. 1989. 59.95 (0-8151-0513-4) Mosby Yr Bk.

Advances in Pediatrics, Vol. 39. Barness. 505p. 1992. 59.95 (0-8151-0529-0) Mosby Yr Bk.

Advances in Pediatrics, Vol. 40. Barness. 475p. 1993. 59.95 (0-8151-0527-4) Mosby Yr Bk.

Advances in Pediatrics, Vol. 41. Barness. 475p. 1994. 59.95 (0-8151-0530-4) Mosby Yr Bk.

Advances in Pediatrics, Vol. 42. Barness. 576p. 1995. 59.95 (0-8151-0531-2) Mosby Yr Bk.

Advances in Pediatrics, Vol. 43. Barness. 475p. 1996. 59.95 (0-8151-0532-0, Yr Bk Med Pubs) Mosby Yr Bk.

Advances in Pediatrics, 1986, Vol. 33. Advances in Pediatrics Staff. Ed. by Lewis A. Barness. LC 42-22236. (Illus.). 433p. reprint ed. pap. 123.50 (0-8357-5560-6, 2035189) Bks Demand.

Advances in Penicillium & Aspergillus Systematics. Ed. by Robert A. Samson & John I. Pitt. LC 85-28329. (NATO ASI Series A, Life Sciences: Vol. 102). 494p. 1985. 115.00 (0-306-42222-0, Plenum Pr) Plenum.

Advances in Peptic Ulcer Pathogenesis. W. D. Rees. 250p. 1988. lib. bdg. 103.00 (0-7462-0062-5) Kluwer Ac.

Advances in Perinantal Medicine. Ermelando V. Cosmi et al. 324p. 1988. text ed. 79.00 (3-7186-0463-9) Gordon & Breach.

Advances in Perinatal Medicine, Vol. 1. Ed. by Aubrey Milunsky et al. LC 80-20701. 456p. 1981. 85.00 (0-306-40482-6, Plenum Med Bk) Plenum.

Advances in Perinatal Medicine, Vol. 2. Ed. by Aubrey Milunsky et al. LC 80-20701. 400p. (C). 1982. 85.00 (0-306-40763-9, Plenum Med Bk) Plenum.

Advances in Perinatal Medicine, Vol. 3. Ed. by Aubrey Milunsky et al. LC 80-20701. 272p. 1983. 85.00 (0-306-41208-X, Plenum Med Bk) Plenum.

Advances in Perinatal Medicine, Vol. 4. Ed. by Aubrey Milunsky et al. LC 80-20701. 350p. 1985. 85.00 (0-306-41840-1, Plenum Med Bk) Plenum.

Advances in Perinatal Medicine, Vol. 5. Ed. by Aubrey Milunsky et al. LC 80-20701. 298p. 1986. 89.50 (0-306-42331-6, Plenum Med Bk) Plenum.

Advances in Perinatal Medicine: Proceedings of the First International Congress of Perinatal Medicine, Tokyo, 5-8 November 1991. Ed. by Shoichi Sakamoto & Yoshihiko Takeda. LC 92-49279. (International Congress Ser.: No. 92). 1992. write for info. (0-444-89312-1, Excerpta Medica) Elsevier.

Advances in Perinatal Thyroidology. Ed. by B. B. Bercu & D. I. Shulman. (Advances in Experimental Medicine & Biology Ser.: Vol. 299). (Illus.). 264p. 1991. 75.00 (0-306-44006-7, Plenum Pr) Plenum.

Advances in Periodontics. Ed. by Thomas Wilson et al. (Illus.). 384p. 1992. text ed. 120.00 (0-86715-250-8) Quint Pub Co.

Advances in Permanent Magnetism. Rollin J. Parker. 1990. text ed. 114.00 (0-471-82293-0) Wiley.

Advances in Personal Construct Psychology, Vol. 1. Ed. by Greg J. Neimeyer & Robert A. Neimeyer. 287p. 1989. 73.25 (1-55938-081-0) Jai Pr.

Advances in Personal Relationships, Vol. 2. Ed. by Warren H. Jones & Daniel Perlman. 300p. 1990. 79.00 (1-85302-077-X, Pub. by J Kingsley Pubs UK) Taylor & Francis.

Advances in Personal Relationships, Vol. 3. Ed. by Warren H. Jones & Daniel Perlman. 300p. 1991. 79.00 (1-85302-078-8, Pub. by J Kingsley Pubs UK) Taylor & Francis.

Advances in Personal Relationships, Vol. 4. Ed. by Warren H. Jones & Daniel Perlman. 300p. 1992. pap. 85.00 (1-85302-102-4, Pub. by J Kingsley Pubs UK) Taylor & Francis.

Advances in Personal Relationships, Vol. 5: Attachment Processes in Adulthood. Ed. by Daniel Perlman & Kim Bartholomew. 300p. 1993. 75.00 (1-85302-172-5, Pub. by J Kingsley Pubs UK) Taylor & Francis.

Advances in Personality Assessment, Vol. 1. Ed. by Charles D. Spielberger & James N. Butcher. 256p. 1982. text ed. 49.95 (0-89859-151-1) L Erlbaum Assocs.

Advances in Personality Assessment, Vol. 2. Ed. by James N. Butcher & Charles D. Spielberger. 208p. (C). 1983. text ed. 49.95 (0-89859-216-X) L Erlbaum Assocs.

Advances in Personality Assessment, Vol. 3. Charles D. Spielberger & James N. Butcher. 216p. (C). 1983. text ed. 49.95 (0-89859-313-1) L Erlbaum Assocs.

Advances in Personality Assessment, Vol. 4. Ed. by James N. Butcher & Charles D. Spielberger. 288p. (C). 1985. text ed. 59.95 (0-89859-341-7) L Erlbaum Assocs.

Advances in Personality Assessment, Vol. 5. Ed. by Charles D. Spielberger & James Butcher. 224p. (C). 1985. text ed. 49.95 (0-89859-559-2) L Erlbaum Assocs.

Advances in Personality Assessment, Vol. 6. Ed. by James Butcher & Charles Spielberger. 176p. 1987. text ed. 39.95 (0-89859-660-2) L Erlbaum Assocs.

Advances in Personality Assessment, Vol. 7. Ed. by Charles D. Spielberger & James N. Butcher. 248p. 1988. 49.95 (0-8058-0217-7) L Erlbaum Assocs.

Advances in Personality Assessment, Vol. 8. Ed. by J. Butcher & C. Spielberger. 296p. (C). 1990. text ed. 59.95 (0-8058-0503-6) L Erlbaum Assocs.

Advances in Personality Assessment, Vol. 9. Ed. by Charles D. Spielberger & James N. Butcher. 232p. 1992. text ed. 49.95 (0-8058-1226-1) L Erlbaum Assocs.

***Advances in Personality Assessment, Vol. 10.** Ed. by James N. Butcher & Charles D. Spielberger. (Advances in Personality Assessment Ser.). 200p. 1995. text ed. 49.95 (0-8058-1804-9) L Erlbaum Assocs.

Advances in Pesticide Formulation Technology. Herbert B. Scher. LC 84-6394. (ACS Symposium Ser.: No. 254). 264p. 1984. lib. bdg. 49.95 (0-8412-0840-9) Am Chemical.

Advances in Pesticide Science: Abstracts & Addendum. H. Geissbuhler & P. C. Kearney. LC 79-40363. 1979. 160.00 (0-08-023930-7, Pub. by Pergamon Repr UK) Franklin.

Advances in Petri Nets, 1984. Ed. by Grzegorz Rozenberg. (Lecture Notes in Computer Science Ser.: Vol. 188). vii, 467p. 1985. pap. 45.00 (0-387-15204-0) Spr-Verlag.

Advances in Petri Nets, 1985. Ed. by Grzegorz Rozenberg. (Lecture Notes in Computer Science Ser.: Vol. 222). vi, 498p. 1986. pap. 53.00 (0-387-16480-4) Spr-Verlag.

Advances in Petri Nets, 1987. Ed. by Grzegorz Rozenberg. (Lecture Notes in Computer Science Ser.: Vol. 266). vi, 451p. 1987. pap. text ed. 49.00 (0-387-18086-9) Spr-Verlag.

Advances in Petri Nets, 1988. Ed. by Grzegorz Rozenberg. (Lecture Notes in Computer Science Ser.: Vol. 340). vi, 439p. 1988. pap. 45.00 (0-387-50580-6) Spr-Verlag.

Advances in Petri Nets, 1989. Ed. by Grzegorz Rozenberg et al. (Lecture Notes in Computer Science Ser.: Vol. 424). vi, 524p. 1990. pap. 48.60 (0-387-52494-0) Spr-Verlag.

Advances in Petri Nets, 1990. Ed. by Grzegorz Rozenberg et al. (Lecture Notes in Computer Science Ser.: Vol. 483). vi, 515p. 1991. pap. 51.00 (0-387-53863-1) Spr-Verlag.

Advances in Petri Nets, 1991. Ed. by Grzegorz Rozenberg et al. (Lecture Notes in Computer Science Ser.: Vol. 524). viii, 572p. 1991. pap. 52.00 (0-387-54398-8) Spr-Verlag.

Advances in Petri Nets, 1992. Ed. by Grzegorz Rozenberg et al. (Lecture Notes in Computer Science Ser.: Vol. 609). viii, 472p. 1992. pap. 61.00 (0-387-55610-9) Spr-Verlag.

Advances in Petri Nets, 1993. Ed. by Grzegorz Rozenberg. (Lecture Notes in Computer Science Ser.: Vol. 674). vii, 457p. 1993. pap. 65.00 (0-387-56689-9) Spr-Verlag.

Advances in Petroleum Geochemistry, Vol. 1. Jim Brooks & Dietrich H. Welte. (Serial Publication Ser.). 1984. text ed. 115.00 (0-12-032001-0) Acad Pr.

Advances in Petroleum Geochemistry, Vol. 2. Ed. by Jim Brooks & Dietrich H. Welte. (Serial Publication Ser.). 260p. 1987. text ed. 115.00 (0-12-032002-9) Acad Pr.

***Advances in Pharmaceutical Science, Vol. 7.** Ed. by David Ganderton et al. (Illus.). 383p. 1995. text ed. write for info. (0-12-032307-9) Acad Pr.

Advances in Pharmaceutical Sciences, Vol. 5. H. S. Bean et al. LC 64-21676. 1982. text ed. 158.00 (0-12-032305-2) Acad Pr.

Advances in Pharmaceutical Sciences, Vol. 6. Ed. by D. Ganderton & J. Jones. (Illus.). 197p. 1991. text ed. 94.00 (0-12-032306-0) Acad Pr.

Advances in Pharmacological Research & Practice: Proceedings of the Third Congress of the Hungarian Pharmacological Society, Budapest. Ed. by J. Knoll. (Advances in Pharmacological Research & Practice Ser.). 1981. 920.00 (0-08-026385-2); Special. 300.00 (0-08-027363-7) Franklin.

Advances in Pharmacology, Vol. 21. Ed. by M. W. Anders et al. 364p. 1990. text ed. 105.00 (0-12-032921-2) Acad Pr.

Advances in Pharmacology, Vol. 22. Ed. by J. Thomas August et al. (Illus.). 374p. 1991. text ed. 99.00 (0-12-032922-0) Acad Pr.

Advances in Pharmacology, Vol. 23. Ed. by J. Thomas August et al. (Illus.). 348p. 1992. text ed. 80.00 (0-12-032923-9) Acad Pr.

Advances in Pharmacology, Vol. 24. Ed. by J. Thomas August et al. (Illus.). 301p. 1993. text ed. 89.95 (0-12-032924-7) Acad Pr.

Advances in Pharmacology, Vol. 25. Ed. by J. Thomas August et al. (Illus.). 468p. 1994. text ed. 110.00 (0-12-032925-5) Acad Pr.

Advances in Pharmacology, Vol. 28. Ed. by J. Thomas August et al. (Illus.). 361p. 1994. text ed. 99.00 (0-12-032928-X) Acad Pr.

Advances in Pharmacology, Vol. 30. Ed. by J. Thomas August et al. (Illus.). 399p. 1994. text ed. 95.00 (0-12-032931-X) Acad Pr.

***Advances in Pharmacology, Vol. 32.** Ed. by J. Thomas August et al. (Illus.). 583p. 1995. boxed 99.00 (0-12-032933-6) Acad Pr.

***Advances in Pharmacology, Vol. 33.** Ed. by J. Thomas August et al. (Illus.). 448p. 1995. boxed write for info. (0-12-032934-4) Acad Pr.

Advances in Pharmacology Vol. 29A: DNA Topoisomerases. Ed. by Ferid Myrad et al. (Illus.). 320p. 1994. text ed. 79.00 (0-12-032929-8) Acad Pr.

Advances in Pharmacology Vol. 31: Anesthesia & Cardiovascular Disease. Ed. by Zeljko J. Bosnjak et al. (Illus.). 666p. 1994. text ed. 99.00 (0-12-032932-8) Acad Pr.

***Advances in Pharmacology Vol. 31: Anesthesia & Cardiovascular Disease.** Ed. by Zeljko J. Bosnjak et al. (Illus.). 666p. 1994. pap. 59.95 (0-12-118860-4) Acad Pr.

Advances in Pharmacology & Chemotherapy, Vol. 20. Ed. by Silvio Garattini et al. (Serial Publication Ser.). 1984. text ed. 120.00 (0-12-032920-4) Acad Pr.

Advances in Pharmacology & Chemotherapy, Vols. 7-11 & 14-16. Ed. by Silvio Garattini et al. Incl. Vol. 15. 1978. (0-318-50209-7); Vol. 15. 1978. 60.00 (0-12-032981-6); Vol. 15. 1978. (0-12-032982-4); Vol. 16. 1979. lib. bdg. 70.00 (0-685-00041-9); (Serial Publication Ser.). write for info. (0-318-50208-9) Acad Pr.

Advances in Pharmacology & Therapeutics: Proceedings of Eighth International Congress of Pharmacology, Tokyo, Japan, 19-24 July 1981, Ser. 2, Vol. 3. Ed. by H. Hagihara Yoshida & Setsuro Ebashi. (Illus.). 346p. 1982. 140.00 (0-08-028023-4, Pub. by Pergamon Repr UK) Franklin.

Advances in Pharmacology & Therapeutics: Proceedings of the Eighth International Congress of Pharmacology, Tokyo, Japan, 19-24 July, 1981, Series No. 2, Vol. 4. Ed. by H. Hagihara Yoshida & Y. Gigihara. (Illus.). 310p. 1982. 117.00 (0-08-028024-2, Pub. by Pergamon Repr UK) Franklin.

Advances in Pharmacology & Therapeutics: Proceedings of the Eighth International Congress of Pharmacology, Tokyo, Japan, 19-24 July, 1981, Series No. 2, Vol. 5. Ed. by H. Hagihara Yoshida & Setsuro Ebashi. (Illus.). 380p. 1982. 150.00 (0-08-028025-0, Pub. by Pergamon Repr UK) Franklin.

Advances in Pharmacology & Therapeutics: Proceedings of 8th International Congress of Pharmacology, Tokyo, Japan, July 19-24, 1981, Series No. 2, Vol. 6. Ed. by H. Hagihara Yoshida & Setsuro Ebashi. (Illus.). 310p. 1982. 132.00 (0-08-028026-9, Pub. by Pergamon Repr UK) Franklin.

Advances in Pharmacology & Therapeutics II, 6-Vol. set. Ed. by Yoshida Hagihara et al. 1982. 535.00 (0-317-66812-9, Pergamon Pr) Elsevier.

Advances in Pharmacology & Therapeutics II. Ed. by H. Hagihara Yoshida. 1983. 320.00 (0-317-66813-7, Pergamon Pr) Elsevier.

Advances in Pharmacology & Therapeutics 2, 6 vols., Set. H. Hagihara Yoshida & Yoshida Hagihara. 1982. 794.00 (0-08-027975-9, Pub. by Pergamon Repr UK) Franklin.

Advances in Pharmacology, Vol. 26: Cyclic GMP: Synthesis, Metabolism, & Function. Ed. by J. Thomas August et al. (Illus.). 335p. 1994. text ed. 95.00 (0-12-032926-3) Acad Pr.

Advances in Pharmacology, Vol. 27: Conjugation-Dependent Carcinogenicity & Toxicity of Foreign Compounds. Ed. by J. Thomas August et al. (Illus.). 519p. 1994. text ed. 99.00 (0-12-032927-1) Acad Pr.

Advances in Pharmacology, Vol. 29B: DNA Topoisomerases. Ed. by Ferid Myrad et al. (Illus.). 315p. 1994. text ed. 74.95 (0-12-032930-1) Acad Pr.

Advances in Phase Change Heat Transfer: Proceedings of the International Symposium on Phase Change Heat Transfer, Chongqing University, China, 20-23 May 1988. Ed. by Xin Mingdao. (International Academic Publishers Ser.). 724p. 1989. 205.00 (0-08-036625-2, Pergamon Pr) Elsevier.

Advances in Phenylketonuria Research. Ed. by V. Romano. (Journal: Developmental Brain Dysfunction: Vol. 6, Nos. 1-3, 1993). (Illus.). 192p. 1993. pap. 78.50 (3-8055-5759-0) S Karger.

Advances in Phosphate Fertilizer Technology. Gordon F. Palm. Ed. by Wes Atwood et al. LC 93-12275. (Symposium Ser.: No. 292, Vol. 89). 1993. 75.00 (0-8169-0593-2) Am Inst Chem Eng.

Advances in Photochemistry, Vol. 7. Advances in Photochemistry Staff. LC 63-13592. 424p. reprint ed. pap. 120.90 (0-8357-5175-9, 2006493) Bks Demand.

Advances in Photochemistry, Vol. 13. Ed. by David H. Volman et al. 500p. 1986. text ed. 195.00 (0-471-81523-3) Wiley.

Advances in Photochemistry, Vol. 14. Ed. by David H. Volman et al. 340p. 1988. text ed. 140.00 (0-471-81524-1) Wiley.

An Asterisk (*) at the beginning of an entry indicates that the title is appearing in BIP for the first time.

An Asterisk (*) at the beginning of an entry indicates that the title is appearing in BIP for the first time.

97

A

Advances in Probability & Related Topics, 2 vols., 3. Ed. by Peter Ney & Sidney Port. LC 75-79066. 422p. pap. 120.30 (*0-8357-8391-X*, 2027071) Bks Demand.

Advances in Probability & Related Topics, 2 vols., Vol. 1. Ed. by Peter Ney & Sidney Port. LC 75-79066. 229p. pap. 65.30 (*0-8357-8390-1*, 2027071) Bks Demand.

Advances in Probability & Related Topics, Vol. 2. Ed. by Peter Ney. LC 75-79066. 262p. reprint ed. pap. 74.70 (*0-8357-5178-3*, 2027071) Bks Demand.

Advances in Probability Distributions with Given Marginals: Beyond the Copulas. Ed. by G. Dall'Aglio et al. (C). 1991. lib. bdg. 94.00 (*0-7923-1156-6*) Kluwer Ac.

Advances in Probability Theory: Limit Theorems & Related Problems. Ed. by A. V. Balakrishnan & A. A. Borovkov. LC 84-2366. (Translations Series in Mathematics & Engineering). 392p. 1984. text ed. 98.00 (*0-911575-03-0*) Optimization Soft.

Advances in Probability Theory: Limit Theorems for Sums of Random Variables. Ed. by A. V. Balakrishnan & A. A. Borovkov. LC 85-27931. (Translations Series in Mathematics & Engineering). 313p. 1985. text ed. 80.00 (*0-911575-17-0*) Optimization Soft.

Advances in Processing & Finishing of Plastics in Business Machines: Proceedings of the Society of Plastics Engineers, Genesee Plaza Holiday Inn, Rochester, New York, October 19-20, 1982. Society of Plastics Engineers Staff. 178p. reprint ed. pap. 50.80 (*0-8357-5180-5*, 2019656) Bks Demand.

Advances in Processing & Finishing of Plastics in Business Machines: Rochester Retec 85: October 1 & 2, 1985, Genesee Plaza Holiday Inn, Rochester, New York SPE, Rochester Section. Society of Plastics Engineers Staff. 224p. reprint ed. pap. 63.90 (*0-8357-5179-1*, 2027692) Bks Demand.

Advances in Production Management Systems: Proceedings of the IFIP TC5 - WG5.7 Fifth International Conference on Advances in Production Management Systems, APMS '93, Athens, Greece, 28-30 September 1993. Ed. by Ioannis A. Pappas & Ilias P. Tatsiopoulos. LC 93-27019. (IFIP Transactions B: Applications in Technology Ser.: Vol. B-13). 1993. write for info. (*0-444-81598-8*, North Holland) Elsevier.

Advances in Production Management Systems: Proceedings of the IFIP TC5 International Conference, 4th, APMS, Espoo, Finland, 20-22 Aug. 1990. Ed. by E. Eloranta. 584p. 1991. 125.50 (*0-444-88919-1*, North Holland) Elsevier.

Advances in Production Management Systems '82: Production Management Systems in the Eighties; Proceedings of the IFIP WG 5.7 Working Conference, Bordeaux, France, Aug. 1982. Ed. by Guy Doumeingts & William A. Carter. xiv, 528p. 1984. 79.50 (*0-444-86827-5*, I-026-84, North Holland) Elsevier.

Advances in Production Management Systems '85. Ed. by E. Szelke & James J. Browne. 396p. 1986. 77.00 (*0-444-87975-7*, North Holland) Elsevier.

Advances in Program Theory. Ed. by Leonard Bickman. LC 85-644749. (New Directions for Program Evaluation Ser.: No. 47). 1990. 17.95 (*1-55542-813-4*) Jossey-Bass.

Advances in Programming Non-Numerical Applications to Computing Machines. Ed. by L. Fox. 1966. 95.00 (*0-08-011356-7*, Pub. by Pergamon Repr UK) Franklin.

Advances in Progressive Supranuclear Palsy. Ed. by E. Tolosa et al. (Journal of Neural Transmission Ser.: Vol. 42). (Illus.). 1994. pap. 88.00 (*0-387-82523-1*) Spr-Verlag.

Advances in Progressive Supranuclear Palsy. Ed. by E. Tolosa et al. (Journal of Neural Transmission Ser.: Vol. 42). (Illus.). 320p. 1994. pap. 90.00 (*0-387-82541-X*) Spr-Verlag.

Advances in Project Scheduling. Ed. by Roman Slowinski & J. Weglarz. (Studies in Production & Engineering Economics: Vol. 9). 544p. 1989. 138.50 (*0-444-87358-9*) Elsevier.

***Advances in Prostaglandin & Thromboxane Research: 1976, Vol. 1.** Ed. by Bengt Samuelsson & Rodolfo Paoletti. LC 75-14588. Date not set. reprint ed. pap. 148.80 (*0-7837-9509-2*, 2060259) Bks Demand.

***Advances in Prostaglandin & Thromboxane Research: 1980, Vol. 6.** Ed. by Bengt Samuelsson et al. LC 75-14588. Date not set. reprint ed. pap. 180.00 (*0-7837-9510-6*, 2060259) Bks Demand.

Advances in Prostaglandin, Thromboxane, & Leukotriene Research, Vol. 15: Proceedings of the Kyoto Conference on Prostaglandins. Ed. by Osamu Hayaishi & Shozo Yamamoto. 776p. 1985. text ed. 142.50 (*0-88167-113-4*) Raven.

Advances in Protein Chemistry, Vol. 34. Ed. by Christian B. Anfinsen et al. 1981. 128.00 (*0-12-034234-0*) Acad Pr.

Advances in Protein Chemistry, Vol. 35. (Serial Publication Ser.). 396p. 1982. text ed. 128.00 (*0-12-034235-9*) Acad Pr.

Advances in Protein Chemistry, Vol. 36. (Serial Publication Ser.). 1984. text ed. 116.00 (*0-12-034236-7*) Acad Pr.

Advances in Protein Chemistry, Vol. 38. Ed. by Christian B. Anfinsen et al. (Serial Publication Ser.). 389p. 1986. text ed. 121.00 (*0-12-034238-3*) Acad Pr.

Advances in Protein Chemistry, Vol. 39. Ed. by Christian B. Anfinsen et al. (Serial Publication Ser.). 265p. 1988. text ed. 92.00 (*0-12-034239-1*) Acad Pr.

Advances in Protein Chemistry, Vol. 40. Ed. by Christian B. Anfinsen et al. (Serial Publication Ser.). 403p. 1990. text ed. 108.00 (*0-12-034240-5*) Acad Pr.

Advances in Protein Chemistry, Vol. 41. Ed. by Christian B. Anfinsen et al. (Illus.). 352p. 1991. text ed. 83.00 (*0-12-034241-3*) Acad Pr.

Advances in Protein Chemistry, Vol. 42. Ed. by Christian B. Anfinsen et al. (Illus.). 396p. 1991. text ed. 94.00 (*0-12-034242-1*) Acad Pr.

Advances in Protein Chemistry, Vol. 43. Ed. by Christian B. Anfinsen et al. (Illus.). 392p. 1992. text ed. 80.00 (*0-12-034243-X*) Acad Pr.

***Advances in Protein Chemistry, Vol. 47.** Ed. by Christian B. Anfinsen et al. (Illus.). 350p. 1995. text ed. write for info. (*0-12-034247-2*) Acad Pr.

Advances in Protein Chemistry, Vols. 1-28, 31. Incl. Vol. 29. 1975. lib. bdg. 90.00 (*0-12-034274-X*); Vol. 30. 1976. lib. bdg. 90.00 (*0-12-034276-6*); Vols. 3-4. LC 44-8853. 1948. 85.00 (*0-685-00042-7*); Vol. 15. LC 44-8853. 1961. 75.00 (*0-12-034215-4*); Vol. 21. , 2 vols. LC 44-8853. 1966. text ed. (*0-12-034221-9*); Vol. 22. , 2 vols. LC 44-8853. 1967. text ed. (*0-12-034222-7*); Vol. 23. LC 44-8853. 1968. 75.00 (*0-12-034223-5*); Vol. 25. LC 44-8853. 1971. 75.00 (*0-12-034225-1*); Vol. 31. LC 44-8853. 1977. lib. bdg. 90.00 (*0-12-034278-2*); LC 44-8853. (Serial Publication Ser.). Vols 1-28, 31. write for info. (*0-318-50214-3*) Acad Pr.

Advances in Protein Chemistry, Vols. 29-30. Incl. Vol. 29. 1975. lib. bdg. 90.00 (*0-12-034274-X*); Vol. 30. 1976. lib. bdg. 90.00 (*0-12-034276-6*); Vols. 3-4. LC 44-8853. 1948. 85.00 (*0-685-00042-7*); Vol. 15. LC 44-8853. 1961. 75.00 (*0-12-034215-4*); Vol. 21. , 2 vols. LC 44-8853. 1966. text ed. (*0-12-034221-9*); Vol. 22. , 2 vols. LC 44-8853. 1967. text ed. (*0-12-034222-7*); Vol. 23. LC 44-8853. 1968. 75.00 (*0-12-034223-5*); Vol. 25. LC 44-8853. 1971. 75.00 (*0-12-034225-1*); Vol. 31. LC 44-8853. 1977. lib. bdg. 90.00 (*0-12-034278-2*); (Serial Publication Ser.). write for info. (*0-318-50213-5*) Acad Pr.

Advances in Protein Chemistry: Accessory Folding Proteins, Vol. 44. Ed. by George Lorimer et al. (Illus.). 218p. 1993. text ed. 59.00 (*0-12-034244-8*) Acad Pr.

Advances in Protein Chemistry: Lipoproteins, Apolipoproteins, & Lipases, Vol. 45. Ed. by Verne N. Schumaker. (Illus.). 464p. 1994. text ed. 90.00 (*0-12-034245-6*) Acad Pr.

***Advances in Protein Chemistry Vol. 46: Protein Stability.** Ed. by C. B. Anfinsen et al. (Illus.). 334p. 1995. boxed 69.00 (*0-12-034246-4*) Acad Pr.

Advances in Protein Design: International Workshop 1988. Ed. by H. Blocker et al. (Society for Biotechnology Research Monograph Ser.: Vol. 12). 217p. 1989. pap. text ed. 95.00 (*0-89573-953-4*) VCH Pubs.

Advances in Protoplast Research: Proceedings of the International Protoplast Symposium, 5th, Szeged, Hungary, 1979. International Protoplast Symposium Staff. Ed. by L. Ferenczy & G. L. Farks. LC 79-41251. 550p. 1980. 217.00 (*0-08-025528-0*, Pub. by Pergamon Repr UK) Franklin.

***Advances in Protozoological Research: Proceedings of the 1st International Conference of Hungary on Protozoology & Memorial Session for Joz.** M. C. Bereczky. 549p. (C). 1986. 174.00x (*963-05-4437-7*, Pub. by Akad Kiado HU) St Mut.

Advances in Psychoanalytic Sociology: A Text & Reader. Jerome Rabow et al. LC 83-86. 379p. (C). 1987. text ed. 35.50 (*0-89874-608-6*) Krieger.

Advances in Psychobiology, Vol. 3. A. H. Riesen & R. F. Thompson. LC 70-178148. 509p. reprint ed. pap. 145.10 (*0-8357-9831-3*, 2015177) Bks Demand.

Advances in Psychological Assessment, Vol. 3. Ed. by Paul McReynolds. LC 73-21077. (Jossey-Bass Behavioral Science Ser.). 572p. reprint ed. pap. 163.10 (*0-8357-5181-3*, 2021088) Bks Demand.

Advances in Psychological Assessment, 3 vols., Vol. 4. Ed. by Paul McReynolds. LC 78-647160. (Jossey-Bass Social & Behavioral Science Ser.). (Illus.). 611p. reprint ed. pap. 174.20 (*0-8357-4714-X*, 2021088) Bks Demand.

Advances in Psychological Assessment, 3 vols., Vol. 5. Ed. by Paul McReynolds. LC 78-647160. (Jossey-Bass Social & Behavioral Science Ser.). (Illus.). 582p. reprint ed. pap. 165.90 (*0-8357-4715-8*, 2021088) Bks Demand.

Advances in Psychological Assessment, 3 vols., Vol. 6. Ed. by Paul McReynolds. LC 78-647160. (Jossey-Bass Social & Behavioral Science Ser.). (Illus.). 399p. reprint ed. pap. 113.80 (*0-8357-4716-6*, 2021088) Bks Demand.

Advances in Psychological Assessment, Vol. 7. Ed. by P. McReynolds et al. LC 78-647160. (Illus.). 330p. 1990. 55.00 (*0-306-43399-0*, Plenum Pr) Plenum.

Advances in Psychological Assessment, Vol. 8. Ed. by J. C. Rosen & P. McReynolds. (Illus.). 260p. (C). 1992. 55.00 (*0-306-44251-5*, Plenum Pr) Plenum.

Advances in Psychology & Education, Vol. 1. Ed. by Charles A. Maher. 1988. 73.25 (*0-89232-842-8*) Jai Pr.

Advances in Psychoneuroendocrinology. Ed. by F. G. Brambilla et al. (Giovanni Lorenzini Foundation Symposia Ser.: Vol. 8). 1980. 127.25 (*0-444-80294-0*) Elsevier.

***Advances in Psychoneuroimmunology.** Ed. by Istvan Berczi & Judith Szelenyi. LC 94-47537. (Hans Selye Symposia on Neuroendocrinology & Stress Ser.: Vol. 3). 360p. 1995. 95.00 (*0-306-44883-1*, Plenum Pr) Plenum.

Advances in Psychopharmacology: Predicting & Improving Treatment Response. Ed. by Mark S. Gold et al. 344p. 1984. 156.00 (*0-8493-5680-6*, RC483) CRC Pr.

Advances in Psychopharmacology & Behavioral Neurology. Birnbaum. 1990. 74.95 (*0-8151-0824-9*, Yr Bk Med Pubs) Mosby Yr Bk.

Advances in Psychophysiology, Vol. 4. Ed. by J. Richard Jennings. 300p. 1991. 88.00 (*1-85302-079-6*, Pub. by J Kingsley Pubs UK) Taylor & Francis.

Advances in Psychophysiology, Vol. 5. Ed. by J. Richard Jennings et al. 300p. 1993. 99.00 (*1-85302-191-1*, Pub. by J Kingsley Pubs UK) Taylor & Francis.

Advances in Psychosomatic Obstetrics & Gynecology, Berlin 1980: Proceedings. Ed. by H. J. Prill & M. Stauber. (Illus.). 560p. 1982. pap. 59.00 (*0-387-11710-5*) Spr-Verlag.

Advances in Public Interest Accounting, Vol. 1. Ed. by Marilyn Neimark. 1986. 73.25 (*0-89232-516-X*) Jai Pr.

Advances in Public Interest Accounting, Vol. 2. Ed. by Marilyn Neimark et al. 1987. 73.25 (*0-89232-698-0*) Jai Pr.

Advances in Public Interest Accounting, Vol. 3. Ed. by Marilyn Neimark et al. 275p. 1990. 73.25 (*0-89232-784-7*) Jai Pr.

Advances in Public Interest Accounting, Vol. 4. Ed. by Cheryl Lehman et al. 1991. 73.25 (*1-55938-254-6*) Jai Pr.

Advances in Qualitative Psychology: Themes & Variations. F. J. Van Zuuren et al. 210p. 1987. pap. 22.00 (*90-265-0849-2*, Pub. by Swets Pub Serv NE) Taylor & Francis.

Advances in Quantitative Analysis of Finance & Accounting, Vol. 1, Pt. A: Methodologies. Ed. by Cheng-Few Lee. 1990. 73.25 (*1-55938-026-8*) Jai Pr.

Advances in Quantitative Analysis of Finance & Accounting, Vol. 1, Pt. B: Applications. Ed. by Cheng-Few Lee. 1990. 73.25 (*1-55938-138-8*) Jai Pr.

Advances in Quantitative Coronary Arteriography. Ed. by Johan H. Reiber & Patrick W. Serruys. LC 92-20819. (Developments in Cardiovascular Medicine Ser.: Vol. 137). 1993. lib. bdg. 299.00 (*0-7923-1863-3*) Kluwer Ac.

Advances in Quantum Chemistry, Vol. 17. Ed. by Per-Olov Lowdin. (Serial Publication Ser.). 1985. text ed. 189.00 (*0-12-034817-9*) Acad Pr.

Advances in Quantum Chemistry, Vol. 18. Ed. by Per-Olov Lowdin. (Serial Publication Ser.). 1986. text ed. 176.00 (*0-12-034818-7*) Acad Pr.

Advances in Quantum Chemistry, Vol. 19. Ed. by Per-Olov Lowdin et al. (Serial Publication Ser.). 365p. 1988. text ed. 134.00 (*0-12-034819-5*) Acad Pr.

Advances in Quantum Chemistry, Vol. 20. Ed. by Per-Olov Lowdin et al. (Serial Publication Ser.). 453p. 1989. text ed. 128.00 (*0-12-034820-9*) Acad Pr.

Advances in Quantum Chemistry, Vol. 22. Ed. by Per-Olov Lowdin et al. (Illus.). 385p. 1991. text ed. 94.00 (*0-12-034822-5*) Acad Pr.

Advances in Quantum Chemistry, Vol. 23. Ed. by Per-Olov Lowdin et al. (Illus.). 363p. 1992. text ed. 85.00 (*0-12-034823-3*) Acad Pr.

Advances in Quantum Chemistry, Vol. 24. Ed. by Per-Olov Lowdin et al. (Illus.). 298p. 1992. text ed. 75.00 (*0-12-034824-1*) Acad Pr.

Advances in Quantum Chemistry, Vol. 25. Ed. by Per-Olov Lowdin. 320p. 1994. text ed. 79.00 (*0-12-034825-X*) Acad Pr.

***Advances in Quantum Chemistry, Vol. 26.** Ed. by John R. Sabin et al. (Illus.). 392p. 1995. boxed write for info. (*0-12-034826-8*) Acad Pr.

Advances in Quantum Chemistry, Vols. 1-11. Incl. Vol. 1. 1964. 85.00 (*0-12-034801-2*); Vol. 2. 1966. 85.00 (*0-12-034802-0*); Vol. 3. 1967. 85.00 (*0-12-034803-9*); Vol. 4. 1968. 85.00 (*0-12-034804-7*); Vol. 5. 1970. 85.00 (*0-12-034805-5*); Vol. 6. 1972. 85.00 (*0-12-034806-3*); Vol. 7. 1973. 85.00 (*0-12-034807-1*); Vol. 8. 1974. 85.00 (*0-12-034808-X*); Vol. 10. 1977. 85.00 (*0-12-034810-1*); (Serial Publication Ser.). write for info. (*0-318-50217-8*) Acad Pr.

Advances in Quantum Chemistry, Vol. 21: Density Functional Theory of Many-Fermion Systems. Samuel B. Trickey. Ed. by Per-Olov Lowdin. 405p. 1990. text ed. 99.00 (*0-12-034821-7*) Acad Pr.

Advances in Quantum Flux Parametron Computer Design. Ed. by E. Goto et al. LC 92-19667. (Studies in Josephson Supercomputers). 500p. (C). 1992. text ed. 81.00 (*981-02-0826-X*) World Scientific Pub.

***Advances in Quantum Phenomena: Proceedings of an International Course Held in Erice, Sicily, February 16-18, 1994.** Ed. by Enrico E. Beltrametti & Jean-Marc Levy-Leblond. (NATO ASI Series B, Physics: Vol. 347). 375p. 1995. 115.00 (*0-306-45072-0*) Plenum.

Advances in Quasi-Experimental Design & Analysis. Ed. by William M. Trochim. LC 85-81899. (New Directions for Program Evaluation Ser.: No. PE 31). (Orig.). 1986. pap. 17.95 (*1-55542-990-4*) Jossey-Bass.

***Advances in Queuing Models, Methods, & Problems.** Ed. by Jewgeni H. Dshalalow. 496p. 1995. 69.95 (*0-8493-8074-X*, 8074) CRC Pr.

Advances in Radiation Biology, Vol. 10. (Serial Publication Ser.). 1983. text ed. 158.00 (*0-12-035410-1*) Acad Pr.

Advances in Radiation Biology, Vol. XI. (Serial Publication Ser.). 1984. text ed. 158.00 (*0-12-035411-X*) Acad Pr.

Advances in Radiation Biology, Vol. 12. Ed. by Ann B. Cox & Ursula K. Ehmann. (Serial Publication Ser.). 296p. 1987. text ed. 158.00 (*0-12-035412-8*) Acad Pr.

Advances in Radiation Biology, Vol. 13. Ed. by John T. Lett et al. (Serial Publication Ser.). 414p. 1987. text ed. 158.00 (*0-12-035413-6*) Acad Pr.

Advances in Radiation Biology: Relative Radiation Sensitivities of Human Organ Systems, Vol. 18, Pt. IV. Ed. by John T. Lett et al. (Illus.). 232p. 1994. text ed. 110.00 (*0-12-035418-7*) Acad Pr.

Advances in Radiation Biology Vol. 18: Relative Radiation Sensitivities of Human Organ Systems, Pt. IV. Ed. by John T. Lett et al. (Illus.). 232p. 1994. boxed 110.00 (*0-12-034518-8*) Acad Pr.

Advances in Radiation Biology, Vol. 14: Relative Radiation Sensitivities of Human Organ Systems, Pt. II. Ed. by Kurt I. Altman & John T. Lett. 324p. 1990. text ed. 128.00 (*0-12-035414-4*) Acad Pr.

Advances in Radiation Biology, Vol. 15: Relative Radiation Sensitivities of Human Organ Systems, Pt. III. Ed. by John T. Lett & Kurt I. Altman. (Illus.). 328p. 1992. text ed. 125.00 (*0-12-035415-2*) Acad Pr.

Advances in Radiation Biology, Vol. 16: Effects of Low Dose & Low Dose Rate Radiation. Ed. by John T. Lett et al. (Illus.). 336p. 1992. text ed. 105.00 (*0-12-035416-0*) Acad Pr.

Advances in Radiation Biology, Vol. 17: DNA & Chromatin Damage Caused by Radiation. Ed. by John T. Lett & Warren K. Sinclair. (Illus.). 507p. 1993. text ed. 130.00 (*0-12-035417-9*) Acad Pr.

Advances in Radiation Oncology Physics: Dosimetry, Treatment Planning, & Brachytherapy. Ed. by James A. Purdy. LC 92-81653. (American Association of Physicists in Medicine Symposium Ser.: No. 19). 1099p. 1993. 75.00 (*1-56396-054-0*) Am Inst Physics.

Advances in Radiation Processing: Transactions of the Second International Meeting on Radiation Processing Held at Miami, Florida 22-26 Oct. 1978, 2 vols., Set. Ed. by Joseph Silverman. 948p. 1980. pap. 160.00 (*0-08-025025-4*, Pergamon Pr) Elsevier.

Advances in Radiation Protection. Ed. by Martin Oberhofer. (C). 1991. lib. bdg. 127.00 (*0-7923-1232-5*) Kluwer Ac.

Advances in Radiation Research: Biology & Medicine, 3 vols., Vol. 2. Ed. by J. F. Duplan & A. Chapiro. LC 72-92724. 490p. 1973. Vol. 1, 490p. text ed. 272.00 (*0-677-30880-9*); text ed. 289.00 (*0-677-30890-6*) Gordon & Breach.

Advances in Radiation Research: Biology & Medicine, 3 vols., Vol. 3. Ed. by J. F. Duplan & A. Chapiro. LC 72-92724. 1564p. 1973. Set, 1564p. text ed. 585.00 (*0-677-15770-3*); text ed. 241.00 (*0-677-30900-7*) Gordon & Breach.

Advances in Radiation Research: Physics & Chemistry, 2 vols., Set. Ed. by J. F. Duplan & A. Chapiro. LC 72-92724. 668p. 1973. 238.00 (*0-677-15780-0*) Gordon & Breach.

Advances in Radiation Research: Physics & Chemistry, 2 vols., Vol. 1. Ed. by J. F. Duplan & A. Chapiro. LC 72-92724. 360p. 1973. text ed. 220.00 (*0-677-30640-7*) Gordon & Breach.

Advances in Radiation Research: Physics & Chemistry, 2 vols., Vol. 2. Ed. by J. F. Duplan & A. Chapiro. LC 72-92724. 308p. 1973. text ed. 216.00 (*0-677-30650-4*) Gordon & Breach.

Advances in Radiation Therapy Treatment Planning: Proceedings of the AAPM Summer School Held at Southeastern Louisiana University, Hammond, Louisiana, July 26-30, 1982. Ed. by Ann E. Wright & Arthur L. Boyer. (American Association of Physicists in Medicine Symposium Ser.: No. 9). 635p. 1983. 60.00 (*0-88318-423-0*) Am Inst Physics.

Advances in Radiopharmaceutical Design, Vol. 1. Ed. by Hank F. Kung. 1991. 90.25 (*1-55938-175-2*) Jai Pr.

***Advances in Radiosurgery I.** C. Lindquist. 124p. 1995. 94.00 (*3-211-82612-2*) Spr-Verlag.

Advances in Raman Spectorscopy: Proceedings of the Third International Conference on Raman Spectroscopy: University of Reims, France, September, 1972. Ed. by J. P. Mathieu. LC 73-76120. 655p. reprint ed. pap. 180.00 (*0-8357-5182-1*, 2023996) Bks Demand.

Advances in Range Management in Arid Lands: Proceedings of the First International Conference on Range Management in the Arabian Gulf. Ed. by Riad Halwagy et al. 300p. 1990. 79.95 (*0-7103-0360-2*, A3919) Routledge Chapman & Hall.

Advances in Reactor Physics & Radiation Protection & Shielding, Chicago, IL, Sept. 17-19, 1984, 2 vols., Set. 901p. 1984. 75.00 (*0-89448-113-4*, 700095) Am Nuclear Soc.

Advances in Reading-Language Research, Vol. 1. Ed. by Barbara Hutson. 1982. 73.25 (*0-89232-197-0*) Jai Pr.

Advances in Reading-Language Research, Vol. 2. Ed. by Barbara Hutson. 1983. 73.25 (*0-89232-200-4*) Jai Pr.

Advances in Reading-Language Research, Vol. 3. Ed. by Barbara Hutson. 1985. 73.25 (*0-89232-389-2*) Jai Pr.

Advances in Reading-Language Research, Vol. 4. Ed. by Barbara Hutson. 1986. 73.25 (*0-89232-631-X*) Jai Pr.

Advances in Reading-Language Research, Vol. 5. Ed. by Barbara Hutson. 1988. 73.25 (*0-89232-813-4*) Jai Pr.

Advances in Ready Mixed Concrete Technology. R. K. Dhir. 1976. text ed. 209.00 (*0-08-020415-5*, Pub. by Pergamon Repr UK) Franklin.

***Advances in Real-Time Systems.** Ed. by Sang H. Son. LC 94-26844. 1994. text ed. 60.00 (*0-13-083348-7*) P-H.

Advances in Real-Time Systems. John A. Stankovic & Krithi Ramamritham. LC 93-2243. 792p. 1993. text ed. 88.00 (*0-8186-3792-7*, 3792) IEEE Comp Soc.

***Advances in Red Blood Cell Biology.** fac. ed. D. J. Weatherall et al. LC 81-47975. (Illus.). 442p. Date not set. pap. 126.00 (*0-7837-7354-4*, 2047163) Bks Demand.

Advances in Refractories for the Metallurgical Industries: Proceedings of the International Symposium, Winnipeg, August 1987. Ed. by M. A. Rigaud. (CIM Ser.: No. 4). (Illus.). 327p. 1988. Delegates. 26.25 (*0-08-035881-0*, Pergamon Pr); 45.00 (*0-08-035880-2*, Pergamon Pr) Elsevier.

Advances in Regional Cancer Therapy. Ed. by J. Kreidler et al. (Illus.). x, 228p. 1988. 53.75 (*3-8055-4842-7*) S Karger.

Advances in Regional Demography: Forecasts, Information, Models. Peter Congdon & Peter Batey. 256p. 1989. 55.00 (*1-85293-046-2*, Pub. by Pinter Pubs UK) St Martin.

***Advances in Relationship Marketing.** Ed. by Adrian Payne. (Cranfield Management Ser.). 240p. 1995. pap. 32.50 (*0-7494-1636-X*, Pub. by Kogan Pg UK) Cassell.

Advances in Reliability: A Selection of Papers from the International Research Conference on Reliability, Missouri, Columbia, 19-22 June, 1991. Ed. by Asit P. Basu. LC 93-3047. 471p. 1993. 165.75 (*0-444-89645-7*, North Holland) Elsevier.

Advances in Reliability & Quality Control: Proceedings of IASTED Symposium, Paris, June 22 & 23, 1988, & in Los Angeles, December 12-14, 1988. Ed. by M. H. Hamza. 200p. 1988. 68.00 (*0-88986-109-9*, 124) Acta Pr.

An Asterisk (*) at the beginning of an entry indicates that the title is appearing in BIP for the first time.

Advances in Reliability & Stress Analysis: Presented at the ASME Winter Annual Meeting, San Francisco, CA, December, 1978. American Society of Mechanical Engineers. Ed. by John J. Burns, Jr. LC 79-50208. 258p. reprint ed. pap. 73.60 (*0-8357-5183-X*, 2056308) Bks Demand.

Advances in Remote Sensing Retrieval Methods. Ed. by Adarsh Deepak et al. LC 86-2057. (Illus.). 737p. 1985. 71.00 (*0-937194-07-7*) A Deepak Pub.

Advances in Renal Medicine. Ed. by A. E. Raine. LC 92-49499. (Oxford Medical Publications). 1993. 105.00 (*0-19-262102-5*); pap. 52.50 (*0-19-262101-7*) OUP.

Advances in Reproductive Endocrinology Vol. 1: Endometriosis. Ed. by R. W. Shaw. (Advances in Reproductive Endocrinology Ser.: Vol. 1). (Illus.). 230p. (C). 1990. 68.00 (*1-85070-297-7*) Prthnon Pub.

Advances in Reproductive Endocrinology Vol. 2: Dysfunctional Uterine Bleeding. Ed. by R. W. Shaw. (Advances in Reproductive Endocrinology Ser.: Vol. 2). (Illus.). 164p. (C). 1990. 68.00 (*1-85070-296-9*) Prthnon Pub.

Advances in Research & Practice in Self-Directed Learning. Huey B. Long et al. 295p. (Orig.). (C). 1990. pap. 19.95 (*0-9622488-2-7*) U OK PMC.

Advances in Research & Technology of Seeds, Pts. I & II. PUDOC Staff et al. (C). 1991. text ed. 2,500.00 (*0-89771-631-0*, Pub. by Intl Bk Distr II) St Mut.

Advances in Research & Technology of Seeds, 2 vols., Set. J. Thomson & S. Matthews. (C). 1991. 2,500.00 (*81-7089-153-1*, Pub. by Intl Bk Distr II) St Mut.

Advances in Research & Technology of Seeds, XPudoc. Incl. Pt. 6. Ed. by J. R. Thomas. 124p. 1981. pap. 21.00 (*90-220-0786-3*, PDC234); Pt. 7. Ed. by J. R. Thomsom. 140p. 1982. pap. 20.00 (*90-220-0802-9*, PDC249); Pt. 8. Ed. by J. R. Thomson. 124p. 1983. pap. 25.00 (*90-220-0834-7*, PDC263); Pt. 9. Ed. by J. R. Thomson. 131p. 1984. pap. 25.00 (*90-220-0861-4*, PDC276); write for info. (*0-318-60630-5*) UNIPUB.

Advances in Research on Cholera & Related Diarrheas. Ed. by S. Kuwahara. (New Perspectives in Clinical Microbiology Ser.). 1983. lib. bdg. 117.00 (*0-89838-592-X*) Kluwer Ac.

Advances in Research on Cholera & Related Diarrheas, Vol. 2. Ed. by S. Kuwahara & N. F. Pierce. (New Perspectives in Clinical Microbiology Ser.). 1985. lib. bdg. 134.50 (*0-89838-680-2*) Kluwer Ac.

***Advances in Research on Mineral Resources, 1994.** Ed. by Byron R. Berger. (U. S. Geological Survey Bulletin Ser.: Vol. 2081). 1995. write for info. (*0-615-00244-7*) US Geol Survey.

***Advances in Research on Neurodegeneration Vol. II: Etiopathogenesis.** Ed. by Y. Mizuno et al. (Illus.). xiii, 221p. 1994. text ed. 95.00 (*0-8176-3762-1*) Birkhauser.

Advances in Research on Neurodegeneration, I: Definitions, Clinical Features, & Morphology. Ed. by D. B. Calne et al. (Advances in Research on Neurodegeneration Ser.). (Illus.). 280p. 1993. 95.00 (*0-8176-3631-5*) Birkhauser.

Advances in Research on Plant Pathogenic Bacteria. S. S. Gnanamanickam & A. Mahadevan. (International Bioscience Ser.: Vol. XIII). (Illus.). 250p. 1988. 65.00 (*1-55528-147-8*, Messers Today & Tomorrow) Scholarly Pubns.

Advances in Research on the Strength & Fracture of Materials, 6 Vols. D. M. Taplin. Incl. Vol. 1. Overview. LC 77-15623. 1978. 349.00 (*0-08-022136-X*); Vol. 2a. Physical Metallurgy of Fracture. LC 77-15623. 1978. 284.00 (*0-08-022138-6*); Vol. 2b. Fatigue. LC 77-15623. 1978. 297.00 (*0-08-022140-8*); Vol. 3a. LC 77-15623. 1978. 221.00 (*0-08-022142-4*); Vol. 3b. Applications & Non-Metals. LC 77-15623. 1978. Incl. index. 318.00 (*0-08-022144-0*); LC 77-15623. 1978. 1,616.00 (*0-08-022130-0*, Pub. by Pergamon Repr UK) Franklin.

Advances in Reservoir Geology. Ed. by M. Ashton. (Geological Society Special Publications: No. 69). (Illus.). viii, 240p. (C). 1993. 84.00 (*0-903317-84-2*, Pub. by Geol Soc Pub Hse UK) AAPG.

Advances in Resist Technology & Processing, No. IV. Ed. by Bowden. 373p. 1987. 57.00 (*0-89252-806-0*, 771) SPIE.

Advances in Resist Technology & Processing, No. V. Ed. by MacDonald. 1988. 65.00 (*0-89252-955-5*, 920) SPIE.

Advances in Resist Technology & Processing, No. VII. Ed. by M. P. Watts. 603p. 1990. 70.00 (*0-8194-0309-1*, VOL. 1262) SPIE.

Advances in Resist Technology & Processing IX. Ed. by A. E. Novembre. 1992. 86.00 (*0-8194-0827-1*, 1672) SPIE.

Advances in Resist Technology & Processing VI. Ed. by Else Reichmanis. 629p. 1989. 86.00 (*0-8194-0121-8*, VOL. 1086) SPIE.

Advances in Resist Technology & Processing VIII, Vol. 1466. H. Ito. 1991. 86.00 (*0-8194-0565-5*) SPIE.

***Advances in Resource Mangement: Tributes to W. R. Derrick Sewell.** Ed. by Harold D. Foster. 1994. text ed. 74.95 (*0-471-94602-8*) Wiley.

Advances in Reversal Theory. Ed. by John H. Kerr et al. LC 93-12666. 1993. 60.00 (*90-265-1202-3*, Pub. by Swets Pub Serv NE) Taylor & Francis.

Advances in Rheology: Proceedings of the Ninth International Congress on Rheology Acapulco, Mexico, October 8-13, 1984, 4 vols. Ed. by B. Mena et al. 1985. pap. 300.00 (*0-444-99576-5*) Elsevier.

Advances in Robot Kinematics. Ed. by S. Stifter & J. Lenarcic. (Illus.). xiv, 484p. 1991. pap. 99.00 (*0-387-82302-6*) Spr-Verlag.

Advances in Robot Kinematics & Computational Geometry. Ed. by Jadran Lenarcic & Bahram Ravani. LC 94-21074. (Diversity & Direction in Children's Literature Ser.). 520p. (C). 1994. lib. bdg. 216.00 (*0-7923-2983-X*) Kluwer Ac.

Advances in Robotics: Algorithmic & Geometric Aspects of Robotics. Ed. by J. T. Schwartz & C. K. Yap. (Advances in Robotics Ser.). 320p. 1987. 59.95 (*0-89859-554-1*) L Erlbaum Assocs.

Advances in Robotics - 1992. Ed. by H. Kazerooni. (DSC Ser.: Vol. 42). 256p. 1992. 62.50 (*0-7918-1107-7*, G00751) ASME.

Advances in Robotics & Automation '84: Proceedings, IASTED Symposium, San Francisco, U. S. A., May 23-24, 1984 & Amsterdam, Netherlands, June 27-29, 1984. Ed. by M. H. Hamza. 144p. 1984. 65.00 (*0-88986-059-9*, 074) Acta Pr.

Advances in Robotics, Mechatronics & Haptic Interfaces 1993. Ed. by H. Kazerooni et al. LC 93-73727. 367p. Date not set. pap. 75.00 (*0-7918-1019-4*) ASME.

Advances in Robotics '85: Proceedings, IASTED Symposium, Santa Barbara, U. S. A., May 29-31, 1985. Ed. by M. H. Hamza. 155p. 1985. 75.00 (*0-88986-075-0*, 078) Acta Pr.

Advances in Robust & Nonlinear Control Systems. Ed. by E. A. Misawa. LC 93-73654. 131p. Date not set. pap. 45.00 (*0-7918-1259-6*) ASME.

Advances in Robust & Nonlinear Control Systems. Ed. by E. A. Misawa. (DSC Ser.: Vol. 43). 96p. 1992. 30.00 (*0-7918-1114-X*, G00758) ASME.

Advances in Rockfill Structures. Ed. by E. Maranha Das Neves. (C). 1991. lib. bdg. 202.50 (*0-7923-1267-8*) Kluwer Ac.

Advances in Role & Reference Grammar. Ed. by Robert D. Van Valin, Jr. LC 92-42015. (Current Issues in Linguistic Theory Ser.: No. 82). xii, 569p. 1992. 148.00x (*1-55619-137-5*); pap. 29.95 (*1-55619-552-4*) Benjamins North Am.

***Advances in Roumanian Linguistics.** Ed. by Guglielmo Cinque & Giuliana Giusti. LC 95-9960. (Linguistik Aktuell/Linguistics Today Ser.: No. 10). xi, 172p. 1995. lib. bdg. 53.00 (*1-55619-228-2*) Benjamins North Am.

Advances in School Effectiveness Research & Practice. David Reynolds et al. LC 94-15705. 1994. text ed. 72.00 (*0-08-042392-2*, Pergamon Pr) Elsevier.

Advances in School Management, Vol. 1. Ed. by Samuel B. Bacharach. 1988. 73.25 (*0-89232-767-7*) Jai Pr.

Advances in School Psychology, Vol. 1. Thomas R. Kratochwill. 368p. 1981. text ed. 79.95 (*0-89859-076-0*) L Erlbaum Assocs.

Advances in School Psychology, Vol. 2. Ed. by T. R. Kratochwill. (Illus.). 400p. (C). 1982. text ed. 79.95 (*0-89859-162-7*) L Erlbaum Assocs.

Advances in School Psychology, Vol. 4. Ed. by Thomas R. Kratochwill. 336p. 1985. text ed. 69.95 (*0-89859-454-5*) L Erlbaum Assocs.

Advances in School Psychology, Vol. 5. Ed. by Thomas Kratochwill. 264p. 1986. text ed. 59.95 (*0-89859-708-0*) L Erlbaum Assocs.

Advances in School Psychology, Vol. 6. Ed. by T. R. Kratochwill. 320p. 1988. 59.95 (*0-8058-0067-0*) L Erlbaum Assocs.

Advances in School Psychology, Vol. 7. Ed. by Thomas R. Kratochwill. 192p. 1990. 39.95 (*0-8058-0350-5*) L Erlbaum Assocs.

Advances in School Psychology, Vol. 8. Ed. by Thomas Kratochwill et al. (Advances in School Psychology Ser.). 216p. 1992. text ed. 49.95 (*0-8058-1118-4*) L Erlbaum Assocs.

Advances in School Psychology, Vol.3. Ed. by Thomas R. Kratochwill. 384p. 1983. text ed. 79.95 (*0-89859-280-1*) L Erlbaum Assocs.

Advances in Scientific Visualization. Ed. by Eurographics Association Staff et al. LC 92-11412. (Focus on Computer Graphics Ser.). 232p. 1993. pap. 89.00 (*0-387-55203-0*) Spr-Verlag.

Advances in Seafood Biochemistry: Composition & Quality. Ed. by George J. Flick & Roy E. Martin. LC 92-60029. 410p. 1992. text ed. 98.00 (*0-87762-931-5*) Technomic.

Advances in Seafood Technology. Rodrick. 1995. write for info. (*0-8493-4526-X*) CRC Pr.

Advances in Seat Belt Restraints: Design, Performance & Usage. 1984. 98.00 (*0-89883-097-4*, P141) Soc Auto Engineers.

Advances in Second Messenger & Phosphoprotein Research, Vol. 22. Ed. by Paul Greengard & G. Alan Robison. (Illus.). 400p. 1988. text ed. 108.50 (*0-88167-441-9*) Raven.

Advances in Second Messenger & Phosphoprotein Research, Vol. 23. Paul Greengard & G. Alan Robison. 304p. 1991. 121.50 (*0-88167-687-X*) Raven.

Advances in Self-Psychology. Arnold Goldberg. 562p. 1980. 60.00 (*0-8236-0098-X*) Intl Univs Pr.

Advances in Separation Processes. K. Davies. (Institution of Chemical Engineers Symposium Ser.: No. 118). 168p. 1990. 68.00 (*1-56032-077-X*) Hemisp Pub.

Advances in Serials Management, Vol. 1. Ed. by Marcia Tuttle & Jean G. Cook. 238p. 1986. lib. bdg. 73.25 (*0-89232-568-2*) Jai Pr.

Advances in Serials Management, Vol. 2. Marcia Tuttle. Ed. by Jean G. Cook. 1987. lib. bdg. 73.25 (*0-89232-672-7*) Jai Pr.

Advances in Serials Management, Vol. 3. Ed. by Marcia Tuttle & Jean G. Cook. 265p. 1989. 73.25 (*0-89232-965-3*) Jai Pr.

Advances in Sexually Transmitted Diseases: Diagnosis & Treatment. Ed. by R. Morisset & E. Kurstak. 237p. 1986. lib. bdg. 110.00 (*90-6764-059-X*, Pub. by VSP NE) Coronet Bks.

Advances in Shannon's Sampling Theory. Ahmed I. Zayed. LC 93-19506. 352p. 1993. 59.95 (*0-8493-4293-7*, QA276) CRC Pr.

Advances in Shuttle Imaging Radar-B Research. Ed. by J. P. Ford. 214p. 1988. 42.00 (*0-85066-878-6*) Taylor & Francis.

Advances in Signal Processing for Nondestructive Evaluation of Materials: Proceedings of the NATO Advanced Research Workshop, Quebec City, Quebec, Canada, August 17-20, 1993. Ed. by X. P. Maldague. LC 94-6394. (NATO Advanced Study Institutes Series E, Applied Sciences: Vol. 262). 504p. (C). 1994. lib. bdg. 199.50 (*0-7923-2765-9*) Kluwer Ac.

Advances in Silicon Chemistry, Vol. 1. Ed. by Gerald L. Larson. 1991. 90.25 (*1-55938-176-0*) Jai Pr.

Advances in Silicon Chemistry, Vol. 2. Ed. by Gerald L. Larson. 1992. 90.25 (*1-55938-177-9*) Jai Pr.

Advances in Site Characterization: Data Acquisition, Data Management, & Data Interpretation: Proceedings of a Symposium - Sponsored by the Committee on Engineering Geology & the Committee on Soil Properties of the Geotechnical Engineering Division of the Americaan Society of Civil Engineers in Conjunction with the ASCE Convention in Dallas, Texas, October 27-28, 1993. Ed. by Carlton L. Ho & Roman D. Hryciw. LC 93-31661. (Geotechnical Special Publication Ser.: No. 37): 1993. write for info. (*0-87262-984-8*) Am Soc Civil Eng.

Advances in Small Animal Practice: Proceedings of the 6th Conference on British Small Animal Veterinary Association London 4-63, Vol. 5. Brent D. Jones. LC 60-10840. 1964. 76.00 (*0-08-010953-5*, Pub. by Pergamon Repr UK) Franklin.

Advances in Small Business Finance. Ed. by Rassoul Yazdipour. (C). 1991. lib. bdg. 84.00 (*0-7923-1135-3*) Kluwer Ac.

Advances in Small Millets. Ed. by Kenneth Riley et al. (Illus.). 575p. (C). 1994. text ed. 70.00 (*1-881570-07-X*) Intl Sci Pub.

Advances in Smoking of Foods. Ed. by Rutkowski. 1978. 42.00 (*0-08-022002-9*, Pub. by Pergamon Repr UK) Franklin.

Advances in Social Network Analysis: Research in the Social & Behavioral Sciences. Ed. by Stanley Wasserman & Joseph Galaskiewicz. (Focus Editions Ser.: Vol. 173). 280p. 1994. 49.95 (*0-8039-4302-4*); pap. 24.95 (*0-8039-4303-2*) Sage.

Advances in Social Science Methodology, Vol. 1. Ed. by Bruce Thompson. 1988. 73.25 (*0-89232-736-7*) Jai Pr.

Advances in Social Science Methodology, Vol. 2. Ed. by Bruce Thompson. 1991. 73.25 (*1-55938-073-X*) Jai Pr.

Advances in Social Science Methodology, Vol. 3. Bruce Thompson. 1992. 73.25 (*1-55938-379-8*) Jai Pr.

Advances in Software: Theory & Applications, Vol. 1. Ed. by Roy Campbell. 1989. 73.25 (*0-89232-874-6*) Jai Pr.

Advances in Software Engineering & Knowledge Engineering. V. Ambriola & G. Tortora. (Series on Software Engineering & Knowledge). 180p. 1993. text ed. 53.00 (*981-02-1594-0*) World Scientific Pub.

Advances in Software Science & Technology, Vol. 1. Ed. by Japanese Society for Science & Technology Staff. 216p. 1989. text ed. 80.00 (*0-12-037101-4*) Acad Pr.

Advances in Software Science & Technology, Vol. 2. Ed. by Japan Society for Software Science & Technology Staff. (Illus.). 218p. 1991. text ed. 72.00 (*0-12-037102-2*) Acad Pr.

Advances in Software Science & Technology, Vol. 3. Ed. by Japan Society for Software Science & Technology. (Illus.). 184p. 1991. text ed. 72.00 (*0-12-037103-0*) Acad Pr.

Advances in Software Science & Technology, Vol. 4. Ed. by Japan Society of Software Science & Technology Staff. (Illus.). 198p. 1993. text ed. 69.95 (*0-12-037104-9*) Acad Pr.

Advances in Software Science & Technology, Vol. 5. Ed. by Japan Society for Software Science & Technology Staff. (Illus.). 255p. 1994. text ed. 89.00 (*0-12-037105-7*) Acad Pr.

***Advances in Soil Dynamics Vol. 1.** LC 94-72088. 330p. 1994. 42.00 (*0-929355-52-0*) Am Soc Ag Eng.

Advances in Soil Science, Vol. 1. Ed. by B. A. Stewart. (Illus.). 375p. 1984. 99.00 (*0-387-96027-9*) Spr-Verlag.

Advances in Soil Science, Vol. 2. Ed. by B. A. Steward. (Illus.). 220p. 1985. 99.00 (*0-387-96114-3*) Spr-Verlag.

Advances in Soil Science, Vol. 3. Ed. by B. A. Stewart. (Illus.). 240p. 1985. 99.00 (*0-387-96116-X*) Spr-Verlag.

Advances in Soil Science, Vol. 4. Ed. by B. A. Stewart. (Illus.). 240p. 1986. 99.00 (*0-387-96247-6*) Spr-Verlag.

Advances in Soil Science, Vol. 5. Ed. by B. A. Stewart. (Illus.). 270p. 1986. 99.00 (*0-387-96321-9*) Spr-Verlag.

Advances in Soil Science, Vol. 6. Ed. by B. A. Stewart. (Illus.). 235p. 1987. 99.00 (*0-387-96432-0*) Spr-Verlag.

Advances in Soil Science, Vol. 7. Ed. by B. A. Stewart. (Illus.). 250p. 1987. 99.00 (*0-387-96551-3*) Spr-Verlag.

Advances in Soil Science, Vol. 8. Ed. by B. A. Stewart. (Illus.). 225p. 1988. 99.00 (*0-387-96670-6*) Spr-Verlag.

Advances in Soil Science, Vol. 9. Ed. by B. A. Stewart. (Illus.). 215p. 1988. 109.00 (*0-387-96781-8*) Spr-Verlag.

Advances in Soil Science, Vol. 10. Ed. by B. A. Stewart. (Illus.). 225p. 1989. 109.00 (*0-387-96900-4*) Spr-Verlag.

Advances in Soil Science, Vol. 12. Ed. by B. A. Stewart. (Illus.). ix, 221p. 1989. 109.00 (*0-387-97121-1*, 3242) Spr-Verlag.

Advances in Soil Science, Vol. 13. Ed. by B. A. Stewart et al. (Illus.). xiv, 373p. 1990. 98.00 (*0-685-46310-9*) Spr-Verlag.

Advances in Soil Science, Vol. 14. Ed. by B. A. Stewart. ix, 196p. 1990. 109.00 (*0-387-97193-9*) Spr-Verlag.

Advances in Soil Science, Vol. 15. Ed. by B. A. Stewart. (Illus.). 264p. 1991. 109.00 (*0-387-97354-0*) Spr-Verlag.

Advances in Soil Science, Vol. 16. Ed. by B. A. Stewart. (Illus.). ix, 240p. 1991. 109.00 (*0-387-97519-5*) Spr-Verlag.

Advances in Soil Science, Vol. 18. Ed. by B. A. Stewart. (Illus.). 320p. 1992. 109.00 (*0-387-97697-3*) Spr-Verlag.

Advances in Soil Science, Vol. 20. Ed. by B. A. Stewart. (Illus.). 320p. 1992. 99.00 (*0-387-97828-3*) Spr-Verlag.

Advances in Solar Energy, Vol. 1. Ed. by Karl W. Boer & John A. Duffie. LC 85-646250. 320p. 1985. 135.00 (*0-306-42019-8*, Plenum Pr) Plenum.

Advances in Solar Energy, Vol. 2. Ed. by Karl W. Boer & John A. Duffie. LC 85-646250. 510p. 1985. 135.00 (*0-306-42064-3*, Plenum Pr) Plenum.

Advances in Solar Energy, Vol. 3. Ed. by Karl W. Boer. LC 85-646250. 502p. 1986. 135.00 (*0-306-42364-2*, Plenum Pr) Plenum.

Advances in Solar Energy, Vol. 4. Ed. by Karl W. Boer. LC 85-646250. (Illus.). 534p. 1988. 145.00 (*0-306-42810-5*, Plenum Pr) Plenum.

Advances in Solar Energy, Vol. 5. (Illus.). 472p. 1989. 145.00 (*0-306-43323-0*, Plenum Pr) Plenum.

Advances in Solar Energy, Vol. 6. Ed. by Karl W. Boer. LC 85-646250. (Illus.). 630p. 1990. 145.00 (*0-306-43727-9*, Plenum Pr) Plenum.

Advances in Solar Energy: An Annual Review of Research & Development in 1981, Vol. I. Ed. by Karl W. Boer & John A. Duffie. (Illus.). 1982. pap. text ed. 125.00 (*0-89553-040-6*) Am Solar Energy.

Advances in Solar Energy Technology, 3 Vols., Set. H. P. Garg. 1987. lib. bdg. 199.00 (*90-277-2443-4*) Kluwer Ac.

Advances in Solar Energy Technology, Vol. 1: Collection & Storage Systems. H. P. Garg. 1987. lib. bdg. 172.50 (*90-277-2430-X*) Kluwer Ac.

Advances in Solar Energy Technology, Vol. 2: Industrial Applications of Solar Energy. H. P. Garg. 1987. lib. bdg. 147.00 (*90-277-2431-8*) Kluwer Ac.

Advances in Solar Energy Technology, Vol. 3: Heating, Agriculture & Photovoltaic Applic. H. P. Garg. 1987. lib. bdg. 79.00 (*0-317-57392-6*) Kluwer Ac.

Advances in Solar Energy Technology: Proceedings of the Biennial Congress of the International Solar Energy Society, Hamburg, FRG, 13-18 September 1987, 4 vols., Set. W. H. Bloss & F. Pfisterer. LC 88-17824. 4070p. 1988. 1,644.00 (*0-08-034315-5*, Pub. by Pergamon Repr UK); pap. 75.00 (*0-08-034316-3*, Pub. by Pergamon Repr UK) Franklin.

Advances in Solar System Magnetohydrodynamics. Ed. by Eric R. Priest & Alan W. Hood. (Illus.). 452p. (C). 1991. 59.95 (*0-521-40325-1*) Cambridge U Pr.

Advances in Solid-Liquid Flow in Pipes & Its Application. Ed. by I. Zandi. LC 77-120000. 1971. 131.00 (*0-08-015767-X*, Pub. by Pergamon Repr UK) Franklin.

Advances in Solid Liquid Separation. Ed. by H. S. Muralidhara. LC 86-26569. 494p. 1986. 79.50 (*0-85186-363-9*) Battelle.

Advances in Solid-Liquid Separation: Supplement. Ed. by H. S. Muralidhara. 180p. 1986. pap. 26.50 (*0-685-40037-9*) Battelle.

Advances in Solid-State Chemistry, Vol. 1. Ed. by C. R. Catlow. 1988. 73.25 (*0-89232-867-3*) Jai Pr.

Advances in Solid-State Chemistry, Vol. 2. Ed. by C. R. Catlow. 394p. 1991. 90.25 (*0-89232-954-8*) Jai Pr.

Advances in Solid-State Chemistry, Vol. 3. Ed. by C. R. Catlow. 1992. 90.25 (*1-55938-271-6*) Jai Pr.

Advances in Solid State Chemistry: Proc of the Insa Golden Jubilee Symp. C. N. Rao. 428p. 1987. 85.00 (*9971-5-0137-6*) World Scientific Pub.

Advances in Solid State Physics, 32 - Festkorperprobleme: Plenary Lectures of the Divisions Semiconductor Physics, Thin Films, Dynamics & Statistical Physics of the German Physical Society (DPG), Regensburg, March 16-20, 1992. Ed. by Ulrich Rossler. viii, 372p. 1992. 124.00 (*3-528-08040-X*, Pub. by Vieweg & Sohn GW) Ballen Bkslr.

Advances in Solidification Processes. Ed. by H. Fredriksson et al. (European Materials Research Society Symposia Proceedings Ser.: Vol. 44). 424p. 1994. 171.50 (*0-444-81821-9*, North Holland) Elsevier.

Advances in Some Aspects of Osteoporosis. Ed. by J. L. Ambrus et al. 1985. pap. 35.00 (*0-915340-13-5*) PJD Pubns.

Advances in Sonochemistry, Vol. 1. Ed. by Timothy J. Mason. 275p. 1990. 90.25 (*1-55938-178-7*) Jai Pr.

Advances in Sonochemistry, Vol. 2. Ed. by Timothy J. Mason. 1991. 90.25 (*1-55938-267-8*) Jai Pr.

Advances in Soviet Tube Manufacture: The Institute VNITI. Israil M. Sukonnik. Ed. by John Williams. 152p. (Orig.). 1987. pap. text ed. 75.00 (*1-55831-048-7*) Delphic Associates.

Advances in Space Biology & Medicine, Vol. 1. Ed. by Sjoerd L. Bonting. 1991. 90.25 (*1-55938-296-1*) Jai Pr.

Advances in Space Plasma Physics: Proceedings of the ICTP College on Plasma Physics, Trieste, Itlay, 1985. Ed. by B. Buti. 500p. 1985. 115.00 (*9971-5-0016-7*) World Scientific Pub.

Advances in Space Research. T. M. Tabanera. LC 63-23209. (Proceedings of the First Interamerican Symposium on Space Research Ser.). 1964. 188.00 (*0-08-010293-X*, Pub. by Pergamon Repr UK) Franklin.

Advances in Space Research, Vol. 9, No. 3 see Cometary Environments: Proceedings of Symposium 5, Workshop IV & Topical Meeting of the Interdisciplinary Scientific Commission (Meeting C2) of COSPAR Plenary Meeting

Advances in Space Research, Vol. 9, No. 5 see Ionospheric Incoherent Scatter Results: Proceedings of Workshop V of the COSPAR Plenary Meeting, Espoo, Finland, 18-29 July 1988

Advances in Spatial Databases: Proceedings of the Third International Symposium, SSD '93, Singapore, June 23-25, 1993. Ed. by D. Abel & B. C. Ooi. (Lecture Notes in Computer Science Ser.: Vol. 692). xiii, 529p. 1993. pap. 72.00 (*0-387-56869-7*) Spr-Verlag.

Advances in Spatial Databases: 2nd Symposium, SSD '91 Zurich, Switzerland, August 28-30, 1991 Proceedings. Ed. by O. Gunther et al. (Lecture Notes in Computer Science Ser.: Vol. 525). xi, 471p. 1991. pap. 44.00 (*0-387-54414-3*) Spr-Verlag.

An Asterisk (*) at the beginning of an entry indicates that the title is appearing in BIP for the first time.

A

Advances in Spatial Information Extraction & Analysis for Remote Sensing. 128p. 1990. 10.00 (0-944426-37-9) ASP & RS.

Advances in Spatial Reasoning, Vol. I. Ed. by Su-shing Chen. 312p. (C). 1990. text ed. 59.50 (0-89391-572-6) Ablex Pub.

Advances in Spatial Reasoning, Vol. II. Ed. by Su-shing Chen. 312p. (C). 1990. text ed. 59.50 (0-89391-573-4) Ablex Pub.

Advances in Spatial Theory & Dynamics. Ed. by A. Andersson et al. (Studies in Regional Science & Urban Economics: Vol. 20). 318p. 1989. 87.25 (0-444-87357-0, North Holland) Elsevier.

Advances in Special Education, Vol. 1. Ed. by Barbara K. Keogh. 1980. lib. bdg. 73.25 (0-89232-077-X) Jai Pr.

Advances in Special Education, Vol. 3. Ed. by Barbara K. Keogh. 325p. 1981. 73.25 (0-89232-202-0) Jai Pr.

Advances in Special Education, Vol. 6. Ed. by Jay Gottlieb & Barbara W. Gottlieb. 1988. 73.25 (0-89232-632-8) Jai Pr.

Advances in Special Education: Annual, Vol. 2. Ed. by Barbara Keogh. 350p. (Orig.). 1980. lib. bdg. 73.25 (0-89232-144-X) Jai Pr.

Advances in Special Education & Rehabilitation. Ed. by Ronald C. Eaves & Phillip J. McLaughlin. 240p. 1993. 49.95 (1-56372-064-7, Andover Med Pubs) Buttrwrth-Heinemann.

Advances in Speciation in Ion Chromatography, Vol. 1. Ed. by Isai T. Urasa. 1992. 90.25 (1-55938-179-5) Jai Pr.

Advances in Spectrum Analysis & Array Processing, Vol. II. Simon Haykin. 336p. 1990. text ed. 76.00 (0-13-008574-X) P-H.

Advances in Spider Taxonomy 1988-1991: With Synonymies & Transfers 1940-1980. Norman I. Platnick. Ed. by P. Merrett. 864p. 1993. text ed. 75.00 (0-913424-10-2) Am Mus Natl Hist.

Advances in Spoken Discourse Analysis. Ed. by Malcolm Coulthard. LC 91-40402. 256p. 1992. 69.95 (0-415-06686-7, A7477); pap. 22.50 (0-415-06687-5, A7481) Routledge.

Advances in Sport Psychology. Ed. by Thelma S. Horn. LC 91-42061. (Illus.). 320p. (C). 1992. text ed. 44.00x (0-87322-364-0, BHOR0364) Human Kinetics.

Advances in Sports Medicine & Fitness, Vol. 4. Grana. 1990. 54.95 (0-8151-3581-5, Yr Bk Med Pubs) Mosby Yr Bk.

Advances in Statistical Analysis & Statistical Computing, Vol. 1. Roberto Mariano. 1986. 73.25 (0-89232-467-8) Jai Pr.

Advances in Statistical Analysis & Statistical Computing, Vol. 2. Ed. by Roberto S. Mariano. 1987. 73.25 (0-89232-826-6) Jai Pr.

Advances in Statistical Analysis & Statistical Computing, Vol. 3. Ed. by Roberto S. Mariano. 1991. 73.25 (1-55938-069-1) Jai Pr.

Advances in Statistical Methods for Genetic Improvement of Livestock. Ed. by D. Gianola & K. Hammond. (Advanced Series in Agricultural Sciences: Vol. 18). (Illus.). 560p. 1990. 99.00 (0-387-50809-0) Spr-Verlag.

Advances in Statistical Physics of Solids & Liquids. Shamsher Prakash & K. N. Pathak. 422p. 1991. text ed. 63.95 (0-470-21710-3) Halsted Pr.

Advances in Statistical Signal Processing, Vol. 1: Estimation. H. Vincent Poor. 73.25 (0-89232-570-4) Jai Pr.

***Advances in Steam Turbine Technology for the Power Generation Industry: Proceedings of the International Joint Power Generation Conference, Phoenix, AZ, 1994.** Ed. by W. G. Moore. 330p. 1994. pap. 65.00 (0-7918-1382-7) ASME.

Advances in Stereotactic & Functional Neurosurgery, Vol. 8. Ed. by G. Broggi et al. (Illus.). 130p. 1989. 94.00 (0-387-82120-1) Spr-Verlag.

Advances in Stereotactic & Functional Neurosurgery, Vol. 10. Ed. by B. Meyerson et al. 200p. 1993. 132.00 (0-387-82478-2) Spr-Verlag.

Advances in Stereotactic & Functional Neurosurgery, No. 9: Proceedings of the 9th Meeting of the European Society for Stereotactic & Functional Neurosurgery, Malaga 1990, Acta Naurochirurgica - Supplementum, No. 52. Ed. by E. R. Hirchcock et al. (Illus.). 160p. 1991. 104.00 (0-387-82283-6) Spr-Verlag.

Advances in Steroid Analysis. S. Gorog. 492p. (C). 1991. 180.00 (0-89771-834-8, Pub. by Collets) St Mut.

***Advances in Steroid Analysis 1990: Proceedings of the 4th Symposium on the Analysis of Steroids.** S. Gorog & E. Heftmann. 505p. (C). 1991. 180.00x (963-05-6034-8, Pub. by Akad Kiado HU) St Mut.

Advances in Steroid Analysis '93: Proceedings of the 5th Symposium on the Analysis of Steroids Held at Szombathely, Hungary, May 3-5, 1993. Ed. by S. Gorog. 608p. Date not set. pap. 85.00 (963-05-6721-0, Pub. by A K HU) Intl Spec Bk.

Advances in Steroid Biochemistry & Pharmacology, Vols. 1-7. Ed. by M. H. Briggs & G. A. Christie. Incl. Vol. 4. 1974. 70.00 (0-12-037504-4); Vol. 6. 1978. text ed. 139.00 (0-12-037506-0); write for info. (0-318-50218-6) Acad Pr.

***Advances in Stochastic Modelling & Data Analysis.** Ed. by Jacques Janssen. (Diverse Ser.). 440p. (C). 1995. lib. bdg. 219.00 (0-7923-3564-3) Kluwer Ac.

Advances in Strain in Organic Chemistry, Vol. 1. Ed. by Brian Halton. 1991. 90.25 (1-55938-180-9) Jai Pr.

Advances in Strategic Management, Vol. 1. Ed. by Robert B. Lamb. 1983. 73.25 (0-89232-408-2) Jai Pr.

Advances in Strategic Management, Vol. 2. Ed. by Robert B. Lamb. 1983. 73.25 (0-89232-409-0) Jai Pr.

Advances in Strategic Management, Vol. 3. Robert Lamb. 1985. 73.25 (0-89232-506-2) Jai Pr.

Advances in Strategic Management, Vol. 4. Ed. by Robert Lamb & Paul Shrivastava. 1986. 73.25 (0-89232-668-9) Jai Pr.

Advances in Strategic Management, Vol. 5. Ed. by Robert Lamb & Paul Shrivastava. 1988. 73.25 (0-89232-766-9) Jai Pr.

Advances in Stroke Prevention: Sanofi-Winthrop Symposium, Second European Stroke Conference, Lausanne, June 1992. Ed. by J. M. Orgogozo & M. Dyken. (Journal: Cerebrovascular Diseases: Vol. 3, Suppl. 1, 1993). (Illus.). iv, 44p. 1993. pap. 19.25 (3-8055-5787-6) S Karger.

Advances in Stroke Rehabilitation. Ed. by Wayne A. Gordon. 288p. 1993. 49.50 (1-56372-035-3, Andover Med Pubs) Buttrwrth-Heinemann.

***Advances in Stroke Rehabilitation.** Ed. by Wayne A. Gordon et al. LC 94-40389. 1995. write for info. (0-89079-656-4) PRO-ED.

Advances in Stroke Therapy. Ed. by F. Clifford Rose. 348p. 1982. text ed. 134.00 (0-89004-847-9) Raven.

Advances in Structural & Syntactic Pattern Recognition: Proceedings of the International Workshop on Structural & Syntactic Pattern Recognition, Bern, Switzerland, August 26-28, 1992. Ed. by H. Bunke. LC 92-41024. (Series in Machine Perception & Artificial Intelligence: Vol. 5). 636p. 1993. text ed. 121.00 (981-02-1183-X) World Scientific Pub.

Advances in Structural Biology, Vol. 1. Ed. by Sudarshan Malhotra. 1991. 90.25 (1-55938-292-9) Jai Pr.

Advances in Structural Ceramics. Ed. by P. F. Becher et al. (MRS Symposium Proceedings Ser.: Vol. 78). 1987. text ed. 38.00 (0-931837-43-X) Materials Res.

***Advances in Structural Optimization.** Ed. by Jose Herskovitz. LC 95-13513. (Solid Mechanics & Its Applications Ser.: Vol. 25). 1995. write for info. (0-7923-2510-9) Kluwer Ac.

Advances in Structural Reliability. Ed. by Alfredo C. Lucia. 1987. lib. bdg. 101.50 (90-277-2429-6) Kluwer Ac.

Advances in Structure Research by Diffraction Methods, Vol. 3. R. Brill & R. Mason. LC 73-99027. 1970. 113.00 (0-08-017543-0, Pub. by Pergamon Repr UK) Franklin.

Advances in Structure Research by Diffraction Methods, Vol. 4. W. Hoppe & R. Mason. LC 73-99027. 1972. 91.00 (0-08-017595-3, Pub. by Pergamon Repr UK) Franklin.

Advances in Structure Research by Diffraction Methods, Vol. 5. W. Hoppe & R. Mason. LC 64-3554. 1974. 50.00 (0-08-017287-3, Pub. by Pergamon Repr UK) Franklin.

Advances in Structure Research by Diffraction Methods, Vol. 6. W. Hoppe & R. Mason. LC 64-3554. (Fortschritte der Strukturforschung mit Beugungsemethoden Ser.). 1975. 111.00 (0-08-019921-6, Pub. by Pergamon Repr UK) Franklin.

Advances in Structured & Heterogeneous Continua: Selected Papers from the Proceedings of the International Symposium, Moscow, Russia, August 22-26, 1993. Ed. by D. A. Siginer & Y. G. Yanovsky. LC 94-10698. 1994. 180.00 (0-89864-071-7) Allerton Pr.

Advances in Subsea Pipeline Engineering & Technology: Papers Presented at Aspect '90. Ed. by C. P. Ellinas. (C). 1990. lib. bdg. 133.00 (0-7923-0794-1) Kluwer Ac.

Advances in Substance Abuse, Vol. 4. Ed. by Nancy K. Mello. 300p. (Orig.). 1991. 88.00 (1-85302-080-X, Pub. by J Kingsley Pubs UK) Taylor & Francis.

Advances in Sugarbeet Production: Proceedings of the Sugarbeet Congress on Principles & Practices, Salt Lake City, 1969. Sugarbeet Congress Staff. Ed. by Russell Johnson & John T. Alexander. LC 75-137094. 480p. reprint ed. pap. 136.80 (0-8357-5184-8, 2023006) Bks Demand.

Advances in Sulfur Chemistry, Vol. 1. Ed. by Eric Block. 1988. 73.25 (0-89232-868-1) Jai Pr.

Advances in Superconductivity. Ed. by K. Kiyazawa & T. Ishiguro. (Illus.). xxiv, 920p. 1989. 141.00 (0-387-70039-0) Spr-Verlag.

Advances in Superconductivity: Proceedings of the 3rd International Symposium on Superconductivity (ISS '90) November 6-9, 1990, Sendai, Vol. III. Ed. by K. Kajimura & H. Hayakawa. (Illus.). 1352p. 1991. 169.00 (0-387-70071-4) Spr-Verlag.

Advances in Superconductivity II: Proceedings of the 2nd International Symposium on Superconductivity (ISS '89) November 14-17, 1989, Tsukuba. Ed. by T. Ishiguro & K. Kajimura. (Illus.). 1120p. 1990. 128.00 (0-387-70059-5) Spr-Verlag.

Advances in Superconductivity IV: Proceedings of the Fourth International Symposium on Superconductivity, ISS '91, October 14-17, 1991, Tokyo. Ed. by H. Hayakawa & N. Koshizuka. (Illus.). 1148p. 1992. 179.00 (0-387-70097-8) Spr-Verlag.

***Advances in Superconductivity VI.** T. Fujita. 1427p. 1994. 235.00 (0-387-70138-9) Spr-Verlag.

Advances in Superconductivity 5: Proceedings of the 5th International Symposium on Superconductivity (ISS '92), November 16-19, 1992, Kobe. Ed. by Yoshichika Bando & Hisao Yamauchi. LC 93-1409. 1993. 240.00 (0-387-70122-2) Spr-Verlag.

Advances in Superplasticity & Superplastic Forming. Ed. by N. Chandra et al. LC 93-79176. 165p. 1993. 42.00 (0-87339-250-7) Minerals Metals.

Advances in Supramolecular Chemistry, Vol. 1. Ed. by George W. Gokel. 197p. 1990. 90.25 (1-55938-181-7) Jai Pr.

Advances in Supramolecular Chemistry, Vol. 2. Ed. by George W. Gokel. 1991. 90.25 (1-55938-329-1) Jai Pr.

Advances in Surface & Thin Film Diffraction: Materials Research Society Symposium Proceedings, Vol. 208. Ed. by P. I. Cohen et al. 367p. 1991. text ed. 50.00 (1-55899-100-X) Materials Res.

***Advances in Surface Research: Proceedings of the International Surface Physics Symposium, Held in Leipzig, Germany, September 1989.** International Surface Physics Symposium Staff. Ed. by Ch. Kleint et al. 394p. 1991. text ed. 166.00 (3-908044-08-1, Pub. by Trans Tech SZ) LPS Dist Ctr.

Advances in Surface Treatments: Proceedings of the AST World Conference, December 3-4, 1986, Paria. Ed. by A. Niku-Lari. (AST Ser.: No. 5). (Illus.). 446p. 1987. 221.00 (0-08-034923-4) Franklin.

Advances in Surface Treatments: Residual Stresses. Ed. by A. Niku-Lari. (Advances in Surface Treatments Ser.: Vol. 4). 400p. 1987. 239.00 (0-08-034062-8, Pub. by PPL UK) Franklin.

Advances in Surface Treatments: Technology, Applications, Effects, Vol. 1. Ed. by A. Niku-Lari. (Illus.). 240p. 1984. 124.00 (0-08-031126-1, Pub. by Pergamon Repr UK) Franklin.

Advances in Surface Treatments II: Technology, Applications, Effects. Ed. by A. Niku Lari. (Illus.). 294p. 1986. 118.00 (0-08-032535-1, Pub. by PPL UK) Franklin.

Advances in Surface Treatments III: Technology, Applications, Effects, III. Ed. by A. Niku-Lari. (Advances in Surface Treatments Ser.: Vol. 3). 270p. 1986. 116.00 (0-08-033464-4) Franklin.

Advances in Surgery, Vol. 20. Mannick. 1986. 59.95 (0-8151-5751-7, Yr Bk Med Pubs) Mosby Yr Bk.

Advances in Surgery, Vol. 21 - 1987. Advances in Surgery Staff. LC 65-29931. (Illus.). 320p. reprint ed. pap. 91.20 (0-8357-7676-X, 2057004) Bks Demand.

Advances in Surgery, Vol. 23. Tompkins. 344p. 1989. 59.95 (0-8151-8812-9, Yr Bk Med Pubs) Mosby Yr Bk.

Advances in Surgery, Vol. 24. Cameron. 424p. 1990. 59.95 (0-8151-1489-3, Yr Bk Med Pubs) Mosby Yr Bk.

Advances in Surgery, Vol. 25. Cameron. 371p. 1991. 59.95 (0-8151-1490-7) Mosby Yr Bk.

Advances in Surgery, Vol. 26. Cameron. 419p. 1992. 59.95 (0-8151-1491-5) Mosby Yr Bk.

Advances in Surgery, Vol. 27. Cameron. 425p. 1993. 59.95 (0-8151-1492-3, Yr Bk Med Pubs) Mosby Yr Bk.

Advances in Surgery, Vol. 28. Cameron. 452p. 1994. 59.95 (0-8151-1493-1, Yr Bk Med Pubs) Mosby Yr Bk.

Advances in Surgery, Vol. 29. Cameron. 452p. 1995. 59.95 (0-8151-1495-8, Yr Bk Med Pubs) Mosby Yr Bk.

Advances in Surgery, Vol. 30. Cameron. 452p. 1996. 59.95 (0-8151-1496-6, Yr Bk Med Pubs) Mosby Yr Bk.

Advances in Systemic Linguistics: Recent Theory & Practice. Ed. by Martin Davies & Louise Ravelli. 300p. 1992. text ed. 69.00 (0-86187-070-0, Pub. by Pinter Pubs UK) St Martin.

Advances in Taxation, 1. Ed. by Sally M. Jones. 1987. 73.25 (0-89232-782-0) Jai Pr.

Advances in Taxation, 2. Ed. by Sally M. Jones. 1987. write for info. (0-89232-783-9) Jai Pr.

Advances in Taxation, Vol. 3. Ed. by Jerrold J. Stern. 1991. 73.25 (1-55938-120-5) Jai Pr.

Advances in Teacher Education, Vol. 1. Ed. by Lilian G. Katz & James Raths. (Advances in Teacher Education Ser.). 272p. (C). 1985. text ed. 65.00 (0-89391-185-2) Ablex Pub.

Advances in Teacher Education, Vol. 2. Ed. by Lilian G. Katz & James Raths. (Advances in Teacher Education Ser.). 296p. 1986. text ed. 65.00 (0-89391-275-1) Ablex Pub.

Advances in Teacher Education, Vol. 3. Ed. by Martin Haberman & Julie Backus. (Advances in Teacher Education Ser.). 288p. (C). 1987. text ed. 65.00 (0-89391-396-0) Ablex Pub.

Advances in Teacher Education, Vol. 4. Ed. by Lilian G. Katz & James Raths. 192p. (C). 1990. text ed. 45.00 (0-89391-564-5) Ablex Pub.

Advances in Technology Yield Profitability: Papers from the SPE Pacific Technical Conference, February 1983, Anaheim, California. (Illus.). 436p. 1983. 43.00 (0-938648-33-0, 1510) T-C Pubns CA.

Advances in Technology Yield Profitability: 7th Annual Pacific Technical Conference, Feb. 22-24, 1983. Society of Plastics Engineers Staff. 444p. reprint ed. pap. 126.60 (0-8357-5185-6, 2021699) Bks Demand.

***Advances in Telecommunications Networks.** William S. Lee & Derrick C. Brown. LC 94-44499. 1995. write for info. (0-89006-606-X) Artech Hse.

Advances in Telematics, Vol 1. Ed. by Indu B. Singh & Janice Hanson. 288p. (C). 1991. text ed. 65.00 (0-89391-555-6) Ablex Pub.

***Advances in Telematics, Vol. 2.** Gina Daddario et al. Ed. by Jarice Hanson. 216p. 1994. 55.00 (0-89391-865-2) Ablex Pub.

***Advances in Telematics Vol. 3.** John M. Artz et al. Ed. by Jarice Hanson & Jay Liebowitz. (Illus.). 248p. 1995. write for info. (1-56750-118-4) Ablex Pub.

Advances in Test Anxiety Research, Vol. 1. Ed. by R. Schwarzer et al. xii, 164p. 1982. 17.75 (90-265-0414-4, Pub. by Swets Pub Serv NE) Taylor & Francis.

Advances in Test Anxiety Research, Vol. 2. Ed. by H. M. Van der Ploeg et al. x, 222p. 1983. 22.00 (90-265-0454-3, Pub. by Swets Pub Serv NE) Taylor & Francis.

Advances in Test Anxiety Research, Vol. 3. Ed. by H. M. Van der Ploeg et al. xii, 286p. 1984. 27.75 (90-265-0556-6, Pub. by Swets Pub Serv NE) Taylor & Francis.

Advances in Test Anxiety Research, Vol. 4. Ed. by H. M. Van der Ploeg et al. xiv, 262p. 1985. 24.00 (90-265-0596-5, Pub. by Swets Pub Serv NE) Taylor & Francis.

Advances in Test Anxiety Research, Vol. 5. Ed. by R. Schwarzer et al. xii, 278p. 1986. 27.90 (90-265-0673-2, Pub. by Swets Pub Serv NE) Taylor & Francis.

Advances in Test Anxiety Research, Vol. 7. Ed. by K. A. Hagtvet & T. Backer Johnsen. 424p. 1992. pap. 44.75 (90-265-1168-X, Pub. by Swets Pub Serv NE) Taylor & Francis.

Advances in Test Measurement see Instrumentation in the Aerospace Industry, Vol. 30: Proceedings of the International Instrumentation Symposium, 30th, 1984

Advances in Thanatology, Vol. 4. 1978. 15.00 (0-8422-7305-0) Irvington.

Advances in Thanatology, Vol. 4, No. 1. 1979. 19.95 (0-405-12507-0) Ayer.

Advances in Thanatology, Vol. 5, No. 1. 19.95 (0-405-12641-7) Ayer.

Advances in Thanatology, Vol. 5, No. 2. 19.95 (0-405-14221-8, 745) Ayer.

***Advances in the Applications of Membrane-Mimetic Chemistry.** Ed. by Teh Fu Yen et al. LC 94-48496. 280p. 1995. 89.50 (0-306-44828-9, Plenum Pr) Plenum.

Advances in the Art of Testing Soils under Cyclic Conditions: Proceedings of a Session Sponsored by the Geotechnical Engineering Division. Ed. by Vijay Khosla. 289p. 1985. 32.00 (0-87262-497-8) Am Soc Civil Eng.

Advances in the Astronautical Sciences. Incl. Vol. 6. Sixth Annual Meeting, New York, 1960. Ed. by H. Jacobs & E. Burgess. 1961. 45.00 (0-87703-007-3); Vol. 9. Fourth Western Regional Meeting, San Francisco, 1961. Ed. by H. Jacobs. 1963. 45.00 (0-87703-010-3); Vol. 11. Eighth Annual Meeting, Washington, 1962. Ed. by H. E. Jacobs. 1963. 45.00 (0-87703-012-X); Vol. 13. Ninth Annual Meeting, Interplanetary Missions, Los Angeles, 1963. Ed. by E. Burgess. 1963. 45.00 (0-87703-014-6); write for info. (0-318-50452-9, Am Astronaut) Univelt Inc.

Advances in the Behavioral Assessment of Children & Families, Vol. 5. Ed. by Ronald J. Prinz. 320p. 1991. 85.00 (1-85302-069-9, Pub. by J Kingsley Pubs UK) Taylor & Francis.

***Advances in the Biology of Shrews.** Ed. by Joseph F. Merritt et al. (Special Publications of CMNH Ser.: 18). x458p. (Orig.). 1994. pap. 40.00x (0-911239-44-8) Carnegie Mus.

Advances in the Biology of Turbellarians & Related Plathelminths. Ed. by Seth Taylor. (Developments in Hydrobiology Ser.). 1986. lib. bdg. 205.00 (90-6193-542-3) Kluwer Ac.

Advances in the Biomechanics of the Hand & Wrist. Ed. by F. Schuind et al. LC 93-43655. (NATO ASI Series A, Life Sciences: Vol. 256). (Illus.). 522p. 1994. 129.50 (0-306-44580-8, Plenum Pr) Plenum.

Advances in the Biosciences. Incl. Vol. 2. Schering Symposium on Biodynamics & Mechanism of Action of Steroid Hormones, Berlin 1968. Ed. by G. Raspe et al. 1970. 97.00 (0-08-006942-8); Vol. 4. Schering Symposium on Mechanisms Involved in Conception, Berlin 1969. Ed. by G. Raspe et al. 1970. 201.00 (0-08-017546-5); Vol. 5. Schering Workshop in Pharmacokinetics, Berlin 1969. Ed. by G. Raspe et al. 1970. 120.00 (0-08-017548-1); Vol. 6. Schering Symposium on Intrinsic & Extrinsic Factors in Early Mammalian Development, Venice 1970. Ed. by G. Raspe et al. 1971. 274.00 (0-08-017571-6); Vol. 7. Schering Workshop on Steroid Hormone "Receptors," Berlin, 1970. Ed. by G. Raspe et al. 1971. 179.00 (0-08-017578-3); Vol. 8. Ed. by G. Raspe et al. 1972. 206.00 (0-08-017290-3); Vol. 9. International Conference of Prostaglandins, Vienna 1972. Ed. by Bergstrom et al. 1973. 366.00 (0-08-017291-1); Vol. 11. Schering Workshop on Virus - Cell Interaction. Ed. by G. Raspe et al. 1974. 112.00 (0-08-017296-2); Vol. 12. Schering Symposium on Immunopathology. Ed. by G. Raspe et al. 1974. 294.00 (0-08-017297-0); Vol. 13. Hormones & Embryonic Development. Ed. by G. Raspe et al. 1974. 113.00 (0-08-018239-9); Vol. 14. Schering Workshop on Prognostic Factors in Human Acute Leukemia. Ed. by G. Raspe et al. 1975. 97.00 (0-08-019621-7); Vol. 15. Schering Workshop on Central Action of Estrogenic Hormones. Ed. by G. Raspe et al. 1975. 150.00 (0-08-019726-4); Vol. 16. Dahlem Workshop of Myelofibrosis-Osteosclerosis. Ed. by Bernhard et al. 1975. 200.00 (0-08-019728-0); write for info. (0-318-55130-6, Pub. by Pergamon Repr UK) Franklin.

Advances in the Chemistry & Processing of Various Elastomers. Ed. by Melvyn A. Kohudic. LC 94-60613. (Advances in Elastomers Ser.). 220p. 1994. pap. text ed. 49.00 (1-56676-192-1) Technomic.

***Advances in the Chemistry of Insect Control III: Proceedings of the 3rd International Symposium, Cambridge, UK, 1993.** Ed. by G. G. Briggs. 256p. 1994. 89.95 (0-85186-992-0, R6992, Pub. by Royal Soc Chem UK) CRC Pr.

Advances in the Control of Human Extremities, Vol. 10. Ed. by Dejan B. Popovic. 616p. 1991. 84.95 (86-7621-001-2) Demos Vermande.

Advances in the Control of Theileriosis: Current Topics in Veterinary Medicine & Animal Science, No. 14. Ed. by A. D. Irvin et al. xiv, 428p. 1981. lib. bdg. 117.00 (90-247-2575-5) Kluwer Ac.

Advances in the Creation & Revision of Writing Systems. J. Fishman. 1977. 106.95 (90-279-7552-3) Mouton.

Advances in the Dempster-Shafer Theory of Evidence. Ronald R. Yager. 608p. 1994. text ed. 59.95 (0-471-55248-8) Wiley.

Advances in the Drug Therapy of Mental Illness: Proceedings of the WHO-International Task Force on World Health Manpower Symposiums, Geneva, 1973. WHO Staff & International Task Force on World Health Manpower Staff. 1976. pap. 12.00 (92-4-156051-7) World Health.

An Asterisk (*) at the beginning of an entry indicates that the title is appearing in BIP for the first time.

An Asterisk (*) at the beginning of an entry indicates that the title is appearing in BIP for the first time.

101

Advances in Urethane Science & Technology, Vol. 9. Ed. by Kurt C. Frisch & Daniel Klempner. LC 75-150348. 191p. 1984. pap. 38.50 (*0-87762-350-3*) Technomic.

Advances in Urethane Science & Technology, Vol. 10. Ed. by Kurt C. Frisch & Daniel Klempner. LC 85-641251. 200p. 1987. pap. 40.00 (*0-87762-527-1*) Technomic.

Advances in Urethane Science & Technology, Vol. 11. Ed. by Daniel Klempner & Kurt Frisch. 250p. 1992. pap. text ed. 75.00 (*0-87762-896-3*) Technomic.

Advances in Urethane Science & Technology, Vol. 12. Ed. by Daniel Klempner & Kurt Frisch. 215p. 1992. pap. text ed. 75.00 (*0-87762-970-6*) Technomic.

Advances in Urologic Oncology. Richard D. Williams. 1987. text ed. 49.50 (*0-07-105329-8*) McGraw.

Advances in Urology, Vol. 2. Lytton. 272p. 1989. 64.95 (*0-8151-5669-3*, Yr Bk Med Pubs) Mosby Yr Bk.

Advances in Urology, Vol. 3. Lytton. 232p. 1990. 64.95 (*0-8151-5667-7*, Yr Bk Med Pubs) Mosby Yr Bk.

Advances in Urology, Vol. 4. Lytton. 220p. 1991. 69.95 (*0-8151-5692-8*, Yr Bk Med Pubs) Mosby Yr Bk.

Advances in Urology, Vol. 5. Lytton. 262p. 1992. 69.95 (*0-8151-5693-6*) Mosby Yr Bk.

Advances in Urology, Vol. 6. Lytton et al. 288p. 1993. 69.95 (*0-8151-5694-4*, Yr Bk Med Pubs) Mosby Yr Bk.

Advances in Urology, Vol. 7. Lytton et al. 300p. 1994. 69.95 (*0-8151-5695-2*, Yr Bk Med Pubs) Mosby Yr Bk.

Advances in Urology, Vol. 8. Lytton. 240p. 1995. 69.95 (*0-8151-5696-0*, Yr Bk Med Pubs) Mosby Yr Bk.

Advances in Vaccination Against Virus Diseases. Ed. by R. Purtschert. (Monographs in Pediatrics: Vol. 11). (Illus.). 1979. pap. 27.25 (*3-8055-3046-3*) S Karger.

Advances in Vacuum Science & Technology, 2 vols., Set. E. Thomas. 1960. 380.00 (*0-08-009211-X*, Pub. by Pergamon Repr UK) Franklin.

Advances in Vacuum Science & Technology: Proceedings of the Israeli Vacuum Congress, 5th, Israel, April, 1978. Israeli Vacuum Congress Staff. Ed. by J. Yarwood & Y. Margoninski. 1979. pap. 15.75 (*0-08-024238-3*, Pergamon Pr) Elsevier.

Advances in Vascular Pathology Nineteen Eighty-Nine: Proceedings of the 15th World Congress of the International Union of Angiology, Rome, Italy, 17-22 Sept., 1988, 2 vols., Set. Ed. by A. Strano & S. Novo. (International Congress Ser.: No. 868). 1456p. 1989. 277.00 (*0-444-81136-2*, Excerpta Medica) Elsevier.

Advances in Vascular Surgery, Vol. 1. Whittemore. 1993. 69.95 (*0-8151-9405-6*, Yr Bk Med Pubs) Mosby Yr Bk.

Advances in Vascular Surgery, Vol. 2. Whittemore. 350p. 1994. 69.95 (*0-8151-9406-4*, Yr Bk Med Pubs) Mosby Yr Bk.

Advances in Vascular Surgery, Vol. 3. Whittemore. 350p. 1995. 69.95 (*0-8151-9407-2*, Yr Bk Med Pubs) Mosby Yr Bk.

Advances in Vascular Surgery, Vol. 4. Whittemore. 350p. 1996. 69.95 (*0-8151-9408-0*, Yr Bk Med Pubs) Mosby Yr Bk.

Advances in Vascular Surgery, Vol. 5. Whittemore. 350p. 1997. 69.95 (*0-8151-9409-9*, Yr Bk Med Pubs) Mosby Yr Bk.

Advances in Veterinary Immunology, 1981. F. Kristensen & D. F. Antczak. (Developments in Animal & Veterinary Science Ser.: Vol. 9). 282p. 1982. 77.00 (*0-444-42051-7*) Elsevier.

Advances in Veterinary Immunology, 1982. F. Kristensen & D. F. Antczak. (Developments in Animal & Veterinary Science Ser.: No. 12). 1983. 84.75 (*0-444-42191-2*) Elsevier.

Advances in Veterinary Immunology, 1983. Ed. by F. J. Bourne & Neil T. Gorman. (Developments in Animal & Veterinary Science Ser.: Vol. 16). 260p. 1985. 105.25 (*0-444-42367-2*) Elsevier.

Advances in Veterinary Science, Vol. 28. Ed. by C. A. Brandly & E. L. Jungherr. (Serial Publication Ser.). 1984. text ed. 134.00 (*0-12-039228-3*) Acad Pr.

Advances in Veterinary Science, Vols. 1-12. Ed. by C. A. Brandly & E. L. Jungherr. Incl. Vol. 2. 1955. 80.00 (*0-12-039202-X*); write for info. (*0-318-50220-8*) Acad Pr.

Advances in Veterinary Science & Comparative Medicine, Vol. 27. Ed. by Charles E. Cornelius & Charles F. Simpson. (Serial Publication Ser.). 1983. text ed. 134.00 (*0-12-039227-5*) Acad Pr.

Advances in Veterinary Science & Comparative Medicine, Vol. 29. Ed. by Charles E. Cornelius & Charles F. Simpson. (Serial Publication Ser.). 1985. text ed. 134.00 (*0-12-039229-1*) Acad Pr.

Advances in Veterinary Science & Comparative Medicine, Vol. 30. Ed. by Charles E. Cornelius & Charles F. Simpson. (Serial Publication Ser.). 1985. text ed. 134.00 (*0-12-039230-5*) Acad Pr.

Advances in Veterinary Science & Comparative Medicine, Vols. 13-22. Incl. Vol. 19. LC 53-7098. 1976. lib. bdg. 90.00 (*0-12-039274-7*); Vol. 21. LC 53-7098. 1977. lib. bdg. 95.00 (*0-12-039278-X*); Vol. 22. LC 53-7098. 1978. lib. bdg. 90.00 (*0-12-039280-1*); LC 53-7098. (Serial Publication Ser.). write for info. (*0-318-50221-6*) Acad Pr.

Advances in Veterinary Science & Comparative Medicine: Experimental & Comparative Toxicology, Vol. 31. Andre G. Rico. 1987. text ed. 106.00 (*0-12-039231-3*) Acad Pr.

Advances in Veterinary Science & Comparative Medicine Vol. 38, Pt. B: Comparative Vertebrate Exercise Physiology: Phyletic Adaptations. Ed. by James H. Jones et al. (Illus.). 236p. 1994. text ed. 80.00 (*0-12-039239-9*) Acad Pr.

Advances in Veterinary Science & Comparative Medicine Vol. 38A: Comparative Vertebrate Exercise Physiology: Unifying Physiological Principles. Ed. by C. E. Cornelius et al. (Illus.). 291p. 1994. text ed. 80.00 (*0-12-039238-0*) Acad Pr.

***Advances in Veterinary Science & Comparative Medicine Vol. 39: Veterinary Medical Specialization: Bridging Science & Medicine.** Ed. by W. Jean Dodds. (Illus.). 300p. 1995. boxed write for info. (*0-12-039240-2*) Acad Pr.

Advances in Veterinary Science & Comparative Medicine, Vol. 32: Immunodeficiency Disorders & Retroviruses. Ed. by Kalman Perk et al. 262p. 1988. text ed. 99.00 (*0-12-039232-1*) Acad Pr.

Advances in Veterinary Science & Comparative Medicine, Vol. 33: Vaccine Biotechnology. Ed. by James L. Bittle et al. 444p. 1989. text ed. 109.00 (*0-12-039233-X*) Acad Pr.

Advances in Veterinary Science & Comparative Medicine, Vol. 34: Animal Cytogenetics. Ed. by Richard A. McFeely. 322p. 1990. text ed. 96.00 (*0-12-039234-8*) Acad Pr.

Advances in Veterinary Science & Comparative Medicine, Vol. 35: Immunomodulation in Domestic Food Animals. Ed. by Charles E. Cornelius et al. 334p. 1990. text ed. 99.00 (*0-12-039235-6*) Acad Pr.

Advances in Veterinary Science & Comparative Medicine, Vol. 36: Comparative Transfusion Medicine. Ed. by Susan M. Cotter et al. (Illus.). 343p. 1991. text ed. 88.00 (*0-12-039236-4*) Acad Pr.

Advances in Veterinary Science & Comparative Medicine, Vol. 37: Animal Models in Liver Research. Ed. by Charles E. Cornelius et al. (Illus.). 479p. 1993. text ed. 99.00 (*0-12-039237-2*) Acad Pr.

Advances in Veterinary Virology: Proceedings of the Congress of the European Society for Veterinary Virology, 1st, Univ. of Liege, Liege, Belgium, 5-7 April, 1989. Ed. by S. Edwards & P. P. Pastoret. 395p. 1990. 128.25 (*0-444-88783-0*) Elsevier.

***Advances in Vibration Control for Intelligent Structures Vol. 1.** Ed. by Melvyn A. Kohudic. LC 94-60737. (Advances in Intelligent Material Systems & Structures Ser.). 166p. 1994. pap. text ed. 49.00 (*1-56676-195-6*) Technomic.

Advances in Vibrational Spectrocopy & Dynamics, Vol. 1. Ed. by Joel M. Bowman. 1988. 73.25 (*0-89232-870-3*) Jai Pr.

Advances in Virus Research, Vol. 28. Ed. by Max A. Lauffer & Karl Maramorosch. (Serial Publication Ser.). 1983. text ed. 151.00 (*0-12-039828-1*) Acad Pr.

Advances in Virus Research, Vol. 29. Ed. by Kenneth M. Smith & Max Lauffler. (Serial Publication Ser.). 1984. text ed. 151.00 (*0-12-039829-X*) Acad Pr.

Advances in Virus Research, Vol. 30. Ed. by Karl Maramorosch et al. (Serial Publication Ser.). 368p. 1986. text ed. 128.00 (*0-12-039830-3*) Acad Pr.

Advances in Virus Research, Vol. 31. Ed. by Karl Maramorosch et al. (Serial Publication Ser.). 464p. 1986. text ed. 128.00 (*0-12-039831-1*) Acad Pr.

Advances in Virus Research, Vol. 32. Ed. by Karl Maramorosch et al. (Serial Publication Ser.). 300p. 1987. text ed. 109.00 (*0-12-039832-X*) OneOnOne Comp Trng.

Advances in Virus Research, Vol. 33. Ed. by Karl Maramorosch et al. (Serial Publication Ser.). 300p. 1987. text ed. 109.00 (*0-12-039833-8*) Acad Pr.

Advances in Virus Research, Vol. 34. Ed. by Karl Maramorosch et al. (Serial Publication Ser.). 327p. 1988. text ed. 109.00 (*0-12-039834-6*) Acad Pr.

Advances in Virus Research, Vol. 35. Ed. by Karl Maramorosch et al. (Serial Publication Ser.). 501p. 1988. text ed. 109.00 (*0-12-039835-4*) Acad Pr.

Advances in Virus Research, Vol. 36. Ed. by Karl Maramorosch et al. (Serial Publication Ser.). 356p. 1989. text ed. 109.00 (*0-12-039836-2*) Acad Pr.

Advances in Virus Research, Vol. 37. Ed. by Karl Maramorosch et al. (Serial Publication Ser.). 349p. 1989. text ed. 99.00 (*0-12-039837-0*) Acad Pr.

Advances in Virus Research, Vol. 38. Karl Maramorosch et al. (Serial Publication Ser.). 457p. 1990. text ed. 110.00 (*0-12-039838-9*) Acad Pr.

Advances in Virus Research, Vol. 39. Ed. by Karl Maramorosch et al. (Illus.). 355p. 1991. text ed. 94.00 (*0-12-039839-7*) Acad Pr.

Advances in Virus Research, Vol. 40. Ed. by Karl Maramorosch et al. (Illus.). 291p. 1991. text ed. 72.00 (*0-12-039840-0*) Acad Pr.

Advances in Virus Research, Vol. 41. Ed. by Karl Maramorosch et al. (Illus.). 472p. 1992. text ed. 95.00 (*0-12-039841-9*) Acad Pr.

Advances in Virus Research, Vol. 42. Ed. by Karl Maramorosch et al. (Illus.). 421p. 1992. text ed. 90.00 (*0-12-039842-7*) Acad Pr.

Advances in Virus Research, Vol. 43. Ed. by Karl Maramorosch et al. (Illus.). 398p. 1994. text ed. 90.00 (*0-12-039843-5*) Acad Pr.

Advances in Virus Research, Vol. 44. Ed. by Karl Maramorosch et al. (Illus.). 473p. 1994. text ed. 99.00 (*0-12-039844-3*) Acad Pr.

***Advances in Virus Research, Vol. 45.** Ed. by Karl Maramorosch et al. (Illus.). 327p. 1995. boxed 75.00 (*0-614-05260-2*) Acad Pr.

Advances in Virus Research, Vols. 1-18 & 21-24. Karl Maramorosch et al. Ed. by Max A. Lauffer & Karl Maramonosch. Incl. Vol. 1. 1953. 66.00 (*0-12-039801-X*); Vol. 5. 1958. 70.00 (*0-12-039805-2*); (Serial Publication Ser.). write for info. (*0-318-50222-4*) Acad Pr.

***Advances in Virus Research Vol. 45, Vol. 45.** Ed. by Karl Maramorosch et al. (Illus.). 347p. 1995. boxed 75.00 (*0-12-039845-1*) Acad Pr.

***Advances in Visual Semiotics: The Semiotic Web 1992-93.** Ed. by Thomas A. Sebeok & Jean Umiker-Seboek. (Approaches to Semiotics Ser.: No. 118). 679p. (C). 1994. lib. bdg. 275.40 (*3-11-013001-7*, 239-94) Mouton.

Advances in Vocational Psychology Vol. 1: The Assessment of Interests. Ed. by W. Bruce Walsh & Samuel H. Osipow. 216p. (C). 1986. 39.95 (*0-89859-755-2*, P9224) L Erlbaum Assocs.

Advances in Volcanic Seismology. Ed. by Emile A. Okal. 248p. 1988. reprint ed. 41.00 (*0-8176-1927-5*) Birkhauser.

Advances in Water Engineering: Proceedings of the International Symposium Advances in Water Engineering Held at the University of Birmingham July 15-19, 1985. Ed. by T. H. Tebbutt. 368p. 1985. 84.75 (*0-85334-374-8*, Pub. by Elsevier Applied Sci UK) Elsevier.

Advances in Water Pollution Research: Proceedings 4th International Conference, Prague 1969. S. H. Jenkins. LC 62-22109. 1969. 387.00 (*0-08-012999-4*, Pub. by Pergamon Repr UK) Franklin.

Advances in Water Pollution Research: Proceedings 5th International Conference Held in San Francisco & Hawaii 1970, Set. S. H. Jenkins. LC 62-22109. 1971. 578.00 (*0-08-016375-0*, Pub. by Pergamon Repr UK) Franklin.

Advances in Water Pollution Research: Proceedings 6th International Conference Jerusalem 6-72. S. H. Jenkins. LC 62-22109. 1973. 393.00 (*0-08-017005-6*, Pub. by Pergamon Repr UK) Franklin.

Advances in Water Pollution Research, Vols. 1-3: Proceedings of the International Conference, London, September, 1962. W. Wesley Eckenfelder. LC 62-22109. 1964. 163.00 (*0-08-010297-2*, Pub. by Pergamon Repr UK) Franklin.

Advances in Water Resources Technology: Proceedings of the European Conference on Advances in Water Resources Technology, Athens, 20-23 March 1991. Ed. by G. Tsakiris. (Illus.). 686p. (C). 1991. text ed. 130.00 (*90-6191-184-2*, Pub. by A A Balkema NE) Ashgate Pub Co.

***Advances in Water Resources Technology & Management: Proceedings of the Second European Conference, Lisbon, Portugal, June 1994.** 2nd ed. Ed. by G. Tsakiris & M. A. Santos. (Illus.). 512p. (C). 1994. text ed. 95.00 (*90-5410-389-2*, Pub. by A A Balkema NE) Ashgate Pub Co.

Advances in Water Treatment & Environmental Management. G. Thomas & R. King. 1991. 93.50 (*1-85166-632-X*) Elsevier.

Advances in Welding Processes (WI) AWP. 414p. 1978. 120.00 (*0-686-95639-7*) Am Welding.

Advances in Well Test Analysis. R. C. Earlougher, Jr. 264p. 1977. 35.00 (*0-89520-204-2*, 30405) Soc Petrol Engineers.

Advances in Wind Engineering: Proceedings of the 7th International Congress on Wind Engineering, Aachen, Aachen, FRG, July 6-10, 1987, 3 vols., Set. Ed. by C. Kramer & H. J. Gerhardt. 1188p. 1989. 400.00 (*0-444-87156-X*) Elsevier.

Advances in Wind Farming: Proceedings of the International Conference, 13-16 Oct., 1987, Leeuwarden, the Netherlands. Ed. by G. G. Piepers. 476p. 1988. 138.50 (*0-444-42952-2*) Elsevier.

Advances in Working Capital Management, Vol. 1. Ed. by Yong H. Kim & V. Srinivasan. 1988. 73.25 (*0-89232-827-4*) Jai Pr.

Advances in Working Capital Management, Vol. 1. Ed. by Yong H. Kim. 1991. 73.25 (*0-89232-664-6*) Jai Pr.

Advances in World Archaeology, Vol. 3. Fred Wendorf & Angela E. Close. (Serial Publication Ser.). 1984. text ed. 114.00 (*0-12-039903-2*) Acad Pr.

Advances in World Archaeology, Vol. 5. Ed. by Fred Wendorf & Angela E. Close. (Serial Publication Ser.). 1986. pap. text ed. 60.00 (*0-12-000009-1*) Acad Pr.

Advances in World Diabetes Research. F. Belfiore & Silvia Iannello. (Frontiers in Diabetes Ser.: Vol. 5). x, 258p. 1984. 132.00 (*3-8055-3810-3*) S Karger.

Advances in Wound Management. Ed. by T. D. Turner et al. LC 86-22423. 157p. reprint ed. pap. 44.80 (*0-8357-6306-4*, 2035579) Bks Demand.

Advances in Writing Research: Childrens Early Writing Development, Vol. 1. Ed. by Marcia Farr. (Writing Research Ser.). 372p. 1985. text ed. 67.50 (*0-89391-179-8*) Ablex Pub.

Advances in Writing Research: Writing in Academic Disciplines, Vol. 2. David A. Jolliffe. Ed. by Marcia Farr. (Writing Research Ser.). 272p. 1988. text ed. 67.50 (*0-89391-434-7*) Ablex Pub.

Advances in Written Text Analysis. Ed. by Malcolm Coulthard. LC 93-25182. 1994. write for info. (*0-04-150519-0*); pap. write for info. (*0-415-09520-4*) Routledge.

***Advances in X-Ray Analysis, 37.** Ed. by J. V. Gilfrich et al. (Illus.). 778p. (C). 1994. 145.00 (*0-306-44901-3*, Plenum Pr) Plenum.

Advances in X-Ray Analysis, Vol. 28. Ed. by Charles S. Barrett et al. LC 58-35928. 408p. 1985. 85.00 (*0-306-41939-4*, Plenum Pr) Plenum.

Advances in X-Ray Analysis, Vol. 29. Ed. by Charles S. Barrett et al. LC 58-35928. 618p. 1986. 95.00 (*0-306-42287-5*, Plenum Pr) Plenum.

Advances in X-Ray Analysis, Vol. 30. Ed. by Charles S. Barrett et al. LC 58-35928. (Illus.). 620p. 1987. 95.00 (*0-306-42690-0*, Plenum Pr) Plenum.

Advances in X-Ray Analysis, Vol. 31. Charles S. Barrett et al. LC 58-35928. (Illus.). 542p. 1988. 110.00 (*0-306-42932-2*, Plenum Pr) Plenum.

Advances in X-Ray Analysis, Vol. 32. Charles S. Barrett et al. (Illus.). 708p. 1989. 125.00 (*0-306-43236-6*, Plenum Pr) Plenum.

Advances in X-Ray Analysis, Vol. 33. Ed. by Charles S. Barrett et al. (Illus.). 724p. 1990. 125.00 (*0-306-43615-9*, Plenum Pr) Plenum.

Advances in X-Ray Analysis, Vol. 34. Ed. by Charles S. Barrett et al. (Illus.). 732p. 1991. 125.00 (*0-306-44003-2*, Plenum Pr) Plenum.

Advances in X-Ray Analysis, Vol. 35. Ed. by Charles S. Barrett et al. (Illus.). 1312p. (C). 1992. 185.00 (*0-306-44249-3*, Plenum Pr) Plenum.

Advances in X-Ray Analysis, Vol. 36. Ed. by J. V. Gilfrich et al. 678p. 1993. 125.00 (*0-306-44571-9*, Plenum Pr) Plenum.

Advances in X-Ray Analysis: Proceedings of the Fourteenth Annual Conference of X-Ray Analysis held August 25-27, 1965 - Sponsored by University of Denver, Denver Research Institute, Vol. 9. Conference on Applications of X-Ray Analysis (14th: 1965, Denver). Ed. by Gavin Mallett et al. LC 58-35928. 554p. reprint ed. pap. 157.90 (*0-8357-5192-9*, 2026282) Bks Demand.

Advances in X-Ray Analysis: Proceedings of the Seventh Annual Conference on Applications of X-Ray Analysis held August 13-15, 1958 - Sponsored by University of Denver, Denver Research Institute, Vol. 2. Conference on Applications of X-Ray Analysis (7th: 1958). Ed. by William M. Mueller. LC 58-35928. 359p. reprint ed. pap. 102.40 (*0-8357-5194-5*, 2026279) Bks Demand.

Advances in X-Ray Analysis: Proceedings of the Sixth Annual Conference on Applications of X-Ray Analysis held August 7-9, 1957 - Sponsored by University of Denver, Denver Research Institute, Vol. 1. Conference on Applications of X-Ray Analysis (6th-1957-Denver). Ed. by William M. Mueller. LC 58-35928. 504p. reprint ed. pap. 143.70 (*0-8357-5193-7*, 2026278) Bks Demand.

Advances in X-Ray Analysis: Proceedings of the Tenth Annual Conference on Applications of X-Ray Analysis held August 7-9, 1961 - Sponsored by University of Denver, Denver Research Institute, Vol. 5. Conference on Application of X-Ray Analysis (10th, 1961, Denver). Ed. by William M. Mueller. LC 58-35928. 576p. reprint ed. pap. 164.20 (*0-8357-5195-3*, 2026280) Bks Demand.

Advances in X-Ray Analysis: Proceedings of the Twelfth Annual Conference on Applications of X-Ray Analysis held August 7-9, 1963 - Sponsored by University of Denver, Denver Research Institute, Vol. 7. Conference on Applications of X-Ray Analysis (12th: 1963, Denver). Ed. by William M. Mueller et al. LC 58-35928. 672p. reprint ed. pap. 180.00 (*0-8357-5196-1*, 2026281) Bks Demand.

Advances in X-Ray Analysis, Vol. 3: Proceedings of the Eighth Annual Conference on Applications of X-Ray Analysis Held August 12-14, 1959. Conference on Applications of X-Ray Analysis. Ed. by William M. Mueller. LC 58-35928. (Illus.). 384p. reprint ed. pap. 109.50 (*0-8357-5197-X*, 2019407) Bks Demand.

Advances in X-Ray Spectroscopy: A Reference Text in Honour of Professor Y. Cauchois. Ed. by C. Bonnelle & C. Mande. LC 82-12300. (Illus.). 400p. 1982. 199.00 (*0-08-025266-4*, Pub. by Pergamon Repr UK) Franklin.

***Advances of Bryology: Biology of Sphagnum, Vol. 5.** Ed. by E. B. Carother et al. 338p. 1993. pap. 120.00 (*0-614-00103-X*, Pub. by Cramer-Borntraeger GW) Lubrecht & Cramer.

***Advances of Bryology, Vol. 5: Biology of Sphagnum.** Ed. by E. B. Carother et al. 338p. 1993. pap. 120.00 (*0-614-00208-7*) Lubrecht & Cramer.

Advances of Phase Transitions & Disorder Phenomena: Proceedings of the International Conference, Amalfi, Salerno, June 25-27, 1987. Ed. by G. Busiello et al. 588p. 1987. pap. 62.00 (*9971-5-0173-2*) World Scientific Pub.

Advances on the AIDS Horizon. 3rd ed. Lauren Russel. 86p. 1989. pap. 9.95 (*0-942028-41-4*); student ed 18.97 (*0-942028-42-2*) R D Anderson.

***Advances Related to United States & International Mineral Resources: Developing Frameworks & Exploration Technologies.** Ed. by R. W. Scott, Jr. et al. (Illus.). 277p. (Orig.). (C). 1994. pap. text ed. 95.00x (*0-7881-1244-9*) Diane Pub.

Advancing A Levels: Report of a Committee Appointed by the Secretary of State for Education & Science & the Secretary of State for Wales. (Illus.). 51p. 1988. pap. 8.00 (*0-11-270652-5*, HM3841, Pub. by HMSO UK) UNIPUB.

Advancing American Art: Painting, Politics, & Cultural Confrontation at Mid-Century. Taylor Littleton & Maltby Sykes. LC 88-27655. (Illus.). 176p. (C). 1989. pap. 19.95 (*0-8173-0426-6*) U of Ala Pr.

Advancing American Art: Politics & Aesthetics in the U. S. State Department Exhibition, 1946-48. Virginia Mecklenburg & Margaret L. Ausfeld. LC 83-19301. (Illus.). 120p. (Orig.). (ps-12). 1984. pap. 12.00 (*0-89280-021-6*) Montgomery Mus.

Advancing Beyond the Techniques in Fund Raising. Maurice G. Gurin. 149p. 1991. pap. 26.95 (*0-930807-14-6*, 600220) Fund Raising.

Advancing Business Concepts in a JAD Workshop Setting. Anthony Crawford. LC 93-29395. (Yourdon Press Computing Ser.). 256p. 1994. text ed. 45.00 (*0-13-146226-1*) P-H.

Advancing Classical Guitarist, Vol. 1. Rene Gonzalez. 96p. 1992. teacher ed 24.95 (*1-879542-07-2*); audio 18.95 (*1-879542-24-2*) Ellis Family Mus.

Advancing Classical Guitarist, Vol. 1. Rene Gonzalez. 96p. (gr. 6 up). 1992. student ed 19.95 (*1-879542-15-3*) Ellis Family Mus.

Advancing Classical Guitarist, Vol. 1. Rene Gonzalez. 96p. (YA). (gr. 6 up). 1993. 22.95 (*1-879542-16-1*) Ellis Family Mus.

Advancing Communication Science: Merging Mass & Interpersonal Processes. Ed. by Robert P. Hawkins et al. LC 88-823. (Sage Annual Reviews of Communication Research Ser.: No. 16). 312p. reprint ed. pap. 89.00 (*0-7837-6581-9*, 2046146) Bks Demand.

102

An Asterisk (*) at the beginning of an entry indicates that the title is appearing in BIP for the first time.

An Asterisk (*) at the beginning of an entry indicates that the title is appearing in BIP for the first time.

103

Adventure in Reasoning. Elbert R. Moses, Jr. 80p. 1988. 15.00 (0-9621305-0-8) Moses Pubns.

Adventure in Reform. John A. Gable. (Breaking New Ground Lecture Ser.: No. 1). (Illus.). 46p. 1986. pap. 2.95 (0-938549-02-2) Grey Towers Pr.

Adventure in Space: The Flight to Fix the Hubble. large type ed. Elaine Scott. LC 94-7756. (Illus.). 64p. (J). (gr. 3-7). 1995. 16.95 (0-7868-0038-0) Hyprn Child.

Adventure in Space: The Flight to Fix the Hubble. large type ed. Elaine Scott. LC 94-7756. (Illus.). 64p. (J). (gr. 3-7). 1995. lib. bdg. 16.89 (0-7868-2031-4) Hyprn Child.

Adventure in Spiritual Direction: A Prophetic Pattern. Roman Ginn. 117p. (Orig.). 1979. pap. 4.95 (0-914544-27-6) Living Flame Pr.

Adventure in Splendid China. Erika Fabian. (Illus.). 64p. (J). (gr. 4 up). 1994. 16.95 (0-9638417-0-X) Eriako Assocs.
ADVENTURE IN SPLENDID CHINA: Five children, Billy, an African-American; Pablo, a Mexican-American; Amy & Kirk, two Caucasians; & Ying, a girl from Hong Kong, join the legendary Monkey King on a magical journey in China. Through the people they meet, they learn about Chinese beliefs, customs, & art such as why brides wear red, why the horse-head violin is played in Mongolia, & why tigers are friends of the Yi people. This is an entertaining as well as educational book to be enjoyed by anyone curious about China. Charming, full-color illustrations combined with photography make each page a visual surprise. Ages 9 & up. 64 p. hardback. January 1994. $16.95. ISBN 0-9638417-0-X. COSTUMES OF SPLENDID CHINA: A paper doll book that features full-color regional costumes from China. Five American children of various ethnic backgrounds & the Monkey King of China, each have three pre-cut outfits. Included is a booklet describing the costumes & customs from each region, plus a full-color map of China that highlights these locations. Ages 6 & up. 24 p. March 1994 $6.95. ISBN 0-9638417-1-8. Orders for both books may be placed by contacting The Book People: 800-999-4650 or The Distributors: 800-955-7032 or China Books: Phone 415-282-2994 or FAX 415-282-0994. ***Publisher Provided Annotation.***

*Adventure in Suicide.** Frank R. Vivelo. 230p. 1995. pap. 8.95 (1-56901-722-0) NW Pub.

Adventure in the Amazon. Cousteau Society Staff. LC 91-34167. (Illus.). 48p. (J). (gr. 3-7). 1992. pap. 15.00 (0-671-77071-3, S&S Bks Young Read) S&S Childrens.

Adventure in the Arctic Circle. Christopher Carrie. (Crayola Color & Activity Ser.). (Illus.). 40p. (J). (gr. k up). 1990. 1.59 (0-86696-249-2) Binney & Smith.

Adventure in the Desert. Herbert Kaufmann. (Illus.). (J). (gr. 7 up). 1961. 10.95 (0-8392-3000-1) Astor-Honor.

Adventure in the Haunted House. Page McBrier. LC 85-8436. (Oliver & Company Ser.). (Illus.). 96p. (J). (gr. 3-6). 1986. lib. bdg. 9.89 (0-8167-0539-9); pap. text ed. 2.95 (0-8167-0540-2) Troll Assocs.

*Adventure in the High Andes.** Natalie Barber. 90p. Date not set. pap. 7.95 (1-56901-646-1) NW Pub.

Adventure in the Lost World. R. W. Stroh. LC 85-2530. (Illus.). 96p. (J). (gr. 3-6). 1985. lib. bdg. 9.49 (0-8167-0535-6); pap. text ed. 2.95 (0-8167-0536-4) Troll Assocs.

Adventure in the Wilderness. Wunderli & Watts. (J). pap. 5.95 (0-88494-648-7) Bookcraft Inc.

Adventure in Vedanta: J. D. Salingers The Glass Family. Som. P. Ranchan. 1989. 14.50 (81-202-0245-7, Pub. by Ajanta II) S Asia.

Adventure into BBC Basic. Miles Ellis & David Ellis. LC 83-16998. 325p. reprint ed. pap. 92.70 (0-8357-5200-3, 2032656) Bks Demand.

Adventure Inward: Christian Growth Through Personal Journal Writing. Morton T. Kelsey. LC 80-65551. 224p. (Orig.). 1980. pap. 13.99 (0-8066-1796-9, 10-0166, Augsburg) Augsburg Fortress.

Adventure Language. Frank Hill. (Pocket Pac Ser.). 1991. Incl. 10 phrasecards. 4.00 (0-88699-058-0) Travel Sci.

Adventure Magazine Index, 2 vols. Richard J. Bleiler. LC 90-10407. 1085p. (Orig.). 1990. lib. bdg. 150.00 (1-55742-189-7) Borgo Pr.

Adventure Mountain Biking: Touring, Sport & Expeditions. Carlton Reid. (Illus.). 160p. 1991. 34.95 (1-85223-388-5, Pub. by Crowood Pr UK) Trafalgar.

Adventure, Mystery, & Romance: Formula Stories As Art & Popular Culture. John G. Cawelti. LC 75-5077. (Phoenix Ser.). 336p. 1976. reprint ed. pap. 15.95x (0-226-09867-2, P732) U Ch Pr.

Adventure of Black Peter & The 'Gloria Scott, Vol. I. Illus. by George Overlie. (Match Wits with Sherlock Holmes Ser.). (J). (gr. 4-7). 1990. lib. bdg. 17.50 (0-87614-385-0, Carolrhoda) Lerner Group.

Adventure of Blueberrying: On Cape Ann Massachusetts. Merrill F. McLane. (Illus.). (Orig.). 1994. pap. 12.95 (0-938813-06-4) Carderock Pr.

Adventure of Christian Fast. Don Oakley. LC 88-8001. (Illus.). 279p. (Orig.). (YA). (gr. 9 up). 1989. 12.95 (0-9619465-1-2); pap. 8.95 (0-9619465-2-0) Eyrie Pr.

Adventure of Consciousness. Satprem. Tr. by Luc Venet. LC 83-22725. (Works of Satprem-Institute for Evolutionary Research). 385p. 1984. reprint ed. pap. 11.50 (0-938710-04-4) Inst Evolutionary.

Adventure of Criticism. K. R. Iyengar. 691p. 1986. reprint ed. text ed. 50.00 (0-685-11915-7, Pub. by Sterling Pubs II) Apt Bks.

Adventure of Difference: Philosophy after Nietzsche & Heidegger. Gianni Vattimo. Tr. by Cyprian Blamires & Thomas Harrison. LC 92-40885. (Parallax). 210p. 1993. text ed. 29.95 (0-8018-4643-9) Johns Hopkins.

Adventure of Elizabeth in Rugen. Elizabeth Von Arnim. 299p. 1992. pap. 10.95 (1-85381-223-4, Pub. by Virago Pr UK) Trafalgar.

Adventure of Faith: When Religion Is Just the Beginning. John Luongo. LC 92-15128. 176p. 1992. pap. 5.95 (0-8091-3313-X) Paulist Pr.

Adventure of Fifi's Honey Bee Bears & the Big Bee Hive. Ruth Schroeder. (Illus.). 28p. (J). (gr. k-5). 1987. lib. bdg. 8.95 (0-935087-24-9) R & D Bks.

Adventure of George the Dinosaur (La Adventura de Jorge il Dinosaurio) Doron W. Blake. Ed. by Winafred B. Lucas. Tr. by Anna Gremard. (Illus.). 32p. (J). (gr. k-3). 1994. 11.95 (1-882530-04-7); 11.95 (1-882530-05-5) Deep Forest Pr.

Adventure of Hajji Baba of Ispahan. J. Morier. 464p. 1987. 100.00 (1-85077-145-6, Darf Pubs Ltd) St Mut.

Adventure of Interviewing. Janice G. Franzen. 204p. (Orig.). (C). 1989. pap. text ed. 9.95 (0-9622197-0-3) Christian Writers.

Adventure of Intimacy: A Journey Through Broken Circles. Thomas Tyrrell. LC 92-60891. 112p. (Orig.). 1993. pap. 7.95 (0-89622-532-1) Twenty-Third.

Adventure of Leadership. Hap Klopp & Brian Tarcy. 1992. 18.95 (0-681-41406-5) Longmeadow Pr.

*Adventure of Leadership.** Hap Klopp. Ed. by Brian Tarcy. 208p. 1994. reprint ed. pap. 10.00 (0-425-14376-7, Berkley Trade) Berkley Pub.

Adventure of Learning. William P. Tolley. 1977. 14.95x (0-8156-0142-5) Syracuse U Pr.

Adventure of Living God's Will. Marion Wilson. 48p. 1980. teacher ed 1.00 (0-89114-094-8); pap. 1.50 (0-89114-093-X) Baptist Pub Hse.

Adventure of Marriage. Harry Silverstone. 1967. 7.50 (0-87948-006-8) Beatty.

Adventure of Mr. Mocker. Thornton Burgess. 120p. 1977. reprint ed. lib. bdg. 17.95 (0-89966-271-4) Buccaneer Bks.

Adventure of Reason: The Uses of Philosophy in Sociology. Ed. by H. P. Rickman. LC 83-5622. (Contributions in Sociology Ser.: No. 46). xi, 172p. 1983. text ed. 49.95 (0-313-23871-5, RAR/, Greenwood Pr) Greenwood.

*Adventure of Retirement: It's about More Than Just Money.** Guild A. Fetridge. (Golden Age Bks.). 250p. (C). 1994. 24.95 (0-87975-921-6) Prometheus Bks.

*Adventure of Retirement: It's about More Than Just Money.** Guild A. Fetridge. (Golden Age Bks.). (C). 1994. pap. 16.95 (0-87975-941-0) Prometheus Bks.

Adventure of Self-Discovery: Dimensions of Consciousness & New Perspectives in Psychotherapy & Inner Exploration. Stanislav Grof. LC 87-17967. (SUNY Series in Transpersonal & Humanistic Psychology). 321p. 1988. 49.50 (0-88706-540-6); pap. 16.95 (0-88706-541-4) State U NY Pr.

Adventure of Spiritual Healing. large type ed. Michael Drury. 304p. 1985. pap. 9.95 (0-8027-2493-0) Walker & Co.

Adventure of Squeek the Rabbit. Joel Reinheimer. (J). 1990. 6.95 (0-533-08900-X) Vantage.

Adventure of Tangerine Island. Gordon R. Forrer. LC 81-81615. 1982. 10.95 (0-87212-148-8) Libra.

Adventure of the Backyard Sleepout. Nancy McArthur. 80p. (J). 1992. pap. 2.95 (0-590-45033-6) Scholastic Inc.

Adventure of the Cardboard Box & Scandal in Bohemia, Vol. II. Illus. by George Overlie. (Match Wits with Sherlock Holmes Ser.). (J). (gr. 4-6). 1990. lib. bdg. 14.95 (0-87614-386-9, Carolrhoda) Lerner Group.

Adventure of the Copper Beeches & The Redheaded League, Vol. IV. Illus. by George Overlie. (Match Wits with Sherlock Holmes Ser.). (J). (gr. 4-7). 1990. lib. bdg. 17.50 (0-87614-388-5, Carolrhoda) Lerner Group.

Adventure of the Dancing Men: The Three Garridebs. Illus. by George Overlie. LC 92-21787. (Match Wits with Sherlock Holmes Ser.: Vol. 7). (J). 1993. pap. 4.95 (0-87614-555-1, Carolrhoda) Lerner Group.

Adventure of the Dancing Men: The Three Garridebs. Illus. by George Overlie. LC 92-21787. (Match Wits with Sherlock Holmes Ser.: Vol. 7). (J). (gr. 4-7). 1993. lib. bdg. 17.50 (0-87614-716-3, Carolrhoda) Lerner Group.

Adventure of the Discerning Thespian. Frank Ramirez. LC 82-91140. (Illus.). 64p. 1983. 28.00 (0-88014-064-X) Mosaic Pr OH.

Adventure of the Eleven Cuff-Buttons. James F. Thierry. 1979. pap. 6.50 (0-915230-14-3) Rue Morgue.

*Adventure of the Missing Brother.** Eugene E. Snyder. LC 94-79993. 168p. 1995. pap. 12.95 (0-8323-0510-3) Binford Mort.

Adventure of the Priory School: A Facsimile of the Original Manuscript in the Marvin P. Epstein Sherlock Holmes Collection. Arthur Conan Doyle. 100p. 1987. 85.00 (0-944166-00-8) Santa Teresa Pr.

Adventure of the Six Napoleons & the Blue Carbuncle, Vol. III. Illus. by George Overlie. (Match Wits with Sherlock Holmes Ser.). (J). (gr. 4-7). 1990. lib. bdg. 17.50 (0-87614-387-7, Carolrhoda) Lerner Group.

Adventure of the Solitary Cyclist. Arthur Conan Doyle. (Classic Short Stories Ser.). (J). 1991. lib. bdg. 13.95 (0-88682-472-9) Creative Ed.

Adventure of the Speckled Band. Arthur Conan Doyle. (Classic Short Stories Ser.). 64p. (J). (gr. 6). 1990. lib. bdg. 13.95 (0-88682-301-3) Creative Ed.

Adventure of the Speckled Band. Tim Kelly. 52p. (J). (gr. 4 up). 1981. pap. 4.00 (0-88680-000-5) I E Clark.

Adventure of the Squib Owl: Squib Ser., 5 vols. Larry Shles. (Illus.). (J). 1988. pap. 7.95 (0-915190-85-0) Jalmar Pr.

Adventure of the Stone Man. Frances Hamerstrom. (Illus.). (J). (gr. 4-7). 1990. pap. 10.95 (1-55821-084-9) Lyons & Burford.

Adventure of the Wandering Wolves in Vulcan's Vent. Karla Kelly et al. Ed. by Harriet Crosby. (Tales of Terratopia Ser.). (Illus.). 40p. (Orig.). (J). (gr. 1-6). 1993. pap. 6.95 (1-883871-01-8) Nature Co.

Adventure on the Graveyard of the Wrecks. Olga Cossi. LC 90-20686. 144p. (Orig.). (YA). (gr. 9-12). 1991. pap. 6.95 (0-88289-808-6) Pelican.

Adventure on the Island. (Key Words Readers Ser.: A Series, No. 641-10a). (Illus.). (J). (ps-5). 3.50 (0-7214-0010-8) Ladybird Bks.

Adventure on the Santa Fe Trail. Ed. by Leo E. Oliva. LC 88-50922. (Illus.). 127p. 1988. pap. 7.95 (0-87726-033-8) Kansas St Hist.

*Adventure on Thunder Island.** Edna King & Jordan Wheeler. (Blue Kite Adventure Ser.). (Illus.). (J). (gr. 2 up). 1995. pap. 8.95 (1-55028-133-X) Formac Dist Ltd.

*Adventure on Thunder Island.** Edna King & Jordan Wheeler. (Blue Kite Adventure Ser.). (Illus.). (J). (gr. 2 up). 1995. bds. 16.95 (1-55028-135-6) Formac Dist Ltd.

Adventure or Experience: Four Essays on Certain Writers & Readers of Novels. Dorothy Brewster & Angus Burrell. LC 67-23185. (Essay Index Reprint Ser.). 1977. reprint ed. 19.95 (0-8369-0252-1) Ayer.

Adventure Playground of Mechanisms & Novel Reactions. Rolf Huisgen. LC 94-13957. (Profiles, Pathways & Dreams Ser.). 279p. 1994. 24.95 (0-8412-1832-3) Am Chemical.

*Adventure Radio.** (Stereo Boom Box Ser.: Vol. 3). 160p. (J). (gr. 1-6). 1994. 149.95 (1-57405-050-8) CharismaLife Pub.

Adventure Roads North. Alaska Geographic Staff. Ed. by Robert Henning. (Alaska Geographic Ser.: Vol. 10, No. 1). (Illus.). 144p. 1978. reprint ed. pap. 19.95 (0-88240-114-9) Alaska Geog Soc.

Adventure Stories. Ed. by Clive King. LC 92-26452. (Story Library). Orig. Title: Selected by. (Illus.). (J). 1993. pap. 6.95 (1-85697-882-6, Kingfisher LKC) LKC.

Adventure Stories. Walter Swan. Ed. by Deloris Swan. (Illus.). 252p. (J). (gr. k-5). 1991. 19.95 (0-927176-08-4) Swan Enterp.

Adventure Tales of Arkansas: A Cartoon History of a Spirited People. C. Fred Williams. (Illus.). x, 38p. (Orig.). (J). (gr. 5-7). 1986. teacher ed 3.50 (0-9616677-1-0); pap. 5.95 (0-9616677-0-2) Signal Media.

Adventure Teacher's Resource Guide. Irene Welch. Ed. by Liz Parker. (Take Ten Bks.). 35p. (Orig.). 1992. pap. text ed. 14.95 (1-56254-060-2) Saddleback Pubns.

Adventure Therapy: Therapeutic Applications of Adventure Programming. Michael Gass. 528p. 1995. 29.95 (0-8403-8272-3) Assn Exper Ed.

Adventure Through Khyber. Victor Bayley. (C). 1988. 39.00 (81-212-0142-X, Pub. by Gian Publng Hse II) S Asia.

*Adventure to Contarrian.** Mike Michaelson. Orig. Title: Lightyears. 118p. (Orig.). (J). 1994. spiral bd. 16.95 (0-9635636-0-2) Humanform Robot.

Adventure to Entrepreneurship: A Journey to Self-Discovery for Young Women. Cynthia Iannarelli & Wendy J. Peters. 200p. (YA). (gr. 7-12). Date not set. pap. 24.00 (1-885043-02-3) Nat Educ Ctr Women.

Adventure to Orbital. Cynthia M. Kreuger & Kirsten M. Kreuger. LC 92-61367. 45p. (J). (gr. k-4). 1993. pap. 5.95 (1-55523-558-1) Winston-Derek.

Adventure Trails in Montana. 7th rev. ed. John Willard. (Illus.). 250p. reprint ed. pap. 10.95 (0-9612398-1-6) J A Willard.

Adventure Travel Abroad. Pat Dickerman. (Illus.). 1986. pap. 12.95 (0-685-45255-7) Farm Ranch Ctry Vac.

Adventure Travel in Africa. Pamela McKinstry. 224p. (C). 1990. 140.00 (0-907151-98-1, Pub. by IMMEL Pubng UK) St Mut.

Adventure Travel in Latin America: Where to Backpack, Camp & Find Adventure in Mexico, the Caribbean, Central America & South America. Scott Graham. LC 90-37146. (Illus.). 200p. (Orig.). 1990. pap. 12.95 (0-89997-105-9) Wilderness Pr.

Adventure Travel North America. 9th ed. Ed. by Pat Dickerman. (Illus.). 288p. 1993. pap. 16.95 (0-913216-01-1) Adven Guides.

Adventure Travel Photography: How to Shoot Great Pictures off the Beaten Track. Nevada Wier. (Illus.). 144p. 1992. pap. 22.50 (0-8174-3276-0, Amphoto) Watsn-Guptill.

Adventure Treks: Western North America. Chris Townsend. (Illus.). 160p. 1990. pap. 24.95 (0-938567-23-3) Cloudcap.

Adventure Unlimited: Searching the Globe with Francis Raymond Line. Francis R. Line. (Illus.). 206p. (Orig.). 1988. pap. 8.95 (0-938109-05-7) Wide Horiz Pr.

*Adventure Vacations: A 50-State Guide to Rock Climbing, Horseback Riding, Spelunking, Whitewater Rafting, Snorkeling, Hang Gliding & Ballooning.** Stephanie Ocko. (Illus.). 256p. 1995. pap. 14.95 (0-8065-1632-1, Citadel Pr) Carol Pub Group.

Adventure Vacations: From Trekking in New Guinea to Swimming in Siberia. Ed. by Richard Bangs. (Illus.). 256p. (Orig.). 1990. pap. 17.95 (0-945465-76-9) John Muir.

*Adventure with Billy Bunny.** Maurice Pledger. (Illus.). 20p. (J). (ps). 1995. 14.50 (1-881445-47-X) Sandvik Pub.

Adventure with Children. Mary H. Lewis. Ed. by Eugene F. Provenzo, Jr. & Therese M. Provenzo. LC 85-15821. (Illus.). 124p. 1985. reprint ed. lib. bdg. 52.00 (0-8191-4911-X) U Pr of Amer.

Adventure with Crom. (Illus.). (J). (ps-2). 1991. lib. bdg. 8.99 (0-8136-5162-X); pap. 4.79 (0-8136-5662-1) Modern Curr.

Adventure with Eagles. David Hancock. (Illus.). 56p. 1989. pap. 5.95 (0-88839-217-6) Hancock House.

Adventure World Sourcebook, Series I. Paul McMenamin. (Illus.). 432p. 1991. pap. 24.95 (0-685-48070-4) Boken Commns.

*Adventurer.** Diana Whitney. (Special Edition Ser.). 1995. pap. 3.50 (0-373-09934-7, 1-09934-0) Silhouette.

Adventurer: The Fate of Adventure in the Western World. Paul Zweig. LC 81-47798. 288p. (Orig.). 1981. reprint ed. 42.50 (0-691-06451-2); reprint ed. pap. 14.95 (0-691-01387-X) Princeton U Pr.

Adventurer II Stamp Album. Ed. by David S. Macdonald. (Illus.). 272p. 1986. pap. 6.95 (0-937458-44-9) Harris & Co.

Adventurer in Spain. Samuel R. Crockett. LC 70-106282. (Short Story Index Reprint Ser.). 1977. 21.95 (0-8369-3319-2) Ayer.

Adventurer. Nos. 1-140, 2 vols. 1753-1754, Set. Adventurer Magazine Staff. LC 68-58000. reprint ed. 125.00 (0-404-19300-5) AMS Pr.

Adventurer of the North. Gilbert Parker. LC 74-98589. (Short Story Index Reprint Ser.). 1977. 19.95 (0-8369-3163-7) Ayer.

Adventurers. Ernest Haycox. 1976. 21.95 (0-89190-971-0) Amereon Ltd.

Adventurers. Ernest Haycox. 320p. 1993. pap. 3.50 (1-55817-707-8, Pinnacle NY) Windsor NY.

Adventurers. Jane A. Hodge. 1977. pap. 1.95 (0-449-23451-7, Crest) Fawcett.

Adventurers. Robbins. 1993. pap. 6.99 (0-671-87482-9) PB.

Adventurers. large type ed. Vivian Stuart. 704p. 1984. 23.95 (0-7089-8196-8, Charnwood) Ulverscroft.

*Adventurers: A Year in the Life of a Venture Capital House.** Anthea Masey. 184p. (Orig.). 1995. pap. 14.95 (0-563-36771-7, Pub. by BBC UK) Parkwest Pubns.

Adventurers Afloat - A Nautical Bibliography: A Comprehensive Guide to Books in English Recounting the Adventures of Amateur Sailors upon the Waters of the World in Yachts, Boats, & Other Devices & Including Works on the Arts & Sciences of Cruising, Racing, Seamanship, Navigation, Design, Building, etc. from the Earliest Writings Through 1986, 2 vols., Set. Ernest W. Toy, Jr. LC 88-31209. 1193p. 1988. 89.50 (0-8108-2189-3) Scarecrow.

Adventurers & Proletarians: The Story of Migrants in Latin America. Magnus Morner. Tr. by Harold Sims. LC 84-19597. (Latin American Ser.). (Illus.). 195p. 1985. 49.95 (0-8229-3505-8) U of Pittsburgh Pr.

*Adventurers & Prophets: American Autobiographers in Mexican California, 1828-1847.** Charles B. Churchill. LC 94-47236. (Western Frontiersmen Ser.: No. 24). (Illus.). 1995. 35.00 (0-87062-228-5) A H Clark.

Adventurers for Another World: Jonathan Trumble's Commonplace Book. Albert E. Van Dusen. 42p. 1983. pap. 5.95 (0-940748-87-8) Conn Hist Soc.

Adventurer's Guide to Dana Point. Doris Walker. (Illus.). 64p. (Orig.). 1992. pap. 10.95 (0-9606476-4-3) To-the-Point.

Adventurer's Guide to Interleaf Lisp. David Weinberger. 334p. 1994. disk, pap. 49.95 (1-56690-042-5, OnWord Pr) High Mtn.

Adventurer's Guide to Laser Play. Dean Lorey & Fran Rizzo. 256p. 1987. pap. 3.50 (0-8217-2229-8) Zebra.

Adventurer's Guide to Number Theory. Richard Friedberg. (Illus.). 228p. 1994. reprint ed. pap. 7.95 (0-486-28133-7) Dover.

*Adventurer's Guide to the Magdalen Islands.** George Fischer. (Illus.). 128p. 1995. pap. 14.95 (1-55109-088-0, Pub. by Nimbus Publishing Ltd CN) Chelsea Green Pub.

*Adventurer's Guide to the Sierra Nevada Mountains.** Claire Hiester. (Illus.). 1994. 19.95 (0-9619827-4-8) DesignWorks.

Adventurer's Guide to the Sierra Nevada Mountains. Claire Hiester & Marty Hiester. (Illus.). (C). 1994. pap. text ed. 9.95 (0-9619827-3-X) DesignWorks.

Adventurer's Hawaii. Peter Caldwell. LC 92-80609. (Illus.). 144p. 1992. pap. 19.95 (0-9626124-1-3) Taote Pub.

Adventurers in the Eighteenth Century. Peter Wilding. LC 76-93387. (Essay Index Reprint Ser.). 1977. 26.95 (0-8369-1434-1) Ayer.

*Adventurers of Purse & Person: Order of First Families of Virginia.** 1956. 85.00 (0-87517-066-8) Dietz.

Adventures. Thomas J. Tansey. LC 92-81380. (Illus.). 342p. 1993. pap. 14.95 (0-935834-83-4) Rainbow Books.

Adventures: Reading Level 2-3. Illus. by Bob Doucet. LC 93-12039. (Timeless Tales Ser.). 1993. 4.25 (0-88336-458-1); audio 10.50 (0-88336-523-5) New Readers.

Adventures Abroad: Exploring the Travel-Retirement Option. Allene Symons & Jane Parker. 252p. (Orig.). 1991. pap. 12.95 (0-933469-10-1) Gateway Bks.

Adventures among Birds. William H. Hudson. reprint ed. 64.50 (0-404-03407-1) AMS Pr.

Adventures among Books. Andrew Lang. LC 73-105023. (Essay Index Reprint Ser.). 1977. 23.95 (0-8369-1474-0) Ayer.

An Asterisk (*) at the beginning of an entry indicates that the title is appearing in BIP for the first time.

Adventures among the Toroids. 2nd ed. B. M. Stewart. LC 73-14167. 1980. pap. 13.50 (*0-686-11936-3*) B M Stewart.

***Adventures & Accidents.** Baden-Powell. (Illus.). 184p. 1995. pap. 16.95 (*1-885529-18-X*) Stevens Pub.

Adventures & Achievements of Americans. Henry Howe. (Notable American Authors Ser.). 1992. reprint ed. lib. bdg. 75.00 (*0-7812-3206-6*) Rprt Serv.

Adventures & Advice about Acting in TV Commercials. Gwen H. Wilson. 1994. pap. text ed. 12.95 (*0-533-10751-2*) Vantage.

Adventures & Confessions. William L. Phelps. LC 71-121497. (Essay Index Reprint Ser.). 1977. 19.95 (*0-8369-1771-5*) Ayer.

Adventures & Letters of Richard Harding Davis. Charles B. Davis. (American Newspapermen 1790-1933 Ser.). (Illus.). iii, 417p. 1974. reprint ed. 29.00 (*0-8464-0024-3*) Beekman Pubs.

Adventures & Letters of Richard Harding Davis. Richard Davis. (American Biography Ser.). 417p. 1991. reprint ed. lib. bdg. 89.00 (*0-7812-8101-6*) Rprt Serv.

Adventures & Mis-Adventures of Antique Dealers & Collectors. 162p. 1993. 25.00 (*0-916528-07-3*) J M Pearson.

Adventures & Misadventures of Peter Beard in Africa. Jon Bowermaster. LC 92-18212. (Illus.). 224p. 1993. 40.00 (*0-8212-1907-3*) Bulfinch Pr.

Adventures & Misgivings. Edward V. Lucas. LC 78-105027. (Essay Index Reprint Ser.). 1977. 18.95 (*0-8369-1523-2*) Ayer.

Adventures & Missionary Labours in Several Countries in the Interior of Africa from 1849-1856. 2nd rev. ed. T. J. Bowen. 359p. 1968. reprint ed. 35.00 (*0-7146-1863-2*, Pub. by F Cass Pubs UK) Intl Spec Bk.

Adventures & Philosophy of a Pennsylvania Dutchman: An Autobiography in a Broad Setting. Homer T. Rosenberger. LC 79-165295. (Illus.). 665p. 1971. lib. bdg. 15.00 (*0-917264-03-7*) Rose Hill.

***Adventures Around Kilauea: Kilauea Volcano.** Faith Roelofs. (Exploring the Islands: Island of Hawai'i Ser.). 1994. pap. write for info. (*1-882163-30-3*) Moanalua Grdns Fnd.

Adventures at Sea in the Great Age of Sail: Five Firsthand Narratives. Ed. by Elliot Snow. 353p. 1986. reprint ed. pap. 8.95 (*0-486-25177-2*) Dover.

Adventures Captain Bonneville, U. S. A. 54.95 (*0-8488-0222-5*, J M C & Co) Amereon Ltd.

Adventures down the Mississippi. 2nd rev. ed. Karen C. Kendrick & Cynthia C. Black. 266p. (Orig.). 1993. pap. 23.95 (*1-878631-12-8*) S Kovalik.

Adventures for Growing Families. Wes Haystead & Sheryl Haystead. 360p. (Orig.). 1993. pap. 17.99 (*1-56476-120-7*, Victor Books) SP Pubns.

Adventures for the Soul. Natalie Sleeth. 139p. 1987. pap. 5.95 (*0-916642-30-5*, 785) Hope Pub.

Adventures from the Pentateuch. J. Curtis Manor. 1994. 17.95 (*1-56794-068-4*) Star Bible.

Adventures Greek Heroes. Mollie McLean. 1972. pap. 5.95 (*0-395-13714-4*) HM.

Adventures in a New Land. Joseph H. Anway & Carol A. Anway. 216p. 1987. pap. 19.00 (*0-8309-0487-5*) Herald Hse.

Adventures in Acrylics & Oils, No. 1. Bob Bates. (How to Draw & Paint Ser.). (Illus.). 32p. (Orig.). 1989. pap. 5.95 (*0-929261-42-9*, HT186) W Foster Pub.

Adventures in Acrylics & Oils, No. 2. Bob Bates. (How to Draw & Paint Ser.). (Illus.). 32p. (Orig.). 1989. pap. 5.95 (*0-929261-45-3*, HT200) W Foster Pub.

Adventures in Afghanistan. Louis Palmer. 239p. 1990. 24.00 (*0-86304-053-5*, Pub. by Octagon Pr UK); pap. 11.00 (*0-86304-057-8*, Pub. by Octagon Pr UK) ISHK Bk Service.

Adventures in America. John A. Trickel. 272p. 1990. per. 24.95 (*0-8403-5718-4*) Kendall-Hunt.

Adventures in America: Readings in Early American History to 1877. 2nd ed. John A. Trickel. 304p. 1991. per. 15.95 (*0-8403-6744-9*) Kendall-Hunt.

Adventures in an American's Literature. Norbert Blei. 224p. (Orig.). 1982. pap. 5.95 (*0-933180-41-1*) Ellis Pr.

Adventures in Arabia. Seabrook. 1994. pap. 12.95 (*1-56924-905-9*) Marlowe & Co.

Adventures in Arithmetic for the Pre-Algebra Student. Boyd Henry. 51p. 1994. pap. 19.95 (*0-939765-66-7*) Janson Pubns.

Adventures in Arizona: An Illustrated History. Linda Lawrence & Kate Thorne. Ed. by Aliza Caillou. LC 91-65779. (Illus.). 48p. (Orig.). (J). (gr. 4 up). 1991. pap. 6.95 (*0-9628329-3-6*) Thorne Enterprises.

Adventures in Arkham Country: Five Adventures along the Miskatonic Valley. Hassal et al. Ed. by Keith Herber. (Call of Cthulhu Roleplaying Game Ser.). (Illus.). 125p. (Orig.). 1993. pap. 18.95 (*1-56882-004-6*, 2342) Chaosium.

Adventures in Art, Bk. 1. Laura Chapman. (Discover Art Ser.). (J). (gr. 1-6). 1994. text ed. 17.20 (*0-87192-251-7*); teacher ed, spiral bd. 31.10 (*0-87192-257-6*) Davis Mass.

Adventures in Art, Bk. 2. Laura Chapman. (Discover Art Ser.). (J). (gr. 1-6). 1994. teacher ed 31.10 (*0-87192-258-4*); text ed. 17.20 (*0-87192-252-5*) Davis Mass.

Adventures in Art, Bk. 3. Laura Chapman. (Discover Art Ser.). (J). (gr. 1-6). 1994. text ed. 20.20 (*0-87192-253-3*); teacher ed, spiral bd. 31.10 (*0-87192-259-2*) Davis Mass.

Adventures in Art, Bk. 4. Laura Chapman. (Discover Art Ser.). (J). (gr. 1-6). 1994. text ed. 20.20 (*0-87192-254-1*); teacher ed, spiral bd. 31.10 (*0-87192-260-6*) Davis Mass.

Adventures in Art, Bk. 5. Laura Chapman. (Discover Art Ser.). (J). (gr. 1-6). 1994. text ed. 20.20 (*0-87192-255-X*); teacher ed, spiral bd. 31.10 (*0-87192-261-4*) Davis Mass.

Adventures in Art, Bk. 6. Laura Chapman. (Discover Art Ser.). (J). (gr. 1-6). 1994. text ed. 20.20 (*0-87192-256-8*); teacher ed, spiral bd. 31.10 (*0-87192-262-2*) Davis Mass.

Adventures in Art: Art & Crafts Experiences for 7- to 14-Year Olds. Susan Milord. Ed. by Susan Williamson. LC 90-39031. (Kids Can! Ser.: No. 3). (Illus.). 160p. (Orig.). (J). (gr. 2-8). 1990. pap. 12.95 (*0-913589-54-3*) Williamson Pub Co.

Adventures in Artificial Life. Clayton Walnum. 1993. disk, pap. 24.95 (*1-56529-356-8*) Que.

Adventures in Being. Alfredo Rubio. 138p. 1992. pap. 12.95 (*0-85244-212-2*, Pub. by Gracewing UK) Morehouse Pub.

Adventures in Blueprinting: Cyanotype. Patri Feher. Ed. by P. A. Feher. (Illus.). 50p. 1994. student ed, pap. text ed. 49.95 (*0-685-67868-7*) Spinach Pubns.

Adventures in Bubby Irma's Kitchen. Bubby Irma. 183p. 1992. 14.95 (*0-944070-95-7*) Targum Pr.

Adventures in Card Play. Geza Ottlik & Hugh Kelsey. (Master Bridge Ser.). (Illus.). 288p. 1983. pap. 19.95 (*0-575-03365-7*, Pub. by V Gollancz UK) Trafalgar.

Adventures in Careering: A Twin Cities Field Guide. Joan P. Pasiuk. 187p. 1991. pap. 12.95 (*0-9631399-0-8*) Basswood Pr.

Adventures in Caucasia. Alexandre Dumas. Ed. by Alma E. Murch. LC 75-16415. (Illus.). 205p. 1975. reprint ed. text ed. 55.00 (*0-8371-8187-9*, DUAC, Greenwood Pr) Greenwood.

Adventures in Celestial Mechanics: A First Course in the Theory of Orbits. Victor G. Szebehely. (Illus.). 191p. (C). 1989. text ed. 30.00x (*0-292-75105-2*) U of Tex Pr.

Adventures in Chaos: American Intervention for Reform in the Third World. Douglas J. Macdonald. 361p. 1992. 45.00 (*0-674-00577-5*) HUP.

Adventures in Cheap Eating: Hawaii: The Comprehensive Guide to Righteous Deals & Authentic. March Egerton. LC 93-60643. 1994. pap. 9.95 (*0-9637709-0-X*) Tsunami Pr.

Adventures in Close-up Photography. Lief Ericksenn & Els Sincebaugh. (Illus.). 144p. 1985. pap. 22.50 (*0-8174-3502-6*, Amphoto) Watsn-Guptill.

Adventures in Colors & Shapes. Walt Disney Productions Staff. (Walt Disney's Fun-to-Learn Library Ser.: Vol. 3). (Illus.). 44p. (J). (gr. 1-6). reprint ed. 2.99 (*0-9619525-4-7*) Advance Pubs.

***Adventures in Consciousness.** Jane Roberts. 1994. lib. bdg. 24.95x (*1-56849-496-3*) Buccaneer Bks.

Adventures in Consciousness. Friend Stuart. 1962. pap. 6.95 (*0-912132-00-0*) Dominion Pr.

Adventures in Consciousness: An Introduction to Aspect Psychology. Jane Roberts. 1978. 7.95 (*0-13-013953-X*) P-H.

Adventures in Conservation: Painting the Cows & Other Tales. T. A. Roberts. LC 88-63984. 176p. 1989. pap. 12.95 (*0-913276-53-7*) Stone Wall Pr.

Adventures in Contentment. David Grayson, pseud. LC 87-26428. (Illus.). 1987. pap. 14.95 (*0-939650-18-5*) R H Pub.

Adventures in Cooking: A Gourmet Primer. Christel Augl. 464p. (Orig.). 1993. pap. write for info. (*1-56167-130-4*) Am Literary Pr.

Adventures in Creating Earrings. Laura Reid. Ed. by Monte Smith. LC 90-82647. (Illus.). 96p. 1990. per. 9.95 (*0-943604-28-1*) Eagles View.

Adventures in Criticism. Arthur T. Quiller-Couch. 1975. 59.95 (*0-87968-578-6*) Gordon Pr.

Adventures in Criticism. Arthur T. Quiller-Couch. (BCL1-PR English Literature Ser.). 408p. 1992. reprint ed. lib. bdg. 99.00 (*0-7812-7017-0*) Rprt Serv.

Adventures in Criticism. Arthur T. Quiller-Couch. LC 12-37963. 1969. reprint ed. 9.00 (*0-403-00064-5*) Scholarly.

Adventures in Diving: Advanced Training for Open Water Divers. rev. ed. Bob Wohlers et al. Ed. by Drew Richardson & Joe De La Torre. (Illus.). 284p. (C). 1991. pap. text ed. 22.95 (*1-878663-08-9*) PADI.

Adventures in Earth Science. Margy Kuntz. 1987. pap. 6.99 (*0-8224-2318-9*) Fearon Teach Aids.

Adventures in Eating: A Guide to Denver's Ethnic Markets, Bakeries & Gourmet Stores. Susan E. Permut. (Illus.). 160p. (Orig.). 1993. pap. 9.95 (*0-9638153-1-8*) Better Busn Communs.

Adventures, in Egypt & Nubia. Giovanni Belzoni. 1843. 49.00 (*0-403-00454-3*) Scholarly.

Adventures in Fern Hollow. John Patience. (Illus.). 64p. (J). (ps-1). 1985. 2.98 (*0-517-45856-X*) Random Hse Value.

Adventures in Flight Simulator. Timothy Trimble. 1993. disk, pap. 22.95 (*1-55615-582-4*) Microsoft.

Adventures in Friendship. David Grayson. LC 89-3616. (Illus.). 240p. 1989. reprint ed. pap. 14.95 (*1-55838-081-7*) R H Pub.

Adventures in Fugawiland: A Computer Simulation in Archeology. Doug Price & Gette Gebauer. 106p. (C). 1990. disk, pap. text ed. 19.95 (*0-87484-948-9*) Mayfield Pub.

***Adventures in Genealogy: Case Studies in the Unusual.** Norman E. Wright. (Illus.). 163p. 1994. 24.95 (*0-614-00876-X*, 9495) Clearfield Co.

Adventures in Geology. Jack Hassard. (Illus.). 40p. (Orig.). 1989. pap. text ed. 6.95 (*0-922152-04-7*) Am Geol.

Adventures in God. rev. ed. John G. Lake. 96p. 1991. pap. 4.95 (*0-89274-819-2*, HH-819) Harrison Hse.

Adventures in Good Company: The Complete Guide to Women's Tours & Outdoor Trips. Thalia Zepatos. LC 94-8440. 432p. (Orig.). 1994. pap. 16.95 (*0-933377-27-4*) Eighth Mount Pr.

Adventures in Good Company: The Complete Guide to Women's Tours & Outdoor Trips. Thalia Zepatos. LC 94-8440. 432p. (Orig.). 1994. lib. bdg. 24.95 (*0-933377-28-2*) Eighth Mount Pr.

Adventures in Greater Puget Sound: An Educational Guide Exploring the Marine Environment of Greater Puget Sound. Dawn Ashbach & Janice Veal. (Illus.). 56p. (Orig.). (J). (gr. 3-9). 1991. 7.95 (*0-9629778-0-2*) NW Island.

***Adventures in Growing up: I Really Do Love My Brothers.** Brian Berlage. (Illus.). (Orig.). 1994. pap. 12.95 (*0-9644367-0-1*) Brian Berlage.

Adventures in Growth. 18th ed. SMI Staff. (Illus.). (J). (gr. 3-7). 1988. text ed. 120.00 (*0-924121-00-9*) LMI TX.

Adventures in Healing. Parnell Bradbury. 22.50 (*0-89979-000-3*) British Am Bks.

Adventures in Healthful Cooking. Peggy R. Scribner. LC 85-71158. (Illus.). 212p. (Orig.). 1985. vinyl bd. 9.95 (*0-9614978-0-7*) Dogwood Pr.

Adventures in Heaven. Charles Angoff. LC 76-132110. (Short Story Index Reprint Ser.). 1977. 15.95 (*0-8369-3667-1*) Ayer.

Adventures in Hell, Vol. 1: Vietnam War Stories by Vietnam Vets. David Andersen et al. 254p. (Orig.). 1991. pap. 11.95 (*0-9627904-3-5*) Ritz Pub.

Adventures in Hiking. Barbara McMartin. 110p. (J). 1993. pap. 12.50 (*0-925168-25-4*) North Country.

Adventures in Hypnosis. limited ed. William Beigl. Ed. & Illus. by Wayne Strnad. LC 89-92466. (Adventure in Hypnosis Reprint Ser.: Vol. I). 200p. (Orig.). 1990. pap. text ed. 500.00 (*0-9624961-0-3*) Rainbow News.

***Adventures in Hypnosis.** 2nd ed. William Beigl. Ed. by Wayne Strong. LC 91-7651. (Adventure in Hypnosis Reprint Ser.: Vol. 2). (Illus.). 200p. (Orig.). 1991. pap. text ed. 19.95 (*0-9624961-1-1*) Rainbow News.

Adventures in Idaho's Sawtooth Country: Sixty-Three Trips for Hikers & Mountain Bikers. Lynne Stone. (Illus.). 256p. (Orig.). 1990. pap. 12.95 (*0-89886-192-6*) Mountaineers.

Adventures in Idealism: A Personal Record of the Life of Professor Sabsovich. Katherine Sabsovich. LC 74-29520. (Modern Jewish Experience Ser.). (Illus.). 1975. reprint ed. 25.95 (*0-405-06745-3*) Ayer.

Adventures in Improvisation at the Keyboard. Glenn Mack. 64p. 1970. pap. text ed. 9.95 (*0-87487-076-3*) Summy-Birchard.

Adventures in Indian Cooking. M. Atwood. 256p. 1978. 9.95 (*0-318-36281-3*) Asia Bk Corp.

Adventures in Indian Cooking. Ron Nunn & Kay Marten. (Illus.). 61p. (Orig.). 1990. pap. text ed. 5.95 (*0-936731-10-9*) Devel Self Rel.

Adventures in Interviewing. Isaac F. Marcosson. LC 80-130996. reprint ed. 21.50 (*0-404-04186-8*) AMS Pr.

Adventures in Kinship with All Life. 3rd ed. J. Allen Boone & Paul H. Leonard. 128p. 1994. pap. text ed. 9.95 (*0-930852-27-3*) Tree Life Pubns.

Adventures in Lesbian Philosophy. Ed. by Claudia Card. LC 94-3921. (Hypatia Bks.). 320p. 1994. text ed. 35.00 (*0-253-31308-2*); pap. 15.95 (*0-253-20899-8*) Ind U Pr.

Adventures in Life Science. Margy Kuntz. (J). (gr. 4-6). 1987. pap. 6.99 (*0-8224-2317-0*) Fearon Teach Aids.

Adventures in Living, from Cato to George Sand. Murial Jaeger. LC 79-121480. (Essay Index Reprint Ser.). 1977. 20.95 (*0-8369-1758-8*) Ayer.

Adventures in Living Plants. Edwin B. Kurtz & Chris Allen. 120p. reprint ed. pap. 34.20 (*0-8357-5201-1*, 2055330) Bks Demand.

Adventures in Medialand: Behind the News, Beyond the Pundits. Jeff Cohen & Norman Solomon. 1993. 29.95 (*1-56751-015-9*); pap. 11.95 (*1-56751-014-0*) Common Courage.

Adventures in Medical Research: A Century of Discovery at Johns Hopkins. A. McGehee Harvey. LC 75-36955. (Illus.). 480p. reprint ed. 136.80 (*0-8357-9259-5*, 2017573) Bks Demand.

Adventures in Medicine: One Doctor's Life Amid the Great Discoveries of 1940-1990. Sibley W. Hoobler. LC 91-92240. 199p. reprint ed. pap. 56.80 (*0-7837-6406-5*, AU00446) Bks Demand.

***Adventures in MicroStation 3D.** Thomas Synnott. (Illus.). 500p. 1995. disk, pap. 49.95 (*1-56690-068-9*, 1435, OnWord Pr) High Mtn.

Adventures in Modern Painting. (Illus.). 16p. 1992. pap. text ed. 52.50 (*0-935493-62-X*) Modern Learn Pr.

Adventures in Modern Painting Text & Prints, Pt. 2. (Illus.). 16p. 1992. pap. text ed. 52.00 (*0-935493-73-5*) Modern Learn Pr.

Adventures in Modes & Keys. Glenn Mack. 32p. 1991. pap. text ed. 5.95 (*0-87487-625-7*) Summy-Birchard.

Adventures in Nepal - The Last Home of Mystery. E. A. Powell. (C). 1991. text ed. 90.00 (*0-7855-0127-4*, Pub. by Ratna Pustak Bhandar) St Mut.

Adventures in Neural Networks. California Scientific Software Staff. (Illus.). 356p. (Orig.). 1993. pap. 24.95 (*1-56529-470-X*) Que.

Adventures in Nutrition. Fredrick J. Stare. LC 91-70698. 1991. 24.95 (*0-8158-0470-9*) Chris Mass.

***Adventures in Odyssey Bible: Includes The Entire Text, International Children's Bible.** Focus on the Family Staff. LC 94-31398. (J). 1994. 22.99 (*0-8499-5024-4*) Word Pub.

Adventures in Oz: Ozma of Oz & Marvelous Land of Oz, The Original Editions Complete & Unabridged. L. Frank Baum. (Juveniles Ser.). 575p. (J). (gr. 2 up). 1985. pap. 11.90 (*0-486-24880-1*) Dover.

Adventures in Oz: Wonderful Wizard of Oz Pop-Ups. L. Frank Baum. (J). 1991. 2.99 (*0-517-05267-9*) Random Hse Value.

Adventures in Patchwork. Dorothea Nield. 84p. 1976. 8.95 (*0-263-05591-4*) Transatl Arts.

Adventures in Pennsylvania. H. Bess Shires & Rita N. March. (J). (gr. 5-6). 1984. pap. 4.95 (*0-931992-12-5*) Penns Valley.

Adventures in Philosophy & Religion. James B. Pratt. LC 75-3323. reprint ed. 16.00 (*0-404-59319-4*) AMS Pr.

Adventures in Physical Science. Margy Kuntz. (J). (gr. 4-6). 1987. pap. 6.99 (*0-8224-2319-7*) Fearon Teach Aids.

Adventures in Political Science. Remigio E. Agpalo. 402p. 1994. pap. text ed. 24.00 (*971-542-018-4*, Pub. by U of Philippines Pr) UH Pr.

Adventures in Porkland: How Washington Wastes Your Money. Brian Kelly. LC 92-53649. 1992. 22.50 (*0-679-40656-5*, Villard Bks) Random.

Adventures in Porkland: How Washington Wastes Your Money & Why They Won't Stop. Brian Kelly. 1994. pap. 13.00 (*0-8129-2313-8*, Times Bks) Random.

Adventures in Pragmatic Problem-Solving: Stories & Language Activities for Children. Larry J. Mattes & Debe Eddo. (Illus.). 174p. 1989. pap. text ed. 22.95 (*0-930951-11-5*) Acad Comm.

Adventures in Prayer. Catherine Marshall. 1987. mass mkt. 4.95 (*0-345-34755-2*) Ballantine.

Adventures in Prayer. Catherine Marshall. LC 75-15720. 112p. 1985. pap. 6.99 (*0-8007-9105-3*) Chosen Bks.

Adventures in Prehistoric Archaeology: Differentiated Curriculum for Elementary & Intermediate Level Gifted Students. Robert Bleiweiss. 1989. 14.00 (*0-910609-18-7*) Gifted Educ Pr.

Adventures in Radiography: (From the Inside Out) Phyllis B. Irwin & Ann H. Watson. (Illus.). 475p. (C). 1987. text ed. 89.00 (*0-9619895-0-5*) Adventures TN.

Adventures in Ray Tracing. Alfonso Hermida. 1993. pap. 27.95 (*1-56529-555-2*) Que.

Adventures in Religious Life. Swami Yatiswarananda. pap. 3.95 (*0-87481-498-7*, Pub. by Ramakrishna Math II) Vedanta Pr.

Adventures in Retrieval: Han Murals & Shang Bronze Molds. Wilma Fairbank. LC 79-173410. (Harvard-Yenching Institute Studies: No. 28). 211p. 1972. pap. 8.50 (*0-674-00575-9*) HUP.

Adventures in Rhyme: Children's Stories in Verse & Adult Poems. Eugene L. Vickery. (Illus.). 96p. (Orig.). 1986. pap. 5.95 (*0-937775-01-0*) Stonehaven Pubs.

Adventures in Sakaeland, Comprising Harilek: Wrexham's Romance, Being a Continuation of "Harilek", 2 vols. in 1. Martin L. Gompertz. Ed. by R. Reginald & Douglas Melville. LC 77-84226. (Lost Race & Adult Fantasy Ser.). 1978. reprint ed. lib. bdg. 58.95 (*0-405-10978-4*) Ayer.

Adventures in Scale Modeling. Don Godish & Mike Lech. LC 94-10690. 1994. 23.00 (*0-688-04575-8*) Hearst Bks.

Adventures in Science & Math: Integrated Activities for Young Children. Julie G. Whitney & Linda J. Sheffield. 96p. (J). (ps-2). 1991. pap. text ed. 9.95 (*0-938587-18-8*) Cuisenaire.

***Adventures in Scuba Diving CD-ROM.** Naui & Tophook Staff. 1995. cd-rom write for info. (*0-916974-63-4*, 296) NAUI.

Adventures in SeeLogo: Course Code 192-1. Sandra Kennedy & James MacDonald. Ed. by Bonnie Schroeder. (Illus.). 12p. (Orig.). (gr. 4). 1989. student ed 6.95 (*0-917531-43-4*) CES Compu-Tech.

Adventures in SeeLogo: Course Code 192-2. Sandra Kennedy & James MacDonald. Ed. by Bonnie Schroeder. (Illus.). 91p. (Orig.). (J). (gr. 4). 1989. student ed 6.95 (*0-917531-44-2*) CES Compu-Tech.

Adventures in SeeLogo, Pt. 1: Lab Pack. Sandra Kennedy & James MacDonald. Ed. by Bonnie Schroeder. (Illus.). 229.95 (*1-56177-024-8*, L192-1); disk 15.95 (*1-56177-022-1*, D192-1) CES Compu-Tech.

Adventures in SeeLogo, Pt. 2: Lab Pack. Sandra Kennedy & James MacDonald. Ed. by Bonnie Schroeder. (Illus.). 229.95 (*1-56177-025-6*, L192-2); disk 15.95 (*1-56177-023-X*, D194-2) CES Compu-Tech.

Adventures in SeeLogo Teacher Edition: Course Code 192-1. Sandra Kennedy & Irene Danziger. Ed. by Bonnie Schroeder. (Illus.). 140p. (Orig.). 1989. 19.95 (*0-917531-68-X*) CES Compu-Tech.

Adventures in See Logo Teacher Edition: Course Code 192-2. Irene Danziger & Sandra Kennedy. Ed. by Bonnie Schroeder. (Illus.). 120p. (Orig.). 1989. 19.95 (*0-917531-69-8*) CES Compu-Tech.

Adventures in Simple Living: A Creation-Centered Spirituality. Rich Heffern. LC 93-45875. 160p. (Orig.). 1994. pap. 11.95 (*0-8245-1400-9*) Crossroad NY.

Adventures in Singing: A Process for Exploring, Discovering & Developing Vocal Potential. Clifton Ware. LC 94-18002. 1994. 19.96 (*0-07-068272-0*) McGraw.

Adventures in Social Research: Data Analysis Using SPSS. Earl Babbie & Fred Halley. 300p. 1993. disk, pap. 28.95 (*0-8039-9007-3*) Pine Forge.

***Adventures in Social Research: Data Analysis Using SPSS for Windows.** Earl Babbie & Fred Halley. LC 94-48281. 1995. pap. write for info. (*0-8039-9055-3*) Pine Forge.

Adventures in Socialism: New Lanark Establishment & Orbiston Community. Alexander Cullen. LC 70-134404. reprint ed. 27.50 (*0-404-08448-6*) AMS Pr.

Adventures in Socialism: New Lanark Establishment & Orbiston Community. Alexander Cullen. LC 68-55519. (Illus.). 329p. 1972. reprint ed. 37.50 (*0-678-00804-3*) Kelley.

Adventures in Solitude. David Grayson. (Illus.). 1990. pap. 14.95 (*1-55838-111-2*) R H Pub.

Adventures in Sound for Piano. Emma L. Diemer. 32p. 1989. pap. text ed. 5.95 (*0-87487-662-1*) Summy-Birchard.

Adventures in Sourdough Cooking & Baking. 2nd ed. Charles D. Wilford. (Illus.). 275p. 1971. pap. 5.00 (*0-912936-00-2*) Gold Rush.

Adventures in Sourdough Cooking & Baking. Charles D. Wilfred. (Illus.). 210p. 1990. reprint ed. 10.00 (*0-685-66158-X*) Gold Rush.

Adventures in South Carolina. Linda Hirschmann & Sharon Applebaum. 1974. pap. 4.95 (*0-87844-031-3*) Sandlapper Pub Co.

An Asterisk (*) at the beginning of an entry indicates that the title is appearing in BIP for the first time.

Adventures in Stochastic Processes. S. Resnick. xii, 626p. 1994. 64.50 (*0-8176-3591-2*) Spr-Verlag.

Adventures in Successful Thinking. 2nd ed. Richard A. Gunnell. 1982. reprint ed. pap. text ed. 5.95 (*0-939530-01-5*) Burtis Ent.

Adventures in Taste: The Wines & Folk Food of Spain. D. E. Pohren. (Illus.). 302p. 1972. 19.95 (*0-933224-13-3*, Pub. by Soc Sp Studies SP) Bold Strummer Ltd.

Adventures in Texas History: Texas History Classroom Resource & Activities Guide. 24p. 1987. pap. 4.95 (*0-88415-406-8*) Gulf Pub.

Adventures in the Alaskan Skin Trade. John Hawkes. 400p. 1986. mass mkt. 10.95 (*0-14-009283-8*, Penguin Bks) Viking Penguin.

Adventures in the Apache Country: A Tour Through Arizona & Sonora, with Notes on the Silver Regions of Nevada. John R. Browne. LC 72-9430. (Far Western Frontier Ser.). (Illus.). 540p. 1973. reprint ed. 39.95 (*0-405-04961-7*) Ayer.

Adventures in the Apache Country: A Tour through Arizona & Sonora, 1864. John R. Browne. LC 74-83332. 313p. reprint ed. pap. 89.30 (*0-8357-5202-X*, 2025551) Bks Demand.

Adventures in the Berkshires: Places to Go with Children. Patti Silver. 1993. pap. 7.95 (*0-936399-44-9*) Berkshire Hse.

Adventures in the Big Thicket. Ken Gire. (Illus.). 112p. (J). (gr. k-5). 1990. 14.99 (*0-929608-72-0*) Focus Family.

Adventures in the Biology Laboratory. 3rd ed. Daniel N. Anderson. (Illus.). vi, 107p. 1990. student ed. 10.00 (*0-942788-17-6*) Iris Visual.

Adventures in the Deeps of the Mind: The Cuchulain Cycle of W. B. Yeats. Barton Friedman. LC 76-45897. (Essays in Literature Ser.). 204p. 1977. 29.95x (*0-691-06325-7*) Princeton U Pr.

Adventures in the High Wind: Poetic Observations & Other Lore. Robert Nichols. 144p. (Orig.). (C). 1990. pap. 7.95 (*0-9627615-0-8*) Mntn Muse Pub.

Adventures in the Kitchen. Wolfgang Puck. (Illus.). 320p. 1991. 30.00 (*0-394-55895-2*) Random.

Adventures in the Land of Canaan. R. L. Berry. 128p. pap. 1.50 (*0-686-29096-8*) Faith Pub Hse.

Adventures in the Land of Me. Eva Thayer. (Illus.). 65p. (Orig.). (J). (gr. 4-8). 1989. student ed, pap. 6.95 (*0-9616432-4-2*) TES Pub.

Adventures in the Middle East: Excursions & Incursions. Donald N. Wilber. LC 86-8826. (Illus.). 256p. 1986. 17. 95 (*0-87850-053-7*) Darwin Pr.

Adventures in the Navy, in Education, Science, Engineering & the War: A Life Story. William F. Durand. LC 53-2031. 228p. reprint ed. pap. 65.00 (*0-8357-5203-8*, 2013306) Bks Demand.

Adventures in the Northern Wilderness. Kevin Siembieda et al. Ed. by Alex Marciniszyn. (Fantasy Ser.: Bk. IV). (Illus.). 96p. (Orig.). (YA). (gr. 8 up). 1989. pap. 9.95 (*0-916211-39-8*, 456) Palladium Bks.

***Adventures in the Santa Fe Trade, 1844-1847.** James J. Webb. Ed. by Ralph P. Bieber. LC 94-43638. (Illus.). 312p. 1995. pap. 12.00 (*0-8032-9772-6*, Bison Books) U of Nebr Pr.

Adventures in the Screen Trade: A Personal View of Hollywood & Screenwriting. William Goldman. LC 82-17602. 432p. (Orig.). 1989. 15.99 (*0-446-39117-4*) Warner Bks.

Adventures in the Skin Trade. Andrew Sinclair. LC 68-15883. 1968. 4.50 (*0-8112-0383-2*) New Directions.

Adventures in the Skin Trade & Other Stories. Dylan Thomas. LC 55-7367. (C). 1955. pap. 8.95 (*0-8112-0202-X*, NDP183) New Directions.

Adventures in the Space Trade or with a Richard Wilson Checklist. Richard Wilson. (Drumm Booklet Ser.: No. 23). 36p. (Orig.). 1986. pap. 2.00 (*0-936055-24-3*) C Drumm Bks.

Adventures in the Space Trade or with a Richard Wilson Checklist. limited ed. Richard Wilson. (Drumm Booklet Ser.: No. 23). 36p. (Orig.). 1986. 5.00 (*0-936055-25-1*) C Drumm Bks.

***Adventures in the Twilight Zone.** Ed. by Carol Serling. 336p. 1995. pap. 4.99 (*0-88677-662-7*) DAW Bks.

Adventures in the Unknown Interior of America. Alvar N. Cabeza de Vaca. Tr. & Anno. by Cyclone Covey. LC 82-21897. 160p. (C). 1983. pap. 9.95 (*0-8263-0656-X*) U of NM Pr.

Adventures in the West. Jane V. Barker & Sybil Downing. (Colorado Heritage Ser.). (Illus.). 40p. (J). reprint ed. pap. 5.95 (*1-878611-05-4*) Silver Rim Pr.

Adventures in the Wild. John G. Samson. 1990. 19.98 (*0-88486-034-5*) Arrowood Pr.

Adventures in the Wilderness. Clark Wissler. 1925. 100.00 (*0-686-83455-0*) Elliots Bks.

Adventures in the Wilderness. William H. Murray. Ed. by William K. Verner. LC 72-132972. (Illus.). 332p. 1989. reprint ed. pap. text ed. 13.95 (*0-8156-2466-2*) Syracuse U Pr.

Adventures in the Wilderness: The American Journals of Louis Antoine de Bougainville, 1756-1760. Louis A. Bougainville. Ed. & Tr. by Edward P. Hamilton. LC 64-11318. (American Exploration & Travel Ser.: Vol. 42). (Illus.). 384p. 1990. pap. 15.95 (*0-8061-2248-X*) U of Okla Pr.

Adventures in Thinking. Edith Neimark. 360p. (C). 1987. pap. text ed. 20.00 (*0-15-501895-7*) HB Coll Pubs.

Adventures in Tripoli. G. H. Griffin. 312p. 1984. 200.00 (*1-85077-010-7*, Darf Pubs Ltd) St Mut.

Adventures in Two Worlds. large type ed. A. J. Cronin. 599p. 1974. 15.95 (*0-85456-306-7*) Ulverscroft.

Adventures in Understanding. Manly P. Hall. pap. 10.00 (*0-89314-809-1*) Philos Res.

Adventures in Understanding. Lois Lenski. 1968. 4.95 (*0-9607778-1-4*) Friends Fla St.

Adventures in Understanding. deluxe ed. Lois Lenski. 1968. 12.50 (*0-9607778-2-2*) Friends Fla St.

Adventures in Unhistory: Conjectures on the Factual Foundations of Several Ancient Legends. Avram Davidson. (Illus.). 1993. 24.75 (*0-913896-29-2*) Owlswick Pr.

Adventures in Unhistory: Conjectures on the Factual Foundations of Several Ancient Legends. deluxe ed. Avram Davidson. (Illus.). 1993. 50.00 (*0-913896-33-0*) Owlswick Pr.

Adventures in UNIX Network Application. Bill Rieken. 464p. 1992. pap. text ed. 44.95 (*0-471-52858-7*) Wiley.

Adventures in UNIX Network Applications Programming. Bill Rieken & Lyle Weiman. (Illus.). 464p. 1992. text ed. 39.95 (*0-471-52859-5*) Wiley.

Adventures in Virtual Reality. Tom Hayward. (Illus.). 160p. (Orig.). 1993. disk, pap. 24.95 (*1-56529-208-1*) Que.

Adventures in West Virginia. Ann Stowers & Ellen Wilkerson. LC 88-70451. 320p. (Orig.). 1988. pap. 9.95 (*0-916383-59-8*) Aegina Pr.

Adventures in Windows. Bryan Affenberger. 1993. pap. 16. 95 (*1-55958-449-1*) Prima Pub.

Adventures in Wine Cookery. 2nd ed. California Winemakers Staff. Ed. by Donna Bottrell et al. (Wine Cookbook Ser.). (Illus.). 144p. 1986. pap. 7.95 (*0-932664-10-5*) Wine Appreciation.

Adventures in Wine Cookery by California Winemakers. Wine Advisory Board Staff. LC 65-27205. (Illus.). 1965. 5.95 (*0-685-22257-8*, WAB-2) Piper.

***Adventures in Woodturning: Techniques & Projects.** David Springett. (Illus.). 240p. 1995. pap. 24.95 (*0-946819-57-2*) Sterling.

Adventures in Yap. Clyman Otis. 1994. 13.95 (*0-533-10762-8*) Vantage.

Adventures in Your National Parks. Ed. by Donald J. Crump. (Books for World Explorers Series 10: No. 2). (J). (gr. 3-8). 1989. 8.95 (*0-87044-702-5*) Natl Geog.

Adventures in Your National Parks. National Geographic Society Staff. Ed. by Donald J. Crump. (Books for World Explorers Series 10: No. 2). (J). (gr. 3-8). 1994. pap. 12.50 (*0-87044-707-6*) Natl Geog.

Adventures in 3D. Doug Wolfgram. (Illus.). 224p. (Orig.). 1993. pap. 27.95 (*1-56529-355-X*) Que.

Adventures of a Bubble-Bellied Bloopy Droopy Detective. Vestavia Elementary School Fourth Grade Class & Marcille Cockrell. (Illus.). 32p. (J). (gr. k-5). 1989. pap. 3.95 (*0-943487-22-6*) Sevgo Pr.

Adventures of a Bus Driver. Harry Jordan & Kay Jordan. 81p. (C). 1989. text ed. 50.00 (*0-685-63534-1*, Pub. by Pentland Pr UK) St Mut.

Adventures of a Bystander. Peter F. Drucker. 360p. (C). 1994. pap. 21.95 (*1-56000-738-9*) Transaction Pubs.

***Adventures of a Chemist Collector.** Alfred Bader. (Illus.). 288p. 1995. 29.95 (*0-297-83461-4*, Pub. by Weidenfeld) Trafalgar.

Adventures of a Deep Sea Angler, Set. 2nd ed. R. C. Grey. (Zane Grey Famous Fishing Library). 300p. 1991. write for info. (*1-56416-084-X*) Derrydale Pr.

Adventures of a Fakir. Vsevolod V. Ivanov. LC 74-10085. (Soviet Literature in English Translation Ser.). viii, 300p. 1974. reprint ed. 20.35 (*0-88355-172-1*) Hyperion Conn.

Adventures of a Freelancer: The Literary Exploits & Autobiography of Stanton A. Coblentz. Stanton A. Coblentz & Jeffrey M. Elliot. Ed. by Scott A. Burgess. LC 93-189506. (Borgo Bioviews Ser.: No. 2). 160p. 1993. lib. bdg. 27.00 (*0-89370-338-9*, 10323058); pap. 17.00x (*0-89370-438-5*, 10323058) Borgo Pr.

Adventures of a Frontier Naturalist: The Life & Times of Dr. Gideon Lincecum. Ed. by Jerry B. Lincecum. LC 94-11122. (Illus.). 344p. 1994. 35.00 (*0-89096-592-7*); pap. 14.95 (*0-89096-603-6*) Tex A&M Univ Pr.

Adventures of a Greenhorn: An Autobiographical Novel. Robert Reitzel. Tr. by Jacob Erhardt. LC 91-28511. (New German-American Studies - Neue Deutsch-Amerikanische Studien: Vol. 3). 94p. (C). 1992. text ed. 35.95 (*0-8204-1330-5*) P Lang Pubs.

Adventures of a High School Hunk. Gordon Hoban. LC 89-92322. 350p. (Orig.). 1990. pap. 16.95 (*0-944204-08-2*) Omniun.

Adventures of a Jeeponary. Carolyn London. (J). (ps-3). 1982. pap. 2.50 (*0-915374-19-6*) Rapids Christian.

Adventures of a Librarian. Harlan Ballard. 1973. 59.95 (*0-87968-579-4*) Gordon Pr.

Adventures of a Literary Historian: A Collection of His Writings Presented to H. C. Lancaster by His Former Students & Other Friends in Anticipation of His Sixtieth Birthday November 10, 1942. Henry C. Lancaster. LC 68-14907. (Essay Index Reprint Ser.). 1977. 23.95 (*0-8369-0605-5*) Ayer.

Adventures of a Mathematician. S. M. Ulam. (Illus.). 384p. 1991. pap. 18.00 (*0-520-07154-9*) U CA Pr.

Adventures of a Missionary: Or, Rivers of Water in a Dry Place. Robert Moffat. LC 70-89387. (Black Heritage Library Collection). 1977. 17.95 (*0-8369-8635-0*) Ayer.

Adventures of a Mountain Man: The Narrative of Zenas Leonard. Zenas Leonard. Ed. by Milo M. Quaife. LC 78-17427. (Illus.). xx, 274p. 1978. reprint ed. 25.00 (*0-8032-2853-8*); reprint ed. pap. 9.95 (*0-8032-7903-5*) U of Nebr Pr.

Adventures of a Nature Guide & Essays in Interpretation. 2nd ed. Enos A. Mills. Ed. by Enda M. Kiley & Michael J. Goc. (Illus.). 248p. 1991. reprint ed. pap. 10.95 (*0-938627-12-0*) New Past Pr.

Adventures of a New York Telegraph Boy. Horatio Alger, Jr. (Works of Horatio Alger Jr.). 1989. reprint ed. lib. bdg. 79.00 (*0-685-27609-0*) Rprt Serv.

Adventures of a Novelist. Gertrude Atherton. 1992. reprint ed. lib. bdg. 75.00 (*0-7812-5001-3*) Rprt Serv.

Adventures of a Novelist. Gertrude F. Atherton. Ed. by Annette K. Baxter. LC 79-8769. (Signal Lives Ser.). 1980. reprint ed. lib. bdg. 68.95 (*0-405-12819-3*) Ayer.

Adventures of a Parapsychologist. Susan Blackmore. LC 86-20466. 249p. 1986. 28.95 (*0-87975-360-9*) Prometheus Bks.

Adventures of a Psychic. Sylvia Brown & Antoinette May. (Illus.). 256p. 1991. reprint ed. pap. 4.99 (*0-451-16987-5*, Sig) NAL-Dutton.

Adventures of a San Francisco Newsman. Baron Muller. 100p. 1991. pap. 8.95 (*0-917583-21-3*) Lexikos.

Adventures of a Self-Managing Team. Mark Kelly. (Illus.). 121p. (Orig.). 1990. pap. 15.00 (*1-882133-02-1*) Barefoot Pr.

Adventures of a Self-Managing Team. Mark Kelly. LC 91-71465. 120p. (Orig.). 1991. pap. 16.95 (*0-88390-058-0*) Pfeiffer & Co.

Adventures of a Treasure Hunter: A Rare Bookman in Search of American History. Charles P. Everitt. 296p. 1987. reprint ed. pap. 12.50 (*0-916638-12-X*) Meyerbooks.

Adventures of a Verbivore. Richard Lederer. LC 93-32287. 1994. 21.00 (*0-671-70941-0*) PB.

***Adventures of a Verbivore.** Richard Lederer. Ed. by Jane Rosenman. 288p. 1995. pap. 10.00 (*0-671-70942-9*) PB.

Adventures of a White-Collar Man. Alfred P. Sloan, Jr. Ed. by Boyden Sparkes. LC 74-126258. (Select Bibliographies Reprint Ser.). 1977. 21.95 (*0-8369-5485-8*) Ayer.

Adventures of a "Wild" Plants Woman: In Pursuit of Native Plant Preservation. Norma Phillips. LC 88-51160. (Illus.). 236p. (Orig.). (C). 1988. pap. text ed. 12.95 (*0-9622758-1-6*) Little Bridge.

Adventures of a Woman Homesteader: The Life & Letters of Elinore Pruitt Stewart. Susanne K. George. LC 92-1206. (Illus.). xiv, 227p. (C). 1992. pap. 9.95 (*0-8032-7042-9*) U of Nebr Pr.

Adventures of a Young Swiss in California: The Gold Rush Account of Theophile de Rutte. Theophile De Rutte. Ed. & Tr. by Mary G. Paquette. (Illus.). 128p. 1992. lib. bdg. 40.00 (*0-9617334-2-X*) Sacto Bk Collectors.

Adventures of a Younger Son. Edward J. Trelawny. LC 70-177569. (Illus.). reprint ed. 45.00 (*0-404-07448-0*) AMS Pr.

Adventures of a Younger Son. Edward J. Trelawny. (BCL1-PR English Literature Ser.). 544p. 1992. reprint ed. lib. bdg. 99.00 (*0-7812-7520-2*) Rprt Serv.

Adventures of Achilles Jones. (Orig.). 1979. 10.00 (*0-914476-81-5*); pap. 5.00 (*0-914476-80-7*) Thorp Springs.

Adventures of Albert, the Running Bear. Barbara Isenberg & Susan Wolf. (J). (gr. k-3). 1985. audio 22.95 (*0-941078-90-6*); audio, pap. 14.95 (*0-941078-88-4*) Live Oak Media.

Adventures of Albert the Running Bear. Barbara Isenberg & Susan Wolf. LC 82-1311. (Illus.). 32p. (J). (ps-3). 1982. pap. 6.95 (*0-89919-125-8*, Clarion Bks) HM.

Adventures of Albert, the Running Bear, 4 bks., Set. Barbara Isenberg & Susan Wolf. (J). (gr. k-3). 1985. audio, pap. 35.95 (*0-941078-89-2*) Live Oak Media.

Adventures of Alexander Barclay: Mountain Man in Colorado & New Mexico & Builder of Barclay's Fort on the Santa Fe Trail in 1848. Ed. by George P. Hammond. 1976. 50.00 (*0-912094-19-2*) Old West.

Adventures of Ali Baba Bernstein. Johanna Hurwitz. LC 84-27387. (Illus.). 96p. (J). (gr. 2-5). 1985. 15.00 (*0-688-04161-2*); lib. bdg. 14.93 (*0-688-04345-3*) Morrow Jr Bks.

***Adventures of Ali Baba Bernstein.** Johanna Hurwitz. 96p. (J). 1995. pap. 3.50 (*0-380-72349-2*, Camelot) Avon.

***Adventures of Ali Baba Bernstein.** Elizabeth Spencer. Ed. by J. Friedland & R. Kessler. (Novel-Ties Ser.). (J). (gr. 2-4). 1995. pap. text ed. 15.95 (*1-56982-274-3*) Lrn Links.

Adventures of Alice in Nutritionland: A Nutritional Storybook for Children. Larry Thill. (Illus.). 31p. (Orig.). (J). (gr. k-6). 1989. pap. 8.00 (*0-317-93500-3*) Impressive Pubns.

Adventures of Alonso: Containing Some Striking Anecdotes of the Present Minister of Portugal. Thomas A. Digges. (C). 1986. reprint ed. pap. text ed. 5.95 (*0-8290-1896-4*) Irvington.

Adventures of Alonso: Containing Some Striking Anecdotes of the Present Minister of Portugal. Thomas A. Digges. LC 43-13609. (Monograph Ser.: No. 18). 1943. reprint ed. 12.00 (*0-930060-01-6*) US Cath Hist.

Adventures of Alonso: Continuing Some Striking Anecdotes of the Present Minister of Portugal. Thomas A. Digges. LC 74-104439. 1988. 11.00 (*0-8398-0362-1*) Irvington.

***Adventures of Alonzo Woodchuck.** Robert E. Klein. (Illus.). 65p. (J). (gr. 3-6). 1995. pap. 3.95 (*1-896209-08-4*, Pub. by Bayeaux Arts CN) Trafalgar.

Adventures of Amos 'n' Andy: A Social History of an American Phenomenon. Melvin P. Ely. 350p. 1991. text ed. 27.95 (*0-02-909502-6*) Free Pr.

Adventures of Amos 'n' Andy: A Social History of an American Phenomenon. Melvin P. Ely. 322p. 1992. pap. 12.95 (*0-02-909503-4*) Free Pr.

***Adventures of an Attorney in Search of Practice.** Samuel Warren. 422p. 1994. reprint ed. lib. bdg. 45.00x (*0-8377-2777-4*) Rothman.

Adventures of an Innocent in the Spanish Civil War. Antonio Candela. 224p. (C). 1988. 65.00 (*1-85200-020-1*, Pub. by United Writers Pubns UK) St Mut.

Adventures of an Older Man. David G. Cohen. Ed. by James B. Van Treese. Tr. by Ingram. 208p. 1994. pap. 8.95 (*1-56901-123-0*) NW Pub.

Adventures of Andrew Byerly, American Frontiersman, Ranger & Courier. Charles R. Freeble, Jr. (Illus.). 72p. (Orig.). 1993. pap. 8.95 (*0-934616-47-7*) Valkyrie Pub Hse.

Adventures of Antar: An Early Arab Epic Approaches to Arabic. Norris. 1980. 39.95 (*0-85668-161-X*, Pub. by Aris & Phillips UK) David Brown.

Adventures of Anybody. Richard Bandler. LC 93-84506. 1993. 12.95 (*0-916990-29-X*) META Pubns.

Adventures of Augie March. Saul Bellow. 544p. 1984. pap. 11.00 (*0-14-007272-1*, Penguin Bks) Viking Penguin.

Adventures of Baby Penrose-the Richest Infant in the World: Being the Tales of Life in Silicone City in the Early Nineteen Nineties. 2nd ed. Daniel Dove. (Orig.). 1980. pap. 10.00 (*0-686-27614-0*) Tetragrammaton.

Adventures of Baron Munchausen: The Novel. Terry Gilliam & Charles McKeown. (Illus.). 192p. (Orig.). (J). 1989. pap. 12.95 (*1-55783-039-8*) Applause Theatre Bk Pubs.

Adventures of Baron Munchausen: The Screenplay. Charles McKeown & Terry Gilliam. (Illus.). 256p. (Orig.). 1989. pap. 8.95 (*1-55783-041-X*) Applause Theatre Bk Pubs.

***Adventures of Beatrix Potter & Her Friends - Musical.** Adapt. by Joseph Robinette. Date not set. 5.50 (*0-87129-523-7*, A56) Dramatic Pub.

Adventures of Belzoni. Belzoni. 1988. reprint ed. lib. bdg. 75.00 (*0-7812-0342-2*) Rprt Serv.

Adventures of Bermuda. Henry C. Wilkinson. 1976. lib. bdg. 34.95 (*0-8490-1402-6*) Gordon Pr.

Adventures of Big Bird in Dinosaur Days. Sarah Roberts. LC 83-61891. (Sesame Street Mini-Storybooks Ser.). (Illus.). 32p. (J). (ps-3). 1984. pap. 1.50 (*0-394-85926-X*) Random Bks Yng Read.

Adventures of Big-Foot Wallace, Texas Ranger & Hunter. John C. Duval. 1993. reprint ed. lib. bdg. 75.00 (*0-7812-5877-4*) Rprt Serv.

***Adventures of Billy Bee: Billy & Friends.** Peter Thomas. (Illus.). 32p. (J). (gr. k-6). 1995. 14.95 (*1-886919-00-3*) Billy Bee.

Adventures of Bishop Delgazo. Tom Nelson. LC 90-72008. (Illus.). 96p. (Orig.). 1992. pap. 8.00 (*1-56002-089-X*, Univ Edtns) Aegina Pr.

Adventures of Blaze. Paul Tell. LC 92-80452. (Illus.). 64p. (J). (gr. 2-6). 1992. lib. bdg. 12.95 (*1-878893-19-X*); pap. 5.95 (*1-878893-18-1*) Telcraft Bks.

Adventures of Bob White. Thornton W. Burgess. 18.95 (*0-88411-776-6*, Aeonian Pr) Amereon Ltd.

Adventures of Bob White. Thornton Burgess. (J). 1992. reprint ed. lib. bdg. 17.95 (*0-89966-994-8*) Buccaneer Bks.

Adventures of Bobby Coon. Thornton W. Burgess. (J). 18. 95 (*0-8488-0383-3*) Amereon Ltd.

Adventures of Bobby Coon. Thornton Burgess. (J). 1992. reprint ed. lib. bdg. 17.95 (*0-89966-992-1*) Buccaneer Bks.

***Adventures of Bobby Raccoon.** Thornton W. Burgess. LC 94-44605. (Illus.). 96p. (J). 1995. pap. text ed. 1.00 (*0-486-28617-7*) Dover.

Adventures of Boo: The Journey Begins. Julie Cox. LC 90-62757. (Illus.). 32p. (J). 1990. write for info. (*0-9627586-0-4*); audio write for info. (*0-9627586-1-2*) Mango Entrps.

Adventures of Boo, Vol. 2: Circus. Julia Cox. (Illus.). 32p. (J). 1992. write for info. (*0-9627586-2-0*) Mango Entrps.

Adventures of Boone Barnaby. Joe Cottonwood. 224p. (J). (gr. 4-7). 1990. 13.95 (*0-590-43546-9*) Scholastic Inc.

Adventures of Boone Barnaby. Joe Cottonwood. (J). 1992. pap. 2.95 (*0-590-43547-7*, Apple Paperbacks) Scholastic Inc.

Adventures of Bro & Tracy. Joyce Fay. 1993. 16.95 (*0-00-255111-X*) Collins SF.

***Adventures of Buck Felner.** John McPherson. LC 94-43860. 1995. pap. 7.99 (*0-310-48681-5*) Zondervan.

Adventures of Budgie. Duchess of York. LC 92-11218. (Illus.). (J). 1992. audio 20.00 (*0-685-59712-1*, S&S Bks Young Read) S&S Childrens.

***Adventures of Budgie.** deluxe ed. Duchess of York, pseud. (Illus.). (J). (ps-1). 1992. boxed 60.00 (*0-671-79392-6*, S&S Bks Young Read) S&S Childrens.

Adventures of Budgie. limited ed. Duchess of York. LC 92-11218. (Illus.). (J). 1992. 60.00 (*0-685-59711-3*, S&S Bks Young Read) S&S Childrens.

***Adventures of Buffalo Bill & Cody: Meeting in the Mountains. Elisabeth P. Longbotham & Jack H. Longbotham. (Young West Collection: Bk. 1). (Illus.). 28p. (J). (ps-3). 1995. 8.95 (*0-9645947-0-6*) West Heritage Pub. THE ADVENTURES OF BUFFALO BILL & CODY is a delightful story of two real live buffalo written as children's fiction. It is a tale which centers around the basic instincts of the largest native mammal of the American West. This book will be enjoyed by any age child who loves animal stories. It will stir their imagination from the very beginning through an encounter with the traditional enemy-the wolf-& on to their lifetime companionship, it will excite the youngster. This first book of the Young West Collection deals with the adventures of these two buffalo. It provides understanding of one of America's most beloved animals, which almost became extinct. The authors have written & designed the book for the young reader at pre-school & primary grade levels. At the same time, it provides a learning opportunity for**

An Asterisk (*) at the beginning of an entry indicates that the title is appearing in BIP for the first time.

the early reader to make the association & meaning between words & pictures. The beautiful four color illustrations preserve both color & dimension & capture the authenticity of the Buffalo. The authors are Christian educators & writers who own their own ranch where quarter horses, cattle & buffalo are raised - including Buffalo Bill & Cody. To order: Western Heritage Publishers, P.O. Box 3703, Abilene, TX 79604. Phone: 915-893-4345. ***Publisher Provided Annotation.***

Adventures of Bum & Carey Bear: A Christmas Tale. Robert E. Perron. (Illus.). 48p. (J). 1994. pap. 8.00 (*0-8059-3578-9*) Dorrance.

Adventures of Buster Bear. Thornton W. Burgess. (J). 19.95 (*0-8488-0354-X*) Amereon Ltd.

Adventures of Buster Bear. Thornton Burgess. (Bedtime Story Bks.). (J). 1986. reprint ed. lib. bdg. 17.95 (*0-89966-525-X*) Buccaneer Bks.

Adventures of Buster Bear. Thornton W. Burgess. LC 92-36949. (Children's Thrift Classics Ser.). (Illus.). 96p. (J). 1993. reprint ed. pap. 1.00 (*0-486-27564-7*) Dover.

Adventures of Buster the Puppy, 6 vols., Set. Hisako Madokoro. (Illus.). 96p. (J). (gr. k-2). 1991. lib. bdg. 103.60 (*0-8368-0488-0*) Gareth Stevens Inc.

Adventures of C S Elliot. abr. ed. Seward Whitfield. 242p. 1994. pap. 9.95 (*1-56901-139-7*) NW Pub.

Adventures of Captain America, No. 1. Fabian Nicieza et al. 48p. 1991. 4.95 (*0-87135-811-5*) Marvel Entmnt.

Adventures of Captain America, No. 2. Fabian Nicieza et al. 48p. 1991. 4.95 (*0-87135-812-3*) Marvel Entmnt.

Adventures of Captain America, No. 3. Fabian Nicieza et al. 48p. 1991. 4.95 (*0-87135-813-1*) Marvel Entmnt.

Adventures of Captain Bonneville. Washington Irving. 1976. 29.95 (*0-8488-0286-1*) Amereon Ltd.

Adventures of Captain Bonneville. Washington Irving. (Illus.). 375p. 1954. 19.95 (*0-8323-0100-0*) Binford Mort.

Adventures of Captain Bonneville, U. S. A: In the Rocky Mountains & the Far West. Washington Irving. Ed. by Edgeley W. Todd. LC 86-40088. (Illus.). 496p. 1986. reprint ed. pap. 14.95 (*0-8061-2015-0*) U of Okla Pr.

Adventures of Captain Horn. Frank R. Stockton. 23.95 (*0-8488-0320-5*) Amereon Ltd.

***Adventures of Captain Morgan & Other Stories & Poems.** Michael Normandin. (J). 1995. 8.95 (*0-8062-5267-7*) Carlton.

Adventures of Captain Rhema. rev. ed. Barbara G. Castle. LC 91-6082. (J). (gr. 5-9). 1991. pap. 4.00 (*0-915541-61-0*) Star Bks Inc.

Adventures of Captain Simon Suggs. Johnson J. Hooper. (Southern Classics Ser.). (Illus.). 280p. (C). 1993. reprint ed. pap. 10.95 (*1-879941-16-3*) J S Sanders.

Adventures of Captain Simon Suggs, Late of the Tallapoosa Volunteers: Together with "Taking the Census" & Other Alabama Sketches. Johnson J. Hooper. (Library of Alabama Classics). 272p. 1993. pap. 14.95 (*0-8173-0706-0*) U of Ala Pr.

Adventures of Cardigan. Frederick Nebel. LC 88-5233. (Dime Detective Bk.). 208p. 1988. pap. 9.95 (*0-89296-950-4*) Mysterious Pr.

Adventures of Charlie the Cat. Christina Singh. (Flying Classics Ser.). 1990. pap. 6.95 (*0-938991-69-8*) Colonial Pr AL.

Adventures of Chatrat. Venetia Spicer. (Illus.). 48p. (J). 1981. 9.95 (*0-7043-2269-2*, Pub. by Quartet UK) Charles River Bks.

Adventures of Chatterer the Red Squirrel. Thornton W. Burgess. (J). 18.95 (*0-8488-0376-0*) Amereon Ltd.

Adventures of Chatterer the Red Squirrel. unabridged ed. Thornton W. Burgess. LC 92-14627. (Children's Thrift Classics Ser.). (Illus.). 96p. (J). 1992. reprint ed. pap. 1.00 (*0-486-27399-7*) Dover.

Adventures of Christabel Crocodile. Helga Knuppel. LC 90-21029. (Illus.). 32p. (J). (ps-5). 1991. 13.95 (*0-940793-74-1*, Crocodile Bks) Interlink Pub.

Adventures of Christopher Bear & His Friends. Anne Gerrard. (Illus.). 32p. (J). (gr. 3). 1993. pap. 8.95 (*0-8059-3329-8*) Dorrance.

Adventures of Christopher Hawkins. Christopher Hawkins. LC 67-29042. (Eyewitness Accounts of the American Revolution Ser., No. 1). (Illus.). 1976. reprint ed. 28.95 (*0-405-01111-3*) Ayer.

Adventures of Clifford the Big Red Dog. Norman Bridwell. (Comes to Life Bks.). 16p. (J). (ps-2). 1994. write for info. (*1-883366-42-9*) YES Ent.

Adventures of Clyde Cockroach. Dolores Bersen. 26p. (J). (ps-4). 1994. 13.95 (*0-9640986-0-1*); lib. bdg. 14.95 (*0-9640986-1-X*); pap. 4.95 (*0-9640986-4-4*) DUB Pubng.

Adventures of Colonel Gracchus Vanderbomb. John B. Jones. (Notable American Authors Ser.). 1992. reprint ed. lib. bdg. 75.00 (*0-7812-3517-0*) Rprt Serv.

Adventures of Connie & Diego. Garcia. (J). (gr. 4-7). 1994. pap. 6.95 (*0-89239-124-3*) Childrens Book Pr.

Adventures of Connie & Diego Audiocassette. Ed. by Anna Olivarez. (ENG & SPA.). (J). 1989. 8.95 (*0-89239-051-4*) Childrens Book Pr.

Adventures of Connie & Diego (Los aventuras de Connie y Diego) Maria Garcia. LC 86-17132. (Fifth World Tales Ser.). (Illus.). 32p. (ENG & SPA.). (J). (gr. 2-9). 1987. 13.95 (*0-89239-028-X*) Childrens Book Pr.

Adventures of Connie & Diego Read-Along. Maria Garcia. (J). 1988. audio 22.95 (*0-89239-033-6*) Childrens Book Pr.

***Adventures of Crawfish Dan.** Dustin Green. 36p. (J). 1992. pap. 5.00 (*1-886210-04-7*) Tyketoon Yng Author.

Adventures of Crawfish-Man. Timothy J. Edler. (Tim Edler's Tales from the Atchafalaya Ser.). (Illus.). 40p. (J). (gr. k-8). 1979. pap. 6.00 (*0-931108-04-7*) Little Cajun Bks.

Adventures of Curious Eric: Learning Concepts. Marilyn J. Shearer. LC 90-60397. (Illus.). 16p. (J). (ps-6). 1990. 19.95 (*0-685-33064-8*); pap. 10.95 (*1-878389-01-7*) L Ashley & Joshua.

***Adventures of Curious George, 3 Vols., Set.** H. A. Rey. 1995. pap. 10.00 (*0-395-73518-1*) HM.

Adventures of Danny Meadow Mouse. Thornton W. Burgess. (J). 18.95 (*0-8488-0377-9*) Amereon Ltd.

Adventures of Danny Meadow Mouse. Thornton W. Burgess. LC 92-36950. (Illus.). 96p. (J). 1993. reprint ed. pap. 1.00 (*0-486-27565-5*) Dover.

Adventures of David Simple: Containing an Acocunt of His travels Through the Cities of London & Westminster in the Search of a Real Friend. Sarah Fielding. (World's Classics Ser.). (Illus.). 466p. 1987. pap. 8.95 (*0-19-281766-3*) OUP.

***Adventures of Dinkytown Daycare Kids: Believing in Yourself.** Bob Williams. Ed. by Jacob R. Miles, 3rd. (Illus.). 38p. (J). 1995. text ed. 14.99 (*0-9635529-3-7*) Cult Exchange.

Adventures of Diode Dude. T. L. Hutson & B. K. Hixson. 60p. 1992. pap. text ed. 12.99 (*1-57156-009-2*) Wild Goose UT.

Adventures of Doctor Eszterhazy. Avram Davidson. (Illus.). 1991. 24.50 (*0-913896-28-4*) Owlswick Pr.

Adventures of Doctor Eszterhazy. deluxe ed. Avram Davidson. (Illus.). 1991. 50.00 (*0-913896-30-6*) Owlswick Pr.

Adventures of Dolly Dingle Paper Dolls. Grace G. Drayton. (J). 1985. pap. 3.95 (*0-486-24809-7*) Dover.

***Adventures of Donnechad's Piper.** Edith S. Weigand. LC 95-90281. (Illus.). vi, 76p. (Orig.). (J). (ps-3). 1995. pap. 12.95 (*0-9618904-3-6*) Zhera Pubns.

Adventures of Down & Out Dawg. James Sturm. 1993. pap. 8.95 (*0-9626258-5-X*) Cheshire Iguana.

***Adventures of Dr. Alphabet: 104 Unusual Ways to Write Poetry in the Classroom & the Community.** Dave Morice. (Illus.). 276p. (Orig.). 1995. pap. 15.95 (*0-915924-44-7*) Tchrs & Writers Coll.

Adventures of Dr. Huckleberry. E. R. Huckleberry. (Illus.). 288p. 1980. 7.95 (*0-87595-025-6*) Oregon Hist.

Adventures of Dudley Dormouse. Judy Taylor. LC 91-58717. (Illus.). 80p. (J). (ps up). 1992. 9.95 (*1-56402-043-6*) Candlewick Pr.

Adventures of Dusty. M. M. Dee. LC 84-81557. (Illus.). 48p. (J). (gr. k-4). 1985. 9.95 (*0-937460-14-1*) Hendrick-Long.

***Adventures of Dusty Sourdough: A Gift for Dusty.** Glen E. Guy. Ed. by Sandy I. Guy. (Illus.). 54p. (Orig.). 1994. pap. 5.95 (*0-9644491-0-2*) Old Alaska.

Adventures of Dusty Sourdough: The Trail to Wrangell, Vol. 2. Glen Guy. (Illus.). 152p. (Orig.). (J). 1995. pap. 7.95 (*0-9644491-3-7*) Old Alaska. THE ADVENTURES OF DUSTY SOURDOUGH is a story for all ages. Travel along the trails of THE LAST FRONTIER, on Dusty's trail to destiny. Through Dusty's eyes you will feel & see Alaska in the 1800s. Ride down the white waters of the Kenai River, come face to face with a raging grizzly & even live through a ground shaking earthquake. Be there when he finally marries his love, Aura Lee. Enjoy some of the well-known characters he meets along the way (Soapy Smith, Wyatt Earp, One Eyed Reilly & others). Fall in love with his great wolf dog, Shadow Spirit. Sit high on a mountain pass, watching a majestic Eagle soar in the azure blue skies. In Dusty's first book (A GIFT OF DUSTY ISBN 0-9644491-0-1) you found out what it was like to get trapped in a blizzard. This time look death in the face in another form. Heighten your enjoyment of these fast moving adventure stories with the compatible, dramatized version of them, available on audio cassette. Be sure to travel along with Dusty & Aura Lee on other forthcoming adventures, soon to be available wherever fine books are sold. For more information, or to order contact: Old Alaska Today, P.O. Box 201355, Anchorage, AK 99520-1355. Phone (907) 345-6811.** ***Publisher Provided Annotation.

Adventures of Ecomunk: Mr. Beaver Builds a Dam. D. Morgans Bell. (J). 1992. 8.95 (*0-533-10212-X*) Vantage.

Adventures of Eggbert Egghead. Michelle Olson. Ed. by James B. Van Treese. Tr. by Ingram. (Illus.). (J). 1993. 9.95 (*1-880416-27-1*) NW Pub.

Adventures of Ernie & Bert at the South Pole. Dan Elliott. LC 84-60187. (Sesame Street Mini-Storybooks Ser.). (Illus.). 32p. (J). (ps-3). 1984. pap. 1.50 (*0-394-86299-6*) Random Bks Yng Read.

Adventures of Ernie & Bert in Twiddlebug Land. Dan Elliott. LC 83-61719. (Sesame Street Mini-Storybooks Ser.). (Illus.). 32p. (J). (ps-3). 1984. pap. 1.50 (*0-394-85925-1*) Random Bks Yng Read.

Adventures of Eros & Psyche. I. M. Richardson. LC 82-16057. (Illus.). 32p. (J). (gr. 4-8). 1983. lib. bdg. 11.79 (*0-89375-861-2*); pap. text ed. 2.95 (*0-89375-862-0*) Troll Assocs.

Adventures of Ferdinand Count Fathom. Tobias Smollett. Ed. by Jerry C. Beasley. LC 87-26368. (Works of Tobias Smollett Ser.). (Illus.). 504p. 1988. 40.00 (*0-8203-1010-7*) U of Ga Pr.

Adventures of Ferdinand Count Fathom. Tobias Smollett. Ed. by Jerry C. Beasley. LC 87-26368. (Works of Tobias Smollett Ser.). (Illus.). 528p. 1992. pap. 20.00 (*0-8203-1435-8*) U of Ga Pr.

Adventures of Ferdinand Count Fathom. Tobias G. Smollett. (Classics Ser.). 512p. 1990. pap. 10.95 (*0-14-043307-4*, Penguin Classics) Viking Penguin.

Adventures of Finspot. Zane Grey. 1976. 19.95 (*0-8488-0805-3*) Amereon Ltd.

***Adventures of Fred & Ned.** Cheri Moser. 1995. 9.95 (*0-8062-5300-2*) Carlton.

Adventures of Freddie. John H. Perry. (C). 1989. 30.00 (*0-7223-2347-6*, Pub. by A H S Ltd UK) St Mut.

Adventures of Frenchy & Joe. Lisa K. (YA). 1993. 12.95 (*0-533-10415-7*) Vantage.

***Adventures of Froggy.** H. L. Wehrle, Jr. (Illus.). x, 170p. (Orig.). (J). (gr. 3 up). 1995. pap. 12.95 (*1-887285-00-8*) Noggleman Pr.

***Adventures of Gesso Martin.** Karl Roeseler. 111p. (Orig.). 1994. pap. 8.95 (*0-9639192-1-0*) Trip St Pr.

Adventures of Gilly, the Guitar, Bk. 1. Cathy Ellis. (Illus.). 40p. (J). (ps-2). 1991. student ed, audio 15.95 (*1-879542-04-8*) Ellis Family Mus.

Adventures of Gluckel of Hameln. Bea Stadtler. LC 67-18814. (J). (gr. 6-10). 3.75 (*0-8381-0731-1*, 10-731) United Syn Bk.

Adventures of God. Richard Morris. 1993. 2.00 (*0-939520-04-4*) Ghost Dance.

Adventures of Grandfather Frog. Thornton W. Burgess. (J). (gr. 5-6). 18.95 (*0-88411-777-4*, Aeonian Pr) Amereon Ltd.

Adventures of Grandfather Frog. unabridged ed. Thornton W. Burgess. LC 92-13146. (Children's Thrift Classics Ser.). (Illus.). 96p. (J). 1992. reprint ed. pap. text ed. 1.00 (*0-486-27400-4*) Dover.

Adventures of Greek Heroes. Mollie McLean & Anne Wiseman. LC 61-10628. (Merit Ser.). (Illus.). 192p. (J). (ps-3). 1973. 16.95 (*0-395-06913-0*, Sandpiper); pap. 5.95 (*0-685-42189-9*, Sandpiper) HM.

Adventures of Growing Up. Arletta R. Howell. Ed. by James B. Van Treese. 80p. 1994. pap. 7.95 (*1-56901-195-8*) NW Pub.

Adventures of Growl. Walter F. Zeltmann. LC 89-51220. 175p. 1989. 24.90 (*0-9622705-1-2*) Yellow Hook Pr.

Adventures of Grubber Bug. William G. Duffy, Jr. LC 82-71946. 45p. (J). (ps-3). 1984. pap. 3.50 (*0-943864-33-X*) Davenport.

***Adventures of Hacker Vols. 1-3, 3 bks., Set.** Harry Heuston. (Illus.). 480p. (J). (gr. 4-8). 1995. pap. 9.25 (*1-57414-014-0*) Value Network.

Adventures of Harlequin. William Glennon & Susan Grote. 37p. (Orig.). 1963. reprint ed. 3.45 (*0-87129-058-8*, A42) Dramatic Pub.

Adventures of Harry Franco: A Tale of the Great Panic. Charles F. Briggs. 1972. reprint ed. 26.50 (*0-8422-8010-3*) Irvington.

Adventures of Harry Franco: A Tale of the Great Panic. Charles F. Briggs. (C). 1986. reprint ed. pap. text ed. 7.95 (*0-8290-1898-0*) Irvington.

Adventures of Harry Richmond. George Meredith. Ed. by L. T. Hergenhan. LC 78-88088. xxxviii, 613p. 1970. 35.00 (*0-8032-0712-3*) U of Nebr Pr.

Adventures of Heart Longing. Julie Klassen. LC 86-82881. 128p. (J). (gr. 1-6). 1987. pap. 2.95 (*0-88243-557-4*, 02-0557) Gospel Pub.

Adventures of Henry Turnbuckle: Detective Comedies by Jack Ritchie. Ed. by Francis M. Nevins, Jr. & Martin H. Greenberg. LC 86-31372. (Mystery Makers Ser.). 386p. 1987. 29.95 (*0-8093-1397-9*) S Ill U Pr.

Adventures of Herby. William F. Burt. (J). 1993. 7.95 (*0-8062-4782-7*) Carlton.

Adventures of Hercules. I. M. Richardson. LC 82-16557. (Illus.). 32p. (J). (gr. 4-8). 1983. lib. bdg. 11.79 (*0-89375-865-5*); pap. text ed. 2.95 (*0-89375-866-3*) Troll Assocs.

***Adventures of Herman & Hurby.** Ingrid D. Larson. LC 94-90281. (Illus.). 64p. (Orig.). (J). 1995. pap. 10.00 (*1-56002-485-2*, Univ Edtns) Aegina Pr.

***Adventures of Hershel of Ostropol.** Illus. by Trina S. Hyman. 64p. (J). 1995. pap. 15.95 (*0-8234-1210-5*) Holiday.

Adventures of Huckleberry Finn. Samuel L. Clemens. Ed. by E. Sculley Bradley et al. LC 76-30648. (Critical Editions Ser.). (C). 1977. pap. text ed. 7.95 (*0-393-09146-5*) Norton.

Adventures of Huckleberry Finn. Clare Dwiggins. Ed. by Chris Ulm & Mickie Villa. (Illus.). 177p. 1990. pap. 12.95 (*0-944735-55-X*) Malibu Graphics.

***Adventures of Huckleberry Finn.** Gerald Graff & James Phelan. (Case Studies in Contemporary Criticism). 528p. 1995. 35.00 (*0-312-12261-6*) St Martin.

Adventures of Huckleberry Finn. Randal Myler. 1990. 4.95 (*0-87129-141-X*, A50) Dramatic Pub.

Adventures of Huckleberry Finn. Mark Twain. LC 85-9576. (J). (gr. 5 up). 1962. pap. 2.75 (*0-8049-0004-3*, CL-4) Airmont.

Adventures of Huckleberry Finn. Mark Twain. Ed. by Lionel Trilling. LC 48-8523. (Rinehart Editions Ser.). 274p. (C). 1948. pap. text ed. 19.75 (*0-03-009770-3*) HB Coll Pubs.

Adventures of Huckleberry Finn. Mark Twain. 288p. (YA). (gr. 9-12). 1959. pap. 2.95 (*0-451-52373-3*, Sig Classics) NAL-Dutton.

***Adventures of Huckleberry Finn.** Mark Twain. (Puffin Classics Ser.). 336p. (J). 1995. pap. 3.50 (*0-14-036676-8*) Puffin Bks.

Adventures of Huckleberry Finn. Mark Twain. LC 92-10194. (Children's Classics Ser.). (Illus.). (YA). 1992. 12.99 (*0-517-08128-8*, Child Classics) Random Hse Value.

Adventures of Huckleberry Finn. Mark Twain. 1993. 15.50 (*0-679-42470-9*, Modern Lib) Random.

Adventures of Huckleberry Finn. Mark Twain. (World's Great Bks.). 325p. 1991. 19.95 (*1-879329-00-X*) Time Warner Libraries.

Adventures of Huckleberry Finn. Mark Twain. LC 84-40712. (Pennyroyal-California Edition Ser.). (Illus.). 1985. 38.00 (*0-520-05338-9*) U CA Pr.

Adventures of Huckleberry Finn. Mark Twain. Ed. by Walter Blair & Victor Fischer. LC 83-40713. (Mark Twain Library: No. 6). (Illus.). 432p. 1985. pap. 12.00 (*0-520-05337-0*); pap. 12.00 (*0-520-05520-9*) U CA Pr.

Adventures of Huckleberry Finn. Mark Twain. LC 85-9576. 384p. (YA). (gr. 4-6). 1986. mass mkt. 4.95 (*0-14-039046-4*, Penguin Classics) Viking Penguin.

Adventures of Huckleberry Finn. Mark Twain, pseud. Ed. by Henry N. Smith. LC 85-9576. (J). (gr. 9 up). 1972. pap. 9.96 (*0-395-05114-2*, RivEd) HM.

Adventures of Huckleberry Finn. Samuel L. Clemens. (Works of Samuel Clemens). 1989. reprint ed. lib. bdg. 79.00 (*0-7812-1118-2*) Rprt Serv.

Adventures of Huckleberry Finn. Mark Twain. 1982. reprint ed. lib. bdg. 15.95 (*0-89967-047-4*) Harmony Raine.

Adventures of Huckleberry Finn. Mark Twain, pseud. LC 94-4522. (Thrift Editions Ser.). 224p. 1994. reprint ed. pap. 2.00 (*0-486-28061-6*) Dover.

Adventures of Huckleberry Finn: A Study Guide. Joy Leavitt. (Novel-Ties Ser.). (YA). (gr. 10-12). 1983. 15.95 (*0-88122-020-5*) Lrn Links.

Adventures of Huckleberry Finn: American Comic Vision. David E. Sloane. (Masterwork Studies: No. 18). 184p. 1988. text ed. 22.95 (*0-8057-7963-9*, Twayne); pap. 12.95 (*0-8057-8016-5*, Twayne) Macmillan.

***Adventures of Huckleberry Finn: Critical Controversies.** Mark Twain, pseud. Ed. by Gerald Graff & James Phelan. 416p. 1995. pap. text ed. 6.65 (*0-312-11225-4*) St Martin.

Adventures of Huckleberry Finn see Mississippi Writings

Adventures of Huckleberry Finn see Adventures of Tom Sawyer

Adventures of Huckleberry Finn Centennial. Mark Twain. (C). 1990. text ed. 10.75 (*0-06-046722-3*) HarpCollege.

Adventures of Huckleberry Finn Notes. James L. Roberts. 1971. pap. 3.95 (*0-8220-0606-5*) Cliffs.

Adventures of Ibn Battuta, a Muslim Traveler of the Fourteenth Century. Ross E. Dunn. 1986. 48.00 (*0-520-05771-6*); pap. 15.00 (*0-520-06743-6*) U CA Pr.

Adventures of Ideas. Alfred N. Whitehead. 310p. 1967. pap. 12.95 (*0-02-935170-7*) Free Pr.

Adventures of Immanence. Yirmiyahu Yovel. 360p. 1989. 35.00 (*0-685-30560-0*) Princeton U Pr.

Adventures of Inquisitive Englebert. Wick Hutchison. (Illus.). 64p. (J). (gr. k-3). 1991. pap. 7.95 (*0-929690-11-7*) Herit Pubs AZ.

Adventures of Isabel. Ogden Nash. (Illus.). (J). (ps-3). 1991. 14.95 (*0-316-59874-7*) Little.

Adventures of Isabel. Ogden Nash. (J). (ps-3). 1994. 4.95 (*0-316-59883-6*) Little.

Adventures of Jack: Or Life on A Wave. Charles L. Newhall. 93p. 1981. 10.95 (*0-87770-263-2*) Ye Galleon.

Adventures of Jacob. Zev Paamoni. (Shulsinger Biblical Ser.). (Illus.). (J). (gr. 5-10). 1970. 3.00 (*0-914080-26-1*) Shulsinger Sales.

Adventures of James Capen Adams. Theodore H. Hittell. LC 78-39492. (Select Bibliographies Reprint Ser.). 1977. reprint ed. 22.95 (*0-8369-9914-2*) Ayer.

Adventures of Jamie. Tom Bowie. LC 78-62815. (Illus.). 1978. 18.95 (*0-932508-00-6*); pap. 4.95 (*0-932508-01-4*) Seven Oaks.

Adventures of Jason. Christopher Quinn. Ed. by Stanley C. Coy. (Illus.). 36p. (Orig.). (J). (gr. 3-5). 1994. pap. 5.95 (*1-881459-13-6*) Eagle Pr SC.

Adventures of Jason: Mythical Magical Journey into Self-Discovery. Pamela Edgar & Dale Matz. LC 85-9695. (Illus.). 64p. (Orig.). (J). (gr. 1-5). 1985. pap. 7.95 (*0-941992-05-5*) Los Arboles Pub.

Adventures of Jason Ashley. (Christian Living Bks.). (J). (gr. 4-6). 1990. 1.55 (*0-89636-119-5*) Accent CO.

Adventures of Jason Jackrabbit. LC 89-2164. 48p. (J). (gr. k-4). 1990. 9.95 (*0-937460-60-5*) Hendrick-Long.

Adventures of Jeremy Levy. 1981. 9.95 (*0-87306-319-8*) Feldheim.

Adventures of Jerry Muskrat. Thornton W. Burgess. (J). (gr. 5-6). 18.95 (*0-88411-782-0*, Aeonian Pr) Amereon Ltd.

Adventures of Jerry Muskrat. Thornton W. Burgess. (Illus.). 96p. (J). 1993. reprint ed. pap. text ed. 1.00 (*0-486-27817-4*) Dover.

Adventures of Jimmy Jack Jones. abr. ed. Russel Cabral. 82p. 1993. pap. 7.95 (*1-56901-377-2*) NW Pub.

Adventures of Jimmy Skunk. Thornton W. Burgess. (Illus.). 128p. (J). (ps-3). 1987. pap. 2.95 (*0-316-11662-9*) Little.

Adventures of Jimmy Skunk. Thornton W. Burgess. (J). 18.95 (*0-8488-0384-1*) Amereon Ltd.

An Asterisk (*) at the beginning of an entry indicates that the title is appearing in BIP for the first time.

107

A

Adventures of Jimmy Skunk. Thornton Burgess. (J). 1992. reprint ed. lib. bdg. 17.95 (0-89966-993-X) Buccaneer Bks.

Adventures of Jimmy Skunk. Thornton W. Burgess. (Children's Thrift Stories Ser.). (Illus.). 96p. (J). 1994. reprint ed. pap. 1.00 (0-486-28023-3) Dover.

***Adventures of Jocko & Gip.** Jane C. Reich. (We're Heroes Too! Ser.). (Illus.). 50p. (J). 1995. 9.95 (0-9636703-6-0) RCR Ent.

***Adventures of John Wetherell.** John Wetherell. Ed. & Intro. by C. S. Forester. 276p. 1995. pap. 11.95 (0-7181-3844-9, Penguin Bks) Viking Penguin.

Adventures of Johnny Chuck. Thonrton W. Burgess. (J). (gr. 5-6). 18.95 (0-88411-787-1, Aeonian Pr) Amereon Ltd.

***Adventures of Johnny Chuck.** unabridged ed. Thornton W. Burgess. LC 94-29788. (Children's Thrift Classics Ser.). (Illus.). 96p. (J). 1995. pap. text ed. 1.00 (0-486-28353-4) Dover.

Adventures of Johnny Chuck. Thornton Burgess. (J). 1992. reprint ed. lib. bdg. 17.95 (0-89966-991-3) Buccaneer Bks.

Adventures of Jozedek. Bishop & Leechman. LC 86-72946. (Illus.). 62p. (Orig.). (J). (gr. 4-5). 1987. pap. 6.00 (0-916383-23-7) Aegina Pr.

Adventures of Juan Chicaspatas. Rudolfo Anaya. LC 84-72301. (Orig.). (C). 1984. pap. 5.00 (0-934770-45-X) Arte Publico.

Adventures of Justin Clay. Telfair. 182p. 1981. pap. 3.95 (0-9609502-0-6) Perilous Pr.

Adventures of Kalakoa: A Hawaiian Rainbow Fantasy. Akiko Masuda. (Illus.). 32p. (J). (gr. k-7). 1991. 7.95 (0-9629842-1-3) Stew & Rice.

Adventures of Kauyumari. Venado Azul. LC 93-71712. (Shamanic Library: No. 2). 50p. (Orig.). pap. 10.00 (0-943907-06-3) Bruce Finson.

Adventures of King Midas. Lynne R. Banks. 160p. (J). (gr. 4). 1993. pap. 3.99 (0-380-71564-3, Camelot) Avon.

Adventures of King Midas. Lynne R. Banks. LC 92-3795. (Illus.). 160p. (J). (gr. 3 up). 1992. 14.00 (0-688-10894-6) Morrow Jr Bks.

Adventures of Kitten & Pachyderm. L. E. Ferraris. (J). 1992. 11.95 (0-533-10132-8) Vantage.

Adventures of Lightfoot the Deer. Thornton W. Burgess. (J). 19.95 (0-8488-0393-0) Amereon Ltd.

***Adventures of Lily & Her Old Fool.** Dana Elam. (Illus.). 96p. (Orig.). 1995. pap. 12.50 (0-9645694-0-X) Leigh Creat.

***Adventures of Little Creatures for Young People.** Juanita A. White. (Illus.). 1995. 7.95 (0-533-11382-2) Vantage.

***Adventures of Little Poodle Droodle the Pup by Uncle Mickey.** M. H. Clark. Ed. by Corlys Disbrow & Henry Ceperich. LC 94-96341. (Illus.). 84p. (Orig.). (J). (gr. 3-5). 1994. pap. 5.00 (1-885591-26-8) Morris Pubng.

Adventures of Little Red. J. David Jones. Ed. by Kathleen Krull. (Illus.). 64p. (J). 1993. write for info. (1-883088-01-1) Source CA.

***Adventures of Lowly Worm.** Scarry. LC 94-67787. 1995. 12.00 (0-679-87248-5) Random.

Adventures of Lucius Leffing. Joseph P. Brennan. (Illus.). 1989. 30.00 (0-937986-95-X) D M Grant.

***Adventures of Lulu, Queen of Everything.** Marael Johnson. 1994. pap. 8.95 (971-19-0161-7) Paper Dreams.

Adventures of Mabel. Harry T. Peck. (Illus.). 236p. (J). (gr. k-5). 1986. reprint ed. 21.95 (0-9616844-0-2) Greenhouse Pub.

Adventures of Maqroll. Alvaro Mutis. 320p. 1995. 24.00 (0-06-017004-2, HarpT) HarpC.

***Adventures of Maqroll: Four Novellas.** Alvaro Mutis & Edith Grossman. 369p. Date not set. 24.00 (0-615-00587-X) HarpC.

Adventures of Max Latin. Norbert Davis. 272p. 1988. pap. 8.95 (0-89296-932-6) Mysterious Pr.

Adventures of Maynard, a Maine Moose. Marybeth Baker. (Illus.). 48p. 1984. pap. 7.95 (0-930096-60-6) G Gannett.

Adventures of Micki Microbe. Maurine B. Guymon. (Illus.). 88p. (J). (gr. 2-5). 1987. 15.00 (0-9618650-0-8) MoDel Pubs.

Adventures of Mike Blair. Hank Searls. LC 87-73209. (Dime Detective Bk.). 224p. 1988. 8.95 (0-89296-918-0) Mysterious Pr.

Adventures of Miles Diamond: The Case of the Missing Twin. Derek Adams. (Orig.). 1993. pap. text ed. 4.95 (1-56333-118-7) Masquerade.

Adventures of Millie. Elizabeth Kontoyiannaki. (Illus.). 15p. (J). (gr. 1-3). 1992. pap. 10.95 (1-56606-012-5) Bradley Mann.

***Adventures of Missus Beckaling.** J. B. Langer. 160p. 1996. pap. 7.95 (0-7610-0506-4) NW Pub.

Adventures of Mister Mocker. Thornton W. Burgess. (J). 18.95 (0-8488-0378-7) Amereon Ltd.

Adventures of Moccasin Joe: The True Life Story of Sgt. George S. Howard. Susan C. Reneau. Ed. by Jack Strohm. LC 91-73719. (Illus.). 224p. (Orig.). 1994. pap. 19.95 (0-9611376-1-4) Colo Big Game.

Adventures of Mohan. Ella Grove. 144p. 1990. 6.30 (0-317-02910-X) Rod & Staff.

Adventures of Momotaro, the Peach Boy. Ralph F. McCarthy. Ed. by Ogawa & Pockell. LC 93-18501. (Children's Classics Ser.). (Illus.). 48p. (J). 1994. 13.00 (4-7700-1755-3) Kodansha.

***Adventures of Mona Pinsky.** Harriet Ziskin. 200p. (Orig.). 1995. 24.95 (0-934971-44-7); pap. 12.95 (0-934971-43-9) Calyx Bks.

Adventures of Monka the Monkey. Nancy B. Irland. 79p. 1990. pap. 3.99 (0-8163-0881-0) Pacific Pr Pub Assn.

Adventures of Monkey King. Tr. by R. L. Gao. (Illus.). 132p. (Orig.). (J). (gr. 2-5). 1989. pap. 6.95 (0-9620765-1-1) Victory Press.

***Adventures of Mr. Hugo.** Patricia G. Cutie. LC 93-94975. (Illus.). 64p. (Orig.). (J). 1994. pap. 6.00 (1-56002-404-6) Aegina Pr.

***Adventures of Mr. Lewis in Russia: A Ten Act Situational Play.** Klara K. Lewis. (In the Shoes of the Traveler Ser.). (Illus.). (Orig.). (RUS.). 1995. pap. 11.95 (1-886821-08-9); audio, pap. 24.99 (1-886821-09-7); pap. text ed. 11.95 (1-886821-21-6) Pavleen.

Adventures of Mr. Nicholas Wisdom. Ignacy Krasicki. Tr. by Thomas H. Hoisington. 175p. (Orig.). 1992. 25.95 (0-8101-1014-8); pap. 12.95 (0-8101-1039-3) Northwestern U Pr.

Adventures of Mustard. Brian J. Foley. (J). 1993. 7.95 (0-533-10662-1) Vantage.

Adventures of My Grandfather. John L. Peyton. LC 65-27156. 270p. 1972. reprint ed. 18.95 (0-405-03680-9) Ayer.

Adventures of Mycroft Holmes. Quinn Fawcett. 1994. pap. 12.99 (1-56171-316-3, S P I Bks) Sure Sellers.

Adventures of Nelda Navajo & Her Forest Friends. Beverly Schulz. (J). 1993. 7.95 (0-8062-4818-1) Carlton.

Adventures of Nicolet. Betty Brandt. Ed. by Laura Brandt. 160p. (Orig.). (YA). (gr. 8-12). 1991. 12.95 (0-9622014-2-1) Beaver Valley.

Adventures of Notationman: A Computerized Introduction to Labanotation. G. W. Gorchoff. (Illus.). 1992. 3.5 hd 50.00 (1-878084-05-4) Danscores.

***Adventures of Obatala: Ifa & Santeria God of Creativity.** Ifayemi Eleburuibon. Ed. by Anthony K. Andoh & Kali Sichen. (Illus.). 90p. 1988. pap. 9.95 (0-916299-08-2) North Scale Co.

Adventures of Ol' Mistah Buzzard. Thornton W. Burgess. (J). (gr. 5-6). 18.95 (0-88411-784-7, Aeonian Pr) Amereon Ltd.

Adventures of Olaudah, the African Boy; Move Feet Move **see Black History Series 1**

Adventures of Old Man Coyote. Thornton W. Burgess. (J). (gr. 5-6). 18.95 (0-88411-781-2, Aeonian Pr) Amereon Ltd.

Adventures of Old Mr. Toad. Thornton W. Burgess. (J). (gr. 5-6). 18.95 (0-88411-785-5, Aeonian Pr) Amereon Ltd.

Adventures of Oliver Twist **see Oxford Illustrated Dickens**

Adventures of Ol'Mistah Buzzard. Thornton Burgess. (J). 1992. reprint ed. lib. bdg. 17.95 (0-89966-995-6) Buccaneer Bks.

***Adventures of Opal & Cupid.** T. Tryon. 1994. pap. 4.99 (0-517-12652-4) Random.

Adventures of Oregon: A Chronicle of the Fur Trade. Constance L. Skinner. (BCL1 - United States Local History Ser.). 290p. 1991. reprint ed. lib. bdg. 79.00 (0-7812-6344-1) Rprt Serv.

Adventures of Paddy the Beaver. Thornton W. Burgess. (J). 18.95 (0-8488-0379-5) Amereon Ltd.

Adventures of Paul Pry, Vol. 1. large type ed. Erle Stanley Gardner. (Nightingale Ser.). 264p. (Orig.). 1991. pap. 13.95 (0-8161-5105-9) G K Hall.

Adventures of Paul Pry, Vol. 2. large type ed. Erle Stanley Gardner. (Nightingale Ser.). 310p. (Orig.). 1991. pap. 14.95 (0-8161-5106-7) G K Hall.

Adventures of Paz in the Land of Numbers. Miriam Bowden. LC 89-71741. (Illus.). 32p. (J). (ps-3). 1992. 10.95 (0-89334-150-9, 150-9) Humanics Ltd.

Adventures of Peela & Keela: Visit to Woodland. Padi Hollen. (Illus.). 64p. (J). 1994. pap. 9.95 (0-8059-3564-9) Dorrance.

Adventures of Pepe the Poodle & Other Stories. Maureen Points. (Illus.). (J). 1978. pap. 3.50 (0-9601594-1-X) Maureen Points.

Adventures of Peter Cottontail. Thornton W. Burgess. (J). 18.95 (0-8488-0353-1) Amereon Ltd.

Adventures of Peter Cottontail. large type ed. Thornton W. Burgess. (Children's Thrift Classics Ser.). 96p. (J). 1992. reprint ed. pap. 1.00 (0-486-26929-9) Dover.

Adventures of Peter Cottontail. Thornton Burgess. (Illus.). (J). (ps-8). 1990. reprint ed. lib. bdg. 18.95 (0-89966-664-7) Buccaneer Bks.

Adventures of Peter Rabbit (& His Friends) Beatrix Potter. 1994. 4.95 (0-87129-356-0, A53) Dramatic Pub.

Adventures of Phineous. Dumas F. Frick. (Illus.). 96p. (J). (gr. 1-3). 1993. 21.95 (1-56167-112-6) Noble Hse MD.

Adventures of Pinocchio. C. Collodi. Tr. by Carol D. Chiesa. LC 88-26684. (Illus.). 280p. (Orig.). (J). (gr. 3 up). 1989. text ed., lib. bdg. 24.95 (0-02-722821-5, Mac Bks Young Read) S&S Childrens.

Adventures of Pinocchio. Carlo Collodi. (Airmont Classics Ser.). (Illus.). (J). (gr. 4 up). 1966. pap. 1.75 (0-8049-0101-5, CL-101) Airmont.

Adventures of Pinocchio. Carlo Collodi. (Illus.). (J). (gr. 4-6). 1982. 12.95 (0-448-06001-9, G&D) Putnam Pub Group.

Adventures of Pinocchio. Carlo Collodi. 256p. (Orig.). 1984. lib. bdg. 25.95 (0-89968-257-X, Lghtyr Pr) Buccaneer Bks.

Adventures of Pinocchio. Carlo Collodi. LC 92-2503. (Pictureback Ser.). (Illus.). 32p. (Orig.). (J). (ps-2). 1992. pap. 2.25 (0-679-83466-4) Random Bks Yng Read.

Adventures of Pinocchio: Le Avventure di Pinocchio. Carlo Collodi. Tr. & Intro. by Nicolas J. Perella. pap. 16.00 (0-520-07782-2) U CA Pr.

Adventures of Pinocchio: The Ultimate Illustrated Edition. Carlo Colladi. (Illus.). 160p. (J). (ps up). write for info. (0-318-62823-6) Bantam.

Adventures of Pinto Bean & Chapulin. Frederick Hayes & Jean Hayes. (Chili Pot Ser.: Vol. 1, Bk. 1). (Illus.). 20p. (Orig.). (J). (gr. 1-8). 1988. pap. text ed. 6.95 (0-317-93098-2) Pinto Pub.

***Adventures of Pocket Malone.** Dave Blanchette. (Illus.). 32p. (J). (gr. 4-4). 1995. 12.95 (1-886428-00-X) Pockets Press.

Adventures of Poor Mrs. Quack. Thornton W. Burgess. (J). (gr. 5-6). 18.95 (0-88411-775-8, Aeonian Pr) Amereon Ltd.

Adventures of Poor Mrs. Quack. Thornton W. Burgess. (Illus.). 96p. (J). 1993. reprint ed. pap. text ed. 1.00 (0-486-27818-2) Dover.

Adventures of Prickly Porky. Thornton W. Burgess. (J). (gr. 5-6). 18.95 (0-88411-783-9, Aeonian Pr) Amereon Ltd.

Adventures of Prince Albert & the Royal Dinosaurs. Frank A. Manson. (Prince Albert Ser.: No. 1). (Illus.). 144p. (J). (gr. 2-7). 1990. 11.95 (0-918339-17-0) Vandamere.

***Adventures of Pudgie Duck.** Carolyn Shaw. (Illus.). 40p. (J). (gr. k-3). 1995. pap. 8.00 (0-8059-3742-0) Dorrance.

Adventures of Pussycat Wizzy Willums. Lizzy Pearl. LC 92-9475. (Illus.). 26p. (J). (ps-3). 1992. 6.98 (1-56566-020-X) Thomasson-Grant.

Adventures of Race Williams. Carroll J. Daly. 352p. 1989. 9.95 (0-89296-959-8) Mysterious Pr.

Adventures of Rama. Milo C. Beach. LC 83-1473. (Illus.). 64p. (Orig.). 1983. 15.00 (0-934686-51-3) Freer.

Adventures of Ranald Bannerman. rev. ed. George MacDonald. Ed. by Michael Phillips. (George MacDonald Classics for Young Readers Ser.: Bk. 4). 192p. (J). (gr. 3 up). 1991. 10.99 (1-55661-223-0) Bethany Hse.

Adventures of Ratman. Ellen Weiss & Mel Friedman. LC 89-10869. (Stepping Stone Bks.). (Illus.). 64p. (Orig.). (J). (gr. 2-4). 1990. pap. 2.99 (0-679-80531-1) Random Bks Yng Read.

Adventures of Reddy Fox. Thornton W. Burgess. (J). 18.95 (0-8488-0380-9) Amereon Ltd.

Adventures of Reddy Fox. large type ed. Thornton W. Burgess. (Children's Thrift Classics Ser.). 96p. (J). 1992. reprint ed. pap. 1.00 (0-486-26930-2) Dover.

Adventures of Reddy Fox. Thornton Burgess. (J). 1992. reprint ed. lib. bdg. 17.95 (0-89966-990-5) Buccaneer Bks.

***Adventures of Road Kill Kitty.** Staefan E. Rada. LC 95-68016. (Illus.). 32p. (Orig.). 1995. pap. 6.95 (1-886023-10-7) Coyote Pr NM.

Adventures of Robin Day. Robert M. Bird. (Works of Robert Montgomery Bird). 1989. reprint ed. lib. bdg. 79.00 (0-7812-1993-0) Rprt Serv.

***Adventures of Robin Hood.** (Classic Fables, Myths & Legends Ser.). 56p. (J). Date not set. 3.50 (0-7214-1758-2) Ladybird Bks.

Adventures of Robin Hood. Ed. by Rudy Behlmer & Tino Balio. LC 79-3971. (Warner Bros. Screenplay Ser.). (Illus.). 210p. 1979. pap. 10.95 (0-299-07944-9) U of Wis Pr.

Adventures of Robin Hood. Roger L. Green. (Orig.). (J). (gr. 2-5). 1984. pap. 3.99 (0-14-035034-9, Puffin) Puffin Bks.

Adventures of Robin Hood. Ret. by Roger L. Green. LC 94-5862. (Everyman's Library Children's Classics). (J). 1994. 13.95 (0-679-43636-7, Evrymans Lib Childs) Knopf.

***Adventures of Robin Hood.** Roger L. Green. (Puffin Classics Ser.). 320p. (YA). (gr. 5 up). 1995. pap. 3.99 (0-14-036700-4) Puffin Bks.

Adventures of Robin Hood. E. Charles Vivian. (Airmont Classics Ser.). (Illus.). (J). (gr. 5 up). 1965. pap. 1.75 (0-8049-0067-1, CL-67) Airmont.

Adventures of Robin Hood. Illus. & Told by Marcia Williams. LC 94-10436. 1995. 17.95 (1-56402-535-7) Candlewick Pr.

Adventures of Robin Hood & His Merry Men. Howard Pyle. Ed. by Kay Reynolds. (Illus.). 160p. 1988. pap. 12.95 (0-89865-602-8, Starblaze) Donning Co.

Adventures of Robin Hood & His Merry Men. limited ed. Howard Pyle. Ed. by Kay Reynolds. (Illus.). 160p. 1988. 40.00 (0-89865-601-X, Starblaze) Donning Co.

Adventures of Robina by Herself. Emma Tennant. LC 87-7921. 1988. 14.95 (0-89255-126-7) Persea Bks.

Adventures of Roderick Random. Tobias G. Smollett. Ed. by Paul-Gabriel Bouce. (World's Classics Ser.). 1982. pap. 6.95 (0-19-281261-0) OUP.

Adventures of Rondy. Frederick J. Schwartz. Ed. by Wayne Olson. 148p. (J). (gr. k-7). 1985. 7.95 (0-9616638-0-4) Rondy Pubns.

Adventures of Roundup & the Sacred Cow Cattle Drive. Knots Lessen. 145p. (Orig.). 1992. pap. 8.50 (0-9632144-0-3) Unidox Print.

Adventures of Sammy Jay. Thornton W. Burgess. (J). 15.95 (0-8488-0381-7) Amereon Ltd.

Adventures of Samuel Swartwout in the Age of Jefferson & Jackson. B. R. Brunson. LC 88-13702. (Studies in American History: Vol. 2). 275p. 1989. lib. bdg. 89.95 (0-88946-097-3) E Mellen.

Adventures of Sandy Wert, Private Eye. Stephen Wright. 1986. pap. 9.50 (0-317-99814-5) Stephen Wright.

Adventures of Sandy West, Private Eye. Stephen Wright. LC 86-90688. 244p. (Orig.). 1986. pap. 9.50 (0-9601904-1-4, Mystery Notebk Edns) Stephen Wright.

Adventures of Satan Hall. Carroll J. Daly. 304p. 1988. pap. 8.95 (0-89296-938-5) Mysterious Pr.

Adventures of Science Fiction, Vol. 3. Isaac Asimov. 21.95 (0-88411-587-9, Aeonian Pr) Amereon Ltd.

Adventures of Sherlock Holmes. Arthur Conan Doyle. 1982. lib. bdg. 25.95 (0-89966-385-0) Buccaneer Bks.

Adventures of Sherlock Holmes. Arthur Conan Doyle. 272p. (YA). (gr. 9-12). 1989. pap. 2.50 (0-8125-0424-0) Tor Bks.

Adventures of Sherlock Holmes. Arthur Conan Doyle. 304p. (J). (gr. 10 up). 1986. pap. 3.99 (0-425-09838-9) Berkley Pub.

***Adventures of Sherlock Holmes.** Arthur Conan Doyle. 144p. (J). 1994. 12.98 (0-86112-972-5) Brimax Bks.

Adventures of Sherlock Holmes. Arthur Conan Doyle. LC 91-39632. (Books of Wonder). (Illus.). 352p. (YA). 1992. 20.00 (0-688-10782-6) Morrow Jr Bks.

Adventures of Sherlock Holmes. Arthur Conan Doyle. Ed. by Richard L. Green. (Oxford Sherlock Holmes Ser.). 448p. (C). 1993. 11.00 (0-19-212318-1, 14613) OUP.

Adventures of Sherlock Holmes. Arthur Conan Doyle. 288p. 1981. mass mkt. 6.00 (0-14-005724-2, Penguin Bks) Viking Penguin.

Adventures of Sherlock Holmes. large type ed. Arthur Conan Doyle. (Large-Print Ser.). 494p. 1986. reprint ed. lib. bdg. 22.00 (0-939495-30-9) North Bks.

Adventures of Sherlock Holmes. Arthur Conan Doyle. (World's Classics Ser.). 448p. 1995. reprint ed. pap. 5.95 (0-19-282378-7) OUP.

Adventures of Sherlock Holmes: A Scandal in Bohemia. Arthur Conan Doyle. write for info. (0-318-59569-9) S&S Trade.

Adventures of Sherlock Holmes: Blue Carbuncle. Arthur Conan Doyle. write for info. (0-318-59715-2) S&S Trade.

Adventures of Sherlock Holmes: Dancing Men. Arthur Conan Doyle. write for info. (0-318-59716-0) S&S Trade.

***Adventures of Sherlock Holmes: Detecting Social Order.** Rosemary Jann. (Twayne's Masterwork Studies Ser.: No. 152). 176p. 1994. text ed. 22.95x (0-8057-8384-9, Twayne); pap. 12.95 (0-8057-8385-7, Twayne) Macmillan.

Adventures of Sherlock Holmes: The Speckled Band. Arthur Conan Doyle. write for info. (0-318-59570-2) S&S Trade.

Adventures of Sherlock Holmes, Bk. 1. Arthur Conan Doyle. (Illus.). 140p. (Orig.). (J). (gr. 4-7). 1981. pap. 3.50 (0-380-78089-5, Camelot) Avon.

Adventures of Sherlock Holmes, Bk. 2. Arthur Conan Doyle. (Illus.). 156p. (Orig.). (J). (gr. 4-7). 1981. pap. 2.95 (0-380-78097-6, Camelot) Avon.

Adventures of Sherlock Holmes, Bk. 3. Arthur Conan Doyle. (Illus.). 112p. (Orig.). (J). (gr. 4-7). 1981. pap. 2.95 (0-380-78105-0, Camelot) Avon.

Adventures of Sherlock Holmes, Bk. 4. Arthur Conan Doyle. (Illus.). 112p. (Orig.). (J). (gr. 4-7). 1988. pap. 3.50 (0-380-78113-1, Camelot) Avon.

Adventures of Simple Shmerel. Solomon Simon. (Illus.). (J). (gr. 3-7). 1942. pap. 4.95 (0-87441-127-0) Behrman.

Adventures of Simple Simon. Chris Conover. 1989. pap. 4.95 (0-374-40096-2) FS&G.

Adventures of Simplicius Simplicissimus. rev. ed. Hans J. Von Grimmelshausen. LC 92-33514. (Studies in German Literature, Linguistics & Culture). 1993. pap. 18.95 (1-879751-38-0) Camden Hse.

Adventures of Simplicius Simplicissimus. 2nd rev. ed. Hans J. Von Grimmelshausen. LC 92-33514. (Studies in German Literature, Linguistics & Culture). 1993. 47.00 (1-879751-37-2) Camden Hse.

Adventures of Sir Wellington Boots. Cliff Peterson & Anne Peterson. (J). 1993. 7.95 (0-533-10328-2) Vantage.

Adventures of Small Head, Square Head & Fat Head. Sonia Sanchez. (Illus.). 32p. (J). (gr. 2-6). 1973. 11.95 (0-89388-094-9) Okpaku Communications.

Adventures of Snail at School. John Stadler. LC 91-45403. (I Can Read Bk.). (Illus.). 64p. (J). (gr. k-3). 1993. 14.95 (0-06-021041-9); lib. bdg. 14.89 (0-06-021042-7) HarpC Child Bks.

Adventures of Speedy. Thelma Osborne. Ed. by Mary Caroland. LC 90-71229. (Illus.). 44p. (J). (gr. k-3). 1991. 5.95 (1-55523-383-X) Winston-Derek.

Adventures of Spero the Orthodox Church Mouse: The Nativity of Our Lord Christ's Birth. Jane Sarlas-Fontana. (Illus.). 20p. (J). (ps-4). 1992. pap. 6.95 (0-937032-91-3) Light&Life Pub Co MN.

Adventures of Spider: West African Folk Tales. Illus. by Jerry Pinkney. LC 92-444. (J). 1992. 7.95 (0-316-05107-1) Little.

Adventures of Stout Mama. Sibyl James. LC 93-18338. 131p. 1993. 14.00 (0-918949-34-3); pap. 9.00 (0-918949-33-5) Papier-Mache Press.

***Adventures of Sugar & Junior.** Angela S. Medearis. LC 94-42368. (Illus.). 32p. (J). 1995. lib. bdg. 15.95 (0-8234-1182-6) Holiday.

***Adventures of Superman.** George Lowther. LC 94-43029. (Illus.). 228p. (YA). (gr. 5 up). 1995. 16.95 (1-55709-228-1) Applewood.

Adventures of Sweet Gwendoline. John Willie. LC 74-6328. (Illus.). 144p. 1974. 20.00 (0-914646-01-X) Belier Pr.

Adventures of Talldorf & Small: The Myth, Bk. 1. Franklin Dunlap & John H. Perrill. 546p. (Orig.). 1990. pap. 9.95 (0-9626555-0-3) Wilderness Road.

Adventures of Tara. Rheya Swanet. 200p. (Orig.). 1993. pap. text ed. 10.95 (1-883457-19-X) Mouseion Pub.

Adventures of Taxi Dog. Sal Barracca & Debra Barracca. Ed. by Phyllis J. Fogelman. LC 89-1056. (Illus.). 32p. (J). (ps-3). 1990. 14.99 (0-8037-0671-5); lib. bdg. 12.89 (0-8037-0672-3) Dial Bks Young.

Adventures of Telemachus. Louis R. Aragon. Tr. by Renee R. Hubert & Judd D. Hubert. LC 87-18208. (French Modernist Library). xxx, 102p. 1988. 25.00 (0-8032-1021-3) U of Nebr Pr.

Adventures of the Amazing Mazers: Hidden Pictures & Maze Games. Christine San Jose & Jody Taylor. (Illus.). 32p. (J). (gr. 2-7). 1994. pap. 4.95 (1-56397-335-9) Boyds Mills Pr.

Adventures of the Animal Town Aviators, Bk. I. H. Boylston Dummer. (Illus.). 118p. (J). (ps-3). 1989. 17.95 (0-87510-198-4) Christian Sci.

Adventures of the Animal Town Aviators, Bk. II. H. Boylston Dummer. (Illus.). 118p. (J). (ps-3). 1989. 17.95 (0-87510-199-2) Christian Sci.

***Adventures of the Ballenger Bears.** Sharon Ballenger. 60p. (Orig.). Date not set. pap. 9.95 (0-7610-0422-X) NW Pub.

An Asterisk (*) at the beginning of an entry indicates that the title is appearing in BIP for the first time.

An Asterisk (*) at the beginning of an entry indicates that the title is appearing in BIP for the first time.

Adventuring in Alaska: The Ultimate Travel Guide to the Great Land. rev. ed. Peggy Wayburn. LC 87-23578. (Adventure Travel Guide Ser.). (Illus.). 416p. (Orig.). 1994. pap. 14.00 (*0-87156-472-6*) Sierra.

Adventuring in Arizona: The Sierra Club Travel Guide to the Grand Canyon State. John Annerino. LC 91-14186. (Adventure Travel Guide Ser.). (Illus.). 384p. (Orig.). 1991. pap. 15.00 (*0-87156-681-8*) Sierra.

Adventuring in Art. Lois B. Tracy. LC 90-7000. (Illus.). 224p. (Orig.). 1990. pap. 19.95 (*0-910923-79-5*) Pineapple Pr.

Adventuring in Australia. Eric Hoffman. LC 90-33703. 1990. pap. 15.00 (*0-87156-742-3*) Sierra.

Adventuring in Belize: The Sierra Club Travel Guide to the Islands, Waters & Inland Parks of Central America's Tropical Paradise. Eric Hoffman. LC 93-5569. (Adventure Travel Guide Ser.). (Illus.). 416p. (Orig.). 1994. pap. 15.00 (*0-87156-592-7*) Sierra.

Adventuring in British Columbia. Isabel Nanton & Mary Simpson. LC 91-10193. (Adventure Travel Guide Ser.). (Illus.). 368p. 1992. reprint ed. pap. 15.00 (*0-87156-674-5*) Sierra.

***Adventuring in Central America: Guatemala, Belize, Honduras, El Salvador, Nicaragua, Costa Rica, Panama.** David R. Wallace. LC 95-1174. (Illus.). 512p. (Orig.). 1995. pap. 16.00 (*0-87156-473-4*) Sierra.

Adventuring in East Africa: The Sierra Club Travel Guide to the Great Safaris of Kenya, Tanzania, Rwanda, Eastern Zaire & Uganda. Allen Bechky. LC 89-10572. (Adventure Travel Guide Ser.). (Illus.). 464p. 1990. pap. 15.00 (*0-87156-747-4*) Sierra.

Adventuring in Florida: The Sierra Club Travel Guide to the Sunshine State. Sierra Club Staff & Allen De Hart. LC 91-12430. (Adventure Travel Guide Ser.). (Illus.). 400p. (Orig.). 1991. pap. 14.00 (*0-87156-602-8*) Sierra.

***Adventuring in Florida: The Sierra Club Travel Guide to the Sunshine State - Includes the Georgia Sea Islands & the Okefenokee Swamp.** rev. ed. Allen De Hart. LC 91-12430. (Illus.). 448p. (Orig.). 1995. pap. 15.00 (*0-87156-373-8*) Sierra.

Adventuring in New Zealand: The Sierra Club Travel Guide to the Pearl of the Pacific. Margaret Jefferies. LC 93-12366. (Adventure Travel Guide Ser.). (Illus.). 480p. (Orig.). 1993. pap. 15.00 (*0-87156-571-4*) Sierra.

Adventuring in North Africa: The Sierra Club Travel Guide to Morocco, Algeria, Tunisia & the Maltese Islands. Scott Wayne. LC 90-45253. (Adventure Travel Guide Ser.). (Illus.). 464p. 1991. pap. 16.00 (*0-87156-745-8*) Sierra.

Adventuring in the Alps: The Sierra Club Travel Guide to the Alpine Regions of France, Switzerland, Germany, Austria, Liechtenstein, Italy & Yugoslavia. William Reifsnyder. LC 85-18471. 1986. pap. 10.95 (*0-87156-754-7*) Sierra.

Adventuring in the Andes: The Sierra Club Travel Guide to Ecuador, Peru, Bolivia, the Amazon Basin, & Galapagos Islands. Charles Frazier & Donald Secreast. LC 84-22219. (Adventure Travel Guide Ser.). (Illus.). 384p. (Orig.). 1985. pap. 10.95 (*0-87156-833-0*) Sierra.

Adventuring in the California Desert: The Sierra Club Travel Guide to the Great Basin, Mojave, & Colorado Desert Regions of California. Lynne Foster. LC 87-4720. (Adventure Travel Guide Ser.). (Illus.). 448p. (Orig.). 1987. pap. 14.00 (*0-87156-721-0*) Sierra.

Adventuring in the Caribbean. Carrol Fleming. LC 89-6143. (Adventure Travel Guide Ser.). 1989. pap. 15.00 (*0-87156-789-X*) Sierra.

Adventuring in the Chesapeake Bay Area. John Bowen. LC 89-10551. (Adventure Travel Guide Ser.). (Illus.). 400p. 1990. pap. 14.00 (*0-87156-680-X*) Sierra.

Adventuring in the Pacific: The Sierra Club Travel Guide to the Islands of Polynesia, Melanesia, & Micronesia. Susanna Margolis. LC 87-23558. (Adventure Travel Guide Ser.). (Illus.). 400p. 1988. pap. 12.95 (*0-87156-780-6*) Sierra.

Adventuring in the Rockies: The Sierra Club Travel Guide to the Rocky Mountain Regions of Canada & the U. S. A. rev. ed. Jeremy Schmidt. LC 92-34644. (Adventure Travel Guide Ser.). (Illus.). 336p. (Orig.). 1993. pap. 15.00 (*0-87156-534-X*) Sierra.

Adventuring in the San Francisco Bay Area. Peggy Wayburn. LC 86-22095. (Adventure Travel Guide Ser.). (Illus.). 448p. (Orig.). 1987. pap. 12.00 (*0-87156-711-3*) Sierra.

***Adventuring in the San Francisco Bay Area.** rev. ed. Peggy Wayburn. LC 86-22095. (Orig.). 1995. pap. 15.00 (*0-87156-353-3*) Sierra.

Adventuring into Vermont's Past. Faye S. Moulton. LC 90-80145. (Illus.). 84p. (Orig.). 1990. pap. 8.95 (*0-914960-81-4*) Academy Bks.

Adventuring with Books: A Booklist for Pre-K - Grade 6. 10th ed. Ed. by Julie M. Jensen & Nancy L. Roser. LC 93-30112. (Bibliography Ser.). 1993. 19.95 (*0-8141-0079-1*) NCTE.

***Adventuring with Children.** Nan Jeffrey. (Illus.). 1995. pap. 14.95 (*0-9627562-4-5*) Menasha Ridge.

Adventuring with Christ. 2nd ed. Lester Sumrall. 161p. (YA). 1988. reprint ed. text ed. 11.95 (*0-937580-13-9*) LeSEA Pub Co.

Adventurings in the Physical. H. A. Bruce. 1976. 59.95 (*0-87968-581-6*) Gordon Pr.

Adventurous Americans. Ed. by Devere Allen. LC 71-156604. (Essay Index Reprint Ser.). 1977. reprint ed. 28.95 (*0-8369-2264-6*) Ayer.

Adventurous Aquanaut. Ed. by Hillary Hauser. 508p. 1990. 28.95 (*0-941332-14-4*) Best Pub Co.

Adventurous Bowmen. Saxton Pope. 1991. 36.00 (*1-879356-06-6*) Wolfe Pub Co.

Adventurous Gardener's Sourcebook of Rare & Unusual Plants. William C. Mulligan. LC 92-12060. (Illus.). 1993. 40.00 (*0-671-75104-2*) S&S Trade.

***Adventurous Life of Philip Mazzei.** Margherita Marchione. LC 95-6188. (ENG & ITA.). 1995. pap. write for info. (*0-8191-9927-3*) U Pr of Amer.

Adventurous Male: Chapters in the History of the White Male Mind. Martin Green. LC 92-26085. 256p. (C). 1993. 28.50 (*0-271-00875-X*) Pa St U Pr.

Adventurous Muse: The Poetics of American Fiction, 1789-1900. William C. Spengemann. LC 76-26936. 300p. reprint ed. pap. 85.50 (*0-8357-8008-2*, 2033894) Bks Demand.

Adventurous Simplicissimus: Being the Description of the Life of a Strange Vagabond Named Melchoir Sternfels von Fuchshaim. Hans J. Grimmelshausen. Tr. by A. T. Goodrick. LC 62-8406. (Bison Book Ser.: No. BB134). 432p. reprint ed. pap. 123.20 (*0-7837-6145-7*, 2043916) Bks Demand.

Adventurous Spirit: A Story about Ellen Swallow Richards. Ethlie A. Vare. (J). (gr. 3-6). 1992. 15.95 (*0-87614-733-3*, Carolrhoda) Lerner Group.

Adventurous Story of General Hannibal the Conqueror. Charles Hinton. LC 94-96003. (Illus.). 112p. (Orig.). 1994. pap. text ed. 12.95 (*0-9639934-0-2*) C Hinton.

Adventurous Thirties: A Chapter in the Women's Movement. Janet E. Courtney. LC 67-26728. (Essay Index Reprint Ser.). 1977. 20.95 (*0-8369-0341-2*) Ayer.

Adverbial Modification. Maxwell J. Cresswell. 1985. lib. bdg. 97.50 (*90-277-2059-2*) Kluwer Ac.

Adverbial Relations in Russian & Their English Equivalents. V. Beldiushkin. 240p. (C). 1988. 40.00 (*0-685-33702-2*, Pub. by Collets) St Mut.

Adverbials of Time & Location in English. C. J. Daswani. 140p. 1977. pap. 4.95 (*0-86125-004-4*, Pub. by Orient Longman Ltd II) Apt Bks.

***Adverbien und Partikeln: Woerterbuch Deutsch-Englisches.** Ekkehard Koenig. 275p. (ENG & GER.). 1990. 49.95 (*0-7859-8696-0*, 387276635x) Fr & Eur.

Adverbs & Comparatives: An Analytical Bibliography. Conrad Sabourin. (Library & Information Sources in Linguistics: No. 2). vii, 208p. 1977. 52.00x (*90-272-0993-6*) Benjamins North Am.

Adverbs of Quantification: A Generalized Quantifier Approach. Henriette De Swart. LC 93-6928. (Outstanding Dissertations in Linguistics Ser.). 360p. 1993. 77.00 (*0-8153-1430-2*) Garland.

Adversaria. Timothy Russell. (TriQuarterly Bks.). 87p. (Orig.). 1993. 25.00 (*0-8101-5027-1*); pap. 10.95 (*0-8101-5002-6*) Northwestern U Pr.

Adversaria. Bannatyne Club Staff. Ed. by David Laing. LC 78-158230. (Bannatyne Club, Edinburgh. Publications: No. 120). reprint ed. 27.50 (*0-404-52879-1*) AMS Pr.

Adversaria Critica Ad Scriptores Graecos et Latinos, 3 vols., Set. Johan N. Madvig. viii, 1703p. 1967. reprint ed. write for info. (*0-318-70779-9*, Pub. by Georg Olms GW) Lubrecht & Cramer.

Adversaria, Notae et Emendationes in Poetas Graecos. Richard Porson. xviii, 354p. 1982. reprint ed. write for info. (*3-487-07198-3*, Pub. by Georg Olms GW) Lubrecht & Cramer.

Adversarial Justice: The American Approach to Adjudication. Stephan A. Landsman. (American Casebook Ser.). 217p. (C). 1990. reprint ed. pap. text ed. 18.50 (*0-314-36115-4*) West Pub.

***Adversaries.** Jack Cavanaugh. 500p. 1996. pap. 11.99 (*1-56476-535-0*, 6-3535) SP Pubns.

Adversario. Mark I. Bubeck. Orig. Title: The Adversary. 160p. (SPA.). 1988. pap. 5.99 (*0-8254-1093-2*) Kregel.

Adversary. Mark I. Bubeck. (C). 1975. pap. 7.99 (*0-8024-0143-0*) Moody.

Adversary. A. M. Kabal. 1987. 15.95 (*0-8027-0952-4*) Walker & Co.

Adversary. Julian May. (Saga of Pliocene Exile Ser.: Vol. IV). 512p. 1987. mass mkt. 4.95 (*0-345-35244-0*, Del Rey) Ballantine.

Adversary see Adversario

Adversary Economy: Business Responses to Changing Government Requirements. Alfred A. Marcus. LC 83-17674. (Illus.). xvi, 260p. 1984. text ed. 65.00 (*0-89930-055-3*, MAV/, Quorum Bks) Greenwood.

Adversary in Heaven: Satan in the Hebrew Bible. Peggy L. Day. LC 88-19170. (Harvard Semitic Monographs). 177p. 1988. 18.95 (*1-55540-248-8*, 04 00 43) Scholars Pr GA.

Adversary Politics & Land: The Conflict over Land & Property Policy in Post-War Britain. Andrew Cox. LC 83-14483. 296p. 1984. 64.95 (*0-521-25517-1*) Cambridge U Pr.

Adversary Press: A Modern Media Institute Ethics Center Seminar. 112p. 1983. pap. 3.00 (*0-935742-06-9*) Poynter Inst.

Adversary System: An Annotated Bibliography. Franklin D. Strier & Edith Greene. vii, 218p. 1990. 35.00 (*0-8377-1159-2*) Rothman.

Adverse Consequences for the Enjoyment of Human Rights of Political, Military, Economic & Other Forms of Assisstance Given to the Racist Colonialist Regime of South Africa. 183p. 1987. 15.50 (*92-1-154061-5*, E.86. XIV.4) UN.

Adverse Consequences for the Enjoyment of Human Rights of Political, Military, Economic & Other forms of Assistance Given to the Racist & Colonialist Regime of South Africa. 164p. 1985. 19.00 (*92-1-154046-1*, E.85. XIV.4) UN.

Adverse Drug Reactions. Ed. by R. D. Mann. (Illus.). 240p. 1987. 65.00 (*1-85070-137-7*) Prthnon Pub.

Adverse Drug Reactions: A Practical Guide to Diagnosis & Management. Ed. by Christian Benichou. LC 94-6102. 1994. pap. text ed. 44.95 (*0-471-94211-1*) Wiley.

Adverse Drug Reactions & the Skin. S. M. Breathnach & H. Hintner. (Illus.). 408p. 1992. 135.00 (*0-632-03349-5*) Blackwell Sci.

Adverse Drug Reactions in Dentistry. R. A. Seymour & J. G. Walton. 216p. 1989. 45.00 (*0-19-261617-X*) OUP.

Adverse Effects of Air Pollutants: Medical Subject Analysis & Research Bibliography. Lillian B. Sheridan. LC 84-45660. 150p. 1985. 39.50 (*0-88164-210-X*); pap. 34.50 (*0-88164-211-8*) ABBE Pubs Assn.

***Adverse Effects of Antiepileptic Drugs.** Dieter Schmidt. LC 82-14027. (Illus.). Date not set. reprint ed. pap. 67.90 (*0-7837-9540-8*, 2060289) Bks Demand.

Adverse Effects of Aspirin: Medical & Scientific Guide for Reference & Research. Charlene P. Singh. LC 83-46099. 150p. 1985. 39.50 (*0-88164-130-8*); pap. 34.50 (*0-88164-131-6*) ABBE Pubs Assn.

Adverse Effects of Foods. Ed. by E. F. Jelliffe & Derrick B. Jelliffe. LC 82-566. 630p. 1982. 125.00 (*0-306-40870-8*, Plenum Pr) Plenum.

Adverse Effects of Herbal Drugs, Vol. 1. Ed. by P. A. De Smet et al. 264p. 1992. pap. 72.00 (*0-387-53100-9*) Spr-Verlag.

Adverse Effects of Herbal Drugs, Vol. 2. Ed. by P. A. De Smet et al. (Illus.). 256p. 1993. pap. 72.00 (*0-387-55800-4*) Spr-Verlag.

Adverse Effects of Lithium: Medical Subject Analysis with Reference Bibliography. Roy R. Zimmerman. LC 85-48083. 150p. 1987. 39.50 (*0-88164-438-2*); pap. 34.50 (*0-88164-439-0*) ABBE Pubs Assn.

Adverse Effects of Pertussis & Rubella Vaccines. Ed. by Christopher P. Howson et al. 382p. 1991. 39.95 (*0-309-04499-5*) Natl Acad Pr.

Adverse Effects of Psychotropic Drugs. Ed. by John M. Kane & Jeffrey A. Lieberman. LC 92-1519. 511p. 1992. lib. bdg. 65.00 (*0-89862-885-7*) Guilford Pr.

Adverse Effects of Radiotherapy: Medical Subject Analysis with Reference Bibliography. Judy J. Hallcrest. LC 85-48102. 150p. 1987. 39.50 (*0-88164-476-5*); pap. 34.50 (*0-88164-477-3*) ABBE Pubs Assn.

Adverse Events Associated with Childhood Vaccines: Evidence Bearing on Causality. Institute of Medicine, Vaccine Safety Committee Staff. 480p. (Orig.). (C). 1993. 49.95 (*0-309-04895-8*) Natl Acad Pr.

Adverse Health Consequences of Cocaine Abuse. Ed. by A. Arif. 47p. 1987. pap. 5.40 (*92-4-156107-6*) World Health.

Adverse Neurological Effects of Cancer Therapy. 1994. lib. bdg. 250.75 (*0-8490-8517-9*) Gordon Pr.

***Adverse Neurological Effects of Cancer Therapy.** 1995. lib. bdg. 251.95 (*0-8490-7585-8*) Gordon Pr.

Adverse Nutrition Effects of Taxing Export Crops in Malawi. CFNPP Staff et al. (Working Paper Ser.). (C). 1992. pap. 7.00 (*1-56401-129-1*) Cornell Food.

Adverse Possession: A Conveyancer's Guide. Andrew J. Pain. 224p. 1992. 84.00 (*1-85190-183-3*, Pub. by Tolley Pubng UK) St Mut.

***Adverse Possession & the South Carolina Land Surveyor.** John E. Keen. 23p. (C). 1995. pap. text ed. 20.00 (*1-56569-006-0*) Land Survey.

Adverse Reactions. Thomas Maeder. LC 93-31896. 1994. 27.95 (*0-688-11682-5*) Morrow.

Adverse Reactions to Anesthetic Drugs. J. A. Thornton. (Monographs in Anaesthesiology: Vol. 8). 1981. 126.00 (*0-685-05918-9*) Elsevier.

Adverse Reactions to Anesthetic Drugs. J. A. Thornton. (Monographs in Anaesthesiology: Vol. 8). 336p. 1981. 152.00 (*0-444-80213-4*) Elsevier.

Adverse Reactions to Cosmetics. Anton C. De Grott. Ed. by Gordon L. Lackie. (Illus.). 241p. 1989. text ed. 75.00 (*0-685-74191-5*) Scholium Intl.

Adverse Reactions to Drug Formulations Agents: A Handbook of Excipients. Weiner & Bernstein. (Clinical Pharmacology Ser.: Vol. 14). 480p. 1989. 175.00 (*0-8247-7944-4*) Dekker.

Adverse Reactions to Food. Therese Beaudette. LC 91-31708. 1991. pap. 7.65 (*0-88091-093-3*, 0154) Am Dietetic Assn.

Adverse Reactions to Foods. 117p. 1984. pap. 9.50 (*0-16-002624-5*, S/N 017-044-00045-1) USGPO.

Adverse Reactions to Non-Steroidal Anti-Inflammatory Drugs: Clinical Pharmacoepidemiology. Ed. by M. Kurowski. LC 92-17629. (Advances in Pharmacological Sciences Ser.). vii, 103p. 1992. 64.50 (*0-8176-2628-X*, Pub. by Birkhauser Vlg SZ) Birkhauser.

Adverse Report. large type ed. Gerald Hammond. 1990. 21.95 (*0-7089-2119-1*) Ulverscroft.

Adversity. Elaine Cannon. 9.95 (*0-88494-630-4*) Bookcraft Inc.

Adversus Judaeos: A Bird's-Eye View of Christian Apologiae until the Renaissance. A. Lukyn Williams. LC 36-11257. 446p. reprint ed. pap. 127.20 (*0-8357-5204-6*, 2051943) Bks Demand.

Advertise! An Assessment of Fundamentals for Small Business. Keith F. Luscher. LC 90-91596. (Illus.). 140p. (Orig.). 1991. pap. 14.95 (*0-9625977-9-1*) K & L Pubns.

***Advertise Poems: Italian Antipoems.** Ignazio Apolloni. (Illus.). 80p. 1978. 10.00 (*0-89304-652-3*) Cross-Cultrl NY.

Advertisement Digest: Library & Information Services, 1978. Chung I. Park. 89p. 1979. pap. 5.00 (*0-939670-06-2*) Info Digest.

Advertisements & Notices of Interest from Norristown, PA Newspapers, Vol. 6: 1844-1848. Judith A. Meier. 324p. 1992. pap. 22.95 (*1-55856-108-0*) Closson Pr.

Advertisements & Notices of Interest from Norristown, Pennsylvania Newspapers, Vol. 3. Comp. by Judith A. Meier. 199p. 1990. pap. text ed. 19.95 (*1-55856-057-2*) Closson Pr.

Advertisements & Notices of Interest from Norristown, Pennsylvania Newspapers, 1799-1821. Judith A. Meier. 1988. pap. text ed. 19.95 (*0-933227-89-2*) Closson Pr.

Advertisements & Notices of Interest from Norristown, Vol. II: 1822-1827. Comp. by Judith Meier. 187p. 1989. pap. text ed. 19.95 (*1-55856-031-9*) Closson Pr.

Advertisements for Myself. Norman Mailer. 532p. 1992. reprint ed. pap. text ed. 15.95 (*0-674-00590-2*) HUP.

Advertisements for the Unexperienced Planters of New England. John Smith. LC 77-171792. (English Experience Ser.: No. 356). 40p. 1971. reprint ed. 25.00 (*90-221-0356-0*) Walter J Johnson.

Advertiser's Copy Prompter. Grant L. Bourn. 28p. 1985. reprint ed. pap. 5.00 (*0-931061-07-5*) Mail Trade.

Advertiser's Guide to the Successful Use of Computers. 65p. (Orig.). 1991. pap. 32.50 (*1-56318-005-7*) Assn Natl Advertisers.

Advertiser's Handbook for Budget Determination. Simon Broadbent. LC 87-46448. 256p. 1988. text ed. 52.95 (*0-669-18139-0*) Free Pr.

Advertising. Courtland L. Bovee et al. LC 94-12495. (Series in Marketing). 1994. text ed. write for info. (*0-07-006847-X*) McGraw.

Advertising. Mark Dunster. 12p. (Orig.). 1991. pap. 4.00 (*0-89642-201-1*) Linden Pubs.

Advertising. C. Frisch. (Communication: Today & Tomorrow Ser.). (Illus.). 48p. (J). (gr. 4-8). 1989. lib. bdg. 17.27 (*0-86592-078-8*); lib. bdg. 12.95 (*0-685-58626-X*) Rourke Corp.

Advertising. S. William Pattis. (VGM Career Planner Ser.). 128p. 1989. pap. 7.95 (*0-8442-8675-3*, VGM Career Bks) NTC Pub Grp.

Advertising. Susan Wake. Ed. by Rebecca Stefoff. LC 90-3895. (Media Story Ser.). (Illus.). 32p. (J). (gr. 4-8). 1991. lib. bdg. 17.26 (*0-944483-95-X*) Garrett Ed Corp.

Advertising. Roderick White. 1989. pap. text ed. 12.95 (*0-07-707077-1*) McGraw.

Advertising. 2nd ed. William Antrim. Ed. by Eugene L. Dorr. (Occupational Manuals & Projects in Marketing Ser.). (Illus.). (gr. 11-12). 1978. text ed. 12.28 (*0-07-002114-7*) McGraw.

Advertising. 4th ed. James D. Norris. 496p. (C). 1989. pap. text ed. write for info. (*0-13-016056-3*) P-H.

Advertising: A Decision-Making Approach. Charles H. Patti & Charles F. Frazer. (Illus.). 592p. (C). 1988. text ed. 56.00 (*0-03-071687-X*) Dryden Pr.

Advertising: Concept & Copy. George Felton. LC 93-31862. 1993. pap. text ed. write for info. (*0-13-189655-5*) P-H.

Advertising: Concepts & Strategies. Christopher Gilson & Harold W. Berkman. 596p. 1980. text ed. write for info. (*0-394-32265-7*) Random.

Advertising: Concepts, Strategies & Issues. Edward C. Applegate et al. 352p. 1993. per. 29.99 (*0-8403-8345-2*) Kendall-Hunt.

Advertising: Distinguishing Between Fact & Opinion. Neal Bernards. LC 91-28266. (Opposing Viewpoints Juniors Ser.). (Illus.). 32p. (J). (gr. 4-7). 1991. lib. bdg. 11.95 (*0-89908-614-4*) Greenhaven.

Advertising: From Fundamentals to Strategies. Michael Rothschild. LC 86-80487. (Illus.). 776p. (C). 1987. text ed. 38.00 (*0-669-07213-3*); Instr.'s guide with test items. teacher ed 2.00 (*0-669-07212-5*); Archive testing prog. IBM-PC. 150.00 (*0-669-11317-4*); Archive testing prog. Apple. 150.00 (*0-669-11319-0*) Heath.

Advertising: Identification & Price Guide. Dawn E. Reno. 572p. (Orig.). 1993. pap. 15.00 (*0-380-76884-4*, Confident Collect) Avon.

Advertising: Its Role in Modern Marketing. 7th ed. S. Watson Dunn et al. 672p. (C). 1990. text ed. 57.75 (*0-03-030748-1*) Dryden Pr.

Advertising: Planning, Implementation, & Control. 4th ed. David W. Nylen. LC 92-42795. 1993. text ed. 60.95 (*0-538-80918-3*) S-W Pub.

Advertising: Policy & Practice. John Priver & Gordon R. Foxall. LC 84-40336. 172p. 1984. text ed. 39.95 (*0-312-00731-0*) St Martin.

Advertising: Principles & Practice. William Wells et al. 704p. (C). 1989. text ed. 52.00 (*0-13-014549-1*) P-H.

***Advertising: Principles & Practice.** 3rd ed. William Wells et al. LC 94-30364. 1994. text ed. 69.33 (*0-13-722869-4*) P-H.

Advertising: Sword Arm of Business. Theodore MacManus. 9.50 (*0-8159-6832-9*) Devin.

Advertising: What It Is & How to Do It. 3rd ed. Roderick White. LC 92-46380. 1993. 16.95 (*0-07-707764-4*) McGraw.

Advertising Advantage. Harvard Business Review Staff. (Marketing & Advertising Essentials Ser.). 100p. 1991. pap. 19.95 (*0-87584-280-1*) Harvard Busn.

Advertising Advantage. Harvard Business School Press Staff. 1991. pap. text ed. 19.95 (*0-07-103340-8*) McGraw.

Advertising Age: The Principles of Advertising at Work. Esther Thorson. 192p. 1989. pap. 11.95 (*0-8442-3175-4*, NTC Busn Bks) NTC Pub Grp.

Advertising Age Classics, 5 vols., Set. 1987. boxed 56.80 (*0-8442-3009-X*, NTC Busn Bks) NTC Pub Grp.

Advertising Agency Business. rev. ed. Herbert S. Gardner, Jr. 224p. 1988. 29.95 (*0-8442-3167-3*, Crain Bks) NTC Pub Grp.

Advertising Agency Management. Jay McNamara. 225p. 1989. text ed. 35.00 (*1-55623-230-6*) Irwin Prof Pubng.

Advertising, Alcohol Consumption, & Abuse: A Worldwide Survey. Joseph C. Fisher. LC 93-9316. (Contributions to the Study of Mass Media & Communications Ser.: No. 41). 216p. 1993. text ed. 55.00 (*0-313-28959-X*, GM8959, Greenwood Pr) Greenwood.

Advertising & a Democratic Press. Edwin Baker. LC 93-2177. 208p. 1994. text ed. 24.95 (*0-691-03258-0*) Princeton U Pr.

Advertising & Children. IAA Global Products-Services Commission & Elhanan C. Stone. 19p. 1985. 10.00 (*0-318-22257-4*) Intl Advertising Assn.

Advertising & Consumer Psychology, Vol. 3. Ed. by Jerry C. Olson & Keith Sentis. LC 86-12219. 302p. 1986. text ed. 55.00 (*0-275-92154-9*, C21543, Praeger Pubs) Greenwood.

An Asterisk (*) at the beginning of an entry indicates that the title is appearing in BIP for the first time.

Advertising & Democracy in the Mass Age. Terence H. Qualter. LC 91-11299. 200p. 1991. text ed. 49.95 (*0-312-06507-8*) St Martin.

Advertising & Display: Promotion in Agribusiness. James E. McGuire & Jasper S. Lee. (Career Preparation for Agriculture-Agribusiness Ser.). (Illus.). 1979. text ed. 16. 96 (*0-07-045129-X*) McGraw.

Advertising & Market Power. William S. Comanor & Thomas A. Wilson. LC 73-90849. (Economic Studies: No. 144). 270p. 1974. 17.50 (*0-674-00580-5*) HUP.

Advertising & Marketing Checklists: One Hundred Seven Proven Checklists to Save Time & Boost Advertising Effectiveness. 2nd ed. Ron Kaatz. Ed. by Anne Knudsen. LC 94-14171. (Orig.). 1994. pap. 22.95 (*0-8442-3520-2*, NTC Busn Bks) NTC Pub Grp.

Advertising & Marketing Communication Management. John H. Murphy & Isabella C. Cunningham. LC 92-43667. 528p. (C). 1993. text ed. 49.00 (*0-03-051069-4*) Dryden Pr.

***Advertising & Marketing to the New Majority: A Case Study Approach.** Gail B. Woods. LC 94-27899. 182p. 1995. pap. 20.95 (*0-534-24192-1*) Intl Thomson.

Advertising & Medicine: Guidebook for Reference & Research. Pauline N. Opekola. LC 83-46107. 150p. 1984. 39.50 (*0-88164-148-0*); pap. 34.50 (*0-88164-149-9*) ABBE Pubs Assn.

Advertising & Popular Culture: Studies in Variety & Versatility. Ed. by Sammy R. Danna. LC 91-77257. (Illus.). 180p. (C). 1992. text ed. 29.95 (*0-87972-527-3*); pap. text ed. 14.95 (*0-87972-528-1*) Bowling Green Univ.

Advertising & Promotion Management. John R. Rossiter. 1987. text ed. write for info. (*0-07-053907-3*) McGraw.

Advertising & Promotion Management. Paul W. Farris & John A. Quelch. LC 87-15902. 314p. 1987. reprint ed. lib. bdg. 29.50 (*0-89464-238-3*); reprint ed. pap. 21.50 (*0-89464-261-8*) Krieger.

Advertising & Promotion Management: A Manager's Guide to Theory & Practice. Paul W. Farris & John A. Quelch. LC 81-70915. 313p. reprint ed. pap. 89.30 (*0-8357-5205-4*, 2029394) Bks Demand.

Advertising & Public Relations. E. Pokress. 8.40 (*0-685-22752-9*) Aurea.

***Advertising & Public Relations for a Small Business.** 6th ed. Diane Bellavance. LC 94-68753. (Illus.). 100p. (Orig.). 1994. pap. 15.95 (*0-9605276-7-2*) DBA Bks.

Advertising & Publicity Resources for Scholarly Books. Association of American University Presses Staff. 1988. pap. text ed. 200.00 (*0-945103-00-X*) Assn Am Univ.

Advertising & the First Amendment: A Twentieth Century Fund Paper. Michael G. Gartner. 69p. 1989. 18.95 (*0-87078-237-1*); pap. 9.95 (*0-87078-236-3*) TCFP-PPP.

Advertising & the Market Process: A Modern Economic View. Robert B. Ekelund & David S. Saurman. LC 87-63450. 220p. (C). 1988. 29.95 (*0-936488-20-4*); pap. 12. 95 (*0-936488-21-2*) PRIPP.

Advertising & the Mind of the Consumer: What Works, What Doesn't & Why. Max Sutherland. 1994. pap. 14. 95 (*1-86373-358-2*, Pub. by Allen & Unwin Aust Pty AT) IPG Chicago.

Advertising & the Promotion Industry. Maggie-Jo St. John. LC 93-16330. (International English Language Teaching Professional Reading Skills Ser.). 1993. 10.00 (*0-13-720038-2*) P-H Gen Ref & Trav.

Advertising & the Public Interest: Selected Papers from the Conference on Advertising & the Public Interest Held in Washington D.C., May 1973. Ed. by S. F. Divita. LC 74-82870. 280p. reprint ed. pap. 79.80 (*0-8357-5206-2*, 2017780) Bks Demand.

Advertising & the Transformation of American Society, 1865-1920. James D. Norris. LC 90-2760. 224p. 1990. text ed. 45.00 (*0-313-26801-0*, Greenwood Pr) Greenwood.

***Advertising & the Use of Alcohol: An Empirical Study.** Joseph C. Fisher & Peter A. Cook. LC 95-9874. (Contributions to the Study of Mass Media & Communications Ser.). 184p. 1995. text ed. 55.00 (*0-313-29457-7*, Greenwood Pr) Greenwood.

Advertising Art in the Art Deco Style. Ed. by Theodore Menten. LC 74-27703. (Pictorial Archive Ser.). (Illus.). 153p. 1975. pap. 8.95 (*0-486-23164-X*) Dover.

Advertising Art of Coca-Cola. Gerry Rosentswieg. 192p. 1994. (*0-942604-46-6*) Madison Square.

***Advertising Art of Coca-Cola.** Gerry Rosentswieg. 256p. 1996. 59.95 (*0-942604-52-0*) Madison Square.

Advertising As a Business Force: A Compilation of Experience Records. Paul T. Cherington. LC 75-39238. (Getting & Spending The Consumer's Dilemma Ser.). (Illus.). 1976. reprint ed. 26.50 (*0-405-08015-8*) Ayer.

Advertising As Communication. Gillian Dyer. (Studies in Communication). 250p. 1982. pap. 14.95 (*0-416-74530-X*, NO. 3662) Routledge.

Advertising Black Markets: A Directory of Slang, Jargon & Chocolate Grammar. Lamp Light Press Staff. 70p. 1993. ring bd. 49.95 (*0-917593-21-9*, Lamp Light Pr) Prosperity & Profits.

Advertising British Cars of the 1950's. Heon Stevenson. (Illus.). 96p. 1991. 24.95 (*0-85429-898-3*) Haynes Pubns.

Advertising Campaign Planning: Developing and Advertising-Based Marketing Plan. Jim Avery & Bruce B. Bendinger. 208p. (C). 1993. pap. 19.50 (*0-9621415-5-0*) Copy Wrkshp.

Advertising Career Directory. R. Fry. 1992. pap. 17.95 (*0-8103-9429-4*) Visible Ink Pr.

Advertising Career Directory. 5th ed. Ed. by Bradley J. Morgan. (Career Advisor Ser.). 300p. 1992. pap. 39.00 (*0-8103-5606-6*, 101578) Visible Ink Pr.

Advertising Catering & Other Businesses Creatively with Rhyming Recipes, Menu Rhymes, Greetings; Includes Site Licensing Forms & Fee: Includes Site Licensing Forms & Fee. Alpha Pyramis Research Division Staff. (Recipe & Recipe Recitals Ser.). 1993. ring bd. 179.00 (*0-913597-79-1*) Prosperity & Profits.

Advertising Character Collectibles: An Identification & Value Guide. Warren Dotz. 176p. 1993. pap. 17.95 (*0-89145-531-0*, 3427) Collector Bks.

Advertising Cheaper with Telemarketing: Script Presentations Directory. Lamp Light Press Staff. 200p. (C). 1993. ring bd. 94.95 (*0-917593-18-9*, Lamp Light Pr) Prosperity & Profits.

Advertising Children's Events with Story Rhymes: Samples Directory. Story Rhyme Staff. 50p. 1993. ring bd. 59.95 (*1-56820-097-8*) Story Time.

***Advertising Clocks: America's Timeless Heritage: with Price Guide.** Michael Bruner. LC 95-6994. (Collectors Bks.). (Illus.). 128p. (Orig.). 1995. pap. 29.95 (*0-88740-790-0*) Schiffer.

Advertising, Communication, Economics. Diane Sylvester. (Enrichment & Gifted Ser.). 112p. (J). (gr. 4-6). 1986. 9.95 (*0-88160-129-2*, LW907) Learning Wks.

Advertising, Competition, & Public Policy Theories & New Evidence. Robert E. McAuliffe. 128p. 1986. text ed. 32. 95 (*0-669-12391-9*) Free Pr.

Advertising Compliance Handbook. Kenneth A. Plevan & Miriam L. Siroky. LC 88-62454. 527p. 1988. text ed. 10. 00 (*0-318-41230-6*, G1-1008) PLI.

Advertising Compliance Handbook. 2nd ed. Kenneth A. Plevan et al. 860p. 1992. text ed. 125.00 (*0-87224-025-8*, G6-2003) PLI.

Advertising Compliance Law: Handbook for Marketing Professionals & Their Counsel. John Lichtenberger. LC 85-31248. 224p. 1986. text ed. 59.95 (*0-89930-122-3*, LAD/, Quorum Bks) Greenwood.

Advertising Controversy: Evidence on the Economic Effects of Advertising. Mark S. Albion & Paul W. Farris. LC 80-24645. 226p. (C). 1981. text ed. 55.00 (*0-86569-057-X*, Auburn Hse) Greenwood.

Advertising Copywriting. 400p. 1990. 39.95 (*0-8442-3200-9*, NTC Busn Bks) NTC Pub Grp.

Advertising Copywriting: Techniques for Improving Your Writing Skills. James L. Marra. 240p. 1993. pap. text ed. write for info. (*0-13-007774-7*) P-H.

Advertising Creativity. James L. Marra. 208p. (C). 1989. pap. text ed. write for info. (*0-13-015009-6*) P-H.

Advertising Designs of Walter Dorwin Teague. Ed. by Clarence P. Hornung. LC 91-74126. (Illus.). 128p. 1991. text ed. 27.50 (*0-88108-094-2*) Art Dir.

Advertising Directions, 3 vols., Vol. 2. LC 59-14827. (Illus.). 1964. Vol.2. 12.50 (*0-910158-12-6*) Art Dir.

Advertising Directions, 3 vols., Vol. 3. LC 59-14827. (Illus.). 1964. Vol.3. 12.50 (*0-910158-13-4*) Art Dir.

Advertising Directions, 3 vols., Vol. 4. LC 59-14827. (Illus.). 1964. Vol.4. 12.50 (*0-910158-14-2*) Art Dir.

Advertising Dolls. Joleen Robison. 1980. pap. 9.95 (*0-89145-134-X*) Collector Bks.

Advertising Exposure, Memory & Choice. Ed. by Andrew Mitchell. (Advertising & Consumer Psychology Ser.). 352p. 1992. text ed. 69.95 (*0-8058-0685-7*) L Erlbaum Assocs.

Advertising Fashions with Poetry. Alpha Pyramis Research Division Staff. 38p. 1994. ring bd. 19.95 (*0-913597-60-0*) Prosperity & Profits.

Advertising Festivals, Fairs & Annual Events with Story Rhymes: Samples Directory. Story Rhyme Staff. 50p. 1993. ring bd. 59.95 (*1-56820-098-6*) Story Time.

Advertising Fictions: Literature, Advertisement, & Social Reading. Jennifer A. Wicke. (Social Foundations of Aesthetic Forms Ser.). (Illus.). 224p. 1988. text ed. 39.50 (*0-231-06604-X*) Col U Pr.

Advertising Financial Products & Services: Proven Techniques & Principles for Banks, Investment Firms, Insurance Companies, & Their Agencies. Alec Benn. LC 85-24406. (Illus.). 256p. 1986. text ed. 59.95 (*0-89930-103-7*, BNH, Quorum Bks) Greenwood.

Advertising Food Businesses with Recipe Greetings: Samples Directory for Licensing. Lamp Light Press Staff. 60p. 1993. ring bd. 39.95 (*0-917593-19-7*, Lamp Light Pr) Prosperity & Profits.

***Advertising for a Small Business Made Simple.** Bernard Ryan, Jr. Ed. by New England Publishing Associates, Inc. Staff. LC 95-11876. (Made Simple Bks.). 1996. write for info. (*0-385-47567-5*) Doubleday.

Advertising Freelancers: Everything about This Promising Work Style as Told by Successful Copy Writers & Art Directors. 2nd rev. ed. Sue Fulton & Ed Buxton. (Illus.). 210p. 1989. pap. 20.00 (*0-917168-10-0*) Executive Comm.

Advertising from the Desktop: The Desktop Publisher's Guide to Designing Ads That Work. Elaine Floyd & Lee Wilson. (Illus.). 464p. 1994. pap. 24.95 (*1-56604-064-7*) Ventana Pr.

Advertising Greeting Cards, No. 3. P. I. E. Books Staff. (Illus.). 224p. 1993. 79.95 (*4-938586-41-X*, Pub. by PIE Bks JA) Bks Nippan.

Advertising Growth Trends. 218p. 1992. pap. text ed. 325. 00 (*1-878339-20-6*) Schonfeld & Assocs.

Advertising Growth Trends. 218p. 1993. pap. text ed. 325. 00 (*1-878339-26-5*) Schonfeld & Assocs.

Advertising Growth Trends. 218p. 1994. pap. text ed. 325. 00 (*1-878339-34-6*) Schonfeld & Assocs.

***Advertising Growth Trends.** 240p. 1995. pap. text ed. 325. 00 (*1-878339-41-9*) Schonfeld & Assocs.

***Advertising Handbook.** Sean Brierly. LC 94-48378. (Media Practice Ser.). 1995. write for info. (*0-415-10713-X*) Routledge.

Advertising Handbook for Health Care Services. Ed. by William J. Winston. LC 85-27013. (Health Marketing Quarterly Ser.: Supplement No. 1). 287p. 1986. text ed. 49.95 (*0-86656-390-3*) Haworth Pr.

Advertising Handbook for Small Business: Make a Big Impact with a Small Budget. 2nd ed. Dell Dennison. (Business Ser.). 296p. 1994. pap. 10.95 (*0-88908-798-9*) Self-Counsel Pr.

Advertising in Contemporary Society. 2nd ed. Kim B. Rotzoll. (C). 1989. pap. text ed. write for info. (*0-318-65184-X*, SJ70BA) S-W Pub.

Advertising in Our Economy. Neil H. Borden. Ed. by Henry Assael. LC 78-239. (Century of Marketing Ser.). 1979. reprint ed. lib. bdg. 26.95 (*0-405-11172-X*) Ayer.

Advertising in Society: Classic & Contemporary Readings on Advertising's Role in Society. Roxanne Hovland & Gary Wilcox. 544p. 1989. pap. 24.95 (*0-8442-3177-0*, NTC Busn Bks) NTC Pub Grp.

Advertising in the Marketplace. 2nd ed. John D. Burke. 1980. text ed. 35.95 (*0-07-009035-1*) McGraw.

Advertising Injury Endorsement in Insurance Disputes: Its Scope, Application, & Coverage. (Commercial Law & Practice Course Handbook Ser.). 192p. 1992. pap. 70.00 (*0-685-69377-5*) PLI.

Advertising Injury Endorsement in Insurance Disputes 1993: Its Scope & Application. (Commercial Law & Practice Course Handbook Ser.: Vol. 661). 204p. 1993. 70.00 (*0-685-69708-8*, A4-4418) PLI.

Advertising International: The Globalisation of Consumer Culture. Armand Mattelart. Tr. by Michael Chanan. (Comedia Bk.). 208p. 1991. 49.95 (*0-415-05063-4*, A5739); pap. 15.95 (*0-415-05064-2*, A5767) Routledge.

Advertising Is A Waste of Money. Robert Ranson. 1994. pap. 12.95 (*0-87425-971-1*) Human Res Dev Pr.

Advertising Kit: A Complete Guide for Small Businesses. Jeanette Smith. 200p. 1994. text ed. 19.95 (*0-02-929515-7*) Free Pr.

Advertising Language: A Pragmatic Approach to Advertisements in Britain & Japan. Keiko Tanaka. LC 93-24963. 1994. write for info. (*0-415-07647-1*) Routledge.

Advertising Law Anthology, 3 vols., Set. (National Law Anthology Ser.). 3000p. 1995. 299.95 (*0-914250-62-0*) Intl Lib.

Advertising Law Anthology, 7 vols., Set. 7500p. 41.95 (*0-686-40890-X*) Thompson Pub Group.

***Advertising Law Anthology, 19 vols., Set.** (National Law Anthology Ser.). 18000p. 1995. 1,475.00 (*1-57024-025-6*) Intl Lib.

***Advertising Law Anthology Vol. XVII, Pt. 1: Jan.-June 1995.** Ed. by Allison P. Zabriskie. (National Law Anthology Ser.). 1995. 154.95 (*1-57024-020-5*) Intl Lib.

Advertising Law Anthology, January-June 1994, Vol. XVII, Pt. I. Ed. by Donald J. Hoyes. (National Law Anthology Ser.). 1994. 154.95 (*1-57024-007-8*) Intl Lib.

Advertising Law Anthology, Vol. XVII, Pt. II: July-Dec. 1994. Ed. by Allison P Zabriskie. (National Law Anthology Ser.). 1995. 154.95 (*1-57024-010-8*) Intl Lib.

Advertising Layout Basics: Ad Kit 4. Larry Notman. 43p. (C). 1981. pap. 5.00 (*0-918488-09-5*) Newspaper Serv.

Advertising Management. 3rd ed. David A. Aaker & John G. Myers. (Illus.). 528p. 1986. text ed. 70.00 (*0-13-016023-7*) P-H.

Advertising Management. 4th ed. David A. Aaker et al. 592p. 1991. text ed. 70.00 (*0-13-014101-1*) P-H.

Advertising Management. C. Nugent Wedding & Richard S. Lessler. LC 62-19340. (Illus.). 637p. reprint ed. pap. 180. 00 (*0-8357-5207-0*, 2012397) Bks Demand.

Advertising Management & the Business Publishing Industry. Albert N. Greco. (Business Magazine Publishing Ser.). 320p. 1991. text ed. 40.00 (*0-8147-3040-X*); pap. 16.50x (*0-8147-3041-8*) NYU Pr.

Advertising Manager's Handbook. Robert W. Bly. LC 92-26107. 1992. write for info. (*0-13-007345-8*) P-H.

Advertising Manager's Handbook. Richard H. Stansfield. 1088p. 1982. 49.95 (*0-85013-128-6*) Dartnell Corp.

Advertising Media: Strategy & Tactics. Donald W. Jugenheimer et al. 488p. (C). 1992. boxed write for info. (*0-697-11791-X*) Brown & Benchmark.

Advertising Media Models: A Practical Guide. Roland T. Rust. 176p. 1986. text ed. 37.95 (*0-669-09375-0*) Free Pr.

Advertising Media Planning. 2nd ed. Surmanek. 1987. pap. 34.95 (*0-8442-3157-6*, NTC Busn Bks) NTC Pub Grp.

Advertising Media Planning. 3rd rev. ed. Jack Z. Sissors & Lincoln Bumba. 480p. 1989. 39.95 (*0-8442-3158-4*, NTC Busn Bks) NTC Pub Grp.

Advertising Media Planning. 4th ed. Jack Z. Sissors & Lincoln Bumba. LC 92-11405. 480p. 1993. 44.95 (*0-8442-3508-3*, NTC Busn Bks) NTC Pub Grp.

Advertising Media Sourcebook: How to Find & Evaluate Essential Media Resources. Arnold Barban et al. 192p. 1989. pap. 17.95 (*0-8442-3159-2*, NTC Busn Bks) NTC Pub Grp.

Advertising of Micropublications. (National Information Standards Ser.). 1981. 10.00 (*0-88738-976-7*, Z39.26) Transaction Pubs.

Advertising on Trial: Managing Your Agency for Effective Results. Jim Ring. (Financial Times Management Ser.). 224p. 1993. 77.50x (*0-273-03970-9*, Pub. by Pitman Pub Ltd UK) Trans-Atl Phila.

Advertising Portfolio. 128p. 1990. 14.95 (*0-8442-3126-6*, NTC Busn Bks) NTC Pub Grp.

Advertising Principles. Daniel Starch. Ed. by Henry Assael. LC 78-310. (Century of Marketing Ser.). 1979. reprint ed. lib. bdg. 51.95 (*0-405-11173-8*) Ayer.

Advertising Promotion Challenge: Vaguely Right or Precisely Wrong. Leonard M. Lodish. (Illus.). 192p. 1986. 25.00 (*0-19-503702-2*) OUP.

Advertising Pure & Simple: The New Edition. 2nd ed. Hank Seiden. LC 90-55209. 240p. 1990. 21.95 (*0-8144-5981-1*) AMACOM.

Advertising Ratios & Budgets. 200p. 1992. pap. text ed. 325.00 (*1-878339-15-X*) Schonfeld & Assocs.

Advertising Ratios & Budgets. 200p. 1993. pap. text ed. 325.00 (*1-878339-22-2*) Schonfeld & Assocs.

Advertising Ratios & Budgets. 200p. 1994. pap. text ed. 325.00 (*1-878339-30-3*) Schonfeld & Assocs.

***Advertising Ratios & Budgets.** 216p. 1995. pap. text ed. 325.00 (*1-878339-37-0*) Schonfeld & Assocs.

Advertising Ratios & Budgets: 1990 Edition. Schonfeld & Associates Staff. 200p. (C). 1990. pap. text ed. 295.00 (*1-878339-05-2*) Schonfeld & Assocs.

Advertising Ratios & Budgets, 1989. Schonfeld & Associates, Inc. Staff. 207p. (C). 1989. pap. text ed. 295. 00 (*1-878339-00-1*) Schonfeld & Assocs.

Advertising Ratios & Budgets, 1991. Schonfeld & Associates, Inc. Staff. 200p. (C). 1991. pap. text ed. 295. 00 (*1-878339-10-9*) Schonfeld & Assocs.

***Advertising Reach & Frequency: Maximizing Advertising Results Through Effective Frequency.** Colin McDonald. Date not set. 39.95 (*0-614-06754-5*) Assn Natl Advertisers.

Advertising Realities: A Practical Guide to Agency Management. Wes Perrin. 184p. (C). 1991. pap. text ed. 19.95 (*0-87484-999-3*) Mayfield Pub.

Advertising Recycled Clothing Fashions with Poetry. Alpha Pyramis Research Division Staff. 70p. 1994. pap. text ed. 19.95 (*0-913597-61-9*) Prosperity & Profits.

Advertising Regulation. Shenagh Barnes & Michael Blakeney. lii, 612p. 1982. pap. 97.00 (*0-455-20545-0*, Pub. by Law Bk Co) W W Gaunt.

Advertising Research. Neil Holbert. LC 75-33820. (American Marketing Association Monograph Ser.: No. 1). 21p. reprint ed. pap. 25.00 (*0-8357-5208-9*, 2023357) Bks Demand.

Advertising Research. Percival White. Ed. by Henry Assael. LC 78-266. (Century of Marketing Ser.). (Illus.). 1979. reprint ed. lib. bdg. 56.95 (*0-405-11178-9*) Ayer.

Advertising Resource Handbook. Keith Adler. (Illus.). 248p. (Orig.). (C). 1988. pap. text ed. 14.95 (*0-923044-01-9*) Ad Resources Inc.

Advertising Revenues Per Television Household: A Market by Market Analysis. National Association of Broadcasters Staff. 51p. (Orig.). 1993. pap. 100.00 (*0-89324-209-8*) Natl Assn Broadcasters.

Advertising Rights: The Neglected Freedom - Toward a New Doctrine of Commercial Speech. Richard T. Kaplar. LC 91-60930. 105p. 1991. 16.95 (*0-937790-45-1*, 4380) Media Institute.

Advertising Salesmanship. Arnold A. DeLuca. (Illus.). 500p. (C). 1990. text ed. 49.50 (*1-878666-01-0*) Dynamo Intl.

Advertising Salesmanship. Arnold A. DeLuca. (Illus.). 500p. 1992. 49.50 (*0-685-49849-2*) Dynamo Intl.

Advertising Salesmanship Student Work Book. Arnold A. DeLuca. 83p. (C). 1992. student ed, pap. text ed. 10.00 (*1-878666-02-9*) Dynamo Intl.

Advertising Self-Regulation: Sixteen Advanced Systems. J. J. Boddewyn. 105p. 1986. 65.00 (*0-318-22260-4*) Intl Advertising Assn.

Advertising Self-Regulation & Outside Participation: A Multinational Comparison. Jean J. Boddewyn. LC 87-24939. 385p. 1988. text ed. 69.50 (*0-89930-295-5*, BAV/, Quorum Bks) Greenwood.

Advertising Services. Ralph Wray. Ed. by Richard L. Lynch. (Career Competencies in Marketing Ser.). (Illus.). 1979. text ed. 12.04 (*0-07-071900-4*) McGraw.

Advertising Services: Full Service Agency, a La Carte, or In-House? rev. ed. 42p. 1991. pap. 37.50 (*1-56318-004-9*) Assn Natl Advertisers.

Advertising Slogans of America. Comp. by Harold S. Sharp. LC 83-20431. 554p. 1984. 39.50 (*0-8108-1681-4*) Scarecrow.

Advertising Spot Illustrations of the Twenties & Thirties. Leslie Cabarga. 1989. pap. 5.95 (*0-486-26098-4*) Dover.

Advertising Strategy: A Communication Theory Approach. Larry Percy & John R. Rossiter. LC 79-25228. 314p. 1980. text ed. 49.95 (*0-275-91692-8*, C1692, Praeger Pubs) Greenwood.

Advertising Survival Kit. Lain. 64p. 1992. 1.75 (*0-318-60010-2*) Quill & Scroll.

Advertising Techniques & Consumer Fraud. Northwest Regional Educational Laboratory Staff. (Lifeworks Ser.). (Illus.). 1979. text ed. 13.96 (*0-07-047308-0*) McGraw.

Advertising That Sells: A Primer for Product Managers. Miner Raymond. (Illus.). 160p. (Orig.). 1989. pap. 24.95 (*0-685-28874-9*) Blk Rose Pub.

Advertising That Sells: A Primer for Product Managers. Miner Raymond. Ed. by Elizabeth Raymond. (Illus.). 160p. (Orig.). 1990. write for info. (*0-9624575-0-7*) Blk Rose Pub.

Advertising the American Dream: Making Way for Modernity, 1920-1940. Roland Marchand. LC 84-28082. 1985. 50.00 (*0-520-05253-6*); pap. 19.00 (*0-520-05885-2*) U CA Pr.

Advertising, the Uneasy Persuasion: Its Dubious Impact on American Society. Michael Schudson. 292p. 1986. pap. text ed. 15.00 (*0-465-00080-0*) Basic.

Advertising Via Telemarketing Script Presentations Encyclopaedia. Data Notes Publishing Staff. 150p. 1991. 125.00 (*0-911569-73-1*) Prosperity & Profits.

Advertising with Flowers: Clip Art Directory. Lamp Light Staff. (Illus.). 60p. 1993. ring bd. 39.95 (*0-917593-20-0*, Lamp Light Pr) Prosperity & Profits.

Advertising with Story Rhymes: Review Collection for Licensing. Story Time Staff. (Illus.). 38p. 1993. ring bd. 21.95 (*1-56820-096-X*) Story Time.

Advertising Worldwide. 2nd ed. Marieke DeMooij. 1994. pap. text ed. 33.00 (*0-13-288598-0*) P-H.

An Asterisk (*) at the beginning of an entry indicates that the title is appearing in BIP for the first time.

111

A

Advertising Worldwide: Concepts, Theories & Practice of International Multinational & Global Advertising. Marieke De Mooij & Warren Keegan. 400p. 1991. pap. text ed. 39.00 (0-13-471897-6) P-H.

Advertising Writing. 3rd ed. W. Keith Hafer & Gordon E. White. (Illus.). 338p. 1988. text ed. 57.00 (0-314-46532-4) West Pub.

Advertising's Benevolent Dictators. Bart Cummings. LC 83-72178. Orig. Title: Benevolent Dictators. (Illus.). 344p. 1984. 24.95 (0-8442-3191-6, Crain Bks) NTC Pub Grp.

Advertising's Hidden Effects: Manufacturers' Advertising & Retailing Pricing. Mark S. Albion. LC 82-6776. 330p. 1983. text ed. 24.95 (0-86569-111-8, Auburn Hse) Greenwood.

Advertising's Role in Society. John S. Wright & John E. Mertes. LC 74-1325. 522p. reprint ed. pap. 148.80 (0-8357-5209-7, 2022846) Bks Demand.

Advice. Nachman of Breslov. Tr. by Avraham Greenbaum. LC 83-70202. 522p. 1983. 16.00 (0-930213-04-1) Breslov Res Inst.

Advice, a High Profit Business: A Guide to Consultants & Other Entrepreneurs. Herman R. Holtz. 1986. 29.95 (0-13-011958-X) P-H.

Advice after Appomattox: Letters to Andrew Johnson, 1865-1866. Ed. by Brooks D. Simpson et al. LC 87-5961. (Papers of Andrew Johnson Ser.: No. 1). (Illus.). 286p. (C). 1988. lib. bdg. 35.00x (0-87049-536-4); pap. 16.00x (0-87049-549-6) U of Tenn Pr.

Advice among Masters: The Ideal in Slave Management in the Old South. Ed. by James O. Breeden. LC 79-54054. (Contributions in Afro-American & African Studies: No. 51). (Illus.). xxvi, 350p. 1980. text ed. 59.95 (0-313-20658-9, BRS/) Greenwood.

Advice & Consent: Clarence Thomas, Robert Bork & the Intriguing History of the Supreme Court's Nomination Battles. Paul Simon. 1992. 23.95 (0-915765-98-5) Natl Pr Bks.

Advice & Consent: The Development of the Policy Sciences. Peter DeLeon. LC 88-32140. 141p. 1989. 19.95 (0-87154-215-3) Russell Sage.

Advice & Consent of the Senate: A Study of the Confirmation of Appointments by the United States Senate. Joseph P. Harris. LC 68-23294. (Illus.). 457p. 1968. reprint ed. text ed. 35.00 (0-8371-0095-X, HAAS, Greenwood Pr) Greenwood.

Advice & Consent: The Selection of United States Supreme Court Justices: Proceedings of a Symposium. Ed. by A. Darby Dickerson. (Institute & Seminar Proceedings Ser.). 94p. 1994. 9.00 (0-89940-106-6) LBJ Sch Pub Aff.

Advice & Support: The Early Years of U. S. Army in Vietnam, 1941-1960. Ronald H. Spector. (Illus.). 415p. (C). 1985. pap. 14.95 (0-02-930370-2) Free Pr.

Advice & Support: The Final Years, 1965-1973. Jeffrey J. Clarke. LC 87-600379. (United States Army in Vietnam CMH Publication Ser.: CMH Pub No. 91-3). (Illus.). 583p. 1988. 25.00 (0-16-001960-5, S/N 008-029-00157-8); pap. 21.00 (0-318-42874-1, S/N 008-029-00158-6) USGPO.

Advice & Support, the Early Years 1941-1960. Ronald H. Spector. LC 83-600103. (United States Army in Vietnam Ser.). (Illus.). 407p. 1983. 18.00 (0-16-001591-X, 008-020-00967-9); pap. 11.00 (0-318-22759-2, S/N 008-020-00933-4) USGPO.

Advice Book: A Question-Answer Book for Those Who Love. Ken Magid. 247p. (Orig.). 1993. pap. 19.95 (1-883590-50-7) K M Prods.

Advice for Conscientious Objectors in the Armed Forces. 5th ed. Ed. by Robert A. Seeley. LC 74-27602. 189p. 1984. 3.00 (0-933368-06-2) CCCO.

Advice for Seekers. Charles H. Spurgeon. 85p. 1993. reprint ed. 3.95 (0-85151-651-3) Banner of Truth.

Advice for Students. Swami Jyotir Maya Nanda. (Illus.). 1972. pap. 0.49 (0-934664-00-5) Yoga Res Foun.

Advice from a Sojourner: Humility & Dominion in Proverbs 30. James B. Jordan. 95p. 1993. pap. 7.00 (1-883690-02-1) Transfig Pr.

Advice from a Spiritual Friend. rev. ed. Geshe Rabten & Geshe Dhargyey. Ed. & Tr. by Brian Beresford. (Wisdom Basic Book, Orange Ser.). (Illus.). 160p. 1994. pap. 8.95 (0-86171-017-7) Wisdom MA.

Advice from the Diamond Headache Clinic. Seymour Diamond & Judi Diamond-Falk. LC 82-8973. ix, 194p. 1982. 25.00 (0-8236-0119-6) Intl Univs Pr.

Advice from the Masters: A Compendium for Writers. Barnaby Conrad. Ed. by Shelly Lowenkopf. (Santa Barbara Writers Conference Shop Talk Ser.: Bk. II). (Illus.). 72p. (Orig.). 1991. pap. text ed. 7.95 (1-880093-01-4) Charters W.

Advice from the Soccer Pros. David Faries. LC 79-64730. (Illus.). 176p. 1980. pap. 5.95 (0-89037-219-5) Anderson World.

Advice Limited. Edward P. Oppenheim. LC 74-134972. (Short Story Index Reprint Ser.). 1977. 20.95 (0-8369-3703-1) Ayer.

***Advice on Marriage Between Equals: Peer Marriage.** Schwartz. 1995. pap. 12.00 (0-02-874061-0) Free Pr.

Advice on the Art of Governance (Mau'izah-i Jahangiri) of Muhammad Baqir Najm-i Sani: An Indo-Islamic Mirror for Princes. Ed. by Sajida S. Alvi. LC 88-16342. (SUNY Series in Near Eastern Studies). 215p. (ENG & PER.). 1989. 64.50 (0-88706-918-5); pap. 21.95 (0-88706-919-3) State U NY Pr.

Advice on the Study of the Law: With Directions for the Choice of Books, Addressed to Attorneys' Clerks, with Additional Notes for the American Student. LC 94-17735. 167p. 1994. reprint ed. lib. bdg. 45.00 (0-8377-1910-0) Rothman.

Advice to a Daughter, 1687 see **Free Life: Essays & Vignettes, 1926-1987**

Advice to a Freshman. John R. Conners. 104p. 1984. pap. text ed. 12.25 (0-89917-416-7) Tichenor Pub.

Advice to a Friend. S. A. Rauf. pap. 3.95 (0-935782-25-7) Kazi Pubns.

Advice to a Young Man on the Choice of a Mistress. Benjamin Franklin. 1973. 250.00 (0-87968-097-0) Gordon Pr.

Advice to a Young Scientist. P. B. Medawar. 128p. 1981. reprint ed. pap. 13.00 (0-465-00092-4) Basic.

***Advice to a Young Wife from an Old Mistress.** Michael Drury. LC 94-29664. 1995. 15.00 (0-679-43872-6) Random.

Advice to a Young Wife from an Old Mistress. 2nd ed. Michael Drury. 204p. 1993. 17.95 (0-9627659-5-3) Four Directions.

Advice to Doctors & Other Big People...from Kids. Center for Attitudinal Healing Staff. (Illus.). 164p. (Orig.). (YA). (gr. 8-12). 1990. pap. 7.95 (0-89087-618-5) Celestial Arts.

Advice to Farm Women. Ed. by Jeanne H. Delgado. (Wisconsin Stories Ser.). 27p. pap. 1.25 (0-87020-186-7) State Hist Soc Wis.

Advice to Householders. Swami Jyotirmayananda. (Illus.). 174p. 1989. 5.95 (0-934664-54-4) Yoga Res Foun.

Advice to Parents of a Cleft Palate Child. 2nd fac. ed. Donna K. Wicka & Mervyn L. Falk. (Illus.). 80p. 1982. Photocopy ed. 21.95 (0-398-04704-9) C C Thomas.

Advice to Seekers. C. H. Spurgeon. 1994. pap. 2.00 (1-56186-431-5) Pilgrim Pubns.

Advice to Students. Swami Jyotir Maya Nanda. (Illus.). 236p. 1991. pap. 5.95 (0-934664-55-2) Yoga Res Foun.

Advice to the Minister of Music: Get a Giant Hat Rack! Cheri Walters. 160p. (Orig.). 1994. pap. 8.95 (0-88243-339-3, 02-339) Gospel Pub.

Advice to the Officers of the British Army: With the Addition of Some Hints to the Drummer & Private Soldier. Frances Grose. 134p. 1992. pap. 8.00 (0-9633659-0-8) US Hist Res Srv.

Advice to the Players. Robert Lewis. LC 79-3291. 192p. 1989. reprint ed. pap. 8.95 (1-55936-003-8) Theatre Comm.

Advice to Travellers: Selected Poems. Stanley R. Green. 96p. 1990. pap. text ed. 14.00 (0-08-037973-7, Pub. by Aberdeen U Pr) Macmillan.

Advice to Violin Students. Wallace Ritchie. 110p. 1991. reprint ed. lib. bdg. 69.00 (0-7812-9353-7) Rprt Serv.

Advice to Young Christians: Exploring Paul's Letters. Paul Woods. (Active Bible Curriculum Ser.). (Illus.). 48p. 1992. pap. 9.99 (1-55945-146-7) Group Pub.

Advice to Youth see **Consejos a la Juventud**

Advice...Southern Style. Date not set. write for info. (0-9615622-1-8) McElyea Pubns.

Advise & Consent. Allen Drury. 1991. lib. bdg. 45.95 (1-56849-060-7) Buccaneer Bks.

Advise & Dissent: Memoirs of South Dakota & the U. S. Senate. James G. Abourezk. LC 89-15354. 288p. 1989. 18.95 (1-55652-066-2) L Hill Bks.

Advise & Invent: The Lawyer as Counselor-Strategist & Other Essays. James C. Freund. 312p. 1990. 60.00 (0-13-009069-7) Aspen Law.

Advise to Improvisers. Tchicai. Date not set. pap. 9.95 (0-685-69293-0, Pub. by Wilhelm Hansen DK) Music Sales.

Adviser-Advisee Programs: Why, What, & How. Michael James. 70p. (Orig.). (C). 1986. pap. text ed. 10.00 (1-56090-029-6) Natl Middle Schl.

Advisers: Scientists in the Policy Process. Bruce L. Smith. 238p. 1992. 36.95 (0-8157-7990-9); pap. 16.95 (0-8157-7989-5) Brookings.

Adviser's Manual of Federal Regulations Affecting Foreign Students & Scholars. rev. ed. ring bd. 75.00 (0-912207-63-9) NAFSA Washington.

Advising California Condominium & Homeowners Associations. Curtis C. Sproul & Katharine N. Rosenberry. Ed. by Gordon Graham & Craig H. Scott. LC 91-71136. 849p. 1991. 160.00 (0-88124-371-X, RE31630) Cont Ed Bar-CA.

Advising California Employers. California Continuing Education of the Bar Staff et al. LC 81-65536. (Illus.). xiv, 635p. 1981. 100.00 (0-88124-078-8, BU-35510) Cont Ed Bar-CA.

Advising California Employers: May 1993 Update. Wayne E. Barlow et al. Ed. by Janette Tom. LC 81-65536. 482p. 1993. pap. text ed. 55.00 (0-88124-617-4, BU-35516) Cont Ed Bar-CA.

Advising California Nonprofit Corporations. Kenneth L. Guernsey et al. Ed. by Michael C. Hone. LC 84-45135. 676p. 1984. text ed. 105.00 (0-88124-128-8, BU-36620) Cont Ed Bar-CA.

Advising California Partners & Sole Proprietors. Robert Petersen & Jerold Freedland. 1992. write for info. (0-318-69517-0) Bender.

Advising California Partnerships. 2nd ed. Curtis M. Karplus. LC 87-72943. 658p. 1988. text ed. 125.00 (0-88124-159-8, BU-35630) Cont Ed Bar-CA.

***Advising Clients on Retirement Plans.** Sophie M. Korczyk et al. LC 94-31796. (Retirement Plans Workbook & Tax Practice Ser.). 1994. 95.00 (0-615-00184-X) Clark Boardman Callaghan.

Advising Corporations on Merger, Acquisition, & Takeover Situations. Law & Business Inc. Staff. LC 85-242505. (Illus.). iv, 442p. 40.00 (0-685-13426-1) HarBrace.

Advising Ike: The Memoirs of Attorney General Herbert Brownell. Herbert Brownell & John P. Burke. LC 92-37584. (Illus.). 416p. 1993. 29.95 (0-7006-0590-8) U Pr of KS.

***Advising Minnesota Corporations and Other Business Organizations.** suppl. ed. Martin J. Costello et al. 1994. ring bd. 48.50 (0-614-03161-3) Butterworth Legal Pubs.

Advising Premedical Students: Symposium, Friday, October 11, 1991. LC 92-48380. (C). 1992. 19.95 (0-924143-02-9) NY Acad Med.

Advising Small Businesses, 3 vols., Set. Steven Alberty. 1990. 350.00 (0-685-30632-1) Clark Boardman Callaghan.

Advising the Elderly Client, 3 vols., Set. Louis A. Mezzullo & Mark Woolpert. LC 92-72717. 1992. ring bd. 395.00 (0-685-59858-6) Clark Boardman Callaghan.

Advising the Elderly Or Disabled Client: Legal - Financial - Estate Planning. Lawrence A. Frolik & Melissa C. Brown. 1992. text ed. 140.00 (0-685-69653-7, AEDC) Warren Gorham & Lamont.

Advising the Older Client. Ed. by Lynn P. Chard. LC 90-85065. 600p. 1990. ring bd. 110.00 (0-685-39003-9, 90-035) U MI Law CLE.

Advising the Older Client. suppl. ed. Ed. by Lynn P. Chard. LC 90-85065. 600p. 1991. 60.00 (0-685-58919-6) U MI Law CLE.

Advising the Older Client. suppl. ed. Ed. by Lynn P. Chard. LC 90-85065. 600p. 1992. 55.00 (0-685-58920-X) U MI Law CLE.

***Advising the Public about Radiation Emergencies: A Document for Public Comment.** Intro. by Charles B. Meinhold. (NCRP Commentaries Ser.). 25p. (Orig.). Date not set. pap. text ed. 15.00 (0-929600-38-X) NCRP Pubns.

Advising West European Governments: Inquiries, Expertise, & Public Policy. Ed. by Guy Peters & Anthony Barker. (Policy & Institutional Studies). 240p. (C). 1993. text ed. 49.95 (0-8229-1172-8); pap. text ed. 19.95 (0-8229-6099-0) U of Pittsburgh Pr.

Advisor (Da Co-Van) Porfirio Torres-Gonzales. 1993. 16.95 (0-533-10481-5) Vantage.

Advisors: Oppenheimer, Teller, & the Superbomb. Herbert F. York. LC 88-62671. (Nuclear Age Ser.). xvi, 201p. 1989. reprint ed. 35.00 (0-8047-1713-3); reprint ed. pap. 9.95 (0-8047-1714-1) Stanford U Pr.

***Advisory Comments for Growth & Profitability: A Guide for Accountants & Consultants.** Peter F. Stone & Mark L. Frigo. LC 94-19477. 201p. 1994. 50.00 (0-7863-0241-0) Irwin Prof Pubng.

***Advisory Committee Advantage: Creating an Effective Strategy for Programmatic Improvement.** Lee Teitel. Ed. & Frwd. by Jonathan D. Fife. (ASHE-ERIC Higher Education Report: No. 1, 1994). 101p. (Orig.). (C). 1994. pap. 18.00x (1-878380-57-5) GWU Schl E&HD.

Advisory Committee on the Microbiological Safety of Food: Campylobacter. 108p. 1993. pap. 20.00 (0-11-321662-9, HM216629, Pub. by HMSO UK) UNIPUB.

Advisory Entities: Utilization by the Alabama Judicial System. National Center for State Courts Staff. 54p. 1975. 3.24 (0-685-15096-8, MAB-004) Natl Ctr St Courts.

Advisory Group on the Medical Aspects of Air Pollution Episodes: Sulphur Dioxide. HMSO Staff. 161p. 1992. pap. 65.00 (0-11-321532-0, HM15320, Pub. by HMSO UK) UNIPUB.

Advisory Memorandum on Office Automation Security Guideline. 60p. (Orig.). (C). 1993. pap. text ed. 30.00 (1-56806-531-0) Diane Pub.

Advisory Notes on Lifeline Earthquake Engineering. 242p. 1983. pap. 27.00 (0-87262-377-7) Am Soc Civil Eng.

Advisory Panel on Alzheimer's Disease: Third Report. (Illus.). 75p. (Orig.). (C). 1994. pap. text ed. 34.95 (0-7881-0527-2) Diane Pub.

Advocacy: Legal Practice Handbook. Avrom Sherr. 127p. (C). 1993. pap. 26.00 (1-85431-172-7, Pub. by Blackstone Pr UK) W W Gaunt.

Advocacy: The Art of Pleading a Cause. 2nd ed. Richard A. Givens. 1985. text ed. 95.00 (0-07-023371-3) McGraw.

Advocacy: The Art of Pleading a Cause. 2nd ed. Richard A. Givens. LC 79-26332. (Trial Practice Ser.). xxi, 857p. 1980. text ed. 70.00 (0-07-023355-1) Shepards-McGraw.

***Advocacy: The Essentials of Argumentation & Debate.** Dean Fadely. 336p. (C). 1994. per., pap. text ed. 35.85 (0-8403-9808-5) Kendall-Hunt.

Advocacy & Empowerment: Mental Health Care in Community. Stephen M. Rose & Bruce Black. LC 85-1802. 256p. 1985. 27.50 (0-7100-9963-0, RKP) Routledge.

***Advocacy & Indigenous Film-Making Number One of Intervention: Nordic Papers in Critical Anthropology.** Ed. by Birgitte Markussen & Hans Henrik. 74p. 1995. pap. 15.00 (87-89825-09-8) Smyrna.

Advocacy & Negotiation in Industrial Relations. 3rd ed. W. J. Holdsworth. xi, 272p. 1987. pap. 29.50 (0-455-20778-X, Pub. by Law Bk Co) W W Gaunt.

Advocacy & Opposition: An Introduction to Argumentation. 2nd ed. Karyn C. Rybacki & Donald J. Rybacki. 304p. (C). 1990. pap. text ed. write for info. (0-13-016130-6) P-H.

Advocacy & Social Change: A Study of Welfare Rights Workers. Tony Simpson. 1978. 30.00 (0-317-05752-9, Pub. by Natl Inst Soc Work) St Mut.

Advocacy & the Litigation Process in Hong Kong. Wilkinson. 1991. 106.00 (0-409-99597-5) Butterworth Legal Pubs.

Advocacy at the Bar. Keith Evans. 200p. 1983. pap. 24.00 (0-906322-23-5, Pub. by Blackstone Pr UK) W W Gaunt.

Advocacy at the Bar. Keith Evans. 212p. 1993. 26.00 (1-85431-236-7, Pub. by Blackstone Pr UK) W W Gaunt.

Advocacy Basics for Solicitors. Keith Tronc & Ian Dearden. 1993. pap. write for info. (0-455-21198-1, Pub. by Law Bk Co) W W Gaunt.

Advocacy for Children. Barbara Howard. 56p. 1987. pap. 6.50 (0-8309-0492-1) Herald Hse.

Advocacy for Deaf Children. Ed. by Hugh T. Prickett. (Illus.). 114p. (C). 1989. text ed. 32.95x (0-398-05610-2) C C Thomas.

***Advocacy for Deaf Children.** Ed. by Hugh T. Prickett. (Illus.). 114p. 1989. pap. 18.95 (0-398-06332-X) C C Thomas.

Advocacy for Senior Citizens Practice Manual. 6th ed. 1989. 75.00 (0-932622-30-5) Ctr Public Rep.

Advocacy in America: Case Studies in Social Change. Ed. by Gladys W. Hall et al. LC 86-32499. (Illus.). 214p. (Orig.). (C). 1987. lib. bdg. 44.50 (0-8191-6110-1); pap. text ed. 22.50 (0-8191-6111-X) U Pr of Amer.

***Advocacy in Court: A Beginner's Guide.** Keith Evans. 206p. 1995. pap. 28.00 (1-85431-458-0, Pub. by Blackstone Pr UK) W W Gaunt.

Advocacy in Health Care. Ed. by Joan H. Marks. LC 86-283. (Contemporary Issues in Biomedicine, Ethics, & Society Ser.). 160p. 1986. 39.50 (0-89603-092-X) Humana.

Advocacy, Negotiation & Conference Skills. 3rd ed. Inns of Court School of Law Teaching Staff et al. xix, 394p. 1992. pap. 52.00 (1-85431-156-5, Pub. by Blackstone Pr UK) W W Gaunt.

Advocacy Planning for Urban Development: With Analysis of Six Demonstration Programs. Earl Blecher. LC 77-146890. (Special Studies in U. S. Economic, Social & Political Issues). 1971. 39.50 (0-89197-650-7) Irvington.

***Advocacy, Self-Advocacy & Special Needs.** Ed. by Philip Garner & Sarah Sandow. 176p. 1995. pap. text ed. 24.95x (1-85346-349-3, Pub. by D Fulton UK) Taylor & Francis.

Advocacy Skills. Michael Hyam. 162p. 1990. pap. 26.00 (1-85431-061-5, Pub. by Blackstone Pr UK) W W Gaunt.

Advocacy Skills. 2nd ed. Michael Hyam. 168p. 1992. pap. 22.00 (1-85431-204-9, Pub. by Blackstone Pr UK) W W Gaunt.

Advocacy Skills: A Handbook for Human Service Professionals. Neil Bateman. 176p. 1995. pap. 25.95 (1-85742-200-7, Pub. by Arena UK) Ashgate Pub Co.

Advocacy, the Art of Pleading a Cause. 3rd ed. Richard A. Givens. LC 92-15008. (Trial Practice Ser.). 2500p. 1992. text ed. 249.00 (0-07-172398-6) Shepards-McGraw.

Advocate Adviser. Pat Califia. 240p. (Orig.). 1991. pap. 8.95 (1-55583-169-9) Alyson Pubns.

Advocate & Activist: Memoirs of an American Communist Lawyer. John Abt & Michael Myerson. LC 92-47040. 400p. 1993. 39.95 (0-252-02030-8) U of Ill Pr.

Advocate for Texas: Thomas Wilson. Francis W. Wilson. (Illus.). 180p. (Orig.). 1987. pap. 14.83 (0-9619215-1-X) F W Wilson.

Advocate of Understanding: Sidney Gulick & the Search for Peace with Japan. Sandra C. Taylor. LC 84-12272. 274p. 1985. 25.00 (0-87338-307-9) Kent St U Pr.

Advocates. David Pannick. 320p. 1993. reprint ed. pap. 12.95 (0-19-285289-2) OUP.

Advocate's Deskbook: The Essentials of Trying a Case. Irving Younger. 376p. 1988. 65.00 (0-13-018169-2) Aspen Law.

Advocate's Devil. Alan M. Dershowitz. 352p. 1994. 22.95 (0-446-51759-3) Warner Bks.

***Advocate's Devil.** Alan M. Dershowitz. 384p. 1995. mass mkt. 6.50 (0-446-60291-4) Warner Bks.

Advocate's Guide to Auditing the Compliance of Hill-Burton Facilities. 90p. 1988. 15.00 (0-317-02678-X, 44,325) NCLS Inc.

Advocate's Guide to Home Care for the Elderly. Peter Komlos-Hrobsky. 132p. 1988. 15.00 (0-941077-18-7, 43,200) NCLS Inc.

Advocate's Guide to Lobbying & Political Activity for Non-Profits: What You Can & Cannot Do. Children's Defense Fund Staff. 24p. (Orig.). 1991. pap. 4.95 (0-938008-88-9) Childrens Defense.

Advocate's Guide to Medicaid Case Management Programs. 1988. 15.00 (0-941077-20-9, 44,300) NCLS Inc.

Advocate's Guide to Medicare & Medicare Appeals. 23p. 1988. pap. 4.00 (0-317-02679-8, 44,270) NCLS Inc.

Advocate's Guide to the Media. Children's Defense Fund Staff. 24p. (Orig.). 1990. pap. 4.95 (0-938008-75-7) Childrens Defense.

Advocate's Guide to the Medicaid Program. Roger Schwartz. 66p. (Orig.). 1985. pap. 8.00 (0-941077-00-4, 40,200) NCLS Inc.

Advocate's Guide to the Medically Needy Program. Jane Perkins & Lucien Wulsin. (Illus.). 120p. 1985. pap. 10.00 (0-941077-01-2, 40,250) NCLS Inc.

***Advocate's Guide to the Summer Food Service Program.** Children's Defense Fund Staff. 36p. 1994. pap. write for info. (1-881985-07-5) Childrens Defense.

Advocate's Guide to Using Data. Children's Defense Fund Staff. 20p. (Orig.). 1990. pap. 5.95 (0-938008-80-3) Childrens Defense.

Advocate's Introduction to Guaranteed Service Plans & Service Limiters. 203p. 1985. 11.00 (0-685-30188-5, 37, 271) NCLS Inc.

Advocates' Library. Roger Crail & John St. Clair. 80p. 1989. pap. 14.00 (0-11-493499-1, HM9491) UNIPUB.

Advocates of God. Martha M. Wall. (Illus.). 326p. (Orig.). 1987. pap. 12.95 (0-944632-00-9) Chateau Pubs.

Advocates of God. Martha M. Wall. (Illus.). 326p. 1987. write for info. (0-944632-01-7) Chateau Pubs.

Advocates of Peace in Antebellum America. Valarie H. Ziegler. LC 91-16318. (Religion in North America Ser.). 260p. 1992. text ed. 35.00 (0-253-36864-2) Ind U Pr.

***Advocating Archives: An Introduction to Public Relations.** Ed. by Elsie Finch. 208p. 1994. pap. 45.00 (0-614-01639-8) Soc Am Archivists.

***Advocating Archives: An Introduction to Public Relations for Archivists.** Ed. by Elsie F. Finch. LC 94-3797. (Society of American Archivists Ser.). 202p. 1994. 39.50 (0-8108-2935-5) Scarecrow.

An Asterisk (*) at the beginning of an entry indicates that the title is appearing in BIP for the first time.

A

***Advocating for Self: Women's Decisions Concerning Contraception.** Peggy Matteson. LC 95-14297. (Illus.). 146p. (C). 1995. lib. bdg. 29.95 (*1-56024-948-X*); pap. 12.95 (*1-56023-868-2*) Haworth Jrnl Co-Edits.

Advocating for the Child in Protection Proceedings: A Guide for Child Advocates. Donald N. Duquette. 192p. 1990. text ed. 24.95 (*0-669-21465-5*) Free Pr.

Ady Es Kincs Gyula: Biography of Hungarian Poet Ady. Elek Kincs. LC 68-150338. 1970. pap. 3.50 (*0-911862-20-X*) Hungarian Rev.

Adytum of the Heart: The Literary Criticism of Charlotte Bronte. Patricia H. Wheat. LC 90-56414. 128p. 1992. 28.50 (*0-8386-3443-5*) Fairleigh Dickinson.

AEA Technology - Annual Review: 1992-93, 2 vols., Set. 88p. 1993. pap. 35.00 (*0-11-984000-6*, HM40006, Pub. by HMSO UK) UNIPUB.

***AEA Technology Pages, 1994.** 162p. 1994. pap. write for info. (*0-614-04924-5*) Venture Pub NA.

AEC Drafting Fundamentals. Jules Ciavaroli. LC 93-48079. 320p. 1994. pap. text ed. 27.25 (*0-314-93452-9*) West Pub.

AED Membership Directory. annuals 72p. 10.00 (*0-318-13416-0*); 5.00 (*0-318-13417-9*) Assn Equip Distrs.

Aedificiorum Figurae: Untersuchungen Zu Den Architekturdarstellungen Des Fruhen Zweiten Stils. Rolf A. Tybout. (Dutch Monographs on Ancient History & Archaeology: Vol. VII). (Illus.). ix, 462p. (GER.). 1989. 127.00 (*90-5063-042-1*, Pub. by Gieben NE) Benjamins North Am.

AEE Directory of Energy Professionals, 1982-83. rev. ed. Association of Energy Engineers. 1982. text ed. 28.00 (*0-915586-58-4*) Fairmont Pr.

AEF & Coalition Warmaking, 1917-1918. David F. Trask. LC 93-7992. (Modern War Studies). (Illus.). 248p. (C). 1993. 29.95 (*0-7006-0619-X*) U Pr of KS.

Aegean Bronze Age. Oliver Dickinson. LC 93-2666. (World Archaeology Ser.). (Illus.). 368p. (C). 1994. 64.95 (*0-521-24280-0*) Cambridge U Pr.

Aegean Bronze Age. Oliver Dickinson. LC 93-2666. (World Archaeology Ser.). (Illus.). 368p. (C). 1994. pap. 27.95 (*0-521-45664-9*) Cambridge U Pr.

Aegean Crossroads. James Trilling et al. LC 83-18284. (Illus.). 150p. 1983. pap. 25.00 (*0-87405-022-7*) Textile Mus.

Aegean Crossroads: Greek Island Embroideries in the Textile Museum. James Trilling et al. (Illus.). 150p. 1989. pap. 25.00 (*0-295-96593-2*) U of Wash Pr.

Aegean Mission: Allied Operations in the Dodecanese, 1943. Jeffrey Holland. LC 88-5659. (Contributions in Military Studies: No. 77). 208p. 1988. text ed. 49.95 (*0-313-26283-7*, HDM/, Greenwood Pr) Greenwood.

Aegean Painting in the Bronze Age. Sara A. Immerwahr. LC 87-43123. (Illus.). 304p. 1990. lib. bdg. 55.00 (*0-271-00628-5*) Pa St U Pr.

Aegean Summer: A Family Odyssey. Mimi L. Summerskill. LC 90-36781. (Illus.). 304p. 1990. 22.50 (*0-8397-0105-5*) Eriksson.

Aegean World. Alfred Nawrath. LC 77-87872. (Illus.). 1977. 30.00 (*0-88331-097-X*) J J Binns.

Aegidius Romanus, De Renunciatione Pape. Ed. by John R. Eastman. LC 92-39792. (Texts & Studies in Religion: Vol. 52). 428p. 1992. text ed. 109.95 (*0-7734-9623-8*) E Mellen.

Aegina. Thomas J. Figueira. Ed. by W. R. Connor. LC 80-2649. (Monographs in Classical Studies). 1981. lib. bdg. 39.00 (*0-405-14036-3*) Ayer.

Aegis: Selected Poems Nineteen Seventy-Nineteen to Eighty. Cid Corman. LC 82-16923. 112p. (Orig.). 1983. 14.95 (*0-930794-57-5*); pap. 5.95 (*0-930794-58-3*) Station Hill Pr.

Aegis - Guardian of the Fleet: Official Strategy Guide. Ed Dille. 1994. pap. 19.95 (*1-55958-625-7*) Prima Pub.

Aegis Gd Missile Cruiser. Dennis Bailey & Arnold Meisner. (Illus.). 96p. 1991. pap. 9.95 (*0-87938-545-6*) Motorbooks Intl.

Aegypt. John Crowley. 1994. pap. 12.95 (*0-553-37430-3*) Bantam.

Aegyptiaca, Etc. Manetho. Ed. by E. H. Warmington. Bd. with Tetrabiblios (Loeb Classical Library: No. 350). (ENG & GRE.). 15.50 (*0-674-99385-3*) HUP.

Aegyptian Logic: A Curriculum Guide. A. W. Evans. LC 90-91656. (Illus.). 72p. (Orig.). 1990. pap. text ed. 19.95 (*0-9626253-1-0*) AWE Pub.

Aegyptischen Personennamen. Hermann Ranke. Incl. List of Names. 90.00 (*0-685-71722-4*); Form, Meaning, History of Names. 128.00 (*0-685-71723-2*); List of Components. 75.00 (*0-685-71721-6*); write for info. (*0-318-53734-6*) J J Augustin.

AEI Studies on Contemporary Economic Problems, 1976. Ed. by William J. Fellner. LC 76-21977. 379p. reprint ed. pap. 108.10 (*0-8357-4455-8*, 2037293) Bks Demand.

Aeiolian Sediments. Ed. by K. Pye & N. Lancaster. LC 92-36454. (International Association of Sedimentologists Special Publication Ser.: No. 16). 1993. pap. 65.00 (*0-632-03544-7*) Blackwell Sci.

Aekyung's Dream. Min Paek. LC 88-18928. (Illus.). 24p. (ENG & KOR.). (J). (gr. 2-7). 1988. 13.95 (*0-89239-042-5*) Childrens Book Pr.

Aelfric: An Annotated Bibliography. Luke M. Reinsma. LC 85-45125. (Reference Library of the Humanities: Vol. 617). 328p. 1987. lib. bdg. 60.00 (*0-8240-8665-1*) Garland.

Aelfric's First Series of Catholic Homilies see Early English Manuscripts in Facsimile

Aelfwine's Prayerbook. Intro. by Beate Gunsel. (Henry Bradshaw Society Ser.: Vol. 108). (Illus.). 196p. (C). 1993. text ed. 63.00 (*1-870252-04-7*) Boydell & Brewer.

Aelius Aristides, Klage Uber Eleusis (Oratio 22) Ein Kommentar. Achilles Humbel. Bd. 52. (GER.). Date not set. write for info. (*0-318-70632-6*, Pub. by Georg Olms GW) Lubrecht & Cramer.

Aelred of Rievaulx: A Study. Aelred Squire. (Cistercian Studies: No. 50). 192p. 1981. 10.95 (*0-87907-850-2*); pap. 5.00 (*0-686-85802-6*) Cistercian Pubns.

Aelred of Rievaulx, Historical Works. Aelred of Rievaulx. Ed. by Jane P. Freeland & Marsha Dutton. LC 93-46002. (Cistercian Fathers Ser.: No. 56). 1994. write for info. (*0-87907-256-3*); pap. write for info. (*0-87907-288-1*) Cistercian Pubns.

Aelred of Rievaulx's Spiritual Friendship. Tr. by Mark F. Williams. LC 93-63036. 1994. write for info. (*0-940866-30-7*) U Scranton Pr.

***Aelteren Greichischen Katenen zum Buch Hiob Band 1: Einleitung, Prologe und Epiloge, Fragmente zu Hiob 1, 1-8, 22.** Ed. by Ursula Hagedorn & Dieter Hagedorn. (Patristische Texte Und Studien Ser.: No. 40). xv, 457p. (GER.). (C). 1994. lib. bdg. 183.10 (*3-11-014483-2*) De Gruyter.

Aemilius Paullus, Conquerer of Greece. William A. Reiter. 160p. 1988. lib. bdg. 55.00 (*0-7099-4285-0*, Pub. by Croom Helm UK) Routledge Chapman & Hall.

Aeneas: Virgil's Epic Retold for Young Readers. E. Frenkel. 184p. 1986. 14.95 (*0-86292-198-8*, Pub. by Brstl Class Pr UK) Focus Info Gr.

Aeneas' Arrival in Latium. Henriette Boas. Vol. VI. 263p. Date not set. write for info. (*0-318-71077-3*, Pub. by Georg Olms GW) Lubrecht & Cramer.

Aeneas, Sicily & Rome. Gotthard K. Galinsky. LC 69-18059. (Princeton Monographs in Art & Archaeology: 40). 394p. reprint ed. pap. 112.30 (*0-8357-5210-0*, 2055272) Bks Demand.

Aeneas to Augustus: A Beginning Latin Reader for College Students. 2nd ed. Mason Hammond & Anne R. Amory. LC 67-12104. 474p. (Orig.). (C). 1967. pap. 19.95 (*0-674-00600-3*) HUP.

Aeneid. Robert Fitzgerald. 1984. pap. 10.95 (*0-394-72596-4*) Random.

Aeneid. Virgil. Tr. by James H. Mantinband. LC 64-15700. 200p. 1964. pap. text ed. 10.95 (*0-8044-6952-0*, F Ungar Bks) Continuum.

Aeneid. Virgil. 1992. 17.00 (*0-679-41335-9*, Everymans Lib) Knopf.

Aeneid. Virgil. Ed. by Ahl. (Classical Texts Ser.: Bk VI). write for info. (*0-85668-417-1*, Pub. by Aris & Phillips UK); pap. write for info. (*0-85668-418-X*, Pub. by Aris & Phillips UK) David Brown.

***Aeneid.** Virgil. 1995. pap. 2.00 (*0-486-28749-1*) Dover.

Aeneid. Virgil. Tr. by Robert Fitzgerald. LC 89-40605. 448p. 1990. pap. 8.00 (*0-679-72952-6*, Vin) Random.

Aeneid. Virgil. Tr. by William F. Knight. (Classics Ser.). 1956. mass mkt. 8.95 (*0-14-044051-8*, Penguin Classics) Viking Penguin.

Aeneid. Virgil. (Book Notes Ser.). (C). 1984. pap. 2.50 (*0-8120-3400-7*) Barron.

Aeneid. Virgil. (Illus.). 1991. 40.00 (*0-937986-71-2*) D M Grant.

Aeneid. Virgil. Tr. by Patric Dickinson. 1961. pap. 3.99 (*0-451-62277-4*, ME2277, Ment) NAL-Dutton.

Aeneid. Virgil. Tr. by Robert Fitzgerald. LC 83-3101. 1983. 39.95 (*0-394-52827-1*) Random.

Aeneid. Virgil. Tr. & Intro. by David West. (Illus.). 288p. 1991. mass mkt. 8.95 (*0-14-044457-2*, Penguin Classics) Viking Penguin.

Aeneid, Bk. VIII. Virgil. Ed. by K. W. Gransden. LC 76-12729. (Cambridge Greek & Latin Classics Ser.). (Illus.). 1976. pap. 21.95 (*0-521-29047-3*) Cambridge U Pr.

Aeneid, Bk. IX. Virgil. Ed. by Philip Hardie. LC 93-44010. (Cambridge Greek & Latin Classics Ser.). 264p. (C). 1995. 59.95 (*0-521-35126-X*); pap. 22.95 (*0-521-35952-X*) Cambridge U Pr.

Aeneid, Bks. 7-12. Virgil. Ed. by R. D. Williams. (Classical Ser.). 1973. pap. text ed. 20.00 (*0-312-84840-4*) St Martin.

Aeneid, No. XII. Virgil. Ed. by McKay. 1992. write for info. (*0-85668-518-6*, Pub. by Aris & Phillips UK); pap. write for info. (*0-85668-519-4*, Pub. by Aris & Phillips UK) David Brown.

Aeneid II Selections. Virgil. Ed. by C. H. Craddock. (Cambridge Latin Texts Ser.). 1975. pap. 7.50 (*0-521-20827-0*) Cambridge U Pr.

Aeneid IV Selections. Virgil. (Cambridge Latin Texts Ser.). 1977. pap. 8.95 (*0-521-21581-1*) Cambridge U Pr.

Aeneid Notes. Robert Milch. 1982. pap. 3.95 (*0-8220-0119-5*) Cliffs.

Aeneid of Virgil. 381p. (C). 1983. pap. write for info. (*0-02-358500-5*, Scribners) S&S Trade.

Aeneid of Virgil. Rolfe Humphries. 1983. pap. write for info. (*0-684-18085-5*, SL6, Scribners) S&S Trade.

Aeneid of Virgil. Rolfe Humphries. 1984. pap. 6.95 (*0-684-71816-2*, Scribners) S&S Trade.

***Aeneid of Virgil.** Tr. by Edward McCrorie. 1994. 39.50 (*0-472-09595-1*) U of Mich Pr.

***Aeneid of Virgil.** Tr. by Edward McCrorie. 1995. pap. 14.95 (*0-472-06595-5*) U of Mich Pr.

Aeneid of Virgil. Virgil. Ed. by Edward M. Forster. Tr. by Edward F. Taylor. LC 70-177561. (Temple Greek & Latin Classics: No. 3). 1906. 30.00 (*0-404-07903-2*) AMS Pr.

Aeneid of Virgil. Virgil. LC 82-45105. 1953. mass mkt. 10.95 (*0-385-09318-7*, A20, Anchor NY) Doubleday.

Aeneid of Virgil. Virgil. Tr. by Allen Mandelbaum. (Bantam Classics Ser.). 416p. (gr. 9-12). 1981. pap. 3.95 (*0-553-21041-6*) Bantam.

Aeneid of Virgil: A Verse Translation. Rolfe Humphries. 416p. (C). 1987. pap. write for info. (*0-02-427780-0*) Macmillan.

Aeneid of Virgil: A Verse Translation. Virgil. Tr. by Allen Mandelbaum. (Illus.). 415p. 1981. pap. 15.00 (*0-520-04550-5*) U CA Pr.

Aeneid of Virgil Translated into Scottish Verse, 2 Vols, Set. Virgil. Ed. by George Dundas. Tr. by Gawin Douglas. LC 73-144418. (Bannatyne Club, Edinburgh. Publications: No. 64). reprint ed. 82.50 (*0-404-52775-2*) AMS Pr.

Aeneid Second Vergil. Frank O. Copley. 352p. (C). 1975. pap. write for info. (*0-02-325340-1*) Macmillan.

Aeneid VI Selections. Virgil. Ed. by Anne Haward. LC 82-12760. (Cambridge Latin Texts Ser.). 64p. 1983. pap. 8.50 (*0-521-28694-8*) Cambridge U Pr.

Aeneid VIII Selections. Virgil. Ed. by C. H. Craddock. (Cambridge Latin Texts Ser.). 48p. (C). 1973. pap. 7.50 (*0-521-20280-9*) Cambridge U Pr.

Aeneid XI. Virgil & McKay. (Classical Texts Ser.). 1991. write for info. (*0-85668-516-X*, Pub. by Aris & Phillips UK); pap. write for info. (*0-85668-517-8*, Pub. by Aris & Phillips UK) David Brown.

Aeneida, or Critical, Exegetical, & Aesthetical Remarks on the Aeneis, 4 vols., Set. James Henry. 1969. reprint ed. 559.00 (*0-685-66477-5*, 05102006, Pub. by Georg Olms GW) Lubrecht & Cramer.

Aeneidos: Liber Primus. Virgil. (LAT.). 1984. 24.95 (*0-19-872117-X*) OUP.

Aeneidos: Liber Quartus. Virgil. Ed. by R. G. Austin. (C). 1983. reprint ed. 19.95 (*0-19-872111-0*) OUP.

Aeneidos: Liber Secundus. Virgil. Ed. by R. G. Austin. 1980. pap. 19.95 (*0-19-872106-4*) OUP.

Aeneidos: Liber Sextus. Virgil. Ed. by R. G. Austin. (Illus.). 316p. 1986. pap. 19.95 (*0-19-872128-5*) OUP.

Aenied, Bk. XI. Virgil. Ed. by K. W. Grandsen. (Greek & Latin Classics Ser.). 160p. (C). 1991. pap. 19.95 (*0-521-27816-3*) Cambridge U Pr.

Aenied, Bk. XI. Virgil. Ed. by K. W. Grandsen. (Greek & Latin Classics Ser.). 160p. (C). 1991. 49.95 (*0-521-26040-X*) Cambridge U Pr.

***Aeolian & Adhesion Morphodynamics & Phytoecology in Recent Coastal & Inland Sand & Snow Flats & Dunes from Mainly North Sea & Baltic Sea to Mars & Venus, 2 vols.** Detlef Mader. LC 94-41210. 2348p. 1994. 225.95 (*0-8204-2814-0*) P Lang Pubs.

Aeolian Dust & Dust Deposits. Kenneth Pye. (Orig.). 1987. text ed. 102.00 (*0-12-568690-0*); pap. text ed. 49.00 (*0-12-568691-9*) Acad Pr.

Aeolian Grain Transport, Vol. 1: Mechanics. O. E. Barndorff-Nielsen & B. B. Willets. (Acta Mechanical, Supplementum Ser.: No. 1-2). (Illus.). ix, 181p. 1991. 142.00 (*0-387-82269-0*) Spr-Verlag.

Aeolian Grain Transport, Vol. 2: The Erosional Environment. O. E. Barndorff-Nielsen & B. B. Willets. (Acta Mechanical, Supplementum Ser.: No. 1-2). (Illus.). ix, 181p. 1991. 142.00 (*0-387-82274-7*) Spr-Verlag.

Aeolian Islands. Philip Ward. (Travel Bks.: Vol. 4). (Illus.). 1974. pap. 12.50 (*0-902675-43-5*) Oleander Pr.

Aeolian Sand & Sand Dunes. Kenneth Pye & Haim Tsoar. 416p. 1990. 115.00 (*0-04-551125-X*) Routledge Chapman & Hall.

Aeonic Delusions of Money. (Money Reform Ser.). 1994. lib. bdg. 250.00 (*0-8490-5656-X*) Gordon Pr.

Aepinus's Essay on the Theory of Electricity & Magnetism. R. W. Home. Tr. by P. J. Connor. LC 78-10105. 1979. 85.00 (*0-691-08222-7*) Princeton U Pr.

***Aepinus's Essay on the Theory of Electricity & Magnetism: Introductory Monograph & Notes by R. W. Home.** Franz U. Aepinus. LC 78-10105. reprint ed. pap. 150.50 (*0-7837-9324-3*, 2060064) Bks Demand.

AEPS Curriculum for Birth to Three Years. Ed. by Juliann J. Cripe et al. (Assessment, Evaluation, & Programming System (AEPS) for Infants & Children Ser.: Vol. 2). 496p. (C). 1992. spiral bd. 59.00 (*1-55766-096-4*) P H Brookes.

AEPS Curriculum for Birth to Three Years, Family Interest Survey, pkg. of 30. Ed. by Juliann J. Cripe et al. (Assessment, Evaluation, & Programming System (AEPS) for Infants & Children Ser.: Vol. 2). 496p. (C). 1992. 10.00 (*1-55766-098-0*) P H Brookes.

Aequanimitas: With Other Addresses to Medical Students, Nurses & Practitioners of Medicine. 3rd ed. William Osler. 421p. 1932. text ed. 50.00 (*0-07-047915-1*) Hlth Prof Div.

Aeration. Water Pollution Control Federation Staff. (MOP Ser.: No. MFD13). 167p. 1988. pap. 37.50 (*0-943244-73-0*) Water Environ.

Aeration: A Wastewater Treatment Process. (ASCE Manual & Report on Engineering Practice Ser.: No. 68). 178p. 1988. 50.00 (*0-87262-673-3*) Am Soc Civil Eng.

Aeration of Activated Sludge in Sewage Treatment. D. L. Gibbon. LC 74-8138. 126p. 1974. 56.00 (*0-08-018156-2*, Pub. by Pergamon Repr UK) Franklin.

***Aeration Technology.** Ed. by R. E. Arndt & A. Prosperetti. LC 94-71359. (Fluid Engineering Division Conference Ser.: Vol. 187). 67p. 1994. pap. 25.00 (*0-7918-1370-3*) ASME.

Aerea in the Forests of Manhattan. Emmanuel Hocquard. Tr. by Lydia Davis. LC 92-60853. 128p. 1992. 16.95 (*0-910395-88-8*) Marlboro Pr.

Aerial, No. 5. Ed. by Rod Smith. 184p. (Orig.). 1989. pap. 7.50 (*0-9619097-2-2*) Edge Bks.

Aerial America: From Sea to Shining Sea. Jim Doane, Jr. (J). (ps-12). 1981. 2.95 (*0-936672-11-0*) Aerial Photo.

Aerial Anomalies International Directory: Aerial Anomalies International Associate Directory, 1990. Robert D. Boyd. (Illus.). (Orig.). (C). 1990. per. 10.00 (*0-9620197-4-7*) R D Boyd.

Aerial Atlas of Ancient Crete. Ed. by J. Wilson Myers et al. LC 91-20649. (Centennial Book Ser.). (C). 1992. 110.00 (*0-520-07382-7*) U CA Pr.

Aerial Combat Escapades. J. Hunter Reinburg. Ed. by Michael J. Ebersole. 280p. 1988. pap. 12.95 (*0-9613218-2-2*) GCBA.

Aerial Discovery Manual. Carl H. Strandberg. LC 67-19945. (Wiley Series on Photographic Science & Technology & the Graphic Arts). (Illus.). 285p. reprint ed. pap. 81.30 (*0-8357-5211-9*, 2056445) Bks Demand.

***Aerial Freestyle Guidebook.** Dale Stuart. (Illus.). 72p. 1993. pap. 29.95 (*0-9607814-9-8*) Aero Graphics.

Aerial Gunners: The Unknown Aces of World War II. Charles A. Watry & Duane L. Hall. LC 85-91368. (Illus.). 256p. (Orig.). (J). 1986. pap. 12.95 (*0-914379-01-1*) C Watry.

Aerial Interdiction: Air Power & the Land Battle in Three American Wars. 1992. text ed. write for info. (*0-912799-74-9*); pap. text ed. write for info. (*0-912799-73-0*) Off Air Force.

Aerial Mapping: Methods & Applications. Edgar Falkner. LC 94-15243. (Mapping Sciences Ser.). 1994. write for info. (*1-56670-103-1*) Lewis Pubs.

Aerial Perception. Margret Dreikausen. LC 82-65880. (Illus.). 1985. 35.00 (*0-87982-040-3*) Art Alliance.

Aerial Photography & Image Interpretation for Resource Management. David P. Paine. LC 81-4287. 571p. 1981. Net. text ed. write for info. (*0-471-01857-0*) Wiley.

Aerial Photography in Anthropological Field Research. Ed. by Evon Z. Vogt. LC 73-90850. (Illus.). 204p. reprint ed. pap. 57.60 (*0-7837-1732-6*, 2057262) Bks Demand.

Aerial Pioneers: The U. S. Air Mail Service, 1918-1927. William M. Leary. LC 85-600033. (Illus.). 310p. 1986. 29.95 (*0-87474-610-8*, LEAP) Smithsonian.

Aerial Piracy & Aviation Security. Ed. by Yonah Alexander & Eugene Sochor. (International Studies on Terrorism). 224p. 1990. lib. bdg. 92.00 (*0-7923-0932-4*) Kluwer Ac.

Aerial Reconnaissance for Verification of Arms Limitation Agreements, an Introduction. 166p. 1991. 35.00 (*92-9045-044-4*, E.GV.90.0.11) UN.

Aerial Search: The C. A. P. Story. Frank Burnham. 208p. 1982. pap. 2.95 (*0-8168-0054-5*, 28907, TAB-Aero) TAB Bks.

Aerial Six - Seven: Art Is Either a Complaint or Do Something Else. John Cage et al. Ed. by Rod Smith. 224p. (Orig.). 1991. pap. 15.00 (*0-9619097-3-0*) Edge Bks.

Aerial Studies: A Collection of Poems. Sandra A. Witt. LC 93-83980. (Minnesota Voices Project Ser.). 72p. (Orig.). 1994. pap. 7.95 (*0-89823-157-4*) New Rivers Pr.

Aerial Suppression of Bushfires. I. T. Loane & J. S. Gould. 1986. pap. 40.00 (*0-643-04023-4*, Pub. by CSIRO AT) Intl Spec Bk.

Aerial Tide Coming In. Frannie Lindsay. (Illus.). 16p. 1981. pap. 3.00 (*0-934714-24-X*); bds. 25.00 (*0-934714-23-1*) Swamp Pr.

Aerial View of Louisiana. Cleopatra Mathis. LC 79-90841. 77p. 1979. 9.95 (*0-935296-00-X*) Sheep Meadow.

***Aerial 8: Barrett Watten.** Barrett Watten et al. Ed. & Intro. by Rod Smith. (Contemporary Poetics As Critical Theory Ser.). 320p. (Orig.). 1995. pap. 12.95 (*0-9619097-4-9*) Edge Bks.

Aero Engined Racing Cars. Bill Boddy. (Illus.). 160p. 1992. 39.95 (*0-85429-867-3*) Haynes Pubns.

Aero-Hydrodynamics of Sailing. Zeslaw A. Marchaj. 1980. 40.00 (*0-396-07739-0*, Putnam) Putnam Pub Group.

Aero-Hydrodynamics of Sailing. exp. rev. ed. C. A. Marchaj. (Illus.). 746p. 1988. text ed. 59.95 (*0-87742-993-6*) Intl Marine.

Aero into the Aether: Surrealist Comics & Poems. Hal Rammel. (Illus.). 28p. 1980. pap. 12.00 (*0-941194-14-0*) Black Swan Pr.

Aero Nursing News. Ed. by Darlene M. Sredl. 1985. pap. 2.50 (*0-930835-02-6*) Med Res Assocs.

Aero-Optical Phenomena. Ed. by Keith G. Gilbert et al. LC 81-20490. (PAAS Ser.: Vol. 80). (Illus.). 412p. 1982. 65.95 (*0-915928-60-4*) AIAA.

Aeroassisted Orbital Transfer: Guidance & Control Strategies. D. Subbaram Naidu. LC 93-38670. 1993. 44.00 (*0-387-19819-9*) Spr-Verlag.

Aerobatics. Neil Williams. (Illus.). 266p. 1991. 29.95 (*0-9504543-0-3*) Specialty Pr.

Aerobic Biological Treatment of Waste Waters: Principles & Practice; a Monograph. Arthur W. Busch. LC 70-155639. (Illus.). 432p. reprint ed. pap. 123.20 (*0-8357-8009-0*, 2034171) Bks Demand.

Aerobic Chic & Other Delusions. John L. Parker. (Orig.). 1983. pap. 3.95 (*0-915297-03-5*) Cedarwinds.

***Aerobic Dance.** Donna Gardner et al. 48p. (C). 1994. pap. text ed. 9.56 (*0-8403-9728-3*) Kendall-Hunt.

Aerobic Dance. Phyllis C. Jacobson. (Sport for Life Ser.). (C). 1988. pap. text ed. 11.00 (*0-673-18522-2*) HarpCollege.

Aerobic Dance: Fitness for College & Beyond. Bibik et al. 192p. 1993. per. 16.95 (*0-8403-8229-4*) Kendall-Hunt.

Aerobic Dance: Fitness for College & Beyond. Janice Bibik et al. 192p. (C). 1994. per. 18.95 (*0-8403-9402-0*) Kendall-Hunt.

Aerobic Dance: Fitness for Life. Martha A. Quillin. 128p. (C). 1992. pap. text ed. 24.95 (*0-8403-7626-X*) Kendall-Hunt.

Aerobic Dance: Handbook. 128p. (C). 1992. spiral bd. 12.95 (*0-8403-7943-9*) Kendall-Hunt.

Aerobic Dance-Exercise Instructor Manual: An Official Publication of the International Dance-Exercise (IDEA) Foundation. Ed. by Naneene VanGelder & Sheryl Marks. LC 87-80343. (Illus.). 389p. 1987. pap. 24.95 (*0-9618161-0-4*) Am Coun Exer.

Aerobic Dance for Effective Performance. Anita J. Simms et al. 144p. (C). 1994. per. 25.56 (*0-8403-9551-5*) Kendall-Hunt.

An Asterisk (*) at the beginning of an entry indicates that the title is appearing in BIP for the first time.

A

Aerobic Dance for Health & Fitness. Lorna Francis. 144p. (C). 1993. pap. text ed. write for info. (*0-697-10492-3*) Brown & Benchmark.

Aerobic Exercise for Life. Teresa J. Landis. 80p. (C). 1991. pap. text ed. 12.95 (*0-8403-6281-1*) Kendall-Hunt.

Aerobic Fitness & Health. Roy J. Shephard. LC 93-457. (Illus.). 368p. 1994. text ed. 48.00x (*0-87322-417-5*, BSHE0417) Human Kinetics.

Aerobic Fitness Everyone. Stokes & Trapp. 260p. 1989. pap. text ed. 12.95 (*0-88725-114-5*) Hunter Textbks.

Aerobic Gram-Negative Bronchopneumonias: Proceedings of the Symposium, Brussels, Sept. 22, 1978. Aerobic Gram-Negative Bronchopneumonias Symposium Staff. Ed. by J. Thys et al. LC 79-42759. (Illus.). 120p. 1980. 86.00 (*0-08-025533-7*, Pub. by Pergamon Repr UK) Franklin.

***Aerobic Heterotrophic Biodegradation in Polluted Drains & Sewers: The Drain & Sewers As Dual-Phase Biological Reactors.** Ye-Shi Cao. 138p. 1994. 39.00 (*90-5410-402-3*) Balkema RSA.

Aerobic-Isometric Exercises for Men & Women over Sixty. Morton Edell & Norman Wall. 105p. 1993. pap. text ed. 8.95 (*0-9639683-0-0*) Vitality Corp.

Aerobic Running: Help Yourself to Fitness & Fun. George R. Colfer et al. 144p. (C). 1993. per. 10.95 (*0-8403-8906-X*) Kendall-Hunt.

Aerobic Walking: The Best & Safest Weight Loss & Cardiovascular Exercise for Everyone Overweight or Out of Shape. Casey Meyers. LC 87-40076. 224p. 1987. pap. 10.00 (*0-394-75440-9*, Vin) Random.

Aerobic Weight Training. 181p. 1982. 11.95 (*0-89037-230-6*) Anderson World.

Aerobic Weight Training. Sobey. (Runner's World Ser.). 1982. pap. 9.95 (*0-02-499490-1*) Macmillan.

Aerobic Workbook: A Self Study Manual for College Students. Jackie Tally. 112p. (C). 1993. pap. text ed. 15.95 (*0-8403-8351-7*) Kendall-Hunt.

***Aerobics.** Jeff Savage. (Illus.). (YA). (gr. 5 up). 1995. pap. 7.95 (*0-382-24945-3*, Crstwood Hse) Silver Burdett Pr.

Aerobics. Jeff Savage. LC 93-37296. (Working Out Ser.). (J). 1995. text ed. 13.95 (*0-89686-853-2*, Crstwood Hse) Silver Burdett Pr.

Aerobics: A Guide for Participants. 2nd ed. Shanna M. Chastain. 80p. 1993. per. 10.50 (*0-8403-8492-0*) Kendall-Hunt.

Aerobics: The Way to Fitness. Karen S. Mazzeo. (Illus.). 200p. (C). 1992. pap. text ed. 14.95x (*0-89582-221-0*) Morton Pub.

***Aerobics: Basic & Creative: The ABCs of Instructor Training 3 Complete Courses.** Pam Germain. (Illus.). 175p. (Orig.). (C). 1995. pap. text ed. 24.95 (*1-886924-25-2*) BodyBasics.

***Aerobics: Basic & Creative: The ABCs of Instructor Training-3 Complete Courses.** Pam Germain. (Illus.). 175p. (Orig.). (C). 1995. student ed 7.95 (*1-886924-26-0*) BodyBasics.

Aerobics for Fiddlers. Date not set. 5.95 (*0-7866-0000-4*, 95166); audio 9.98 (*0-7866-0001-2*, 95166C) Mel Bay.

Aerobics for the Spirit. Robert Morley. 1990. pap. write for info. (*0-8499-3224-6*) Word Inc.

Aerobics Instructor Manual: The Resource for Fitness Professionals. Ed. by Richard T. Cotton & Robert L. Goldstein. (Illus.). 536p. (C). 1993. text ed. 39.95 (*0-9618161-3-9*) Am Coun Exer.

Aerobics Program. Kenneth H. Cooper. 1985. pap. 16.95 (*0-553-34677-6*) Bantam.

Aerobics Today. Carole M. Casten & Peg Jordan. Ed. by Clyde Perlee. 151p. (C). 1990. pap. text ed. 20.00 (*0-314-68953-2*) West Pub.

Aerobie Book. rev. ed. John Cassidy. (Illus.). 1985. pap. 12.95 (*0-932592-30-9*) Klutz Pr.

Aerobiological Pathway of Microorganisms. C. S. Cox. 293p. 1987. text ed. 110.00 (*0-471-91170-4*) Wiley.

Aerobiological Pathway of Microorganisms. C. S. Cox. LC 86-15710. (Wiley-Interscience Publication Ser.). 305p. reprint ed. pap. 87.00 (*0-7837-3229-5*, 2043247) Bks Demand.

Aerobiology. Muilenbery. 1995. write for info. (*0-87371-724-4*) Lewis Pubs.

Aerobix Plus: How to Sweat with Class. Sue Block. LC 81-80789. (Illus.). 240p. (Orig.). 1982. pap. text ed. 14.00 (*0-918438-72-1*, PBLO0072) Human Kinetics.

Aerobox: A High Performance Fitness Program. Michael Olajide, Jr. & Phil Berger. 192p. (Orig.). 1995. pap. 12.99 (*0-446-67116-9*) Warner Bks.

Aerocrafter: Homebuilt Aircraft Sourcebook. Ed. by Don Purdy. 200p. 1993. pap. 12.95 (*0-9636409-0-9*) BAI Pub.

AeroCrafter: Homebuilt Aircraft Sourcebook. 2nd ed. Ed. by Don Purdy. (Illus.). 300p. 1994. pap. 20.00 (*0-9636409-1-7*) BAI Pub.

***AeroCrafter: Homebuilt Aircraft Sourcebook.** 3rd ed. Don Purdy. 400p. 1995. pap. 25.00 (*0-9636409-2-5*) BAI Pub.

Aerodays 1993: Second Community Aeronautics RTD Conference, EUR 14977. 576p. 1993. pap. 65.00 (*92-826-6301-9*, CD-NA-14977-EN-C, Pub. by Europ Com) UNIPUB.

Aerodrome: A Love Story. Rex Warner. LC 93-11245. 312p. 1993. reprint ed. pap. 12.95 (*1-56663-025-8*) I R Dee.

Aerodynamic Characteristics of Atmospheric Boundary Layers. Erich J. Plate. LC 70-611329. (AEC Critical Review Ser.). 190p. 1971. pap. 12.75 (*0-87079-132-X*, TID-25465); fiche 9.00 (*0-87079-133-8*, TID-25465) DOE.

Aerodynamic Design of Aircraft: In SI Metric Units. D. Kuchemann. 1978. 233.00 (*0-08-020515-1*, Pub. by Pergamon Repr UK) Franklin.

Aerodynamic Noise: Proceedings of AFOSR-UTIAS Symposium, Held at Toronto, 1968. AFOSR-UTIAS Symposium on Aerodynamic Noise Staff. LC 70-443978. 454p. reprint ed. pap. 129.40 (*0-8357-5212-7*, 2014382) Bks Demand.

Aerodynamic Theory: A General Review of Progress, 5 vols., Set. Ed. by W. Frederick Durand. Incl. Vol. 1. Aerodynamic Theory: A General Review of Progress Vol. 1: Mathematical Aids, Fluid Mechanics, Historical Sketch. 1995. 16.00 (*0-8446-0603-0*); Vol. 2. Aerodynamic Theory: A General Review of Progress Vol. 2: General Aerodynamic Theory, Perfect Fluids. 1995. 16.00 (*0-8446-0604-9*); Vol. 3. Aerodynamic Theory: A General Review of Progress Vol. 3: Theory of Single Burbling, Mechanics of Viscous Fluids, Etc. 1995. 16.00 (*0-8446-0605-7*); Vol. 5. Aerodynamic Theory: A General Review of Progress Vol. 5: Dynamics of the Airplane, Airplane Performance. 1995. 16.00 (*0-8446-0607-3*); Vol. 6. Aerodynamic Theory: A General Review of Progress Vol. 6: Airplanes As a Whole, Aerodynamics of Airships, Etc. 1995. 16.00 (*0-8446-0739-8*); 1995. 80.00 (*0-8446-0602-2*) Peter Smith.

***Aerodynamics, Aeronautics & Fight Mechanics.** 2nd ed. Barnes W. McCormick. LC 94-222312. 1994. text ed. write for info. (*0-471-57506-2*) Wiley.

Aerodynamics, Aeronautics & Flight Mechanics. Barnes W. McCormick, Jr. LC 79-11073. 652p. 1979. Net. text ed. write for info. (*0-471-03032-5*) Wiley.

Aerodynamics & Aeroacoustics: Proceedings of the Symposium. K. Y. Fung. (Advanced Series on Fluid Mechanics). 384p. 1994. text ed. 91.00 (*981-02-1732-3*) World Scientific Pub.

Aerodynamics for Engineering Students. 4th ed. E. L. Houghton & P. W. Carpenter. 515p. 1993. pap. text ed. 52.95 (*0-470-22130-5*) Halsted Pr.

Aerodynamics for Engineers. 2nd ed. John J. Bertin & Michael L. Smith. 624p. 1988. text ed. 81.00 (*0-13-018243-5*) P-H.

Aerodynamics for Naval Aviation. Chief of Naval Operations. (Illus.). 416p. (C). 1987. reprint ed. pap. text ed. 12.95 (*0-317-65919-7*) Astro Pubs.

Aerodynamics for Naval Aviators: Chief of Naval Operations. (Illus.). 416p. 1987. pap. 12.95 (*0-317-65393-8*) Astro Pubs.

Aerodynamics for Naval Aviators. H. H. Hurt, Jr. LC 92-25028. (Illus.). 432p. 1992. pap. 16.95 (*1-56027-140-X*, ASA-ANA) Av Suppl & Acad.

Aerodynamics for Naval Aviators. rev. ed. H. H. Hurt, Jr. 416p. 1965. reprint ed. pap. text ed. 15.95 (*0-685-05990-1*) Flightshops.

Aerodynamics for Naval Aviators. rev. ed. H. H. Hurt, Jr. (Illus.). 432p. (C). 1991. reprint ed. pap. text ed. 15.95 (*0-89100-370-3*, EA-ANA) IAP.

Aerodynamics for Naval Aviators: Workbook. Fred Calfior. 1994. pap. text ed. 22.95 (*0-89100-433-5*, EA-ANA-W) IAP.

Aerodynamics for the Professional Pilot. Richard Bowyer. 1993. pap. 26.95 (*1-85310-326-8*, Pub. by Airlife Pub Ltd UK) Voyageur Pr.

Aerodynamics of Large Bridges: Proceedings of the First International Symposium, Copenhagen, Denmark, 19-21 February 1992. Ed. by Allan Larsen. (Illus.). 313p. (C). 1992. text ed. 85.00 (*90-5410-042-7*, Pub. by A A Balkema NE) Ashgate Pub Co.

Aerodynamics of the Helicopter. Alfred Gessow & Garry C. Myers, Jr. LC 67-26126. 1967. 39.50 (*0-8044-4275-4*, F Ungar Bks) Continuum.

Aerodynamics of Transportation II. Ed. by T. Morel & J. Miller. 89p. 1983. pap. text ed. 24.00 (*0-317-03525-8*, H00282) ASME.

Aerodynamics of Turbines & Compressors. Ed. by W. R. Hawthorne. (High Speed Aerodynamics & Jet Propulsion Ser.: Vol. 10). 1964. 95.00x (*0-691-07904-8*) Princeton U Pr.

Aerodynamics of V-STOL Flight. Ed. by Barnes W. McCormick, Jr. 1967. text ed. 66.00 (*0-12-482350-5*) Acad Pr.

Aerodynamics of Wind Turbines. R. F. Wilson & P. B. Lissaman. Vol. 1. write for info. (*0-318-56679-6*) Elsevier.

Aerodynamics of Wings & Bodies. Holt Ashley & Marten Landahl. LC 85-6992. 288p. 1985. reprint ed. pap. 7.95 (*0-486-64899-0*) Dover.

Aerodynamik der Reinen Unterschallstromung. (Flugtechnische Reihe Ser.: No. 1). (Illus.). 324p. (GER.). 1979. 48.95 (*0-8176-1073-1*) Birkhauser.

***Aeroelasticity & Fluid Structure Interaction Problems: 1994 International Mechanical Engineering Congress & Exposition, Chicago, Illinois - November 6-11, 1994.** (AD Ser.: Vol. 44). 260p. 1994. 88.00 (*0-7918-1453-X*, G00948) ASME.

Aeroelasticity of Plates & Shells. E. H. Dowell. (Mechanics: Dynamical Systems Ser.: No. 1). 154p. 1974. lib. bdg. 55.00 (*90-286-0404-9*) Kluwer Ac.

Aeroflot: An Airline & Its Aircraft. R. E. Davies. (Great Airlines of the World Ser.). (Illus.). 96p. 1995. 37.50 (*0-9626483-1-0*) Paladwr Pr.

Aerogels. Ed. by J. Fricke. (Proceedings in Physics Ser.: Vol. 6). (Illus.). 216p. 1986. 73.00 (*0-387-16256-9*) Spr-Verlag.

Aerogels - a New Generation of Foam Materials, (Seminar Notes - Dec. 1992) ring bd. 75.00 (*1-56676-051-8*) Technomic.

Aerogeology. H. Von Bandat. LC 62-18077. 362p. reprint ed. 103.20 (*0-8357-9145-9*, 2011715) Bks Demand.

Aerogrammes of Australia & Its Dependencies, 1944-1980. Robert C. Stein. (Illus.). 192p. 1984. 20.00 (*0-933580-12-6*) Am Philatelic Society.

Aerology. V. A. Belinskii. 400p. 1967. text ed. 98.00 (*0-7065-0371-6*, Pub. by Keter Pub IS) Coronet Bks.

Aerology of the Polar Regions. S. S. Gaigerov. 288p. 1967. text ed. 74.50 (*0-7065-0441-0*, Pub. by Keter Pub IS) Coronet Bks.

***Aeromedical Training for Flight Personnel.** 1995. lib. bdg. 266.95 (*0-8490-6568-2*) Gordon Pr.

Aeronautic Dictionary: English-Russian-Serbian. Cistogradov Djordje. (ENG, RUS & SER.). 1989. 95.00 (*0-8288-8226-6*) Fr & Eur.

Aeronautic Engineering Dictionary: English-French-German-Arabic. M. A. Zimaity. Ed. by A. M. Abd-El-Wahed. 369p. (ARA, ENG, FRE & GER.). 1976. 75.00 (*0-8288-5572-2*, M9764) Fr & Eur.

Aeronautical Chart Users Guide. National Oceanic & Atmospheric Administration Staff. (Government Reprints Ser.). (Illus.). 104p. (C). 1994. pap. text ed. 13.95 (*1-56027-192-2*, ASA-CUG) Av Suppl & Acad.

Aeronautical Decision Making for Helicopter Pilots. (Illus.). 134p. 1987. pap. 24.95 (*0-685-24697-3*) Aviation.

Aeronautical Dictionary: With Emphasis on A. T. C. Communications, 2 vols., 1. J. Deborah Balter. 653p. (Orig.). 1994. pap. text ed. write for info. (*0-941456-08-0*) Aviation Lang Sch.

Aeronautical Dictionary: With Emphasis on A. T. C. Communications, 2 vols., 2. J. Deborah Balter. 653p. (Orig.). 1994. pap. text ed. write for info. (*0-941456-09-9*) Aviation Lang Sch.

Aeronautical Dictionary: With Emphasis on A. T. C. Communications, 2 vols., Set. J. Deborah Balter. 653p. (Orig.). 1994. pap. text ed. 65.00 (*0-941456-10-2*) Aviation Lang Sch.

Aeronautical Stories: A Reader with Questions. 1994. 10.00 (*0-941456-12-9*) Aviation Lang Sch.

Aeronautical Technologies for the Twenty-First Century. National Research Council, Commission on Engineering & Technical Systems Staff. (Illus.). 314p. (Orig.). (C). 1992. pap. text ed. 38.00 (*0-309-04732-3*) Natl Acad Pr.

Aeronautics: An Abridgement of Aeronautical Specifications Filed at the Patent Office from 1815 to 1891. G. Brewer & P. Y. Alexander. (Illus.). 166p. reprint ed. pap. text ed. 20.00 (*90-6078-010-8*, Pub. by B M Israel NE) Coronet Bks.

Aeronautics & Space Flight. Ed. by Catherine D. Scott. LC 84-15725. (Special Collections Ser.: Vol. 3, Nos. 1 & 2). 229p. 1985. text ed. 49.95 (*0-86656-251-6*) Haworth Pr.

Aeronautics in the Union & Confederate Armies: With a Survey of Military Aeronautics Prior to 1861, Vol. I. Frederick S. Haydon. Ed. by James B. Gilbert. LC 79-7271. (Flight: Its First Seventy-Five Years Ser.). (Illus.). 1980. reprint ed. lib. bdg. 41.95 (*0-405-12181-4*) Ayer.

Aeronautique, Astronautique, Aerodynamique: Anglais Technique. Demazet. 268p. (ENG & FRE.). 1976. pap. 59.95 (*0-8288-5573-0*, M6000) Fr & Eur.

Aeronca: A Photo History. Bob Hollenbaugh & John Houser. (Illus.). 138p. 1993. pap. text ed. 16.95 (*0-943691-10-9*) Aviation Heritage.

Aeronca, Best of Paul Matt. Paul Matt. (Illus.). 96p. 1993. pap. text ed. 19.95 (*0-943691-02-8*) Aviation Heritage.

Aeronca C-2: The Story of the Flying Bathtub. Jay P. Spenser. LC 78-606098. (Famous Aircraft of the National Air & Space Museum Ser.: No. 2). (Illus.). 72p. 1978. pap. 12.95 (*0-87474-879-8*, SPA2P) Smithsonian.

Aeronca 7AC Champion: Service Manual. 1992. pap. 8.00 (*0-911139-08-7*) Flying Bks.

Aeronomy. P. M. Banks & G. Kockarts. Incl. Set. 1973. 50.00 (*0-686-77004-8*); write for info. (*0-318-50223-2*) Acad Pr.

Aeronomy of the Middle Atmosphere. rev. ed. Guy Brasseur & Susan Solomon. 1986. pap. text ed. 59.50 (*90-277-2344-3*) Kluwer Ac.

Aeronomy of the Middle Atmosphere. 2nd rev. ed. Guy Brasseur & Susan Solomon. 1986. lib. bdg. 121.50 (*90-277-2343-5*) Kluwer Ac.

Aeroplane Structure. Alfred C. Kermode. LC 41-8677. 190p. reprint ed. pap. 54.20 (*0-8357-5213-5*, 2013678) Bks Demand.

Aeroplani C. Studi-Progetti-Realizzazioni dal 1908 al 1935. Gianni Caproni. Ed. by James B. Gilbert. LC 79-7234. (Flight: Its First Seventy-Five Years Ser.). (Illus.). (ITA.). 1980. reprint ed. lib. bdg. 68.95 (*0-405-12150-4*) Ayer.

***Aeroscout Procedures.** 1995. lib. bdg. 250.75 (*0-8490-6622-0*) Gordon Pr.

Aeroscouts. Charles Holley. Ed. by Eric Tobias. 256p. (Orig.). 1992. mass mkt. 4.99 (*0-671-76055-6*) PB.

***Aerosmith: Life in the Fast Lane.** Malcolm Doom. 1994. pap. 14.95 (*1-898141-75-4*, Pub. by Castle Communs UK) Viking Penguin.

***Aerosmith: Live!** Mark Putterford. (Illus.). (Orig.). (YA). (gr. 9 up). 1994. pap. 9.95 (*0-7119-4246-3*, OP47707) Omnibus NY.

Aerosmith: The Fall & Rise of Aerosmith. Mark Putterford. (Illus.). 80p. 1991. pap. 19.95 (*0-7119-2303-5*, OP46028) Omnibus NY.

***Aerosmith: The Fall & Rise of Rock's Greatest Band.** Martin Huxley. 1995. pap. 12.95 (*0-312-11737-X*) St Martin.

Aerosmith - Pump: Easy Guitar Transcriptions Complete with Lessons. (Easy Guitar Recorded Versions Ser.). 64p. (Orig.). 1990. pap. 14.95 (*0-7935-0284-5*, HL00660134) H Leonard.

Aerosol-Cloud-Climate Interactions. Ed. by Peter V. Hobbs. LC 92-41627. (International Geophysics Ser.: Vol. 54). (Illus.). 235p. 1993. text ed. 65.00 (*0-12-350725-1*) Acad Pr.

Aerosol Effects on Climate. Ed. by S. Gerard Jennings. LC 92-29967. (Illus.). 304p. 1993. 40.00 (*0-8165-1362-7*) U of Ariz Pr.

***Aerosol Forcing of Climate: Report of the Dahlem Workshop on Aerosol Forcing of Climate, Berlin 1994, April 24-29.** Ed. by R. J. Charlson & J. Heintzenberg. LC 95-14231. (Environmental Sciences Research Report Ser., Vol. 17; Dahlem Workshop Reports Ser.). 1995. text ed. 125.00 (*0-471-95693-7*) Wiley.

Aerosol Measurement. Aerosol Measurement Workshop Staff. Ed. by Dale A. Lundgren et al. LC 78-15424. (Illus.). 740p. reprint ed. pap. 180.00 (*0-8357-6719-1*, 2035354) Bks Demand.

Aerosol Measurement: Principles, Techniques, & Application. Ed. by Klaus Willeke & Paul A. Baron. LC 92-11371. 1993. text ed. 99.95 (*0-442-00486-9*) Van Nos Reinhold.

Aerosol R & D in the Soviet Union: The Measurement of Main Parameters. Lev Ruzer. (Illus.). 160p. (Orig.). 1989. pap. 75.00 (*0-685-35188-2*) Delphic Associates.

Aerosol Resuspension in the Reactor Cooling System for LWR's under Severe Accident Conditions. A. Alonso et al. 64p. 1992. pap. 9.00 (*92-826-2857-4*, CD-NA-13789-EN-C, Pub. by Europ Com) UNIPUB.

Aerosol Sampling: Science & Practice. James Vincent. 450p. 1989. text ed. 375.00 (*0-471-92175-0*) Wiley.

Aerosol Science & Technology. 2nd ed. Parker Reist. 1992. text ed. 59.00 (*0-07-051882-3*) McGraw.

***Aerosol Science for Industrial Hygienists.** James H. Vincent. LC 95-4232. 1995. text ed. write for info. (*0-08-042029-X*, Pergamon Pr) Elsevier.

Aerosol Science: Theory & Practice: With Special Applications to the Nuclear Industry. M. M. Williams & Sudarshan K. Loyalka. 466p. 1991. 125.00 (*0-08-037209-0*, Pergamon Pr) Elsevier.

Aerosol Technology: Properties, Behavior, & Measurement of Airborne Particles. William C. Hinds. LC 82-1889. 424p. 1982. text ed. 94.95 (*0-471-08726-2*, Wiley-Interscience) Wiley.

Aerosol Therapy. Saint Elizabeth Hospital Medical Center Staff. (Respiratory Patient Education Ser.). (Illus.). 24p. 1992. pap. text ed. 5.95 (*1-56077-237-9*) Ctr Learning.

Aerosols: An Industrial & Environmental Science (Monograph) George M. Hidy. 1984. text ed. 165.00 (*0-12-347260-1*) Acad Pr.

Aerosols: Anthropogenic & Natural, Sources & Transport. Ed. by Theo J. Kneip & Paul J. Lioy. LC 80-12891. (Annals Ser.: Vol. 338). 618p. 1980. 110.00 (*0-89766-064-1*); pap. 110.00 (*0-89766-065-X*) NY Acad Sci.

Aerosols, Airways & Asthma. Ed. by J. Trautlein. 121p. 1981. text ed. 20.00 (*0-88331-109-7*) Luce.

Aerosols & Climate. Ed. by Peter V. Hobbs & M. Patrick McCormick. LC 88-29946. (Illus.). 486p. 1988. 84.00 (*0-937194-11-5*) A Deepak Pub.

Aerosols & Their Climatic Effects. Ed. by Hermann E. Gerber & Adarsh Deepak. LC 85-1651. (Illus.). 297p. 1984. 66.00 (*0-937194-06-9*) A Deepak Pub.

Aerosols in Medicine: Principles, Diagnosis, & Therapy. 2nd ed. Ed. by F. Moren et al. LC 93-36576. 1993. 218.75 (*0-444-81332-2*) Elsevier.

Aerosols in Medicine Principles Diagnosis & Therapy. Ed. by F. Moren et al. 336p. 1985. 128.75 (*0-444-80610-5*) Elsevier.

Aerosols in Science, Medicine & Technology: Proceedings of the Tenth Annual Conference of the Association for Aerosol Research (Gesellschaft fur Aerosolforschung), Bologna, Italy, 14-17 September 1982. Ed. by H. Fissan. 225p. 1983. pap. 32.00 (*0-08-030260-2*, Pergamon Pr) Elsevier.

Aerosols: Science, Industry, Health & Environment: Proceedings of the Third International Aerosol Conference, Kyoto, Japan, 24-27 September 1990, 2 vols., Set. Ed. by S. Masuda & Koichiro Takahashi. (Illus.). 1388p. 1990. pap. 55.25 (*0-08-037525-1*, Pergamon Pr) Elsevier.

Aerospace. Joseph H. Hughes, Jr. & James S. Priamos. LC 77-926280. 1977. pap. 4.95 (*0-686-22888-X*) Aaron-Jenkins.

Aerospace, 3 vols., Set. 175.00 (*0-685-67790-7*, AEROPKG) Soc Computer Sim.

Aerospace, Vol. 1: Proceedings of First Workshop. write for info. (*0-318-70642-3*, WNN90-1) Soc Computer Sim.

Aerospace, Vol. 2: Proceedings of Second Workshop. write for info. (*0-318-70643-1*, WNN91-1) Soc Computer Sim.

Aerospace, Vol. 3: Proceedings of Conference. write for info. (*0-318-70644-X*, SS19-1) Soc Computer Sim.

Aerospace Abbreviations: French-English-German-Spanish. Groupe Aerospatiale. 298p. (FRE, GER & SPA.). 1987. pap. 62.50 (*0-7859-7452-0*, 285608026X) Fr & Eur.

Aerospace Agencies & Organizations: A Guide for Business & Government. George V. D'Angelo. LC 93-293. 192p. 1993. text ed. 52.95 (*0-89930-842-2*, Q842, Quorum Bks) Greenwood.

Aerospace America, Vol. 32. Ed. by Elaine Camhi. 1994. 70.00 (*0-685-63109-5*) AIAA.

Aerospace & Defense Seminar Proceedings. LC 85-72346. 142p. 1985. 10.00 (*0-935406-70-0*) Am Prod & Inventory.

Aerospace & Defense Specific Industry Group. American Production & Inventory Control Society Staff & Herb Langthorp. 166p. 1992. 12.00 (*1-55822-091-7*) Am Prod & Inventory.

Aerospace & Defense Symposium Proceedings. (Illus.). 182p. 1988. 25.00 (*1-55822-000-3*) Am Prod & Inventory.

Aerospace & Defense Symposium Proceedings. LC 88-83819. (Illus.). 461p. 1989. 25.00 (*1-55822-015-1*) Am Prod & Inventory.

Aerospace & Defense Symposium Proceedings. American Production & Inventory Control Society Staff. 237p. 1991. 25.00 (*1-55822-034-8*) Am Prod & Inventory.

An Asterisk (*) at the beginning of an entry indicates that the title is appearing in BIP for the first time.

An Asterisk (*) at the beginning of an entry indicates that the title is appearing in BIP for the first time.

115

Aesop's Fables, 4 vols., III. Ed. by Kathryn T. Hegeman. (J). (gr. 1-4). 1984. pap. 5.00 (0-89824-053-0) Trillium Pr.

Aesop's Fables, 4 vols., IV. Ed. by Kathryn T. Hegeman. (J). (gr. 1-4). 1984. pap. 5.00 (0-89824-054-9) Trillium Pr.

Aesop's Fables, 4 vols., Set. Ed. by Kathryn T. Hegeman. (J). (gr. 1-4). 1984. pap. 16.00 (0-89824-050-6) Trillium Pr.

Aesop's Fables: A Classic Illustrated Edition. Ed. by Bernard Higton. (Illus.). (J). 1990. 15.95 (0-87701-780-8) Chronicle Bks.

Aesop's Fables: Literature Mini-Unit. Jo E. Moore. (Illus.). 16p. 1989. pap. 5.95 (1-55799-145-6, EMC518) Evan-Moor Corp.

Aesop's Fables: Plays for Young Children. Albert Cullum. (J). (gr. k-3). 1993. pap. 13.99 (0-86653-940-9) Fearon Teach Aids.

Aesop's Fables: Santore Edition. Aesop. 1988. 14.00 (0-517-64115-1) Random Hse Value.

Aesop's Fables: With a Life of Aesop. Tr. by John E. Keller & L. Clark Keating. (Studies in Romance Languages: No. 34). (Illus.). 256p. (C). 1993. text ed. 45.00 (0-8131-1812-3) U Pr of Ky.

Aesops Fables-Color Book. Aesop. (J). 1978. pap. 2.95 (0-486-21040-5) Dover.

Aesop's Fables in Song. Ralph Martell. (Illus.). 21p. (J). (gr. k-5). 1987. audio 9.95 (0-941977-00-5, RTB-1) Ralmar Enter.

Aesop's Falables: Musical. Ed Graczyk. (J). 1969. 5.00 (0-87602-100-3) Anchorage.

Aesop's Forest; The Plot of the Mice. Robert Coover & Brian Swann. (Capra Back-to-Back Ser.: No. 8). 115p. (C). 1988. reprint ed. lib. bdg. 25.00x (0-8095-4107-6) Borgo Pr.

Aesop's Four Footed Fables. Aesop. (Illus.). 48p. 1985. pap. 4.95 (0-932458-29-7) Star Rover.

Aesop's Garden. Don Byrd. 1976. pap. 4.00 (0-913028-42-8) North Atlantic.

Aesopus - Index Aesopi Fabularum. Ed. by Francisco M. Garcia & Alfredo R. Lopez. (Alpha-Omega, Reihe A Ser.: Bd. CXVIII). viii, 170p. (GER.). 1991. write for info. (3-487-09354-5, Pub. by Georg Olms GW) Lubrecht & Cramer.

Aesthete in the City: The Philosophy & Practice of American Abstract Painting in the 1980s. David Carrier. (Illus.). 304p. (C). 1994. 45.00 (0-271-00943-8) Pa St U Pr.

Aesthetes & Decadents of the Eighteen Nineties. Ed. & Intro. by Karl Beckson. (Illus.). 337p. 1981. reprint ed. pap. 14.00 (0-89733-044-7) Academy Chi Pubs.

Aesthetic & Ethical Values in Japanese Culture. Ronald McLaren et al. (Occasional Papers, Institute for Education on Japan: Vol. 1, No. 4). 48p. (C). 1990. reprint ed. pap. 5.00 (0-9619977-6-1) Earlham College Pr.

Aesthetic & Philosophical Issues in Afro-American Art. Ed. by Vattel T. Rose. (Papers on Afro-American, African, & Caribbean Studies). (Illus.). 150p. 1985. pap. 6.00 (0-911393-04-8) Ctr Afro Stud Ohio.

Aesthetic & Reconstructive Otoplasty. J. Davis. (Illus.). 582p. 1987. 274.00 (0-387-96308-1) Spr-Verlag.

Aesthetic & Reconstructive Surgery of the Scalp. Fleming & Mayer. (Illus.). 384p. 1991. 120.00 (0-8016-1593-3) Mosby Yr Bk.

Aesthetic Arsenal: Socialist Realism under Stalin. Joseph Bakshtein et al. LC 93-61431. (Illus.). 300p. 1993. write for info. (1-884229-00-X) Inst For Contemp.

***Aesthetic as Science of Expression & General Linguistic.** Benedetto Croce. Tr. by Douglas Ainslie. LC 94-44020. 1995. pap. write for info. (1-56000-818-0) Transaction Pubs.

Aesthetic as the Science of Expression & of the Linguistic in General (ESTETICA), Pt. I: Theory. Benedetto Croce. Tr. by Colin Lyas. 224p. (C). 1992. 64.95 (0-521-35216-9); pap. 18.95 (0-521-35996-1) Cambridge U Pr.

Aesthetic Aspects of Recent Experimental Film. Barry W. Moore. Ed. by Garth S. Jowett. LC 79-6680. (Dissertations on Film, 1980 Ser.). 1980. lib. bdg. 15.95 (0-405-12913-0) Ayer.

***Aesthetic Attitude.** David E. Fenner. 208p. (C). 1996. text ed. 45.00 (0-391-03934-2) Humanities.

Aesthetic Autobiography: From Life to Art in Marcel Proust, James Joyce, Virginia Woolf, & Anais Nin. Suzanne Nalbantian. LC 94-9925. 1994. text ed. 35.00 (0-312-12170-9) St Martin.

***Aesthetic Blepharoplasty.** Francis G. Wolfort & William R. Kanter. LC 94-21952. 1994. 185.00 (0-316-95091-2) Little.

***Aesthetic Code of Don Ramon del Valle-Inclan.** Gerard Flynn. LC 94-90113. (Illus.). 240p. (Orig.). 1995. pap. 10.95 (1-56002-445-3, Univ Edtns) Aegina Pr.

Aesthetic Contouring of the Craniofacial Skeleton. Ousterhout. 1991. 340.00 (0-316-67410-9) Little.

Aesthetic Dentistry with Indirect Resins. Howard Stean. (Illus.). 95p. 1992. text ed. 68.00 (1-85097-026-2) Quint Pub Co.

Aesthetic Dermatology. Lawrence C. Parish. 400p. 1991. text ed. 115.00 (0-07-048476-7) Hlth Prof Div.

***Aesthetic Design for Ceramic Restorations.** David Korson. 159p. 1994. 78.00 (1-85097-034-3) Quintessence.

Aesthetic Dimension: Toward a Critique of Marxist Aesthetics. Herbert Marcuse. LC 76-9001. 1978. reprint ed. pap. 12.00 (0-8070-1519-9, BPA17) Beacon Pr.

Aesthetic Element in Morality & Its Place in a Utilitarian Theory of Morals. Frank C. Sharp. LC 75-3363. 1976. reprint ed. 10.00 (0-404-59360-7) AMS Pr.

Aesthetic Experience: An Anthropologist Looks at the Visual Arts. Jaques P. Maquet. LC 85-8232. (Illus.). 277p. 1986. text ed. 50.00 (0-300-03342-7) Yale U Pr.

Aesthetic Experience: An Anthropologist Looks at the Visual Arts. Jaques P. Maquet. LC 85-8232. (Illus.). 277p. 1988. pap. 22.00 (0-300-04134-9) Yale U Pr.

Aesthetic Experience & the Humanities. F. Shoemaker. LC 70-176013. reprint ed. 22.50 (0-404-05987-2) AMS Pr.

Aesthetic Face of Being: Art in the Theology of Pavel Florensky. Victor Bychkov. Tr. by Richard Peaver & Larissa Valokhonsky. LC 93-15303. 1993. 7.95 (0-88141-127-2) St Vladimirs.

Aesthetic Facial Surgery. Charles J. Krause et al. (Illus.). 794p. 1991. text ed. 225.00 (0-397-50955-3) Lippincott.

Aesthetic Facial Surgery. Peter McKinney & Bruce L. Cunningham. (Illus.). 234p. 1992. text ed. 134.00 (0-443-08703-2) Churchill.

Aesthetic Facial Surgery. John Q. Owsley. LC 93-2826. (Illus.). 416p. 1993. text ed. 165.00 (0-7216-3364-1) Saunders.

Aesthetic Facial Surgery. Tardy & Thomas. 400p. 1993. 175.00 (0-8016-7508-1) Mosby Yr Bk.

Aesthetic Facial Surgery: A Clinical & Surgical Atlas. H. George Brennan. 304p. 1991. 205.00 (0-88167-642-X) Raven.

Aesthetic Factors in Natural Science. Ed. by Nicholas Rescher. LC 89-35898. 110p. (C). 1990. lib. bdg. 37.50 (0-8191-7576-5) U Pr of Amer.

Aesthetic Form of Education. Ed. by Michael F. Andrews. LC 58-11799. (Illus.). 115p. reprint ed. pap. 32.80 (0-8357-5216-X, 2019471) Bks Demand.

Aesthetic Frontiers: The Machiavellian Tradition & the Southern Imagination. Richard Nelson. LC 90-32055. 336p. 1990. 39.50 (0-87805-439-1) U Pr of Miss.

Aesthetic Headaches: Women & a Masculine Poetics in Poe, Melville, & Hawthorne. Leland S. Person, Jr. LC 87-12536. 208p. 1988. 25.00 (0-8203-0985-0) U of Ga Pr.

Aesthetic Illusion: Theoretical & Historical Approaches. Ed. by Frederick Burwick & Walter Pape. x, 478p. (C). 1990. lib. bdg. 163.10 (3-11-011750-9) De Gruyter.

Aesthetic Imperative: Relevance & Responsibility in Arts Education. Malcolm Ross. (Curriculum Issues in Arts Education Ser.: Vol. 2). 187p. 1981. 83.00 (0-08-026766-1, Pub. by Pergamon Repr UK) Franklin.

Aesthetic Impulse. M. Ross. 250p. 1984. 64.00 (0-08-030234-3, 3400-3, 2600-2, Pub. by Pergamon Repr UK) Franklin.

Aesthetic Individualism & Practical Intellect: American Allegory in Emerson, Thoreau, Adams & James. Olaf Hansen. 261p. (Orig.). 1990. text ed. 35.00 (0-691-06823-2) Princeton U Pr.

***Aesthetic Judgement & the Moral Image of the World: Studies in Kant.** Dieter Henrich. 1994. pap. 12.95 (0-8047-2367-2) Stanford U Pr.

Aesthetic Judgment. D. Prall. 1972. 59.95 (0-87968-583-2) Gordon Pr.

Aesthetic Judgment & the Moral Image of the World: Studies in Kant. Dieter Henrich. LC 92-10124. (Series in Philosophy). 200p. (C). 1993. 35.00 (0-8047-2054-1) Stanford U Pr.

Aesthetic Knowledge. Stephen L. Albaugh. 94p. (C). 1989. text ed. write for info. (0-318-65315-X) Iowa Inst Philos.

Aesthetic Legacies. Lucian Krukowski. LC 92-19307. (Arts & Their Philosophies Ser.). 264p. (C). 1992. 44.95 (0-87722-972-4) Temple U Pr.

Aesthetic Method in Self-Conflict: Accompanied by Psychiatry, Economics, Aesthetics. 2nd ed. Eli Siegel. LC 79-55196. 91p. 1976. pap. write for info. (0-910492-29-8) Definition.

Aesthetic Movement in England. Walter Hamilton. LC 76-144633. reprint ed. 18.00 (0-404-03091-2) AMS Pr.

Aesthetic Nature of Tennyson. J. Paul Smith. LC 77-122998. (Studies in Tennyson: No. 27). 1970. reprint ed. lib. bdg. 53.95 (0-8383-1131-8) M S G Haskell Hse.

Aesthetic of Isolation in Film Theory--Hugo Munsterberg. Donald L. Fredericksen. 1977. 24.95 (0-405-09889-8, 11484) Ayer.

Aesthetic Plastic Surgery, 5 vols., Set. M. Gonzalez-Ulloa et al. 1765p. 1988. text ed. 1,000.00 (1-57235-007-5) Piccin NY.

Aesthetic Plastic Surgery, 2 vols., Set. 2nd ed. Thomas D. Rees & Gregory S. LaTrenta. (Illus.). 1384p. 1994. text ed. 395.00 (0-7216-3712-4) Saunders.

Aesthetic Plastic Surgery, Vol. I. M. Gonzalez-Ulloa et al. 322p. 1988. text ed. 250.00 (1-57235-002-4) Piccin NY.

Aesthetic Plastic Surgery, Vol. II. M. Gonzalez-Ulloa et al. 334p. 1988. text ed. 200.00 (1-57235-003-2) Piccin NY.

Aesthetic Plastic Surgery, Vol. III. M. Gonzalez-Ulloa et al. 448p. 1988. text ed. 260.00 (1-57235-004-0) Piccin NY.

Aesthetic Plastic Surgery, Vol. IV. M. Gonzalez-Ulloa et al. 353p. 1988. text ed. 250.00 (1-57235-005-9) Piccin NY.

Aesthetic Plastic Surgery, Vol. V. M. Gonzalez-Ulloa et al. 308p. 1988. text ed. 250.00 (1-57235-006-7) Piccin NY.

Aesthetic Plastic Surgery: Principles & Techniques. Paule Regnault & Rollin K. Daniel. 800p. 1984. 230.00 (0-316-73851-4) Little.

Aesthetic Plastic Surgery - Rhinoplasty. Ed. by Rollin K. Daniel. LC 92-48728. (Illus.). 1000p. 1993. 425.00 (0-316-17251-0) Little.

Aesthetic Plastic Surgery of Head & Body. I. Pitanguy. (Illus.). 425p. 1981. 654.00 (0-387-08706-0) Spr-Verlag.

Aesthetic Point of View: Selected Essays. Monroe C. Beardsley & Michael Wreen. Ed. by Donald M. Callen. LC 82-71601. 385p. 1982. 49.95 (0-8014-1250-1) Cornell U Pr.

Aesthetic Process. Bertram Morris. LC 75-12900. (Northwestern University. Humanities Ser.: No. 8). reprint ed. 25.00 (0-404-50708-5) AMS Pr.

Aesthetic Quality: A Contextualistic Theory of Beauty. Stephen C. Pepper. LC 79-110052. 239p. 1970. reprint ed. text ed. 45.00 (0-8371-4437-X, PEAQ, Greenwood Pr) Greenwood.

Aesthetic Realism: We Have Been There, Six Artists on the Siegel Theory of Opposites. Ed. by Sheldon Kranz. LC 69-17523. (Illus.). 119p. (Orig.). 1969. 6.95 (0-910492-11-5) Definition.

Aesthetic Realism: We Have Been There, Six Artists on the Siegel Theory of Opposites. Ed. by Sheldon Kranz. LC 69-17523. (Illus.). 119p. (Orig.). (C). 1969. pap. 4.95 (0-910492-24-7) Definition.

Aesthetic Restoration of Nasal Defects. Burget & Menick. 400p. 1993. 169.00 (0-8016-7443-3) Mosby Yr Bk.

Aesthetic Rhinoplasty. Gilbert Aiach & Jacque Levignac. Tr. by S. Anthony Wolfe. (Illus.). 124p. 1991. text ed. 115.00 (0-443-04398-1) Churchill.

Aesthetic Rhinoplasty. 2nd ed. Sheen. (Illus.). 1504p. 1987. 399.00 (0-8016-4580-8) Mosby Yr Bk.

Aesthetic Rhinoplasty, 2 vols., Set. G. Zaoli. 590p. 1994. text ed. 385.00 (1-57235-065-2) Piccin NY.

Aesthetic Studies: Architecture & Poetry. Katharine Gilbert. LC 79-124762. reprint ed. 27.50 (0-404-02765-2) AMS Pr.

Aesthetic Surgery see Plastic & Reconstructive Surgery of the Face & Neck

Aesthetic Theories of French Artists, from Realism to Surrealism. Charles E. Gauss. LC 69-66657. (Johns Hopkins Paperbacks Ser.: No. JH-23). 123p. reprint ed. pap. 35.10 (0-8357-5217-8, 2007635) Bks Demand.

Aesthetic Theories of India, Vol. II. Padma Sudhi. (C). 1988. 44.00 (81-7076-012-7, Pub. by Intellectual Pub Hse II) S Asia.

Aesthetic Theories of India, Vol. III. Padma Sudhi. 1990. 54.00 (81-7076-024-0, Pub. by Intellectual II) S Asia.

Aesthetical Essays: Studies in Aesthetics; Hindustani Music & Kathak Dance. S. K. Saxena. 1982. 18.00 (0-8364-0898-5, Pub. by Chanakya II) S Asia.

Aestheticienne: Helping Poeple Look & Feel Good. Ann Hagman & W. E. Arnould-Taylor. (Illus.). 192p. (Orig.). 1981. pap. 27.50 (0-85950-308-9, Pub. by Stanley Thornes UK) Trans-Atl Phila.

Aestheticism. Leon Chai. 1990. text ed. 32.50 (0-231-07224-4) Col U Pr.

***Aestheticism.** Steinberg. 1994. 26.95 (0-8057-8616-3, Twayne); pap. 14.95 (0-8057-8641-4, Twayne) Macmillan.

Aestheticism: The Religion of Art in Post-Romantic Literature. Leon Chai. 352p. 1990. text ed. 32.00 (0-685-34737-0) Col U Pr.

Aestheticism & Deconstruction: Pater, Derrida, & De Man. Jonathan Loesberg. 276p. 1991. text ed. 32.50 (0-691-06884-4) Princeton U Pr.

Aestheticism & the Canadian Modernists: Aspects of a Poetic Influence. Brian Trehearne. 384p. (C). 1989. text ed. 49.95 (0-7735-0710-8, Pub. by McGill CN) U of Toronto Pr.

Aesthetics: A Critical Anthology. George Dickie & Richard J. Sclafani. Ed. by Ronald Roblin. LC 88-60543. 875p. (C). 1989. pap. text ed. 42.00 (0-312-00309-9) St Martin.

Aesthetics: A Critical Anthology. Ed. by George Dickie et al. 669p. (C). 1989. text ed. write for info. (0-318-68122-6) St Martin.

Aesthetics: An Introduction. George Dickie. LC 72-12659. (Traditions in Philosophy Ser.). 1971. pap. 7.20 (0-672-63500-3) Pegasus.

Aesthetics: An Introduction to the Philosophy of Art. Anne Sheppard. (Illus.). 192p. 1987. 35.00 (0-19-219180-2); pap. 9.95 (0-19-289164-2) OUP.

Aesthetics: Issues & Inquiry. E. Louis Lankford. 106p. 1992. pap. 15.00 (0-937652-60-1) Natl Art Ed.

Aesthetics: Lectures & Essays. Edward Bullough. Ed. by Elizabeth M. Wilkinson. LC 77-21814. 158p. 1977. reprint ed. text ed. 49.75 (0-8371-9789-9, WIAE, Greenwood Pr) Greenwood.

Aesthetics: Lectures on Fine Art by G. W. F. Hegel, Vol. II. Georg W. Hegel. Tr. by T. M. Knox. 696p. 1988. 120.00 (0-19-824499-1) OUP.

Aesthetics: Or the Science of Beauty. rev. ed. John Bascom. LC 75-3030. (Philosophy in America Ser.). reprint ed. 42.00 (0-404-59029-2) AMS Pr.

Aesthetics: Problems in the Philosophy of Criticism. 2nd ed. Monroe C. Beardsley. LC 80-28899. (Illus.). 688p. (C). 1981. reprint ed. 37.95 (0-915145-09-X); reprint ed. pap. text ed. 24.50 (0-915145-08-1) Hackett Pub.

Aesthetics after Modernism. Peter Fuller. pap. 2.95 (0-86316-044-1) Writers & Readers.

Aesthetics & Art in the Astree of Honore d'Urfe. M. Catharine McMahon. LC 78-94197. (Catholic University of America. Studies in Romance Languages & Literatures: No. 1). reprint ed. 21.00 (0-404-50301-2) AMS Pr.

Aesthetics & Arts Education. Alan Simpson. Ed. by Ralph A. Smith. 408p. 1991. 39.95 (0-252-01752-8); pap. 16.95 (0-252-06141-1) U of Ill Pr.

Aesthetics & Criticism. Harold Osborne. LC 73-3756. 341p. 1973. reprint ed. text ed. 65.00 (0-8371-6847-3, OSAC, Greenwood Pr) Greenwood.

Aesthetics & Economics. Gianfranco Mossetto. LC 93-15476. 232p. (C). 1993. Acid-free paper. lib. bdg. 104.00 (0-7923-2296-7) Kluwer Ac.

Aesthetics & Education. Michael J. Parsons & H. Gene Blocker. LC 92-21377. (Disciplines in Art Education Ser.). 208p. 1993. 39.95 (0-252-01988-1); pap. 15.95 (0-252-06293-0) U of Ill Pr.

Aesthetics & Education. G. Ramesh. (C). 1988. 17.50 (81-7003-094-3, Pub. by S Asia Pubs II) S Asia.

Aesthetics & History. Bernard Berenson. LC 52-1732. 242p. reprint ed. pap. 69.00 (0-8357-5218-6, 2012984) Bks Demand.

Aesthetics & History. Bernhard Berenson. LC 52-1732. 242p. 1955. reprint ed. 49.00 (0-403-03882-0) Somerset Pub.

Aesthetics & Ideology. Ed. by George Levine. LC 93-31173. 325p. (C). 1994. text ed. 48.00 (0-8135-2058-4); pap. text ed. 20.00 (0-8135-2059-2) Rutgers U Pr.

Aesthetics & Revolution: Nicaraguan Poetry, 1979-1990. Greg Dawes. 224p. (C). 1992. text ed. 29.95 (0-8166-2146-2) U of Minn Pr.

Aesthetics & Ritual in the United Arab Emirates: The Anthropology of Food & Personal Adornment among Arabian Women. Aida S. Kanafani. (Illus.). 134p. 1983. text ed. 22.50 (0-8156-6068-5, Am U Beirut) Syracuse U Pr.

Aesthetics & Technology in Building. Pier L. Nervi. Tr. by R. Einaudi. LC 65-16686. (Charles Eliot Norton Lectures: 1961-1962). (Illus.). 210p. 1965. 22.00 (0-674-00701-8) HUP.

***Aesthetics & the Art of Musical Composition in the German Enlightment: Selected Writings of Johann Georg Sulzer & Heinrich Christoph Koch.** Ed. by Nancy Baker & Thomas Christensen. (Cambridge Studies in Music Theory & Analysis: No. 7). (Illus.). 250p. (C). 1992. write for info. (0-521-36035-8) Cambridge U Pr.

Aesthetics & the Good Life. Marcia M. Eaton. LC 87-46420. (Illus.). 216p. 1989. 37.50 (0-8386-3336-6) Fairleigh Dickinson.

Aesthetics & the Literature of Ideas: Essays in Honor of A. Owen Aldridge. Ed. by Francois Jost & Melvin J. Friedman. LC 88-46185. (Illus.). 288p. 1990. 36.50 (0-87413-363-7) U Delaware Pr.

Aesthetics & the Search for Political Authority. Tracy B. Strong. 225p. 1929. text ed. 34.95 (0-8133-0395-8) Westview.

Aesthetics & the Sociology of Art. Janet Wolff. 136p. (C). 1992. text ed. 27.95 (0-472-09499-8); pap. 13.95 (0-472-06499-1) U of Mich Pr.

Aesthetics & the Theory of Criticism: Selected Essays of Arnold Isenberg. Arnold Isenberg. Ed. by William Calleghan et al. (Illus.). xl, 322p. 1988. pap. text ed. 14.95 (0-226-38512-4) U Ch Pr.

Aesthetics for Art Educators. E. F. Kaelin. 256p. 1989. text ed. 36.95 (0-8077-2961-2); pap. text ed. 18.95 (0-8077-2960-4) Tchrs Coll.

***Aesthetics for the Tehrapist.** Ann Hagman. 224p. 1991. pap. 42.00 (0-7487-0566-X, Pub. by S Thornes Pubs UK) St Mut.

Aesthetics from Classical Greece to the Present: A Short History. Monroe C. Beardsley. LC 75-20138. (Studies in the Humanities: No. 13). 416p. 1975. reprint ed. pap. 14.50 (0-8173-6623-7) U of Ala Pr.

Aesthetics in Feminist Perspective. Ed. by Hilde Hein & Carolyn Korsmeyer. LC 92-23948. 320p. 1993. 39.95 (0-253-32861-6); pap. 14.95 (0-253-20774-6) Ind U Pr.

Aesthetics in Scotland. Hugh MacDiarmid. Ed. by Alan Bold. LC 84-28469. (Illus.). 100p. 1985. 31.00 (0-389-20558-3, N8120) B&N Imports.

Aesthetics in Twentieth-Century Poland: Selected Essays. Ed. by Jean Harrell & Alina Wierzbianska. 285p. 1973. 39.50 (0-8387-1100-6) Bucknell U Pr.

Aesthetics in Washington. Horatio Greenough. (Notable American Authors Ser.). 1992. reprint ed. lib. bdg. 90.00 (0-7812-2953-7) Rprt Serv.

Aesthetics, Mind, & Nature: A Communication Approach to the Unity of Matter & Consciousness. Asghar T. Minai. LC 92-36548. 352p. 1993. text ed. 69.50 (0-275-94296-1, C4296, Praeger Pubs) Greenwood.

Aesthetics of Action: Continuity & Change in a West African Town. Kris L. Hardin. LC 92-20747. (Ethnographic Inquiry Ser.). (Illus.). 352p. (C). 1993. text ed. 47.00 (1-56098-235-7) Smithsonian.

Aesthetics of Ambivalence: Rethinking Science Fiction Film in the Age of Electronic (Re) Production. Brooks Landon. LC 92-4048. (Contributions to the Study of Science Fiction & Fantasy Ser.: No. 52). 224p. 1992. text ed. 49.95 (0-313-25687-X, LAA/, Greenwood Pr) Greenwood.

Aesthetics of Architecture. Roger Scruton. LC 79-84026. (Essays on the Arts Ser.: No. 8). (Illus.). 1980. pap. 18.95 (0-691-00322-X) Princeton U Pr.

Aesthetics of Artifice: Villiers' Future Eve. Marie Lathers. LC 91-58691. (AMS Studies in the Nineteenth Century: No. 13). 1992. 39.50 (0-404-61493-0) AMS Pr.

Aesthetics of Bridge Design. (PCI Journal Reprints Ser.). 20p. 1968. pap. 6.00 (0-686-40001-1, JR62) P-PCI.

Aesthetics of Built Form. Alan Holgate. (Illus.). 304p. 1992. 90.00 (0-19-856336-1) OUP.

Aesthetics of Change. Bradford P. Keeney. LC 82-15720. (Guilford Family Therapy Ser.). 217p. 1983. lib. bdg. 25.00 (0-89862-043-0, 2043) Guilford Pr.

Aesthetics of Chaosmos: The Middle Ages of James Joyce. Umberto Eco. Tr. by Ellen Esrock. LC 88-21315. 112p. 1989. pap. 14.50 (0-674-00635-6) HUP.

Aesthetics of Communication: Pramatics & Beyond. Herman Parret. (Library of Rhetorics Ser.). 184p. (C). 1993. lib. bdg. 79.50 (0-7923-2198-7) Kluwer Ac.

Aesthetics of Contemporary Spanish American Social Protest Poetry. Frederic W. Murray. LC 90-19948. (Hispanic Literature Ser.: Vol. 9). 224p. 1990. lib. bdg. 89.95 (0-88946-591-6) E Mellen.

Aesthetics of Dedalus & Bloom. Marguerite Harkness. LC 82-45564. 300p. 1984. 39.50 (0-8387-5050-8) Bucknell U Pr.

Aesthetics of Disappearance. Paul Virilio. 130p. 1991. pap. 9.00 (0-936756-42-X) Autonomedia.

Aesthetics of Discontent: Politics & Reclusion in Medieval Japanese Literature. Michele Marra. LC 90-25540. (Illus.). 248p. 1991. text ed. 35.00 (0-8248-1336-7); pap. text ed. 14.95 (0-8248-1364-2) UH Pr.

An Asterisk (*) at the beginning of an entry indicates that the title is appearing in BIP for the first time.

***Aesthetics of Disturbance: Anti-Art in Avant-Garde Drama.** David Graver. LC 95-16289. (Theater--Theory-Text-Performance Ser.). 1995. write for info. (*0-472-10507-8*) U of Mich Pr.

Aesthetics of Environment. Arnold Berleant. 256p. (C). 1992. 34.95 (*0-87722-993-7*) Temple U Pr.

Aesthetics of Excess. Allen S. Weiss. LC 88-39379. (Aesthetics & the Philosophy of Art Ser.). 211p. 1989. 64.50 (*0-7914-0052-2*); pap. 21.95 (*0-7914-0053-0*) State U NY Pr.

Aesthetics of Film. Jacques Aumont et al. Tr. by Richard Neupert. LC 91-33706. (Film Studies). (Illus.). 279p. (Orig.). 1992. text ed. 40.00 (*0-292-70428-3*); pap. 17.95 (*0-292-70437-2*) U of Tex Pr.

Aesthetics of French Photography Studies. Ed. by Peter C. Bunnell. LC 76-24672. (Sources of Modern Photography Ser.). (Illus.). (FRE.). 1979. lib. bdg. 38.95 (*0-405-09983-5*) Ayer.

Aesthetics of James Joyce. Jacques Aubert. 208p. 1992. text ed. 30.00 (*0-8018-4349-9*) Johns Hopkins.

Aesthetics of Junk Fiction. Thomas J. Roberts. LC 89-4911. 288p. 1990. 30.00 (*0-8203-1149-9*) U of Ga Pr.

Aesthetics of Landscape. Steven C. Bourassa. 168p. 1992. text ed. 43.95 (*0-470-21889-4*) Halsted Pr.

Aesthetics of Landscape. Steven C. Bourassa. (Illus.). 186p. 1992. text ed. 55.00 (*1-85293-071-3*, Pub. by Pinter Pubs UK) St Martin.

***Aesthetics of Landscape.** Steven C. Bourassa. 1993. text ed. 49.95 (*0-471-94487-4*) Wiley.

Aesthetics of Loss & Lessness. Angela Moorjani. LC 91-22390. 260p. 1991. text ed. 49.95 (*0-312-06827-1*) St Martin.

Aesthetics of Movement. Paul Souriau. Ed. & Tr. by Manon Souriau. LC 83-10366. Orig. Title: L' Esthetique du Mouvement. (Illus.). 184p. 1983. lib. bdg. 25.00 (*0-87023-412-9*) U of Mass Pr.

Aesthetics of Murder: A Study in Romantic Literature & Contemporary Culture. Joel Black. LC 91-8595. (Parallax: Re-Visions of Culture & Society Ser.). (Illus.). 224p. 1991. text ed. 45.00x (*0-8018-4180-1*); pap. text ed. 14.95 (*0-8018-4181-X*) Johns Hopkins.

Aesthetics of Musical Art. Ferdinand Hand. 187p. 1991. reprint ed. lib. bdg. 69.00 (*0-7812-9346-4*) Rprt Serv.

Aesthetics of Pianoforte-Playing. Adolph Kullak. LC 69-16652. (Music Reprint Ser.). 340p. 1972. reprint ed. lib. bdg. 39.50 (*0-306-71095-1*) Da Capo.

Aesthetics of Power: Essays in Critical Art History. Carol Duncan. LC 92-20448. (New Art History & Criticism Ser.). (Illus.). 256p. (C). 1993. pap. 17.95 (*0-521-42187-X*) Cambridge U Pr.

Aesthetics of Power: Essays in Critical Art History. Carol Duncan. LC 92-20448. (New Art History & Criticism Ser.). (Illus.). 256p. (C). 1993. 54.95 (*0-521-42044-X*) Cambridge U Pr.

Aesthetics of Primitive Art. H. Gene Blocker. (Illus.). 342p. (Orig.). (C). 1994. lib. bdg. 62.50 (*0-8191-9316-X*); pap. text ed. 48.00 (*0-8191-9317-8*) U Pr of Amer.

Aesthetics of Progress: Forms of the Future in American Design 1930's-1980's. Katy Kline. (Illus.). 28p. (Orig.). 1984. pap. 5.00 (*0-938437-10-0*) MIT List Visual Arts.

Aesthetics of Robert Schumann. Thomas A. Brown. LC 73-16607. (Illus.). 207p. 1975. reprint ed. text ed. 55.00 (*0-8371-7184-9*, BRAS, Greenwood Pr) Greenwood.

Aesthetics of Rock. Richard Meltzer. 1987. pap. 11.95 (*0-306-80287-2*) Da Capo.

Aesthetics of Stephane Mallarme in Relation to His Public. Paula G. Lewis. LC 74-5898. 260p. (C). 1976. 25.00 (*0-8386-1615-1*) Fairleigh Dickinson.

***Aesthetics of Textiles & Clothing: Advancing Multi-Disciplinary Perspectives, 7.** Marilyn R. DeLong & Ann M. Fiore. (ITAA Special Publication: No. 7). (C). 1994. pap. text ed. 35.00 (*1-885715-03-X*) Intl Textile.

Aesthetics of the Critical Theorists: Studies on Benjamin, Adorno, Marcuse, & Habermas. Ed. by Ronald Roblin. LC 90-30955. (Problems in Contemporary Philosophy Ser.: Vol. 23). 532p. 1990. lib. bdg. 119.95 (*0-88946-368-9*) E Mellen.

Aesthetics of the Greek Banquet: Images of Wine & Ritual. Francois Lissarrague. Tr. by Andrew Szegedy-Maszak. (Illus.). 165p. (C). 1990. text ed. 26.95 (*0-691-03595-4*) Princeton U Pr.

Aesthetics of the Popular Arts. Sung-Bong Park. (Aesthetica Upsaliensia Ser.: No. 5). 188p. (Orig.). 1993. pap. 47.50x (*91-554-3047-3*, Pub. by Uppsala Universitet SW) Coronet Bks.

Aesthetics of Thomas Aquinas. Umberto Eco. Tr. by Hugh Bredin. LC 88-658. 304p. 1988. pap. 14.00 (*0-674-00676-3*) HUP.

Aesthetics of Townscape. Robert J. Goakes. 168p. (C). 1990. pap. 90.00 (*0-86439-031-9*, Pub. by Boolarong Pubns AT) St Mut.

Aesthetics of Visual Poetry, 1914-1928. Willard Bohn. (Illus.). 250p. 1986. 59.95 (*0-521-30697-3*) Cambridge U Pr.

Aesthetics of Visual Poetry, 1914-1928. Willard Bohn. (Illus.). 304p. 1993. pap. text ed. 14.95 (*0-226-06325-9*) U Ch Pr.

Aesthetics of Wonder. A. V. Subramanian. (C). 1988. 17.50 (*81-208-0444-9*, Pub. by Motilal Banarsidass II) S Asia.

Aesthetik. 2nd ed. Nicolai Hartmann. (C). 1966. 123.10 (*3-11-000146-2*) De Gruyter.

Aestimanda: Practical Criticism of Latin & Greek Poetry & Prose. Maurice G. Balme & M. S. Warman. 1965. pap. 9.95 (*0-19-831766-2*) OUP.

Aestiuation. Mike Newell. (Illus.). 56p. (Orig.). 1992. pap. 5.00 (*1-880977-02-8*) Watusi.

***Aether Madness: An Offbeat Guide to the Online World.** Michael Stein & Gary Wolf. 350p. 1994. pap. 21.95 (*1-56609-020-2*) Peachpit Pr.

Aethicus Ister, Aethici Istrici Cosmographia Ab Hieronymo Ex Graeco Latinum Breviarium Redacta. Ed. by Heinrich Wuttke. cxcv, 136p. 1991. reprint ed. write for info. (*3-487-09497-5*, Pub. by Georg Olms GW) Lubrecht & Cramer.

Aethiopian History. Heliodorus. Tr. by Thomas Underdowne. LC 07-3349. (Tudor Translations, First Ser.: No. 5). reprint ed. 57.50 (*0-404-51852-4*) AMS Pr.

Aetia, Iambi, Lyric Poems, Hecale, Minor Epic & Elegiac Poems, Fragments of Epigrams, Fragments of Uncertain Location. Callimachus. (Loeb Classical Library: No. 421). 440p. 1958. 18.95 (*0-674-99463-9*) HUP.

Aetiogical Studies of Isolated Common Congenital Abnormalities in Hungary. A. Czeizel & G. Tusnady. 360p. 1984. 147.00 (*0-569-08808-9*, Pub. by Collets UK) Pro-Am Music.

***Aetiological Studies of Isolated Common Congenital Abnormalities in Hungary.** E. Czeizel & G. Tusnady. 358p. (C). 1984. 90.00x (*963-05-3223-9*, Pub. by Akad Kiado HU) St Mut.

Aetiology - Idiopathic Scoliosis. Ed. by Robin. 1990. 78.95 (*0-8493-6722-0*, R) CRC Pr.

Aetiology of Compressed Air Intoxication & Inert Gas Narco. P. Bennett & G. A. Kerkut. LC 65-22882. (International Series of Monographs on Pure & Applied Mathematics: Vol. 31). 1966. 55.00 (*0-08-011396-6*, Pub. by Pergamon Repr UK) Franklin.

Aetolia: Its Geography, Topography, & Antiquities. William J. Woodhouse. LC 72-7909. (Greek History Ser.). 1977. reprint ed. 41.95 (*0-405-04805-X*) Ayer.

AFA Specialized Catalog, 1981-1982: Bicolored Issues, 1870-1905. Ed. by George B. Koplowitz & Alan Warren. Tr. by S. Mejdal. (Illus.). 156p. (Orig.). 1988. pap. text ed. 25.00 (*0-936493-12-7*) Scand Philatelic.

AFA Specialized Catalog 1981-1982: Denmark & Greenland. Ed. by George B. Koplowitz. Tr. by Majp S. Mejdal. (Illus.). 222p. (Orig.). 1986. pap. text ed. 27.50 (*0-936493-09-7*) Scand Philatelic.

***AFAA Reference Manual.** AFAA Staff. 192p. 1994. per., pap. text ed. 19.95 (*0-7872-0009-3*) Kendall-Hunt.

AFB Directory of Services for Blind & Visually Impaired Persons in the United States & Canada. 24th ed. 1993. 75.00 (*0-89128-242-4*); cd-rom 100.00 (*0-89128-243-2*) Am Foun Blind.

AFBTR Dictionary. 1991. write for info. (*0-944093-15-9*) Am Brain Tumor.

***Affable Savages: An Anthropologist among the Urubu Indians of Brazil.** Francis Huxley. 285p. (C). 1995. pap. text ed. 9.95 (*1-879215-27-6*) Sheffield WI.

Affacombe Affair. large type ed. Elizabeth Lemarchand. 1979. 12.00 (*0-7089-0280-4*) Ulverscroft.

Affair: The Case of Alfred Dreyfus. Jean-Denis Bredin. 1987. pap. 19.95 (*0-8076-1175-1*) Braziller.

Affair at Barwold. large type ed. Laurence Meynell. 1990. 21.95 (*0-7089-2142-6*) Ulverscroft.

Affair at Claife Manor. large type ed. Newlyn Nash. (Linford Romance Library). 272p. 1988. pap. 11.95 (*0-7089-6576-8*, Linford) Ulverscroft.

Affair at Honey Hill. Berry Fleming. LC 81-65833. 93p. 1981. 8.95 (*0-9604810-2-8*, Pub. by Cotton Lane) Pelican.

Affair at Honey Hill. Berry Fleming. LC 89-62516. 96p. 1990. 22.00 (*0-932966-96-9*) Permanent Pr.

Affair in Black Tie. Abbolyn B. Byrd. Ed. by James B. Van Treese. 326p. 1994. pap. 9.95 (*1-56901-210-5*) NW Pub.

Affair of the Heart. Phyllis Denny. LC 87-1092. 1988. 17.95 (*0-87949-278-3*) Ashley Bks.

Affair of the Jade Monkey. Clifford Knight. (Illus.). 239p. 1994. pap. 9.95 (*0-939666-71-5*) Yosemite Assn.

Affair on the Rhine. Dennis Weber. 1981. pap. 1.95 (*0-8439-0906-4*) Dorchester Pub Co.

Affair Prevention. Kreitler. 1981. 10.95 (*0-02-566710-6*) Macmillan.

Affair to Remember: My Life with Cary Grant. large type ed. Maureen Donaldson & William Royce. (General Ser.). (Illus.). 441p. 1990. 19.95 (*0-8161-4896-1*, Large Print Bks) Hall.

***Affair with a Log Cabin.** Larren Wood. LC 94-61686. 149p. (Orig.). 1995. pap. 9.95 (*0-9636546-2-4*) Woodstock North.

Affaire Calas et Autres Affaires. Voltaire. (Folio Ser.: No. 672). 416p. 1975. 9.95 (*2-07-036672-3*) Schoenhof.

Affaire de Coeur. 2nd rev. ed. Rene C. Du Gard. Tr. by Chantal. (Illus.). 356p. (FRE.). 1983. 19.00 (*0-939586-10-X*) Edns des Deux Mondes.

Affaire de Coeur. 3rd ed. Rene C. Du Gard. Tr. by Chantal. (Illus.). 290p. (FRE.). 1986. pap. 16.00 (*0-939586-12-6*) Edns des Deux Mondes.

Affaire de la Rue de Lourcine. Eugene Labiche. 64p. (FRE.). 1989. pap. 13.95 (*0-7859-1551-6*, 2851812416) Fr & Eur.

Affaire Dreyfus: La Verite en Marche. Avec: Choix de Lettres et d'Extraits des Impressions d'Audience. Emile Zola. 240p. (FRE.). 1988. pap. 18.95 (*0-7859-1558-3*, 2870272634) Fr & Eur.

Affaire N'Gustro. Jean-Patrick Manchette. 224p. (FRE.). 1987. pap. 10.95 (*0-7859-4270-X*, 2070378543) Fr & Eur.

Affaire Tournesol. Herge. (Illus.). 64p. (FRE.). (J). (gr. 7-9). 1992. reprint ed. write for info. (*0-7859-4692-6*) Fr & Eur.

Affaires du conte de Boduel. James H. Bothwell. LC 71-39513. (Bannatyne Club, Edinburgh. Publications: No. 29). reprint ed. 17.50 (*0-404-52735-3*) AMS Pr.

Affairs: A Novel. J. Eddie Infante. 169p. (Orig.). (C). 1984. pap. 9.50 (*971-10-0162-4*, Pub. by New Day Pub PH) Cellar.

Affairs in Order: A Complete Resource Guide to Death & Dying. Patricia Anderson. LC 92-34748. 315p. 1993. reprint ed. pap. 12.00 (*0-02-030280-0*, Collier S&S) S&S Trade.

Affairs in Order: A Complete Resource Guide to Wills & Other Financial-Legal Plans - Terminal Care & Counseling; Bioethics; Funeral & Disposition Options; Notification & Documents; Executor-Survivor Aid; Bereavement Help & More. Patricia Anderson. 256p. 1991. text ed. 21.95 (*0-02-501991-0*) Macmillan.

Affairs in the Late Insurrectionary States. U. S. House of Representatives Staff. LC 71-90199. (Mass Violence in America Ser.). 1969. reprint ed. 43.95 (*0-405-01321-3*) Ayer.

Affairs of Arabia: 1905-1906, 2 vols., Set. Ed. by Robin Bidwell. 1971. 250.00 (*0-7146-2694-5*, Pub. by F Cass Pubs UK) Intl Spec Bk.

Affairs of Party: The Political Culture of Northern Democrats in the Mid-19th Century. Jean H. Baker. (Illus.). 368p. 1983. pap. 16.95 (*0-8014-9883-X*) Cornell U Pr.

Affairs of State. Margot Arnold. 352p. 1982. pap. 3.50 (*0-449-12384-7*, GM) Fawcett.

Affairs of State: Public Life in Late Nineteenth Century America. Morton Keller. LC 76-21676. 640p. 1979. pap. text ed. 18.95 (*0-674-00710-7*) Belknap Pr.

Affairs of the Heart. Bobbi. (Illus.). 120p. (Orig.). 1990. pap. 9.95 (*0-9626608-0-9*) Magik NY.

Affairs of the Heart. large type ed. Sarah Franklin. 1992. 16.95 (*0-263-13150-5*, MB077, Pub. by Mills & Boon Ltd UK) Chivers N Amer.

Affairs of the Heart: How to Start & Operate a Successful Special Event Planning Service. Nancy D. Gluck. 144p. 1993. pap. 69.00 (*0-9638085-0-8*) Humbug Assocs.

Affairs of the Heart: Women & Men Reveal the Truth about Extramarital Affairs. Virginia Lee. 200p. 1993. 10.95 (*0-89594-621-1*) Crossing Pr.

Affairs of the Hearth: Victorian Poetry, Domestic Ideology & Narrative Form. Rod Edmond. (Illus.). 240p. 1988. 45.00 (*0-415-00656-2*) Routledge.

Affairs of West Africa. E. D. Morel. (Illus.). 382p. 1968. reprint ed. 35.00 (*0-7146-1702-4*, Pub. by F Cass Pubs UK) Intl Spec Bk.

Affairs to Remember: The Hollywood Comedy of the Sexes. Bruce Babington. 1992. text ed. 19.95 (*0-7190-2291-6*, Pub. by Manchester Univ Pr UK) St Martin.

Affect: Psychoanalytic Perspectives. Ed. by Theodore Shapiro & Robert N. Emde. LC 92-49359. 514p. (C). 1992. text ed. 65.00 (*0-8236-0116-1*) Intl Univs Pr.

Affect & Accuracy in Recall: Studies of "Flashbulb" Memories. Ed. by Eugene Winograd & Ulric Neisser. (Emory Symposia in Cognition Ser.: No. 4). (Illus.). 288p. (C). 1992. 44.95 (*0-521-40188-7*) Cambridge U Pr.

Affect & Attachment in Family: A Family-Based Treatment of Major Psychiatric Disorders. Jeri A. Doane & Diana Diamond. 320p. 1994. text ed. 35.00 (*0-465-00536-5*) Basic.

Affect & Cognition: Seventeenth Annual Carnegie Symposium on Cognition. Ed. by Margaret S. Clark & Susan T. Fiske. (Ongoing Ser.). 368p. (C). 1982. text ed. 75.00 (*0-89859-212-7*) L Erlbaum Assocs.

Affect & Creativity: The Role of Affect & Play in the Creative Process. Sandra Russ. (Spielberger: Personality Assessment Ser.). 160p. 1993. text ed. 36.00 (*0-8058-0986-4*) L Erlbaum Assocs.

Affect & Emotion Journal: Psychopathology, Vol. 21, No. 2-3, 1988. Ed. by P. Berner & E. Gabriel. (Illus.). 92p. 1989. pap. 59.25 (*3-8055-5005-7*) S Karger.

Affect & Mathematical Problem Solving. Ed. by D. B. McLeod & V. M. Adams. (Illus.). 280p. 1989. 53.00 (*0-387-96924-1*) Spr-Verlag.

Affect & Memory: A Reformulation. S. Dutta & R. N. Kanunga. LC 75-8628. 148p. 1975. 67.00 (*0-08-018270-4*, Pub. by Pergamon Repr UK) Franklin.

Affect & Social Behavior. Bert S. Moore & Alice M. Isen. (Studies in Emotion & Social Interaction). (Illus.). 288p. (C). 1990. 59.95 (*0-521-32768-7*) Cambridge U Pr.

***Affect & the Developmental Process.** E. Virginia Demos & Samuel Kaplan. Date not set. write for info. (*0-88163-075-6*) Analytic Pr.

Affect, Cognition & Personality: Empirical Studies. Ed. by Silvan S. Tomkins & Carroll E. Izard. LC 65-17489. (Illus.). 464p. 1965. 30.00 (*0-8261-0771-0*) Springer Pub.

Affect, Cognition & Social Behavior: New Evidence & Integrative Attempts. Ed. by K. Fiedler & J. L. Forgas. LC 87-26602. 392p. (C). 1988. text ed. 59.00 (*0-88937-016-8*) Hogrefe & Huber Pubs.

Affect, Cognition, & Stereotyping: Interactive Processes in Group Perception. Ed. by Diane Mackie & David Hamilton. (Illus.). 389p. 1993. text ed. 59.95 (*0-12-464410-4*) Acad Pr.

Affect, Conditioning & Cognition: Essays on the Determinants of Behavior. Robert Brush & Bruce J. Overmier. LC 85-15862. 400p. (C). 1985. text ed. 79.95 (*0-89859-586-X*) L Erlbaum Assocs.

Affect, Imagery, & Consciousness, Vol. 1: The Positive Affects. Silvan S. Tomkins. LC 62-16410. (Illus.). 544p. 1963. 49.95 (*0-8261-0541-6*) Springer Pub.

Affect, Imagery, & Consciousness, Vol. 2: The Negative Affects. Silvan S. Tomkins. LC 62-16410. (Illus.). 580p. 1963. 46.95 (*0-8261-0542-4*) Springer Pub.

Affect, Imagery, Consciousness: Cognition: Duplication & Transformation of Information, Vol. 4. Silvan S. Tomkins. LC 62-16410. 464p. 1992. 58.00 (*0-8261-0544-0*) Springer Pub.

Affect, Imagery, Consciousness, Vol. 3: The Negative Affects: Anger & Fear. Silvan S. Tomkins. 592p. 1991. 74.00 (*0-8261-0543-2*) Springer Pub.

Affect in Psychoanalytic Theory & Practice: A Clinical Synthesis. Charles Spezzano. (Relational Perspectives Book Ser.: Vol. 2). 256p. 1993. 36.00 (*0-88163-128-0*) Analytic Pr.

Affect in the Curriculum: Toward Democracy, Dignity, & Diversity. James A. Beane. 232p. (C). 1990. pap. text ed. 17.95 (*0-8077-2999-X*) Tchrs Coll.

Affect, Object, & Character Structure. Morton Kissen. 312p. 1994. text ed. 45.00 (*0-8236-0114-5*) Intl Univs Pr.

Affect Regulation & the Origin of Self: The Neurobiology of Emotional Development. Allan N. Schore. 693p. 1993. text ed. 135.00 (*0-8058-1396-9*) L Erlbaum Assocs.

***Affected with the Public Interest.** 172p. 1994. 30.00 (*0-614-06940-8*) NARUC.

Affecting Change: Social Workers in the Political Arena. 2nd ed. Karen S. Haynes & James S. Mickelson. 192p. (C). 1991. pap. text ed. 25.50 (*0-8013-0669-8*, 78656) Longman.

Affecting Performance: Meaning, Movement, & Experience in Okiek Women's Initiation. Corinne A. Kratz. LC 92-35663. (Ethnographic Inquiry Ser.). (Illus.). 480p. (C). 1993. text ed. 69.00 (*1-56098-234-9*); pap. text ed. 24.95 (*1-56098-273-X*) Smithsonian.

Affectionately, Rachel: Letters from India, 1860-1884. Ed. by Barbara M. Tull. LC 92-4014. (Illus.). 368p. 1992. lib. bdg. 35.00 (*0-87338-463-6*) Kent St U Pr.

Affectionately Yours. Carla J. Tenret. (Illus.). 56p. 1990. 5.00 (*0-9625973-0-9*) Carlagraphics.

Affective & Cognitive Domains: Integration for Instruction & Research. Barbara L. Martin & Leslie J. Briggs. LC 85-16143. (Illus.). 500p. 1986. 39.95 (*0-87778-193-1*) Educ Tech Pubns.

Affective & Schizoaffective Disorders: Similarities & Differences. Ed. by A. Marneros & Ming T. Tsuang. 304p. 1990. 96.00 (*0-387-52071-6*) Spr-Verlag.

Affective Correlates of Learning Disabilities. Ed. by J. W. Chapman & F. J. Boersma. (Modern Approaches to the Diagnosis & Instruction of Multi-Handicapped Children Ser.: Vol. 15). vi, 110p. 1980. 26.50 (*90-265-0341-5*, Pub. by Swets Pub Serv NE) Taylor & Francis.

Affective Development & the Creative Arts: A Process Approach to Early Childhood Education. George C. Edwards, III. 288p. (C). 1990. pap. write for info. (*0-675-21023-2*, Merrill Pub Co) Macmillan.

Affective Development in Infancy. T. Berry Brazelton & Michael E. Yogman. LC 85-3396. 168p. 1986. text ed. 39.50 (*0-89391-345-6*) Ablex Pub.

Affective Disorders. Ed. by Frederic F. Flach. (Directions in Psychiatry Monograph Ser.: No. 3). 1988. 29.95 (*0-393-70055-0*) Norton.

Affective Disorders. Ed. by John M. Davis & James W. Maas. LC 83-3731. 445p. reprint ed. pap. 126.90 (*0-8357-7854-1*, 2036231) Bks Demand.

Affective Disorders: Perspectives on Basic Research & Clinical Practice. Ed. by Tetsuhiko Kariya & Michio Nakagawara. LC 92-48745. (Illus.). 160p. 1993. 20.95 (*0-87630-674-1*) Brunner-Mazel.

Affective Disorders: Psychoanalytic Contributions to Their Study. Ed. by Phyllis Greenacre. LC 53-11058. 211p. 1961. text ed. 30.00 (*0-8236-0100-5*) Intl Univs Pr.

Affective Disorders & the Family: Assessment & Treatment. Ed. by John F. Clarkin et al. LC 87-28175. (Guilford Family Therapy Ser.). 263p. 1988. lib. bdg. 35.00 (*0-89862-101-1*) Guilford Pr.

Affective Disorders in Childhood & Adolescence: An Update. Ed. by D. Cantwell & G. Carlson. (Child Behavior & Development Ser.: Vol. 5). 500p. 1983. 39.95 (*0-89335-189-X*) PMA Pub Corp.

Affective Disorders, Psychopathology & Treatment. Ed. by Eduardo R. Val et al. LC 81-19777. 509p. 1982. reprint ed. pap. 145.10 (*0-8357-7634-4*, 2056957) Bks Demand.

Affective Disorders Reassessed, 1983. Ed. by Frank Ayd et al. 250p. (Orig.). 1983. text ed. 35.00 (*0-931858-05-4*) Ayd Medical Comm.

Affective Education: Methods & Techniques. Ed. by Isadore L. Sonnier. LC 88-24407. (Illus.). 260p. 1989. pap. 24.95 (*0-87778-212-1*) Educ Tech Pubns.

Affective Education: Self Concept & the Gifted Student. Elinor Katz. (Professional Development Series, Current Themes in Gifted Education). 100p. 1994. pap. text ed. write for info. (*0-9638228-7-X*) Open Space Comn.

Affective Expression Guide. Bob Eberle. 16p. (Orig.). 1983. teacher ed. pap. 1.50 (*0-88047-032-1*, 8316) DOK Pubs.

Affective Self-Esteem: Lesson Plans for Affective Education. Katherine Krefft. LC 92-55064. 248p. 1993. pap. text ed. 18.95 (*1-55959-048-3*) Accel Devel.

Affectivity & Learning see Science of Education

***Affects as Process: An Inquiry into the Centrality of Affect in Psychological Life.** Joseph M. Jones. 320p. 1995. text ed. 39.95 (*0-88163-125-6*) Analytic Pr.

Afferent Control of Posture & Locomotion. Ed. by J. H. Allum & M. Hulliger. (Progress in Brain Research Ser.: No. 80). 532p. 1990. 283.25 (*0-444-81225-3*) Elsevier.

Affibility Blues. Albert Cook. LC 93-36166. 204p. 1994. pap. 24.95 (*0-7734-2799-6*, Mellen Poetry Pr) E Mellen.

Affiches et Art Publicitaire see Annual of Auction Prices for Posters

***Affine Analysis of Image Sequences.** Larry S. Shapiro. (Distinguished Dissertations in Computer Science Ser.: No. 10). 200p. (C). 1995. write for info. (*0-521-55063-7*) Cambridge U Pr.

***Affine & Projective Geometry.** M. K. Bennett. Date not set. text ed. 44.95 (*0-471-11315-8*) Wiley.

Affine Differential Geometry. Su Buchin. 254p. (C). 1983. text ed. 169.00 (*0-677-31060-9*) Gordon & Breach.

Affine Differential Geometry: Geometry of Affine Immersions. Katsumi Nomizu & Takeshi Sasaki. LC 93-46712. (Cambridge Tracts in Mathematics Ser.: Vol. 111). (Illus.). 250p. (C). 1995. 49.95 (*0-521-44177-3*) Cambridge U Pr.

Affine Kac-Moody Algebras, Weight Multiplicities, & Branching Rules, Vols. 1 & 2. S. N. Kass et al. 1989. 75.00 (*0-520-06768-1*) U CA Pr.

A

An Asterisk (*) at the beginning of an entry indicates that the title is appearing in BIP for the first time.

117

Affine Lie Algebras & Quantum Groups: An Introduction: With Applications in Conformal Field Theory. Jurgen Fuchs. (Cambridge Monographs on Mathematical Physics). (Illus.). 448p. (C). 1992. 100.00 (*0-521-41593-4*) Cambridge U Pr.

*__Affine Lie Algebras & Quantum Groups: An Introduction, with Applications in Conformal Field Theory.__ Jurgen Fuchs. (Cambridge Monographs on Mathematical Physics). (Illus.). 448p. (C). 1995. pap. 39.95 (*0-521-48412-X*) Cambridge U Pr.

Affine Representations of Grothendieck Groups & Applications to Rickart C-Algebras & Aleph O-Continuous Regular Rings. K. R. Goodearl et al. LC 80-17018. (Memoirs Ser.: No. 26/234). 163p. 1980. pap. 16.00 (*0-8218-2234-9*, MEMO 26/234) Am Math.

Affinitas Linguae Hungaricae Cum Linguis Fennicae Originis, Grammatice Demonstrata, 1799. Samuel Gyarmathi. LC 67-66171. (Uralic & Altaic Ser.: Vol. 95). 380p. 1968. pap. text ed. 13.00 (*0-87750-040-1*) Res Inst Inner Asian Studies.

Affinities. Rachel Perez. (Orig.). 1993. pap. text ed. 4.95 (*1-56333-113-6*) Masquerade.

Affinities: Myron Stout, Bill Jensen, Brice Marden & Terry Winters. Kathy Halbreich. (Illus.). 44p. (Orig.). 1983. pap. 6.00 (*0-938437-06-2*) MIT List Visual Arts.

Affinities & Extremes: Crisscrossing the Bittersweet Ethnology of East Indies History, Hindu-Balinese Culture & Indo-European Allure. James A. Boon. LC 89-20326. (Illus.). 280p. 1990. lib. bdg. 45.00 (*0-226-06461-1*) U Ch Pr.

Affinities & Extremes: Crisscrossing the Bittersweet Ethnology of East Indies History, Hindu-Balinese Culture & Indo-European Allure. James A. Boon. LC 89-20326. (Illus.). 280p. 1990. pap. text ed. 14.95 (*0-226-06463-8*) U Ch Pr.

Affinities & Intuitions: The Gerald S. Elliott Collection of Contemporary Art. Ed. by Neal Benezra. LC 89-51745. (Illus.). 312p. 1990. 60.00 (*0-500-23577-5*) Art Inst Chi.

Affinities & Medieval Transposition. Dolores Pesce. LC 86-45398. (Music: Scholarship & Performance Ser.). (Illus.). 256p. 1987. 17.95 (*0-253-30460-1*) Ind U Pr.

Affinity & Matter: Elements of Chemical Philosophy, 1800-1865. Trevor H. Levere. LC 92-45001. (Classics in the History & Philosophy of Science Ser.: Vol. 12). 1993. pap. text ed. 36.00 (*2-88124-583-8*) Gordon & Breach.

Affinity As a Value: Marriage Alliance in South India with Comparative Essays on Australia. Louis Dumont. LC 82-13468. (Illus.). 248p. (C). 1983. 22.00 (*0-226-16964-2*) U Ch Pr.

Affinity Chromatography. Jaroslava Turkova. (Journal of Chromatography Library: Vol. 12). 406p. 1978. 120.50 (*0-444-41605-6*) Elsevier.

Affinity Chromatography. Christopher R. Lowe & P. D. Dean. LC 73-17598. 284p. reprint ed. pap. 81.00 (*0-8357-5219-4*, 2023997) Bks Demand.

Affinity Chromatography: A Practical Approach. Ed. by P. D. Dean et al. (Practical Approach Ser.). 232p. 1985. pap. 39.00 (*0-904147-71-1*, IRL Pr) OUP.

Affinity Chromatography: Practical & Theoretical Aspects. Mohr & Pomerening. (Chromatographic Science Ser.: Vol. 33). 320p. 1985. 150.00 (*0-8247-7468-X*) Dekker.

Affinity Chromatography: Proceedings of an International Symposium Held in Vienna, 1977. Ed. by O. Hoffman-Ostenhof et al. LC 78-40289. 1978. 162.00 (*0-08-022632-9*, Pub. by Pergamon Repr UK) Franklin.

Affinity Chromatography: Template Chromatography of Nucleic Acids & Proteins. Schott. (Chromatographic Science Ser.: Vol. 27). 248p. 1984. 125.00 (*0-8247-7111-7*) Dekker.

Affinity Chromatography & Related Techniques: Theoretical Aspects. Ed. by T. C. Gribnau et al. (Analytical Chemistry Symposia Ser.: Vol. 9). 584p. 1981. 125.75 (*0-444-42031-2*) Elsevier.

Affinity Electrophoresis: Principles & Clinical Application. Breborowicz & Mackiewi. 1991. 179.00 (*0-8493-6665-8*, QP519) CRC Pr.

Affinity Labelling & Cloning of Steroid & Thyroid Hormone Receptors. Ed. by H. Gronemeyer. (Ellis Horwood Series in Biomedicine). 322p. 1988. lib. bdg. 165.00 (*0-89573-579-2*) VCH Pubs.

Affinity (Love) rev. ed. James J. Carter. Ed. by Margaret Verhulst. (Illus.). 96p. (Orig.). 1986. 9.95 (*0-685-08017-X*); pap. 4.95 (*0-937004-02-2*) Unicorn PA.

Affinity Membranes: Their Chemistry & Performance in Adsorptive Separation Processes. Elias Klein. 152p. 1991. text ed. 110.00 (*0-471-52765-3*) Wiley.

Affinity Modification of Biopolymers. Dimitri G. Knorre & Valentin V. Vlassov. 272p. 1988. 159.00 (*0-8493-6925-8*, QP519, CRC Reprint) Franklin.

*__Affinity Reference for BioMedical.__ Marquette Electronics Staff. 256p. 1995. boxed 24.95 (*0-7872-0065-4*) Kendall-Hunt.

Affinity Techniques: Enzyme Purification see Methods in Enzymology

Affinity Technology, No. C-130. Business Communications Co., Inc. Staff. 180p. 1991. 2,650.00 (*0-89336-800-8*) BCC.

Affinties Electives. W. Goethe. 352p. (FRE.). 1980. pap. 11.95 (*0-7859-2437-X*, 2070372375) Fr & Eur.

Affirm Yourself Day by Day: Begin Your Day With Seed Thoughts for Loving Yourself. Suzanne E. Harrill. 416p. (Orig.). 1992. pap. 11.95 (*0-9625996-1-1*); audio 10.95 (*0-9625996-9-7*); 12.95 (*0-9625996-2-X*) Innerworks Pub.

*__Affirmation: The AIDS Odyssey of Dr. Peter.__ Daniel Gawthrop. (Illus.). 268p. (Orig.). 1994. pap. 12.00 (*0-921586-35-3*, Pub. by New Star Bks CN) InBook.

Affirmation & Denial: Construction of Femininity on Indian Television. Prabha Krishnan & Anita Dighe. 128p. (C). 1990. text ed. 22.50 (*0-8039-9643-8*) Sage.

Affirmation in a Moral Wasteland: A Comparison of Ford Madox Ford & Graham Greene. Ed. by Karen M. Radell. (American University Studies: English Language & Literature: Ser. IV, Vol. 54). 233p. (C). 1987. text ed. 33.00 (*0-8204-0499-3*) P Lang Pubs.

Affirmation of Life: A Reichian Energetic Perspective. John Lawson. LC 91-75113. 128p. 1991. pap. 7.95 (*0-9630338-1-6*) Ardengrove.

Affirmation of Ministry. Hoyt Stone. 1991. pap. 7.99 (*0-87148-034-4*) Pathway Pr.

*__Affirmations.__ Stuart Wilde. Ed. by Jill Kramer. Date not set. pap. 9.95 (*1-56170-167-X*, 188) Hay House.

Affirmations. Stuart Wilde. (Illus.). 164p. 1988. 14.95 (*0-930603-02-8*); pap. 9.95 (*0-930603-36-2*) White Dove NM.

Affirmations: Living Day by Day. 1991. 7.95 (*0-89954-511-4*) Antioch Pub Co.

Affirmations: Poems in Scots & English. M. S. Lumsden. (Illus.). 76p. 1990. text ed. 19.00 (*0-08-040929-6*, Pub. by Aberdeen U Pr) Macmillan.

Affirmations: The Messages of the Flowers in Transformative Words for the Soul. Patricia Kaminski. (Illus.). 320p. (Orig.). 1995. pap. 12.95 (*0-9631306-2-5*) Flower Essence.

*__Affirmations & Meditations: The Invisible Forces.__ Jerry W. Whitley. 100p. 1995. pap. 10.95 (*0-9646984-0-4*) Moonlight Prodns.

Affirmations, by a Group of American Anglo-Catholics, Clerical & Lay. Ed. by Bernard I. Bell. LC 68-16906. (Essay Index Reprint Ser.). 1977. 18.95 (*0-8369-0185-1*) Ayer.

Affirmations Can Change your Life. 3.00 (*0-318-37760-8*) Transitions.

Affirmations, Declarations & Blues. NoNyaniso Zinza. 1989. pap. 7.00 (*0-933033-01-X*) Du Ewa.

Affirmations Especially for Women. 1991. 7.95 (*0-89954-681-1*) Antioch Pub Co.

Affirmations for a Year-Round Kwanzaa. Gwynelle Dismukes. LC 92-84104. 50p. 1993. pap. 4.95 (*1-55523-585-9*) Winston-Derek.

Affirmations for Adult Children. Dianne Mackie. 1991. 6.95 (*0-9622150-0-7*) Aurora VA.

Affirmations for Parents: How to Nurture Your Children. Tian Dayton. (Orig.). 1991. pap. 6.95 (*1-55874-151-8*) Health Comm.

Affirmations for Self Healing. rev. ed. J. Donald Walters. 132p. 1992. reprint ed. pap. 7.95 (*1-878265-40-7*) Crystal Clarity.

Affirmations for the Inner Child. Rokelle Lerner. 1989. pap. 6.95 (*1-55874-054-6*) Health Comm.

Affirmations for Your Healthy Pregnancy. Cheryl Kilvington. 288p. 1992. pap. text ed. 10.00 (*0-9633188-0-2*) Affirmative.

*__Affirmations, Meditations.__ L. Dackman. 1994. pap. 3.99 (*0-517-13241-9*) Random Hse Value.

Affirmations of a Skeptical Believer. G. Avery Lee. (C). 1993. pap. 14.95 (*0-86554-395-X*) Mercer Univ Pr.

Affirmations of Reality. Richard Schain. 120p. (Orig.). 1982. pap. 5.00 (*0-9609922-0-0*) Garric Pr.

Affirmative Action? National Association for Women Deans, Administrators & Counselors. 1976. pap. 6.00 (*0-686-15381-2*) Natl Assn Women.

Affirmative Action: Opportunity for All? Trudy J. Hanmer. LC 92-44972. (Issues in Focus Ser.). (Illus.). 128p. (J). (gr. 6 up). 1993. lib. bdg. 17.95 (*0-89490-451-5*) Enslow Pubs.

Affirmative Action After the Johnson Decision: Practical Guidance for Planning & Compliance. Douglas S. McDowell. 166p. 1988. 25.00 (*0-916559-14-9*) EPF.

Affirmative Action & Justice: A Philosophical & Constitutional Inquiry. Michel Rosenfeld. 384p. (C). 1991. text ed. 40.00 (*0-300-04781-9*) Yale U Pr.

Affirmative Action & Justice: A Philosophical & Constitutional Inquiry. Michel Rosenfeld. 384p. (C). 1993. reprint ed. pap. text ed. 19.00 (*0-300-05508-0*) Yale U Pr.

Affirmative Action & Preferential Admissions in Higher Education. Kathryn Swanson. LC 81-45. 344p. 1981. 29.50 (*0-8108-1411-0*) Scarecrow.

Affirmative Action & Principles of Justice: Contributions in Legal Studies, No. 53. Kathanne W. Greene. LC 89-2121. 208p. 1989. text ed. 45.00 (*0-313-26678-6*, GAA/, Greenwood Pr) Greenwood.

Affirmative Action & the University: A Philosophical Inquiry. Ed. by Steven M. Cahn. LC 92-18787. 320p. 1993. 37.95 (*1-56639-030-3*) Temple U Pr.

Affirmative Action & the Woman Worker: Guidelines for Personnel Management. Jennie Farley. LC 78-11719. 237p. reprint ed. pap. 67.60 (*0-8357-5220-8*, 2023886) Bks Demand.

Affirmative Action at Work: Law, Politics, & Ethics. Bron R. Taylor. LC 90-24450. (Policy & Institutional Studies). 288p. (C). 1991. text ed. 49.95 (*0-8229-3674-7*); pap. text ed. 16.95 (*0-8229-5453-2*) U of Pittsburgh Pr.

Affirmative Action Federal Contract Compliance Manual: Desk Audit, Onsite & Corporate Management Review. U. S. Department of Labor, Employment Standards Administration Staff. 320p. 1992. pap. 59.00 (*0-86587-323-2*) Gov Insts.

*__Affirmative Action Handbook.__ 500p. (Orig.). 1995. pap. 1,295.00 (*0-7605-1483-6*) Rector Pr.

Affirmative Action Handbook. Venable, Baetjer & Howard Staff & Berkshire Associates Staff. 160p. 1991. pap. text ed. 65.00 (*0-86587-274-0*) Gov Insts.

Affirmative Action in Action: Strategies for Enchancing Employment Prospects of Qualified Handicapped Individuals. Henry McCarthy & Lana Smart. LC 79-90291. 40p. 1979. 3.75 (*0-686-38808-9*) Human Res Ctr.

Affirmative Action in Higher Education: A Sourcebook. rev. ed. Lois Vander Waerdt. 320p. 1989. write for info. (*0-318-65503-9*) Higher Educ Exec Pubns.

Affirmative Action in Perspective. Ed. by F. A. Blanchard & F. J. Crosby. (Recent Research in Psychology Ser.). (Illus.). 240p. 1989. pap. 53.00 (*0-387-96971-3*) Spr-Verlag.

Affirmative Action Officer. Jack Rudman. (Career Examination Ser.: C-2647). 1994. pap. 29.95 (*0-8373-2647-8*) Nat Learn.

Affirmative Action on Campus. Ed. by Joseph G. Ponterotto et al. LC 85-644751. (New Directions for Student Services Ser.: No. 52). 1990. 16.95 (*1-55542-816-9*) Jossey-Bass.

Affirmative Action Programs after Bakke. Ron Simmons. 210p. 1982. 19.95 (*0-87073-516-0*); pap. 11.95 (*0-87073-517-9*) Schenkman Bks Inc.

Affirmative Action Reconsidered: Was It Necessary in Academia? Thomas Sowell. LC 75-42779. 45p. 1975. pap. 10.00 (*0-8447-3199-4*) Am Enterprise.

Affirmative Action Specialist. Jack Rudman. (Career Examination Ser.: C-2581). 1991. pap. 20.00 (*0-8373-2581-1*) Nat Learn.

Affirmative Aging: A Resource for Ministry. Episcopal Society for Ministry on Aging Staff. 200p. (Orig.). 1994. pap. 14.95 (*0-8192-1623-2*) Morehouse Pub.

Affirmative Discrimination: Ethnic Inequality & Public Policy. Nathan Glazer. LC 87-8378. 272p. 1987. pap. 13.95 (*0-674-00730-1*) HUP.

Affirmative Dynamic Psychotherapy with Gay Men. Ed. by Carlton Cornett. LC 93-12886. 264p. 1993. 35.00 (*1-56821-001-9*) Aronson.

Affirmative Marketing Handbook. 87p. write for info. (*0-318-15167-7*) Natl Assoc Realtors.

Affirmative Marketing Handbook. 87p. 4.50 (*0-318-59950-3*, 111-827) Natl Assoc Realtors.

Affirmative Rhetoric, Negative Action: African-American & Hispanic Faculty at Predominantly White Institutions. Valora Washington. Ed. by William Harvey. LC 89-83593. (ASHE-ERIC Higher Education Report Ser.: No. 2, 1989). 115p. (Orig.). (C). 1989. pap. text ed. 15.00 (*0-9623882-1-1*) GWU Schl E&HD.

Affirmative Talk, Affirmative Action: A Comparative Study of the Politics of Affirmative Action. Augustus J. Jones, Jr. LC 90-24157. 208p. 1991. text ed. 45.00 (*0-275-93681-3*, C3681, Praeger Pubs) Greenwood.

Affirmative Word Power: Interpretations on a Metaphysical Vocabulary. Virginia A. McIntire. 64p. 1992. pap. 7.50 (*0-9634894-1-0*) V A McIntire.

*__Affirming Children's Roots: Cultural & Linguistic Diversity in Early Care & Education.__ Hedy N. Chang & Laura Sakai. 101p. 1993. pap. 17.00 (*1-887039-08-2*) Calif Tomorrow.

Affirming Cosmic Unity: Awakening Universal Spirituality. Kathleen L. Mendel. Ed. by Candy K. Brethauer. LC 93-71317. 64p. (Orig.). (C). 1993. pap. 6.10 (*1-878142-31-3*) Telstar TX.

Affirming Cultural Citizenship in the Community: Critical Literacy & the el Barrio Popular Education Program. Rosa M. Torruellas et al. 73p. 1991. lib. bdg. 7.00 (*1-878483-01-3*) Hunter Coll CEP.

Affirming Diversity: The Sociopolitical Context of Multicultural Education. Sonia Nieto. 335p. (Orig.). (C). 1992. pap. text ed. 35.95 (*0-8013-0529-2*, 78406) Longman.

*__Affirming Diversity: The Sociopolitical Context of Multicultural Education.__ 2nd ed. Sonia Nieto. LC 95-7931. (C). 1996. pap. text ed. 33.95 (*0-8013-1420-8*) Longman.

Affirming Equity: A Framework for Teachers & Schools. Fred Rodriquez. 336p. (C). 1993. per. 24.76 (*0-8403-9024-6*) Kendall-Hunt.

Affirming Flame: Religion, Language, Literature. David Patterson. LC 87-30026. (Illus.). 192p. 1988. 29.95 (*0-8061-2109-2*) U of Okla Pr.

Affirming Life. Seymour Cohen. 350p. 1987. 20.00 (*0-88125-112-7*) Ktav.

Affirming Limits: Essays on Mortality, Choice, & Poetic Form. Robert Pack. LC 85-2768. 272p. (Orig.). 1985. 30.00 (*0-87023-483-8*); pap. 16.95 (*0-87023-653-9*) U of Mass Pr.

Affirming Love: Affirmations to Bring More Love into Your Life & into Your Relationship. Willie C. Hooks. 100p. (Orig.). 1990. pap. 7.95 (*0-9623440-3-6*) JTE Assocs.

Affirming the Soul: Remarkable Conversations Between Mental Health Professionals & an Ordained Minister. Jeffrey H. Boyd. 275p. (Orig.). 1994. pap. 14.95 (*0-9636990-3-2*) Soul Res Inst.

*__Affirming the Will of God.__ Paul Little. Tr. by Y. P. Chen. 42p. (CHI.). 1988. pap. 0.75 (*1-56582-074-6*) Christ Renew Min.

Affirmist Manifesto. rev. ed. Andre Bacard. 50p. 1986. 2.95 (*0-935539-00-X*) Heroica Bks.

Affliction. Russell Banks. LC 89-45075. 368p. 1990. pap. 12.00 (*0-06-092007-6*, PL) HarpC.

Affliction. Edith Schaeffer. (Raven's Ridge Imprint Ser.). 252p. 1993. reprint ed. pap. 11.99 (*0-8010-8355-9*) Baker Bk.

Affluence & Anxiety: America since Nineteen Forty-Five. 2nd ed. Carl N. Degler. (C). 1975. pap. text ed. 15.00 (*0-673-07956-2*) HarpCollege.

Affluence & Cultural Survival, 1981. Ed. by Richard F. Salisbury & Elisabeth Tooker. (Proceedings of the American Ethnological Society Ser.). 1984. 14.00 (*0-942976-03-7*) Am Anthro Assn.

Affluence & the French Worker in the Fourth Republic. Richard F. Hamilton. LC 67-11033. (Illus.). 335p. reprint ed. pap. 95.50 (*0-8357-3842-6*, 2036574) Bks Demand.

Affluent Investor: Investment Strategies for All Markets. Stephen P. Rappaport. 1990. 24.95 (*0-13-018375-X*) P-H.

Affluent Investor: Investment Strategies for All Markets. Stephen P. Rappaport. 1990. 24.95 (*0-317-03937-7*) NY Inst Finance.

Affluent Market. 2nd ed. Ed. by Peter Allen. 250p. 1987. pap. 995.00 (*0-941285-00-6*) FIND-SVP.

Affluent Society. rev. ed. John Kenneth Galbraith. 320p. 1963. pap. 4.95 (*0-451-62394-0*, ME2186, Ment) NAL-Dutton.

Affluent Workers Revisited: Privatism & the Working Class. Fiona Devine. (Edinburgh Education & Society Ser.). 336p. 1992. text ed. 49.00 (*0-7486-0370-0*, Pub. by Edinburgh U Pr UK) Col U Pr.

Affordable Caribbean: How to See the Best for Less. 1993. pap. 16.00 (*0-679-02559-6*) Fodors Travel.

*__Affordable Caribbean 1996.__ 2nd ed. Fodor's Staff. 1995. pap. 16.50 (*0-679-02948-6*) Fodors Travel.

Affordable City: Toward a Third Sector Housing Policy. Ed. by John E. Davis. LC 93-705. (Conflicts in Urban & Regional Development Ser.). 320p. 1993. 44.95 (*1-56639-109-1*) Temple U Pr.

Affordable Community: Adapting Today's Communities to Tomorrow's Needs: The Report of the Council on Development Choices for the '80's. Urban Land Institute Staff. (Illus.). 132p. reprint ed. pap. 37.70 (*0-8357-6766-3*, 2035427) Bks Demand.

Affordable Computer: The Microcomputer for Business & Industry. Ed. by Claire Summer & Walter A. Levy. LC 78-23754. 185p. reprint ed. pap. 52.80 (*0-8357-5221-6*, 2023887) Bks Demand.

*__Affordable Decorating.__ Home Decorating Institute Staff. (Arts & Crafts for Home Decorating Ser.). 128p. 1995. 18.95 (*0-86573-376-7*); pap. 15.95 (*0-86573-377-5*) Cy De Cosse.

*__Affordable Development? Biotechnology in the Third World.__ Mila Avramovic. 224p. (C). 1995. text ed. 59.95 (*1-85649-333-4*, Pub. by Zed Books UK); pap. 22.50 (*1-85649-334-2*, Pub. by Zed Books UK) Humanities.

Affordable Dreams: The Goetsch-Winckler House & Frank Lloyd Wright. Elizabeth Halsted et al. Ed. by Susan J. Bandes. (Illus.). 109p. (Orig.). 1991. pap. 21.95 (*1-879147-12-2*) Kresge Art Mus.

Affordable Employee Health Care: Options for a Model Benefits Plan. Larry S. Chapman. 400p. 1991. 69.95 (*0-8144-5047-4*) AMACOM.

Affordable Europe: How to See the Best for Less. 2nd ed. 1993. pap. 18.00 (*0-679-02491-3*) Fodors Travel.

Affordable Florida: How to See the Best for Less. 1993. pap. 16.00 (*0-679-02560-X*) Fodors Travel.

Affordable Flying: How to Use General Aviation Products & Services Affordably. rev. ed. Don Gladney. (Illus.). 270p. 1989. pap. write for info. (*0-318-65360-5*) ATDI.

Affordable France: How to See the Best for Less. 3rd ed. 1993. pap. 16.00 (*0-679-02492-1*) Fodors Travel.

Affordable Furs: Combining Fur & Leather with Knitting. Janet W. Mysse. LC 83-62505. (Illus.). 150p. 1983. spiral bd. 16.50 (*0-934318-21-2*) Falcon Pr MT.

Affordable Germany. 3rd ed. 1993. pap. 16.00 (*0-679-02493-X*) Fodors Travel.

Affordable Great Britain: How to See the Best for Less. 3rd ed. 1993. pap. 16.00 (*0-679-02494-8*) Fodors Travel.

Affordable Great Britain 1992: How to See the Best for Less. 1992. 14.00 (*0-679-02140-X*) Fodors Travel.

Affordable Health Insurance & Wellness Programs. Charles Youngblood. LC 93-80041. 75p. (Orig.). 1993. pap. 19.95 (*0-935927-01-8*) Hascom Pubs.

*__Affordable Heirlooms.__ Edna Powers & Gaye Kriegel. LC 95-10550. (Creative Machine Arts Ser.). 128p. 1995. pap. 15.95 (*0-8019-8647-8*) Chilton.

Affordable Home Plans: 430 Home Designs for Modest & Medium Budgets. (Illus.). 320p. 1990. pap. 8.95 (*0-918894-78-6*) Home Planners.

Affordable Homes Collection: New Home Plan Books for the Professional Builder. Building News Staff. 1994. pap. 29.95 (*1-55701-106-0*) BNI Pubns.

Affordable Horse: A Guide to Low-Cost Ownership. Sharon B. Smith. LC 93-36774. 1994. 17.00 (*0-87605-966-3*) Howell Bk.

Affordable Housing: A Challenge for Civil Engineers. Ed. by Oktay Ural & L. David Shen. 272p. 1989. pap. text ed. 32.00 (*0-87262-738-1*) Am Soc Civil Eng.

Affordable Housing: A Resource Guide to Alternative & Factory-Built Homes, New Technologies, & the Owner-Builder Option. Grant Burns. LC 89-42707. 196p. 1989. pap. 27.50x (*0-89950-419-1*) McFarland & Co.

Affordable Housing: Twenty Examples from the Private Sector. Douglas R. Porter & Susan Cole. LC 82-83409. (Illus.). 112p. reprint ed. pap. 32.00 (*0-8357-3185-5*, 2039455) Bks Demand.

Affordable Housing Alternatives. 1991. lib. bdg. 250.00 (*0-8490-4671-8*) Gordon Pr.

Affordable Housing & Public Policy: Strategies for Metropolitan Chicago. Ed. by Lawrence B. Joseph. (Chicago Assembly Ser.). 350p. (C). 1992. pap. text ed. 14.95 (*0-9626755-2-0*) UC Ctr UR&PS.

Affordable Housing & the Homeless. Ed. by Juergen Friedrichs. 191p. (C). 1988. lib. bdg. 46.95 (*3-11-011611-1*) De Gruyter.

*__Affordable Housing & the Homeless.__ Ed. by Juergen Friedrichs. 191p. (C). 1988. lib. bdg. 44.95 (*0-89925-451-9*) De Gruyter.

*__Affordable Housing for Everyone.__ Vartan Vahramian. 16p. 1994. 3.75 (*0-9643071-0-3*) Homelnd Bldg.

Affordable Housing in London. Ed. by C. M. Whitehead & D. T. Cross. (Progress in Planning Ser.: No. 36). (Illus.). 96p. 1991. pap. 57.00 (*0-08-041157-6*, Pergamon Pr) Elsevier.

Affordable Housing Mediation: Building Consensus for Regional Agreements in the Hartford & Greater Bridgeport Regions. Lawrence E. Susskind & Susan L. Podziba. 144p. 1990. pap. 9.40 (*1-55844-113-1*) Lincoln Inst Land.

An Asterisk (*) at the beginning of an entry indicates that the title is appearing in BIP for the first time.

A

An Asterisk (*) at the beginning of an entry indicates that the title is appearing in BIP for the first time.

119

A

Africa: A Study Guide to Better Understanding. Ed. by Charles A. Geoffrion. (African Humanities Ser.). (Orig.). 1970. pap. text ed. 2.00 (*0-941934-03-9*) Indiana Africa.

Africa: A Study in Tropical Development. 3rd ed. L. Dudley Stamp & W. T. Morgan. LC 75-178152. 534p. reprint ed. 152.20 (*0-8357-9832-1*, 2011881) Bks Demand.

Africa: Art & Culture of the Upper Volta. Laurent Van Ham & Robert Van Dijk. (Illus.). 96p. (DUT & ENG.). 1981. 39.95 (*90-70218-09-7*, Pub. by Schuurman Prod NE) Ethnographic Arts Pubns.

Africa: Dimensions of the Economic Crisis. Shanti S. Ali & Anirudha Gupta. 240p. (C). 1988. text ed. 32.50 (*81-207-0727-3*, Pub. by Sterling Pubs II) Apt Bks.

Africa: Dispatches from a Fragile Continent. Blaine Harden. (Illus.). 352p. 1991. pap. 11.95 (*0-395-59746-3*) HM.

Africa: Encyclopaedic Handbook, Vol. 1, 2 vols. Ed. by A. Gromyko. 672p. (C). 1986. 210.00 (*0-685-37158-1*, Pub. by Collets) St Mut.

Africa: Endurance & Change South of the Sahara. Catherine Coquery-Vidrovitch. Tr. by David Maisel. (Illus.). 448p. 1988. 50.00 (*0-520-05679-5*); pap. 16.00 (*0-520-07881-0*) U CA Pr.

Africa: Geography of a Changing Continent. J. M. Pritchard. LC 71-145838. 248p. 1971. 39.50 (*0-8419-0071-X*, Africana) Holmes & Meier.

Africa: Her History, Lands, & People Told with Pictures. John A. Williams. LC 62-19529. (Illus.). 127p. (Orig.). pap. 27.00 (*0-8154-0258-9*) Cooper Sq.

Africa: History of Exploration & Adventure. Charles H. Jones. LC 70-89399. (Black Heritage Library Collection). 1977. 32.95 (*0-8369-8614-8*) Ayer.

Africa: Its Geography, People & Products, 2 vols. in 1. W. E. B. Du Bois. Ed. & Intro. by Herbert Aptheker. Bd. with Its Place in Modern HistoryLC 76-53579. LC 76-53579. (C). 1977. reprint ed. Set lib. bdg. 8.00 (*0-527-25260-3*) Kraus Intl.

Africa: Mother of Western Civilization. Yosef Ben-Jochannan. LC 88-72105. 760p. 1988. reprint ed. pap. 34.95 (*0-933121-25-3*) Black Classic.

***Africa: On a Shoestring.** 7th ed. Geoff Crowther et al. (Illus.). 1024p. 1995. pap. 27.95 (*0-86442-288-1*) Lonely Planet.

Africa: Opposing Viewpoints. Ed. by Carol Wekesser. LC 91-42292. (Opposing Viewpoints Ser.). (Illus.). 264p. (YA). (gr. 10 up). 1992. lib. bdg. 19.95 (*0-89908-186-X*); pap. text ed. 11.55 (*0-89908-161-4*) Greenhaven.

Africa: Progress, Problems & Prospects (An Analysis of the 1960's-1970's) Anatoly Gromyko. 254p. 1983. 15.00 (*0-317-39471-1*, Pub. by Collets UK) St Mut.

Africa: Selected Readings. rev. ed. Hyman Kublin. (World Regional Studies). 1974. pap. 24.52 (*0-395-17743-X*) HM.

***Africa: The Art of a Continent.** (Illus.). 540p. 1995. text ed. 85.00 (*3-7913-1603-6*) Pegasus.

Africa: The Challenge of Transformation. Stephen McCarthy. 256p. 1994. text ed. 55.00 (*1-85043-821-8*, Pub. by I B Tauris UK) St Martin.

Africa: The History of Exploration & Adventure. Ed. by Charles H. Jones. 1875. 25.00 (*0-403-00375-X*) Scholarly.

Africa: The Legacy of Slavery & Colonialism in the Modern World. Paul E. Lovejoy & Toyin Falola. (C). 1929. text ed. 35.00 (*0-8133-0441-5*); pap. text ed. 16.95 (*0-8133-0442-3*) Westview.

Africa: The People & Politics of an Emerging Continent. 3rd ed. Sanford J. Ungar. 1989. pap. 15.95 (*0-671-67565-6*, Touchstone Bks) S&S Trade.

Africa: The Struggle for Independence. Dennis Wepman. (World History Library). (Illus.). 128p. 1993. 16.95 (*0-8160-2820-6*) Facts on File.

Africa: The Sub-Saharan Economies. (C). 1990. 295.00 (*1-870031-23-7*, Pub. by Euromoney UK) St Mut.

Africa: Through the Eyes of Women Artists. Betty LaDuke. LC 91-72496. (Illus.). 1991. 45.95 (*0-685-56372-3*); pap. 15.95 (*0-86543-199-X*) Africa World.

Africa: Troubled Continent -- A Problem Approach. Harry A. Gailey. LC 82-23342. 158p. (Orig.). 1983. pap. 9.50 (*0-89874-342-7*) Krieger.

***Africa: Women's Art, Women's Lives.** Betty LaDuke. 1995. pap. 18.95 (*0-86543-435-2*) Africa World.

***Africa Vol. 1.** Herb Ritts. (Illus.). 136p. 1994. 75.00 (*0-8212-2121-3*) Bulfinch Pr.

***Africa, a Bibliography of Geography & Related Disciplines: A Selected Listing of Recent Literature Published in the English Language.** 3rd fac. ed. Sanford H. Bederman. LC 74-22175. 342p. 1994. pap. 97.50 (*0-7837-7677-2*, 2047430) Bks Demand.

Africa, A Modern History: Eighteen Hundred to Nineteen Seventy Five. J. O. Sagay & D. A. Wilson. LC 79-16594. (Illus.). 425p. (C). 1981. 45.00 (*0-8419-0542-8*, Africana) Holmes & Meier.

Africa Adjustments. Ed. by Lewis B. Sckolnick. 350p. (Orig.). (C). 1994. pap. 125.00 (*1-57205-414-X*) Rector Pr.

Africa Adorned. Angela Fisher. LC 84-461. (Illus.). 304p. 1984. 65.00 (*0-8109-1823-4*) Abrams.

Africa Alone: Odyssey of an American Traveller. 2nd ed. Sandy S. McMath. (Illus.). 383p. 1989. reprint ed. 24.95 (*0-9622515-0-X*); reprint ed. pap. 9.95 (*0-9622515-1-8*) Columbus & Co.

Africa & Africans. 3rd ed. Paul Bohannan & Philip Curtin. (Illus.). 435p. (Orig.). 1988. pap. text ed. 15.95 (*0-88133-347-6*) Waveland Pr.

***Africa & Africans.** 4th rev. ed. Paul Bohannan & Philip Curtin. (Illus.). 301p. (Orig.). (C). 1995. pap. text ed. 15.95x (*0-88133-840-0*) Waveland Pr.

Africa & Africans As Seen by Classical Writers: The William Leo Hansberry African History Notebook, Vol. 2. Ed. by Joseph E. Harris. LC 77-6214. 1981. pap. 9.95 (*0-88258-089-2*) Howard U Pr.

Africa & Africans in the Formation of the Atlantic World, 1400-1680. John Thornton. (Studies in Comparative World History). (Illus.). 416p. (C). 1992. 59.95 (*0-521-39233-0*); pap. 17.95 (*0-521-39864-9*) Cambridge U Pr.

Africa & America. Alex Crummel. LC 72-79009. (Black Heritage Library Collection). 1977. 36.95 (*0-8369-8550-8*) Ayer.

Africa & America: Addresses & Discourses. Alex Crummell. 468p. Date not set. reprint ed. 45.00 (*0-933121-74-1*) Black Classic.

Africa & America: Addresses & Discourses. Alexander Crummell. 1977. reprint ed. 18.00 (*0-403-07784-2*) Scholarly.

Africa & Asia: Can High Rates of Economic Growth be Replicated? Peter B. Robinson & Somsak Tambunlertchai. LC 93-10021. (Occasional Papers - International Center for Economic Growth: No. 40). 1993. pap. 6.95 (*1-55815-261-X*) ICS Pr.

Africa & Christianity. Diedrich Westermann. LC 74-15102. (Duff Lectures, 1935). reprint ed. 32.50 (*0-404-12151-9*) AMS Pr.

Africa & Empire: W. H. MacMillan, Historian & Social Critic. Hugh MacMillan. Ed. by Shula Marks. (Commonwealth Papers: No. 25). 351p. 1989. text ed. 59.95 (*0-566-05494-9*, Pub. by Dartmth Pub UK) Ashgate Pub Co.

***Africa & Europe: Relations of Two Continents in Transition.** Ed. by Stefan Brune. (African Studies). (C). 1994. pap. text ed. 22.25 (*3-89473-714-X*) Westview.

Africa & Europe from Roman Times to National Independence. 2nd ed. Norman R. Bennett. 160p. 1984. 34.95 (*0-8419-0900-8*, Africana); pap. 16.95 (*0-8419-0901-6*, Africana) Holmes & Meier.

Africa & Her Flags. Michael Faul. (J). (gr. 1-9). 1992. pap. 3.95 (*0-88388-160-8*) Bellerophon Bks.

Africa & India's Foreign Policy. Ed. by Verinder Grover. (C). 1992. 72.00 (*81-7100-347-8*, Pub. by Deep) S Asia.

Africa & Its Explorers: Motives, Methods, & Impact. Robert I. Rotberg. LC 77-134327. 351p. 1970. pap. 15.50 (*0-674-00777-8*) HUP.

Africa & Law: Developing Legal Systems in African Commonwealth Nations. Ed. by Thomas W. Hutchison et al. 174p. 1968. 20.00 (*0-299-04610-9*) U of Wis Pr.

Africa & the Afro-American Experience: Eight Essays. Ed. by Lorraine A. Williams. LC 74-34584. 1981. pap. 9.95 (*0-88258-087-6*) Howard U Pr.

Africa & the American Negro. Congress On Africa. Ed. by J. W. Bowen. LC 74-79020. (Black Heritage Library Collection). 1977. 26.95 (*0-8369-8547-8*) Ayer.

***Africa & the Birth of Science & Technology: A Brief Overview.** Charles S. Finch, 3rd. 40p. 1993. pap. 5.00 (*0-9629444-2-4*) Khenti.

Africa & the Caribbean: The Legacies of a Link. Ed. by Margaret E. Crahan & Franklin W. Knight. LC 78-20531. (Johns Hopkins Studies in Atlantic History & Culture Ser.). 173p. reprint ed. pap. 49.40 (*0-8357-5222-4*, 2027898) Bks Demand.

Africa & the Challenge of Development: Acquiescence & Dependency Versus Freedom & Development. Ahmad Abubakar. LC 88-32290. 160p. 1989. text ed. 49.95 (*0-275-93221-4*, C3221, Praeger Pubs) Greenwood.

Africa & the Common Market. Pius N. Okigbo. LC 67-18007. 199p. reprint ed. pap. 56.80 (*0-8357-5223-2*, 2016718) Bks Demand.

Africa & the Communist World. Ed. by Zbigniew K. Brzezinski. xii, 272p. 1963. 37.50 (*0-8047-0179-2*) Stanford U Pr.

Africa & the Development of International Law. 2nd rev. ed. T. O. Elias. Ed. by Richard Akinjide. (C). 1988. lib. bdg. 133.00 (*90-247-3796-6*) Kluwer Ac.

Africa & the Disciplines: The Contributions of Research in Africa to the Social Sciences & Humanities. Ed. by Robert H. Bates et al. LC 93-3770. 232p. 1993. lib. bdg. 24.95 (*0-226-03900-5*); pap. text ed. 9.95 (*0-226-03901-3*) U Ch Pr.

Africa & the Discovery of America. Leo Wiener & John H. Clarke. 280p. 1992. pap. text ed. 10.00 (*1-881316-02-5*) A&B Bks.

Africa & the European Community after Nineteen Ninety-Two. Dermot McAleese et al. LC 92-43305. (EDI Seminar Report Ser.). 108p. 1993. 7.95 (*0-8213-2368-7*, 12368) World Bank.

Africa & the European Economic Community, 1957-1992. Charles O. Chikeka. LC 93-905. 236p. 1993. 89.95 (*0-7734-9259-3*) E Mellen.

Africa & the First World War. Ed. by Melvin E. Page. LC 86-29831. 270p. 1987. text ed. 45.00 (*0-312-00411-7*) St Martin.

Africa & the International Law of the Sea: A Study of the Contribution of the African States to the Third United Nations Conference on the Law of the Sea. N. S. Rembe. (Series on Ocean Development: No. 6). 272p. 1980. lib. bdg. 91.50 (*90-286-0639-4*) Kluwer Ac.

Africa & the International Monetary Fund. Ed. by Gerald K. Helleiner. 277p. 1986. pap. 10.00 (*0-939934-61-2*) Intl Monetary.

Africa & the International Monetary Fund: Papers Presented at a Symposium Held in Nairobi, Kenya, May 13-15, 1985. Ed. by Gerald K. Helleiner. LC 86-10415. 289p. reprint ed. pap. 82.40 (*0-8357-5224-0*, 2029547) Bks Demand.

Africa & the Middle East see Developing Areas: A Classed Bibliography of the Joint Bank-Fund Library, World Bank Group & International Monetary Fund

Africa & the Middle East Conflict. Arye Oded. LC 87-9576. 244p. 1987. lib. bdg. 40.00 (*1-55587-057-0*) Lynne Rienner.

Africa & the Modern World. Immanuel Wallerstein. LC 85-71384. 290p. 1986. 32.00 (*0-86543-021-7*); pap. 10.95 (*0-86543-022-5*) Africa World.

Africa & the Origin of Humans. (History of the World Ser.). (Illus.). 80p. (J). (gr. 4 up). 1988. lib. bdg. 25.67 (*0-8172-3301-6*) Raintree Steck-V.

***Africa & the Renaissance: Art in Ivory.** Ezio Bassani & William B. Fagg. Ed. by Susan Vogel. (Illus.). 256p. 1988. text ed. 60.00 (*0-614-06951-3*) Museum African.

Africa & the Renaissance: Art in Ivory. Ezio Bassani & William Fagg. (Illus.). 256p. 1988. 85.00 (*3-7913-0880-7*, Pub. by Prestel) TeNeues.

Africa & the Rise of Capitalism. Wilson E. Williams & Robert E. Martin. Bd. with Negro Disenfranchisement in Virginia. LC 79-144702. LC 79-144702. reprint ed. 32.50 (*0-404-06987-8*) AMS Pr.

Africa & the United States: Vital Interests. Ed. by Jennifer S. Whitaker. LC 77-92753. 1978. 45.00x (*0-8147-9181-6*) NYU Pr.

Africa & the United States, 1981. (African-American Conferences Ser.). 1981. pap. 3.00 (*0-89192-342-X*) Interbk Inc.

Africa & the West. Jerah Johnson. LC 77-2737. (Berkshire Studies). 176p. 1978. reprint ed. pap. 8.50 (*0-88275-564-1*) Krieger.

Africa & the West: Intellectual Responses to European Culture. Ed. by Philip D. Curtin. LC 77-176409. 272p. 1972. 35.00 (*0-299-06121-3*) U of Wis Pr.

Africa & the West: Intellectual Responses to European Culture. Ed. by Philip D. Curtin. LC 77-176409. 272p. 1974. pap. 16.50 (*0-299-06124-8*) U of Wis Pr.

Africa & the West: The Legacies of Empire. Ed. by Isaac J. Mowoe & Richard Bjornson. LC 85-5618. (Contributions in Afro-American & African Studies: No. 92). (Illus.). 284p. 1986. text ed. 55.00 (*0-313-24109-0*, MOW/, Greenwood Pr) Greenwood.

Africa & World Peace. George Padmore. 285p. 1972. reprint ed. 35.00 (*0-7146-1764-4*, BHA-01764, Pub. by F Cass Pubs UK) Intl Spec Bk.

Africa, Asia, & South America since 1800: A Bibliographical Guide. Comp. by A. J. H. Latham. LC 93-47152. 1994. text ed. write for info. (*0-7190-1877-3*, Pub. by Manchester Univ Pr UK) St Martin.

Africa Betrayed. George B. Ayittey. 432p. 1993. text ed. 19.95 (*0-312-10400-6*) St Martin.

Africa Between East & West. John Dumoga. LC 76-77360. (Background Ser.). 1969. 16.95 (*0-8023-1214-4*) Dufour.

***Africa Beyond Adjustment.** N. Limpumba. LC 94-36132. (Policy Essay Ser.: Vol. 15). 1994. pap. 9.95 (*1-56517-016-4*) Overseas Dev Council.

Africa Brothers & Sisters. Virginia Kroll. LC 91-20346. (Illus.). 32p. (J). (ps-2). 1993. text ed., lib. bdg. 14.95 (*0-02-751166-9*, Four Winds Pr) S&S Childrens.

***Africa Business & Political Handbook.** (Illus.). 600p. (Orig.). 1994. pap. 2,400.00 (*0-7605-1336-8*) Rector Pr.

Africa by Four: Coloring Book. Russell J. Larson. (Illus.). 14p. (Orig.). (J). (gr. k-6). 1992. pap. text ed. 1.85 (*1-881087-01-8*) Storm Moutain.

Africa Calling: Isolate the Racists! the Liberation Struggle in Southern Africa. John Pittman. 32p. 1973. pap. 0.60 (*0-87898-107-1*) New Outlook.

Africa Can Compete! Export Opportunities & Challenges for Garments & Home Products in the U. S. Market. Tyler Biggs et al. LC 94-16198. (Discussion Papers; Africa Technical Department Ser.: Vol. 242). 84p. 1994. write for info. (*0-8213-2838-7*) World Bank.

Africa Contemporary Record, Vol. 8:1975-76. Ed. by Colin Legum. LC 70-7957. (Illus.). 1220p. 1976. 345.00 (*0-8419-0157-0*, Africana) Holmes & Meier.

Africa Contemporary Record, Vol. 10:1977-78. Ed. by Colin Legum. LC 70-7957. 1472p. 1979. 345.00 (*0-8419-0159-7*, Africana) Holmes & Meier.

Africa Contemporary Record, Vol. 11:1978-79. Ed. by Colin Legum. LC 70-7957. 1354p. 1980. 345.00 (*0-8419-0160-0*, Africana) Holmes & Meier.

Africa Contemporary Record, Vol. 12:1979-80. Colin Legum. LC 70-7957. 1294p. 1981. 345.00 (*0-8419-0550-9*, Africana) Holmes & Meier.

Africa Contemporary Record, Vol. 13:1980-81. Ed. by Colin Legum. LC 70-7957. 1300p. 1982. 345.00 (*0-8419-0551-7*, Africana) Holmes & Meier.

Africa Contemporary Record: Annual Survey & Documents, 1985-1986, Volume XVIII. Ed. by Colin Legum. 1392p. 1987. 345.00 (*0-8419-0556-8*, Africana) Holmes & Meier.

Africa Contemporary Record: Annual Survey & Documents 1986-1987, Vol. XIX. Colin Legum. LC 70-7957. 1000p. 1988. lib. bdg. 345.00 (*0-8419-0557-6*, Africana) Holmes & Meier.

Africa Contemporary Record Annual Survey & Documents: Volume XVII: 1984-85. Ed. by Colin Legum. 1100p. 1986. 345.00 (*0-8419-0555-X*, Africana) Holmes & Meier.

Africa Contemporary Record Annual Survey & Documents, Vol. I, 1968-69. Ed. by Colin Legum. 1970. 345.00 (*0-8419-0150-3*, Africana) Holmes & Meier.

Africa Contemporary Record Annual Survey & Documents, Vol. III, 1970-71. Ed. by Colin Legum. 1972. 345.00 (*0-8419-0152-X*, Africana) Holmes & Meier.

Africa Contemporary Record Annual Survey & Documents, Vol. IV, 1971-72. Ed. by Colin Legum. 1973. 345.00 (*0-8419-0153-8*, Africana) Holmes & Meier.

Africa Contemporary Record Annual Survey & Documents, Vol. IX, 1976-77. Ed. by Colin Legum. LC 70-7957. (Illus.). 1293p. 1978. 345.00 (*0-8419-0158-9*, Africana) Holmes & Meier.

Africa Contemporary Record Annual Survey & Documents, Vol. V, 1972-73. Ed. by Colin Legum. 1974. 345.00 (*0-8419-0154-6*, Africana) Holmes & Meier.

Africa Contemporary Record Annual Survey & Documents, Vol. VII, 1974-75. Ed. by Colin Legum. LC 70-7957. (Illus.). 1185p. 1975. 345.00 (*0-8419-0156-2*, Africana) Holmes & Meier.

Africa Contemporary Record Annual Survey & Documents, Vol. XX, 1987-88. Ed. by Colin Legum & Marion Doro. 1182p. 1990. 359.00 (*0-8419-0558-4*, Africana) Holmes & Meier.

Africa Contemporary Record Annual Survey & Documents, Vol. XXI, 1988-89. Ed. by Marion Doro. 1200p. 1992. 375.00 (*0-8419-0559-2*, Africana) Holmes & Meier.

Africa Contemporary Record, Vol. 14: 1981-82. Ed. by Colin Legum. 1280p. 1983. 345.00 (*0-8419-0552-5*, Africana) Holmes & Meier.

Africa Contemporary Record, Vol. 15: 1982-1983. Ed. by Colin Legum. 1216p. 1984. 345.00 (*0-8419-0553-3*, Africana) Holmes & Meier.

Africa Contemporary Record, Vol. 16: 1983-84. Ed. by Colin Legum. (Illus.). 1344p. 1985. 345.00 (*0-8419-0554-1*, Africana) Holmes & Meier.

Africa Contemporary Record, Vol. 6: 1973-74. Ed. by Colin Legum. LC 70-7957. (Illus.). 1255p. 1974. 345.00 (*0-8419-0155-4*, Africana) Holmes & Meier.

Africa Counts. Claudia Zaslavsky. LC 72-91248. (Illus.). 336p. 1979. pap. 11.95 (*1-55652-075-1*) L Hill Bks.

Africa, Development & Public Policy. Ed. by Stuart S. Nagel. LC 93-26989. 1994. text ed. 69.95 (*0-312-10383-2*) St Martin.

Africa, Disarmament & Security (Algiers, 24-25 March) 1990. 127p. 1991. 36.00 (*92-9045-045-2*, GV.91.0.1) UN.

Africa Dream. Eloise Greenfield. LC 77-5080. (Illus.). 32p. (J). (ps-3). 1989. lib. bdg. 14.89 (*0-690-04776-2*, Crowell Jr Bks) HarpC Child Bks.

Africa Dream. Eloise Greenfield. LC 77-5080. (Trophy Picture Bk.). (Illus.). 32p. (J). (ps-3). 1992. pap. 4.95 (*0-06-443277-7*, Trophy) HarpC Child Bks.

Africa, Eighteen Eighty to Nineteen Eighty: An Economic History. Peter L. Wickins. 321p. 1987. 38.00 (*0-19-570416-9*) OUP.

Africa Explores: Twentieth Century African Art. Susan Vogel & Ima Ebong. LC 90-26683. (Illus.). 1991. pap. 39.00 (*0-945802-09-9*) Museum African.

Africa Explores: Twentieth Century African Art. Susan Vogel et al. (Illus.). 300p. 1991. 70.00 (*3-7913-1143-3*, Pub. by Prestel) TeNeues.

Africa Facing Its Priorities. B. Schneider. 111p. 1989. text ed. 85.00 (*1-85148-023-4*, Tycooly Pub) Weidner & Sons.

Africa for the Africans. G. Mennen Williams. LC 75-75103. (Illus.). 218p. reprint ed. pap. 62.20 (*0-8357-5225-9*, 2012765) Bks Demand.

Africa for the Africans: Selected Speeches of Marcus Mosiah Garvey, Malcolm X & Nelson R. Mandela. Ed. by Edward W. Crosby & Linus A. Hoskins. 115p. (Orig.). (C). 1991. pap. text ed. 9.95 (*0-9613067-4-2*) L A Hoskins.

Africa, from People to People: Six Short Stories from Contemporary Africa. S. Henry Cordor. 71p. 1979. 8.50 (*0-686-33168-0*) Arden Assocs.

Africa from the Twelfth to Sixteen Century see UNESCO General History of Africa

Africa, Human Rights, & the Global System: The Political Economy of Human Rights in a Changing World. Ed. by Eileen McCarthy-Arnolds et al. LC 93-1643. 288p. 1993. text ed. 57.95 (*0-313-29007-5*, Greenwood Pr) Greenwood.

***Africa in America: Slave Acculturation & Resistance in the American South & the British.** Michael Mullin. 1994. pap. 15.95 (*0-252-06446-1*) U of Ill Pr.

Africa in America: Slave Acculturation & Resistance in the American South & the British Caribbean, 1736-1831. Michael Mullin. (Blacks in the New World Ser.). 432p. (C). 1992. 37.50 (*0-252-01889-3*) U of Ill Pr.

***Africa in an Era of Crisis.** Hadjor. Date not set. per. 11.95 (*0-86543-150-7*) Africa World.

Africa in Antiquity: The Arts of Ancient Nubia & the Sudan -- The Essays, Vol. 1. LC 78-10925. (Illus.). 1978. pap. text ed. 8.00 (*0-87273-065-4*) Bklyn Mus.

Africa in Crisis: The Causes, the Cures of Environmental Bankruptcy. Lloyd Timberlake. 240p. 1986. lib. bdg. 39.95 (*0-86571-081-3*); pap. 16.95 (*0-86571-082-1*) New Soc Pubs.

Africa in Economic Crisis. Ed. by John Ravenhill. LC 85-26972. 320p. 1986. text ed. 52.50 (*0-231-06382-2*); pap. text ed. 18.50 (*0-231-06383-0*) Col U Pr.

Africa in History. rev. ed. Basil Davidson. 406p. 1992. pap. 15.00 (*0-02-042791-3*, Collier S&S) S&S Trade.

Africa in History: Themes & Outlines. enl. rev. ed. Basil Davidson. 1974. pap. 11.95 (*0-02-031260-1*, Collier S&S) S&S Trade.

Africa in Latin America. Ed. by Manuel M. Fraginals. Tr. by Leonor Blum. LC 84-639. 342p. 1984. 49.50 (*0-8419-0748-X*) Holmes & Meier.

***Africa in Literature for Children & Young Adults: An Annotated Bibliography of English Language Books.** Meena Khorana. LC 94-34223. (Bibliographies & Indexes in World Literature Ser.: Vol. 46). 368p. 1994. text ed. 59.95 (*0-313-25488-5*, Greenwood Pr) Greenwood.

Africa in Retrospect. A. B. Assensoh. 76p. 1986. 40.00 (*0-7223-1764-6*, Pub. by A H S Ltd UK) St Mut.

Africa in Retrospect. A. B. Assensoh. 76p. 1987. pap. 35.00 (*0-317-62465-2*, Pub. by A H S Ltd UK) St Mut.

Africa in Scott Joplin's Music. Carol Lems-Dworkin. (Illus.). 27p. (Orig.). 1991. pap. 11.00 (*0-9637048-0-X*) C Lems-Dworkin Pubs.

An Asterisk (*) at the beginning of an entry indicates that the title is appearing in BIP for the first time.

Africa in Soviet Studies. A. Gromyko. 256p. (C). 1988. 95.00 (*0-685-31625-4*, Pub. by Collets UK) Pro-Am Music.

Africa in Soviet Studies: 1983 Annual. 378p. 1983. 40.00 (*0-685-16981-2*, Pub. by Collets UK) Pro-Am Music.

Africa in Struggle: National Liberation & Proletarian Revolution. 2nd ed. Daniel Fogel. LC 82-82655. (Illus.). 428p. (Orig.). 1986. reprint ed. pap. 8.00 (*0-910383-00-6*) Ism Pr.

Africa in the Iron Age. Roland Oliver & Brian M. Fagan. LC 74-25639. (Illus.). 300p. 1975. pap. 19.95 (*0-521-09900-5*) Cambridge U Pr.

Africa in the Nineteen Eighties: Results & Prospects of Development. Ed. by P. Fedoseyev. 172p. (C). 1986. 40.00 (*0-685-31624-6*, Pub. by Collets UK) Pro-Am Music.

Africa in the Nineteen Nineties & Beyond: U. S. Policy Opportunities & Choices. Ed. by Robert I. Rotberg. LC 88-6724. (Illus.). 300p. (Orig.). 1988. text ed. 24.95 (*0-917256-43-3*); pap. 12.95 (*0-917256-44-1*) Ref Pubns.

Africa in the Post-Decolonization Era. Ed. by Richard E. Bissell & Michael Radu. 278p. 1984. 34.95 (*0-87855-496-3*) Transaction Pubs.

Africa in the Roman Empire. I. M. Barton. 84p. 1972. 11.95 (*0-87676-144-9*, Pub. by Brstl Class Pr UK) Focus Info Gr.

Africa in the United Nations. Thomas Hovet, Jr. LC 62-17804. (African Studies Ser.: No. 10). (Illus.). 350p. reprint ed. 99.80 (*0-8357-9444-X*, 2014774) Bks Demand.

Africa in the United Nations System. Wellington W. Nyangoni. LC 81-72033. 288p. 1985. 46.50 (*0-8386-3118-5*) Fairleigh Dickinson.

Africa in the Wider World. David Brokensha & M. Crowder. 1967. 117.00 (*0-08-012673-1*, Pub. by Pergamon Repr UK) Franklin.

Africa in Transition. Ed. by Marvin E. Wolfgang & Richard D. Lambert. LC 77-183. (Annals Ser.: No. 432). 1977. pap. 18.00 (*0-87761-217-X*) Am Acad Pol Soc Sci.

Africa in U. S. Schools, K-12: A Survey. Susan J. Hall. 39p. (Orig.). 1978. pap. text ed. 4.00 (*0-89192-292-X*) Interbk Inc.

Africa in World Affairs: The Next Thirty Years. Ali A. Mazrui & Hasu H. Patel. LC 72-80184. 286p. (C). 1973. 25.00 (*0-89388-046-9*) Okpaku Communications.

***Africa in World History: Old, New, Then, & Now.** Ed. by Michael W. Coy, Jr. & Leonard Plotnicov. LC 94-62224. (Ethnology Monographs: No. 16). x, 164p. (Orig.). (C). 1995. pap. text ed. 10.00 (*0-945428-09-X*) Ethnology Monographs.

***Africa in World Politics: Post-Cold War Challenges.** 2nd ed. Ed. by John W. Harbeson & Donald Rothchild. LC 94-35035. (C). 1995. text ed. 74.00 (*0-8133-2102-6*); pap. text ed. 21.95 (*0-8133-2103-4*) Westview.

Africa Is Not a Country: It's a Continent. Lewing Arthur. 100p. 1991. pap. 9.95 (*0-9628911-1-8*) Clarendon NJ.

Africa, Its Empires, Nations, & People: A Reader for Young Adults. Mary P. Motley. LC 72-96720. (Illus.). 165p. reprint ed. pap. 47.10 (*0-7837-3592-8*, 2043456) Bks Demand.

Africa, Land of Diversity: An Ethnographic Exhibit at the Cleveland Museum of Natural History, March 4-October 31, 1977. Esther Bockhoff. (Illus.). 64p. (Orig.). 1977. pap. 3.50 (*1-878600-02-8*) Cleve Mus Nat Hist.

Africa Must Change: An African Manifesto. Thomas N. Kanza. LC 78-21067. 25p. 1979. text ed. 5.50 (*0-87073-914-X*); pap. 2.50 (*0-87073-915-8*) Schenkman Bks Inc.

Africa Must Unite. Kwame Nkrumah. 229p. (C). 1963. pap. 11.95 (*0-901787-13-2*, Pub. by Panaf Bks UK) Humanities.

Africa News Cookbook. Africa News Staff & Tami Hultman. (Cookbook Ser.). 208p. 1986. pap. 17.00 (*0-14-046751-3*, Penguin Bks) Viking Penguin.

Africa Notebook. C. W. Gusewelle. LC 86-82805. (Illus.). 212p. (Orig.). 1986. pap. 9.95 (*0-932845-24-X*) Lowell Pr.

Africa, O Africa. Louise R. Chapman. 88p. 1989. pap. text ed. 4.50 (*0-8341-1330-9*) Nazarene.

Africa O-Ye! A Celebration of African Music. Graeme Ewens. (Illus.). 215p. (Orig.). 1992. pap. 27.95 (*0-306-80461-1*) Da Capo.

Africa on Film: Beyond Black & White. Kenneth Cameron. (Illus.). 288p. 1994. 27.50 (*0-8264-0658-0*) Continuum.

Africa Policy in Transition. Ed. by H. Noviki. (African American Conferences Ser.). 52p. (Orig.). 1983. pap. 10.00 (*0-89192-386-1*) Interbk Inc.

Africa Policy Update. Jane W. Jacqz. 43p. (Orig.). (C). 1978. pap. text ed. 10.95 (*0-87855-727-X*) Transaction Pubs.

Africa Projected: From Recession to Renaissance by the Year 2000? Ed. by Timothy M. Shaw & Olajide Aluko. LC 84-40444. 298p. 1985. text ed. 39.95 (*0-312-00951-8*) St Martin.

Africa Religions & Culture: A Focus on the Ashanti People. Grace Chavis-Butler. (Illus.). 304p. 1994. text ed. 16.95 (*0-8059-3501-0*) Dorrance.

Africa Remembered: Narratives by West Africans from the Era of the Slave Trade. Ed. by Philip D. Curtin. (Illus.). 376p. 1968. pap. 16.95 (*0-299-04284-7*) U of Wis Pr.

Africa Revisited: A Diary of a Sentimental Journey of Return. H. J. Schueler. 1990. 15.95 (*0-533-08636-1*) Vantage.

***Africa Revisited 1972-1990.** Bilal Abdurahman. (Illus.). 55p. (YA). 1993. pap. text ed. 10.00 (*0-9619070-3-7*) Ethno Modes Folkloric Workshop Inc.

Africa since 1800. Anthony Atmore & Roland Oliver. LC 93-9779. (Illus.). 400p. (C). 1994. 64.95 (*0-521-41946-8*); pap. 18.95 (*0-521-42970-6*) Cambridge U Pr.

Africa Since 1914: A Historical Bibliography. LC 83-27153. (Clio Bibliography Ser.: No. 17). 402p. 2984. lib. bdg. 105.00 (*0-87436-395-0*) ABC-CLIO.

Africa South. Harm J. De Blij. LC 62-14295. 409p. reprint ed. 116.60 (*0-8357-9445-8*, 2014770) Bks Demand.

Africa-South America Connection. Ed. by Wilma George & Rene Lavocat. LC 92-27733. (Oxford Monographs on Biogeography: No. 7). (Illus.). 245p. 1993. 61.00 (*0-19-854577-0*, Clarendon Pr) OUP.

Africa South of the Sahara: A Geographical Interpretation. Robert F. Stock. LC 94-34329. (Regional Geography Ser.). 1995. lib. bdg. 45.00 (*0-89862-406-1*, 2406) Guilford Pr.

Africa South of the Sahara: Index to Periodical Literature, First Supplement. Library of Congress Staff. 1973. lib. bdg. 120.00 (*0-8161-1048-4*, Hall Library) G K Hall.

Africa South of the Sahara: Index to Periodical Literature, 1900-1970, 4 vols, Set. Library of Congress Staff. 1974. lib. bdg. 400.00 (*0-8161-0892-7*, Hall Library) G K Hall.

Africa South of the Sahara: The Challenge to Western Security. L. H. Gann & Peter Duignan. LC 80-82750. (Publication Ser.: No. 238). 155p. 1981. pap. 9.95 (*0-8179-7382-6*) Hoover Inst Pr.

Africa South of the Sahara - 1992. 21th ed. 1994. write for info. (*0-8103-9810-9*, Pub. by Europa UK) Gale.

Africa South of the Sahara, 1992. 21th ed. 1144p. 1992. lib. bdg. 275.00 (*1-55888-776-8*, Pub. by Europa Pubns UK) Omnigraphics Inc.

Africa South of the Sahara, 1993. 22th ed. 1994. 17.95 (*0-8103-9963-6*, Pub. by Europa UK) Gale.

***Africa South of the Sahara, 1995.** 24th ed. 1200p. 1994. 320.00x (*0-946653-97-6*, Pub. by Europa UK) Gale.

Africa That Never Was: Four Centuries of British Writing about Africa--an Anthropological View Contrasting the Africa of Fact & the Africa of Fiction. rev. ed. Dorothy Hammond & Alta Jablow. (Illus.). 251p. (C). 1992. reprint ed. pap. text ed. 11.95 (*0-88133-690-4*) Waveland Pr.

Africa, the American Intelligentsia, & the Shadow of Vietnam. Martin Staniland. (CISA Working Paper Ser.: No. 35). 34p. (Orig.). Date not set. pap. 10.00 (*0-86682-046-9*) Ctr Intl Relations.

Africa, the Atlantic Slave Trade & the West Indies: African Background to West Indian History. V. B. Thompson. LC 79-89012. write for info. (*0-88357-085-8*); pap. text ed. 4.95 (*0-88357-086-6*) NOK Pubs.

Africa: the Land & Its People: Learning Center. Irene Handberg. (Multicultural Education Ser.). 96p. 1992. teacher ed write for info. (*1-56831-311-X*) Lrning Connect.

Africa: the Land & Its People: Learning Center, Set. Irene Handberg. (Multicultural Education Ser.). 96p. 1992. write for info. (*1-56831-300-4*) Lrning Connect.

Africa, the Wonder & the Glory. Anna M. Graves. 43p. 1980. reprint ed. pap. text ed. 3.00 (*0-933121-12-1*) Black Classic.

Africa Today. Ed. by Charles G. Haines. LC 68-8736. (Illus.). 510p. 1969. reprint ed. text ed. 55.00 (*0-8371-0094-1*, HAAT, Greenwood Pr) Greenwood.

***Africa Today: An Atlas of Reproducible Papers.** rev. ed. (World Eagle's Today Ser.). (Illus.). 209p. 1994. ring bd. 33.45 (*0-930141-56-3*) World Eagle.

Africa under Colonial Domination, 1880-1935 see UNESCO General History of Africa

Africa View. Julian S. Huxley. LC 68-23300. 1979. reprint ed. text ed. 75.00 (*0-8371-0112-3*, HUAV, Greenwood Pr) Greenwood.

Africa Within the World: Beyond Dispossession & Dependence. Ed. by Adebayo Adedeji. LC 94-1574. 234p. (C). 1993. text ed. 49.95 (*1-85649-249-4*, Pub. by Zed Books UK); pap. 19.95 (*1-85649-250-8*, Pub. by Zed Books UK) Humanities.

***Africa Wo/Man Palava: The Nigerian Novel by Women.** Chikwenye O. Ogunyemi. (Women in Culture & Society Ser.). 336p. 1995. 37.50 (*0-226-62084-0*); pap. 15.95 (*0-226-62085-9*) U Ch Pr.

Africa, 1500-1900. Constance Jones. LC 92-22677. (World History Library). (Illus.). 144p. (J). (gr. 5-12). 1993. 17.95x (*0-8160-2774-9*) Facts on File.

***Africa 1995.** 30th ed. Pierre E. Dostert. 234p. 1995. pap. 9.50 (*0-943448-89-1*) Stryker-Post.

Africam. Olagoke F. Adoboyde & Harry McKenzie. 305p. (Orig.). 1994. pap. 16.95 (*0-86626-003-X*) McKinzie Pub.

African. Harold Courlander. LC 93-13923. 320p. 1993. pap. 12.95 (*0-8050-3000-X*) H Holt & Co.

African. Thomas Watson. 1982. lib. bdg. 69.95 (*0-87700-384-X*) Revisionist Pr.

African: His Antecedents, His Genius, & His Destiny. G. K. Osei. 1971. 5.95 (*0-8216-0051-6*, Univ Bks) Carol Pub Group.

***African: Photo Essay on Black Women.** Joseph Franklin. (Illus.). Date not set. pap. 12.00 (*0-614-04063-9*) Three Continents.

African - American Social & Political Thought 1850-1920. Ed. by Howard Brotz. 641p. (C). 1991. pap. text ed. 24.95 (*1-56000-563-7*) Transaction Pubs.

African Achievements: Leaders, Civilizations & Cultures of Ancient Africa. rev. ed. Lester Brooks. LC 75-105341. (Illus.). 275p. (YA). (gr. 8-12). 1992. reprint ed. pap. 18.95 (*0-9626946-2-2*) De Gustibus Pr.

African Adventurers. Peter H. Captstick. 1993. mass mkt. 5.99 (*0-312-95084-5*) St Martin.

African Adventurers: A Return to the Silent Places. Peter H. Capstick. 288p. 1992. 22.95 (*0-312-07622-3*) St Martin.

African Adventures. J. F. Burger. (Illus.). 222p. 1993. 35.00 (*0-940143-77-1*) Safari Pr.

African Aesthetic: Keeper of the Traditions. Ed. by Kariamu Welsh-Asante. LC 92-5438. (Contributions in Afro-American & African Studies: No. 153). 280p. 1993. text ed. 55.00 (*0-313-26549-6*, WLH, Greenwood Pr) Greenwood.

***African Aesthetic: Keeper of the Traditions.** Kariamu Welsh-Asante. LC 92-5438. p. 1994. pap. text ed. 18.95 (*0-275-95117-0*, Praeger Pubs) Greenwood.

African Aesthetics: The Carlo Monzino Collection. Susan Vogel. LC 86-4151. (Illus.). 1986. write for info. (*0-9614587-2-0*); pap. text ed. 115.00 (*0-685-69232-9*) Museum African.

African Affair. Carolyn M. Radcliffe. 1994. 15.95 (*0-533-10866-7*) Vantage.

African Agriculture: The Critical Choices. Ed. by H. A. Amara & B. Founou-Tchuigoua. LC 89-35869. (UNU Studies in African Political Economy: Vol. 6). 320p. (C). 1990. text ed. 55.00 (*0-86232-798-9*, Pub. by Zed Books UK); pap. 17.50 (*0-86232-799-7*, Pub. by Zed Books UK) Humanities.

African America: Heralding a Heritage. (J). 9.95 (*0-932991-05-X*) Place in the Woods.

African America: Portrait of People. 1993. 18.95 (*0-8103-9453-7*, 089205) Visible Ink Pr.

African-American. Jerry Evans. LC 93-79055. 186p. (Orig.). (YA). (gr. 11 up). 1993. pap. 9.95 (*0-9623698-8-8*) Magnum Pr.

African American: Harriet Tubman. Ret. by Beth Lyons. (Graphic Learning Multicultural Literature Program Ser.). (Illus.). (ENG & SPA.). (J). (gr. k-5). 1994. 39.00 (*0-87746-401-4*) Graphic Learning.

African American: John Henry. Ret. by G. Davis. (Graphic Learning Multicultural Literature Program Ser.). (Illus.). (ENG & SPA.). (J). (gr. k-5). 1994. 39.00 (*0-87746-407-3*) Graphic Learning.

African American: Mr. Knee-High Man. Ret. by G. Davis. (Graphic Learning Multicultural Literature Program Ser.). (Illus.). (ENG & SPA.). (J). (gr. k-5). 1994. 39.00 (*0-87746-404-9*) Graphic Learning.

African American: The Name of the Tree. Ret. by Beth Lyons. (Graphic Learning Multicultural Literature Program Ser.). (Illus.). (ENG & SPA.). (J). (gr. k-5). 1994. 39.00 (*0-87746-410-3*) Graphic Learning.

***African-American Address Book.** Tabatha Crayton. LC 94-30205. 304p. (Orig.). 1995. pap. 14.00 (*0-399-52148-8*, Perigee Bks) Berkley Pub.

***African American Aesthetic in the Visual Arts & Postmodernism.** Ed. by David Driskell. LC 95-10256. 1995. write for info. (*1-56098-605-0*) Smithsonian.

African-American Almanac, 3 Vols., Set. (African-American Reference Library). (Illus.). 576p. (J). (gr. 6-9). 1994. 84.00 (*0-8103-9239-9*, 021503, UXL) Gale.

***African-American Almanac, Vol. 2.** Ed. by Jay P. Pederson & Kenneth Estell. (African-American Reference Library). (Illus.). (J). (gr. 6-9). 1994. write for info. (*0-8103-9241-0*, UXL) Gale.

***African-American Almanac, Vol. 3.** Ed. by Jay P. Pederson & Kenneth Estell. (African-American Reference Library). (Illus.). (J). (gr. 6-9). 1994. write for info. (*0-8103-9242-9*, UXL) Gale.

***African-American Almanac, Vol.1.** Ed. by Jay P. Pederson & Kenneth Estell. (African-American Reference Library). (Illus.). 576p. (J). (gr. 6-9). 1994. write for info. (*0-8103-9240-2*, UXL) Gale.

***African American Almanac: Day-by-Day Black History.** Kenneth A. Mimms & Leon T. Ross. 240p. 1995. lib. bdg. 29.95 (*0-89950-675-5*) McFarland & Co.

African-American & Hispanic Children's Concept of Death. Sydney C. Butts. Ed. by Hugh F. Butts. LC 90-84289. 56p. (C). 1991. 19.95 (*0-9623987-1-3*) Clementine Pub Co.

***African American Answer Book: Science & Discovery.** R. S. Rennert. (Illus.). 64p. (YA). (gr. 5 up). 1995. 7.95 (*0-7910-3207-8*) Chelsea Hse.

***African-American Answer Book: Sports.** R. S. Rennert. (Illus.). 64p. (YA). (gr. 5 up). 1995. 7.95 (*0-7910-3205-1*); pap. 4.95 (*0-7910-3208-6*); pap. 4.95 (*0-7910-3206-X*) Chelsea Hse.

***African American Answer Book, Arts & Entertainment: 325 Questions Drawn from the Expertise of Harvard's Du Bois Institute.** R. S. Rennert. LC 94-29999. (Illus.). 64p. (YA). (gr. 5 up). 1995. 12.95 (*0-7910-3201-9*) Chelsea Hse.

***African American Answer Book, Arts & Entertainment: 325 Questions Drawn from the Expertise of Harvard's Du Bois Institute.** Richard S. Rennert. LC 94-29999. (J). 1995. pap. write for info. (*0-7910-3202-7*) Chelsea Hse.

***African American Answer Book, Biography: Three Hundred Twenty-Five Questions Drawn from the Expertise of Harvard's Du Bois Institute.** LC 94-30201. 1995. pap. write for info. (*0-7910-3204-3*) Chelsea Hse.

***African American Answer Book, Biography: Three Hundred Twenty-Five Questions Drawn from the Expertise of Harvard's Du Bois Institute.** Richard S. Rennert. LC 94-30201. (J). 1995. write for info. (*0-7910-3203-5*) Chelsea Hse.

***African American Answer Book, Facts & Trivia: 325 Questions Drawn from the Experience of Harvard's Du Bois Institute.** Richard S. Rennert. LC 94-30203. 1995. pap. write for info. (*0-7910-3212-4*) Chelsea Hse.

***African American Answer Book, Facts & Trivia: 325 Questions Drawn from the Expertise of Harvard's Du Bois Institute.** Ed. by Richard S. Rennert. LC 94-30203. (YA). (gr. 10 up). 1995. write for info. (*0-7910-3211-6*) Chelsea Hse.

***African American Answer Book, History: Three Hundred Twenty-Five Questions Drawn from the Expertise of Harvard's Du Bois Institute.** R. S. Rennert. LC 94-30202. 1995. pap. write for info. (*0-7910-3210-8*) Chelsea Hse.

***African American Answer Book, History: Three Hundred Twenty-Five Questions Drawn from the Expertise of Harvard's Du Bois Institute.** R. S. Rennert. LC 94-30202. (J). (gr. 1-8). 1995. write for info. (*0-7910-3209-4*) Chelsea Hse.

African-American Architects in Current Practice. Jack Travis. LC 91-25113. (Illus.). 1992. 22.95 (*1-878271-38-5*) Princeton Arch.

African-American Architectural Presence in Arizona. 2nd ed. Anthony V. Brown et al. 44p. 1993. pap. 20.00 (*1-884320-00-7*) ASU Herberger Ctr.

African American Art. Leilani L. Duke. 22p. 1991. teacher ed write for info. (*1-56290-025-0*, 6011) Crystal.

African American Art & Artists. Samella Lewis. LC 93-40781. 1994. 50.00 (*0-520-08788-7*); pap. 25.00 (*0-520-08532-9*) U CA Pr.

African American Artists: Affirmation Today. 208p. 1994. student ed, sl. 85.00 (*1-56290-103-6*, 6047) Crystal.

African American Autobiography: A Collection of Critical Essays. William L. Andrews. 1992. pap. 12.95 (*0-13-019845-5*) P-H.

African American Bibliography: History. 18p. 1992. 2.00 (*0-317-05245-4*) NYS Library.

African American Bibliography: Science Medicine & Allied Fields. 14p. 1991. 2.00 (*0-317-05530-5*) NYS Library.

African American Bibliography: The Arts. New York State Library Staff. 21p. 1990. 2.00 (*0-317-05244-6*) NYS Library.

African American Biographies: Profiles of 558 Current Men & Women. Walter L. Hawkins. LC 91-50938. 496p. 1992. lib. bdg. 39.95 (*0-89950-664-X*) McFarland & Co.

African American Biographies, Vol. 2: Profiles of 332 Current Men & Women. Walter L. Hawkins. LC 93-44998. 379p. 1994. lib. bdg. 35.00 (*0-89950-921-5*) McFarland & Co.

African-American Biography, 4 vols., Set. (African-American Reference Library). (Illus.). 832p. (J). (gr. 6-9). 1993. 112.00 (*0-8103-9234-8*, 021502, UXL) Gale.

African-American Business Leaders: A Biographical Dictionary. John N. Ingham & Lynne B. Feldman. LC 93-20430. 824p. 1993. text ed. 99.50 (*0-313-27253-0*, IBL) Greenwood.

African-American Cemeteries & Their History of Choctaw County, Alabama. Nova Law Staff. (Illus.). 113p. (Orig.). 1993. pap. text ed. 29.95 (*1-882804-01-5*) Legacy Pub AL.

African American Children's Day Book. Terry Williams. Ed. by Maria Mallory. (Black Parents Press - Kujichagalia Ser.). (Illus.). 36p. (Orig.). 1994. pap. write for info. (*0-937913-08-1*) W Stery.

African American Children's Religious Sourcebook: Christian Resources for African American Children. Terry Williams. Ed. by Maria Mallory. (Black Parents Press - Kujichagalia Ser.). (Illus.). 32p. 1994. pap. write for info. (*0-937913-05-7*) W Stery.

African-American Child's Heritage Cookbook. Vanessa R. Parham. Ed. by R. Rolle-Whatley. LC 92-60006. (Illus.). 296p. (Orig.). (J). 1992. pap. 19.95 (*0-9627756-2-2*) Sandcastle Pub.

African American Christian Worship. Melva W. Costen. LC 93-13826. 144p. (Orig.). 1993. pap. 12.95 (*0-687-00931-6*) Abingdon.

African-American Christianity: Essays in History. Paul E. Johnson. LC 93-3895. 1994. 35.00 (*0-520-07593-5*); pap. 12.00 (*0-520-07594-3*) U CA Pr.

African-American Chronology: A Subseries of American-American Reference Library, 2 vols., Set. LC 93-38944. (African-American Reference Library). (Illus.). 320p. (J). (gr. 6-9). 1993. 55.00 (*0-8103-9231-3*, 021501, UXL) Gale.

African American Chronology, Vol. 1: 1492-1972. Alton Hornsby, Jr. & Deborah G. Straub. LC 93-38944. (J). 1993. write for info. (*0-8103-9232-1*, UXL) Gale.

African American Chronology, Vol. 2: 1973-1993. Alton Hornsby, Jr. & Deborah G. Straub. LC 93-38944. (J). 1993. write for info. (*0-8103-9233-X*, UXL) Gale.

African American Church Growth: 12 Principles of Prophetic Ministry. Carlyle F. Stewart. LC 93-5062. 176p. (Orig.). 1994. pap. 10.95 (*0-687-16541-5*) Abingdon.

African American Communication: Ethnic Identity & Cultural Interpretation. Michael L. Hecht et al. (Language & Language Behaviors Ser.: Vol. 2). (Illus.). 233p. (C). 1993. text ed. 48.00 (*0-8039-4515-9*); pap. text ed. 21.95 (*0-8039-4516-7*) Sage.

African American Communications: An Anthology in Traditional & Contemporary Studies. James W. Ward. 352p. 1992. per. 34.95 (*0-8403-8292-8*) Kendall-Hunt.

African-American Community Studies from North America: A Classified, Annotated Bibliography. Fred J. Hay. LC 91-8158. (Applied Social Science Bibliographies Ser.: Vol. 5). 258p. 1991. 40.00 (*0-8240-6643-X*, SS420) Garland.

African American Consciousness: Reclaiming Your History! John Ballard. (Illus.). 304p. 1995. 14.95 (*0-932279-99-6*) World Citizens.

African-American Culture & Life Search. John C. Cothran. LC 92-61350. (Illus.). 400p. 1996. 24.95 (*0-9634002-0-7*); text ed. 24.95 (*0-9634002-2-3*); lib. bdg. 24.95 (*0-9634002-1-5*) Stardate Pub.

African-American Culture & Life Search. John C. Cothran. LC 92-61350. (Illus.). 400p. 1997. pap. 12.95 (*0-9634002-3-1*) Stardate Pub.

An Asterisk (*) at the beginning of an entry indicates that the title is appearing in BIP for the first time. 121

A

African-American Cultures: Myths & Legends from Ghana for Children. Rute Larungu. LC 92-81116. (Illus.). 96p. (J). (gr. 3 up). 1992. lib. bdg. 14.95 (*1-878893-21-1*); pap. 8.95 (*1-878893-20-3*) Telcraft Bks.

*__African American Educators' Hall of Fame: Educators' Hall of Fame.__ Patricia A. Adelekan et al. (African American Educators' Hall of Fame Ser.). 24p. (Orig.). 1993. pap. 4.99 (*0-9620036-4-6*) Adelekan Pub Co.

*__African American Educators' Hall of Fame: 1994 Edition, a Multi-Cultural Selection.__ Patricia A. Adelekan. 24p. (Orig.). 1994. pap. 4.99 (*0-9620036-5-4*) Adelekan Pub Co.

*__African American Educators' Hall of Fame: 1995 Edition, a Multi-Cultural Selection.__ Patricia A. Adelekan. 24p. (Orig.). 1995. pap. 4.99 (*0-9620036-6-2*) Adelekan Pub Co.

African American Encyclopedia. Ed. by Michael W. Williams. LC 93-141. 1993. 449.95 (*1-85435-545-7*, Pub. by M Cavendish Bks UK) Marshall Cavendish.

African-American Exodus: The Segregation of the Southern Churches. Katharine L. Dvorak. LC 90-23383. (Chicago Studies in the History of American Religion Ser.: Vol. 4). 256p. 1991. 50.00 (*0-926019-25-2*) Carlson Pub.

African-American Exodus & White Migration 1950 to 1970: A Comparative Analysis of Populations' Movements & Their Relations Labor. Sam J. Dennis. (Studies in Historical Demography). 368p. 1989. reprint ed. 35.00 (*0-8240-3351-5*) Garland.

African American Experience. Thomas J. Haley et al. 432p. Date not set. boxed write for info. (*0-13-019969-9*) P-H.

African-American Experience: Issues & Analysis. Cottee J. White. 208p. (C). 1993. per. 29.95 (*0-8403-8497-1*) Kendall-Hunt.

African-American Families: Issues, Insights & Directions. Wade W. Nobles et al. 1987. 10.00 (*0-939205-04-1*) Blk Fam Inst Pub.

*__African American Family Album.__ Dorothy Hoobler & Thomas Hoobler. (American Family Album Ser.). (Illus.). 128p. (J). 1995. text ed. 19.95 (*0-19-509460-3*); lib. bdg. 22.50 (*0-19-508128-5*) OUP.

African American Family City Profile - Atlanta: Places to Go & Things to Do for Today's African American Families in Atlanta. Terry Williams. Ed. by Maria Mallory. (Black Parents Press - Kujichagalia Ser.). (Illus.). 24p. 1994. pap. write for info. (*0-937913-03-0*) W Stery.

African-American Family in the South, 1861-1900. Intro. by Donald G. Nieman. LC 93-37087. (African American Life in the Post-Emancipation South Ser.: Vol. 8). (Illus.). 368p. 1994. 64.00 (*0-8153-1445-0*) Garland.

African-American Family Reunion. JimmieLee Denton-Hatten. 1992. write for info. (*0-9638137-0-6*) AA Family.

African-American Firsts: Famous, Little-Known, & Unsung Triumphs of Blacks in America. Joan Potter & Constance Claytor. LC 93-84716. (Illus.). 352p. (Orig.). (YA). (gr. 7 up). 1994. pap. 14.95 (*0-9632476-1-1*) Pinto Pr.

African-American Folktales. Richard Young & Judy D. Young. 176p. (J). 1993. 19.95 (*0-87483-308-6*); pap. 10.95 (*0-87483-309-4*) August Hse.

African-American Gardens & Yards in the Rural South. Richard Westmacott. LC 92-16555. (Illus.). 216p. (Orig.). 1992. 39.95 (*0-87049-761-8*); pap. 24.95 (*0-87049-762-6*) U of Tenn Pr.

*__African American Genealogical Sourcebook.__ Ed. by Paula K. Byers. LC 95-2263. (Genealogy Sourcebook Ser.). 228-250p. 1995. 69.00 (*0-8103-9226-7*) Gale.

African-American Genealogy: Workbook for Beginners. 2nd ed. Nova Law Staff. (Illus.). 113p. 1993. 19.95 (*1-882804-02-3*) Legacy Pub AL.

African-American Genealogy Workbook: Finding Your Roots. 3rd ed. Nova Law. (Illus.). 118p. 1992. student ed 17.95 (*1-882804-03-1*) Legacy Pub AL.

African-American Genealogy Workbook for Beginners: Tracing Your Ancestry Historically & Genetically. Nova Law Staff. 75p. 1992. 10.95 (*1-882804-00-7*) Legacy Pub AL.

African American Generals & Flag Officers: Biographies of over 120 Blacks in the United States Military. Walter L. Hawkins. LC 92-50886. 272p. 1993. lib. bdg. 29.95x (*0-89950-774-3*) McFarland & Co.

African American Good News (Gospel) Music. Sherry S. DuPree & Herbert C. DuPree. LC 92-37092. (Illus.). 156p. (Orig.). 1993. pap. 19.95 (*1-877971-08-1*) Mid Atl Reg Pr.

African-American Guide to Better English: A Speaking & Writing Survival Manual for African-Americans. 2nd ed. Garrard O. McClendon. LC 93-80308. (Illus.). 79p. (Orig.). 1995. pap. 7.95 (*0-9639329-0-X*) Positive People.

*__African American Guide to Tennessee.__ (Illus.). 60p. (Orig.). 1994. pap. 14.95 (*1-57205-733-5*) Rector Pr.

African-American Health Book: A Prescription for Improvement. Veliere Alcena. LC 93-44652. 1994. 18.95 (*1-55972-214-2*, Birch Ln Pr) Carol Pub Group.

*__African-American Heritage of Florida.__ Ed. by David R. Colburn & Jane L. Landers. LC 94-40977. (Illus.). 352p. 1995. lib. bdg. 49.95 (*0-8130-1332-1*) U Press Fla.

African-American Hidden Treasure Resources. Willie E. Box, Jr. 73p. (Orig.). 1993. lib. bdg. write for info. (*1-882901-37-1*) W Box & Assocs.

*__African American Historic Places.__ National Park Service Staff & National Register of Historic Places Staff. Ed. by Beth L. Savage et al. LC 94-33218. (Illus.). 623p. (Orig.). 1994. pap. 25.95 (*0-89133-253-7*) Preservation Pr.

*__African-American History.__ Richard Beck. 1994. student ed, pap. 15.00 (*0-88092-152-8*) Royal Fireworks.

*__African-American History.__ Richard Beck. 1994. teacher ed, pap. 10.00 (*0-88092-153-6*) Royal Fireworks.

African-American History. Thomas C. Holt. (New American History Ser.). 30p. (C). 1991. reprint ed. 5.00 (*0-87229-060-3*) Am Hist Assn.

African-American History: Heroes in Hardship. Lisbeth G. Stevenson. (Illus.). 352p. (Orig.). (YA). (gr. 8-9). 1991. pap. text ed. 12.50 (*0-944348-01-7*) Cambdgport Pr.

African-American History Facts (1619-1974) P. Hilton Taylor. 114p. 1991. pap. 9.99 (*0-9638528-2-5*) Brainpower Pubng.

African-American History for Young Readers. 2nd ed. Julia A. Davis. (Illus.). 336p. (J). (gr. 5-9). 1992. 30.00 (*0-9631110-5-1*) Epps-Alford.

African American Holiday of Kwanzaa: A Celebration of Family, Community & Culture. Maulana Karenga. 116p. (Orig.). 1989. pap. 9.95 (*0-943412-09-9*) Univ Sankore Pr.

African American Holidays: A Historical Research & Resource Guide to Cultural Celebrations. James C. Anyike. 85p. (C). 1991. pap. text ed. 7.95 (*0-9631547-0-2*) Pop Truth.

African-American Holiness Pentecostal Movement: An Annotated Bibliography. Sherry S. DuPree. LC 94-20225. (Religious Information Systems Ser.: Vol. 4). (Illus.). 710p. 1995. 95.00 (*0-8240-1449-9*, SS526) Garland.

African-American Humanism: An Anthology. Ed. by Norm R. Allen, Jr. 286p. (Orig.). (C). 1991. pap. 18.95 (*0-87975-658-6*) Prometheus Bks.

African-American Husbands: A Study of Black Family Life. Ron Stewart. LC 91-50746. vi, 108p. (Orig.). (C). 1992. pap. text ed. 14.95 (*1-55605-192-1*) Wyndhall Pr.

African-American Identity Crisis. Horus M. Alkebu-Can et al. 54p. (Orig.). 1991. pap. text ed. 7.00 (*0-9628788-0-4*) Alkebu-Lan & Assocs.

African-American Image in Crisis. Sidney R. Sharif. (Illus.). 148p. (Orig.). 1985. pap. 6.95 (*0-933821-03-4*) New Mind Prod.

African-American in South Africa: The Travel Notes of Ralph J. Bunche, September 28, 1937 - January 1, 1938. Ralph J. Bunche. Ed. by Robert R. Edgar. (Illus.). 405p. 1992. text ed. 40.00 (*0-8214-1021-0*) Ohio U Pr.

African-American Index: Journals & Magazines 1989, Vol. 1, No. 1. Ed. by Norman Harris & Clarissa Myrick-Harris. 144p. 1990. write for info. (*1-878531-01-8*) Black Res Ctr.

African-American Index - 1994. Ed. by Norman Harris. 350p. (C). 1994. lib. bdg. 85.00 (*1-878531-06-9*) Black Res Ctr.

African American Index 1990. Ed. by Norman Harris & Clarissa Myrick-Harris. 1991. lib. bdg. write for info. (*1-878531-04-2*) Black Res Ctr.

African American Inventor Math Pack Workbook. Dexter Akinsheye. Ed. by Dayo Akinsheye. (Illus.). 20p. (Orig.). (J). (gr. 2-5). 1992. pap. text ed. 2.50 (*1-877835-53-6*) TD Pub.

African-American Inventors. Patricia McKissack & Fredrick McKissack. LC 93-42625. (Proud Heritage Ser.). (Illus.). 96p. (J). (gr. 4-6). 1994. lib. bdg. 17.90 (*1-56294-468-1*) Millbrook Pr.

African American Inventors Study Print Series: Two Teacher's Guides & a Set of 40 study prints. Dexter Akinsheye. Ed. by Dayo Akinsheye. 1992. 72.00 (*1-877835-84-6*) TD Pub.

African American Islam. Aminah B. McCloud. LC 94-18313. 200p. 1995. 49.95 (*0-415-90785-3*, B0634); pap. 16.95 (*0-415-90786-1*, B0638) Routledge.

African-American Kitchen: Cooking from Our Heritage. Angela S. Mederis. LC 94-1323. 1994. 23.95 (*0-525-93834-6*) NAL-Dutton.

African-American Legacies for the 21st Century: A Bibliography of Biographies for Children about Notable African-Americans. Jeanette Lambert. 25p. (Orig.). (J). (gr. k-8). 1994. pap. 4.95 (*0-9632736-5-5*) Edit Cetera.

African-American Literary Tradition. Patricia L. Hill. 1995. text ed. write for info. (*0-07-028896-8*) McGraw.

*__African-American Literature.__ Young. (Literary Mosiac Ser.). (C). 1995. text ed. write for info. (*0-673-99017-6*) HarpCollege.

African American Literature: An Anthology of Nonfiction, Fiction, Poetry & Drama. Demetrice A. Worley. 1993. pap. 23.95 (*0-8442-5727-3*) NTC Pub Grp.

African-American Male: A Need for Family Empowerment: A Town Meeting. Ed. by S. Adele Doherty. 128p. (C). 1992. pap. 10.00 (*0-9630511-3-X*) DSH Pub.

African American Males: A Critical Link in the African American Family. Ed. by Dionne J. Jones. 95p. (C). 1994. pap. 19.95 (*1-56000-744-3*) Transaction Pubs.

African-American Market Handbook. Charles Wimbley. Ed. by Peggy Bessette. 450p. 1993. 64.95 (*0-8103-8996-7*, 101783) Gale.

*__African American Market Handbook 1993.__ 150p. (Orig.). 1995. pap. 2,195.00 (*0-7605-2007-0*) Rector Pr.

*__African-American Medical Pioneers.__ Charles H. Epps, Jr. et al. 272p. 1994. 60.00 (*0-941406-46-6*) Betz Pub Co Inc.

African-American Mosaic: A Library of Congress Resource Guide for the Study of Black History & Culture. Ed. by Debra N. Ham et al. LC 93-21605. 1993. write for info. (*0-8444-0800-X*) Lib Congress.

African American Mothers & Urban Schools: The Power of Participation. Wendy G. Winters. LC 93-11154. 1993. text ed. 25.95 (*0-669-28201-4*) Free Pr.

African-American Movement Today. Geoffrey Jacques. LC 92-17086. (African-American Experience Ser.). (Illus.). 144p. (YA). (gr. 9-12). 1992. lib. bdg. 14.98 (*0-531-11033-8*) Watts.

African-American Novel in the Age of Reaction: Three Classics. Frances E. Harper et al. 592p. (Orig.). 1992. pap. 5.99 (*0-451-62849-7*, Ment) NAL-Dutton.

African American Parents Resource Guide: Places Things & Services for Today's Families. Terry Williams. Ed. by Maria Mallory. (Illus.). 64p. (Orig.). 1994. pap. write for info. (*0-318-72776-5*) W Stery.

African-American Pastoral Care. Edward P. Wimberly. LC 90-26646. 1991. pap. 10.95 (*0-687-00933-2*) Abingdon.

African-American Perspectives on Biomedical Ethics. Ed. by Harley E. Flack & Edmund D. Pellegrino. LC 92-17638. 224p. (Orig.). 1992. pap. text ed. 25.00 (*0-87840-532-1*) Georgetown U Pr.

African-American Perspectives on Crime Causation, Criminal Justice Administration, & Crime Prevention. Ed. by Anne T. Sulton. LC 93-87085. 220p. 1994. 49.95 (*0-9639633-0-9*); pap. 24.95 (*0-9639633-1-7*) A T Sulton.

African-American Poetry of the Nineteenth Century: An Anthology. Ed. by Joan R. Sherman. 512p. (C). 1992. 44.95 (*0-252-01917-2*); pap. 16.95 (*0-252-06246-9*) U of Ill Pr.

African American Political Thought: DuBois, Washington, Randolph, & Garvey. Ed. by Cary D. Wintz. 272p. 1995. 45.00 (*1-56324-178-1*); pap. 19.95 (*1-56324-179-X*) M E Sharpe.

African-American Principals: School Leadership & Success. Kofi Lomotey. LC 89-1881. (Contributions in Afro-American & African Studies: No. 124). 188p. 1989. text ed. 45.00 (*0-313-26375-2*, LBP, Greenwood Pr) Greenwood.

African American Psychology: Theory, Research, & Practice. Ed. by A. Kathleen Burlew et al. (Illus.). 400p. (C). 1992. 52.00 (*0-8039-4765-8*); pap. 24.95 (*0-8039-4766-6*) Sage.

*__African American Quiltmaking in Michigan.__ Ed. by Marsha MacDowell. 375p. 1996. 45.00 (*0-87013-410-8*) Mich St U Pr.

African-American Reactions to War in Ethiopia, 1936-1941. Joseph E. Harris. LC 93-10343. (Illus.). xiv, 248p. 1994. text ed. 35.00 (*0-8071-1832-X*) La State U Pr.

African-American Reference Library, 10 Vols., Set. (Illus.). (J). (gr. 6-9). 1993. 195.00 (*0-8103-9230-5*, 021500, UXL) Gale.

African-American Reflections on Brazil's Racial Paradise. Ed. by David J. Hellwig. 285p. (C). 1992. 34.95 (*0-87722-892-2*) Temple U Pr.

African-American Relations in the 80's. (African-American Conferences Ser.). 1981. pap. 3.00 (*0-89192-344-6*) Interbk Inc.

African American Religion: Research Problems & Resources for the 1990s. 159p. 1992. write for info. (*0-87104-432-3*) NY Pub Lib.

African-American Religion in the Twentieth Century: Varieties of Protest & Accommodation. Hans A. Baer & Merrill Singer. LC 91-40209. 296p. (Orig.). 1992. lib. bdg. 34.00x (*0-87049-746-4*); pap. text ed. 16.00x (*0-87049-747-2*) U of Tenn Pr.

African American Religious Studies: An Interdisciplinary Anthology. Ed. by Gayraud S. Wilmore. LC 88-33567. xxii, 468p. 1989. 55.50 (*0-8223-0904-1*); pap. 21.95 (*0-8223-0926-2*) Duke.

African-American Resource Guide. Anita D. Diggs. LC 93-47551. 1994. pap. 12.99 (*1-56980-006-5*) Barricade Bks.

African-American Scientists. Patricia McKissack & Fredrick McKissack. LC 93-11226. (Proud Heritage Ser.). (Illus.). 96p. (J). (gr. 4-6). 1994. lib. bdg. 17.90 (*1-56294-372-3*) Millbrook Pr.

*__African American Single Mothers.__ Bette J. Dickerson. (Sage Series on Race & Ethnic Relations). 272p. 1995. text ed. 49.95 (*0-8039-4911-1*); pap. text ed. 24.00 (*0-8039-5912-5*) Sage.

African-American Sites & Insights: A Guide to Places to Go & People to Know, 1994. Naida M. Davidson. 125p. (Orig.). 1993. pap. 7.95 (*0-9638924-0-1*) Grace Commun.

African-American Social Change: A Philosophical Approach. Norman Harris. 214p. (Orig.). (C). 1990. pap. text ed. write for info. (*1-878531-03-4*) Black Res Ctr.

African American Soldiers in the National Guard: Recruitment & Deployment During Peacetime & War. Charles Johnson, Jr. LC 91-44510. (Contributions in Afro-American & African Studies: No. 149). 232p. 1992. text ed. 49.95 (*0-313-20706-2*, JBS/, Greenwood Pr) Greenwood.

*__African-American Soldiers Series, 9 vols., Set.__ (Illus.). 80p. (J). (gr. 4-7). 1994. lib. bdg. 134.82 (*0-8050-3661-X*) TFC Bks NY.

*__African-American Sports Greats: A Biographical Dictionary.__ Ed. by David L. Porter. LC 95-7189. 1995. text ed. 59.95 (*0-313-28987-5*, Greenwood Pr) Greenwood.

African American Sunday School & It's Origins. Oneal Sandidge. LC 94-76373. 104p. 1994. pap. 9.95 (*1-55523-698-7*) Winston-Derek.

African American Task Force Report on the Year 2000: Health Promotion Objectives & Recommendations for California. 77p. (Orig.). (C). 1993. pap. text ed. 40.00 (*0-7881-0090-4*) Diane Pub.

African American Television Experience: A Researcher's Bibliography of Scholarly Writings. George H. Hill et al. 78p. (Orig.). 1987. pap. text ed. 8.00 (*0-685-13975-1*) Daystar Co Carson.

*__African American Theater: Out of Bondage (1876) & Peculiar Sam; or The Underground Railroad (1879)__ Ed. by Eileen Southern. LC 94-20285. (Nineteenth-Century American Musical Theater Ser.: No. 9). 254p. 1994. 86.00 (*0-8153-1367-5*) Garland.

African-American Theatre: An Historical & Critical Analysis. Samuel A. Hay. (Studies in American Theatre & Drama Ser.: No. 1). 272p. (C). 1994. pap. 18.95 (*0-521-46585-0*) Cambridge U Pr.

African-American Traditions in Song, Sermon, Tale & Dance, 1600s-1920: An Annotated Bibliography of Literature, Collections & Artworks. Ed. by Josephine Wright. LC 90-34101. (Encyclopedia of Black Music Ser.). 416p. 1990. text ed. 65.00 (*0-313-24918-0*, SUN, Greenwood Pr) Greenwood.

*__African American Voices.__ Ed. by Ruth W. Johnson. 1995. pap. 32.95 (*0-88737-625-8*) Natl League Nurse.

*__African-American Voices.__ Michele Stepto. LC 94-16081. (Writers of America Ser.). (Illus.). 160p. (YA). (gr. 7 up). 1995. lib. bdg. 16.90 (*1-56294-474-6*) Millbrook Pr.

African American Voices: The Life Cycle of Slavery. Intro. by Steven Mintz. 202p. (Orig.). (C). 1993. Net. pap. text ed. 10.96 (*1-881089-11-8*) Brandywine Press.

African-American Voices: Tradition, Transition, Transformation. Ed. by Karen P. Smith. LC 94-13800. 1994. 45.00 (*0-8108-2907-X*) Scarecrow.

African American Wisdom. Reginald McKnight. LC 93-33729. (Classic Wisdom Collection). 96p. 1994. 12.95 (*1-880032-34-1*) New Wrld Lib.

African American Woman: Social & Economic Conditions: A Bibliography. Ed. by Joan Nordquist. (Contemporary Social Issues: A Bibliographic Ser.: No. 32). 64p. (Orig.). 1993. pap. 15.00 (*0-937855-62-6*) Ref Rsch Serv.

African American Women: A Biographical Dictionary. Ed. by Dorothy C. Salem. LC 92-45727. (Biographical Directories of Minority Women Ser.: Vol. 2). (Illus.). 664p. 1993. 75.00 (*0-8240-9782-3*, SS706) Garland.

African American Women: A Study of Will & Success. Elizabeth A. Peterson. LC 92-54088. 144p. 1992. pap. 24.95x (*0-89950-730-1*) McFarland & Co.

African-American Women Fiction Writers, 1859-1986: An Annotated Bio-Bibliography. Sharon M. Howard. 350p. Date not set. 49.00 (*0-8240-6646-4*, H788) Garland.

*__African American Women Speak Out on Anita Hill-Clarence Thomas.__ Ed. by Geneva Smitherman. (African American Life Ser.). (Illus.). 330p. (Orig.). 1995. pap. 18.95 (*0-8143-2530-0*) Wayne St U Pr.

African-American Writers. Valerie Smith et al. LC 90-52918. 576p. 1991. text ed. 95.00 (*0-684-19058-3*, Scribners) S&S Trade.

African American Youth: Their Social & Economic Status in the United States. Ed. by Ronald L. Taylor. LC 94-8565. 376p. 1994. text ed. 59.95 (*0-275-94886-2*, Praeger Pubs); pap. text ed. 19.95 (*0-275-94940-0*, Praeger Pubs) Greenwood.

African Americans. Ed. by David Cohen & Charles Collins. LC 93-1574. (Illus.). 240p. 1993. 45.00 (*0-670-84982-0*, Viking Studio) Studio Bks.

*__African Americans.__ Donna Evert et al. (Thematic Units Ser.). 1995. pap. text ed. 8.95 (*1-55734-590-2*) Tchr Create Mat.

African-Americans. Richard A. Long. 1993. 17.99 (*0-517-08792-8*) Random Hse Value.

African Americans. Shelia Payton. LC 94-12631. (Cultures of America Ser.). (J). (gr. 4-7). 1994. 19.95 (*1-85435-787-5*) Marshall Cavendish.

*__African Americans.__ Smead. 1995. (*0-7910-3369-4*) Chelsea Hse.

*__African Americans: A Celebration of Achievement.__ Ed. by Charles M. Collins & David Cohen. (Illus.). 240p. 1995. pap. 22.95 (*0-14-024918-4*, Viking Studio) Studio Bks.

African-Americans: Essential Perspectives. Ed. by Wornie L. Reed et al. LC 92-31298. 184p. 1993. text ed. 49.95 (*0-86569-221-1*, T221, Auburn Hse); pap. text ed. 16.95 (*0-86569-222-X*, R222, Auburn Hse) Greenwood.

African Americans: Social & Economic Conditions: A Bibliography. Ed. by Joan Nordquist. (Contemporary Social Issues: A Bibliographic Ser.: No. 27). 68p. (Orig.). (C). 1992. pap. 15.00 (*0-937855-52-9*) Ref Rsch Serv.

African-Americans: Their Impact on U. S. History. Doris Metcalf. (Illus.). 240p. (J). (gr. 5-9). 1992. 16.95 (*0-86653-670-1*, GA1345) Good Apple.

*__African Americans, Alcohol, Tobacco & Other Drugs: A Resource Guide.__ 1995. lib. bdg. 251.95 (*0-8490-6784-7*) Gordon Pr.

African Americans & Education in the South, 1865-1900. Ed. by Donald G. Nieman. LC 93-38436. (African American Life in the Post-Emancipation South Ser.: Vol. 10). (Illus.). 464p. 1994. reprint ed. 70.00 (*0-8153-1447-7*) Garland.

*__African-Americans & Jewish-Americans: A History of Struggle.__ Hedda Garza. (African-American Experience Ser.). (Illus.). (YA). (gr. 9-12). 1995. lib. bdg. 14.98 (*0-531-11217-9*) Watts.

African-Americans & Non-Agricultural Labor in the South, 1865-1900. Intro. by Donald G. Nieman. LC 93-37339. (African American Life in the Post-Emancipation South Ser.: Vol. 4). 400p. 1994. 64.00 (*0-8153-1441-8*) Garland.

African-Americans & Other Myths: Confusing Racism with Cultural Diversity. Kenneth Brooks. LC 93-73899. 160p. (Orig.). 1993. pap. 13.98 (*0-9639042-3-X*) Amper Pubng.

African Americans & Rise of Buffalo's Post-Industrial City, 1940-1980. Ed. by Henry L. Taylor, Jr. 320p. (Orig.). 1990. pap. text ed. 15.00 (*0-9626940-0-2*) Buffalo Urban.

African-Americans & Southern Politics from Redemption to Disfranchisement. Intro. by Donald G. Nieman. LC 93-36874. (African American Life in the Post-Emancipation South Ser.: Vol. 6). 360p. 1994. 58.00 (*0-8153-1443-4*) Garland.

African-Americans & the American Political System. Lucius J. Barker & Mack H. Jones. 1994. write for info. (*0-318-72280-1*) P-H.

African-Americans & the American Political System. 3rd ed. Lucius J. Barker & Mack Jones. 400p. (C). 1994. pap. text ed. write for info. (*0-13-084575-2*) P-H.

African-Americans & the Doctoral Experience: Implications for Policy. Charles V. Willie et al. 128p. (C). 1991. text ed. 21.95 (*0-8077-3087-4*) Tchrs Coll.

An Asterisk (*) at the beginning of an entry indicates that the title is appearing in BIP for the first time.

African-Americans & the Emergence of Segregation, 1865-1900. Intro. by Donald G. Nieman. LC 93-29264. (African American Life in the Post-Emancipation South Ser.: Vol. 11). (Illus.). 464p. 1994. 65.00 (*0-8153-1448-5*) Garland.

African-Americans & the Law: General Themes. Ed. by Paul Finkelman. LC 91-37462. (Race, Law & American History, 1700-1990 Ser.: Vol. 1). 648p. 1992. 97.00 (*0-8153-0534-6*) Garland.

African-Americans & the Legal Professions in Historical Perspective. Ed. by Paul Finkelman. LC 91-39440. (Race, Law & American History, 1700-1990 Ser.: Vol. 10). 544p. 1992. 79.00 (*0-8153-0543-5*) Garland.

***African Americans & the Living Constitution.** John H. Franklin & Genna R. McNeil. LC 94-30724. 1995. boxed write for info. (*1-56098-472-4*) Smithsonian.

***African Americans & the Living Constitution.** Ed. by John H. Franklin & Genna R. McNeil. LC 94-30724. 1995. pap. write for info. (*1-56098-471-6*) Smithsonian.

African Americans & the New Policy Consensus: Retreat of the Liberal State? Ed. by Marilyn E. Lashley & Melanie N. Jackson. LC 94-872. (Contributions in Political Science Ser.: No. 347). 264p. 1994. text ed. 55.00 (*0-313-28880-1*, Greenwood Pr) Greenwood.

African Americans & the Quest for Civil Rights, 1900-1990. Sean D. Cashman. (Illus.). 360p. 1991. 40.00 (*0-8147-1440-4*) NYU Pr.

African-Americans & the Quest for Civil Rights, 1900-1990. Sean D. Cashman. (Illus.). 321p. (C). 1993. pap. text ed. 16.95 (*0-8147-1441-2*) NYU Pr.

African-Americans & the Right to Vote. Ed. by Paul Finkelman. LC 91-39438. (Race, Law & American History, 1700-1990 Ser.: Vol. 6). 592p. 1992. 90.00 (*0-8153-0539-7*) Garland.

African Americans & the Visual Arts: A Resource Guide to Books, Articles & Dissertations 1900-1990. Florence J. Staats. 36p. (Orig.). 1990. pap. text ed. 9.95 (*0-9627366-0-0*) Arts & Comns NY.

African Americans & U. S. Policy Toward Africa: In Defense of Black Nationality, 1850-1924. Elliott P. Skinner. LC 92-17588. 1992. 34.95 (*0-88258-142-2*); pap. 24.95 (*0-88258-159-7*) Howard U Pr.

***African American's Art Lesson on Portraits: How to Paint a Portrait with the Use of Oil Paint.** rev. ed. Charles Jones. (Illus.). 97p. (C). pap. 25.95 (*0-9643501-1-4*) C & C Jones.

African Americans at the Crossroads: The Restructuring of Black Leadership & the 1992 Elections. Clarence Lusane. 160p. (Orig.). 1993. 40.00 (*0-89608-469-8*); pap. text ed. 16.00 (*0-89608-468-X*) South End Pr.

***African American's Guide to Financial Fitness.** Caryn Johnson. 100p. 1994. pap. 9.95 (*0-9642742-0-5*) Jenco Pubng.

***African Americans in Alaska Resource Guide: Promoting Alaska Where We Live.** Abram Abraham Production & Management Staff. Ed. by Sheryl K. Bailey et al. (Sixth Annual Ser.). 44p. (Orig.). 1994. pap. text ed. 15.95 (*0-614-00760-7*) A Abraham.

African Americans in Alaska Resource Guide & Calendar - Booklet 1992. 3rd ed. Sheryl K. Bailey et al. 40p. (Orig.). 1991. pap. text ed. 12.00 (*0-9630369-0-4*) A Abraham.

African Americans in Alaska Resource Guide & Calendar 1993. 4th ed. Sheryl K. Bailey et al. 40p. (Orig.). 1992. pap. text ed. 15.95 (*0-9630369-1-2*) A Abraham.

African Americans in Alaska Resource Guide & Calendar 1994. 5th ed. Sheryl K. Bailey et al. 40p. (Orig.). 1993. pap. text ed. 15.95 (*0-9630369-2-0*) A Abraham.

African-Americans in Boston: More Than 350 Years. Robert C. Hayden. (Illus.). 187p. (Orig.). 1992. pap. 15.00 (*0-89073-083-0*) Boston Public Lib.

African-Americans in Florida: An Illustrated History. Maxine D. Jones & Kevin M. McCarthy. LC 93-27737. (Illus.). (J). (gr. 4-8). 1993. 24.95 (*1-56164-030-1*); pap. 17.95 (*1-56164-031-X*) Pineapple Pr.

***African Americans in Iowa: A Chronicle of Contributions, 1830-1992.** Frances E. Hawthorne. 1993. pap. 5.00 (*0-9641663-1-3*) African Am Hist.

African Americans in Pennsylvania. Charles L. Blockson. 230p. (Orig.). Date not set. pap. 14.95 (*0-933121-85-7*) Black Classic.

African-Americans in the Colonial Era: From African Origins Through the American Revolution. Donald R. Wright. Ed. by John H. Franklin & A. S. Eisenstadt. LC 89-23633. (American History Ser.). (Illus.). 140p. (C). 1990. pap. text ed. write for info. (*0-88295-832-1*) Harlan Davidson.

African-Americans in the Early Republic, 1789-1831. Donald R. Wright. Ed. by John H. Franklin & A. S. Eisenstadt. LC 92-27210. (American History Ser.). 264p. (C). 1993. pap. text ed. write for info. (*0-88295-897-6*) Harlan Davidson.

African Americans in the Maritime Trades: A Guide to Resources in New England. Mary Malloy. (Museum Monograph Ser.). (Illus.). 1990. pap. text ed. 6.50 (*0-937854-30-1*) Kendall Whaling.

African Americans in the New Millennium: Blueprinting the Future. Erskine Peters. (Orig.). 1991. pap. 9.95 (*0-916147-18-5*) Regent Pr.

African Americans in the South: Issues of Race, Class, & Gender. Ed. by Hans A. Baer & Yvonne Jones. LC 91-17728. 192p. 1992. 30.00 (*0-8203-1376-9*); pap. 15.00 (*0-8203-1377-7*) U of Ga Pr.

African Americans in the Spanish Civil War: This Ain't Ethiopia, but It'll Do. Ed. by Danny D. Collum. 256p. 1992. text ed. 39.95 (*0-8161-7378-8*, Hall Reference) Macmillan.

African Americans of Mars Bluff, South Carolina. Amelia W. Vernon. LC 93-15834. (Illus.). 344p. 1994. 29.95 (*0-8071-1846-X*) La State U Pr.

African Americans Struggle for Equality. Anna Wilson. LC 92-16282. (Discrimination Ser.). (J). 1992. 22.60 (*0-86593-184-4*); lib. bdg. 16.95 (*0-685-59724-5*) Rourke Corp.

African-Americans; Tradition & Culture: Learning Center. Irene Handberg. (Multicultural Education Ser.). 96p. 1992. teacher ed write for info. (*1-56831-911-8*) Lrning Connect.

African-Americans; Tradition & Culture: Learning Center, Set. Irene Handberg. (Multicultural Education Ser.). 96p. 1992. write for info. (*1-56831-900-2*) Lrning Connect.

African-Americans under Segregation - Our Own Brand of Apartheid: An Overview of Race Prejudice: It Was Like This. Westwood Winfree. 1993. 13.95 (*0-533-10470-X*) Vantage.

***African Anarchism: The History of a Movement.** Samuel Mbah & I. G. Igariwey. 1995. pap. 12.95 (*1-884365-05-1*) See Sharp Pr.

***African & African-American Sensibility.** Ed. by Michael W. Coy, Jr. & Leonard Plotnicov. LC 94-62223. (Ethnology Monographs: No. 15). (Illus.). xiv, 122p. (Orig.). (C). 1995. pap. 10.00 (*0-945428-08-1*) Ethnology Monographs.

African & African American Studies. (Ethnic Studies Reviews). 152p. 1992. 22.00 (*0-8389-7692-1*) Assn Coll & Res Libs.

African & Afro-American History. Jack Rudman. (College Proficiency Examination Ser.: CPEP-36). 1994. pap. 23.95 (*0-8373-5436-6*) Nat Learn.

African & Afro-American History. Jack Rudman. (ACT Proficiency Examination Program Ser.: PEP-1). 1994. pap. 23.95 (*0-8373-5501-X*) Nat Learn.

African & Caribbean Historical Novel. Paschal B. K. Kyoore. LC 94-16864. (Francophone Cultures & Literature Ser.: Vol. 3). Date not set. write for info. (*0-8204-2555-9*) P Lang Pubs.

African & the Cinema. L. A. Notcott & G. C. Latham. 1976. lib. bdg. 69.95 (*0-8490-1403-4*) Gordon Pr.

***African Animal Giants.** James M. Dietz. LC 94-25393. (National Geographic Action Bk.). (Illus.). (J). (gr. 2). 1994. 24.50 (*0-7922-2783-2*) Natl Geog.

African Animal Tales. Rogerio A. Barbosa. Tr. by Feliz Guthrie. LC 92-42378. (Illus.). 60p. (J). (gr. 1-3). 1993. 17.95 (*0-912078-96-0*) Volcano Pr.

African Animals. John W. Purcell. LC 82-9541. (New True Bks.). (Illus.). 48p. (J). (gr. k-4). 1982. 12.90 (*0-516-01665-2*); pap. 4.95 (*0-516-41665-0*) Childrens.

***African Animals ABC.** Philippa-Alys Browne. (Illus.). 32p. (J). (ps-2). 1995. 15.95 (*0-87156-372-X*) Sierra.

African Animals Discovery Library, 6 bks., Set. Lynn Stone. (Illus.). 144p. (J). (gr. k-5). 1990. lib. bdg. 71.64 (*0-86593-047-3*); lib. bdg. 53.70 (*0-685-36343-0*) Rourke Corp.

African Animals in Origami. John Montroll. LC 91-76400. (Illus.). 160p. (Orig.). (YA). 1993. pap. 9.95 (*1-877656-09-7*) Antroll Pub.

African Animals in Origami. John Montroll. (Illus.). 160p. (Orig.). pap. 9.95 (*0-486-26977-9*) Dover.

African Animals of William R. Leigh. Forrest Fenn. (Illus.). 32p. (Orig.). 1980. pap. 10.00 (*0-937634-01-8*) Fenn Pub Co.

African Answer: The Key to Global Productivity. Edgar J. Ridley. LC 92-14518. 100p. (Orig.). 1992. 24.95 (*0-86543-358-5*); pap. 8.95 (*0-86543-359-3*) Africa World.

African Apostles: Ritual & Conversion in the Church of John Maranke. Bennetta Jules-Rosette. LC 75-8437. (Symbol, Myth & Ritual Ser.). (Illus.). 352p. 1975. 45.00 (*0-8014-0846-6*) Cornell U Pr.

African-Arab Conflict in the Sudan. Dunstan M. Wai. LC 80-15410. 240p. 1981. 39.50 (*0-8419-0631-9*, Africana) Holmes & Meier.

African-Arab Relations. Hilmi S. Yousuf. LC 84-72245. 220p. (Orig.). 1986. 12.50 (*0-915597-06-3*); pap. 9.95 (*0-915597-12-8*) Amana Bks.

African Archaeology. 2nd ed. David W. Phillipson. LC 92-35021. (Cambridge World Archaeology Ser.). (Illus.). 300p. (C). 1994. 59.95 (*0-521-44103-X*); pap. 19.95 (*0-521-44658-9*) Cambridge U Pr.

African Archaeology: A Selected Bibliography. Robert B. Ridinger. (G. K. Hall Reference Ser.). 550p. 1993. text ed. 55.00 (*0-8161-9086-0*, Hall Reference) Macmillan.

African Aristocracy. Hilda Kuper. LC 79-24794. 269p. 1980. reprint ed. 45.00 (*0-8419-0581-9*, Africana) Holmes & Meier.

African Ark: People & Ancient Cultures of Ethiopia & the Horn of Africa. Photos by Carol Beckwith & Angela Fisher. (Illus.). 320p. 1990. 65.00 (*0-8109-1902-8*) Abrams.

African Arms & Armor. Christopher Spring. LC 93-84191. (Illus.). 192p. 1993. 45.00 (*1-56098-317-5*) Smithsonian.

African Art. (Illus.). 1986. 19.95 (*0-8148-0736-4*, Apollo) L Amiel Pub.

African Art. 1991. 29.99 (*0-517-05411-6*) Random Hse Value.

African Art. rev. ed. Frank Willet. LC 93-60124. (World of Art Ser.). 1993. pap. 14.95 (*0-500-20267-2*) Thames Hudson.

African Art: A Bibliographic Guide. 2nd ed. (Smithsonian Institution Libraries Research Guide Ser.: No. 4). 55p. 1985. 7.25 (*0-8419-1030-8*, Africana) Holmes & Meier.

African Art: Activity Workbook. Jay Monteith. (Illus.). 24p. (Orig.). (J). 1993. pap. text ed. 8.75 (*0-9627366-4-3*) Arts & Comns NY.

African Art: From Crocodiles to Convertibles in the Collection of the Seattle Art Museum. Pamela McClusky. LC 87-61752. (Illus.). 32p. 1987. pap. 4.95 (*0-932216-24-2*) Seattle Art.

African Art: The Barbier-Mueller Collection. Ed. by Werner Schmalenbach. (Illus.). 320p. 1989. 70.00 (*3-7913-0849-1*, Pub. by Prestel) TeNeues.

African Art: The Years Since 1920. Marshall W. Mount. (Quality Paperbacks Ser.). (Illus.). 254p. 1989. pap. 16.95 (*0-306-80373-9*) Da Capo.

African Art: Virginia Museum of Fine Arts. Richard B. Woodward. Ed. by Monica S. Rumsey. (Illus.). 94p. (Orig.). 1994. pap. 9.00 (*0-917046-37-4*) Va Mus Arts.

African Art & Culture Coloring Book. Sidney R. Holston. 24p. 1991. 4.95 (*1-880569-00-0*) Authentic Des.

African Art & Leadership. Ed. by Douglas Fraser & Herbert M. Cole. LC 72-157391. (Illus.). 350p. reprint ed. pap. 99.80 (*0-8357-5226-7*, 2007667) Bks Demand.

***African Art at the Harn Museum: Spirit Eyes, Human Hands.** Robin Poynor. LC 94-25648. (Illus.). 256p. 1995. lib. bdg. 49.95 (*0-8130-1325-9*) U Press Fla.

African Art from the Harrison Eiteljorg Collection. Peggy S. Gilfoy. (Illus.). 83p. 1976. 6.00 (*0-317-29202-1*) Ind Mus Art.

African Art in Cultural Perspective: An Introduction. William R. Bascom. (Illus.). 192p. (C). 1973. pap. text ed. 9.95 (*0-393-09375-1*) Norton.

African Art in the Cycle of Life. Roy Sieber & Roslyn A. Walker. LC 87-43079. (Illus.). 155p. (C). 1987. 39.95 (*0-87474-822-4*); pap. 29.95 (*0-87474-821-6*) Smithsonian.

African Art in Transit: The Production of Value & Mediation of Knowledge in the African Art Trade. Christopher B. Steiner. LC 92-47387. (Studies in Social & Cultural Anthropology). 1994. 59.95 (*0-521-43447-5*); pap. 19.95 (*0-521-45752-1*) Cambridge U Pr.

African Art in Washington Collections. (Publication of the Museum of African Art). (Illus.). 60p. 1972. pap. 4.00 (*0-89192-230-X*) Interbk Inc.

African Art Masterpieces. George N. Preston. (Illus.). 120p. 1991. 35.00 (*0-88363-801-0*) H L Levin.

African Art Portfolio, an Illustrated Introduction: Masterpieces from the Eleventh to the Twentieth Centuries. Carol Thompson. LC 93-27015. 24p. 1993. pap. 17.95 (*1-56584-112-3*) New Press NY.

African Artists in America. Tritobia H. Benjamin. (Illus.). 1977. pap. 2.00 (*0-685-07657-1*) Interbk Inc.

African Arts & Cultures. Jacqueline Chanda. LC 93-73930. (Illus.). 152p. 1994. 24.95 (*0-87192-249-5*) Davis Mass.

African Assortment, African Art in Museums in England & Scotland. Michael Pennie. (Illus.). 303p. (Orig.). 1991. pap. 39.95 (*0-9513023-2-9*, Pub. by Bath Coll High Educ UK) Ethnographic Arts Pubns.

African Authors: A Companion to Black African Writing 1300-1973, Vol. 1. Ed. by Donald E. Herdeck. LC 73-172338. (Illus.). 605p. 1973. 70.00 (*0-8103-0076-1*) Gale.

African Background Outlined: Or, Handbook for the Study of the Negro. Carter G. Woodson. LC 68-55922. (Illus.). 478p. 1969. reprint ed. text ed. 35.00 (*0-8371-0760-1*, WOB&, Negro U Pr) Greenwood.

***African Banjo Echoes in Appalachia: A Study of Folk Traditions.** Cecelia Conway. LC 94-18762. (Publications of the American Folklore Society). 1995. write for info. (*0-87049-892-4*); pap. write for info. (*0-87049-893-2*) U of Tenn Pr.

African Beer Gardens of Bulawayo: Integrated Drinking in a Segregated Society. H. F. Wolcott. LC 73-620218. (Monograph Ser.: No. 10). 1974. 6.50 (*0-911290-42-7*) Rutgers Ctr Alcohol.

***African Biographical Dictionary.** Norbert Brockman. LC 94-31361. 1994. 60.00 (*0-87436-748-4*) ABC-CLIO.

African Birds of Prey. Warwick Tarboton. LC 90-1462. (Illus.). 228p. 1990. 48.50 (*0-8014-2515-8*) Cornell U Pr.

African Birds of Prey. Warwick Tarboton. 228p. (C). 1989. 210.00 (*1-85368-064-8*, Pub. by New Holland Pubs UK) St Mut.

African Blossoms. Dorothy Hargreaves & Bob Hargreaves. LC 72-85425. (Illus.). 64p. 1972. pap. 3.85 (*0-910690-06-5*) Ross-Hargreaves.

African Book World & Press: A Director Repertoire Du Livre et de la Presse en Afrique. 4th rev. ed. Ed. by Hans M. Zell. 336p. 1989. lib. bdg. 135.00 (*0-905450-50-7*, Pub. by H Zell Pubs UK) Bowker-Saur.

African Books in Print Livres Africains Disponibles, 2 vols., Set. 4th ed. Ed. by Hans Zell. 1520p. 1993. 400.00 (*1-873836-11-2*, Pub. by H Zell Pubs UK) Bowker-Saur.

African Bourgeoisie: Race, Class & Politics in South Africa. Leo Kuper. LC 64-20925. 478p. reprint ed. pap. 136.30 (*0-8357-5229-1*, 2022009) Bks Demand.

African Buffalo. Lynn Stone. (African Animals Discovery Library). (Illus.). 24p. (J). (gr. k-5). 1990. lib. bdg. 11.94 (*0-86593-052-X*); lib. bdg. 8.95 (*0-685-36344-9*) Rourke Corp.

African Buffalo: A Study of Resource Limitations of Populations. A. R. Sinclair. LC 76-22955. (Wildlife Behavior & Ecology Ser.). (Illus.). 1977. 20.00 (*0-226-76030-8*) U Ch Pr.

African Business Handbook: A Practical Guide to Business Resources for U. S.-Africa Trade & Investment 1993-94. 2nd ed. Michael E. Sudarkasa. 420p. 1993. 35.00 (*0-9638197-0-4*) Twty-Fst Cent.

***African Calliope: A Journey to the Sudan.** Edward Hoagland. 256p. 1995. pap. 14.95 (*1-55821-370-8*) Lyons & Burford.

African Campfire Nights. J. Burger. (Illus.). 192p. 1993. 32.50 (*0-940143-82-8*) Safari Pr.

African Campfires. Stewart E. White. (Illus.). 456p. 1987. reprint ed. 25.00 (*0-935632-44-1*) Wolfe Pub Co.

African Canvas: The Art of West African Women. Margaret Courtney-Clarke. LC 89-24037. (Illus.). 204p. 1990. 60.00 (*0-8478-1166-2*) Rizzoli Intl.

African Capacity Building Initiative: Toward Improved Policy Analysis & Development Management in Sub-Saharan Africa. 64p. (ENG & FRE.). 1991. English. 6.95 (*0-8213-1735-0*, 11736); French. write for info. (*0-8213-1736-9*) World Bank.

African Capitalists in African Development. Ed. by Bruce J. Berman & Colin T. Leys. LC 93-28585. 288p. 1993. lib. bdg. 45.00 (*1-55587-417-7*) Lynne Rienner.

African Catholicism: Essays in Discovery. Adrian Hastings. LC 89-4506. 1989. pap. 14.95 (*0-334-00019-X*) TPI PA.

African Centered Child-Rearing: Hidden Legacy of Black Women. Yuhaayaa L. Kaahena. Ed. by Latifa Ismail. 45p. (Orig.). (C). 1993. pap. 5.00 (*1-883781-05-1*) Yuhaaya.

***African Centered Interdisciplinary Multi Level Hands-on Science.** Bernida Thompson. 293p. Date not set. pap. 75.00 (*0-9632940-2-4*) Roots Act.

African Childhood: Poor Social & Economic Environments. John E. Eberegbulam Njoku. LC 93-10122. (Illus.). 164p. 1993. text ed. 79.95 (*0-7734-9271-2*) E Mellen.

***African Children's & Youth Literature.** Osayimwense Osa. LC 94-44450. (Twayne's World Authors Ser.: Vol. 853). (YA). 1995. lib. bdg. 23.95x (*0-8057-4524-6*, Twayne) Macmillan.

African Christian Spirituality. Ed. by Aylward Shorter. LC 79-23063. 172p. (Orig.). reprint ed. pap. 49.10 (*0-8357-8791-5*, 2033555) Bks Demand.

African Christian Theology: The Quest for Self-hood. K. Gordon Molyneux. LC 93-16622. 432p. 1993. pap. 89.95 (*0-7734-1946-2*) E Mellen.

African Christianity: Patterns of Religious Continuity. Ed. by George D. Bond et al. LC 79-51668. (Studies in Anthropology). 1979. text ed. 63.00 (*0-12-113450-4*) Acad Pr.

***African Cichlids Vol. II: Cichlids from Eastern Africa.** Staeck. 1995. 28.95 (*1-56465-167-3*) Tetra Pr.

African Cichlids of Lakes Malawi & Tanganyika. Herbert R. Axelrod. (Illus.). 224p. 1988. 22.95 (*0-685-62699-7*, PS-703) TFH Pubns.

African Cinema: Politics & Culture. Manthia Diawara. LC 91-24579. (Blacks in the Diaspora Ser.). (Illus.). 208p. 1992. text ed. 29.95 (*0-253-31704-5*); pap. text ed. 10.95 (*0-253-20707-X*, MB-707) Ind U Pr.

African Cities & Towns Before the European Conquest. Richard W. Hull. LC 76-16038. (C). 1977. pap. text ed. 7.95 (*0-393-09166-X*) Norton.

African City. Anthony M. O'Connor. LC 83-10648. (Illus.). 360p. (C). 1983. 32.50 (*0-8419-0881-8*); pap. 17.50 (*0-8419-0882-6*) Holmes & Meier.

African Civilization: The Aksumite Kingdom of Northern Ethiopia. Stuart Munro-Hay. 256p. 1989. 45.00 (*0-7486-0106-6*, Pub. by Edinburgh U Pr UK) Col U Pr.

African Civilization Revisited: From Antiquity to Modern Times. rev. ed. Basil Davidson. LC 88-83120. Orig. Title: The African Past. 460p. (C). 1990. pap. 14.95 (*0-86543-124-8*) Africa World.

African Civilization Revisited: From Antiquity to Modern Times. 2nd rev. ed. Basil Davidson. LC 88-83120. Orig. Title: The African Past. 460p. (C). 1990. 39.95 (*0-86543-123-X*) Africa World.

African Civilizations: Precolonial Cities & States in Tropical Africa - An Archaeological Perspective. Graham Connah. (Illus.). 288p. 1987. pap. 19.95 (*0-521-31992-7*) Cambridge U Pr.

African Colonial State in Comparative Perspective. Crawford Young. LC 94-11020. 384p. 1994. 40.00 (*0-300-05802-0*) Yale U Pr.

African Company Presents Richard III. Carlyle Brown. 1994. pap. 4.75 (*0-8222-1378-8*) Dramatists Play.

African Concept of Life & Death. G. K. Osei. Ed. by Al I. Obaba. (Illus.). 49p. (Orig.). (YA). 1991. pap. text ed. 3.00 (*0-916157-64-4*) African Islam Miss Pubns.

African Condition. Ali A. Mazrui. LC 79-9657. 192p. 1980. 42.95 (*0-521-23265-1*); pap. 14.95 (*0-521-29884-9*) Cambridge U Pr.

***African Conflict Resolution: The U. S. Role in Peacemaking.** David R. Smock & Chester A. Crocker. (Orig.). 1995. pap. text ed. write for info. (*1-878379-00-3*) US Inst Peace.

African Connection: A Study of Black Behavior. Wallace Y. McNair. 150p. (Orig.). (C). 1993. pap. text ed. write for info. (*0-9627600-5-6*) Wstrn Images.

African Cookbook. Bea Sandler. LC 92-37570. 1993. reprint ed. pap. 12.95 (*0-8065-1398-5*) Carol Pub Group.

African Cookery. Annette Merson. LC 86-40283. 80p. (Orig.). 1987. pap. 8.95 (*1-55523-027-X*) Winston-Derek.

African Countries' Foreign Policy. Anatoly Gromyko. 222p. 1983. 25.00 (*0-685-16978-2*, Pub. by Collets UK) Pro-Am Music.

African Country Reports. 20p. (Orig.). 1993. pap. 250.00 (*0-934393-60-5*) Rector Pr.

African Crafts. Judith H. Corwin. LC 90-12493. (Illus.). 48p. (J). (gr. k-4). 1990. lib. bdg. 13.27 (*0-531-10846-5*) Watts.

African Crafts. Jane Kerina. LC 69-18916. (Illus.). (J). (gr. 2-6). 1970. lib. bdg. 13.95 (*0-87460-084-7*) Lion Bks.

African Crisis Areas & U. S. Foreign Policy. Gerald J. Bender et al. 400p. 1985. pap. 16.00 (*0-520-05628-0*) U CA Pr.

African Crossroads. Charles Dundas. LC 76-45443. 242p. 1977. reprint ed. text ed. 59.75 (*0-8371-9089-4*, DUAF, Greenwood Pr) Greenwood.

African Cry. Jean-Marc Ela. Tr. by Robert R. Barr. LC 92-17041. 160p. (Orig.). 1986. pap. 16.95 (*0-88344-259-0*) Orbis Bks.

African Cry. Jean M. Ela. Tr. by Robert R. Barr. LC 86-12429. 160p. (Orig.). reprint ed. pap. 45.60 (*0-8357-8549-1*, 2034870) Bks Demand.

A

An Asterisk (*) at the beginning of an entry indicates that the title is appearing in BIP for the first time.

African Culture: The Rhythms of Unity. Ed. by Molefi K. Asante & Kariamu W. Asante. LC 89-84609. 280p. (C). 1989. pap. 12.95 (*0-86543-134-5*) Africa World.

African Culture: The Rhythms of Unity. Molefi K. Asante & Kariamu W. Asante. LC 84-9015. (Contributions in Afro-American & African Studies: No. 81). (Illus.). x, 270p. 1985. text ed. 55.00 (*0-313-24404-9*, ASA/, Greenwood Pr) Greenwood.

African Culture & the Christian Church: An Introduction to Social & Pastoral Anthropology. Aylward Shorter. LC 73-79481. 241p. reprint ed. pap. 68.70 (*0-8357-5230-5*, 2025114) Bks Demand.

African Custom & Western Law: The Development of the Rhodesian Criminal Law for Africans. Emmet V. Mittlebeeler. LC 73-86268. 250p. (C). 1976. 49.50 (*0-8419-0107-4*, Africana) Holmes & Meier.

African Dance: An Artistic, Historical & Philosophical Inquiry. Ed. by Kariamu Welsh-Asante. 350p. (Orig.). (C). 1994. 49.95 (*0-86543-196-5*); pap. 16.95 (*0-86543-197-3*) Africa World.

African Dawn. Millicent Gordon et al. 352p. 1989. mass mkt. 4.50 (*0-380-75393-6*) Avon.

African Debt & Financing. Ed. by Carol Lancaster & John Williamson. LC 86-7421. (Institute for International Economics. Special Report Ser.: No. 5). 236p. (Orig.). reprint ed. pap. 67.30 (*0-7837-4219-3*, 2043908) Bks Demand.

African Debt Crisis. Trevor Parfitt & Stephen Riley. 256p. 1989. 49.95 (*0-415-00441-1*) Routledge.

African Decameron. Peter Fuchs. Tr. by Robert Meister. 1964. 12.95 (*0-8392-1000-0*) Astor-Honor.

African Decolonization. H. S. Wilson. (Contemporary History Ser.). 224p. 1994. pap. 17.95 (*0-340-55929-2*, B0091, Pub. by E Arnold UK) Routledge Chapman & Hall.

African Desert. Bernard Plossu. LC 87-5021. (Illus.). 91p. 1987. pap. 6.95 (*0-8165-0934-4*) U of Ariz Pr.

African Designs from the Congo, Nigeria, the Cameroons & the Guinea Coast. Caren Caraway. (International Design Library). (Illus.). 144p. (Orig.). 1987. pap. 15.95 (*0-88045-093-2*) Stemmer Hse.

African Designs from Traditional Sources. Geoffrey Williams. LC 76-162027. (Pictorial Archive Ser.). (Illus.). (Orig.). 1971. pap. 6.95 (*0-486-22752-9*) Dover.

African Designs of Guinea Coast. Caren Caraway. (International Design Library). (Illus.). 48p. 1985. pap. 5.95 (*0-88045-064-9*) Stemmer Hse.

African Designs of Nigeria & the Cameroons. Caren Caraway. (International Design Library). (Illus.). 48p. (Orig.). 1984. pap. 5.95 (*0-88045-060-6*) Stemmer Hse.

African Designs of the Congo. Caren Caraway. (International Design Library). (Illus.). 48p. (Orig.). 1986. pap. 5.95 (*0-88045-083-5*) Stemmer Hse.

African Development: Adebayo Adedeji's Alternative Strategies. S. K. Asante. 248p. 1991. 70.00 (*0-905450-49-3*, Pub. by H Zell Pubs UK) Bowker-Saur.

African Development: Lessons from Asia. Aft. by Robert Wade. 240p. (Orig.). (C). 1991. pap. 14.95 (*0-933595-55-7*) Winrock Intl.

African Development & Europe. T. Burley & P. Tregear. 1970. 83.00 (*0-08-006669-0*, Pub. by Pergamon Repr UK) Franklin.

African Development & Policy Issues: Implications for California. (African-American Conferences Ser.). 1982. pap. 3.00 (*0-89192-355-1*) Interbk Inc.

***African Development Handbook.** 700p. (Orig.). 1994. pap. 195.00 (*0-7605-0989-1*) Rector Pr.

African Development Indicators. United Nations Development Programme & World Bank Staff. 377p. 1992. 21.95 (*0-8213-2044-0*, 12044) World Bank.

***African Development Indicators 1994-95.** 420p. 1995. 24.95 (*0-8213-3127-2*, 13127) World Bank.

African Development, OAU-ECA & Lagos Plan of Action. Ed. by Ralph A. Onwuka et al. LC 85-70677. (Illus.). 242p. 1985. 21.50 (*0-931494-58-3*); pap. 12.50 (*0-931494-57-5*) Brunswick Pub.

***African Development Perspectives Vol. 2, Vol. 2.** (C). 1994. pap. text ed. 67.50 (*3-89473-234-2*) Westview.

African Diary. Naka Pillman. LC 89-42868. 304p. 1990. 18.95 (*0-937552-31-3*) Quail Ridge.

African Diaspora. Heywood-Howard University Staff. 1991. 22.00 (*0-536-57585-1*) Ginn Pr.

African Diaspora: Interpretive Essays. Ed. by Martin L. Kilson & Robert I. Rotberg. LC 75-30643. 523p. reprint ed. pap. 150.00 (*0-7837-2287-7*, 2057375) Bks Demand.

African Diaspora & the Black Experience in New World Slavery. Okon Uya. 320p. 1992. 35.95 (*0-89388-224-0*); pap. 19.95 (*0-89388-225-9*) Okpaku Communications.

African Dilemma Tales. Ed. by William R. Bascom. (World Anthropology Ser.). xiv, 162p. 1975. 26.95 (*90-279-7509-4*) Mouton.

African Divination Systems: Ways of Knowing. Ed. by Philip M. Peek. LC 90-39421. (African Systems of Thought Ser.). (Illus.). 240p. 1991. 35.00 (*0-253-34309-7*); pap. 14.95 (*0-253-20653-7*, MB-653) Ind U Pr.

African Dream: Themes & Images of John Muafangejo. Orde Levinson. LC 92-70865. (Illus.). 120p. 1993. pap. 14.95 (*0-500-27682-X*) Thames Hudson.

African Economic Handbook. 350p. 1986. 90.00 (*0-86338-088-3*, Pub. by Euromonitor Pubns UK) Gale.

African Economic History: Internal Development & External Dependency. Ralph A. Austen. LC 86-25639. x, 294p. (Orig.). 1987. pap. text ed. 25.00 (*0-435-08017-2*, 08017) Heinemann.

African Economic Reform: The External Dimension. Carol Lancaster. LC 91-21933. (Policy Analysis in International Economics Ser.: No. 33). (Illus.). 82p. 1991. pap. 10.00 (*0-88132-096-X*) Inst Intl Eco.

African Education & Identity: Proceedings of the 5th Session of the International Congress of African Studies, Held at Ibadan, December, 1985. Ed. by Abiola Irele. LC 92-11213. 448p. 1992. 100.00 (*0-905450-81-7*, Pub. by H Zell Pubs UK) Bowker-Saur.

African Elephant. Alison Tibbitts & Alan Roocroft. (Animals, Animals, Animals Ser.). (Illus.). 32p. (J). (ps-2). 1992. lib. bdg. 12.95 (*1-56065-100-8*) Capstone Pr.

African Elephant: Last Days of Eden. Boyd Norton. (Illus.). 128p. 1991. 29.95 (*0-89658-158-6*) Voyageur Pr.

African Elephant: Twilight in Eden. Roger L. DiSilvestro. 224p. 1991. text ed. 34.95 (*0-471-53207-X*) Wiley.

***African Elephants.** Roland Smith. LC 94-34313. (Early Bird Nature Bks.). (J). 1995. 18.95 (*0-8225-3006-6*, Lerner Publctns) Lerner Group.

African Elephants. Eduard Zingg. Ed. by Bob Italia. LC 93-3699. 40p. (J). (gr. 5 up). 1993. lib. bdg. 14.96 (*1-56239-216-6*) Abdo & Dghtrs.

African Elephants: Giants of the Land. Dorothy H. Patent. LC 91-55028. (Illus.). 40p. (J). (gr. 3-7). 1991. lib. bdg. 14.95 (*0-8234-0911-2*) Holiday.

African Elephants & Rhinos: Status Survey & Conservation Action Plan. D. H. Cumming et al. (Illus.). 72p. (Orig.). 1990. pap. 15.00 (*2-88032-975-2*, Pub. by IUCN SZ) Island Pr.

African Elite: The Big Men of a Small Town. Joan Vincent. LC 79-132691. (Illus.). 1973. text ed. 50.00 (*0-231-03353-2*); pap. text ed. 19.50 (*0-231-08332-7*) Col U Pr.

African Emigres in the United States: A Missing Link in Africa's Social & Economic Development. Kofi K. Apraku. LC 90-24130. 192p. 1991. text ed. 49.95 (*0-275-93799-2*, C3799, Praeger Pubs) Greenwood.

African Encounter: A Selected Bibliography of Books, Films, & Other Materials for Promoting an Understanding of Africa among Young Adults. American Library Association, Young Adult Services Division Staff. LC 63-22444. 80p. reprint ed. pap. 25.00 (*0-8357-5231-3*, 2001782) Bks Demand.

African Encounters with Domesticity. Ed. by Karen T. Hansen. LC 91-32144. 325p. (C). 1992. text ed. 42.00 (*0-8135-1803-2*); pap. text ed. 16.00 (*0-8135-1804-0*) Rutgers U Pr.

African Energy Policies. AFREPREN Staff. LC 89-48786. (Illus.). 192p. (C). 1990. text ed. 49.95 (*0-86232-912-4*, Pub. by Zed Books UK); pap. 19.95 (*0-86232-913-2*, Pub. by Zed Books UK) Humanities.

African-English, English-African Dictionary. A. Coetzee. 39.50 (*0-87559-000-4*); 44.50 (*0-87559-001-2*) Shalom.

African English Literature. Ed. by Anne Tibble. 1969. pap. 7.95 (*0-8079-0139-3*) October.

African Entrepreneurs: Pioneers of Development. Keith Marsden. (IFC Discussion Paper Ser.: No. 9). 76p. 1990. English. pap. 7.95 (*0-8213-1693-1*, 11693); French. pap. 7.95 (*0-8213-1782-2*, 11782) World Bank.

African Environment: Problems & Perspectives. Ed. by Paul Richards & Nicola Harris. LC 76-371759. (African Environment: Special Report Ser.: Vol. 1). 131p. reprint ed. pap. 37.40 (*0-8357-5232-1*, 2055389) Bks Demand.

African Environments & Resources. L. A. Lewis & L. Berry. (Illus.). 352p. 1988. 49.95 (*0-04-916010-9*); pap. 19.95 (*0-04-916011-7*) Routledge Chapman & Hall.

African Exchange: Toward a Biological History of Black People. Ed. by Kenneth F. Kiple. LC 87-30333. (Illus.). vi, 280p. (C). 1988. lib. bdg. 39.50 (*0-8223-0731-6*) Duke.

African Experience. Roland Oliver. (Illus.). 304p. 1992. pap. 15.00 (*0-06-430218-0*, PL) HarpC.

African Experience, Vol. 3-A, Bibliography. Ed. by John N. Paden & Edward W. Soja. LC 70-98466. reprint ed. pap. 120.00 (*0-8357-5233-X*, 2016720) Bks Demand.

African Experience, Vol. 3-B, Guide to Resources. Ed. by John N. Paden & Edward W. Soja. LC 70-98466. 149p. reprint ed. pap. 42.50 (*0-8357-5234-8*) Bks Demand.

African Experience: An Education Officer in North Rhodesia (Zambia). T. E. Dorman. 240p. (C). 1993. text ed. 39.50 (*1-85043-568-5*, Pub. by I B Tauris UK) St Martin.

African Experience: An Introduction. Vincent Khapoya. LC 93-29596. 1993. pap. text ed. 18.00 (*0-13-019662-2*) P-H.

African Experience: Volume 3B, Guide to Resources. Ed. by John N. Paden & Edward W. Soja. 141p. 1970. 35.00 (*0-89771-005-3*) St Mut.

African Experience in Community Development: The Continuing Struggle in Africa & the Americas, Vol. 1. Ed. by Edward Crosby et al. 420p. (Orig.). (C). 1981. pap. text ed. 18.95 (*0-89894-025-7*) Advocate Pub Group.

African Experience in Literature & Ideology. Abiola Irele. LC 89-24586. 234p. 1990. 29.95 (*0-253-33124-2*); pap. 12.95 (*0-253-20569-7*, MB-569) Ind U Pr.

African Explains Apartheid. Jordan K. Ngubane. LC 75-35338. (Illus.). 243p. 1977. reprint ed. text ed. 59.75 (*0-8371-8565-3*, NGAE, Greenwood Pr) Greenwood.

African External Finance in the 1990s: A World Bank Symposium. Ed. by Ishrat Husain & John Underwood. 200p. 1991. 16.95 (*0-8213-1926-4*, 11926) World Bank.

***African Fables.** Helen Palmer. 1995. 10.95 (*0-8062-5074-7*) Carlton.

African Farmers in Rhodesia: Old & New Peasant Communities in Karangaland. A. K. Weinrich. LC 75-319028. 360p. reprint ed. pap. 102.60 (*0-8357-6978-X*, 2039038) Bks Demand.

African Fever: A Study of British Science, Technology, & Politics in West Africa, 1787-1864. Dennis G. Carlson. LC 81-5621. 1984. 15.95 (*0-88202-196-6*) Watson Pub Intl.

African Finance: Research & Reform. Ed. by Lawrence White. 1993. 34.95 (*1-55815-274-1*); pap. 15.95 (*1-55815-275-X*) ICS Pr.

African Folk. Ed. by Wolfgang Hageney. (Graphic Spirit of Native Designs Ser.). (Illus.). 112p. (Orig.). 1993. pap. 24.95 (*88-7070-196-4*) Belvedere USA.

***African Folktales.** (Tell Tale Theater Pop-up Bks. & Story Tape). (Illus.). 12p. 1995. digital audio, pap. 12.95 (*1-56138-501-8*) Running Pr.

African Folktales. Paul Radin. LC 74-106800. (Bollingen Ser., Vol. 32). 338p. (Orig.). reprint ed. 96.40 (*0-8357-9491-1*, 2013034) Bks Demand.

African Folktales. Ed. by Paul Radin. LC 82-10475. 344p. (Orig.). 1987. reprint ed. pap. 14.95 (*0-8052-0732-5*) Schocken.

African Folktales: Traditional Stories of the Black World. Ed. by Roger D. Abrahams. LC 83-2474. (Fairy Tale & Folklore Library). 384p. 1983. pap. 16.00 (*0-394-72117-9*) Pantheon.

African Folktales in the New World. William R. Bascom. LC 91-46789. (Folkloristics Ser.). (Illus.). 272p. 1992. 35.00 (*0-253-31128-4*); pap. 14.95 (*0-253-20736-3*) Ind U Pr.

African Folktales with Foreign Analogues. May A. Klipple. LC 91-37764. (Folklore Library: Vol. 3). 514p. 1992. 77.00 (*0-8240-7147-6*, H1287) Garland.

African Food Systems in Crisis, Pt. 1: Microperspectives. Ed. by Rebecca Huss-Ashmore & Solomon H. Katz. 350p. 1989. text ed. 59.00 (*2-88124-306-1*); pap. text ed. 30.00 (*2-88124-332-0*) Gordon & Breach.

African Foundations of Judaism & Christianity. E. Curtis Alexander. LC 84-48679. (Alkelbulan Historical Research Society Monograph Ser.: No. 3). 84p. (Orig.). 1985. pap. 6.95 (*0-938818-08-2*) ECA Assoc.

African Frontier: The Reproduction of Traditional African Societies. Ed. by Igor Kopytoff. LC 85-45468. (Illus.). 296p. 1986. 35.00 (*0-253-30252-8*); pap. 12.95 (*0-253-20539-5*, MB-539) Ind U Pr.

African Fundamentalism: A Literary & Cultural Anthology of Garvey's Harlem Renaissance. Tony Martin. (New Marcus Garvey Library: No. 5). (Illus.). xviii, 363p. (Orig.). (C). 1991. pap. text ed. 14.95 (*0-912469-09-9*) Majority Pr.

African Furniture & Household Objects. Roy Sieber. LC 79-5340. (Illus.). 279p. reprint ed. pap. 79.60 (*0-8357-5235-6*, 2056719) Bks Demand.

***African Game-Lands: A Grahic Itinerary in Kenya & along the Livingstone Trail in Tanganyika, Belgian Congo & Angola, 1929.** Prentiss N. Gray. Ed. by Theodore J. Holsten, Jr. & Susan C. Reneau. (Illus.). 200p. 1995. 39.95 (*0-940864-23-1*) Boone & Crockett.

African Game Trails. Theodore Roosevelt, Jr. (Peter Capstick Library). (Illus.). 620p. 1988. 19.95 (*0-312-02151-8*) St Martin.

African Genesis. Leo Frobenius & Douglas C. Fox. LC 66-29780. (Illus.). 1972. 23.95 (*0-405-08539-7*, Pub. by Blom Pubns UK) Ayer.

African Genius: An Introduction to Social & Cultural History. Basil Davidson. (Illus.). 1970. pap. 13.95 (*0-316-17432-7*) Little.

African Geology Reviews. Ed. by P. Bowden & J. Kinnaird. (Geological Journals: Vol. 22, Winter Thematic Issue 1987). 592p. reprint ed. pap. 168.80 (*0-7837-3223-6*, 2043240) Bks Demand.

African Glory. J. C. Degraft-Johnson. 210p. 1986. reprint ed. pap. text ed. 14.95 (*0-933121-03-2*) Black Classic.

African Gold Ornament Designs: The International Design Library. Diane V. Horn. (Illus.). 48p. (Orig.). 1992. pap. 5.95 (*0-88045-124-6*) Stemmer Hse.

African Gray Parrots. Annette Wolter. (Illus.). 64p. (J). (gr. 4 up). 1987. pap. 5.95 (*0-8120-3773-1*) Barron.

African Grey Parrots. Al David. (Illus.). 128p. 1989. 14.95 (*0-86622-957-4*, TS-111) TFH Pubns.

African Grey Parrots. E. J. Mulawka. (Illus.). 128p. 19.95 (*0-86622-975-2*, PS-780) TFH Pubns.

African Grey Parrots. Paul R. Paradise. (Illus.). 1979. 9.95 (*0-86622-721-0*, KW-018) TFH Pubns.

African Grey Parrots As a Hobby. H. Pinter. (Illus.). 96p. 1994. pap. 7.95 (*0-7938-0093-5*, TT036) TFH Pubns.

African Hairstyles: Styles of Yesterday & Today. Esi Sagay. (Illus.). 108p. (Orig.). 1983. pap. 16.50 (*0-435-89830-2*) Heinemann.

African Healer: I Want to Say Another Story. Ed. by Julianna Freehand. Tr. by Howell Wechsler. (Maddo Pandanzyla's Stories Ser.). (Illus.). (Orig.). (J). (gr. k-8). 1994. teacher ed 35.00 (*0-9605700-9-8*); pap. text ed. 22.00 (*0-9605700-7-1*) Lifeline Res.

***African Healer: I Want to Say Another Story.** Ed. by Julianna Freehand. Tr. by Howell Wechsler. (Maddo Pandanzyla's Stories Ser.). (Illus.). (J). (gr. k-8). 1994. pap. 9.50 (*0-9605700-8-X*) Lifeline Res.

African Health & Healing Systems: Proceedings of a Symposium. Ed. by P. Stanley Yoder. 252p. 1982. 30.00 (*0-918456-34-7*, Crossroads) African Studies Assn.

African Heritage. Stanley H. Barkan & Raymond R. Patterson. 1991. boxed 75.00 (*0-89304-947-6*); boxed 50.00 (*0-89304-976-X*) Cross-Cultrl NY.

African Heritage. P. J. Larkin. 64p. (C). 1988. 50.00 (*0-685-33811-8*, Pub. by S Thornes Pubs UK) St Mut.

African Heritage. rev. ed. P. J. Larkin. (Illus.). 64p. 1980. pap. 10.95 (*0-7175-0613-4*) Dufour.

African Heritage in Black American Churches. Kisa Djawotho & Peter K. Quansah. LC 93-78754. (Illus.). 120p. (Orig.). 1994. pap. 6.95 (*0-9637667-0-8*) Int Christ Assn.

African Heritage of American English. Joseph E. Holloway & Winifred K. Vass. LC 92-18270. 240p. 1993. 24.95 (*0-253-32838-1*) Ind U Pr.

African Heritage Study Bible. Ed. by James Peebles. 2048p. 1993. 39.99 (*0-529-10067-3*) World Bible.

African Heritage Study Bible: King James Version. Ed. & Intro. by Cain H. Felder. (Illus.). 2200p. 1993. boxed 42.50 (*1-55523-371-6*) Winston-Derek.

***African Heritage Study Bible: King James Version.** Ed. & Intro. by Cain H. Felder. (Illus.). 2200p. 1993. pap. 32.00 (*1-55523-711-8*) Winston-Derek.

***African Heritage Study Bible: King James Version, Black Bonded Leather.** deluxe ed. Ed. & Intro. by Cain H. Felder. (Illus.). 2200p. 1993. 59.95 (*1-55523-674-X*) Winston-Derek.

African Heritage Study Bible: King James Version, Black Leatherette. Ed. & Intro. by Cain H. Felder. (Illus.). 2200p. 1993. Black leatherette. 44.50 (*1-55523-373-2*) Winston-Derek.

***African Heritage Study Bible: King James Version, Burgundy Bonded Leather.** deluxe ed. Ed. & Intro. by Cain H. Felder. (Illus.). 2200p. 1993. 59.95 (*1-55523-675-8*) Winston-Derek.

***African Heritage Study Bible: King James Version, Burgundy Leatherette.** deluxe ed. Ed. & Intro. by Cain H. Felder. (Illus.). 2200p. 1993. 45.50 (*1-55523-372-4*) Winston-Derek.

African Heroes & Heroines. Carter G. Woodson. (Illus.). (YA). 1990. 12.95 (*0-87498-077-1*); pap. 9.95 (*0-87498-076-3*) Assoc Pubs DC.

African Historical Religions: A Conceptual & Ethical Foundation for Western Religions. E. Curtis Alexander. LC 83-83096. (Alkelbulan Historical Research Society Monograph Ser.: No. 2). (Illus.). 70p. 1984. pap. 6.95 (*0-938818-05-8*) ECA Assoc.

African Historical Studies. E. A. Avandele. 314p. 1979. 35.00 (*0-7146-2942-1*, Pub. by F Cass Pubs UK) Intl Spec Bk.

African Historiography: Essays in Honour of Jacob Ade Ajayi. Ed. by Toyin Faldla. 256p. (C). 1993. text ed. 76.95 (*0-582-07935-7*, 76450) Longman.

African History. Ed. by Philip D. Curtin et al. 612p. (C). 1978. pap. text ed. 27.95 (*0-582-64663-4*, 74644) Longman.

African History. 2nd ed. Philip Curtin et al. LC 93-47290. (C). 1995. text ed. 79.95 (*0-582-05071-5*, 74644, Pub. by Longman UK) Longman.

African History. 2nd ed. Ed. by Daniel Smith. (Selected Course Outlines in History from American Colleges & Universities Ser.). 298p. 1993. pap. text ed. 16.95 (*1-55876-063-6*) Wiener Pubs Inc.

African History - Text & Readings, Vol. I: Western Africa. Robert O. Collins. LC 89-70619. (Topics in World History Ser.). (Illus.). 220p. (Orig.). (C). 1990. pap. text ed. 16.95 (*1-55876-015-6*) Wiener Pubs Inc.

African History - Text & Readings, Vol. II: Eastern Africa. Robert O. Collins. LC 89-70615. (Topics in World History Ser.). 260p. (Orig.). (C). 1991. 16.95 (*1-55876-016-4*) Wiener Pubs Inc.

African History - Text & Readings, Vol. III: Central & South Africa. Robert O. Collins. LC 89-70617. (Topics in World History Ser.). 240p. 1990. pap. text ed. 16.95 (*1-55876-017-2*) Wiener Pubs Inc.

African History & Culture. Ed. by Richard Olaniyan. (Illus.). 259p. (Orig.). (C). 1982. pap. text ed. 23.95 (*0-582-64369-4*, 74594) Longman.

African History & Literatures. Harvard University Library Staff. LC 70-128716. (Widener Library Shelflist: No. 34). 1990. 37.50 (*0-674-00780-8*) HUP.

African History for Beginners, Part 1: African Dawn - A Diasporan View. Herb Boyd. (Writers & Readers Documentary Comic Bks.). (Illus.). 176p. (Orig.). 1991. pap. 7.95 (*0-86316-144-8*) Writers & Readers.

African History in Maps. Kwamena-Poh et al. LC 81-675343. (Illus.). 76p. (Orig.). (C). 1984. pap. text ed. 18.50 (*0-582-60331-5*, 74486) Longman.

African History On File. Diagram Group Staff. LC 93-10078. (Illus.). 288p. 1993. 155.00 (*0-8160-2910-5*) Facts on File.

African Holistic Health. rev. ed. Llaila O. Afrika. Ed. by T. Nokwari Adesegun. (Illus.). 300p. 1989. pap. 14.95 (*1-877610-00-3*) Sea Island.

African Holistic Health. Llaila O. Afrika. 418p. 1993. reprint ed. pap. text ed. write for info. (*1-881316-71-8*) A&B Bks.

African Honey Bee. David J. Fletcher & Michael D. Breed. Ed. by Marla Spivak. 435p. (C). 1991. text ed. 83.00 (*0-8133-7209-7*) Westview.

African Hunter. Bror Von Blixen-Finecke. Tr. by F. H. Lyon. (Peter Capstick Library). (Illus.). 304p. 1985. 15.95 (*0-312-00959-3*) St Martin.

African Husbandman. William Allan. LC 75-17188. (Illus.). 505p. 1977. reprint ed. text ed. 55.00 (*0-8371-8287-5*, ALAH, Greenwood Pr) Greenwood.

***African Icons of Power: An Illustrated Curriculum Guide.** Bowers Museum of Cultural Art Staff. Ed. by Daniella B. Walsh. 84p. (J). (gr. k-12). 1994. pap. text ed. write for info. (*0-9633959-2-0*) Bowers Mus.

African Identity in Crisis. R. Osoro. (African Identity, Negation Freedom Ser.). (C). 1993. pap. text ed. 17.95 (*0-9636956-0-6*) Bayana Pubs.

African Images: Art & Ornament. (Illus.). 68p. 1981. pap. 5.00 (*0-912303-23-9*) Michigan Mus.

African in America. Lemuel E. Bentley. LC 76-20830. (Illus.). 72p. 1976. 5.00 (*0-686-27414-8*) Du Sable Mus.

African in Greenland. large type ed. Tete-Michel Kpomassie. (Illus.). 496p. 1986. 15.95 (*0-7089-1461-6*) Ulverscroft.

African in Me. Howard Gordon. LC 92-21535. 176p. 1993. 19.95 (*0-8076-1296-0*) Braziller.

African in Paris. Bernard B. Dadie. Tr. by Karen C. Hatch. LC 93-30915. 136p. (ENG.). 1994. 27.95 (*0-252-02040-5*) U of Ill Pr.

An Asterisk (*) at the beginning of an entry indicates that the title is appearing in BIP for the first time.

African Placenames: Origins & Meanings of the Names for over 2000 Natural Features, Towns, Cities, Provinces & Countries. Adrian Room. LC 93-40261. 245p. 1994. lib. bdg. 49.95 (*0-89950-943-6*) McFarland & Co.

African Poetry of the Living Dead: Igbo Masquerade Poetry. Romanus N. Egudu. LC 92-26780. 1992. 89.95 (*0-7734-9170-8*) E Mellen.

African Poison Murders. large type ed. Elspeth Huxley. (Mainstream Ser.). 312p. 1988. reprint ed. lib. bdg. 9.47 (*1-85089-209-1*, Pub. by ISIS UK) Transaction Pubs.

African Policies of Gabriel Hanotaux, 1894-1898. Alf A. Heggoy. LC 78-145888. 169p. reprint ed. pap. 48.20 (*0-8357-5239-9*, 2031146) Bks Demand.

African Policy in the Eighties. Ed. by Margaret Noviki. (African-American Conferences Ser.). 40p. (Orig.). 1984. pap. 5.00 (*0-89192-387-X*) Interbk Inc.

African Political Facts since Nineteen Forty-Five. 2nd ed. Chris Cook & David Killingray. 272p. 1990. lib. bdg. 35.00 (*0-8160-2418-9*) Facts on File.

***African Political Leadership.** Assensoh. (Anvil Ser.). 1996. pap. text ed. write for info. (*0-89464-911-6*) Krieger.

African Political Systems. Ed. by M. Fortes & Sir Edward Evans-Prichard. 305p. (C). 1994. pap. 25.50 (*0-7103-0245-2*, Pub. by Kegan Paul Intl UK) Routledge Chapman & Hall.

African Politics: Crises & Challenges. J. Gus Liebenow. LC 85-45469. (Illus.). 320p. 1986. 35.00 (*0-253-30275-7*); pap. 12.95 (*0-253-20388-0*, MB-388) Ind U Pr.

African Politics & British Policy in the Gold Coast 1868-1900: A Study in the Forms & Force of Protest. Francis Agbodeka. LC 73-175916. (Legon History Ser.). 218p. reprint ed. 62.20 (*0-8357-9446-6*, 2015285) Bks Demand.

African Politics & Problems in Development. Richard L. Sklar & C. S. Whitaker. LC 90-49540. 374p. 1991. lib. bdg. 45.00 (*1-55587-244-1*) Lynne Rienner.

African Polyphony & Polyrhythm: Musical Structure & Methodology. Simha Arom. Tr. by Raymond Boyd et al. (Illus.). 672p. (C). 1991. 155.00 (*0-521-24160-X*) Cambridge U Pr.

African Poor: A History. John Iliffe. (African Studies: No. 58). 400p. 1987. pap. 27.95 (*0-521-34877-3*) Cambridge U Pr.

***African Popular Theatre: From Precolonial Times to the Present Day.** David Kerr. LC 95-10210. (Studies in African Literature). 1995. write for info. (*0-435-08967-6*); pap. write for info. (*0-435-08969-2*) Heinemann.

African Population & Capitalism: Historical Perspectives. Ed. by Dennis D. Cordell & Joel W. Gregory. LC 93-39164. 1994. 40.00 (*0-299-14270-1*); pap. 17.95 (*0-299-14274-4*) U of Wis Pr.

African Portraits. Dorothy Hoobler & Thomas Hoobler. LC 92-17284. (Images Across the Ages Ser.). (Illus.). 96p. (J). (gr. 7-8). 1992. lib. bdg. 24.26 (*0-8114-6378-8*) Raintree Steck-V.

***African Prayer Book.** Desmond Tutu. 1995. 15.00 (*0-385-47730-9*) Doubleday.

African Preacher: An Authentic Narrative. William S. White. LC 72-3105. (Black Heritage Library Collection). 1977. reprint ed. 16.95 (*0-8369-9092-7*) Ayer.

African Presence in Early America. Ivan Van Sertima. 250p. 1987. pap. 12.50 (*0-88738-715-2*) Transaction Pubs.

African Presence in Early Asia. rev. ed. Ivan Van Sertima. Ed. by Runoko Rashidi. 224p. 1987. pap. 15.00 (*0-88738-717-9*) Transaction Pubs.

African Presence in Early Europe. Ed. by Ivan Van Sertima. 260p. 1986. pap. 12.50 (*0-88738-664-4*) Transaction Pubs.

African Presence in the Americas: 1492-1992. (Illus.). 1992. ring bd. 85.00 (*0-685-65642-X*) NY Pub Lib.

African Press. Martin Ochs. 155p. 1987. pap. 17.50 (*977-424-128-2*, Pub. by Am Univ Cairo Pr UA) Col U Pr.

***African Pride: From the Other Side.** Nilene O. Foxworth. (Illus.). 132p. 1994. pap. text ed. 10.75 (*0-9644137-0-1*) NOA Intl.

African Princess. large type ed. Princess Elizabeth of Toro. 464p. 1985. 15.95 (*0-7089-1336-9*) Ulverscroft.

African Professional Women in Agriculture: An Analysis of Two Roundtable Discussions. Cheryl R. Doss. (Development Studies Paper). 22p. (Orig.). 1991. pap. 6.00 (*0-933595-58-1*) Winrock Intl.

African Proverbs. 1962. 7.99 (*0-88088-025-2*) Peter Pauper.

African Psychology: Toward its Reclamation, Reascension & Revitalization. Wade W. Nobles. 134p. 1986. 10.00 (*0-939205-02-5*) Blk Fam Inst Pub.

***African Psychology in Historical Perspective.** Ed. by Azibo. Date not set. per. 14.95 (*0-86543-293-7*) Africa World.

African Pygmies. Ed. by Luigi L. Cavalli-Sforza. 1986. pap. text ed. 70.00 (*0-12-164481-2*) Acad Pr.

African Queen. large type ed. C. S. Forester. LC 94-13169. 1994. 19.95 (*0-8161-7459-8*) Hall.

African Queen. C. S. Forester. 316p. 1992. reprint ed. lib. bdg. 21.95 (*0-89966-903-4*) Buccaneer Bks.

African Queen. C. S. Forester. 1984. reprint ed. pap. 11.95 (*0-316-28910-8*) Little.

African Queen. C. S. Forester. 136p. 1977. reprint ed. lib. bdg. 24.95 (*0-89244-065-1*) Queens Hse-Focus Serv.

African Quest for Freedom & Identity: Cameroonian Writing & the National Experience. Richard Bjornson. LC 90-39423. (Illus.). 528p. 1994. text ed. 29.95 (*0-253-31194-2*) Ind U Pr.

***African Quest for Freedom & Identity: Cameroonian Writing & the National Experience.** Richard Bjornson. LC 90-39423. (Illus.). 528p. 1994. reprint ed. pap. 18.95 (*0-253-20908-0*) Ind U Pr.

African Question Collection. Linda Schwartz. 120p. (J). (gr. 4-8). 1994. 7.95 (*0-88160-264-7*, LW228) Learning Wks.

African Reactions to Missionary Education. Edward H. Berman. LC 74-22497. (Publications of the Center for Education in Africa). 255p. reprint ed. pap. 72.70 (*0-8357-5240-2*, 2030137) Bks Demand.

African Recipes: Liberian Cookbook. Selena H. Hoffman. 65p. (Orig.). 1990. pap. 11.50 (*0-910363-07-2*) EBONICS.

African Reflections: Art from Northeastern Zaire. Enid Schildkrout & Curtis Keim. LC 90-11990. (Illus.). 272p. 1990. 50.00 (*0-295-96961-X*) U of Wash Pr.

African Reflections: Art from Northeastern Zaire. Enid Schildkrout & Curtis Keim. LC 90-11990. (Illus.). 272p. (C). 1993. pap. 29.95 (*0-295-96962-8*) U of Wash Pr.

African Refugees. Ed. by Howard Adelman & John Sorenson. 225p. (C). 1994. text ed. 52.50 (*0-8133-8460-5*) Westview.

African Refugees: Reflections on the African Refugee Problem. Gaim Kibreab. LC 84-81772. 140p. (C). 1985. 25.00 (*0-86543-006-3*); pap. 7.95 (*0-86543-007-1*) Africa World.

African Refugees & Human Rights in Host Countries: The Long Term Demographic, Environmental, Economic, Social, & Psychological Impacts of Angolan Refugees in Zambia. Nsolo J. Mijere. 1994. 16.95 (*0-533-10621-4*) Vantage.

African Religions: A Symposium. Newell S. Booth. LC 73-88062. 390p. 1977. text ed. 21.50 (*0-88357-012-2*) NOK Pubs.

African Religions: Symbol, Ritual & Community. Benjamin C. Ray. 1975. pap. text ed. write for info. (*0-13-018622-8*) P-H.

African Religions & Philosophy. 2nd ed. John S. Mbiti. LC 89-48596. 288p. (C). 1990. pap. 21.50 (*0-435-89591-5*, 89591) Heinemann.

African Religions in European Scholarship. Okot P'Bitek. (African Heritage Classical Research Studies). 140p. reprint ed. 15.00 (*0-938818-29-5*) ECA Assoc.

African Responses. Mokwugo Okoye. 420p. 1987. 40.00 (*0-7223-0018-2*, Pub. by A H S Ltd UK) St Mut.

African Rhapsody: Short Stories of the Contemporary African Experience. Ed. by Nadezda Obradovic. LC 93-21132. 1994. 12.95 (*0-385-46816-4*, Anchor NY) Doubleday.

African Rhinoceros. Mary L. Samuelson & Gloria Schlaepfer. LC 91-40953. (Remarkable Animals Ser.). (Illus.). 60p. (J). (gr. 4 up). 1992. text ed., lib. bdg. 13.95 (*0-87518-505-3*, Dillon Silver Burdett) Silver Burdett Pr.

African Rhinos. Carl R. Green & William R. Sanford. (Wildlife Habits & Habitats Ser.). (Illus.). 48p. (J). (gr. 5). 1987. text ed., lib. bdg. 12.95 (*0-89686-327-1*, Crstwood Hse) Silver Burdett Pr.

***African Rhythm: A Northern Ewe Perspective.** Kofi Agawu. (Illus.). 250p. (C). 1995. write for info. (*0-521-48084-1*) Cambridge U Pr.

African Rhythm & African Sensibility: Aesthetics & Social Action in African Musical Idioms. John M. Chernoff. LC 79-189. xviii, 262p. 1981. lib. bdg. 15.00 (*0-226-10346-3*) U Ch Pr.

African Rhythm & African Sensibility: Aesthetics & Social Action in African Musical Idioms. John M. Chernoff. LC 79-189. xviii, 262p. 1981. pap. 13.95 (*0-226-10345-5*) U Ch Pr.

African Rifles & Cartridges. Taylor. LC 80-82384. 35.00 (*0-88227-013-3*) Gun Room.

***African Rifles & Cartridges.** J. Taylor. (Illus.). 430p. 1994. 35.00 (*1-57157-009-8*) Safari Pr.

African River Basin Development. Thayer Scudder. 192p. (C). 1929. pap. text ed. 25.00 (*0-8133-7790-0*) Westview.

African Roots. Comp. by Jerry Silverman. (Traditional Black Music Ser.). (Illus.). 64p. (YA). (gr. 5 up). 1994. lib. bdg. 15.95 (*0-7910-1828-8*, Am Art Analog); pap. 9.95 (*0-7910-1844-X*, Am Art Analog) Chelsea Hse.

***African Roots: Towards an Afrocentric Christian Witness.** Ed. by Michael I. Dash et al. (Illus.). (Orig.). (C). 1994. pap. text ed. 14.95 (*0-913491-39-X*) SCP Third.

African Roots in Britain. Imekada J. Alleyne. 1994. pap. 4.95 (*0-86543-425-5*) Africa World.

African Rural-Urban Migration: The Movement to Ghana's Towns. John C. Caldwell. LC 69-17496. 257p. 1969. text ed. 40.50 (*0-231-03269-2*) Col U Pr.

African Safari. Richard Brightfield. (Young Indiana Jones Chronicles Ser.: No. 5). (J). (gr. 4-7). 1993. pap. 3.25 (*0-553-29953-0*) Bantam.

African Safari. Moira Butterfield. (Wildlife World Ser.). (Illus.). 16p. (Orig.). (J). (gr. 1-4). 1994. pap. 7.95 (*1-57102-010-1*, Ideals Child) Hambleton-Hill.

African Safari: The Complete Travel Guide to 10 Top Game Viewing Countries. Mark W. Nolting. LC 87-8481. (Illus.). 256p. (Orig.). 1987. pap. 15.95 (*0-939895-00-5*) Global Travel Pubs.

African Saga. Blaise Cendrars. Tr. by Margery Bianco. LC 75-97359. 378p. 1969. reprint ed. text ed. 35.00 (*0-8371-2419-0*, CEA&, Negro U Pr) Greenwood.

African Savanna: Synthesis of the Nylsvley Study. R. J. Scholes & B. H. Walker. LC 92-46453. (Studies in Applied Ecology & Resource Management). (Illus.). 300p. (C). 1993. 69.95 (*0-521-41971-9*) Cambridge U Pr.

African Sayings. Issy K. Tindimwebwa. 66p. 1982. 6.95 (*0-9607296-0-7*); pap. 4.95 (*0-9607296-1-5*) Akili Bks of Amer.

African Sculpture. Ladislas Segy. 1975. pap. 7.95 (*0-486-20396-4*) Dover.

African Sculpture from the Collection of the Society of African Missions. 48p. 1980. 10.00 (*0-317-93947-5*) Arden Assocs.

African Sculpture from the University Museum. Allen Wardwell. LC 86-22489. (Illus.). 152p. 1986. pap. 14.95 (*0-87633-067-7*) Phila Mus Art.

African Sculpture Speaks. 4th rev. ed. Ladislas Segy. LC 75-14323. (Art History Paperbacks). (Illus.). 360p. 1975. pap. 17.95 (*0-306-80018-7*) Da Capo.

***African Seats.** Ed. by Sandro Bocola. (Illus.). 208p. 1995. 60.00 (*3-7913-1426-2*, Pub. by Prestel) TeNeues.

African Short Stories. Ed. by Chinua Achebe & C. L. Innes. (African Writers Ser.). 159p. (Orig.). (C). 1988. pap. 9.95 (*0-435-90536-8*) Heinemann.

African Short Stories. Joan S. Kenna. 68p. (C). 1989. 69.00 (*0-7223-2339-5*, Pub. by A H S Ltd UK) St Mut.

African Silences. Peter Matthiessen. 1991. 21.00 (*0-679-40021-4*) Random.

African Silences. Peter Matthiessen. 1992. pap. 11.00 (*0-679-73102-4*, Vin) Random.

African Slave in Colonial Peru, 1524-1650. Frederick P. Bowser. LC 73-80619. (Illus.). 456p. 1974. 52.50 (*0-8047-0840-1*) Stanford U Pr.

African Slave Trade. Rufus W. Clark. LC 70-133151. (Black Heritage Library Collection). 1977. 21.95 (*0-8369-8706-3*) Ayer.

African Slave Trade. enl. rev. ed. Basil Davidson. 304p. 1988. pap. 12.95 (*0-316-17438-6*) Little.

African Slave Trade & American Courts: The Pamphlet Literature, 2 vols. Ed. by Paul Finkelman. (Slavery, Race & the American Legal System, 1700-1872 Ser.). 832p. 1988. lib. bdg. 87.00 (*0-8240-6722-3*) Garland.

African Slave Trade & Its Suppression: A Classified & Annotated Bibliography. Ed. by Peter Hogg. 427p. 1973. 65.00 (*0-7146-2775-5*, Pub. by F Cass Pubs UK) Intl Spec Bk.

African Slavery in Latin America & the Caribbean. Herbert S. Klein. (Illus.). 336p. 1988. pap. 18.95 (*0-19-503838-X*) OUP.

African Sleeping Sickness: Political Ecology, Colonialism, & Control in Uganda. Jonathan Musere. LC 90-44199. (Studies in African Health & Medicine: Vol. 5). 224p. 1990. lib. bdg. 89.95 (*0-88946-280-1*) E Mellen.

African Sleeping Sickness: Stories & Poems. Wanda Coleman. LC 90-1294. 332p. 1993. reprint ed. pap. 13.00 (*0-87685-812-4*) Black Sparrow.

African Social Psychology: Review & Annotated Bibliography. Michael Armer. LC 74-23711. (African Bibliography Ser.: Vol. 2). 400p. 1975. 45.00 (*0-8419-0164-3*, Africana) Holmes & Meier.

African Social Situation: Crucial Factors of Development & Transformation. Adebayo Adedeji et al. (African Social Challenges Ser.: No. 2). 221p. 1990. lib. bdg. 60.00 (*0-905450-78-7*, Pub. by H Zell Pubs UK) Bowker-Saur.

African Social Studies Programme: A Handbook for Teachers. Kemoh Salia-Bao. 208p. 1992. 13.95 (*0-237-51110-X*, Pub. by Evans Bros Ltd UK) Trafalgar.

African Socialism. Ed. by William H. Friedland & Carl G. Rosberg, Jr. xi, 313p. 1964. pap. 13.95 (*0-8047-0204-7*) Stanford U Pr.

African Socio-Economic Indicators. 80p. 1986. 20.00 (*92-1-125054-4*, EF89.11.K.1) UN.

African Socio-Economic Indicators. 69p. 1987. 25.00 (*92-1-025023-0*) UN.

African Socio-Economic Indicators, 1985. 80p. 1987. pap. 25.00 (*92-1-125050-1*, EF90.11.K.9) UN.

African Spaces: Designs for Living in Upper Volta. Jean-Paul Bourdier & Trinh T. Minh-ha. (Illus.). 275p. (C). 1985. 69.50 (*0-8419-0890-7*, Africana) Holmes & Meier.

African Speaks for His People. Parmenas G. Mockerie. LC 74-15068. reprint ed. 27.50 (*0-404-12110-1*) AMS Pr.

African Stars: Studies in Black South African Performance. Veit Erlmann. (Chicago Studies in Ethnomusicology Ser.). (Illus.). 280p. 1991. lib. bdg. 34.95 (*0-226-21722-1*); pap. 15.95 (*0-226-21724-8*) U Ch Pr.

African State in Transition. Ed. by Zaki Ergas. LC 87-4727. 320p. 1987. text ed. 45.00 (*0-312-00768-X*) St Martin.

African States & Rulers: An Encyclopedia of Native, Colonial & Independent States & Rulers Past & Present. John Stewart. LC 88-7945. 415p. 1989. lib. bdg. 49.95x (*0-89950-390-X*) McFarland & Co.

African Statistical Yearbook, Pt. 3. 400p. 1987. 46.00 (*92-1-025021-4*) UN.

African Statistical Yearbook 1985, Pt. 1: North Africa. Part 1: North Africa. 24.00 (*92-1-025009-5*, EF.88.II.K.3) UN.

African Statistical Yearbook 1985, Pt. 2: West Africa. 408p. Part 2: West Africa, 408 pgs. 50.00 (*92-1-025010-9*, EF.88.II.K.4) UN.

African Statistical Yearbook 1985, Pt. 3: Eastern & Southern Africa. 165p. Part 3: Eastern & Southern Africa, 165 pgs. 55.00 (*92-1-025011-7*, EF.88.II.K.5) UN.

African Statistical Yearbook 1985, Pt. 4: Central Africa & Other African Countries. Part 4: Central Africa & Other African Countries. 37.00 (*92-1-025012-5*, EF.88.II.K.6) UN.

African Statistical Yearbook, 1986, Pt. 1: North Africa. 20.00 (*92-1-025014-1*, EF88.11.K.7) UN.

African Statistical Yearbook, 1986, Pt. 2: West Africa. 35.00 (*92-1-025016-8*, EF88.11.K.8) UN.

African Statistical Yearbook, 1986, Pt. 3: Eastern & Southern Africa. 48.00 (*92-1-025017-6*, EF88.11.K.9) UN.

African Statistical Yearbook, 1986, Pt. 4: Central Africa & Other African Countries. 149p. 1986. 30.00 (*92-1-025018-4*, EF88.11.K.10) UN.

African Statistical Yearbook 1987 Pt. 1: North Africa. 150p. 1987. 24.00 (*92-1-025019-2*) UN.

African Statistical Yearbook 1987 Pt. 4: Central Africa & Other African Countries. 236p. 1987. 39.00 (*92-1-025022-2*) UN.

African Stories. Robert Hull. LC 92-40632. (Tales from Around the World Ser.). (Illus.). 48p. (J). (gr. 5-9). 1993. 15.95 (*1-56847-004-5*) Thomson Lrning.

***African Stories.** Donna Washington. LC 94-18697. (Illus.). (J). 1997. 18.00 (*0-06-024929-3*); lib. bdg. 17.89 (*0-06-024932-3*) HarpC Child Bks.

African Studies: Dedicated to the 5th International Congress of African Studies in Nigeria. G. Brehme & T. Buttner. 286p. 1983. 37.50 (*0-685-16959-6*, Pub. by Collets UK) Pro-Am Music.

African Studies & the Undergraduate Curriculum. Ed. by Patricia Alden et al. LC 93-50942. 340p. 1994. pap. text ed. 25.00 (*1-55587-445-2*) Lynne Rienner.

African Studies Companion: A Resource Guide & Directory. Hans M. Zell. 200p. 1989. lib. bdg. 55.00 (*0-905450-80-9*, Pub. by H Zell Pubs UK) Bowker-Saur.

***African Studies Companion: A Resource Guide & Directory.** 2nd rev. ed. Hans Zell. 192p. 1995. 49.95 (*1-873836-41-4*) Bowker-Saur.

African Studies Handbook for Teachers. 3rd ed. 221p. (C). 1983. teacher ed 8.00 (*0-932288-69-3*) Ctr Intl Ed U of MA.

African Studies Information Resources Directory. Ed. by Jean E. Gosebrink. xii, 572p. 1986. lib. bdg. 98.00 (*3-598-10657-2*) K G Saur.

African Studies Thesaurus: Subject Headings for Library Users. Freda E. Otchere. LC 92-12523. (Bibliographies & Indexes in Afro-American & African Studies: No. 29). 480p. 1992. text ed. 79.50 (*0-313-27437-1*, OAB/, Greenwood Pr) Greenwood.

African Successes: Four Public Managers of Kenyan Rural Development. David K. Leonard. LC 90-11089. (Illus.). 390p. 1991. 55.00 (*0-520-07075-5*); pap. 19.00 (*0-520-07076-3*) U CA Pr.

African Swine Fever. Ed. by Yechiel Becker. (Developments in Veterinary Virology Ser.). 1986. lib. bdg. 77.50 (*0-89838-848-1*) Kluwer Ac.

African Swine Fever Virus. W. R. Hess. Bd. with Bluetongue Virus. (Virology Monographs: Vol. 9). 1971. 25.00 (*0-387-81006-4*) Spr-Verlag.

African Symbols, Proverbs & Myths: The Hermeneutics of Destiny. Raphael O. Madu. LC 91-42866. (Studies in African & African-American Culture: Vol. 3). 327p. (C). 1993. text ed. 59.80 (*0-8204-1863-3*) P Lang Pubs.

***African Synod.** Ed. by Africa Faith & Justice Network Staff. 240p. (Orig.). 1995. pap. 21.95 (*1-57075-038-6*) Orbis Bks.

African Systems of Kinship & Marriage. Ed. by A. R. Radcliffe-Brown & Daryll Forde. (Illus.). 400p. 1994. pap. text ed. 25.50 (*0-7103-0234-7*, 02347, Pub. by Kegan Paul Intl UK) Routledge Chapman & Hall.

African Systems of Thought: Studies Presented & Discussed at the Third International African Seminar in Salisbury, December, 1960. International African Seminar Staff. LC 65-2218. 400p. reprint ed. pap. 114.00 (*0-8357-3219-3*, 2057091) Bks Demand.

African Tales: Folklore of the Central African Republic. Polly Strong. LC 91-66693. (Illus.). 96p. (J). (gr. 2 up). 1992. 10.95 (*1-878893-15-7*); pap. 6.95 (*1-878893-14-9*) Telcraft Bks.

African Textiles. 1989. pap. 0.99 (*0-517-68807-7*) Random Hse Value.

African Textiles. John Picton. 1989. pap. text ed. 25.00 (*0-06-430190-7*, Icon Edns) HarpC.

African Theatre: A Checklist of Critical Materials. Ed. by N. B. East. LC 70-96260. 47p. (C). 1970. pap. 7.50 (*0-8419-0025-6*, Africana) Holmes & Meier.

African Theatre Today. Martin Banham & Clive Wake. LC 77-350062. 111p. reprint ed. pap. 31.70 (*0-8357-5241-0*, 2032488) Bks Demand.

African Theology: A Critical Analysis & Annotated Bibliography. Josiah U. Young. LC 92-38979. (Bibliographies & Indexes in Religious Studies: No. 26). 288p. 1993. text ed. 55.00 (*0-313-26487-2*, YAT/) Greenwood.

African Theology: Inculturation & Liberation. Emmanuel Martey. LC 93-16262. 184p. (Orig.). 1993. pap. 18.95 (*0-88344-861-0*) Orbis Bks.

African Theology en Route: Papers from the Pan African Conference of Third World Theologians, December 17-23, 1977, Accra, Ghana. Ed. by Kofi Appiah-Kubi & Sergio Torres. LC 78-10604. 224p. reprint ed. pap. 63.90 (*0-8357-8792-3*, 2033461) Bks Demand.

African Theology in Its Social Context. Benezet Bujo. (Faith & Cultures Ser.). 1992. 16.95 (*0-88344-805-X*) Orbis Bks.

African Theology of Mission. Gwinyai H. Muzorewa. LC 89-78555. (Studies in History of Missions: Vol. 5). (Illus.). 256p. 1990. lib. bdg. 89.95 (*0-88946-073-6*) E Mellen.

African Trade Unions. Ioan Davies. LC 76-44461. 1977. reprint ed. 35.00 (*0-8371-9081-9*, DAATU, Greenwood Pr) Greenwood.

African Traditional Architecture. Susan Denyer. LC 77-16428. (Illus.). 210p. (C). 1978. 44.50 (*0-8419-0287-9*, Africana); pap. 21.95 (*0-8419-0336-0*, Africana) Holmes & Meier.

African Traditional Religion. 3rd ed. Geoffrey Parrinder. LC 76-22490. (Illus.). 156p. 1970. reprint ed. text ed. 48.50 (*0-8371-3401-3*, PAF&, Greenwood Pr) Greenwood.

African Traditional Religion in Contemporary Society. Intro. by Jacob K. Olupona. LC 89-77137. 212p. 1991. pap. 12.95 (*0-89226-079-3*, New Era Bks) Paragon Hse.

African Tree of Life. Thomas G. Christensen. LC 89-72148. (American Society of Missiology Ser.). 1990. pap. 19.95 (*0-88344-656-1*) Orbis Bks.

African Trees. Dorothy Hargreaves & Bob Hargreaves. LC 72-85426. (Illus.). 64p. 1972. pap. 3.85 (*0-910690-07-3*) Ross-Hargreaves.

African Triumph. LC 67-29693. (Encounter Ser.). (J). (gr. 3-7). 1978. 3.00 (*0-8198-0225-5*); pap. 2.00 (*0-8198-0226-3*) Pauline Bks.

An Asterisk (*) at the beginning of an entry indicates that the title is appearing in BIP for the first time.

A

Afrique Francaise du Nord: Bibliographie Militaire des Ouvrages Francaise Ou Traduits En Francais et des Articles des Principales Revues Francaises Relatifs a L'algerie, a la Tunisie et Au Maroc De 1830-1927, 4 parts in 2 vols., Set. France Armee Etat Major Staff. (FRE.). reprint ed. pap. 155.00 (*0-404-56206-X*) AMS Pr.

Afrique Two: New Plays from Madagascar, Mauritania, Togo, 6 plays. Incl. Singing Tortoise & Yevi's Adventures in Monsterland. Senouvo A. Zinsou. Tr. by Townsend Brewster & Danielle Brunon. LC 91-65893. 1991. (*0-318-68406-3*); Crossroads. Josue K. Efoui. Tr. by Jill MacDougall. LC 91-65893. 1991. (*0-318-68407-1*); Prophet & the President. Jean-Luc Raharimahara. Tr. by Stephen J. Vogel. LC 91-65893. 1991. (*0-318-68408-X*); Herd. Charlotte-Arrisoa Rafenomanjato. Tr. by Marjolijn De Jager. LC 91-65893. 1991. (*0-318-68409-8*); Legend of Wagadu: The Legend of Wagadu as Seen by Sia Yatabere. Moussa Diagana. Tr. by Richard Miller. LC 91-65893. 309p. 1991. (*0-318-68410-1*); LC 91-65893. (Orig.). (C). 1991. Set pap. 15.95 (*0-913745-33-2*) Ubu Repertory.

Afro - Tots Numbers 1-2-3. Oswald Gift. (Illus.). 24p. 1992. pap. text ed. write for info. (*1-881316-25-4*) A&B Bks.

Afro-American & East German Fiction: A Comparative Study of Alienation, Identity & the Development of Self. Vernessa C. White. LC 83-48138. (American University Studies: Comparative Literature: Ser. III, Vol. 4). 210p. (C). 1983. pap. text ed. 17.90 (*0-8204-0016-5*) P Lang Pubs.

Afro-American & the Second World War. Neil Wynn. LC 76-3767. 182p. 1979. 37.50 (*0-8419-0232-1*) Holmes & Meier.

Afro-American & the Second World War. rev. ed. Neil Wynn. 208p. 1993. pap. 19.95 (*0-8419-1333-1*) Holmes & Meier.

Afro-American Artists: A Bio-Bibliographical Directory. Theresa Cederholm. 1973. 10.00 (*0-89073-007-5*) Boston Public Lib.

Afro-American Artists New York & Boston. Intro. by Edmund B. Gaither. (Illus.). 90p. 1970. pap. 6.95 (*0-87846-216-3*) Mus Fine Arts Boston.

Afro-American Authors. Ed. by William Adams et al. LC 74-160035. (Multi-Ethnic Literature Ser.). (Illus.). 165p. (gr. 10-12). 1976. pap. 18.32 (*0-395-24043-3*); teacher ed 8.24 (*0-685-02278-1*) HM.

Afro-American Cinematic Experience: An Annotated Bibliography & Filmography. Ed. by Marshall Hyatt. LC 82-22974. 260p. 1983. lib. bdg. 40.00 (*0-8420-2213-9*) Scholarly Res Inc.

Afro-American Copy Color Fun. Zenobia M. Johnson. (Illus.). 32p. (Orig.). (J). (ps-1). 1979. student ed 3.00 (*0-9617411-2-0*) Z M Johnson.

Afro-American Demography & Urban Issues: A Bibliography. Robert A. Obudho & Jeannine B. Scott. LC 85-17752. (Bibliographies & Indexes on Afro-American & African Studies Ser.: No. 8). xl, 433p. 1985. text ed. 65.00 (*0-313-24656-4*, OAA/) Greenwood.

Afro-American Education, 1907-1932: A Bibliographic Index. Richard Newman. LC 83-24869. 198p. 1995. 45.00 (*0-931186-05-6*) Lambeth Pr.

Afro-American Encyclopedia; or, The Thoughts, Doings, & Sayings of the Race, Vols. I & II. Ed. by James T. Haley. LC 92-61737. (Illus.). 600p. 1992. reprint ed. pap. 24.95 (*1-55523-538-7*) Winston-Derek.

Afro-American Fiction Writers after Nineteen Fifty-Five, Vol. 33. Ed. by Trudier Harris & Thadious Davis. (Dictionary of Literary Biography Ser.: Vol. 33). 368p. 1984. 128.00 (*0-8103-1711-7*) Gale.

Afro-American Folk Culture: An Annotated Bibliography of Materials from North, Central & South America & the West Indies, 2 vols., Pt. 1. John F. Szwad & Roger D. Abrahams. LC 77-16567. (Publications of the American Folklore Society, Bibliographical & Special Ser.: Vol. 31 & 32). reprint ed. pap. 89.00 (*0-8357-5244-5*, 2025712) Bks Demand.

Afro-American Folk Culture: An Annotated Bibliography of Materials from North, Central & South America & the West Indies, 2 vols., Pt. 2. John F. Szwad & Roger D. Abrahams. LC 77-16567. (Publications of the American Folklore Society, Bibliographical & Special Ser.: Vol. 31 & 32). 414p. reprint ed. pap. 118.00 (*0-8357-5245-3*) Bks Demand.

Afro-American Folklore. Abigail M. Christensen. LC 71-157364. (Black Heritage Library Collection). 1977. 10.95 (*0-8369-8802-7*) Ayer.

Afro-American Folklore: Told Round Cabin Fires on the Sea Islands of South Carolina. Abigail M. Christensen. LC 73-78761. (Illus.). 116p. 1969. text ed. 35.00 (*0-8371-1387-3*, CHA&, Negro U Pr) Greenwood.

Afro-American Folktales: Stories from Black Traditions in the New World. Roger D. Abrahams. LC 84-16601. (Fairy Tale & Folklore Library). 352p. 1985. pap. 16.00 (*0-394-72885-8*) Pantheon.

Afro-American Griot Speaks: Afro-American Names. Sharon R. Munoz. LC 93-61423. 140p. 1994. pap. 6.95 (*1-55523-671-5*) Winston-Derek.

Afro-American History. Jack Rudman. (College Level Examination Ser.: CLEP-36). 1994. 39.95 (*0-8373-5386-6*); pap. 23.95 (*0-8373-5336-X*) Nat Learn.

Afro-American History: Primary Sources. 2nd ed. Thomas R. Frazier. 464p. (C). 1988. pap. 24.95 (*0-534-10530-0*) Intl Thomson.

Afro-American History: Separate or Interracial. Meyer Weinberg. 1968. pap. 0.90 (*0-912008-16-4*) Equity & Excel.

Afro-American History: The Modern Era. Herbert C. Aptheker. 1971. reprint ed. pap. 10.95 (*0-8065-0362-9*, Citadel Pr) Carol Pub Group.

Afro-American in New York City, 1827-1860. George E. Walker. LC 92-46183. (Studies in African American History & Culture). (Illus.). 248p. 1993. 58.00 (*0-8153-1010-2*) Garland.

Afro-American Jeremiad: Appeals for Justice in America. David Howard-Pitney. 260p. 1990. 44.95 (*0-87722-673-3*) Temple U Pr.

Afro-American Jeremiad: Appeals for Justice in America. David Howard-Pitney. 260p. 1993. pap. 16.95 (*1-56639-086-9*) Temple U Pr.

Afro-American Literary Study in the 1990s. Ed. by Houston A. Baker, Jr. & Patricia Redmond. LC 89-31971. (Black Literature & Culture Ser.). 280p. 1989. 24.95 (*0-226-03537-9*) U Ch Pr.

Afro-American Literary Study in the 1990s. Ed. by Houston A. Baker, Jr. & Patricia Redmond. LC 89-31971. (Black Literature & Culture Ser.). 252p. 1991. pap. text ed. 11.95 (*0-226-03543-3*) U Ch Pr.

Afro-American Literature: Drama. Ed. by William Adams et al. (Afro-American Literature Ser.). (gr. 9-12). 1970. pap. 18.32 (*0-395-01973-7*) HM.

Afro-American Literature: The Reconstruction of Instruction. Ed. by Dexter Fisher & Robert B. Stepto. LC 78-62061. viii, 256p. 1979. pap. 19.75 (*0-87352-351-2*, B1020) Modern Lang.

Afro-American Literature in the Twentieth Century: The Achievement of Intimacy. Michael G. Cooke. LC 84-5066. 256p. 1986. pap. 15.00x (*0-300-03624-8*, Y-561) Yale U Pr.

Afro-American Music, South Africa, & Apartheid. Charles Hamm. LC 88-80431. (I.S.A.M. Monographs: No. 28). 52p. (Orig.). 1988. pap. 11.00 (*0-914678-31-0*) Inst Am Music.

Afro-American Novel & Its Tradition. Bernard W. Bell. LC 86-25070. 448p. 1987. pap. 18.95 (*0-87023-688-1*) U of Mass Pr.

Afro-American Novel since Nineteen-Sixty: A Collection of Critical Essays. Ed. by Peter Bruck & Wolfgang Karrer. viii, 327p. 1982. pap. 35.00 (*90-6032-219-3*, Pub. by B R Gruener NE) Benjamins North Am.

***Afro-American Periodical Press, 1838-1909.** fac. ed. Penelope L. Bullock. LC 81-1712. (Illus.). 344p. 1981. reprint ed. pap. 98.10 (*0-7837-7938-0*, 2047694) Bks Demand.

Afro-American Poetics: Revisions of Harlem & the Black Aesthetic. Houston A. Baker, Jr. LC 88-27274. (Illus.). 212p. (Orig.). (C). 1988. text ed. 21.95 (*0-299-11500-3*) U of Wis Pr.

Afro-American Poets after 1955, Vol. 41. (Dictionary of Literary Biography Ser.: Vol. 41). 428p. 1985. 128.00 (*0-8103-1719-2*) Gale.

Afro-American Press & Its Editors. I. Garland Penn. LC 69-18574. (American Negro: His History & Literature, Ser. No. 2). 1969. reprint ed. 36.95 (*0-405-01887-8*) Ayer.

***Afro-American Readings.** Rhonda Williams. 288p. (C). 1995. pap. text ed., spiral bd. 49.95 (*0-7872-1107-9*) Kendall-Hunt.

Afro-American Reference: An Annotated Bibliography of Selected Resources. Ed. by Nathaniel Davis. LC 85-21942. (Bibliographies & Indexes in Afro-American & African Studies: No. 9). xiii, 288p. 1985. text ed. 79.50 (*0-313-24930-X*, DRS/) Greenwood.

Afro-American Religious History: A Documentary Witness. Ed. by Milton C. Sernett. LC 84-24686. xii, 506p. (C). 1985. text ed. 52.95 (*0-8223-0591-7*); pap. text ed. 20.95 (*0-8223-0594-1*) Duke.

Afro-American Religious Music: A Bibliography & a Catalogue of Gospel Music. Comp. by Irene V. Jackson. LC 78-60527. (Illus.). 210p. 1979. text ed. 42.95 (*0-313-20560-4*, JGM/, Greenwood Pr) Greenwood.

Afro-American Short Story: A Comprehensive, Annotated Index with Selected Commentaries. Comp. by Preston M. Yancy. LC 85-27132. (Bibliographies & Indexes in Afro-American & African Studies: No. 10). 185p. 1986. text ed. 49.95 (*0-313-24355-7*, YAF/) Greenwood.

Afro-American Slaves: Community or Chaos? Ed. by Randall M. Miller. LC 80-24034. 152p. (Orig.). (C). 1981. pap. 9.50 (*0-89874-078-9*) Krieger.

Afro-American Sources in Virginia: A Guide to Manuscripts. Michael Plunkett. LC 89-16616. (Carter G. Woodson Institute Series in Black Studies). 323p. 1990. text ed. 35.00 (*0-8139-1251-2*) U Pr of Va.

Afro-American Studies. Nathan I. Huggins. LC 84-24714. 96p. (Orig.). (C). 1985. pap. (*0-916584-25-9*) Ford Found.

Afro-American Tradition in Decorative Arts. John M. Vlach. LC 89-20574. (Illus.). 184p. 1990. reprint ed. 50.00 (*0-8203-1232-0*); reprint ed. pap. 19.95 (*0-8203-1233-9*) U of Ga Pr.

Afro-American Ugly Duckling. Tim Kumanu. 1994. 10.95 (*0-8062-5004-6*) Carlton.

Afro American View of the Women's Liberation Movement. Barbara M. Sims. 21p. (C). 1985. pap. text ed. 6.90 (*0-935543-02-3*) Inst Political Res.

Afro-American Vocal Music: A Select Guide to Fifteen Composers. Frank Perry, Jr. LC 91-751616. 142p. (C). 1991. 24.95 (*0-9628916-2-2*) Vande Vere.

Afro-American Women of the South & the Advancement of the Race, 1895-1925. Cynthia Neverdon-Morton. LC 88-17481. (Illus.). 288p. 1989. text ed. 41.00x (*0-87049-583-6*); pap. 18.95 (*0-87049-684-0*) U of Tenn Pr.

Afro-American Women Writers, 1746-1933: An Anthology & Critical Guide. Ann A. Schockley. (G. K. Hall Reference Bks.). 420p. 1988. text ed. 42.50 (*0-8161-8823-8*, Hall Reference) Macmillan.

Afro-American Women Writers, 1746-1933: An Anthology & Critical Guide. Ed. by Ann A. Shockley. 1989. 15.00 (*0-452-00981-2*, Mer) NAL-Dutton.

Afro-American Writers. Darwin T. Turner. LC 72-79171. (Goldentree Bibliographies Series in Language & Literature). (C). 1970. pap. text ed. write for info. (*0-88295-527-6*) Harlan Davidson.

Afro-American Writers after 1955: Dramatists & Prose Writers, Vol. 38. Ed. by Trudier Harris & Thadious Davis. (Dictionary of Literary Biography Ser.: Vol. 38). 392p. 1985. 128.00 (*0-8103-1716-8*) Gale.

Afro-American Writers Before the Harlem Renaissance, Vol. 50. Ed. by Trudier Harris. (Dictionary of Literary Biography Ser.: Vol. 50). 369p. 1986. 128.00 (*0-8103-1728-1*) Gale.

Afro-American Writers from the Harlem Renaissance to 1940, Vol. 51. Ed. by Trudier Harris. (Dictionary of Literary Biography Ser.: Vol. 51). 386p. 1986. 128.00 (*0-8103-1729-X*) Gale.

Afro-American Writers, Nineteen Forty to Nineteen Fifty-Five, Vol. 76. Ed. by Trudier Harris. (Dictionary of Literary Biography Ser.: Vol. 76). 389p. 1988. pap. 128.00 (*0-8103-4554-4*, 006544-M99348) Gale.

Afro-American Writing: An Anthology of Prose & Poetry. 2nd enl. ed. Ed. by Richard A. Long & Eugenia W. Collier. 784p. 1990. 15.95 (*0-271-00376-6*) Pa St U Pr.

Afro-American Writing Today: An Anniversary Issue of the Southern Review. Ed. by James Olney. LC 88-39021. (Illus.). 328p. 1989. text ed. 34.95 (*0-8071-1482-0*) La State U Pr.

Afro-Americans. Howard Smead. (Peoples of North America Ser.). (Illus.). 120p. (J). (gr. 5 up). 1989. lib. bdg. 17.95 (*0-87754-854-4*); pap. 9.95 (*0-7910-0256-X*) Chelsea Hse.

Afro-Americans & Africa: Black Nationalism at the Crossroads. Comp. by William B. Helmreich. LC 76-56621. (Special Bibliographic Series, New Ser.: No. 3). 74p. 1977. text ed. 47.95 (*0-8371-9439-3*, HAA/, Greenwood Pr) Greenwood.

Afro-Americans in Antebellum Boston: An Analysis of Probate Records. Carol Buchalter Stapp. LC 92-40357. 336p. 1993. 73.00 (*0-8153-1194-X*) Garland.

Afro-Americans in California. 2nd ed. Rudolph M. Lapp. Ed. by Norris Hundley, Jr. & John A. Schutz. (Golden State Ser.). (Illus.). 128p. 1987. pap. 10.00 (*0-87835-152-3*) MTL.

Afro-Americans Seventy-Six. Eugene Winslow. LC 75-23936. (Illus.). 80p. 1975. 14.95 (*0-910030-20-0*); pap. 9.95 (*0-910030-21-9*) Afro-Am.

Afro-Arabian Geology: A Kinematic View. Robert T. Bower & Ulrick Jux. 300p. 1987. text ed. 75.00 (*0-412-29700-0*) Chapman & Hall.

Afro-Argentines of Buenos Aires, Eighteen Hundred to Nineteen Hundred. G. Reid Andrews. LC 80-5105. 304p. 1980. 31.50 (*0-299-08290-3*) U of Wis Pr.

Afro-Asian Dimension of Brazilian Foreign Policy, 1956-1972. Wayne A. Selcher. LC 73-19968. (Latin American Monographs: Ser. 2, No. 13). 261p. reprint ed. pap. 74.40 (*0-7837-4968-6*, 2044634) Bks Demand.

Afro-Asian Publishing: Contemporary Trends. Ed. by Narendra Kumar & S. K. Ghai. xvi, 189p. 1992. 30.00 (*81-207-1290-0*, Pub. by Sterling Pubs II) Apt Bks.

Afro-Asian World in Transition. Ed. by Se-Jin Kim. LC 74-75645. 160p. 1974. 2.00 (*0-686-09055-1*) NC Central Pol Sci.

Afro-Bets: Book of Colors. Margery W. Brown. LC 91-76334. (Illus.). 24p. (Orig.). (J). (ps-1). 1991. pap. 3.95 (*0-940975-28-9*) Just Us Bks.

Afro-Bets: Book of Shapes. Margery W. Brown. LC 91-76333. (Illus.). 24p. (Orig.). (J). (ps-1). 1991. pap. 3.95 (*0-940975-29-7*) Just Us Bks.

Afro-Bets A B C Book. Cheryl W. Hudson. LC 87-81580. (Afro-Bets Bks.: Vol. 1). (Illus.). 24p. (J). (ps-3). 1987. pap. 3.95 (*0-940975-00-9*) Just Us Bks.

Afro-Bets A B C Coloring & Activity Book. Dwayne Ferguson. (J). (ps-3). 1989. pap. 3.95 (*0-940975-13-0*) Just Us Bks.

Afro-Bets Activity & Enrichment Guide: Book of Black Heroes from A to Z. Vernell C. Farrand & Brent Farrand. (J). Date not set. pap. 7.95 (*0-940975-05-X*) Just Us Bks.

Afro-Bets Activity & Enrichment Guide: First Book about Africa. Veronica F. Ellis. (J). (gr. 1-4). Date not set. pap. 7.95 (*0-940975-07-6*) Just Us Bks.

Afro-Bets Alphabet Rap Song. Wade Hudson. 1990. pap. write for info. (*0-940975-04-1*) Just Us Bks.

Afro-Bets Book of Black Heroes from A to Z: An Introduction to Important Black Achievers. Wade Hudson & Valerie W. Wesley. LC 87-82951. (Illus.). 64p. (J). (gr. 3-6). 1988. pap. 7.95 (*0-940975-02-5*) Just Us Bks.

AFRO-Bets Book of Black Heroes from A-Z: An Introduction to Important Black Achievers. Wade Hudson & Valerie W. Wesley. (J). (gr. 3 up). 1993. 14.95 (*0-940975-46-7*) Just Us Bks.

Afro-Bets First Book about Africa. Veronica F. Ellis. LC 89-85157. (Illus.). 32p. (Orig.). (J). (gr. 1-4). 1990. lib. bdg. 13.95 (*0-940975-12-2*); pap. 6.95 (*0-940975-03-3*) Just Us Bks.

Afro-Bets Kids: I'm Gonna Be! Wade Hudson. LC 92-72000. (Illus.). 32p. (Orig.). (J). (ps up). 1992. pap. 6.95 (*0-940975-40-8*) Just Us Bks.

Afro-Bets Kids Christmas Fun: An Activity & Coloring Book. Dwayne Ferguson. LC 92-72003. (Illus.). 48p. (J). (gr. k-3). 1992. pap. 2.95 (*0-940975-41-6*) Just Us Bks.

Afro-Bets 1 2 3 Book. Cheryl W. Hudson. LC 87-82952. (Afro-Bets Bks.: Vol. 2). (Illus.). 24p. (J). (ps-3). 1988. pap. 3.95 (*0-940975-01-7*) Just Us Bks.

***Afro-Centric Guide to: Reflections, Affirmations, Meditations & Prayers.** Jamilla Powers & Tyson Gibbs. 130p. (Orig.). 1994. pap. 10.95 (*0-9638548-0-1*) Jamilla Powers.

Afro-Christian Religion & Healing in Southern Africa. Ed. by G. C. Oosthuizen et al. LC 88-8894. (African Studies: Vol. 8). 450p. 1989. lib. bdg. 109.95 (*0-88946-282-8*) E Mellen.

Afro-Christian Religion at the Grassroots in Southern Africa. Ed. by G. C. Oosthuizen & Irving Hexham. LC 91-10173. (African Studies: Vol. 19). 440p. 1991. lib. bdg. 109.95 (*0-88946-226-7*) E Mellen.

Afro-Christian Vision: OZOVEHE (Toward a More Humanized World) George O. Ehusani. 276p. (Orig.). (C). 1991. lib. bdg. 49.50 (*0-8191-8114-5*); pap. text ed. 32.50 (*0-8191-8115-3*) U Pr of Amer.

***Afro-Christianity at the Grassroots: Bits Dynamics & Strategies.** Ed. by G. C. Oosthuizen & H. J. Becken. LC 94-26023. (Studies of Religion in Africa: 9). 1994. 74.50 (*90-04-10035-0*) E J Brill.

Afro-Classic Folk Tales, Bk. 1: A Rattlesnake Tale. Floyd E. Norman. Ed. by Lyn Stewart. (Illus.). 28p. (Orig.). (J). (gr. 4-7). 1992. pap. 9.95 (*1-881368-00-9*) Vignette.

Afro-Classic Folk Tales, Bk. 2: Anancy & the Tiger. Leo Sullivan. Ed. by Lyn Stewart. (Illus.). 28p. (Orig.). (J). (gr. 4-7). 1992. pap. 9.95 (*1-881368-19-X*) Vignette.

Afro-Classic Folk Tales, Bk. 3: Bro Rabbit. Leo Sullivan & Floyd Norman. Ed. by Lyn Stewart. (Illus.). 28p. (Orig.). (J). (gr. 4-7). 1992. pap. 9.95 (*1-881368-20-3*) Vignette.

Afro-Classic Folk Tales, Bk. 4: High John. Floyd Norman. Ed. by Lyn Stewart. (Illus.). 28p. (Orig.). (J). (gr. 4-7). 1992. pap. 9.95 (*1-881368-21-1*) Vignette.

Afro-Classic Folk Tales, Bk. 5: Anancy's Riding Horse. Leo Sullivan & Floyd Norman. Ed. by Lyn Stewart. (Illus.). 28p. (Orig.). (J). (gr. 4-7). 1992. pap. 9.95 (*1-881368-22-X*) Vignette.

Afro-Classic Folk Tales, Bk. 6: Work-Let-Me-See. Floyd Norman & Leo Sullivan. Ed. by Lyn Stewart. (Illus.). 28p. (Orig.). (J). (gr. 4-7). 1992. pap. 9.95 (*1-881368-23-8*) Vignette.

Afro-Cuban Poetry. Claudio Freixas. LC 78-57695. 1978. pap. 5.00 (*0-89729-192-1*) Ediciones.

Afro-Cuban Poetry. Ramon Guirao & Marcelino Arozarena. (B. E. Ser.: No. 7). 1966. Two works in one unit. 35.00 (*0-8115-2958-4*) Periodicals Srv.

Afro Hair: A Salon Handbook. Phillip Hatton. (Illus.). 224p. 1994. pap. write for info. (*0-632-02285-X*) Blackwell Sci.

Afro-Hispanic Literature: An Anthology of Hispanic Writers of Hispanic Ancestry. Ingrid W. Miller. LC 91-84525. (Coleccion Ebano y Canela Ser.). 143p. (Orig.). 1991. pap. 19.00 (*0-89729-582-X*) Ediciones.

Afro-Latin Rhythm Dictionary. Thomas A. Brown. (Alfred Handy Guides Ser.). 48p. (Orig.). 1992. pap. text ed. 4.95 (*0-88284-151-3*, 2427) Alfred Pub.

Afro-Marxist Regimes: Ideology & Public Policy. Ed. by Edmond J. Keller & Donald Rothchild. LC 87-16776. 280p. 1987. pap. text ed. 17.95 (*1-55587-100-3*) Lynne Rienner.

Afro-Spanish American Author II, the 1980s: An Annotated Bibliography of Recent Criticism. Richard L. Jackson. LC 89-2685. 154p. (C). 1989. lib. bdg. 25.00 (*0-933951-26-4*) Locust Hill Pr.

Afro-Trinidadian: Reflections on an Endangered Species. Tony Martin. LC 93-43662. 80p. (Orig.). (C). Date not set. pap. text ed. 9.95 (*0-912469-31-5*) Majority Pr.

Afro-Victorian Feminist: The Life & Times of Adelaide Smith Casely Hayford, 1868-1960. Adelaide M. Cromwell. (Illus.). 275p. 1986. 38.00 (*0-7146-3226-0*, Pub. by F Cass Pubs UK) Intl Spec Bk.

Afro-Yankees: Providence's Black Community in the Antebellum Era. Robert J. Cottrol. LC 81-23717. (Contributions in Afro-American & African Studies: No. 68). (Illus.). xviii, 200p. 1982. text ed. 49.95 (*0-313-22936-8*, CBL/, Greenwood Pr) Greenwood.

Afroasiatic: A Survey. Ed. by Carlton T. Hodge. LC 78-181828. (Janua Linguarum, Series Practica: No. 163). 130p. (Orig.). 1971. pap. text ed. 34.65 (*90-279-1844-9*) Mouton.

***Afrocentric Architecture.** David Hughes. (Illus.). 212p. (C). 1994. pap. text ed. 39.95 (*1-57074-100-X*) Greyden Pr.

Afrocentric Educational Manual: Toward a Non-Deficit Perspective in Services to Families & Children. Jualynne E. Dodson. 169p. (Orig.). 1983. 7.00 (*0-89695-010-7*) U Tenn CSW.

Afrocentric Guide to a Spiritual Union. Ra U. Amen. (Illus.). 129p. (Orig.). 1992. pap. 9.95 (*1-877662-07-0*) Khamit.

***Afrocentric Guide to Selected Black Studies Terms & Concepts.** Katherine K. Bankole. (Illus.). 205p. (Orig.). 1995. pap. 20.00x (*1-878045-73-3*) Whittier Pubns.

Afrocentric Idea. Molefi K. Asante. LC 86-30046. 232p. 1988. pap. 14.95 (*0-87722-573-7*) Temple U Pr.

***Afrocentric Myth: Islam: The Liberator of the American People.** Abubakr B. Salahuddin. 121p. (Orig.). 1995. pap. 9.95 (*0-9645005-0-7*) New Wrld Order.

Afrocentric Self-Inventory & Discovery Workbook. Useni E. Perkins. 1990. 5.95 (*0-88378-043-7*) Third World.

Afrocentric Sermons: The Beauty of Blackness in the Bible. Kenneth L. Waters, Sr. 104p. 1993. pap. 9.00 (*0-8170-1199-4*) Judson.

Afrocentric Shopping Guide: Where to Find African-American Products in Houston & Surrounding Areas. Beverly J. Mackie. 44p. (Orig.). 1994. pap. 6.95 (*1-884509-05-3*) Creat Info.

Afrocentric Theory & Application, Vol. 2: Advances in the Adolescent Rite of Passage. Nsenga Warfield-Coppock & Bertram A. Coppock. 205p. (Orig.). 1992. pap. text ed. 18.00 (*0-9625647-3-7*) Baobab Assocs.

Afrocentric Theory & Applications, Vol. 1: Adolescent Rites of Passage. Nsenga Warfield-Coppock. (Illus.). 147p. 1990. pap. 16.00 (*0-9625647-1-0*); pap. text ed. 20.00 (*0-9625647-0-2*); student ed 4.00 (*0-9625647-2-9*) Baobab Assocs.

An Asterisk (*) at the beginning of an entry indicates that the title is appearing in BIP for the first time.

A

Afrocentricity: The Theory of Social Change. 2nd ed. Molefi K. Asante. LC 87-72779. 145p. (Orig.). 1990. reprint ed. pap. 9.95 (*0-86543-067-5*) Africa World.
Afrocentricity, Malcolm X & Al-Islam. Mustafa El-Amin. (Illus.). 150p. (Orig.). 1994. pap. text ed. 8.00 (*0-9638597-1-4*) El-Amin Prods.
***Afrocentrism & World Politics: Towards a New Paradigm.** Errol A. Henderson. LC 94-46170. 240p. 1995. text ed. 55.00 (*0-275-95127-8*) Greenwood.
Afrocommunism. 2nd ed. Marina Ottaway & David Ottaway. (Illus.). 280p. (C). 1986. text ed. 39.50 (*0-8419-1034-0*); pap. text ed. 18.95 (*0-8419-1035-9*) Holmes & Meier.
AfroCuba. Ed. by Pedro P. Sarduy & Jean Stubbs. (Illus.). 309p. 1994. pap. 17.95 (*1-875284-41-9*, Pub. by Ocean Pr AT) Talman.
AfroCuba. Ed. by Jean Stubbs & Pedro P. Sarduy. (Illus.). 280p. 1992. 34.95 (*1-875284-40-0*, Pub. by Ocean Pr AT) Talman.
Afrotina & the Three Bears: (A Retold Story) Fred Crump. LC 88-51222. (Illus.). 44p. (J). (gr. k-2). 1991. pap. 6.95 (*1-55523-195-0*) Winston-Derek.
AFS-CMI Conference on Thermal Analysis of Molten Aluminum: Proceedings. (Illus.). 347p. 1987. pap. 50.00 (*0-317-59822-8*, NF8502) Am Foundrymen.
AFSC vs. Thornburgh: Immigration, Employment & Religious Freedom. American Friends Service Committee Staff. 27p. 1990. pap. 1.50 (*0-910082-20-0*) Am Fr Serv Comm.
Afstand In der Wuste. Thomas E. Lawrence. (Illus.). 402p. 1988. reprint ed. write for info. (*3-487-08300-0*, Pub. by Georg Olms GW) Lubrecht & Cramer.
AFTA: The Way Ahead. Ed. by Pearl Imada & Seiji Naya. 145p. 1993. 22.75 (*981-3016-51-5*, Pub. by Inst SE Asian Studies SI); pap. 15.25 (*981-3016-50-7*, Pub. by Inst SE Asian Studies SI) Ashgate Pub Co.
After. Ann Douglas. LC 89-25277. 72p. 1991. 16.95 (*0-932576-80-X*); pap. 9.95 (*0-932576-81-8*) Breitenbush Bks.
After a California Earthquake: Attitude & Behavior Change. Risa I. Palm & Michael E. Hodgson. LC 91-857. (Illus.). 144p. 1992. pap. text ed. 15.00 (*0-226-64499-5*) U Ch Pr.
After a Child Dies: Counseling Bereaved Families. Sherry E. Johnson. LC 87-16637. 232p. 1987. 28.95 (*0-8261-5690-8*) Springer Pub.
After a Cremation. Edward McCrorie. 1974. pap. 3.00 (*0-914476-32-7*) Thorp Springs.
After a Fashion: How to Reproduce, Restore, & Wear Vintage Styles. Frances Grimble. (Illus.). 352p. (Orig.). 1993. pap. 35.00 (*0-9636517-0-6*) Lavolta Pr.
***After a Loss: Thoughts, Feelings & Behaviors.** Bill Steele. 47p. (YA). (gr. 7-12). 1994. pap. write for info. (*1-57515-048-4*) PPI Pubng.
After a Lost Original. David Shapiro. 112p. 1994. 19.95 (*0-87951-527-9*); pap. 12.95 (*0-87951-528-7*) Overlook Pr.
After a Stroke: A Support Book for Patients, Caregivers, Families & Friends. 2nd ed. Geoffrey A. Donnan & Carol Burton. (Illus.). 144p. 1992. reprint ed. pap. 9.95 (*1-55643-130-9*) North Atlantic.
After Abuse: Papers on Caring & Planning for a Child Who Has Been Sexually Abused. J. Robson et al. (C). 1989. 400.00 (*0-903534-82-7*, Pub. by Brit Ag for Adopt & Fost UK) St Mut.
After Afghanistan: The Long Haul. Harlan Cleveland et al. (Atlantic Council Policy Papers). 71p. 1980. 6.00 (*0-317-33689-4*) Atl Coun US.
After Africa: Extracts from British Travel Accounts & Journals of the Seventeenth, Eighteenth, & Nineteenth Centuries Concerning the Slaves, Their Manners, & Customs in the British West Indies. Ed. by Roger D. Abrahams & John F. Szwed. LC 82-20110. 480p. 1983. text ed. 57.00 (*0-300-02748-6*) Yale U Pr.
After Algiers. Proctor Jones. LC 89-91213. 295p. (Orig.). 1990. pap. 4.95 (*0-9608860-4-4*) Proctor Jones.
After Alice. Margaret Bingley. 1989. mass mkt. 3.95 (*0-445-20528-8*, Mysterious Paperbk) Warner Bks.
After Alice: Exploring Children's Literature. Ed. by Morag Styles et al. 196p. 1992. text ed. 60.00 (*0-304-32412-4*); pap. text ed. 19.95 (*0-304-32431-0*) Cassell.
After Alienation. Marcus Klein. LC 70-128267. (Essay Index Reprint Ser.). 1980. 23.95 (*0-8369-1969-6*) Ayer.
After Alinsky - In Illinois: Community Organizing in Illinois. Ed. by Peg Knoepfle. 176p. (Orig.). (C). 1990. pap. 11.95 (*0-9620873-3-5*) Illinois Issues.
***After All.** Jill M. Landis. 336p. (Orig.). 1995. pap. text ed. 5.50 (*0-515-11501-0*) Jove Pubns.
After All. Gren Seibels. LC 83-91428. (Illus.). 208p. 1983. pap. 15.00 (*0-9613056-0-6*) G Seibels.
After All: From Colonial Times to the 20th Century. Elsie De Wolfe. LC 74-3938. (Women in America Ser.). (Illus.). 310p. 1974. reprint ed. 28.95 (*0-405-06085-8*) Ayer.
After All, It's Only a Game. Willie Morris. LC 92-19542. (Author & Artist Ser.). (Illus.). 100p. 1992. 25.00 (*0-87805-600-9*) U Pr of Miss.
After All These Years. Susan Isaacs. LC 93-27046. 1994. mass mkt. 6.99 (*0-06-109179-0*, Harp PBks) HarpC.
***After All These Years.** Susan Isaacs. Date not set. pap. 5.98 (*0-8317-0029-7*) Smithmark.
After All These Years. large type ed. Susan Isaacs. LC 93-27046. 1993. 25.95 (*1-56895-035-7*) Wheeler Pub.
After All These Years. Sam Moskowitz. 96p. 1991. reprint ed. lib. bdg. 23.00x (*0-8095-6857-8*) Borgo Pr.
After All These Years: Sixties Ideals in a Different World. Lauren Kessler. 210p. 1990. pap. 13.95 (*0-938410-92-X*) Thunders Mouth.
After Amnesia: Tradition & Change in Indian Literary Criticism. D. N. Devy. 1993. 22.50 (*0-86311-267-6*, Pub. by Orient Longman Ltd II) Apt Bks.
After & Before the Lightning. Simon J. Ortiz. LC 94-5761. (Sun Tracks Ser.: Vol. 28). 160p. (Orig.). 1994. lib. bdg. 32.50 (*0-8165-1423-2*); pap. 15.95 (*0-8165-1448-8*) U of Ariz Pr.
***After Angel Comes.** Sophy Burnham. Date not set. write for info. (*0-345-39507-7*) Ballantine.
After Angola: The War over Southern Africa. Colin Legum & Tony Hodges. LC 76-17076. (Current Affairs Ser.). (C). 1976. pap. 6.95 (*0-8419-0279-8*, Africana) Holmes & Meier.
After Apartheid: Renewal of the South African Economy. Ed. by John Suckling & Landeg White. LC 88-71830. 230p. (C). 1988. 35.00 (*0-86543-112-4*); pap. 11.95 (*0-86543-113-2*) Africa World.
After Apartheid: The Future of South Africa. Sebastian Mallaby. LC 91-50190. (Illus.). 275p. 1992. 21.50 (*0-8129-1938-6*, Times Bks) Random.
After Apartheid: The Future of South Africa. Sebastian Mallaby. 1993. pap. 14.00 (*0-8129-2204-2*, Times Bks) Random.
***After Apocalypse: Four Japanese Plays of Hiroshima & Nagasaki.** Tr. by David G. Goodman. (Cornell East Asia Ser.: No. 71). (Illus.). 344p. (C). 1994. pap. text ed. 15.00 (*0-939657-71-6*, 71) Cornell East Asia Pgm.
After Apocalypse: Four Japanese Plays of Hiroshima & Nagasaki. David G. Goodman. LC 85-17051. 347p. reprint ed. pap. 98.90 (*0-7837-0433-X*, 2040756) Bks Demand.
***After Appomattox: How the South Won the War.** Stetson Kennedy. (Illus.). 368p. 1995. lib. bdg. 49.95 (*0-8130-1341-0*) U Press Fla.
***After Art: Rethinking 150 Years of Photography: Essays.** Chris Bruce & Andy Grundberg. LC 94-25923. (Illus.). 120p. 1995. pap. 37.50 (*0-295-97415-X*) U of Wash Pr.
After Asia. Michael Stephens. 82p. (Orig.). 1993. write for info. (*1-881471-04-7*); pap. write for info. (*1-881471-05-5*) S Duyvil.
***After Assessment: Facilitator Instructions II.** Meredith M. Bell. 48p. 1994. pap. text ed. 25.00 (*1-886713-05-7*) Perform Support Systs.
After Auschwitz: History, Theology, & Contemporary Judaism. 2nd ed. Richard L. Rubenstein. (Jewish Studies). 416p. 1992. text ed. 48.50 (*0-8018-4284-0*); pap. text ed. 14.95 (*0-8018-4285-9*) Johns Hopkins.
***After Auschwitz: Responses to the Holocaust in Contemporary Art.** Monica Bohm-Duchen. (Illus.). 160p. 1995. pap. 39.95 (*0-85331-666-X*, Pub. by Lund Humphries UK) Antique Collect.
***After Authoritarianism: Democracy or Disorder?** Ed. by Daniel N. Nelson. LC 95-5267. (Contributions in Political Science Ser.: Vol. 360). 200p. 1995. text ed. 59.95 (*0-313-29393-7*, Greenwood Pr) Greenwood.
***After Authoritarianism: Democracy or Disorder?** Ed. by Daniel N. Nelson. 200p. 1995. pap. text ed. 18.95 (*0-275-95330-0*, Greenwood Pr) Greenwood.
***After Autumn Rain: Haiku, Senryu, Sketches.** Francine Porad. (Illus.). 28p. (Orig.). (C). 1987. pap. text ed. 5.00 (*0-9618009-2-5*) Vandina Pr.
After Aztlan: Latino Poets of the Nineties. Ed. by Ray Gonzalez. 1992. pap. 15.95 (*0-87923-932-8*) Godine.
After Babel: Aspects of Language & Translation. George Steiner. LC 92-13874. 560p. 1993. pap. 16.95 (*0-19-282874-6*) OUP.
After Bakhtin: Essays on Fiction & Criticism. David Lodge. 208p. 1990. 49.95 (*0-415-05037-5*, A4556); pap. 14.95 (*0-415-05038-3*, A4560) Routledge.
After Becoming a Christian What's Next? Dick Andrew. 1991. pap. write for info. (*0-914936-29-8*) Bible Temple.
After Big Game in Central Africa. Edouard Foa. 1989. 16.95 (*0-312-03274-9*) St Martin.
After Big Game in Central Africa. limited ed. Edouard Foa. (Illus.). 330p. 1986. boxed 45.00 (*0-940143-04-6*) Safari Pr.
***After Bipolarity: The Vanishing Threat, Theories of Cooperation & the Future of the Atlantic Alliance.** Fred Chernoff. 326p. 1994. text ed. 44.50x (*0-472-10550-7*) U of Mich Pr.
After Black Monday: Extract Painfree Profits from Wall Street Without Fear or Guilt. John V. Kamin. 174p. 1988. 35.00 (*0-911353-11-9*) Forecaster Pub.
After Brecht: British Epic Theater. Janelle Reinelt. LC 94-17613. (Theater -- Theory-Text-Performance Ser.). (Illus.). 212p. 1994. 39.50 (*0-472-10321-0*) U of Mich Pr.
After Brezhnev: Sources of Soviet Conduct in the 1980s. Ed. by Robert F. Byrnes. LC 82-48614. (CSIS Publication Series on the Soviet Union in the 1980's; Midland Bks.). 475p. reprint ed. pap. 135.40 (*0-8357-3939-2*, 2057034) Bks Demand.
After Brockman: A Symposium. LC 74-84162. 69p. (Orig.). 1974. pap. 2.00 (*0-911856-14-5*) Abyss.
After Calculus. Craig Watson. (Poetry Ser.). 72p. (Orig.). 1988. pap. 7.00 (*0-930901-40-1*) Burning Deck.
After Calculus. limited ed. Craig Watson. (Poetry Ser.). 72p. (Orig.). 1988. pap. 15.00 (*0-930901-46-0*) Burning Deck.
After Cancer: A Guide to Your New Life. Wendy S. Harpham. LC 93-44553. 1994. 23.00 (*0-393-03664-2*) Norton.
After Chartism: Class & Nation in English Radical Politics, 1848-1884. Margot C. Finn. LC 92-30241. (Past & Present Publications). (Illus.). 350p. (C). 1993. 59.95 (*0-521-40496-7*) Cambridge U Pr.
After Chernobyl. Cornelia Hesse-Honegger et al. (Illus.). 66p. 1991. 35.00 (*3-906700-46-1*, Pub. by Lars Muller SZ) Dist Art Pubs.
After China. Brian Castro. 145p. (Orig.). 1993. pap. 14.95 (*1-86373-243-8*, Pub. by Allen & Unwin Aust Pty AT) IPG Chicago.
After Christendom: How the Church Is to Behave If Freedom, Justice, & a Christian Nation Are Bad. Stanley Hauerwas. 1991. pap. 12.95 (*0-687-00929-4*) Abingdon.
After Christmas Tree. Linda W. Tyler. (J). (ps-3). 1990. 12.95 (*0-670-83045-3*) Viking Child Bks.
After-Christmas Tree. Linda W. Tyler. LC 92-8616. (J). (gr. 4 up). 1992. 3.99 (*0-14-054191-8*) Puffin Bks.
***After Colette.** Joan Lingard. 315p. 1995. 24.95 (*1-85619-328-4*, Sinclair-Stevenson) Trafalgar.
After College: The Business of Getting Jobs. Jack Falvey. Ed. by Susan Williamson. LC 85-22640. 192p. (Orig.). 1986. pap. 9.95 (*0-913589-17-9*) Williamson Pub Co.
After College Guide to Life. Carole B. Everett & Tracy C. Harkins. LC 92-74814. (Illus.). 192p. (Orig.). 1993. pap. 12.95 (*0-9634987-0-3*) Alcove Pr.
***After Colonialism: Imperial Histories & Postcolonial Displacements.** Ed. by Gyan Prakash. LC 94-21310. 1994. 16.95 (*0-691-03742-6*) Princeton U Pr.
After Columbus: Essays in the Ethnohistory of Colonial North America. James Axtell. (Illus.). 320p. 1990. reprint ed. pap. 17.95 (*0-19-505376-1*) OUP.
After Columbus: The Horse's Return to America. Herman J. Viola. LC 92-11038. (Smithsonian Wild Heritage Collection). (Illus.). 32p. (J). (gr. 2-5). 1992. 11.95 (*0-924483-61-X*); audio 16.95 (*0-924483-60-1*); audio 25.95 (*0-924483-59-8*); audio write for info. (*0-924483-74-1*) Soundprints.
After Columbus: The Horse's Return to America. Herman J. Viola. LC 92-11038. (Smithsonian Wild Heritage Collection). (Illus.). 32p. (J). (gr. 2-5). 1992. audio 39.95 (*0-924483-58-X*) Soundprints.
After Columbus: The Smithsonian Chronicle of the North American Indian. Herman J. Viola. (Illus.). 1990. 45.00 (*0-517-58108-6*, Orion Bks) Crown Pub Group.
After Columbus: The Smithsonian Chronicle of the North American Indian. Herman J. Viola. LC 90-9990. (Illus.). 288p. 1993. pap. 24.95 (*0-89599-031-8*) Smithsonian Bks.
***After Columbus: The Smithsonian Chronicle of the North American Indians.** Herman J. Viola. 1993. pap. 24.95 (*0-89599-028-8*) Smithsonian Bks.
After Communion. 144p. (Orig.). 1988. pap. 5.95 (*0-85182-032-8*, Pub. by Four Courts Pr EIRE) Scepter Pubs.
After Communion: Book of Devotions. 144p. 1988. 4.95 (*0-912414-51-0*) Lumen Christi.
After Communism; from the Atlantic to the Urals. Jacques Lesourne & Bernard Lecomte. 271p. 1991. text ed. 58.00 (*3-7186-5211-0*, HX) Gordon & Breach.
After Damien: Dutton, Yankee Soldier at Molokai. Howard E. Crouch & Mary Augustine. LC 81-67534. (Illus.). 144p. (Orig.). 1981. pap. 5.00 (*0-9606330-0-6*) Damien-Dutton Soc.
***After Darin.** Travis A. Haskins. 224p. 1994. 14.95 (*0-9641576-1-6*) Soulprint Pubng.
After Dark. Louis Baum. LC 89-16123. (Illus.). 32p. (J). (ps-3). 1990. 11.95 (*0-87951-382-9*) Overlook Pr.
***After Dark.** Phillip Margolin. LC 94-41997. 384p. 1995. 23.95 (*0-385-47548-9*) Doubleday.
After Dark, My Sweet. Jim Thompson. LC 90-50250. (Vintage Crime - Black Lizard Ser.). 160p. 1990. pap. 7.95 (*0-679-73247-0*, Vin) Random.
After Dark, My Sweet. Jim Thompson. LC 85-72391. 160p. 1986. reprint ed. pap. 3.95 (*0-88739-005-6*, Blk Lizard) Creat Arts Bk.
After Death: Judgment or Recycling? Ralph Rath. (Get the Facts Ser.: Series I). 30p. (Orig.). 1993. pap. 2.95 (*0-9640167-3-7*) Peter Pubns.
After Death: The Disembodiment of Man. Paschal B. Randolph. reprint ed. spiral bd. 7.70 (*0-7873-0701-7*) Mokelumne.
After Death: The Immortality of Man. Paschal B. Randolph. 272p. 1970. write for info. (*0-932785-00-X*) Philos Pub.
After Death Experience. Ian Wilson. LC 88-23474. (Illus.). 234p. 1990. reprint ed. pap. 8.95 (*0-688-09419-8*, Quill) Morrow.
After Death Tax Planning: Minimizing Tax Liabilities. Jerry A. Kasner & Robert Whitman. LC 90-55159. 140p. 1990. text ed. 90.00 (*0-8318-0498-X*, B498) Am Law Inst.
After Death, What? rev. ed. Leoline L. Wright. Ed. by W. Emmett Small & Helen Todd. (Theosophical Manual Ser.: No. 5). 96p. 1974. pap. 3.95 (*0-913004-15-4*) Point Loma Pub.
***After Derrida.** Nicholas Royle. LC 94-5404. 1995. text ed. write for info. (*0-7190-4378-6*, Pub. by Manchester Univ Pr UK); text ed. write for info. (*0-7190-4379-4*, Pub. by Manchester Univ Pr UK) St Martin.
After Deschooling, What? Ivan Illich. (Education Ser.). 64p. (Orig.). 1980. pap. 2.50 (*0-904613-36-4*) Writers & Readers.
After Desert Storm: Rethinking U. S. Defense Requirements. Carl Conetta & Charles Knight. (Briefing Report Ser.: No. 2). 26p. 1991. reprint ed. pap. 5.50 (*1-881677-00-1*) Commonwlth Inst.
After Dinner & Other Speeches. John D. Long. LC 72-4550. (Essay Index Reprint Ser.). 1977. reprint ed. 20.95 (*0-8369-2958-6*) Ayer.
***After-Dinner Devotions: Family Devotions Your Kids Will Love!** 1995. 8.99 (*0-8423-1671-X*) Tyndale.
After-Dinner Gardening Book. rev. ed. Richard W. Langer. (Illus.). 208p. 1992. pap. 9.95 (*0-89815-450-2*) Ten Speed Pr.
After Dinner Jokes. Bill Stott. Ed. by Helen Exley & Samantha Armstrong. (Joke Bks.). (Illus.). 60p. 1991. 6.99 (*1-85015-260-8*) Exley Giftbooks.
After Dinner Speeches. Martin Nicholls. (Work Matters Ser.). 96p. 1991. pap. 4.95 (*0-7063-6816-9*, Pub. by Ward Lock UK) Sterling.
After Dinner Speeches & Stories. Foulsham Editors. 128p. 1995. pap. 7.95 (*0-572-00021-9*, Pub. by Foulsham UK) Atrium Pubs.
After Dinner's Sleep. large type ed. Stanley Middleton. 448p. 1988. 15.95 (*0-7089-1903-0*) Ulverscroft.
After Dionysus: An Essay on Where We Are Now. Henry Ebel. LC 70-156321. 136p. 1975. 22.50 (*0-8386-7958-7*) Fairleigh Dickinson.
After Divestiture: The Political Economy of State Telecommunications Regulation. Paul Teske. LC 89-21851. (SUNY Series in Public Administration). 162p. 1990. 59.50 (*0-7914-0323-8*); pap. 19.95 (*0-7914-0324-6*) State U NY Pr.
After Divestiture: What the AT&T Settlement Means for Business & Residential Telephone Service. Samuel A. Simon. LC 84-21301. (Professional Librarian Ser.). 138p. 1985. text ed. 38.95 (*0-86729-110-9*, Hall Reference) Macmillan.
After Doomsday. Conleth Ellis. (Raven Long Poems Ser.). 1981. 8.95 (*0-906897-45-9*); pap. 7.95 (*0-906897-46-7*) Dufour.
After Duwagan: Deforestation, Succession & Adaptation in Upland Luzon, Philippines. J. Peter Brosius & Karl L. Hutterer. LC 89-81764. (Michigan Studies on South & Southeast Asia: No. 2). (Illus.). 188p. (Orig.). 1990. pap. 16.95 (*0-89148-061-7*) Ctr S&SE Asian.
After Earth Day: Continuing the Conservation Effort. Ed. by Max Oelschlaeger. LC 92-922. (Philosophy & the Environment Ser.: No. 1). 264p. 1992. text ed. 24.50 (*0-929398-44-0*); pap. text ed. 15.95 (*0-929398-40-8*) UNTX Pr.
After Easter. Anne Devlin. 96p. (Orig.). 1994. pap. 9.95 (*0-571-17394-2*) Faber & Faber.
***After Eden.** Glen Enloe. (Petite Ser.). 56p. 1994. pap. 4.00 (*1-884754-09-0*) Potpourri Pubns.
After Eden: Facing the Challenge of Gender Reconciliation. Mary S. Van Leeuwen et al. 640p. (Orig.). 1993. pap. 29.99 (*0-8028-0646-5*) Eerdmans.
After Eden: The Secularization of American Space in the Fiction of Willa Cather & Theodore Dreiser. Conrad E. Ostwalt, Jr. LC 89-42505. 160p. 1990. 32.50 (*0-8387-5168-7*) Bucknell U Pr.
After Eli. Terry P. Kay. 1992. 16.50 (*1-56145-068-5*) Peachtree Pubs.
After Ellis Island: A Nineteen Ten Census Monograph. Ed. by Susan C. Watkins. (Illus.). 448p. 1994. 49.95 (*0-87154-910-7*) Russell Sage.
After Every Wedding Comes a Marriage. Florence Littauer. LC 81-80023. 208p. (Orig.). 1981. pap. 7.99 (*0-89081-289-6*) Harvest Hse.
After Fifteen Years. Leon Jaworski. LC 61-14514. (Illus.). 168p. reprint ed. pap. 47.90 (*0-8357-8010-4*, 2034170) Bks Demand.
After Fifteen Years: Artificial Liver & Artificial Pancreas. 2nd ed. K. N. Matsumura & William L. Hamilton. LC 78-56092. (Illus.). 1978. 6.95 (*0-9606924-0-1*) Alin Found Pr.
After Fifth Grade, the World! Claudia Mills. LC 88-26664. 128p. (J). (gr. 3-7). 1989. text ed., lib. bdg. 13.95 (*0-02-767041-4*, Mac Bks Young Read) S&S Childrens.
After Fifth Grade, the World! Claudia Mills. (J). (gr. 3-7). 1991. reprint ed. pap. 2.95 (*0-380-70894-9*, Camelot) Avon.
After Fifty Thousand Miles. Hal Roth. (Illus.). 1977. 24.95 (*0-393-03202-7*) Norton.
After Fifty Thousand Miles. Hal Roth. 352p. 1993. pap. 16.95 (*0-393-30948-7*) Norton.
After First Principles. Gary Underwood & Marylyn Underwood. 1984. pap. 5.75 (*0-89137-710-7*) Quality Pubns.
After Five Cook. Thayer Wine. 1987. pap. 10.95 (*0-9618910-0-9*) Jackson Sun.
After Forty: The Time for Achievement? Cary Cooper & Derek P. Torrington. 211p. 1981. text ed. 63.95 (*0-471-28043-7*, Wiley-Interscience) Wiley.
After Forty: The Time for Achievement? Ed. by Cary L. Cooper & Derek P. Torrington. LC 82-105750. (Illus.). 219p. reprint ed. pap. 62.50 (*0-8357-4911-8*, 2037841) Bks Demand.
After Foucault Humanistic Knowledge, Postmodern Challenges. Ed. by Jonathan Arac. 224p. (Orig.). (C). 1988. text ed. 35.00 (*0-8135-1329-4*); pap. text ed. 15.00 (*0-8135-1330-8*) Rutgers U Pr.
After Freedom: A Cultural Study in the Deep South. Hortense Powdermaker. LC 92-56923. (New Directions in Anthropological Writing Ser.). 462p. (C). 1993. reprint ed. lib. bdg. 42.50 (*0-299-13780-5*); reprint ed. pap. 17.95 (*0-299-13784-8*) U of Wis Pr.
After Frost, the Spring. large type ed. Janet Beaton. (Linford Romance Library). 1991. pap. 13.95 (*0-7089-7097-4*) Ulverscroft.
After Fundamentalism: The Future of Evangelical Theology. Bernard L. Ramm. LC 82-47792. 226p. 1984. pap. 9.95 (*0-06-066789-3*) Harper SF.
After Goodbye: How to Begin Again after the Death of Someone You Love. Ted Menten. LC 93-85506. 128p. 1994. 12.95 (*1-56138-295-7*) Running Pr.
After Gorbachev? Ernest Raiklin. (Journal of Social, Political & Economic Studies Monograph Ser.: No. 20). 128p. (Orig.). 1989. pap. 15.00 (*0-930690-23-0*) Coun Soc Econ.
After Gorbachev. 4th ed. Stephen White. (Soviet Paperbacks Ser.: No. 3). 368p. (C). 1993. 49.95 (*0-521-45264-3*); pap. 13.95 (*0-521-45896-X*) Cambridge U Pr.
After Great Pain: The Inner Life of Emily Dickinson. John Cody. LC 79-148937. 552p. reprint ed. pap. 157.40 (*0-7837-1511-0*, 2041788) Bks Demand.
After Gregory. Austin Wright. 275p. 1994. 20.00 (*1-880909-12-X*) Baskerville.

An Asterisk (*) at the beginning of an entry indicates that the title is appearing in BIP for the first time. 129

After Hard Guns. Eli Mitchell. 272p. (Orig.). 1980. pap. 1.95 (*0-89083-699-X*) Zebra.

After Hegemony: Cooperation & Discord in the World Political Economy. Robert O. Keohane. LC 84-42576. 290p. 1984. text ed. 45.00x (*0-691-07676-6*); pap. 14.95 (*0-691-02228-3*) Princeton U Pr.

After Henry. Joan Didion. LC 92-50640. 1993. pap. 12.00 (*0-679-74539-4*, Vin) Random.

After Hiroshima: America since 1945. 2nd ed. Albert C. Ganley et al. (Illus.). 356p. (Orig.). (C). (gr. 11-12). 1985. pap. text ed. 18.17 (*0-88334-121-2*, 76095) Longman.

After History? Francis Kukuyama & His Critics. Ed. by Timothy Burns. 240p. 1994. lib. bdg. 54.50 (*0-8476-7926-8*); pap. 16.95 (*0-8226-3035-4*) Rowman.

***After Hours: Conversations with Lawrence Block.** Lawrence Block & Ernest Bulow. LC 94-34718. 170p. (C). 1995. 19.95 (*0-8263-1583-6*) U of NM Pr.

After Hours: Modern Japan & the Search for Enjoyment. David W. Plath. LC 83-22869. xi, 222p. 1984. reprint ed. text ed. 55.00 (*0-313-24297-6*, PLAF, Greenwood Pr) Greenwood.

After Hours with P. G. Wodehouse. Richard Usborne. 201p. 1995. 21.95 (*0-87008-128-4*) JAS Heineman.

After House. Mary R. Rinehart. 21.95 (*0-8488-1140-2*) Amereon Ltd.

After House. Mary R. Rinehart. 1989. mass mkt. 3.99 (*0-8217-4242-6*) Zebra.

After I Fall: Collected Poems. Ronald Alexander et al. 64p. (Orig.). 1991. pap. 8.95 (*0-941017-22-2*) Bombshelter Pr.

***After Identity: A Reader in Law & Culture.** Ed. by Dan Danielsen & Karen Engle. 400p. 1994. 59.95 (*0-415-90996-1*, B3877) Routledge.

***After Identity: A Reader in Law & Culture.** Ed. by Dan Danielsen & Karen Engle. 400p. 1994. pap. 18.95 (*0-415-90997-X*, B3881) Routledge.

After Ideology: Recovering the Spiritual Foundations of Freedom. David Walsh. LC 89-46470. 336p. 1990. 29.95 (*0-685-45875-X*) Harper SF.

After I'm Dead, Will My Life Begin? James Humphrey. Ed. by Saroyan Humphrey. 150p. (Orig.). 1985. pap. 10.50 (*0-936641-00-2*) Poets Alive Pr.

After Images: The Collected Poems of Kingsley Tufts. Kingsley Tufts. 365p. (Orig.). 1994. 19.95 (*1-56474-084-6*) Fithian Pr.

After Imperialism: The Search for a New Order in the Far East, 1921-1931. Akira Iriye. LC 90-84056. 392p. (C). 1990. reprint ed. pap. text ed. 15.95 (*1-879176-00-9*) Imprint Pubns.

After Innocence. Brenda Joyce. 432p. (Orig.). 1994. mass mkt. 5.99 (*0-380-77572-7*) Avon.

After Jesus: The Triumph of Christianity. Reader's Digest Editors. LC 91-8873. (Illus.). 352p. 1992. 30.00 (*0-89577-392-9*, Random) RD Assn.

After Jews & Arabs: Remaking Levantine Culture. Ammiel Alcalay. 288p. (C). 1992. text ed. 44.95 (*0-8166-2154-3*); pap. text ed. 16.95 (*0-8166-2155-1*) U of Minn Pr.

After Kafka: The Influence of Kafka's Fiction. Shimon Sandbank. LC 88-24995. 192p. 1989. 25.00 (*0-8203-1105-7*) U of Ga Pr.

After Khomeini: New Directions in Iran's Foreign Policy. K. L. Afrasiabi. (C). 1994. text ed. 54.95 (*0-8133-2115-8*) Westview.

***After Khomeini: The Iranian Second Republic.** Anoushiravan Ehteshami. LC 94-37691. 256p. 1995. 65.00x (*0-415-10878-0*, C0169); pap. 17.95 (*0-415-10879-9*, C0170) Routledge.

After King Fahd: Succession in Saudi Arabia. Simon Henderson. LC 94-12154. (Policy Papers Series: No. 37). 1994. write for info. (*0-944029-55-8*) Wash Inst NEP.

After Lazarus: A Filmscript. limited ed. Robert Coover. 1980. 50.00 (*0-89723-020-5*) Bruccoli.

After Leaving Mr. Mackenzie. Jean Rhys. 191p. 1990. pap. 8.95 (*0-88184-585-X*) Carroll & Graf.

After Leningrad: A Diary of Survival. Elena Skrjabina. Tr. & Intro. by Norman Luxenburg. (Soviet Union at War Ser.: Vol. 2). 193p. (Orig.). 1988. pap. 21.95x (*0-88738-749-7*) Transaction Pubs.

***After Liberalism.** Immanuel Wallerstein. LC 95-7424. 288p. 1995. pap. 14.95 (*1-56584-304-5*) New Press NY.

After Life. Andrew Neiderman. 1993. mass mkt. 4.99 (*0-425-13974-3*) Berkley Pub.

***After Life, What? A Post-Death Quest.** Robert Pinansky. 105p. (Orig.). 1995. pap. 11.95 (*1-885395-12-4*) Book Tree.

After Livingstone: An African Trade Romance. Frederick L. Moir. 1977. 17.95 (*0-8369-9212-1*, 9068) Ayer.

After London, or, Wild England, 2 pts. Richard Jefferies. Incl. Pt 1. Relapse into Barbarism. LC 74-16503. 1975. (*0-318-50782-X*); Pt 2. Wild England. LC 74-16503. 1975. (*0-318-50783-8*); LC 74-16503. (Science Fiction Ser.). 450p. 1975. reprint ed. 36.95 (*0-405-06301-6*) Ayer.

After Loss: Survival Lessons From an Author Who Learned. Robert DiGiulio. (Illus.). 160p. 1993. pap. 10.95 (*1-56796-022-7*) WRS Group.

***After Lydia.** Sandra Tyler. LC 94-27359. 1995. 22.00 (*0-15-193111-9*) HarBrace.

***After Maastricht: American & European Perspectives.** Ed. by Paul M. Lutzeler. LC 94-33658. 320p. (C). 1994. 29.95 (*1-57181-020-X*) Berghahn Bks.

***After Mabo.** Tim Rowse. 1995. pap. text ed. 19.95 (*0-522-84492-8*) Intl Spec Bk.

After Machiavelli: "Re-Writing" & the "Hermeneutic Attitude" Barbara Godorecci. LC 93-15905. (Studies in Romance Literatures: Vol. 3). 224p. 1993. 36.00 (*1-55753-045-9*) Purdue U Pr.

After MacIntyre: Critical Perspectives on the Work of Alasdair MacIntyre. Ed. by John Horton & Susan Mendus. LC 94-76358. (C). 1994. text ed. 39.95 (*0-268-00642-3*) U of Notre Dame Pr.

***After MacIntyre: Critical Perspectives on the Work of Alasdair MacIntyre.** Ed. by John Horton & Susan Mendus. LC 94-76358. (C). Date not set. reprint ed. pap. text ed. 19.50 (*0-268-00643-1*) U of Notre Dame Pr.

After Many a Summer Dies the Swan. Aldous Huxley. 1977. reprint ed. lib. bdg. 23.95 (*0-89190-395-X*, Queens House) Amereon Ltd.

After Many a Summer Dies the Swan. Aldous Huxley. 360p. 1993. reprint ed. pap. 14.95 (*1-56663-018-5*) I R Dee.

After Many Days. Lucy M. Montgomery. 1992. mass mkt. 3.99 (*0-553-29184-X*) Bantam.

After Many Years. Mario Luzi. (C). 1990. 26.00 (*0-948268-77-8*, Pub. by Dedalus Pr IE); pap. 18.00 (*0-948268-76-X*, Pub. by Dedalus Pr IE) St Mut.

After Mao: Chinese Literature & Society, 1978-1981. Ed. by Jeffrey C. Kinkley. (East Asian Monographs: No. 115: Vol. 1). 375p. 1985. pap. 18.00 (*0-674-00885-5*) HUP.

After Marriage Ends: Economic Consequences for Midlife Women. Leslie A. Morgan. (New Perspectives on Family Ser.). (Illus.). 240p. 1991. 46.00 (*0-8039-3548-X*); pap. 21.95 (*0-8039-3549-8*) Sage.

After Marx, Before Lenin: Marxism & Socialist Working-Class Parties in Europe, 1884-1914. Gary P. Steenson. LC 90-21489. 368p. (C). 1991. 49.95 (*0-8229-3673-9*) U of Pittsburgh Pr.

After Marxism. Ronald Aronson. 344p. 1994. pap. 18.95 (*0-89862-416-9*) Guilford Pubns.

***After Marxism.** Ronald Aronson. LC 94-23009. (Critical Perspectives Ser.). 322p. 1994. lib. bdg. 40.00 (*0-89862-417-7*) Guilford Pr.

After Materialism-What? Richard C. Tute. LC 72-13176. (Essay Index Reprint Ser.). 1977. reprint ed. 18.95 (*0-8369-8175-8*) Ayer.

After Matisse. Tiffany Bell et al. (Illus.). 64p. 1986. 18.00 (*0-916365-19-0*) Ind Curators.

After Metaphysics: Toward a Grammar of Interaction & Discourse. Harvey Sarles. (Studies in Semiotics: No. 13). 286p. 1977. pap. 35.00 (*90-316-0134-9*, Pub. by Gruner NE) Benjamins North Am.

After Middle Age: A Limitless Sky. Osho Rajneesh. Ed. by Mary Amoore. (Introduction to the Teachings of Osho Ser.). 96p. 1992. 6.95 (*0-918963-02-8*) Osho Chidvilas.

After Midnight. Martha Albrand. 1976. pap. 0.95 (*0-380-01009-7*) Avon.

After Midnight. Susan Kyle. 352p. (Orig.). 1993. mass mkt. 5.50 (*0-446-36361-8*) Warner Bks.

***After Midnight.** Warren. (Loveswept Ser.: No. 737). 1995. mass mkt. 3.50 (*0-553-44404-2*, Loveswept) Bantam.

After Midnight. large type ed. Eva Burfield. 432p. 1987. 16.95 (*0-7089-1651-1*) Ulverscroft.

After Midnight Stories, Bk. 4. large type ed. Ed. by Amy Meyers. 1990. 21.95 (*0-7089-2290-2*) Ulverscroft.

After Modernism: Global Restructuring & the Changing Boundaries of City Life. Ed. by Michael P. Smith. (Comparative Urban & Community Research Ser.: Vol. 4). 156p. (C). 1992. pap. 21.95 (*1-56000-598-X*) Transaction Pubs.

After Modernity... What? Thomas C. Oden. 1992. pap. 16.99 (*0-310-75391-0*) Zondervan.

After Moondog. Shapiro. 1992. 22.95 (*0-15-193096-1*) HarBrace.

After Moondog. Jane Shapiro. 336p. 1993. pap. 9.99 (*0-446-39526-9*) Warner Bks.

After Mormonism, What? Latayne C. Scott. LC 93-10784. 160p. (Orig.). 1993. pap. 7.99 (*0-8010-8350-8*) Baker Bk.

After Nature's Revolt: Eco-Justice & Theology. Dieter T. Hessel. LC 91-44441. 232p. (Orig.). 1992. pap. 16.00 (*0-8006-2532-3*, 1-2532, Fortress Pr) Augsburg Fortress.

After Newton: Essays on Natural Philosophy. P. M. Harman. (Collected Studies: Vol. CS389). 237p. 1993. 89.95 (*0-86078-348-0*, Pub. by Variorum UK) Ashgate Pub Co.

After Nine Hundred Years: The Background of the Schism Between the Eastern & Western Churches. Yves M. Conger. LC 78-6154. 150p. 1978. reprint ed. text ed. 35.00 (*0-313-20493-4*, COAN, Greenwood Pr) Greenwood.

After Nineteen Eighty-Four: Prospects for a Better World. Frank George. (Abacus Bks.). 208p. 1984. text ed. 40.00 (*0-85626-443-1*) Gordon & Breach.

After Nineteen NInety-Two: The United States of Europe. Ernest Wistrich. 1989. 35.00 (*0-415-04451-0*) Routledge.

After Nineteen Ninety-Two: The United States of Europe. Ernest Wistrich. 176p. 1991. pap. 16.95 (*0-415-06457-0*, A5650) Routledge.

After Ninety. Imogen Cunningham. LC 77-73306. (Illus.). 80p. 1977. pap. 24.95 (*0-295-95673-9*) U of Wash Pr.

After Nostradamus. A. Voldben. 186p. 1974. 6.95 (*0-8065-0431-5*, Citadel Pr) Carol Pub Group.

After Oedipus: Shakespeare in Psychoanalysis. Julia R. Lupton & Kenneth Reinhard. LC 92-54975. (Illus.). 288p. 1993. 37.50 (*0-8014-2407-0*); pap. 14.95 (*0-8014-9687-X*) Cornell U Pr.

***After Ovid: New Metamorphoses.** Michael Hofmann. 1995. 25.00 (*0-374-10197-3*) FS&G.

After Oz. Michael J. Bugeja. LC 92-32274. 80p. (Orig.). 1993. pap. 11.95 (*0-914061-32-1*) Orchises Pr.

After Pa Was Shot. Judy Alter. LC 89-12176. (Illus.). 192p. (Orig.). (J). (gr. 4-9). 1991. reprint ed. pap. 5.95 (*0-936650-12-5*) E C Temple.

After Patriarchy: Feminist Transformations of the World Religions. Ed. by Paula Cooey et al. LC 91-3287. (Faith Meets Faith Ser.). 175p. (Orig.). 1991. 39.95 (*0-88344-749-5*); pap. 16.95 (*0-88344-748-7*) Orbis Bks.

After Perestroika: Democracy in the Soviet Union. Ed. by Brad Roberts & Nina Belyaeva. (Significant Issues Ser.). 130p. (Orig.). 1991. pap. text ed. 6.95 (*0-89206-173-1*) CSI Studies.

After Perestroika: Kithenmaids of Stateswomen. Independent Curators Editors. 1994. pap. 17.95 (*0-916365-38-7*) Ind Curators.

After Philosophy: End or Transformation? Ed. by Kenneth Baynes et al. 300p. (Orig.). (C). 1986. pap. 20.00 (*0-262-52113-X*) MIT Pr.

After Plastic Surgery: Adaptation & Adjustment. Frances C. Macgregor. LC 79-11808. (Praeger Special Studies). 160p. 1979. text ed. 45.00 (*0-275-90383-4*, C0383, Praeger Pubs) Greenwood.

After Plastic Surgery: Adaptation & Adjustment. Francis C. McGregor. 160p. (C). 1979. 39.95 (*0-03-052131-9*) Phoenix Soc.

After Play, Acting Ed. Anne Meara. 1995. pap. 4.75 (*0-8222-0459-2*) Dramatists Play.

***After Political Correctness: The Humanities & Society in the 1990s.** Ed. by Christopher Newfield & Ronald Strickland. LC 94-33692. (Cultural Studies - Politics & Culture Subs). 1995. text ed. 79.95 (*0-8133-2336-3*) Westview.

***After Political Correctness: The Humanities & Society in the 1990s.** Ed. by Christopher Newfield & Ronald Strickland. LC 94-33692. (Cultural Studies - Politics & Culture Subs). (C). 1995. pap. text ed. 24.95 (*0-8133-2337-1*) Westview.

After Polygamy Was Made a Sin. John Cairncross. 1974. 22.00 (*0-7100-7730-0*) Dufour.

After Polygamy Was Made a Sin: The Social History of Christian Polygamy. John Cairncross. 236p. 1974. 17.95 (*0-318-39996-2*, Pub. by Colin Smythe Ltd UK) Dufour.

***After Postmodernism: Education, Politics, & Identity.** Ed. by Richard Smith & Philip Wexler. LC 95-7251. 1995. 36.00 (*0-7507-0441-1*, Falmer Pr); pap. 13.95 (*0-7507-0442-X*, Falmer Pr) Taylor & Francis.

After Postmodernism: Reconstructing Ideology Critique. Herbert W. Simons. Ed. by Michael Billig. (Inquiries in Social Construction Ser.). 272p. 1994. 69.95 (*0-8039-8877-X*) Sage.

After Postmodernism: Reconstructing Ideology Critique. Ed. by Herbert W. Simons & Michael Billig. (Inquiries in Social Construction Ser.). 272p. 1994. pap. 22.95 (*0-8039-8878-8*) Sage.

After Poststructuralism: Interdisciplinarity & Literary Theory. Ed. by Nancy Easterlin & Barbara Riebling. (Rethinking Theory Ser.). 300p. (Orig.). 1993. 45.95 (*0-8101-1096-2*); pap. 19.95 (*0-8101-1097-0*) Northwestern U Pr.

After Principles. Garrett Barden. LC 89-40743. (Revisions: A Series of Books on Ethics: Vol. 9). 160p. (C). 1990. text ed. 19.95 (*0-268-00626-1*) U of Notre Dame Pr.

After Ratification: Material Life in Delaware, 1789-1820. J. Ritchie Garrison et al. (Illus.). 143p. (Orig.). (C). 1989. pap. text ed. 12.50 (*0-925050-00-8*) U Del Mus Studies Prog.

After Reagan: Confronting the Changed World Economy. C. Michael Aho & Marc Levinson. 160p. 1988. pap. 11.95 (*0-87609-041-2*) Coun Foreign.

After Reagan: False Starts, Missed Opportunities & New Beginnings. Simon Serfaty. LC 88-31090. 80p. 1989. pap. 11.50 (*0-941700-47-X*, JH FPI SAIS) U Pr of Amer.

After Redundancy: The Experience of Economic Insecurity. John Westergaard et al. (Illus.). 240p. (C). 1989. 64.95 (*0-7456-0151-0*) Blackwell Pubs.

***After Reengineering: Measuring Profit Through Real Time Cost Management.** Ernst & Gragoo. Date not set. text ed. 34.95 (*0-471-12617-9*) Wiley.

After Removal: The Choctaw in Mississippi. Ed. by Samuel J. Wells & Roseanna Tubby. LC 85-26538. 200p. 1986. 30.00 (*0-87805-289-5*) U Pr of Miss.

After Roy. Mary Tannen. 256p. 1991. mass mkt. 4.95 (*0-8041-0704-1*) Ivy Books.

After Russia-Posle Rossii. Marina I. Tsvetaeva. Tr. & Intro. by Michael Naydan. 1992. 32.50 (*0-87501-076-8*) Ardis Pubs.

After Saigon Fell: Daily Life under the Vietnamese Communists. Nguyen Long & Harry H. Kendall. LC 81-85304. (Research Papers & Policy Studies: No. 4). (Illus.). (Orig.). 1981. pap. 4.00 (*0-912966-46-7*) IEAS.

After Sales Service in the European Economic Community. Bureau Europeen des Unions de Consommateurs Staff. 281p. 1977. pap. text ed. 43.50 (*0-86010-056-1*) G & T Inc.

After San Jacinto: The Texas-Mexican Frontier, 1836-1841. Joseph M. Nance. LC 62-9789. (Illus.). 681p. reprint ed. pap. 180.00 (*0-8357-5246-1*, 2027908) Bks Demand.

After Sanctification. T. M. Anderson. 1984. pap. 4.99 (*0-88019-003-5*) Schmul Pub Co.

After School. Jack Ridl. 1988. pap. 1.50 (*0-318-37519-2*) Samisdat.

***After-School & Parent Education Programs for At-Risk Youths & Their Families: A Guide to Organizing & Operating Community-Based Center for Basic Educational Skills Reinforcement, Homework Assistance, Cultural Enrichment & A Parent Involvement Focus.** Tommie Morton-Young. LC 94-38716. (Illus.). 144p. (C). 1995. text ed. 37.95x (*0-398-05961-6*); pap. text ed. 22.95x (*0-398-05962-4*) C C Thomas.

After-School Care of School-Age Children: December 1984. Rosalind R. Bruno. (Current Population Reports Series P-23, Special Studies: No. 149). 31p. (Orig.). 1987. pap. 1.75 (*0-16-013379-3*, S/N 803-005-10002-2) USGPO.

After-School Crafts. Barbara L. Dondiego. (Anytime Crafts Bk.). (Illus.). 144p. (J). 1992. 22.95 (*0-8306-3868-7*, 4138); pap. 12.95 (*0-8306-3869-5*, 4138) TAB Bks.

After School Crafts. Barbara L. Dondiego. 1992. pap. text ed. 12.95 (*0-07-017578-0*) McGraw.

After-School Monster. Marissa Moss. LC 90-49416. (Illus.). 32p. (J). (gr. k up). 1991. 13.95 (*0-688-10116-X*); lib. bdg. 13.88 (*0-688-10117-8*) Lothrop.

After-School Monster. Marissa Moss. 32p. (J). (ps-3). 1993. pap. 4.99 (*0-14-054829-7*, Puffin) Puffin Bks.

After Secession: Jefferson Davis & the Failure of Confederate Nationalism. Paul D. Escott. LC 78-5726. 295p. (C). 1992. pap. text ed. 12.95 (*0-8071-1807-9*) La State U Pr.

After Seven Years. Raymond Moley. LC 71-168390. (FDR & the Era of the New Deal Ser.). 446p. 1972. reprint ed. lib. bdg. 55.00 (*0-306-70327-0*) Da Capo.

After Seymour's Funeral. Roy McFadden. 61p. 1990. pap. 13.95 (*0-85640-434-9*, Pub. by Blackstaff Pr IE) Dufour.

After Shocks. Burton Goodman. 151p. (J). (gr. 5). 1994. pap. 9.00 (*0-89061-751-1*) Jamestown Pubs.

After Shocks - Near Escapes. Stephen Dobyns. 1992. pap. 10.00 (*0-14-015358-6*, Penguin Bks) Viking Penguin.

After Silence. Jonathan Carroll. LC 93-38874. 1994. 12.00 (*0-385-47351-6*) Doubleday.

After Slavery: The Negro in South Carolina During Reconstruction, 1861-1877. Joel Williamson. LC 90-50317. 454p. 1990. pap. 22.95 (*0-8195-6236-X*, Wesleyan Univ Pr) U Pr of New Eng.

After Some Years: Reflection on the Ministry of the Priest. Carlo C. Martini. 125p. 1991. pap. 9.95 (*1-85390-038-9*, Pub. by Veritas Publns IE) Ignatius Pr.

***After Sorrow: An American Among the Vietnamese.** Lady Borton. LC 94-39146. 1995. 23.95 (*0-670-84332-6*, Viking) Viking Penguin.

After Spring Came Winter. Helsinki Watch et al. (Illus.). 104p. 1985. 7.00 (*0-938579-96-7*, Fund Free Exp) Hum Rts Watch.

After Stephen: From Hurting to Healed. Norma R. Lantz. LC 87-70625. (Illus.). 175p. (Orig.). 1987. pap. 9.95 (*0-942419-00-6*) Ana Pub.

After Strange Fruit: Changing Literary Tastes in Post-World-War II Boston. P. Albert Duhamel. 1980. 4.00 (*0-89073-063-6*) Boston Public Lib.

***After Strange Texts: The Role of Theory in the Study of Literature.** Ed. by Gregory S. Jay & David L. Miller. LC 84-160. 07p. 1985. pap. 59.00 (*0-7837-8385-X*, 2059195) Bks Demand.

After Such Pleasures. Frances Mayes. LC 79-14984. 1979. 9.95 (*0-913282-20-0*); pap. 4.75 (*0-913282-21-9*) Seven Woods Pr.

After Suicide. John H. Hewett. LC 79-24373. (Christian Care Bks.: Vol. 4). 118p. 1980. pap. 10.99 (*0-664-24296-0*, Westminster) Westminster John Knox.

After Suicide. Samuel E. Wallace. LC 73-9793. 285p. reprint ed. 81.30 (*0-8357-9833-X*, 2012586) Bks Demand.

After Suicide: A Ray of Hope. 2nd rev. ed. Eleanora "Betsy" Ross. 230p. 1990. per. 16.95 (*0-940179-01-6*) Lynn Pubns.

After Suicide: A Unique Grief Process. Eleanora "Betsy" Ross. 24p. 1987. pap. 4.95 (*0-940179-02-4*) Lynn Pubns.

After Supper Ghost Stories: And Other Tales. Jerome K. Jerome. (Jerome K. Jerome Ser.). 176p. (YA). (gr. 6-9). 1990. pap. 8.00 (*0-86299-762-3*) A Sutton Pub.

After Tet: The Bloodiest Year. Ronald H. Spector. LC 92-23853. (Illus.). 1992. text ed. 27.95 (*0-02-930380-X*) Free Pr.

After Tet: The Bloodiest Year in Vietnam. Ronald H. Spector. 1994. pap. 13.00 (*0-679-75046-0*) Random.

After the Adoption. Elizabeth Hormann. LC 86-27992. 1987. 9.99 (*0-8007-1516-0*) Revell.

After the Altar. Melanie Jongsma. (Friendship Ser.). (Illus.). 48p. (Orig.). 1993. pap. write for info. (*1-882536-16-9*, A100-0057) Bible League.

After the Apostles: Christianity in the Second Century. Walter H. Wagner. 296p. 1993. pap. 16.00 (*0-8006-2567-6*, 1-2567) Augsburg Fortress.

After the Applause: Life after Hockey with Esposito, Richard, Geoffrion, Skack, Gasby, Howe, Hull, Mikita, Hay, & Worsley. Colleen Howe et al. (Illus.). 232p. 1991. pap. 5.95 (*0-7710-4227-2*, Pub. by McClelland & Stewart CN) Firefly Bks Ltd.

After the Australopithecines: Stratigraphy, Ecology, & Culture Change in the Middle Pleistocene. Ed. by Karl W. Butzer & Glynn L. Isaac. (World Anthropology Ser.). xvi, 912p. 1975. 90.00 (*90-279-7629-5*) Mouton.

***After the Autogolpe: Human Rights in Peru & the U. S. Response.** 63p. Date not set. pap. text ed. 6.00 (*0-929513-28-2*) WOLA.

After the Avant-Garde. Robert Boyers. LC 86-43029. 250p. 1988. 30.00 (*0-271-00609-9*) Pa St U Pr.

After the Baby's Birth: A Woman's Way to Wellness. Robin Lim. LC 90-1802. 272p. (Orig.). 1990. pap. 14.95 (*0-89087-590-1*) Celestial Arts.

After the Ball. large type ed. Eileen Dewhurst. 320p. 1989. pap. 13.95 (*0-8161-4759-0*) G K Hall.

After the Ball. large type ed. Catherine George. (Harlequin Ser.). 1993. 17.95 (*0-263-13420-2*) Thorndike Pr.

After the Ball. Charles K. Harris. (Music Ser.). 376p. 1987. reprint ed. lib. bdg. 39.50 (*0-306-76282-X*) Da Capo.

After the Ball: How America Will Conquer Its Fear & Hatred of Homosexuals in the '90s. Marshall Kirk & Hunter Madsen. 432p. 1990. pap. 12.95 (*0-452-26498-7*, Plume) NAL-Dutton.

After the Ball: Pop Music from Rag to Rock. rev. ed. Ian Whitcomb. LC 85-30131. 324p. 1986. reprint ed. pap. 17.95 (*0-87910-063-X*) Limelight Edns.

After the Banquet. Yukio Mishima. Tr. by Donald Keene. (Perigee Japanese Library). 288p. 1981. pap. 10.50 (*0-399-50486-9*, Perigee Bks) Berkley Pub.

After the Bargain: The Hungarian Reform. L. Gubcsi. 170p. (C). 1988. 100.00 (*0-569-09127-6*, Pub. by Collets UK) Pro-Am Music.

A

An Asterisk (*) at the beginning of an entry indicates that the title is appearing in BIP for the first time.

A

After the Miracle: The Amazin' Mets - Two Decades Later. Maury Allen. 1991. mass mkt. 4.95 (*0-312-92432-1*) St Martin.

After the New Criticism. Frank Lentricchia. LC 79-23715. 1981. 21.00 (*0-226-47197-7*); pap. text ed. 18.95 (*0-226-47198-5*) U Ch Pr.

After the Nightmare. Liang Heng & Judith Shapiro. 1986. 16.95 (*0-394-55153-2*) Knopf.

After the Nightmare: The Treatment of Non-Offending Mothers of Sexually Abused Children. Wendy Ovaris. 1991. pap. 16.95 (*1-55691-041-X*) Learning Pubns.

After the Noise of Saigon. Walter McDonald. LC 87-20582. 80p. (Orig.). (C). 1988. lib. bdg. 17.50 (*0-87023-600-8*); pap. 9.95 (*0-87023-601-6*) U of Mass Pr.

After the Oil Price Collapse: OPEC, the United States, & the World Oil Market. Ed. by Wilfrid L. Kohl. LC 90-46169. 256p. 1991. text ed. 39.95 (*0-8018-4097-X*) Johns Hopkins.

After the Peewits. Camilla Campbell. (C). 1988. 60.00 (*0-317-91161-9*, Pub. by Granary UK) St Mut.

After the People Vote: A Guide to the Electoral College. enl. rev. ed. Ed. by Walter Berns. 115p. (C). 1992. text ed. 22.50 (*0-8447-3803-4*); pap. text ed. 7.95 (*0-8447-3802-6*) Am Enterprise.

After the Promise. Debbi Bedford. (Superromance Ser.). 1993. mass mkt. 3.39 (*0-373-70546-8*, 1-70546-6) Harlequin Bks.

After the Quake: Poems 1972-79. Taylor Graham. 28p. (Orig.). 1991. pap. 3.00 (*1-880575-06-X*) Hot Pepper.

After the Rain. Jared Carter. LC 92-70728. (CSU Poetry Ser.: XXXVII). 98p. (Orig.). 1993. pap. 8.00 (*0-914946-97-8*) Cleveland St Univ Poetry Ctr.

After the Rain. Norma F. Mazer. 240p. 1987. mass mkt. 3.99 (*0-380-75025-2*, Flare) Avon.

After the Rain. Norma F. Mazer. LC 86-33270. 304p. (YA). (gr. 7 up). 1987. 15.00 (*0-688-06867-7*) Morrow Jr Bks.

After the Rain. large type ed. Norma F. Mazer. 408p. (J). (gr. 7 up). 1989. 14.95 (*0-8161-4807-4*, Large Print Bks) Hall.

***After the Rain: A Play in Three Acts.** John Bowen. 93p. 1967. 12.95 (*0-910278-90-3*) Boulevard.

After the Raj: British Novels of India since 1947. David G. Rubin. LC 86-40115. 211p. 1986. text ed. 25.00 (*0-87451-383-9*) U Pr of New Eng.

After the Reforms: Education & Policy in Northern Ireland. Ed. by Robert D. Osbourne et al. 304p. 1993. 59.95 (*1-85628-401-8*, Pub. by Avebury Pub UK) Ashgate Pub Co.

After the Rehabilitation Centre: A Study into the Course of Functioning after Discharge from Rehabilitation. Luc De Witte. 248p. 1991. pap. 40.00 (*90-265-1206-6*, Pub. by Swets Pub Serv NE) Taylor & Francis.

After the Resurrection. Alexander Maclaren. LC 91-21642. 160p. 1992. pap. 9.99 (*0-8254-3199-9*) Kregel.

***After the Return.** Mordechai Becher & Moshe Newman. LC 94-30794. 1994. write for info. (*0-87306-688-X*) Feldheim.

After the Reunion: Poems by David Baker. David Baker. LC 94-1308. 80p. 1994. 20.00 (*1-55728-352-4*); pap. 12.00 (*1-55728-353-2*) U of Ark Pr.

After the Revival-What? Robert L. Sumner. 1980. pap. 3.95 (*0-914012-22-3*) Sword of Lord.

After the Revolution. Diego Abad De Santillan. 1976. lib. bdg. 59.95 (*0-8490-1404-2*) Gordon Pr.

***After the Revolution: A Citizen's Guide to the First Republican Congress in Forty Years.** James W. Robinson & Russ Colliau. LC 94-47409. 1995. pap. 9.95 (*0-7615-0072-3*) Prima Pub.

After the Revolution? Authority in a Good Society. rev. ed. Robert A. Dahl. 168p. (C). 1990. text ed. 27.00 (*0-300-04963-3*); pap. 11.00x (*0-300-04964-1*) Yale U Pr.

After the Revolution: Profiles of Early American Culture. Joseph J. Ellis. (Illus.). 272p. (C). 1981. pap. text ed. 10.95 (*0-393-95200-2*) Norton.

After the Revolution: Studies in the Contemporary Jewish-American Imagination. Mark Shechner. LC 85-45977. 272p. 1987. 29.95 (*0-253-30450-4*) Ind U Pr.

After the Revolution: The New Political Landscape in East Germany. Daniel Hamilton. LC 90-82606. (German Issues Ser.: No. 7). (Orig.). 1990. pap. 5.00 (*0-941441-03-2*) Am Inst Contemp Ger Studies.

After the Revolution: Waking to Global Capitalism. Arif Dirlik. LC 93-39490. 143p. (C). 1994. text ed. 29.95 (*0-8195-5274-7*, Wesleyan Univ Pr); pap. 12.95 (*0-8195-6279-3*, Wesleyan Univ Pr) U Pr of New Eng.

After the Revolution: Who Rules? 1977. pap. text ed. 0.75 (*0-935534-01-6*) NY Labor News.

After the Revolutions: East-West Trade & Technology Transfer in the 1990's. Ed. by Gary K. Bertsch et al. 227p. (C). 1991. pap. text ed. 45.00 (*0-8133-8278-5*) Westview.

After the Rhymer's Guild. Peter Klappert. 1972. 5.00 (*0-936814-05-5*) New Collage.

After the Rights Revolution: Reconceiving the Regulatory State. Cass R. Sunstein. (Illus.). 284p. 1990. 35.00x (*0-674-00908-8*) HUP.

After the SATs: An Insider's Guide to Freshman Year. Michele A. Paige. 240p. 1991. pap. 9.95 (*0-8120-4477-0*) Barron.

After the School Bell Rings. Carl A. Grant & Christine E. Sleeter. 352p. 1986. pap. 29.00 (*1-85000-086-7*, Falmer Pr) Taylor & Francis.

After the Second Flood: Essays on German Post-War Literature. Michael Hamburger. LC 86-22008. 288p. 1986. 35.00 (*0-312-00087-1*); pap. 12.95 (*0-312-00088-X*) St Martin.

***After the Smoke Clears - Surviving the Police Shooting: An Analysis of the Post Officer-Involved Shooting Trauma.** Clarence E. Jones, Jr. (Illus.). 122p. 1989. pap. 19.95 (*0-398-06187-4*) C C Thomas.

After the Smoke Clears--Surviving the Police Shooting: An Analysis of the Post Officer-Involved Shooting Trauma. Clarence E. Jones, Jr. (Illus.). 122p. (C). 1989. text ed. 34.95x (*0-398-05527-0*) C C Thomas.

After the Solstice. Fred Dings. LC 93-18470. 64p. (Orig.). 1993. pap. 12.95 (*0-914061-34-8*) Orchises Pr.

After the Soviet Union. Ed. by Timothy J. Colton & Robert H. Legvold. 240p. 1992. 21.95 (*0-393-03420-8*) Norton.

After the Soviet Union: From Empire to Nations. Ed. by Timothy J. Colton & Robert H. Legvold. (American Assembly Book Ser.). 240p. (C). 1992. pap. text ed. 9.95 (*0-393-96359-4*) Norton.

After the Splendid Display. Don Bogen. LC 85-8826. (Wesleyan New Poets Ser.). 64p. 1986. pap. 10.95 (*0-8195-1128-5*, Wesleyan Univ Pr) U Pr of New Eng.

After the Storm. Rebecca Flanders. (Men Made in America Ser.). 1994. mass mkt. 3.59 (*0-373-45174-1*, 1-45174-9) Silhouette.

After the Storm. Bob Italia. Ed. by Rosemary Wallner. LC 92-17392. (War in the Gulf Ser.). (J). (gr. 4 up). 1992. lib. bdg. 13.99 (*1-56239-147-X*) Abdo & Dghtrs.

After the Storm. Judith Richards. 354p. 1987. 14.95 (*0-934601-17-8*) Peachtree Pubs.

***After the Storm.** Ed. by Diana Zeiger. 750p. 1995. 69.95 (*1-56167-262-9*) Nat Lib Poetry.

After the Storm. Annie G. Nelson. LC 76-14493. 131p. 1976. reprint ed. 10.00 (*0-87152-243-8*) Reprint.

After the Storm: Learning to Abide. Nanette Thorsen-Snipes. (Orig.). 1990. pap. 4.00 (*0-915541-56-4*) Star Bks Inc.

After the Storm: Lessons from the Gulf War. Ed. by Joseph S. Nye & Roger K. Smith. 426p. 1992. 24.95 (*0-8191-8529-9*) Madison Bks UPA.

After the Storm: Lessons from the Gulf War. Ed. by Joseph S. Nye & Roger K. Smith. 426p. 1993. pap. 14.95 (*1-56833-015-4*) Madison Bks UPA.

After the Storm: Poems on the Persian Gulf War. Ed. by F. D. Reeve & Jay Meek. LC 92-11673. 1992. pap. 10.95 (*0-944624-16-2*) Maisonneuve Pr.

After the Storm: The Changing Military Balance in the Middle East. Anthony H. Cordesman. 811p. (C). 1993. text ed. 68.50 (*0-8133-1692-8*) Westview.

After the Storm Comes the Rainbow. Paul H. Dunn. 11.95 (*0-88494-662-2*) Bookcraft Inc.

After the Storm, the Rainbow: The Church of the Nazarene in Cuba. H. T. Reza. 88p. 1994. pap. write for info. (*0-8341-1475-5*) Nazarene.

After the Story's Over: Your Enrichment Guide to 88 Read-Aloud Children's Classics, K-Grade 3. Linda K. Garrity. 1990. pap. 14.95 (*0-673-38836-0*) GdYrBks.

After the Stroke. May Sarton. 1990. pap. 5.95 (*0-393-30630-5*) Norton.

After the Stroke: Coping with America's Third Leading Cause of Death. Evelyn Shirk. (Golden Age Books - Perspectives on Aging Ser.). 114p. 1991. 21.95 (*0-87975-693-4*); pap. 15.95 (*0-87975-694-2*) Prometheus Bks.

After the Tassel Is Moved. rev. ed. Louis O. Caldwell. 1990. pap. 8.99 (*0-8010-2553-2*) Baker Bk.

After the Tears: Parents Talk about Raising a Child with a Disability. Robin Simons. (Illus.). 1987. 14.95 (*0-15-103963-1*, Harvest Bks); pap. 7.95 (*0-15-602900-6*, Harvest Bks) HarBrace.

After the Tears: Reclaiming the Personal Losses of Childhood. Jane Middelton-Moz & Lorie Dwinell. 146p. (Orig.). 1986. pap. 7.95 (*0-932194-36-2*) Health Comm.

After the Tempest: The Tempest, or, the Enchanted Island: the Mock- Tempest, or the Enchanted Castle: the Tempest, an Opera. Intro. by George R. Guffey. LC 92-2371. (Augustan Reprints Ser.: No. 4 (1969)). 1992. 50.00 (*0-404-70104-3*) AMS Pr.

After the Thousand Years: Resurrection & Judgment in Revelation 20. Webb J. Mealy. (JSNT Supplement Ser.: No. 70). 275p. (C). 1992. 35.00 (*1-85075-363-6*, Pub. by Sheffield Acad UK) CUP Services.

After the Trade Is Made: Processing Securities Transactions. David Weiss. LC 85-30997. (Illus.). 464p. 1986. text ed. 24.95 (*0-13-018581-7*) NY Inst Finance.

After the Trade is Made: Processing Securities Transactions. 2nd ed. David M. Weiss. LC 93-25716. 1993. 39.95 (*0-13-177601-0*) NY Inst Finance.

After the Trade Is Made - An Operation Training Manual: Study Guide. New York Institute of Finance Staff. (Illus.). 224p. 1987. 24.95 (*0-13-858721-3*) NY Inst Finance.

After the Trail of Tears: The Cherokees' Struggle for Sovereignty, 1839-1880. William G. McLoughlin. LC 93-18532. xvi, 440p. (C). 1994. 39.95 (*0-8078-2111-X*); pap. 17.95 (*0-8078-4433-0*) U of NC Pr.

After the Trees: Living on the Transamazon Highway. Douglas I. Stewart. LC 93-49553. (Illus.). 200p. 1994. text ed. 30.00 (*0-292-77678-0*); pap. 12.95 (*0-292-77680-2*) U of Tex Pr.

After the Twelve Days. Hollis Summers. 48p. 1987. pap. 6.00 (*0-912592-25-7*) Ashland Poetry.

***After the Twinkling of an Eye.** Noah W. Hutchings et al. 30p. (Orig.). 1994. pap. 2.50 (*1-879366-44-4*) Hearthstone OK.

After the Velvet Revolution: Vaclav Havel & the New Leaders of Czechoslovakia Speak Out. Ed. by Tim D. Whipple. LC 90-49104. (Focus on Issues Ser.: No. 14). (Illus.). 342p. (C). 1991. 27.95 (*0-932088-62-7*); pap. 14.95 (*0-932088-61-9*) Freedom Hse.

After the Victorians. Amy Cruse. 1988. reprint ed. lib. bdg. 49.00 (*0-685-55954-8*) Rprt Serv.

After the Victorians. Amy Cruse. LC 76-158495. 1971. reprint ed. 39.00 (*0-403-01315-1*) Scholarly.

After the Victorians: Private Conscience & Public Duty in Modern Britain. Ed. by Peter Mandler & Susan Pedersen. LC 93-17693. 1994. write for info. (*0-415-07056-2*) Routledge.

After the Vows Were Spoken: Marriage in American Literary Realism. Allen F. Stein. LC 84-16552. 339p. 1984. 42.50 (*0-8142-0382-5*) Ohio St U Pr.

After the Wake. Brendan Behan. Ed. by Peter Fallon. LC 82-159911. (Classic Irish Fiction Ser.). 156p. 1983. 15.95 (*0-905140-97-4*) Devin.

After the Wake. Brendan Behan. 156p. 1981. pap. 8.95 (*0-86278-031-4*, Pub. by OBrien Pr IE) Dufour.

After the Wall. Ed. by Geoffrey Nowell-Smith & Tana Wollen. (European Media Monograph: No. 1). (Illus.). 96p. 1992. pap. 9.95 (*0-85170-296-1*, Pub. by British Film Inst UK) Ind U Pr.

After the Wall: American Policy Toward Germany - A Twentieth Century Fund Paper. Elizabeth Pond. 111p. (Orig.). (C). 1990. pap. 9.95 (*0-87078-323-8*) TCFP-PPP.

***After the Wall: Germany, the Germans, & the Burdens of History.** Marc Fisher. LC 95-3892. 1995. 25.00 (*0-684-80291-0*) S&S Trade.

After the War. Lily Brett. (Illus.). 137p. 1990. 29.95 (*0-522-84415-4*) Intl Spec Bk.

After the War. H. R. Coursen. LC 81-4241. (Illus.). 1981. 13.95 (*0-918606-06-3*); pap. 8.95 (*0-918606-05-5*) Heidelberg Graph.

After the War. Debeauvoir. 1994. pap. 14.95 (*1-56924-982-2*) Marlowe & Co.

After the War. Daniel Stern. LC 94-13174. (Modern Masters Ser.). 243p. 1994. 22.50 (*0-89263-331-X*) Rice Univ.

After the War. Daniel Stern. LC 94-13174. (First Rediscovered Modern Masterpieces Edition Ser.). 243p. (C). 1994. pap. 11.95 (*0-89263-332-8*) Rice Univ.

After the War. Richard Marius. LC 94-2927. 640p. (J). 1994. reprint ed. pap. 14.95 (*1-55853-273-0*) Rutledge Hill Pr.

After the War: A Novel. Richard C. Marius. 1992. 24.50 (*0-394-58322-1*) Knopf.

After the War: Essays on Recent Spanish Poetry. Ed. by Salvador J. Fajardo & John C. Wilcox. LC 88-61768. 128p. 1988. pap. 35.00 (*0-89295-055-2*) Society Sp & Sp-Am.

***After the War: Poems & Stories.** Andy Wainwright. 80p. 1995. lib. bdg. 25.00 (*0-8095-4523-3*) Borgo Pr.

After the War: The Novel & England since 1945. D. J. Taylor. 304p. 1994. 34.95 (*0-7011-6054-3*, Pub. by Chatto & Windus UK) Trafalgar.

***After the War: The Novel & England since 1945.** D. J. Taylor. 304p. 1994. 34.95 (*0-7011-3769-X*, Pub. by Chatto & Windus UK) Trafalgar.

***After the War Was Over.** Sheehan. 1994. pap. 4.99 (*0-517-13040-8*) Random.

After the War Was Over: Hanoi & Saigon. Neil Sheehan. LC 92-50617. 1993. pap. 9.00 (*0-679-74507-6*, Vin) Random.

After the Wars: Reconstruction in Afghanistan, Indochina, Central America, Southern Africa, & the Horn of Africa. Anthony Lake et al. (U. S. Third World Policy Perspectives Ser.: No. 16). 240p. (C). 1990. 32.95 (*0-88738-392-0*); pap. 17.95 (*0-88738-880-9*) Transaction Pubs.

After the Waste Land: A Democratic Economics for the Year 2000. Samuel Bowles et al. LC 90-9078. 288p. 1991. text ed. 46.95 (*0-87332-644-X*); pap. text ed. 20.95 (*0-87332-645-8*) M E Sharpe.

After the West Was Won: Homesteaders & Town-Builders in Western South Dakota, 1900-1917. Paula M. Nelson. LC 86-11405. (Illus.). 238p. (C). 1986. reprint ed. pap. 13.95 (*0-87745-250-4*) U of Iowa Pr.

***After the Whale: Melville in the Wake of Moby-Dick.** Clark Davis. LC 94-43179. (Illus.). 256p. (C). 1995. pap. text ed. 29.95 (*0-8173-0774-5*) U of Ala Pr.

After the World Broke in Two: The Later Novels of Willa Cather. Merrill M. Skaggs. 208p. 1990. 28.50 (*0-8139-1300-4*) U Pr of Va.

After the Zap. Michael Armstrong. 256p. (Orig.). 1987. pap. 2.95 (*0-445-20438-9*) Warner Bks.

After Theory: Postmodernism - Postmarxism. Thomas Docherty. 240p. 1990. 55.00 (*0-415-04179-1*, A4166) Routledge.

After This Manner Pray. Mark Copeland. LC 92-70135. 164p. (Orig.). 1992. pap. 7.95 (*0-88270-653-5*) Bridge Pub.

After Thoughts. large type ed. Max Bygraves. 1990. 21.95 (*0-7089-2279-1*) Ulverscroft.

After Timur: Qur'ans of the Fifteenth & Sixteenth Centuries AD. David James. (Nassar D. Khalili Collection of Islamic Art: Vol. III). (Illus.). 256p. 1992. 275.00 (*0-19-727602-4*) OUP.

After Tippecanoe. Ed. by Philip P. Mason. LC 73-7076. (Illus.). 106p. 1973. reprint ed. text ed. 38.50 (*0-8371-6903-8*, MAAT, Greenwood Pr) Greenwood.

After Tomorrow. LC 90-82434. 1990. 11.95 (*0-685-34699-4*) Makin Do Ent.

After Tragedy & Triumph: Modern Jewish Thought & the American Experience. Michael Berenbaum. 224p. (C). 1990. 39.95 (*0-521-38057-X*) Cambridge U Pr.

After Truth: Explorations in Life Sense. Mervyn Sprung. LC 92-45189. 189p. 1993. 57.50 (*0-7914-1703-4*); pap. 18.95 (*0-7914-1704-2*) State U NY Pr.

After Tut 'Ankhamun: Research & Excavation in the Royal Necropolis at Thebes. C. N. Reeves. LC 90-43443. 211p. 1992. 95.00 (*0-7103-0406-4*, Pub. by Kegan Paul Intl UK) Routledge Chapman & Hall.

After Twelve Thousand Years. Coblentz. 5.00 (*0-686-00464-7*); pap. 2.00 (*0-686-00465-5*) Fantasy Pub Co.

After Two Hundred Years: Photographic Essays of Aboriginal & Islander Australia Today. Ed. by Penny Taylor. (Illus.). 384p. (C). 1989. 84.95 (*0-521-37013-2*) Cambridge U Pr.

***After Tylor: British Social Anthropology, 1888-1951.** George W. Stocking, Jr. LC 95-6365. 1995. write for info. (*0-299-14580-8*) U of Wis Pr.

After Uelsmann see Three by Three: Bloom Blood

After Vasari: History, Art, & Patronage in Late Medici Florence. Edward L. Goldberg. 359p. 1989. text ed. 60.00 (*0-691-04066-4*) Princeton U Pr.

After Virtue: A Study in Moral Theory. 2nd ed. Alasdair MacIntyre. LC 83-40601. 320p. 1984. pap. text ed. 12.95 (*0-268-00611-3*) U of Notre Dame Pr.

After Walden: Thoreau's Changing Views on Economic Man. Leo Stoller. 163p. 1957. 22.50 (*0-8047-0500-3*) Stanford U Pr.

After We Die, What Then? George W. Meek. LC 79-90909. (Life's Energy Fields Ser.: Vol. 3). (Illus.). (Orig.). 1980. 8.95 (*0-935436-00-6*) Metascience.

After We Die, What Then? rev. ed. George W. Meek. LC 79-909. (Illus.). 216p. (Orig.). 1987. reprint ed. pap. 11.95 (*0-89804-099-X*, Metasci) Ariel GA.

After Wild Sheep in the Altai & Mongolia. deluxe limited ed. E. Demidoff. 324p. 1993. ring bd. 100.00 (*0-940143-99-2*) Safari Pr.

After Wilson: The Struggle for the Democratic Party, 1920-1934. Douglas B. Craig. LC 92-53629. xviii, 406p. (C). 1993. 45.00 (*0-8078-2058-X*) U of NC Pr.

After Winning: The Legacy of the New Jersey Suffragists, 1920-1947. Felice D. Gordon. LC 85-11745. 240p. (C). 1986. 35.00 (*0-8135-1137-2*) Rutgers U Pr.

***After Wounded Knee: Correspondence of Major & Surgeon John Vance Lauderdale While Serving with the Army Occupying the Pine Ridge Indian Reservation, 1890-1891.** Ed. by Jerry Green. 250p. 1995. 34.95 (*0-87013-405-1*) Mich St U Pr.

***After Yesterday's Crash: The Avant-Pop Anthology.** Ed. by Larry McCaffery. LC 94-48772. 1995. write for info. (*0-01-402485-3*, Penguin Bks) Viking Penguin.

***After Yesterday's Crash: The Avant-Pop Anthology.** Ed. & Intro. by Larry McCaffery. 320p. (Orig.). 1995. pap. 12.95 (*0-14-024085-3*, Penguin Bks) Viking Penguin.

After You. Janet Riehecky. (Manners Matter Ser.). (Illus.). 32p. (J). (ps-2). 1989. lib. bdg. 18.50 (*0-89565-538-1*) Childs World.

After You Graduate: Answers to Twenty-Seven Most Frequently Asked Questions. rev. ed. Ed. by Steve Lawhead. 160p. 1991. pap. 12.99 (*0-310-71211-4*) Zondervan.

After You, Mark Twain: A Modern Journey Around the Equator. Betty Wetzel. LC 90-37972. (Illus.). 238p. 1990. pap. 11.95 (*1-55591-069-6*) Fulcrum Pub.

After You Say Goodbye: When Someone You Love Dies of Aids. Paul K. Froman. 288p. (Orig.). 1992. pap. text ed. 10.95 (*0-8118-0088-1*) Chronicle Bks.

After You Say I Do. Norm Wright & Wes Roberts. LC 79-66960. 80p. (Orig.). (C). 1979. pap. 7.99 (*0-89081-205-5*) Harvest Hse.

After You with the Pistol. Kyril Bonfiglioli. LC 92-70419. 181p. 1992. reprint ed. pap. 6.95 (*1-55882-123-6*, Lib Crime Classics) Intl Polygonics.

After Your First Six Words ... I Know You: A Guide to Tooling, up the Great You. Evelyn Bowling. Ed. by Jack Brown. 232p. (Orig.). 1988. pap. 15.00 (*0-923834-06-0*) Shenandoah Val Bk.

After You've Gone. braille ed. Alice Adams. 364p. 1992. vinyl bd. 29.12 (*1-56956-033-1*, BR8350) W A T Braille.

After You've Said Goodbye: How to Recover after Ending a Relationship. Trudy Helmlinger. 292p. 1977. 18.95 (*0-87073-791-0*) Schenkman Bks Inc.

After You've Said Goodbye: Learning How to Stand Alone. Trudy Helmlinger. LC 82-9472. 288p. (C). 1982. reprint ed. pap. 8.95 (*0-932370-36-5*) Brooks Pub Co.

After You've Said I Do. Hardy R. Denham, Jr. 96p. (Orig.). 1983. pap. 7.95 (*0-939298-18-X*) J M Prods.

After You've Tried Everything Else: A "More Excellent Way" to Freedom from Addictions. Chuck Makela. 32p. (Orig.). 1987. pap. 1.00 (*0-9618532-0-4*) Just Pub Hse.

Afterbeats. D. Jayne McPherson. Ed. by Edward Mycue. (Took Modern Poetry in English Ser.: No. 20). (Illus.). 28p. (Orig.). 1991. pap. 3.00 (*1-879457-19-9*) Norton Coker Pr.

AfterCulture: Detroit & the Humiliation of History. Jerry Herron. LC 93-10873. 216p. 1993. text ed. 19.95 (*0-8143-2070-8*) Wayne St U Pr.

***AfterCulture: Detroit & the Humiliation of History.** Jerry Herron. 216p. 1995. pap. 14.95 (*0-8143-2071-6*) Wayne St U Pr.

Afterglow. Catherine Coulter. 1993. mass mkt. 4.50 (*0-373-48260-4*, 5-48260-9) Silhouette.

Afterglow. Genevieve Parker. LC 93-86984. 248p. 1994. 22.95 (*0-9638987-0-1*) Parker Homestead.

Afterglow. Judith Plowden. 320p. 1986. reprint ed. pap. 3.50 (*0-8439-2353-9*) Dorchester Pub Co.

Afterglow: More Stories of Lesbian Desire. Ed. by Karen Barber. 189p. (Orig.). 1993. pap. 8.95 (*1-55583-315-2*, Lace MA) Alyson Pubns.

Afterglow & Nightfall: The Brothers of Gwynedd IV. Edith Pargeter. 342p. 1991. pap. 10.95 (*0-7472-3030-7*, Pub. by Headline UK) Trafalgar.

Afterglow & Other Undergraduate Writings of John Dos Passos. Ed. by Richard Layman. (Archive of Literary Documents Ser.). xviii, 277p. 1990. lib. bdg. 125.00 (*1-55888-265-0*) Omnigraphics Inc.

***Afterimage.** Phillis Levin. 63p. (Orig.). 1995. pap. 9.95 (*0-914278-67-3*) Copper Beech.

Afterimage. Kristine K. Rusch & Kevin J. Anderson. 288p. 1992. 4.99 (*0-451-45175-9*, ROC) NAL-Dutton.

An Asterisk (*) at the beginning of an entry indicates that the title is appearing in BIP for the first time.

Afterimages: Poems by Cathryn Hankla. Cathryn Hankla. LC 90-27598. 64p. 1991. text ed. 14.95 (*0-8071-1684-X*); pap. 7.95 (*0-8071-1685-8*) La State U Pr.

Afterimages of Modernity: Structure & Indifference in Twentieth-Century Literature. Henry Sussman. LC 89-15478. 256p. 1990. text ed. 36.00x (*0-8018-3887-8*) Johns Hopkins.

Afterlife. Paul Monette. 288p. 1991. pap. 10.00 (*0-380-71197-4*) Avon.

Afterlife. Paul Monette. 1990. 19.95 (*0-517-57339-3*, Crown) Crown Pub Group.

Afterlife. braille ed. Paul Monette. 563p. 1991. vinyl bd. 45.04 (*1-56956-360-8*, BR8410) W A T Braille.

Afterlife. Jenny Randles & Peter Hough. 240p. 1994. reprint ed. pap. 10.00 (*0-425-14212-4*, Berkley Trade) Berkley Pub.

Afterlife: Poems. Larry Levis. LC 77-8598. 61p. reprint ed. pap. 25.00 (*0-8357-3840-X*, 2036572) Bks Demand.

Afterlife: The Complete Guide to Life after Death. Emily Goldman. LC 94-9625. 224p. 1994. 22.95 (*0-670-85732-7*, Viking Studio) Studio Bks.

Afterlife: The Final Answer. David Darling. LC 94-12489. 1995. 20.00 (*0-679-41845-8*, Villard Bks) Random.

***Afterlife & Other Stories.** Updike. pap. write for info. (*0-449-22391-4*) Fawcett.

Afterlife & Other Stories. John Updike. LC 94-9818. 1994. 24.00 (*0-679-43583-2*) Knopf.

Afterlife Connection, Heavenly Reflection. A. G. Caputo. (Illus.). 144p. 1988. 12.95 (*0-929484-00-2*) Crystal Pl Inc.

***Afterlife Diet.** Daniel Pinkwater. LC 94-21540. 1995. 21.00 (*0-679-41936-5*) Random.

Afterlife for Children. Barbara Ganzel. (Amherst Writers & Artists Chapbook Ser.). 32p. (Orig.). 1988. pap. 8.00 (*0-941895-02-5*) Amherst Wri Art.

Afterlife of Plays. Jonathan Miller. (Distinguished Graduate Research Lecture Ser.: No. 5). 48p. 1992. 12.50 (*1-879691-12-4*) SDSU Press.

Afterlife of Property: Domestic Security & the Victorian Novel. Jeff Nunokawa. LC 93-30912. 1994. 24.95 (*0-691-03320-X*) Princeton U Pr.

Afterlight. Marc Hudson. LC 83-10441. 80p. 1983. lib. bdg. 15.00 (*0-87023-413-7*); pap. 9.95 (*0-87023-414-5*) U of Mass Pr.

***AfterLoss: A Recovery Companion for Those Who Are Grieving.** Barbara H. LesStrang. 240p. (Orig.). 1995. pap. 12.95 (*1-879560-36-4*) Harbor Hse West.

***Afterman & Baxt's Cases & Materials on Corporations & Associations.** 6th ed. R. Baxt & K. L. Fletcher. 1016p. 1992. pap. 96.00 (*0-409-30329-1*, Austral) Butterworth Legal Pubs.

***Aftermarketing: How to Keep Customers for Life Through Relationship Marketing.** Terry G. Vavra. 292p. 1995. pap. 15.00 (*0-7863-0405-7*) Irwin Prof Pubng.

Aftermarketing: Strategies to Keep Customers for Life. Terry G. Vavra. 292p. 1992. 30.00 (*1-55623-605-0*) Irwin Prof Pubng.

Aftermath. Edward Doyle & Terrence Maitland. Ed. by Robert Manning. (Vietnam Experience Ser.: Vol. 17). (Illus.). 192p. 1985. 16.95 (*0-939526-17-4*) Boston Pub Co.

Aftermath. Editors of Flying Magazine. 1994. text ed. 24.95 (*0-07-021429-8*) McGraw.

Aftermath. Flying Magazine Editors. LC 93-27575. 1993. 24.95 (*0-8306-4283-8*); pap. 15.95 (*0-8306-4282-X*) TAB Bks.

Aftermath. O. T. Jackson. 1979. pap. 1.50 (*0-8439-0609-X*) Dorchester Pub Co.

Aftermath. James L. Allen. (Principle Works of James Lane Allen). 1989. reprint ed. lib. bdg. 79.00 (*0-7812-1730-X*) Rprt Serv.

Aftermath, Vol. 3. Editors of Flying Magazine. 1993. text ed. 26.95 (*0-07-021431-X*) McGraw.

Aftermath: A Supplement to The Golden Bough. James G. Frazer. LC 75-41104. reprint ed. 34.00 (*0-404-14543-4*) AMS Pr.

Aftermath: Along the Way...One Man's War & Peace (1940-1990) Ed. by Graham Burrell. (C). 1990. text ed. 35.00 (*0-7223-2544-4*, Pub. by A H S Ltd UK) St Mut.

Aftermath: An Anthology. 1977. pap. 4.00 (*0-912678-22-4*, Greenfld Rev Pr); per. 10.00 (*0-912678-44-5*, Greenfld Rev Pr) Greenfld Rev Lit.

***Aftermath: An Anthology of Post-Vietnam Fiction.** Ed. by Donald Anderson. LC 94-33932. 304p. 1995. 25.00 (*0-8050-3655-5*); pap. 12.95 (*0-8050-3656-3*) H Holt & Co.

***Aftermath: Living with the Holocaust.** Aaron Hass. 272p. (C). 1995. 22.95 (*0-521-47429-9*) Cambridge U Pr.

Aftermath: Tarnished Outcomes of American Foreign Policy. Frwd. by John D. Montgomery & William Sullivan. LC 85-11176. 200p. (C). 1985. text ed. 45.00 (*0-86569-126-6*, Auburn Hse) Greenwood.

Aftermath: The Legacy of War, 1975-1985. Ed. by Robert Manning. (Vietnam Experience Ser.). (Illus.). 192p. 1986. 16.30 (*0-201-11273-6*) Addison-Wesley.

Aftermath of Chernobyl: History's Worst Nuclear Power Reactor Accident. 2nd ed. Charles C. Bailey. 208p. 1993. per. 26.95 (*0-8403-8562-5*) Kendall-Hunt.

Aftermath of Defeat: Societies, Armed Forces, & the Challenge of Recovery. Ed. by George J. Andreopoulos & Harold E. Selesky. LC 94-3989. 1994. 22.50 (*0-300-05853-5*) Yale U Pr.

Aftermath of Non-Cooperation & Emergence of Swaraj Partay. Sreekuraran. (C). 1991. 36.00 (*81-7023-130-2*, Pub. by Allied II) S Asia.

Aftermath of Operation Bluestar, 2 vols., Set. Ed. by M. S. Deora. (Political Developments in Punjab Ser.: No. 2). (C). 1992. text ed. 78.50 (*81-7041-645-0*, Pub. by Anmol II) S Asia.

Aftermath of Revolt India, 1857-1870. Thomas R. Metcalf. 352p. (C). 1990. reprint ed. 25.00 (*81-85054-99-1*) Riverdale Co.

Aftermath of Revolution: British Policy Toward the United States, 1783-1795. Charles R. Ritcheson. LC 77-86328. 519p. reprint ed. pap. 148.00 (*0-8357-8793-1*, 2033426) Bks Demand.

Aftermath of Slavery: A Study of the Condition & Environment of the American Negro. William A. Sinclair. LC 69-18548. (American Negro: His History & Literature, Ser. No. 2). 1968. reprint ed. 28.95 (*0-405-01894-0*) Ayer.

Aftermath of Stroke: The Experience of Patients & Their Families. Robert Anderson. 296p. (C). 1992. 74.95 (*0-521-40196-8*) Cambridge U Pr.

Aftermath of the Civil War, in Arkansas. Powell Clayton. LC 79-89029. 378p. 1969. reprint ed. text ed. 35.00 (*0-8371-1820-4*, CLA&, Negro U Pr) Greenwood.

Aftermath of the Gulf War: An Assessment of U. N. Action. Ian Johnstone. LC 93-38921. (International Peace Academy Occasional Paper Ser.). 84p. (C). 1994. pap. text ed. 7.95 (*1-55587-487-8*) Lynne Rienner.

Aftermath of the Lost Labourers' Revolt: 1830-1831. LC 72-2518. (British Labour Struggles Before 1850 Ser.). 1974. reprint ed. 40.95 (*0-405-04411-9*) Ayer.

Aftermath of War. Robin Cross. LC 93-50154. (World War II Ser.). (Illus.). 48p. (J). (gr. 5-9). 1994. 14.95 (*1-56847-178-5*) Thomson Lrning.

Aftermath of War: Americans & the Remaking of Japan, 1945-1952. Howard B. Schonberger. LC 88-30585. (American Diplomatic History Ser.: No. 1). 347p. 1989. pap. 18.00 (*0-87338-382-6*) Kent St U Pr.

Aftermath of War: Bainbridge Colby & Wilsonian Diplomacy, 1920-1921. Daniel M. Smith. LC 77-115881. (American Philosophical Society, Memoirs Ser.: Vol. 80). 183p. reprint ed. pap. 52.20 (*0-8357-5248-8*, 2025138) Bks Demand.

Aftermath of War: Everyone Must Go Home. Carol Mather. (Illus.). 272p. 1992. 29.95 (*0-08-037708-4*, Pub. by Brasseys UK) Brasseys Inc.

Aftermath of War: Experiences of a Quaker Relief Officer, No. 20. Henry Hamilton. 1982. 25.00 (*0-89029-306-6*) Morningside Bkshop.

Afternoon at Emmi's. Gail . Griffin. (Hippy Ser.). (Illus.). 24p. (Orig.). (J). (ps). 1992. pap. text ed. 3.00 (*1-56134-163-0*) Dushkin Pub.

Afternoon at Tavern MacTavish: My Wallet's in the Highlands. Frances A. Hogg. (Illus.). 13p. 1994. pap. 3.00 (*0-88680-399-3*) I E Clark.

Afternoon in the Jungle: The Selected Short Stories of Albert Maltz. Albert Maltz. 1971. pap. 2.75 (*0-87140-256-4*) Liveright.

Afternoon in Waterloo Park. Gerald Dumas. LC 87-31731. (Great Lakes Bks.). (Illus.). 140p. 1988. reprint ed. pap. 12.95 (*0-8143-2039-2*, Great Lakes Bks) Wayne St U Pr.

Afternoon Neighbors. Hamlin Garland. (Collected Works of Hamlin Garland). 1988. reprint ed. lib. bdg. 59.00 (*0-7812-1255-3*) Rprt Serv.

Afternoon Neighbors see Collected Works of Hamlin Garland

Afternoon of a Writer. Peter Handke. Tr. by Ralph Manheim. 96p. 1989. 14.95 (*0-374-10207-4*) FS&G.

Afternoon of an Author. F. Scott Fitzgerald. 1972. pap. 9.95 (*0-684-12734-2*, SL332, Scribners) S&S Trade.

Afternoon of an Author. F. Scott Fitzgerald. (Hudson River Editions Ser.). 1981. text ed. 22.50 (*0-684-16469-8*, Scribners) S&S Trade.

Afternoon of an Author. F. Scott Fitzgerald. (Twentieth Century Classics Ser.). 240p. 1987. pap. 4.95 (*0-02-019860-4*, Collier S&S) S&S Trade.

Afternoon of March 30: A Contemporary Historical Novel. Nathaniel Blumberg. LC 84-90141. 378p. 1984. 15.00 (*0-9613338-0-4*) Wood Fire.

Afternoon of Mr. Andesmas see Four Novels

Afternoon of the Elves. Janet T. Lisle. LC 88-35099. 128p. (J). (gr. 4-6). 1989. 14.95 (*0-531-05837-9*); lib. bdg. 14.99 (*0-531-08437-X*) Orchard Bks Watts.

Afternoon of the Elves. Janet T. Lisle. (J). (gr. 4-7). 1991. pap. 2.75 (*0-590-43944-8*, Apple Paperbacks) Scholastic Inc.

Afternoon of the Gosling. Marlys Huffman. 1989. pap. 3.95 (*0-8217-2841-5*) Zebra.

***Afternoon on the Amazon.** Mary P. Osborne. LC 95-3237. (Magic Tree House Ser.: No. 6). (Illus.). 1995. 3.99 (*0-679-86372-9*); pap. 9.99 (*0-679-96372-3*) Random.

Afternoon on the Potomac: A British View of America's Changing Position in the World. Roy H. Jenkins. LC 77-188329. (Henry L. Stimson Lecture Ser.). 64p. 1972. 20.00x (*0-300-01586-0*) Yale U Pr.

Afternoon Regard for Photography. Eli Siegel. (Illus.). 14p. 1967. Photographs, 6 hslftones. pap. 3.00 (*0-911492-08-9*) Aesthetic Realism.

***Afternoon Tea.** Koren Trygg. 1993. 7.95 (*0-89954-830-X*) Antioch Pub Co.

Afternoon Tea & Other Stories. Tina Peralta. 102p. (Orig.). 1993. pap. 6.50 (*971-10-0457-7*, Pub. by New Day Pub PH) Cellar.

Afternoon Tea Book. Michael Smith. LC 86-47681. (Illus.). 320p. 1986. text ed. 21.95 (*0-689-11592-X*, Atheneum S&S) S&S Trade.

Afternoon Tea Book. Michael Smith. 304p. 1989. pap. 10.95 (*0-02-010351-4*, Collier S&S) S&S Trade.

Afternoon Tea Delicacies: Recipe Post Card Book. Grace Young. 1993. mass mkt. 7.95 (*0-385-42586-4*) Doubleday.

***Afternoon Tea Guide.** Ellen Easton. 200p. (Orig.). 1995. pap. write for info. (*1-885591-75-6*) Morris Pubng.

Afternoon Teas: Recipes, History, Menus. Pam McKee et al. (Between Friends Cookbook Ser.). (Illus.). 64p. (Orig.). 1995. pap. 7.95 (*1-56523-040-X*) Fox Chapel Pub.

Afternoon to Kill. Shelley Smith. 192p. 1984. pap. 5.95 (*0-89733-122-2*) Academy Chi Pubs.

Afternoon to Kill. large type ed. Shelley Smith. 272p. 1988. 15.95 (*0-7089-1920-0*) Ulverscroft.

Afternoons of a Woman of Leisure. Elizabeth Bennett. 1993. pap. 5.95 (*1-56201-029-8*, 126) Blue Moon Bks.

***Afterrimages.** Joan Retallack. 112p. 1995. 25.00x (*0-8195-2219-8*, Wesleyan Univ Pr); pap. 12.95 (*0-8195-1223-0*, Wesleyan Univ Pr) U Pr of New Eng.

Afterschooling & Enrichment. Mary Pride. LC 89-81254. (Big Book of Home Learning Ser.: Vol. 4). 320p. 1991. pap. 20.00 (*0-89107-551-8*) Crossway Bks.

Aftershock. Lynn Michaels. (Temptation Ser.). 1994. mass mkt. 2.99 (*0-373-25581-0*, 1-25581-9) Harlequin Bks.

Aftershock. Lillian O'Donnell. 1982. pap. 2.50 (*0-449-24479-2*) Fawcett.

Aftershock: Helping Your People Through Corporate Change. Wilson Learning Corporation Staff & Harry Woodward. 233p. 1987. text ed. 24.95 (*0-471-62478-0*) Wiley.

Aftershock: Poems & Prose from the Vietnam War. Jim Nye. LC 91-372302. 80p. (Orig.). 1991. pap. 8.95 (*0-938317-14-8*) Cinco Puntos.

Aftershock: The Loma Prieta Earthquake & Its Impact on San Benito County. James Z. McCann. Ed. by Adele Churchill. LC 90-63594. (Illus.). 80p. (Orig.). 1990. pap. 14.95 (*0-9628177-0-8*) J Churchill.

Aftershocks. Catherine Coulter. 1993. mass mkt. 4.50 (*0-373-48259-0*, 5-48259-1) Silhouette.

AfterShocks: A Novel. Jess Wells. LC 92-7959. 240p. (Orig.). 1992. pap. 10.95 (*1-879427-08-7*) Third Side Pr.

Aftersight & Foresight: Selected Essays. Gerhart Niemeyer. LC 87-33418. 374p. (Orig.). (C). 1988. lib. bdg. 48.00 (*0-8191-6840-8*); pap. text ed. 32.00 (*0-8191-6841-6*) U Pr of Amer.

Aftertexts - Prose Pieces. Richard Kostelanetz. 148p. 1987. 20.00 (*0-912377-11-9*); pap. 12.95 (*0-912377-12-7*) Atticus Pr.

Afterthoughts. George W. Russell. LC 68-16975. (Essay Index Reprint Ser.). 1977. reprint ed. 23.95 (*0-8369-0843-0*) Ayer.

Afterthoughts on Material Civilization & Capitalism. Fernand Braudel. Tr. by Patricia M. Ranum. LC 76-47368. (Symposia in Comparative History Ser.). (Illus.). 136p. 1977. pap. 10.95x (*0-8018-2217-3*) Johns Hopkins.

Afterward. large type ed. Catherine M. Rae. LC 92-11681. 273p. 1992. reprint ed. lib. bdg. 19.95 (*1-56054-422-8*) Thorndike Pr.

Afterwards. Amy Bartlett. (National Poetry Ser.). 66p. (Orig.). 1985. 13.95 (*0-89255-090-2*); pap. 7.95 (*0-89255-091-0*) Persea Bks.

Afterwards. Patricia Cumming. LC 73-94068. 64p. 1974. pap. 9.95 (*0-914086-02-2*) Alicejamesbooks.

Afterwards, & Other Stories. John B. Watson. LC 75-150565. (Short Story Index Reprint Ser.). 1977. reprint ed. 23.95 (*0-8369-3863-1*) Ayer.

Afterwords. James R. Nichols. 52p. 1986. pap. 4.95 (*0-89697-272-0*) Intl Univ Pr.

Afterwords: An English Prof's Reflections on a Campus Career. Lyle Crist. (Illus.). 198p. (Orig.). 1989. pap. write for info. (*0-9624800-0-2*) Mt Union Coll.

Afterworld. Christine Garren. LC 92-32680. (Phoenix Poets Ser.). 64p. (C). 1993. lib. bdg. 20.00 (*0-226-28408-5*); pap. 7.95 (*0-226-28409-3*) U Ch Pr.

Afton of Margate Castle. Angela Hunt. LC 93-7201. 1993. 9.99 (*0-8423-1222-6*) Tyndale.

AFV Retrofit Systems see Jane's Armour & Artillery Upgrade

AFVA Evaluations, 1991. American Film & Video Association Staff. (Illus.). 340p. 1992. 25.00 (*0-917846-07-9*, 95507) Highsmith Pr.

AFVA Evaluations, 1992. American Film & Video Association Staff. (Illus.). 336p. 1993. 25.00 (*0-917846-13-3*, 95524) Highsmith Pr.

***Aga.** Jake G. Young. Ed. by Charlotte Stone. (Illus.). 32p. 1994. 6.95 (*0-8118-0623-5*) Chronicle Bks.

AGA Gas Handbook: Properties & Uses of Industrial Gases. Ed. by Kersti Ahlberg. (Illus.). 582p. 1985. text ed. 121.00x (*91-970061-1-4*) Coronet Bks.

Aga Khan Awards for Architecture, Bk. 2. Ed. by James Steele. (Illus.). 150p. 1994. 60.00 (*1-85490-207-5*, Academy Edits) St Martin.

Aga Khan Rural Support Program in Pakistan: Second Interim Evaluation. (Operations Evaluation Study Ser.). 144p. 1990. 9.95 (*0-685-74577-5*, 11612) World Bank.

AGA Line Pipe Research Symposium Proceedings. Incl. Dallas, 19653rd ed. 214p. pap. 5.00 (*0-318-12672-9*, L30000); Houston, 19796th ed. 200p. pap. 35.00 (*0-318-12675-3*, L30175); write for info. (*0-318-62029-4*) Am Gas Assn.

Agada: The Language of Jewish Faith. Samuel E. Karff. LC 79-15610. (Alumni Series of the Hebrew Union College Press). 228p. reprint ed. pap. 65.00 (*0-8357-8011-2*, 2034161) Bks Demand.

Again. Kathleen G. Seidel. 384p. (Orig.). 1994. pap. 5.50 (*0-451-40502-1*, Onyx) NAL-Dutton.

***Again & Twenty-four Top Movie & TV Hits.** 120p. (Orig.). 1994. pap. 12.95 (*0-89724-214-9*) Warner Brothers.

Again Calls the Owl. Margaret Craven. 1984. mass mkt. 4.99 (*0-440-30074-6*) Dell.

Again for the First Time. Rosemary Catacalos. 72p. 1984. pap. 6.00 (*0-940510-07-3*) Tooth of Time.

Again the Gemini Are in the Orchard. Gail Wronsky. 64p. 1991. 6.95 (*0-932616-35-6*) New Poets Chestnut Hills.

Again the Three Just Men. Edgar Wallace. LC 75-130077. (Short Story Index Reprint Ser.). 1977. 20.95 (*0-8369-3658-2*) Ayer.

***Again to the Life of Eternity: William Blake's Illustrations to the Poems of Thomas Gray.** Frank A. Vaughan. LC 95-9928. Date not set. write for info. (*0-945636-74-1*) Susquehanna U Pr.

Against a Darkening Sky. Janet Lewis. LC 85-9770. 302p. 1985. reprint ed. text ed. 22.50 (*0-8040-0865-5*); reprint ed. pap. 9.95 (*0-8040-0866-3*) Swallow.

Against a Field Sinister. Edith Jenkins. 144p. (Orig.). 1991. pap. 7.95 (*0-87286-263-1*) City Lights.

Against Academia: The History of the Popular Culture Association - American Culture Association & Popular Culture Movement 1967-1988. Ray B. Browne. (Illus.). 195p. 1989. 34.95 (*0-87972-451-X*); pap. 17.95 (*0-87972-452-8*) Bowling Green Univ.

Against All Enemies: Interpretations of American Military History from Colonial Times to the Present. Ed. by Kenneth J. Hagan & William R. Roberts. LC 85-17660. (Contributions in Military Studies: No. 51). (Illus.). 411p. 1986. text ed. 65.00 (*0-313-21197-3*, HOR/); pap. text ed. 19.95 (*0-313-25280-7*, HORPB/) Greenwood.

Against All Hope: Resistance in the Nazi Concentration Camps, 1938-1945. Hermann Langbein. Tr. by Henry Zohn. LC 93-16247. 1993. 29.95 (*1-55778-363-2*) Paragon Hse.

***Against All Odds.** John C. Allen. LC 94-27434. (C). 1994. pap. text ed. 19.95 (*0-8133-8842-2*) Westview.

***Against All Odds.** John C. Allen. LC 94-27434. (C). 1994. text ed. 19.95 (*0-8133-8821-X*) Westview.

***Against All Odds.** Franklin W. Dixon. Ed. by Anne Greenberg. (Hardy Boys Case Files Ser.: No. 96). 160p. (Orig.). (J). 1995. mass mkt. 3.99 (*0-671-88207-4*, Archway) PB.

Against All Odds. Eichler. 1991. pap. 15.95 (*0-8384-2855-X*) Heinle & Heinle.

Against All Odds. Eichler. 1991. audio 25.00 (*0-8384-2856-8*); audio 25.00 (*0-8384-2858-4*) Heinle & Heinle.

***Against All Odds.** Dave Jackson et al. LC 94-69842. 128p. 1995. pap. 4.95 (*0-89221-287-X*) New Leaf.

Against All Odds. Marion F. Lansing. LC 78-84318. (Essay Index Reprint Ser.). 1977. 21.95 (*0-8369-1149-0*) Ayer.

Against All Odds. Jim Stier. 1995. pap. 8.99 (*0-927545-44-6*) YWAM Pub.

Against All Odds. Julia A. Whitaker. 1992. 11.95 (*0-533-10056-9*) Vantage.

Against All Odds. J. Llewellyn Youmans. Ed. by Ann B. McKellips. LC 82-90749. 220p. 1983. 14.95 (*0-9609670-0-1*) J-Y Ent.

Against All Odds: A Chronicle of the Eritrean Revolution. Dan Connell. LC 93-1010. (Illus.). 312p. 1993. 24.95 (*0-932415-89-X*) Red Sea Pr.

Against All Odds: A Tale of Two Survivors. Norman Salsitz & Amalie P. Salsitz. Ed. by Richard Skolnick et al. LC 90-20281. (Illus.). 325p. 1991. 24.95 (*0-89604-148-4*); pap. 12.95 (*0-89604-149-2*) Holocaust Pubns.

Against All Odds: Breaking the Poverty Trap. Ed. by Donatus De Silva. LC 89-4258. 186p. 1989. text ed. 24.95 (*0-932020-69-0*); pap. 11.95 (*0-932020-70-4*) Seven Locks Pr.

Against All Odds: Case Studies on Library Financial Management. Ed. by Linda Crismond. 246p. 1994. text ed. 35.00 (*0-917846-28-1*, 95574) Highsmith Pr.

***Against All Odds: Football's Great Comebacks & Upsets.** William Shanklin. 1994. pap. 14.95 (*0-935016-13-9*, Barclay House) Excelsior Music Pub Co.

Against All Odds: The Feminist Movement in Mexico to 1940. Anna Macias. LC 81-6201. (Contributions in Women's Studies: No. 30). xv, 195p. 1982. text ed. 42.95 (*0-313-23028-5*, MAO/, Greenwood Pr) Greenwood.

Against All Odds: The Story of the Toyota Motor Corporation & the Family That Created It. Yukiyasu Togo & William Wartman. (Illus.). 272p. 1993. 22.95 (*0-312-09733-6*) St Martin.

Against All Opposition: Black Explorers in America. Jim Haskins. 128p. (YA). 1992. 13.95 (*0-8027-8137-3*); lib. bdg. 14.85 (*0-8027-8138-1*) Walker & Co.

Against All Wounds. Judson Crews. (Backpocket Poets Ser.). 36p. (Orig.). 1987. pap. 2.50 (*0-916155-06-4*) Trout Creek.

Against Architecture: The Writings of Georges Bataille. Denis Hollier. (Illus.). 201p. 1992. pap. 14.95 (*0-262-58113-2*) MIT Pr.

Against Aristotle on the Eternity of the World. John Philoponus. Ed. & Tr. by Christian Wildberg. LC 86-47973. (Ancient Commentators on Aristotle Ser.). 160p. 1987. 39.95 (*0-8014-2052-0*) Cornell U Pr.

***Against Biblical Counseling: For the Bible.** Martin Bobgan & Deidre Bobgan. LC 94-92307. 200p. (Orig.). 1994. pap. 10.95 (*0-941717-09-7*) EastGate Pubs.

Against Borders: Promoting Books for a Multicultural World. Hazel Rochman. LC 93-17840. 288p. (Orig.). (YA). (gr. 5-12). 1993. pap. text ed. 18.95 (*0-8389-0601-X*) ALA.

Against Capitalism. rev. ed. David Schweickart. LC 92-47480. (Studies in Marxism & Social Theory). 480p. (C). 1993. 69.95 (*0-521-41851-8*) Cambridge U Pr.

Against Criminology. Stanley Cohen. 352p. 1988. 39.95x (*0-88738-153-7*); pap. 21.95x (*0-88738-689-X*) Transaction Pubs.

Against Deconstruction. John M. Ellis. 152p. (Orig.). 1990. pap. text ed. 10.95 (*0-691-01484-1*) Princeton U Pr.

Against Democracy & Equality: The European New Right. Tomislav Sunic. (American University Studies: Political Science: Ser. X, Vol. 25). xii, 196p. 1990. 39.95 (*0-8204-1294-5*) P Lang Pubs.

Against Dirigisme: The Case for Unshackling Economic Markets. Deepak Lal. LC 94-1702. 1994. pap. 14.95 (*1-55815-324-1*) ICS Pr.

Against Dreaming: Poems. C. G. Hanzlicek. LC 93-33656. 64p. 1994. text ed. 18.95 (*0-8262-0932-7*); pap. 9.95 (*0-8262-0933-5*) U of Mo Pr.

***Against Empire.** Michael Parenti. 256p. (Orig.). 1995. pap. text ed. 12.95 (*0-87286-298-4*) City Lights.

A

An Asterisk (*) at the beginning of an entry indicates that the title is appearing in BIP for the first time.

A

Against Ethics: Contributions to a Poetics of Obligation with Constant Reference to Deconstruction. John D. Caputo. LC 92-41567. (Studies in Continental Thought). 1993. write for info. (0-253-31313-9); pap. write for info. (0-253-20816-5) Cambridge U Pr.

Against Every Human Law: The Terrorist Threat to Diplomacy. Andrew Selth. (ANUP Ser.). 208p. 1989. pap. text ed. 21.95 (0-08-034404-6, Pergamon Pr) Elsevier.

Against Excess: Drug Policy for Results. Mark A. Kleiman. LC 91-55459. 496p. 1993. reprint ed. pap. 17.00 (0-465-00086-X) Basic.

Against False Union. Alexandre Kalomiros. Tr. by George Gabriel. LC 90-61948. (Illus.). 170p. (Orig.). 1990. reprint ed. pap. 7.50 (0-913026-70-0) St Nectarios.

Against Fascism & War. George Dimitrov. LC 86-20121. 130p. (C). 1987. pap. 4.25 (0-7178-0643-X) Intl Pubs Co.

Against Fate. Glenn Tinder. LC 81-50462. (Loyola Lecture Series in Political Analysis). 173p. (C). 1984. pap. text ed. 9.95 (0-268-00607-5) U of Notre Dame Pr.

Against Finality: Inaugural Lecture, Delivered 4th February 1993. John Beer. 42p. (C). 1994. pap. 9.95 (0-521-45954-0) Cambridge U Pr.

Against Forgetting: Twentieth-Century Poetry of Witness. Ed. by Carolyn Forche. 500p. 1993. pap. 19.95 (0-393-30976-2) Norton.

Against Gravity. Ed McCabe. 1991. pap. 15.95 (0-446-39239-1) Warner Bks.

Against Great Odds: The History of Alcorn State University. Josephine M. Posey. LC 93-38375. (Illus.). 224p. 1994. 29.50 (0-87805-681-5) U Pr of Miss.

***Against Her Will.** Watkins. 1995. mass mkt. (0-7860-0145-3, Pinnacle NY) Windsor NY.

***Against Her Will.** Ronald J. Watkins. 480p. 1995. pap. 4.99 (0-8217-0145-2) Zebra.

Against His-Story, Against Leviathan! Fredy Perlman. (Illus.). 1983. pap. 4.00 (0-934868-25-5) Black & Red.

Against History. Fredy Perlman. 1986. lib. bdg. 79.95 (0-8490-3849-9) Gordon Pr.

Against Individual Terrorism. Leon Trotsky. 1987. reprint ed. pap. 2.50 (0-87348-334-0) Pathfinder NY.

Against Infinity. Gregory Benford. 1983. 25.00 (0-671-46491-4) Ultramarine Pub.

Against Infinity: An Anthology of Contemporary Mathematical Poetry. Ed. by E. Robson & J. Wimp. LC 79-90106. 1979. 17.00 (0-934982-00-7); pap. 8.95 (0-934982-01-5) Primary Pr.

Against Information. John Lane. Ed. by Thomas R. Crowe. (Illus.). 8p. 1994. 1.00 (1-883197-04-X) New Native Pr.

***Against Information & Other Poems.** John Lane. LC 94-69299. 68p. (Orig.). 1995. pap. 7.95 (1-883197-06-6) New Native Pr.

Against Instinct: From Biology to Philosophical Psychology. Dennis M. Senchuk. 200p. 1991. 44.95 (0-87722-815-9) Temple U Pr.

Against Interpretation. Susan Sontag. 1990. mass mkt. 9.95 (0-385-26708-8, Anchor NY) Doubleday.

***Against Itself: The Federal Theater & Writers' Projects in the Midwest.** Paul Sporn. (Illus.). 392p. 1995. text ed. 24.95x (0-8143-2590-4) Wayne St U Pr.

***Against Itself: The Federal Theater & Writers' Projects in the Midwest.** Paul Sporn. LC 94-43427. 1995. write for info. (0-8143-2461-4) Wayne St U Pr.

Against Julian. St. Augustine. LC 77-81347. (Fathers of the Church Ser.: Vol. 35). 407p. 1957. 21.95 (0-8132-0035-0) Cath U Pr.

Against Language? Dissatisfaction with Language As Theme & As Impulse Towards Experiments in Twentieth Century Poetry. Rosemarie Waldrop. (De Proprietatibus Litterarum, Ser. Minor: No. 6). 132p. (Orig.). 1971. pap. text ed. 65.40 (90-279-1789-2) Mouton.

Against Leviathan. Norman Kreitman. 39p. 1989. pap. text ed. 5.75 (0-08-037735-1, 6202, Pub. by Aberdeen U Pr) Macmillan.

Against Liberation: Putting Animals in Perspective. Michael Leahy. 272p. 1991. 59.95 (0-415-03584-8, A5672) Routledge.

Against Literature. John Beverley. LC 92-46356. 192p. 1993. text ed. 34.95 (0-8166-2248-5); pap. text ed. 14.95 (0-8166-2249-3) U of Minn Pr.

Against Lord & State: Religion & Peasant Uprisings in Malabar (1836-1921) K. N. Panikkar. (Illus.). 248p. 1989. 28.00 (0-19-562139-5) OUP.

Against Machismo: Rubem Alves, Leonardo Boff, Gustavo Gutierrez, Jose Miguez Bonino, Juan Luis Segundo...& Others Talk about the Struggle of Women. Alves. Ed. by Elsa Tamez. Tr. by John Eagleson. LC 87-21981. 160p. (Orig.). 1987. 11.95 (0-940989-12-3) Meyer Stone Bks.

Against Mechanism: Protecting Economics from Science. Philip Mirowski. 264p. 1988. pap. 18.95 (0-8476-7695-1) Rowman.

Against Mechanism: Why Economics Needs Protection from Science. Philip Mirowski. 264p. (C). 1988. 57.00 (0-8476-7436-3) Rowman.

Against Mediocrity: The Humanities in America's High Schools. Ed. by Chester E. Finn, Jr. et al. LC 83-22819. 276p. 1984. 32.50 (0-8419-0944-X); pap. 13.95 (0-8419-0945-8) Holmes & Meier.

Against Meidias, Vol. III. Demosthenes. Ed. by E. H. Warmington. Bd. with Against Androtion; Against Aristocrates.; Against Timocrates.; Against Aristogeiton 1 & 2, 21-26. (Loeb Classical Library: No. 299). (ENG & GRE.). (C). 15.50 (0-674-99330-6) HUP.

Against Meidias (Oration 21) Demosthenes. Ed. by Douglas M. MacDowell. (Illus.). 456p. 1990. 105.00 (0-19-814763-5) OUP.

Against Method. Paul K. Feyerabend. 352p. 1988. 50.00 (0-86091-222-1, Pub. by Verso UK); pap. 16.95 (0-86091-934-X, Pub. by Verso UK) Routledge Chapman & Hall.

Against Method: Outline of an Anarchistic Theory of Knowledge. 3rd ed. Paul K. Feyerabend. 352p. 1993. 64.95 (0-86091-481-X, B2484, Pub. by Verso UK); pap. 18.95 (0-86091-646-4, B2488, Pub. by Verso UK) Routledge Chapman & Hall.

Against Nature. Joris-Karl Huysmans. Tr. by Robert Baldick. (Classics Ser.). 220p. 1959. pap. 9.95 (0-14-044086-0, Penguin Classics) Viking Penguin.

Against Nature: A Group Show of Work by Homosexual Men. Ed. by Richard Hawkins. (Illus.). 36p. (Orig.). (C). 1989. 2.50 (0-685-25226-4) LA Contemp Exhib.

Against Nature: And Other Essays on History, Sexuality & Identity. Jeffrey Weeks. 256p. (Orig.). (C). 1991. text ed. 49.95 (1-85489-028-X, Pub. by Rivers Oram Pr UK); pap. text ed. 19.95 (1-85489-004-2, Pub. by Rivers Oram Pr UK) Paul & Co Pubs.

Against Nature: Japanese Art in the 80s. (Illus.). 90p. 1991. pap. 15.00 (0-685-50523-5) Grey Art Gallery Study Ctr.

Against Nature: Wilderness Poems. Judith McCombs. (American Dust Ser.: No. 9). 1979. 7.95 (0-913218-83-9); pap. 2.95 (0-913218-84-7) Dustbooks.

Against Our Vanishing: Winter Conversations with Allen Grossman. Allen Grossman. Ed. by Mark Halliday. LC 81-51048. (Poetics Ser.: No. 1). 128p. (Orig.). 1981. pap. 7.95 (0-937672-04-1) Rowan Tree.

Against Our Will: Men, Women & Rape. Susan Brownmiller. 480p. 1993. pap. 12.50 (0-449-90820-8, Columbine) Fawcett.

***Against Paradise.** Jonathan Holden. LC 89-27667. (University of Utah Press Poetry Ser.). 69p. (Orig.). 1989. pap. 25.00 (0-7837-8556-9, 2049371) Bks Demand.

Against Patriarchal Thinking: Women Philosophers in Europe 1992; a Future Without Discrimination? Ed. by Maja Pellikaan & Hannelore Schroder. 400p. (Orig.). 1993. pap. text ed. 45.00 (90-5383-102-9, Pub. by VU Univ Pr NE) Paul & Co Pubs.

Against Pornography: The Evidence of Harm. Diana E. Russell. LC 93-92610. (Illus.). 169p. 1994. pap. 12.95 (0-9634776-1-7) Russell CA.

Against Post-Modernism: A Marxist Critique. Alex Callinicos. 200p. 1990. text ed. 55.00 (0-312-04224-8); pap. 15.95 (0-312-04225-6) St Martin.

Against Principalities & Powers: Letters from a Brazilian Jail. Carlos Christo. Tr. by John Drury. LC 76-43030. 255p. reprint ed. pap. 72.70 (0-8357-8794-X, 2033556) Bks Demand.

Against Pure Reason: Writings on Religion, Language, & History. J. G. Herder. Tr. & Intro. by Marcia Bunge. LC 92-360. (Texts in Modern Theology Ser.). 288p. (Orig.). 1992. pap. 20.00 (0-8006-3212-5, 1-3212, Fortress Pr) Augsburg Fortress.

Against Racism: Unpublished Essays, Papers, Addresses, 1887-1961. W. E. B. Du Bois. Ed. by Herbert Aptheker. LC 84-16173. (Illus.). 304p. 1985. pap. 17.95 (0-87023-624-5) U of Mass Pr.

Against Relativism: A Philosophical Defense of Method. James F. Harris. LC 92-21019. 244p. 1992. 54.95 (0-8126-9201-2); pap. 19.95 (0-8126-9202-0) Open Court.

Against Sadomasochism: A Radical Feminist Analysis. Ed. by Robin R. Linden et al. LC 81-15284. 224p. (Orig.). (C). 1981. pap. 7.95 (0-9603628-3-5) Frog in Well.

Against Silence: The Voice & Vision of Elie Wiesel, 3 vols., 1. Irving Abrahamson. 1188p. 1985. write for info. (0-89604-075-5) Holocaust Pubns.

Against Silence: The Voice & Vision of Elie Wiesel, 3 vols., 2. Irving Abrahamson. 1188p. 1985. write for info. (0-89604-076-3) Holocaust Pubns.

Against Silence: The Voice & Vision of Elie Wiesel, 3 vols., 3. Irving Abrahamson. 1188p. 1985. write for info. (0-89604-077-1) Holocaust Pubns.

Against Silence: The Voice & Vision of Elie Wiesel, 3 vols., Set. Irving Abrahamson. 1188p. 1987. 95.00 (0-685-08779-4) Holocaust Pubns.

Against the Academicians. St. Augustine. Tr. by M. Patricia Garvey. (Medieval Philosophical Texts in Translation Ser.: No. 1). 1957. pap. 10.00 (0-87462-202-6) Marquette.

Against the American Dream: Essays on Charles Bukowski. Russell Harrison. LC 94-35255. 323p. (Orig.). (C). 1994. 30.00 (0-87685-960-0); pap. 15.00 (0-87685-959-7) Black Sparrow.

Against the American Grain: Essays on the Effects of Mass Culture. Dwight Macdonald. LC 83-7665. (Quality Paperbacks Ser.). (Illus.). xvi, 429p. 1983. reprint ed. pap. 9.95 (0-306-80205-8) Da Capo.

Against the American Grain: Myth & History in William Carlos Williams, Jay Wright & Nicolas Guillen. Vera M. Kutzinski. LC 86-18504. 312p. 1986. text ed. 45.00 (0-8018-3330-2) Johns Hopkins.

Against the Apocalypse: Responses to Catastrophe in Modern Jewish Culture. David G. Roskies. (Illus.). 352p. 1984. 32.00 (0-674-00915-0) HUP.

Against the Apocalypse: Responses to Catastrophe in Modern Jewish Culture. David G. Roskies. LC 83-18663. (Illus.). 352p. 1986. pap. text ed. 12.50 (0-674-00916-9) HUP.

Against the Barbarians & Other Reflections on Familiar Themes. M. E. Bradford. 280p. (C). 1992. text ed. 37.50 (0-8262-0804-5) U of Mo Pr.

Against the Blues. Alvin Aubert. 1972. pap. 4.00 (0-910296-73-1) Broadside Pr.

Against the Bomb: The British Peace Movement 1958-1965. Richard Taylor. 384p. 1988. 75.00 (0-19-827537-4) OUP.

Against the Christians & Upon the Sovereign Sun. Thomas Taylor. 119p. 1980. 15.00 (0-89005-301-4) Ares.

Against the Current. Frances K. Ring. 160p. (Orig.). 1987. pap. 6.95 (0-88739-015-3) Creat Arts Bk.

Against the Current: As I Remember F. Scott Fitzgerald. Frances K. Ring. LC 84-47682. (Illus.). 160p. (C). 1985. 14.95 (0-88739-001-3) Creat Arts Bk.

Against the Evidence: Selected Poems, 1934-1994. David Ignatow. LC 93-4303. 196p. 1994. 30.00 (0-8195-2211-2, Wesleyan Univ Pr); pap. 14.95 (0-8195-1214-1, Wesleyan Univ Pr) U Pr of New Eng.

Against the Faith. James Herrick. LC 85-43040. (Skeptic's Bookshelf Ser.). 250p. 1985. 27.95 (0-87975-288-2) Prometheus Bks.

Against the Few: Struggles of India's Rural Poor. Arun Sinha. LC 89-8869. 288p. (C). 1991. text ed. 55.00 (0-86232-718-0, Pub. by Zed Books UK); pap. 17.50 (0-86232-719-9, Pub. by Zed Books UK) Humanities.

***Against the Grain.** Simon Jenkins. 208p. 1995. 39.95 (0-7195-5570-1, Pub. by John Murray UK) Trafalgar.

Against the Grain. Joris K. Huysmans. Orig. Title: A Rebours. 1969. reprint ed. pap. 4.95 (0-486-22190-3) Dover.

Against the Grain: Bentwood Furniture from the Collection of Fern & Manfred Steinfeld. Ghenete Zelleke et al. Tr. by Matthew Heintzelmann. LC 93-11194. (Illus.). 124p. 1993. 29.95 (0-86559-113-X) Art Inst Chi.

Against the Grain: Essays Nineteen Seventy-Five to Nineteen Eighty-Five. Terry Eagleton. 200p. 1986. text ed. 50.00 (0-86091-134-9, Pub. by Verso UK); pap. 14.95 (0-86091-841-6, Pub. by Verso UK) Routledge Chapman & Hall.

Against the Grain: Interviews with Maverick American Publishers. Ed. by Robert Dana. LC 86-1457. (Illus.). 288p. 1986. 34.95x (0-87745-146-X) U of Iowa Pr.

Against the Grain: New Approaches to Professional Ethics. Michael Goldberg. LC 93-3917. 1993. pap. 15.00 (1-56338-058-7) TPI PA.

Against the Grain: Southern Radicals & Prophets, 1929-1959. Anthony P. Dunbar. LC 81-1782. (Illus.). ix, 306p. 1981. 32.50 (0-8139-0892-2) U Pr of Va.

Against the Grain: The Contemporary Women's Movement in Northern Ireland. Eileen Evason. 64p. (Orig.). (C). 1991. pap. 7.99 (1-85594-019-1, Pub. by Attic IE) InBook.

***Against the Grain: The New Criterion on Art & Intellect at the End of the Twentieth Century.** Ed. by Hilton Kramer & Roger Kimball. LC 94-31977. 1995. 35.00 (1-56663-069-X); pap. 16.95 (1-56663-070-3) I R Dee.

***Against the Grain: The Slightly Eccentric Guide to Living Well Without Gluten or Wheat.** Jax P. Lowell. LC 94-39985. 320p. 1995. 22.50 (0-8050-3624-5) H Holt & Co.

Against the Horizon: Feminism & Postwar Austrian Women Writers. Jacqueline Vansant. LC 87-24951. (Contributions in Woman's Studies: No. 92). 192p. 1988. text ed. 49.95 (0-313-25863-5, VFM/, Greenwood Pr) Greenwood.

***Against the House.** Jack Finney. 1994. lib. bdg. 27.95x (1-56849-411-4) Buccaneer Bks.

***Against the Law.** Michael C. Eberhardt. LC 94-46565. 320p. 1995. 21.95 (0-525-93994-6) NAL-Dutton.

Against the Manichees. Serapion. Ed. by Robert P. Casey. (Harvard Theological Studies: Vol. 15). 1931. pap. 15.00 (0-527-01015-4) Periodicals Srv.

Against the Market: Political Economy, Market Socialism & the Marxist Critique. David McNally. 280p. 1993. 59.95 (0-86091-431-3, B2496, Pub. by Verso UK); pap. 18.95 (0-86091-606-5, B2500, Pub. by Verso UK) Routledge Chapman & Hall.

Against the Meanwhile: 3 Elegies. Mark Irwin. LC 87-27244. (Wesleyan Poetry Ser.). 79p. 1988. 22.50 (0-8195-2150-7, Wesleyan Univ Pr); pap. 10.95 (0-8195-1151-X, Wesleyan Univ Pr) U Pr of New Eng.

Against the Moon. Jane G. Rushing. LC 91-3111. (Texas Tradition Ser.: No. 17). 222p. 1991. reprint ed. pap. 14.95 (0-87565-094-5) Tex Christian.

Against the Musicians (Adversus Musicos) Sextus Empiricus. Ed. & Tr. by Denise D. Greaves. LC 85-28850. (Greek & Latin Music Theory Ser.). x, 213p. 1986. 25.00 (0-8032-4168-2) U of Nebr Pr.

Against the Nations: War & Survival in a Liberal Society. Stanley Hauerwas. LC 92-50408. (Orig.). (C). 1992. reprint ed. pap. text ed. 12.95 (0-268-00638-5) U of Notre Dame Pr.

Against the Night: Living in the New Dark Ages. Charles M. Colson. 205p. (Orig.). 1991. reprint ed. pap. 8.99 (0-89283-732-2, Vine Bks) Servant.

Against the Odds. Tina Darragh. 72p. (Orig.). 1989. pap. 8.00 (0-937013-28-5) Potes Poets.

Against the Odds. L. M. Montgomery. (YA). 1994. mass mkt. 4.50 (0-553-56592-3) Bantam.

Against the Odds. Created by Francine Pascal. (Sweet Valley High Ser.: No. 51). 160p. (J). 1989. pap. 2.95 (0-553-27650-6) Bantam.

Against the Odds. large type ed. Francine Pascal. (Sweet Valley High Ser.: No. 51). 151p. (J). (gr. 5-8). 1989. reprint ed. 9.50 (1-55905-006-3, Gareth Stevens Inc); reprint ed. lib. bdg. 10.50 (1-55905-016-0, Gareth Stevens Inc) Grey Castle.

Against the Odds: Adopting Mentally Handicapped Children. C. Macaskill. (C). 1989. 60.00 (0-903534-58-4, Pub. by Brit Ag for Adopt & Fost UK) St Mut.

Against the Odds: African-American Artists & the Harmon Foundation. Gary A. Reynolds & Beryl J. Wright. LC 89-27552. 298p. 1990. 40.00 (0-932828-21-3); pap. 20.00 (0-932828-22-1) Newark Mus.

Against the Odds: African-American Artists & the Harmon Foundation. Gary A. Reynolds & Beryl J. Wright. (Illus.). 256p. 1990. pap. 22.50 (0-295-96976-8) U of Wash Pr.

Against the Odds: Battles at Sea, 1591-1949. Alexander McKee. (Illus.). 288p. 1991. 25.95 (1-55750-025-8) Naval Inst Pr.

***Against the Odds: The True Story of Michele a Cancer Survivor.** Patrick Nolan. 256p. 1995. pap. 18.25 (1-887170-05-7) Alchemy Pub.

***Against the Panzers: United States Infantry vs. German Tanks, 1944-1945: A History of Eight Battles Told Through Diaries, Unit Histories & Interviews.** Allyn R. Vannoy & Jay Karamales. 336p. 1995. lib. bdg. 42.50 (0-7864-0129-X) McFarland & Co.

Against the Protestant Gnostics. Philip J. Lee. 368p. 1993. reprint ed. pap. 19.95 (0-19-508436-5) OUP.

Against the Rules. Francine Pascal. (Sweet Valley Twins Ser.: No. 9). (Orig.). (J). 1987. 3.25 (0-553-15676-4) Bantam.

Against the Rules. large type ed. Jamie Suzanne. (Sweet Valley Twins Ser.: No. 9). 104p. (YA). (gr. 7-12). 1991. reprint ed. 9.95 (1-55905-072-1) Grey Castle.

Against the Season. Jane Rule. 224p. 1984. reprint ed. pap. 8.95 (0-930044-48-7) Naiad Pr.

Against the Self-Images of the Age: Essays on Ideology & Philosophy. Alasdair MacIntyre. LC 78-1571. 1978. reprint ed. pap. text ed. 12.95 (0-268-00587-7) U of Notre Dame Pr.

***Against the Sickle Moon.** Jennifer Music. 320p. 1995. pap. 9.95 (0-7610-0092-5) NW Pub.

***Against the Simple.** Robert Miltner. LC 94-33223. (Wick Poetry Chapbook Ser.: No. 6). 24p. (Orig.). 1995. pap. 3.00 (0-87338-521-7) Kent St U Pr.

Against the Specter of a Dragon: The Campaign for American Military Preparedness, 1914-1917. John P. Finnegan. LC 74-288. (Contributions in Military History Ser.: No. 7). (Illus.). 253p. 1975. text ed. 69.50 (0-8371-7376-0, FSD/, Greenwood Pr) Greenwood.

Against the State. David E. Apter & Nagayo Sawa. (Illus.). 296p. 1986. pap. 14.95 (0-674-00921-5) HUP.

Against the State: Politics & Social Protest in Japan. David E. Apter & Nagayo Sawa. LC 83-15338. (Illus.). 296p. 1984. 37.50 (0-674-00920-7) HUP.

Against the State of Nuclear Terror. Joel Kovel. LC 84-50942. 250p. 1983. 30.00 (0-89608-220-2); pap. 9.50 (0-89608-219-9) South End Pr.

Against the Storm. Sean Dunne. 1985. pap. 9.95 (0-85105-440-4, Pub. by Colin Smythe Ltd UK) Dufour.

Against the Storm. Gaye Hicyilmaz. (J). 1993. pap. 3.50 (0-440-40892-X) Dell.

Against the Storm. Gaye Hicyilmaz. 176p. (YA). (gr. 7 up). 1992. 14.95 (0-316-36078-3, Joy St Bks) Little.

Against the Tide. Angus Kinnear. (Illus.). 332p. pap. 5.99 (0-8423-0045-7) Tyndale.

Against the Tide. Tim LaHaye & Beverly LaHaye. 288p. 1993. 16.99 (0-88070-578-7, Multnomah Bks) Questar Pubs.

Against the Tide. Harry Weinberg. LC 89-43229. 144p. 1989. 18.95 (0-88400-138-5) Shengold.

Against the Tide: An Autobiography. Adam C. Powell, Sr. Ed. by Edwin S. Gaustad. LC 79-52603. (Baptist Tradition Ser.). 1980. reprint ed. 33.95 (0-405-12468-6) Ayer.

Against the Tide: Jewish Nonconformist Views of Israel & Zionism. Bezalel Chaim. 1979. lib. bdg. 42.95 (0-686-24783-3) M Buber Pr.

Against the Tide: Pro-Feminist Men in the United States, 1776-1990, a Documentary History. Ed. by Michael S. Kimmel & Thomas E. Mosmiller. (Men & Masculinity Ser.). (Illus.). 560p. 1993. reprint ed. pap. 20.00 (0-8070-6767-9) Beacon Pr.

Against the Tide: Watchman Nee. Angus Kinnear. 1992. pap. 5.95 (0-87508-408-7) Chr Lit.

Against the Tide: Whites in the Struggle Against Apartheid. Joshua Lazerson. 1994. text ed. 39.95 (0-8133-8487-7) Westview.

Against the Wall. Julia Vinograd. 50p. (Orig.). 1992. pap. 4.95 (0-929730-39-9) Zeitgeist Pr.

Against the Wind. J. F. Freedman. 464p. 1992. 5.99 (0-451-17308-2, Sig) NAL-Dutton.

Against the Wind. Edwin T. Holland & Enid M. Holland. 1990. write for info. (0-9628017-0-4) E T Holland.

Against the Wind. Richard Pini. 288p. 1992. mass mkt. 4.99 (0-8125-2274-5) Tor Bks.

***Against the Wind: "Trials, Tragedy & Rewards - Growing up on a Montana Frontier Homestead"** Park York. (Illus.). 83p. (Orig.). 1995. pap. 8.95 (0-9645881-0-2) Eagle Wings Pr.

Against the Wind: The Evolution of U.S. Policy Toward China, 1945-1950; Perspectives of a Chinese Scholar. Zhongyun Zi. 250p. 1992. 40.00 (1-879176-09-2); pap. 19.95 (1-879176-12-2) Imprint Pubns.

Against the World: A Behind the Scenes Look at the Portland Trail Blazers' Chase for the NBA Championship. Kerry Eggers & Dwight Jaynes. LC 92-82549. (Illus.). 250p. 1992. 19.95 (0-915611-67-8) Sagamore Pub.

***Against Their Wills: Children Board Affected by Drugs.** Harold L. Hodgkinson & Janice H. Outtz. 20p. 1993. 10.00 (0-937846-53-8) Inst Educ Lead.

***Against Theory: Continental & Analytic Challenges in Moral Philosophy.** Dwight Furrow. 256p. 1995. 59.95x (0-415-91079-X, B4806, Routledge NY); pap. 17.95 (0-415-91080-3, B4810, Routledge NY) Routledge.

Against Theory: Literary Studies & the New Pragmatism. Ed. by W. J. Mitchell. LC 84-29127. vi, 146p. 1985. pap. text ed. 9.95 (0-226-53227-5) U Ch Pr.

Against Therapy. Jeffrey M. Masson. LC 93-26695. 1993. reprint ed. 29.95 (1-56751-023-X); reprint ed. pap. 15.95 (1-56751-022-1) Common Courage.

Against This Ground. Donna Ashworth. (Illus.). (Orig.). 1994. pap. write for info. (0-9630364-2-4) Small Mtn.

An Asterisk (*) at the beginning of an entry indicates that the title is appearing in BIP for the first time.

An Asterisk (*) at the beginning of an entry indicates that the title is appearing in BIP for the first time.

135

A

Age, Health & Employment. James E. Birren et al. 192p. (C). 1986. text ed. 49.00 (*0-13-018524-8*) P-H.

Age in Motion: Popular Radicalism in Java, 1912-1926. Takashi Shiraishi. LC 89-37476. (Asia East by South Ser.). (Illus.). 392p. 1990. 36.50 (*0-8014-2188-8*) Cornell U Pr.

Age Ingrat. Jose Cabanis. 320p. (FRE.). 1974. pap. 10.95 (*0-7859-1788-8*, 2070366006) Fr & Eur.

Age Markers in the Human Skeleton. Ed. by M. Yasar Iscan. (Illus.). 378p. (C). 1989. text ed. 79.95x (*0-398-05614-5*) C C Thomas.

***Age Markers in the Human Skeleton.** Ed. by M. Yasar Iscan. (Illus.). 378p. 1989. pap. 42.95 (*0-614-02185-5*) C C Thomas.

Age Misreporting & Age-Selective Underenumeration: Sources, Patterns, & Consequences for Demographic Analysis. Douglas C. Ewbank. LC 81-81759. (Committee on Population & Demography Report Ser.: No. 4). 130p. reprint ed. pap. 37.10 (*0-8357-7699-9*, 2036052) Bks Demand.

Age, Nativity, & Citizenship for the U. S., States & Counties. (Orig.). 60p. (Orig.). (C). 1994. pap. text ed. 40.00 (*1-56806-266-4*) Diane Pub.

Age of Adam. James Lees-Milne. 1988. reprint ed. lib. bdg. 59.00 (*0-7812-0146-2*) Rprt Serv.

Age of Adventure: The Renaissance Philosophers. Ed. by George De Santillana. LC 71-117839. (Essay Index Reprint Ser.). 1977. reprint ed. 25.95 (*0-8369-1850-9*) Ayer.

Age of Aetherius. 2nd rev. ed. Kevin Q. Avery & George King. LC 86-198666. 96p. 1982. pap. 6.30 (*0-937249-08-4*) Aetherius Soc.

Age of Aging: A Reader in Social Gerontology. Ed. by Abraham Monk. LC 79-2727. 367p. (C). 1979. 22.95 (*0-87975-111-8*); pap. 12.95 (*0-87975-114-2*) Prometheus Bks.

Age of Agony: The Art of Healing 1700-1800. Guy Williams. (Illus.). 264p. 1986. reprint ed. pap. 12.00 (*0-89733-203-2*) Academy Chi Pubs.

Age of Alexander. Plutarch. Tr. by Ian Scott-Kilvert. (Classics Ser.). 1973. pap. 10.95 (*0-14-044286-3*, Penguin Classics) Viking Penguin.

Age of Ambivalence: A New Generation Reckons with Motherhood. Judith D. Schwartz. 368p. 1993. pap. 22.00 (*0-671-76768-2*) S&S Trade.

Age of Analysis. Horton White. 1955. mass mkt. 10.95 (*0-452-00830-1*, Mer) NAL-Dutton.

Age of Analysis. Ed. by Morton G. White. LC 70-117860. (Essay Index Reprint Ser.). 1977. 21.95 (*0-8369-1858-4*) Ayer.

***Age of Anxiety.** W. H. Auden. 1994. lib. bdg. 24.95x (*1-56849-387-8*) Buccaneer Bks.

***Age of Anxiety: A Reassessment.** Malcolm Lader. 24p. 1984. pap. 4.00 (*0-904674-09-6*, Pub. by Octagon Pr UK) ISHK Bk Service.

Age of Anxiety: Security & Politics in Soviet & Post-Soviet Russia. Mark Galeotti. LC 94-9874. (C). 1994. text ed. 38.95 (*0-582-21853-5*, 76903, Pub. by Longman UK) Longman.

Age of Anxiety: Security & Politics in Soviet & Post-Soviet Russia. Mark Galeotti. LC 94-9874. 240p. (C). 1995. pap. text ed. 16.95 (*0-582-21852-7*, 76888, Pub. by Longman UK) Longman.

Age of Aristocracy: 1688 to 1830, 4 vols. 5th ed. William B. Wilcox & Walter L. Arnstein. Ed. by Lacey B. Smith. LC 87-81186. (History of England Ser.: Vol. III). 352p. (C). 1987. pap. text ed. 13.00 (*0-669-13423-6*) Heath.

Age of Aristocracy: 1688 to 1830, 4 vols. 6th ed. William B. Willcox & Walter L. Arnstein. Ed. by Lacey B. Smith. (History of England Ser.: Vol. III). 336p. (C). 1992. pap. text ed. write for info. (*0-669-24459-7*) Heath.

Age of Atilla. C. Gordon. 1992. 19.95 (*0-88029-788-3*) Marboro Bks.

Age of Atonement: The Influence of Evangelicalism on Social & Economic Thought 1785-1865. Boyd Hilton. 428p. 1992. reprint ed. pap. 29.95 (*0-19-820295-4*) OUP.

***Age of Automation: Technical Genius, Social Dilemma.** George M. Hall. LC 94-44175. 256p. 1995. text ed. 49.95 (*0-275-95194-4*, Praeger Pubs) Greenwood.

Age of Baroque in Portugal. Ed. by Jay A. Levenson. LC 93-5424. 303p. 1994. pap. 25.00 (*0-89468-198-2*) Natl Gallery Art.

Age of Battles: The Quest for Decisive Warfare from Breitenfeld to Waterloo. Russell F. Weigley. LC 90-4757. (Illus.). 602p. 1991. 35.00 (*0-253-36380-2*) Ind U Pr.

Age of Bede. Tr. by J. F. Webb & David H. Farmer. 256p. 1983. pap. 8.95 (*0-14-044437-8*, Penguin Classics) Viking Penguin.

Age of Behemoths: The Globalization of Mass Media Firms. Anthony Smith. 83p. 1991. pap. 8.95 (*0-87078-325-4*) TCFP-PPP.

Age of Belief. Ed. by Anne Fremantle. LC 75-117793. (Essay Index Reprint Ser.). 1977. 20.95 (*0-8369-1829-0*) Ayer.

Age of Belief: The Medieval Philosophers. Ed. by Anne Fremantle. (Orig.). 1955. pap. 3.95 (*0-452-00720-8*, Mer) NAL-Dutton.

Age of Birds. Alan Feduccia. LC 80-11926. (Illus.). 208p. 1980. 34.50 (*0-674-00975-4*) HUP.

Age of Birds. Alan Feduccia. (Illus.). 208p. 1987. pap. text ed. 15.95 (*0-674-00976-2*) HUP.

Age of Bluff: Paradox & Ambiguity in Rabelais & Montaigne. Barbara C. Bowen. LC 71-165041. (Illinois Studies in Language & Literature: No. 62). 180p. reprint ed. pap. 51.30 (*0-8357-6008-1*, 2034427) Bks Demand.

Age of Bruegel: Netherlandish Drawings in the Sixteenth Century. John O. Hand et al. (Illus.). 352p. 1987. 95.00 (*0-521-34196-5*) Cambridge U Pr.

Age of Calamity, (1300-1400 AD) (Time Frame Ser.). (Illus.). 176p. 1989. 19.93 (*0-8094-6441-1*); lib. bdg. 25.93 (*0-8094-6442-X*) Time-Life.

Age of Changing Priorities for Land & Water: Irrigation & Drainage Division Specialty Conference, Spokane, Washington, September 26-28, 1972. American Society of Civil Engineers, Irrigation & Drainage Division Staff. LC 73-155132. 492p. reprint ed. pap. 140.30 (*0-8357-5251-8*, 2007866) Bks Demand.

Age of Charisma. Arthur Schweitzer. LC 83-17268. 430p. 1983. lib. bdg. 37.95 (*0-8304-1015-5*) Nelson-Hall.

Age of Charlemagne. David Nicolle. (Men-at-Arms Ser.: No. 150). (Illus.). 48p. pap. 11.95 (*0-85045-042-X*, 9082, Pub. by Osprey UK) Stackpole.

Age of Chaucer. John A. Brendon. LC 72-179301. (Illus.). reprint ed. 39.50 (*0-404-01070-9*) AMS Pr.

Age of Chaucer. Arthur T. Quiller-Couch. LC 75-155616. reprint ed. 29.00 (*0-404-05201-0*) AMS Pr.

Age of Chaucer: 1346-1400. Frederick J. Snell. LC 72-128754. reprint ed. 29.50 (*0-404-06138-9*) AMS Pr.

Age of Chivalry. Thomas Bulfinch. (Airmont Classics Ser.). (YA). (gr. 8 up). 1965. pap. 1.95 (*0-8049-0061-2*, CL-61) Airmont.

Age of Chivalry. Thomas Bulfinch. 1971. 250.00 (*0-87968-585-9*) Gordon Pr.

Age of Chivalry. Abigail Frost. LC 89-17396. (Myths & Legends Ser.). (Illus.). 48p. (J). (gr. 4-8). 1990. lib. bdg. 9.95 (*1-85435-235-0*) Marshall Cavendish.

Age of Chivalry. Ed. by Nigel Saul. LC 92-6509. 1992. text ed. 39.95 (*0-312-08115-4*) St Martin.

Age of Chivalry. Thomas Bulfinch. (Works of Thomas Bulfinch). 1989. reprint ed. lib. bdg. 79.00 (*0-7812-2163-3*) Rprt Serv.

Age of Chivalry & Legends of Charlemagne. Thomas Bulfinch. 1992. pap. 19.95 (*0-88029-750-6*) Marboro Bks.

***Age of Churchill & Eden: A History of the Conservative Party, 1940-1957.** John Ramsden. LC 95-9778. 368p. (C). 1996. text ed. 69.95 (*0-582-50463-5*) Longman.

***Age of Computer.** (Young Scientist Ser.). (J). (gr. 4-6). 1995. write for info. (*0-7166-6304-X*) World Bk.

Age of Conflict: Readings in Twentieth Century European History. Leslie Derfler. 384p. (C). 1990. pap. text ed. 18.75 (*0-15-502076-5*) HB Coll Pubs.

Age of Consciousness. Milton Ward. LC 65-92058. 164p. 1985. 9.95 (*0-939835-02-9*) Optimus Bks.

***Age of Consent.** Geoffrey Wolff. LC 94-29334. 1995. 22.00 (*0-679-40638-7*) Knopf.

Age of Constantine the Great. Jacob Burckhardt. Tr. by Moses Hadas. 400p. 1983. pap. 14.00 (*0-520-04680-3*) U CA Pr.

Age of Constantine the Great. Jacob Burckhardt. (Reprints Ser.). 300p. 1989. 17.95 (*0-88029-323-3*) Dorset Pr.

Age of Correggio & the Carracci: Painting in Emilia in the Sixteenth & Seventeenth Centuries. National Gallery Art Staff. 602p. 1987. 90.00 (*0-521-34019-5*) Cambridge U Pr.

Age of Crisis: Man & World in Eighteenth Century French Thought. Lester G. Crocker. LC 59-14233. (Goucher College Ser.). 516p. reprint ed. pap. 147.10 (*0-8357-9260-9*, 2011983) Bks Demand.

Age of Curiosity: Especially for Grandmothers. Randolph Curtice. (Illus.). 1978. 7.50 (*0-9601722-0-3*) North Lake Prod.

Age of Desire. Clive Barker. 1992. pap. 7.95 (*1-56060-139-6*) Eclipse Bks.

Age of Diminished Expectations: U. S. Economic Policy in the 1990s. rev. ed. Paul R. Krugman. LC 93-6411. (Illus.). 239p. 1990. pap. 12.95x (*0-262-61092-2*) MIT Pr.

Age of Dinosaurs. Glynis Langley. (Illus.). 64p. (J). (gr. k-5). 1992. per. 6.95 (*0-8249-8537-0*, Ideals Child) Hambleton-Hill.

Age of Dinosaurs. David Noll. (Arts & Letters Ser.). 44p. 1993. pap. text ed. 3.95 (*1-883515-00-9*) Computer Support.

Age of Dinosaurs: A Fact-Filled Coloring Book. Donald F. Glut. (Start Exploring Ser.). (Illus.). 128p. (J). 1994. pap. text ed. 8.95 (*1-56138-456-9*) Running Pr.

Age of Discontinuity: Guidelines to Our Changing Society. Peter F. Drucker. 420p. (C). 1992. pap. 21.95 (*1-56000-618-8*) Transaction Pubs.

Age of Discovery. P. J. Larkin. 64p. (C). 1988. 35.00 (*0-685-33808-8*, Pub. by S Thornes Pubs UK) St Mut.

Age of Discovery. rev. ed. P. J. Larkin. (Illus.). 64p. 1976. pap. 9.95 (*0-7175-0761-0*) Dufour.

Age of Discovery: From the Renaissance to American Independence. Brian Williams & Brenda Williams. LC 94-18459. (Timelink Ser.). (Illus.). 64p. (YA). (gr. 5 up). 1994. lib. bdg. 17.95 (*0-87226-311-8*) P Bedrick Bks.

***Age of Discovery & the Slave Trade.** Ed. by Darlene C. Hine et al. (Milestones in Black American History Ser.). (Illus.). 144p. (YA). (gr. 5 up). 1995. lib. bdg. 18.95 (*0-7910-2257-9*) Chelsea Hse.

***Age of Discovery & the Slave Trade.** Ed. by Darlene C. Hine et al. (Milestones in Black American History Ser.). (Illus.). 144p. (YA). (gr. 5 up). 1995. pap. 7.95 (*0-7910-2683-3*) Chelsea Hse.

Age of Discovery, 1500-1650. Hazel M. Martell. LC 92-18621. (Illustrated History of the World Ser.). (Illus.). 80p. (J). (gr. 2-6). 1993. 17.95 (*0-8160-2789-7*) Facts on File.

Age of Doubt: American Thought & Culture in the 1940s. William Graebner. 216p. 1990. text ed. 26.95 (*0-8057-9061-6*, Twayne); pap. 14.95 (*0-8057-9070-5*, Twayne) Macmillan.

Age of Dryden. Donald F. Bond. LC 72-118855. (Goldentree Bibliographies Series in Language & Literature). 120p. (C). 1970. pap. text ed. write for info. (*0-88295-502-0*) Harlan Davidson.

Age of Dryden. Richard Garnett. LC 70-164601. (Select Bibliographies Reprint Ser.). 1977. reprint ed. 23.95 (*0-8369-5885-3*) Ayer.

Age of Electronic Messages. John G. Truxal. 1990. 40.00x (*0-262-20074-0*) MIT Pr.

Age of Electronic Messages. John G. Truxal. 1990. pap. text ed. write for info. (*0-07-065319-4*) McGraw.

Age of Elegance. A. F. Scott. 276p. 1984. 40.00 (*0-905418-78-6*, Pub. by Gresham Bks UK) St Mut.

Age of Elizabeth: England under the Later Tudors, 1547-1603. 2nd ed. D. M. Palliser. 516p. (C). 1992. pap. text ed. 32.50 (*0-582-01322-4*, 79279) Longman.

Age of Emperor Wu, 140 to c. 100 B.C. see Records of the Grand Historian of China

Age of Empire. Eric J. Hobsbawm. 1989. pap. 14.00 (*0-679-72175-4*, V175, Vin) Random.

Age of Enlightenment. Ed. by Isaiah Berlin. LC 72-117760. (Essay Index Reprint Ser.). 1980. 19.95 (*0-8369-1822-3*) Ayer.

Age of Enlightenment: The Eighteenth Century Philosophers. Ed. by Isaiah Berlin. (Orig.). 1984. pap. 10.00 (*0-452-00904-9*, Mer) NAL-Dutton.

Age of Excess: The United States from 1877-1914. 2nd ed. Ray Ginger. (Illus.). 419p. (C). 1989. reprint ed. pap. text ed. 14.95 (*0-88133-462-6*) Waveland Pr.

***Age of Extremes: A History of the World, 1914-1991.** Eric Hobsbawn. LC 94-28981. (Illus.). 627p. 1995. 30.00 (*0-394-58575-5*) Pantheon.

Age of Exuberance: Backgrounds to Eighteenth Century Literature, 1660-1785. Donald Greene. (Language & Literature Studies). (Orig.). (C). 1970. pap. text ed. write for info. (*0-07-553580-7*) McGraw.

Age of Fable. Thomas Bulfinch. (Works of Thomas Bulfinch). 1989. reprint ed. lib. bdg. 79.00 (*0-7812-2162-5*) Rprt Serv.

Age of Faith. Will Durant. (Story of Civilization Ser.: Vol. 4). (Illus.). 1983. 35.00 (*0-671-01200-2*) S&S Trade.

Age of Faith, Vol. IV. Will Durant. (Story of Civilization Ser.: Vol. 4). 1994. 17.98 (*1-56731-015-X*, MJF Bks) Fine Comms.

Age of Federalism. Stanley Elkins & Eric L. McKitrick. LC 92-33660. 944p. 1993. 39.95 (*0-19-506890-4*) OUP.

Age of Federalism: The Early American Republic, 1788-1800. Stanley Elkins & Eric McKitrick. 926p. 1995. reprint ed. pap. 19.95 (*0-19-509381-X*) OUP.

Age of Feudalism. Timothy L. Biel. LC 93-19290. (World History Ser.). (J). (gr. 6-9). 1994. 16.95 (*1-56006-232-0*) Lucent Bks.

***Age of Fighting Sail: The Story of the Naval War of 1812.** Cecil S. Forester. 288p. 1995. pap. 17.85 (*0-939218-06-2*) Chapman Billies.

Age of Flowers-Nature: Sense & Sentiment in Victorian America. Doris L. Swarthout. LC 75-21061. (Illus.). 160p. 1975. 9.95 (*0-85699-127-9*) Chatham Pr.

Age of German Liberation, 1795-1815. Friedrich Meinecke. Tr. by Peter Paret & Helmut Fischer. LC 74-79767. Orig. Title: Das Zeitalter der Deutschen Erhebung. 1977. 45.00 (*0-520-02792-2*); pap. 13.00 (*0-520-03454-6*) U CA Pr.

Age of Giant Corporations: A Microeconomic History of American Business, 1914-1992. 3rd ed. Robert Sobel. LC 92-33304. (Contributions in Economics & Economic History Ser.: No. 146). 328p. 1993. text ed. 55.00 (*0-313-28730-9*, GM8730, Greenwood Pr); pap. text ed. 18.95 (*0-275-94470-0*, B4470, Praeger Pubs) Greenwood.

Age of God Kings, (3000-1500 BC) (Time Frame Ser.). (Illus.). 176p. 1987. lib. bdg. 25.93 (*0-8094-6401-2*) Time-Life.

Age of Gold. Sotere Torregian. reprint ed. 7.00 (*0-686-20818-8*); reprint ed. pap. 3.50 (*0-686-20819-6*) Kulchur Foun.

Age of Gold, Age of Iron: Renaissance Spain & Symbols of Monarchy, Set. Barbara Von Barghahn. (Imperial Legacy of Charles V & Philip II Royal Castles, Palace-Monasteries, Princely Houses Ser.: 2 vols.). (Illus.). 1036p. 1985. lib. bdg. 377.50 (*0-8191-4739-7*) U Pr of Amer.

Age of Grace: Charis in Early Greek Poetry. Bonnie MacLachlan. LC 92-37031. (Illus.). 192p. (C). 1993. text ed. 29.95 (*0-691-06974-3*) Princeton U Pr.

***Age of Grandeur & a Woman Who Lived It: Artist Evelyn Metzger.** Brett Topping & Nancy Heller. LC 94-37120. (Illus.). 200p. 1995. 29.95 (*0-940979-29-2*) Natl Museum Women.

***Age of Grandeur & a Woman Who Lived It: Artist Evelyn Metzger.** Brett Topping et al. LC 94-37120. 1995. pap. write for info. (*0-940979-28-4*) Natl Museum Women.

Age of Great Dreams: America in the 1960s. David Farber. Ed. by Eric Foner. LC 93-32266. 1994. 25.00 (*0-8090-2401-2*); pap. 10.95 (*0-8090-1567-6*) Hill & Wang.

Age of Grief. Jane Smiley. LC 87-45120. 1987. 15.95 (*0-394-55848-0*) Knopf.

Age of Grief. Jane Smiley. 224p. 1992. pap. 10.00 (*0-449-90795-3*, Columbine) Fawcett.

Age of Grief. Jane Smiley. 192p. 1988. mass mkt. 4.99 (*0-8041-0368-2*) Ivy Books.

Age of Gunpowder Empires, 1450-1800. William H. McNeill. Ed. by Michael Adas. LC 89-84997. (Essays on Global & Comparative History Ser.). 49p. 1989. pap. 6.00 (*0-87229-043-3*) Am Hist Assn.

Age of "Hair" Evolution & Impact of Broadway's First Rock Musical. Barbara L. Horn. LC 91-15984. (Contributions in Drama & Theatre Studies: No. 42). 192p. 1991. text ed. 45.00 (*0-313-27564-5*, HAV, Greenwood Pr) Greenwood.

Age of Hate: Andrew Johnson & the Radicals. George F. Milton. (History - United States Ser.). 787p. 1992. reprint ed. lib. bdg. 109.00 (*0-7812-6205-4*) Rprt Serv.

Age of Hereos Sourcebook. Nicky Rea & TSR, Inc. Staff. (Illus.). 1994. 18.00 (*1-56076-814-2*) TSR Inc.

Age of Heroes: The Incredible Adventures of a Pan Am Pilot & His Greatest Triumph - Earhart. Henri Keyzer-Andre & Hy Steirman. (Illus.). 350p. 1993. 22.50 (*0-8038-9351-5*) Hastings.

Age of Hirohito: In Search of Modern Japan. Daikichi Irokawa. 1995. 25.00 (*0-02-915665-3*) Free Pr.

Age of Hogarth. Elizabeth Einberg & Judy Egerton. (Illus.). 256p. 1990. 90.00 (*0-295-96956-3*) U of Wash Pr.

***Age of Homo Sapiens Sapiens.** Edward E. Bruessaro. 300p. (Orig.). (C). 1995. pap. 42.95 (*0-9630815-9-4*) BIIP.

Age of Ideology. Ed. by Henry D. Aiken. LC 77-117748. (Essay Index Reprint Ser.). 1977. 21.95 (*0-8369-1821-5*) Ayer.

Age of Ideology. Ed. by Henry D. Aiken. 1989. mass mkt. 4.95 (*0-452-00792-5*) NAL-Dutton.

***Age of Imagery.** Mary A. White. (Illus.). 246p. (C). 1995. lib. bdg. 37.50 (*0-89341-759-9*); pap. text ed. 19.50 (*0-89341-760-2*) Hollowbrook.

Age of Imperialism. Harry Magdoff. LC 69-19788. 1969. 6.00 (*0-85345-082-X*); pap. 9.00 (*0-85345-101-X*) Monthly Rev.

Age of Improvement, 1783 to 1867. Asa Briggs. (History of England Ser.). (Illus.). (C). 1988. pap. text ed. 25.95 (*0-582-49100-2*, 73478) Longman.

Age of Individuality: America's Kinship with the Brooklyn Bridge. Karl Roebling. 190p. 1983. 10.95 (*0-942910-05-2*) Dynapress.

Age of Information. Stephen Saxby. 288p. 1991. 55.00 (*0-8147-7922-0*) NYU Pr.

Age of Information: An Interdisciplinary Survey of Cybernetics. T. C. Helvey. LC 78-125870. 224p. 1971. 34.95 (*0-87778-008-0*) Educ Tech Pubns.

***Age of Innocence.** David Hamilton. (Illus.). 220p. Date not set. 39.99 (*1-85410-304-0*, London Bridge) Genl Dist Srvs.

Age of Innocence. Edith Wharton. LC 93-38688. 1994. pap. 14.95 (*0-8161-5916-5*) Hall.

Age of Innocence. Edith Wharton. 1994. 21.95 (*0-8161-5915-7*) Hall.

***Age of Innocence.** Edith Wharton. Date not set. pap. 11.99 (*0-517-12418-1*) Random.

Age of Innocence. Edith Wharton. LC 68-27785. 1976. text ed. 40.00 (*0-684-14659-2*, Scribners); pap. 14.00 (*0-684-71925-8*, Scribners) S&S Trade.

Age of Innocence. Edith Wharton. 384p. 1982. pap. 4.95 (*0-684-17818-4*, Scribners) S&S Trade.

Age of Innocence. Edith Wharton. (Twentieth Century Classics Ser.). 378p. 1987. pap. 5.95 (*0-02-059890-4*, Collier S&S) S&S Trade.

Age of Innocence. Edith Wharton. 383p. 1992. pap. 9.00 (*0-02-026476-3*, Collier S&S) S&S Trade.

Age of Innocence. Edith Wharton. 384p. 1993. pap. 5.95 (*0-02-026478-X*, Collier S&S) S&S Trade.

Age of Innocence. Edith Wharton. 24.95 (*0-89190-508-1*, Am Repr) Amereon Ltd.

Age of Innocence. Edith Wharton. 366p. 1993. text ed. 20.00 (*0-684-19719-7*, Scribners) S&S Trade.

Age of Innocence. large type ed. Edith Wharton. 1993. 39.95 (*0-7066-1028-8*, Pub. by Remploy Pr CN) St Mut.

Age of Innocence: A Portrait of the Film Based on the Novel by Edith Wharton. Martin Scorsese & Jay Cocks. (Illus.). 1993. 49.50 (*1-55704-143-1*) Newmarket.

***Age of Innocence: Paintings & Drawings by Jeffrey Jones.** Jeffrey Jones. 1994. pap. 14.95 (*0-88733-185-8*) Underwood-Miller.

Age of Innocence see Novels

Age of Innovation: The World of Electronics, 1930-2000. Electronics Magazine Editors. LC 80-14816. (Illus.). 274p. 1980. text ed. 18.50 (*0-07-606688-6*) McGraw.

Age of Intelligent Machines. Ray Kurzweil. (Illus.). 584p. 1992. pap. 27.50x (*0-262-61079-5*) MIT Pr.

Age of Interdependence: Economic Policy in a Shrinking World. Michael Stewart. 208p. 1984. pap. 9.95 (*0-262-69103-5*) MIT Pr.

Age of Iron. J. M. Coetzee. 1992. 10.00 (*0-679-73292-6*) McKay.

Age of Iron & Other Interludes, Vol. 1. Arlene Zekowski. LC 73-77095. (Archives of Post-Modern Literature Ser.). 1973. pap. 22.95 (*0-913844-01-2*) Am Canadian.

Age of Jackson. Arthur M. Schlesinger, Jr. 578p. 1988. pap. 15.95 (*0-316-77343-3*) Little.

***Age of Johnson, Vol. 6.** annuals Ed. by Paul J. Korshin. LC 85-48058. 580p. 1992. 59.50 (*0-404-62756-0*) AMS Pr.

Age of Johnson, Vols. 1-6. Ed. by Paul J. Korshin. LC 85-48058. 59.50 (*0-404-62750-1*) AMS Pr.

Age of Johnson: Essays Presented to Chauncey Brewster Tinker. Ed. by F. W. Hilles. LC 75-41004. reprint ed. 27.50 (*0-404-14770-4*); reprint ed. 50.00 (*0-685-00365-5*) AMS Pr.

Age of Johnson, 1740-1789. John Butt. Ed. by Geoffrey Carnall. (Oxford History of English Literature Ser.: Vol. 10). 688p. 1990. 59.00 (*0-19-812236-5*) OUP.

Age of Krypton. Carol J. Pierman. LC 88-70389. (Carnegie Mellon Poetry Ser.). 1989. pap. 9.95 (*0-685-30813-8*) Carnegie-Mellon.

Age of Leif Eriksson. Richard Humble. LC 89-8867. (Exploration Through the Ages Ser.). (Illus.). 32p. (J). (gr. 5-8). 1989. lib. bdg. 13.23 (*0-531-10741-8*) Watts.

Age of Liberty: Sweden 1719-1772. Michael Roberts. 185p. 1986. 49.95 (*0-521-32092-5*) Cambridge U Pr.

Age of Louis the Fourteenth. Will Durant & Ariel Durant. (Story of Civilization Ser.: Vol. 8). (Illus.). 1983. 35.00 (*0-671-01215-0*) S&S Trade.

Age of Louis the Fourteenth. rev. ed. Laurence B. Packard. (Illus.). 64p. (C). 1991. pap. text ed. 2.25 (*1-877891-04-5*) Paperbook Pr Inc.

An Asterisk (*) at the beginning of an entry indicates that the title is appearing in BIP for the first time.

An Asterisk (*) at the beginning of an entry indicates that the title is appearing in BIP for the first time.

Age of Wonders: Exploring the World of Science Fiction. David Hartwell. LC 84-15392. 205p. 1984. 25.00 (*0-89366-163-5*); pap. 3.95 (*0-89366-164-3*) Ultramarine Pub.

Age of Wordsworth. Charles H. Herford. LC 79-164606. (Select Bibliographies Reprint Ser.). 1977. reprint ed. 24.95 (*0-8369-5890-X*) Ayer.

Age One - Part One: For Parents or Teachers of Children One Year of Age or Older. Solon W. McDonald. 1993. pap. 7.95 (*0-533-10361-4*) Vantage.

Age Pages. rev. ed. 100p. 1985. pap. 3.50 (*0-16-002786-1*, S/N 017-062-00137-5) USGPO.

***Age Plus Wisdom: The ARt of Thriving in a Retirement Community.** Libby Rollin. 276p. 1995. 23.00 (*1-885420-07-2*) Peradam Pr.

Age Projection Test: Short-Term Imagery Treatment of Hysterias Phobias & Other Themes. Akhter Ahsen. LC 88-62767. 71p. 1988. pap. text ed. write for info. (*0-913412-17-1*) Brandon Hse.

Age, Race & Ethnicity: A Comparative Approach. Ken Blakemore & Margaret Boneham. (Rethinking Aging Ser.). 160p. 1993. 79.00 (*0-335-19234-3*, Open Univ Pr); pap. 29.50 (*0-335-19086-3*, Open Univ Pr) Taylor & Francis.

Age-Related Cataract. Richard W. Young. (Illus.). 304p. 1990. 55.00 (*0-19-506383-X*) OUP.

Age-Related Dopamine-Dependent Disorders. Ed. by M. Segawa & Y. Nomura. (Monographs in Neural Sciences: Vol. 14). (Illus.). x, 256p. 1994. 192.00 (*3-8055-5960-7*) S Karger.

Age-Related Factors in Carcinogenesis: Proceedings of a Symposium Organized by the IARC & the N. N. Petrov Research Institute of Oncology, Held in Leningrad, 7-9 December 1983. International Agency for Research on Cancer Staff. Ed. by A. Likhachev et al. LC 86-192218. (IARC Scientific Publications: No. 58). 300p. reprint ed. pap. 85.50 (*0-7837-4005-0*, 2043835) Bks Demand.

Age-Related Factors in Radionuclide Metabolism & Dosimetry. Ed. by G. B. Gerber et al. (Developments in Nuclear Medicine Ser.). (C). 1987. lib. bdg. 169.50 (*0-89838-953-4*) Kluwer Ac.

Age-Related Macular Degeneration: Principles & Practice. Ed. by Robert G. Hampton & Philip T. Nelsen. 320p. 1992. 88.50 (*0-88167-916-X*) Raven.

Age Relations in High-Grade Metamorphic Terrains. Ed. by H. R. Wynne-Edwards. LC 75-505974. (Geological Association of Canada. Special Paper Ser.: No. 5). 235p. reprint ed. pap. 67.00 (*0-8357-5252-6*, 2027840) Bks Demand.

Age Relationships of the Golconda Thrust Fault, Sonoma Range, North-Central Nevada. Norman J. Silberling. LC 74-31780. (Geological Society of America, Special Paper Ser.: No. 163). 48p. reprint ed. pap. 25.00 (*0-8357-5253-4*, 2025034) Bks Demand.

Age Search: How to Search Vital Records for Your Age. 1991. lib. bdg. 79.00 (*0-8490-4485-5*) Gordon Pr.

Age Structuring in Comparative Perspective. Ed. by D. Kertzer & K. W. Schaie. 296p. 1989. 59.95 (*0-8058-0202-9*) L Erlbaum Assocs.

Age, Time & Fertility: Applications of Exploratory Data Analysis. Mary B. Breckenridge. (Studies in Population). 1983. text ed. 72.00 (*0-12-128750-5*) Acad Pr.

Age Wave: Choices & Challenges for Our New Future. Ken Dychtwald. 1990. pap. 12.95 (*0-553-34806-X*) Bantam.

Age, Work & Automation. Ed. by P. M. Paillat & M. E. Bunch. (Interdisciplinary Topics in Gerontology Ser.: Vol. 6). 1970. 24.00 (*3-8055-0507-8*) S Karger.

Age, Work, & Social Security. Ed. by A. B. Atkinson & Martin Rein. LC 92-18004. 1993. text ed. 79.95 (*0-312-08548-6*) St Martin.

Agean Fun. Kosta Kontoyiannaki. (Illus.). 16p. (J). (gr. k-3). 1992. pap. 12.95 (*1-895583-23-3*) MAYA Pubs.

Aged & Society. Ed. by Milton Derbers & Leon Stein. LC 79-8665. (Growing Old Ser.). (Illus.). 1980. reprint ed. lib. bdg. 24.95 (*0-405-12783-9*) Ayer.

Aged & the Depression. Incl. Care of the Aged. I. M. Rubino. LC 71-169363. 1972. (*0-318-50784-6*); More Security for Old Age. Margaret G. Schneider. LC 71-169363. 1972. (*0-318-50785-4*); LC 71-169363. (Family in America Ser.). 368p. 1980. 41.95 (*0-405-03881-X*) Ayer.

Aged & the Elderly: Social & Medical Subject Analysis with Reference Bibliography. Rosetta R. Hardine. LC 85-48097. 150p. 1987. 39.50 (*0-88164-466-8*); pap. 34.50 (*0-88164-467-6*) ABBE Pubs Assn.

Aged & the Mentally Disabled: Housing Persons with Mental Disabilities & the Elderly. (Illus.). 165p. (Orig.). (C). 1993. pap. text ed. 30.00x (*1-56806-181-1*) Diane Pub.

Aged Client & the Law. John Regan. 1990. text ed. 35.00 (*0-231-06978-2*) Col U Pr.

Aged in India. R. N. Pati & B. Jena. 1989. 38.50 (*81-7024-264-9*, Pub. by Ashish II) S Asia.

Aged in Rural America. John A. Krout. LC 85-17740. (Contributions to the Study of Aging Ser.: No. 5). (Illus.). 198p. 1986. text ed. 45.00 (*0-313-24511-8*, KAG/, Greenwood Pr) Greenwood.

Aged in Salt Water: A Journey Through the Pacific Islands. Richard K. Williams. Ed. by Lewis L. Baldwin & Fred Harrison. 300p. 1991. write for info. (*0-9622551-3-0*); pap. write for info. (*0-9622551-2-2*) Sea Hse Pubs.

Aged in the Community: Managing Senility & Deviance. Dwight Frankfather. LC 77-8327. (Praeger Special Studies). 236p. 1977. text ed. 55.00 (*0-275-90264-1*, C0264, Praeger Pubs) Greenwood.

Aged Patient: A Sourcebook for the Allied Health Professional. Nora S. Ernst & Hilda R. Glazer-Waldman. LC 82-10917. 357p. reprint ed. pap. 101.80 (*0-8357-5254-2*, 2030841) Bks Demand.

Aged Person & the Nursing Process. 3rd ed. Ann G. Yurick et al. 809p. (C). 1989. boxed 46.95 (*0-8385-0084-6*, A0084-2) Appleton & Lange.

Aged to Perfection. Ed. by Mac Anderson. (Illus.). 78p. (Orig.). 1989. pap. 7.95 (*0-931089-27-1*) Great Quotations.

Agee. Peter Ohlin. 1965. 19.95 (*0-8392-1146-5*); pap. 7.95 (*0-8392-5011-8*) Astor-Honor.

Agee: A Record of the Agee Family. P. M. Agee. (Illus.). 330p. 1991. reprint ed. lib. bdg. 62.50 (*0-8328-1863-1*); reprint ed. pap. 52.50 (*0-8328-1864-X*) Higginson Bk Co.

Agee & Actuality: Artistic Vision in His Work. Victor A. Kramer. LC 90-70214. 167p. 1990. 17.50 (*0-87875-395-8*) Whitston Pub.

Ageing: Challenges & Opportunities. A. M. Ghadirian. 144p. 1991. pap. 10.95 (*0-85398-329-1*) G Ronald Pub.

Ageing: Debates over Demographic Transition & Social Policy. Kasturi Sen. LC 94-41477. 192p. (C). 1995. text ed. 49.95 (*1-85649-259-1*, Pub. by Zed Books UK); pap. 17.50 (*1-85649-260-5*, Pub. by Zed Books UK) Humanities.

Ageing: The Facts. 2nd ed. Nicholas Coni et al. (Facts Ser.). (Illus.). 216p. 1992. 18.95 (*0-19-262150-5*) OUP.

***Ageing, a Biomedical Perspective.** Denis Bellamy. LC 95-10483. 1995. pap. write for info. (*0-471-92067-3*) Wiley.

Ageing & Life Course Transitions: An Interdisciplinary Perspective. Ed. by Tamara K. Hareven & Kathleen J. Adams. 301p. reprint ed. pap. 85.80 (*0-7837-1207-3*, 2041739) Bks Demand.

Ageing & Stabilisation of Polymers. Ed. by A. S. Duz'minskii & B. N. Leyland. (Illus.). xiv, 280p. 1971. 55.00 (*0-444-20076-2*, Pub. by Elsevier Applied Sci UK) Elsevier.

Ageing & the Care of Older People in Europe. Richard Hugman. LC 94-7205. 1994. text ed. 39.95 (*0-312-12193-8*, Pub. by Macm UK) St Martin.

Ageing & Urbanization. 1991. write for info. (*92-1-151233-6*, 91.XIII.12) UN.

Ageing, Healthy, & in Control: An Alternative Approach to Maintaining the Health of Older People. Steve Scrutton. LC 92-21681. 1992. write for info. (*1-56593-032-0*) Singular Publishing.

Ageing in Cold-Blooded Vertebrates. Ed. by B. K. Patnaik. (Journal: Gerontology Ser.: Vol. 40, Nos. 2-4, 1994). (Illus.). 166p. 1994. pap. 121.00 (*3-8055-5995-X*) S Karger.

Ageing in East & Southeast Asia. Ed. by David R. Phillips. (Research Studies in Gerontology). 224p. 1992. 59.95 (*0-340-54367-1*, A9633, Pub. by E Arnold UK) Routledge Chapman & Hall.

Ageing in Industry: An Inquiry, Based on Figures Derived from Census Reports. Clark F. Le Gros & Agnes C. Dunne. LC 75-136890. (Illus.). 146p. 1971. reprint ed. text ed. 49.75 (*0-8371-5332-8*, CLAI, Greenwood Pr) Greenwood.

Ageing, Independence & the Life Course. Ed. by Sara Arber & Maria Evandrou. 256p. 1993. pap. 37.50 (*1-85302-180-6*, Pub. by J Kingsley Pubs UK) Taylor & Francis.

Ageing Population: A Reader & Sourcebook. Ed. by Vida Carver & Penny Liddiard. LC 78-26607. 434p. 1979. 49.50 (*0-8419-0474-X*) Holmes & Meier.

Ageing Populations: The Economic Future of Social Welfare. Paul Johnson & Jane Falkingham. (Illus.). 224p. (C). 1992. 55.00 (*0-8039-8248-8*); pap. 19.95 (*0-8039-8249-6*) Sage.

Ageing Spine. Ed. by D. W. Hukins & M. A. Nelson. 176p. 1988. text ed. 55.00 (*0-7190-2574-5*, Pub. by Manchester Univ Pr UK) St Martin.

Ageing Surgical Patient: Anaesthetic, Operative & Medical Management. D. L. Crosby et al. 457p. 1992. text ed. 185.00 (*0-471-92847-X*, Wiley-Liss) Wiley.

***Ageism.** Bill Bytheway. LC 94-27686. 1994. write for info. (*0-335-19176-2*); pap. write for info. (*0-335-19175-4*, Open Univ Pr) Taylor & Francis.

Ageism: Negative & Positive. Erdman Palmore. LC 90-9775. (Adulthood & Aging Ser.: Vol. 25). 232p. 1990. 29.95 (*0-8261-7000-5*) Springer Pub.

Ageless: Living Younger Longer. Ben H. Douglas. LC 89-70325. 204p. 1990. 14.95 (*0-937552-33-X*) Quail Ridge.

Ageless Adobe: History & Preservation in Southwestern Architecture. Jerome Iowa. LC 84-16337. (Illus.). 158p. (Orig.). 1985. pap. 16.95 (*0-86534-034-X*) Sunstone Pr.

Ageless Beauty the Natural Way. Anita Guyton. 1993. pap. 14.00 (*0-7225-2774-8*) Thorsons SF.

***Ageless Body.** Chris Griscom. 174p. 1992. pap. 15.00 (*0-9623696-1-6*) Light Inst Fndtn.

Ageless Body, Timeless Mind. Deepak Chopra. 1993. 12.50 (*0-517-59818-3*) Crown Pub Group.

Ageless Body, Timeless Mind: The Quantum Alternative to Growing Old. Deepak Chopra. LC 93-16766. 1993. 23.00 (*0-517-59257-6*, Harmony) Crown Pub Group.

Ageless Body, Timeless Mind: The Quantum Alternative to Growing Old. Deepak Chopra. 1994. pap. 13.00 (*0-517-88212-4*, Crown) Crown Pub Group.

Ageless Chinese: A History. 3rd ed. Iun J. Li. LC 73-159451. 629p. (C). 1978. pap. write for info. (*0-02-370550-7*, Scribners) S&S Trade.

Ageless Counsel for Modern Life: Profound Commentaries on the I Ching by an Achieved Taoist Master. Hua-Ching Ni. LC 91-53212. 256p. (Orig.). 1992. pap. 15.95 (*0-937064-50-5*) SevenStar Comm.

Ageless Exercise: A Gentle Approach for the Inactive or Physically Limited. Joan Laird. LC 93-60903. (Illus.). 64p. 1994. spiral bd. 10.95 (*0-9638390-0-4*) Angelwood Pr.

Ageless Inspirations: A Collection of Spiritual Favorites. Comp. by Ellie Busha. LC 90-19569. 288p. (Orig.). 1990. pap. 11.95 (*0-926284-04-5*) Evergreen MI.

Ageless Mysteries: Karma, Reincarnation, Spiritualism, Astrology. F. Hart. 1971. 59.95 (*0-87968-586-7*) Gordon Pr.

Ageless Prose: A Study of the Media-Projected Images of Aging. Bridget C. Loetterle. LC 93-34528. 328p. 1993. 72.00 (*0-8153-1534-1*) Garland.

Ageless Purity. Wayde K. Brown. (Illus.). 26p. (Orig.). 1991. pap. text ed. 6.95 (*1-56315-051-4*) Sterling Hse.

Ageless Remedies from Mothers Kitchen. Hanna Kroeger. 94p. 1981. pap. 3.50 (*1-883713-04-8*) Kroeger Herb. AGELESS REMEDIES FROM MOTHERS KITCHEN is part of sixteen amazing books on the topic of natural health & healing published by Hanna Kroeger Publications. For over fifty years Hanna Kroeger has been constantly exploring & discovering healing techniques from around the world & has helped thousands of people through her consultations. Hannah shares her findings through her books drawing from an extensive, eclectic background to help people help themselves. Her books range from simple home remedies to homeopathy, herbs, massage & special diets. Hanna's books include: AGELESS REMEDIES FROM MOTHERS KITCHEN (1-883713-04-8), ALLERGY BAKING RECIPES (1-883713-02-1), ALZHEIMER'S, SCIENCE & GOD (1- 883713-10-2), ARTERIOSCLEROSIS & HERBAL CHELATION (1-883713-03-X), CANCER: TRADITIONAL & NEW CONCEPTS (1-883713-06-4), COOKBOOK FOR ELECTRO-CHEMICAL ENERGIES (1-883713-13-7), GOD HELPS THOSE THAT HELP THEMSELVES (1-883713-11-0), GOOD HEALTH THROUGH SPECIAL DIETS (1-883713-14-5), HOW TO COUNTERACT ENVIRONMENTAL POISONS (1-883713- 15-3), INSTANT HERBAL LOCATOR (1-883713-16-1), INSTANT VITAMIN- MINERAL LOCATOR (1883713-01-3), NEW DIMENSIONS IN HEALING YOURSELF (1-883713-09-9), OLD TIME REMEDIES FOR MODERN AILMENTS (1-883713-05-6), PARASITES: THE ENEMY WITHIN (1-883713-07-2), THE PENDULUM, THE BIBLE & YOUR SURVIVAL (1-883713-08-0), SPICES TO THE RESCUE (1-883713-12-9). To order any of these books call 800-206-6722. Also distributed through Summit Beacon Int. 800-823-8330 & Royal Publications 800-279-2048. Distributors please contact Hanna Kroeger Publications 800-225-8787.** ***Publisher Provided Annotation.

Ageless Self: Sources of Meaning in Late Life. Sharon R. Kaufman. LC 86-40053. (Life Course Studies). 220p. 1994. text ed. 24.50 (*0-299-10860-0*) U of Wis Pr.

***Ageless Self: Sources of Meaning in Late Life.** Sharon R. Kaufman. LC 86-40053. (Life Course Studies). 220p. 1995. pap. text ed. 11.95 (*0-299-10864-3*) U of Wis Pr.

Ageless Spirit. Phillip L. Berman & Connie Goldman. 272p. 1992. pap. 9.00 (*0-345-36956-4*, Ballantine Trade) Ballantine.

Ageless Wisdom. Torkom Saraydarian. LC 89-51507. 336p. 1989. pap. 16.00 (*0-929874-13-7*) TSG Pub Found.

***Ageless Wisdom of Life.** Codd. 1995. 12.95 (*81-7059-112-0*, Quest) Theos Pub Hse.

***Ageless Wisdom of Life.** Codd. 1995. 17.95 (*81-7059-219-4*, Quest) Theos Pub Hse.

Agence Thompson & Company. Jules Verne. (Illus.). 440p. (FRE.). 1982. pap. 18.95 (*0-7859-1221-5*, 2010054695) Fr & Eur.

Agences Regionales Du Credit Lyonnais: Annees 1870-1914. Jacques Dagneau. Ed. by Stuart Bruchey. LC 77-81826. (Dissertations in European Economic History Ser.). (Illus.). (FRE.). 1978. lib. bdg. 65.95 (*0-405-10778-1*) Ayer.

Agencies for Project Assistance: Sources of Support for Small Church & or Lay Sponsored Projects in Africa, Asia, Latin America & the Pacific. 2nd ed. Pierre Aubin & George Cotter. (Illus.). 330p. 1986. pap. 50.00 (*0-913671-03-7*) Mission Proj Serv.

Agencies for Project Assistance: Sources of Support for Small Church & or Lay Sponsored Projects in Africa, Asia, Latin America & the Pacific. 3rd ed. Pierre Aubin & George Cotter. 340p. 1988. write for info. (*0-913671-04-5*) Mission Proj Serv.

***Agency.** John McNamara. 211p. 1995. 22.00 (*0-9646347-0-8*) Possiblts Pr.

Agency. Sell. 1975. text ed. 19.95 (*0-88277-416-6*) Foundation Pr.

Agency: The Rise & Decline of the CIA. John Ranelagh. 1987. pap. 17.00 (*0-671-63994-3*, Touchstone Bks) S&S Trade.

***Agency: The William Morris Agency & the Hidden History of Show Business.** Frank Rose. 1995. 30.00 (*0-88730-749-3*) Harper Busn.

Agency & Alienation: A Theory of Human Wholeness. Jerome M. Segal. 224p. 1991. 46.50 (*0-8476-7628-5*, R 7628) Rowman.

***Agency & Distribution Agreements: An International Survey.** Ed. by Jausas Agustin. LC 94-29307. (International Bar Association Ser.). 1995. 115.00 (*1-85966-100-9*) G & T Inc.

Agency & Ethics. Anthony Schools Corporation Staff. (Continuing Education in Real Estate Ser.). 48p. (Orig.). 1993. pap. text ed. 12.00 (*0-941833-44-5*) Anthony Schools.

Agency & Integrality: Philosophical Themes in the Ancient Discussions of Determinism & Responsibility. Michael J. White. 1985. lib. bdg. 97.50 (*90-277-1968-3*) Kluwer Ac.

Agency & Organization: Towards an Organizational Theory of Society. Goran Ahrne. 160p. 1991. 45.00 (*0-8039-8292-5*); pap. 19.95 (*0-8039-8293-3*) Sage.

Agency & Outside Work. rev. ed. W. Herriott & J. E. Reed. 26p. 1987. pap. 60.00 (*0-948691-08-5*, Pub. by Witherby & Co UK) St Mut.

Agency & Partnership. Conrad et al. 1987. text ed. 30.95 (*0-88277-598-7*) Foundation Pr.

Agency & Partnership. Myron Hill, Jr. et al. (Smith's Review Ser.). 222p. 1989. pap. text ed. 11.95 (*1-56542-105-1*) E Law Outlines.

Agency & Partnership: Cases, Materials & Problems. 3rd ed. J. Dennis Hynes. (Contemporary Legal Education Ser.). 720p. 1989. 36.00 (*0-87473-443-6*) Michie Butterworth.

Agency & Partnership - Adaptable to Courses Utilizing Hynes' Casebook on Agency & Partnership. Casenotes Publishing Co., Inc. Staff. Ed. by Goldenberg, Tenen & Switzer Staff. (Legal Briefs Ser.). 1991. pap. write for info. (*0-87457-168-5*, 1351) Casenotes Pub.

Agency & Partnership, an Introduction To. Melvin A. Eisenberg. 131p. 1987. pap. text ed. 10.95 (*0-88277-577-4*) Foundation Pr.

***Agency & Partnership & Other Forms of Business Associations.** William A. Gregory. Ed. by Thomas R. Hurst. (American Casebook Ser.). 130p. 1994. pap. text ed. write for info. (*0-314-05277-1*) West Pub.

Agency & Partnership Law: Cases & Materials. Gary Rosin & Michael Closen. LC 92-71956. 1992. 45.00 (*0-89089-515-5*); write for info. (*0-318-69288-0*) Carolina Acad Pr.

Agency & Partnership Law: Cases & Materials. suppl. ed. Gary Rosin & Michael Closen. 1993. write for info. (*0-318-69289-9*) Carolina Acad Pr.

Agency & Structure: Dialectics in the Administration of Education. Peter Watkins. 124p. (C). 1985. 48.00 (*0-7300-0186-5*, Pub. by Deakin Univ AT) St Mut.

Agency & Structure: Reorienting Social Theory, Vol. 4. Ed. by Piotr Sztompka. LC 93-19945. (International Studies in Global Change). 1993. write for info. (*2-88124-592-7*) Gordon & Breach.

Agency & Urgency: The Origin of Moral Obligation. Thomas E. Wren. 169p. 1974. 21.95 (*0-685-43095-2*) Transaction Pubs.

Agency-Based Social Work: Neglected Aspects of Clinical Practice. Harold Weissman et al. LC 83-9314. (C). 1983. pap. text ed. 22.95 (*0-87722-330-0*) Temple U Pr.

Agency Company Relationships in Manpower Operations for the Hard to Employ. Louis A. Ferman & Roger Manela. 1973. pap. 6.50 (*0-87736-329-3*) U of Mich Inst Labor.

***Agency Compensation: A Guidebook.** Robert Lundin. 1995. pap. 37.50 (*1-56318-018-9*) Assn Natl Advertisers.

***Agency for Health Care Policy Research: An Annotated Bibliography.** 1995. lib. bdg. 251.95 (*0-8490-6781-2*) Gordon Pr.

Agency, Free Will, & Moral Responsibility. Mark P. Strasser. LC 91-41673. 212p. (C). 1993. text ed. 35.00 (*0-89341-704-1*) Hollowbrook.

Agency in Action: The Practical Rational Agency Machine. S. C. Coval & P. G. Campbell. (Studies in Cognitive Systems). 224p. 1992. lib. bdg. 94.00 (*0-7923-1661-4*) Kluwer Ac.

Agency Merger & Bureaucratic Redesign. Karen M. Hult. LC 86-19349. (Series in Policy & Institutional Studies). 232p. 1987. 49.95 (*0-8229-3549-X*) U of Pittsburgh Pr.

Agency Nurse. large type ed. Lilian Woodward. (Linford Romance Library). 1991. pap. 13.95 (*0-7089-7058-3*) Ulverscroft.

Agency of Fear: Opiates & Political Power in America. rev. ed. Edward J. Epstein. 384p. 1990. pap. 17.95 (*0-86091-529-8*, A4973, Pub. by Verso UK) Routledge Chapman & Hall.

Agency Operations & Sales Management, 2 vols. 3rd ed. Carol A. Hammes et al. LC 92-71750. (C). 1992. text ed. 26.00 (*0-89462-069-X*) IIA.

Agency-Partnership. Roscoe T. Steffen. (Nutshell Ser.). 364p. 1993. reprint ed. pap. text ed. 15.00 (*0-314-33236-7*) West Pub.

Agency, Partnership & Employment: A Transactional Approach. Slain et al. 1980. write for info. (*0-8205-0011-9*, 013) Bender.

Agency-Partnership Cases & Materials. 4th ed. Roscoe T. Steffen & Thomas R. Kerr. LC 79-28206. (American Casebook Ser.). 859p. 1993. reprint ed. text ed. 44.50 (*0-8299-2077-3*) West Pub.

***Agency Performance Results Study, 1994-95.** Academy of Producer Insurance Studies, Inc. Staff. 244p. (Orig.). 1994. pap. text ed. 29.50 (*1-878204-51-3*) APIS Inc.

An Asterisk (*) at the beginning of an entry indicates that the title is appearing in BIP for the first time.

An Asterisk (*) at the beginning of an entry indicates that the title is appearing in BIP for the first time.

139

A

***Agglomeration 77: Proceedings of the 2nd International Symposium on Agglomeration, Atlanta, GA, March 6-10, 1977, Vol. 2.** fac. ed. Intl. Symposium on Agglomeration Staff. Ed. by K. V. Sastry. (Illus.). 594p. 1977. reprint ed. pap. 169.30 (*0-7837-7839-2*, 2047598) Bks Demand.

Agglutination Analyses: Characteristics of Antibody, Methodology, Limitations, & Clinical Validation, Vol. 6. National Committee for Clinical Laboratory Standards Staff. (Tentative Guideline Ser.: Vol. 6). 1986. 40.00 (*1-56238-066-4*, DI3-T) Natl Comm Clin Lab Stds.

Aggravating the Conscience: Jewish-American Literary Mothers in the Promised Land. Rose Y. Kamel. (American University Studies: English Language & Literature: Ser. IV, Vol. 64). 203p. (C). 1988. 30.50 (*0-8204-0554-X*) P Lang Pubs.

Aggregate Amount of Each Description of Persons, 1810. U. S. Census Office Staff. LC 75-22847. (America in Two Centuries Ser.). 1976. reprint ed. 18.95 (*0-405-07751-3*) Ayer.

Aggregate & Industry-Level Productivity Analysis. Ali Dogramaci & Nabil R. Adam. (Productivity Analysis Studies: Vol. 2). 204p. 1981. lib. bdg. 49.50 (*0-89838-037-5*) Kluwer Ac.

Aggregate & Pavement-Related Research. LC 92-33728. (Transportation Research Record Ser.: No. 1362). 1992. 24.00 (*0-309-05402-8*) Transport Res Bd.

Aggregate Inventory Management Training Aid. Donald W. Fogarty & John M. Burnham. LC 83-73024. 18p. 1984. 25.00 (*0-935406-38-7*) Am Prod & Inventory.

Aggregate Personal Income of the Black Population in the United States: 1947-1980. David H. Swinton & Julian Ellison. 75p. (Orig.). 1974. pap. text ed. 18.95 (*0-87855-600-1*) Transaction Pubs.

Aggregate Production Planning: Text & Cases. Robert D. Landel & James R. Freeland. (C). 1984. teacher ed write for info. (*0-8359-0032-0*, Reston) P-H.

Aggregates: Sand, Gravel & Crushed Rock Aggregates for Construction Purposes. Ed. by M. R. Smith & L. Collis. (Geological Society Engineering Geology Special Publications: No. 9). (Illus.). 360p. 1993. 65.00 (*0-903317-89-3*, Pub. by Geol Soc Pub Hse UK) AAPG.

***Aggregates: Waste & Recycled Materials; New Rapid Evaluation Technology (TRR 1437)** Ed. by Naomi Kassabian. (Transportation Research Record Ser.). (Illus.). 72p. 1994. pap. text ed. 21.00 (*0-309-05515-6*) Transport Res Bd.

***Aggregates (Construction) Market.** 400p. (Orig.). 1994. pap. 2,500.00 (*1-57205-986-9*) Rector Pr.

Aggregation: Aggregate Production Functions & Related Topics. Franklin M. Fisher. Ed. by John Monz. LC 92-25515. 400p. 1993. 47.50x (*0-262-06152-X*) MIT Pr.

Aggregation & Disaggregation in the Social Sciences. Michael T. Hannan. (Issues in Organization & Management Ser.). 160p. 1991. text ed. 39.95 (*0-669-20490-0*) Free Pr.

Aggregation & Fractal Aggregates. R. Jullien & R. Botet. 132p. 1987. text ed. 32.00 (*9971-5-0248-8*) World Scientific Pub.

Aggregation & Representation of Preferences: Introduction to Mathematical Theory of Democracy. A. S. Tanguine. (Illus.). 352p. 1991. 84.00 (*0-387-53845-3*) Spr-Verlag.

Aggregation, Consumption & Trade: Essays in Honor of H.S. Houthakker. Ed. by Louis Phlips & Lester D. Taylor. LC 92-33114. (Advanced Studies in Theoretical & Applied Econometrics: Vol. 27). (C). 1992. lib. bdg. 90.50 (*0-7923-2001-8*) Kluwer Ac.

Aggregation Phenomena of Point Defects in Silicon: Proceedings of the Satellite Symposium to ESSDERC '82, Munich. Satellite Symposium to ESSDERC '82 (1982: Munich, Germany) Staff. Ed. by Erhard Sirtl et al. LC 83-80790. (Electrochemical Society Proceedings Ser.: No. 83-4). (Illus.). 222p. reprint ed. pap. 63.30 (*0-8357-5257-7*, 2027973) Bks Demand.

Aggregation Processes in Solution. Ed. by E. Wyn-Jones & J. Gormally. (Studies in Physical & Theoretical Chemistry: Vol. 26). 632p. 1983. 187.25 (*0-444-42187-4*) Elsevier.

Aggression: Its Causes, Consequences, & Control. Leonard Berkowitz. 1992. pap. 33.50 (*0-07-004883-5*) McGraw.

Aggression: Its Causes, Consequences, & Control. Leonard Berkowitz. LC 92-31862. 496p. 1993. 49.95 (*1-56639-033-8*) Temple U Pr.

Aggression: Its Causes, Consequences & Control. Leonard Berkowitz. LC 92-33589. (Series in Social Psychology). (C). 1992. pap. text ed. write for info. (*0-07-004874-6*) McGraw.

Aggression: Myths & Models. Knud S. Larsen. LC 76-5882. 416p. 1976. 37.95 (*0-911012-71-0*) Nelson-Hall.

Aggression: Psychological, Behavioral & Medical Subject Analysis with Research Index & Bibliography. Willard T. Brainard. LC 83-71647. 141p. 1984. 39.50 (*0-88164-028-X*); pap. 34.50 (*0-88164-029-8*) ABBE Pubs Assn.

Aggression: The Myth of the Beast Within. John Klama. Ed. by John Durant et al. LC 87-2765. 169p. 1988. text ed. 36.95 (*0-470-20790-6*) Wiley.

Aggression: Theoretical & Methodologic Issues. Ed. by Russell Geen & Edward Donnerstein. LC 82-24348. 1983. 45.00 (*0-685-06540-5*); Vol. 2: Issues in Research. text ed. 60.00 (*0-12-278802-8*) Acad Pr.

Aggression: Theoretical & Methodologic Issues, Vol. 1: Theoretical Issues. Ed. by Russell Geen & Edward Donnerstein. LC 82-24348. 1983. text ed. 60.00 (*0-12-278801-X*) Acad Pr.

Aggression & Behavior Change: Biological & Social Processes. Ed. by Seymour Feshbach & Adam Fraczek. LC 79-17934. (Praeger Special Studies). (Illus.). 316p. 1979. text ed. 65.00 (*0-275-90352-4*, C0352, Praeger Pubs) Greenwood.

Aggression & Community: Paradoxes of Andalusian Culture. David D. Gilmore. LC 86-24576. 236p. reprint ed. pap. 67.30 (*0-7837-4543-5*, 2080321) Bks Demand.

Aggression & Conflict. David Levinson. (Human Experience Ser.). 240p. 1994. lib. bdg. 49.50 (*0-87436-728-X*) ABC-CLIO.

Aggression & Crimes of Violence. 2nd ed. Jeffrey H. Goldstein. (Illus.). 1986. pap. 12.95 (*0-19-503944-0*) OUP.

Aggression & Dangerousness. Ed. by David P. Farrington & John Gunn. LC 84-13112. (Wiley Series on Current Research in Forensic Psychiatry & Psychology). 281p. reprint ed. pap. 80.10 (*0-7837-4395-5*, 2044135) Bks Demand.

Aggression & Peacefulness in Humans & Other Primates. James Silverberg & J. Patrick Gray. (Illus.). 496p. 1992. 55.00 (*0-19-507119-0*, 12373) OUP.

Aggression & Repression in the Individual & Society. Hans E. Lauer. Tr. by K. Castelliz & Saunders Davies. 111p. 1981. pap. 9.95 (*0-85440-359-0*, Steinerbks) Anthroposophic.

Aggression & Violence. Waln K. Brown et al. 20p. 1989. 2.95 (*1-56456-008-2*, 204) W Gladden Found.

Aggression & Violence: Social Interactionist Perspectives. Ed. by Richard B. Felson & James T. Tedeschi. (Illus.). 278p. 1993. text ed. 40.00 (*1-55798-190-6*) Am Psychol.

Aggression & Violence Throughout the Life Span. Ray D. Peters & Robert J. McMahon. (Illus.). 342p. (C). 1992. 52.00 (*0-8039-4550-7*); pap. 24.00 (*0-8039-4551-5*) Sage.

Aggression & World Order. Julius Stone. LC 76-4567. 226p. 1976. reprint ed. text ed. 35.00 (*0-8371-8806-7*, STWO, Greenwood Pr) Greenwood.

Aggression, Family Violence & Chemical Dependency. Ed. by Ronald T. Potter-Efron & Patricia Potter-Efron. LC 89-24737. (Journal of Chemical Dependency Treatment: Vol. 3, No. 1). (Illus.). 226p. 1989. text ed. 39.95 (*0-86656-964-2*); pap. text ed. 17.95 (*0-86656-977-4*) Haworth Pr.

Aggression in Children & Youth. Ed. by Robert M. Kaplan et al. 1983. lib. bdg. 136.50 (*90-247-2903-3*) Kluwer Ac.

Aggression in Our Children: Coping with It Constructively. Henri Parens. LC 87-19547. 224p. 1993. pap. 25.00x (*1-56821-076-0*) Aronson.

Aggression in Personality Disorders & Perversions. Otto F. Kernberg. 384p. (C). 1993. text ed. 37.50 (*0-300-05003-8*) Yale U Pr.

Aggression Replacement Training: A Comprehensive Intervention for Aggressive Youth. Arnold P. Goldstein et al. LC 86-61551. 376p. (Orig.). 1987. pap. 18.95 (*0-87822-283-9*, 2839) Res Press.

Aggression, Subversion, Seduction: Young German Painters. Steven S. High & Donald B. Kuspit. LC 86-71564. (Orig.). 1986. 7.50 (*0-939799-00-6*) Portland Schl Baxter.

Aggression Systems: Human Aspects; Evolution; Brain Mechanisms; & Dynamics. David Adams. (Illus.). 414p. 1989. lib. bdg. 49.50 (*0-9619209-4-7*) D Adams.

Aggressive Adolescent: A Clinical Perspective. Ed. by Charles R. Keith. LC 83-48750. 544p. (C). 1984. text ed. 45.00 (*0-02-916720-5*) Free Pr.

Aggressive Behavior. Goldstein. (Practitioner Guidebook Ser.). (C). 1987. pap. 25.95 (*0-205-14336-9*, H4336, Longwood Div) Allyn.

Aggressive Behavior: Current Perspectives. Ed. by L. R. Huesmann. (Social-Clinical Psychology Ser.). (Illus.). 270p. (C). 1994. 45.00 (*0-306-44553-0*, Plenum Pr) Plenum.

Aggressive Behavior: Genetic & Neural Approaches. Ed. by Edward C. Simmel et al. 224p. 1983. text ed. 49.95 (*0-89859-253-4*) L Erlbaum Assocs.

Aggressive Campaign for Automatic Commodity Trading. Joseph Hadad. 1980. 65.00 (*0-930233-37-9*) Windsor.

Aggressive Political Participation. Edward N. Muller. LC 78-70309. 1979. 47.50 (*0-691-07605-7*) Princeton U Pr.

***Aggressive Political Participation.** Edward N. Muller. LC 78-70309. Date not set. reprint ed. pap. 90.10 (*0-7837-9396-0*, 2060141) Bks Demand.

***Aggressive Tax Avoidance for Real Estate Investors: How to Make Sure You Aren't Paying One.** 14th enl. ed. John T. Reed. 267p. 1995. pap. 23.95 (*0-939224-34-8*) John T Reed.

Aggressive Unilateralism: America's 301 Trade Policy & the World Trading System. Ed. by Jagdish Bhagwati & Hugh T. Patrick. 270p. 1990. 47.50 (*0-472-09455-6*); pap. 17.95 (*0-472-06455-X*) U of Mich Pr.

Aggressive Ways of the Casual Stranger. Rosmarie Waldrop. LC 73-37084. 92p. 1980. reprint ed. 10.00 (*0-930900-74-X*) Burning Deck.

Aggressor. Nick Cook. 1993. 239.40 (*0-312-07925-7*) St Martin.

Aggressor Six. Wil McCarthy. 256p. (Orig.). 1994. pap. 4.99 (*0-451-45405-7*, ROC) NAL-Dutton.

Aggrey of Africa. Edwin W. Smith. LC 70-173617. (Black Heritage Library Collection). 1977. reprint ed. 22.95 (*0-8369-8909-0*) Ayer.

Agha: The Terrible Demon. 2nd ed. Karen Wilson. Ed. by Joshua Greene. Tr. by A. C. Prubhupada. (Classics from India for Children Ser.). (Illus.). 32p. (J). (gr. 1-4). 1989. pap. 6.95 (*0-89647-023-7*) Bala Bks.

Agha, Shaikh & State: The Social & Political Structures of Kurdistan. Martin Van Bruinessen. LC 91-23906. 400p. (C). 1992. text ed. 70.00 (*1-85649-018-1*, Pub. by Zed Books UK); pap. 35.00 (*1-85649-019-X*, Pub. by Zed Books UK) Humanities.

Agharta. Robert E. Dickoff. 106p. 1964. reprint ed. spiral bd. 6.60 (*0-7873-1239-8*) Mokelumne.

Agharta, the Subterranean World. Raymond Bernard. 59p. 1960. reprint ed. spiral bd. 5.50 (*0-7873-0099-3*) Mokelumne.

Aghora: At the Left Hand of God. Robert E. Svoboda. 326p. (Orig.). 1986. pap. 21.95 (*0-914732-21-8*) Bro Life Inc.

Aghora Two: Kundalini. Robert E. Svoboda. (Illus.). 320p. (Orig.). 1993. pap. 18.95 (*0-914732-31-5*) Bro Life Inc.

AGI Data Sheets. 3rd rev. ed. Ed. by J. T. Dutro, Jr. et al. LC 89-32854. (Illus.). 1990. pap. 34.95 (*0-922152-01-2*) Am Geol.

AGI Yearbook 1989. Ed. by Roger Moore. 250p. 1989. 105.00 (*0-85066-793-3*); pap. 53.00 (*0-85066-794-1*) Taylor & Francis.

AGI Yearbook, 1990. Foster & Shand. 1990. 53.00 (*0-85066-826-3*) Taylor & Francis.

***Agikuyu.** Wanjiku M. Kabira. LC 94-26118. (J). (ps-8). 1994. write for info. (*0-8239-1762-2*) Rosen Group.

Agile at Eighty. Robert L. Whiteside. LC 89-90278. (Illus.). 128p. (Orig.). 1989. pap. 7.95 (*0-9623385-0-8*) R L Whiteside.

***Agile Competitors & Virtual Organizations: Strategies for Enriching the Customer.** Kenneth Preiss et al. (Industrial Engineering Ser.). 250p. 1994. text ed. 29.95 (*0-442-01903-3*) Van Nos Reinhold.

Agile Customer-Supplier Relations. Ed. by Kenneth Preiss. (Report Ser. in Agility). 75p. (Orig.). 1994. pap. 25.00 (*1-885166-00-1*) Agile Manufact.

***Agile-Lean: A Common Strategy for Success.** Daniel Roos. (Perspectives on Agility Ser.). 10p. (Orig.). 1995. pap. 10.00 (*1-885166-01-X*) Agile Manufact.

***Agile Manufacturing & an Equipment Portfolio Systems Strategy.** Larry Streng. (Perspectives on Agility Ser.). (Illus.). 16p. (Orig.). 1995. pap. 10.00 (*1-885166-05-2*) Agile Manufact.

Agile Servant: Community Leadership by Community Foundations. Ed. by Richard Magat. LC 89-38377. 1989. 24.95 (*0-87954-330-2*); pap. 15.95 (*0-87954-332-9*) Foundation Ctr.

***Agility Forum Fourth Annual Conference Proceedings, Vol. 1.** Ed. by Joyce J. Barker. (Agility Forum Conference Proceedings Ser.). 516p. (Orig.). 1995. pap. write for info. (*1-885166-02-8*) Agile Manufact.

***Agility Forum Fourth Annual Conference Proceedings, Vol. 2.** Ed. by Joyce J. Barker. (Agility Forum Conference Proceedings Ser.). 537p. (Orig.). 1995. pap. write for info. (*1-885166-03-6*) Agile Manufact.

Agility Training: The Fun Sport for All Dogs. Jane Simmons-Moake. (Illus.). 256p. 1992. 25.95 (*0-87605-402-5*) Howell Bk.

Agincourt. 2nd ed. Christopher Hibbert. (Illus.). 176p. 1986. reprint ed. 22.50 (*0-88029-054-4*) Dorset Pr.

Agincourt War. Alfred H. Burne. LC 75-17190. 359p. 1976. reprint ed. text ed. 41.50 (*0-8371-8300-6*, BUAW, Greenwood Pr) Greenwood.

Agincourt War: A Military History of the Latter Part of the Hundred Years War, 1369-1453. Alfred H. Burne. 368p. 37.50 (*1-85367-087-1*, 5457) Stackpole.

Agincourt 1415. M. Bennett. (Campaign Ser.: No. 9). (Illus.). 96p. pap. 14.95 (*1-85532-132-7*, 9508, Pub. by Osprey UK) Stackpole.

Aging. Bliss. (Troubled Society Ser.: Set II). (J). 1991. 12.95 (*0-86593-114-3*) Rourke Corp.

Aging. Edward Edelson. (Life Cycle Ser.). (Illus.). 112p. (YA). (gr. 6-12). 1991. 18.95 (*0-7910-0035-4*) Chelsea Hse.

Aging. Helen Lancaster. 1980. pap. 6.50 (*0-8309-0290-2*) Herald Hse.

Aging, Vol. 3. Ed. by Eleanor C. Goldstein. (Social Issues Resources Ser.). 1991. Incl. 1986-1990 Supplements. 95.00 (*0-89777-084-6*) Sirs Inc.

Aging: A Challenge to Science & Society, Vol. 3: Behavioral Sciences & Conclusions. Ed. by James E. Birren. (Illus.). 1983. text ed. 85.00 (*0-19-261256-5*) OUP.

Aging: A Guide to Public Policy. Bennett M. Rich & Martha Baum. LC 84-40228. (Contemporary Community Health Ser.). (Illus.). 288p. 1984. 19.95 (*0-8229-5364-1*) U of Pittsburgh Pr.

***Aging: A Natural History.** Robert E. Ricklefs & Caleb E. Finch. LC 95-2334. 1995. text ed. write for info. (*0-7167-5056-2*) W H Freeman.

Aging: A Source Guide. 1991. lib. bdg. 250.00 (*0-8490-4850-8*) Gordon Pr.

Aging: An Exploration. David P. Barash. LC 82-48868. 232p. 1983. 25.00 (*0-295-95993-2*) U of Wash Pr.

Aging: An Introduction to Gerontology. Lewis R. Aiken. 450p. 1994. 55.00 (*0-8039-5445-X*) Sage.

Aging: Binder Evaluation. Chris A. Bell & Don Sosnovski. 81p. (Orig.). (C). 1994. pap. text ed. 15.00 (*0-685-75330-1*, SHRP-A-384) SHRP.

Aging: Canadian Perspectives. Ed. by Victor Marshall & Barry McPherson. 240p. 1994. pap. text ed. 19.95 (*1-55111-012-1*) Broadview Pr.

Aging: Concepts & Controversies. Harry R. Moody, Jr. 512p. 1994. pap. 31.95 (*0-8039-9013-8*) Pine Forge.

Aging: Continuity & Change. 2nd ed. Robert C. Atchley. 324p. (C). 1987. pap. 24.95 (*0-534-06960-6*) Intl Thomson.

Aging: Issues & Policies for the 1980's. Ed. by Ted Tedrick. LC 84-26328. 256p. 1985. text ed. 49.95 (*0-275-90173-4*, C0173, Praeger Pubs) Greenwood.

Aging: Its History & Literature. Joseph T. Freeman. LC 79-11839. 161p. 1979. 29.95 (*0-87705-251-4*) Human Sci Pr.

Aging: Proceedings Symposium, University of Oregon Medical School, 1964. W. Montagna. LC 60-10839. (Advances in Biology of Skin Ser.: Vol. 6). 1965. 120.00 (*0-08-011387-7*, Pub. by Pergamon Repr UK) Franklin.

Aging: Psychological Changes. Sue H. Erp & Jean D. Freeman. 60p. (Orig.). (C). 1971. pap. text ed. 3.00 (*0-87678-416-3*) Continuing Ed Pr.

Aging: Stability & Change in the Family. Ed. by Robert Fogel et al. LC 81-12804. 1981. pap. text ed. 48.00 (*0-12-040023-5*) Acad Pr.

Aging: The Burden Study on Foundation Grantmaking Trends. Barbara R. Greenberg et al. Ed. by Loren Renz. (Benchmark Studies). 131p. (Orig.). 1991. pap. text ed. 40.00 (*0-87954-389-2*) Foundation Ctr.

Aging: The Fulfillment of Life. Henri J. Nouwen & Walter J. Gaffney. LC 74-1773. 160p. 1976. mass mkt. 8.95 (*0-385-00918-6*, Image Bks) Doubleday.

Aging: The Health Care Challenge. 2nd ed. Ed. by Carole B. Lewis. LC 89-25679. (Illus.). 427p. (C). 1990. text ed. 38.00 (*0-8036-5615-7*) Davis Co.

***Aging: The Health Care Challenge.** 3rd ed. Carole B. Lewis. (Illus.). 500p. (C). 1995. pap. text ed. 38.00 (*0-8036-0042-9*) Davis Co.

Aging: The Universal Human Experience; Selected Papers from the XIIth Congress of the International Association of Gerontology. Ed. by George L. Maddox & E. W. Busse. LC 87-26624. 688p. 1987. 75.00 (*0-8261-5490-5*) Springer Pub.

Aging Vol. 4: (Incl. 1991-94 Supplements) Ed. by Eleanor C. Goldstein. (Social Issues Resources Ser.). 1995. 76.00 (*0-89777-166-4*) Sirs Inc.

Aging Adult in Children's Books & Nonprint Media: An Annotated Bibliography. Catherine T. Horner. LC 81-14446. 266p. 1982. 25.00 (*0-8108-1475-7*) Scarecrow.

Aging Aircraft: Second Annual International Conference, October 3-5, 1989, Grand Ballroom, Marriott Inner Harbor Hotel, Baltimore, Maryland. International Conference on Aging Aircraft Staff. 262p. reprint ed. pap. 74.70 (*0-8357-2648-7*, 2040136) Bks Demand.

Aging America: Issues Facing An Aging Society. Karen A. Conner. 240p. (C). 1991. pap. text ed. write for info. (*0-13-019621-5*) P-H.

Aging American: An Introduction to Social Gerontology & Geriatrics. Milton L. Barron. LC 74-8874. (Illus.). 269p. 1974. reprint ed. text ed. 55.00 (*0-8371-7595-X*, BAAG, Greenwood Pr) Greenwood.

***Aging & Active: Dimensions of Productive Engagement among Older Americans.** Ed. by Scott A. Bass. LC 95-4262. 1995. write for info. (*0-300-06326-1*) Yale U Pr.

Aging & Behavior: A Comprehensive Integration of Research Findings. 3rd ed. Jack Botwinick. LC 84-1376. 448p. 1984. 39.95 (*0-8261-1443-1*) Springer Pub.

Aging & Cancer. F. F. Holmes. (Recent Results in Cancer Research Ser.: Vol. 87). (Illus.). 88p. 1983. 44.00 (*0-387-12656-2*) Spr-Verlag.

Aging & Caregiving: Theory, Research & Policy. Ed. by David E. Biegel & Arthur Blum. (Focus Editions Ser.: Vol. 110). (Illus.). 296p. (C). 1990. text ed. 49.95 (*0-8039-3566-8*); pap. text ed. 24.95 (*0-8039-3567-6*) Sage.

Aging & Cell Function. Ed. by John E. Johnson, Jr. LC 83-27167. 298p. 1984. 85.00 (*0-306-41420-1*, Plenum Pr) Plenum.

Aging & Cell Structure, Vol. 1. Ed. by John E. Johnson, Jr. LC 81-17886. 402p. (C). 1981. 89.50 (*0-306-40695-0*, Plenum Pr) Plenum.

Aging & Cell Structure, Vol. 2. Ed. by John E. Johnson, Jr. LC 81-17886. 238p. 1984. 79.50 (*0-306-41455-4*, Plenum Pr) Plenum.

Aging & Cellular Defense Mechanisms. Ed. by Claudio Franceschi et al. LC 92-49531. 1992. write for info. (*0-89766-729-8*); pap. write for info. (*0-89766-730-1*) NY Acad Sci.

Aging & Clinical Practice: Depression & Coexisting Disease. Robert G. Robinson. LC 88-28444. 248p. 1989. 52.00 (*0-89640-152-9*) Igaku-Shoin.

Aging & Cognition: Knowledge Organization & Utilization. Ed. by T. M. Hess. (Advances in Psychology Ser.: No. 71). 514p. 1990. 145.75 (*0-444-88369-X*, North Holland) Elsevier.

Aging & Cognition: Mental Processes, Self-Awareness & Interventions. Ed. by E. A. Lovelace. (Advances in Psychology Ser.: No. 72). 452p. 1991. 137.25 (*0-444-88367-3*, North Holland) Elsevier.

Aging & Cognitive Processes. Ed. by Fergus Craik & Sandra E. Trehub. LC 82-18129. (Advances in the Study of Communication & Affect Ser.: Vol. 8). 396p. 1982. 80.00 (*0-306-40946-1*, Plenum Pr) Plenum.

***Aging & Cohabitation.** Rebecca G. Hatch. LC 94-47353. (Studies on the Elderly in America). (Illus.). 192p. 1995. 53.00 (*0-8153-1910-X*) Garland.

Aging & Communication: Problems in Management. Ed. by Carol N. Wilder & Barbara Weinstein. LC 83-26545. (Advanced Models & Practice in Aged Care Ser.: No. 3). 83p. 1984. text ed. 19.95 (*0-86656-156-0*) Haworth Pr.

Aging & Cultural Diversity: New Directions & Annotated Bibliography. Heather Strange et al. LC 86-3571. 352p. 1987. text ed. 65.00 (*0-89789-103-1*, Bergin & Garvey) Greenwood.

***Aging & Death No. 4.** Vickie Kaczmarek. 12p. 1993. pap. text ed. 4.00 (*1-882472-13-6*) Comm Grief Ctr.

Aging & Disabilities: Seeking Common Ground. Ed. by Edward F. Ansello & Nancy N. Eustis. LC 92-28829. (Generations & Aging Ser.). 204p. 1992. pap. text ed. 14.95 (*0-89503-108-6*) Baywood Pub.

Aging & Drug Effects: A Planning Manual for Medication & Alcohol Abuse Treatment of the Elderly. Douglas H. Ruben. LC 89-43687. 224p. 1990. pap. 27.50x (*0-89950-472-8*) McFarland & Co.

Aging & Environmental Toxicology: Biological & Behavioral Perspectives. Ed. by Ralph L. Cooper et al. LC 90-5134. (Series in Environmental Toxicology). (Illus.). 312p. 1991. text ed. 70.00 (*0-8018-4105-4*) Johns Hopkins.

Aging & Ethics. Ed. by Nancy S. Jecker. LC 91-10792. (Contemporary Issues in Biomedicine, Ethics, & Society Ser.). 408p. 1991. 39.50 (*0-89603-201-9*) Humana.

Aging & Ethics. Ed. by Nancy S. Jecker. LC 91-10792. (Contemporary Issues in Biomedicine, Ethics, & Society Ser.). 408p. 1992. pap. 19.50 (*0-89603-255-8*) Humana.

An Asterisk (*) at the beginning of an entry indicates that the title is appearing in BIP for the first time.

An Asterisk (*) at the beginning of an entry indicates that the title is appearing in BIP for the first time.

141

A

Aging in Minnesota: A Report of the Minnesota Planning Committee for the White House Conference on Aging, Governor's Citizens Council on Aging. Ed. by Arnold M. Rose. LC 63-13884. 334p. reprint ed. pap. 95.20 (*0-8357-5260-7*, 2055904) Bks Demand.

Aging in Muscle. Ed. by George Kaldor & William J. DiBattista. LC 78-4356. (Aging Ser.: Vol. 6). 244p. 1978. 59.00 (*0-89004-097-4*) Raven.

Aging in North America see Aging in All Nations: A Special Report on the United Nations World Assembly on Aging

Aging in Place. Ed. by James J. Callahan, Jr. LC 92-41721. (Generations & Aging Ser.). 145p. 1993. pap. text ed. 14.95 (*0-89503-113-2*) Baywood Pub.

Aging in Place: The Role of Housing & Social Supports. Leon A. Pastalan. LC 90-34022. (Journal of Housing for the Elderly: Vol. 6, Nos. 1-2). 130p. 1990. text ed. 29.95 (*0-86656-981-2*) Haworth Pr.

Aging in Place with Dignity: International Solutions Relating to the Low-Income & Frail Elderly. Ed. by Leonard F. Heumann & Duncan P. Boldy. LC 92-36552. 216p. 1993. text ed. 55.00 (*0-275-94356-9*, C4356, Praeger Pubs) Greenwood.

Aging in Rural America. C. Neil Bull. (Focus Editions Ser.: Vol. 162). (Illus.). 296p. (C). 1993. text ed. 49.95 (*0-8039-4885-9*); pap. text ed. 24.95 (*0-8039-4886-7*) Sage.

Aging in Rural Mid-America: A Symposium on Values for an Evolving Quality of Life, June 5-6, 1978. Frwd. by Lloyd Foerster. LC 78-19579. 1978. pap. 3.00 (*0-916030-04-0*) Bethany Coll KS.

Aging in Society: An Introduction to Social Gerontology. Ed. by John Bond & Peter Coleman. (Illus.). 338p. (C). 1990. text ed. 45.00 (*0-8039-8282-8*); pap. text ed. 19.95 (*0-8039-8283-6*) Sage.

Aging in Society: Selected Reviews of Recent Research. Ed. by Matilda W. Riley et al. 288p. (C). 1983. text ed. 59.95 (*0-89859-267-4*) L Erlbaum Assocs.

Aging in the Designed Environment. Margaret A. Christenson. LC 90-4421. (Physical & Occupational Therapy in Geriatrics Ser.: Vol. 8, Nos. 3 & 4). 133p. 1990. text ed. 29.95 (*1-56024-031-8*) Haworth Pr.

Aging in the Eighties & Beyond. Manfred Bergener et al. LC 83-6747. 416p. 1983. 46.00 (*0-8261-3690-7*) Springer Pub.

Aging in the Lord. Mary H. Valentine. LC 94-16327. 144p. 1994. pap. 7.95 (*0-8091-3486-1*) Paulist Pr.

Aging in the Past: Demography, Society, & Old Age. Ed. by David I. Kertzer & Peter Laslett. LC 93-33288. (Studies in Demography: Vol. 7). 1995. 50.00 (*0-520-08465-9*); pap. 18.00 (*0-520-08466-7*) U CA Pr.

Aging in the United States & Japan: Economic Trends. Ed. by Yukio Noguchi & David A. Wise. LC 94-14101. (National Bureau of Economic Research Conference Report Ser.). (Illus.). 208p. 1994. 39.95 (*0-226-59018-6*) U Ch Pr.

Aging in the Urban Community. Dan W. Edwards & Sloan T. Letman. 120p. 1983. pap. text ed. 12.50 (*0-934872-05-8*) Carlinshar.

Aging in the Western Pacific: A Four-Country Study. G. R. Andrews et al. (Western Pacific Reports & Studies: No. 1). 165p. 1987. pap. 15.00 (*92-9061-161-8*) World Health.

Aging in the 1980s: Psychological Issues. Ed. by Leonard W. Poon et al. LC 80-18515. 656p. reprint ed. pap. 180.00 (*0-7837-0482-8*, 2040806) Bks Demand.

Aging into the Twenty-First Century: The Exploration of Aspirations & Values. Rachelle A. Dorfman. LC 93-11673. 240p. 1994. 27.95 (*0-87630-643-1*) Brunner-Mazel.

Aging Is a Lifelong Affair. Ben Weininger & Eva L. Menkin. LC 89-31052. 120p. (C). 1988. reprint ed. lib. bdg. 25.00x (*0-8095-4005-3*) Borgo Pr.

Aging-Its Chemistry: Proceedings of the Third Arnold O. Beckman Conference in Clinical Chemistry. Ed. by A. A. Dietz. LC 80-65825. 448p. 1980. 20.00 (*0-915274-10-8*) Am Assn Clinical Chem.

Aging Lung: Normal Function. J. R. Edge et al. LC 73-1458. 1974. 19.00 (*0-8422-7165-1*) Irvington.

Aging, Money & Life Satisfaction: Aspects of Financial Gerontology. Ed. by Neal E. Cutler et al. LC 91-5230. 208p. 1992. 34.95 (*0-8261-7700-X*) Springer Pub.

Aging Motor System, Vol. 3. Ed. by James Mortimer et al. LC 82-598. 270p. 1982. text ed. 55.00 (*0-275-90865-8*, C08653, Praeger Pubs) Greenwood.

Aging Mouth. Ed. by D. B. Ferguson. (Frontiers of Oral Physiology Ser.: Vol. 6). (Illus.). viii, 176p. 1987. 95.25 (*3-8055-4513-4*) S Karger.

Aging, Musculoskeletal Disorders, & Care of the Frail Elderly. Ed. by Horace M. Perry, III et al. LC 93-1426. 392p. 1993. 48.95 (*0-8261-7930-4*) Springer Pub.

Aging Network: Programs & Services. 3rd ed. Donald E. Gelfand. (Adulthood & Aging Ser.: Vol. 8). 320p. 1988. pap. 24.95 (*0-8261-3054-2*) Springer Pub.

Aging Network: Programs & Services. 4th ed. Donald E. Gelfand. LC 93-19615. 440p. 1993. 37.95 (*0-8261-3056-9*) Springer Pub.

Aging Nuclear Power Plants: Managing Plant Life & Decommissioning. 1994. lib. bdg. 250.00 (*0-8490-8550-0*) Gordon Pr.

Aging of Connective Tissues-Skin: Proceedings of the International Colloquium of Dermo-Chemistry on Aging of Skin, Paris. International Colloquium of Dermo-Chemistry on Aging of Skin Staff. Ed. by L. Robert & Barbara Robert. (Frontiers of Matrix Biology Ser.: Vol. 1). (Illus.). 250p. 1973. 78.50 (*3-8055-1633-9*) S Karger.

Aging of Reproductive Organs. Ed. by Y. Taketani & S. Kawagoe. (Journal: Hormone Research: Vol. 39, Suppl. 1, 1993). (Illus.). vi, 38p. 1993. pap. 17.75 (*3-8055-5797-3*) S Karger.

Aging of the American Work Force: Problems, Programs, Policies. Ed. by Irving Bluestone et al. LC 89-5572. (Labor Economics & Policy Ser.). (Illus.). 434p. (C). 1990. pap. text ed. 21.95 (*0-8143-2175-5*) Wayne St U Pr.

Aging of the Autonomic Nervous System. Ed. by Francesco Amenta. 1993. 179.95 (*0-8493-6981-9*, QP368) CRC Pr.

Aging of the Brain. Ed. by David Samuel et al. (Aging Ser.: Vol. 22). 410p. 1983. text ed. 100.50 (*0-89004-870-3*) Raven.

Aging of the Brain: Cellular & Molecular Aspects of Brain Aging & Alzheimer's Disease. Ed. by T. Nagatsu & O. Hayaishi. (Taniguchi Symposia on Brain Sciences Ser.: Vol. 13). (Illus.). x, 302p. 1991. 134.50 (*3-8055-5334-X*) S Karger.

Aging of the Brain & Alzheimer's Disease: Proceedings of the Fourteenth International Summer School, Amsterdam, The Netherlands, August 26-30, 1985. Ed. by D. F. Swaab et al. (Progress in Brain Research Ser.: No. 70). 525p. 1987. 206.25 (*0-444-80793-4*) Elsevier.

Aging of the Central Nervous System. V. V. Frolkis & V. V. Bezrukov. (Interdisciplinary Topics in Gerontology Ser.: Vol. 16). (Illus.). 1979. pap. 53.00 (*3-8055-2995-3*) S Karger.

Aging Parent: A Guide for Program Planners. LC 80-65407. 48p. 1980. pap. 1.50 (*0-87495-021-X*) Am Jewish Comm.

Aging Parents, Ambivalent Baby Boomers: A Critical Approach to Gerontology. Jayne E. Maugans. LC 93-79472. 192p. (Orig.). 1994. text ed. 34.95 (*0-930390-49-0*); pap. text ed. 18.95 (*0-930390-23-7*) Gen Hall.

Aging Parents & You. rev. ed. 1993. 9.95 (*0-942361-58-X*) MasterMedia Ltd.

Aging Parents & You: A Complete Handbook to Help You Help Your Elders Maintain a Healthy, Productive & Independent Life. rev. ed. Eugenia Anderson-Ellis. pap. 9.95 (*0-942361-05-9*) MasterMedia Ltd.

Aging Pigment: Current Research, Vol. 1. B. S. Nanda et al. 191p. 1974. text ed. 25.50 (*0-8422-7197-X*) Irvington.

Aging Pigment: Current Research, Vol. 2. William B. Weglicki et al. 268p. 1974. text ed. 28.50 (*0-8422-7198-8*) Irvington.

***Aging Political Activists: Personal Narratives from the Old Left.** David P. Shuldiner. LC 94-33258. 312p. 1995. text ed. 55.00 (*0-275-95045-X*, Praeger Pubs) Greenwood.

Aging Population. A. P. Huijser & P. D. Van Loo. 1986. pap. text ed. 37.00 (*90-247-3376-6*) Kluwer Ac.

Aging Population in the Twenty-First Century: Statistics for Health Policy. 340p. 1988. pap. text ed. 27.95 (*0-309-03881-2*) Natl Acad Pr.

Aging Populations: The Social Policy Implications. 90p. 1988. 22.00 (*92-64-13113-2*) OECD.

Aging Process: Therapeutic Implications. Ed. by Robert N. Butler & Alexander G. Bearn. (MEDAC, 1984 Ser.). 352p. 1985. text ed. 88.00 (*0-88167-065-0*) Raven.

Aging Process: Implications for ACE Inhibition: Proceedings of a Symposium held in Montreux, March 1987. Ed. by H. Brunner. (Journal: Gerontology: Vol. 33, Suppl. 1). (Illus.). x, 56p. 1988. pap. 17.00 (*3-8055-4729-3*) S Karger.

Aging Process of Population. E. Rosset & I. Dobosz. LC 63-19956. 1964. 208.00 (*0-08-010402-9*, Pub. by Pergamon Repr UK) Franklin.

Aging Public Policy: Bonding the Generations. Theodore H. Koff & Richard W. Park. LC 92-39350. (Society & Aging Ser.). 367p. 1993. text ed. 39.95 (*0-89503-111-6*); pap. text ed. 29.95 (*0-89503-112-4*) Baywood Pub.

Aging, Race & Culture: Issues in Long Term Care. Ed. by Geralyn G. Magan. LC 82-72776. 77p. 1982. 6.50 (*0-685-06337-2*) Am Assn Homes.

***Aging, Religion & Spirituality: A Handbook.** Ed. by Melvin A. Kimble et al. LC 95-6351. 1995. write for info. (*0-8006-2667-2*, Fortress Pr) Augsburg Fortress.

Aging, Reproduction, & the Climacteric. Ed. by Luigi Mastroianni, Jr. & C. Alvin Paulsen. LC 85-28299. 332p. 1986. 69.50 (*0-306-42142-9*, Plenum Pr) Plenum.

Aging Sensory Systems & Perception. John F. Corso. LC 80-39579. 302p. 1981. text ed. 65.00 (*0-275-90599-3*, C0599, Praeger Pubs) Greenwood.

Aging Services Representative. Jack Rudman. (Career Examination Ser.: C-2880). 1994. pap. 27.95 (*0-8373-2880-2*) Nat Learn.

Aging, Sex, & DNA Repair. Carol Bernstein & Harris Bernstein. (Illus.). 382p. 1991. text ed. 59.95 (*0-12-092860-4*) Acad Pr.

Aging Skeleton: Aspects of Human Bone Involution. Spencer L. Rogers. (Illus.). 120p. (C). 1982. 24.95 (*0-398-04710-3*) C C Thomas.

Aging Skin: Properties & Functional Changes. Jean-Luc Leveque & Agache. (Basic & Clinical Dermatology Ser.: Vol. 4). 320p. 1993. 150.00 (*0-8247-8791-9*) Dekker.

Aging Slowly. Prevention Magazine Editors & Myron Brenton. LC 83-13975. (Prevention Total Health System Ser.). (Illus.). 176p. 1984. 17.95 (*0-87857-465-4*, 05-129-0) Rodale Pr Inc.

Aging Smarter. Thomas L. Nolan, Jr. (Illus.). 156p. (Orig.). 1991. pap. 12.95 (*0-9630727-0-6*) Spring Brook.

Aging, Some Social & Biological Aspects: Proceedings of the American Association for the Advancement of Science, Symposia presented at the Chicago Meeting. American Association for the Advancement of Science Staff. Ed. by Nathan W. Shock. LC 73-167305. (Essay Index Reprint Ser.). 1977. reprint ed. 36.95 (*0-8369-2735-4*) Ayer.

Aging Spine: Essentials of Pathophysiology, Diagnosis & Treatment. William E. Boden & Sam W. Wiesel. (Illus.). 384p. 1991. text ed. 79.50 (*0-7216-3538-5*) Saunders.

Aging Stress & Health. Kyriacos C. Markides et al. 290p. 1989. text ed. 101.50 (*0-471-92157-2*) Wiley.

***Aging, the Individual & Society.** Georgia M. Barrow. Ed. by Schonebaum. 380p. 1995. pap. text ed. write for info. (*0-314-04444-2*) West Pub.

Aging, the Individual, & Society. 5th ed. Georgia M. Barrow & Guy Shuttlesworth. Ed. by LaMarre. 380p. (C). 1993. pap. text ed. 47.25 (*0-314-93332-8*) West Pub.

Aging Two Thousand: Our Health Care Destiny, Vol. 2. Ed. by C. M. Gaitz et al. (Illus.). 400p. 1985. 88.00 (*0-387-96070-8*) Spr-Verlag.

Aging with a Disability. Roberta B. Trieschmann. LC 86-72100. (Illus.). 148p. 1987. 42.95 (*0-939957-01-9*) Demos Vermande.

Aging with Confidence. American Institute for Preventive Medicine Staff. LC 93-40576. (For Your Information Ser.). 1993. 5.95 (*1-56420-017-5*); audio 16.00 (*1-56420-018-3*) New Readers.

Aging with Joy. Ruth Morrison & Dawn Radtke. LC 87-51567. 112p. (Orig.). 1988. pap. 5.95 (*0-89622-360-4*) Twenty-Third.

Aging with Passionate Pleasure. Gladys Hotchkiss. LC 92-61374. 140p. 1992. pap. 14.95 (*0-88100-077-9*) Natl Writ Pr.

Aging with Spinal Cord Injury. Whiteneck et al. 374p. 1992. 94.95 (*0-939957-48-5*) Demos Vermande.

Aging Work Force. Ed. by Nancy Julius & Herbert Krauss. 270p. 1993. 49.00 (*1-878240-19-6*) Coll & U Personnel.

Aging World, No. II. (Illus.). 100p. (Orig.). (C). 1993. pap. text ed. 40.00 (*1-56806-468-3*) Diane Pub.

Agit-Pop: Political Culture & Communication Theory. Arthur A. Berger. 254p. 1989. 32.95 (*0-88738-315-7*) Transaction Pubs.

Agita: Fatal Affliction: the "Hits" Recipe Book. Joseph Giambra. (Orig.). 1991. pap. 6.00 (*1-880631-00-8*) Shuffaloff Bks.

Agitator: A Collection of Diverse Opinions from America's Not So Popular Press. Ed. by Donald L. Rice. LC 74-178271. (Schism Anthology Ser.). 462p. reprint ed. pap. 131.70 (*0-8357-5261-5*, 2024188) Bks Demand.

Agitprop: The Life of an American Working-Class Radical: The Autobiography of Eugene V. Dennett. Eugene V. Dennett. LC 88-31668. (American Labor History Ser.). 270p. 1990. 59.50 (*0-7914-0078-6*); pap. 19.95 (*0-7914-0079-4*) State U NY Pr.

Aglow with the Spirit. Robert Frost. 1986. pap. 3.95 (*0-912106-64-6*) Bridge Pub.

Aglow with the Spirit: How to Receive the Baptism in the Holy Spirit. rev. ed. Robert C. Frost. 127p. 1992. pap. 6.95 (*0-88270-651-9*) Bridge Pub.

AGMA Design Manual for Enclosed Epicyclic Metric Module Gear Drives. (AGMA Ser.: No. 6123-A88). (Illus.). 55p. 1989. pap. text ed. 50.00 (*1-55589-505-0*) AGMA.

AGMA Design Manual for Epicyclic Gear Drives. (AGMA Ser.: No. 6023-A88). (Illus.). 55p. 1989. pap. text ed. 50.00 (*1-55589-504-2*) AGMA.

Agneau. Francois Mauriac. 12.95 (*0-685-73251-7*, F112540) Fr & Eur.

Agneau. Francois Mauriac. (FRE.). 1985. pap. 10.95 (*0-7859-2986-X*, F112540) Fr & Eur.

Agnes & Sally. Lewis Warsh. LC 83-16543. 111p. 1984. pap. 6.95 (*0-914590-81-2*) Fiction Coll.

Agnes' Cardboard Piano. Linda P. Silbert & Alvin J. Silbert. (Little Twirps Understanding People Bks.). (Illus.). (J). (gr. k-4). 1978. pap. 4.98 (*0-89544-054-7*) Silbert Bress.

Agnes Day. Lionel Fenn. 256p. (Orig.). 1987. pap. 2.95 (*0-8125-3789-0*) Tor Bks.

Agnes De Mille. Margaret Speaker-Yuan. (American Women of Achievement Ser.). (Illus.). 112p. (J). (gr. 5 up). 1990. lib. bdg. 17.95 (*1-55546-648-6*) Chelsea Hse.

Agnes de Mille: Dancing off the Earth. Beverly Gherman. LC 93-26606. (Great Achievers Ser.). (Illus.). 160p. (J). (gr. 7 up). 1994. reprint ed. pap. 5.95 (*0-02-043240-2*, Collier Bks Young) S&S Childrens.

Agnes Denes. Ed. by Jill Hartz. (Illus.). 208p. 1993. 60.00 (*0-295-97277-7*); pap. 35.00 (*0-295-97278-5*) U of Wash Pr.

Agnes Grey. Anne Bronte. Ed. by Hilda Marsden & Robert Inglesfield. (Clarendon Edition of the Novels of the Brontes Ser.). 256p. 1988. 72.00 (*0-19-812693-X*) OUP.

Agnes Grey. Anne Bronte. Ed. by Hilda Marsden. (World's Classics Ser.). 248p. 1991. pap. 5.95 (*0-19-282711-1*, 12022) OUP.

Agnes Grey. Anne Bronte. 272p. 1989. mass mkt. 5.95 (*0-14-043210-8*, Penguin Classics) Viking Penguin.

Agnes Grey & Poems. Anne Bronte. 208p. 1914. pap. 4.95 (*0-460-87121-8*, Everyman's Classic Lib) C E Tuttle.

Agnes Martin. Barbara Haskell. LC 92-17968. 1992. write for info. (*0-87427-082-0*) Whitney Mus.

***Agnes Martin.** Barbara Haskell. (Illus.). 188p. 1995. pap. 35.00 (*0-8109-6817-7*) Abrams.

Agnes Martin: Writings. Agnes Martin. (Illus.). 176p. 1994. pap. 24.95 (*3-89322-375-4*, Pub. by Edition Cantz GW) Dist Art Pubs.

Agnes Moorehead: A Bio-Bibliography. Lynn Kear. LC 92-28064. (Bio-Bibliographies in the Performing Arts Ser.: No. 36). 320p. 1992. text ed. 45.00 (*0-313-28155-6*, KAE/, Greenwood Pr) Greenwood.

Agnes of Sorrento. Harriet Beecher Stowe. 1890. 16.00 (*0-403-00279-6*) Scholarly.

Agnes of Sorrento. Harriet Beecher Stowe. LC 72-144691. reprint ed. 17.50 (*0-404-06289-X*) AMS Pr.

Agnes of Sorrento. Harriet Beecher Stowe. (BCL1-PS American Literature Ser.). 412p. 1992. reprint ed. lib. bdg. 99.00 (*0-7812-6870-2*) Rprt Serv.

***Agnes Pelton: Poet of Nature.** Michael Zakian. (Illus.). 128p. (C). 1995. pap. 29.95 (*0-295-97451-6*) U of Wash Pr.

Agnes Smedley: The Life & Times of an American Radical. Janice R. MacKinnon & Stephen R. MacKinnon. 460p. (C). 1988. 32.00 (*0-520-05966-2*); pap. 14.00 (*0-520-06614-6*) U CA Pr.

Agnes the Sheep. William Taylor. 176p. (J). (gr. 5 up). 1991. 13.95 (*0-590-43365-2*, Scholastic Hardcover) Scholastic Inc.

Agnes the Sheep. William Taylor. (J). (gr. 4-7). 1994. pap. 3.25 (*0-590-43364-4*) Scholastic Inc.

Agnew: The Coining of a Household Word. Ed. by Robert W. Peterson. LC 70-183844. (Interim History Ser.). 187p. reprint ed. pap. 53.30 (*0-8357-5262-3*, 2022893) Bks Demand.

Agnew: The Hereditary Sheriffs of Galloway, Their Forebears & Friends, Their Courts & Customs of Their Times With Notes of the Early History, 2 vols., Set. Andrew Agnew. (Illus.). 1992. reprint ed. lib. bdg. 153.00 (*0-8328-2474-7*); reprint ed. pap. 143.00 (*0-8328-2475-5*) Higginson Bk Co.

Agni. Robert E. Miller. (Writers Workshop Redbird Ser.). 1975. 8.00 (*0-88253-492-0*); pap. text ed. 4.80 (*0-88253-491-2*) Ind-US Inc.

Agni: Issue Focuses on State Control & the Arts. Ed. by Askold Melnyczuk. 322p. (C). 1990. write for info. (*0-318-66933-1*) New Cambrdge.

Agni: The Used World. Ed. by Askold Melnyczuk. 312p. (Orig.). (C). 1989. pap. write for info. (*0-318-66934-X*) New Cambrdge.

Agni: The Vedic Ritual of the Fire Altar, 2 vols. Fritz Staal. (Illus.). (C). 1983. 300.00 (*0-89581-450-1*, Asian Human Pr) Jain Pub Co.

Agni Purana, Pt. III. (Ancient Indian Tradition & Mythology Ser.: Vol. 29). 1991. 26.00 (*0-685-35375-3*, Pub. by Motilal Banarsidass II) S Asia.

Agni Purana, Pt. IV. Ed. by N. Gangadharan. (C). 1987. 26.00 (*81-208-0306-X*, Pub. by Motilal Banarsidass II) S Asia.

Agnon's Art of Indirection: Uncovering Latent Content in the Fiction of S. Y. Agnon. Nitza Ben-Dov. LC 93-30732. (Jewish Studies: Vol. 7). x, 167p. 1993. 57.25 (*90-04-09863-1*) E J Brill.

Agnos Years. Warren Hinckle. 96p. 1991. text ed. 12.95 (*0-9631643-0-9*); pap. text ed. 2.95 (*0-9631643-1-7*) SF Ind Newspaper.

Agnosia & Apraxia: Selected Papers of Liepman, Lange, & Potzl. Ed. by Jason W. Brown. (Institute for Research in Behavioral Neuroscience Ser.). 336p. 1988. 69.95 (*0-8058-0286-X*) L Erlbaum Assocs.

Agnostic Spirit As a Common Motif in Liberal Theology & Liberal Skepticism. James Woelfel. LC 90-21357. 136p. 1990. lib. bdg. 69.95 (*0-7734-9921-0*) E Mellen.

Agnosticism & Anecdotes: With Some Personal Medical Experiences & Self-Help Ideas. Bronislav R. Mehl. 1991. 16.95 (*0-533-08959-X*) Vantage.

Agnosticism & Christianity & Other Essays. Thomas H. Huxley. (Great Minds Ser.). 232p. (Orig.). (C). 1991. pap. 10.95 (*0-87975-749-3*) Prometheus Bks.

Agnosticism & Theism in the Nineteenth Century. Richard A. Armstrong. 1977. lib. bdg. 59.95 (*0-8490-1406-9*) Gordon Pr.

Agnosticism Is Also Faith. George G. Strem. LC 85-90970. 1986. 15.00 (*0-87212-194-1*) Libra.

AGO Ninetieth Anniversary Anthology of American Organ Music. Ed. by Philip Brunelle. 184p. 1988. 35.00 (*0-19-385788-X*) OUP.

Agon: Towards a Theory of Revisionism. Harold Bloom. 1983. pap. 11.95 (*0-19-503354-X*) OUP.

Agon in Euripides. Michael Lloyd. 224p. 1992. 45.00 (*0-19-814778-3*) OUP.

Agonies of the Intellectual: Commitment, Subjectivity, & the Performative in the Twentieth-Century French Tradition. Allan Stoekl. LC 91-17143. xii, 384p. 1992. 40.00 (*0-8032-4215-8*) U of Nebr Pr.

***Agonistic Imperative: The Rational Burden of Africa-Centeredness.** Kwesi Otabil. 250p. (Orig.). (C). Date not set. pap. text ed. 24.95 (*1-55605-244-8*) Wyndhall Pr.

***Agonistic Imperative: The Rational Burden of Africa-Centeredness.** Kwesi Otabil. 250p. (Orig.). (C). Date not set. text ed. 34.95x (*1-55605-245-6*) Wyndhall Pr.

Agonistic Poetry: The Pindaric Mode in Pindar, Horace, Holderlin, & the England Ode. Wiliam Fitzgerald. LC 86-30923. 225p. 1987. 35.00 (*0-520-05765-1*) U CA Pr.

Agonizingly Gross Jokes. Julius Alvin. 1991. pap. 3.50 (*0-8217-3648-5*) Zebra.

Agony: The Untold Tale of the Nigerian Society. Richard O. Nwachukwu. 118p. (Orig.). 1987. pap. 6.95 (*0-941823-00-8*) Good Hope Enterp.

Agony & Death on a Gold Rush Steamer: Disastrous Sinking of the Side-Wheeler Yankee Blade. Donald G. Knight & Eugene D. Wheeler. LC 90-7139. 144p. (Orig.). 1990. pap. 7.95 (*0-934793-27-1*) Pathfinder CA.

Agony & Death on a Gold Rush Steamer: Disastrous Sinking of the Side-Wheeler Yankee Blade. Donald G. Knight & Eugene D. Wheeler. (Illus.). 144p. (Orig.). 1991. reprint ed. lib. bdg. 25.00x (*0-8095-5910-2*) Borgo Pr.

Agony & the Ecstasy. Irving Stone. 766p. 1987. pap. 5.95 (*0-451-15947-0*, AE2643, Sig) NAL-Dutton.

Agony & the Ecstasy. Irving Stone. 1994. reprint ed. lib. bdg. 39.95 (*1-56849-340-1*) Buccaneer Bks.

Agony & the Ego: The Art & Strategy of Fiction Writing Explored. Ed. by Clare Boylan. 272p. 1994. pap. 10.00 (*0-14-016975-X*, Penguin Bks) Viking Penguin.

Agony & the Glory. Vinayak K. Gokak. (C). 1992. 19.50 (*81-7018-713-3*, Pub. by BR Pub II) S Asia.

Agony at Galloway: One Church's Struggle with Social Change. W. J. Cunningham. LC 79-56698. 181p. reprint ed. pap. 51.60 (*0-7837-1400-9*, 2041581) Bks Demand.

Agony Column. Earl D. Biggers. 1976. reprint ed. lib. bdg. 21.95 (*0-89966-074-6*) Buccaneer Bks.

An Asterisk (*) at the beginning of an entry indicates that the title is appearing in BIP for the first time.

Agony Dance: Death of the Dancing Dolls. Besmilr Brigham. 30p. (Orig.). 1969. pap. 2.50 (*0-932264-11-5*) Trask Hse Bks.

Agony in Education: The Importance of Struggle in the Process of Learning. Edward L. Kuhlman. LC 93-362126. 224p. 1994. text ed. 49.95 (*0-89789-374-3*, Bergin & Garvey) Greenwood.

Agony in Limbo. Abdullatif A. Akel. Ed. by A. J. Ciulla. (Illus.). 388p. (C). 17.95 (*0-913791-01-6*) Rubicon Bks.

Agony in the Garden. Lawrence J. Babin. LC 75-158476. 1971. 3.00 (*0-912492-25-2*); pap. 1.00 (*0-912492-00-7*) Pyquag.

***Agony in the Garden: The Story of a Gay Minister.** Howard Hannon. 224p. 1995. pap. 12.95 (*1-887092-01-3*) Tzedakah Pubns.

Agony of Alice. Phyllis R. Naylor. LC 85-7957. 144p. (J). (gr. 4-9). 1985. text ed., lib. bdg. 13.95 (*0-689-31143-5*, Atheneum Bks Young) S&S Childrens.

Agony of Alice. Phyllis Naylor-Reynolds. (J). (gr. k-6). 1988. pap. 3.50 (*0-440-40051-1*, YB) Dell.

Agony of De-Feet: A Podiatrist's Guide to Footcare. Burton S. Schuler. (Illus.). 128p. 1982. 15.95 (*0-686-32827-2*); pap. 13.95 (*0-686-32828-0*) La Luz Pr.

Agony of Deceit. Michael Horton. 1990. pap. 8.99 (*0-8024-8778-5*) Moody.

Agony of Flies: Notes & Notations. Elias Canetti. 1994. 27.50 (*0-374-10254-6*); pap. 14.00 (*0-374-52410-6*) FS&G.

Agony of Grief. Jewell N. Jackson. LC 85-52320. (Illus.). 96p. (Orig.). 1986. pap. 8.95 (*0-934955-02-6*) Watercress Pr.

***Agony of Hell.** Turner Publishing Company Staff. LC 94-60251. 200p. 1994. 48.00 (*1-56311-139-X*) Turner Pub KY.

Agony of Jesus. Padre Pio. 40p. 1974. pap. 1.50 (*0-89555-097-0*) TAN Bks Pubs.

Agony of Lewis Carroll. Richard Wallace. LC 90-90304. (Illus.). 308p. (Orig.). 1990. pap. 13.00 (*0-9627195-5-2*) Gemini MA.

Agony of Modernization: Labor & Industrialization in Spain. Benjamin Martin. LC 89-77909. (Cornell International Industrial & Labor Relations Reports: No. 16). 576p. 1990. 45.00 (*0-87546-165-4*) ILR Pr.

Agony of Survival. Albert A. Hutler. LC 89-83455. (Illus.). 229p. 1990. 18.95 (*0-944435-06-8*) Glenbridge Pub.

Agony of Uganda: From Idi Amin to Obote. Francis A. Bwengye. 1986. 39.00 (*0-7212-0717-0*, Pub. by Regency Press) St Mut.

***Agora, Academy, & the Conduct of Philosophy.** Debra Nails. (Philosophical Studies Ser.). 284p. (C). 1995. lib. bdg. 130.00 (*0-7923-3543-0*) Kluwer Ac.

Agora of Athens. Homer A. Thompson & R. E. Wycherley. LC 75-327835. (Athenian Agora Ser.: Vol. 14). (Illus.). xxiii, 257p. 1972. 45.00 (*0-87661-214-1*) Am Sch Athens.

Agora Que Voce E De Cristo. David Shibley. 96p. (POR.). 1991. 3.95 (*0-8297-1654-8*) Life Pubs Intl.

Agora Services Guide. MZ Media Group, Inc. Staff. Date not set. 14.95 (*1-885313-01-2*) MZ Group.

Agoraphobia. Peter Ganick. 144p. (Orig.). 1993. pap. 11.00 (*0-9628456-1-2*) Drogue Pr.

Agoraphobia: A Clinical & Personal Account. J. C. Clarke. (Illus.). 202p. 1985. text ed. 39.00 (*0-08-029866-4*, PPA); pap. text ed. 21.00 (*0-08-029846-X*, PPA) Elsevier.

Agoraphobia: Coming to Terms with the World Outside. Muriel Frampton. 96p. (C). 1990. reprint ed. lib. bdg. 23.00x (*0-8095-7072-6*) Borgo Pr.

Agoraphobia: Current Perspectives on Theory & Treatment. Kevin Gournay. 256p. 1989. 67.50 (*0-415-01886-2*, A3459) Routledge.

Agoraphobia: Fear of Fear. Adele Paolino. 256p. 1985. pap. text ed. 8.95 (*0-9611448-1-5*) A Paolino.

Agoraphobia: How I Overcame This Crippling Disease. Adele Paolino. 80p. 1983. pap. 5.95 (*0-9611448-0-7*) A Paolino.

Agoraphobia: Multiple Perspectives on Theory & Treatment. Ed. by Dianne L. Chambless & Alan J. Goldstein. LC 82-7087. (Wiley Series on Personality Processes). 239p. reprint ed. pap. 68.20 (*0-7837-2391-1*, 2040076) Bks Demand.

Agoraphobia: Nature & Treatment. Andrew M. Mathews et al. LC 80-29038. (Guilford Clinical Psychology & Psychotherapy Ser.). 233p. 1981. lib. bdg. 32.00 (*0-89862-003-1*) Guilford Pr.

Agoraphobia & Panic: A Guide to Psychological Treatment. Jeffrey E. Hecker & Geoffrey L. Thorpe. 273p. (C). 1992. text ed. 49.95 (*0-205-12906-4*, Longwood Div) Allyn.

Agostino Agazzari & Music at Siena Cathedral, 1597-1641. Colleen Reardon. (Oxford Monographs on Music). (Illus.). 224p. 1994. 45.00 (*0-19-816272-3*) OUP.

Agostino Soderini: Canzoni a 4. & 8. Voci...Libro Primo (Milan, 1608) Ed. by James Ladewig. LC 91-760648. (Italian Instrumental Music of the Sixteenth & Early Seventeenth Centuries Ser.: Vol. 19). 264p. 1992. 75.00 (*0-8240-4518-1*) Garland.

Agotado (Burnout) Ayudas-Vidas Desequilibradas. Myron Rush. (SPA.). 1992. 5.99 (*1-56063-242-9*, 497706) Editorial Unilit.

Agotamiento Espiritual. Malcolm Smith. 240p. (SPA.). 1990. pap. 4.95 (*0-8297-0923-1*) Life Pubs Intl.

Agrammatic Aphasia: A Cross-Language Narrative Sourcebook, 1. Ed. by Lise Menn & Loraine K. Obler. LC 89-18418. 2100p. 1990. write for info. (*1-55619-025-5*) Benjamins North Am.

Agrammatic Aphasia: A Cross-Language Narrative Sourcebook, 2. Ed. by Lise Menn & Loraine K. Obler. LC 89-18418. 2100p. 1990. write for info. (*1-55619-026-3*) Benjamins North Am.

Agrammatic Aphasia: A Cross-Language Narrative Sourcebook, 3. Ed. by Lise Menn & Loraine K. Obler. LC 89-18418. 2100p. 1990. write for info. (*1-55619-027-1*) Benjamins North Am.

Agrammatic Aphasia: A Cross-Language Narrative Sourcebook, Set. Ed. by Lise Menn & Loraine K. Obler. LC 89-18418. 2100p. 1990. 690.00 (*1-55619-024-7*) Benjamins North Am.

Agraphcs Nomos & der Charakter in der Sprache der Fruhgriechischen Dichtung, 2 vols. in one. Rudolf Hirzel & Walter Marg. Ed. by Gregory Vlastos. LC 78-14615. (Morals & Law in Ancient Greece Ser.). (GER & GRE.). 1979. reprint ed. lib. bdg. 21.95 (*0-405-11590-3*) Ayer.

Agrarian Bengal: Economy, Society & Politics, 1919-1947. Sugata Bose. (Cambridge South Asian Studies: No. 36). (Illus.). 250p. 1987. 69.95 (*0-521-30448-2*) Cambridge U Pr.

Agrarian Capitalism & the World Market: Buenos Aires in the Pastoral Age, 1840-1890. Hilda Sabato. LC 90-12635. 330p. 1990. 50.00 (*0-8263-1218-7*) U of NM Pr.

Agrarian Capitalism in Theory & Practice. Susan A. Mann. LC 89-22656. (Illus.). xvi, 212p. (C). 1990. 34.95 (*0-8078-1885-2*) U of NC Pr.

Agrarian Change in Communist Laos. Grant Evans. 88p. 1988. pap. text ed. 13.60 (*981-3035-16-1*, Pub. by Inst SE Asian Studies SI) Ashgate Pub Co.

Agrarian Change in Sri Lanka. James Brow. Ed. by Joe Weeraamunda. 400p. (C). 1992. text ed. 39.95 (*0-8039-9415-X*) Sage.

Agrarian China: Selected Source Materials from Chinese Authors. Institute of Pacific Relations Staff. LC 75-30060. (Institute of Pacific Relations Ser.). reprint ed. 55.00 (*0-404-59532-4*) AMS Pr.

Agrarian China: Selected Source Materials from Chinese Authors. Tr. by Richard H. Tawney. LC 75-32310. (Studies in Chinese History & Civilization). 281p. 1976. reprint ed. text ed. 55.00 (*0-313-26969-6*, U6969, Greenwood Pr) Greenwood.

Agrarian Crisis in India: The Case of Bihar. F. Tomasson Jannuzi. LC 73-19811. 245p. reprint ed. pap. 69.90 (*0-8357-4280-6*, 2037079) Bks Demand.

Agrarian Economy in Andhra under Vijayanagar. K. Jayasree. (C). 1991. 15.00 (*81-7013-084-0*, Pub. by Navrang) S Asia.

Agrarian Economy of Tamilnadu, 1820-1855. Arun Bandopadhyaya. (C). 1992. 28.00 (*81-7074-108-4*, Pub. by KP Bagchi IA) S Asia.

Agrarian Elites & Italian Fascism: The Province of Bologna, 1901-1926. Anthony L. Cardoza. LC 82-47585. 495p. reprint ed. pap. 141.10 (*0-8357-7892-4*, 2036311) Bks Demand.

***Agrarian Feminism: The Politics of Ontario Farm Women.** Louise I. Carbert. (Illus.). 304p. 1995. 50.00 (*0-8020-2931-0*); pap. 19.95 (*0-8020-7756-0*) U of Toronto Pr.

Agrarian History of England & Wales, Vol. 3, 1350-1500. Ed. by Edward Miller. (Illus.). 750p. (C). 1991. 150.00 (*0-521-20074-1*) Cambridge U Pr.

Agrarian History of England & Wales, Vol. 1, Pt. 1: Prehistory. Ed. by Stuart Piggott. LC 66-19763. (Agrarian History of England & Wales Ser.). 1981. 125.00 (*0-521-08741-4*) Cambridge U Pr.

Agrarian History of England & Wales, Vol. 2: 1042-1348. Ed. by H. E. Hallam. (Illus.). 960p. 1989. 175.00 (*0-521-20073-3*) Cambridge U Pr.

Agrarian History of England & Wales, Vol. 6: 1750-1850. Ed. by G. E. Mingay. 1280p. 1989. 185.00 (*0-521-22726-7*) Cambridge U Pr.

Agrarian India Between the World Wars. R. Ulianovsky. 296p. (C). 1985. 50.00 (*0-685-31623-8*, Pub. by Collets UK) Pro-Am Music.

Agrarian Kentucky. Thomas D. Clark. LC 77-73703. (Kentucky Bicentennial Bookshelf Ser.). 147p. reprint ed. pap. 41.90 (*0-7837-5821-9*, 2045488) Bks Demand.

Agrarian Land Law in the Western World. Ed. by Wim Brussaard & Margaret R. Grossman. 280p. 1992. text ed. 94.00 (*0-85198-727-3*) CAB Intl.

Agrarian Legislation in India, 1793-1966, Vol. 1. D. C. Wakhwa. 865p. 1973. text ed. 30.00 (*0-86125-376-0*, Pub. by Orient Longman Ltd II) Apt Bks.

Agrarian Movement in North Dakota. Paul R. Fossum. LC 78-64116. (Johns Hopkins University. Studies in the Social Sciences. Thirtieth Ser. 1912: 1). 184p. reprint ed. 37.50 (*0-404-61231-8*) AMS Pr.

Agrarian Movements & Congress Politics in Bihar, 1927-1947. K. K. Sharma. 1989. 23.00 (*81-85150-10-9*, Pub. by Usha II) S Asia.

Agrarian Movements in India: Studies on 20th Century Bihar. Ed. by Arvind N. Das. (Library of Peasant Studies: No. 5). (Illus.). 200p. 1982. text ed. 35.00 (*0-7146-3216-3*, Pub. by F Cass Pubs UK) Intl Spec Bk.

Agrarian Origins of American Capitalism. Allan Kulikoff. LC 92-11395. (Illus.). 400p. (C). 1992. text ed. 49.50 (*0-8139-1388-8*); pap. text ed. 18.95 (*0-8139-1420-5*) U Pr of Va.

Agrarian Origins of Commerce & Industry: A Study of Peasant Marketing to Indonesia. Yujiro Hayami & Toshihiko Kawagoe. LC 92-18420. 1993. text ed. 69.95 (*0-312-08621-0*) St Martin.

Agrarian Origins of Modern Japan. Thomas C. Smith. LC 59-7429. xiv, 250p. 1959. 35.00 (*0-8047-0530-5*); pap. 11.95 (*0-8047-0531-3*) Stanford U Pr.

Agrarian Policies & Problems in Communist & Noncommunist Countries. Ed. by W. A. Jackson. LC 75-103292. (Publications on Russia & Eastern Europe of the School of International Studies: No. 2). (Illus.). 497p. 1971. 35.00 (*0-295-95063-3*) U of Wash Pr.

Agrarian Policies in Communist Europe: A Critical Introduction, Vol. 1. Karl-Eugen Wadekin. Ed. by Everett M. Jacobs. LC 79-55000. (Studies in East European & Soviet Russian Agrarian Policy: Vol. 1). (Illus.). 336p. 1982. text ed. 43.00 (*0-916672-40-9*); pap. 18.25 (*0-86598-084-5*) Rowman.

Agrarian Policy of the Chinese Communist Party, Nineteen Twenty-One to Nineteen Fifty-Nine. Chao Kuo-Chun. LC 77-14587. 1978. reprint ed. text ed. 59.75 (*0-8371-9861-5*, CHAP, Greenwood Pr) Greenwood.

Agrarian Policy of the Russian Socialist-Revolutionary Party from Its Origins Through the Revolution of 1905-1907. Maureen Perrie. LC 76-644. (Soviet & East European Studies). 228p. reprint ed. pap. 65.00 (*0-8357-5263-1*, 2030613) Bks Demand.

Agrarian Question & Reformism in Latin America. Alain De Janvry. LC 81-4147. (Illus.). 352p. 1981. pap. text ed. 15.95x (*0-8018-2532-6*) Johns Hopkins.

Agrarian Question & the Peasant Movement in Colombia: Struggles of the National Peasant Association, 1967-1981. Leon Zamosc. (Cambridge Latin American Studies: No. 58). (Illus.). 336p. 1986. 69.95 (*0-521-32010-0*) Cambridge U Pr.

Agrarian Question in India: Some Perspectives. M. Kistaiah & M. Srinivasulu. 1993. text ed. 22.50 (*81-207-1477-6*, Pub. by Sterling Pubs II) Apt Bks.

Agrarian Question in North Vietnam, 1974-1979: A Study of Cooperator Resistance to State Policy. Adam Fforde. LC 88-6726. 288p. 1989. text ed. 62.95 (*0-87332-486-2*) M E Sharpe.

Agrarian Question in Socialist Transitions. Ed. by Ashwani Saith. 256p. 1986. 30.00 (*0-7146-3276-7*, Pub. by F Cass Pubs UK) Intl Spec Bk.

Agrarian Questions. Ed. by Kaushik Basu. (Oxford in India Readings: Themes in Economics). 256p. 1994. 24.00 (*0-685-69207-8*) OUP.

Agrarian Radicalism in China, 1968-1981. David Zweig. LC 88-21261. (East Asian Ser.: No. 102). (Illus.). 288p. 1989. 37.00x (*0-674-01175-9*) HUP.

Agrarian Radicalism in South India. Marshall M. Bouton. LC 85-3411. (Illus.). 336p. 1985. pap. 57.50 (*0-691-07686-3*) Princeton U Pr.

***Agrarian Radicalism in South India.** Marshall M. Bouton. LC 85-3411. reprint ed. pap. 99.20 (*0-7837-9302-2*, 2060042) Bks Demand.

Agrarian Radicalism in Veracruz, 1920-38. Heather F. Salamini. LC 77-26106. 259p. reprint ed. pap. 73.90 (*0-8357-3813-2*, 2036540) Bks Demand.

Agrarian Reform & Grassroots Development: Ten Case Studies. Ed. by Roy L. Prosterman et al. LC 90-8493. 342p. 1990. lib. bdg. 40.00 (*1-55587-231-X*) Lynne Rienner.

Agrarian Reform & Official Development Assistance in the Philippines: Four Papers. J. Putzel et al. (Occasional Papers). (Illus.). 135p. 1990. 15.00 (*0-317-05274-8*, Pub. by CSEAS UK) Cellar.

Agrarian Reform & Peasant Economy in Southern Peru. David Guillet. LC 78-19644. (Illus.). 244p. 1979. text ed. 30.00 (*0-8262-0263-2*) U of Mo Pr.

Agrarian Reform & Peasant Organization on the Ecuadorian Coast. M. R. Redclift. (Institute of Latin American Studies Monographs: No. 8). (Illus.). 186p. (C). 1978. text ed. 44.50 (*0-485-17708-0*, Pub. by Athlone Pr UK) Humanities.

Agrarian Reform & Rural Reconstruction: A Seminar Report. Edward P. Reed. 66p. pap. text ed. 6.50 (*0-942717-00-7*) Intl Inst Rural.

Agrarian Reform & Social Transformation: Preconditions for Development. Rehman Sobhan. LC 92-42280. (Illus.). 160p. (C). 1993. text ed. 49.95 (*1-85649-169-2*, Pub. by Zed Books UK); pap. 17.50 (*1-85649-170-6*, Pub. by Zed Books UK) Humanities.

Agrarian Reform As Unfinished Business: The Selected Papers of Wolf Ladejinsky. Wolf Ladejinsky. Ed. by Louis Walinsky. (World Bank Research Publications Ser.). 1977. 35.00 (*0-19-920095-5*) OUP.

Agrarian Reform in Contemporary Developing Countries. Ed. by Ajit K. Ghose. LC 83-13703. 384p. 1983. text ed. 39.95 (*0-312-01445-7*) St Martin.

Agrarian Reform in El Salvador: A Program of Rural Pacification. 21p. 1980. pap. 2.50 (*0-317-03387-5*) EPICA.

***Agrarian Reform in Ethiopia.** Rahmato. Date not set. per. 7.95 (*0-932415-07-5*) Red Sea Pr.

Agrarian Reform in Latin America: An Annotated Bibliography. LC 74-29076. (Land Economics Monographs: No. 5). 684p. 1975. 40.00 (*0-299-95030-1*); pap. 20.00 (*0-299-95034-4*) U of Wis Pr.

***Agrarian Reform in the Philippines: Democratic Transitions & Redistributive Reform.** Jeffrey M. Riedinger. LC 94-44005. 386p. 1995. 45.00x (*0-8047-2530-6*) Stanford U Pr.

Agrarian Reforms in India: Critical Analysis. D. S. Sastry. (C). 1991. 44.00 (*0-685-54510-5*, Pub. by Anmol II) S Asia.

Agrarian Relation in Transition: Caste - Class Relation & Dynamics of Land Transfer, Vol. 1. Binoy N. Verma. (Illus.). xviii, 170p. 1993. 24.00 (*81-7024-571-0*, Pub. by Ashish Pub Hse II) Nataraj Bks.

Agrarian Relation Institutional Change & Colonial Legacy: The Case of Eastern India, Vol. 3. Binoy N. Verma. (Illus.). xiv, 355p. 1993. 24.00 (*81-7024-573-7*, Pub. by Ashish Pub Hse II) Nataraj Bks.

Agrarian Relations & Accumulation: The "Mode of Production" Debate in India. Ed. by Utsa Patnaik. 280p. 1991. 24.95 (*0-19-562565-X*) OUP.

Agrarian Relations & Peasant in Modern Andhra. D. Subramanyam Reddy. 1990. 16.00 (*81-7035-073-5*, Pub. by Daya Pub Hse II) S Asia.

Agrarian Relations & Rural Exploitation. B. C. Mehta. 268p. (C). 1987. 31.50 (*81-7024-163-4*, Pub. by Ashish II) S Asia.

Agrarian Relations in India. Arvind Dass. 1980. 18.50 (*0-685-04705-9*, Pub. by Manohar II) S Asia.

Agrarian Relations in the Ottoman Empire in the Fifteenth & Sixteenth Centuries. Vera P. Moutafchieva. (East European Monographs: No. 251). 200p. 1988. text ed. 34.50 (*0-88033-148-8*) East Eur Quarterly.

Agrarian Relations in West Bengal. Ashok Rudra & P. K. Barhan. 1982. 12.50 (*0-8364-0922-1*, Pub. by Somaiya) S Asia.

Agrarian Revolt in a Mexican Village. Paul Friedrich. LC 77-89627. (Illus.). 1977. reprint ed. pap. text ed. 9.95 (*0-226-26481-5*, P832) U Ch Pr.

Agrarian Revolution: Social Movements & Export Agriculture in the Underdeveloped World. Jeffery M. Paige. LC 74-25601. 1978. pap. 14.95 (*0-02-923550-2*) Free Pr.

Agrarian Revolution in Georgia, 1865-1912. Robert P. Brooks. LC 72-181919. reprint ed. 31.50 (*0-404-00007-X*) AMS Pr.

Agrarian Revolution in Georgia, 1865-1912. Robert P. Brooks. LC 73-129939. 129p. 1970. reprint ed. text ed. 35.00 (*0-8371-1603-1*, BRG&, Negro U Pr) Greenwood.

Agrarian Social Structure: Continuity & Change in Bihar, 1786-1920. Manoshi Mitra. 1986. 27.00 (*0-8364-1622-8*, Pub. by Manohar II) S Asia.

Agrarian Society of the Punjab, 1849-1901. Himadri Banerjee. 1983. 24.00 (*0-8364-0968-X*, Pub. by Manohar II) S Asia.

Agrarian Sociology of Ancient Civilizations. Max M. Weber. 384p. 1988. pap. text ed. 18.95 (*0-86091-938-2*, Pub. by Verso UK) Routledge Chapman & Hall.

Agrarian Structure & Economic Underdevelopment. K. Basu. (Fundamentals of Pure & Applied Economics Ser.: Vol. 37). x, 102p. 1990. pap. text ed. 27.00 (*3-7186-4993-4*) Gordon & Breach.

Agrarian Structure & Labor Migration in Rural Mexico. Kenneth D. Roberts. (Research Report Ser.: No. 30). 46p. (Orig.). (C). 1981. ring bd. 5.00 (*0-935391-29-0*, RR-30) UCSD Ctr US-Mex.

***Agrarian Structure & Political Power: Landlord & Peasant in the Making of Latin America.** Ed. by Evelyne Huber & Frank Safford. LC 95-16082. (Latin American Ser.). 1995. write for info. (*0-8229-3880-4*); pap. write for info. (*0-8229-5564-4*) U of Pittsburgh Pr.

Agrarian Structure & Political Power in Mexico. Roger Bartra. Tr. by Stephen K. Ault. LC 92-11605. 256p. 1993. text ed. 45.00 (*0-8018-4398-7*); pap. text ed. 14.95 (*0-8018-4542-4*) Johns Hopkins.

Agrarian Structure & Productivity in Developing Countries. Albert R. Berry & William R. Cline. LC 78-20524. 1979. text ed. 38.50x (*0-8018-2190-8*) Johns Hopkins.

Agrarian Structure in Central India & the Northern Decca, 300-500 A.D. A Study of Lakataka Inscriptions. K. M. Shrimali. 134p. (C). 1987. 20.00 (*81-215-0050-8*, Pub. by Munshiram Manoharial II) S Asia.

Agrarian Structure of Bangladesh. F. T. Jannuzi & James T. Peach. 156p. 1982. pap. text ed. 11.95 (*0-86131-434-4*, Pub. by Orient Longman Ltd II) Apt Bks.

Agrarian Structures & Agrarian Reform. Suleiman Cohen. (Studies in Development & Planning: Vol. 8). 1978. lib. bdg. 37.00 (*90-207-0764-7*) Kluwer Ac.

***Agrarian System in Eastern Bengal C 1870-1910.** Nariaki Nakazato. (C). 1994. 27.50x (*81-7074-145-9*, Pub. by KP Bagchi IA) S Asia.

Agrarian System of Eastern Rajasthan. Satya P. Gupta. 352p. (C). 1986. 32.00 (*81-85054-11-8*, Pub. by Manohar II) S Asia.

Agrarian System of Moslem India. William H. Moreland. 314p. reprint ed. text ed. 27.50 (*0-685-13416-4*) Coronet Bks.

Agrarian System of the Sikhs Seventeen Fifty-Nine to Eighteen Forty-Nine. Indu Banga. 1979. 18.50 (*0-88386-758-3*) S Asia.

Agrarian Systems & Rural Development. Ed. by Dharam Ghai et al. LC 79-16547. 375p. 1980. 49.50 (*0-8419-0541-X*) Holmes & Meier.

Agrarian Tension & Conflict, Vol. 2. Binoy N. Verma & Neelam Verma. (Illus.). xviii, 199p. 1993. 24.00 (*81-7024-572-9*, Pub. by Ashish Pub Hse II) Nataraj Bks.

Agrarian Transformations: Local Processes & the State in Southeast Asia. Ed. by Gillian Hart et al. (C). 1989. pap. 15.00 (*0-520-07884-5*) U CA Pr.

Agrarian Transition in America: Dualism & Change. Wayne Rohrer & Louis H. Douglas. LC 68-15586. 1969. 29.50 (*0-672-60806-5*) Irvington.

Agrarian Unrest & Socio-Economic Change, 1900-1980. Arvind Das. 1983. 28.00 (*0-8364-0967-1*, Pub. by Manohar II) S Asia.

Agrarian Unrest in Karnataka. D. Murahari Naik. (Sociological Publications in Honour of Dr. K. Ishwaran: No. 4). xiv, 134p. 1990. text ed. 25.00 (*81-85047-45-6*, Pub. by Reliance Pub Hse II) Apt Bks.

Agrarian Unrest in the Philippines: Guardia de Honor - Revitalization within the Revolution & Rizalistas - Contemporary Revitalization Movements in the Philippines. LC 71-42704. (Papers in International Studies: Southeast Asia Ser.: No. 8). 50p. reprint ed. pap. 25.00 (*0-8357-5264-X*, 2004379) Bks Demand.

Agrarian Urban Economy & Social Change. Gita Bajpal. (C). 1989. 29.50 (*81-7035-053-0*, Pub. by Daya Pub Hse II) S Asia.

Agrarian Warlord: Saturnino Cedillo & the Mexican Revolution in San Luis Potosi. Dudley Ankerson. LC 84-20683. 303p. 1985. 32.00 (*0-87580-101-3*) N Ill U Pr.

An Asterisk (*) at the beginning of an entry indicates that the title is appearing in BIP for the first time.

143

Agrarian Women: Wives & Mothers in Rural Nebraska, 1880-1940. Deborah Fink. LC 91-31410. (Studies in Rural Culture). (Illus.). xxiv, 242p. (C). 1992. 37.50 (0-8078-2019-9); pap. 13.95 (0-8078-4364-4) U of NC Pr.

Agrarianism & Reconstruction Politics: The Southern Homestead Act. Michael L. Lanza. LC 89-12137. 184p. 1990. text ed. 25.00 (0-8071-1545-2) La State U Pr.

Agrarians & Aristocrats: Party Political Ideology in the United States, 1837-1846. John Ashworth. (Royal Historical Society Ser.: No. 37). 327p. 1983. 59.00 (0-901050-87-3) Boydell & Brewer.

Agreed Frontier: Ladakh & India's Northernmost Borders. Parshotam Mehra. (Illus.). 264p. 1993. 23.00 (0-19-562758-X) OUP.

Agreement. Douglas Taylor. 1967. pap. 2.75 (0-8222-0011-2) Dramatists Play.

Agreement: An Attitude of Prayer. Virginia Stephenson. 88p. 1991. reprint ed. pap. 6.95 (0-87516-638-5) DeVorss.

Agreement & Anti-Agreement. Susan Steele. (C). 1990. lib. bdg. 170.50 (0-7923-0260-5) Kluwer Ac.

Agreement, & Back. Theodore Enslin. 1969. 5.00 (0-685-00999-8) Elizabeth Pr.

Agreement & Innovation. Vittorio Dimartino & Peter Cressey. 256p. 53.33 (0-13-019548-0) P-H.

Agreement Between EEC & Polish Peoples Republic on Trade & Comm & Econ Co-Op...EC, No. 10. HMSO Staff. (Command Paper Ser.: No. 1421). 60p. 1991. pap. 18.00 (0-10-114212-9, HM8127) UNIPUB.

Agreement Between the Inuit of the Nunavut Settlement Area & Her Majesty the Queen in Right of Canada. (Illus.). 282p. (Orig.). (C). 1994. pap. text ed. 60.00 (0-7881-0487-X) Diane Pub.

Agreement in Natural Language: Approaches, Theories, Descriptions. Ed. by Michael Barlow & Charles A. Ferguson. LC 86-71109. 355p. (Orig.). 1988. text ed. 35.00 (0-937073-02-4) Ctr Study Language.

Agreement of Indemnity: Practical Applications by the Surety. LC 89-82253. 230p. 1990. pap. 44.95 (0-89707-516-1, 519-0126) Amer Bar Assn.

Agreement on the European Economic Area (EEA) A Guide to the Free Movement of Goods & Competition Rules. Therese Blanchet et al. 500p. 1994. 79.00 (0-19-825892-5); pap. 39.95 (0-19-825884-4) OUP.

Agreement on the European Economic Area with Final Act & Declaration E. C., No. 7 (92) HMSO Staff. (Command Paper Ser.: No. 2073). 567p. 1992. pap. 75.00 (0-10-120732-8, HM07328, Pub. by HMSO UK) UNIPUB.

Agreement Relating to Community Patents: (European Communities, 1991, No. 22) HMSO Staff. (Command Paper Ser.: No. 1452). 72p. 1991. pap. 18.00 (0-10-114522-5, HM5252) UNIPUB.

Agreement to Seek Reconciliation Through Christian Mediation (Agreeing to Agree in Obedience to God, Jo. 14: 21, 23; ICor. 6: 1-10; Jo. 15: 12) Robert Abarno. 1991. write for info. (0-9631575-9-0) R Abarno.

Agreements & Working Arrangements with Other International Organizations: Basic Documents, No. 3. World Meteorological Organization Staff. (WMO Ser.: No. 60). 1988. 35.00 (0-685-47335-X, Pub. by Wrld Meteorological SZ); ring bd. 20.00 (92-63-10060-8, Pub. by Wrld Meteorological SZ) Am Meteorological.

Agreements for Employee Leasing. T. Joe Willey. (Illus.). 208p. (C). Date not set. student ed, audio 150.00 (0-944308-08-2) Aegis Consulting.

Agreements of the People's Republic of China. 2nd rev. ed. Wolfgang Bartke. 660p. 1992. lib. bdg. 135.00 (3-598-10840-0) K G Saur.

Agreements of the People's Republic of China: A Calendar of Events, 1966-1980. Hungdah Chiu. LC 81-8686. 350p. 1981. text ed. 75.00 (0-275-90594-2, C0594, Praeger Pubs) Greenwood.

Agrest & Gandelsonas, Works. Diana Agrest & Mario Gandelsonas. LC 94-30361. (Illus.). 304p. 1994. 60.00 (0-910413-28-2); pap. 40.00 (1-878271-90-3) Princeton Arch.

Agri-Culture: Farmers, Artists of New Jersey. Ori Z. Soltes & Marion Monk. (Illus.). (Orig.). Date not set. pap. text ed. write for info. (1-881456-05-6) B B K Natl Jew Mus.

Agri-Diagnostics Markets. (Market Research Reports: No. 242). (Illus.). 96p. 1992. 295.00 (0-317-04976-3) Theta Corp.

Agri Selling. 2nd ed. W. David Downey et al. LC 82-73827. 238p. 1984. 21.95 (0-930264-50-9) Century Comm.

Agribusiness. Boy Scouts of America. (Illus.). 72p. (Orig.). (YA). (gr. 6-12). 1987. pap. 1.85 (0-8395-3272-5, 3272) BSA.

Agribusiness: An Entrepreneurial Approach. William H. Hamilton. 1991. text ed. 29.50 (0-8273-4447-3); teacher ed 10.00 (0-8273-4448-1) Delmar.

Agribusiness: An Entrepreneurial Approach Workbook. William H. Hamilton & Donald F. Connelly. 98p. 1993. 15.95 (0-8273-5961-6) Delmar.

Agribusiness - An Entrepreneurial Approach: Instructor's Guide to Accompany Workbook. William H. Hamilton & Donald F. Connelly. 39p. 1993. 10.00 (0-8273-6480-6) Delmar.

Agribusiness Accounting & Taxation: (Including '86 TRA Supplement) Maydew. 368p. 1986. 39.50 (0-318-33074-1, 5421) Commerce.

Agribusiness & Rural Enterprise. B. H. Kinsey. 240p. 1987. 59.95 (0-7099-1558-6, Pub. by Croom Helm UK) Routledge Chapman & Hall.

Agribusiness Education in Transition: Strategies for Change, Report of the National Agribusiness Education Commission, June 1989. Lincoln Institute of Land Policy Staff. Ed. by W. David Downey. 80p. reprint ed. pap. 25.00 (0-7837-2162-5, 2042467) Bks Demand.

Agribusiness Finance. Gary T. Devino. 166p. 1981. pap. 18.60x (0-8134-2191-8) Interstate.

***Agribusiness Finance.** Gary T. Devino. 166p. 1981. pap. text ed. 13.95x (0-685-02528-4) Interstate.

Agribusiness in Africa. Barbara Dinham et al. 224p. (C). 1984. 29.95 (0-86543-003-9); pap. text ed. 9.95 (0-86543-004-7) Africa World.

***Agribusiness in Peru 1990-91.** Ed. by Jonathan Cavanagh. 208p. (ENG & SPA.). 1990. pap. 50.00 (1-886617-12-0) Peru Rept.

***Agribusiness in Peru 1995.** Ed. by Jonathan Cavanagh. 208p. (ENG & SPA.). 1995. pap. 85.00 (1-886617-04-X) Peru Rept.

Agribusiness in the Americas. Roger Burbach & Patricia Flynn. (Illus.). 314p. 1980. lib. bdg. 16.00 (0-916024-40-7); pap. 7.50 (0-916024-41-5) NA Cong Lat Am.

***Agribusiness in the Americas.** Roger Burbach & Patricia Flynn. LC 80-17114. reprint ed. pap. 89.50 (0-7837-9609-9, 2060366) Bks Demand.

Agribusiness Management. 2nd ed. David Downey & Steven Erickson. 1987. text ed. write for info. (0-07-017667-1) McGraw.

Agribusiness Marketing: The Management Perspective. James G. Beierlein & Michael W. Woolverton. 352p. 1990. text ed. 77.00 (0-13-019480-8) P-H.

Agribusiness Procedures & Practices. Delene W. Lee & Jasper S. Lee. (Career Preparation for Agriculture-Agribusiness Ser.). (Illus.). 1980. text ed. 16.96 (0-07-036737-X) McGraw.

***Agribusiness Reforms in China: The Case of Wool.** J. W. Longworth & C. G. Brown. 280p. 1995. 70.00x (0-85198-951-9) CAB Intl.

Agribusiness Safety. Center for Occupational Research & Development Staff. (Job Safety & Health Instructional Materials Ser.). (Illus.). 38p. (C). 1981. pap. text ed. 3.25 (1-55502-093-3) CORD Commns.

***Agricide: The Hidden Crisis That Affects Us All.** Michael W. Fox. 1995. write for info. (0-89464-945-0) Krieger.

Agricola. Tacitus. Ed. by D. Soulsby. (Cambridge Latin Texts Ser.). (Illus.). 64p. 1973. pap. 7.50 (0-521-20308-2) Cambridge U Pr.

Agricola: A Study of Agriculture & Rustic Life in the Greco-Roman World from the Point of View of Labour. William E. Heitland. LC 69-13929. 492p. 1970. reprint ed. text ed. 41.50 (0-8371-4088-9, HEAG, Greenwood Pr) Greenwood.

Agricola & the Germania. Tacitus. Tr. by Hugh Mattingly. (Classics Ser.). 1971. mass mkt. 9.95 (0-14-044241-3, Penguin Classics) Viking Penguin.

Agricola, Vol. I: Germania, Agricola. Tacitus. (Loeb Classical Library: No. 35). 374p. 1994. 18.95 (0-674-99039-0) HUP.

Agricultrual Land Evaluation & Site Assessment: Status of State & Local Programs. Frederick Steiner et al. 400p. 1991. pap. text ed. 45.00 (1-884320-01-5) ASU Herberger Ctr.

Agricultura: Spanish Take-Home Parent Pack, Set. (Take-Home Parent Packs Ser.). (Illus.). (Orig.). (SPA.). 1993. pap. 11.95 (1-56334-389-4) Hampton-Brown.

Agricultura: Teacher's Theme Guide. (Que Maravilla! Ser.). (Illus.). (Orig.). (SPA.). 1992. pap. 29.95 (1-56334-166-2) Hampton-Brown.

Agricultural Adjustment. Adjustment Administration, U. S. Department of Agriculture Staff. LC 75-27634. (World Food Supply Ser.). (Illus.). 1976. reprint ed. 35.95 (0-405-07776-9) Ayer.

Agricultural Alcohol & Social Change in the Third World. T. Kortteinen. (Finnish Foundation for Alcohol Studies: Vol. 38). 1989. 20.00 (951-9192-42-5) Rutgers Ctr Alcohol.

Agricultural Alternatives & Nutritional Self-Sufficiency: Proceedings of the 7th International Scientific Conference of IFOAM in Burkina Faso. Ed. by A. Djigma et al. 429p. (Orig.). 1989. pap. 29.95 (3-927080-13-6, Pub. by IFOAM SZ) Ag Access.

Agricultural & Animal Sciences Journals & Serials: An Analytical Guide. Richard D. Jensen & Nathan M. Smith. LC 85-27133. (Annotated Bibliographies of Serials: A Subject Approach Ser.: No. 4). 234p. 1986. text ed. 65.00 (0-313-24331-X, JA) Greenwood.

Agricultural & Environmental Policies: Opportunities for Integration. OECD Staff. 200p. (Orig.). Date not set. pap. text ed. 22.00 (92-64-13127-2, 97-88-04-1) OECD.

Agricultural & Environmental Policy Integration: Recent Progress & New Directions. OECD Staff. 112p. (Orig.). 1993. pap. 24.00 (92-64-13820-X) OECD.

Agricultural & Environmental Resource Economics. Ed. by Gerald A. Carlson et al. LC 92-21524. (Oxford Biological Resource Management Ser.). 544p. 1993. 45.00 (0-19-507651-6) OUP.

Agricultural & Food Marketing in Developing Countries: Selected Readings. Ed. by John Abbott. 408p. (C). 1993. pap. text ed. 46.50 (0-85198-804-0) CAB Intl.

***Agricultural & Food Policy.** 3rd ed. Ronald D. Knutson et al. LC 94-35147. 480p. 1995. text ed. 70.00 (0-13-019860-9) P-H.

Agricultural & Food Processing Wastes: Proceedings of the 6th International Symposium on Agricultural & Food Processing Wastes. LC 90-85958. 547p. 1990. 57.00 (0-929355-10-5, P0590) Am Soc Ag Eng.

Agricultural & Food Sector in the New Global Era. Alessandro Bonanno. 1993. 28.00 (81-7022-464-0, Pub. by Concept II) S Asia.

Agricultural & Horticultural Engineering. Clifford J. Studman. 500p. 1990. pap. text ed. 59.95 (0-409-60469-0) Buttrwrth-Heinemann.

Agricultural & Hunting Methods of the Navaho Indians. Willard W. Hill. LC 76-43742. (Yale Univ. Publications in Anthropology: No. 18). reprint ed. 32.50 (0-404-15583-9) AMS Pr.

Agricultural & Socioeconomic Perspectives of Arkansas Counties & Regions. Ralph O. Gunderson & Enrique Ospina. (Illus.). 129p. 1987. per. 7.00 (0-933595-13-1) Winrock Intl.

Agricultural & Synthetic Polymers: Buiodegradability & Utilization. Ed. by Haas Company Staff et al. LC 90-39043. (ACS Symposium Ser.: No. 433). (Illus.). 328p. (C). 1990. 69.95 (0-8412-1816-1) Am Chemical.

Agricultural & Urban Considerations in Irrigation & Drainage: Selected Papers from Specialty Conference, Fort Collins, Colorado, April 22-24. American Society of Civil Engineers Staff. 808p. reprint ed. pap. 180.00 (0-8357-5265-8, 2022520) Bks Demand.

***Agricultural & Veterinary Sciences International Who's Who.** 5th ed. 1248p. 1994. 595.00 (1-56159-121-1, Stockton Pr) Groves Dictionaries.

Agricultural & Veterinary Sciences International Who's Who, 2 Vols., Set. 3rd ed. 1400p. 1987. 450.00 (0-582-90159-6, Pub. by Longman Grp UK) Gale.

Agricultural Approach to Family Planning. Demetrio M. Maglalang. 159p. 1976. pap. text ed. 9.00 (0-942717-01-5) Intl Inst Rural.

Agricultural Aspects of Soil Disinfestation: Proceedings of the International Symposium, Louvain, 1973. Ed. by C. Van Assche. (Agro-Ecosystems Ser.: Vol. 1, No. 3). 1974. 20.50 (0-686-43413-7) Elsevier.

Agricultural Aviation. Miles E. Gibson. 100p. (Orig.). 1974. pap. 9.95 (0-942306-02-3) Diversified Pub Co.

Agricultural Bioethics: Implications of Agricultural Biotechnology. Ed. by Steven M. Gendel et al. LC 89-15598. (Illus.). 382p. 1990. text ed. 37.95 (0-8138-0129-X) Iowa St U Pr.

***Agricultural Biotechnology: An Economic Perspective.** M. F. Caswell et al. 52p. (Orig.). (C). 1994. pap. text ed. 35.00x (0-7881-1282-1) Diane Pub.

Agricultural Biotechnology: Country Case Studies. G. J. Persley. 450p. Date not set. write for info. (0-85198-816-4) CAB Intl.

Agricultural Biotechnology: Opportunities for International Development. Gabrielle J. Persley. (Biotechnology in Agriculture Ser.: No. 2). 528p. 1991. text ed. 119.50 (0-85198-643-9) CAB Intl.

Agricultural Biotechnology: Prospects for the Third World. Ed. by John W. Farrington. 88p. (C). 1990. pap. text ed. 31.00 (0-8133-1082-2) Westview.

Agricultural Biotechnology: Staggering Opportunities in World's Largest Market. Market Intelligence Staff. 323p. (Orig.). 1992. 1,895.00 (1-56753-037-0) Frost & Sullivan.

Agricultural Biotechnology: Strategies for National Competitiveness. National Research Council Staff. LC 87-12181. 221p. reprint ed. pap. 63.00 (0-7837-2776-3, 2043167) Bks Demand.

Agricultural Biotechnology: The Next "Green Revolution"? (Technical Paper Ser.: No. 133). 62p. 1991. pap. 6.95 (0-8213-1741-5, 11741) World Bank.

***Agricultural Biotechnology Markets.** Market Intelligence Staff. 263p. 1994. 1,995.00 (0-7889-0071-4) Frost & Sullivan.

Agricultural Buildings & Structures. Whitaker. (Illus.). 1979. teacher ed write for info. (0-8359-0177-7, Reston) P-H.

Agricultural Change. Tony McAleavy. (C). 1988. 40.00 (0-7157-2769-9) St Mut.

Agricultural Change: Policy & Practice, 1500-1750. Ed. by Joan Thirsk. (C). 1990. pap. 34.95 (0-521-36882-0) Cambridge U Pr.

Agricultural Change & Rural Poverty: Variations on a Theme by Dharm Narain. Ed. by John W. Mellor & Gunvant M. Desai. LC 85-50. 256p. 1985. 28.50 (0-8018-3275-6) Johns Hopkins.

Agricultural Change & the Peasant Economy of South China. Evelyn S. Rawski. LC 77-173407. (Harvard East Asian Ser.: No. 66). 300p. reprint ed. pap. 85.50 (0-7837-1525-0, 2041802) Bks Demand.

Agricultural Change, Environment & Economy: Essays in Honour of W. B. Morgan. Ed. by Keith Hoggard. (Global Development & the Environment Ser.). 272p. 1992. text ed. 90.00 (0-7201-2127-2, Mansell Pub) Cassell.

Agricultural, Chemical, & Pesticide Hazards. Center for Occupational Research & Development Staff. (Job Safety & Health Instructional Materials Ser.). (Illus.). 28p. (C). 1981. pap. text ed. 2.50 (1-55502-148-4) CORD Commns.

Agricultural Chemical Products. Ernest W. Flick. LC 88-23284. 327p. 1989. 48.00 (0-8155-1174-4) Noyes.

Agricultural Chemicals: Herbicides 1993, Bk. II. rev. ed. W. T. Thomson. 330p. (C). 1993. pap. 19.50 (0-913702-40-4) Thomson Pubns.

Agricultural Chemicals Book One: 1994-95: Insecticides. rev. ed. W. T. Thomson. 302p. 1994. pap. 24.95 (0-913702-33-1) Thomson Pubns.

Agricultural Chemicals Book Three: 1994-95: Fumigants, Growth Regulators, Repellents, Rodenticides. rev. ed. 210p. 1992. per., pap. 24.95 (0-913702-37-4) Thomson Pubns.

Agricultural Chemicals-Hazard Response Handbook. Euan Wallace. 334p. 1990. pap. 50.00 (0-318-19715-4) Thomson Pubns.

Agricultural Chemicals Ind. Regulations, Tech. Economics Change. 186p. 1991. 1,950.00 (0-685-49394-6, C119) BCC.

Agricultural Chemicals of the Future (BARC VIII) James L. Hilton. LC 84-9936. (Illus.). 480p. (C). 1985. text ed. 81.00 (0-86598-138-8) Rowman.

Agricultural Chemicals, 1993 Bk. 4: Fungicides. rev. ed. W. T. Thomson. LC 64-24795. 198p. 1993. pap. 19.50 (0-913702-48-X) Thomson Pubns.

Agricultural Choice & Change: Decision Making in a Costa Rican Community. Peggy F. Barlett. LC 81-13835. (Illus.). 206p. reprint ed. pap. 59.30 (0-8357-7940-8, 2057013) Bks Demand.

Agricultural Colonization of the Zionist Organization in Palestine. Arthur Ruppin. Tr. by R. J. Feiwel. LC 75-6451. (Rise of Jewish Nationalism & the Middle East Ser.). vii, 209p. 1975. reprint ed. 20.35 (0-88355-337-6) Hyperion Conn.

Agricultural, Commercial & Financial Interests of Ceylon: With an Appendix; Containing Some of the Principal Laws & Usages of the Candians. Anthony Bertolacci. 1993. reprint ed. 45.00 (81-7013-102-2, Pub. by Navrang) S Asia.

Agricultural Commercialization & Government Policy in Africa. Jan Hinderink & J. J. Sterkenburg. (Monographs from the African Studies Centre, Leiden). 1987. text ed. 65.00 (0-7103-0205-3, Pub. by Kegan Paul Intl UK) Routledge Chapman & Hall.

Agricultural Commercialization, Economic Development, & Nutrition. Ed. by Joachim Von Braun & Eileen Kennedy. LC 93-30256. 1994. text ed. 57.50 (0-8018-4759-1) Johns Hopkins.

Agricultural Commercialization, Nutrition, & the Rural Poor: A Study of Philippine Farm Households. Howarth E. Bouis & Lawrence J. Haddad. LC 90-8074. 190p. 1990. lib. bdg. 32.00 (1-55587-206-9) Lynne Rienner.

Agricultural Commodity Markets: A Guide to Futures Trading. Michael Atkin. (Commodities Ser.). 240p. 1989. 79.95 (0-415-01887-0, A3204) Routledge.

Agricultural Communication Networks. D. P. Gogoi. 200p. 1989. text ed. 25.00 (81-7027-128-2, Pub. by Radiant Pubs II) S Asia.

Agricultural Compendium: For Rural Development in the Tropics & Subtropics. Euroconsult Staff. 740p. 1989. 64.00 (0-444-42905-0) Elsevier.

Agricultural Cooperation: Selected Readings. Ed. by Martin A. Abrahamsen & Claud L. Scroggs. LC 57-7008. 590p. reprint ed. pap. 168.20 (0-8357-5266-6, 2055833) Bks Demand.

Agricultural Cooperatives: Their Why & Their How. Glynn McBride. (Illus.). 1986. text ed. 62.95 (0-87055-534-0) AVI.

Agricultural Cooperatives in Transition. Ed. by Yoav Kislev & Csaba Csaki. LC 93-15758. (C). 1993. Alk. paper. pap. text ed. 69.50 (0-8133-8759-0) Westview.

Agricultural Credit: A Global Enigma. Jack D. Hartman. 158p. 1985. pap. 8.95x (0-8134-2446-1, 2246) Interstate.

***Agricultural Credit: A Global Enigma.** Jack D. Hartman. 158p. 1985. pap. text ed. 8.95x (0-685-10592-X) Interstate.

Agricultural Credit & Finance. H. Clay Little. 112p. 1988. per., pap. 22.95 (0-8403-4726-X) Kendall-Hunt.

Agricultural Credit & Rural Development in Drought Regions: A Study of Cooperative Banks of A. P. C. S. Rayudu. (C). 1992. text ed. 21.00 (81-7022-385-7, Pub. by Concept II) S Asia.

Agricultural Credit Bibliography. Incl. 43p. 1979. pap. 8.00 (92-5-000689-6, F1821, FAO); 204p. (J). (gr. 2). 86.15 (0-317-02295-4, 4-09020-00); 1985 56p. 1984. pap. 10.00 (92-5-002146-1, F2681 ,FAO); 1985 56p. 1984. pap. 10.00 (92-5-002146-1, F2681 ,FAO); write for info. (0-318-60632-1) UNIPUB.

Agricultural Credit Bibliography, No. 4. Incl. 43p. 1979. pap. 8.00 (92-5-000689-6, F1821, FAO); 204p. (J). (gr. 2). 86.15 (0-317-02295-4, 4-09020-00); 1985 56p. 1984. pap. 10.00 (92-5-002146-1, F2681 ,FAO); 1985 56p. 1984. pap. 10.00 (92-5-002146-1, F2681 ,FAO); (Agricultural Credit Bibliography). 44p. (ENG, FRE & SPA.). 1985. write for info. (92-5-002259-X, F2800) UNIPUB.

Agricultural Crisis: A Crisis of Culture. Wendell Berry. 41p. (gr. 8-12). 1977. write for info. (0-913098-28-0) Myrin Institute.

Agricultural Crisis in America. Barbara McEwan. (Contemporary World Issues Ser.). 260p. 1995. lib. bdg. 39.50 (0-87436-737-9) ABC-CLIO.

Agricultural Crop Issues & Policies. National Research Council, Committee on Managing Global Genetic Resources Staff. (Managing Global Genetic Resources Ser.). 480p. (C). 1994. text ed. 49.95 (0-309-04430-8) Natl Acad Pr.

Agricultural Database Management. Dick Landis & Edward Schmisseur. (C). 1985. text ed. 23.95 (0-8359-9130-X, Reston); pap. 19.95 (0-8359-9129-6, Reston) P-H.

Agricultural Decision Analysis. Jock R. Anderson et al. LC 76-46456. 354p. reprint ed. pap. 100.90 (0-8357-5267-4, 2029720) Bks Demand.

Agricultural Decision Making. Barlett. 1984. pap. text ed. 54.00 (0-12-078882-9) Acad Pr.

Agricultural Development: An International Perspective. rev. ed. Yujiro Hayami & Vernon W. Ruttan. LC 84-23386. (Studies in Development). 512p. 1985. text ed. 65.00 (0-8018-2348-X); pap. text ed. 22.95x (0-8018-2376-5) Johns Hopkins.

***Agricultural Development: Command Area Approach.** Raja Ram. (C). 1993. 32.00x (81-7017-299-3, Pub. by Abhinav II) S Asia.

Agricultural Development: Soil, Food, People, Work. Charles E. Kellogg. (Illus.). 233p. 1975. 8.75 (0-89118-763-4) Soil Sci Soc Am.

Agricultural Development & Economic Growth. Ed. by Herman M. Southworth & Bruce F. Johnston. (Illus.). 623p. 1967. 47.50 (0-8014-0405-3) Cornell U Pr.

Agricultural Development & Employment Patterns in India: A Comparative Analysis of Punjab & Bihar. M. R. Khurana. 1992. 20.00 (81-7022-439-X, Pub. by Concept II) S Asia.

An Asterisk (*) at the beginning of an entry indicates that the title is appearing in BIP for the first time.

Agricultural Development & Productivity: Lessons from the Chilean Experience. Pierre R. Crosson. LC 74-128181. (Resources for the Future Ser.). (Illus.). 214p. 1970. 16.50 (*0-8018-1216-X*) Johns Hopkins.

Agricultural Development & Productivity: Lessons from the Chilean Experience. Pierre R. Crosson. LC 74-128181. 216p. reprint ed. pap. 61.60 (*0-8357-5268-2*, 2030197) Bks Demand.

Agricultural Development & Rural Employment: A Mexican Dilemma. August Schumacher. (Research Report Ser.: No. 21). 37p. (Orig.). (C). 1981. ring bd. 5.00 (*0-935391-20-7*, RR-21) UCSD Ctr US-Mex.

Agricultural Development & Rural Labour: A Case Study of Punjab & Haryana. Harbans S. Sidhu. 1991. 28.50 (*81-7022-336-9*, Pub. by Concept II) S Asia.

Agricultural Development & Rural Poverty. Ajit K. Singh. 1986. 45.00 (*0-317-56199-5*, Pub. by Ashish II) S Asia.

Agricultural Development & Rural-Urban Disparities. Ed. by J. Mahendra Reddy & S. Kishen Rao. 288p. (C). 1991. text ed. 27.95 (*81-207-1315-X*, Pub. by Sterling Pubs II) Apt Bks.

Agricultural Development & Tenancy Disputes in Japan, 1870-1940. Richard J. Smethurst. LC 85-43313. (Illus.). 450p. 1986. text ed. 70.00x (*0-691-05468-1*) Princeton U Pr.

Agricultural Development Council: A History. Russell Stevenson & Virginia O. Locke. LC 88-28175. (Illus.). 226p. (Orig.). 1989. pap. 17.50 (*0-933595-15-8*) Winrock Intl.

Agricultural Development in Assam, 1950-85. Umananda Phukan. 1990. 21.50 (*81-7099-202-8*, Pub. by Mittal II) S Asia.

Agricultural Development in China. Ge Xiao-Jia & Shu-Min Huang. (Bibliographies in Technology & Social Change Ser.: No. 4). 46p. (Orig.). (C). 1988. pap. 6.00 (*0-945271-07-7*) ISU-TSCP.

Agricultural Development in India. D. S. Bisht. 332p. 1989. 140.00 (*81-7041-161-0*, Pub. by Scientific Pubs II) St Mut.

Agricultural Development in India: An Analytical State-Wide Study. M. Idris Siddiqi. 1990. 22.50 (*0-86132-215-0*, Pub. by Popular Prakashan II) S Asia.

Agricultural Development in India's Districts. Dorris D. Brown. LC 71-131467. (Center for International Affairs Ser.). 182p. 1971. 25.00 (*0-674-01230-5*) HUP.

Agricultural Development in Japan: The Land Improvement District in Concept & Practice. Gil Latz. (Research Papers Ser.: No. 225). (Illus.). 1989. pap. 12.00 (*0-89065-129-9*) U Chicago Comm Geo.

Agricultural Development in North-East India: Constraints & Prospects. Ed. by K. Alam. 1993. 30.00 (*81-7100-471-7*, Pub. by Deep) S Asia.

Agricultural Development in Southern Africa: Farm Household-Economics & the Food Crisis. Allan Low. 218p. 1989. pap. text ed. 22.50 (*0-435-08027-X*, 08027) Heinemann.

Agricultural Development in the Mekong Basin: Goals, Priorities, & Strategies: A Staff Study. Resources for the Future, Inc. Staff. LC 70-158820. 116p. reprint ed. pap. 33.10 (*0-8357-5269-0*, 2023810) Bks Demand.

***Agricultural Development in the Middle East.** fac. ed. Ed. by Peter Beaumont & Keith McLachlan. LC 85-6414. 361p. Date not set. pap. 102.90 (*0-7837-7372-2*, 2047182) Bks Demand.

Agricultural Development in the Third World. rev. ed. Ed. by Carl K. Eicher & John M. Staatz. LC 90-31729. (Johns Hopkins Studies in Development). 560p. 1990. pap. text ed. 65.00x (*0-8018-4000-7*) Johns Hopkins.

Agricultural Development in the Third World. 2nd rev. ed. Ed. by Carl K. Eicher & John M. Staatz. LC 90-31729. (Johns Hopkins Studies in Development). 560p. 1990. text ed. 62.50 (*0-8018-3999-8*) Johns Hopkins.

Agricultural Development of India. S. Giriappa & M. Vivekananda. 1985. 12.50 (*0-8364-1306-7*, Pub. by Ashish II) S Asia.

Agricultural Development of Japan. Ed. by Yujiro Hayami & Saburo Yamada. 250p. 1991. text ed. 59.50 (*0-86008-476-0*, Pub. by U of Tokyo JA) Col U Pr.

Agricultural Development of Zaire. David Shapiro & Eric Tollens. 215p. 1992. 63.95 (*1-85628-244-9*, Pub. by Avebury Pub UK) Ashgate Pub Co.

Agricultural Development, Planning & Implementation: Israel Case Study. R. Weitz & A. Rokach. 404p. 1967. lib. bdg. 80.00 (*90-277-0102-4*) Kluwer Ac.

Agricultural Development Price Policy & Marketed Surplus in India. Ramesh Ghand. (C). 1991. text ed. 14.00 (*81-7022-241-9*, Pub. by Concept II) S Asia.

Agricultural Development Principles: Economic Theory & Empirical Evidence. Robert D. Stevens & Cathy L. Jabara. LC 87-31076. 464p. (C). 1988. pap. text ed. 19.95x (*0-8018-3582-8*) Johns Hopkins.

Agricultural Developments in Africa & Supply of Manufactured Goods. OECD Staff et al. 130p. (Orig.). 1989. pap. 24.00 (*92-64-13273-2*) OECD.

Agricultural Dictionary in Eight Languages, 2 vols., Set. N. D. Pume & A. V. Magnyickij. 1720p. (BUL, CZE, ENG, GER, HUN, POL, RUM & RUS.). 1970. write for info. (*0-8288-7191-4*) Fr & Eur.

Agricultural Dictionary in Eight Languages, 2 vols., Set. N. D. Pume. 1721p. (BUL, CZE, ENG, GER, HUN, POL, RUM & RUS.). 1970. 72.00 (*0-88431-080-9*) IBD Ltd.

Agricultural Dimensions of Global Climate Change. Ed. by Harry M. Kaiser & Thomas E. Drennen. LC 93-28519. (Illus.). 311p. 1993. 69.95 (*0-9634030-3-6*) St Lucie Pr.

Agricultural Diversification: Policies & Issues from East Asian Experience. Agriculture & Rural Development Department Staff. (Policy & Research Ser.: No. 11). 54p. 1990. 6.95 (*0-8213-1517-X*, 11517) World Bank.

Agricultural Diversity in Wisconsin. Tom McKay & Deborah Kmetz. LC 87-6482. (Illus.). 93p. 1987. pap. 4.00 (*0-87020-250-2*) State Hist Soc Wis.

Agricultural Ecology. Joy Tivy. 1990. pap. text ed. 47.95 (*0-470-21480-5*) Halsted Pr.

***Agricultural Ecology.** S. S. Yadav. 1993. 250.00 (*81-7132-066-X*, Pub. by Print Hse II) St Mut.

Agricultural Ecology & Environment: Proceedings of an International Symposium, Padova, Italy, 5-7 April, 1988. Ed. by M. G. Paoletti et al. 644p. 1990. reprint ed. 143.75 (*0-444-88610-9*) Elsevier.

Agricultural Economics. Kenneth Casavant & Craig Infanger. (C). 1985. text ed. 18.95 (*0-8359-0185-8*, Reston) P-H.

***Agricultural Economics.** Ed. by George H. Peters. LC 95-13218. (International Library of Critical Writings in Economics: Vol. 55). 1995. 115.00 (*1-85278-301-X*, Pub. by E Elgar Pub UK) Ashgate Pub Co.

Agricultural Economics. 2nd ed. John W. Goodwin. (Illus.). 400p. 1982. teacher ed write for info. (*0-8359-0183-1*, Reston) P-H.

Agricultural Economics & Agribusiness. 6th ed. Gail L. Cramer & Clarence W. Jensen. LC 93-35984. 1994. text ed. write for info. (*0-471-59552-7*) Wiley.

***Agricultural Economics & Agriculture in Economic Development.** Comp. by Edward Tower. (Economics Reading Lists, Exams, Puzzles & Problems Ser.: 23). (Illus.). 231p. (Orig.). (C). 1995. pap. text ed. 25.00 (*0-88024-303-1*) Eno River Pr.

Agricultural Economics & Policy: International Challenges for the Nineties: Essays in Honour of Prof. J. De Veer. Ed. by K. Burger et al. (Developments in Agricultural Economics Ser.: No. 7). 226p. 1991. 97.25 (*0-444-88974-4*) Elsevier.

Agricultural Economics & Rural Sociology: The Contemporary Core Literature. Wallace C. Olsen. 304p. 1991. 53.95 (*0-8014-2677-4*) Cornell U Pr.

Agricultural Economics Bibliography, 14 vols., Set. U. S. Department of Agriculture, Bureau of Agricultural Economics Editors. LC 74-15150. 1975. 850.00 (*0-405-06249-4*) Ayer.

Agricultural Economy of Northeast Brazil. Gary P. Kutcher & Pasquale L. Scandizzo. LC 81-47615. (World Bank Research Publication Ser.). 285p. reprint ed. pap. 81.30 (*0-7837-5383-7*, 2045147) Bks Demand.

Agricultural Economy of the Danubian Countries, 1935-45. S. D. Zagoroff et al. xiv, 478p. 1955. 57.50 (*0-8047-0467-8*) Stanford U Pr.

Agricultural Ecosystem Effects on Trace Gases & Global Climate Change: Proceedings of a Symposium. Ed. by Dennis E. Rolston et al. LC 92-45593. (ASA Special Publication: No. 55). 1993. write for info. (*0-89118-113-X*) Am Soc Agron.

Agricultural Ecosystems: Unifying Concepts. Ed. by Richard Lowrance et al. LC 83-23504. (Wiley-Interscience Publication Ser.). 245p. reprint ed. pap. 69.90 (*0-7837-2400-4*, 2040085) Bks Demand.

Agricultural Education: Review & Synthesis of the Research. 4th ed. Jasper S. Lee. 38p. 1985. text ed. 4.75 (*0-318-20330-8*, IN298) Ctr Educ Trng Employ.

Agricultural Education for Development in the Middle East. Ed. by John Ryan & Adib T. Saad. 1980. 24.95 (*0-8156-6057-X*) Syracuse U Pr.

Agricultural Education in a Technical Society: An Annotated Bibliography of Resources. Mary Brown et al. LC 72-7501. 240p. reprint ed. pap. 68.40 (*0-8357-5270-4*, 2024189) Bks Demand.

Agricultural Engineering: Proceedings of the 11th International Congress, Dublin,m 4 - 8 September 1989, 4 vols., Set. Ed. by Vincent A. Dodd & Patrick Grace. (Illus.). 3175p. (C). 1989. text ed. 375.00 (*90-6191-980-0*, Pub. by A A Balkema NE) Ashgate Pub Co.

Agricultural Engineering Conference, 1990. Intro. by Malcolm McKay. (Illus.). 533p. (Orig.). 1990. pap. 96.00 (*0-85825-509-X*) Accents Pubns.

Agricultural Engineering Dictionary: English-French-German-Arabic. Abd El Nassar. 446p. (ARA, ENG, FRE & GER.). 1977. 75.00 (*0-8288-5288-X*, M9761) Fr & Eur.

Agricultural Engineering in Development: Selection of Mechanization Inputs. (Agricultural Services Bulletin Ser.: No. 84). 110p. 1991. pap. 14.00 (*92-5-103018-9*, F0030) UNIPUB.

Agricultural Engineering Index, 1981-1985. James A. Basselman. Ed. by Carl W. Hall. 232p. 1987. text ed. 27.50 (*0-317-64893-4*) Am Soc Ag Eng.

Agricultural Engineering Index 1986-1990, Vol. V. 454p. 1991. 35.00 (*0-685-72648-7*, N0391) Am Soc Ag Eng.

Agricultural Engineering Soil Mechanics. E. McKyes. (Developments in Agricultural Engineering Ser.: Vol. 10). 292p. 1989. 57.50 (*0-444-88080-1*) Elsevier.

Agricultural Entomology. Dennis S. Hill. LC 91-39244. (Illus.). 1994. 89.95 (*0-88192-223-4*) Timber.

Agricultural Entrepreneurship in India. G. Anjaneya Swamy. (C). 1988. 36.00 (*81-85076-39-1*, Pub. by Chugh Pubns II) S Asia.

Agricultural Equipment Financing. Howard G. Diesslin. (Occasional Papers: No. 50). 111p. 1955. reprint ed. 28.90 (*0-87014-364-6*) Natl Bur Econ Res.

Agricultural Equipment Industry. Ed. by ICC Information Group Staff. 1990. 650.00 (*1-85319-032-2*, Pub. by ICC Info Group Ltd UK) St Mut.

***Agricultural Ethics - Issues for the 21st Century: Proceedings of a Symposium Sponsored by the Soil Science Society of America, American Society of Agronomy & the Crop Science Society of America in Minneapolis, MN, Oct. 31-Nov. 5, 1992.** Peter G. Hartel et al. Ed. by Horace D. Skipper & Thomas A. Ruehr. LC 94-25924. (Special Publications: Vol. 57). 70p. 1994. pap. 21.00 (*0-89118-121-0*) Am Soc Agron.

Agricultural Expansion & Pioneer Settlements in the Humid Tropics. (United Nations University (UNU) Publications). 305p. 1989. 20.00 (*0-685-28279-1*, E.88. III.A.4) UN.

Agricultural Experimentation Design & Analysis: Design & Analysis. T. M. Little. Ed. by F. J. Hills. LC 77-26745. 350p. (C). 1978. Net. pap. text ed. write for info. (*0-471-02352-3*) Wiley.

Agricultural Exports & Economic Growth. Michael Hubbard. 1987. 65.00 (*0-7103-0121-9*, Pub. by Kegan Paul Intl UK) Routledge Chapman & Hall.

Agricultural Exports, Farm Income, & the Eisenhower Administration. Trudy H. Peterson. LC 79-15825. 236p. reprint ed. pap. 67.30 (*0-8357-3810-8*, 2036537) Bks Demand.

Agricultural Exports Strategy: Problems & Prospects. Economic & Scientific Research Foundation, Staff & D. H. Panandiker. 326p. 1986. text ed. 37.50 (*81-7027-098-7*, Pub. by Radiant Pubs II) S Asia.

Agricultural Extension: A Step Beyond the Next Step. Charles Ameur. LC 94-16437. (World Bank Technical Paper Ser.: No. 247). 44p. 1994. write for info. (*0-8213-2843-3*) World Bank.

Agricultural Extension: The Next Step. (Policy & Research Ser.: No. 13). 56p. 1990. 6.95 (*0-8213-1673-7*, 11673) World Bank.

Agricultural Extension for Women Farmers in Africa. Katrine A. Saito & C. Jean Weidemann. (Discussion Paper Ser.: No. 103). 74p. 1990. English. 7.95 (*0-8213-1657-5*, 11657); French. 7.95 (*0-8213-1746-6*) World Bank.

Agricultural Extension in Africa. Aruna Bagchee. LC 93-45658. (Discussion Paper, Africa Technical Department Ser.: Vol. 231). 1994. write for info. (*0-8213-2756-9*) World Bank.

Agricultural Extension in Africa. Ed. by Nigel Roberts. (Symposium Ser.). 114p. 1989. 11.95 (*0-8213-1195-6*, BK1195) World Bank.

Agricultural Extension in Changing World Perspective. R. K. Samantha. (C). 1991. text ed. 21.00 (*81-85565-00-7*, Pub. by Uppal Pub Hse II) S Asia.

Agricultural Extension in East Africa. Lisa A. Schwartz & Jacob Kampen. (Technical Paper Ser.: No. 164). 72p. 1992. 6.95 (*0-8213-1989-2*, 11989) World Bank.

Agricultural Extension in India. Michael Macklin. LC 92-38463. (Technical Paper Ser.: No. 190). 37p. 1992. 6.95 (*0-8213-2291-5*, 12291) World Bank.

***Agricultural Extension Systems in Asia & the Pacific.** Asian Productivity Organization Staff. 381p. 1994. pap. 15.00 (*92-833-2148-0*, APO321480, Pub. by Asian Prod Organ) UNIPUB.

Agricultural Extension Worldwide: Factors for Success. Ed. by W. M. Rivera. (International Perspectives on Adult & Continuing Education Ser.). 272p. 1986. 35.00 (*0-7099-4238-9*, Pub. by Croom Helm UK) Routledge Chapman & Hall.

Agricultural Fair. Wayne C. Neely. LC 73-181962. reprint ed. 17.50 (*0-404-04669-X*) AMS Pr.

Agricultural Field Experiment: A Statistical Examination of Theory & Practice. S. C. Pearce. LC 82-13711. 335p. 1983. text ed. 142.95 (*0-471-10511-2*, Wiley-Interscience) Wiley.

Agricultural Field Experiment: A Statistical Examination of Theory & Practice. Stanley C. Pearce. LC 82-13711. 351p. reprint ed. pap. 100.10 (*0-7837-4731-4*, 2044516) Bks Demand.

Agricultural Field Experiments: Design & Analysis. Petersen. (Books in Soils, Plants & the Environment: Vol. 31). 416p. 1994. 150.00 (*0-8247-8912-1*) Dekker.

Agricultural Finance. 8th rev. ed. Warren F. Lee et al. LC 87-31081. 480p. (C). 1988. text ed. 36.95 (*0-8138-0051-X*) Iowa St U Pr.

Agricultural Finance: Theory & Practice. J. P. Singh. 1988. 28.50 (*81-7024-175-8*, Pub. by Ashish II) S Asia.

Agricultural Finance & Development. N. Thirpalu. (C). 1987. 26.00 (*81-85076-33-2*, Pub. by Chugh Pubns II) S Asia.

Agricultural Futures & Options. Wayne Purcell. 384p. (C). 1991. write for info. (*0-02-397011-1*) Macmillan.

Agricultural Geography. T. S. Chouhan. (C). 1987. text ed. 150.00 (*0-685-61673-8*, Pub. by Scientific Pubs II) St Mut.

Agricultural Geography: A Study of Rajasthan State. T. S. Chauhan. 342p. (C). 1988. 300.00 (*0-317-92353-6*, Scientific) St Mut.

Agricultural Geography: Issues & Applications. R. S. Dube. 208p. 1987. 10.00 (*81-212-0083-0*, Pub. by Gian Publng Hse II) S Asia.

Agricultural Geography of Denmark. A. H. Kampp. 88p. 1974. 40.00 (*0-569-08235-8*, Pub. by Collets UK) Pro-Am Music.

***Agricultural Geography of Denmark.** A. H. Kampp. (Geography of World Agriculture Ser.: No. 5). 88p. (C). 1975. 23.00x (*963-05-0673-4*, Pub. by Akad Kiado HU) St Mut.

Agricultural Growth & Assistance to Africa: Lessons of a Quarter Century. Uma Lele. LC 89-48873. 106p. 1990. pap. 9.95 (*1-55815-063-3*) ICS Pr.

Agricultural Growth & Equity. C. H. Shah. (C). 1991. 18.00 (*81-7022-358-X*, Pub. by Concept II) S Asia.

Agricultural Growth & Non-Agricultural Growth: Dynamics of National Development. T. K. Meti. 170p. 1989. write for info. (*81-212-0272-8*, Pub. by Gian Publng Hse II) S Asia.

Agricultural Growth & Structural Changes in the Punjab. G. S. Bhalla et al. 119p. 1990. 10.00 (*0-89629-085-9*) Intl Food Policy.

Agricultural Growth in Japan, Taiwan, Korea, & the Philippines. Ed. by Yujiro Hayami et al. LC 77-26819. 414p. reprint ed. pap. 118.00 (*0-7837-3978-8*, 2043808) Bks Demand.

Agricultural Growth Linkages in Madagascar. CFNPP Staff et al. (Working Paper Ser.). (C). 1992. pap. text ed. 7.00 (*1-56401-122-4*) Cornell Food.

Agricultural Growth, Rural Poverty & Environmental Degradation in India. C. H. Rao. (Illus.). 288p. 1994. 23.00 (*0-19-563343-1*) OUP.

Agricultural History of the Genesee Valley, 1790-1860. Neil A. McNall. LC 75-25260. (Illus.). 276p. 1976. reprint ed. text ed. 59.75 (*0-8371-8396-0*, MCGV, Greenwood Pr) Greenwood.

***Agricultural Household Modelling & Family Economics.** Ed. by France Caillavet et al. LC 94-37299. (Developments in Agricultural Economics Ser.: Vol. 10). 314p. 1994. 205.75 (*0-444-81969-X*) Elsevier.

Agricultural Household Models: Extensions, Applications, & Policy. Inderjit Singh et al. LC 85-45102. 320p. 1986. text ed. 37.95 (*0-8018-3149-0*) Johns Hopkins.

***Agricultural Income: 1993.** Eurostat Staff. 137p. 1994. pap. 30.00 (*92-826-7551-3*, CA-82-94-496-EN, Pub. by Europ Com) UNIPUB.

***Agricultural Income: 1994.** Eurostat Staff. 137p. 1995. pap. 30.00 (*92-826-9965-X*, CA-87-95-442-EN, Pub. by Europ Com) UNIPUB.

Agricultural Income Situation in Less Favoured Areas of the EC. 208p. 1994. pap. 45.00 (*92-826-7341-3*, CH-82-94-400-EN, Pub. by Europ Com) UNIPUB.

Agricultural Income, 1989. 112p. 1990. pap. 25.00 (*92-826-1248-1*, CA-58-90-271-EN-C) UNIPUB.

Agricultural Income, 1990. 112p. 1991. pap. 40.00 (*92-826-2444-7*, CA-60-91-789-EN, Pub. by Europ Com) UNIPUB.

Agricultural Income 1992. Eurostat Staff. 137p. 1992. pap. 45.00 (*92-826-5630-6*, CA-77-93-902-EN-C, Pub. by Europ Com) UNIPUB.

Agricultural Indebtedness & Institutional Finance, India. R. K. Panda. 1985. 24.00 (*0-8364-1385-7*, Pub. by Ashish II) S Asia.

Agricultural Individuality: A Picture of the Human Being. Martin Pfeiffer. 64p. (Orig.). (C). 1990. pap. text ed. 4.75 (*0-938250-27-2*) Bio-Dynamic Farm.

Agricultural, Industrial & Urban Dynamism under the Sultans of Delhi, 1206-1555. Hamida K. Nazvi. 1986. 26.00 (*81-215-0002-8*, Pub. by Munshiram Manoharial II) S Asia.

Agricultural Information Resource Centers: A World Directory 1990. International Association of Agricultural Librarians & Documentalists (IAALD) Staff. LC 89-83416. 641p. 1990. text ed. 140.00 (*0-9624052-0-5*) IAAL&D.

Agricultural Innovation in Colonial Africa: Kenya & the Great Depression. I. D. Talbott. LC 90-45710. (African Studies: Vol. 18). 204p. 1991. lib. bdg. 89.95 (*0-88946-262-3*) E Mellen.

Agricultural Input Policies under Structural Adjustment: Their Distributional Implications. CFNPP Staff et al. (Working Paper Ser.). (C). 1992. pap. 7.00 (*1-56401-131-3*) Cornell Food.

Agricultural Insect Pests of Temperate Regions & Their Control. D. S. Hill. (Illus.). 600p. 1987. 145.00 (*0-521-24013-1*) Cambridge U Pr.

Agricultural Instability in China, 1931-1990. Y. Y. Kueh. (Studies on Contemporary China). 325p. 1995. 72.00 (*0-19-828777-1*) OUP.

Agricultural Insurance: A New Policy for Developing Countries. Syed M. Ahsan. LC 85-8035. 1985. text ed. 59.95 (*0-566-00800-9*) Ashgate Pub Co.

Agricultural Insurance: A New Policy for Developing Countries. Syed M. Ashan. (C). 1985. 270.00 (*0-685-33799-5*, Pub. by Witherby & Co UK) St Mut.

Agricultural Insurance: Principles & Organization & Application to Developing Countries. P. K. Ray. LC 66-178100. 1967. 141.00 (*0-08-011513-6*, Pub. by Pergamon Repr UK) Franklin.

Agricultural Insurance: Theory & Practice & Application to Developing Countries. 2nd ed. P. K. Ray. (Illus.). 360p. 1981. 190.00 (*0-08-025787-9*, Pub. by Pergamon Repr UK) Franklin.

Agricultural Intensification & Prehistoric Health in the Valley of Oaxaca, Mexico. Denise C. Hodges. LC 88-38162. (Memoirs Ser.: No. 22). (Illus.). xii, 132p. (Orig.). 1989. pap. 16.00 (*0-915703-16-5*) U Mich Mus Anthro.

Agricultural Inventions Directory. 158p. (Orig.). (C). 1992. pap. text ed. 60.00 (*1-56806-055-6*) Diane Pub.

Agricultural Involution: The Processes of Ecological Change in Indonesia. Clifford Geertz. LC 63-20356. 1963. pap. 14.00 (*0-520-00459-0*) U CA Pr.

Agricultural Issues of the 1990s. Ed. by Lisa Barbus et al. 266p. 1991. 15.95 (*0-8213-1890-X*, 11890) World Bank.

Agricultural Labour Markets & Structural Adjustment in Sub-Saharan Africa. Lawrence D. Smith. (Economic & Social Development Papers: No. 99). 92p. 1991. pap. 9.00 (*92-5-102863-X*, F863X) UNIPUB.

Agricultural Land: Assessment, Taxation & Preservation. Stuart W. Miller. (Bibliographic Ser.). 44p. 1981. pap. 10.50 (*0-88329-048-0*) IAAO.

Agricultural Land Conversion in the Urban-Rural Fringe. Robert E. Coughlin. Ed. by Benjamin H. Stevens. (Discussion Paper Ser.: No. 11). 39p. 1979. pap. 10.00 (*1-55869-139-1*) Regional Sci Res Inst.

Agricultural Land in an Urban Society. Owen J. Furuseth & John T. Pierce. Ed. by C. Gregory Knight. LC 82-18424. (Resource Publications in Geography). 89p. (Orig.). 1982. pap. 10.00 (*0-89291-149-2*) Assn Am Geographers.

Agricultural Larousse: Larousse Agricole. J. M. Clement. 1207p. (FRE.). 1981. 195.00 (*0-8288-1174-1*, M14293) Fr & Eur.

Agricultural Law, 15 vols. Neil E. Harl. 1981. Updates. ring bd. write for info. (*0-8205-1303-2*) Bender.

An Asterisk (*) at the beginning of an entry indicates that the title is appearing in BIP for the first time.

A

Agricultural Law. Julian C. Juergensmeyer & James B. Wadley. LC 81-82512. 1472p. 1982. 160.00 (*0-316-47612-9*) Little.

Agricultural Law. Christopher P. Rodgers & Clive V. Margrave-Jones. 1991. U.K. pap. 99.00 (*0-406-11269-X*) Butterworth Legal Pubs.

Agricultural Law, 1. Julian C. Juergensmeyer & James B. Wadley. LC 81-82512. 1472p. 1982. 85.00 (*0-316-47610-2*) Little.

Agricultural Law, 2. Julian C. Juergensmeyer & James B. Wadley. LC 81-82512. 1472p. 1982. 85.00 (*0-316-47611-0*) Little.

Agricultural Law: A Lawyer's Guide to Representing Farm Clients. 630p. 1989. pap. 49.95 (*0-89707-538-2*, 515-0202) Amer Bar Assn.

Agricultural Law: Cases & Materials. Keith G. Meyer et al. LC 84-19692. (American Casebook Ser.). 931p. 1984. text ed. 51.00 (*0-314-85082-1*) West Pub.

Agricultural Law: Principles & Cases. Donald L. Uchtmann & J. W. Looney. (Illus.). 688p. (C). 1981. text ed. write for info. (*0-07-065746-7*) McGraw.

Agricultural Law: Principles & Cases. 2nd ed. J. W. Looney & Donald L. Uchtman. LC 93-1644. 1993. text ed. write for info. (*0-07-038720-6*) McGraw.

Agricultural Law Graphics. Harold W. Hannah. (Illus.). 132p. (C). 1990. pap. text ed. 9.80 (*0-87563-346-3*) Stipes.

***Agricultural Law in a Nutshell.** Donald B. Pedersen & Keith G. Meyer. (Nutshell Ser.). 460p. (C). 1995. pap. text ed. 19.00 (*0-314-06454-0*) West Pub.

Agricultural Law Manual. Neil E. Harl. 1985. Looseleaf updates available. write for info. (*0-8205-1069-6*) Bender.

Agricultural Literacy Workbook. Ray Herren. 1992. 15.95 (*0-8273-5345-6*) Delmar.

Agricultural Literacy Workbook Instructors Guide. Ray Herren. 1992. 10.00 (*0-8273-5346-4*) Delmar.

Agricultural Literature: Proud Heritage-Future Promise. Ed. by Alan Fusonie & Leila Moran. (Illus.). 320p. 1976. 13.50 (*0-87771-011-2*); pap. 9.95 (*0-87771-010-4*) Grad School.

Agricultural Location Theory: A Review & Bibliography of Theory & Applications. Aharon Kellerman. Ed. by Benjamin H. Stevens. (Discussion Paper Ser.: No. 129). 72p. (Orig.). 1983. pap. 10.00 (*1-55869-006-9*) Regional Sci Res Inst.

Agricultural Machinery Management. Comp. by Charles L. Peterson. LC 88-70148. 170p. 1988. spiral bd. 29.00 (*0-916150-90-9*, S1387) Am Soc Ag Eng.

Agricultural Machines: Theory of Operation, Computation of Controlling Parameters & the Conditions of Operation. Ed. by N. I. Klenin et al. Tr. by A. Jaganmohan. 650p. (C). 1985. text ed. 190.00 (*90-6191-448-5*, Pub. by A A Balkema NE) Ashgate Pub Co.

Agricultural Management Economics: Activity Analysis & Decision Making. Ed. by A. Rae. 358p. 1994. pap. 41.50 (*0-85198-768-0*) CAB Intl.

Agricultural Marketing. 2nd ed. J. W. Barker. (Illus.). 264p. 1990. 59.95 (*0-19-859493-3*) OUP.

Agricultural Marketing: The World Bank's Experience. (Operations Evaluation Study Ser.). 102p. 1990. 7.95 (*0-8213-1535-8*, 11535) World Bank.

Agricultural Marketing in India. Gulab N. Singh. (C). 1987. 35.00 (*81-85076-25-1*, Pub. by Chugh Pubns II) S Asia.

***Agricultural Marketing System.** 4th ed. V. James Rhodes. 496p. 1993. pap. write for info. (*0-89787-130-8*) Gorsuch Scarisbrick.

Agricultural Markets & Trade, 1500-1750. Ed. by John Chartres. (C). 1990. pap. 37.95 (*0-521-36881-2*) Cambridge U Pr.

Agricultural Mathematics. 2nd ed. Roger Higgs et al. 297p. 1981. 2.00 (*0-8134-2131-4*, 2131); pap. 26.60 (*0-8134-2130-6*) Interstate.

***Agricultural Mathematics.** 2nd ed. Roger Higgs et al. 297p. 1991. pap. text ed. 19.95 (*0-685-02529-2*) Interstate.

Agricultural Mechanics: Fundamentals & Applications. 2nd ed. Elmer L. Cooper & William Hamilton. LC 85-20568. 532p. 1994. teacher ed 14.00 (*0-8273-3470-2*); 15.95 (*0-8273-3471-0*); text ed. 39.95 (*0-8273-3469-9*) Delmar.

***Agricultural Mechanics: Fundamentals & Applications.** 3rd ed. Elmer L. Cooper. LC 95-15152. 1996. text ed. write for info. (*0-8273-6854-2*) Delmar.

Agricultural Mechanics Fundamentals & Applications: Instructor's Guide to Accompany Lab Manual. 2nd ed. William Hamilton. 35p. 1994. 12.00 (*0-8273-6380-X*) Delmar.

Agricultural Mechanization: Issues & Options (A World Bank Policy Study) World Bank Staff. 96p. 1987. 9.95 (*0-8213-0903-X*, 10903) World Bank.

Agricultural Mechanization & the Evolution of Farming Systems in Sub-Saharan Africa. Prabhu L. Pingali et al. LC 86-27523. 208p. 1987. text ed. 25.95 (*0-8018-3502-X*) Johns Hopkins.

Agricultural Mechanization Policy & Strategy. A. G. Rijk. 283p. 1989. text ed. 39.75 (*92-833-1111-6*, 0208, Pub. by APO JA) Qual Resc.

Agricultural Meteorology. (Meteorological Monograph Ser.: No. 28). 1965. 27.00 (*0-933876-18-1*) Am Meteorological.

***Agricultural Meteorology.** N. Gopalaswamy. (C). 1994. 22.50x (*81-7033-225-7*, Pub. by Rawat II) S Asia.

Agricultural Meteorology. Paul E. Waggoner et al. (Meteorological Monograph Ser.: Vol. 6, No. 28). (Illus.). 188p. 1965. pap. 25.00 (*0-933876-19-X*) Am Meteorological.

Agricultural Meteorology of Japan. Ed. by Yoshiaki Mihara. LC 74-78859. (East-West Center Book Ser.). 225p. reprint ed. pap. 64.20 (*0-7837-3985-0*, 2043815) Bks Demand.

Agricultural Modernization in India. S. Khan. 1989. 22.00 (*81-7041-211-0*, Pub. by Anmol II) S Asia.

Agricultural Modernization, Poverty & Inequality. David Gibbons & Rodolphe De Koninck. 256p. 1979. text ed. 58.00 (*0-566-00331-7*) Ashgate Pub Co.

Agricultural Nonpoint Source Pollution: Model Selection & Application. Ed. by A. Giorgini et al. 380p. 1986. 105.25 (*0-444-99505-6*) Elsevier.

Agricultural Options: Trading, Risk Management & Hedging. Christopher A. Bobin. 1990. text ed. 49.95 (*0-471-52429-8*) Wiley.

Agricultural Organization in the United States. Edward Wiest. LC 74-30666. (American Farmers & the Rise of Agribusiness Ser.). 1975. reprint ed. 59.95 (*0-405-06842-5*) Ayer.

Agricultural Origins & Development in the Midcontinent. Ed. by William Green. LC 93-7119. (Office of the State Archaeologist Report Ser.: Vol. 19). 1993. 15.00 (*0-87414-090-0*) U IA Pubns Dept.

***Agricultural Outlook 1995-2000.** 100p. (Orig.). 1995. pap. 29.00x (*92-64-14389-0*) OECD.

Agricultural Pilot & Chemicals. Miles E. Gibson. (Illus.). 75p. (Orig.). 1974. pap. 9.95 (*0-942306-05-8*) Diversified Pub Co.

***Agricultural Planning & Technology in Rural Development.** A. K. Mitra & B. Sahoo. 266p. (C). 1994. 75.00x (*81-85880-49-2*, Pub. by Print Hse II) St Mut.

Agricultural Planning Handbook. J. P. Mulligan. (Illus.). 400p. 1986. text ed. write for info. (*0-408-10797-9*) Buttrwrth-Heinemann.

Agricultural Plants. 2nd ed. G. D. Hill & R. H. Langer. (Illus.). 377p. (C). 1991. 105.00 (*0-521-40545-9*); pap. 32.95 (*0-521-40563-7*) Cambridge U Pr.

Agricultural Policies for the Nineteen Nineties. OECD Staff & Sartaj Aziz. 136p. (Orig.). 1990. pap. 25.00 (*92-64-13350-X*) OECD.

Agricultural Policies in a New Decade. Ed. by Kristen Allen. LC 89-43667. 356p. 1990. pap. 20.00 (*0-915707-54-3*) Resources Future.

Agricultural Policies in Developing Countries. Frank Ellis. (Wye Studies in Agricultural & Rural Development). (Illus.). 364p. (C). 1992. 69.95 (*0-521-40004-X*); pap. 32.95 (*0-521-39584-4*) Cambridge U Pr.

Agricultural Policies in Vermont, 1860-1945. Edwin C. Rozwenc. 190p. 1981. pap. 9.50 (*0-934720-24-X*) VT Hist Soc.

Agricultural Policies, Markets & Trade: Monitoring & Outlook, 1992. 490p. (Orig.). 1992. pap. 50.00 (*92-64-13655-X*) OECD.

Agricultural Policies, Markets & Trade: Monitoring & Outlook 1993. OECD Staff. 380p. (Orig.). 1993. pap. 52.00 (*92-64-13902-8*) OECD.

***Agricultural Policies, Markets & Trade: Monitoring & Outlook, 1994.** OECD Staff. 365p. (Orig.). 1994. pap. 50.00 (*92-64-14140-5*) OECD.

***Agricultural Policies, Markets & Trade in OECD Countries: Monitoring & Outlook 1995.** 298p. (Orig.). 1995. pap. 57.00 (*92-64-14419-6*, Pub. by Econ & Coop Dev FR) OECD.

Agricultural Policies, Markets & Trade in the Central & East European Countries, the New Independent States & China. OECD Staff. 150p. (Orig.). 1993. pap. 22.00 (*92-64-13916-8*) OECD.

***Agricultural Policies, Markets & Trade in the Central & Eastern European Countries, Selected New Independent States, Mongolia & China: Monitoring & Outlook 1995.** 232p. (Orig.). 1995. pap. 37.00 (*92-64-14434-X*, Pub. by Econ & Coop Dev FR) OECD.

Agricultural Policies of the World Markets. Alex F. McCalla & Timothy E. Josling. 1985. text ed. 43.00 (*0-07-044795-0*) McGraw.

***Agricultural Policy Analysis in Egypt: Selected Papers.** F. K. Bishay et al. (Economic & Social Development Papers: No. 129). 186p. 1994. pap. 17.00 (*92-5-103594-6*, F35946, Pub. by FAO IT) UNIPUB.

Agricultural Policy & Performance in Zambia: History, Prospects, & Proposals for Change. Doris J. Dodge. LC 77-620042. (Research Ser.: No. 32). (Illus.). xiii, 285p. 1977. pap. 4.95 (*0-87725-132-0*) U of Cal IAS.

Agricultural Policy & Sustainability: Case Studies from India, Chile, the Philippines, & the United States. large type ed. Paul Faeth et al. 75p. 1993. Large format. pap. 14.95 (*0-915825-94-5*, FAAPP) World Resources Inst.

Agricultural Policy & the Environment: Iron Fist & Open Hand. Ed. by Louis Swanson. 200p. 1994. pap. text ed. 33.95 (*0-935734-35-X*) Soil & Water Conserv.

Agricultural Policy & Trade: Adjusting Domestic Programs in an International Framework. D. Gale Johnson et al. (Triangle Papers). 1985. 6.00 (*0-8147-4168-1*) Trilateral Comm.

Agricultural Policy & U. S.-Taiwan Trade. D. Gale Johnson et al. 200p. Date not set. pap. write for info. (*0-8447-3826-3*) Am Enterprise.

Agricultural Policy & U. S.-Taiwan Trade. D. Gale Johnson et al. 200p. 1993. 34.75 (*0-8447-3827-1*) Am Enterprise.

Agricultural Policy Formation in the European Community: The Birth of Milk Quotas & CAP Reform. M. Petit et al. (Developments in Agricultural Economics Ser.: Vol. 4). 176p. 1987. 66.75 (*0-444-42894-1*) Elsevier.

Agricultural Policy Implementation: A Case Study from Western Kenya. Kathleen Staudt. LC 84-29737. (Kumarian Press Case Studies on Women's Roles & Gender Differences in Development: No. 3). 67p. 1985. pap. 8.95 (*0-931816-18-1*) Kumarian Pr.

***Agricultural Policy in Kenya: Applications of the Policy Analysis Matrix.** Scott Pearson et al. (Food Systems & Agrarian Change Ser.). (Illus.). 328p. 1996. 45.00x (*0-8014-3085-2*) Cornell U Pr.

Agricultural Policy Issues. (C). 1978. pap. 12.00 (*0-918592-27-5*) Pol Studies.

Agricultural Policy Model for the U. K. Michael Burton. 329p. 1991. 68.95 (*1-85628-295-3*, Pub. by Avebury Pub UK) Ashgate Pub Co.

***Agricultural Policy Reform: New Approaches, the Role of Direct Income Payments.** 192p. (Orig.). 1995. pap. 47.00x (*92-64-14291-6*) OECD.

Agricultural Policy Reform: Politics & Process in the EC & U. S. A. H. Wayne Moyer. LC 89-48550. (Illus.). 256p. 1990. text ed. 29.95 (*0-8138-1371-9*) Iowa St U Pr.

***Agricultural Policy Reform & Adjustment: The Swedish Experience.** 118p. (Orig.). 1995. pap. 34.00 (*92-64-14342-4*, Pub. by Econ & Coop Dev FR) OECD.

***Agricultural Policy Reform in the United States.** Ed. by Daniel A. Sumner. (Studies in Agricultural Policy). 236p. (Orig.). 1995. pap. 19.95 (*0-8447-3913-8*) Am Enterprise.

Agricultural Policy Reforms & Regional Market Integration in Malawi, Zambia, & Zimbabwe. Ed. by Alberto Valdes & Kay Muir-Leresche. LC 93-18029. 1993. write for info. (*0-89629-327-0*) Intl Food Policy.

Agricultural Policy under Economic Development. Earl O. Heady. LC 62-9124. 682p. 1962. pap. 24.95 (*0-8138-2265-3*) Iowa St U Pr.

Agricultural Pollution, 2 vols., Set. Ed. by S. G. Misra & Dinesh Mani. (Illus.). 1994. 25.00 (*0-685-72742-4*, Pub. by Ashish Pub Hse II) Nataraj Bks.

Agricultural Pollution, Vol. 1. Ed. by S. G. Misra & Dinesh Mani. (Illus.). iv, 98p. 1994. write for info. (*81-7024-574-5*, Pub. by Ashish Pub Hse II) Nataraj Bks.

Agricultural Pollution, Vol. 2. Ed. by S. G. Misra & Dinesh Mani. (Illus.). vi, 188p. 1994. write for info. (*81-7024-601-6*, Pub. by Ashish Pub Hse II) Nataraj Bks.

Agricultural Power & Machinery. C. O. Jacobs & W. R. Harrell. 480p. 1983. text ed. 29.96 (*0-07-032210-4*) McGraw.

Agricultural Price Analysis & Forecasting. John W. Goodwin. LC 93-21449. 1994. text ed. write for info. (*0-471-30447-6*) Wiley.

Agricultural Price Policies & the Developing Countries. George S. Tolley et al. LC 81-47614. 256p. 1982. pap. 12.95 (*0-8018-3124-5*) Johns Hopkins.

Agricultural Price Policies in the Near East: Lessons of Experience. (Economic & Social Development Papers: No. 82). (Illus.). 91p. 1989. pap. 12.00 (*92-5-102780-3*, F7803) UNIPUB.

Agricultural Price Policy: A Practitioner's Guide to Partial Equilibrium Analysis. Isabelle Tsakok. LC 89-45978. (Illus.). 344p. 1990. 57.50 (*0-8014-2363-5*); pap. 19.95 (*0-8014-9596-2*) Cornell U Pr.

Agricultural Price Policy & Production in India, 1956-1990. Sitesh Bhatia. viii, 221p. (C). 1991. text ed. 27.50 (*81-220-0210-2*) Advent Bks Div.

Agricultural Price Policy for Developing Countries. Ed. by John W. Mellor & Raisuddin Ahmed. LC 87-26862. 352p. 1988. text ed. 35.00 (*0-8018-3586-0*) Johns Hopkins.

Agricultural Price Policy in India: An Econometric Approach. Ashok Gulati. 1987. 21.50 (*0-8364-2235-X*, Pub. by Concept II) S Asia.

Agricultural Prices & Its Impact on the Indian Economy. S. K. Goyal. (C). 1992. 14.00 (*81-7054-153-0*, Pub. by Classics India Pubns II) S Asia.

Agricultural Prices Price - Indices & Absolute Prices 1982-1991. 363p. 1992. pap. 40.00 (*92-826-4495-2*, CA-75-92-413-3A-C, Pub. by Europ Com) UNIPUB.

Agricultural Prices, Price - Indicies & Absolute Prices: 1983-1992. 363p. 1993. pap. 35.00 (*92-826-6182-2*, CA-79-93-691-3A-C) UNIPUB.

Agricultural Prices, 1980-1989. (Illus.). 363p. (ENG, FRE, GER & ITA.). 1990. pap. 30.00 (*92-826-1271-6*, CA-59-90-306-2A-C) UNIPUB.

Agricultural Pricing Policy in Eastern Africa: A Macroeconomic Simulation for Kenya, Malawi, Tanzania, & Zambia. Christopher D. Gerrard et al. LC 93-3078. (EDI Technical Materials Ser.). 94p. 1993. 7.95 (*0-8213-1967-1*, 11967) World Bank.

Agricultural Problems in Ethiopia. Harjinder Singh. 266p. 1987. 13.00 (*81-212-0078-4*, Pub. by Gian Publng Hse II) S Asia.

Agricultural Process Engineering. 3rd ed. Henderson. 1976. text ed. 39.95 (*0-87055-212-0*) Chapman & Hall.

Agricultural Process Engineering. 3rd ed. S. M. Henderson & R. L. Perry. (Illus.). (C). 1976. text ed. 29.95 (*0-87055-300-3*) AVI.

Agricultural Processing for Development: Enterprise Management in Agricultural & Fish Processing. John C. Abbott. 275p. 1988. text ed. 68.95 (*0-566-05553-8*, Pub. by Avebury Pub UK) Ashgate Pub Co.

Agricultural Producers & Their Markets. Ed. by Thorald K. Warley. LC 67-6960. 1967. 49.50 (*0-678-06263-3*) Kelley.

Agricultural Product Prices. 3rd ed. William G. Tomek & Kenneth L. Robinson. LC 89-70779. (Illus.). 384p. 1990. 29.95 (*0-8014-2451-8*) Cornell U Pr.

***Agricultural Production & Indian History.** Ed. by David Ludden. (Oxford in India Readings Ser.). 400p. 1995. 29.95 (*0-19-563268-0*) OUP.

Agricultural Production Economics. David L. Debertin. 623p. (C). 1986. write for info. (*0-02-328060-3*) Macmillan.

Agricultural Production Functions: An Appraisal. Venkata R. Katla. 1990. 32.00 (*81-202-0255-4*, Pub. by Ajanta II) S Asia.

Agricultural Production in Communist China, Nineteen Forty-Nine to Nineteen Sixty-Five. Kang Chao. LC 70-121766. (Illus.). 374p. 1970. 30.00 (*0-299-05770-4*) U of Wis Pr.

Agricultural Productivity & Economic Development in France: Eighteen Fifty-Two to Nineteen Fifty. Louis-Marie Goreux. Ed. by Stuart Bruchey. LC 77-77171. (Dissertations in European Economic History Ser.). (Illus.). (ENG & FRE.). 1978. lib. bdg. 26.95 (*0-405-10784-6*) Ayer.

Agricultural Productivity Measurement & Explanation. Ed. by Susan M. Capalbo & John M. Antle. LC 87-27224. 404p. 1988. 30.00 (*0-915707-37-3*) Resources Future.

Agricultural Productivity, Sustainability, & Fertilizer Use. Dennis H. Parish. LC 93-16931. (Paper Ser.: No. P-18). (Illus.). 21p. (Orig.). 1993. pap. text ed. 4.00 (*0-88090-102-0*) Intl Fertilizer.

Agricultural Project Management: Monitoring & Control of Implementation. Ed. by P. Smith. (Illus.). ix, 190p. 1984. 57.75 (*0-85334-282-2*, I-322-84, Pub. by Elsevier Applied Sci UK) Elsevier.

Agricultural Protectionism in the Industrialized World. Ed. by Fred H. Sanderson. LC 90-34094. 488p. 1990. pap. 45.00 (*0-915707-57-8*) Resources Future.

***Agricultural Recycling of Sewage Sludge & the Environment.** S. R. Smith. 380p. 1995. 90.00 (*0-85198-980-2*) CAB Intl.

***Agricultural Reform & Its Impact on the Fruit & Vegetables Sector in OECD Countries.** 172p. (Orig.). 1995. pap. 41.00x (*92-64-14253-3*) OECD.

Agricultural Reform in China. Simon G. Powell. (Studies on East Asia). 256p. 1992. text ed. 79.95 (*0-7190-3382-9*, Pub. by Manchester Univ Pr UK) St Martin.

Agricultural Reform in Taiwan: From Here to Modernity? Irene Bain. 582p. 1994. 87.50 (*962-201-543-3*, Pub. by Chinese Univ HK) Coronet Bks.

Agricultural Reform in the U. S. S. R. Contract & Lease Farming Implications for Perestroika. Gene Davidovich. Ed. by Jonathan Gallant. (Illus.). 126p. (Orig.). 1989. pap. 75.00 (*1-55831-112-2*) Delphic Associates.

***Agricultural Reforms & Grain Production in China.** Shujie Yao. LC 94-21687. 1994. text ed. 79.95 (*0-312-12370-1*) St Martin.

Agricultural Research Alternatives. William Lockeretz & Molly D. Anderson. LC 92-37613. (Our Sustainable Future Ser.: Vol. 3). x, 248p. 1993. 30.00 (*0-8032-2901-1*) U of Nebr Pr.

Agricultural Research & Technology in Economic Development. Per Pinstrup-Anderson. LC 81-14297. (Illus.). 304p. (C). 1982. text ed. 39.95 (*0-582-46048-4*) Longman.

Agricultural Research & Technology Transfer. Isaac Arnon. 844p. 1989. 153.00 (*1-85166-275-8*) Elsevier.

***Agricultural Research Centers: A Worldwide Directory of Organizations & Programs.** 12th ed. 1000p. 1995. 595.00 (*1-56159-128-9*, Stockton Pr) Groves Dictionaries.

Agricultural Research Centres. 11th ed. 1993. 500.00 (*0-8103-9668-8*, 076048, Pub. by Longman Grp UK) Gale.

Agricultural Research Centres, Vol. 1. 11th ed. 1992. write for info. (*0-8103-9669-6*, 100786, Pub. by Longman Grp UK) Gale.

Agricultural Research Centres, Vol. 2. 11th ed. 1992. 595.00 (*0-8103-9670-X*, 100787, Pub. by Longman Grp UK) Gale.

Agricultural Research for Development: The Hamulonge Contribution. Ed. by M. H. Arnold. LC 75-31400. 375p. reprint ed. pap. 106.90 (*0-8357-5271-2*, 2024411) Bks Demand.

***Agricultural Research in an Era of Adjustment: Policies, Institutions, & Progress.** Ed. by Steven R. Tabor. LC 95-5538. (EDI Seminar Ser.). 1995. write for info. (*0-8213-3197-3*) World Bank.

Agricultural Research in Southern Africa: A Framework for Action. Andrew Spurling et al. LC 92-35157. (Discussion Paper, Africa Technical Department Ser.: No. 184). 81p. 1992. 7.95 (*0-8213-2282-6*, 12282) World Bank.

Agricultural Research in the Northeastern United States: Critical Review & Future Perspectives: Proceedings of the 1992 Symposium, Northeastern Branch, American Society of Agronomy: June 29-30, 1992, University of Connecticut, Storrs, CT. Ed. by J. T. Sims. LC 93-17496. 139p. 1993. pap. 22.00 (*0-89118-117-2*) Am Soc Agron.

Agricultural Research Policy. Vernon W. Ruttan. LC 81-16396. (Illus.). 384p. reprint ed. pap. 109.50 (*0-8357-6537-7*, 2035899) Bks Demand.

Agricultural Research Policy: International Quantitative Perspectives. Ed. by Philip G. Pardey et al. (Illus.). 484p. (C). 1991. 47.95 (*0-521-40009-0*) Cambridge U Pr.

***Agricultural Research Through International Cooperation: The Indian Experience.** Roli Srivastava. (C). 1993. 18.00x (*81-204-0777-6*, Pub. by Oxford IBH II) S Asia.

Agricultural Research to Protect Water Quality: Proceedings of the Conference, February 21-24, 1993, Minneapolis, Minnesota, USA. LC 94-1818. 1994. write for info. (*0-935734-34-1*) Soil & Water Conserv.

Agricultural Resources & Planning in India. R. K. Singh. 1990. 40.00 (*81-85076-88-X*, Pub. by Chugh Pubns II) S Asia.

Agricultural Resources of California Counties. Ann Scheuring et al. LC 82-71076. 136p. (Orig.). 1982. pap. text ed. 5.00 (*0-931876-57-5*, 3275) ANR Pubns CA.

An Asterisk (*) at the beginning of an entry indicates that the title is appearing in BIP for the first time.

An Asterisk (*) at the beginning of an entry indicates that the title is appearing in BIP for the first time.

147

Agriculture & the State: Market Processes & Bureaucracy. Ernest C. Pasour, Jr. LC 89-11067. (Independent Institute Ser.). 288p. (Orig.). 1990. 39.95 (*0-8419-1272-6*) Holmes & Meier.

Agriculture & the State: Market Processes & Bureaucracy. Ernest C. Pasour, Jr. (Independent Studies in Political Economy). 279p. (Orig.). (C). 1993. reprint ed. pap. 16.95 (*0-945999-29-1*) Independent Inst.

Agriculture & the State in Ancient Mesopotamia: An Introduction to Problems of Land Tenure. Maria deJ Ellis. (Occasional Publications of the Babylonian Fund: No. 1). xii, 194p. 1990. reprint ed. 35.00 (*0-934718-28-8*) U PA Mus Pubns.

Agriculture & the Trade Cycle: Their Mutual Relations with Special Reference to the Period 1926-1931. John H. Kirk. LC 68-30531. (Reprints of Economic Classics Ser.). 1972. reprint ed. 37.50 (*0-678-00887-6*) Kelley.

Agriculture & the Undergraduate: Proceedings. National Research Council, Board on Agriculture Staff. 268p. (C). 1992. pap. text ed. 33.00 (*0-309-04682-3*) Natl Acad Pr.

Agriculture & Trade in China & India: Policies & Performance since 1950. T. N. Srinivasan. 1993. pap. 14.95 (*1-55815-281-4*) ICS Pr.

Agriculture & Trade in the Pacific: Toward the Twenty-First Century. Ed. by William T. Coyle et al. (C). 1992. text ed. 61.00 (*0-8133-8277-7*) Westview.

Agriculture & Vegetation of the World. Ed. by Scott Morris. LC 92-22290. (Using & Understanding Maps Ser.). (Illus.). (J). 1993. pap. write for info. (*0-7910-1817-2*, Am Art Analog) Chelsea Hse.

Agriculture & Vegetation of the World. Ed. by Scott Morris. LC 92-22290. (Using & Understanding Maps Ser.). (Illus.). 48p. (YA). (gr. 5 up). 1993. lib. bdg. 15.95 (*0-7910-1804-0*, Am Art Analog) Chelsea Hse.

Agriculture & Water Quality. DeWitt John. Ed. by Karen Glass. 40p. (Orig.). 1989. pap. text ed. 10.00 (*1-55877-054-2*) Natl Governor.

Agriculture & Water Quality: International Perspectives. Ed. by John B. Braden & Stephen B. Lovejoy. LC 89-10811. 224p. 1989. lib. bdg. 35.00 (*1-55587-183-6*) Lynne Rienner.

Agriculture, Bureaucracy & Military Government in Peru. Peter S. Cleaves & Martin J. Scurrah. (Illus.). 336p. 1980. 42.50 (*0-8014-1300-1*) Cornell U Pr.

Agriculture-Commodities-Fisheries-Food-Plants, Pt. 2. Amos J. Peaslee. (International Governmental Organizations Constitutional Documents Ser.). 1975. lib. bdg. 257.50 (*90-247-1687-X*) Kluwer Ac.

Agriculture Development of a Tropical Delta: A Study of the Chao Phraya Delta. Yoshikazu Takaya. Tr. by Peter Hawkes. (Center for Southeast Asian Studies, Kyoto University). (Illus.). 288p. 1986. text ed. 30.00 (*0-8248-1072-4*) UH Pr.

Agriculture Dictionary. Ray V. Herren. 1990. text ed. 29.95 (*0-8273-4095-8*) Delmar.

Agriculture Dictionary. Ray V. Herren. 1991. teacher ed 9.00 (*0-8273-4096-6*) Delmar.

Agriculture, Economics & Resource Management. 2nd ed. Milton M. Snodgrass & Tim Wallace. (Illus.). 1980. text ed. 48.20 (*0-13-018820-4*) P-H.

Agriculture, Environment, & Health: Sustainable Development in the 21st Century. Ed. by Vernon W. Ruttan. LC 93-8527. 384p. (C). 1993. text ed. 44.95 (*0-8166-2291-4*); pap. text ed. 19.95 (*0-8166-2292-2*) U of Minn Pr.

Agriculture, External Trade & International Co-Operation (Est. e Inf. 73) 88p. 4.00 (*92-1-121144-1*, E.88.II.G.15) UN.

***Agriculture Fact Book 1994.** (Illus.). 216p. (Orig.). (C). 1994. pap. text ed. 35.00x (*0-7881-1489-1*) Diane Pub.

***Agriculture-Fertilizer Interface in Asia: Issues of Growth & Sustainability.** Saleem Ahmed. 172p. 1995. text ed. 48.00 (*1-886106-26-6*) Science Pubs.

Agriculture, Fisheries & Forestry Aspects of Britain. 73p. 1993. pap. 9.00 (*0-11-701724-8*, HM17248, Pub. by HMSO UK) UNIPUB.

***Agriculture, Foraging, & Wildlife Resource Use in Africa: Cultural & Political Dynamics in Zambezi Valley.** Richard Hasler. LC 95-14863. 1995. write for info. (*0-7103-0515-X*, Pub. by Kegan Paul Intl UK) Routledge Chapman & Hall.

Agriculture, Forestry, & Allied Terminology Dictionary: English-Arabic with Arabic Glossary. Chihabi. Ed. by A. Khatib. (ARA & ENG.). 1978. 65.00 (*0-86685-072-4*) Intl Bk Ctr.

Agriculture, Forestry & Global Climate Change: A Reader, 2 vols., Set. 1991. lib. bdg. 175.95 (*0-8490-4393-X*) Gordon Pr.

Agriculture-Forestry-Horticulture Dictionary: English-German. Peter Muhle. 144p. (ENG & GER.). 1990. lib. bdg. 150.00 (*0-8288-3597-7*, F92570) Fr & Eur.

***Agriculture-Forestry-Horticulture Dictionary: English-German.** Peter Muhle. 732p. (ENG & GER.). 1990. 225.00 (*0-7859-8516-6*, 3861170124) Fr & Eur.

Agriculture, Geology, & Society in Antebellum South Carolina: The Private Diary of Edmund Ruffin, 1843. Edmund Ruffin. Ed. by William M. Mathew. LC 90-24718. (Illus.). 424p. 1992. 50.00 (*0-8203-1324-6*) U of Ga Pr.

Agriculture, Growth & Redistribution of Income. N. S. Narayana et al. (Contributions to Economic Analysis Ser.: Vol. 190). 1991. 72.50 (*0-444-88667-2*, CEA 190) Elsevier.

Agriculture in a Turbulent World Economy: Proceedings of the 19th International Conference of Agricultural Economists. Ed. by Allen Maunder. 740p. 1986. text ed. 62.95 (*0-566-05225-3*, Pub. by Avebury Pub UK) Ashgate Pub Co.

Agriculture in an Interdependent World: U. S. & Canadian Perspectives. T. K. Warley. LC 77-73919. (Canadian-American Committee Ser.). 104p. 1977. 4.00 (*0-89068-040-X*) Natl Planning.

Agriculture in Britain: Changing Pressures & Policies. Ed. by Dennis Britton. 214p. (Orig.). 1990. pap. text ed. 32.00 (*0-85198-655-2*) CAB Intl.

Agriculture in Britain & America, 1660-1820: An Annotated Bibliography of the Eighteenth-Century Literature. Ed. by Samuel J. Rogal. LC 94-12323. (Bibliographies & Indexes in World History Ser.: No. 33). 280p. 1994. text ed. 75.00 (*0-313-29352-X*, Greenwood Pr) Greenwood.

Agriculture in China's Modern Economic Development. Nicholas R. Lardy. LC 82-23555. (Illus.). 285p. 1983. 69.95 (*0-521-25246-6*) Cambridge U Pr.

Agriculture in Development Theory. Ed. by Lloyd G. Reynolds. LC 74-20085. (Economic Growth Center, Yale University Publication Ser.). 522p. reprint ed. pap. 148.80 (*0-8357-8013-9*, 2033867) Bks Demand.

Agriculture in Dry Lands: Principles & Practice. Isaac Arnon. LC 92-12960. (Developments in Agricultural & Managed-Forest Ecology Ser.: Vol. 26). xii, 980p. 1992. write for info. (*0-444-88912-4*) Elsevier.

Agriculture in Economic Development: 1940's to 1990's: A Survey of Agriculture Economics Literature, Vol. 4. Ed. by Lee R. Martin. (Illus.). 1064p. (C). 1991. text ed. 59.95 (*0-8166-1942-3*) U of Minn Pr.

Agriculture in England: Eighteen Seventy to Nineteen Forty Seven. Jonathan Brown. 1988. text ed. 65.00 (*0-7190-1759-9*, Pub. by Manchester Univ Pr UK) St Martin.

Agriculture in Europe - Development Constraints & Perspectives. 97p. 1992. pap. 10.00 (*92-826-0476-4*, CM-60-90-418-EN-C, Pub. by Europ Com) UNIPUB.

Agriculture in Flood Prone Region: A Geographical Perspective. Ganga P. Jha. (C). 1989. 42.00 (*81-210-0225-7*, Pub. by Inter-India Pubns) S Asia.

Agriculture in France on the Eve of the Railway Age. Hugh Clout. (Illus.). 239p. 1980. 44.00 (*0-389-20017-4*, N6790) B&N Imports.

Agriculture in Iron Age Israel: The Evidence from Archaeology & the Bible. Oded Borowski. LC 86-24237. xxii, 215p. 1987. 22.50 (*0-931464-27-7*) Eisenbrauns.

Agriculture in Lanarkshire, 1760-1820. (C). 1989. 35.00 (*0-903915-12-X*, Pub. by Jordanhill College UK) St Mut.

Agriculture in New Jersey: A Three Hundred Year History. Hubert G. Schmidt. (Illus.). 352p. 1973. 45.00 (*0-8135-0756-1*) Rutgers U Pr.

Agriculture in North Carolina Before the Civil War. Cornelius O. Cathey. (Illus.). viii, 46p. 1974. pap. 3.00 (*0-86526-073-7*) NC Archives.

Agriculture in Scotland: Report for 1987. (Illus.). 45p. 1988. pap. 16.00 (*0-10-104352-X*, HM352X, Pub. by HMSO UK) UNIPUB.

Agriculture in Scotland, Report for 1986. 41p. (Orig.). 1987. pap. text ed. 16.00 (*0-10-101442-2*, HM3410, Pub. by HMSO UK) UNIPUB.

Agriculture in Secondary Schools: Case Studies of Botswana, Kenya & Tanzania. James R. Sheffield et al. LC 76-11330. 124p. (Orig.). 1976. pap. 2.75 (*0-686-66072-2*) AAI.

Agriculture in Semi-Arid Environments. Ed. by G. H. Cannell et al. (Ecological Studies: Vol. 34). (Illus.). 1979. 95.00 (*0-387-09414-8*) Spr-Verlag.

Agriculture in the City's Countryside. C. Bryant & T. Johnson. 256p. 1989. 39.00 (*1-85293-027-6*, Pub. by Pinter Pubs UK) St Martin.

Agriculture in the City's Countryside. C. R. Bryant & T. R. Johnston. 256p. 1992. 45.00 (*0-8020-2842-X*); pap. 18.95 (*0-8020-7723-4*) U of Toronto Pr.

Agriculture in the Malaysian Region. R. D. Hill. 234p. 1982. 154.00 (*0-569-08721-X*, Pub. by Collets UK) Pro-Am Music.

***Agriculture in the Malaysian Region.** R. D. Hill. (Geography of World Agriculture Ser.: No. 11). 234p. (C). 1982. 72.00x (*963-05-2825-8*, Pub. by Akad Kiado HU) St Mut.

***Agriculture in the Middle Ages.** Del Sweeney. (Middle Ages Ser.). (Illus.). 416p. 1995. text ed. 48.95 (*0-8122-3282-8*); pap. text ed. 18.95 (*0-8122-1511-7*) U of Pa Pr.

Agriculture in the Middle East. Ed. by Adel Salman. LC 89-72105. 417p. (C). 1990. 34.95 (*0-943852-80-3*) Prof World Peace.

Agriculture in the Postbellum South: The Economics of Production & Supply. Stephen J. Decanio. 1975. 37.50 (*0-262-04047-6*) MIT Pr.

***Agriculture in the Republic Ireland.** D. A. Gillmor. (Geography of World Agriculture Ser.: No. 7). 202p. (C). 1977. 39.00x (*963-05-1218-1*, Pub. by Akad Kiado HU) St Mut.

Agriculture in the Republic of Ireland. D. Gillmore. 201p. 1977. 74.00 (*0-569-08405-9*, Pub. by Collets UK) Pro-Am Music.

Agriculture in the Twentieth Century. LC 77-90597. (Essay Index Reprint Ser.). 1977. 30.95 (*0-8369-1268-3*) Ayer.

Agriculture in the U. S. A Documentary History, 4 vols., 1. David W. Rasmussen. (Documentary Reference Collections). 1977. text ed. 95.00 (*0-313-20148-X*, RAAG1) Greenwood.

Agriculture in the U. S. A Documentary History, 4 vols., Set. David W. Rasmussen. LC 74-9643. (Documentary Reference Collections). 1977. text ed. 295.00 (*0-313-20147-1*, RAAG) Greenwood.

Agriculture in the U. S. A Documentary History, 4 vols., Vol. 2. David W. Rasmussen. (Documentary Reference Collections). 1977. text ed. 95.00 (*0-313-20149-8*, RAAG2) Greenwood.

Agriculture in the U. S. A Documentary History, 4 vols., Vol. 3. David W. Rasmussen. (Documentary Reference Collections). 1977. text ed. 95.00 (*0-313-20150-1*, RAAG3) Greenwood.

Agriculture in the U. S. A Documentary History, 4 vols., Vol. 4. David W. Rasmussen. (Documentary Reference Collections). 1977. text ed. 95.00 (*0-313-20151-X*, RAAG4) Greenwood.

Agriculture in the U. S. A. Today. Donald J. Murphy. LC 92-3516. (Illus.). 156p. 1992. pap. text ed. 49.95 (*0-7734-9910-5*) E Mellen.

Agriculture in the United Kingdom. 42p. (Orig.). 1987. pap. text ed. 17.00 (*0-10-100672-1*, HM1352, Pub. by HMSO UK) UNIPUB.

Agriculture in the United Kingdom. 86p. 1994. pap. 30.00 (*0-11-242956-4*, HM29564, Pub. by HMSO UK) UNIPUB.

Agriculture in the United Kingdom: 1988. (Illus.). 57p. 1989. pap. 19.00 (*0-11-242866-5*, HM8665, Pub. by HMSO UK) UNIPUB.

Agriculture in the United Kingdom 1992. Orig. Title: Annual Review of Agriculture. 81p. 1993. pap. 25.00 (*0-11-242938-6*, HM29386, Pub. by HMSO UK) UNIPUB.

Agriculture in the Uruguay Round. Ed. by K. A. Ingersent et al. LC 93-29433. 1994. text ed. 75.00 (*0-312-10632-7*) St Martin.

Agriculture in the West. Ed. by Edward L. Schapsmeier & Frederick H. Schapsmeier. (Illus.). 116p. 1980. pap. text ed. 15.00 (*0-89745-005-1*) Sunflower U Pr.

Agriculture in Virginia, 1607-1699. Lyman Carrier. (Jamestown 350th Anniversary Historical Booklet Ser.: No. 14). 43p. reprint ed. pap. 25.00 (*0-8357-5272-0*, 2026220) Bks Demand.

Agriculture, Liberalisation, & Economic Growth in Ghana & Cote D'Ivoire. OECD Staff. 144p. (Orig.). 1993. pap. 27.00 (*92-64-13936-2*) OECD.

Agriculture, Libraries & Information. K. W. Russel & Maria G. Pisa. (C). 1992. text ed. 200.00 (*81-7233-034-0*, Pub. by Scientific Pubs II) St Mut.

Agriculture Marketing: Systems, Coordination, Cash & Future Prices. Wayne Purcell. (Illus.). 1979. teacher ed write for info. (*0-8359-0196-3*, Reston) P-H.

Agriculture, Marketing & Pricing in Sub-Saharan Africa. John DeWilde. 1984. pap. 18.50 (*0-918456-48-7*) African Studies Assn.

Agriculture of China. Ed. by Xu Guohua & L. J. Peel. (Centre for Agricultural Strategy Ser.: No. 2). (Illus.). 320p. 1991. 90.00 (*0-19-859208-6*) OUP.

Agriculture of Egypt. Ed. by Gillian M. Craig. (Centre for Agricultural Strategy Ser.: No. 3). 536p. 1993. 90.00 (*0-19-859203-5*) OUP.

Agriculture of the Hidatsa Indians: An Indian Interpretation. Gilbert L. Wilson. LC 76-43892. (Univ. of Minnesota Studies in the Social Sciences: No. 9). reprint ed. 47.50 (*0-404-15754-8*) AMS Pr.

Agriculture of the Sudan. G. M. Craig. (Centre for Agricultural Strategy Ser.: No. 1). (Illus.). 490p. 1991. 120.00 (*0-19-859210-8*) OUP.

***Agriculture of the World.** Anna Burger. 320p. 1994. 59.95 (*1-85628-609-6*, Pub. by Avebury Pub UK) Ashgate Pub Co.

***Agriculture on the Road to Industrialization.** Ed. by John W. Mellor. (International Food Policy Research Institute Ser.). 488p. 1994. text ed. 57.50x (*0-8018-5012-6*) Johns Hopkins.

Agriculture Paraprofessionals in the Philippines: Farmer Scholars, Agricultural Counselors & the Samahang Nayon Development Project. Douglas Gritzinger. (Special Series on Paraprofessionals). 55p. (Orig.). (C). 1981. pap. 3.50 (*0-86731-052-9*) Cornell CIS RDC.

***Agriculture, Poverty, & Policy Reform in Sub-Saharan Africa.** Kevin M. Cleaver & W. Graeme Donovan. LC 95-2574. (World Bank Discussion Paper Ser.: No. 280). 60p. 1995. 7.95 (*0-8213-3189-2*, 13189) World Bank.

Agriculture Productivity in India: Impact of Chemical Fertilizers. Dhiam S. Bhau & Singh Bhau. 1990. 21.00 (*81-7041-290-0*, Pub. by Anmol II) S Asia.

Agriculture, Projects & Development: Papers in Honour of David Edwards. John D. MacArthur & John Weiss. 400p. 1994. 68.95 (*1-85628-647-9*, Pub. by Avebury Pub UK) Ashgate Pub Co.

Agriculture State of the Kingdom, 1816. Great Britain Board of Agriculture Staff. LC 78-108849. xvi, 436p. 1970. reprint ed. lib. bdg. 49.50 (*0-678-07767-3*) Kelley.

Agriculture, the Environment & Trade - Conflict or Cooperation? Ed. by Caroline T. Williamson. LC 93-77535. 287p. (Orig.). 1993. 45.00 (*0-9636143-0-4*) IPC Agri & Trade.

Agriculture Trade, Protectionism & the Problems of Development: A Legal Perspective. Joseph A. McMahon. 240p. 1992. text ed. 55.00 (*0-312-07608-8*) St Martin.

Agriculture Two-Thousand: A Look at the Future. Battelle Memorial Institute Staff. Ed. by Mary Bucher. LC 82-25308. (Illus.). 199p. 1983. pap. 8.95 (*0-935470-15-8*) Battelle.

Agriculture under the Common Agriculture Policy: A Geography. Ian R. Bowler. LC 84-25041. 255p. 1985. pap. 15.00 (*0-685-09209-7*, Pub. by Manchester Univ Pr UK) St Martin.

Agriculture's Futures: America's Food System. L. T. Wallace. (Illus.). x, 93p. 1987. pap. 35.00 (*0-387-96482-7*) Spr-Verlag.

AgriData's Week-by-Week Marketing Journal. AgriData Staff. 64p. 1986. pap. 10.95 (*0-910939-16-0*) AgriData.

Agrimed Research Programme Enrichment of Wine in the European Community. Ed. by J. De Hoogh et al. 151p. 1992. pap. 17.00 (*92-826-2000-X*, CD-NA-13239-EN-C) UNIPUB.

Agrimonetary System of the European Economic Community & Its Prospects. European Communities Staff. 107p. 1992. pap. 10.00 (*92-823-0353-5*, AX-72-91-819-EN, Pub. by Europ Com) UNIPUB.

***Agrippa: The Man, the Magician.** Lewis Spence. 1994. pap. 6.95 (*1-55818-293-4*, Sure Fire) Holmes Pub.

Agrippa & the Crisis of Renaissance Thought. Charles G. Nauert. LC 65-63002. (Illinois, University, Illinois Studies in the Social Sciences Ser.: Vol. 55). 382p. reprint ed. pap. 108.90 (*0-8357-5273-9*, 2019027) Bks Demand.

Agrippa d'Aubigne. Keith Cameron. LC 77-540. (Twayne's World Authors Ser.). 169p. (C). 1977. 17.95 (*0-8057-6280-9*) Irvington.

Agrippa d'Aubigne, Poete des Tragiques. Bailbe. (Publ. Fac. des Lettres et Sc. Hum. Universite de Caen). 38.95 (*0-8288-6088-2*, F28350) Fr & Eur.

Agrippa d'Aubigne's "Les Tragiques" A Study of the Baroque Style in Poetry. Imbrie Buffum. LC 75-41042. reprint ed. 12.50 (*0-404-14804-2*) AMS Pr.

Agrippa First: The Last King of Judaea. Daniel R. Schwartz. (Texte und Studien zum Antiken Judentum Ser.: No. 23). 270p. 1990. lib. bdg. 87.50 (*3-16-145341-7*, Pub. by J C B Mohr GW) Coronet Bks.

Agrippina. Claire Bretecher. 50p. (YA). 1992. pap. 9.95 (*0-7493-0812-5*, Pub. by Mandarin UK) Heinemann.

Agrippina: Empress of Depravity. Frederick W. Farrar. (Golden Age of Rome Ser.). 1978. pap. 2.50 (*0-89083-354-0*) Zebra.

***Agriscience: Fundamentals & Applications.** 2nd ed. Elmer L. Cooper. LC 95-15156. (J). 1995. text ed. write for info. (*0-8273-6278-1*) Delmar.

Agriscience & Technology. L. DeVere Burton. 1991. text ed. 28.50 (*0-8273-4016-8*) Delmar.

Agriscience & Technology: Lab Manual. L. DeVere Burton. 199p. 1994. 15.95 (*0-8273-4018-4*); teacher ed 10.00 (*0-8273-4017-6*) Delmar.

Agriscience & Technology Instructor's Guide to Accompany Laboratory Manual. Walter York. 24p. 1994. 10.00 (*0-8273-6419-9*) Delmar.

Agriscience: Fundamentals & Applications: Lab Manual Instructor's Guide. Elmer Cooper. 1991. teacher ed 8.00 (*0-8273-5321-9*) Delmar.

AgriScience in Our Lives. 6th ed. Alfred H. Krebs. (Illus.). 788p. 1994. teacher ed 9.95 (*0-8134-2966-8*); text ed. 29.95 (*0-8134-2965-X*, 2349) Interstate.

Agriscience Lab Manual. Walter York. 1991. 15.95 (*0-8273-3391-9*) Delmar.

Agro-Climatic Atlas of Europe. Ed. by P. Thran & S. Brockhuizen. (Agro-Ecological Atlas Ser.: Vol. 1). 294p. 1965. 243.75 (*0-444-40569-0*) Elsevier.

Agro-Ecological Aspects of Soil Disinfestation. Ed. by C. Van Assche. (Agro-Ecosystems Ser.: Vol. 1, No. 2). 1974. 18.00 (*0-686-43414-5*) Elsevier.

Agro-Forestry in the Pacific Islands: Systems for Sustainability. Ed. by W. C. Clark & R. R. Thaman. 307p. 1993. pap. 35.00 (*92-808-0824-9*, UNUP-824, Pub. by UN Univ JA) UNIPUB.

Agro-Industrial Complexes & Types of Agriculture in Eastern Siberia. V. P. Shotski. 131p. 1979. 75.00 (*0-569-08581-0*, Pub. by Collets UK) Pro-Am Music.

Agro-Pastoralism in Chad As a Strategy for Survival. Angelo M. Bonfiglioli. (Social Dimensions of Adjustment in Sub-Saharan Africa Working Paper Ser.: No. 11). 64p. 1992. 6.95 (*0-8213-1667-2*, 11667) World Bank.

Agro-Pastoralisme au Tchad Comme Strategie de Survie: Essai Sur la Relation Entre l'Anthropologie & la Statistique. Angelo M. Bonfiglioli. (SDA Working Paper Ser.: No. 11F). 61p. 1992. pap. 6.95 (*0-8213-2008-4*, 12008) World Bank.

Agro-Processing: Strategy for Acceleration & Exports. Ed. by Srivastava & Vathsala. (C). 1989. 40.00 (*81-204-0410-6*, Pub. by Oxford IBH II) S Asia.

Agro-Technological System Towards 2000: A European Perspective - Contributions to Economic Analysis. Ed. by G. Antonelli & A. Quadrio-Curzio. 298p. 1988. 89.75 (*0-444-70461-2*, North Holland) Elsevier.

***Agrobacterium Protocols, Vol. 44.** Ed. by Kevan M. Gartland & Michael R. Davey. LC 95-15031. (Methods in Molecular Biology Ser.). (Illus.). 432p. 1995. spiral bd. 69.50 (*0-89603-302-3*) Humana.

***Agrochemical Environmental Fate Studies: State of the Art.** Marguerite L. Leng et al. LC 94-38029. 416p. 1995. 75.00 (*1-56670-034-5*, L1034) Lewis Pubs.

Agrochemicals: Preparation & Mode of Action. 2nd ed. R. J. Cremlyn. 396p. 1991. pap. text ed. 74.95 (*0-471-92992-1*) Wiley.

Agrochemicals Desk Reference. John H. Montgomery. 1993. 89.95 (*0-87371-738-4*, TD427) Lewis Pubs.

***Agrochemicals from Natural Products.** Ed. by C. Godfrey. LC 94-35411. (Books in Soils, Plants & the Environment). 1994. 165.00 (*0-8247-9553-9*) Dekker.

Agrochemicals in Soils: Selected Papers. Soil Chemistry, Soil Fertility & Soil Clay Mineralogy Commissions of the International Society of Soil Science, 13-18 July 1976, Jerusalem. Ed. by A. Banin & U. Kafkafi. LC 79-41750. 500p. 1980. 192.00 (*0-08-025914-6*, Pub. by Pergamon Repr UK) Franklin.

Agroclimatology of the Sugar-Cane Crop. B. C. Biswas. (WMO, No. 703 & Technical Note Ser.: No. 193). xvi, 90p. 1988. pap. 23.00 (*92-63-10703-3*, Pub. by Wrld Meteorological SZ) Am Meteorological.

Agroecological Constraints to Crop Production in West Asia & North Africa, & Their Impact on Fertilizer Use. Peter Cooper et al. Ed. by E. N. Roth. LC 89-15447. (Paper Ser.: No. P-9). (Illus.). 30p. (Orig.). 1989. pap. text ed. 4.00 (*0-88090-074-1*) Intl Fertilizer.

Agroecology. C. Ronald Carroll et al. (Biological Resource Management Ser.). 640p. 1990. text ed. 93.00 (*0-07-052923-X*) McGraw.

An Asterisk (*) at the beginning of an entry indicates that the title is appearing in BIP for the first time.

Agroecology. Ed. by S. R. Gliessman. (Ecological Studies: Vol. 78). (Illus.). xiv, 380p. 1991. 98.00 (*0-387-97028-2*, 2942) Spr-Verlag.

***Agroecology: The Science of Sustainable Agriculture.** 2nd ed. Miguel A. Altieri. (C). 1995. text ed. 65.00 (*0-8133-1717-7*); pap. text ed. 24.95 (*0-8133-1718-5*) Westview.

Agroecology: The Scientific Basis of Alternative Agriculture. Miguel A. Altieri. 227p. (C). 1987. pap. text ed. 41.00 (*0-8133-7284-4*) Westview.

Agroecology & Small Farm Development. Ed. by Miguel A. Altieri & Susanna B. Hecht. 336p. 1990. 69.00 (*0-8493-4885-4*, SB) CRC Pr.

Agroforestry: Classification & Management. Ed. by Kenneth G. Macdicken & Napoleon T. Vergara. 416p. 1990. text ed. 84.95 (*0-471-83781-4*) Wiley.

Agroforestry: Indian Perspective. Ed. by L. K. Jha & P. K. Sen Sarma. (Illus.). x, 341p. 1993. 38.00 (*81-7024-543-5*, Pub. by Ashish Pub Hse II) Nataraj Bks.

Agroforestry Education & Training: Present & Future. Ed. by P. K. Nair et al. (Forestry Sciences Ser.). (C). 1990. lib. bdg. 65.00 (*0-7923-0864-6*) Kluwer Ac.

Agroforestry for Soil Conservation. Anthony Young. 280p. (Orig.). 1989. pap. text ed. 33.25 (*0-85198-648-X*) CAB Intl.

Agroforestry in Irrigated Lands. A. M. Stepanov. 205p. (C). 1993. 75.00 (*81-85880-12-3*, Pub. by Print Hse II) St Mut.

Agroforestry in South Asia: Problems & Applied Research Perspectives. William Bentley et al. (Winrock Ser.). 390p. (C). 1993. text ed. 55.00 (*1-881570-16-9*) Intl Sci Pub.

Agroforestry in South Asia: Problems & Applied Research Perspectives. Ed. by William R. Bentley. (Winrock-Oxford & IBH Ser.). (C). 1993. text ed. 34.00 (*81-204-0755-5*, Pub. by Oxford IBH II) S Asia.

Agroforestry in Sub-Saharan Africa: A Farmer's Perspective. Cynthia C. Cook & Mikael Grut. (Technical Paper Ser.: No. 112). 104p. 1989. 7.95 (*0-8213-1389-4*, 11389) World Bank.

***Agroforestry Systems for Degraded Lands, 2 vols., Set.** Ed. by Panjab Singh et al. 1009p. 1995. text ed. 144.00 (*1-886106-20-7*) Science Pubs.

***Agroforestry Systems for Sustainable Land Use.** Ed. by Panjab Singh et al. 292p. 1994. text ed. 72.00 (*1-886106-19-3*) Science Pubs.

Agroforestry Systems in the Tropics. Ed. by P. K. Nair. (Forestry Sciences Ser.). (C). 1989. lib. bdg. 211.50 (*90-247-3790-7*) Kluwer Ac.

Agroforestry Technology Information Kit. 1991. 23.00 (*0-942717-31-7*) Intl Inst Rural.

Agroindustrial Investment & Operations. James G. Brown. LC 93-3077. 1993. write for info. (*0-8213-2345-8*) World Bank.

Agroindustrial Project Analysis. James E. Austin. LC 80-550. (World Bank Research Publication Ser.). (Illus.). 224p. 1981. text ed. 23.95 (*0-8018-2412-5*) Johns Hopkins.

Agroindustrial Project Analysis: Critical Design Factors. 2nd ed. James E. Austin. 272p. 1992. pap. text ed. 23.95x (*0-8018-4530-0*, 44530) Johns Hopkins.

Agrometeorological Aspects of Crops in the United Kingdom & Ireland, EUR 13039. M. N. Hough. 310p. 1991. pap. 35.00 (*92-826-1649-5*, CD-NA-13039-EN-C) UNIPUB.

Agrometeorological Aspects of Operational Crop Protection: Report of the Working Group on Agrometeorological Aspects of Operational Crop Protection of the Commission for Agricultural Meteorology. World Meteorological Organization Staff. (WMO Ser.: No. 687). (Illus.). xiv, 165p. 1988. pap. 30.00 (*92-63-10687-8*, Pub. by Wrld Meteorological SZ) Am Meteorological.

Agrometeorology. G. Z. Ventskevich. 304p. 1958. text ed. 76.00 (*0-317-46406-X*, Pub. by Keter Pub IS) Coronet Bks.

Agromyzidae (Diptera) of Fenno-scandia & Denmark, 2 pts., Set. K. A. Spencer. (Fauna Entomologica Scandinavica Ser.: No. 5). (Illus.). 922p. 1976. pap. 60.00 (*87-87491-08-7*) Lubrecht & Cramer.

Agronomic & Economic Evaluation of Urea Placement & Sulfur-Coated Urea for Irrigated Paddy in Farmers' Fields in Eastern India, P-4. Adolfo Martinez et al. Ed. by Ernest D. Frederick & E. N. Roth. LC 83-10874. (Paper Ser.). (Illus.). 36p. 1983. pap. text ed. 4.00 (*0-88090-044-X*) Intl Fertilizer.

Agronomic Evaluation of Partially Acidulated Phosphate Rocks in the Tropics: IFDC's Experience. S. H. Chien & L. L. Hammond. Ed. by E. N. Roth. LC 88-32883. (Paper Ser.: No. P-7). (Illus.). 10p. (Orig.). 1988. pap. text ed. 4.00 (*0-88090-070-9*) Intl Fertilizer.

Agronomy: From World Hunger to Biotech. Harry Cralle. 1991. spiral bd. 26.00 (*0-88252-130-6*) Paladin Hse.

Agronomy: Science & Technology of Crop Growth, Breeding & Production. Harry Cralle. 1986. spiral bd. 27.75 (*0-88252-128-4*) Paladin Hse.

Agronomy of Grassland Systems. Craig J. Pearson & Ray L. Ison. (Illus.). 200p. 1987. pap. 24.95 (*0-521-31009-1*) Cambridge U Pr.

Agrophydrology - Recent Developments: Proceedings of the Symposium at the International Agricultural Centre IAC, Wageningen, the Netherlands, 29 September to 1 October 1987. Ed. by J. W. Van Hoorn. 550p. 1988. 141.00 (*0-444-43028-8*) Elsevier.

Agropolitics in the European Community: Interest Groups & the Common Agricultural Policy. William F. Averyt, Jr. LC 77-10619. 144p. 1977. 31.95 (*0-03-039666-2*, Praeger Pubs) Greenwood.

Aground. James E. Minnoch. 1985. 12.95 (*0-07-155319-3*) McGraw.

Aground: Coping with Emergency Groundings. James E. Minnoch. LC 85-71609. (Illus.). 160p. 1985. 12.95 (*0-8286-0098-8*) J De Graff.

***AGS: A History.** Audrey N. Slate. LC 94-24722. 1994. write for info. (*0-9643240-0-8*) Assn Grad Schls.

Agta of Northeastern Luzon: Recent Studies. Agnes Estioko-Griffin. Ed. by P. Bion Griffin. (San Carlos Humanities Ser.: No. 16). (Illus.). xiv, 187p. (C). 1986. 15.75 (*0-317-01355-6*, Pub. by San Carlos Univ PH); pap. 12.50 (*0-317-01356-4*, Pub. by San Carlos Univ PH) Cellar.

Agu, Agu, Agu: Murmel, Murmel, Murmel. Robert Munsch. (Illus.). 32p. (SPA.). (J). (ps-2). 1991. pap. 5.95 (*1-55037-095-2*, Pub. by Annick CN) Firefly Bks Ltd.

Agua. Jo E. Moore & Joy Evans. Tr. by Dora Ficklin & Liz Wolfe. (Science Mini-Units Ser.). (Illus.). 16p. (SPA.). (J). (gr. 1-3). 1992. pap. text ed. 5.95 (*1-55799-234-7*) Evan-Moor Corp.

Agua. J. M. Parramon et al. (Four Elements Ser.). 32p. (SPA.). (J). (ps). 1985. pap. 6.95 (*0-8120-3621-2*) Barron.

Agua, Agua, Agua. 2nd ed. Pat Mora. (Let Me Read Ser.). 16p. (J). (ps-1). 1994. text ed. 2.95 (*0-673-36195-0*) GdYrBks.

***Agua Agua Agua.** 3rd ed. Pat Mora. Tr. by Alma F. Ada. (Let Me Read, Level 2, Ser.). (Illus.). (SPA.). (J). 1995. bds. 2.95 (*0-673-36292-2*) GdYrBks.

Agua De Fuego. Nicolas E. Alvarez. LC 90-84744. (Coleccion Espejo de Paciencia Ser.). 60p. (Orig.). (SPA.). 1991. pap. 9.00 (*0-89729-583-8*) Ediciones.

Agua Fresca. Estevan A. Rodriguez et al. (Illus.). 59p. 1980. pap. 3.50 (*0-918358-10-8*) Pajarito Pubns.

Agua Negra. 4th ed. Leo Romero. Ed. by Dale Boyer. LC 81-68459. (Ahsahta Press Modern & Contemporary Poets of the West Ser.). 55p. 1981. pap. 6.95 (*0-916272-17-6*) Ahsahta Pr.

Agua Quieta. Rodrigo R. Rosa. 108p. (Orig.). (SPA.). (C). 1991. pap. 6.95 (*0-9626221-2-5*) Vista Pubns FL.

***Agua Santa: Holy Water.** Pat Mora. LC 95-6024. 160p. (C). 1995. 17.95 (*0-8070-6828-4*) Beacon Pr.

Agua Viva see Stream of Life

Agua Viva - Living Water: El Nuevo Testamento - Bilingual New Testament. (ENG & SPA.). 1987. pap. 5.70 (*0-311-48690-8*) Casa Bautista.

Agua y Espejos: Imagenes. Amelia del Castillo. LC 86-80921. (Coleccion Espejo de Paciencia Ser.). (Illus.). 69p. (Orig.). (SPA.). 1986. pap. 9.00 (*0-89729-402-5*) Ediciones.

Agua y Tu. Clarita Kohen. (Illus.). 16p. (SPA.). (J). (gr. k-5). 1993. lib. bdg. 7.50 (*1-56492-101-8*) Laredo.

Aguahega. Kathleen Snow. LC 90-578. 496p. 1990. 9.95 (*0-934745-13-7*) Acadia Pub Co.

Aguas Refrescantes. T. S. Nee. Orig. Title: Through the Year. 270p. (SPA.). 1992. pap. 5.25 (*0-8254-1500-4*) Kregel.

***Aguazuque: Evidencias de Cazadores, Recolectores y Plantadores en la Altiplanicie de la Cordillera Oriental.** Gonzalo Correal. (Illus.). 307p. (SPA.). 1990. pap. 8.50 (*1-877812-11-0*) UPLAAP.

Aguedo Mojica: La Luminosa Entrega. Luis Mojica-Sandoz. LC 83-82447. 336p. 1983. pap. 12.95 (*0-940238-70-5*) Ediciones Huracan.

Aguiar Collection in the Arizona Pioneers' Historical Society. Paul Ezell & Greta Ezell. 1964. pap. 12.50 (*0-916304-00-0*) SDSU Press.

Aguila del Viento. Lada J. Kratky. (Que Maravilla! Ser.: Level 2). (Illus.). 16p. (Orig.). (SPA.). (J). (gr. 2-4). 1992. pap. text ed. 29.95 (*1-56334-172-7*); pap. text ed. 6.00 (*1-56334-173-5*) Hampton-Brown.

Aguila Del Viento: Level 2. (Que Maravilla! Ser.). 16p. (Orig.). (SPA.). 1992. pap. write for info. (*1-56334-214-6*) Hampton-Brown.

***Aguilar, Colorado.** Josephine Cuzzetto. (Illus.). 226p. 1994. 57.50 (*0-88107-245-1*) Curtis Media.

Aguilas. Eduardo Mallea. Bd. with Rodeada Esta de Ensueno.; Retorno.; Vinculo.; Enemigos del Alma.; Torre. (SPA.). 12.95 (*0-7859-0128-0*, S2130); Bd. with 12.95 (*0-8288-6089-0*, S2130) Fr & Eur.

Aguilas. LC 92-8454. (YA). 1992. 12.67 (*0-86593-196-8*); 9.50 (*0-685-59292-8*) Rourke Corp.

Aguilas. Christine Butterworth & Donna Bailey. LC 91-22808. (Animales Ser.). (Illus.). 32p. (SPA.). (J). (gr. 1-4). 1992. lib. bdg. 19.97 (*0-8114-2660-2*) Raintree Steck-V.

Aguirre. Stephen Minta. 256p. 1995. pap. 11.95 (*0-8050-3104-9*) H Holt & Co.

Aguirre: The Re-Creation of a Sixteenth-Century Journey Across South America. Stephen Minta. LC 93-11679. 208p. 1994. 20.00 (*0-8050-3103-0*) H Holt & Co.

Agunah. Chaim Grade. Tr. by Curt Leviant. 1978. reprint ed. pap. 5.95 (*0-932232-00-0*) Menorah Pub.

***Agunah: A Sourcebook on the "Chained Wife"** Jack N. Porter. LC 95-9843. 1995. pap. write for info. (*1-56821-440-5*) Aronson.

Agustin Acosta: El Modernista y Su Isla. Maria Capote. LC 89-81546. (Coleccion Polymita Ser.). (Illus.). 260p. (Orig.). (SPA.). 1990. pap. 19.00 (*0-89729-550-1*) Ediciones.

Agustin De Rojas el Natural Desdichado. Intro. by James White Cromwell. lxxi, 201p. (ENG & SPA.). 1939. text ed. 2.60 (*0-318-14233-3*) Hispanic Inst.

Agustin Duran: A Bibliography & Literary Appreciation. David T. Gies. (Serie A: Monagrafias, XLVIII). 197p. (Orig.). (C). 1975. 45.00 (*0-7293-0000-5*, Pub. by Tamesis Bks Ltd UK) Boydell & Brewer.

Agustin Yanez Y Sus Cuentos. Richard A. Young. (Serie A: Monagrafias, LXVIII). 169p. (SPA.). (C). 1978. 45.00 (*0-7293-0068-4*, Pub. by Tamesis Bks Ltd UK) Boydell & Brewer.

Agustine: "Confessions" Gillian Clark. LC 92-41452. (Landmarks of World Literature Ser.). (Illus.). 128p. (C). 1993. 29.95 (*0-521-40104-6*); pap. 10.95 (*0-521-40942-X*) Cambridge U Pr.

AGV Handbook: A Handbook for the Selection of Automated Guided Vehicle Systems. Guy A. Castleberry. LC 90-82031. (Illus.). 288p. 1991. 110.00 (*0-9627038-1-8*) AGV Decisions.

AGV System Specification, Procurement, & Implementation Guide: A Step-by-Step Guide to Selecting & Installing an Automated Guided Vehicle System. Guy A. Castleberry. LC 90-83341. (Illus.). 227p. 1992. 250.00 (*0-9627038-2-6*) AGV Decisions.

Agviq. Michael Armstrong. 1990. mass mkt. 4.50 (*0-445-20848-1*) Warner Bks.

Agweddau Ar Dwf Piwritaniaeth Yng Nghymru Yn Yr Ail Ganrif Ar Bymtheg. Ed. by J. Gwynfor Jones. LC 91-42424. (Welsh Studies: Vol. 6). 252p. (WEL.). 1992. lib. bdg. 89.95 (*0-7734-9452-9*) E Mellen.

Agyar. Steven Brust. 256p. 1994. mass mkt. 4.99 (*0-8125-1521-8*) Tor Bks.

Agyptisches Kulturgut im Phonikischen und Punischen Sardinien, Tomes I und II, 2 vols., Gunther Holbl. (Etudes Preliminaires aux Religions Orientales dans l'Empire Romain Ser.: Tome 102). (Illus.). 1986. 183.00 (*90-04-07182-2*); Vol. I, xxi, 430. write for info. (*0-318-61849-4*); Vol. II, v, 245. write for info. (*0-318-61850-8*) E J Brill.

Ah! Josse Coffin. (Illus.). 28p. 1992. 14.95 (*0-8109-1910-9*) Abrams.

***AH.** Walter Lee. (Illus.). 200p. 1995. write for info. (*0-615-00661-2*) Faun Pub Co.

***Ah.** Walter Lee. 200p. 1995. write for info. (*1-887409-01-7*); pap. write for info. (*1-887409-00-9*) Faun Pub Co.

Ah, Assyria...Studies in Assyrian History & Ancient Near Eastern Historiography: Presented to Hayim Tadmor. Ed. by Mordechai Cogan & Israel Ephal. (Scripta Hiersolymitana Ser.: No. 33). 347p. 1991. 33.00 (*0-685-53241-0*, Pub. by Magnes Press IS) Eisenbrauns.

Ah Bak's Strange New Crop. Illus. by Fabricio Vanden Broeck. LC 92-11322. (J). 1995. text ed. 14.95 (*0-02-775657-2*) Macmillan.

Ah! Berlin et Autres Recits. Patrick Besson. 342p. (FRE.). 1989. pap. 12.95 (*0-7859-2237-7*, 207038117X) Fr & Eur.

Ah, but Your Land Is Beautiful. Alan Paton. 280p. 1983. pap. 13.95 (*0-684-17830-3*, Scribners) S&S Trade.

Ah-Choo. Mercer Mayer. (Pied Piper Bks.). (Illus.). (J). (gr. k-2). 1977. lib. bdg. 4.58 (*0-8037-4895-7*) Dial Bks Young.

Ah-Chooo Book. Linda Pohl. (Illus.). 20p. (J). (ps-2). 1990. 3.95 (*0-9625453-0-9*) L P Pohl.

Ah, Eurydice! A Lyrical Fantasy in One Act. Stanley Taikeff. 1977. pap. 2.75 (*0-8222-0012-0*) Dramatists Play.

Ah Julian! A Memoir of Julian Brodetsky. Leonard Wibberley. LC 84-307. (Borgo Bioviews Ser.: No. 5). 154p. 1987. lib. bdg. 27.00x (*0-89370-341-9*) Borgo Pr.

Ah King. W. Somerset Maugham. LC 75-26127. (Works of W. Somerset Maugham Ser.). 1977. reprint ed. 23.95 (*0-405-07850-1*) Ayer.

Ah, Mediterranean: Twentieth Century Classicism in America, Vol. 2. Ed. by Charles W. Moore & Wayne Attoe. (Illus.). 128p. 1986. pap. 15.00 (*0-8478-5414-0*) Ctr Study of Amer Archit.

Ah Mo. ARthur Griffin. Ed. by Tren J. Griffin. (Illus.). 64p. (Orig.). 1990. pap. 7.95 (*0-88839-244-3*) Hancock House.

Ah Mo: Indian Legends from Washington State. Ed. by Arthur E. Griffin. (Illus.). 75p. (Orig.). (J). (gr. 2-5). 1989. pap. write for info. (*0-318-65297-8*) Bainbridge Pr.

Ah Q, & Others: Selected Stories of Lusin. Shu-Jen Chou. Tr. by Chi-Chen Wang. LC 70-150542. (Short Story Index Reprint Ser.). 1977. reprint ed. 19.95 (*0-8369-3839-9*) Ayer.

Ah Q & Others: Selected Stories of Lusin. Chou Shu-Jen. Tr. by Chi-Chen Wang. LC 75-143310. 1971. reprint ed. text ed. 55.00 (*0-8371-5965-2*, CHAQ, Greenwood Pr) Greenwood.

Ah, Sweet Mystery. Celestine Sibley. 1992. mass mkt. 4.50 (*0-06-109083-2*, Harp PBks) HarpC.

Ah, Sweet Mystery of Life. Roald Dahl. 176p. 1991. pap. 6.95 (*0-14-011847-0*) Viking Penguin.

Ah This! Osho Rajneesh. Ed. by Rajneesh Foundation International Staff. LC 82-24026. (Zen Ser.). 268p. (Orig.). 1982. pap. 8.95 (*0-88050-502-8*) Osho Chidvilas.

Ah, Treachery! Ross Thomas. 288p. 1994. 21.95 (*0-89296-452-9*) Mysterious Pr.

***Ah, Treachery!** Ross Thomas. 272p. 1995. mass mkt. 5.99 (*0-446-40031-9*, Mysterious Paperbk) Warner Bks.

***Ah, Treachery!** large type ed. Ross Thomas. LC 94-39241. 423p. 1995. 22.95 (*0-7862-0384-6*) Thorndike Pr.

Ah, Treasure! David Drew. LC 92-21455. (Voyages Ser.). (Illus.). (J). 1993. 3.75 (*0-383-03611-9*) SRA Schl Grp.

Ah Wisconsin. Smith & Mead. 1990. 19.95 (*0-915024-35-7*) WI Trails.

Ah, You Iowans! At Home, at Work, at Play, at War. Chuck Offenburger. LC 92-20994. (Illus.). 316p. 1992. pap. 14.95 (*0-8138-1833-8*) Iowa St U Pr.

AH-64 Apache. Doug Richardson. (Combat Aircraft Ser.). 1992. 9.99 (*0-517-06739-0*) Random Hse Value.

AH-64 Apache in Action. Al Adcock. (Aircraft in Action Ser.). (Illus.). 50p. 1989. pap. 8.95 (*0-89747-223-3*, 1095) Squad Sig Pubns.

AHA. Aleister Crowley. LC 83-82342. 80p. 1986. reprint ed. pap. 9.95 (*1-56184-035-1*) New Falcon Pubns.

Aha! A Puzzle Approach to Creative Thinking. Morgan Worthy. LC 75-23143. 152p. 1975. 23.95 (*0-88229-271-4*) Nelson-Hall.

Aha! The Realization Book. Janet McClure & Lillian Harben. 120p. (Orig.). 1990. pap. 11.95 (*0-929385-14-4*) Light Tech Comns Servs.

Aha! Gotcha: Paradoxes to Puzzle & Delight. Martin Gardner. (Illus.). 164p. (C). 1995. pap. text ed. write for info. (*0-7167-1361-6*) W H Freeman.

AHA Guide to the Health Care Field. American Hospital Association Staff. (Illus.). 830p. (Orig.). 1994. pap. 195.00 (*0-87258-662-6*, 010094) Am Hospital.

AHA Guide to the Health Care Field: 1993 Edition. American Hospital Association Staff. (Illus.). 830p. (Orig.). 1993. pap. 195.00 (*0-87258-639-1*, 010093) Am Hospital.

AHA Hospital Statistics. American Hospital Association Staff. (Illus.). 112p. (Orig.). 1994. pap. 139.00 (*0-87258-663-4*, 082094) Am Hospital.

AHA Hospital Statistics, 1993-94. (Illus.). 112p. (Orig.). 1993. pap. 139.00 (*0-87258-658-8*, 082093) Am Hospital.

Aha! Insight. Martin Gardner. LC 78-51259. (Illus.). 179p. 1995. pap. text ed. write for info. (*0-7167-1017-X*) W H Freeman.

AHA Low Fat Low Cholesterol Cookbook. large type ed. Scott Grundy. LC 90-11242. 1990. reprint ed. lib. bdg. 22.95 (*1-56054-032-X*) Thorndike Pr.

Aha! The Ice Cream Koans Answer Book: Solutions to 101 Problems in Child Maintenance. Michael Pastore. LC 92-82028. (Orig.). 1993. pap. 14.95 (*0-927379-19-8*, ZP 120) Zorba Pr.

Ahab. Ed. by Harold Bloom. (Major Literary Characters Ser.). 264p. 1991. lib. bdg. 34.95 (*0-7910-0933-5*) Chelsea Hse.

Ahab. Robert E. Campbell. 40p. (Orig.). (C). 1989. Letter press edition. pap. 12.95 (*0-9621912-0-5*, TXV 324 342) Leviathan Bks.

Ahab & Other Poems. Aleister Crowley. 1973. lib. bdg. 250.00 (*0-87968-221-3*) Krishna Pr.

Ahapius Honcharenko & the Alaska Hearald: The Editor's Life & an Analysis of His Newspaper. Wasyl Luciw. LC 65-923. pap. text ed. 10.00 (*0-918884-10-1*) Slavia Lib.

Ahare Mot Qedoshim, Emor, Behar & Behuqotai see Sifra: An Analytical Translation

Aharon Appelfeld: The Holocaust & Beyond. Gila Ramras-Rauch. LC 93-5016. 1994. 35.00 (*0-253-34831-5*) Ind U Pr.

Aharonov-Bohm Effect. M. Peshkin & A. Tonomura. (Lecture Notes in Physics Ser.: Vol. 340). vi, 152p. 1989. 31.00 (*0-387-51567-4*, 3455) Spr-Verlag.

Ahavat Chesed - Love Mercy: Reader. Abraham Shumsky & Adaia Shumsky. (Mah Tov Hebrew Teaching Ser.: Bk. 2). (Illus.). (J). (gr. 4-6). 1970. student ed 6.00 (*0-8074-0177-3*, 405303); text ed. 6.00 (*0-8074-0175-7*, 405304) UAHC.

Ahavath Chesed: The Love of Kindness As Required by G-D. 2nd rev. ed. Hafetz Hayyim, pseud. Tr. by Leonard Oschry. 1976. 14.95 (*0-87306-110-1*) Feldheim.

AHD Larousse Span-Eng. 1987. pap. 4.95 (*0-395-44146-3*) HM.

AHEA: A History of Excellence. Helen M. Pundt. 1980. write for info. (*0-8461-5042-5*) Am Home Eco.

***Ahead of All Parting: The Selected Poetry & Prose of Rainer Maria Rilke.** Rainer Rilke. 1995. 18.00 (*0-679-60161-9*) Random.

Ahead of Her Time: Abby Kelly & the Politics of Antislavery. Dorothy Sterling. 1994. pap. 14.95 (*0-393-31131-7*) Norton.

Ahead of His Time: Michel T. Halbouty Speaks to the People. Michel T. Halbouty. Ed. by James A. Clark. LC 73-187217. 380p. reprint ed. pap. 108.30 (*0-8357-5274-7*, 2051871) Bks Demand.

Ahead of Time: My Early Years As a Foreign Correspondent. Ruth Gruber. LC 90-22414. 384p. 1991. 19.99 (*0-922066-64-7*, Wynwood Pr) Revell.

Ahearn Tradition. David Smale. Ed. by Richard Silverman. 152p. 1988. 22.75 (*0-9624679-0-1*) SportMemories.

AHFS Drug Information, 1994. rev. ed. Ed. by Gerald K. McEvoy. 2500p. 1994. pap. text ed. 115.00 (*1-879907-35-6*) Am Soc Hlth-Syst.

***AHFS Drug Information, 1995.** rev. ed. Gerald K. McEvoy. 2500p. 1995. per., pap. text ed. 115.00 (*1-879907-53-4*) Am Soc Hlth-Syst.

Ahi Ni Nikisheegiizh. Mazii Dineltsoi. 38p. (Orig.). (NAV.). 1988. pap. 5.00 (*0-317-91235-6*) Princeton Collects W Americana.

Ahimsa: Buddhist & Gandhian. Indu M. Ghosh. 1989. 26.00 (*81-85004-07-2*, Indian Biblio Bureau) S Asia.

Ahmad B, 'Ali B, Mas'ud on Arabic Morphology, Marah al-Arwah, Pt. 1: The Strong Verb, As-Sahih. Tr. & Intro. by Joyce Akesson. LC 90-2470. (Studia Orientalia Lundensia: Vol. 4). xxx, 125p. (ARA & ENG.). 1990. pap. 43.00 (*90-04-09311-7*) E J Brill.

Ahmad B. at-Tayyib as-Sarahsi. Franz Rosenthal. (American Oriental Ser.: Vol. 26). 1943. pap. 5.00 (*0-940490-26-9*) Am Orient Soc.

Ahmadabad. Ed. by George Michell. (C). 1988. 48.50 (*81-85026-03-3*, Pub. by Marg) S Asia.

Ahmadiya Movement. H. A. Walter. (C). 1991. 25.00 (*81-85425-36-1*, Pub. by Manohar II) S Asia.

Ahmadu Bello: Sardauna of Sokoto Values & Leadership in Nigeria. Ed. by John N. Paden. xvi, 800p. 1986. pap. 13.50 (*0-340-38967-2*, 00589) Heinemann.

Ahmed. Mark Dunster. 25p. (Orig.). 1986. pap. 4.00 (*0-89642-140-6*) Linden Pubs.

Ahony en Lattam see As I Saw It: The Tragedy of Hungary

Ahora, Leamos. 2nd ed. Jackie Jarest & Marsha Robinson. 171p. 1990. pap. 28.95 (*0-8384-1876-7*) Heinle & Heinle.

Ahora que Creo. Robert Cook. Orig. Title: Now That I Believe. 128p. (SPA.). 1984. pap. 3.99 (*0-8254-1137-8*) Kregel.

An Asterisk (*) at the beginning of an entry indicates that the title is appearing in BIP for the first time.

Ahora Que Soy Cristiano: Now That I Am a Christian, Vol. 1. Chuck Miller. (SPA.). 3.95 (84-7228-489-1, 220013, Pub. by Edit Clie SP) TSELF.

Ahora Que Soy Cristiano: Now That I Am a Christian, Vol. 2. Chuck Miller. (SPA.). 3.95 (84-7228-490-5, 220014, Pub. by Edit Clie SP) TSELF.

***Ahoy There, Little Polar Bear.** Hans De Beer. (Illus.). 32p. (J). (gr. k-3). 1988. lib. bdg. 13.88 (1-55858-240-1) North-South Bks NYC.

Ahoy There, Little Polar Bear. Hans De Beer. LC 88-42533. (Illus.). 32p. (J). (gr. k-3). 1988. 13.95 (1-55858-028-X) North-South Bks NYC.

Ahrends, Burton & Koralek: An Architectural Monograph. Peter B. Jones et al. (Academy Editions Ser.). (Illus.). 176p. (Orig.). 1991. 45.00 (0-312-06191-9); pap. 29.95 (0-312-06192-7) St Martin.

Ahrens-Fox: The Rolls Royce of Fire Engines. 2nd ed. Ed Hass. (Illus.). 160p. 1983. reprint ed. pap. text ed. 30.00 (0-9611166-0-9) E Hass.

Ahrimanic Deception. Rudolf Steiner. 20p. (Orig.). 1985. pap. 2.95 (0-88010-146-6) Anthroposophic.

Ahtna Athabaskan Dictionary. Ed. by James Kari. xii, 702p. (Orig.). 1990. text ed. 50.00 (1-55500-035-5); pap. text ed. 25.00 (1-55500-033-9) Alaska Native.

Ah...To Be A Kid: Three Dozen Aikido Games for Children of All Ages. Michael Friedl. (Illus.). 55p. (Orig.). (J). 1994. pap. 9.95 (0-9638530-1-5) Magical Michael.

***Ahwinma: Following the Sun & Moon.** Alph H. Secakuku. LC 94-46844. 1994. write for info. (0-934351-48-1); pap. write for info. (0-934351-49-X) Heard Mus.

Ahyoka & the Talking Leaves. Peter Roop & Connie Roop. LC 91-3036. (Illus.). 48p. (J). (gr. 1 up). 1992. text ed. 14.00 (0-688-10697-8) Lothrop.

Ahyoka & the Talking Leaves. Peter Roop & Connie Roop. Ed. by Amy Cohn. LC 91-30366. (Illus.). 64p. (J). (gr. 3 up). 1994. reprint ed. pap. 3.95 (0-688-13082-8, Pub. by Beech Tree Bks) Morrow.

Ai: A Social Vision. Charles S. Daniel. LC 70-154438. (Utopian Literature Ser.). 1976. reprint ed. 26.95 (0-405-03521-7) Ayer.

AI: The Tumultuous History of the Search for Artificial Intelligence. Daniel Crevier. (Illus.). 432p. 1994. pap. 14.00 (0-465-00104-1) Basic.

AI & Cognitive Science Ninety-One: University College, Cork, 19-20 September 1991. Ed. by Humphrey Sorensen. LC 92-18611. (Workshops in Computing Ser.). 1993. 69.00 (0-387-19785-0) Spr-Verlag.

AI & Cognitive Science '89: Proceedings of the Second Irish Conference on Artificial Intelligence & Cognitive Science, September 14-15, 1989, Dublin City University, Ireland. Ed. by A. F. Smeaton et al. (Workshops in Computing Ser.). (Illus.). 288p. 1990. pap. 39.00 (0-387-19608-0) Spr-Verlag.

AI & Cognitive Science '90: Proceedings of the Third Irish Conference on Artificial Intelligence & Cognitive Science 20-22 September 1990, Ulster. Ed. by M. McTear & N. Creaney. (Workshops in Computing Ser.). xv, 392p. 1991. pap. 59.00 (0-387-19653-6) Spr-Verlag.

AI & Cognitive Science '92. Ed. by Kevin Ryan & R. F. Sutcliffe. (Workshops in Computing Ser.). (Illus.). 385p. 1993. pap. write for info. (3-540-19799-0) Spr-Verlag.

AI & Cognitive Science '92: University of Limerick, 10-11 September, 1992. Ed. by Kevin Ryan & F. E. Sutcliffe. LC 93-26018. (Workshops in Computing Ser.). 1993. 79.00 (0-387-19799-0) Spr-Verlag.

***AI & Collaborative Design: Papers from the 1993 Workshop.** Ed. by John Gero & Mary L. Maher. (Technical Reports). (Illus.). 320p. (Orig.). 1994. pap. 25.00x (0-929280-67-9) Amer Artificial.

AI & Expert Systems: A Comprehensive Guide, C Version. Robert Levine. 1990. pap. text ed. 29.95 (0-07-037500-3) McGraw.

AI & Simulation. Luker & Brirtwistle. 100p. 1987. 40.00 (0-685-66775-8, SS18-3) Soc Computer Sim.

AI & Simulation: Theory & Applications, 1990. Ed. by Wade Webster & Ranjeet J. Uttamsingh. (Simulation Ser.: Vol. 22, No. 3). 336p. 1990. 60.00 (0-911801-68-5, SS22-3) Soc Computer Sim.

AI & the Eye. Ed. by Andrew Blake & Tom Troscianko. 1990. text ed. 116.95 (0-471-92194-7) Wiley.

***AI & Theories of Groups & Organizations: Conceptual & Empirical Research: Papers from the 1993 Workshop.** Ed. by Mike Prietula. (Technical Reports). (Illus.). 102p. (Orig.). 1994. pap. 25.00x (0-929280-55-5) Amer Artificial.

Ai-Chan's Secret. Irene Hope. (J). 1989. pap. 2.95 (9971-972-85-9) OMF Bks.

***AI in Intelligent Vehicle Highway Systems: Papers from the 1993 Workshop.** Ed. by Yukiko Sekine. (Technical Reports). (Illus.). 95p. (Orig.). 1994. pap. 25.00x (0-929280-64-4) Amer Artificial.

AI in Process Control. Michael J. Stock. 352p. 1989. text ed. 47.00 (0-07-061590-X) McGraw.

Ai: Japan Through John Lennon's Eyes: A Personal Sketchbook. John Lennon. Ed. by Seiji Horibuchi. Tr. by Satoru Fujii. (Illus.). 194p. (Orig.). 1992. pap. 21.95 (0-929279-78-6, Cadence Bks) Viz Commns Inc.

AI Methods in Statistics see Interactions in Artificial Intelligence & Statistical Methods

AI 'Ninety-One Frontiers in Innovative Computing for the Nuclear Industry Topical Meeting, Jackson Lake, WY, Sept. 15-18, 1991, 2 vols., Set. 922p. 1991. 100.00 (0-89448-171-1, 700172) Am Nuclear Soc.

AI Papers, 1988: (ESC 1988, Orlando) (Simulation Ser.: Vol. 20, No. 1). 162p. 1988. 48.00 (0-911801-35-9, SS20-1) Soc Computer Sim.

AI Programming Systems. Richard K. Miller & Terri C. Walker. LC 88-81893. (Survey on Technology & Markets Ser.: No. 95). 50p. 1989. pap. text ed. 200.00 (1-55865-095-4) Future Tech Surveys.

AI Review. Ed. by American Association for Artificial Intelligence Staff. (Illus.). 80p. (C). 1988. pap. text ed. 15.00x (0-929280-27-X) Amer Artificial.

AI, Simulation & Planning in High Autonomy Systems, 3rd Conference. LC 91-77320. 306p. 1992. 70.00 (0-8186-2675-5, 2675) IEEE Comp Soc.

***AI, Simulation & Planning in High Autonomy Systems, 5th Conference.** LC 94-76639. 304p. 1994. 70.00 (0-8186-6440-1, PR06440) IEEE Comp Soc.

AI Technology. Ed. by Fumio Mizoguchi. x, 187p. 1991. 80.00 (90-5199-050-2, Pub. by IOS Pr NE) IOS Press.

AI Theory & Applications in the VAX Environment. Michael Stock. (Computing That Works Ser.). 1988. 43.00 (0-07-061574-8) McGraw.

AI Theory & Applications in the Vax Environment. Michael J. Stock. (Illus.). 300p. 1988. pap. text ed. 26.95 (0-07-061573-X) McGraw.

AI Tools & Techniques. Ed. by Mark Richer. LC 88-21983. 384p. (C). 1989. text ed. write for info. (0-89391-494-0) Ablex Pub.

AI Workbench: Babylon: An Open & Portable Development Environment for Expert Systems. Ed. by Thomas Christaller et al. (Knowledge Based Systems Ser.). (Illus.). 474p. 1992. pap. text ed. 85.00 (0-12-174235-0) Acad Pr.

AI, 1988. Ed. by V. C. Barter & M. Brooks. (Lecture Notes in Computer Science Ser.: Vol. 406). viii, 463p. 1990. pap. 45.10 (0-387-52062-7) Spr-Verlag.

AI, 1993: Proceedings of the 6th Australian Joint Conference on Artificial Intelligence. C. Rowles et al. 450p. 1993. text ed. 114.00 (981-02-1526-6) World Scientific Pub.

AI, '92: Proceedings of the Fifth Australian Joint Conference on Artificial Intelligence: Hobart, Tasmania, 16-18 November 1992. Ed. by Anthony Adams & Leon S. Sterling. LC 92-38726. 408p. 1992. text ed. 109.00 (981-02-1250-X) World Scientific Pub.

Aia: Fields of Sleep & People of the Darkness, 2 vols. in 1. Charles E. Vivian. Ed. by R. Reginald & Douglas Melville. LC 77-84272. (Lost Race & Adult Fantasy Ser.). 1978. lib. bdg. 50.95 (0-405-11011-1) Ayer.

***AIA: The Story of the Artists International Association 1933-1953.** Lynda Morris & Robert Radford. 96p. 1983. 32.00 (0-905836-35-9, Pub. by Museum Modern Art UK) St Mut.

AIA Architectural Guide to Nassau & Suffolk Counties, Long Island. American Institute of Architects, Long Island Chapter & Society for the Preservation of Long Island Antiquities Staff. (Illus.). 176p. (Orig.). 1992. pap. 11.95 (0-486-26946-9) Dover.

AIA Awards Program, 1985. American Institute of Architects, Chicago Chapter Staff. (Illus.). 121p. 1991. pap. 15.00 (1-55652-011-5) Chicago Review.

AIA Awards Program 1986. American Institute of Architects, Chicago Chapter Staff. (Illus.). 121p. 1987. pap. 15.00 (1-55652-000-X) Chicago Review.

AIA Awards Program, 1987. American Institute of Architects, Chicago Chapter Staff. (Illus.). 121p. 1991. pap. 15.00 (1-55652-024-7) Chicago Review.

AIA Energy Design Handbook. Donald Watson. (Illus.). 600p. 1993. pap. 29.95 (1-55835-094-2) AIA Press.

AIA Guide to Chicago. Alice Sinkevitch. 1993. pap. 22.95 (0-15-637975-9) HarBrace.

AIA Guide to Chicago. Alice Sinkevitch. 1993. 34.95 (0-15-138018-X) HarBrace.

AIA Guide to New York City. 3rd ed. Elliot Willensky & Norval White. (Illus.). 999p. 1988. 34.95 (0-15-104040-0); pap. 21.95 (0-15-603600-2) HarBrace.

AIA Guide to the Architecture of Atlanta. Isabelle Gournay. LC 91-28973. (Illus.). 384p. 1993. 45.00 (0-8203-1439-0); pap. 19.95 (0-8203-1450-1) U of Ga Pr.

AIA Guide to the Architecture of Washington, D. C. 3rd ed. Christopher Weeks. LC 93-34867. 1994. 39.95 (0-8018-4712-5); pap. 19.95 (0-8018-4713-3) Johns Hopkins.

AIAA - AAS Astrodynamics Conference: Proceedings. 1986. pap. 125.00 (0-317-55338-0, CP867) AIAA.

AIAA - AAS Astrodynamics Conference: Proceedings. 1992. 220.00 (0-685-63113-3, CP9210) AIAA.

AIAA - AHS Biennial Flight Test Conference: Proceedings. 1992. 130.00 (0-685-63114-1, CP9212) AIAA.

AIAA - ASME - ASCE - AHS - ASC Structures Structural Dynamics, & Materials Conference: Proceedings. 1992. 290.00 (0-685-59648-6, CP922) AIAA.

AIAA - ASME - ASCE - AHS - ASC Structures, Structural Dynamics, & Materials Conference: Proceedings, 6 vols. 3725p. 1993. 380.00 (0-685-65317-X, CP931) AIAA.

AIAA - IKI Microgravity Science Symposium: Proceedings. 382p. 1991. 69.95 (1-56347-001-2, 01-2) AIAA.

AIAA - NASA International Symposium on Space Information Systems: Proceedings, 2nd, 2 vols. 1214p. 1991. 125.00 (0-930403-89-4) AIAA.

AIAA - RAES Aerodynamic Decelerator Systems Technology Conference & Seminar: Proceedings. 1993. 184.00 (0-685-65320-X, CP932) AIAA.

AIAA - USAF - NASA - OAI Symposium on Multidisciplinary Analysis & Optimization: Proceedings. 1992. 300.00 (0-685-63115-X, CP9213) AIAA.

***AIAA-AAS Astrodynamics Conference: A Collection of Technical Papers, Scottsdale, AZ, August 1-3, 1994.** LC 94-25999. 1994. pap. 260.00 (1-56347-090-X) AIAA.

AIAA Aerodynamic Decelerator Systems Technology Conference: Proceedings, 11th. 1991. 120.00 (0-685-63116-8, CP912) AIAA.

AIAA Aerospace Computer Security Conference: Proceedings, 2nd. 1986. 75.00 (0-317-55337-2) AIAA.

AIAA Aerospace Design Engineers Guide. 3rd ed. LC 92-29652. 294p. 1993. 49.95 (1-56347-045-4) AIAA.

AIAA Applied Aerodynamics Conference: Proceedings. 1992. 240.00 (0-685-63111-7, CP926) AIAA.

AIAA Applied Aerodynamics Conference: Proceedings, 2 vols., Set. 1116p. 1993. 260.00 (0-685-70340-1, CP935) AIAA.

AIAA Applied Aerodynamics Conference: Proceedings, 5th. 1987. 80.00 (0-317-66168-X, CP875) AIAA.

AIAA Applied Aerodynamics Conference: Proceedings, 9th. 9th ed. 1991. 190.00 (0-685-63110-9, CP918) AIAA.

AIAA-ASME Adaptive Structures Forum: April 21-22, 1994, Hilton Head, South Carolina, 1 Vol. LC 94-13441. 65p. 1994. 160.00 (1-56347-102-7, CP944(890)) AIAA.

AIAA-ASME-ASCE-AHS-ASC 35th Structures, Structural Dynamics & Materials Conference: April 18-20, 1994, Hilton Head, South Carolina, 5 Vols. LC 94-13439. 350p. 1994. 350.00 (1-56347-101-9, CP942(890)) AIAA.

AIAA Atmospheric Flight Mechanics Conference. 1987. 80.00 (0-317-66170-1, CP876) AIAA.

AIAA Atmospheric Flight Mechanics Conference. 1991. 160.00 (0-685-63117-6, CP916) AIAA.

AIAA Atmospheric Flight Mechanics Conference. 617p. 1993. 240.00 (0-685-70341-X, CP936) AIAA.

AIAA Atmospheric Flight Mechanics Conference: Proceedings. 1992. 220.00 (0-685-63112-5, CP929) AIAA.

AIAA Atmospheric Flight Mechanics Conference: Proceedings. American Institute of Aeronautics & Astronautics Staff. (Orig.). 1985. pap. 85.00 (0-317-38982-3, CP857) AIAA.

AIAA Atmospheric Flight Mechanics Conference, 11th. 1984. 50.00 (0-317-36840-0, CP849) AIAA.

AIAA Communication Satellite Systems Conference: Proceedings, 11th. 1986. 100.00 (0-317-43145-5, CP862) AIAA.

AIAA Communications Satellite Systems Conference: Proceedings of the AIAA Conference, 10th, 1984. 743p. 1984. 95.00 (0-317-36844-3, CP842) AIAA.

AIAA Computers in Aerospace Conference, 4th, 1983. 1984. 85.00 (0-317-06655-2, CP837) AIAA.

AIAA Computers in Aerospace, 6th. 1987. 90.00 (0-317-66165-5, CP8710) AIAA.

AIAA Computing in Aerospace: Proceedings, 9th. 1993. 370.00 (0-685-70342-8, CP939) AIAA.

AIAA Computing in Aerospace, 8th. 1991. 190.00 (0-685-63119-2, CP9110) AIAA.

AIAA Dynamics Specialist Conference: April 21-22, 1994, Hilton Head, South Carolina, 1 Vol. LC 94-13442. 65p. 1994. 160.00 (1-56347-103-5, CP943(890)) AIAA.

AIAA Dynamics Specialist Conference: Proceedings. 1992. 210.00 (0-685-59649-4, CP923) AIAA.

AIAA Flight Simulation Technologies Conference: Proceedings. 1991. 110.00 (0-685-63120-6, CP917) AIAA.

AIAA Flight Simulation Technologies Conference: Proceedings. 1992. 130.00 (0-685-63123-0, CP9211) AIAA.

AIAA Flight Simulation Technologies Conference: Proceedings. 347p. 1993. 130.00 (0-685-70343-6, CP937) AIAA.

AIAA Flight Simulation Technology Conference. 1987. 75.00 (0-317-66167-1, CP877) AIAA.

AIAA Guidance & Control Conference: Proceedings. 1991. 290.00 (0-685-63121-4, CP915) AIAA.

AIAA Guidance, Navigation & Control Conference: Proceedings. 1992. 290.00 (0-685-63122-2, CP928) AIAA.

AIAA Guide for Berthing - Docking - Grasping Interfaces for Serviceable Spacecraft: Standard. 32p. 1992. 29.95 (1-56347-052-7, G-056-92) AIAA.

AIAA Guide for Estimating & Budgeting Weight & Power Contingencies for Spacecraft Systems: Standard. 1991. pap. 24.95 (0-930403-86-X, G-020-91) AIAA.

AIAA Guide for Human Performance Measurements: Standard. 156p. 1992. 79.95 (1-56347-026-8, G-035-92) AIAA.

AIAA Guide for Implementing Software Development Files Conforming to DoD-Std-2167A: Standard. 20p. 1991. 24.95 (0-930403-81-9, G-009-91) AIAA.

AIAA Guide for Life-Cycle Development of Knowledge Based Systems with DoD-Std-2167A: Standard. 40p. 1992. 29.95 (1-56347-025-X, G-031-92) AIAA.

AIAA Guide for Reusable Software: Assessment Criteria for Aerospace Applications: Standard. 28p. 1993. 24.95 (0-685-70081-X) AIAA.

AIAA Guide for the Preparation of Operational Concept Documents: Standard. 32p. 1992. 29.95 (1-56347-049-7) AIAA.

AIAA Guide: Human Factors Taxonomy: Standard. 1993. write for info. (0-318-69930-3) AIAA.

AIAA Guide: Terminology for Space Launch Systems: Standard. Date not set. write for info. (0-318-72355-7) AIAA.

AIAA Guide to Design for On-Orbit Spacecraft Servicing. 400p. 1991. pap. 39.95 (1-56347-028-4, G-042-91) AIAA.

AIAA Guide to Reference & Standard Atmosphere Models: Standard. 80p. 1990. pap. 79.95 (0-930403-84-3, G-003-90) AIAA.

AIAA International Balloon Technology Conference: Proceedings. 1991. 144.00 (0-685-63125-7, CP919) AIAA.

AIAA International Powered Lift Conference: Proceedings. 1993. 190.00 (0-685-70348-7, CP9310) AIAA.

AIAA Journal, Vol. 32. Ed. by George W. Sutton. 1994. 435.00 (0-685-30528-7) AIAA.

AIAA Lighter-Than-Air Systems Technology Conference: Proceedings. 104p. 1993. 120.00 (0-685-70345-2, CP938) AIAA.

AIAA Lighter-Than-Air Technology Conference. 1991. 100.00 (0-685-63124-9, CP913) AIAA.

AIAA Lighter-Than-Air Technology Conference, 8th. 1987. 75.00 (0-317-66166-3, CP879) AIAA.

AIAA Materials Specialist Conference - Coating Technology for Aerospace Systems: Proceedings. 1992. 210.00 (0-685-59650-8, CP924) AIAA.

***AIAA Recommended Practice Part 1: Astrodynamics-Concepts, Terms & Symbols.** 56p. 1994. pap. text ed. 29.95 (1-56347-098-5, A-064-94(890)) AIAA.

AIAA Recommended Practice for Astrodynamics, Pt. 1: Concepts, Quantities, & Symbols. 1994. write for info. (0-318-72891-5) AIAA.

AIAA Recommended Practice for Atmospheric & Space Flight Vehicle Coordinate Systems: Standard. 62p. 1991. pap. 44.95 (0-930403-82-7, R-004-92) AIAA.

AIAA Recommended Practice for Human-Computer Interfaces for Space Systems Operations: Standard. 32p. 1991. pap. 24.95 (0-930403-91-6, R-023-91) AIAA.

AIAA Recommended Practice for Reporting Earth-to-Orbit Mission Profiles: Standard. 1993. 14.95 (1-56347-053-5) AIAA.

AIAA Recommended Practice for Software Reliability: Standard. 76p. 1992. 49.95 (1-56347-024-1, R-013-92) AIAA.

AIAA Recommended Practice for Space Operations & Support Documentation: Standard. LC 93-28271. 20p. 1993. pap. 24.95 (1-56347-070-5, R-024093) AIAA.

AIAA Recommended Practice for Spacecraft System Design in SI Units. 8p. 1991. pap. 14.95 (0-685-49458-6, R-021-91) AIAA.

***AIAA Special Report: Contemporary Models of the Orbital Environment.** 112p. 1994. pap. text ed. 39.95 (1-56347-108-6, SP-069-94(890)) AIAA.

AIAA Special Report: Future Air Traffic Control & Navigation Systems. Ed. by James E. French. 160p. 1991. pap. 29.95 (1-56347-030-6, SP-050) AIAA.

***AIAA Special Report: Guidance, Navigation & Control Information Interface Standards.** 200p. 1994. pap. text ed. 24.95 (1-56347-109-4, SP-073-94(890)) AIAA.

***AIAA Special Report: Strategic Issues in Aerospace Standardization.** 80p. 1994. pap. text ed. 14.95 (1-56347-110-8, SP-074-94(890)) AIAA.

AIAA Special Report: Future of Aerospace: Standard. 36p. 1990. pap. 14.95 (0-930403-88-6, SP-039-90) AIAA.

AIAA Special Report Nineteen Ninety-One Earth Observations Directory: A Worldwide Listing of Government Institutions & Related Groups. 172p. 1990. pap. 89.95 (0-930403-80-0, SP-012-90) AIAA.

AIAA Special Report: Orbital Debris Mitigation: Technical, Legal, & Economic Aspects. (Illus.). 50p. 1992. pap. 29.95 (1-56347-023-3, SP-016-92) AIAA.

AIAA Special Report: Standardization for Commercial Space Transportation Operations: Standard. 40p. 1993. 24.95 (1-56347-076-4) AIAA.

AIAA Standard for Aerodynamic Decelerator Drawings. 56p. 1991. pap. 49.95 (0-930403-94-0, S-017-91) AIAA.

AIAA Standard Terminology for Space Structures. 32p. 1991. pap. 24.95 (0-930403-83-5, S-001-91) AIAA.

AIAA Structures, Structural Dynamics & Materials Conference, 28th: Proceedings, 1987, 2 vols., Set. 1987. pap. 200.00 (0-317-58630-0, CP872) AIAA.

AIAA Structures, Sturctural Dynamics & Materials Conference: Proceedings, 32nd. 1991. 245.00 (0-685-63128-1, CP911) AIAA.

AIAA Student Journal, Vol. 32. Ed. by Patrick Gouhin. 1994. 18.00 (0-685-63126-5) AIAA.

***AIAA/USAF/NASA/ISSMO Symposium on Multidisciplinary Analysis & Optimization: A Collection of Technical Papers, September 7-9, 1994, Panama City Beach, FL.** LC 94-34446. 1994. write for info. (1-56347-097-7) AIAA.

Aiax. Sophocles. (Illus.). viii, 430p. (GER.). 1976. reprint ed. write for info. (3-487-05932-0, Pub. by Georg Olms GW) Lubrecht & Cramer.

AIBD Home Designs, Vol. 1, No. 1. 34p. 1988. pap. 7.00 (0-931518-29-6) W D Farmer.

AIC Directory. 38.00 (0-318-18693-4) Am Inst Conser Hist.

AIChE Applications Software Survey for Personal Computers, 1985-86. 290p. 1985. pap. 70.00 (0-8169-0345-X, D-14) Am Inst Chem Eng.

AIChE Forest Products Division Sessions, 1988: November 27-December 2, Washington Hilton Hotel, Washington, D. C. Technical Association of the Pulp & Paper Industry Staff. (TAPPI Proceedings Ser.). 239p. pap. 68.20 (0-8357-6316-1, 2035589) Bks Demand.

AIChE Forest Products Symposium, 1991: Westin Bonaventure, Los Angeles, CA, November 17-22. Technical Association of the Pulp & Paper Association Staff. Ed. by Douglas W. Bousfield et al. (TAPPI Proceedings Ser.). (Illus.). 193p. reprint ed. pap. 52.20 (0-7837-4383-1, 2044123) Bks Demand.

AIChE Pocket Handbook. Ed. by Thomas R. Hanley. 50p. 1985. pap. 12.00 (0-8169-0342-5, X-60) Am Inst Chem Eng.

AICP First Annual Reports Investigating Poverty, Nos. 1-10. New York Association for Improving the Condition of the Poor Staff. LC 77-137179. (Poverty U. S. A. Historical Record Ser.). 1978. reprint ed. 35.95 (0-405-03117-3) Ayer.

AICPA Audit & Accounting Guide: Audit Sampling. 120p. 1992. pap. 20.00 (0-685-67103-8, 4813) Commerce.

AICPA Audit & Accounting Guide: Audits of Agricultural Producers & Agricultural Cooperatives with Conforming Changes As of May 1, 1992. 144p. 1992. pap. 24.00 (0-685-67081-3, 4767) Commerce.

AICPA Audit & Accounting Guide: Audits of Brokers & Dealers in Securities with Conforming Changes As of May 1, 1992. 184p. 1992. pap. 24.00 (0-685-67082-1, 4760) Commerce.

An Asterisk (*) at the beginning of an entry indicates that the title is appearing in BIP for the first time.

An Asterisk (*) at the beginning of an entry indicates that the title is appearing in BIP for the first time.

151

*AIDS: A Guide to the Law. Ed. by Richard Haigh & Dai Harris. 1994. pap. 17.95 (0-415-09699-5, B4514) Routledge.

AIDS: A Guide to the Law. Ed. by Dai Harris & Richard Haigh. 208p. 1990. 52.50 (0-415-04667-X, A4205) Routledge.

*AIDS: A Guide to the Law. 2nd ed. Ed. by Richard Haigh & Dai Harris. 208p. 1994. 55.00x (0-415-11511-6, B4510) Routledge.

AIDS: A Handbook for Housestaff. King K. Holmes et al. 160p. 1990. pap. text ed. 35.00 (0-07-029678-2) Hlth Prof Div.

AIDS: A Health Care Management Response. Kevin D. Blanchet. 319p. 1987. 61.00 (0-87189-877-2) Aspen Pub.

AIDS: A Multimedia Sourcebook. John J. Miletich. LC 92-39121. 288p. 1993. pap. text ed. 15.95 (0-89789-362-X, Greenwood Pr) Greenwood.

AIDS: A Multimedia Sourcebook. Comp. by John J. Miletich. LC 93-10830. (Bibliographies & Indexes in Medical Studies: No. 10). 288p. 1993. text ed. 59.95 (0-313-28669-8) Greenwood.

AIDS: A Nutritional Approach. Louise Tenney. (Todays Health Ser.: No. 6). 30p. 1987. pap. 3.95 (0-913923-62-1) Woodland UT.

AIDS: A Pilgrimage to Healing. Peter Todd. 176p. pap. 8.95 (0-85574-902-4, Pub. by E J Dwyer AT) Morehouse Pub.

AIDS: A Problem for Sociological Research. Ed. by Michael Pollak et al. (Special Issue of Current Sociology Ser.). (Illus.). 144p. (C). 1993. text ed. 55.00 (0-8039-8841-9); pap. text ed. 22.95 (0-8039-8840-0) Sage.

AIDS: A Program for Catholic Schools. 56p. teacher ed 9.95 (0-914070-86-X, 710) ACTA Pubns.

AIDS: A Program for Catholic Schools. 40p. (gr. 7-8). 5.95 (0-914070-89-4, 711) ACTA Pubns.

AIDS: A Program for Catholic Schools. 32p. (gr. 9-10). 5.95 (0-914070-90-8, 712) ACTA Pubns.

AIDS: A Special Issue of the New England Journal of Public Policy. Ed. by Padraig O'Malley. 526p. 1988. pap. 20.95x (0-87023-657-1) U of Mass Pr.

AIDS: Abstracts of the Psychological & Behavioral Literature, 1983-1991. 3rd ed. Ed. by John R. Anderson et al. LC 91-22115. (Bibliographies in Psychology Ser.: No. 6). 312p. 1991. pap. 27.50 (1-55798-148-5) Am Psychol.

AIDS: Acquired Immune Deficiency Syndrome. Ed. by David A. Tyckoson. LC 85-3061. (Science Bibliographies Ser.: Vol. 1). 64p. 1985. pap. 17.75 (0-89774-203-6) Oryx Pr.

AIDS: An African Perspective. Williams. 1991. 161.00 (0-8493-6437-X, RA644) CRC Pr.

AIDS: An Epidemic of Ethical Puzzles. Hastings Center Staff. (Hastings Center: Issues in Bioethics: No. 1). 120p. 1991. text ed. 59.95 (1-85521-206-4, Pub. by Dartmth Pub UK) Ashgate Pub Co.

AIDS: Answers for Everyone. Stephen J. Manfredi. 96p. (Orig.). (YA). (gr. 6-12). 1989. pap. text ed. 9.95 (0-929496-01-9) Treehaus Comns.

AIDS: Blunt Talk on How to Avoid It. Randolph Norman. 32p. 1985. pap. 5.95 (0-86668-057-8) ARCsoft.

AIDS: CDC's Investigation of HIV Transmissions by a Dentist. (Illus.). 50p. (Orig.). (C). 1993. pap. text ed. 40.00 (1-56806-908-1) Diane Pub.

AIDS: Crisis in Professional Ethics. Ed. by Elliot D. Cohen & Michael Davis. 320p. (C). 1994. text ed. 49.95 (1-56639-164-4); pap. 22.95 (1-56639-165-2) Temple U Pr.

AIDS: Cultural Analysis - Cultural Activism. Ed. by Douglas Crimp. (October Bks.). 275p. (Orig.). 1988. pap. 16.95 (0-262-53079-1) MIT Pr.

AIDS: Diagnosis with Medical Subject Analysis & Reference Bibliography. Martin D. Raber. LC 85-48191. 156p. 1985. reprint ed. 39.50 (0-88164-488-9); reprint ed. pap. 34.50 (0-88164-489-7) ABBE Pubs Assn.

AIDS: Diseases & Diets the Authorities Fail to Tell You: the Incorrectness of the Pasteur Germ Theory & Its Relationship with AIDS. 1991. lib. bdg. 250.00 (0-8490-4254-2) Gordon Pr.

AIDS: Distinguishing Between Fact & Opinion. Teresa Opheim. LC 89-12006. (Opposing Viewpoints Juniors Ser.). (Illus.). 32p. (J). (gr. 3-6). 1990. lib. bdg. 11.95 (0-89908-633-0) Greenhaven.

AIDS: Effective Health Communicaton for the 90's. Ed. by Scott C. Ratzan. LC 92-17933. 1992. 39.50 (1-56032-273-X) Hemisp Pub.

AIDS: Ethical Guidelines for Healthcare Providers. Diana Bader & Elizabeth McMillan. 32p. 1987. pap. 2.75 (0-87125-141-8) Cath Health.

AIDS: Ethics & Public Policy. Ed. by Christine Pierce & Donald VanDeVeer. 241p. (C). 1988. pap. 19.95 (0-534-08286-6) Intl Thomson.

AIDS: Etiology, Diagnosis, Treatment & Prevention. 3rd ed. Vincent T. DeVita, Jr. et al. 544p. 1992. text ed. 79.50 (0-397-51229-5) Lippincott.

AIDS: Examining the Crisis. Tom Flynn & Karen Lound. LC 94-13326. (Frontline Ser.). (Illus.). 112p. (YA). (gr. 6 up). 1995. lib. bdg. 17.50 (0-8225-2625-5, Lerner Publctns) Lerner Group.

AIDS: Facts & Issues. Ed. by Victor Gong & Norman Rudnick. LC 86-20415. 408p. reprint ed. pap. 116.30 (0-7837-5670-4, 2059097) Bks Demand.

AIDS: Foundations for the Future. Ed. by Peter Aggleton et al. LC 94-14183. (Social Aspects of AIDS Ser.). 240p. 1994. 75.00x (0-7484-0227-6); pap. 27.50x (0-7484-0228-4) Taylor & Francis.

AIDS: Helping Families Cope. Joan L. Zlotnik et al. 26p. 1988. 5.95 (0-685-24562-4, A51); vhs 45.00 (0-685-24563-2, A55) Natl Assn Soc Wkrs.

AIDS: Images of the Epidemic. WHO Staff. (Illus.). 154p. 1994. 28.50 (92-4-156163-7) World Health.

AIDS: Impact on Schools. Roberta Weiner. LC 86-81456. 274p. (Orig.). 1986. 45.50 (0-937925-02-0, AIDS) Capitol VA.

AIDS: In Search of a Killer. Suzanne LeVert. LC 86-33218. (Illus.). 128p. (YA). (gr. 6 up). 1987. lib. bdg. 12.98 (0-671-62840-2, Julian Messner); lib. bdg. 5.95 (0-671-65662-7, Julian Messner) Silver Burdett Pr.

AIDS: Individual, Cultural & Policy Dimensions. Ed. by Peter M. Aggleton et al. 262p. 1990. 70.00 (1-85000-763-2, Falmer Pr); pap. 33.00 (1-85000-764-0, Falmer Pr) Taylor & Francis.

AIDS: Insights & Strategies. (RC Squared Ser.). pap. 10.00 (0-685-72151-5) UAHC.

AIDS: Intervening with Hidden Grievers. Barbara O. Dane & Samuel O. Miller. LC 92-10959. 240p. 1992. text ed. 47.95 (0-86569-028-6, T028, Auburn Hse) Greenwood.

AIDS: It May Not Be Too Late. Joe J. Cardot. 56p. (Orig.). 1989. pap. 4.99 (0-685-28032-2) Srch Fndtn.

AIDS: Just the Facts Jack. Tim Jackson. (What Are Friends For? Ser.: No. 6). (Illus.). (Orig.). (J). (gr. 5 up). 1988. pap. 1.95 (0-942675-06-1, 6) Creative License.

AIDS: Legal Implications for Healthcare Providers. rev. ed. Mark A. Kadzielski. 16p. 1988. pap. 2.00 (0-87125-128-0, 105) Cath Health.

AIDS: Legal, Legislative, & Policy Issues. Ed. by Norman Quist. (Special Studies on AIDS). 448p. 1989. pap. text ed. 58.00 (1-55572-020-X) Univ Pub Group.

AIDS: Lessons from the First Decade. Appleman & Dellacorte. 176p. (C). 1992. pap. text ed. 29.95 (0-8403-7206-X) Kendall-Hunt.

Aids: Meeting the Community Challenge. Ed. by Vicky Cossick. 190p. 1989. pap. 27.00 (0-86217-288-8, Pub. by Veritas IE) St Mut.

AIDS: Meeting the Community Challenge. Ed. by Vicky Cosstick. (C). 1988. 39.00 (0-85439-264-5, Pub. by St Paul Pubns UK) St Mut.

AIDS: Ministry in the Midst of an Epidemic - A Medical-Theological Perspective. Wendell W. Hoffman & Stanley J. Grenz. LC 89-32312. 336p. (Orig.). 1990. pap. 12.99 (0-8010-4346-8) Baker Bk.

AIDS: Modern Concepts & Therapeutic Challenges. Ed. by Samuel Broder. 384p. 1987. 110.00 (0-8247-7649-6) Dekker.

AIDS: Myths, Facts & Ethics. Elizabeth Prior-Jonson. 165p. 1989. pap. text ed. 17.00 (0-08-034434-8, Pergamon Pr) Elsevier.

AIDS: One Thousand Full-Text Statistical Abstracts from the "A Matter of Fact" Database, 1984-1992. Ed. by C. Edward Wall et al. (Statistical Perspectives Ser.). 112p. 1993. pap. 15.00 (0-87650-329-6) Pierian.

AIDS: Opposing Viewpoints. Ed. by Michael D. Biskup & Karin L. Swisher. LC 92-19874. (Opposing Viewpoints Ser.). 240p. (YA). (gr. 10 up). 1992. lib. bdg. 19.95 (0-89908-190-8); pap. text ed. 11.55 (0-89908-165-7) Greenhaven.

AIDS: Origins, Prevention & Cure, 4 Vols. (AIDS Ser.). 1987. lib. bdg. 800.00 (0-8490-3958-4) Gordon Pr.

AIDS: Papers from Science, 1982-1985. Ed. by Ruth Kulstad. LC 85-28776. (AAAS Publication Ser.: No. 85-23). (Illus.). 659p. reprint ed. pap. 180.00 (0-7837-6739-0, 2046367) Bks Demand.

AIDS: Passageway to Transformation. C. Norman Shealy & Caroline M Myss. LC 87-62669. (Creation of Health Ser.). 96p. (Orig.). 1988. 10.95 (0-913299-47-2) Stillpoint.

AIDS: Pathogenesis & Treatment. Levy. (Immunology Ser.: Vol. 44). 720p. 1989. 125.00 (0-8247-7684-4) Dekker.

AIDS: Personal Stories in Pastoral Perspective. Earl E. Shelp et al. LC 86-21209. 206p. (Orig.). 1986. pap. 10.95 (0-8298-0739-X) Pilgrim OH.

*AIDS: Plague or Panic? Ed. by Oliver Trager. LC 88-6889. (Editorials on File Book Ser.). (Illus.). 224p. 1988. reprint ed. pap. 63.90 (0-7837-8099-0, 2047854) Bks Demand.

AIDS: Policies & Programs for the Workplace. Kathleen C. Brown & Joan G. Turner. 1989. text ed. 34.95 (0-442-23353-1) Van Nos Reinhold.

AIDS: Political, Social, International Aspects: A Bibliography. Ed. by Joan Nordquist. (Contemporary Social Issues: A Bibliographic Ser.: No. 10). 60p. (Orig.). 1988. pap. 15.00 (0-937855-19-7) Ref Rsch Serv.

AIDS: Prevention & Treatment. Seligson & Peterson. 1991. pap. 31.00 (1-56032-093-1) Hemisp Pub.

AIDS: Principles, Practices & Politics. Ed. by Inge B. Corless & Mary Pittman-Lindeman. (Death Education, Aging & Health Care Ser.). 780p. 1989. 58.00 (0-89116-716-1, 66-56086) Hemisp Pub.

AIDS: Principles, Practices & Politics. abr. ed. Ed. by Inge B. Corless & Mary Pittman-Lindeman. (Death Education, Aging & Health Care Ser.). 400p. 1987. 55.00 (0-89116-795-1, 66-57001); pap. 26.00 (0-89116-772-2, 66-56813) Hemisp Pub.

AIDS: Problems & Prospects. Ed. by Lawrence Corey. LC 92-49045. (Hospital Practice Book Ser.). 1993. pap. 19.95 (0-393-71015-7) Norton.

AIDS: Public Health & Legal Dimensions. D. C. Jayasuriya. (C). 1988. lib. bdg. 75.50 (90-247-3686-2) Kluwer Ac.

*AIDS: Readings on a Global Crisis. Elizabeth R. Bethel. (Illus.). 448p. 1994. pap. write for info. (0-02-309192-4, Merrill Pub Co) Macmillan.

AIDS: Responses, Interventions & Care. Ed. by Peter Aggleton et al. (Social Aspects of AIDS Ser.). 256p. 1991. 65.00 (1-85000-871-X, Falmer Pr); pap. 31.00 (1-85000-872-8, Falmer Pr) Taylor & Francis.

AIDS: Rights, Risk & Reason. Peter Aggleton et al. Ed. by Peter M. Davies & Graham Hart. LC 92-112687. (Social Aspects of AIDS Ser.). 224p. 1992. 80.00 (0-7507-0039-4, Falmer Pr); pap. 27.00 (0-7507-0040-8, Falmer Pr) Taylor & Francis.

AIDS: Scare or Scam? Evan C. Lambrou. 1994. 10.95 (0-533-10709-1) Vantage.

*AIDS: Science & Society. Hung Fan et al. (Health Science Ser.). 1995. pap. 29.95 (0-86720-913-5) Jones & Bartlett.

AIDS: Scientific & Social Issues. Peter Aggleton et al. (Illus.). 128p. 1989. pap. text ed. 17.00 (0-443-04182-2) Churchill.

AIDS: Setting a Feminist Agenda. Ed. by Lesley Doyal et al. LC 94-4132. (Gender & Society Ser.). 1994. write for info. (0-7484-0162-8, Pub. by Tay Francis Ltd UK); pap. 27.00 (0-7484-0163-6) Taylor & Francis.

AIDS: Sharing the Pain, a Guide for Caregivers. Bill Kirkpatrick. LC 89-22997. 152p. (Orig.). 1990. pap. 10.95 (0-8298-0831-0) Pilgrim OH.

AIDS: Silent Killer. Don Boys. 1991. pap. 10.00 (1-879805-00-6) Freedom FL.

AIDS: Social Representations, Social Practices. Ed. by Peter Aggleton & Graham Hart. 226p. 1989. 70.00 (1-85000-430-7, Falmer Pr); pap. 33.00 (1-85000-431-5, Falmer Pr) Taylor & Francis.

AIDS: Spirits Share Understanding & Comfort from the "Other" Side. Ed. by Molli Nickell. 110p. 1986. 9.95 (0-938283-99-5) Spirit Speaks.

AIDS: Testing & Privacy. Gunderson et al. LC 88-39245. (Ethics in a Changing World Ser.: Vol. 2). 256p. 1989. pap. 20.00 (0-87480-317-9) U of Utah Pr.

AIDS: The American Roads of Denial. Richard Carper. Ed. by Joella Ewing. (Illus.). 200p. (Orig.). 1990. pap. 11.50 (0-930693-05-1) Cross-Cultrl NY.

AIDS: The Biological Basis. I. Edward Alcamo. 304p. (C). 1992. pap. text ed. write for info. (0-697-12061-9) Wm C Brown Pubs.

AIDS: The Burdens of History. Ed. by Elizabeth Fee & Daniel M. Fox. 340p. 1988. 48.00 (0-520-06395-3); pap. 15.00 (0-520-06396-1) U CA Pr.

AIDS: The End of Civilization. William C. Douglass. (Orig.). 1989. pap. write for info. (0-932298-68-0) Tri-State Pr Corp.

AIDS: The End of Civilization. William C. Douglass. 256p. (Orig.). 1989. pap. 9.95 (1-877652-13-X) Valet Pub.

AIDS: The Epidemic of Kaposi's Sarcoma & Opportunistic Infections. Ed. by Alvin E. Friedman-Kien & Linda J. Laubenstein. LC 83-25578. (Illus.). 371p. 1984. 62.00 (0-89352-217-1, Yr Bk Med Pubs) Mosby Yr Bk.

AIDS: The Facts. John J. Langone. 192p. 1988. pap. 8.95 (0-316-51412-8) Little.

AIDS: The Facts. rev. ed. John J. Langone. 1991. pap. 10.95 (0-316-51414-4) Little.

AIDS: The HIV Myth. Jad Adams. 256p. 1989. 16.95 (0-312-02859-8) St Martin.

AIDS: The Impact on the Criminal Justice System. Mark Blumberg. 336p. (C). 1990. pap. write for info. (0-675-21183-2, Merrill Pub Co) Macmillan.

AIDS: The Law. 60p. 1990. 10.00 (0-932622-37-2); 10.00 (0-932622-36-4) Ctr Public Rep.

AIDS: The Literary Response. Emmanuel S. Nelson. 360p. 1992. text ed. 23.95 (0-8057-9029-2, Twayne); pap. 14.95 (0-8057-9032-2, Twayne) Macmillan.

AIDS: The Lonely Voyage. Nancy L. Shands. LC 87-51279. 175p. (Orig.). 1988. pap. 10.95 (0-933174-54-3) Wide World-Tetra.

AIDS: The Making of a Chronic Disease. Ed. by Elizabeth Fee & Daniel M. Fox. LC 91-731. (Illus.). 417p. 1992. 45.00 (0-520-07569-2); pap. 15.00 (0-520-07778-4) U CA Pr.

AIDS: The Mystery & the Solution. (AIDS Ser.). 1987. lib. bdg. 250.00 (0-8490-3924-X) Gordon Pr.

AIDS: The Mystery & the Solution. rev. ed. Alan Cantwell, Jr. Ed. by Jim Highland. LC 86-1210. (Illus.). 210p. 1994. pap. 9.95 (0-917211-16-2) Aries Rising.

AIDS: The Pathology of the Nervous System. Ed. by Francesco Scaravilli. LC 92-2222. 1993. write for info. (3-540-19739-7); 265.00 (0-387-19739-7) Spr-Verlag.

AIDS: The Politics of Survival. Ed. by Nancy Krieger & Glen Margo. LC 94-372. (Policy, Politics, Health & Medicine Ser.). 296p. 1994. text ed. 28.00 (0-89503-122-1); pap. text ed. 21.00 (0-89503-123-X) Baywood Pub.

AIDS: The Second Decade. Ed. by Peter Aggleton et al. LC 93-16013. (Social Aspects of AIDS Ser.). 1993. 85.00 (0-7507-0131-5, Falmer Pr); pap. 29.00 (0-7507-0132-3, Falmer Pr) Taylor & Francis.

AIDS: The Second Decade. Ed. by Heather G. Miller et al. 512p. 1990. pap. 39.95 (0-309-04287-9) Natl Acad Pr.

AIDS: The Ultimate Challenge. Elisabeth Kubler-Ross. LC 93-16078. 348p. 1993. pap. 10.00 (0-02-089143-1, Collier S&S) S&S Trade.

Aids: Trading Fear for Facts; A Guide for Young People. 3rd ed. Karen Hein. (YA). 1994. pap. 5.95 (0-89043-721-1) Consumers Union.

AIDS: What Does It Mean to You? rev. ed. Margaret O. Hyde. 128p. (YA). (gr. 7 up). 1987. 12.95 (0-8027-6699-4); lib. bdg. 13.85 (0-8027-6705-2); pap. 6.95 (0-8027-6747-8) Walker & Co.

AIDS: What Does It Mean to You? rev. ed. Margaret O. Hyde & Elizabeth Forsyth. 124p. (YA). (gr. 7 up). 1990. lib. bdg. 14.85 (0-8027-6898-9) Walker & Co.

AIDS: What Does It Mean to You? rev. ed. Margaret O. Hyde & Elizabeth Forsyth. LC 92-14670. 128p. (J). 1992. lib. bdg. 14.85 (0-8027-8203-5) Walker & Co.

AIDS: What Does It Mean to You? 3rd rev. ed. Margaret O. Hyde & Elizabeth Forsyth. 124p. (YA). (gr. 7 up). 1990. 13.95 (0-8027-6897-0) Walker & Co.

*AIDS: What Does It Mean to You? 4th ed. Margaret O. Hyde & Elizabeth Forsyth. (Illus.). 124p. (YA). (gr. 6 up). 1995. 14.95 (0-8027-8396-1) Walker & Co.

AIDS: What Does It Mean to You? 4th rev. ed. Margaret O. Hyde & Elizabeth Forsyth. LC 92-14670. 128p. (J). 1992. 13.95 (0-8027-8202-7) Walker & Co.

*AIDS: What Does It Mean to You? 5th ed. Margaret O. Hyde & Elizabeth Forsyth. (Illus.). 124p. (YA). (gr. 6 up). 1995. lib. bdg. 15.85 (0-8027-8398-8) Walker & Co.

*AIDS: What Is It All About? Ed. by Norma Jones et al. (Compact Reference Ser.). 48p. (YA). 1994. pap. text ed. 11.95 (1-878623-74-5) Info Plus TX.

AIDS: What the Government Isn't Telling You. Lorraine Day. LC 91-75346. (Illus.). 301p. 1991. per., pap. 22.95 (0-9630940-0-9) Rockford Pr.

AIDS: What Young Adults Should Know. 1990. Student guide. student ed 2.50 (0-88314-406-9); teacher ed 10.95 (0-88314-410-7) AAHPERD.

AIDS: Women, Drugs & Social Care. Ed. by Nicholas Dorn et al. (Social Aspects of AIDS Ser.: Vol. 1). 224p. 1992. 70.00 (1-85000-873-6, Falmer Pr); pap. 25.00 (1-85000-874-4, Falmer Pr) Taylor & Francis.

AIDS: You Can't Catch It Holding Hands. Niki De Saint Phalle. (Illus.). 52p. 1987. reprint ed. 13.00 (0-932499-52-X) Lapis Pr.

*AIDS Vol. 3: Including 1994 Supp. Ed. by Eleanor Goldstein. (Social Issues Resources Ser.). 1995. 19.00 (0-614-01897-8) Sirs Inc.

AIDS - From Fear to Hope: Channeled Teachings Offering Insight & Inspiration. Ed. by Spirit Speaks Staff. LC 87-61682. 275p. (Orig.). 1987. pap. 9.95 (0-934619-02-6) New Age FL Pub.

AIDS - STD Barriers: Benefits & Risks. John J. Riordan. 112p. 1993. 39.95 (1-56167-110-X) Noble Hse MD.

AIDS - The End of Civilization: The Greatest Biological Disaster in the History of Mankind. William C. Douglass. 256p. 1992. reprint ed. pap. text ed. write for info. (1-881316-00-9) A&B Bks.

AIDS - The Last Great Plague. Sananda et al. (Phoenix Journals). 149p. (Orig.). (C). 1990. pap. 10.00 (0-922356-04-1) Amer West Pubs.

AIDS - Today, Tomorrow: An Introduction to the HIV Epidemic in America. 2nd rev. ed. Robert S. Walker. LC 94-17975. (C). 1994. pap. 14.95 (0-391-03859-1) Humanities.

AIDS - Vol. II of XII: Index of Modern Authors & Scientific Reviews for Inclusions in Current Research. American Health Research Institute Staff. LC 90-56331. 243p. 1991. 44.50 (1-55914-224-3); 39.50 (1-55914-225-1) ABBE Pubs Assn.

AIDS - Zmowa Milczenia. Gene Antonio. Tr. by Jacek Szacki. 190p. (Orig.). (POL.). 1992. pap. text ed. 8.50 (0-9632313-1-6) Global Comm Netwk.

AIDS: A Comprehensive Manual of Legal & Policy Issues: A Legal & Policy Manual Designed to Provide Attorneys, AIDS Services Organizations, Activists, & Volunteers with the Tools Necessary to Respond to the Needs of People with AIDS-Related Legal Problems. Ed. by Jeff G. Peters. (Illus.). 1326p. 1992. 85.00 (0-9626786-1-9) FL AIDS LD&EF.

AIDS, A Manual for Pastoral Care. Ronald H. Sunderland & Earl E. Shelp. LC 87-15957. 76p. (Orig.). 1988. pap. 6.99 (0-664-24088-7, Westminster) Westminster John Knox.

AIDS: A Moral Issue: The Ethical, Legal & Social Aspects. Ed. by Brenda Almond. 288p. 1990. text ed. 35.00 (0-312-04204-3) St Martin.

*AIDS, a Teacher Resource Package. Jill Golick et al. 96p. (C). 1990. spiral bd., pap. 150.00x (0-7478-0450-8, Pub. by S Thornes Pubs UK) St Mut.

AIDS Agenda: Emerging Issues in Civil Rights. Nan D. Hunter. 320p. 1992. 27.95 (1-56584-001-1) New Press NY.

AIDS & Accusation: Haiti & the Geography of Blame. Paul Farmer. 1992. 35.00 (0-520-07701-6) U CA Pr.

AIDS & Accusation: Haiti & the Geography of Blame. Paul Farmer. (C). 1993. pap. 13.00 (0-520-08343-1) U CA Pr.

AIDS & Alcohol-Drug Abuse: Psychosocial Research. Ed. by Dennis G. Fisher. LC 90-5311. (Drugs & Society Ser.). (Illus.). 109p. 1990. text ed. 29.95 (1-56024-041-5); pap. text ed. 9.95 (0-918393-85-X) Haworth Pr.

AIDS & Associated Cancers in Africa. Ed. by G. Giraldo et al. (Illus.). x, 346p. 1988. 238.50 (3-8055-4701-3) S Karger.

AIDS & Behavior: An Integrated Approach. Institute of Medicine, Committee on Substance Abuse & Mental Health Issues in AIDS Research Staff. Ed. by Judith D. Auerbach et al. 360p. (C). 1994. text ed. 39.95 (0-309-05093-6) Natl Acad Pr.

*AIDS & Beyond: Dietary & Lifestyle Guidelines for New Viral & Bacterial Disease. Kushi. 96p. (Orig.). 1995. pap. text ed. 5.95 (1-882984-09-9) One Peaceful World.

AIDS & Biological Warfare. (Nikola Tesla Ser.). 1991. lib. bdg. 250.00 (0-8490-4328-X) Gordon Pr.

AIDS & Canadian Law. Rozovsky. 160p. 1992. boxed 50.00 (0-409-88935-0) Butterworth Legal Pubs.

AIDS & Chemical Dependency. 1991. lib. bdg. 250.00 (0-8490-4367-0) Gordon Pr.

AIDS & Children. Waln K. Brown. 20p. 1989. 2.95 (1-56456-041-4, 214) W Gladden Found.

AIDS & Chinese Medicine. Qingkai Zhang. 1993. pap. 19.95 (0-941942-31-7) Orient Heal Arts.

*AIDS & Chinese Medicine. Qingcai Zang & Hong-Yen Hsu. LC 94-47451. 256p. 1995. reprint ed. pap. 14.95 (0-87983-673-3) Keats.

AIDS & Community-Based Drug Intervention Programs: Evaluation & Outreach. Ed. by Dennis G. Fisher. LC 93-23471. (Drugs & Society Ser.). (Illus.). 233p. 1993. lib. bdg. 39.95 (1-56024-510-7); pap. text ed. 14.95 (1-56023-050-9) Haworth Pr.

AIDS & Contemporary History. Ed. by Virginia Berridge & Philip Strong. LC 92-14276. (Cambridge History of Medicine Ser.). 295p. (C). 1993. 54.95 (0-521-41477-6) Cambridge U Pr.

An Asterisk (*) at the beginning of an entry indicates that the title is appearing in BIP for the first time.

An Asterisk (*) at the beginning of an entry indicates that the title is appearing in BIP for the first time.

A

AIDS-HIV: A Prescription for Survival, Vol. 1: Hyperthermia, Autoimmune Therapy & Drugs. T. R. Shantha. (Illus.). 317p. 1991. 29.95 (*1-879144-01-8*) Internatl Pub Hse.

AIDS, HIV, & Mental Health. Michael B. King. LC 92-48544. (Psychiatry & Medicine Ser.). (Illus.). 179p. (C). 1993. pap. 21.95 (*0-521-42356-2*) Cambridge U Pr.

AIDS, HIV, & Mental Health. Michael B. King. LC 92-48544. (Psychiatry & Medicine Ser.). (Illus.). 179p. (C). 1994. 42.95 (*0-521-45294-5*) Cambridge U Pr.

AIDS, HIV, & School Health Education: State Policies & Programs 1990. 142p. 1991. 12.50 (*0-317-05337-X*) NASBE.

***AIDS-HIV in the Workplace: A Fact Sheet for Employees.** Nadya Aswad. 8p. 1994. pap. text ed. 0.95 (*0-87179-840-9*) BNA.

***AIDS Home Care Handbook.** (Illus.). 178p. (Orig.). (C). 1994. pap. 34.95x (*0-7881-1011-X*) Diane Pub.

AIDS Hysteria. Arthur F. Ide. LC 85-29651. (Illus.). 117p. (Orig.). 1986. pap. 5.00 (*0-930383-08-7*) Monument Pr.

AIDS Hysteria. 2nd ed. Arthur F. Ide. LC 88-9166. (Illus.). 154p. (Orig.). (C). 1988. pap. 7.00 (*0-930383-12-5*) Monument Pr.

***AIDS, Identity, & Community Vol. 2: Contributions from Lesbian & Gay Psychology.** Gregory Herek & Beverly Greene. (Psychological Perspectives on Lesbian & Gay Issues Ser.). (Illus.). 232p. 1995. 39.95 (*0-8039-5360-7*); pap. 18.95 (*0-8039-5361-5*) Sage.

AIDS: Impact on Public Policy: An International Forum - Policy, Politics & AIDS. Ed. by Robert F. Hummel et al. LC 86-30516. 180p. 1987. 65.00 (*0-306-42540-8*, Plenum Pr) Plenum.

AIDS in Africa. Ed. by Max Essex et al. 752p. 1994. 160.00 (*0-7817-0110-4*) Raven.

AIDS in Africa: A Manual for Physicians. P. Piot et al. (Illus.). viii, 125p. 1992. pap. text ed. 14.40 (*92-4-154435-X*) World Health.

AIDS in Africa: Its Present & Future Impact. Tony Barnett & Piers Blaikie. 200p. (Orig.). 1992. pap. text ed. 18.95 (*0-89862-880-6*) Guilford Pr.

AIDS in Africa: The Social Impact & Policy Issues. Ed. by Norman Miller. LC 88-12750. (Studies in African Health & Medicine: Vol. 1). 350p. 1989. lib. bdg. 99.95 (*0-88946-187-2*) E Mellen.

AIDS in America. C. H. Russell. xi, 147p. 1991. 54.00 (*0-387-97462-8*) Spr-Verlag.

AIDS in America: Our Chances, Our Choices (A Survival Guide for the Individual & Society) Robert E. Lee. LC 87-51105. 200p. 1987. 18.50 (*0-87875-355-9*); pap. 9.95 (*0-87875-357-5*) Whitston Pub.

AIDS in an Aging Society: What We Need to Know. Ed. by Matilda W. Riley et al. 240p. 1989. 28.95 (*0-8261-7060-9*) Springer Pub.

AIDS in Developing Countries: Cost Issues & Policy Tradeoffs. Maureen Lewis et al. LC 89-35241. (Report Ser.: No. 89-5). 92p. (Orig.). (C). 1989. lib. bdg. 41.00 (*0-87766-426-9*); pap. text ed. 15.50 (*0-87766-427-7*) Urban Inst.

***AIDS in Global Perspective.** Hraf. 1995. 25.00 (*0-8161-1613-X*); pap. 14.95 (*0-8161-1614-8*) G K Hall.

***AIDS in India: Myth & Reality.** Gracious Thomas. (C). 1994. 22.00x (*81-7033-218-4*, Pub. by Rawat II) S Asia.

***AIDS in Post Communist Russia & Its Successor States.** Christopher Williams. 230p. (C). 1995. boxed, pap. text ed. 59.95 (*1-85628-570-7*, Pub. by Avebury Pub UK) Ashgate Pub Co.

AIDS in Prison. Philip A. Thomas & Martin Moerings. (Socio-Legal Studies). 160p. 1994. 57.95 (*1-85521-297-8*, Pub. by Dartmth Pub UK) Ashgate Pub Co.

Aids in Probation & Parole. (Illus.). 108p. (Orig.). (C). 1993. pap. text ed. 40.00 (*1-56806-816-6*) Diane Pub.

AIDS in Sport. Gregory L. Landry. 32p. 1989. pap. (*0-88011-353-7*, PLAN0353) Human Kinetics.

AIDS in the Dental Office? The Story of Kimberly Bergalis & Dr. David Acer. Robert R. Runnells. Ed. by Katherine Newman. (Illus.). 325p. 1993. 29.95 (*0-936751-11-8*) Infection Control.

AIDS in the Industrialized Democracies: Passions, Politics, & Policies. Ed. by David L. Kirp & Ronald Bayer. LC 91-40630. 406p. (C). 1992. text ed. 45.00 (*0-8135-1821-0*); pap. text ed. 16.00 (*0-8135-1822-9*) Rutgers U Pr.

AIDS in the Nervous System. Richard Lechtenberg & Joan H. Sher. (Illus.). 136p. 1988. text ed. 55.95 (*0-443-08616-8*) Churchill.

AIDS in the Netherlands up to the Year 2000. Scenario Committee on AIDS Staff. (Future Health Scenarios Ser.). 1992. pap. text ed. 94.00 (*0-7923-1895-1*) Kluwer Ac.

AIDS in the Workplace. 88p. 1990. pap. 15.00 (*0-685-67114-3*, 4978) Commerce.

AIDS in the Workplace. Neil Reichenberg. (Monograph Ser.). 1989. 10.00 (*0-685-41304-7*) Intl Personnel Mgmt.

AIDS in the Workplace: Legal Questions & Practical Answers. William F. Banta. LC 86-46309. 288p. 1987. text ed. 45.00 (*0-669-15334-6*) Free Pr.

AIDS in the Workplace: Legal Questions & Practical Solutions. enl. rev. ed. William F. Banta. 1992. 29.95 (*0-669-28056-9*) Heath.

AIDS in the Workplace: The Complete Resource Guide. 3rd rev. ed. 1989. 75.00 (*1-55871-111-2*) BNA.

AIDS in the World, 1992. Ed. by Jonathan Mann et al. 1037p. 1992. text ed. 50.00 (*0-674-01265-8*); pap. text ed. 24.95 (*0-674-01266-6*) HUP.

AIDS Inc: Scandal of the Century. Jon Rappoport. LC 88-80560. (Illus.). 275p. 1988. pap. 13.95 (*0-941523-03-9*) Human Energy Pr.

AIDS Information Sourcebook, 1991-92. 3rd ed. H. Robert Malinowsky & Gerald J. Perry. 312p. 1991. pap. 39.95 (*0-89774-598-1*) Oryx Pr.

***AIDS is a Woman's Nightmare.** Mary Lee. Ed. by Barbara King. (Orig.). (YA). Date not set. pap. text ed. write for info. (*1-881242-00-5*) Pyramid Educ Inc.

AIDS Is for Death. Jack Van Impe. 266p. 1988. pap. 9.00 (*0-934803-67-6*) J Van Impe.

AIDS Issues: A Handbook. David E. Newton. LC 92-10071. (Issues in Focus Ser.). 144p. (J). (gr. 6 up). 1992. lib. bdg. 18.95 (*0-89490-338-1*) Enslow Pubs.

AIDS Issues: Confronting the Challenge. Ed. by David G. Hallman. LC 88-25508. 316p. (Orig.). 1989. pap. 16.95 (*0-8298-0793-4*) Pilgrim OH.

AIDS Issues in the Workplace: A Response Model for Human Resource Management. Dale A. Masi. LC 90-8912. 232p. 1990. text ed. 55.00 (*0-89930-516-4*, MAQ/, Quorum Bks) Greenwood.

AIDS Knowledge & Attitudes for April-June 1990 Provisional Data from the National Health Interview Survey: PHS 91-1250. No. 195. 1991. write for info. (*0-318-69600-2*) Natl Ctr Health Stats.

AIDS Knowledge & Attitudes for January-March 1990: PHS 90-1250. No. 193. write for info. (*0-318-69617-7*) Natl Ctr Health Stats.

AIDS Knowledge & Attitudes for July-September 1989: PHS 90-1250. No. 183. write for info. (*0-318-69626-6*) Natl Ctr Health Stats.

AIDS Knowledge & Attitudes for October-December 1989: PHS 90-1250. No. 186. write for info. (*0-318-69623-1*) Natl Ctr Health Stats.

***AIDS Knowledge & Attitudes for 1992.** National Center for Health Statistics Staff. (Advance Data Ser.: No. 243). 16p. Date not set. write for info. (*0-614-02930-9*) Natl Ctr Health Stats.

AIDS Knowledge & Attitudes of Black Americans: United States, 1990 PHS 92-1250. No. 206. 1991. write for info. (*0-318-69614-2*) Natl Ctr Health Stats.

AIDS Knowledge & Attitudes of Hispanic Americans: United States, 1990 PHS 92-1250. No. 207. 1991. write for info. (*0-318-69615-0*) Natl Ctr Health Stats.

AIDS Law & Litigation Reporter, 5 vols., Set. 1995. ring bd. 3,425.00 (*1-55572-003-X*) Univ Pub Group.

***AIDS Law & Policy.** 2nd ed. A. Leonard et al. LC 94-72965. 562p. 1995. write for info. (*0-916081-35-4*) J Marshall Pub Co.

AIDS Law for Mental Health Professionals. Gary J. Wood. 272p. (Orig.). 1990. pap. 19.95 (*0-89087-601-0*) Celestial Arts.

AIDS Law in a Nutshell. Robert M. Jarvis et al. (Nutshell Ser.). 349p. 1992. reprint ed. pap. text ed. 17.50 (*0-314-80908-2*) West Pub.

AIDS Law Today: A New Guide for the Public. 2nd ed. Ed. by Yale AIDS Law Project Staff et al. LC 92-35572. 464p. (C). 1993. text ed. 45.00 (*0-300-05505-6*); pap. 16.00 (*0-300-05512-9*) Yale U Pr.

AIDS Legal Bibliography. Comp. by Arthur S. Leonard. (Legal Bibliography Ser.: No. 33). 25p. 1989. 40.00 (*0-935630-28-7*) U of Tex Tarlton Law Lib.

AIDS Legal Bibliography. 2nd ed. Comp. by Arthur S. Leonard. (Tarlton Law Library Legal Bibliography Ser.: No. 37). 97p. 1993. 40.00 (*0-935630-39-2*) U of Tex Tarlton Law Lib.

AIDS Literature. (AIDS Reference & Research Collection Ser.). 825p. 1993. ring bd. 95.00 (*1-55572-005-6*) Univ Pub Group.

AIDS Litigation Digest 1992. Ed. by Nancy J. Johnson & Jennifer F. Vaughan. 92p. pap. text ed. 34.50 (*0-9616858-4-0*) Strafford Pubns.

AIDS Litigation Digest 1994. Ed. by Nancy J. Johnson & Jennifer F. Vaughan. 117p. 1994. pap. text ed. 34.50 (*0-9616858-5-9*) Strafford Pubns.

***AIDS Litigation Digest 1995.** Ed. by Jennifer F. Vaughan & Zahna L. Ellis. 117p. 1995. pap. text ed. 34.50 (*0-9616858-9-1*) Strafford Pubns.

***AIDS Litigation Project I.** Lawrence Gostin. 200p. 1994. 45.00 (*1-55572-013-7*) Univ Pub Group.

***AIDS Litigation Project II.** Lawrence Gostin. 200p. 1994. 45.00 (*1-55572-014-5*) Univ Pub Group.

AIDS, Macrobiotics, & Natural Immunity. Michio Kushi & Martha C. Cottrell. LC 86-81560. (Illus.). 359p. 1989. pap. 19.95 (*0-87040-680-9*) Japan Pubns USA.

AIDS: Mystery Solved: AIDS - HIV Is Not a Death Sentence. Terrance Jackson. LC 92-97075. (Illus.). 160p. (Orig.). 1992. pap. 14.95 (*0-9630013-1-0*) AKASA Pr.

AIDS Ninety Summary: A Practical Synopsis of the VI International Conference. J. Arbeit et al. (Illus.). 350p. (Orig.). 1991. pap. 85.00 (*0-924236-05-1*) Phila Scis Group.

AIDS Notebooks. Stephen Schecter. LC 89-21824. 166p. 1990. 59.50 (*0-7914-0333-5*); pap. 19.95 (*0-7914-0334-3*) State U NY Pr.

AIDS on the College Campus - an ACHA Special Report. 2nd ed. American College Health Association Task Force on AIDS. 189p. 1989. pap. text ed. 15.00 (*1-877918-02-4*) Am Coll Hlth.

AIDS Pandemic: A Global Emergency. Ed. by R. Bolton. xii, 118p. 1989. pap. text ed. 26.00 (*2-88124-374-6*) Gordon & Breach.

AIDS Pandemic: Social Perspectives. Yole G. Sills. LC 93-25064. (Contributions in Medical Studies: No. 38). 264p. 1993. text ed. 55.00 (*0-313-28606-X*, ZAP/, Greenwood Pr) Greenwood.

AIDS Pastoral Care: An Introductory Guide. Sean Connolly. 96p. (Orig.). 1994. pap. 7.95 (*0-9636183-1-8*) Arc Res.

AIDS, Philosophy & Beyond: Philosophical Dilemmas of a Modern Pandemic. Joseph W. Smith. (Avebury Series in Philosophy). 347p. 1991. text ed. 68.95 (*1-85628-138-8*, Pub. by Avebury Pub UK) Ashgate Pub Co.

AIDS Plague. (AIDS Ser.). 1987. lib. bdg. 250.00 (*0-8490-3923-1*) Gordon Pr.

AIDS Plague. James McKeever. 180p. 1986. write for info. (*0-86694-104-5*) Omega Pubns OR.

AIDS Practice Manual. 3rd ed. Ed. by Paul Albert et al. 1990. pap. write for info. (*0-9602188-7-4*) Natl Lawyers Guild.

AIDS Prevention & Control: Invited Presentations & Papers from the World Summit of Ministers of Health on Programmes for AIDS Prevention - Jointly Organized by the WHO & the UK Government, London, 26-28 January, 1988. World Health Organization Staff. 192p. 1988. 69.00 (*0-08-036142-0*, Pergamon Pr) Elsevier.

AIDS Prevention & Services: Community Based Research. Ed. by Johannes P. Van Vugt. LC 93-207. 296p. 1993. Alk. paper. text ed. 59.95 (*0-89789-264-X*, Bergin & Garvey); Alk. paper. pap. text ed. 19.95 (*0-89789-265-8*) Greenwood.

AIDS Prevention in the Community: Lessons from the First Decade. Ed. by Nicholas Freudenberg & Marc A. Zimmerman. 238p. 1995. pap. 48.00 (*0-87553-219-5*) Am Pub Health. This book describes in detail a variety of community-based AIDS prevention programs & synthesizes the experience with such programs in the United States during the late 1980s & early 1990s. It offers AIDS educators, program planners, & policymakers a summary of the lessons learned about planning, implementing & managing AIDS prevention programs for the diverse population that can be reached in community settings. The book differs from other recent books on AIDS in that it is written primarily for practitioners & program planners & presents practical advice in the broader framework of what is known about changing health behavior & social environments. Nonmembers: $48.00 APHA Members: $33.60** ***Publisher Provided Annotation.

AIDS: Prevention Through Education: A World View. Ed. by Jaime Sepulveda et al. LC 92-49655. 384p. 1993. pap. 29.95 (*0-19-508207-9*) OUP.

AIDS-Proofing Your Kids: A Step-by-Step Guide. Loren E. Acker et al. Ed. by Michelle Roehm. 150p. 1992. pap. 8.95 (*0-941831-72-8*) Beyond Words Pub.

AIDS Public Policy Dimensions. Ed. by John Griggs. 304p. 1987. 30.00 (*0-934459-35-5*) United Hosp Fund.

AIDS Questions & Answers for Kids. rev. ed. Linda Schwartz. (Health Ser.). (Illus.). 24p. (J). (gr. 4-6). 1993. 3.95 (*0-88160-154-3*, LW272) Learning Wks.

AIDS: Rage & Reality: Why Silence Is Deadly. Gene Antonio. 336p. (Orig.). 1992. pap. 19.95 (*0-9634774-3-9*) Anchor Bks.

AIDS Reader, Vol. I. Loren K. Clarke & Malcolm Potts. 350p. 1988. pap. 17.95 (*0-8283-1918-9*) Branden Pub Co.

AIDS Reader: Privacy, Poverty, Community. Ed. by Nancy F. McKenzie. 1990. pap. 9.95 (*0-452-01048-9*, Mer) NAL-Dutton.

AIDS Reader: Social, Political, & Ethical Issues. Ed. by Nancy F. McKenzie. 484p. 1991. pap. 15.00 (*0-452-01072-1*, Mer) NAL-Dutton.

AIDS Reference & Research Collection. 7000p. 1994. ring bd. 925.00 (*1-55572-002-1*) Univ Pub Group.

AIDS Reference Guide: A Sourcebook for Planners & Decision Makers. Ed. by Steven J. Goodwin. 2400p. 1988. ring bd. 335.00 (*0-929156-01-3*) Atlantic Info Services Inc.

***AIDS-Related Behavior among Women 15-44 Years of Age: United States, 1988 & 1990.** National Center for Health Statistics Staff. (Advance Data Ser.: No. 239). 16p. Date not set. write for info. (*0-614-02926-0*) Natl Ctr Health Stats.

AIDS-Related Neoplasis. Ed. by L. Schmid & H. J. Senn. (Recent Results in Cancer Research Ser.: Vol. 112). (Illus.). 130p. 1988. 66.00 (*0-387-19227-1*) Spr-Verlag.

AIDS Related Products in Western Europe. (Market Research Reports: No. 281). (Illus.). 107p. 1992. 295.00 (*0-317-04974-7*) Theta Corp.

AIDS-Related Psychotherapy. Winiarski. (C). 1991. 37.95 (*0-205-14511-6*, H4511, Longwood Div) Allyn.

***AIDS, Reproductive Technology, & Ethics.** Julien S. Murphy. 160p. (C). 1995. text ed. 44.50x (*0-7914-2517-7*); pap. text ed. 14.95 (*0-7914-2518-5*) State U NY Pr.

AIDS Research at E. C. Level: Results of the 4th E. C. Biomedical & Health Research Program. A. E. Baert & M. C. Razquin. LC 94-75420. (Biomedical & Health Research Ser.). 400p. 1994. 99.00 (*90-5199-159-2*) IOS Press.

AIDS Research in the Netherlands. Dutch Program Committee for Aids Research. 213p. 1992. pap. 24.50 (*90-5356-008-4*) IBD Ltd.

AIDS Research Program of the National Institutes of Health. Institute of Medicine, Committee to Study the AIDS Research Program of the National Institutes of Health Staff. 156p. 1991. pap. text ed. 24.00 (*0-309-04436-7*) Natl Acad Pr.

AIDS Research Reviews, Vol. 1. Ed. by Wayne C. Koff et al. 480p. 1991. 180.00 (*0-8247-8502-9*) Dekker.

AIDS Research Reviews, Vol. 2. Ed. by Koff et al. 416p. 1992. 155.00 (*0-8247-8665-3*) Dekker.

AIDS Research Reviews, Vol. 3. Koff et al. 416p. 1993. 195.00 (*0-8247-9045-6*) Dekker.

AIDS Scam: Science & Hoax, How Special Interests Benefit. 1994. lib. bdg. 250.00 (*0-8490-5623-3*) Gordon Pr.

AIDS, Sexual Behavior, & Intravenous Drug Use. Ed. by Charles F. Turner et al. 608p. 1989. 39.95 (*0-309-03976-2*); pap. 29.95 (*0-309-03948-7*) Natl Acad Pr.

***AIDS-SIDA: A Comparison Between Europe & Africa.** Matthias Schrappe. 1993. pap. text ed. 74.95 (*0-471-02511-9*) Wiley.

***AIDS Sourcebook.** Karen Bellenir. Ed. by Peter D. Dresser. LC 95-5997. (Health Reference Ser.: No. 4). 1995. lib. bdg. 80.00x (*0-7808-0031-1*) Omnigraphics Inc.

AIDS, Stories of Living Longer. Ed. by C. Ray. 32p. (Orig.). 1991. pap. 3.25 (*0-9616792-9-8*) Taterhill.

AIDS Summary: In-Depth Review & Update. B. Wallace & J. Lasker. (Illus.). 156p. (Orig.). 1989. pap. 55.00 (*0-924236-01-9*) Phila Scis Group.

AIDS Testing: A Comprehensive Guide to Technical, Medical, Social, Legal, & Management Issues. Ed. by G. Schochetman & J. R. George. LC 94-7986. 1994. 49.00 (*0-387-94291-2*) Spr-Verlag.

AIDS Testing: Methodology & Management Issues. Ed. by G. Schochetman & J. R. George. (Illus.). 232p. 1991. 54.00 (*0-387-97534-9*) Spr-Verlag.

AIDS Testing with Its Uses & Abuses: Index of New Information with Authors & Subjects. American Health Research Institute Staff. LC 92-54210. 180p. 1992. 44.50 (*1-55914-572-2*); pap. 39.50 (*1-55914-573-0*) ABBE Pubs Assn.

***AIDS Testing with Its Uses & Abuses: Index of New Information with Authors & Subjects.** Contrib by American Health Research Institute Staff. LC 94-31244. 1994. 44.50 (*0-7883-0438-0*); pap. 39.50 (*0-7883-0439-9*) ABBE Pubs Assn.

AIDS; the Challenge: Understanding, Education, & Care. Neil Small. LC 93-24408. 192p. 1993. 54.95 (*1-85628-455-7*, Pub. by Avebury Pub UK) Ashgate Pub Co.

AIDS the Expanding Epidemic - What the Public Needs to Know: A Multicultural Overview. Valiere Alcena. 204p. (Orig.). 1994. 24.99 (*0-9633365-1-7*) Alcena Med Comms.

AIDS the Last Great Plague. 1992. lib. bdg. 250.00 (*0-8490-8707-4*) Gordon Pr.

AIDS, the Spiritual Dilemma. John E. Fortunato. 1987. pap. 7.95 (*0-685-18065-4*) Harper SF.

AIDS-The True Story: A Comprehensive Guide. Balamurali Ambati & Jayakrishna Ambati. 176p. (Orig.). (C). 1989. pap. 14.95 (*0-924385-00-6*) B J Pubns MD.

AIDS, the Unnecessary Epidemic: America under Seige. Stanley Monteith. 392p. 1991. pap. 14.95 (*0-925591-17-3*) Covenant Hse Bks.

AIDS, the Winter War. Arthur D. Kahn. LC 92-15423. 224p. (C). 1993. 27.95 (*1-56639-018-4*) Temple U Pr.

AIDS Therapies: 1992 Edition. Daniel J. DeNoon & Charles W. Henderson. 350p. 1992. reprint ed. 899.00 (*0-9631698-0-7*) C W Henderson.

Aids to Access: Resources for Educators of Adults. A. Charters. (MS Ser.). 1978. 4.25 (*0-686-52208-7*, MSS 1) Syracuse U Cont Ed.

Aids to Anaesthesia, No. 1: Basic Sciences. 3rd ed. T. E. Healy et al. (Illus.). 272p. (Orig.). 1991. pap. 29.95 (*0-443-04231-4*) Churchill.

Aids to Anatomy. Simon Paterson-Brown & Rupert Eckersley. (Illus.). 288p. 1988. pap. text ed. 23.00 (*0-443-03624-1*) Churchill.

Aids to Anatomy & Physiology for Nurses. J. Joseph. (C). 1984. 75.00 (*0-685-33798-7*, Pub. by Witherby & Co UK) St Mut.

Aids to Biological Communication: Prosthesis & Synthesis. Ed. by Diane M. Ramsey-Klee. 392p. 1970. 173.00 (*0-677-13410-X*) Gordon & Breach.

Aids to Clinical Examination. 2nd ed. Peter L. Hayes & McWalter. (Illus.). 144p. (Orig.). 1992. pap. text ed. 19.95 (*0-443-04572-0*) Churchill.

Aids to Clinical Haematology. 2nd ed. J. A. Child. (Illus.). 194p. (Orig.). 1992. pap. text ed. 16.95 (*0-443-04192-X*) Churchill.

Aids to Clinical Pharmacology & Therapeutics. 3rd ed. John Rees et al. LC 92-49325. (Illus.). 350p. 1993. pap. text ed. write for info. (*0-443-04698-0*) Churchill.

Aids to Ethics & Professional Conduct for Student Radiologic Technologists. 2nd ed. James Ohnysty. 176p. 1979. spiral bd., pap. 27.95x (*0-398-01419-1*) C C Thomas.

Aids to General Practice. 2nd ed. Michael Mead. (Illus.). 170p. 1991. pap. text ed. 22.00 (*0-443-04589-5*) Churchill.

***Aids to General Practice.** 3rd ed. Michael Mead. LC 94-43949. 1995. write for info. (*0-443-05277-8*) Churchill.

Aids to Geographical Research: Bibliographies, Periodicals, Atlases, Gazetteers & Other Reference Books. rev. ed. John K. Wright. LC 73-106702. 331p. 1971. reprint ed. text ed. 59.75 (*0-8371-3384-X*, WRGR, Greenwood Pr) Greenwood.

Aids to Historical Research. John M. Vincent. LC 70-88035. (Essay Index Reprint Ser.). 1977. 19.95 (*0-8369-1160-1*) Ayer.

Aids to Microbiology & Infectious Diseases. R. A. Benn. 208p. (Orig.). 1986. pap. text ed. 22.95 (*0-443-03127-4*) Churchill.

Aids to Obstetrics & Gynaecology: For MRCOG Part 2. 3rd ed. Gordon M. Stirrat. 306p. (Orig.). 1991. pap. text ed. 23.00 (*0-443-04382-5*) Churchill.

An Asterisk (*) at the beginning of an entry indicates that the title is appearing in BIP for the first time.

Aids to Operative Surgery. Graeme J. Poston. LC 86-8320. (Illus.). 224p. (Orig.). (C). 1987. pap. 28.00 (0-443-03566-0) Churchill.

Aids to Ophthalmology. P. T. Khaw et al. (Illus.). 296p. 1989. pap. text ed. 29.95 (0-443-04012-5) Churchill.

Aids to Paediatrics. 3rd ed. Alex Habel. LC 93-322. 244p. 1993. pap. write for info. (0-443-04714-6) Churchill.

Aids to Pathology. 4th ed. Michael F. Dixon & Philip Quirke. LC 93-18262. 1993. pap. 27.00 (0-443-04442-2) Churchill.

Aids to Pharmacology. 3rd rev. ed. Steven Sacks & Roy Spector. LC 92-21013. 1993. 29.00 (0-443-04695-6) Churchill.

Aids to Physiology. 2nd ed. Thomas Scratcherd. 320p. 1989. pap. text ed. 25.00 (0-443-03973-9) Churchill.

Aids to Physiotherapy. 2nd ed. Ed. by Jennifer M. Lee. (Illus.). 216p. 1989. pap. text ed. 15.00 (0-443-03438-9) Churchill.

Aids to Postgraduate Medicine. 5th ed. J. L. Burton. (Illus.). 272p. 1988. pap. text ed. 16.95 (0-443-03548-2) Churchill.

Aids to Postgraduate Medicine. 6th ed. J. L. Burton. 1994. pap. 19.95 (0-443-04913-0) Churchill.

Aids to Postgraduate Surgery. 3rd ed. Roger M. Watkins & J. Meirion Thomas. 276p. 1989. text ed. 28.00 (0-443-03807-4) Churchill.

Aids to Psychiatry. 3rd ed. H. G. Morgan. (Illus.). 224p. 1989. pap. text ed. 24.00 (0-443-03928-3) Churchill.

Aids to Radiological Differential Diagnosis. 2nd ed. Stephen Chapman & Richard Nakielny. (Illus.). 336p. 1990. pap. text ed. 29.50 (0-7020-1440-0, Bailliere-Tindall) Saunders.

Aids to "Revelation" Watchman Nee. Tr. by Stephen Kaung. 122p. 1983. pap. 4.00 (0-935008-60-8) Christian Fellow Pubs.

Aids to Scoutmastership: A Handbook for Scoutmasters on the Theory of Scout Training. Robert Baden-Powell. 127p. (Orig.). 1992. pap. 14.95 (0-9632054-2-0) Stevens Pub.

Aids to the Psalms, Cycle A. Hugh H. Drennan. 1992. pap. 10.75 (1-55673-435-2, 9238) CSS OH.

Aids to Undergraduate Medicine. 5th ed. J. L. Burton. (Aids to... Ser.). (Illus.). 172p. 1990. pap. text ed. 19.95 (0-443-04191-1) Churchill.

Aids to Undergraduate Obstetrics & Gynaecology. 2nd ed. Christopher Sinclair & J. Beverley Webb. LC 92-49138. (Illus.). 224p. 1993. pap. text ed. 27.00 (0-443-04785-5) Churchill.

Aids to Undergraduate Surgery. 4th ed. Peter M. Mowschenson. LC 93-34955. 1994. 19.95 (0-443-04966-1) Churchill.

AIDS: Trading Fears for Facts: A Guide for Young People. rev. ed. Consumer Reports Books Editors et al. (Illus.). 176p. (YA). (gr. 8 up). 1992. pap. 4.95 (0-89043-481-6) Consumer Reports.

AIDS, Trading Fears for Facts: A Guide for Young People. 3rd ed. Ed. by Consumer Reports Books Editors et al. LC 93-27881. 1993. write for info. (0-89043-272-4) Consumer Reports.

AIDS Treatment News. John S. James. LC 89-7399. 400p. (Orig.). 1989. pap. 12.95 (0-89087-553-7) Celestial Arts.

AIDS Treatment News, Vol. 3. Ed. by John S. James. 567p. (Orig.). 1994. pap. 14.95 (1-55583-261-X) Alyson Pubns.

AIDS Treatment News, Vol. 2: Issues 76-125. John S. James. 300p. (Orig.). 1991. pap. 16.95 (0-89087-614-2) Celestial Arts.

AIDS "Trivia" The AIDS Prevention Game. Ed. by Thomas Rundquist. 12p. (Orig.). (C). 1988. pap. 6.95 (0-9618567-2-6) Nova Media.

AIDS Trivia: Update for 90's Updated. 2nd ed. Ed. by Thomas J. Rundquist. (Illus.). 42p. (Orig.). (C). 1994. pap. text ed. 12.95 (0-9618567-6-9) Nova Media.

***AIDS Trivia: Update for 90's Updated.** 3rd ed. Ed. by Thomas J. Rundquist. (Illus.). 42p. (Orig.). 1995. teacher ed, pap. text ed. 14.95 (1-884239-01-3); disk 39.95 (1-884239-02-1) Nova Media.

AIDS Vaccine Research & Clinical Trials. Putney & Bolognesi. 504p. 1990. 125.00 (0-8247-8221-6) Dekker.

AIDS War: Propaganda, Profiteering & Genocide from the Medical-Industrial Complex. John Lauritsen. (Illus.). 480p. (Orig.). 1993. pap. 20.00 (0-943742-08-0, Asklepios) Pagan Pr.

AIDS, Women, & the Next Generation: Towards a Morally Acceptable Public Policy for HIV Testing of Pregnant Women & Newborns. Ed. by Ruth Faden et al. (Illus.). 400p. 1991. 39.95 (0-19-506572-7) OUP.

AIDS World in Nineteen Ninety-Nine: A Modern Plague That May Destroy the World if We Stay Naive, Passive, Unaware,... Mura Editors Staff & Tonci Kodbov. 250p. (Orig.). (ENG & JPN.). 1989. pap. write for info. (0-929602-02-1) Mura Pub Co.

AIDS-Zits: A "Sextionary" for Kids. Carole Marsh. (Smart Sex Stuff Ser.). (Orig.). (J). (gr. 2-12). 1994. 24.95 (1-55609-263-6); pap. 14.95 (1-55609-210-5) Gallopade Pub Group.

AIDS, 1981-1983: An Annotated Bibliography. Rhoda Garoogian. LC 84-1736. (CompuBibs Ser.: No. 2). 92p. 1984. pap. 15.00 (0-914791-05-2) Vantage Info.

AIDS 1986 (Acquired Immune Deficiency Syndrome) 2nd ed. Ed. by David A. Tyckoson. LC 86-42747. (Science Bibliographies Ser.: Vol. 7). 96p. 1986. pap. 17.75 (0-89774-323-7) Oryx Pr.

AIDS, 1989, Pt. 1. Ed. by David A. Tyckoson. (AIDS Bibliographies Ser.). 144p. 1989. pap. 21.50 (0-89774-578-7) Oryx Pr.

AIDS 88 Summary: A Practical Synopsis of the IV International Conference. B. Wallace & J. Lasker. (Illus.). 156p. (Orig.). 1988. pap. 75.00 (0-924236-00-0) Phila Scis Group.

AIDS 89 Summary: A Practical Synopsis of the V International Conference. B. Wallace & J. Lasker. (Illus.). 350p. (Orig.). 1989. pap. 85.00 (0-924236-02-7) Phila Scis Group.

AIDS 91 Summary: A Practical Synopsis of the VII International Conference. J. Arbeit et al. (Illus.). 350p. 1992. pap. 85.00 (0-924236-07-8) Phila Scis Group.

Aie Aie De la Corne De Brume. Florence Delay. (FRE.). 1984. pap. 11.95 (0-7859-1994-5, 2070375544) Fr & Eur.

Aiea Loop Trail & Keaiwa Heiau. Faith M. Roelofs. (Exploring Oahu: Field Site Guides for Teachers Ser.). 24p. 1992. pap. write for info. (1-882163-02-8) Moanalua Grdns Fnd.

***Aiea Loop Trail & Keaiwa Heiau Field Site Guide for Teachers.** Faith Roelofs. (Exploring the Islands Ser.). 1992. teacher ed write for info. (1-882163-38-9) Moanalua Grdns Fnd.

AIENG '95--Applications of Artificial Intelligence in Engineering X: Proceedings of the Tenth International Conference. Ed. by R. A. Adey & G. Rzevski. (AIENG Ser.: Vol. 10). 650p. 1995. 275.00 (1-56252-240-X) Computational Mech MA.

AIFLD: Agents As Organizers. rev. ed. Tom Barry & Deb Preusch. 76p. 1990. 5.95 (0-911213-11-2) Interhemisp Res Ctr.

AIFLD: U. S. Trojan Horse in Latin America & the Caribbean. (Illus.). 47p. (ENG & SPA.). 1983. pap. 2.00 (0-317-03384-0) EPICA.

Aigle a Deaux Tetes. Jean Cocteau. (FRE.). 1973. pap. 10.95 (0-7859-1732-2, 2070363287) Fr & Eur.

Aigle a Deux Tetes. Jean Cocteau. (Folio Ser.: No. 328). (FRE.). 1973. 6.95 (2-07-036328-7) Schoenhof.

Aigle a Deux Tetes see Theatre

Aigle de Fer. Jean Orieux. (FRE.). 1985. pap. 17.95 (0-7859-4234-3) Fr & Eur.

Aiglon. Edmond Rostand. (Illus.). 434p. (FRE.). 1986. 15.95 (0-685-74006-4, 2070377644) Fr & Eur.

Aiglon. Edmond Rostand. (Folio Ser.: No. 1764). 434p. 1986. pap. 13.95 (2-07-037764-4) Schoenhof.

Aiglon see Chefs-d'Oeuvre

Aiiieeeee! An Anthology of Asian American Writers. Ed. by Jeffrey P. Chan et al. 304p. 1991. pap. 5.99 (0-451-62836-5, Ment) NAL-Dutton.

AIIM Government Affairs Annual Report. 1992. 20.00 (0-89258-259-6, Y401) Assn Inform & Image Mgmt.

AIIM Speakers Directory 1992-1993. 278p. 1992. pap. 95.00 (0-89258-270-7, D406) Assn Inform & Image Mgmt.

Aiki. John Gilbert. LC 86-81474. 288p. 1986. 17.95 (0-917657-86-1) D I Fine.

Aikido. Jerry Craven. LC 94-4093. (J). 1994. write for info. (0-86593-364-2) Rourke Corp.

***Aikido.** Bill Gutman. (Action Sports Ser.). 48p. (J). (gr. 3-9). 1995. lib. bdg. 13.35 (1-56065-268-3) Capstone Pr.

Aikido. Morihei Uyeshiba & Kisshomaru Uyeshiba. (Illus.). 190p. 1985. 28.00 (0-87040-629-9) Japan Pubns USA.

Aikido: A Supplement to Dojo Training. Jeffrey I. Baygents. LC 81-69692. (Illus.). 150p. 1981. pap. text ed. 14.00 (0-9607326-0-8) M E Benefield Pub.

Aikido: Its Heart & Appearance. 1976. 11.95 (0-685-88117-2) Wehman.

Aikido: The Heavenly Road. Kenji Shimizu. LC 94-10356. (Illus.). 175p. 1994. 29.95 (1-883695-02-3) Edition Q.

Aikido: The Way of Harmony. John Stevens & Shirata Rinjiro. LC 82-42680. (Illus.). 200p. (Orig.). 1984. pap. 20.00 (0-394-71426-1) Shambhala Pubns.

Aikido: The Way of Harmony. John Stevens. (Orig.). 1986. pap. 20.00 (0-87773-229-9) Shambhala Pubns.

Aikido: Traditional Art & Modern Sport. Brian N. Bagot. (Illus.). 224p. 1993. pap. 29.95 (1-85223-715-5, Pub. by Crowood Pr UK) Trafalgar.

Aikido & Bokata. Bruce Tegner. LC 83-4871. (Illus.). 128p. (Orig.). 1983. pap. 7.00 (0-87407-039-2, T-39) Thor.

***Aikido & Chinese Martial Arts.** Tetsutaka Sugawara et al. 212p. Date not set. 29.00 (0-87040-963-8) FS&G.

Aikido & Chinese Martial Arts. Tetsutaka Sugawara. (Illus.). 180p. 1994. pap. 19.00 (0-87040-934-4) Japan Pubns USA.

Aikido & the Dynamic Sphere. A. M. Westbrook & O. Ratti. LC 69-16180. (Illus.). 376p. 1970. 29.95 (0-8048-0004-9) C E Tuttle.

Aikido & the Dynamic Sphere. A. M. Westbrook & O. Ratti. 29.95 (0-685-63742-5) Wehman.

Aikido & the Harmony of Nature. Mitsugi Saotome. LC 92-56440. (Illus.). 248p. 1993. reprint ed. pap. 25.00 (0-87773-855-6) Shambhala Pubns.

Aikido & the New Warrior. Ed. by Richard S. Heckler. 256p. 1985. pap. 12.95 (0-938190-51-2) North Atlantic.

Aikido Complete. Y. Yamada. 10.95 (0-685-70666-4) Wehman.

Aikido Complete. Yoshimitsu Yamada. LC 67-24707. 1970. 7.95 (0-8184-0001-3) Carol Pub Group.

Aikido Complete. Yoshimitsu Yamada. (Illus.). 128p. 1984. pap. 8.95 (0-8065-0914-7, Citadel Pr) Carol Pub Group.

Aikido for Life. Gaku Homma. (Illus.). 120p. (Orig.). 1990. reprint ed. pap. 9.95 (1-55643-078-7) North Atlantic.

***Aikido in America.** Ed. by John Stone. 250p. (Orig.). (C). 1995. pap. 16.95 (1-883319-27-7) Frog CA.

Aikido in Everyday Life: Giving in to Get Your Way. Terry Dobson & Victor Miller. (Illus.). 257p. (Orig.). 1992. reprint ed. pap. 14.95 (1-55643-151-1) North Atlantic.

Aikido in Training: A Manual of Traditional Aikido Practice & Principles. R. Crane & K. Crane. LC 93-71042. 336p. 1993. 34.95 (0-9636429-5-2) Cool Rain Prods.

Aikido Student Handbook. Greg O'Connor. LC 93-25763. (Illus.). 108p. (Orig.). 1993. pap. 9.95 (1-883319-04-8) Frog CA.

AILA Consular Post Handbook. 3rd ed. Ed. by Seymour Rosenberg & Richard S. Goldstein. 125p. 1990. pap. text ed. 18.00 (1-878677-14-4) Amer Immi Law Assn.

AILA's Labor Department Directory for Immigration Lawyers. 2nd ed. Ed. by Jane W. Goldblum & Amy R. Novick. 92p. 1993. pap. text ed. 16.00 (1-878677-51-9) Amer Immi Law Assn.

AILA's Labor Department Directory for Immigration Lawyers: A Guide to Finding DOL, SESA, & Job Service Offices. Ed. by Jane W. Goldblum & Amy R. Novick. 94p. 1992. pap. text ed. 16.00 (1-878677-38-1) Amer Immi Law Assn.

Aileen: Ozark Pioneering Spirit. Aileen M. Hatch & Iris C. Meadows. Ed. by Roy W. Meadows & Dan Hatch. LC 92-93038. (Illus.). 187p. (Orig.). 1992. pap. 7.00 (0-9624710-2-X) Culver-Meadows.

Ailes de la Colombe, Tome I. Henry James. 440p. (FRE.). 1979. pap. 11.95 (0-7859-2416-7, 2070370976) Fr & Eur.

Ailes de la Colombe, Tome II. Henry James. 372p. (FRE.). 1979. pap. 11.95 (0-7859-2417-5, 2070370984) Fr & Eur.

Aileurs. Henri Michaux. (FRE.). 1986. pap. 11.95 (0-7859-2802-2) Fr & Eur.

Ailing, Aging, & Addicted Leaders: Studies of Compromised Leadership. Bert E. Park. LC 93-19550. 288p. 1993. 29.00 (0-8131-1853-0) U Pr of Ky.

Ailing Empire: Germany from Bismarck to Hitler. Sebastian Haffner. Tr. by Jean Steinberg. LC 88-33491. Orig. Title: Von Bismarck zu Hitler. 266p. 1991. pap. 9.95 (0-88064-127-4) Fromm Intl Pub.

Ailing Spine: A Holistic Approach to Rehabilitation. Hans Tilscher & Manfred Eder. (Manuelle Medizin Ser.). (Illus.). 176p. 1991. pap. 64.00 (0-387-53008-8) Spr-Verlag.

Ailing Steel: The Transatlantic Quarrel. Ed. by Walter H. Goldberg. LC 83-40527. 559p. 1986. text ed. 49.95 (0-312-01502-X) St Martin.

Ailment & Other Psychoanalytic Essays. Tom Main. 256p. 1989. 40.00 (1-85343-104-4) Col U Pr.

Aim: From Concept to Reality. C. Wedemeyer & R. Najem. 1969. 2.50 (0-8156-7040-0, NES 61) Syracuse U Cont Ed.

Aim & Structure of Physical Theory. Pierre Duhem. Tr. by Philip P. Wiener. 344p. 1991. pap. 14.95 (0-691-02524-X) Princeton U Pr.

Aim-Far 1988. TAB-Aero Staff. 416p. 1987. pap. 11.60 (0-8306-8388-7, 24388P, TAB-Aero) TAB Bks.

AIM-FAR, 1989. TAB-Aero Staff. (Illus.). 464p. 1989. 16.95 (0-8306-8089-6, 24389, TAB-Aero); pap. 11.60 (0-8306-8889-7, 24389, TAB-Aero) TAB Bks.

AIM-FAR 1990. TAB-Aero Staff. (Illus.). 464p. 1989. 19.95 (0-8306-4390-7, TAB-Aero); pap. 11.95 (0-685-26498-X, TAB-Aero) TAB Bks.

Aim-Far, 1991. Tab Publishing Staff. (Aero Ser.). (Illus.). 608p. 1991. 19.95 (0-8306-5391-0, 24391, TAB-Aero) TAB Bks.

AIM-FAR 1992. TAB-Aero Staff. 576p. 1991. 21.95 (0-8306-2150-4, TAB-Aero); pap. 12.95 (0-8306-2149-0, TAB-Aero) TAB Bks.

Aim Far, 1992. TAB Books Staff. 1991. 21.95 (0-07-157958-3); pap. 12.95 (0-07-157957-5) McGraw.

AIM-FAR 1992 Midyear Update. 20p. 1992. pap. write for info. (0-318-69179-5) TAB Bks.

Aim Far, 1993. TAB-Aero Editors. 1992. 22.95 (0-07-062860-2); pap. 12.95 (0-07-062861-0) McGraw.

AIM-FAR, 1993. TAB-Aero Staff. 592p. 1992. 22.95 (0-8306-4221-8, 24396, TAB-Aero); pap. 12.95 (0-8306-4220-X, 24396, TAB-Aero) TAB Bks.

Aim Far, 1994. 1993. pap. 12.95 (0-8306-4380-X, TAB-Aero) TAB Bks.

Aim Far, 1994. Tab-Aero Editors. 1993. text ed. 23.95 (0-07-062872-6); pap. text ed. 12.95 (0-07-062873-4) McGraw.

***Aim Far, 1995.** 1994. pap. text ed. 12.95 (0-07-063084-4, TAB-Aero) TAB Bks.

***Aim First! Because You Can't Reach a Goal You Don't Have.** Lee T. Silber. (Illus.). 128p. (Orig.). 1995. pap. 11.95 (0-9628771-3-1) Tales From Tropics.

Aim for a Job As a Waiter or Waitress. Peggy O'Connell. LC 79-15014. (Arco's Career Guidance Ser.). (Illus.). 1980. lib. bdg. 7.95 (0-668-04767-4, Arco Test); pap. 4.50 (0-668-04771-2, Arco Test) P-H Gen Ref & Trav.

Aim High: An Olympic Decathlete's Inspiring Story. Dave Johnson & Verne Becker. LC 94-13716. 1994. 18.99 (0-310-46190-1) Zondervan.

Aim Higher. 2nd ed. Maximilian Kolbe. Ed. by Marion Goodwin. Tr. by Dominic Wisz. Orig. Title: Do Ideata. 167p. 1994. pap. text ed. 4.95 (0-913382-59-0, 101-42) Prow Bks-Franciscan.

***Aim Maps: Orlando Street Guide.** 200p. Date not set. pap. 9.95 (1-886751-00-5) AIM Maps.

***Aim Maps: Orlando Street Guide.** 200p. Date not set. pap. 11.95 (1-886751-01-3) AIM Maps.

Aim of the Game. A Lauffer. LC 73-84873. 132p. 1974. 9.95 (0-88437-052-6) Psych Dimensions.

AIM, 1989. TAB-Aero Staff. (Illus.). 288p. 1989. pap. 6.95 (0-8306-8369-0, 21369, TAB-Aero) TAB Bks.

***AIM 95.** FAA Series: FAR-AIM Series Staff. (Illus.). 1995. 14.95 (1-56027-208-2, ASA-95-AIM) Av Suppl & Acad.

Aimales Domesticos. LC 92-61169. (Spanish Chunky Bks.). 28p. (SPA.). (J). (ps). 1993. 3.25 (0-679-84169-5) Random Bks Yng Read.

Aime Cesaire. L. Kesteloot. (Coll. Poetes d'aujourd'hui Ser.). pap. 24.95 (0-8288-6090-4, F92520) Fr & Eur.

Aime Cesaire. Janis L. Pallister. (Twayne's World Authors Ser.: No. 821). 130p. 1992. text ed. 24.95 (0-8057-8266-4, Twayne) Macmillan.

AIME 'Eighty-Nine. Ed. by J. Hunter et al. (Lecture Notes in Medical Informatics Ser.: Vol. 38). x, 330p. 1989. pap. 55.00 (0-387-51543-7, 3394) Spr-Verlag.

AIME International Symposium: Mining & Metallurgy of Lead & Zinc, Set. LC 78-132404. 1970. 20.00 (0-89520-040-6) SMM&E Inc.

AIME International Symposium: Mining & Metallurgy of Lead & Zinc, Vol. 1. LC 78-132404. 1017p. 1970. 10.00 (0-685-73437-4) SMM&E Inc.

AIME International Symposium: Mining & Metallurgy of Lead & Zinc, Vol. 2. LC 78-132404. 1099p. 1970. 20.00 (0-685-42353-0) SMM&E Inc.

Aimed at Nobody: Poems from Notebooks. W. S. Graham. 96p. (Orig.). 1993. pap. 8.95 (0-571-16745-4) Faber & Faber.

Aimee Semple McPherson: Everybody's Sister. Edith L. Blumhofer. LC 93-39149. (Library of Religious Biography Ser.). (Illus.). xiv, 434p. (C). 1994. 24.99 (0-8028-3752-2); pap. 14.99 (0-8028-0155-2) Eerdmans.

Aimez-Vous Brahms? Francoise Sagan. 1963. 10.95 (0-685-23930-6, F123361) Fr & Eur.

***Aimilia-Georgios - Emily-George.** Helen Z. Papanikolas. LC 86-28266. (Utah Centennial Ser.: No. 3). 341p. (ENG & GRE.). 1987. pap. 97.20 (0-7837-8552-6, 2049367) Bks Demand.

Aiming for the Jugular in New Orleans. W. Hardy Davis. LC 75-16561. 1976. 21.95 (0-87949-035-7) Ashley Bks.

AIMS: Developmental Indicators of Emotional Health. Susan Partridge. 1991. write for info. (0-939561-10-7) Univ South ME.

Aims & Means. John Boynton. LC 64-8214. (Background Ser.). (Illus.). 1964. 16.95 (0-8023-1015-X) Dufour.

Aims & Methods in Neuroethology. Ed. by D. M. Guthrie. (Studies in Neuroscience). 320p. 1988. text ed. 75.00 (0-7190-2213-4, Pub. by Manchester Univ Pr UK) St Martin.

Aims & Modes in the Writing Process. 2nd ed. Polnac & Wilkerson. 208p. (C). 1992. pap. text ed. 13.95 (0-8403-7811-4) Kendall-Hunt.

Aims & Motives in Clinical Medicine: A Practical Approach to Medical Ethics. B. P. Bliss & A. G. Johnson. 150p. 1975. pap. text ed. 25.00 (0-8464-0123-1) Beekman Pubs.

Aims & Prospects of Semiotics: To Honor A. J. Greimas, 2 Vols., 1. Ed. by Herman Parret & H. Ruprecht. LC 85-11049. lxxxv, 550p. 1985. write for info. (90-272-2020-4) Benjamins North Am.

Aims & Prospects of Semiotics: To Honor A. J. Greimas, 2 Vols., 2. Ed. by Herman Parret & H. Ruprecht. LC 85-11049. lxxxv, 550p. 1985. write for info. (90-272-2021-2) Benjamins North Am.

Aims & Prospects of Semiotics: To Honor A. J. Greimas, 2 Vols., Set. Ed. by Herman Parret & H. Ruprecht. LC 85-11049. lxxxv, 550p. 1985. 260.00 (90-272-2019-0) Benjamins North Am.

***Aims of Argument: A Brief Rhetoric.** Timothy Crusius & Carolyn Channell. (C). 1994. teacher ed, pap. text ed. write for info. (0-614-01950-8) Mayfield Pub.

***Aims of Argument: A Brief Rhetoric.** Timothy W. Crusius & Carolyn E. Channell. LC 94-21888. 267p. (C). 1994. pap. text ed. 12.95 (1-55934-440-7) Mayfield Pub.

***Aims of Argument: A Rhetoric & Reader.** 3rd ed. Timothy W. Crusius & Carolyn E. Channell. 672p. (C). 1994. pap. text ed. 26.95 (1-55934-114-9) Mayfield Pub.

Aims of College Teaching. Kenneth E. Eble. LC 83-48157. (Higher & Adult Education Ser.). 205p. 1983. 30.95x (0-87589-575-1) Jossey-Bass.

Aims of Education. Alfred N. Whitehead. LC 29-10164. 1967. pap. 15.95 (0-02-935180-4) Free Pr.

Aims of Education: Early Twentieth Century. Jack Harrington. LC 74-7167. 297p. 1974. text ed. 24.50 (0-8422-5176-6); pap. text ed. 12.50 (0-8422-0419-9) Irvington.

Aims of Education in India: Vedic Buddhist, Medieval, British & Post Independence. Bhanu P. Singh. 1990. 29.50 (81-202-0282-1, Pub. by Ajanta II) S Asia.

Aims of Primary Education & the National Curriculum. Ed. by Nigel Proctor. (Contemporary Analysis in Education Ser.). 220p. 1990. 70.00 (1-85000-559-1); pap. 33.00 (1-85000-560-5) Taylor & Francis.

Aims of Representation: Subject - Text - History. Ed. by Murray Krieger. LC 92-80808. 280p. (C). 1993. pap. 14.95 (0-8047-2098-3) Stanford U Pr.

Aims of the Essay: A Reader & Guide. Don Knefel. 450p. 1990. pap. text ed. write for info. (0-205-12655-3, H26552) Allyn.

Aims, Values & Education. F. W. Garforth. 191p. (C). 1985. pap. 39.95 (0-948340-00-2, Pub. by Christygate Pr UK) St Mut.

A'in-i Akbari, 3 vols., Set. Abul-Fazl Allami. (C). 1989. 90.00 (0-8364-2426-3, Pub. by Usha II) S Asia.

AIN Symposium Proceedings, Nutrition '87. Ed. by Orville A. Levander. (Illus.). 157p. (Orig.). 1987. pap. 15.00 (0-943029-01-5) Am Inst Nutrition.

Aine des Ferchaux. Georges Simenon. (FRE.). 1977. pap. 13.95 (0-7859-4076-6) Fr & Eur.

Aineias the Tactician: How to Survive under Siege. Tr. & Intro. by David Whitehead. (Clarendon Ancient History Ser.). 240p. 1990. 59.00 (0-19-814878-X) OUP.

Aineias the Tactician: How to Survive under Siege. Tr. & Intro. by David Whitehead. (Clarendon Ancient History Ser.). 240p. 1990. pap. 19.95 (0-19-814744-9) OUP.

Ainesworth Prowler. Peggy Albrecht. (gr. 6-8). 1984. pap. 3.95 (0-87508-658-6) Chr Lit.

Aino Folk Tales. Basil H. Chamberlain. (Folk Lore Society, London Ser.: Vol. 22). 1972. reprint ed. pap. 15.00 (0-8115-0509-X) Periodicals Srv.

Ainsi des Exiles. Viviane Forrester. 179p. (FRE.). 1985. pap. 10.95 (0-7859-2507-4, 2070376729) Fr & Eur.

Ainsi Soit-Il ou les Jeux Sont Faits: Essai. Andre Gide. 200p. (FRE.). 1952. 27.95 (0-7859-4587-3) Fr & Eur.

A

Ainsi va la France. R. Steele & J. Gaillard. (C). 1985. 60.00 (*0-85950-298-8*, Pub. by S Thornes Pubs UK); audio 220.00 (*0-85950-749-1*, Pub. by S Thornes Pubs UK) St Mut.

Ainsi Va Toute Chair, Tome I. Samuel Butler. 237p. (FRE.). 1977. pap. 10.95 (*0-7859-1845-0*, 2070369145) Fr & Eur.

Ainsi Va Toute Chair, Tome II. Samuel Butler. (FRE.). 1977. pap. 10.95 (*0-7859-1846-9*, 2070369153) Fr & Eur.

Ainslie Meares Compendium: Dialogue on Meditation, from the Quiet Place & a Kind of Believing. Ainslie Meares. 156p. (Orig.). 1994. pap. 10.95 (*0-85572-195-2*, Pub. by Hill Content Pubng AT) Seven Hills Bk.

Ainslie's Complete Guide to Thoroughbred Racing. Tom Ainslie. (Illus.). 352p. 1988. pap. 11.95 (*0-671-65655-4*, Fireside) S&S Trade.

Ainslie's Complete Hoyle. Tom Ainslie. LC 74-32023. 544p. 1979. pap. 15.00 (*0-671-24779-4*) S&S Trade.

Ainslie's Encyclopedia of Thoroughbred Handicapping. Tom Ainslie. LC 78-9755. 1978. 20.45 (*0-688-03345-8*) Morrow.

Ainslie's Encyclopedia of Thoroughbred Handicapping. Tom Ainslie. LC 78-9755. 1981. pap. 15.45 (*0-688-00466-0*, Quill) Morrow.

Ainsworth & Bisby's Dictionary of the Fungi. 7th ed. Ed. by D. L. Hawksworth et al. 445p. 1983. text ed. 31.50 (*0-85198-515-7*) CAB Intl.

Ain't Broadway Grand - A Brand New 1948 Musical. Ed. by Milton Okun. pap. 14.95 (*0-89524-747-X*) Cherry Lane.

Ain't, but It Can Be: Persistence & Faith Overcoming Racist-Related Adversities. William D. Phears. LC 93-72874. 323p. 1993. pap. 12.95 (*1-878398-37-7*) Blue Note Pubns.

***Ain't Gonna Be the Same Fool Twice.** April Sinclair. 256p. 1996. 19.95 (*0-7868-6069-3*) Hyperion.

Ain't Gonna Let Nobody Turn Me Round: The Pursuit of Racial Justice in the Rural South. Richard A. Couto. 310p. 1991. 44.95 (*0-87722-806-X*) Temple U Pr.

Ain't Gonna Let Nobody Turn Me Round: The Pursuit of Racial Justice in the Rural South. Richard A. Couto. 421p. 1992. pap. 18.95 (*1-56639-004-4*) Temple U Pr.

Ain't Gonna Study War No More: Biblical Ambiguity & the Abolition of War. Albert C. Winn. LC 92-33997. 112p. (Orig.). 1993. pap. 10.99 (*0-664-25207-9*) Westminster John Knox.

Ain't Got Time to Die. Nolan Davis. (Orig.). 1993. pap. 3.95 (*0-685-69520-4*) Holloway.

Ain't I a Woman! Comp. by Illona Linthwaite. LC 87-35577. 214p. 1991. pap. 7.95 (*0-87226-209-X*) P Bedrick Bks.

Ain't I a Woman! A Book of Women's Poetry from Around the World. Ed. by Illona Linthwaite. LC 93-13201. 1993. 7.99 (*0-517-09365-0*, Pub. by Wings Bks) Random Hse Value.

Ain't I a Woman? Black Women & Feminism. Bell Hooks. LC 81-51392. 205p. 1981. 25.00 (*0-89608-130-3*); pap. 12.00 (*0-89608-129-X*) South End Pr.

Ain't It Great to Be Crazy! (Illus.). 32p. 1986. pap. 7.95 (*0-685-65814-7*, AM67042) Music Sales.

Ain't Misbehavin' (Illus.). 1983. 12.95 (*0-88188-534-7*, 00359040) H Leonard.

Ain't Misbehavin: The Story of Fats Waller. Ed Kirkeby. LC 76-14124. (Roots of Jazz Ser.). 248p. 1975. reprint ed. lib. bdg. 27.50 (*0-306-70683-0*); reprint ed. pap. 8.95 (*0-306-80015-2*) Da Capo.

Ain't No Big Thing: Coping Strategies in a Hawaiian-American Community. Alan Howard. LC 73-86029. 339p. reprint ed. pap. 96.70 (*0-8357-5276-3*, 2017218) Bks Demand.

Ain't No Cure for Rock & Roll. Al Blair. 6p. 1988. pap. 3.95 (*0-930366-21-2*) Northcountry Pub.

Ain't No Help on the Way. Hermand Bennette. 76p. 1990. 10.00 (*0-8187-0121-8*) Harlo Press.

Ain't No Makin' It: Leveled Aspirations in a Low-Income Neighborhood. Jay MacLeod. 198p. (C). 1987. pap. text ed. 15.95 (*0-8133-7163-5*) Westview.

Ain't No Makin' It: Leveled Aspirations in a Low-Income Neighborhood. 2nd rev. ed. Jay Macleod. 338p. (C). 1995. text ed. 55.00 (*0-8133-1514-X*); pap. text ed. 15.95 (*0-8133-1515-8*) Westview.

***Ain't Nobody Here but Us Typewriters.** Wendell Metzger. 48p. (Orig.). 1993. 4.95 (*1-878116-29-0*) JVC Bks.

***Ain't Nobody's Business If You Do.** Peter McWilliams. 1995. pap. 5.95 (*0-931580-58-7*) Prelude Press.

Ain't Nobody's Business If You Do: The Absurdity of Consensual Crimes in a Free Society. Peter McWilliams. 818p. 1993. 11.47 (*0-931580-53-6*) Prelude Press.

Ain't You Got a Right to the Tree of Life! The People of Johns Island, South Carolina - Their Faces, Their Words & Their Songs. enl. rev. ed. Ed. by Guy Carawan & Candie Carawan. (Brown Thrasher Bks.). (Illus.). 256p. 1994. reprint ed. pap. 19.95 (*0-8203-1643-1*) U of Ga Pr.

Ainu & Their Folklore. John Batchelor. 1972. lib. bdg. 250.00 (*0-87968-478-X*) Krishna Pr.

Ainu Folktales. B. H. Chamberlain. 1976. lib. bdg. 250.00 (*0-8490-1407-7*) Gordon Pr.

Ainu Language: The Morphology & Syntax of the Shizunai Dialect. Kirsten Refsing. 301p. 1986. 73.00x (*87-7288-020-1*) Coronet Bks.

Ainu of Japan: The Religion, Superstitions, & General History of the Hairy Aborigines of Japan. John Batchelor. 1977. 28.95 (*0-8369-7153-1*, 7985) Ayer.

Ainu of the Northwest Coast of Southern Sakhalin. Emiko Ohnuki-Tierney. (Illus.). 127p. (C). 1984. reprint ed. pap. text ed. 8.95 (*0-88133-092-2*) Waveland Pr.

Ainu Speak: The Land Was a Forest. Kayano & Shigeru. (Transitions Series: Asia & the Pacific). (C). 1994. pap. text ed. 15.95 (*0-8133-1880-7*) Westview.

Aioaeuie Ntnlnqrr. Jim Shaw. (Illus.). 1986. 8.95 (*0-9607640-1-1*) End is Here Pubns.

AIP Conference Proceedings, No. 134. Ed. by Melvin Month et al. LC 85-73170. 382p. 1985. lib. bdg. 46.00 (*0-88318-333-1*) Am Inst Physics.

AIP Conference Proceedings, No. 137. Rabin. LC 85-73915. 302p. 1986. lib. bdg. 53.75 (*0-88318-336-6*) Am Inst Physics.

***AIP Handbook of Condenser Microphones: Theory, Calibration & Measurements.** George S. Wong & Tony F. Embleton. LC 94-28421. (AIP Series in Modern Acoustics & Signal Processing). (Illus.). 400p. 1994. text ed. 85.00 (*1-56396-284-5*, AIP Pr) Am Inst Physics.

AIP Handbook of Modern Sensors: Physics, Designs, & Applications. Jacob Fraden. (Modern Instrumentation & Measurements in Physics & Engineering Ser.). 552p. 1993. 80.00 (*1-56396-108-3*) Am Inst Physics.

Air. Michael Allaby. (Elements Ser.). (Illus.). 208p. 1992. 35.00 (*0-8160-2525-8*) Facts on File.

Air. Kitty Benedict. (My First Nature Bks.). (J). (gr. 5 up). 1992. lib. bdg. 10.95 (*0-88682-547-4*) Creative Ed.

Air. Keith Brandt. LC 84-2608. (Illus.). 32p. (J). (gr. 3-6). 1985. lib. bdg. 9.49 (*0-8167-0130-X*); pap. text ed. 2.95 (*0-8167-0131-8*) Troll Assocs.

Air. Andrew Charman. LC 93-31748. (First Starts Ser.). (J). 1994. lib. bdg. 19.97 (*0-8114-5509-2*) Raintree Steck-V.

Air. Hilary Devonshire. LC 91-34421. (Science Through Art Ser.). (Illus.). 32p. (J). (gr. 3-5). 1992. lib. bdg. 13.23 (*0-531-14134-9*) Watts.

Air. Terry Jennings. LC 89-453. (Young Scientist Investigates Ser.). (Illus.). 32p. (J). (gr. 3-6). 1989. pap. 4.95 (*0-516-48435-4*) Childrens.

Air. Wendy Larson. (My World Poke & Look Bks.). (Illus.). 14p. (J). (ps-1). 1994. bds. 4.95 (*0-448-40569-5*, G&D) Putnam Pub Group.

Air. Chris Oxlade. LC 94-5547. (Science Magic Ser.). (Illus.). 30p. (J). (gr. 2-5). 1994. 12.95 (*0-8120-6444-5*); pap. 4.95 (*0-8120-1983-0*) Barron.

Air. J. M. Parramon et al. (Four Elements Ser.). 32p. (J). (ps). 1985. pap. 6.95 (*0-8120-3597-6*) Barron.

Air. E. N. Ramsden & R. E. Lee. 64p. (C). 1987. 39.00 (*0-85950-388-7*, Pub. by S Thornes Pubs UK) St Mut.

Air. Joy Richardson. LC 91-42612. (Picture Science Ser.). (Illus.). 30p. (J). (gr. k-4). 1992. lib. bdg. 12.25 (*0-531-14201-9*) Watts.

Air. Robbins. (J). 1996. 16.95 (*0-8050-2292-9*) H Holt & Co.

Air. Philip Sauvain. LC 91-27905. (Way It Works Ser.). (Illus.). 48p. (J). (gr. 6 up). 1992. text ed. 13.95 (*0-02-781076-3*, Mac Bks Young Read) S&S Childrens.

Air. Bonita Searle-Barnes. (Wonder of God's World Ser.). (Illus.). 32p. (J). (gr. k-3). 1993. 6.99 (*0-7459-2694-0*) Lion USA.

Air. Su Swallow. LC 90-31033. (Starting Points Ser.). (Illus.). 32p. (J). (gr. k-4). 1991. lib. bdg. 12.60 (*0-531-14097-0*) Watts.

Air. Paul Vangelisti. 1973. pap. 2.50 (*0-685-04492-0*) Invisible-Red Hill.

Air: All about Cyclones, Rainbows, Clouds, Ozone & More. David Allen. (Illus.). 32p. (J). 1993. pap. 5.95 (*1-895688-08-6*, Pub. by Greey dePencier CN) Firefly Bks Ltd.

***Air: Hands on Elementary School Science.** Linda Poore. 18p. 1994. teacher ed 35.00 (*1-883410-18-5*) L Poore.

Air: Simple Experiments for Young Scientists. Larry White. LC 94-9837. (Gateway Science Ser.). (Illus.). 48p. (J). (gr. 2-4). 1995. lib. bdg. 13.90 (*1-56294-471-1*) Millbrook Pr.

Air Accidents Investigation Branch: Report on the Incident of Boeing 747, N605PE, at Gatwick Airport, Sussex on 1 February 1988. 40p. 1989. pap. 15.00 (*0-11-550925-9*, HM9259, Pub. by HMSO UK) UNIPUB.

Air Aces of the Austro-Hungarian Empire, 1914-1918. Martin O'Connor. LC 86-8237. (Illus.). 336p. 1994. reprint ed. 49.95 (*0-9637110-1-6*) Flying Machines.

Air Acoustics: Applications in Engineering. Ed. by H. M. Atassi. LC 92-43206. 904p. 1993. 99.00 (*0-387-97977-8*); write for info. (*3-540-97977-8*) Spr-Verlag.

Air, Air, Air. Lawrence Jefferies. LC 82-15808. (Question & Answer Bks.). (Illus.). 32p. (J). (gr. 3-6). 1983. lib. bdg. 10.59 (*0-89375-880-9*); pap. text ed. 2.95 (*0-89375-881-7*) Troll Assocs.

Air All Around. Joanne Barkan. Ed. by Bonnie Brook. (First Facts Ser.). (Illus.). 32p. (J). (ps-1). 1990. 4.95 (*0-671-68659-3*); lib. bdg. 6.95 (*0-671-68655-0*) Silver Pr.

Air, Air Everywhere. Tom Johnston. LC 87-42752. (Science in Action Ser.). (Illus.). 32p. (J). (gr. 4-6). 1988. lib. bdg. 17.27 (*1-55532-406-1*) Gareth Stevens Inc.

Air Almanac. 1990. lib. bdg. 300.00 (*0-8490-4012-4*) Gordon Pr.

Air Almanac, 2 vols., Set. 1994. lib. bdg. 600.00 (*0-8490-5712-4*) Gordon Pr.

Air Almanac, 1989. (Illus.). 902p. 1988. text ed. 50.00 (*0-16-002105-7*, S/N 008-054-00126-2) USGPO.

Air Almanac, 1991. (Illus.). 900p. 1990. pap. 36.00 (*0-16-002115-4*) USGPO.

Air Almanac, 1993. 904p. 1992. pap. 85.00 (*0-11-772653-2*, HM26532, Pub. by HMSO UK) UNIPUB.

Air Almanac 1994. 904p. 1993. pap. 80.00 (*0-11-772743-1*, HM27431, Pub. by HMSO UK) UNIPUB.

Air Analysis for Health & Dangers at Home, Work or Play in the U. S. A. Index of New Information with Authors & Subjects. Arlene A. Slattner. 180p. 1993. 49.50 (*1-55914-892-6*); pap. 39.50 (*1-55914-893-4*) ABBE Pubs Assn.

Air & Angels. large type ed. Susan Hill. (Romance Ser.). 336p. 1992. 23.95 (*0-7089-8651-X*) Ulverscroft.

Air & Armor. 1987. 25.00 (*0-87431-049-0*) West End Games.

Air & Dreams: An Essay on the Imagination of Movement. Gaston Bachelard. Tr. by Edith Farrell & Frederick Farrell. LC 88-25704. (Bachelard Translation Ser.). 298p. 1988. pap. 18.00 (*0-911005-13-7*) Dallas Inst Pubns.

***Air & Fire.** Thomson. 1995. pap. 12.00 (*0-679-74730-3*) Random.

Air & Fire. Rupert Thomson. LC 93-8429. 1994. 23.00 (*0-679-42506-3*) Knopf.

Air & Flying. David Evans & Claudette Williams. (Let's Explore Science Ser.). (Illus.). 32p. (J). (gr. k-4). 1993. 9.95 (*1-56458-343-0*) Dorling Kindersley.

Air & Flying. Barbara Taylor. LC 90-46261. (Science Starters Ser.). (Illus.). 32p. (J). (gr. 4-6). 1991. lib. bdg. 13.23 (*0-531-14183-7*) Watts.

***Air & Minuet for Three Recorders (SAT: Composed 1928)** Rudolph Dolmetsch. (Contemporary Consort Ser.: No. 29). 3p. 1994. 1.00 (*1-56571-099-1*) PRB Prods.

Air & Other Gases. Robert Mebane & Thomas Rybolt. (Everyday Material Science Experiments Ser.). (Illus.). 64p. (J). (gr. 5-8). 1995. lib. bdg. 15.98 (*0-8050-2839-0*) TFC Bks NY.

Air & Salt. Eve Shellnut. LC 82-74301. 1983. 16.95 (*0-915604-80-9*); pap. 9.95 (*0-915604-81-7*) Carnegie-Mellon.

Air & Space. (Time Travel Activity Book Ser.). 48p. (J). (gr. 3 up). 1992. 1.95 (*0-88679-915-5*) Educ Insights.

Air & Space. Lynn Cohen. 64p. (J). (ps-2). 1988. 6.95 (*0-912107-80-4*, MM984) Monday Morning Bks.

Air & Space Catalog. Joel Makower. LC 89-40133. 336p. 1990. pap. 16.95 (*0-679-72038-3*, Vin) Random.

Air & Space History: An Annotated Bibliography. Ed. by Lewis Pisano. LC 88-342. 571p. 1988. 88.00 (*0-8240-8543-4*, H00834) Garland.

Air & Space Law: De Lege Ferenda: Essays in Honour of Henri A. Wassenbergh. Ed. by Tanja L. Masson-Zwaan & Pablo M. Mendes de Leon. LC 92-18235. 344p. (C). 1992. lib. bdg. 122.00 (*0-7923-1626-6*) Kluwer Ac.

Air & Space Library. 34.95 (*0-86545-117-6*) Spizzirri.

Air & Space Spacecraft, 10 vols., Set. (Smithsonian Postcard Bks.). 1988. pap. 49.50 (*0-87474-759-7*) Smithsonian.

***Air & Waste Management: A Laboratory-Field Handbook.** Howard E. Hesketh. LC 94-61075. 260p. 1994. pap. text ed. 35.00 (*1-56676-111-5*) Technomic.

Air & Water: The Biology & Physics of Life's Media. Mark W. Denny. LC 92-20969. (Illus.). 360p. (C). 1993. text ed. 39.50 (*0-691-08734-2*); pap. 24.95 (*0-691-02518-5*) Princeton U Pr.

Air & Water Activities. Dorothy Diamond. 72p. (C). 1987. pap. 70.00 (*0-7175-1187-1*, Pub. by S Thornes Pubs UK) St Mut.

Air & Water Analysis: New Techniques & Data. Ed. by R. W. Frei & J. Albaiges. (Current Topics In Environmental & Toxicological Chemistry Ser.: Vol. 9). 319p. 1986. text ed. 119.00 (*2-88124-183-2*) Gordon & Breach.

Air & Water Pollution: Proceedings of the Summer Workshop, August 3 to August 15, 1970, University of Colorado. Ed. by Wesley E. Brittin et al. LC 72-165367. (Illus.). 631p. reprint ed. pap. 179.90 (*0-8357-5514-2*, 2035130) Bks Demand.

Air & Water Pollution Regulation: Accomplishments & Economic Consequences. Martin Freedman & Bikki Jaggi. LC 92-34948. 288p. 1993. text ed. 65.00 (*0-89930-721-3*, FRE, Quorum Bks) Greenwood.

***Air Arizona.** Tom Smith. 180p. 1995. pap. 7.95 (*0-7610-0100-X*) NW Pub.

Air Around Us. Eleonore Schmid. LC 92-9830. (Illus.). 32p. (J). (gr. k-3). 1992. 14.95 (*1-55858-165-0*); lib. bdg. 14.88 (*1-55858-166-9*) North-South Bks NYC.

Air Around Us: An Air Pollution Primer. Jon R. Luoma. (Illus.). 20p. (YA). (gr. 5 up). 1989. 9.95 (*0-935577-10-6*) Acid Rain Found.

Air Assault Operations. 1989. lib. bdg. 79.95 (*0-8490-3983-5*) Gordon Pr.

***Air Assault Operations.** 1995. lib. bdg. 251.99 (*0-8490-6675-1*) Gordon Pr.

***Air Bag Guide.** (Illus.). 600p. (C). 1994. pap. 225.00 (*0-7605-0404-0*) Rector Pr.

Air Battle Central Europe. Alfred Price. 200p. 1987. text ed. 22.95 (*0-02-925451-5*) Free Pr.

Air Brake Technology. M. N. Homewood. (C). 1982. 90.00 (*0-9505410-1-X*, Pub. by S Thornes Pubs UK) St Mut.

Air Brake Technology. 3rd ed. Martin Homewood. (Illus.). 300p. (C). 1991. pap. 48.00x (*0-7487-0564-3*, Pub. by S Thornes Pubs UK) St Mut.

Air Brakes from the Driver's Seat. Allan Wright. 30p. 1988. pap. text ed. 7.95 (*1-884566-05-7*) Inst Police Tech.

Air-Breathing Fishes of India: Their Structure Function & Life History. G. M. Hughes & J. S. Datta Munshi. (Illus.). 358p. (C). 1992. text ed. 95.00 (*90-6191-954-1*, Pub. by A A Balkema NE) Ashgate Pub Co.

Air Campaign: Planning for Combat. John A. Warden, III. (Illus.). 186p. 1989. 14.95 (*0-08-036735-6*) Brasseys Inc.

Air Campaign: Planning for Combat. John A. Warden, III. (Illus.). 193p. (C). 1994. pap. text ed. 34.95 (*0-7881-0809-3*) Diane Pub.

Air Campaign: Planning for Combat. John A. Warden, III. LC 88-19556. (Illus.). 217p. 1988. per., pap. 6.00 (*0-16-001684-3*, S/N 008-020-011) USGPO.

Air Campaign Against the Iraqi Army in the Kuwaiti Theater of Operations. Fred L. Frostic. LC 94-10057. 1994. write for info. (*0-8330-1529-X*, MR-357-AF) Rand Corp.

Air Camping. Don Downie & Julia Downie. (Illus.). 160p. (Orig.). 1985. pap. 12.95 (*0-8306-2380-9*, 2380P) TAB Bks.

Air Cargo & the Opening of China: New Opportunities for Hong Kong. Joseph P. Schwieterman. 114p. (Orig.). 1993. pap. 29.50 (*962-201-612-X*, Pub. by Chinese Univ HK) Coronet Bks.

Air Carrier Voluntary Flight Operational Quality Assurance Program - Prepared under Contract to the Federal Aviation Administration by Flight Safety Foundation Contract No. DTFA01-92-C-00010. Flight Safety Foundation Staff. 195p. reprint ed. pap. 55.60 (*0-7837-7032-4*, 2046847) Bks Demand.

Air Change Rate & Airtightness in Buildings, No. 1067. Ed. by M. H. Sherman. LC 89-18598. (Special Technical Publication (STP) Ser.). (Illus.). 315p. 1990. text ed. 62.00 (*0-8031-1451-6*, 04-010670-10) ASTM.

Air Charlie. Shari Lewis. (Lamb Chop's Play-Along Adventures Ser.). (J). (ps-3). 1994. 2.99 (*0-553-37391-9*) Bantam.

***Air Charters: Audit Technique Guides.** (IRS Tax Audit Information Ser.). 25p. 1994. pap. 6.50 (*1-57402-101-X*) Athena Info Mgt.

Air Combat. Time-Life Books Editors. (New Face of War Ser.). (Illus.). 176p. 1991. write for info. (*0-8094-8604-0*); lib. bdg. write for info. (*0-8094-8605-9*) Time-Life.

Air Commandos: The Quiet Professionals. Randy Jolly. (Illus.). 208p. 1994. 29.95 (*0-9624862-7-2*) Aero Graphics.

***Air Composition & Chemistry.** 2nd ed. Peter Brimblecombe. (Cambridge Environmental Chemistry Ser.: No. 1). (Illus.). 250p. (C). Date not set. write for info. (*0-521-45366-6*); pap. write for info. (*0-521-45972-9*) Cambridge U Pr.

***Air Compressor License.** (Career Examination Ser.: Series 1). Date not set. pap. 23.95 (*0-8373-3761-5*) Nat Learn.

Air-Conditioned Nightmare. Henry Miller. LC 45-11390. 1970. pap. 10.95 (*0-8112-0106-6*, NDP302) New Directions.

Air Conditioners: Home & Commercial. Miller. 1986. 15.95 (*0-02-501930-9*) Macmillan.

Air Conditioning. 2nd ed. Edwin P. Anderson. Ed. by Rex Miller. (Illus.). 1984. write for info. (*0-318-58077-2*) Macmillan.

Air Conditioning. 8th rev. ed. Ed. by Deere & Company Staff. (Fundamentals of Service Ser.). (Illus.). 104p. 1994. pap. text ed. 15.95 (*0-86691-190-1*, FOS5708B); Slide set. sl. 65.95 (*0-685-75058-2*) Deere & Co. This comprehensive text covers servicing of air conditioning systems, primarily for farm & industrial equipment. Most of the information is also applicable to automotive systems. Course teaches "how it works," "why it fails," & "what to do about it." Text begins with basic principles of heat & matter & adds on step-by-step. Tells how each component works. Explains use of various types of servicing equipment. Tells how to visually inspect, diagnose, & test the system. Includes glossary of terms & symbols. CONTENTS: Basic principles, refrigeration cycle, refrigerants, basic refrigeration system, compressors, condensers, expansion valves, evaporators, dehydrators, controls, service equipment, visual inspection, diagnosis, testing, evacuating & charging, troubleshooting charts & glossary. This edition includes EPA concerns & the Refrigerants section will have a vs. R12. *Publisher Provided Annotation.*

Air Conditioning: A Practical Introduction. David V. Chadderton. LC 92-39664. 1993. write for info. (*0-419-15380-2*, E & FN Spon) Routledge Chapman & Hall.

Air Conditioning: Home & Commercial. 2nd ed. Edwin P. Anderson. 1984. 15.95 (*0-672-23397-5*, Audel) Macmillan.

Air Conditioning: Home & Commercial. 4th ed. Edwin P. Anderson. 528p. 1990. text ed. 24.00 (*0-02-584885-2*, Audel) Macmillan.

Air Conditioning - Refrigeration Toolbox Manual. David Tenenbaum. (Illus.). 352p. 1990. pap. 12.00 (*0-13-770264-7*) P-H.

Air Conditioning & Heating. Bill Savage. 124p. (C). 1992. 19.53 (*1-56870-019-9*) RonJon Pub.

Air Conditioning & Heating Labor Guide 1991-93. 144p. 1993. pap. 15.00 (*0-8019-8482-3*) Chilton.

Air Conditioning & Heating Manual, 1991-93. Ed. by Chilton Staff. 2304p. 1993. text ed. 95.00 (*0-8019-8444-0*) Chilton.

***Air Conditioning & Heating Reference Notebook.** Don Swenson. Ed. by Joanna Turpin. LC 94-34531. 190p. (Orig.). 1995. pap. text ed. 11.95 (*0-912524-99-5*) Busn News.

Air Conditioning & Mechanical Trades: Preparing for the Contractor's License Examination. 2nd rev. ed. John Gladstone. (Illus.). 422p. 1990. reprint ed. pap. text ed. 27.95 (*0-930644-13-1*) Engineers Pr.

An Asterisk (*) at the beginning of an entry indicates that the title is appearing in BIP for the first time.

An Asterisk (*) at the beginning of an entry indicates that the title is appearing in BIP for the first time.

157

A

Air Pollutants & Their Effects on the Terrestrial Ecosystem. Ed. by Sagar V. Krupa & Allan H. Legge. LC 85-6461. (Advances in Environmental Science & Technology Ser.). 662p. 1986. text ed. 155.00 (*0-471-08312-7*) Wiley.

Air Pollutants Effects on Forest Ecosystems: Proceedings of a Symposium, May 8-9, 1985. Ed. by Harriett Stubbs. (Illus.). 439p. 1985. 49.00 (*0-935577-01-7*) Acid Rain Found.

Air Pollutants' Effects on Forests, 2 vols., Set. Edward W. Hessler & Acid Rain Foundation Staff. 1990. 14.95 (*0-935577-24-6*) Acid Rain Found.

***Air Pollutants' Effects on Forests, Vol. I: Trees & the Forest Environment.** E. Hessler. 92p. 1990. write for info. (*0-614-06684-0*) Acid Rain Found.

***Air Pollutants' Effects on Forests, Vol. II: Trees & Air Pollution.** E. Hessler. 60p. 1990. write for info. (*0-614-06685-9*) Acid Rain Found.

Air Pollution. D. M. Bowen. 1991p. (C). 1991. text ed. 350.00 (*0-89771-564-0*, Pub. by Intl Bk Distr II) St Mut.

Air Pollution. Kathlyn Gay. LC 91-17780. (Impact Bks.). (Illus.). 144p. (YA). (gr. 9-12). 1991. lib. bdg. 14.98 (*0-531-13002-9*) Watts.

Air Pollution. Ed. by O. Hutzinger. (Handbook of Environmental Chemistry Ser.: Vol. 4, Pt B). (Illus.). 270p. 1989. 141.00 (*0-387-50915-1*, 2774) Spr-Verlag.

Air Pollution. Ed. by O. Hutzinger. (Handbook of Environmental Chemistry Ser.: Vol. 4, Pt. C). (Illus.). xi, 185p. 1991. 109.00 (*0-387-53999-9*) Spr-Verlag.

Air Pollution. Gary Lopez. (Images Ser.). (J). (gr. 5 up). 1992. lib. bdg. 16.95 (*0-88682-427-3*) Creative Ed.

Air Pollution. Gary Lopez. (J). (gr. 4-7). 1993. 15.95 (*1-56846-050-3*) Creative Ed.

Air Pollution. Henry C. Perkins. (Illus.). 448p. (C). 1974. text ed. write for info. (*0-07-049302-2*) McGraw.

Air Pollution. R. S. Scorer. 1968. 68.00 (*0-08-013345-2*, Pub. by Pergamon Repr UK) Franklin.

Air Pollution. Ashok K. Sriasava. 1991. 35.00 (*81-7024-419-6*, Pub. by Ashish II) S Asia.

Air Pollution. Darlene Stille. LC 89-25348. (New True Bks.). (Illus.). 48p. (J). (gr. k-4). 1990. lib. bdg. 12.90 (*0-516-01181-2*); pap. 4.95 (*0-516-41181-0*) Childrens.

Air Pollution. Ed. by P. Zannetti & C. A. Brebbia. LC 92-75803. (Air Pollution Ser.: Vol. 1). 808p. 1993. 360.00 (*1-56252-146-2*) Computational Mech MA.

Air Pollution. Ed. by Paolo Zannetti et al. 808p. 1993. 320.00 (*1-85166-836-5*, Pub. by Elsevier Applied Sci UK) Elsevier.

Air Pollution, Vol. 2. 3rd ed. Arthur C. Stern. (Environmental Science Ser.). 1977. text ed. 176.00 (*0-12-666602-4*) Acad Pr.

Air Pollution, Vol. 5. 3rd ed. Arthur C. Stern. (Environmental Science Ser.). 1977. text ed. 151.00 (*0-12-666605-9*) Acad Pr.

Air Pollution: Actions to Promote Radon Testing. (Illus.). 35p. (Orig.). (C). 1993. pap. text ed. 15.00 (*1-56806-314-8*) Diane Pub.

***Air Pollution: Allowance Trading Offers an Opportunity to Reduce Emissions at Less Cost.** (Illus.). 77p. (Orig.). (C). 1995. pap. text ed. 35.00x (*0-7881-1689-4*) Diane Pub.

Air Pollution: Environmental Issues & Health Effects. Ed. by Shyamal K. Majumdar et al. LC 91-61996. (Illus.). x, 496p. (C). 1991. text ed. 45.00 (*0-945809-05-0*) Penn Science.

Air Pollution: Handbook of Environment Chemistry. (Handbook of Environmental Chemistry Ser.: Vol. 4 Pt. A). (Illus.). 250p. 1986. 141.00 (*0-387-15041-2*) Spr-Verlag.

Air Pollution: Its Effect on the Urban Man & His Adaptive Strategies. Kaiman Lee. LC 74-182905. 52p. 1974. 12.00 (*0-915250-13-6*) Environ Design.

Air Pollution: Its Origin & Control. 2nd ed. Kenneth Wark & Cecil F. Warner. 526p. (C). 1990. text ed. 82.00 (*0-7002-2534-X*) HarpCollege.

Air Pollution: Supplement Part A - Air Pollutants, Their Transformation, Transport & Effects, Vol. VI. 3rd ed. Ed. by Arthur C. Stern. 1986. text ed. 134.00 (*0-12-666606-7*) Acad Pr.

Air Pollution - Health Management: Proceedings of the Joint IIASA-WHO-EURO Workshop, Laxenburg, Austria, 27-30 July, 1982. M. J. Suess. Ed. by W. Klug et al. 176p. 1984. pap. 46.00 (*0-08-031429-5*, Pergamon Pr) Elsevier.

Air Pollution, Acid Rain & the Environment. Ed. by K. Mellanby. 126p. 1989. pap. 72.00 (*1-85166-222-7*) Elsevier.

Air Pollution, Acid Rain, & the Future of Forests. Sandra Postel. LC 84-50653. (Worldwatch Papers). 1984. pap. 5.00 (*0-916468-57-7*) Worldwatch Inst.

Air Pollution & Acid Rain. 1986. lib. bdg. 250.00 (*0-8490-3804-9*) Gordon Pr.

Air Pollution & Cancer in Man: Proceedings of the Second Hanover International Carcinogenesis Meeting Held in Hanover, 22-24 October, 1975. Hanover International Carcinogenesis Meeting Staff. Ed. by U. Mohr et al. LC 77-371605. (IARC Scientific Publications: No. 16). 346p. reprint ed. pap. 98.70 (*0-7837-3996-6*, 2043826) Bks Demand.

Air Pollution & Climate Change: The Biological Impact. 2nd rev. ed. Alan Wellburn. LC 93-31701. 1994. pap. text ed. 39.95 (*0-470-20006-5*) Halsted Pr.

Air Pollution & Community Health: A Critical Review & Data Sourcebook. Frederick W. Lipfert. LC 93-1364. 1994. text ed. 69.95 (*0-442-01444-9*) Van Nos Reinhold.

Air Pollution & Conservation: Safeguarding Our Architectural Heritage. Ed. by J. Rosvall & S. Aleby. 432p. 1989. 143.75 (*0-444-87131-4*) Elsevier.

Air Pollution & Control. P. Mowli & N. V. Subbaya. (C). 1990. text ed. 135.00 (*0-685-63521-X*, Pub. by Scientific Pubs II) St Mut.

Air Pollution & Control. P. Pratapa Mowli & V. Venkata Subbayya. (C). 1988. 260.00 (*81-85312-02-8*, Scientific) St Mut.

Air Pollution & Ecosystems. Ed. by P. Mathy. (C). 1987. lib. bdg. 267.50 (*90-277-2611-6*) Kluwer Ac.

Air Pollution & Forest Decline: Is There a Link? Jon R. Luoma & Kimberly C. Joyner. (USDA Forest Service Agriculture Information Bulletin Ser.: No. 595). (Illus.). 20p. 1990. write for info. (*0-935577-23-8*) Acid Rain Found.

Air Pollution & Forests. W. H. Smith. (Environmental Management Ser.). (Illus.). 379p. 1981. 47.00 (*0-387-90501-4*) Spr-Verlag.

Air Pollution & Forests. 2nd ed. W. H. Smith. (Environmental Management Ser.). (Illus.). 512p. 1989. 129.00 (*0-387-97084-3*, 3109) Spr-Verlag.

Air Pollution & Historic Monuments in Cracow: Report of the U. S. National Park Service Delegation to Poland. US & Polish Delegation Staff. (U. S. - ICOMOS Occasional Paper Ser.: No. 1). (Illus.). 154p. (Orig.). (C). 1991. pap. text ed. 18.00 (*0-911697-07-1*) US ICOMOS.

Air Pollution & Human Health. Lester B. Lave & Eugene Seskin. LC 74-6830. 388p. reprint ed. pap. 110.60 (*0-8357-5282-8*, 2030740) Bks Demand.

Air Pollution & Industry. R. Ross. 1995. text ed. write for info. (*0-442-00125-8*) Van Nos Reinhold.

Air Pollution & Its Influence on Vegetation: Causes-Effects-Prophylaxis & Therapy. Ed. by H. G. Dassler & S. Bortitz. (Tasks for Vegetation Science Ser.). (C). 1987. lib. bdg. 110.50 (*90-6193-619-5*) Kluwer Ac.

Air Pollution & Lung Diseases in Adults. Witorsch. 1994. write for info. (*0-8493-0181-5*) CRC Pr.

Air Pollution & Plant Metabolism: Proceedings of the 2nd International Symposium on Air Pollution & Plant Metabolism, Munich, F.R.G., April 6-9, 1987. Ed. by S. Schulte-Hostede & N. M. Darrall. 382p. 1991. 108.00 (*1-85166-230-8*) Elsevier.

***Air Pollution & Road Transport.** Dhulasi B. Varadarajan & V. Subramanian. 111p. (C). 1993. 100.00x (*81-7024-549-4*, Pub. by Print Hse II) St Mut.

Air Pollution & the Lung: Proceedings of the "Oholo" Biological Conference, 20th Annual. Ed. by E. Ahronson et al. 328p. 1975. text ed. 82.50 (*0-7065-1553-6*, Pub. by Keter Pub IS) Coronet Bks.

Air Pollution & the Market for Monitors & Sensors. 225p. 1992. 2,250.00 (*0-89336-916-0*, E-049R) BCC.

Air Pollution & the Politics of Control. Elliot Goldstein et al. 182p. (C). 1973. text ed. 23.50 (*0-8422-7136-8*) Irvington.

Air Pollution & the Social Sciences: Formulating & Implementing Control Programs. Ed. by Paul B. Downing. LC 75-153390. (Special Studies in U. S. Economic, Social & Political Issues). 1971. 46.50 (*0-89197-652-3*) Irvington.

Air Pollution & Tree Health in the United Kingdom. HMSO Staff. 88p. 1993. pap. 40.00 (*0-11-752636-3*, HM26363, Pub. by HMSO UK) UNIPUB.

Air Pollution by Nitrogen Oxides: Proceedings of the U. S.-Dutch International Symposium, Maastricht, May 24-28, 1982. Ed. by T. Schneider & L. D. Grant. (Studies in Environmental Science: No. 21). 1118p. 1983. 248.75 (*0-444-42127-0*) Elsevier.

Air Pollution by Photochemical Oxidants. I. Colbeck & A. R. MacKenzie. LC 94-16255. (Air Quality Monographs Ser.: Vol. 1). 1994. write for info. (*0-444-88542-0*) Elsevier.

Air Pollution by Photochemical Oxidants. Ed. by R. Guderian. (Ecological Studies, Analysis & Synthesis: Vol. 52). (Illus.). 380p. 1985. 128.00 (*0-387-13966-4*) Spr-Verlag.

Air Pollution Chemistry. J. D. Butler. 1979. text ed. 184.00 (*0-12-147950-1*) Acad Pr.

Air Pollution Control. BNA's Environment & Safety Services Staff. 1980. ring bd. 707.00 (*0-87179-914-6*) BNA.

Air Pollution Control, Pt. 4. Ed. by Werner Strauss & Gordon Bragg. LC 79-28773. (Environmental Science & Technology Ser.). (Illus.). 368p. reprint ed. pap. 104.90 (*0-8357-5283-6*, 2056447) Bks Demand.

Air Pollution Control: A Design Approach. 2nd rev. ed. C. David Cooper & F. C. Alley. (Illus.). 694p. (C). 1994. text ed. 54.95 (*0-88133-758-7*) Waveland Pr.

Air Pollution Control: Internal Combustion Engines - Exhaust Treatment 1976. James R. Critser, Jr. (Ser. 41C-76). 1977. pap. 115.00 (*0-914428-40-3*) Lexington Data.

Air Pollution Control: Traditional & Hazardous Pollutants. Howard E. Hesketh. LC 90-72057. 485p. 1991. 75.00 (*0-87762-763-0*) Technomic.

Air Pollution Control & Design for Industry. Ed. by Paul N. Cheremisinoff. LC 93-18115. 608p. 1993. Alk. paper. 165.00 (*0-8247-9057-X*) Dekker.

Air Pollution Control & Design Handbook, Pt. 1. Ed. by Cheremisinoff & Young. (Pollution Engineering & Technology Ser.: Vol. 2). 624p. 1977. 190.00 (*0-8247-6444-7*) Dekker.

Air Pollution Control & Design Handbook, Pt. 2. Ed. by Paul N. Cheremisinoff & Richard A. Young. LC 76-588. (Pollution Engineering & Technology Ser.: No. 2). (Illus.). 423p. reprint ed. pap. 120.60 (*0-7837-3418-2*, 2052464) Bks Demand.

Air Pollution Control Chemist. Jack Rudman. (Career Examination Ser.: C-1084). 1994. pap. 29.95 (*0-8373-1084-9*) Nat Learn.

Air Pollution Control Engineer. Jack Rudman. LC 94-38034. (Career Examination Ser.: C-76). 1994. pap. 29.95 (*0-8373-0076-2*) Nat Learn.

Air Pollution Control Engineering. Noel De Nevers. LC 94-12074. (Series in Water Resources & Environmental Engineering, Chemical Engineering Ser.). 1995. text ed. write for info. (*0-07-061397-4*) McGraw.

Air Pollution Control Engineering: Basic Calculations for Particulate Collection. 2nd ed. Licht. 496p. 1988. 140.00 (*0-8247-7898-7*) Dekker.

Air Pollution Control Engineering Trainee. Jack Rudman. (Career Examination Ser.: C-1926). 1994. pap. 27.95 (*0-8373-1926-9*) Nat Learn.

Air Pollution Control Equipment. H. Brauer & Y. B. Varma. (Illus.). 388p. 1981. 271.00 (*0-387-10463-1*) Spr-Verlag.

Air Pollution Control Equipment, 2 vols., Vol. I. Louis Theodore & Anthony J. Buonicore. 208p. 1988. 173.00 (*0-8493-5818-3*, TD889) CRC Pr.

Air Pollution Control Equipment, 2 vols., Vol. II. Louis Theodore & Anthony J. Buonicore. 176p. 1988. 173.00 (*0-8493-5819-1*, TD889) CRC Pr.

Air Pollution Control Equipment: (Selection, Design, Operation & Maintenance) Louis Theodore & Anthony J. Buonicore. 429p. 1992. reprint ed. text ed. 70.00 (*1-882767-00-4*) ETS.

***Air Pollution Control Equipment: A Self-Instructional Problem Workbook.** Louis Theodore & Robert Allen. 379p. 1994. pap. text ed. 50.00 (*1-882767-09-8*) ETS.

***Air Pollution Control Equipment: Selection, Design, Operation & Equipment.** Ed. by L. Theodore & A. Buonicore. LC 94-36100. (Environmental Engineering Ser.). 1994. write for info. (*0-387-57998-2*) Spr-Verlag.

Air Pollution Control Equipment Markets. Market Intelligence Staff. 202p. 1993. 2,900.00 (*1-56753-543-7*) Frost & Sullivan.

Air Pollution Control in the European Community: Implementation of the EC Directives in the Twelve Member States. Ed. by Graham Bennett. 224p. (C). 1991. lib. bdg. 85.00 (*1-85333-567-3*, Pub. by Graham & Trotman UK) Kluwer Ac.

Air Pollution Control Manual. Air & Waste Management Association Staff. (Illus.). 1008p. 1992. text ed. 129.95 (*0-442-00843-0*) Van Nos Reinhold.

Air Pollution Control-Processes, Equipment, Instrumentation. James R. Critser, Jr. Incl. Indexes & Abstracts 1967-19711972. 310.00 (*0-914428-08-X*, 4-6771B); write for info. (*0-318-54071-1*) Lexington Data.

Air Pollution Control Technician. Jack Rudman. (Career Examination Ser.: C-1085). 1991. pap. 22.00 (*0-8373-1085-7*) Nat Learn.

Air Pollution Control Techniques, Equipment, & Services in Europe. 115p. 1992. 1,500.00 (*0-89336-967-5*, E-064) BCC.

Air Pollution Control Technology. B. Bretschneider & J. Kurfurst. (Fundamental Aspects of Pollution Control & Environmental Science Ser.: No. 8). 270p. 1987. 92.50 (*0-444-98985-4*) Elsevier.

Air Pollution Control Waste Incineration. L. Theodore. 1990. text ed. 74.95 (*0-442-00398-6*) Van Nos Reinhold.

Air Pollution Damage to Vegetation. Ed. by N. Neegele. (C). 1991. text ed. 375.00 (*0-89771-612-4*, Pub. by Intl Bk Distr II) St Mut.

Air Pollution Effects on Biodiversity. Ed. by Jerry Barker & David T. Tingey. (Illus.). 304p. 1992. text ed. 59.95 (*0-442-00748-5*) Chapman & Hall.

Air Pollution Effects on Crops & Forests: Bibliography 1986-1991. 101p. (Orig.). (C). 1993. pap. text ed. 50.00 (*1-56806-660-0*) Diane Pub.

Air Pollution Effects on Plant Growth. Ed. by Mack Dugger. LC 74-26543. (ACS Symposium Ser.: No. 3). 1974. 21.95 (*0-8412-0223-0*) Am Chemical.

Air Pollution Experiments for Junior & Senior High School Science Classes. 2nd ed. Air Pollution Control Association Staff. Ed. by Donald C. Hunter & Henry C. Wohlers. 128p. (gr. 7-12). 1972. 1.50 (*0-318-12242-1*, APX) Air & Waste.

Air Pollution II, 2 vols., Set. Ed. by C. A. Brebbia et al. LC 94-72461. (Air Pollution Ser.: Vol. 2). 1184p. 1994. text ed. 372.00 (*1-56252-195-0*) Computational Mech MA.

***Air Pollution II Vol. 1: Computer Simulation.** Ed. by J. H. Baldasano et al. LC 94-72961. (Air Pollution Ser.: Vol. 2). 1994. 210.00 (*1-56252-284-1*) Computational Mech MA.

***Air Pollution II Vol. 2: Pollution Control & Monitoring.** Ed. by J. H. Baldasano et al. LC 94-72961. (Air Pollution Ser.: Vol. 2). 1994. 199.00 (*1-56252-285-X*) Computational Mech MA.

Air Pollution III: Proceedings of the Third International Conference. Ed. by C. A. Brebbia et al. (Air Pollution Ser.: Vol. 3). 1100p. 1995. 358.00 (*1-56252-235-3*) Computational Mech MA.

Air Pollution in Mines: Theory, Hazards & Controls. G. D Lidin. 304p. 1966. text ed. 79.50 (*0-7065-0411-9*, Pub. by Keter Pub IS) Coronet Bks.

Air Pollution Inspector. Jack Rudman. (Career Examination Ser.: C-11). 1994. pap. 29.95 (*0-8373-0011-8*) Nat Learn.

Air Pollution Instrumentation. Richard K. Miller & Marcia E. Rupnow. LC 90-83884. (Survey on Technology & Markets Ser.: No. 180). 50p. 1991. pap. text ed. 200.00 (*1-55865-204-3*) Future Tech Surveys.

Air Pollution Laboratory Maintainer. Jack Rudman. (Career Examination Ser.: C-1086). 1994. pap. 29.95 (*0-8373-1086-5*) Nat Learn.

Air Pollution Meteorology. Joe R. Eagleman. LC 90-71552. (Illus.). 255p. (C). 1991. pap. text ed. 37.95 (*1-877696-04-8*) Trimedia Pub.

Air Pollution Modeling. Paolo Zannetti. 437p. 1991. text ed. 72.95 (*0-442-30805-1*) Chapman & Hall.

Air Pollution Modeling. Paolo Zannetti. LC 90-62205. 448p. 1990. 135.00 (*0-945824-84-X*) Computational Mech MA.

Air Pollution Modeling & Its Application, VIII. Ed. by Han Van Dop & D. G. Steyn. (NATO - Challenges of Modern Society Ser.: Vol. 15). (Illus.). 766p. 1991. 175.00 (*0-306-43828-3*, Plenum Pr) Plenum.

Air Pollution Modeling & Its Application, Vol. VI. Ed. by Han Van Dop. LC 88-2333. (NATO - Challenges of Modern Society Ser.: Vol. 11). (Illus.). 714p. 1988. 145.00 (*0-306-42814-8*, Plenum Pr) Plenum.

Air Pollution Modeling & Its Application, Vol. VII. Ed. by Han Van Dop. (NATO - Challenges of Modern Society Ser.: Vol. 13). (Illus.). 636p. 1989. 175.00 (*0-306-43225-0*, Plenum Pr) Plenum.

Air Pollution Modeling & Its Application IX. Ed. by Han Van Dop & George Kallos. LC 92-22699. (NATO - Challenges of Modern Society Ser.: Vol. 17). 1992. 175.00 (*0-306-44248-5*, Plenum Pr) Plenum.

Air Pollution Modeling & Its Application V. Ed. by C. De Wispelaere et al. LC 86-14239. (NATO - Challenges of Modern Society Ser.: Vol. 10). 786p. 1986. 135.00 (*0-306-42293-X*, Plenum Pr) Plenum.

***Air Pollution Modeling & Its Application X.** Ed. by Sven-Erik Gryning & Millan M. Millan. LC 94-47051. (NATO Challenges of Modern Society Ser.: Vol. 18). 700p. 1995. 165.00 (*0-306-44888-2*, Plenum Pr) Plenum.

***Air Pollution of Humans with Bacteria, Fungus & Molds in Homes, Offices & Hospitals: Index of New Information with Authors & Subjects.** rev. ed. George R. Bonadio. 157p. 1995. 49.50 (*0-7883-0404-6*); pap. 39.50 (*0-7883-0405-4*) ABBE Pubs Assn.

Air Pollution, Part 1: Analysis. Joe O. Ledbetter. LC 77-160112. (Environmental Health Engineering Textbooks Ser.: Vol. 2). (Illus.). 440p. reprint ed. pap. 125.40 (*0-8357-5284-4*, 2029001) Bks Demand.

Air Pollution, Part 2: Prevention & Control. Joe O. Ledbetter. LC 77-160112. (Environmental Health Engineering Textbooks Ser.: Vol. 2). 304p. pap. 86.70 (*0-7837-0024-5*, 2029001) Bks Demand.

Air Pollution Permitting Reference & Workbook. J. Laznow. 1992. text ed. write for info. (*0-442-01446-5*) Van Nos Reinhold.

Air Pollution Primer. (Illus.). 105p. 6.50 (*0-685-11546-1*) Am Lung Assn.

Air Pollution, the Automobile, & Public Health. Ed. by Donald Kennedy & Richard R. Bates. 704p. 1988. text ed. 69.95 (*0-309-03726-3*) Natl Acad Pr.

Air Pollution, Vol. 1: Air Pollutants, Their Transformation & Transport. 3rd ed. Arthur C. Stern. (Environmental Science Ser.). 715p. 1976. text ed. 176.00 (*0-12-666601-6*) Acad Pr.

Air Pollution, Vol. 3: Measuring, Monitoring & Surveillance. 3rd ed. Arthur C. Stern. (Environmental Science Ser.). 799p. 1976. text ed. 176.00 (*0-12-666603-2*) Acad Pr.

Air Pollution, Vol. 7: Supplement, Part B: Measurement, Monitoring, Surveillance, & Engineering Control of Air Pollution. 3rd ed. Arthur C. Stern. 1986. text ed. 134.00 (*0-12-666607-5*) Acad Pr.

Air Pollution, Vol. 8: Supplement, Part C: Management of Air Quality. 3rd ed. Ed. by Arthur C. Stern. 1986. text ed. 85.00 (*0-12-666608-3*) Acad Pr.

Air Pollution's Toll on Forests. James J. Mackenzie. 1990. text ed. 45.00 (*0-300-04569-7*) Yale U Pr.

Air Pollution's Toll on Forests & Crops. James J. MacKenzie & Mohamed T. El-Ashry. 384p. (C). 1992. reprint ed. pap. text ed. 22.00 (*0-300-05232-4*) Yale U Pr.

***Air Polutants & the Leaf Cuticle.** Ed. by Kevin E. Percy et al. LC 94-21967. (NATO ASI, Series G, Ecological Sciences: 36). 1994. 168.00 (*0-387-58146-4*) Spr-Verlag.

Air Power: A Concise History. 3rd enl. rev. ed. Robin Higham. (Illus.). 204p. 1988. 18.95 (*0-89745-115-5*) Sunflower U Pr.

Air Power: An Overview of Roles. R. A. Mason. (Air Power: Aircraft, Weapons Systems & Technology Ser.: Vol. 1). (Illus.). 151p. 1987. 40.00 (*0-08-031195-4*, Pub. by Brasseys UK) Brasseys Inc.

Air Power: An Overview of Roles. R. A. Mason. (Air Power: Aircraft, Weapons Systems & Technology Ser.: Vol. 1). (Illus.). 151p. 1987. pap. 15.95 (*0-08-031194-6*, Pub. by Brasseys UK) Brasseys Inc.

Air Power: Global Developments & Australian Perspectives. D. Ball. (Illus.). 659p. 1989. 40.00 (*0-08-034417-8*, Pergamon Pr) Elsevier.

Air Power & Armies. John C. Slessor. LC 76-29428. (Illus.). 240p. reprint ed. 42.00 (*0-404-15342-9*) AMS Pr.

Air Power & Colonial Control: The Royal Air Force 1919-1939. David E. Omissi. LC 90-40817. (Studies in Imperialism). 288p. 1990. text ed. 79.95 (*0-7190-2960-0*, Pub. by Manchester Univ Pr UK) St Martin.

Air Power & Desert Storm. Ed. by Richard B. Clark. (Illus.). 96p. (Orig.). (C). 1993. pap. text ed. 40.00 (*1-56806-446-2*) Diane Pub.

Air Power & the Fight for Khe Sanh. Bernard C. Nalty. (Illus.). 134p. 1986. reprint ed. pap. write for info. (*0-912799-20-X*) Off Air Force.

Air Power & the Ground War in Vietnam: Ideas & Actions. Donald J. Mrozek. LC 87-31931. (Orig.). 1988. pap. 9.00 (*0-16-002237-1*, S/N 008-070-00601-4) USGPO.

Air Power in Modern Warfare. Jasjit Singh. 1988. 34.00 (*81-7062-047-3*, Pub. by Lancer II) S Asia.

Air Power in the Nuclear Age. 2nd ed. M. J. Armitage & R. A. Mason. LC 82-17551. 334p. reprint ed. pap. 95.20 (*0-8357-6354-4*, 2035629) Bks Demand.

Air Power in Three Wars: World War Two, Korea & Vietnam. William W. Momyer. (Illus.). 358p. 1986. reprint ed. pap. write for info. (*0-912799-33-1*) Off Air Force.

Air Power Unleashed: The Air War, 1968-1975. John Morrocco. Ed. by Boston Publishing Company Editors. (Illus.). 192p. 1985. 16.30 (*0-201-11268-X*) Addison-Wesley.

Air Pressures for Pneumatic Controllers, Transmitters, & Transmission Systems. 1984. pap. 20.00 (*0-87664-336-5*, S7.4) Instru Soc.

An Asterisk (*) at the beginning of an entry indicates that the title is appearing in BIP for the first time.

An Asterisk (*) at the beginning of an entry indicates that the title is appearing in BIP for the first time.

159

A

Airborne: The Struggle & Triumph of Michael Jordan. Jesse Kornbluth. LC 94-12553. (J). 1994. text ed. 14.95 (0-02-750922-2) Macmillan.

Airborne Album, Vol. 1. John C. Andrews. Ed. by James M. Philips. LC 81-82475. (Illus.). 52p. 1981. 5.95 (0-932572-07-3) Phillips Pubns.

Airborne Album, 1943-45: From Normandy to Victory Parade. John C. Andrews. Ed. by Jim Phillips. (Illus.). 125p. 1993. 29.95 (0-932572-16-2) Phillips Pubns.

Airborne & Spaceborne Lasers for Terrestrial Geophysical Sensing. Ed. by Allario. 1988. 45.00 (0-89252-924-5, 889) SPIE.

Airborne Contagion: Proceedings of the New York Academy of Sciences, Nov. 7-9, 1979, Vol. 353. New York Academy of Sciences Staff. Ed. by Ruth B. Kundsin. LC 80-27061. (Annals Ser.). 341p. 1980. 69.00 (0-89766-095-1); pap. 69.00 (0-89766-096-X) NY Acad Sci.

Airborne Early Warning. David Baker. (Military Aircraft Library). (Illus.). 48p. (J). (gr. 3-8). 1989. lib. bdg. 18.60 (0-86592-533-X) Rourke Corp.

Airborne Early Warning Systems Concepts. Ed. by Maurice W. Long. (Radar Library). 528p. 1992. text ed. 89.00 (0-89006-491-1) Artech Hse.

***Airborne Geophysics & Precise Positioning: Scientific Issues & Future Directions.** National Research Council Staff. 200p. (Orig.). (C). 1994. pap. text ed. 30.00 (0-309-05183-5) Natl Acad Pr.

Airborne Missions in the Mediterranean, 1942-1945. John C. Warren. (USAF Historical Studies: No. 74). 137p. 1953. pap. text ed. 22.95 (0-89126-023-4) MA-AH Pub.

Airborne Operations: A German Appraisal. Hellmuth Reinhardt. (Center for Military History Publication German Report Series, DA Pam: Nos. 104-13 & 20-232). 64p. 1989. reprint ed. pap. 2.00 (0-16-001976-1, S/N 008-029-00174-8) USGPO.

Airborne Operations in World War Two, European Theater. John C. Warren. (USAF Historical Studies: No. 97). 239p. 1956. pap. text ed. 29.95 (0-89126-015-3) MA-AH Pub.

Airborne Particles in Museums: Research in Conservation, No. 2. W. W. Nazaroff et al. LC 92-35622. (Illus.). 144p. (Orig.). 1993. pap. 25.00 (0-89236-187-5) J P Getty Trust.

Airborne Patient Care Management: A Multidisciplinary Approach. Darlene M. Sredl. LC 84-60070. (Illus.). 331p. (Orig.). pap. text ed. 27.95 (0-930835-00-X) Med Res Assocs.

Airborne Pollutants: Characteristics & Detection. Dale A. Lundgren et al. (Air Pollution Ser.: Vol. 7). 153p. (C). 1974. text ed. 24.00 (0-8422-7158-9) Irvington.

Airborne Pollutants from Coal Fired Power Plants - Water Pollution: Part of an IAWPRC International Conference on Coal Fired Power Plants & the Aquatic Environment, 16-18 August 1982, Copenhagen. Ed. by S. H. Jenkins & P. Schjodtz Hansen. LC 83-19445. (Illus.). 144p. 1984. pap. 44.00 (0-08-031024-9, Pergamon Pr) Elsevier.

Airborne Pulsed Doppler Radar. Guy V. Morris. (Radar Library). 416p. 1988. text ed. 79.00 (0-89006-272-2) Artech Hse.

Airborne Rangers. Alan M. Landau & Frieda W. Landau. LC 92-7488. (Power Ser.). (Illus.). 128p. 1992. pap. 14.95 (0-87938-606-1) Motorbooks Intl.

Airborne Reconnaissance, No. XI. Ed. by LaGesse & Henkel. 1987. 38.00 (0-89252-868-0, 833) SPIE.

Airborne Reconnaissance Fifteen. 1992. 53.00 (0-8194-0666-X, 1538) SPIE.

Airborne Reconnaissance Fourteen, Vol. 1342. P. A. Henkel et al. 1990. 70.00 (0-8194-0403-9) SPIE.

Airborne Reconnaissance XII, Vol. 979. Ed. by P. A. Henkel et al. 1988. 45.00 (0-8194-0014-9) SPIE.

Airborne Reconnaissance XIII. Ed. by Paul A. Henkel et al. 327p. 1990. 62.00 (0-8194-0192-7, VOL. 1156) SPIE.

***Airborne Remote Sensing of Coastal Waters.** S. Boxall et al. (R & D Report Ser.: No. 4). 72p. 1994. pap. 75.00 (0-11-885827-0, HM58270, Pub. by HMSO UK) UNIPUB.

Airborne Weather Radar: A User's Guide. James C. Barr. LC 93-17077. (Illus.). 128p. 1993. pap. 17.95 (0-8138-1363-8) Iowa St U Pr.

Airbrake Maintainer. Jack Rudman. (Career Examination Ser.: C-12). 1994. pap. 23.95 (0-8373-0012-6) Nat Learn.

Airbridge to Berlin: The Berlin Crisis of 1948, Its Origins & Aftermath. D. M. Giangreco & Robert E. Griffin. (Illus.). 304p. 1988. 14.95 (0-89141-329-4) Presidio Pr.

Airbrush: The Complete Studio Handbook. Radu Vero. Ed. by Barbara Wood. (Illus.). 192p. 1983. 27.50 (0-8230-0166-0, Watsn-Guptill) Watsn-Guptill.

***Airbrush Action.** Date not set. pap. 29.99 (1-56496-127-3) Rockport Pubs.

***Airbrush Action, No. 3.** Steiglitz. 1995. pap. text ed. 29.99 (1-56496-162-1) North Light Bks.

***Airbrush Action, No. 4.** (Illus.). 192p. 1995. pap. 39.99 (1-56496-208-3) Rockport Pubs.

Airbrush Action: The Best New Airbrush Illustration. Airbrush Action Magazine Editors. (Illus.). 192p. 1992. 39.99 (1-56496-028-5, 30466) Rockport Pubs.

Airbrush Action 2. 192p. 1993. 39.99 (1-56496-067-6) Rockport Pubs.

Airbrush Action 2: The Best New Airbrush Illustration. Airbrush Action Magazine Editors. 1994. pap. 29.99 (1-56496-130-3) Rockport Pubs.

***Airbrush Action 3 No. 3.** Cliff Steiglitz. 1995. 29.99 (1-56496-137-0) Rockport Pubs.

***Airbrush & Colored Pencil Techniques.** James Deaton. Ed. by Jennifer Carder. LC 93-84873. (Illus.). 48p. (Orig.). (C). Date not set. pap. text ed. 24.95 (1-883602-03-3) Atlantic Digital.

Airbrush Book. S. Tombs-Curtis & C. Hunt. 1980. text ed. 44.95 (0-442-21213-5) Van Nos Reinhold.

Airbrush Maintenance. Peter Owen & John Sutcliffe. (On the Spot Guides Ser.). (Illus.). 96p. 1994. 7.95 (1-56970-500-3, Nippan Pubns) Bks Nippan.

Airbrush Painting. Miguel Ferron. (Artist's Library). (Illus.). 112p. 1989. pap. 14.95 (0-8230-0168-7, Watsn-Guptill) Watsn-Guptill.

Airbrush Painting: Art, Techniques & Projects. Norman Fullner. LC 82-73301. (Illus.). 208p. 1983. 31.95 (0-87192-138-3) Davis Mass.

Airbrush Rendering. Gary Buckley. (How to Draw & Paint Ser.). (Illus.). 32p. (Orig.). 1989. pap. 5.95 (1-56010-025-7, HT212) W Foster Pub.

Airbrush Techniques: Liquids. Mark Riedy. (Graphic Workbook Ser.). 1988. 9.95 (0-89134-241-9, 30056) North Light Bks.

Airbrush Techniques: Textured Surfaces. Mark Riedy. (Graphic Workbook Ser.). 1988. 9.95 (0-89134-239-7, 30054) North Light Bks.

Airbrush Techniques: Transparent-Translucent Objects. Mark Riedy. (Graphic Workbook Ser.). 1988. 9.95 (0-89134-240-0, 30055) North Light Bks.

Airbrushing. Peter West. (Artist's Library). (Illus.). 64p. (Orig.). 1989. pap. 6.95 (0-929261-09-7, AL09) W Foster Pub.

Airbrushing & Spray Painting Manual. Ian Peacock. (Illus.). 175p. 1983. pap. 20.95 (0-85242-802-2, Pub. by Argus Pubs UK) Motorbooks Intl.

Airbrushing Shadows. (Airbrush Artist's Library). (Illus.). 64p. 1989. pap. 12.95 (0-89134-279-6, 30125) North Light Bks.

Airbrushing Techniques for Waterfowl Carving. Michael Veasey & Douglas Congdon-Martin. LC 92-60643. (Illus.). 96p. 1992. pap. 12.95 (0-88740-384-0) Schiffer.

Airburst. Steven L. Thompson. (Orig.). 1988. mass mkt. 3.95 (0-373-97056-0) Harlequin Bks.

Airbus. P. R. Smith. (Airline Markings Ser.: Vol. 4). 1993. 14.95 (1-85310-204-0, Pub. by Airlife Pub Ltd UK) Voyageur Pr.

***Airbus Industrie: The Politics of an International Industrial Collaboration.** David W. Thornton. LC 94-43407. 1995. text ed. write for info. (0-312-12441-4) St Martin.

Aircover: Airborne Radar Vertical Coverage Calculation Software & User's Manual, Set. William A. Skillman. (Artech House Radar Software Library). 120p. 1990. ring bd. 190.00 (0-89006-442-3) Artech Hse.

Aircraft. Bob Munro. LC 93-19868. (Pointers Ser.). (Illus.). 32p. (J). (gr. 4-6). 1993. lib. bdg. 19.97 (0-8114-6161-0) Raintree Steck-V.

Aircraft, 10 vols., Set. (Smithsonian Coloring Bks.). (Illus.). 32p. (J). (ps-6). 1983. pap. 29.50 (0-87474-825-9, AICBP) Smithsonian.

Aircraft: An Educational Coloring Book. Spizzirri Publishing Co. Staff. Ed. by Linda Spizzirri. (Illus.). 32p. (J). (gr. 1-8). 1981. pap. 1.75 (0-86545-033-1) Spizzirri.

Aircraft: Structures for Engineering Students. 2nd ed. T. H. Megson. 1990. pap. text ed. 64.95 (0-470-21653-0) Halsted Pr.

Aircraft: Superfacts. (J). 1992. pap. 4.99 (0-517-07324-2) Random Hse Value.

Aircraft see Rand McNally Fact Books

Aircraft Accident Inquiry in the Netherlands. A. A. Van Wijk. 420p. 1974. pap. 72.00 (90-268-0737-6) Kluwer Law Tax Pubs.

Aircraft Acquisition Finance: Aircraft Acquisition Finance & Airline Credit Analysis. Stephen Holloway. 284p. (C). 1992. 195.00x (0-273-03893-1) Krieger.

Aircraft Air Conditioning Systems: Vapor Cycle. 2nd ed. Ed. by IAP Inc. LC 92-24620. (Aviation Technician Training Ser.). (Illus.). 25p. 1985. pap. 6.95 (0-89100-051-8, EA-AAC-1) IAP.

Aircraft Basic Science. Michael J. Kroes & James R. Rardon. LC 92-35355. (Aviation Technology Ser.). 1993. 35.50 (0-02-801814-1) Glencoe.

Aircraft Basic Science. 5th ed. Ralph D. Bent & James L. McKinley. 1980. text ed. 39.95 (0-07-004791-X) McGraw.

Aircraft Basic Science. 6th ed. Michael Kroes et al. 1988. text ed. write for info. (0-07-035710-2) McGraw.

Aircraft Basic Science. 6th ed. Michael J. Kroes et al. 400p. 1988. text ed. 36.95 (0-07-004799-5) McGraw.

Aircraft Batteries: Lead Acid & Nickel Cadmium. International Aviation Publishers Staff. Ed. by IAP, Inc. LC 92-24619. (Aviation Technician Training Ser.). 25p. 1985. pap. 5.95 (0-89100-052-6, EA-AB-1) IAP.

Aircraft Bonded Structure. International Aviation Publishers Staff. LC 92-24392. (Aviation Technician Training Ser.). (Illus.). 48p. 1977. pap. 6.95 (0-89100-065-8, EA-NMR) IAP.

Aircraft Cabin: Managing the Human Factor. Mary Edwards & Elwyn Edwards. (Illus.). 200p. 1990. text ed. 59.95 (0-566-09056-2, Pub. by Avebury Pub UK); pap. text ed. 27.95 (0-566-09091-0, Pub. by Avebury Pub UK) Ashgate Pub Co.

Aircraft Cabin Cleaning & Refurbishing Operations. (Four Hundred Ser.). 1994. pap. 20.25 (0-685-58232-9, 410-89) Natl Fire Prot.

Aircraft Carrier. large type ed. John Winton. 528p. 1987. 16.95 (0-7089-1649-X) Ulverscroft.

Aircraft Carrier Intrepid. John Roberts. LC 82-81105. (Anatomy of the Ship Ser.). (Illus.). 96p. 1982. 36.95 (0-87021-901-4) Naval Inst Pr.

Aircraft Carrier Victorious. Ross Watton. (Anatomy of the Ship Ser.). (Illus.). 128p. 1991. 36.95 (1-55750-026-6) Naval Inst Pr.

***Aircraft Carriers.** Norman. 1991. pap. 4.95 (0-516-95136-X) Childrens.

Aircraft Carriers. C. J. Norman. LC 85-51452. (Picture Library). (Illus.). 32p. (J). (gr. 3-6). 1989. pap. 4.95 (0-531-15136-0) Watts.

Aircraft Carriers. Anthony Preston. LC 84-9669. (Modern Military Techniques Ser.). (Illus.). 48p. (J). (gr. 5 up). 1985. pap. 4.95 (0-8225-9504-4, Lerner Publctns) Lerner Group.

Aircraft Carriers. Anthony Preston. LC 84-9669. (Modern Military Techniques Ser.). (Illus.). 48p. (YA). (gr. 5 up). 1985. lib. bdg. 14.95 (0-8225-1377-3, Lerner Publctns) Lerner Group.

Aircraft Carriers. Christopher Tunney. LC 79-64384. (Lerner Question & Answer Bks.). (Illus.). 36p. (J). (gr. 3-6). 1980. lib. bdg. 13.50 (0-8225-1176-2, Lerner Publctns) Lerner Group.

Aircraft Carriers & the Role of Naval Power in the Twenty-First Century. Jacquelyn K. Davis. LC 93-27011. (National Security Papers: No. 13). 1993. 15.00 (0-89549-099-4) Inst Foreign Policy Anal.

Aircraft Carriers of the World: 1914 to the Present. Roger Chesneau. (Illus.). 256p. 1984. 42.95 (0-87021-902-2) Naval Inst Pr.

Aircraft Certification: Limited Progress on Developing International Design Standards. 80p. (Orig.). (C). 1993. pap. text ed. 40.00 (1-56806-674-0) Diane Pub.

Aircraft Control & Simulation. Brian L. Stevens & Frank L. Lewis. 544p. 1992. text ed. 84.95 (0-471-61397-5) Wiley.

Aircraft Conversions for Airfix Magazine. Alan W. Hall. 32p. 1983. 25.00 (0-905418-71-9, Pub. by Gresham Bks UK) St Mut.

Aircraft Corrosion Control. Ed. by IAP, Inc. LC 92-24628. (IAP Training Ser.). (Illus.). 48p. 1979. pap. text ed. 8.45 (0-89100-111-5, EA-CC-1) IAP.

Aircraft Crashworthiness. Ed. by Kenneth Saczalski et al. LC 75-26665. 713p. reprint ed. pap. 180.00 (0-8357-5286-0, 2055727) Bks Demand.

Aircraft Design. E. Heinemann et al. LC 83-26885. (Illus.). 130p. 1985. 34.95 (0-933852-15-0) Nautical & Aviation.

Aircraft Design: A Conceptual Approach. 2nd ed. Daniel P. Raymer. (Educ Ser.). 739p. 1992. 66.95 (0-930403-51-7) AIAA.

Aircraft Detail Design Manual. 3rd ed. Stanley J. Dzik. Ed. by Michael S. Rice. (Illus.). 100p. 1977. pap. 18.50 (0-87994-011-5) Aviat Pub.

Aircraft Dope & Fabric. Ruth Spencer. 1970. pap. 4.95 (0-8306-2203-9, 2203) TAB Bks.

Aircraft Dynamic Stability & Response. A. W. Babister. (Illus.). 230p. 1980. 99.00 (0-08-024769-5, Pub. by Pergamon Repr UK) Franklin.

Aircraft Dynamics & Automatic Control. Duane McRuer et al. LC 73-134350. 624p. (Orig.). 1990. 135.00x (0-691-08083-6); pap. text ed. 42.50 (0-691-02440-5) Princeton U Pr.

Aircraft Electrical Systems: Single & Twin Engine. J. E. Bygate. Ed. & Illus. by IAP Staff. LC 92-24372. 128p. 1990. reprint ed. pap. text ed. 12.95 (0-89100-357-6, EA-357) IAP.

Aircraft Electricity & Electronics. 3rd rev. ed. Ralph D. Bent & James L. McKinley. (Aviation Technology Ser.). (Illus.). 432p. (C). 1981. text ed. 39.95 (0-07-004793-6) McGraw.

Aircraft Electricity & Electronics. 4th ed. Thomas K. Eismin et al. 368p. 1988. pap. text ed. 39.95 (0-07-004800-2); pap. text ed. write for info. (0-07-004803-7) McGraw.

Aircraft Electricity & Electronics. 5th ed. Thomas K. Eismin. LC 93-43328. (Aviation Technology Ser.). 1994. write for info. (0-02-801859-1) Glencoe.

Aircraft Encyclopedia. (Illus.). 192p. (J). (gr. 3 up). 1985. pap. 7.95 (0-671-55337-2, S&S Bks Young Read) S&S Childrens.

Aircraft Engine Design. J. Mattingly et al. (Educ Ser.). 600p. 1987. Book. 61.95 (0-930403-23-1); Disks. disk 27.00 (0-930403-31-2) AIAA.

Aircraft Engine Design, Set. J. Mattingly et al. (Educ Ser.). 600p. 1987. 86.95 (0-685-73870-1) AIAA.

Aircraft Engine Operating Guide. Belvoir Publications Staff & Kas Thomas. (Illus.). 224p. 1988. pap. 15.95 (0-8306-2431-7, 2431P) TAB Bks.

Aircraft Engines & Gas Turbines. 2nd ed. Jack L. Kerrebrock. (Illus.). 748p. 1992. 52.00x (0-262-11162-4) MIT Pr.

Aircraft Fabric Covering. Neal Carlson. Ed. by IAP, Inc. LC 93-20622. (Aviation Maintenance Training Course Ser.). (Illus.). 54p. (C). 1978. pap. 7.95 (0-89100-077-1, EA-ADF) IAP.

Aircraft Financing. (C). 1990. 325.00 (1-870031-12-1, Pub. by Euromoney UK) St Mut.

Aircraft Fire & Explosion Investigators. National Fire Protection Association Staff. 1991. 16.75 (0-317-63438-0, 422M-91) Natl Fire Prot.

Aircraft Flight Control Actuation System Design. E. T. Raymond & C. C. Chenoweth. 325p. 1993. 85.00 (1-56091-376-2, R-123) Soc Auto Engineers.

***Aircraft for the Many: A Detailed Story of the RAF's in Aircraft in 1944.** Michael J. Bowyer. (Illus.). 256p. 1995. 44.95 (1-85260-427-1, Pub. by J H Haynes & Co UK) Motorbooks Intl.

Aircraft Fuel Metering Systems. Ed. by IAP, Inc. LC 92-24622. (Aviation Maintenance Training Course Ser.). (Illus.). 70p. (C). 1985. pap. 7.95 (0-89100-057-7, EA-FMS) IAP.

Aircraft Fuel Servicing. (Four Hundred Ser.). 28p. 1990. pap. 20.25 (0-685-44139-3, 407) Natl Fire Prot.

Aircraft Fueling Ramp Drainage. National Fire Protection Association Staff. 1992. 16.75 (0-317-63430-5, 415-92) Natl Fire Prot.

Aircraft Gas Turbine Engine Monitoring Systems: An Update. 1988. 19.00 (0-89883-999-8, SP728) Soc Auto Engineers.

Aircraft Gas Turbine Engine Technology. 2nd ed. Irwin Treager. (Illus.). 1978. text ed. 46.95 (0-07-065158-2) McGraw.

Aircraft Gas Turbine Engine Technology. 2nd ed. Irwin E. Treager. 1979. text ed. write for info. (0-07-065199-X) McGraw.

Aircraft Gas Turbine Engines of the World & Dictionary of the Gas Turbine. Charles E. Otis & Peter A. Vosbury. LC 91-28478. (Illus.). 455p. 1991. pap. text ed. 22.95 (0-89100-390-8, EA-390) IAP.

Aircraft Gas Turbine Powerplants. 2nd ed. Charles E. Otis. LC 91-14478. (Aviation Maintenance Training Course Ser.). (Illus.). 468p. 1989. reprint ed. pap. 17.95 (0-89100-255-3, EA-TEP-2) IAP.

Aircraft Gas Turbine Powerplants Workbook. Charles E. Otis. Ed. by IAP Staff. (Illus.). 188p. (Orig.). (C). 1989. pap. 9.95 (0-89100-342-8, EA-TEP-2W) IAP.

Aircraft Governors. Frank Delp. LC 92-24618. (Aviation Technician Training Ser.). 50p. (Orig.). 1982. pap. text ed. 6.95 (0-89100-156-5, EA-AGV) IAP.

Aircraft Hand Fire Extinguishers. (Four Hundred Ser.). 1994. pap. 16.75 (0-685-58062-8, 408) Natl Fire Prot.

Aircraft Hangars. National Fire Protection Association Staff. 31p. 1990. 20.25 (0-317-63425-9, 409-90) Natl Fire Prot.

Aircraft Hardware Standards Manual & Engineering Reference. (Illus.). 138p. 1974. pap. 14.95 (0-87994-012-3) Aviat Pub.

Aircraft Hijacking & the Developing Law. S. K. Ghosh. 160p. 1985. 22.95 (0-317-66150-7) Asia Bk Corp.

Aircraft Hydraulic Systems. Ed. by IAP, Inc. LC 92-24617. (Aviation Technician Training Ser.). (Illus.). 93p. 1985. pap. text ed. 9.45 (0-89100-058-5, EA-AH-1) IAP.

Aircraft Hydraulic Systems. 3rd ed. William A. Neese. 526p. (C). 1991. 48.95 (0-89464-562-5) Krieger.

Aircraft Hydraulic Systems: An Introduction to the Analysis of Systems & Components. W. L. Green. LC 85-12385. 137p. 1986. text ed. 64.95 (0-471-90848-7) Wiley.

Aircraft Ignition & Electrical Power Systems. Ed. by IAP, Inc. LC 92-24787. (Aviation Technician Training Ser.). (Illus.). 133p. 1977. pap. 8.95 (0-89100-063-1, EA-IGS) IAP.

***Aircraft in Warfare: The Dawn of the Fourth Arm.** F. W. Lanchester. LC 95-77628. (Illus.). 224p. (C). 1995. 24.95 (1-57321-002-1) Lanchester Pr.

Aircraft Industry Dynamics. Barry Bluestone et al. LC 81-2118. 208p. 1981. text ed. 55.00 (0-86569-053-7, Auburn Hse) Greenwood.

Aircraft Inspection & Maintenance Records. John Enga. LC 92-24396. (Aviation Technician Training Ser.). 94p. (Orig.). 1979. pap. text ed. 7.95 (0-89100-094-1, EA-IAR) IAP.

Aircraft Inspection, Repair & Alterations AC 43.13-1A-2A-3: Acceptable Methods, Techniques & Practices. 2nd ed. Department of Transportation, Federal Aviation Administration Staff. (Illus.). 439p. (Orig.). 1992. reprint ed. pap. 14.95 (1-56027-098-5, ASA-AC43.13) Av Suppl & Acad.

Aircraft Inspection, Repair & Alterations Handbook (Including Change Three for Part 43.13, 1A) rev. ed. FAA Staff & IAP, Inc. Staff. 486p. (C). 1988. pap. 14.95 (0-89100-306-1, EA-AC43.13-1A/3) IAP.

Aircraft Inspection Repair & Alterations Study Guide. 1988. student ed. pap. 12.95 (0-940732-63-7, ASA-AC43.13-SG) Av Suppl & Acad.

Aircraft Instrument Systems. Ed. by IAP, Inc. LC 92-24616. (Aviation Technician Training Ser.). (Illus.). 81p. 1985. pap. 9.45 (0-89100-062-3, EA-AIS) IAP.

Aircraft Instruments & Avionics for A & P Technicians. Max F. Henderson. (Illus.). 204p. 1993. pap. text ed. 18.95 (0-89100-422-X, EA-422) IAP.

Aircraft Landing Gear Design: Principles & Practices. Norman S. Currey. (Educ Ser.). (Illus.). 373p. 1988. 67.95 (0-930403-41-X) AIAA.

Aircraft Landing Gear Systems (PT-37) 1991. 29.00 (1-56091-074-7) Soc Auto Engineers.

Aircraft Lift-the-Flap Book. Illus. by Gerard Browne. 18p. (J). (gr. 2-5). 1992. 13.00 (0-525-67351-2, Lodestar Bks) Dutton Child Bks.

Aircraft Loading Walkways. (Four Hundred Ser.). 1990. pap. 16.75 (0-685-58236-1, 417) Natl Fire Prot.

Aircraft Log. Ed. by ASA Staff. (Logbook Ser.). (Orig.). 1991. 9.95 (1-56027-049-7, ASA-SA-2); pap. 5.95 (1-56027-048-9, ASA-SA-1) Av Suppl & Acad.

Aircraft Logbook. IAP, Inc. Staff. 32p. 1988. pap. 4.95 (0-89100-330-4, EA-ALB) IAP.

Aircraft Maintenance & Repair. 4th ed. Ralph D. Bent & James L. McKinley. (Aviation Technology Ser.). 1979. text ed. 39.95 (0-07-004794-4) McGraw.

Aircraft Maintenance & Repair. 5th ed. Ralph D. Bent & James L. McKinley. 1987. text ed. write for info. (0-07-004812-6) McGraw.

Aircraft Maintenance & Repair. 5th ed. Frank Delp et al. 576p. 1987. text ed. 33.95 (0-07-004798-7) McGraw.

Aircraft Maintenance & Repair. 6th rev. ed. Michael J. Kroes et al. LC 92-18146. (Aviation Technology Ser.). 1992. pap. write for info. (0-02-803459-7) Glencoe.

Aircraft Maintenance Regulations. Stephen Luddington. 120p. 1991. 49.95 (0-7506-0043-8) Buttrwrth-Heinemann.

Aircraft Noise. Mike Smith. (Cambridge Aerospace Ser.). (Illus.). 240p. 1989. 99.95 (0-521-33186-2) Cambridge U Pr.

***Aircraft of the Luftwaffe Fighter Aces, Vol. I.** (Illus.). 256p. 1995. 39.95 (0-88740-751-X) Schiffer.

***Aircraft of the Luftwaffe Fighter Aces, Vol. II.** Bernd Barbas. (Illus.). 256p. 1995. 39.95 (0-88740-752-8) Schiffer.

Aircraft of the Luftwaffe, 1939-1945. World Airpower Journal Staff. 1992. 29.95 (1-880588-10-2) AIRtime Pub.

An Asterisk (*) at the beginning of an entry indicates that the title is appearing in BIP for the first time.

Aircraft of the National Air & Space Museum. 4th rev. ed. LC 91-27296. (Illus.). 180p. 1992. pap. 9.95 (*1-56098-153-9*) Smithsonian.

Aircraft of the Royal Air Force since 1918. Owen Thetford. 684p. 1990. 44.95 (*0-933852-69-X*) Nautical & Aviation.

Aircraft of the Royal Navy since Nineteen Forty-Five. Maritime Books Staff. (C). 1986. 59.00 (*0-907771-06-8*, Pub. by Maritime Bks UK) St Mut.

Aircraft of the Spanish Civil War, 1936-1939. Gerald Howson. LC 90-61731. (Illus.). 256p. (C). 1991. 60.00 (*1-56098-015-X*) Smithsonian.

Aircraft of the World. William Green & Gerald Pollinger. Ed. by James B. Gilbert. LC 79-7262. (Flight: Its First Seventy-Five Years Ser.). (Illus.). 1980. reprint ed. lib. bdg. 37.95 (*0-405-12172-5*) Ayer.

***Aircraft of World War II.** (Jane's Gem Ser.). (Illus.). 256p. (Orig.). 1995. pap. 8.00 (*0-00-470849-0*) HarpC.

Aircraft Painting & Finishing. 2nd ed. IAP Staff & Neal Carlson. LC 93-24822. (Aviation Maintenance Training Course Ser.). (Illus.). 67p. (C). 1985. pap. 7.95 (*0-89100-152-2*, EA-AP-2) IAP.

Aircraft-Pavement Interaction. Ed. by Paul T. Foxworthy. LC 91-26813. 423p. 1991. pap. text ed. 41.00 (*0-87262-819-1*) Am Soc Civil Eng.

Aircraft Performance. Donald Layton. 224p. 1988. 39.95 (*0-916460-40-1*) Weber Systems.

Aircraft Performance. W. Austyn Mair & David L. Birdsall. (Aerospace Ser.: No. 5). (Illus.). 304p. (C). 1992. 89.95 (*0-521-36264-4*) Cambridge U Pr.

Aircraft Performance: The Forces Without. Ed. by Richard Taylor. (Command Decisions Ser.). 171p. 1991. 21.95 (*1-879620-07-3*) Belvoir Pubns.

Aircraft Performance Engineering. Wagenmakers. 200p. 1991. text ed. 26.00 (*0-13-019217-1*) P-H.

Aircraft Powerplant Handbook: Cam-107. Ed. by S. H. Schmid. (Illus.). 350p. reprint ed. pap. 9.95 (*0-940000-88-1*, 21-13470) EAA Aviation.

Aircraft Powerplants. 4th ed. Ralph D. Bent & James L. McKinley. Orig. Title: Powerplants for Aerospace Vehicles. (Illus.). 1978. text ed. 39.95 (*0-07-004792-8*) McGraw.

Aircraft Powerplants. 5th ed. Ralph D. Bent & James L. McKinley. Orig. Title: Powerplants for Aerospace Vehicles. 608p. 1985. text ed. 34.95 (*0-07-004797-9*); text ed. write for info. (*0-07-004811-8*) McGraw.

Aircraft Powerplants. 6th ed. Michael J. Kroes et al. (Aviation Technology Ser.). 640p. 1989. pap. text ed. write for info. (*0-07-035569-X*) McGraw.

Aircraft Powerplants. 7th rev. ed. Michael J. Kroes & Thomas W. Wild. LC 93-34445. (Aviation Technology Ser.). 1994. write for info. (*0-02-801874-5*) Glencoe.

Aircraft Production Technology. Douglas F. Horne. (Illus.). 350p. 1986. 115.00 (*0-521-26553-3*) Cambridge U Pr.

Aircraft Propeller-Rotor Logbook. IAP, Inc. Staff. 32p. 1988. pap. 4.95 (*0-89100-333-9*, EA-PLB) IAP.

Aircraft Propellers & Controls. Frank Delp. LC 92-24615. (Aviation Technician Training Ser.). (Illus.). 156p. 1979. pap. text ed. 9.95 (*0-89100-097-6*, EA-APC) IAP.

Aircraft Propulsion Systems Technology & Design. G. C. Oates. (Educ Ser.). 1989. 57.95 (*0-930403-24-X*) AIAA.

Aircraft Radio Logbook. IAP, Inc. Staff. 32p. 1988. pap. 4.95 (*0-89100-332-0*, EA-RLB) IAP.

Aircraft Radio Systems. James Powell. LC 92-46754. (Illus.). 255p. 1990. reprint ed. pap. text ed. 24.95 (*0-89100-356-8*, EA-356) IAP.

Aircraft Reciprocating Engines. Ed. by IAP Staff. LC 92-24625. (Illus.). 113p. 1985. pap. 8.95 (*0-89100-075-5*, EA-ARE) IAP.

***Aircraft Recognition Training for Ground Observers.** 1995. lib. bdg. 255.99 (*0-8490-6636-0*) Gordon Pr.

Aircraft Rescue & Fire Fighting. 3rd ed. IFSTA Committee Staff. Ed. by Lynne C. Murnane & Carl E. Goodson. LC 91-77965. (Illus.). 247p. 1992. pap. text ed. 22.00 (*0-87939-099-9*) IFSTA.

Aircraft Rescue & Fire Fighting Operational Procedures. National Fire Protection Association Staff. 110p. 1991. 26.50 (*0-317-63421-6*, 402M-91) Natl Fire Prot.

Aircraft Rescue & Fire Fighting Services at Airports & Heliports. (Four Hundred Ser.). 24p. 1993. pap. 20.25 (*0-685-44138-5*, 403) Natl Fire Prot.

Aircraft Rescue & Fire Fighting Vehicles. (Four Hundred Ser.). 69p. 1990. pap. 22.25 (*0-685-46037-1*, 414) Natl Fire Prot.

***Aircraft Service Worker.** (Career Examination Ser.: Series 1). Date not set. pap. 27.95 (*0-8373-3691-0*) Nat Learn.

Aircraft Sheet Metal. Nick Bonacci. LC 92-24394. (Illus.). 134p. (C). 1987. pap. 10.45 (*0-89100-296-0*, EA-SM) IAP.

Aircraft Structures. 2nd ed. David J. Peery & J. J. Azar. 1982. text ed. write for info. (*0-07-049196-8*) McGraw.

Aircraft Systems: Really Knowing Your Airplane. Ed. by Richard Taylor. (Command Decisions Ser.). 221p. 1991. 21.95 (*1-879620-04-9*) Belvoir Pubns.

Aircraft Systems: Understanding Your Airplane. David A. Lombardo. 1988. pap. text ed. 19.95 (*0-07-155265-0*) McGraw.

Aircraft Systems: Understanding Your Airplane. David A. Lombardo. (Practical Flying Ser.). (Illus.). 304p. pap. 19.95 (*0-8306-0823-0*, 2423) TAB Bks.

Aircraft Systems: Understanding Your Airplane. David A. Lombardo. (Practical Flying Ser.). (Illus.). 208p. 1988. 27.95 (*0-8306-9426-9*, 2423H); pap. 16.95 (*0-8306-2426-0*, 2423P) TAB Bks.

Aircraft Systems & Components. D. F. Garrett. LC 92-180220. (Illus.). 320p. 1993. pap. text ed. 24.95 (*0-89100-393-2*, EA-393) IAP.

Aircraft Systems for Pilots. Dale De Remer. LC 91-58613. (Illus.). 450p. 1992. pap. text ed. 24.95 (*0-89100-384-3*, EA-384) IAP.

Aircraft Technical Dictionary. 3rd ed. IAP Staff & James Foye. LC 92-234959. (Illus.). 502p. 1992. pap. text ed. 12.95 (*0-89100-410-6*, EA-ATD-3) IAP.

Aircraft Tires & Tubes. 2nd ed. Ed. by IAP, Inc. LC 92-24626. (Aviation Technician Training Ser.). (Illus.). 46p. 1985. pap. text ed. 6.95 (*0-89100-178-6*, EA-ATT-2) IAP.

***Aircraft Turbine Engine Technology.** 3rd ed. Irwin E. Treager. LC 95-10190. (Aviation Technology Ser.). 1995. write for info. (*0-02-801828-1*); teacher ed write for info. (*0-02-801831-1*) McGraw.

Aircraft Types & Price Guidelines 1994-1995. Comp. by Lloyd's Aviation Dept. Staff. 1994. 80.00 (*1-85044-463-3*) Lloyds London Pr.

Aircraft vs. Aircraft. Norman Franks. 1990. 19.95 (*0-685-33407-4*); pap. 12.99 (*0-517-69497-2*) Random Hse Value.

Aircraft Weaponry of Today. Roy Braybrook. (Illus.). 14.98 (*0-85429-634-4*, F634, Pub. by G T Foulis Ltd) Haynes Pubns.

Aircraft Weight & Balance. Joseph Schafer. LC 92-24629. (Aviation Technician Training Ser.). (Illus.). 104p. 1979. pap. text ed. 7.95 (*0-89100-096-8*, EA-BAL) IAP.

Aircraft Welding. rev. ed. Ed. by Paul Poberezny & S. H. Schmid. (How to Aircraft Building Ser.). (Illus.). 116p. 1991. pap. 11.95 (*0-940000-49-0*) EAA Aviation.

Aircraft Wheels, Brakes & Antiskid Systems. Ed. by IAP, Inc. LC 92-24627. (Aviation Technician Training Ser.). (Illus.). 61p. 1979. pap. text ed. 7.95 (*0-89100-099-2*, EA-AWB) IAP.

Aircraft World Wars I & II. Jeff Daniels. (Concise Color Guides Ser.). (Illus.). 240p. 1988. pap. 4.50 (*0-681-40431-0*) Longmeadow Pr.

***Aircraft Wrecks in the Mountains & Deserts of California, 1908-1990.** Gary P. Macha. (Illus.). 150p. 1991. 17.95 (*0-9630073-0-0*) Aviat Arch Pr.

***Aircrafts & Air Transportation in Commerce & Medicine: Index of New Information for Research & Progress.** Jack Klingenhagen. 175p. 1995. 37.50 (*0-7883-0646-4*); pap. 34.50 (*0-7883-0647-2*) ABBE Pubs Assn.

Aircrew Survival. Ed. by R. E. Penoff. (AF Pam Ser.: No. 64-5). (Illus.). 121p. 1985. spiral bd. 6.50 (*0-16-002209-6*, S/N 008-070-00565-4) USGPO.

Aircrew Unlimited: The Commonwealth Air Training Plan During WWII. John Golley. (Illus.). 192p. 1993. 32.95 (*1-85260-243-0*, Pub. by J H Haynes & Co UK) Motorbooks Intl.

Airdrie Weavers. (C). 1989. 45.00 (*0-903915-23-5*, Pub. by Jordanhill College UK) St Mut.

Aire. J. M. Parramon et al. (Four Elements Ser.). 32p. (SPA.). (J). (ps). 1985. pap. 5.95 (*0-8120-3620-4*) Barron.

Aire y Otras Mentiras. Wilfredo Alvelo. 42p. (Orig.). (SPA.). 1989. pap. 6.00 (*0-9623552-0-8*) Ed Arcas.

AIREA Financial Tables. Ed. by James J. Mason. 473p. 1981. 27.50 (*0-911780-54-8*) Appraisal Inst.

Airedale Terrier Champions: 1952-1986. Camino E. E. & B. Co. Staff. (Illus.). 187p. 1987. pap. 36.95 (*0-940808-45-5*) Camino E E & Bk.

Airedale Terriers. 1990. 11.95 (*0-86622-511-0*, KW-165) TFH Pubns.

Airedale Terriers. Evelyn Miller. (Illus.). 160p. 1989. 11.95 (*0-86622-674-5*, KW165) TFH Pubns.

Airedale Terriers: An Owner's Companion. Mary Swash & Donald Millar. (Illus.). 176p. 1991. 39.95 (*1-85223-315-X*, Pub. by Crowood Pr UK) Trafalgar.

Aireon Coronet 400, Type 1209A Service Manual of 1948. rev. ed. Ed. by Frank Adams. (Illus.). 110p. reprint ed. 32.50 (*1-56642-002-4*, R-3) AMR Pub Co.

Aireon of 1946-48: Service Manual - Covers Aireon Super Deluxe & Fiesta Deluxe. rev. ed. Ed. by Frank Adams. (Illus.). 114p. reprint ed. 29.50 (*1-56642-075-X*, R-419) AMR Pub Co.

Airfare Secrets Exposed: The How-to Resource Guide to the Absolute Lowest Fares on the Market. Sharon Tyler & Matthew Wunder. LC 93-61753. 192p. (Orig.). 1994. pap. 16.95 (*1-881999-26-2*) Univ Info Corp.

Airfields Safety Code, Vol. 7. Institute of Petroleum Staff. 1971. 25.25 (*0-444-39969-0*, Pub. by Elsevier Applied Sci UK) Elsevier.

Airfix Magazine, 1978-1979. 672p. 1983. 45.00 (*0-905418-73-5*, Pub. by Gresham Bks UK) St Mut.

Airflow. Martin Simons. 122p. (C). 1985. 110.00 (*0-86787-045-1*, Pub. by S Thornes Pubs UK) St Mut.

Airfoil Design & Data. R. Eppler. (Illus.). viii, 562p. 1992. 85.00 (*0-387-52505-X*) Spr-Verlag.

Airfoil Selection: Understanding & Choosing Airfoils for Light Aircraft. Barnaby Wainfan. (Illus.). 57p. 1988. pap. 15.50 (*0-916413-18-7*) Aviation.

Airframe & Power Plant Mechanics: Airframe Handbook. rev. ed. (Advisory Circular Ser.: No. 65-15A). (Illus.). 613p. 1976. pap. 20.00 (*0-16-005149-5*, S/N 050-007-00391-9) USGPO.

Airframe & Powerplant Mech Powerplant Study Guide: Powerplant Study Guide. Dale Crane. Ed. by ASA Staff. (Mechanic Ser.). 125p. (Orig.). (C). 1988. pap. 12.95 (*0-940732-60-2*, ASA-AC65-12A-SG) Av Suppl & Acad.

Airframe & Powerplant Mechanics: Airframe Study Guide. Dale Crane. 1988. pap. 12.95 (*0-940732-58-0*, ASA-AC65-15A-SG) Av Suppl & Acad.

Airframe & Powerplant Mechanics: Powerplant Workbook. Dale Crane. 1988. pap. 9.95 (*0-940732-71-8*, ASA-AC65-12A-WK) Av Suppl & Acad.

Airframe & Powerplant Mechanics Airframe Handbook (Including Index) AC 65-15A. Federal Aviation Administration Staff. 615p. 1979. pap. 20.00 (*0-89100-080-1*) IAP.

Airframe & Powerplant Mechanics Airframe Workbook: Airframe Workbook. Dale Crane. 1988. pap. 9.95 (*0-940732-72-6*, ASA-AC65-15A-WK) Av Suppl & Acad.

Airframe & Powerplant Mechanics Certification Guide. Flight Standards Service, Federal Aviation Administration Staff. (Illus.). 64p. (Orig.). 1992. reprint ed. pap. 6.00 (*1-56027-097-7*, ASA-AC-65-2D) Av Suppl & Acad.

Airframe & Powerplant Mechanics General Handbook (Including Index) AC 65-9A. Federal Aviation Administration Staff. 561p. 1979. pap. 22.00 (*0-89100-078-X*) IAP.

Airframe & Powerplant Mechanics General Study Guide: General Study Guide. Dale Crane. (Illus.). 1988. pap. text ed. 12.95 (*0-940732-59-9*, ASA-AC65-9A-SG) Av Suppl & Acad.

Airframe & Powerplant Mechanics Powerplant Handbook (Including Index) AC 65-12A. Federal Aviation Administration Staff. 519p. 1979. pap. 18.00 (*0-89100-079-8*) IAP.

Airframe Mechanics FAA Exam Book, 1992-94. Federal Aviation Administration Staff & International Aviation Publishers, Inc. Staff. (Illus.). 230p. 1992. pap. text ed. 10.95 (*0-89100-419-X*, EA-FAA-T-8080-12DX) IAP.

Airframe or Powerplant Mechanics. Jack Rudman. (Occupational Competency Examination Ser.: OCE-2). 1994. pap. 23.95 (*0-8373-5702-0*, OCE-2) Nat Learn.

Airframe Test Guide: Aviation Mechanic. Dale Crane. (Fast Track Ser.). (Illus.). 192p. (Orig.). 1994. pap. 11.95 (*1-56027-197-3*, ASA-AMA-12E) Av Suppl & Acad.

Airfreighters. Osprey. 1990. 12.99 (*0-517-01220-0*) Random Hse Value.

Airguide Manual. 2nd ed. Ed. by Newton W. Miller & Monty Navarre. 1207p. 1987. pap. write for info. (*0-934754-01-2*) Airguide Pubns.

***Airienteering with "13MIKE" A Microsoft Flight Simulator Action Book, Bk. 3, Level A.** Fred J. Calfior & Douglas W. Miller. LC 94-72676. 280p. 1995. 19.95 (*0-9639052-3-6*) CalMil Pubng.

Airing Dirty Laundry. Ishmael Reed. LC 93-13874. 1993. 19.23 (*0-201-62462-1*) Addison-Wesley.

***Airing Dirty Laundry.** Ishmael Reed. 304p. 1995. pap. 11.54 (*0-201-40832-5*) Addison-Wesley.

***Airland Combat: An Organization for Joint Warfare.** 1995. lib. bdg. 251.95 (*0-8490-7560-2*) Gordon Pr.

Airless: What's the Secret? Robert C. Walker. Ed. by Don F. Haslam & Michael L. Steinman. (Illus.). 157p. (Orig.). 1988. write for info. (*0-318-64841-5*) Haslam & Walker.

Airlift. David Baker. (Military Aircraft Library). (Illus.). 48p. (J). (gr. 3-8). 1989. lib. bdg. 18.60 (*0-86592-531-3*) Rourke Corp.

Airlift & Other Stories. Jan E. Seale. LC 91-42107. 176p. 1992. 21.95 (*0-87565-100-3*) Tex Christian.

Airlift Bioreactors. M. Y. Chisti. 350p. 1989. 74.00 (*1-85166-320-7*) Elsevier.

Airline: A Strategic Management Simulation. 3rd ed. Jerald R. Smith & Peggy A. Golden. LC 94-20589. 1994. pap. text ed. write for info. (*0-13-105875-4*) P-H.

Airline Artistry: Vintage Posters & Publicity. Don Thomas. (Illus.). 64p. 1992. pap. 18.00 (*0-9618642-4-9*) D Thomas.

Airline Automation Systems. Pat Wharton. 100p. (Orig.). 1986. pap. 14.00 (*0-911563-04-0*) Brdgwtr Pub Co.

Airline Bibliography: The Salem College Guide to Sources on Commercial Aviation, the United States. Myron J. Smith, Jr. LC 86-7149. (Illus.). xxxii, 464p. 1988. lib. bdg. 75.00 (*0-933951-12-4*) Locust Hill Pr.

Airline Career Opportunities. Barry E. Monteiro. 52p. 1994. pap. 12.95 (*0-9639973-0-0*) Airline Career.

Airline Competition: A Study of the Effects of Competition on the Quality & Price of Airline Service & the Self-Sufficiency of the United States Domestic Airlines. F. W. Gill & G. L. Bates. 1949. 294.00 (*0-08-018738-2*, Pub. by Pergamon Repr UK) Franklin.

Airline Competition: Impact of Changing Foreign Investment & Control Limits on U. S. Airlines. (Illus.). 75p. (Orig.). (C). 1993. pap. text ed. 35.00 (*1-56806-313-X*) Diane Pub.

Airline Deregulation. Kenneth Button. 224p. 1991. 55.00 (*0-8147-1157-X*) NYU Pr.

Airline Deregulation: The Early Experience. John R. Meyer, Jr. et al. LC 81-3620. 287p. 1981. text ed. 49.95 (*0-86569-078-2*, Auburn Hse) Greenwood.

Airline Deregulation & Laissez Faire Mythology. Paul S. Dempsey & Andrew R. Goetz. LC 91-35688. 264p. 1992. text ed. 59.95 (*0-89930-693-4*, DAK/, Quorum Bks) Greenwood.

Airline Handbook. 9th ed. Ed. by Paul K. Martin. (Illus.). 608p. (Orig.). 1985. pap. 16.00 (*0-914553-85-2*) AeroTravel Res.

Airline Handbook. 10th ed. Ed. by Paul K. Martin. (Illus.). 700p. (Orig.). 1987. pap. 17.50 (*0-914553-86-0*) AeroTravel Res.

Airline Handbook: 7th Annual. Ed. by Paul K. Martin. (Illus.). 476p. (Orig.). 1982. pap. 14.00 (*0-686-32833-7*) AeroTravel Res.

Airline Handbook: 8th Annual. Ed. by Paul K. Martin. (Illus.). 500p. (Orig.). 1983. pap. 15.00 (*0-914553-83-6*) AeroTravel Res.

Airline Industry. Ed. by William M. Leary. (Encyclopedia of American Business History & Biography Ser.). (Illus.). 352p. 1992. lib. bdg. 85.00 (*0-8160-2675-0*) Facts on File.

***Airline Industry & the Impact of Deregulation.** rev. ed. George Williams. 1994. 59.95 (*0-291-39824-3*, Pub. by Avebury Pub UK) Ashgate Pub Co.

***Airline Industry Jobs.** 5th rev. ed. Richard M. Zink. (Illus.). 64p. (YA). (gr. 9 up). 1994. pap. 9.95 (*0-939469-43-X*) Zinks Career Guide.

Airline Labor Law: The Railway Labor Act & Aviation after Deregulation. William E. Thoms & Frank J. Dooley. LC 90-8450. 216p. 1990. text ed. 55.00 (*0-89930-470-2*, TLL, Quorum Bks) Greenwood.

***Airline Labor Relations in the Global Era: The New Frontier.** Ed. by Peter Cappelli. 304p. 1995. 45.00 (*0-87546-343-6*) ILR Pr.

***Airline Labor Relations in the Global Era: The New Frontier.** Ed. by Peter Cappelli. 304p. 1995. pap. 19.95 (*0-87546-344-4*) ILR Pr.

Airline Management. Charles Banfe. 240p. 1991. text ed. 59.00 (*0-13-019183-3*, 320701) P-H.

***Airline Marketing & Management.** Stephen Shaw. 352p. (C). 1990. 90.00x (*0-273-03208-9*, Pub. by Pitman Pubng UK) St Mut.

Airline Marketing & Management. 3rd ed. Stephen Shaw. 270p. (C). 1993. reprint ed. 29.50 (*0-89464-854-3*) Krieger.

***Airline Markets International to the Year 2000 Handbook.** (Illus.). 550p. (Orig.). 1994. pap. 8,900.00 (*0-7605-0949-2*) Rector Pr.

Airline Medical Manual. Ed. by Peter Chapman. (Illus.). 125p. 1991. pap. 18.95 (*0-442-31313-6*) Chapman & Hall.

***Airline Odyssey: The World's Airline Turbulent Flight into the Future.** James D. Ott & Raymond E. Neidl. 1995. text ed. 22.95 (*0-07-048030-3*) McGraw.

Airline Operations Research. D. Teodorovic. 457p. 1988. text ed. 131.00 (*2-88124-672-9*) Gordon & Breach.

Airline Passenger's Guerrilla Handbook: Strategies & Tactics for Beating the Air Travel System. George A. Brown. (Illus.). 416p. (Orig.). 1989. pap. 14.95 (*0-924022-04-3*) Blakes Pub Group.

Airline Pilot. Future Aviation Professionals of America Staff. (Illus.). 256p. 1990. pap. 16.00 (*0-13-115015-4*) P-H.

Airline Pilot Employment Interview. Clark St. John. 70p. 1988. pap. 10.95 (*0-942397-03-7*) Buckeye Aviat Bk.

Airline Pilot Employment Interview. Clark St. John. 100p. 1991. pap. 12.95 (*0-942397-25-8*) Buckeye Aviat Bk.

Airline Pilot Employment Testing Kit. Clark St. John. 155p. 1989. pap. 22.95 (*0-942397-10-X*) Buckeye Aviat Bk.

Airline Pilot Interviews: How You Can Succeed in Getting Hired. I. Jasinski. LC 87-70680. (Illus.). 152p. (C). 1987. pap. 14.95 (*0-942195-01-9*) Career Adv Pub.

Airline Re-Regulation. Laurence E. Gesell. LC 90-82939. (Illus.). 286p. 1990. text ed. 28.00 (*0-9606874-6-7*) Coast Aire.

Airline Regulation in America: Effects & Imperfections. William A. Jordan. LC 79-4194. 352p. 1979. reprint ed. text ed. 69.50 (*0-313-20997-9*, JOAR, Greenwood Pr) Greenwood.

Airline Safety: A View from the Cockpit. William Heller. 120p. 1984. 11.95 (*0-917613-00-7*) Rulorca.

Airline Safety: A View from the Cockpit. William Heller. 148p. 1986. 11.95 (*0-685-60190-0*) Rulorca.

Airline Safety: An Annotated Bibliography. Comp. by John J. Miletich. LC 90-13988. (Bibliographies & Indexes in Psychology Ser.: No. 7). 240p. 1990. text ed. 59.95 (*0-313-27391-X*, MRS/, Greenwood Pr) Greenwood.

Airline Testing Study Kit. FAPA Staff. 60p. 1988. audio, pap. 32.95 (*0-685-44542-9*) FAPA Inc.

***Airline Training Pilot.** Tony Smallwood & Michael Fraser. 200p. 1995. boxed 51.95 (*0-291-39816-2*) Ashgate Pub Co.

Airline Transport Pilot, Aircraft Dispatcher, & Flight Navigator Question Book. (Illus.). 158p. 1989. per., pap. 16.00 (*0-16-005272-6*, S/N 050-007-008) USGPO.

Airline Transport Pilot Airplane-FAR Pt. 121: Aircraft Dispatcher, Flight Navigator with Answers (FAA T-8070-5A) Department of Transportation Staff. (Illus.). 264p. (Orig.). 1986. reprint ed. pap. text ed. 13.95 (*0-941272-27-3*) Astro Pubs.

Airline Transport Pilot & Type Rating: Practical Test Standards (Airplane-Helicopter) FAA Reprint Staff. 50p. (C). 1989. reprint ed. pap. 4.95 (*0-89100-336-3*, EA-FAA-S-8081-5) IAP.

Airline Transport Pilot FAA Written Exam. 2nd ed. Irvin N. Gleim. LC 93-79478. 690p. (Orig.). 1994. pap. text ed. 23.95 (*0-917539-42-7*) Gleim Pubns.

Airliner Cabin Environment: Air Quality & Safety. National Research Council Staff. 318p. 1986. pap. text ed. 29.95 (*0-309-03690-9*) Natl Acad Pr.

Airliners in Colour. Mach III Plus Staff. (C). 1993. pap. 59.00 (*0-9515462-4-4*, Mach III Plus) St Mut.

Airlines of the United States since 1914. R. E. Davies. LC 82-600203. (Illus.). 746p. 1983. reprint ed. text ed. 60.00 (*0-87474-356-7*, DAAU) Smithsonian.

Airlines of the World. Leyson K. Phillips. 1979. lib. bdg. 250.00 (*0-8490-1359-3*) Gordon Pr.

Airlines Worldwide. B. I. Hengi. (Illus.). 306p. 1994. pap. 27.95 (*1-85780-021-4*) Voyageur Pr.

Airmail Antics. Fred Boughner. (Illus.). 186p. 1988. 20.00 (*0-940403-19-6*); pap. 9.95 (*0-940403-08-0*) Linns Stamp News.

Airmail Special Delivery Stamps of the United States. 2nd ed. Ralph L. Sloat. (Illus.). 86p. 1990. pap. text ed. 12.00 (*0-930412-01-X*) Bureau Issues.

Airmail to the Moon. Tom Birdseye. LC 87-21199. (Illus.). 32p. (J). (ps-3). 1988. lib. bdg. 14.95 (*0-8234-0683-0*); pap. 5.95 (*0-8234-0754-3*) Holiday.

Airman at the Helm. Eric Blackman. 116p. 1987. 40.00 (*0-85937-167-0*, Pub. by K Mason Pubns Ltd UK) St Mut.

Airman Far Away: The Story of an Australian Dambuster. Eric Fry. (Illus.). 248p. 1993. 29.95 (*0-86417-501-9*, Pub. by Kangaroo Pr AT) Seven Hills Bk.

Airman Mortensen. Michael Blake. 1991. 20.00 (*0-9627387-7-8*) Seven Wolves.

A

An Asterisk (*) at the beginning of an entry indicates that the title is appearing in BIP for the first time. 161

A

Airman's Guide. 3rd ed. Wayne A. Valey. (Illus.). 296p. 1994. pap. 16.95 (*0-8117-2402-6*) Stackpole.

Airman's Information Manual (Aim 1988) TAB-Aero Staff. 288p. 1987. pap. 6.70 (*0-8306-8368-2*, 21368, TAB-Aero) TAB Bks.

Airman's Odyssey. Antoine de Saint-Exupery. Tr. by Stuart Gilbert & Lewis Galantiere. LC 84-10479. 444p. 1984. pap. 12.00 (*0-15-603733-5*, Harvest Bks) HarBrace.

***Airmanship Technique & Safety: The Best of Dan Manningham.** Manningham. 1995. pap. text ed. 18.95 (*0-07-009426-8*) TAB Bks.

Airmobile Operations. 1989. lib. bdg. 79.95 (*0-8490-3984-3*) Gordon Pr.

Airola Diet & Cookbook. Paavo Airola & Anni M. Lines. (Illus.). 288p. 1981. 12.95 (*0-932090-11-7*) Health Plus.

Airola Diet & Cookbook. Paavo O. Airola & Anni M. Lines. (Health Plus Book Ser.). 1984. 12.95 (*0-685-53936-9*) Contemp Bks.

Airplane Activities: A Coloring Book with Games & Projects That Kids Can Do Again & Again. Jennifer W. McIntosh. Ed. by Kathleen Gavin & Marshall Gavin. (Kids on the Go Ser.). (Illus.). 56p. (Orig.). (J). (ps-8). 1994. pap. 3.95 (*1-885437-00-5*) B dazzle.

Airplane Book. Cheryl W. Bellville. (Photo Bks.). (Illus.). 48p. (J). (ps-5). 1991. lib. bdg. 19.95 (*0-87614-686-8*, Carolrhoda) Lerner Group.

Airplane Book. Cheryl W. Bellville. (J). (ps-5). 1993. pap. 5.95 (*0-87614-618-3*, Carolrhoda) Lerner Group.

Airplane Book. Edith Kunhardt. (Golden Super Shape Bks.). (Illus.). 24p. (J). (ps-00). 1987. pap. write for info. (*0-307-10083-9*, Golden Bks) Western Pub.

Airplane Design: A Series of Articles Printed First in Kitplanes Magazine. Donald Crawford. LC 86-72617. (Illus.). 1986. pap. 25.00 (*0-9603934-1-2*) Crawford Aviation.

Airplane Five Views, Vol. 1. Bernhard Klein. (Illus.). 40p. (Orig.). 1987. pap. 3.50 (*0-9618861-0-2*) BCFK Pubns.

***Airplane Ownership.** Ron Wanttaja. LC 94-3509. 1994. pap. 17.95 (*0-07-068157-0*) McGraw.

***Airplane Ownership.** Ronald J. Wanttaja. 1994. pap. 17.95 (*0-07-068158-9*) McGraw.

***Airplane Performance.** Grady Jones & Jean Jack. 128p. (C). 1995. pap. text ed. 19.95 (*0-7872-0751-9*) Kendall-Hunt.

Airplane Performance, Stability & Control. Courtland D. Perkins & Robert E. Hage. 493p. 1949. Net. text ed. write for info. (*0-471-68046-X*) Wiley.

Airplane Ride. (Kitten Tales Ser.). (Illus.). 28p. (J). (ps-2). 1992. 3.95 (*0-7214-5311-2*, S915-4 SER.) Ladybird Bks.

Airplane Ride over Newport. Richard Grosvenor. (Birds Pack Ser.). 8p. (J). (gr. k-2). 1993. pap. write for info. (*1-882563-02-6*) Lamont Bks.

Airplane Stained Glass Coloring Book. John Green. (Illus.). (J). (gr. k-3). 1993. pap. 1.00 (*0-486-27528-0*) Dover.

Airplane Talk: Complete Book of VFR & IFR Communications. 2nd ed. Glenn E. Carlson. (Illus.). 276p. (C). 1993. pap. 16.95 (*0-9611954-0-1*) Aviation.

***Airplane Talk: Complete Book of VFR & IFR Communications.** 2nd ed. Glenn E. Carlson. (Illus.). 276p. (C). 1993. pap. 17.95 (*0-614-03028-5*) Watosh Pub.

Airplanes. Byron Barton. LC 85-47899. (Illus.). 32p. (J). (ps-00). 1986. 6.95 (*0-694-00060-4*, Crowell Jr Bks); lib. bdg. 13.89 (*0-690-04532-8*, Crowell Jr Bks) HarpC Child Bks.

Airplanes. J. Cooper. (Traveling Machines Ser.). (J). 1991. 8.95 (*0-86592-493-7*) Rourke Enter.

***Airplanes.** Gini Holland. (Inventors & Inventions Ser.). 64p. (J). (gr. 3-5). 1995. lib. bdg. write for info. (*0-7614-0068-0*, Benchmark NY) Marshall Cavendish.

Airplanes. Patricia Lantier-Sampon. LC 91-50344. (Wings Ser.). (Illus.). 24p. (J). (ps-2). 1993. lib. bdg. 15.93 (*0-8368-0539-9*) Gareth Stevens Inc.

Airplanes. David Peterson. LC 81-7671. (New True Bks.). (Illus.). 48p. (J). (gr. k-4). 1981. lib. bdg. 12.90 (*0-516-01606-7*) Childrens.

Airplanes. Joy Richardson. LC 93-42184. (Picture Science Ser.). (Illus.). (J). 1994. lib. bdg. 12.25 (*0-531-14324-4*) Watts.

Airplanes: The Lure of Flight. Tom Stacey. LC 90-6471. (Encyclopedia of Discovery & Invention Ser.). (Illus.). 96p. (J). (gr. 5-8). 1990. lib. bdg. 17.95 (*1-56006-203-7*) Lucent Bks.

Airplanes & Balloons. rev. ed. Howard W. Kanetzke. LC 87-23230. (Read about Science Ser.). (Illus.). 48p. (J). (gr. 2-6). 1987. lib. bdg. 10.95 (*0-8172-3251-6*) Raintree Steck-V.

Airplanes & Flying Machines. Illus. by Donald Grant. (First Discovery Bks.). (J). (ps). 1992. bds. 11.95 (*0-590-45267-3*, 037, Cartwheel) Scholastic Inc.

Airplanes & Income Tax. 3rd rev. ed. Daniel J. O'Connor. Ed. by Michael J. Ebersole. 85p. 1984. spiral bd. 14.95 (*0-685-46436-9*) GCBA.

Airplanes & Income Tax. 4th ed. Daniel J. O'Connor. Ed. by Michael J. Ebersole. 85p. 1985. spiral bd. 14.95 (*0-9613218-1-4*) GCBA.

Airplanes & Income Tax. 5th ed. Daniel J. O'Connor. Ed. by Michael J. Ebersole. 85p. 1986. spiral bd. 12.95 (*0-9613218-3-0*) GCBA.

Airplanes & Income Tax. 6th ed. Daniel J. O'Conner. 75p. 1994. pap. 12.95 (*0-9613218-5-7*) Aviation.

Airplanes & Other Things That Fly. Steven Kelley. (Deluxe Golden Bks.). (Illus.). 48p. (J). (ps-2). 1990. write for info. (*0-307-17867-6*, Golden Bks) Western Pub.

Airplanes & Things That Fly. Gina Ingoglia. (Golden Little Look-Look Book Ser.). (Illus.). 24p. (J). (ps-00). 1989. pap. write for info. (*0-307-11807-X*, Golden Bks) Western Pub.

Airplayers. Sara G. Armstrong. (Illus.). 80p. (Orig.). 1990. vinyl bd. 30.00 (*0-930279-17-4*) Willis Locker & Owens.

Airport. (Fiction Ser.). (Orig.). (YA). 1993. pap. text ed. 6.50 (*0-582-08479-2*, 79815) Longman.

***Airport.** (Mighty Machines Ser.: No. 3). 32p. (J). 1995. 6.95 (*0-7894-0211-4*, 5-70624) Dorling Kindersley.

Airport. Byron Barton. LC 79-7816. (Illus.). 32p. (J). (ps-00). 1982. 15.00 (*0-690-04168-3*, Crowell Jr Bks); lib. bdg. 14.89 (*0-690-04169-1*, Crowell Jr Bks) HarpC Child Bks.

Airport. Byron Barton. LC 79-7816. (Trophy Picture Bk.). (Illus.). 32p. (J). (ps-1). 1987. pap. 4.95 (*0-06-443145-2*, Trophy) HarpC Child Bks.

Airport. Arthur Hailey. LC 68-11755. 1986. mass mkt. 5.95 (*0-440-10066-6*) Dell.

***Airport.** Arthur Hailey. LC 68-11755. 1994. reprint ed. lib. bdg. 27.95x (*1-56849-562-5*) Buccaneer Bks.

Airport: Terminal Nights & Runway Days at John F. Kennedy International Airport. James Kaplan. LC 93-48715. 1994. 23.00 (*0-688-09247-0*) Morrow.

Airport - Community Emergency Planning. National Fire Protection Association Staff. 68p. 1991. 22.25 (*0-317-63441-0*, 424M-91) Natl Fire Prot.

Airport, Aircraft & Airline Security. 2nd ed. Kenneth C. Moore. 424p. 1991. 49.95 (*0-7506-9019-4*) Buttrwrth-Heinemann.

Airport & Terminal-Area Operations of the Future. (Transportation Research Circular Ser.: No. 325). 111p. 1987. 6.00 (*0-685-38558-2*) Transport Res Bd.

Airport Attendant. Jack Rudman. (Career Examination Ser.: C-306). 1994. pap. 23.95 (*0-8373-0306-0*) Nat Learn.

Airport Book: The Passenger's Guide to Major Airports in the United States & Canada. Albert Diaz. (Illus.). 1979. pap. 3.95 (*0-935866-00-0*) Airport Bk Pr.

Airport Business. Rigas Doganis. LC 91-44797. 256p. 1992. 74.50 (*0-415-07877-6*, A7485); pap. 25.00 (*0-415-08117-3*, A7489) Routledge.

Airport Cafe. Ed. by Elsa Cameron. (Illus.). 80p. 1986. write for info. (*0-9617165-0-9*) Cmnty Arts.

Airport Cities Twenty-One: The New Global Transport Centers of the Twenty-First Century. McKinley Conway. (Illus.). 113p. 1992. write for info. (*0-910436-32-0*) Conway Data.

Airport City: Development Concepts for the Twenty-First Century. rev. ed. McKinley Conway. LC 80-65254. (Illus.). 288p. 1980. 11.95 (*0-910436-14-2*) Conway Data.

Airport Drainage. 1994. lib. bdg. 259.95 (*0-8490-9060-1*) Gordon Pr.

Airport Drainage: Guidance for Engineers, Airport Managers, & the Public in the Design & Maintenance of Airport Drainage Systems. 1993. lib. bdg. 265.75 (*0-8490-8924-7*) Gordon Pr.

Airport Engineering. 3rd ed. Norman J. Ashford & Paul H. Wright. 500p. 1992. text ed. 94.95 (*0-471-52755-6*) Wiley.

Airport Finance. Norman J. Ashford & Clifton A. Moore. (Illus.). 240p. 1992. text ed. 64.95 (*0-442-00192-4*) Chapman & Hall.

Airport Fire Fighter Professional Qualifications. National Fire Protection Association Staff. 1994. 16.75 (*0-317-63522-0*, 1003-94) Natl Fire Prot.

Airport for Tacoma. Patrick M. Steele. Ed. by Val Dumond. (Illus.). 280p. (Orig.). 1992. pap. 19.95 (*0-9613673-5-0*) V Dumond.

Airport Growth: Creating New Economic Opportunities. Sarah Eilers. Ed. by Jenny Murphy. 44p. (Orig.). 1989. pap. 21.50 (*0-317-04807-4*) Natl Coun Econ Dev.

Airport Growth & Safety: Executive Summary of the Schiphol Project. Richard Hillestad et al. LC 93-37700. 1993. write for info. (*0-8330-1463-3*, MR-297-EAC) Rand Corp.

Airport Guide. 4th ed. Randall L. Voight. 1986. pap. 7.95 (*0-930318-01-3*) Intl Res Eval.

Airport Hotel Directory. Ed. by Stuart J. Faber. (Illus.). 176p. (Orig.). 1987. pap. text ed. 12.00 (*0-89074-102-6*) Charing Cross.

Airport Humor. Jonathon Maas. 120p. 1992. pap. 6.95 (*0-9632230-0-3*) Travelers Pub.

Airport Landside Capacity. (Special Report Ser.: No. 159). 294p. 1975. 12.00 (*0-309-02462-5*) Transport Res Bd.

Airport Landside Planning & Operations. LC 92-43573. (Transportation Research Record Ser.: No. 1373). 1993. 17.00 (*0-309-05415-X*) Transport Res Bd.

Airport Maintenance Supervisor. Jack Rudman. (Career Examination Ser.: C-3381). 1994. pap. 27.95 (*0-8373-3381-4*) Nat Learn.

Airport Master Plans. (Advisory Circular Ser.: No. 50-5070-6A). (Illus.). 86p. 1985. pap. 4.75 (*0-16-005216-5*, S/N 050-007-00703-5) USGPO.

Airport Nineteen Hundred Four. Eddie Cope & Buster Cearley. (Illus.). 40p. 1981. pap. 3.50 (*0-88680-002-1*); 10.00 (*0-88680-003-X*) I E Clark.

Airport Operations. Norman Ashford et al. 480p. (C). 1991. 150.00x (*0-273-03445-6*, Pub. by Pitman Pub Ltd UK) Trans-Atl Phila.

Airport Passenger Terminal. Walter Hart. LC 91-11700. 264p. (C). 1992. reprint ed. lib. bdg. 64.50 (*0-89464-612-5*) Krieger.

Airport Pavement Innovations - Theory to Practice: Proceedings of the Conference, Vicksburg, Mississippi, September 8-10, 1993. Ed. by Jim W. Hall, Jr. LC 93-11968. 432p. 1993. 40.00 (*0-87262-925-2*) Am Soc Civil Eng.

Airport Pavement Maintenance Field Manual. M. Hahin. 1990. pap. write for info. (*0-442-23820-7*) Van Nos Reinhold.

Airport Planning: Nineteen Sixty-Five to Nineteen Seventy-Five, No. 1140. Sarojini Balachandran. 1976. 5.00 (*0-686-20412-3*) CPL Biblios.

Airport Planning & Management. Ed. by Alexander T. Wells. (Illus.). 432p. (C). 1986. 32.95 (*0-8306-2189-X*, TAB NO. 2389) TAB Bks.

Airport Planning & Management. 2nd ed. Alexander T. Wells. 512p. 1992. 39.95 (*0-8306-3086-4*, 3977) TAB Bks.

Airport Planning & Management. 2nd ed. Alexander T. Wells. 1992. 39.95 (*0-07-069260-2*) McGraw.

Airport Planning, Operation, & Management (TRR 1423) Ed. by Anna Rigamer. (Transportation Research Record Ser.). (Illus.). 68p. 1994. pap. text ed. 22.00 (*0-309-05570-9*) Natl Res Coun.

Airport Pocket Guide: United States Edition. Andy Migliorini. (Illus.). 186p. (C). 1992. pap. 14.95 (*0-943265-17-7*) AM Data Services.

Airport Regulation, Law, & Public Policy: The Management & Growth of Infrastructure. Robert M. Hardaway. LC 90-22126. 264p. 1991. text ed. 59.95 (*0-89930-474-5*, HAQ, Quorum Bks) Greenwood.

Airport Security Guard. Jack Rudman. (Career Examination Ser.: C-456). 1994. pap. 23.95 (*0-8373-0456-3*) Nat Learn.

Airport Security Supervisor. Jack Rudman. (Career Examination Ser.: C-2153). 1994. 27.95 (*0-8373-2153-0*) Nat Learn.

Airport Site: A Multicomponent Site in the Sangamon River Drainage. Donna C. Roper. (Research Series: Papers in Anthropology: No. 4). (Illus.). 32p. 1978. pap. 2.00 (*0-89792-074-0*) Ill St Museum.

Airport Supervisor. Jack Rudman. (Career Examination Ser.: C-3219). 1994. pap. 27.95 (*0-8373-3219-2*) Nat Learn.

Airport System Capacity: Strategic Choices. (Special Report Ser.: No. 226). 134p. 1990. 17.00 (*0-309-04956-3*) Transport Res Bd.

Airport Terminal & Landside Design & Operation 1990. (Transportation Research Record Ser.: No. 1273). 54p. 1990. 12.00 (*0-309-05020-0*) Transport Res Bd.

Airport Terminal Buildings. (Four Hundred Ser.). 1993. pap. 16.75 (*0-685-58235-3*, 416) Natl Fire Prot.

Airport Terminal Facilities: ASCE-AOCI Specialty Conference, Houston, Texas. American Society of Civil Engineers Staff. 335p. reprint ed. pap. 95.50 (*0-8357-5287-9*, 2004909) Bks Demand.

Airport Terminals. Christopher Blow. (Illus.). 200p. 1991. 99.95 (*0-7506-1278-9*, Butterwrth Archit) Buttrwrth-Heinemann.

Airports. (Illus.). 88p. 1990. 70.00 (*0-317-04133-9*, Pub. by Parkett Pubs SZ) Dist Art Pubs.

Airports. Jason Cooper. LC 92-8677. (Great Places to Visit Ser.). (J). 1992. 12.67 (*0-86593-208-5*); lib. bdg. 9.50 (*0-685-59384-3*) Rourke Corp.

Airports. Helmut Jahn. Ed. by Werner Blaser. (Illus.). 180p. 1991. pap. 98.00 (*0-8176-2613-1*) Birkhauser.

Airports. Joy Richardson. (Picture Science Ser.). (Illus.). 32p. (J). (gr. 2-4). 1994. lib. bdg. 12.25 (*0-531-14292-2*) Watts.

Airports: Challenges of the Future. American Society of Civil Engineers Staff. LC 76-371620. 219p. reprint ed. pap. 62.50 (*0-8357-5288-7*, 2010119) Bks Demand.

Airports: Proceedings of the Airports Conference, Atlanta 1971. Airports Conference Staff. LC 73-171782. 297p. reprint ed. pap. 84.70 (*0-8357-5289-5*, 2010118) Bks Demand.

Airports & Automation: Proceedings of the 9th World Airports Conference, Organized by the Institution of Civil Engineers, London, England, September 10-12, 1991. Ed. by G. M. Crook. 136p. 1992. 95.00 (*0-7277-1680-8*, Pub. by T Telford UK) Am Soc Civil Eng.

Airports for People. (Conference Proceedings Ser.). 160p. 1988. 97.00 (*0-7277-1327-2*) Am Soc Civil Eng.

Airports Full of People a Long Time Dead. Ivan Kershner. LC 94-11947. 68p. 1994. pap. 14.95 (*0-7734-0015-X*, Mellen Poetry Pr) E Mellen.

Airports of Columbia: A Photographic History. Russell Maxey. (Illus.). 300p. 1987. 19.50 (*0-317-56064-6*) Palmetto Pub.

Airports Survey. Civil Aeronautics Authority Staff. LC 77-74965. (American Federalism Ser.). (Illus.). 1978. reprint ed. lib. bdg. 23.95 (*0-405-10507-X*) Ayer.

Airpower: A Centennial Appraisal. Tony Mason. 226p. 1994. 45.00 (*1-85753-069-1*) Macmillan.

Airpower: The Decisive Force in Korea. Ed. by James T. Stewart & James B. Gilbert. LC 79-7298. (Flight: Its First Seventy-Five Years Ser.). (Illus.). 1980. reprint ed. lib. bdg. 27.95 (*0-405-12204-7*) Ayer.

***Airpower: Theory & Practice.** John Gooch. LC 95-14978. 1995. pap. write for info. (*0-7146-4186-3*, Pub. by F Cass Pubs UK) Intl Spec Bk.

***Airpower: Theory & Practice.** Ed. by John Gooch. LC 95-14978. 1995. write for info. (*0-7146-4657-1*, Pub. by F Cass Pubs UK) Intl Spec Bk.

Airpower & Russian Partisan Warfare. Karl Drum. LC 68-22553. (German Air Force in World War 2 Ser.). (Illus.). 1968. reprint ed. 16.95 (*0-405-00041-3*) Ayer.

Airpower & the Airlift Evacuation of Kham Duc. Alan L. Gropman. (USAF Southeast Asia Monograph Ser.: Vol. 5, Monograph 7). (Illus.). 87p. 1986. reprint ed. pap. write for info. (*0-912799-30-7*) Off Air Force.

Airpower & the Nineteen Seventy-Two Spring Invasion. John A. Doglione et al. (USAF Southeast Asia Monograph Ser.: Vol. 2, Monograph 3). (Illus.). 113p. 1986. reprint ed. pap. write for info. (*0-912799-27-7*) Off Air Force.

Airpower in the Gulf. 2nd ed. James P. Coyne. (Illus.). 224p. 1992. pap. 12.60 (*0-9608492-1-1*) Aero Ed Found.

Airpower in Three Wars. William W. Momyer. Ed. by James B. Gilbert. LC 79-7287. (Flight: Its First Seventy-Five Years Ser.). (Illus.). 1980. lib. bdg. 27.95 (*0-405-12196-2*) Ayer.

***Airpower in U. S. Light Combat Operations.** Kenneth Watman & Dan Raymer. LC 94-26398. 1994. write for info. (*0-8330-1562-1*, MR457AF) Rand Corp.

Airs. Brutus. 1989. 1.50 (*0-685-25947-1*) Whirlwind Pr.

Airs above Ground. Mary Stewart. 1988. mass mkt. 5.99 (*0-449-21564-4*) Fawcett.

Airs & Tributes. Dennis Brutus. Ed. by Gil Ott. (Illus.). 32p. (Orig.). 1989. pap. 10.00 (*0-922827-00-1*) Whirlwind Pr.

Airs de plusiers musiciens reduits a quatre parties see Monuments de la musique francaise au temps de la Renaissance

Airs et Villanelles see Florilege du Concert Vocal de la Renaissance

Airs from Arcadia & Elsewhere. Henry C. Bunner. 1971. 59.95 (*0-87968-587-5*) Gordon Pr.

Air's Nearly Perfect Elasticity. Richard Duerden. 1979. pap. 3.50 (*0-939180-08-1*) Tombouctou.

Airs of Providence. Jean McGarry. LC 85-8905. (Poetry & Fiction Ser.). 144p. 1985. 16.95 (*0-8018-2909-7*) Johns Hopkins.

Airship. Ken Forsse. (Teddy Ruxpin Adventure Ser.). (Illus.). 26p. (J). (ps). 1985. audio 9.95 (*0-934323-00-3*) Alchemy Comms.

Airshipmen, Businessmen, & Politics, 1890-1940. Henry C. Meyer. LC 90-22345. (History of Aviation Ser.). (Illus.). 276p. (C). 1991. text ed. 45.00 (*1-56098-031-1*) Smithsonian.

***Airships.** Patrick Abbott. (C). 1989. pap. 25.00x (*0-7478-0084-7*, Pub. by Shire UK) St Mut.

Airships. Barry Hannah. LC 93-43713. 288p. 1994. pap. 11.00 (*0-8021-3388-6*) Grove-Atltic.

Airships. Barry Hannah. (Vintage Contemporaries Ser.). 1985. pap. 5.95 (*0-394-72913-7*, Vin) Random.

Airships Cardington. Geoffrey Chamberlain. 239p. 1994. 48.00 (*0-86138-025-8*, Pub. by T Dalton UK) St Mut.

Airships, History & Technology. Louis Gerken. LC 90-4. (Illus.). 480p. 1990. 50.00 (*0-9617163-3-9*) Amer Scientific.

Airshow. 1990. 19.99 (*0-517-01221-9*) Random Hse Value.

Airshow: The World's Classic Air on Display. Jon Davison. (Virgin Publishing Ser.). (Illus.). 160p. 1993. pap. 19.95 (*0-86369-509-4*) Motorbooks Intl.

Airspace. Larry D. Griffin. Ed. by Chuck Taylor. (Everybody Books Ser.). 35p. (Orig.). 1990. pap. 4.00 (*0-685-45161-5*) Slough Pr TX.

Airspeed: The Company & Its Aeroplanes. D. H. Middleton. 216p. (C). 1988. 120.00 (*0-86138-009-6*, Pub. by T Dalton UK) St Mut.

Airtight Willie & Me. Iceberg Slim. 1988. pap. 4.95 (*0-87067-754-3*) Holloway.

Airwalker: A Date with Destiny! Rocket-Belt History & Construction Plans Exhaustive Study Manual. Derwin Beushausen. (Illus.). 160p. (Orig.). 1993. pap. 29.95 (*0-9637097-0-4*) Airwalker Soc.

Airwaves of Zion: Radio & Religion in Appalachia. Howard Dorgan. LC 92-40704. (Illus.). 248p. (Orig.). (C). 1993. text ed. 31.95 (*0-87049-796-0*); pap. 18.95 (*0-87049-797-9*) U of Tenn Pr.

Airwaves over Alaska: Story of Pioneer Broadcaster Augie Hiebert. Robin A. Chlupach. (Illus.). 266p. 1992. 19.95 (*0-942381-09-2*) Sammamish Pr.

Airway: Emergency Management. Robert H. Dailey et al. 397p. 1992. 64.00 (*0-8016-1270-5*) Mosby Yr Bk.

Airway Calibre in Health & Disease: The Pathophysiology of Upper & Lower Airway Narrowing. Ed. by A. H. Campbell et al. 354p. 1988. 152.50 (*0-444-80923-6*) Elsevier.

Airway Epithelium: Physiology, Pathophysiology & Pharmacology. Ed. by Farmer & Hay. (Lung Biology in Health & Disease Ser.: Vol. 55). 680p. 1991. 210.00 (*0-8247-8510-X*) Dekker.

Airway Obstruction & Inflammation: Present Status & Perspectives. Ed. by D. Olivieri & S. Bianco. (Progress in Respiration Research Ser.: Vol. 24). (Illus.). viii, 288p. 1990. 223.25 (*3-8055-5006-5*) S Karger.

Airway Responsiveness & Atopy in the Development of Chronic Lung Disease. Scott T. Weiss & David Sparrow. 344p. 1989. 109.50 (*0-88167-535-0*) Raven.

Airway Secretions. Ed. by Takishima & Shimura. 688p. 1994. 195.00 (*0-8247-8843-5*) Dekker.

Airway Smooth Muscle: Mod of Receptors & Response. Ed. by Asrawal. 1990. 190.00 (*0-8493-5904-X*, QP121) CRC Pr.

Airway to Everywhere: A History of All American Aviation 1937-1953. W. David Lewis & William F. Trimble. LC 87-25176. (Illus.). 240p. (C). 1988. 29.95 (*0-8229-3579-1*) U of Pittsburgh Pr.

Airways: Neural Control in Health & Disease. Kaliner & Barnes. (Lung Biology in Health & Disease Ser.: Vol. 33). 688p. 1988. 210.00 (*0-8247-7779-4*) Dekker.

Airways: Rising to the Challenge of Managing COPD. Barb Markey & Tad Hunt. Ed. by Susan D. Allen & Colleen A. Holloran. (Illus.). 56p. Date not set. pap. text ed. 3.50 (*0-916999-13-0*) HERC Inc.

Airways: The History of Commercial Aviation in the United States. Henry L. Smith. (Airlines History Project Ser.). (Illus.). reprint ed. 52.50 (*0-404-19335-8*) AMS Pr.

Airways: The History of Commercial Aviation in the United States. Henry L. Smith. LC 90-21853. (History of Aviation Ser.). 448p. (C). 1991. reprint ed. pap. 19.95 (*1-56098-052-4*) Smithsonian.

Airways Abroad: The Story of American World Air Routes. Henry L. Smith. (Airlines History Project Ser.). reprint ed. 40.00 (*0-404-19336-6*) AMS Pr.

Airways Abroad: The Story of American World Air Routes. Henry L. Smith. LC 90-21379. (History of Aviation Ser.). 356p. (C). 1991. reprint ed. 17.50 (*1-56098-053-2*) Smithsonian.

An Asterisk (*) at the beginning of an entry indicates that the title is appearing in BIP for the first time.

Airways & Vascular Remodelling in Asthma & Cardiovascular Disease: Implications for Therapeutic Intervention. Ed. by Clive Page & Judith Black. (Illus.). 189p. 1994. boxed 82.50 (*0-12-543540-1*) Acad Pr.

Airways Hyperresponsiveness, Is It Really Important for Asthma? C. P. Page & P. J. Gardiner. (Illus.). 384p. 1993. 135.00 (*0-632-03061-5*) Blackwell Sci.

Airways Smooth Muscle: Biochemical Control of Contraction & Relaxation. Ed. by David Raeburn & Mark A. Giembycz. LC 94-20775. (Respiratory Pharmacology & Pharmacotherapy Ser.). viii, 351p. 1994. text ed. 159.00 (*0-8176-5043-1*) Birkhauser.

Airways Smooth Muscle: Development, & Regulation of Contractility. Ed. by D. Raeburn & M. A. Giembycz. LC 94-8800. (Respiratory Pharmacology & Pharmacotherapy Ser.). 1994. 169.00 (*0-8176-5011-3*, Pub. by Birkhauser Vlg SZ) Birkhauser.

***Airways Smooth Muscle: Peptide Receptors, Ion Channels & Signal Transduction.** Ed. by D. Raeburn & M. A. Giembycz. LC 94-48621. (Respiratory Pharmacology & Pharmacotherapy Ser.). 1995. write for info. (*0-8176-5140-3*) Birkhauser.

***Airways Smooth Muscle: Structure, Innervation & Neurotransmission.** D. Raeburn & M. A. Giembycz. (Respiratory Pharmacology & Pharmacotherapy Ser.). 336p. 1994. 149.00 (*0-8176-5010-5*) Spr-Verlag.

***Airwise.** Kahn. 1995. pap. 7.95 (*0-85207-264-3*) Atrium Pubs.

Airwise. Farrol S. Kahn. 96p. (Orig.). 1993. pap. 7.95 (*0-8464-4171-3*) Beekman Pubs.

***Airy Plumeflights: A Beginner's Guide to Celtic Script & Design.** Tim O'Neill. (Illus.). 48p. (Orig.). 1994. pap. 11.95 (*1-874675-35-X*, Pub. by Lilliput Pr Ltd IE) Irish Bks Media.

AI's Concerns February - June 1991. 1991. pap. 2.00 (*0-685-53238-0*) Amnesty Intl USA.

AIS New Car Cost Guide, 1986. 6th ed. Ed. by Christine Boldt. 1986. 73.00 (*0-88098-076-1*, H M Gousha) P-H Gen Ref & Trav.

AISB Ninety One: Proceedings of the Eighth Conference of the Society for the Study of Artificial Intelligence & Simulation of Behaviour, 16-19 April 1991, University of Leeds. Ed. by L. L. Steels & B. M. Smith. (Illus.). 272p. 1991. pap. 59.50 (*0-387-19671-4*) Spr-Verlag.

AISB-89: Proceedings of the Seventh Conference of SSAISB. Ed. by Antony G. Cohn. 256p. (C). 1989. text ed. 250.00 (*0-273-08808-4*, Pub. by Pitman Pubng UK) St Mut.

Aischines von Sphettos: Studien zur Literaturgeschichte der Sokratiker. Heinrich Dittmar. LC 75-13262. (History of Ideas in Ancient Greece Ser.). (GER.). 1976. reprint ed. 23.95 (*0-405-07304-6*) Ayer.

Aischylos Interpretationen. Ulrich Von Wilamowitz-Moellendorff. v, 260p. 1967. write for info. (*3-296-16030-2*, Pub. by Georg Olms GW) Lubrecht & Cramer.

Aisha: The Truthful. Fazl Ahmad. (Heroes of Islam Ser.: Bk. 11). 140p. (Orig.). (YA). (gr. 7-12). 1984. pap. 3.50 (*1-56744-238-2*) Kazi Pubns.

***Aisha Goes Wild.** Katherine Applegate. (Boyfriends & Girlfriends Ser.: No. 8). (YA). 1994. pap. 3.99 (*0-06-106251-0*) HarpC Child Bks.

Aishah: The Beloved of Mohammed. Nabia Abbott. LC 73-6264. (Middle East Ser.). 1973. reprint ed. 20.95 (*0-405-05318-5*) Ayer.

***Aishel: Stories of Contemporary Jewish Hospitality.** Meir Wikler. LC 94-27092. 1994. write for info. (*0-87306-676-6*) Feldheim.

AISI American Genealogical Census Catalog. (Illus.). lib. bdg. 50.00 (*0-89593-206-7*) Accelerated Index.

AISI American Genealogical Library Census Catalog: Over 200,000 Census Entries. 1983. 50.00 (*0-89593-627-5*) Accelerated Index.

AISI Catalog Immigrant & Passenger Lists Microfilms. 1980. 10.00 (*0-685-45822-9*) Accelerated Index.

AISI Catalog of Published Indexes for U. S., 1965-1991. Limit 1. write for info. (*0-318-67061-5*) Accelerated Index.

AISI Microfiche Data Base List & Manual, 1983. 1983. 10.00 (*0-89593-625-9*) Accelerated Index.

AISI Microfiche Data Base, October 1983. 1991. 2,500.00 (*0-89593-626-7*) Accelerated Index.

AISI Mortality Indexes & Microfilms Catalog. 1982. 4.00 (*0-685-45823-7*) Accelerated Index.

AISI State & Special Census Microfilms. 1990. 10.00 (*0-89593-640-2*) Accelerated Index.

AISI State Tax Lists & Special Microfilms. 1984. write for info. (*0-89593-641-0*) Accelerated Index.

Aisling. Louise Cooper. (Indigo Saga Ser.: Vol. 7). 384p. (Orig.). 1994. mass mkt. 4.99 (*0-8125-0808-4*) Tor Bks.

Ait Ayash of the High Molouuya Plain: Rural Social Organization in Morocco. John P. Chiapuris. (Anthropological Papers: No. 69). 1980. pap. 3.00 (*0-932206-83-2*) U Mich Mus Anthro.

Ait Ndhir of Morocco: A Study of the Social Transformation of a Berber Tribe. Amal R. Vinogradov. (Anthropological Papers: No. 55). (Illus.). 1974. pap. 2.00 (*0-932206-53-0*) U Mich Mus Anthro.

Aitareya Brahmanam of Rigveda: Containing the Earliest Speculations of the Brahmans on the Meaning of the Sacrificial Prayers, & on the Origin, Performance & Sense of the Rites of the Vedic Religion. Ed. & Tr. by Martin Haug. LC 73-3830. (Sacred Books of the Hindus: Extra Vol. 4). reprint ed. 35.00 (*0-404-57848-9*) AMS Pr.

Aitareya Upanisat,, 2 pts. in 1. Tr. by Srisa Chandra Vidyarnava & Mohan L. Sandal. LC 73-3823. (Sacred Books of the Hindus: No. 30, Pts. 1-2). reprint ed. 18.00 (*0-404-57830-6*) AMS Pr.

Aitareya Upanishad. Tr. by Swami Gambhirananda. (Upanishads with Shankara's Commentary Ser.). 75p. 1993. pap. 1.25 (*0-87481-200-3*, Pub. by Advaita Ashrama II) Vedanta Pr.

Aitareyopanisad. Tr. by Swami Sarvananda. (C). 1978. Bilingual ed. pap. 1.50 (*0-87481-463-4*, Pub. by Ramakrishna Math II) Vedanta Pr.

Aith Waryaghar of the Moroccan Rif: An Ethnography & History. David M. Hart. LC 75-12254. (Viking Fund Publications in Anthropology: No. 55). 580p. reprint ed. pap. 165.30 (*0-8357-5290-9*, 2052224) Bks Demand.

AIUM-SDMS Annual Convention Proceedings, 1984. 230p. 15.00 (*0-318-12814-4*, 315) Am Inst Ultrasound.

AIVF Guide to International Film & Video Festivals. rev. ed. Intro. by Kathryn Bowser. 149p. (C). 1988. pap. 19.50 (*0-9622448-0-5*) FIVF.

***AIX - 6000 Developer's Tool Kit.** Leininger. 1995. cd-rom, pap. text ed. 49.95 (*0-07-911993-X*) McGraw.

***AIX - 6000 System Guide.** Graubart-Cervone. 1995. pap. text ed. 40.00 (*0-07-024129-5*) McGraw.

AIX Command Summary. Leslie Cummings et al. (Orig.). 1991. disk, spiral bd. 99.95 (*0-9628940-0-1*) Secutron.

Aix Companion (Book) David Cohn. 496p. 1994. Incl. disk. pap. text ed. 40.00 (*0-13-291220-1*) P-H.

AIX for RS6000: System & Administration Guide. James W. DeRoest. (Ranade Workstation Ser.). 1994. pap. text ed. 39.95 (*0-07-036439-7*) McGraw.

Aizer Knegdo: Jewish Woman's Guide to Happiness in Marriage. Sarah C. Radcliffe. 254p. 1989. 16.95 (*0-944070-08-6*) Targum Pr.

A.J. Greimas & the Nature of Meaning: Linguistics, Semiotics & Discourse Theory. Ronald Schleifer. LC 87-5087. (Critics of the Twentieth Century Ser.). xxvi, 233p. 1987. pap. 10.95 (*0-8032-9180-9*) U of Nebr Pr.

Ajatasatru: The Story of Who We Are. Shoji Matsumoto & Ruth M. Tabrah. LC 88-16813. 84p. (Orig.). 1988. pap. 7.95 (*0-938474-08-1*) Buddhist Study.

Ajax. Sophocles. Ed. by W. R. Connor. LC 78-18609. (Greek Texts & Commentaries Ser.). (ENG & GRE.). 1979. reprint ed. lib. bdg. 33.95 (*0-405-11449-4*) Ayer.

Ajax see Sophocles Two

Ajeemah & His Son. James Berry. LC 92-6615. (Willa Perlman Bks.). 96p. (YA). (gr. 7 up). 1992. 13.95 (*0-06-021043-5*); lib. bdg. 13.89 (*0-06-021044-3*) HarpC Child Bks.

Ajeemah & His Son. James Berry. LC 92-6615. (Willa Perlman Bks.). 96p. (YA). (gr. 7 up). 1994. pap. 3.95 (*0-06-440523-0*, Trophy) HarpC Child Bks.

Ajitena: Symbols of the Orishas. Oba Ecun. (Illus.). 170p. (Orig.). 1992. write for info. (*0-926603-08-6*) Obaecun Bks.

AJN: Five Year Cumulative Index, 1951-55 (XAO2. Incl. AJN: Five Year Cumulative Index, 1956-60. 117p. 1961. pap. text ed. 4.50 (*0-937126-94-2*); AJN: Five Year Cumulative Index, 1966-70. 1971. pap. text ed. 6.00 (*0-937126-92-6*, XA05); AJN: Five Year Cumulative Index, 1971-75. 128p. 1976. pap. text ed. 8.00x (*0-937126-91-8*, XA06); 134p. 1956. Set pap. text ed. 3.90 (*0-937126-95-0*) Am Journal Nurse.

AJN - Mosby Nursing Boards Review, No. 9. American Journal of Nursing Company Staff. 713p. 1993. pap. 26.95 (*0-8016-7781-5*) Mosby Yr Bk.

AJN - NBR: (RAI Edition Only), No. 8. AJN - Mosby Staff. 704p. 1991. pap. 25.95 (*0-685-65098-7*) Mosby Yr Bk.

AJN: Five Year Cumulative Index, 1956-60 see AJN: Five Year Cumulative Index, 1951-55 (XAO2

AJN: Five Year Cumulative Index, 1966-70 see AJN: Five Year Cumulative Index, 1951-55 (XAO2

AJN: Five Year Cumulative Index, 1971-75 see AJN: Five Year Cumulative Index, 1951-55 (XAO2

AJ's Best Friends. Karla Erickson. 1993. pap. 5.95 (*0-88494-906-0*) Bookcraft Inc.

AJ's Promise. Karla Erickson. 1992. pap. 5.95 (*0-88494-849-8*) Bookcraft Inc.

***AJ's World.** Mary E. Richardson-Hawkins. (J). 1995. 7.95 (*0-533-11093-9*) Vantage.

Ajuna's Star. Dean McMahan. LC 90-82569. (Illus.). 24p. (SPA.). (J). (ps-2). 1990. pap. 4.95 (*0-9626254-3-4*) Ajuna Unlimited.

Ajuna's Star. Dean McMahan & Willi Rose. 1990. English version. audio 8.95 (*0-9626254-5-0*); Spanish version. audio 8.95 (*0-9626254-6-9*) Ajuna Unlimited.

Ajuna's Star. rev. ed. Dean McMahan & Willi Rose. LC 90-80841. (Illus.). 24p. (J). (ps-2). 1990. reprint ed. pap. 4.95 (*0-9626254-1-8*); reprint ed. audio write for info. (*0-9626254-2-6*) Ajuna Unlimited.

Ajustamento e Crescimento na Actual Conjuntura Economica Mundial. Ed. by Jose Lopes Da Silva. xii, 200p. 1985. pap. 10.00 (*0-939934-47-7*) Intl Monetary.

Ajustarse o Autodestruirse. Craig Massey. Orig. Title: Adjust or Self-Destruct. 144p. (SPA.). 1983. pap. 3.99 (*0-8254-1470-9*) Kregel.

Ajuste Con Crecimiento y Finanzas Publicas en America Latina. Eugenio Diaz-Bonilla. (EDI Policy Seminar Report Ser.: No. 27). 48p. (SPA.). 1991. 5.95 (*0-8213-1722-9*, 11722) World Bank.

AK. Peter Dickinson. (YA). 1992. 15.00 (*0-385-30608-3*) Doubleday.

AK. Pter Dickinson. (YA). 1994. mass mkt. 3.99 (*0-440-21897-7*) Dell.

***Ak Va Thap-Gia.** Phan-Phat-Huon. 303p. 1994. pap. text ed. 20.00 (*1-885550-06-5*) Du-Sinh St Joseph.

AKA. B. E. Jones. 1981. 12.95 (*0-02-559870-8*) Macmillan.

Aka Plunkitt of Tammany Hall see Honest Graft: The World of George Washington Plunkitt

Akademie der Wissenschaften - The Academy of Sciences & Technology in Berlin-Jahrbuch - Yearbook 1988. viii, 599p. (C). 1989. lib. bdg. 103.10x (*3-11-012301-0*) De Gruyter.

Akademie der Wissenschaften zu Berlin - The Academy of Sciences & Technology in Berlin: Jahrbuch - Yearbook 1990-1992. (Illus.). xii, 814p. (GER.). (C). 1993. lib. bdg. 198.50 (*3-11-013891-3*) De Gruyter.

Akademie der Wissenschaften zu Berlin (The Academy of Sciences & Technology in Berlin) Jahrbuch Yearbook 1989. (Illus.). vii, 429p. (GER.). (C). 1991. lib. bdg. 106.15 (*3-11-012146-8*) De Gruyter.

Akademische Deutschland, 4 vols., Set. Michael Doeberl. reprint ed. write for info. (*0-318-71899-5*, Pub. by Georg Olms GW) Lubrecht & Cramer.

Akademishce Kunstmuseum der Universitat Bonn: Unter der Direktion von Reinhard Kekule. Wilfred Geominy. x, 253p. (GER.). 1989. 35.00 (*90-6032-077-8*, Pub. by B R Gruener NE) Benjamins North Am.

Akaike Information Criterion Statistics. Y. Sakamoto et al. 1986. lib. bdg. 157.50 (*90-277-2253-6*) Kluwer Ac.

Akali Agitation to Operation Bluestar, 2 vols. M. S. Deora. (C). 1991. 94.00 (*81-7041-450-4*, Pub. by Anmol II) S Asia.

***Akali Politics in Punjab (1964-1985)** Devinder Singh. (C). 1993. 28.00 (*81-85135-70-3*, Pub. by National Bk Organ) S Asia.

Akamba. Tiyambe Zeleza. LC 94-13614. (Heritage Library of African Peoples). 1994. 15.95 (*0-8239-1768-1*) Rosen Group.

***Akan - The Royal Bear.** Deborah Easton. (Illus.). (Orig.). 1995. pap. 7.95 (*1-885821-01-8*) Identity Toys.

Akan Arts & Aesthetics: Elements of Change in a Ghanaian Indigenous Knowledge System. Ed. by D. M. Warren. (Studies in Technology & Social Change: No. 16). (Illus.). 60p. (Orig.). (C). 1990. pap. 7.00 (*0-945271-25-5*) ISU-TSCP.

Akan-Ashanti Folk-Tales. Robert S. Rattray. LC 78-63214. (Folktale Ser.). (Illus.). 320p. 1983. reprint ed. 34.50 (*0-404-16155-3*) AMS Pr.

Akan Trickster Cycle: Myth or Folktale. Kwesi Yankah. (Graduate Student Term Paper Co-Winner Ser.). 17p. 1983. pap. text ed. 2.00 (*0-941934-43-8*) Indiana Africa.

Akanthos: A Book of Channeled Insights. Marcy Foley. 306p. 1992. pap. 14.95 (*0-9631452-0-7*) M Foley.

***Akashic Brotherhood.** White Wolf Staff. 72p. 1994. per., pap. 10.00 (*1-56504-410-X*, 4057) White Wolf.

Akashic Record Player: A Non-Stop Geomantic Conspiracy. Antero Alli. LC 88-83350. 200p. (Orig.). 1988. pap. 12.95 (*0-941404-91-9*) New Falcon Pubns.

***Akathisia & Restless Legs.** Perminder Sachdev. (Illus.). 220p. (C). 1995. 69.95 (*0-521-44426-8*) Cambridge U Pr.

Akathist Hymn to Our Most Holy Lady the Theotokos, the Joy of All That Sorrow. 1993. pap. 1.00 (*0-89981-144-2*) Eastern Orthodox.

Akathist to Great Martyr George. Orthodox Eastern Church Staff. 1993. pap. 0.50 (*0-89981-142-6*) Eastern Orthodox.

Akathist to Sts. Martha & Mary. Bethany Community of the Resurrection of Christ Staff. 1991. pap. 1.00 (*0-89981-112-4*) Eastern Orthodox.

Akathistos Hymn. Tom Peters. (Illus.). 35p. 1990. pap. 4.95 (*1-879516-01-2*) Betterpub Pr.

Akatokamanava: Myth, History, & Society in the Southern Cook Islands. Jukka Siikala. 154p. (C). 1992. pap. text ed. 18.95 (*0-473-01133-6*, Pub. by Polynesian Soc) UH Pr.

Akavak. James R. Houston. 80p. (J). (gr. 5 up). 1990. pap. 8.95 (*0-15-201731-3*) HarBrace.

Akayna, Sachem's Daughter. Mildred E. Riley. 1992. pap. 4.75 (*1-878634-07-0*) Odyssey Bks.

Akbar: The Greatest Mogul. S. M. Burke. 262p. 1989. reprint ed. 24.00 (*0-317-99945-1*, Pub. by M Manoharial II) Coronet Bks.

Akbar & Jeff's Guide to Life. Matt Groening. (Illus.). 1989. pap. 7.95 (*0-679-72680-2*) Pantheon.

***Akbar & the Jesuits: An Account of the Jesuit Missions to the Court of Akbar.** Intro. by C. H. Payne. (Curzon Travellers Ser.). (C). 1995. text ed. 70.00 (*0-7007-0349-7*, Pub. by Curzon Pr UK) Humanities.

Akbar Behkalam: Movement & Change, Paintings & Sketches. Akbar Behkalam. (Illus.). 117p. (Orig.). 1989. pap. 25.00 (*0-939214-37-7*) Mazda Pubs.

Akbar Nama of Abu-I-Fazal, 3 vols., Set. Tr. by Henry Beveridge. 1989. reprint ed. 72.50 (*81-85395-03-9*) S Asia.

Akbar the Greatest Mogul. S. M. Burke. (C). 1989. 44.00 (*0-685-30707-7*, Pub. by Munshiram Manoharial II) S Asia.

Akdamus. Avrohon Y. Salamon & Nosson Scherman. (Art Scroll Mesorah Ser.). 160p. 1978. 16.95 (*0-89906-154-0*) Mesorah Pubns.

Ake: The Years of Childhood. Wole Soyinka. LC 83-48035. (Library of Contemporary World Literature). 240p. 1983. 14.95 (*0-394-52807-7*) Random.

Ake: The Years of Childhood. Wole Soyinka. (Vintage International Ser.). 1989. pap. 12.00 (*0-679-72540-7*, Vin) Random.

Akenfield: Portrait of an English Village. Ronald Blythe. (Village Ser.). 1980. pap. 9.56 (*0-394-73847-0*) Pantheon.

Akeres Habayis: Realizing Your Potential as a Jewish Homemaker. Sarah C. Radcliffe. 228p. 1991. 15.95 (*0-944070-64-7*) Targum Pr.

Akers' Simple Library Cataloging. 7th rev. ed. Arthur Curley et al. LC 83-14423. 1985. 27.50 (*0-8108-1649-0*) Scarecrow.

Akewa Is a Woman: And Other Poems. Beatriz Badikian. Ed. by Carlos Cumpian. (Illus.). 24p. (Orig.). 1989. reprint ed. pap. 4.00 (*1-877636-07-X*) March Abrazo.

Akha & Miao: Problems of Applied Ethnography in Farther India. Hugo A. Bernatzik. LC 73-114702. (Monographs). 780p. 1970. 30.00x (*0-87536-027-0*) HRAFP.

Akha-English Dictionary. Paul Lewis. LC 73-14371. (Cornell University, Southeast Asia Program, Data Paper Ser.: No. 70). 403p. reprint ed. pap. 114.90 (*0-8357-5291-7*, 2010475) Bks Demand.

***Akhbar Ibrahim al Mausuli II.** Tr. by A. Wormhoudt. (Arab Translation Ser.: No. 139). 170p. 1995. pap. 6.50 (*0-940307-42-1*) Wormhoudt.

***Akhbar Ibrahim Mausuli I.** Tr. by A. Wormhoudt. (Arab Translation Ser.: No. 137). 160p. 1995. pap. 6.50 (*0-940307-40-5*) Wormhoudt.

A

Akhenaten: King of Egypt. Cyril Aldred. LC 87-51153. (Illus.). 320p. 1991. reprint ed. pap. 24.95 (*0-500-27621-8*) Thames Hudson.

Akhenaten: The Heretic King. Donald B. Redford. LC 83-22960. (Illus.). 281p. 1987. pap. 19.95 (*0-691-00217-7*) Princeton U Pr.

Akhenaten Temple Project, Vol. 1: Initial Discoveries. Smith. (Akhenaten Temple Project Ser.: Vol. 1). 1977. 85.00 (*0-85668-034-6*, Pub. by Aris & Phillips UK) David Brown.

Akhenaten's Egypt. Angela P. Thomas. (Shire Egyptology Ser.: No. 10). (Illus.). 68p. 1988. pap. text ed. 10.50 (*0-85263-973-2*, Pub. by Shire Pubns UK) Lubrecht & Cramer.

Akhenaten's Sed-Festival at Karnak. Jocelyn Gohary. (Studies in Egyptology). 256p. (C). 1991. text ed. 99.95 (*0-7103-0380-7*, A4701, Pub. by Kegan Paul Intl UK) Routledge Chapman & Hall.

Akhenaton: Torchbearer of Light. AESOP Enterprises, Inc. Staff & Gwendolyn J. Crenshaw. (Heroes & Sheroes Ser.). 14p. (J). (gr. 3-12). 1991. audio, pap. write for info. (*1-880771-12-8*) AESOP Enter.

Akhundzadeh As a Modern Literary Critic. Iraj Parsinejad. (Middle Eastern Ser.: No. 17). (Illus.). 125p. (Orig.). 1986. pap. 9.00 (*0-936665-03-3*) Jahan Bk Co.

Aki & the Banner of Names: And Other Stories from Japan. Atsuko G. Lolling. (Orig.). (J). (gr. 1-6). pap. 4.95 (*0-377-00218-6*) Friendship Pr.

AKIA Spa Cookbook. Wilhelmina Maguire. 71p. (Orig.). 1992. pap. 13.50 (*0-9639039-0-X*) AKIA.

Akiba: Scholar, Saint & Martyr. Louis Finkelstein. LC 90-31767. 392p. 1990. 30.00 (*0-87668-806-7*) Aronson.

***Akiba Rubinstein: Uncrowned King.** John Donaldson & Nikolay Miner. Ed. by Eric Woro. 336p. (Orig.). 1994. text ed. 34.95 (*1-879479-20-6*); pap. 27.95 (*1-879479-19-2*) ICE WA.

Akin to Anne: Tales of Other Orphans. Lucy M. Montgomery. 1990. mass mkt. 3.99 (*0-553-28387-1*) Bantam.

Akionalitatsklassen des Deutchen. Erwin P. Tschirner. LC 90-5928. (Berkeley Insights in Linguistics & Semiotics Ser.: Vol. 5). 200p. (GER.). (C). 1990. text ed. 35.95 (*0-8204-1340-2*) P Lang Pubs.

Akiouin's: Le Fleur de Lys Ne Se Fane Pas. Aharon Ben-Haim. (Illus.). 230p. (Orig.). (FRE.). 1989. 24.95 (*0-317-94011-2*); lib. bdg. 19.95 (*0-317-94012-0*); pap. 14.95 (*0-317-94013-9*) Four N Language.

Akira, No. 1. Otomo & Jo Duffy. 64p. 1988. 3.95 (*0-87135-584-1*) Marvel Entmnt.

Akira, No. 2. Otomo & Jo Duffy. 64p. 1988. 3.95 (*0-87135-585-X*) Marvel Entmnt.

Akira, No. 11. Otomo & Jo Duffy. 64p. 1989. 3.50 (*0-87135-586-8*) Marvel Entmnt.

Akira, No. 12. Otomo & Jo Duffy. 64p. 1989. 3.50 (*0-87135-587-6*) Marvel Entmnt.

Akira, No. 13. Otomo & Jo Duffy. 64p. 1989. 3.50 (*0-87135-588-4*) Marvel Entmnt.

Akira, No. 14. Otomo & Jo Duffy. 64p. 1989. 3.50 (*0-87135-589-2*) Marvel Entmnt.

Akira, No. 15. Otomo & Jo Duffy. 64p. 1989. 3.50 (*0-87135-590-6*) Marvel Entmnt.

Akira, No. 16. Otomo & Jo Duffy. 64p. 1989. 3.95 (*0-87135-591-4*) Marvel Entmnt.

Akira, No. 17. Otomo & Jo Duffy. 64p. 1990. 3.95 (*0-87135-618-X*) Marvel Entmnt.

Akira, No. 18. Otomo & Jo Duffy. 64p. 1990. 3.95 (*0-87135-619-8*) Marvel Entmnt.

Akira, No. 19. Otomo & Jo Duffy. 64p. 1990. 3.95 (*0-87135-620-1*) Marvel Entmnt.

Akira, No. 20. Otomo & Jo Duffy. 64p. 1990. 3.95 (*0-87135-621-X*) Marvel Entmnt.

Akira, No. 21. Otomo & Jo Duffy. 64p. 1990. 3.95 (*0-87135-622-8*) Marvel Entmnt.

Akira, No. 22. Otomo & Jo Duffy. 64p. 1990. 3.95 (*0-87135-623-6*) Marvel Entmnt.

Akira, No. 23. Otomo & Jo Duffy. 64p. 1990. 3.95 (*0-87135-624-4*) Marvel Entmnt.

Akira, No. 24. Otomo & Jo Duffy. 64p. 1990. 3.95 (*0-87135-683-X*) Marvel Entmnt.

Akira, No. 25. Otomo & Jo Duffy. 64p. 1990. 3.95 (*0-87135-684-8*) Marvel Entmnt.

Akira, No. 26. Otomo & Jo Duffy. 64p. 1990. 3.95 (*0-87135-685-6*) Marvel Entmnt.

Akira, No. 27. Otomo & Jo Duffy. 64p. 1991. 3.95 (*0-87135-686-4*) Marvel Entmnt.

Akira, No. 28. Otomo & Jo Duffy. 64p. 1991. 3.95 (*0-87135-687-2*) Marvel Entmnt.

Akira, No. 29. Otomo & Jo Duffy. 64p. 1991. 3.95 (*0-87135-688-0*) Marvel Entmnt.

Akira, No. 30. Otomo & Jo Duffy. 64p. 1991. 3.95 (*0-87135-689-9*) Marvel Entmnt.

Akira, No. 31. Otomo & Jo Duffy. 64p. 1991. 3.95 (*0-87135-690-2*) Marvel Entmnt.

Akira, No. 32. Otomo & Jo Duffy. 64p. 1991. 3.95 (*0-87135-793-3*) Marvel Entmnt.

Akira, No. 33. Otomo & Jo Duffy. 1993. 3.95 (*0-87135-794-1*) Marvel Entmnt.

Akira, No. 34. Otomo & Jo Duffy. 64p. Date not set. 3.95 (*0-87135-795-X*) Marvel Entmnt.

Akira, No. 35. Otomo & Jo Duffy. 64p. Date not set. 3.50 (*0-87135-796-8*) Marvel Entmnt.

An Asterisk (*) at the beginning of an entry indicates that the title is appearing in BIP for the first time. 163

A

Akira, No. 36. Otomo & Jo Duffy. 64p. Date not set. 4.50 (*0-87135-797-6*) Marvel Entmnt.

Akira, No. 37. Otomo & Jo Duffy. 64p. Date not set. 4.50 (*0-87135-910-3*) Marvel Entmnt.

Akira, Vol. 2. Otomo & Jo Duffy. 192p. 1991. pap. 14.95 (*0-87135-782-8*) Marvel Entmnt.

Akira, Vol. 3. Otomo & Jo Duffy. 192p. 1991. pap. 14.95 (*0-87135-831-X*) Marvel Entmnt.

Akira, Vol. 4. Otomo & Jo Duffy. 192p. 1992. pap. 14.95 (*0-87135-832-8*) Marvel Entmnt.

Akira, Vol. 5. Otomo & Jo Duffy. 192p. 1992. pap. 14.95 (*0-87135-900-6*) Marvel Entmnt.

Akira, Vol. 6. Otomo & Jo Duffy. 192p. 1992. pap. 14.95 (*0-87135-901-4*) Marvel Entmnt.

Akira Kurosawa & Intertextual Cinema. James Goodwin. LC 93-15618. (Illus.). 264p. (C). 1993. text ed. 45.00 (*0-8018-4660-9*); pap. text ed. 14.95 (*0-8018-4661-7*) Johns Hopkins.

Akita. Gerald Mitchell & Kath Mitchell. (Illus.). 160p. 1993. 22.95 (*0-948955-11-2*, Pub. by Ringpr Bks UK) Seven Hills Bk.

Akita Champions, 1973-1981. Jan L. Freund. (Illus.). 106p. 1986. pap. 36.95 (*0-940808-14-5*) Camino E E & Bk.

Akita Champions, 1982-1986. Camino E. E. & B. Co. Staff. (Illus.). 82p. 1987. pap. 28.95 (*0-940808-54-4*) Camino E E & Bk.

Akita Champions, 1987-1992. Camino E. E. & Book Co. Staff. (Illus.). 145p. 1994. pap. 32.95 (*1-55893-028-0*) Camino E E & Bk.

Akita Holy Mother & Modern Miracles. Francis Fukushima. 244p. 1994. pap. text ed. 8.50 (*1-882972-30-9*) Queenship Pub.

Akita, Treasure of Japan. Barbara Bouyet. 318p. 1992. 39.95 (*0-9617204-3-3*) MIP Pub.

***Akitas.** Van. 1994. (*0-7938-1060-4*) TFH Pubns.

Akitas. Edita Van der Lyn. (Illus.). 128p. 1981. 11.95 (*0-86622-598-6*, KW-107) TFH Pubns.

***Akkadian Chrestomathy Vol. 1: Selected Cuneiform Texts.** Franz M. Bohl. xvi, 166p. 1947. pap. text ed. 32.25 (*0-614-03990-8*, Pub. by Netherlands Inst NE) Eisenbrauns.

Akkadian Grammar. Arthur Ungnad. Tr. by Harry Hoffner. (Society of Biblical Literature Resources for Biblical Study). 185p. 1992. 39.95 (*1-55540-800-1*, 060330); pap. 24.95 (*1-55540-801-X*, 060330) Scholars Pr GA.

Akkadian Grammar: A Translation of Lehrbuch Des Akkadischen. 3rd ed. Thomas Caldwell et al. 1978. pap. 20.00 (*0-87462-444-4*) Marquette.

Akkadian Handbook: Paradigms, Helps, Logograms, & Sign Lists. Douglas B. Miller & R. Mark Shipp. 1995. pap. text ed. write for info. (*0-931464-86-2*) Eisenbrauns.

Akkadian of Ugarit. John Huehnergard. LC 88-4143. (Harvard Semitic Studies). 473p. 1989. pap. 31.95 (*1-55540-316-6*, 04-04-34) Scholars Pr GA.

Akkadien de Boghaz-Koi. Rene Labat. LC 78-72748. (Ancient Mesopotamian Texts & Studies). reprint ed. 37.50 (*0-685-91790-8*) AMS Pr.

***Aklat Ni Juan.** Charles Brock. 177p. (Orig.). (TAG.). 1989. pap. 3.75 (*1-885504-25-X*) Church Gwth.

***Akmola Kazakhstan City Plan, 1992.** (Illus.). 60p. (Orig.). 1994. pap. 59.95 (*0-7605-0518-7*) Rector Pr.

Akokoaso, a Survey of a Gold Coast Village. W. H. Beckett. LC 76-44689. reprint ed. 32.50 (*0-404-15905-2*) AMS Pr.

***Ako'y Ipinanganak Na Muli Ano Ang Susunod?** Charles Brock. 81p. (Orig.). (TAG.). 1983. pap. 2.50 (*1-885504-20-9*) Church Gwth.

***Akrobaty i Philatelisty.** Mikhail Ivanov. (Illus.). 78p. (Orig.). (RUS.). 1994. pap. 5.99 (*0-9643971-1-0*) Isometry.

***Akron: City at the Summit.** George W. Knepper. (Illus.). 223p. 1994. text ed. 32.95 (*0-89865-893-4*) Summit Cty Hist Soc.

Akron & Summit Co. (Ohio) Karl H. Grismer. (Illus.). 834p. 1993. reprint ed. lib. bdg. 83.50 (*0-8328-2805-X*) Higginson Bk Co.

Akron Genesis of Alcoholics Anonymous: An A.A.-Good Book Connection. Dick B. LC 92-97026. 429p. (Orig.). 1994. reprint ed. pap. text ed. 16.00 (*1-881212-03-3*, 0942) Good Bk Pub.

***Akron's Library: Commemorating Twenty-Five Years on Main Street.** Margaret N. Dietz. (Illus.). 148p. 1994. 9.40 (*0-9643208-0-0*) Akron-Summit.

Aksara: A Forgotten Chapter in the History of Indian Philosophy. 2nd ed. P. M. Modi. 187p. 1985. reprint ed. 18.50 (*81-7030-041-X*, Pub. by Sri Satguru Pubns II) S Asia.

***Aksayamatinirdesasutra: The Tradition of Imperishability in Buddhist Thought, Vol. 1.** Jens Braarvig. 290p. Date not set. 39.50 (*82-560-0916-0*) Intl Spec Bk.

***Aksayamatinirdesasutra: The Tradition of Imperishability in Buddhist Thought, Vol. 2.** Jens Braarvig. 591p. Date not set. 39.50 (*82-560-0917-9*) Intl Spec Bk.

Aksel Sandemose: Exile in Search of a Home. Randi Birn. LC 83-13034. (Contributions to the Study of World Literature Ser.: No. 2). xii, 137p. 1984. text ed. 45.00 (*0-313-24163-5*, BAS/, Greenwood Pr) Greenwood.

Akston: Monumental Bronzes & Tapestries. (Illus.). 1982. pap. 1.50 (*0-943411-01-7*) Norton Gal Art.

Aksum: An African Civilization of Late Antiquity. Stuart Munro-Hay. 288p. 1992. pap. 29.50 (*0-7486-0209-7*, Pub. by Edinburgh U Pr UK) Col U Pr.

Aktionsfeld Osmanisches Reich: Die Wirtschaftsinteressen des Deutschen Kaiserreiches in der Turkei 1871-1908 (Unter Besonderer Berucksichtigung Europaischer Literatur) Armin Kossler. Ed. by Stuart Bruchey. LC 80-2814. (Dissertations in European Economic History Ser.). (Illus.). 1981. lib. bdg. 46.95 (*0-405-13998-5*) Ayer.

Aktives Biomonitoring Mit der Flechte Hypogymnia Physodes zur Ermittlung der Luftqualitaet in Hannover. Andreas Werner. (Bibliotheca Lichenologica Ser.: Vol. 49). (Illus.). 111p. (GER.). 1993. pap. text ed. 45.75 (*0-685-67202-6*, Pub. by Cramer-Borntraeger GW) Lubrecht & Cramer.

Aktualisierende Konkordanz Zu Dittenbergers Orientis Graeci Inscriptiones Selectae (OGIS) vi, 316p. (GER.). 1977. write for info. (*3-487-06447-2*, Pub. by Georg Olms GW) Lubrecht & Cramer.

Aktuell und Interessant. 2nd ed. Griesbach. 224p. 1993. 17.50 (*3-468-49563-3*) Langenscheidt.

Aktuelle Aspekte der Hormonalen Kontrazeption. Ed. by P. J. Keller. (Illus.). 104p. (GER.). 1991. pap. 36.00 (*3-8055-5264-5*) S Karger.

Aktuelle Entwicklung und Standard der kuenstlichen Ernaehrung. Ed. by R. Doelp & D. Loehlein. (Beitraege zur Infusionstherapie und Klinische Ernaehrung Ser.: Vol. 16). (Illus.). viii, 156p. 1986. 46.50 (*3-8055-4353-0*) S Karger.

Aktuelle klinische Zytologie. Ed. by U. Bonk. (Beitraege zur Onkologie, Contributions to Oncology Ser.: Vol. 38). (Illus.). x, 350p. 1990. 63.25 (*3-8055-5230-0*) S Karger.

Aktuelle Probleme der Haematologie und Onkologie. Ed. by W. Wilmanns & R. Hartenstein. (Beitraege zur Onkologie, Contributions to Oncology Ser.: Vol. 13). (Illus.). xii, 388p. 1982. pap. 63.25 (*3-8055-3506-6*) S Karger.

Aktuelle Probleme der Paediatrischen Hepatologie. Ed. by R. Landolt. (Paediatrische Fortbildungskurse fuer die Praxis Ser.: Band 44). (Illus.). 1977. 76.00 (*3-8055-2662-8*) S Karger.

Aktuelle Themen: An Intermediate Reader for Expanding Skills & Perspectives. Renate A. Schulz et al. 269p. (C). 1987. pap. text ed. 22.75 (*0-03-063072-X*) HB Coll Pubs.

Aktueller Stand der Diagnostik und Therapie von Hodentumoren. Ed. by N. J. Jaeger & J. H. Hartlapp. (Beitraege zur Onkologie, Contributions to Oncology Ser.: Vol. 40). (Illus.). viii, 264p. 1990. 63.25 (*3-8055-5232-7*) S Karger.

Akushiyon de Gaku Shiuu Suru Nihongo. Bertha E. Segal. (JAP.). 1992. teacher ed 24.99 (*0-938395-29-7*) B Segal.

Akutagawa: An Introduction. Beongcheon Yu. LC 75-37579. 161p. reprint ed. pap. 45.90 (*0-7837-3651-7*, 2043522) Bks Demand.

Akutagawa & Dazai: Instances of Literary Adaptation. James O'Brien. LC 88-70040. (Arizona State University Center for Asian Studies Monograph Ser.: No. 21). 150p. 1988. pap. 10.00 (*0-939252-18-X*) ASU Ctr Asian.

Akute Pankreatitis - Transplantatpankreatitis. Ed. by U. T. Hopt et al. (Illus.). viii, 216p. 1994. 92.00 (*3-8055-5811-2*) S Karger.

AK47: The Complete Kalashnikov Family of Assault Rifles. Duncan Long. (Illus.). 192p. 1988. pap. 14.00 (*0-87364-477-8*) Paladin Pr.

***Al.** Hoddy Allen. (Orig.). 1995. pap. text ed. 4.95 (*1-56333-302-3*) Masquerade.

Al: Star in the Sky. Marvin G. Goldman. Ed. by John Wegg. LC 90-70242. (Illus.). 160p. 1990. 29.95 (*0-9626730-0-5*) World Transport.

Al-Andalus: The Islamic Arts of Spain. Jerrilyn D. Dodds. (Illus.). 464p. 1992. 60.00 (*0-8109-6413-9*, Abrams); pap. 29.95 (*0-87099-637-1*, Abrams) Metro Mus Art.

Al-Anon: A Message of Hope. Joseph L. Kellermann. 16p. (Orig.). 1976. pap. 1.30 (*0-89486-025-9*, 1135B) Hazelden.

Al-Anon: On Sex & Sobriety Series. Al-Anon Family Group Headquarters, Inc., Staff. 144p. 1993. Homeward Bound. pap. 2.50 (*0-910034-85-0*); Living with Sobriety: Another Beginning. pap. 2.50 (*0-910034-58-3*); Sexual Intimacy & the Alcoholic Relationship. pap. 2.50 (*0-910034-87-7*) Al-Anon.

Al-Anon: On Sex & Sobriety Series, Set. Al-Anon Family Group Headquarters, Inc., Staff. 144p. 1993. pap. 7.50 (*0-910034-88-5*) Al-Anon.

Al-Anon Faces Alcoholism. 2nd ed. Al-Anon Family Group Headquarters, Inc. Staff. LC 84-70190. 265p. 1984. 7.50 (*0-910034-55-9*) Al-Anon.

Al-Anon Family Groups. Al-Anon Family Group Headquarters, Inc. Staff. LC 84-7019. 177p. 1984. 6.50 (*0-910034-54-0*) Al-Anon.

Al-Anon's Twelve Steps & Twelve Traditions. Al-Anon Family Group Headquarters, Inc. Staff. LC 80-28087. 142p. 1981. 6.50 (*0-910034-24-9*) Al-Anon.

Al-Aqrabadhin al-Saghir: Dispensatorium Parvum. Sabur ibn Sahl. LC 93-47287. (Islamic Philosophy, Theology & Science, Studies & Texts Ser.: Vol. 16). (ARA & ENG.). 1994. 83.00 (*90-04-10004-0*) E J Brill.

***Al Arabiyya No. 2: AATA Monographs in Arabic Studies.** Ed. by Mahmoud Al-Batal. (C). Date not set. pap. text ed. 29.00 (*0-9621530-1-X*) AM Assn Teach.

Al-Arif: A Dictionary of Grammatical Terms, Arabic-English, English-Arabic. Pierre Cachia. 1974. 16.95 (*0-86685-119-4*) Intl Bk Ctr.

Al-Azhar: A Millennium of Muslim Learning. Bayard Dodge. (Illus.). 1974. 3.50 (*0-916808-11-4*) Mid East Inst.

Al-Azhar: A University Between Two Ages. Mohammed Misbah. (TWEC World Education Monographs). 1983. 2.50 (*0-685-09456-1*) I N Thut World Educ Ctr.

Al Azmah al Fikriyah al Mu'asirah: (The Contemporary Intellectual Crisis) Taha Jabir al Alwani. LC 89-7434. (Silsilat al Muhadarat Ser.: No. 1). (Illus.). 52p. (Orig.). (ARA.). 1989. pap. text ed. 3.00 (*0-912463-35-X*) IIIT VA.

Al Borde de la Cerca. Nicolas A. Felippe. (Biblioteca Cubana Contemporanea Ser.). 194p. (Orig.). (SPA.). 1987. pap. 9.95 (*84-359-0488-1*, Pub. by Editorial Playor SP) Ediciones.

Al Borde del Abismo. Pablo Rodriguez. LC 91-77144. 221p. (Orig.). (C). 1992. pap. text ed. 8.00 (*0-9622522-9-8*) Editorial Academica.

Al Capone: The Biography of a Self-Made Man. Fred Pasley. LC 78-150196. (Select Bibliographies Reprint Ser.). 1977. reprint ed. 30.95 (*0-8369-5709-1*) Ayer.

Al Capone - The Hawk - Prohibition. Leon H. Tashjian. 137p. 1989. 13.95 (*0-533-08095-9*) Vantage.

Al Capp Remembered. Elliott Caplin. LC 93-79503. (Illus.). 148p. (C). 1994. text ed. 21.95 (*0-87972-629-6*); pap. text ed. 10.95 (*0-87972-630-X*) Bowling Green Univ.

Al Capsella & the Watchdogs. J. Clarke. LC 90-26090. 160p. (YA). (gr. 6 up). 1991. 14.95 (*0-8050-1598-1*, Bks Young Read) H Holt & Co.

Al Colegio. Charles M. Schulz. (Peanuts Ser.). 64p. (J). 1971. 1.50 (*0-686-56186-4*); 4.95 (*0-8288-4506-9*) Fr & Eur.

Al Corriente: Curso Intermedio de Espanol. Martha Marks & Robert Blake. 1993. Realia kit. write for info. (*0-07-040472-0*) McGraw.

Al Corriente: Curso Intermedio de Espanol. 2nd ed. Martha Marks & Robert Blake. 1993. pap. text ed. write for info. (*0-07-040467-4*) McGraw.

Al Corriente: Curso Intermedio de Espanol. 2nd ed. Martha Marks & Robert Blake. 1993. Tapescript. write for info. (*0-07-040471-2*) McGraw.

Al Corriente: Curso Intermedio de Espanol. 2nd ed. Martha Marks & Robert Blake. 1993. Wkbk. & lab bk. student ed, pap. text ed. write for info. (*0-07-040469-0*) McGraw.

Al-Damurdashi's Chronicle of Egypt 1688-1755: Al-Durra al-Musana fi Akhbar al-Kinana. Daniel Crecelius & 'Abd Al-Wahhab Bakr. LC 91-10886. (Arab History & Civilization, Studies & Texts: Vol. 2). (Illus.). 424p. 1991. 125.75 (*90-04-09408-3*) E J Brill.

Al Dente: Italian Cooking Done Just Right. Tullia Barbanti. (Illus.). 209p. (Orig.). 1987. pap. text ed. 15.99 (*0-9620558-0-8*) T Barbanti.

Al Dia de los Negocios: Habla. Ella Gomez-Quintero & Maria Perez. 288p. (SPA.). (C). 1984. pap. text ed. write for info. (*0-07-554495-4*) McGraw.

Al Dia in los Negocios: Escribamos. Ela R. Gomez-Quintero & Maria E. Perez. 1984. pap. text ed. write for info. (*0-07-554494-6*) McGraw.

Al Encuentro de Nueva Vida (Finding New Life, Spanish Edition) 64p. 1987. pap. 1.99 (*0-89283-500-1*) Servant.

Al Fakhri. G. E. Whitting. 336p. (C). 1988. 200.00 (*0-685-21322-6*, Darf Pubs Ltd) St Mut.

Al Fakhri. G. E. Whitting. 336p. 1989. 60.00 (*1-85077-184-7*, Darf Pubs Ltd) St Mut.

Al-Fakhri: On the Systems of Government and the Moslem Dynasties. Ibn Al-Titaka. Tr. by C. E. Whitting. LC 80-2201. reprint ed. 35.00 (*0-404-18968-7*) AMS Pr.

***Al-Farabi & Aristotelian Syllogistics: Greek Theory & Islamic Practice.** Joep Lameer. 1994. 74.50 (*90-04-09884-4*) E J Brill.

Al-Farabi & His School. Ian R. Netton. LC 91-42233. (Arabic Thought & Culture Ser.). 208p. 1992. 62.50 (*0-415-03594-5*, A7566); pap. 16.95 (*0-415-03595-3*, A7570) Routledge.

Al-Farabi's Commentary & Short Treatise on Aristotle's De Interpretatione. Ed. by F. W. Zimmermann. (Classical & Medieval Logic Texts Ser.: No. III). 440p. 1988. pap. 52.00 (*0-19-726066-7*) OUP.

Al Fara'id: Gems from the Arabic Classical Dictionaries. Ibrahim As-Samarra'i. (ARA.). 1984. 17.95 (*0-86685-357-X*) Intl Bk Ctr.

Al-Faruq: Life of Umar the Great, Vol. 1. Allama Shibli Numani. 350p. 1985. 14.50 (*1-56744-213-7*) Kazi Pubns.

Al-Faruq: Life of Umar the Great, Vol. 2. Allama Shibli Numani. 360p. (C). 1985. 14.50 (*1-56744-214-5*) Kazi Pubns.

Al Filo de un Cansancio Apatrida: Poemas; On the Edge of a Countryless Weariness: Poems. Victoria Miranda & Camilo Fenini. Tr. by Daniel Fogel et al. LC 86-21022. 56p. (Orig.). (ENG & SPA.). 1986. Bilingual ed. pap. 5.00 (*0-910383-24-3*) Ism Pr.

Al filo del agua see Edge of the Storm

Al Filo del Poder: Subalternos y Dominantes en PR, 1739-1910. Fernando Pico. (Caribbean Collection). 1993. pap. 11.95 (*0-8477-0180-8*) U of PR Pr.

***Al Fin, Mujer.** 4th ed. Jacinto Benavente. 170p. 1981. pap. write for info. (*0-7859-5155-5*) Fr & Eur.

Al Final de las Palabras. David Cortes-Caben. Ed. by SLUSA Staff. 110p. (Orig.). (SPA.). 1984. pap. 4.50 (*0-9606758-9-2*) SLUSA.

***Al Frank's New Prudent Speculator: A Proven Method for Building Wealth in the Stock Market.** rev. ed. Al Frank. 300p. 1995. 24.95 (*1-55738-873-3*) Probus Pub Co.

***Al Fresco in Athens: The Owl Bay Guide to Georgia Bulldog Tailgating.** Lucy Littleton. 1994. pap. 8.95 (*0-9638568-6-3*) Owl Bay Pubs.

Al Fustat: Its Foundation & Early Urban Development. W. B. Kubiak. 1987. pap. 25.00 (*977-424-100-2*, Pub. by Am Univ Cairo Pr UA) Col U Pr.

Al Ghazali: On the Duties of Brotherhood. Tr. by Muhtar Holland. LC 76-8057. 96p. 1979. pap. 8.95 (*0-87951-083-8*) Overlook Pr.

Al-Ghazali & the Asharite School. Richard M. Frank. LC 93-40005. 136p. 1994. text ed. 29.95 (*0-8223-1427-4*) Duke.

Al-Ghazali on Islamic Guidance. Muhammad A. Quasem. 1979. 12.00 (*0-318-00409-7*) Quasem.

Al Ghazzali on Repentance. M. S. Stern. 1990. text ed. 22.50 (*81-207-1184-X*, Pub. by Sterling Pubs II) Apt Bks.

Al-Ghazzali's Alchemy of Happiness. C. Field. 4.50 (*0-935782-28-1*) Kazi Pubns.

Al Gore: United States Vice President. Betty M. Burford. LC 93-47475. (People to Know Ser.). (Illus.). 128p. (J). (gr. 6 up). 1994. lib. bdg. 17.95 (*0-89490-496-5*) Enslow Pubs.

Al Gore: Vice President. Rebecca Stefoff. (Gateway Biographies Ser.). (Illus.). 48p. (J). (gr. 2-4). 1994. lib. bdg. 13.90 (*1-56294-433-9*) Millbrook Pr.

Al Gore: Vice President of the United States. Bob Italia. LC 93-26099. (All the President's Men & Women Ser.). (J). (gr. 5 up). 1993. lib. bdg. 13.99 (*1-56239-253-0*) Abdo & Dghtrs.

Al Gore Jr. Born to Lead. Hank Hillin. Ed. by Willene Hall. (Illus.). 200p. (Orig.). 1988. pap. 8.95 (*0-9615022-1-5*) Pine Hall.

Al Gore Jr. His Life & Career. Hank Hillin. LC 92-30976. 1992. 16.95 (*1-55972-159-6*, Birch Ln Pr) Carol Pub Group.

Al Hadj: The Pilgrimage. David A. Wilson. 84p. (Orig.). 1981. pap. 5.00 (*0-934852-22-7*) Lorien Hse.

Al-Halal Wal-Haram Fil Islam see Lawful & the Prohibited in Islam

Al-Hallaj. Herbert W. Mason. (Curzon Sufi Ser.: No. 2). 228p. (C). 1995. pap. 18.50 (*0-7007-0311-X*, Pub. by Curzon Pr UK) Humanities.

Al Hasetumot Bamizmor: Commentary on the Book of Psalms. Aharon Pollack. Ed. by Osnath Nizri. 556p. (HEB.). 1991. text ed. 65.00 (*965-222-230-5*, Pub. by Nezer Pubng IS) Edit Orphee.

Al Held. Richard Armstrong. LC 91-52792. (Illus.). 128p. 1991. 24.95 (*0-8478-1413-0*) Rizzoli Intl.

Al Held. Irving Sandler. LC 84-10752. (Illus.). 192p. 1984. 75.00 (*0-933920-38-5*) Hudson Hills.

Al Held: After Paris 1953 to 1955. (Illus.). 64p. (Orig.). 1990. pap. 20.00 (*0-944680-05-4*) R Miller Gal.

Al Held: Paintings & Drawings, 1973 - 1978. (Illus.). 1978. pap. 2.50 (*0-910663-15-7*) ICA Inc.

Al Held: Paintings from the Years 1954-1959. Irving Sandler. (Illus.). 42p. 1982. pap. 10.00 (*0-944680-17-8*) R Miller Gal.

Al Held: Taxi Cabs Nineteen Fifty-Nine. Donald Kuspit. (Illus.). 1987. pap. 10.00 (*0-944680-19-4*) R Miller Gal.

Al Held 1959-1961. Irving Sandler. (Illus.). 38p. 1980. pap. 10.00 (*0-944680-18-6*) R Miller Gal.

Al-Hind - The Making of the Indo-Islamic World, Vol. 1: Early Medieval India & the Expansion of Islam 7th-11th Centuries. Andre Wink. (Illus.). viii, 396p. 1991. 94.50 (*90-04-09249-8*) E J Brill.

Al-Hizb al-Azam: A Collection of Prayers. Sunnah. Tr. by M. Abdul Hamid Siddiqi. 175p. (Orig.). 1985. pap. 3.50 (*1-56744-291-9*) Kazi Pubns.

Al Hold That Flight. Sarah Tyberg. 1992. 10.95 (*0-87306-591-3*); pap. 8.95 (*0-87306-592-1*) Feldheim.

Al 'Ilm wa al Iman - Science & Faith: Madkhal ila Nazariyat al Ma'rifah fi al Islam: (Introduction to the Theory of Knowledge in Islam) Ibrahim A. Umar. LC 91-48411. (Silsilat Abhath 'Ilmiyah Ser.: No. 5). (Illus.). 77p. (Orig.). (ARA.). 1992. pap. 5.00 (*0-685-70433-5*) IIIT VA.

Al-Islam: Unity & Leadership. Imam W. Mohammed. LC 91-61449. (Illus.). 176p. (Orig.). 1992. pap. 7.95 (*1-879698-00-5*) Sense Maker.

Al-Islam, Christianity, & Freemasonry. Mustafa El-Amin & Muhammad A. Nu'man. 214p. (Orig.). 1985. pap. 6.95 (*0-933821-05-0*) New Mind Prod.

Al Islam wa al Tanmiyah al Ijtima'iyah: (Islam & Social Development) 2nd ed. Muhsin Abd al Hamid. (Silsilat Qadaya al Fikr al Islami Ser.: No. 3). 153p. (ARA.). 1992. pap. 5.00 (*1-56564-049-7*) IIIT VA.

Al Jalala: A Calligraphic Celebration of "God" A. Ganima. 544p. (C). 1990. 120.00 (*0-685-74643-7*, Pub. by IMMEL Pubng UK) St Mut.

Al Jolson: A Bio-Bibliography. James Fisher. LC 93-37192. (Bio-Bibliographies in the Performing Arts Ser.: No. 48). 321p. 1994. text ed. 59.95 (*0-313-28620-5*, Greenwood Pr) Greenwood.

Al Jolson: A Bio-Discography. Larry F. Kiner & Philip R. Evans. (Illus.). 832p. 1992. 79.50 (*0-8108-2633-X*) Scarecrow.

Al-Jurjanis Theory of Poetic Imagery, Vol. I: Approaches to Arabic Literature. Deeb. 1990. pap. 32.50 (*0-85668-280-2*, Pub. by Aris & Phillips UK) David Brown.

Al-Kamil Arabic-French-English Dictionary: Al-Kamil Dictionnaire Arabe-Francais-Anglais. Moustafa Chouemi & C. H. Pellat. 64p. (ARA, ENG & FRE.). 1981. write for info. (*0-8288-4426-7*, M9286) Fr & Eur.

Al-Kashi's Geographical Table. E. S. Kennedy & M. H. Kennedy. LC 87-72865. (Transactions Ser.: Vol. 77, Pt. 7). 50p. 1988. pap. 12.00 (*0-87169-778-5*, T777-KEE) Am Philos.

Al Kashshaf al Iqtisadi li Ayat al Qur'an al Karim: Economic Index to the Verses of the Noble Qur'an. Muhi D. Atiyah. LC 91-28510. (Silsilat al Ma'ajim wa al Adillah wa al Kashshafat Ser.: No. 1). 598p. (Orig.). (ARA.). 1991. 25.00 (*0-912463-98-8*); pap. 15.00 (*0-912463-97-X*) IIIT VA.

Al Kashshaf al Mawdu'i li Ahadith Sahih al Bukhari: Subject Index to the Hadiths of Sahih al Bukhari. Muhi D. Atiyah. LC 91-31964. (Silsilat al Ma'jim wa al Adillah wa al Kashshafat: No. 2). 766p. (Orig.). (ARA.). 1992. 25.00 (*0-685-70434-3*); pap. 20.00 (*1-56564-100-0*) IIIT VA.

Al-Kasim B. Ibrahim on the Proof of God's Existence: Kitab al-Dalil al-Kabir. Ed. by Binyamin Abrahamov. (Islamic Philosophy, Theology & Science, Studies & Texts Ser.: Vol. V). xiii, 201p. 1989. 63.00 (*90-04-08985-3*) E J Brill.

Al-Kemi: A Memoir. Andre Vandenbroeck. 256p. 1989. 22.95 (*0-940262-30-4*); pap. 14.95 (*0-940262-31-2*) Lindisfarne Pr.

An Asterisk (*) at the beginning of an entry indicates that the title is appearing in BIP for the first time.

Al Khitab al 'Arabi al Mu'asir: Qira'ah Naqdiyah fi Mafahim al Nahdah wa al Taqaddum wa al Hadathah, 1978-1987 - The Contemporary Arab Discourse. Fadi Isma'il. LC 91-12591. (Silsilat al Rasa'il al Jami'iyah Ser.: No. 3). 181p. (Orig.). (ARA.). 1991. 15.00 (0-912463-85-6); pap. 7.95 (0-912463-86-4) IIIT VA.

Al-Khulafe al-Rashidoon. A. S. Hashim. (Islamic Books for Children: Bk. 6). (J). pap. 5.95 (0-935782-29-X) Kazi Pubns.

***Al-Kiama (The Life after)** Moustafa Moukarim. 100p. Date not set. pap. 7.95 (0-7610-0424-6) NW Pub.

Al-Kindi: The Philosopher of the Arabs. George M. Attiyah. 16.50 (0-935782-30-3) Kazi Pubns.

Al-Kindi's Metaphysics: A Translation of the Treatise on First Philosophy. Ya'Qub I. Al-Kindi. Tr. by Alfred L. Ivry. LC 70-171182. 207p. 1974. 59.50 (0-87395-092-5) State U NY Pr.

***Al-Kitab: A Textbook for Beginning Arabic.** Mahmoud Al-Batal et al. LC 95-6982. Orig. Title: Textbook for Beginning Arabic. 1995. pap. write for info. (0-87840-291-8) Georgetown U Pr.

Al-Majd. Daly. 1991. pap. 21.50 (0-86372-051-X, Pub. by Ithaca UK) Paul & Co Pubs.

Al-Manar: An English-Arabic Dictionary. Hasan Karmi. 1986. text ed. 18.95x (0-86685-071-6) Intl Bk Ctr.

Al-Maqasid: Imam Nawawi's Manual of Islam. Yahya ibn Sharaf Al-Nawawi. Ed. & Tr. by Nuh Ha Mim Keleer. LC 93-87727. xiii, 134p. (Orig.). 1994. pap. 9.95 (0-9638342-1-5) Sunna Bks.

Al Margen de la Vida: Poblacion y Pobreza en America Central. J. Mayone Stycos. LC 72-90916. Orig. Title: The Margin of Life. (Illus.). (SPA.). 1974. reprint ed. pap. text ed. 12.95 (0-89197-653-1) Irvington.

Al-Mawrid: Dictionary. M. Balbaki. 69.00 (0-935782-34-6) Kazi Pubns.

Al-Mawrid al-Muyassir (Dictionary) Munir Al-Balbaki. 22.50 (0-935782-31-1) Kazi Pubns.

Al-Mawrid Al-Qareb Pocket Size Dictionary. M. Balbaki. 8.50 (0-935782-32-X) Kazi Pubns.

Al-Mawrid Al-Sagher Pocket Size Dictionary. M. Balbaki. 1992. 6.50 (0-935782-33-8) Kazi Pubns.

Al Mufid: Learner's English-Arabic Dictionary. Khatib Nasr. 1983. 28.00 (0-86685-376-6) Intl Bk Ctr.

Al Mughni Al-Akbar English-Arabic Dictionary. Husan Karmi. 1800p. 1987. 69.95 (0-86685-420-7) Intl Bk Ctr.

Al-Mughni Al-Kabir: English - Arabic Dictionary. Hasan S. Karmi. 1991. 49.95 (0-86685-466-5) Intl Bk Ctr.

***Al-Mughtaribun: American Law & the Transformation of Muslim Life in the United States.** Kathleen M. Moore. (Middle Eastern Studies Ser.). 208p. (C). 1995. text ed. 49.50x (0-7914-2579-7); pap. text ed. 16.95x (0-7941-2580-8) State U NY Pr.

Al Muharraq: Architecture, Urbanism & Society in a Historic Arabian Town. John Yarwood. 230p. (C). 1991. 25.00 (1-85075-334-2, Pub. by Sheffield Acad UK) CUP Services.

Al Muslimun wa Kitabat al Tarikh: Dirasah fi al Ta'sil al Islami li 'Ilm al Tarikh - (The Muslims & the Writing of History) A. Rahman Khidr. LC 92-14770. (Silsilat al Manhajiyah al Islamiyah Ser.: No. 6). 319p. (Orig.). (ARA.). 1992. pap. 10.00 (1-56564-040-3) IIIT VA.

Al-Muwatta of Imam Malik Ibn Anas: The First Formulation of Islamic Law. Imam Malik Ibn Anas. Tr. by Aisha A. Bewley. 500p. 1989. 65.00 (0-7103-0361-0, A3920) Routledge Chapman & Hall.

Al Norte: Agricultural Workers in the Great Lakes Region, 1917-1970. Dennis N. Valdes. (Mexican American Monographs: No. 13). (Illus.). 315p. (Orig.). 1991. text ed. 35.00x (0-292-70413-5); pap. 16.95 (0-292-70420-8) U of Tex Pr.

Al Pacino: A Life on the Wire. Andrew Yule. 1992. pap. 5.50 (1-56171-161-6) Sure Sellers.

Al Packer: A Colorado Cannibal. Jo Mazzula. 3.50 (0-686-16037-1) F&J Mazzulla.

Al Partir. Omar Torres. LC 84-72305. 160p. (Orig.). (SPA.). 1985. pap. 8.50 (0-934770-47-6) Arte Publico.

Al Pasar el Tiempo (Seasons of a Marriage) Etapas Del Matrimonio. Norman Wright. (SPA.). 1992. 5.99 (1-56063-389-1, 498543) Editorial Unilit.

Al Phillip Bettle. Linda Bruce. (Illus.). (J). (gr. k-3). 1965. 8.95 (0-8392-3050-8) Astor-Honor.

Al Pie de la Gloria: The Starting Place of Glory. David M. McIntyre. (SPA.). 3.25 (84-7228-931-1, 220997, Pub. by Edit Clie SP) TSELF.

Al Purdy: An Annotated Bibliography. Marianne Micros. 277p. (C). 1980. pap. text ed. 9.00 (0-920763-61-8, Pub. by ECW Press CN) Genl Dist Srvs.

Al Purdy & His Works. Louis Mackendrick. 56p. (C). 1990. pap. text ed. 9.95 (1-55022-058-6, Pub. by ECW Press CN) Genl Dist Srvs.

Al-Qadim: Arabian Adventures. Jeff Grubb & A. Hayday. (Advanced Dungeons & Dragons, Second Edition; Al-Qadim Ser.). (Illus.). 1992. 18.00 (1-56076-358-2) TSR Inc.

Al Qoyawayma: Hopi Potter. Al Qoyawayma & Bruce Berger. Ed. by Alma S. King. (Illus.). 32p. (Orig.). 1984. pap. 5.00 (0-941430-07-3) Santa Fe E Gallery.

Al-Qur'an: A Contemporary Translation. Ahmed Ali. 576p. 1988. 75.00 (0-691-07329-5); pap. text ed. 16.95 (0-691-02046-9) Princeton U Pr.

Al-Quran: The Ultimate Miracle. Ahmed Deedat. 75p. (Orig.). 1989. pap. 3.50 (1-56744-368-0) Kazi Pubns.

Al Quran the Ultimate Miracle. Ahmed Deedat. 96p. 1970. pap. text ed. 4.95 (0-916157-75-X) African Islam Miss Pubns.

Al Qur'an wa al Nazar al 'Aqli: (The Qur'an & the Rational View) Fatimah I. Isma'il. LC 91-44548. (Silsilat al Rasa'il al Jami'iyah Ser.: No. 7). 351p. (Orig.). (ARA.). 1993. pap. 10.00 (1-56564-021-7) IIIT VA.

Al-Qur'anal-Karim, the Holy Qur'an, Pt. 30: Surah Al-Fatiha, Section 1 of Surah Bagarah, Ayatul Kursi, Surah Nas thru Surah Naba, with Modern English Translations, & Reading Guide, Prayer Modes & Qaidah. Muhammad S. Haque. LC 84-63148. (Illus.). viii, 80p. (Orig.). (ARA & ENG.). 1993. pap. text ed. 4.50 (0-933057-02-4) Namuk Intl Inc.

Al Rasa'El. Molana-al-Moazam Hazrat Shah & Maghsoud Sadegh-ibn-Mohammad Angha. 146p. (Orig.). 1986. pap. 19.50 (0-8191-5332-X) U Pr of Amer.

Al-Rasa'el. 22th ed. Shah Maghsoud Sadegh Angha. LC 86-5490. 200p. (ARA, ENG & PER.). 1987. text ed. 22.00 (0-910735-33-6) MTO Printing & Pubn Ctr.

Al-Rawd al-Mi'tar FiKhabar al-Aqtar. Ibn Al-Himyari. (ARA.). 1975. 40.00 (0-86685-358-8) Intl Bk Ctr.

Al Raychard's Fly Fishing in Maine: The Complete Guide to the Best Fly Fishing in Maine. rev. ed. Al Raychard. LC 80-12126. (Illus.). 184p. 1990. pap. 9.95 (0-945980-20-5) Nrth Country Pr.

Al Raychard's Guide to Remote Trout Ponds in Maine. Al Raychard. LC 88-22524. (Illus.). 211p. (Orig.). 1984. pap. 9.95 (0-945980-06-X) Nrth Country Pr.

Al Sabah History. Rush. 1991. 80.00 (0-86372-081-1, Pub. by Ithaca UK) Paul & Co Pubs.

Al-Saheefa Al-Sajjadiyyah. Zainul A. Imam. Tr. by Syed A. Ali. 366p. (C). 1984. pap. 8.00 (0-940368-41-2, 159) Tahrike Tarsile Quran.

Al-Salat. 3rd ed. Shah Maghsoud Sadegh Angha. 116p. (Orig.). (PER.). 1978. pap. 5.00 (0-318-37656-3) MTO Printing & Pubn Ctr.

Al-Salat in Quran. B. Ali. 270p. 1991. 45.00 (1-56744-375-3) Kazi Pubns.

Al-Seerat An-Nabwi - Life of Prophet Muhammad, the Final Messenger: With His Sermons & Treaties. M. Shamsul Haque. (Illus.). 160p. (Orig.). 1993. 11.95 (0-933057-09-1); pap. 8.95 (0-933057-10-5) Namuk Intl Inc.

Al-Shafi'i's Risala: Treatise on the Foundations of Islamic Jurisprudence. Tr. by Majid Khadduri. 379p. 1995. 19.95 (0-946621-15-2, Pub. by Islamic Texts UK) Atrium Pubs.

***Al Sieber: Chief of Scouts.** Dan L. Thrapp. LC 95-8305. 1995. write for info. (0-8061-2770-8) U of Okla Pr.

Al, Simulation & Planning in High Autonomy Systems, 4th Conference. LC 93-77040. 344p. 1993. pap. text ed. 70.00 (0-8186-4020-0, 4020) IEEE Comp Soc.

Al Smith & His America. Oscar Handlin. 224p. 1987. reprint ed. pap. text ed. 12.95 (1-55553-021-4) NE U Pr.

Al Son del Tipley et Guiro . . . Manuel Cachan. LC 86-83336. (Caniqui Ser.). 59p. (Orig.). 1987. pap. 6.00 (0-89729-423-8) Ediciones.

***Al Stevens Teaches C: An Interactive Tutorial.** Al Stevens. LC 94-31623. 294p. 1994. pap. 24.95 (1-55828-387-0) MIS Press.

AL Study Guide for RE Fundamentals. 6th ed. Wade E. Gaddy, Jr. 1994. pap. 12.95 (0-7931-1039-4, 151305-06) Dearborn Finan.

Al-Tabari, the Early Abbasi Empire, Vol. 1. Tr. by John A. Williams. (Illus.). 266p. 1988. 69.95 (0-521-32662-1) Cambridge U Pr.

Al-Tabari, the Early Abbasi Empire, Vol. 2. Tr. by John A. Williams. (Illus.). 343p. 1989. 69.95 (0-521-35001-8) Cambridge U Pr.

Al Tafakhur min al Mushahadah ila al Shuhud: Dirasah Nafsiyah Islamiyah - (Contemplation, from Witnessing to Testifying: An Islamic Psychological Perspective) 3rd rev. ed. Malik Badri. LC 91-38924. (Silsilat Abhath 'Ilmiyah Ser.: No. 3). (ARA.). 1993. pap. text ed. 5.00 (1-56564-007-1) IIIT VA.

***Al-Tajweed Al-Muyassar - Easy Tajweed: Rules for Reciting Qur'aan Correctly & Beautifully.** Muhammad S. Haque. LC 95-68801. (Illus.). 128p. (Orig.). 1995. per., pap. 9.95 (0-933057-11-3) Namuk Intl Inc.

Al Tanto. 2nd ed. Gene Kupferschmid. (C). 1991. write for info. (0-395-54004-6) HM Soft Schl Col Div.

Al-Tawahhujwal-Uful. Rose Ghurayyib. 290p. (Orig.). (ARA.). 1978. 14.00 (0-89410-151-X) Three Continents.

Al Usus al Islamiyah lil 'Ilm: (The Islamic Foundations of Science) Moinuddin Siddiqi. (Silsilat Rasa'il Islamiyat al Ma'rifah: No. 3). (Illus.). 65p. (ARA.). 1989. pap. 2.00 (1-56564-162-0) IIIT VA.

Al Wajiz fi Islamiyat al Ma'rifah (Synopsis of Islamization of Knowledge) (Silsilat Islamiyat al Ma'rifah Ser.: No. 3). 132p. (Orig.). (ARA.). 1987. pap. text ed. 3.00 (1-56564-148-5) IIIT VA.

ALA Filing Rules. American Library Association Resources & Technical Services Division Filing Committee. LC 80-22186. 59p. 1980. pap. 14.00 (0-8389-3255-X) ALA.

***ALA Fingertip Guide to National Health-Information Resources.** Beatrice Kovacs. LC 94-38095. 150p. (Orig.). 1994. pap. text ed. 12.00x (0-8389-0645-1) ALA.

ALA Glossary of Library & Information Science. Ed. by Heartsill Young & Terry Belanger. LC 82-18512. 261p. reprint ed. pap. 74.40 (0-7837-6156-2, 2045878) Bks Demand.

ALA Guide to Information Access: A Complete Research Handbook & Directory. Sandy Whiteley. 1994. pap. 19.00 (0-679-75075-4) Random.

ALA Rules for Filing Catalog Cards. abr. ed. Ed. by Pauline A. Seely. LC 68-21019. 272p. 1968. pap. 14.00 (0-8389-0001-1) ALA.

Ala Story Collection of International Modern Art. rev. ed. Santa Barbara Museum of Art Staff. LC 84-27552. (Illus.). 88p. (Orig.). 1984. reprint ed. pap. 12.00 (0-89951-056-6) Santa Barb Mus Art.

ALA Survey of Librarian Salaries, 1991. Mary J. Lynch et al. 63p. reprint ed. pap. 25.00 (0-7837-5913-4, 2045712) Bks Demand.

ALA Survey of Librarian Salaries, 1994. Mary Jo Lynch et al. 57p. 1994. pap. text ed. 45.00 (0-8389-7719-7) ALA.

ALA Target Packet for Preservation Microfilming. Debra McKern & Sherry Byrne. LC 91-8677. (Illus.). (C). 1991. pap. text ed. 32.00 (0-8389-7492-9) ALA.

ALA World Encyclopedia of Library & Information Services. 2nd ed. Ed. by Robert Wedgeworth. LC 86-10894. (Illus.). 921p. reprint ed. pap. 180.00 (0-7837-5909-6, 2045707) Bks Demand.

ALA Worldwide Directory & Fact Book 1985-86. 3rd rev. ed. Ed. by Alan Goldstein. (Illus.). 250p. 1985. pap. 50.00 (0-915959-00-3) Am Logistics Assn.

ALA Yearbook 1976: Centennial Edition. Ed. by Robert Wedgeworth. Incl. ALA Yearbook 1977: A Review of Library Events 1976. LC 76-647548. 474p. 1977. 60.00 (0-8389-0233-2, 76-647548); ALA Yearbook 1978: A Review of Library Events 1977. LC 76-647548. 480p. 1978. 60.00 (0-8389-0261-8, 76-647548); ALA Yearbook 1979: A Review of Library Events 1978. LC 76-647548. 432p. 1979. 60.00 (0-8389-0292-8, 76-647548); ALA Yearbook 1980: A Review of Library Events 1979. LC 76-647548. 432p. 1980. 60.00 (0-8389-0306-1, 76-647548); Vol. 6. ALA Yearbook 1981: A Review of Library Events 1980. LC 76-647548. 390p. 1981. 60.00 (0-8389-0335-5, 76-647548); Vol. 7. ALA Yearbook 1982: A Review of Library Events 1981. LC 76-647548. 390p. 1982. pap. text ed. 25.00 (0-8389-0378-9, 76-647548); ALA Yearbook 1983: A Review of Library Events 1982. LC 76-647548. 380p. 1983. 65.00 (0-8389-0369-X, 76-647548); LC 76-647548. 510p. 1976. 65.00 (0-8389-0223-5) ALA.

ALA Yearbook 1977: A Review of Library Events 1976 see ALA Yearbook 1976: Centennial Edition

ALA Yearbook 1978: A Review of Library Events 1977 see ALA Yearbook 1976: Centennial Edition

ALA Yearbook 1979: A Review of Library Events 1978 see ALA Yearbook 1976: Centennial Edition

ALA Yearbook 1980: A Review of Library Events 1979 see ALA Yearbook 1976: Centennial Edition

ALA Yearbook 1981: A Review of Library Events 1980 see ALA Yearbook 1976: Centennial Edition

ALA Yearbook 1982: A Review of Library Events 1981 see ALA Yearbook 1976: Centennial Edition

ALA Yearbook 1983: A Review of Library Events 1982 see ALA Yearbook 1976: Centennial Edition

Alaawich. Lucy Arvidson. 1978. 3.00 (0-939046-01-6) Malki Mus Pr.

Alabama. Dottie Brown. LC 93-37796. (Hello U. S. A. Ser.). (Illus.). (J). (gr. 3-6). 1994. lib. bdg. 17.50 (0-8225-2741-3, Lerner Publctns) Lerner Group.

Alabama. Dennis B. Fradin. LC 92-37047. (From Sea to Shining Sea Ser.). (Illus.). 64p. (J). (gr. 3-5). 1993. lib. bdg. 16.50 (0-516-03801-X) Childrens.

Alabama. Sylvia McNair. LC 88-11744. (America the Beautiful Ser.). (Illus.). 144p. (J). (gr. 4 up). 1988. lib. bdg. 20.55 (0-516-00447-6) Childrens.

Alabama. Kathleen Thompson. LC 87-26486. (Portrait of America Library). 48p. (J). (gr. 3 up). 1988. 21.36 (0-8174-4613-3) Raintree Steck-V.

Alabama. braille ed. Sylvia McNair. 178p. (J). 1993. vinyl bd. 15.40 (1-56956-159-1, BR9022) W A T Braille.

***Alabama.** 2nd ed. Gay N. Martin. LC 95-17675. (Off the Beaten Path Ser.). (Illus.). 160p. 1995. pap. 10.95 (1-56440-731-4) Globe Pequot.

Alabama. Joseph Wheeler. Ed. by Clement A. Evans. (Confederate Military History Extended Edition Ser.: Vol. VIII). (Illus.). 863p. 1988. reprint ed. 50.00 (1-56837-027-X) Broadfoot.

Alabama: A Guide to the Deep South. Federal Writers' Project Staff & Writers Program-WPA Staff. (American Guide Ser.). 1989. reprint ed. lib. bdg. 69.00 (0-7812-1001-1) Rprt Serv.

Alabama: A Guide to the Deep South. Federal Writers' Project Staff. (American Guidebook Ser.). 1941. reprint ed. 79.00 (0-403-02153-7) Somerset Pub.

Alabama: A History. Virginia Van der Veer Hamilton. (States & the Nation Ser.). (Illus.). 1984. pap. 11.00 (0-393-30172-9) Norton.

Alabama: A Picture Book to Remember Her By. (Illus.). 1991. 6.99 (0-517-62358-7) Random Hse Value.

Alabama: Cheap Seats. (Illus.). 52p. (Orig.). 1993. pap. 16.95 (0-89724-037-5) Warner Brothers.

Alabama: Documentary History to 1900. Lucille Griffith. LC 73-169499. 688p. 1987. pap. 29.95 (0-8173-5221-X) U of Ala Pr.

***Alabama: Documentary History to 1900.** Ed. by Lucille Griffith. LC 73-169499. 688p. 1987. pap. 29.95 (0-8173-0371-5) U of Ala Pr.

Alabama: Mine, Mill & Microchip. Wayne Flint. LC 87-9192. 368p. 1987. 29.95 (0-89781-215-8) Preferred Mktg.

Alabama: One Big Front Porch. Kathryn T. Windham. 168p. 1991. pap. 14.95 (0-8173-0562-9) U of Ala Pr.

Alabama: The History of a Deep South State. William W. Rogers et al. LC 93-27240. (Illus.). 768p. 1994. 49.95 (0-8173-0712-5); pap. 29.95 (0-8173-0714-1) U of Ala Pr.

Alabama - Collected Works of Federal Writers Project. Federal Writers Project Staff. 1991. reprint ed. lib. bdg. 98.00 (0-7812-5500-7) Rprt Serv.

Alabama - Northwest Florida Golf. Michelle Segrest. 208p. (Orig.). 1994. pap. 11.95 (1-878561-23-5) Seacoast AL.

Alabama Affair: The British Shipyards Conspiracy in the American Civil War. David Hollett. 180p. (Orig.). 1993. pap. 27.50 (1-85058-385-4, Pub. by Sigma Press UK) Coronet Bks.

Alabama, an Index to the U. S. Census, 1830. Pauline J. Gandrud & Bobbie J. McLane. 382p. (Orig.). 1973. pap. 30.00 (0-929604-25-3) Arkansas Ancestors.

Alabama & Other State Greats (Biographies) Carole Marsh. (Carole Marsh Alabama Bks.). (Illus.). (YA). (gr. 3-12). 1994. lib. bdg. 24.95 (1-55609-469-8); pap. 14.95 (1-55609-468-X); disk 29.95 (0-7933-1338-4) Gallopade Pub Group.

***Alabama & the Borderlands: From Prehistory to Statehood.** fac. ed. Ed. by R. Reid Badger & Lawrence A. Clayton. LC 83-17957. (Illus.). 266p. 1985. pap. 75.90 (0-7837-8362-0, 2059171) Bks Demand.

Alabama Angels. Mary Barwick. (Illus.). 64p. 1993. 15.00 (0-345-38574-8, Ballantine Trade) Ballantine.

Alabama Angels. 3rd ed. Mary Barwick. (Illus.). 28p. (J). (gr. 1-6). 1989. pap. 8.95 (0-9622815-1-4) Black Belt Pr.

Alabama Angels in Anywhere, L. A. (Lower Alabama) Mary Barwick. (Illus.). 32p. (Orig.). (J). 1991. pap. 8.95 (0-9622815-6-5) Black Belt Pr.

Alabama Appellate Court Automation Requirements Analysis. Doug Walker et al. 139p. 1989. 8.00 (0-685-34849-0, SERO-051) Natl Ctr St Courts.

Alabama Arbitration. Thomas W. Balch. LC 74-95063. (Select Bibliographies Reprint Ser.). 1977. 21.95 (0-8369-5065-8) Ayer.

Alabama-Auburn Jokes. Sally Walton & Faye Wilkinson. (Illus.). 72p. (Orig.). 1981. pap. 4.95 (0-937552-07-0) Quail Ridge.

Alabama Automotive Directory. Ed. by T. L. Spelman. 1985. 24.95 (1-55527-000-X) Auto Contact Inc.

Alabama Bandits, Bushwackers, Outlaws, Crooks, Devils, Ghosts, Desperadoes & Other Assorted & Sundry Characters! Carole Marsh. (Carole Marsh Alabama Bks.). (Illus.). (YA). (gr. 3-12). 1994. lib. bdg. 24.95 (0-7933-0041-X); pap. 14.95 (0-7933-0040-1); disk 29.95 (0-7933-0042-8) Gallopade Pub Group.

Alabama Biking Guide. Barb McCaig. Ed. by Chris Boyce. (Illus.). 80p. (Orig.). 1989. pap. text ed. 5.95 (0-935201-81-5) Affordable Adven.

Alabama Bookstore Book: A Surprising Guide to Our State's Bookstores & Their Specialties for Students, Teachers, Writers & Publishers. Carole Marsh. (Carole Marsh Alabama Bks.). (Illus.). 1994. lib. bdg. 24.95 (0-7933-2855-1); pap. 14.95 (0-7933-2856-X); disk 29.95 (0-7933-2857-8) Gallopade Pub Group.

Alabama Bound. Melissa Hurt. 1988. 9.95 (0-932298-67-2) Tri-State Pr Corp.

***Alabama Bound: Contemporary Stories of a State.** Ed. by James E. Colquitt. LC 95-76058. 224p. 1994. text ed. 24.95 (0-942979-25-7) Livingston U Pr.

***Alabama Bound: Contemporary Stories of a State.** Ed. by James E. Colquitt. LC 95-76058. 224p. (C). 1994. pap. 14.50 (0-942979-26-5) Livingston U Pr.

***Alabama Business Directory, 1995-96.** rev. ed. 1995. 250.00 (1-56105-759-2) Am Busn Direct.

Alabama Canoe Rides & Float Trips. John Foshee. LC 86-19192. 264p. 1986. pap. 14.95 (0-8173-0334-0) U of Ala Pr.

Alabama Catalog Historic American Buildings Survey: A Guide to the Early Architecture of the State. Robert S. Gamble. LC 82-20288. (Illus.). 472p. 1986. 55.00 (0-8173-0148-8) U of Ala Pr.

Alabama Census Index 1850 Mortality Schedules. (Illus.). 1984. lib. bdg. 48.00 (0-89593-078-1) Accelerated Index.

Alabama Census Index, 1850 Slave Schedule. (Illus.). 1988. lib. bdg. 66.00 (0-89593-084-6) Accelerated Index.

Alabama Census Index 1860 Mortality Schedules. (Illus.). 1987. lib. bdg. 68.00 (0-89593-091-9) Accelerated Index.

Alabama Census Index 1860 Slave Schedule. (Illus.). 1990. lib. bdg. 86.00 (0-89593-121-4) Accelerated Index.

Alabama Census Index, 1880. (Illus.). lib. bdg. write for info. (0-89593-164-8) Accelerated Index.

Alabama Census Tax Lists Index, 1811-1819. Ronald V. Jackson. (Illus.). 1983. lib. bdg. 49.00 (0-89593-701-8) Accelerated Index.

Alabama Census Tax Lists Index, 1820-1829. Ronald V. Jackson. (Illus.). 1983. lib. bdg. 51.00 (0-89593-703-4) Accelerated Index.

Alabama Census Tax Lists Index, 1831-1839. Ronald V. Jackson. (Illus.). 1983. lib. bdg. 53.00 (0-89593-704-2) Accelerated Index.

Alabama Civil Practice Forms, 2 vols., Set. 2nd suppl. ed. Allen W. Howell. 1100p. 1994. 140.00 (0-87473-993-4) Michie Butterworth.

Alabama Civil Procedure. suppl. ed. Jerome A. Hoffman & Sandra C. Guin. 1051p. 1993. pap. 85.00 (0-87473-712-5) Michie Butterworth.

Alabama Classic Christmas Trivia: Stories, Recipes, Activities, Legends, Lore & More! Carole Marsh. (Carole Marsh Alabama Bks.). (Illus.). (YA). (gr. 3-12). 1994. lib. bdg. 24.95 (0-7933-0044-4); pap. 14.95 (0-7933-0043-6); disk 29.95 (0-7933-0045-2) Gallopade Pub Group.

Alabama Coastales! Carole Marsh. (Carole Marsh Alabama Bks.). (J). 1994. lib. bdg. 24.95 (0-7933-6938-X) Gallopade Pub Group.

Alabama Coastales! Carole Marsh. (Carole Marsh Alabama Bks.). (Illus.). (YA). (gr. 3-12). 1994. lib. bdg. 24.95 (1-55609-465-5); pap. 14.95 (1-55609-120-6); disk 29.95 (0-7933-1334-1) Gallopade Pub Group.

Alabama Confederate Reader. Ed. by Malcolm C. McMillan. LC 92-8817. (Library of Alabama Classics). 512p. (C). 1992. reprint ed. pap. 24.95 (0-8173-0595-5) U of Ala Pr.

Alabama Crime Perspective, 1994. Ed. by Kathleen O. Morgan et al. 24p. 1994. 18.00 (1-56692-250-X) Morgan Quitno Corp.

***Alabama Crime Perspective, 1995.** Ed. by Kathleen O. Morgan et al. 24p. 1995. 18.00 (1-56692-350-6) Morgan Quitno Corp.

Alabama Criminal Code. Michie Company Staff. 1991. pap. 29.00 (0-87473-529-7) Michie Butterworth.

***Alabama Criminal Code: 1993 Edition.** annot. ed. Date not set. 30.00 (0-614-05772-8) Michie Butterworth.

A

An Asterisk (*) at the beginning of an entry indicates that the title is appearing in BIP for the first time.

165

A

Alabama "Crinkum-Crankum" A Funny Word Book about Our State. Carole Marsh. (Carole Marsh Alabama Bks.). (Illus.). (J). 1994. lib. bdg. 24.95 (*0-7933-4810-2*); pap. 14.95 (*0-7933-4811-0*); disk 29.95 (*0-7933-4812-9*) Gallopade Pub Group.

Alabama Dingbats! Bk. 1: A Fun Book of Games, Stories, Activities & More about Our State That's All in Code! for You to Decipher. Carole Marsh. (Carole Marsh Alabama Bks.). (Illus.). (J). (gr. 3-12). 1994. lib. bdg. 24.95 (*0-7933-3773-9*); pap. 14.95 (*0-7933-3774-7*); disk 29.95 (*0-7933-3775-5*) Gallopade Pub Group.

Alabama Early Census, Vol. 1. Ronald V. Jackson. (Illus.). 1981. lib. bdg. 38.00 (*0-89593-865-0*) Accelerated Index.

Alabama Early Census, Vol. 2. Ronald V. Jackson. (Illus.). lib. bdg. 38.00 (*0-89593-718-2*) Accelerated Index.

Alabama Economic Outlook, 1990, No. 10. William D. Gunther et al. (Illus.). 1990. pap. 10.00 (*0-943394-05-8*) U of Ala Ctr Bus.

Alabama Economy: Critical Issues for the 1990s. (Illus.). 1990. pap. 15.00 (*0-943394-07-4*) U of Ala Ctr Bus.

Alabama Eighteen Forty Census Index: Vol. 1, The Counties Formed from the Creek & Cherokee Sessions of the 1830s. Betty Drake. 93p. 1983. reprint ed. 15.00 (*0-89308-331-3*) Southern Hist Pr.

Alabama Energy & Environmental Agencies. University of Alabama, Law Center Staff. ii, 97p. write for info. (*0-318-61629-7*) U AL Law.

Alabama Environmental Law Handbook. 2nd ed. Maynard et al. (State Environmental Law Ser.). 120p. 1992. pap. 69.00 (*0-86587-320-8*) Gov Insts.

Alabama Fan's Guidebook to Understanding Auburn Mentality. Eula M. Smitten. (Illus.). 104p. (Orig.). 1991. pap. 4.95 (*0-9630297-0-3*) Sassafras Creek.

Alabama Federal Census Index, 1810. Ronald V. Jackson. (Illus.). 1987. lib. bdg. 38.00 (*0-89593-700-X*) Accelerated Index.

Alabama Federal Census Index, 1820. Ronald V. Jackson. (Illus.). 1981. lib. bdg. 54.00 (*0-89593-702-6*) Accelerated Index.

Alabama Federal Census Index, 1830. Ronald V. Jackson. LC 77-85644. (Illus.). 1976. lib. bdg. 50.00 (*0-89593-000-5*) Accelerated Index.

Alabama Federal Census Index, 1840. Ronald V. Jackson. LC 77-85789. 1982. lib. bdg. 53.00 (*0-89593-001-3*) Accelerated Index.

Alabama Federal Census Index, 1850. Ronald V. Jackson. LC 77-85798. (Illus.). 1981. lib. bdg. 78.00 (*0-89593-002-1*) Accelerated Index.

Alabama Federal Census Index, 1860. (Illus.). 1989. lib. bdg. 150.00 (*0-89593-090-0*) Accelerated Index.

Alabama Federal Census Index, 1870. (Illus.). 1986. lib. bdg. 350.00 (*0-89593-163-X*) Accelerated Index.

Alabama Festival Fun for Kids! Carole Marsh. (Carole Marsh Alabama Bks.). (Illus.). (YA). (gr. 3-12). 1994. lib. bdg. 24.95 (*0-7933-3926-X*); pap. 14.95 (*0-7933-3927-8*); disk 29.95 (*0-7933-3928-6*) Gallopade Pub Group.

Alabama Folk Lyric: A Study in Origins & Media of Dissemination. Ed. by Ray B. Browne. LC 78-61076. 1979. 26.00 (*0-87972-129-4*) Bowling Green Univ.

Alabama Football Trivia. Wayne Hester. (Illus.). 80p. (Orig.). 1992. pap. 6.00 (*1-878561-10-3*) Seacoast AL.

*__Alabama Gang.__ Clyde Bolton. 1994. pap. 9.95 (*0-9635413-3-1*) Birm News.

Alabama Gardener's Almanac. Barbara Pleasant. 64p. 1992. pap. 5.95 (*0-9633210-0-5*) Southern Ground.

Alabama Government & Politics. James D. Thomas & William H. Stewart. LC 87-16242. (Politics & Governments of the American States Ser.). xxvi, 230p. 1988. 30.00 (*0-8032-4182-8*); pap. 15.00 (*0-8032-9181-7*) U of Nebr Pr.

Alabama Government's Performance Standards, 1990. Ed. by Greg Michels. (Governments Performance Standards Ser.). (Illus.). 150p. 1990. text ed. 125.00 (*1-55507-474-X*) Municipal Analysis.

Alabama Health Care Perspective, 1994. Ed. by Kathleen O. Morgan et al. 24p. 1994. 18.00 (*1-56692-150-3*) Morgan Quitno Corp.

*__Alabama Health Care Perspective 1995.__ Ed. by Kathleen O. Morgan et al. 24p. 1995. 18.00 (*1-56692-400-6*) Morgan Quitno Corp.

Alabama Herb Gardener. Nadine Johnson. (Illus.). 128p. (Orig.). 1993. pap. 9.95 (*1-882616-01-4*) Advertiser.

Alabama Heritage Cookbook. Susan D. Rush & Katherine C. Durham. LC 83-82791. (Illus.). 164p. 1984. 19.95 (*0-9612868-1-4*); spiral bd. 12.95 (*0-9612868-0-6*) Heritage Pubns.

Alabama Historical & Biographical Index, Vol. 1. Ronald V. Jackson. LC 78-53685. (Illus.). 1984. lib. bdg. 30.00 (*0-89593-170-2*) Accelerated Index.

Alabama Hot Air Balloon Mystery. Carole Marsh. (Carole Marsh Alabama Bks.). (Illus.). (J). (gr. 2-9). 1994. 24.95 (*0-7933-2318-5*); pap. 14.95 (*0-7933-2319-3*); disk 29.95 (*0-7933-2320-7*) Gallopade Pub Group.

*__Alabama Impact: Contemporary Artists with Alabama Ties.__ Mobile Museum of Art Staff & Huntsville Museum of Art Staff. (Illus.). 84p. (Orig.). (YA). 1995. pap. text ed. 20.00 (*1-885820-01-1*) Huntsville.

Alabama in Perspective, 1994. Ed. by Kathleen O. Morgan et al. 26p. 1994. pap. 18.00 (*1-56692-200-3*) Morgan Quitno Corp.

*__Alabama in Perspective 1995.__ Ed. by Kathleen O. Morgan et al. 26p. 1995. pap. 18.00 (*1-56692-450-2*) Morgan Quitno Corp.

Alabama in the Fifties: A Social Study. Minnie C. Boyd. LC 31-33199. (Columbia University. Studies in the Social Sciences: No. 353). reprint ed. 21.00 (*0-404-51353-0*) AMS Pr.

Alabama in the 1830's. Ed. by Walter B. Posey. (Illus.). 5.95 (*0-317-68073-0*) Southern U Pr.

Alabama Jeopardy! Answers & Questions about Our State! Carole Marsh. (Carole Marsh Alabama Bks.). (Illus.). (J). (gr. 3-12). 1994. lib. bdg. 24.95 (*0-7933-4079-9*); pap. 14.95 (*0-7933-4080-2*); disk 29.95 (*0-7933-4081-0*) Gallopade Pub Group.

Alabama "Jography" A Fun Run Thru Our State! Carole Marsh. (Carole Marsh Alabama Bks.). (Illus.). (YA). (gr. 3-12). 1994. lib. bdg. 24.95 (*1-55609-461-2*); pap. 14.95 (*1-55609-092-7*); disk 29.95 (*0-7933-1327-9*) Gallopade Pub Group.

Alabama Judicial Article: Judicial Administration of Trial Courts, Rule-Making Power, Jury & Grand Jury, Entry & Withdrawal of Municipal Courts; Technical Assistance Report. National Center for State Courts Staff. 1974. 1.50 (*0-685-15015-1*, MAB-005) Natl Ctr St Courts.

Alabama Judicial Facility Plan: Case Processing, Records Management, & Technology Assessment. 52p. 1986. 3.00 (*0-685-18267-3*, SERO-019) Natl Ctr St Courts.

Alabama Kid's Cookbook: Recipes, How-to, History, Lore & More! Carole Marsh. (Carole Marsh Alabama Bks.). (Illus.). (YA). (gr. 3-12). 1994. lib. bdg. 24.95 (*0-7933-0082-7*); pap. 14.95 (*0-7933-0081-9*); disk 29.95 (*0-7933-0083-5*) Gallopade Pub Group.

*__Alabama Land Surveying Law: Questions & Answers.__ John E. Keen. 49p. (C). 1995. pap. text ed. 20.00 (*1-56569-014-1*) Land Survey.

Alabama Law: Land Surveying & Boundaries Statutes & Case Law. Comp. & Intro. by Donald A. Wilson. 876p. (C). 1990. text ed. 125.00 (*0-685-48818-7*) Coffeetable.

*__Alabama Law of Evidence.__ suppl. ed. Joseph A. Colquitt. 813p. 1994. 85.00 (*0-87473-645-5*) Michie Butterworth.

Alabama Legislation. Alabama Law Institute Staff et al. 1985. write for info. (*0-318-60678-X*) AL Law Inst.

Alabama Library Book: A Surprising Guide to the Unusual Special Collections in Libraries Across Our State for Students, Teachers, Writers & Publishers - Includes Reproducible Mailing Labels Plus Activities for Young People! Carole Marsh. (Carole Marsh Alabama Bks.). (Illus.). 1994. lib. bdg. 24.95 (*0-7933-3008-4*); pap. 14.95 (*0-7933-3009-2*); disk 29.95 (*0-7933-3010-6*) Gallopade Pub Group.

Alabama Life & Health Course. James J. Smith. Date not set. 24.00 (*1-56461-089-6*, 26262) Rough Notes.

Alabama Life Course. James J. Smith. Date not set. 32.00 (*1-56461-090-X*, 26293) Rough Notes.

*__Alabama Love Scene.__ Pat Deshane. Date not set. pap. 9.95 (*0-89716-457-1*) Peanut Butter.

Alabama Manufacturers' Register, 1991. 288p. 1991. 75.00 (*0-317-03049-3*) Manufacturers.

Alabama Marriages, Early to Eighteen Twenty-Five. Liahona Research, Inc. Staff. Ed. by Jordan Dodd. 158p. 1991. lib. bdg. 35.00 (*1-877677-36-1*) Precision Indexing.

Alabama Media Book: A Surprising Guide to the Amazing Print, Broadcast & Online Media of Our State for Students, Teachers, Writers & Publishers - Includes Reproducible Mailing Labels Plus Activities for Young People! Carole Marsh. (Carole Marsh Alabama Bks.). (Illus.). 1994. lib. bdg. 24.95 (*0-7933-3161-7*); pap. 14.95 (*0-7933-3162-5*); disk 29.95 (*0-7933-3163-3*) Gallopade Pub Group.

Alabama Memories. Chip Cooper. (Illus.). 192p. 1995. 25.00 (*0-317-06157-7*) Alabama Mem.
ALABAMA MEMORIES is a rich & varied collection of the extraordinary beauties of Alabama with photos by Chip Cooper & essays by Maridith Walker. Chip Cooper crisscrossed the state countless times, stopping in unlikely & unexpected places. In ALABAMA MEMORIES he shows us an Alabama most of us have forgotten how to see. In this book he reminds us again & again that attention must be paid to the landscapes & artifacts of a passing way of life - not for their sake as much as for our own. From fading porches to stately mansions, from pecan orchards to a formal garden, from abandoned warehouses to a solitary cotton buggy, he has captured in ALABAMA MEMORIES the rich texture of a commonly held visual past. He trains us to see in a new way, to understand that there is much more to Alabama than Deep South stereotypes. The common signs of a commonly held past - unprententious as the land itself - find their way into image after image that Cooper shoots. The results is a book that is stunning for both its immediate visual impact & for the memories, recollections & shared histories it will suggest. ***Publisher Provided Annotation.***

---

*__Alabama Miracles: Real Life Stories to Warm the Heart & Lift the Spirit.__ Lynn G. Fuliman. 128p. 1994. pap. 7.95 (*1-878561-24-3*) Seacoast AL.

Alabama Motor Vehicle Laws. Michie Company Staff. 1991. 25.00 (*0-87473-521-1*) Michie Butterworth.

*__Alabama Motor Vehicle Laws: 1993 Edition.__ annot. ed. Date not set. 27.50 (*0-614-05773-6*) Michie Butterworth.

Alabama Mystery Van Takes Off! Book 1: Handicapped Alabama Kids Sneak Off on a Big Adventure. Carole Marsh. (Carole Marsh Alabama Bks.). (Illus.). (J). (gr. 3-12). 1994. 24.95 (*0-7933-4964-8*); pap. 14.95 (*0-7933-4965-6*); disk 29.95 (*0-7933-4966-4*) Gallopade Pub Group.

*__Alabama Myths, Mysteries & Legends.__ Elaine Miller. 1995. pap. write for info. (*1-878561-36-7*) Seacoast AL.

*__Alabama Newspaper Tradition: Grover C. Hall & the Hall Family.__ Daniel W. Hollis. LC 82-13582. (Illus.). 207p. 1983. pap. 59.00 (*0-7837-8382-5*, 2059192) Bks Demand.

Alabama Notes, 2 vols. in 1, Vols. 1 & 2. Flora D. England. 1990. reprint ed. 20.00 (*0-685-60364-4*, 1680) Clearfield Co.

Alabama Notes, Vols. 3 & 4. Flora D. England. 280p. 1993. reprint ed. pap. 24.00 (*0-685-69967-6*, 1681) Clearfield Co.

Alabama on My Mind. Wayne Greenhaw. (People, Politics, History & Ghost Stories Sers.). 160p. 1987. 11.95 (*0-944404-00-6*) Sycamore AL.

Alabama Pattern Jury Instructions: Civil. Alabama Pattern Jury Instructions Committee. LC 73-93831. 644p. 1974. 95.00 (*0-317-04336-6*) Lawyers Cooperative.

Alabama Pattern Jury Instructions: Civil. suppl. ed. Alabama Pattern Jury Instructions Committee. LC 73-93831. 644p. 1990. Suppl. 1990. 46.50 (*0-317-03223-2*) Lawyers Cooperative.

Alabama Poets: A Contemporary Anthology. Ed. by Ralph Hammond. LC 90-60311. 180p. (Orig.). 1990. 18.95 (*0-942979-06-0*); pap. 12.95 (*0-942979-07-9*) Livingston U Pr.

*__Alabama Population Projections 1990-2015.__ Carolyn Trent. Ed. by William Gunther et al. (Illus.). 148p. 1994. 20.00 (*0-614-03533-3*) U of Ala Ctr Bus.

Alabama Practice Series, 2 vols. 2nd ed. Champ Lyons, Jr. 1250p. 1986. 120.00 (*0-317-52097-0*) West Pub.

Alabama Project on Medicaid. Alabama Law Institute Staff & Richard A. Thigpen. write for info. (*0-318-57196-X*) AL Law Inst.

Alabama Property & Casualty Course. James J. Smith. Date not set. 50.00 (*1-56461-091-8*, 26978) Rough Notes.

*__Alabama Property Rights & Remedies.__ Jesse Evans. 925p. 1994. 95.00 (*1-55834-171-4*) Michie Butterworth.

Alabama Quiz Bowl Crash Course! Carole Marsh. (Carole Marsh Alabama Bks.). (Illus.). (YA). (gr. 3-12). 1994. lib. bdg. 24.95 (*1-55609-467-1*); pap. 14.95 (*1-55609-466-3*); disk 29.95 (*0-7933-1333-3*) Gallopade Pub Group.

*__Alabama Rain.__ Heather McCutchen. Date not set. 5.00 (*0-87129-566-0*, A62) Dramatic Pub.

Alabama Retail Sales, Nineteen Seventy-Eight to Nineteen Eighty-Eight. Carolyn Trent & Kathryn Rivers. (Illus.). 109p. (Orig.). 1990. pap. 20.00 (*0-943394-06-6*) U of Ala Ctr Bus.

Alabama Rollercoasters! Carole Marsh. (Carole Marsh Alabama Bks.). (Illus.). (YA). (gr. 3-12). 1994. lib. bdg. 24.95 (*0-7933-5224-X*); pap. 14.95 (*0-7933-5225-8*); disk 29.95 (*0-7933-5226-6*) Gallopade Pub Group.

*__Alabama Rules: 1994 Edition, 2 vols., Set.__ annot. ed. Date not set. pap. 40.00 (*1-55834-039-4*) Michie Butterworth.

Alabama Rules Annotated. Michie Company Editorial Staff. 1549p. 1992. pap. 37.50 (*0-87473-839-3*) Michie Butterworth.

*__Alabama Rules of Criminal Procedure, 2 vols., Set.__ 2nd suppl. ed. Hugh Maddox. 1994. 130.00 (*0-87473-636-6*) Michie Butterworth.

Alabama School Trivia: An Amazing & Fascinating Look at Our State's Teachers, Schools & Students! Carole Marsh. (Carole Marsh Alabama Bks.). (Illus.). (YA). (gr. 3-12). 1994. lib. bdg. 24.95 (*0-7933-0079-7*); pap. 14.95 (*0-7933-0049-5*); disk 29.95 (*0-7933-0080-0*) Gallopade Pub Group.

Alabama Scrapbook. Marie Jemison. Ed. by Ellen Sullivan. LC 88-83561. (Illus.). 200p. 1988. write for info. (*0-9621455-0-5*) Crane Hill AL.

Alabama Showdown. Geoffrey Norman. 1987. pap. 3.95 (*0-8217-2157-7*) Zebra.

Alabama Silly Basketball Sportsmysteries, Vol. I. Carole Marsh. (Carole Marsh Alabama Bks.). (Illus.). (YA). (gr. 3-12). 1994. lib. bdg. 24.95 (*0-7933-0047-9*); pap. 14.95 (*0-7933-0046-0*); disk 29.95 (*0-7933-0048-7*) Gallopade Pub Group.

Alabama Silly Basketball Sportsmysteries, Vol. II. Carole Marsh. (Carole Marsh Alabama Bks.). (Illus.). (YA). (gr. 3-12). 1994. lib. bdg. 24.95 (*0-7933-1562-X*); pap. 14.95 (*0-7933-1563-8*); disk 29.95 (*0-7933-1564-6*) Gallopade Pub Group.

Alabama Silly Football Sportsmysteries, Vol. I. Carole Marsh. (Carole Marsh Alabama Bks.). (Illus.). (YA). (gr. 3-12). 1994. lib. bdg. 24.95 (*1-55609-464-7*); pap. 14.95 (*1-55609-463-9*); disk 29.95 (*0-7933-1329-5*) Gallopade Pub Group.

Alabama Silly Football Sportsmysteries, Vol. II. Carole Marsh. (Carole Marsh Alabama Bks.). (Illus.). (YA). (gr. 3-12). 1994. lib. bdg. 24.95 (*0-7933-1339-2*); pap. 14.95 (*0-7933-1340-6*); disk 29.95 (*0-7933-1341-4*) Gallopade Pub Group.

Alabama Silly Trivia! Carole Marsh. (Carole Marsh Alabama Bks.). (Illus.). (YA). (gr. 3-12). 1994. lib. bdg. 24.95 (*1-55609-460-4*); pap. 14.95 (*1-55609-038-2*); disk 29.95 (*0-7933-1326-0*) Gallopade Pub Group.

Alabama Sketchbook: Alabama Scenic & Historical Drawings with Captions. Joseph Stone. (Illus.). 70p. (Orig.). 1993. pap. 18.00 (*0-9638708-0-7*) J Stone.

Alabama Soldiers (Revolution, War of 1812 & Indian Wars) Vol. 16: Surnames Lacey Thru Lewis. Bobbie J. McLane & Pauline J. Gandrud. 89p. (Orig.). 1995. pap. 15.00 (*0-929604-74-1*) Arkansas Ancestors.

*__Alabama Soldiers (Revolution, War of 1812 & Indian Wars) Vol. 17: Surnames Lightfoot Thru Lynn.__ Bobbie J. McLane & Pauline J. Gandrud. 89p. (Orig.). 1995. 15.00 (*0-614-04067-1*) Arkansas Ancestors.

Alabama Soldiers (Revolution, War of 1812 & Indian Wars), Vol. 1: Surnames A through Ba. Bobbie J. McLane & Pauline J. Gandrud. 107p. (Orig.). 1975. pap. 15.00 (*0-929604-46-6*) Arkansas Ancestors.

Alabama Soldiers (Revolution, War of 1812 & Indian Wars), Vol. 10: Surnames Grace through Hamner. Bobbie J. McLane & Pauline J. Gandrud. 109p. (Orig.). 1986. pap. 15.00 (*0-929604-55-5*) Arkansas Ancestors.

Alabama Soldiers (Revolution, War of 1812 & Indian Wars), Vol. 11: Surnames Hanby through Henderson. Bobbie J. McLane & Pauline J. Gandrud. 100p. (Orig.). 1988. pap. 15.00 (*0-929604-56-3*) Arkansas Ancestors.

Alabama Soldiers (Revolution, War of 1812 & Indian Wars), Vol. 12: Surnames Hendon through Holland. Bobbie J. McLane & Pauline J. Gandrud. 104p. (Orig.). 1989. pap. 15.00 (*0-929604-60-1*) Arkansas Ancestors.

Alabama Soldiers (Revolution, War of 1812 & Indian Wars), Vol. 13: Surnames Holley through End Hs. Bobbie J. McLane & Pauline J. Gandrud. 100p. (Orig.). 1990. pap. 15.00 (*0-929604-66-0*) Arkansas Ancestors.

Alabama Soldiers (Revolution, War of 1812 & Indian Wars), Vol. 14: Surnames I through Jones, James. Bobbie J. McLane & Pauline J. Gandrud. 102p. (Orig.). 1991. pap. 15.00 (*0-929604-71-7*) Arkansas Ancestors.

Alabama Soldiers (Revolution, War of 1812 & Indian Wars), Vol. 15: Surnames Jones, John Through K. Bobbie J. McLane & Pauline J. Gandrud. 108p. (Orig.). 1992. pap. 15.00 (*0-929604-73-3*) Arkansas Ancestors.

Alabama Soldiers (Revolution, War of 1812 & Indian Wars), Vol. 2: Surnames Be through Bond. Bobbie J. McLane & Pauline J. Gandrud. 100p. (Orig.). 1977. pap. 15.00 (*0-929604-47-4*) Arkansas Ancestors.

Alabama Soldiers (Revolution, War of 1812 & Indian Wars), Vol. 3: Surnames Bonner through Brynes. Bobbie J. McLane & Pauline J. Gandrud. 152p. (Orig.). 1977. pap. 15.00 (*0-929604-48-2*) Arkansas Ancestors.

Alabama Soldiers (Revolution, War of 1812 & Indian Wars), Vol. 4: Surnames Ca through Coker. Bobbie J. McLane & Pauline J. Gandrud. 102p. (Orig.). 1978. pap. 15.00 (*0-929604-49-0*) Arkansas Ancestors.

Alabama Soldiers (Revolution, War of 1812 & Indian Wars), Vol. 5: Surnames Cole through End Cs. Bobbie J. McLane & Pauline J. Gandrud. 90p. (Orig.). 1978. pap. 15.00 (*0-929604-50-4*) Arkansas Ancestors.

Alabama Soldiers (Revolution, War of 1812 & Indian Wars), Vol. 6: Surnames D. Bobbie J. McLane & Pauline J. Gandrud. 128p. (Orig.). 1979. pap. 15.00 (*0-929604-51-2*) Arkansas Ancestors.

Alabama Soldiers (Revolution, War of 1812 & Indian Wars), Vol. 7: Surnames E through Fl. Bobbie J. McLane & Pauline J. Gandrud. 115p. (Orig.). 1983. pap. 15.00 (*0-929604-52-0*) Arkansas Ancestors.

Alabama Soldiers (Revolution, War of 1812 & Indian Wars), Vol. 8: Surnames Forbes through Gary. Bobbie J. McLane & Pauline J. Gandrud. 103p. (Orig.). 1983. pap. 15.00 (*0-929604-53-9*) Arkansas Ancestors.

Alabama Soldiers (Revolution, War of 1812 & Indian Wars), Vol. 9: Surnames Gassaway through Gower. Bobbie J. McLane & Pauline J. Gandrud. 98p. (Orig.). 1984. pap. 15.00 (*0-929604-54-7*) Arkansas Ancestors.

*__Alabama State Business Handbook.__ 400p. (C). 1995. text ed. 395.00 (*0-7605-1915-3*) Rector Pr.

Alabama State Census Index, 1855. (Illus.). lib. bdg. 90.00 (*0-89593-165-6*) Accelerated Index.

Alabama State Census, 1866. 1990. 160.00 (*0-89593-611-9*) Accelerated Index.

Alabama State Constitution: A Reference Guide. William H. Stewart. LC 94-7616. (Reference Guides to the State Constitutions of the United States Ser.: No. 20). 288p. 1994. text ed. 79.50 (*0-313-27551-3*, Greenwood Pr) Greenwood.

Alabama State Court System (Proposed) Personnel Rules. National Center for State Courts Staff. 1976. 2.28 (*0-685-15202-2*, MAB-006) Natl Ctr St Courts.

Alabama State Parks. McCaig & Boyce. 100p. (Orig.). 1989. pap. text ed. 5.95 (*0-935201-62-9*) Affordable Adven.

Alabama Story: State History & Geography. Robert J. Norrell. (Illus.). 304p. (J). (gr. 4). 1993. 22.95 (*1-882700-00-7*) Yellowhammer.

Alabama Survival. Betty L. Hall & Ellen Burchfield. 160p. (Orig.). (YA). (gr. 10-12). 1979. pap. text ed. 5.84 (*0-03-055461-6*) Westwood Pr.

Alabama Tales: Anecdotes, Legends, & Stories from the Past. Drue Duke. LC 93-32590. (Illus.). 168p. (Orig.). 1994. pap. 9.95 (*0-9630700-5-3*) Vision AL.

Alabama Timeline: A Chronology of Alabama History, Mystery, Trivia, Legend, Lore & More. Carole Marsh. (Carole Marsh Alabama Bks.). (Illus.). (J). (gr. 3-12). 1994. lib. bdg. 24.95 (*0-7933-5875-2*); pap. 14.95 (*0-7933-5876-0*); disk 29.95 (*0-7933-5877-9*) Gallopade Pub Group.

*__Alabama Tort Law Handbook.__ suppl. ed. Michael L. Roberts & Gregory S. Cusimano. 1065p. 1994. 90.00 (*0-87473-581-5*) Michie Butterworth.

Alabama Torts Case Finder. suppl. ed. Allen W. Howell. 559p. 1993. 85.00 (*0-87473-426-6*) Michie Butterworth.

Alabama Trails. Patricia S. Sharpe. LC 93-1640. 168p. (Orig.). (C). 1993. pap. 17.95 (*0-8173-0690-0*) U of Ala Pr.

Alabama Trivia. Jill Couch & Ernie Couch. LC 87-4491. 192p. (Orig.). 1987. pap. 5.95 (*0-934395-44-6*) Rutledge Hill Pr.

Alabama Twilight. Danette Chartier. 480p. 1993. mass mkt. 4.50 (*1-55817-700-0*, Pinnacle NY) Windsor NY.

An Asterisk (*) at the beginning of an entry indicates that the title is appearing in BIP for the first time.

Alabama Unified Judicial System Affirmative Action Evaluation: Technical Assistance Report. National Center for State Courts Staff. 42p. 1979. 2.52 (0-685-15305-3, NCRO, T/A-503) Natl Ctr St Courts.

Alabama Writers: Titles in Print. Ruth Waldrop. LC 87-61390. 95p. (Orig.). 1987. pap. 10.95 (0-317-59023-5) RuSK Inc.

Alabama's Covered Bridges. Tom Sangster & Dess L. Sangster. LC 80-68408. (Illus.). 162p. (Orig.). 1980. 29.50 (0-686-69146-6); pap. 25.00 (0-938252-00-3) Coffeetable.

Alabama's (Most Devastating!) Disasters & (Most Calamitous!) Catastrophies! Carole Marsh. (Carole Marsh Alabama Bks.). (Illus.). (YA). (gr. 3-12). 1994. lib. bdg. 24.95 (0-7933-0038-X); pap. 14.95 (0-7933-0037-1); disk 29.95 (0-7933-0039-8) Gallopade Pub Group.

Alabama's State & Local Governments. 3rd ed. David L. Martin. (Illus.). 256p. (C). 1994. pap. text ed. 17.95 (0-8173-0738-9) U of Ala Pr.

Alabama's Unsolved Mysteries (& Their "Solutions") Includes Scientific Information & Other Activities for Students. Carole Marsh. (Carole Marsh Alabama Bks.). (Illus.). (J). (gr. 3-12). 1994. lib. bdg. 24.95 (0-7933-5722-5); pap. 14.95 (0-7933-5723-3); disk 29.95 (0-7933-5724-1) Gallopade Pub Group.

Alabama's Youngest Admirals. James L. Estes. Ed. by Mary E. Krauel. (Illus.). 132p. (Orig.). (J). (gr. 4-12). 1991. pap. 8.95 (0-9628634-0-8) J L Estes.

Alabanza a la Disciplina. Richard Foster. Tr. by M. Francisco Lievano. 224p. (SPA.). 1986. pap. 4.95 (0-88113-012-5) Edit Betania.

Alabanza Da Resultado: Praise Works. Merlin Carothers. (SPA.). 5.50 (84-7228-501-4, 360020, Pub. by Edit Clie SP) TSELF.

Alabanza Es Dinamita. Don Gossett. 90p. (SPA.). 1989. pap. 3.95 (0-938127-07-1) Gospel Pr FL.

Alabanza Que Libera. Judson Cornwall. 160p. 1976. 3.50 (0-88113-002-8) Edit Betania.

***Alabaster & Leopard Jasper.** Sharon R. Amos. 24p. 1994. write for info. (0-914620-05-3) Alpha Pr.

Alabaster Box. James L. Allen. (Principle Works of James Lane Allen). 1989. reprint ed. lib. bdg. 79.00 (0-7812-1744-X) Rprt Serv.

***Alabaster Doves: True Stories of Women Whose Lives Were Characterized by Strength & Gentleness.** Holland. 1995. pap. 8.99 (0-8024-0861-3) Moody.

Alabaster Jar. Frederick L. Saur. 40p. 1989. pap. 3.25 (0-687-00946-4) Abingdon.

Alabaster Shrine of King Amenhotep the Second. Charles C. Van Siclen, III. (Brooklyn Museum Mut Expedition Ser.: Vol. I). (Illus.). xvi, 58p. (Orig.). 1986. pap. 25.00 (0-933175-05-1) Van Siclen Bks.

Alabi's World. Richard Price. LC 89-15488. (Illus.). 480p. 1990. text ed. 65.00x (0-8018-3862-2); pap. 19.95 (0-8018-3956-4) Johns Hopkins.

Aladdin. (Illus.). 64p. (J). 1993. pap. 16.95 (0-7935-1782-6, 00312480) H Leonard.

Aladdin. (Xylotone Fun! Ser.). (Illus.). 16p. (J). 1993. spiral bd. 9.95 (0-7935-1827-X, 00824025); spiral bd. 9.95 (0-7935-1825-3, 00710370); spiral bd. 9.95 (0-7935-1828-8, 00821007) H Leonard.

Aladdin. (Piano Fun! Ser.). (Illus.). 16p. (J). 1993. pap. 19.95 (0-7935-2809-7, HL00826003) H Leonard.

Aladdin. (Ladybird Stories Ser.). (Illus.). (ARA.). (J). (gr. 5-12). 1987. 3.95 (0-86685-182-8) Intl Bk Ctr.

Aladdin. (Play - a - Sound Ser.). (Illus.). 24p. (J). 1993. 12.98 (0-7853-0131-3) Pubns Intl Ltd.

***Aladdin.** (Little Library). 8p. (J). 1994. 4.98 (0-8317-5526-1) Smithmark.

***Aladdin.** (Little Library Ser.). 126p. (J). 1993. write for info. (1-57082-010-4) Mouse Works.

***Aladdin.** Adapt. by Sarah Harris. (Comes to Life Bks.). 16p. (ENG & FRE.). (J). (ps-2). 1995. write for info. (1-57234-043-6) YES Ent.

***Aladdin.** Adapt. by Sarah Harris. (Comes to Life Bks.). 16p. (DUT & ENG.). (J). (ps-2). 1995. write for info. (1-57234-034-7) YES Ent.

Aladdin. L. Spencer Humphrey. 32p. (J). 1995. pap. 2.95 (0-8125-2319-9) Tor Bks.

Aladdin. Andrew Lang. (Illus.). 32p. (J). (gr. k-3). 1983. pap. 5.99 (0-14-050389-7, Puffin) Puffin Bks.

***Aladdin.** Little Golden Books Staff. (J). Date not set. 1.59 (0-307-00124-5, Golden Pr) Western Pub.

***Aladdin.** Slott. 1995. pap. (0-7851-0105-5) Marvel Entmnt.

***Aladdin.** Eric Suben. (Storytime Ser.). (Illus.). 24p. (J). (ps-2). 1995. pap. 0.99 (1-56293-542-9) McClanahan Bk.

Aladdin. Illus. by Diana Wakeman. LC 91-58974. (Pop-up Bk.). 12p. (J). (ps-3). 1993. 11.95 (1-56282-242-X) Disney Pr.

***Aladdin.** Walt Disney Company Staff. (FRE.). Date not set. pap. 9.95 (0-7859-8852-1) Fr & Eur.

Aladdin. Walt Disney Staff. (Penguin-Disney Ser.). (J). (ps-3). 1992. 6.98 (0-453-03058-0) Mouse Works.

Aladdin. rev. ed. William Glennon. 63p. 1990. 3.45 (0-87129-072-3, A46) Dramatic Pub.

Aladdin: A Participation Play. Moses Goldberg. (J). 1977. 5.00 (0-87602-101-1) Anchorage.

Aladdin: And Other Tales from the Arabian Nights. N. J. Dawood. 176p. (J). (gr. 4 up). 1990. pap. 3.50 (0-14-035105-1, Puffin) Puffin Bks.

Aladdin: Little Library. Walt Disney. (J). (ps). 1993. 5.98 (0-453-03170-6) Mouse Works.

Aladdin: Master of the Lamp. Ed. by Mike Resnick & Martin H. Greenberg. 352p. (Orig.). 1992. mass mkt. 4.99 (0-88677-545-0) DAW Bks.

Aladdin: Peek Abu. Illus. by Vaccaro Associates Staff & Dennis Durrell. LC 92-53496. (Surprise Lift-the-Flap Ser.). 18p. (J). (ps-1). 1993. 9.95 (1-56282-389-2) Disney Pr.

Aladdin: The Genie Gets Wet. (Bath Book Ser.). 4p. (J). 1993. 5.98 (1-57082-011-2) Mouse Works.

Aladdin: The Genie Gets Wet Bath Book. Walt Disney. (J). (ps). 1993. 5.98 (0-453-03169-2) Mouse Works.

Aladdin: The Magic Carpet Ride. Illus. by Vaccaro Associates Staff & Garparo Vaccaro. LC 92-54878. (Tiny Changing Pictures Bks.). 10p. (J). (ps-00). 1993. 4.95 (1-56282-396-5) Disney Pr.

Aladdin: Travels with Genie. Walt Disney. (J). (ps-3). 1993. 6.98 (0-453-03138-2) Mouse Works.

***Aladdin: U. K. English.** Adapt. by Sarah Harris. (Comes to Life Bks.). 16p. (J). (ps-2). 1995. write for info. (1-57234-028-2) YES Ent.

***Aladdin - Magic Carpet Ride.** Little Golden Books Staff. (J). Date not set. 1.59 (0-307-30144-3, Golden Pr) Western Pub.

Aladdin & Other Favorite Arabian Nights Stories. Ed. by Philip Smith. LC 93-22073. (Children's Thrift Classics Ser.). (Illus.). 96p. (J). (gr. 3 up). 1993. reprint ed. pap. 1.00 (0-486-27571-X) Dover.

Aladdin & Other Tales from the Arabian Nights. LC 93-55071. (Everyman's Library of Children's Classics). (J). 1993. 12.95 (0-679-42533-0) Knopf.

Aladdin & the Magic Lamp. (Fun-to-Read Fairy Tales Series II). (Illus.). 24p. (J). (gr. k-3). 1992. pap. 2.50 (1-56144-169-4, Honey Bear Bks) Modern Pub NYC.

Aladdin & the Magic Lamp. Patricia Daniels. LC 79-27304. (Fairy Tales Ser.). (Illus.). 24p. (J). (gr. k-5). 1980. lib. bdg. 9.95 (0-8393-0257-6) Raintree Steck-V.

Aladdin & the Magic Lamp. Ret. by Patricia Daniels. LC 79-27304. (Fairy Tale Clippers Ser.). (Illus.). 24p. (J). (gr. k-5). 1981. lib. bdg. 29.28 (0-8393-1832-4) Raintree Steck-V.

Aladdin & the Magic Lamp. Deborah Hautzig. LC 92-1608. (Step into Reading Bks.: Step 3). (Illus.). 48p. (Orig.). (J). (gr. 2-3). 1993. pap. 3.99 (0-679-83241-6) Random Bks Yng Read.

Aladdin & the Magic Lamp. Deborah Hautzig. LC 92-1608. (Step into Reading Bks.: Step 3). (Illus.). 48p. (Orig.). (J). (gr. 2-3). 1993. lib. bdg. 7.99 (0-679-93241-0) Random Bks Yng Read.

Aladdin & the Magic Lamp. Illus. by Greg Hildebrandt. (Read-to-Me Ser.). 48p. (J). (ps-2). 1992. 5.95 (0-88101-266-1) Unicorn Pub.

Aladdin & the Magic Lamp. Jordan Horowitz. (J). (ps-3). 1993. pap. 2.50 (0-590-46417-5) Scholastic Inc.

***Aladdin & the Magic Lamp.** Kuntsler. 1995. pap. 19.95 (0-689-80063-0) S&S Trade.

***Aladdin & the Magic Lamp: Full-Color Picture Book.** Pat Stewart. LC 94-44518. (Illus.). 16p. (Orig.). (J). 1995. pap. text ed. 1.00 (0-486-28524-3) Dover.

Aladdin & the Wonderful Lamp. James Norris. (J). 1940. 5.00 (0-87602-102-X) Anchorage.

Aladdin & the Wonderful Lamp. Illus. by Bryna Waldman. LC 87-13756. 32p. (J). (gr. 1-4). 1988. lib. bdg. 9.79 (0-8167-1073-2); pap. text ed. 2.50 (0-8167-1074-0) Troll Assocs.

Aladdin Bath Book. Walt Disney Staff. (Penguin-Disney Ser.). (J). (ps-3). 1992. 5.98 (0-453-03060-2) Mouse Works.

***Aladdin "Built in a Day" House Catalog, 1917.** Aladdin Company Staff. (Illus.). 128p. 1995. pap. text ed. 11.95 (0-486-28591-X) Dover.

Aladdin Effect. Michelinie et al. 64p. 1985. 5.95 (0-87135-081-5) Marvel Entmnt.

Aladdin Electric Lamps. J. W. Courter. (Illus.). (C). 1987. 24.95 (0-9618879-0-7) J W Courter.

***Aladdin en Espanol.** (Spanish Classics Ser.). 96p. (J). 1993. 6.98 (1-57082-015-5) Mouse Works.

Aladdin en Espanol. Walt Disney. (J). 1993. 6.98 (0-453-03164-1) Mouse Works.

Aladdin Illustrated Songbook. (Illus.). 48p. (Orig.). 1994. 14.95 (0-7935-3412-7, HL00312503) H Leonard.

Aladdin-Imperial Labels: A Discography. Comp. by Michel Ruppli. LC 90-22696. (Discographies Ser.: No. 42). 760p. 1991. text ed. 89.50 (0-313-27821-0, RAH, Greenwood Pr) Greenwood.

Aladdin Junior Graphic Novel. Walt Disney. (J). (gr. 4-7). 1993. pap. 3.95 (0-8167-3062-8) Troll Assocs.

Aladdin Literature Mini-Unit. Janet Lovelady. (Illus.). 32p. (J). (gr. 3-5). 1990. student ed 4.95 (1-56096-016-7) Mari.

Aladdin Little Library. Walt Disney Staff. (Penguin-Disney Ser.). (J). (ps-3). 1992. 5.98 (0-453-03059-9) Mouse Works.

Aladdin McFaddin. Wil Denson & Michael Cunningham. (Illus.). 44p. (J). (gr. 2 up). 1977. pap. 4.00 (0-88680-004-8); 7.50 (0-88680-005-6) I E Clark.

Aladdin n' His Magic Lamp. rev. ed. William-Alan Landes. LC 89-43679. (Wondrawhopper Ser.). 52p. (J). (gr. 3-12). 1985. pap. 6.00 (0-88734-102-0); 30.00 (0-88734-003-2) Players Pr.

Aladdin n' His Magic Lamp: Music & Lyrics. rev. ed. William-Alan Landes. (Wondrawhopper Ser.). (J). (gr. 3-12). 1985. pap. text ed. 15.00 (0-88734-002-4) Players Pr.

***Aladdin Postcard Book.** Walt Disney's Feature Animation Department Staff. (Illus.). 64p. 1995. pap. 8.95 (0-7868-8059-7) Hyperion.

Aladdin's Lamp: A Classic Tale. Tr. by Diane D. Suire. LC 88-35312. (Illus.). 32p. (J). (gr. 1-4). 1988. lib. bdg. 19.93 (0-89565-481-4) Childs World.

Aladdin's Lamp: The Wealth of the American People. Gorham Munson. (Social Credit Ser.). 420p. 1982. lib. bdg. 75.00 (0-8490-3222-9) Gordon Pr.

Aladdin's Problem. Ernst Junger. Tr. by Joachim Neugroschel. LC 92-82648. 144p. 1992. 19.00 (0-941419-58-4, Eridanos Library) Marsilio Pubs.

***Aladura: A Religious Movement.** J. D. Peel. (Classics in African Anthropology Ser.). (C). 1995. text ed. 58.00 (3-89473-688-7); pap. text ed. 25.50 (3-89473-877-4) Westview.

***Alae Supra Canalem.** Turner Publishing Company Staff. LC 95-60553. 200p. 1995. 48.00 (1-56311-210-8) Turner Pub KY.

ALAHOW-to-Parent Group Manual. Alahow-to-Parent. 172p. (Orig.). 1989. pap. text ed. write for info. (0-318-66436-4) Alahow-To-Parent.

***Alain Locke.** Perry. 1997. text ed. 22.95 (0-8057-4023-6) Macmillan.

Alain Locke: Reflections on a Modern Renaissance Man. Ed. by Russell J. Linnemann. LC 82-7211. xv, 146p. (C). 1982. text ed. 27.50 (0-8071-1036-1) La State U Pr.

Alain Locke & Philosophy: A Quest for Cultural Pluralism. Johnny Washington. LC 85-9873. (Contributions in Afro-American & African Studies: No. 94). (Illus.). 328p. 1986. text ed. 55.00 (0-313-22957-0, WL, Greenwood Pr) Greenwood.

Alain Robbe-Grillet: An Annotated Bibliography of Critical Studies, 1953-1972. Dale W. Fraizer. LC 73-13874. (Author Bibliographies Ser.: No. 13). 286p. 1973. 27.50 (0-8108-0645-2) Scarecrow.

Alain Robbe-Grillet: The Body of the Text. Ben Stoltzfus. LC 83-49342. (Illus.). 192p. 1985. 36.50 (0-8386-3212-2) Fairleigh Dickinson.

Alakananda. Monika Varma. 1976. 8.00 (0-89253-823-6); 4.80 (0-89253-824-4) Ind-US Inc.

Alalakh: An Account of the Excavations at Tell Atchana in the Hatav, 1937-1949. Leonard Woolley et al. (Society of Antiquaries of London, Research Committee Reports: No. 18). (Illus.). 562p. reprint ed. pap. 160.20 (0-8357-5292-5, 2013144) Bks Demand.

Alalakh Tablets. Donald J. Wiseman. LC 78-72775. (Ancient Mesopotamian Texts & Studies). 232p. 1983. reprint ed. 49.50 (0-404-18237-2) AMS Pr.

***Alamance County, North Carolina 1850 Census with Ancestors & Descendants of Selected Families.** Marian D. Chiarito. 240p. 1987. lib. bdg. 51.00 (0-8095-8266-X); pap. 24.00 (0-8095-8502-2) Borgo Pr.

Alamance County, North Carolina 1850 Census with Ancestors & Descendants of Selected Families. Marian D. Chiarito. 240p. 1987. 25.00 (0-945503-12-1) Clarkton Pr.

Alameda - Contra Costa Counties Street Guide & Directory Census Tract Edition, 1991. Thomas Bros. Maps Staff. (Illus.). 314p. 1991. pap. 49.95 (0-88130-461-1) Thomas Bros Maps.

Alameda - Contra Costa Counties Street Guide & Directory Zip Code Edition, 1991. Thomas Bros. Maps Staff. (Illus.). 314p. 1991. pap. 27.95 (0-88130-462-X) Thomas Bros Maps.

Alameda - Contra Costa Counties Street Guide & Directory, 1991. Thomas Bros. Maps Staff. (Illus.). 312p. 1990. pap. 21.95 (0-88130-459-X) Thomas Bros Maps.

Alameda - Santa Clara Counties Street Guide & Directory. Thomas Bros. Maps Staff. (Illus.). 316p. 1991. pap. 21.95 (0-88130-460-3) Thomas Bros Maps.

Alameda-Contra Costa Counties Street Guide & Directory: 1992 Census Tract Edition. (Illus.). 314p. pap. 59.95 (0-88130-525-1) Thomas Bros Maps.

Alameda-Contra Costa Counties Street Guide & Directory: 1994 Edition. (Illus.). 312p. 1994. pap. 21.95 (0-88130-623-1) Thomas Bros Maps.

***Alameda-Contra Costa Counties Street Guide & Directory: 1995 Edition.** Thomas Bros. Maps Staff. (Illus.). 312p. 1994. pap. 21.95 (0-88130-686-X) Thomas Bros Maps.

Alameda County: California Crossroads: An Illustrated History. Ruth H. Willard. 128p. 1988. 27.95 (0-89781-283-2, 5300) Preferred Mktg.

Alameda County Clerk Criminal-Corpus Division Workload Analysis. National Center for State Courts Staff. 101p. 1978. 6.06 (0-685-15442-4, WRO-020) Natl Ctr St Courts.

Alameda County Commerce & Industry Directory, 1994. rev. ed. 352p. 1994. disk write for info. (0-318-72184-8) Database Pub Co.

Alameda County Commerce & Industry Directory, 1994. 24th rev. ed. 352p. 1995. pap. 75.00 (0-929695-69-0) Database Pub Co.

Alameda County Street Guide & Directory: 1994 Edition. (Illus.). 176p. 1994. pap. 12.95 (0-88130-622-3) Thomas Bros Maps.

***Alameda County Street Guide & Directory: 1995 Edition.** Thomas Bros. Maps Staff. (Illus.). 176p. 1994. pap. 12.95 (0-88130-685-1) Thomas Bros Maps.

Alameda County Street Guide & Directory, 1991. Thomas Bros. Maps Staff. (Illus.). 176p. 1990. pap. 12.95 (0-88130-458-1) Thomas Bros Maps.

Alameda County 1994 McCormack's Guides. 1994. pap. 6.95 (0-931299-41-1) McCormacks Guides.

***Alameda County 1995: McCormack's Guides.** 1995. pap. 8.95 (0-931299-46-2) McCormacks Guides.

***Alameda County 1996: McCormack's Guides.** 1995. pap. 8.95 (0-931299-54-3) McCormacks Guides.

Alameda-Santa Clara Counties Street Guide & Directory: 1994 Edition. (Illus.). 312p. 1994. pap. 21.95 (0-88130-624-X) Thomas Bros Maps.

***Alameda-Santa Clara Counties Street Guide & Directory: 1995 Edition.** Thomas Bros. Maps Staff. (Illus.). 312p. 1994. pap. 21.95 (0-88130-687-8) Thomas Bros Maps.

Alamein. Philip Sauvain. LC 91-28378. (Great Battles & Sieges Ser.). (Illus.). 32p. (J). (gr. 6 up). 1992. text ed. 13.95 (0-02-781081-X, Mac Bks Young Read) S&S Childrens.

Alamein to Zem Zem. Keith Douglas. (Illus.). 156p. 1994. pap. 10.95 (0-571-16264-9) Faber & Faber.

***Alamkara: 5000 Years of Indian Art.** R. C. Sharma et al. LC 94-77448. (Illus.). 144p. (C). 1995. pap. 35.00 (0-944142-97-4) U of Wash Pr.

Alamo. Herma Silverstein. LC 91-42461. (Places in American History Ser.). (Illus.). 72p. (J). (gr. 4 up). 1992. text ed. 14.95 (0-87518-502-9, Dillon Silver Burdett) Silver Burdett Pr.

Alamo. Lynda Sorensen. LC 94-7054. (American Symbols Ser.). (J). 1994. write for info. (1-55916-049-7) Rourke Bk Co.

Alamo. John M. Myers. LC 48-5208. (Illus.). 240p. 1973. reprint ed. pap. 8.95 (0-8032-5779-1) U of Nebr Pr.

Alamo: An In-Depth Study of the Battle. C. D. Huneycutt. (Illus.). 120p. (Orig.). 1986. pap. 9.95 (0-915153-12-2) Gold Star Pr.

Alamo: And the Texas War for Independence, 1835-1836. Albert A. Nofi. (Illus.). 240p. 1992. 18.95 (0-938289-10-1) Combined Bks.

Alamo: Battle of Honor & Freedom. L. Wade. (Doors to America's Past Ser.). (J). 1991. 11.95 (0-86592-470-8) Rourke Enter.

Alamo Across Texas. Jill Stover. LC 91-47572. (Illus.). (J). (ps-3). 1993. 12.93 (0-688-11713-9) Lothrop.

Alamo Across Texas. Jill Stover. LC 91-47572. (Illus.). 32p. (J). (ps up). 1993. 13.00 (0-688-11712-0) Lothrop.

Alamo & the Texan War of Independence. Philip Haythornthwaite. (Men-at-Arms Ser.: No. 173). (Illus.). 48p. 1986. pap. 11.95 (0-85045-684-3, Pub. by Osprey UK) Stackpole.

Alamo & the Texas War of Independence: Heroes, Myths & History. Albert A. Nofi. LC 93-33619. (Illus.). 234p. 1994. reprint ed. pap. 13.95 (0-306-80563-4) Da Capo.

Alamo Battle: Eight Essays. C. D. Huneycutt. (Illus.). 100p. (Orig.). 1987. pap. 4.80 (0-915153-26-2) Gold Star Pr.

Alamo Battle: Seven More Essays. C. D. Huneycutt. (Illus.). 80p. (Orig.). 1989. pap. 4.80 (0-915153-33-5) Gold Star Pr.

Alamo Cat. Kerr. (Illus.). 64p. (J). (gr. 4-6). 1988. 10.95 (0-89015-639-5) Sunbelt Media.

Alamo Defenders, a Genealogy: The People & Their Words. Bill Groneman. Ed. by Edwin M. Eakin. (Illus.). 224p. 1990. 12.95 (0-89015-757-X) Sunbelt Media.

Alamo Jefferson. large type ed. Mark Carrel. 304p. 1992. pap. 14.95 (0-7089-7149-0, Linford) Ulverscroft.

Alamo Movies. Frank Thompson. LC 93-49611. 128p. (Orig.). 1994. pap. 14.95 (1-55622-375-7, Rep of TX Pr) Wordware Pub.

***Alamo Remembered: Tejano Accounts.** Timothy M. Matovina. LC 95-10131. 1995. write for info. (0-292-75185-0); pap. write for info. (0-292-75186-9) U of Tex Pr.

***Alamodome Murders.** Aubrey Smith. 300p. 1995. pap. 9.95 (0-7610-0153-0) NW Pub.

Alamos Before the Bomb & Other Stories. Charles S. Pearce. 1990. 9.50 (0-533-06948-3) Vantage.

Alamos Primer: The First Lectures on How to Build an Atomic Bomb. Robert Serber. Ed. by Richard Rhodes. 1992. 25.00 (0-520-07576-5) U CA Pr.

Alamosa, Salida & the Valley Line. Richard L. Dorman. LC 91-91427. (Illus.). 224p. 1992. 41.95 (0-9616656-5-3) RD Pubns.

Alamo...the Price of Freedom. George A. McAlister. (Illus.). 230p. (Orig.). 1988. pap. text ed. 7.95 (0-924307-00-5) Docutex Inc.

Alamut Ambush. large type ed. Anthony Price. (Adventure Suspense Ser.). 406p. 1988. 15.95 (0-7089-1854-9) Ulverscroft.

Alan & Naomi. Myron Levoy. LC 76-41522. (Trophy Bk.). 176p. (J). (gr. 6 up). 1987. pap. 3.95 (0-06-440209-6, Trophy) HarpC Child Bks.

Alan & Naomi: A Study Guide. Marcia Tretler. (Novel-Ties Ser.). (J). (gr. 4-6). 1989. student ed, teacher ed 15.95 (0-88122-055-8) Lrn Links.

Alan & the Baron. Ron Hamilton. (Illus.). 50p. (Orig.). (J). (gr. 3-7). 1983. pap. 2.95 (0-913072-54-0) Natl Assn Deaf.

Alan Ayckborn: A Casebook. Bernard F. Dukore. LC 91-17093. (Casebooks on Modern Dramatists Ser.: Vol. 11). 228p. 1991. 30.00 (0-8240-5759-7, 1361) Garland.

Alan Ayckbourn. 2nd ed. Michael Billington. Ed. by Bruce King & Adele King. LC 89-70086. (Modern Dramatists Ser.). 240p. 1990. text ed. 29.95 (0-312-04242-6) St Martin.

***Alan Ayckbourn Plays, No. 1.** Alan Ayckbourn. 384p. (Orig.). 1995. pap. 13.95 (0-614-06710-3) Faber & Faber.

Alan Ayckbourns Dramenfiguren. Uta Bartsch. (Anglistische und Amerikanistische Texte und Studien Ser.: Vol. 1). x, 296p. 1986. write for info. (3-487-07746-9, Pub. by Georg Olms GW) Lubrecht & Cramer.

Alan Barbour's Screen Facts & Screen Nostalgia Illustrated Collection. Ed. by Mary E. Morrison. (Guide to the Microfiche Collection Ser.). 11p. (Orig.). 1987. 10.00 (0-685-46000-2) Univ Microfilms.

Alan Bible: Recollections of a Nevada Native Son: The Law, Politics, the Nevada Attorney General's Office, & the United States Senate. Ed. by Mary E. Glass. 357p. 1982. lib. bdg. 49.00 (1-56475-216-X); fiche write for info. (1-56475-217-8) U NV Oral Hist.

Alan Davie. Ed. by Douglas Hall. (Illus.). 200p. (C). 1992. 80.00 (0-85331-597-3, Pub. by Lund Humphries UK) Antique Collect.

Alan Davie: Quest for the Miraculous. Michael Tucker. (Illus.). 96p. (C). 1993. pap. 39.95 (0-85331-636-8, Pub. by Lund Humphries UK) Antique Collect.

Alan F. Griffin on Teaching. NCSS Staff. 92p. 1992. per. 14.95 (0-8403-8147-6) Kendall-Hunt.

Alan Feltus: Recent Works. Howard D. Spencer. LC 87-51360. (Illus.). 24p. 1987. pap. 5.00 (0-939324-32-6) Wichita Art Mus.

An Asterisk (*) at the beginning of an entry indicates that the title is appearing in BIP for the first time.

167

A

*Alan Gottlieb's Celebrity Address Book. Alan M. Gottlieb. LC 94-76475. 194p. 1994. pap. 14.95 (0-936783-11-7) Merril Pr.

Alan Leo's Dictionary of Astrology. Alan Leo & Vivian E. Robson. 224p. 1981. pap. 12.00 (0-89540-101-0, SB-101, Sun Bks) Sun Pub.

Alan Magee 1981-1991: Selected Works. Farnsworth Art Museum Staff et al. (Illus.). 64p. 1991. pap. 25.00 (0-918749-01-8); pap. 19.95 (0-918749-02-6) W A Farnsworth.

Alan of Lille's Grammar of Sex: The Meaning of Grammar to a Twelfth-Century Intellectual. Jan Ziolkowski. LC 83-62358. (Speculum Anniversary Monographs: No. 10). 171p. 1985. 20.00 (0-910956-85-5); pap. 12.00 (0-910956-86-3) Medieval Acad.

Alan Oken's Complete Astrology. rev. ed. Alan Oken. LC 87-47885. (Illus.). 640p. 1988. pap. 15.95 (0-553-34537-0) Bantam.

Alan Paton. rev. ed. Edward Callan. (World Authors Ser.: No. 40). 1982. text ed. 22.95 (0-8057-6512-3, Twayne) Macmillan.

Alan Paton: A Biography. Peter F. Alexander. (Illus.). 528p. 1994. 35.00 (0-19-811237-8) OUP.

*Alan Pinkerton. Carl R. Green & William R. Sanford. LC 94-33473. (Outlaws & Lawmen of the Wild West Ser.). (Illus.). 48p. (J). (gr. 4-10). 1995. lib. bdg. 14.95 (0-89490-590-2) Enslow Pubs.

Alan Saret. 1983. 3.50 (0-914782-48-7) Buffalo Acad.

Alan Sillitoe. William Hutchings. (Milford Ser.: Popular Writers of Today). 128p. Date not set. lib. bdg. write for info. (0-8095-5203-5); pap. write for info. (0-8095-5228-0) Borgo Pr.

Alan Sillitoe: An Annotated Bibliography. David Gerard. 197p. 1988. text ed. 55.00 (0-313-27672-2) Greenwood.

Alan Silverstein's Home Buying Strategies: Newly Built Homes. Alan Silverstein. 304p. 1987. 19.95 (0-7737-2089-8, Pub. by Stoddart Pubng CN) Genl Dist Srvs.

*Alan Simpson's Easy Guide to Windows 95. Alan Simpson et al. 1995. 19.99 (0-7821-1708-2) Sybex.

Alan Vega. Kyoichi Tsuzuki. (Art Random Ser.: No. 91). (Illus.). 48p. 1991. 32.95 (4-7636-8592-9, Pub. by Kyoto Shoin JA) Bks Nippan.

Alana & the Dolphins. Wendy Mateja. Orig. Title: Alana, Lady of Light. (Illus.). 16p. (Orig.). 1978. pap. text ed. 4.95 (0-9601836-0-4) Magic Unicorn Pubns.

Alana, Lady of Light see Alana & the Dolphins

Alana's Secret Friend. Jess Christopher. LC 93-74754. (Little Mermaid Novels Ser.: No. 12). (Illus.). 80p. (J). (gr. 1-4). 1994. pap. 3.50 (0-7868-4002-1) Disney Pr.

Alankaratnakara of Sobhakaramitra: A Study. G. Parthasardhy Rao. (C). 1992. text ed. 50.00 (81-7099-406-3, Pub. by Mittal II) S Asia.

Alanna: The First Adventure Song of the Lioness, Bk. One. Tamora Pierce. LC 83-2595. 252p. (YA). (gr. 6 up). 1983. text ed. 16.95 (0-689-30994-5, Atheneum Bks Young) S&S Childrens.

Alaric Watts: A Narrative of His LIfe, 2 vols., Set. Alaric A. Watts. LC 79-148326. (Illus.). reprint ed. 67.50 (0-404-07495-2) AMS Pr.

Alarm. Rick Taylor. (Illus.). 48p. Date not set. pap. 9.95 (0-7119-0831-1) Omnibus NY.

Alarm & Interlock Systems. Thomas G. Fisher. LC 84-170231. (Instructional Resource Package Ser.). 218p. 1984. Student Text: 218p. student ed, pap. text ed. 35.00 (0-87664-736-0, 1736-0) Instru Soc.

Alarm & Interlock Systems: Instructor's Guide. Thomas G. Fisher. LC 84-170231. (Instructional Resource Package Ser.). 27p. reprint ed. pap. 25.00 (0-7837-5136-2, 2044864) Bks Demand.

Alarm Book: A Guide to Burglar & Fire Alarms. Dan McTague & Doug Smith. 192p. 1991. pap. 24.95 (0-7506-9316-9) Buttrwrth-Heinemann.

Alarm Clock see Three Little Friends Series

Alarm Dealers Guide. John Sanger. 300p. 1985. text ed. 32.95 (0-409-95088-2) Buttrwrth-Heinemann.

Alarm, Sensor, & Security Circuit Cookbook. Thomas Petruzellis. LC 93-27562. 1993. 29.95 (0-8306-4314-1); pap. 17.95 (0-8306-4312-5) TAB Bks.

Alarm, Sensor & Security Circuit Cookbook. Thomas Petruzellis. 1993. pap. text ed. 17.95 (0-07-049707-9) McGraw.

Alarm, Sensor & Security Circuit Cookbook. Thomas Petruzellis. 1994. text ed. 29.95 (0-07-049706-0) McGraw.

Alarm Set, Anti-Intrusion, Restricted Areas. (Security Ser.). 1991. lib. bdg. 79.95 (0-8490-4123-6) Gordon Pr.

Alarm to the Unconverted see Sure Guide to Heaven

*Alarming Animals. Parker. (Illus.). (J). 1995. pap. text ed. (0-8114-6332-X) Raintree Steck-V.

Alarming Animals. Steve Parker. LC 93-6651. (Creepy Creatures Ser.). (Illus.). 38p. (J). (gr. 3-6). 1993. lib. bdg. 21.36 (0-8114-0658-X) Raintree Steck-V.

Alarming Heat. Regine Sands. 96p. (Orig.). 1991. pap. 7.95 (1-55583-311-X) Alyson Pubns.

Alarming History of Medicine: Amusing Anecdotes from Hippocrates to Heart Transplants. Richard Gordon. (Illus.). 272p. 1993. 22.95 (0-312-10411-1) St Martin.

Alarms. Richard Laymon. 1986. 25.00 (0-929480-72-4) Mark Ziesing.

Alarms. limited ed. Richard Laymon. 1986. 60.00 (0-929480-71-6) Mark Ziesing.

Alarms: Fifty-Five Electronic Projects & Circuits. Charles D. Rakes. (Illus.). 160p. 1988. 19.95 (0-8306-2096-6, 2996) TAB Bks.

Alarms & Epitaphs: The Art of Eric Ambler. Peter Wolfe. LC 92-74552. 230p. (C). 1993. 40.95 (0-87972-602-4); pap. 15.95 (0-87972-603-2) Bowling Green Univ.

Alarms & Mirrors. Adam Atkin. LC 91-67356. 188p. (Orig.). 1991. pap. 7.95 (0-9631360-3-8) Sea Tree Pr.

Alarums & Excursions. James Agate. LC 67-30169. (Essay Index Reprint Ser.). 1977. 20.95 (0-8369-0138-X) Ayer.

Alaryngeal Speech Rehabilitation. Ed. by Shirley Salmon & Kay Mount. LC 90-9164. 1991. pap. text ed. 28.00 (0-89079-415-4, 1817) PRO-ED.

Alas, Alas, Kongo: A Social History of Indentured African Immigration into Jamaica, 1841-1865. Monica Schuler. LC 79-3681. (Johns Hopkins Studies in Atlantic History & Culture Ser.). 199p. reprint ed. pap. 56.80 (0-8357-6625-X, 2035271) Bks Demand.

Alas, Babylon. Pat Frank. 280p. 1990. reprint ed. lib. bdg. 25.95x (0-89966-744-9) Buccaneer Bks.

Alas, Babylon. Pat Frank. 320p. 1993. reprint ed. mass mkt. 6.00 (0-06-081254-0, PL) HarpC.

Alas in Blunderland. Peter Gunning. (Illus.). 32p. (Orig.). (J). (gr. 5-7). 1991. pap. 10.95 (0-86278-271-6, Pub. by OBrien Pr IE) Dufour.

Alas, Poor Yorick. Alfred H. Bill. LC 71-110180. (Short Story Index Reprint Ser.). 1977. 20.95 (0-8369-3331-1) Ayer.

Alascattalo Tales: A Treasury of Alaskan Humor. Steven C. Levi. LC 92-56660. 264p. 1993. pap. 25.95 (0-89950-864-2) McFarland & Co.

Alasdair MacIntyre: Critic of Modernity. Peter McMylor. LC 93-3490. 1993. write for info. (0-415-04426-X); pap. write for info. (0-415-04427-8) Routledge.

Alaska. 1991. 9.99 (0-517-64410-X) Random Hse Value.

Alaska. 1988. pap. 16.00 (0-394-57078-2) Random.

Alaska. Cheryl K. Barger. (Illus.). 32p. (Orig.). 1993. pap. 4.95 (0-9637540-0-9) Wassillie Ent.

Alaska. M. Falk. (World Bibliographical Ser.). 1994. lib. bdg. 80.00 (1-85109-141-6) ABC-CLIO.

Alaska. Jennifer Grambs. (American Traveler Ser.). 1992. 7.98 (0-8317-8827-5) Smithmark.

Alaska. Ann Heinrichs. LC 90-33847. (America the Beautiful Ser.). (Illus.). 144p. (J). (gr. 4 up). 1990. lib. bdg. 20.55 (0-516-00448-4) Childrens.

Alaska. Fred Hirschmann. 1994. 39.95 (1-55868-160-4) Gr Arts Ctr Pub.

Alaska. Joyce Johnston. LC 93-25401. (Hello U. S. A. Ser.). (J). (gr. 3-6). 1994. lib. bdg. 17.50 (0-8225-2735-9, Lerner Publctns) Lerner Group.

Alaska. James A. Michener. 1088p. 1989. mass mkt. 6.99 (0-449-21726-4, Crest) Fawcett.

Alaska. James A. Michener. 1994. mass mkt. 6.99 (0-449-45313-8, Crest) Fawcett.

Alaska. James A. Michener. LC 87-43232. 1100p. 1988. 22.00 (0-394-55154-0) Random.

Alaska. Outlet Book Company Staff. (Picture Memory Ser.). (Illus.). 1992. 7.99 (0-517-07270-X) Random Hse Value.

Alaska. Kathleen Thompson. LC 87-26487. (Portrait of America Library). 48p. (J). (gr. 3 up). 1988. 21.36 (0-8174-4710-5) Raintree Steck-V.

Alaska. braille ed. Ann Heinrichs. 201p. (J). 1993. vinyl bd. 15.40 (1-56956-127-3, BR9049) W A T Braille.

Alaska, 4 bks., Set. Ed. by Leslie Kusz. (Illus.). (Orig.). 1991. pap. 13.50 (1-878654-54-3) Lit Coun AK.

*Alaska: A Golden Past, a Rich Future. Scott Foster et al. (Illus.). 320p. (C). 1995. text ed. 49.95 (0-9634100-3-2) Wyndham Pubns.

Alaska: A Guide to Alaska, Last American Frontier. Federal Writers' Project Staff & Writers Program-WPA Staff. (American Guide Ser.). 1989. reprint ed. lib. bdg. 79.00 (0-7812-1002-X) Rprt Serv.

Alaska: A Guide to Alaska, Last American Frontier. Federal Writers' Project Staff. LC 72-84457. (American Guidebook Ser.). 1981. reprint ed. lib. bdg. 89.00 (0-403-02154-5) Somerset Pub.

Alaska: A History of the 49th State. 2nd ed. Claus M. Naske & Herman E. Slotnick. LC 87-40215. (Illus.). 368p. 1994. pap. 16.95 (0-8061-2573-X) U of Okla Pr.

Alaska: A Photographic Journey. Stevens D. Bunker. 1990. 14.99 (0-517-00178-0) Random Hse Value.

Alaska: A Travel Survival Kit. 4th ed. Jim DuFresne. (Illus.). 448p. (Orig.). 1994. pap. 14.95 (0-86442-213-X) Lonely Planet.

*Alaska: Anchorage & South Central. Ed. by J. B. Anderson. 32p. (Orig.). 1995. pap. 4.99 (1-886462-08-9) J & H Sales.

Alaska: Business & Industry. Robert R. Richards. 1989. 34.95 (0-89781-265-4) Preferred Mktg.

Alaska: Images of the Country. John McPhee. 1992. 19.98 (0-88394-060-4) Promntory Pr.

Alaska: Images of the Country. deluxe limited ed. Galen Rowell & John McPhee. LC 81-5265. (Illus.). 160p. 1981. 100.00 (0-87156-293-6) Sierra.

Alaska: Insight Guide. write for info. (0-318-59688-1) S&S Trade.

Alaska: Past & Present. 3rd ed. Clarence C. Hulley. LC 80-25274. (Illus.). 477p. 1981. reprint ed. text ed. 75.00 (0-313-22845-0, HUAL, Greenwood Pr) Greenwood.

Alaska: Reflections on Land & Spirit. Ed. by Robert Hedin & Gary Holthaus. LC 88-27803. (Illus.). 322p. 1989. 8.95 (0-8165-1093-8) U of Ariz Pr.

Alaska: Reflections on Land & Spirit. Ed. by Robert Hedin & Gary Holthaus. LC 88-27803. (Illus.). 322p. 1994. reprint ed. pap. 16.95 (0-8165-1442-9) U of Ariz Pr.

Alaska: Southeast to McKinley. Andrew Jaffe et al. LC 85-43485. (Illus.). 184p. 1986. 45.00 (0-8478-0690-1); pap. 29.95 (0-8478-0703-7) Rizzoli Intl.

*Alaska: The Catalog for Independent Travellers. Alaska Rainforest Tours Staff. 68p. 1994. pap. 4.95 (0-9643593-0-8) Alaska Rainforest.

Alaska: The Cruise Lover's Guide. Paul Grescoe & Audrey Grescoe. LC 93-41276. (Illus.). 272p. (Orig.). 1994. pap. 16.95 (0-88240-452-0) Alaska Northwest.

Alaska: The Great Land. Penny Rennick & L. J. Campbell. (Alaska Geographic Ser.: Vol. 19, No. 2). (Illus.). 112p. 1992. pap. 18.95 (1-56661-002-8) Alaska Geog Soc.

Alaska: The Harriman Expedition, 1899. John Burroughs et al. 21.50 (0-8446-6259-3) Peter Smith.

Alaska: The Harriman Expedition, 1899. John Burroughs et al. 576p. 1986. reprint ed. pap. 11.95 (0-486-25109-8) Dover.

Alaska: The Outsiders. rev. ed. John R. Hall. (Illus.). 135p. 1986. pap. 12.95 (0-685-44601-8) Ulu Pub.

Alaska: Trail Tales & Eccentric Detours. Lucinda Bunnen & Virginia W. Smith. (Illus.). 80p. 1992. 75.00 (1-882313-00-3) Ice Hse Pr.

*Alaska: Twenty Poems & a Journal. Brod Bagert. (Illus.). 67p. (Orig.). 1988. pap. 10.00 (0-9614228-3-1) Juliahouse Pubs.

*Alaska - From Sea to Shining Sea. Dennis B. Fradin. LC 93-15709. (From Sea to Shining Sea Ser.). (Illus.). 64p. (J). (gr. 3-5). 1993. pap. 5.95 (0-516-43802-6) Childrens.

Alaska - From Sea to Shining Sea. Dennis B. Fradin. (From Sea to Shining Sea Ser.). (Illus.). 64p. (J). (gr. 3-5). 1993. lib. bdg. 16.50 (0-516-03802-8) Childrens.

Alaska A to Z: The Most Comprehensive Book of Facts & Figures Ever Compiled about Alaska. Milepost Editors. (Illus.). 200p. (Orig.). 1993. pap. 9.95 (1-878425-75-7) Vernon Pubns.

Alaska ABC Book. Charlene Kreeger. (Illus.). 36p. (Orig.). (J). (gr. k-1). 1978. pap. 8.95 (0-933914-01-6) Paws Four Pub.

*Alaska ABC Book. Charlene Kreeger & Shannon Cartwright. (Illus.). 32p. (J). (gr. k-3). 1978. 13.95 (0-934007-17-9) Paws Four Pub.

Alaska Administrative Code, 6 vols. suppl. ed. Butterworth Staff. 9000p. 1993. 125.00 (0-685-75306-9) Butterworth Legal Pubs.

Alaska Administrative Code, 7 vols., Set. Butterworth Staff. 9000p. 1993. ring bd. 350.00 (0-87473-454-1) Michie Butterworth.

*Alaska Adventure. Cynthia Blair. 1995. pap. 4.50 (0-449-70439-4) Fawcett.

Alaska Adventure Book. Ed. by Kevin Cassity. LC 87-70492. 120p. (Orig.). 1987. pap. 13.95 (0-9617945-0-X) Alaska Illus.

*Alaska Airmen's Association Logbook: For Alaska, NW Canada & Russia. 2nd ed. Alaska Airmen's Assoc. Staff. Ed. by Don Bowers. (Illus.). 198p. 1994. pap. 29.95 (1-884646-04-2) Maverick Dist.

Alaska Almanac. 17th ed. Alaska Northwest Books Staff. (Illus.). 240p. 1993. pap. 9.95 (0-88240-446-6) Alaska Northwest.

Alaska Almanac: Facts about Alaska. 18th ed. Alaska Northwest Books Staff. Ed. by Carolyn Smith. (Illus.). 240p. (Orig.). 1994. pap. 9.95 (0-88240-459-8) Alaska Northwest.

*Alaska Alphabet: Stories & Activities. Marilyn Morgan. (Illus.). 423p. (Orig.). (C). 1994. teacher ed, pap. text ed. 34.95 (1-878051-18-0) Circumpolar Pr.

Alaska & Beyond. John Zeigler. LC 84-51299. 59p. 1984. pap. 10.00 (0-937684-31-7) Tradd St Pr.

Alaska & Its Resources. William H. Dall. LC 72-125736. (American Environmental Studies). (Illus.). 1974. reprint ed. 40.95 (0-405-02661-7) Ayer.

Alaska & Japan: Perspectives of Past & Present. Ed. by Tsuguo Arai. (Alaskana Ser.: No. 16). 172p. 1972. 6.00 (0-685-49380-6, 16); pap. 4.00 (0-685-49381-4) Alaska Pacific.

Alaska & Other State Greats (Biographies) Carole Marsh. (Carole Marsh Alaska Bks.). (Illus.). (YA). (gr. 3-12). 1994. lib. bdg. 24.95 (1-55609-483-3); pap. 14.95 (1-55609-482-5); disk 29.95 (0-7933-1354-6) Gallopade Pub Group.

Alaska & the Pacific Rim. Morgan B. Sherwood. (Illus.). 198p. (Orig.). 1989. pap. 15.00 (0-943712-21-1) Alaska Hist.

Alaska & the Yukon. Joyce Walker. (Bertinetti Ser.). 1992. 14.98 (0-8317-0212-5) Smithmark.

Alaska Association of Small Press Catalog: 1985. Ed. by Constance Taylor. 48p. 1985. pap. 4.50 (0-9607358-4-4) Fathom Pub.

*Alaska at War, 1941-1945: The Forgotten Front Remembered Papers from the Alaska at War Symposium Anchorage, Alaska, November 11-13, 1993. Fern Chandonnet. (Illus.). 1995. lib. bdg. write for info. (0-9646980-0-5) Alaska at War.

Alaska Atlas & Gazetteer. DeLorme. 152p. (Orig.). 1992. pap. 19.95 (0-89933-201-3) DeLorme Map.

Alaska Backyard Wines. Jan O'Meara. (Illus.). 60p. (Orig.). 1988. pap. 6.50 (0-9621543-1-8) Wizard Works.

*Alaska Backyard Wines. Jan O'Meara. (Illus.). 64p. (Orig.). 1988. pap. 7.95 (0-9621543-5-0) Wizard Works.

Alaska Bandits, Bushwackers, Outlaws, Crooks, Devils, Ghosts, Desperadoes & Other Assorted & Sundry Characters! Carole Marsh. (Carole Marsh Alaska Bks.). (Illus.). (YA). (gr. 3-12). 1994. lib. bdg. 24.95 (0-7933-0094-0); pap. 14.95 (0-7933-0093-2); disk 29.95 (0-7933-0095-9) Gallopade Pub Group.

Alaska Barber Tales. Arlen E. Johnson. (Illus.). 100p. (Orig.). 1995. pap. 8.95 (0-9645610-0-X) Dixieland Pr. These 54 short stories are all true events in the author's life that happened over a period of many years. These events are all well within the range of experiences that happen to most people, the difference is in the reporting of those events. Everyone has a good story & with a little effort a good story can become an epic. The reader can easily identify with each of these stories & in all probability after reading the book, many scenarios will appear in his mind that he knows would make a good story. These stories depict a lifestyle of observation & also, not as apparent, they depict a theme of the joy of living & of participating in interesting activities. The stories are mostly humorous & are not meant to teach anything, they are meant to gently nudge the reader to go out & become involved in Life beyond the ho-hum routine of get-up-go-to-work-eat supper-watch TV until bedtime. To order: Dixieland Press, 6311 Debarr Rd., Suite 265, Anchorage, AK 99504. Price $8.95 plus $1.50 shipping & handling.** ***Publisher Provided Annotation.

Alaska Bear Tales. Larry Kaniut. LC 83-5974. 324p. 1983. pap. 12.95 (0-88240-232-3) Alaska Northwest.

Alaska Benchbook. National Center for State Courts Staff. 118p. 1978. 7.00 (0-685-15064-X, WRO-060) Natl Ctr St Courts.

Alaska Bibliography: An Introductory Guide to Alaskan Historical Literature. Melvin Ricks. LC 77-80570. 288p. 1977. 20.00 (0-8323-0292-9) Binford Mort.

Alaska Bicycle Touring Guide: Including Parts of the Yukon Territory & Northwest Territories. 2nd ed. Pete Praetorius & Alys Culhane. (Illus.). 320p. 1992. pap. 17.50 (0-938737-27-9) Denali Press.

Alaska Bookstore Book: A Surprising Guide to Our State's Bookstores & Their Specialties for Students, Teachers, Writers & Publishers. Carole Marsh. (Carole Marsh Alaska Bks.). (Illus.). 1994. lib. bdg. 24.95 (0-7933-2858-6); pap. 14.95 (0-7933-2859-4); disk 29.95 (0-7933-2860-8) Gallopade Pub Group.

Alaska Bound: A Life of Travel & Adventure in the Far North. Michael P. Dixon. LC 94-93911. 225p. 1996. pap. 9.95 (0-9639981-0-2) Dixon Paperback.

Alaska Broker. Edward M. Boyd. LC 88-72058. (Illus.). 364p. (Orig.). 1988. pap. 13.95 (0-8323-0464-6) Binford Mort.

*Alaska Business Directory, 1995-96. rev. ed. 432p. 1995. 180.00 (1-56105-745-2) Am Busn Direct.

Alaska Calls. Virginia L. Neely. (Illus.). 208p. (Orig.). 1983. pap. 9.95 (0-88839-970-7) Hancock House.

Alaska Cat, 3 bks. JoAnn Roe. (Illus.). 64p. (J). (gr. k-5). Alaska Cat. lib. bdg. 11.95 (0-931551-05-6); Alaska Cat. pap. 6.95 (0-931551-04-8) Montevista Pr.

Alaska Census of Transportation. John T. Gray & J. Phillip Rowe. (ISER Reports: No. 54). (Illus.). 84p. 1982. pap. 7.50 (0-88353-032-5) U Alaska Inst Res.

Alaska Classic Christmas Trivia: Stories, Recipes, Activities, Legends, Lore & More! Carole Marsh. (Carole Marsh Alaska Bks.). (Illus.). (YA). (gr. 3-12). 1994. lib. bdg. 24.95 (0-7933-0097-5); pap. 14.95 (0-7933-0096-7); disk 29.95 (0-7933-0098-3) Gallopade Pub Group.

Alaska Coastales. Carole Marsh. (Carole Marsh Alaska Bks.). (J). 1994. lib. bdg. 24.95 (0-7933-7266-6) Gallopade Pub Group.

Alaska Coastales. Carole Marsh. (Carole Marsh Alaska Bks.). (Illus.). (YA). (gr. 3-12). 1994. lib. bdg. 24.95 (1-55609-479-5); pap. 14.95 (1-55609-478-7); disk 29.95 (0-7933-1353-8) Gallopade Pub Group.

Alaska Cooking Classics: A Treasury of Lodge & Bed & Breakfast Favorite Recipes. Mary Gerkin. Ed. by Cass Crandall. (Illus.). 245p. 1991. pap. 14.95 (0-9626071-3-4) Kachemak Pub.

Alaska Corporation Manual: How to Form an Alaska Corporation Without a Lawyer for 80 Dollars or Less. Welmon Walker, Jr. LC 76-58671. (Illus.). 1979. 17.95 (0-918270-03-0) That New Pub.

Alaska Crime Perspective, 1994. Ed. by Kathleen O. Morgan et al. 24p. 1994. 18.00 (1-56692-251-8) Morgan Quitno Corp.

*Alaska Crime Perspective 1995. Ed. by Kathleen O. Morgan et al. 24p. 1995. 18.00 (1-56692-351-4) Morgan Quitno Corp.

*Alaska Criminal & Traffic Law Manual: 1993 Edition. Date not set. 25.00 (0-614-05774-4) Michie Butterworth.

Alaska "Crinkum-Crankum" A Funny Word Book about Our State. Carole Marsh. (Carole Marsh Alaska Bks.). (Illus.). (J). 1994. lib. bdg. 24.95 (0-7933-4813-7); pap. 14.95 (0-7933-4814-5); disk 29.95 (0-7933-4815-3) Gallopade Pub Group.

Alaska Days with John Muir. S. Hall Young. LC 74-174351. (Illus.). 1972. reprint ed. 19.95 (0-405-09110-9) Ayer.

Alaska Deception. William M. Brinton. LC 84-60271. 277p. 1984. 15.95 (0-916515-00-1) Mercury Hse Inc.

Alaska Dictionary & Pronunciation Guide. Jan O'Meara. (Illus.). 156p. (Orig.). 1988. pap. 8.50 (0-9621543-0-X) Wizard Works.

Alaska Dingbats! Bk. 1: A Fun Book of Games, Stories, Activities & More about Our State That's All in Code! for You to Decipher. Carole Marsh. (Carole Marsh Alaska Bks.). (Illus.). (J). (gr. 3-12). 1994. lib. bdg. 24.95 (0-7933-3776-3); pap. 14.95 (0-7933-3777-1); disk 29.95 (0-7933-3778-X) Gallopade Pub Group.

Alaska Directory of Attorneys (Spring 1990 Edition) rev. ed. 224p. 1990. spiral bd. 20.00 (1-878100-00-9) Todd Commns.

*Alaska Dog Mushing Guide: Facts & Legends. Ron Wendt. 70p. 1994. pap. text ed. 9.95 (1-886574-05-7) Goldstream Pubns.

Alaska Dragon. Benjamin A. Shaine. 365p. (Orig.). 1991. lib. bdg. 21.95 (0-914221-12-4); pap. 10.95 (0-914221-11-6) Fireweed Pr AK.

*Alaska Earthquake. 32p. 1995. pap. 4.95 (1-886462-09-7) J & H Sales.

An Asterisk (*) at the beginning of an entry indicates that the title is appearing in BIP for the first time.

An Asterisk (*) at the beginning of an entry indicates that the title is appearing in BIP for the first time.

171

A

Albert Schweitzer: A Biography. George Marshall & David Poling. 1990. 4.00 (*0-317-02831-6*) Albert Schweitzer.

Albert Schweitzer: An Adventurer for Humanity. Harold Robles. (Illus.). 64p. (J). (gr. 4-6). 1994. lib. bdg. 15.40 (*1-56294-352-9*) Millbrook Pr.

Albert Schweitzer: Friend of All Life. Carol Greene. LC 93-12975. (Rookie Biographies Ser.). (Illus.). 48p. (J). (gr. k-3). 1993. lib. bdg. 12.90 (*0-516-04258-0*); pap. 4.95 (*0-516-44258-9*) Childrens.

Albert Schweitzer: Sketches for a Portrait. Jackson Ice. LC 93-40728. 1994. 34.00 (*0-8191-9400-X*) U Pr of Amer.

Albert Schweitzer: The Doctor Who Devoted His Life to Africa's Sick. James Bentley. LC 90-9974. (People Who Made a Difference Ser.). (Illus.). 64p. (J). (gr. 3-4). 1991. lib. bdg. 21.26 (*0-8368-0457-0*) Gareth Stevens Inc.

Albert Schweitzer: The Doctor Who Gave up a Brilliant Career to Serve the People of Africa. James Bentley. LC 88-17731. (Illus.). 68p. (J). (gr. 5-6). 1989. lib. bdg. 21.26 (*1-55532-823-7*) Gareth Stevens Inc.

Albert Schweitzer & Alice Ehlers: A Friendship in Letters. Ed. by Kurt Bergel & Alice R. Bergel. Tr. by Alice R. Bergel. 132p. (C). 1991. lib. bdg. 39.00 (*0-8191-8327-X*) U Pr of Amer.

Albert Schweitzer Jubilee Book. Ed. by A. A. Roback. LC 79-97392. (Illus.). 508p. 1971. reprint ed. text ed. 65.00 (*0-8371-2670-3*, ASJB, Greenwood Pr) Greenwood.

Albert Schweitzer, Musician. Michael Murray. 176p. 1994. 44.95 (*1-85928-031-5*, Pub. by Scolar Pr UK) Ashgate Pub Co.

Albert Schweitzers Kulturphilosophie Im Horizont Saekularer Ethik. Wolfgang E. Mueller. (Theologische Bibliothek Toepelmann Ser.: Vol. 59). ix, 331p. (GER.). (C). 1993. lib. bdg. 113.85 (*3-11-013966-9*) De Gruyter.

Albert Sidney Johnston: Soldier of Three Republics. Charles P. Roland. (Illus.). 408p. (Orig.). 1987. reprint ed. pap. 18.95 (*0-292-70399-6*) U of Tex Pr.

***Albert Speer: His battle with truth.** Gitta Sereny. LC 94-19764. (Illus.). 784p. 1995. pap. 35.00 (*0-394-52915-4*) Knopf.

Albert Speer & the Nazi Ministry of Arms: Economic Institutions & Industrial Production in the German War Economy. Edward R. Zilbert. LC 76-17030. 304p. 1981. 35.00 (*0-8386-1709-3*) Fairleigh Dickinson.

Albert Stewart: The Artist, Teacher & Friend. Frwd. by Douglas McClellan et al. (Illus.). 125p. 1966. 30.00 (*0-915478-05-6*) Galleries Coll.

Albert Stewart Sculpture. Ed. by Frederick Hard. (Illus.). 1963. 1.00 (*0-915478-03-X*) Galleries Coll.

Albert the Albatross. Syd Hoff. LC 61-5767. (Early I Can Read Bk.). (Illus.). 32p. (J). (gr. k-3). 1961. lib. bdg. 14.89 (*0-06-022446-0*) HarpC Child Bks.

Albert the Great: His Life & Scholastic Labours. Joachim Sighart. Tr. by T. A. Dixon. reprint ed. lib. bdg. 45.00 (*0-697-00016-8*) Irvington.

Albert the Great: Man & the Beasts: De animalibus (Books 22-26) Tr. by James J. Scanlan. LC 87-7964. (Medieval & Renaissance Texts & Studies: Vol. 47). (Illus.). 528p. 1987. 30.00 (*0-86698-032-6*) MRTS.

Albert the Running Bear Gets the Jitters. Barbara Isenberg & Susan Wolf. 40p. (J). (gr. k-4). 1987. 13.95 (*0-89919-517-2*, Clarion Bks) HM.

Albert Thomas DeRome, 1885-1959: Being a Story of His Life & a Picture Diary of His Oils & Watercolors. Walter A. Nelson-Rees. LC 87-51379. (Illus.). 164p. 1988. 60.00 (*0-938842-06-4*) WIM Oakland.

***Albert Watson: Cyclops, Vol. 1.** Albert Watson. (Illus.). 192p. 1994. 75.00 (*0-8212-2141-8*) Bulfinch Pr.

Albert Wesselski & Recent Folk-Tale Theories. Emma E. Kiefer. LC 72-6828. (Studies in Comparative Literature: No. 35). 1972. reprint ed. lib. bdg. 56.95 (*0-8383-1654-9*) M S G Haskell Hse.

Alberta. Edna Bakken. LC 91-951144. (Discover Canada Ser.). (Illus.). 144p. (J). (gr. 5-8). 1992. lib. bdg. 21.23 (*0-516-06611-0*) Childrens.

Alberta. Suzanne LeVert. (Let's Discover Canada Ser.). (Illus.). 64p. (J). (gr. 3 up). 1991. lib. bdg. 16.95 (*0-7910-1026-0*) Chelsea Hse.

***Alberta.** Sarah Yates. LC 94-45478. (Hello Canada Ser.). (J). 1995. write for info. (*0-8225-2763-4*) Lerner Group.

Alberta Alone. Cora Sandel, pseud. Tr. by Elizabeth Rokkan. LC 83-19323. (Alberta Trilogy Ser.). 297p. 1984. reprint ed. 15.95 (*0-8214-0760-0*); reprint ed. pap. 9.95 (*0-8214-0761-9*) Ohio U Pr.

Alberta & Freedom. Cora Sandel, pseud. Tr. by Elizabeth Rokkan. LC 83-19322. (Alberta Trilogy Ser.). 254p. 1984. reprint ed. 15.95 (*0-8214-0758-9*); reprint ed. pap. 9.95 (*0-8214-0759-7*) Ohio U Pr.

***Alberta & the Northwest Territories Handbook: Including Banff, Jasper & the Canadian Rockies.** Andrew Hempstead & Nadina Purdon. (Moon Travel Handbooks Ser.). (Illus.). 450p. (Orig.). 1995. pap. 17.95 (*1-56691-067-6*) Moon Pubns CA.

***Alberta Business Directory 1995-96.** rev. ed. 1136p. 1995. 220.00 (*1-56105-803-3*) Am Busn Direct.

Alberta Hailstorms. A. J. Chisolm & Marianne English. (Meteorological Monograph Ser.: Vol. 14, No. 36). (Illus.). 98p. 1973. 23.00 (*0-933876-39-4*) Am Meteorological.

Alberta Infant Motor Scale (AIMS) Martha C. Piper & Johanna Darrah. (Illus.). 1994. 20.95 (*0-7216-4721-9*) Saunders.

Alberta on My Mind. Intro. by Andy Russell. (America on My Mind Ser.). (Illus.). 120p. 1990. 29.50 (*1-56044-028-7*) Falcon Pr MT.

***Alberta Temple: Centre & Symbol of Faith.** Vi A. Wood. (Illus.). (Orig.). 1989. 25.95 (*0-920490-95-6*, Pub. by Detselig CN); pap. 16.95 (*0-920490-94-8*, Pub. by Detselig CN) Temeron Bks.

Albertanus of Brescia: The Pursuit of Happiness in the Early Thirteenth Century. James M. Powell. LC 91-29777. (Middle Ages Ser.). 168p. (C). 1992. text ed. 24.95 (*0-8122-3138-4*) U of Pa Pr.

***Alberta's Revolutionary Leaders.** T. C. Byrne. (Illus.). 247p. (Orig.). 1991. pap. 17.95 (*1-55059-024-3*) Temeron Bks.

Albertina Anda Arriba: El Abecedario: Albertina Goes Up: An Alphabet Book. Nancy M. Grande Tabor. (Illus.). 32p. (J). (ps-3). 1993. lib. bdg. 15.88 (*0-88106-638-9*); pap. 6.95 (*0-88106-418-1*) Charlesbridge Pub.

Albertine Disparu La Fugitive, Bk. 7: A la Recherche du Temps Perdu. Marcel Proust. (FRE.). 1990. pap. 15.95 (*0-8288-3759-7*, F119550) Fr & Eur.

Albertine Disparue: (La Fugitive) Marcel Proust. (Folio Ser.: No. 2139). 374p. (FRE.). 1984. pap. 9.95 (*2-07-038233-8*, 2127) Schoenhof.

Albertine, in Five Times. Tremblay. (NFS Canada Ser.). Date not set. pap. 9.95 (*0-88922-234-7*, Pub. by Talonbooks CN) InBook.

Alberto Ghiraldo: A Chronology. V. Munoz. Tr. by W. Scott Johnson. (Libertarian & Anarchist Chronology Ser.). 1979. lib. bdg. 59.95 (*0-8490-3033-1*) Gordon Pr.

***Alberto Giacometti: Early Works in Paris (1922 - 1930)** Casimiro Di Crescenzo. Ed. by Craig S. Hayes. Tr. by Camilla B. Rudolph et al. (Illus.). 148p. (Orig.). 1994. pap. 25.55 (*0-9626731-7-X*) Yoshii Gallery.

Alberto Giacometti: Sculptures - Paintings - Drawings. Ed. & Contrib by Angela Schneider. (Illus.). 224p. 1994. 60.00 (*3-7913-1371-1*, Pub. by Prestel) TeNeues.

***Alberto Moravia.** Peterson. 1995. 26.95 (*0-8057-8296-6*, Twayne) Macmillan.

Alberto Moravia. Luciano Rebay. LC 77-126544. (Columbia Essays on Modern Writers Ser.: No. 52). (Orig.). 1971. pap. text ed. 7.50 (*0-231-02762-1*) Col U Pr.

Alberto Morrocco. Victoria Keller & Clara Young. (Illus.). 96p. 1994. 34.95 (*1-85158-590-7*, Pub. by Mnstream UK) Trafalgar.

***Alberto Savinio: Musician Writer & Painter.** Paolo Baldacci et al. Tr. by Margaret Poser et al. (Illus.). 125p. (Orig.). Date not set. pap. 30.00 (*1-887157-00-X*) P Baldacci.

Alberto Savinio: Speaking to Clio. Tr. by John Shepley. LC 86-63743. 1988. 14.95 (*0-910395-22-5*); pap. 9.00 (*0-910395-23-3*) Marlboro Pr.

Albertosaurus. Swann. (Dinosaur Library: Set V). (Illus.). 24p. (J). 1984. lib. bdg. 14.00 (*0-86592-527-5*) Rourke Enter.

Albert's Alphabet. Leslie Tryon. LC 90-38883. (Illus.). 40p. (J). (ps-1). 1991. text ed. 14.95 (*0-689-31642-9*, Atheneum Bks Young) S&S Childrens.

Albert's Alphabet. Leslie Tryon. LC 93-48408. (Illus.). 32p. (J). (ps-2). 1994. pap. 4.95 (*0-689-71799-7*, Aladdin Paperbacks) S&S Childrens.

Albert's Bridge & Other Plays. Tom Stoppard. Incl. If You're Glad I'll Be Frank. 1977. (*0-318-52808-8*); Artist Descending a Staircase. 1977. (*0-318-52809-6*); Where Are They Now? 1977. (*0-318-52810-X*); Separate Peace. 1977. (*0-318-52811-8*); 1977. Set pap. 3.95 (*0-394-17000-8*, E686) Grove-Atltic.

Albert's Field Trip. Leslie Tryon. LC 92-43686. (Illus.). 32p. (J). (gr. k-3). 1993. text ed. 14.95 (*0-689-31821-9*, Atheneum Bks Young) S&S Childrens.

Albert's Hair. Slightly Off-Center Writers Group, Ltd. Staff. (Spark of Life Ser.). (Illus.). 60p. (J). (gr. 4-6). 1994. pap. 6.95 (*1-56721-081-3*) Twenty-Fifth Cent Pr.

Albert's Horoscope Almanac. Albert Goldbarth. 1986. pap. 30.00 (*0-931460-27-1*) Bieler.

***Albert's Nap.** Michael Grejniec. LC 94-45628. (Illus.). 32p. (J). (ps-3). 1995. 14.95 (*1-55858-279-7*); lib. bdg. 14.88 (*1-55858-280-0*) North-South Bks NYC.

Albert's Play. Leslie Tryon. LC 91-23145. (Illus.). 32p. (J). (gr. k-3). 1992. text ed. 13.95 (*0-689-31525-2*, Atheneum Bks Young) S&S Childrens.

Albert's Riddle. Seth McEvoy & Nancy Wartik. (Illus.). 224p. (J). (gr. 6-8). 1989. 9.95 (*0-318-37482-X*) Kipling Pr.

Albert's Thanksgiving. Leslie Tryon. LC 94-8025. 32p. (J). 1994. text ed. 14.95 (*0-689-31865-0*, Atheneum S&S) S&S Trade.

Albert's Toothache. Barbara Williams. LC 74-4040. (Unicorn Paperbacks Ser.). (Illus.). 32p. (J). (ps-1). 1988. pap. 3.95 (*0-525-44363-0*, 0383-120, DCB) Dutton Child Bks.

Albert's Toothache. Barbara Williams. LC 74-4040. (Unicorn Paperbacks Ser.). (Illus.). 32p. (J). (ps-1). 1974. pap. 3.95 (*0-525-45037-8*, Dutton) NAL-Dutton.

Albert's Toothache. Barbara Williams. (Illus.). (J). (ps-3). 1992. pap. 4.99 (*0-14-054733-9*, Puff Unicorn) Puffin Bks.

Albertsen's - International Edition, 1991: Directory Guide to English-Language Foreign Magazines & Newspapers World-Wide. Comp. by Ken Albertsen. 176p. (Orig.). 1991. pap. text ed. 45.00 (*1-879338-06-8*) Albertsens.

Albertsen's U. S. & Foreign Diplomatic Contacts, 1991. Comp. by Ken Albertsen. (Illus.). 50p. (Orig.). 1990. pap. text ed. 15.00 (*1-879338-08-4*) Albertsens.

Albertson Site: A Deeply & Clearly Stratified Ozark Bluff Shelter. Don R. Dickson. (Research Ser.: No. 41). (Illus.). 300p. (Orig.). 1991. pap. text ed. 25.00 (*0-685-50316-X*) AR Archaeol.

Albertus Magnus: Egyptian Secrets. Albertus Magnus. 9.95 (*0-685-72555-3*) Wehman.

Albertus Magnus: Egyptian Secrets, White & Black Art for Man & Beast. L. W. De Laurence. 208p. 1972. spiral bd. 8.25 (*0-7873-0264-3*) Mokelumne.

Albertville '92. (Illus.). 208p. Date not set. 34.95 (*1-56486-015-9*) Prof Team.

Alberuni's India: An Account of the Religion, Philosophy, Literature, Geography, Chronology, Astronomy , Customs, Laws & Astrology of India about AD 1030, 2 vols. in 1. Al-Biruni. Tr. by Edward C. Sachau. reprint ed. text ed. 54.00 (*0-685-13423-7*) Coronet Bks.

***Albie & Billy the Sky-Pilot - & Other Stories.** Wayne Short. 184p. (Orig.). 1995. pap. 13.95 (*0-9644980-4-9*) Devils Thumb.

Albie the Lifeguard. Louise Borden. LC 91-11327. (Illus.). 32p. (J). (ps-3). 1993. 14.95 (*0-590-44585-5*) Scholastic Inc.

***Albietz Powers & Duties of Lay Justices of the Peace in Queensland.** 8th ed. Keith Tronc. 206p. 1994. pap. 49.00 (*0-455-21272-4*, Pub. by Law Bk Co) W W Gaunt.

Albigen Papers. rev. ed. Richard Rose. 240p. 1978. reprint ed. pap. 9.00 (*1-878683-00-4*) TAT Found.

Albigen Papers. 3rd rev. ed. Richard Rose. 240p. 1978. reprint ed. 12.00 (*1-878683-07-1*) TAT Found.

Albigenses: A Romance, 4 vols., Set. Charles R. Maturin. LC 73-22768. (Gothic Novels II Ser.). 1979. reprint ed. 96.95 (*0-405-06017-3*) Ayer.

Albigensian Crusade: An Historical Essay. Jacques Madaule. Tr. by Barbara Wall. LC 66-23621. 191p. reprint ed. pap. 54.50 (*0-7837-0455-0*, 2040778) Bks Demand.

Albigensian Crusades. Joseph Strayer. (Ann Arbor Paperbacks Ser.). 250p. (C). 1992. reprint ed. text ed. 39.50 (*0-472-09476-9*, Ann Arbor Bks); reprint ed. pap. text ed. 16.95 (*0-472-06476-2*, Ann Arbor Bks) U of Mich Pr.

Albigeois. 2nd ed. Celestin Douais. LC 78-63182. (Heresies of the Early Christian & Medieval Era Ser.: Second Ser.). reprint ed. 64.50 (*0-404-16221-5*) AMS Pr.

Albina Redner: A Shoshone Life. Ed. by Helen M. Blue & R. T. King. (Illus.). 162p. 1990. lib. bdg. 34.00 (*1-56475-346-8*); fiche write for info. (*1-56475-347-6*) U NV Oral Hist.

***Albino Joe.** Jack Cauley. 1995. 9.95 (*0-533-11211-7*) Vantage.

Albino Knife. Steve Perry. 1991. mass mkt. 4.99 (*0-441-01391-0*) Ace Bks.

Albinus on Anatomy. Robert B. Hale. 1989. pap. 11.95 (*0-486-25836-X*) Dover.

Albion & Ariel Vol. 166: British Puritanism & the Birth of Political Zionism. Dennis J. Culver. LC 94-16473. (American University Studies: No. VII). 238p. (C). 1994. text ed. 48.95 (*0-8204-2303-3*) P Lang Pubs.

***Albion, Michigan.** (Illus.). 138p. 1991. 34.95 (*0-88107-193-5*) Curtis Media.

Albion W. Tourgee. Theodore L. Gross. LC 63-10956. (Twayne's United States Authors Ser.). 1963. lib. bdg. 17.95 (*0-89197-654-X*); pap. text ed. 3.95 (*0-89197-999-9*) Irvington.

Albion's England. William Warner. 1971. reprint ed. 138.00 (*3-487-03325-9*) Adlers Foreign Bks.

Albion's England. William Warner. (Anglistica & Americana Ser.: No. 102). xvi, 399p. 1971. reprint ed. 89.70 (*0-685-66528-3*, 05103325, Pub. by Georg Olms GW) Lubrecht & Cramer.

Albion's Fatal Tree: Crime & Society in Eighteenth-Century England. Edward P. Thompson et al. (Illus.). 1976. pap. 13.56 (*0-394-73085-2*) Pantheon.

Albion's People: English Society, 1714-1815. John Rule. (Social & Economic History of England Ser.). 269p. (C). 1991. pap. text ed. 28.50 (*0-582-08916-6*, 79212) Longman.

Albion's Seed: Four British Folkways in America. David H. Fischer. (America: A Cultural History Ser.: Vol. I). (Illus.). 970p. 1989. 40.00 (*0-19-503794-4*) OUP.

Albion's Seed: Four British Folkways in America. David H. Fischer. (America: A Cultural History Ser.: Vol. 1). (Illus.). 972p. 1991. reprint ed. pap. 22.50 (*0-19-506905-6*, 12055) OUP.

***Albion's Story.** Kate Grenville. LC 94-27277. 1994. 21.95 (*0-15-100122-7*) HarBrace.

***Albizu Campos & the Ponce Massacre.** Juan A. Corretjer. 26p. 1993. pap. 2.50 (*0-89567-115-8*) World View Forum.

Albizuri Among the Lyngams: A Brief History of the Catholic Mission Among the Lyngams on North East India. Sebastian Karotemprel. 1986. 17.50 (*0-8364-1569-8*, KL Mukhopadhyay) S Asia.

Albnius & the History of Middle Platonism. R. E. Witt. 159p. 1937. reprint ed. lib. bdg. 36.00 (*0-685-13618-3*, Pub. by A M Hakkert SP) Coronet Bks.

Albores Historicos del Capitalismo en Puerto Rico. 2nd ed. Arturo Morales-Carrion. (UPREX, Humanidades Ser.: No. 9). 140p. (C). 1980. pap. 1.50 (*0-8477-0009-7*) U of PR Pr.

Albori Del Melodramma, 3 vols., Set. Angelo Solerti. xxi, 902p. 1969. reprint ed. write for info. (*0-318-71588-0*, Pub. by Georg Olms GW) Lubrecht & Cramer.

Albrecht Altdorfer & the Origins of Landscape. Christopher S. Wood. LC 93-13123. (Illus.). 1993. 65.00 (*0-226-90601-9*) U Ch Pr.

Albrecht Durer. E. Ullmann. 72p. (GER.). 1982. 39.00 (*0-317-57245-8*, Pub. by Collets UK) St Mut.

Albrecht Durer. Ernest Raboff. LC 87-17702. (Trophy Nonfiction Art for Children Ser.). (Illus.). 32p. (J). (gr. 1 up). 1988. reprint ed. pap. 5.95 (*0-06-446071-1*, Trophy) HarpC Child Bks.

Albrecht Durer: A Biography. Jane C. Hutchison. (Illus.). 288p. (C). 1992. text ed. 39.50 (*0-691-03978-X*); pap. text ed. 12.95 (*0-691-00297-5*) Princeton U Pr.

Albrecht Durer: Engravings & Etchings. Campbell Dodgson. LC 67-27451. (Graphic Art Ser.). 1967. reprint ed. 35.00 (*0-306-70976-7*) Da Capo.

Albrecht Durer: Master Printmaker. Ed. by Boston Museum of Fine Arts Staff. LC 87-80023. 1988. reprint ed. lib. bdg. 75.00 (*0-87817-316-1*) Hacker.

Albrecht Durer: Paintings, Prints & Drawings. Peter Streider. 1990. 95.00 (*0-89835-317-3*) Abaris Bks.

Albrecht Durer: Selected Woodcuts from the Collection of the Hermitage. Ed. by Collet's Holdings, Ltd. Staff. 1979. 175.00 (*0-317-39475-4*, Pub. by Collets UK) St Mut.

Albrecht Durer: Selected Woodcuts from the Hermitage. Charmian Mezentseva. 1976. 550.00 (*0-317-61185-2*, Pub. by Collets UK) Pro-Am Music.

Albrecht Durer, Paintings, Prints & Drawings. Peter Strieder. 1990. 95.00 (*0-89835-057-3*) Abaris Bks.

Albrecht Durer, The Painter's Manual. Tr. by Walter S. Strauss. LC 77-86240. (Illus.). 1978. 59.50 (*0-913870-52-8*) Abaris Bks.

Albrecht Papers, Vol. III. William A. Albrecht. Ed. by Charles Walters, Jr. LC 88-82608. (Illus.). 397p. 1989. 20.00 (*0-911311-18-1*) Halcyon Hse.

Albrecht Papers, Vol. IV. William A. Albrecht. LC 92-71281. 250p. 1992. pap. 20.00 (*0-911311-23-8*) Halcyon Hse.

Albrecht Papers, Vol. II. William A. Albrecht. Ed. by Charles Walters, Jr. LC 83-81673. 192p. 1983. 15.00 (*0-911311-07-6*) Halcyon Hse.

Albrecht Ritschl & the Problem of the Historical Jesus. Clive Marsh. LC 92-3639. 248p. 1992. lib. bdg. 89.95 (*0-7734-9822-2*) E Mellen.

Albrecht Von Eyb, Medieval Moralist. Joseph A. Hiller. LC 70-140027. (Catholic University Studies in German: No. 13). 1970. reprint ed. 37.50 (*0-404-50233-4*) AMS Pr.

Albrecht von Hallers Ruhm als Dichter. Franz R. Kempf. (American University Studies: Germanic Languages & Literature: Ser. I, Vol. 52). 178p. (GER.). 1987. text ed. 27.00 (*0-8204-0332-6*) P Lang Pubs.

Albucasis on Surgery & Instruments: A Definitive Edition of the Arabic Text with English Translation & Commentary. M. S. Spink & G. L. Lewis. LC 68-10498. 866p. reprint ed. pap. 180.00 (*0-8357-5297-6*, 2031499) Bks Demand.

Albucius. Pascal Quignard. (FRE.). 1992. pap. 10.95 (*0-7859-3169-4*, 2253059560) Fr & Eur.

Albucius. Pascal Quignard. Tr. by Bruce Boone. (Illus.). 188p. (C). 1993. 35.00 (*0-932499-69-4*) Lapis Pr.

***Album.** Louise Bourgeois. (Illus.). 123p. 1994. text ed. 125.00 (*0-935875-13-1*) P Blum Edit.

Album. Kenwald Elmslie. (Illus.). 56p. pap. 3.50 (*0-686-09746-7*) Kulchur Foun.

Album. David Rimmer. 1981. pap. 4.75 (*0-8222-0013-9*) Dramatists Play.

Album. Mary R. Rinehart. 1988. pap. 3.50 (*0-8217-2334-0*) Zebra.

Album. Rebecca M. Valette & Jean-Paul Valette. 208p. (SPA.). (C). 1990. pap. text ed. 17.00 (*0-669-06782-2*) Heath.

Album: Cuentos del Mundo Hispanico. 2nd ed. Rebecca M. Valette & Joy Renjilian-Burgy. 240p. (SPA.). (C). 1993. Shrinkwrapped with free student cassette. pap. text ed. write for info. (*0-669-29485-3*) Heath.

Album: The Portraits of Duane Michals, 1958-1988. (Illus.). 144p. 1988. 55.00 (*0-942642-31-7*) Twelvetrees Pr.

Album Amicorum Kenneth C. Lindsay: Essays on Art & Literature, Vol. X1. Ed. by Susan A. Stein & George D. McKee. (Illus.). 392p. (C). 1990. 40.00 (*0-9621899-9-5*) MRTS.

Album Cover, Album 6. (Illus.). 144p. (GER.). Date not set. write for info. (*3-283-00261-4*, Pub. by Georg Olms GW) Lubrecht & Cramer.

Album De Cinelandia. L. A. Villegas. 1976. lib. bdg. 105.00 (*0-8490-1408-5*) Gordon Pr.

Album de la Familia. Ed. by Isabel Pico. 45p. 1984. pap. 5.75 (*0-8477-2473-5*) U of PR Pr.

Album de Vers Anciens see Poesies

Album Elemer Malyusz. 406p. (FRE & GER.). 1982. 52.30 (*0-685-06606-1*) P Lang Pubs.

Album ex libres medicorum. Wasyl Luciw. (Illus.). 31p. 1961. 25.00 (*0-918884-09-8*) Slavia Lib.

Album Familiar: Bajarse Al Moro. Jose L. Alonso de Santos. Ed. by Andres Amoros. (Nueva Austral Ser.: No. 260). (SPA.). 1993. pap. text ed. 24.95x (*84-239-7260-7*) Elliots Bks.

Album Francais - Morceaux Reserves: 24 Vocal Pieces (7 Additional Pieces in Appendix) Gioachino Rossini. Ed. by Rossana Dalmonte. xlii, 404p. 1991. 100.00 (*0-226-72843-9*) U Ch Pr.

Album Francois Dumont. 309p. (FRE.). 1982. 44.60 (*0-685-06618-5*) P Lang Pubs.

Album Lyrique & Dernieres Pensees. Maria Malibran & Charlotte Grernspan. LC 83-7841. (Women Composers Ser.: No. 14). 62p. 1983. reprint ed. lib. bdg. 26.50 (*0-306-76194-7*) Da Capo.

Album Maya. Ed. by Rolfe. F. Schell. Tr. by Rolfe F. Schell & Pierre-Albert Camus. LC 73-87109. (Illus.). (ENG, FRE & SPA.). 1973. 4.50 (*0-87208-020-X*); pap. 2.95 (*0-87208-019-6*) Island Pr Pubs.

Album of American Battle Art, 1755-1918. Donald H. Mugridge & Helen F. Conover. LC 72-6278. (Illus.). 340p. 1972. reprint ed. lib. bdg. 55.00 (*0-306-70523-0*) Da Capo.

Album of American History, 3 vols., Set. rev. ed. James T. Adams. LC 74-91746. 2512p. 1981. text ed. 295.00 (*0-684-16848-0*, Scribners) S&S Trade.

Album of American History Supplement I. LC 82-42761. (Illus.). 280p. 1985. text ed. 70.00 (*0-684-17440-5*, Scribners) S&S Trade.

Album of Bible Characters. John Waddey. 1983. pap. 6.25 (*0-89137-542-2*) Quality Pubns.

Album of Carte-de-Visite & Cabinet Portrait Photographs 1854-1914. Oliver Mathews. (Illus.). 148p. 1987. 14.95 (*0-85945-002-3*, Pub. by Bishopsgte Pr UK) Intl Spec Bk.

An Asterisk (*) at the beginning of an entry indicates that the title is appearing in BIP for the first time.

Album of Chinese Brush Painting - Eighty Paintings & Ideas: Ning Yeh's Second Art Album. Ning Yeh. (Illus.). 184p. (C). 1987. 29.95 (*0-9618307-0-0*) Ning & Ling Yeh.

Album of Chinese Contemporary Paintings. 214p. (CHI & ENG.). 1994. pap. 94.95 (*92-3-002841-X*, U2841, Pub. by UNESCO FR) UNIPUB.

Album of Civil War Battle Art. Library of Congress Staff. 128p. 1988. reprint ed. pap. 12.95 (*1-55709-111-0*) Applewood.

Album of Curious Houses. Lucinda Lambton. 1989. 24.95 (*0-7011-3119-5*) Random.

Album of Finnish Halls. Reino Hannula. Ed. by Amy W. Van Hazinza & Toini P. Laakso. (Illus.). 196p. 1991. 29.00 (*0-9626860-1-8*) Finn Heritage.

Album of Fluid Motion. Milton Van Dyke. LC 81-83088. (Illus.). 176p. 1982. text ed. 25.00 (*0-915760-03-7*); pap. text ed. 15.00 (*0-915760-02-9*) Parabolic Pr.

Album of Fragrance: With Complete Instructions for Making Your Own Perfume, Potpourri, Sachet, Herbal Moth Repellant & Incense. Edith G. Bailes. (Illus.). 100p. (Orig.). 1983. pap. 9.95 (*0-9611118-0-1*) Cardamom.

Album of Horses. Marguerite Henry. LC 92-33009. (Illus.). 112p. (J). (gr. 2-5). 1993. reprint ed. pap. 9.95 (*0-689-71709-1*, Aladdin Paperbacks) S&S Childrens.

Album of Indian Paintings. Mulk R. Anand. (Illus.). 1979. 7.50 (*0-89744-191-5*); pap. 10.00 (*0-89744-192-3*) Auromere.

Album of Indian Sculpture. C. Sivaramamurti. (Illus.). 1979. pap. 7.50 (*0-89744-194-X*) Auromere.

Album of Map Projections. John P. Snyder & Philip M. Voxland. LC 86-600253. 256p. 1989. pap. 14.00 (*0-16-003368-3*, S/N 024-001-03568-5) USGPO.

Album of Maya Architecture. Tatiana Proskouriakoff. LC 63-17166. 1976. reprint ed. pap. 18.95 (*0-8061-1351-0*) U of Okla Pr.

Album of Nine Songs. Nielsen. Date not set. pap. 19.95 (*0-685-69294-9*, Pub. by Wilhelm Hansen DK) Music Sales.

Album of Nineteen Dances. J. S. Bach. Date not set. pap. 8.95 (*0-685-69295-7*, Pub. by Wilhelm Hansen DK) Music Sales.

Album of Nineteenth Century Homes: Shawnee County. 72p. 4.95 (*0-686-79874-0*, 51) Shawnee County Hist.

Album of Old Arundel. Nicholas Thornton. (C). 1989. 50.00 (*1-85455-010-1*, Pub. by Ensign Pubns & Print UK) St Mut.

Album of Old Beaulieu & Bucklers Hard. Ed. by Susan Tomkins. (C). 1989. 39.00 (*1-85455-046-2*, Pub. by Ensign Pubns & Print UK) St Mut.

Album of Old Horsham. Tony Wales. (C). 1989. 39.00 (*1-85455-011-X*, Pub. by Ensign Pubns & Print UK) St Mut.

Album of Old Lymington & Milford-on-Sea. Chris Hobby. (C). 1989. 39.00 (*1-85455-020-9*, Pub. by Ensign Pubns & Print UK) St Mut.

Album of Rhode Island History. Patrick T. Conley. (Illus.). 284p. (Orig.). 1986. 24.95 (*0-317-55271-6*) Donning Co.

Album of Science, 5 vols., Set. Ed. by I. Bernard Cohen. 1989. text ed. 395.00 (*0-684-19074-5*, Scribners) S&S Trade.

Album of Science: From Leonardo to Lavoisier, 1450-1800. I. Bernard Cohen. LC 80-15542. (Illus.). 320p. 1980. text ed. 85.00 (*0-684-15377-7*, Scribners) S&S Trade.

Album of Science: The Biological Sciences in the 20th Century. Merriley Borell. Ed. by I. Bernard Cohen. LC 88-14715. 320p. 1988. text ed. 85.00 (*0-684-16483-3*, Scribners) S&S Trade.

Album of Science: The Nineteenth Century. L. Pearce Williams. LC 77-3907. 432p. 1978. text ed. 85.00 (*0-684-15047-6*, Scribners) S&S Trade.

Album of Science: The Physical Sciences in the 20th Century. Owen Gingerich. Ed. by I. Bernard Cohen. LC 88-24007. 320p. 1989. text ed. 85.00 (*0-684-15497-8*, Scribners) S&S Trade.

Album of Science, Vol. 1: Antiquity & the Middle Ages. John E. Murdoch. LC 84-1400. (Illus.). 375p. 1984. text ed. 85.00 (*0-684-15496-X*, Scribners) S&S Trade.

Album of Scottish Families, 1694-1696: Being the First Installment of George Home's Diary, Supplemented by Much Further Research into the Edinburgh & Border Families Forming His Extensive Social Network. Helen Kelsall & Keith Kelsall. 1990. pap. text ed. 25.00 (*0-08-040930-X*, Pub. by Aberdeen U Pr) Macmillan.

Album of Secrets & Memories, for Piano Solo. Kristof Vigh. (Contemporary Keyboard Ser.: No. 5). 8p. 1993. 14.00 (*1-56571-078-9*, CK005) PRB Prods.

Album of Selected Bookbindings. Clara L. Penney. (Illus.). 132p. 1967. 11.00 (*0-317-00602-9*, Hispanic Soc) Interbk Inc.

Album of Six Pieces. Francis Poulenc. Date not set. pap. 13.95 (*0-685-68971-9*, Chester Music) Music Sales.

Album of Songs. Arnold Box. Date not set. pap. 11.95 (*0-685-68970-0*, Chester Music) Music Sales.

Album of Songs, Vol. I. Cecile Chaminade. LC 84-1799. (Women Composers Ser.: No. 17). 96p. 1985. reprint ed. lib. bdg. 26.50 (*0-306-76245-5*) Da Capo.

Album of Tazewell County, Virginia. LC 89-63032. (Illus.). 212p. 1989. text ed. 25.00 (*0-929521-28-5*) Pictorial Hist.

Album of the Bannatyne Club. Bannatyne Club Staff. LC 72-160005. (Bannatyne Club, Edinburgh. Publications: No. 117). reprint ed. 15.00 (*0-404-52875-9*) AMS Pr.

Album of the Great Wave of Immigration. April Koral. LC 92-15009. (Picture Album Ser.). (Illus.). 64p. (J). (gr. 6-8). 1992. lib. bdg. 14.77 (*0-531-11123-7*) Watts.

Album of the Heart. Mabel N. Floyd. 1994. 8.95 (*0-533-11092-0*) Vantage.

Album of the Yiddish Theatre. Z. Zylberzweig. (Judaica Ser.). 1992. lib. bdg. 329.95 (*0-8490-5318-8*) Gordon Pr.

Album of Twenty-Six Pieces. Frederic Chopin. Date not set. pap. 15.95 (*0-685-68972-7*, Pub. by Wilhelm Hansen DK) Music Sales.

Album of Violin Pieces, EFS6. (Illus.). 192p. 1934. pap. 11.95 (*0-8256-2006-6*, AM40056) Music Sales.

Album of Virginia: Or Illustrations of the Old Dominion. Edward Beyer. (Illus.). vii, 40p. 1980. text ed. 39.95 (*0-88490-091-6*) VA State Lib.

Album of War Refugees. April Koral. LC 89-30948. (Picture Album Ser.). (Illus.). 96p. (J). (gr. 6-9). 1989. lib. bdg. 14.77 (*0-531-10765-5*) Watts.

Albumen & Salted Paper Book. James Reilly. LC 80-14340. (Extended Photo Media Ser.: No. 2). (Illus.). 1980. pap. text ed. 8.95 (*0-87992-014-9*) Light Impressions.

Albumin & Systematic Circulation. Ed. by P. Lundsgaard-Hansen & B. Blauhut. (Current Studies in Hematology & Blood Transfusion: No. 53). (Illus.). xiv, 234p. 1986. 141.75 (*3-8055-4367-0*) S Karger.

Albumin Structure Biosynthesis Function. T. Peters & I. Sjoholm. LC 77-30609. (Proceedings 11th FEBS Meeting, Copenhagen 1977 Ser.: Vol. 50: B9). 1978. 40.00 (*0-08-022631-0*, Pub. by Pergamon Repr UK) Franklin.

Albumin: Structure, Function & Uses. Ed. by Victor Rosenoer et al. 1977. 173.00 (*0-08-019603-9*, Pub. by Pergamon Repr UK) Franklin.

Albums of James Tissot. Willard E. Misfeldt. (Illus.). 134p. 1982. 25.95 (*0-87972-209-6*); pap. 13.95 (*0-87972-210-X*) Bowling Green Univ.

Albuquerque. Rudolfo Anaya. LC 91-43597. 288p. 1992. 22.50 (*0-8263-1359-0*) U of NM Pr.

Albuquerque: A Narrative History. Marc Simmons. LC 82-11124. 459p. reprint ed. pap. 130.90 (*0-8357-5298-4*, 2032585) Bks Demand.

Albuquerque: Coming Back to the U. S. A. Margaret Randall. 350p. (Orig.). 1986. pap. 12.95 (*0-919573-53-3*) Left Bank.

Albuquerque Colors: A Closer Look at the Colorful City on the Rio Grand, Vol. 1. Carol C. Smith. LC 90-60357. (Illus.). 48p. 1990. write for info. (*0-9625761-0-7*) Albuquer Econ Dev.

Albuquerque Meeting (Dpf 94) The Proceedings of the 8th Meeting O T Aps Division of Part & Fields. S. Seidel. 2080p. 1995. text ed. 213.00 (*981-02-2072-3*) World Scientific Pub.

Albuquerque Trivia: A Treasury of Niceties. Cynthia Romero & Arthur Romero. (Illus.). 101p. (Orig.). 1993. pap. text ed. 7.95 (*1-880047-06-3*) Creative Des.

Albuquerque '50s. Deborah Boll et al. (Illus.). 60p. (Orig.). 1989. pap. 10.00 (*0-944282-06-7*) UNM Art Mus.

Alburquerque. Rudolfo Ananya. 304p. 1994. mass mkt. 5.99 (*0-446-36544-0*) Warner Bks.

Alcala-Zamora, Diccionario Frances-Espanol, Espanol-Frances. Pedro De Alcala-Zamora. 960p. (FRE & SPA.). 1982. pap. 28.95 (*0-7859-5110-5*, S50399) Fr & Eur.

Alcalde de Zalamea. Calderon. 134p. (SPA.). 1977. 3.50 (*0-8288-7150-7*, S8830) Fr & Eur.

Alcalde de Zalamea. Pedro Calderon De La Barca. Ed. by Jose M. Ruano De La Haza. (Nueva Austral Ser.: Vol. 50). (SPA.). 1991. pap. text ed. 12.95x (*84-239-1850-5*) Elliots Bks.

Alcalde de Zalamea. 2nd ed. Pedro Calderon De La Barca. 192p. 1990. pap. write for info. (*0-7859-5178-4*) Fr & Eur.

Alcan & Canol. Stan Cohen. 1992. pap. 19.95 (*0-929521-50-1*) Pictorial Hist.

Alcan Trail Blazers. Sidney J. Navratil et al. Ed. by John K. Lloyd & Helen Navratil. (Illus.). 68p. (Orig.). 1992. pap. 14.00 (*0-9633018-0-2*) Six Hund Forty-Eight Mem.

Alcanzando al Mundo (Consumer Catalog) (Illus.). (SPA.). Date not set. write for info. (*0-318-72874-5*, 499603) Editorial Unilit.

Alcar, the Captive Creole. M. Roland Markham. LC 77-170701. (Black Heritage Library Collection). 1977. reprint ed. 21.95 (*0-8369-8891-4*) Ayer.

Alcatraz. Robert W. Cameron. 1983. 8.95 (*0-918684-39-0*) Cameron & Co.

Alcatraz. Richard Cecil. LC 91-23326. 96p. 1992. pap. 8.50 (*1-55753-015-7*) Purdue U Pr.

Alcatraz. large type ed. Max Brand. LC 90-26041. 309p. 1991. reprint ed. lib. bdg. 16.95 (*1-56054-139-3*) Thorndike Pr.

Alcatraz: Indian Land Forever. Ed. by Troy R. Johnson. LC 94-77967. (Native American Politics Ser.: 4). 144p. 1994. pap. 15.00 (*0-935626-40-9*) U Cal AISC.

Alcatraz: Indian Land Forever. Ed. by Troy R. Johnson. LC 94-77967. (Native American Politics Ser.: 4). 144p. 1994. 25.00 (*0-935626-41-7*) U Cal AISC.

Alcatraz: Island of Change. James P. Delgado. (Illus.). 48p. (Orig.). 1992. pap. 7.95 (*0-9625206-6-7*) Gldn Gate Natl Park Assoc.

Alcatraz: The Story Behind the Scenery. James P. Delgado. LC 85-80214. (Illus.). 48p. (Orig.). 1984. pap. text ed. 6.95 (*0-88714-001-7*) KC Pubns.

Alcatraz! Alcatraz! The Indian Occupation of 1969-1971. Adam F. Eagle. LC 91-70320. (Illus.). 160p. (Orig.). 1992. pap. 9.95 (*0-930588-51-7*) Heyday Bks.

Alcatraz! Alcatraz! The Indian Occupation of 1969-1971. Adam Fortunate Eagle. 160p. 1991. reprint ed. lib. bdg. 27.00x (*0-8095-4954-9*) Borgo Pr.

Alcatraz from Inside. Jim Quillen. (Illus.). 164p. (Orig.). 1992. pap. 11.95 (*0-9625206-1-6*) Gldn Gate Natl Park Assoc.

Alcatraz Island: Maximum Security. Donald J. Hurley. (Illus.). 130p. (Orig.). 1989. pap. 9.95 (*0-9620546-1-5*) D J Hurley.

Alcatraz Island: Maximum Security. rev. ed. Donald J. Hurley. LC 89-80985. (Illus.). 140p. (Orig.). (C). 1989. pap. text ed. 11.95 (*0-9620546-2-3*) D J Hurley.

Alcatraz Island: Memories. 2nd rev. ed. Donald J. Hurley. LC 88-91097. (Illus.). 150p. 1988. reprint ed. pap. 8.49 (*0-9620546-0-7*) D J Hurley.

Alcatraz Merry-Go-Round. Leon W. Thompson. (Illus.). 234p. 1995. pap. write for info. (*0-9646402-0-1*) Winter Bks.

Alceste. Christoph M. Wieland. Ed. by Thomas Bauman. Bd. with Alcymist. August Gottlieb.; Ariadne auf Naxos. Johann C. Brandes.; Belmont und Constanze. Carl F. Bretzner. (German Opera Ser., 1770-1800: Vol. 3). 540p. 1986. Set lib. bdg. 15.00 (*0-8240-8852-2*) Garland.

Alceste. Jean-Baptiste Lully. Ed. by Theodore D. De Lajarte. (Chefs-d'oeuvre classiques de l'opera francaise Ser.: Vol. 16). (Illus.). 314p. (FRE.). 1970. reprint ed. pap. 35.00 (*0-8450-1116-2*) Broude.

Alcest: The Tragedie of Alceste & Eliza. Tr. by Francisco Bracciolini. LC 79-84082. (English Experience Ser.: No. 902). 80p. 1979. reprint ed. lib. bdg. 20.00 (*90-221-0902-X*) Walter J Johnson.

Alcester. David Green. (Towns & Villages of England Ser.). (Illus.). 1994. pap. 12.50 (*0-7509-0466-6*) A Sutton Pub.

Alcestis & Other Plays. rev. ed. Euripides. Tr. by Philip Vellacott. (Classics Ser.). 1953. pap. 6.95 (*0-14-044031-3*, Penguin Classics) Viking Penguin.

Alcestis Barcinonensis: Text & Commentary. Ed. by Miroslav Marcovich. LC 87-37212. (Mnemosyne, Bibliotheca Classica Batava Ser.: No. 103). 117p. (Orig.). 1988. pap. 25.25 (*90-04-08600-5*) E J Brill.

Alchemical Essence: An Episode in the Quest for the Unchanging. M. M. P. Muir. 1994. pap. 8.95 (*1-55818-291-8*) Holmes Pub.

Alchemical Imagery in Bosch's Garden of Delights. Laurinda S. Dixon. LC 81-14673. (Studies in the Fine Arts: Iconography: No. 2). (Illus.). 249p. reprint ed. pap. 71.00 (*0-8357-1247-8*, 2070204) Bks Demand.

Alchemical Mandala: A Survey of the Mandala in the Western Esoteric Traditions. Adam McLean. LC 89-34803. (Hermetic Research Ser.: No. 3). (Illus.). 145p. (Orig.). 1989. 25.00 (*0-933999-79-8*); pap. 14.95 (*0-933999-80-1*) Phanes Pr.

Alchemical Medicine. Paracelsus. 1986. pap. 4.95 (*0-916411-30-3*) Holmes Pub.

Alchemical Poetry from the English Renaissance & Restoration: Previously Unpublished Texts, 1575-1700. Ed. by Robert M. Schuler. LC 95-13704. (English Renaissance Hermeticism Ser.: Vol. 5). (Illus.). 712p. 1995. 95.00 (*0-8240-7599-4*, H1087) Garland.

Alchemical Society. Journal, Vols. 1-3 In 1. LC 79-8591. reprint ed. 29.50 (*0-404-18445-6*) AMS Pr.

Alchemical Symbols & Secret Alphabets. C. J. Thompson. 1986. pap. 3.95 (*0-916411-98-2*) Holmes Pub.

Alchemical Tradition in the Late Twentieth Century. 5th ed. Ed. by Richard Grossinger. (Illus.). 330p. 1992. pap. 14.95 (*1-55643-133-3*) North Atlantic.

Alchemical Treatrise on the Great Art. Antoine-Joseph Pernety. 272p. 1995. pap. 35.00 (*0-87728-725-2*) Weiser.

Alchemical Wedding of Christian Rosycross: Esoteric Analysis of the Chymische Hoch Zeit Christiani Rosencreutzed Anno 1459, Pt. 1. (Secrets of the Rosicrucian Brotherhood Ser.: Vol. 3). 1991. 35.00 (*90-6732-058-7*) Rosycross Pr.

Alchemical Wedding of Christian Rosycross: Esoteric Analysis of the Chymische Hoch Zeit Christiani Rosencreutzed Anno 1459, Pt. 2. (Secrets of the Rosicrucian Brotherhood Ser.: Vol. 4). 1991. 35.00 (*90-6732-078-1*) Rosycross Pr.

Alchemical Wedding of Christian Rosycross (Chymische Hochzeit Christiani Rosencreutz, Anno 1459, Part I) see Secrets of the Rosicrucian Brotherhood

Alchemical Wedding of Christian Rosycross (Chymische Hochzeit Christiani Rosencreutz, Anno 1459, Part II) see Secrets of the Rosicrucian Brotherhood

Alchemical Works: Eirenaeus Philalethes Compiled. Eirenaeus Philalethes. Ed. by S. Merrow Broddle. 592p. 1994. 60.00 (*0-9640067-0-7*) Cinnabar.

Alchemical Works of Geber. Richard Russell. (Illus.). 320p. (Orig.). 1994. text ed. 35.00 (*0-87728-811-9*) Weiser.

Alchemical World of the German Court: Occult Philosophy & Chemical Medicine in the Circle of Moritz of Hessen 1572-1632. Von Bruce T. Moran. 193p. (Orig.). 1991. pap. 49.50 (*3-515-05369-7*) Coronet Bks.

Alchemical Writings of Edward Kelly: Two Excellent Treatises on the Philosopher's Stone Together with the Theatre of Terrestrial Astronomy. Arthur E. Waite. 219p. 1992. pap. 19.95 (*1-56459-166-2*) Kessinger Pub.

Alchemist. Ben Jonson. Ed. by Gerald E. Bentley. (Crofts Classics Ser.). 128p. 1947. pap. text ed. write for info. (*0-88295-048-7*) Harlan Davidson.

Alchemist. Ben Jonson. Ed. by Peter Bement. (English Texts Ser.). 270p. 1988. pap. 9.95 (*0-416-30480-X*) Routledge Chapman & Hall.

Alchemist. Ben Jonson. Ed. by Alvin B. Kernan. LC 73-86901. 1974. pap. 13.00 (*0-300-01736-7*, Y-268) Yale U Pr.

Alchemist. Les Whitten. 416p. 1986. pap. 3.95 (*0-8217-1865-7*) Zebra.

Alchemist. Leslie H. Whitten. 1976. pap. 1.75 (*0-380-00078-4*) Avon.

Alchemist. large type ed. Paulo Coelho. Tr. by Alan R. Clarke. LC 94-42789. 165p. 1995. 19.95 (*0-7838-1195-0*, Large Print Bks) Hall.

Alchemist. Ben Jonson. LC 74-25830. (English Experience Ser.: No. 330). 96p. 1971. reprint ed. 30.00 (*90-221-0330-7*) Walter J Johnson.

Alchemist: A Fable about Following Your Dream. Paulo Coelho. LC 92-56413. 1993. 16.00 (*0-06-250217-4*) Harper SF.

Alchemist: A Fable about Following Your Dreams. Paulo Coelho. Tr. by Alan R. Clarke. 192p. 1995. pap. 10.00 (*0-06-250218-2*) Harper SF.

Alchemist: Founders of Modern Chemistry, Vol. 1. Frank S. Taylor. LC 74-361. (Gold Ser.). (Illus.). 246p. 1974. reprint ed. 29.95 (*0-405-05922-1*) Ayer.

Alchemist: The Formula for Turning Your Life into Gold. Monty Farber & Amy Zerner. 52p. 1991. 24.95 (*0-312-06181-1*, Pub. by Thomas Dunne Bks) St Martin.

Alchemist & Other Plays. Ben Jonson. Ed. by Gordon Campbell. 560p. 1995. 65.00 (*0-19-812150-4*); pap. 7.95 (*0-19-282252-7*) OUP.

Alchemist in Life, Literature, & Art. John Read. (Illus.). 120p. 1992. pap. text ed. 17.95 (*1-56459-210-3*) Kessinger Pub.

Alchemist in Life, Literature & Art. John Read. LC 79-8620. reprint ed. 29.50 (*0-404-18486-3*) AMS Pr.

Alchemist of Time, Bk. 3. Karen Ripley. (Orig.). 1994. pap. 4.99 (*0-345-38118-1*, Del Rey Discovery) Ballantine.

Alchemist to Mercury. Robert Kelly. 230p. 1981. 30.00 (*0-913028-82-7*); pap. 7.95 (*0-913028-83-5*) North Atlantic.

Alchemists: Founders of Modern Chemistry. F. Sherwood Taylor. 246p. 1992. reprint ed. pap. 24.95 (*1-56459-002-X*) Kessinger Pub.

Alchemist's Handbook. Frater Albertus. LC 74-21127. (Illus.). 124p. (Orig.). 1987. pap. 12.50 (*0-87728-655-8*) Weiser.

Alchemist's Retort. Anna K. Vogel. (Amherst Writers & Artists Chapbook Ser.). 32p. (Orig.). 1995. pap. 12.00 (*0-941895-06-8*) Amherst Wri Art.

Alchemists Through the Ages. Arthur E. Waite. LC 76-130814. 320p. 1986. pap. 14.00 (*0-89345-235-1*, Steinerbks) Garber Comm.

Alchemists Through the Ages: Together with a Study of the Principles & Practice of Alchemy, Including a Bibliography of Alchemical & Hermetic Philosophy. Arthur E. Waite. 320p. 1994. pap. 19.95 (*1-56459-457-2*) Kessinger Pub.

Alchemy. Franz Von. 1995. pap. 18.00 (*0-919123-04-X*) Atrium Pubs.

Alchemy. Dana Wildsmith. 40p. 1995. pap. 6.00 (*1-885912-05-6*) Sows Ear Pr.

Alchemy. Franz Hartmann. 1984. reprint ed. pap. 2.95 (*0-916411-24-9*, Sure Fire) Holmes Pub.

Alchemy: A Comprehensive Bibliography of the Manly P. Hall Collection of Books & Manuscripts. Ed. by Ron C. Hogart. 1985. 125.00 (*0-89314-542-4*) Philos Res.

Alchemy: A Reference. Alpha Pyramis Research Division Staff. 50p. 1990. pap. 3.75 (*0-913597-40-6*) Prosperity & Profits.

Alchemy: The Secret Art. Stanislas K. De Rola. LC 85-50803. (Art & Imagination Ser.). (Illus.). (Orig.). 1986. pap. 14.95 (*0-500-81003-6*) Thames Hudson.

Alchemy: The Third Column of Medicine. Paracelsus. Tr. by A. E. Waite. 1989. pap. 3.95 (*1-55818-120-2*) Holmes Pub.

Alchemy Ancient & Modern. H. Stanley Redgrove. 141p. 1992. pap. 17.95 (*1-56459-143-3*) Kessinger Pub.

Alchemy & Academe. Anne McCaffrey. 1987. mass mkt. 4.95 (*0-345-34419-7*, Del Rey) Ballantine.

Alchemy & Chemistry in the Sixteenth & Seventeenth Centuries: Proceedings Warburg Colloquium 1989. Ed. by Antonio Clericuzio & Piyo Rattansi. LC 93-33464. (Archives Internationales d'Histoire des Idees (International Archives of the History of Ideas) Ser.: No. 140). 224p. (C). 1994. lib. bdg. 105.50 (*0-7923-2573-7*) Kluwer Ac.

Alchemy & Finnegans Wake. Barbara DiBernard. LC 79-22809. 163p. 1980. 64.50 (*0-87395-388-6*); pap. 21.95 (*0-87395-429-7*) State U NY Pr.

Alchemy & Other Chemical Achievements of the Ancient Orient. Masumi Chikashige. LC 79-8602. reprint ed. 27.50 (*0-404-18456-1*) AMS Pr.

Alchemy & the Alchemists. Ethan A. Hitchcock. 18.00 (*0-89314-400-2*) Philos Res.

Alchemy & the Alchemists. Chambers. 50p. 1992. reprint ed. pap. 9.95 (*1-56459-005-4*) Kessinger Pub.

Alchemy & the Alchemists, 3 vols., Set. Reuben S. Clymer. LC 79-8603. reprint ed. 105.00 (*0-404-18457-X*) AMS Pr.

Alchemy in Europe: A Guide to Research. Claudia Kren. LC 90-2899. 144p. 1990. 25.00 (*0-8240-8538-8*, H692) Garland.

Alchemy in "The Sun Also Rises" Hidden Gold in Hemingway's Narrative. Wolfgang E. Rudat. LC 92-25021. 288p. 1992. text ed. 89.95 (*0-7734-9579-7*) E Mellen.

Alchemy, Its Science & Romance. John E. Mercer. LC 79-8617. (Illus.). reprint ed. 27.50 (*0-404-18481-2*) AMS Pr.

Alchemy of Awareness. Lorraine Sinkler. reprint ed. pap. 12.95 (*0-9629119-3-3*) Valor Fndtn.

Alchemy of English: The Spread, Functions, & Models of Non-Native Englishes. Braj B. Kachru. (English in the Global Context Ser.). 216p. (C). 1990. pap. 12.95 (*0-252-06172-1*) U of Ill Pr.

Alchemy of Finance: Reading the Mind of the Market. George Soros. 1994. pap. text ed. 19.95 (*0-471-04206-4*) Wiley.

Alchemy of Finance: Reading the Mind of the Market. George Soros. LC 94-6764. 1994. text ed. 45.00 (*0-471-04313-3*) Wiley.

Alchemy of Genres: Cross-Genre Writing by American Feminist Poet-Critics. Diane P. Freedman. (C). 1992. text ed. 27.50 (*0-8139-1377-2*); pap. 12.95 (*0-8139-1378-0*) U Pr of Va.

Alchemy of Glory: The Dialectic of Truthfulness & Untruthfulness in Medieval Arabic Literary Criticism. Mansour Ajami. 150p. (Orig.). 1988. 30.00 (*0-89410-632-5*); pap. 16.00 (*0-89410-633-3*) Three Continents.

An Asterisk (*) at the beginning of an entry indicates that the title is appearing in BIP for the first time.

173

A

Alchemy of Happiness. Al-Ghazzali. Tr. by Claud Field. 122p. 1983. 16.00 (0-900860-71-5, Pub. by Octagon Pr UK) ISHK Bk Service.

Alchemy of Happiness. annot. rev. ed. Abu Hamid al-Ghazzali. Tr. by Claud Field. LC 91-9523. (Sources & Studies in World History Ser.). 160p. (C). 1991. 41.95 (1-56324-004-1); pap. text ed. 18.95 (1-56324-005-X) M E Sharpe.

Alchemy of Healing: Psyche & Soma. Edward C. Whitmont. 250p. (Orig.). 1992. pap. 14.95 (1-55643-146-5) North Atlantic.

***Alchemy of Illness.** Duff. 3.99 (0-517-13773-9) Random Hse Value.

Alchemy of Illness. Kat Duff. LC 92-50474. 176p. 1993. 19.00 (0-679-42053-3) Pantheon.

Alchemy of Illness. Kat Duff. 1994. 11.00 (0-517-88097-0, Bell Tower) Crown Pub Group.

***Alchemy of Love & Sex.** Lee Lozowick. 298p. (C). 1995. pap. 16.95 (0-934252-58-0) Hohm Pr.

Alchemy of Race & Rights. Patricia J. Williams. LC 90-48439. 263p. 1991. text ed. 27.50 (0-674-01470-7, WILALC) HUP.

Alchemy of Race & Rights. Patricia J. Williams. LC 90-48439. 320p. 1992. pap. text ed. 12.00 (0-674-01471-5) HUP.

Alchemy of Revolution: Gerrard Winstanley's Occultism & Seventeenth-Century English Communism. David Mulder. LC 89-34745. (American University Studies: History: Ser. IX, Vol. 77). 364p. 1990. text ed. 60.95 (0-8204-1173-6) P Lang Pubs.

Alchemy of Sex Ecstasy. 1991. lib. bdg. 250.00 (0-8490-4586-X) Gordon Pr.

Alchemy of Survival: One Woman's Journey. John E. Mack & Rita S. Rogers. (Radcliffe Biography Ser.). (Illus.). 1988. 17.26 (0-201-12682-6) Addison-Wesley.

Alchemy of Survival: One Woman's Journey. John E. Mack & Rita S. Rogers. (Radcliffe Biography Ser.). (Illus.). 1989. pap. 13.41 (0-201-51800-7) Addison-Wesley.

Alchemy of the Heart. Reshad Feild. 1990. pap. 14.95 (1-85230-171-6) Element MA.

***Alchemy of the Heart: The Transformative Power of Love in Everyday Life.** Mary M. Morrissey. LC 95-67928. 208p. 1995. pap. 12.00 (0-89716-562-4) P B Pubng.

***Alchemy of the Heavens: Searching for Meaning in the Milky Way.** Ken Crowswell. LC 94-30452. (Illus.). 1995. 24.95 (0-385-47213-7, Anchor NY) Doubleday.

Alchemy of the Word: Language & the End of Theology. Carl A. Raschke. LC 79-15490. (American Academy of Religion. Studies in Religion: No. 20). 106p. reprint ed. pap. 30.30 (0-7837-5476-0, 2045241) Bks Demand.

Alchemy of Thought. Lawrence P. Jacks. LC 68-8473. (Essay Index Reprint Ser.). 1977. 23.95 (0-8369-0562-8) Ayer.

Alchemy of Will & Desire. Joanne H. Stroud. 192p. 1994. 22.95 (0-8264-0646-7) Continuum.

Alchemy Rediscovered & Restored. A. Cochren. (Orig.). 1992. lib. bdg. 79.95 (0-8490-5279-3) Gordon Pr.

Alchemy Rediscovered & Restored. A. Cochren. 141p. 1992. pap. 17.95 (1-56459-148-4) Kessinger Pub.

Alchemy Rediscovered & Restored. A. Cochren. 158p. (Orig.). 1963. reprint ed. spiral bd. 6.60 (0-7873-0187-6) Mokelumne.

Alchemy Unlimited. Douglas W. Clark. 320p. 1990. pap. 3.50 (0-380-75726-5) Avon.

Alchohol & Health: Sixth Special Report to the United States Congress. LC 87-1519. (DHHS Publication ADM Ser.). (Illus.). 167p. 1987. pap. 8.00 (0-317-67393-9, 017-024-01326-9) US HHS.

Alchymist: Dresden, Seventeen Seventy-Eight see Romeo und Julie: Gotha, Seventeen Seventy-Six

Alchymist's Journal. Evan S. Connell. 224p. 1991. 19.95 (0-86547-464-8, North Pt Pr) FS&G.

Alchymist's Journal. Evan S. Connell. 224p. 1992. reprint ed. pap. 10.00 (0-14-016932-6, Penguin Bks) Viking Penguin.

Alcibiades. Walter M. Ellis. 176p. 1989. 49.95 (0-415-00993-6); pap. 14.95 (0-415-00994-4) Routledge.

***Alcibiades at the Door: Gay Discourses in French Literature.** Lawrence R. Schehr. LC 94-46646. 242p. 1995. 32.50x (0-8047-2467-9) Stanford U Pr.

Alcidamas, Aristophanes & the Beginnings of Greek Stylistic Theory. Neil O'Sullivan. 176p. (Orig.). 1992. pap. 54.00 (3-515-05420-0) Coronet Bks.

Alco-Calculator: An Educational Instrument. 1983. 4.95 (0-911290-04-4); 0.95 (0-911290-16-8) Rutgers Ctr Alcohol.

Alco Line. Eric Hirsimaki. (Illus.). 128p. 1993. 45.00 (0-929886-06-2) Mileposts Pub.

Alco RSD Seven & Fifteen. John Nelsen & Scott Law. Ed. by Robert L. Hundman & Cathy H. Lee. (Dataseries Ser.). (Illus.). 100p. 1988. 14.50 (0-945434-09-X) Hundman Pub.

Alcoa, an American Enterprise. Charles C. Carr. LC 72-5039. (Technology & Society Ser.). (Illus.). 292p. 1972. reprint ed. 26.95 (0-405-04692-8) Ayer.

Alcohol. Charles Carroll & William Bock. 352p. 1995. pap. text ed. write for info. (0-697-20018-3) Brown & Benchmark.

Alcohol. Pamela Holmes. LC 91-30344. (Drugs: the Complete Story Ser.). (Illus.). 64p. (YA). (gr. 6-12). 1991. lib. bdg. 24.26 (0-8114-3203-3); pap. text ed. write for info. (0-8114-3206-8) Raintree Steck-V.

Alcohol. N. S. Miller & M. S. Gold. LC 91-2391. (Drugs of Abuse: A Comprehensive Series for Clinicians: Vol. 2). (Illus.). 260p. 1991. 37.50 (0-306-43641-8, Plenum Med Bk) Plenum.

Alcohol. Judy Monroe. LC 93-28607. (Drug Library Ser.). (Illus.). 128p. (YA). (gr. 6 up). 1994. lib. bdg. 17.95 (0-89490-470-1) Enslow Pubs.

Alcohol. Ellen Wijnberg. LC 93-25156. (Teen Hotline Ser.). (Illus.). (J). (gr. 6-9). 1993. lib. bdg. 22.80 (0-8114-3528-8) Raintree Steck-V.

Alcohol. 2nd ed. Brent Q. Hafen & Molly J. Brog. (Illus.). 290p. (C). 1983. pap. text ed. 36.50 (0-314-69652-0) West Pub.

Alcohol: A Family Destroyer. Jerry Hull. (Christian Living Ser.). 53p. 1991. pap. 2.50 (0-8341-1386-4) Beacon Hill.

Alcohol: Customs & Rituals. Thomas Babor. (Encyclopedia of Psychoactive Drugs Ser.: No. 1). (Illus.). (YA). (gr. 5 up). 1992. lib. bdg. 19.95 (0-685-52235-0) Chelsea Hse.

Alcohol: How It Affects Your Health. rev. ed. 1994. pap. 0.25 (0-89230-191-0) Do It Now.

Alcohol: How to Give It up & Be Glad You Did, a Sensible Approach. Philip Tate. 1992. pap. 14.95 (0-9634275-1-2) Rat Self Help.

Alcohol: Simple Facts about Combinations with Other Drugs. rev. ed. 1988. pap. 0.25 (0-317-38033-8) Do It Now.

Alcohol: Teenage Drinking. Alan R. Lang. (Encyclopedia of Psychoactive Drugs Ser.: No. 1). (Illus.). (YA). (gr. 5 up). 1992. lib. bdg. 19.95 (0-685-52236-9) Chelsea Hse.

Alcohol: The Beloved Enemy. Jack Van Impe. 190p. 1980. pap. 7.00 (0-934803-07-2) J Van Impe.

Alcohol: The Development of Sociological Perspectives on Use & Abuse. Paul M. Roman. 401p. 1991. 27.95 (0-911290-23-0) Rutgers Ctr Alcohol.

Alcohol: Understanding Words in Context. Carol O'Sullivan. LC 89-11712. (Opposing Viewpoints Juniors Ser.). (Illus.). 32p. (J). (gr. 3-6). 1990. lib. bdg. 11.95 (0-89908-634-9) Greenhaven.

Alcohol: What It Is, What It Does. Judith S. Seixas. LC 76-43344. (Illus.). 56p. (J). (gr. k up). 1977. pap. 6.95 (0-688-00462-8, Mulberry) Morrow.

Alcohol Vol. 5: (Incl. 1992-94 Supplement) Ed. by Eleanor C. Goldstein. (Social Issues Resources Ser.). 1995. 57.00 (0-89777-172-9) Sirs Inc.

Alcohol - the Nationalized Sin. Gordon Lindsay. 1962. per. 2.95 (0-89985-274-2) Christ for the Nations.

***Alcohol- & Drug-Related Visits to Hospital Emergency Departments: 1992 National Hospital Ambulatory Medical Care Survey.** National Center for Health Statistics Staff. (Advance Data Ser.: No. 251). 16p. Date not set. write for info. (0-614-02938-4) Natl Ctr Health Stats.

Alcohol Abuse: Geographical Perspectives. Christopher J. Smith & Robert Q. Hanham. Ed. by C. Gregory Knight. LC 82-25529. (Resource Publications in Geography). 85p. (Orig.). 1983. pap. 10.00 (0-89291-166-2) Assn Am Geographers.

Alcohol Abuse: How to Help a Loved One. Pippa Sales Staff. LC 94-94058. 120p. (Orig.). 1994. pap. 10.95 (1-884633-01-3) DISA Pubns.

Alcohol Abuse in Indians of North & South America: Cultural Difference in the Conflict with Western Civilization - Journal: Confinia Psychiatrica, Vol. 21, No. 4. (Illus.). 1978. pap. 9.75 (3-8055-3043-9) S Karger.

Alcohol Abuse Treatment. Ed. by Ronald R. Watson. LC 92-1569. (Drug & Alcohol Abuse Reviews Ser.). (Illus.). 336p. 1992. 59.50 (0-89603-242-6) Humana.

Alcohol, Accidents, Injuries. 1986. 35.00 (0-89883-737-5, P 173) Soc Auto Engineers.

Alcohol Addiction & Chronic Alcoholism. E. M. Jellinek. Ed. by Gerald N. Grob. LC 80-1272. (Addiction in America Ser.). 1981. reprint ed. lib. bdg. 35.95 (0-405-13593-9) Ayer.

Alcohol Addiction & Self-Regulation: A Controlled Trial of a Relapse Prevention Program for Finnish Inpatient Alcoholics. Anja Koski-Jannes. (Finnish Foundation for Alcohol Studies: Vol. 41). 198p. 1992. pap. 35.00 (951-9192-53-0) Rutgers Ctr Alcohol.

Alcohol & Adolescent Abuse: The Alcan Family Services Treatment Model. Jerry P. Flanzer & Kinly Sturkie. LC 86-82355. (Research Based Evaluation Ser.). 96p. 1986. pap. 19.95 (0-918452-97-X) Learning Pubns.

Alcohol & Aggression: Proceedings of the Symposium on Alcohol & Aggression Held at the Center of Alcohol Studies, Rutgers University, October 1992. Ed. by Larissa A. Pohorecky et al. (Journal of Studies on Alcohol: Suppl. No. 11). 200p. 1993. pap. 26.95 (0-911290-52-4, AJS-106) Rutgers Ctr Alcohol.

***Alcohol & Aging.** Ed. by Thomas P. Beresford & Edith Gomberg. (Illus.). 304p. 1995. text ed. 49.95 (0-19-508090-4) OUP.

Alcohol & Alcoholism. Ross Fishman. (Encyclopedia of Psychoactive Drugs Ser.: No. 1). (Illus.). (YA). (gr. 5 up). 1992. lib. bdg. 19.95 (0-685-52234-2) Chelsea Hse.

Alcohol & Biological Membranes. Walter A. Hunt. LC 84-25317. (Guilford Alcohol Studies). 214p. 1985. lib. bdg. 40.00 (0-89862-165-8) Guilford Pr.

Alcohol & Blacks: An Overview. Frederick D. Harper. 21p. (gr. 10-12). 1976. pap. text ed. 1.75 (0-935392-03-3) Douglass Pubs.

Alcohol & Brain Development. James R. West. (Illus.). 456p. 1986. 60.00 (0-19-503706-5) OUP.

Alcohol & Cancer. Watson. 1992. 95.00 (0-8493-7938-5, RC268) CRC Pr.

Alcohol & Conflict. U. G. Ahlfors. 1969. 4.00 (951-9192-06-9) Rutgers Ctr Alcohol.

Alcohol & Criminal Violence: Time Series Analyses in a Comparative Perspective. Leif Lenke. 187p. (Orig.). 1990. pap. 47.50x (91-22-01415-2, Pub. by Almqv & Wiksell SW) Coronet Bks.

Alcohol & Culture: Comparative Perspectives from Europe & America, Vol. 472. Ed. by Thomas F. Babor. 60.00 (0-89766-339-X); pap. 60.00 (0-89766-340-3) NY Acad Sci.

Alcohol & Disease. Ed. by Niels Tygstrup & Rolf Olsson. (Illus.). 290p. 1985. text ed. 109.00x (91-22-00786-5, Pub. by Almqv & Wiksell SW) Coronet Bks.

Alcohol & Drug Abuse as Encountered in Office Practice. Frank L. Iber & Edward Hines, Jr. (Illus.). 224p. 1990. 75.00 (0-8493-0166-1, RC564) CRC Pr.

Alcohol & Drug Abuse Funding: An Analysis of Foundation Grants, 1983-1987. Foundation Center Staff. Ed. by Loren Renz. 1989. pap. text ed. 45.00 (0-87954-286-1) Foundation Ctr.

Alcohol & Drug Abuse Handbook. Roland E. Herrington. (Allied Health Professions Monograph). 516p. 1987. 55.00 (0-87527-274-6) Green.

Alcohol & Drug Abuse in Old Age. Ed. by Roland M. Atkinson. LC 84-6271. (Clinical Insights Ser.). 82p. reprint ed. pap. 25.00 (0-8357-7810-X, 2036182) Bks Demand.

Alcohol & Drug Abuse in the Affluent. Ed. by Barry Stimmel. LC 84-19164. (Advances in Alcohol & Substance Abuse Ser.: Vol. 4, No. 2). 106p. 1984. text ed. 29.95 (0-86656-332-6) Haworth Pr.

Alcohol & Drug Abuse in the Workplace: The Complete Resource Guide. 2nd ed. 1989. ring bd. 95.00 (1-55871-143-0, BSP 132) BNA.

Alcohol & Drug Abuse Prevention Education in Oregon: K-12 Infused Lesson Guide. Dan Mielke & Peggy Holstedt. (Illus.). 762p. (Orig.). (C). 1993. pap. text ed. 49.95 (0-7881-0081-5) Diane Pub.

Alcohol & Drug Education for Parents. Sally S. Crawford. 86p. 1992. spiral bd., pap. 15.00 (1-882802-00-4) Healthy Life.

Alcohol & Drugs. Ed. by Martin Plant et al. 1991. text ed. 50.00 (0-7486-0113-9, Pub. by Edinburgh U Pr UK) Col U Pr.

Alcohol & Drugs: The Scottish Experience. Ed. by Martin Plant et al. (Illus.). 216p. 1992. pap. text ed. 24.50 (0-7486-0377-8, Pub. by Edinburgh U Pr UK) Col U Pr.

Alcohol & Drugs Are Women's Issues, 2 vols., Set. Ed. by Paula Roth. LC 90-49988. (Illus.). 155p. 1991. 50.00 (0-8108-2437-X) Scarecrow.

Alcohol & Drugs Are Women's Issues: The Model Program Guide, Vol. 2. Ed. by Paula Roth. (Illus.). 155p. 1991. 29.50 (0-8108-2389-6) Scarecrow.

Alcohol & Drugs Are Women's Issues, Vol. 1: A Review of the Issues. Ed. by Paula Roth. LC 90-49988. (Copublished with Women's Action Alliance Ser.). (Illus.). 202p. 1991. 32.50 (0-8108-2360-8) Scarecrow.

Alcohol & Drugs in the Public Schools: Implications for School Leaders. 60p. 1988. write for info. (0-318-68342-3) Natl Sch Boards.

Alcohol & Drugs in the Workplace. Barbara Butler. 298p. 1993. pap. 45.00 (0-409-90544-5, CN) Butterworth Legal Pubs.

Alcohol & Drugs in the Workplace: Costs, Controls, & Controversies. (Special Report Ser.). 136p. 1986. 30.00 (0-87179-905-7, LDSR 39) BNA.

Alcohol & Health. 1991. lib. bdg. 75.00 (0-8490-4373-5) Gordon Pr.

Alcohol & Health: Seventh Special Report to the United States Congress. (Illus.). 317p. 1990. per., pap. 16.00 (0-16-021365-7, S/N 017-024-013) USGPO.

Alcohol & Highway Safety: Proceedings of the North American Conference on Alcohol & Highway Safety. Ed. by T. B. Turner et al. (Journal of Studies on Alcohol: Suppl. No. 10). 1985. pap. 20.00 (0-911290-17-6) Rutgers Ctr Alcohol.

Alcohol & Homicide: A Deadly Combination of Two American Traditions. Robert N. Parker & Linda-Anne Rebhun. (Violence Ser.). 160p. (C). 1995. text ed. 49.50 (0-7914-2463-4); pap. 16.95 (0-7914-2464-2) State U NY Pr.

***Alcohol & Hormones.** Ed. by Ronald R. Watson. LC 94-38231. (Drug & Alcohol Abuse Reviews Ser.: Vol. 6). 352p. 1995. text ed. 89.50 (0-89603-290-6) Humana.

Alcohol & Human Behavior: Theory, Research, & Practice. Clayton P. Rivers. LC 93-33821. 1993. pap. text ed. write for info. (0-13-019878-1) P-H.

Alcohol & Illness: Health & Society. Ed. by John Duffy. 224p. 1992. text ed. 55.00 (0-7486-0353-0, Pub. by Edinburgh U Pr UK) Col U Pr.

Alcohol & Longevity. Raymond Pearl. Ed. by Gerald N. Grob. LC 80-1245. (Addiction in America Ser.). (Illus.). 1981. reprint ed. lib. bdg. 30.95 (0-405-13615-3) Ayer.

Alcohol & Man: The Effects of Alcohol on Man in Health & Disease. Ed. by Haven Emerson & Gerald N. Grob. LC 80-1227. (Addiction in America Ser.). 1981. reprint ed. lib. bdg. 41.95 (0-405-13585-8) Ayer.

Alcohol & Marijuana Use in Texas. Ralph O. Marshall et al. 24p. 1981. 2.00 (0-318-02511-6) S Houston Employ.

Alcohol & Neurobiology: Brain Development & Hormone Regulation. Watson. 1992. 95.00 (0-8493-7935-0, QP801) CRC Pr.

Alcohol & Neurobiology: Receptors, Membrances & Channels. Watson. 1993. 85.00 (0-685-70119-0, QP801) CRC Pr.

Alcohol & Other Drug Abuse Strategy: A Report to the Minnesota State Legislature. 52p. (Orig.). (C). 1993. pap. text ed. 25.00 (1-56806-584-1) Diane Pub.

***Alcohol & Other Drug Related Periodicals: An Annotated Bibliography & Resource Guide.** 1995. lib. bdg. 251.95 (0-8490-6785-5) Gordon Pr.

Alcohol & Other Drugs. Bosworth et al. (Body Awareness Resource Network Ser.). (YA). (gr. 7-12). Date not set. disk 120.00 (0-912899-59-X) Lrning Multi-Systs.

Alcohol & Other Drugs: Issues in Arbitration. Tia S. Denenberg & R. V. Denenberg. 404p. 1991. text ed. 47.00 (0-87179-687-2, 0687) BNA.

Alcohol & Other Drugs: Self Responsibility. Ruth C. Engs. (C). 1987. reprint ed. pap. text ed. 22.95 (0-89917-473-6) Tichenor Pub.

Alcohol & Other Drugs: Use, Abuse, & Disabilities. Peter E. Leone. (Exceptional Children at Risk Ser.). 33p. 1991. 8.90 (0-86586-215-X, P358) Coun Exc Child.

Alcohol & Poetry: John Berryman & the Booze Talking. Lewis Hyde. LC 86-13595. 20p. (Orig.). 1987. pap. 4.00 (0-911005-10-2) Dallas Inst Pubns.

Alcohol & Pregnancy: A Retrieval Index & Bibliography of the Fetal Alcohol Syndrome. Leslie P. Gartner. LC 84-11311. 80p. 1984. pap. text ed. 35.00 (0-910841-03-9) Jen Hse Pub Co.

Alcohol & Public Policy: Beyond the Shadow of Prohibition. National Research Council (U. S.), Panel on Alternative Policies Affecting the Prevention of Alcohol Abuse & Alcoholism Staff. Ed. by Mark H. Moore & Dean R. Gerstein. LC 81-11217. 477p. reprint ed. pap. 136.00 (0-7837-0351-1, 2040670) Bks Demand.

***Alcohol & Public Policy: Evidence & Issues.** Ed. by Harold Holder & Griffith Edwards. (Illus.). 300p. 1995. 95.00 (0-19-262635-3) OUP.

Alcohol & Reproduction: A Bibliography. Comp. by Ernest L. Abel. LC 82-6202. ix, 219p. 1982. text ed. 49.95 (0-313-23474-4, AAR/, Greenwood Pr) Greenwood.

Alcohol & Seizures: Basic Mechanisms & Clinical Concepts. Ed. by Roger J. Porter et al. LC 90-2712. (Illus.). 342p. (C). 1990. text ed. 75.00 (0-8036-7008-7) Davis Co.

Alcohol & Sexuality. Carlotta L. Schuster. LC 87-7182. (Sexual Medicine Ser.: No. 7). 142p. 1988. text ed. 55.00 (0-275-92559-5, C2559, Praeger Pubs) Greenwood.

Alcohol & Sexuality: The Effects of Alcohol on Both the Physiological & the Psychological Components of Sexuality & Reproduction. (Illus.). 168p. (C). 1992. pap. text ed. 29.95 (1-56806-002-5) Diane Pub.

***Alcohol & Society: Patterns & Attitudes.** Knud-Erik Sabroe. 198p. 1994. pap. 27.50 (87-981549-9-0, Pub. by Aarhus Univ Pr DK) Coronet Bks.

Alcohol & Substance Abuse in Adolescence. Ed. by Judith S. Brook et al. LC 84-29004. (Advances in Alcohol & Substance Abuse Ser.: Vol. 4, Nos. 3 & 4). 206p. 1985. text ed. 49.95 (0-86656-333-4) Haworth Pr.

Alcohol & Substance Abuse in Women & Children. Barry Stimmel. LC 86-251. (Advances in Alcohol & Substance Abuse Ser.: Vol. 5, No. 3). 148p. 1986. 39.95 (0-86656-575-2) Haworth Pr.

Alcohol & Teens. Jane C. Miner. LC 84-658. (Jem (High Interest-Low Reading Level) Ser.). (Illus.). 64p. (YA). (gr. 7-11). 1984. lib. bdg. 9.29 (0-671-44890-0, Julian Messner) Silver Burdett Pr.

Alcohol & the Addictive Brain: New Hope for Alcoholics from Biogenetic Research. Kenneth Blum & James E. Payne. 300p. 1991. text ed. 29.95 (0-02-903701-8) Free Pr.

Alcohol & the Brain. (Illus.). 87p. (Orig.). (C). 1993. pap. text ed. 39.95 (0-7881-0032-7) Diane Pub.

Alcohol & the Brain: Chronic Effects. Ed. by Ralph E. Tarter & David H. Van Thiel. LC 85-12068. 366p. 1985. 65.00 (0-306-41998-X, Plenum Med Bk) Plenum.

Alcohol & the Cardiovascular System. (Illus.). 86p. (Orig.). (C). 1993. pap. text ed. 35.00 (1-56806-418-7) Diane Pub.

Alcohol & the Cell. Pref. by Emanuel Rubin. (Annals Ser.: Vol. 492). (Illus.). 412p. 1987. 103.00 (0-89766-380-2) NY Acad Sci.

Alcohol & the Church: Developing an Effective Ministry. Margaret A. Fuad. LC 91-42493. 230p. (C). 1992. lib. bdg. 18.95 (0-932727-51-4); pap. 12.95 (0-932727-50-6) Hope Pub Hse.

Alcohol & the Constitution of Man. Edward L. Youmans. Ed. by Gerald N. Grob. LC 80-1255. (Addiction in America Ser.). 1981. reprint ed. lib. bdg. 18.95 (0-405-13625-0) Ayer.

Alcohol & the Developing Brain: Proceedings of the Third International Berzelius Symposium. Ed. by Ulf Rydberg et al. (Illus.). 240p. 1985. text ed. 94.00 (0-88167-127-4) Raven.

Alcohol & the Elderly: A Comprehensive Bibliography. Grace M. Barnes et al. LC 80-1786. xvii, 138p. 1980. text ed. 49.95 (0-313-22132-4, BAE/, Greenwood Pr) Greenwood.

Alcohol & the Family: A Comprehensive Bibliography. Comp. by Grace M. Barnes & Diane K. Augustino. LC 86-27112. (Bibliographies & Indexes in Sociology Ser.: No. 9). 474p. 1987. text ed. 69.50 (0-313-24782-X, BFA/, Greenwood Pr) Greenwood.

Alcohol & the Family: Research & Clinical Perspectives. Ed. by R. Lorraine Collins et al. LC 89-37204. (Substance Abuse Ser.). 386p. 1990. lib. bdg. 42.95 (0-89862-169-0) Guilford Pr.

Alcohol & the Fetus: A Clinical Perspective. Henry L. Rosett & Lyn Weiner. LC 84-919. (Illus.). 1984. text ed. 37.50 (0-19-503458-9) OUP.

***Alcohol & the Gastrointestinal Tract.** Victor R. Preedy & Ronald R. Watson. 336p. 1995. 159.95 (0-8493-2480-7, 2480) CRC Pr.

Alcohol & the Impaired Driver: A Manual on the Medicolegal Aspects of Chemical Tests for Intoxication with Supplement on Breath-Alcohol Tests. American Medical Association, Committee on Medicolegal Problems Staff. LC 75-183674. (Illus.). 292p. reprint ed. pap. 83.30 (0-8357-5299-2, 2030325) Bks Demand.

Alcohol & the Jews: A Cultural Study of Drinking & Sobriety. Charles R. Snyder. LC 77-24885. (Arcturus Books Paperbacks). 240p. 1978. reprint ed. pap. 9.95 (0-8093-0846-0) S Ill U Pr.

Alcohol & Tobacco. Mary Turck. LC 88-20253. (Facts About Ser.). (Illus.). 48p. (J). (gr. 5-6). 1988. text ed. 12.95 (0-89686-411-1, Crstwood Hse) Silver Burdett Pr.

Alcohol & You. rev. ed. Jane Claypool. Ed. by Lorna Greenberg. LC 88-10258. (Impact Bks.). (Illus.). 112p. (J). 1988. lib. bdg. 14.42 (0-531-10566-0) Watts.

Alcohol & Youth: A Comprehensive Bibliography. Comp. by Grace M. Barnes. LC 82-15397. xvi, 432p. 1982. text ed. 65.00 (0-313-23136-2, BAY/, Greenwood Pr) Greenwood.

A

A

Alcoholism: A Perspective. Ed. by Messiha & Tyner. LC 80-80209. 512p. 1980. 49.95 (*0-915340-02-X*) PJD Pubns.

Alcoholism: A Practical Treatment Guide. 2nd ed. Ed. by Stanley E. Gitlow & Herbert Peyser. 304p. 1988. pap. text ed. 32.50 (*0-8089-1912-1*; 791555, Grune) Saunders.

Alcoholism: A Source Guide. 1991. lib. bdg. 250.00 (*0-8490-4908-3*) Gordon Pr.

Alcoholism: A Treatment Manual. Wayne Poley et al. LC 78-13455. 1979. text ed. 25.00 (*0-89876-063-1*) Gardner Pr.

Alcoholism: Analysis of a World Wide Problem. P. Golding. 560p. 1983. lib. bdg. 144.00 (*0-85200-713-2*) Kluwer Ac.

Alcoholism: Biomedical & Genetic Aspects. H. W. Goedde & Dharam P. Agarwal. 1989. text ed. 67.00 (*0-07-105273-9*) McGraw.

Alcoholism: Causes, Effects, & Treatment. Joseph F. Perez. LC 92-53191. 312p. 1992. pap. text ed. 21.95 (*1-55959-039-4*) Accel Devel.

Alcoholism: Development, Consequences & Intervention. 3rd ed. Estes & Heinmann. 1986. 27.95 (*0-8016-1604-2*) Mosby Yr Bk.

Alcoholism: Introduction to Theory & Treatment. 3rd ed. David A. Ward. 528p. (Orig.). 1990. per. 34.95 (*0-8403-5758-3*) Kendall-Hunt.

Alcoholism: Modern Psychological Approaches to Treatment. Eva M. Blum & Richard H. Blum. LC 67-13278. (Jossey-Bass Behavioral Science Ser.). 391p. reprint ed. pap. 111.50 (*0-8357-4967-3*, 2037900) Bks Demand.

Alcoholism: New Light on the Disease. John Wallace. 1990. pap. 9.95 (*0-933741-01-4*) Edgehill Pubns.

Alcoholism: New Light on the Disease. John Wallace. LC 85-80595. 164p. 1990. reprint ed. pap. 9.95 (*0-926028-08-1*) Edgehill Pubns.

Alcoholism: Origins & Outcome. Ed. by Robert M. Rose & James E. Barrett. (American Psychopathological Association Ser.). (Illus.). 314p. 1988. text ed. 104.00 (*0-88167-333-1*) Raven.

Alcoholism: The Curse, the Causes & the "Cures" William A. Sanderson. LC 85-70769. (Illus.). 180p. (Orig.). 1985. pap. 12.95 (*0-9614833-0-X*) Azure Zephyr.

Alcoholism: The Facts. Donald W. Goodwin. LC 93-33957. (Facts Ser.). (Illus.). 192p. 1994. pap. 12.95 (*0-19-262338-9*) OUP.

Alcoholism: The Nutritional Approach. Roger J. Williams. 130p. 1959. pap. 4.95 (*0-292-70301-5*) U of Tex Pr.

Alcoholism: Treatment, Vol. 2. Cedric M. Smith. (Alcohol Research Review Ser.). 107p. 1980. reprint ed. 30.95 (*0-87705-968-3*) Human Sci Pr.

*__Alcoholism: Your Questions Answered.__ Liz Hodgkinson. 128p. 1995. pap. 8.95 (*0-7063-7402-9*, Pub. by Ward Lock UK) Sterling.

Alcoholism - a Terminal Disease. Richard Kay. (C). 1989. text ed. 35.00 (*0-902662-92-9*, Pub. by R K Pubns UK) St Mut.

Alcoholism - The Genetic Inheritance. rev. ed. Kathleen W. Fitzgerald. (Illus.). 234p. reprint ed. pap. 14.95 (*1-882195-01-9*) Whales Tale Pr.

Alcoholism, a Multidisciplinary Approach: Proceedings of the Symposium on Alcoholism, Amsterdam, May 1978. Alcoholism Symposium Staff. Ed. by J. Mendlewicz & Herman M. Van Praag. (Advances in Biological Psychiatry Ser.: Vol. 3). (Illus.). 1979. pap. 44.00 (*3-8055-2977-5*) S Karger.

Alcoholism & Addiction. S. Swinson & E. Eaves. 1990. pap. 35.00 (*0-7121-0161-6*, Pub. by Northcote UK) St Mut.

Alcoholism & Affective Disorders: Clinical, Genetic, & Biochemical Studies with Emphasis on Alcohol-Lithium Interaction. Ed. by Donald W. Goodwin & Carlton K. Erickson. (Illus.). 298p. 1979. 40.00 (*0-88331-110-0*) Luce.

Alcoholism & Aging: Advances in Research. Ed. by W. Gibson Wood & Merrill F. Elias. 240p. 1982. 92.00 (*0-8493-5832-9*, HV5138) CRC Pr.

*__Alcoholism & Aging: An Annotated Bibliography & Review.__ Ed. by Nancy J. Osgood et al. LC 94-41371. (Bibliographies & Indexes in Gerontology Ser.: Vol. 24). 264p. 1995. text ed. 65.00 (*0-313-28398-2*, Greenwood Pr) Greenwood.

Alcoholism & Clinical Psychiatry. Ed. by Joel Solomon. LC 81-22701. 250p. 1982. 45.00 (*0-306-40794-9*, Plenum Med Bk) Plenum.

Alcoholism & Drug Abuse in the Workplace: Employee Assistance Programs. Walter F. Scanlon. 160p. 1985. 35.00 (*0-275-92043-7*, C2043, Praeger Pubs) Greenwood.

Alcoholism & Drug Abuse in the Workplace: Managing Care & Costs Through Employee Assistance Programs. 2nd ed. Walter F. Scanlon. LC 90-49202. 208p. 1991. text ed. 55.00 (*0-275-93675-9*, C3675, Praeger Pubs); pap. text ed. 17.95 (*0-275-93676-7*, B3676, Praeger Pubs) Greenwood.

Alcoholism & Drug Abuse Treatment Centers Directory. 47.50 (*0-685-04287-1*) Ready Ref Pr.

Alcoholism & Homosexuality. Ed. by Thomas O. Ziebold & John E. Mongeon. LC 82-9217. (Journal of Homosexuality: Vol. 7, No. 4). 107p. 1982. text ed. 32.95 (*0-917724-93-3*) Haworth Pr.

*__Alcoholism & Human Sexuality.__ Gary G. Forrest. LC 94-37991. 412p. 1994. pap. text ed. 35.00 (*1-56821-404-9*) Aronson.

Alcoholism & Its Treatment in Industry. Carl J. Schramm. LC 77-4783. 204p. reprint ed. pap. 58.20 (*0-8357-5300-X*, 2017028) Bks Demand.

Alcoholism & Mortality. Per Sundby. 1967. 16.00 (*0-685-04408-4*) Rutgers Ctr Alcohol.

Alcoholism & Other Drug Dependence Services Standards Scoring Guidelines. 68p. 1987. 25.00 (*0-86688-137-9*) Joint Comm Hlthcare.

*__Alcoholism & Other Drug Problems.__ 2nd ed. Royce. 1995. 34.00 (*0-02-874049-1*) Free Pr.

Alcoholism & Problem Drinking: Treating Addiction or Modifying Bad Habits? J. C. Clarke. 152p. 1988. text ed. 24.51 (*0-08-034432-1*, Pergamon Pr); pap. text ed. 28.00 (*0-08-034433-X*, Pergamon Pr) Elsevier.

Alcoholism & Recovery: A Manual for Pastoral Ministry. Ed. by Steven L. Berg. 200p. (Orig.). 1989. pap. 8.95 (*0-685-27224-9*) Guest Hse Inc.

Alcoholism & Related Problems: Issues for the American People. Ed. by Louis J. West. LC 84-13451. 224p. 1984. 12.95 (*0-13-021486-8*); pap. 6.95 (*0-13-021478-7*) Am Assembly.

Alcoholism & Related Problems: Issues for the American Public. American Assembly Staff. LC 84-13451. 226p. reprint ed. pap. 64.50 (*0-8357-5301-8*, 2029859) Bks Demand.

Alcoholism & Sexual Dysfunction: Issues in Clinical Management. Ed. by David J. Powell. LC 89-1998. (Alcoholism Treatment Quarterly Ser.: Vol. 1, No. 3). 145p. 1984. text ed. 32.95 (*0-86656-365-2*) Haworth Pr.

Alcoholism & Spirituality: Stress Management & Serenity During Recovery. Charles L. Whitfield. 150p. (Orig.). 1985. pap. 13.00 (*0-933825-12-9*) T W Perrin.

Alcoholism & Substance Abuse: Strategies for Intervention. Ed. by Thomas E. Bratter & Gary G. Forrest. 640p. (C). 1985. text ed. 55.00 (*0-02-904260-7*) Free Pr.

Alcoholism & Substance Abuse in Special Populations. Gary W. Lawson & Ann W. Lawson. LC 88-7600. 370p. (C). 1989. 58.00 (*0-8342-0007-4*) Aspen Pub.

Alcoholism & the Family. Gilda Berger. LC 93-10898. (Changing Family Ser.). (Illus.). 128p. (YA). (gr. 7-12). 1993. lib. bdg. 14.49 (*0-531-12548-3*) Watts.

Alcoholism & the Family. Saturo Saitoh et al. LC 90-2644. 324p. 1992. 25.95 (*0-87630-626-1*) Brunner-Mazel.

Alcoholism & the Family: A Guide to Treatment & Prevention. Gary W. Lawson et al. LC 82-24352. 296p. (C). 1983. 38.00 (*0-87189-606-0*) Aspen Pub.

Alcoholism & the Identification of Alcoholics. H. G. Giles et al. 160p. 1990. 22.95 (*0-669-24923-8*) Heath.

*__Alcoholism & Women.__ Bauer. 1995. pap. 16.00 (*0-919123-10-4*) Atrium Pubs.

Alcoholism As a Medical Problem. Ed. by H. D. Kruse & Gerald N. Grob. LC 80-1266. (Addiction in America Ser.). 1981. reprint ed. lib. bdg. 15.95 (*0-405-13600-5*) Ayer.

Alcoholism Chemical Dependency & the College Student. Intro. by Timothy M. Rivinus. LC 88-9443. (Journal of College Student Psychotherapy: Vol. 2, Nos. 3-4). (Illus.). 257p. (Orig.). 1988. text ed. 49.95 (*0-86656-734-8*); pap. text ed. 14.95 (*0-86656-812-3*) Haworth Pr.

Alcoholism Counselor. Jack Rudman. (Career Examination Ser.: C-2145). 1994. pap. 29.95 (*0-8373-2145-X*) Nat Learn.

Alcoholism Educator. (Career Examination Ser.: C-3282). 1994. pap. 29.95 (*0-8373-3282-6*) Nat Learn.

Alcoholism Etiology & Treatment: Issues for Theory & Practice Treatment. Ed. & Pref. by Bernard Segal. LC 88-16358. (Drugs & Society Ser.: Vol. 2, Nos. 3-4). 131p. 1989. text ed. 32.95 (*0-86656-845-X*) Haworth Pr.

Alcoholism Facts Explored. Gary Stone. (Illus.). 164p. 1984. spiral bd. 15.95 (*0-930427-00-9*) Alcohol Con Serv.

Alcoholism for Beginners. David Berger. 1994. pap. 9.95 (*0-86316-163-4*) Writers & Readers.

Alcoholism in America. Harrison M. Trice. LC 77-2665. 168p. 1978. reprint ed. pap. 6.95 (*0-88275-479-3*) Krieger.

Alcoholism in North America, Europe, & Asia. John E. Helzer & Glorisa J. Canino. (Illus.). 208p. 1992. 49.95 (*0-19-505090-8*) OUP.

Alcoholism in the Elderly: Social & Biomedical Issues. Ed. by James T. Hartford & T. Samorajski. (Aging Ser.: Vol. 25). 304p. 1984. text ed. 104.50 (*0-89004-924-6*) Raven.

Alcoholism in the Professions. LeClair Bissell & Paul W. Haberman. 214p. 1984. 35.00 (*0-19-503459-7*) OUP.

*__Alcoholism, Narcissism & Psychopathology.__ Gary G. Forrest. LC 94-34542. 324p. 1994. pap. text ed. 30.00 (*1-56821-377-8*) Aronson.

Alcoholism Problems: Selected Issues. Sidney Cohen. LC 83-179. 193p. 1983. text ed. 39.95 (*0-86656-209-5*); pap. text ed. 19.95 (*0-86656-179-X*) Haworth Pr.

Alcoholism Programs in Industry: The Patient's View. Margaret M. Heyman. LC 77-620066. (Monograph Ser.: No. 12). 1978. 7.50 (*0-911290-45-1*) Rutgers Ctr Alcohol.

Alcoholism Rehabilitation: Methods & Experiences of Private Rehabilitation Centers. Ed. by Vincent Groupe. LC 78-620026. (NIAAA-RUCAS Alcoholism Treatment Ser.: No. 3). 1978. pap. 6.00 (*0-911290-49-4*) Rutgers Ctr Alcohol.

Alcoholism Rehabilitation Consultant. Jack Rudman. (Career Examination Ser.: C-2772). 1994. pap. 29.95 (*0-8373-2772-5*) Nat Learn.

Alcoholism Research Project of Mexican Americans in Scottsbluff, Nebraska. Jesse Cervantes & David R. DiMartino. 35p. (Orig.). 1980. pap. 3.00 (*1-55719-051-8*) U NE CPAR.

Alcoholism Syndrome in Finland. P. Kiviranta. (Finnish Foundation for Alcohol Studies: Vol. 17). 1969. 5.50 (*951-9192-07-7*) Rutgers Ctr Alcohol.

Alcoholism the Biochemical Connection: A Breakthrough Seven-Week Self-Treatment Program. Joan Mathews-Larsen. 1992. 22.50 (*0-679-41493-2*, Villard Bks) Random.

*__Alcoholism Treatment: A Social Work Perspective.__ Katherine. LC 94-43291. 1995. write for info. (*0-8034-1387-4*) Nelson-Hall.

Alcoholism Treatment: Context, Process, & Outcome. Rudolf H. Moos et al. (Illus.). 304p. 1990. 45.00 (*0-19-504362-6*) OUP.

Alcoholism Treatment for Impaired Drivers: An Evaluation. Paul C. Whitehead et al. LC 90-6104. (Interdisciplinary Studies in Alcohol Use & Abuse: Vol. 3). 150p. 1990. lib. bdg. 69.95 (*0-88946-284-4*) E Mellen.

Alcoholism Treatment Matching Research: Methodological & Clinical Approaches. Dennis M. Donovan & Margaret E. Mattson. (Journal of Studies on Alcohol: Suppl. No. 12). 1994. pap. 26.95 (*0-911290-53-2*, AJS-107) Rutgers Ctr Alcohol.

Alcoholismo: Un Carrusel Llamado Negacion. Joseph A. Kellermann. 20p. (Orig.). (SPA.). 1983. pap. 1.30 (*0-89486-199-9*) Hazelden.

Alcoholism's Children: ACoAs in Priesthood & Religious Life. Sean D. Sammon. LC 88-39524. 100p. (Orig.). 1989. pap. 4.95 (*0-8189-0545-X*) Alba.

Alcohols & Derivatives, 2 vols. Ed. by J. Tremolieres. 1970. Set. 128.00 (*0-08-006937-1*, Pub. by Pergamon Repr UK) Franklin.

Alcohols with Water. A. S. Burton. Ed. by A. F. Barton. (Solubility Data Ser.: Vol. 15). 465p. 1984. 184.00 (*0-08-025276-1*, Pub. by Pergamon Repr UK) Franklin.

Alcools. annot. ed. Guillaume Apollinaire. Tr. & Anno. by Anne H. Greet. LC 65-20148. 1966. pap. 12.00 (*0-520-00029-3*) U CA Pr.

Alcools: Guillaume Apollinaire. Guillaume Apollinaire. Ed. by Garnet Rees. (French Poets Ser.). 192p. (FRE.). (C). 1975. pap. 12.50 (*0-485-12708-3*, Pub. by Athlone Pr UK) Humanities.

*__Alcools: Poems.__ Guillaume Apollinaire. Tr. by Donald Revell. LC 95-2294. (ENG & FRE.). 1995. write for info. (*0-8195-2224-4*, Wesleyan Univ Pr); pap. write for info. (*0-8195-1228-1*, Wesleyan Univ Pr) U Pr of New Eng.

Alcools, le Bestaire: Vitam Impendere Amori. Guillaume Apollinaire. (Poesie Ser.). (FRE.). 1971. pap. 9.95 (*2-07-030007-2*) Schoenhof.

Alcools, le Bestiare Vitam Impendere Amori. Guillaume Apollinaire. 192p. (FRE.). 1971. pap. 11.95 (*0-7859-2753-0*, F82040) Fr & Eur.

Alcott Family Arrives. Ann Struthers. LC 93-72268. (Illus.). 80p. (Orig.). 1993. pap. 10.00 (*0-9636959-0-8*) Coe Review Pr.

Alcott Memoirs. Frederic E. Willis. 108p. 1970. reprint ed. pap. 5.00 (*0-910120-04-8*) Americanist.

Alcuin. Charles B. Brown. Ed. by Cynthia Kierner. (Masterworks of Literature Ser.). 1994. pap. (*0-8084-0448-2*) NCUP.

Alcuin: A Dialogue. Charles B. Brown. (Works of Charles Brockden Brown). 1989. reprint ed. lib. bdg. 79.00 (*0-7812-2065-3*) Rprt Serv.

Alcuin & the Rise of the Christian Schools. Andrew F. West. LC 73-149674. reprint ed. 24.50 (*0-404-06908-8*) AMS Pr.

Alcuin & the Rise of the Christian Schools. Andrew F. West. 1892. reprint ed. 9.00 (*0-403-00031-9*) Scholarly.

Alcuin of York: The Life & Letters of the Saxon Scholar, AD 732 to 804. Stephen Allott. (C). 1988. 68.00 (*1-85072-021-5*, Pub. by W Sessions UK) St Mut.

Alcymist see Alceste

Alcyone: Nietzsche on Gifts, Noise, & Women. Gary Shapiro. LC 90-48444. (SUNY Series in Contemporary Continental Philosophy). 170p. (C). 1991. 59.50 (*0-7914-0741-1*); pap. 19.95 (*0-7914-0742-X*) State U NY Pr.

Aldea Perdida. Armando Palacio Valdes. Ed. by Alvaro Ruiz de la Pena. (Nueva Austral Ser.: Vol. 180). (SPA.). 1991. pap. text ed. 24.95x (*84-239-1980-3*) Elliots Bks.

Aldeanismo en la Poesia de Luis Pales Matos. Luz V Romero Garcia. (UPREX, Estudios Literarios Ser.: No. 42). 119p. (C). 1976. pap. 1.50 (*0-8477-0042-9*) U of PR Pr.

*__Alden: Descendents of Polly & Ebenezer Alden, Who were 6th in Descent from John Alden, the Pilgrim.__ E. Alden & H. Shaw. 100p. 1994. reprint ed. lib. bdg. 29.50 (*0-8328-4287-7*); reprint ed. pap. 19.50 (*0-8328-4288-5*) Higginson Bk Co.

*__Alden: The Story of a Pilgrim Family from the Mayflower to the Present Time (1899), with Autobiography, Recollections, Letters, Incidents & Genealogy.__ John Alden. (Illus.). 441p. 1994. lib. bdg. 78.00 (*0-8328-4285-0*) Higginson Bk Co.

*__Alden: The Story of a Pilgrim Family from the Mayflower to the Present Time (1899), with Autobiography, Recollections, Letters, Incidents & Genealogy.__ John Alden. (Illus.). 441p. 1994. reprint ed. pap. 68.00 (*0-8328-4286-9*) Higginson Bk Co.

*__Alden Aaroe: Voice of the Morning.__ Steve Clark. 168p. 1994. 15.95 (*0-87517-072-2*) Dietz.

Alden Coll - The King's Daughter. Isabella M. Alden. 1992. pap. 7.99 (*0-88419-308-X*, Creation Hse) Strang Comms Co.

Alden Collection - As in a Mirror. Isabella M. Alden. LC 92-72776. 308p. 7.99 (*0-88419-319-5*) Strang Comms Co.

Alden Collection - Ester Ried's Awakening. Isabella M. Alden. LC 92-72777. 266p. 7.99 (*0-88419-320-9*) Strang Comms Co.

Alden Nowlan & His Works. Michael Oliver. 58p. (C). 1990. pap. text ed. 9.95 (*1-55022-067-5*, Pub. by ECW Press CN) Genl Dist Srvs.

Alder Gulch. Ernest Haycox. 288p. 1992. pap. 3.50 (*1-55817-634-9*, Pinnacle NY) Windsor NY.

Alderian Family Counseling: A Manual for Counselor, Educator, & Psychotherapist. rev. ed. Ed. by Oscar C. Christensen. LC 93-70537. 186p. 1993. pap. text ed. 9.95 (*0-932796-56-7*) Ed Media Corp.

Aldermanbury Trust PLC - Investigation under Section 432(2) Companies Act, 1985. G. W. Staple & T. G. Tress. 330p. 1991. pap. 85.00 (*0-11-515280-6*, HM2860) UNIPUB.

Alderney at War. Brian Bonnard. (Illus.). 192p. 1993. 30.00 (*0-7509-0343-0*) A Sutton Pub.

Alderson Story: My Life As a Political Prisoner. Elizabeth G. Flynn. LC 63-10863. 223p. 1972. pap. 2.25 (*0-7178-0002-4*) Intl Pubs Co.

Aldhelm: The Poetic Works. Ed. by James L. Rosier & M. Lapidge. Tr. by Michael Lapidge & James Rosier. LC 84-29781. 274p. 1985. 63.00 (*0-85991-146-2*) Boydell & Brewer.

Aldhelm: The Prose Works. Aldhelm. Ed. by Michael Lapidge & James L. Rosier. Tr. by James L. Rosier. 210p. 1970. 70.00 (*0-85991-041-5*) Boydell & Brewer.

Aldhelm: The Prose Works. Tr. by Michael Lapidge & Michael Herren. 210p. 1979. 52.25 (*0-8476-6090-7*) Rowman.

Aldiss Unbound: The Science Fiction of Brian W. Aldiss. Richard Mathews. LC 77-24582. (Milford Series: Popular Writers of Today: Vol. 9). 64p. 1977. lib. bdg. 20.00 (*0-89370-113-0*); pap. 10.00 (*0-89370-213-7*) Borgo Pr.

Aldo. John Burningham. LC 91-19589. (Illus.). 32p. (J). (ps-2). 1992. 15.00 (*0-517-58701-7*); lib. bdg. 15.99 (*0-517-58699-1*) Crown Bks Yng Read.

Aldo Applesauce. Johanna Hurwitz. LC 79-16200. (Illus.). 128p. (J). (gr. 4-6). 1979. 15.00 (*0-688-22199-8*); lib. bdg. 14.93 (*0-688-32199-2*) Morrow Jr Bks.

Aldo Applesauce. Johanna Hurwitz. (Illus.). 128p. (J). (gr. 3-5). 1989. pap. 3.99 (*0-14-034083-1*, Puffin) Puffin Bks.

Aldo Ice Cream. Johanna Hurwitz. LC 80-24371. (Illus.). 128p. (J). (gr. 4-6). 1981. 15.00 (*0-688-00375-3*); lib. bdg. 14.93 (*0-688-00374-5*) Morrow Jr Bks.

Aldo Ice Cream. Johanna Hurwitz. (Illus.). 128p. (J). (gr. 3-7). 1989. pap. 3.99 (*0-14-034084-X*, Puffin) Puffin Bks.

*__Aldo Leopold: American Ecologist.__ Peter Anderson. LC 95-2596. (First Bks.). (J). 1995. lib. bdg. 13.93 (*0-531-20203-8*) Watts.

Aldo Leopold: His Life & Work. Curt Meine. LC 87-40367. (Illus.). 654p. 1988. 35.00 (*0-299-11490-2*) U of Wis Pr.

Aldo Leopold: His Life & Work. Curt Meine. LC 87-40367. (Illus.). 654p. 1991. reprint ed. pap. 21.95 (*0-299-11494-5*) U of Wis Pr.

Aldo Leopold: Living with the Land. Julie Dunlap. (Earth Keepers Ser.). (Illus.). 80p. (J). (gr. 4-7). 1993. lib. bdg. 14.98 (*0-8050-2501-4*) TFC Bks NY.

Aldo Leopold: The Man & His Legacy. Ed. by Thomas Tanner. LC 87-9493. (Illus.). 170p. (Orig.). 1987. pap. text ed. 12.00 (*0-935734-13-9*) Soil & Water Conserv.

*__Aldo Leopold's Southwest.__ Ed. by David E. Brown & Neil B. Carmony. LC 94-48678. (Illus.). 259p. 1995. pap. 17.95 (*0-8263-1580-1*) U of NM Pr.

*__Aldo Moro Murder Case.__ Richard Drake. (Illus.). 336p. (C). 1995. text ed. 45.00 (*0-674-01481-2*) HUP.

Aldo Peanut Butter. Johanna Hurwitz. LC 90-35366. (Illus.). 128p. (J). (gr. 2 up). 1990. 12.95 (*0-688-09751-0*) Morrow Jr Bks.

Aldo Peanut Butter. Johanna Hurwitz. (Illus.). 112p. (J). (gr. 3-7). 1992. pap. 3.99 (*0-14-036020-4*) Puffin Bks.

Aldo Rossi. (Architecture & Urbanism Extra Edition Ser.). (Illus.). 232p. (Orig.). (ENG & JPN.). (C). pap. text ed. 68.00 (*4-900211-06-0*, Pub. by Japan Architect JA) Gingko Press.

Aldo Rossi. Gianni Braghieri. (Illus.). 272p. (ENG & SPA.). 1992. pap. 18.95 (*84-252-1539-0*) Rizzoli Intl.

Aldo Rossi. Hans G. Hannesen. (Illus.). 249p. 1995. pap. 40.00 (*1-85490-364-0*, Academy Edits) St Martin.

Aldo Rossi: Architecture. Ed. by Morris Adjmi. LC 91-27398. (Illus.). 304p. 1991. 60.00 (*1-878271-15-6*); pap. 40.00 (*1-878271-16-4*) Princeton Arch.

Aldo Rossi: Buildings & Projects. Ed. by Peter Arnell et al. LC 83-42923. (Illus.). 320p. 1985. pap. 35.00 (*0-8478-0499-2*) Rizzoli Intl.

Aldo Rossi: Drawings & Paintings 1981-1991. Ed. by Morris Adjmi & Giovanni Bertolotto. LC 93-21052. (Illus.). 224p. Date not set. Italian ed. pap. 40.00 (*1-878271-91-1*) Princeton Arch.

Aldo Rossi: Drawings & Paintings 1981-1991. Ed. by Morris Adjmi & Giovanni Bertolotto. LC 93-21052. (Illus.). 224p. 1993. English ed. 60.00 (*1-878271-49-0*); English ed. pap. 40.00 (*1-878271-50-4*) Princeton Arch.

*__Aldobrandini Wedding.__ Frank G. Muller. (Iconological Studies in Roman Art: Vol. 3). (Illus.). xii, 208p. 1994. lib. bdg. 49.00x (*90-5063-266-1*, Pub. by Gieben NE) Benjamins North Am.

Aldosterone. Edith Glaz & Paul Vecsei. LC 70-138666. 628p. 1971. 263.00 (*0-08-013368-1*, Pub. by Pergamon Repr UK) Franklin.

Aldous Huxley. Harold H. Watts. (English Authors Ser.: No. 79). 184p. 1969. text ed. 22.95 (*0-8057-1284-4*, Twayne) Macmillan.

Aldous Huxley & Film. Virginia M. Clark. LC 87-12308. (Filmmakers Ser.: No. 16). (Illus.). 185p. 1987. 20.00 (*0-8108-2002-1*) Scarecrow.

Aldous Huxley & the Way to Reality. Charles M. Holmes. LC 77-16216. (Illus.). 238p. 1978. reprint ed. text ed. 35.00 (*0-313-20016-5*, HOAH, Greenwood Pr) Greenwood.

*__Aldous Huxley Recollected.__ David Dunaway. 304p. 1995. 22.00 (*0-7867-0189-7*) Carroll & Graf.

Aldous Huxley's Brave New World, 10. Berthold Thiel. (Bochum Studies in English). ii, 346p. (Orig.). 1980. pap. 35.00 (*90-6032-193-6*, Pub. by B R Gruener NE) Benjamins North Am.

An Asterisk (*) at the beginning of an entry indicates that the title is appearing in BIP for the first time.

A

An Asterisk (*) at the beginning of an entry indicates that the title is appearing in BIP for the first time.

177

Alex Katz: Echoes. Jacques Bellefroid & Vilma Fuentes. Tr. by James Strancel. (Other Monograph Ser.). (Illus.). 200p. 1992. 39.95 (*1-878552-01-5*) Ptmanteau Pr.

Alex Katz: The Complete Prints, 1947-1983. Nicholas P. Maravell. (Illus.). 252p. 1983. 125.00 (*1-55660-063-1*) A Wofsy Fine Arts.

Alex Katz from the Early Sixties. Text by Michael Scholnick. (Illus.). 65p. 1987. pap. 20.00 (*0-944680-13-5*) R Miller Gal.

Alex Katz, Small Paintings 1952-1991. Michael Kohn. (Illus.). 22p. (Orig.). 1991. 15.00 (*1-880086-00-X*) M Kohn Gallery.

Alex Livingston, the Tomato Man. Cornelia M. Parkinson. (Illus.). 20p. (J). (gr. 4 up). 1985. pap. 1.50 (*0-938404-05-9*, AWL) Hist Tales.

***Alex Lord's British Columbia: Recollections of a Rural School Inspector.** 212p. 1991. pap. 15.95 (*0-7748-0385-1*) U of Wash Pr.

Alex Posey: Creek Poet, Journalist, & Humorist. Daniel F. Littlefield, Jr. LC 91-14538. (American Indian Lives Ser.). viii, 331p. 1992. 39.95 (*0-8032-2899-6*) U of Nebr Pr.

Alex Randall's Used Computer Handbook. Alexander Randall & Steven J. Bennett. 1990. pap. 14.95 (*1-55615-267-1*) Microsoft.

Alex Sanders Lectures. Ed. by Alex Sanders. (Illus.). 90p. 1989. pap. 6.95 (*0-939708-05-1*) Magickal Childe.

Alex Stewart: Portrait of a Pioneer. John R. Irwin. LC 85-62592. (Illus.). 298p. 1985. pap. 14.95 (*0-88740-053-1*) Schiffer.

Alex Sweet's Texas: The Lighter Side of Lone Star History. Alexander E. Sweet. Ed. by Virginia Eisenhour. LC 85-22746. (Illus.). 224p. (C). 1986. 19.95 (*0-292-70382-1*); pap. 11.95 (*0-292-70390-2*) U of Tex Pr.

Alex the Great. Barbara Cole. 1989. 12.95 (*0-8239-0941-7*) Rosen Group.

Alex, the Kid with AIDS. Linda W. Girard. Ed. by Abby Levine. LC 89-77592. (Albert Whitman Concept Bks.). (Illus.). 32p. (J). (gr. 2-5). 1991. lib. bdg. 13.95 (*0-8075-0245-6*); pap. 5.95 (*0-8075-0247-2*) A Whitman.

Alex Wants to Call It Love. Silvia Sanza. LC 90-64193. 176p. (Orig.). 1991. pap. 14.95 (*1-85242-214-9*) Serpents Tail.

Alex, Who Won His War. Chester Aaron. 144p. (J). (gr. 5 up). 1991. 17.95 (*0-8027-8098-9*) Walker & Co.

***Alex You're Growing!** Diana G. Gallagher. Ed. by Lisa Clancy. (Secret World of Alex Mack Ser.: No. 1). 144p. (Orig.). (YA). 1995. mass mkt. 3.99 (*0-671-52599-9*, Minstrel Bks) PB.

***Alexakis Bride.** Anne McAllister. 1995. mass mkt. 3.25 (*0-373-11769-8*, 1-11769-6) Harlequin Bks.

Alexandar Stoddard's Tea Celebrations. Alexandra Stoddard. LC 94-17054. 1994. 18.00 (*0-688-13427-0*) Morrow.

Alexander. (Deutsche Volksbucher in Faksimiledrucken, Reihe A Ser.: Bd. 1). 362p. 1975. reprint ed. write for info. (*3-487-05471-X*, Pub. by Georg Olms GW) Lubrecht & Cramer.

Alexander. Duncan Townson. Ed. by Margaret Killingray et al. (World History Ser.). (Illus.). 32p. (YA). (gr. 6-11). 1980. reprint ed. pap. text ed. 4.35 (*0-89908-014-6*) Greenhaven.

Alexander. Ulrich Von Eschenbach. Ed. by Wendlin Toiscsher. (Bibliothek Des Literarischen Vereins in Stuttgart Ser.: Bd. 182). xxii, 867p. 1974. reprint ed. write for info. (*3-487-04437-4*, Pub. by Georg Olms GW) Lubrecht & Cramer.

Alexander: A History of the Origin & Growth of the Art of War from the Earliest Times to the Battle of Ipsus, 301 B.C., with a Detailed Account of the Campaigns of the Great Macedonian. Theodore A. Dodge. 721p. 1994. 59.95 (*1-85367-178-9*, 5400) Stackpole.

Alexander: Descent of the Scottish Alexanders, a Genealogical Sketch, with Discussions of Some Historic Matters. F. A. Sondley. 73p. 1992. reprint ed. lib. bdg. 25.00 (*0-8328-2619-7*); reprint ed. pap. 15.00 (*0-8328-2620-0*) Higginson Bk Co.

Alexander: El Libro De Alixandre. (Gesellschaft Fur Romanische Literatur Ser.: Vol. 10). xxviii, 333p. 1978. reprint ed. write for info. (*3-487-06543-6*, Pub. by Georg Olms GW) Lubrecht & Cramer.

Alexander: Family Biographies of the Families of Alexander, Wilkinson, Sparr & Guthrie, with Sketches & Memorials. William G. Alexander. (Illus.). 180p. 1994. reprint ed. lib. bdg. 39.00 (*0-8328-4187-0*); reprint ed. pap. 29.00 (*0-8328-4188-9*) Higginson Bk Co.

***Alexander: Record of the Descendants of John Alexander of Lanarkshire, kScotland, & His Wife Margaret Glasson, Who Emigrated from Co. Armagh, Ireland, to Chester Co. PA.** J. A. Alexander. 220p. 1994. reprint ed. lib. bdg. 46.00 (*0-8328-4289-3*); reprint ed. pap. 36.00 (*0-8328-4290-7*) Higginson Bk Co.

Alexander A. Friedmann: The Man Who Made the Universe Expand. Eduard A. Tropp et al. Tr. by Alexander Dron & Michael Burov. LC 92-28315. (Illus.). 336p. (C). 1993. 49.95 (*0-521-38470-2*) Cambridge U Pr.

Alexander A. Potebnja's Psycholinguistic Theory of Literature: A Metacritical Inquiry. John Fizer. LC 87-80688. (Harvard Ukrainian Research Institute Monograph). (Illus.). 164p. (C). 1990. 7.50 (*0-916458-16-4*) Harvard Ukrainian.

***Alexander Alekhine's Chess Games, 1902-1946: Nearly 2500 Games of the Former World Champion, Many Fully Annotated byy Alekhine, with 1500 Diagrams, Fully Indexed.** Leonard M. Skinner & Robert G. Verhoeven. (Illus.). 800p. 1995. lib. bdg. 95.00 (*0-7864-0117-6*) McFarland & Co.

Alexander & the Dragon. Katharine Holabird. (Illus.). 24p. (J). (ps-2). 1988. 14.00 (*0-517-56996-5*, Clarkson Potter) Crown Bks Yng Read.

Alexander & the Greeks. Victor Ehrenberg. Tr. by Ruth Fraenkel Von Velson. LC 79-4913. 1985. reprint ed. 17.00 (*0-88355-963-3*) Hyperion Conn.

Alexander & the Greeks: Mini-Play & Activities. Lawrence Stevens. (World History Ser.). (YA). (gr. 7 up). 1981. 6.50 (*0-89550-339-5*) Stevens & Shea.

Alexander & the Magic Boat. Katharine Holabird. (Illus.). 24p. (J). (ps-2). 1990. 11.95 (*0-517-58142-6*); lib. bdg. 12.99 (*0-517-58149-3*) Crown Bks Yng Read.

***Alexander & the Terrible, Horrible No Good, Very Bad Day.** Garrett Christopher. Ed. by J. Friedland & R. Kessler. (Novel-Ties Ser.). (J). (gr. k-1). 1992. student ed, pap. text ed. 14.95 (*0-88122-732-3*) Lrn Links.

Alexander & the Terrible, Horrible, No Good, Very Bad Day. Judith Viorst. LC 72-75289. (Illus.). 32p. (J). (gr. k-4). 1972. text ed. 13.95 (*0-689-30072-7*, Atheneum Bks Young) S&S Childrens.

Alexander & the Terrible, Horrible, No Good, Very Bad Day. Judith Viorst. LC 87-1087. (Illus.). 32p. (J). (gr. k-4). 1987. reprint ed. pap. 3.95 (*0-689-71173-5*, Aladdin Paperbacks) S&S Childrens.

Alexander & the Wind-up Mouse. Leo Lionni. LC 76-77423. (Illus.). 32p. (J). (ps-2). 1969. 15.00 (*0-394-80914-9*); lib. bdg. 15.99 (*0-394-90914-3*) Knopf Bks Yng Read.

Alexander & the Wind-up Mouse. Leo Lionni. LC 74-2088. (Pinwheel Bks.). (Illus.). 32p. (J). (ps-3). 1974. reprint ed. pap. 5.99 (*0-394-82911-5*) Pantheon.

Alexander Anderson's Life & Engravings with a Checklist of Publications Drawn from His Diary. Jane R. Pomeroy. (Illus.). 75p. 1990. 8.00 (*0-944026-25-7*) Am Antiquarian.

Alexander Andreyevich Ivanov. M. M. Allenov. 204p. 1980. 35.00 (*0-317-14213-5*, Pub. by Collets UK) St Mut.

***Alexander Baxter.** Leonard S. Berman. 32p. (J). (gr. 3-7). 1995. 14.95 (*0-929999-16-9*) Tzedakah Pubns.

Alexander Bestuzhev-Marlinsky & Russian Byronism. Lewis Bagby. LC 93-47591. (Illus.). 376p. 1995. 45.00 (*0-271-01336-2*) Pa St U Pr.

Alexander Blok: Selected Poems. Ed. by Avril Pyman. LC 67-31506. 388p. (C). 1972. 155.00 (*0-08-012185-3*, Pub. by Pergamon Repr UK) Franklin.

Alexander Book in Ethiopia. Ernest A. Budge. LC 73-18834. (Illus.). reprint ed. 37.50 (*0-404-11307-9*) AMS Pr.

Alexander Botts: Great Stories from the Saturday Evening Post. William H. Upson. LC 77-90937. 320p. 1977. 22.95 (*0-89387-011-0*, Queens House) Amereon Ltd.

***Alexander Brest Museum & Gallery: A Guide to the Collections.** David Lauderdale. Ed. by Cheryl Sowder. LC 94-78736. 112p. (Orig.). 1994. pap. write for info. (*0-9643165-0-1*) Jacksnvl Univ.

Alexander Brook (1898-1980) Looking Back. Alma S. King. (Important American Artists, Limited Ed. Exhibition Catalogues Ser.). (Illus.). 32p. (Orig.). (C). 1981. lib. bdg. 35.00 (*0-941430-01-4*); pap. 10.00 (*0-941430-00-6*) Santa Fe E Gallery.

Alexander Bryan Johnson: Philosophical Banker. Charles L. Todd & Robert Sonkin. 1977. 34.95x (*0-8156-2188-4*) Syracuse U Pr.

Alexander Calder. Joan M. Marter. (Monographs on American Artists). (Illus.). 288p. (C). 1992. 80.00 (*0-521-33038-6*) Cambridge U Pr.

Alexander Calder. Richard J. Wattenmaker & Christopher R. Young. LC 82-84524. (Illus.). 39p. (Orig.). 1983. pap. 4.50 (*0-939896-05-2*) Flint Inst Arts.

Alexander Calder: A Survey of Works from the Greenberg Gallery. Ed. by Sally Vogt. 32p. (Orig.). 1980. 17.50 (*0-942779-05-3*) Greenberg Gallery.

***Alexander Calder: The Major Sculptures.** 168p. Date not set. write for info. (*3-89322-552-8*) Dist Art Pubs.

Alexander Calder & His Magical Mobiles. Jean Lipman & Margaret Aspinwall. LC 81-1811. (Illus.). 96p. (J). (ps up). 1981. 19.95 (*0-933920-17-2*) Hudson Hills.

Alexander Calder from the Collection of the Ruth & Leonard J. Horwich Family. Lynne Warren. Ed. by Tom Fredrickson. (Illus.). 24p. (Orig.). 1992. pap. 12.95 (*0-933856-35-0*) Mus Art Chicago.

Alexander Campbell Reader. Lester G. McAllister. 128p. (Orig.). 1988. pap. 10.99 (*0-8272-0017-X*) Chalice Pr.

Alexander Cheves Haskell: The Portrait of a Man. Louise H. Daly. (Illus.). 267p. 1989. reprint ed. 25.00 (*0-916107-13-2*) Broadfoot.

Alexander Collection: Floral Painting with Lowell Speers. John Hartman. (Illus.). 24p. 1992. pap. text ed. write for info. (*1-883576-28-8*, FLKT-001) Alexander Art.

Alexander Collection: Oil Painting Landscapes. Toby Willis-Camp. (Illus.). 24p. 1992. pap. text ed. write for info. (*1-883576-27-X*, NO. LSKT-001) Alexander Art.

Alexander Collection: Oil Painting Projects. John Hartman. (Illus.). 32p. 1992. pap. text ed. write for info. (*1-883576-29-6*, SS-800) Alexander Art.

Alexander Crummell: Pioneer in Nineteenth-Century Pan-African Thought. Gregory U. Rigsby. LC 86-15034. (Contributions in Afro-American & African Studies: No. 101). 249p. 1987. text ed. 55.00 (*0-313-25570-9*, RYC/, Greenwood Pr) Greenwood.

Alexander Crummell (Eighteen Nineteen to Eighteen Ninety-Eight) & the Creation of an African-American Church in Liberia. J. R. Oldfield. LC 90-31353. (Studies in the History of Missions: Vol. 6). 180p. 1990. lib. bdg. 79.95 (*0-88946-074-4*) E Mellen.

Alexander Deineka Paintings, Graphic Works, Sculptures, Mosaics, Excerpts from the Artist's Writings. Vladimir Sysoev. 308p. 1982. 248.00 (*0-317-57217-2*, Pub. by Collets UK) St Mut.

***Alexander Dolls Collection Price Guide, Vol. 2.** Glenn Mandeville. 128p. 1995. pap. 11.95 (*0-87588-435-0*) Hobby Hse.

Alexander Dovzhenko: The Poet As Filmmaker. Alexander Dovzhenko. Tr. by Marco Carynnyk. LC 73-2934. 384p. 1973. pap. 6.95 (*0-262-54019-3*) MIT Pr.

Alexander Dubcek. Ina Navazelskis. (World Leaders - Past & Present Ser.). (Illus.). 112p. (YA). (gr. 5 up). 1991. 17.95 (*1-55546-831-4*) Chelsea Hse.

Alexander Families of Upper South Carolina. Peggy B. Rich et al. (Illus.). 1100p. 1988. 45.00 (*0-9620691-0-8*) Rich SC.

Alexander Fleming. Richard Tames. LC 89-70492. (Lifetimes Ser.). (Illus.). 32p. (J). (gr. 5-8). 1990. lib. bdg. 12.95 (*0-531-14005-9*) Watts.

Alexander Fleming: Conquering Disease with Penicillin. Steven Otfinoski. LC 92-9910. (Makers of Modern Science Ser.). (Illus.). 128p. (J). (gr. 5 up). 1993. lib. bdg. 16.95 (*0-8160-2752-8*) Facts on File.

Alexander Fleming: The Man & the Myth. Gwyn Macfarlane. LC 83-18358. (Illus.). 352p. 1984. 32.00 (*0-674-01490-1*) HUP.

***Alexander Forbes of Brechin: The First Tractarian Bishop.** Rowan Strong. 296p. 1995. text ed. 56.00 (*0-19-826357-0*) OUP.

Alexander Foster McIlraith (1858-1945) Genealogy: Including the Foster, Charland, Gavin & Love Lines; Ontario, North Dakota, Washington, Quebec, Manitoba & Alberta. Comp. by Terence T. Quirke, Jr. LC 87-60962. (Illus.). 275p. (Orig.). 1987. pap. 20.00 (*0-944113-00-1*) Quirke Quirke Assocs.

Alexander Gifford, or, Vi'let's Boy: A Story of Negro Life. Henry A. Merrill. LC 72-1821. (Black Heritage Library Collection). 1977. reprint ed. 31.95 (*0-8369-9036-6*) Ayer.

Alexander Glazounov, His Life & Works. Donald J. Venturini. 104p. 1992. pap. 14.95 (*0-9635451-0-8*) Aero Print.

Alexander Graham Bell. Kathy Pelta. (Pioneers in Change Ser.). (Illus.). 144p. (J). (gr. 5-9). 1989. lib. bdg. 13.95 (*0-382-09529-4*) Silver Burdett Pr.

Alexander Graham Bell. Richard Tames. LC 89-29281. (Life & Times Ser.). (Illus.). 32p. (J). (gr. 5-8). 1990. lib. bdg. 12.95 (*0-531-14003-2*) Watts.

Alexander Graham Bell: Man of Sound. Elizabeth Rider Montgomery. (Discovery Biographies Ser.). (Illus.). 80p. (J). (gr. 2-6). 1993. reprint ed. lib. bdg. 12.95 (*0-7910-1423-1*) Chelsea Hse.

Alexander Graham Bell: the Man Who Contracted Space. Catherine MacKenzie. LC 77-150193. (Select Bibliographies Reprint Ser.). 1977. reprint ed. 33.95 (*0-8369-5706-7*) Ayer.

Alexander "Greek" Thomson. 48p. 1984. 24.00 (*0-904503-52-6*, Pub. by Third Eye Centre UK) St Mut.

Alexander Gumberg & Soviet-American Relations, 1917-1933. James K. Libbey. LC 77-73704. 241p. reprint ed. pap. 68.70 (*0-7837-5777-8*, 2045443) Bks Demand.

Alexander H. Stephens of Georgia: A Biography. Thomas E. Schott. LC 87-12487. (Southern Biography Ser.). (Illus.). 552p. 1988. text ed. 45.00 (*0-8071-1373-5*) La State U Pr.

Alexander Hamilton. Steve O'Brien. (World Leaders - Past & Present Ser.). (Illus.). 112p. (YA). (gr. 5 up). 1989. 17.95 (*1-55546-810-1*) Chelsea Hse.

Alexander Hamilton. Henry C. Lodge. Ed. by John T. Morse, Jr. LC 72-128971. (American Statesmen Ser.: No. 7). reprint ed. 35.00 (*0-404-50857-X*) AMS Pr.

Alexander Hamilton. Henry C. Lodge. (BCL1 - U. S. History Ser.). 317p. 1991. reprint ed. lib. bdg. 89.00 (*0-7812-6125-2*) Rprt Serv.

Alexander Hamilton: A Biography. Forrest McDonald. (Illus.). 480p. 1982. pap. 14.95 (*0-393-30048-X*) Norton.

Alexander Hamilton: A Concise Biography. Broadus Mitchell. LC 75-16899. (Illus.). 1976. 29.95 (*0-19-501979-2*) OUP.

Alexander Hamilton: Architect of American Nationalism. Gerald Kurland. Ed. by D. Steve Rahmas. LC 73-190245. (Outstanding Personalities Ser.: No. 27). 32p. (J). (gr. 7-12). 1972. lib. bdg. 4.95 (*0-87157-527-2*) SamHar Pr.

Alexander Hamilton: Selections Representing His Life, His Thought, & His Style. Alexander Hamilton. Ed. by Bower Aly. 1957. 5.00 (*0-672-61272-0*, AHS20, Bobbs) Macmillan.

Alexander Hamilton & the Idea of Republican Government. Gerald Stourzh. LC 79-18496. 115p. reprint ed. pap. 30.00 (*0-8357-3730-6*, 2036455) Bks Demand.

Alexander Hamilton & the Political Order: An Interpretation of His Political Thought & Practice. Morton J. Frisch. 130p. (C). 1991. lib. bdg. 24.00 (*0-8191-8049-1*) U Pr of Amer.

Alexander Hamilton (1762-1824) A Chapter in the Early History of Sanskrit Philology. Rosane Rocher. (American Oriental Ser.: Vol. 51). 1968. pap. 8.00 (*0-940490-51-X*) Am Orient Soc.

Alexander Hamilton's Financial Policies. Mildred B. Otenasek. Ed. by Stuart Bruchey. LC 76-39837. (Nineteen Seventy-Seven Dissertations Ser.). 1977. lib. bdg. 20.95 (*0-405-09917-7*) Ayer.

Alexander Holley & the Makers of Steel. Jeanne McHugh. LC 79-27414. (Johns Hopkins Studies in the History of Technology; New Ser.: No. 4). 416p. reprint ed. pap. 118.60 (*0-7837-2199-4*, 2042537) Bks Demand.

Alexander I. Janet M. Hartley. LC 93-11656. (Profiles in Power Ser.). 256p. (C). 1994. pap. text ed. 17.95 (*0-685-72576-6*, 73434) Longman.

Alexander I: A Post-Communist Reappraisal. Ludmila Evreinov. (Illus.). 656p. 1995. 35.00 (*0-7145-4276-8*) Riverrun NY.

Alexander Ivanov. M. Neklyudova. (Illus.). (C). 1988. 50.00 (*0-569-51981-0*, Pub. by Collets UK) Pro-Am Music.

Alexander Jackson Davis, American Architect, 1803-1892. Ed. by Amelia Peck. LC 92-8479. (Illus.). 1992. 45.00 (*0-8478-1484-X*); pap. 29.95 (*0-8478-1485-8*) Rizzoli Intl.

Alexander Jackson Davis, Romantic Architect, 1803-1892. John Donoghue. 1981. 32.95 (*0-405-14078-9*) Ayer.

Alexander James Dallas, Lawyer-Politician-Financier. Raymond Walters. LC 75-86582. (American Scene Ser.). 1969. reprint ed. lib. bdg. 32.50 (*0-306-71814-6*) Da Capo.

Alexander Kerensky: The First Love of the Revolution. Richard Abraham. 448p. 1987. text ed. 47.50 (*0-231-06108-0*) Col U Pr.

Alexander Kerensky: The First Love of the Revolution. Richard Abraham. 1990. pap. text ed. 17.50 (*0-231-06109-9*) Col U Pr.

Alexander Kluge. Jan Dawson & Alexander Kluge. (Illus.). (Orig.). 1977. pap. 6.95 (*0-918432-03-0*) Baseline Bks.

Alexander Letters, 1787-1900. Marion A. Boggs. (American Biography Ser.). 387p. 1991. reprint ed. lib. bdg. 79.00 (*0-7812-8028-1*) Rprt Serv.

***Alexander Lipson in Memoriam.** Ed. by Charles E. Gribble et al. (Illus.). 313p. 1994. 19.95 (*0-89357-246-2*) Slavica.

Alexander MacDonald: Leader of the Miners. G. M. Wilson. 244p. 1982. text ed. 31.00 (*0-08-028455-8*, Pergamon Pr) Elsevier.

Alexander Mackenzie. Ed. by Fred Rendell. (C). 1989. 30.00 (*1-85098-075-6*, Pub. by Jordanhill College UK) St Mut.

Alexander Mackenzie & the Explorers of Canada. Georgia Xydes. (World Explorers Ser.). (Illus.). 112p. (YA). (gr. 5 up). 1992. lib. bdg. 18.95 (*0-7910-1314-6*) Chelsea Hse.

Alexander Meiklejohn: Teacher of Freedom. Cynthia S. Brown. Ed. by Ann F. Ginger. LC 81-81355. (Studies in Law & Social Change: No. 2). (Illus.). 304p. 1981. 13.95 (*0-913876-16-X*, 176); pap. 7.95 (*0-913876-17-8*, 177) Meiklejohn Civ Lib.

Alexander Montgomerie: A Selection from His Songs & Poems. Helena M. Shire. 1989. 35.00 (*0-85411-014-3*, Pub. by Saltire Soc) St Mut.

***Alexander Neil & the Last Shenandoah Valley Campaign: Letters of an Army Surgeon to This Family, 1864.** Ed. by Richard R. Duncan. (Illus.). 156p. (C). 1995. 19.95 (*0-942597-95-8*) White Mane Pub.

Alexander of Macedon, 356-323 B.C. A Historical Biography. Peter Green. LC 91-7292. 650p. 1991. 40.00 (*0-520-07165-4*) U CA Pr.

Alexander of Macedon, 356-323 B.C. A Historical Biography. Peter Green. 1992. pap. 15.00 (*0-520-07166-2*) U CA Pr.

Alexander Phimister Proctor, Sculptor in Buckskin: An Autobiography. Alexander P. Proctor. Ed. by Hester E. Proctor. LC 77-108803. (Illus.). 281p. reprint ed. 80.10 (*0-8357-9716-3*, 2016251) Bks Demand.

Alexander Plays. Adrienne Kennedy. (Emergent Literatures Ser.). 128p. 1992. 15.95 (*0-8166-2077-6*) U of Minn Pr.

Alexander Pope. Alexander Pope. Ed. by Pat Rogers. (Oxford Poetry Library). 256p. 1994. pap. 7.95 (*0-19-282270-5*) OUP.

Alexander Pope. Bonamy Dobree. LC 72-94604. 125p. 1969. reprint ed. text ed. 45.00 (*0-8371-2459-X*, DOAP, Greenwood Pr) Greenwood.

Alexander Pope. Edith Sitwell. LC 72-7190. (Select Bibliographies Reprint Ser.). 1977. reprint ed. 26.95 (*0-8369-6953-7*) Ayer.

Alexander Pope. Leslie Stephen. (BCL1-PR English Literature Ser.). 216p. 1992. reprint ed. lib. bdg. 79.00 (*0-7812-7394-3*) Rprt Serv.

Alexander Pope: A Bibliography, 2 pts. in 1 vol. Reginald H. Griffith. LC 77-161771. reprint ed. 45.00 (*0-404-09020-6*) AMS Pr.

Alexander Pope: A Life. Maynard Mack. LC 85-2941. (Illus.). 1986. 25.95 (*0-393-02208-0*) Norton.

Alexander Pope: A Life. Maynard Mack. LC 85-2941. (Illus.). 1988. pap. 14.95 (*0-393-30529-5*) Norton.

Alexander Pope: A Life. Maynard Mack. LC 85-40466. (Illus.). 976p. 1985. 40.00 (*0-300-03391-5*) Yale U Pr.

Alexander Pope: A Life. Maynard Mack. LC 85-40466. (Illus.). 976p. 1988. pap. 22.00 (*0-300-04303-1*) Yale U Pr.

Alexander Pope: A Literary Life. Felicity Rosslyn. LC 89-24045. 220p. 1990. text ed. 39.95 (*0-312-04021-0*) St Martin.

Alexander Pope: An Annotated Bibliography, 1945-1967. Cecilia L. Lopez. LC 78-99213. 164p. reprint ed. pap. 46.80 (*0-8357-5302-6*, 2007585) Bks Demand.

Alexander Pope: Essays for the Tercentenary. Colin Nicholson. (Illus.). 280p. 1988. text ed. 30.00 (*0-08-036394-6*, Pub. by Aberdeen U Pr) Macmillan.

Alexander Pope: Selected Poetry & Prose. Ed. by Robin Sowerby. (English Texts Ser.). 160p. 1988. pap. 10.95 (*0-415-00665-1*) Routledge.

Alexander Pope: The Genius of Sense. David B. Morris. LC 83-18577. 384p. reprint ed. pap. 109.50 (*0-7837-4474-9*, 2044182) Bks Demand.

Alexander Pope: The Poet in Poems. Dustin H. Griffin. LC 78-51167. 1978. 47.50x (*0-691-06371-0*) Princeton U Pr.

Alexander Pope: The Poet in the Poems. Dustin H. Griffen. LC 78-51167. 304p. reprint ed. pap. 86.70 (*0-7837-1932-9*, 2042147) Bks Demand.

Alexander Pope: Tradition & Identity. John P. Russo. LC 70-188354. 255p. 1972. 32.00 (*0-674-01520-7*) HUP.

Alexander Pope & His Eighteenth-Century Women Readers. Claudia N. Thomas. LC 92-42647. 344p. (C). 1994. 39.95 (*0-8093-1886-5*) S Ill U Pr.

Alexander Pope & the Traditions of Formal Verse Satire. Howard D. Weinbrot. LC 81-47957. 375p. 1982. 57.50x (*0-691-06510-1*) Princeton U Pr.

An Asterisk (*) at the beginning of an entry indicates that the title is appearing in BIP for the first time.

An Asterisk (*) at the beginning of an entry indicates that the title is appearing in BIP for the first time.

179

Alexandrian, African, & Spanish Wars. Julius Caesar. Tr. by A. G. Way. (Loeb Classical Library: No. 402). 440p. 1955. text ed. 15.50 (*0-674-99443-4*) HUP.

Alexandrian Citizenship During the Roman Principate. Diana Delia. (American Philological Association, American Classical Studies). 222p. (C). 1991. 29.95 (*1-55540-525-8*, 400423); pap. 19.95 (*1-55540-526-6*, 400423) Scholars Pr GA.

Alexandrian Notebook. Desmond O'Grady. 32p. 1990. pap. 7.95 (*1-85186-064-9*) Dufour.

Alexandrian Poetry under the First Three Ptolemies, 324-222 BC. A. Couat. Tr. by James Loeb. xx, 638p. (C). 1993. reprint ed. pap. text ed. 30.00 (*0-89005-500-9*) Ares.

Alexandrina: The Agony & the Glory. Francis Johnston. (Illus.). 120p. 1982. pap. 4.00 (*0-89555-179-9*) TAN Bks Pubs.

Alexandrine Scripts: A Stretch of Sand & Other Stories. Daniel Ray. 168p. 1989. 19.95 (*0-86327-177-4*, Pub. by Wolfhound Pr IE) Dufour.

Alexandros Expedition. Patricia Sitkin. 224p. (Orig.). 1983. pap. 5.95 (*0-932870-35-X*) Alyson Pubns.

Alexandru D. Xenopol & the Development of Romanian Historiography. Paul A. Hiemstra. Ed. by William H. McNeill & Charles Jelavich. (Modern European History Ser.). 224p. 1987. lib. bdg. 15.00 (*0-8240-8026-2*) Garland.

Alexa's Vineyard. Rosemary Enright. 480p. 1991. mass mkt. 5.95 (*0-8041-0631-2*) Ivy Books.

Alexei Savrasov. F. Malseva. 407p. 1977. 60.00 (*0-317-14216-X*, Pub. by Collets UK) St Mut.

Alexei the Gangster. Yuri Herman, pseud. Tr. by Stephen Garry. LC 74-10084. (Soviet Literature in English Translation Ser.). 288p. 1974. reprint ed. 19.25 (*0-88355-171-3*) Hyperion Conn.

Alexei Venetsianov. D. Sarab'ianov. (Illus.). (C). 1988. text ed. 50.00 (*0-685-40258-4*, Pub. by Collets) St Mut.

*__Alexei von Jawlensky.__ Karel Schampers. (Illus.). 292p. 1995. pap. 40.00 (*90-6918-135-5*) U of Wash Pr.

Alexej Jawlensky, Vol. 2. Maria Jawlensky et al. (Illus.). 550p. 1992. 395.00 (*0-85667-406-0*, Pub. by P Wilson Pubs) Sothebys Pubns.

Alexej Jawlensky, 1890-1914, Vol. 1: Catalogue Raisonne of the Oil Paintings. Lucia Maria et al. (Illus.). 560p. 1991. 395.00 (*0-85667-398-6*) Sothebys Pubns.

Alexej von Jawlensky: Catalogue Raisonne of the Oil Paintings, Vol. III: 1934-1937. Maria Jawlensky et al. (Illus.). 560p. 1993. 395.00 (*0-85667-420-6*, Pub. by P Wilson Pubs) Sothebys Pubns.

Alexej Von Jawlensky's Life & Graphic Work. Detlev Rosenbach. (Illus.). 176p. (GER.). 1985. 120.00 (*0-915346-96-6*) A Wofsy Fine Arts.

Alexiad of Anna Comnena. Tr. by E. R. Sewter. (Classics Ser.). 1979. pap. 10.95 (*0-14-044215-4*, Penguin Classics) Viking Penguin.

Alexiad of the Princess Anna Comnena. Anna Comnena. Tr. by Elizabeth A. Dawes. LC 76-29821. reprint ed. 48.00 (*0-404-15414-X*) AMS Pr.

Alexis. Marguerite Yourcenar. Tr. by Walter Kaiser. LC 84-6009. 105p. 1984. 12.95 (*0-374-10263-5*) FS&G.

Alexis. Marguerite Yourcenar. Tr. by Walter Kaiser. LC 84-6009. 105p. 1985. pap. 6.95 (*0-374-51906-4*, Noonday) FS&G.

Alexis. large type ed. Mary Delorme. (General Fiction Ser.). 304p. 1992. 21.95 (*0-7089-2659-2*) Ulverscroft.

Alexis Bespaloff New Signet Book of Wine. rev. ed. Alexis Bespaloff. 368p. 1971. pap. 4.50 (*0-451-14401-5*, Sig) NAL-Dutton.

Alexis Bespaloff's Complete Guide to Wine. rev. ed. Alexis Bespaloff. 400p. 1994. pap. 5.99 (*0-451-18169-7*, Sig) NAL-Dutton.

Alexis Carrel: Visionary Surgeon. W. Sterling Edwards & Peter D. Edwards. (Illus.). 160p. 1974. 13.95x (*0-398-03130-4*) C C Thomas.

Alexis de Tocqueville. Matthew Mancini. (Twayne's World Authors Ser.). 184p. 1993. text ed. 22.95 (*0-8057-4305-7*, Twayne) Macmillan.

Alexis de Tocqueville. J. P. Mayer. LC 78-67399. (European Political Thought Ser.). (GER.). 1980. reprint ed. lib. bdg. 17.95 (*0-405-11716-7*) Ayer.

Alexis de Tocqueville: Threats to Freedom in Democracy. Michael Hereth. Tr. by George F. Bogardus. LC 85-20594. xi, 196p. 1986. 31.95 (*0-8223-0541-0*) Duke.

Alexis de Tocqueville & the New Science of Politics: An Interpretation of Democracy in America. John C. Koritansky. LC 84-70753. 170p. 1986. lib. bdg. 17.50 (*0-89089-285-7*) Carolina Acad Pr.

Alexis de Tocqueville Livre du Centenaire (1859-1959) Mantoux. 8.95 (*0-8288-6094-7*, F74630) Fr & Eur.

Alexis de Tocqueville on Democracy, Revolution, & Society. Alexis De Tocqueville. Ed. by John Stone et al. LC 79-21204. (Heritage of Sociology Ser.). 392p. (C). 1982. pap. text ed. 15.95 (*0-226-80527-1*) U Ch Pr.

Alexis de Tocqueville's Journey to Ireland. Ed. by Emmet Larkin. LC 89-23851. 157p. 1990. 26.95 (*0-8132-0718-5*); pap. 14.95 (*0-8132-0719-3*) Cath U Pr.

Alexis in the Saint Albans Psalter: A Look into the Heart of the Matter. Rachel Bullington. LC 91-22717. (Studies in Medieval Literature: Vol. 4). 296p. 1991. 40.00 (*0-8240-4038-4*, H1229) Garland.

Alexis Jean Fournier: The Last American Barbizon. Rena N. Coen. LC 85-15281. (Illus.). 41p. (Orig.). 1985. pap. 8.95 (*0-87351-190-5*) Minn Hist.

Alexis Lichine's Guide to the Wines & Vineyards of France. 3rd ed. Alexis Lichine. 1986. 25.00 (*0-394-55335-7*) Knopf.

Alexis Lichine's Guide to the Wines & Vineyards of France. 4th ed. Alexis Lichine. 1989. pap. 18.95 (*0-679-72285-8*) Knopf.

Alexis Lichine's New Encyclopedia of Wines & Spirits. 5th ed. LC 87-2590. 752p. 1987. 45.00 (*0-394-56262-3*) Knopf.

Alexis Ou le Traite du Vain Combat: Coup de Grace. M. Yourcenar. (FRE.). 1978. pap. 10.95 (*0-8288-3803-8*, F132580) Fr & Eur.

Alexis ou le Traite du Vain Combat; Le Coup de Grace. Marguerite Yourcenar. (Folio Ser.: No. 1041). (FRE.). pap. 8.95 (*2-07-037041-0*) Schoenhof.

Alexis Ou le Traite Du Vain Combat, le Coup De Grace. Marguerite Yourcenar. (FRE.). 1978. pap. 10.95 (*0-7859-0462-X*, 2070370410) Fr & Eur.

*__Alexis Rockman: Second Nature.__ (Illus.). 96p. Date not set. pap. 19.95 (*0-945558-23-6*) ISU Univ Galls.

Alexis Smith: Whitney Museum of American Art. Richard Armstrong. (Illus.). 288p. 1991. 50.00 (*0-8478-1446-7*) Rizzoli Intl.

Alex's Journey: The Story of a Child with a Brain Tumor. 1994. write for info. (*0-944093-29-9*) Am Brain Tumor.

Alex's Restaurant: Cartoons. Peter Sinclair. LC 93-25853. 144p. 1993. pap. 8.95 (*0-89594-579-7*) Crossing Pr.

Alf. Gallagher & Severin. 64p. 1990. 4.95 (*0-87135-655-4*) Marvel Entmnt.

Alf Francis: Racing Mechanic, 1948-58. Peter Lewis. 1991. 49.95 (*0-85429-937-8*, Pub. by G T Foulis Ltd) Haynes Pubns.

Alf 'N Bet. Illus. by Pam Adams. LC 92-14641. (J). 1992. 5.95 (*0-85953-167-8*) Childs Play.

Alf 'n Bet's Handwriting Book. Pam Adams. (J). (ps-3). 1993. pap. 5.95 (*0-85953-168-6*) Childs Play.

Alfa Romeo: Ninety Years of Success on Road & Track. David Owen. (Illus.). 160p. 1993. 39.95 (*1-85260-446-8*, Pub. by J H Haynes & Co UK) Motorbooks Intl.

Alfa Romeo: The Complete Story. David Styles. (Crowood Autoclassics Ser.). (Illus.). 192p. 1992. 35.95 (*1-85223-636-1*, Pub. by Crowood UK) Motorbooks Intl.

Alfa Romeo Duetto. Text by Giancenzo Madaro. (Illus.). 96p. 1988. 24.95 (*88-7911-063-2*, Pub. by Giorgio Nada Editore IT) Howell Pr VA.

Alfa Romeo Giulia: History & Restoration. Pat Braden & Weber. (Illus.). 192p. 1991. pap. text ed. 24.95 (*0-87938-529-4*) Motorbooks Intl.

Alfa Romeo Giulia Coupe GT & GTA. John Tipler. (Illus.). 160p. 1992. 39.95 (*1-874105-00-6*, Pub. by Veloce Pub UK) Motorbooks Intl.

Alfa Romeo Giulia GT. Text by Brizio Pignacca. (Cars That Made History Ser.). (Illus.). 84p. 24.95 (*88-7911-055-1*, Pub. by Giorgio Nada Editore IT) Howell Pr VA.

Alfa Romeo Legend Revived. David Styles. 1990. 84.95 (*0-901564-75-3*) Auto Quarterly.

Alfa Romeo Owner's Bible. Braden. 1993. pap. 29.95 (*0-8376-0707-8*) Bentley.

*__Alfa-Romeo Spider.__ David Sparrow & Adrienne Kessel. (Osprey Color Library). (Illus.). 128p. 1995. pap. 15.95 (*1-85532-523-3*, Pub. by Osprey UK) Motorbooks Intl.

Alfa Romeo Spider, Nineteen Fifty-Five - Nineteen Eighty-Six. Walter Zeichner. LC 89-84167. (Automotive Ser.). (Illus.). 96p. 1989. 19.95 (*0-88740-195-3*) Schiffer.

Alfa Romeo Spiders & Coupes. Richard Bremmer. (Illus.). 160p. 1991. 39.95 (*0-947981-59-4*, Pub. by Motor Racing UK) Motorbooks Intl.

Alfa Romeo Tradition. Griffith Borgeson. 208p. 1990. 69.95 (*0-685-41180-X*, 3-AQ-0076) Auto Quarterly.

Alfa Romeo Veloce: The Racing Giuliettas, 1956-63. Donald Hughes & Witting. (Illus.). 250p. 1989. 49.95 (*0-85429-731-6*, Pub. by J H Haynes & Co UK) Motorbooks Intl.

Alfa Romeo 6C 1500, 1750, 1900. Angela Cherrett. (Veloce Ser.). (Illus.). 229p. 1989. 49.95 (*0-85429-720-0*, Pub. by J H Haynes & Co UK) Motorbooks Intl.

Alfa y el Bebe Sucio: Alpha & the Dirty Baby. Brock Cole. Tr. by T. Gottlieb. (Mirasol Ser.). (Illus.). 32p. (SPA.). (J). (ps-3). 1991. 14.95 (*0-374-30242-1*) FS&G.

Alfabetische Catalogus van de Boeken en Brochures van Het Internationaal Instituut voor Sociale Geschiedenis (Alphabetical Catalog of the Books & Pamphlets of the International Institute of Social History) Amsterdam, 1st Supplement, 2 vols, Set. Instituut voor Sociale Geschiedenis Staff. 1974. lib. bdg. 275.00 (*0-8161-1033-6*, Hall Library) G K Hall.

Alfabetische Catalogus Van De Boeken En Brochures Van Het International: Alphabetical Catolog of the Books & Pamphlets of the International Institute of Social History, 12 vols, Set. Institut Voor Sociale Geschiedenis Staff. 1970. lib. bdg. 1,340.00 (*0-8161-0807-2*, Hall Library) G K Hall.

Alfabeto: A Child's Introduction to the Letters & Sounds of Spanish. Illus. by Gwen Connelly. 32p. (J). (gr. 1-6). 1991. 7.95 (*0-8442-7564-6*, Passport Bks) NTC Pub Grp.

Alfabeto: Mentes Activas. Tr. by University of Mexico City Staff. (Mentes Activas-Spanish Ser.). (Illus.). 24p. (SPA.). (J). (ps-8). 1992. lib. bdg. 11.95 (*1-56674-036-3*) Forest Hse.

Alfabeto: Mayusculas: Alphabet: Uppercase. Barbara Gregorich. Ed. by Joan Hoffman. Tr. by Shepherd-Bartram. (Illus.). 32p. (Orig.). (SPA.). (J). (ps). 1987. student ed 1.99 (*0-938256-75-0*) Sch Zone Pub Co.

Alfabeto: Minusculas: Alphabet: Lowercase. Barbara Gregorich. Ed. by Joan Hoffman. Tr. by Shepherd-Bartram. (Illus.). 32p. (Orig.). (SPA.). (J). (ps). 1987. student ed 1.99 (*0-938256-76-9*) Sch Zone Pub Co.

Alfalfa. A. I. Ivanov. Ed. by D. D. Brezhnev. Tr. by A. K. Dhote. (Russian Translation Ser.: No. 63). (Illus.). 327p. 1988. text ed. 85.00 (*90-6191-910-X*, Pub. by A A Balkema NE) Ashgate Pub Co.

Alfalfa. A. I. Ivanov & D. D. Brezhnev. (C). 1988. 34.00 (*81-7087-018-6*, Pub. by Oxford IBH II) S Asia.

Alfalfa & Alfalfa Improvement. Ed. by A. A. Hanson et al. (Illus.). 1110p. 1988. 66.00 (*0-89118-016-8*) Am Soc Agron.

Alfalfa Management Guide. Dan Undersander et al. LC 92-17964. 1992. pap. 4.50 (*0-89118-111-3*) Am Soc Agron.

Alfalfabet. Phillips Winslow. (Cityscapes Ser.). 26p. (J). (gr. k). 1992. pap. text ed. 23.00 (*1-56843-015-9*); pap. text ed. 4.50 (*1-56843-065-5*) BGR Pub.

Alfarabi, Avicenna, & Averroes on Intellect: Their Cosmologies, Theories of Active Intellect & Theories of the Human Intellect. Herbert A. Davidson. 384p. 1992. 49.95 (*0-19-507423-8*) OUP.

Alfarabi's Abhandlung der Musterstaat & Der Musterstaat von Alfarabi. Al Farabi. xv, 85p. 1985. reprint ed. write for info. (*3-487-07683-7*, Pub. by Georg Olms GW) Lubrecht & Cramer.

Alfarabi's Theory of Communication. Fuad Haddad. 220p. (Orig.). 1989. pap. text ed. 19.95 (*0-8156-6082-0*) Syracuse U Pr.

*__Alferd Packer's High Protein Cookbook.__ Wendy Spurr & Kimberly Spurr. 48p. 1995. spiral bd., pap. 8.95 (*1-882418-19-0*) Centenn Pubns.

Alferd Packer's Wilderness Cookbook. James E. Banks. LC 70-15764. (Wild & Woolly West Ser., No. 9). (Illus.). (Orig.). 1969. pap. 3.00 (*0-910584-09-5*) Filter.

Alfi & the Dark. Sally Miles. LC 88-1043. (Illus.). 32p. (J). (ps-1). 1988. 13.95 (*0-87701-527-9*) Chronicle Bks.

Alfie Collection: Alfie's Feet; An Evening at Alfie's; Alfie Gives a Hand; Alfie Gets in First, 4 bks., Set. Shirley Hughes. (Illus.). (J). (ps up). 1993. boxed 16.95 (*0-688-12750-9*, Tupelo Bks) Morrow.

Alfie Gets in First. Shirley Hughes. LC 81-8427. (Illus.). 32p. (J). (ps-1). 1982. 16.00 (*0-688-00848-8*); lib. bdg. 15.93 (*0-688-00849-6*) Lothrop.

Alfie Gets in First. Shirley Hughes. LC 81-8427. (Illus.). 32p. (J). (ps up). 1987. pap. 4.95 (*0-688-07036-1*, Mulberry) Morrow.

Alfie Gives a Hand. Shirley Hughes. LC 83-14883. (Illus.). 32p. (J). (ps-1). 1984. 15.00 (*0-688-02386-X*); lib. bdg. 14.93 (*0-688-02387-8*) Lothrop.

Alfie Gives a Hand. Shirley Hughes. LC 83-14883. (Illus.). (J). (ps up). 1986. 4.95 (*0-688-06521-X*, Mulberry) Morrow.

Alfieri's Ode to America's Independence. Adolph Caso. LC 76-6244. 1976. pap. 11.95 (*0-8283-1667-8*) Branden Pub Co.

Alfie's Feet. Shirley Hughes. LC 82-13012. (Illus.). 32p. (J). (ps-1). 1983. 14.95 (*0-688-01658-8*); lib. bdg. 14.88 (*0-688-01660-X*) Lothrop.

Alfie's Feet. Shirley Hughes. LC 82-13012. (Illus.). 32p. (J). (ps up). 1988. pap. 3.95 (*0-688-07812-5*, Mulberry) Morrow.

Alfie's Home. Richard A. Cohen. LC 93-78368. (Illus.). 30p. (J). (gr. 3-12). 1993. 14.95 (*0-9637058-0-6*) Intl Healing.

Alfon Ivri, a Hebrew Primer. Schlomo Haramati. (Illus.). 1979. pap. text ed. 8.95x (*0-87441-321-4*) Behrman.

Alfons Paquet, Prophecies. Tr. by H. M. Waidson. LC 82-84465. (Studies in German Literature, Linguistics & Culture: Vol. 10). (Illus.). xx, 140p. 1983. 35.00 (*0-938100-08-4*) Camden Hse.

Alfons Spies: Militat Omnis Amons see Bruno Lier: Ad Topica Carminum Amatorium Symbolae

Alfonse Borysewicz: Exhibition Catalogue of Artwork. (Illus.). 20p. (Orig.). 1993. 10.00 (*0-9626731-2-9*) Yoshii Gallery.

*__Alfonse, Where Are You?__ Linda Wikler. LC 95-3670. (J). 1996. write for info. (*0-517-70045-X*); lib. bdg. write for info. (*0-517-70046-8*) Crown Pub Group.

Alfonsina Storni: Anthology of Poems. Tr. by Dorothy S. Loos. (Illus.). 200p. (Orig.). (SPA.). 1986. pap. 5.95 (*0-915597-31-4*) Amana Bks.

Alfonsina Storni: From Poetess to Poet. Rachel Phillips. (Serie A: Monografias, LII). 131p. (Orig.). (C). 1975. pap. 36.00 (*0-7293-0001-3*, Pub. by Tamesis Bks Ltd UK) Boydell & Brewer.

Alfonso Dalla Viola: Il Secondo Libro Di Madrigali (4) (Ferrara, 1540) Ed. by Jessie A. Owens. LC 90-754166. (Sixteenth Century Madrigal Ser.: Vol. 6). 240p. 1991. 86.00 (*0-8240-5506-3*) Garland.

Alfonso Dalla Viola: Primo Libro Di Madrigali (4) (Ferrara, 1539) Ed. by Jessie A. Owens. LC 90-750439. (Sixteenth Century Madrigal Ser.: Vol. 5). 275p. 1990. 86.00 (*0-8240-5505-5*) Garland.

Alfonso Reyes y la Literatural Espanola. Jorge L. Morales. LC 79-19455. (Mante y Palabra Ser.). 193p. (SPA.). (C). 1980. 5.00 (*0-8477-0558-7*); pap. 4.00 (*0-8477-0559-5*) U of PR Pr.

Alfonso Sastre. Farris Anderson. LC 78-125251. (Twayne's World Authors Ser.). 1971. lib. bdg. 17.95 (*0-8057-2802-3*) Irvington.

Alfonso X & the Jews: An Edition of & Commentary on Siete Partidas 7.24 "De los Judios" Dwayne E. Carpenter. LC 86-11425. (Publications in Modern Philology: No. 115). 1987. pap. 22.00 (*0-520-09951-6*) U CA Pr.

*__Alfonso X & the Jews: An Edition of & Commentary on Siete Partidas 7.24 "De los Judios"__ fac. ed. Dwayne E. Carpenter. LC 86-11425. (University of California Publications in Entomology: No. 115). 173p. 1986. reprint ed. pap. 49.40 (*0-7837-8130-X*, 2047937) Bks Demand.

Alfonso X, el Sabio. John E. Keller. LC 66-29183. (Twayne's World Authors Ser.). 1967. lib. bdg. 17.95 (*0-8057-2032-4*) Irvington.

*__Alfonso X, el Sabio, Estoria De Alexandre el Grand, General Estoria (Quarta Parte) - The Life of Alexander the Great As Narrated by King Alfonso X the Wise, of Castile, in the General Estoria: Manuscript U. Vatican Urb. Lat. 539.__ Ed. by Joseph A. Levi. LC 95-14847. (Hispanic Literature Ser.: Vol. 26). (Illus.). 224p. 1996. text ed. 89.95 (*0-7734-8900-2*) E Mellen.

Alfonso X of Castile, Patron of Literature & Learning. Evelyn S. Procter. LC 80-10508. (Norman Macoll Lectures Ser.: 1949). vi, 149p. 1980. reprint ed. text ed. 35.00 (*0-313-22347-5*, PRAL, Greenwood Pr) Greenwood.

Alfonso XIII. Vicente R. Pilapil. LC 78-77035. (Twayne's Rulers & Statesmen of the World Ser.). 242p. (C). 1969. lib. bdg. 17.95 (*0-8290-1749-6*) Irvington.

Alfonso's Dream. Susan A. Couture. LC 93-5784. (J). 1996. text ed. 14.95 (*0-02-724827-5*, Mac Bks Young Read) S&S Childrens.

*__Alford Brothers: We All Must Dye Sooner Or Later.__ Ed. by Richard S. Skidmore. (Illus.). 1995. pap. write for info. (*0-9623292-6-6*) Nugget IN.

Alfred. Bronwen Scarffe. LC 92-21442. (Voyages Ser.). (Illus.). (J). 1993. 3.75 (*0-383-03612-7*) SRA Schl Grp.

Alfred Adler. Joseph Rattner. Tr. by Harry Zohn. LC 82-40251. (Literature & Life Ser.). 226p. (C). 1983. 19.95 (*0-8044-5988-6*, F Ungar Bks) Continuum.

Alfred Adler: As We Remember Him. 2nd ed. Ed. by Genevieve Painter et al. (Illus.). 122p. 1988. pap. write for info. (*0-926164-00-7*) N Am Soc Adlerian.

Alfred Adler Revisited. Heinz L. Ansbacher. 400p. 1988. write for info. (*0-318-55345-7*, C2650, Praeger Pubs) Greenwood.

Alfred Adler's Basic Concepts & Implications. Robert W. Lundin. LC 88-71464. 166p. (Orig.). 1989. pap. text ed. 17.95 (*0-915202-83-2*) Accel Devel.

Alfred Andersch (1914-1980) & the Reception of French Thought in the Federal Republic of Germany. Margaret Littler. LC 91-26228. (Studies in German Language & Literature: Vol. 8). 404p. 1991. lib. bdg. 109.95 (*0-7734-9679-3*) E Mellen.

Alfred Bester. Carolyn Wendell. Ed. by Roger C. Schlobin. LC 80-19655. (Starmont Reader's Guide Ser.: Vol. 6). 72p. 1982. lib. bdg. 21.00x (*0-916732-17-7*) Borgo Pr.

Alfred de Musset. Margaret A. Rees. LC 73-120495. (Twayne's World Authors Ser.). 1971. lib. bdg. 17.95 (*0-8057-2646-2*) Irvington.

Alfred de Vigny's Chatterton: A 3-Act Play. Tr. by Philip A. Fulvi. 90p. 1990. pap. 12.00 (*0-918680-45-X*) Bagehot Council.

Alfred Deakin: A Biography, 2 Vols. John A. LaNauze. 1965. 45.00 (*0-522-83884-7*) Intl Spec Bk.

Alfred Doeblin: Erzaehlkunst im Umbruch. Erwin Kobel. x, 423p. (GER.). 1985. 100.80 (*3-11-010339-7*) De Gruyter.

Alfred E. Smith: A Critical Study. Henry F. Pringle. LC 75-101271. reprint ed. 20.00 (*0-404-00627-2*) AMS Pr.

Alfred E. Smith: A Critical Study. Henry F. Pringle. (History - United States Ser.). 402p. 1992. reprint ed. lib. bdg. 99.00 (*0-7812-6217-8*) Rprt Serv.

Alfred Einstein on Music: Selected Music Criticisms. Catherine Dower. LC 90-13997. (Contributions to the Study of Music & Dance Ser.: No. 21). 328p. 1991. text ed. 55.00 (*0-313-27363-4*, DEK/, Greenwood Pr) Greenwood.

Alfred G. Graebner Memorial High School Handbook of Rules & Regulations. Ellen Conford. (J). (gr. 7-12). 1976. 14.95 (*0-316-15293-5*) Little.

Alfred Gilbert. Richard Dorment. LC 84-52241. (Illus.). 320p. 1986. pap. 30.00 (*0-300-03698-1*) Yale U Pr.

Alfred Goes to the Hospital. Lawrence Balter. (Stepping Stone Stories Ser.). (Illus.). 40p. (J). (gr. 3-7). 1990. 5.95 (*0-8120-6150-0*) Barron.

Alfred Gong: Early Poems: A Selection from the Years 1941-45. Ed. by Jerry Glenn et al. LC 87-71128. (Studies in German Literature, Linguistics & Culture: Vol. 38). (Illus.). 151p. 1987. 31.00 (*0-938100-59-9*) Camden Hse.

Alfred Henry Lewis. Abe C. Ravitz. LC 78-52560. (Western Writers Ser.: No. 32). 46p. 1978. pap. 3.95 (*0-88430-056-0*) Boise St U W Writ Ser.

Alfred Hitchcock. Peter Noble. (Film Ser.). 1979. lib. bdg. 250.00 (*0-8490-2862-0*) Gordon Pr.

Alfred Hitchcock. Gene D. Phillips. LC 83-22786. (Filmmakers Ser.). 233p. 1984. text ed. 22.95 (*0-8057-9293-7*, Twayne) Macmillan.

Alfred Hitchcock. Gene D. Phillips. LC 83-22786. (Filmmakers Ser.). 233p. 1984. pap. 14.95 (*0-8057-9301-1*, Twayne) Macmillan.

Alfred Hitchcock: A Guide to References & Resources. Jane E. Sloan. LC 92-15103. (Reference Publication in Film Ser.). 400p. 1993. text ed. 65.00 (*0-8161-9057-7*, Hall Reference) Macmillan.

Alfred Hitchcock: Best of Mystery. Alfred Hitchcock. 1990. 9.98 (*0-88365-644-2*) Galahad Bks.

Alfred Hitchcock: Filmography & Biography. Jane E. Sloan. LC 92-15103. 1995. 18.00 (*0-520-08904-9*) U CA Pr.

Alfred Hitchcock: Portraits of Murder. Alfred Hitchcocks Mystery Magazine Staff. 1993. pap. 12.95 (*0-88486-085-X*) Arrowood Pr.

Alfred Hitchcock: Portraits of Murder. Alfred Hitchcock. 1989. 9.98 (*0-88365-727-9*) Galahad Bks.

*__Alfred Hitchcock: The Legacy of Victorianism.__ Paula M. Cohen. LC 95-2325. (Illus.). 224p. (Orig.). 1995. text ed. 36.95 (*0-8131-1930-8*); pap. 14.95 (*0-8131-0850-0*) U Pr of Ky.

Alfred Hitchcock & the British Cinema. Tom Ryall. LC 86-11361. (Illus.). 208p. 1986. 24.95 (*0-252-01374-3*) U of Ill Pr.

Alfred Hitchcock & the Making of Psycho. Stephen Rebello. LC 89-30988. 1990. 24.95 (*0-942637-14-3*, Dembner NY) Barricade Bks.

Alfred Hitchcock & the Making of Psycho. Stephen Rebello. LC 90-55514. (Illus.). 224p. 1991. reprint ed. pap. 12.00 (*0-06-097366-8*, PL) HarpC.

An Asterisk (*) at the beginning of an entry indicates that the title is appearing in BIP for the first time.

Alfred Hitchcock & the Three Investigators, 4 bks. Incl. Mystery of the Fiery Eye. Robert Arthur. 1978. (0-318-55411-9); Mystery of the Moaning Cave. William Arden. 1978. (0-318-55412-7); Mystery of the Silver Spider. Robert Arthur. 1978. (0-318-55413-5); Secret of Terror Castle. Robert Arthur. 1978. (0-318-55414-3); (J). (gr. 4-7). 1978. Boxed Set. Set pap. 7.80 (0-394-84005-4) Random Bks Yng Read.

Alfred Hitchcock Murder Case. George Baxt. (Library of Crime Classics). 277p. 1987. pap. 5.95 (0-930330-55-2) Intl Polygonics.

Alfred Hitchcock Presents: Stories That Go Bump in the Night. Alfred Hitchcock. 23.95 (0-88411-707-3, Aeonian Pr) Amereon Ltd.

Alfred Hitchcock Presents: The Master's Choice. Ed. by Alfred Hitchcock. (J). 1979. 12.95 (0-394-50419-4) Random Bks Yng Read.

Alfred Hitchcock Quote Book. Laurent Bouzereau. LC 92-37554. 1993. pap. 8.95 (0-8065-1390-X) Carol Pub Group.

Alfred Hitchcock's Borrowers of the Night. large type ed. Ed. by Cathleen Jordan. LC 92-44512. 1993. 21.95 (0-7927-1515-2, Curley Lrg Print); pap. 19.95 (0-7927-1514-4, Curley Lrg Print) Chivers N Amer.

Alfred Hitchcock's Daring Detectives. Ed. by Alfred Hitchcock. LC 76-79077. (Illus.). (J). (gr. 5 up). 1982. pap. 4.99 (0-394-84902-7) Random Bks Yng Read.

Alfred Hitchcock's Ghostly Gallery. Ed. by Alfred Hitchcock. LC 62-14298. (Illus.). 272p. (J). (gr. 5 up). 1984. pap. 4.99 (0-394-86762-9) Random Bks Yng Read.

Alfred Hitchcock's Haunted Houseful. Ed. by Alfred Hitchcock. LC 84-15949. (Illus.). 272p. (J). (gr. 4-9). 1985. pap. 4.99 (0-394-87041-7) Random Bks Yng Read.

Alfred Hitchcock's High Vernacular. Stefan Sharff. 1991. text ed. 32.50 (0-231-06914-6) Col U Pr.

Alfred Hitchcock's Home Sweet Homicide. Ed. by Cathleen Jordan. 288p. 1991. 18.95 (0-8027-5798-7) Walker & Co.

Alfred Hitchcock's Monster Museum. Ed. by Alfred Hitchcock. LC 81-13883. (Illus.). 224p. (J). (gr. 5 up). 1982. pap. 4.99 (0-394-84899-3) Random Bks Yng Read.

Alfred Hitchcock's More Crime Watch. large type ed. Ed. by Cathleen Jordan. LC 94-4516. 1994. 17.95 (0-7927-2030-X, Curley Lrg Print) Chivers N Amer.

Alfred Hitchcock's More Crime Watch. large type ed. Ed. by Cathleen Jordan. LC 94-4516. 1994. pap. 18.95 (0-7927-2029-6, Curley Lrg Print) Chivers N Amer.

Alfred Hitchcock's Solve-Them-Yourself Mysteries. Ed. by Alfred Hitchcock. LC 63-7818. (Illus.). 256p. (J). (gr. 6-9). 1986. pap. 4.99 (0-394-88240-7) Random Bks Yng Read.

Alfred Hitchcock's Spellbinders in Suspense. Alfred Hitchcock. (Illus.). (J). (gr. 7-11). 1982. 4.99 (0-394-84900-0) Random Bks Yng Read.

Alfred Hitchcock's Supernatural Tales of Terror & Suspense. Ed. by Alfred Hitchcock. (Illus.). (J). (gr. 5 up). 1983. pap. 4.99 (0-394-85622-8) Random Bks Yng Read.

Alfred Hitchcock's Tales of the Supernatural & the Fantastic. Ed. by Cathleen Jordan. LC 93-20152. (Illus.). 480p. 1993. 9.98 (0-8317-0437-3) Smithmark.

Alfred Hitchcock's Tales to be Read With Caution. Alfred Hitchcock. Ed. by Eleanor Sullivan. 23.95 (0-88411-706-5, Aeonian Pr) Amereon Ltd.

***Alfred Hitchcock's Tales To Be Read with Caution.** large type ed. Ed. by Eleanor Sullivan. LC 94-41624. 1995. write for info. (0-7862-0380-3) Thorndike Pr.

Alfred Hugenberg: The Radical Nationalist Campaign Against the Weimar Republic. John A. Leopold. LC 77-4026. (Illus.). 314p. reprint ed. pap. 89.50 (0-8357-5303-4, 2032135) Bks Demand.

Alfred Hutty & the Charleston Renaissance. Boyd Saunders & Ann McAden. (Illus.). 128p. 1990. 24.95 (0-87844-089-5) Sandlapper Pub Co.

Alfred I. Du Pont: The Man & His Family. Joseph F. Wall. 718p. 1990. 35.00 (0-19-504349-9) OUP.

Alfred Jacob Miller: Artist on the Oregon Trail. Ed. by Ron Tyler. LC 81-69175. (Illus.). 480p. 1982. 25.00 (0-88360-042-0) Amon Carter.

Alfred Jarry: The Man with the Axe. Nigey Lennon. 1991. pap. 9.95 (0-86719-382-4) Last Gasp.

Alfred Jarry: The Man with the Axe. Nigey Lennon. (Illus.). 120p. 1984. 15.95 (0-915572-74-5); pap. 6.95 (0-915572-73-7) Panjandrum.

Alfred Jensen: Paintings & Diagrams from the Years 1957-1977. Linda L. Cathcart. LC 77-83756. 1977. 12.00 (0-914782-15-0) Buffalo Acad.

Alfred Khouri Collection II. (Illus.). 1969. pap. 2.00 (0-940744-06-6) Chrysler Museum.

Alfred Khouri Memorial Collection I. Frwd. by Henry B. Caldwell. (Illus.). 42p. 1963. pap. 2.00 (0-940744-05-8) Chrysler Museum.

Alfred Korzybski: Collected Writings, 1920-1950. Comp. by M. Kendig. xxv, 915p. 1990. 55.00 (0-910780-08-0); pap. 45.00 (0-685-40616-4) Inst Gen Seman.

Alfred Kubin. Ed. by Serge Sabarsky. (Illus.). 96p. pap. 16.00 (0-918825-45-8) Moyer Bell.

Alfred Kubin: Visions from the Other Side. Jane Kallir. (Illus.). 48p. (Orig.). 1983. pap. 7.00 (0-910810-22-2) Johannes.

Alfred Leslie: The Grisaille Paintings 1962-1967. (Illus.). 104p. 1992. pap. 25.00 (0-9624258-8-5) Flynn Gallery.

Alfred Leslie: The Killing Cycle. Alfred Leslie. (Illus.). 96p. 1992. pap. 29.95 (0-89178-036-X) Flynn Gallery.

Alfred Lord Tennyson. Intro. by Harold Bloom. (Modern Critical Views Ser.). 1985. 29.95 (0-87754-615-0) Chelsea Hse.

Alfred, Lord Tennyson. Alfred Tennyson. (Poets Ser.). 146p. 1993. 5.95 (0-7117-0402-3, Pub. by Jarrold Pub UK) Seven Hills Bk.

Alfred Lord Tennyson: A Memoir by His Son, 2 vols., Set. Hallam T. Tennyson. 1899. 32.00 (0-403-00274-5) Scholarly.

Alfred Lord Tennyson: A Memoir by His Son, 4 vols., Set. Hallam T. Tennyson. LC 74-176139. reprint ed. 34.50 (0-404-06380-2) AMS Pr.

Alfred Lord Tennyson; a Memoir, by His Son, 4 vols., Set. Hallam Tennyson. (BCL1-PR English Literature Ser.). 1992. reprint ed. lib. bdg. 300.00 (0-7812-7699-3) Rprt Serv.

Alfred Lunt & Lynn Fontanne: A Bibliography. Phillip M. Runkel. (Illus.). (C). 1978. pap. 4.50 (0-916120-03-1) Carroll Coll.

***Alfred Marshall: Critical Assessments.** Ed. by John C. Wood. LC 95-3275. (Critical Assessments of Leading Economists Ser.). 1996. write for info. (0-415-08735-X) Routledge.

Alfred Marshall: Progress & Politics. David Reisman. LC 87-4811. 500p. 1987. text ed. 49.95 (0-312-00773-6) St Martin.

Alfred Marshall in Retrospect. Rita Tullberg. 256p. 1990. text ed. 67.95 (1-85278-344-3, Pub. by E Elgar Pub UK) Ashgate Pub Co.

Alfred Marshall (1842-1924) & Francis Edgeworth (1845-1926) Ed. by Mark Blaug. (Pioneers in Economics Ser.: No. 29). 384p. 1992. 123.95 (1-85278-492-X, Pub. by E Elgar Pub UK) Ashgate Pub Co.

Alfred Morang: A Neglected Master. Walt Wiggins. LC 79-87716. (Art Book Ser.: No. 1). (Illus.). 1979. 25.00 (0-934116-01-6) Pintores Pr.

Alfred Morang: A Neglected Master. deluxe ed. Walt Wiggins. LC 79-87716. (Art Book Ser.: No. 1). (Illus.). 1979. 150.00 (0-934116-00-8) Pintores Pr.

Alfred Nobel. Kenne Fant. Tr. by Marianne Ruuth. (Illus.). 400p. 1993. 24.95 (1-55970-222-2) Arcade Pub Inc.

Alfred North Whitehead: A Primer of His Philosophy. Nathaniel Lawrence. 192p. 1974. 59.50 (0-685-63209-1) Elliots Bks.

Alfred North Whitehead: Essays on His Philosophy. George L. Kline. 216p. (C). 1989. reprint ed. pap. text ed. 22.50 (0-8191-7283-9) U Pr of Amer.

Alfred North Whitehead: The Man & His Work, Vol. II; 1910-1917. Victor Lowe. 1990. 39.95 (0-8018-3960-2) Johns Hopkins.

Alfred North Whitehead: The Man & His Work, Vol. 1: 1861-1910. Victor Lowe. LC 84-15467. 392p. 1985. 39.95 (0-8018-2488-5) Johns Hopkins.

Alfred R. Waud: Special Artist on Assignment. Historic New Orleans Collection Staff. (Illus.). ii, 22p. 1979. pap. 3.00 (0-917860-03-9) Historic New Orleans.

Alfred Russel Wallace: An Anthology of His Shorter Writings. Ed. by Charles H. Smith. (Illus.). 568p. 1991. 79.00 (0-19-857725-7) OUP.

Alfred Russel Wallace: Letters & Reminiscences. James Marchant. LC 74-26273. (History, Philosophy & Sociology of Science Ser.). 1975. reprint ed. 38.95 (0-405-06601-5) Ayer.

Alfred Schutz on Phenomenology & Social Relations: Selected Writings. Alfred Schutz. Ed. by Helmut R. Wagner. LC 73-102072. (Heritage of Sociology Ser.). 1972. pap. text ed. 17.00 (0-226-74153-2, P360) U Ch Pr.

Alfred Sisley. A. Babin. (Illus.). (C). 1988. text ed. 50.00 (0-569-09107-1, Pub. by Collets UK) Pro-Am Music.

Alfred Sisley. Ed. by Mary A. Stevens. (Illus.). 312p. (C). 1992. 55.00 (0-300-05244-8); 35.00 (0-300-05245-6) Yale U Pr.

Alfred Sisley in the Musee du Louvre. Pierre Du Colombies. (Illus.). 1947. lib. bdg. 9.95 (0-8288-3979-4) Fr & Eur.

Alfred Stevens. William Coles. (Illus.). 152p. 1977. pap. 12.50 (0-912303-12-3) Michigan Mus.

Alfred Stieglitz. Norman. 1991. 29.95 (0-89381-429-6) Aperture.

Alfred Stieglitz. Comp. by Dorothy Norman. (Masters of Photography Ser.: Vol. 6). (Illus.). 1989. 22.95 (0-89381-308-7); pap. 14.95 (0-89381-309-5) Aperture.

Alfred Stieglitz. Eva Weber. 1994. 15.99 (0-517-10332-X) Random Hse Value.

***Alfred Stieglitz: A Biography.** Richard Whelan. LC 94-39372. 1995. 29.95 (0-316-93404-6) Little.

Alfred Stieglitz: An American Seer. Dorothy Norman. 1990. pap. 16.95 (0-89381-425-3) Aperture.

Alfred Stieglitz: Scientist, Photographer, & Avatar of Modernism, 1880-1913. Geraldine W. Kiefer. LC 91-14136. (Garland Publications in the Fine Arts). (Illus.). 672p. 1991. 150.00 (0-8153-0114-6) Garland.

Alfred Stieglitz Talking: Notes on Some of His Conversations, 1925-1931 with a Foreword. Herbert J. Seligmann. LC 66-21942. 151p. reprint ed. pap. 43.10 (0-8357-5304-2, 2032137) Bks Demand.

Alfred Stieglitz's Camera Notes. Ed. by Christian A. Peterson. LC 93-12089. (Illus.). 192p. 1993. 39.95 (0-393-03534-4) Norton.

Alfred Summer. Jan Slepian. LC 79-24097. 132p. (J). (gr. 6 up). 1980. text ed. 13.95 (0-02-782920-0, Mac Bks Young Read) S&S Childrens.

Alfred Sutro: A Man with a Heart. Lewis Sawin. 208p. 1989. 29.95 (0-87081-200-9) Univ Pr Colo.

Alfred Tennyson. James D. Kissane. (English Authors Ser.: No. 110). 184p. 1970. text ed. 21.95 (0-8057-1544-4, Twayne) Macmillan.

Alfred Tennyson. Alan Sinfield. 208p. 1986. pap. 21.95 (0-631-13583-9) Blackwell Pubs.

Alfred Tennyson. 2nd ed. Andrew Lang. LC 70-111615. reprint ed. 27.50 (0-404-03856-5) AMS Pr.

Alfred Tennyson. Arthur C. Benson. LC 69-13820. 243p. 1969. reprint ed. text ed. 35.00 (0-8371-1071-8, BENA, Greenwood Pr) Greenwood.

Alfred Tennyson. Arthur C. Benson. (BCL1-PR English Literature Ser.). 243p. 1992. reprint ed. lib. bdg. 79.00 (0-7812-7693-4) Rprt Serv.

Alfred Tennyson: A Literary Life. Leonee Ormond. LC 93-2626. (Literary Lives Ser.). 240p. 1993. text ed. 35.00 (0-312-09597-X) St Martin.

Alfred Tennyson: A Saintly Life. Robert F. Horton. LC 72-10628. (Studies in Tennyson: No. 27). 1973. reprint ed. lib. bdg. 66.95 (0-8383-1687-5) M S G Haskell Hse.

Alfred the Ant, An Ant Who Lives in Central Park: The First Storytelling "Flip Over" Picture Book. Jehan Clements. LC 89-61138. (Illus.). 48p. (J). (gr. k-3). 1994. 19.95 (0-9622500-0-7) Strytllr Co.

Alfred the Great. Israel Horovitz. 1992. pap. 4.75 (0-8222-1297-8) Dramatists Play.

Alfred the Great. Tr. by Simon Keynes & Michael Lapidge. (Classics Ser.). 368p. (C). 1984. pap. 11.95 (0-14-044409-2, Penguin Classics) Viking Penguin.

Alfred the Great. Frederic Harrison. Ed. by Alfred Bowker. LC 78-154144. (Select Bibliographies Reprint Ser.). 1977. reprint ed. 21.95 (0-8369-5760-1) Ayer.

Alfred the Great: The King & His England. Eleanor S. Duckett. LC 56-13050. 1958. pap. text ed. 12.95 (0-226-16779-8, P29) U Ch Pr.

Alfred True on Agricultural Experimentation & Research: An Original Anthology. Alfred C. True. Ed. by I. Bernard Cohen. LC 79-8001. (Three Centuries of Science in America Ser.). (Illus.). 1980. lib. bdg. 70.95 (0-405-12589-5) Ayer.

Alfred V. Fedak Hymnary. Alfred V. Fedak. 48p. 1990. pap. 4.50 (0-9622553-2-7, 125-012) Selah Pub Co.

Alfred V. Kidder. Richard B. Woodbury. LC 72-10082. (Leaders of Modern Anthropology Ser.). 225p. (C). 1978. pap. text ed. 16.00 (0-231-03485-7) Col U Pr.

Alfred Vincent Kidder & the Development of Americanist Archaeology. Douglas R. Givens. LC 91-43853. 224p. 1992. 32.50x (0-8263-1351-5) U of NM Pr.

Alfred Waterhouse & the Natural History Museum. Mark Girouard. LC 80-53742. (Illus.). 1981. 30.00x (0-300-02578-5) Yale U Pr.

Alfred Waterhouse, 1830-1905: Biography of a Practice. Colin Cunningham & Prudence Waterhouse. (Clarendon Studies in the History of Art). (Illus.). 436p. 1992. 185.00 (0-19-817511-6) OUP.

Alfred Williams: His Life & Work. Leonard Clark. LC 69-13754. (Illus.). xv, 206p. 1969. reprint ed. 29.50 (0-678-05512-2) Kelley.

***Alfreda's Stories, Tales & Myths - 20 Plus.** Alfreda C. Doyle. 64p. (Orig.). (J). (gr. 3-9). 1995. pap. text ed. 15.95 (1-56820-125-7) Story Time.

Alfredo De Palchi: Sessions with My Analyst. Alfredo De Palchi. Tr. by I. L. Salomon. 1971. 8.95 (0-8079-0167-9); pap. 4.95 (0-8079-0168-7) October.

Alfredo Jaar: Geography Equals War. H. Ashley Kistler et al. Ed. by Anne Barriault. LC 91-21091. (Illus.). 49p. 1991. pap. 10.00 (0-917046-32-3) Va Mus Arts.

Alfredo Viazzi's Italian Cooking: More Than 150 Inspired Interpretations of Great Italian Cuisine. Alfredo Viazzi. LC 83-47818. (Illus.). 240p. 1983. 12.95 (0-394-50167-5) Random.

Alfred's Alphabet Antics. Elizabeth Gregory. (Illus.). (J). 1981. 6.95 (0-933184-07-7); pap. 4.95 (0-933184-08-5) Flame Intl.

Alfred's Basic Adult Piano Course: Lesson Book, Level One. Willard A. Palmer et al. (Alfred's Basic Piano Library). 96p. (Orig.). 1983. pap. text ed. 8.50 (0-88284-616-7, 2236) Alfred Pub.

Alfred's Metres of Boethius. Ed. by Bill Griffiths. 212p. (Orig.). 1992. pap. text ed. 25.00 (0-9516209-5-9, Pub. by Anglo-Saxon Bks UK) Paul & Co Pubs.

Alfred's Pocket Dictionary of Music. Sandy Feldstein. (Illus.). 240p. 1986. pap. text ed. 4.95 (0-88284-349-4, 2400) Alfred Pub.

Alfresco: Over One Hundred Recipes with Menus for Memorable Outdoor Meals. Rosamond Richardson. (Illus.). 1992. 35.00 (0-517-58482-4, C P Pubs) Crown Pub Group.

Alfven Wave. Akira Hasegawa & Chanchal Uberoi. LC 81-607894. (DOE Critical Review Ser.: Advances in Fusion Science & Engineering). 137p. 1981. pap. 13.50 (0-87079-125-7, DOE/TIC-11197); fiche 9.00 (0-87079-236-9, DOE/TIC-11197) DOE.

Algae: A Review. Gerald W. Prescott. (Illus.). xi, 436p. 1984. reprint ed. ring bd. 85.00 (3-87429-244-4) Koeltz Sci Bks.

Algae: A Source Guide. 1991. lib. bdg. 250.00 (0-8490-4856-7) Gordon Pr.

Algae: An Introduction to Phycology. Christiaan Van Den Hoek et al. (Illus.). 576p. (C). 1994. write for info. (0-521-30419-9); pap. write for info. (0-521-31687-1) Cambridge U Pr.

Algae: Form & Function. G. S. Venketaraman et al. 578p. 1974. 25.00 (0-88065-201-2, Messers Today & Tomorrow) Scholarly Pubns.

Algae Abstracts: A Guide to the Literature, 3 vols. Comp. by Office of Water Resources Research Staff. Incl. Vol. 1. To 1969. 586p. 1973. 95.00 (0-306-67181-6); Vol. 2. 1970 to 1972. 694p. 1973. 95.00 (0-306-67182-4); Vol. 3. 1972 to 1974. 890p. 1976. 95.00 (0-306-67183-2); write for info. (0-318-53513-0, IFI-Plenum) Plenum.

Algae & Element Cycling in Wetlands. Vymazal. 1994. write for info. (0-87371-899-2) Lewis Pubs.

Algae & Human Affairs. Ed. by Carole A. Lembi & J. Robert Waaland. (Illus.). 585p. 1989. 84.95 (0-521-32115-8) Cambridge U Pr.

Algae & Symbiosis: Plants-Animals-Fungi-Viruses-Interactions Explored. Ed. by W. Reisser. (Illus.). 746p. 1992. lib. bdg. 199.00 (0-948737-15-8, Pub. by Biopress Ltd UK) Lubrecht & Cramer.

Algae & the Aquatic Environment: Contributions in Honour of J. W. G. Lund. Ed. by F. E. Round. (Illus.). 460p. 1988. lib. bdg. 106.00 (0-948737-06-9, Pub. by Biopress Ltd UK) Lubrecht & Cramer.

***Algae & Water Pollution.** Ed. by L. C. Rai & J. P. Gaur. (Advances in Limnology Ser.: No. 42). (Illus.). 304p. 1994. pap. text ed. 110.00 (3-510-47043-5, Pub. by Schweitzerbart'sche GW) Lubrecht & Cramer.

Algae As Ecological Indicators. Ed. by L. E. Shubert. 1984. text ed. 137.00 (0-12-640620-0) Acad Pr.

Algae Italianae e Dalmatiche illustrata. Giuseppe Meneghini. (Illus.). 1970. 55.00 (90-6123-094-2) Lubrecht & Cramer.

Algae of New Zealand Thermal Areas. Together With: Taxonomic Guide to Thermally Associated Algae (Excluding Diatoms) in New Zealand. V. Cassie & R. C. Cooper. (Bibliotheca Phycologica Ser.: Vol. 78). (Illus.). 261p. 1989. spiral bd. 85.00 (3-443-60005-0, Pub. by Cramer GW) Lubrecht & Cramer.

Algae of Southern Victorialand, Antarctica, Taxonomic & Distributional Study. K. G. Seaburg et al. (Illus.). 1980. lib. bdg. 33.00 (3-7682-1249-1) Lubrecht & Cramer.

Algae of the Indian Subcontinent: A Collection of Papers. (Bibliotheca Phycologica Ser.: Vol. 66). (Illus.). 446p. 1984. lib. bdg. 90.00 (3-7682-1398-6) Lubrecht & Cramer.

Algae of the Western Great Lakes Area: With Illustrated Key to the Genera of Desmids on Freshwater Diatoms. Gerald W. Prescott. (Illus.). 977p. 1983. pap. text ed. 89.00 (3-87429-205-3) Koeltz Sci Bks.

Algae of Western Lake Erie. Clarence E. Taft & Celeste W. Taft. (Bulletin New Ser.). (Illus.). 189p. 1990. reprint ed. 15.00 (0-86727-060-8) Ohio Bio Survey.

Algal Assays & Monitoring Eutrophication. P. Marvan et al. (Illus.). 253p. 1979. 33.50 (3-510-65091-3) Lubrecht & Cramer.

Algal Biofertilizers & Rice Cultivation. G. S. Venketaraman et al. 83p. 1972. 8.00 (0-88065-202-0, Messers Today & Tomorrow) Scholarly Pubns.

Algal Biofouling: Proceedings of a Symposium, Gainesville, FL, August, 1985. Phycological Society of America. Ed. by K. D. Hoagland & L. V. Evans. (Studies in Environmental Science: No. 28). 328p. 1987. 105.25 (0-444-42705-8) Elsevier.

Algal Biomass Technologies, an Interdisciplinary Approach: Proceedings of a Workshop on the Present Status & Future Directions for Biotechnologies Based on Algal Biomass Production, 1984, at the University of Colorado. Ed. by Wm. R. Barclay & R. P. McIntosh. (Nova Hedwigia Beiheft Ser.: No. 83). (Illus.). 274p. 1986. pap. 76.00 (3-443-51003-5) Lubrecht & Cramer.

Algal Biotechnology: Proceedings of the 4th International Meeting of the SAA, Villeneuve D'Ascq, France, September 15-17, 1987. Ed. by T. Stadler et al. 522p. 1988. 108.00 (1-85166-233-2) Elsevier.

Algal Cell Motility. Ed. by Michael Melkonian & Matthew J. Dring. (Current Phycology Ser.). 192p. 1991. 42.00 (0-412-02431-4, A4037, Chap & Hall NY) Chapman & Hall.

Algal Culture: From Laboratory to Pilot Plant. Ed. by John S. Burlew. (Illus.). 366p. 1953. 20.00 (0-87279-611-6, 600) Carnegie Inst.

Algal Cultures & Phytoplankton Ecology. 2nd ed. G. E. Fogg. LC 74-27308. (Illus.). 192p. 1975. 25.00 (0-299-06760-2) U of Wis Pr.

Algal Cultures & Phytoplankton Ecology. 3rd ed. G. E. Fogg & Brenda Thake. LC 85-40895. (Illus.). 320p. 1987. text ed. 27.50 (0-299-10560-1) U of Wis Pr.

Algal Limestones Within the Minturn Formation, Meeker to Dotsero Area, Western Colorado. Ed. by Jon Raese & J. H. Goldberg. (Colorado School of Mines Quarterly Ser.: Vol. 78, No. 2). (Illus.). 14p. 1983. pap. 10.00 (0-686-45171-6) Colo Sch Mines.

Algal Photosynthesis: The Measurement of Algal Gas Exchange. Richard J. Geider & Bruce A. Osborne. Ed. by Matthew J. Dring & Michael Melkonian. (Current Phycology Ser.). (Illus.). 192p. 1991. 38.00 (0-412-02351-2, A4041, Chap & Hall NY) Chapman & Hall.

Algal Symbiosis: A Continuum of Interaction Strategies. Ed. by Lynda J. Goff. LC 83-7275. (Illus.). 224p. 1984. 64.95 (0-521-25541-4) Cambridge U Pr.

Algal Toxins in Seafood & Drinking Water. Ed. by Ian Falconer. (Illus.). 224p. 1993. text ed. 59.95 (0-12-247990-4) Acad Pr.

Algarve. Ulrich Fleischmann. (Windsor Destination Guides Ser.). (Illus.). 56p. (Orig.). 1993. pap. 12.95 (1-874111-09-X, Pub. by Windsor Bks UK) Seven Hills Bk.

Algarve & Southern Portugal. Thomas Cook. (Passport's Illustrated Travel Guides from Thomas Cook Ser.). (Illus.). 192p. 1993. pap. 12.95 (0-8442-9044-0, Passport Bks) NTC Pub Grp.

Algarve Plants & Landscapes: Passing Tradition & Ecological Change. D. J. Mabberley & P. J. Placito. LC 92-26904. (Illus.). 336p. 1993. 49.95 (0-19-858702-3) OUP.

Algarve Pocket Guide. Berlitz Editors. (Pocket Guides Ser.). 1989. pap. 7.95 (2-8315-1435-5) Berlitz.

Algarve, Travel & Property Guide. Brian Nuttall. (Illus.). 192p. (Orig.). 1990. pap. 19.95 (1-85365-177-X, Pub. by McCarta UK) Seven Hills Bk.

Alge im System der Pflanzen: Nanochlorum Eucaryotum - Eine Alge mit Minimalen Eukaryotischen Kriterien. M. Reitz. (Illus.). 273p. (GER.). 1986. lib. bdg. 55.35 (3-437-30523-9) Lubrecht & Cramer.

Algebra. Michael Artin. 664p. 1991. text ed. 72.00 (0-13-004763-5, 540201) P-H.

Algebra. I. Gelfand & A. Shen. 153p. 1993. 24.50 (0-8176-3737-0); pap. 18.50 (0-8176-3677-3) Birkhauser.

A

Algebra. Larry C. Grove. (Pure & Applied Mathematics Ser.). (C). 1983. text ed. 70.00 (*0-12-304620-3*) Acad Pr.

Algebra. Thomas W. Hungerford. (Graduate Texts in Mathematics Ser.: Vol. 73). 502p. 1993. 42.00 (*0-387-90518-9*) Spr-Verlag.

Algebra. L. E. Sigler. (Undergraduate Texts in Mathematics Ser.). (Illus.). 1976. 39.00 (*0-387-90195-7*) Spr-Verlag.

Algebra. Mark Steinberger. LC 93-5104. (Prindle, Weber & Schmidt Series in Advanced Mathematics). 1994. text ed. 69.95 (*0-534-93678-4*) PWS Pubs.

Algebra. 2nd ed. Serge A. Lang. 714p. (C). 1984. text ed. 63.50 (*0-201-05487-6*, Adv Bk Prog) Addison-Wesley.

Algebra. 3rd ed. Serge A. Lang. (Illus.). 892p. (C). 1993. text ed. 64.50 (*0-201-55540-9*) Addison-Wesley.

Algebra. 3rd ed. Saunders Mac Lane & Garrett Birkhoff. xv, 630p. (C). 1987. text ed. 32.50 (*0-8284-0330-9*) Chelsea Pub.

***Algebra.** 4th ed. Charuhas. (Essential Mathematics for Life Ser.: No. 6). 1995. pap. text ed. 7.95 (*0-02-802612-8*) Glencoe.

Algebra. S. N. Cernikov et al. (Translations Ser.: No. 1, Vol. 1). 473p. 1968. reprint ed. 35.00 (*0-8218-1601-2*, TRANS 1-1) Am Math.

***Algebra, No. 111.** Anthony Nicolaides. (C). 1990. pap. 39.95x (*1-872684-13-0*, Pub. by P A S S Pubns UK) St Mut.

Algebra, Vol. 1. L. Redei. 1967. 337.00 (*0-08-010954-3*, Pub. by Pergamon Repr UK) Franklin.

Algebra, Vol. 1. B. L. Van der Waerden. xiv, 265p. 1993. 34.50 (*0-387-97424-5*) Spr-Verlag.

Algebra, Vol. 1. 2nd ed. P. M. Cohn. LC 81-21932. 410p. 1982. pap. text ed. 77.95 (*0-471-10169-9*, Wiley-Interscience) Wiley.

Algebra, Vol. 2. B. L. Van der Waerden. xii, 284p. 1993. 34.50 (*0-387-97425-3*) Spr-Verlag.

Algebra, Vol. 2. 2nd ed. P. M. Cohn. 1989. text ed. 115.00 (*0-471-92234-X*) Wiley.

Algebra, Vol. 2. Paul M. Cohn. LC 73-2780. 497p. reprint ed. pap. 141.70 (*0-8357-5305-0*, 2026687) Bks Demand.

Algebra, Vol. 3. 2nd ed. P. M. Cohn. 1991. text ed. 175.00 (*0-471-92840-2*) Wiley.

Algebra: A First Course. 3rd ed. John D. Baley & Martin Holstege. 529p. (C). 1990. text ed. 48.95 (*0-534-10332-4*) PWS Pubs.

***Algebra: A Graphing Approach.** Elaine Hubbard & Ronald D. Robinson. 864p. (C). 1995. text ed. write for info. (*0-669-33318-2*) Heath.

***Algebra: A Traditional Approach to Problem Solving.** John Gorham. 1994. text ed. 21.75 (*0-9637658-2-5*) Davis-Gorham Pr.

Algebra: An Algorithmic Treatment. K. E. Iverson. (Illus.). (Orig.). 1977. reprint ed. pap. text ed. 15.00 (*0-917326-09-1*) APL Pr.

Algebra: An Approach Via Module Theory. William A. Adkins & Steven H. Weintraub. Ed. by J. H. Ewing et al. LC 92-11951. (Graduate Texts in Mathematics Ser.: Vol. 136). (Illus.). 536p. 1992. 44.50 (*0-387-97839-9*); write for info. (*3-540-97839-9*) Spr-Verlag.

Algebra: An Elementary Course. 2nd ed. Raymond A. Barnett & Thomas J. Kearns. 1987. pap. text ed. write for info. (*0-07-003923-2*) McGraw.

Algebra: An Elementary Course. 2nd ed. Raymond A. Barnett & Thomas J. Kearns. 1987. Student solution manual. student ed, pap. text ed. write for info. (*0-07-003770-1*) McGraw.

Algebra: An Incremental Approach, Vol. I. John H. Saxon, Jr. (Illus.). 1979. Reference ed. pap. text ed. write for info. (*0-13-021600-3*) P-H.

Algebra: An Intermediate Course. 2nd ed. Raymond Barnett & Thomas J. Kearns. 1987. pap. text ed. write for info. (*0-07-003749-3*) McGraw.

Algebra: An Intermediate Course. 2nd ed. Mervin L. Keedy. 425p. (C). 1986. text ed. write for info. (*0-318-59745-4*) Addison-Wesley.

Algebra: An Introductory Course. Mervin L. Keedy. (Illus.). 512p. 1983. text ed. write for info. (*0-201-14798-X*) Addison-Wesley.

Algebra: Create & Discover. Carla Oblas. 328p. (C). 1991. pap. text ed. 19.00 (*0-89801-021-7*) NE Univ Pub.

Algebra: Groups, Rings, & Fields. Louis Rowen. LC 93-39371. 264p. 1995. text ed. 49.95 (*1-56881-028-8*) AK Peters.

Algebra: Its Elements & Structure, Bk. 2. 3rd rev. ed. Max A. Sobel & J. Houston Banks. 624p. (gr. 11). 1977. text ed. 32.36 (*0-07-059585-2*) McGraw.

Algebra, a Graduate Course. I. Martin Isaacs. LC 93-21157. 1994. text ed. 65.95 (*0-534-19002-2*) Brooks-Cole.

Algebra Acrobatic Puzzles. Morris Bureloff. (Illus.). (J). (gr. 7-12). 1988. pap. 7.95 (*0-918932-93-9*) Activity Resources.

Algebra, Algebraic Topology & Their Interactions. Ed. by J. E. Roos. (Lecture Notes in Mathematics Ser.: Vol. 1183). xi, 396p. 1986. pap. 53.40 (*0-387-16453-7*) Spr-Verlag.

Algebra & Analysis: Evolution of the Number Concept & Determinants-Equations-Logarithms-Limits see Fundamentals of Mathematics from an Advanced Viewpoint

Algebra & Elementary Functions. 2nd ed. H. S. Bear. LC 76-184869. (Page-Ficklin Math Ser). 1976. pap. text ed. write for info. (*0-8087-2855-5*) Burgess MN Intl.

Algebra & Its Applications. Manocha & Srivastava. (Lecture Notes in Pure & Applied Mathematics Ser.: Vol. 91). 416p. 1984. 140.00 (*0-8247-7165-6*) Dekker.

Algebra & Number Theory: Proceedings of a Conference Held at the Institute of Experimental Mathematics, Universtiy of Essen (Germany), December 2-4, 1992. Ed. by Gerhard Frey & Jurgen Ritter. LC 94-5598. x, 296p. 1994. 119.95 (*3-11-014250-3*) De Gruyter.

Algebra & Practical Applications. rev. ed. J. L. McCabe. (Illus.). 133p. 1994. reprint ed. pap. text ed. 13.95 (*0-942465-03-2*, 2-038-778) Summertree Bks.

***Algebra & Tiling.** Sherman Stein & Sandor Szabo. (Carus Mathematical Monographs: No. 25). 224p. (C). 1994. text ed. 38.00 (*0-88385-028-1*) Math Assn.

Algebra & Trigonometry. Marvin L. Bittinger & Judith A. Beecher. (Illus.). 768p. (C). 1989. text ed. 49.50 (*0-201-09152-6*) Addison-Wesley.

Algebra & Trigonometry. Philip W. Gillett. (C). 1988. text ed. 37.50 (*0-673-18311-4*) HarpCollege.

Algebra & Trigonometry. Dennis Zill & Jacqueline Dewar. 650p. (C). 1989. text ed. 42.95 (*0-394-35673-X*) Random.

Algebra & Trigonometry. 2nd ed. Stanley I. Grossman. 752p. (C). 1992. text ed. 51.00 (*0-03-052167-X*) SCP.

Algebra & Trigonometry. 2nd ed. Thomas W. Hungerford & Richard Mercer. 672p. (C). 1991. teacher ed write for info. (*0-03-054247-2*); text ed. 51.00 (*0-03-046928-7*) SCP.

Algebra & Trigonometry. 2nd ed. Roland E. Larson. 736p. (C). 1990. teacher ed 2.00 (*0-669-16270-1*); text ed. 33.00 (*0-669-16269-8*); 8.50 (*0-669-16271-X*); 10.50 (*0-669-16272-8*) Heath.

Algebra & Trigonometry. 2nd ed. John Tobey, Jr. et al. 720p. (C). 1986. write for info. (*0-697-06921-4*) Wm C Brown Pubs.

Algebra & Trigonometry. 2nd ed. John Tobey, Jr. et al. 720p. (C). 1986. text ed. write for info. (*0-697-06898-6*) Wm C Brown Pubs.

Algebra & Trigonometry. 2nd ed. Dennis Zill & Jacqueline Dewar. 784p. (C). 1990. write for info. (*0-318-65086-X*); text ed. write for info. (*0-07-557095-5*); teacher ed, pap. text ed. 13.54 (*0-07-557006-8*) McGraw.

Algebra & Trigonometry. 3rd annot. ed. Roland E. Larson & Robert P. Hostetler. 818p. (C). 1993. Instr.'s annotated ed. teacher ed write for info. (*0-669-33234-8*) Heath.

Algebra & Trigonometry. 3rd ed. David C. Cohen. Ed. by Marshall. LC 92-11099. 725p. (C). 1993. text ed. 60.75 (*0-314-93363-8*) West Pub.

Algebra & Trigonometry. 3rd ed. Roland E. Larson & Robert P. Hostetler. 818p. (C). 1993. text ed. write for info. (*0-669-28298-7*); Study & soultions guide. student ed write for info. (*0-669-28300-2*); Transparencies. trans. write for info. (*0-318-70104-9*); Complete solutions guide. write for info. (*0-669-28301-0*); Test item file/ Resource guide. write for info. (*0-669-28302-9*) Heath.

Algebra & Trigonometry. 3rd ed. Paul K. Rees et al. (Illus.). 576p. (C). 1975. text ed. write for info. (*0-07-051723-1*) McGraw.

Algebra & Trigonometry. 4th ed. Dennis T. Christy. 688p. (C). 1988. text ed. write for info. (*0-697-05322-9*) Wm C Brown Pubs.

Algebra & Trigonometry. 4th ed. Dennis T. Christy. 688p. (C). 1989. write for info. (*0-697-05625-2*) Wm C Brown Pubs.

Algebra & Trigonometry. 4th ed. Max A. Sobel & Norbert Lerner. 848p. (C). 1991. text ed. write for info. (*0-13-025818-0*) P-H.

Algebra & Trigonometry. 5th ed. Mervin L. Keedy & Marvin L. Bittinger. (Illus.). 640p. (C). 1990. pap. text ed. 49.50 (*0-201-14995-8*) Addison-Wesley.

Algebra & Trigonometry. 5th ed. Max Sobel & Norbert Lerner. LC 94-11438. 1995. text ed. write for info. (*0-13-299124-1*) P-H.

Algebra & Trigonometry. 6th ed. Margaret L. Lial et al. LC 93-26181. 654p. (C). 1994. 61.50 (*0-673-46739-2*) HarpCollege.

Algebra & Trigonometry: A Functions Approach. Mervin L. Keedy & Marvin L. Bittinger. 550p. (C). 1986. teacher ed write for info. (*0-201-13326-1*); pap. text ed. write for info. (*0-201-13325-3*); student ed write for info. (*0-201-13327-X*); write for info. (*0-201-13328-8*); write for info. (*0-318-59744-6*) Addison-Wesley.

Algebra & Trigonometry: A Problem Solving Approach. 4th ed. Walter Fleming et al. 720p. (C). 1991. text ed. write for info. (*0-318-68773-9*) P-H.

Algebra & Trigonometry: A Straightforward Approach. 2nd ed. (Illus.). 573p. 1985. 29.95 (*0-912675-49-7*); student ed 16.95 (*0-912675-51-9*); teacher ed 16.95 (*0-912675-50-0*); 16.95 (*0-912675-52-7*); write for info. (*0-912675-53-5*) Ardsley.

Algebra & Trigonometry: Right Triangle. 2nd ed. Marvin L. Bittinger et al. (Illus.). 672p. (C). 1993. pap. text ed. 50.50 (*0-201-52510-0*) Addison-Wesley.

Algebra & Trigonometry: Unit Circle. 6th ed. Mervin L. Keedy et al. (Illus.). 896p. (C). 1993. pap. text ed. 50.50 (*0-201-52517-8*) Addison-Wesley.

***Algebra & Trigonometry & Their Applications.** 2nd ed. Larry Goldstein. 768p. (C). 1995. text ed. write for info. (*0-697-26533-1*) Wm C Brown Pubs.

***Algebra & Trigonometry & Their Applications.** 2nd ed. Larry Goldstein. 256p. (C). 1995. student ed write for info. (*0-697-26536-6*) Wm C Brown Pubs.

Algebra & Trigonometry for College Students. 2nd ed. Richard S. Paul & Ernest F. Haeussler, Jr. 1983. text ed. write for info. (*0-8359-0178-5*, Reston); write for info. (*0-8359-0179-3*, Reston) P-H.

Algebra & Trigonometry Problem Solver. rev. ed. Research & Education Association Staff. LC 76-334. (Illus.). 924p. (C). 1994. pap. text ed. 23.95 (*0-87891-508-7*) Res & Educ.

Algebra & Trigonometry Refresher for Calculus Students. Loren C. Larson. LC 79-20633. (Mathematical Sciences Ser.). (Illus.). 192p. (C). 1995. pap. text ed. write for info. (*0-7167-1110-9*) W H Freeman.

Algebra & Trigonometry with Analytic Geometry. Karl J. Smith. 568p. (C). 1987. text ed. 54.95 (*0-534-06684-4*) Brooks-Cole.

Algebra & Trigonometry with Analytic Geometry. 3rd ed. Walter Fleming & Dale E. Varberg. 720p. (C). 1989. text ed. write for info. (*0-13-023441-9*) P-H.

Algebra & Trigonometry with Analytic Geometry. 8th ed. Earl W. Swokowski & Jefferey Cole. LC 92-29045. 896p. 1993. text ed. 57.95 (*0-534-93190-1*) PWS Pubs.

Algebra & Trigonometry with Applications. Jagdish C. Arya & Robin W. Lardner. (Illus.). 272p. (C). 1983. text ed. write for info. (*0-13-021675-5*) P-H.

Algebra & Trigonometry with Applications. 3rd ed. M. A. Munem & David Foulis. (Illus.). 738p. 1991. text ed. 55.95x (*0-87901-498-9*); student ed, pap. 11.95x (*0-87901-513-6*) Worth.

Algebra & Trigonometry with Applications. 4th ed. Bernard Rice & Jerry Strange. (Illus.). 552p. (C). 1989. student ed, disk write for info. (*0-318-63833-9*) Brooks-Cole.

Algebra Arcade. 1983. IBM-PC. write for info. (*0-534-02973-6*); Atari 800. write for info. (*0-318-58327-5*); Commodore 64. write for info. (*0-534-02972-8*); 49.95 (*0-685-09666-1*) COMPress.

Algebra; Beginning; Syllabus. 2nd ed. Al Gray. 1976. pap. text ed. 8.25 (*0-89420-033-X*, 367015); audio 164.35 (*0-89420-125-5*, 367007) Natl Book.

Algebra by Design. Russell F. Jacobs. 48p. (YA). (gr. 8-10). 1990. student ed 11.95 (*0-918272-17-3*) Jacobs.

Algebra, Combinatorics & Logic in Computer Science: Colloquia Matthematica Societatis Janos Bolyai, 2 Vols. Ed. by J. Demetrovics et al. (Colloquia Mathematica Societatis Janos Bolyai Ser.: Vol. 42). 888p. 1986. 187.25 (*0-444-87869-6*) Elsevier.

Algebra Eight: Representations of Finite-Dimensional Algebras. Ed. by A. I. Kostrikin et al. (Encyclopaedia of Mathematical Sciences Ser.: Vol. 73). (Illus.). 192p. 1992. 79.00 (*0-387-53732-5*) Spr-Verlag.

Algebra Facts: A Survival Guide to Basic Algebra. Szymanski. 1993. pap. 8.95 (*0-534-19986-0*) PWS Pubs.

Algebra Flipper, Vol. 2. Jay Clark. 49p. (YA). (gr. 8 up). 1993. 6.25 (*1-878383-21-3*) C Lee Pubns.

Algebra Flipper Vol. 1. Eric R. Churchill. 49p. (J). (gr. 5 up). 1989. reprint ed. 6.25 (*1-878383-03-5*) C Lee Pubns.

Algebra for College Students. Raymond A. Barnett & Thomas J. Kearsn. LC 94-18497. (C). 1994. text ed. write for info. (*0-07-005001-5*) McGraw.

Algebra for College Students. Marvin L. Bittinger & David Ellenbogen. (Illus.). 700p. (C). 1992. text ed. 51.75 (*0-201-19657-3*) Addison-Wesley.

Algebra for College Students. Robert F. Blitzer & Jack C. Gill. (Illus.). 976p. (C). 1991. Addtl. materials avail. text ed. write for info. (*0-02-343040-0*) Macmillan.

Algebra for College Students. Robert F. Blitzer & Jack C. Gill. (Illus.). 976p. (C). 1992. write for info. (*0-02-343031-1*) Macmillan.

***Algebra for College Students.** Edward Doran & Raymond Boersema. 694p. (Orig.). (C). 1995. pap. text ed. 48.00 (*0-941775-09-7*) Finesse Pub.

Algebra for College Students. James W. Hall. 704p. (C). 1988. text ed. 46.95 (*0-87150-191-0*) PWS Pubs.

Algebra for College Students. Margaret L. Lial & Charles D. Miller. (C). 1988. text ed. 37.00 (*0-673-18866-3*) HarpCollege.

Algebra for College Students. Margaret L. Liall et al. (C). 1991. text ed. 59.00 (*0-673-46469-5*) HarpCollege.

Algebra for College Students. Margaret L. Liall et al. (C). 1991. 21.50 (*0-673-46471-7*); 18.50 (*0-673-46470-9*) HarpCollege.

Algebra for College Students. Gilbert M. Peter & C. Lee Welch. (C). 1988. text ed. 58.00 (*0-673-18798-5*) HarpCollege.

Algebra for College Students. Norman Siever. (C). 1990. text ed. 45.16 (*0-395-53281-7*) HM.

Algebra for College Students. D. Franklin Wright & Bill D. New. 592p. (C). 1990. student ed write for info. (*0-697-11107-5*) Wm C Brown Pubs.

Algebra for College Students. D. Franklin Wright & Bill D. New. 592p. (C). 1990. write for info. (*0-697-07870-1*) Wm C Brown Pubs.

Algebra for College Students. D. Franklin Wright & Bill D. New. 592p. (C). 1990. write for info. (*0-697-10879-1*) Wm C Brown Pubs.

***Algebra for College Students.** 2nd ed. Robert F. Blitzer. LC 94-37712. (C). 1995. text ed. write for info. (*0-02-310861-4*) P-H.

Algebra for College Students. 2nd ed. James Hall. 1994. text ed. 53.95 (*0-534-93348-3*) PWS Pubs.

Algebra for College Students. 2nd ed. M. A. Munem & W. Tschirhart. 609p. (C). 1988. text ed. 49.95x (*0-87901-384-2*); student ed, pap. 11.95x (*0-87901-386-9*) Worth.

Algebra for College Students. 3rd ed. R. David Gustafson & Peter D. Frisk. LC 91-13290. 672p. (C). 1992. text ed. 50.95 (*0-534-16710-1*) Brooks-Cole.

Algebra for College Students. 3rd ed. Ernest F. Haeussler, Jr. & Richard S. Paul. (C). 1985. text ed. write for info. (*0-8359-9179-2*, Reston) P-H.

Algebra for College Students. 3rd ed. Bernard Kolman & Arnold L. Shapiro. 650p. (C). 1990. text ed. 47.25 (*0-15-502162-1*) SCP.

***Algebra for College Students.** 3rd ed. Margaret L. Lial et al. LC 95-8117. (Illus.). (C). 1995. text ed. write for info. (*0-673-99061-3*) HarpCollege.

Algebra for College Students. 3rd ed. Terry H. Wesner & Harry L. Nustad. 816p. (C). 1992. text ed. write for info. (*0-697-07654-7*) Wm C Brown Pubs.

Algebra for College Students. 3rd ed. Terry H. Wesner & Harry L. Nustad. 816p. (C). 1992. write for info. (*0-697-11390-6*) Wm C Brown Pubs.

***Algebra for College Students.** 4th ed. R. David Gustafson & Peter D. Frisk. LC 94-29954. 650p. (C). 1995. text ed. 49.95 (*0-534-25188-9*) Brooks-Cole.

Algebra for College Students. 4th ed. Jerome E. Kaufmann. 752p. 1992. text ed. 55.95 (*0-534-92860-9*) PWS Pubs.

Algebra for College Students. 4th ed. Max A. Sobel & Norbert Lerner. 640p. (C). 1991. text ed. write for info. (*0-13-025933-0*) P-H.

Algebra for College Students: An Intermediate Approach. 3rd ed. Margaret H. Babcock. (Illus.). (C). 1986. pap. text ed. write for info. (*0-13-021643-7*) P-H.

Algebra for Computer Science. L. Garding & T. Tambour. (Universitext Ser.). (Illus.). 210p. 1988. pap. 43.00 (*0-387-96780-X*) Spr-Verlag.

Algebra for Everyone. Ed. by Edgar L. Edwards, Jr. LC 90-6272. (Illus.). 89p. (Orig.). 1990. pap. 7.00 (*0-87353-297-X*) NCTM.

Algebra for Everyone In-Service Handbook. David J. Glatzer & Stuart A. Choate. Ed. by Albert P. Shulte. (Illus.). 44p. (Orig.). 1992. pap. 8.00 (*0-87353-347-X*) NCTM.

Algebra-Geometric & Lie Theoretic Techniques in Systems Theory, Pt. A. Robert Herman. (Interdisciplinary Mathematics Ser.: No. 13). 256p. 1977. 40.00 (*0-915692-17-1*, 991600185) Math Sci Pr.

Algebra Geometrica. Paolo Bonasoni. Ed. & Tr. by Robert Schmidt. LC 85-80178. (Illus.). 202p. 1985. lib. bdg. 36.00 (*0-931267-01-3*) Golden Hind Pr.

Algebra I. Ed. by A. I. Kostrikin & I. R. Shafarevich. (Encyclopaedia of Mathematical Sciences Ser.: Vol. 11). (Illus.). 272p. 1989. 69.00 (*0-387-17006-5*) Spr-Verlag.

Algebra I: In a Flash. Elizabeth Burchard & Peter Bernstock. (Exambusters Ser.). 436p. (J). (gr. 7-12). 1994. pap. 9.95 (*1-881374-13-0*) Flash Blasters.

Algebra I: Rings, Modules, & Categories. Carl Faith. LC 72-96724. (Grundlehren der Mathematischen Wissenschaften Ser.: Vol. 190). (Illus.). xxiii, 565p. 1981. 89.00 (*0-387-05551-7*) Spr-Verlag.

***Algebra I: Written by Teachers for Students.** Gary L. Cavender & Marshall Falgout. (Power Algebra Ser.). (Illus.). 520p. (YA). (gr. 8-12). 1995. 30.00 (*0-9645613-0-1*) Power Pubs.

Algebra I Quick Review. Cliff Staff & Jerry Bobrow. 1994. pap. text ed. 7.95 (*0-8220-5302-0*) Cliffs.

Algebra II: Chapters Four-Seven. N. Bourbaki. 460p. 1990. 98.00 (*0-387-19375-8*) Spr-Verlag.

Algebra II: Noncommutative Rings, Identities, Vol. 18. Ed. by A. I. Kostrikin & I. R. Shafarevich. Tr. by E. Behr. (Encyclopaedia of Mathematical Sciences Ser.). (Illus.). vii, 234p. 1991. 65.00 (*0-387-18177-6*) Spr-Verlag.

Algebra II-Trigonometry: A Guided Inquiry. rev. ed. Sherman K. Stein et al. 600p. 1986. text ed. 21.20 (*1-55636-757-0*); 14.31 (*1-55636-758-9*) Sunburst Comm.

Algebra in a Localic Topos with Applications to Ring Theory. F. Borceux & G. Van Den Bossche. (Lecture Notes in Mathematics Ser.: Vol. 1038). 240p. 1983. pap. 27.00 (*0-387-12711-9*) Spr-Verlag.

***Algebra in a Technological World.** M. Kathleen Heid et al. LC 95-10254. (Addenda Ser.). 168p. (Orig.). (YA). (gr. 9-12). 1995. pap. 15.00 (*0-87353-326-7*) NCTM.

Algebra in Concrete. Mary Laycock & Reuben Schadler. (J). (gr. 6-10). 1973. pap. 7.95 (*0-918932-00-9*) Activity Resources.

Algebra IV: Infinite Groups, Linear Groups. Ed. by A. I. Kostrikin & I. R. Shafarevich. Tr. by J. Wiegold. (Encyclopaedia of Mathematical Sciences Ser.: Vol. 37). (Illus.). 215p. 1993. write for info. (*3-540-53372-9*) Spr-Verlag.

Algebra IV: Infinite Groups, Linear Groups, with Nine Figures. Ed. by A. I. Kostrikin & I. R. Shafarevich. LC 92-34231. (Encyclopaedia of Mathematical Sciences Ser.: Vol. 37). 1993. 98.00 (*0-387-53372-9*) Spr-Verlag.

Algebra L Sub T: An Interactive, Group-Oriented Approach, Pt. 1. 2nd ed. Clarence Taylor. 512p. (C). 1993. per., pap. text ed. 44.95 (*0-8403-9054-8*) Kendall-Hunt.

Algebra Lineal. 4th ed. Orlando E. Villamayor. (Serie de matematica Monografia: No. 5). 129p. (C). 1981. pap. text ed. 3.50 (*0-8270-1413-9*) OAS.

Algebra Lineal e Geometria Euclidiana. (Serie de Matematica: No. 6). (POR.). 1969. pap. 3.50 (*0-8270-6245-1*) OAS.

Algebra, Mathematical Logic, Number Theory, Topology: A Collection of Survey Papers on the 50th Anniversary of the Institute, Pt. I. Ed. by Vinogradov. LC 86-26522. (STEKLO Ser.: Vol. 168). 267p. 1986. pap. text ed. 124.00 (*0-8218-3096-1*, STEKLO-168) Am Math.

Algebra of Abu Kamil, in a Commentary by Mordecai Finzi. Abukamil Shuja Ibn Aslam. Tr. by Martin Levey. (Medieval Science Publications: No. 10). 240p. 1966. 37.50 (*0-299-03800-9*) U of Wis Pr.

***Algebra of Communicating Processes: Proceedings of ACP94, the First Workshop on the Algebra of Communicating Processes, Utrecht, The Netherlands, 16-17 May 1994.** First Workshop on the Algebra of Communicating Processes Staff. Ed. by A. Ponse et al. (Workshops in Computing Ser.). 357p. 1995. 69.00 (*3-540-19909-8*) Spr-Verlag.

***Algebra of Communicating Processes: Proceedings of the First Workshop on the Algebra of Communicating Processes, Utrecht, the Netherlands, 16-17 May 1994.** British Computer Society Staff. Ed. by A. Ponse et al. LC 94-39829. (Workshops in Computing Ser.). 357p. 1994. pap. 69.00 (*0-387-19909-8*) Spr-Verlag.

Algebra of Conscience. Vladimir A. Lefebvre. 1982. lib. bdg. 84.00 (*90-277-1301-4*) Kluwer Ac.

Algebra of Econometrics. D. S. Pollack. LC 78-27237. (Wiley Series in Probability & Mathematical Statistics). 375p. reprint ed. pap. 106.90 (*0-8357-6709-4*, 2035340) Bks Demand.

An Asterisk (*) at the beginning of an entry indicates that the title is appearing in BIP for the first time.

Algebra of Mohammed Ben Musa, 2 pts. in 1. Al K. Muhammad Ibn Musa. Ed. & Tr. by Frederic Rosen. xvi, 208p. 1986. reprint ed. lib. bdg. 63.70 (*3-487-07722-1*, Pub. by Georg Olms GW) Lubrecht & Cramer.

Algebra of Need: William Burroughs & the Gods of Death. 2nd enl. ed. Eric Mottram. 320p. 1994. pap. 19.95 (*0-7145-2916-8*) M Boyars Pubs.

Algebra of Omar Khayyam. Omar Khayyam. Ed. by Daoud S. Kasir. LC 70-177135. (Columbia University. Teachers College. Contributions to Education Ser.: No. 385). reprint ed. 37.50 (*0-404-55385-0*) AMS Pr.

Algebra of Quantics. 2nd ed. Edwin B. Elliott. LC 63-11320. 24.95 (*0-8284-0184-5*) Chelsea Pub.

Algebra of Soviet Power: Elite Circulation in the Belorussian Republic, 1966-1986. Michael E. Urban. (Cambridge Russian, Soviet & Post-Soviet Studies: No. 67). (Illus.). (C). 1989. 54.95 (*0-521-37256-9*) Cambridge U Pr.

Algebra One: Chapters 1-3. N. Bourbaki. 736p. 1989. 79.00 (*0-387-19373-1*) Spr-Verlag.

Algebra Programmed, 2 pts., Pt. I. 3rd ed. Robert H. Alwin & Robert D. Hackworth. (Illus.). 480p. 1986. pap. text ed. write for info. (*0-13-021908-8*) P-H.

Algebra Programmed, 2 pts., Pt. II. 3rd ed. Robert H. Alwin & Robert D. Hackworth. (Illus.). 480p. 1987. pap. text ed. write for info. (*0-13-021916-9*) P-H.

Algebra Programmed, Pt. 3. 3rd ed. Robert H. Alwin et al. (Illus.). 624p. (C). 1987. pap. text ed. write for info. (*0-13-021940-1*) P-H.

Algebra Seven: Combinatorial Group Theory. Applications to Geometry. Ed. by A. N. Parshin & I. R. Shafarevich. LC 92-13652. (Encyclopaedia of Mathematical Sciences Ser.: Vol. 58). 1993. 89.00 (*0-387-54700-2*) Spr-Verlag.

Algebra Some Current Trends. Ed. by L. L. Avramov & K. B. Tchakerian. (Lecture Notes in Mathematics Ser.: Vol. 1352). ix, 240p. 1988. 24.00 (*0-387-50371-4*) Spr-Verlag.

Algebra the Easy Way. 2nd ed. Douglas Downing. (Easy Way Ser.). 304p. 1989. pap. 10.95 (*0-8120-4194-1*) Barron.

Algebra, Theory of Numbers & Their Applications. Ed. by A. N. Andrianov et al. LC 80-28539. (STEKLO Ser.: No. 148). 283p. 1980. 137.00 (*0-8218-3046-5*, STEKLO-148) Am Math.

Algebra Through Practice, Bk. 4. T. S. Blyth & E. F. Robertson. 1985. pap. 12.95 (*0-521-27289-0*) Cambridge U Pr.

Algebra Thru Practice, Bk. 1. T. S. Blyth & E. F. Robertson. 1984. pap. 12.95 (*0-521-27285-8*) Cambridge U Pr.

Algebra Thru Practice, Bk. 2. T. S. Blyth & E. F. Robertson. 1984. pap. 12.95 (*0-521-27286-6*) Cambridge U Pr.

Algebra Thru Practice, Bk. 3. T. S. Blyth & E. F. Robertson. 1984. pap. 12.95 (*0-521-27288-2*) Cambridge U Pr.

Algebra Thru Practice, Bk. 5. T. S. Blyth & E. F. Robertson. 1985. pap. 12.95 (*0-521-27290-4*) Cambridge U Pr.

Algebra Thru Practice, Bk. 6. T. S. Blyth & E. F. Robertson. 1985. pap. 12.95 (*0-521-27291-2*) Cambridge U Pr.

Algebra Two - Trigonometry: In a Flash. Elizabeth Burchard & Matthew Soroka. (Exambusters Ser.). 450p. (J). (gr. 7-12). 1994. pap. 9.95 (*1-881374-14-9*) Flash Blasters.

Algebra V: Homological Algebra. Ed. by A. I. Kostrikin & I. R. Shararevich. Tr. by S. I. Gel'fand & Yu I. Manin. LC 93-33442. (Encyclopaedia of Mathematical Sciences Ser.: Vol. 38). 227p. 1994. 99.00 (*0-387-53373-7*) Spr-Verlag.

Algebra VI: Combinatorial & Asymptotic Methods of Algebra - Nonassociative Structures. Ed. by A. I. Kostrikin & I. R. Shafarevich. Tr. by R. Dimitric. LC 93-25596. (Encyclopaedia of Mathematical Sciences Ser.: Vol. 57). (Illus.). 272p. 1994. 99.00 (*0-387-54699-5*) Spr-Verlag.

***Algebra with Applications.** William Adams. 275p. (C). 1995. per., pap. text ed. 29.95 (*0-7872-0996-1*) Kendall-Hunt.

Algebra with Trigonometry. Richard N. Aufmann et al. (C). 1991. write for info. (*0-395-54437-8*) HM Soft Schl Col Div.

Algebra with Trigonometry for College Students. 2nd ed. Charles P. McKeague. 714p. (C). 1988. text ed. 42.75 (*0-15-502120-6*) SCP.

Algebra with Trigonometry for College Students. 3rd ed. Jerome E. Kaufmann. 896p. 1992. text ed. 55.95 (*0-534-92840-4*) PWS Pubs.

Algebra 1: An Incremental Development. 2nd ed. John H. Saxon, Jr. (YA). (gr. 7-12). 1990. text ed. 31.00 (*0-939798-42-5*); teacher ed 31.00 (*0-939798-43-3*); disk 180.00 (*0-939798-96-4*); 39.00 (*0-939798-44-1*); 17.00 (*0-939798-98-0*) Saxon Pubs OK.

***Algebra 1 Handbook: 1000 Problems Solved Simply & Clearly.** Alice M. Martin. 200p. 1995. pap. text ed. 12.95 (*0-9642188-8-7*) Four Seasns.

Algebra 1-2: An Incremental Development. 2nd ed. John H. Saxon, Jr. (YA). (gr. 7-12). 1990. text ed. 31.00 (*0-939798-45-X*); teacher ed 31.00 (*0-939798-46-8*); disk 180.00 (*0-939798-95-6*); 39.00 (*0-939798-47-6*); 17.00 (*1-56577-000-5*) Saxon Pubs OK.

Algebra 2: An Incremental Development. John H. Saxon, Jr. (YA). (gr. 9-12). 1991. teacher ed 33.75 (*0-939798-63-8*) Saxon Pubs OK.

Algebra 2: An Incremental Development. rev. ed. John H. Saxon, Jr. (YA). (gr. 9-12). 1991. disk 180.00 (*0-939798-97-2*); 39.00 (*0-939798-64-6*); 17.00 (*0-939798-99-9*) Saxon Pubs OK.

Algebra 2: An Incremental Development. 2nd rev. ed. John H. Saxon, Jr. (YA). (gr. 9-12). 1991. student ed 33.75 (*0-939798-62-X*) Saxon Pubs OK.

Algebraic Algorithms & Error-Correcting Codes. Ed. by J. Calmet. (Lecture Notes in Computer Science Ser.: Vol. 229). vii, 416p. 1986. pap. 45.00 (*0-387-16776-5*) Spr-Verlag.

Algebraic Analysis. Dauta Przeworska-Rolewicz. (C). 1988. lib. bdg. 229.50 (*90-277-2443-1*) Kluwer Ac.

Algebraic Analysis: Papers Dedicated to Professor Mikio Sato on the Occasion of His Sixtieth Birthday, Vol. 1. Ed. by Masaki Kashiwara & Takahiro Kawai. 472p. 1989. text ed. 97.00 (*0-12-400465-2*) Acad Pr.

Algebraic Analysis: Papers Dedicated to Professor Mikio Sato on the Occasion of His Sixtieth Birthday, Vol. 2. Ed. by Masaki Kashiwar & Takahiro Kawai. 480p. 1989. text ed. 97.00 (*0-12-400466-0*) Acad Pr.

Algebraic Analysis, Geometry & Number Theory: Proceedings of the JAMI Inaugural Conference. Ed. by Jun-Ichi Igusa. (American Journal of Mathematics Supplement Ser.). 448p. 1989. text ed. 55.00x (*0-8018-3841-X*) Johns Hopkins.

***Algebraic Analysis of Solvable Lattice Models.** Michio Jimbo & Tetsuji Miwa. LC 94-23840. (Regional Conference Series in Mathematics: No. 85). 1994. pap. 38.00 (*0-8218-0320-4*) Am Math.

Algebraic Analysis of Storage Fragmentation. Terry Betteridge. LC 82-11194. (Computer Science: Systems Programming Ser.: No. 15). (Illus.). 232p. reprint ed. pap. 66.20 (*0-8357-1364-4*, 2070359) Bks Demand.

Algebraic & Analytic Aspects of Operator Algebras. I. Kaplansky. LC 74-145635. (CBMS Regional Conference Series in Mathematics: Vol. 1). 20p. 1980. reprint ed. 17.00 (*0-8218-1650-0*, CMBS/1) Am Math.

***Algebraic & Analytic Geometry of Fans.** Carlos Andradas & Jesus M. Ruiz. LC 95-1556. (Memoirs Ser.: No. 553). 1995. write for info. (*0-8218-2612-3*) Am Math.

Algebraic & Automata-Theoretic Properties of Formal Languages. S. Ginsburg. LC 73-86082. (Fundamental Studies in Computer Science: Vol. 2). 313p. 1975. 77.00 (*0-444-10586-7*, North Holland) Elsevier.

Algebraic & Combinatorial Methods in Operations Research: Proceedings of the Workshop on Algebraic Structures in Operations Research. R. E. Burkard et al. (Mathematics Studies, Vol. 95; Annals of Discrete Mathematics: No. 19). 382p. 1984. 95.00 (*0-444-87571-9*, North Holland) Elsevier.

Algebraic & Diagrammatic Methods in Many-Fermion Theory. Frank E. Harris et al. (Illus.). 416p. (C). 1992. text ed. 75.00 (*0-19-506130-6*) OUP.

Algebraic & Geometric Combinatorics. Ed. by E. Mendelsohn. 378p. 1982. pap. 125.75 (*0-444-86365-6*, I-194-82, North Holland) Elsevier.

Algebraic & Geometric Methods in Linear Systems Theory. Ed. by Christopher I. Byrnes & Clyde F. Martin. LC 80-27354. (Lectures in Applied Mathematics: Vol. 18). 327p. 1980. 44.00 (*0-8218-1118-5*, LAM-18) Am Math.

Algebraic & Geometric Methods in Nonlinear Control Theory. Ed. by M. Fliess & Michiel Hazewinkel. 1986. lib. bdg. 166.50 (*90-277-2286-2*) Kluwer Ac.

Algebraic & Geometric Structures in Current Algebra Theory. Robert Hermann. LC 77-133441. 120p. 1970. 22.00 (*0-403-04504-5*) Scholarly.

Algebraic & Geometric Topology. Ed. by A. A. Ranicki et al. (Lecture Notes in Mathematics Ser.: Vol. 1126). v, 423p. 1985. pap. 49.60 (*0-387-15235-0*) Spr-Verlag.

Algebraic & Geometric Topology, 2 pts., Pt. 1. 3rd ed. Ed. by James R. Milgram. LC 78-14304. (Proceedings of Symposia in Pure Mathematics Ser., Humboldt State University, Arcata, CA, July 29-August 16, 1974: Vol. 32). 412p. 1989. 36.00 (*0-8218-1432-X*, PSPUM 32.1) Am Math.

Algebraic & Geometric Topology, 2 pts., Pt. 2. 3rd ed. Ed. by James R. Milgram. LC 78-14304. (Proceedings of Symposia in Pure Mathematics Ser., Humboldt State University, Arcata, CA, July 29-August 16, 1974: Vol. 32). 322p. 1989. 36.00 (*0-8218-1433-8*, PSPUM 32.2) Am Math.

Algebraic & Geometric Topology, 2 pts., Set. 3rd ed. Ed. by James R. Milgram. LC 78-14304. (Proceedings of Symposia in Pure Mathematics Ser., Humboldt State University, Arcata, CA, July 29-August 16, 1974: Vol. 32). 734p. 1989. 60.00 (*0-8218-1473-7*, PSPUM 32) Am Math.

Algebraic & Logic Programming. Ed. by J. Grabowski et al. (Lecture Notes in Computer Science Ser.: Vol. 343). 278p. 1989. pap. 37.00 (*0-387-50667-5*, 2573) Spr-Verlag.

Algebraic & Logic Programming: Proceedings of the Third International Conference, Pisa, Italy, September 1992. Ed. by H. Kirchner & Giorgio Levi. LC 92-23272. (Lecture Notes in Computer Science Ser.: Vol. 632). ix, 457p. 1992. pap. write for info. (*3-540-55873-X*); pap. 67.00 (*0-387-55873-X*) Spr-Verlag.

***Algebraic & Logic Programming: Proceedings of the 4th International Conference, ALP '94, Madrid, Spain, September 1994.** Giorgio Levi & Mario R. Artalejo. LC 94-33286. (Series Lecture Notes in Computer Science Ser.: 850). 1994. write for info. (*0-387-58431-5*) Spr-Verlag.

***Algebraic & Logic Programming: 4th International Conference, ALP '94, Madrid, Spain, September 14 16, 1994. Proceedings.** Ed. by G. Levi & M. Rodriguez-Artalejo. (Lecture Notes in Computer Science Ser.: Vol. 850). 304p. 1994. pap. 47.00 (*3-540-58431-5*) Spr-Verlag.

Algebraic & Structural Automata Theory. M. P. Heble. (Annals of Discrete Mathematics Ser.: No. 44). 564p. 1989. 131.75 (*0-685-27176-5*, North Holland) Elsevier.

Algebraic & Structural Automata Theory. Mikolajczak. (Annals of Discrete Mathematics Ser.: Vol. 44). 1991. 143.00 (*0-444-87458-5*, ADM 44) Elsevier.

Algebraic Approach to Simple Quantum Systems: With Applications to Perturbation Theory. Barry G. Adams. (Illus.). 467p. 1994. Incl. 3 1/2" diskette. pap. 49.00 (*0-387-57801-3*) Spr-Verlag.

Algebraic Approaches to Nuclear Structure: Interacting Boson & Fermion Models. Ed. by Richard F. Casten. LC 92-26649. (Contemporary Concepts in Physics Ser.: Vol. 6). 1993. text ed. 88.00 (*3-7186-0537-6*); pap. text ed. 38.00 (*3-7186-0538-4*) Gordon & Breach.

Algebraic Approaches to Program Semantics. Ernest G. Manes & Michael A. Arbib. (Texts & Monographs in Computer Science). (Illus.). 355p. 1986. 85.00 (*0-387-96324-3*) Spr-Verlag.

Algebraic Calculation of the Rainbow. Benedictus De Spinoza. (Illus.). 26p. 1963. reprint ed. text ed. 38.50 (*90-6004-175-5*, Pub. by B De Graaf NE) Coronet Bks.

Algebraic Calculation of the Rainbow & Calculation of Chances. Spinoza. Ed. by Michael Petry. 1986. lib. bdg. 89.00 (*90-247-3149-6*) Kluwer Ac.

Algebraic Characterization of Geometric Four-Manifolds. J. A. Hillman. (London Mathematical Society Lecture Note Ser.: No. 198). 180p. (C). 1994. pap. 34.95 (*0-521-46778-0*) Cambridge U Pr.

Algebraic Cobordism & K-Theory. V. P. Snaith. LC 79-17981. (Memoirs Ser.: No. 21/221). 152p. 1979. pap. 19.00 (*0-8218-2221-7*, MEMO 21/221) Am Math.

Algebraic Cobordism & K-Theory. Victor P. Snaith. LC 79-17981. (Memoirs of the American Mathematical Society Ser.: No. 221). 159p. reprint ed. pap. 45.40 (*0-7837-5926-6*, 2045725) Bks Demand.

Algebraic Coding: First French-Israeli Workshop, Paris, France, July 1993. Ed. by G. Cohen et al. LC 94-8268. (Lecture Notes in Computer Science Ser.: Vol. 781). xii, 326p. 1994. pap. 45.00 (*0-387-57843-9*) Spr-Verlag.

Algebraic Coding: First French-Soviet Workshop, Paris, France, July 22-24, 1991 Proceedings. Ed. by G. Cohen et al. (Lecture Notes in Computer Science Ser.: Vol. 573). x, 158p. 1992. pap. 35.00 (*0-387-55130-1*) Spr-Verlag.

Algebraic Coding Theory. rev. ed. Elwyn R. Berlekamp. 474p. 1984. reprint ed. pap. 40.80 (*0-89412-063-8*) Aegean Park Pr.

Algebraic Coding Theory & Application. Ed. by G. Longo & C. R. Hartmann. (CISM Courses & Lectures Ser.: Vol. 258). (Illus.). 529p. 1980. pap. 68.00 (*0-387-81544-9*) Spr-Verlag.

Algebraic Combinatorics. C. D. Godsil. LC 92-41097. 1993. 29.95 (*0-412-04131-6*) Chapman & Hall.

Algebraic Computing in Control: Proceedings of the First European Conference Paris, March 13-15, 1991. Ed. by G. Jacob & F. Lamnabhi-Lagarrigue. (Lecture Notes in Control & Information Sciences Ser.: Vol. 165). (Illus.). 392p. 1992. pap. 76.00 (*0-387-54408-9*) Spr-Verlag.

***Algebraic Computing in General Relativity: Lecture Notes from the First Brazilian School on Computer Algebra, Vol. 2.** Malcolm A. MacCallum et al. Ed. by Marcelo J. Reboucas & Waldir L. Roque. 400p. 1995. text ed. 63.00 (*0-19-853646-1*) OUP.

Algebraic Computing with REDUCE. Malcolm A. MacCallum & Francis J. Wright. 320p. 1992. 59.95 (*0-19-853444-2*); pap. 29.95 (*0-19-853443-4*) OUP.

Algebraic Curves. R. J. Walker. LC 78-11956. x, 201p. 1991. reprint ed. pap. 32.00 (*0-387-90361-5*) Spr-Verlag.

Algebraic Curves: An Introduction to Algebraic Geometry. William Fulton. (Math Lecture Notes Ser.: No. 30). (C). 1974. pap. 34.50 (*0-8053-3082-8*, Adv Bk Prog) Addison-Wesley.

Algebraic Curves & Projective Geometry. E. Ballico & C. Ciliberto. (Lecture Notes in Mathematics Ser.: Vol. 1389). v, 288p. 1989. pap. 37.30 (*0-387-51509-7*, 3437) Spr-Verlag.

***Algebraic Curves & Riemann Surfaces.** Rick Miranda. LC 95-1947. (Graduate Studies in Mathematics: Vol. 5). 1995. write for info. (*0-8218-0268-2*) Am Math.

Algebraic Curves over Finite Fields: Error-Correcting Codes & Exponential Sums. Ed. by Carlos Moreno. (Tracts in Mathematics Ser.: No. 97). 272p. (C). 1991. 59.95 (*0-521-34252-X*) Cambridge U Pr.

Algebraic Curves over Finite Fields: Error-Correcting Codes & Exponential Sums. Carlos Moreno. (Tracts in Mathematics Ser.: No. 97). 255p. (C). 1994. pap. 27.95 (*0-521-45901-X*) Cambridge U Pr.

***Algebraic Cycles & Hodge Theory: Lectures Given at the 2nd Session of the Centro Internazionale Matematico Estivo (C. I. M. E.) Held in Torino, Italy, June 21-29, 1993.** M. Green et al. Ed. by A. Albano & F. Bardelli. LC 94-39109. (Lecture Notes in Mathematics: Vol. 1594). 1994. 45.00 (*3-540-58692-X*) Spr-Verlag.

***Algebraic Cycles & Hodge Theory: Lectures Given at the 2nd Session of The Centro Internazionale Mathematicoestivo (C. I. M. E.) Held in Torino, Italy, June 21-29, 1993.** M. Green et al. Ed. by A. Albano & F. Bardelli. LC 94-39109. (Lecture Notes in Mathematics: Vol. 1594). 1994. write for info. (*0-387-58692-X*) Spr-Verlag.

Algebraic D-Modules. Armand Borel. (Perspectives in Mathematics Ser.). 368p. 1987. text ed. 66.00 (*0-12-117740-8*) Acad Pr.

Algebraic Eigenvalue Problem. J. Harvie Wilkinson. (Monographs on Numerical Analysis). 680p. 1988. pap. 55.00 (*0-19-853418-3*) OUP.

Algebraic Extensions of Fields. Paul J. McCarthy. 1991. pap. 6.95 (*0-486-66651-4*) Dover.

Algebraic, Extremal & Metric Combinatorics 1986. Ed. by M. M. Deza et al. (London Mathematical Society Lecture Note Ser.: No. 131). 300p. 1988. pap. 47.95 (*0-521-35923-6*) Cambridge U Pr.

Algebraic Fantasies & Realistic Romances: More Masters of Science Fiction. Brian M. Stableford. LC 94-31347. (Milford Series: Popular Writers of Today: Vol. 54). 128p. 1995. lib. bdg. 25.00x (*0-89370-183-1*); pap. 15.00x (*0-89370-283-8*) Borgo Pr.

Algebraic Function Fields & Codes. Henning Stichtenoth. LC 93-7182. (Universitext Ser.). 260p. 1993. pap. 34.00 (*0-387-56489-6*) Spr-Verlag.

Algebraic Functions. Kenkichi Iwasawa. Tr. by Goro Kato. LC 92-39922. (Translations of Mathematical Monographs: Vol. 118). 287p. 1993. 131.00 (*0-8218-4595-0*) Am Math.

Algebraic-Geometric Codes. M. A. Tsfasman & S. G. Vladut. (C). 1991. lib. bdg. 229.00 (*0-7923-0727-5*) Kluwer Ac.

Algebraic Geometry. Ed. by I. Dolgachev. (Lecture Notes in Mathematics Ser.: Vol. 1008). 138p. 1983. pap. 22.00 (*0-387-12337-7*) Spr-Verlag.

Algebraic Geometry. Ed. by Jun-Ichi Igusa. LC 77-4603. (Centennial Lectures Ser.). 140p. 1977. text ed. 17.50 (*0-8018-2021-9*) Johns Hopkins.

Algebraic Geometry. Masayoshi Miyanishi. LC 94-2018. (Translations of Mathematical Monographs: Vol. 135). 1994. write for info. (*0-8218-4615-9*) Am Math.

Algebraic Geometry. Ed. by M. Raynaud & T. Shioda. (Lecture Notes in Mathematics Ser.: Vol. 1016). 528p. 1983. pap. 49.60 (*0-387-12685-6*) Spr-Verlag.

Algebraic Geometry. Ed. by A. J. Sommese et al. (Lecture Notes in Mathematics Ser.: Vol. 1417). v, 320p. 1990. pap. 44.20 (*0-387-52217-4*) Spr-Verlag.

Algebraic Geometry. rev. ed. R. Hartshorne. (Graduate Texts in Mathematics Ser.: Vol. 52). (Illus.). 496p. 1993. 54.50 (*0-387-90244-9*) Spr-Verlag.

Algebraic Geometry: A First Course. James R. Harris. Ed. by J. H. Ewing et al. (Graduate Texts in Mathematics Ser.: Vol. 133). (Illus.). 344p. 1993. 39.95 (*0-387-97716-3*) Spr-Verlag.

Algebraic Geometry: Proceedings of the Conference at Berlin, 9-15 March, 1988. Ed. by H. Kurke & J. H. Steenbrink. (C). 1990. lib. bdg. 109.50 (*0-7923-0934-0*) Kluwer Ac.

Algebraic Geometry: Proceedings of the U. S.-U. S. S. R. Symposium Held in Chicago, June 20-July 14, 1989. Ed. by S. Bloch et al. (Lecture Notes in Mathematics Ser.: Vol. 1479). vii, 300p. 1991. pap. 41.00 (*0-387-54456-9*) Spr-Verlag.

Algebraic Geometry: Sendai, Nineteen Eighty-Five. Tadao Oda. (Advanced Studies in Pure Mathematics: Vol. 10). 794p. 1988. 231.00 (*0-444-70313-6*, North Holland) Elsevier.

Algebraic Geometry: Sitges (Barcelona) 1983. Ed. by E. Casa-Alvero et al. (Lecture Notes in Mathematics Ser.: Vol. 1124). xi, 416p. 1985. pap. 49.60 (*0-387-15232-6*) Spr-Verlag.

Algebraic Geometry: Sundance 1988. Harbourne & Speiser. LC 90-29884. (CONM Ser.: Vol. 116). 146p. 1991. 59.00 (*0-8218-5124-1*, CONM-116) Am Math.

Algebraic Geometry - Arcata 1974. Pure Mathematics Symposium Staff. Ed. by Robin Hartshorne. LC 75-9530. (Proceedings of Symposia in Pure Mathematics Ser., Humboldt State University, Arcata, CA, July 29-August 16, 1974: Vol. 29). 642p. 1982. 62.00 (*0-8218-1429-X*, PSPUM-29) Am Math.

Algebraic Geometry & Algebraic Number Theory. K. Q. Feng. (Nankai Series in Pure, Applied Mathematics & Theoretical Physics). 250p. 1992. text ed. 81.00 (*981-02-0946-0*) World Scientific Pub.

Algebraic Geometry & Commutative Algebra, Vol. 1: In Honor of Masayoshi Nagata. Ed. by Hiroaki Hijikata et al. 400p. 1989. text ed. 116.00 (*0-12-348031-0*) Acad Pr.

Algebraic Geometry & Commutative Algebra, Vol. 2: In Honor of Masayoshi Nagata. Ed. by Hiroaki Hijikata et al. 400p. 1989. text ed. 116.00 (*0-12-348032-9*) Acad Pr.

Algebraic Geometry & Complex Analysis. Ed. by E. Ramirez de Arellano. (Lecture Notes in Mathematics Ser.: Vol. 1414). vi, 180p. 1990. pap. 30.60 (*0-387-52175-5*, 3875) Spr-Verlag.

Algebraic Geometry & Its Applications. Ed. by A. I. Kostrikin et al. LC 85-28762. (Proceedings of the Steklov Institute of Mathematics Ser.: Vol. 165). 251p. 1986. reprint ed. 115.00 (*0-8218-3092-9*, STEKLO/165C) Am Math.

Algebraic Geometry & It's Applications: Collection of Papers from Shreeram Abhyankar's 60th Birthday Conference. Ed. by Chanderjit Bajaj. LC 93-33433. 1994. 69.00 (*0-387-94176-2*) Spr-Verlag.

Algebraic Geometry & Its Applications: Proceedings of the 8th Algebraic Geometry Conference, Yaroslavl 1992; a Publication from the Steklov Institute of Mathematics; Adviser: Sergeev, Armen. Ed. by Alexander Tikhomirov & Andrej Tyurin. (Aspects of Mathematics Ser.: Vol. E25). xii, 251p. 1994. 63.00 (*3-528-06599-0*, Pub. by Vieweg & Sohn GW) Ballen Bkslr.

Algebraic Geometry & Related Topics. Ed. by Y. Namikawa et al. (Series in Algebraic Geometry). 208p. 1994. 22.00 (*1-57146-013-6*) Intl Pr Boston.

Algebraic Geometry & Theta Functions. Arthur B. Coble. LC 30-12679. (American Mathematical Society, Colloquium Publications: No. 10). 290p. reprint ed. pap. 82.70 (*0-8357-3329-7*, 2039553) Bks Demand.

Algebraic Geometry-Bowdoin 1985, 2 pts., Pt. I. S. P. Bloch. LC 87-12306. (PSPUM Ser.: Vol. 46). 481p. 1987. 74.00 (*0-8218-1476-1*, PSPUM-46.1) Am Math.

Algebraic Geometry-Bowdoin 1985, 2 pts., Pt. II. S. P. Bloch. LC 87-12306. (PSPUM Ser.: Vol. 46). 513p. 1987. pap. 80.00 (*0-8218-1480-X*, PSPUM-46.2) Am Math.

Algebraic Geometry-Bowdoin 1985, 2 pts., Set. S. P. Bloch. LC 87-12306. (PSPUM Ser.: Vol. 46). 994p. 1987. 146.00 (*0-8218-1481-8*) Am Math.

A

An Asterisk (*) at the beginning of an entry indicates that the title is appearing in BIP for the first time. 183

Algebraic Geometry, Bucharest 1982: Proceedings of the International Conference, Held in Bucharest, Romania, August 2-7, 1982. Ed. by L. Badescu & D. Popescu. (Lecture Notes in Mathematics Ser.: Vol. 1056). vii, 380p. 1984. 37.00 (*0-387-12930-8*) Spr-Verlag.

Algebraic Geometry for Scientists & Engineers. Shreeram S. Abhyanker. LC 90-815. (SURV Ser.: Vol. 35). 295p. 1992. 90.00 (*0-8218-1535-0*, SURV-35) Am Math.

***Algebraic Geometry I: Complex Projective Varieties.** 2nd ed. David Mumford. LC 94-39113. (Classics in Mathematics Ser.). 1994. write for info. (*3-540-58657-1*) Spr-Verlag.

Algebraic Geometry IV: Linear Algebraic Groups, Invariant Theory. Ed. by A. N. Parshin & I. R. Shafarevich. LC 93-13928. (Encyclopaedia of Mathematical Sciences Ser.: Vol. 55). (Illus.). 291p. 1994. 99.00 (*0-387-54682-0*) Spr-Verlag.

Algebraic Geometry 1: Algebraic Curves, Algebraic Manifolds & Schemes. Ed. by I. R. Shafarevich. LC 93-4995. (Encyclopaedia of Mathematical Sciences Ser.: vol. 23). 1994. 99.00 (*0-387-51995-5*) Spr-Verlag.

Algebraic Graph Theory. 2nd ed. Norman Biggs. LC 73-86042. (Cambridge Mathematical Library). (Illus.). 214p. (C). 1994. pap. 24.95 (*0-521-45897-8*) Cambridge U Pr.

Algebraic Groups: Lecture Notes in Mathematics, Vol. 1271. Ed. by A. M. Cohen et al. 284p. 1987. pap. 39.30 (*0-387-18234-9*) Spr-Verlag.

Algebraic Groups & Class Fields. Jean-Pierre Serre. (Graduate Texts in Mathematics Ser.: Vol. 107). ix, 207p. 1987. 39.00 (*0-387-96648-X*) Spr-Verlag.

Algebraic Groups & Discontinuous Subgroups: Proceedings. Pure Mathematics Symposium Staff. Ed. by A. Borel & G. D. Mostow. LC 66-18581. (Proceedings of Symposia in Pure Mathematics Ser., Humboldt State University, Arcata, CA, July 29-August 16, 1974: Vol. 9). 426p. 1986. reprint ed. pap. 49.00 (*0-8218-1409-5*, PSPUM-9) Am Math.

Algebraic Groups & Modular Lie Algebras. J. E. Humphreys. (Memoirs Ser.: No. 1/71). 76p. 1967. pap. 16.00 (*0-8218-1271-8*, MEMO 1/71) Am Math.

Algebraic Groups & Number Theory. Vladimir Platonov & Andrei Rapinchuk. Tr. by Rachel Rowen. LC 92-35876. (Pure & Applied Mathematics Ser.: Vol. 139). (Illus.). 614p. (ENG & RUS.). 1993. text ed. 99.95 (*0-12-558180-7*) Acad Pr.

Algebraic Groups & Related Topics: Proceedings of Symposium Held in Kyoto, Japan 5-7 Sept. 1983 & Nagoya, Japan 11-14 Oct 1983. Ed. by R. Hotta. (Advanced Studies in Pure Mathematics: Vol. 6). 544p. 1985. 210.25 (*0-444-87711-8*, North Holland) Elsevier.

Algebraic Groups & Their Generalizations, 2 vols., Set. Ed. by William J. Haboush & Brian J. Parshall. LC 93-28132. (Proceedings of Symposia in Pure Mathematics Ser., Humboldt State University, Arcata, CA, July 29-August 16, 1974). 1994. 133.00 (*0-8218-1497-4*) Am Math.

Algebraic Groups & Their Generalizations, Vol. 1. Ed. by William J. Haboush & Brian J. Parshall. LC 93-28132. (Proceedings of Symposia in Pure Mathematics Ser., Humboldt State University, Arcata, CA, July 29-August 16, 1974). 1994. 68.00 (*0-8218-1540-7*) Am Math.

Algebraic Groups & Their Generalizations, Vol. 2. Ed. by William J. Haboush & Brian J. Parshall. LC 93-28132. (Proceedings of the Symposia in Pure Mathematics Ser.). 1994. 72.00 (*0-8218-1541-5*) Am Math.

Algebraic Homotopy. Hans J. Baues. 400p. 1989. 125.00 (*0-521-33376-8*) Cambridge U Pr.

Algebraic Hyperstructures & Applications. Ed. by T. Vougiouklis. 236p. (C). 1991. text ed. 84.00 (*981-02-0479-5*) World Scientific Pub.

***Algebraic Hyperstructures & Applications: Proceedings of the Fifth International Congress on Algebraic Hyperstructures & Applications.** Mirela Stefanescu. (Illus.). 276p. (Orig.). (C). 1994. pap. 80.00 (*0-911767-76-2*) Hadronic Pr Inc.

Algebraic Ideas in Ergodic Theory. K. Schmidt. LC 90-877. (CBMS Regional Conference Series in Mathematics: No. 76). 94p. 1990. pap. text ed. 31.00 (*0-8218-0727-7*, CBMS-76) Am Math.

Algebraic Information Theory. V. D. Goppa & E. N. Gozodnichev. (Series on Soviet & East European Mathematics: No. 11). 200p. 1994. text ed. 48.00 (*981-02-0943-6*) World Scientific Pub.

***Algebraic Introduction to Complex Projective Geometry Vol. 1: Commutative Algebra.** Christian Peskine. (Studies in Advanced Mathematics: No. 47). 240p. (C). Date not set. write for info. (*0-521-48072-8*) Cambridge U Pr.

***Algebraic K-Theory.** Hvedri Inassaridze. LC 94-35621. (Mathematics & Its Application: Vol. 311). 1994. lib. bdg. 189.00 (*0-7923-3185-0*) Kluwer Ac.

Algebraic K-Theory. V. Srinivas. (Progress in Mathematics Ser.). 450p. 1990. 42.50 (*0-8176-3529-7*) Birkhauser.

Algebraic K-Theory. A. A. Suslin. (ADVSOV Ser.: No. 4). 170p. 1991. 83.00 (*0-8218-4103-3*, ADVSOV-4) Am Math.

Algebraic K-Theory. 2nd ed. V. Srinivas. LC 93-9417. (Progress in Mathematics Ser.: Vol. 90). (Illus.). 380p. 1993. 49.50 (*0-8176-3702-8*) Birkhauser.

Algebraic K-Theory: Connections with Geometry & Topology. Ed. by J. F. Jardine & V. P. Snaith. (C). 1989. lib. bdg. 175.50 (*0-7923-0292-3*) Kluwer Ac.

Algebraic K-Theory & Algebraic Number Theory. Ed. by M. R. Stein & R. K. Dennis. LC 88-38151. (CONM Ser.: Vol. 83). 488p. 1989. pap. 57.00 (*0-8218-5090-3*, CONM-83) Am Math.

Algebraic K-Theory & Algebraic Topology: Proceedings of the NATO Advanced Study Institute, Lake Louise, Alberta, Canada, December 12-16, 1991. Ed. by P. G. Goerss. (NATO Advanced Science Institutes Series C: Mathematical & Physical Sciences). 340p. (C). 1993. lib. bdg. 156.00 (*0-7923-2391-2*) Kluwer Ac.

Algebraic K-Theory & Its Applications. Jonathan Rosenberg. LC 94-8077. (Graduate Texts in Mathematics Ser.: Vol. 147). (Illus.). 408p. 1994. 49.95 (*0-387-94248-3*) Spr-Verlag.

Algebraic K-Theory & Localised Stable Homotopy Theory. V. P. Snaith. LC 83-3726. (Memoirs of the American Mathematical Society Ser.: No. 43/280). 102p. 1983. pap. 19.00 (*0-8218-2280-2*, MEMO 43/280) Am Math.

Algebraic K-Theory, Commutative Algebra, & Algebraic Geometry. R. K. Dennis et al. LC 91-45311. 230p. 1992. 59.00 (*0-8218-5130-6*, CONM-126) Am Math.

Algebraic K-Theory, Number Theory, Geometry & Analysis: Proceedings of July 26-30, 1982. International Conference, Bielefeld, West Germany Staff. Ed. by A. Bak. (Lecture Notes in Mathematics Ser.: Vol. 1046). ix, 464p. 1984. pap. 48.40 (*0-387-12891-3*) Spr-Verlag.

Algebraic K-Theory 1: Higher K-Theories. Ed. by H. Bass. LC 73-13419. (Lecture Notes in Mathematics Ser.: Vol. 341). xv, 335p. 1986. pap. 49.30 (*0-387-06434-6*) Spr-Verlag.

Algebraic K-Theory 2: Classical Algebraic K-Theory, & Connections with Arithmetic. Ed. by H. Bass. LC 73-13420. (Lecture Notes in Mathematics Ser.: Vol. 342). xv, 527p. 1986. pap. 67.50 (*0-387-06435-4*) Spr-Verlag.

Algebraic L-Theory & Topological Manifolds. A. Ranicki. (Tracts in Mathematics Ser.: No. 102). 350p. (C). 1993. 69.95 (*0-521-42024-5*) Cambridge U Pr.

Algebraic Logic. P. R. Halmos. LC 61-17955. 1962. 18.95 (*0-8284-0154-3*) Chelsea Pub.

Algebraic Logic: Problem Books in Mathematics. S. G. Gindikin. Tr. by R. H. Silverman. (Illus.). xviii, 356p. 1985. 59.90 (*0-387-96179-8*) Spr-Verlag.

Algebraic Logic & Predicate Functors. Willard V. Quine. LC 71-157092. 1971. reprint ed. pap. text ed. 3.95 (*0-672-61267-4*) Irvington.

Algebraic Logic & Universal Algebra in Computer Science: Conference, Ames, Iowa, U. S. A., June 1-4, 1988 Proceedings. Ed. by C. H. Bergman et al. (Lecture Notes in Computer Science Ser.: Vol. 425). xii, 292p. 1990. pap. 31.00 (*0-387-97288-9*) Spr-Verlag.

Algebraic Method: Theory, Tools & Applications. Ed. by M. Wirsing & J. A. Bergstra. (Lecture Notes in Computer Science Ser.: Vol. 394). vi, 558p. 1989. pap. 59.00 (*0-387-51698-0*, 3576) Spr-Verlag.

Algebraic Methodology & Software Technology (AMAST '91) Proceedings of the Second International Conference on Algebraic Methodology & Software Technology, Iowa City, U. S. A. 22-25 May 1991. Ed. by Maurice Nivat et al. LC 92-33753. (Workshops in Computing Ser.). 1993. 89.00 (*0-387-19797-4*) Spr-Verlag.

Algebraic Methodology Software Technology (AMAST'91) Proceedings of the Third International Conference on Algebraic Methodology & Software Technology. M. Nivat et al. LC 93-38672. (Workshops in Computing Ser.). 1994. 76.00 (*0-387-19852-0*) Spr-Verlag.

Algebraic Methods for Toeplitz-Like Matrices & Operators. Ed. by Collet's Holdings, Ltd. Staff. 1986. 63.00 (*0-317-46570-8*, Pub. by Collets UK) Pro-Am Music.

Algebraic Methods for Toeplitz-Like Matrices & Operators. Heinig & Rost. (Operator Theory Ser.: No. 13). 1985. text ed. 61.00 (*0-8176-1643-8*) Birkhauser.

Algebraic Methods II: Theory, Tools & Applications. Ed. by J. A. Bergstra & Loe M. Feijs. (Lecture Notes in Computer Science Ser.: Vol. 490). vi, 434p. 1991. pap. 43.00 (*0-387-53912-3*) Spr-Verlag.

Algebraic Methods in Molecular & Nuclear Structure Physics. Alejandro Frank & Pieter Van Isacker. LC 93-41843. 488p. 1994. text ed. 69.95 (*0-471-52640-1*) Wiley.

Algebraic Methods in Nonlinear Perturbation Theory. V. N. Bogaevski & A. Y. Povzner. (Applied Mathematical Sciences Ser.: Vol. 88). (Illus.). 263p. 1991. 65.00 (*0-387-97491-1*) Spr-Verlag.

Algebraic Methods in Operator Theory. Ed. by Raul E. Curto et al. LC 94-5179. 1994. 84.50 (*0-8176-3745-1*) Birkhauser.

Algebraic Methods in Quantum Chemistry & Physics. Francisco M. Fernandez & Eduardo A. Castro. 208p. 1995. 89.95 (*0-8493-8292-0*, 8292) CRC Pr.

Algebraic Models for Social Networks. Philippa Pattison. (Structural Analysis in the Social Sciences Ser.: No. 7). (Illus.). 272p. (C). 1993. 39.95 (*0-521-36568-6*) Cambridge U Pr.

Algebraic Number Theory. Ed. by J. W. Cassels & A. Frohlich. 384p. 1986. pap. text ed. 47.00 (*0-12-163251-2*) Acad Pr.

Algebraic Number Theory. Ed. by John Coates. (Advanced Studies in Pure Mathematics: Vol. 17). 492p. 1989. text ed. 140.00 (*0-12-177370-1*) Acad Pr.

Algebraic Number Theory. A. Frohlich & M. J. Taylor. (Cambridge Studies in Advanced Mathematics: No. 27). 300p. (C). 1992. 89.95 (*0-521-36664-X*) Cambridge U Pr.

Algebraic Number Theory. A. Frohlich & M. J. Taylor. (Cambridge Studies in Advanced Mathematics: No. 27). 355p. (C). 1993. pap. 32.95 (*0-521-43834-9*) Cambridge U Pr.

Algebraic Number Theory. Robert Long. (Pure & Applied Mathematics Ser.: Vol. 41). 208p. 1977. 110.00 (*0-8247-6540-0*) Dekker.

Algebraic Number Theory. 2nd ed. Serge Lang. LC 93-50625. (Graduate Texts in Mathematics Ser.: Vol. 110). 376p. 1994. text ed. 39.00 (*0-387-94225-4*) Spr-Verlag.

Algebraic Number Theory. Serge A. Lang. (Graduate Texts in Mathematics Ser.: Vol. 110). 370p. 1993. reprint ed. 29.80 (*0-387-96375-8*) Spr-Verlag.

Algebraic Number Theory & Representations. Steklov Institute of Mathematics, Academy of Sciences, U. S. S. R. Staff. Ed. by D. K. Faddeev. (Proceedings of the Steklov Institute of Mathematics Ser.: No. 80). 215p. 1968. 69.00 (*0-8218-1880-5*, STEKLO-80) Am Math.

Algebraic Numbers & Algebraic Functions. E. Artin. 364p. 1967. pap. text ed. 104.00 (*0-677-00635-7*) Gordon & Breach.

Algebraic Numbers & Algebraic Functions. P. M. Cohn. (Mathematics Ser.). 250p. 1991. 45.00 (*0-412-36190-6*, A6162) Chapman & Hall.

Algebraic Potential Theory. Maynard Arsove & Heinz Leutwiler. LC 79-24384. (Memoirs of the American Mathematical Society Ser.: Vol. 23/226). 130p. 1983. reprint ed. pap. 18.00 (*0-8218-2226-8*, MEMO 23/226) Am Math.

Algebraic Probability Theory. Imre Z. Ruzsa. LC 87-25444. (Probability & Mathematical Statistics Ser.). 251p. 1988. text ed. 175.00 (*0-471-91803-2*) Wiley.

***Algebraic Renormalization: Perturbative Renormalization, Symmetries & Anomalies.** Olivier Piguet & Silvio P. Sorella. LC 95-15984. (Lecture Notes in Physics: New Series M, Monographs: Vol. 28). 1995. write for info. (*3-540-59115-X*) Spr-Verlag.

***Algebraic Riccati Equations.** P. Lancaster & L. Rodman. (Oxford Mathematical Monographs). 491p. 1995. 104.00 (*0-19-853795-6*) OUP.

Algebraic Semantics. Irene Guessarian. (Lecture Notes in Computer Science Ser.: Vol. 99). 158p. 1981. pap. 23.00 (*0-387-10284-1*) Spr-Verlag.

***Algebraic Set Theory.** I. Moerdijk & A. Joyal. (Studies in Publishing & Printing: No. 220). (Illus.). 200p. (C). Date not set. pap. write for info. (*0-521-55830-1*) Cambridge U Pr.

Algebraic Specification of Communication Protocols. S. Mauw & G. J. Veltink. (Tracts in Theoretical Computer Science Ser.: No. 36). 200p. (C). 1993. 42.95 (*0-521-41883-6*) Cambridge U Pr.

Algebraic Specification Techniques in Object Oriented Programming Environments. R. Breu. Ed. by G. Goos & J. Hartmanis. (Lecture Notes in Computer Science Ser.: Vol. 562). xi, 228p. 1991. pap. 39.00 (*0-387-54972-2*) Spr-Verlag.

Algebraic Specifications: Case Studies in Programming in Language Definition. J. A. Bergstra. 1989. text ed. 39.75 (*0-201-41635-2*) Addison-Wesley.

Algebraic Specifications in Software Engineering. I. Van Horebeek & Paul J. Lewi. (Illus.). 368p. 1989. 49.00 (*0-387-51626-3*, 3487) Spr-Verlag.

Algebraic Structure of Crossed Products. Gregory Karpilovsky. 348p. 1987. 87.25 (*0-444-70239-3*, North Holland) Elsevier.

Algebraic Structure of Group Rings. Donald S. Passman. LC 84-15403. 750p. (C). 1985. reprint ed. lib. bdg. 73.50 (*0-89874-789-9*) Krieger.

Algebraic Structures & Operator Calculus. Philip Feinsilver & Rene Schott. LC 92-44824. (Mathematics & Its Applications Ser.: Vol. 241). 1993. Alk. paper. lib. bdg. 93.50 (*0-7923-2116-2*) Kluwer Ac.

***Algebraic Structures & Operator Calculus Vol. II: Special Functions & Computer Science.** Philip Feinsilver. (Mathematics & Its Applications Ser.: Vol. 292). 160p. (C). 1994. lib. bdg. 70.00 (*0-7923-2921-X*) Kluwer Ac.

Algebraic Structures, Extensions, & Homomorphisms. Secondary School Mathematics Curriculum Improvement Study Staff. LC 73-154476. (Unified Modern Mathematics Ser.; Course 6, Bklet. C). 88p. reprint ed. pap. 25.10 (*0-8357-5306-9*, 2051821) Bks Demand.

Algebraic Structures in Automata & Database Theory. B. I. Plotkin et al. 300p. 1992. text ed. 61.00 (*981-02-0936-3*) World Scientific Pub.

Algebraic Structures of Symmetric Domains. Ichiro Satake. LC 80-7551. (Publications of the Mathematical Society of Japan: No. 14). 315p. 1981. 65.00 (*0-691-08271-5*) Princeton U Pr.

Algebraic Surfaces. 2nd ed. O. Zariski. LC 70-148144. (Ergebisse der Mathematik und Ihrer Grenzgebiete Ser.: Vol. 61). 1971. 69.00 (*0-387-05335-2*) Spr-Verlag.

***Algebraic Surfaces.** 3rd ed. Oscar Zariski. LC 94-39107. (Classics in Mathematics Ser.). 1994. write for info. (*3-540-58658-X*) Spr-Verlag.

Algebraic Surfaces: Proceedings. Steklov Institute of Mathematics, Academy of Sciences, U. S. S. R. Staff. Ed. by I. R. Safarevic. (Proceedings of the Steklov Institute of Mathematics Ser.: No. 75). 281p. 1982. reprint ed. 82.00 (*0-8218-1875-9*, STEKLO-75) Am Math.

Algebraic System Specification & Development: A Survey & Annotated Bibliography. J. Kreowski. Ed. by M. Bidoit et al. (Lecture Notes in Computer Science Ser.: Vol. 501). vi, 98p. 1991. pap. 22.00 (*0-387-54060-1*) Spr-Verlag.

Algebraic Systems. A. I. Mal'cev. Tr. by B. D. Seckler & A. P. Doohovskoy. (Grundlehren der Mathematischen Wissenschaften Ser.: Vol. 192). 320p. 1973. 79.00 (*0-387-05792-7*) Spr-Verlag.

Algebraic Systems & Computational Complexity Theory. Z. Wang. LC 93-31541. (Mathematics & Its Applications Ser.). 256p. (C). 1994. lib. bdg. 112.00 (*0-7923-2533-8*) Kluwer Ac.

***Algebraic Theory of Automata.** F. Gecseg & I. Peak. (Disquisitiones Mathematicae Hungaricae Ser.). 326p. (C). 1972. 57.00x (*0-614-00702-X*, Pub. by Akad Kiado HU) St Mut.

Algebraic Theory of Automata. F. Gecseg & I. Peak. 326p. 1986. 65.00 (*0-685-19908-8*, Pub. by Collets UK) Pro-Am Music.

Algebraic Theory of Automata. Abraham Ginzburg. LC 68-23492. (ACM Monograph Ser.). 1968. text ed. 91.00 (*0-12-285050-5*) Acad Pr.

Algebraic Theory of Linear Feedback Systems with Full & Decentralized Compensators. A. N. Gundes & C. A. Desoer. Ed. by M. Thoma & A. Wyner. (Lecture Notes in Control & Information Sciences Ser.: Vol. 142). (Illus.). v, 176p. 1990. pap. 34.00 (*0-387-52476-2*) Spr-Verlag.

Algebraic Theory of Measure & Integration. 2nd ed. Constantin Caratheodory. Ed. by P. Finsler et al. Tr. by Fred E. Linton. LC 63-13094. 378p. (C). 1986. 27.50 (*0-8284-0161-6*) Chelsea Pub.

Algebraic Theory of Modular Systems. F. S. Macaulay. (Mathematical Library). 144p. (C). 1994. pap. 19.95 (*0-521-45562-6*) Cambridge U Pr.

Algebraic Theory of Molecules. F. Iachello & R. D. Levine. LC 93-37702. (Topics in Physical Chemistry Ser.). (Illus.). 224p. 1995. 59.95 (*0-19-508091-2*) OUP.

Algebraic Theory of Numbers. rev. ed. Hermann Weyl. (Annals of Mathematics Studies: No. 1). (Orig.). (C). 1954. pap. 35.00x (*0-691-07908-0*) Princeton U Pr.

Algebraic Theory of Processes. Matthew Hennessy. (Foundations of Computing Ser.). 272p. 1988. 45.00x (*0-262-08171-7*) MIT Pr.

Algebraic Theory of Quadratic Forms. T. Y. Lam. 343p. (C). 1980. pap. text ed. 36.75 (*0-8053-5666-5*, Adv Bk Prog) Addison-Wesley.

Algebraic Theory of Semigroups. Ed. by G. Pollak. (Colloquia Mathematica Societatis Janos Bolyai Ser.: Vol. 20). 754p. 1979. 146.25 (*0-444-85282-4*, North Holland) Elsevier.

Algebraic Theory of Semigroups, 2 Vols, Vol. 1. A. H. Clifford & G. B. Preston. LC 61-15686. (Mathematical Surveys Ser.). 224p. 1990. 38.00 (*0-8218-0271-2*, SURV-7.1) Am Math.

Algebraic Theory of Semigroups, 2 Vols, Vol. 2. A. H. Clifford & G. B. Preston. LC 61-15686. (Mathematical Surveys Ser.). 352p. 1988. 49.00 (*0-8218-0272-0*, SURV-7.2) Am Math.

Algebraic Theory of Switching Circuits. G. Moisil & I. N. Sneddon. LC 63-10024. (International Series of Monographs on Pure & Applied Mathematics: Vol. 41). 1969. 292.00 (*0-08-010148-8*, Pub. by Pergamon Repr UK) Franklin.

Algebraic Theory of the Bianchi Groups. Fine. (Pure & Applied Mathematics Ser.: Vol. 129). 264p. 1989. 110.00 (*0-8247-8192-9*) Dekker.

Algebraic Topics in Systems Theory. Robert Hermann. (Interdisciplinary Mathematics Ser.: No. 3). 177p. 1973. 25.00 (*0-915692-02-3*) Math Sci Pr.

Algebraic Topology. Ed. by G. Carlsson et al. (Lecture Notes in Mathematics Ser.: Vol. 1370). ix, 456p. 1989. pap. 55.00 (*0-387-51118-0*) Spr-Verlag.

Algebraic Topology. M. Glezerman et al. (Translations Ser.: No. 1, Vol. 7). 449p. 1991. 35.00 (*0-8218-1607-1*, TRANS 1-7) Am Math.

***Algebraic Topology.** E. Spanier. 544p. 1994. 39.00 (*0-387-94426-5*) Spr-Verlag.

Algebraic Topology. E. H. Spanier. 528p. 1990. 49.00 (*0-387-90646-0*) Spr-Verlag.

Algebraic Topology. Solomon Lefschetz. LC 41-6147. (Colloquium Publications: Vol. 27). 389p. 1986. reprint ed. pap. 57.00 (*0-8218-1027-8*, COLL-27) Am Math.

Algebraic Topology, 153. W. Fulton & P. R. Halmos. Ed. by J. H. Ewing et al. LC 94-21786. (Undergraduate Texts in Mathematics Ser.). 432p. 1994. pap. text ed. 29.95 (*0-387-94327-7*) Spr-Verlag.

Algebraic Topology, Vol. 22. Pure Mathematics Symposium Staff. Ed. by Arunas Liulevicius. LC 72-167684. (Proceedings of Symposia in Pure Mathematics Ser., Humboldt State University, Arcata, CA, July 29-August 16, 1974). 294p. 1971. text ed. 55.00 (*0-8218-1422-2*, PSPUM-22) Am Math.

Algebraic Topology, Vol. 1286. Ed. by H. R. Miller & D. C. Ravenel. (Lecture Notes in Mathematics Ser.). vii, 341p. 1987. pap. 45.30 (*0-387-18481-3*) Spr-Verlag.

Algebraic Topology: (Proceedings of the International Conference) M. Mahowald & S. Priddy. LC 89-15023. (CONM Ser.: Vol. 96). 350p. 1989. pap. 49.00 (*0-8218-5102-0*, CONM96) Am Math.

Algebraic Topology: A First Course. M. J. Greenberg & J. R. Harper. 311p. (C). 1981. pap. 35.95 (*0-8053-3557-9*, Adv Bk Prog) Addison-Wesley.

Algebraic Topology: A First Course. Max K. Agoston. LC 75-18033. (Pure & Applied Mathematics Ser.: No. 32). (Illus.). 376p. reprint ed. pap. 107.20 (*0-8357-5307-7*, 2032241) Bks Demand.

***Algebraic Topology: A First Course, 153.** W. Fulton. Ed. by J. H. Ewing et al. (Graduate Texts in Mathematics Ser.). 432p. 1994. 59.50 (*0-387-94326-9*) Spr-Verlag.

Algebraic Topology: An Introduction. W. S. Massey. LC 77-22206. (Graduate Texts in Mathematics Ser.: Vol. 56). (Illus.). xxi, 261p. 1990. 39.00 (*0-387-90271-6*) Spr-Verlag.

Algebraic Topology: Oaxtepec 1991 (Proceedings of an International Conference in Algebraic Topology Held on July 4-11, 1991 with Support from the National Science Foundation & the Consejo Nacional de Ciencia y Technologia, Mexico) Ed. by Martin C. Tangora. LC 93-15227. 481p. 1993. 71.00 (*0-8218-5162-4*, CONM/146) Am Math.

Algebraic Topology - Homotopy & Group Cohomology: Proceedings of a Conference Held in Barcelona, Spain, June 6-12, 1990. Ed. by J. Aguade et al. (Lecture Notes in Mathematics Ser.: Vol. 1509). x, 330p. 1992. pap. 49.00 (*0-387-55195-6*) Spr-Verlag.

An Asterisk (*) at the beginning of an entry indicates that the title is appearing in BIP for the first time.

An Asterisk (*) at the beginning of an entry indicates that the title is appearing in BIP for the first time.

185

Algorithmic Learning Theory II: Proceedings of ALT'91, Tokyo, October 23-25, 1991. Ed. by S. Arikawa et al. LC 92-53256. 320p. 1992. 88.00 (*90-5199-088-X*, Pub. by IOS Pr NE) IOS Press.

Algorithmic Logic. C. Mirkowska & Andrzej Salwicki. 1987. lib. bdg. 136.50 (*90-277-1928-4*) Kluwer Ac.

Algorithmic Methods in Algebra & Number Theory. Ed. by Michael E. Pohst. 135p. 1988. text ed. 37.00 (*0-12-559190-X*) Acad Pr.

***Algorithmic Number Theory: Proceedings of the First International Symposium, ANTS-I, Ithaca, NY, U. S. A., May 6-9, 1994.** Ed. by Leonard M. Adleman et al. LC 94-238714. (Lecture Notes in Computer Science: Vol. 877). 1994. write for info. (*3-540-58691-1*); write for info. (*0-387-58691-1*) Spr-Verlag.

***Algorithmic Probability: A Collection of Problems.** Marcel F. Neuts. 1995. write for info. (*0-412-99691-X*) Chapman & Hall.

Algorithmic Properties of Structures: Selected Papers of E. Engeler. E. Engeler. 250p. 1994. text ed. 61.00 (*981-02-0872-3*) World Scientific Pub.

Algorithmic Skeletons: Structural Management of Parallel Computation. Murray I. Cole. (Research Monographs in Parallel & Distributed Computing). 224p. 1989. pap. 27.95 (*0-262-53086-4*) MIT Pr.

Algorithmic Skeletons: Structured Management of Parallel Computation. Ed. by Murray I. Cole. 208p. (C). 1989. pap. text ed. 200.00 (*0-273-08807-6*, Pub. by Pitman Pubng UK) St Mut.

Algorithmic Theory of Numbers, Graphs, & Convexity. Laszlo Lovasz. LC 86-61532. (CBMS-NSF Regional Conference Ser.: No. 50). v, 91p. 1986. pap. 18.25 (*0-89871-203-3*) Soc Indus-Appl Math.

Algorithmic Trends in Computational Fluid Dynamics for the 1990s. Ed. by M. Yousuff Hussaini et al. LC 92-44294. 440p. 1993. 59.00 (*0-387-94014-6*) Spr-Verlag.

Algorithmically Specialized Parallel Computers. Ed. by Lawrence Synder et al. 1985. text ed. 65.00 (*0-12-654130-2*) Acad Pr.

Algorithmics: The Spirit of Computing. David Harel. 450p. (C). 1987. pap. text ed. 24.75 (*0-201-19240-3*) Addison-Wesley.

Algorithmics: The Spirit of Computing. 2nd ed. David Harel. (Illus.). 512p. (C). 1992. pap. text ed. 37.75 (*0-201-50401-4*) Addison-Wesley.

Algorithmics for VLSI. C. Trullemans. (International Lecture Series in Computer Mathematics). 1986. text ed. 60.00 (*0-12-701230-3*) Acad Pr.

Algorithmization in Learning & Instruction. L. N. Landa. Ed. by Felix F. Kopstein. Tr. by Virginia Bennett. LC 73-11044. 752p. 1974. reprint ed. 44.95 (*0-87778-063-3*) Educ Tech Pubns.

Algorithms. Ivan Horabin & Brian Lewis. Ed. by Danny G. Langdon. LC 78-2307. (Instructional Design Library). (Illus.). 80p. 1978. 23.95 (*0-87778-106-0*) Educ Tech Pubns.

Algorithms. Robert Sedgewick. (Computer Science Ser.). (Illus.). 560p. 1983. 43.25 (*0-201-06672-6*) Addison-Wesley.

Algorithms: A-W Computer Science. 2nd ed. Robert Sedgewick. 672p. (C). 1988. text ed. 48.50 (*0-201-06673-4*) Addison-Wesley.

Algorithms: International Symposium SIGAL '90, Tokyo, Japan, August 16-18, 1990 Proceedings. Ed. by T. Asano et al. (Lecture Notes in Computer Science Ser.: Vol. 450). viii, 479p. 1990. pap. 46.00 (*0-387-52921-7*) Spr-Verlag.

Algorithms: Main Ideas & Applications. Vladimir Uspensky. (Mathematics & Its Applications Ser.). 288p. (C). 1993. lib. bdg. 116.00 (*0-7923-2210-X*) Kluwer Ac.

Algorithms: The Construction, Proof & Analysis of Programs. Pierre Berlioux & Philippe Bizard. LC 85-18000. 145p. 1986. pap. text ed. 56.50 (*0-471-90844-4*) Wiley.

Algorithms: Their Complexity & Efficiency. 2nd ed. Lydia Kronsjo. (Series in Computing). 1987. text ed. 87.95 (*0-471-91201-8*) Wiley.

Algorithms - ESA '93: First Annual European Symposium, Bad Honnef, Germany, September 30-October 2, 1993 Proceedings. Ed. by Thomas Lengauer. LC 93-34004. (Lecture Notes in Computer Science Ser.: Vol. 726). 1993. 60.00 (*0-387-57273-2*) Spr-Verlag.

***Algorithms - ESA '94: Second Annual European Symposium, Utrecht, the Netherlands, September 26-28, 1994. Proceedings.** Ed. by J. Van Leeuwen. (Lecture Notes in Computer Science: Vol. 855). 510p. 1994. pap. 69.00 (*3-540-58434-X*) Spr-Verlag.

Algorithms, Abstraction & Implementation. Carol Foster. (Cognitive Science Ser.). (Illus.). 232p. 1992. text ed. 64.95 (*0-12-262660-5*) Acad Pr.

Algorithms & Applications on Vector & Parallel Computers. Ed. by T. Te Riele et al. (Special Topics in Supercomputing Ser.: Vol. 3). 458p. 1987. 97.50 (*0-444-70322-5*) Elsevier.

Algorithms & Architecture: Proceedings of the 2nd NEC Research Symposium. Ed. by T. Ishiguro. (Proceedings in Applied Mathematics Ser.: No. 65). x, 282p. 1993. 37.50 (*0-89871-312-9*) Soc Indus-Appl Math.

Algorithms & Architectures for Real-Time Control: Preprints of the IFAC Workshop, Seoul, Korea, 31 August-2 September 1992. Ed. by P. J. Fleming & W. H. Kwon. LC 92-40443. 1993. pap. 115.00 (*0-08-042050-8*, Pergamon Pr) Elsevier.

Algorithms & Classification in Combinatorial Group Theory. Ed. by Gilbert Baumslag et al. (Mathematical Sciences Research Institute Publications: Vol. 23). (Illus.). viii, 232p. 1991. 47.00 (*0-387-97685-X*) Spr-Verlag.

Algorithms & Complexity. Herbert S. Wilf. 240p. 1986. text ed. 49.00 (*0-13-021973-8*) P-H.

Algorithms & Complexity: New Directions & Recent Results. Ed. by Joseph F. Traub. 1976. text ed. 114.00 (*0-12-697540-X*) Acad Pr.

Algorithms & Complexity: Proceedings of the Second Italian Conference, CIAC '94, Rome, Italy, February 23-25, 1994. Ed. by M. Bonuccelli et al. LC 94-3186. (Lecture Notes in Computer Science Ser.: Vol. 778). viii, 222p. 1994. pap. 35.00 (*0-387-57811-0*) Spr-Verlag.

Algorithms & Complexity: Proceedings of the 1st Italian Conference. D. P. Bovet & R. Petreschi. Ed. by G. Ausiello et al. 228p. 1990. pap. 28.00 (*981-02-0399-3*) World Scientific Pub.

***Algorithms & Computation, 834.** Ed. by D. Z. Du et al. (Lecture Notes in Computer Science: Vol. 834). 687p. 1994. pap. text ed. 96.00 (*0-387-58325-4*) Spr-Verlag.

Algorithms & Computation: Proceedings, Fourth International Symposium, ISAAC '93, Hong Kong, December 1993. K. W. Ng et al. LC 93-44957. (Lecture Notes in Computer Science Ser.: Vol. 762). 1994. 78.00 (*0-387-57568-5*) Spr-Verlag.

Algorithms & Computation: Third International Symposium, ISAAC '92, Nagoya, Japan, December 16-18, 1992, Proceedings. Ed. by T. Ibaraki et al. LC 92-39212. (Lecture Notes in Computer Science Ser.: Vol. 650). 1992. 70.00 (*0-387-56279-6*) Spr-Verlag.

Algorithms & Data Structures. Ed. by Frank Dehne et al. (Lecture Notes in Computer Science Ser.: Vol. 382). ix, 592p. 1989. pap. 63.00 (*0-387-51542-9*, 3415) Spr-Verlag.

Algorithms & Data Structures: Proceedings of the Third Workshop on Algorithms & Data Structures, Montreal, Canada, August 11-13, 1993. Third Workshop on Algorithms & Data Structures Staff. Ed. by Frank Dehne et al. (Lecture Notes in Computer Science Ser.: Vol. 709). xii, 634p. 1993. pap. write for info. (*3-540-57155-8*) Spr-Verlag.

Algorithms & Data Structures: Proceedings of the Third Workshop, WADS 93, Montreal, Canada, August 11-13, 1993. Frank Dehne et al. LC 93-28887. (Lecture Notes in Computer Science Ser.: Vol. 709). 1993. 86.00 (*0-387-57155-8*) Spr-Verlag.

Algorithms & Data Structures: Second Workshop, WADS '91, Ottawa, Canada, August 14-16, 1991 Proceedings. Ed. by Frank Dehne et al. (Lecture Notes in Computer Science Ser.: Vol. 519). x, 495p. 1991. pap. 48.00 (*0-387-54343-0*) Spr-Verlag.

Algorithms & Data Structures: With Applications to Graphics & Geometry. Jurg Nievergelt & Klaus H. Hinrichs. 336p. 1992. text ed. 62.00 (*0-13-489428-6*) P-H.

Algorithms & Data Structures in C Plus Plus. Parker. 1993. 49.95 (*0-8493-7171-6*, QA) CRC Pr.

Algorithms & Model Formulations in Mathematical Programming. Ed. by S. W. Wallace. (NATO Asi Series F: Vol. 51). ix, 208p. 1989. 51.00 (*0-387-50842-2*) Spr-Verlag.

Algorithms & Order. Ivan Rival. (C). 1988. lib. bdg. 165.50 (*0-7923-0007-6*) Kluwer Ac.

***Algorithms & Parallel VLSI Architectures III: Proceedings of The International Workshop, Algorithms & Parallel VLSI Architectures III, Leuven, Belgium, August 29-31, 1994.** Ed. by Marc Moonen & Francky Catthoor. LC 94-44668. 1995. write for info. (*0-444-82106-6*) Elsevier.

Algorithms & Techniques for VLSI Layout & Synthesis. Dwight D. Hill et al. (C). 1988. lib. bdg. 77.50 (*0-89838-301-3*) Kluwer Ac.

Algorithms & Theory in Filtering & Control. D. Sorenson & Roger J. Wets. (Mathematical Programming Studies: Vol. 18). 160p. 1982. pap. 51.50 (*0-444-86399-0*, I-125-82, North Holland) Elsevier.

Algorithms C Plus Plus. Robert Sedgewick. (Illus.). 660p. (C). 1992. text ed. 46.25 (*0-201-51059-6*) Addison-Wesley.

Algorithms for Approximation. J. C. Mason & M. G. Cox. 350p. 1990. 99.95 (*0-412-34580-3*, A3805) Chapman & Hall.

Algorithms for Approximation. Ed. by J. C. Mason & M. G. Cox. (Institute of Mathematics & Its Applications Conference Series, New Ser.: New Series 10). (Illus.). 710p. 1987. 125.00 (*0-19-853612-7*) OUP.

Algorithms for Chemists. Jure Zupan. 290p. 1989. text ed. 173.00 (*0-471-92173-4*) Wiley.

Algorithms for Computer Aided Design of Linear Microwave Circuits. Stanislaw Rosloniec. (Microwave Library). 256p. 1990. 49.00 (*0-89006-354-0*); disk 49.00 (*0-685-45614-5*) Artech Hse.

Algorithms for Computer-Aided Design of Multivariable Control Systems. Stanoje Bingulac & Hugh F. Van Landingham. LC 93-10191. (Electrical Engineering & Electronics Ser.: Vol. 84). 424p. 1993. disk 140.00 (*0-8247-8913-X*) Dekker.

Algorithms for Computer Algebra. Ed. by Keith O. Geddes. LC 92-18660. 608p. 1992. lib. bdg. 145.50 (*0-7923-9259-0*) Kluwer Ac.

Algorithms for Constrained Minimization of Smooth Nonlinear Functions. A. G. Buckley & J. L. Goffin. (Mathematical Programming Studies: Vol. 16). 190p. 1982. reprint ed. pap. 51.50 (*0-444-86390-7*, North Holland) Elsevier.

Algorithms for Continuous Optimization: The State of the Art. Ed. by Emilio Spedicato. LC 94-15437. (NATO ASI Series C: Mathematical & Physical Sciences: Vol. 434). 584p. (C). 1994. lib. bdg. 215.00 (*0-7923-2859-0*) Kluwer Ac.

Algorithms for Discrete Fourier Transform & Convolution. Richard Tolimieri et al. xv, 350p. 1991. reprint ed. 65.00 (*0-387-97118-1*, 3231) Spr-Verlag.

Algorithms for Games. G. M. Adelson-Velsky et al. 125p. 1987. 81.00 (*0-387-96629-3*) Spr-Verlag.

Algorithms for Graphics & Image Processing. Theo Pavlidis. LC 81-9832. (Principles of Computer Science Ser.). (Illus.). 416p. (C). 1995. text ed. 46.95 (*0-7167-8106-9*, Computer Sci Pr) W H Freeman.

Algorithms for HVAC Acoustics. Ed. by M. Geshwiler. 204p. (C). 1990. pap. 68.00 (*0-910110-75-1*) Am Heat Ref & Air Eng.

Algorithms for Modular Elliptic Curves. J. E. Cremona. (Illus.). 300p. (C). 1992. 59.95 (*0-521-41813-5*) Cambridge U Pr.

Algorithms for Mutual Exclusion. Michel Raynal. (Scientific Computation Ser.). 160p. 1985. 30.00x (*0-262-18119-3*) MIT Pr.

Algorithms for Parallel Polygon Rendering. T. Theoharis. (Lecture Notes in Computer Science Ser.: Vol. 373). viii, 147p. 1989. pap. 31.00 (*0-387-51394-9*, 3239) Spr-Verlag.

Algorithms for Personal Computing. Dave MacCormack & Toni Michael. (Essential Algorithms Ser.). (Illus.). 250p. (Orig.). 1985. pap. 14.95 (*0-931145-07-4*) Sandlight Pubns.

Algorithms for Predicting Noise Generated by Grilles, Louvres, Dampers & Bends with Turning Vanes. 1977. 60.00 (*0-86022-049-4*, Pub. by Build Servs Info Assn UK) St Mut.

Algorithms for Random Generation & Counting: A Markov Chain Approach. Alistair Sinclair. LC 92-34616. (Progress in Theoretical Computer Science Ser.). viii, 146p. 1992. 49.50 (*0-8176-3658-7*) Birkhauser.

Algorithms for Some Design Automation Problems. James P. Cohoon. LC 84-24101. (Computer Science: Computer Architecture & Design Ser.: No. 3). (Illus.). 114p. reprint ed. pap. 32.50 (*0-8357-1615-5*, 2070372) Bks Demand.

Algorithms for Synthesis & Testing of Asynchronous Circuits. Luciano Lavagno & Alberto L. Sangiovanni-Vincentelli. LC 93-19510. (International Series in Engineering & Computer Science, VLSI, Computer Architecture, & Digital Screen Processing). 360p. (C). 1993. lib. bdg. 97.50 (*0-7923-9364-3*) Kluwer Ac.

Algorithms for VLSI Physical Design Automation. Naveed A. Sherwani. LC 92-38496. 512p. (C). 1993. lib. bdg. 105.00 (*0-7923-9294-9*) Kluwer Ac.

***Algorithms for VLSI Physical Design Automation.** 2nd ed. Naveed Sherwani. 568p. (C). 1995. lib. bdg. 120.00 (*0-7923-9592-1*) Kluwer Ac.

Algorithms from P to NP: Design & Efficiency, Vol. I. Bernard Moret. 450p. (C). 1991. text ed. 52.75 (*0-8053-8008-6*) Benjamin-Cummings.

Algorithms, Graphs & Computers. Richard E. Bellman et al. (Mathematics in Science & Engineering Ser.: Vol. 62). 1970. text ed. 73.00 (*0-12-084840-6*) Acad Pr.

Algorithms in C. Robert Sedgewick. (Computer Science Ser.). (Illus.). 672p. (C). 1990. text ed. 46.25 (*0-201-51425-7*) Addison-Wesley.

Algorithms in Combinatorial Design Theory. Ed. by C. J. Colbourn & M. J. Colbourn. LC 85-10371. (Mathematics Studies: Vol. 114). 334p. 1985. 74.50 (*0-444-87802-5*, North Holland) Elsevier.

Algorithms in Combinatorial Geometry. H. Edelsbrunner. (AETCS Ser.: Vol. 10). 440p. 1987. 69.00 (*0-387-13722-X*) Spr-Verlag.

Algorithms in Invariant Theory. Bernd Sturmfels. (Texts & Monographs in Symbolic Computation). (Illus.). 300p. 1993. pap. write for info. (*3-211-82445-6*) Spr-Verlag.

Algorithms in Invariant Theory. Bernd Sturmfels. LC 93-26772. (Texts & Monographs in Symbolic Computation). 1994. 39.50 (*0-387-82445-6*) Spr-Verlag.

Algorithms in Modula Three. Robert Sedgewick. (Illus.). 672p. (C). 1993. text ed. 46.25 (*0-201-53351-0*) Addison-Wesley.

Algorithms in Real Algebraic Geometry. Denis S. Arnon. 1988. text ed. 47.00 (*0-12-063880-0*) Acad Pr.

Algorithms in SNOBOL4. James F. Gimpel. 506p. 1985. reprint ed. disk 44.95 (*0-939793-02-4*); reprint ed. text ed. 39.95 (*0-939793-01-6*); reprint ed. pap. text ed. 29.95 (*0-939793-00-8*) Catspaw Inc.

Algorithms on Graphs. H. T. Lau. 180p. 1989. 29.95 (*0-8306-3429-0*, TAB/TPR) TAB Bks.

Algorithms on Graphs. H. T. Lau. 1991. 24.95 (*0-8306-5429-1*) TAB Bks.

Algorithms Plus Data Structures Equals Programs. Niklaus Wirth. (Illus.). 400p. (C). 1975. text ed. 74.00 (*0-13-022418-9*) P-H.

Algorithms, Software, Architecture: Information Processing 92: Proceedings of the IFIP 12th World Computer Congress, Madrid, Spain, 7-11 September 1992. Ed. by Jan Van Leeuwen. LC 92-24976. (IFIP Transactions A: Computer Science & Technology Ser.: Vol. 12). 1992. write for info. (*0-444-89747-X*, North Holland) Elsevier.

Algorithms Two: Data Structures & Search Algorithms. Pierre Berlioux & Philippe Bizard. 1990. pap. text ed. 64.95 (*0-471-92417-2*) Wiley.

***Alguans Nubes.** Paco I. Taibo, II. 1995. pap. 12.50 (*0-679-76332-5*, Vin) Random.

Algues D'Eau Douce: Complements Au Tome 1. Pierre Bourrelly. (Illus.). 182p. (FRE.). 1988. text ed. 65.00 (*0-685-32242-4*, Pub. by Editions Boubees FR) Lubrecht & Cramer.

Algues d'Eau Douce de la Partie Amazonienne de la Bolivie: 1. Cyanophycees, Euglenophycees Chrysophycees, Xanthophycees, Dinophycees.. 2. Chlorophytes: Troisieme Contribution. Y. Therezien. (Bibliotheca Phycologica Ser.: Vol. 82). (Illus.). 140p. (FRE.). 1989. spiral bd. 49.00 (*3-443-60009-3*, Pub. by Cramer GW) Lubrecht & Cramer.

Algues D'Eau Douce De Porto Alegre, Bresil (les Diatomophyceae Exclus) I. M. Franceschini. (Bibliotheca Phycologica Ser.: Vol. 92). (Illus.). 128p. (FRE.). 1992. pap. text ed. 49.00 (*3-443-60019-0*, Pub. by Cramer-Borntraeger GW) Lubrecht & Cramer.

Algues d'Eau Douce des Iles Kerguelen et Crozet. Y. Therezien & A. Coute. (Comite National Francais des Recherches Antartique, Territoire des Terres Australes et Antartique Ser.). (Illus.). 90p. (FRE.). 1982. pap. text ed. 60.00 (*3-87429-207-X*) Koeltz Sci Bks.

Algues d'Eau Douce des Mares d'Alpage de la Region de Lunz am See, Autriche. Pierre Bourrelly. (Bibliotheca Phycologica Ser.: Vol. 76). (Illus.). (FRE.). 1987. pap. 105.00 (*3-443-60003-4*) Lubrecht & Cramer.

Algues d'Eau douce. Initiation a la Systematique Volume 1. rev. ed. Pierre Bourrelly. (Faunes et Flores Actuelles Ser.). (Illus.). 511p. (FRE.). 1988. lib. bdg. 130.00 (*0-685-43966-6*) Lubrecht & Cramer.

Algues d'Eau douce. Initiation a la Systematique Volume 2: Algues jaunes et brunes. Generalities sur les Chromophytes-Crysophysees-Pheophycees-Zantophycees-Diamophycees. rev. ed. Pierre Bourrelly. (Faunes et Flores Actuelles Ser.). (Illus.). 440p. (FRE.). 1981. lib. bdg. 130.00 (*2-85004-029-0*) Lubrecht & Cramer.

Algues d'Eau douce. Initiation a la Systematique. Volume 3: Algues bleues et rouges. Pyrrophytes-Algues rouges ou Rhodophytes-Algues bleues on Cyanophycees-Systematics des Algues d'Eau douce. rev. ed. Pierre Bourelly. (Fannes et Flores Actuelles Ser.). (Illus.). 544p. (FRE.). 1983. lib. bdg. 130.00 (*2-85004-040-1*) Lubrecht & Cramer.

Algues des Cotes Francaises: Manche et Atlantique. P. Gayral. (Illus.). 632p. (Orig.). (FRE.). 1982. reprint ed. pap. text ed. 66.00 (*3-87429-204-5*) Koeltz Sci Bks.

Alguien a Quien Amar (Creacion) Marilyn Lashbrook. Orig. Title: Someone to Love. 32p. (SPA.). 1994. pap. 3.25 (*0-8254-1427-X*) Kregel.

Alguien Mas en el Espejo. Carlos M. Suarez-Ardillo. Ed. by SLUSA Staff. 224p. (Orig.). (SPA.). 1984. pap. 12.00 (*0-917129-00-8*) SLUSA.

Alguien Se Preocupa. Edwin D. Roels. Tr. by John Cosby. (Friendship Ser.). (Illus.). 48p. (SPA.). 1992. pap. write for info. (*1-882536-27-4*, A110-0016) Bible League.

Alguien Va a Nacer: Poems for Expectant Mothers. Gloria Santamaria. (SPA.). 3.25 (*84-7228-487-5*, 220016, Pub. by Edit Clie SP) TSELF.

Algunas Cruces Altas (Some High Crosses) A. Lockward. (SPA.). Date not set. 6.99 (*1-56063-159-7*, 490218) Editorial Unilit.

Algunos Analisis: (El Terreriamo, Derecho Internacional) Eduardo De Acha. 104p. (Orig.). (SPA.). 1987. pap. 9.00 (*0-89729-436-X*) Ediciones.

Algunos Muchachos. 3rd ed. Ana M. Ausejo. 170p. (SPA.). 1990. pap. 11.95 (*0-7859-4993-3*) Fr & Eur.

Algunos Pensamientos. Carlos Gonzalez. (SPA.). 1982. write for info. (*1-56491-003-2*) Imagine Pubs.

Alhaji: A Peace Corps Adventure in Nigeria. Jane B. Hirsch. 80p. (Orig.). 1994. pap. 8.95 (*1-56474-098-6*) Fithian Pr.

Alhambra. W. Irving. 456p. 1986. 300.00 (*1-85077-093-X*, Darf Pubs Ltd) St Mut.

Alhambra, 2 vols. Washington Irving. 1976. 500.00 (*0-8490-1409-3*) Gordon Pr.

Alhambra. 2nd rev. ed. Oleg Grabar. (Illus.). xiv, 196p. (C). 1992. 25.00 (*0-944940-04-8*) Solipsist Pr.

Alhambra. Washington Irving. (BCL1-PS American Literature Ser.). 436p. 1992. reprint ed. lib. bdg. 99.00 (*0-7812-6752-8*) Rprt Serv.

Alhambra. Washington Irving. LC 82-5644. (Illus.). 464p. 1982. reprint ed. 23.95 (*0-912882-48-4*) Sleepy Hollow.

Alhambra: A Cycle of Studies on the Eleventh Century in Moorish Spain. Fredrick P. Bargebuhr. (C). 1968. 215.40 (*3-11-000524-7*) De Gruyter.

Alhambra: Plans, Elevations, Sections & Drawings. Owen Jones. (Illus.). 630p. 1994. 200.00 (*0-86356-466-6*, Pub. by Saqi Bks UK) Interlink Pub.

Alhambra: A Series of Tales & Sketches of the Moors & Spaniards (1982) The Complete Works of Washington Irving. Ed. by William Lenehan & Andrew B. Myers. (Complete Works of Washington Irving Ser.). 1983. text ed. 50.00 (*0-8057-8512-4*, Twayne) Macmillan.

Alhambra Decree. David Raphael. LC 88-71589. 360p. (C). 1988. 18.00 (*0-9620772-0-8*) Carmi Hse Pr.

ALI-ABA Course of Study on Defense of Drug Cases. Ed. by Brian E. Appel. 406p. 1971. pap. 2.50 (*0-317-30871-8*, B187) Am Law Inst.

ALI-ABA Course of Study on SEC Rule 144: Restricted Securities & Non-Underwritten Distributions. 243p. 1972. pap. 10.00 (*0-317-30780-0*, B156) Am Law Inst.

ALI-ABA Report on the Survey of Bridge-the-Gap Programs. ALI-ABA Committee on Continuing Professional Education. LC 85-71317. 78p. (Orig.). 1985. pap. 19.00 (*0-8318-0503-X*, B503) Am Law Inst.

ALI-ABA's Practice Checklist Manual for Drafting Leases: Checklists, Forms, & Drafting Advice from The Practical Lawyer & The Practical Real Estate Lawyer. Intro. by Mark T. Carroll. LC 94-71722. (Practical Checklist Ser.). x, 328p. (Orig.). 1994. pap. 70.00 (*0-8318-1400-4*, F140) Am Law Inst.

***ALI-ABA's Practice Checklist Manual on Taking Deposition: Checklists & Advice from The Practical Lawyer & The Practical Litigator.** Ed. by Mark T. Carroll. LC 95-75486. 170p. (Orig.). 1995. pap. 70.00 (*0-8318-1401-2*, F141) Am Law Inst.

ALI-ABA...XL! Paul A. Wolkin. 282p. 1988. 55.00 (*0-8318-0616-8*, B616) Am Law Inst.

Ali & Me: Through the Ropes. Richard Kaletsky. LC 82-73549. (Illus.). 88p. (Orig.). 1982. pap. 4.65 (*0-9610534-0-2*) Adrienne Pubns Inc.

Ali & the Golden Eagle. Wayne Grover. LC 91-43736. (Illus.). 160p. (J). (gr. 7 up). 1993. 13.00 (*0-688-11385-0*) Greenwillow.

Ali Baba: In Arabic. (Ladybird Stories Ser.). (Illus.). (J). (gr. 4-12). 1987. 3.95 (*0-86685-184-4*) Intl Bk Ctr.

An Asterisk (*) at the beginning of an entry indicates that the title is appearing in BIP for the first time.

An Asterisk (*) at the beginning of an entry indicates that the title is appearing in BIP for the first time.

187

A

Alice Walker. Donna H. Winchell. (Twayne's United States Authors Ser.). 150p. (C). 1992. text ed. 20.95 (*0-8057-7642-7*, Twayne) Macmillan.

Alice Walker: An Annotated Bibliography. Erma D. Banks & Keith Byerman. LC 89-1251. 242p. 1989. 36.00 (*0-8240-5734-1*, H889) Garland.

***Alice Walker: Author of The Color Purple.** Barbara Kramer. LC 95-5809. (People to Know Ser.). (Illus.). 128p. (YA). (gr. 6 up). 1995. lib. bdg. 17.95 (*0-89490-620-8*) Enslow Pubs.

Alice Walker: Black Americans of Achievement. Tony Gentry. (J). (gr. 4-7). 1992. pap. 7.95 (*0-7910-1913-6*) Chelsea Hse.

Alice Walker: Critical Perspectives Past & Present. Henry L. Gates, Jr. & K. A. Appiah. LC 92-45754. (Literary Ser.). 368p. 1993. 24.95 (*1-56743-013-9*); pap. 14.95 (*1-56743-026-0*) Amistad Pr.

Alice Walker & Zora Neale Hurston: The Common Bond. Ed. by Lillie P. Howard. LC 93-20324. (Contributions in Afro-American & African Studies: No. 163). 184p. 1993. text ed. 49.95 (*0-313-25790-6*, HDE) Greenwood.

Alice Walker Boxed Set-Fiction: The Third Life of Grange Copeland, You Can't Keep a Good Woman Down, & In Love & Trouble. Alice Walker. 1985. pap. 12.95 (*0-15-694101-5*, Harvest Bks) HarBrace.

Alice Walker Boxed Set-Poetry: Good Night, Willie Lee, I'll See You in the Morning; Revolutionary Petunias & Other Poems; Once, Poems. Alice Walker. 1985. pap. 12.95 (*0-15-694102-3*, Harvest Bks) HarBrace.

Alice Waynewright & More. B. Edward Mullins. 65p. (Orig.). 1989. pap. 4.95 (*0-929880-00-5*) Gall Pr Intl.

Alice's Abenteuer im Wunderland. Lewis Carroll. Tr. by Antonie Zimmermann. (Illus.). 178p. 1974. reprint ed. 5.95 (*0-486-20668-8*) Dover.

Alice's Adventures. Chilton Designs Publishers Staff. (C). 1992. pap. 35.00 (*0-9503527-6-4*, Pub. by Chilton Designs UK) St Mut.

Alice's Adventures In Jurisprudencia. Peter F. Sloss. LC 82-70520. (Illus.). 87p. (Orig.). 1982. pap. 4.95 (*0-9608246-0-X*) Borogove Pr.

Alice's Adventures in Wonderland. Lewis Carroll. (Illus.). pap. 3.95 (*0-8283-1423-3*, 19, Intl Pocket Lib) Branden Pub Co.

Alice's Adventures in Wonderland. Lewis Carroll & Moser. (J). 1991. 34.95 (*0-15-104230-6*); pap. 16.95 (*0-15-604426-9*, Harvest Bks) HarBrace.

Alice's Adventures in Wonderland. Lewis Carroll. LC 85-856. 128p. (J). (gr. 4-6). 1985. 19.95 (*0-8050-0212-X*, Bks Young Read) H Holt & Co.

Alice's Adventures in Wonderland. Lewis Carroll. LC 94-15229. (Children's Library). (J). 1994. 10.95 (*0-681-00644-7*) Longmeadow Pr.

Alice's Adventures in Wonderland. Lewis Carroll. LC 91-31482. (Illus.). 208p. (J). 1992. 15.00 (*0-688-11087-8*) Morrow Jr Bks.

Alice's Adventures in Wonderland. Lewis Carroll. LC 82-242973. (Classics Ser.). (Illus.). (J). (gr. 7 up). 1985. pap. 2.25 (*0-14-035038-1*, Puffin) Puffin Bks.

Alice's Adventures in Wonderland. Lewis Carroll. (Classics Ser.). 160p. (J). (gr. 5 up). 1994. pap. 2.99 (*0-14-036675-X*) Puffin Bks.

Alice's Adventures in Wonderland. Lewis Carroll. LC 82-242973. (Illus.). 160p. (J). (gr. 3 up). 1984. 3.99 (*0-517-55591-3*) Random Hse Value.

Alice's Adventures in Wonderland. Lewis Carroll. LC 92-50804. (Miniature Editions Ser.). (Illus.). 192p. (J). 1993. 4.95 (*1-56138-246-9*) Running Pr.

Alice's Adventures in Wonderland. Lewis Carroll. LC 93-72323. (Illus.). 96p. (J). (gr. 2 up). 1994. text ed. 16.95 (*0-689-31864-2*, Atheneum Bks Young) S&S Childrens.

Alice's Adventures in Wonderland. Lewis Carroll. 1992. pap. 2.50 (*0-8125-0418-6*) Tor Bks.

Alice's Adventures in Wonderland. Lewis Carroll. LC 89-33889. (Illustrated Classics Ser.). (Illus.). 48p. (J). (gr. 3-6). 1990. lib. bdg. 12.89 (*0-8167-1861-X*); pap. text ed. 3.95 (*0-8167-1862-8*) Troll Assocs.

Alice's Adventures in Wonderland. Lewis Carroll, pseud. & John Tenniel. LC 82-242973. (Illus.). (J). (gr. 5 up). 1977. 14.95 (*0-312-01821-5*) St Martin.

Alice's Adventures in Wonderland. Lewis Carroll. Bd. with Through the Looking Glass. LC 82-242973. LC 82-242973. 315p. (J). (gr. 4-6). 1962. Set pap. 2.95 (*0-02-042350-0*, Collier Bks Young) S&S Childrens.

Alice's Adventures in Wonderland. Lewis Carroll. Bd. with Through the Looking Glass. 1950. Set pap. 3.95 (*0-14-030169-0*, Puffin) Puffin Bks.

Alice's Adventures in Wonderland. Lewis Carroll. Bd. with Through the Looking Glass. LC 82-242973. LC 82-242973. (Airmont Classics Ser.). (J). (gr. 5 up). 1965. Set pap. 1.95 (*0-8049-0079-5*, CL-79) Airmont.

Alice's Adventures in Wonderland. Lewis Carroll. Bd. with Through the Looking Glass. LC 82-242973. LC 82-242973. (Bantam Classics Ser.). (Illus.). 256p. (gr. 6-12). 1985. Set pap. 1.95 (*0-553-21173-0*) Bantam.

Alice's Adventures in Wonderland. large type ed. Lewis Carroll. Bd. with Through the Looking Glass. LC 82-242973. LC 82-242973. (Reader's Request Ser.). (J). 1980. 11.95 (*0-8161-3070-1*, Large Print Bks) Hall.

Alice's Adventures in Wonderland. Lewis Carroll. LC 93-571. (Little Barefoot Books). (Illus.). 230p. (J). 1993. reprint ed. 6.00 (*1-56957-900-8*) Barefoot Bks.

Alice's Adventures in Wonderland. Lewis Carroll. LC 93-4056. (Thrift Editions Ser.). (Illus.). 80p. 1993. reprint ed. pap. 1.00 (*0-486-27543-4*) Dover.

Alice's Adventures in Wonderland. Lewis Carroll. Bd. with Through the Looking Glass: And What Alice Found There. LC 82-242973.; Hunting of the Snark: An Agony in Eight Fits. LC 82-242973. LC 82-242973. (Illus.). (YA). (gr. 10 up). 1987. reprint ed. Set pap. 5.95 (*0-8052-0594-2*) Schocken.

Alice's Adventures in Wonderland: An 1865 Printing Re-Described. Justin G. Schiller. (Illus.). 112p. 1990. 75.00 (*0-9627110-0-4*) Battledore Ltd.

Alice's Adventures in Wonderland: The Ultimate Illustrated Edition. Lewis Carroll. (J). (ps up). 1989. 22.50 (*0-553-05385-X*) Bantam.

Alice's Adventures in Wonderland & Through the Looking Glass. Lewis Carroll. LC 92-53181. (Illus.). 336p. (J). 1992. 12.95 (*0-679-41795-8*, Evrymans Lib Childs) Knopf.

Alice's Adventures in Wonderland & Through the Looking Glass. Lewis Carroll. (Illus.). 256p. (J). 1984. 2.95 (*0-553-21345-8*, Bantam Classics) Bantam.

Alice's Adventures in Wonderland & Through the Looking Glass. Lewis Carroll. (J). (gr. 4). 1960. pap. 2.95 (*0-451-52320-2*, Sig Classics) NAL-Dutton.

Alice's Adventures in Wonderland & Through the Looking Glass. Lewis Carroll. Ed. by Roger L. Green. (World's Classics Ser.). (Illus.). 1983. pap. 3.50 (*0-19-281620-9*) OUP.

Alice's Adventures in Wonderland & Through the Looking Glass, 2 bks., Set. Lewis Carroll. (Illus.). (J). 1993. boxed 29.95 (*0-688-12050-4*) Morrow Jr Bks.

Alice's Adventures in Wonderland & Through the Looking Glass: And What Alice Found There. Lewis Carroll. (Illus.). 416p. (J). 1992. mass mkt. 3.99 (*0-440-40743-5*, Yearling Classics) Dell.

Alice's Adventures in Wonderland & Through the Looking Glass: Nonsense, Sense & Meaning. Donald Rackin. (Twayne's Masterworks Ser.: No. 81). 176p. 1991. pap. 12.95 (*0-8057-8553-1*, Twayne) Macmillan.

Alice's Adventures in Wonderland & Through the Looking Glass: Nonsense, Sense & Meaning. Donald Rackin. (Twayne's Masterworks Ser.: No. 81). 176p. 1991. text ed. 21.95 (*0-8057-9430-1*, Twayne) Macmillan.

Alice's Adventures in Wonderland, Through the Looking-Glass, & the Hunting of the Snark. Charles L. Dodgson. (BCL1-PR English Literature Ser.). 351p. 1992. reprint ed. lib. bdg. 89.00 (*0-7812-7517-2*) Rprt Serv.

***Alice's Adventures under Ground.** Christopher Hampton. (Orig.). 1995. pap. 11.95 (*0-614-06707-3*) Faber & Faber.

Alice's Adventures under Ground: The Story That Became Alice in Wonderland. Lewis Carroll. (Illus.). 112p. (J). 1992. 17.95 (*1-85145-471-3*, Pub. by Pavilion UK) Trafalgar.

Alice's Adventures Underground. Lewis Carroll. (Illus.). 128p. (J). (gr. 4-9). 1965. pap. 2.95 (*0-486-21482-6*) Dover.

Alice's Amazing Butterfly. Alex N. Holland. (Illus.). 15p. (J). (gr. 1-3). 1992. pap. 11.95 (*1-56606-001-X*) Bradley Mann.

***Alice's Brady Bunch Cookbook.** Ann B. Davis. (Illus.). 256p. 1994. 12.95 (*1-55853-307-9*) Rutledge Hill Pr.

Alice's Diary. Chilton Designs Publishers Staff. (C). 1989. pap. 35.00 (*0-9503527-1-3*, Pub. by Chilton Designs UK) St Mut.

Alice's Flip Book. Ed Rayher. (Illus.). 38p. (J). 1982. per., pap. 1.75 (*0-934714-19-3*) Swamp Pr.

***Alice's Masque.** Lindsay Clarke. 246p. 1995. 24.95 (*0-224-03287-9*, Pub. by Jonathan Cape UK) Trafalgar.

ALice'S WonDerland. Greg West. (Illus.). 23p. 1994. pap. 3.00 (*0-88680-397-7*) I E Clark.

Alice's World: The Life & Photography of an American Original: Alice Austen, 1866-1952. Ann Novotny. LC 76-18489. (Illus.). (J). (gr. 7-9). 1976. 22.50 (*0-85699-128-7*) Chatham Pr.

Alicia. Laura Matthews. (Regency Romance Ser.). 256p. (Orig.). 1992. pap. 3.99 (*0-451-17197-7*, Sig) NAL-Dutton.

Alicia: My Story. Alicia Appleman-Jurman. 1990. mass mkt. 5.99 (*0-553-28218-2*) Bantam.

Alicia: My Story. large type ed. Appleman-Jurman. 1990. 23.95 (*0-7089-8533-5*, Charnwood) Ulverscroft.

Alicia Alonso: At Home & Abroad. Tana De Gamez. 1970. 10.00 (*0-8065-0218-5*, Citadel Pr) Carol Pub Group.

Alicia Alonso: First Lady of the Ballet. Sandra M. Arnold. LC 93-18098. 104p. (YA). (gr. 7 up). 1993. 14.95 (*0-8027-8242-6*); lib. bdg. 15.85 (*0-8027-8243-4*) Walker & Co.

***Alicia en el Pais de las Maravillas.** (Illus.). (SPA.). (J). 1995. pap. 2.95 (*0-486-28177-9*) Dover.

Alicia Has a Bad Day. Lisa Jahn-Clough. LC 94-4520. (J). 1994. 13.95 (*0-395-69454-X*) HM.

Alicia in Blunderland. P. Schuyler Miller. 10.00 (*1-880418-22-3*) D M Grant.

Alicia, the Newest Stockholder. Phyllis Evelyn. (Illus.). 1995. pap. 14.98 (*1-883579-00-7*) Nordic Goddess.

Alicyclic Chemistry, Vols. 2-6. Ed. by W. Parker. Incl. 1972 LiteratureLC 72-83459. 1974. Vol. 2, 1974. 47.00 (*0-85186-522-4*); Vol. 3. 1973 Literature. LC 72-82047. 1973. 61.00 (*0-85186-552-6*); 1974 LiteratureLC 72-83459. 1976. 70.00 (*0-85186-582-8*); 1975 LiteratureLC 72-83459. 1977. 72.00 (*0-85186-612-3*); 1976 LiteratureLC 72-23822. 1978. 73.00 (*0-85186-632-8*); LC 72-82047. write for info. (*0-318-50459-6*) Am Chemical.

Alida: An Erotic Novel. Edna MacBrayne. LC 81-80486. 180p. (Orig.). 1981. pap. 9.00 (*0-939500-00-0*) Parkhurst.

Alida Roochvarg Collection of Books About Books. Ed. by Alida Roochvarg. (Illus.). 300p. 1981. 45.00 (*0-938768-00-X*) Oak Knoll.

***Alien.** Mayer. (J). 1995. pap. text ed. 3.50 (*0-307-16661-9*, Golden Pr) Western Pub.

Alien. Jane O'Brien. (Tales of Terror Ser.). (Illus.). 48p. (J). (gr. 5-6). 1991. text ed. 13.95 (*0-89686-573-8*, Crstwood Hse) Silver Burdett Pr.

***Alien Abduction Survival Guide: How to Cope with Your ET Experience.** Michelle LaVigne. Ed. by Amy E. Owen & Marc Davenport. 106p. (Orig.). 1995. pap. 12.95 (*0-926524-27-5*, Wild Flower Pr) Blue Wtr Pubng.

Alien Abductions. Jenny Randles. 1990. pap. 10.95 (*0-938294-65-2*) Glob Comm-Inner Lght.

Alien Affair, No. 4. L. Ron Hubbard. (Mission Earth Ser.: No. 4). 1993. pap. 4.95 (*0-88404-285-5*) Bridge Pubns Inc.

Alien Agenda. Clifford Wilson. 256p. 1975. pap. 3.95 (*0-451-15706-0*, Sig) NAL-Dutton.

Alien Alert! Debra Hess. LC 95-528. (Spy from Outer Space Ser.). (Illus.). 128p. (J). (gr. 3-6). 1993. pap. 3.50 (*1-56282-567-4*) Hyprn Child.

Alien Alphabet. Rob Chaplin. LC 94-16630. (J). 1994. 11.95 (*0-8118-0701-0*) Chronicle Bks.

Alien & the Immigration Law: A Study of 1446 Cases Arising under the Immigration & Naturalization Laws of the United States. Common Council for American Unity. LC 72-6923. 388p. reprint ed. lib. bdg. 22.50 (*0-8371-6503-2*, ALIL) Greenwood.

Alien Art. Gordon R. Dickson. 192p. 1986. reprint ed. pap. 2.95 (*0-8125-3577-4*) Tor Bks.

***Alien Attack.** Pawnee Elementary School Third-Graders. (Wee Write Bks.: No. 4). (Illus.). 25p. (J). (ps-3). 1994. 17.95 (*1-884987-15-X*) WeWrite.

***Alien Attack.** Pawnee Elementary School Third-Graders. (Wee Write Bks.: No. 4). (Illus.). 25p. (J). (ps-3). 1994. pap. 7.95 (*1-884987-16-8*) WeWrite.

***Alien Attack, Big Bk.** Pawnee Elem. School Third-Graders. (Wee Write Bks.: No. 4). (Illus.). 25p. (J). (ps-3). 1994. 32.95 (*1-884987-17-6*) WeWrite.

Alien Blues. Lynn S. Hightower. 256p. 1992. pap. text ed. 4.99 (*0-441-64460-0*) Ace Bks.

Alien Book of Truth: Who Am I? What Am I Doing? Why Am I Here? Ida Kannenberg. Ed. by Brian Crissey. (UFO Chronicles Ser.). (Illus.). 128p. (Orig.). 1993. pap. 7.95 (*0-926524-15-1*, Wild Flower Pr) Blue Wtr Pubng.

Alien Bootlegger & Other Stories. Rebecca Ore. 1993. mass mkt. 3.99 (*0-8125-1278-2*) Tor Bks.

Alien Bootlegger & Other Stories. Rebecca Ore. 320p. 1993. 19.95 (*0-312-85549-4*) Tor Bks.

Alien Bootlegger & Other Stories. Rebecca Ore. 1995. pap. 14.95 (*0-312-89030-3*) Tor Bks.

***Alien Cantica: An American Journey (1964-1993)** Giose Rimanelli. Ed. & Tr. by Luigi Bonaffini. LC 94-37736. (Southern Italian & Italian-American Culture Ser.: Vol. 7). 1995. write for info. (*0-8204-2650-4*) P Lang Pubs.

Alien Contact: Top Secret UFO Files Revealed. Timothy Good. LC 92-26856. 1993. 22.00 (*0-688-12223-X*) Morrow.

Alien Contact: Top-Secret UFO Files Revealed. Timothy Good. 1994. pap. 12.00 (*0-688-13510-2*, Quill) Morrow.

Alien Contacts & Abductions: The Real Story from the Other Side. Jenny Randles. LC 94-20750. (Illus.). 196p. 1994. pap. 9.95 (*0-8069-0751-7*) Sterling.

Alien Corn: A Novel. Edith L. Tiempo. 135p. (Orig.). 1993. pap. 7.75 (*971-10-0492-5*, Pub. by New Day Pub PH) Cellar.

Alien Dark. Diana G. Gallagher. LC 89-52096. (TSR Bks.). 320p. (Orig.). 1990. pap. 3.95 (*0-88038-928-1*) TSR Inc.

Alien Diaries. Maris Bishofs. LC 86-1080. (Illus.). 116p. 1986. pap. text ed. 9.95 (*0-915361-44-2*) Modan-Adama Bks.

***Alien Discussions: Proceedings of the Abduction Study Conference Held at M. I. T. Cambridge, MA.** Ed. by Andrea Pritchard et al. (Illus.). 684p. 1994. 69.95 (*0-9644917-0-2*) N Cambridge Pr.

Alien Doctors: Foreign Medical Graduates in American Hospitals. Rosemary Stevens et al. LC 77-12934. (Health, Medicine & Society Ser.). 383p. reprint ed. 109.20 (*0-8357-9834-8*, 2016472) Bks Demand.

Alien Encounters. Ed. by Jim Hicks. LC 92-13265. (Mysteries of the Unknown Ser.). (Illus.). 144p. 1992. 12.95 (*0-8094-6545-0*); lib. bdg. 17.45 (*0-8094-6546-9*) Time-Life.

Alien Encounters: Anatomy of Science Fiction. Mark Rose. LC 81-683. 220p. 1982. pap. text ed. 11.95 (*0-674-01566-5*) HUP.

***Alien Encounters: The Deception Menace.** James L. Thompson. 1995. 18.98 (*0-88290-516-3*, 1048) Horizon Utah.

Alien Enemies. Scott Heine. Ed. by Rob Bell. (Champions Ser.). (Illus.). 64p. (Orig.). (C). 1990. pap. text ed. 12.00 (*1-55806-112-6*, 413) Iron Crown Ent Inc.

Alien Entities. Lester Sumrall. 111p. (Orig.). (C). 1983. pap. text ed. 10.00 (*0-937580-76-7*) LeSEA Pub Co.

Alien Equation. Annie Maccoby & Jeff Church. 47p. 1986. reprint ed. 3.45 (*0-87129-024-3*, A45) Dramatic Pub.

Alien Eyes. Lynn S. Hightower. 256p. (Orig.). 1993. pap. text ed. 4.99 (*0-441-01688-X*) Ace Bks.

Alien Factor. Franklin W. Dixon. Ed. by Anne Greenberg. (Hardy Boys - Tom Swift Ultra Thriller Ser.). 224p. (Orig.). (J). 1993. mass mkt. 3.99 (*0-671-79532-5*, Archway) PB.

***Alien Game.** Catherine Dexter. LC 94-33240. 192p. (YA). (gr. 5 up). 1995. 15.00 (*0-688-11332-X*) Morrow Jr Bks.

Alien, Go Home. Seddon Johnson. (Choose Your Own Adventure Ser.: No. 101). (J). 1990. pap. 3.25 (*0-553-28482-7*) Bantam.

***Alien, Go Home!** large type ed. Seddon Johnson. (Choose Your Own Adventure Ser.: No. 101). (Illus.). 128p. (J). 1995. lib. bdg. 15.93 (*0-8368-1304-9*) Gareth Stevens Inc.

Alien Harvest: Further Evidence Linking Animal Mutilations & Human Abductions to Alien Life Forms. Linda M. Howe. (Illus.). 456p. 1993. reprint ed. pap. 40.00 (*0-9620570-1-0*) L M Howe Prodns.
Television producer-director-writer Linda Moulton Howe received her Masters Degree from Stanford University with a focus on science, medicine & the environment. When animals, especially cattle & horses, were found throughout the world in the 1970s with the same pattern of bizarre, bloodless, excisions of tissue, she investigated the story as an environmental contamination until eyewitness testimonies forced her to confront the possibility that non-human intelligences are interacting with us, our animals & our plant life. The result was her 1980 Emmy Award-winning documentary A STRANGE HARVEST. A decade later, Howe has synthesized her research & contacts with alleged government insiders in AN ALIEN HARVEST. One Air Force intelligence officer told her: "That documentary you did upset some people in Washington. They don't want animal mutilations & UFO's connected together in the public's mind." REVIEWS: "This book comes as close as any yet toward boring right into the heart of what the UFO mystery has become... By following Linda Howe's odyssey through an American West littered the carcasses of mutilated livestock, by discovering with her the distinct UFO connection to these mutilations which have not gone away by any means, & by becoming involved with the U.S. government itself to the point of being shown a briefing paper prepared for none less than the President of the U.S., you will learn what UFOlogy is REALLY about now some 42 years after its arrival into our consciousness. The book has the impact of a runaway freight train."--Bob Girard, Arcturus Books. "If seeing is believing, then here's what you've been looking for: a large format, 476 page volume with many graphic color pictures."--Martin Burkey, The Huntsville Times. "If books could convince, skeptics would be an endangered species after reading AN ALIEN HARVEST."--Dennis Stacy, New Age Journal. 4th printing, May 1995. ***Publisher Provided Annotation.***

Alien Heart. K. S. Duggal. 1990. text ed. 6.95 (*0-86131-997-4*, Pub. by Orient Longman Ltd II) Apt Bks.

Alien Heat. Lynn S. Hightower. 240p. (Orig.). 1994. pap. text ed. 4.99 (*0-441-00072-X*) Ace Bks.

Alien Homage - Edward Thompson & Rabindranath Tagore: With an Appendix on Edward Thomspon's "Notebook of Converstaions with Rabindranath" by Uma das Gupta. E. P. Thompson. 188p. 1993. 16.95 (*0-19-563011-4*) OUP.

Alien Identities: Ancient Insights into Modern UFO Phenomenon. Richard L. Thompson. LC 92-76167. 512p. (Orig.). 1993. pap. 19.95 (*0-9635309-1-7*) Govardhan Hill.

Alien Immigrants to England. 2nd ed. William Cunningham. (Illus.). 286p. 1969. reprint ed. 35.00 (*0-7146-1295-2*, Pub. by F Cass Pubs UK) Intl Spec Bk.

Alien Immigrants to England. William Cunningham. LC 72-94541. (Reprints of Economic Classics Ser.). (Illus.). 1969. reprint ed. lib. bdg. 37.50 (*0-678-05098-8*) Kelley.

Alien in Israelite Law. Van Houten. (JSOT Supplement Ser.). 165p. (C). 1991. 22.50 (*1-85075-317-2*, Pub. by Sheffield Acad UK) CUP Services.

Alien Ink: The FBI's War on Freedom of Expression. Natalie Robins. LC 92-36943. (Illus.). 495p. (C). 1993. reprint ed. pap. 14.95 (*0-8135-1954-3*) Rutgers U Pr.

Alien Invasions. Benjamin Kendall. Ed. by Nancy R. Thatch. LC 93-13423. (Books for Students by Students Ser.). (Illus.). 29p. (J). (gr. 2-4). 1993. lib. bdg. 14.95 (*0-933849-42-7*) Landmark Edns.

Alien Labor Contracts. John P. Carney. 148p. 1994. pap. 5.75 (*1-879861-06-2*) Consensus Pubs.

Alien Legacy. Paul Estenson. LC 94-70719. 456p. (Orig.). 1994. pap. 11.95 (*1-885185-00-6*) Alta Pr.

***Alien Legacy: Official Players Guide.** John Sauer. (Illus.). 224p. (Orig.). 1994. pap. 18.95 (*1-57280-006-2*) IFTW Bks.

Alien Legion: A Grey Day to Die. Potts et al. 64p. 1986. 5.95 (*0-87135-207-9*) Marvel Entmnt.

Alien Legion: Jugger Grimrod. Chuck Dixon & Mike McMahon. 48p. 1992. 4.95 (*0-87135-897-2*) Marvel Entmnt.

Alien Legion: One Planet at a Time, No. 1. 1992. write for info. (*0-87135-898-0*) Marvel Entmnt.

Alien Legion: One Planet at a Time, No. 2. 1992. write for info. (*0-87135-899-9*) Marvel Entmnt.

An Asterisk (*) at the beginning of an entry indicates that the title is appearing in BIP for the first time.

An Asterisk (*) at the beginning of an entry indicates that the title is appearing in BIP for the first time.

Alimentary Tract Radiology, No. 4. Margulis. (Illus.). 2216p. 1989. 299.00 (*0-8016-3191-2*) Mosby Yr Bk.
Alimentation Clinique des Petits Animaux, No. III. 3rd ed. Lon D. Lewis et al. Tr. by Philippe Moreau. (Illus.). 470p. (C). 1989. 18.00 (*0-945837-00-3*) M Morris Assocs.
***Alimentation des Femmes: Etape essentielle au Development de l'Enfant.** Ed. by Anne-Marie Masse-Raimbault et al. 152p. (Orig.). (FRE.). 1994. pap. text ed. write for info. (*0-89492-107-X*) Acad Educ Dev.
Alimento de Fe Devocionales Diarios Para Invierno. Kenneth E. Hagin. 96p. (SPA.). 1992. pap. 2.50 (*0-89276-141-5*) Hagin Ministries.
Alimony. Faith Baldwin. 1976. reprint ed. 21.95 (*0-88411-616-6*, Aeonian Pr) Amereon Ltd.
Alimony: New Strategies for Pursuit & Defense. LC 88-70998. 228p. 1988. pap. 39.95 (*0-89707-369-X*, 513-0024-01) Amer Bar Assn.
Alimony or Death of the Clock. Lynn Watson. Ed. by Laura Israel. (Illus.). 97p. (Orig.). 1981. pap. 7.95 (*0-9607328-0-2*) Keegan Pr.
Alin Learns to Use His Imagination. Ilona Selke. 48p. (YA). 1994. pap. 11.95 (*1-884246-01-X*) Liv from Vis.
Alina: A Russian Girl Comes to Israel. Mira Meir. Tr. by Zeva Shapiro. (Illus.). 48p. (J). (gr. 2-4). 1982. 9.95 (*0-8276-0208-1*) JPS Phila.
Aline et Valcourt. Donatien A. Sade. 480p. (FRE.). 1986. pap. 45.00 (*0-7859-1544-3*, 2720201995) Fr & Eur.
Aline Meyer Liebman: Pioneer Collector & Artist. Margaret L. Berger. LC 81-80753. (Illus.). 148p. 1982. 25.00 (*0-9605914-0-0*) M L Berger.
Alineas - l'Art D'Ecrire. Ronald St. Onge & Maguy Albet. 228p. 1990. text ed. 36.95 (*0-8384-2094-X*) Heinle & Heinle.
***Alington Inheritance.** P. Wentworth. Date not set. pap. 3.99 (*0-517-13220-6*) Random.
Alington Inheritance. Patricia Wentworth. 19.95 (*0-88411-730-8*, Aeonian Pr) Amereon Ltd.
Alinor. Roberta Gellis. 560p. 1994. reprint ed. pap. 5.99 (*0-8439-3607-X*) Dorchester Pub Co.
Alinsky Legacy: Alive & Kicking. Louis Kriesberg et al. (Research in Social Movement, Conflicts & Change Ser.: Suppl. 1). 1987. 73.25 (*0-89232-722-7*) Jai Pr.
Aliocha. Henri Troyat. (FRE.). 1993. pap. 4.95 (*0-7859-3290-9*, 2277234095) Fr & Eur.
Aliphatic Chemistry, Vol. 2. A. McKillop. 1972. 41.00 (*0-85186-512-7*, Pub. by Royal Soc Chem UK) Am Chemical.
Aliphatic Chemistry, Vol. 3. A. McKillop. 1973. 43.00 (*0-85186-542-9*, Pub. by Royal Soc Chem UK) Am Chemical.
Aliphatic Chemistry, Vol. 4. A. McKillop. 1974. 45.00 (*0-85186-572-0*, Pub. by Royal Soc Chem UK) Am Chemical.
Aliphatic Chemistry, Vol. 5. A. McKillop. 1975. 61.00 (*0-85186-602-6*, Pub. by Royal Soc Chem UK) Am Chemical.
Aliphatic Derivatives. V. St. Georgiev. (Survey of Drug Research in Immunologic Disease Ser.: Vol. 1). (Illus.). x, 542p. 1982. 392.00 (*3-8055-3503-1*) S Karger.
Aliphatic Ketones, Ammonium Salts, Atmosphere, Potassium Chloride: Corrosive Agents & Their Interaction with Materials. Dieter Behrens. (Dechema Corrision Handbook Ser.: Vol. 7). 338p. 1990. lib. bdg. 575.00 (*0-89573-628-4*) VCH Pubs.
Alismataceae. Robert R. Haynes & Lauritz B. Holm-Nielson. (Flora Neotropica Ser.: Vol. 64). (Illus.). 1994. pap. text ed. 17.50 (*0-89327-387-2*) NY Botanical.
Alismataceae to Orchidaceae see Flora Europaea
***Alison.** Raleigh Rogers. LC 93-94366. 208p. (Orig.). 1995. pap. 12.00 (*1-56002-433-X*, Univ Edtns) Aegina Pr.
Alison: A Father's Search for His Missing Daughter. Quentin Macfarlane. (Illus.). 192p. 1994. pap. 17.95 (*1-85158-624-5*, Pub. by Mnstream UK) Trafalgar.
Alison: Principles of the Criminal Law of Scotland (1832) & Practice of the Criminal Law in Scotland (1833), 2 vols., Set. J. Irvine Smith. (Scottish Legal Classics Ser.). 1990. boxed 200.00 (*0-406-17898-4*, UK) Butterworth Legal Pubs.
***Alison Goes for the Gold.** Nancy Lamb. Ed. by Judit Bodnar & Betsy Gould. (Magic Attic Club Ser.). (Illus.). 64p. (Orig.). (J). (gr. 2-6). 1995. 12.95 (*1-57513-002-5*); pap. 5.95 (*1-57513-003-3*) Magic Attic Club.
Alison Lurie. Richard H. Costa. 160p. (C). 1992. text ed. 22.95 (*0-8057-7634-6*, Twayne) Macmillan.
***Alison on the Trail.** Nancy Lamb. Ed. by Judit Bodnar & Betsy Gould. (Magic Attic Club Ser.). (Illus.). 64p. (Orig.). (J). (gr. 2-6). 1995. 12.95 (*1-57513-010-6*); pap. 5.95 (*1-57513-011-4*) Magic Attic Club.
Alison's Zinnia. Anita Lobel. LC 89-23700. (Illus.). 32p. (J). (ps up). 1990. 15.00 (*0-688-08865-1*); lib. bdg. 15.93 (*0-688-08866-X*) Greenwillow.
Alistair & the Alien Invasion. Marilyn Sadler. LC 92-22828. (Illus.). (J). 1994. pap. 15.00 (*0-671-75957-4*, S&S Bks Young Read) S&S Childrens.
Alistair in Outer Space. Marilyn Sadler. LC 84-4896. (J). 1984. pap. 15.00 (*0-671-66678-9*, S&S Bks Young Read) S&S Childrens.
Alistair in Outer Space. Marilyn Sadler. LC 84-4896. (J). 1989. pap. 6.95 (*0-671-67938-4*, S&S Bks Young Read) S&S Childrens.
Alistair Maclean. Jack Webster. (Illus.). 328p. 1993. pap. 8.95 (*1-85592-576-1*, Pub. by Chapmans UK) Trafalgar.
Alistair Maclean: A Biography of a Master Storyteller. large type ed. Jack Webster. (Illus.). 496p. 1993. 23.95 (*0-7089-8687-0*, Charnwood) Ulverscroft.
Alistair MacLean: The Key Is Fear. Robert A. Lee. LC 76-29047. (Milford Series: Popular Writers of Today: Vol. 2). 60p. 1976. lib. bdg. 20.00 (*0-89370-103-3*); pap. 10.00 (*0-89370-203-X*) Borgo Pr.
***Alistair MacLean's Golden Girl.** Simon Gandolfi. 1994. mass mkt. 5.99 (*0-449-14888-2*, GM) Fawcett.
Alistair Maclean's Time of the Assassins. Alastair MacNeill. 1993. mass mkt. 5.99 (*0-06-104229-3*, Harp PBks) HarpC.
Alistair Underwater. Marilyn Sadler. (J). 1990. pap. 15.00 (*0-671-69406-5*, S&S Bks Young Read) S&S Childrens.
Alistair Underwater. Marilyn Sadler. LC 89-3658. (J). (ps-3). 1992. pap. 5.95 (*0-671-79246-6*, S&S Bks Young Read) S&S Childrens.
Alistair's Elephant. Marilyn Sadler & Roger Bollen. LC 82-23091. (Illus.). 48p. (J). (gr. k-4). 1991. pap. 14.00 (*0-671-66680-0*, S&S Bks Young Read); pap. 5.95 (*0-671-66681-9*, S&S Bks Young Read) S&S Childrens.
Alistair's Time Machine. Marilyn Sadler. (Illus.). 40p. (J). (ps up). 1989. pap. 5.95 (*0-671-68493-0*, S&S Bks Young Read) S&S Childrens.
Alistair's Time Machine. Marilyn Sadler. (Illus.). 40p. (J). (ps up). 1992. pap. 15.00 (*0-671-66679-7*, S&S Bks Young Read) S&S Childrens.
Alistar MacLean's Red Alert. large type ed. Alistair MacNeill. 1992. 18.95 (*0-7927-1255-2*, E0036, Eagle Lrg Print) Chivers N Amer.
Aliteracy: People Who Can Read but Won't. Ed. by Nick Thimmesch. 59p. 1984. pap. 12.50 (*0-8447-2247-2*) Am Enterprise.
Alitji in Dreamland: Alitjinya Ngura Tjukurmankuntjala: An Aboriginal Version of Lewis Carroll's Alice's Adventures in Wonderland. Illus. by Donna Leslie. LC 92-17640. 104p. (J). (gr. 6 up). 1992. 16.95 (*0-89815-478-2*) Ten Speed Pr.
Alive: Daily Devotions for Young People. S. Rickly Christian. (Illus.). (YA). 1990. pap. 9.99 (*0-310-71031-6*) Zondervan.
Alive! God in Intimate Relationship with You. Churches Alive, Inc. Staff. (God in You Bible Study Ser.). (Illus.). 72p. (Orig.). 1986. 5.00 (*0-89109-093-2*) NavPress.
Alive: The Story of the Andes Survivors. Piers P. Read. 1979. mass mkt. 5.99 (*0-380-00321-X*) Avon.
***Alive No. 1: Daily Devotions.** rev. ed. S. Rickly Christian. 272p. (YA). 1995. pap. 9.99 (*0-310-49901-1*) Zondervan.
***Alive No. 2: Daily Devotions.** rev. ed. S. Rickly Christian. 272p. (YA). 1995. pap. 9.99 (*0-310-49911-9*) Zondervan.
Alive Again! Bill Banks. 168p. (Orig.). 1977. pap. 4.95 (*0-89228-048-4*) Impact Christian.
Alive Alive O: Conversations with Dublin Women. Marvin Johnston. (Illus.). 160p. (Orig.). (C). 1989. pap. 11.95 (*0-946211-49-3*, Pub. by Attic IE) InBook.
Alive All Day. Richard Jackson. LC 92-70725. (CSU Poetry Ser.: XXXVI). 96p. (Orig.). 1992. 15.00 (*0-914946-95-1*); pap. 10.00 (*0-914946-96-X*) Cleveland St Univ Poetry Ctr.
Alive & Dead. large type ed. Elizabeth X. Ferrars. 1978. 12.00 (*0-7089-0131-X*) Ulverscroft.
***Alive & Kicking.** Date not set. (*0-8317-5826-0*) Smithmark.
Alive & Kicking: A Novel. Michael Levin. 368p. 1993. 21.00 (*0-671-73190-4*) S&S Trade.
Alive & Kicking: Towards a Practical Theology of Illness & Healing. Stephen Pattison. 208p. (C). 1989. pap. text ed. 15.95 (*0-334-01871-4*, SCM Pr) TPI PA.
***Alive & Kicking Vol. 1.** Michael Levin. 1994. pap. 4.99 (*0-312-95305-4*) St Martin.
Alive & Well: A Path of Healing in a Time of HIV. Peter A. Hendrickson. (Illus.). 150p. 1990. 24.95 (*0-8290-2450-6*); pap. 12.95 (*0-8290-2460-3*); audio 19.95 (*0-8290-2475-1*) Irvington.
Alive & Well: A Study of the Church - First John. Randal E. Denny. 192p. (Orig.). 1993. per., pap. 10.95 (*0-8341-1453-4*, 45516) Beacon Hill.
***Alive & Well: A Workbook for Recovering Your Body.** Rita Justice. 304p. 1995. pap. write for info. (*0-9605376-3-5*) Peak Pr.
Alive & Well: Decisions in Health. Arlene Eisenberg & Howard Eisenberg. 1979. pap. text ed. write for info. (*0-07-019136-0*) McGraw.
***Alive & Well: One Doctor's Experience with Nutrition in the Treatment of Cancer Patients.** Philip E. Binzel. (Illus.). 144p. (Orig.). (C). 1994. pap. 9.95 (*0-912986-17-4*) Am Media.
Alive & Well? A Research & Policy Review of Health Programs for Poor Young Children. Lorraine V. Klerman. LC 90-20002. (Illus.). 132p. (Orig.). 1991. pap. 11.95 (*0-926582-02-X*) NCCP.
Alive & Well in the Fast Lane. Carolyn Coats & Pamela Smith. (Illus.). 156p. 1987. pap. 10.00 (*1-878722-03-4*) C Coats Bestsellers.
Alive & Writing: Interviews with American Authors of the 1980s. Ed. by Larry McCaffery & Sinda Gregory. LC 86-25075. (Illus.). 296p. (C). 1987. 29.95 (*0-252-01385-9*) U of Ill Pr.
***Alive Beyond Blue.** Thomas Williams. LC 94-42342. 64p. 1995. pap. 12.95 (*0-7734-2740-6*, Mellen Poetry Pr) E Mellen.
Alive for God in Christ Jesus. Edmund J. Elbert. 1993. 16.95 (*0-533-10655-9*) Vantage.
***Alive in Christ.** Stuart Olyott. 1994. pap. 8.99 (*0-85234-315-9*, Pub. by Evangel Pr UK) Presby & Reformed.
Alive in Christ. David Womack. LC 75-22609. (Radiant Life Ser.). 128p. 1975. teacher ed 4.50 (*0-88243-162-5*, 32-0162); pap. 2.95 (*0-88243-888-3*, 02-0888) Gospel Pub.
***Alive in Christ: How to Find Renewed Spiritual Power.** Charles W. Price. LC 94-37821. 160p. 1995. pap. 5.99 (*0-8254-3551-X*) Kregel.
Alive in Christ, Alert to Life. John Weborg. 1985. pap. 5.95 (*0-910452-63-6*) Covenant.
Alive in Him. Phyllis M. Carson. (Illus.). 32p. 1993. write for info. (*1-883331-01-3*) Anderie Poetry.
Alive in the Risen Christ: First Corinthians 8-16. Werner Kliewer & Marilyn Kliewer. Ed. by Maynard Shelly. LC 87-81721. (Faith & Life Bible Studies). 148p. (Orig.). 1987. pap. 4.95 (*0-87303-119-9*) Faith & Life.
Alive in the Spirit: A Study of the Nature & Work of the Holy Spirit. Jimmy Jividen. 146p. 1990. pap. 6.99 (*0-89225-368-1*) Gospel Advocate.
Alive in the Twentieth Century: or, How Existence Seems to Me. David Holden. 1992. 15.95 (*0-533-10062-3*) Vantage.
Alive on Men's Lips. Dora Pym & Nancy Silver. 150p. (C). 1982. pap. text ed. 50.00 (*0-685-44231-4*, Pub. by Old Vicarage UK) St Mut.
Alive or Dead. Heinz Piontek. Tr. by Richard Exner. LC 72-77917. (German Ser.: Vol. 4). 64p. 1975. 17.50 (*0-87775-041-6*); pap. 7.95 (*0-87775-089-0*) Unicorn Pr.
Alive to God: Studies in Spirituality Presented to James M. Houston. Ed. by J. I. Packer & Loren Wilkinson. LC 92-31340. 314p. 1992. pap. 19.99 (*0-8308-1767-0*) InterVarsity.
Alive Two. S. Rickly Christian. (Illus.). (YA). 1990. pap. 9.99 (*0-310-71041-3*) Zondervan.
***Alivio de la Pobreza y Fondos de Inversion Social: La Experiencia Latinoamericana.** Philip J. Glaessner et al. (Discussion Papers: Vol. 261). 84p. (SPA.). 1995. 7.95 (*0-8213-3172-8*, 13172) World Bank.
Aliya. Aliza Auerbach. (Illus.). 220p. 1993. 38.00 (*0-317-05858-4*, Pub. by Israel Ministry Def IS) Gefen Bks.
Alizarin Lake Reader. Alizarin Lake. (Orig.). 1993. pap. text ed. 4.95 (*1-56333-106-3*) Masquerade.
***ALJ Handbook: An Insider's Guide to Becoming a Federal Administrative Law Judge.** 2nd ed. Ed. by Richard L. Hermann & Linda P. Sutherland. 90p. 1994. 34.95 (*0-929728-25-4*) Federal Reports Inc.
Aljeksjej Theodorovich L'vov-director Imperatorskoj pridvornoj pevcheskoj kapelli i dukhovnij kompozitor. Johann V. Gardner. 90p. 1970. pap. 3.00 (*0-317-30387-2*) Holy Trinity.
Alkali- & Alkaline-Earth Metal Oxides & Hydroxides in Water: Solubilities of Solids. Bauman. (Solubility Data Ser.). 1992. 130.00 (*0-08-023920-X*, Pergamon Pr) Elsevier.
Alkali-Aggregate Reaction: Eighth International Conference, Kyob, Japan, 17-20 July 1989. Ed. by K. Okada et al. 890p. 1990. 176.50 (*1-85166-417-3*) Elsevier.
Alkali Cation Transport Systems in Prokaryotes. Bakker. 1992. 219.00 (*0-8493-6982-7*, QH509) CRC Pr.
Alkali County Tales. John R. Erickson. (Illus.). 100p. (Orig.). (J). (gr. 3-p). 1984. 9.95 (*0-916941-06-X*); pap. 5.95 (*0-9608612-8-9*) Maverick Bks.
Alkali Metal, Alkaline-Earth Metal & Ammonium Halides in Amide Solvents. Ed. by Scrosati & Colin A. Vincent. (IUPAC Solubility Data Ser.: Vol. 11). 374p. 1980. 154.00 (*0-08-023917-X*, Pub. by Pergamon Repr UK) Franklin.
Alkali Metal & Ammonium Chlorides in Water & Heavy Water (Binary Systems) Ed. by R. Cohen-Adad & J. W. Lorimer. (Solubility Data Ser.: Vol. 47). 330p. 1991. 145.00 (*0-08-023918-8*, Pergamon Pr) Elsevier.
Alkali Metal Halates, Ammonium Iodate & Iodic Acid. A. S. Miyamoto & M. Salamon. (Solubility Data Ser.: No. 30). 1987. 170.00 (*0-08-029210-0*, Pergamon Pr) Elsevier.
Alkali Metal Halates, Ammonium Iodate & Iodic Acid. A. S. Miyamoto & M. Salamon. (Solubility Data Ser.: No. 30). 1999. Japanese ed. 130.00 (*0-08-029211-9*, Pergamon Pr) Elsevier.
Alkali Metal Orthophosphates. Ed. by J. Eysseltova & T. P. Dirkse. (IUPAC Solubility Data Ser.: Vol. 31). (Illus.). 368p. 1988. 170.00 (*0-08-035937-X*, Pergamon Pr) Elsevier.
Alkali-Silica Reaction in Concrete. D. W. Hobbs. 192p. 1988. 54.00 (*0-7277-1317-5*, Pub. by T Telford UK) Am Soc Civil Eng.
Alkali-Silica Reactivity: An Overview of Research. Richard Helmut et al. 105p. (Orig.). (C). 1993. pap. text ed. 15.00 (*0-309-05602-0*, SHRP-C-342) SHRP.
Alkali Soils: Their Reclamation & Productivity. L. L. Somani. 331p. (C). 1990. 125.00 (*81-85312-05-2*, Scientific) St Mut.
Alkali Trails. William Holden. 1993. reprint ed. lib. bdg. 75.00 (*0-7812-5936-3*) Rprt Serv.
Alkalies in Concrete, STP 930. Ed. by Vance H. Dodson. LC 86-20564. (Special Technical Publication (STP) Ser.). (Illus.). 90p. pap. text ed. 24.00 (*0-8031-0498-7*, 04-930000-07) ASTM.
Alkaline Earth Metal Halates. Ed. by H. Miyamoto et al. 352p. 1983. 130.00 (*0-08-029213-5*, Pergamon Pr) Elsevier.
Alkaline Earth Metal Perchlorates. Ed. by Chan Chee-Yan et al. LC 85-641351. (Solubility Data Ser.: No. 41). 304p. 1989. 120.00 (*0-08-040198-8*, Pergamon Pr) Elsevier.
Alkaline Papermaking: A TAPPI Press Anthology of Published Papers, 1982-1992. Ed. by Dan W. Manson. LC 92-28279. 1992. 148.00 (*0-89852-271-4*, 0101R204) TAPPI.
Alkaline Papermaking: A TAPPI Press Anthology of Published Papers, 1982-1992. Technical Associaton of the Pulp & Paper Industry Staff. Ed. by Dan W. Manson. LC 92-28279. 437p. reprint ed. pap. 124.60 (*0-7837-3940-0*, 2043695) Bks Demand.
Alkaline Papermaking, 1985: Notes of TAPPI, Denver Marriott, Denver, CO, April 17-19. Technical Association of the Pulp & Paper Industry Staff. 139p. reprint ed. pap. 39.70 (*0-8357-5309-3*, 2025286) Bks Demand.
Alkaline Ring Complexes in Africa: Proceedings of the International Conference Held in Zaria, Nigeria, Dec. 6-10, 1983. Ed. by R. Black & Peter Boden. 286p. 1985. pap. 51.00 (*0-08-032613-7*, Pub. by PPL UK) Elsevier.
Alkaline Rocks. Ed. by Henning Sorensen. LC 72-5725. (Illus.). 634p. reprint ed. pap. 180.00 (*0-8357-5310-7*, 2030422) Bks Demand.
Alkaline Rocks & Carbonatites of the World: Pt. 1, North & South America. Alan R. Woolley. (Illus.). 222p. 1987. text ed. 65.00 (*0-292-70389-9*) U of Tex Pr.
***Alkalize Or Die.** Theodore A. Baroody. (Illus.). 242p. (Orig.). 1991. pap. 14.95 (*0-9619595-3-3*) Eclectic Pr NC.
Alkaloids. Ed. by J. F. Jackson & H. F. Linskens. (Modern Methods of Plant Analysis Ser.: Vol. 15). (Illus.). 304p. 1994. 196.00 (*0-387-52738-9*) Spr-Verlag.
Alkaloids, Vol. 23. Arnold Brossi. Ed. by R. H. Manske & H. L. Holmes. (Serial Publication Ser.). 1984. text ed. 169.00 (*0-12-469523-X*) Acad Pr.
Alkaloids, Vol. 27. Arnold Brossi. (Serial Publication Ser.). 1986. text ed. 169.00 (*0-12-469527-2*) Acad Pr.
Alkaloids, Vol. 28. Ed. by Arnold Brossi. (Serial Publication Ser.). 1986. text ed. 158.00 (*0-12-469528-0*) Acad Pr.
Alkaloids, Vol. 30. Ed. by Arnold Brossi. (Serial Publication Ser.). 387p. 1987. text ed. 143.00 (*0-12-469530-2*) Acad Pr.
Alkaloids, Vol. 31. Ed. by Arnold Brossi. (Serial Publication Ser.). 395p. 1987. text ed. 154.00 (*0-12-469531-0*) Acad Pr.
Alkaloids, Vol. 32. Arnold Brossi. (Serial Publication Ser.). 454p. 1988. text ed. 162.00 (*0-12-469532-9*) Acad Pr.
Alkaloids, Vol. 34. Ed. by Arnold Brossi. (Serial Publication Ser.). 400p. 1988. text ed. 136.00 (*0-12-469534-5*) Acad Pr.
Alkaloids, Vol. 42. Ed. by Geoffrey A. Cordell. (Illus.). 314p. 1992. text ed. 110.00 (*0-12-469542-6*) Acad Pr.
Alkaloids, Vol. 43. Ed. by Geoffrey A. Cordell. (Illus.). 301p. 1993. text ed. 99.00 (*0-12-469543-4*) Acad Pr.
Alkaloids, Vols. 1-8. Ed. by M. F. Grundon. Incl. Vol. 1. 1969-70 Literature. LC 70-616637. 1971. 43.00 (*0-85186-257-8*); Vol. 3. 1971-72 Literature. LC 70-616637. 1973. 37.00 (*0-85186-277-2*); Vol. 4. 1972-73 Literature. LC 70-616637. 1974. 43.00 (*0-85186-287-X*); Vol. 5. 1973-74 Literature. LC 70-616637. 1975. 47.00 (*0-85186-297-7*); Vol. 6. 1974-75 Literature. LC 70-616637. 1976. 50.00 (*0-85186-307-8*); Vol. 7. 1975-76 Literature. LC 70-616637. 1977. 65.00 (*0-85186-317-5*); Vol. 8. 1976-77 Literature. LC 79-67610. 1978. 61.00 (*0-85186-327-2*); LC 70-616637. write for info. (*0-318-50460-X*) Am Chemical.
Alkaloids: Chemical & Biological Perspectives, Vol. 2. Ed. by S. William Pelletier. LC 82-11071. 504p. 1984. text ed. 63.00 (*0-471-89299-8*) Krieger.
Alkaloids: Chemical & Biological Perspectives, Vol. 3. Ed. by S. William Pelletier. 336p. 1990. text ed. 75.00 (*0-471-89302-1*) Krieger.
Alkaloids: Chemical & Biological Perspectives, Vol. 4. Pelletier. (Chemical & Biological Perspectives Ser.). 460p. 1986. text ed. 100.00 (*0-471-89301-3*) Krieger.
Alkaloids: Chemical & Biological Perspectives, Vol. 5. Ed. by S. William Pelletier. 730p. 1987. text ed. 125.00 (*0-471-85372-0*) Krieger.
Alkaloids: Chemical & Biological Perspectives, Vol. 6. Ed. by S. William Pelletier. 542p. 1988. text ed. 199.00 (*0-471-60298-1*) Wiley.
***Alkaloids: Chemical and Biological Perspectives, Vol. 9.** Pelletier. (Alkaloids Chemical & Biological). 273p. 1994. text ed. 140.00 (*0-08-042089-3*, Pergamon Pr) Elsevier.
Alkaloids: Chemistry & Pharmacology, Vol. 20. Ed. by R. Manske & R. G. Rodrigo. (Serial Publication Ser.). 1982. text ed. 148.00 (*0-12-469520-5*) Acad Pr.
Alkaloids: Chemistry & Pharmacology, Vol. 21. Ed. by R. F. Manske & H. L. Holmes. (Serial Publication Ser.). 1983. text ed. 148.00 (*0-12-469521-3*) Acad Pr.
Alkaloids: Chemistry & Pharmacology, Vol 22. Ed. by R. H. Manske. (Serial Publication Ser.). 1983. text ed. 148.00 (*0-12-469522-1*) Acad Pr.
Alkaloids: Chemistry & Pharmacology, Vol. 24. Ed. by Arnold Brossi. (Serial Publication Ser.). 1985. text ed. 169.00 (*0-12-469524-8*) Acad Pr.
Alkaloids: Chemistry & Pharmacology, Vol. 36. Ed. by Arnold Brossi. (Serial Publication Ser.). 337p. 1989. text ed. 130.00 (*0-12-469536-1*) Acad Pr.
Alkaloids: Chemistry & Physiology. Ed. by R. H. Manske et al. write for info. (*0-318-50224-0*) Acad Pr.
Alkaloids: Chemistry & Physiology, Vol. 18. Ed. by R. H. Manske & R. G. Rodrigo. LC 50-5522. 1981. text ed. 170.00 (*0-12-469518-3*) Acad Pr.
Alkaloids: The Fundamental Chemistry: A Biogenetic Approach. David R. Dalton. LC 79-4538. (Studies in Organic Chemistry: No. 7). (Illus.). 803p. reprint ed. pap. 180.00 (*0-7837-4423-4*, 2052483) Bks Demand.
***Alkaloids Vol. 46: Chemistry & Pharmacology.** Ed. by Geoffrey A. Cordell. (Illus.). 308p. 1995. boxed write for info. (*0-12-469546-9*) Acad Pr.
***Alkaloids Vol. 47: Chemistry & Pharmacology, Vol. 47.** Ed. by Geoffrey A. Cordell. (Illus.). 284p. 1995. text ed. write for info. (*0-12-469547-7*) Acad Pr.
Alkaloids, Vol. 19: Chemistry & Physiology. Ed. by R. G. Manske. 1981. text ed. 148.00 (*0-12-469519-1*) Acad Pr.
Alkaloids, Vol. 33: Chemistry & Pharmacology. Ed. by Arnold Brossi. 360p. 1988. text ed. 162.00 (*0-12-469533-7*) Acad Pr.
Alkaloids, Vol. 35: Chemistry & Pharmacology. Ed. by Arnold Brossi. 321p. 1989. text ed. 140.00 (*0-12-469535-3*) Acad Pr.
Alkaloids, Vol. 37: Antitumor Bisindole Alkaloids from Catharanthus Roseus (L) Ed. by Arnold Brossi & Matthew Suffness. 250p. 1990. text ed. 116.00 (*0-12-469537-X*) Acad Pr.

An Asterisk (*) at the beginning of an entry indicates that the title is appearing in BIP for the first time.

An Asterisk (*) at the beginning of an entry indicates that the title is appearing in BIP for the first time.

191

All about Finches. Ian Harman & Matthew M. Vriends. (Illus.). 1978. 16.95 (*0-87666-965-8*, PS-765) TFH Pubns.

***All about Florida Almanac: Instant Information about Hundreds of Subjects.** Ed. by Harry Shay. (Illus.). (Orig.). 1995. per., pap. text ed. 17.95 (*1-883351-04-9*) Instant Info.

All about Football. George Sullivan. (Illus.). 128p. (J). (gr. 3-7). 1990. pap. 7.95 (*0-399-21907-2*, Putnam) Putnam Pub Group.

All about FORTH. 3rd ed. Glen B. Haydon. (MVP-Forth Bks.: Vol. 1). 600p. 1990. pap. 90.00 (*0-685-62537-0*) Mntn View Pr.

***All about Frogs.** Larry Block. 30p. (J). Date not set. 6.95 (*0-7610-0296-0*) NW Pub.

All about Futures: From the Inside Out. Thomas A. McCafferty & Russell R. Wasendorf. 300p. 1992. 19.95 (*1-55738-296-4*) Probus Pub Co.

All about Goals & How to Achieve Them. Jack E. Addington. LC 77-80016. 1977. pap. 8.95 (*0-87516-237-1*) DeVorss.

All about Goats. 2nd ed. Lois Hetherington. (Illus.). 196p. 1979. 24.95 (*0-85236-094-0*, Pub. by Farming Pr UK) Diamond Farm Bk.

All about God. Mary R. Pearson. LC 93-7692. (J). 1993. 8.99 (*0-8423-1215-3*) Tyndale.

All about God: His-Story, Vol. 1. Richard E. Culp. 112p. 1991. pap. 19.95 (*1-880736-00-4*) His-Story Pubs.

All about God's Church: His-Story, Vol. 6. Richard E. Culp. 160p. 1992. pap. 19.95 (*1-880736-05-5*) His-Story Pubs.

All about God's Past: His-Story, Vol. 2. Richard E. Culp. 128p. 1991. pap. 19.95 (*1-880736-01-2*) His-Story Pubs.

All about Ground Covers. rev. ed. Monica Brandies. Ed. by Nancy Arbuckle. LC 92-61735. (Illus.). 112p. 1993. pap. 9.95 (*0-89721-254-1*, 05280A) Ortho Info.

All about Growing Fruits, Berries, & Nuts. Ortho Staff. Ed. by Barbara Ferguson. LC 87-70194. (Illus.). 112p. (Orig.). 1987. pap. 9.95 (*0-89721-096-4*) Ortho Info.

All about Growing Orchids. Rick Bond. LC 87-72816. 96p. 1988. pap. 9.95 (*0-89721-151-0*) Ortho Info.

All about H. Hatterr. rev. ed. G. V. Desani. LC 86-18119. 320p. 1986. 20.00 (*0-914232-79-7*); pap. 12.00 (*0-914232-78-9*) McPherson & Co.

All about Ham Radio. Harry L. Helms. 300p. 1992. pap. 19.95 (*1-878707-04-3*) HighText.

All about Hand-Held & Briefcase Portable Computers. C. Louis Hohenstein. 320p. 1984. pap. text ed. 9.95 (*0-07-029452-6*, BYTE Bks) McGraw.

All about Hands. Illus. by Roberta K. Loman. (Happy Day Bks.). 28p. (J). (ps). 1992. 2.50 (*0-87403-951-7*, 24-03591) Standard Pub.

All about Hanukkah. Judye Groner & Madeline Wikler. LC 88-13435. (Illus.). (J). (gr. k-5). 1988. 10.95 (*0-930494-81-4*); pap. 4.95 (*0-930494-82-2*) Kar Ben.

All about Harvard Square - A Guide: Historic Walking Tours, Museums, Restaurants, Shopping & Entertainment. Richard Curran & Allan Curran. LC 89-50283. (Illus.). 112p. (Orig.). 1989. pap. 4.95 (*0-9622433-0-2*) Basement Graphics.

***All about Hawaiian: A Guide to the Language.** Albert J. Schutz. LC 95-1632. (Illus.). 80p. 1995. pap. 5.95 (*0-8248-1686-2*) UH Pr.

***All about Her: A Personal Reference from the Woman in My Life.** Beverly Clark. 1995. pap. 7.95 (*0-934081-10-7*) Wlshre Pubns.

All about Herbs. James Wilson & Mike Smith. LC 90-80069. 112p. 1990. pap. 9.95 (*0-89721-224-X*) Ortho Info.

***All about Him: A Personal Reference from the Man in My Life.** Beverly Clark. 1995. pap. 7.95 (*0-934081-11-5*) Wlshre Pubns.

All about Hock. Andre L. Simon. (All about Wines Ser.: Vol. 4). 7.50 (*0-87559-180-9*) Shalom.

All about Home Care: A Consumer's Guide. 1982. 2.00 (*0-318-03442-5*) Natl Homecaring.

All about Houseplants. rev. ed. Susan Lammers. Ed. by ORTHO Books Editorial Staff. LC 81-86183. (Illus.). 96p. (Orig.). 1982. pap. 9.95 (*0-89721-002-6*) Ortho Info.

All about Houseplants. rev. ed. Susan Lauwers et al. Ed. by Marianne Lipanovich. LC 93-86235. (Illus.). 112p. 1994. pap. 9.95 (*0-89721-264-9*, UPC 05223A) Ortho Info.

***All about How Things Are Made.** (Inspector McQ Ser.). (J). (ps-2). 1995. write for info. (*0-7166-1627-0*) World Bk.

All about Hulk Hogan. (WWF Fact Bks.). (Illus.). 24p. (J). 1991. pap. 1.95 (*1-56288-123-5*) Checkerboard.

All about Iguanas. Mervin F. Roberts & Martha D. Roberts. (Orig.). 1976. 9.95 (*0-86622-747-4*, PS-311) TFH Pubns.

All about Implants & Spiritual Limitation Devices. August Stahr. 60p. (Orig.). 1993. pap. 10.00 (*1-884686-01-X*) Living Lght.

All about Intelligence: Human, Animal & Artificial. Robert Howard. 1991. pap. 16.95 (*0-86840-252-4*, Pub. by New South Wales Univ Pr AT) Intl Spec Bk.

All about Internet FTP: Learning & Teaching to Transfer Files on the Internet. David F. Robinson. (Internet Workshop Ser.: Vol. 2). 1994. spiral bd. 30.00 (*1-882208-04-8*) Library Solns.

All about Internet FTP Plus: Learning & Teaching to Transfer Files on the Internet. David F. Robinson. (Internet Workshop Ser.: Vol. 2). 1994. disk, spiral bd. 45.00 (*1-882208-06-4*) Library Solns.

***All about Interviewing: A Collection of Articles about the Interview Process.** Ed. by Sharon Feinroth. 64p. (Orig.). Date not set. pap. 15.00 (*0-938369-19-9*) Ntl Assn Legal Srch.

All about Ireland: Facts & Figures. Hugh Oram. (Pocket Guide Ser.). (Illus.). 72p. (Orig.). 1990. pap. 7.95 (*0-86281-231-3*, Pub. by Appletree Pr IE) Irish Bks Media.

All about Islands. Wendy Rydell. LC 83-4833. (Question & Answer Bks.). (Illus.). 32p. (J). (gr. 3-6). 1984. lib. bdg. 10.59 (*0-89375-975-9*); pap. text ed. 2.95 (*0-89375-976-7*) Troll Assocs.

All about Israel: His-Story, Vol. 4. Richard E. Culp. 160p. 1992. pap. 19.95 (*1-880736-03-9*) His-Story Pubs.

All about Judo. Geof Gleeson & Gerry Hicks. (EP Sports Ser.). (Illus.). 1975. 6.95 (*0-7158-0590-8*) Charles River Bks.

All about Junk: How to Cash in on Other Peoples Junk & Make a Fortune. Jay B. Decker. LC 84-60970. 63p. (Orig.). (C). 1984. pap. text ed. 4.95 (*0-88247-741-2*) R & E Pubs.

All about Katakana. Anne M. Stewart. Ed. by Brase & Suzuki. (Power Japanese Ser.). (Illus.). 128p. (Orig.). (ENG & JPN.). 1993. pap. 9.00 (*4-7700-1696-4*) Kodansha.

***All about Keno.** John Gollehon. (Orig.). 1985. pap. 4.50 (*0-914839-07-1*) Gollehon Pr.

All about Kids & Eating Disorders. Alan Dubro. (Family Forum Library Ser.). 16p. 1992. 1.95 (*1-56688-016-5*) Bur For At-Risk.

***All about Klondike.** H. A. Beicher. 40p. 1995. pap. 5.95 (*1-881147-15-0*) Lowell Print.

All about Lamps: Construction, Repair & Restoration. Frank W. Coggins. (Illus.). 256p. 1986. 24.95 (*0-8306-0258-5*, 2658) TAB Bks.

All about Land Hermit Crabs. Mervin F. Roberts. (Illus.). 96p. 1989. pap. 9.95 (*0-86622-793-8*, PS-767) TFH Pubns.

All about Landscaping. rev. ed. Alvin Horton. Ed. by Ortho Books Editorial Staff. LC 88-71152. (Illus.). 112p. 1988. pap. 9.95 (*0-89721-150-2*) Ortho Info.

All about Lawns. rev. ed. Cathy Haas & Michael Mac Caskey. Ed. by Janet Goldenberg. LC 93-86234. (Illus.). 112p. 1994. pap. 9.95 (*0-89721-265-7*, UPC 05303A) Ortho Info.

All about Letters. rev. ed. Intro. by William F. Bolger. LC 82-600601. (Illus.). 64p. (J). (gr. 9-12). 1982. pap. 2.50 (*0-685-06202-3*, 01135) USPS.

All about Life & Death, Vol. 1. Cho Chikun Nine-Dan. Tr. by Bruce Olsen. (Illus.). 192p. (Orig.). 1993. pap. 14.95 (*4-87187-042-1*, G42) Ishi Pr Intl.

All about Life & Death, Vol. 2. Cho Chikun Nine-Dan. Tr. by Bruce Olsen. (Illus.). 192p. (Orig.). 1993. pap. 14.95 (*4-87187-043-X*, G43) Ishi Pr Intl.

***All about Light: A Do-It-Yourself Science Book.** Berger. 1995. pap. (*0-590-48076-6*) Scholastic Inc.

All about Lightning. Martin A. Uman. 192p. 1986. reprint ed. pap. 5.95 (*0-486-25237-X*) Dover.

All about Living in Hawaii. Norvelle Sannebeck. LC 77-23732. (Illus.). 1977. 14.95 (*0-87015-224-6*) Pacific Bks.

All about Lizards. Robert Sprackland, Jr. (Illus.). 128p. 1989. 9.95 (*0-87666-764-7*, PS-316) TFH Pubns.

All about Lobsters, Crabs, Shrimps, & Their Relatives. Richard Headstrom. LC 84-18786. (Nature Ser.). 144p. 1985. reprint ed. pap. 4.95 (*0-486-24795-3*) Dover.

All about Lovebirds. P. M. Soderberg. Orig. Title: Foreign Birds for Cage & Aviary; Lovebirds, Cardinals & Buntings. (Illus.). 1977. pap. 7.95 (*0-87666-957-7*, PS-742) TFH Pubns.

All about Magnets. Stephen Krensky. (J). (ps-3). 1993. pap. 4.95 (*0-590-45567-2*) Scholastic Inc.

All about Magnifying Glasses. Melvin Berger. (J). (ps-3). 1993. pap. 4.95 (*0-590-45510-9*) Scholastic Inc.

All about Mandan, Michigan. (Copper Country Local History Ser.: Vol. 19). (Illus.). 83p. 1982. 3.00 (*0-942363-18-3*) C J Monette.

All about Me. Lynn Brown. (Illus.). 92p. (J). (ps-1). 1993. 14.95 (*0-9640001-0-5*) Jikani Pr.

All about Me. Catherine Bruzzone & Lone Morton. (Illus.). 24p. (Orig.). (J). (gr. k-3). 1993. pap. 3.95 (*0-8249-8605-9*, Ideals Child) Hambleton-Hill.

All about Me. Donna Frinks. (J). (gr. k). 1989. 160.00 (*0-318-41077-X*) Southwinds Pr.

All about Me. Debbie MacKinnon & Anthea Sieveking. LC 93-23143. (Illus.). 32p. (J). (ps). 1994. 11.95 (*0-8120-6348-1*) Barron.

All about Me. Michaela Muntean. (Illus.). 48p. (J). (ps-3). 1984. 5.95 (*0-8193-1123-5*) Parents.

All about Me. Shereen G. Rutman. (Learn Today for Tomorrow Ser.). (Illus.). 32p. (J). (ps). 1992. student ed 1.95 (*1-56293-174-1*) McClanahan Bk.

All about Me: Developing Self Image & Self-Esteem with Hands-On Learning Activities. Wendy Pfeffer. Ed. by Mary B. Minucci & Mary L. Johansen. (Creative Concept Ser.). (Illus.). 48p. 1990. pap. 6.95 (*1-878727-01-X*) First Teacher.

***All about Me Activity Book.** Gloria Truitt. 1994. pap. 3.49 (*0-570-04767-6*) Concordia.

All about Me Activity Guide. Bobbie Kalman. (In My World Ser.). (Illus.). 96p. (J). (gr. k-2). 1985. pap. 15.95 (*0-86505-066-X*) Crabtree Pub Co.

All about Medicare, 1992. William W. Thomas, III. 100p. (Orig.). (C). 1992. pap. 7.95 (*0-87218-493-5*) Natl Underwriter.

All about Medicare, 1992. 6th ed. Ed. by William W. Thomas, III. 100p. (Orig.). 1992. pap. 7.95 (*0-685-57336-2*) Natl Underwriter.

All about Medicare, 1993. 7th ed. National Underwriter Staff. 100p. 1993. pap. 8.95 (*0-87218-107-3*, N97) Natl Underwriter.

All about Meters: How to Build Simple Electrical Meters. Charles Green. (Illus.). 60p. (Orig.). 1985. pap. 9.95 (*0-930003-01-2*) Allabout Bks.

All about Method Acting. Ned Manderino. 192p. (Orig.). 1985. pap. 10.95 (*0-9601194-3-4*) Manderino Bks.

***All about Michigan Almanac: Instant Information about Hundreds of Subjects.** 2nd ed. Ed. by Harry Shay. (Annual-Individual States Ser.). (Illus.). 164p. (Orig.). 1993. per., pap. 9.95 (*1-883351-00-6*) Instant Info.

***All about Michigan Almanac - 1995: Instant Information about Hundreds of Subjects.** 3rd ed. Ed. by Harry Shay. (Annual-Individual States Ser.). (Illus.). 292p. (Orig.). 1995. per., pap. 17.95 (*1-883351-03-0*) Instant Info.

***All about Micrographics.** Don M. Avedon & Rodd Exelbert. (Illus.). 20p. 1990. pap. text ed. 15.00 (*1-879391-00-7*) Avedon Assocs.

All about Mortgages. Julie Garton-Good. 320p. 1994. pap. 19.95 (*0-7931-0949-3*, 1905-9201) Dearborn Finan.

All about Mountains & Volcanoes. Elizabeth Marcus. LC 83-4834. (Question & Answer Bks.). (Illus.). 32p. (J). (gr. 3-6). 1984. lib. bdg. 10.59 (*0-89375-969-4*); pap. text ed. 2.95 (*0-89375-970-8*) Troll Assocs.

***All about Mutual Funds: From the Inside Out.** Bruce Kacobs. 1994. pap. 19.95 (*1-55738-807-5*) Probus Pub Co.

All about My School. Linda Schwartz. LC 93-86209. 32p. (J). (gr. 1-6). 1994. 4.95 (*0-88160-236-1*, LW331) Learning Wks.

All about Myth: An Introduction to Mythanalysis. David Carney. LC 90-85386. 147p. (Orig.). 1990. pap. 10.00 (*1-879320-00-2*) Adastra.

All about Noah. Jodi Holley. 1990. pap. 5.95 (*0-940754-97-5*, 5880) Ed Ministries.

***All about Ohio Almanac - 1994: Instant Information about Hundreds of Subjects.** Ed. by Harry Shay. (Annual-Individual States Ser.). (Illus.). 292p. (Orig.). 1994. per., pap. 14.95 (*1-883351-01-4*) Instant Info.

***All about Ohio Almanac - 1995: Instant Information about Hundreds of Subjects.** 2nd ed. Ed. by Harry Shay. (Illus.). 292p. Date not set. per., pap. 17.95 (*1-883351-06-5*) Instant Info.

All about One Russell. Charles C. Cook. 48p. 1988. reprint ed. pap. 2.95 (*1-883858-37-2*) Witness CA.

All about Options: From the Inside Out. Thomas A. McCafferty & Russell R. Wasendorf. 225p. 1993. pap. 19.95 (*1-55738-434-7*) Probus Pub Co.

All about Our Bodies, Our Digestion. (Illus.). 14p. (J). (gr. k-6). 1990. pap. 4.50 (*0-89346-297-7*) Heian Intl.

All about Our Bodies, Our Eyes, Ears & Noses. (Illus.). 14p. (J). (gr. k-6). 1990. pap. 4.50 (*0-89346-299-3*) Heian Intl.

All about Our Bodies, Our Hearts & Lungs. (Illus.). 14p. (J). (gr. k-6). 1990. pap. 4.50 (*0-89346-298-5*) Heian Intl.

All about Our Bodies, Our Teeth. (Illus.). 14p. (J). (gr. k-6). 1990. pap. 4.50 (*0-89346-296-9*) Heian Intl.

***All about Outlets: The Guide to Factory & Off-Price Shopping in New England.** 2nd ed. Andrea Brox. (Illus.). Date not set. pap. 12.95 (*0-924771-30-5*) Brick Hse Pub.

All about Paperweights. Lawrence H. Selman. (Illus.). 120p. (Orig.). 1992. pap. 24.95 (*0-933756-17-8*) Paperwght Pr.

All about Parties. Edith Gilbert. LC 68-8522. 1968. 8.95 (*0-9600786-0-6*) Jetiquette.

All about Pennsylvania. Lucille Wallower. Ed. by Ellen J. Wholey. (Illus.). (J). (gr. 3-4). 1984. pap. 4.55 (*0-931992-05-2*) Penns Valley.

All about Pentecost. William S. Deal. 1983. pap. 3.95 (*0-318-18716-7*) Crusade Pubs.

All about Pentecost. William S. Deal. 1983. pap. 4.99 (*0-88019-051-5*) Schmul Pub Co.

***All about People.** LC 94-22406. (First Encyclopedia Ser.). (Illus.). (J). 1995. 12.95 (*0-590-47525-8*); pap. write for info. (*0-590-47526-6*) Scholastic Inc.

All about Perennials. rev. ed. Ortho Books Staff. Ed. by Sara Godwin. LC 92-70588. (Illus.). 112p. 1992. pap. 9.95 (*0-89721-247-9*) Ortho Info.

***All about Pets.** (Inspector McQ Ser.). (J). (ps-2). 1995. write for info. (*0-7166-1625-4*) World Bk.

All about Plants Activity Book. Justine Korman. (J). (ps-3). 1994. pap. 1.95 (*0-590-47590-8*) Scholastic Inc.

All about Pockets: Storytime Activities for Early Childhood. Christine P. Kallevig. LC 93-83415. (Illus.). 128p. (Orig.). 1993. pap. 9.95 (*0-9628769-6-8*) Storytime Ink.

All about Ponds. Jane Rockwell. LC 83-4835. (Question & Answer Bks.). (Illus.). 32p. (J). (gr. 3-6). 1984. lib. bdg. 10.59 (*0-89375-971-6*); pap. text ed. 2.95 (*0-89375-972-4*) Troll Assocs.

All about Prophecy: His-Story, Vol. 5. Richard E. Culp. 416p. 1991. pap. 39.95 (*1-880736-04-7*) His-Story Pubs.

All about Prosperity & How You Can Prosper. Cornelia Addington & Jack Addington. LC 83-73342. (Orig.). 1984. pap. 6.95 (*0-87516-533-8*) DeVorss.

All about Pruning. rev. ed. Ortho Books Editorial Staff. LC 88-63844. (Illus.). 112p. 1989. pap. 9.95 (*0-89721-198-7*) Ortho Info.

All about Rabbits. Howard Hirschhorn. (Illus.). 96p. (Orig.). 1974. 9.95 (*0-86622-693-1*, M-543) TFH Pubns.

All about Radiation. L. Ron Hubbard. 20.00 (*0-686-30790-9*) Church Scient NY.

All about Radiation. Medicus Staff & L. Ron Hubbard. 1989. 20.00 (*0-88404-446-7*) Bridge Pubns Inc.

All about Raising Children. Helen B. Andelin. 410p. 1981. 12.95 (*0-911094-07-5*) Pacific Santa Barbara.

***All about Real Estate Investing: From the Inside Out.** William Benke & John M. Fowler. 200p. 1995. 19.95 (*1-55738-882-2*) Probus Pub Co.

All about Rivers. Jane Emil. LC 83-4868. (Question & Answer Bks.). (Illus.). 32p. (J). (gr. 3-6). 1984. lib. bdg. 10.59 (*0-89375-979-1*); pap. text ed. 2.95 (*0-89375-980-5*) Troll Assocs.

All about Rivkah. 1981. pap. 2.95 (*0-87306-236-1*) Feldheim.

All about Roses. rev. ed. Rex Wolf & James McNair. Ed. by Susan Lang. LC 90-80073. (Illus.). 112p. 1990. pap. 9.95 (*0-89721-217-7*) Ortho Info.

***All about Roses.** rev. ed. Rex Wolfe & James McNair. Ed. by Michael D. Smith. LC 94-69601. (Illus.). 112p. 1995. pap. 9.95 (*0-89721-256-8*, 05338A) Ortho Info.

All about Roulette. John Gollehon. (Perigee Casino Library). 64p. 1987. reprint ed. pap. 4.50 (*0-399-51460-0*, Perigee Bks) Berkley Pub.

All about Saguaros. Carle Hodge. 64p. 1991. pap. 8.50 (*0-916179-31-1*) Ariz Hwy.

All about Salvation. Paul Trinchard. 119p. (Orig.). 1994. pap. 8.95 (*0-685-71270-2*) Cath Treas.

All about Sam. Lois Lowry. (Illus.). 144p. (J). (gr. k-6). 1989. pap. 3.50 (*0-440-40221-2*, YB) Dell.

All about Sam. Lois Lowry. (Illus.). 144p. (J). (gr. 1-5). 1988. 13.95 (*0-395-48662-9*) HM.

All about Sam. Lucina B. Moxley. LC 91-58050. 175p. 1991. pap. 13.95 (*1-878208-09-8*) Guild Pr IN.

All about Satellite TV: A Technical Guide for Home Dish Owners. Karl Fincke. Ed. by James E. Scott. 128p. 1993. pap. 9.95 (*1-879804-01-8*) Fortuna Commns.

All about Sauternes. Andre L. Simon. (All about Wines Ser.: Vol. 2). 7.50 (*0-87559-182-5*) Shalom.

All about Scarecrows. Bobi Martin. (Illus.). 64p. (Orig.). 1990. pap. 7.95 (*0-9617357-5-9*) Tomato Enter.

All about Science Fairs. John Carratello & Patty Carratello. (Illus.). 96p. (J). (gr. 1-8). 1989. student ed 10.95 (*1-55734-228-8*) Tchr Create Mat.

All about Seals, Sea Lions & Walruses. Jane Resnick. (Sea World All about Library). (Illus.). 32p. (J). (gr. 1-6). 1994. pap. 3.95 (*1-884506-13-5*) Third Story.

All about Seeds. Susan Kuchalla. LC 81-11480. (Now I Know Ser.). (Illus.). 32p. (J). (gr. k-2). 1982. lib. bdg. 11.59 (*0-89375-658-X*); pap. 2.95 (*0-89375-659-8*) Troll Assocs.

All about Seeds: A Hands-On Science Book. Melvin Berger. 32p. (J). 1992. pap. 2.95 (*0-590-44909-5*) Scholastic Inc.

All about Sewing Machines. Robert Johanson. (Illus.). 1970. pap. 7.95 (*0-933261-01-2*) Twin Peaks Pr.

All About Sex Therapy. Peter R. Kilmann & Katherine H. Mills. LC 82-2257. 228p. 1983. 18.95 (*0-306-41317-5*, Plenum Pr) Plenum.

All about Shanghai: A Basic Guidebook. Henry J. Lethbridge. (Oxford in Asia Paperbacks Ser.). (Illus.). 264p. 1986. pap. 8.95 (*0-19-581594-7*) OUP.

All about Shapes. (Sing & Learn Ser.). (Illus.). 32p. (Orig.). (J). 1994. audio, pap. 8.95 (*0-7935-2381-8*, 00330504) H Leonard.

All about Sharks. Jane Resnick. (Sea World All about Library). (Illus.). 32p. (Orig.). (J). (gr. 1-8). 1994. pap. 3.95 (*1-884506-10-0*) Third Story.

All about Sherry. Andre L. Simon. (All about Wines Ser.: Vol. 6). 7.50 (*0-87559-183-3*) Shalom.

All About Siamese Cats. Barbara Burns. (Illus.). 160p. 1993. 19.95 (*0-86622-665-6*, TS-129) TFH Pubns.

All about Silk: A Fabric Dictionary & Swatchbook. Julie Parker. LC 93-117999. (Fabric Reference Ser.). 92p. 1992. pap. 29.95 (*0-9637612-0-X*) Rain City.

All about Slots & Video Poker! John Gollehon. (Perigee Casino Library). 64p. 1987. reprint ed. pap. 4.50 (*0-399-51458-9*, Perigee Bks) Berkley Pub.

All about Sound. Melvin Berger. (Do-It-Yourself Science Ser.). (J). (ps-3). 1994. pap. 3.95 (*0-590-46760-3*) Scholastic Inc.

All about Sound. David C. Knight. LC 82-17387. (Question & Answer Bks.). (Illus.). 32p. (J). (gr. 3-6). 1983. lib. bdg. 10.59 (*0-89375-878-7*); pap. text ed. 2.95 (*0-89375-879-5*) Troll Assocs.

All about South Africa. Andre L. Simon. (All about Wines Ser.: Vol. 8). 7.50 (*0-87559-184-1*) Shalom.

All about Sports Betting. John Gollehon. (Perigee Casino Library). 64p. (Orig.). 1989. pap. 4.50 (*0-399-51505-4*, Perigee Bks) Berkley Pub.

All about Stacy. Patricia R. Giff. (New Kids at the Polk Street School Ser.: No. 3). 80p. (Orig.). (J). (gr. k-6). 1988. pap. 3.50 (*0-440-40088-0*, YB) Dell.

All about Stamp Collecting. rev. ed. Howard G. Treacher & Walter F. Gray. (Illus.). Date not set. pap. 2.95 (*0-937458-25-2*) Harris & Co.

All about Stars. Lawrence Jefferies. LC 82-20027. (Question & Answer Bks.). (Illus.). 32p. (J). (gr. 3-6). 1983. lib. bdg. 10.59 (*0-89375-888-4*); pap. text ed. 2.95 (*0-89375-889-2*) Troll Assocs.

All about Stepparenting. Jane C. Sacknowitz. (Family Forum Library Ser.). 16p. 1992. 1.95 (*1-56688-044-0*) Bur For At-Risk.

***All about Stocks: From Inside Out.** Esme Faerber. 1994. pap. 19.95 (*1-55738-806-7*) Probus Pub Co.

All about Successful Parenting. Maryanne Driscoll. (Family Forum Library Ser.). 16p. 1992. 1.95 (*1-56688-009-2*) Bur For At-Risk.

All about Suing & Being Sued. Arthur J. Sabin. LC 80-23991. (Illus.). 91p. (Orig.). 1981. pap. 8.95 (*0-89037-185-7*); 12.95 (*0-89037-191-1*) Anderson World.

All about Tarantulas. Dale Lund. (Illus.). 1977. 9.95 (*0-87666-909-7*, PS-749) TFH Pubns.

All about Teaching Peace. Elaine M. Ward. 36p. (Orig.). 1989. pap. 6.95 (*0-940754-69-X*) Ed Ministries.

All about the Alphabet: Fun with Letters A-Z. Steven Traugh. (Sing & Learn Ser.). (Illus.). 32p. (Orig.). (J). (ps-3). 1993. audio, pap. 8.95 (*0-7935-2260-9*, 00330500) H Leonard.

All About the Angels. Paul O'Sullivan. LC 90-70122. 148p. 1990. reprint ed. pap. 5.00 (*0-89555-388-0*) TAN Bks Pubs.

All about the Bible. 7.99 (*1-55748-082-6*, Christian Lib) Barbour & Co.

An Asterisk (*) at the beginning of an entry indicates that the title is appearing in BIP for the first time.

All about the Boston Harbor Islands. 4th ed. Emily Kales & David Kales. Ed. by Nancy Witting. (Illus.). 120p. 1993. pap. 9.95 (*0-9636000-0-1*) Hewitts Cove.

All about the Boxer. John F. Gordon. (Pets - Animals Ser.). (Illus.). 144p. 1988. 14.95 (*0-317-67305-X*, Penguin Bks) Viking Penguin.

All about the Cairn Terrier. John F. Gordon. (Illus.). 240p. 1988. 14.95 (*0-317-67306-8*, Penguin Bks) Viking Penguin.

***All about the Chinese Automobile Industry.** Ed. by David Andrews & Jack Bernstein. Tr. by Interlingua Staff. (Illus.). 146p. 1995. 875.00 (*1-884730-02-7*) JB & Me.

All about the End Time: His-Story, Vol. 7. Richard E. Culp. 160p. 1992. pap. 19.95 (*1-880736-06-3*) His-Story Pubs.

All about the Fifty States: A Picture Puzzle Book. Nancy E. Krulik. (J). 1992. pap. 1.95 (*0-590-45223-1*) Scholastic Inc.

All about the Fila. Clelia Kruel. Ed. by Julie Stevenson. (Illus.). 142p. (Orig.). 1992. pap. 7.95 (*0-945402-01-5*) Kruel Pubns.

All about the Frog. William White, Jr. LC 91-40812. (Color Nature Book Ser.). (Illus.). 72p. (YA). (gr. 7-12). 1992. 14.95 (*0-8069-8274-8*) Sterling.

All about the Heart & Blood. Donna Bailey. LC 90-10052. (Health Facts Ser.). (Illus.). 48p. (J). (gr. 2-6). 1990. lib. bdg. 21.36 (*0-8114-2779-X*) Raintree Steck-V.

All about the Jack Russell Terrier. Gerry Huxham. (Pets - Animals Ser.). (Illus.). 176p. 1987. 14.95 (*0-7207-1201-7*, Penguin Bks) Viking Penguin.

All about the Moon. David Adler. LC 82-17422. (Question & Answer Bks.). (Illus.). 32p. (J). (gr. 3-6). 1983. lib. bdg. 10.59 (*0-89375-886-8*); pap. text ed. 2.95 (*0-89375-887-6*) Troll Assocs.

All about the Moravians. Edwin A. Sawyer. LC 89-69836. (Illus.). 80p. (Orig.). 1990. pap. text ed. 5.00 (*1-878422-00-6*) Moravian Ch in Amer.

All about the Origin of Man: His-Story, Vol. 3. Richard E. Culp. 160p. 1991. pap. 19.95 (*1-880736-02-0*) His-Story Pubs.

All about the Seasons Activity Book. Tara Doyle. (J). (ps-3). 1993. pap. 1.95 (*0-590-46296-2*) Scholastic Inc.

All about the Turtle. William White, Jr. LC 91-41301. (Illus.). 72p. (YA). (gr. 7-12). 1992. 14.95 (*0-8069-8276-4*) Sterling.

All about the U. S. A. Peter Murphy & Milada Broukal. 96p. 1991. pap. text ed. 12.95 (*0-8013-0637-X*, 78572) Longman.

All About the U.S.A: The Rugged Northeast; Dynamic East Central; The Industrious Southeast; The Heartland; The Central Core; The Lofty Ones; Ocean Lands, 7 Bks. (J). (gr. 5-9). 1987. 139.00 (*0-8347-3385-4*) Ency Brit Ed.

All about the Weather. Beth Goodman. 1989. pap. 1.95 (*0-590-41978-1*) Scholastic Inc.

All about Theatre. rev. ed. Helen Sheehy. (Illus.). 272p. (Orig.). 1944. teacher ed 9.76 (*0-8013-0326-5*, 78097); pap. text ed. 9.28 (*0-88334-147-6*, 76115) Longman.

All about Thickness. Nine-Dan Ishida Yoshio. 1990. 24.95 (*0-685-35687-6*, G34H); pap. 14.95 (*4-87187-034-0*, G34) Ishi Pr Intl.

***All About Time.** Illus. by Celine Bour-Chollet et al. LC 94-49120. (First Discovery Bk.). (ENG & FRE.). (J). 1995. write for info. (*0-590-42793-8*, Cartwheel) Scholastic Inc.

All about Training Shamu. Jane Resnick. (Sea World All about Library). (Illus.). 32p. (Orig.). (J). (gr. 1-8). 1994. pap. 3.95 (*1-884506-11-9*) Third Story.

All about Trees. Jane Dickinson. LC 82-17382. (Question & Answer Bks.). (Illus.). 32p. (J). (gr. 3-6). 1983. lib. bdg. 10.59 (*0-89375-892-2*); pap. text ed. 2.95 (*0-89375-893-0*) Troll Assocs.

All about Trees. rev. ed. Ortho Books Staff. Ed. by Nancy Arbuckle & Cederick Crocker. LC 92-70589. (Illus.). 112p. 1992. pap. 9.95 (*0-89721-248-7*) Ortho Info.

***All about Trout.** John Holt. LC 91-60836. (Complete Angler's Library). 264p. 1991. write for info. (*0-914697-38-2*) N Amer Outdoor Grp.

All about Turtles. Andrea Ross. LC 89-92455. 24p. (J). (ps-3). 1990. audio, pap. 5.95 (*0-943864-59-3*) Davenport.

All about Twins. Gillian Leigh. 1985. pap. 8.95 (*0-7100-9888-X*, RKP) Routledge.

All about Twins: A Handbook for Parents. Gillian Leigh. (Illus.). 253p. (Orig.). 1984. pap. 14.95 (*0-415-04287-9*, 9888-X) Routledge.

All about Ultimate Warrior. (WWF Fact Bks.). (Illus.). 24p. (J). 1991. pap. 1.95 (*1-56288-124-8*) Checkerboard.

All about Underage Drinking. Charles Gleason & Maryanne Driscoll. (Family Forum Library Ser.). 16p. 1992. 1.95 (*1-56688-014-9*) Bur For At-Risk.

All about Us. Dina Rosenfeld. (Illus.). 32p. (J). (ps-1). 1989. 8.95 (*0-922613-02-8*); pap. 6.95 (*0-922613-03-6*) Hachai Pubns.

All about Us - Nous Autres: Creative Writing & Painting by & for Young People. Ed. by Betty Nickerson. (Illus.). 36p. (ENG & FRE.). (J). 1992. pap. 4.95 (*0-685-61052-7*) All About Us.

***All about Variable Annuities: From the Inside Out.** Bruce F. Wells. 200p. 1995. 18.95 (*1-55738-874-1*) Probus Pub Co.

All about Vegetables. rev. ed. Walter Doty. Ed. by Mike Smith. LC 90-80068. 160p. 1990. reprint ed. pap. 9.95 (*0-89721-222-3*) Ortho Info.

All About Vertical Antennas. William I. Orr & Stuart D. Cowan. LC 86-61499. (Illus.). 192p. 1986. 10.95 (*0-933616-09-0*) Radio Pubns.

All about Vertical Antennas. William I. Orr & Stuart D. Cowan. (Illus.). 192p. pap. 11.95 (*0-8230-8710-7*, RAC Bks) Watsn-Guptill.

All about VHF Amateur Radio. William I. Orr. 1991. pap. 11.95 (*0-933616-10-4*) Radio Pubns.

All about VHF Amateur Radio. William I. Orr. (Illus.). 172p. pap. 11.95 (*0-8230-8705-0*, RAC Bks) Watsn-Guptill.

All About Vitamins & Minerals: Key Nutrients for Optimum Health. Ed. by Prevention Magazine Staff. (No Nonsense Health Guide Ser.). (Illus.). 88p. 1989. pap. 4.95 (*0-681-40715-8*) Longmeadow Pr.

All about Water. Melvin Berger. (Do-It-Yourself Science Ser.). (J). (ps-3). 1994. pap. 3.95 (*0-590-46761-1*) Scholastic Inc.

All about Weeds. Edwin R. Spencer. LC 73-91485. (Illus.). 352p. 1974. reprint ed. pap. 7.95 (*0-486-23051-1*) Dover.

All about Whales. Deborah Kovacs. (Sea World All about Library). (Illus.). 32p. (Orig.). (J). (gr. 1-8). 1994. pap. 3.95 (*1-884506-08-9*) Third Story.

All about Where. Tana Hoban. LC 90-30849. (Illus.). 32p. (J). (ps up). 1991. 13.95 (*0-688-09697-2*); lib. bdg. 13.88 (*0-688-09698-0*) Greenwillow.

All about Wills & Trusts for Florida Residents. 11th rev. ed. Ralph Richards. Ed. by Sandra F. Diamond & Laurie W. Valentine. LC 64-25300. 1994. pap. text ed. 5.95 (*0-88251-085-1*) Trend Bk Div.

All about Wills for Florida Residents. rev. ed. Ralph Richard. (Illus.). 1983. pap. 4.95 (*0-88251-078-9*) Trend Bk Div.

All about Wines, 8 bks. 55.00 (*0-87559-138-8*) Shalom.

All about Wines Ser. Andre L. Simon. (All about Wines: Vol. 3). pap. 7.50 (*0-87559-181-7*) Shalom.

All about Women. Andrew M. Greeley. 1991. mass mkt. 4.95 (*0-8125-0570-0*) Tor Bks.

All about Women. Girija Khanna. (C). 1992. pap. 5.95 (*0-7069-5955-8*, Pub. by Vikas II) S Asia.

All about Women: How to Get a Woman No Matter How You Look? How to Please a Woman Physically & Mentally-Mind, Body & Soul? Bobby R. Stanley & Dorothea A. Hobson. LC 87-90520. (Illus.). 202p. (C). 14.95 (*0-318-22827-0*) Lerai Enterprises.

All about Wool. Claire Jobin. Tr. by Sarah Matthews. LC 87-31751. (Illus.). 38p. (J). (gr. k-5). 1988. 5.95 (*0-944589-18-9*, 189) Young Discovery Lib.

***All about Wool: A Fabric Dictionary & Swatchbook.** Julie Parker. (Fabric Reference Ser.). Date not set. pap. write for info. (*0-9637612-2-6*) Rain City.

All about WWF Superstars. (WWF Fact Bks.). (Illus.). 24p. (J). 1991. pap. 1.95 (*1-56288-126-4*) Checkerboard.

All about WWF Tag Teams. (WWF Fact Bks.). (Illus.). 24p. (J). 1991. pap. 1.95 (*1-56288-125-6*) Checkerboard.

All about You. Catherine Anholt & Laurence Anholt. (Illus.). 32p. (J). (ps). 1992. 14.00 (*0-670-84488-8*) Viking Child Bks.

All about You. Laurence Anholt. (Illus.). 32p. (J). (ps-1). 1994. pap. 4.99 (*0-14-055319-3*) Puffin Bks.

***All about You.** (Inspector McQ Ser.). (J). (ps-2). 1995. write for info. (*0-7166-1612-2*) World Bk.

All about You. Walt Disney Productions Staff. (Walt Disney's Fun-to-Learn Library Ser.: Vol. 11). (Illus.). 44p. (J). (gr. 1-6). reprint ed. 2.99 (*1-885222-02-5*) Advance Pubs.

All about You: A Religious Physiology & Hygiene for Parents to Read to Their Children. Helen R. Reed. (J). 1992. 7.95 (*0-533-10079-8*) Vantage.

All about You: A Simple Yet Powerful Guide to Confidence, Love & Success. Robert Silhan. LC 92-74941. 112p. 1993. pap. 9.95 (*0-9634930-0-0*) Lumen Displays.

All about You: An Adventure of Self-Discovery. Aylette Jenness. LC 92-50699. (J). (gr. 4 up). 1993. pap. 8.95 (*1-56584-053-4*) New Press NY.

All about You: Learning about Yourself. Mary J. Haugen. (Life Skills Educational Board Game Ser.: No. 4). 50p. 1991. teacher ed, text ed. 49.95 (*1-884074-03-0*) Program Concepts.

All about Your Brain. Donna Bailey. LC 90-41008. (Health Facts Ser.). (Illus.). 48p. (J). (gr. 2-6). 1990. lib. bdg. 21.36 (*0-8114-2778-1*) Raintree Steck-V.

All about Your Lungs. Donna Bailey. LC 90-41009. (Health Facts Ser.). (Illus.). 48p. (J). (gr. 2-6). 1990. lib. bdg. 21.36 (*0-8114-2782-X*) Raintree Steck-V.

All about Your Senses. Donna Bailey. LC 90-10051. (Health Facts Ser.). (Illus.). 48p. (J). (gr. 2-6). 1990. lib. bdg. 21.36 (*0-8114-2776-5*) Raintree Steck-V.

All about Your Skeleton. Donna Bailey. LC 90-10114. (Health Facts Ser.). (Illus.). 48p. (J). (gr. 2-6). 1990. lib. bdg. 21.36 (*0-8114-2780-3*) Raintree Steck-V.

All about Your Skin, Hair & Teeth. Donna Bailey. LC 90-10050. (Health Facts Ser.). (Illus.). 48p. (J). (gr. 2-6). 1990. lib. bdg. 21.36 (*0-8114-2783-8*) Raintree Steck-V.

***All about Your 401K Plan: Simple Answers to Securing Your Financial Future.** Ellie Williams. 1994. pap. 19.95 (*1-55738-805-9*) Probus Pub Co.

All about Zora: Views & Reviews by Colleagues & Scholars: Proceedings of the First Annual Zora Neale Hurston Festival of the Arts, January 26-27, 1990. Ed. by Alice M. Grant. 140p. 1991. pap. 19.95 (*0-9625423-4-2*) Four-G Pubs.

***All Acts Are Simply Acts.** Edward Foster. 111p. 1995. lib. bdg. 27.00 (*1-887289-06-2*); pap. 7.00 (*1-887289-03-8*) Rodent Pr.

All Alone. Claire H. Bishop. (Illus.). 96p. (J). (gr. 2-5). 1953. 15.00 (*0-670-11336-0*) Viking Child Bks.

***All Alone: Surviving the Loss of Your Spouse.** Kathleen R. Buntin. LC 94-40691. iv, 155p. 1995. write for info. (*0-87579-933-7*) Deseret Bk.

All Alone after School. Muriel Stanek. Ed. by Ann Fay. LC 84-17243. (Albert Whitman Concept Bks.). (Illus.). 32p. (J). (gr. 1-4). 1985. lib. bdg. 11.95 (*0-8075-0278-2*) A Whitman.

All Alone in the Eighth Grade. Suzanne Weyn. LC 91-10162. (Midway Junior High Ser.). 128p. (J). (gr. 6-9). 1992. lib. bdg. 9.89 (*0-8167-2394-X*); pap. text ed. 2.95 (*0-8167-2395-8*) Troll Assocs.

All Alone with Daddy: A Young Girl Plays the Role of Mother. Joan Fassler. LC 76-80120. (Illus.). 32p. (J). (ps-3). 1975. 16.95 (*0-87705-009-0*) Human Sci Pr.

All along the Danube: Recipes from Germany, Austria, Czechoslovakia, Yugoslavia, Hungary, Romania & Bulgaria. Marina Polvay. (International Cookbook Classics Ser.). (Illus.). 349p. 1992. pap. 11.95 (*0-7818-0098-6*) Hippocrene Bks.

All along the River. Allan Fowler. LC 93-39646. (Rookie Read-about Science Ser.). (Illus.). 32p. (J). (ps-2). 1994. lib. bdg. 10.80 (*0-516-06019-8*) Childrens.

***All along the River.** Allan Fowler. (J). (ps-2). 1994. pap. 11.93 (*0-516-46019-6*) Childrens.

All-America: The Complete Roster of Football's Heroes. Bernie McCarty. 300p. 1991. pap. 19.95 (*0-685-48956-6*) B McCarty.

All-America: the Complete Roster of Football's Heroes, Vol. 1: 1889-1945. Bernie McCarty. (Illus.). 300p. (Orig.). 1991. pap. 19.95 (*0-9629969-0-4*) B McCarty.

All-American. John R. Tunis. 261p. (J). (gr. 3-7). 1989. pap. 3.95 (*0-15-202292-9*, Odyssey) HarBrace.

All American: Musical. Mel Brooks. 1962. 5.45 (*0-87129-312-9*, A02) Dramatic Pub.

All American Apple Cookbook. Sharon K. Alexander & Kay Fairbairn. LC 82-70679. (Die-Cut Cookbooks Ser.: No. 2). (Illus.). 105p. 1982. pap. text ed. 12.95 (*0-9608126-1-X*) ABC Enterprises.

All-American Barbeque Cookbook. 1990. spiral bd., pap. 6.99 (*0-517-01999-X*) Random Hse Value.

All-American Bean Book. F. H. Waskey. (Illus.). 192p. 1988. pap. 11.00 (*0-671-64403-3*, Fireside) S&S Trade.

***All-American Boy: A Gay Son's Search for His Father.** Scott Peck. LC 94-45480. 1995. 22.00 (*0-02-595362-1*, Scribners) S&S Trade.

All American Boys. Frank Mosca. 116p. (Orig.). (J). (gr. 7-12). 1983. pap. 5.95 (*0-932870-44-9*) Alyson Pubns.

All American Cars & Trucks (A Consumer's Guidebook to...) Warren Brown. (Illus.). 192p. 1994. pap. 12.95 (*1-882605-05-5*) Natl Pr Bks.

***All-American Chili Book: The Official Cookbook of the International Chili Society.** Jenny Kellner & Richard Rosenblatt. LC 94-24269. 1995. 14.95 (*0-688-13693-1*) Hearst Bks.

All American Cooking: Savory Recipes from Savvy Creative Cooks Across America. Meryl Nelson. LC 91-6652. 125p. 1992. pap. 7.95 (*0-88247-902-4*, 902-4) R & E Pubs.

***All-American Cowboy Cookbook.** Jim Clark & Ken Beck. (Illus.). 256p. 1995. 14.95 (*1-55853-365-6*) Rutledge Hill Pr.

All-American Dinosaur Family: Meet the Hoadleys. Ed King. (Illus.). 24p. (J). (gr. k-12). 1993. 3.95 (*1-56288-387-9*) Checkerboard.

All-American Dinosaur Family: The Hoadleys in Town. Ed King. (Illus.). 24p. (J). (ps-12). 1993. 3.95 (*1-56288-390-9*) Checkerboard.

All-American Dinosaur Family: The Hoadleys on Vacation. Ed King. (Illus.). 24p. (J). (ps-12). 1993. 3.95 (*1-56288-388-7*) Checkerboard.

All-American Dinosaur Family: The Hoadleys Travel in Time. Ed King. (Illus.). 24p. (J). (ps-12). 1993. 3.95 (*1-56288-389-5*) Checkerboard.

All-American Girl: The Ideal of Real Womanhood in Mid-Nineteenth Century America. Frances B. Cogan. LC 88-8590. (Illus.). 312p. 1989. pap. 16.00 (*0-8203-1063-8*) U of Ga Pr.

All-American Girls Professional Baseball League. Trudy Hanmer. LC 94-1233. (American Events Ser.). (YA). 1994. text ed. 15.95 (*0-02-742595-9*) Macmillan.

All American Guide to Country Music. Frank Eichenlaub & Patricia Eichenlaub. LC 91-77862. (Illus.). 144p. (Orig.). 1992. pap. 12.95 (*1-56626-000-0*) Country Rds.

All American Hero: A Story about the Meaning of Veterans Day. Louise Mandrell. (Louise Mandrell's Holiday Adventure Ser.). (J). (gr. 4-7). 1993. 12.95 (*1-56530-010-6*) Summit TX.

***All-American Hippie Comix.** Dan Steffan et al. Ed. by Dave Schreiner & Phil Amara. (Illus.). 160p. Date not set. 29.95 (*0-87816-299-2*) Kitchen Sink.

All-American Hippie Comix. Dan Steffan et al. Ed. by Dave Schreiner & Phil Amara. (Illus.). 160p. 1994. reprint ed. pap. 14.95 (*0-87816-298-4*) Kitchen Sink.

All-American Low-Fat Meals in Minutes. M. J. Smith. LC 90-21955. 1990. pap. 12.95 (*0-937721-73-5*) Chronimed.

***All American Mafioso: The Johnny Rosselli Story.** rev. ed. Charles Rappleye & Ed Becker. LC 94-46832. 1995. pap. 14.95 (*1-56980-027-8*) Barricade Bks.

All-American Map: Wax Engraving & Its Influence on Cartography. David Woodward. LC 76-8099. (Illus.). 1977. lib. bdg. 15.00 (*0-226-90725-2*) U Ch Pr.

***All-American Quote Book.** Michael Reagan & Bob Phillips. LC 94-48344. (Orig.). 1995. pap. 8.99 (*1-56507-346-0*) Harvest Hse.

***All-American Skin Game, or, The Decoy of Race: The Long & Short of It, 1990-1994.** Stanley Crouch. LC 95-10142. 1995. 25.00 (*0-679-44202-2*) Pantheon.

All American Sports Fan Cookbook. Elisa Garin & Cynthia Gomes. (Illus.). 183p. 1989. pap. 9.95 (*0-89716-300-1*) P B Pubng.

All-American Stamp Album. rev. ed. Ed. by Ben Blumenthal. (Illus.). 500p. 1992. 45.00 (*0-912236-34-5*, Minkus Pubns) Novus Debut.

***All-American Vegetarian: A Regional Harvest of Low-Fat Recipes.** Barbara Grunes & Virginia Van Wynckt. LC 94-23879. 368p. 1995. 25.00 (*0-8050-3509-5*) H Holt & Co.

All American Women: Lines That Divide, Ties That Bind. Johnnetta B. Cole. 448p. 1986. pap. 19.95 (*0-02-906460-0*) Free Pr.

All American Wonder, Vol. 1. Ray Cowdery. (Illus.). 144p. 1993. reprint ed. pap. 19.95 (*0-910667-10-1*) Northstar Bks.

All-American Wonder, Vol. 2: The Military Jeep 1941-1945. Ray R. Cowdery. (Illus.). 144p. 1990. pap. text ed. 20.00 (*0-910667-20-9*) Northstar Bks.

All-Americans. James R. Parish & Don E. Stanke. (Illus.). 1978. pap. 12.95 (*0-89508-011-7*) Rainbow Bks.

All Americans, 82d Airborne. John B. Wildman & James J. Lindsay. (Illus.). 400p. 1983. 20.00 (*0-912081-00-7*) Delmar Co.

ALL (Analysis of the Language of Learning) Elizabeth G. Blodgett & Eugene B. Cooper. 1987. pap. 36.00 (*1-55999-014-7*) LinguiSystems.

All & Everything: Beelzebub's Tales to His Grandson. G. Gundjieff. 1238p. 1993. reprint ed. 45.00 (*0-89756-018-3*) Two Rivers.

All Animals are Equal. (Gamma World Adventure Ser.: GWQ2). 1993. pap. 9.95 (*1-56076-638-7*) TSR Inc.

***All Anybody Ever Wanted of Me Was to Work: The Memoirs of Edith Bradley Rendleman.** Edith B. Rendleman. Ed. & Intro. by Jane Adams. LC 94-37252. (Shawnee Bks.). (Illus.). 232p. (C). 1996. 39.95 (*0-8093-1931-4*) S Ill U Pr.

All Are Alike unto God. E. Dale LeBaron. 9.95 (*0-88494-738-6*) Bookcraft Inc.

All-Around Man: Selected Letters of Percy Grainger, 1914-1961. Ed. by Malcolm Gillies. (Illus.). 288p. 1994. 39.95 (*0-19-816377-0*) OUP.

***All Around Me.** Sally Hewitt. (Now I Know Ser.). (Illus.). 48p. (J). (gr. 3-6). 1995. 15.95 (*1-56847-266-8*) Thomson Lrning.

All Around the House. Bank Street College of Education Editors. (Bunny Bks.). (Illus.). 64p. (J). (ps-00). 1985. 2.95 (*0-8120-3613-1*) Barron.

All Around the Neighborhood. Bank Street College of Education Editors. (Bunny Bks.). (Illus.). 64p. (J). (ps-00). 1985. 2.95 (*0-8120-3612-3*) Barron.

All Around the Town. Mary Higgins Clark. 1994. reprint ed. lib. bdg. 32.95 (*1-56849-264-2*) Buccaneer Bks.

All Around the Town. Mary Higgins Clark. Ed. by Julie Rubenstein. 352p. 1993. reprint ed. pap. 6.99 (*0-671-79348-9*) PB.

All Around the World: A Bedtime Book. Caroline A. Glyman. (Forest House First Ser.). (Illus.). 32p. (J). (gr. k-3). Date not set. lib. bdg. 12.95 (*1-878363-77-8*) Forest Hse.

All Around the Year: Holidays & Celebrations in American Life. Jack Santino. LC 93-1516. (Illus.). 256p. (C). 1994. 24.95 (*0-252-02049-9*) U of Ill Pr.

***All Around the Year: Holidays & Celebrations in American Life.** Jack Santino. (Illus.). 256p. (C). 1995. pap. 14.95 (*0-252-06516-6*) U of Ill Pr.

***All Around Town.** Lois Becker & Mark Stratton. Ed. by Mary Becker et al. (Teddy Ruxpin Tell Me Again Ser.). (Illus.). 24p. (J). 1995. audio, pap. 11.99 (*0-934323-81-X*) Alchemy Comms.

All Around Us. Eric Carle. LC 86-9354. (Illus.). (J). (ps up). 1991. boxed 11.95 (*0-88708-016-2*, Picture Book Studio) S&S Childrens.

All Asia Guide. 16th ed. Far Eastern Economic Review Staff. (Illus.). 512p. (Orig.). 1994. pap. 23.95 (*962-7010-50-2*) C E Tuttle.

All at Sea. Ambrose Greenway & William Shakespeare. 64p. 1987. 35.00 (*0-85937-289-8*, Pub. by K Mason Pubns Ltd UK) St Mut.

All Babies. Maureen Connelly. Ed. by Janet Sieff. (Illus.). 16p. (J). (ps-3). 1993. pap. 1.50 (*1-56123-063-4*) Centering Corp.

All Backs Were Turned. Marek Hlasko. Tr. by Tomasz Mirkowicz. LC 90-84230. 118p. (Orig.). (C). 1991. pap. 8.95 (*0-943433-07-X*) Cane Hill Pr.

All-Bank Statistics, United States, 1896-1955. Federal Reserve System, Board of Governors Staff. LC 75-22816. (America in Two Centuries Ser.). 1976. reprint ed. 107.95 (*0-405-07688-6*) Ayer.

All Beautiful Things. 2nd ed. Naomi F. Faust. LC 82-83853. 104p. (YA). (gr. 7-12). 1983. per., pap. 5.00 (*0-916418-49-9*) Lotus.

All Because of Agatha. Jonathan Troy. 1964. pap. 4.75 (*0-8222-0015-5*) Dramatists Play.

All Because of Raizy. Miriam L. Elias. 1990. 11.95 (*0-87306-535-2*); pap. 9.95 (*0-87306-540-9*) Feldheim.

All Before Them: 1660-1780, Vol. 1. John McVeagh. LC 88-7489. (English Literature & the Wider World Ser.). (Illus.). 320p. (C). 1990. text ed. 55.00 (*0-948660-08-2*, Pub. by Ashfield Pr UK) Humanities.

All Better Book. Suzy Becker et al. LC 92-50282. (Illus.). (J). 1992. pap. 5.95 (*1-56305-314-4*, 3314) Workman Pub.

All Bisque & Half Bisque Dolls. Genevieve Angione. LC 76-77265. (Illus.). 357p. 1981. reprint ed. 25.00 (*0-916838-39-0*) Schiffer.

All-Breed Dictionary of Unusual Names. Gloria Jarrett. 240p. (Orig.). 1988. pap. 10.95 (*0-931866-32-4*) Alpine Pubns.

All Breed Dog Grooming. 87p. 1988. 14.95 (*0-86622-938-8*, TS-101) TFH Pubns.

All-Breed Dog Grooming. (Illus.). 160p. 1989. spiral bd. 34.95 (*0-86622-925-6*, H-1095) TFH Pubns.

***All Breed Dog Grooming Guide.** Sam Kohl. 265p. 1987. pap. text ed. 19.95 (*0-9646072-0-4*) Aaronco.

All Breed Dog Grooming (132) (Illus.). 240p. 1987. 24.95 (*0-86622-937-X*, PS-872) TFH Pubns.

All Bucks Are Trophies. Myrland Grimm. 132p. 1990. write for info. (*0-9637947-0-1*) M Grimm.

All Businesses Communicate: A Manual. Robert H. Sheldon. 273p. 1988. 60.00 (*0-946796-21-1*) St Mut.

An Asterisk (*) at the beginning of an entry indicates that the title is appearing in BIP for the first time. 193

A

All but Alice. Phyllis R. Naylor. LC 91-28722. 160p. (J). (gr. 4-8). 1992. text ed. 13.95 (*0-689-31773-5*, Atheneum Bks Young) S&S Childrens.

All but Love. Ann H. White. 224p. (Orig.). 1993. pap. 2.95 (*1-56597-049-7*, Kismet) Meteor Pub.

***All but My Life.** Gerda W. Klein. LC 94-43065. 272p. 1995. pap. 10.00 (*0-8090-1580-3*) Hill & Wang.

***All but My Life.** expanded ed. Gerda W. Klein. LC 94-43065. 272p. 1995. 21.00 (*0-8090-2460-8*) Hill & Wang.

All but the Waltz: Essays on a Montana Family. Mary C. Blew. 240p. 1992. pap. 10.00 (*0-14-012892-1*, Penguin Bks) Viking Penguin.

All by Myself. June M. Milam & Kathy Gaston. Ed. by Chris Gilmer & Amy L. Wilson. (Drugless Douglass Tales Ser.). (Illus.). 24p. (Orig.). (J). (ps-00). 1993. pap. text ed. 42.95 (*1-884307-00-0*); student ed 4.95 (*1-884307-01-9*) Dev Res Educ.

All By Myself. Mercer Mayer. (Golden Look-Look Bks.). (Illus.). 24p. (J). (ps-3). 1985. reprint ed. pap. write for info. (*0-307-11938-6*, Golden Bks) Western Pub.

All Cats Are Gray in the Dark: A Graphic Play. Robert Schoolcraft. Ed. by Manuela Menendez. (Limited Edition Ser.). (Illus.). 88p. (Orig.). (YA). (gr. 9 up). 1994. pap. 7.50 (*0-9640414-0-5*) MS Bks Pubng.

All Change. Charles McLeod. 222p. 1970. 29.95 (*0-8464-1454-6*) Beekman Pubs.

All Change at Work: The Human Dimension. Ed. by Theon Wilkinson. 160p. (C). 1989. 100.00 (*0-85292-414-3*, Pub. by IPM Hse UK) St Mut.

***All Children Are Special: Creating an Inclusive Classroom.** Greg Lang & Chris Berberich. (Illus.). 152p. (Orig.). (C). 1995. pap. text ed. 18.50 (*1-57110-017-2*) Stenhse Pubs.

All Children Create: Levels Four to Six, an Elementary Art Curriculum, Vol. II. Paula Sefkow & Helen Berger. LC 80-82018. (Illus.). 204p. (Orig.). (J). (gr. 4-6). 1981. pap. 24.95 (*0-918452-25-2*) Learning Pubns.

All Children Create: Levels One to Three, an Elementary Art Curriculum, Vol. I. Paula Sefkow & Helen Berger. LC 80-82018. (Illus.). 204p. (J). (gr. 1-3). 1981. pap. 24. 95 (*0-918452-24-4*) Learning Pubns.

All Children Successful: Real Answers for Helping At-Risk Elementary Students. Vito Germinario et al. LC 92-53827. 210p. 1992. text ed. 29.00 (*0-87762-921-8*) Technomic.

All China. 2nd ed. China Guides Editors. (China Guides Ser.). 144p. 1988. 9.95 (*0-8442-9802-6*, Passport Bks) NTC Pub Grp.

All Clear: Idioms in Context. 2nd ed. Helen K. Fragiadakis. LC 92-27549. 1992. pap. 19.95 (*0-8384-3966-7*) Heinle & Heinle.

All Clear: Idioms in Context. 2nd ed. Helen K. Fragiadakis. LC 92-27549. 1993. audio 20.00 (*0-8384-4126-2*) Heinle & Heinle.

All Clear: Idioms in Context. 2nd ed. Helen K. Fragiadakis. LC 92-27549. 1993. audio 21.95 (*0-8384-4224-2*); cd-rom 21.95 (*0-8384-4223-4*); cd-rom 20.00 (*0-8384-5092-X*) Heinle & Heinle.

All Clever Men, Who Make Their Way: Critical Discourse in the Old South. Ed. by Michael O'Brien. LC 92-17539. (Brown Thrasher Bks.). 480p. 1992. reprint ed. pap. 19.95 (*0-8203-1490-0*) U of Ga Pr.

***All Cloudless Glory Vol. 1: The Life of George Washington: From Boyhood to Valley Forge, 2 vols., Set.** E. Harrison Clark. (Illus.). 608p. (C). 1995. 35.00 (*0-89526-466-8*) Regnery Pub.

All Color Auto Library: Jaguar. Bron Kowal. 1988. 4.98 (*0-671-09396-7*) S&S Trade.

***All Color Bass Fishing Guide.** Bill Herzog. (Illus.). 48p. 1995. pap. 15.95 (*1-57188-003-8*) F Amato Pubns.

All Color Book of the Body. write for info. (*0-318-59588-5*) S&S Trade.

All-Colour Chinese Recipes. Date not set. write for info. (*0-318-72222-4*) Atrium Pubs.

All-Colour Food Combining Recipes. Ursula Summ. 1994. 19.95 (*0-572-01942-4*, Pub. by W Foulsham UK) Trans-Atl Phila.

All Colour Vegetarian Recipes. Ed. by Christopher Conil & Jean Conil. (Illus.). 128p. 1995. 9.95 (*0-572-01715-4*, Pub. by Foulsham UK) Atrium Pubs.

All Colour Wok Cookbook. Peter Nikolay. (Illus.). 128p. 1995. 9.95 (*0-572-01767-7*, Pub. by Foulsham UK) Atrium Pubs.

All Compact Orientable Three Dimensional Manifolds Admit Total Foliations. Detlef Hardorp. LC 80-16612. (Memoirs Ser.: No. 23/233). 74p. 1980. pap. 16.00 (*0-8218-2233-0*, MEMO 23/233) Am Math.

All Consuming Images: The Politics of Style in Contemporary Culture. Stuart Ewen. LC 88-47684. (Illus.). 320p. 1990. pap. 15.00 (*0-465-00101-7*) Basic.

All Contraries Confounded: The Lyrical Fiction of Virginia Woolf, Djuna Barnes, & Marguerite Duras. Karen Kaivola. LC 90-24358. 184p. (C). 1991. text ed. 25.95x (*0-87745-323-3*); pap. 11.95x (*0-87745-324-1*) U of Iowa Pr.

All Cotton Briefs. M. Kasper. 64p. 1985. pap. 3.95 (*0-915996-10-3*) North Am Rev.

All Creatures. Pauline Cartwright. LC 90-10021. (Highgate Collection). (Illus.). 16p. (J). (gr. 1-4). 1990. lib. bdg. 14. 64 (*0-8114-2695-5*) Raintree Steck-V.

***All Creatures Great & Small.** 1995. 4.50 (*0-679-87218-3*) Random.

All Creatures Great & Small. Isabelle Brent. (J). (ps-3). 1994. 14.95 (*0-316-10869-3*) Little.

All Creatures Great & Small. James Herriot. (J). (gr. 6 up). 1985. mass mkt. 6.99 (*0-553-26812-0*) Bantam.

All Creatures Great & Small. James Herriot. 1972. 17.95 (*0-312-01960-2*, A20000) St Martin.

All Creatures Great & Small. 20th aniversary ed. James Herriot. 448p. 1992. 18.95 (*0-312-08498-6*) St Martin.

All Creatures Great & Small: Bible Pop-Up. Ed. by Henrietta Gambill. (Illus.). 10p. (J). (ps). 1994. 3.99 (*0-7847-0205-5*, 24-03145) Standard Pub.

All Cultivated People: A History of the United States Arts Club, Dublin. Patricia Boylan. (Illus.). 1989. 26.00 (*0-86140-266-9*, Pub. by Colin Smythe Ltd UK) Dufour.

All Dads on Deck. Judy Delton. (Pee Wee Scouts Ser.: No. 23). (J). (ps-3). 1994. pap. 3.25 (*0-440-40943-8*) Dell.

All-Day Care: Exploring the Options for You & Your Child. Susan M. Zitzman. 236p. (Orig.). 1990. pap. 7.99 (*0-87788-039-5*) Shaw Pubs.

All Day, Every Day: Factory & Family in the Making of Women's Lives. Sallie Westwood. LC 84-23989. 280p. 1985. 29.95 (*0-252-01191-0*); pap. 11.95 (*0-252-01192-9*) U of Ill Pr.

All Day Long: Fifty Rhymes of the Never Was & Always Is. David McCord. (J). (gr. 4-7). 1992. mass mkt. 6.95 (*0-316-55532-0*) Little.

***All Day Suckers.** Gordon Kent. LC 92-12843. (Widgets Ser.). (J). (gr. 2). 1992. lib. bdg. 13.99 (*1-56239-155-0*) Abdo & Dghtrs.

***All Day...All God.** Doris Pharrams & Anna Charles. 52p. (Orig.). 1995. pap. 5.95 (*0-9645558-0-8*) Gift of Love.

***All Days & Nights.** William Maxwell. 1995. pap. write for info. (*0-679-76102-0*) Random.

All Deliberate Speed: Segregation & Exclusion in California Schools, 1855-1977. Charles M. Wollenberg. 1978. pap. 10.00 (*0-520-03728-6*) U CA Pr.

All Desires Known. Malcolm Macdonald. 352p. 1993. 21.95 (*0-312-10415-4*) St Martin.

All Desires Known. enl. ed. Janet Morley. LC 93-45039. 128p. 1994. pap. 10.95 (*0-8192-1610-0*) Morehouse Pub.

All Down to a River. Nichola Manning. 64p. (Orig.). 1984. pap. 5.95 (*0-89807-112-7*) Illuminati.

All Dressed Up. Mariette Buckle. LC 92-21447. (Voyages Ser.). (Illus.). (J). 1993. 3.75 (*0-383-03613-5*) SRA Schl Grp.

All Dressed Up & Nowhere to Go. Daniel M. Joseph. (J). (ps-3). 1993. 14.95 (*0-395-60196-7*) HM.

All Dressed up to Die. Robert Nordan. 224p. 1989. pap. 3.50 (*0-449-14576-X*, GM) Fawcett.

***All Ears.** Alvin Meyer & Kitty Meyer. Tr. by Cal Huiping. (Illus.). 32p. (Orig.). (CHI.). 1995. pap. write for info. (*0-9645121-0-6*) US China Invest.

All Ears: A Christmas Story. Judy L. Vernon. 25p. (Orig.). (J). (gr. 2-8). 1989. pap. 4.95 (*0-9617776-4-8*) J Vernon.

All Electric Motional Electric Field Generator. 1987. 8.75 (*0-914119-12-5*) Tesla Bk Co.

All Else in Bondage: Non-Volitional Living. Wei Wu-wei. 68p. (C). 1982. pap. text ed. 22.00 (*962-209-025-7*, Pub. by Hong Kong U Pr HK) St Mut.

All England Law Reports, 1936-1993, 171 vols., Set. boxed 9,889.00 (*0-406-86861-1*, U.K.) Butterworth Legal Pubs.

All Eyes & Blind: Parable Stories for Sunday Scriptures, Cycle B. Francis P. Sullivan. LC 90-61960. 224p. (Orig.). (C). 1990. pap. 14.95 (*1-55612-354-X*) Sheed & Ward MO.

All Eyes on the Pond. Michael J. Rosen. LC 93-11743. (Illus.). 32p. (J). (ps-2). 1994. 14.95 (*1-56282-475-9*); lib. bdg. 14.89 (*1-56282-476-7*) Hyprn Child.

***All Eyes on the Pond.** Michael J. Rosen. LC 93-11743. (Illus.). 32p. (J). (ps-2). 1995. pap. 4.95 (*0-7868-1078-5*) Hyprn Ppbks.

All Faithful People: Change & Continuity in Middletown's Religion. Theodore Caplow et al. LC 82-24759. 390p. reprint ed. pap. 111.20 (*0-7837-2972-3*, 2057482) Bks Demand.

All Fall Down. Lee Gruenfeld. LC 93-40482. 448p. 1994. 21.95 (*0-446-51714-3*) Warner Bks.

All Fall Down. Lee Gruenfeld. 512p. 1995. mass mkt. 5.99 (*0-446-60186-1*) Warner Bks.

All Fall Down. James L. Herlihy. 1990. pap. 8.95 (*1-55611-192-4*, Primus Lib Contemp) D I Fine.

All Fall Down. Wendy Lill. 108p. 1994. pap. 10.95 (*0-88922-336-X*, Pub. by Talonbooks CN) InBook.

All Fall Down. Helen Oxenbury. (Macmillan Big Board Bks.). (Illus.). 10p. (J). (ps-00). 1987. pap. 6.95 (*0-02-769040-7*, Aladdin Paperbacks) S&S Childrens.

All Fall Down. Carlene Thompson. 304p. (Orig.). 1993. mass mkt. 4.99 (*0-380-77021-0*) Avon.

All Fall Down. Brian Wildsmith. (Illus.). 16p. (J). 1987. pap. 3.50 (*0-19-272135-6*) OUP.

All Falling Down. Gene Zion. LC 51-12571. (Illus.). 32p. (J). (ps-1). 1951. lib. bdg. 13.89 (*0-06-026831-X*) HarpC Child Bks.

***All Feelings Are OK: It's What You Do with Them That Counts.** Lawrence E. Shapiro. Ed. by Hennie M. Shore. (Play & Read Ser.). (Illus.). 200p. (Orig.). (J). (ps-5). 1993. pap. 23.95 (*0-614-07239-5*) Ctr Applied Psy.

All Feelings Are Ok - It's What You Do with Them That Counts. Lawrence E. Shapiro. Ed. by Hennie M. Shose. (Play-&-Read Ser.). (Illus.). 100p. (Orig.). (J). (gr. k-4). 1993. 14.95 (*1-882732-04-9*) Ctr Applied Psy.

All-Fellows & the Cloak of Friendship. Laurence Housman. LC 74-122721. (Short Story Index Reprint Ser.). 1977. 17.95 (*0-8369-3554-3*) Ayer.

All Flesh Is Grass. Clifford D. Simak. 256p. (YA). (gr. 7 up). 1978. pap. 3.50 (*0-380-39933-4*, 39933) Avon.

All Flesh Is Grass. Clifford D. Simak. 256p. 1993. 4.95 (*0-7867-0045-9*) Carroll & Graf.

***All Fools.** fac. ed. George Chapman. Ed. by Frank Manley. LC 68-10664. (Regents Renaissance Drama Ser.). 123p. 1994. pap. 35.10 (*0-7837-7336-6*, 2047289) Bks Demand.

All for a Lark. large type ed. Madeline Lark. (Ulverscroft Ser.). 208p. 1994. 20.95 (*0-7089-3046-8*) Ulverscroft.

All for Art: the Ricketts & Shannon Collection: Fitzwilliam Museum, Cambridge, 9 October-3 December 1979. Ed. by Joseph Darracott. LC 79-14089. 135p. reprint ed. pap. 38.50 (*0-8357-5311-5*, 2031650) Bks Demand.

All for Hecuba. Michael MacLiammoir. (Illus.). 25.95 (*0-8283-1137-4*) Branden Pub Co.

All for Jesus. Ed. by John S. Sawin & Samuel J. Stoesz. LC 86-72007. (Illus.). 322p. 1986. 14.99 (*0-87509-383-3*) Chr Pubns.

All for Jesus: or The Easy Ways of Divine Love. Frederick W. Faber. LC 90-70239. 308p. 1991. reprint ed. pap. 13. 50 (*0-89555-401-1*) TAN Bks Pubs.

All for Love. Pat Booth. LC 93-9890. 1993. 21.00 (*0-517-58416-6*, Crown) Crown Pub Group.

All for Love. Ed. & Illus. by Tasha Tudor. LC 83-21959. 96p. (J). (gr. 6-8). 1984. 16.95 (*0-399-21012-1*, Philomel Bks) Putnam Pub Group.

All for Love. large type ed. Pat Booth. LC 94-9506. 1994. 23.95 (*0-7927-2062-8*, Eagle Lrg Print) Chivers N Amer.

All for Love. large type ed. Pat Booth. LC 94-9506. 1995. pap. 22.95 (*0-7927-2061-X*, Paragon Lrg Print) Chivers N Amer.

***All for Maine: A Biography of Governor Percy Baxter.** Liz Soares. Ed. by Jane Weinberger. (Illus.). 160p. (YA). 1995. pap. 8.95 (*1-883650-17-8*) Windswept Hse.

All for Money. Thomas Lupton. LC 79-133700. (Tudor Facsimile Texts. Old English Plays Ser.: No. 51). reprint ed. 49.50 (*0-404-53351-5*) AMS Pr.

All for Nothing & Another Story. W. P. Farnfield. (C). 1989. pap. 23.00 (*0-7223-2358-1*, Pub. by A H S Ltd UK) St Mut.

All for Strings: Conductor Score. Gerald Anderson & Robert Frost. 180p. 1986. 14.95 (*0-8497-3226-3*, 78F) Kjos.

***All for Strings: Conductor Score, Bk. 1: Parts.** Gerald Anderson & Robert Frost. 1986. 4.95 (*0-614-03101-X*) Kjos.

All for Strings: Conductor Score, Bk. 3. Gerald Anderson & Robert Frost. 180p. 1986. 17.95 (*0-8497-3309-X*, 80F) Kjos.

***All for Strings: Conductor Score, Bk. 3: Parts.** Gerald Anderson & Robert Frost. 1986. 4.95 (*0-614-03102-8*) Kjos.

All for Strings, Bk. 2: Conductor Score. Gerald Anderson & Robert Frost. 180p. 1986. 14.95 (*0-8497-3240-9*, 79F); 4.95 (*0-685-74719-0*) Kjos.

All for Strings Theory Workbook, No. 1: Conductor Answer Key. Gerald Anderson & Robert Frost. 32p. 1988. 3.45 (*0-8497-3265-4*, 84F); 3.45 (*0-685-74720-4*) Kjos.

All for Strings Theory Workbook, No. 2: Conductor Answer Key. Gerald Anderson & Robert Frost. 32p. 1989. 3.45 (*0-8497-3266-2*, 85F); 3.45 (*0-685-74721-2*) Kjos.

***All for the Best.** Ruchoma Shain. LC 94-27091. 1994. write for info. (*0-87306-687-1*) Feldheim.

All for the Better: A Story of el Barrio. Nicholasa Mohr. LC 92-23639. (Stories of America Ser.). (Illus.). 56p. (J). (gr. 2-5). 1992. lib. bdg. 21.36 (*0-8114-7220-5*) Raintree Steck-V.

All for the Boss. Ruchoma Shain. 439p. 1984. 17.95 (*0-87306-346-5*); (*0-318-60357-8*) Feldheim.

All for the Love of That Boy. Linda Lewis. 224p. (J). (gr. 7-9). 1989. pap. 2.95 (*0-671-68243-1*, Archway) PB.

All for the Love of You. large type ed. Claire Hamilton. 1990. pap. 12.95 (*0-7089-6880-5*, Linford) Ulverscroft.

All for the Union: The Civil War Diary & Letters of Elisha Hunt Rhodes. Ed. by Robert H. Rhodes. (Illus.). 256p. 1991. 21.00 (*0-517-58427-1*, Orion Bks) Crown Pub Group.

All for the Union: The Civil War Diary & Letters of Elisha Hunt Rhodes. Robert H. Rhodes. 1992. pap. 11.00 (*0-679-73828-2*, Vin) Random.

All for the Wolves: Selected Poems, 1947-1975. Peter Russell. Ed. by Peter Jay. (Literary Ser.). 151p. 1984. 25.00 (*0-933806-20-5*) Black Swan CT.

All "Fore Golf" Laurie Wax & Martin Wax. (Illus.). 45p. (Orig.). 1986. pap. text ed. 3.95 (*0-9617857-0-5*) All Fore Golf.

All Four Feet & a Snout in the Trough: 200 Alleged Ethics Violations by Reagan Administration Appointees. (Ethics in Government Ser.: No. 1). 80p. 1987. pap. 14. 95 (*0-941375-09-9*) Diane Pub.

All Fourteen Eight-Thousanders. Reinhold Messner. Tr. by Audrey Salkeld. (Illus.). 247p. 1988. 40.00 (*0-938567-05-5*) Cloudcap.

All Fulness Dwells. Bob Jones. 152p. 1971. 6.95 (*0-89084-002-4*) Bob Jones Univ Pr.

All Generations Shall Call Me Blessed. Ed. by Francis A. Eigo. LC 94-4971. 1994. 8.95 (*0-87723-061-7*) Villanova U Pr.

All-Girl Football Team. Lewis Nordan. (Contemporaries Ser.). 1989. pap. 5.95 (*0-394-75701-7*, Vin) Random.

All God's Children. Alexander La Perchia. LC 86-91204. 1987. 9.95 (*0-87212-197-6*) Libra.

All God's Children: Ministry with Disabled Persons. rev. ed. Gene Newman & Joni E. Tada. LC 92-28627. 128p. 1993. pap. 10.99 (*0-310-59381-6*) Zondervan.

***All God's Children: The Bosket Family & the American Tradition of Violence.** Fox Butterfield. (Illus.). 1995. pap. 27.50 (*0-394-58286-1*) Knopf.

All God's Children & Blue Suede Shoes: Christians & Popular Culture. Ken Myers. LC 87-71899. (Turning Point Christian Worldview Ser.). 224p. 1989. pap. 12.99 (*0-89107-538-0*) Crossway Bks.

All God's Children Got Gum in Their Hair. Steve Phelps. LC 94-16538. 1994. write for info. (*0-8308-1822-7*) InterVarsity.

All God's Children, Great & Small: The Solution to the Abortion Debate. Mark Emershaw. (Orig.). 1991. pap. 6.95 (*0-9626784-1-4*) Comforter Pub.

All God's Children Need Traveling Shoes. Maya Angelou. LC 85-19351. 162p. 1986. 19.95 (*0-394-52143-9*) Random.

All God's Children Need Traveling Shoes. Maya Angelou. LC 86-46173. 1987. pap. 7.00 (*0-394-75077-2*, Vin) Random.

All God's Children Need Traveling Shoes. Maya Angelou. LC 90-55700. 224p. 1991. pap. 9.00 (*0-679-73404-X*, Vin) Random.

All God's Chillun Got Soul. Morrie Turner. 64p. (J). (gr. 6). 1980. pap. 7.00 (*0-8170-0892-6*) Judson.

All God's Creatures. Gary Richmond. 1991. 8.99 (*0-8499-3251-3*) Word Inc.

All God's Creatures. Susan S. Swartz. (J). (ps-3). 1994. pap. 4.99 (*0-8066-2687-9*) Augsburg Fortress.

All God's Critters Got a Place in the Choir. Bill Staines. LC 88-31696. (Illus.). 32p. (J). (ps-2). 1989. 14.99 (*0-525-44469-6*, DCB) Dutton Child Bks.

All God's Critters Got a Place in the Choir. Bill Staines. (Illus.). 32p. (J). (ps-2). 1993. pap. 4.99 (*0-14-054838-6*) Puffin Bks.

***All God's Critters Got a Place in the Choir: Giving Voice to the Differences That Unite Women.** Laurel T. Ulrich & Emma L. Thayne. LC 94-48846. 228p. 1995. 14.95 (*1-56236-226-7*) Aspen Bks.

All God's Dangers: The Life of Nate Shaw. Theodore Rosengarten. 1984. pap. 12.95 (*0-394-72245-0*) Random.

All God's Dangers: The Life of Nate Shaw. Theodore Rosengarten. LC 83-19828. 608p. 1989. pap. 14.00 (*0-679-72761-2*, Vin) Random.

All God's Mistakes: Genetic Counseling in a Pediatric Hospital. Charles L. Bosk. LC 91-36938. 222p. 1992. 24.95 (*0-226-06681-9*) U Ch Pr.

***All God's Mistakes: Genetic Counseling in a Pediatric Hospital.** Charles L. Bosk. 196p. 1995. pap. text ed. 12. 95 (*0-226-06682-7*) U Ch Pr.

***All God's People.** David Smith. 440p. 1996. 19.99 (*1-56476-382-X*, 6-3382, Bridgepoint) SP Pubns.

All God's People Are Ministers: Equipping Church Members for Ministry. Patricia N. Page. LC 93-19835. 112p. 1993. pap. 9.99 (*0-8066-2643-7*, 9-2643) Augsburg Fortress.

All Gone! Sarah Garland. (J). (ps). 1991. pap. 3.95 (*0-14-054409-7*, Puffin) Puffin Bks.

All Gone: Eighteen Short Stories. Stephen Dixon. 1990. 17. 95 (*0-8018-4010-4*) Johns Hopkins.

All Gone Book. Norma J. Stodden & Linda McCormick. Ed. by Gail Levy. (Baby Sign Bks.). (Illus.). 18p. (J). (ps). 1988. bds. 3.95 (*0-943693-05-5*) TRI Pubns.

All Good Greetings: Letters of Geraldine Farrar to Ilka Marie Stotler, 1946-1958. Ed. by Aida C. Truxall. (Illus.). 314p. (C). 1991. text ed. 22.95 (*0-8229-7016-3*) U of Pittsburgh Pr.

All Good Men. Thomas J. Fleming. LC 76-6341. (Irish Americans Ser.). 1976. reprint ed. 34.95 (*0-405-09336-5*) Ayer.

All Good Things. Michael J. Friedman. (Star Trek: The Next Generation Ser.). 1994. 20.00 (*0-671-50014-7*) PB.

***All Good Things.** Michael J. Friedman. Ed. by Kevin Ryan. (Star Trek: The Next Generation Ser.). 256p. 1995. mass mkt. 5.99 (*0-671-52148-9*) PB.

All Ground Is Holy: A Guide to the Christian Retreat. Jeannette L. Angell. LC 92-35258. 80p. (Orig.). 1993. pap. 7.95 (*0-8192-1597-X*) Morehouse Pub.

All Grown Up & No Place to Go: Teenagers in Crisis. David Elkind. LC 84-6388. 1984. pap. 13.46 (*0-201-11379-1*, 861) Addison-Wesley.

All Hail King Jesus. Marty Parks. 1991. 5.25 (*0-8341-9205-5*, ME-41); audio 10.98 (*0-685-68615-9*, TA-9138C) Lillenas.

All Hail the Power of Jesus' Name: The History of Christ Cathedral. Ed. by Joseph Kimmett & Jo Reed. (Illus.). (C). 1992. 25.00 (*0-9635141-0-5*) Christ Cathedral.

All Hallows, Barking-by-the-Tower, Pt. II. Ed. by Francis H. Sheppard. (Survey of London Ser.: Vol. XV). (C). 1934. pap. 75.00 (*0-485-48215-0*, Pub. by Athlone Pr UK) Humanities.

All Hallows Eve. Annette N. Ashbaugh. (Illus.). 15p. 1988. 5.95 (*0-943480-66-3*) Friis-Pioneer Pr.

All Hallows' Eve. Charles W. Williams. 274p. 1981. pap. 9.99 (*0-8028-1250-3*) Eerdmans.

All Hallow's Eve. Charles Williams. 1993. reprint ed. lib. bdg. 18.95 (*0-89968-414-9*, Lghtyr Pr) Buccaneer Bks.

All Hallow's Eve: Tales of Love & the Supernatural. Ed. by Mary E. Allen. LC 92-11147. 214p. 1992. 21.95 (*0-8027-1252-5*) Walker & Co.

All Hallow's Evil. Valerie Wolzien. (Orig.). 1992. mass mkt. 3.99 (*0-449-14745-2*, GM) Fawcett.

All Have the Same God. Walbert Buhlmann. (C). 1988. 39. 00 (*0-685-22281-0*, Pub. by St Paul Pubns UK) St Mut.

All He Fears. Howard Barker. 28p. (Orig.). 1994. pap. 5.95 (*0-7145-4235-0*) Riverrun NY.

All Heads Turn When the Hunt Goes By. John Farris. 1993. reprint ed. lib. bdg. 18.95 (*0-89968-427-0*, Lghtyr Pr) Buccaneer Bks.

All Heaven Can Give. Ronald S. Joseph. 416p. (Orig.). 1991. pap. 5.99 (*0-451-40267-7*, Onyx) NAL-Dutton.

All Heavens Ranges. Fred W. Readel. (Orig.). 1986. pap. 4.95 (*0-9616822-3-X*) F W Readel.

All Hell Broke Loose. William H. Hull. (Illus.). 236p. (Orig.). 1985. pap. 8.95 (*0-939330-01-6*) W H Hull.

All Hell Needs Is Water. Budge Ruffner. (Illus.). 96p. reprint ed. pap. 27.40 (*0-8357-5312-3*, 2025555) Bks Demand.

All Her Children. Dave Wakefield. 1977. pap. 1.75 (*0-380-00920-X*) Avon.

All Her Dreams. Barbara Harrison. 1994. 22.00 (*0-7278-4600-0*) Severn Hse.

All Her Dreams. Alexandra Lyle. 448p. 1993. mass mkt. 4.99 (*1-55817-703-5*, Pinnacle NY) Windsor NY.

All Her Lovely Companions. large type ed. Stella Kent. 304p. 1987. 16.95 (*0-7089-1657-0*) Ulverscroft.

All Her Paths Are Peace: Women Pioneers in Peacemaking. Michael Henderson. LC 94-14748. (Kumarian Press Books for a World That Works). (Illus.). 188p. 1994. 42.00 (*1-56549-035-5*); pap. 14.95 (*1-56549-034-7*) Kumarian Pr.

An Asterisk (*) at the beginning of an entry indicates that the title is appearing in BIP for the first time.

An Asterisk (*) at the beginning of an entry indicates that the title is appearing in BIP for the first time.

All My Dreams. Debra W. Alexander. 16p. (YA). (gr. 6-12). 1993. 3.95 (*1-56688-067-X*) Bur For At-Risk.

All My Dreams. Victoria Chancellor. 1992. mass mkt. 4.50 (*0-06-108015-2*, Harp PBks) HarpC.

All My Feelings. Debra W. Alexander. 23p. (J). (gr. k-5). 1992. 3.95 (*1-56688-055-6*) Bur For At-Risk.

All My Feelings Are OK: An Innovative Program Using Stories, Skits, & Games to Help Families Identify & Express Their Feelings. Linda Kondracki. LC 92-41974. (Guides for Growing a Healthy Family Ser.). 128p. (Orig.). 1993. pap. 7.99 (*0-8007-5441-7*) Revell.

All My Friends Are Going to Be Strangers. Larry McMurtry. 1989. pap. 7.95 (*0-671-68103-6*, Touchstone Bks) S&S Trade.

All My Friends Are Going to Be Strangers. Larry McMurtry. Ed. by Bill Grose. 288p. 1992. reprint ed. pap. 6.50 (*0-671-75871-3*) PB.

All My Heroes Are Crazy. People's Bridge Action Inc. Staff. 104p. 1992. pap. 9.00 (*1-881467-00-7*) Peoples Bdge Act.

All My Life. Edward Fortner. 1993. 12.95 (*0-533-10550-1*) Vantage.

All My Life with Hunting Birds. L. DeBastyai. (Illus.). 256p. 1984. 45.00 (*0-87556-590-5*) Saifer.

All My Little Ducklings. Monica Wellington. LC 88-22841. (Illus.). 32p. (J). (ps-00). 1989. 11.95 (*0-525-44459-9*, DCB) Dutton Child Bks.

***All My Little Ducklings Board Book.** Monica Wellington. (Illus.). 7p. (J). (ps). 1995. bds. 5.99 (*0-525-45360-1*) Dutton Child Bks.

All My Love. Peggy W. Cozzi. (Illus.). 80p. 1988. pap. 5.00 (*0-942568-21-4*) Canyon Pub Co.

All My Men. Bernard Ashley. LC 78-12683. (J). (gr. 6 up). 1978. 22.95 (*0-87599-228-5*) S G Phillips.

***All My Octobers.** Mantle. 1995. mass mkt. 5.99 (*0-06-109212-6*, Harp PBks) HarpC.

All My Octobers: My Memories of 12 World Series When the Yankees Ruled Baseball. Mickey Mantle. 272p. 1994. 23.00 (*0-06-017747-0*, HarpT) HarpC.

All My Own Work! Adventures in Art. Carole Armstrong & Anthea Peppin. (Illus.). 48p. (J). (gr. 2-7). 1993. pap. 6.95 (*0-8120-1755-2*) Barron.

All My Patients Are under the Bed. Louis J. Camuti. 1985. pap. 8.95 (*0-671-55450-6*, Fireside) S&S Trade.

All My Pretty Ones see Heart of Anne Sexton's Poetry

All My Relations. Christopher McIlroy. LC 93-23006. (Flannery O'Connor Award for Short Fiction Ser.). 200p. 1994. 19.95 (*0-8203-1602-4*) U of Ga Pr.

All My Relations: An Anthology of Contemporary Canadian Native Fiction. Ed. by Thomas King. LC 92-54145. (American Indian Literature & Critical Studies: Vol. 4). 236p. 1992. reprint ed. pap. 14.95 (*0-8061-2429-6*) U of Okla Pr.

All My Road Before Me. C. S. Lewis. 1992. pap. 14.95 (*0-15-604643-1*, Harvest Bks) HarBrace.

All My Road Before Me: The Diary of C. S. Lewis (1922-1927) C. S. Lewis. 1991. 24.95 (*0-15-104609-3*) HarBrace.

***All My Sins Are Relatives.** William Penn. (North American Indian Prose Award: Vol. 3). (Illus.). 270p. (C). 1995. 25.00 (*0-8032-3709-X*) U of Nebr Pr.

All My Sins Remembered. Joe W. Haldeman. 224p. 1978. pap. 2.95 (*0-380-39321-2*) Avon.

All My Sins Remembered. Joe W. Haldeman. LC 76-62773. 184p. 1977. 25.00 (*0-89366-145-7*) Ultramarine Pub.

All My Sins Remembered: Another Part of Life - The Other Side of Genius: Family Letters. Wilfred R. Bion. 246p. 1985. reprint ed. pap. 31.95 (*0-9507895-1-8*, Pub. by Karnac Bks UK) Brunner-Mazel.

All My Sons. Christer Kihlman. Tr. by Joan Tate. 1984. 22.00 (*0-7206-0628-4*) Dufour.

All My Stars & Animals. Ken Fontenot. Ed. by Chuck Taylor. 120p. (Orig.). 1988. 14.95 (*0-318-33441-0*); pap. 7.95 (*0-941720-61-6*) Slough Pr TX.

***All My Suspects.** Louise Shaffer. 224p. 1995. pap. text ed. 4.99 (*0-425-14770-3*, Prime Crime) Berkley Pub.

All My Suspects: A Daytime Crime Mystery. Louise Shaffer. LC 94-9495. 224p. 1994. 19.95 (*0-399-13965-6*, Putnam) Putnam Pub Group.

All My Things. Photos by Laura Dwight. (Baby Photo Board Bks.). (Illus.). 28p. (J). (ps). 1992. bds. 2.95 (*1-56288-185-X*) Checkerboard.

All My Tomorrows. Sally Hawthorne. 175p. (Orig.). 1988. pap. 6.95 (*0-89265-131-8*) Randall Hse.

All My Tomorrows, Vol. I. Ed. by Shirley Mikkelson. (Illus.). 148p. (Orig.). 1993. pap. 24.95 (*0-943536-73-1*) Quill Bks.

All My Tomorrows, Vol. II. Ed. by Shirley Mikkelson. (Illus.). 148p. (Orig.). 1993. pap. 24.95 (*0-943536-74-X*) Quill Bks.

All My Tomorrows, Vol. III. Ed. by Shirley Mikkelson. (Illus.). 148p. (Orig.). 1993. pap. 24.95 (*0-943536-75-8*) Quill Bks.

All My Toys Are on the Floor. Mary Blocksma. LC 85-27000. (Just One More Ser.). (Illus.). 24p. (J). (ps-2). 1986. pap. 4.50 (*0-516-41579-4*) Childrens.

All My Trials. John W. Corrington. LC 86-6905. 233p. 1983. pap. 10.95 (*0-938626-73-6*) U of Ark Pr.

***All My Trials, Lord: Selections from Women's Slave Narratives.** Mary Young. (African-American Experience Ser.). (Illus.). (YA). (gr. 9-12). 1995. lib. bdg. 14.98 (*0-531-11219-5*) Watts.

All My Yesterdays: An Autobiography. Cecil Lewis. LC 93-14870. 1993. 24.95 (*1-85230-405-7*) Element MA.

***All Names Spoken.** Kobayashi & Oikawa. 1993. per. 11.95 (*0-920813-88-7*, Pub. by Sister Vision CN) InBook.

All Nations Christian Home & School Dictionary. Morris G. Watkins & Lois I. Watkins. 914p. 1992. 12.95 (*0-9628789-2-8*) All Nations.

All Nations English Dictionary. Morris G. Watkins & Lois I. Watkins. 914p. (Orig.). 1992. 12.95 (*0-9628789-3-6*) All Nations.

All Nations English Dictionary. Morris G. Watkins & Lois I. Watkins. 914p. (Orig.). 1992. pap. 7.95 (*0-9628789-0-1*) All Nations.

All Natural Pogo. Norman Hale. (Illus.). 96p. (Orig.). 1993. pap. 9.95 (*0-87816-150-3*) Pubs Dist MI.

All-Natural Sugar-Free Dessert Cookbook. Linda R. Leahy. 1992. mass mkt. 4.99 (*0-440-21100-X*) Dell.

All Natural Things: Archaeology & the Green Debate. Ed. by Lesley Macinnes & Caroline R. Wickham-Jones. (Oxbow Monographs in Archaeology: No. 21). (Illus.). 203p. 1992. pap. 31.50 (*0-946897-45-X*, Pub. by Oxbow Bks UK) David Brown.

All Nature Is but Art: The Coincidence of Opposites in English Romantic Literature. Mark T. Smith. LC 93-27166. (Locust Hill Literary Studies: No. 12). (Illus.). 282p. (C). 1993. lib. bdg. 32.00 (*0-933951-44-2*) Locust Hill Pr.

All Nature Is My Bride: Selections from Thoreau. Ed. by William M. White. LC 74-27954. (Illus.). 1975. 12.95 (*0-85699-113-9*) Chatham Pr.

All Nature Sings. Edith M. Clarkson. LC 86-16529. 148p. (Orig.). reprint ed. pap. 42.20 (*0-7837-3194-9*, 2042798) Bks Demand.

All Necessary Means: Inside the Gulf War. Ben Brown & David Shukman. (Illus.). 198p. (Orig.). 1994. pap. 14.95 (*0-563-36304-5*, BBC-Parkwest) Parkwest Pubns.

All New Advanced Custom Rod Building. rev. ed. Dale P. Clemens. (Illus.). 320p. 1988. 27.95 (*0-8329-0436-8*, Winchester Pr) New Win Pub.

***All-New Allstar Hockey Activity Book.** Noah Ross & Julian Ross. (Illus.). 48p. (Orig.). (J). (gr. 4-8). 1993. pap. 5.95 (*0-919591-89-2*, Pub. by Polestar Bk Pubs CN) Orca Bk Pubs.

All New Beautiful Braids. Judy Rambert. (Illus.). 64p. 1993. spiral bd. 5.98 (*1-56173-231-1*, 3612102) Pubns Intl Ltd.

All New Borden Pies: American Favorites Kit. Outlet Book Co Staff. 1992. pap. 6.99 (*0-517-06674-2*) Random Hse Value.

All-New Clean Joke Book. Bob Phillips. LC 90-36617. 192p. (Orig.). 1990. mass mkt. 3.99 (*0-89081-830-4*) Harvest Hse.

All-New Cookbook for Diabetics & Their Families. (Illus.). 224p. 1989. pap. 12.95 (*0-8487-0750-8*) Oxmoor Hse.

All New Diet Cookbook. (Illus.). 224p. 1993. 19.98 (*1-56173-549-3*, 2015800) Pubns Intl Ltd.

All New Dinosaurs. Robert A. Long & Samuel P. Welles. (J). (gr. 7 up). 1975. pap. 3.95 (*0-88388-031-8*) Bellerophon Bks.

All-New Edition of Our American Presidents. Joan Bumann & John Patterson. 176p. (J). (gr. 5 up). 1993. pap. 2.99 (*0-87406-644-1*) Willowisp Pr.

All New Free to Be Thin: The Successful Weight-Management Plan that Links How to Eat with How. Neva Coyle. 1993. 13.99 (*1-55661-312-1*) Bethany Hse.

***All-New Free to Be Thin: The Successful Weight-Management Plan That Links How to Eat with How...** Neva Coyle & Marie Chapian. 224p. 1994. pap. 8.99 (*1-55661-534-5*) Bethany Hse.

All New Free to Be Thin Lifestyle Plan: The Successful Weight-Management Plan That Links How To. Neva Coyle. 1993. pap. 8.99 (*1-55661-343-1*) Bethany Hse.

All New Jonah Twist. Natalie Honeycutt. 128p. (J). (gr. 3-5). 1987. pap. 3.50 (*0-380-70317-3*, Camelot) Avon.

All New Jonah Twist. Natalie Honeycutt. LC 85-28048. 128p. (J). (gr. 3-5). 1986. text ed. 13.95 (*0-02-744840-1*, Bradbury S&S) S&S Childrens.

***All-New Mighty Morphin Power Rangers Scrapbook, No. 02.** Scholastic. 1995. pap. (*0-590-50950-0*) Scholastic Inc.

All New Nineteen Ninety-One Meal Planner. John Schlife. 256p. (C). 1990. spiral bd. 14.95 (*0-8403-6388-5*) Kendall-Hunt.

All New Official Cheerleader's Handbook. International Cheerleading Foundation Staff et al. 1986. pap. 14.95 (*0-671-61210-7*, Fireside) S&S Trade.

All New People. Anne Lamott. LC 89-15954. 192p. 1989. 16.95 (*0-86547-394-3*, North Pt Pr) FS&G.

All-New Ultimate Football Quiz Book. Warren Etheredge. 176p. (Orig.). (YA). 1993. pap. 3.99 (*0-451-17616-2*, Sig) NAL-Dutton.

All Night, All Day: A Child's First Book of African-American Spirituals. Ashley Bryan. LC 90-753145. (Illus.). 48p. (J). (ps-4). 1991. text ed. 14.95 (*0-689-31662-3*, Atheneum Bks Young) S&S Childrens.

All Night Long. (Sweet Valley High Ser.: No. 5). 128p. (Orig.). (YA). (gr. 7-12). 1984. pap. 3.50 (*0-553-27568-2*) Bantam.

All Night Long. large type ed. Francine Pascal. (Sweet Valley High Ser.: No. 5). 134p. (J). (gr. 5-8). 1989. reprint ed. 9.50 (*1-55905-004-7*, Gareth Stevens Inc); reprint ed. lib. bdg. 10.50 (*1-55905-014-4*, Gareth Stevens Inc) Grey Castle.

All Night near the Water. Jim Arnosky. LC 93-31078. (Illus.). 32p. (J). (ps-1). 1994. lib. bdg. 15.95 (*0-399-22629-X*, Putnam) Putnam Pub Group.

All-Night Visitors. Clarence Major. 203p. 1973. pap. 7.50 (*0-685-32466-4*) Univ Place.

All Night Yemenite Cafe. Diane Frank. 80p. 1993. pap. 10.00 (*1-884226-01-9*) Dark River.

All-Nite Cafe. Philip Gross. (J). (gr. 4 up). 1993. pap. 5.95 (*0-571-16753-5*) Faber & Faber.

All Occasion, Any Occasion, Promise, Favor Card Plaque Gift Instruction Workbook. Greetings Etc. by Alfreda Staff. 1984. pap. text ed. 19.95 (*0-318-04360-2*, Greetings) Prosperity & Profits.

All-Occasion Cookbook: Books for Cooks. Ed. by Reader's Digest Editors. LC 94-64. 1994. 19.95 (*0-89577-592-1*) RD Assn.

All-of-a-Kind Family. Sydney Taylor. (Illus.). 192p. (J). (gr. k-6). 1980. mass mkt. 3.99 (*0-440-40059-7*, YB) Dell.

All-of-a-Kind Family. Sydney Taylor. (J). (gr. 2-6). 17.25 (*0-8446-6253-4*) Peter Smith.

All of a Kind Family: A Study Guide. Beatrice G. Davis. (Novel-Ties Ser.). (J). (gr. 3-6). 1984. student ed, teacher ed 15.95 (*0-88122-072-8*) Lrn Links.

All-of-a-Kind Family Uptown. braille ed. Sydney Taylor. 166p. (J). 1992. vinyl bd. 13.28 (*1-56956-106-0*, BR8727) W A T Braille.

All of a Piece: A Life with Multiple Sclerosis. Barbara D. Webster. LC 88-29343. 112p. 1989. 15.95 (*0-8018-3733-2*) Johns Hopkins.

All of a Piece: New Essays. Edward V. Lucas. LC 68-22923. (Essay Index Reprint Ser.). 1977. reprint ed. 19.95 (*0-8369-0627-6*) Ayer.

All of Grace. C. H. Spurgeon. 1978. pap. 3.50 (*1-56186-329-7*) Pilgrim Pubns.

All of Grace. Charles Spurgeon. Tr. by Ruth T. Chen & Peter Chou. 142p. (CHI.). 1984. pap. write for info. (*0-941598-22-5*) Living Spring Pubns.

All of Grace. Charles H. Spurgeon. (Moody Classics Ser.). 1984. pap. 3.99 (*0-8024-0001-9*) Moody.

All of Grace. C. H. Spurgeon. 144p. 1981. reprint ed. pap. 3.99 (*0-88368-097-1*) Whitaker Hse.

All of Grace see Solamente Por Gracia

All of Heaven. large type ed. Petra Nash. (Masquerade Historical Romance Ser.). 1993. 18.95 (*0-263-13753-8*, Pub. by Mills & Boon Ltd UK) Chivers N Amer.

All of It. Jeannett Haien. LC 87-45623. 160p. 1988. reprint ed. pap. 10.00 (*0-06-097147-9*, PL-7147, PL) HarpC.

All of Mine for Him. Damon C. Dodd. 1977. pap. 3.95 (*0-89265-045-1*) Randall Hse.

All of One Peace. Colman McCarthy. LC 93-45521. 256p. (C). 1994. text ed. 37.00 (*0-8135-2096-7*); pap. text ed. 15.00 (*0-8135-2097-5*) Rutgers U Pr.

All of Our Noses Are Here & Other Noodle Tales. Alvin Schwartz. LC 84-48330. (Harper I Can Read Bk.). (Illus.). 64p. (J). (gr. k-3). 1985. lib. bdg. 14.89 (*0-06-025288-X*) HarpC Child Bks.

All of Our Noses Are Here & Other Noodle Tales. Alvin Schwartz. LC 84-48330. (Trophy I Can Read Bk.). (Illus.). 64p. (J). (gr. k-3). 1987. pap. 3.50 (*0-06-444108-3*, Trophy) HarpC Child Bks.

All of Shakespeare. Maurice Charney. LC 93-6660. (C). 1993. write for info. (*0-231-06862-X*) Col U Pr.

All of Shakespeare. Maurice Charney. 1993. pap. 14.00 (*0-231-06863-8*) Col U Pr.

All of the Above. Dorothy Barresi. LC 90-20532. (Barnard New Women Poets Ser.). 1991. pap. 12.00 (*0-8070-6815-2*) Beacon Pr.

***All of the Above: Your Choice to Collegiate Success.** Ed. by David W. Eggebrecht et al. 256p. (C). 1992. pap. text ed. 29.95 (*0-614-00486-1*) Concordia U Pr.

All of the People, All the Time: Strategic Communication & American Politics. Jarol B. Manheim. LC 90-39657. 272p. 1991. text ed. 36.95 (*0-87332-796-9*) M E Sharpe.

All of the Women of the Bible. Edith Deen. LC 55-8521. 432p. 1988. pap. 15.00 (*0-06-061852-3*) Harper SF.

All of the Women of the Bible. braille ed. Edith Deen. 834p. 1991. vinyl bd. 66.72 (*1-56956-180-X*, BR7765) W A T Braille.

All of Us Are Present: The Stephens College Symposium Women's Education the Future. Ed. by Eleanor M. Bender et al. (C). 1984. pap. 15.00 (*0-916767-01-9*) J M Wood Res.

All of Us Here. limited ed. Irving Feldman. Ed. by John Wheatcroft. (Bucknell University Fine Editions: Series in Contemporary Poetry). (Illus.). 60p. 1990. 150.00 (*0-916375-13-7*) Press Alley.

All of Us Together: The Story of Inclusion at the Kinzie School. Jeri Banks. LC 94-7508. 200p. 1994. 24.95 (*1-56368-028-9*) Gallaudet Univ Pr.

All of You Was Singing. Richard Lewis. LC 89-18263. (Illus.). 32p. (J). 1991. text ed. 13.95 (*0-689-31596-1*, Atheneum Bks Young) S&S Childrens.

All of You Was Singing. Richard Lewis. LC 93-44589. (Illus.). 32p. (J). (gr. k-3). 1994. pap. 4.95 (*0-689-71853-5*, Aladdin Paperbacks) S&S Childrens.

***All on a Mardi Gras Day: Episodes in the History of New Orleans Carnival.** Reid Mitchell. LC 94-28098. (Illus.). 255p. 1995. text ed. 29.95 (*0-674-01622-X*, MITALL) HUP.

All on a Mountain Day. Aileen Fisher. 127p. 1956. 4.90 (*0-686-05600-0*) Rod & Staff.

***All on a Saturday Night.** Sandra Passwaters. 130p. Date not set. pap. 7.95 (*0-7610-0205-7*) NW Pub.

All on a Summer's Day. John Wainwright. 290p. 1989. pap. 3.95 (*0-88184-452-7*) Carroll & Graf.

All on a Summer's Day. large type ed. Judy Gardiner. 491p. 1992. 21.95 (*0-7505-0290-8*, Pub. by Magna Print Bks) Ulverscroft.

All on a Winter's Day. Nola Thacker. 144p. (YA). (gr. 7 up). 1990. pap. 2.95 (*0-590-43416-0*) Scholastic Inc.

All on C. Ken Pugh. (C). 1989. pap. text ed. 35.50 (*0-673-18603-2*) HarpCollege.

All on the Irish Shore. Edith A. Somerville & Violet F. Martin. LC 70-81275. (Short Story Index Reprint Ser.). 1977. 20.95 (*0-8369-3027-4*) Ayer.

All One System: Demographics of Education - Kindergarten Through Graduate School. Harold L. Hodgkinson. 22p. (Orig.). 1985. pap. 5.50 (*0-937846-93-7*) Inst Educ Lead.

***All One Universe.** Poul Anderson. 1996. 22.95 (*0-312-85873-6*) Tor Bks.

All or Nothing. Catherine Lanigan. 400p. (Orig.). 1989. mass mkt. 4.50 (*0-380-75459-2*) Avon.

All or Nothing: The Axis & the Holocaust, 1941-1943. Jonathan Steinberg. 320p. 1990. 27.50 (*0-415-04757-9*) Routledge.

All or Nothing: The Axis & the Holocaust, 1943-1945. Jonathan Steinberg. (Illus.). 336p. 1994. pap. 17.95 (*0-415-07142-9*, B2227) Routledge.

***All Or Nothing-Rainbow's End.** Lori Copeland. 368p. 1995. mass mkt., pap. text ed. 4.99 (*0-505-52028-1*) Dorchester Pub Co.

All Organizations Are Public: Bridging Public & Private Organizational Theories. Barry Bozeman. LC 86-27699. (Public Administration Ser.). 203p. 1987. 29.95x (*1-55542-036-2*) Jossey-Bass.

All Organizations Need to Manage Disaster Effectively. Zenobia A. James. 70p. (Orig.). 1993. pap. 10.75 (*0-9635708-1-1*) Z James.

All Other Perils. large type ed. Robert MacLeod. 1978. 15.95 (*0-7089-0138-7*) Ulverscroft.

All Our Children. Carnegie Council on Children Staff & Kenneth Keniston. LC 77-84900. (Illus.). 255p. 1978. pap. 5.95 (*0-15-604700-4*, Harvest Bks) HarBrace.

All Our Days. W. E. McCumber. 1989. pap. 2.95 (*0-8341-1320-1*) Beacon Hill.

All Our Fault. Daniel Mornin. 218p. 1992. 22.95 (*0-09-174678-7*, Pub. by Hutchinson & Co UK) Heinemann.

All Our Kin: Strategies for Survival in a Black Community. Carol B. Stack. 1983. pap. text ed. 12.00 (*0-06-131982-1*, TB1982, Torch) HarpC.

All Our Labours: Oral Histories of Working Life in 20th Century Sydney. Ed. by John Shields. 1992. pap. 29.95 (*0-86840-117-X*, Pub. by New South Wales Univ Pr AT) Intl Spec Bk.

***All Our Lives.** Nancy Wagner. 336p. (Orig.). 1995. mass mkt. 5.50 (*0-380-77808-4*) Avon.

***All Our Lives.** Alice D. Miller. 1994. reprint ed. lib. bdg. 21.95x (*1-56849-519-6*) Buccaneer Bks.

All Our Losses, All Our Griefs: Resources for Pastoral Care. Kenneth R. Mitchell & Herbert Anderson. LC 83-19851. 180p. (Orig.). (C). 1983. pap. 10.99 (*0-664-24493-9*, Westminster) Westminster John Knox.

All Our People: Population Policy with a Human Face. Klaus Leisinger. LC 93-50647. 350p. 1994. text ed. 45.00 (*1-55963-292-5*); pap. text ed. 24.95 (*1-55963-293-3*) Island Pr.

All Our Tomorrows. Ted Allbeury. 272p. 1989. 18.95 (*0-89296-183-X*) Mysterious Pr.

All Our Vows. Ruth Shamir. LC 82-61795. 1983. 11.95 (*0-88400-090-7*) Shengold.

All Our Yesterdays. Natalia Ginzburg. 1989. pap. 8.95 (*1-55970-026-2*) Arcade Pub Inc.

All Our Yesterdays. Robert B. Parker. LC 94-2583. 1994. 22.95 (*0-385-30437-4*) Delacorte.

***All Our Yesterdays.** Robert B. Parker. 1994. 27.95 (*0-385-31374-8*) Delacorte.

All Our Yesterdays: A Brief History of Detroit. Frank B. Woodford & Arthur M. Woodford. LC 68-27691. (Illus.). 412p. (Orig.). 1969. pap. 14.95 (*0-8143-1381-7*) Wayne St U Pr.

All Our Yesterdays: A Pictorial Record of the London Borough of Sutton Over the Last Century. Ed. by J. Broughton. 58p. 1988. 29.00 (*0-9503224-2-3*, Pub. by Sutton Libs & Arts) St Mut.

All Our Yesterdays: Ninety Years of British Cinema. Ed. by Charles Barr. (Illus.). 446p. 1986. 29.95 (*0-85170-179-5*, Pub. by British Film Inst UK) Ind U Pr.

All Over see Plays

All over but the Shooting. Richard Powell. (Black Dagger Crime Ser.). 192p. 1989. reprint ed. text ed. 16.50 (*0-86220-764-9*, Black Dagger) Chivers N Amer.

All over the Keys. D. Carr Glover. (Easy Piano Ser.). 1990. 4.95 (*0-685-32024-3*, H201) Hansen Ed Mus.

All over the Map. David Jouris. 96p. 1994. pap. 9.95 (*0-89815-649-1*) Ten Speed Pr.

All over the Town. large type ed. Ronald F. Delderfield. 1979. 12.00 (*0-7089-0297-9*) Ulverscroft.

All over Town. Murray Schisgal. 1975. pap. 4.75 (*0-8222-0017-1*) Dramatists Play.

All Passion Spent. Vita Sackville-West. 304p. 1991. pap. 9.95 (*0-88184-794-1*) Carroll & Graf.

All Passion Spent. V. Sackville-West. 296p. 1990. reprint ed. lib. bdg. 29.95 (*0-89966-745-7*) Buccaneer Bks.

All Paths Lead to Bethlehem. Patricia McKissack & Frederick McKissack. LC 87-70472. (Illus.). 32p. (Orig.). (J). (ps-3). 1987. pap. 5.99 (*0-8066-2265-2*, 10-0220, Augsburg) Augsburg Fortress.

All Patients Sick & Crazy: The Madcap Memoirs of a Family Doctor. Philip H. Smith. 256p. (Orig.). 1993. pap. 4.99 (*1-56171-235-3*, S P I Bks) Sure Sellers.

All Pieces of a Legacy. Charles Entrekin. 54p. (Orig.). 1975. pap. 5.95 (*0-917658-03-5*) BPW & P.

All Pigs Are Beautiful. Dick King-Smith. LC 92-53136. (Illus.). 32p. (J). (ps-3). 1993. 14.95 (*1-56402-148-3*) Candlewick Pr.

***All Pigs Are Beautiful.** Dick King-Smith. (J). (ps-3). 1995. pap. 5.99 (*1-56402-431-8*) Candlewick Pr.

All Points Bulletin. Mike Weiss. 176p. (Orig.). 1989. pap. 3.50 (*0-380-75715-X*) Avon.

***All Politics Is Local: And Other Rules of the Game.** Tip O'Neill & Gary Hymel. 1995. pap. 7.95 (*1-55850-470-2*) Adams Pubng.

All Politics is Local & Other Rules of the Game. Thomas O'Neill & Gary Hymel. LC 93-29988. 1993. 15.00 (*0-8129-2297-2*, Times Bks) Random.

All Possible Surprises. Gene Knudsen-Hoffman. 57p. 1990. pap. 8.00 (*0-938077-31-7*) Parallax Pr.

All Possible Worlds: A History of Geographical Ideas. 3rd ed. Geoffrey J. Martin & Preston E. James. 608p. 1993. Net. text ed. write for info. (*0-471-63414-X*) Wiley.

An Asterisk (*) at the beginning of an entry indicates that the title is appearing in BIP for the first time.

All Practical Purposes. Comap. LC 93-30027. (C). Date not set. text ed. write for info. (*0-7167-2520-7*) W H Freeman.

***All-Pro Cookbook.** (Illus.). 224p. (Orig.). 1995. pap. 14.95 (*1-57028-058-4*) Masters Pr IN.

All Quiet on the Eastern Front: The Death of South Vietnam. Ed. by Anthony T. Bouscaren. LC 76-18443. 1976. 12.00 (*0-8159-5018-7*); pap. 7.95 (*0-8159-5019-5*) Devin.

All Quiet on the Western Front. Erich M. Remarque. 16.95 (*0-8488-1459-2*) Amereon Ltd.

All Quiet on the Western Front. Erich M. Remarque. (Book Notes Ser.). (C). 1984. pap. 2.50 (*0-8120-3401-5*) Barron.

All Quiet on the Western Front. Erich M. Remarque. 1987. mass mkt. 4.95 (*0-449-21394-3*, Crest) Fawcett.

All Quiet on the Western Front. Erich M. Remarque. (YA). (gr. 7 up). 1929. 21.95 (*0-316-73992-8*) Little.

All Quiet on the Western Front. Erich M. Remarque. 391p. 1981. reprint ed. lib. bdg. 21.95x (*0-89966-292-7*) Buccaneer Bks.

All Quiet on the Western Front: A Study Guide. Joy Leavitt. (Novel-Ties Ser.). (J). 1983. student ed, teacher ed 15.95 (*0-88122-035-3*) Lrn Links.

All Quiet on the Western Front: Literary Analysis & Cultural Context. Richard A. Firda. LC 93-3872. (Twayne's Masterworks Ser.: No. 129). 168p. 1993. text ed. 22.95 (*0-8057-8386-5*, Twayne); pap. 12.95 (*0-8057-8387-3*, Twayne) Macmillan.

All Quiet on the Western Front Notes. Mary E. Snodgrass & Rollin O. Glaser. (Cliffs Notes Ser.). (Illus.). 82p. (Orig.). (YA). (gr. 10-12). 1995. pap. text ed. 4.25 (*0-8220-0155-1*) Cliffs.

All Quiet on the Yamhill: The Civil War in Oregon. Royal A. Bensell. Ed. by Gunter Barth. LC 60-63172. 1959. 5.00 (*0-87114-005-5*) U of Oreg Bks.

***All Quilt Blocks Are Not Square.** Deb Wagner. (Illus.). 192p. 1995. pap. 21.95 (*0-8019-8643-5*) Chilton.

All Right for Some! The Problem of Sexism. J. L. Thompson. (C). 1989. 75.00 (*0-09-164721-5*, Pub. by S Thornes Pubs UK) St Mut.

***All Right for Some! The Problem of Sexism.** Jane L. Thompson. 96p. (C). 1986. pap. 30.00x (*0-7478-1009-5*, Pub. by S Thornes Pubs UK) St Mut.

All Risk Policy: Its Problems, Perils & Practical Applications. TIPS Property Insurance Law Committee & American Bar Association Staff. LC 86-71672. 390p. 1986. pap. 29.95 (*0-89707-255-3*, 519-0062) Amer Bar Assn.

All Risks Mortality. Peter Cunningham. 1988. 17.95 (*0-316-16460-7*) Little.

All Rites Reversed: Ritual Technology for New Age. Antero Alli. (Orig.). 1988. pap. 9.95 (*0-941404-81-1*) New Falcon Pubns.

All Roads Are Good: Native Voices on Life & Culture. Frwd. by W. Richard West. LC 94-8236. (Illus.). 224p. 1994. 55.00 (*1-56098-451-1*); pap. 29.95 (*1-56098-452-X*) Smithsonian.

All Roads Lead to Bushy Fork. Virginia L. Long. Ed. by Michael Hathaway. (Illus.). 63p. (Orig.). 1992. pap. 6.00 (*0-943795-22-2*) Chiron Rev.

All Roads Lead to the United States. Michael Dzandza. 1992. 16.95 (*0-533-10130-1*) Vantage.

All-Romanized English-Japanese Dictionary. Hyojun R. Kai. LC 73-90232. 732p. (ENG & JPN.). 1973. pap. 9.95 (*0-8048-1118-0*) C E Tuttle.

All-Romanized English-Japanese Dictionary. 9th ed. Hyojun Romaji Kai. 732p. (ENG & JPN.). 1980. pap. 14.95 (*0-8288-1611-5*, M9548) Fr & Eur.

All Round Compass. Ron Brown. 1993. 19.95 (*1-85756-081-7*, Pub. by Janus Pub UK) Intl Spec Bk.

All Round Ministry. C. H. Spurgeon. 1978. pap. 11.95 (*0-85151-181-3*) Banner of Truth.

All-Round Ministry. C. H. Spurgeon. 1983. pap. 6.95 (*1-56186-311-4*) Pilgrim Pubns.

All Said & Done. Debeauvoir. 1994. pap. 16.95 (*1-56924-981-4*) Marlowe & Co.

***All Saints among the Churches.** Ed. by Blair G. Meeks. (Liturgy Ser.). (Illus.). 70p. (Orig.). 1995. pap. 10.95 (*0-918208-69-6*) Liturgical Conf.

***All Saints Church, Waccamaw, 1739-1968 with Updates to Which Have Been Added Additional Text, Parish Register Updates, Appendixes, & Index 1948.** Henry D. Bull. LC 94-42749. (Illus.). 400p. 1995. 37.50 (*0-87152-488-0*) Reprint.

All Scientists Now: The Royal Society in the Nineteenth Century. Marie B. Hall. LC 84-7705. (Illus.). 272p. 1985. 69.95 (*0-521-26746-3*) Cambridge U Pr.

All-Season Guide to Minnesota's Parks, Canoe Routes & Trails. Jim Umhoefer. LC 84-8066. (Illus.). 104p. (Orig.). 1984. pap. 9.95 (*1-55971-015-2*, Heartlnd Pr) NorthWord.

All-Season Investor: Successful Strategies for Every Stage in the Business Cycle. Martin J. Pring. 352p. 1992. text ed. 29.95 (*0-471-54977-0*) Wiley.

All Season Tourism: Analysis of Experience Suitable Products & Clientele. 72p. 1993. pap. 16.00 (*92-826-5986-0*, CT-79-93-243-EN, Pub. by Europ Com) UNIPUB.

***All Set about with Fever Trees, & Other Stories.** Pam Durban. LC 95-13562. 1995. write for info. (*0-8203-1775-6*) U of Ga Pr.

***All Shadows Fled.** Ed Greenwood. (Shadow of the Avatar Ser.). 320p. (Orig.). 1995. pap. 4.95 (*0-7869-0302-3*) TSR Inc.

***All Shall Be Well.** Deborah Crombie. 272p. Date not set. pap. text ed. 4.99 (*0-425-14771-1*) Berkley Pub.

All Shall Be Well: A Superintendent Duncan Kincaid - Sergeant Gemma James Mystery. Deborah Crombie. 256p. 1994. text ed. 20.00 (*0-684-19654-9*, Scribners) S&S Trade.

All Shall Be Well: Daily Readings from Julian of Norwich. Abr. by Sheila Upjohn. LC 93-50573. 208p. (Orig.). 1994. pap. 14.95 (*0-8192-1614-3*) Morehouse Pub.

***All Shall Be Well: <.** large type ed. Deborah Crombie. (Cloak & Dagger Ser.). 351p. 1994. 19.95 (*0-7862-0298-X*) Thorndike Pr.

All Shapes & Sizes. Shirley Hughes. LC 86-2734. (Illus.). 24p. (J). (ps). 1986. 4.95 (*0-688-04205-8*) Lothrop.

All She Can Be. Fern Michaels. 1991. reprint ed. 17.95 (*0-7278-4139-4*) Severn Hse.

All Shook Up: Elvis Day-by-Day, 1954-1977. Lee Cotten. (Rock & Roll Reference Ser.: No. 13). (Illus.). 606p. 1993. reprint ed. 39.50 (*1-56075-033-2*) Popular Culture.

***All Shook Up: Mississippi Roots of American Popular Music.** Ed. by Christine Wilson. (Illus.). 120p. 1995. pap. write for info. (*0-938896-65-2*) Mississippi Archives.

All Sickness Is Home Sickness. Diane M. Connelly. (Illus.). 167p. (Orig.). 1987. pap. 12.00 (*0-912379-02-2*) Ctr Traditional Acupuncture.

All Sickness Is Homesickness. Dianne M. Connelly. (Illus.). Date not set. reprint ed. pap. 14.00 (*0-912381-02-7*) Trad Acupuncture.

All Sides of the Issue: Activities for Cooperative Jigsaw Groups. Coelho et al. 160p. 1989. teacher ed 19.95 (*0-13-019498-0*) Alemany Pr.

All Sides of the Subject: Women & Biography. Ed. by Teresa Iles. (Athene Ser.). 192p. (C). 1992. text ed. 37.00 (*0-8077-6256-3*); pap. text ed. 16.95 (*0-8077-6255-5*) Tchrs Coll.

All Signs Rising. Elbert Wade. 80p. 1984. 7.00 (*0-86690-281-3*, W2555-014) Am Fed Astrologers.

All Silver & No Brass: An Irish Christmas Mumming. Henry Glassie. LC 82-21937. (Illus.). 224p. 1976. 17.95 (*0-8122-1139-1*) U of Pa Pr.

All Slave-Keepers That Keep the Innocent in Bondage, Apostates Pretending to Lay Claim to the Pure & Holy Christian Religion. Benjamin Lay. LC 72-82203. (Anti-Slavery Crusade in America Ser.). 1970. reprint ed. 15.95 (*0-405-00642-X*) Ayer.

All Small. David McCord. (Illus.). (J). (gr. 6-8). 1986. lib. bdg. 12.95 (*0-316-55519-3*); mass mkt. 4.95 (*0-316-55520-7*) Little.

All Smiles. Bruce Velick. LC 94-17326. 1995. 12.95 (*0-8118-0590-5*) Chronicle Bks.

***All Sold Out! How to Sneak into Sporting Events & Concerts.** Scott J. Kerman. 120p. (Orig.). 1995. pap. 8.95 (*1-887448-00-4*) Ya Gotta Laugh.

All Sorts of Good Sufficient Cloth. LC 79-92225. (Illus.). 1979. 8.00 (*0-937474-00-2*) Mus Am Textile Hist.

All Souls. John Brady. 304p. 1993. 20.95 (*0-312-09735-2*) St Martin.

All Souls. Javier Marias. Tr. by Marguaret J. Costa. 210p. (Orig.). 1993. pap. 12.00 (*0-00-271283-0*, Pub. by HarperCollins UK) Harper SF.

***All Souls' Rising.** Madison S. Bell. LC 95-12339. 1995. 25.00 (*0-679-43989-7*) Pantheon.

All Spelled Out: Basic Spelling Patterns for Learners of English. H. Elaine Kirn. (Illus.). 94p. (Orig.). (gr. 7 up). 1981. 2.00 (*0-87789-207-5*); audio 16.95 (*0-87789-217-2*) ELS Educ Servs.

All Spelled Out: Basic Spelling Patterns for Learners of English. H. Elaine Kirn. (Illus.). 94p. (Orig.). (YA). (gr. 7 up). 1981. pap. text ed. 3.95 (*0-89285-153-8*) ELS Educ Servs.

***All-Sport Autograph Guide.** Mark A. Baker. 1994. pap. 12.95 (*0-87341-316-4*) Krause Pubns.

All Standards for All Organs, 4 vols. pap. 5.95 (*0-685-73404-8*, Peer-Southern) CPP Belwin.

***All Star Circuit of Champions: A Quarter Century of Racing Thrill.** Bill Holder. 140p. (Orig.). 1995. pap. 12.00 (*1-886613-01-X*) Holder Comm.

All Star Comics Archives, Vol. 1. Ed. by Michael C. Hill & Bob Kahan. (Illus.). 272p. 1992. 49.95 (*1-56389-019-4*) DC Comics.

All Star Comics Archives, Vol. 2. Gardner Fox. Ed. by Bob Kahan. 256p. 1993. 49.95 (*0-930289-12-9*) DC Comics.

***All Star Country Cookout.** 326p. 1994. 14.95 (*1-885507-00-3*) Fundco Printers.

***All-Star Fever: A Peach Street Mudders Story.** Matt Christopher. LC 94-34184. (Illus.). (J). 1995. 13.95 (*0-316-14265-4*) Little.

All-Star Game. Steve Potts. (Great Moments in Sports Ser.). (YA). (gr. 5 up). 1992. lib. bdg. 14.95 (*0-88682-537-7*) Creative Ed.

***All-Star Line-up.** Nathan Aaseng. (J). (gr. 4-7). 1994. pap. 9.99 (*0-7814-0203-4*) Cook.

All-Star Mystery Athlete Puzzle Book. Andrew Lerner. (J). (gr. 4-7). 1994. 3.50 (*0-553-48163-0*) Bantam.

All-Stars All-Star Baseball Book. Nick Acocella. 23.95 (*0-8488-1571-8*) Amereon Ltd.

All State Career School Student Manual: Without Trucks America Stops. All State Career Staff. 304p. 1993. 9.75 (*0-8403-8568-4*) Kendall-Hunt.

All States Tax Guide. ring bd. write for info. (*0-318-57357-1*) P-H.

All States Tax Handbook. Prentice-Hall Editorial Staff. 320p. 1987. 17.50 (*0-13-022799-4*) P-H.

All States Tax Handbook. rev. ed. RIA In-House Professional Staff. 400p. 1992. pap. text ed. 25.00 (*0-7811-0062-3*) Res Inst Am.

All States Tax Handbook 1989. Prentice-Hall Editorial Staff. 300p. 1988. 18.95 (*0-13-023219-X*, Busn) P-H.

All States Tax Handbook 1992. 300p. 1992. 23.95 (*0-7811-0006-2*, Maxwell Macmillan) Macmillan.

All States Tax Handbook 1994. rev. ed. Research Institute of America Staff. 410p. 1993. pap. text ed. 30.00 (*0-7811-0079-8*) Res Inst Am.

***All States Tax Handbook 1995.** rev. ed. RIA In-House Professional Staff. 410p. 1994. pap. text ed. 29.95 (*0-7811-0092-5*) Res Inst Am.

All Stories Are True. John E. Wideman. LC 92-50616. 1993. pap. 10.00 (*0-679-73752-9*, Vin) Random.

All Strange Away. Samuel Beckett. 1991. pap. 6.95 (*0-7145-3858-2*) Riverrun NY.

All Stuck Up. Linda Hayward. LC 89-34675. (Step into Reading Bks.). (Illus.). 32p. (Orig.). (J). (ps-1). 1990. pap. 3.50 (*0-679-80216-9*) Random Bks Yng Read.

All Stuck Up. Linda Hayward. LC 89-34675. (Step into Reading Bks.). (Illus.). 32p. (Orig.). (J). (ps-1). 1990. lib. bdg. 7.99 (*0-679-90216-3*) Random Bks Yng Read.

All-Stud. Clay Caldwell. (Orig.). 1993. pap. text ed. 4.95 (*1-56333-104-7*) Masquerade.

All Sufficient Christ: Studies in Paul's Letters to the Colossians. William Barclay. 142p. 1993. pap. 21.00 (*0-7152-0389-4*) St Mut.

All Suite Hotel Guide. 5th ed. Pamela Lanier. (Orig.). 1991. pap. 14.95 (*0-89815-445-6*) Ten Speed Pr.

All Suite Hotel Guide. 6th ed. Pamela Lanier. (Illus.). 236p. (Orig.). 1992. pap. 14.95 (*0-89815-512-6*) Ten Speed Pr.

All-Suite Hotel Guide. 7th ed. Pamela Lanier. 1993. pap. 14.95 (*0-89815-580-0*) Ten Speed Pr.

***All-Suite Hotel Guide.** 8th ed. Pamela Lanier. 336p. 1995. pap. 14.95 (*0-89815-725-0*) Ten Speed Pr.

All Summer Long. Bob Greene. LC 93-20143. 1993. 23.00 (*0-385-42589-9*) Doubleday.

All Talk. Huizenga & Ruzic. 1992. pap. 18.95 (*0-8384-3979-9*) Heinle & Heinle.

All Talk: The Talkshow in Media Culture. Wayne Munson. LC 92-9389. (Culture & the Moving Image Ser.). 232p. (C). 1994. pap. 18.95 (*1-56639-194-6*) Temple U Pr.

All Tangled up with the Living. Louis Jenkins. 64p. 1991. pap. 6.95 (*0-915408-42-2*, PS3560.E488A75) Ally Pr.

All Teams Are Not Created Equal: How Employee Empowerment Really Works. Lyman Ketchum & Eric Trist. (Illus.). 288p. (C). 1992. 31.50 (*0-8039-4652-X*) Sage.

All-Terrain Bicycling. Charles Coombs. LC 86-14980. (Illus.). 144p. (J). (gr. 5-9). 1987. 14.95 (*0-8050-0204-9*) H Holt & Co.

All Terrain Biking: Skills & Techniques for Mountain Bikers. 2nd ed. Jim Zarka. LC 91-70409. (Illus.). 157p. (Orig.). 1992. pap. 7.95 (*0-933201-38-9*) Bicycle Books.

All Terrain Vehicle Service Manual. 2nd ed. Intertec Publishing Staff. LC 87-81179. (Illus.). 434p. 1988. pap. 24.95 (*0-87288-277-2*, ATV1-2) Intertec Pub.

***All-Terrain Vehicles (ATV's)** Smith. (J). 1995. pap. 5.95 (*0-516-40218-8*) Childrens.

***All-Terrain Vehicles (ATVs)** Jay H. Smith. (Wheels Ser.). 48p. (J). (gr. 3-4). 1994. lib. bdg. 13.35 (*1-56065-218-7*) Capstone Pr.

ALL Test (Analysis of the Language of Learning) Elizabeth G. Blodgett & Eugene B. Cooper. 1987. 54.95 (*1-55999-013-9*) LinguiSystems.

All That Autumn. Eileen Silver-Lillywhite. LC 83-13002. 63p. (Orig.). 1983. pap. 5.00 (*0-87886-122-X*, Greenfld Rev Pr) Greenfld Rev Lit.

All That Comes to Light. Lisa Steinman. (Orig.). 1989. 22.00 (*0-934847-10-X*); pap. 9.00 (*0-934847-11-8*) Arrowood Bks.

***All That Ever Was.** David Heilpern. (Illus.). 60p. (Orig.). 1994. pap. text ed. 16.00 (*0-937025-04-6*) Shadowood Pubns.

All That Evolve. Richard Brenner. Ed. by Sherry Brenner. (Illus.). (Orig.). 1984. pap. 4.95 (*0-317-03255-0*) Applause Pub.

All That Fall see **Krapp's Last Tape & Other Dramatic Pieces**

***All That Glitters.** V. C. Andrews. Ed. by Linda Marrow. 352p. 1995. 23.00 (*0-671-87574-4*) PB.

***All That Glitters.** V.C. Andrews. (Illus.). (J). 1995. mass mkt. 6.50 (*0-671-87319-9*) PB.

All That Glitters. Michael Anthony. (Caribbean Writers Ser.). 208p. (Orig.). 1983. pap. 7.95 (*0-435-98034-3*, Pub. by H & S UK) Heinemann.

All That Glitters. Manning Coles. 196p. 1988. pap. 3.95 (*0-88184-338-5*) Carroll & Graf.

***All That Glitters.** Catrin Collier. 432p. 1995. 26.00 (*0-7126-5850-5*, Pub. by Century UK) Trafalgar.

All That Glitters. Bill Hegner. 1994. write for info. (*0-312-85379-3*) Tor Bks.

All That Glitters. Susan Kyle. 341p. (Orig.). 1995. mass mkt. 5.99 (*0-446-36362-6*) Warner Bks.

All That Glitters. Ruth Langan. 1994. mass mkt. 4.99 (*0-06-108177-9*, Harp PBks) HarpC.

All That Glitters. J. L. Lynnlee. LC 86-61197. (Illus.). 128p. 1986. pap. 9.95 (*0-88740-069-8*) Schiffer.

All That Glitters. Dawn Reno. 512p. 1993. mass mkt. 4.99 (*1-55817-694-2*, Pinnacle NY) Windsor NY.

All That Glitters. rev. ed. J. L. Lynnlee. LC 86-61197. (Illus.). 128p. 1993. pap. 12.95 (*0-88740-504-5*) Schiffer.

All That Glitters. F. P. Keyes. 358p. 1981. reprint ed. lib. bdg. 18.95 (*0-89968-238-3*, Lghtyr Pr) Buccaneer Bks.

All That Glitters: A Newsperson Explores the World of Television. Coleen Cook. 1992. text ed. 15.99 (*0-8024-0736-6*) Moody.

All That Glitters: Country Music in America. George H. Lewis. LC 92-74544. 340p. 1993. 44.95 (*0-87972-573-7*); pap. 21.95 (*0-87972-574-5*) Bowling Green Univ.

***All That Glitters: Men & Women of the Gold & Silver Rushes.** Phyllis R. Emert. LC 94-69885. (Perspectives on History Ser.). (Illus.). 64p. (Orig.). (J). (gr. 5-12). 1995. pap. 4.95 (*1-878668-49-8*) Disc Enter Ltd.

All That Glitters on Water. Carol Langille. Ed. by Clarinda H. Raymond. 64p. 1990. pap. 5.95 (*0-932616-29-1*) New Poets Chestnut Hills.

All That God Has Given: Faithful Stewardship As Followers of Jesus. Hartland H. Gifford. LC 92-31987. 112p. 1993. pap. 8.99 (*0-8066-2655-0*, 9-2655) Augsburg Fortress.

All That God Hath Done with Them: The Narration of the Works of God in the Early Christian Community as Described in the Acts of the Apostles. Linda M. Maloney. LC 90-40424. (American University Studies: Theology & Religion: Ser. VII, Vol. 91). 238p. (C). 1991. text ed. 42.95 (*0-8204-1410-7*) P Lang Pubs.

All That Heat in a Cold Sky. Elizabeth Libbey. (Poetry Ser.). (Orig.). 1992. lib. bdg. 16.95 (*0-88748-144-2*); pap. 9.95 (*0-88748-145-0*) Carnegie-Mellon.

All That Hollywood Allows: Re-reading Gender in 1950s Melodrama. Jackie Byars. LC 90-46738. (Gender & American Culture Ser.). (Illus.). x, 326p. (C). 1991. 45.00 (*0-8078-1953-0*); pap. 14.95 (*0-8078-4312-1*) U of NC Pr.

All That I Am: A Healing from Within. Marilyn R. Kern. LC 90-70532. 106p. 1990. pap. 6.95 (*1-55523-344-9*) Winston-Derek.

All That I Have Met. Frances E. Beddington. LC 79-8050. reprint ed. 29.50 (*0-404-18361-1*) AMS Pr.

All That Is Native & Fine: The Politics of Culture in an American Region. David Whisnant. LC 82-24851. (Illus.). xv, 340p. 1986. reprint ed. pap. 14.95 (*0-8078-4143-9*) U of NC Pr.

All That Is Solid Melts into Air: The Experience of Modernity. Marshall Berman. 384p. 1988. pap. 12.95 (*0-14-010962-5*, Penguin Bks) Viking Penguin.

All That Is Solid Melts Into the Air: The Experience of Modernity. Marshall Berman. 21.25 (*0-8446-6681-5*) Peter Smith.

All That Jazz! Jack Wheaton. (Illus.). 379p. (C). 1994. pap. text ed. 38.95 (*0-912675-92-6*) Ardsley.

All That Jazz & More... 2nd ed. LDI Productions Staff. 160p. 1994. per., pap. text ed. 21.95 (*0-8403-9020-3*) Kendall-Hunt.

***All That Matters: (March Madness)** Elizabeth Mayne. (Historical Ser.). 1995. pap. 4.50 (*0-373-28859-X*, 1-28859-6) Harlequin Bks.

All That Matters: The Texas Plains in Photographs & Poems. Ed. by Janet M. Neugebauer. LC 92-16575. 144p. 1992. 22.50 (*0-89672-291-0*) Tex Tech Univ Pr.

***All That Matters: What Is It We Value in School & Beyond?** Ed. by Linda Rief & Muareen Barbieri. LC 95-6643. 1995. pap. text ed. write for info. (*0-435-08848-3*) Heinemann.

***All That Once Was Good: Inside America's National Pastime.** Howard Rothman. LC 95-16199. 1995. write for info. (*0-9644849-0-0*) Pendleton Clay.

***All That Our Hands Have Done: A Pictorial History of the Hamilton Workers.** Craig Heron et al. (Illus.). 192p. 1995. lib. bdg. 37.00 (*0-8095-4922-0*) Borgo Pr.

All That Remains. Patricia D. Cornwell. (Kay Scarpetta Mystery Ser.). 416p. 1995. mass mkt. 6.50 (*0-380-71833-2*) Avon.

All That Remains. large type ed. Patricia D. Cornwell. (General Ser.). 447p. 1992. 21.95 (*0-8161-5526-7*, Large Print Bks) Hall.

All That Remains. large type ed. Patricia D. Cornwell. 416p. 1992. text ed. 21.95 (*0-684-19515-1*, Scribners) S&S Trade.

All That Remains: A Novel. Patricia D. Cornwell. 416p. 1992. text ed. 20.00 (*0-684-19395-7*, Scribners) S&S Trade.

All That Remains: A West Virginia Archaeologist's Discoveries. Robert Pyle. Ed. by Betty L. Wiley. 84p. (C). 1991. pap. write for info. (*0-9623153-2-X*) Cannon Graphics.

All That Remains: Palestinian Villages Occupied & Depopulated by Israel in 1948. Ed. by Walid Khalidi et al. LC 92-10109. (Illus.). (Orig.). (C). 1992. 59.00 (*0-88728-224-5*) Inst Palestine. The first detailed compendium of the 418 villages destroyed during the 1948 war & its aftermath. Entries for each village give a statistical, topographical, historical & economic history; the circumstances of military occupation; & the current state of the site including Jewish settlements on village lands. OTHER TITLES: ROY, SARA, THE GAZA STRIP: THE POLITICAL ECONOMY OF DEVELOPMENT, 350pp, + illus. ISBN 0-88728-260-1, $27.95 cloth. Sara Roy examines the political economy of the Gaza Strip since the Israeli occupation. She argues that despite certain economic benefits to the Gaza Strip, Israeli policy has been guided by political concerns that blocked internal economic development. NEFF, DONALD, FALLEN PILLARS: U.S. POLICY TOWARDS PALESTINE & ISRAEL SINCE 1945, 280pp + illus. ISBN: 0-88728-259-8, $12.00 paperback. FALLEN PILLARS is a concise summary of the evolution of American foreign policy towards Palestine & Israel, particularly with regard to Jerusalem, Israeli settlements, Palestinian refugees, security, & borders. ORDER TITLES FROM THE INSTITUTE FOR PALESTINE STUDIES, 1-800-874-3614 or 202-342-3990. ***Publisher Provided Annotation.***

An Asterisk (*) at the beginning of an entry indicates that the title is appearing in BIP for the first time. 197

A

All that She Can Be: Helping Your Daughter Achieve Her Full Potential & Maintain Her Self-Esteem During the Critical Years of Adolescence. Carol J. Eagle & Carol Colman. LC 93-6791. 288p. 1993. 22.00 (*0-671-78948-1*) S&S Trade.

All That She Can Be: Helping Your Daughter Maintain Her Self-Esteem During the Critical Years. Carol J. Eagle. 1994. pap. 11.00 (*0-671-88554-5*, Fireside) S&S Trade.

All That, So Simple. Neil Myers. LC 78-71637. 72p. 1980. pap. 7.95 (*0-911198-56-3*) Purdue U Pr.

All That the Rain Promises & More... A Hip Pocket Guide to Western Mushrooms. David Arora. (Illus.). 256p. (Orig.). 1990. pap. 15.95 (*0-89815-388-3*) Ten Speed Pr.

All That Was Ever Ours. Elisabeth Elliott. LC 87-37669. 192p. 1988. 10.99 (*0-8007-1588-8*) Revell.

All That We Are We Give. James G. Fairfield. LC 77-14510. 192p. 1977. pap. 5.95 (*0-8361-1839-1*) Herald Pr.

All That You Are. Mary. 1959. pap. 8.95 (*0-87516-055-7*) DeVorss.

All That's Practical about Wood: Stoves, As a Fuel, Heating. Ralph W. Ritchie. (Illus.). 136p. (Orig.). 1992. pap. 9.95 (*0-939656-11-6*) Ritchie Unltd.

All the Above. Peggy Forster. LC 86-90536. 95p. (Orig.). 1987. pap. 5.95 (*0-317-53266-9*) J E Stopp.

All the Animals. (J). (ps-1). 1990. bds. 6.99 (*0-7459-1838-7*) Lion USA.

All the Banners Wave: Art & War in the Romantic Era, 1792-1851. Brown University, Department of Art Staff. LC 81-71834. (Illus.). 125p. (Orig.). 1982. pap. text ed. 14.00 (*0-933519-04-4*) D W Bell Gallery.

***All the Bells on Earth.** James P. Blaylock. LC 95-7142. 1995. write for info. (*0-441-00247-1*) Ace Bks.

All the Best Chicken Dinners. Joie Warner. 1992. pap. 8.00 (*0-688-11657-4*) Hearst Bks.

***All the Best Contests.** Joan Bergstrom & Craig Bergstrom. LC 91-37659. 288p. (J). (gr. 1-7). 1995. pap. 8.95 (*1-883672-29-5*) Tricycle Pr.

All the Best Contests for Kids, No. 4. Joan Bergstrom. (Orig.). 1994. pap. 7.95 (*0-89815-604-1*) Ten Speed Pr.

All the Best Contests for Kids, 1992-1993. 3rd ed. Joan M. Bergstrom & Craig Bergstrom. 288p. (J). (gr. k-9). 1992. pap. 9.95 (*0-89815-451-0*) Ten Speed Pr.

All the Best Cookies. Joie Warner. LC 94-20767. 1994. 8.00 (*0-688-13346-0*) Hearst Bks.

All the Best Mexican Meals. Joie Warner. 1992. pap. 8.00 (*0-688-11656-6*) Hearst Bks.

All the Best Muffins & Quick Breads. Joie Warner. 1992. pap. 8.00 (*0-688-11658-2*) Hearst Bks.

All the Best Pasta Sauces. Joie Warner. Ed. by Andrew Ambraziejus. 96p. 1991. pap. 8.00 (*0-688-10127-5*) Hearst Bks.

All the Best Pasta Sauces II. Joie Warner. LC 94-20764. 1994. 8.00 (*0-688-13348-7*) Hearst Bks.

All the Best Pizzas. Joie Warner. Ed. by Andrew Ambraziejus. 96p. 1991. pap. 7.95 (*0-688-10125-9*) Hearst Bks.

All the Best Potatoes. Joie Warner. LC 93-14991. 1993. 8.00 (*0-688-12705-3*) Hearst Bks.

All the Best Rice. Joie Warner. LC 94-19234. 1994. 8.00 (*0-688-13345-2*) Hearst Bks.

All the Best Rock & Roll. (Mixed Folios - Pop Ser.). 256p. (Orig.). 1994. pap. 16.95 (*0-89724-124-X*) Warner Brothers.

All the Best Salads. Joie Warner. Ed. by Andrew Ambraziejus. 96p. 1991. pap. 8.00 (*0-688-10126-7*) Hearst Bks.

All the Best Standard Love Songs. 160p. (Orig.). 1993. pap. 14.95 (*0-89724-074-X*) Warner Brothers.

All the Best Stir-Fries. Joie Warner. LC 93-14981. 1993. 8.00 (*0-688-12704-5*) Hearst Bks.

All the Better to See You With. Margaret Wild. Ed. by Kathy Tucker. LC 92-39127. (Illus.). 32p. (J). (gr. 1-3). 1993. lib. bdg. 13.95 (*0-8075-0284-7*) A Whitman.

All the Birds of the Bible. Alice Parmelee. 1988. pap. 9.95 (*0-87983-468-4*) Keats.

All the Bloks Are Geese. Mary S. Suit. LC 93-33692. (Illus.). 1994. 17.95 (*1-56477-049-4*) That Patchwork.

All the Brave Promises: Memories of Aircraft Woman 2nd Class 2146391. Mary L. Settle. (Signature Editions Ser.). (Illus.). 1988. pap. 8.95 (*0-684-18756-6*, Scribners) S&S Trade.

All the Bright Sons of Morning. Nancy N. Baxter. 500p. 1992. pap. 14.95 (*1-878208-14-4*) Guild Pr IN.

All the Colors of Earth. Sheila Hamanaka. LC 93-27118. (Illus.). 32p. (J). 1994. 15.00 (*0-688-11131-9*); lib. bdg. 14.93 (*0-688-11132-7*) Morrow Jr Bks.

All the Colors of the Race. Arnold Adoff. LC 81-11777. (Illus.). 64p. (J). (gr. 5 up). 1982. 15.00 (*0-688-00879-8*); lib. bdg. 14.93 (*0-688-00880-1*) Lothrop.

All the Colors of the Race. Arnold Adoff. LC 81-11777. (Illus.). 56p. (J). (gr. 5 up). 1992. pap. 4.95 (*0-688-11496-2*, Pub. by Beech Tree Bks) Morrow.

All the Colors We Are-Todos los Colores de Nuestra Piel: The Story of How We Get Our Skin Color-La Historia de por que Tenemos Differentes Colores de Piel. Katie Kissinger. Ed. by Prisma International Staff. LC 94-17091. (Illus.). 32p. (Orig.). (J). (ps-5). 1994. pap. 9.95 (*0-934140-80-4*) Redleaf Pr.

All the Conspirators. Christopher Isherwood. LC 58-12798. 1979. reprint ed. pap. 7.95 (*0-8112-0725-0*, NDP480) New Directions.

***All the Corporate & Legal Forms You'll Ever Need to Properly Run Your Corporation: The National Corporate Forms Kit.** Benji O. Anosike. 250p. (Orig.). 1995. pap. text ed. 29.95 (*0-932704-39-5*) Do It Yourself Legal Pubs.

All the Crazy Winters. Deborah Adams. 1992. mass mkt. 3.99 (*0-345-37076-7*) Ballantine.

All the Dark Disguises. Deborah Adams. 1993. mass mkt. 3.99 (*0-345-37765-6*) Ballantine.

***All the Days & Nights: The Collected Stories of William Maxwell.** William Maxwell. LC 94-27509. 415p. 1995. 25.00 (*0-679-43829-7*) Knopf.

All the Days of Her Life. Lurlene McDaniel. (One Last Wish Ser.: No. 10). (YA). 1994. pap. 3.50 (*0-553-56264-9*) Bantam.

All the Days of My Life. Hilary Bailey. 1986. mass mkt. 4.95 (*0-449-13154-8*) Fawcett.

All the Days of My Life. Amelia Barr. Ed. by Annette K. Baxter. LC 79-8772. (Signal Lives Ser.). (Illus.). 1980. reprint ed. lib. bdg. 63.95 (*0-405-12822-3*) Ayer.

All the Days of My Life: An Autobiography. Amelia E. Barr. 1993. reprint ed. lib. bdg. 75.00 (*0-7812-5863-4*) Rprt Serv.

All the Devils Are Here. Ed. by David D. Deyo, Jr. (Illus.). x, 118p. 1986. pap. 8.50 (*0-934227-02-0*) Unnameable Pr.

All the Difference: A Development Economist's Quest. Benjamin Higgins. 280p. 1992. 55.00 (*0-7735-0904-6*, Pub. by McGill CN) U of Toronto Pr.

All the Divine Names & Titles. Herbert Lockyer. 1988. pap. 17.99 (*0-310-28041-9*, 10077P) Zondervan.

All the Doctrines. Herbert Lockyer. 1988. pap. 17.99 (*0-310-28051-6*, 10082P) Zondervan.

All the Drowning Seas. large type ed. Alexander Fullerton. 560p. 1984. 15.95 (*0-7089-1159-5*) Ulverscroft.

All the Errors. Giorgio Manganelli. Tr. by Henry Martin. LC 90-5489. 158p. 1990. 20.00 (*0-929701-07-0*); pap. 10.00 (*0-929701-06-2*) McPherson & Co.

All the Famous Battles That Have Been Fought in Our Age. John Poleman. LC 68-54658. (English Experience Ser.: No. 64). 337p. 1968. reprint ed. 55.00 (*90-221-0064-2*) Walter J Johnson.

All the Fulness of God: Essays on Orthodoxy, Ecumenism & Modern Society. Thomas Hopko. LC 82-5454. 188p. (Orig.). 1982. pap. 9.95 (*0-913836-96-6*) St Vladimirs.

All the Girls. O'Brien. 1983. pap. 3.50 (*0-449-20251-8*) Fawcett.

All the Gods Are Dying Gods. Mary C. Smith. 191p. 1983. reprint ed. 13.95 (*0-9609286-0-X*) St Peters Pr.

All the Good Gifts: On Doing Bible Stewardship. Wallace E. Fisher. LC 79-50077. 112p. 1979. pap. 7.99 (*0-8066-1702-0*, 10-0227, Augsburg) Augsburg Fortress.

All the Great Pretenders. Deborah Adams. (Orig.). 1991. mass mkt. 4.99 (*0-345-37075-9*) Ballantine.

All the Greek Verbs. Ed. by N. Marinone. 352p. 1990. pap. text ed. 17.50 (*0-89341-629-0*, Longwood Academic) Hollowbrook.

All The Hungry Mothers. Deborah Adams. (Southern Mysteries Ser.). (Orig.). 1994. mass mkt. 4.99 (*0-345-38552-7*) Ballantine.

All the Janata Men. J. Thakur. 170p. 1978. 11.95 (*0-318-37289-4*) Asia Bk Corp.

***All the King's Animals: The Return of Endangered Wildlife to Swaziland.** Cristina Kessler. LC 94-79621. (Illus.). 64p. (J). (gr. 3-7). 1995. 17.95 (*1-56397-364-2*, Wordsong) Boyds Mills Pr.

All the King's Falcons: Rumi on Prophets & Revelation. John Renard. LC 94-2307. 236p. (C). 1994. text ed. 57.50x (*0-7914-2221-6*); pap. text ed. 18.95x (*0-7914-2222-4*) State U NY Pr.

All the King's Horses. Jeffrey A. Nesbit. 192p. (Orig.). (YA). (gr. 9-12). 1990. pap. 6.99 (*0-87788-040-9*) Shaw Pubs.

All the King's Ladies: Actresses of the Restoration. John H. Wilson. LC 58-11962. 216p. reprint ed. pap. 61.60 (*0-8357-5314-X*, 2024072) Bks Demand.

All the King's Men. Robert Penn Warren. 13.95 (*0-8488-1504-1*) Amereon Ltd.

All the King's Men. Robert Penn Warren. LC 83-51770. (Book Notes Ser.). 1985. pap. 2.50 (*0-8120-3500-3*) Barron.

All the King's Men. Robert Penn Warren. 1961. pap. 4.75 (*0-8222-0018-X*) Dramatists Play.

All the King's Men. Robert Penn Warren. LC 46-6144. 438p. 1983. pap. 11.00 (*0-15-604762-4*, Harvest Bks) HarBrace.

All the King's Men. Robert Penn Warren. 576p. 1990. 15.95 (*0-15-104772-3*) HarBrace.

All the King's Men. Robert Penn Warren. 1960. 15.95 (*0-394-40502-1*) Random.

All the King's Men. Robert Penn Warren. 350p. 1981. reprint ed. lib. bdg. 35.95 (*0-89966-290-0*) Buccaneer Bks.

All the King's Men: Confrontation Between the Old & the New South. Harold Woodell. LC 92-45601. (Masterwork Studies: No. 112). 160p. 1993. text ed. 22.95 (*0-8057-9411-5*, Twayne); pap. 12.95 (*0-8057-8580-9*, Twayne) Macmillan.

All the Kings Men Notes. Robert H. Lynn. 1982. pap. 3.75 (*0-8220-0146-2*) Cliffs.

All the King's Things: The Ultimate Elvis Memorabilia Book. Robin Rosaaen. (Illus.). 40p. 1993. text ed. 12.95 (*0-912517-04-2*) Bluewood Bks.

All the Letters. Michele P. Hofbauer. LC 93-77607. (Illus.). 56p. (J). (ps-2). 1993. 15.95 (*1-880851-08-3*) Greene Bark Pr.

All the Lights in the Night. Arthur A. Levine. LC 90-47496. (Illus.). 32p. (J). (ps-3). 1991. 14.95 (*0-688-10107-0*, Tambourine Bks); lib. bdg. 14.88 (*0-688-10108-9*, Tambourine Bks) Morrow.

All the Little Live Things. Wallace Stegner. (Contemporary American Fiction Ser.). 352p. 1991. reprint ed. pap. 11.95 (*0-14-015441-8*, Penguin Bks) Viking Penguin.

All the Livelong Day: The Meaning & Demeaning of Routine Work. rev. ed. Barbara Garson. 256p. 1994. pap. 11.95 (*0-14-023491-8*, Penguin Bks) Viking Penguin.

All the Love Poems of Shakespeare. William Shakespeare. (Illus.). 176p. (C). 1993. reprint ed. pap. 6.95 (*0-8065-0855-8*, Citadel Pr) Carol Pub Group.

All the Magic in the World. Wendy Hartmann. LC 92-38289. (Illus.). 32p. (J). (gr. k-3). 1993. 12.99 (*0-525-45092-0*, DCB) Dutton Child Bks.

All the Marbles: A Novel. J. Bruce Monson. LC 91-11721. 288p. (Orig.). 1991. pap. 10.95 (*0-931832-91-8*) Fithian Pr.

***All the Math That's Fit to Print: Articles from the Manchester Guardian.** Keith Devlin. LC 94-77346. 345p. Date not set. pap. 32.50 (*0-88385-515-1*, ATMA) Math Assn.

All the Math You'll Ever Need. Steven L. Slavin. 1989. pap. text ed. 12.95 (*0-471-50636-2*) Wiley.

All the Messianic Prophecies. Herbert Lockyer. 1988. pap. 17.99 (*0-310-28091-5*, 10076P) Zondervan.

All the Miracles of the Bible. Herbert Lockyer. 1988. pap. 17.99 (*0-310-28101-6*, 10066P) Zondervan.

All the Money in the World. Bill Brittain. LC 77-25635. (Illus.). 160p. (J). (gr. 3-7). 1979. lib. bdg. 14.89 (*0-06-020676-4*) HarpC Child Bks.

All the Money in the World. Bill Brittain. LC 77-25635. (Trophy Bk.). (Illus.). 160p. (J). (gr. 4-7). 1982. pap. 3.95 (*0-06-440128-6*, Trophy) HarpC Child Bks.

All the Mothers Are One: Hindu India & the Cultural Reshaping of Psychoanalysis. Stanley N. Kurtz. 1994. pap. 17.50 (*0-231-07869-2*) Col U Pr.

All the Mothers Are One: Hindu India & the Cultural Reshaping of Psychoanalysis. Stanley R. Kurtz. (Illus.). 384p. 1992. text ed. 45.00 (*0-231-07868-4*) Col U Pr.

All the Muscle You Need. Diana McRae. LC 88-23954. 288p. (Orig.). 1988. pap. 8.95 (*0-933216-59-9*) Spinsters Ink.

***All the Nations under Heaven: An Ethnic & Racial History of New York City.** Frederick M. Binder & David M. Reimers. LC 94-45085. 1995. write for info. (*0-231-07878-1*) Col U Pr.

All the News. Mark Pawlak. LC 84-12956. 1984. pap. 4.00 (*0-914610-37-6*) Hanging Loose.

***All the Obscenities of the Bible.** Gene Kasmar. 501p. (Orig.). 1995. pap. 9.95 (*0-9645995-0-3*) Kasmar Pub.

***All the Old Lions.** Carol Caverly. 214p. 1994. 18.95 (*1-885173-00-8*) Write Way.

All the Orations of Demosthenes. 2nd ed. Demosthenes. Tr. by Thomas Leland. LC 76-161787. (Augustan Translators Ser.). reprint ed. 59.00 (*0-404-54113-5*) AMS Pr.

All the Pain That Money Can Buy: The Life of Christina Onassis. William Wright. 1992. mass mkt. 5.99 (*0-312-92833-5*) St Martin.

All the Parables. Herbert Lockyer. 1988. pap. 17.99 (*0-310-28111-3*, 10075P) Zondervan.

All the Pieces Fit. Gillian Hunt. 1987. pap. 4.95 (*9971-972-57-3*) OMF Bks.

All the Pieces Will Fit. R. L. La Barge. LC 86-71712. (Illus.). 195p. (Orig.). 1986. pap. 6.95 (*0-9617796-0-8*) Allfit.

All the Places to Love. Patricia MacLachlan. LC 92-794. (Charlotte Zolotow Bk.). (Illus.). 32p. (J). (gr. 1 up). 1994. 15.00 (*0-06-021098-2*) HarpC Child Bks.

All the Places to Love. Patricia MacLachlan. LC 92-794. (Charlotte Zolotow Bk.). (Illus.). 32p. (J). (gr. 1 up). 1994. lib. bdg. 14.89 (*0-06-021099-0*) HarpC Child Bks.

All the Polarities: Comparative Studies in Contemporary Canadian Novels in French & English. Philip Stratford. 150p. (C). 1986. pap. text ed. 15.00 (*0-920763-05-7*, Pub. by ECW Press CN) Genl Dist Srvs.

All the Possibilities. Nora Roberts. 1992. mass mkt. 3.59 (*0-373-51015-2*, 5-51015-1) Harlequin Bks.

***All the Powerful Invisible Things: A Sportswoman's Notebook.** Gretchen Legler. 180p. (Orig.). 1995. text ed. 20.95 (*1-878067-70-2*); pap. text ed. 12.95 (*1-878067-69-9*) Seal Pr Feminist.

All the Prayers of the Bible. Herbert Lockyer. 1990. pap. 17.99 (*0-310-28121-0*) Zondervan.

All the President's Men. Carl Bernstein & Bob Woodward. 1994. pap. 12.00 (*0-685-71044-0*, Touchstone Bks) S&S Trade.

All the President's Men. Bob Woodward & Carl Bernstein. (Illus.). 368p. 1987. pap. 9.95 (*0-671-64644-3*, Touchstone Bks) S&S Trade.

***All the President's Men.** Carl Bernstein & Bob Woodward. 1994. reprint ed. lib. bdg. 29.95x (*1-56849-568-4*) Buccaneer Bks.

All the Pretty Horses. Cormac McCarthy. 1992. 21.00 (*0-394-57474-5*) Random.

All the Pretty Horses. Cormac McCarthy. LC 92-50836. 1993. pap. 12.00 (*0-679-74439-8*, Vin) Random.

All the Pretty Horses. large type ed. Cormac McCarthy. LC 93-7017. 1993. pap. 22.95 (*0-7927-1575-6*, Curley Lrg Print) Chivers N Amer.

All the Prime Minister's Men. J. Thakur. 182p. 1977. 11.95 (*0-318-37293-2*) Asia Bk Corp.

All the Promises of the Bible. Herbert Lockyer. 1990. pap. 17.99 (*0-310-28131-8*) Zondervan.

All the Questions You Ever Wanted to Ask American Atheists with All the Answers. 2nd ed. Jon Murray & Madalyn O'Hair. 248p. (Orig.). 1986. pap. 9.00 (*0-910309-24-8*, 5356) Am Atheist.

All the Rage. Time-Life Books Editors. LC 92-26513. (Library of Curious & Unusual Facts). (Illus.). 128p. 1993. 17.27 (*0-8094-7739-4*); lib. bdg. 23.27 (*0-8094-7740-8*) Time-Life.

All the Riches of Job, a True Story of Success, & What Came After. Chuck Lewis. LC 93-83590. (Illus.). 128p. (Orig.). (C). 1993. pap. text ed. 8.95 (*0-9635854-0-1*) Serendipty Pr.

***All the Right Answers.** David L. Mathieu. 1995. 17.95 (*0-533-11111-0*) Vantage.

All the Right Answers. Robert Noah. 320p. 1988. 17.95 (*0-15-104779-0*) HarBrace.

All the Right Enemies: The Life & Murder of Carlo Tresca. Dorothy Gallagher. 300p. 1988. 24.95 (*0-8135-1310-3*) Rutgers U Pr.

***All the Right Men.** Michelle Ogbankwa. 503p. 1995. pap. 22.95 (*0-9644230-5-7*) Diamond Pubng.

All the Right Moves: A VLSI Architecture for Chess. Carl Ebeling. (ACM Doctoral Dissertation Award Ser.). (Illus.). 175p. 1987. 27.50x (*0-262-05035-8*) MIT Pr.

All the Right Places: Traveling Light Through China, Japan, & Russia. Bradley Newsham. 1989. 16.95 (*0-394-57410-9*, Villard Bks) Random.

All the Right Reasons: The Power of Charitable Giving. Marcus C. Cherry, III. LC 89-62016. (Illus.). 136p. (Orig.). 1989. pap. 24.00 (*0-87218-070-0*) Natl Underwriter.

All the Saints Adore Thee: Insight from Christian Classics. 2nd ed. Bruce Shelley. LC 88-14913. 288p. 1994. pap. 11.99 (*0-8010-8364-8*) Baker Bk.

***All the Secrets of Magic Revealed: The Tricks & Illusions of the World's Greatest Magicians.** Herbert L. Becker. LC 94-32605. 1995. 18.95 (*0-8119-0794-5*) LIFETIME.

All the Secrets of Palmistry for Profession & Popularity. Dayanand. (C). 1992. 10.00 (*0-8364-2857-9*, Pub. by UBS Pubs Dist II) S Asia.

All the Shining Young Men. Gilbert Morris & Bobby Funderburk. LC 93-24235. (Price of Liberty Ser.: No. 3). 1993. 8.99 (*0-8499-3496-6*) Word Pub.

All the Small Poems. Valerie Worth. (Illus.). 192p. (J). (gr. 3 up). 1987. pap. 4.95 (*0-374-40344-9*) FS&G.

***All the Small Poems & Fourteen More.** Valerie Worth. (Illus.). 206p. (J). (ps up). 1994. 18.00 (*0-374-30211-1*) FS&G.

All the Southwest. 2nd ed. Thomas B. Lesure. (Illus.). 364p. 4.95 (*0-686-63832-8*) Allsport Pub.

All the Spiritualism of the Christian Bible & the Scripture Directly Opposing It. E. W. Sprague. 392p. 1969. reprint ed. spiral bd. 11.05 (*0-7873-0812-9*) Mokelumne.

All the Stars Are Snowflakes. Ralph Wright. LC 92-73080. 1992. 9.00 (*0-8233-0482-5*) Golden Quill.

All the Strange Hours. Loren Eiseley. 1983. 20.25 (*0-8446-5978-9*) Peter Smith.

All the Strange Hours. Loren Eiseley. 288p. 1987. pap. 11.00 (*0-684-18907-0*, Scribners) S&S Trade.

All the Strange Hours: The Excavation of a Life. Loren Eiseley. LC 75-22433. 1977. pap. 8.95 (*0-684-14868-4*, SL690, Scribners) S&S Trade.

All the Sweet Tomorrows. Bertrice Small. 1986. mass mkt. 4.99 (*0-345-33473-6*) Ballantine.

All the Tea in China. Kit Chow & Ione Kramer. LC 89-60878. (Illus.). 160p. (Orig.). 1990. pap. 14.95 (*0-8351-2194-1*) China Bks.

All the Teachings of Jesus. Herbert Lockyer. 1991. pap. 14.00 (*0-06-065274-8*) Harper SF.

All the Time in the World. Margery Larrabee. 1971. pap. 2.00 (*0-911214-21-6*) Rational Isl.

All the Time We Need. Megan Daniel. 400p. (Orig.). 1993. pap. 4.99 (*0-505-51909-7*, Love Spell) Dorchester Pub Co.

All the Traps of Earth. Clifford D. Simak. 1979. pap. 3.50 (*0-380-45500-5*, 45500) Avon.

All the Trouble in the World: The Lighter Side of Overpopulation, Famine, Plague, Ecological Disaster, Ethnic Hatred, & Poverty. P. J. O'Rourke. 240p. 1994. 22.00 (*0-87113-580-9*) Grove-Atltc.

All the Troubles of World. Isaac Asimov. (Isaac Asimov Ser.). 40p. (J). (gr. 5). 1989. lib. bdg. 13.95 (*0-88682-233-5*) Creative Ed.

All the Visions. Rudy Rucker. (Doubles Ser.). (Illus.). 224p. 1993. pap. 14.95x (*0-938075-12-8*) Ocean View Bks.

All the Visions. deluxe limited ed. Rudy Rucker. (Doubles Ser.). (Illus.). 224p. 1993. 40.00 (*0-938075-37-3*) Ocean View Bks.

All the Visions & The Secret of Life, 2 vols., Set. deluxe limited ed. Rudy Rucker. (Illus.). 1993. boxed 60.00 (*0-938075-09-8*) Ocean View Bks.

All the Way. (Orig.). 1992. pap. 4.95 (*1-56333-023-7*) Masquerade.

All the Way. Felice Buckvar. (Orig.). 1980. pap. 2.25 (*0-89083-571-3*) Zebra.

All the Way: German. Heidi Singer. 1994. Incl. CD. 80.00 (*0-517-59779-1*, Living Language) Crown Pub Group.

All the Way: Italian. Salvatore Bancheri. 1994. CD. cd-rom 80.00 (*0-517-59781-0*, Living Language) Crown Pub Group.

All the Way: Spanish. Irwin Stern. 1994. Incl. cassettes. 60.00 (*0-517-58372-0*, Living Language); Incl. CD. 80.00 (*0-517-59782-9*, Living Language) Crown Pub Group.

All the Way: Spanish. Irwin Stern. 1994. 15.00 (*0-517-58373-9*, Living Language) Random.

All the Way Home. Jim Hanyen. 230p. (Orig.). 1995. 10.75 (*1-880664-06-2*) E M Pr.

All the Way Home. Keith J. Karren. 9.95 (*0-88494-586-3*) Bookcraft Inc.

All the Way Home. Tad Mosel. 1961. 15.00 (*0-8392-1003-5*) Astor-Honor.

All the Way Home. Mary Pride. LC 87-71897. 284p. 1989. pap. 13.99 (*0-89107-465-1*) Crossway Bks.

All the Way Home. Lore Segal. (Sunburst Ser.). (Illus.). 32p. (J). (ps up). 1988. pap. 3.95 (*0-374-40355-4*) FS&G.

All the Way to China. K. D. Pyne. (Illus.). 16p. (J). (ps). 1993. 4.95 (*1-882185-06-4*) Crnrstone Pub.

***All the Ways Home: Parenting & Children in the Lesbian & Gay Communities - A Collection of Short Fiction.** Ed. by Cindy Rizzo et al. 200p. (Orig.). 1995. pap. 10.95 (*0-934678-65-0*) New Victoria Pubs.

***All the Ways Home: Parenting & Children in the Lesbian & Gay Communities - A Collection of Short Fiction.** Ed. by Cindy Rizzo et al. 200p. 1995. 19.95 (*0-934678-68-5*) New Victoria Pubs.

All the Western Stars. Philip L. Williams. 240p. 1988. 15.95 (*0-934601-47-X*) Peachtree Pubs.

An Asterisk (*) at the beginning of an entry indicates that the title is appearing in BIP for the first time.

All the Western States & Territories. Henry Howe. (Notable American Authors Ser.). 1992. reprint ed. lib. bdg. 75.00 (*0-7812-3208-2*) Rprt Serv.

All the Weyrs of Pern. Anne McCaffrey. 1992. mass mkt. 5.99 (*0-345-36893-2*, Del Rey) Ballantine.

***All the Winters That Have Been: A Novel.** Evan Maxwell. 192p. 1995. 15.00 (*0-06-017633-4*) HarpC.

All the Women Are White, All the Blacks Are Men, but Some of Us Are Brave: Black Women's Studies. Ed. by Gloria T. Hull et al. LC 81-689180. (Illus.). 432p. (C). 1982. pap. 15.95 (*0-912670-95-9*) Feminist Pr.

All the Women of the Bible. Herbert Lockyer. 1988. pap. 17.99 (*0-310-28151-2*, 10038P) Zondervan.

All the Words of Jesus. Comp. by George R. Long. 510p. 1993. text ed. 9.95 (*1-56794-041-2*, C-2323) Star Bible.

All the World's a Fair: Visions of Empire at American International Expositions, 1876-1916. Robert W. Rydell. LC 84-2674. (Illus.). x, 334p. (C). 1987. pap. text ed. 15.95 (*0-226-73240-1*) U Ch Pr.

All the World's a Stage. William Shakespeare. 1984. 2.50 (*0-87129-227-0*, A32) Dramatic Pub.

All the World's a Stage. David H. Wilson. 1969. pap. 2.75 (*0-8222-0019-8*) Dramatists Play.

All the World's a Stage... Art & Pageantry in the Renaissance & Baroque, 2 pts. Ed. by Susan S. Munshower. (Papers in Art History: Vol. VI). (Illus.). 575p. (Orig.). 1990. boxed, pap. 45.00 (*0-915773-05-8*) Penn St Univ Dept Art Hist.

All the World's a Stage: Memoirs. Hershel Zohn. LC 92-61290. (Illus.). 352p. 1992. 16.95 (*1-881325-01-6*) Yucca Tree Pr.

All the World's an Interview: Complete, Concise, Resumes, Cover Letters, Self-Marketing, Interviewing, Following up, Negotiating, Problem Solving, Closing Deals, Getting Raises. Bob Finnie & Gloria Finnie. 101p. (Orig.). 1990. pap. 7.98 (*1-879977-50-8*, TX2-956-305) Finnie & Assocs.

All the World's Mornings: A Novel. Pascal Quignard. Tr. by James Kirkup. LC 93-2161. 112p. 1993. pap. 9.00 (*1-55597-203-9*) Graywolf.

All the Wrong Places: Adrift in the Politics of the Pacific Rim. James Fenton. (Travel Ser.). 288p. 1988. pap. 9.95 (*0-87113-204-4*) Grove-Atltic.

All the Young Men. Oliver La Farge. LC 75-41169. reprint ed. 36.00 (*0-404-14566-3*) AMS Pr.

All Their Kingdoms. large type ed. Madeleine A. Polland. 592p. 1983. 21.95 (*0-7089-0934-5*) Ulverscroft.

***All Their Kings Have Fallen.** Jonathan L. Snare. 270p. 1995. pap. 8.95 (*1-56901-798-0*) NW Pub.

***All There Is To Know.** Coleman Alexander. 1995. pap. 15.00 (*0-671-50005-8*, Touchstone Bks) S&S Trade.

All There Is to Know: Readings from the Illustrious of the Encyclopaedia Britannica. 11th ed. Ed. by Alexander Coleman & Charles Simmons. LC 93-5297. 1994. 30.00 (*0-671-76747-X*) S&S Trade.

All There Is to Know...Is Inside. Daya Devi-Doolin. 50p. (Orig.). 1989. pap. text ed. write for info. (*0-318-65569-1*) Padaran Pubns.

All These. Paul R. Frothingham. LC 70-86752. (Essay Index Reprint Ser.). 1977. 21.95 (*0-8369-1182-2*) Ayer.

All These Lands You Call One Country: Poems. Stephen Corey. 64p. (C). 1992. text ed. 18.95 (*0-8262-0837-1*); pap. 9.95 (*0-8262-0838-X*) U of Mo Pr.

All These Splendid Sins. Lee Rogers. (Orig.). 1979. pap. 2.50 (*0-89083-480-6*) Zebra.

All These Things Added. James Allen. 192p. 1983. pap. 17.50 (*0-89540-129-0*, SB-129) Sun Pub.

All These Things Shall Give Thee Experience. Neal A. Maxwell. LC 79-26282. 138p. 1979. 10.95 (*0-87747-796-5*) Deseret Bk.

***All These Trees.** Tom Earley. 84p. 1992. pap. 20.00 (*0-86383-866-9*, Pub. by Gomer Pr UK) St Mut.

All These Voices: New & Selected Poems. Faye Kicknosway. LC 86-24493. 175p. 1986. pap. 9.95 (*0-918273-26-9*) Coffee Hse.

All These Wonderful Names: A Potpourri of People, Places, & Things. J. N. Hook. 1991. pap. text ed. 10.95 (*0-471-53011-5*) Wiley.

***All These Years.** Patricia Gangas. 70p. (Orig.). 1995. pap. 9.95 (*1-887312-00-5*) P Gangas.

All Things Are Holy. limited ed. Gustav Davidson. LC 78-146980. (Living Poets' Library Ser.). (Illus.). pap. 2.50 (*0-686-01280-1*) Dragons Teeth.

All Things Are Possible. Yvonne Duffy. LC 81-83657. (Illus.). 1981. pap. 8.95 (*0-9607252-0-2*) A J Garvin.

All Things Are Possible. Sue M. Kidd. (Illus.). 60p. 1988. 8.50 (*0-8378-1814-1*) Gibson.

All Things Are Possible: The Charles Cullum Lessons. Charles G. Cullum. LC 86-5819. 176p. (Orig.). 1986. pap. 7.95 (*0-937641-00-6*) Stone Canyon Pr.

All Things Are Possible: The Healing & Charismatic Revivals in Modern America. David E. Harrell, Jr. LC 75-1937. (Illus.). 320p. 1976. 29.95 (*0-253-10090-9*); pap. 12.95 (*0-253-20221-3*, MB-221) Ind U Pr.

***All Things Are Possible - Pass the Word.** Barbara M. Ohrbach. LC 94-37344. (J). 1995. pap. 7.00 (*0-517-88426-7*, Clarkson Potter) Crown Bks Yng Read.

All Things Are Possible & Penultimate Words & Other Essays. Lev Shestov. LC 76-8303. xiii, 239p. 1977. 16.95x (*0-8214-0237-4*) Ohio U Pr.

All Things Are Possible Through Prayer: The Faith-Filled Guidebook That Can Change Your Life. Charles L. Allen. LC 58-11022. reprint ed. pap. 3.99 (*0-8007-8000-0*) Revell.

***All Things Are Possible to Believers: Reflections on the Lord's Prayer & the Sermon on the Mount.** Rudolph Schnackenburg. Tr. by James S. Currie. LC 94-22146. 112p. (Orig.). 1995. pap. 12.99 (*0-664-25517-5*) Westminster John Knox.

All Things Beautiful. Cathy Maxwell. 1994. mass mkt. 4.50 (*0-06-108278-3*, Harp PBks) HarpC.

All Things Bright & Beautiful. Cecil Alexander. LC 91-28428. (Illus.). 32p. (Orig.). (J). (ps-2). 1992. 11.95 (*0-8249-8544-3*, Ideals Child) Hambleton-Hill.

All Things Bright & Beautiful. Cecil F. Alexander. (All Aboard Bks.). (Illus.). 32p. (Orig.). (J). (ps-2). 1989. pap. 1.95 (*0-448-34304-5*, Platt & Munk Pubs) Putnam Pub Group.

All Things Bright & Beautiful. James Herriot. 1984. mass mkt. 6.99 (*0-553-26970-4*) Bantam.

All Things Bright & Beautiful. James Herriot. LC 73-87407. 400p. 1974. 18.95 (*0-312-02030-9*) St Martin.

All Things Bright & Beautiful. Laura Lanier. (Illus.). 64p. 1993. 9.50 (*0-8378-6946-3*) Gibson.

All Things Change: Maylene the Mermaid. braille ed. Trenna Daniells. (One to Grow On! Ser.). (Illus.). (Orig.). (J). (gr. 1). 1992. vinyl bd. 10.95 (*1-56956-004-8*, BI0005) W A T Braille.

All Things Change: Maylene the Mermaid. braille ed. Trenna Daniells. (One to Grow On! Ser.). (Illus.). (Orig.). (J). (gr. 2). 1992. vinyl bd. 10.95 (*1-56956-029-3*, BI0005) W A T Braille.

All Things Chocolate. Ariel Books Staff. 1994. 4.95 (*0-8362-3061-2*) Andrews & McMeel.

All Things Come of Age & the Test of Courage. Liam O'Flaherty. (Illus.). 39p. 1984. pap. 5.95 (*0-86327-044-1*, Pub. by Wolfhound Pr IE) Dufour.

All Things Common: The Hutterian Way of Life. Victor Peters. LC 65-28661. (Illus.). 245p. reprint ed. pap. 69.90 (*0-8357-5315-8*, 2033282) Bks Demand.

***All Things Connected: Native American Creations.** Museum of Natural History, Roger Williams Park Staff. 65p. 1995. pap. 14.95x (*0-9646544-0-7*) Mus Nat Hist.

All Things Considered. Gilbert K. Chesterton. LC 70-84060. 1969. 16.95 (*0-8023-1225-X*) Dufour.

All Things Considered. Y. Ganz. 1993. 17.95 (*0-89906-572-4*); 14.95 (*0-89906-573-2*) Mesorah Pubns.

***All Things Considered.** Debbie Macomber. (Western Lovers Ser.). 1996. mass mkt. 3.99 (*0-373-88535-0*, 1-88535-9) Harlequin Bks.

All Things Considered. Gilbert K. Chesterton. LC 74-156629. (Essay Index Reprint Ser.). 1977. reprint ed. 21.95 (*0-8369-2275-1*) Ayer.

***All Things Considered.** Howard O'Brien. (American Autobiography Ser.). 345p. 1995. reprint ed. lib. bdg. 89.00 (*0-7812-8601-8*) Rprt Serv.

All Things for Good. Thomas Watson. (Puritan Paperbacks Ser.). 128p. (Orig.). 1986. pap. 4.95 (*0-85151-478-2*) Banner of Truth.

All Things Heal in Time. Jeanette Gilge. LC 88-3580. (Pioneer Family Ser.). 192p. 1988. pap. 6.99 (*1-55513-474-2*, LifeJourney) Chariot Family.

***All Things Herriot: James Herriot & His Peaceable Kingdom.** Sanford Sternlicht. LC 94-39523. (Illus.). 220p. 1995. 24.95 (*0-8156-0322-3*) Syracuse U Pr.

All Things in Their Time. LaWant P. Jack. pap. 4.95 (*0-89036-145-2*) Hawkes Pub Inc.

All Things Made New: A Comprehensive Outline of the Baha'i Faith. rev. ed. John Ferraby. 1975. 26.50 (*0-900125-23-3*, 332-016); pap. 14.50 (*0-900125-24-1*, 332-017) Bahai.

***All Things Made New (B) Homilies for Sundays & Holy Days Cycle B.** Harold A. Buetow. (Orig.). 1996. pap. write for info. (*0-8189-0728-2*) Alba.

All Things Natural: The Dallas Edition. Dejavu & D. Byrne. (Illus.). 160p. (Orig.). 1989. pap. text ed. 11.95 (*0-685-30390-X*) Deja vu TX.

All Things New. Arthur E. Bloomfield. LC 42-5300. 1959. pap. 8.99 (*0-87123-007-0*); student ed 1.99 (*0-87123-520-X*) Bethany Hse.

All Things New: A Celebration of Forgiveness Family Book. Ed. by James Bitney. (Illus.). 48p. 1992. reprint ed. pap. text ed. 6.30 (*1-55944-016-3*, 2536316) Franciscan Comns.

All Things New: American Communes & Utopian Movements, 1860-1914. Robert S. Fogarty. (Illus.). 264p. 1990. 34.50 (*0-226-25654-5*) U Ch Pr.

All Things New: Essays in Honor of Roy A. Harrisville. Ed. by Arland J. Hultgren et al. LC 91-78425. (Word & World Supplement Ser.: No. 1). 200p. (Orig.). 1992. pap. text ed. 14.95 (*0-9632389-0-6*) Luther Seminary.

All Things Nice. Sharman Macdonald. 80p. (Orig.). 1991. pap. 9.95 (*0-571-16429-3*) Faber & Faber.

All Things Nuclear. James C. Warf. (Illus.). 303p. (Orig.). (C). 1989. pap. 24.00 (*0-9626706-0-X*) SC Fed Scientists.

All Things Possible. Roy E. Davis. 192p. 1991. pap. 4.95 (*0-87707-231-0*) CSA Pr.

All Things to All Men: An Introduction to Missions in Filipino Culture. Ed. by Evelyn Miranda-Feliciano. 63p. (Orig.). (C). 1989. pap. 5.00 (*971-10-0387-2*, Pub. by New Day Pub PH) Cellar.

***All Things to All People.** Jeffrey D. Allen. 1995. 14.95 (*0-533-11175-7*) Vantage.

All Things to All People: A Primer for K-12 ESL Teachers in Small Programs. Donald N. Flemming et al. LC 92-63213. 224p. 1993. pap. 17.95 (*0-939791-44-7*) Tchrs Eng Spkrs.

All Things to All People: The Catholic Church Confronts the AIDS Crisis. Mark R. Kowalewski. 167p. (C). 1994. 44.50 (*0-7914-1777-8*); pap. 16.95 (*0-7914-1778-6*) State U NY Pr.

All Things Touched by Wind. John Daniel. 65p. (Orig.). (C). 1994. pap. 9.95 (*0-934000-5-3*) Salmon Run.

All Things under the Moon. Robert Morgan. 224p. (Orig.). 1994. pap. text ed. 4.99 (*0-425-14302-3*, Prime Crime) Berkley Pub.

All Things Vain: Religious Satirists & Their Art. Robert A. Kantra. LC 83-43029. (Illus.). 240p. 1984. 30.00 (*0-271-00358-8*) Pa St U Pr.

All Things Wise & Wonderful. James Herriot. LC 77-76640. 1977. 17.95 (*0-312-02031-7*) St Martin.

All Things Wonderful. James Herriot. 1981. mass mkt. 6.99 (*0-553-26605-5*) Bantam.

All This, & Heaven Too. Rachel Field. 1976. 32.95 (*0-8488-0269-1*) Amereon Ltd.

All This & Heaven Too. Rachel Field. 320p. 1983. reprint ed. lib. bdg. 35.95 (*0-89966-323-0*) Buccaneer Bks.

All This Change. Susan Hertel. 1994. pap. 9.95 (*0-942396-69-3*) Blackberry ME.

All This Every Day. Joanne Kyger. (Orig.). 1975. 4.00 (*0-929844-04-1*) Big Sky Bolinas.

All This Was Bataan. Silvestre L. Tagarao. 141p. (Orig.). (C). 1992. pap. 8.75 (*971-10-0445-3*, Pub. by New Day Pub PH) Cellar.

All Those Bells. Lois Van Houten. (Poetry Ser.: No. 13). (Illus.). 104p. (Orig.). 1981. pap. 6.95 (*0-930020-12-X*) Stone Country.

All Those Cessna One Fifty's. 363p. 1980. pap. text ed. 12.95 (*0-939158-01-9*) Flightshops.

All Those Secrets of the World. Jane Yolen. (J). (ps-3). 1991. 14.95 (*0-316-96891-9*) Little.

All Those Secrets of the World. Jane Yolen. (J). (ps-3). 1993. mass mkt. 4.95 (*0-316-96895-1*) Little.

All Through the House. Janice Bartlett. 224p. (Orig.). 1992. pap. 2.95 (*1-56597-002-0*, Kismet) Meteor Pub.

All Through the House. Heritage House, Inc. Staff. 1993. write for info. (*0-87197-378-2*) Favorite Recipes.

All Through the Night. Teny Nudson. (Illus.). 36p. (Orig.). 1990. pap. 13.95 (*0-935133-38-0*) CKE Pubns.

All Through the Night. Grace L. Hill. 1976. reprint ed. lib. bdg. 20.95 (*0-89190-001-2*, Rivercity Pr) Amereon Ltd.

All Through the Night, No. 6. Grace L. Hill. 224p. 1989. pap. 4.99 (*0-8423-0018-X*) Tyndale.

***All Through the Week with Cat & Dog.** Rozanne Williams. (Emergent Reader Bks.). 16p. 1994. 2.49 (*0-916119-64-5*) Creat Teach Pr.

All Thumbs Guide to Car Care. Robert W. Wood. 1993. pap. text ed. 9.95 (*0-07-071754-0*) McGraw.

All Thumbs Guide to Compact Disc Players. Gene B. Williams. 1993. pap. text ed. 9.95 (*0-07-070587-9*) McGraw.

All Thumbs Guide to Fixing Furniture. Robert W. Wood. 1993. pap. text ed. 9.95 (*0-8306-4433-4*) TAB Bks.

All Thumbs Guide to Home Computers. Gene B. Williams. 1993. pap. text ed. 9.95 (*0-07-070591-7*) McGraw.

All Thumbs Guide to Home Energy Savings. Robert W. Wood. 1992. pap. text ed. 9.95 (*0-07-071752-4*) McGraw.

All Thumbs Guide to Home Security. Robert W. Wood. LC 92-41243. (Illus.). 1993. 9.70 (*0-8306-4166-1*) TAB Bks.

All Thumbs Guide to Telephones & Answering Machines. Gene B. Williams. 1993. pap. 9.95 (*0-8306-4435-0*) TAB Bks.

All Thumbs Guide to VCRs. Gene B. Williams. 1992. pap. text ed. 9.95 (*0-07-070589-5*) McGraw.

All Thy Love. large type ed. Jean Ure. 432p. 1985. 15.95 (*0-7089-1260-5*) Ulverscroft.

***All Time American Favorites.** Frances Cleary. (Illus.). 128p. 1995. 14.98 (*0-8317-2759-4*) Smithmark.

All-Time Awesome Bible Search. Sandy Silverthorne. (Illus.). 32p. (Orig.). (J). 1991. 11.99 (*0-89081-920-3*) Harvest Hse.

All-Time Baking Favorites. Family Circle Editors. 1977. 12.95 (*0-405-11406-0*) Ayer.

All-Time Baking Favorites. Ed. by Nancy H. Fitzpatrick. LC 74-76331. (Family Circle Bks.). (Illus.). 144p. 1976. 7.98 (*0-405-06686-4*) Ayer.

***All Time Favorite Recipes.** Malcolm Page. 1994. 16.99 (*0-376-02158-6*) Sunset Menlo Pk.

All-Time Great Cakes: Rare & Unusual Cakes from All over the U. S. A. Ed. by Louise Surland. (Illus.). 64p. 1986. pap. 5.95 (*0-938592-02-5*) Harriets Kitchen.

All-Time Great World Series. Andrew Gutelle. LC 93-35668. (All Aboard Reading Ser.). (Illus.). 48p. (J). (gr. 2-3). 1994. 7.99 (*0-448-40472-9*, G&D); pap. 3.50 (*0-448-40471-0*, G&D) Putnam Pub Group.

All Time Greats. Bernardo Barden. LC 92-12053. (Basketball Heroes Ser.). (J). 1992. 17.26 (*0-86593-163-1*); lib. bdg. 12.95 (*0-685-59373-8*) Rourke Corp.

All Time Greats of Boxing. Peter Arnold. 1993. 14.98 (*1-55521-957-8*) Bk Sales Inc.

All-Time Hits: One Hundred Favorite Standards. (Ultimate Ser.). 256p. 1982. pap. 17.95 (*0-7935-1875-X*, 00361424) H Leonard.

All Times, All Peoples: A World History of Slavery. Milton Meltzer. LC 79-2810. (Illus.). 80p. (J). (gr. 5-9). 1980. lib. bdg. 15.89 (*0-06-024187-X*) HarpC Child Bks.

All Together. Jim Boulden. (Illus.). 32p. (Orig.). (J). (gr. 1-7). 1991. pap. 4.95 (*1-878076-10-8*) Boulden Pub.

All Together: A Manual of Cooperative Games. Ruth Cornelius. 1950. 3.00 (*0-933061-00-5*) Lentz Peace Res.

All Together Now: Let's Write! Joyce C. Bumgardner. (Illus.). 1989. spiral bd. write for info. (*0-318-65793-7*) Froggie Pr.

All Tutus Should Be Pink. Sheri Brownrigg. (Illus.). 32p. (J). 1992. pap. 2.95 (*0-590-43904-9*, Cartwheel) Scholastic Inc.

All under Heaven... Sun Yat-sen & His Revolutionary Thought. Sidney H. Chang & Leonard H. Gordon. (Publication Ser.: No. 400). 240p. (C). 1991. text ed. 29.95 (*0-8179-9081-X*); pap. text ed. 20.95 (*0-8179-9082-8*) Hoover Inst Pr.

All under Heaven: Transforming Paradigms in Confucian-Christian Dialogue. John Berthrong. LC 93-17291. (Chinese Philosophy & Culture Ser.). 273p. (C). 1994. 64.50 (*0-7914-1857-X*); pap. 21.95 (*0-7914-1858-8*) State U NY Pr.

***All Visitors Welcome: Accessibility in State Park Interpretive Programs & Facilities.** Erika R. Porter. Ed. by Mary A. Helmich & Donna C. Pozzi. (Illus.). 262p. (Orig.). (C). 1994. pap. 20.00 (*0-941925-16-1*) Cal Parks Rec.

All-Volunteer Force: A Study of Ideology in the Military. Jerald G. Bachman et al. LC 77-5631. 220p. 1977. reprint ed. pap. 62.70 (*0-7837-4710-1*, 2059062) Bks Demand.

All-Volunteer Force & American Society. Ed. by John B. Keeley. LC 78-18420. 224p. reprint ed. pap. 63.90 (*0-8357-5316-6*, 2011981) Bks Demand.

All-Waldo Comics. Kim Deitch. 64p. 1992. per., pap. 7.95 (*1-56097-078-2*) Fantagraph Bks.

All Was Light: An Introduction to Newton's Opticks. A. Rupert Hall. LC 92-43731. 1993. 52.50 (*0-19-853985-1*, Clarendon Pr) OUP.

All We Are Saying: Popular Musicians & the Struggle for Peace. Ed. by Don McLeese & Marianne Philbin. (Illus.). 1987. pap. write for info. (*0-394-75626-6*) Pantheon.

***All We Excellent Kittens.** Edna Kimball. 64p. (J). 1994. pap. text ed. 7.50 (*1-879260-31-X*) Evanston Pub.

All We Had Was Us. Robert Whittemore. (Illus.). 112p. (Orig.). 1992. pap. 6.50 (*0-9634247-0-X*) R E Whittemore.

***All We Hold Dear.** Kathryn L. Davis. LC 94-33241. 1995. 22.00 (*0-671-73603-5*) PB.

All We Know of Heaven. large type ed. Dore Mullen. 608p. 1985. 15.95 (*0-7089-1339-3*) Ulverscroft.

All We Like Sheep. Mary G. Peeples. 104p. 1989. write for info. (*0-9634836-0-9*) Sheep Shoppe.

***All We Need of Hell.** Rika Lesser. 83p. 1995. 15.95 (*0-929398-85-8*); pap. 10.95 (*0-929398-92-0*) UNTX Pr.

All-Weather Warriors: The Search for the Ultimate Fighter Aircraft. Mike Spick. (Illus.). 160p. 1994. 24.95 (*1-85409-202-2*) Sterling.

***All Weather Yachtsman.** Peter Haward. (Illus.). 224p. Date not set. pap. 18.50 (*0-7136-3560-6*) Sheridan.

All Went Willingly 1941-1945: World War II. J. J. Glasgow. LC 94-96493. 229p. (Orig.). (C). (gr. 13). 1994. pap. 13.95 (*0-9643299-0-5*) J J Glasgow. A very personal autobiography of a young boy from a provincial Indiana town who enlists in the army during World War II & acclimates himself to military life & its violence during his two-year journey throughout British & Dutch New Guinea & Leyte & Luzon in the Philippines. His activities are dovetailed with the experiences of Norm, a childhood friend & a seaman on the U.S.S. CLEVELAND. Several chapters are devoted to the childhood of Beckie, an eight-year-old Dutch girl, who, raised in Java in the Netherlands East Indies, lived through the invasions by the Japanese. Time-paralleled with that of the author, it follows her life, with her mother & six older sisters, during their three-year internment in six different Japanese concentration camps. Frequent flash backs describing childhood experiences or flash forwards to post-war stories related to the veteran's mind set, along with detailed descriptions of war experiences, comrades, & stories creating humor or pathos, adds a human flavor to the manuscript. LITTLE PROFESSOR BOOK CO., Fort Wayne, IN: ALL WENT WILLINGLY "...is one of our top ten best-selling books in our history section." Order direct from: J. J. Glasgow, 1531 Magnolia Ln., Fort Wayne, IN 46825; 219-482-5125.** ***Publisher Provided Annotation.

***All We're Meant to Be: Biblical Feminism for Today.** 3rd ed. Letha D. Scanzoni & Nancy A. Hardesty. LC 93-120683. 440p. (Orig.). 1992. reprint ed. pap. 125.40 (*0-7837-7973-9*, 2047729) Bks Demand.

All What Jazz: A Record Diary. Philip Larkin. 316p. 1985. 19.95 (*0-374-10340-2*); pap. 9.95 (*0-374-51908-0*) FS&G.

All Wheel Drive High Performance Handbook. Jay W. Lamm. (Illus.). 144p. 1990. pap. 9.98 (*0-87938-419-0*) Motorbooks Intl.

All Where Each Is. Andrew Crozier. (Agneau 2 Paperbook Ser.: 2). 320p. (Orig.). 1985. 26.00 (*0-907954-02-2*, Pub. by Allardyce Barnett UK); pap. 15.00 (*0-907954-03-0*, Pub. by Allardyce Barnett UK) SPD-Small Pr Dist.

***All White World of Children's Books & African American Children's Literature.** Ed. by Osayimwense Osa. 1995. pap. 14.95 (*0-86543-477-8*) Africa World.

***All Will Be Well: Based on the Classic Spirituality of Julian of Norwich.** Richard Chilson. (30 with a Great Spiritual Teacher Ser.). 216p. (Orig.). 1995. pap. 6.95 (*0-87793-563-7*) Ave Maria.

An Asterisk (*) at the beginning of an entry indicates that the title is appearing in BIP for the first time.

All Will Yet Be Well: The Diary of Sarah Gillespie Huftalen, 1873-1952. Suzanne L. Bunkers. LC 93-32516. (Bur Oak Original Ser.). (Illus.). 346p. 1993. text ed. 46.95x (*0-87745-421-3*); pap. 17.95 (*0-87745-422-1*) U of Iowa Pr.

All Women Are Healers: A Comprehensive Guide to Natural Healing. Diane Stein. 425p. (Orig.). 1990. pap. 12.95 (*0-89594-409-X*) Crossing Pr.

All Women Are Lunch: How Learning to be a Bastard with Women Can Enrich Your Life. Gary Brodsky. 144p. 1987. 5.95 (*1-55601-009-5*) Great Sky.

***All Women's Health in the 90s Series. Celina Poy-Wing. Date not set. write for info. (*0-9638783-4-4*) All Womens Hlth.**
A series of books dealing with women's health & sexuality by Celina Poy-Wing, MD, a practicing gynecologist. Just out, CLIMAXX!! ORGASMIC SEX (9.95, ISBN 0-9638783-1-X), deals with sexual joy & potency. From the essential facts to exotic, erotic tips, Dr. Celina Poy-Wing covers the wide territory of orgasmic sex. Can a woman ejaculate (& how)? Giving oral sex, responding to petit mort, & getting sexual energy flowing with aphrodisiacs & fantasies are just a few of the topics covered. CLIMAXX!! is the second book in Dr. Poy-Wing's series on All Women's Health in the 90s. Her first book, TAME THE YEAST BEAST! (4.95, ISBN 0-9638783-0-1), is a comprehensive & easily read "must" for any woman who suffers from recurring yeast infections. An upcoming book called SEX-ED MANUAL (6.95, ISBN 0-9638783-2-8), answers questions that address the concerns & expectations of teenagers ages 12-17. HAZARDOUS LOVE: STDs (5.95, ISBN 0-9638783-3-6), a clinically-based exploration of sexually-transmitted diseases, is scheduled for release in October 1995. To order Dr. Poy-Wing's books, write: All Women's Health Publishers Corporation (AWHP Corp.), 817 S. University Dr., Suite 101, Plantation, FL 33324 or call 910-656-3700. ***Publisher Provided Annotation.***

All Work & No Pay. (Money Reform Ser.). 1994. lib. bdg. 250.95 (*0-8490-5657-8*) Gordon Pr.

All Work & No Play? The Sociology of Women & Leisure. Rosemary Deem. 160p. 1986. pap. 32.00 (*0-335-15354-2*, Open Univ Pr) Taylor & Francis.

All Year Long. Nancy Tafuri. LC 82-9275. (Illus.). 32p. (J). (gr. k-2). 1983. lib. bdg. 13.88 (*0-688-01416-X*) Greenwillow.

***All Year Projects & Patterns: Animal Bulletin Boards.** Karen Sevaly. (Illus.). 48p. (J). 1994. teacher ed, pap. 6.95 (*0-943263-51-4*, TF-1353) Teachers Friend Pubns.

***All Year Projects & Patterns: Everyday Bulletin Boards.** Karen Sevaly. (Illus.). 48p. (J). 1994. teacher ed, pap. 6.95 (*0-943263-54-9*, TF-1356) Teachers Friend Pubns.

***All Year Projects & Patterns: Holiday Bulletin Boards.** Karen Sevaly. (Illus.). 48p. (J). (ps-6). 1994. teacher ed, pap. 6.95 (*0-943263-52-2*, TF-1354) Teachers Friend Pubns.

***All Year Projects & Patterns: Make Your Own Games!** Karen Sevaly. (Illus.). 48p. (J). (ps-6). 1994. teacher ed, pap. 6.95 (*0-943263-56-5*, TF-1358) Teachers Friend Pubns.

***All Year Projects & Patterns: Masks, Visors & More!** Karen Sevaly. (All Year Ser.). (Illus.). 48p. (Orig.). (J). (gr. k-5). 1994. pap. 6.95 (*0-943263-49-2*, TF-1351) Teachers Friend Pubns.

***All Year Projects & Patterns: Mobiles.** Karen Sevaly. (All Year Ser.). (Illus.). 48p. (Orig.). (J). (gr. k-5). 1994. pap. 6.95 (*0-943263-50-6*, TF-1352) Teachers Friend Pubns.

***All Year Projects & Patterns: Seasonal Bulletin Boards.** Karen Sevaly. (Illus.). 48p. (J). (ps-6). 1994. teacher ed, pap. 6.95 (*0-943263-53-0*, TF-1355) Teachers Friend Pubns.

***All Year Projects & Patterns: Stand Up Characters.** Karen Sevaly. (Illus.). 48p. (J). (ps-6). 1994. teacher ed, pap. 6.95 (*0-943263-55-7*, TF-1357) Teachers Friend Pubns.

All Year Round Magic Pen Book. (J). (gr. 2 up). 1991. pap. 1.97 (*1-56297-133-6*) Lee Pubns KY.

***All Year Round with Little Frog.** Muff Singer. LC 94-67563. (Squeeze & Squeak Books Ser.). (Illus.). 18p. (J). 1995. bds. 4.99 (*0-89577-657-X*) RD Assn.

All You Can Do Is All You Can. 1989. pap. 11.00 (*0-394-57928-3*) Random.

All You Can Do Is All You Can Do But All You Can Do Is Enough. A. L. Williams. 1989. mass mkt. 5.99 (*0-8041-0499-9*) Ivy Books.

All You Can Eat: Stories. Robin Hemley. Ed. by Anne Rumsey. (Atlantic Monthly Press Fiction Ser.). 228p. (Orig.). 1988. pap. 7.95 (*0-87113-261-3*) Grove-Atltic.

All You Can Eat Diet. Anthony Newbury. (Orig.). 1986. pap. 14.95 (*0-9601978-4-2*) Health Res Las Vegas.

All You Could Forget about Older People. Leo E. Missinne & Ed Fischer. LC 81-51459. (Illus.). 150p. (C). 1981. per. 9.95 (*0-88247-600-9*) R & E Pubs.

All You Ever Wanted to Know about Microscopy & Were Afraid to Ask. Jim Hilton. (Illus.). 120p. (Orig.). (C). 1984. pap. text ed. 11.95 (*0-917441-00-1*) Altitude.

All You Ever Wanted to Know about Zoning... Sheldon W. Damsky & James A. Coon. Ed. by Patricia Salkin. (Illus.). 195p. (Orig.). (C). 1989. pap. text ed. 55.00 (*0-8113-0000-5*) NY Plan Fed.

All You Have in Common. Dara Wier. LC 84-70179. (Poetry Ser.). 64p. 1984. 16.95 (*0-88748-004-7*); pap. 9.95 (*0-88748-005-5*) Carnegie-Mellon.

***All You Need Is a Friend.** Mary Engelbreit. (Illus.). 1995. 4.95 (*0-8362-0782-3*) Andrews & McMeel.

All You Need Is Ears. George Martin. (Illus.). 288p. 1982. pap. 12.95 (*0-312-02044-9*) St Martin.

All You Need Is Ears. George Martin & Jeremy Hornsby. (Illus.). 288p. 1994. pap. 13.95 (*0-312-11482-6*) St Martin.

All You Need to Know. Donald Passman. 1994. 25.00 (*0-685-68780-5*) S&S Trade.

All You Need to Know about Bidding. Terence Reese & David Bird. (Illus.). 128p. 1993. 24.95 (*0-575-05378-X*, Pub. by V Gollancz UK) Trafalgar.

***All You Need to Know about Copyrights & Trademarks.** David M. Monchan. 105p. 1994. 29.95 (*1-57002-035-3*); pap. 19.95 (*0-614-03065-X*) Univ Publng Hse.

All You Need to Know about Dinosaurs. Mark Norell. LC 91-21701. (Illus.). 96p. (J). (gr. 2-9). 1991. 13.95 (*0-8069-8396-5*) Sterling.

All You Need to Know about Joint Replacement. W. B. Maguire. (C). 1990. pap. 24.00 (*0-86439-101-3*, Pub. by Boolarong Pubns AT) St Mut.

All You Need to Know about Microcomputers: The Small Business Manager's Advisory. Shirley Daniels. LC 79-64577. (Illus.). 144p. 1979. pap. text ed. 9.95 (*0-89914-003-3*) Third Party Pub.

All You Need to Know about Play. Terence Reese & David Bird. 128p. 1994. 24.95 (*0-575-05670-3*, Pub. by V Gollancz UK) Trafalgar.

***All You Need to Know about Play.** Terence Reese & David Bird. LC 94-45165. (Master Bridge Ser.). 120p. 1995. pap. 9.95 (*0-395-72861-4*) HM.

All You Need to Know about the Lottery: Play to Win. M. N. Manougian. LC 91-3240. (Illus.). 114p. 1991. 12.95 (*0-931541-23-9*); pap. 5.95 (*0-931541-24-7*) Mancorp Pub.

All You Need to Know about the Music Business. Donald S. Passman. 1991. pap. 24.95 (*0-671-76139-0*) S&S Trade.

All You Need to Know about the Music Business. 2nd ed. Donald S. Passman. 1994. 25.00 (*0-671-88304-6*) S&S Trade.

***All You Need to Know Before Buying a Home.** Wasfi Youssef. (Illus.). 360p. (Orig.). 1995. pap. 19.95 (*0-9632423-1-8*) Alpha Pub.

All You Really Need to Know to Interpret Arterial Blood Gases. Lawrence Martin. (Illus.). 224p. 1992. pap. 23.95 (*0-8121-1572-4*) Williams & Wilkins.

***All You Wanted to Know about Mathematics but Were Afraid to Ask Vol. 1: Mathematics Applied to Science.** Louis Lyons. (Illus.). 240p. (C). 1995. write for info. (*0-521-43465-3*); pap. write for info. (*0-521-43600-1*) Cambridge U Pr.

***All You Who Labor: Work & the Sanctification of Daily Life.** Stefan Wyszynski. LC 94-46757. 190p. (ENG & POL.). 1995. 16.95 (*0-918477-26-3*) Sophia Inst Pr.

All You Who Sleep Tonight. Vikram Seth. LC 90-50627. 80p. 1991. 7.00 (*0-679-73025-7*, Vin) Random.

Alla Breve. Carl Engel. LC 71-128238. (Essay Index Reprint Ser.). 1977. 23.95 (*0-8369-1919-X*) Ayer.

Alla en el Pesebre. Guillermo Woggon. Tr. by Nola Cranberry. (Libros Para Colorear Ser.). (Illus.). 16p. (SPA.). (J). (ps-2). 1987. reprint ed. pap. 1.40 (*0-311-38562-1*) Casa Bautista.

***Alla Scoperta Dei Dinosauri.** Alice Jablonsky. Tr. by DigiPro Staff. (Comes to Life Bks.). 16p. (ITA.). (J). (ps-2). 1994. write for info. (*1-57234-000-2*) YES Ent.

Alla Tratoria: More than One Hundred Eighty Recipes from Italian Chefs. Lori Carangelo. 1991. pap. 10.95 (*0-89594-450-2*) Crossing Pr.

***Alladin & the Lamp.** Illus. by Jonathon Heap. 1993. 8.95 (*0-86685-589-0*) Intl Bk Ctr.

Allagash. Lew Dietz. LC 78-8326. (Illus.). 264p. 1978. reprint ed. pap. 9.95 (*0-945980-34-5*) Nrth Country Pr.

Allagash Abductions: Undeniable Evidence of Alien Intervention. Raymond E. Fowler. Ed. by Lisa Oister. LC 93-17654. (Illus.). 376p. (Orig.). 1993. Casebound. 23.95 (*0-926524-23-2*, Wild Flower Pr); boxed 16.95 (*0-926524-22-4*, Wild Flower Pr) Blue Wtr Pubng.

Allagash Incident. Jack Weiner & Charles Rak. Ed. by Mark Martin et al. (Illus.). 32p. (Orig.). 1993. pap. 2.95 (*1-56862-020-9*) Tundra MA.

Allagash, Maine's Wild & Scenic River. Dean Bennett. LC 94-14451. (Illus.). 112p. 1994. 35.00 (*0-89272-332-7*) Down East.

***Allah Created Everything.** C. Alta. (Illus.). 28p. (J). (gr. 1-3). 1995. 14.95 (*1-884187-09-9*) AMICA Pub Hse.

***Allah Created Everything.** C. Alta. Ed. by Rafiah Khokhar. LC 94-71172. (Illus.). 28p. (J). (ps-2). 1995. pap. 14.95 (*1-884187-04-8*) AMICA Pub Hse.

***Allah O Akbar: A Journey Through Militant Islam.** Abbas Magnum. (Illus.). 320p. (C). 1994. 60.00 (*0-7148-3162-X*, Pub. by Phaidon Press UK) Chronicle Bks.

Allah Transcendant: Studies in the Structure & Semiotics of Islamic Philosophy, Theology & Cosmology. Ian R. Netton. 448p. (C). 1994. pap. 29.95 (*0-7007-0287-3*, Pub. by Curzon Pr UK) Humanities.

Allahu Akbar. Edward Nash. (Illus.). 500p. (Orig.). 1988. 29.95 (*0-918266-21-1*); pap. 15.00 (*0-918266-20-3*) Smyrna.

Allamvezetok Titkos Levelei Az 1944 Ev Elotti Es Az 1944 Evbol see Secrete Correspondences of the Leaders of Governments in the Year Nineteen Forty-Four & Earlier Years

Allan & the Ice-Gods: A Tale of Beginnings. H. Rider Haggard. Ed. by R. Reginald & Douglas Menville. LC 75-46274. (Supernatural & Occult Fiction Ser.). 1976. lib. bdg. 26.95 (*0-405-08132-4*) Ayer.

Allan Armitage on Perennials. Allan Armitage. LC 92-16353. (Burpee Expert Gardener Ser.). 1993. 18.00 (*0-13-095225-7*, P-H Gardening) P-H Gen Ref & Trav.

Allan Armitage on Perennials. Allan Armitage. (Burpee Expert Gardener Ser.). (Illus.). 176p. 1993. bds. 18.00 (*0-671-84722-8*, P-H Gardening) P-H Gen Ref & Trav.

Allan Bakke Versus Regents of the University of California, 6 vols., Set. Council on Legal Education Opportunity Staff. Ed. by Alfred A. Slocum. LC 78-3573. 1978. lib. bdg. 264.00 (*0-379-20297-2*) Oceana.

Allan Borushek's Pocket Calorie & Fat Counter. Allan Borushek. 1992. pap. 4.95 (*0-9587991-1-3*) A Borushek.

***Allan Created Everything.** C. Alta. (Illus.). 28p. (J). (gr. 1-3). 1995. bds. 4.95 (*1-884187-02-1*) AMICA Pub Hse.

Allan Greenberg. Ed. by Allan Greenberg & Richard Economakis. (Architectural Monographs: No. 33). (Illus.). 144p. (Orig.). 1995. pap. 38.00 (*1-85490-262-8*, Academy Edits) St Martin.

Allan Houser: Ha-o-zous. Barbara H. Perlman. LC 86-26605. (Illus.). 266p. (C). 1991. reprint ed. 75.00 (*1-56098-102-4*) Smithsonian.

Allan Kardec's Doctrine of Spiritism: A Phenomenological Study. Juan J. Santiago. 97p. 1988. write for info. (*0-318-64713-3*) Ed Astrolabio.

Allan McCollum. Ed. by William S. Bartman & Miyoshi Barosh. (Explores the Work of Artists in Mid-Career Ser.). (Illus.). 80p. 1995. pap. text ed. 25.00 (*0-923183-14-0*) ART Pr CA.

Allan McCollum. Allan McCollum & Thomas Lawson. (Illus.). 64p. 1993. pap. 25.00 (*0-932183-14-X*) ART Pr CA.

Allan McCollum. Allan McCollum. (Illus.). 68p. 1988. 35.00 (*3-88375-100-6*, Pub. by Walther Konig GW) Dist Art Pubs.

Allan Pinkerton: America's First Private Eye. Richard Wormser. (Illus.). 119p. (YA). (gr. 5 up). 1990. 19.95 (*0-8027-6964-0*); lib. bdg. 18.85 (*0-8027-6965-9*) Walker & Co.

***Allan Pinkerton: The Original Private Eye.** Judith P. Josephson. LC 95-13222. (J). 1996. write for info. (*0-8225-4923-9*, Lerner Publctns) Lerner Group.

***Allan Quatermain.** H. Rider Haggard. Ed. by Dennis Butts. (The World's Classics Ser.). (Illus.). 336p. 1995. pap. 8.95 (*0-19-282297-7*) OUP.

Allan Quatermain. H. Rider Haggard. reprint ed. lib. bdg. 19.95 (*0-89190-712-2*, Aeonian Pr) Amereon Ltd.

Allan Quatermain. H. Rider Haggard. 1994. reprint ed. lib. bdg. 29.95 (*1-56849-286-3*) Buccaneer Bks.

Allan Ramsay. Alastair Smart. (Illus.). 176p. 1993. pap. 49.50 (*0-903598-19-1*, Pub. by Natl Port Gall UK) Antique Collect.

Allan Ramsay. Alastair Smart. (Illus.). 320p. (C). 1992. text ed. 75.00 (*0-300-05690-7*) Yale U Pr.

Allan Ramsay. William H. Smeaton. LC 77-144486. reprint ed. 29.50 (*0-404-08599-7*) AMS Pr.

Allan "Rocky" Lane Book. 184p. 1990. 20.00 (*0-944019-09-9*) Empire NC.

***Allan Sekula: Fish Story.** Benjamin Buchloh. (Illus.). 186p. Date not set. 65.00 (*3-928762-28-1*) Dist Art Pubs.

Allan Wexler: Table-Building-Landscape & Proposals for a Picnic Area. Rachel R. Lafo. (Illus.). 8p. (Orig.). 1992. pap. 1.00 (*0-945506-10-4*) DeCordova Mus.

Allan's Wife: With Hunter Quatermain's Story, A Tale of Three Lions, & Long Odds. H. Rider Haggard. Ed. by R. Reginald. LC 80-8671. (Forgotten Fantasy Library: Vol. 24). 240p. 1981. lib. bdg. 27.00x (*0-89370-523-3*) Borgo Pr.

Allcanplay: Music for People Who Don't Read Music. Mike Weinberg. (Orig.). (gr. 6 up). 1985. audio, pap. 12.95 (*0-933073-00-3*) Allcanplay.

Alle Kunstler-War-Revolution-Weimar: German Expressionist Prints, Drawings, Posters & Periodicals from the Robert Gore Rifkind Foundation. Ida K. Rigby. LC 83-60977. (Illus.). 118p. 1987. pap. 18.75 (*0-916304-62-0*) SDSU Press.

Alle Mesholim Fun, 2 vols., Set. Dubner Magid. 19.50 (*0-88482-720-8*) Hebrew Pub.

***Allegan County: A Bibliography.** (Illus.). 40p. (Orig.). 1994. pap. 6.00 (*1-877703-08-7*) Pavilion Pr.

***Allegany County & Its People: A Centennial Memorial History of Allegany County, Also, Histories of the Towns of the County.** Ed. by Georgia D. Merrill. (Illus.). 951p. 1995. reprint ed. lib. bdg. 95.00 (*0-8328-4707-0*) Higginson Bk Co.

Allegany County, Maryland Rural Cemeteries. Genealogical Society of Allegany County, Maryland Staff. 264p. 1990. 25.00 (*0-9627264-0-0*) McClain.

Allegations of Police Torture in Chicago, Illinois. 1990. pap. 2.00 (*0-685-53239-9*) Amnesty Intl USA.

Alleged Discrepancies of the Bible. John W. Haley. 480p. 1984. pap. text ed. 6.99 (*0-88368-157-9*) Whitaker Hse.

Alleged Imagery Errors. Brian Madison. (C). 1992. pap. text ed. 10.95 (*0-913412-56-2*) Brandon Hse.

***Alleged Transnational Criminal: The Second Biennial International Criminal Law Seminar.** International Criminal Law Seminar Staff. Ed. by Richard D. Atkins. LC 95-12468. 1995. write for info. (*0-7923-3409-4*, Pub. by M Nijhoff) Kluwer Ac.

Allegemeiner Bildniskatalog, 14 Vols. H. W. Singer. 1972. pap. 1,120.00 (*0-8115-3501-0*) Periodicals Srv.

Allegeries A-Z. Tova Navarra & Myron Lipkowitz. LC 93-33379. 352p. 1994. 40.00 (*0-8160-2824-9*) Facts on File.

***Alleghany County, Virginia Marriages, 1822-1854.** John Vogt & T. William Kethley, Jr. 120p. 1994. lib. bdg. 47.00 (*0-8095-8267-8*); pap. 20.00 (*0-8095-8505-7*) Borgo Pr.

Allegheny Captive. Caroline Bourne. 1990. mass mkt. 4.50 (*0-8217-3138-6*) Zebra.

Allegheny Cemetery: A Romantic Landscape in Pittsburgh. Walter C. Kidney. Ed. by Louise K. Ferguson. LC 90-62613. (Illus.). xvi, 156p. 1991. 34.95 (*0-916670-14-7*) Pitt Hist & Landmks Found.

Allegheny County Archives, Vol. 4. K. T. McFarland. 157p. 1991. text ed. 19.95 (*1-55856-068-8*) Closson Pr.

Allegheny County, PA Archives, Vol. 1. K. T. McFarland. 185p. 1991. text ed. 19.95 (*1-55856-052-1*) Closson Pr.

Allegheny County, PA Archives, Vol. 2. K. T. McFarland. 136p. 1990. text ed. 19.95 (*1-55856-065-3*) Closson Pr.

Allegheny County, PA Archives, Vol. 3. K. T. McFarland. 174p. 1991. text ed. 19.95 (*1-55856-067-X*) Closson Pr.

Allegheny County, PA Archives, Vol. 5. K. T. McFarland. 117p. 1991. text ed. 19.95 (*1-55856-069-6*) Closson Pr.

Allegheny County, PA Archives, Vol. 6. K. T. McFarland. 167p. 1991. text ed. 19.95 (*1-55856-060-2*) Closson Pr.

Allegheny County, PA Archives, Vol. 8: Partition Dockets 4-7, 1873-1884. K. T. McFarland. 127p. 1994. text ed. 19.95 (*1-55856-166-8*) Closson Pr.

Allegheny County, Pa. Cemeteries, Vol. II. Ed. by Sharon Kraynek. 147p. (Orig.). pap. text ed. 10.00 (*0-933227-50-7*) Closson Pr.

Allegheny County, Pa. Cemeteries, Vol. VI. Sharon Kraynek. 69p. (Orig.). per. 7.00 (*0-933227-14-0*) Closson Pr.

Allegheny County, Pa. Cemeteries, Vol. IX. Sharon Kraynek. 185p. (Orig.). 1985. per. 14.00 (*0-933227-10-8*) Closson Pr.

Allegheny County, Pa. Cemeteries, Vol. XII. Comp. by Sharon Kraynek. 137p. (Orig.). 1988. pap. text ed. 10.00 (*0-933227-77-9*) Closson Pr.

Allegheny County, Pa. Cemetery Records, Vol. X. Ed. by Sharon Kraynek. 106p. per., pap. text ed. 9.00 (*0-933227-28-0*) Closson Pr.

Allegheny County, Pa. Cemetery Records, Vol. XIII. Ed. by Sharon Kraynek. 112p. 1989. pap. text ed. 9.00 (*1-55856-021-1*) Closson Pr.

Allegheny County, Pa. Court of Common Pleas Minute Clerks' Manual: Civil Division. Daniel Valluzzi. 70p. 1984. 4.00 (*0-685-15097-6*, NERO-158) Natl Ctr St Courts.

Allegheny County, Pa. Court of Common Pleas Minute Clerks' Manual: Criminal Division. Daniel Valluzzi. 187p. 1984. 11.00 (*0-685-15098-4*, NERO-159) Natl Ctr St Courts.

Allegheny County, Pa. Orphans' Court Management Review. T. K. Farley et al. 92p. 1989. 6.00 (*0-685-33606-9*, NERO-227) Natl Ctr St Courts.

Allegheny Ecstasy. Caroline Bourne. 1990. mass mkt. 4.50 (*0-8217-2957-8*) Zebra.

Allegheny General: Portrait of an Urban Medical Center. Ed. by Mary J. Bent et al. 1991. 40.00 (*0-9628790-0-2*) Allegheny Health.

Allegheny-Lima's Finest. rev. ed. Gene Huddleston & Tom Dixon. Ed. by Robert L. Hundman. LC 88-81151. (Illus.). 246p. 1988. 28.50 (*0-945434-03-0*) Hundman Pub.

Allegheny Passage: Churches & Families of Western Maryland & Virginia Church of the Brethren 1752-1990. Emmert F. Bittinger. LC 90-60242. (Illus.). 880p. 1990. 45.00 (*0-929539-66-4*, 1166, Penobscot Pr) Picton Pr.

Allegheny Portage Railroad. Sylvester Welch. (Illus.). 26p. (C). 1993. pap. text ed. 2.00 (*0-939631-65-2*) Thomas Publications.

Allegheny River: Watershed of a Nation. Photos by Jim Schafer. (Keystone Bks.). (Illus.). 320p. 1992. 45.00 (*0-271-00836-9*) Pa St U Pr.

Allegiances. Adelyn Bonin. (Illus.). 352p. 1993. pap. 12.95 (*1-56474-036-6*) Fithian Pr.

Allegmeine SS. Robin Lumsden. (Men-at-Arms Ser.). (Illus.). 48p. 1993. pap. 11.95 (*1-85532-358-3*, 9237, Pub. by Osprey UK) Stackpole.

Allegoria und Anagoge bei Didymos dem Blinden von Alexandria. Wolfgang A. Bienert. (Patristische Texte und Studien Ser.: Vol. 13). xii, 188p. (C). 1972. 52.30x (*3-11-003715-7*) De Gruyter.

Allegoriae Iliades Acc. Pselli Allegoriae. Tzetza. Ed. by Boissonade. viii, 414p. 1967. reprint ed. write for info. (*0-318-71056-0*, Pub. by Georg Olms GW) Lubrecht & Cramer.

Allegorical & Metaphorical Language in the Autos Sacramentales of Calderon. M. Frances McGarry. LC 79-94165. (Catholic University of America. Studies in Romance Languages & Literatures: No. 16). reprint ed. 23.00 (*0-404-50316-0*) AMS Pr.

Allegorical Epic: Essays in Its Rise & Decline. Michael Murrin. LC 79-20832. 1980. lib. bdg. 23.00 (*0-226-55402-3*) U Ch Pr.

Allegorical Imagery: Some Mediaeval Books & Their Posterity. Rosemond Tuve. LC 65-14312. (Illus.). 474p. reprint ed. pap. 135.10 (*0-8357-6009-X*, 2034298) Bks Demand.

***Allegorical Impulse in the Works of Julien Gracq: History As Rhetorical Enactment in le Rivage des Syrtes & un Balcon en Foret.** Carol J. Murphy. LC 95-2416. (Studies in the Romance Languages & Literatures: No. 250). 1995. write for info. (*0-8078-9254-8*) U of NC Pr.

An Asterisk (*) at the beginning of an entry indicates that the title is appearing in BIP for the first time.

An Asterisk (*) at the beginning of an entry indicates that the title is appearing in BIP for the first time.

201

A

Allergy & Inflammation. Ed. by A. Barry Kay. 1987. text ed. 154.00 (0-12-402745-8) Acad Pr.

Allergy & Inflammation Nineteen Eighty-Eight: From Gene Cloning to Clinical Practice - Journal: International Archives of Allergy & Applied Immunology, Vol. 88, Nos. 1 & 2. Ed. by A. Sehon. (Illus.). 260p. 1989. pap. 96.00 (3-8055-4988-1) S Karger.

Allergy & Molecular Biology: Proceedings of the International Symposium on Allergy & Molecular Biology, Laguna Niguel, CA, U. S. A., 11-12 April 1988. Ed. by A. Said El Shami & T. G. Merrett. (Advances in the Biosciences Ser.: No. 74). (Illus.). 444p. 1989. 155.00 (0-08-036883-2, Pergamon Pr) Elsevier.

***Allergy, Asthma, & Immunology from Infancy to Adulthood: Management in Infants, Children, & Adults.** 3rd ed. Warren Bieman et al. (Illus.). 784p. 1995. text ed. 115.00 (0-7216-5587-4) Saunders.

Allergy; Audiology. Jack B. Anon & Aaron Thornton. (Current Opinion in Otolaryngology & Head & Neck Surgery Ser.). (Illus.). 216p. (Orig.). 1994. pap. text ed. write for info. (1-85922-631-0) Current Science.

Allergy Baker. 3rd ed. Carol Rudoff. LC 89-85111. (Illus.). 128p. 1990. pap. 8.95 (0-944569-00-5) Allergy Pubns.

Allergy Cookbook. Ruth R. Shattuck. 1986. pap. 5.99 (0-451-16517-9, Sig) NAL-Dutton.

Allergy Cookbook: Recipes Free from Eggs, Milk, Cheese, Butter, Wheat Flour, Chocolate, Salt, Sugar, Baking Powder, & Cornflower. Patricia Carter. LC 93-1969. (Orig.). 1993. 15.00 (0-88734-629-4) Players Pr.

Allergy Cookie Jar. Carol Rudoff. LC 85-60322. (Illus.). 128p. 1985. pap. 7.95 (0-9616708-3-5) Allergy Pubns.

Allergy Cooking with Ease: The No Wheat, Milk, Eggs, Corn, Soy, Yeast, Sugar, Grain & Gluten Cookbook. Nicolette M. Dumke. 320p. 1992. pap. 12.95 (0-914984-42-X) Starburst.

Allergy Cures Your Allergist Never Mentioned. Sterling R. Booth, Jr. LC 80-20698. 1989. 22.95 (0-87949-191-4) Ashley Bks.

Allergy Encyclopedia. Ed. by Craig T. Norback. 258p. 1981. pap. 7.95 (0-318-13534-5) Asthma & Allergy.

Allergy Encylopedia. Ed. by Asthma & Allergy Foundation of America Editors & Craig T. Norback. (Mosby Medical Library). (Illus.). 336p. 1981. pap. 8.95 (0-452-25629-1, Z5629, Plume) NAL-Dutton.

Allergy-Free Cooking: How to Survive the Elimination Diet & Eat Happily Ever After. Eileen Yoder. LC 86-32136. 224p. 1987. pap. 13.41 (0-201-09797-4) Addison-Wesley.

***Allergy-Free Eating.** Liz Reno & Joanna Devrais. 400p. 1995. pap. 14.95 (0-89087-745-9) Celestial Arts.

Allergy Free Vegetarian Cookbook. Claude A. Frazier & Dara Llewellyn. LC 94-12369. 136p. (Orig.). 1994. pap. 12.00 (0-87573-033-7) Jain Pub Co.

Allergy Gourmet: A Collection of Wheat-Free, Milk-Free, Egg-Free, Corn-Free & Soy-Free Recipes. Carol Rudoff. LC 83-61902. (Illus.). 225p. 1983. pap. 12.95 (0-930048-11-3) Allergy Pubns.

Allergy in Children. 15p. 0.50 (0-318-13535-3) Asthma & Allergy.

Allergy Oven. Carol Rudoff. LC 88-70472. (Allergy Kitchen Ser.: Vol. 3). (Illus.). 112p. (Orig.). 1988. pap. 7.95 (0-9616708-9-4) Allergy Pubns.

Allergy Plants. Mary Jelks. 64p. 18.95 (0-911977-12-0); pap. 9.95 (0-911977-04-X) World FL.

***Allergy Products Directory.** Carol Rudoff. Ed. by Joann Blessing-Moore. 1995. 34.95 (0-944569-02-1) Allergy Pubns.

***Allergy Products Directory Vol. 1: Controlling Your Environment.** Carol Rudoff. Ed. by Joann Blessing-Moore. LC 95-75930. 288p. (ENG & SPA.). 1995. pap. 34.95 (0-944569-03-X) Allergy Pubns.

***Allergy Products Directory Vol. 2: Asthma Resources Directory.** Carol Rudoff. Ed. by Joann Blessing-Moore. LC 95-75929. 256p. (ENG & SPA.). 1995. pap. 29.95 (0-944569-05-6) Allergy Pubns.

***Allergy Products Directory Vol. 3: Allergy Asthma Finding Help.** Carol Rudoff. Ed. by Joann Blessing-Moore. LC 95-79543. 240p. (ENG & SPA.). 1995. pap. 29.95 (0-944569-04-8) Allergy Pubns.

***Allergy Products Directory Vol. 4: Protecting Your Skin.** Carol Rudoff. Ed. by Joseph F. Fowler, Jr. LC 95-75928. 160p. 1995. pap. 19.95 (0-944569-06-4) Allergy Pubns.

Allergy Self-Help Book: A Complete Guide to Nondrug Relief of Asthma, Hay Fever, Headaches, Fatigue, Digestive Problems & over 50 Other Allergy-Related Problems. Prevention Magazine Editors & Sharon Faelten. LC 83-11197. 384p. 1983. 21.95 (0-87857-458-1, 05-121-0) Rodale Pr Inc.

Allergy Self-Help Cookbook: Over 325 Natural Foods Recipes, Free of Wheat, Milk, Eggs, Corn, Yeast, Sugar & Other Common Food Allergens. Marjorie H. Jones. 400p. 1992. pap. 14.95 (0-87596-109-6) Rodale Pr Inc.

Allergy Self-Help Cookbook: Over 325 Natural Foods Recipes Free of Wheat, Milk, Eggs, Corn, Yeast, Sugar & Other Common Foods Allergens. Marjorie H. Jones. LC 94-7391. 1994. reprint ed. write for info. (0-517-12002-X, Pub. by Wings Bks) Random Hse Value.

Allergy Shots. Robert B. Litman. LC 92-70081. 254p. (Orig.). 1993. pap. text ed. 9.95 (0-918921-04-X) Ivy League Pr.

***Allergy Sourcebook: Everything You Need to Know.** Merla Zellerbach. LC 94-43948. 240p. 1995. 25.00 (1-56565-208-8) Lowell Hse.

Allergy Survival Guide & Cookbook to Your Good Health. Carolyn Stone & Janice Beima. 251p. 1988. 19.95 (0-9622246-0-X) C C & Co Pub.

Allerlei zum Lesen. Herman Teichert & Lovette Teichert. 204p. (GER.). (C). 1992. pap. text ed. write for info. (0-669-20143-X); Text shrinkwrapped with free student cassette. pap. text ed. write for info. (0-669-27640-5) Heath.

Alles Beginnt im Positiven Denken. Herbert L. Beierle. 1981. 10.00 (0-940480-14-X) UNI Press.

Alles Gute! Basic German for Communication. Jeanine Briggs & John E. Crean. LC 81-23417. 350p. (C). 1983. text ed. write for info. (0-394-32872-8); write for info. (0-394-32873-6); write for info. (0-394-33028-5); write for info. (0-394-33013-7) Random.

Alles Gute! Basic German for Communication. 2nd ed. Jeanine Briggs & John E. Crean. (C). 1986. student ed 12.95 (0-685-10328-5); 11.50 (0-685-10329-3) McGraw.

Alles Gute! Basic German for Communication. 3rd ed. Jeanine Briggs et al. 1990. text ed. write for info. (0-07-540826-0) McGraw.

Alles Gute! Basic German for Communication. 3rd ed. Jeanine Briggs et al. 1990. student ed 29.95 (0-07-540830-9); pap. text ed. 12.61 (0-07-540827-9); Incl. 1 tapescript. audio 100.00 (0-07-540832-5); write for info. (0-07-909499-6); write for info. (0-07-540831-7); write for info. (0-07-909500-3) McGraw.

Alles Gute! Basic German for Communication. 4th ed. Jeanine Briggs et al. LC 93-36233. 1994. text ed. write for info. (0-07-007864-5) McGraw.

Alles Gute: Basic German for Communication. 4th ed. Jeanine Briggs et al. 1994. pap. text ed. write for info. (0-07-007866-1) McGraw.

Alles Gute: Basic German for Communication. 4th ed. Jeanine Briggs et al. 1994. pap. text ed. write for info. (0-07-007867-X) McGraw.

Alles Gute: Companion Guide. 1989. 13.25 (3-468-96870-1); teacher ed 38.95 (3-468-96890-6); student ed 19.95 (3-468-96880-9) Langenscheidt.

Alles in Allem. Jeanine Briggs & Beate T. Engel-Doyle. 1994. pap. text ed. write for info. (0-07-007832-7); pap. text ed. write for info. (0-07-007833-5) McGraw.

Alles in Allem: An Intermediate German Course: Grammar. Jeanine Briggs & Beate Engel-Doyle. LC 94-4402. (ENG & GER.). 1995. pap. text ed. write for info. (0-07-007837-8) McGraw.

Alleviating Soil Fertility Constraints to Increase Crop Production in West Africa. Ed. by A. Uzo Mokwunye. (Developments in Plant & Soil Sciences Ser.). 264p. (C). 1991. lib. bdg. 129.00 (0-7923-1221-X) Kluwer Ac.

Alleviation of Poverty under Structural Adjustment. Lionel Demery & Tony Addison. 48p. 1987. 6.95 (0-8213-0956-0, 10956) World Bank.

Alley. abr. ed. Robert A. Bimson. 120p. 1994. pap. 6.95 (1-56901-325-X) NW Pub.

***Alley Alligator's Awesome Smile.** Timothy E. McNutt, Sr. (Illus.). (J). (ps). 1994. pap. text ed. 3.95 (0-9642475-0-X) T E McNutt.

Alley Cat. Yves Beauchemin. (C). 1989. 39.00 (0-948353-18-X, Pub. by Oldcastle Bks UK) St Mut.

Alley Cat on the Page. (Chapbook Series II: No. 1). 40p. 1980. pap. 3.00 (1-880649-07-1) Writ Ctr Pr.

Alley in Chicago: Biography of Jack Egan. Margery Frisbie. LC 91-61105. 300p. (Orig.). 1991. pap. 13.95 (1-55612-463-5, LL1463) Sheed & Ward MO.

***Alley Kat Blues.** Karen Kijewski. LC 94-35200. 1995. 22.95 (0-385-46852-0) Doubleday.

Alley Life in Washington: Family, Community, Religion, & Folklife in the City, 1850-1970. James Borchert. LC 80-12375. (Blacks in the New World Ser.). (Illus.). 352p. 1982. pap. 12.95 (0-252-01003-5) U of Ill Pr.

Alley of Flashing Spears & Other Stories. Donn B. Byrne, pseud. LC 70-103501. (Short Story Index Reprint Ser.). 1977. 19.95 (0-8369-3243-9) Ayer.

Alley Oop. V. T. Hamlin. Ed. & Intro. by Frank Stack. LC 90-44079. (Illus.). 156p. 1990. 25.00 (0-87816-111-2); pap. 13.95 (0-87816-112-0) Kitchen Sink.

Alley Oop: The Sawalla Chronicles. V. T. Hamlin. Ed. by Herb Galewitz. (U. S. Classics Ser.). (Illus.). 80p. (Orig.). 1983. pap. 5.95 (0-912277-02-5) K Pierce Inc.

Alley Oop, Vol. 2: The Mystery of the Sphinx. V. T. Hamlin. Ed. & Intro. by Frank Stack. LC 91-40079. (Illus.). 160p. 1991. 25.00 (0-87816-137-6); pap. 13.95 (0-87816-138-4) Kitchen Sink.

Alley Strewn Phrases. Bill Miller. 56p. (Orig.). 1986. pap. 5.00 (0-940584-04-2) Gull Bks.

Alley Urchin. large type ed. Josephine A. Cox. 544p. 1994. 21.95 (0-7089-3039-5) Ulverscroft.

***Alleyn & Others.** Ngaio Marsh. 1995. pap. 10.95 (1-55882-028-0) Intl Polygonics.

Alleyn Papers: A Collection of Original Documents Illustrative of the Life & Times of Edward Alleyn & of the Early English Stage. Edward Alleyn. LC 79-113543. reprint ed. 37.50 (0-404-00329-X) AMS Pr.

***Alleys & Back Buildings of Galveston.** Ellen Beasley. (Illus.). 300p. 1995. 39.95 (0-89263-328-X) Rice Univ.

Alleys of Eden. Robert O. Butler. LC 93-28540. 256p. 1994. pap. 11.00 (0-8050-3141-3, Owl) H Holt & Co.

Alleys of Eden. Robert O. Butler. 256p. 1994. 25.00 (0-8050-3199-5) H Holt & Co.

Alleys of the Heart. Robert M. Petersen. 130p. 1988. 16.95 (0-938493-11-6) Hulogosi Inc.

Allez Jouer Ailleurs. Pascal Bruckner. 256p. (FRE.). 1989. pap. 12.95 (0-7859-2109-5, 2070381072) Fr & Eur.

ALLG Australian Law Librarians' Group Newsletter. LC 92-33113. 1992. 225.00 (0-89941-808-2, 307660) W S Hein.

Allgemeine Deutsche Bibliothek, 118 vols. Ed. by Friedrich Nicolai. reprint ed. write for info. (0-318-71727-1, Pub. by Georg Olms GW) Lubrecht & Cramer.

Allgemeine Deutsche Seeversicherungs Bedingungen. 80p. (GER.). 1985. pap. 15.40x (3-11-010413-X) De Gruyter.

Allgemeine Geomorphologie: Methodik - Grundvorstellungen - Ausblick auf den Landschaftshaushalt. Hanna Bremer. (Illus.). 450p. (GER.). 1989. pap. text ed. 40.95 (3-443-01026-1, Pub. by Gebrueder Borntraeger GW) Lubrecht & Cramer.

Allgemeine Hydrogeologie. Grundwasserhaushalt. G. Matthess & K. Ubell. (Lehrbuch der Hydrogeologie Ser.: Vol. 1). (Illus.). 438p. (GER.). 1983. text ed. 77.00 (3-443-01005-9, Pub. by Gebrueder Borntraeger GW) Lubrecht & Cramer.

Allgemeine Hydrologie. Quantitative Hydrologie. 1990. A. Baumgartner & J. J. Liebscher. (Lehrbuch der Hydrologie Ser.: Vol. 1). (Illus.). 673p. (GER.). 1990. text ed. 105.00 (3-443-30001-4, Pub. by Gebrueder Borntraeger GW) Lubrecht & Cramer.

Allgemeine Krankheitsbezeichnungen im Corpus Hippocraticum: Bedeutung und Gebrauch von Nousos und Nosema. Gerd Preiser. (Ars Medica, Abt. 2, Griechisch Lateinische Medizin Ser.). (C). 1976. text ed. 97.75 (3-11-001830-6) De Gruyter.

Allgemeine Litteratur der Musik. Johann N. Forkel. xxiv, 540p. 1962. reprint ed. write for info. (0-318-71779-4, Pub. by Georg Olms GW) Lubrecht & Cramer.

Allgemeine Methodenlehre der Statistik, Pt. 1. 6th ed. Johann Pfanzagl. 254p. (GER.). 1983. 17.55 (3-11-009674-9) De Gruyter.

Allgemeine Musikalische Zeitung, mit Besonderer Rucksich auf den Osterreichischen Kaiserstaat 1817-1824, 2 vols., Set. Ed. by H. Robert Cohen. (Repertoire International de la Presse Musicale Ser.). (GER.). 1992. lib. bdg. 240.00 (0-8357-2218-X) Univ Microfilms.

Allgemeine Mythologie und Ihre Ethnologischen Grundlagen. Paul Ehrenreich. Ed. by Kees W. Bolle. LC 77-79125. (Mythology Ser.). 1978. reprint ed. lib. bdg. 37.95 (0-405-10536-3) Ayer.

Allgemeine Plastische Chirurgie see Handbuch der Plastischen Chirurgie

Allgemeine Staatengeographie. Martin Schwind. (Lehrbuch der Allgemeinen Geographie Ser. Vol. 12: Vol. 8). (Illus.). xxii, 585p. (C). 1972. 72.35 (3-11-001634-6) De Gruyter.

Allgemeine und Anorganische Chemie: Ein Lehrbuch fuer Studenten mit Nebenfach Chemie. 3rd ed. Erwin Riedel. (Illus.). x, 346p. (GER.). 1985. pap. text ed. 37.70x (3-11-010269-2) De Gruyter.

Allgemeine Wiener Musik-Zeitung, 4 vols. Ed. by H. Robert Cohen. (Repertoire International de la Presse Musicale Ser.). 1990. 480.00 (0-8357-0892-6) Univ Microfilms.

Allgemeiner Portrait Katalog. Wilhelm E. Drugulin. (GER.). 1972. reprint ed. 92.00 (0-685-07030-1) Periodicals Srv.

Allgemeiner Teil und Einfuehrung in den Speziellen Teil see Atlas der Plastischen Chirurgie

Allgemeines Bibliographisches Lexikon, 2 vols., Set. Friedrich A. Ebert. 1965. reprint ed. write for info. (0-318-71768-9, Pub. by Georg Olms GW) Lubrecht & Cramer.

Allgemeines Bucherlexikon Oder Vollstandiges Verzeichnis Aller Von 1700 Bix Ende 1892 Erschienenen Bucher, 19 vols., Set. Wilhelm Heinsius. reprint ed. write for info. (0-318-71798-0, Pub. by Georg Olms GW) Lubrecht & Cramer.

Allgemeines Gelehrten-Lexicon. Christian G. Jocher. 1961. reprint ed. write for info. (0-318-70764-0, Pub. by Georg Olms GW) Lubrecht & Cramer.

Allgemeines Gelehrten-Lexicon, 4 vols., Set. Christian G. Jocher. 1961. reprint ed. write for info. (0-318-71918-5, Pub. by Georg Olms GW) Lubrecht & Cramer.

Allgemeines Historisches Kunstler-Lexikon. Gottfried J. Dlabacz. xii, 1752p. 1973. reprint ed. write for info. (3-487-05014-5, Pub. by Georg Olms GW) Lubrecht & Cramer.

Allgemeines Kunstler Lexikon. Collet's Staff. 1024p. 1983. 545.00 (0-317-57196-6, Pub. by Collets UK) St Mut.

***Allgemeines Kunstlerlexikon: Benech-C.** 750p. 1994. 295.00 (3-598-22749-3) K G Saur.

Allgemeines Kunstlerlexikon: Biographical Dictionary of Artists. Incl. Vol. 1. A-Alanson. 744p. 1991. lib. bdg. 240.00 (3-598-22741-8); Vol. 2. Alanson-Alvarez. 743p. 1991. lib. bdg. 240.00 (3-598-22742-6); Vol. 3. Alvarez-Angelin. 755p. 1991. lib. bdg. 240.00 (3-598-22743-4); Vol. 4. Angelin-Ardon. 736p. 1991. lib. bdg. 240.00 (3-598-22744-2); Vol. 5. Ardos-Avogaro. 748p. 1991. lib. bdg. 240.00 (3-598-22745-0); Vol. 6. Avogaro-Barbieri. 736p. 1992. lib. bdg. 240.00 (3-598-22746-9); Vol. 7. Barbieri-Bayona. 750p. 1993. lib. bdg. 240.00 (3-598-22747-7); Vol. 8. Bayona- 750p. 1993. lib. bdg. 250.00 (3-598-22748-5); Set lib. bdg. write for info. (0-318-69470-0) U Pubns Amer.

Allgemeines Lexikon der Bildenden: Kunstler Von Der Antike Bis Zur Gegenwart, 37 vols., Set. Ulrich Theime & Felix Becker. 1983. 9,990.00 (0-317-57199-0, Pub. by Collets UK) St Mut.

***Allgemeines Lexikon der Bildenden Kunstler, 25 vols.** Ulrich Thieme. (GER.). Date not set. 2,395.00 (0-7859-8354-6, 3423059079) Fr & Eur.

Allgemeines Repertorium der Mineralogischen, Bergwerks- und Salzwerkswissenschaftlichen Literatur. Christoph W. Gatterer. Vols. I-II. reprint ed. write for info. (0-318-71783-2, Pub. by Georg Olms GW) Lubrecht & Cramer.

Allgemeines Repertorium der Mineralogischen, Bergwerks- und Salzwerkswissenschaftlichen Literatur, Vol. 1. Christoph W. Gatterer. reprint ed. Von der Mineralogie Uberhaupt. write for info. (0-318-71784-0, Pub. by Georg Olms GW) Lubrecht & Cramer.

Allgemeines Sachregister Uber die Wichtigsten Deutschen Zeitund Wochenschriften, 2 vols., Set. Johann H. Beutler & Johann C. Gutsmuth. 1976. reprint ed. write for info. (3-487-05934-7, Pub. by Georg Olms GW) Lubrecht & Cramer.

Allgemeines Verwaltungsarchiv, Archiv der Republik, Vienna. Ed. by Loren Mikoletsky. LC 94-45841. (Archives of the Holocaust Ser.: Vol. 21). 435p. 1995. 125.00 (0-8240-6465-8) Garland.

Allgemeinpraxis: Das Zentrum der Psychosozialen Grundversorgung? Gottlieb Duttweiler Institut Staff. 97p. (GER.). 1984. pap. 6.00 (0-89192-363-2) Interbk Inc.

Alli Gator Gets a Bump on His Nose. Margaret Z. Searcy. LC 78-61369. (Illus.). (J). (gr. 2-4). 1978. 7.50 (0-916620-20-4) Portals Pr.

Alliance Against Hitler: The Origins of the Franco-Soviet Pact. William E. Scott. LC 62-20214. (Duke Historical Publications). 312p. reprint ed. pap. 89.00 (0-8357-8900-4, 2026215) Bks Demand.

Alliance & Classification among the Lamet see Lamet: Hill Peasants in French Indochina

Alliance & Labor Songster. Illus. by Vincent Leopold. LC 74-30660. (American Farmers & the Rise of Agribusiness Ser.). 1975. reprint ed. 16.95 (0-405-06837-9) Ayer.

Alliance Capitalism: The Social Organization of Japanese Business. Michael L. Gerlach. LC 92-16619. 350p. 1993. 35.00 (0-520-07688-5) U CA Pr.

Alliance for Change: A Plan for Community Action on Adolescent Drug Abuse. James F. Crowley. LC 84-71356. (Illus.). 226p. (Orig.). 1984. pap. 8.95 (0-9613416-0-2) Comm Intervention.

Alliance for Murder: The Nazi-Ukrainian Nationalist Partnership in Genocide. Ed. by B. F. Sabrin. (Illus.). 320p. 1992. 21.95 (0-9627613-0-3) Sarpedon.

Alliance for Murder: The Nazi-Ukrainian Nationalist Partnership in Genocide. B. F. Sabrin. (Illus.). 290p. 1990. 21.95 (1-56171-020-2) Sure Sellers.

Alliance for Progress: Past, Present, & Future. Ed. by L. Ronald Scheman. LC 88-6035. 297p. 1988. text ed. 52.95 (0-275-92763-6, C2763, Praeger Pubs) Greenwood.

Alliance for Progress: Problems & Perspectives. Ed. by John C. Oreier. LC 62-18508. 166p. reprint ed. pap. 47.40 (0-8357-5319-0, 2020765) Bks Demand.

Alliance, Illinois. Dave Etter. 240p. 1983. 14.95 (0-933180-43-8) Spoon Riv Poetry.

Alliance in Eskimo Society: American Ethnological Society Proceedings, 1971. Ed. by D. L. Guemple. LC 84-45507. 1988. reprint ed. pap. 45.00 (0-404-62665-3) AMS Pr.

Alliance Israelite Universelle & the Jewish Communities of Morocco, 1862-1962. Michael M. Laskier. LC 82-5892. (Modern Jewish History Ser.). 384p. 1984. 64.50 (0-87395-656-7); pap. 21.95 (0-87395-655-9) State U NY Pr.

Alliance of Divine Offices. Hamon L'Estrange. LC 71-172316. (Library of Anglo-Catholic Theology: No. 12). reprint ed. 27.50 (0-404-52104-5) AMS Pr.

Alliance of Iron & Wheat in the Third French Republic, 1860-1914: Origins of the New Conservatism. Herman Lebovics. LC 87-21386. 240p. 1988. text ed. 32.50 (0-8071-1350-6) La State U Pr.

Alliance of Musick, Poetry & Oratory. Anselm Bayly. (Anglistica & Americana Ser.: Vol. 108). vi, 384p. 1989. reprint ed. 63.70 (3-487-09068-6, Pub. by Georg Olms GW) Lubrecht & Cramer.

Alliance or Compliance: Implications of the Chilean Experience for the Catholic Church in Latin America. Virginia M. Bouvier. LC 83-960. (Foreign & Comparative Studies Program, Latin American Ser.: No. 3). (Orig.). 1983. pap. text ed. 7.00 (0-915984-94-6) Syracuse U Foreign Comp.

Alliance Policy in the Cold War. Ed. by Arnold Wolfers. LC 76-42310. 314p. 1976. reprint ed. text ed. 45.00 (0-8371-9275-7, WOAP, Greenwood Pr) Greenwood.

***Alliance Response to Nuclear Weapons Proliferation: Deterrence, Defense, & Cooperative Options.** L. Paul Bremer et al. (Institute for Foreign Policy Analysis Special Report Ser.). 130p. (Orig.). 1995. pap. 11.95 (1-57488-044-6) Brasseys Inc.

Alliance Security: NATO & the No-First-Use Question. Ed. by John D. Steinbruner & Leon V. Sigal. LC 83-72566. (Studies in Defense Policy). 222p. 1983. 29.95 (0-8157-8118-0); pap. 10.95 (0-8157-8117-2) Brookings.

Alliance Strategy & Navies: The Evolution & Scope of NATO's Maritime Dimension. Robert Jordan. 256p. 1990. text ed. 49.95 (0-312-04827-0) St Martin.

Alliance under Tension: The Evolution of South Korean-U. S. Relations. Chung-In Moon et al. 229p. (C). 1988. text ed. 63.00 (0-8133-0835-6) Westview.

Alliance Within the Alliance? Franco-German Military Cooperation & the European Pillar of Defense. David G. Haglund. 213p. (C). 1991. pap. text ed. 48.00 (0-8133-0976-X) Westview.

Alliances: Strategies for Building Integrated Delivery Systems. Goldstein & McKell. 336p. 0994. 175.00 (0-8342-0531-9, 20602) Aspen Pub.

Alliances: Strategies for Building Integrated Delivery Systems. Douglas E. Goldstein. 336p. 1994. ring bd. 175.00 (0-8342-0602-1) Aspen Pub.

Alliances & Coalitions: Your Key to Personal & Business Success. Edward Levin. 170p. 1984. text ed. 15.95 (0-07-037283-7) McGraw.

Alliances & Small Powers. Robert L. Rothstein. LC 68-28401. (Institute of War & Peace Studies). 1968. text ed. 50.00 (0-231-03113-0) Col U Pr.

Alliances & the Third World. George Liska. LC 68-17254. (Washington Center of Foreign Policy Research. Studies in International Affairs: No. 5). 71p. reprint ed. pap. 25.00 (0-8357-5320-4, 2023128) Bks Demand.

An Asterisk (*) at the beginning of an entry indicates that the title is appearing in BIP for the first time.

***Alliances in International Construction.** (Illus.). 153p. (Orig.). (C). 1994. pap. 65.00x (*0-7881-1355-0*) Diane Pub.

Allianzen und Vertrage Zwischen Frankischen und Islamischen Herrschern Im Vorderen Orient: Eine Studie Uber das Zwischenstaatliche Zusammenleben Vom 12. Bis Ins 13. Jahrhundert. Michael A. Kohler. (Studien zur Sprache, Geschichte und Kultur des Islamischen Orients: Vol. 12). (Illus.). xix, 478p. (GER.). (C). 1991. lib. bdg. 206.15 (*3-11-011959-5*) De Gruyter.

Allie. Nancy E. Wild. 1992. 18.95 (*0-533-10179-4*) Vantage.

***Allied & American Naval Operations in the European Theater, World War I.** Paolo E. Coletta. LC 95-46440. (Studies in American History: Vol. 7). (Illus.). 604p. 1996. text ed. 129.95 (*0-7734-8883-9*) E Mellen.

Allied Artists Checklist: The Feature Films & Short Subjects of Allied Artists Pictures Corporation, 1947-1978. Len D. Martin. LC 92-56665. (Illus.). 232p. 1993. lib. bdg. 45.00 (*0-89950-782-4*) McFarland & Co.

Allied Artists of America, Inc. Annual Exhibition 78. 64p. 1978. pap. 3.50 (*0-317-05506-2*) Allied Artists America.

Allied Battle Tanks. Yves Debay. (Europa Militaria Ser.: No. 4). (Illus.). 64p. 1990. pap. 15.95 (*1-872004-35-0*) Motorbooks Intl.

Allied Bomber War. Spellmount Ltd. Publishers Staff. (C). 1992. 125.00 (*0-685-60242-7*, Pub. by Spellmount UK) St Mut.

***Allied Bomber War 1939-45.** Maurice Harvey. (Illus.). 207p. 1994. 29.95 (*1-885119-07-0*) Sarpedon.

Allied Bomber War 1939-45. Maurice Harvey. 216p. (C). 1991. 125.00 (*0-946771-33-2*, Pub. by Spellmount UK) St Mut.

Allied Coastal Forces of World War II, Vol. 1. John Lambert & Al Ross. (Illus.). 256p. 1994. 43.95 (*1-55750-034-7*) Naval Inst Pr.

Allied Coastal Forces of World War II, Vol. 2. John Lambert & Al Ross. (Illus.). 256p. 1994. 43.95 (*1-55750-035-5*) Naval Inst Pr.

Allied Commanders of World War II. Anthony Kemp. (Men-at-Arms Ser.: No. 120). (Illus.). 48p. 1990. pap. 11.95 (*0-85045-420-4*, 9172, Pub. by Osprey Pubng Ltd UK) Stackpole.

Allied Escort Carriers. Kenneth Poolman. LC 88-60817. (Illus.). 272p. 1988. 34.95 (*0-87021-005-X*) Naval Inst Pr.

Allied Health Aptitude Tests (AHAT) Jack Rudman. (Admission Test Ser.: ATS-78). 1994. pap. 23.95 (*0-8373-5078-6*) Nat Learn.

Allied Health Education: Instructor Resource Guide. Center for Occupational Research & Development Staff. (Job Safety & Health Instructional Materials Ser.). 88p. (C). 1981. pap. text ed. 20.00 (*1-55502-034-8*) CORD Commns.

Allied Health Education Directory. 19th ed. 1993. 36.00 (*0-89970-436-0*, OP417593) AMA.

Allied Health Entrance Examination (AHEE) Jack Rudman. (Admission Test Ser.: ATS-79). 1994. pap. 23.95 (*0-8373-5079-4*) Nat Learn.

Allied Health Guide to Risk Management: Risk-Management for the Allied Health Practitioner. Ricardo Scott. 110p. (Orig.). 1994. write for info. (*1-883427-11-8*) Crnerstone GA.

Allied Health Professions. Arco Editorial Board Staff. 176p. 1993. pap. 18.00 (*0-671-84708-2*, Arco Test) P-H Gen Ref & Trav.

Allied Health Professions Admission Test. (Admission Test Ser.: ATS-99). 1994. 23.95 (*0-8373-5099-9*) Nat Learn.

Allied Health Professions Admission Test (AHPAT) Practice Examination Number 1 - Annotated Answers. David M. Tarlow. (Practice Examination Ser.). 1992. pap. 6.95 (*0-317-30190-X*) Datar Pub.

Allied Health Professions Admission Test (AHPAT) Practice Examination Number 3. David M. Tarlow. (Practice Examination Ser.). 40p. 1992. pap. 16.95 (*0-317-30193-4*) Datar Pub.

Allied Health Professions Admission Test (AHPAT) Practice Examination Number 5 - Annotated Answers. David M. Tarlow. (Practice Examination Ser.). 20p. 1992. pap. 4.95 (*0-317-30197-7*) Datar Pub.

***Allied Health Professions Admission Test (AHPAT) The Betz Guide.** Aftab Hassan et al. (Betz Guide Ser.: No. 4). (Illus.). 320p. (Orig.). (YA). (gr. 10 up). 1994. pap. 24.95 (*0-941406-36-9*) Betz Pub Co Inc.

Allied Health Professions Admissions Test (AHPAT) Practice Examination Number 1. David M. Tarlow. (Practice Examination Ser.). 40p. 1992. pap. 16.95 (*0-931572-30-4*) Datar Pub.

Allied Health Professions Admissions Test (AHPAT) Practice Examination Number 2. David M. Tarlow. (Practice Examination Ser.). 1992. pap. 16.95 (*0-931572-31-2*) Datar Pub.

Allied Health Professions Admissions Test (AHPAT) Practice Examination Number 3 - Annotated Answers. David M. Tarlow. 20p. 1992. pap. 4.95 (*0-317-30194-2*) Datar Pub.

Allied Health Professions Admissions Test (AHPAT) Practice Examination Number 4. David M. Tarlow. (Practice Examination Ser.). 40p. 1992. pap. 16.95 (*0-317-30195-0*) Datar Pub.

Allied Health Professions Admissions Test (AHPAT) Practice Examination Number 5. David M. Tarlow. (Practice Examination Ser.). 40p. 1992. pap. 16.95 (*0-317-30196-9*) Datar Pub.

Allied Health Professions Admissions Test (AHPAT) Student Guide. David M. Tarlow. (Student Guide Ser.). 140p. 1993. pap. 15.95 (*0-931572-29-0*) Datar Pub.

***Allied Health Professions Career Planning Guide.** Zubie Metcalf. (Planning Guide Ser.). 160p. (Orig.). (YA). (gr. 10 up). 1995. pap. 14.95 (*0-941406-53-9*) Betz Pub Co Inc.

Allied Health Reading Vocabulary Workbook. Frances McMurtray. 122p. 1978. pap. text ed. 7.95x (*0-89641-008-0*) American Pr.

Allied Health Services: Avoiding Crises. Institute of Medicine (U. S.) Staff. LC 88-37922. 360p. reprint ed. pap. 102.60 (*0-7837-5565-1*, 2045340) Bks Demand.

Allied in Victory. Con Sellers. Ed. by Paul McCarthy. (Men at Arms Ser.: No. 4). 320p. (Orig.). 1992. mass mkt. 5.99 (*0-671-66768-8*) PB.

Allied Military Fighting Knives & the Men Who Made Them Famous. 2nd ed. Robert A. Buerlein. LC 85-70203. (Illus.). 194p. (Orig.). 1985. 34.95 (*0-933489-00-5*); pap. 19.95 (*0-933489-01-3*) Amer Hist Found.

Allied Military Fighting Knives & the Men Who Made Them Famous. 2nd limited ed. Robert A. Buerlein. LC 85-70203. (Illus.). 194p. (Orig.). 1985. write for info. (*0-933489-02-1*) Amer Hist Found.

Allied Propaganda & the Collapse of the German Empire in 1918. George G. Bruntz. LC 72-4658. (International Propaganda & Communications Ser.). (Illus.). 246p. 1977. reprint ed. 19.95 (*0-405-04741-X*) Ayer.

Allied Relations in Iran, 1941-1945. David S. Painter. (Pew Case Studies in International Affairs). 50p. (C). 1986. pap. text ed. 2.50 (*1-56927-425-8*) Geo U Inst Dplmcy.

***Allied-Signal Inc. A Report on the Company's Environmental Policies & Practices.** (Illus.). 50p. (C). 1994. reprint ed. pap. text ed. 200.00x (*0-7881-0900-6*, Coun on Econ) Diane Pub.

Allies. Bob Shapiro & Edouard Mabe. Ed. by Allyn Brodsky. (Illus.). 80p. (Orig.). (gr. 7). 1983. pap. 6.95 (*0-9614082-1-9*) With Love Foun.

Allies, Adversaries, & International Trade. Joanne Gowa. LC 93-2178. 176p. 1993. text ed. 24.95 (*0-691-03355-2*) Princeton U Pr.

Allies Against Axis. Steins. 256p. (J). 1993. lib. bdg. write for info. (*0-8050-3165-0*) H Holt & Co.

Allies Against the Axis: World War II (1940-1950) Richard Steins. (First Person America Ser.). (Illus.). 64p. (J). (gr. 5-8). 1994. lib. bdg. 15.98 (*0-8050-2586-3*) TFC Bks NY.

Allies & Adversaries: The Impact of Managed Care on Mental Services. Ed. by Robert K. Schreter et al. LC 94-368. 1994. 36.00 (*0-88048-677-5*) Am Psychiatric.

***Allies & Aliens.** Roger M. Allen. 736p. 1995. mass mkt. 5.99 (*0-671-87658-9*) Baen Bks.

Allies & Arms Control. Ed. by Fen O. Hampson et al. LC 91-17666. (Perspectives on Security Ser.). 408p. 1991. text ed. 55.00 (*0-8018-4201-8*) Johns Hopkins.

Allies & East-West Economic Relations: Past Conflicts & Present Choices. Ed. by Henry R. Nau & Kevin F. Quigley. 42p. 1989. pap. 4.00 (*0-87641-306-8*) Carnegie Ethics & Intl Affairs.

Allies & Mates: An American Soldier with the Australians & New Zealanders in Vietnam, 1966-67. Gordon L. Steinbrook. LC 94-1287. 1995. 25.00 (*0-8032-4238-7*) U of Nebr Pr.

Allies at War: The Soviet, American, & British Experience, 1939-1945. Ed. by David Reynolds et al. LC 93-22957. (Franklin & Eleanor Roosevelt Institute Series on Diplomatic & Economic History: Vol. 7). 1994. text ed. 59.95 (*0-312-10259-3*) St Martin.

Allies for Enterprise: Highlights of the 1987-88 National Conferences on Higher Education & Economic Development. 142p. (Orig.). 1988. lib. bdg. 37.25 (*0-88044-097-X*); pap. text ed. 18.25 (*0-88044-096-1*) AASCU Press.

Allies in Adversity: The Frontline States in Southern African Security, 1975-1993. Gilbert M. Khadiagala. 380p. (C). 1994. text ed. 50.00 (*0-8214-1097-0*) Ohio U Pr.

Allies in Apartheid: Western Capitalism in Occupied Namibia. Ed. by Allan D. Cooper. LC 87-27016. 224p. 1988. text ed. 45.00 (*0-312-01197-0*) St Martin.

Allies in Crisis: Meeting Global Challenges to Western Security. Elizabeth D. Sherwood. LC 89-35260. 272p. (C). 1990. 30.00 (*0-300-04170-5*) Yale U Pr.

Allies in Educational Reform: How Teachers, Unions, & Administrators Can Join Forces for Better Schools. Jerome M. Rosow et al. LC 88-46095. (Education-Higher Education Ser.). 353p. 1989. 36.95x (*1-55542-158-X*) Work in Amer.

Allies in Healing: When the Person You Love Was Sexually Abused As a Child, a Support Book for Partners. Laura Davis. LC 90-56423. 256p. (Orig.). 1991. pap. 14.00 (*0-06-096883-4*, PL) HarpC.

Allies of a Kind: The United States, Britain, & the War Against Japan, 1941-1945. Christopher Thorne. LC 79-14921. (Illus.). 1979. reprint ed. pap. 13.95 (*0-19-520173-6*) OUP.

Allies on the Rhine, 1945-1950. Elena Skrjabina. (Soviet Union at War Ser.: Vol. 3). 171p. 1980. 37.95 (*0-8093-0939-4*) Transaction Pubs.

Allies or Adversaries? U. S. - European Relations in the Paul-Henri Spaak Lectures, Harvard University, 1985-1992. Harvard University, Center for International Affairs Staff. 248p. (Orig.). (C). 1993. lib. bdg. 56.00 (*0-8191-9053-5*) U Pr of Amer.

Alligator - Monarch of the Marsh. rev. ed. Connie Toops. (Illus.). (C). 1988. reprint ed. pap. 5.95 (*0-945142-00-5*) FL Natl Parks.

Alligator Alley. Jenna McKnight. (American Romance Ser.). 1993. mass mkt. 3.50 (*0-373-16512-9*, 1-16512-5) Harlequin Bks.

Alligator & the Everglades. Dave Taylor. (Animals & Their Ecosystems Ser.). (Illus.). 32p. (J). (gr. 3-4). 1990. lib. bdg. 15.95 (*0-86505-367-7*); pap. 7.95 (*0-86505-397-9*) Crabtree Pub Co.

Alligator & the Toothfairy. Jo-Anna Roberts. (Illus.). 56p. (J). (ps-2). 1991. 11.50 (*1-879212-00-5*) Desert Star Intl.

Alligator Arrived with Apples: A Potluck Alphabet Feast. Crescent Dragonwagon. LC 86-37. (Illus.). 40p. (J). (gr. k-3). 1987. text ed. 15.95 (*0-02-733090-7*, Mac Bks Young Read) S&S Childrens.

Alligator Arrived with Apples: A Potluck Alphabet Feast. Crescent Dragonwagon. LC 91-38490. (Illus.). 40p. (J). (gr. k-3). 1992. reprint ed. pap. 4.95 (*0-689-71613-3*, Aladdin Paperbacks) S&S Childrens.

Alligator at the Airport. Kaye Wiley. 1994. pap. 9.53 (*0-201-58818-8*) Addison-Wesley.

Alligator Dance. Janet Peery. LC 93-18694. (Southwest Life & Letters Ser.). 224p. (Orig.). 1993. 22.50 (*0-87074-353-8*); pap. 10.95 (*0-87074-366-X*) SMU Press.

Alligator Inventions. Dan Guillory. 64p. 1991. 14.95 (*0-935153-14-4*) Stormline Pr.

Alligator Man. Jack A. Kaplan. 1975. pap. 2.75 (*0-8222-0020-1*) Dramatists Play.

Alligator Mound: An Effigy or Symbolic Mound in Licking County, Ohio. Isaac Smucker. (Archaeology, Ohio History, Prehistoric Indians Ser.). (Illus.). 7p. 1994. reprint ed. pap. 1.30 (*1-56651-108-9*); reprint ed. spiral bd. 2.00 (*1-56651-109-7*) A W McGraw.

Alligator Mouse & Other Disasters. Rita Benson. LC 93-18052. (J). 1994. write for info. (*0-383-03674-7*) SRA Schl Grp.

Alligator Named...Alligator. Lois Grambling. (Illus.). 32p. (J). (ps-1). 1991. lib. bdg. 12.95 (*0-8120-6224-8*); pap. 5.95 (*0-8120-4756-7*) Barron.

Alligator Region River System: Murgenella & Cooper's Creeks; East, South & West Alligator Rivers & Wildman River see Survey of Tidal River Systems in the Northern Territory & Their Crocodile Populations: Monographs

Alligator Report. W. P. Kinsella. LC 85-17412. (Illus.). 125p. (Orig.). 1985. pap. 9.95 (*0-918273-10-2*) Coffee Hse.

Alligator Shoes. Arthur Dorros. LC 82-2409. (Unicorn Paperbacks Ser.). (Illus.). 24p. (J). (ps-00). 1988. pap. 3.95 (*0-525-44428-9*) Dutton Child Bks.

Alligator Shoes. Arthur Dorros. LC 82-2409. (Unicorn Paperbacks Ser.). (Illus.). (J). (ps-00). 1982. 3.95 (*0-525-44001-1*, Dutton) NAL-Dutton.

Alligator Snapping Turtle: Biology & Conservation. Peter C. Pritchard. LC 89-13935. (Illus.). 104p. 1989. pap. text ed. 29.95 (*0-89326-124-6*) Milwaukee Pub Mus.

Alligator Sticker Paper Doll. Judy M. Johnson. (Illus.). (J). (gr. k-3). 1994. pap. 1.00 (*0-486-27924-3*) Dover.

Alligator with a Toothache. Mary J. Wiles. (J). (ps-3). 1978. pap. 1.75 (*0-8198-0355-3*) Pauline Bks.

Alligator Wrestling & You: An Impractical Guide to an Impossible Sport. Louis Phillips. 96p. (Orig.). (J). (gr. 7-12). 1992. pap. 3.50 (*0-380-76303-6*, Camelot) Avon.

Alligators. Dick Bothwell. LC 62-52731. (Orig.). 1962. pap. 3.95 (*0-8200-0302-6*) Great Outdoors.

Alligators. Christine Butterworth. LC 90-9927. (Animal World Ser.). (Illus.). 32p. (J). (gr. 1-4). 1990. lib. bdg. 19.97 (*0-8114-2639-4*); pap. 3.95 (*0-8114-4608-5*) Raintree Steck-V.

Alligators. L. Martin. (Reptile Discovery Library). (Illus.). 24p. (J). (gr. k-5). 1989. lib. bdg. 11.94 (*0-86592-579-8*) Rourke Corp.

***Alligators.** Frank Staub. LC 94-39112. (Early Bird Nature Books Ser.). (J). 1995. write for info. (*0-8225-5300-7*) Lerner Group.

***Alligators.** Frank J. Staub. LC 94-39112. (Early Bird Nature Books Ser.). (J). 1995. write for info. (*0-8225-3007-4*) Lerner Group.

Alligators. John Updike. (Creative Short Stories Ser.). (J). (gr. 4-12). 1989. 13.95 (*0-88682-358-7*, 97211-098) Creative Ed.

Alligators: A Success Story. Patricia Lauber. LC 93-3302. (Illus.). 64p. (J). (gr. 2-4). 1994. 14.95 (*0-8050-1909-X*, Bks Young Read) H Holt & Co.

Alligators All Around. Maurice Sendak. (Illus.). 32p. (J). (ps-3). 1962. lib. bdg. 13.89 (*0-06-025530-7*) HarpC Child Bks.

Alligators All Around: An Alphabet. Maurice Sendak. LC 62-13315. (Trophy Picture Bk.). (Illus.). 32p. (J). (ps-3). 1991. pap. 3.95 (*0-06-443254-8*, Trophy) HarpC Child Bks.

Alligators All Around see Nutshell Library

Alligators & Crocodiles. Lesley Dow. (Great Creatures of the World Ser.). 72p. (YA). 1990. 17.95 (*0-8160-2273-9*) Facts on File.

Alligators & Crocodiles. Michael George. (Nature Books Ser.). (Illus.). 32p. (J). 1991. lib. bdg. 22.79 (*0-89565-720-1*) Childs World.

Alligators & Crocodiles. James E. Gerholdt. LC 94-14053. (Remarkable Reptiles Ser.). (J). 1994. lib. bdg. 13.99 (*1-56239-309-X*) Abdo & Dghtrs.

Alligators & Crocodiles. Malcolm Penny. 1991. 14.99 (*0-517-07012-X*) Random Hse Value.

Alligators & Crocodiles. Jim Rothaus. (Zoobooks Ser.). 24p. (J). (gr. 3). 1988. lib. bdg. 14.95 (*0-88682-220-3*) Creative Ed.

Alligators & Crocodiles. Lynn M. Stone. LC 89-9985. (New True Bks.). 48p. (J). (gr. k-4). 1989. lib. bdg. 12.90 (*0-516-01170-7*); pap. 4.95 (*0-516-41170-5*) Childrens.

Alligators & Crocodiles. Erik D. Stoops & Debbie L. Stone. LC 94-15691. (Illus.). 80p. (J). 1994. 16.95 (*0-8069-0422-4*) Sterling.

Alligators & Crocodiles. Wildlife Education, Ltd. Staff. (Zoobooks Ser.). (Illus.). 20p. (Orig.). (YA). (gr. 5 up). 1984. pap. 2.75 (*0-937934-25-9*) Wildlife Educ.

Alligators & Music. Donald Elliott. LC 84-13862. (Illus.). (J). (gr. 8). 1984. pap. 8.95 (*0-87645-118-0*) Gambit Inc Pubs.

Alligators & Others All Year Long: A Book of Months. Crescent Dragonwagon. LC 91-2831. (Illus.). 32p. (J). (gr. k-3). 1993. text ed. 14.95 (*0-02-733091-5*, Mac Bks Young Read) S&S Childrens.

Alligators in China. Fauvel. 1992. write for info. (*0-916984-25-7*) SSAR.

Alligator's Life History. McIlhenny. LC 76-6228. 1976. write for info. (*0-916984-01-X*); pap. write for info. (*0-916984-00-1*) SSAR.

Alligator's Life History. E. A. McIlhenny. 128p. 1987. pap. 7.95 (*0-89815-230-5*) Ten Speed Pr.

Alligators, Monsters & Cool School Poems. Addie M. Sanders. (Illus.). 80p. (Orig.). (J). (gr. 3-10). 1994. pap. 9.00 (*0-911943-38-2*) Leadership Pub.

Alligators to Zebras! Whole Language Activities for the Primary Grades. Elizabeth C. Stull. 352p. 1991. pap. text ed. 24.95 (*0-87628-150-1*) Ctr Appl Res.

Alligators to Zooplankton: A Dictionary of Water Babies. Les Kaufman & NEA Staff. (New England Aquarium Bks.). (Illus.). 64p. (J). (gr. 5-7). 1991. lib. bdg. 16.87 (*0-531-10995-X*) Watts.

Allingham Case Book. Margery Allingham. 18.95 (*0-89190-915-X*, Am Repr) Amereon Ltd.

Allingham Case-Book. Margery Allingham. 224p. 1993. 19.95 (*1-56723-000-8*) Yestermorrow.

Allingham Case-Book. 2nd ed. Margery Allingham. 240p. 1992. 3.95 (*0-88184-889-1*) Carroll & Graf.

***Allis-Chalmers Farm Equipment 1914-1985.** Norm Swinford. LC 94-72224. 384p. 1994. 39.75 (*0-929355-54-7*) Am Soc Ag Eng.

Allis-Chalmers Story. C. H. Wendel. LC 93-7694. (Crestline Ser.). 1993. reprint ed. 29.95 (*0-87938-828-5*) Motorbooks Intl.

Allis Chalmers Tractors. Andrew Morland & C. H. Wendel. (Illus.). 128p. 1992. pap. 19.95 (*0-87938-628-2*) Motorbooks Intl.

Allison & the Big Apple. Mallory Tarcher. (Adventurers, Inc Ser.: No. 4). 144p. 1994. pap. 3.50 (*0-8217-4767-3*) Zebra.

***Allison & the Sunken Treasure.** Mallory Tarcher. (Adventurers, Inc. Ser.: No. 8). 144p. 1995. mass mkt. 3.50 (*0-8217-4881-5*) Zebra.

Allison's Affair with the High School Principal. Ben Rowland. LC 92-239897. 141p. 1993. reprint ed. 21.95 (*0-9636632-0-8*) GI Pub.

Allison's Grandfather. large type ed. Linda Peavy. 40p. (J). (gr. 3-4). 1984. reprint ed. 9.50 (*0-317-01866-3*, J-00780-00) Am Printing Hse.

***Allison's Happy Summer.** Jonathan Roach. 1995. 8.95 (*0-8062-5264-2*) Carlton.

Allison's Shadow. Tracy Leddy. LC 82-61020. 124p. (Orig.). 1982. pap. 12.00 (*0-89142-040-1*) Sant Bani Ash.

All'Italiana. Rosaria D. Bhacca. Ed. by Cheryl J. Stevens. LC 81-84607. (Illus.). 133p. (Orig.). 1981. pap. 6.95 (*0-88127-001-6*) Oracle Pr LA.

Alliterations A-Z Potluck Poetry. Wanda S. Dieckow. 60p. 1993. 10.00 (*1-882560-10-8*) W Dieckow.

Alliterative Morte Arthure: A New Verse Translation. Valerie Krishna. LC 82-24838. 144p. (Orig.). 1983. pap. text ed. 18.50 (*0-8191-3036-2*) U Pr of Amer.

Alliterative Morte Arthure, The Owl & the Nightingale, & Five Other Middle English Poems: In a Modernized Version with Comments on the Poems & Notes. John C. Gardner. LC 73-7728. (Arcturus Books Paperbacks). 310p. 1973. pap. 19.95 (*0-8093-0648-4*) S Ill U Pr.

Alliterative Poem on the Deposition of King Richard Second. Ed. by Thomas Wright. LC 17-1185. (Camden Society, London. Publications, First Ser.: No. 3). reprint ed. 18.00 (*0-404-50103-6*, A17-1185) AMS Pr.

Alliterative Poetry of the Later Middle Ages: An Anthology. Ed. by Thorlac Turville-Petre. 261p. 1989. 39.95 (*0-8132-0674-X*); pap. 19.95 (*0-8132-0675-8*) Cath U Pr.

Alliterative Revival. Thorlac Turville-Petre. 152p. 1970. 63.00 (*0-85991-019-9*) Boydell & Brewer.

Alliterative Tradition in the Fourteenth Century. Ed. by Bernard S. Levy & Paul E. Szarmach. LC 80-28821. 227p. reprint ed. pap. 64.70 (*0-7837-0293-0*, 2040614) Bks Demand.

***Allitt Inquiry - Independent Inquiry Relating to Deaths & Injuries on Children's.** HMSO Staff. 140p. 1994. pap. 12.00 (*0-11-321714-5*, HM17145, Pub. by HMSO UK) UNIPUB.

Alliums: The Ornamental Onions. Dilys Davies. (Illus.). 168p. 1992. 29.95 (*0-88192-224-2*) Timber.

Alliums: The Ornamental Onions. Dilys Davies. (Illus.). 168p. 1993. pap. 22.95 (*0-88192-241-2*) Timber.

Allo Allo: The Complete War Diaries of Rene Artois. Rene Artois. (Illus.). 360p. (Orig.). 1992. pap. 10.95 (*0-563-36327-4*, BBC-Parkwest) Parkwest Pubns.

Allo la France. S. Dietiker & G. Burger. 256p. (Orig.). (C). 1985. pap. 28.95 (*0-8384-1292-0*) Heinle & Heinle.

Alloantigen System of Human Leucocytes & Platelets. Lili F. Aszodi. 336p. 1979. 120.00 (*0-569-08562-4*, Pub. by Collets UK) Pro-Am Music.

***Alloantigen Systems of Human Leukocytes & Platelets.** L. Fulop-Aszodi. 336p. (C). 1979. 90.00x (*963-05-1721-3*) St Mut.

Allocating Credit & Receivable Costs. Credit Research Foundation Staff. 16p. 1984. 40.00 (*0-939050-03-X*) Credit Res NYS.

***Allocating Health Care Resources: Biomedical Ethics Reviews, 1994.** Ed. by James M. Humber & Robert F. Almeder. LC 84-640015. (Contemporary Issues in Biomedicine, Ethics & Society Ser.). 223p. 1995. 44.50 (*0-89603-260-4*) Humana.

Allocation Models & Their Use in Economic Planning. A. R. Heesterman. LC 78-14694. 203p. 1971. lib. bdg. 65.50 (*90-277-0182-2*) Kluwer Ac.

An Asterisk (*) at the beginning of an entry indicates that the title is appearing in BIP for the first time.

Allocation of Corporate Indirect Costs. James M. Fremgen & Shu S. Liao. 103p. pap. 15.95 (*0-86641-006-6*, 81130) Inst Mgmt Account.

Allocation of Economic Resources. Moses Abramovitz et al. LC 59-7420. x, 244p. 1959. pap. 11.95 (*0-8047-0569-0*) Stanford U Pr.

Allocation of Income Within the Household. Edward P. Lazear & Robert T. Michael. (Illus.). 200p. 1988. 34.95 (*0-226-46966-2*) U Ch Pr.

Allocation of Industry in the Andean Common Market. Jan Ter Wengel. (Studies in Development & Planning: Vol. 11). 1980. lib. bdg. 49.50 (*0-89838-020-0*) Kluwer Ac.

Allocation of Road Capital in Two-Dimensional Space: A Continuous Approach. Tonu Puu. (Studies in Regional Science & Urban Economics: Vol. 5). 216p. 1979. 51.50 (*0-444-85324-3*, North Holland) Elsevier.

Allocation of Time & Goods over the Life Cycle. Gilbert R. Ghez & Gary S. Becker. (Studies in Human Behavior & Social Institutions: No. 6). 172p. 1975. 44.80 (*0-87014-514-2*) Natl Bur Econ Res.

Allocation of Time for Transit Bus Maintenance Functions. (National Cooperative Transit Research Program Synthesis Ser.: No. 4). 25p. 1984. 6.40 (*0-309-03865-0*) Transport Res Bd.

Allocation Problem: Part Two, Vol. 9. Arthur L. Thomas. (Studies in Accounting Research). 194p. 1974. 12.00 (*0-86539-021-5*) Am Accounting.

Allocation Problem in Financial Accounting Theory, Vol. 3. Arthur L. Thomas. (Studies in Accounting Research). 122p. 1969. 12.00 (*0-86539-015-0*) Am Accounting.

Allocations: Art for a Natural & Artificial Environment. Thomas McEvilley et al. (Illus.). 1992. 55.00 (*90-800914-2-1*) Dist Art Pubs.

Allochthonous Terranes. Ed. by J. F. Dewey et al. (Illus.). 150p. (C). 1991. 69.95 (*0-521-40461-4*) Cambridge U Pr.

Allografts in Orthopaedic Practice. Andrei A. Czitrom & Allan E. Gross. (Illus.). 240p. 1992. 75.00 (*0-683-02300-4*) Williams & Wilkins.

Alloimmunity: 1993 & Beyond. Ed. by Sandra T. Nance. 1993. text ed. 35.00 (*1-56395-025-1*) Am Assn Blood.

Allometry of Growth & Reproduction. Michael J. Reiss. (Illus.). 168p. (C). 1989. 54.95 (*0-521-36091-9*) Cambridge U Pr.

Allometry of Growth & Reproduction. Michael J. Reiss. (Illus.). 182p. (C). 1991. pap. 22.95 (*0-521-42358-9*) Cambridge U Pr.

Allons Voir. Bragger & Rice. 1992. pap. 32.95 (*0-8384-2136-9*) Heinle & Heinle.

Allons Voir. Bragger & Rice. 1992. 32.95 (*0-8384-3913-6*) Heinle & Heinle.

Allons Voir. Bragger & Rice. 1992. vhs 100.00 (*0-8384-2137-7*) Heinle & Heinle.

Allons-Y! Le Francais par Etapes. 2nd ed. J. Bragger & D. Rice. 1990. pap. 32.95 (*0-8384-2162-8*) Heinle & Heinle.

Allons-Y! Le Francais par Etapes. 3rd ed. 1992. audio, text ed. 49.95 (*0-8384-2621-2*) Heinle & Heinle.

Allons-Y! Le Francais par Etapes. 3rd ed. 1992. pap. 29.95 (*0-8384-2427-9*) Heinle & Heinle.

Allons-Y! Le Francais par Etapes. 3rd ed. 1992. vhs 100.00 (*0-8384-3914-4*) Heinle & Heinle.

Allos: Forty-One Writings by Forty-One Writers. Ed. by Kenneth Gaburo et al. LC 80-80809. (Illus.). 448p. (C). 1980. pap. 16.95 (*0-939044-26-9*) Lingua Pr.

***Allosaurus.** Janet Riehecky. LC 80-1693. (Illus.). 32p. (ENG & SPA.). (J). (ps-2). 1988. text ed. 21.36 (*1-56766-134-3*) Childs World.

Allosaurus. Janet Riehecky. LC 88-1693. (Dinosaurs Bks.). (Illus.). 32p. (ENG & SPA.). (J). (ps-2). 1988. lib. bdg. 21.36 (*0-89565-421-0*) Childs World.

Allosaurus. Wilson. (Dinosaur Library: Set II). (Illus.). 24p. (J). 1984. lib. bdg. 14.00 (*0-86592-206-3*) Rourke Enter.

Allosteric Enzymes. Ed. by Heroe. 1989. 230.00 (*0-8493-6854-5*, QP601) CRC Pr.

Allosteric Enzymes: Kinetic Behaviour. Boris I. Kurganov. Ed. by V. A. Yakovlev. Tr. by R. F. Brookes. LC 81-21861. (Illus.). 362p. reprint ed. pap. 103.20 (*0-8357-5321-2*, 2030526) Bks Demand.

Allosteric Modulation of Amino Acid Receptors: Therapeutic Implications. E. A. Barnard & E. Costa. (Fidia Research Foundation Symposium Ser.: Vol. 1). 422p. 1989. 101.00 (*0-88167-482-6*) Raven.

Allotment Movement in Britain. Denis M. Moran. (American University Studies: Geography: Ser. XXV, Vol. 1). 200p. (C). 1989. text ed. 44.50 (*0-8204-0812-3*) P Lang Pubs.

Allotments. R. P. Lister. (Illus.). (C). 1989. 75.00 (*1-85183-025-1*, Silent Bks) St Mut.

Allouez, New Allouez, & Bumbletown. (Copper Country Local History Ser.: Vol. 47). (Illus.). 132p. 1994. 3.00 (*0-942363-46-9*) C J Monette.

Allover Patterns for Designers & Craftsmen. Clarence P. Hornung. (Illus.). 96p. 1975. pap. 6.00 (*0-486-23179-8*) Dover.

Allover Patterns with Letter Forms. Jean Larcher. LC 85-4544. 48p. (Orig.). 1985. pap. 3.50 (*0-486-24908-5*) Dover.

Allow Divine Energy to Help You. George Snelling. 181p. pap. 4.95 (*0-934142-03-3*) Vancento Pub.

Allowable Stress Design of Simple Shear Connections. 1990. 16.00 (*1-56424-009-6*, S337) Am Inst Steel Construct.

Allowable Stress Design Specification for Structural Joints Using ASTM A325 or A490 Bolts. 48p. 1985. 5.00 (*1-56424-015-0*, S329) Am Inst Steel Construct.

Allowance for Loan & Lease Losses for Community Banks. Mikkalya W. Walton & James S. Watrous. Ed. by Shelley W. Geehr. LC 93-39456. (Illus.). 120p. (Orig.). 1993. pap. text ed. 37.00 (*1-57070-001-X*, 35041) Robt Morris Assocs.

***Alloway Strange: Alva Extranea de Virginia.** 2nd ed. Ed. by John R. Mayer. LC 90-148997. (Extraneus Ser.: Vol. III, Bk. X). (Illus.). xxiv, 256p. (C). 1994. pap. 22.00 (*0-9638665-3-2*) Arapacana Pr.

Allowing the Creator to Deal with the Creature: An Approach to the Spiritual Exercises of Ignatius of Loyola. William A. Barry. LC 94-16220. 128p. (Orig.). 1994. pap. 6.95 (*0-8091-3465-9*) Paulist Pr.

Alloy Eight Hundred: Proceedings of the Petten International Conference, the Netherlands, 14-16 March, 1978. Ed. by W. Betteridge et al. 1979. 100.00 (*0-444-85228-X*, North Holland) Elsevier.

***Alloy Finder.** cd-rom 1,200.00 (*0-614-03596-1*, 7542U) ASM Intl.

Alloy Phase Diagrams, ASM Handbook, Vol. 3. (Illus.). 512p. 1992. 147.00 (*0-87170-381-5*) ASM.

Alloy Phase Stability. Ed. by G. M. Stocks & A. Gonis. (C). 1989. lib. bdg. 211.50 (*0-7923-0142-0*) Kluwer Ac.

Alloy Phase Stability & Design. Ed. by G. M. Stocks et al. (MRS Symposium Proceedings Ser.: Vol. 186). 1991. text ed. 44.00 (*1-55899-075-5*) Materials Res.

Alloying Behavior & Effects in Concentrated Solid Solutions. Ed. by T. B. Massalski. LC 65-18398. (Metallurgical Society Conference Ser.: Vol. 29). 455p. reprint ed. pap. 129.70 (*0-8357-5322-0*, 2001517) Bks Demand.

Alloying Elements in Steel. 2nd ed. Harold W. Paxton & Edgar C. Bain. LC 65-29304. 301p. reprint ed. pap. 85.80 (*0-8357-5323-9*, 2026990) Bks Demand.

Alloys, IPNs, Liquid Crystals. 246p. 1991. 2,450.00 (*0-89336-602-1*, PO75U) BCC.

Alloys of Niobium. D. A. Prokoshin & E. V. Vasil'eva. 352p. 1965. text ed. 88.50 (*0-7065-0578-6*, Pub. by Keter Pub IS) Coronet Bks.

All's Fair. Anne Avery. 400p. (Orig.). 1994. pap. 4.99 (*0-505-51937-2*, Love Spell) Dorchester Pub Co.

All's Fair. Richard E. Wormser. LC 74-22825. (Labor Movement in Fiction & Non-Fiction Ser.). reprint ed. 20.00 (*0-404-58484-5*) AMS Pr.

***All's Fair: Love, War, & Running for President.** Mary Matalin & James Carville. 1995. pap. 13.00 (*0-684-80133-7*, Touchstone Bks) S&S Trade.

All's Fair - Come Love, Call My Name. Anne N. Reisser. 368p. 1990. pap. 3.95 (*0-8439-2978-2*) Dorchester Pub Co.

All's Faire. Pamela F. Service. 1993. mass mkt. 3.99 (*0-449-70421-1*) Fawcett.

All's Well. Joan McIntyre. (Illus.). 48p. 1981. 24.00 (*0-88014-040-2*) Mosaic Pr OH.

***All's Well Story from Boccaccio to Shakespeare.** fac. ed. Howard C. Cole. LC 81-2474. 159p. 1994. pap. 45.40 (*0-7837-7615-2*, 2047367) Bks Demand.

All's Well That Ends Well. Ed. by Barbara Everett. (New Penguin Shakespeare Ser.). 1981. mass mkt. 5.50 (*0-14-070720-4*, Penguin Classics) Viking Penguin.

All's Well That Ends Well. Ed. by A. L. Rowse. LC 85-678. (Contemporary Shakespeare Ser.: Vol. III). 124p. (Orig.). (C). 1985. pap. text ed. 3.45 (*0-8191-3917-3*) U Pr of Amer.

All's Well That Ends Well. Shakespeare. (Illus.). 128p. 1981. pap. 4.95 (*0-563-17874-4*, Pub. by BBC UK) Parkwest Pubns.

All's Well That Ends Well. William Shakespeare. LC 85-4167. (Airmont Shakespeare Ser.). (J). (gr. 9 up). 1968. pap. 0.60 (*0-8049-1022-7*, S22) Airmont.

All's Well That Ends Well. William Shakespeare. Ed. by Russell A. Fraser. (New Cambridge Shakespeare Ser.). (Illus.). 168p. 1986. 39.95 (*0-521-22150-1*); pap. 9.95 (*0-521-29365-0*) Cambridge U Pr.

All's Well That Ends Well. William Shakespeare. Ed. by Elizabeth Huddlestone & Sheila Innes. (School Shakespeare Ser.). (Illus.). 192p. (C). 1993. pap. 7.50 (*0-521-44583-3*) Cambridge U Pr.

All's Well That Ends Well. William Shakespeare. 1988. pap. 2.95 (*0-671-66923-0*) Folger.

All's Well That Ends Well. William Shakespeare. pap. 2.95 (*0-451-51944-2*, CJ1657, Sig Classics) NAL-Dutton.

All's Well That Ends Well. William Shakespeare. Ed. by Susan Snyder. LC 93-32341. (World's Classics; The Oxford Shakespeare Ser.). (Illus.). 256p. 1994. pap. 6.95 (*0-19-281459-1*) OUP.

All's Well That Ends Well. William Shakespeare. Ed. by J. L. Styan. LC 83-11246. (Shakespeare in Performance Ser.). (Illus.). 144p. 1988. text ed. 11.95 (*0-7190-0999-5*, Pub. by Manchester Univ Pr UK) St Martin.

All's Well That Ends Well. Ed. by Susan Snyder. LC 92-23243. (C). 1993. 45.00 (*0-19-812931-9*, Clarendon Pr) OUP.

All's Well That Ends Well. Sheldon Zitner. (Twayne's New Critical Introduction to Shakespeare Ser.: No. 10). 208p. 1989. pap. 13.95 (*0-8057-8719-4*, Twayne) Macmillan.

All's Well That Ends Well. Sheldon Zitner. (Twayne's New Critical Introduction to Shakespeare Ser.: No. 10). 208p. 1989. text ed. 22.95 (*0-8057-8718-6*, Twayne) Macmillan.

All's Well That Ends Well. rev. ed. William Shakespeare. 1965. pap. 3.95 (*0-451-52261-3*, Sig Classics) NAL-Dutton.

All's Well That Ends Well. 3rd ed. William Shakespeare. Ed. by George K. Hunter. (Arden Shakespeare Ser.). 1966. reprint ed. 49.95 (*0-416-47560-4*, NO.2440); reprint ed. pap. 8.95 (*0-416-49610-5*, NO.2441) Routledge Chapman & Hall.

All's Well That Ends Well & The Merry Wives of Windsor Notes. Denis Calandra. 71p. (Orig.). (C). 1985. pap. text ed. 4.50 (*0-8220-0004-0*) Cliffs.

***Allstar Hockey Activity Book.** Noah Ross & Julian Ross. (Illus.). 48p. (Orig.). (J). (gr. 4-8). 1990. pap. 5.95 (*0-919591-60-4*, Pub. by Polestar Bk Pubs CN) Orca Bk Pubs.

Alltaksverb im Blickpunkt. Kenneth M. Ralston & Mechtild Schwed. 1995. pap. text ed. write for info. (*0-07-051325-2*) McGraw.

Allumette Facile. David Goodis. 256p. (FRE.). 1987. pap. 10.95 (*0-7859-2536-8*, 2070378268) Fr & Eur.

Allure. Jan Butlin. 1992. mass mkt. 4.99 (*0-06-100352-2*, Harp PBks) HarpC.

Allure de Morand: Du Modernisme au Petainisme. Bruno Thibault. LC 92-64402. (Illus.). 166p. (FRE.). 1993. lib. bdg. 33.95 (*0-917786-90-4*) Summa Pubns.

***Allure of Bronze: Masterpieces from the Walters Art Gallery.** Joaneath Spicer. (Illus.). 30p. (Orig.). 1995. pap. write for info. (*0-911886-40-0*) Walters Art.

Allure of Discus. Herbert R. Axelrod & Bernd Degen. (Illus.). 192p. 1991. 59.95 (*0-86622-544-7*, TS-162) TFH Pubns.

***Allure of Gnosticism: The Gnostic Experience in Jungian Psychology & Contemporary Culture.** Ed. by Robert A. Segal et al. 250p. 1995. text ed. 38.95 (*0-8126-9277-2*) Open Court.

***Allure of Gnosticism: The Gnostic Experience in Jungian Psychology & Contemporary Culture.** Ed. by Robert A. Segal et al. 250p. 1995. pap. text ed. 17.95 (*0-8126-9278-0*) Open Court.

Allure of Love. large type ed. Honor Vincent. (Linford Romance Library). 285p. 1984. pap. 11.95 (*0-7089-6034-0*, Linford) Ulverscroft.

Allure of the Cat. Richard H. Gebhardt. 1992. 69.95 (*0-86622-194-8*, TS173) TFH Pubns.

Alluring Deceit. Melissa L. Jones. 320p. 1993. mass mkt. 3.99 (*0-8217-4411-9*) Zebra.

Alluring Imagery Details. Roger Stark. (C). 1992. pap. text ed. 14.95 (*0-913412-61-9*) Brandon Hse.

Alluring Lady. Meg-Lynn Roberts. 1992. mass mkt. 3.99 (*0-8217-3757-0*) Zebra.

Allusion: A Literary Craft. Allan H. Pasco. (Theory - Culture Ser.). 272p. (C). 1994. 55.00 (*0-8020-0449-0*) U of Toronto Pr.

Allusions -- Cultural, Literary, Biblical & Historical: A Thematic Dictionary. 2nd ed. Ed. by Laurence Urdang. 634p. 1986. 89.00 (*0-8103-1828-8*) Gale.

Allusions in Ulysses: An Annotated List. Weldon Thornton. LC 68-14359. ix, 554p. 1982. pap. 17.95 (*0-8078-4089-0*) U of NC Pr.

Alluvial Archaeology in Britain. Ed. by Stuart Needham & Mark G. Macklin. (Oxbow Monographs in Archaeology: No. 27). (Illus.). 276p. 1992. pap. 61.00 (*0-946897-52-2*, Pub. by Oxbow Bks UK) David Brown.

Alluvial Channel Data on PC. K. Mahmood et al. 1989. disk 350.00 (*0-318-41785-5*) WRP.

Alluvial Fans: A Field Approach. Ed. by Andrzej H. Rachocki & Michael Church. 391p. 1990. text ed. 255.00 (*0-471-91694-3*) Wiley.

Alluvial Fans: An Attempt at an Empirical Approach. Andrzej Rachocki. LC 80-42061. (Illus.). 171p. reprint ed. pap. 48.80 (*0-8357-3081-6*, 2039338) Bks Demand.

Alluvial Fans & Fan Deltas: An Exploration Guide. Fraser & Suttner. 223p. 1988. text ed. 42.00 (*0-13-023581-4*) P-H.

Alluvial Fans & Fan Deltas: An Exploration Guide. Gordon S. Fraser & Lee J. Suttner. (Illus.). 223p. 1986. 40.00 (*0-88746-096-8*) Intl Human Res.

Alluvial Prospecting & Mining. 2nd ed. S. Griffith. LC 60-11192. 1960. 104.00 (*0-08-009331-0*, Pub. by Pergamon Repr UK) Franklin.

Alluvial River Problems: Proceedings of the Third International Workshop on Alluvial River Problems, University of Roorkee, India, 2-4 March 1989. 340p. (C). 1989. text ed. 90.00 (*90-6191-958-4*, Pub. by A A Balkema NE) Ashgate Pub Co.

Alluvial Sedimentation. Ed. by M. Marzo & C. Puigdefabergas. LC 92-36455. (International Association of Sedimentologists Special Publication Ser.: No. 17). 1994. pap. write for info. (*0-632-03545-5*) Blackwell Sci.

Allversoehnung: Ein Transzendentaltheologischer Grundlegungsversuch. Hartmut Rosenau. (Theologische Bibliothek Toepelmann Ser.: No. 57). x, 544p. (GER.). 1993. lib. bdg. 163.10 (*3-11-013738-0*) De Gruyter.

Ally Versus Ally: America, Europe, & the Siberian Pipeline Crisis. Anthony J. Blinken. LC 86-25222. 206p. 1987. text ed. 55.00 (*0-275-92410-6*, C2410, Praeger Pubs); pap. text ed. 14.95 (*0-685-18009-3*, B2616, Praeger Pubs) Greenwood.

Allyl Compounds, Aldehydes, Epoxides & Peroxides. (IARC Monographs on the Evaluation of the Carcinogenic Risk of Chemicals to Humans: No. 36). 369p. 1985. pap. 42.00 (*92-832-1536-2*) World Health.

Allyn & Bacon Detecting & Correcting Series. Joyce S. Choate et al. 180p. 1989. Science. pap. 18.00 (*0-685-74174-5*, H21504) Allyn.

Allyn & Bacon Handbook. Leonard J. Rosen & Laurence Behrens. 864p. (C). 1992. text ed. 23.00 (*0-205-13347-9*) Allyn.

Allyn & Bacon Handbook. 2nd ed. Leonard J. Rosen & Laurence Behrens. LC 93-39768. 1994. text ed. 25.00 (*0-205-15327-5*) Allyn.

Allyn & Bacon Molecular Model Set for Organic Chemistry. 1983. write for info. (*0-205-08136-3*, 688136) P-H.

Allyn & Bacon Molecular Model Set for Stereochemistry. (Illus.). 1991. write for info. (*0-205-12886-6*, H28863) P-H.

Allyn & Bacon Reading Program: Pathfinder. large type ed. R. Ruddell et al. Incl. Level 8. Surprises & Prizes. (gr. 1). 1979. Text 84p. pap. 9.46 (*0-317-02066-8*, 4-0026); Level 8. Surprises & Prizes. (gr. 1). 1979. Wkbks., 2 vols., 264p. 29.37 (*0-317-04356-0*, 4-0027); Level 9. Upside & Down. 164p. (gr. 1). 1979. 22.19 (*0-317-02068-4*, 4-0028); Level 9. Upside & Down. 164p. (gr. 1). 1979. 33.55 (*0-317-04357-9*, 4-0029); Level 10. Inside & Out. 128p. (gr. 1-2). 1979. 19.25 (*0-317-02070-6*, 4-0031); Level 10. Inside & Out. 128p. (gr. 1-2). 1979. 37.73 (*0-317-04358-7*, 4-0030); Level 11. Moon Magic. 264p. (gr. 2). 1979. 33.83 (*0-317-02072-2*, 4-0032); Level 11. Moon Magic. 264p. (gr. 2). 1979. 33.55 (*0-317-04359-5*, 4-0033); Level 12. Riding Rainbow. 264p. (gr. 2-3). 1979. 33.85 (*0-317-02074-9*, 4-0034); Level 12. Riding Rainbow. 264p. (gr. 2-3). 1979. 33.55 (*0-317-04360-9*, 4-0035); Level 13. Sunshine Days. 356p. (gr. 3). 1979. 50.16 (*0-317-02076-5*, 4-0036); Level 13. Sunshine Days. 356p. (gr. 3). 1979. 37.73 (*0-317-04361-7*, 4-0037); Level 14. Handstands, 2 vols. 356p. (gr. 3-4). 1979. 50.16 (*0-317-02078-1*, 4-0038); Level 14. Handstands, 2 vols. 356p. (gr. 3-4). 1979. 41.81 (*0-317-04362-5*, 4-0039); Level 15. Person to Person, 2 vols. 288p. (gr. 4). 1979. 38.50 (*0-317-02080-3*, 4-0040); Level 15. Person to Person, 2 vols. 288p. (gr. 4). 1979. 31.46 (*0-317-04363-3*, 4-0041); Level 16. Free Rein, 2 vols. 288p. 1979. 38.50 (*0-317-02082-X*, 4-0042); Level 16. Free Rein, 2 vols. 288p. 1979. 31.46 (*0-317-04364-1*, 4-0043); Level 17. Majesty & Mystery, 2 vols. 352p. (gr. 5). 1979. 50.16 (*0-317-02084-6*, 4-0044); Level 17. Majesty & Mystery, 2 vols. 352p. (gr. 5). 1979. 31.46 (*0-317-04365-X*, 4-0045); Level 18. Standing Strong, 2 vols. 344p. (gr. 5-6). 1979. 44.33 (*0-317-02086-2*, 4-0046); Level 18. Standing Strong, 2 vols. 344p. (gr. 5-6). 1979. 31.46 (*0-317-04366-8*, 4-0047); Level 19. Widening Path, 2 vols. 344p. (gr. 6). 1979. 44.33 (*0-317-02088-9*, 4-0048); Level 19. Widening Path, 2 vols. 344p. (gr. 6). 1979. 31.46 (*0-317-04367-6*, 4-0049); (J). (gr. 1-6). 1979. reprint ed. write for info. (*0-318-66083-0*) Am Printing Hse.

Allyn & Bacon Workbook. 2nd ed. Kathleen S. Cain. LC 93-42555. 1994. pap. text ed. 15.00 (*0-205-15564-2*) Allyn.

Alma Amortalhada: Mario de Sa-Carneiro's Use of Metaphor & Image. Pamela Bacarisse. (Serie A: Monografias, CV). 191p. (C). 1984. 45.00 (*0-7293-0189-3*, Pub. by Tamesis Bks Ltd UK) Boydell & Brewer.

Alma at the Waters of Mormon. Sherrie Johnson. 1994. pap. 4.95 (*0-87579-855-1*) Deseret Bk.

Alma Brava. Carmen Chiesa. LC 91-77459. (Illus.). 62p. (C). 1992. 7.50 (*0-685-54728-0*) Editorial Academica.

Alma Lynne's Country Cross-Stitch. Alma Lynne. 1990. 24.95 (*0-8487-1014-2*) Oxmoor Hse.

Alma Lynne's Country Needlecrafts: From Cross-Stitch Bunnies to Easy Christmas Quilts, over 50 Projects to Warm Hearts & Homes. Ed. by Karen Bolesta. LC 94-13872. 1994. 26.95 (*0-87596-636-5*) Rodale Pr Inc.

Alma Lynnes Cross-Stitch for Special Occasions. LC 93-84607. 144p. 1993. 24.99 (*0-8487-1121-1*) Oxmoor Hse.

Alma Mahler: Or the Art of Being Loved. Francoise Giroud. Ed. & Tr. by R. M. Stock. (Illus.). 176p. 1992. 25.00 (*0-19-816156-5*) OUP.

Alma Mater: A College Homecoming. P. F. Kluge. LC 93-19823. (Illus.). 320p. 1993. 22.07 (*0-201-56793-8*) Addison-Wesley.

Alma Mater: Design & Experience in the Women's Colleges from Their Nineteenth-Century Beginnings to the 1930's. Helen L. Horowitz. LC 84-47506. (Illus.). 448p. 1984. 25.00 (*0-394-53439-5*) Knopf.

Alma Mater: Design & Experience in the Women's Colleges from Their Nineteenth-Century Beginnings to the 1930's. 2nd ed. Helen L. Horowitz. LC 93-4393. (Illus.). 448p. 1993. reprint ed. pap. 17.95 (*0-87023-869-8*) U of Mass Pr.

Alma Mater: The Gothic Age of the American College. Henry S. Canby. LC 75-1835. (Leisure Class in America Ser.). (Illus.). 1975. reprint ed. 23.95 (*0-405-06904-9*) Ayer.

Alma on the Mississippi, 1848-1932. Barbara Anderson-Sannes. Ed. by Michael Doyle et al. LC 80-68241. (Illus.). 198p. (Orig.). 1980. pap. 11.95 (*0-9604684-0-4*) Alma Hist Soc.

Alma Rose. Edith Forbes. LC 92-42985. 336p. (Orig.). 1993. pap. 10.95 (*1-878067-33-8*) Seal Pr Feminist.

ALMACA International Resource Directory. ALMACA Staff. pap. 5.00 (*0-318-22972-2*) ALMACA.

Almacen de Dios: Exodo, 16 Lecciones, Vol. 2. Bernice C. Jordan. (Pasos De Fe Ser.). (SPA.). 1961. teacher ed, pap. text ed. 3.95 (*0-86508-403-3*); 11.95 (*0-86508-404-1*) BCM Pubn.

Almadas & Alamos, Seventeen Eighty-Three to Eighteen Sixty-Seven. Albert Stagg. LC 77-74317. (Illus.). 183p. reprint ed. pap. 52.20 (*0-8357-5324-7*, 2029658) Bks Demand.

***Almain & Other Measures in England: Their History & Choreography.** Ian Payne. 220p. 1995. 59.95 (*0-85967-965-9*, Pub. by Scolar Pr UK) Ashgate Pub Co.

Almanac Branch. Bradford Morrow. 288p. 1992. pap. 8.95 (*0-393-30921-5*) Norton.

Almanac-Calendar Edition, 1992. Frank A. Taucher. 1992. pap. 109.00 (*1-879591-03-0*) Mkt Movements.

Almanac for Americans. Willis Thornton. 418p. 1993. reprint ed. lib. bdg. 44.00 (*1-55888-889-6*) Omnigraphics Inc.

Almanac for Computers, 1990. 100p. 1990. per., pap. text ed. 4.50 (*0-16-018420-7*, S/N 008-054-001) USGPO.

Almanac for Computers, 1991. Leroy E. Doggett & William J. Tangren. 100p. 1991. per., pap. 4.00 (*0-16-028552-6*) USGPO.

An Asterisk (*) at the beginning of an entry indicates that the title is appearing in BIP for the first time.

Almanac for Moderns. Donald C. Peattie. LC 79-90410. (Non Pareil Ser.). (Illus.). 416p. 1995. reprint ed. pap. 15.95 (*0-87923-314-1*) Godine.

Almanac for Twilight. Jack Matthews. (Classic Contemporaries Ser.). 1992. reprint ed. pap. 10.95 (*0-88748-143-4*) Carnegie-Mellon.

Almanac of America Cook Book. Nancy Otto. LC 86-90559. (Illus.). 263p. 1986. 16.95 (*0-9617435-0-6*) N L Otto.

Almanac of American Employers, 1994-95. rev. ed. Jack W. Plunkett. 1994. pap. 110.00 (*0-9638268-0-8*) Corp Jobs Outlk.

Almanac of American Government Jobs & Careers. Ronald L. Krannich & Caryl R. Krannich. 289p. 1991. 27.95 (*0-942710-45-2*); pap. 14.95 (*0-942710-39-8*) Impact VA.

Almanac of American Politics: 1990 Edition. rev. ed. Michael Barone. Ed. by Grant Ujifusa. (Illus.). 1500p. 1989. 56.95 (*0-89234-043-6*, Macmillan); pap. 44.95 (*0-89234-044-4*, Macmillan) Natl Journal.

Almanac of American Politics, 1988. Michael Barone. Ed. by Grant Ujifusa. (Illus.). 1500p. 1987. text ed. 42.95 (*0-89234-037-1*) Natl Journal.

Almanac of American Politics, 1994. Michael Barone. 1993. 59.95 (*0-89234-057-6*); pap. 48.95 (*0-89234-058-4*) Natl Journal.

Almanac of American Presidents: From 1789 to the Present. Thomas Connolly. (Illus.). 384p. 1991. 45.00 (*0-8160-2219-4*) Facts on File.

Almanac of American Women in the 20th Century. Judith Clark. (Illus.). 320p. (Orig.). 1987. pap. 15.95 (*0-685-18014-X*) P-H.

Almanac of Anniversaries. Kim Long. LC 92-28945. 1992. lib. bdg. 40.00 (*0-87436-675-5*) ABC-CLIO.

Almanac of Back Pain Treatments. Julie Zimmerman. LC 90-85650. (Illus.). 190p. (Orig.). 1991. pap. 9.95 (*1-879418-03-7*) Biddle Pub.

Almanac of British Politics. Robert Waller. LC 83-3100. 600p. 1983. text ed. 29.95 (*0-312-02136-4*) St Martin.

Almanac of British Politics. 3rd ed. Robert Waller. 640p. 1987. pap. 22.50 (*0-7099-2798-3*, Pub. by Croom Helm UK) Routledge Chapman & Hall.

Almanac of British Politics. 4th ed. Robert Waller. 640p. 1991. 89.95 (*0-415-06434-1*, A5868) Routledge.

Almanac of Business & Industrial Financial Ratios. Leo Troy. LC 72-181403. 373p. 1986. pap. text ed. 39.95 (*0-13-022963-6*, Busn) P-H.

Almanac of Business & Industrial Financial Ratios: 1989 Edition. Leo Troy. 432p. 1989. pap. text ed. 49.95 (*0-13-021312-8*) P-H.

Almanac of Business & Industrial Financial Ratios, 1987. Leo Troy. 416p. 1987. pap. text ed. 39.95 (*0-13-023045-6*) P-H.

Almanac of Business & Industrial Financial Ratios, 1990. Leo Troy. 1990. pap. 49.95 (*0-13-025800-8*) P-H.

Almanac of Business & Industrial Financial Ratios, 1991. 20th ed. Leo Troy. 432p. 1991. pap. 49.95 (*0-13-026451-2*, 130501) P-H.

Almanac of Business & Industrial Financial Ratios, 1993. Leo Troy. 1993. pap. 69.95 (*0-13-137449-4*) P-H.

***Almanac of Business & Industrial Ratios.** Leo Troy. 1995. pap. text ed. 89.95 (*0-13-349531-0*) P-H.

Almanac of California Government & Politics. 7th ed. Ed. by Thomas R. Hoeber. (Biennial Ser.). (Illus.). 192p. (Orig.). 1989. pap. 8.95 (*0-930302-70-2*) Cal Journal.

Almanac of California Government & Politics: 1985-86. Ed. by Thomas R. Hoeber. (Biennial Ser.). (Illus.). 176p. (Orig.). 1985. pap. 5.95 (*0-930302-57-5*) Cal Journal.

Almanac of California Government & Politics: 1987-88. Ed. by Thomas R. Hoeber. (Biennial Ser.). (Illus.). 192p. (Orig.). 1987. pap. 8.95 (*0-930302-60-5*) Cal Journal.

***Almanac of Canadian Politics.** 2nd ed. Ed. by Munroe Eagles et al. (Illus.). 768p. 1995. 89.00 (*0-19-541140-4*) OUP.

***Almanac of Canadian Politics.** 2nd ed. Ed. by Munroe Eagles et al. (Illus.). 768p. 1995. pap. 33.00 (*0-19-541141-2*) OUP.

***Almanac of Childhood & Children: Customs, Superstitions, Theories & Facts.** Joan B. Geddes. Ed. by Nick Bakalar. (Illus.). 640p. 1995. pap. 49.50 (*0-89774-880-8*, 2201) Oryx Pr.

Almanac of China's Economy, 1949-1981. Economic Research Centre Staff et al. Ed. by Xue Muqiao. 155.00 (*0-88410-894-5*) Eurasia Pr NY.

***Almanac of European Politics, 1994.** Matthew Cossolotto. LC 94-32762. 1994. 49.95 (*0-87187-914-X*); pap. text ed. 29.95 (*0-87187-913-1*) Congr Quarterly.

Almanac of Famous People, 3 vols. 5th ed. Susan L. Stetler. 1993. 99.00 (*0-8103-6988-5*) Gale.

Almanac of Famous People, Vol. 1, A-I. 5th ed. Susan L. Stetler. 1993. write for info. (*0-8103-6989-3*) Gale.

Almanac of Famous People, Vol. 2, J-Z. 5th ed. Susan L. Stetler. 1993. write for info. (*0-8103-6990-7*) Gale.

Almanac of Fascinating Beginnings: From the Academy Awards to the Xerox Machine. Norman King. LC 94-20161. 1994. 9.95 (*0-8065-1549-X*, Citadel Pr) Carol Pub Group.

Almanac of Federal PACs: 1988. Edward P. Zuckerman. 500p. 1988. pap. 69.50 (*0-939676-07-9*) Amward Pubns.

Almanac of Federal PACs: 1990. Edward P. Zuckerman. 660p. 1990. pap. 79.50 (*0-939676-08-7*) Amward Pubns.

Almanac of Federal Pacs: 1994-95. Edward P. Zuckerman. 512p. 1994. pap. 97.50 (*0-939676-11-7*) Amward Pubns.

Almanac of Federal PACs, 1986. Edward P. Zuckerman. 424p. 1986. pap. 49.50 (*0-939676-06-0*) Amward Pubns.

Almanac of Federal PACs, 1992-93. Edward P. Zuckerman. 700p. 1992. pap. 79.50 (*0-939676-09-5*) Amward Pubns.

***Almanac of Higher Education, 1995.** Chronicle of Higher Education Editors. 350p. 1995. pap. text ed. 18.95 (*0-226-18460-9*) U Ch Pr.

Almanac of Illinois Politics - 1992. Ed. by Jack R. Van Der Slik. LC 92-7183. 442p. (Orig.). 1992. pap. 38.00 (*0-9620873-7-8*) Illinois Issues.

Almanac of Illinois Politics - 1994. Ed. by Jack R. Van Der Slik. 460p. (Orig.). 1994. pap. 43.00 (*0-938943-06-5*) Sangamon Pub Affairs.

Almanac of Illinois Politics-1990. Ed. by Jack R. Van Der Slik. LC 90-82302. 394p. (Orig.). 1990. pap. 35.00 (*0-9620873-4-3*) Illinois Issues.

Almanac of International Jobs & Careers. Ronald L. Krannich & Caryl R. Krannich. 348p. 1991. 27.95 (*0-942710-46-0*); pap. 14.95 (*0-942710-40-1*) Impact VA.

Almanac of International Jobs & Careers: A Guide to over 1001 Employers. 2nd ed. Ronald L. Krannich & Caryl R. Krannich. LC 94-9323. 1994. 34.95 (*0-942710-99-1*); pap. 19.95 (*0-942710-95-9*) Impact VA.

Almanac of Modern Terrorism. Jay M. Shafritz et al. 288p. 1991. 29.95 (*0-8160-2123-6*) Facts on File.

Almanac of Quotable Quotes from 1990. Ron Pasqariello. 300p. 1991. 29.95 (*0-685-38168-4*, Busn); pap. 9.95 (*0-685-38169-2*, Busn) P-H.

Almanac of Quotable Quotes from 1990. Ron Pasquariello. 1991. 29.95 (*0-13-026386-9*); pap. 9.95 (*0-685-47732-0*); pap. 9.95 (*0-13-026378-8*) P-H.

Almanac of Quotable Quotes from 1991. Ronald D. Pasquaiello. 1992. pap. 12.95 (*0-13-031717-9*, Busn) P-H.

***Almanac of Renewable Energy: The Complete Guide to Emerging Energy Technologies.** Richard Golob & Eric Brus. LC 94-13963. (Reference Bks Ser.). 368p. 1994. pap. 19.95 (*0-8050-3392-0*) H Holt & Co.

Almanac of Rural Living. Harvey C. Neese. (Illus.). 1976. per. 6.95 (*0-686-16740-6*) N & N Resources.

Almanac of Science & Technology: What's New & What's Known. Richard Golob. 1990. 59.95 (*0-15-105050-3*); pap. 29.95 (*0-15-600049-0*) HarBrace.

***Almanac of Seapower, 1995.** George C. Wilson et al. Ed. by Vincent C. Thomas, Jr. (Illus.). 320p. 1995. 19.95x (*0-944433-14-6*); pap. 12.95 (*0-944433-15-4*) Navy League US.

Almanac of Soviet Manned Space Flight. Dennis Newkirk. (Illus.). 378p. 1990. 29.95 (*0-87201-848-2*) Gulf Pub.

Almanac of Sports Contacts: The Global Resource Guide for Addresses in the Sports Marketplace. Greg J. Cylkowski. 345p. (Orig.). (C). 1994. pap. text ed. 23.50 (*0-9636449-1-2*) Athletic Achieve.

Almanac of State Government & Politics: 1979-1980. Comp. by Ed Salzman. (Illus.). 1979. pap. 3.95 (*0-930302-20-6*) Cal Journal.

Almanac of State Government & Politics, 1983-1984. Ed. by Thomas R. Hoeber. (Biennial Ser.). (Illus.). 200p. (Orig.). 1983. pap. 4.95 (*0-930302-52-4*) Cal Journal.

Almanac of the Bible. Geoffrey Wigoder & Benedict T. Viviano. (Illus.). 448p. 1991. 40.00 (*0-13-026899-2*) P-H Gen Ref & Trav.

Almanac of the Canning, Freezing, Preserving Industries, 1990-91. 75th ed. Edward E. Judge & Sons, Inc. Staff. Ed. by Daniel P. Judge. 706p. 1991. pap. 43.00 (*1-880821-02-8*) E E Judge & Sons.

Almanac of the Dead. Leslie M. Silko. (Contemporary American Fiction Ser.). 792p. 1992. reprint ed. pap. 13.95 (*0-14-017319-6*, Penguin Bks) Viking Penguin.

***Almanac of the Executive Branch, 1995.** Jeffrey B. Trammell & Gary P. Osifchin. (Illus.). 600p. (C). 1995. pap. 125.00 (*0-88622-200-1*) Almanac Pub.

Almanac of the Federal Judiciary, 2 Vols. Prentice-Hall Editorial Staff. 1994. Vol. 1. ring bd. 295.00 (*0-13-288854-8*) Aspen Law.

Almanac of the Federal Judiciary: Profiles of All Active United States Circuit Judges. (Almanac of the Federal Judiciary Ser.: Vol. II). 1988. 130.00 (*0-318-35158-7*) LawLetters.

Almanac of the Federal Judiciary: Profiles of All Active United States District Judges. (Almanac of the Federal Judiciary Ser.: Vol. I). 1988. 170.00 (*0-914239-02-3*) LawLetters.

Almanac of the Fifty States, 1994: Basic Data Profiles with Comparative Tables. rev. ed. Intro. by Edith R. Hornor. 464p. 1994. pap. 47.00 (*0-931845-37-8*) Info Pubns.

Almanac of the Gross, Disgusting & Totally Repulsive: Odious Information for Oddball Bibliophiles. Eric Elfman. LC 93-48678. (Illus.). 80p. (J). (gr. 4-7). 1994. pap. 4.99 (*0-679-85805-9*) Random Bks Yng Read.

***Almanac of the 50 States, 1995: Basic Data Profiles with Comparative Tables.** rev. ed. Ed. & Intro. by Edith R. Hornor. 464p. 1995. pap. 47.00 (*0-931845-42-4*) Info Pubns.

***Almanac of the 50 States, 1995: Basic Data Profiles with Comparative Tables.** rev. ed. Ed. & Intro. by Edith R. Hornor. 464p. 1995. lib. bdg. 55.00 (*0-931845-43-2*) Info Pubns.

Almanac of Virginia Politics: 1977. Incl. Almanac of Virginia Politics: 1978 Supplement. Flora et al. Crater. LC 76-24321. (Illus.). 1978. pap. 2.00 (*0-917560-09-4*); Almanac of Virginia Politics: 1979. 2nd ed. Flora et al. Crater. LC 76-24321. 1979. pap. 5.95 (*0-685-05436-5*, 78-6331); Almanac of Virginia Politics: 1980 Supplement. Flora Crater. LC 76-24321. (Illus.). 1977. pap. 3.95 (*0-685-05437-3*); Almanac of Virginia Politics: 1981. 3rd ed. Flora et al. Crater. LC 76-24321. (Illus.). 1981. pap. 7.95 (*0-917560-16-7*, 80-71076); Almanac of Virginia Politics: 1982 Supplement. Flora et al. Crater. LC 76-24321. (Illus.). 1982. pap. 4.95 (*0-917560-17-5*); Almanac of Virginia Politics: 1983 Edition. Flora at al. Crater. LC 76-24321. (Illus.). 1983. pap. 9.95 (*0-917560-18-3*); Almanac of Virginia Politics: 1985 Edition. Flora Crater & Greg Williams. LC 76-24321. 1977. 16.95 (*0-917560-20-5*); LC 76-24321. (Illus.). 1977. Set pap. 3.95 (*0-917560-07-8*) Woman Activist.

Almanac of Virginia Politics: 1986 Supplement. Flora Crater et al. write for info. (*0-917560-21-3*) Woman Activist.

Almanac of Virginia Politics: 1987 Regular. Flora Crater et al. 13.95 (*0-917560-22-1*) Woman Activist.

Almanac of Virginia Politics: 1988 Supplement. Flora Crater et al. pap. 5.95 (*0-917560-23-X*) Woman Activist.

Almanac of Virginia Politics: 1989 Regular. Flora Crater et al. 1990. pap. 17.95 (*0-917560-24-8*) Woman Activist.

Almanac of Virginia Politics: 1990 Supplement. Flora Crater. 1990. pap. 11.95 (*0-917560-50-7*) Woman Activist.

Almanac of Virginia Politics: 1991 Regular. Flora Crater et al. 1990. 19.95 (*0-917560-25-6*) Woman Activist.

Almanac of Virginia Politics: 1992 Supplement. Flora Crater et al. 13.95 (*0-917560-26-4*) Woman Activist.

Almanac of Virginia Politics: 1993 Supplement. Flora Crater et al. 21.95 (*0-917560-27-2*) Woman Activist.

Almanac of Virginia Politics: 1994 Supplement. Flora Crater et al. 1995. pap. 15.95 (*0-917560-28-0*) Woman Activist.

Almanac of Virginia Politics: 1978 Supplement see Almanac of Virginia Politics: 1977

Almanac of Virginia Politics: 1979 see Almanac of Virginia Politics: 1977

Almanac of Virginia Politics: 1980 Supplement see Almanac of Virginia Politics: 1977

Almanac of Virginia Politics: 1981 see Almanac of Virginia Politics: 1977

Almanac of Virginia Politics: 1982 Supplement see Almanac of Virginia Politics: 1977

Almanac of Virginia Politics: 1983 Edition see Almanac of Virginia Politics: 1977

Almanac of Virginia Politics: 1985 Edition see Almanac of Virginia Politics: 1977

Almanac of World Crime. J. Robert Nash. (Illus.). 464p. 1988. 7.99 (*0-517-62530-X*) Random Hse Value.

Almanac of 1988 Presidential Politics. American Political Network, Inc. Staff & LTV Corporation Staff. Ed. by Gary Maloney. (Illus.). 164p. (Orig.). 1989. pap. 12.95 (*0-9621971-0-6*) APN Inc.

Almanac, 1980. 1980. 7.95 (*0-685-22648-4*) RWCPH.

Almanac, 1981. 1981. 7.95 (*0-685-44308-6*) RWCPH.

Almanac, 1987. 1987. 8.95 (*0-685-22668-9*) RWCPH.

Almanach des Dyspepsies. A. L. Blum et al. LC 92-28887. 1992. 45.00 (*0-387-55674-5*) Spr-Verlag.

Almanache der Romantik. Raimund Pissin. Vol. 5. xii, 450p. 1970. reprint ed. write for info. (*0-318-71856-1*, Pub. by Georg Olms GW) Lubrecht & Cramer.

Almanachs du Pere Ubu see Tout Ubu

Al'Manakh Bibliofila. Ed. by Collet's Holdings, Ltd. Staff. 434p. (RUS.). 1985. 125.00 (*0-317-40847-X*, Pub. by Collets UK) Pro-Am Music.

***Almanaque De la Musica Latinoamericana.** Frank M. Figueroa. (Illus.). 75p. (SPA.). Date not set. pap. write for info. (*0-9643201-3-4*) Pillar Publns.

Almanaque Mundial, 1988. Ed. by Carlos Roman. LC 55-22432. (Illus.). (Orig.). (SPA.). 1986. pap. text ed. 6.00 (*0-944499-07-4*) Editorial Amer.

Almanaque Mundial, 1990. Ed. by Carlos Roman. (Illus.). 592p. (Orig.). (SPA.). 1989. pap. 6.00 (*0-944499-61-9*) Editorial Amer.

Almanaque Mundial, 1991. Ed. by Carlos Roman. (Illus.). 608p. (Orig.). (SPA.). 1990. pap. write for info. (*0-944499-85-6*) Editorial Amer.

Almanaque Mundial, 1992. Editorial America, S. A. Staff. Ed. by Carlos Roman. (Illus.). 592p. (SPA.). 1991. pap. 6.00 (*1-56259-008-1*) Editorial Amer.

Almanaque Mundial, 1993. Editorial America, S. A. Staff. Ed. by Carlos Roman. (Illus.). 592p. (SPA.). 1992. pap. 6.00 (*1-56259-024-3*) Editorial Amer.

Almanaque Mundial, 1994. Ed. by Carlos Roman. (Illus.). 592p. (SPA.). 1993. pap. 6.00 (*1-56259-026-X*) Editorial Amer.

Almanaque Mundial, 1995. Editorial America, S. A. Staff. Ed. by Carlos Roman. (Illus.). 608p. (SPA.). 1994. pap. 6.00 (*1-56259-032-4*) Editorial Amer.

***Almanaque Mundial, 1996.** Editorial America, S. A. Staff. Ed. by Carlos Roman. (Illus.). 608p. (SPA.). 1995. pap. 6.00x (*1-56259-033-2*) Editorial Amer.

Almanaque Universal 1990. Ed. by Carlos Roman. (Illus.). 608p. (Orig.). (SPA.). 1989. pap. 6.00 (*0-944499-65-1*) Editorial Amer.

Almanaque Universal 1991. Ed. by Carlos Roman. (Illus.). 608p. (Orig.). (SPA.). 1990. pap. write for info. (*0-944499-86-4*) Editorial Amer.

Almanzar. James F. Davis. LC 70-144153. (Short Story Index Reprint Ser.). (Illus.). 1977. reprint ed. 19.95 (*0-8369-3768-6*) Ayer.

Almayer's Folly. Joseph Conrad. 1976. 17.95 (*0-8488-0460-0*) Amereon Ltd.

Almayer's Folly. Joseph Conrad. 321p. 1983. lib. bdg. 15.95 (*0-89966-056-8*) Buccaneer Bks.

Almayer's Folly. Joseph Conrad. 1976. mass mkt. 4.95 (*0-14-000036-4*, Penguin Bks) Viking Penguin.

Almayer's Folly. Joseph Conrad. LC 79-184735. 224p. 1971. reprint ed. lib. bdg. 20.00 (*0-8376-0408-7*) Bentley.

Almayer's Folly: A Story of an Eastern River. Joseph Conrad. Ed. by David L. Higdon et al. (Cambridge Edition of the Works of Joseph Conrad). (Illus.). 450p. (C). 1994. 69.95 (*0-521-43205-7*) Cambridge U Pr.

Almayer's Folly: A Story of an Eastern River. Joseph Conrad. Ed. by Jacques Berthoud. (World's Classics Ser.). (Illus.). 320p. 1992. pap. 5.95 (*0-19-281697-7*) OUP.

Almendros y Hucares. write for info. (*0-318-72522-3*) Instit Nacional.

Almighty & the Dollar Workbook. Jim McKeever. 1980. 23.95 (*0-685-07327-0*) Omega Pubns OR.

Almighty Chance. Ya B. Zeldovich et al. (Lecture Notes in Physics Ser.: Vol. 20). 328p. 1990. text ed. 86.00 (*9971-5-0916-4*); pap. text ed. 43.00 (*9971-5-0917-2*) World Scientific Pub.

Almighty Dollar Bill. Adrienne Golday. LC 85-51078. (Illus.). 64p. 1985. 15.00 (*0-930509-10-2*) Wisdom Bk Pubs.

Almighty One Guide Catalogue. Cecil E. Bower. (Illus.). 256p. (Orig.). 1989. write for info. (*0-9623894-0-4*) C E Bower.

Almighty Wall: The Architecture of Henry Vaughan. William N. Morgan. 1982. 40.00 (*0-262-13187-0*) MIT Pr.

***Almodovar on Almodovar.** Frederic Strauss. (Directors & Directors Ser.). 160p. 1995. 22.95 (*0-571-17544-9*) Faber & Faber.

Almond Cookies & Dragon Well Tea. Cynthia Chin-Lee. LC 92-21518. (Illus.). 36p. (J). (gr. k-3). 1993. 12.95 (*1-879965-03-8*) Polychrome Pub.

Almond Orchard. Laura J. Coats. LC 90-38009. (Illus.). 32p. (J). (gr. 1-4). 1991. text ed. 14.95 (*0-02-719041-2*, Mac Bks Young Read) S&S Childrens.

***Almond Production Manual.** Ed. by Warren Micke. (Illus.). 200p. 1995. pap. write for info. (*1-879906-22-8*, 3364) ANR Pubns CA.

Almond Tree: The Collected Poems of George Edgar Wolfe. Edgar Wolfe. (Orig.). 1989. per., pap. 7.50 (*0-939391-13-9*) Cottonwood KS.

***Almond Tree Speaks: New & Selected Writings 1974-1994.** Murray Bodo. 160p. 1994. 7.95 (*0-86716-237-6*) St Anthony Mess Pr.

Almonds & Raisins. Maisie Mosco. 1991. mass mkt. 5.50 (*0-06-100142-2*, PL) HarpC.

Almoner at Anson's. large type ed. Kathleen Treves. (Linford Romance Library). 304p. 1985. pap. 11.95 (*0-7089-6132-0*, Linford) Ulverscroft.

Almost a Gentleman, Vol. II: An Autobiography, 1955-1956. John Osborne. (Illus.). 304p. 1994. pap. 10.95 (*0-571-16635-0*) Faber & Faber.

***Almost a Hero.** John Neufeld. LC 94-12785. (J). 1995. 15.00 (*0-689-31971-1*, Atheneum S&S) S&S Trade.

Almost a Lady. Sonya Birmingham. 400p. (Orig.). 1993. mass mkt. 4.50 (*0-380-76766-X*) Avon.

Almost a Layman. Samuel L. Hoard. 1981. 6.50 (*0-9610678-0-2*) Drake's Ptg & Pub.

Almost a Layman. Samuel L. Hoard. 1982. pap. 4.95 (*0-9610678-1-0*) Drake's Ptg & Pub.

Almost a Rainbow: A Book of Poems. Joan W. Anglund. (Illus.). 64p. 1980. 12.00 (*0-394-50072-5*) Random.

Almost a Revolution: Mental Health Law & the Limits of Change. Paul S. Appelbaum. 268p. 1994. pap. 34.95 (*0-19-506880-7*) OUP.

Almost a Territory: America's Attempt to Annex the Dominican Republic. William J. Nelson. LC 89-40204. (Illus.). 152p. 1990. 32.50 (*0-87413-380-7*) U Delaware Pr.

Almost a Whisper. Charlene Cross. 1994. mass mkt. 5.50 (*0-671-79431-0*) PB.

Almost Adult: Devotions for 9-12 Year Olds. Charles Mueller. LC 92-27014. 160p. (Orig.). (J). (gr. 4-7). 1993. pap. 6.99 (*0-570-04598-3*) Concordia.

Almost Alchemy. David R. Morgan & David Caddy. 52p. (C). 1988. 75.00 (*0-947612-31-9*, Pub. by Rivelin Grapheme Pr) St Mut.

Almost All Lies Are Pocket Size. limited ed. Lionel Ziprin. (Illus.). 22p. 1990. 55.00 (*0-9623585-3-3*) Flockophobic Pr.

Almost at the End. Yevgeny Yevtushenko. Tr. by Antonina W. Bouis & Albert C. Todd. LC 86-22800. 160p. 1988. pap. 8.95 (*0-8050-0785-7*, Owl) H Holt & Co.

Almost Awful Play. Patricia R. Giff. (J). (gr. 2-4). 1989. audio, pap. 14.95 (*0-87499-115-3*) Live Oak Media.

Almost Awful Play. Patricia R. Giff. LC 84-17922. (Illus.). 32p. (J). (ps-3). 1985. pap. 4.99 (*0-14-050530-X*, Puffin) Puffin Bks.

Almost Awful Play, 4 bks., Set. Patricia R. Giff. (J). (gr. 2-4). 1989. audio, pap. 29.95 (*0-87499-117-X*) Live Oak Media.

***Almost, But Not Quite (the Secret Evolution)** Helen A. Englsman. 1994. 10.00 (*0-533-11029-7*) Vantage.

Almost Chosen People: Oblique Biographies in the American Grain. Michael Zuckerman. LC 92-5779. 1993. 30.00 (*0-520-06651-0*) U CA Pr.

Almost Chosen People: The Moral Aspirations of Americans. Ed. by Walter Nicgorski & Ronald Weber. LC 76-41343. 170p. reprint ed. pap. 48.50 (*0-8357-5325-5*, 2022062) Bks Demand.

Almost Christian Discovered: The False Professor Tried & Cast. Matthew Mead. Ed. by Don Kistler. 172p. 1994. 16.95 (*1-877611-72-7*) Soli Deo Gloria.

Almost Coffee: Coffee Substitutes Poetry Book. Center for Self-Sufficiency, Research Division Staff. 11p. 1983. pap. text ed. 4.00 (*0-910811-66-0*) Ctr Self Suff.

Almost Complete 78 RPM Record Dating Guide. Steven C. Barr. 177p. 1992. spiral bd. 15.95 (*0-9640687-2-9*) Promar Pubng.

Almost Complex & Complex Structures. C. C. Hsiung. (Series in Pure Mathematics). 220p. 1995. text ed. 48.00 (*981-02-1712-9*) World Scientific Pub.

Almost Complex Homogeneous Spaces & Their Submanifolds. K. Yang. 124p. (C). 1987. text ed. 40.00 (*9971-5-0377-8*) World Scientific Pub.

***Almost Complex Structures: Proceedings of the International Workshop.** K. Sekigawa & S. Dimiev. 232p. 1994. text ed. 86.00 (*981-02-2101-0*) World Scientific Pub.

Almost Coping. Terri Auchter. LC 83-61876. (Illus.). 160p. 1983. pap. 2.95 (*0-931762-20-0*) Phunn Pubs.

***Almost Eden.** Dorothy Garlock. 336p. (Orig.). 1995. pap. 5.99 (*0-446-36372-3*, Warner Vision) Warner Bks.

A

An Asterisk (*) at the beginning of an entry indicates that the title is appearing in BIP for the first time.

205

***Almost Elvis.** M. Bowser. Ed. by Alister MacLean. (Cartoon Ser.). (Illus.). 110p. (CHI, FRE & GER.). 1995. lib. bdg. 20.00 (0-940178-29-X) Sitare.

***Almost Everthing You Need to Know about Guitar Chords: A Practical Method for Construction, Memorization & Utilization.** rev. ed. RalphL. Scicchitano. 75p. 1995. pap. 10.95 (0-9646652-8-X) Anytime Pubns.

Almost Every Answer for Practically Any Teacher. Bruce Wilkinson. (Seven Laws of the Learner Resource Guide Ser.). (Illus.). 272p. 1992. pap. text ed. 12.99 (0-88070-473-X, Multnomah Bks) Questar Pubs.

Almost Everything Teens Want Parents to Know: But Are Afraid to Tell Them. Bill Sanders. LC 87-9550. 160p. (Orig.). (YA). 1987. pap. 7.99 (0-8007-5245-7) Revell.

Almost Everywhere Convergence. Ed. by Gerald A. Edgar & Louis Sucheston. 400p. 1989. text ed. 80.00 (0-12-231050-0) Acad Pr.

Almost Everywhere Convergence 2: Proceedings of the International Conference on Almost Everywhere Convergence in Probability & Ergodic Theory, Evanston, Illinois, October 16-20, 1989. Ed. by Alexandra Bellow & Roger Jones. 273p. 1991 text ed. 69.95 (0-12-085520-8) Acad Pr.

Almost Famous. Sally Demay. Ed. by Gwen Costa. 254p. 1992. 29.95 (0-87949-365-8) Ashley Bks.

Almost Famous. David Getz. 192p. (J). (gr. 4-7). 1993. 13. 95 (0-8050-1940-5, Bks Young Read) H Holt & Co.

***Almost Famous.** David Getz. 192p. (J). 1994. pap. 5.95 (0-8050-3464-1) H Holt & Co.

Almost Famous: A Novel. David Small. 1990. pap. 9.95 (0-393-30666-6) Norton.

Almost Famous: Personal Growth & Other Adventures In & Out of Show Biz. Pam Munter. LC 85-13621. (Illus.). 275p. 1985. 16.95 (0-9614926-0-0) Westgate Oregon.

Almost Fifteen. Marilyn Sachs. 144p. 1988. pap. 2.95 (0-380-70357-2, Flare) Avon.

Almost Finished. Cedric Vallet. (Illus.). 18p. (J). (gr. k-3). 1992. pap. 11.95 (1-895583-28-4) MAYA Pubs.

Almost Forever. Linda Howard. 1994. mass mkt. 4.50 (0-373-48306-6, 5-48306-0) Harlequin Bks.

***Almost Forever.** Linda Howard. 1994. pap. 4.99 (1-55166-011-3, 1-66011-7, Mira Bks) Harlequin Bks.

Almost Forever. Karen Harper. 432p. 1992. reprint ed. 20. 00 (0-7278-4335-4) Severn Hse.

Almost Free Land: Guide to the Acquisition of Land at Property Tax Auctions. Phillip P. Karagan. LC 83-90399. 129p. (Orig.). 1983. pap. 7.95 (0-9612394-0-9) P P Karagan.

Almost Free Modules: Set-Theoretic Methods. P. C. Eklof & A. H. Mekler. (North-Holland Mathematical Library: No. 46). 482p. 1990. 115.50 (0-444-88502-1, North Holland) Elsevier.

Almost Golden: Jessica Savitch & the Selling of Television News. Gwenda Blair. 368p. 1989. mass mkt. 4.50 (0-380-70752-7) Avon.

Almost Good. James E. Tyvoll. LC 94-60124. 326p. 1993. 11.95 (1-55523-683-9) Winston-Derek.

Almost Heaven. Sandra James. (Superromance Ser.: No. 435). 1991. pap. 2.95 (0-373-70435-6) Harlequin Bks.

Almost Heaven. Judith McNaught. Ed. by Linda Marrow. 528p. 1991. pap. 6.50 (0-671-74255-8) PB.

***Almost Heaven.** Becky L. Wevrich. 448p. 1995. mass mkt. 5.99 (0-8217-4929-3) Windsor NY.

Almost Heaven. large type ed. Judith McNaught. LC 91-18384. 882p. 1991. reprint ed. lib. bdg. 20.95 (1-56054-209-8) Thorndike Pr.

Almost History. Christopher Bram. 1992. 22.50 (1-55611-231-9) D I Fine.

Almost History. Christopher Bram. 412p. 1993. pap. 12.95 (0-452-26966-0, Plume) NAL-Dutton.

Almost Home: Romance from the Heart of America. Debra S. Cowan. 304p. (Orig.). 1994. mass mkt. 4.99 (1-55773-978-1) Diamond.

Almost Homogeneous Functions: A Theoretical & Empirical Analysis with Special Emphasis on Labour Input-The Case of Swedish Manufacturing Industries. Epaminondas E. Panas. (Studia Oeconomica Upsaliensia: No. 11). 130p. (Orig.). 1987. pap. text ed. 35.50x (91-554-1972-0, Pub. by Uppsala Univ Acta Univ Uppsaliensis SW) Coronet Bks.

Almost Human: A Journey into the World of Baboons. Shirley C. Strum. LC 86-29712. (Illus.). 320p. 1987. 22. 50 (0-394-54724-1) Random.

Almost Human: A Journey into the World of Baboons. Shirley C. Strum. 1990. pap. 12.95 (0-393-30708-5) Norton.

Almost Human Gesture. Louis Jenkins. 1987. pap. 6.95 (0-915408-32-5) Ally Pr.

Almost Inkfish. N. J. Pierotti. 105p. 1993. pap. 10.00 (0-9638096-0-1) Inkfish Pr.

Almost Innocent. Kate Bradley. (Silhouette Romance Ser.). 1993. pap. 2.75 (0-373-08951-1, 5-08951-1) Silhouette.

Almost Like Being see America Hurrah & Other Plays

Almost Married. Francine Pascal. (Sweet Valley High Ser.: No. 102). (YA). (gr. 7 up). 1994. pap. 3.50 (0-553-29859-3) Bantam.

Almost Meat: Nutritional Foods that Can Be Prepared to Taste Like Meat. rev. ed. Ed. by Bibliotheca Press Research Division Staff. 50p. 1993. ring bd. 21.95 (0-939476-60-6, Biblio Pr) Prosperity & Profits.

Almost No Cholesterol Gourmet Cookbook. Jeanette Seaver. 1990. 19.95 (0-517-57518-3, Crown) Crown Pub Group.

Almost-No Cholesterol Gourmet Cookbook. Jeanette M. Seaver. LC 94-14276. (Illus.). 1994. pap. 14.95 (1-55970-274-5) Arcade Pub Inc.

Almost No Fat Cookbook: Everyday Vegetarian Recipes. Bryanna C. Grogan. LC 94-9594. 192p. (Orig.). 1994. pap. text ed. 10.95 (0-913990-12-4) Book Pub Co.

***Almost No Fat Holiday Cookbook: Festive Vegetarian Recipes.** Branna C. Melina. 192p. 1995. 12.95 (1-57067-009-9) Book Pub Co.

Almost One Year. Aldo Fallai. (Illus.). 192p. 1993. 49.50 (1-883489-00-8) Takarajima.

Almost Out of the World: Scenes from Washington Territory. James G. Swan. Ed. by William A. Katz. LC 75-148061. (Illus.). 126p. 1971. 7.50 (0-917048-10-5) Wash St Hist Soc.

Almost Paradise? Patricia L. Eachus-Cox. 1990. 10.00 (0-533-07335-9) Vantage.

Almost Paradise. Susan Isaacs. 576p. 1985. mass mkt. 5.99 (0-345-31677-0) Ballantine.

***Almost Perfect.** Adams. 5.99 (0-517-13752-6) Random Hse Value.

Almost Perfect. Alice Adams. LC 92-54797. 1993. 23.00 (0-679-42398-2) Knopf.

Almost Perfect. Alice Adams. 1994. mass mkt. 5.99 (0-449-14892-0, GM) Fawcett.

Almost Perfect. large type ed. Alice Adams. LC 93-49647. 1994. 22.95 (0-7862-0180-0) Thorndike Pr.

Almost Perfect: How a Bunch of Regular Guys Built WordPerfect Corporation. W. E. Peterson. LC 93-34366. 1993. 18.95 (1-55958-477-7) Prima Pub.

***Almost Perfect Crimes: Mini-Mysteries for You to Solve.** Hy Conrad. LC 95-20065. (Illus.). 96p. 1995. pap. 5.95 (0-8069-3807-2) Sterling.

***Almost Perfect Game.** Stephen Manes. LC 94-18192. 1995. 14.95 (0-590-44432-8) Scholastic Inc.

Almost Periodic Functions. Harald Bohr. LC 47-5500. 1980. 12.00 (0-8284-0027-X) Chelsea Pub.

Almost Periodic Functions. 2nd rev. ed. Constantin Corduneau. Tr. by Eugene Tomer. LC 87-72946. (Illus.). 261p. (C). 1988. 19.95 (0-8284-0331-7, 331) Chelsea Pub.

Almost Periodic Functions & Differential Equations. B. M. Levitan & V. V. Zhikov. Tr. by L. V. Longdon. LC 82-4352. 150p. 1983. 59.95 (0-521-24407-2) Cambridge U Pr.

Almost Periodic Measures. L. N. Argabright & J. G. De Lamadrid. LC 90-31823. (Memoirs Ser.: Vol. 85/428). 219p. 1991. text ed. 28.00 (0-8218-2490-2, MEMO 85/428) Am Math.

Almost Periodic Operators & Related Nonlinear Integral Systems. V. A. Chulaevsky. (Nonlinear Science: Theory & Applications Ser.). 152p. 1992. text ed. 105.00 (0-471-93517-4) Wiley.

Almost Persuaded: American Physicians & Compulsory Health Insurance, 1912-1920. Ronald L. Numbers. LC 77-17254. (Henry E. Sigerist Supplements to the Bulletin of the History of Medicine, New Ser.: No. 1). 173p. reprint ed. pap. 49.40 (0-7837-6425-1, 2046423) Bks Demand.

Almost Sisters: The Sisters Scheme. Kathryn Makris. 144p. (Orig.). (YA). 1991. pap. 2.99 (0-380-76035-5, Camelot) Avon.

Almost Sisters: The Sisters Team. Kathryn Makris. 176p. (Orig.). (J). (gr. 5 up). 1992. pap. 3.50 (0-380-76056-8, Camelot) Avon.

Almost Sisters, No. 2: The Sisters War. Kathryn Makris. 160p. (Orig.). (YA). 1991. pap. 3.50 (0-380-76055-X, Camelot) Avon.

Almost Snow White. Jeffrey Blount. LC 91-67219. 93p. (Orig.). 1992. pap. 8.00 (1-56002-125-X) Aegina Pr.

Almost Sugar & Not Quite Butter - Alternative Sugar & Butter Reference. Alpha Pyramis Research Division Staff. 1989. pap. 4.95 (0-913597-02-3) Prosperity & Profits.

Almost Sure Convergence. William F. Stout. 1974. text ed. 121.00 (0-12-672750-3) Acad Pr.

Almost Sure Invariance Principles for Partial Sums of Weakly Dependent Random Variables. Walter Philipp & William Stout. (Memoirs Ser.: No. 2/161). 140p. 1987. reprint ed. pap. 26.00 (0-8218-1861-9, MEMO 2/161) Am Math.

Almost the Real Thing: Simulation in Your High-Tech World. Gloria Skurzynski. (Illus.). 64p. (J). (gr. 9 up). 1991. text ed. 16.95 (0-02-778072-4, Bradbury S&S) S&S Childrens.

Almost the Truth. Margaret Yorke. 288p. 1995. 18.95 (0-89296-582-7) Mysterious Pr.

***Almost the Truth.** Margaret Yorke. 240p. 1996. mass mkt. 5.99 (0-446-40479-9, Mysterious Paperbk) Warner Bks.

***Almost the Truth.** large type ed. Margaret Yorke. LC 94-44493. 419p. 1995. 19.95 (0-7862-0391-9) Thorndike Pr.

Almost to the Presidency. Albert Eisele. LC 76-187432. 1972. 20.00 (0-87832-005-9) Piper.

Almost Too Late see Four Against the Wilderness: The True Story of a Father & His Three Teenage Children Shipwrecked off the Coast of Alaska in Winter

Almost Transparent Blue. Ryu Murakami. Ed. by Shaw. Tr. by Nancy Andrew. LC 77-75959. 128p. 1992. reprint ed. pap. 8.00 (0-87011-469-7) Kodansha.

Almost Twelve. Kenneth N. Taylor. 64p. 1989. pap. 3.99 (0-8423-1649-3) Tyndale.

Almost Vegetarian. Diana Shaw. LC 93-41748. 1994. pap. 18.00 (0-517-88206-X, C P Pubs) Crown Pub Group.

Almost World. Hans Koning. LC 72-3632. 224p. 1975. reprint ed. pap. 2.95 (0-85345-362-4) Monthly Rev.

Almost...but Lost. Carolyn Reno. pap. 0.25 (1-56632-013-5) Revival Lit.

***Almostism in Christianity: A Look at the Lukewarm Christian in Need of Total Commitment.** Jerome T. Nolan. 96p. 1994. per., pap. 9.00 (0-8059-3629-7) Dorrance.

ALMS: A Budget Based Library Management System. Ed. by Betty J. Mitchell. LC 82-81208. (Foundations in Library & Information Science: Vol. 16). 235p. 1983. lib. bdg. 73.25 (0-89232-246-2) Jai Pr.

Alms & Charity. John Chrysostom. 1990. pap. 1.95 (0-89981-216-3) Eastern Orthodox.

Alms & Vagabonds: Buddhist Temples & Popular Patronage in Medieval Japan. Janet R. Goodwin. LC 93-31406. 1994. text ed. 27.00 (0-8248-1547-5) UH Pr.

Alms at Beautiful Gate. Larry Stenzel. 92p. (Orig.). 1991. pap. 8.00 (0-910021-04-X) Samuel P Co.

Alms for Jude. Scott E. Sprecher. Tr. by Ingram. 400p. 1994. pap. 9.95 (1-56901-251-2) NW Pub.

Alms for Oblivion. Fata S. Malifa. 1993. 17.95 (0-533-10466-1) Vantage.

ALMS for Oblivion, Essays. Edward Dahlberg. LC 64-13767. 176p. reprint ed. pap. 50.20 (0-8357-5326-3, 2033214) Bks Demand.

Almshouse Experience: Collected Papers. Philadelphia Board of Guardians Staff & Massachusetts General Court Staff. LC 74-137197. (Poverty U. S. A. Historical Record Ser.). 1974. reprint ed. 23.95 (0-405-03092-4) Ayer.

Almuerzo Entre Dioses y Otros Relatos. Armando M. Molina. Ed. by Solaris Staff. Tr. by Lalo Borja. 110p. (SPA.). 1989. write for info. (0-318-65310-9) Ed Solaris.

Almuric: An Adaptation of the Novel by Robert E. Howard. Illus. by Tim Conrad. 72p. (Orig.). 1991. pap. 10.95 (1-878574-18-3) Dark Horse Comics.

Alnilam. James Dickey. 768p. 1988. mass mkt. 4.95 (1-55817-086-3, Pinnacle NY) Windsor NY.

Alnwick Castle, with Other Poems. Fitz-Greene Halleck. (Notable American Authors Ser.). 1992. reprint ed. lib. bdg. 75.00 (0-7812-2989-5) Rprt Serv.

Alo Raun Bibliography. E. J. Brill Koln. (Arcadia Bibliographica Virorum Eruditorum Ser.: Fasc. 2). 29p. 1980. 18.00 (0-931922-02-X) Eurolingua.

Aloe - Myth, Magic, Medicine: Aloe Vera across Time. 2nd ed. Odus M. Hennessee & Bill R. Cook. Ed. by Marilyn Krebs. LC 89-50558. (Illus.). 186p. 1990. lib. bdg. 9.95 (1-878491-00-8) Universal Graphics.

Aloe - Myth, Magic, Medicine: Aloe Vera across Time. 2nd ed. Odus M. Hennessee & Bill R. Cook. Ed. by Marilyn Krebs. LC 89-50558. (Illus.). 186p. (YA). (gr. 8 up). 1990. pap. 4.95 (0-685-74192-3) Universal Graphics.

Aloe Vera. Carol M. Kent. LC 78-74978. (Illus.). 114p. 1979. pap. 6.00 (0-9604886-0-X) C M Kent.

Aloe Vera: Literature Index & Abstract 1980-1992. E. M. Morsy. 450p. 1992. 285.00 (0-937425-06-0) CITA Intl.

Aloe Vera: Stabilization & Processing for the Cosmetic, Food & Beverage Industries. 3rd ed. Esam M. Morsy. LC 82-84430. (Illus.). 1985. lib. bdg. 85.00 (0-317-14729-3) CITA Intl.

Aloe Vera: The Miracle Plant. Fit Magazine Editors. 64p. 1983. pap. 3.95 (0-89037-261-6) Anderson World.

Aloe Vera, Farming, Processing & Applications, A Technical Guide. E. M. Morsy. 400p. 1992. write for info. (0-937425-07-9) CITA Intl.

Aloe Vera, Jojoba & Yucca. John Heinerman. (Good Health Guide Ser.). 32p. (Orig.). 1982. pap. 2.50 (0-87983-269-X) Keats.

Aloe Vera, Science & Technology, 1980-1993. 7th ed. E. M. Morsy. (Illus.). 579p. 1993. pap. text ed. 285.00 (0-937425-26-5) CITA Intl.

Aloe Vera, Stabilization & Processing for the Cosmetic & Beverage. 1,992th rev. ed. E. M. Morsy. 200p. 1992. 135.00 (0-937425-05-2) CITA Intl.

Aloe Vera Use Poetry Pages. Data Notes Research Project. 6p. (C). 1985. pap. text ed. 3.00 (0-911569-81-2) Prosperity & Profits.

Aloes: Poems from Hollywood. Mark Dunster. 63p. (Orig.). 1985. pap. 6.00 (0-89642-119-8) Linden Pubs.

Aloes of South Africa. Gilbert W. Reynolds. 616p. (C). 1982. text ed. 135.00 (90-6191-230-X, Pub. by A A Balkema NE) Ashgate Pub Co.

Aloft: A Meditation on Pigeons & Pigeon-Flying. Stephen Bodio. LC 93-9819. 88p. 1993. pap. 12.95 (0-87108-837-1) Pruett.

Aloft: A Meditation on Pigeons & Pigeon Flying. Stephen J. Bodio. 100p. 1990. 15.95 (1-55821-054-7) Lyons & Burford.

Aloha. Mark Christensen. 1994. 21.00 (0-685-70985-X) S&S Trade.

Aloha. Christensen Mark. 1994. 21.00 (0-671-87023-8) S&S Trade.

***Aloha!** Chieko N. Okazaki. 1995. 14.95 (0-87579-979-5) Deseret Bk.

Aloha! Fabulous Foods from Hawaii. Maxine S. Sommers. (Illus.). 15p. (Orig.). 1995. pap. 2.95 (0-943991-38-2) Pound Sterling Pub.

Aloha Bear: Color & Activity Book. Mark A. Wagenman. (Illus.). 24p. (J). (ps-00). 1988. pap. 2.95 (0-89610-023-5) Island Heritage.

Aloha Bear ABC: Coloring & Activity Book. Mark A. Wagenman. (Illus.). 24p. (J). (ps-00). 1989. pap. 2.95 (0-89610-146-0) Island Heritage.

Aloha Bear & Maui the Whale (the Adventures of) Mark A. Wagenman. (Illus.). 28p. (J). (ps-2). 1989. 7.95 (0-89610-148-7) Island Heritage.

Aloha Bear & the Meaning of Aloha. Dick Adair. (Illus.). 24p. (J). (ps-00). 1987. 7.95 (0-89610-077-4) Island Heritage.

Aloha Cowboy. Virginia Cowan-Smith & Bonnie D. Stone. LC 87-25574. (Illus.). 160p. 1988. 19.95 (0-8248-1085-6) UH Pr.

***Aloha from Hawaii.** Bonnie Warren. (Illus.). 24p. (J). (ps-3). 1987. 8.95 (0-9643494-0-X) Warren OR.

***Aloha Love.** Kremer. (Sweet Dreams Ser.: No. 226). 1995. mass mkt. 3.50 (0-553-56680-6) Bantam.

Aloha Means Come Back: The Story of a World War II Girl. Dorothy Hoobler & Thomas Hoobler. (Her Story Ser.). (Illus.). 64p. (J). (gr. 4-6). 1992. 5.95 (0-382-24156-8); lib. bdg. 7.95 (0-382-24148-7); pap. 3.95 (0-382-24349-8) Silver Burdett Pr.

***Aloha, My Love to You.** Armine Tempski. (American Autobiography Ser.). 235p. 1995. reprint ed. lib. bdg. 79. 00 (0-7812-8651-4) Rprt Serv.

Aloha, My Love to You. Armine Von Tempski. LC 87-36894. vi, 235p. 1988. reprint ed. 27.50 (0-918024-63-3); reprint ed. pap. 14.95 (0-918024-59-5) Ox Bow.

Aloha O Kalapana. Dorian Weisel & Frankie Stapleton. (Illus.). 154p. 1992. pap. 29.95 (0-930897-69-2) Bishop Mus.

Aloha Oe Sing-Along: You Can Play Uke. (Uke & Harmonica Ser.). 1990. 2.95 (0-685-32014-6, G019) Hansen Ed Mus.

Aloha Waikiki. DeSoto Brown. (Illus.). 96p. (Orig.). 1985. pap. 9.95 (0-9607938-9-5) Editions Ltd.

Aloha...Forever!! Mark Yasuhara & Diana Yasuhara. LC 75-21285. 140p. 1976. pap. 1.95 (0-89221-036-2) New Leaf.

Aloineae: A Biosystematic Survey. Herbert P. Riley & Shyamal K. Majumdar. LC 77-92927. (Illus.). 192p. 1980. 28.00 (0-8131-1376-8) U Pr of Ky.

Alois Riegl: Art History & Theory. Margaret Iversen. (Illus.). 240p. 1993. 35.00 (0-262-09030-9) MIT Pr.

***Alone.** Richard E. Byrd & Daniel J. Boorstin. Ed. by Philip Turner. (Illus.). 304p. 1995. pap. 13.00 (1-56836-068-1, Kodansha Globe) Kodansha.

Alone: A Fascinating Study of Those Who Have Survived Long, Solitary Ordeals. Richard Logan. LC 92-44228. 240p. 1993. pap. 16.95 (0-8117-2500-6) Stackpole.

Alone: A Search for Joy. Katie F. Wiebe. 220p. 1987. pap. 7.95 (0-919797-59-8) Kindred Prods.

Alone: The Man Who Braved the Vast Pacific - & Won. Gerard D'Aboville. Tr. by Richard Seaver. (Illus.). 176p. 1994. pap. 11.95 (1-55970-246-X) Arcade Pub Inc.

Alone after School: A Self-Care Guide for Latchkey Children & Their Parents. Helen L. Swan & Victoria Houston. LC 85-3442. 200p. 1987. 17.95 (0-13-023011-1, Busn); 8.95 (0-13-023003-0, Busn) P-H.

Alone, Again! Hildreth Scott. (Uplook Ser.). 1976. pap. 0.99 (0-8163-0251-0, 01496-9) Pacific Pr Pub Assn.

Alone, Alive, Fulfilled. large type ed. write for info. (0-318-68640-6, 7025) LBW.

Alone among the Living. Richard G. Hoard. LC 93-33746. 224p. 1994. 24.95 (0-8203-1610-5) U of Ga Pr.

Alone at Home. Barbara S. Hazen. LC 91-15878. (Illus.). 64p. (J). (gr. 2-4). 1992. text ed. 13.95 (0-689-31691-7, Atheneum Bks Young) S&S Childrens.

Alone at Last. Rita Rainville. (Silhouette Romance Ser.: No. 873). 1992. pap. 2.69 (0-373-08873-6, 5-08873-7) Silhouette.

***Alone but Not Lonely.** Karen Dockrey. Ed. by Becky Nelson. 22p. (Orig.). (YA). (gr. 10-12). 1994. pap. text ed. 1.95 (1-56309-070-8, Wrld Changers Res) Womans Mission Union.

***Alone in a Crowd.** Bockoven. 1995. mass mkt. 4.99 (0-06-108216-3, Harp PBks) HarpC.

Alone in a Crowd: Women in the Trades Tell Their Stories. Jean R. Schroedel. Ed. by Ronnie J. Steinberg. LC 84-16159. (Women in the Political Economy Ser.). 280p. 1985. 32.95 (0-87722-378-5) Temple U Pr.

Alone in a Crowd: Women in the Trades Tell Their Stories. Jean R. Schroedel. (Women in the Political Economy Ser.). 280p. 1986. pap. 14.95 (0-87722-397-1) Temple U Pr.

Alone in Arabian Nights. rev. ed. Sirdar I. Ali Shah. 215p. 1992. 24.00 (0-86304-063-2, Pub. by Octagon Pr UK) ISHK Bk Service.

Alone in China & Other Stories. Julian Ralph. LC 70-101819. (Short Story Index Reprint Ser.). 1977. 30.95 (0-8369-3207-2) Ayer.

Alone in My Kayak. Agnes Rodli. 280p. (Orig.). 1993. pap. 8.95 (1-56043-768-5) Destiny Image.

Alone in the Ashes. William W. Johnstone. 1989. mass mkt. 3.99 (0-8217-4019-9) Zebra.

Alone in the Crowd. Francine Pascal. (Orig.). (YA). 1986. pap. 2.99 (0-553-28087-2) Bantam.

Alone in the Crowd: One Man's Struggle with Obsessive Compulsive Disorder. Joe H. Vaughan. 136p. (Orig.). 1993. pap. text ed. 9.95 (0-9636863-6-4, 566369) J Vaughan Assocs.

Alone in the Crowd: The Jim Gilmore Story. William Neely. LC 88-70765. (Illus.). 192p. 1988. 18.50 (0-89404-083-9) Aztex.

***Alone in the Dark.** Parker. (Baby-Sitter's Nightmares Ser.: No. 1). 1995. mass mkt. 3.50 (0-06-106302-9, Harp PBks) HarpC.

Alone in the Dark: Official Strategy Guide. Johan Rodson. 1994. pap. 19.95 (1-55958-604-4) Prima Pub.

***Alone in the Dark No. 3: The Official Strategy Guide.** Schwartz. 1995. pap. text ed. 19.95 (1-55958-792-X) Prima Pub.

Alone in the Dawn: The Life of Adelaide Crapsey. Karen Alkalay-Gut. LC 87-25575. (Illus.). 368p. 1988. 35.00 (0-8203-1016-6) U of Ga Pr.

Alone in the House. Edmund Plante. 176p. (Orig.). (J). (gr. 5). 1991. pap. 3.50 (0-380-76424-5, Flare) Avon.

Alone in the Sierra. Marcel P. Fraser. LC 91-19319. 80p. (Orig.). 1991. pap. 8.00 (0-931832-98-5) Fithian Pr.

Alone in the Valley. Kenneth W. Baker. LC 91-42101. 296p. 1992. 22.00 (1-877946-17-6) Permanent Pr.

Alone of All Her Sex: The Myth & the Cult of the Virgin Mary. Marina Warner. 1983. pap. 18.00 (0-394-71155-6) Knopf.

Alone of All Her Sex: The Myth & the Cult of the Virgin Mary. Marina Warner. LC 82-40051. (Illus.). 488p. 1983. pap. 10.95 (0-685-53901-6, Vin) Random.

Alone on the Great Wall. William Lindesay. LC 91-71367. 234p. 1991. pap. 14.95 (1-55591-079-3) Fulcrum Pub.

Alone Through China & Tibet. large type ed. Helena Drysdale. (Illus.). 384p. 1988. 15.95 (0-7089-1831-X) Ulverscroft.

Alone Together. Elena Bonner. LC 87-40092. 320p. 1988. pap. 8.95 (0-394-75538-3, Vin) Random.

Alone Together. Jim Boulden. (Illus.). 32p. (Orig.). (J). (gr. 1-7). 1991. pap. 4.95 (1-878076-09-4) Boulden Pub.

An Asterisk (*) at the beginning of an entry indicates that the title is appearing in BIP for the first time.

An Asterisk (*) at the beginning of an entry indicates that the title is appearing in BIP for the first time.

A

Alpha Box & Dictionary. Brigid Gaynor. (Illus.). 28p. (J). (ps). Date not set. 14.95 (*1-56828-008-4*) Red Jacket Pr.

***Alpha Bugs.** David Carter. (J). 1994. 16.95 (*0-671-86631-1*, Litl Simon S&S) S&S Childrens.

Alpha-Bytes Count with Computers. Sherry Kinkoph. (J). (ps up). 1993. disk, pap. 16.95 (*1-56761-031-5*) Alpha Bks IN.

Alpha-Bytes Draw with Computers. Sherry Kinkoph. (J). (ps up). 1993. 16.95 (*1-56761-032-3*) Alpha Bks IN.

Alpha-Bytes Fun with Computers. Sherry Kinkoph. (J). (ps up). 1992. disk, pap. 16.95 (*0-672-30238-1*) Alpha Bks IN.

Alpha Chi Recorder. annuals 100p. write for info. (*0-318-59897-3*) Alpha Chi.

Alpha Children: Right Brained & Gifted. Jack Fadely & Virginia Hosler. (Illus.). 141p. 1985. pap. text ed. 7.00 (*0-934293-04-X*) Huber-Copeland Pub.

Alpha Control Reference Manual. William E. Anchors, Jr. & Gary Stork. 102p. 1986. pap. 11.95 (*1-880417-00-6*) Star Tech.

Alpha-Emitting Particles in Lungs. LC 75-17147. (Report Ser.: No. 46). 1975. 15.00 (*0-913392-28-6*) NCRP Pubns.

Alpha Encyclopedia, 17 vols., Set. 6240p. (FRE.). 1,495.00 (*0-8288-6098-X*, M6002) Fr & Eur.

Alpha-Glucosidease Inhibition: Potential Use in Diabetes: Proceedings of the First Preclinical Workshop on Acarbose. Ed. by C. A. Maggio & A. Scriabine. (Drugs in Development Ser.). (Illus.). 285p. (Orig.). 1994. pap. text ed. 75.00 (*0-9637603-0-0*) Neva Pr.

Alpha Hand ABC Shorthand: Notetaking & Secretarial. Steve Rosen & Rose Palmer. (Alpha Hand Ser.). 172p. 1989. 14.00 (*0-936862-02-5*, AH-1); teacher ed 10.00 (*0-936862-49-1*, AHM); student ed 6.00 (*0-936862-09-2*, AHWB); audio 7.50 (*0-936862-33-5*, 98) DDC Pub.

Alpha Hand Dictionary. Steve Rosen. (Alpha Hand Ser.). 63p. 1980. 4.00 (*0-936862-08-4*, AHD) DDC Pub.

Alpha Hand Shorthand Two. (Alpha Hand Ser.). 1985. 10.00 (*0-936862-28-9*, 2468) DDC Pub.

Alpha Hand: Transcription & Review: Second Semester Textbook & Cassette. Minni Richardson. (Alpha Hand Ser.). 148p. 1989. 15.00 (*0-936862-47-5*, AH-22); teacher ed 9.00 (*0-936862-46-7*, AH2-TM) DDC Pub.

Alpha Junior. (Voyageur Starfinder Ser.). 1993. pap. 9.95 (*0-89658-187-X*) Voyageur Pr.

Alpha Kat. William B. Lovejoy. 384p. 1992. mass mkt. 4.50 (*0-8217-3958-1*) Zebra.

Alpha Man: Postcards from Europe. Kay Thorpe. (Presents Ser.). 1994. mass mkt. 2.99 (*0-373-11619-5*, 1-11619-3) Harlequin Bks.

Alpha Olefins Applications Handbook. Lappin & Sauer. (Chemical Industries Ser.: Vol. 37). 480p. 1989. 155.00 (*0-8247-7895-2*) Dekker.

Alpha Omega. Max Childers. 1993. 18.95 (*0-941711-21-8*) Wyrick & Co.

Alpha One. (Voyageur Starfinder Ser.). 1993. pap. 9.95 (*0-89658-185-3*) Voyageur Pr.

Alpha-Phonics: A Primer for Beginning Readers. 8th ed. Samuel L. Blumenfeld. LC 82-12873. 168p. 1991. reprint ed. pap. 24.95 (*0-941995-00-3*) Paradigm ID.

***Alpha Raid.** large type ed. Alan Scholefield. 1994. 21.95 (*0-7089-3173-1*) Ulverscroft.

Alpha Stories. Mary B. Spann. Ed. by Lisa L. Durkin & Kathleen Hyson. (Illus.). 124p. 1987. pap. 10.95 (*0-9615005-6-5*) First Teacher.

ALPHA Test (Assessment Link Between Phonology & Articulation) Robert J. Lowe. 1986. 36.00 (*1-55999-012-0*) LinguiSystems.

Alpha to Omega. Jane Lippy. LC 88-50832. 17p. 1988. pap. 5.95 (*1-55523-162-4*) Winston-Derek.

Alpha, Trans, Chung: A Photographic Model: Semiotics, Film & Interpretation. Peter D'Agostino. LC 78-73214. (Illus.). 1978. pap. 10.95 (*0-917986-09-1*) NFS Pr.

Alpha Two. (Voyageur Starfinder Ser.). 1993. pap. 14.95 (*0-89658-186-1*) Voyageur Pr.

Alpha-1 Adrenergic Receptors. Ed. by R. R. Ruffolo. LC 87-17006. (Receptors Ser.). 568p. 1987. 99.50 (*0-89603-110-1*) Humana.

***Alpha 1-Antitrypsin Deficiency.** Ed. by Crystal. 473p. 1995. write for info. (*0-8247-8848-6*) Dekker.

Alpha-2 Adrenergic Receptors. Ed. by Lee E. Limbird. LC 88-6833. (Receptors Ser.). (Illus.). 384p. 1988. 99.50 (*0-89603-135-7*) Humana.

***Alpha 94 Literacy & Cultural Development Strategies in Rural Areas.** Jean-Paul Hautecoeur. 347p. 1994. pap. 35.00 (*92-820-1067-8*, U0678, Pub. by UNESCO FR) UNIPUB.

***Alphabake: A Cookbook & Cookie Cutter Set.** Debora Pearson. LC 95-13379. (Illus.). 32p. (J). (ps-3). 1995. 15.99 (*0-525-45461-6*, DCB) Dutton Child Bks.

Alphabatics. Suse MacDonald. LC 85-31429. (Illus.). 64p. (J). (ps up). 1986. text ed. 16.95 (*0-02-761520-0*, Bradbury S&S) S&S Childrens.

Alphabatics. Suse MacDonald. LC 91-38497. (Illus.). 56p. (J). (ps-1). 1992. reprint ed. pap. 6.95 (*0-689-71625-7*, Aladdin Paperbacks) S&S Childrens.

Alphabatty: Riddles from A to Z. Ann Walton & Rick Walton. (You Must Be Joking! Riddle Bks.). (Illus.). 32p. (J). (gr. 1-4). 1991. lib. bdg. 13.50 (*0-8225-2335-3*, Lerner Publctns) Lerner Group.

Alphabatty: Riddles from A to Z. Rick Walton. (J). (gr. 1-4). 1991. pap. 3.95 (*0-8225-9593-1*, Lerner Publctns) Lerner Group.

Alphabatty Animals & Funny Foods. Mimi Mazzarella. LC 83-81449. (Illus.). 96p. (Orig.). (J). (gr. k-3). 1984. pap. 5.95 (*0-89709-045-4*) Liberty Pub.

Alphabears. Kathleen Hague. (J). (ps-2). 1985. audio, lib. bdg. 22.95 (*0-941078-99-X*) Live Oak Media.

Alphabears: An ABC Book. Kathleen Hague. LC 83-26476. (Illus.). 32p. (J). (ps-2). 1984. 12.95 (*0-8050-0841-1*, Bks Young Read) H Holt & Co.

Alphabears: An ABC Book. Kathleen Hague. LC 83-26476. (Illus.). 32p. (J). (ps-2). 1991. pap. 4.95 (*0-8050-1637-6*, Bks Young Read) H Holt & Co.

Alphabeasts. Durga Bernhard. LC 92-24980. (Illus.). 32p. (J). (ps-3). 1993. lib. bdg. 14.95 (*0-8234-0993-7*) Holiday.

Alphabeasts. Dick King-Smith. LC 91-38435. (Illus.). 64p. (J). (gr. 1 up). 1992. text ed. 14.95 (*0-02-750720-3*, Mac Bks Young Read) S&S Childrens.

***Alphabestiary: Animal Poems from A to Z.** Jane Yolen. (Illus.). 64p. (J). (ps-2). 1995. 16.95 (*1-56397-222-0*, Wordsong) Boyds Mills Pr.

Alphabet. (Honey Bear Shaped Ser.). (Illus.). 12p. (J). (gr. k-2). 1982. bds. 3.95 (*0-87449-175-4*) Modern Pub NYC.

Alphabet. (Active Minds Ser.). (Illus.). 24p. (J). 1993. 4.98 (*1-56173-485-3*) Pubns Intl Ltd.

***Alphabet.** 1995. 9.99 (*0-88705-641-5*) Joshua Morris.

Alphabet. Walter Anderson. LC 84-7291. (Illus.). 64p. 1992. pap. 10.95 (*0-87805-573-8*) U Pr of Miss.

Alphabet. Bearl Brooks. (Early Education Ser.). 26p. (ps-1). 1979. student ed 5.00 (*0-8209-0199-7*, K-1) ESP.

Alphabet. Christopher Carrie. (Crayola Kinder Art BKs.). (Illus.). 12p. (Orig.). (J). (gr. 3-6). 1987. pap. 4.70 (*0-86696-204-2*) Binney & Smith.

Alphabet. M. R. Doty. (Illus.). 1979. pap. 3.50 (*0-934184-00-3*) Alembic Pr.

Alphabet. Illus. & Created by Monique Felix. (Mouse Bks.). (J). (gr. 5 up). 1992. lib. bdg. 10.95 (*0-88682-563-6*) Creative Ed.

Alphabet. Joan Hoffman. (I Know It! Bks.). (Illus.). 32p. (J). (ps-1). 1987. student ed 1.99 (*0-938256-03-3*) Sch Zone Pub Co.

Alphabet. Stuart Z. Perkoff. 1973. 4.00 (*0-88031-010-3*) Invisible-Red Hill.

Alphabet. Fiona Pragoff. LC 87-635. (Illus.). (J). (ps-00). 1987. mass mkt. 6.95 (*0-385-24171-2*) Doubleday.

Alphabet. Schaffer, Frank, Publications Staff. (Help Your Child Learn Ser.). (Illus.). 24p. (J). (ps-2). 1978. student ed 3.98 (*0-86734-001-0*, FS-3002) Schaffer Pubns.

Alphabet. Annette Taulbee. (Be Smart Bks.). (Illus.). 24p. (J). (ps-00). 1986. 3.98 (*0-86734-059-2*, FS-3051) Schaffer Pubns.

Alphabet. Paul Valery. (Illus.). (FRE.). 1976. 350.00 (*0-7859-1565-6*, 2900200024) Fr & Eur.

Alphabet. William Nicholson. LC 75-14747. (Illus.). 1975. reprint ed. 30.00 (*0-915346-02-8*) A Wofsy Fine Arts.

Alphabet: A Child's Introduction to the Letters & Sounds of French. Roger Pare. (Illus.). 32p. (J). 1991. 7.95 (*0-8442-1395-0*, Natl Textbk) NTC Pub Grp.

Alphabet: A Handbook of ABC Books & Book Extensions for the Elementary Classroom. 2nd ed. Patricia L. Roberts. LC 93-42444. 1994. 32.50 (*0-8108-2823-5*) Scarecrow.

Alphabet: Active Minds. Photos by George Siede & Donna Preis. (Active Minds-English Ser.). (Illus.). 24p. (J). (ps-3). 1992. lib. bdg. 9.95 (*1-56674-000-2*, HTS Bks) Forest Hse.

***Alphabet: An Account of the Origin & Development of Letters, 2 vols.** Isaac Taylor. Incl. Aryan Alphabets. (C). 1991. reprint ed. (*0-318-70306-8*, Pub. by Asian Educ Servs II); Semitic Alphabets, 2 vols. (C). 1991. reprint ed. (*0-318-70305-X*, Pub. by Asian Educ Servs II); 70.00x (*81-206-0694-9*, Pub. by Asian Educ Servs II) S Asia.

Alphabet: Individual Sets. Marion W. Stuart. Date not set. text ed. write for info. (*0-943343-12-7*) Lrn Wrap-Ups.

Alphabet: Its Rise & Development. Martin Sprengling. 1975. 250.00 (*0-87968-589-1*) Gordon Pr.

Alphabet: Lowercase. Barbara Gregorich. Ed. by Joan Hoffman. (Get Ready! Bks.). (Illus.). 32p. (J). (ps). 1983. student ed 1.99 (*0-938256-66-1*) Sch Zone Pub Co.

***Alphabet: The History, Evolution, & Design of the Letters We Use Today.** Allan Haley. LC 94-39682. 1995. 24.95 (*0-8230-0170-9*) Watsn-Guptill.

Alphabet: Uppercase. Barbara Gregorich. Ed. by Joan Hoffman. (Get Ready! Bks.). (Illus.). 32p. (J). (ps). 1983. student ed 1.99 (*0-938256-65-3*) Sch Zone Pub Co.

Alphabet A-Z. Walt Disney Productions Staff. (Walt Disney's Fun-to-Learn Library Ser.: Vol. 1). (Illus.). 44p. (J). (gr. 1-6). reprint ed. 0.99 (*0-9619525-2-0*) Advance Pubs.

Alphabet Aa to Zz. Renee Z. Novit. (Kidz & Katz Educational Learning Book Ser.). (Illus.). 16p. (J). (ps-00). Date not set. pap. 7.95 (*1-883371-00-7*) Kidz & Katz.

Alphabet Abecedarium: Some Notes on Letters. Richard A. Firmage. LC 93-26544. 1993. 40.00 (*0-87923-987-5*); pap. 19.95 (*0-87923-998-0*) Godine.

***Alphabet about Kids with Cancer.** Rita Berglund. (Illus.). 89p. (J). 1994. 19.95 (*0-9629365-3-7*) Childrens Lgcy.

Alphabet Activities. Jill M. Coudron. (J). (ps-3). 1982. pap. 11.99 (*0-8224-0297-1*) Fearon Teach Aids.

Alphabet & Elements of Lettering. Frederick W. Goudy. (Illus.). 1922. pap. 6.95 (*0-486-20792-7*) Dover.

Alphabet & Elements of Lettering. Frederic W. Goudy. (Reprints Ser.). (Illus.). 101p. 1989. reprint ed. 29.95 (*0-88029-330-6*) Dorset Pr.

Alphabet & Image: A Quarterly of Typography & Graphic Arts, 2 vols., Set. Ed. by Robert Harling. LC 75-138686. (Contemporary Art Ser.). (Illus.). 1975. reprint ed. 151.95 (*0-405-00766-3*) Ayer.

***Alphabet & Number Rhymes.** (Take-Home Rhyme Bks.). (Illus.). 160p. (J). (ps-1). 1995. 14.95 (*0-614-06832-0*, WPH 1102) Totline Bks.

Alphabet & Number Rhymes. Jean Warren. Ed. by Gayle Bittinger. (Take-Home Ser.). (Illus.). 160p. (Orig.). (J). (ps-1). 1989. pap. text ed. 14.95 (*0-911019-27-8*) Warren Pub Hse.

Alphabet & the Brain. Ed. by D. De Kerdhove. (Illus.). 490p. 1988. 113.00 (*0-387-18122-9*) Spr-Verlag.

Alphabet & Words. Marilyn Hayes. (Early Education Ser.). 24p. (gr. 1). 1982. student ed 5.00 (*0-8209-0214-4*, K-16) ESP.

Alphabet Animals. Charles Sullivan. (J). 1991. 15.95 (*0-8478-1377-0*) Rizzoli Intl.

Alphabet Art: Thirteen ABCs from Around the World. Leonard E. Fisher. LC 84-28752. (Illus.). 64p. (J). (gr. 3-7). 1984. reprint ed. text ed. 16.95 (*0-02-735230-7*, Four Winds Pr) S&S Childrens.

Alphabet Arts. Kathy Faggella et al. (Illus.). 122p. 1987. pap. 10.95 (*0-9615005-7-3*) First Teacher.

Alphabet Avalanche. Barbara Gregorich. Ed. by Joan Hoffman. (Fast Forward Enrichment Ser.). 32p. (Orig.). (J). (ps-1). student ed 1.99 (*0-88743-128-3*) Sch Zone Pub Co.

***Alphabet Band.** (J). Date not set. 16.98 (*0-7853-0565-3*) Pubns Intl Ltd.

Alphabet Bandits: An ABC Book. Marcia Leonard. LC 89-4933. (Illus.). 24p. (J). (gr. k-2). 1990. lib. bdg. 9.59 (*0-8167-1718-4*); pap. text ed. 2.50 (*0-8167-1719-2*) Troll Assocs.

Alphabet Between. Marni McGee. LC 91-25489. (Illus.). 32p. (J). (ps-1). 1995. text ed. 14.95 (*0-689-31753-0*, Atheneum Bks Young) S&S Childrens.

Alphabet Book. (Sunbird Ser.: No. 792-1). (Illus.). (J). (ps-00). 3.50 (*0-7214-8100-0*) Ladybird Bks.

Alphabet Book. P. D. Eastman. LC 73-16859. (Illus.). 32p. (J). (ps-3). 1974. pap. 2.50 (*0-394-82818-6*) Random Bks Yng Read.

Alphabet Book. Arthur Geisert. (J). (ps-1). 1985. write for info. (*0-318-60128-1*) HM.

***Alphabet Book: An ABC Book of AA, Rhymes, Patterns, & Activities.** Sharon Ralph. Ed. by Leslie Britt. (Illus.). 96p. (Orig.). (J). (gr. k-2). 1995. pap. text ed. 9.95 (*0-86530-307-X*, 1P307-0) Incentive Pubns.

Alphabet Book Mobile. Illus. by Miriam Schapiro. (Book Mobiles Ser.). 28p. 1993. 7.95 (*1-56640-582-3*) Pomegranate Calif.

Alphabet Books As a Key to Language Patterns. Patricia L. Roberts. LC 87-3216. ix, 263p. 1988. 36.00 (*0-208-02151-5*, Lib Prof Pubns) Shoe String.

Alphabet Careers: A Career Awareness Program for Grades Two Through Four. Judith Sahlin. 16p. (J). 1994. 10.95 (*1-884063-15-2*) Mar Co Prods.

Alphabet City. Geoffrey Biddle. 1992. 50.00 (*0-520-07360-6*); pap. 18.00 (*0-520-07949-3*) U CA Pr.

***Alphabet City.** Stephen T. Johnson. LC 95-12335. (Illus.). 32p. (J). 1995. 14.99 (*0-670-85631-2*, Viking) Viking Penguin.

Alphabet Connections. (Illus.). 24p. (J). 1991. write for info. (*0-318-69689-4*, RR-001) Wonder Well.

Alphabet Connections. Shirley Ross et al. (Illus.). 352p. 1993. pap. 24.95 (*1-878279-52-1*) Monday Morning Bks.

***Alphabet Connections.** Shirley Ross et al. (Illus.). 352p. 1993. teacher ed, pap. 24.95 (*0-87827-952-0*, MM 1969) Evan-Moor Corp.

Alphabet Cookbook. Mary Buckman. (One in a Series of Cook & Learn Books). (Illus.). (J). (gr. k-2). 1988. pap. text ed. 9.95 (*1-879414-03-1*) Mary Bee Creat.

Alphabet Cooking Cards. Cheryl Olmsted. (J). (gr. k-1). 1990. pap. 11.99 (*0-8224-0454-0*) Fearon Teach Aids.

Alphabet Dot-to-Dot. Annette Taulbee. (Be Smart Bks.). (Illus.). 24p. (J). (ps-00). 1986. 3.98 (*0-86734-062-2*, FS-3054) Schaffer Pubns.

Alphabet Drawings. Schomer Lichtner. (Illus.). 88p. (Orig.). (J). (gr. k up). 1973. pap. 4.50 (*0-686-97176-0*) Lichtner.

Alphabet for Gourmets. M. F. Fisher. LC 88-32966. 256p. 1989. reprint ed. pap. 12.95 (*0-86547-391-9*, North Pt Pr) FS&G.

Alphabet for Positive Living: Play with Words to Improve Your Emotional Fitness. Inez P. Exton. (Illus.). 60p. 1987. pap. text ed. 7.50 (*0-961891 5-0-5*) Zebra Comns.

***Alphabet for Young ECKists.** Jean Lucchese. 26p. 1995. 6.00 (*1-57043-104-3*) ECKANKAR.

Alphabet from Z to A: With Much Confusion on the Way. Judith Viorst. LC 91-39338. (Illus.). 32p. (J). (gr. 2-5). 1994. text ed. 14.95 (*0-689-31768-9*, Atheneum Bks Young) S&S Childrens.

***Alphabet Fun.** Julie Orr. Ed. by Joan Hoffman. (Jump Ahead Book Ser.). (Illus.). 32p. (J). (ps-k). 1994. student ed 1.99 (*0-88743-115-1*) Sch Zone Pub Co.

Alphabet Fun & Games. Jill M. Coudron. LC 83-62563. (J). (ps-3). 1984. pap. 11.99 (*0-8224-0295-5*) Fearon Teach Aids.

Alphabet Garden. Laura J. Coats. LC 92-6235. (Illus.). 32p. (J). (ps-1). 1993. text ed. 13.95 (*0-02-719042-0*, Mac Bks Young Read) S&S Childrens.

Alphabet Hidden Picture Coloring Book. Anna Pomaska. (Illus.). (J). (gr. k-3). 1992. pap. 2.50 (*0-486-27261-3*) Dover.

Alphabet House. (Little Golden Sound Story Bks.). (Illus.). 24p. (J). (ps up). 1992. write for info. (*0-307-74811-1*, 64811, Golden Pr) Western Pub.

Alphabet in Five Acts. Karen B. Andersen. LC 92-26947. (Illus.). 32p. (J). 1993. 13.99 (*0-8037-1440-8*); lib. bdg. 13.89 (*0-8037-1441-6*) Dial Bks Young.

Alphabet in Signs: ABC's in Fingerspelling. Michael Geiger. (Illus.). 60p. (Orig.). (J). (ps-3). 1984. pap. 5.00 (*0-916708-13-6*) Modern Signs.

Alphabet in the Park. Adelia Prado. Tr. by Ellen Watson. LC 89-38463. (Wesleyan Poetry in Translation Ser.). 80p. 1990. 22.50 (*0-8195-2175-2*, Wesleyan Univ Pr); pap. 10.95 (*0-8195-1177-3*, Wesleyan Univ Pr) U Pr of New Eng.

Alphabet Kids. Kathleen Tompkins. (Illus.). 23p. (Orig.). 1978. pap. 6.95 (*0-915248-15-8*) Wedgehouse.

Alphabet Kids: Reading Readiness Book. Kathleen Tompkins. (Illus.). 26p. (Orig.). (J). 1994. pap. text ed. 6.00 (*0-944073-01-8*) Wedgehouse.

Alphabet Kids Coloring Sticker Book. Kathleen Tompkins. (Illus.). 31p. (Orig.). 1987. pap. 3.50 (*0-944073-00-X*) Wedgehouse.

Alphabet Makers: A Presentation from the Museum of the Alphabet. Katie Voightlander. (Illus.). 96p. (Orig.). (C). 1990. pap. write for info. (*0-938978-13-6*) Wycliffe Bible.

Alphabet Man: A Novel. Richard Grossman. 443p. 1993. 22.95 (*0-932511-76-7*); pap. 11.95 (*0-932511-77-5*) Fiction Coll.

Alphabet Mastery: Cursive, Level 2, Reusable Edition. Enid L. Huelsberg. 32p. 1975. 6.50 (*0-87879-786-6*, Ann Arbor Div) Acad Therapy.

Alphabet Mastery Manuscript, Level 1: Reusable Edition. Enid L. Huelsberg. 32p. (J). (ps-3). 1977. 6.50 (*0-87879-785-8*, Ann Arbor Div) Acad Therapy.

Alphabet of Angels. Nancy Willard. LC 93-48836. (J). 1994. 16.95 (*0-590-48480-X*, Blue Sky Press) Scholastic Inc.

Alphabet of Animal Signs. S. Harold Collins. (Beginning Sign Language Ser.). (Illus.). 15p. (J). (ps-00). 1994. pap. text ed. 2.95 (*0-931993-65-2*, GP-065) Garlic Pr OR.

Alphabet of Animals. Illus. by Isabelle Brent. LC 92-54652. (J). 1993. 12.95 (*0-316-10852-9*) Little.

Alphabet of Attributes. Harold Downs. LC 72-107695. (Essay Index Reprint Ser.). 1977. 20.95 (*0-8369-1498-8*) Ayer.

Alphabet of Bible Creatures. Marni S. McKenzie. (Illus.). 56p. (J). (ps-8). 1993. 14.95 (*1-882630-00-9*) Mercy Pr.

***Alphabet of Books: Literature Based Activities for Schools & Libraries.** Robin W. Davis. (Illus.). 120p. (J). (ps-2). 1995. student ed 11.95 (*0-917846-38-9*, 33918, Alleyside) Highsmith Pr.

Alphabet of Civility. Virginia C. Clarkson. LC 93-15686. (Illus.). (J). 1993. 9.95 (*0-913515-86-8*, Starrhill) Elliott & Clark.

Alphabet of Desire. Ken Norris. 70p. (C). 1991. pap. 12.00 (*1-55022-148-5*, Pub. by ECW Press CN) Genl Dist Srvs.

Alphabet of Dinosaurs. Peter Dodson. LC 94-15522. (J). 1995. 14.95 (*0-590-46486-8*) Scholastic Inc.

Alphabet of Economic Science: Elements of Theory of Value or Worth. Philip H. Wicksteed. LC 75-15410. (Reprints of Economic Classics Ser.). (Illus.). xiii, 142p. 1970. reprint ed. 27.50 (*0-678-00379-3*) Kelley.

Alphabet of Girls. rev. ed. Leland Jacobs. LC 93-8328. (Illus.). 32p. (J). 1994. 14.95 (*0-8050-3018-2*) H Holt & Co.

Alphabet of Grace. Frederick Buechner. LC 84-48765. 128p. 1989. pap. 10.00 (*0-06-061179-0*) Harper SF.

***Alphabet of Grace.** Chuck Sullivan. 72p. (Orig.). 1994. pap. 9.95 (*1-885926-01-4*) Sandstone NC.

Alphabet of Lili. Mike Glier. 40p. 1992. pap. 10.00 (*0-942324-05-6*) Visual Studies.

Alphabet of Mission. Alfred H. Jones. (Orig.). 1991. pap. 3.95 (*0-377-00238-0*) Friendship Pr.

***Alphabet of Murder.** Bad Otis Link. 32p. 1994. 4.95 (*1-885730-03-9*) Verotik.

Alphabet of the Heart: Sacred Geometry: Genesis in Principle of Language & Feeling. rev. ed. Daniel Winter. (Illus.). 440p. 1993. pap. 22.00 (*0-9640980-0-8*) Crystal Hill.

Alphabet Orders & Fun Feelings. Staci Coblentz. LC 93-93509. (Illus.). 64p. (Orig.). (J). 1994. pap. 6.00 (*1-56002-368-6*, Univ Edtns) Aegina Pr.

Alphabet Out Loud. Ruth G. Bragg. LC 91-14546. (Illus.). 32p. (J). (gr. k up). 1991. pap. 14.95 (*0-88708-172-X*, Picture Book Studio) S&S Childrens.

Alphabet Pal. Robin Q. Buschemeyer. (Professor Elly Fun's Back to Basics Ser.). 64p. (Orig.). (J). (ps-3). 1986. pap. 2.99 (*0-935609-01-6*) Eduplay.

Alphabet Parade. Seymour Chwast. 30p. (J). (ps-2). 1991. 13.95 (*0-15-200351-7*, HB Juv Bks) HarBrace.

***Alphabet Parade.** Seymour Chwast. (J). (PS-1). 1994. pap. 4.95 (*0-15-200115-8*) HarBrace.

Alphabet Patterns. Linda Milliken. (Illus.). 64p. (J). (ps-2). 1993. Grades ps-2. pap. text ed. 6.95 (*1-56472-008-X*) Edupress.

Alphabet Picture Key Word Cards. Monica Foltzer. (Illus.). 38p. (J). 1987. 4.60 (*0-9607918-5-X*, A 505419) St Ursula.

Alphabet Pocket Fun: Letter Sound & Word Recognition Activities. Linda Milliken. (Illus.). 64p. 1994. student ed 6.95 (*1-56472-019-5*) Edupress.

Alphabet Puppets. Jill M. Coudron. LC 78-72077. (J). (gr. k-3). 1979. pap. 9.99 (*0-8224-0298-X*) Fearon Teach Aids.

***Alphabet Puppets & More!** Karen Sevaly. (Illus.). 48p. (J). (ps-6). 1994. teacher ed, pap. 6.95 (*0-943263-70-0*, TF-1359) Teachers Friend Pubns.

Alphabet Puzzle. Jill Downie. LC 88-80278. (Illus.). 64p. (J). (ps-1). 1988. 16.00 (*0-688-08044-8*) Lothrop.

Alphabet Roots: A Glimpse of the Alphabet Museum. Wally Kennicutt. (Illus.). 32p. (Orig.). 1989. pap. text ed. 1.00 (*0-9615959-5-7*) JAARS Inc.

***Alphabet Seekers.** Julie Orr. Ed. by Joan Hoffman. (Jump Ahead Book Ser.). (Illus.). 32p. (J). (ps-k). 1994. student ed 1.99 (*0-88743-112-7*) Sch Zone Pub Co.

Alphabet Sequence. Fred Justus. (Early Education Ser.). 24p. (gr. 1). 1980. student ed 5.00 (*0-686-42826-9*) ESP.

Alphabet Sounds & Pictures see Let's Learn Set

Alphabet Soup. Carol J. Anderson. (Illus.). 60p. (J). (gr. k-4). 1989. 12.95 (*0-935317-26-0*) Blue Heron WA.

Alphabet Soup. Kate Banks. (Dragonfly Bks.). (Illus.). 32p. (J). (ps-2). 1994. pap. 5.99 (*0-679-86723-6*) Knopf Bks Yng Read.

***Alphabet Soup: A Feast of Letters.** Scott Gustafson. LC 94-30729. (Illus.). (J). 1994. 19.95 (*0-86713-025-3*) Greenw Pr Ltd.

An Asterisk (*) at the beginning of an entry indicates that the title is appearing in BIP for the first time.

Alphabet Soup: A Recipe for Understanding & Treating Attention Deficit Disorder. James Javorsky. 50p. (Orig.). 1994. pap. text ed. 6.95 (*0-934695-00-8*) Minerva Pr MI.

Alphabet Soup: A Tablature Primer for Viols. Carol Herman. (Educational Ser.: No. 2). vi, 40p. (Orig.). 1990. pap. text ed. 14.00 (*1-56571-043-6*) PRB Prods.

Alphabet Soup: An Orderly Collection of Disorderly Thought. Stanley Berne. Ed. by Albert Scharf. (Illus.). 240p. (Orig.). 1994. 22.00 (*0-913844-20-9*, Bookpeople); pap. 13.95 (*0-913844-21-7*, Bookpeople) Danrus Pubs.

Alphabet Soup: Jewish Family Cooking from A to Z. Ed. by Karen B. Sager. (Illus.). 416p. 1990. write for info. (*0-9627058-0-2*) S Schechter Day Schls.

Alphabet Soup Isn't Supposed to Make Sense. Tom Wilson. 256p. 1984. pap. 3.95 (*0-8362-1222-3*) Andrews & McMeel.

***Alphabet Stitchery by Hand & Machine.** (Illus.). 168p. 1995. pap. 19.95 (*0-8019-8527-7*) Chilton.

Alphabet Stories. Jill M. Coudron. (J). (ps-3). 1982. pap. 11.99 (*0-8224-0299-8*) Fearon Teach Aids.

Alphabet Symphony. Bruce McMillan. (Illus.). 32p. (J). (gr. k-2). 1977. 15.00 (*0-688-80112-9*) Apple Isl Bks.

Alphabet Tale. Jan Garten. LC 93-4879. (Illus.). 32p. (J). (ps up). 1994. 15.00 (*0-688-12702-9*); lib. bdg. 14.93 (*0-688-12703-7*) Greenwillow.

Alphabet Talk: Gospel Rhymes for Each Letter of the Alphabet. Rayola C. Larsen. LC 89-83429. (Illus.). 32p. (Orig.). (J). (gr. k-3). 1989. reprint ed. pap. 4.98 (*0-88290-147-8*) Horizon Utah.

Alphabet-ter Letter Rhymes. Ruth I. Dowell. 32p. (Orig.). (J). (ps-2). 1987. pap. 6.00 (*0-945842-05-8*) Pollyanna Prodns.

Alphabet-ter Letter Rhymes Activity Book. Ruth I. Dowell. (Move Over, Mother Goose Ser.). (J). (ps-2). 1991. pap. 6.00 (*0-945842-14-7*) Pollyanna Prodns.

***Alphabet Theme-a-Saurus.** Jean Warren. (Theme-a-Saurus Ser.). (Illus.). 280p. (J). 1995. teacher ed 19.95 (*0-614-06855-X*, WPH 1004) Totline Bks.

Alphabet Theme-a-Saurus: The Great Big Book of Letter Recognition. Ed. by Elizabeth McKinnon & Gayle Bittinger. LC 90-71272. (Theme-A-Saurus Ser.). (Illus.). 280p. (J). (ps-1). 1991. pap. text ed. 19.95 (*0-911019-38-3*) Warren Pub Hse.

Alphabet Times Four: An International ABC. Ruth Brown. LC 91-3162. (Illus.). 32p. (J). (ps up). 1991. 13.95 (*0-525-44831-4*, DCB) Dutton Child Bks.

Alphabet Town. Stephen H. Lemberg. (Illus.). (J). (ps). 1993. Incl. cass. 7.95 (*1-882500-02-4*) SmartSong.

Alphabet Town Picnic. Singin' Steve. (Smart Song Adventures Ser.). (Illus.). 16p. (J). (gr. k-1). 1994. bds. write for info. (*1-882500-06-7*) SmartSong.

Alphabet Witch. Irene Smalls-Hector. LC 94-6196. (Illus.). (J). 1994. 7.95 (*0-681-00542-4*) Longmeadow Pr.

Alphabet Year. Kathryn H. Kidd. 244p. (Orig.). 1991. pap. 7.95 (*0-9624049-3-4*) Hatrack River.

Alphabet Zoo. Laird. LC 74-190264. (Illus.). 32p. (J). (ps-2). 1972. lib. bdg. 9.95 (*0-87783-053-3*) Oddo.

Alphabet Zoo: A Rhyming Menagerie. Stephen Holmes. (J). 1994. 5.98 (*0-8317-0454-3*) Smithmark.

Alphabetic Filing Rules. 40p. 1986. pap. 21.00 (*0-933887-00-0*, A4511) Assn Recs Mgrs & Admin.

Alphabetic Key Punch Operator, (IBM) Jack Rudman. (Career Examination Ser.: C-13). 1994. pap. 23.95 (*0-8373-0013-4*) Nat Learn.

Alphabetic Labyrinth: The Alphabet in History, Mysticism & Imagination. Johanna Drucker. LC 93-61369. (Illus.). 328p. 1995. 45.00 (*0-500-01608-9*) Thames Hudson.

Alphabetic Writing & the Old Georgian Script: A Typology & Provenience of Alphabetic Writing Systems. Thomas V. Gamkrelidze. LC 94-15617. (Anatolian & Caucasian Studies Ser.). 1995. 75.00 (*0-88206-082-1*) Caravan Bks.

Alphabetical Africa. Walter Abish. 160p. 1974. pap. 8.95 (*0-8112-0533-9*, NDP375) New Directions.

Alphabetical & Chronological Review of Announced U. S. Nuclear Tests: July 1945-December 1983. 72p. (Orig.). 1984. 6.95 (*0-914677-01-2*) Contemp Issues.

Alphabetical & Numerical Index to Wallace Nutting Pictures. Michael Ivankovich. Ed. by Susan Di Marco. LC 88-71204. (Illus.). 275p. (Orig.). (C). 1988. pap. 14.95 (*0-9615843-5-1*) Diamond Pr PA.

Alphabetical Arrangement of Main Entries from the Shelf List of the Union Theological Seminary Library, 10 Vols, Set. Union Theological Seminar Library Staff. 1970. lib. bdg. 1,555.00 (*0-8161-0595-2*, Hall Library) G K Hall.

Alphabetical Bible: King James Version. Intro. by D. Lewis Staton. 1510p. 1994. 24.95 (*0-9620578-1-9*) Hilton Hse Pubs.

Alphabetical Catalog of the Books & Pamphlets of the International Institute of Social History: Library Catalogs-Bibliography Guides 2nd Supplement. International Institute of Social History, Amsterdam Staff. 1979. lib. bdg. 450.00 (*0-8161-0297-X*, Hall Library) G K Hall.

Alphabetical City. Steven Holl. (Pamphlet Architecture Ser.: No. 5). (Illus.). 72p. 1987. pap. 10.95 (*0-910413-16-9*) Princeton Arch.

Alphabetical First & Last Name Index, Vol. 1: History of Columbia Co. New York by Capt. Benjamin F. Ellis. Albert L. Divine. 105p. 1991. lib. bdg. 22.00 (*1-56012-087-8*) Kinship Rhinebeck.

Alphabetical Index of Patentees of Inventions 1617-1852. Great Britain, Patent Office Staff. Ed. by Bennett Woodcroft. LC 68-58945. 650p. 1969. reprint ed. lib. bdg. 57.50 (*0-678-07755-X*) Kelley.

Alphabetical Index of Revolutionary Pensioners Living in Maine. Charles A. Flagg. 91p. 1992. reprint ed. pap. 12.00 (*0-685-62564-8*, 1860) Clearfield Co.

Alphabetical Index to Breton & Leroux Canadian Coin Catalogues. James G. Hirtle. 50p. (Orig.). 1989. pap. text ed. 20.00 (*0-921937-0-4*) Chesapeake Coin.

Alphabetical Index to the New Testament. Samuel A. Allibone. (Principle Works of Samuel Austin Allibone). 1989. reprint ed. lib. bdg. 79.00 (*0-7812-1785-7*) Rprt Serv.

***Alphabetical Label Book.** 1991. 13.50 (*0-934715-03-3*) San Franciscana.

Alphabetical List of Battles, 1754-1900. Newton A. Strait. text ed. 19.95 (*0-8488-0039-7*, J M C & Co); pap. 12.95 (*0-8488-0229-2*, J M C & Co) Amereon Ltd.

Alphabetical List of U. S. Battles, 1754-1900. N. A. Stuart. 1976. 69.95 (*0-87968-590-5*) Gordon Pr.

Alphabetical List of Villages in the Taluks & Districts of the Madras Presidency. (C). 1992. reprint ed. 70.00 (*81-206-0575-6*, Pub. by Asian Educ Servs II) S Asia.

***Alphabetical Soup.** Suzy Spafford. 32p. (J). 1994. 14.95 (*0-9643588-0-8*) Suzys Zoo.

Alphabetical Table of Contents to Shelley's Poetical Works. F. S. Ellis. LC 74-30275. (Shelley Society, Fourth Ser.: No. 6). reprint ed. 20.00 (*0-404-11517-9*) AMS Pr.

Alphabetical Vocabularies of the Clallam & Lumni. George Gibbs. LC 75-168115. (Library of American Linguistics: No. 11). reprint ed. 42.75 (*0-404-50991-6*) AMS Pr.

Alphabetical Vocabulary of the Chinook Language. George Gibbs. LC 72-168141. (Library of American Linguistics: No. 13). (CHN.). reprint ed. 42.75 (*0-404-50993-2*) AMS Pr.

Alphabetics: A History of Our Alphabet. rev. ed. Sally J. Patton. 92p. (J). (gr. 2-8). 1989. reprint ed. pap. text ed. 14.95 (*0-913705-40-3*) Zephyr Pr AZ.

Alphabetischer Katalog der Bibliothek, 5 Vols, Set. Herder, Johann Gottfried Institut Staff. 1971. lib. bdg. 545.00 (*0-8161-0698-3*, Hall Library) G K Hall.

Alphabetischer Katalog der Bibliothek, 2 vols., Set. suppl. ed. Herder, Johann Gottfried Institut Staff. 1971. lib. bdg. 235.00 (*0-8161-0808-0*, Hall Library) G K Hall.

Alphabetischer Katalog der Bibliothek des Johann Gottfried Herder-Instituts: Second Supplement. Herder, Johann Gottfried Institut Staff. 1981. lib. bdg. 400.00 (*0-8161-0277-5*, Hall Library) G K Hall.

Alphabetischer Katalog der Deutschen Staatsbibliothek Berlin. 1987. write for info. (*0-318-71809-X*, Pub. by Georg Olms GW) Lubrecht & Cramer.

Alphabetischer Katalog der Kinder- und Jugendbuchabteilung. fiche write for info. (*0-318-71812-X*, Pub. by Georg Olms GW) Lubrecht & Cramer.

Alphabetischer Katalog der Musiksammlung der Deutschen Staatsbibliothek Berlin. 1990. fiche write for info. (*0-318-71813-8*, Pub. by Georg Olms GW) Lubrecht & Cramer.

Alphabetischer Katalog der Stadt- und Universitatsbibliothek Bern. 1991. fiche write for info. (*0-318-71814-6*, Pub. by Georg Olms GW) Lubrecht & Cramer.

Alphabetischer Katalog der Universitatsbibliothek Graz. 1983. fiche write for info. (*0-318-71821-9*, Pub. by Georg Olms GW) Lubrecht & Cramer.

Alphabetischer Zentralkatalog der Zuricherischen Bibliotheken. 1990. fiche write for info. (*0-318-71830-8*, Pub. by Georg Olms GW) Lubrecht & Cramer.

ALPHABETivities: 175 Ready-to-Use Activities from A to Z. Claudia Krause. LC 85-30912. 1986. pap. text ed. 24.95 (*0-87628-149-8*) Ctr Appl Res.

Alphabets. Phyllis Fitzgerald. LC 87-51494. (Illus.). 30p. (J). (gr. k-2). 1988. 6.95 (*1-55523-130-6*) Winston-Derek.

Alphabets - Lettering with Historical Descriptions. 3rd ed. E. Strange. (Illus.). 335p. 1987. reprint ed. pap. 25.00 (*0-87556-688-X*) Saifer.

Alphabets & Birthdays, Vol. Seven Of Unpublished Works Of Gertrude Stein. Gertrude Stein. LC 79-103660. (Select Bibliographies Reprint Ser.). 1980. 30.95 (*0-8369-5160-3*) Ayer.

Alphabets & Numbers. Patrick Spielman & Sherri S. Valitchka. LC 93-48072. (Woodworker's Pattern Library). (Illus.). 128p. 1994. pap. 9.95 (*0-8069-0487-9*) Sterling.

Alphabets & Numerals. A. A. Turbayne. 64p. 1992. pap. 19.95 (*0-9632921-0-2*) Godolphin Pr.

Alphabets & Ornaments. Ernst Lehner. (Pictorial Archive Ser.). (Illus.). 1968. pap. 8.95 (*0-486-21905-4*) Dover.

Alphabets & Samplers: Forty Cross-Stitch & Needlepoint Projects. Brenda Keyes. (Illus.). 128p. 1993. 24.95 (*0-7153-9983-7*, Pub. by D & C Pub UK) Sterling.

***Alphabets from Early Samplers: Sixty-Four Examples from Samplers Dating from 1590 to 1868, with Charts & Authentic Color Schemes.** Marsha Van Valin. (Illus.). 44p. 1994. pap. 15.00 (*0-9644764-0-1*) Scarlet Let.

Alphabets Old & New. Lewis F. Day. 1974. 59.95 (*0-87968-591-3*) Gordon Pr.

Alphabetum Narrationum: An Alphabet of Tales. Ed. by M. M. Banks. (EETS, OS Ser.: Nos. 126-7). 1972. reprint ed. 65.00 (*0-527-00122-8*) Periodicals Srv.

Alphabetyping: Look As You Learn. rev. ed. Ruth C. Weyer. Ed. by Margaret Malsam. 26p. (Orig.). 1995. pap. 12.95 (*0-9616108-3-2*) Beaumont Bks.

Alphabite! A Funny Feast from A to Z. Charles Reasoner. LC 89-65563. 36p. (J). (ps). 1989. 9.95 (*0-8431-2361-3*) Price Stern.

AlphaBlack Culture Beginning Activity Book. 2nd ed. Mia Isaac. 64p. 1991. student ed 16.95 (*0-9630229-1-1*) IGIA.

Alphaboo! A Hidden Letter ABC Book. Carol Thompson. LC 93-26925. (All Aboard Reading Ser.). (Illus.). 32p. (J). (ps-3). 1994. pap. 2.25 (*0-448-40213-0*, G&D) Putnam Pub Group.

Alphabox. Walker. 64p. (J). 1995. 16.95 (*0-8050-1581-7*) H Holt & Co.

AlphaBuddies Coloring & Reading Book, No. 1. Sarah Shepherd & Thomas Shepherd. 56p. (J). (gr. 1-2). 1992. student ed 4.95 (*0-9634846-0-5*) AlphaBuddies.

Alphagator. Mary Buckman. (Illus.). 32p. (J). (ps). 1992. pap. 8.95 (*1-879414-10-4*) Mary Bee Creat.

ALPHanauts. Mel Davis. 182p. 1985. 7.25 (*0-89697-246-1*) Intl Univ Pr.

Alphanumeric COM Quality Test Slide: ANSI-AIIM MS28-1987. Association for Information & Image Management Staff. 1987. pap. 30.00 (*0-89258-124-7*, MS28) Assn Inform & Image Mgmt.

Alphanumeric Filing Rules for Business Documents. Herbert H. Hoffman. LC 77-357152. 118p. 1977. pap. 4.00 (*0-89537-001-8*) Headway Pubns.

Alphard: Form & Content. Ed. by Mary Shaw. 321p. 1981. pap. 49.00 (*0-387-90663-0*) Spr-Verlag.

Alphaville. Jean-Luc Godard. (Illus.). 102p. (Orig.). 1988. pap. 8.95 (*0-571-12553-0*) Faber & Faber.

AlphaZoo Christmas. Susan Harrison. LC 93-20351. (Illus.). 40p. (J). (ps-2). 1993. 13.95 (*0-8249-8623-7*, Ideals Child); lib. bdg. 14.00 (*0-8249-8632-6*, Ideals Child) Hambleton-Hill.

Alpha2-Agents in Animals Sedation, Analgesia & Anaesthesia. Charles E. Short. LC 92-64484. 85p. (Orig.). 1993. pap. text ed. 25.00 (*0-9603534-2-9*) Vet Practice.

Alphita, a Medico-Botanical Glossary. Ed. by J. L. Mowat. (Anecdota Oxoniensia Ser.: No. 2). 1988. reprint ed. 67.40 (*0-404-63952-6*) AMS Pr.

Alphonse: A One Man Play in the Words of Al Capone (with a Chronology of His Life) Kenan Heise. 52p. (Orig.). 1989. pap. text ed. 6.95 (*0-924772-00-X*) CH Bookworks.

Alphonse Bertillon's Instructions for Taking Descriptions for the Identification of Criminals, & Others by Means of Anthropometric Indications. Alphonse Bertillon. LC 72-156004. (Foundations of Criminal Justice Ser.). reprint ed. 41.50 (*0-404-09104-0*) AMS Pr.

Alphonse Daudet. Alphonse Roche. LC 75-25549. (Twayne's World Authors Ser.). (C). 1976. lib. bdg. 17.95 (*0-317-38183-0*) Irvington.

Alphonse Daudet: Great Short Stories from Around the World I. Illus. by James Balkovek. LC 94-75344. (Classic Short Stories Ser.). 80p. 1994. pap. 4.50 (*1-56103-043-0*) Lake Pub Co.

Alphonse de Lamartine: A Political Biography. William Fortescue. LC 82-42927. 304p. 1983. text ed. 35.00 (*0-312-02138-0*) St Martin.

***Alphonse Has an Accident.** 4th ed. Susan Hiebert. (Illus.). 30p. (J). (gr. 4-6). 1990. pap. 6.95 (*0-919566-29-4*) Peguis Pubs Ltd.

Alphonse in Austin. Ed. by Katherine Hart. 1972. 20.00 (*0-88426-005-4*) Encino Pr.

Alphonse Juilland: D'une passion l'autre. Ed. by Brigitte Cazelles & Rene Girard. (Stanford French & Italian Studies: No. 53). 290p. 1987. pap. 46.50 (*0-915838-69-9*) Anma Libri.

Alphonse Knows...A Circle Is Not a Valentine. H. Werner Zimmermann. (Alphonse Knows Ser.). (Illus.). 24p. (J). (ps-2). 1991. bds. 9.95 (*0-19-540744-X*) OUP.

Alphonse Mattia Bookshelves Any Size: Peter Joseph Gallery, New York. Michael Bierut. LC 93-84101. (Illus.). 1993. write for info. (*1-881658-06-6*) P J Gallery.

Alphonso de Espina & the Fortalitium Fidei. Steven McMichael. (USF Studies in the History of Judaism: Vol. 96). 1994. write for info. (*0-614-03783-2*) Scholars Pr GA.

Alphonsus de Liguori: The Saint of Bourbon Naples 1696-1787. Frederick M. Jones. LC 92-73646. (Illus.). 513p. (C). 1993. 39.95 (*0-87061-195-X*, CC-00195) Chr Classics.

Alphonsus Liguori: The Redeeming Love of Christ. Ed. by Joseph Oppitz. 136p. (Orig.). 1992. pap. 8.95 (*0-911782-97-4*) New City.

Alphonsus Liguori: Tireless Worker for the Most Abandoned. 700p. 1989. 36.00 (*0-911782-68-0*) New City.

Alphra Behn. Sue Wiseman. 1990. 39.00 (*0-7463-0704-7*, Pub. by Northcote UK); pap. 21.00 (*0-685-67969-1*, Pub. by Northcote UK) St Mut.

Alpine: Four Thousand Meter Peaks by the Classic Routes. Richard Goedeke. LC 91-21684. (Illus.). 240p. 1991. 24.95 (*0-89732-111-1*) Menasha Ridge.

***Alpine: History of a Mountain Settlement.** 6th ed. Beatrice La Force. (Illus.). 529p. 1994. reprint ed. pap. 25.00 (*0-9643749-0-0*) Sky Mesa Pr.

Alpine Advocate. Mary R. Daheim. (Orig.). 1992. mass mkt. 4.99 (*0-345-37672-2*) Ballantine.

Alpine Advocate. large type ed. Mary Daheim. LC 93-18807. (Orig.). 1993. 17.95 (*1-56054-732-4*) Thorndike Pr.

Alpine & Sub-Alpine Vegetation of South East Sikkim. W. W. Smith. 108p. (C). 1977. text ed. 100.00 (*0-89771-655-8*, Pub. by Intl Bk Distr II) St Mut.

Alpine & Sub-Alpine Vegetation of South East Sikkim. W. Smith. 108p. (C). 1977. reprint ed. 110.00 (*0-685-21813-9*, Pub. by Intl Bk Distr II) St Mut.

***Alpine Angler: A Fly Fisher's Guide to the Western Wilderness.** John Shewey. (Illus.). 80p. 1995. 34.95 (*1-878175-99-8*); pap. 24.95 (*1-878175-98-X*) F Amato Pubns.

Alpine Betrayal. Mary R. Daheim. 1993. mass mkt. 4.50 (*0-345-37937-3*) Ballantine.

Alpine Betrayal. large type ed. Mary Daheim. LC 93-22678. 1993. 17.95 (*1-56054-874-6*) Thorndike Pr.

Alpine Christ & Other Poems. Robinson Jeffers. Ed. by William Everson. 1974. 20.00 (*0-9600372-4-1*) Cayucos.

Alpine Christmas. Mary R. Daheim. 1993. mass mkt. 4.99 (*0-345-38270-6*) Ballantine.

Alpine Christmas. large type ed. Mary Daheim. LC 93-38619. 1993. pap. 17.95 (*0-7862-0001-4*) Thorndike Pr.

Alpine Decoy. Mary Daheim. (Northwest Mysteries Ser.). 1994. mass mkt. 4.99 (*0-345-38841-0*) Ballantine.

***Alpine Escape.** Mary Daheim. (Orig.). 1995. mass mkt. 5.99 (*0-345-38842-9*) Ballantine.

Alpine Flora of Kashmir Himalaya. U. Dhar & P. Kachroo. 280p. 1983. 210.00 (*81-85046-08-5*, Scientific) St Mut.

Alpine Flora of New Guinea, 4 vols., Set. P. Van Royen. Incl. Vol. 1. General Part. 1980. lib. bdg. 66.00 (*3-7682-1243-2*); Vol. 2. Taxonomic Part 1: Cupressaceae to Poaceae. 1980. lib. bdg. 198.00 (*3-7682-1244-0*); Vol. 3. Taxonomic Part 2: Winteraceae to Polygonaceae. 1982. lib. bdg. 198.00 (*3-7682-1245-9*); Vol. 4. Taxonomic Part 3: Fagaceae to Asteraceae. 1983. lib. bdg. 198.00 (*3-7682-1246-7*); 660.00 (*3-7682-1247-5*) Kelley.

Alpine Flower Designs for Artists & Craftsmen. Francois Gos & Karen Baldauski. (Illus.). 64p. (Orig.). 1980. pap. 4.95 (*0-486-23982-9*) Dover.

***Alpine Flower Finder: A Guide to Wildflowers Found above Treeline in the Rocky Mountains.** rev. ed. Loraine Yeats. (Illus.). 128p. 1995. pap. 5.95 (*1-57098-026-8*) R Rinehart.

***Alpine Folly.** Mary Daheim. Date not set. pap. write for info. (*0-345-38843-7*) Ballantine.

Alpine Gardening. Roy Elliot. (Illus.). 1978. reprint ed. 15.00 (*0-913728-13-6*) Theophrastus.

Alpine Glow. Peter Turrini. Tr. by Richard Dixon. LC 94-16234. (Studies in Austrian Literature, Culture & Thought; Translation Ser.). 69p. 1994. pap. 10.00 (*0-929497-95-3*) Ariadne CA.

Alpine House: Its Plants & Purposes. Robert Rolfe. (Illus.). 144p. 1991. 27.50 (*0-88192-185-8*) Timber.

Alpine-Mediterranean Geodynamics. Ed. by H. Berckhemer & K. Hsu. (Geodynamics Ser.: Vol. 7). 216p. 1982. 22.00 (*0-87590-503-X*) Am Geophysical.

Alpine Ski Maintenance & Repair. rev. ed. Seth Masia. (Illus.). 128p. 1987. pap. 10.95 (*0-8092-4718-6*) Contemp Bks.

Alpine Skiing. 2nd ed. Robert E. Leach. LC 93-26993. (Handbook of Sports Medicine & Science Ser.). (Illus.). 144p. (Orig.). 1994. pap. text ed. write for info. (*0-632-03033-X*) Blackwell Sci.

Alpine Skiing: Steps to Success. John Yacenda. LC 91-31380. (Illus.). 176p. 1993. pap. 13.95 (*0-88011-455-X*, PYAC0455) Human Kinetics.

Alpine Tavern: Photographs of a Social Gathering Place. James Cloutier. LC 77-77899. (Illus.). 1977. pap. 9.95 (*0-918966-00-0*) Image West.

Alpine to Alkali. Marie E. Freeman & Maria H. Davis. LC 83-80807. (Nevada: Its Land & Communities Ser.). (Illus.). 150p. (Orig.). (J). (gr. 7-12). 1983. pap. text ed. 3.98 (*0-913205-01-X*) Grace Dangberg.

Alpine Vegetation of the Indian Peaks Area, Front Range, Colorado Rocky Mountains. V. Komarkova. (Flora et Vegetatio Mundi Ser.: No. 7). (Illus.). 1979. lib. bdg. 120.00 (*3-7682-1208-4*) Lubrecht & Cramer.

Alpine Wild Flowers. Dee Strickler. (Illus.). 112p. (Orig.). 1990. pap. 9.95 (*1-56044-011-2*) Falcon Pr MT.

Alpine Wildflowers. J. E. Underhill. (Illus.). 64p. pap. 6.95 (*0-88839-975-8*) Hancock House.

Alpine Wildflowers of the Rocky Mountains. Joseph F. Duft & Robert K. Moseley. LC 89-30719. 206p. 1989. pap. 14.00 (*0-87842-238-2*) Mountain Pr.

Alpines. Will Ingwersen. 320p. 1991. 65.00 (*0-88192-193-9*) Timber.

Alpine's. O. O'Banion. (Illus.). 223p. (Orig.). 1994. pap. 8.95 (*0-9637174-2-1*) Two O Bks.

Alpines: An Illustrated Dictionary. Clive Innes. (Illus.). 195p. 1995. 39.95 (*0-88192-290-0*) Timber.

Alpines: Step by Step to Growing Success. Mary A. Robinson. (Crowood Gardening Guides Ser.). (Illus.). 128p. 1992. pap. 16.95 (*1-85223-669-8*, Pub. by Crowood Pr UK) Trafalgar.

Alpines & Bog Plants. Reginald Farrer. LC 75-42433. 1976. reprint ed. 12.50 (*0-913728-10-1*) Theophrastus.

Alpines & Rockplants. Howard Drury. 96p. 1988. 60.00 (*1-85283-227-4*, Pub. by Boxtree Ltd UK) St Mut.

Alpines in the Open Garden. Jack Elliott. (Illus.). 154p. 1991. 29.95 (*0-88192-200-5*) Timber.

Alpines the Easy Way. Joe Elliott. (Wisley Ser.). (Illus.). 64p. 1991. pap. 5.95 (*0-304-32007-2*, Pub. by Cassell UK) Sterling.

***Alpines Woeterbuch: German-English-French-Italian.** Rudolf Weiss. 452p. (ENG, FRE & GER.). 1989. 95.00 (*0-7859-6978-0*) Fr & Eur.

***Alps & Jura.** 3rd ed. (Visitor's Guides Ser.). (Illus.). 256p. 1995. pap. 14.95 (*0-86190-562-8*) Hunter NJ.

Alps & Their People. Susan Bullen. LC 93-42277. (People & Places Ser.). (Illus.). 48p. (J). (gr. 5-8). 1994. 15.95 (*1-56847-165-3*) Thomson Lrning.

Alps, Apennines, Hellenides: Geodynamics Investigations along Geotraverses by an International Group of Geoscientists. Ed. by H. Closs et al. (Illus.). 638p. (Orig.). 1978. pap. text ed. 97.50 (*3-510-65083-2*, Pub. by E Schweizerbartsche GW) Lubrecht & Cramer.

Alps of the New Testament. James A. Stewart. 1964. pap. 1.99 (*1-56632-033-X*) Revival Lit.

***Alps 4000: 75 Peaks in 52 Days.** Martin Moran. (Pevensey Island Guides Ser.). (Illus.). 288p. 1995. 24.95 (*0-7153-0268-X*, Pub. by D & C Pub UK) Sterling.

ALPUK Ninety-Two: Proceedings of the 4th U. K. Annual Conference on Logic Programming, London, 30 March - 01 April 1992. Ed. by Krysia Broda. LC 92-39256. (Workshops in Computing Ser.). 1993. 79.00 (*0-387-19783-4*); 57.00 (*3-540-19783-4*) Spr-Verlag.

An Asterisk (*) at the beginning of an entry indicates that the title is appearing in BIP for the first time.

209

ALPUK 91: Proceedings of the Third U. K. Annual Conference on Logic Programming, Edinburgh, 10-12 April, 1991. Ed. by G. A. Wiggins et al. (Workshops in Computing Ser.). (Illus.). 256p. 1992. pap. 54.00 (0-387-19734-6) Spr-Verlag.
Alquimista: Una Fabula Para Seguir Tus Suenos. Paulo Coelho. Tr. by Juan G. Costa. 192p. (SPA.). 1994. pap. 10.00 (0-06-251140-8) Harper SF.
ALR Federal: American Law Reports, 106 vols. Suppl. 1993. write for info. (0-318-57182-X) Lawyers Cooperative.
ALR Federal: American Law Reports, 106 vols. suppl. ed. 1992. Suppl. 1992. write for info. (0-318-57181-1) Lawyers Cooperative.
ALR Federal: American Law Reports, 106 vols., Set. suppl. ed. 1990. write for info. (0-318-57180-3) Lawyers Cooperative.
ALR Index: Covering ALR 2d, ALR3d, ALR 4th, ALR Fed. suppl. ed. Lawyers Co-Operative Publishing Staff & Bancroft-Whitney Company. 1993. Suppl. 1993. write for info. (0-318-62121-5) Lawyers Cooperative.
ALR Medical Malpractice, 12 vols. Lawyers Co-Operative Publishing Company Staff. LC 70-1405. 1987. 824.00 (0-686-14517-8) Lawyers Cooperative.
ALR Medical Malpractice, 12 vols. suppl. ed. Lawyers Co-Operative Publishing Company Staff. LC 70-1405. 1993. Suppl. 1993. 75.00 (0-317-03150-3) Lawyers Cooperative.
ALR 3rd: American Law Reports, 100 vols. suppl. ed. 1993. Suppl. 1993. write for info. (0-318-57177-3) Lawyers Cooperative.
ALR 4th: American Law Reports, 90 vols. suppl. ed. 1993. write for info. (0-318-57179-X) Lawyers Cooperative.
ALR 4th: American Law Reports, 90 vols., Set. 1991. write for info. (0-318-57178-1) Lawyers Cooperative.
Alraune. Hanns H. Ewers. Ed. by R. Reginald & Douglas Menville. Tr. by S. Guy Endore. LC 75-46269. (Supernatural & Occult Fiction Ser.). 1976. lib. bdg. 28.95 (0-405-08130-8) Ayer.
***Already the World: Poems.** Victoria Redel. LC 95-4151. (Wick Poetry First Bks.: No. 1). 128p. 1995. text ed. 17.00x (0-87338-530-6); pap. 9.50 (0-87338-531-4) Kent St U Pr.
Already to Harvest. Hartman Rector, Jr. 91p. 1985. pap. 5.95 (0-934126-73-9) CFI Dist.
Alrededor del Mundo Con Logos (Around the World with Logos) (SPA.). Date not set. 5.99 (1-56063-098-1, 490360) Editorial Unilit.
Alrightniks Row: The Making of a Professional Jew, Haunch, Paunch & Jowl. Samuel Ornitz. LC 85-40730. (Masterworks of Modern Jewish Writing Ser.). 323p. 1986. reprint ed. 18.95 (0-910129-49-5); reprint ed. pap. 9.95 (0-910129-46-0) Wiener Pubs Inc.
Alroy: Or, the Prince of the Captivity see Works of Benjamin Disraeli, Earl of Beaconsfield
ALS: A Guide for Librarians & Systems Managers. Rod Cowley. 100p. 1988. text ed. 54.95 (0-566-03541-3, Pub. by Gower UK) Ashgate Pub Co.
***ALS-AS Logic Handbook.** 200p. (Orig.). 1995. pap. 125.00 (0-7605-1821-1) Rector Pr.
Al's Blind Date. Constance C. Greene. (Illus.). 128p. (YA). (gr. 5-9). 1991. pap. 3.95 (0-14-034171-4, Puffin) Puffin Bks.
ALS Guide to Australian Writers: A Bibliography 1963-1990. Ed. by Martin Duwell et al. LC 93-226785. (Studies in Australian Literature). 366p. 1993. pap. 29.95 (0-7022-2439-1, Pub. by Univ Queensland Pr AT) Intl Spec Bk.
Alsace. (Insight Guides Ser.). 1993. pap. 21.95 (0-395-66299-0) HM.
***Alsace.** Hubrecht Duijker. (Wine Lover's Touring Guides Ser.). (Illus.). 144p. (Orig.). 1995. pap. 15.95 (1-85365-301-2, Pub. by Spectrum UK) Seven Hills Bk.
Alsace & Lorraine from Caesar to Kaiser 58 B.C.-1871 A.D. Ruth Putnam. LC 75-160988. (Select Bibliographies Reprint Ser.). 1977. reprint ed. 33.95 (0-8369-5856-X) Ayer.
***Alsace et Lorraine Green Guide French Edition.** Michelin Staff. (FRE.). Date not set. pap. 17.95 (0-7859-7219-6, 2067003720) Fr & Eur.
Alsace et Lorraine Green Guide (Vosges) 4th ed. (FRE.). Date not set. pap. 18.00 (2-06-700372-0, 372) Michelin.
Alsace-Lorraine. deluxe ed. Fanny Howe. Ed. by Maureen Owen. (Summer Ser.). (Illus.). 64p. (Orig.). 1982. pap. 10.00 (0-916382-28-1) Telephone Bks.
Alsace-Lorraine under German Rule. Charles D. Hazen. LC 78-164603. (Select Bibliographies Reprint Ser.). 1977. reprint ed. 20.95 (0-8369-5887-X) Ayer.
Alsace Wines & Spirits. Pamela V. Price & Christopher Fielden. LC 84-50547. (Illus.). 216p. 1984. 29.95 (0-85667-183-5, Pub. by P Wilson Pubs) Sothebys Pubns.
Alsatian Acts of Identity: Language Use & Language Attitudes in Alsace. Liliane M. Vassberg. LC 92-29031. (Multilingual Matters Ser.: No. 90). 1993. 79.00 (1-85359-173-4, Pub. by Multilingual Matters UK); pap. 29.95 (1-85359-172-6, Pub. by Multilingual Matters UK) Taylor & Francis.
***Alsatian Connections, Vol. I.** Doris Wesner. 474p. 1995. text ed. 39.95 (1-55856-185-4) Closson Pr.
***Alsea Texts & Myths.** Leo J. Frachtenberg. (Bureau of American Ethnology Bulletins Ser.). 304p. 1995. lib. bdg. write for info. (0-7812-4067-0) Rprt Serv.
Alsino Vol. 21: Pedro Prado. Pedro Prado. Tr. by Guillermo I. Castillo-Feliu. LC 93-22219. (American University Studies: No. XXII). 191p. (SPA.). (C). 1994. text ed. 39.95 (0-8204-2148-0) P Lang Pubs.
Also a Mother: Work & Family As Theological Dilemma. Bonnie Miller-McLemore. LC 93-44713. 224p. (Orig.). 1994. pap. 15.95 (0-687-11020-3) Abingdon.
Also Known As Sam Poisson. John J. Heldt. (Illus.). 72p. (Orig.). 1985. pap. 19.95 (0-933931-04-2) Hitchcock Pub.
Also My Journey: A Personal Story of Alzheimer's. Marguerite H. Atkins. LC 84-62378. 160p. 1985. pap. 8.95 (0-8192-1385-3) Morehouse Pub.
Also Rans: Great Men Who Missed Making the Presidential Goal. Don C. Seitz. (Essay Index Reprint Ser.). 1977. 23.95 (0-8369-0863-5) Ayer.
Also Sprach Zarathustra: Ein Buch fuer Alle und Keinen, 1883-85 see Nietzsche Werke
Alson Skinner Clark, 1876-1949. Jean Stern. LC 83-62425. (Illus.). 115p. 1983. 35.00 (0-8227-8042-9) DeRu's Fine Art.
Alstons & Allstons of North & South Carolina. Joseph A. Groves. (Illus.). 1976. reprint ed. 40.00 (0-89308-013-6) Southern Hist Pr.
Alt Babylonische Briefe aus dem Museum zu Philadelphia. Arthur Ungnad. LC 78-72770. (Ancient Mesopotamian Texts & Studies). reprint ed. 22.50 (0-404-18226-7) AMS Pr.
***Alt. Culture: From Acid Jazz to Zippies: the UnderGround Bible Complete with Online Info.** 1995. pap. 16.00 (0-06-273383-4, Harper Ref) HarpC.
ALTA. Peter Forbes. 370p. (Orig.). 1995. pap. 12.00 (0-9628750-7-4) Cyclosunshine.
Alta California, 1840-1842: The Journal & Observations of William Dane Phelps. William D Phelps. Ed. by Briton C Busch. LC 82-71376. (Western Lands & Waters Ser.: XIII). (Illus.). 364p. 1983. 29.50 (0-87062-143-2) A H Clark.
Alta Toquima Village Project, 1981: A Preliminary Report. David H. Thomas. (Social Sciences Center Technical Report Ser.: No. 27). (Illus.). 105p. (C). 1982. spiral bd. 10.00 (0-945920-27-X) Desert Rsch Inst.
***ALTA/ACSM Land Title Surveys, the Cadillac of Surveys: Questions & Answers.** John E. Keen. 95p. (C). 1995. pap. text ed. 30.00 (1-56569-007-9) Land Survey.
Altamira. Myra Sklarew. LC 86-51523. (Series Eleven). 82p. 1987. pap. 7.00 (0-931846-30-7) Wash Writers Pub.
Altar. Susan Bright. 24p. 1984. 6.00 (0-911051-10-4) Plain View.
Altar & Pew. Ed. by John Betjeman. (Pocket Poet Ser.). 1960. pap. 3.50 (0-8023-9041-2) Dufour.
Altar & the City: A Reading of Virgil's Aeneid. Mario Di Cesare. LC 74-3436. 278p. 1974. text ed. 43.00 (0-231-03830-5); pap. text ed. 17.50 (0-231-03831-3) Col U Pr.
Altar & the Crown. Marian Niven. LC 73-175112. (Seekers Ser.: Pt. I). 413p. 1971. 10.00 (0-8164-0099-7) Univ South Pr.
Altar de la Unidad: The Altar of Unity. Benjamin Angurell. (SPA.). 3.95 (84-7645-223-3, 223270, Pub. by Edit Clie SP) TSELF.
Altar Guild Book. Barbara Gent & Betty Sturges. LC 82-80469. (Illus.). 104p. 1982. pap. 6.95 (0-8192-1305-5) Morehouse Pub.
Altar Guild Handbook. S. Anita Stauffer. LC 85-47713. 128p. 1985. pap. 9.00 (0-8006-1868-8, 1-1868, Fortress Pr) Augsburg Fortress.
Altar Guild Manual. 3rd rev. ed. Edith W. Perry. 72p. 1992. reprint ed. pap. 5.95 (0-8192-1067-6) Morehouse Pub.
Altar of the Dead. Henry James, Jr. (Notable American Authors Ser.). 1992. reprint ed. lib. bdg. 75.00 (0-7812-3405-0) Rprt Serv.
Altar of the Dead. Henry James. Bd. with Beast in the Jungle. LC 74-158796.; Birthplace. LC 74-158796.; Private Life. LC 74-158796.; Owen Wingrave. LC 74-158796.; Friend of the Friends. LC 74-158796.; Sir Edmund Orme. LC 74-158796.; Real Right Thing. LC 74-158796.; Jolly Corner. LC 74-158796.; Julia Bride. LC 74-158796. LC 74-158796. (Novels & Tales of Henry James Ser.: Vol. 17). xxviii, 541p. 1971. reprint ed. 45.00 (0-678-02817-6) Kelley.
Altar of the Earth. Peter Gold. LC 87-12941. (Illus.). 221p. (Orig.). 1987. pap. 14.95 (0-937938-44-0) Snow Lion Pubns.
Altar of Venus. 309p. 1983. reprint ed. pap. 4.50 (0-88184-001-7) Carroll & Graf.
Altar Pieces. Jerome Rothenberg. (Illus.). 1982. pap. 5.50 (0-930794-48-6) Station Hill Pr.
Altar Pieces of St. Nicholas from Janosret. G. Torok. (Illus.). (C). 1990. text ed. 80.00 (0-685-40253-3, Pub. by Collets) St Mut.
Altar Prayer Workbook A. rev. ed. Earl Albrecht. Ed. by Michael L. Sherer. 1986. 8.95 (0-89536-812-9, 6841) CSS OH.
Altar Prayer Workbook B: (Common-Luth) Earl Albrecht. 1984. 8.95 (0-89536-688-6, 4865) CSS OH.
Altar Prayer Workbook C (C-L-RC) Earl Albrecht. 1985. 8.95 (0-89536-758-0, 5864) CSS OH.
Altar Service of the Protestant Episcopal Church. write for info. (0-318-54802-X) OUP.
Altared States: Portrait of a Fiancee. Jennie Nash. 1992. 16.00 (0-517-58497-2, Crown) Crown Pub Group.
Altarity. Mark C. Taylor. (Illus.). 352p. (C). 1987. pap. text ed. 17.95 (0-226-79138-6) U Ch Pr.
Altarity. Mark C. Taylor. (Illus.). 352p. (C). 1987. lib. bdg. 42.50 (0-226-79137-8) U Ch Pr.
Altarmenisches Elementarbuch. Antoine Meillet. LC 80-24325. (Anatolian & Caucasian Studies). 228p. 1980. reprint ed. 50.00 (0-88206-043-0) Caravan Bks.
Altarpiece in Renaissance Venice. Peter Humfrey. LC 92-36349. (Illus.). 352p. (C). 1993. text ed. 65.00 (0-300-05358-4) Yale U Pr.
Altarpiece in the Renaissance. Ed. by Peter Humfrey & Martin Kemp. (Illus.). 256p. (C). 1991. 69.95 (0-521-36061-7) Cambridge U Pr.
Altars & Offerings Unto the Most High. Lester Sumrall. 55p. (C). 1983. pap. text ed. 6.00 (0-937580-69-4) LeSEA Pub Co.
Altars of the World: Practical Altar Construction. Allen Kus. (Illus.). 210p. (Orig.). Date not set. 25.00 (1-57179-036-5) Intern Guild ASRS.
Altars of Unhewn Stone: Science & the Earth. Wes Jackson. LC 86-62837. 176p. 1987. pap. 9.95 (0-86547-287-4, North Pt Pr) FS&G.
***Alta's Visit to Nebraska.** Virginia H. Inness. (Illus.). 56p. (C). 1995. pap. 7.95 (1-886225-01-X) Dageforde Pub.
Altassyrischen Rechtsurkunden von Kueltepe, 2 vols., Set. George Eisser & Julius Lewy. LC 78-72733. (Ancient Mesopotamian Texts & Studies). reprint ed. 62.50 (0-404-18170-8) AMS Pr.
Altazor. Vicente Huidobro. Tr. by Eliot Weinberger. LC 87-83082. (Palabra Sur Ser.). 114p. 1988. pap. 8.50 (1-55597-106-7) Graywolf.
Altchristliche Literatur und Ihre Erforschung Seit, 1880. Albert Ehrhard. (Straburger Theologische Studien Ser.: Vol. I, 4/5). 258p. 1982. reprint ed. write for info. (3-487-07255-6, Pub. by Georg Olms GW) Lubrecht & Cramer.
Alte Legenden und Neue Literatur. Karen C. Kossuth & David R. Antal. 368p. (C). 1986. pap. text ed. 22.00 (0-03-063877-1) HB Coll Pubs.
Alte Pinakothek, Munich. Erich Steingraber. LC 84-52513. (Illus.). 128p. 1991. 25.00 (0-85667-222-X) Scala Books.
Alten Postpositionen des Nenzischen Juraksamojedischen. Tibor Mikola. (Janua Linguarum, Series Practica: No. 240). 242p. 1975. pap. text ed. 53.50 (90-279-3087-2) Mouton.
Alten Uebersetzungen des Neuen Testaments, die Kirchenvaeterzitate und Lektionare: Der Gegenwaertige Stand Ihrer Erforschung und Ihre Bedeutung fuer die Griechische Textgeschichte. Ed. by Kurt Aland. (Arbeiten zur Neutestamentlichen Textforschung Ser.: No. 5). xxiv, 590p. (C). 1972. 142.35 (3-11-004121-9) De Gruyter.
Altenglisches Elementarbuch: Einfuehrung, Grammatik, Text mit Uebersetzung und Woerterbuch. 9th rev. ed. Martin Lehnert. (Sammlung Goeschen Ser.: No. 2210). (GER.). (C). 1978. 9.85 (3-11-007643-8) De Gruyter.
***Altenglisches Elementarbuch: Einfuhrung, Grammatik, Woerterbuch.** 10th ed. Martin Lehnert. 179p. (ENG & GER.). 1990. 29.95 (0-7859-8274-4, 3110124718) Fr & Eur.
Alter Ego: Eduardo Sanguinetti. 1986. 30.00 (0-946270-17-1, Pub. by Pentland Pr UK) St Mut.
Alter Katalog der Musikdrucke. 1985. fiche write for info. (0-318-71828-6, Pub. by Georg Olms GW) Lubrecht & Cramer.
Alter Sonnets. Paul Jacob. 8.00 (0-89253-481-8); 4.00 (0-89253-482-6) Ind-US Inc.
***Alter und Altern: Ein Interdisziplinaerer Studientext zur Gerontologie.** Ed. by Paul B. Baltes et al. (Sonderausgabe des 1992 Ershienenen 5. Forschungsberichtes der Akademie der Wissenschaft zu Berlin Ser.). 822p. (GER.). (C). 1994. pap. text ed. 36.95 (3-11-014408-5) De Gruyter.
Alter Your Life. Emmet Fox. LC 93-23918. 256p. 1994. pap. 10.00 (0-06-250897-0) Harper SF.
Alteration. Kingsley Amis. 210p. 1988. pap. 3.95 (0-88184-432-2) Carroll & Graf.
Alteration & Interference of Feelings see Mental & Physical Measurements of Working Children
Alteration of Orthodoxy. Ed. by Jacob Neusner. LC 92-37155. (Judaism in Cold War America, 1945-1990 Ser.: Vol. 8). 264p. 1993. 46.00 (0-8153-0077-8) Garland.
Alteration Workroom Manual. pap. 25.00 (0-87102-025-4, 50-6840) Natl Ret Merch.
Alterations & Adaptions of Shakespeare. Frederick W. Kilbourne. LC 79-171065. reprint ed. 34.50 (0-404-03674-0) AMS Pr.
Alterations in Defenses During Psychoanalysis. Ed. by Bernard D. Fine & Herbert F. Waldhorn. Bd. with Aspects of Psychoanalytic Intervention. LC 74-21186. LC 74-21186. (Kris Study Group Monograph: No. 6). 97p. 1975. Set text ed. 25.00 (0-8236-0143-9) Intl Univs Pr.
Alterations in the Neuronal Cytoskeleton in Alzheimer's Disease. Ed. by G. Perry. LC 87-29256. (Advances in Behavioral Biology Ser.: Vol. 34). 240p. 1987. 69.50 (0-306-42766-4, Plenum Pr) Plenum.
Alterations of Personality, Vol. 5. Alfred Binet. Tr. by Helen G. Baldwin. Bd. with On Double-Consciousness. LC 77-72191. LC 77-72191. (Contributions to the History of Psychology Ser.). 499p. 1977. reprint ed. Set text ed. 75.00 (0-313-26944-0, U6944, Greenwood Pr) Greenwood.
Alteratives. Ed. by Warren Motte & Gerald Prince. LC 93-76190. (French Forum Monographs: No. 82). 229p. (Orig.). 1993. pap. 17.95 (0-917058-87-9) French Forum.
Altere Pythagoreismus. Wilhelm Bauer. (Berner Studien Zur Philosophie und Ihrer Geschichte Ser.: Bd. VIII). viii, 232p. 1976. reprint ed. write for info. (3-487-05553-8, Pub. by Georg Olms GW) Lubrecht & Cramer.
Altered Ambitions: What's Next in Your Life? Betsy Jaffe. 1991. 19.95 (1-55611-266-1) D I Fine.
Altered Body Image: The Nurse's Role. Mave Salter. (Illus.). 204p. 1988. pap. 20.00 (0-471-91042-2) Ishiyaku Euro.
Altered Brand. J. Jay Myers. LC 92-45715. 142p. 1993. 19.95 (0-8027-1271-1) Walker & Co.
***Altered Conditions: Disease, Medicine, & Storytelling.** Julia Epstein. 320p. 1994. 59.95 (0-415-90717-9, A9837); pap. 17.95 (0-415-90718-7, A9841) Routledge.
Altered Egos. Karen Moss. Ed. by Scott Boberg. (Illus.). 84p. (Orig.). 1994. pap. 25.00 (0-9624941-2-7) SM Mus Art.
Altered Egos. Adrian Too. (Illus.). 222p. (Orig.). 1990. pap. 9.95 (0-9627725-0-X) Blind Chameleon.
Altered Egos: Authority in American Autobiography. G. Thomas Couser. 304p. 1989. 45.00 (0-19-505833-X) OUP.
Altered Fates: The Genetic Re-Engineering of Human Life. Jeff Lyon & Peter Gorner. 800p. 1995. 27.50 (0-393-03596-4) Norton.
Altered I: Ursula K. Le Guin's Science Fiction Writing Workshop. Ursula K. Le Guin. Ed. by Lee Harding. 1978. pap. 7.50 (0-425-03849-1) Ultramarine Pub.
Altered Landscapes: The Photographs of John Pfahl. Intro. by Bill Woods. LC 81-66455. (Illus.). 1981. 20.00 (0-933286-23-6) Frnds Photography.
Altered Proteins & Aging. Ed. by Richard C. Adelman & George S. Roth. 192p. 1983. 104.00 (0-8493-5812-4, QP86) CRC Pr.
***Altered Reality of Philip K. Dick: Selected Writings.** Philip K. Dick. Ed. by Lawrence Sutin. LC 94-27812. 1995. 27.50 (0-679-42644-2) Pantheon.
Altered Sensation & Pain. Ed. by M. R. Dimitrijevic et al. (Recent Achievements in Restorative Neurology Ser.: Vol. 3). (Illus.). xiv, 214p. 1990. 158.50 (3-8055-5036-7) S Karger.
Altered States. (Illus.). 75p. pap. 8.00 (0-685-72792-0) Kent Gallery.
Altered States: A Reader in the New World Order. Ed. by Phyllis Bennis & Michel Moushabeck. LC 93-4299. 540p. 1993. 39.95 (1-56656-115-9, Olive Branch Pr); pap. 16.95 (1-56656-112-4, Olive Branch Pr) Interlink Pub.
Altered States: Alcohol & Other Drugs in America. Patricia M. Tice. LC 92-36241. 1992. write for info. (0-940365-05-7) Strong Mus.
Altered States: Postmodernism, Politics, Culture. Ed. by Mark Perryman. 192p. (C). 1994. pap. 25.00 (0-85315-793-6, Pub. by Lawrence & Wishart UK) Humanities.
Altered States of Consciousness. 3rd rev. ed. Ed. by Charles T. Tart. (Illus.). 691p. 1992. reprint ed. pap. 16.95 (0-685-59684-2) Psych Processes Inc.
Altered States of Consciousness & Mental Health. Ed. by Colleen A. Ward. (Cross-Cultural Research & Methodology Ser.: Vol. 12). 320p. 1989. text ed. 49.95 (0-8039-3277-4) Sage.
Altered States of Consciousness & PSI: An Historical Survey & Research Prospectus. Edward F. Kelly & Ralph G. Locke. LC 81-82545. (Parapsychological Monograph Ser.: No. 18). 91p. (Orig.). (C). 1981. pap. text ed. 8.00 (0-912328-34-7) Parapsych Foun.
Altered States of Mind: A Critical Observation of the Drug War. Ed. by Peter B. Kraska. LC 93-7387. 1993. 43.00 (0-8153-0898-1) Garland.
Altering & Repairing Pressurized Pipe Systems Symposium, November 1978. (Piping Ser.). 234p. 1979. 25.00 (0-910091-07-2) Inst Gas Tech.
Altering Eye: Contemporary International Cinema. Robert P. Kolker. LC 81-22488. (Illus.). 1983. pap. 15.95 (0-19-503302-7) OUP.
Altering Manufactured Apparel to the Invisible Body. Rosalie Stevens. (Illus.). (Orig.). 1992. teacher ed 10.95 (0-9622771-0-X) R Stevens.
Altering Men's Ready-to-Wear. Mary A. Roehr. (Illus.). 150p. (Orig.). 1987. pap. 14.95 (0-685-71938-3) M Roehr Cust Tailor.
Altering Men's Ready-to-Wear. Mary A. Roehr. (Illus.). 150p. (Orig.). (C). 1987. pap. text ed. 17.95 (0-9619229-1-5) M Roehr Cust Tailor.
Altering Ready-to-Wear Fashions. Ann Aletti & Jeanne Brinkley. (gr. 10-12). 1976. teacher ed 1.28 (0-317-00011-X); text ed. 20.48 (0-317-00010-1) Bennett IL.
Altering the Earth's Chemistry: Assessing the Risks. Sandra Postel. LC 86-61917. (Worldwatch Papers). 68p. (Orig.). 1986. pap. 5.00 (0-916468-72-0) Worldwatch Inst.
Altering the Image of AIDS. Maria De Bruyn. 96p. 1994. pap. 16.00 (90-5383-259-9, Pub. by VU Univ Pr NE) Paul & Co Pubs.
Altering Women's Ready-to-Wear. Mary A. Roehr. (Illus.). 190p. (Orig.). (C). 1987. pap. 19.95 (0-9619229-0-7) M Roehr Cust Tailor.
Alternaria: Biology, Plant Diseases, & Metabolites. Ed. by J. Chelkowski & A. Visconti. LC 92-14792. (Topics in Secondary Metabolism Ser.: Vol. 3). 1992. write for info. (0-444-88998-1) Elsevier.
Alternate Alloying for Environmental Resistance. Ed. by G. R. Smolik & S. K. Banerji. LC 86-31207. (Illus.). 485p. 1987. 10.00 (0-87339-057-1) Minerals Metals.
***Alternate Alloying for Environmental Resistance: Proceedings of the Symposium Sponsored by the Corrosion & Environmental Effects Committee of the Metallurgical Society of AIME & Held at the TMS-AIME Annual Meeting in New Orleans, Louisiana, from March 2-6, 1986.** fac. ed. Metallurgical Society of AIME Staff. Ed. by G. R. Smolik & S. K. Banerji. LC 86-31207. 497p. 1987. reprint ed. pap. 141.70 (0-7837-8301-9, 2049087) Bks Demand.
Alternate Asimov. Isaac Asimov. 1988. pap. 3.95 (0-451-15370-7, ROC) NAL-Dutton.
Alternate Casts. Marsh Cassady. 180p. (Orig.). 1990. pap. 8.95 (0-934411-33-6, Banned Bks) Edward-William Austin.
Alternate Cite Acute Care Equipment & Supply Markets: Quest for Cost Reductions Foster Ambulatory Center Group. Market Intelligence Staff. 260p. 1993. 1,695.00 (1-56753-495-3) Frost & Sullivan.

An Asterisk (*) at the beginning of an entry indicates that the title is appearing in BIP for the first time.

*Alternate Cite Respiratory Therapy Markets. Market Intelligence Staff. 250p. 1994. 2,195.00 (0-7889-0072-2) Frost & Sullivan.

Alternate Computers. (Understanding Computers Ser.). (Illus.). 128p. (YA). (gr. 7 up). 1989. 19.93 (0-8094-5745-8); lib. bdg. 25.93 (0-8094-5746-6) Time-Life.

Alternate Conceptions of Work & Society: Implications for Professional Nursing. Ed. by Carol A. Lindeman. 225p. (Orig.). 1988. pap. 20.00 (0-922148-00-7) AACN.

Alternate Court Reporting Techniques for Connecticut. National Center for State Courts Staff. 184p. 1979. 11.04 (0-685-15843-8, NERO-031) Natl Ctr St Courts.

Alternate Dispute Resolution & Public Policy. Ed. by Miriam Mills. (Orig.). 1988. pap. 12.00 (0-944285-01-5) Pol Studies.

Alternate Dispute Resolution in Florida, Vol. I. Florida Bar Legal Education Staff. LC 89-80981. 580p. 1991. ring bd. 70.00 (0-945979-02-9, 221) FL Bar Legal Ed.

Alternate Dispute Resolution in Florida, Vol. II. Florida Bar Legal Education Staff. 446p. 1992. ring bd. 75.00 (0-945979-35-5, 221) FL Bar Legal Ed.

Alternate Education, K-12, 2 vols. Dorie A. Erickson. LC 80-51385. (Illus.). 55p. 1980. Set incls. Start Your Own Private School-Legally!. pap. 11.00 (0-937242-01-2) Scandia Pubs.

Alternate Endings. Frances Jaffer. (HOW (ever) Bk.: No. 1). 80p. (Orig.). 1985. pap. 6.00 (0-933539-00-2) HOWever.

Alternate Energy-Solar Energy. Vincent Robertson & Roin Robertson. 1977. pap. 3.95 (0-685-59747-4) Alternate Energy.

Alternate Forms of Energy. Jeffrey Feinman. 1981. pap. text ed. 1.95 (0-89083-834-8) Zebra.

*Alternate Fuels: A Decade of Success & Promise. Ed. by Reda M. Bata. Date not set. pap. 79.00 (1-56091-593-5, PT48) Soc Auto Engineers.

Alternate Fuels, Engine Performance, & Emissions. Ed. by M. R. Goyal. (ICE Ser.: Vol. 20). 236p. 1993. 45.00 (0-7918-0692-8, 100355) ASME.

*Alternate Geneologies: Self-Portraits & Family Romances of Antonin Artaud. John C. Stout. 120p. (C). 1995. text ed. 29.95 (0-88920-249-4, Pub. by Wilfrid Laurier CN) Humanities.

Alternate Healing Methods: An Overview. Angela Plum. LC 93-85295. (Illus.). 128p. (Orig.). 1993. pap. 8.50 (1-56664-051-2) WorldComm.

Alternate Identities for Fun Profit & Survival. 3rd ed. (Illus.). 50p. 1993. pap. 20.00 (1-877884-07-3) Tech Group.

Alternate Kennedys. Ed. by Mike Resnick. 416p. 1992. mass mkt. 4.99 (0-8125-1955-8) Tor Bks.

Alternate Methods in the Treatment of Benign Prostatic Hyperlasia. Ed. by Nicholas A. Romas & E. Darracott Vaughan. LC 92-48354. 1993. write for info. (3-540-56389-X); 109.00 (0-387-56389-X) Spr-Verlag.

*Alternate Modernity: The Technical Turn in Philosophy & Social Theory. Andrew Feenberg. LC 95-8666. 1995. write for info. (0-520-08985-5); pap. write for info. (0-520-08986-3) U CA Pr.

Alternate Mortgage Instruments & Financing Techniques. Intro. by John R. Johnsich. (Orig.). 1981. pap. 6.95 (0-914256-14-9) Real Estate Pub.

*Alternate MUniverses: Exploration of the World of MUDS, Mucks, Tiny MUDS, & MUSHes. David Ciskowski. (Illus.). (Orig.). 1995. pap. 19.99 (1-56686-246-9) Brady Compu Bks.

Alternate Outlaws. Ed. by Mike Resnick. 544p. (Orig.). (C). 1994. mass mkt. 4.99 (0-8125-3344-5) Tor Bks.

Alternate Presidents. Ed. by Mike Resnick. 1992. mass mkt. 4.99 (0-8125-1192-1) Tor Bks.

Alternate Realities: Mathematical Models of Nature & Man. John L. Casti. 300p. 1989. text ed. 68.95 (0-471-61842-X) Wiley.

Alternate Roots: Plays from the Southern Theatre. Valetta Anderson & Denobriga. LC 93-20879. 300p. (C). 1994. pap. 17.95 (0-435-08632-4) Heinemann.

*Alternate Sides. Marissa Piesman. 1995. write for info. (0-385-31355-1) Delacorte.

*Alternate Site Acute Care Equipment & Supplies Markets. (Market Report Ser.: No. 440). (Illus.). 155p. 1994. 795.00 (0-614-01240-6) Theta Corp.

Alternate Sources of Energy: A Bibliography of Solar, Geothermal, Wind & Tidal Energy, & Environmental Architecture. Barbara K. Harrah & David F. Harrah. LC 75-17853. 216p. 1975. 20.00 (0-8108-0839-0) Scarecrow.

Alternate Style: Options in Composition. Winston Weathers. LC 80-18325. 144p. 1980. text ed. 12.50 (0-8104-6130-7) Boynton Cook Pubs.

Alternate Test Manual to Accompany Gerald C. Davison, John M. Neale Abnormal Psychology. 2nd ed. Robert Emery et al. LC 77-13940. 105p. reprint ed. pap. 30.00 (0-8357-5328-X, 2016477) Bks Demand.

Alternate Tunings Guide for Guitar. Mark Hanson. (Illus.). 40p. 1991. pap. 4.95 (0-8256-1251-9, AM72521) Music Sales.

*Alternate Tyrants. Ed. by Mike Resnick. 544p. (Orig.). 1996. pap. 5.99 (0-614-05546-6) Tor Bks.

Alternate Voices in the Contemporary Latin American Narrative. David W. Foster. LC 85-1411. 184p. 1985. text ed. 23.00 (0-8262-0481-3) U of Mo Pr.

Alternate Warriors. Ed. by Mike Resnick. 448p. (Orig.). 1993. mass mkt. 4.99 (0-8125-2346-6) Tor Bks.

*Alternate Work Schedules: Experience of Federal Agencies. (Illus.). 62p. (Orig.). (C). 1994. pap. text ed. 40.00x (0-7881-0897-2) Diane Pub.

Alternating Copolymers. Ed. by J. M. Cowie. LC 84-24812. (Specialty Polymers Ser.). 294p. 1985. 85.00 (0-306-41779-0, Plenum Pr) Plenum.

Alternating Current. Octavio Paz. 1991. pap. 9.95 (1-55970-136-6) Arcade Pub Inc.

Alternating Current Analysis. Robert G. Seippel & Roger L. Nelson. LC 74-24890. (Illus.). reprint ed. pap. 33.80 (0-8357-5329-8, 2011570) Bks Demand.

Alternating Current Circuit. Heinz Rieger. (Siemens Programmed Insturction Ser.: 13). 68p. reprint ed. pap. 25.00 (0-8357-5330-1, 2052103) Bks Demand.

Alternating Current Circuit Analysis through Experimentation. 3rd ed. Kenneth A. Fiske & James H. Harter. 176p. 1985. pap. 10.50 (0-911908-41-2) Tech Ed Pr.

*Alternating Current Fundamentals. Tom Adamson. Ed. by Kelly Gorham. 24p. Date not set. student ed write for info. (0-8064-0366-7, E17) Bergwall.

Alternating Current Fundamentals. John R. Duff & Stephen L. Herman. LC 94-4887. 1995. write for info. (0-8273-6844-5); pap. write for info. (0-8273-6624-8) Delmar.

Alternating Current Fundamentals. 3rd ed. John R. Duff & Stephen L. Herman. 576p. 1986. teacher ed 12.00 (0-8273-2240-2); text ed. 33.95 (0-8273-2239-9); pap. text ed. 24.95 (0-8273-2238-0) Delmar.

Alternating Current Fundamentals. 4th ed. John R. Duff & Stephen L. Herman. 1990. text ed. 33.95 (0-8273-4156-3); pap. text ed. 29.95 (0-8273-4157-1) Delmar.

Alternating Current Fundamentals IG. 4th ed. John R. Duff & Steven L. Herman. 1990. teacher ed 12.00 (0-8273-4159-8) Delmar.

Alternating Current Machines. 5th ed. M. G. Say. LC 83-10719. 632p. 1984. pap. text ed. 76.95 (0-470-27451-4) Halsted Pr.

Alternating Currents: Nationalized Power in France, 1946-1970. Robert L. Frost. LC 90-55727. 288p. 1991. 42.50 (0-8014-2351-1) Cornell U Pr.

Alternating Currents of Love & Friendship. Jerry Buchanan. LC 85-73609. 1986. pap. 6.95 (0-930668-02-2) Towers Club.

Alternating Hemiplegia of Childhood. Frederick Andermann et al. (International Review of Child Neurology Ser.). 240p. 1995. 85.00 (0-7817-0163-5) Raven.

Alternating Sequential: Parallel Processing. Yehuda Wallach. (Lecture Notes in Computer Science Ser.: Vol. 127). 327p. 1982. pap. 30.00 (0-387-11194-8) Spr-Verlag.

Alternating Voltage & Current. Heinz Rieger. (Siemens Programmed Instruction Ser.: No. 12). 80p. reprint ed. pap. 25.00 (0-8357-5331-X, 2052089) Bks Demand.

Alternation of Native Hawaiian Vegetation: Effects of Humans, Their Activities & Introductions. Linda W. Cuddihy & Charles P. Stone. 128p. (Orig.). 1990. pap. text ed. 18.00 (0-8248-1308-1) UH Pr.

Alternativa Liberal: Una Vision Historica De Puerto Rico. Juan M. Garcia Passalacqua. (UPREX, Ensayo Ser.: No. 27). 164p. (C). 1974. pap. 1.50 (0-8477-0027-5) U of PR Pr.

Alternativas. Stacy Rinehart. (SPA.). Date not set. pap. 6.99 (0-88113-111-3) Edit Betania.

*Alternative. Dennis M. Lee. (Illus.). 360p. (Orig.). 1994. pap. 19.95 (0-9644068-0-2) Better Wrld Tech.

Alternative. Oswald E. Mosley. 1972. 59.95 (0-87968-592-1) Gordon Pr.

Alternative Agriculture. Committee on the Role of Alternative Farming Methods in Modern Production Agriculture Staff. 464p. 1989. pap. text ed. 28.95 (0-309-03985-1) Natl Acad Pr.

Alternative Alcott. Louisa May Alcott. Ed. by Elaine Showalter. (American Women Writers Ser.). 400p. 1988. 45.00 (0-8135-1271-9); pap. 15.00 (0-8135-1272-7) Rutgers U Pr.

Alternative America. Richard Gardner. LC 83-244775. 275p. 1985. pap. 19.95 (0-933342-04-7) Resources MA.

Alternative America. Richard Gardner. LC 83-244775. 275p. 1987. pap. 19.95 (0-933342-09-8) Resources MA.

Alternative America: Henry George, Edward Bellamy, Henry Demarest Lloyd & the Adversary Tradition. John L. Thomas. LC 82-15448. (Illus.). 432p. 1983. 38.00 (0-674-01676-9) HUP.

Alternative American Schools: Ideals in Action. Claire V. Korn. LC 90-32304. 170p. 1991. 64.50 (0-7914-0471-4); pap. 21.95 (0-7914-0472-2) State U NY Pr.

Alternative Americas. Mildred J. Loomis. LC 81-19775. (Universe Bks.). 175p. 1982. 5.00 (0-87663-375-0); pap. 3.00 (0-87663-567-2) Schalkenbach.

Alternative Americas: The Historical Case for Decentralization. 1992. lib. bdg. 250.00 (0-8490-8761-9) Gordon Pr.

Alternative Analyses of Phonemic System in Central South-Lappish. Gustav Hasselbrink. LC 65-63390. (Uralic & Altaic Ser.: Vol. 49). (Orig.). 1965. pap. text ed. 7.00 (0-87750-015-0) Res Inst Inner Asian Studies.

Alternative & Holistic Health Care for AIDS & Its Prevention: A Sourcebook of Descriptions, Bibliography, & Practitioners in the Washington, D.C.-Baltimore, Maryland Area. Paul N. Van Ness. 76p. (Orig.). 1988. pap. 5.00 (0-9619604-0-X) Whitman Walker.

Alternative Animals for Fibre Protection, No. EUR 14808. Ed. by A. J. Russel. 118p. 1993. pap. 19.00 (92-826-6299-3, CH-NA-14808-EN-C, Pub. by Europ Com) UNIPUB.

Alternative Answers to Hot Political Issues. Whitcher. 1994. 13.95 (1-881116-25-5) Black Forrest Pr.

Alternative Approach to Allergies: The New Field of Clinical Ecology Unravels the Environmental Causes of Mental & Physical Ills. rev. ed. Theron G. Randolph & Ralph W. Moss. LC 88-45902. 352p. 1990. reprint ed. pap. 13.00 (0-06-091693-1, PL) HarpC.

Alternative Approach to General Revenue Sharing: A Needs-Based Allocation Formula. Gregory Schmid et al. 89p. 1975. 9.00 (0-318-14408-5, R34) Inst Future.

Alternative Approaches to a Theory of Economic Growth: Marx, Marshall & Schumpeter. Sukhamoy Chakravarty. (R. C. Dutt Lectures on Political Economy: 1980). 1982. pap. text ed. 4.95 (0-86131-355-0, Pub. by Orient Longman Ltd II) Apt Bks.

Alternative Approaches to British Defence Policy. Ed. by John Baylis. LC 83-40164. 272p. 1984. text ed. 32.50 (0-312-02146-1) St Martin.

Alternative Approaches to Economic Planning. Martin Cave & Paul Hare. 1981. text ed. 39.95 (0-312-02147-X) St Martin.

Alternative Approaches to Financing Business Development. Jody Tompros. Ed. by Jenny Murphy. 118p. (Orig.). 1989. pap. 26.00 (0-317-04842-2) Natl Coun Econ Dev.

Alternative Approaches to Life Safety. 85p. 1994. 20.00 (0-685-64968-7, 101M-94) Natl Fire Prot.

Alternative Approaches to Lithic Analysis. Ed. by Donald O. Henry & George H. Odell. 1989. 13.50 (0-913167-30-4) Am Anthro Assn.

Alternative Approaches to Meeting Basic Health Needs in Developing Countries: A Joint UNICEF-WHO Study. Ed. by V. Djukanovic & E. P. Mach. 1975. pap. 9.60 (92-4-156048-7) World Health.

Alternative Approaches to Pollution Control & Waste Management: Regulatory & Economic Instruments. Janis D. Bernstein. LC 93-16297. (Urban Management Ser.: No. 3). 80p. 1993. 7.95 (0-8213-2344-X, 12344) World Bank.

Alternative Approaches to the Comprehensive Adjudication of Drug Arrestees (CADA) Thomas Henderson et al. 156p. 1991. 9.50 (0-685-55339-6, WPO-028) Natl Ctr St Courts.

Alternative Approaches to the Problem of Development: A Selected & Annotated Bibliography. Charles W. Bergquist. LC 77-88665. 264p. 1979. lib. bdg. 22.75 (0-89089-081-1); pap. 9.95 (0-89089-083-8) Carolina Acad Pr.

Alternative Approaches to the Study of Sexual Behavior. Donn Byrne & Kathryn Kelley. 240p. (C). 1986. text ed. 49.95 (0-89859-677-7) L Erlbaum Assocs.

Alternative Approaches to Tuition Financing. Robert A. Foose & Joel M. Myerson. Ed. by Laurie Denton. 80p. 1987. pap. 13.00 (0-915164-33-7) NACUBO.

*Alternative Assessment of Performance in the Language Arts: Proceedings. Ed. by Carl B. Smith. (Illus.). (Orig.). (C). 1991. pap. 21.95 (0-927516-24-1) ERIC-REC.

*Alternative Assessment Techniques for Reading & Writing. Wilma H. Miller. LC 95-826. 1995. spiral bd. 29.95 (0-87628-141-2) Ctr Appl Res.

Alternative Bypass Conduits & Methods for Surgical Coronary Revascularization. Ed. by Ronald K. Grooters & Hiroshi Nishida. (Illus.). 336p. 1994. 65.00 (0-87993-577-4) Futura Pub.

*Alternative Care Programs in Hospice. National Hospice Organization, Alternative Care Task Force Staff. 29p. 1991. 10.50 (0-931207-11-8) Natl Hospice.

Alternative Careers for Humanities Ph.D.s. Ed. by Lewis Solmon et al. LC 79-16049. 243p. 1979. text ed. 55.00 (0-275-90426-1, C0426, Praeger Pubs) Greenwood.

Alternative Careers for Ph.D.'s in the Humanities: A Selected Bibliography. Christine F. Donaldson & Elizabeth A. Flynn. LC 82-3399. 48p. reprint ed. pap. 25.00 (0-8357-5332-8, 2030789) Bks Demand.

Alternative Careers for Political Scientists. Ed. by James P. McGregor. 114p. (C). 1984. pap. text ed. 5.00x (0-915654-63-6) Am Political.

Alternative Careers for Teachers. rev. ed. Sandy Pollack. LC 84-19727. 176p. 1984. pap. 9.95 (0-916782-60-3) Harvard Common Pr.

Alternative Cars in the Twenty-First Century: A New Personal Transportation Paradigm. Robert Q. Riley. 400p. 1994. 39.00 (1-56091-519-6, R139) Soc Auto Engineers.

Alternative Christianity. John Punshon. LC 81-85560. (C). 1982. pap. 3.00 (0-87574-245-9) Pendle Hill.

Alternative Clauses to Standard Construction Contracts. Ed. by James E. Stephenson. (Construction Law Library). 1990. text ed. 123.00 (0-471-51088-2) Wiley.

Alternative Clauses to Standard Construction Contracts Disk Library. Wiley Staff. (Construction Law Library). 32p. 1993. 3.5 hd 210.00 (0-471-59475-X); 5.25 hd 210.00 (0-471-59592-6) Wiley.

Alternative Coca Reduction Strategies in the Andean Region. (Illus.). 175p. (Orig.). (C). 1994. pap. text ed. 60.00 (0-7881-0362-8) Diane Pub.

Alternative Coca Reduction Strategies in the Andean Region. (Orig.). 1994. lib. bdg. 250.00 (0-8490-8551-9) Gordon Pr.

Alternative Conceptions of Phrase Structure. Mark R. Baltin & Anthony S. Kroch. LC 88-34327. (Illus.). 336p. 1989. lib. bdg. 60.00 (0-226-03641-3); pap. text ed. 19.95 (0-226-03642-1) U Ch Pr.

Alternative Constitutions for the United States: A Documentary History. Steven R. Boyd. LC 91-38208. (Contributions in American History Ser.: No. 145). 308p. 1992. text ed. 59.95 (0-313-25419-2, BDE, Greenwood Pr) Greenwood.

Alternative Conventional Defense, Vol. 1. Baruch & Robert Kennedy. 200p. 1990. 58.00 (0-8448-1598-5, Crane Russak); pap. 37.00 (0-8448-1599-3, Crane Russak) Taylor & Francis.

Alternative Conventional Defense, Vol. 2. Baruch & Robert Kennedy. 1991. 52.00 (0-8448-1600-0, Crane Russak) Taylor & Francis.

Alternative Conventional Defense Postures in the European Theater, Vol. 3: Military Alternatives for Europe after the Cold War. Ed. by Hans G. Brauch & Robert Kennedy. 240p. 1992. 54.50 (0-8448-1728-7, Crane Russak) Taylor & Francis.

Alternative Cooking Facilities Cookbook. Center for Self-Sufficiency, Research Division Staff. LC 83-90718. 50p. 1983. ring bd. 19.95 (0-910811-08-3) Ctr Self Suff.

Alternative Courses for Secondary School Mathematics. Ed. by Marilyn N. Suydam. LC 85-4835. 57p. (YA). (gr. 7-12). 1985. Grades 7-12. pap. 7.50 (0-87353-222-8) NCTM.

Alternative Culture: Socialist Labor in Imperial Germany. Vernon L. Lidtke. (Illus.). 299p. 1985. 45.00 (0-19-503507-0) OUP.

Alternative Delivery Systems: Approaches for the Health Care Executive. Ed. by Samuel Levey & James Hill. LC 88-16298. (Case Studies in Health Administration: Vol. 7). 95p. 1988. pap. 25.00 (0-910701-40-7, 0115) Health Admin Pr.

Alternative Detective. Robert Sheckley. 256p. 1993. 19.95 (0-312-85023-9) Forge NYC.

Alternative Development Strategies in Sub-Saharan Africa. Ed. by Frances Stewart et al. LC 91-19525. 496p. 1992. text ed. 65.00 (0-312-06738-0) St Martin.

Alternative Directory of Non-Governmental Organizations in South Asia. Ed. by Todd Nachowitz. LC 89-83678. (Orig.). (C). 1989. pap. 15.00 (0-9622716-0-8) Fourth Wrld Pr.

Alternative Directory of Nongovernmental Organizations in South Asia. rev. ed. Todd Nachowitz. (Foreign & Comparative Studies Program, South Asian Ser.: No. 14). 1990. pap. text ed. 15.00 (0-915984-41-5) Syracuse U Foreign Comp.

Alternative Disposal Methods of Associated Gas from Marginal Fields. A. V. Drew. (C). 1989. 110.00 (0-89771-736-8, Pub. by Lorne & MacLean Marine) St Mut.

Alternative Disposal Methods of Association Gas from Marginal Fields. A. V. Drew. 1989. 125.00 (90-6314-561-6, Pub. by Lorne & MacLean Marine) St Mut.

Alternative Dispute Resolution. Ed. by James L. Branton & Jim D. Lovett. (Trial Lawyer's Ser.: Vol. 10). 1992. ring bd. 135.00 (1-878337-32-7) Knowles Law.

*Alternative Dispute Resolution. Michael Freeman. (International Library of Essays in Law & Legal Theory: No. 26). 500p. 1995. 150.00 (0-8147-2636-4) NYU Pr.

Alternative Dispute Resolution, 1 vol. George P. Haldeman. 1993. ring bd. 135.00 (0-685-68846-1) Clark Boardman Callaghan.

Alternative Dispute Resolution: Cases & Materials. Leo Kanowitz. LC 85-22453. (American Casebook Ser.). 1024p. (C). 1985. text ed. 47.00 (0-314-94475-3); teacher ed, pap. text ed. write for info. (0-314-98314-7) West Pub.

Alternative Dispute Resolution: Cases & Materials, 1990 Supplement. Leo Kanowitz. (American Casebook Ser.). 162p. 1990. pap. text ed. 14.00 (0-314-71823-0) West Pub.

Alternative Dispute Resolution: How to Prepare the Case & Represent Your Client. Michael Landrum. 1988. audio 150.00 (1-55917-009-3); vhs 750.00 (1-55917-010-7) Natl Prac Inst.

Alternative Dispute Resolution: Melting the Lances & Dismounting the Steeds. Thomas E. Carbonneau. LC 89-4703. 352p. 1989. 34.95 (0-252-01640-8) U of Ill Pr.

Alternative Dispute Resolution: Practice & Perspective. (BNA Special's Report Ser.). 288p. 1991. 35.00 (1-55871-209-7, BSP149) BNA.

Alternative Dispute Resolution (ADR) Digest: 3rd. 1992. 27.50 (0-685-53123-6) Graduate Group.

*Alternative Dispute Resolution in a Contemporary South African Context. A. T. Trollip. 109p. 1991. pap. 45.00 (0-409-05850-5, SA) Butterworth Legal Pubs.

Alternative Dispute Resolution in a Nutshell. Jacqueline M. Nolan-Haley. (Nutshell Ser.). 298p. 1992. pap. text ed. 15.00 (0-314-00781-4) West Pub.

Alternative Dispute Resolution in the Construction Industry. Ed. by Robert F. Cushman & G. Christian Hedemann. (Construction Law Library). 727p. 1991. text ed. 128.00 (0-471-52127-2) Wiley.

Alternative Dispute Resolution in the Construction Industry. suppl. ed. Ed. by Robert F. Cushman & G. Christian Hedemann. (Construction Law Library). 88p. 1992. Suppl. 1992, 88p. 45.00 (0-471-59215-3) Wiley.

*Alternative Dispute Resolution in the Employment Context. Date not set. 80.00 (0-929576-90-X) Busn Laws Inc.

Alternative Dispute Resolution in the Public Sector. Miriam Mills. (Political Science Ser.). 300p. 1991. 28.95 (0-8304-1258-1) Nelson-Hall.

Alternative Dispute Resolution Practice Guide. American Arbitration Association Staff. 400p. 1993. ring bd. write for info. (0-8403-9146-3) Kendall-Hunt.

Alternative Dispute Resolution Sourcebook, 1993-94. Ed. by Want Publishing Co. Staff. (Your Nation's Courts Ser.). 145p. 1993. text ed. 21.95 (0-942008-65-0) Want Pub.

Alternative Dispute Resolution Techniques: Options & Guidelines to Meet Your Company's Needs. Douglas S. McDowell. (Orig.). 1993. pap. 25.00 (0-916559-43-2) EPF.

Alternative Draft of a Penal Code for the Federal Republic of Germany. Tr. by Joseph J. Darby. (American Series of Foreign Penal Codes: Vol. 21). xvi, 157p. 1977. text ed. 17.50 (0-8377-0041-8) Rothman.

Alternative Economic Indicators. Victor Anderson. (Illus.). 128p. 1991. 64.95 (0-415-04163-5, A5866); pap. 16.95 (0-415-04164-3, A5870) Routledge.

An Asterisk (*) at the beginning of an entry indicates that the title is appearing in BIP for the first time.

A

Alternative Economic Perspectives: A Primer on the Streams of Economic Analysis, 1994-95. W. Robert Brazelton et al. 256p. (C). 1994. per., pap. text ed. 23.95 (0-8403-9225-7) Kendall-Hunt.

Alternative Economic Strategies: The Case of Greece. Euclid Tsakalotos. 328p. 1991. text ed. 68.95 (1-85628-183-3, Pub. by Avebury Pub UK) Ashgate Pub Co.

Alternative Egg Cookbook. Foulsham Editors. 128p. 1995. pap. 7.95 (0-572-01570-4, Pub. by Foulsham UK) Atrium Pubs.

Alternative Energy, 5 vols., Set. Graham Houghton & Graham Rickard. (Illus.). 32p. (J). (gr. 4-6). 1991. lib. bdg. 86.35 (0-8368-0712-X) Gareth Stevens Inc.

*Alternative Energy: Earth, Air, Fire, Water. Allen Kus. Ed. & Pref. by Thor Templar. 98p. (Orig.). 1994. 25.00 (1-57179-044-6) Intern Guild ASRS.

Alternative Energy Handbook. Fairmont Press Staff & Paul Rosenberg. 1993. text ed. 74.00 (0-13-029117-X) P-H.

Alternative Energy Handbook. Paul Rosenberg. LC 92-30937. 1992. write for info. (0-88173-140-4) Fairmont Pr.

Alternative Energy in Agriculture, 2 vols., Set. Ed. by D. Yogi Goswami. 1986. 336.00 (0-8493-6349-7, TJ808, CRC Reprint) Franklin.

Alternative Energy in Agriculture, 2 vols., Vol. I. Ed. by D. Yogi Goswami. 256p. 1986. 180.00 (0-8493-6347-0, TJ808, CRC Reprint) Franklin.

Alternative Energy in Agriculture, 2 vols., Vol. II. Ed. by D. Yogi Goswami. 192p. 1986. 168.00 (0-8493-6348-9, TJ808, CRC Reprint) Franklin.

Alternative Energy Sourcebook 1990: The Complete Guide to Renewable Energy Technologies & Sustainable Living. 8th ed. Real Goods Staff & John Schaeffer. (Real Goods Independent Living Bks.). (Illus.). 672p. (Orig.). 1994. pap. 23.00 (0-930031-68-7) Real Goods Pub.

Alternative Energy Sources for the Steel Industry: Proceedings of the Sixth C. C. Furnas Memorial Conference. Furnas (C C) Memorial Conference Staff. Ed. by Julian Szekely. LC 76-40365. (Illus.). 133p. reprint ed. pap. 38.00 (0-7837-0814-9, 2041129) Bks Demand.

Alternative Energy Sources for the United States. Richard J. Anderson et al. 19p. (C). 1975. pap. 19.95x (0-87855-743-1) Transaction Pubs.

Alternative Energy Sources V: Energy Research, 6 vols., Set. Ed. by T. Nejat Veziroglu. Incl. Pt. A. Solar Radiation-Collection-Storage. 500p. 1984. 164.00 (0-444-42256-0, I-432-83); Pt. B. Solar Applications. 500p. 1984. 164.00 (0-444-42257-9, I-433-83); Pt. C. Indirect Solar-Geothermal. 470p. 1984. 164.00 (0-444-42258-7, I-434-83); Pt. D. Biomass-Hydrocarbons-Hydrogen. 500p. 1984. 164.00 (0-444-42259-5, I-435-83); Pt. E. Nuclear-Conservation-Environment. 450p. 1984. 164.00 (0-444-42260-9, I-436-83); Pt. F. Energy Economics-Planning-Education. 500p. 1984. 166.00 (0-685-08060-9, I-437-83); 1984. 738.50 (0-444-42262-5) Elsevier.

Alternative Energy Sources, VIII: Proceedings of the Miami International Conference, 8th, 2 vols. Ed. by T. Nejat Veziroglu. 2000p. 1988. 338.00 (0-89116-898-2) Hemisp Pub.

Alternative Energy Sources VIII: Research Development, Vol. 2. Ed. by T. Nejat Veziroglu. 1070p. 1988. 172.00 (0-89116-210-0) Hemisp Pub.

Alternative Energy Sources VIII: Solar Energy Fundamentals & Applications, Vol. 1. Ed. by T. Nejat Veziroglu. 1088p. 1988. 172.00 (0-89116-186-4) Hemisp Pub.

Alternative Energy Systems: Electrical Integration & Utilization: Proceedings of the International Conference, Coventry (Lanchester) Polytechnic, U. K., September 10-12, 1984. Ed. by M. J. West et al. (Illus.). 350p. 1984. 128.00 (0-08-031639-5, Pub. by Pergamon Repr UK) Franklin.

Alternative Engines for Road Vehicles. Ed. by M. L. Poulton. LC 94-70408. 192p. 1994. text ed. 89.00 (1-56252-224-8) Computational Mech MA.

Alternative English: Literature Coursework for ages 16-19. C. Swatridge. 160p. (C). 1989. 49.00 (0-7487-0065-X, Pub. by S Thornes Pubs UK) St Mut.

*Alternative Factor. Stacey Enderle. 1995. 16.95 (0-8062-5211-1) Carlton.

Alternative Farm Enterprises. 2nd ed. Bill Slee. (Illus.). 252p. 1989. 27.95 (0-85236-192-0, Pub. by Farming Pr UK) Diamond Farm Bk.

Alternative Farming Systems - Economic Aspects, Bibliography. K. Schnieder. 70p. (Orig.). (C). 1994. pap. text ed. 30.00 (0-7881-0765-8) Diane Pub.

*Alternative Fuel Developments & Overseas Design Influences on North American Bus Operations. 1994. pap. 36.00 (1-56091-577-3, SP1058) Soc Auto Engineers.

*Alternative-Fueled Vehicles: Progress Made in Accelerating Federal Purchases, but Benefits & Costs Remain Uncertain. Victor S. Rezendes. (Illus.). 120p. (Orig.). (C). 1994. pap. text ed. 45.00x (0-7881-1370-4) Diane Pub.

*Alternative-Fueled Vehicles: Progress Made in Accelerating Federal Purchases, but Benefits & Costs Remain Uncertain. (Illus.). 120p. (Orig.). (C). 1995. pap. text ed. 40.00x (0-7881-1725-4) Diane Pub.

Alternative Fuels: Alcohols, Hydrogen, Natural Gas & Propane. (Future Transportation Technology Conference & Exposition, 1993 Ser.). 1993. pap. 57.00 (1-56091-410-6, SP-982) Soc Auto Engineers.

Alternative Fuels: Emissions, Economics & Performance. Timothy T. Maxwell & Jesse C. Jones. 243p. 1994. 49.00 (1-56091-523-4, R143) Soc Auto Engineers.

Alternative Fuels: Experiences of Countries Using Alternative Motor Fuels. 104p. (Orig.). (C). 1993. pap. text ed. 30.00 (1-56806-671-6) Diane Pub.

Alternative Fuels & the Environment. Ed. by Frances Sterrett. LC 94-25419. 1994. write for info. (0-87371-978-6) Lewis Pubs.

Alternative Fuels for CI & SI Engines. 200p. 1992. pap. 39.00 (1-56091-217-0, SP-900) Soc Auto Engineers.

*Alternative Fuels for Low Emissions & Improved Performance in CI & Heavy Duty Engines: 1995 International Congress & Exposition Meeting. 1995. pap. 56.00 (1-56091-643-5, SP1093) Soc Auto Engineers.

Alternative Fuels for Road Vehicles. Ed. by M. L. Poulton. LC 94-70407. 232p. 1994. text ed. 89.00 (1-56252-225-6) Computational Mech MA.

Alternative Fuels in CI & Heavy Duty Engines: SAE International Congress & Exposition 1994, 10 papers. (Special Publications). 1994. pap. 31.00 (1-56091-479-3, SP-1027) Soc Auto Engineers.

Alternative Fuels in the Nineties. 83p. 1991. pap. 45.00 (1-56091-159-X, SP-876) Soc Auto Engineers.

Alternative Fuels in Transportation: Eight Papers. 1992. 35.00 (1-56091-301-0, SP-937) Soc Auto Engineers.

*Alternative Futures: Challenging Designs for Arts Philanthropy. Ed. by Andrew Patner. LC 94-79005. 117p. (Orig.). 1994. pap. 11.95 (0-9643011-0-5) Grantmakers Arts.

Alternative Futures & Postsecondary Education in Pennsylvania. Robert Johansen & Maureen McNulty. 188p. 1977. 12.00 (0-318-14409-3, R- 39) Inst Future.

Alternative Futures for Worship, 7 vols. Incl. Vol. 1. General Introduction. Michael A. Cowan et al. Ed. by Regis A. Duffy. 192p. 1987. pap. (0-8146-1493-0); Vol. 2. Baptism & Confirmation. Andrew D. Thompson et al. 192p. 1987. pap. (0-8146-1494-9); Vol. 3. Eucharist. John H. Westerhoff, III et al. 176p. 1987. pap. (0-8146-1495-7); Vol. 4. Reconciliation. Denis J. Woods et al. Ed. by Peter E. Fink. 176p. 1987. pap. (0-8146-1496-5); Vol. 5. Christian Marriage. William Roberts et al. Ed. by Bernard Cooke. 96p. 1987. pap. (0-8146-1497-3); Vol. 6. Leadership Ministry in Community. David N. Power et al. Ed. by Michael A. Cowan. 184p. 1987. pap. (0-8146-1498-1); Vol. 7. Anointing of the Sick. Mary F. Duffy et al. 160p. 1987. pap. (0-8146-1499-X); (C). 1987. write for info. (0-318-61651-3) Liturgical Pr.

Alternative Futures for Worship, 7 vols., Set. Incl. Vol. 1. General Introduction. Michael A. Cowan et al. Ed. by Regis A. Duffy. 192p. 1987. pap. (0-8146-1493-0); Vol. 2. Baptism & Confirmation. Andrew D. Thompson et al. 192p. 1987. pap. (0-8146-1494-9); Vol. 3. Eucharist. John H. Westerhoff, III et al. 176p. 1987. pap. (0-8146-1495-7); Vol. 4. Reconciliation. Denis J. Woods et al. Ed. by Peter E. Fink. 176p. 1987. pap. (0-8146-1496-5); Vol. 5. Christian Marriage. William Roberts et al. Ed. by Bernard Cooke. 96p. 1987. pap. (0-8146-1497-3); Vol. 6. Leadership Ministry in Community. David N. Power et al. Ed. by Michael A. Cowan. 184p. 1987. pap. (0-8146-1498-1); Vol. 7. Anointing of the Sick. Mary F. Duffy et al. 160p. 1987. pap. (0-8146-1499-X); (C). 1987. Set pap. 56.95 (0-8146-1491-4) Liturgical Pr.

Alternative Futures of Special Education. 204p. 1986. 10.00 (0-86586-160-9, P306) Coun Exc Child.

Alternative Goals in Religion: Love, Freedom, Truth. George B. Burch. LC 72-82248. 128p. reprint ed. pap. 36.50 (0-7837-6907-5, 2046737) Bks Demand.

*Alternative Gospel. Baldock. 1995. pap. text ed. 14.95 (1-85230-643-2) Element MA.

Alternative Hardy. Ed. by Lance St. John Butler. LC 88-23655. 192p. 1989. text ed. 45.00 (0-312-02518-1) St Martin.

Alternative Healing: Opposing Viewpoints. Gail B. Stewart. LC 90-3807. (Great Mysteries Ser.). (Illus.). 112p. (J). (gr. 5-8). 1990. lib. bdg. 16.95 (0-89908-083-9) Greenhaven.

Alternative Healing: The Complete A-Z Guide to Over 160 Different Alternative Therapies. Mark Kastner & Hugh Burroughs. LC 93-77385. 368p. (Orig.). 1993. pap. 15.00 (0-9635997-1-2) Halcyon CA.

*Alternative Health & Medicine Encyclopedia. James Marti. LC 94-34460. 400p. 1994. 45.00 (0-8103-9580-0) Gale.

Alternative Health Care for Women. Patsy Wescott & Leyardia Black. LC 87-19432. 192p. (Orig.). 1987. pap. 12.95 (0-89281-245-1, Heal Arts VT) Inner Tradit.

Alternative Health Care Resources: A Directory & Guide. Brett J. Sinclair. LC 92-28096. 1992. 24.95 (0-13-030073-X); pap. 12.95 (0-13-156522-2) P-H.

Alternative Health Maintenance & Healing Systems for Families. Ed. by Doris Y. Wilkinson & Marvin B. Sussman. LC 87-31198. (Marriage & Family Review Ser.: Vol. 11, Nos. 3-4). (Illus.). 171p. 1988. text ed. 39.95 (0-86656-701-1) Haworth Pr.

Alternative Healthcare: A Comprehensive Guide. Jack Raso. 267p. (C). 1994. 26.95 (0-87975-891-0) Prometheus Bks.

Alternative Housebuilding. Mike McClintock. LC 88-38140. (Popular Science Ser.). (Illus.). 299p. 1989. pap. 19.95 (0-8069-6995-4) Sterling.

Alternative Housebuilding. Mike McClintock. (Illus.). 384p. (C). 1989. reprint ed. lib. bdg. 45.00x (0-8095-7530-2) Borgo Pr.

Alternative Houses: Building Your Own House. 1991. lib. bdg. 250.00 (0-8490-4675-0) Gordon Pr.

Alternative Hydrocarbon Fuels: Combustion & Chemical Kinetics. Ed. by Craig T. Bowman & Jorgen Birkeland. LC 78-7278. (PAAS Ser.: Vol. 62). (Illus.). 463p. 1978. 65.95 (0-915928-25-6) AIAA.

*Alternative Ideas in Real Estate Investment. Ed. by Arthur L. Schwartz. (Research Issues in Real Estate Ser.). 224p. (C). 1995. lib. bdg. 59.95 (0-7923-9497-6) Kluwer Ac.

Alternative Identities: The Self in Literature, History, Theory. Ed. by Linda M. Brooks. LC 94-4895. (Wellesley Studies in Critical Theory, Literary History & Culture: Vol. 7). 368p. 1994. 55.00 (0-8153-1721-2, H1848) Garland.

*Alternative Image: An Aesthetic & Technical Exploration of Nonconventional Photographic Printing Processes. Contrib by Patricia G. Fuller. (Illus.). 156p. 1983. pap. 21.95 (0-932718-13-2) Kohler Arts.

*Alternative Image II: Photography on Nonconventional Supports. (Illus.). 120p. 1984. pap. 18.95 (0-932718-16-7) Kohler Arts.

Alternative in Eastern Europe. Rudolf Bahro. Ed. by David Fernbach. 463p. 1978. pap. text ed. 18.95 (0-86091-734-7, Pub. by Verso UK) Routledge Chapman & Hall.

Alternative in Small Business Finance. Dimitri Papadimitriou et al. (Public Policy Brief Ser.: No. 12). (Illus.). 48p. (Orig.). 1994. pap. write for info. (0-941276-00-7, Edith C Blum Inst) Bard Coll Pubns.

Alternative Influence: The Impact of Investigative Reporting Groups on America's Media. Philip F. Lawler. LC 84-15274. 100p. (Orig.). 1985. pap. text ed. 13.50 (0-8191-4234-4, Media Institute) U Pr of Amer.

Alternative Investments. Rachel S. Epstein. (Basic Investors Library). (Illus.). 48p. 1988. lib. bdg. 12.95 (1-55546-633-8) Chelsea Hse.

*Alternative Jam Trak. Contrib by Ralph Agresta. 1994. 11.95 (0-8256-1373-6, AM91469) Music Sales.

Alternative Japanese Drama: Ten Plays. Ed. by Robert T. Rolf & John K. Gillespie. LC 92-5185. (Illus.). 520p. 1992. text ed. 38.00 (0-8248-1347-2); pap. 14.95 (0-8248-1379-0) UH Pr.

Alternative Knot Book. Harry Asher. (Illus.). 96p. 1989. pap. 12.95 (0-911378-95-2) Sheridan.

Alternative Learning Styles in Business Education, 1979. (Yearbook Ser.). 213p. 5.00 (0-933964-00-5) Natl Busn Ed Assoc.

Alternative Library Literature, 1984-1985: A Biennial Anthology. Ed. by Sanford Berman & James P. Danky. LC 84-646841. 255p. 1986. pap. 35.00 (0-89950-234-2) McFarland & Co.

Alternative Library Literature, 1986-1987: A Biennial Anthology. Ed. by Sanford Berman & James P. Danky. LC 84-646841. (Illus.). 295p. 1988. pap. 35.00 (0-89950-336-5) McFarland & Co.

Alternative Library Literature, 1988-1989: A Biennial Anthology. Ed. by Sanford Berman & James P. Danky. LC 84-646841. (Illus.). 398p. 1990. pap. 35.00 (0-89950-530-9) McFarland & Co.

Alternative Library Literature, 1990-1991: A Biennial Anthology. Ed. by Sanford Berman & James P. Danky. LC 84-646841. (Illus.). 272p. 1992. pap. 35.00 (0-89950-726-3) McFarland & Co.

Alternative Library Literature, 1992-1993: A Biennial Anthology. Ed. by Sanford Berman & James P. Danky. LC 84-646841. (Illus.). 383p. 1994. pap. 35.00 (0-89950-970-3) McFarland & Co.

Alternative Life: History Styles of Animals. Ed. by Michael N. Bruton. (Perspectives in Vertebrate Science Ser.). (C). 1989. lib. bdg. 281.50 (90-6193-662-4) Kluwer Ac.

Alternative Life-History Styles of Fishes. Ed. by Michael N. Bruton. (C). 1990. lib. bdg. 188.50 (0-7923-0801-8) Kluwer Ac.

Alternative Lifestyle: Living & Traveling Full-Time in a Recreational Vehicle. 2nd rev. ed. Ron Hofmeister & Barb Hofmeister. LC 94-185084. 292p. 1994. reprint ed. pap. 12.95 (0-9637319-0-4) R & B Pubns.

Alternative Lifestyles: A Guide to Research Collections on International Communities, Nudism, & Sexual Freedom. Jefferson P. Selth. LC 85-17727. (Bibliographies & Indexes in Sociology Ser.). xii, 133p. 1985. text ed. 49.95 (0-313-24773-0, SAV/) Greenwood.

Alternative Liquid Fuels in Transportation. 148p. 1991. pap. 35.00 (0-685-59696-6, SP-889) Soc Auto Engineers.

Alternative Literary Publishing: Five Modern Histories. Sally Dennison. LC 84-8700. 248p. (Orig.). reprint ed. pap. 70.70 (0-7837-1620-6, 2041913) Bks Demand.

Alternative Lives. Constance Urdang. LC 90-33962. (Poetry Ser.). 72p. 1990. pap. 10.95 (0-8229-5439-7) U of Pittsburgh Pr.

*Alternative Man: Poems & Stories by Michael Phillips. Michael Phillips. 1995. pap. 8.95 (0-9636829-5-4) Mother Road.

Alternative Management Programs: A Housing Resource Guide. LC 85-105290. 31p. 1983. pap. 3.00 (0-88156-081-2) Comm Serv Soc NY.

*Alternative Market. Golden Gate Chapter CPCU Society Staff. 108p. 1994. pap. 29.98 (1-886813-01-9) Intl Risk Mgt.

Alternative Materials for the Reinforcement & Prestressing of Concrete. Ed. by John L. Clarke. LC 93-1468. 1993. write for info. (0-7514-0007-6) Routledge Chapman & Hall.

Alternative Materials in Libraries. Ed. by James P. Danky & Elliott Shore. LC 81-21353. 255p. 1982. 22.50 (0-8108-1508-7) Scarecrow.

Alternative Mathematical Model of Linguistic Semantics. V. Novak. (IFSR International Series on Systems Science: Vol. 8). (Illus.). 230p. (C). 1992. 69.50 (0-306-44269-8, Plenum Pr) Plenum.

Alternative Medicine: A Bibliography of Books in English. R. West & J. Trevelyan. 224p. 1985. text ed. 90.00 (0-7201-1721-6, Mansell Pub) Cassell.

Alternative Medicine: The Definitive Guide. Burton Goldberg Group Staff. LC 93-74059. (Illus.). 1068p. 1993. 59.95 (0-9636334-3-0) Future Md Pub.

Alternative Medicine & American Religious Life. Robert C. Fuller. (Illus.). 182p. 1989. 24.95 (0-19-505775-9) OUP.

*Alternative Medicine: Healing the Self: Toward a Revolution in Health Care. Paul H. Skinner. 160p. (Orig.). (C). 1995. pap. 19.95 (1-886769-00-1) Gld Leaf Pr.

Alternative Medicine in Britain. Ed. by Mike Saks. 272p. 1992. 65.00 (0-19-827278-2) OUP.

Alternative Medicine Yellow Pages: The Comprehensive Guide to the New World of Health. Ed. by Melinda Bonk. 225p. (Orig.). 1994. pap. 12.95 (0-9636334-2-2) Future Md Pub.

*Alternative Methodologies for the Safety Evaluation of Chemicals in the Cosmetic Industry. Nicola Loprieno. Ed. by Mannfred Hollinger. LC 95-2335. (Basic & Clinical Aspects Ser.). 304p. 1995. 149.95 (0-8493-8546-6, 8546) CRC Pr.

*Alternative Methods for Fluid Delivery & Recovery. Larry Murdoch & David Wilson. (Illus.). 87p. (Orig.). (C). 1995. pap. text ed. 45.00 (0-7881-1616-9) Diane Pub.

Alternative Methods of Regression. David Birkes & Yadolah Dodge. LC 92-31165. (Probability & Mathematical Statistics Ser.). 240p. 1993. text ed. 64.95 (0-471-56881-3, Wiley-Interscience) Wiley.

Alternative Minimum Tax. Daniel J. Lathrope. 1993. ring bd. 155.00 (0-685-69582-4, ALMT) Warren Gorham & Lamont.

*Alternative Minimum Tax. Daniel J. Lathrope. 672p. 1994. 155.00 (0-7913-1978-4) Warren Gorham & Lamont.

Alternative Minimum Tax: 1993 Edition. Stewart S. Karlinsky. (Professional Tax Advisor's Guide Ser.). (Illus.). 512p. 1992. pap. text ed. 56.00 (0-7811-0057-7) Res Inst Am.

Alternative Minimum Tax, 1992. Stewart S. Karlinsky. 450p. 1992. 54.95 (0-7811-0005-4, Maxwell Macmillan) Macmillan.

Alternative Modeling Techniques in Computer-Assisted Mass Appraisal. David L. Jenson. (Lincoln Institute Monograph Ser.: No. 83-5). 83p. reprint ed. pap. 25.00 (0-7837-2167-6, 2042484) Bks Demand.

*Alternative Models of Family Preservation: Family-Based Services in Context. Kristine E. Nelson & Miriam J. Landsman. 266p. 1992. pap. 30.95 (0-398-06303-6) C C Thomas.

Alternative Models of Family Preservation: Family-Based Services in Context. Kristine E. Nelson & Miriam J. Landsman. 266p. (C). 1992. text ed. 51.95x (0-398-05810-5) C C Thomas.

Alternative Models of Mennonite Pastoral Formation. Paul Zehr & Jim Egli. (Occasional Papers: No. 15). (Illus.). 134p. (Orig.). (C). 1992. pap. 10.00 (0-936273-19-4) Inst Mennonite.

Alternative Monetary Regimes. Ed. by Colin D. Campbell & William R. Dougan. LC 85-30034. 288p. 1986. pap. text ed. 15.95 (0-8018-2889-9) Johns Hopkins.

Alternative Oxidants for the Removal of Soluble Iron & Manganese. 150p. 1990. pap. 20.50 (0-89867-511-1) Am Water Wks Assn.

Alternative Paradigms: The Impact of Islamic & Western Weltanschauungs on Political Theory. Ahmet Davutoglu. LC 92-46275. 1993. 55.00 (0-8191-9046-2); pap. 34.00 (0-8191-9047-0) U Pr of Amer.

Alternative Paradigms in Environmental Education Research. Ed. by Rick Mrazek. (Monograph Ser.: Vol. 9). (Illus.). 332p. (Orig.). 1993. pap. 20.00 (1-884008-04-6) NAAEE.

Alternative Paths: Soviet-American Relations, 1917-1920. David W. McFadden. LC 92-17949. 464p. 1993. 60.00 (0-19-507187-5) OUP.

*Alternative Paths to Teaching: A Directoru of Post-baccalaureate Programs. 1993. 25.00 (0-89333-114-7) AACTE.

Alternative Pathways to Healing: The Recovery Medicine Wheel. Kip Coggins. 1990. pap. 7.95 (1-55874-089-9) Health Comm.

Alternative Perspectives in Assessing Children's Language & Literacy. David Bloome et al. 240p. (C). 1994. text ed. 49.50 (0-89391-864-4); pap. 24.50 (0-89391-914-4) Ablex Pub.

Alternative Perspectives on School Improvement. Ed. by D. W. Hopkins & Marvin F. Wideen. LC 83-25497. 215p. 1984. 48.00 (0-905273-82-6, Falmer Pr); pap. 30.00 (0-905273-81-8, Falmer Pr) Taylor & Francis.

*Alternative Pick, 1992. Ed. by Maria Ragusa & Juliette Wolf. 390p. 1995. boxed 50.00 (0-9632606-3-4) Storm Music.

Alternative Pleasures: Post-Realist Fiction & the Tradition. Philip Stevick. LC 80-25900. 184p. 1981. 24.95 (0-252-00877-4) U of Ill Pr.

*Alternative Pleasures: Postrealist Fiction & the Tradition. fac. ed. Philip Stevick. LC 80-25900. 171p. 1981. reprint ed. pap. 48.80 (0-7837-8062-1, 2047815) Bks Demand.

Alternative Policies for the Control of Air Pollution in Poland. Robin Bates et al. LC 94-45657. (Environment Paper Ser.: No. 7). 84p. 1994. write for info. (0-8213-2753-4) World Bank.

Alternative Policing Styles: Cross-Cultural Perspectives. Ed. by Mark Findlay & Ugljesa Zvekic. LC 93-15573. 1993. write for info. (90-6544-710-5) Kluwer Law Tax Pubs.

Alternative Politics: The German Green Party. Thomas Poguntke. (Environment, Politics, & Society Ser.). 288p. 1993. text ed. 75.00 (0-7486-0393-X, Pub. by Edinburgh U Pr UK) Col U Pr.

An Asterisk (*) at the beginning of an entry indicates that the title is appearing in BIP for the first time.

An Asterisk (*) at the beginning of an entry indicates that the title is appearing in BIP for the first time.

A

A

Alternatives to Imprisoning Young Offenders: Noteworthy Programs. Margaret L. Woods. 1982. 10.45 (*0-318-02055-6*) Natl Coun Crime.

Alternatives to Imprisonment. Ulla Bondeson. 322p. (C). 1994. text ed. 52.50 (*0-8133-2011-9*) Westview.

Alternatives to Imprisonment in Comparative Perspective. Ed. by Ugljesa Zvekic. LC 92-39832. 1993. text ed. 49.95 (*0-8304-1329-4*); text ed. 49.95 (*0-8304-1330-8*); pap. text ed. 27.95 (*0-8304-1403-7*) Nelson-Hall.

Alternatives to Incarceration: An Annotated Bibliography, 1978-80. National Center for State Courts. 97p. 1981. 5.82 (*0-685-43728-0*, SRO-007) Natl Ctr St Courts.

Alternatives to Incarceration: Resource Directory. National Center for State Courts Staff. 184p. 1981. 11.04 (*0-685-43729-9*, SRO-017) Natl Ctr St Courts.

Alternatives to Intensive Husbandry Systems. 1981. 45.00 (*0-317-43809-3*) St Mut.

Alternatives to Lean Production: Work Organization in the Swedish Auto Industry. 2nd ed. Christian Berggren. LC 92-20986. (Cornell International Industrial & Labor Relations Reports: No. 22). 312p. 1993. pap. 21.95 (*0-87546-317-7*) ILR Pr.

Alternatives to Lumber & Plywood in Home Construction. Eric Lund. (Illus.). 61p. (Orig.). (C). 1994. pap. text ed. 45.00 (*0-7881-0264-8*) Diane Pub.

Alternatives to Master Metering in Multifamily Housing. LC 80-84530. 131p. 1981. pap. 6.47 (*0-912104-50-3*, 899) Inst Real Estate.

Alternatives to Open Vascular Surgery. Ed. by Morris D. Kerstein. (Illus.). 448p. (C). 1994. text ed. 125.00 (*0-397-51324-0*, Lippincott Medical) Lippincott.

Alternatives to Positivism: Criticism of Bourgeois Ideology & Revisionism. Igor Naletov. 470p. 1984. 30.00 (*0-685-17082-9*) St Mut.

Alternatives to Prison: An Examination of Non-Custodial Sentencing of Offenders. Stephen Stanley & Mary Baginsky. (Contemporary Issues Ser.). 192p. 1984. 30.00 (*0-7206-0522-9*, Pub. by P Owen Ltd UK); 25.00 (*0-317-61345-6*, Pub. by P Owen Ltd UK); pap. 15.95 (*0-7206-0626-8*, Pub. by P Owen Ltd UK) Dufour.

Alternatives to Prison: Issues & Options, Criminal Justice Prisons. Ed. by Rodger O. Darnell et al. 100p. (C). 1979. pap. 4.95 (*0-934936-01-3*) U of Iowa Sch Soc Wk.

Alternatives to Prison: Punishment, Custody & the Community. Anthony A. Vass. (Contemporary Criminology Ser.). 224p. (C). 1990. 45.00 (*0-8039-8263-1*); pap. 19.95 (*0-8039-8264-X*) Sage.

Alternatives to Psychiatric Hospitalization: With Annotated Readers Guide. Harry Gottesfeld. 1977. 24.95 (*0-89876-057-7*) Gardner Pr.

Alternatives to Punishment: Non-Aversive Strategies for Solving Behavior Problems. Gary W. LaVigna & Anne Donnellan-Walsh. 220p. 1986. text ed. 27.50 (*0-8290-1245-1*) Irvington.

Alternatives to Social Assistance in Indian Communities. Ed. by Frank Cassidy & Shirley B. Seward. 120p. 1991. pap. text ed. 17.00 (*0-88645-137-X*, Pub. by Inst Res Pub CN) Ashgate Pub Co.

Alternatives to the Automobile. Marcia D. Lowe. 70p. (Orig.). 1990. pap. 5.00 (*0-916468-99-2*) Worldwatch Inst.

Alternatives to the Central Bank in the Developing World. Charles Collyns. (Occasional Paper Ser.: No. 20). 23p. 1983. pap. 5.00 (*1-55775-057-2*) Intl Monetary.

Alternatives to the Current Use of Nitrite in Foods: Part 2 of a 2-Part Study. Assembly of Life Sciences (U. S.), Committee on Nitrite & Alternative Curing Agents in Food Staff. LC 82-81677. 283p. reprint ed. pap. 80.70 (*0-8357-6814-7*, 2035497) Bks Demand.

Alternatives to the Ditto: Resources for the Reading-Language Arts Teacher. Calvin Greatsinger. (Illus.). 1977. 3.50 (*0-914634-46-1*, 7712) DOK Pubs.

***Alternatives to the Hospital for Acute Psychiatric Treatment.** Ed. by Richard Warner. LC 95-34. (Clinical Practice Ser.: No. 32). 307p. 1995. boxed 34.00 (*0-88048-484-5*, 8484) Am Psychiatric.

Alternatives to the Internal Combustion Engine: Impacts on Environmental Quality. Robert U. Ayres & Richard P. McKenna. LC 74-181555. (Resources for the Future Ser.). 340p. 1972. 27.50 (*0-8018-1369-7*) Johns Hopkins.

Alternatives to the Internal Combustion Engine: Impacts on Environmental Quality. Robert U. Ayres & Robert P. McKenna. LC 74-181555. (Illus.). 340p. reprint ed. pap. 96.90 (*0-8357-5334-4*, 2030190) Bks Demand.

Alternatives to the Peace Corps: A Directory of Third World & U. S. Volunteer Opportunities. 6th ed. Ed. by Annette Olson. 88p. 1994. reprint ed. pap. 6.95 (*0-935028-62-5*) Inst Food & Develop.

Alternatives to the Welfare Hotel: Using Emergency Assistance to Provide Decent Transitional Shelter for Homeless Families. Victor Bach & Renee Steinhagen. LC 87-402526. (Illus.). 54p. (Orig.). 1987. pap. text ed. 7.00 (*0-88156-047-2*) Comm Serv Soc NY.

***Alternatives to Tracking & Ability Grouping.** Anne Wheelock. 80p. 1994. pap. 7.95 (*0-87652-199-5*, 21-00447) Am Assn Sch Admin.

Alternatives to Traditional Family Living. Ed. by Harriet Gross & Marvin B. Sussman. LC 82-9250. (Marriage & Family Review Ser.: Vol. 5, No. 2). 128p. 1982. text ed. 39.95 (*0-917724-59-3*) Haworth Pr.

Alternatives to Traditional Regulation: Options for Reform: Proceedings of the Institute of Public Utilities Nineteenth Annual Conference. Michigan State University, Institute of Public Utilities Conference Staff. Ed. by Harry M. Trebing & Patrick C. Mann. LC 88-83141. (MSU Public Utilities Papers: No. 1987). 616p. reprint ed. pap. 175.60 (*0-7837-6268-2*, 2045980) Bks Demand.

***Alternatives to Traditional Transportation Fuels: An Overview.** (Illus.). 164p. (Orig.). (C). 1994. pap. text ed. 45.00x (*0-7881-0833-6*) Diane Pub.

Alternatives to Universities. OECD Staff. 85p. (Orig.). 1991. pap. 22.00 (*92-64-13530-8*) OECD.

Alternatives to Violence: A Manual for Teaching Peacemaking to Youth & Adults. 2nd ed. Kathy Bickmore et al. Ed. by Kathy Soltis et al. (Illus.). 126p. 1987. reprint ed. pap. text ed. 6.95 (*0-9619819-2-X*) Peace Grows.

Alternatives to Violence: Interdisciplinary Perspectives on Filipino People Power. Ed. by Douglas J. Elwood. 124p. (Orig.). (C). 1989. pap. 7.50 (*971-10-0315-5*, Pub. by New Day Pub PH) Cellar.

Alternatives to Violence Workbook. 2nd ed. John Looney. Ed. by Danene Bender & Waring Smith. (Illus.). 440p. 1987. teacher ed 19.90 (*0-9619819-3-8*) Peace Grows.

Alternatives to Violence Workbook: A Course in Solving Conflict Peaceably for Happier Relationships, Safer Communities, a More Peaceful World. John Looney. Ed. by Danene Bender & Waring Smith. (Illus.). 278p. (Orig.). (YA). (gr. 9 up). 1986. ring bd. 12.95 (*0-9619819-1-1*) Peace Grows.

Alternatives to Women's Imprisonment. Pat Carlen. 1990. 85.00 (*0-335-09926-2*, Open Univ Pr); pap. 29.00 (*0-335-09925-4*, Open Univ Pr) Taylor & Francis.

Alternatives, Yes, Lower Standards, No! Minimum Standards for Alternative Teacher Certification Programs. Association of Teacher Educators Staff. 1989. pap. 3.75 (*0-685-41074-9*) Assn Tchr Ed.

Alternator Explained. Peter Novellino. LC 80-730752. 1980. student ed 6.00 (*0-8064-0143-5*, 439); audio 319.00 (*0-8064-0144-3*) Bergwall.

Altertuemer von Pergamon. Incl. Vol. 8, Pt. 3. Inschriften des Asklepieions. Christian Habicht. (Illus.). xii, 202p. (C). 1969. 92.35x (*3-11-001197-2*); Vol. 11, Pt. 1. Asklepieion: Der Suedliche Temenosbezirk in Hellenistischer & Fruehroemischer Zeit. Oskar Ziegenaus & Gioia De Luca. (Illus.). xii, 188p. (C). 1968. 120.00 (*3-11-001196-4*); (Deutsches Archaeologisches Institut Ser.). (GER.). (C). write for info. (*0-318-51609-8*) De Gruyter.

Altertumer von Pergamon, Die Stadtgrabung, Band XV-2: Teil 2: Die Byzantinische Wohnstadt. Klaus Rheidt. (Illus.). xviii, 253p. (GER.). (C). 1991. lib. bdg. 229.25 (*3-11-012621-4*) De Gruyter.

Altes Testament - Literatursammlung und Heilige Schrift: Gesammelte Aufsaetze zur Entstehung, Geschichte und Auslegung des Alten Testaments. Ed. by Julis Maennchen & Ernst-Joachim Waschke. (Beihefte zur Zeitschrift fuer die Alttestamentliche Wissenschaft Ser.: Bd. 212). viii, 306p. (GER.). (C). 1993. lib. bdg. 106.15 (*3-11-013982-0*) De Gruyter.

Altes und Neues uber Konvexe Korper. H. Hadwiger. (Elemente der Mathematik Vom Hoeheren Standpunkt Aus Ser.: Vol. 3). 116p. (GER.). 1980. pap. 18.00 (*0-8176-0160-0*) Birkhauser.

Altfranzosiches Ubungsbuch. W. Foerster & K. Koschwitz. (Romance Monographs Reprint: No. 1). 1973. reprint ed. pap. 13.00 (*0-317-01688-1*) Romance.

Altfranzosische Liedersammlung, Ermanonyme Teil der Liederhandschriften Knpx. Ed. by Hans Spanke. LC 80-2161. reprint ed. 57.50 (*0-404-19025-1*) AMS Pr.

Altfranzosischen Liederhandschriften: Ihr Verhaltniss, Ehre Entstehung und Ihre Bestimmung. Eduard Schwan. LC 80-2169. reprint ed. 39.50 (*0-404-19033-2*) AMS Pr.

Altgeld's America: The Lincoln Ideal Versus Changing Realities. 2nd ed. Ray Ginger. LC 86-40364. (History Ser.). 400p. 1986. reprint ed. pap. text ed. 16.95 (*0-910129-48-7*) Wiener Pubs Inc.

Altgermanische Religionsgeschichte: History of Ancient Germanic Religion. Richard M. Meyer. Ed. by Kees W. Bolle. LC 77-79143. (Mythology Ser.). (GER.). 1978. reprint ed. lib. bdg. 54.95 (*0-405-10552-5*) Ayer.

Althea. J. M. Alonso. LC 76-2875. 1976. 15.95 (*0-914590-24-3*); pap. 6.95 (*0-914590-25-1*) Fiction Coll.

Althea Gibson. Tom Biracee. 1990. pap. 3.95 (*0-87067-563-X*, Melrose Sq) Holloway.

Althea Gibson. Tom Biracree. (American Women of Achievement Ser.). (Illus.). 112p. (J). (gr. 5 up). 1990. lib. bdg. 17.95 (*1-55546-654-0*) Chelsea Hse.

Althea's Grand Tour. Emily Hendrickson. 224p. (Orig.). 1994. pap. 3.99 (*0-451-17936-6*, Sig) NAL-Dutton.

Althochdeutsche Sprache & Literatur: Eine Einfuehrung in das Aelteste Deutsch. Darstellung & Grammatik. Stefan Sonderegger. (Sammlung Goeschen Ser.: Vol. 8005). 272p. (C). 1983. 15.25x (*3-11-004559-1*) De Gruyter.

Althochdeutschen Glossen der Handschrift Leipzig Rep. II. 6. Irmgard Frank. (Arbeitem zur Fruehmittelalterforschung Ser.: Vol. 7). 294p. (C). 1973. 115.40 (*3-11-004370-X*) De Gruyter.

Althochdeutscher Sprachschatz, 6 vols., Set. Eberhard G. Graff. 1963. reprint ed. write for info. (*0-318-71787-5*, Pub. by Georg Olms GW) Lubrecht & Cramer.

***Althochdeutsches Woerterbuch, 2 vols.** Jochen Splett. 1860p. (GER.). 1993. 1,195.00 (*0-7859-8273-6*, 3110124629) Fr & Eur.

***Althochdeutsches Woerterbuch.** 4th ed. Rudolf Schutzeichel. 309p. (GER.). 1989. 65.00 (*0-7859-8396-1*, 3484106360) Fr & Eur.

Althodeutsches Woerterbuch: Analyse der Wortfamilienstrukturen Des Althochdeutschen, Zugleich Grundlegung Einer Zukuenftigen Strukturgeschichte Des Deutschen Wortschatzes, 3 vols., Set. Jochen Splett. (GER.). 1992. lib. bdg. 607.70 (*3-11-012462-9*) De Gruyter.

Although... Those Who Overcame. Barbara G. Smith. LC 81-1038. (Illus.). 168p. (Orig.). 1981. pap. 9.95 (*0-914598-03-1*) Padre Prods.

Althusser: A Critical Reader. Ed. by Gregory Elliott. 256p. (Orig.). 1994. text ed. 49.95 (*0-631-18806-1*); pap. text ed. 19.95 (*0-631-18807-X*) Blackwell Pubs.

Althusser: The Detour of Theory. Gregory Elliott. 360p. 1988. text ed. 60.00 (*0-86091-818-1*, Pub. by Verso UK); pap. text ed. 16.95 (*0-86091-900-5*, Pub. by Verso UK) Routledge Chapman & Hall.

Althusser & Feminism. Alison Assiter. 180p. (C). 1993. text ed. 55.50 (*0-7453-0294-7*, Pub. by Pluto Pr UK) Westview.

***Althusser & the End of Leninism?** Margaret A. Majumdar. LC 95-3741. 6p. (C). 1995. text ed. 69.95 (*0-7453-0888-0*, Pub. by Pluto Pr UK); pap. text ed. 22.95 (*0-7453-0887-2*, Pub. by Pluto Pr UK) Westview.

Althusser & the Renewal of Marxist Social Theory. Robert P. Resch. LC 91-3014. (C). 1992. 42.00 (*0-520-06082-2*) U CA Pr.

Althusserian Legacy. Ed. by Michael Sprinker & E. Ann Kaplan. 240p. 1992. 59.95 (*0-86091-399-6*, A9769, Pub. by Verso UK); pap. 18.95 (*0-86091-594-8*, A9722, Pub. by Verso UK) Routledge Chapman & Hall.

Altiora Peto. Laurence Oliphant. LC 79-8183. reprint ed. 44.50 (*0-404-62079-5*) AMS Pr.

Altitude Illness: Prevention & Treatment. Stephen Bezruchka. (Illus.). 80p. 1994. pap. 6.95 (*0-89886-402-X*) Mountaineers.

Altitude-Rated Places: A Medical Atlas, Vol. 1. 2nd rev. ed. Blake Mooney. Ed. by Juliette Landry. (Illus.). 225p. (Orig.). 1994. pap. 16.95 (*0-9638226-0-8*) Med-Travel Bks.

Altitude Zero. Hank Searls. 304p. (Orig.). 1993. mass mkt. 4.99 (*0-515-11270-4*) Jove Pubns.

Altitudinal Ecology of Agama Tuberculata Gray in the Western Himalayas. Robert C. Waltner. (Miscellaneous Publications). (Illus.). 74p. 1991. pap. text ed. 5.00 (*0-89338-036-9*) U of KS Mus Nat Hist.

Altkirchenslavisch-Griechisches Worterbuch des Codex Supraliensis. Karl H. Meyer. (GRE.). 25.00 (*0-685-71713-5*) J J Augustin.

Altmann's Tongues: Stories & Novella. Brian Evenson. LC 93-28631. 1994. 22.00 (*0-679-42912-3*) Knopf.

***Altman's Spring & Summer Fashions Catalog.** B. Altman & Co. Staff. LC 94-44617. (Illus.). 1995. pap. write for info. (*0-486-28527-8*) Dover.

Altmesopotamische Weihplatten: Eine Sumerische Denkmalsgattung des Dritten Jahrtausends v. Chr. Johannes Boese. (Untersuchungen zur Assyriologie und Vorderasiatischen Archaeologie Ser.: Vol. 6). (Illus.). 232p. (C). 1971. 184.65 (*3-11-002484-5*) De Gruyter.

Altnordische Heroische Elegie. Ulrike Sprenger. (Ergaenzungsbaende Zum Reallexicon der Germanischen Altertumskunde Ser.: No. 6). xii, 367p. (GER.). (C). 1992. lib. bdg. 149.25 (*3-11-013254-0*) De Gruyter.

***Alto a la Enfermedad! Coma Bien y Viva Mejor.** Susan Powter. (ENG & SPA.). 1995. pap. 11.00 (*0-684-81327-0*) S&S Trade.

Alto Adige, South Tyrol: Italy's Frontier with the German World. Mario Toscano. Ed. by George A. Carbone. LC 75-11349. 297p. reprint ed. pap. 84.70 (*0-8357-8015-5*, 2034151) Bks Demand.

Alto Before the Dawn. Robert L. Rider. LC 91-74091. (Illus.). 409p. 1992. 29.95 (*0-9634116-0-8*) Dawn Pub Co.

Alto Rhapsody: Opus Fifty-Three for Contralto, Men's Chorus, & Orchestra (Text from Goethe's Harzreise im Winter); a Facsimile Edition from the Composer's Autograph Manuscript. Johannes Brahms. LC 82-25959. (Illus.). 76p. 1983. 50.00 (*0-87104-283-5*) NY Pub Lib.

Alto Sax One. Ed. by Bram Wiggins. (Bandstand Junior Album Ser.). Date not set. pap. 5.95 (*0-685-68973-5*, Chester Music) Music Sales.

Alto Sax Two. Ed. by Bram Wiggins. (Bandstand Junior Album Ser.). Date not set. pap. 5.95 (*0-685-68974-3*, Chester Music) Music Sales.

Altogether American: Robert Mills, Architect & Engineer, 1781-1855. Rhodri W. Liscombe. LC 92-40045. 384p. 1994. 45.00 (*0-19-508019-X*) OUP.

Altogether Different Language: Poems 1934-1994. Anne Porter. LC 94-14561. (Illus.). 128p. 1994. 16.95 (*0-944072-44-5*); pap. 10.95 (*0-944072-45-3*) Zoland Bks.

Altogether Elsewhere: Writers in Exile. Ed. by Marc Robinson. LC 93-46457. 360p. 1994. 26.95 (*0-571-19829-5*) Faber & Faber.

Altogether New Book of Top Ten Lists: From "Late Night with David Letterman" Late Night with David Letterman Writers Staff & David Letterman. Ed. by Sally Peters. 160p. (Orig.). 1991. pap. 11.00 (*0-671-74901-3*) PB.

Altogether, One at a Time. E. L. Konigsburg. LC 70-134814. (Illus.). 88p. (J). (gr. 4-7). 1971. text ed. 13.95 (*0-689-20638-0*, Atheneum Bks Young) S&S Childrens.

Altogether, One at a Time. 2nd ed. E. L. Konigsburg. (Illus.). 96p. (J). (gr. 3-7). 1989. reprint ed. pap. 3.95 (*0-689-71290-1*, Aladdin Paperbacks) S&S Childrens.

Alton Locke, Tailor & Poet. Charles Kingsley. 1971. reprint ed. 39.00 (*0-403-01056-X*) Scholarly.

Alton Ochsner, Surgeon of the South. John Wilds & Ira Harkey. LC 89-13524. (Southern Biography Ser.). (Illus.). 264p. 1990. 24.95 (*0-8071-1564-9*) La State U Pr.

Alton Pickens. (Illus.). 1977. pap. 3.00 (*0-89192-354-3*) Interbk Inc.

Alton Trials: Of Winthrop S. Gilman & Others. John F. Trow. LC 73-89440. (Black Heritage Library Collection). 1977. 18.95 (*0-8369-8671-7*) Ayer.

Alton Trials - of Winthrop S. Gilman, Enoch Long & Others. William Lincoln. LC 70-125703. (American Journalists Ser.). 1978. reprint ed. 18.95 (*0-405-01684-0*) Ayer.

***Altra Meta del Cielo: Italian Poetry.** Alberto Cardillo. 31p. 1987. pap. 5.00 (*0-89304-577-2*) Cross-Cultrl NY.

Altruism. David O. Otebele. 1994. 16.95 (*0-533-10768-7*) Vantage.

Altruism. Ed. by Ellen F. Paul et al. LC 93-6963. (Social Philosophy & Policy Ser.: No. 10). 256p. (C). 1993. pap. 19.95 (*0-521-44759-3*) Cambridge U Pr.

Altruism: Contemplation for the Scientific Age. Karma Sonan Senge. Ed. by Karma Chime Wongmo. 100p. (Orig.). 1986. pap. text ed. 6.95 (*0-9602722-3-2*) Open Path.

Altruism & Aggression: Social & Biological Origins. Ed. by Carolyn Zahn-Waxler et al. (Studies in Emotion & Social Interaction). (Illus.). 352p. (C). 1991. pap. 24.95 (*0-521-42367-8*) Cambridge U Pr.

***Altruism & Beyond: An Economic Analysis of Transfers & Exchanges Within Families & Groups.** Oded Stark. (Oscar Morgenstern Memorial Lectures). (Illus.). 100p. (C). 1995. 24.95 (*0-521-47419-1*) Cambridge U Pr.

Altruism & the Elderly. Elizabeth Midlarksy & Eva Kahana. (Library of Social Research: Vol. 196). 320p. 1994. 49.95 (*0-8039-2768-1*); pap. 24.00 (*0-8039-2769-X*) Sage.

Altruism in Social Systems. Ed. by L. Montada & H. W. Bierhoff. (Illus.). 268p. 1991. text ed. 43.00 (*0-88937-045-1*) Hogrefe & Huber Pubs.

Altruism, Morality, & Economic Theory. Ed. by Edmund S. Phelps. LC 74-79448. 242p. 1975. 29.95 (*0-87154-659-0*) Russell Sage.

Altruism Question: Toward a Social-Psychological Answer. C. Daniel Batson. 272p. 1991. text ed. 49.95 (*0-8058-0245-2*) L Erlbaum Assocs.

Altruistic Imagination: A History of Social Work & Social Policy in the United States. John H. Ehrenreich. LC 84-45807. (Illus.). 304p. (C). 1985. 26.95 (*0-8014-1764-3*) Cornell U Pr.

Altruistic Personality: Rescuers of Jews in Nazi Europe. Samuel P. Oliner & Pearl Oliner. LC 87-33223. 432p. 1988. text ed. 27.95 (*0-02-923830-7*) Free Pr.

Altruistic Personality: Rescuers of Jews in Nazi Europe. Samuel P. Oliner. 1992. pap. 14.95 (*0-02-923829-3*) Free Pr.

Altruists & Volunteers: Life Histories. William N. Stephens. 87p. (C). 1991. pap. 18.95 (*0-945795-06-8*) MBA Pub.

Altruria. Titus K. Smith. LC 77-154463. (Utopian Literature Ser.). 1976. reprint ed. 19.95 (*0-405-03545-4*) Ayer.

Alttrakien. Christo Danov. LC 73-75484. (C). 1976. 203.85 (*3-11-003434-4*) De Gruyter.

***Altura: Fusion of the Soul.** Ani Lea. 64p. (Orig.). 1995. pap. text ed. 7.95 (*0-9645725-2-4*) Numina.

Altus of St. Columba. Tr. by John Dowden. 1989. pap. 1.25 (*0-89981-210-4*) Eastern Orthodox.

Altyn-Depe. V. M. Masson. Tr. by Henry N. Michael. (University Museum Monographs: No. 55). (Illus.). xx, 150p. 1989. text ed. 55.00 (*0-934718-54-7*) U PA Mus Pubns.

ALT4.IBM: (Short Reference ALT4.I): New Subsonic & Supersonic Rocket Performance & Drug Programs. Fred Brennlon et al. (Illus.). 68p. (C). 1989. disk, pap. text ed. 69.00 (*0-912468-18-1*) CA Rocketry.

Alum Sludge in the Aquatic Environment. 244p. 1991. pap. 36.50 (*0-89867-531-6*, 90582) Am Water Wks Assn.

Alumina: Processing, Properties & Applications. E. Dorre et al. (Materials Research & Engineering Ser.). (Illus.). 330p. 1984. 95.00 (*0-387-13576-6*) Spr-Verlag.

Alumina as a Ceramic Material. Ed. by Walter H. Gitzen. 254p. 1978. pap. 16.00 (*0-916094-46-4*) Am Ceramic.

Alumina Chemicals: Science & Technology Handbook. Ed. by L. Hart. 617p. 1990. 178.00 (*0-916094-33-2*) Am Ceramic.

***Alumina Plants Worldwide.** Ed. by Errol D. Sehnke. (Illus.). 98p. (Orig.). (C). 1994. pap. text ed. 75.00x (*0-7881-1146-9*) Diane Pub.

***Aluminium Boatbuilding.** 2nd ed. Ernst Sims. (Illus.). 128p. Date not set. 35.00 (*0-7136-3691-2*) Sheridan.

Aluminium Multinationals & the Bauxite Cartel. Steven K. Holloway. LC 87-12991. 256p. 1988. text ed. 49.95 (*0-312-00939-9*) St Martin.

***Aluminium Production: Glossary of Technical Terms English-French-German-Spanish.** J. Nitsche. 361p. (ENG, FRE & GER.). 1992. pap. 120.00x (*3-87017-182-0*) IBD Ltd.

Aluminium Radiators. D. P. Gregory. (C). 1986. 105.00 (*0-86022-178-4*, Pub. by Build Servs Info Assn UK) St Mut.

Aluminium Structures-Advances, Design & Construction: Proceedings of the International Conference on Steel & Aluminium Structures, Cardiff, U. K., 8-10 July, 1987. Ed. by R. Narayanan. 202p. 1987. 59.50 (*1-85166-121-2*, Pub. by Elsevier Applied Sci UK) Elsevier.

Aluminizing of Steel. Vladimir R. Ryabov. (Illus.). 216p. (C). 1985. 28.59x (*81-205-0021-0*, Pub. by Oxford IBH II) S Asia.

Aluminum. V. N. Tikhonov. (Analytical Chemistry of the Elements Ser.). 316p. 1970. text ed. 77.50 (*0-7065-1223-5*, Pub. by Keter Pub IS) Coronet Bks.

Aluminum: Properties & Physical Metallurgy. Ed. by John E. Hatch. 424p. 1984. 134.00 (*0-87170-176-6*, 6236U) ASM.

Aluminum--Index of New Information & Medical Research Bible. Anita E. Funstun. 150p. 1994. 44.50 (*0-7883-0082-2*); pap. 39.50 (*0-7883-0083-0*) ABBE Pubs Assn.

Aluminum Alloys for Packaging. Ed. by H. D. Merchant et al. (Illus.). 352p. 1993. 68.00 (*0-87339-221-3*, 465) Minerals Metals.

Aluminum & Aluminum Alloys. Joseph R. Davis. LC 93-41647. (ASM Specialty Handbook Ser.). (Illus.). 784p. 1993. 159.00 (*0-87170-496-X*, 6610U) ASM.

Aluminum & Health: A Critical Reivew. Gitelman. 314p. 1989. 110.00 (*0-8247-8026-4*) Dekker.

An Asterisk (*) at the beginning of an entry indicates that the title is appearing in BIP for the first time.

Aluminum & Renal Failure. Ed. by Marc E. De Broe. (C). 1990. lib. bdg. 180.50 (*0-7923-0347-4*) Kluwer Ac.

***Aluminum Applications for Automotive Design: 1995 International Congress & Exposition Meeting.** 1995. pap. 34.00 (*1-56091-647-8*, SP1097) Soc Auto Engineers.

Aluminum, Bauxite & Alumina. (Metals & Minerals Ser.). 1993. lib. bdg. 250.95 (*0-8490-8957-3*) Gordon Pr.

Aluminum Cast House Technology. Ed. by Madhu Nilamni. (Illus.). 532p. 1993. 60.00 (*0-87339-198-5*) Minerals Metals.

Aluminum Casting Technology. (Illus.). 296p. 1987. 80.00 (*0-317-59820-1*, NF8501) Am Foundrymen.

Aluminum Casting Technology. 2nd ed. 368p. 140.00 (*0-87433-157-9*, NF9300) Am Foundrymen.

Aluminum in Biology & Medicine. Ed. by Derek J. Chadwick & Julie Whelan. LC 92-14002. (CIBA Foundation Symposia Ser.: Vol. 169). 316p. 1992. 75.00 (*0-471-93413-5*) Wiley.

Aluminum in Building. 150p. 1992. 78.95 (*1-85742-082-9*, Pub. by Ashgate UK) Ashgate Pub Co.

Aluminum-Lithium Alloys: Proceedings of the First International Aluminum-Lithium Conference. International Aluminum-Lithium Conference Staff. Ed. by T. H. Sanders & E. A. Starke, Jr. LC 81-80989. 389p. reprint ed. pap. 110.90 (*0-8357-5336-0*, 2025447) Bks Demand.

Aluminum-Lithium Alloys II: Proceedings of the Second International Aluminun-Lithium Conference. Ed. by E. A. Starke, Jr. et al. LC 83-83124. (Conference Proceedings Ser.). (Illus.). 710p. reprint ed. pap. 180.00 (*0-8357-5335-2*, 2032591) Bks Demand.

Aluminum-Lithium, Vols. 1 & 2: Proceedings of the 6th International Aluminum-Lithium Conference, 2 vols., Set. Ed. by Manfred Peters & Peter Winkler. 1395p. Date not set. lib. bdg. 275.00 (*3-88355-180-5*, Pub. by DGM Metallurgy Info GW) IR Pubns.

Aluminum Recycling. rev. ed. Data Notes Staff. 93p. 1992. pap. text ed. 17.95 (*0-911569-40-5*) Prosperity & Profits.

***Aluminum Structures: A Guide to Their Specifications & Design.** J. Randolph Kissell & Robert L. Ferry. 1995. text ed. 69.95 (*0-471-05385-6*) Wiley.

Aluminum Technology '86. Ed. by T. Sheppard. 850p. 1986. text ed. 50.00 (*0-904357-85-6*, Pub. by Inst Materials UK) Ashgate Pub Co.

Aluminum Transformation Technology & Applications: Proceedings of the International Symposium at Puerto Madryn. Symposium Aluminum Transformation Technology & Its Applications (1978). Ed. by C. A. Pampillo. LC 80-10612. (Materials-Metalworking Technology Ser.). 636p. reprint ed. pap. 180.00 (*0-8357-5337-9*, 2026997) Bks Demand.

Aluminum Transformation Technology & Applications, 1981: Proceedings of the Second International Symposium. American Society for Metals Staff. Ed. by C. A. Pampillo. LC 82-70649. (Materials-Metalworking Technology Ser.). 676p. reprint ed. pap. 180.00 (*0-8357-5338-7*, 2026996) Bks Demand.

Alumni Continuing Education. Steven L. Calvert. (ACE-Oryx Series on Higher Education). 336p. 1987. 31.95 (*0-02-905171-1*, ACE-Oryx) Oryx Pr.

***Alumni Drawings: Celebrating Forty Years of the Visual Arts at Boston University School for the Arts.** Mary D. McInnes et al. (Illus.). 29p. (Orig.). (C). 1995. pap. text ed. 5.00 (*1-881450-05-8*) Boston U Art.

Alumni Invitational Exhibition. Daniel E. Stetson. Ed. by Kevin Boatright. (Illus.). 16p. (Orig.). 1982. pap. text ed. 2.50 (*0-932660-05-3*) U of NI Dept Art.

Alumni Research: Methods & Applications. Ed. by Gerlinda S. Melchiori. LC 85-645339. (New Directions for Institutional Research Ser.: No. IR 60). 1988. 16.95 (*1-55542-889-4*) Jossey-Bass.

Alumni Stimulation by the American College President. Webster S. Stover. LC 74-177818. (Columbia University. Teachers College. Contributions to Education Ser.: No. 432). reprint ed. 37.50 (*0-404-55432-6*) AMS Pr.

Alumni Treasures, Phillips Academy. Intro. by Bartlett H. Hayes. (Illus.). 108p. 1967. 15.00 (*1-879886-17-0*) Addison Gallery.

Alumni Who Collect I: Drawings from the Sixteenth Century to the Present, Vol. I. Frwd. by Edward A. Maser. LC 82-70634. (Illus.). 78p. (Orig.). 1982. pap. text ed. 3.00 (*0-935573-09-7*) D & A Smart Museum.

Alun Hoddinott: A Bio-Bibliography. Stewart R. Craggs. LC 92-38456. (Bio-Bibliographies in Music Ser.: No. 44). 256p. 1993. text ed. 55.00 (*0-313-27321-9*, CGH/) Greenwood.

Alun Lewis: A Life. John Pikoulis. LC 84-62692. (Illus.). 323p. 1984. 30.00 (*0-907476-26-0*, Pub. by Poetry Wales Pr UK) Dufour.

Alun Lewis: A Life. John Pikoulis. 322p. (C). 1989. 59.00 (*0-685-61449-2*, Pub. by D Brown & Sons Ltd UK) St Mut.

Alun Lewis: A Life. rev. ed. John Pikoulis. (Illus.). 290p. 1992. pap. 24.00 (*1-85411-018-7*, Pub. by Seren Bks UK) Dufour.

Alun Lewis: Collected Stories. Alun Lewis. 360p. 1990. 38.00 (*1-85411-012-8*, Pub. by Poetry Wales Pr UK) Dufour.

Alun Llywelyn-Williams. Elwyn Evans. 91p. 1991. pap. 7.00 (*0-7083-1103-2*, Pub. by U of Wales UK) Bks Intl VA.

Alusiones Literarias en la Obra Narrativa de Francisco Ayala. Rosario Hiriart. 1972. 10.50 (*0-88303-016-0*); pap. 7.50 (*0-685-73218-5*) E Torres & Sons.

Alva Community, Oklahoma. Joyce Beagley & Delia Shore. (Illus.). 567p. 1986. 67.70 (*0-88107-075-0*) Curtis Media.

Alva Myrdal: A Daughter's Memoir. Sissela Bok. 375p. 1991. 22.07 (*0-201-57086-6*) Addison-Wesley.

Alva Myrdal: A Daughter's Memoir. Sissela Bok. 1992. pap. 12.45 (*0-201-60815-4*) Addison-Wesley.

Alvah & Arvilla. Mary L. Ray. LC 93-31874. (Illus.). (J). 1994. 14.95 (*0-15-202655-X*) HarBrace.

Alvah Bessie's Short Fictions. Alvah Bessie. LC 82-9739. 312p. (Orig.). 1982. pap. 7.95 (*0-88316-546-5*) Chandler & Sharp.

Alvan Stewart's Writings on Slavery. Alvan Stewart. Ed. by L. R. Marsh. LC 71-128412. (Studies in Black History & Culture: No. 54). 1970. reprint ed. lib. bdg. 66.95 (*0-8383-1153-9*) M S G Haskell Hse.

Alvar. Francesc Miralles & Miquel Alzueta. (Illus.). 359p. (ENG, FRE & JPN.). 1993. 75.00 (*0-9636243-0-X*) E Newman.

Alvar Aalto. (Architecture & Urbanism Extra Edition Ser.). (Illus.). 200p. (Orig.). (ENG & JPN.). (C). pap. text ed. 68.00 (*4-900211-07-9*, Pub. by Japan Architect JA) Gingko Press.

***Alvar Aalto.** Richard Weston. (Illus.). 240p. (C). 1995. 75.00 (*0-7148-3159-X*, Pub. by Phaidon Press UK) Chronicle Bks.

Alvar Aalto: A Bibliography, No. 1190. William C. Miller. 1976. 5.00 (*0-686-19684-8*) CPL Biblios.

Alvar Aalto: A Critical Study. Malcolm Quantrill. (Illus.). 307p. (C). 1989. reprint ed. pap. 30.00 (*0-941533-35-2*) New Amsterdam Bks.

Alvar Aalto: An Academy Architectural Monograph. Ed. by David Dunster. (Illus.). 128p. 1984. pap. 21.95 (*0-312-02150-X*) St Martin.

Alvar Aalto: Synopsis: Painting, Architecture, Sculpture. 2nd ed. (Illus.). 240p. (ENG, FRE & GER.). 1980. 116.95 (*3-7643-1109-6*) Birkhauser.

Alvar Aalto: The Complete Catalogue of Architecture, Design, & Art. Goran Schildt. LC 94-65702. (Illus.). 320p. 1994. 75.00 (*0-8478-1818-7*) Rizzoli Intl.

Alvar Aalto: The Mature Years. Goran Schildt. LC 90-53591. (Illus.). 300p. 1991. 50.00 (*0-8478-1329-0*) Rizzoli Intl.

Alvar Aalto & the International Style. Paul D. Pearson. (Illus.). 240p. 1989. pap. 32.50 (*0-8230-0174-1*, Whitney Lib) Watsn-Guptill.

Alvar Mayor: Death & Silver. Trillo. Ed. by Timothy Truman. Tr. by Enrique Villacran & Charles Dixon. (Illus.). 64p. (Orig.). 1988. pap. 8.98 (*0-922173-01-X*) Four Winds Pub Group.

Alvar Nunez Cabeza de Vaca. Peter Wild. LC 91-55035. (Western Writers Ser.: No. 101). (Illus.). 51p. 1991. 3.95 (*0-88430-100-1*) Boise St U W Writ Ser.

Alvarez on Alvarez. Walter C. Alvarez. LC 76-47216. (Illus.). 160p. (Orig.). 1977. pap. 5.95 (*0-89407-005-3*) Strawberry Hill.

Alvaro Obregon: Power & Revolution in Mexico, 1911-1920. Linda B. Hall. LC 80-6110. (Illus.). 304p. 1981. 28.50 (*0-89096-113-1*) Tex A&M Univ Pr.

***Alvaro Siza: City Sketches = Stadtskizzen = Desendos Urbanos.** Norman Foster. Ed. by Bridgitte Fleck. LC 94-27572. 1994. write for info. (*3-7643-2820-7*) Birkhauser.

Alvaro Siza, 1954-1988. (Architecture & Urbanism Extra Edition Ser.). (Illus.). 244p. (Orig.). (ENG & JPN.). (C). pap. text ed. 75.00 (*4-900211-27-3*, Pub. by Japan Architect JA) Gingko Press.

Alva's World. Alva A. Bader. Ed. by Kathryn L. Hall. (Illus.). 488p. (Orig.). 1992. pap. 21.95 (*1-56664-021-0*) WorldComm.

Alveograph Handbook. Ed. by Hamed Faridi & Vladimir F. Rasper. LC 87-72508. (Illus.). 56p. 1987. 59.00 (*0-913250-52-X*) Am Assn Cereal Chem.

Alveolar Interstitium of the Lung: Pathological & Physiological Aspects: Proceedings of the International Symposium on Pulmonary Interstitium, Paris, May, 1974. International Symposium on Pulmonary Interstitium Staff. Ed. by F. Basset & Robert Geovges. (Progress in Respiration Research Ser.: Vol. 8). viii, 245p. 1975. 122.50 (*3-8055-2193-6*) S Karger.

Alves & Co. Jose M. De Queiros. Tr. by Robert M. Fedorchek. LC 88-22799. 136p. (Orig.). (C). 1988. pap. text ed. 16.50 (*0-8191-7157-3*) U Pr of Amer.

Alvey: Britain's Strategic Computing Initiative. Brian Oakley & Kenneth Owen. 352p. 1990. 44.00x (*0-262-15038-7*) MIT Pr.

Alvin Ailey. Andrea Davis Pinkney. LC 92-54865. (Illus.). 32p. (J). (gr. 1-4). 1993. 13.95 (*1-56282-413-9*); lib. bdg. 13.89 (*1-56282-414-7*) Hyprn Child.

***Alvin Ailey.** Robert Fleming. 208p. 1995. 4.95 (*0-87067-793-4*) Holloway.

***Alvin Ailey.** Andrea D. Pinkney. LC 92-54865. (Illus.). 32p. (J). (gr. k-4). 1995. pap. 4.95 (*0-7868-1077-7*) Hyprn Ppbks.

***Alvin Ailey.** Robert Reid-Pharr. Ed. by Martin Duberman. (Lives of Notable Gay Men & Lesbians Ser.). (Illus.). 168p. (YA). (gr. 9 up). 1995. pap. 9.95 (*0-7910-2886-0*) Chelsea Hse.

***Alvin Ailey.** Robert Reid-Pharr. Ed. by Martin Duberman. (Lives of Notable Gay Men & Lesbians Ser.). (Illus.). 168p. (YA). (gr. 9 up). 1995. lib. bdg. 19.95 (*0-7910-2314-1*) Chelsea Hse.

***Alvin Ailey: Choreographer.** Ed. by Nathan I. Huggins. (Black Americans of Achievement Ser.). (Illus.). 144p. (YA). (gr. 5 up). 1995. 18.95 (*0-7910-1861-X*) Chelsea Hse.

Alvin Ailey American Dance Theater: Jack Mitchell Photographs. Jack Mitchell. LC 93-13582. (Illus.). 144p. (Orig.). 1993. 29.95 (*0-8362-4509-1*); pap. 19.95 (*0-8362-4508-3*) Andrews & McMeel.

Alvin Ailey, Jr. A Life in Dance. Julinda Lewis-Ferguson. LC 93-17906. 64p. (J). (gr. 3-8). 1994. 14.95 (*0-8027-8239-6*); lib. bdg. 15.85 (*0-8027-8241-8*) Walker & Co.

Alvin & the Chipmunks: Alvin's Daydreams. Michael Teitelbaum. Ed. by YES! Entertainment Corporation Staff. (Comes to Life Bks.). 16p. (J). (ps-2). 1993. write for info. (*1-883366-18-6*) YES Ent.

Alvin & the Unruly Elves. Ulf Lofgren. (J). (ps-3). 1992. 18.95 (*0-87614-590-X*, Carolrhoda) Lerner Group.

***Alvin Journeyman.** Orson C. Card. (Alvin Maker Ser.: Vol. 4). 320p. 1995. 23.95 (*0-312-85053-0*) Tor Bks.

Alvin Langdon Coburn: Symbolist Photographer. Mike Weaver. (Illus.). 80p. 1986. 25.00 (*0-89381-240-4*) Aperture.

Alvin Langdon Coburn: Symbolist Photographer, 1882-1966. Mike Weaver. LC 85-52455. 1990. 19.95 (*0-89381-246-3*) Aperture.

Alvin Langdon Coburn, Photographer: An Autobiography. Alvin L. Coburn. Ed. by Helmut & Alison Gernsheim. (Illus.). 1978. pap. 8.95 (*0-486-23685-4*) Dover.

Alvin Lucier. James Tenney et al. (Illus.). 24p. (Orig.). (C). 1988. pap. 8.00 (*0-929687-01-9*) E & C Zilkha Gal.

Alvin Plantinga. Ed. by James E. Tomberlin & Peter Van Inwagen. 1985. pap. text ed. 55.00 (*90-277-2106-8*) Kluwer Ac.

Alvin the Knight. Ulf Lofgren. (J). (ps-3). 1992. 18.95 (*0-87614-698-1*, Carolrhoda) Lerner Group.

Alvin the Pirate. Ulf Lofgren. (Illus.). 32p. (J). (ps-3). 1990. lib. bdg. 18.95 (*0-87614-402-4*, Carolrhoda) Lerner Group.

Alvin the Pirate: Picture Book. Ulf Lofgren. (J). (ps-3). 1991. pap. 5.95 (*0-87614-551-9*, Carolrhoda) Lerner Group.

Alvin the Zookeeper. Ulf Lofgren. (Picture Bks.). (Illus.). 32p. (J). (ps-3). 1991. lib. bdg. 18.95 (*0-87614-689-2*, Carolrhoda) Lerner Group.

Alvin's No Horse. Harding. (J). 1994. pap. 4.95 (*0-8050-3274-6*) H Holt & Co.

Alvis: The Postwar Cars. John P. Williams. (Illus.). 144p. 1993. 39.95 (*0-947981-73-X*, Pub. by Motor Racing UK) Motorbooks Intl.

Always. Ginna Gray. 1994. mass mkt. 3.50 (*0-373-09891-X*, 5-09891-8) Harlequin Bks.

Always... Jeane Renick. 1993. mass mkt. 4.99 (*0-06-108141-8*, Harp PBks) HarpC.

Always. Jeane Renick. 1994. pap. 2.99 (*0-06-108294-5*, Harp PBks) HarpC.

Always. Catherine Sellers. 224p. (Orig.). 1990. pap. 2.75 (*1-878702-00-9*, Kismet) Meteor Pub.

Always a Beginning. Helene W. Stasiulis. 1994. 18.95 (*0-533-10786-5*) Vantage.

Always a Body to Trade. K. C. Constantine. 248p. 1993. pap. 5.95 (*0-87923-952-2*) Godine.

Always a Commander: The Reminiscences of Major General William H. Gill. William H. Gill. (Illus.). 124p. 1974. pap. 10.00 (*0-89839-077-X*) Battery Pr.

Always a Lady. Sharon Sala. 224p. (Orig.). 1993. pap. 2.95 (*1-56597-045-4*, Kismet) Meteor Pub.

Always a Rebel: Ricardo Flores Magon & the Mexican Revolution. Ward S. Albro. LC 92-6074. (Illus.). 220p. 1992. 24.95 (*0-87565-108-9*) Tex Christian.

***Always a Reckoning: And Other Poems.** Jimmy Carter. 1994. 18.00 (*0-8129-2434-7*, Times Bks) Random.

***Always a Reckoning: And Other Poems.** large type ed. Jimmy Carter. LC 95-13851. (Illus.). 126p. 1995. 20.95 (*0-7838-1301-5*, Large Print Bks) Hall.

Always a River: The Ohio River & the American Experience. Ed. & Tr. by Robert L. Reid. LC 90-25293. (Illus.). 270p. 1991. 35.00 (*0-253-34958-3*) Ind U Pr.

Always a Season for Porcelain Painters. Gladys Gilbert. (Illus.). 64p. 1993. 14.95 (*0-86417-476-4*, Pub. by Kangaroo Pr AT) Seven Hills Bk.

***Always a Sister: The Feminism of Lillian D. Wald.** Doris G. Daniels. 224p. 1995. pap. 12.95 (*1-55861-113-4*) Feminist Pr.

Always a Springtime. Helen S. Rice. (Illus.). 96p. 1987. 13.99 (*0-8007-1556-X*) Revell.

Always a Warrior: The Memoir of a Six-War Soldier. Charles W. Sasser. Ed. by Eric Tobias. 320p. (Orig.). 1994. mass mkt. 5.50 (*0-671-78931-7*) PB.

Always a Winner: An Experiment under Grace. Donald S. Bachtell. LC 92-17390. 96p. (Orig.). 1993. pap. 8.95 (*1-56474-028-5*) Fithian Pr.

Always Abounding. John F. Avanzini. 122p. 1989. pap. 5.95 (*0-89274-581-9*, HH581) HIS Publish.

Always Alvin. Diane Van Allen. (Illus.). (Orig.). (J). (ps). 1984. pap. 3.95 (*0-939332-11-6*) J Pohl Assocs.

Always, Always. Crescent Dragonwagon. LC 83-22199. (Illus.). 32p. (J). (gr. 1-4). 1984. text ed. 13.95 (*0-02-733080-X*, Mac Bks Young Read) S&S Childrens.

Always among Us: Images of the Poor in Zwingli's Zurich. Lee P. Wandel. 304p. (C). 1990. 39.95 (*0-521-39096-6*) Cambridge U Pr.

Always & Forever. Cynthia Freeman. 1991. mass mkt. 5.95 (*0-515-10607-0*) Jove Pubns.

Always & Forever. Gina Robins. 448p. 1992. mass mkt. 4.99 (*1-55817-647-0*, Pinnacle NY) Windsor NY.

Always & Forever. braille ed. Cynthia Freeman. 667p. 1991. vinyl bd. 53.36 (*1-56956-181-8*, BR8442) W A T Braille.

Always & Forever. large type ed. Patricia Cavendish. 548p. 1992. 21.95 (*0-7505-0440-4*, Pub. by Magna Print Bks) Ulverscroft.

Always & Forever. large type ed. Cynthia Freeman. 614p. 1991. reprint ed. 22.95 (*1-56054-092-3*) Thorndike Pr.

Always & Forever. large type ed. Cynthia Freeman. 614p. 1991. pap. 14.95 (*1-56054-997-1*) Thorndike Pr.

Always & Forever: A Wedding Treasury. Annette Reynolds. 1992. 7.98 (*0-88486-060-4*) Arrowood Pr.

***Always & Forever: The Life & Times of Mother Franciska Lechner.** M. Clementine Poch. 224p. (Orig.). 1994. pap. text ed. 12.95 (*1-883520-04-5*) Jeremiah Pr.

Always & Forever Friends. C. S. Adler. 176p. (J). 1990. pap. 3.99 (*0-380-70687-3*, Camelot) Avon.

Always Annie. Patty Copeland. 224p. (Orig.). 1992. pap. 2.95 (*1-878702-76-9*, Kismet) Meteor Pub.

Always Anonymous Beast. Lauren W. Douglas. 224p. 1987. pap. 8.95 (*0-941483-04-5*) Naiad Pr.

Always Another Dawn: The Story of a Rocket Test Pilot. A. Scott Crossfield & Clay Blair, Jr. LC 73-169413. (Literature & History of Aviation Ser.). 1972. reprint ed. 43.95 (*0-405-03758-9*) Ayer.

***Always Arthur.** (J). 1995. cd-rom 58.53 (*0-8368-1335-9*) Gareth Stevens Inc.

Always Arthur. Amanda Graham. LC 89-4474. (Quality Time Bks.). (Illus.). 32p. (J). (gr. 2-3). 1990. lib. bdg. 18.60 (*0-8368-0096-6*) Gareth Stevens Inc.

Always Astonished: Selected Prose. Fernando Pessoa. Tr. by Edwin Honig. 160p. (Orig.). 1988. pap. 8.95 (*0-87286-228-3*) City Lights.

Always at Ease. Christopher J. McCullough. 272p. (Orig.). 1993. mass mkt. 5.50 (*0-425-14012-1*) Berkley Pub.

***Always Aware.** James S. Cusack. Ed. & Pref. by J. Colby. LC 95-75583. (Self-Help Ser.). 200p. 1995. pap. text ed. 9.95 (*1-883283-07-8*, 1-800-68-BRICK) Brick Tower.

Always Bear Left: And Other Ways to Get Things Done Faster & Easier. Ken Cooper. 212p. 1982. pap. 5.95 (*0-385-28006-8*) Total Comm.

Always Bear Left: And Other Ways to Get Things Done Faster & Easier. Ken Cooper. LC 81-15279. (Illus.). 212p. 1987. pap. 6.95 (*0-932801-02-1*, HN90.T5C66) Total Comm.

Always Begin Where You Are: Themes in Poetry & Song. Walter Lamb. LC 78-32108. (Illus.). 1979. text ed. 15.20 (*0-07-035921-0*) McGraw.

Always Bet on the Butcher: Warren Nelson & Casino Gaming, 1930s-1980s. Warren L. Nelson et al. LC 94-21183. (Illus.). 242p. 1994. 21.95 (*1-56475-368-9*) U NV Oral Hist.

Always Come Evening. Robert E. Howard. 110p. 1977. 20.00 (*0-89366-137-6*) Ultramarine Pub.

Always Daddy's Girl: Understanding Your Father's Impact on Who You Are. H. Norman Wright. Ed. by Ed Stewart. LC 89-27319. 285p. 1991. pap. 8.99 (*0-8307-1354-9*, 5419798) Regal.

Always Daddy's Girl see Siempre Sere tu Nina Pequena

Always Follow Your Dreams. Ed. by Susan P. Schutz. (Illus.). 93p. 1985. text ed. 16.95 (*0-88396-234-9*) Blue Mtn Pr CO.

Always Getting Ready, Upterrlainarluta: Yup'ik Eskimo Subsistence in Southwest Alaska. Photos & Text by James H. Barker. LC 92-29530. (Illus.). 144p. (C). 1993. pap. 29.95 (*0-295-97235-1*) U of Wash Pr.

***Always Have Popsicles: The Handbook to Help You Be the Best Grandparent.** Harvin. 1994. pap. text ed. 9.00 (*0-9641477-2-6*) R L Harvin.

Always Home. David Ely. 1991. 18.95 (*1-55611-258-0*) D I Fine.

Always Home: Fifty Years of the USO-The Official Photographic History. F. Coffey. (Illus.). 190p. 1991. 29.95 (*0-08-040576-2*) Brasseys Inc.

Always Hungry, Never Greedy: Food & the Expression of Gender in a Melanesian Society. Miriam Kahn. (Illus.). 187p. (C). 1994. reprint ed. pap. text ed. 9.50 (*0-88133-776-5*) Waveland Pr.

Always Hungry, Never Greedy: Food & the Expression of Gender Relations in a Melanesian Society. Miriam Kahn. (Illus.). 208p. 1986. 59.95 (*0-521-32222-7*) Cambridge U Pr.

Always I Was Getting Ready to Go. Susan Kronenberg. 36p. 1989. pap. 6.00 (*0-930773-10-1*) Black Heron Pr.

Always in a Foreign Land. Barbara A. Scott. LC 93-94049. 410p. 1993. pap. 11.50 (*0-9637134-0-X*) Zenar Bks.

Always in Her Heart. Rebecca Marsh. LC 93-20312. 1993. 18.95 (*0-7927-1619-1*, Curley Lrg Print) Chivers N Amer.

Always in Her Heart. large type ed. Rebecca Marsh. LC 93-20312. 1993. pap. 16.95 (*0-7927-1618-3*, Curley Lrg Print) Chivers N Amer.

Always in Love: Life (Not Death) of a Salesman - a Retrospective Novel. John F. Anderson. 1990. 13.95 (*0-533-09039-3*) Vantage.

***Always in My Dreams.** Jo Goodman. 448p. 1995. mass mkt. 4.99 (*0-8217-4961-7*) Windsor NY.

Always in Season: Folk Art & Traditional Culture in Vermont. Ed. by Jane C. Beck. LC 82-70924. (Vermont Council on the Arts Ser.). (Illus.). 144p. (Orig.). 1982. pap. 16.95 (*0-916718-09-3*) U Pr of New Eng.

Always in Season: Folk Art & Traditional Culture in Vermont. Ed. by Jane C. Beck. LC 82-70924. (Illus.). 144p. (Orig.). 1982. pap. 14.95 (*0-685-05821-2*) VT Folklife Ctr.

Always in September. Doris E. Fell. LC 93-11682. (Seasons of Intrigue Ser.). 288p. (Orig.). 1994. pap. 9.99 (*0-89107-760-X*) Crossway Bks.

Always in Style. Doris Pooser. Ed. by Phyllis Avedon. LC 90-55625. (Fifty-Minute Ser.). (Illus.). 214p. 1989. pap. 14.95 (*0-931961-91-2*) Crisp Pubns.

Always Ireland: An Englishman in Ireland. Roy Kerridge. (Illus.). 208p. 1993. pap. 13.95 (*1-85371-256-6*, Pub. by Poolbeg Pr IE) Dufour.

Always Is for Ever. large type ed. Juliet Gray. (Linford Romance Library). 1990. pap. 12.95 (*0-7089-6819-8*, Linford) Ulverscroft.

Always, Julia. Marcia Wood. LC 91-40460. 128p. (J). (gr. 5-9). 1993. text ed. 13.95 (*0-689-31728-X*, Atheneum Bks Young) S&S Childrens.

Always Kiss with Your Whiskers: Love Advice from My Cat. Liz Nickles & Tamara Asseyev. (Illus.). 64p. 1991. pap. 6.00 (*0-671-74983-8*) PB.

Always Know Your Pal: Children on the Erie Canal. Erie Canal Museum Staff. LC 93-11158. 160p. 1993. pap. 14.95 (*1-883582-00-8*) Erie Canal Mus.

Always Movin' On: The Life of Langston Hughes. James S. Haskins. LC 91-78318. 1992. 35.00 (*0-86543-337-2*); pap. 12.95 (*0-86543-338-0*) Africa World.

An Asterisk (*) at the beginning of an entry indicates that the title is appearing in BIP for the first time.

215

A

Always My Dad. Sharon D. Wyeth. LC 93-43755. (Illus.). 40p. (J). (ps-3). 1995. 15.00 (0-679-83447-8, Apple Soup Bks); lib. bdg. 15.99 (0-679-93447-2, Apple Soup Bks) Knopf Bks Yng Read.

Always, My Love. Carla Simpson. 1990. mass mkt. 4.50 (1-55817-433-8, Pinnacle NY) Windsor NY.

Always of Home: A Southern Illinois Childhood. Edgar A. Imhoff. LC 92-5693. (Shawnee Bks.). 191p. (C). 1993. 24.95 (0-8093-1853-9); pap. 12.95 (0-8093-1854-7) S Ill U Pr.

***Always Postpone Meetings with Time-Wasting Morons: A Dilbert Book.** Scott Adams. (Illus.). 111p. 1994. pap. 7.95 (0-8362-1758-6) Andrews & McMeel.

Always Prayer Shawl. Sheldon Oberman. (Illus.). 32p. (J). (gr. 2 up). 1994. 14.95 (1-878093-22-3) Boyds Mills Pr.

***Always Rachel: The Letters of Rachel Carson & Dorothy Freeman, 1952-1964.** Rachel Carson. Ed. by Martha Freeman. LC 94-25849. (Illus.). 640p. 1994. 35.00 (0-8070-7010-6) Beacon Pr.

Always Room for One More. Sorche Nic Leodhas. LC 65-12881. (Illus.). 32p. (J). (ps-2). 1972. pap. 5.95 (0-8050-0330-4, Bks Young Read) H Holt & Co.

Always Room for One More. Sorche NicLeodhas. LC 65-12881. (Illus.). 32p. (J). (ps-2). 1965. 14.95 (0-8050-0331-2, Bks Young Read) H Holt & Co.

Always Running: Gang Days in L. A. Luis J. Rodriguez. LC 92-39002. (Orig.). (J). (gr. 9 up). 1993. 19.95 (1-880684-06-3) Curbstone.

Always Running: La Vida Loca: Gang Days in L.A. Luis J. Rodriguez. 1994. pap. 10.00 (0-671-88231-7, Touchstone Bks) S&S Trade.

Always Seeking the Edge. Mitchell Howard. LC 82-70641. 112p. (Orig.). 1982. pap. 4.96 (0-9608236-0-3) Amphibian Pubns.

Always Something Doing: A History of Boston's Infamous Scollay Square. David S. Kruh. (Illus.). 200p. 1990. pap. 14.95 (0-571-12911-0) Faber & Faber.

Always Stand in Against the Curve & Other Sports Stories. Willie Morris. (Illus.). 144p. 1983. 15.95 (0-916242-25-0) Yoknapatawpha.

Always Stick up for the Underbird. Charles M. Schulz. (Peanuts Classics Ser.). 128p. 1992. pap. 6.95 (0-8050-2397-6) H Holt & Co.

Always Straight Ahead: A Memoir. Alma Neuman. LC 92-20844. viii, 176p. (C). 1993. 24.95 (0-8071-1792-7) La State U Pr.

Always Take Time to Pray. Mitchell Hugh. (Illus.). (J). (gr. k-6). 1973. 4.99 (3-901170-14-6) CEF Press.

***Always, the End.** Brendan Tripp. 52p. 1994. pap. 5.00 (1-57353-025-5) Eschaton Prods.

Always the Young Strangers. Carl Sandburg. LC 52-11351. (Illus.). 1953. 12.95 (0-15-105459-2) HarBrace.

Always the Young Strangers. Carl Sandburg. 1991. pap. 12.95 (0-15-604765-9, Harvest Bks) HarBrace.

Always There: The African-American Presence in American Quilts, 1800-1900. Text by Cuesta Benberry. (Illus.). 100p. (Orig.). 1992. pap. 24.95 (1-880584-02-6) Kent Qult.

Always There for You. Dennis Allen. 1989. 5.25 (0-8341-9257-8, MB-610) Lillenas.

Always There's a Thud: Poems. Rosa M. Magno. 115p. (Orig.). 1987. pap. 8.75 (971-10-0328-7, Pub. by New Day Pub PH) Cellar.

Always to Remember: The Story of the Vietnam Veterans Memorial. Brent Ashabranner. (Illus.). 40p. (J). (gr. 6 up). 1988. 14.95 (0-399-22031-3, Putnam) Putnam Pub Group.

Always to Remember: The Story of the Vietnam Veterans Memorial. Brent Ashabranner. (J). (gr. 4-7). 1992. pap. 2.95 (0-590-44590-1) Scholastic Inc.

Always to Remember, Never to Forget Shantewa. Ken Miller. 142p. (YA). (gr. 11 up). 1984. 7.95 (0-942241-09-6, 8683) Pubs Bk Sales.

Always Victorious. Maria De Strakosch. LC 87-73065. (Illus.). 662p. 1991. 29.95 (0-685-40034-4) Dennis-Landman.

Always Young: A Biography. Frank Dolson. LC 75-20961. (Illus.). 206p. (Orig.). 1975. pap. 3.95 (0-89037-072-9); 4.95 (0-89037-073-7) Anderson World.

Always Young for Liberty: Biography of William Ellery Channing. Arthur W. Brown. 1956. 34.95x (0-8156-0004-6) Syracuse U Pr.

Alwyn Crawshaw Paints Oils. Alwyn Crawshaw. (Illus.). 96p. 1993. 19.95 (0-89134-537-X, 30548) North Light Bks.

Aly Bain: Fiddler on the Loose. Alastair Clark. (Illus.). 192p. 1994. 34.95 (1-85158-431-5, Pub. by Mnstream UK) Trafalgar.

Alyce's Fat Chance: How to Take off 100 Pounds & Keep It Off! Alyce P. Cornyn-Selby. 72p. (Orig.). 1989. pap. text ed. 8.95 (0-941383-13-X) Beynch Pr.

Alyndoria: Tales of Inner Magic. Robin S. Maglione. (Illus.). 71p. (Orig.). (J). (gr. k-12). 1986. pap. 12.00 (0-910609-11-X) Gifted Educ Pr.

***Alyson Almanac 1996 Edition: The Fact Book of the Lesbian & Gay Community.** Ed. by Alyson Publications Staff. (Illus.). 350p. (Orig.). 1995. pap. 9.95 (1-55583-286-5) Alyson Pubns.

Alyssa. Linda L. Bartell. (Avon Romance Ser.). 368p. 1987. pap. 3.95 (0-380-75157-7) Avon.

Alzare Mis Ojos. Santiago Canclini. 316p. (SPA.). 1988. reprint ed. pap. 8.50 (0-311-40047-7) Casa Bautista.

Alzheimer Disease. Ed. by Robert D. Terry et al. LC 93-16682. 496p. 1994. 139.00 (0-7817-0081-7) Raven.

***Alzheimer Disease: Therapeutic Strategies.** Ed. by Ezio Giacobini et al. LC 94-34494. (Advances in Alzheimer Disease Therapy Ser.). 1994. 74.50 (0-8176-3757-5) Birkhauser.

Alzheimer's: A Caregiver's Guide & Sourcebook. Howard Gruetzner. LC 87-37249. 255p. 1988. write for info. (0-471-52203-1) Wiley.

Alzheimer's: A Caregiver's Guide & Sourcebook. 2nd rev. ed. Howard Gruetzner. 320p. 1992. pap. text ed. 14.95 (0-471-56884-8) Wiley.

Alzheimer's: A Handbook for the Caretaker. Eileen H. Driscoll. LC 94-4805. 1994. pap. 12.95 (0-8283-1962-6) Branden Pub Co.

Alzheimer's: Does "the System" Care? Ted Valenti. 208p. 1989. 14.95 (0-914984-17-9) Starburst.

Alzheimer's ... Another Opportunity to Love. Grayce B. Confer. 64p. 1992. pap. 3.95 (0-8341-1403-8) Beacon Hill.

Alzheimer's & Parkinson's Disease: Strategies for Research & Development. Ed. by Abraham Fisher et al. LC 85-32056. (Advances in Behavioral Biology Ser.: Vol. 29). 726p. 1986. 125.00 (0-306-42232-8, Plenum Pr) Plenum.

Alzheimer's & Parkinson's Diseases: Recent Advances in Research & Clinical Management. Ed. by H. J. Altman & B. N. Altman. LC 90-7241. (Illus.). 604p. 1990. 135.00 (0-306-43482-0, Plenum Pr) Plenum.

***Alzheimer's & Parkinson's Diseases - Recent Developments: Proceedings of the Third International Conference on Alzheimer's & Parkinson's Diseases: Basic & Therapeutic Strategies Held in Chicago, Illinois, November 1-6, 1993.** International Conference on Alzheimer's & Parkinson's Diseases: Basic & Therapeutic Strategies Staff. Ed. by Israel Hanin et al. LC 95-14255. (Advances in Behavioral Biology Ser.: Vol. 44). 740p. 1995. 149.50 (0-306-45004-6, Plenum Pr) Plenum.

Alzheimer's Caregiver: Strategies for Support. Ed. by Kathleen O'Conner & Joyce Prothero. LC 85-40979. (Illus.). 150p. 1987. 25.00 (0-295-96385-9) U of Wash Pr.

Alzheimer's Cope Book: The Complete Care Manual for Patients & Their Families. R. E. Markin. 1992. pap. 7.95 (0-8065-1370-5, Citadel Pr) Carol Pub Group.

Alzheimer's Day Care: A Basic Guide. David A. Linderman et al. 152p. 1990. 57.00 (0-89116-106-6); pap. 29.00 (1-56032-152-0) Hemisp Pub.

Alzheimer's Dementia: Dilemmas in Clinical Research. Ed. by V. Melnick & N. Dubler. LC 85-11740. (Contemporary Issues in Biomedicine, Ethics, & Society Ser.). 344p. 1985. 49.50 (0-89603-067-9) Humana.

Alzheimer's Disease. Laurie Beckelman. LC 89-25251. (Facts About Ser.). (Illus.). 48p. (J). (gr. 5-6). 1990. text ed. 12.95 (0-89686-489-8, Crstwood Hse) Silver Burdett Pr.

Alzheimer's Disease. William A. Check. (Medical Disorders & Their Treatment Ser.). (Illus.). 112p. (YA). (gr. 6-12). 1989. 18.95 (0-7910-0056-7); pap. 9.95 (0-7910-0483-X) Chelsea Hse.

***Alzheimer's Disease.** Susan D. Gold. LC 94-27797. (Health Watch Ser.). (J). 1995. 13.95 (0-89686-857-5, Crstwood Hse) Silver Burdett Pr.

Alzheimer's Disease. Hamdy. 282p. 1990. 35.95 (0-8016-2026-0) Mosby Yr Bk.

Alzheimer's Disease. Carly R. Hellen. 168p. 1992. pap. 32.95 (1-56372-018-3, Andover Med Pubs) Buttrwrth-Heinemann.

Alzheimer's Disease. Richard J. Wurtman et al. (Advances in Neurology Ser.: Vol. 51). 304p. 1990. 99.50 (0-88167-574-1, 2046) Raven.

Alzheimer's Disease: A Guide for Families. Lenore S. Powell & Katie Courtice. LC 83-3887. 288p. 1983. pap. 10.53 (0-201-06099-X) Addison-Wesley.

***Alzheimer's Disease: A Guide to Federal Programs.** 113p. (Orig.). (C). 1995. pap. text ed. 35.00 (0-7881-1564-2) Diane Pub.

Alzheimer's Disease: A Handbook for Caregivers, No. 2. Hamdy. 350p. 1994. pap. 25.95 (0-8016-7282-1) Mosby Yr Bk.

***Alzheimer's Disease: A Medical Companion.** Alistair Burns et al. 1995. write for info. (0-632-03731-8) Blackwell Sci.

Alzheimer's Disease: A Practical Guide for Those Who Help Others. Judah L. Ronch. 144p. 1991. 17.95 (0-8245-1283-9); pap. 12.95 (0-8245-1284-7) Crossroad NY.

Alzheimer's Disease: A Source Guide. 1991. lib. bdg. 250.00 (0-8490-4898-2) Gordon Pr.

Alzheimer's Disease: Abstracts of the Psychological & Behavioral Literature. Ed. by Paul T. Costa, Jr. et al. (Bibliographies in Psychology Ser.: No. 4). 158p. 1989. pap. 25.00 (1-55798-049-7) Am Psychol.

Alzheimer's Disease: Activities That Work. Catherine Abrignani & Bill Messenger. (Illus.). 115p. (Orig.). (C). 1991. pap. text ed. 16.95 (1-877735-34-5, 182) M&H Pub Co TX.

Alzheimer's Disease: Advances in Clinical & Basic Research. Ed. by Benedetto Corain et al. LC 92-48709. 633p. 1993. text ed. 294.95 (0-471-93840-8) Wiley.

Alzheimer's Disease: Amyloid Precursor Proteins, Signal Transduction, & Neuronal Transplantation. Ed. by Roger M. Nitsch et al. LC 93-26927. (Annals Ser.: Vol. 695). 1993. write for info. (0-89766-853-7); pap. 100.00 (0-89766-854-5) NY Acad Sci.

Alzheimer's Disease: An Annotated Bibliography. Betty Weiner. (CompuBibs Ser.: No. 15). 1986. pap. 15.00 (0-914791-14-1) Vantage Info.

Alzheimer's Disease: Basic Mechanics Diagnosis & Therapeutic Strategies. Ed. by Khalid Iqbal et al. 1991. text ed. 329.95 (0-471-92927-1) Wiley.

Alzheimer's Disease: Caregiver Practices, Programs & Community-Based Strategies. E. Pfeiffer et al. LC 89-60347. 103p. 1989. pap. 15.00 (0-9622070-0-4) USF SGC.

***Alzheimer's Disease: Clinical & Treatment Perspectives.** Ed. by N. R. Cutler et al. LC 94-22396. 1994. text ed. 65.95 (0-471-95039-4) Wiley.

Alzheimer's Disease: Current Research in Early Diagnosis. Ed. by Robert E. Becker & Ezio Giacobini. 300p. 1990. 62.00 (0-8448-1659-0, Crane Russak) Taylor & Francis.

***Alzheimer's Disease: Lessons from Cell Biology.** Ed. by K. S. Kosik et al. LC 94-41048. (Research & Perspectives in Alzheimer's Disease Ser.). 280p. 1995. 114.00 (0-387-58744-6) Spr-Verlag.

Alzheimer's Disease: New Treatment Strategies. Ed. by Khachaturian & Blass. 248p. 1992. 110.00 (0-8247-8620-3) Dekker.

Alzheimer's Disease: Optimizing Drug Development Strategies. Neal R. Cutler et al. LC 94-10062. 1994. text ed. 66.95 (0-471-95145-5) Wiley.

Alzheimer's Disease: Oryx Science Bibliographies, Vol. 8. Ed. by Margaret Eide & Twyla M. Racz. LC 86-28609. 76p. 1987. pap. 18.75 (0-89774-324-5) Oryx Pr.

Alzheimer's Disease: Problems, Prospects, & Perspectives. Ed. by H. J. Altman. LC 87-15374. (Illus.). 412p. 1987. 95.00 (0-306-42662-5, Plenum Pr) Plenum.

Alzheimer's Disease: The Long Bereavement. Elizabeth Forsythe. 114p. (Orig.). 1990. pap. 9.95 (0-571-14110-2) Faber & Faber.

Alzheimer's Disease: The Silent Epidemic. Julia Frank. (Illus.). 80p. (J). (gr. 5 up). 1985. lib. bdg. 13.50 (0-8225-1578-4, Lerner Publctns) Lerner Group.

Alzheimer's Disease: The Standard Reference Book. Ed. by Barry Reisberg. 120p. (C). 1983. text ed. 80.00 (0-02-926230-5) Free Pr.

Alzheimer's Disease: Treatment & Long Term Management. Cummings & Miller. (Neurological Disease & Therapy Ser.: Vol. 4). 416p. 1990. 175.00 (0-8247-8177-5) Dekker.

***Alzheimer's Disease Vol. I of II: Index of Modern Authors & Scientific Reviews for Inclusions in Current Research.** rev. ed. Michael R. Scarborough. LC 90-56307. 213p. 1994. 44.50 (0-7883-0414-3); pap. 39.50 (0-7883-0415-1) ABBE Pubs Assn.

Alzheimer's Disease & Marriage. Lore K. Wright. LC 92-48987. (Clinical Nursing Research Ser.). 1993. 37.00 (0-8039-4521-3); pap. 16.95 (0-8039-4522-1) Sage.

Alzheimer's Disease & Presenile Dementia: Subject Analysis with Reference Bibliography. Michael R. Scarbrough. LC 85-48179. 150p. 1987. 39.50 (0-88164-492-7); pap. 34.50 (0-88164-493-5) ABBE Pubs Assn.

Alzheimer's Disease & Related Disorders. Ed. by M. Nicolini et al. (Advances in the Biosciences Ser.: Vol. 87). 474p. 1993. 180.00 (0-08-042330-2, Pergamon Pr) Elsevier.

Alzheimer's Disease & Related Disorders: Looking Beyond the Illness. David M. Weinberger. 50p. (Orig.). 1989. pap. text ed. write for info. (0-318-65402-4) Brillig Hse.

Alzheimer's Disease, Down Syndrome, & Their Relationship. Ed. by J. M. Berg et al. LC 93-28474. (Illus.). 320p. 1994. 85.00 (0-19-262382-6) OUP.

Alzheimer's Disease, Down's Syndrome, & Aging: Proceedings of the Kroc Foundation Conference, October 12-16, 1981, Vol. 396. Kroc Foundation Conference Staff. Ed. by F. Marott Sinex & Carl R. Merril. 199p. 1982. 35.00 (0-89766-182-6); pap. 35.00 (0-89766-183-4) NY Acad Sci.

Alzheimer's Disease Epidemiology, Neuropathology, Neurochemistry, & Clinics: Proceedings, International Congress on Alzheimer's Disease, Wurzburg, June 1989. Ed. by Konrad Maurer et al. (Key Topics in Brain Research Ser.). (Illus.). 600p. 1990. pap. 114.00 (0-387-82197-X) Spr-Verlag.

Alzheimer's Disease from Care to Caring. rev. ed. Elinor Ringland. LC 85-81657. (Illus.). 115p. 1988. pap. 8.00 (0-9613775-3-4) Healthcare Pr.

Alzheimer's Disease Treatment & Family Stress: Directions for Research. Ed. by Barry D. Lebowitz. LC 89-600727. (Illus.). 498p. 1989. per., pap. 14.00 (0-16-002499-4, S/N 017-024-013) USGPO.

Alzheimer's Disease Treatment & Family Stress: Directions for Research. Enid Light & Barry Liebowitz. 500p. 1990. 52.00 (1-56032-137-7) Hemisp Pub.

***Alzheimer's: Finding the Words: A Communication Guide for Those Who Care.** Harriet Hodgson. 160p. 1995. pap. 10.95 (1-56561-071-7) Chronimed.

Alzheimer's Sourcebook for Caregivers: A Practical Guide for Getting Through the Day. Frena G. Davidson. 240p. 1993. 23.95 (1-56565-080-8, Anodyne) Lowell Hse.

Alzheimer's Sourcebook for Caregivers: A Practical Guide for Getting Through the Day. Frena G. Davidson. 228p. 1994. pap. 15.00 (1-56565-146-4) Lowell Hse.

Alzheimer's, Stroke & Twenty-Nine Other Neurological Disorders: A Sourcebook Containing Basic Information on Types, Symptoms, Causes, Diagnostic Methods, & Treatments. Frank E. Bair. (Health Reference Ser.: Vol. 2). 600p. 1993. lib. bdg. 80.00 (1-55888-748-2) Omnigraphics Inc.

Alzira: Tragica Lirica in Three Acts, by Salvadore Cammarano. Giuseppe Verdi. Ed. by Stefano Castelvecchi & Jonathan Cheskin. 100p. 1995. lib. bdg. 250.00 (0-226-85314-4) U Ch Pr.

Al2SiO5 Polymorphs. Derrill M. Kerrick. Ed. by Paul H. Ribbe. (Reviews in Mineralogy Ser.: Vol. 22). 406p. 1990. per. 22.00 (0-939950-27-8) Mineralogical Soc.

Am Anfang war die Liebe. Eberhard Arnold. 367p. (GER.). 1986. pap. 10.00 (3-922819-39-7) Plough.

Am Anfang War Die Logik: Hermaneutische Abhandlungen zum Ansatz der Formalen und Transzendentalem Logik Husserls. George Heffernan. (Bochumer Studien zur Philosophie Ser.: Vol. 11). viii, 253p. (GER.). (C). 1989. 50.00x (90-6032-306-8, Pub. by B R Gruener NE) Benjamins North Am.

Am-e-rican. Intro. by Tato Laviera & Wolfgang Binder. LC 83-72577. 80p. (Orig.). (C). 1984. pap. 7.00 (0-934770-31-X) Arte Publico.

Am I a Hindu? The Hinduism Primer. Ed Viswanathan. LC 92-8587. (Illus.). 336p. (Orig.). 1992. pap. 14.95 (1-879904-06-3) Halo Bks.

***Am I Allowed to Cry?** Maureen Oswin. 1995. pap. 10.95 (0-285-65096-3, Pub. by Souvenir UK) Atrium Pubs.

Am I Asking Too Much. Gwendolyn Tait-Dover. 40p. (Orig.). 1992. pap. 5.95 (1-56411-017-6) Untd Bros & Sis.

Am I Beautiful? Else H. Minarik. LC 91-32562. (Illus.). 24p. (J). (ps-4). 1992. 14.00 (0-688-09911-4); lib. bdg. 13.93 (0-688-09912-2) Greenwillow.

Am I Blue. Beth Henley. 1982. pap. 2.75 (0-8222-0021-X) Dramatists Play.

Am I Blue? Coming Out from the Silence. Marion D. Bauer. LC 93-29574. 224p. (YA). (gr. 7 up). 1994. 15.00 (0-06-024253-1); lib. bdg. 14.89 (0-06-024254-X) HarpC Child Bks.

***Am I Blue? Coming Out from the Silence.** Ed. by Marion D. Bauer. LC 93-29574. 288p. (YA). (gr. 7 up). 1995. pap. 5.95 (0-06-440587-7, Trophy) HarpC Child Bks.

***Am I Covered for...? A Comprehensive Guide to Insuring Your Non-Profit Organization.** 2nd ed. Mary Lai et al. (Illus.). 286p. (C). 1992. pap. text ed. 14.95 (0-614-01352-6) Consort Human.

Am I Fat? Helping Young Children Accept Differences in Body Size: Suggestions for Teachers, Parents, & Other Care Providers of Children to age 10. Joanne Ikeda & Priscilla Naworski. LC 92-19011. 1992. write for info. (1-56071-080-2) ETR Assocs.

Am I Fun to Live With? Audrey A. Bentz. 1994. pap. 6.95 (1-55673-590-1, 7989) CSS OH.

Am I Getting an Education? John Dewey et al. LC 75-3114. (Philosophy America Ser.). reprint ed. 15.00 (0-404-59110-8) AMS Pr.

***Am I Glowing Yet? Understanding & Coping with the Common & Not-So-Common Miseries of Pregnancy.** Virginia H. Tobiassen. 168p. (Orig.). 1995. pap. 14.95 (1-55652-244-4) Chicago Review.

Am I Good Enough: Learning to Live by God's Grace. Richard Ramsey. (Illus.). 98p. (Orig.). 1992. student ed, pap. 4.99 (0-87552-395-1) Presby & Reformed.

Am I in Trouble Using Discipline to Teach Young Children Responsibility. Etrw. 1991. pap. 14.95 (1-56071-026-8) ETR Assocs.

Am I My Brother's Keeper? Ananda K. Coomaraswamy. LC 67-23196. (Essay Index Reprint Ser.). 1977. 15.95 (0-8369-0335-8) Ayer.

Am I My Brother's Keeper? The AIDs Crisis & the Church. Michael Malloy. 149p. (Orig.). 1990. pap. 7.95 (0-8341-1329-5) Beacon Hill.

Am I My Parent's Keeper: An Essay on Justice Between the Young & the Old. Norman Daniels. 206p. 1990. pap. 10.95 (0-19-506164-0) OUP.

Am I Normal? Your Personal Guide to Understanding Yourself & Others. Sid Cormier. 224p. (Orig.). 1992. pap. 11.95 (0-88184-873-5) Carroll & Graf.

Am I on the Right Plane? Transcendental Airlines Puts You on a Different Plane. Connie McDonough. Ed. by Patricia M. Chandler. (Illus.). 201p. (Orig.). 1991. pap. 7.95 (0-9630660-0-5) Hagall.

Am I Saved? Theodore Bobosh. 1984. pap. 3.95 (0-937032-38-7) Light&Life Pub Co MN.

Am I Sick? Is It Serious? What Your Symptoms Really Mean. Isadore Rosenfeld. 1989. 18.95 (0-318-41500-3) S&S Trade.

Am I Still a Big Sister? Audrey B. Weir. LC 92-35395. (Illus.). (J). 1992. 4.95 (0-9633243-0-6) Fall Leaf Pr.

Am I Still a Sister? 3rd ed. Alicia M. Sims. LC 87-71613. (Illus.). 48p. (J). (gr. k-9). 1993. pap. 5.00 (0-9618995-0-6) Big A & Co.

Am I That Name? Feminism & the Category of "Women" in History: Feminism & the Category of Women in History. Denise Riley. LC 88-21640. vi, 126p. (Orig.). 1989. pap. text ed. 12.95 (0-8166-1731-7) U of Minn Pr.

Am I the Only Crazy Mom on the Planet? Elizabeth C. Newenhuyse. 1994. pap. 9.99 (0-310-38631-4) Zondervan.

Am I the Only One Here with Faded Genes? Marie Chapian. LC 87-11611. (Teen Devotionals Ser.). (Illus.). 192p. (J). 1987. pap. 7.99 (0-87123-945-0) Bethany Hse.

***Am I the Only One Who's Crazy?** Elizabeth McDonald. 208p. (Orig.). 1995. pap. text ed. 6.50 (1-879331-53-5, Classc Pub) Marciel Pub & Print.

***Am I Worthy?** John D. Nicklas. LC 94-92223. 100p. (Orig.). 1995. pap. 9.00 (0-9641766-0-2) Beauty Within.

A.M. Klein: Literary Essays & Reviews. Ed. by Usher Caplan & M. W. Steinberg. 45.00 (0-8020-5686-5); pap. 19.95 (0-8020-6607-0) U of Toronto Pr.

Am Olam, Vol. 1. Shlomo Rotenberg. 1989. 17.95 (0-87306-483-6) Feldheim.

AM-PM Guide 1987-1988. 1988. write for info. (0-933875-03-7) AM-PM Pub.

AM Stereo & the FCC: Case Study of a Marketplace Shibboleth. Mark J. Braun. LC 93-46342. (Communication & Information Science Ser.). 216p. 1994. pap. 19.50 (1-56750-000-5) Ablex Pub.

AMA: Managing Sales Leads. Bob Donath et al. Ed. by Anne Knudsen. LC 94-16180. 1995. 37.95 (0-8442-3599-7, NTC Busn Bks) NTC Pub Grp.

Ama & the White Crane. Maureen A. O'Toole. (Orig.). (J). 1991. Playscript. pap. 6.00 (0-87602-295-6) Anchorage.

AMA & U. S. Health Policy Since 1940. LC 84-7817. 1990. 27.50 (0-914091-57-3, OP993088) AMA.

AMA Complete Guide to Small Business Advertising. Joe Vitale. Ed. by Anne Knudsen. LC 94-14170. 1994. pap. 29.95 (0-8442-3594-6, NTC Busn Bks) NTC Pub Grp.

AMA Complete Guide to Small Business Marketing. 1994. pap. 17.95 (0-8442-3596-2, NTC Busn Bks) NTC Pub Grp.

An Asterisk (*) at the beginning of an entry indicates that the title is appearing in BIP for the first time.

An Asterisk (*) at the beginning of an entry indicates that the title is appearing in BIP for the first time.

217

Amarna in Retrospect: One Hundred Years of Tell el-Amarna & Amarna Studies. Ed. by Barry Beitzel & Gordon D. Young. Date not set. write for info. (*0-318-72315-8*) Eisenbrauns.

Amarna Letters. William L. Moran. 464p. 1992. text ed. 68.00 (*0-8018-4251-4*) Johns Hopkins.

Amarna Personal Names. Richard S. Hess. LC 93-31470. (American Schools of Oriental Research Dissertation Ser.: Vol. 9). xii, 292p. 1993. pap. text ed. 45.00 (*0-931464-71-4*) Eisenbrauns.

Amarts & Set Function Processes. A. Gut & K. D. Schmidt. (Lecture Notes in Mathematics Ser.: Vol. 1042). 258p. 1983. pap. 35.30 (*0-387-12867-0*) Spr-Verlag.

Amaryllidacea & a Treatise on Cross-Bred Vegetables. William Herbert. (Illus.). 1970. 96.00 (*3-7682-0672-6*) Lubrecht & Cramer.

Amaryllis. large type ed. Priscilla Jenkins. 496p. 1983. 15.95 (*0-7089-1002-5*) Ulverscroft.

Amaryllis: Songs Sung at the Public Theatres or Gardens, 2 vols. in 1. LC 68-21203. (Illus.). 1972. reprint ed. 23.95 (*0-405-08203-7*, Pub. by Blom Pubns UK) Ayer.

Amaryllis at the Fair. Richard Jeffries. (Pocket Classic Ser.). 176p. 1992. pap. 5.00 (*0-7509-0009-1*) A Sutton Pub.

Amaryllis at the Fair. Richard Jeffries. 4.95 (*0-7043-3312-0*, Pub. by Quartet UK) Charles River Bks.

***Amaryllis Fleming.** Fergus Fleming. 270p. 1995. pap. 24.95 (*0-413-69090-3*, Pub. by Methuen UK) Trafalgar.

Amate Siquiera un Poco. Cecil G. Osborne. Tr. by Julio Orozco. LC 78-57808. 182p. (SPA.). 1978. pap. 5.75 (*0-89922-120-3*) Edit Caribe.

Amateur. Hal Hartley. (Illus.). 128p. (Orig.). 1995. pap. 12.95 (*0-571-17213-X*) Faber & Faber.

Amateur & the Professional: Historians, Antiquarians & Archaeologists in Nineteenth-Century England, 1838-1886. P. J. Levine. (Illus.). 220p. 1986. 64.95 (*0-521-30635-3*) Cambridge U Pr.

Amateur Archaeologist. Stephen Wass. (Illus.). 144p. 1993. 34.95 (*0-7134-6896-3*, Pub. by Batsford UK) Trafalgar.

Amateur Artist' Encyclopedia. D. M. Campana. (Illus.). 9.95 (*0-939608-17-0*) Campana Art.

Amateur Astronomer. Patrick Moore. 1990. 35.00 (*0-393-02864-X*) Norton.

Amateur Astronomer: Explorations & Investigations. Fred Schaaf & Alan E. Nourse. LC 93-31788. (Amateur Science Ser.). (Illus.). 144p. 1994. lib. bdg. 13.93 (*0-531-11138-5*) Watts.

Amateur Astronomer: Explorations & Investigations. Fred Schaaf. (Amateur Science Ser.). (Illus.). 144p. (J). (gr. 6-9). 1994. pap. 6.95 (*0-531-15720-2*) Watts.

Amateur Astronomer's Catalog of Five Hundred Deep-Sky Objects: Astronomy for the Serious Amateur. Ronald J. Morales. (Illus.). 128p. 1986. pap. 12.50 (*0-89404-076-6*) Aztex.

Amateur Astronomer's Handbook. J. B. Sidgwick. (Illus.). 576p. 1981. reprint ed. pap. 9.95 (*0-486-24034-7*) Dover.

Amateur Astronomer's Pathfinder. Colin Humphrey. LC 92-15688. 143p. 1992. text ed. 24.95 (*0-471-93452-6*) Wiley.

Amateur at the Keyboard: A Practice & Study Guide for Nonprofessional Pianists. James Higson. LC 90-53498. (Illus.). 222p. 1991. lib. bdg. 23.95x (*0-89950-589-9*) McFarland & Co.

Amateur-Built Aircraft Flight Testing Handbook. (Illus.). 59p. 1989. pap. 3.25 (*0-16-005291-2*, S/N 050-007-00840-6) USGPO.

Amateur City. Katherine V. Forrest. (Kate Delafield Mystery Ser.). 224p. 1984. pap. 10.95 (*0-930044-55-X*) Naiad Pr.

Amateur Corpse. large type ed. Simon Brett. (Nightingale Ser.). 300p. 1990. pap. 13.95 (*0-8161-5040-0*, Nightingale) Hall.

Amateur Cracksman. Ernest W. Hornung. LC 76-98576. (Short Story Index Reprint Ser.). 1977. 19.95 (*0-8369-3150-5*) Ayer.

Amateur Cracksman. Ernest W. Hornung. 289p. 1988. pap. 3.95 (*0-88184-359-8*) Carroll & Graf.

Amateur Dramatics Handbook: A Practical Guide. Jack Cassin-Scott. (Illus.). 144p. 1994. pap. 14.95 (*0-304-34358-7*, Pub. by Cassell UK) Sterling.

Amateur Fiddle Makers Q & A. Harry S. Wake. (Illus.). 50p. (Orig.). 1980. student ed, pap. 13.50 (*0-9607048-3-3*) H S Wake.

Amateur Garden see Collected Works of George W. Cable

Amateur Gentleman. Jeffrey Farnol. 1975. lib. bdg. 24.30 (*0-89966-086-X*) Buccaneer Bks.

Amateur Geologist: Explorations & Investigations. Raymond Wiggers. (Amateur Science Ser.). (Illus.). 144p. (J). (gr. 6-9). 1993. lib. bdg. 13.93 (*0-531-11112-1*) Watts.

Amateur Geologist: Explorations & Investigations. Raymond Wiggers. (Amateur Science Ser.). (Illus.). (J). (gr. 5-8). 1994. pap. 6.95 (*0-531-15695-8*) Watts.

***Amateur Hambook.** William V. Smith. 1995. pap. 14.95 (*0-917963-04-0*) Artsci Inc.

Amateur Horse Breeder. A. Leighton Hardman. 1979. pap. 5.00 (*0-87980-181-6*) Wilshire.

Amateur in Music. Frank H. Shera. LC 74-114894. (Select Bibliographies Reprint Ser.). 1977. 16.95 (*0-8369-5298-7*) Ayer.

Amateur Magician's Handbook. Henry Hay. 432p. (J). (gr. 7). 1983. pap. 5.99 (*0-451-15502-5*, AE2256, Sig) NAL-Dutton.

***Amateur Magician's Handbook.** Henry Hay. 1994. 9.98 (*0-7858-0204-5*) Bk Sales Inc.

Amateur Meteorologist: Explorations & Investigations. H. Michael Mogil & Barbara G. Levine. LC 93-17506. (Amateur Science Ser.). (Illus.). 144p. (J). (gr. 6-9). 1993. lib. bdg. 13.93 (*0-531-11045-1*) Watts.

Amateur Meteorologist: Explorations & Investigations. H. Michael Mogil & Barbara G. Levine. (Amateur Science Ser.). (Illus.). (J). (gr. 5-8). 1994. pap. 6.95 (*0-531-15696-6*) Watts.

Amateur Military Tradition, 1558-1945. Ian F. Beckett. (History of the British Army Ser.). 224p. 1992. text ed. 69.95 (*0-7190-2912-0*, Pub. by Manchester Univ Pr UK) St Martin.

Amateur Naturalist. Gerald Durrell. 1989. pap. 25.00 (*0-679-72837-6*) McKay.

Amateur Naturalist: Explorations & Investigations. Charles Roth. (Amateur Science Ser.). (Illus.). (J). (gr. 5-8). 1994. pap. 6.95 (*0-531-15697-4*) Watts.

Amateur Naturalist: Explorations & Investigations. Charles E. Roth. LC 93-13390. (Amateur Science Ser.). (Illus.). 144p. (J). (gr. 6-9). 1993. lib. bdg. 13.93 (*0-531-11002-8*) Watts.

Amateur Night. K. K. Beck. 288p. 1993. 18.95 (*0-89296-480-4*) Mysterious Pr.

Amateur Night. K. K. Beck. 256p. 1994. mass mkt. 5.50 (*0-446-40145-5*, Mysterious Paperbk) Warner Bks.

Amateur People. Andree Connors. LC 76-47836. 1977. 10.95 (*0-914590-30-8*); pap. 6.95 (*0-914590-31-6*) Fiction Coll.

Amateur Radio: Theory & Practice. Robert L. Shrader. 352p. 1982. text ed. 28.95 (*0-07-057146-5*) McGraw.

Amateur Radio Almanac, 1994. Doug Grant. Ed. by Edith Lennon. (Illus.). 496p. (Orig.). 1993. pap. 19.95 (*0-943016-06-1*) CQ Commns Inc.

Amateur Radio Encyclopedia. Stan Gibilisco. 1993. text ed. 49.95 (*0-07-023561-9*); pap. text ed. 29.95 (*0-07-023562-7*) McGraw.

Amateur Radio Equipment Fundamentals. Albert D. Helfrick. (Illus.). 336p. (C). 1982. pap. text ed. 40.00 (*0-13-023655-1*) P-H.

Amateur Radio Novice Class Theory Course. Martin Schwartz. LC 87-71508. (Illus.). 1990. pap. text ed. 6.95 (*0-912146-18-4*, 23-01) Ameco.

Amateur Radio RV Antennas. Robert K. Benson. 65p. 1992. pap. 14.95 (*0-936653-41-8*) Tiare Pubns.

Amateur Radio Technical Abstracts. Ed. by Graham Thornton. 123p. 1992. 25.00 (*0-685-65931-3*) Thornton LA.

Amateur Radio Telescope. George W. Swenson, Jr. (Astronomy Quarterly Library: Vol. 4). (Illus.). 64p. 1980. pap. 9.95 (*0-912918-06-3*, 0006) Pachart Pub Hse.

Amateur Radio Theory Course. Martin Schwartz. LC 81-66321. (Illus.). 1990. pap. 7.95 (*0-912146-13-3*, 102-01) Ameco.

Amateur Single Sideband. Collins Radio Company Staff. LC 77-71665. (Illus.). 1977. reprint ed. pap. text ed. 4.95 (*0-918232-05-8*, HR-SSB) Comm Tech.

Amateur Spirit. Bliss Perry. LC 70-84332. (Essay Index Reprint Ser.). 1977. 17.95 (*0-8369-1102-4*) Ayer.

Amateur Stage: A Practical Handbook for Directors & Producers. M. Morris. 1990. 30.00 (*0-7463-0646-6*, Pub. by Northcote UK) St Mut.

***Amateur Strategist: Intuitive Deterrence Theories & the Politics of the Nuclear Arms Race.** James DeNardo. (Cambridge Studies in Political Psychology & Public Opinion). (Illus.). 312p. (C). 1995. 59.95 (*0-521-48121-X*); pap. 19.95 (*0-521-48446-4*) Cambridge U Pr.

Amateur Sugar Maker. 20th anniversary ed. Noel Perrin. LC 91-50818. (Illus.). 120p. 1992. pap. 9.95 (*0-87451-579-3*) U Pr of New Eng.

Amateur Wind Instrument Maker. rev. ed. Trevor Robinson. LC 80-5381. (Illus.). 128p. 1981. pap. 10.95 (*0-87023-312-2*) U of Mass Pr.

***Amateur Zoologist: Explorations & Investigations.** Amateur Science Staff. (Amateur Science Ser.). (Illus.). 144p. (YA). (gr. 7-12). 1995. pap. 6.95 (*0-531-15748-2*) Watts.

Amateur Zoologist: Explorations & Investigations. Mary Dykstra. (Amateur Science Ser.). (Illus.). (J). (gr. 6-9). 1994. lib. bdg. 13.93 (*0-531-11162-8*) Watts.

Amateurs. Tom Griffin. 1991. pap. 4.75 (*0-8222-0022-8*) Dramatists Play.

Amateurs & Professionals in British Politics, 1918-59. Philip W. Buck. LC 63-13073. 155p. reprint ed. pap. 44.20 (*0-8357-5339-5*, 2015751) Bks Demand.

Amateur's Guide to Basketball Recruiting. Equilla A. Webb. 60p. (Orig.). (YA). (gr. 9-12). 1989. pap. text ed. 9.95 (*0-9624771-0-9*) Equilla Enterprises.

Amateur's Guide to Football & Recruiting. Equilla B. Webb. 192p. (Orig.). (YA). (gr. 9-12). 1990. pap. text ed. 45.00 (*0-9624771-1-7*) Equilla Enterprises.

Amateur's Guide to the Night. Mary Robison. LC 89-1904. 1989. reprint ed. pap. 9.95 (*0-87923-802-X*) Godine.

Amateur's Lathe. L. H. Sparey. 16.00 (*0-85242-288-1*) Apple Blossom.

Amateurs, Photography, & the Mid-Victorian Imagination. Grace Seiberling & Carolyn Bloore. LC 85-20901. (Illus.). x, 196p. (C). 1986. 39.95 (*0-226-74498-1*) U Ch Pr.

Amateurs, Professionals, & Serious Leisure. Robert A. Stebbins. 172p. 1992. 47.95 (*0-7735-0901-1*, Pub. by McGill CN) U of Toronto Pr.

***Amateurs, to Arms! A Military History of the War of 1812.** John R. Elting. (Illus.). 383p. 1995. reprint ed. pap. 14.95 (*0-306-80653-3*) Da Capo.

Amateurs, to Arms! A Military History of the War of 1812-1815. John R. Elting. (Major Battles & Campaigns Ser.). (Illus.). 364p. 1991. 24.95 (*0-945575-08-4*) Algonquin Bks.

Amateur's Workshop. Ian Bradley. 18.00 (*0-85242-482-5*) Apple Blossom.

***AMATHing Discovery: A Student's Guide to Solving Math Word Problems.** Sam Fiagome. LC 95-68398. (Illus.). 100p. (Orig.). (YA). (gr. 8-12). 1995. student ed, pap. text ed. 17.95 (*0-9643194-6-2*); disk 54.95 (*0-9643194-7-0*) Paideia Pr.

Amativeness. Orson S. Fowler. LC 78-72339. (Free Love in America Ser.). reprint ed. 12.50 (*0-404-60953-8*) AMS Pr.

Amatory Persuasion. Nicolas P. Gross. LC 82-49303. 192p. 1985. 33.50 (*0-87413-234-7*) U Delaware Pr.

Amaurosis Fugax. Ed. by E. F. Bernstein. (Illus.). 480p. 1988. 99.00 (*0-387-96601-3*) Spr-Verlag.

Amazake. John Finnegan & Kathy Cuisak. (Illus.). 96p. (Orig.). 1990. pap. 6.95 (*0-89087-612-6*) Celestial Arts.

Amazake & Amazake Frozen Desserts: Industry & Market in North America. William Shurtleff & Akiko Aoyagi. (Illus.). 117p. (Orig.). 1988. pap. text ed., spiral bd. 95.00 (*0-933332-38-6*) Soyfoods Center.

Amazement Park Adventure. Richie Chevat. (Ghostwriter Ser.). (J). (gr. 1-3). 1994. pap. 1.99 (*0-553-48091-X*) Bantam.

Amazing Activity of Charley Contrare & the Ninety-Eighth Street Gang. Roy London. 1975. pap. 4.75 (*0-8222-0023-6*) Dramatists Play.

***Amazing Acts.** Ivor Powell. LC 87-3627. 478p. 1987. pap. 16.99 (*0-8254-3545-5*) Kregel.

Amazing Acts. Ivor Powell. LC 87-3627. 478p. 1987. 19.99 (*0-8254-3526-9*) Kregel.

Amazing Adventures. 64p. 1988. 4.95 (*0-87135-339-3*) Marvel Entmnt.

Amazing Adventures. Stef Donev. (Hayes Adventure Ser.). (Illus.). 48p. (J). (gr. 5-9). 1985. pap. 5.95 (*0-88625-093-5*) Durkin Hayes Pub.

Amazing Adventures of Abiola. Jeffrey J. Dean & Debra A. Dean. LC 93-30332. (Illus.). 32p. (J). (gr. 6-9). 1994. 12.95 (*0-86543-409-3*); pap. 5.95 (*0-86543-410-7*) Africa World.

Amazing Adventures of Albert & His Flying Machine. Thomas Sant. (Illus.). 160p. (J). (gr. 4-7). 1990. 13.95 (*0-525-67302-4*, Lodestar Bks) Dutton Child Bks.

Amazing Adventures of Amabel. Natalie J. Prior. (Illus.). 112p. (Orig.). (YA). (gr. 6 up). 1993. pap. 7.95 (*0-04-442163-X*, Pub. by Allen & Unwin Aust Pty AT) IPG Chicago.

***Amazing Adventures of Biscuit Prints (TM) An Uncanny Look into a Child's Imagination of the Many Wonders of Bread. Contesse Wall. Ed. by Cassondra Wall. (Biscuit Prints Battles Evil Lord Pumpernickel Ser.: Vol. 1). (Illus.). 48p. (J). (gr. k-9). 1995. lib. bdg. 11.00 (*1-887507-00-0*) Biscuit Prints.**

THE AMAZING ADVENTURES OF BISCUIT PRINTS is a collection of delightful stories for children of all ages & cultures. It opens a child's imagination to the many wonders of bread. THE AMAZING ADVENTURES OF BISCUIT PRINTS is the story of a fictional character named Biscuit Prints who is a great bread hero with magical powers. Those magical powers are used with unique shoes, & always leaves behind unique prints. This legendary character travels to various bread lands to spread goodness & compassion, while sometimes helping fellow bread characters out of dangerous situations. THE AMAZING ADVENTURES OF BISCUIT PRINTS offers pleasurable reading to all who encounter this new & exciting concept. Children ages 7 & up will certainly enjoy reading about all the great triumphs of Biscuit Prints, while younger children will want every parent & teacher to read the adventure stories over & over again. The illustrations of these terrific adventure stories, along with the scintillating & exhilarating story lines is definitely an added plus to the world of children's literature. To order contact: Biscuit Prints Productions, P.O. Box 750167, New Orleans, LA 70175- 0167, Phone: (504) 246-1754, FAX: (504) 246-0174.

Publisher Provided Annotation.

Amazing Adventures of Flash Gordon, 6 vols. King Features Staff. Incl. Vol. 1. 1980. 2.25 (*0-448-17240-2*); Vol. 2. 1980. 2.25 (*0-448-17241-0*); Vol. 3. 192p. 1980. 2.25 (*0-448-17242-9*); Vol. 4. 1980. 2.25 (*0-448-17155-4*); Vol. 5. 1980. 2.25 (*0-448-17208-9*); Vol. 6. 1980. 2.25 (*0-448-17245-3*); (Flash Gordon Cartoon Ser.). 192p. 1980. write for info. (*0-318-50393-X*) Ace Bks.

Amazing Adventures of Teddy Tum Tum. Gillian Breese & Tony Langham. 32p. (J). (ps-3). 1992. 11.95 (*1-55970-185-4*) Arcade Pub Inc.

Amazing Adventures of the Jewish People. Max I. Dimont. LC 84-16806. 175p. (YA). (gr. 8 up). 1984. pap. 6.95 (*0-87441-391-5*) Behrman.

Amazing Air. Henry Smith. LC 82-80991. (Science Club Ser.). (Illus.). 48p. (J). (gr. 3-6). 1983. lib. bdg. 11.93 (*0-688-00973-5*) Lothrop.

Amazing Air. Henry Smith. LC 82-80991. (Science Club Ser.). (Illus.). 48p. (J). (gr. 3 up). 1983. pap. 7.95 (*0-688-00977-8*, Pub. by Beech Tree Bks) Morrow.

Amazing Aircraft Coloring Book. Frank Dimino & Doug Milloff. (Color & Story Bks.). (Illus.). 32p. (Orig.). (J). (gr. k-6). 1989. pap. 4.50 (*0-8431-1958-6*, Troubador) Price Stern.

***Amazing Airplanes Book & Kit.** Regen Dennis. (Illus.). 36p. (J). 1995. pap. 14.95 (*0-8362-4241-6*) Andrews & McMeel.

***Amazing Alligators - Story Hour Friends.** Suzanne Rogers. (Illus.). 193p. (J). (ps-1). 1990. teacher ed, pap. 8.95 (*1-878279-11-4*, MM 193) Monday Morning Bks.

Amazing Alphabet. (J). 1993. 3.99 (*0-517-08759-6*) Random Hse Value.

Amazing Alphabet Animals. Kathy RuDenski. LC 91-65792. (Illus.). 44p. (J). (gr. k-3). 1992. 8.95 (*1-55523-447-X*) Winston-Derek.

Amazing AMC Muscle: Complete Development & Racing History of the Cars from American Motors. Edrie J. Marquez. (Illus.). 224p. 1988. pap. 9.98 (*0-87938-300-3*) Motorbooks Intl.

***Amazing American Women: Forty Fascinating 5-Minute Reads.** Kendall Haven. 320p. 1995. pap. text ed. 24.00 (*1-56308-291-8*) Libs Unl.

Amazing Amos & the Greatest Couch on Earth. Howie Schneider & Susan Seligson. (Illus.). 32p. (J). (ps-3). 1989. 13.95 (*0-316-78033-2*, Joy St Bks) Little.

Amazing Ancient to Modern Useful Plant Aloe Vera. Ed. by Health Research Staff. 87p. 1990. reprint ed. spiral bd. 6.05 (*0-7873-0397-6*) Mokelumne.

Amazing & Death-Defying Diary of Eugene Dingman. Paul Zindel. (YA). (gr. 7 up). 1989. mass mkt. 3.99 (*0-553-27768-5*, Starfire) Bantam.

Amazing & Death-Defying Diary of Eugene Dingman. Paul Zindel. LC 82-47712. (Charlotte Zolotow Bk.). 224p. (YA). (gr. 7 up). 1987. lib. bdg. 14.89 (*0-06-026863-8*) HarpC Child Bks.

***Amazing & Incredible Counting Stories.** Max Grover. LC 94-17837. (J). 1995. write for info. (*0-15-200090-9*) HarBrace.

Amazing & Incredible Special Effects Cookbook. Michael E. Samonek. LC 92-90755. 60p. 1992. pap. 19.95 (*0-9632877-0-2*) MES FX Pub.

Amazing Animal Babies. Chris Maynard. LC 92-23736. (Eyewitness Juniors Ser.: Vol. 25). 32p. (Orig.). (J). (gr. 1-5). 1993. lib. bdg. 10.99 (*0-679-93924-5*); pap. 7.99 (*0-679-83924-0*) Knopf Bks Yng Read.

Amazing Animal Disguises. Sandie Sowler. LC 91-53141. (Eyewitness Juniors Ser.). (Illus.). 32p. (Orig.). (J). (gr. 1-5). 1992. lib. bdg. 9.99 (*0-679-92768-9*); pap. 6.95 (*0-679-82768-4*) Knopf Bks Yng Read.

Amazing Animal Facts. Walter Fortson. LC 89-80109. (Illus.). 128p. (Orig.). (J). (gr. 5). 1989. pap. 6.95 (*0-685-29400-5*) Fortson Pubs.

Amazing Animal Groups see Books for Young Explorers

Amazing Animal Records. Stuart A. Kallen. Ed. by Rosemary Wallner. LC 91-73055. (World Records Library). (J). 1991. lib. bdg. 12.94 (*1-56239-046-5*) Abdo & Dghtrs.

Amazing Animal Senses. Ron Van Der Meer. (YA). (gr. 9-12). 1990. 10.95 (*0-316-89624-1*, Joy St Bks) Little.

Amazing Animals. (Library of Curious & Unusual Facts). (Illus.). 128p. 1990. 17.27 (*0-8094-7695-9*); lib. bdg. 23.27 (*0-8094-7696-7*) Time-Life.

Amazing Animals. Christopher Carrie. (Crayola Color & Activity Ser.). (Illus.). 40p. (J). (gr. k up). 1991. 1.49 (*0-86696-305-7*) Binney & Smith.

Amazing Animals. Ann De la Sota. (BrainBooster Ser.). (Illus.). 32p. (J). (gr. 3 up). 1986. 5.95 (*0-88679-457-9*) Educ Insights.

Amazing Animals. Gerald Legg. LC 93-36703. (X-Ray Picture Bks.). (Illus.). 48p. (J). (gr. 5-8). 1994. lib. bdg. 14.98 (*0-531-14285-X*); pap. 8.95 (*0-531-15708-3*) Watts.

***Amazing Animals.** Philippa Perry. Ed. by Caroline Clayton & Damian Kelleher. (Info Adventure Ser.). (Illus.). 32p. (J). (gr. 4-6). 1995. pap. 5.95 (*1-56847-314-1*) Thomson Lrning.

***Amazing Animals.** Philippa Perry. Ed. by Caroline Clayton & Damian Kelleher. (Info Adventure Ser.). (Illus.). 32p. (J). (gr. 4-6). 1995. 12.95 (*1-56847-407-5*) Thomson Lrning.

Amazing Animals. A. J. Wood. LC 90-85906. (Illus.). 24p. (J). (ps-1). 1991. 8.95 (*1-878093-46-0*) Boyds Mills Pr.

***Amazing Animals: Question & Answer Book.** 1995. 12.99 (*0-88705-693-8*) Joshua Morris.

Amazing Animals: The Fastest, Heaviest, Smallest, Largest, Fiercest, & Funniest. Marlo Gomboli. (Illus.). 48p. (J). 1994. 9.98 (*1-56138-489-5*) Running Pr.

Amazing Animals of Australia. S. L. Barry et al. Ed. by Donald J. Crump. LC 84-29558. (Books for World Explorers Series 6: No. 2). (Illus.). 104p. (J). (gr. 3-8). 1985. 8.95 (*0-87044-515-4*); lib. bdg. 12.50 (*0-87044-520-0*) Natl Geog.

Amazing Animals of the Sea. Judy Rinard. Ed. by Donald J. Crump. LC 80-8796. (Books for World Explorers Series 3: No. 1). (Illus.). 104p. (J). (gr. 3-8). 1981. 8.95 (*0-87044-382-8*); lib. bdg. 12.50 (*0-87044-387-9*) Natl Geog.

Amazing Anthony Ant. Lorna Philpot & Graham Philpot. (Illus.). 24p. (J). (gr. k-3). 1994. 13.00 (*0-679-85622-6*) Random Bks Yng Read.

Amazing Apple Book. Paulette Bourgeois. 1990. pap. 7.64 (*0-201-52333-7*) Addison-Wesley.

Amazing Archaeologists & Their Finds. William Scheller. LC 93-46919. (Profiles Ser.). (Illus.). 160p. (YA). (gr. 5-12). 1994. lib. bdg. 14.95 (*1-881508-17-X*) Oliver Pr MN.

An Asterisk (*) at the beginning of an entry indicates that the title is appearing in BIP for the first time.

Amazing Architecture from Japan. Hiroshi Watanabe. (Illus.). 144p. (Orig.). 1991. pap. 24.95 (*0-8348-0239-2*) Weatherhill.

Amazing Armored Animals. Sandie Sowler. LC 91-53140. (Eyewitness Juniors Ser.). (Illus.). 32p. (Orig.). (J). (gr. 1-5). 1992. lib. bdg. 9.99 (*0-679-92767-0*); pap. 6.95 (*0-679-82767-6*) Knopf Bks Yng Read.

Amazing Art of Pyrography. Robert Boyer. LC 93-70275. (Illus.). 400p. 1993. 50.00 (*1-879260-12-3*) Evanston Pub.

Amazing Aunt Agatha. Sheila Samton. (Ready-Set-Read Ser.). (Illus.). 24p. (J). (ps-2). 1990. lib. bdg. 17.84 (*0-8172-3575-2*); pap. 4.95 (*0-8114-6737-6*) Raintree Steck-V.

Amazing Balloon Book. Jeff Wolf. 1988. pap. 4.95 (*0-943249-33-3*) Terra Firma Bks.

Amazing Balloon Book (with Ball) Jeff Wolf. 1988. pap. 7.95 (*0-943249-34-1*) Terra Firma Bks.

Amazing Balloon Kit with Balloons. Jeff Wolf. 1989. pap. 9.95 (*0-929634-02-0*) Grnleaf Pubs.

Amazing Basketball Book: The First 100 Years. Bob Hill & Randall Baron. (Illus.). 208p. 1991. pap. 8.95 (*0-910791-42-2*) Devyn Pr.

Amazing Bats. Frank Greenaway. LC 91-6517. (Eyewitness Juniors Ser.). (Illus.). 32p. (Orig.). (J). (gr. 1-5). 1991. lib. bdg. 9.99 (*0-679-91518-4*); pap. 7.99 (*0-679-81518-X*) Knopf Bks Yng Read.

Amazing Bears. Theresa Greenaway. LC 92-910. (Eyewitness Juniors Ser.). (Illus.). 32p. (Orig.). (J). (gr. 1-5). 1992. lib. bdg. 9.99 (*0-679-92769-7*); pap. 7.99 (*0-679-82769-2*) Knopf Bks Yng Read.

Amazing Beetles. John Still. LC 91-6516. (Eyewitness Juniors Ser.). (Illus.). 32p. (Orig.). (J). (gr. 1-5). 1991. lib. bdg. 9.99 (*0-679-91519-2*); pap. 6.95 (*0-679-81519-8*) Knopf Bks Yng Read.

Amazing Bible Puzzles: New Testament. Nancy Sanders. (Illus.). 80p. (Orig.). (J). (gr. 3-7). 1993. pap. 4.99 (*0-570-04749-8*) Concordia.

Amazing Bible Puzzles: Old Testament. Nancy Sanders. (Illus.). 80p. (Orig.). (J). (gr. 3-7). 1993. pap. 4.99 (*0-570-04748-X*) Concordia.

Amazing Bikes. Trevor Lord. LC 92-911. (Eyewitness Juniors Ser.). (Illus.). 32p. (Orig.). (J). (gr. 1-5). 1992. lib. bdg. 9.99 (*0-679-92772-7*); pap. 7.99 (*0-679-82772-2*) Knopf Bks Yng Read.

Amazing Biofacts. Susan Goodman. (Illus.). 160p. (YA). (gr. 7 up). 1993. lib. bdg. 18.00 (*0-87226-364-9*); pap. 9.95 (*0-87226-256-1*) P Bedrick Bks.

Amazing Birds. Alexandra Parsons. (J). (ps-3). 1990. lib. bdg. 9.99 (*0-679-90223-6*); pap. 7.99 (*0-679-80223-1*) Knopf Bks Yng Read.

Amazing Birds of Prey. Jemima Parry-Jones. LC 92-909. (Eyewitness Juniors Ser.). (Illus.). 32p. (Orig.). (J). (gr. 1-5). 1992. lib. bdg. 9.99 (*0-679-92771-9*); pap. 7.99 (*0-679-82771-4*) Knopf Bks Yng Read.

Amazing Boats. Margaret Lincoln. LC 92-3045. (Eyewitness Juniors Ser.). (Illus.). 32p. (Orig.). (J). (gr. 1-5). 1992. lib. bdg. 9.99 (*0-679-92770-0*); pap. 7.99 (*0-679-82770-6*) Knopf Bks Yng Read.

Amazing Body. LC 93-85989. (Unfolding World Ser.). (Illus.). 32p. (J). (gr. 3 up). 1994. 5.95 (*1-56138-196-9*) Running Pr.

Amazing Bone. William Steig. LC 76-26479. (Illus.). 32p. (J). (ps-3). 1983. 17.00 (*0-374-30248-0*) FS&G.

Amazing Bone. William Steig. (J). (ps-3). 1993. pap. 4.95 (*0-374-40358-9*, Sunburst Bks) FS&G.

***Amazing Book of Card Tricks.** Jon Tremaine. 1994. 12.98 (*1-55521-995-0*) Bk Sales Inc.

Amazing Book of Jokes. Colin King. (Amazing Ser.). 32p. (J). 1990. 3.50 (*0-517-69192-2*) Random Hse Value.

***Amazing Book of Magic Tricks.** Jon Tremaine. 1994. 12.98 (*1-55521-996-9*) Bk Sales Inc.

Amazing Book of Puzzles & Tricks. Colin King. (Amazing Ser.). 32p. (J). 1990. 3.50 (*0-517-69194-9*) Random Hse Value.

Amazing Book of Quizzes. (Amazing Ser.). 32p. (J). 1990. 3.50 (*0-517-69193-0*) Random Hse Value.

Amazing Book of Shapes. Lydia Sharman. LC 93-34260. (Illus.). 40p. (J). (gr. k-3). 1994. 14.95 (*1-56458-514-X*) Dorling Kindersley.

Amazing Brain. Robert E. Ornstein & Richard F. Thompson. (Illus.). 224p. 1991. pap. 14.95 (*0-395-58572-4*) HM.

Amazing Buildings. Philip Wilkinson. LC 92-54314. (Illus.). 48p. (J). (gr. 3 up). 1993. 16.95 (*1-56458-234-5*) Dorling Kindersley.

Amazing but True. Owl Magazine Editors. (Illus.). 96p. (J). (gr. 3 up). 1992. pap. 3.95 (*0-920775-69-1*, Pub. by Greey dePencier CN) Firefly Bks Ltd.

Amazing but True Cat Tales. Bruce Nash & Allan Zullo. (Illus.). 104p. (Orig.). 1993. pap. 6.95 (*0-8362-8034-2*) Andrews & McMeel.

***Amazing but True Dog Tales.** Bruce Nash et al. LC 94-25535. (J). 1994. pap. 6.95 (*0-8362-8066-0*) Andrews & McMeel.

***Amazing but True Elvis Facts.** Bruce Nash & Allan Zullo. LC 94-45515. (Illus.). 96p. 1995. pap. 6.95 (*0-8362-7028-2*) Andrews & McMeel.

Amazing but True Fishing Stories. Bruce Nash & Allan Zullo. LC 92-34622. 104p. 1993. pap. 6.95 (*0-8362-8022-9*) Andrews & McMeel.

Amazing but True Golf Facts. Bruce Nash & Allan Zullo. 104p. 1992. pap. 6.95 (*0-8362-7994-8*) Andrews & McMeel.

***Amazing but True Mormon Stories.** Joan Oviatt. 144p. 1994. 10.98 (*0-88290-507-4*, 1050) Horizon Utah.

Amazing but True Sports Stories. Phyllis Hollander & Zander Hollander. (Illus.). 128p. (Orig.). (J). (gr. 3 up). 1986. pap. 2.50 (*0-590-43736-4*) Scholastic Inc.

Amazing Butterflies & Moths. John Still. LC 90-19234. (Eyewitness Juniors Ser.: No. 9). (Illus.). 32p. (Orig.). (J). (gr. 1-5). 1991. lib. bdg. 9.99 (*0-679-91515-X*); pap. 7.99 (*0-679-81515-5*) Knopf Bks Yng Read.

Amazing Card Tricks. Kirk Charles. LC 92-5482. (Illus.). (J). (gr. 2-6). 1992. lib. bdg. 21.36 (*0-89565-965-4*) Childs World.

Amazing Card Tricks Made Easy to Do. rev. ed. William L. Croxton. (Illus.). 64p. (J). (gr. 4 up). 1990. pap. 4.95 (*0-9623230-0-4*) WLC Enterprises.

Amazing Careers of Bob Hope. Joe Morella et al. (Illus.). 1978. pap. 5.95 (*0-89508-000-1*) Rainbow Bks.

Amazing Cars. Trevor Lord. LC 91-53138. (Eyewitness Juniors Ser.). (Illus.). 32p. (Orig.). (J). (gr. 1-5). 1992. lib. bdg. 9.99 (*0-679-92766-2*); pap. 6.95 (*0-679-82766-8*) Knopf Bks Yng Read.

Amazing Cats. Alexandra Parsons. LC 90-31885. (Eyewitness Juniors Ser.: No. 5). (Illus.). 32p. (Orig.). (J). (gr. 1-5). 1990. lib. bdg. 9.99 (*0-679-90690-8*); pap. 7.99 (*0-679-80690-3*) Knopf Bks Yng Read.

***Amazing Christmas Extravaganza.** David Shannon. LC 94-31980. 1995. write for info. (*0-590-48090-1*, Blue Sky Press) Scholastic Inc.

Amazing Coin Tricks. Kirk Charles. LC 93-29259. (Umbrella Bks.). (Illus.). (J). (gr. 2-6). 1995. lib. bdg. 21.36 (*1-56766-084-3*) Childs World.

***Amazing Colors.** Nicola Baxter. LC 94-44720. (Toppers Ser.). (Illus.). (J). 1995. lib. bdg. 10.95 (*0-516-09266-9*) Childrens.

Amazing Crocodiles & Other Reptiles. Mary Ling. LC 90-19239. (Eyewitness Juniors Ser.: No. 10). (Illus.). 32p. (Orig.). (J). (gr. 1-5). 1991. lib. bdg. 9.99 (*0-679-90689-4*); pap. 7.99 (*0-679-80689-X*) Knopf Bks Yng Read.

Amazing Dinosaurs: The Fastest, the Smallest, the Fiercest, & the Tallest. (Illus.). (J). (ps-1). 1991. write for info. (*0-307-15747-4*, Golden Pr) Western Pub.

Amazing Dirt Book. Paulette Bourgeois. (J). 1990. pap. 7.64 (*0-201-55096-2*) Addison-Wesley.

Amazing Discoveries. Christopher Carrie. (Crayola Color & Activity Ser.). (Illus.). 40p. (J). (gr. k up). 1991. 1.49 (*0-86696-308-1*) Binney & Smith.

Amazing Discoveries in the Words of Jesus. Gordon Lindsay. 1960. per. 6.95 (*0-89985-112-6*) Christ for the Nations.

Amazing Discoveries Within the Book of Books. Ralph Woodrow. (Illus.). 1979. pap. 4.95 (*0-916938-04-2*) R Woodrow.

Amazing Discovery. Walter Honek & Robert Proden. 200p. 1991. pap. text ed. 25.00 (*0-9630806-0-1*) Beta TX.

Amazing Egg Book. Margaret Griffin. 1990. pap. 6.68 (*0-201-52334-5*) Addison-Wesley.

***Amazing English.** Michael Walker. 1996. student ed, spiral bd. write for info. (*0-201-85367-1*) Addison-Wesley.

***Amazing English: Skills Journal, Bk. C.** Michael Walker. 112p. 1995. per. write for info. (*0-201-85374-4*) Addison-Wesley.

***Amazing English: Skills Journal, Bk. D.** Michael Walker. 112p. 1995. per. write for info. (*0-201-85378-7*) Addison-Wesley.

***Amazing English: Skills Journal, Bk. A.** Michael Walker. 112p. 1995. per. write for info. (*0-201-85344-2*) Addison-Wesley.

***Amazing English: Skills Journal, Bk. B.** Michael Walker. 112p. 1995. per. write for info. (*0-201-85368-X*) Addison-Wesley.

***Amazing English: Skills Journal, Bk. E.** Michael Walker. 112p. 1995. per. write for info. (*0-201-85382-5*) Addison-Wesley.

***Amazing English: The Buddy Book.** Michael Walker. 1995. write for info. (*0-201-85387-6*) Addison-Wesley.

***Amazing English Bk. C.** Michael Walker. 272p. 1995. student ed, spiral bd. write for info. (*0-201-85375-2*) Addison-Wesley.

***Amazing English Bk. C.** Michael Walker. 1996. teacher ed, spiral bd. write for info. (*0-201-85373-6*) Addison-Wesley.

***Amazing English Bk. D.** Michael Walker. 272p. 1995. teacher ed, spiral bd. write for info. (*0-201-85379-5*) Addison-Wesley.

***Amazing English Bk. D.** Michael Walker. 1996. student ed, spiral bd. write for info. (*0-201-85377-9*) Addison-Wesley.

***Amazing English Bk. A.** Michael Walker. 272p. 1995. teacher ed, spiral bd. write for info. (*0-201-85345-0*) Addison-Wesley.

***Amazing English Bk. A.** Michael Walker. 1996. student ed, spiral bd. write for info. (*0-201-85343-4*) Addison-Wesley.

***Amazing English Bk. B.** Michael Walker. 272p. 1995. teacher ed, spiral bd. write for info. (*0-201-85369-8*) Addison-Wesley.

***Amazing English Bk. E.** Michael Walker. 272p. 1995. teacher ed, spiral bd. write for info. (*0-201-85383-3*) Addison-Wesley.

***Amazing English Bk. E.** Michael Walker. 1996. student ed, spiral bd. write for info. (*0-201-85381-7*) Addison-Wesley.

Amazing Experiments. A. Vowles. (I Can Do Ser.). (Illus.). 32p. (J). (gr. 2-6). 1985. pap. 5.95 (*0-88625-073-0*) Durkin Hayes Pub.

Amazing Facts. 1990. 6.99 (*0-517-69109-4*) Random Hse Value.

Amazing Facts. Ed. by Jean Crawford. LC 93-11599. (Child's First Library of Learning). (Illus.). 88p. (J). (gr. k-3). 1994. write for info. (*0-8094-9458-2*); lib. bdg. write for info. (*0-8094-9459-0*) Time-Life.

Amazing Facts: The Indispensable Collection of True Life Facts & Feats. Richard B. Manchester. 1991. pap. 7.95 (*0-88486-043-4*) Arrowood Pr.

***Amazing Facts about Ancient Egypt.** James Putnam. 1994. 9.95 (*0-8109-1953-2*) Abrams.

Amazing Felix. Emily A. McCully. LC 92-10929. 32p. (J). (ps-3). 1993. 14.95 (*0-399-22428-9*, Putnam) Putnam Pub Group.

Amazing Fish. Mary Ling. LC 90-49651. (Eyewitness Juniors Ser.: No. 11). (Illus.). 32p. (Orig.). (J). (gr. 1-5). 1991. pap. 7.99 (*0-679-81516-3*) Knopf Bks Yng Read.

Amazing Fish. Mary Ling. LC 90-49651. (Eyewitness Juniors Ser.: No. 11). (Illus.). 32p. (Orig.). (J). (gr. 1-5). 1991. lib. bdg. 9.99 (*0-679-91516-8*) Knopf Bks Yng Read.

Amazing Floating Zoo, Bk. 2. Dee Sand. LC 93-70743. (Living Adventure Ser.). (Illus.). 60p. (Orig.). (J). (gr. 2-5). 1993. pap. 4.99 (*0-87509-530-5*) Chr Pubns.

Amazing Flying Machines. Robin Kerrod. LC 91-53137. (Eyewitness Juniors Ser.). (Illus.). 32p. (Orig.). (J). (gr. 1-5). 1992. lib. bdg. 9.99 (*0-679-92765-4*); pap. 6.95 (*0-679-82765-X*) Knopf Bks Yng Read.

Amazing Frogs & Toads. Barry Clarke. LC 90-31882. (Eyewitness Juniors Ser.: No. 6). (Illus.). 32p. (Orig.). (J). (gr. 1-5). 1990. pap. 7.99 (*0-679-80688-1*) Knopf Bks Yng Read.

Amazing Frogs & Toads. Barry Clarke. LC 90-31882. (Eyewitness Juniors Ser.: No. 6). (Illus.). 32p. (Orig.). (J). (gr. 1-5). 1991. lib. bdg. 9.99 (*0-679-90688-6*) Knopf Bks Yng Read.

Amazing Grace. 1978. 6.50 (*0-8378-2014-6*) Gibson.

Amazing Grace. James M. Boice. LC 93-15788. 1993. pap. 9.99 (*0-8423-1245-5*) Tyndale.

Amazing Grace. Mary Hoffman. (J). (ps-3). 1991. 14.99 (*0-8037-1040-2*) Dial Bks Young.

***Amazing Grace.** Deborah James. 288p. (Orig.). 1995. pap. 4.99 (*0-7865-0080-8*) Diamond.

***Amazing Grace.** Newton. 1991. 15.95 (*1-56282-998-X*) Hyperion.

Amazing Grace. Janet Quin-Harkin. 1993. mass mkt. 4.50 (*0-06-108020-9*, Harp PBks) HarpC.

Amazing Grace. Robert Drake. LC 80-16873. 168p. reprint ed. 47.90 (*0-8357-9121-1*, 2019320) Bks Demand.

Amazing Grace: An Understanding of God's Great Love for Us. Tom Barkey. (Illus.). 80p. (Orig.). 1993. pap. write for info. (*0-9626910-2-X*) Power Comm Ch.

Amazing Grace: Autobiography of a Survivor. Grace Halloran. 320p. 1992. pap. 14.95 (*1-880823-05-5*) N Star Pubns.

Amazing Grace: Evangelicalism in Australia, Britain, Canada, & the United States. Ed. by George Rawlyk & Mark A. Noll. LC 92-331996. 416p. (Orig.). 1994. pap. 19.99 (*0-8010-7772-9*) Baker Bk.

Amazing Grace: Evangelicalism in Australia, Britain, Canada, & the United States. Ed. by George Rawlyk & Mark A. Noll. (McGill-Queen's Studies in the History of Religion). 416p. (Orig.). (C). 1994. 44.95 (*0-7735-1207-1*, Pub. by McGill CN); pap. text ed. 22.95 (*0-7735-1214-4*, Pub. by McGill CN) U of Toronto Pr.

Amazing Grace: Hymn Texts for Devotional Use. Ed. by Bert Polman et al. 256p. (Orig.). 1994. pap. 14.99 (*0-664-25510-8*) Westminster John Knox.

***Amazing Grace: The Autobiography of a Call Girl.** Ed. by Madeline Bailey. (Illus.). 180p. (Orig.). 1995. pap. 16.95 (*0-9639688-1-5*) Q C C.

Amazing Grace: The Dramatic Life Story of John Newton. John Pollock. LC 78-3142. 192p. 1983. pap. 5.72 (*0-06-066655-2*, RD-477) Harper SF.

***Amazing Grace: The Lives of Children & the Conscience of a Nation.** Joanthan Kozol. 1995. 23.00 (*0-517-79999-5*, Crown) Crown Pub Group.

Amazing Grace: The Story Behind the Song. Jim Haskins. LC 91-20999. (Illus.). 48p. (J). (gr. 3-5). 1992. lib. bdg. 14.90 (*1-56294-117-8*) Millbrook Pr.

Amazing Grace: Twenty-Fifth Anniversary Edition. Robert Drake. LC 89-49335. xxiv, 116p. 1989. 25.00 (*0-86554-364-X*, MUP/H302); pap. 16.95 (*0-86554-372-0*, MUP/P82) Mercer Univ Pr.

Amazing Grace: 366 Hymn Stories for Personal Devotions. Kenneth W. Osbeck. LC 90-37888. 418p. 1990. pap. 12.99 (*0-8254-3425-4*) Kregel.

Amazing Grace Doll & Book Set. Mary Hoffman. (Illus.). 32p. (J). (ps-4). 1994. pap. 19.95 (*0-8037-1726-1*) Dial Bks Young.

Amazing Grace Hymn Stories. Wilbur Konkel. 1986. pap. 6.99 (*0-88019-048-5*) Schmul Pub Co.

Amazing Graces: Meals & Memories from the Parsonage. 256p. 1993. 14.95 (*0-9636854-0-6*) TX Conf UMMS.

Amazing Gracie. A. E. Cannon. 1993. pap. 3.99 (*0-440-21570-6*) Dell.

Amazing Grains: Creating Vegetarian Main Dishes with Whole Grains. Joanne Saltzman. Ed. by Jay Harlow. LC 89-63725. 216p. 1990. pap. 12.95 (*0-915811-21-9*) H J Kramer Inc.

Amazing Impossible Erie Canal. Cheryl Harness. LC 94-11114. (J). 1995. text ed. 17.95 (*0-02-742641-6*, Bradbury S&S) S&S Childrens.

Amazing Indian Children. Kenneth Thomasma. (J). (gr. 3-8). 1991. 9.95 (*1-880114-12-7*); pap. 6.95 (*0-685-49336-9*) Grandview. AMAZING INDIAN CHILDREN is a series of five books, historic fiction written for a third grade read-ability. They are packed with Indian lore, history, geography & high adventure. Each book has a child as the central character who lives during a key time in that tribe's history. Through the Indian child's eyes the reader relives dramatic historic events. These books are accurately researched & are in use in over 1000 schools. They have been translated into Danish, Dutch, Eskimo & Spanish. Over 300,000 have been sold. NAYA NUKI: GIRL WHO RAN-ISBN 1-880114-01-1 cloth; 1-880114-00-3 pbk. With her friend, Sacagewea, a Shoshoni Indian Girl is taken prisoner, escapes & makes a 1000 mile wilderness journey back to her people. SOUN TETOKEN: NEZ PERCE BOY-ISBN 1-880114-08-9 cloth; 1-880114-07-0 pbk. Although mute since the death of his parents in a forest fire a young boy in Chief Joseph's band lives a happy adventurous life until the War of 1877 changes his life forever. OM-KAS-TOE OF THE BLACKFEET-ISBN 1-880114-06-2 cloth; 1-880114-05-4 pbk. Life changes dramatically for the Blackfeet people in the early 1700s when a twin brother & sister discover a strange animal & succeed in capturing it & returning it to their tribe. KUNU: ESCAPE ON THE MISSOURI-ISBN 1-880114-04-6 cloth; 1-880114-03-8 pbk. Following the forced removal of his people from Minnesota to South Dakota, a Winnebago Indian boy & his dying grandfather embark on a dangerous river journey back to their homeland. PATHKI NANA: KOOTENAI GIRL-ISBN 1-880114-10-0 cloth; 1-880114-09-7 pbk. A 9 year-old Kootenai girl with a very poor self-image leaves her village to seek her guardian spirit & finds herself in a life & death struggle with an evil man who seeks to end her life before she can return to her people. MOHO WAT: SHEEPEATER BOY ATTEMPTS A RESCUE; ISBN 1-880114-14-3 cloth; 1-880114-13-5 pbk. To order call 1-800-525-7344. ***Publisher Provided Annotation.***

***Amazing Insect Safari.** Patrick S. Kelly. (Illus.). 56p. 1992. pap. 14.95 (*0-939251-62-0*) Accord CO.

Amazing Insects. LC 92-50789. (Unfolding World Ser.). (Illus.). 32p. (J). (gr. 3 up). 1993. 5.95 (*1-56138-226-4*) Running Pr.

Amazing Insects. Laurence Mound. LC 92-26735. (Eyewitness Juniors Ser.: Vol. 26). 32p. (Orig.). (J). (gr. 1-5). 1993. lib. bdg. 11.99 (*0-679-93925-3*) Knopf Bks Yng Read.

Amazing Insects. Laurence Mound. LC 92-26735. (Eyewitness Juniors Ser.: Vol. 26). 32p. (Orig.). (J). (gr. 1-5). 1993. pap. 7.99 (*0-679-83925-9*) Knopf Bks Yng Read.

Amazing Interlude. Mary R. Rinehart. 22.95 (*0-8488-0311-6*) Amereon Ltd.

Amazing Investigations: Twins. Jay Ingram. (Illus.). (J). (gr. 3 up). 1989. pap. 12.95 (*0-671-66263-5*) S&S Trade.

***Amazing Jessica.** Francine Pascal. (Sweet Valley Kids Ser.: No. 60). (J). 1995. pap. 2.99 (*0-553-48212-2*) Bantam.

Amazing Karate Workbook. Daniel H. McGraw. (Illus.). 136p. (Orig.). 1988. pap. text ed. 10.95 (*0-911929-49-5*) Onami Pubns.

***Amazing Kids!** Paula N. Kessler. LC 94-28961. (KidBacks Ser.). (Illus.). (J). 1995. pap. 4.99 (*0-679-86943-3*) Random.

Amazing L. A. Environment: A Handbook for Change. Mary Nichols & Stanley Young. (Illus.). 160p. (Orig.). 1991. pap. 6.95 (*1-879326-11-6*) Living Planet Pr.

***Amazing Lamb of God.** Richard Eby. 182p. (Orig.). 1994. pap. 8.99 (*1-56043-803-7*) Destiny Image.

Amazing Laws of Cosmic Mind Power. Joseph Murphy. 1989. 6.95 (*0-13-023888-0*) P-H.

Amazing Legume. Alice Jenner. 1989. 14.95 (*0-87951-364-0*) Overlook Pr.

Amazing Legume: Cooking with Lentils, Beans, & Peas. Alice Jenner. (Illus.). 136p. 1990. pap. 8.95 (*0-87951-375-6*) Overlook Pr.

***Amazing Life of Moe Berg: Catcher, Scholar, Spy.** Tricia Andryszewski. LC 95-8828. (J). 1996. lib. bdg. write for info. (*1-56294-610-2*) Millbrook Pr.

Amazing Lizards. Trevor Smith. LC 90-31884. (Eyewitness Juniors Ser.: No. 7). (Illus.). 32p. (Orig.). (J). (gr. 1-5). 1990. pap. 7.99 (*0-679-80819-1*) Knopf Bks Yng Read.

Amazing Lizards. Trevor Smith. LC 90-31884. (Eyewitness Juniors Ser.: No. 7). (Illus.). 32p. (Orig.). (J). (gr. 1-5). 1990. lib. bdg. 9.99 (*0-679-90819-6*) Knopf Bks Yng Read.

Amazing Logic Puzzles. Norman D. Willis. LC 93-39592. (Illus.). 128p. 1994. pap. 4.95 (*0-8069-0564-6*) Sterling.

Amazing Love. John R. Dewitt. 160p. (Orig.). 1981. pap. text ed. 8.95 (*0-85151-328-X*) Banner of Truth.

Amazing Love. Corrie Ten Boom. 1991. pap. 3.95 (*0-87508-018-9*) Chr Lit.

An Asterisk (*) at the beginning of an entry indicates that the title is appearing in BIP for the first time.

Amazing Love: An Easter Celebration of Hope. Created by Tom Fettke. 1992. 5.95 (*0-8341-9206-3*, ME-42); audio 10.98 (*0-685-72872-2*, TA-9146C); audio 60.00 (*0-685-72874-9*, MU-9146C); audio 45.00 (*0-685-72876-5*, MU-9146R); cd-rom 60.00 (*0-685-72875-7*, MU-9146T); 6.00 (*0-685-72873-0*, L-9146C); 8.00 (*0-685-72877-3*, ME-42SF); 187.00 (*0-685-72878-1*, OR-9146) Lillenas.

Amazing Love see Amor, Asombroso Amor

*__Amazing Machine.__ Alex Parsons. (Life Education Ser.). (Illus.). (J). (gr. 5-8). 1995. lib. bdg. 12.25 (*0-531-14380-5*) Watts.

Amazing Magic Show. P. J. Petersen. LC 93-34861. (J). 1994. 14.00 (*0-671-86581-1*, S&S Bks Young Read) S&S Childrens.

*__Amazing Magic Tricks.__ Dave Brown & Paul Reeve. LC 94-34863. (Illus.). 48p. (J). (gr. 1-4). 1995. 12.95 (*1-56458-877-7*) Dorling Kindersley.

Amazing Magnets. David Adler. LC 82-17377. (Question & Answer Bks.). (Illus.). 32p. (J). (gr. 3-6). 1983. lib. bdg. 10.59 (*0-89375-894-9*); pap. text ed. 2.95 (*0-89375-895-7*) Troll Assocs.

Amazing Magnets. Julian Rowe & Molly Perham. LC 94-16942. (First Science Ser.). (Illus.). 32p. (J). (gr. 1-4). 1994. lib. bdg. 13.95 (*0-516-08137-3*); pap. 4.95 (*0-516-48137-1*) Childrens.

Amazing Mammals. Alexandra Parsons. LC 89-38831. (Eyewitness Juniors Ser.). (Illus.). 32p. (J). (gr. 1-5). 1990. 7.99 (*0-679-80224-X*) Knopf Bks Yng Read.

Amazing Mammals. Alexandra Parsons. LC 89-38831. (Eyewitness Juniors Ser.). (Illus.). 32p. (J). (gr. 1-5). 1990. lib. bdg. 9.99 (*0-679-90224-4*) Knopf Bks Yng Read.

Amazing Mammals I. National Wildlife Federation Staff. (J). (gr. k-8). 1991. pap. 7.95 (*0-945051-29-8*, 75023) Natl Wildlife.

Amazing Mammals II. National Wildlife Federation Staff. (J). (gr. k-8). 1991. pap. 7.95 (*0-945051-30-1*, 75024) Natl Wildlife.

*__Amazing Management Styles.__ R. K. Spriggs. Tr. by J. L. Barnes. (Illus.). 108p. (C). 1995. pap. text ed. 11.95 (*0-9637271-2-5*) I B Bold Pubns.

Amazing Marietta. Gladys Bullock. 1994. 8.95 (*0-8062-4874-2*) Carlton.

Amazing Mark. Robyn Supraner. LC 85-14070. (Illus.). 48p. (Orig.). (J). (gr. 1-3). 1986. lib. bdg. 10.59 (*0-8167-0644-1*); pap. text ed. 3.50 (*0-8167-0645-X*) Troll Assocs.

Amazing Mathematical Amusement Arcade. Brian Bolt. (Illus.). 128p. 1984. pap. 15.95 (*0-521-26980-6*) Cambridge U Pr.

Amazing Mazes. Rolf Heimann. (J). (gr. 4-7). 1990. pap. 3.95 (*0-8167-2201-3*) Troll Assocs.

*__Amazing Mazes.__ Ellen S. Ortelt. (Illus.). 40p. (J). 1995. pap. 7.95 (*0-8059-3736-6*) Dorrance.

Amazing Mazes. Simon & Schuster Staff. (Activity Bks.). (Illus.). 64p. (J). (gr. 2-5). 1990. pap. 1.79 (*0-671-72333-2*, Litl Simon S&S) S&S Childrens.

*__Amazing Medicines the Drug Companies Don't Want You to Discover.__ University Medical Research Staff. 1994. 26.95 (*0-9638714-0-4*) U Med Res Pubs.

Amazing Models! Balloon Power. Peter R. Holland. 64p. (Orig.). 1989. pap. 7.95 (*0-8306-3230-1*) TAB Bks.

Amazing Models: Gravity Power. Peter R. Holland. 1990. pap. 7.95 (*0-8306-3501-7*) TAB Bks.

Amazing Models! Rubberband Power. Peter R. Holland. (Illus.). 64p. (Orig.). 1989. pap. 7.95 (*0-8306-3220-4*) TAB Bks.

Amazing Models: Water Power. Peter R. Holland. 64p. 1990. pap. 7.95 (*0-8306-3502-5*) TAB Bks.

Amazing Models! Balloon Power. Peter Holland. 1989. pap. text ed. 7.95 (*0-07-157046-2*) McGraw.

Amazing Moms. Brad Steiger & Sherry H. Steiger. 224p. (Orig.). 1994. pap. 3.99 (*0-451-18037-2*, Sig) NAL-Dutton.

Amazing Monkeys. Scott Steedman. LC 90-19238. (Eyewitness Juniors Ser.: No. 12). (Illus.). 32p. (Orig.). (J). (gr. 1-5). 1991. lib. bdg. 9.99 (*0-679-91517-6*); pap. 9.99 (*0-679-81517-1*) Knopf Bks Yng Read.

Amazing Monkeys see National Geographic Action Books

Amazing Monsters: Verses to Thrill & Chill. Ed. by Robert Fisher. (Illus.). 96p. (J). (gr. k-5). 1982. pap. 5.95 (*0-571-13925-6*) Faber & Faber.

Amazing Mr. Doolittle: A Biography of Lieutenant General James H. Doolittle. Quentin Reynolds. LC 71-169434. (Literature & History of Aviation Ser.). 1976. reprint ed. 25.95 (*0-405-03778-3*) Ayer.

Amazing Mr. Mohs. Bruce B. Mohs. (Illus.). 256p. (Orig.). (C). 1984. pap. 14.95 (*0-931279-00-3*) Mohs Seaplane Co.

Amazing Mrs. Pollifax. Dorothy Gilman. 1985. mass mkt. 5.99 (*0-449-20912-1*, Crest) Fawcett.

Amazing Mrs. Pollifax. large type ed. Dorothy Gilman. (General Ser.). 286p. 1992. pap. 15.95 (*0-8161-5355-8*, Large Print Bks) Hall.

Amazing Musical Moments. Kathy Poelker. (Illus.). 48p. 1985. teacher ed 7.95 (*0-945405-06-5*) LAM Co.

Amazing Mysteries of the World. Catherine O'Neill. Ed. by Donald J. Crump. LC 83-13444. (Books for World Explorers Series 5: No. 1). 104p. (J). (gr. 3-8). 1983. lib. bdg. 12.50 (*0-87044-502-2*) Natl Geog.

Amazing Navel Swing. A. Dominic Antonini. 60p. 1988. pap. text ed. 4.95 (*0-9619939-0-1*) A&A Ent.

Amazing Nellie Bly. Mignon Rittenhouse. LC 74-148227. (Biography Index Reprint Ser.). 1977. 20.95 (*0-8369-8074-3*) Ayer.

Amazing Newborn. Marshall H. Klaus & Phyllis H. Klaus. 22.25 (*0-8446-6268-2*) Peter Smith.

Amazing Newborn: Discovering & Enjoying Your Baby's Natural Abilities. Marshall H. Klaus & Phyllis H. Klaus. LC 85-9048. 1985p. 1985. pap. 14.42 (*0-201-11672-3*) Addison-Wesley.

*__Amazing Odysseys.__ (YA). (gr. 7-12). 1995. pap. text ed. 299.00 (*0-941217-01-9*) Reading Resources Inc.

Amazing Paper Book. Paulette Bourgeois. (J). (gr. 4-8). 1990. pap. 6.68 (*0-201-52377-9*) Addison-Wesley.

Amazing Paper Cuttings of Hans Christian Andersen. Beth W. Brust. LC 93-24532. 80p. (J). (gr. 2-4). 1994. 15.95 (*0-395-66787-9*) Ticknor & Flds Bks Yng Read.

Amazing Paper Planes. Edmond Hui. 1989. pap. 8.95 (*0-312-03210-2*) St Martin.

Amazing Pennsylvania Canals: One Hundred Sixtieth Anniversary Edition. W. H. Shank. 1991. 9.00 (*0-933788-37-1*) Am Canal & Transport.

Amazing People. Christopher Carrie. (Crayola Color & Activity Ser.). (Illus.). 40p. (J). (gr. k up). 1991. 1.49 (*0-86696-307-3*) Binney & Smith.

Amazing Places. Christopher Carrie. (Crayola Color & Activity Ser.). (Illus.). 40p. (J). (gr. k up). 1991. 1.49 (*0-86696-306-5*) Binney & Smith.

Amazing Poetry of Ron Dultz. Ron Dultz. (Illus.). 56p. 1986. pap. 5.95 (*0-9601636-6-2*) R Dultz.

Amazing Poisonous Animals. Alexandra Parsons. LC 90-31883. (Eyewitness Juniors Ser.: No. 8). 32p. (Orig.). (J). (gr. 1-5). 1990. pap. 7.99 (*0-679-80699-7*) Knopf Bks Yng Read.

Amazing Poisonous Animals. Alexandra Parsons. LC 90-31883. (Eyewitness Juniors Ser.: No. 8). 32p. (Orig.). (J). (gr. 1-5). 1991. lib. bdg. 9.99 (*0-679-90699-1*) Knopf Bks Yng Read.

Amazing Potato: A Story in Which the Incas, Conquistadors, Marie Antoinette, Thomas Jefferson, Wars, Famines, Immigrants, & French Fries All Play a Part. Milton Meltzer. LC 91-29610. (Illus.). 128p. (J). (gr. 3-7). 1992. 15.00 (*0-06-020806-6*); lib. bdg. 14.89 (*0-06-020807-4*) HarpC Child Bks.

Amazing Potato Book. Paulette Bourgeois. LC 91-23847. (YA). 1991. pap. 7.64 (*0-201-56761-X*) Addison-Wesley.

Amazing Power of Ashur Fine. Donald J. Sobol. (J). (gr. 4-8). 1987. reprint ed. pap. 2.95 (*0-8167-1049-X*) Troll Assocs.

Amazing Prophecies Prove the Bible. Gordon Lindsay. 1971. 2.95 (*0-89985-053-7*) Christ for the Nations.

*__Amazing Pulp Heroes.__ 2nd expanded ed. Hamilton & Hullas. 1995. write for info. (*0-614-06209-8*) Gryphon Pubns.

Amazing Rain Forest. Lynn M. Stone. LC 94-20909. (Discovering the Rain Forest Ser.). (J). 1994. write for info. (*0-86593-392-8*) Rourke Corp.

Amazing Records. Robert L. Ripley. (Ripley's Believe It Or Not! Ser.). (Illus.). 48p. (J). (gr. 3-6). 1992. lib. bdg. 12.95 (*1-56065-124-5*) Capstone Pr.

Amazing Rescues. George Shea. LC 90-53221. (Step into Reading Bks.: Step 3). (Illus.). 48p. (J). (gr. 2-3). 1992. pap. 3.99 (*0-679-81107-9*) Random Bks Yng Read.

Amazing Rescues. George Shea. LC 90-53221. (Step into Reading Bks.: Step 3). (Illus.). 48p. (J). (gr. 2-3). 1992. lib. bdg. 7.99 (*0-679-91107-3*) Random Bks Yng Read.

Amazing Rescues. Ed. by Janet Stewart & Nadia Pelowich. (Adventure Ser.). (Illus.). 48p. (J). (gr. 4). 1987. lib. bdg. 14.65 (*0-88625-172-9*); pap. 5.95 (*0-88625-151-6*) Durkin Hayes Pub.

Amazing Results of Positive Thinking. Norman Vincent Peale. 1987. mass mkt. 4.95 (*0-449-21519-9*) Fawcett.

Amazing Sandcastle Builder's Book & Kit. Jane Kobayashi & David Ritch. 1994. pap. 12.95 (*0-8362-4220-3*) Andrews & McMeel.

Amazing Schemes within Your Genes. Fran Balkwill. LC 92-42942. (Cells & Things Ser.). (Illus.). (J). (gr. 3-6). 1993. 17.50 (*0-87614-804-6*, Carolrhoda) Lerner Group.

Amazing Schemes Within Your Genes. Fran Balkwill. (J). (gr. 3-6). 1994. pap. 8.95 (*0-87614-635-3*, Carolrhoda) Lerner Group.

Amazing Science Experiments with Everyday Materials. E. Richard Churchill. LC 90-20641. (Illus.). 128p. (J). (gr. 4-12). 1992. pap. 4.95 (*0-8069-7371-4*) Sterling.

Amazing Science Series, 8 bks., Set. Q. L. Pearce. (Illus.). 256p. (J). (gr. 4-6). 1989. lib. bdg. 77.88 (*0-671-94111-9*, Julian Messner); pap. 35.70 (*0-671-94112-7*, Julian Messner) Silver Burdett Pr.

Amazing Science Tricks. Kirk Charles. LC 92-9012. (Illus.). (J). (gr. 2-6). 1992. lib. bdg. 21.36 (*0-89565-964-6*) Childs World.

Amazing Sculptural Illustration. Graphic-Sha Staff. (Illus.). 160p. 1994. pap. 59.95 (*4-7661-0774-8*, Pub. by Graphic Sha JA) Bks Nippan.

Amazing Secrets of Psychic Healing. Benjamin O. Bibb & Joseph J. Weed. 1986. pap. 6.95 (*0-13-023762-0*) P-H.

Amazing Secrets of the Masters of the Far East. Robert Collier. 1991. pap. 7.95 (*0-912576-02-2*) R Collier.

Amazing Secrets of the Psychic World. Raymond Buckland & Hereward Carrington. 1976. pap. 4.95 (*0-686-96839-5*, Reward) P-H.

*__Amazing Sharks.__ Melvin Berger. (Ranger Rick Science Spectacular Ser.). 16p. (J). (gr. 2-4). 1995. pap. text ed. 14.95 (*1-56784-213-5*) Newbridge Comms.

Amazing Snakes. Alexandra Parsons. LC 89-38944. (Eyewitness Juniors Ser.). (Illus.). 32p. (J). (gr. 1-5). 1990. 7.99 (*0-679-80225-8*) Knopf Bks Yng Read.

Amazing Snakes. Alexandra Parsons. LC 89-38944. (Eyewitness Juniors Ser.). (Illus.). 32p. (J). (gr. 1-5). 1990. lib. bdg. 9.99 (*0-679-90225-2*) Knopf Bks Yng Read.

Amazing Spacefacts. Susan Goodman. LC 92-40112. (Illus.). 144p. (YA). (gr. 7 up). 1993. lib. bdg. 18.00 (*0-87226-365-7*); pap. 8.95 (*0-87226-257-X*) P Bedrick Bks.

Amazing Spider-Man. (Look & Find Ser.). (Illus.). 24p. (J). 1993. 7.98 (*1-56173-702-X*) Pubns Intl Ltd.

Amazing Spider-Man. Stan Lee & Steve Ditko. (Marvel Masterworks Ser.: Vol. 10). 264p. 1989. 29.95 (*0-87135-596-5*) Marvel Entmnt.

Amazing Spider-Man. Stan Lee. 128p. (Orig.). 1992. pap. 3.99 (*0-8125-1019-4*) Tor Bks.

Amazing Spiders. Alexandra Parsons. LC 89-38833. (Eyewitness Juniors Ser.). (Illus.). 32p. (J). (gr. 1-5). 1990. 7.99 (*0-679-80226-6*); lib. bdg. 9.99 (*0-679-90226-0*) Knopf Bks Yng Read.

Amazing Spiders. Claudia Schnieper. (Nature Watch Bks.). (Illus.). 48p. (J). (gr. 2-5). 1989. 19.95 (*0-87614-342-7*, Carolrhoda); pap. 6.95 (*0-87614-518-7*, Carolrhoda) Lerner Group.

*__Amazing Sports Photos: Funny, Famous, & Fantastic Photographs from the World of Sports.__ Sports Illustrated for Kids Editors. (Illus.). 32p. (J). (gr. 3-7). 1995. pap. 3.95 (*1-886749-00-3*, Spts Illus Kids) Little.

Amazing States. Margaret Burda. 160p. (J). (gr. 4-8). 1984. student ed 13.95 (*0-86653-205-6*, GA 546) Good Apple.

*__Amazing Stories: The Anthology.__ Ed. by Kim Mohan. 320p. 1995. pap. 13.95 (*0-312-89048-6*) Tor Bks.

Amazing Stories from Exodus. Contrib by Dave Gallagher. LC 94-4981. 1994. 13.99 (*1-55945-198-X*) Group Pub.

Amazing Stories from Genesis. Cindy Smith. 96p. (J). 1992. pap. 13.99 (*1-55945-094-0*) Group Pub.

Amazing Story of Creation: From Science & the Bible. Duane T. Gish. LC 90-82827. (Illus.). 112p. 1990. 18.95 (*0-89051-120-9*) Master Bks.

Amazing Story of the Fantasticks: America's Longest Running Play. Robert Viagas. 1990. 19.95 (*0-8065-1214-8*, Citadel) Carol Pub Group.

Amazing Story of the Tonelli Family: Twelve Thousand Miles in a Buick in Search of Identity, Ethnicity, Geography, Kinship, & Home. Bill Tonelli. (Illus.). 306p. 1994. 19.23 (*0-201-62455-9*) Addison-Wesley.

Amazing Tales from Indiana. Fred D. Cavinder. LC 89-46005. 176p. 1990. 25.00 (*0-253-31329-5*); pap. 9.95 (*0-253-20658-8*, MB-658) Ind U Pr.

Amazing Tension Getters. Lynn Yaconelli. 1988. pap. 9.99 (*0-310-34881-1*, 11372P) Zondervan.

Amazing Texas Monuments & Museums. Ann Ruff. LC 83-18726. 104p. (Orig.). 1984. pap. 9.95 (*0-88415-564-1*, Lone Star Bks) Gulf Pub.

Amazing the Incredible Super Dog. Crosby N. Bonsall. LC 85-45811. (Illus.). 32p. (J). (gr. k-3). 1986. lib. bdg. 14.89 (*0-06-020591-1*) HarpC Child Bks.

Amazing Theatre. James Agate. LC 76-91307. 1972. reprint ed. 24.95 (*0-405-08181-2*, Pub. by Blom Pubns UK) Ayer.

Amazing Things Animals Do. Ed. by Donald J. Crump. (Books for World Explorers Series 10: No. 4). (J). (gr. 3-8). 1989. 8.95 (*0-87044-709-2*); lib. bdg. 12.50 (*0-87044-704-1*) Natl Geog.

Amazing Traveler: Isabella Bird: The Biography of a Victorian Adventurer. Evelyn Kaye. (Illus.). 224p. (Orig.). (C). 1994. pap. 19.95 (*0-9626231-6-4*) Blue Penguin Pubns.

Amazing Tropical Birds. Gerald Legg. LC 91-6515. (Eyewitness Juniors Ser.). (Illus.). 32p. (Orig.). (J). (gr. 1-5). 1991. pap. 6.95 (*0-679-81520-1*) Knopf Bks Yng Read.

Amazing Tropical Birds. Gerald Legg. LC 91-6515. (Eyewitness Juniors Ser.). (Illus.). 32p. (Orig.). (J). (gr. 1-5). 1991. lib. bdg. 9.99 (*0-679-91520-6*) Knopf Bks Yng Read.

Amazing True Stories. Don L. Wulffson. LC 90-28105. (Illus.). 128p. (J). (gr. 4-9). 1991. 13.95 (*0-525-65070-9*, Cobblehill Bks) Dutton Child Bks.

Amazing True Stories. Don L. Wulffson. (J). (gr. 4-7). 1994. pap. 2.95 (*0-590-45958-9*) Scholastic Inc.

Amazing Universe. Herbert Friedman. Ed. by Donald J. Crump. LC 74-28806. (Special Publications Series 10: No. 4). (Illus.). 200p. 1975. 8.95 (*0-87044-179-5*) Natl Geog.

Amazing Valvano & the Mystery of the Hooded Rat. Mary Robinson. 160p. (J). (gr. 5). 1990. pap. 2.75 (*0-380-70713-6*, Camelot) Avon.

Amazing Valvano & the Mystery of the Hooded Rat. Mary Robinson. LC 87-26179. 168p. (J). (gr. 3-7). 1988. 13.95 (*0-395-44314-8*) HM.

Amazing Venison Recipes. Jim Zumbo. (Illus.). 232p. (Orig.). 1994. pap. 16.95 (*0-9624025-4-0*) Wapiti Valley Pub Co. AMAZING VENISON RECIPES is the finest collection of recipes & information on preparing venison available today. With over 200 palate-satisfying recipes this book places special emphasis on gamey tasting venison, sharing simple & easy techniques to make any cut of venison a gourmet's delight. Written by Jim Zumbo, Hunting Editor for Outdoor Life magazine, this cookbook was written for the millions of hunters in America (& their wives) who are faced with the task of preparing meat very different from that found in the grocery store. "I decided to take up the challenge to create & gather recipes that would neutralize the strong flavor of gamey meat & enhance the natural flavor of mild meat," says Zumbo. This book includes chapters for beginning cooks, information on field care, aging, freezing, marinades, foolproof recipes for the gamiest meat, busy day recipes, & chapters on specific cuts of venison which includes deer, elk, moose, antelope & other animals. This book is a valuable contribution to cookbook collections & according to national magazines like American Hunter, "This book deserves a place in every hunter's kitchen." Order directly from Wapiti Valley Publishing, Co., P.O. Box 2390, Cody, WY 82414 307-587-5486 or 800-673-4868, or your distributor.** ***Publisher Provided Annotation.

Amazing Waist, How Sweet the Pounds. Diana Smith. (Illus.). 119p. (Orig.). (C). 1989. student ed 9.95 (*0-9623791-0-7*) Cornerstn Enhancement.

*__Amazing Whitetails.__ Mike Biggs. LC 94-61042. (Illus.). 192p. 1994. 39.95 (*0-9642915-0-9*) T P W.

*__Amazing Whitetails.__ limited ed. Mike Biggs. LC 94-61042. (Illus.). 192p. 1994. 95.00 (*0-9642915-1-7*) T P W.

Amazing Windows Games. Judd Robbins. LC 93-85587. 155p. 1993. disk. pap. 19.99 (*0-7821-1361-3*) Sybex.

Amazing Windows Magic Show. Corey Sandler. 1993. Incl. disk. pap. 32.95 (*1-56686-088-1*) Brady Compu Bks.

Amazing Wolves, Dogs, & Foxes. Mary Ling. LC 91-6514. (Eyewitness Juniors Ser.). (Illus.). 32p. (Orig.). (J). (gr. 1-5). 1991. pap. 7.99 (*0-679-81521-X*) Knopf Bks Yng Read.

Amazing Wolves, Dogs, & Foxes. Mary Ling. LC 91-6514. (Eyewitness Juniors Ser.). (Illus.). 32p. (Orig.). (J). (gr. 1-5). 1991. lib. bdg. 9.99 (*0-679-91521-4*) Knopf Bks Yng Read.

Amazing World of Animals. Lawrence Jefferies. LC 82-20061. (Question & Answer Bks.). (Illus.). 32p. (J). (gr. 3-6). 1983. lib. bdg. 10.59 (*0-89375-898-1*); pap. text ed. 2.95 (*0-89375-899-X*) Troll Assocs.

Amazing World of Ants. Francene Sabin. LC 81-7492. (Illus.). 32p. (J). (gr. 2-4). 1982. lib. bdg. 11.59 (*0-89375-558-3*); pap. text ed. 2.95 (*0-89375-559-1*) Troll Assocs.

Amazing World of Birds. Stephen Caitlin. LC 89-4968. (Illus.). 32p. (J). (gr. 2-4). 1990. lib. bdg. 11.59 (*0-8167-1747-8*); pap. text ed. 2.95 (*0-8167-1748-6*) Troll Assocs.

Amazing World of Butterflies & Moths. Louis Sabin. LC 81-7504. (Illus.). 32p. (J). (gr. 2-4). 1982. lib. bdg. 11.59 (*0-89375-560-5*); pap. text ed. 2.95 (*0-89375-561-3*); audio 9.95 (*0-685-04943-4*) Troll Assocs.

Amazing World of Dinosaurs. Judith Granger. LC 81-7476. (Illus.). 32p. (J). (gr. 2-4). 1982. lib. bdg. 11.59 (*0-89375-562-1*); pap. text ed. 2.95 (*0-89375-563-X*) Troll Assocs.

Amazing World of Dinosaurs. T. Riley. (Illus.). 80p. (J). (gr. 2-6). 1991. 4.99 (*0-517-63993-9*) Random Hse Value.

Amazing World of Night Creatures. Janet Craig. LC 89-5002. (Illus.). 32p. (J). (gr. 2-4). 1990. lib. bdg. 11.59 (*0-8167-1749-4*); pap. text ed. 2.95 (*0-8167-1750-8*) Troll Assocs.

Amazing World of Plants. Elizabeth Marcus. LC 83-4836. (Question & Answer Bks.). (Illus.). 32p. (J). (gr. 3-6). 1984. lib. bdg. 10.59 (*0-89375-967-8*); pap. text ed. 2.95 (*0-89375-968-6*) Troll Assocs.

Amazing World of Spiders. Janet Craig. LC 89-5005. (Illus.). 32p. (J). (gr. 2-4). 1990. lib. bdg. 11.59 (*0-8167-1751-6*); pap. text ed. 2.95 (*0-8167-1752-4*) Troll Assocs.

*__Amazing 3-D Games Adventure Set.__ Lary Myers. 1995. pap. 39.99 (*1-883577-15-2*) Coriolis Grp.

Amazon. Abigail Frost. LC 89-17357. (Myths & Legends Ser.). (Illus.). 48p. (J). (gr. 4-8). 1990. lib. bdg. 13.95 (*1-85435-236-9*) Marshall Cavendish.

*__Amazon.__ Peter Murray. LC 93-7617. (ENG & SPA.). (J). (gr. 2-6). 1993. lib. bdg. 22.79 (*1-56766-039-8*) Childs World.

Amazon. Peter Murray. LC 93-7617. (ENG & SPA.). (J). (gr. 2-6). 1993. lib. bdg. 22.79 (*1-56766-021-5*) Childs World.

Amazon. Ed. by Harold Sioli. (Monographiae Biologicae Ser.). 1984. lib. bdg. 382.50 (*90-6193-108-8*) Kluwer Ac.

Amazon. Julia Waterlow. LC 92-25446. (Rivers of the World Ser.). (Illus.). 48p. (J). (gr. 5-6). 1993. lib. bdg. 22.80 (*0-8114-3101-0*) Raintree Steck-V.

Amazon: A Novel. Barbara G. Walker. LC 91-58145. 192p. 1993. reprint ed. pap. 10.00 (*0-06-250944-6*) Harper SF.

Amazon: A Young Reader's Look at the Last Frontier. Peter Lourie. LC 90-85720. (Illus.). 48p. (J). (gr. 3-7). 1991. 17.95 (*1-878093-00-2*) Boyds Mills Pr.

Amazon: Past, Present, & Future. Alain Gheerbrant. (Discoveries Ser.). (Illus.). 196p. 1992. pap. 12.95 (*0-8109-2860-4*) Abrams.

Amazon: Vanishing Cultures. Jan Reynolds. LC 92-21089. (Vanishing Cultures Ser.). (Illus.). (J). 1993. 16.95 (*0-15-202831-5*, HB Juv Bks); pap. 8.95 (*0-15-202832-3*, HB Juv Bks) HarBrace.

Amazon Adventure. Larry Bischof & William B. Lowry. LC 92-12844. (Widgets Ser.). (J). (gr. 2). 1992. lib. bdg. 13.99 (*1-56239-150-X*) Abdo & Dghtrs.

Amazon & a Donkey. large type ed. Natascha Scott-Stokes. (Non-Fiction Ser.). 368p. 1992. 23.95 (*0-7089-8647-1*) Ulverscroft.

Amazon & Other Stories. Tr. & Intro. by David Margarshack. LC 76-23884. 282p. 1987. reprint ed. 21.00 (*0-88355-495-X*) Hyperion Conn.

*__Amazon & the Americas.__ Tr. by Maureen Walker. (Tintin's Travel Diaries). (J). 1995. write for info. (*0-8120-6489-5*); pap. write for info. (*0-8120-9160-4*) Barron.

An Asterisk (*) at the beginning of an entry indicates that the title is appearing in BIP for the first time.

An Asterisk (*) at the beginning of an entry indicates that the title is appearing in BIP for the first time.

221

A

Ambiguous Frog: The Galvani-Volta Controversy on Animal Electricity. Marcello Pera. Tr. by Jonathan Mandelbaum. (Illus.). 262p. 1992. text ed. 32.50 (*0-691-08512-9*) Princeton U Pr.

Ambiguous Harmony: Family Talk in America. Herve Varenne. Ed. by Roy Freedle. (Advances in Discourse Processes Ser.: Vol. 44). 272p. (C). 1992. text ed. 52.50 (*0-89391-763-X*); pap. 29.50 (*0-89391-930-6*) Ablex Pub.

Ambiguous Iroquois Empire: The Covenant Chain Confederation of Indian Tribes with English Colonies. Francis Jennings. (Illus.). 464p. 1990. reprint ed. pap. 15.95 (*0-393-30302-0*) Norton.

***Ambiguous Legacy of the Enlightenment.** William Rusher. LC 95-15728. 1995. pap. write for info. (*0-8191-9957-5*) U Pr of Amer.

***Ambiguous Legacy of the Enlightenment.** Ed. by William Rusher. LC 95-15728. 1995. write for info. (*0-8191-9956-7*) U Pr of Amer.

Ambiguous Lives: Free Women of Color in Rural Georgia, 1789-1879. Adele L. Alexander. LC 91-10151. (Illus.). 304p. 1991. 23.00 (*1-55728-214-5*); pap. 15.00 (*1-55728-215-3*) U of Ark Pr.

Ambiguous Partnership: Britain & America, 1944-1947. Robert M. Hathaway. LC 81-6153. (Contemporary American History Ser.). 448p. 1981. text ed. 51.50 (*0-231-04452-6*) Col U Pr.

Ambiguous Partnership: Non Zionists & Zionists in America, 1939-1948. Menahem Kaufman. LC 90-63362. (American Jewish Civilization Ser.). 418p. 1991. 39.95 (*0-8143-2370-7*) Wayne St U Pr.

Ambiguous Realities: Women in the Middle Ages & Renaissance. Ed. by Carole Levin & Jeanie Watson. LC 87-21671. 264p. 1987. 39.95 (*0-8143-1872-X*); pap. 16.95 (*0-8143-1873-8*) Wayne St U Pr.

Ambiguous Relations: Kin, Class & Conflict among Komachi Pastoralists. Daniel J. Bradburd. LC 89-39784. (Ethnographic Inquiry Ser.). (Illus.). 240p. 1990. 32.50 (*0-87474-306-0*) Smithsonian.

Ambiguous Relationship: Theodore Roosevelt & Alfred Thayer Mahan. Richard W. Turk. LC 87-222. (Contributions in Military Studies: No. 63). 191p. 1987. text ed. 49.95 (*0-313-25644-6*, TKA/, Greenwood Pr) Greenwood.

***Ambiophonics: Beyond Surround Sound to Virtual Sonic Reality.** Ralph Glasgal & Keith Yates. (Illus.). 105p. 1995. pap. 29.95 (*0-9646634-0-6*) Ambiophonics Inst.

Ambiquous Africa. Georges Balandier. 225p. 1976. pap. 2.25 (*0-380-00560-3*) Avon.

Ambition. Julie Burchill. 1990. mass mkt. 4.95 (*0-06-100048-5*, Harp PBks) HarpC.

Ambition. Mark H. Simon. Ed. by James B. Van Treese. 170p. 1994. pap. 7.95 (*1-56901-042-0*) NW Pub.

Ambition: How We Manage Success & Failure Throughout Our Lives. Gilbert Brim. LC 91-55453. 224p. 1993. pap. 12.00 (*0-465-00118-1*) Basic.

Ambition: The Secret Passion. Joseph Epstein. 324p. 1989. reprint ed. pap. 8.95 (*0-929587-18-9*, Elephant Paperbacks) I R Dee.

Ambition & Beyond: Career Paths of American Politicians. Ed. by Shirley Williams & Edward L. Lascher, Jr. LC 93-9860. 261p. (Orig.). 1993. pap. 21.95 (*0-87772-338-9*) UCB IGS.

Ambition & Love. Just S. Ward. LC 93-33758. 1994. 22.95 (*0-395-68196-0*) HM.

Ambition & Risk Aversion in the Design of Economic Policies. A. S. Brandsma. 200p. 1995. text ed. 61.00 (*981-02-1266-6*) World Scientific Pub.

Ambition, Discrimination & Censorship in Libraries. Jefferson P. Selth. LC 92-56692. (Illus.). 160p. 1993. pap. 20.95 (*0-89950-883-9*) McFarland & Co.

Ambition, Fertility, Loneliness. Samuel Exler. 72p. (Orig.). 1982. pap. 5.95 (*0-931642-11-6*) Lintel.

Ambition for Lovers. Charles Gallagher. (Celebrate Love Ser.). 56p. (Orig.). 1990. pap. text ed. 3.95 (*0-911905-37-5*) Past & Mat Rene Ctr.

Ambition in Ministry: Our Spiritual Struggle with Success, Achievement & Competition. Robert Schnase. LC 92-38155. 144p. 1993. pap. 11.95 (*0-687-30144-0*) Abingdon.

Ambition of Ghosts. Rosmarie Waldrop. (Poetry Chapbooks Ser.: No. 4). 32p. 1979. pap. 2.50 (*0-913282-18-9*) Seven Woods Pr.

Ambition to Rule: Alcibiades & the Politics of Imperialism in Thucydides. Steven Forde. LC 88-47919. 256p. 1989. 33.95 (*0-8014-2138-1*) Cornell U Pr.

Ambitions. William Delligan. 400p. 1988. pap. 3.95 (*1-55817-128-2*, Pinnacle NY) Windsor NY.

Ambitious Angel. large type ed. Barbara Redmayne. (Romance Ser.). 336p. 1988. 15.95 (*0-7089-1855-7*) Ulverscroft.

Ambitious Appetites: Dining, Behavior & Patterns of Consumption in Federal Washington. Barbara G. Carson. (Illus.). 224p. (Orig.). (C). 1990. pap. 9.98 (*1-55835-026-8*) AIA Press.

Ambitious Dreams: The Values Project at Le Moyne College. Donald J. Kirby. LC 90-60900. (Orig.). (C). 1990. 19.95 (*1-55612-362-0*); pap. 14.95 (*1-55612-412-0*) Sheed & Ward MO.

Ambitious Heights: Writing, Friendship, Love: The Jewsbury Sisters, Felicia Hemans & Jane Carlyle. Norma Clarke. 288p. 1990. 65.00 (*0-415-00051-3*, A4233); pap. 17.95 (*0-415-00052-1*, A4237) Routledge.

Ambitious Men: Their Drives, Dreams, & Delusions. Srully Blotnick. 448p. 1988. mass mkt. 4.95 (*0-14-008818-0*, Penguin Bks) Viking Penguin.

Ambitious Sort of Grief: Pregnancy & Neo-Natal Loss. 2nd ed. Marion D. Cohen. LC 86-2894. (Woman in History Ser.: vol. 72). (Illus.). 122p. 1986. pap. 10.00 (*0-934659-03-6*) Liberal Pr.

Ambitious Woman's Guide to a Successful Career. rev. ed. Margaret V. Higginson & Thomas L. Quick. LC 80-65878. 288p. reprint ed. pap. 82.10 (*0-8357-5341-7*, 2023550) Bks Demand.

Ambivalence of Abortion. Linda B. Francke. 1978. 10.00 (*0-394-41080-7*) Random.

Ambivalence of Form: Lukacs, Freud & the Novel. Susan Derwin. 224p. 1992. text ed. 34.00 (*0-8018-4381-2*) Johns Hopkins.

Ambivalent Americans: The Know-Nothing Party in Maryland. Jean H. Baker. LC 76-51813. 224p. reprint ed. pap. 63.90 (*0-8357-5342-5*, 2025826) Bks Demand.

Ambivalent Anti-Colonialism: The United States & the Genesis of West Indian Independence, 1940-1964. Cary Fraser. LC 93-10372. (Contributions in Latin American Studies: No. 3). 248p. 1994. text ed. 55.00 (*0-313-28795-3*, GM8795, Greenwood Pr) Greenwood.

Ambivalent Churchmen & Evangelical Churchwomen: The Religion of the Episcopal Elite in North Carolina, 1800-1860. Richard Rankin. 218p. (C). 1993. text ed. 39.95 (*0-87249-887-5*) U of SC Pr.

Ambivalent Conquests: Maya & Spaniard in Yucatan, 1517-1570. Inga Clendinnen. (Cambridge Latin American Studies: No. 61). (Illus.). 256p. 1987. 59.95 (*0-521-33397-0*) Cambridge U Pr.

Ambivalent Conquests: Maya & Spaniard in Yucatan, 1517-1570. Inga Clendinnen. (Cambridge Latin American Studies: No. 61). (Illus.). 256p. 1989. pap. 14.95 (*0-521-37981-4*) Cambridge U Pr.

Ambivalent Force: Perspectives On the Police. 3rd ed. Abraham S. Blumberg & Elaine Niederhoffer. 452p. (C). 1985. pap. text ed. 29.50 (*0-03-062004-X*) HB Coll Pubs.

Ambivalent Friends: Afro-Americans View the Immigrant. Arnold M. Shankman. LC 81-20309. (Contributions in Afro-American & African Studies: No. 67). (Illus.). xiv, 198p. 1982. text ed. 49.95 (*0-313-23068-4*, SHF/, Greenwood Pr) Greenwood.

Ambivalent Heritage: Euro-American Relations. Peter Duignan & L. H. Gann. LC 94-5916. (Hoover Essays Ser.: No. 7). 1994. write for info. (*0-8179-3702-1*) Hoover Inst Pr.

***Ambivalent Identities: Processes of Mariginalization & Exclusion.** Paula A. Wagoner. Ed. by Victoria Cuffel. (MacArthur Scholar Ser.). 125p. (Orig.). 1994. pap. 4.50 (*1-881157-27-X*) In Ctr Global.

Ambivalent Image: Nineteenth-Century America's Perception of the Jew. Louise A. Mayo. LC 87-45572. 224p. 1988. 32.50 (*0-8386-3318-8*) Fairleigh Dickinson.

***Ambivalent Journey: U. S. Migration & Economic Mobility in North-Central Mexico.** Richard C. Jones. LC 94-18754. 220p. 1995. 45.00x (*0-8165-1473-9*) U of Ariz Pr.

***Ambivalent Magician.** Simon Hawke. (Orig.). 1996. mass mkt. write for info. (*0-446-36521-1*, Aspect) Warner Bks.

Ambivalent Mind: The Neuropsychology of Left & Right. Michael C. Corballis & Ivan L. Beale. LC 83-4026. (Illus.). 328p. 1983. lib. bdg. 39.95 (*0-88229-475-X*) Nelson-Hall.

Ambivalent Moderns: Portraits in Japanese Cultural Identity. Lawrence Olson. 200p. (C). 1992. text ed. 52.00 (*0-8476-7738-9*); pap. text ed. 17.95 (*0-8476-7739-7*) Rowman.

Ambivalent Welcome: Print Media, Public Opinion & Immigration. Rita J. Simon & Susan H. Alexander. LC 92-32671. 288p. 1993. text ed. 52.95 (*0-275-94492-1*, C4492, Praeger Pubs) Greenwood.

Amble Has a Dream. Keith Faulkner. LC 93-86158. (Dino Dudes Ser.). (Illus.). 20p. (J). (ps-1). 1994. 3.95 (*0-8431-3653-7*) Price Stern.

Amblyopia. Ciuffreda. (Illus.). 500p. 1990. 80.00 (*0-409-95171-4*) Buttrwrth-Heinemann.

Amblyopia. Jena Osman. 48p. (Orig.). (C). 1993. pap. text ed. 8.00 (*0-939691-09-4*) Avenue B.

Amblyopia. deluxe ed. Jena Osman. 48p. (Orig.). (C). 1993. pap. text ed. 18.00 (*0-685-66301-9*) Avenue B.

Ambosia Dancing at Mary's. M. W. McGee. Ed. by Joseph F. Lomax & J. Whitebird. (Illus.). 1977. pap. 15.00 (*0-930324-02-1*) Wings Pr.

Amboy Dukes. Irving Shulman. 18.95 (*0-8488-0628-X*) Amereon Ltd.

Ambrogio Lorenzetti: The Palazzo Pubblico, Siena. Randolph Starn. (Great Fresco Cycles of the Renaissance Ser.). 104p. 1994. 23.50 (*0-8076-1313-4*) Braziller.

Ambroise Vollard, Editeur. Una Johnson. (Illus.). 1977. 19.95 (*0-87070-626-8*, 0-8109-6081-8) Mus of Modern Art.

Ambrose Bierce. Vincent Starrett. 1992. reprint ed. lib. bdg. 75.00 (*0-7812-5091-9*) Rprt Serv.

Ambrose Bierce: Great American Short Stories II. Illus. by James McConnell. LC 94-75024. (Classic Short Stories Ser.). 80p. 1994. pap. 4.50 (*1-56103-016-3*) Lake Pub Co.

Ambrose Bierce, a Biography. Carey McWilliams. (BCL1-PS American Literature Ser.). 358p. 1992. reprint ed. lib. bdg. 89.00 (*0-7812-6677-7*) Rprt Serv.

Ambrose Bierce Is Missing: And Other Historical Mysteries. Joe Nickell. LC 91-3049. (Illus.). 192p. 1991. 22.00 (*0-8131-1766-6*) U Pr of Ky.

Ambrose Bierce's Civil War. Ambrose Bierce. Ed. by William McCann. LC 88-32151. 258p. 1956. pap. 9.95 (*0-89526-770-5*) Regnery Pub.

Ambrose of Milan: Church & Court in a Christian Capital. Neil McLynn. LC 94-2261. (Transformation of the Classical Heritage Ser.: Vol. 22). 1994. 45.00 (*0-520-08461-6*) U CA Pr.

***Ambrose of Milan & the End of the Arian-Nicene Conflicts.** Daniel H. Williams. (Oxford Early Christian Studies). 320p. 1995. text ed. 56.00 (*0-19-826464-X*) OUP.

Ambrose Rigge. Charles Kohler. (C). 1989. pap. 21.00 (*1-85072-072-X*, Pub. by W Sessions UK) St Mut.

Ambrose Wathan: Silence. LC 74-188556. (Cistercian Studies: No. 22). 10.95 (*0-87907-822-7*) Cistercian Pubns.

Ambrosia & the Coral Sun. Sherri L. Board. Ed. by Timothy A. Board. LC 93-61236. (Illus.). 256p. (Orig.). (J). 1994. pap. 8.95 (*0-9634767-7-7*) Tug Pr CA.

Ambrosia in an Earthen Vessel: Three Centuries of Audience & Reader Response to the Works of Thomas Middleton. Sara J. Steen. LC 91-11029. (Studies in the Renaissance: No. 31). (Illus.). 245p. 1992. 45.00 (*0-404-62331-X*) AMS Pr.

Ambrosian Cantus. Terence Bailey. (Wissenschaftliche Abhandlungen-Musicological Studies: Vol. 47). 258p. (ENG.). 1987. 52.00 (*0-931902-53-3*) Inst Mediaeval Mus.

Ambrosio. Romulus Linney. 1993. 4.75 (*0-8222-1320-6*) Dramatists Play.

Ambrotype: Old & New. Thomas P. Feldvebel. LC 80-65216. (Illus.). 51p. 1980. pap. 9.95 (*0-89938-001-8*) Tech & Ed Ctr Graph Arts RIT.

Ambrotype & Photographic Instructor; or, Photography on Glass & Paper. M. H. Ellis. 81p. 1991. reprint ed. lib. bdg. 23.00x (*0-8095-5954-4*) Borgo Pr.

Ambulance: The Story of Emergency Transportation of Sick & Wounded Through the Centuries. Katherine T. Barkley. LC 90-62107. 1990. 22.95 (*0-9626357-1-5*); pap. 14.95 (*0-9626357-2-3*) Load N Go Pr.

Ambulance & EMS Driving. James Hanna. 207p. 1982. pap. 18.95 (*0-317-58937-7*) P-H.

Ambulance & EMS Driving. James Hanna. (C). 1983. pap. text ed. 27.00 (*0-8359-0205-6*, Reston) P-H.

Ambulance Attendant. Jack Rudman. (Career Examination Ser.: C-1088). 1994. pap. 29.95 (*0-8373-1088-1*) Nat Learn.

Ambulance Calls: Review Problems in Emergency Care. 2nd ed. Nancy L. Caroline. 1987. pap. text ed. 22.00 (*0-316-12871-6*, Little Med Div) Little.

Ambulance Corpsman. Jack Rudman. (Career Examination Ser.: C-2650). 1994. pap. 29.95 (*0-8373-2650-8*) Nat Learn.

Ambulance Driver. Jack Rudman. (Career Examination Ser.: C-1089). 1994. pap. 27.95 (*0-8373-1089-X*) Nat Learn.

Ambulances. Leslie Geary. (Illus.). 80p. 1991. 17.00 (*0-86025-879-3*, Pub. by Ian Henry Pubns UK) Empire Pub Srvs.

Ambulante Rehabilitation nach Herzinfarkt. K. E. Schenk. 1979. pap. 19.25 (*3-8055-2965-1*) S Karger.

Ambulataory Care Coding. Vickie L. Rogers. 1993. 49.00 (*0-317-05420-1*) Am Hlth Info.

Ambulatory Anesthesia & Sedation. Klepper. 382p. 1991. 99.95 (*0-632-03036-4*) Blackwell Sci.

***Ambulatory Anesthesia Handbook.** Ed. by Rebecca S. Twersky. LC 94-32505. 1994. write for info. (*0-8151-8847-1*) Mosby Yr Bk.

***Ambulatory Anesthesiology: A Problem-Oriented Approach.** Ed. by Kathryn E. McGoldrick. LC 94-1854. 808p. 1994. 89.00 (*0-683-05875-4*) Williams & Wilkins.

Ambulatory Blood Pressure Recording. Hans R. Brunner & Bernard Waeber. 208p. 1992. 58.00 (*0-88167-889-9*) Raven.

***Ambulatory Blood Pressure Recording.** Ed. by Bernard Waeber et al. LC 94-23214. 208p. 1992. 58.00 (*0-7817-0242-9*) Raven.

Ambulatory Care: Organization & Management. Austin Ross et al. LC 83-16709. (Health Services Ser.: No. 1-456). 453p. 1983. text ed. 41.95 (*0-8273-4349-3*) Delmar.

Ambulatory Care: Subject Index & Research Bibliography. Tricia C. Dooley. LC 87-47677. 150p. 1987. 39.50 (*0-88164-656-3*); pap. 34.50 (*0-88164-657-1*) ABBE Pubs Assn.

Ambulatory Care & Insurance Coverage in an Era of Constraint. Ronald M. Andersen et al. LC 87-60398. 250p. 1987. 29.95 (*0-931028-90-6*) Precept Pr.

Ambulatory Care Clinics. Ed. by Peter Allen. 200p. 1989. pap. 1,495.00 (*0-941285-42-1*) FIND-SVP.

Ambulatory Care Documentation. Laura K. Feste. 194p. 1989. 35.00 (*0-317-05421-X*) Am Hlth Info.

Ambulatory Care in New York City 1984, 3 vols., Set. Comp. by Division of Research, Analysis, & Planning Staff. 1985. 60.00 (*0-934459-16-9*) United Hosp Fund.

Ambulatory Care in New York City 1984, Vol. I: Patient Characteristics & Patterns of Hospital Use. Comp. by Division of Research, Analysis, & Planning Staff. 276p. 1985. 25.00 (*0-934459-17-7*) United Hosp Fund.

Ambulatory Care in New York City 1984, Vol. II: Community Profiles: Outpatient Visits & Insurance Coverage. Comp. by Division of Research, Analysis, & Planning Staff. 198p. 1985. 35.00 (*0-934459-18-5*) United Hosp Fund.

Ambulatory Care in New York City 1984, Vol. III: Community Profiles: Emergency Room Visits & Insurance Coverage. Comp. by Division of Research, Analysis, & Planning Staff. 198p. 1985. 35.00 (*0-934459-19-3*) United Hosp Fund.

Ambulatory Care Management. 2nd ed. Austin Ross. 1991. text ed. 41.95 (*0-8273-4613-1*) Delmar.

Ambulatory Care Management & Practice. Ed. by Albert E. Barnett & Gloria G. Mayer. 526p. 1992. 81.00 (*0-8342-0313-8*, 20313) Aspen Pub.

Ambulatory Care Nursing Policies & Procedures Manual. Leigh Emery & Suzanne P. Noone. 1988. 185.00 (*0-87189-790-3*) Aspen Pub.

Ambulatory Care Nursing Standards & Performance Evaluations. Karen Knutson et al. Ed. by Center for Research in Ambulatory Health Care Administration Staff. 83p. 1987. spiral bd. 22.00 (*0-933948-94-8*, 1479) Ctr Res Ambulatory.

Ambulatory Care Quality Assurance Manual. Rowland. 1990. ring bd. 175.00 (*0-8342-0134-8*, 524) Aspen Pub.

Ambulatory Child Health Care Protocols. M. Cohen et al. (Illus.). 518p. (Orig.). 1992. pap. write for info. (*0-924381-02-7*) Sunbelt Med Pubs.

Ambulatory ECG Monitoring: A Monograph. Ed. by Shlomo Stern. LC 78-52542. (Illus.). 207p. reprint ed. pap. 59.00 (*0-8357-6761-2*, 2035422) Bks Demand.

Ambulatory EEG Monitoring. John S. Ebersole. 384p. 1989. 88.50 (*0-88167-505-9*) Raven.

Ambulatory Electrocardiographic Recording. Workshop on Ambulatory ECG Recording, National Heart, Lung & Blood Institute, 1980 et al. LC 80-25268. (Illus.). 476p. reprint ed. pap. 135.70 (*0-8357-5343-3*, 2032303) Bks Demand.

***Ambulatory Electrocardiographs: EC38-1994.** AAMI Staff. (ANSI-AAMI American National Standard Ser.). (Illus.). 40p. (Orig.). 1994. pap. 59.00 (*1-57020-022-X*) Assn Adv Med Instrn.

Ambulatory Esophageal pH Monitoring: Practical Approach & Clinical Applications. Ed. by Joel E. Richter. LC 90-7056. (Illus.). 248p. 1991. text ed. 63.00 (*0-89640-208-8*) Igaku-Shoin.

Ambulatory Externship Manual. Susan Mboya. (C). 1993. 9.50 (*1-56870-066-0*) RonJon Pub.

Ambulatory Family Practice Protocols. Matthew M. Cohen & Anni Lanigan. 264p. 1994. pap. write for info. (*0-924381-18-3*); 3.5 hd write for info. (*0-924381-19-1*) Sunbelt Med Pubs.

Ambulatory Geriatric Care. Yoshikawa et al. 608p. 1993. pap. 45.00 (*0-8016-6543-4*) Mosby Yr Bk.

Ambulatory Gynecologic Surgery. Purvis L. Martin. LC 78-55286. (Illus.). 394p. 1979. 50.00 (*0-88416-209-5*, Yr Bk Med Pubs) Mosby Yr Bk.

Ambulatory Gynecology. 2nd ed. Nichols. 528p. 1995. 52.50 (*0-397-51325-9*) Lippincott.

Ambulatory Health Care Standards Manual, 1990. Ed. by Stephen Berman. 100p. 1987. pap. 50.00 (*0-86688-204-9*) Joint Comm Hlthcare.

Ambulatory Medicine. Ed. by Barry Stimmel. 344p. 1984. pap. text ed. 35.50 (*0-89004-920-3*) Raven.

Ambulatory Medicine: Primary Care of Families. Mark B. Mengel & L. Peter Schweibert. (Illus.). 690p. 1993. pap. text ed. 26.00 (*0-8385-1294-1*, A1294-6) Appleton & Lange.

Ambulatory Monitoring: Cardiovascular System & Applied Applications. Ed. by Carlo Marchesi. (Developments in Cardiovascular Medicine Ser.). 1984. lib. bdg. 145.00 (*0-89838-642-X*) Kluwer Ac.

Ambulatory Monitoring of the Cardiac Patient. Ed. by Daniel David et al. LC 70-6558. (Cardiovascular Clinics Ser.: Vol. 18, No. 3). (Illus.). 218p. (C). 1988. text ed. 50.00 (*0-8036-2344-5*) Davis Co.

Ambulatory Monitoring of the Cardiovascular Patient. Sidney O. Gottlieb. 1992. text ed. 50.00 (*0-07-023918-5*) McGraw.

Ambulatory Obstetrics: Protocols for Nurse Practitioners - Nurse-Midwives. 2nd enl. ed. Winifred Starr et al. 432p. (C). 1990. 62.00 (*0-943671-07-8*) UCSF Schl Nursing.

Ambulatory Obstetrics: Protocols for Nurse Practitioners-Nurse Midwives. Winifred Star et al. 244p. (C). 1987. text ed. 42.00 (*0-943671-05-1*) UCSF Schl Nursing.

***Ambulatory Patient Care.** Linda B. Chitwood. 250p. (Orig.). (C). 1994. pap. 49.95 (*1-878025-63-5*) Western Schls.

Ambulatory Pediatric Care. 2nd ed. Ed. by Robert A. Dershewitz. LC 92-13524. 1992. 59.50 (*0-397-51196-5*) Lippincott.

Ambulatory Pediatrics. 4th ed. J. Green & Haggerty. (Illus.). 544p. 1990. 65.00 (*0-317-99991-5*) Saunders.

Ambulatory Peritoneal Dialysis. Ed. by C. Giordano & M. M. Avram. (Illus.). 318p. 1990. 79.50 (*0-306-43351-6*, Plenum Pr) Plenum.

***Ambulatory Phlebectomy: A Practical Guide for Treating Varicose Veins.** Stefano Ricci et al. 1995. write for info. (*0-8151-7045-9*) Mosby Yr Bk.

Ambulatory Prenatal Nursing Care: Practice Standards for Positive Pregnancy Outcomes. Marjorie R. Berg et al. LC 85-27649. 224p. 1986. pap. 27.95 (*0-8261-5330-5*) Springer Pub.

Ambulatory Services Policy & Procedure Guideline Manual. Joan C. Blanchard & Diane I. Howery. 1991. 75.00 (*1-879575-12-4*) Acad Med Sys.

Ambulatory Surgery & Office Procedures in Head & Neck Surgery. K. J. Lee & Carol Stewart. 352p. 1986. text ed. 125.00 (*0-8089-1803-6*, 792599, Grune) Saunders.

Ambulatory Surgery & the Basics of Surgical Care. 2nd ed. Wolcott. LC 65-9715. 1988. text ed. 59.50 (*0-397-50805-0*, Lippincott Medical) Lippincott.

Ambulatory Surgical Nursing. Nancy Burden. 736p. 1993. text ed. 63.00 (*0-7216-2897-4*) Saunders.

Ambulatory Surgical Nursing: A Nursing Diagnosis Approach. Sharon Summers & Diane W. Ebbert. (Illus.). 352p. 1991. text ed. 39.50 (*0-397-54799-4*) Lippincott.

***Ambulatory Women's Health Care Nursing.** (Certified Nurse Examination Ser.). Date not set. pap. 23.95 (*0-8373-6124-9*) Nat Learn.

***Ambulatory Women's Health Care Nursing.** (Certified Nurse Examination Ser.). Date not set. 39.95 (*0-8373-6174-5*) Nat Learn.

AmbuQual Data Guide: A System for Collecting, Organizing & Scoring Data. Judi Cagiano. (AmbuQual Ser.). 1993. pap. 129.50 (*1-884742-00-9*) Meth Hosp IN.

AmbuQual II: An Ambulatory Quality Assessment & Quality Management System. 2nd ed. Dale S. Benson & Jane A. Miller. (Quality Primary Care Ser.). 345p. 1993. pap. 130.50 (*0-9603164-8-5*) Meth Hosp IN.

AmbuQual IPA. Dale S. Benson. write for info. (*0-9603164-7-7*) Meth Hosp IN.

An Asterisk (*) at the beginning of an entry indicates that the title is appearing in BIP for the first time.

Ambush. 1994. mass mkt. 4.99 (0-373-61438-1, 1-61438-7) Harlequin Bks.

***Ambush.** Lukas. 4.99 (0-679-87025-3) Random.

Ambush. Steve Mackenzie. (Seals Ser.: No. 1). 192p. 1987. pap. 2.50 (0-380-75189-5) Avon.

Ambush. A. L. Marshall. 256p. 1988. pap. 4.50 (0-515-09543-5) Jove Pubns.

Ambush. Herbert E. Read. LC 74-7020. (English Literature Ser.: No. 33). 1974. lib. bdg. 75.00 (0-8383-1996-3) M S G Haskell Hse.

Ambush. large type ed. Donald C. Porter. LC 93-26719. (White Indian Ser.: Bk. VIII). 1993. 21.95 (0-8161-5846-0, Large Print Bks) Hall.

Ambush: The Real Story of Bonnie & Clyde. Larry Grove & Ted Hinton. (Illus.). 1979. 12.50 (0-88319-041-9) Shoal Creek Pub.

***Ambush: The Story of Bill Keys.** Art Kidwell. (Illus.). 200p. 1995. reprint ed. 11.95 (0-914330-31-4); reprint ed. pap. 7.95 (0-9617961-5-4) Desert Moon Pr.

Ambush & Counter Ambush. Australian Military Forces Staff. (Illus.). 80p. 1965. reprint ed. pap. 10.00 (0-87364-098-5) Paladin Pr.

Ambush at Amboseli. Karen Rispin. LC 93-37801. (Anika Scott Ser.). (J). 1994. 4.99 (0-8423-1295-1) Tyndale.

Ambush at Apache Rocks. Jake Logan. (Jake Logan Ser.: No. 177). 1993. pap. 3.99 (0-425-13981-6) Berkley Pub.

***Ambush at Corellia.** Roger M. Allen. Date not set. mass mkt. 5.99 (0-615-00509-8) Bantam.

Ambush at Junction Rock. Robert MacLeod. 1979. pap. 1.75 (0-449-14303-1, GM) Fawcett.

Ambush at Junction Rock. large type ed. Robert Macleod. 1982. 15.95 (0-7089-0855-1) Ulverscroft.

Ambush at Osirak. Herbert Crowder. 1989. mass mkt. 5.99 (0-515-09932-5) Jove Pubns.

Ambush at Rincon. large type ed. Dudley Dean. (Linford Western Library). 304p. 1989. pap. 11.95 (0-7089-6716-7, Linford) Ulverscroft.

Ambush at Skull Pass. Jon Sharpe. (Trailsman Ser.: No. 154). 176p. (Orig.). 1994. pap. 3.99 (0-451-17890-4, Sig) NAL-Dutton.

Ambush at Vladivostok. Phyllis Schlafly & Chester Ward. 1976. 2.00 (0-934640-00-9) Pere Marquette.

Ambush Moon. J. R. Roberts. (Gunsmith Ser.: No. 148). 192p. (Orig.). 1994. pap. 3.99 (0-515-11358-1) Jove Pubns.

Ambush of Ghosts: A Guide to Great Western Film Locations. David Rothel. LC 90-84532. 306p. 1991. 40. 00 (0-944019-10-2) Empire NC.

Ambush Range. Don P. Jenison. 224p. (Orig.). 1980. pap. 1.95 (0-89083-696-5) Zebra.

Ambush Reckoning - Hellbent for a Hangrope - Lurking Gun. D. B. Newton. 416p. 1993. pap. 5.99 (0-8439-3536-7) Dorchester Pub Co.

Ambush Trail. large type ed. Lee Floren. 1992. pap. 16.95 (0-7927-0762-1, Curley Lrg Print) Chivers N Amer.

Ambush Valley. Eric Hammel. 368p. 1990. 22.50 (0-89141-365-0) Presidio Pr.

Ambushed by Grace: The Virtues of a Useless Faith. Thomas W. Currie, III. LC 93-2701. (Princeton Theological Monograph Ser.: No. 32). 1993. pap. 10.00 (1-55635-017-1) Pickwick.

***Ambushed by Love: God's Triumph in Kenya's Terror.** Dorothy Smoker. (Illus.). 284p. 1994. pap. 8.95 (0-87508-740-X) Chr Lit.

Ambushed in Africa. Peter R. Doyle. 1993. write for info. (1-56179-142-3) Focus Family.

Ambushed on the Road to Glory: Finding the Way Through Jesus' Parables. Ed. by Thomas O. Buford. 144p. (Orig.). 1991. pap. 10.95 (0-9628455-6-6) Smyth & Helwys.

AMC Field Guide to Mountain Flowers of New England. Stuart K. Harris et al. LC 64-54301. (Illus.). 192p. 1977. reprint ed. pap. 14.95 (0-910146-12-8) AMC Books.

***AMC Field Guide to New England Alpine Summits.** Slack. 1995. pap. text ed. 12.95 (1-878239-38-4) AMC Books.

AMC Guide to Freshwater Fishing in New England. Brian R. Kologe. LC 91-9522. (Illus.). 288p. 1991. pap. 14.95 (1-878239-07-4) AMC Books.

AMC Guide to Mount Desert Island & Acadia National Park. 5th ed. Ed. by AMC Books Staff. LC 92-47221. (Trail Guide Ser.). (Illus.). 168p. 1993. pap. 10.95 (1-878239-22-8) AMC Books.

AMC Guide to Mount Washington & the Presidential Range. 5th ed. Ed. by Eugene S. Daniell, III. LC 92-7552. (Trail Guide Ser.). 272p. 1992. pap. 10.95 (1-878239-13-9) AMC Books.

AMC Guide to Winter Camping. Stephen Gorman. LC 91-30921. (Illus.). 224p. 1991. pap. 12.95 (1-878239-09-0) AMC Books.

AMC Maine Mountain Guide. 7th ed. Ed. by Elliott M. Bates. (Trail Guide Ser.). 352p. 1993. pap. 15.95 (1-878239-18-X) AMC Books.

AMC Quiet Water Canoe Guide: Massachusetts - Connecticut - Rhode Island. Alex Wilson. LC 93-21820. (Quiet Water Ser.). (Illus.). 240p. 1993. pap. 12. 95 (1-878239-19-8) AMC Books.

AMC Quiet Water Canoe Guide: New Hampshire-Vermont. Alex Wilson. LC 92-4968. (Quiet Water Ser.). (Illus.). 224p. 1992. pap. 12.95 (1-878239-14-7) AMC Books.

AMC River Guide: Maine. 2nd ed. Ed. by Katherine Yates & Carey Philips. LC 91-11409. (River Guide Ser.). (Illus.). 360p. 1991. pap. 11.95 (1-878239-05-8) AMC Books.

AMC River Guide: Massachusetts, Connecticut, Rhode Island. 2nd ed. Appalachian Mountain Club Staff. 1990. pap. 11.95 (0-87823-900-6) Am Soc Eng Ed.

AMC River Guide: Massachusetts, Connecticut, Rhode Island. 2nd ed. Ed. by Steve Tuckerman. LC 90-37338. (River Guide Ser.). (Illus.). 240p. 1990. pap. 11.95 (1-878239-00-7) AMC Books.

AMC River Guide: New Hampshire, Vermont. 2nd ed. Ed. by Victoria Jas. LC 88-27170. (River Guide Ser.). (Illus.). 208p. 1989. pap. 11.95 (0-910146-77-2) AMC Books.

AMC White Mountain Guide. 25th ed. Ed. by Eugene Daniell, III. LC 92-7545. (Trail Guide Ser.). 672p. 1992. pap. 16.95 (1-878239-12-0) AMC Books.

AMC 1975-86. 1987. pap. 16.95 (0-8019-7746-0) Chilton.

AMDP System in Pharmacopsychiatry. Ed. by D. Bobon et al. (Modern Problems of Pharmacopsychiatry Ser.: Vol. 20). (Illus.). vi, 234p. 1983. 105.75 (3-8055-3637-2) S Karger.

Ame du Monde de Platon aux Stoiciens. Joseph Moreau. 200p. 1981. reprint ed. write for info. (3-487-04094-8, Pub. by Georg Olms GW) Lubrecht & Cramer.

Ame et la Danse see Oeuvres

Ame Sensible. Jean Dutourd. 248p. (FRE.). 1985. pap. 11. 95 (0-7859-2018-8, 2070376834) Fr & Eur.

Amebiasis: Human Parasitic Diseases, Vol. 2. Ed. by A. Martinez-Palomo. 270p. 1986. 124.00 (0-444-80728-4) Elsevier.

Amebiasis: Infection & Disease by Entamoeba Histolytica. Ed. by Roberto R. Kretschmer. 288p. 1990. 205.00 (0-8493-5342-4, RC5342) CRC Pr.

Amedee see Three Plays

Amedee see Theatre

Amedeo Amedei. Lee A. Smith. (Greenbird Ser.). 1975. 12. 00 (0-88253-494-7); pap. text ed. 4.80 (0-88253-493-9) Ind-US Inc.

Amedeo Modigliani. (Prestel Postcard Bks.). (Illus.). 18p. 1994. 8.95 (3-7913-1357-6, Pub. by Prestel) TeNeues.

Amedeo Modigliani: Paintings, Sculptures, Drawings. Werner Schmalenbach. (Illus.). 228p. 1990. 65.00 (3-7913-1095-X, Pub. by Prestel) TeNeues.

Ameer Al-Mumineen (Leader of the Believers) 2nd ed. Imam Mohamad Jawad Chirri. 600p. 15.00 (0-317-52359-7) Islamic Ctr.

Amele. John Roberts. 400p. 1987. 72.50 (0-7099-4254-0, Pub. by Croom Helm UK) Routledge Chapman & Hall.

Amelia. Henry Fielding. Ed. & Intro. by David Blewett. 608p. 1987. pap. 7.95 (0-14-043229-9, Penguin Classics) Viking Penguin.

Amelia. Diana Palmer. (Orig.). 1993. mass mkt. 5.99 (0-8041-0974-5) Ivy Books.

Amelia. Fred Wehr. (J). 1994. 15.95 (1-877853-33-X) Nautical & Aviation.

Amelia, a Mid-Nineteenth Century Novel of Kauai. Juliet R. Wichman. LC 79-21726. 1979. pap. 5.95 (0-686-26165-8) Kauai Museum.

***Amelia Absent Amelia Present.** 51p. (Orig.). 1995. pap. 10.95 (0-614-06989-0) Clay Springs.

***Amelia Bedelia.** Garrett Christopher. Ed. by J. Friedland & R. Kessler. (Novel-Ties Ser.). (J). (gr. k-1). 1994. student ed, pap. text ed. 14.95 (1-56982-084-8) Lrn Links.

Amelia Bedelia. Peggy Parish. LC 91-10163. (I Can Read Bk.). (Illus.). 64p. (J). (gr. k-3). 1992. 14.95 (0-06-020186-X); lib. bdg. 14.89 (0-06-020187-8); pap. 3.50 (0-06-444155-5, Trophy) HarpC Child Bks.

Amelia Bedelia & Her Wacky World, 4 vols., Set. 1986. boxed 15.96 (0-380-75238-7, Camelot) Avon.

Amelia Bedelia & the Baby. Peggy Parish. (Snuggle & Read Story Bks.). (Illus.). 64p. (J). (gr. k-3). 1982. pap. 3.99 (0-380-57067-X, Camelot) Avon.

Amelia Bedelia & the Baby. Peggy Parish. LC 80-22263. (Greenwillow Read-Alone Bks.). (Illus.). 64p. (J). (gr. 1-3). 1981. 14.00 (0-688-00316-8); lib. bdg. 13.93 (0-688-00321-4) Greenwillow.

Amelia Bedelia & the Surprise Shower. Peggy Parish. LC 66-18655. (Harper I Can Read Bk.). (Illus.). 64p. (J). (gr. k-3). 1966. 13.95 (0-06-024642-1); lib. bdg. 13.89 (0-06-024643-X) HarpC Child Bks.

Amelia Bedelia & the Surprise Shower. Peggy Parish. LC 66-18655. (Trophy I Can Read Bk.). (Illus.). 64p. (J). (ps-3). 1979. pap. 3.50 (0-06-444019-2, Trophy) HarpC Child Bks.

Amelia Bedelia & the Surprise Shower. unabridged ed. Peggy Parish. (I Can Read Book Ser.). (Illus.). (J). (ps-3). 1990. audio, pap. 6.95 (1-55994-216-9, Caedmon) HarperAudio.

Amelia Bedelia Goes Camping. Peggy Parish. 1986. pap. 3.99 (0-380-70067-0, Camelot) Avon.

Amelia Bedelia Goes Camping. Peggy Parish. LC 84-7979. (Greenwillow Read-Alone Bks.). (Illus.). 56p. (J). (gr. 1-3). 1985. 14.00 (0-688-04058-6); lib. bdg. 13.93 (0-688-04057-8) Greenwillow.

Amelia Bedelia Helps Out. Peggy Parish. (Snuggle & Read Story Bks.). (Illus.). 64p. (J). (gr. k-3). 1981. pap. 3.99 (0-380-53405-3, Camelot) Avon.

Amelia Bedelia Helps Out. Peggy Parish. LC 79-11729. (Greenwillow Read-Alone Bks.). (Illus.). 64p. (J). (gr. 1-3). 1979. 15.00 (0-688-80231-1); lib. bdg. 13.93 (0-688-84231-3) Greenwillow.

Amelia Bedelia Thinking Book. Nancy Polette. (Illus.). 48p. (J). (gr. k-3). 1994. pap. 5.95 (1-879287-10-2) Bk Lures.

Amelia Bedelia's Family Album. Peggy Parish. 48p. (J). 1989. mass mkt. 5.95 (0-380-70760-8, Camelot) Avon.

Amelia Bedelia's Family Album. Peggy Parish. 48p. (J). 1991. pap. 3.99 (0-380-71698-4, Camelot) Avon.

Amelia Bedelia's Family Album. Peggy Parish. LC 87-15641. (Illus.). 48p. (J). (gr. 3-9). 1988. 13.95 (0-688-07676-9); lib. bdg. 11.88 (0-688-07677-7) Greenwillow.

***Amelia County: Virginia Publick Claims.** Janice L. Abercrombie & Richard Slatten. (Virginia Publick Claims Ser.). ix, 107p. 1992. pap. 14.00x (0-8095-8506-5) Borgo Pr.

Amelia County: Virginia Publick Claims. Janice L. Abercrombie & Richard Slatten. (Virginia Publick Claims Ser.). ix, 107p. (C). 1992. reprint ed. lib. bdg. 35. 00x (0-8095-8302-X) Borgo Pr.

***Amelia County, Virginia Deeds, 1759-1765.** T.L.C. Genealogy Staff. LC 90-70914. 188p. (Orig.). 1990. spiral bd., pap. 12.00 (1-886633-40-1) TLC Genealogy.

***Amelia County, Virginia Deeds, 1765-1768.** T.L.C. Genealogy Staff. LC 90-70914. 71p. (Orig.). 1990. spiral bd., pap. 10.00 (1-886633-41-X) TLC Genealogy.

***Amelia County, Virginia, Tax Lists, 1736-1764: An Every-Name Index.** T.L.C. Genealogy Staff. 217p. (Orig.). 1993. spiral bd., pap. 15.00 (1-886633-42-8) TLC Genealogy.

Amelia Earhart. Kathryn S. Miller. 1993. 3.45 (0-87129-291-2, A54) Dramatic Pub.

Amelia Earhart. Eileen Morey. LC 94-556. (Importance of... Biographies Ser.). (Illus.). 112p. (J). (gr. 5-8). 1995. 16.95 (1-56006-065-4) Lucent Bks.

Amelia Earhart. Muriel E. Morrissey. (Illus.). 1977. pap. 3.95 (0-88388-044-X) Bellerophon Bks.

Amelia Earhart. John Parlin. (Illus.). 80p. 1991. pap. 3.50 (0-440-40117-8) Dell.

Amelia Earhart. Blythe Randolph. LC 90-49175. (American Cavalcade Ser.). (Illus.). 160p. (J). (gr. 6-10). 1991. lib. bdg. 9.95 (1-55905-078-0) Marshall Cavendish.

Amelia Earhart. Nancy Shore. (American Women of Achievement Ser.). (Illus.). 112p. (Orig.). (YA). (gr. 5 up). 1987. 17.95 (1-55546-651-6); pap. 9.95 (0-7910-0415-5) Chelsea Hse.

Amelia Earhart. Richard Tames. LC 89-14972. (Life & Times Ser.). (J). (gr. 4-6). 1990. lib. bdg. 12.95 (0-531-10851-1) Watts.

Amelia Earhart. Richard Tames. (Life & Times Ser.). (Illus.). 32p. (J). (gr. 5 up). 1991. pap. 5.95 (0-531-24610-8) Watts.

Amelia Earhart. Carol A. Pearce. LC 87-9102. (Makers of America Ser.). (Illus.). 175p. reprint ed. pap. 49.90 (0-7837-5340-3, 2045082) Bks Demand.

Amelia Earhart: A Biography. Doris L. Rich. (Illus.). 1989. 24.95 (0-87474-836-4) Smithsonian.

Amelia Earhart: Adventure in the Sky. Francene Sabin. LC 82-15987. (Illus.). 48p. (J). (gr. 4-6). 1983. lib. bdg. 10. 79 (0-89375-839-6); pap. text ed. 3.50 (0-89375-840-X) Troll Assocs.

Amelia Earhart: Aviation Pioneer. Roxane Chadwick. (Lerner Achievers Ser.). (Illus.). 56p. (J). (gr. 4-9). 1987. lib. bdg. 13.50 (0-8225-0484-7, Lerner Publctns); pap. 4.95 (0-8225-9515-X, Lerner Publctns) Lerner Group.

***Amelia Earhart: Aviator.** (Junior World Biographies Ser.). (Illus.). 80p. (J). (gr. 3-6). Date not set. lib. bdg. 14.95 (0-7910-2294-3) Chelsea Hse.

Amelia Earhart: Challenging the Skies. Susan Sloate. (" Great Lives" Biography Ser.). (Illus.). 128p. 1989. pap. 4.99 (0-449-90396-6, Columbine) Fawcett.

Amelia Earhart: Courage in the Sky. Mona Kerby. LC 92-19520. (Women of Our Time Ser.). (Illus.). 64p. (J). (gr. 3-5). 1992. pap. 4.99 (0-14-034263-X) Puffin Bks.

Amelia Earhart: Flying for Adventure. Mary D. Wade. (J). (gr. 4-7). 1992. pap. 5.00 (0-395-64539-5) HM.

Amelia Earhart: Flying for Adventure. Mary D. Wade. LC 91-37645. (Gateway Biography Ser.). (Illus.). 48p. (J). (gr. 2-4). 1992. lib. bdg. 13.40 (1-56294-059-7); pap. 6.95 (1-56294-763-X) Millbrook Pr.

Amelia Earhart: Leading Lady of the Air Age. Lillee D. Zierau. Ed. by D. Steve Rahmas. LC 73-190237. (Outstanding Personalities Ser.: No. 19). 32p. (J). (gr. 7-12). 1972. lib. bdg. 4.95 (0-87157-519-1) SamHar Pr.

Amelia Earhart: Lost Legend. Donald M. Wilson. LC 93-72991. (Illus.). 224p. 1995. pap. 12.95 (0-9637777-0-X) Enigma Pr.

Amelia Earhart: Lost Legend. Donald M. Wilson. (Illus.). 224p. 1995. 16.95 (0-9637777-1-8) Enigma Pr.

Amelia Earhart: Missing, Declared Dead. Anita Larsen. LC 91-19246. (History's Mysteries Ser.). (Illus.). 48p. (J). (gr. 5-6). 1992. text ed. 11.95 (0-89686-613-0, Crstwood Hse) Silver Burdett Pr.

Amelia Earhart: Opposing Viewpoints. Jane Leder. LC 89-12028. (Great Mysteries Ser.). (Illus.). 112p. (J). (gr. 5-8). 1989. lib. bdg. 16.95 (0-89908-070-7) Greenhaven.

Amelia Earhart: Pioneer in the Sky. John Parlin. (Discovery Biographies Ser.). (Illus.). 80p. (J). (gr. 2-6). 1992. reprint ed. lib. bdg. 12.95 (0-7910-1437-1) Chelsea Hse.

Amelia Earhart - Charles Lindbergh. Naunerle C. Farr & John N. Fago. (Pendulum Illustrated Biography Ser.). (Illus.). (J). (gr. 4-12). 1979. student ed 1.25 (0-88301-373-8); pap. text ed. 2.95 (0-88301-349-5) Pendulum Pr.

Amelia Earhart Flies Around the World. Kath Davies. LC 93-29954. (Great Twentieth Century Expeditions Ser.). (Illus.). 32p. (J). (gr. 4 up). 1994. text ed. 13.95 (0-87518-531-2, Dillon Silver Burdett) Silver Burdett Pr.

Amelia, My Courageous Sister: Biography of Amelia Earhart. Muriel E. Morrissey & Carol L. Osborne. (Biography Ser.). (Illus.). 320p. 1987. pap. 19.95 (0-940997-02-9) Aviation.

Amelia, My Courageous Sister: Biography of Amelia Earhart, Set. Muriel E. Morrissey & Carol L. Osborne. (Biography Ser.). (Illus.). 320p. 1987. pap. 29.95 (0-685-17989-3) Aviation.

Amelia's Celebration. Jirina Marton. (Illus.). 24p. (J). (ps-3). 1992. lib. bdg. 15.95 (1-55037-221-1, Pub. by Annick CN); pap. 5.95 (1-55037-220-3, Pub. by Annick CN) Firefly Bks Ltd.

Amelia's Fantastic Flight. Rose Bursik. LC 91-28809. (Illus.). 32p. (J). (ps-2). 1992. 14.95 (0-8050-1872-7, Bks Young Read) H Holt & Co.

Amelia's Fantastic Flight. Rose Bursik. LC 91-28809. (J). (ps-3). 1994. pap. 5.95 (0-8050-3386-6) H Holt & Co.

***Amelia's Intrigue.** Judith A. Lansdowne. 352p. 1995. pap. 3.99 (0-8217-5013-5) Zebra.

Amelia's Nine Lives. Lorna Balian. (Illus.). 32p. (J). (ps-3). 1986. lib. bdg. 12.95 (0-687-01250-3) Humbug Bks.

Amelia's Nine Lives. Lorna Balian. (Illus.). 32p. (J). (ps-3). 1987. reprint ed. 7.50 (0-687-37096-5) Humbug Bks.

***Amelia's Notebook.** Marissa Moss. LC 94-5382. (Illus.). 32p. (J). (gr. 2 up). 1995. 14.00 (1-883672-18-X) Tricycle Pr.

***Amelia's Postcard.** EAK, pseud. 44p. 1991. per., pap. 4.00 (1-886206-03-1) Venom Pr.

Amelia's Road. Linda J. Altman. LC 92-59982. (Illus.). 32p. (J). (gr. k-5). 1993. 14.95 (1-880000-04-0) Lee & Low Bks.

***Amelia's Road.** Linda J. Altman. LC 92-59982. (Illus.). 32p. (J). (gr. k-4). 1995. pap. 5.95 (1-880000-27-X) Lee & Low Bks.

Amelie. M. S. Robbins. 1986. pap. 5.00 (0-941240-07-X) Ommation Pr.

Amelioration of the Human Environment: IGU Congress, Moscow, 1976, Proceedings, Pt. 1. Ed. by Yuri Medvedkov. 1977. pap. 23.00 (0-08-021322-7, Pergamon Pr) Elsevier.

Amelioration of the Slaves in the British Empire, 1790-1833. Robert E. Luster. LC 92-27278. (American University Studies: History: Ser. IX, Vol. 134). 1994. write for info. (0-8204-2068-9) P Lang Pubs.

Ameliorez vos Relations. James Hilt. 160p. (FRE.). 1986. 3.95 (0-8297-0541-4) Life Pubs Intl.

***Amen: A Gathering of Forty Prayers & Blessings from Around the World.** Emily Gwathmey & Suzanne Slesin. 1995. 22.95 (0-670-86045-X, Viking) Viking Penguin.

Amen: The Secret Waters of the Great Pyramid. Ridgely A. Mu'Min. (Illus.). 196p. (Orig.). 1988. lib. bdg. 29.95 (0-317-93344-2); pap. 16.95 (0-317-93345-0) AM Distributors.

Amen! An Interrupted Prayer. Ted Gibbons. (Keepsake Bookcards Ser.). 6p. (YA). 1990. pap. text ed. 1.95 (0-929985-00-1) Jackman Pubng.

Amen, Brother Ben: A Mississippi Collection of Children's Rhymes. Marice C. Brown. LC 78-32017. 111p. reprint ed. pap. 31.70 (0-8357-5344-1, 2032001) Bks Demand.

Amen Corner. James Baldwin. 1990. mass mkt. 5.99 (0-440-20662-6, LE) Dell.

Amen! Until Tomorrow. John D. Wolf. 1990. pap. 9.95 (1-55673-226-0, 7734) CSS OH.

Amen-Worte Jesu: Eine Untersuchung zum Problem der Legitimation in Apokalyptischer Rede. Klaus Berger. (Beiheft 39 zur Zeitschrift fuer die Neuetestamentliche Wissenschaft Ser.). (C). 1970. 60.00 (3-11-006445-6) De Gruyter.

Amenability. A. Paterson. LC 88-14485. (SURV Ser.: No. 29). 452p. 1988. 110.00 (0-8218-1529-6, SURV-29) Am Math.

AMEND - Philosophy & Curriculum for Treating Batterers. Michael Lindsey et al. LC 91-73217. (Illus.). 124p. (Orig.). 1993. pap. 16.95 (1-880197-04-9) Gylantic Pub.

AMEND - Philosophy & Curriculum for Treating Batterers, Set. Michael Lindsey et al. LC 91-73217. (Illus.). 124p. (Orig.). 1993. 28.90 (1-880197-06-5) Gylantic Pub.

Amending America. R. Bernstein & J. Agel. Date not set. write for info. (0-8129-6357-1) Random.

Amending America: If We Love the Constitution So Much, Why Do We Keep Trying to Change It? Richard B. Bernstein & Jerome Agel. LC 92-50499. 1993. 25.00 (0-8129-2038-4, Times Bks) Random.

***Amending America: If We Love the Constitution So Much, Why Do We Keep Trying to Change It?** Richard B. Bernstein & Jerome Agel. 416p. 1995. pap. 17.95 (0-7006-0715-3) U Pr of KS.

Amending of the Federal Constitution. Lester B. Orfield. LC 74-146151. (American Constitutional & Legal History Ser). (Illus.). 1971. reprint ed. lib. bdg. 29.50 (0-306-70094-8) Da Capo.

Amending of the Federal Constitution. Lester B. Orfield. LC 42-36735. (Michigan Legal Publications). xxvii, 242p. 1984. reprint ed. lib. bdg. 37.50 (0-89941-324-2, 303160) W S Hein.

Amending Powers & Constitutional Amendments: From First to the Latest Amendment. Paras Diwan & Peeyushi Diwan. (C). 1990. 175.00 (0-89771-207-2) St Mut.

Amending the Equality Laws. Catherine Scorer & Ann Sedley. (C). 1988. 21.00 (0-946088-04-7, Pub. by NCCL UK) St Mut.

***Amending the Federal Constitution to Require a Balance Budget.** Ronald Snell & Scott Mackey. (Legislative Finance Paper Ser.: No. 96). 17p. 1994. 15.00 (1-55516-008-5, 5101-96) Natl Conf State Legis.

Amendment. Sue Robinson. 1990. 17.95 (1-55972-018-2, Birch Ln Pr) Carol Pub Group.

Amendment. Sue Robinson. 256p. 1991. pap. 4.50 (0-8216-2501-2, Carol Paperbacks) Carol Pub Group.

Amendment of the Community Treatise. Tony Venables & David Martin. 215p. 1992. pap. 180.00 (0-406-00269-X, U.K.) Butterworth Legal Pubs.

Amendment to the Constitution: Averting the Decline & Fall of America. James O. Pace. 179p. (Orig.). 1985. pap. text ed. 10.00 (0-9615268-0-7) JP SF.

***Amendment 2 Murder.** Nigel Stevens. 220p. (Orig.). 1994. pap. 12.95 (0-9642911-0-X) Tanner Long.

Amendments to Solas Nineteen Seventy-Four Concerning Radiocommunications for the Global Maritime Distress & Safety System. International Maritime Organization Staff. 1989. text ed. 80.00 (0-89771-858-5, Pub. by Intl Maritime Org UK) St Mut.

Amendments to the Annex of the Protocol of 1978 Relating to Marpol 73, 1984. International Maritime Organization Staff. 1984. text ed. 30.00 (0-89771-947-6, Pub. by Intl Maritime Org UK) St Mut.

***Amendments to the Constitution: A Commentary.** George Anastaplo. 432p. 1994. text ed. 48.50x (0-8018-4959-4); pap. text ed. 16.95x (0-8018-4960-8) Johns Hopkins.

An Asterisk (*) at the beginning of an entry indicates that the title is appearing in BIP for the first time.

223

A

Amendments to the Convention & to the Operating Agreement on the International Maritime Satellite Organization, 1985. IMO Staff. (ENG, FRE, RUS & SPA.). (C). 1985. 35.00 (*0-7855-0014-6*, Pub. by Intl Maritime Org UK) St Mut.

Amendments to the Convention & to the Operating Agreement on the International Maritime Satellite Organization, 1989. IMO Staff. (C). 1989. 50.00 (*0-7855-0015-4*, Pub. by Intl Maritime Org UK) St Mut.

Amends for a Murder. large type ed. M. D. Lake. 1991. 17.95 (*0-7451-8227-5*, AH0252, Curley Lrg Print) Chivers N Amer.

Amends for Murder. M. D. Lake. 224p. (Orig.). 1989. mass mkt. 4.99 (*0-380-75865-2*) Avon.

Amenity & Urban Planning: The Origin & Role of the Aesthetic Element in Modern Practice. David L. Smith. (Illus.). 247p. 1974. 28.00 (*0-8464-0038-3*) Beekman Pubs.

Amenity Grassland: An Ecological Perspective. Ed. by I. H. Rorison & Roderick Hunt. LC 79-40823. (Illus.). 275p. reprint ed. pap. 78.40 (*0-8357-5345-X*, 2030384) Bks Demand.

Amenity Resource Valuation: Integrating Economics with Other Disciplines. George L. Peterson et al. LC 88-50862. 265p. 1988. 27.95 (*0-910251-27-4*) Venture Pub PA.

Amer Best Recipes - 94. Oxmoor Staff. 1994. 17.95 (*0-8487-1163-7*) Oxmoor Hse.

***Amer Jihad.** Steven Barboza. 1995. pap. 14.00 (*0-385-47694-9*) Doubleday.

***Amer Motorcycle Classics.** 1994. 9.98 (*0-7853-0668-4*) Pubns Intl Ltd.

Amer. Woman 1994-95 PA. Stone Costello. 1994. pap. 12.95 (*0-393-31185-6*) Norton.

Amerasia Papers: Some Problems in the History of US-China Relations. John S. Service. LC 72-635322. (University of California, Center for Chinese Studies, China Research Monographs: No. 7). 220p. reprint ed. pap. 62.70 (*0-8357-5346-8*, 2019467) Bks Demand.

AMERCE Business. abr. ed. Luanna C. Blagrove. (AMERCE Business Ser.). 250p. 1987. text ed. 24.95 (*0-939776-36-7*) Blagrove Pubns.

AMERCE Diatribe Covenant Government. abr. ed. Intro. by Luanna C. Blagrove. (Illus.). 250p. 1988. 24.95 (*0-939776-25-1*); text ed. 24.95 (*0-317-55116-7*) Blagrove Pubns.

Amerce Malpractice. abr. ed. Luanna C. Blagrove. 235p. 1988. 24.95 (*0-939776-40-5*) Blagrove Pubns.

AMERCE Management. abr. ed. Intro. by Luanna C. Blagrove. (AMERCE Management Ser.). (Illus.). 250p. 1988. 24.95 (*0-939776-06-5*) Blagrove Pubns.

AMERCE Read, Write, or Arithmetic. abr. ed. Intro. by Luanna C. Blagrove. (Illus.). 250p. 1988. 24.95 (*0-939776-33-2*) Blagrove Pubns.

AMERCE Subcontractor. abr. ed. Intro. by Luanna C. Blagrove. (Illus.). 275p. 1988. 24.95 (*0-939776-24-3*) Blagrove Pubns.

AMERCE Tribute Account. abr. ed. Luanna C. Blagrove. (Illus.). 250p. 1988. Anabasis, 250 pgs. 24.95 (*0-939776-28-6*); Tax, 250 pgs. write for info. (*0-939776-29-4*); Bookkeeping, 250 pgs. write for info. (*0-939776-30-8*) Blagrove Pubns.

AMERCE Tribute Account: Accounting. abr. ed. Luanna C. Blagrove. (AMERCE Tribute Account Ser.). (Illus.). 250p. 1987. text ed. 24.95 (*0-939776-31-6*) Blagrove Pubns.

Amerce Tribute Account: Accounting. abr. ed. Luanna C. Blagrove. (AMERCE Tribute Account Ser.). (Illus.). 235p. 1988. 24.95 (*0-939776-27-8*) Blagrove Pubns.

***Ameresque: The Snap Wyatt Poems.** Robert Fitterman. 52p. 1994. pap. 6.00 (*1-886353-00-X*) B Downs Bks.

America. Jean Baudrillard. Tr. by Chris Turner. 200p. 1989. 29.50 (*0-86091-220-5*, Pub. by Verso UK); pap. text ed. 13.95 (*0-86091-978-1*, Pub. by Verso UK) Routledge Chapman & Hall.

America, 2 vols. Charles M. Dollar. Incl. Vol. 1. Changing Times to 1877. LC 78-12242. 264p. 1979. 7.95 (*0-471-05908-0*); Vol. 2. Changing Times Since 1865. LC 78-12242. 1979. (*0-471-05907-2*); LC 78-12242. 1979. Combined Ed. 23.95 (*0-471-05029-6*) Wiley.

America. Spencer Hart. (Bertinetti Ser.). (Illus.). 128p. 1992. 14.98 (*0-8317-0803-4*) Smithmark.

America. Photos by Fred Hirschmann. (Illus.). 224p. 1994. 50.00 (*1-55868-195-7*) Gr Arts Ctr Pub.

***America.** David Kolenich. 310p. Date not set. pap. 9.95 (*0-7610-0305-3*) NW Pub.

America. Jason Meyers. 1991. 29.99 (*0-517-69507-3*) Random Hse Value.

America. Patrizia Raffin. (Illus.). 128p. 1993. 12.98 (*0-8317-9069-5*) Smithmark.

America. Illus. by Jake Rajs. LC 90-8169. 256p. 1990. 50.00 (*0-8478-1244-8*) Rizzoli Intl.

America. Ralph Steadman. (Illus.). 120p. 1989. reprint ed. 35.00 (*0-930193-95-4*); reprint ed. pap. 14.95 (*0-930193-78-4*) Fantagraph Bks.

America: A Guide to the Experience. David S. Ryan. (Illus.). 144p. 1989. 24.95 (*0-905116-16-X*, Pub. by Kozmik Pr Centre UK); pap. 17.95 (*0-905116-17-8*) Seven Hills Bk.

America: A History of the United States, 2 vols. Norman K. Risjord. (Illus.). (C). 1985. text ed. write for info. (*0-13-024340-X*) P-H.

America: A History of the United States, 2 vols., Vol. I. Norman K. Risjord. (Illus.). 368p. (C). 1985. pap. text ed. write for info. (*0-13-024324-8*) P-H.

***America: A Narrative History.** George Tindall & David Shi. 1996. teacher ed, pap. text ed. write for info. (*0-393-96878-2*) Norton.

America: A Narrative History. George B. Tindall & David Shi. (Illus.). (C). 1992. pap. text ed. write for info. (*0-393-96154-0*) Norton.

America: A Narrative History. George B. Tindall & David Shi. (Illus.). (C). 1992. pap. text ed., trans. write for info. (*0-393-96155-9*) Norton.

America: A Narrative History. abr. ed. George B. Tindall & David E. Shi. (Illus.). (C). 1989. trans. write for info. (*0-318-63405-8*); Computer test item file (upon adoption only). write for info. (*0-318-63404-X*) Norton.

***America: A Narrative History.** 4th ed. George B. Tindall & David E. Shi. 1400p. (C). 1996. text ed. 38.95 (*0-393-96873-1*) Norton.

America: A Narrative History, I. George B. Tindall & David Shi. (Illus.). (C). 1992. pap. text ed. 23.95 (*0-393-96149-4*) Norton.

America: A Narrative History, I. George B. Tindall & David Shi. (Illus.). (C). 1992. student ed, pap. text ed. 13.95 (*0-393-96152-4*) Norton.

America: A Narrative History, II. George B. Tindall & David Shi. (Illus.). (C). 1992. pap. text ed. 23.95 (*0-393-96151-6*) Norton.

America: A Narrative History, II. George B. Tindall & David Shi. (Illus.). (C). 1992. pap. text ed. 13.95 (*0-393-96153-2*) Norton.

America: A Narrative History, Set. 3rd ed. George B. Tindall & David Shi. (Illus.). (C). 1992. text ed. 39.95 (*0-393-96148-6*) Norton.

***America: A Narrative History, Vol. 1.** George Tindall & David Shi. 1996. pap. text ed. write for info. (*0-393-96874-X*); student ed, pap. text ed. write for info. (*0-393-96876-6*) Norton.

***America: A Narrative History, Vol. 2.** George Tindall & David Shi. 1996. pap. text ed. write for info. (*0-393-96875-8*); pap. text ed. write for info. (*0-393-96877-4*) Norton.

America: A Participatory Democracy. Elmer J. Hankes. (Illus.). 124p. (Orig.). 1989. pap. 8.50 (*0-925837-00-8*) Hankes Found.

America: A Photographic Journey. (Illus.). 1991. 14.99 (*0-517-06031-0*) Random Hse Value.

America: A Portrait in History. 2nd ed. David Burner et al. Incl. Vol. 1. 1978. pap. text ed. 16.95 (*0-13-024232-2*); (Illus.). 1978. write for info. (*0-318-54910-7*) P-H.

America: A Practical Handbook. Ronald E. Mitchell. LC 73-13144. (Foreign Travelers in America, 1810-1935 Ser.). 318p. 1974. reprint ed. 26.95 (*0-405-05467-X*) Ayer.

America: A Study in Heritage - an Interdisciplinary Approach. 7th ed. Frank W. Fox & Clayne L. Pope. 800p. 1993. per. 27.16 (*0-8403-8293-6*) Kendall-Hunt.

America: A Study in Heritage - An Interdisciplinary Approach Workbook. 7th ed. Frank W. Fox & Clayne L. Pope. 208p. 1993. spiral bd. 14.36 (*0-8403-8473-4*) Kendall-Hunt.

America: A View from Above. R. O. Mathews. 240p. 1990. 24.99 (*0-517-69508-1*) Random Hse Value.

America: An Aerial View. Jim Doane, Jr. (J). (ps-12). 1986. 5.00 (*0-936672-01-3*) Aerial Photo.

America: Art & the West. Celeste M. Adams et al. (Illus.). 132p. 1987. 27.50 (*0-8109-1856-0*) Abrams.

America: Awaiting the Verdict. Mike Fuselier. LC 91-78321. 96p. 1992. pap. 4.99 (*1-56384-014-6*) Huntington Hse.

America: Early Maps of the New World. Rudiger Finsterwalder et al. Ed. by Hans Wolff. (Illus.). 192p. 1992. 85.00 (*3-7913-1232-4*, Pub. by Prestel) TeNeues.

America: Five Hundred Anos Despues. Alberto Mottesi. 164p. (Orig.). (SPA.). 1992. pap. 10.95 (*0-9633528-0-6*) A Mottesi Evang Assn.

America: From Sea to Shining Sea. Jerry Aten. 160p. (J). (gr. 4 up). 1988. student ed 12.95 (*0-86653-434-2*, GA1044) Good Apple.

America: God's Chosen Land of Liberty. Duane S. Crowther. LC 87-82115. 112p. 1987. 10.98 (*0-88290-320-9*) Horizon Utah.

America: Ideal & Reality. Werner Stark. LC 73-19226. (Illus.). 115p. 1974. reprint ed. text ed. 49.75 (*0-8371-7313-2*, STAM, Greenwood Pr) Greenwood.

***America: Of Thee I Sing.** Ariel Books Staff. (Illus.). 368p. 1995. pap. 4.95 (*0-8362-0715-7*) Andrews & McMeel.

America: Or, a General Survey of the Political Situation of the Several Powers of the Western Continent. Alexander H. Everett. LC 70-111575. 1970. reprint ed. lib. bdg. 45.00 (*0-678-00651-2*) Kelley.

America: Past & Present. 3rd ed. Robert A. Divine et al. (C). 1990. text ed. 58.00 (*0-673-38864-6*) HarpCollege.

America: Past & Present, 2 vols., I. 3rd ed. Robert A. Divine et al. (C). 1990. pap. text ed. 42.00 (*0-673-38865-4*) HarpCollege.

America: Past & Present, 2 vols., II. 3rd ed. Robert A. Divine et al. (C). 1990. pap. text ed. 42.00 (*0-673-38866-2*) HarpCollege.

America: Past & Present, Vol. I. 3rd ed. Robert A. Divine & T. H. Breen. (C). 1993. text ed. 22.50 (*0-673-46759-7*) HarpCollege.

America: Past & Present, Vol. I. 3rd ed. Robert A. Divine & T. H. Breen. (C). 1993. Study guide. 15.50 (*0-673-46762-7*) HarpCollege.

America: Past & Present, Vol II. 3rd ed. Robert A. Divine & T. H. Breen. (C). 1993. text ed. 22.50 (*0-673-46760-0*) HarpCollege.

America: Past & Present, Vol II. 3rd ed. Robert A. Divine & T. H. Breen. (C). 1993. Study guide. 15.50 (*0-673-46763-5*) HarpCollege.

America: Readings in Themes & Eras. Mary S. Sheridan. LC 92-21594. 368p. (Orig.). (C). 1992. pap. text ed. 34.50 (*0-8191-8775-5*) U Pr of Amer.

America: Religions & Religion. 2nd ed. Catherine L. Albanese. 548p. (C). 1992. pap. 31.95 (*0-534-16488-9*) Intl Thomson.

America: The Fifty States. 1985. 34.95 (*0-517-46014-9*) Random Hse Value.

America: The Glorious Republic. Henry F. Graff. 1984. text ed. 54.20 (*0-395-33992-8*) HM.

America: The Glorious Republic. Henry F. Graff. 1984. teacher ed, pap. 24.96 (*0-395-33993-6*) HM.

America: The Glorious Republic. Henry F. Graff. 1984. Voice of America Reasings. pap. 24.80 (*0-395-35986-4*) HM.

America: The Glorious Republic, 2 vols. 2nd ed. Norman K. Risjord. (Illus.). 450p. (C). 1987. To 1877, 450 pgs. pap. text ed. write for info. (*0-13-025156-9*); Since 1865, 400 pgs. pap. text ed. write for info. (*0-13-025198-4*) P-H.

America: The Glorious Republic, from 1877, Vol. 2. Henry F. Graff. 1985. student ed, pap. 10.76 (*0-395-38178-9*); 30.12 (*0-395-38177-0*) HM.

America: The Glorious Republic, from 1877, Vol. 2. Henry F. Graff. 1985. text ed. 46.72 (*0-395-38175-4*) HM.

America: The Glorious Republic, from 1877, Vol. 2. Henry F. Graff. 1985. teacher ed write for info. (*0-318-58981-8*); teacher ed, pap. 23.88 (*0-395-38176-2*) HM.

America: The Glorious Republic, to 1877, Vol. 1. Henry F. Graff. 1985. text ed. write for info. (*0-318-58980-X*); teacher ed, pap. 23.88 (*0-395-38154-1*); teacher ed, pap. 10.76 (*0-395-38156-8*); pap. 11.84 (*0-395-38157-6*); 30.12 (*0-395-38155-X*) HM.

America: The Jewish Experience. Sondra Leiman. Ed. by Jonathan Sarna. (Illus.). (Orig.). (J). (gr. 4-6). 1994. teacher ed 15.00 (*0-8074-0501-9*, 208034); pap. text ed. 12.00 (*0-8074-0500-0*, 123938) UAHC.

America: The Men & Their Guns That Made Her Great. Ed. by Craig Boddington. 200p. 1981. 19.95 (*0-8227-3022-7*) Petersen Pub.

America: The Origin of Her Present Conflict, Her Prospect for the Slave & Her Claim for Anti-Slavery Sympathy. James W. Massie. LC 75-83887. (Black Heritage Library Collection). 1977. 21.95 (*0-8369-8628-8*) Ayer.

America: To Pray or Not to Pray. rev. ed. Charles D. Barton. LC 88-194216. (Illus.). 216p. 1989. reprint ed. pap. 6.95 (*0-925279-00-5*); reprint ed. spiral bd. 8.95 (*0-925279-01-3*) Wallbuilders.

America: Travel & Exploration. Steven Kagle. LC 78-71883. 1979. 12.95 (*0-87972-134-0*); pap. 7.95 (*0-87972-171-5*) Bowling Green Univ.

America: What Went Wrong? Donald L. Barlett & James B. Steele. 216p. 1992. pap. 6.95 (*0-8362-7001-0*) Andrews & McMeel.

America: What Went Wrong? Bartlett. 20.95 (*0-8488-1530-0*) Amereon Ltd.

America: Who Really Pays the Taxes? Donald L. Barlett & James B. Steele. 1994. 9.95 (*0-671-87157-9*, Touchstone Bks) S&S Trade.

America - Land of the Rising Sun. Don Smithana. (Illus.). 256p. (Orig.). 1991. pap. 9.95 (*0-9627877-0-1*) Anasazi Pub.

America! A Concise History. William J. Rorabaugh & Donald T. Critchlow. 626p. 1994. pap. 28.95 (*0-534-13614-1*) Intl Thomson.

America, a Place Called Hope? Conor O'Clery. 222p. 1993. pap. 18.95 (*0-86278-342-9*, Pub. by OBrien Pr IE) Dufour.

America Abandoned: John Singleton Copley's American Years, 1738-1774, an Interpretative History. Richard Klayman. LC 83-10288. (Illus.). 125p. (Orig.). (C). 1983. pap. text ed. 17.50 (*0-8191-3339-6*) U Pr of Amer.

America after Sixty Years: Diaries of Two Generations of Englishmen. Morgan P. Price. LC 73-13146. (Foreign Travelers in America, 1810-1935 Ser.). (Illus.). 242p. 1974. reprint ed. 23.95 (*0-405-05470-X*) Ayer.

America after Vietnam: Legacies of a Hated War. Edward F. Dolan. LC 89-8982. (Illus.). 160p. (YA). (gr. 7-12). 1989. lib. bdg. 14.98 (*0-531-10793-0*) Watts.

America Against Itself: Moral Vision & the Public Order. Richard J. Neuhaus. LC 91-51112. (C). 1992. text ed. 19.95 (*0-268-00633-4*) U of Notre Dame Pr.

America Aid to NATO Allies in the 1950s: The Dutch Case. Ine Megens. 320p. 1994. pap. 30.00 (*90-5170-252-3*, Pub. by Thesis Pubs NE) IBD Ltd.

America Alive: A History. Jean Karl. LC 92-40539. (Illus.). 128p. (J). 1994. lib. bdg. 22.95 (*0-399-22013-5*, Philomel Bks) Putnam Pub Group.

***America Americas: Myth in the Making of U. S. Policy Toward Latin America.** Eldon Kenworthy. LC 94-20971. (Illus.). 216p. 1995. pap. 14.95 (*0-271-01415-6*) Pa St U Pr.

***America Americas: Myth in the Making of U. S. Policy Toward Latin America.** Eldon Kenworthy. LC 94-20971. 1995. 35.00 (*0-271-01414-8*) Pa St U Pr.

America & Americanism. 1986. pap. 6.95 (*0-916786-82-X*, Saint George Pubns) R Steiner Col Pubns.

America & England, 1558-1776. Ed. by Joseph E. Illick. LC 70-11183. (C). 1970. pap. text ed. 8.95 (*0-89197-006-1*) Irvington.

America & Europe. Adam De Gurowski. LC 72-6042. (Select Bibliographies Reprint Ser.). 1977. reprint ed. 31.95 (*0-8369-6912-X*) Ayer.

America & Europe & Other Essays. Alfred E. Zimmern. LC 78-84350. (Essay Index Reprint Ser.). 1977. 18.95 (*0-8369-1117-2*) Ayer.

America & Europe in an Era of Change. Ed. by Helga Haftendorn & Christian Tuschhoff. LC 92-31017. 180p. 1993. text ed. 55.50 (*0-8133-1670-7*) Westview.

America & Europe in an Era of Change. Ed. by Helga Haftendorn & Christian Tuschhoff. LC 92-31017. 180p. (C). 1993. pap. text ed. 17.95 (*0-8133-1671-5*) Westview.

America & French Culture. Howard M. Jones. (BCL1 - U. S. History Ser.). 615p. 1991. reprint ed. lib. bdg. 109.00 (*0-7812-6046-9*) Rprt Serv.

America & French Culture, 1750-1848. Howard M. Jones. LC 73-3015. (Illus.). 615p. 1973. reprint ed. lib. bdg. 29.50 (*0-8371-6834-1*, JOAF, Greenwood Pr) Greenwood.

America & Her Commentators: With a Critical Sketch of Travel in the U. S. Henry T. Tuckerman. LC 74-107911. viii, 460p. 1970. reprint ed. 49.50 (*0-678-00616-4*) Kelley.

America & Her Problems. D'Estaurnelles De Constant. Ed. by H. B. Paul. LC 73-13127. (Foreign Travelers in America, 1810-1935 Ser.). 570p. 1974. reprint ed. 42.95 (*0-405-05449-1*) Ayer.

America & Hostos. Eugenio M. De Hostos. 1976. lib. bdg. 59.95 (*0-8490-1411-5*) Gordon Pr.

America & I: Short Stories by American Jewish Women Writers. Ed. by Joyce Antler. LC 89-78237. 368p. 1991. pap. 14.00 (*0-8070-3607-2*) Beacon Pr.

America & Ireland, 1776-1976: The American Identify & the Irish Connection. Ed. by David N. Doyle & Owen D. Edwards. LC 79-7066. 348p. 1980. text ed. 55.00 (*0-313-21119-1*, DOA/, Greenwood Pr) Greenwood.

America & Island China: A Documentary History. Ed. by Stephen P. Gibert & William M. Carpenter. LC 88-13882. 418p. (C). 1989. lib. bdg. 57.00 (*0-8191-7256-1*) U Pr of Amer.

America & Its People. 2nd ed. James K. Martin et al. LC 92-18011. (C). 1993. 58.00 (*0-673-46363-X*) HarpCollege.

America & Its People, 2 vols. 2nd ed. James K. Martin et al. LC 92-28837. (C). 1995. Vol. 1, to 1877. 22.50 (*0-673-46781-3*); Vol. 2, from 1865. 22.50 (*0-673-46782-1*) HarpCollege.

America & Its People, 2 vols., 1. 2nd ed. Martin. (C). 1993. 43.00 (*0-673-46364-8*) HarpCollege.

America & Its People, 2 vols., 2. Martin. (C). 1993. 43.00 (*0-673-46365-6*) HarpCollege.

America & Its People, 2 vols., I. 2nd ed. Martin. (C). 1993. student ed 17.00 (*0-673-53825-7*) HarpCollege.

America & Its People, 2 vols., II. 2nd ed. Martin. (C). 1993. student ed 17.00 (*0-673-53826-5*) HarpCollege.

America & Its People, Vol. I. James K. Martin et al. (C). 1988. text ed. 35.00 (*0-673-18302-5*); pap. text ed. 25.75 (*0-673-18315-7*) HarpCollege.

America & Its People, Vol. II. James K. Martin et al. (C). 1988. pap. text ed. 25.75 (*0-673-18316-5*) HarpCollege.

America & Other Poems. Jack Greer. 32p. 1993. pap. 5.95 (*0-931848-82-2*) Dryad Pr.

America & Our World Heritage: A Scientist's Appraisal of America's Destiny. G. F. Steffanides. 1967. pap. 1.00 (*0-9600114-1-2*, A-10757) Steffanides.

America & Palestine: The Attitude of Official America & of the American People Toward the Rebuilding of Palestine As a Free & Democratic Jewish Commonwealth. Ed. by Reuben Fink & Davis Moshe. LC 77-70680. (America & the Holy Land Ser.). 1977. reprint ed. lib. bdg. 44.95 (*0-405-10245-3*) Ayer.

America & Russia: From Cold War Confrontation to Coexistence. Ed. by Gary R. Hess. LC 72-10916. (Problem Studies in American History). (C). 1973. pap. text ed. write for info. (*0-88295-743-0*) Harlan Davidson.

America, & the American Church. Henry Caswall. LC 77-83413. (Religion in America, Ser.). 1980. reprint ed. 23.95 (*0-405-00234-3*) Ayer.

America, & the Americans. James Boardman. LC 73-13120. (Foreign Travelers in America, 1810-1935 Ser.). 446p. 1974. reprint ed. 34.95 (*0-405-05443-2*) Ayer.

America & the Americans from a French Point of View. Price Collier. 1977. text ed. 18.95 (*0-8369-9215-6*, 9071) Ayer.

America & the Americans in 1833-1834, by an Emigrant. Richard Gooch. Ed. by Richard T. Widdicombe. LC 94-25157. (Illus.). 332p. (C). 1994. 27.00 (*0-8232-1594-6*) Fordham.

***America & the Americans in 1833-1834, by an Emigrant.** Richard Gooch. Ed. & Intro. by Richard T. Widdicombe. LC 94-25157. 1994. pap. write for info. (*0-8232-1595-4*) Fordham.

***America & the Americas.** Linda W. Beech et al. Ed. by Susan Evento. (Literature Based Reading Activities/Conversion Ser.). 64p. Date not set. pap. text ed. 9.95 (*1-56784-516-9*) Newbridge Comms.

America & the Americas: The United States in the Western Hemisphere. Lester D. Langley. LC 89-31968. (United States & the Americas Ser.). 304p. 1989. 35.00 (*0-8203-1103-0*); pap. 15.00 (*0-8203-1104-9*) U of Ga Pr.

America & the Arab States: An Uneasy Encounter. Robert W. Stookey. LC 75-25874. (America & the World Ser.). 315p. reprint ed. pap. 89.80 (*0-8357-5347-6*, 2020338) Bks Demand.

America & the Asian Revolutions. 2nd ed. Robert J. Lifton. 178p. (C). 1973. reprint ed. 27.95x (*0-87855-065-8*); reprint ed. pap. text ed. 16.95x (*0-87855-562-5*) Transaction Pubs.

America & the Automobile: Technology, Reform & Social Change, 1893-1923. Peter J. Ling. 208p. 1992. pap. 24.95 (*0-7190-3808-1*, Pub. by Manchester Univ Pr UK) St Martin.

America & the Daguerreotype. Ed. by John Wood. LC 90-25764. (Illus.). 287p. 1991. 69.95 (*0-87745-334-9*) U of Iowa Pr.

America & the Fight for Irish Freedom. Charles C. Tansill. 1957. 12.95 (*0-8159-5002-0*) Devin.

America & the Four Japans: Friend, Foe, Model, Mirror. Frederik L. Schodt. LC 93-31450. 200p. 1993. 19.95 (*1-880656-06-X*); pap. 10.95 (*1-880656-10-8*) Stone Bridge Pr.

America & the French Nation, 1939-1945. Julian G. Hurstfield. LC 85-20899. x, 309p. (C). 1986. 37.50 (*0-8078-1685-X*) U of NC Pr.

An Asterisk (*) at the beginning of an entry indicates that the title is appearing in BIP for the first time.

America & the Germans: An Assessment of a Three Hundred Year History, 2 vols., Set. Ed. by Frank Trommler & Joseph McVeigh. Incl. Vol. I. Immigration, Language, Ethnicity. LC 85-1063. 408p. 1985. pap. text ed. 19.95 (*0-8122-1350-5*); Vol. 2. Relationship in the Twentieth Century. LC 85-1063. 378p. 1985. pap. text ed. 19.95 (*0-8122-1351-3*); LC 85-1063. (Illus.). 1985. Set pap. 43.95 (*0-8122-1425-0*) U of Pa Pr.

America & the Holocaust. (American Jewish History Ser.: Vol. 68, Pt. 3). 1979. 6.00 (*0-911934-01-4*) Am Jewish Hist Soc.

America & the Holocaust. (American Jewish History Ser.: Vol. 70, Pt. 3). 1981. 6.00 (*0-911934-20-0*) Am Jewish Hist Soc.

America & the Holocaust, 13 vols. Intro. by David S. Wyman. 1992. Set. 1,163.00 (*0-8153-0023-9*) Garland.

America & the Holocaust, Vol. I. Ed. by Sanford Pinsker & Jack Fischel. (Holocaust Studies Annual). 200p. (C). 1984. lib. bdg. 15.00 (*0-913283-02-9*) Penkevill.

America & the Holy Land Series, 72 vols. Moshe Davis. (Illus.). 1977. reprint ed. lib. bdg. 2,212.50 (*0-405-10220-8*) Ayer.

America & the Image of Europe: Reflections on American Thought. Daniel J. Boorstin. 11.25 (*0-8446-1703-2*) Peter Smith.

America & the Indochina Wars, 1945-1990: A Bibliographical Guide. Ed. by Lester H. Brune & Richard D. Burns. (New War - Peace Bibliographical Ser.). 350p. 1991. lib. bdg. 39.95 (*0-941690-43-1*) Regina Bks.

America & the Iraqi Crisis, 1990-1992: Origins & Aftermath. Lester H. Brune. LC 93-20611. (Guides to Contemporary Issues Ser.: Vol. 8). 1993. 27.95 (*0-941690-53-9*); pap. 12.95 (*0-941690-54-7*) Regina Bks.

America & the Middle East. Parker T. Hart. Ed. by Richard D. Lambert. LC 72-78294. (Annals Ser.: 401). 300p. 1972. pap. 18.00 (*0-87761-148-3*) Am Acad Pol Soc Sci.

America & the Modern World. Stephen Burman. 224p. 1991. text ed. 45.00 (*0-312-01971-8*) St Martin.

America & the Multinational Corporation: The History of a Troubled Partnership. John J. Reardon. LC 92-12211. 194p. 1992. text ed. 49.95 (*0-275-93918-9*, C3918, Praeger Pubs) Greenwood.

America & the New Economy: How New Competitive Standards Are Radically Changing American Workplaces. Anthony P. Carnevale. LC 91-19307. (Management Ser.). 291p. 1991. 31.95 (*1-55542-371-X*) Jossey-Bass.

***America & the Pacific Rim: Coming to Terms with New Realities.** Gerald L. Houseman. 288p. (C). 1995. lib. bdg. 58.50 (*0-8476-8022-3*); pap. text ed. 22.95 (*0-8476-8023-1*) Rowman.

***America & the Persian Gulf: The Third Party Dimension in World Politics.** Steve Yetiv. LC 94-44171. 200p. 1995. text ed. 49.95 (*0-275-94973-7*, Praeger Pubs) Greenwood.

America & the Russo-Finnish War. Andrew J. Schwartz. LC 74-74344. 103p. 1975. reprint ed. text ed. 55.00 (*0-8371-7964-5*, SCAM, Greenwood Pr) Greenwood.

America & the Sea: A Literary History. Ed. by Haskell Springer. LC 93-44385. (Illus.). 400p. (C). 1995. 40.00 (*0-8203-1651-2*) U of Ga Pr.

America & the Shaping of German Society, 1945-1955. Intro. by Michael Ermarth. LC 92-28545. 208p. 1993. 48.00 (*0-85496-327-8*) Berg Pubs.

America & the Survivors of the Holocaust. Leonard Dinnerstein. LC 81-15443. (Contemporary American History Ser.). 222p. 1986. text ed. 43.00 (*0-231-04176-4*); pap. text ed. 19.50 (*0-231-04177-2*) Col U Pr.

America & the World: Diplomacy, Politics, & War. Ed. by Peter S. Onuf. LC 91-15487. (New American Nation, 1775-1820 Ser.: Vol. 9). 472p. 1991. 80.00 (*0-8153-0444-7*) Garland.

America & the World Political Economy: Atlantic Dreams & National Realities. David P. Callao & Benjamin M. Rowland. LC 73-173390. 383p. reprint ed. pap. 109.20 (*0-8357-5348-4*, 2056025) Bks Demand.

America & the World, 1986. Ed. by Foreign Affairs Editors. 280p. 1987. pap. text ed. 16.95 (*0-08-034682-0*, Pergamon Pr) Elsevier.

America & the World 1987-88. Ed. by William G. Hyland. (AATW 87 Ser.). 278p. 1988. pap. text ed. 13.95 (*0-08-036127-7*, Pergamon Pr) Elsevier.

America Armed: Essays on U. S. Military Policy. Ed. by Robert A. Goldwin. LC 74-157338. (Select Bibliographies Reprint Ser.). 1977. reprint ed. 19.95 (*0-8369-5798-9*) Ayer.

America Arms for a New Century: The Making of a Great Military Power. James L. Abrahamson. LC 80-69716. (Illus.). 1981. 19.95 (*0-685-01676-5*) Free Pr.

America As a Civilization. Max Lerner. 1987. pap. 19.95 (*0-8050-0355-X*) H Holt & Co.

America As a Model: The Impact of American Democracy in the World. Klaus Von Beyme. LC 87-4271. 256p. 1987. text ed. 45.00 (*0-312-00422-2*) St Martin.

America As a Multicultural Society. Ed. by Milton M. Gordon & Richard D. Lambert. LC 80-70879. (Annals of the American Academy of Political & Social Science Ser.: No. 454). 250p. (C). 1981. pap. text ed. 18.00 (*0-87761-261-7*) Am Acad Pol Soc Sci.

America As a World Power: A Realist Appraisal from Wilson to Reagan. Norman A. Graebner. LC 84-10706. 336p. (C). 1984. 40.00 (*0-8420-2230-9*); pap. text ed. 14.95 (*0-8420-2232-5*) Scholarly Res Inc.

America As a World Power: Foreign Policy in a Constitutional Framework. Loch K. Johnson. 1991. pap. text ed. write for info. (*0-07-032644-4*) McGraw.

***America as a World Power: Foreign Policy in a Constitutional Framework.** 2nd ed. Loch K. Johnson. LC 94-3729. 1994. write for info. (*0-07-032716-5*) McGraw.

America As a World Power, 1897-1907. John H. Latane. (History - United States Ser.). 350p. 1992. reprint ed. lib. bdg. 89.00 (*0-7812-6213-5*) Rprt Serv.

America As a World Power, 1897-1907. John H. Latane. LC 79-145131. (Illus.). 1971. reprint ed. 49.00 (*0-403-01064-0*) Scholarly.

America As an Ordinary Country: U. S. Foreign Policy & the Future. Ed. by Richard Rosecrance. LC 75-38427. 288p. 1976. 34.00 (*0-8014-1010-X*) Cornell U Pr.

America As Seen by Its First Explorers: The Eyes of Discovery. John Bakeless. (Illus.). 439p. 1989. pap. 7.95 (*0-486-26031-3*) Dover.

America As Story: Historical Fiction for Secondary Schools. Elizabeth F. Howard. LC 83-3453. 156p. 1988. pap. text ed. 23.00 (*0-8389-0492-0*) ALA.

America Asks Bruce. Bruce Williams. 185p. 1988. pap. text ed. 12.95 (*1-882991-00-1*) Mainst Pubs.

America Asleep: The Free Trade Syndrome & the Global Economic Challenge: A New Conservative Foreign Economic Policy for America. Intro. by Patrick J. Buchanan. 205p. (Orig.). (C). 1991. pap. text ed. 6.95 (*0-944468-03-9*) USIC Ed Found.

America at Century's End. James R. Schlesinger. 88p. 1989. text ed. 20.00 (*0-231-06922-7*) Col U Pr.

America at Century's End. Ed. by Alan Wolfe. 567p. 1991. 35.00 (*0-520-07476-9*) U CA Pr.

America at Century's End. Ed. by Alan Wolfe. 1992. pap. 15.00 (*0-520-07477-7*) U CA Pr.

America at D-Day: A Book of Remembrance. Richard Goldstein. LC 93-37889. 1994. pap. 14.95 (*0-385-31283-0*, Delta) Dell.

America at Home. Alfred M. Low. LC 73-13142. (Foreign Travelers in America, 1810-1935 Ser.). (Illus.). 278p. 1974. reprint ed. 21.95 (*0-405-05465-3*) Ayer.

America at Its Best: Opportunities in the National Guard. Robert F. Collins. Ed. by Ruth Rosen. (Military Opportunities Ser.). (YA). (gr. 7-12). 1989. lib. bdg. 14.95 (*0-8239-1024-5*) Rosen Group.

America at Seventeen-Fifty. Richard Hofstadter. 320p. 1973. pap. 8.00 (*0-394-71795-3*, Vin) Random.

***America at the Crossroads.** Jerome Prescott. (Illus.). 128p. 1995. 15.98 (*0-8317-0739-9*) Smithmark.

America at the Movies. Margaret Thorp. LC 75-124039. (Literature of Cinema Ser.). 1970. reprint ed. 17.95 (*0-405-01639-5*) Ayer.

***America at the Polls, 2 vols.** Alice V. McGillivray & Richard M. Scammon. LC 94-30937. 1905p. 1994. 295.00 (*1-56802-051-1*) Congr Quarterly.

America at the Polls: A Handbook of American Presidential Election Statistics 1920-1964. Ed. by Richard M. Scammon. LC 75-22840. (America in Two Centuries Ser.). 1976. reprint ed. 50.95 (*0-405-07711-4*) Ayer.

***America at the Polls: A Handbook of American Presidential Election Statistics Vol. 2: Kennedy to Clinton, 1960-1992.** Ed. by Alice V. McGillivray & Richard M. Scammon. LC 94-30937. 1994. 295.00 (*1-56802-058-9*); 295.00 (*1-56802-059-7*) Congr Quarterly.

***America at the Polls, 1994.** 160p. 1995. pap. 19.95 (*0-614-04960-1*) Roper Ctr User.

***America at the Polls, 1994.** Roper Center for Public Opinion Research Staff & Everett C. Ladd. (Occasional Papers & Monographs Ser.: No. 12). (Illus.). 170p. (Orig.). (C). 1995. pap. text ed. 19.95 (*1-887415-01-7*) RCPOR.

America at the Polls 2. Richard Scammon & Alice McGillivary. 594p. 1988. 114.00 (*0-685-19513-9*) Congr Quarterly.

***America at the Threshold: Report of the Synthesis Group on America's Space Exploration.** 1994. lib. bdg. 250.75 (*0-8490-6447-3*) Gordon Pr.

***America at War: An Anthology of Articles from MHQ: The Quarterly Journal of Military History.** Ed. & Intro. by Calvin L. Christman. 625p. 1995. 35.00 (*1-55750-036-3*) Naval Inst Pr.

America at War: Battles That Turned the Tide. Brian Black. (J). (gr. 4-7). 1992. pap. 3.50 (*0-590-45505-2*) Scholastic Inc.

America at War in Vietnam: Decisions & Consequences. rev. ed. Jerold M. Starr. (Lessons of the Vietnam War Ser.). (Illus.). 32p. (C). 1991. pap. text ed. 5.00 (*0-945919-02-6*) Ctr Social Studies.

America At Your Fingertips, Vol. 1: An Atlas of the History & Geography of the 50 States & Dependencies of the U. S.A. Bruce W. Jooste & Steven L. Jooste. (Illus.). 70p. (Orig.). 1992. pap. text ed. 12.95 (*1-881247-00-7*) Fingertips.

America, B. C. Barry Fell. LC 75-36269. (Illus.). 1976. write for info. (*0-8129-0624-1*, Times Bks) Random.

America Balkanized: Immigration's Challenge to Government. Brent A. Nelson. LC 94-4306. 1994. 10.00 (*0-936247-14-2*) Amer Immigration.

***America Beautiful.** 1993. 14.99 (*0-517-11161-6*) Random Hse Value.

America Becomes a World Power, 1890-1920. Naunerle Farr. Ed. by D'Ann Calhoun & Lawrence W. Bloch. (Basic Illustrated History of America Ser.). (Illus.). (J). (gr. 4-12). 1977. pap. text ed. 2.95 (*0-88301-199-9*); student ed. 1.25 (*0-88301-236-7*) Pendulum Pr.

America Becomes Urban: The Development of U. S. Cities & Towns, 1780-1980. Eric H. Monkkonen. 336p. (C). 1988. 38.00 (*0-520-06191-8*); pap. 14.00 (*0-520-06972-2*) U CA Pr.

America Before Columbus. rev. ed. Barry Fell. 1989. pap. 14.00 (*0-671-67974-0*) PB.

America Begins: Early American Writings. Ed. by Richard M. Dorson. LC 72-5802. (Folklore of the World Ser.). (Illus.). 1981. reprint ed. lib. bdg. 49.95 (*0-8369-2986-1*) Ayer.

America Betrayed. Marlin Maddoux. Orig. Title: Humanism Exposed. 153p. 1984. pap. 6.99 (*0-910311-18-8*) Huntington Hse.

***America Beyond 2001: Opposing Viewpoints.** Ed. by Oliver W. Markley & Walter R. McCuan. LC 94-46738. (Opposing Viewpoints Ser.). 1995. lib. bdg. 19.95 (*1-56510-293-2*); pap. 11.55 (*1-56510-292-4*) Greenhaven.

America Builds. Leland M. Roth. LC 82-48151. (Illus.). 675p. 1983. pap. text ed. 27.00 (*0-06-430122-2*, IN-122, Icon Edns) HarpC.

America by Design. Spiro Kostof. (Illus.). 400p. 1987. 30.00 (*0-19-504283-2*) OUP.

America by Design: Science, Technology, & the Rise of Corporate Capitalism. David F. Noble. (Orig.). 1979. pap. 11.95 (*0-19-502618-7*) OUP.

America by Land. Robert Olmstead. LC 92-50511. 1993. 20.00 (*0-679-41130-5*) Random.

***America by Land.** braille ed. Robert Olmstead. 314p. 1994. text ed., vinyl bd. 25.12 (*1-56956-530-9*, BR9526) W A T Braille.

America by Mail. Arcama Group Staff. 240p. (Orig.). 1990. pap. 14.95 (*0-380-76175-0*) Avon.

America by the Throat: The Bureaucratization of the United States. 1991. lib. bdg. 69.95 (*0-8490-4470-7*) Gordon Pr.

America by the Throat: The Stranglehold of American Bureaucracy. George Roche, III. 1982. 14.95 (*0-686-81784-2*) Devin.

America by the Throat: The Stranglehold of Federal Bureaucracy. George Roche, III. LC 82-12793. 200p. 1983. 14.95 (*0-8159-6844-2*) Devin.

America Calling: A Social History of the Telephone to 1940. Claude S. Fischer. (Illus.). 1992. 25.00 (*0-520-07933-7*) U CA Pr.

America Calling: A Social History of the Telephone to 1940. Claude S. Fischer. (Illus.). 424p. (C). 1994. pap. 16.00 (*0-520-08647-3*) U CA Pr.

America Can Be Number One in Education: The Structural Biodynamic Approach. Radu Buzescu. (Illus.). 160p. (Orig.). 1993. pap. 25.00 (*0-9624144-2-5*) Transdacia Co.

America Celebrates! A Patchwork of Weird & Wonderful Holiday Lore. Henning Cohen. 384p. 1991. pap. 14.95 (*0-8103-9407-3*) Visible Ink Pr.

***America Challenged: Population Change & the Future of the United States.** LC 94-29676. (C). 1995. pap. text ed. 17.95 (*0-8133-1809-2*) Westview.

***America Challenged: Population Change & the Future of the United States.** Steve H. Murdock. LC 94-29676. (C). 1995. text ed. 49.95 (*0-8133-1808-4*) Westview.

America Comes of Age: A French Analysis. 2nd ed. Andre Siegfried. Tr. by Doris Hemming & H. H. Hemming. LC 68-16244. (American Scene Ser.). 368p. 1974. reprint ed. lib. bdg. 42.50 (*0-306-71025-0*) Da Capo.

America Cooks: A Culinary Journey from Coast to Coast. Judith Ferguson. 1994. 17.98 (*0-681-45395-8*) Longmeadow Pr.

America Discovered: A Poem. Jedediah V. Huntington. (Notable American Authors Ser.). 1992. reprint ed. lib. bdg. 75.00 (*0-7812-3292-9*) Rprt Serv.

America Discovers Columbus. Jr. League Staff. 1984. 18.95 (*0-9613621-0-3*) J L C Pubns.

America Discovers Columbus. Junior League of Columbus, Inc. Staff et al. (Illus.). 520p. 1984. 14.95 (*0-685-09594-0*) J L C Pubns.

America Discovers Columbus: How an Italian Explorer Became an American Hero. Claudia L. Bushman. LC 91-50809. 232p. 1992. 24.95 (*0-87451-576-9*) U Pr of New Eng.

America Does Not Have a Drug Problem. Don Schwerdtfeger. 131p. (Orig.). (YA). 1989. pap. 7.95 (*0-9624760-0-5*) Bding Better People.

America Doesn't Owe You a Living: Success Is Your Choice. rev. ed. Robert M. Unger & John H. Upillas. 240p. 1994. reprint ed. pap. 11.99 (*0-922066-91-4*) Revell.

America During the Cold War. Steven M. Gillon & Diane B. Kunz. LC 92-73125. 414p. 1994. pap. 19.00 (*0-15-500415-8*) HarBrace.

America Eats. Nelson Algren. LC 91-41109. (Iowa Szathmary Culinary Arts Ser.). (Illus.). 143p. 1992. 25.95 (*0-87745-361-6*) U of Iowa Pr.

America Eats Out: An Illustrated History of Restaurants, Taverns, Coffee Shops, Speakeasies, & Other Establishments That Have Fed Us for 350 Years. John Mariani. (Illus.). 288p. 1991. 25.00 (*0-688-09996-3*) Morrow.

America en el Horizonte: Una Perspectiva Cultural. Ernesto Ardura. LC 79-54965. (Coleccion de Estudios Hispanicos - Hispanic Studies Collection). (Illus.). 161p. (Orig.). (SPA.). 1981. pap. 10.95 (*0-89729-240-5*) Ediciones.

America en Su Literatura. 2nd ed. Anita Arroyo. LC 77-3041. (Illus.). 676p. 1978. 12.00 (*0-8477-3175-8*); pap. text ed. 9.60 (*0-8477-3182-0*) U of PR Pr.

America Encounters India, Nineteen Forty-One to Nineteen Forty-Seven. Gary R. Heas. LC 72-163196. 224p. reprint ed. pap. 63.90 (*0-8357-5349-2*, 2025844) Bks Demand.

America Encounters Japan: From Perry to MacArthur. William L. Neumann. (Goucher College Ser.). 366p. 1963. reprint ed. 52.00 (*0-8018-0485-X*) Johns Hopkins.

America Entangled: The Persian Gulf Crisis & Its Consequences. Ed. by Ted G. Carpenter. 116p. 1991. pap. 3.00 (*0-932790-85-2*) Cato Inst.

America Enters the Eighties: Some Social Indicators. Ed. by Conrad Taeuber & Richard D. Lambert. LC 80-68056. (Annals of the American Academy of Political & Social Science Ser.: No. 453). (Illus.). 350p. 1981. 27.00 (*0-87761-258-7*); pap. 18.00 (*0-87761-259-5*) Am Acad Pol Soc Sci.

America, Europe, & the Soviet Union: Selected Essays. Walter Laqueur. LC 82-19423. 234p. 1983. 39.95x (*0-87855-362-2*) Transaction Pubs.

America Every Year Evermore. write for info. (*0-918430-05-4*) Happy History.

America Faces the Future. Ed. by Charles A. Beard. LC 73-90608. (Essay Index Reprint Ser.). 1977. 26.95 (*0-8369-1244-6*) Ayer.

America February. William Kistler. LC 91-70168. 64p. 1991. pap. 9.95 (*0-933031-40-8*) Coun Oak Bks.

***America Fever: A Resource Guide.** Jocelyn Riley. 114p. 1995. 20.00 (*1-877933-50-3*) Her Own Words.

America Fights the Tide, 1942. John Devaney. (World War II Ser.). 192p. (YA). (gr. 12 up). 1991. 17.95 (*0-8027-6997-7*); lib. bdg. 18.85 (*0-8027-6998-5*) Walker & Co.

America First. James Magorian. LC 92-70840. 156p. (Orig.). 1992. pap. 6.00 (*0-930674-37-5*) Black Oak.

***America First! Its History, Culture, & Politics.** Bill Kauffman. 300p. 1995. 25.95 (*0-87975-956-9*) Prometheus Bks.

***America Firsthand: From Settlement to Reconstruction.** 3rd ed. Robert D. Marcus & David Burner. 292p. (C). 1994. pap. text ed. 24.66 (*0-312-10162-7*); pap. text ed. 19.95 (*0-312-10163-5*) St Martin.

America for Americans: Economic Nationalism & Anglophobia in the Late Nineteenth Century. Edward P. Crapol. LC 71-176287. (Contributions in American History Ser.: No. 28). 248p. 1973. text ed. 59.95 (*0-8371-6273-4*, CRA/, Greenwood Pr) Greenwood.

America for Sale: Antique Advertising. Douglas Congdon-Martin. LC 91-65650. (Illus.). 160p. 1991. pap. 29.95 (*0-88740-333-6*) Schiffer.

America, France & Vietnam: Cultural History & Ideas of Conflict. Phil Melling & Jon Roper. 250p. 1991. text ed. 63.95 (*1-85628-072-1*, Pub. by Avebury Pub UK) Ashgate Pub Co.

America from A to Z. Salvatore Parlato. Ed. by Art Freifeld. (Illus.). 161p. (C). 1989. student ed, pap. text ed. 14.95 (*0-916177-67-X*) Am Eng Pubns.

America, from Client State to World Power: Six Major Transitions in U. S. Foreign Relations. Paul A. Varg. LC 89-29012. 315p. 1990. 29.95 (*0-8061-2251-X*) U of Okla Pr.

America Germanica. M. D. Learned. 1972. 59.95 (*0-87968-593-X*) Gordon Pr.

America, Germany, & the Future of Europe. Gregory Treverton. 252p. 1993. pap. text ed. 14.95 (*0-691-00077-8*) Princeton U Pr.

America, Germany, & the Future of Europe. Gregory F. Treverton. 1992. 39.50 (*0-691-07859-9*) Princeton U Pr.

America, Germany & the New Europe. G. Treverton & B. Bicksler. (Critical Issues 1991 Ser.: No. 1). 32p. 1991. pap. 4.95 (*0-87609-103-6*) Coun Foreign.

America, God & the Bomb: The Legacy of Ronald Reagan. F. H. Knelman. 478p. 1988. pap. 6.95 (*0-919573-75-4*) Left Bank.

America Goes to Press: The News of Yesterday. Laurence Greene. LC 74-128252. (Essay Index Reprint Ser.). 1977. 23.95 (*0-8369-1929-7*) Ayer.

America Goes to Press: The News of Yesterday. Laurence Green. LC 79-145060. 1971. reprint ed. 29.00 (*0-403-01003-9*) Scholarly.

***America Goes to School: Law, Reform, & Crisis in Public Education.** Robert M. Hardaway. LC 94-46171. 224p. 1995. text ed. 55.00 (*0-275-94951-6*, Praeger Pubs) Greenwood.

America Goes to the Movies: 100 Years of Motion Picture Exhibition. Barbara Stones. Ed. by Jim Kozak. 1993. 39.95 (*0-9638653-0-7*) Nat Assn Theatre.

America Goes to the Polls: C-Span 1992 Election Calendar. 108p. 1992. pap. 8.95 (*1-881846-04-0*) C-Span.

***America Goes to War: A Social History of the Continental Army.** Charles P. Neimeyer. (American Social Experience Ser.). (Illus.). 240p. 1995. 35.00 (*0-8147-5780-4*) NYU Pr.

America Goes to War: An Introduction to the Civil War & Its Meaning to Americans Today. Illus. by Bruce Catton. 1994. 5.98 (*1-56731-006-0*, MJF Bks) Fine Comms.

America Goes to War: The Civil War & Its Meaning in American Culture. Bruce Catton. LC 58-13602. (Illus.). 128p. 1992. reprint ed. pap. 9.95 (*0-8195-6016-2*, Wesleyan Univ Pr) U Pr of New Eng.

America Goes to War, 1941. John Devaney. (World War II Ser.). 192p. (YA). (gr. 12 up). 1991. 16.95 (*0-8027-6979-9*); lib. bdg. 17.85 (*0-8027-6980-2*) Walker & Co.

America, Greece & Pasok: The Politics of Dependence & Independence. Christopher T. Lazakis. LC 89-61079. 110p. (Orig.). (C). 1989. pap. text ed. 14.95 (*0-9622952-0-5*) Ciel Trappe Bks.

America Held Hostage: From the Teheran Embassy Takeover to the Iran-Contra Affair. Don Lawson. LC 90-20515. (Twentieth Century American History Ser.). (Illus.). 144p. (YA). (gr. 9-12). 1991. lib. bdg. 14.77 (*0-531-11009-5*) Watts.

America Hurrah & Other Plays. Jean-Claude Van Itallie. Incl. Almost Like Being. 1978. (*0-318-52812-6*); Fable. 1978. (*0-318-52813-4*); Hunter & the Bird. 1978. (*0-318-52814-2*); Serpent. 1978. (*0-318-52815-0*); 195p. 1978. Set pap. 5.95 (*0-394-17039-3*, E708) Grove-Atltic.

America Hxatal: Two Books of a Poem. Sterling K. Webb. 44p. (Orig.). 1978. lib. bdg. 9.95 (*0-916908-32-1*); pap. 5.00 (*0-916908-10-0*) Place Herons.

A

An Asterisk (*) at the beginning of an entry indicates that the title is appearing in BIP for the first time.

A

America, I Hear You: A Story about George Gershwin. Barbara Mitchell. (Creative Minds Ser.). (Illus.). 64p. (J). (gr. 3-6). 1987. lib. bdg. 15.95 (*0-87614-309-5*, Carolrhoda) Lerner Group.

America, I Love You: But Not Like I Used To. James Kavanaugh. LC 92-61489. (Illus.). 56p. (Orig.). reprint ed. pap. 6.95 (*1-878995-18-9*) S J Nash Pub.

America, I Presume. Wyndham Lewis. LC 72-2158. (American Literature Ser.: No. 49). 1972. reprint ed. lib. bdg. 75.00 (*0-8383-1476-7*) M S G Haskell Hse.

America in an Interdependent World: Problems of United States Foreign Policy. Ed. by David A. Baldwin. LC 75-41909. 372p. reprint ed. pap. 106.10 (*0-8357-5350-6*, 2023232) Bks Demand.

America in Arms. John M. Palmer. Ed. by Richard H. Kohn. LC 78-22392. (American Military Experience Ser.). 1980. reprint ed. lib. bdg. 18.95 (*0-405-11868-6*) Ayer.

America in Bloom. Murray Alcosser. LC 90-50798. (Illus.). 224p. 1991. 45.00 (*0-8478-1326-6*) Rizzoli Intl.

America in Chaos: America's Second Civil War. Thomas Mariano. Ed. by Patricia Huhn. 105p. (Orig.). 1994. pap. 5.00 (*1-877637-10-6*) Mariano Pub.

America in Crisis & Individual Survival: How the Individual Can Survive in a Hostile Economic & Political Environment to Defend Their Family, Money & Property. 1992. lib. bdg. 254.88 (*0-8490-5591-1*) Gordon Pr.

America in Crisis Survival Portfolio. Archibald E. Roberts. 100p. 1992. pap. 14.95 (*0-934120-23-4*) Comm Restore Const.

America in Decline: An Analysis of the Developments Toward War & Revolution, in the U. S. & Worldwide in the 1980's, Vol 1. Raymond Lotta & Frank Shannon. LC 83-22294. (Illus.). 278p. (Orig.). (C). 1984. 21.95 (*0-916650-12-X*); pap. 11.95 (*0-916650-13-8*) Banner Pr.

America in Depression: The Coming Economic Collapse. James R. Von Feldt & Ronald S. Von Feldt. 144p. 1993. pap. 24.95 (*0-9637546-0-2*) Amer Systs.

America in Eighteen Fifty-Seven: A Nation on the Brink. Kenneth M. Stampp. 1990. 29.95 (*0-685-47701-0*) OUP.

America in Eighteen Seventy-Six. LC 73-13141. (Foreign Travelers in America, 1810-1935 Ser.). 350p. 1974. reprint ed. 26.95 (*0-405-05464-5*) Ayer.

America in European Consciousness, 1493-1750. Karen O. Kupperman. LC 94-5725. (Institute of Early American History & Culture Ser.). (Illus.). 428p. 1995. text ed. 49.95x (*0-8078-2166-7*) U of NC Pr.

***America in European Consciousness, 1493-1750.** Ed. by Karen O. Kupperman. LC 94-5725. (Institute of Early American History & Culture Ser.). 428p. 1995. pap. 19.95x (*0-8078-4510-8*) U of NC Pr.

America in Fourteen Ninety-Two: The World of the Indian Peoples Before the Arrival of Columbus. Ed. by Alvin M. Josephy, Jr. (Illus.). 477p. 1991. 35.00 (*0-394-56438-3*) Newberry.

America in France. Frederick Palmer. LC 74-12754. (Illus.). 479p. 1975. reprint ed. text ed. 65.00 (*0-8371-7752-9*, PAAF, Greenwood Pr) Greenwood.

America in France's Hopes & Fears, 1890-1920, 2 Vols., Set. Charles W. Brooks. Ed. by William H. McNeill & David H. Pinkney. (Modern European History Ser.). 930p. 1987. lib. bdg. 20.00 (*0-8240-8031-9*) Garland.

***America in International Trade.** E. Willard Miller & Ruby M. Miller. 300p. 1995. 39.50 (*0-87436-770-0*) ABC-CLIO.

America in Literature. Ed. by Flory J. Schultheiss. Incl. Small Town. 1979. (*0-684-16138-9*); (gr. 9-12). 1979. Set pap. write for info. (*0-318-55711-8*) Macmillan.

America in Literature. George E. Woodberry. LC 73-104602. 253p. reprint ed. lib. bdg. 34.00 (*0-8398-2176-X*) Irvington.

America in Literature. George E. Woodberry. 253p. (C). 1986. reprint ed. pap. text ed. 6.95 (*0-8290-1900-6*) Irvington.

America in Maps Dating from 1500 to 1856. Ed. by Egon Klemp. LC 75-15952. (Illus.). 290p. 1976. 495.00 (*0-8419-0200-3*) Holmes & Meier.

America in Our Time: From World War II to Nixon--What Happened & Why. Godfrey Hodgson. 1978. pap. 12.76 (*0-394-72517-4*, Vin) Random.

America in Passing. Henri Cartier-Bresson. (Illus.). 152p. 1991. 75.00 (*0-8212-1868-9*) Bulfinch Pr.

***America in Poetry: With Paintings, Drawings, Photographs.** Ed. by Charles Sullivan. (Illus.). 208p. 1993. 20.00 (*1-56865-084-1*, GuildAmerica) Dblday Bk Music.

America in Poetry: With Paintings, Drawings, Photographs, & Other Works of Art. Ed. by Charles Sullivan. (Illus.). 208p. 1992. pap. 19.98 (*0-8109-8112-2*) Abrams.

***America in Prophecy.** E. F. Webber. 30p. (Orig.). 1994. pap. 2.50 (*1-879366-43-6*) Hearthstone OK.

America in Ruins: Beyond the Public Works Pork Barrel. Pat Choate & Susan M. Walter. LC 81-66253. 100p. (Orig.). 1981. pap. 9.95 (*0-934842-25-6*) CSPA.

America in Search of Itself: The Making of the President, 1956-1980. Theodore H. White. 480p. 1988. pap. 9.95 (*0-446-37098-3*) Warner Bks.

***America in Space.** Russell R. Tobias. (Magill Bibliographies Ser.). 327p. 1991. 40.00 (*0-8108-2813-8*) Scarecrow.

***America in Space: Pioneers or Aggressors?** fac. ed. Ed. by Oliver Trager. LC 86-32775. (Editorials on File Book Ser.). (Illus.). 191p. 1986. reprint ed. pap. 54.50 (*0-7837-8138-5*, 2047946) Bks Demand.

America in the Age of the Titans: From the Rise of Theodore Roosevelt to the Death of FDR. Sean D. Cashman. (Illus.). 450p. 1988. 50.00 (*0-8147-1410-2*); pap. 18.50 (*0-8147-1411-0*) NYU Pr.

America in the East. William E. Griffis. (Notable American Authors Ser.). 1992. reprint ed. lib. bdg. 75.00 (*0-7812-2964-2*) Rprt Serv.

America in the Era of Limits: Nativist Reaction to the 'New' Immigration. Wayne A. Cornelius. (Research Report Ser.: No. 3). 31p. (Orig.). (C). 1982. pap. 5.00 (*0-935391-02-9*, RR-03) UCSD Ctr US-Mex.

America in the Gilded Age: From the Death of Lincoln to the Rise of Theodore Roosevelt. 3rd ed. Sean D. Cashman. LC 93-12999. (Illus.). 450p. (C). 1994. text ed. 50.00 (*0-8147-1494-3*); pap. text ed. 18.50 (*0-8147-1495-1*) NYU Pr.

America in the Great War: The Rise of the War Welfare State. Ronald Schaffer. 261p. 1991. 27.95 (*0-19-504903-9*) OUP.

America in the Modern World. Denis W. Brogan. LC 79-25851. 117p. 1980. reprint ed. text ed. 49.75 (*0-313-22254-1*, BRAW, Greenwood Pr) Greenwood.

America in the Movies. Michael Wood. (Illus.). 224p. 1989. text ed. 40.50 (*0-231-07098-5*); pap. text ed. 14.50 (*0-231-07099-3*) Col U Pr.

America in the Nineteen Sixties. Irwin Unger & Debi Unger. 1993. Net. 13.50 (*1-881089-07-X*) Brandywine Press.

America in the Pacific. Foster R. Dulles. LC 73-86595. (American Scene Ser.). 1969. reprint ed. 37.50 (*0-306-71431-0*); reprint ed. pap. text ed. 11.95 (*0-685-01351-0*) Da Capo.

America in the Seventies: Some Social Indicators. Ed. by Conrad Taeuber & Richard D. Lambert. LC 77-22914. (Annals of the American Academy of Political & Social Science Ser.: No. 435). 1978. 27.00 (*0-87761-222-6*); pap. 18.00 (*0-87761-223-4*) Am Acad Pol Soc Sci.

America in the Twentieth Century. LC 94-10854. 1994. Multi-volume set. 399.95 (*1-85435-736-0*) Marshall Cavendish.

America in the Twentieth Century. rev. ed. Frank Freidel. (C). 1982. pap. text ed. 21.95 (*0-685-02843-7*) McGraw.

America in the Twentieth Century. 2nd ed. George D. Moss. 544p. 1992. pap. text ed. write for info. (*0-13-031733-0*) P-H.

America in the Twentieth Century. 4th ed. James Patterson. 1993. pap. 30.75 (*0-15-500502-2*) HarBrace.

America in the Twentieth Century. 5th rev. ed. Frank Freidel. (C). 1982. pap. text ed. write for info. (*0-07-554359-1*) McGraw.

America in the Twentieth Century: A History. 3rd ed. James T. Patterson. 534p. (C). 1988. pap. text ed. 30.75 (*0-15-502264-4*) HB Coll Pubs.

America in the World: A Guide to U. S. Foreign Policy. Wallace Irwin. LC 83-1154. 266p. 1983. text ed. 59.95 (*0-275-91015-6*, C1015, Praeger Pubs) Greenwood.

America in the World: A Guide to U. S. Foreign Policy. Wallace Irwin. LC 83-1154. 266p. 1983. pap. text ed. 16.95 (*0-275-91574-3*, B1574, Praeger Pubs) Greenwood.

America in the World Economy. Charles P. Kindleberger. (Headline Ser.: No. 237). (Illus.). 1977. pap. 11.95 (*0-87124-043-2*, 77-86278) Foreign Policy.

America in the World Economy: A Strategy for the 1990s. C. Fred Bergsten. LC 88-39852. 218p. (Orig.). (C). 1988. text ed. 19.95 (*0-88132-089-7*); pap. 13.95 (*0-88132-082-X*) Inst Intl Eco.

America in the World, 1962-1987: A Strategic & Political Reader. Ed. by Walter Laqueur & Brad Roberts. 350p. 1987. text ed. 39.95 (*0-312-01318-3*) St Martin.

America in Theory. Ed. by Leslie C. Berlowitz et al. 320p. 1989. 29.95 (*0-19-505396-6*) OUP.

***America in Transition: How to Profit.** 200p. (Orig.). 1994. pap. 165.00 (*0-7605-0996-4*) Rector Pr.

America in Travail. Edgar H. Brookes. LC 68-8590. (C). 1968. pap. 3.00 (*0-87574-159-2*) Pendle Hill.

America in Two Centuries: An Inventory. Ed. by Daniel J. Boorstin. 1976. 3,571.50 (*0-405-07666-5*) Ayer.

America in Vietnam. Guenter Lewy. 1980. pap. 11.95 (*0-19-502732-9*) OUP.

America in Vietnam: A Documentary History. Ed. by William A. Williams et al. 1989. pap. 10.95 (*0-393-30555-4*) Norton.

America in Vietnam: From the Files of the United Press International. John Gulmartin. (United Press International Library-Bettmann Archives). (Illus.). 208p. 1991. 19.99 (*0-517-69322-4*) Random Hse Value.

America in Vietnam: The Elephant & the Tiger. Albert Marrin. (Illus.). 256p. (YA). (gr. 7 up). 1992. 16.00 (*0-670-84063-7*) Viking Child Bks.

America in World Affairs. Charles O. Lerche, Jr. LC 79-26759. (Foundations of American Government & Political Science Ser.). (Illus.). 118p. 1980. reprint ed. text ed. 49.75 (*0-313-22315-7*, LEAMW, Greenwood Pr) Greenwood.

America in World War II: 1941. Edward F. Dolan. (J). (gr. 4-7). 1992. pap. 6.96 (*0-395-65944-2*) HM.

America in World War II: 1943. Edward F. Dolan. (J). (gr. 4-7). 1992. pap. 6.96 (*0-395-62463-0*) HM.

America in World War II - 1941. Edward F. Dolan. LC 91-30808. (America in World War II Ser.). (Illus.). 72p. (J). (gr. 4-6). 1991. lib. bdg. 16.90 (*1-878841-05-X*) Millbrook Pr.

America in World War II - 1942. Edward F. Dolan. LC 91-30808. (America in World War II Ser.). (Illus.). 72p. (J). (gr. 4-6). 1991. lib. bdg. 16.90 (*1-56294-007-4*); pap. 6.95 (*1-878841-82-3*) Millbrook Pr.

America in World War II - 1943. Edward F. Dolan. (America in World War II Ser.). (Illus.). 72p. (J). (gr. 4-6). 1992. lib. bdg. 16.90 (*1-56294-113-5*) Millbrook Pr.

America in World War II - 1943. Edward F. Dolan. LC 91-30808. (America in World War II Ser.). 1992. pap. 6.95 (*1-878841-62-9*) Millbrook Pr.

America in World War II - 1944. Edward F. Dolan. (America in World War II Ser.). (Illus.). 72p. (J). (gr. 4-6). 1993. lib. bdg. 16.90 (*1-56294-221-2*); pap. 6.95 (*1-878841-81-5*) Millbrook Pr.

America in World War II - 1945. Edward F. Dolan. (America in World War II Ser.). (Illus.). 72p. (J). (gr. 4-6). 1994. lib. bdg. 16.90 (*1-56294-320-0*) Millbrook Pr.

America in 1492: The World of the Indian Peoples Before the Arrival of Columbus. Intro. by Alvin M. Josephy, Jr. LC 92-56363. 1993. pap. 17.00 (*0-679-74337-5*, Vin) Random.

America in 1857: A Nation on the Brink. Kenneth M. Stampp. (Illus.). 416p. 1990. 35.00 (*0-19-503902-5*) OUP.

America in 1857: A Nation on the Brink. Kenneth M. Stampp. (Illus.). 416p. 1992. pap. 14.95 (*0-19-507481-5*) OUP.

America Insecure: Arms Transfers, Global Interventionism & the Erosion of National Security. Miles D. Wolpin. LC 90-52570. (Illus.). 399p. 1991. lib. bdg. 38.50x (*0-89950-529-5*) McFarland & Co.

America Invests in the Future: The Twenty-Fifth Anniversary of Project Head Start, a Briefing. 50p. 1989. pap. 5.00 (*0-937641-08-1*) Stone Canyon Pr.

***America Is in the Heart.** Carlos Bulosan. (American Autobiography Ser.). 326p. 1995. reprint ed. lib. bdg. 89.00 (*0-7812-8467-8*) Rprt Serv.

America Is in the Heart. Carlos Bulosan. LC 73-13007. 352p. 1973. reprint ed. pap. 13.95 (*0-295-95289-X*) U of Wash Pr.

America Is Too Young to Die. Leonard Ravenhill. LC 79-19229. 128p. 1979. pap. 6.99 (*0-87123-013-5*, 210013) Bethany Hse.

America Is West: Anthology of Middlewestern Life & Literature. John Flanagan. (BCL1-PS American Literature Ser.). 677p. 1993. reprint ed. lib. bdg. 109.00 (*0-7812-6599-1*) Rprt Serv.

America Is West: An Anthology of Middle-Western Life & Literature. Ed. by John T. Flanagan. LC 71-106687. (Illus.). vii, 677p. 1971. reprint ed. text ed. 35.00 (*0-8371-3358-0*, FLAW, Greenwood Pr) Greenwood.

America, Its People, Its Pride, & Its Progress. Kimberly Smithson & Linda Conway. 77p. (Orig.). 1991. pap. 7.50 (*1-880461-00-5*) Celebrat Excell.

America! Jesus Is Here! Mel Tari & Cliff Dudley. LC 76-1058. 1976. 4.95 (*0-89221-021-4*) New Leaf.

America: Land of Beauty & Splendor. Reader's Digest Editors. LC 91-27098. (Illus.). 432p. 1992. 35.00 (*0-89577-404-6*, Random) RD Assn.

America Latina: Contrastes E Confrontos. Ruth S. Lamb. 69p. (POR.). 1973. pap. 4.00 (*0-912434-05-8*) Ocelot Pr.

America Latina En Su Cultura see Latin America in Its Literature

America Latina En Su Cultura see Latin America in Its Architecture

America Learns Russian: A History of the Teaching of the Russian Language in the United States. Albert Parry. LC 67-27162. 217p. reprint ed. pap. 61.90 (*0-8357-5351-4*, 2027399) Bks Demand.

America Living with AIDS: Transforming Anger, Fear, & Indifference into Action: Report of the National Commission on AIDS. 165p. (Orig.). (C). 1992. pap. text ed. 27.95 (*1-56806-106-4*) Diane Pub.

America Looks to the Sea. Douglas Brooks. 1984. 19.95 (*0-685-14505-0*) Viking Penguin.

America Loves Chicken. Linda W. Eckhardt. LC 93-8669. (Illus.). 1993. 7.99 (*0-517-09377-4*, Pub. by Wings Bks) Random Hse Value.

America Loves Hamburger: One Hundred One All-Time Best Recipes. Linda W. Eckhardt. LC 94-11873. (Illus.). 1994. write for info. (*0-517-11843-2*, Pub. by Wings Bks) Random Hse Value.

***America Loves Hamburgers.** Linda W. Eckhardt. 144p. 1994. 8.95 (*1-56865-065-5*, GuildAmerica) Dblday Bk Music.

America Loves Salads. Camille Cusumaro. LC 93-8670. (Illus.). 1993. 7.99 (*0-517-09379-0*, Pub. by Wings Bks) Random Hse Value.

America Mainline Religion: Its Changing Shape of the Religious Establishment. Wade C. Roof & William McKinney. 272p. 1987. text ed. 40.00 (*0-8135-1215-8*); pap. text ed. 15.00 (*0-8135-1216-6*) Rutgers U Pr.

America Nineteen Forty-One: A Nation at the Crossroads. Ross Gregory. (Illus.). 400p. 1988. 29.95 (*0-02-912801-3*) Free Pr.

***America Now: Short Readings from Recent Periodicals.** Robert Atwan. 320p. 1994. pap. text ed. 15.00 (*0-312-10285-2*) St Martin.

America Now: The Anthropology of a Changing Culture see Why Nothing Works: The Anthropology of Daily Life

America of Carl Sandburg. Hazel B. Durnell. LC 90-46584. (Illus.). 276p. 1990. reprint ed. 29.95 (*0-87797-206-0*) Cherokee.

America of Eric Sloane: A Collector's Bibliography. Dean L. Mawdsley. 1990. write for info. (*0-918676-24-X*) Conn Hist Com.

America on Death Row. Michael J. Kempf. LC 93-73294. (Illus.). 96p. 1993. pap. 10.00 (*0-9637662-1-X*) From Blues To Bless.

America on Display. Joyce Jurnovoy & David Jenness. LC 86-24394. 300p. reprint ed. pap. 85.50 (*0-8357-3488-9*, 2039747) Bks Demand.

America on Film & Tape: A Topical Catalog of Audiovisual Resources for the Study of United States History, Society, & Culture. Ed. by Howard B. Hitchens & Vidge Hitchens. LC 85-8011. (Bibliographies & Indexes in American History Ser.: No. 3). xvii, 392p. 1985. text ed. 79.50 (*0-313-24778-1*, HFT/) Greenwood.

America on My Mind. Intro. by Jimmy Carter & Rosalynn Carter. (America on My Mind Ser.). (Illus.). 200p. 1991. 39.50 (*1-56044-057-0*) Falcon Pr MT.

America on Paper: The First Hundred Years. enl. rev. ed. Lynn Glaser. LC 89-6846. (Illus.). 288p. 1989. 32.50 (*0-929679-00-7*) Associated Antiquaries.

***America on Record: A History of Recorded Sound.** Andre Millard. (Illus.). 416p. (C). 1995. 59.95 (*0-521-47544-9*); pap. 17.95 (*0-521-47556-2*) Cambridge U Pr.

America on Six Rubles a Day. Yakov Smirnoff. LC 87-40072. (Illus.). 160p. 1987. pap. 5.95 (*0-394-75523-5*, Vin) Random.

America on Stone: The Other Printmakers to the American People. Harry T. Peters. LC 75-22832. (America in Two Centuries Ser.). (Illus.). 1977. reprint ed. 71.95 (*0-405-07703-3*) Ayer.

America on the Attack, 1943. John Devaney. LC 92-8993. (World War II Ser.). (YA). 1992. lib. bdg. 18.85 (*0-8027-8195-0*) Walker & Co.

America on the Edge: Is It Too Late to Turn Back? Thomas D. Elliff. Ed. by Don McMinn. (Illus.). 128p. (Orig.). 1992. pap. write for info. (*0-9634614-0-0*) Natl Christ Minist.

America on the Ice: Antarctic Policy Issues. Frank G. Klotz. LC 90-13300. (Illus.). 371p. 1991. per., pap. 11.00 (*0-16-023190-6*) USGPO.

America on the Rerun. David Story. LC 92-37558. 1993. 14.95 (*0-8065-1410-8*, Citadel Pr) Carol Pub Group.

America, One Land, One People: Noted Historians Look at America. Ed. by Robert C. Baron. LC 86-25670. (History Ser.). 320p. (C). 1986. 20.00 (*1-55591-012-2*) Fulcrum Pub.

***America Online for Windows 95 Membership Kit & Tour Guide.** 3rd ed. Tom Lichty. 600p. 1995. disk 27.95 (*1-56604-253-4*) Ventana Pr.

***America Online for Windows 95 Tour Guide.** 3rd ed. Tom Lichty. 600p. 1995. 19.95 (*1-56604-252-6*) Ventana Pr.

America Online's Internet: Easy, Graphical Access - the AOL Way - Macintosh Edition. Tom Lichty. 1994. Incl. diskette. disk, pap. 24.95 (*1-56604-175-9*) Ventana Pr.

America Online's Internet for Windows: Easy, Graphical Access - the AOL Way. Tom Lichty. 1994. Incl. diskette. disk, pap. 24.95 (*1-56604-176-7*) Ventana Pr.

America Organizes to Win the War: A Handbook on the American War Effort. LC 72-3445. (Essay Index Reprint Ser.). 1977. reprint ed. 23.95 (*0-8369-2885-7*) Ayer.

America Outside the World: The Collapse of U. S. Foreign Policy. Louis R. Beres. LC 86-45598. 192p. 1987. text ed. 22.95 (*0-669-14016-3*) Free Pr.

America Over. Ryder Stacy. (Doomsday Warrior Ser.: No. 16). 1989. pap. 2.95 (*0-8217-2740-0*) Zebra.

America Overcommitted: United States National Interests in the 1980s. Donald E. Nuechterlein. LC 84-17409. 248p. 1985. 18.00 (*0-8131-1529-9*) U Pr of Ky.

America Papers. Dallas Institute Fellows. 45p. 1991. pap. 8.00 (*0-911005-32-3*) Dallas Inst Pubns.

America-Paradisul Diavolului: Jurnal de Emigrant. Florentin Smarandache. Ed. by Florea Miu. 264p. (Orig.). (RUM.). (C). 1992. pap. 14.99 (*1-879585-27-8*) Xiquan Pubng.

America, Past & Present. 3rd ed. Robert A. Divine. LC 93-25161. (C). 1993. text ed. 32.00 (*0-673-46758-9*) HarpCollege.

America: Past & Present, Vols. 1-3. 2nd rev. ed. Katherine Lancelot-Harrington. LC 92-31762. 1992. Vol. 2, The Challenge of New Frontiers. pap. 18.95 (*0-8384-3440-1*); Vol. 3, The Continuing Quest. pap. 18.95 (*0-8384-3441-X*) Heinle & Heinle.

America: Past & Present, Vols. 1-3. 2nd rev. ed. Katherine Lancelot-Harrington. LC 92-31762. 1992. Vol. 1, The Exploration of a Continent. pap. 18.95 (*0-8384-3439-8*) Heinle & Heinle.

America: Past & Present: Study Guide, 2 vols., I. 3rd ed. Robert A. Divine et al. (C). 1991. 20.00 (*0-673-38918-9*) HarpCollege.

America: Past & Present: Study Guide, 2 vols., II. 3rd ed. Robert A. Divine et al. (C). 1991. 20.00 (*0-673-38919-7*) HarpCollege.

America Play. Suzan-Lori Parks. 1995. pap. 4.75 (*0-8222-1423-7*) Dramatists Play.

America Prepares for War. Wallace B. Black & Jean F. Blashfield. LC 90-46581. (World War II 50th Anniversary Ser.). (Illus.). 48p. (J). (gr. 5-6). 1991. text ed. 12.95 (*0-89686-554-1*, Crstwood Hse) Silver Burdett Pr.

America Preserved: A Checklist of Historic Buildings, Structures & Sites. Historic American Buildings Survey - Historic American Engineering Record Staff. 1994. write for info. (*0-318-72955-5*) Lib Congress.

America Recommitted: United States National Interests in a Restructured World. Donald Nuechterlein. LC 91-163. 280p. 1991. 30.00 (*0-8131-1746-1*) U Pr of Ky.

America Rediscovered. Reuel F. Walker, Jr. (Illus.). 256p. 1985. 29.95 (*0-9606984-1-8*); 100.00 (*0-9606984-2-6*) Breezewood Pub.

***America Report: A Common Sense Annual Report to the Citizens of the United States.** Lyle A. Brecht. 32p. 1994. pap. text ed. write for info. (*0-9642575-0-5*) Blue Heron MD.

America Restored. Carol M. Highsmith & Ted Landphair. LC 93-32365. (Illus.). 320p. 1994. 45.00 (*0-89133-228-6*) Preservation Pr.

America Revised. Frances Fitzgerald. LC 80-11239. 256p. 1980. pap. 7.96 (*0-394-74439-X*, Vin) Random.

America Revisited. Frederick E. Birkenhead. LC 68-16911. (Essay Index Reprint Ser.). 1977. reprint ed. 19.95 (*0-8369-0212-2*) Ayer.

America Revisited. Frederick E. Smith. LC 68-16911. (Essay Index Reprint Ser.). 213p. 1982. reprint ed. lib. bdg. 14.00 (*0-8290-0479-3*) Irvington.

An Asterisk (*) at the beginning of an entry indicates that the title is appearing in BIP for the first time.

An Asterisk (*) at the beginning of an entry indicates that the title is appearing in BIP for the first time.

227

American Adventure. Jed Thompson. 1994. pap. 8.95 (*0-533-10966-3*) Vantage.

American Adventure in Bookburning in the Style of 1918. James J. Martin. LC 89-3246. 1988. 8.50 (*0-87926-024-6*) R Myles.

American Adventures: True Stories from America's Past, 1770-1870. Morrie Greenberg. LC 90-2652. (Illus.). 96p. (Orig.). (J). (gr. 4-9). 1991. pap. text ed. 9.95 (*0-9622652-1-7*) Brooke-Richards.

American Advertising Posters of the Nineteenth Century. Mary Black. (Illus.). (Orig.). 1976. pap. 13.95 (*0-486-23356-1*) Dover.

American Aesop: Negro & Other Humor. William Pickens. LC 76-99888. reprint ed. 34.00 (*0-404-00206-4*) AMS Pr.

American, African, & Old European Mythologies. Tr. by Wendy Doniger et al. LC 92-39231. (Illus.). xxiv, 280p. (C). 1993. pap. 25.00 (*0-226-06457-3*) U Ch Pr.

American Age: U. S. Foreign Policy at Home & Abroad, from 1750 to the Present. 2nd ed. Walter LaFeber. (Illus.). (C). 1994. One Vol. Ed.: 1750-Present. pap. text ed. 25.95 (*0-393-96474-4*); Vol. 1: 1750-1920. pap. text ed. 21.95 (*0-393-96475-2*); Vol. 2: 1896-Present. pap. text ed. 21.95 (*0-393-96476-0*) Norton.

American Agricultural Implements, a Review of Invention & Development in the Agricultural Implement Industry of the United States: Pt. 1 - General History of Invention & Improvement, Pt. 2 - Pioneer Manufacturing Centers, 2 pts. Robert L. Ardrey. LC 72-5028. (Technology & Society Ser.). (Illus.). 240p. 1972. reprint ed. 23.95 (*0-405-04681-2*) Ayer.

American Agricultural Press, 1819-1860: Eighteen Nineteen to Eighteen Sixty. abr. ed. Albert L. Demaree. LC 73-16296. (Perspectives in American History Ser.: No. 4). (Illus.). 430p. 1974. lib. bdg. 45.00 (*0-87991-331-2*) Porcupine Pr.

American Agricultural Problems in the Social Studies. Kenneth E. Oberholtzer. LC 73-177125. (Columbia University. Teachers College. Contributions to Education Ser.: No. 718). reprint ed. 37.50 (*0-404-55718-X*) AMS Pr.

American Agriculture: Brief History. R. Douglas Hurt. LC 93-39998. 400p. 1994. 34.95 (*0-8138-2376-5*) Iowa St U Pr.

American Agriculture, Eighteen Ninety-Nine to Nineteen Thirty-Nine: A Study of Output, Employment & Productivity. Harold Barger. LC 75-41017. (BCL Ser. II). reprint ed. 24.50 (*0-404-14640-6*) AMS Pr.

American Agriculture, Eighteen Ninety-Nine to Nineteen Thirty-Nine: A Study of Output, Employment, & Productivity. Harold Barger & Hans H. Landsberg. LC 75-19693. (National Bureau of Economic Research Ser.). (Illus.). 1975. reprint ed. 36.95 (*0-405-07574-X*) Ayer.

American Agriculture, 1899-1939: A Study of Output, Employment & Productivity. Harold Barger & Hans H. Landsberg. (General Ser.: No. 42). 462p. 1942. reprint ed. 120.20 (*0-87014-041-8*); reprint ed. mic. film 60.10 (*0-685-61226-0*) Natl Bur Econ Res.

American Aid to Israel: Nature & Impact. 1991. lib. bdg. 75.00 (*0-8490-4456-1*) Gordon Pr.

American Air Mail Catalogue, 5 vols. Ed. by American Air Mail Society Staff. 2138p. 12.50 (*0-685-67497-5*) Am Air Mail.

American Air Mail Catalogue, 5 vols., 1. Ed. by American Air Mail Society Staff. 2138p. write for info. (*0-939429-04-7*) Am Air Mail.

American Air Mail Catalogue, 5 vols., 2. Ed. by American Air Mail Society Staff. 2138p. 18.00 (*0-939429-05-5*) Am Air Mail.

American Air Mail Catalogue, 5 vols., 3. Ed. by American Air Mail Society Staff. 2138p. write for info. (*0-939429-06-3*) Am Air Mail.

American Air Mail Catalogue, 5 vols., 5. Ed. by American Air Mail Society Staff. 2138p. 18.00 (*0-939429-08-X*) Am Air Mail.

American Air Power: The First Seventy-Five Years. Joe Christy. (Illus.). 208p. 1982. 21.95 (*0-8306-2327-2*, 2327) TAB Bks.

American Airport Designs. Frwd. by Dominick A. Pisano. (Illus.). 96p. 1990. pap. 12.95 (*1-55835-025-X*) AIA Press.

American Albatross: The Foreign Debt Dilemma - A Twentieth Century Fund Paper. Robert D. Hormats. 117p. 1988. 18.95 (*0-87078-220-7*); pap. 8.95 (*0-87078-221-5*) TCFP-PPP.

American Album. Oliver Jensen et al. LC 85-15046. (Illus.). 352p. 1985. pap. 19.95 (*0-685-42995-4*) HM.

American Aliya: Portrait of an Innovative Migration Movement. Chaim I. Waxman. LC 88-38114. 240p. (C). 1989. 34.95 (*0-8143-1936-X*); pap. 16.95 (*0-8143-1937-8*) Wayne St U Pr.

American Alligator. Dorothy H. Patent. LC 93-37704. (J). 1994. 15.95 (*0-395-63392-3*, Clarion Bks) HM.

American Almanac of Jobs & Salaries. John W. Wright & Edward J. Dwyer. 720p. 1990. reprint ed. pap. 16.00 (*0-380-75898-9*) Avon.

American Almanac of Jobs & Salaries 1994-1995. rev. ed. John W. Wright. 704p. 1993. pap. 17.00 (*0-380-77219-1*) Avon.

American Almanac, 1992-1993. 112th ed. Ed. by U. S. Bureau of the Census Staff. LC 04-18089. (Illus.). 980p. 1992. pap. 14.95 (*1-878753-07-X*) Ref Press.

American Almanac 1993-1994: Statistical Abstract of the United States. 113th ed. Ed. by U. S. Bureau of the Census Staff. (Illus.). 980p. 1993. pap. 14.95 (*1-878753-30-4*) Ref Press.

***American Almanac 1994-1995: Statistical Abstract of the United States.** 3rd ed. Comp. by U. S. Bureau of the Census. 1010p. 1994. pap. 17.95 (*1-878753-66-5*) Ref Press.

***American Almanac 1995-1996: Statistical Abstract of the United States.** Ed. by Reference Press Staff. 1010p. 1995. 17.95 (*1-878753-89-4*) Ref Press.

American Alpine Journal, 1989. Ed. by H. Adams Carter. LC 79-63733. (Illus.). 1989. pap. 25.00 (*0-930410-39-4*) Amer Alpine Club.

American Alpine Journal 1990. Ed. by H. Adams Carter. LC 79-63733. (Illus.). 392p. 1990. pap. 25.00 (*0-930410-42-4*) Amer Alpine Club.

American Alpine Journal 1991. Ed. by H. Adams Carter. LC 79-63633. (Illus.). 384p. 1991. pap. 25.00 (*0-930410-46-7*) Amer Alpine Club.

American Alpine Journal 1992. Ed. by H. Adams Carter. LC 79-63633. (Illus.). 328p. 1992. pap. 25.00 (*0-930410-51-3*) Amer Alpine Club.

American Alpine Journal, 1993. Ed. by H. Adams Carter. (Illus.). 326p. 1993. pap. 25.00 (*0-930410-55-6*) Amer Alpine Club.

American Alps: The San Juan Mountains of Southwest Colorado. Donald L. Baars. LC 92-8859. (Illus.). 203p. 1992. pap. 18.95 (*0-8263-1352-3*) U of NM Pr.

American Ambassador. Ward Just. 320p. 1991. mass mkt. 4.95 (*0-8041-0595-2*) Ivy Books.

American Ambassador: Joseph C. Grew & the Development of the United States Diplomatic Tradition. Waldo H. Heinrichs, Jr. 480p. 1986. pap. 22.00 (*0-19-504159-3*) OUP.

American Ambassadors at the U. N. People, Politics, & Bureaucracy in the Making of Foreign Policy. 2nd ed. Seymour M. Finger. LC 86-19524. 336p. 1987. 49.50 (*0-8419-1057-X*) Holmes & Meier.

American Ambassadors in a Troubled World: Interviews with Senior Diplomats. Dayton Mak & Charles S. Kennedy. LC 92-7398. (Contributions in Political Science Ser.: No. 303). 248p. 1992. text ed. 55.00 (*0-313-28558-6*, MKR, Greenwood Pr) Greenwood.

American Ambitions: Selected Essays on Literary & Cultural Themes. Monroe K. Spears. LC 86-21403. 288p. 1987. text ed. 39.50 (*0-8018-3414-7*) Johns Hopkins.

American Amusement Park Industry: A History of Technology & Thrills. Judith A. Adams & Edwin J. Perkins. (Twayne's Evolution of American Business Ser.: No. 7). 280p. 1991. text ed. 27.95 (*0-8057-9821-8*, Twayne); pap. 14.95 (*0-8057-9822-6*, Twayne) Macmillan.

American Anarchist: The Life of Voltairine De Cleyre. Paul Avrich. LC 78-51153. (Illus.). 1978. text ed. 49.50x (*0-691-04657-3*) Princeton U Pr.

***American Anatomies: Theorizing Race & Gender.** Robyn Wiegman. LC 94-36882. (New Americanists Ser.). 288p. 1995. lib. bdg. 45.95 (*0-8223-1576-9*); pap. text ed. 15.95 (*0-8223-1591-2*) Duke.

American Ancestors & Cousins of the Princess of Wales. Gary B. Roberts & William A. Reitwiesner. LC 84-81095. (Illus.). 194p. 1984. 14.95 (*0-8063-1085-5*) Genealog Pub.

American Ancestors of Stephen. Gregory Roberts & Mark E. Roberts. (Illus.). write for info. (*0-9616192-1-X*) Roberts CA.

American Ancestry, Vol. 3. 57p. 1988. reprint ed. pap. 7.00 (*0-935207-80-5*) Danbury Hse Bks.

American Ancestry, Vol. 4. 62p. 1988. reprint ed. pap. 7.50 (*0-935207-81-3*) Danbury Hse Bks.

American Ancestry, Vol. 5. 60p. 1988. reprint ed. pap. 7.00 (*0-935207-82-1*) Danbury Hse Bks.

American & British Genealogy & Heraldry: A Selected List of Books. 3rd rev. ed. P. William Filby. LC 84-865. xix, 940p. 1983. lib. bdg. 49.95 (*0-88082-004-7*) New Eng Hist.

American & British Literature since 1890. enl. rev. ed. Carl Van Doren & Mark Van Doren. 1939. 49.00 (*0-89197-007-X*) Irvington.

American & British Literature, 1945-1975: An Annotated Bibliography of Contemporary Scholarship. John Somer & Barbara E. Cooper. LC 79-19299. xii, 328p. 1980. 29.95 (*0-7006-0195-3*) U Pr of KS.

American & British Poetry: A Guide to the Criticism, 1925-1978. Harriet S. Alexander. Ed. by George Hendrick & Donna Gerstenberger. LC 83-24114. xii, 486p. 1984. text ed. 55.00 (*0-8040-0848-5*, Swallow) Ohio U Pr.

***American & British Poetry: A Guide to the Criticism, 1979-1990.** Harriet S. Alexander. 450p. (C). 1995. text ed. 65.00 (*0-8040-0988-0*) Ohio U Pr.

American & British Pronunciation. E. Ekwall. Bd. with John Campanius' Lutheran Catechism in the Delaware Language (Essays & Studies on American Language & Literature: Vol. 2). 1972. reprint ed. Set pap. 18.00 (*0-8115-0184-1*) Periodicals Srv.

American & British Theatrical Biography: A Directory. J. P. Wearing. LC 78-31162. 1013p. 1979. 60.00 (*0-8108-1201-0*) Scarecrow.

American & Canadian Doctoral Dissertations & Master's Theses on Africa, 1974-1987. Ed. by Alfred Kagan & Gregory Larkin. 1989. 75.00 (*0-918456-63-0*, Crossroads) African Studies Assn.

American & Catholic: A Popular History of Catholicism in the United States. Clyde Crews. 176p. 1994. 11.95 (*0-86716-175-2*) St Anthony Mess Pr.

***American & Chinese Perceptions & Belief Systems: A People's Republic of China - Taiwanese Comparison.** Lorand B. Szalay et al. LC 94-24981. (Cognition & Language Series in Psycholinguistics). 280p. 1995. 69.50 (*0-306-44980-3*, Plenum Pr) Plenum.

American & English Dart Game Including Tournament Rules. Edmund C. Hady & Regina Hady. LC 73-75678. (Illus.). 1973. pap. 3.75 (*0-9600794-1-6*) E C Hady.

American & English Pewter at the Yale University Art Gallery: A Supplementary Checklist. David L. Barquist. LC 85-52296. (Illus.). 80p. (Orig.). 1986. pap. 12.00 (*0-89467-040-9*) Yale Art Gallery.

American & English Studies, 2 Vols. Whitelaw Reid. LC 68-29240. (Essay Index Reprint Ser.). 1977. reprint ed. 41.95 (*0-8369-0815-5*) Ayer.

***American & European Art Pottery Price Guide.** Ed. by Kyle Husfloen. (Illus.). 248p. (Orig.). 1995. pap. 14.95 (*0-930625-41-2*, Antque Trdr Bks) Antique Trader.

***American & European Decorative & Art Glass.** Ed. by Kyle Husfloen. (Illus.). 208p. 1995. pap. 15.95 (*0-614-04497-9*) Antique Trader.

American & European Decorative & Art Glass Price Guide: Cut, Opalescent, Steuben, Lalique & Other Choice Glasswares of the 19th & 20th Centuries. Ed. by Kyle Husfloen. (Illus.). 208p. (Orig.). 1995. pap. text ed. 15.95 (*0-930625-49-8*) Antique Trader.

***American & European Furniture Price Guide.** Michael Regan. 1995. pap. 15.95 (*0-930625-46-3*) Antique Trader.

American & European in the Works of Henry James. Sten Liljegren. LC 71-119080. (Studies in Henry James: No. 17). (C). 1970. reprint ed. lib. bdg. 49.95 (*0-8383-1076-1*) M S G Haskell Hse.

American & European Pressed Glass in the Corning Museum of Glass. Jane S. Spillman. LC 81-69639. (Catalog Ser.). (Illus.). 404p. (Orig.). 1981. 30.00 (*0-87290-103-3*); pap. 25.00 (*0-686-85820-4*) Corning.

***American & French Culture, 1800-1900: Interchanges in Art, Science, Literature, & Society.** fac. ed. Henry Blumenthal. LC 74-27187. 572p. 1975. reprint ed. pap. 163.10 (*0-7837-7936-4*, 2047692) Bks Demand.

American & French Revolutions, 1763-93 see New Cambridge Modern History

American & German Entrepreneur: Economic & Literary Interplay. Lucie Pfaff. (American University Studies: Economics: Ser. XVI, Vol. 4). 183p. (C). 1989. text ed. 32.50 (*0-8204-0807-7*) P Lang Pubs.

American & His Food: A History of Food Habits in the United States. Richard O. Cummings. LC 74-112536. (Rise of Urban America Ser.). (Illus.). 1979. reprint ed. 22.95 (*0-405-02445-2*) Ayer.

American & Japanese Auto Industries in Transition: The Report of the Joint U. S. - Japan Automotive Study. Ed. by Robert E. Cole & Taizo Yakushiji. LC 84-5814. xxvi, 223p. (C). 1984. pap. 17.95 (*0-939512-28-9*) U MI Japan.

American & Japanese Business Discourse: A Comparison of Interactional Styles. Haru Yamada. Ed. by Roy O. Freedle. (Advances in Discourse Processes Ser.: Vol. 45). 192p. (C). 1992. text ed. 42.50 (*0-89391-800-8*) Ablex Pub.

American & Japanese Relocation in World War II: Fact, Fiction & Fallacy. Lillian Baker. Ed. by Bert Webber. LC 89-8868. (Illus.). 240p. (Orig.). (C). 1989. pap. 26.95 (*0-936738-34-0*) Webb Research.

American & National Leagues: A Complete History, 2 bks. Joel Zoss & John S. Bowman. (Illus.). 192p. 1992. Set. 39.95 (*1-56657-001-8*) NDM Pubns.

American & Soviet Aid: A Comparative Analysis. Robert S. Walters. LC 73-117467. 313p. reprint ed. pap. 89.30 (*0-8357-5352-2*, 2017867) Bks Demand.

American & Soviet Intervention: Effects on World Stability. Ed. by Karen A. Feste. 250p. 1990. 46.00 (*0-8448-1631-0*, Crane Russak); pap. 29.00 (*0-8448-1632-9*, Crane Russak) Taylor & Francis.

American & Soviet Military Trends since the Cuban Missile Crisis. John M. Collins. 496p. 1978. boxed 32.95 (*0-89206-003-4*) Transaction Pubs.

American & Soviet Youth: A Comparative Study of Legal Socialization. James O. Finckenhauer et al. 1992. write for info. (*1-56000-028-7*) Transaction Pubs.

American & Wyoming Government: Study Guide. University of Wyoming Staff. 48p. (C). 1993. spiral bd. 9.95 (*0-8403-8749-0*) Kendall-Hunt.

American Angler in Australia. Zane Grey. 1976. 22.95 (*0-8488-0410-4*) Amereon Ltd.

American Angler in Australia. 2nd ed. Zane Grey. (Zane Grey Famous Fishing Library). 300p. 1992. Set. write for info. (*1-56416-083-1*) Derrydale Pr.

American Angler's Guide: or Complete Fisher's Manual for the U. S. John J. Brown. (Fly Fisherman's Gold Ser.: Vol. 5). (Illus.). 332p. 1993. reprint ed. 42.90 (*1-56416-117-X*) Derrydale Pr.

American Animal Hospital Association's Encyclopedia of Cat Health & Care. Les Sussman. LC 94-6622. 1994. 25.00 (*0-688-13454-8*) Hearst Bks.

American Animal Hospital Association's Encyclopedia of Dog Health & Care. Sally Bordwell. LC 94-6618. 1994. 25.00 (*0-688-13455-6*) Hearst Bks.

American Animated Films: The Silent Era, 1897-1929. annot. ed. Denis Gifford. LC 89-43649. 224p. 1990. lib. bdg. 38.50x (*0-89950-460-4*) McFarland & Co.

American Anniversaries: Every Day in the Year; Presenting Seven Hundred & Fifty Events in United States History from the Discovery of America to the Present Day. Philip R. Dillon. vi, 364p. 1991. reprint ed. lib. bdg. 48.00 (*1-55888-890-X*) Omnigraphics Inc.

American Anthology of Contemporary Poetry, Vol. III. Ed. by Chuck Kramer. 40p. (Orig.). 1991. pap. 19.99 (*0-925037-15-X*) Great Lks Poetry.

American Anthology of Contemporary Poetry, 1988. Ed. by Chuck Kramer. 488p. (Orig.). 1988. pap. 24.99 (*0-925037-02-8*) Great Lks Poetry.

American Anthology of Contemporary Poetry, 1989. Ed. by Chuck Kramer. 400p. (Orig.). 1989. pap. 24.99 (*0-925037-09-5*) Great Lks Poetry.

American Anthology of Midwestern Poetry, 1987. Ed. by Charles Kramer. 184p. (Orig.). 1987. pap. 24.99 (*0-925037-00-1*) Great Lks Poetry.

American Anthology of Midwestern Poetry, 1989. Ed. by Chuck Kramer. 324p. (Orig.). 1989. pap. 24.99 (*0-925037-10-9*) Great Lks Poetry.

American Anthology of Southern Poetry, 1987. Ed. by Chuck Kramer. 108p. (Orig.). 1987. pap. 24.99 (*0-925037-01-X*) Great Lks Poetry.

American Anthology of Southern Poetry, 1989. Ed. by Chuck Kramer. 304p. (Orig.). 1989. pap. 24.99 (*0-925037-05-2*) Great Lks Poetry.

American Anthology of Southern Poetry, 1990. Ed. by Chuck Kramer. 240p. (Orig.). 1990. pap. 24.99 (*0-925037-11-7*) Great Lks Poetry.

American Anthology, 1787-1900. Edmund C. Stedman. reprint ed. 75.00 (*0-7812-0791-6*) Rprt Serv.

American Anthology, 1787-1900, 2 vols., Set. Ed. by Edmund C. Stedman. LC 04-14072. 1969. reprint ed. 89.00 (*0-403-00057-2*) Scholarly.

***American Anti-Management Theories of Organization: A Critique of Paradigm Proliferation.** Lex Donaldson. (Cambridge Studies in Management: No. 25). (Illus.). 325p. (C). 1995. 59.95 (*0-521-47359-4*); pap. 18.95 (*0-521-47917-7*) Cambridge U Pr.

American Anti-Nazi Resistance, Nineteen Thirty-Three to Nineteen Forty-One: An Historical Analysis. Moshe R. Gottlieb. LC 81-8144. 426p. 1982. 45.00 (*0-87068-889-8*) Ktav.

American Anticommunism: Combating the Enemy Within, 1830-1970. M. J. Heale. LC 90-36391. (American Moment Ser.). 256p. 1990. text ed. 38.95 (*0-8018-4050-3*); pap. text ed. 12.95 (*0-8018-4051-1*) Johns Hopkins.

***American Antique Collection of Hennage's.** (Illus.). 230p. (C). 1994. 195.00 (*0-7605-0837-2*) Rector Pr.

American Antique Furniture, 2 Vols, 1. Edgar G. Miller, Jr. (Illus.). 1966. pap. 19.95 (*0-486-21599-7*) Dover.

American Antique Furniture, 2 Vols, 2. Edgar G. Miller, Jr. (Illus.). 1966. pap. 19.95 (*0-486-21600-4*) Dover.

American Antique Furniture: Styles & Origins, 1640-1840. Patricia Petraglia. (Illus.). 176p. 1992. 14.98 (*0-8317-0290-7*) Smithmark.

***American Antique Furniture, 1640-1840.** Patricia Petraglia. LC 94-27973. 1995. pap. write for info. (*1-56799-147-5*, Friedman-Fairfax) M Friedman Pub Grp Inc.

American Antique Quilts: Quilts from the Private Collections of Kinuko Fukii & Margaret Cavigga. Kinuko Fujii & Margaret Cavigga. Ed. by Kumiko Sudo. (Illus.). 64p. (JPN.). 1990. 25.00 (*0-9623778-3-X*) Pegasus.

American Antique Rifles. Martin Rywell. 1975. 2.00 (*0-913150-05-3*) Pioneer Pr.

American Antique Weather Vanes: The Complete Illustrated Westervelt Catalog of 1883. A. B. Westervelt & W. T. Westervelt. (Antiques Ser.). (Illus.). 104p. 1982. reprint ed. pap. 4.95 (*0-486-24396-6*) Dover.

American Antiques: The Hennage Collection. Elizabeth Stillinger. LC 90-38796. (Illus.). 162p. (Orig.). 1990. 60.00 (*0-87935-080-6*) Colonial Williamsburg.

***American Antiques Encyclopedia, 10 vols.** (Illus.). 3000p. (C). 1994. 695.00 (*0-7605-0836-4*) Rector Pr.

***American Antiques of Philadelphia-Hornor.** (Illus.). 230p. (C). 1994. 195.00 (*0-7605-0838-0*) Rector Pr.

American Antislavery Songs: A Collection & Analysis. Vicki L. Eaklor. LC 88-15426. (Documentary Reference Collections). 672p. 1988. text ed. 95.00 (*0-313-25413-3*, EAY/, Greenwood Pr) Greenwood.

American Antitrust Laws in Theory & in Practice. M. L. Greenhut & Bruce Benson. 278p. 1989. text ed. 68.95 (*0-566-07013-8*, Pub. by Avebury Pub UK) Ashgate Pub Co.

American Anxieties: A Collective Portrait of the 1930s. Intro. by Louis Filler. LC 92-35736. Orig. Title: The Anxious Years. 420p. (C). 1993. reprint ed. pap. text ed. 21.95 (*1-56000-672-2*) Transaction Pubs.

American Apartheid: Segregation & the Making of the Underclass. Douglas S. Massey & Nancy A. Denton. (Illus.). 292p. (C). 1993. 37.00 (*0-674-01820-6*) HUP.

***American Apartheid: Segregation & the Making of the Underclass.** Douglas S. Massey & Nancy A. Denton. 292p. 1994. pap. text ed. 14.95 (*0-674-01821-4*, MASAMX) HUP.

American Apocalypse: The Great Fire & the Myth of Chicago. Ross Miller. LC 89-20338. (Illus.). 248p. 1990. 24.95 (*0-226-52599-6*) U Ch Pr.

American Apocalypse: Yankee Protestants & the Civil War, 1860-1869. James H. Moorhead. LC 77-14360. 293p. reprint ed. pap. 83.60 (*0-8357-8016-3*, 2033832) Bks Demand.

American Apocalypses: The Image of the End of the World in American Literature. Douglas Robinson. LC 84-28865. 304p. reprint ed. pap. 86.70 (*0-7837-4402-1*, 2044142) Bks Demand.

American Apostles to the Philippines. Arthur S. Pier & W. Cameron Forbes. LC 74-160926. (Biography Index Reprint Ser.). 1977. reprint ed. 20.95 (*0-8369-8089-1*) Ayer.

***American Appaloosa.** Laurie Sale. (J). 1993. write for info. (*0-8362-4230-0*) Andrews & McMeel.

American Appetites. Joyce Carol Oates. 1990. pap. 12.00 (*0-06-097278-5*, PL) HarpC.

American Appraisals of Soviet Russia: 1917-1977. Ed. by Eugene Anschel. LC 78-5920. 404p. 1978. 30.00 (*0-8108-1135-9*) Scarecrow.

American Approach to Foreign Policy. rev. ed. Dexter Perkins. LC 62-11400. 247p. reprint ed. pap. 72.70 (*0-7837-2309-1*, 2057397) Bks Demand.

American Approach to Foreign Policy: A Pragmatic Perspective. Cecil V. Crabb, Jr. LC 84-29087. (Credibility of Institutions, Policies & Leadership Ser.: Vol. 2). 102p. (Orig.). 1985. lib. bdg. 35.50 (*0-8191-4422-3*, Pub. by White Miller Center); pap. text ed. 14.00 (*0-8191-4423-1*) U Pr of Amer.

An Asterisk (*) at the beginning of an entry indicates that the title is appearing in BIP for the first time.

TITLE INDEX

AMERICAN ASSOCIATION OF ARCHITECTURAL

American Approach to the Arab World. John S. Badeau. LC 67-22494. (Policy Books of the Council on Foreign Relations). 223p. reprint ed. pap. 63.60 (*0-8357-5353-0*, 2002941) Bks Demand.

American Approaches to World Affairs: The Credibility of Institutions, Policies & Leadership, Vol. 4. I. L. Claude. Ed. by Kenneth W. Thompson. 80p. (Orig.). (C). 1986. lib. bdg. 32.00 (*0-8191-5303-6*, Pub. by White Miller Center); pap. text ed. 11.50 (*0-8191-5304-4*, Pub. by White Miller Center) U Pr of Amer.

American Arbitration Association Insurance ADR Manual. James B. Boskey et al. LC 93-32246. 1993. text ed. 85.00 (*0-07-172374-9*) Shepards-McGraw.

American Arbitration Law: Reformation - Nationalization - Internationalization. Ian R. Macneil. 288p. 1992. 45.00 (*0-19-507062-3*) OUP.

American Archaeology Past & Future: A Celebration of the Society for American Archaeology, 1935-1985. Ed. by David J. Meltzer et al. LC 85-600308. (Illus.). 480p. (C). 1986. 39.95 (*0-87474-692-2*, MEAA) Smithsonian.

American Archery: A Vade Mecum of the Art of Shooting with the Long Bow. Robert P. Elmer. (Legends of the Longbow Ser.: Vol. 13). (Illus.). 312p. 1993. reprint ed. 39.95 (*1-56416-099-8*) Derrydale Pr.

American Architects & the Mechanics of Fame. Roxanne K. Williamson. (Illus.). 304p. 1991. 35.00 (*0-292-75121-4*) U of Tex Pr.

American Architects from the First World War to the Present: A Guide to Information Sources. Ed. by Lawrence Wodehouse. LC 74-10259. (Art & Architecture Information Guide Ser.: Vol. 4). 320p. 1977. 68.00 (*0-8103-1270-0*) Gale.

American Architectural Books: A List of Books, Portfolios, & Pamphlets on Architecture & Related Subjects Published in America Before 1895. Henry-Russell Hitchcock & Adolph K. Placzek. LC 75-25672. (Architecture & Decorative Art Ser.). xii, 130p. 1975. reprint ed. lib. bdg. 29.50 (*0-306-70742-X*) Da Capo.

American Architectural Masterpieces. Ed. by George E. Thomas & Michael J. Lewis. LC 91-36816. (Illus.). 384p. 1992. reprint ed. 65.00 (*1-878271-20-2*) Princeton Arch.

American Architectural Photographer: The Architecture of Bohlin Cywinski Jackson. 160p. 1994. pap. 39.99 (*1-56496-073-0*) Rockport Pubs.

American Architecture. Fiske Kimball. LC 77-108121. (Illus.). reprint ed. 20.00 (*0-404-03676-7*) AMS Pr.

American Architecture: A Critical History. David Handlin. LC 84-51824. (World of Art Ser.). (Illus.). 288p. (Orig.). 1985. pap. 12.95 (*0-500-20200-1*) Thames Hudson.

American Architecture: A Critical History. Ed. by David P. Handlin. (Illus.). 288p. (Orig.). 1985. 9.95 (*0-317-65731-3*, TH01) Am Soc Civil Eng.

American Architecture: Eighteen Sixty to Nineteen Seventy-Six, Vol. II. Marcus Whiffen & Fredrick Koeper. 296p. 1983. reprint ed. pap. 20.00x (*0-262-73070-7*) MIT Pr.

American Architecture: 1607 to 1860, Vol. I. Marcus Whiffen & Fredrick Koeper. 280p. 1983. reprint ed. pap. 20.00x (*0-262-73069-3*) MIT Pr.

American Architecture & Urbanism. rev. ed. Vincent Scully. (Illus.). 320p. 1988. 29.95 (*0-8050-0105-0*); pap. 17.95 (*0-8050-0813-6*, Owl) H Holt & Co.

American Architecture of Today. George Edgell. 401p. 1993. reprint ed. lib. bdg. 99.00 (*0-7812-5295-4*) Rprt Serv.

American Architecture of Today. George H. Edgell. LC 79-120562. (Illus.). reprint ed. 34.50 (*0-404-02245-6*) AMS Pr.

American Architecture since Seventeen Eighty: A Guide to the Styles. rev. ed. Marcus Whiffen. (Illus.). 328p. 1992. pap. 16.50 (*0-262-73097-9*) MIT Pr.

American Archival Analysis: The Recent Development of the Archival Profession in the United States. Richard J. Cox. 363p. 1990. 37.50 (*0-8108-2338-1*) Scarecrow.

American Archives. Peter Force. (Notable American Authors Ser.). 1992. reprint ed. lib. bdg. 75.00 (*0-7812-2868-9*) Rprt Serv.

American Arctic Lichens, Vol. 1: Microlichens. John W. Thompson. (Illus.). 576p. 1984. text ed. 87.00 (*0-231-05888-8*) Col U Pr.

American Arias for Soprano: A Diverse Selection of Arias from Operas by American Composers. 112p. (Orig.). 1990. pap. 12.95 (*0-7935-0363-9*, HL50481197, G Schirmer) H Leonard.

American Aristides: A Biography of George Wythe. Imogene E. Brown. LC 77-89776. 324p. 1978. 39.50 (*0-8386-2142-2*) Fairleigh Dickinson.

American Armamentarium Chirurgicum. George Tiemann. (Illus.). 846p. 1989. reprint ed. 165.00 (*0-930405-23-4*) Norman SF.

American Armamentarium Chirurgicum George Tiemann & Company 1889: The Centennial Edition. Intro. by James M. Edmonson & F. Terry Hambrecht. LC 89-8686. (Illus.). 846p. 1989. 165.00 (*0-318-49992-4*) Printers Devil.

***American Armies & Battlefields in Europe: A History, Guide & Reference Book, 2 vols.** 1994. lib. bdg. 625.95 (*0-8490-6425-2*) Gordon Pr.

American Arms Changing Europe. Warner R. Schilling. LC 73-4303. 1973. pap. text ed. 18.50 (*0-231-03705-8*) Col U Pr.

American Arms Supermarket. Michael T. Klare. LC 84-13053. (Illus.). 336p. 1985. pap. 12.95 (*0-292-70370-8*) U of Tex Pr.

American Army of Two. Janet Greeson. (On My Own Bks.). (Illus.). 48p. (J). (gr. k-3). 1991. lib. bdg. 15.95 (*0-87614-664-7*, Carolrhoda) Lerner Group.

American Army of Two. Janet Greeson. (J). (gr. k-3). 1991. pap. 5.95 (*0-87614-547-0*, Carolrhoda) Lerner Group.

***American Art.** Diana Vowels. 64p. 1994. write for info. (*0-9640034-6-5*) World Pubns.

***American Art, Vol. 8, No. 2.** 1994. pap. 15.00 (*0-937311-17-0*) Natl Mus Amer Art.

American Art: History & Culture. Wayne Craven. 688p. 1994. pap. write for info. (*0-697-16763-1*) Brown & Benchmark.

American Art: History & Culture. Wayne Craven. 1994. 60.00 (*0-8109-1942-7*) Abrams.

American Art: Painting, Sculpture, Architecture, Decorative Arts, Photography. M. Brown et al. 1979. text ed. 59.95 (*0-13-024653-0*) P-H.

American Art: Painting, Sculpture, Architecture, Decorative Arts, Photography. Milton W. Brown et al. (Illus.). 616p. 1979. 60.00 (*0-8109-0658-9*) Abrams.

American Art: Paintings from the Amon Carter Museum. Sarah Cash. LC 92-54538. (Illus.). 60p. 1992. pap. 17.95 (*0-88360-070-6*) Amon Carter.

American Art: The Los Angeles County Museum of Art Collection. Ilene S. Fort & Michael Quick. (Illus.). 624p. 1990. 75.00 (*0-295-97027-8*) U of Wash Pr.

***American Art No. 4, Set.** National Museum of American Art Staff. 1994. pap. 15.00 (*0-937311-19-7*) Natl Mus Amer Art.

***American Art Vol. 9 No. 1.** Smithsonian Institution Staff. 128p. 1995. pap. 15.00 (*0-937311-21-9*) Natl Mus Amer Art.

***American Art Vol. 9, No. 2: Summer.** (Illus.). 128p. Date not set. pap. 15.00 (*0-937311-22-7*) Natl Mus Amer Art.

***American Art Vol. 9, No. 3: Fall.** (Illus.). 128p. Date not set. pap. 15.00 (*0-937311-23-5*) Natl Mus Amer Art.

American Art see American Etchings

American Art: American Vision: Paintings from a Century of Collecting. Ellen M. Schall et al. LC 89-13806. (Illus.). 164p. pap. 35.00 (*0-295-97312-9*) U of Wash Pr.

American Art at the Nineteenth-Century Paris Salons. Lois M. Fink. (Illus.). 464p. (C). 1990. 69.95 (*0-521-38499-0*) Cambridge U Pr.

American Art Deco. Alastair Duncan. (Illus.). 288p. 1986. 60.00 (*0-8109-1850-1*) Abrams.

American Art Deco. Eva Weber. (American Artists Ser.). 1992. 16.99 (*0-517-06712-9*) Random Hse Value.

American Art Directory 1993-94. 54th ed. Ed. by Bowker, R. R., Staff. 820p. 1993. 186.00 (*0-8352-3202-6*) Bowker.

American Art Directory 1995-96. 55th ed. Ed. by Bowker, R. R., Staff. 825p. 1995. 199.95 (*0-8352-3521-1*) Bowker.

American Art from the Collection of the Worcester Art Museum. Intro. by Richard S. Teitz. LC 79-84788. (Illus.). 120p. 1979. pap. 7.95 (*0-88360-031-5*) Amon Carter.

***American Art from the Currier Gallery of Art.** Karen Blanchfield et al. (Illus.). 176p. (Orig.). 1995. pap. 28.00 (*0-917418-99-9*) Am Fed Arts.

American Art from the New York World's Fair, 1939. 60.00 (*0-938290-05-3*) Apollo.

American Art Glass. John Shuman. (Illus.). 336p. 1988. 29.95 (*0-89145-355-5*, 1810) Collector Bks.

***American Art in Colorado Collections.** Rosenstock Arts Staff. (Documents of Colorado Art Ser.). (Illus.). 30p. (Orig.). 1983. pap. 19.95 (*0-938075-47-0*) Ocean View Bks.

American Art in Private Italian Collections. Caroline Bruzelius et al. Tr. by Paul Blanchard. (American-Italian Contemporary Art Ser.). (Illus.). 100p. (Orig.). (ENG & ITA.). 1994. pap. 15.00 (*1-879549-01-8*) Am Acad Rome.

American Art in the Barbizon Mood. National Museum of American Art Staff & Peter Bermingham. LC 76-14950. 1977. fiche, lib. bdg. 22.50 (*0-226-69413-5*) U Ch Pr.

American Art in the Barbizon Mood. Peter Bermingham. LC 74-26664. (Illus.). 192p. reprint ed. pap. 54.80 (*0-8357-5354-9*, 2011372) Bks Demand.

American Art in the Newark Museum: Paintings, Drawings & Sculpture. Ed. by Mary S. Sweeney & Wilmot T. Bartle. LC 81-18765. (Illus.). 432p. (Orig.). 1982. 24.95 (*0-932828-05-1*); pap. 17.95 (*0-932828-06-X*) Newark Mus.

American Art in the Twentieth Century: Painting & Sculpture 1913-1993. Ed. by Christos M. Joachimides et al. (Illus.). 490p. 1993. 70.00 (*3-7913-1261-8*, Pub. by Prestel) TeNeues.

American Art Nouveau Glass. Albert C. Revi. LC 68-18778. (Illus.). 476p. 1981. reprint ed. 40.00 (*0-916838-40-4*) Schiffer.

American Art Now. Edward Lucie-Smith. LC 85-60441. (Illus.). 160p. 1985. 24.95 (*0-688-05884-1*) Morrow.

American Art of the Great Depression: Two Sides of the Coin. Howard E. Wooden. LC 85-52142. (Illus.). 152p. 1985. pap. 15.00 (*0-939324-22-9*) Wichita Art Mus.

American Art of the Twentieth Century. Sam Hunter & John Jacobus. (Illus.). 580p. (C). 1974. text ed. 60.95 (*0-13-024075-3*) P-H.

American Art of the Twentieth Century: Painting, Sculpture & Architecture. enl. rev. ed. John Jacobus & Sam Hunter. LC 73-10210. (Illus.). 586p. 1974. 55.00 (*0-8109-0135-8*) Abrams.

American Art of the 1960s. John Elderfield. (Studies in Modern Art: No. 01). 1992. 40.00 (*0-8109-6099-0*) Abrams.

American Art of the 1960s: Studies in Modern Art One. Ed. by John Elderfield. (Annual Journals). (Illus.). 184p. 1991. 40.00 (*0-87070-180-0*, 0-8109-6099-0); pap. 25.00 (*0-87070-458-3*) Mus of Modern Art.

American Art Pottery. Kenneth Trapp et al. Ed. by Nancy Aakre. LC 87-72601. (Collection Catalogue Ser.). (Illus.). 144p. (Orig.). 1988. pap. text ed. 24.95 (*0-910503-51-6*) Cooper-Hewitt Museum.

***American Art Pottery: Selections from the Charles Hosmer Morse Museum of American Art.** Alice C. Frelinghuysen. (Illus.). 152p. 1995. pap. 35.00 (*1-880699-04-4*) Orlando Mus Art.

American Art Song & American Poetry: America Comes of Age, Vol. I. Ruth C. Friedberg. LC 81-9047. 175p. 1981. 20.00 (*0-8108-1460-9*) Scarecrow.

American Art Song & American Poetry: Voices of Maturity, Vol. 2. Ruth C. Friedberg. LC 81-9047. 236p. 1984. 20.00 (*0-8108-1682-2*) Scarecrow.

American Art Song & American Poetry, Vol. III: The Century Advances. Ruth C. Friedberg. LC 81-9047. (Illus.). 351p. 1987. 27.50 (*0-8108-1920-1*) Scarecrow.

American Art Songs of the Turn of the Century. Paul Sperry. 1991. pap. 9.95 (*0-486-26749-0*) Dover.

American Art Student in Paris: The Letters of Kenyon Cox, 1877-1882. Ed. by H. Wayne Morgan. LC 86-4702. (Illus.). 226p. 1986. 35.00 (*0-87338-333-8*) Kent St U Pr.

American Art Theory, 1945-1970. Stewart Buettner. LC 81-1812. (Studies in the Fine Arts - Art Theory: No. 1). (Illus.). 225p. reprint ed. pap. 64.20 (*0-8357-1178-1*, 2070680) Bks Demand.

American Art Union. rev. ed. Maybelle Mann. LC 87-70145. (Illus.). 128p. (C). 1987. pap. 14.95 (*0-9618779-0-1*) ALM Assocs.

American Art, 1700-1960: Sources & Documents. Ed. by John W. McCoubrey. (Orig.). 1965. pap. text ed. 37.80 (*0-13-024521-6*) P-H.

***American Artisans: Crafting Social Identity, 1750-1850.** Ed. by Howard B. Rock et al. LC 95-1296. (Illus.). 272p. 1995. text ed. 45.00x (*0-8018-5029-0*); pap. text ed. 16.95x (*0-8018-5030-4*) Johns Hopkins.

American Artist in Africa, 1937: Sketch Book & Diary. Wanda Norstrom. (Illus.). 112p. (Orig.). 1991. pap. 19.00 (*0-9630357-0-3*) P Shedding.

American Artists. (Shorewood Art Programs for Education Ser.). 24p. 1983. teacher ed 214.25 (*0-88185-072-1*); 289.25 (*0-685-42753-6*) Shorewood Fine Art.

American Artists. Royal Cortissoz. LC 74-128228. (Essay Index Reprint Ser.). 1977. 25.95 (*0-8369-1825-8*) Ayer.

American Artists. Ivan Narodny. LC 74-93365. (Essay Index Reprint Ser.). 1977. 20.95 (*0-8369-1311-6*) Ayer.

American Artists. Royal Cortissoz. LC 70-121282. (BCL Ser. I). reprint ed. 12.50 (*0-404-01736-3*) AMS Pr.

American Artists: Signatures & Monograms, 1800-1989. John Castagno. LC 89-28371. (Illus.). 843p. 1990. 145.00 (*0-8108-2249-0*) Scarecrow.

American Artists in Paris, 1919-1929. Elizabeth H. Turner. LC 88-20471. (Studies in the Fine Arts: The Avant-Garde: No. 62). 232p. reprint ed. pap. 66.20 (*0-8357-1877-8*, 2070663) Bks Demand.

***American Artists in Photographic Portraits: From the Peter A. Juley & Son Collection, National Museum of American Art, Smithsonian Institution.** National Museum of American Art, Smithsonian Institution Staff & Joan Stahl. LC 95-3974. (Pictorial Archive Ser.). (Illus.). 96p. (Orig.). 1995. pap. text ed. 13.95 (*0-486-28659-2*) Dover.

***American Artists in Their New York Studios: Conversations about the Creation of Contemporary Art.** Stephan Gotz. (Illus.). 176p. 1995. pap. 29.95 (*3-87135-006-0*, 0060) A Schwartz & Co.

American Artists Materials: A Guide to Stretchers, Panels, Millboards, & Canvas Marks, Vol. 2. Alexander Katlan. (Illus.). 544p. (C). 1992. text ed. 64.00 (*0-932087-19-1*) Sound View Pr.

American Artists' Materials: Suppliers Directory, Nineteenth Century, Vol. 1. Alexander W. Katlan. LC 87-12283. (Illus.). 460p. 1988. 64.00 (*0-8155-5064-2*) Sound View Pr.

American Artists of Italian Heritage, 1776-1945: A Biographical Dictionary. Regina Soria. LC 91-55130. 1994. write for info. (*0-8386-3425-7*) Fairleigh Dickinson.

American Artists of the Bookplate: 1970-1990. Ed. by James P. Keenan & Jacqueline E. Davis. (Illus.). 155p. 1991. pap. 25.00 (*0-9627290-0-0*) Cambridge Bookplate.

American Artists on Art from 1940-1980. Ed. by Ellen H. Johnson. LC 80-8702. (Icon Editions Ser.). (Illus.). 256p. 1982. pap. text ed. 16.00 (*0-06-430112-5*, IN112, Icon Edns) HarpC.

American Arts & Crafts: From the Collection of Alexandra & Sidney Sheldon. Ed. by Katherine P. Hough. LC 92-40714. (Illus.). 104p. pap. 30.00 (*0-295-97280-7*) U of Wash Pr.

American As Anarchist: Reflections on Indigenous Radicalism. David DeLeon. LC 78-58290. (Illus.). 256p. reprint ed. pap. 73.00 (*0-8357-7885-1*, 2036303) Bks Demand.

American As Reformer. Arthur M. Schlesinger. LC 50-14677. 144p. reprint ed. pap. 41.10 (*0-7837-1527-7*, 2041804) Bks Demand.

***American Ascendant: American Foreign Relations Since 1939.** Thomas Paterson et al. 320p. (C). 1995. pap. text ed. write for info. (*0-669-39361-4*) Heath.

American Assassins: The Darker Side of Politics. James W. Clarke. LC 81-47912. (Illus.). 332p. 1984. pap. 14.95 (*0-691-02221-6*) Princeton U Pr.

American Assimilation or Jewish Revival? Steven M. Cohen. LC 87-45374. (Jewish Political & Social Studies). 192p. 1988. 29.95 (*0-253-30608-6*) Ind U Pr.

American Association: A Baseball History, 1902-1991. Bill O'Neal. LC 91-24176. 400p. (Orig.). 1992. pap. 17.95 (*0-89015-812-6*) Sunbelt Media.

American Association for the Advancement of Science: Caribbean Studies, a Symposium. American Association for the Advancement of Science Staff. Ed. by Vera Rubin. LC 84-45529. (American Ethnological Society Monographs: No. 34). 1988. reprint ed. 22.50 (*0-404-62933-4*) AMS Pr.

American Association of Architectural Bibliographers' Papers, Vol. 1. Incl. Henry-Russell Hitchcock. James H. Grady. LC 65-14273. 1965. (*0-318-56191-3*); Walter Gropius. Carol Shillaber. LC 65-14273. 1965. (*0-318-56192-1*); Philip C. Johnson. William O'Neal. LC 65-14273. 1965. (*0-318-56193-X*); Early Architecture of Virginia. Frederick D. Nichols. LC 65-14273. 1965. (*0-318-56194-8*); Sibyl Moholy-Nagy. Philip C. Johnson & William B. O'Neal. LC 65-14273. (*0-318-56195-6*); Holabird & Roche. William Rudd. LC 65-14273. (*0-318-56196-4*); Early Architecture of Virginia. Frederick D. Nichols. LC 65-14273. 1965. (*0-318-56197-2*); Walter Gropius. LC 65-14273. (*0-318-56198-0*); Carroll L. V. Meeks. William B. O'Neal & Frederick D. Nichols. LC 65-14273. (*0-318-56199-9*); Charles-Louis Clerisseau. Thomas J. McCormick. LC 65-14273. (*0-318-56200-6*); Library at Biltmore. Stapleton D. Gooch. LC 65-14273. (*0-318-56201-4*); International Expositions, 1851-1900. Julia F. Davis. LC 65-14273. (*0-318-56202-2*); Henry-Russell Hitchcock. James H. Grady. LC 65-14273. 1965. (*0-318-56203-0*); Architectural Comment in American Magazines, 1783-1815. J. Meredith Neil. LC 65-14273. (*0-318-56204-9*); Adam Style in America, 1770-1820. Sterling M. Boyd. LC 65-14273. (*0-318-56205-7*); Calvert Vaux. John D. Sigle. LC 65-14273. (*0-318-56206-5*); Alvar Aalto. Peter W. Beal. LC 65-14273. (*0-318-56207-3*); Jefferson As an Architect. William B. O'Neal. LC 65-14273. (*0-318-56208-1*); Sir Nikolaus Pevsner. John R. Barr. LC 65-14273. (*0-318-56209-X*); Supplement to the Bibliography of Walter Gropius. Ed. by Ise Gropius. LC 65-14273. (*0-318-56210-3*); Bibliography of Works About Sir Christopher Wren. Ed. by Gail G. Stringer. LC 65-14273. (*0-318-56211-1*); Benjamin Henry Latrobe. Ed. by Paul F. Norton. LC 65-14273. (*0-318-56212-X*); Frank Lloyd Wright in Print 1959-1970. Comp. by James Muggenberg. LC 65-14273. (*0-318-56213-8*); Bibliography of Antonio Gaudi & the Catalan Movement, 1870-1930. Ed. by Maurice E. Farinas. LC 65-14273. (*0-318-56214-6*); LC 65-14273. 128p. 1965. 13.50 (*0-8139-0003-4*) U Pr of Va.

American Association of Architectural Bibliographers' Papers, Vol. 2. Incl. Henry-Russell Hitchcock. James H. Grady. LC 65-14273. 1965. (*0-318-56191-3*); Walter Gropius. Carol Shillaber. LC 65-14273. 1965. (*0-318-56192-1*); Philip C. Johnson. William O'Neal. LC 65-14273. 1965. (*0-318-56193-X*); Early Architecture of Virginia. Frederick D. Nichols. LC 65-14273. 1965. (*0-318-56194-8*); Sibyl Moholy-Nagy. Philip C. Johnson & William B. O'Neal. LC 65-14273. (*0-318-56195-6*); Holabird & Roche. William Rudd. LC 65-14273. (*0-318-56196-4*); Early Architecture of Virginia. Frederick D. Nichols. LC 65-14273. 1965. (*0-318-56197-2*); Walter Gropius. LC 65-14273. (*0-318-56198-0*); Carroll L. V. Meeks. William B. O'Neal & Frederick D. Nichols. LC 65-14273. (*0-318-56199-9*); Charles-Louis Clerisseau. Thomas J. McCormick. LC 65-14273. (*0-318-56200-6*); Library at Biltmore. Stapleton D. Gooch. LC 65-14273. (*0-318-56201-4*); International Expositions, 1851-1900. Julia F. Davis. LC 65-14273. (*0-318-56202-2*); Henry-Russell Hitchcock. James H. Grady. LC 65-14273. 1965. (*0-318-56203-0*); Architectural Comment in American Magazines, 1783-1815. J. Meredith Neil. LC 65-14273. (*0-318-56204-9*); Adam Style in America, 1770-1820. Sterling M. Boyd. LC 65-14273. (*0-318-56205-7*); Calvert Vaux. John D. Sigle. LC 65-14273. (*0-318-56206-5*); Alvar Aalto. Peter W. Beal. LC 65-14273. (*0-318-56207-3*); Jefferson As an Architect. William B. O'Neal. LC 65-14273. (*0-318-56208-1*); Sir Nikolaus Pevsner. John R. Barr. LC 65-14273. (*0-318-56209-X*); Supplement to the Bibliography of Walter Gropius. Ed. by Ise Gropius. LC 65-14273. (*0-318-56210-3*); Bibliography of Works About Sir Christopher Wren. Ed. by Gail G. Stringer. LC 65-14273. (*0-318-56211-1*); Benjamin Henry Latrobe. Ed. by Paul F. Norton. LC 65-14273. (*0-318-56212-X*); Frank Lloyd Wright in Print 1959-1970. Comp. by James Muggenberg. LC 65-14273. (*0-318-56213-8*); Bibliography of Antonio Gaudi & the Catalan Movement, 1870-1930. Ed. by Maurice E. Farinas. LC 65-14273. (*0-318-56214-6*); LC 65-14273. 113p. 1966. 13.50 (*0-8139-0004-2*) U Pr of Va.

An Asterisk (*) at the beginning of an entry indicates that the title is appearing in BIP for the first time.

229

American Association of Architectural Bibliographers' Papers, Vol. 3. Incl. Henry-Russell Hitchcock. James H. Grady. LC 65-14273. 1965. (*0-318-56191-3*); Walter Gropius. Carol Shillaber. LC 65-14273. 1965. (*0-318-56192-1*); Philip C. Johnson. William O'Neal. LC 65-14273. 1965. (*0-318-56193-X*); Early Architecture of Virginia. Frederick D. Nichols. LC 65-14273. 1965. (*0-318-56194-8*); Sibyl Moholy-Nagy. Philip C. Johnson & William B. O'Neal. LC 65-14273. (*0-318-56195-6*); Holabird & Roche. William Rudd. LC 65-14273. (*0-318-56196-4*); Early Architecture of Virginia. Frederick D. Nichols. LC 65-14273. 1965. (*0-318-56197-2*); Walter Gropius. LC 65-14273. (*0-318-56198-0*); Carroll L. V. Meeks. William B. O'Neal & Frederick D. Nichols. LC 65-14273. (*0-318-56199-9*); Charles-Louis Clerisseau. Thomas J. McCormick. LC 65-14273. (*0-318-56200-6*); Library at Biltmore. Stapleton D. Gooch. LC 65-14273. (*0-318-56201-4*); International Expositions, 1851-1900. Julia F. Davis. LC 65-14273. (*0-318-56202-2*); Henry-Russell Hitchcock. James H. Grady. LC 65-14273. 1965. (*0-318-56203-0*); Architectural Comment in American Magazines, 1783-1815. J. Meredith Neil. LC 65-14273. (*0-318-56204-9*); Adam Style in America, 1770-1820. Sterling M. Boyd. LC 65-14273. (*0-318-56205-7*); Calvert Vaux. John D. Sigle. LC 65-14273. (*0-318-56206-5*); Alvar Aalto. Peter W. Beal. LC 65-14273. (*0-318-56207-3*); Jefferson As an Architect. William B. O'Neal. LC 65-14273. (*0-318-56208-1*); Sir Nikolaus Pevsner. John R. Barr. LC 65-14273. (*0-318-56209-X*); Supplement to the Bibliography of Walter Gropius. Ed. by Ise Gropius. LC 65-14273. (*0-318-56210-3*); Bibliography of Works About Sir Christopher Wren. Ed. by Gail G. Stringer. LC 65-14273. (*0-318-56211-1*); Benjamin Henry Latrobe. Ed. by Paul F. Norton. LC 65-14273. (*0-318-56212-X*); Frank Lloyd Wright in Print 1959-1970. Comp. by James Muggenberg. LC 65-14273. (*0-318-56213-8*); Bibliography of Antonio Gaudi & the Catalan Movement, 1870-1930. Ed. by Maurice E. Farinas. LC 65-14273. (*0-318-56214-6*); LC 65-14273. 138p. 1966. 13.50 (*0-8139-0005-0*) U Pr of Va.

American Association of Architectural Bibliographers' Papers, Vol. 4. Incl. Henry-Russell Hitchcock. James H. Grady. LC 65-14273. 1965. (*0-318-56191-3*); Walter Gropius. Carol Shillaber. LC 65-14273. 1965. (*0-318-56192-1*); Philip C. Johnson. William O'Neal. LC 65-14273. 1965. (*0-318-56193-X*); Early Architecture of Virginia. Frederick D. Nichols. LC 65-14273. 1965. (*0-318-56194-8*); Sibyl Moholy-Nagy. Philip C. Johnson & William B. O'Neal. LC 65-14273. (*0-318-56195-6*); Holabird & Roche. William Rudd. LC 65-14273. (*0-318-56196-4*); Early Architecture of Virginia. Frederick D. Nichols. LC 65-14273. 1965. (*0-318-56197-2*); Walter Gropius. LC 65-14273. (*0-318-56198-0*); Carroll L. V. Meeks. William B. O'Neal & Frederick D. Nichols. LC 65-14273. (*0-318-56199-9*); Charles-Louis Clerisseau. Thomas J. McCormick. LC 65-14273. (*0-318-56200-6*); Library at Biltmore. Stapleton D. Gooch. LC 65-14273. (*0-318-56201-4*); International Expositions, 1851-1900. Julia F. Davis. LC 65-14273. (*0-318-56202-2*); Henry-Russell Hitchcock. James H. Grady. LC 65-14273. 1965. (*0-318-56203-0*); Architectural Comment in American Magazines, 1783-1815. J. Meredith Neil. LC 65-14273. (*0-318-56204-9*); Adam Style in America, 1770-1820. Sterling M. Boyd. LC 65-14273. (*0-318-56205-7*); Calvert Vaux. John D. Sigle. LC 65-14273. (*0-318-56206-5*); Alvar Aalto. Peter W. Beal. LC 65-14273. (*0-318-56207-3*); Jefferson As an Architect. William B. O'Neal. LC 65-14273. (*0-318-56208-1*); Sir Nikolaus Pevsner. John R. Barr. LC 65-14273. (*0-318-56209-X*); Supplement to the Bibliography of Walter Gropius. Ed. by Ise Gropius. LC 65-14273. (*0-318-56210-3*); Bibliography of Works About Sir Christopher Wren. Ed. by Gail G. Stringer. LC 65-14273. (*0-318-56211-1*); Benjamin Henry Latrobe. Ed. by Paul F. Norton. LC 65-14273. (*0-318-56212-X*); Frank Lloyd Wright in Print 1959-1970. Comp. by James Muggenberg. LC 65-14273. (*0-318-56213-8*); Bibliography of Antonio Gaudi & the Catalan Movement, 1870-1930. Ed. by Maurice E. Farinas. LC 65-14273. (*0-318-56214-6*); LC 65-14273. 130p. 1967. 13.50 (*0-8139-0006-9*) U Pr of Va.

American Association of Architectural Bibliographers' Papers, Vol. 5. Incl. Henry-Russell Hitchcock. James H. Grady. LC 65-14273. 1965. (*0-318-56191-3*); Walter Gropius. Carol Shillaber. LC 65-14273. 1965. (*0-318-56192-1*); Philip C. Johnson. William O'Neal. LC 65-14273. 1965. (*0-318-56193-X*); Early Architecture of Virginia. Frederick D. Nichols. LC 65-14273. 1965. (*0-318-56194-8*); Sibyl Moholy-Nagy. Philip C. Johnson & William B. O'Neal. LC 65-14273. (*0-318-56195-6*); Holabird & Roche. William Rudd. LC 65-14273. (*0-318-56196-4*); Early Architecture of Virginia. Frederick D. Nichols. LC 65-14273. 1965. (*0-318-56197-2*); Walter Gropius. LC 65-14273. (*0-318-56198-0*); Carroll L. V. Meeks. William B. O'Neal & Frederick D. Nichols. LC 65-14273. (*0-318-56199-9*); Charles-Louis Clerisseau. Thomas J. McCormick. LC 65-14273. (*0-318-56200-6*); Library at Biltmore. Stapleton D. Gooch. LC 65-14273. (*0-318-56201-4*); International Expositions, 1851-1900. Julia F. Davis. LC 65-14273. (*0-318-56202-2*); Henry-Russell Hitchcock. James H. Grady. LC 65-14273. 1965. (*0-318-56203-0*); Architectural Comment in American Magazines, 1783-1815. J. Meredith Neil. LC 65-14273. (*0-318-56204-9*); Adam Style in America, 1770-1820. Sterling M. Boyd. LC 65-14273. (*0-318-56205-7*); Calvert Vaux. John D. Sigle. LC 65-14273. (*0-318-56206-5*); Alvar Aalto. Peter W. Beal. LC 65-14273. (*0-318-56207-3*); Jefferson As an Architect. William B. O'Neal. LC 65-14273. (*0-318-56208-1*); Sir Nikolaus Pevsner. John R. Barr. LC 65-14273. (*0-318-56209-X*); Supplement to the Bibliography of Walter Gropius. Ed. by Ise Gropius. LC 65-14273. (*0-318-56210-3*); Bibliography of Works About Sir Christopher Wren. Ed. by Gail G. Stringer. LC 65-14273. (*0-318-56211-1*); Benjamin Henry Latrobe. Ed. by Paul F. Norton. LC 65-14273. (*0-318-56212-X*); Frank Lloyd Wright in Print 1959-1970. Comp. by James Muggenberg. LC 65-14273. (*0-318-56213-8*); Bibliography of Antonio Gaudi & the Catalan Movement, 1870-1930. Ed. by Maurice E. Farinas. LC 65-14273. (*0-318-56214-6*); LC 65-14273. 106p. 1968. 13.50 (*0-8139-0007-7*) U Pr of Va.

American Association of Architectural Bibliographers' Papers, Vol. 6. Incl. Henry-Russell Hitchcock. James H. Grady. LC 65-14273. 1965. (*0-318-56191-3*); Walter Gropius. Carol Shillaber. LC 65-14273. 1965. (*0-318-56192-1*); Philip C. Johnson. William O'Neal. LC 65-14273. 1965. (*0-318-56193-X*); Early Architecture of Virginia. Frederick D. Nichols. LC 65-14273. 1965. (*0-318-56194-8*); Sibyl Moholy-Nagy. Philip C. Johnson & William B. O'Neal. LC 65-14273. (*0-318-56195-6*); Holabird & Roche. William Rudd. LC 65-14273. (*0-318-56196-4*); Early Architecture of Virginia. Frederick D. Nichols. LC 65-14273. 1965. (*0-318-56197-2*); Walter Gropius. LC 65-14273. (*0-318-56198-0*); Carroll L. V. Meeks. William B. O'Neal & Frederick D. Nichols. LC 65-14273. (*0-318-56199-9*); Charles-Louis Clerisseau. Thomas J. McCormick. LC 65-14273. (*0-318-56200-6*); Library at Biltmore. Stapleton D. Gooch. LC 65-14273. (*0-318-56201-4*); International Expositions, 1851-1900. Julia F. Davis. LC 65-14273. (*0-318-56202-2*); Henry-Russell Hitchcock. James H. Grady. LC 65-14273. 1965. (*0-318-56203-0*); Architectural Comment in American Magazines, 1783-1815. J. Meredith Neil. LC 65-14273. (*0-318-56204-9*); Adam Style in America, 1770-1820. Sterling M. Boyd. LC 65-14273. (*0-318-56205-7*); Calvert Vaux. John D. Sigle. LC 65-14273. (*0-318-56206-5*); Alvar Aalto. Peter W. Beal. LC 65-14273. (*0-318-56207-3*); Jefferson As an Architect. William B. O'Neal. LC 65-14273. (*0-318-56208-1*); Sir Nikolaus Pevsner. John R. Barr. LC 65-14273. (*0-318-56209-X*); Supplement to the Bibliography of Walter Gropius. Ed. by Ise Gropius. LC 65-14273. (*0-318-56210-3*); Bibliography of Works About Sir Christopher Wren. Ed. by Gail G. Stringer. LC 65-14273. (*0-318-56211-1*); Benjamin Henry Latrobe. Ed. by Paul F. Norton. LC 65-14273. (*0-318-56212-X*); Frank Lloyd Wright in Print 1959-1970. Comp. by James Muggenberg. LC 65-14273. (*0-318-56213-8*); Bibliography of Antonio Gaudi & the Catalan Movement, 1870-1930. Ed. by Maurice E. Farinas. LC 65-14273. (*0-318-56214-6*); LC 65-14273. (Illus.). 150p. 1969. 13.50 (*0-8139-0281-9*) U Pr of Va.

American Association of Architectural Bibliographers' Papers, Vol. 7. Incl. Henry-Russell Hitchcock. James H. Grady. LC 65-14273. 1965. (*0-318-56191-3*); Walter Gropius. Carol Shillaber. LC 65-14273. 1965. (*0-318-56192-1*); Philip C. Johnson. William O'Neal. LC 65-14273. 1965. (*0-318-56193-X*); Early Architecture of Virginia. Frederick D. Nichols. LC 65-14273. 1965. (*0-318-56194-8*); Sibyl Moholy-Nagy. Philip C. Johnson & William B. O'Neal. LC 65-14273. (*0-318-56195-6*); Holabird & Roche. William Rudd. LC 65-14273. (*0-318-56196-4*); Early Architecture of Virginia. Frederick D. Nichols. LC 65-14273. 1965. (*0-318-56197-2*); Walter Gropius. LC 65-14273. (*0-318-56198-0*); Carroll L. V. Meeks. William B. O'Neal & Frederick D. Nichols. LC 65-14273. (*0-318-56199-9*); Charles-Louis Clerisseau. Thomas J. McCormick. LC 65-14273. (*0-318-56200-6*); Library at Biltmore. Stapleton D. Gooch. LC 65-14273. (*0-318-56201-4*); International Expositions, 1851-1900. Julia F. Davis. LC 65-14273. (*0-318-56202-2*); Henry-Russell Hitchcock. James H. Grady. LC 65-14273. 1965. (*0-318-56203-0*); Architectural Comment in American Magazines, 1783-1815. J. Meredith Neil. LC 65-14273. (*0-318-56204-9*); Adam Style in America, 1770-1820. Sterling M. Boyd. LC 65-14273. (*0-318-56205-7*); Calvert Vaux. John D. Sigle. LC 65-14273. (*0-318-56206-5*); Alvar Aalto. Peter W. Beal. LC 65-14273. (*0-318-56207-3*); Jefferson As an Architect. William B. O'Neal. LC 65-14273. (*0-318-56208-1*); Sir Nikolaus Pevsner. John R. Barr. LC 65-14273. (*0-318-56209-X*); Supplement to the Bibliography of Walter Gropius. Ed. by Ise Gropius. LC 65-14273. (*0-318-56210-3*); Bibliography of Works About Sir Christopher Wren. Ed. by Gail G. Stringer. LC 65-14273. (*0-318-56211-1*); Benjamin Henry Latrobe. Ed. by Paul F. Norton. LC 65-14273. (*0-318-56212-X*); Frank Lloyd Wright in Print 1959-1970. Comp. by James Muggenberg. LC 65-14273. (*0-318-56213-8*); Bibliography of Antonio Gaudi & the Catalan Movement, 1870-1930. Ed. by Maurice E. Farinas. LC 65-14273. (*0-318-56214-6*); LC 65-14273. 124p. 1970. 13.50 (*0-8139-0299-1*) U Pr of Va.

American Association of Architectural Bibliographers' Papers, Vol. 9. Incl. Henry-Russell Hitchcock. James H. Grady. LC 65-14273. 1965. (*0-318-56191-3*); Walter Gropius. Carol Shillaber. LC 65-14273. 1965. (*0-318-56192-1*); Philip C. Johnson. William O'Neal. LC 65-14273. 1965. (*0-318-56193-X*); Early Architecture of Virginia. Frederick D. Nichols. LC 65-14273. 1965. (*0-318-56194-8*); Sibyl Moholy-Nagy. Philip C. Johnson & William B. O'Neal. LC 65-14273. (*0-318-56195-6*); Holabird & Roche. William Rudd. LC 65-14273. (*0-318-56196-4*); Early Architecture of Virginia. Frederick D. Nichols. LC 65-14273. 1965. (*0-318-56197-2*); Walter Gropius. LC 65-14273. (*0-318-56198-0*); Carroll L. V. Meeks. William B. O'Neal & Frederick D. Nichols. LC 65-14273. (*0-318-56199-9*); Charles-Louis Clerisseau. Thomas J. McCormick. LC 65-14273. (*0-318-56200-6*); Library at Biltmore. Stapleton D. Gooch. LC 65-14273. (*0-318-56201-4*); International Expositions, 1851-1900. Julia F. Davis. LC 65-14273. (*0-318-56202-2*); Henry-Russell Hitchcock. James H. Grady. LC 65-14273. 1965. (*0-318-56203-0*); Architectural Comment in American Magazines, 1783-1815. J. Meredith Neil. LC 65-14273. (*0-318-56204-9*); Adam Style in America, 1770-1820. Sterling M. Boyd. LC 65-14273. (*0-318-56205-7*); Calvert Vaux. John D. Sigle. LC 65-14273. (*0-318-56206-5*); Alvar Aalto. Peter W. Beal. LC 65-14273. (*0-318-56207-3*); Jefferson As an Architect. William B. O'Neal. LC 65-14273. (*0-318-56208-1*); Sir Nikolaus Pevsner. John R. Barr. LC 65-14273. (*0-318-56209-X*); Supplement to the Bibliography of Walter Gropius. Ed. by Ise Gropius. LC 65-14273. (*0-318-56210-3*); Bibliography of Works About Sir Christopher Wren. Ed. by Gail G. Stringer. LC 65-14273. (*0-318-56211-1*); Benjamin Henry Latrobe. Ed. by Paul F. Norton. LC 65-14273. (*0-318-56212-X*); Frank Lloyd Wright in Print 1959-1970. Comp. by James Muggenberg. LC 65-14273. (*0-318-56213-8*); Bibliography of Antonio Gaudi & the Catalan Movement, 1870-1930. Ed. by Maurice E. Farinas. LC 65-14273. (*0-318-56214-6*); LC 65-14273. 132p. 1972. 13.50 (*0-8139-0391-2*) U Pr of Va.

American Association of Architectural Bibliographers' Papers, Vol. 10. Incl. Henry-Russell Hitchcock. James H. Grady. LC 65-14273. 1965. (*0-318-56191-3*); Walter Gropius. Carol Shillaber. LC 65-14273. 1965. (*0-318-56192-1*); Philip C. Johnson. William O'Neal. LC 65-14273. 1965. (*0-318-56193-X*); Early Architecture of Virginia. Frederick D. Nichols. LC 65-14273. 1965. (*0-318-56194-8*); Sibyl Moholy-Nagy. Philip C. Johnson & William B. O'Neal. LC 65-14273. (*0-318-56195-6*); Holabird & Roche. William Rudd. LC 65-14273. (*0-318-56196-4*); Early Architecture of Virginia. Frederick D. Nichols. LC 65-14273. 1965. (*0-318-56197-2*); Walter Gropius. LC 65-14273. (*0-318-56198-0*); Carroll L. V. Meeks. William B. O'Neal & Frederick D. Nichols. LC 65-14273. (*0-318-56199-9*); Charles-Louis Clerisseau. Thomas J. McCormick. LC 65-14273. (*0-318-56200-6*); Library at Biltmore. Stapleton D. Gooch. LC 65-14273. (*0-318-56201-4*); International Expositions, 1851-1900. Julia F. Davis. LC 65-14273. (*0-318-56202-2*); Henry-Russell Hitchcock. James H. Grady. LC 65-14273. 1965. (*0-318-56203-0*); Architectural Comment in American Magazines, 1783-1815. J. Meredith Neil. LC 65-14273. (*0-318-56204-9*); Adam Style in America, 1770-1820. Sterling M. Boyd. LC 65-14273. (*0-318-56205-7*); Calvert Vaux. John D. Sigle. LC 65-14273. (*0-318-56206-5*); Alvar Aalto. Peter W. Beal. LC 65-14273. (*0-318-56207-3*); Jefferson As an Architect. William B. O'Neal. LC 65-14273. (*0-318-56208-1*); Sir Nikolaus Pevsner. John R. Barr. LC 65-14273. (*0-318-56209-X*); Supplement to the Bibliography of Walter Gropius. Ed. by Ise Gropius. LC 65-14273. (*0-318-56210-3*); Bibliography of Works About Sir Christopher Wren. Ed. by Gail G. Stringer. LC 65-14273. (*0-318-56211-1*); Benjamin Henry Latrobe. Ed. by Paul F. Norton. LC 65-14273. (*0-318-56212-X*); Frank Lloyd Wright in Print 1959-1970. Comp. by James Muggenberg. LC 65-14273. (*0-318-56213-8*); Bibliography of Antonio Gaudi & the Catalan Movement, 1870-1930. Ed. by Maurice E. Farinas. LC 65-14273. (*0-318-56214-6*); LC 65-14273. 1973. 15.00 (*0-8139-0477-3*) U Pr of Va.

American Association of Public Accountants: Its First Twenty Years, 1886-1906. Ed. by Richard P. Brief. LC 77-87292. (Development of Contemporary Accounting Thought Ser.). 1978. reprint ed. lib. bdg. 37.95 (*0-405-10919-9*) Ayer.

***American Astronomers: Searches & Wonderers.** Carole A. Camp. LC 95-14472. (Collective Biographies Ser.). 1995. write for info. (*0-89490-631-3*) Enslow Pubs.

***American at Large.** Ferdinand Jelke. (American Autobiography Ser.). 337p. 1995. reprint ed. lib. bdg. 89.00 (*0-7812-8566-6*) Rprt Serv.

American Athletics Annual: 1980 Edition. Ed. by Richard B. Perelman. 694p. (Orig.). (YA). (gr. 12 up). 1980. pap. 15.00 (*0-686-29735-0*) Athletics Cong.

American Athletics Annual: 1981 Edition. Ed. by Richard B. Perelman. 1981. write for info. (*0-318-57618-X*) Athletics Cong.

American Athletics Annual: 1983 Edition. Ed. by Scott Davis. 1983. 10.00 (*0-686-46900-3*) Athletics Cong.

American Athletics Annual: 1984 Edition. Ed. by Scott Davis. 1984. 12.00 (*0-317-11295-3*) Athletics Cong.

American Athletics Annual: 1985 Edition. Ed. by Hal Bateman. 1985. 12.00 (*0-317-41102-0*) Athletics Cong.

American Athletics Annual, 1986. Ed. by Hal Bateman. 1986. 10.00 (*0-317-41105-5*) Athletics Cong.

American Athletics Annual, 1987. Ed. by Hal Bateman. 1987. write for info. (*0-318-63172-5*) Athletics Cong.

American Athletics Annual, 1988. Ed. by Hal Bateman. 1988. write for info. (*0-318-63173-3*) Athletics Cong.

American Athletics Annual, 1989. Ed. by Hal Bateman. 1990. 10.00 (*0-685-33562-3*) Athletics Cong.

American Athletics Annual, 1990. Ed. by Hal Bateman. 1991. 10.00 (*0-685-41037-4*) Athletics Cong.

American Atlas: U. S. Latitudes, Longitudes, Time Changes & Time Zones. 5th exp. ed. Comp. by Thomas G. Shanks. 636p. (Orig.). 1990. pap. 35.95 (*0-935127-13-5*) ACS Pubns.

American Atom: A Documentary History of Nuclear Policies from the Discovery of Fission to the Present. 2nd ed. Ed. by Philip L. Cantelon et al. LC 91-31676. 392p. (Orig.). (C). 1992. text ed. 42.95 (*0-8122-3096-5*); pap. text ed. 17.95 (*0-8122-1354-8*) U of Pa Pr.

American Audience for Art: Proceedings of the Symposium, Wiggin Gallery, Boston Public Library, 1969 & 1970. Character & Extent of the American Audience for Art Symposium Staff. 1972. 5.00 (*0-89073-027-X*) Boston Public Lib.

***American Authenticity: The Dynamics & Consequences of Discrimination.** Adalberto Aguirre, Jr. & Jonathan H. Turner. LC 94-22093. 1994. pap. text ed. write for info. (*0-07-000625-3*) McGraw.

American Authors' Ancestry. John O. Austin. 115p. 1992. reprint ed. pap. 18.00 (*1-55613-558-0*) Heritage Bk.

American Authors & the Literary Marketplace since 1900. James L. West, III. LC 88-20620. 184p. (C). 1988. pap. 17.95 (*0-8122-1330-0*) U of Pa Pr.

American Authors, 1600-1900: A Biographical Dictionary of American Literature. 8th ed. Ed. by Stanley J. Kunitz & Howard Haycraft. LC 38-27938. (Wilson Authors Ser.). (Illus.). 846p. 1977. 76.00 (*0-8242-0001-2*) Wilson.

American Authors, 1795-1895. Patrick K. Foley. 1972. 59.95 (*0-8490-1412-3*) Gordon Pr.

American Autobiography: Retrospect & Prospect. Ed. by Paul J. Eakin. LC 90-12971. (Studies in American Autobiography). 298p. 1991. 42.50 (*0-299-12780-X*); pap. text ed. 17.50 (*0-299-12784-2*) U of Wis Pr.

American Autobiography, 1945-1980: A Bibliography. Mary L. Briscoe. LC 82-70547. 384p. 1982. text ed. 35.00 (*0-299-09090-6*) U of Wis Pr.

An Asterisk (*) at the beginning of an entry indicates that the title is appearing in BIP for the first time.

An Asterisk (*) at the beginning of an entry indicates that the title is appearing in BIP for the first time.

231

American Book Trade Directory 1994-95. 40th ed. Ed. by Bowker, R. R., Staff. 1800p. 1994. 225.00 (*0-8352-3423-1*) Bowker.

***American Book Trade Directory 1995-96. 41th ed. Ed. by Bowker, R. R., Staff. 1800p. 1995. 235.00 (*0-8352-3582-3*) Bowker. "...wonderfully comprehensive & easy to use."--AMERICAN REFERENCE BOOKS ANNUAL. This handy volume captures listings for more than 27,500 retail & antiquarian book dealers, plus almost 1,500 book & magazine wholesalers, distributors, & jobbers. Organized geographically by state & city, entries indicate which businesses handle audiocassettes, software, & other sidelines as well. An Index to Dealers in Foreign Language Books, arranged by language, a Types of Stores Index, listing stores under bookselling categories from Art to Zoology; an Index to Wholesale Remainder Dealers, Paperback Distributors, Exporters & Importers; & an Index to Retailers & Wholesalers are also included.** *Publisher Provided Annotation.*

American Bookmen. M DeWolfe Howe. LC 72-6896. (Essay Index Reprint Ser.). 1977. reprint ed. 53.95 (*0-8369-7248-1*) Ayer.

American Books Abroad: Toward a National Policy. Ed. by William M. Childs & Donald E. McNeil. LC 85-17540. 309p. 1986. 35.00 (*0-916882-05-5*) Heldref Pubns.

***American Booksellers Association: 1995 Membership Directory.** American Booksellers Association Staff. 372p. (Orig.). 1995. pap. 100.00 (*1-879556-17-0*) ABA.

American Bookshelf, Seventeen Fifty-Five. Lawrence C. Wroth. LC 73-87742. (American Education: Its Men, Institutions & Ideas, Ser.). 1975. reprint ed. 23.95 (*0-405-01495-3*) Ayer.

American Border Gardens. Melanie Fleischman. (Illus.). 144p. 1993. 30.00 (*0-517-57646-5*, C P Pubs) Crown Pub Group.

American Bottom Archaeology: A Summary of the FAI-270 Project Contribution to the Culture History of the Mississippi River Valley. Ed. by Charles J. Bareis & James W. Porter. LC 83-15366. (Illus.). 304p. 1984. pap. 24.95 (*0-252-06346-5*) U of Ill Pr.

***American Bounty: Great Contemporary Cooking from the Culinary Institute of America.** Louis Wallach. (Illus.). 208p. 1995. 35.00 (*0-8478-1908-6*) Rizzoli Intl.

***American Bounty: Great Contemporary Cooking from the Culinary Institute of America.** Louis Wallach. (Illus.). 208p. 1995. 35.00 (*0-8478-1923-X*) Rizzoli Intl.

American Boynton Directory: Boyingtons & Byingtons in the U. S. & British Dominions. John Farnham. 147p. 1988. reprint ed. lib. bdg. 32.00 (*0-8328-0298-0*); reprint ed. pap. 22.00 (*0-8328-0299-9*) Higginson Bk Co.

American Boys. Steven P. Smith. 448p. 1984. mass mkt. 4.50 (*0-380-67934-5*) Avon.

American Boy's Handy Book: What to Do & How to Do It. Daniel C. Beard. LC 82-3155. (Illus.). 320p. (J). (gr. 4 up). 1983. reprint ed. pap. 12.95 (*0-87923-449-0*) Godine.

American Brahman: A History of the American Brahman Breed & the American Brahman Breeders Association. Joe Akerman. (Illus.). 384p. 1982. 17.50 (*0-318-12445-9*) Am Brahman Breeders.

American Brahman: A History of the American Brahman Breed & the American Brahman Breeders Association. deluxe ed. Joe Akerman. (Illus.). 384p. 1982. ring bd. 52.50 (*0-318-12446-7*) Am Brahman Breeders.

***American Brands: A Report on the Company's Environmental Policies & Practices.** (Illus.). 27p. (C). 1994. reprint ed. pap. text ed. 200.00x (*0-7881-0988-X*, Coun on Econ) Diane Pub.

***American Brat.** Bapsi Sidhwa. LC 93-27523. 384p. 1993. pap. 14.95 (*0-614-05130-4*) Milkweed Ed.

American Brat. Bapsi Sidhwa. LC 93-27523. 384p. 1993. 21.95 (*0-915943-73-5*) Milkweed Ed.

American Brittany. Nicky Bissell. (Breed Bks.). (Illus.). 1995. 19.95 (*0-87714-153-3*) Denlingers.

American Broadside Verse from Imprints of the 17th & 18th Centuries. Comp. by Ola E. Winslow. LC 77-153361. reprint ed. 67.50 (*0-404-07000-0*) AMS Pr.

American Bronze Sculpture: Eighteen Fifty to the Present. Gary A. Reynolds. Ed. by Mary S. Sweeney. LC 84-22616. (Illus.). 72p. (Orig.). 1984. pap. 12.95 (*0-932828-20-5*) Newark Mus.

American Buddhist Directory. 2nd ed. Kevin O'Neil. 116p. (Orig.). 1985. pap. 20.00 (*0-685-11198-9*) Crises Res Pr.

American Buddhist Directory, 1982. Kevin O'Neil. 96p. 1982. pap. 7.00 (*0-86627-003-5*) Crises Res Pr.

American Buddhist Newsletter: 1981-82, Vol. I. Ed. by Kevin R. O'Neil. 136p. (Orig.). 1982. pap. 35.00 (*0-86627-000-0*) Crises Res Pr.

American Buffalo. David Mamet. LC 77-78079. 128p. 1988. pap. 7.95 (*0-8021-5057-8*) Grove-Atltic.

American Buffalo. limited ed. David Mamet. (Illus.). 118p. 1992. 350.00 (*0-685-70226-X*) Arion Pr.

American Buffet. General Federation of Women's Clubs Staff. LC 93-70636. 1993. write for info. (*0-87197-368-5*) Favorite Recipes.

American Builder's Companion: Or, a System of Architecture, Particularly Adapted to the Present Style of Building. Asher Benjamin. (Illus.). 1969. reprint ed. pap. 8.95 (*0-486-22236-5*) Dover.

American Builder's Companion: 1806 see Works of Asher Benjamin: Boston, 1806-1843

American Building: Materials & Techniques from the Beginning of the Colonial Settlements to the Present. Carl W. Condit. (Illus.). xiv, 330p. (C). 1983. pap. text ed. 18.95 (*0-226-11450-3*, CHAC25) U Ch Pr.

American Building: Materials & Techniques from the Beginning of the Colonial Settlements to the Present. 2nd ed. Carl W. Condit. (Illus.). xiv, 330p. (C). 1983. 16.95 (*0-685-05698-8*) U Ch Pr.

American Buildings & Their Architects, Vol. 1: The Colonial & Neo-Classical Styles. William H. Pierson, Jr. (Illus.). 528p. 1986. pap. 19.95 (*0-19-504216-6*) OUP.

American Buildings & Their Architects, Vol. 2: Technology & the Picturesque, the Corporate & the Early Gothic Styles. William H. Pierson, Jr. (Illus.). 528p. 1986. pap. 16.95 (*0-19-504217-4*) OUP.

American Buildings & Their Architects, Vol. 4: Progressive & Academic Ideals at the Turn of the Twentieth Century. William H. Jordy. (Illus.). 420p. 1986. pap. 19.95 (*0-19-504218-2*) OUP.

American Buildings & Their Architects, Vol. 5: The Impact of European Modernism in the Mid-Twentieth Century. William H. Jordy. (Illus.). 469p. 1986. pap. 19.95 (*0-19-504219-0*) OUP.

American Bull Terriers: A Legacy in Gameness. Frank C. Rocca, II. (Orig.). 1992. pap. write for info. (*0-941223-01-9*) Rocca Ent.

American Bulldog. John Blackwell. (Illus.). 1994. 11.95 (*0-86622-867-5*, KW221) TFH Pubns.

American Bureaucracy. Richard J. Stillman, II. LC 86-23923. 309p. (C). 1987. pap. text ed. 21.95 (*0-8304-1052-X*) Nelson-Hall.

American Bureaucracy. Ed. by Warren G. Bennis. (Society Bks.). 187p. 1970. reprint ed. 27.95x (*0-87855-053-4*); reprint ed. pap. text ed. 16.95x (*0-87855-546-3*) Transaction Pubs.

American Bureaucracy: Public Choice & Public Law. Glen O. Robinson. 276p. (C). 1991. text ed. 42.50 (*0-472-10243-5*) U of Mich Pr.

American Business. (Illus.). 48p. (J). (gr. 6-12). 1975. pap. 1.85 (*0-8395-3325-X*, 33325) BSA.

American Business. abr. ed. Luanna C. Blagrove. (AMERCE Business Ser.). 250p. 1987. text ed. 24.95 (*0-939776-32-4*) Blagrove Pubns.

American Business: An Introduction. 6th ed. Ferdinand F. Mauser & David J. Schwartz. 729p. (C). 1986. pap. text ed. 32.00 (*0-15-502315-2*) Dryden Pr.

American Business: The Last Hurrah? Can We Regain Our Competitive Edge? Terrance S. Hitchcock. LC 81-68094. 220p. reprint ed. pap. 62.70 (*0-8357-5356-5*, 2021656) Bks Demand.

American Business - A Two-Minute Warning: Ten Tough Issues Managers Must Face. C. Jackson Grayson, Jr. & Carla S. O'Dell. 350p. 1988. text ed. 35.00 (*0-02-912680-0*) Free Pr.

American Business Abroad: Ford on Six Continents. Mira Wilkins & Frank E. Hill. LC 64-12747. (Illus.). 559p. 1964. 39.95 (*0-8143-1227-6*) Wayne St U Pr.

American Business Abroad: Six Lectures on Direct Investment. Charles P. Kindleberger. LC 69-12325. (Illus.). 235p. (C). reprint ed. pap. 67.00 (*0-8357-8017-1*, 2033781) Bks Demand.

American Business Abroad Series, 50 vols. Ed. by Stuart Bruchey & Eleanor Bruchey. 1976. reprint ed. 1,451.50 (*0-405-09261-X*) Ayer.

American Business & Insurance Attorneys Directory of Preferred United States, Canadian & International Law Firms. American Business & Insurance Attorneys Association Staff. (Illus.). 1824p. 1992. 59.00 (*0-87218-085-9*) Natl Underwriter.

American Business & the Public School: Case Studies of Corporate Involvement in Public Education. 1988. lib. bdg. 26.95 (*0-87186-338-3*) Comm Econ Dev.

American Business & the Public School: Case Studies of Corporate Involvement in Public Education. Ed. by Marsha Levine & Roberta Trachtman. 296p. 1988. text ed. 27.95 (*0-8077-2880-2*) Tchrs Coll.

American Business Corporations until 1860 with Special Reference to Massachusetts. Edwin M. Dodd. LC 53-9043. 544p. 1954. 35.00 (*0-674-02000-6*) HUP.

American Business Cycle: Continuity & Change. Ed. by Robert J. Gordon. LC 85-29026. (NBER Studies in Business Cycle: Vol. 25). xiv, 868p. 1990. pap. text ed. 35.00 (*0-226-30453-1*) U Ch Pr.

American Business Dictionary. P. H. Collin. 302p. 1991. reprint ed. pap. text ed. 16.95 (*0-948549-11-4*, Pub. by Peter Collin UK) IBD Ltd.

American Business English, No. 1A. Edwin T. Cornelius, Jr. (American Business English (A.B.E.) Satellite Television Program Ser.). (Illus.). 110p. 1987. vhs 60.00 (*0-89209-775-2*) Pace Intl Res.

American Business English, No. 1B. Edwin T. Cornelius, Jr. (American Business English (A.B.E.) Satellite Television Program Ser.). (Illus.). 110p. 1987. vhs 60.00 (*0-89209-776-0*) Pace Intl Res.

American Business English, No. 2A. Edwin T. Cornelius, Jr. (American Business English (A.B.E.) Satellite Television Program Ser.). (Illus.). 133p. 1987. vhs 60.00 (*0-89209-777-9*) Pace Intl Res.

American Business English, No. 2B. Edwin T. Cornelius, Jr. (American Business English (A.B.E.) Satellite Television Program Ser.). (Illus.). 133p. 1987. vhs 60.00 (*0-89209-778-7*) Pace Intl Res.

American Business English, No. 3A. Edwin T. Cornelius, Jr. (American Business English (A.B.E.) Satellite Television Program Ser.). (Illus.). 161p. 1987. vhs 60.00 (*0-89209-779-5*) Pace Intl Res.

American Business English, No. 3B. Edwin T. Cornelius, Jr. (American Business English (A.B.E.) Satellite Television Program Ser.). (Illus.). 161p. 1987. vhs 60.00 (*0-89209-780-9*) Pace Intl Res.

American Business English, No. 4A. Edwin T. Cornelius, Jr. (American Business English (A.B.E.) Satellite Television Program Ser.). (Illus.). 181p. 1987. vhs 60.00 (*0-89209-781-7*) Pace Intl Res.

American Business English, No. 4B. Edwin T. Cornelius, Jr. (American Business English (A.B.E.) Satellite Television Program Ser.). (Illus.). 181p. 1987. vhs 60.00 (*0-89209-782-5*) Pace Intl Res.

American Business English, No. IA. Edwin T. Cornelius, Jr. (American Business English (A.B.E.) Satellite Television Program Ser.). (Illus.). 110p. 1987. audio 12.00 (*0-89209-785-X*) Pace Intl Res.

American Business English, No. IB. Edwin T. Cornelius, Jr. (American Business English (A.B.E.) Satellite Television Program Ser.). (Illus.). 110p. 1987. audio 12.00 (*0-89209-786-8*) Pace Intl Res.

American Business English, No. IIA. Edwin T. Cornelius, Jr. (American Business English (A.B.E.) Satellite Television Program Ser.). (Illus.). 133p. 1987. audio 12.00 (*0-89209-787-6*) Pace Intl Res.

American Business English, No. IIB. Edwin T. Cornelius, Jr. (American Business English (A.B.E.) Satellite Television Program Ser.). (Illus.). 133p. 1987. audio 12.00 (*0-89209-788-4*) Pace Intl Res.

American Business English, No. IIIA. Edwin T. Cornelius, Jr. (American Business English (A.B.E.) Satellite Television Program Ser.). (Illus.). 161p. 1987. audio 12.00 (*0-89209-789-2*) Pace Intl Res.

American Business English, No. IIIB. Edwin T. Cornelius, Jr. (American Business English (A.B.E.) Satellite Television Program Ser.). (Illus.). 161p. 1987. audio 12.00 (*0-89209-790-6*) Pace Intl Res.

American Business English, No. IVA. Edwin T. Cornelius, Jr. (American Business English (A.B.E.) Satellite Television Program Ser.). (Illus.). 181p. 1987. audio 12.00 (*0-89209-791-4*) Pace Intl Res.

American Business English, No. IVB. Edwin T. Cornelius, Jr. (American Business English (A.B.E.) Satellite Television Program Ser.). (Illus.). 181p. 1987. audio 12.00 (*0-89209-792-2*) Pace Intl Res.

American Business English, Vol. I. Edwin T. Cornelius, Jr. (American Business English (A.B.E.) Satellite Television Program Ser.). (Illus.). 110p. 1987. pap. text ed. 8.00 (*0-89209-750-7*) Pace Intl Res.

American Business English, Vol. II. Edwin T. Cornelius, Jr. (American Business English (A.B.E.) Satellite Television Program Ser.). (Illus.). 133p. 1987. pap. text ed. 8.00 (*0-89209-751-5*) Pace Intl Res.

American Business English, Vol. III. Edwin T. Cornelius, Jr. (American Business English (A.B.E.) Satellite Television Program Ser.). (Illus.). 161p. 1987. pap. text ed. 8.00 (*0-89209-752-3*) Pace Intl Res.

American Business English, Vol. IV. Edwin T. Cornelius, Jr. (American Business English (A.B.E.) Satellite Television Program Ser.). (Illus.). 181p. 1987. pap. text ed. 8.00 (*0-89209-753-1*) Pace Intl Res.

American Business Handbook. (Illus.). 450p. (Orig.). (C). 1994. pap. 135.00 (*1-57205-719-X*) Rector Pr.

American Business History: Case Studies. Ed. by Henry C. Dethloff & C. Joseph Pusateri. LC 86-16651. (Illus.). 456p. (C). 1987. pap. text ed. write for info. (*0-88295-845-3*) Harlan Davidson.

***American Business in China.** Davisson K. Chang. (Orig.). 1995. pap. 85.00 (*0-9644322-8-5*) Caravel.

American Business in the Twentieth Century. Thomas C. Cochran. LC 72-78424. 269p. reprint ed. pap. 76.70 (*0-8357-5355-7*, 2019928) Bks Demand.

American Business Law Journal: 1963-1989, 31 vols., Set. 1,392.50 (*0-8377-9014-X*) Rothman.

American Business Leaders. Frank W. Taussig & C. S. Joslyn. LC 70-175040. reprint ed. 29.50 (*0-404-06349-7*) AMS Pr.

American Business Manual, 3 vols., 1. Edward M. Carney, Jr. et al. Ed. by Alfred D. Chandler. LC 79-7536. (History of Management Thought & Practice Ser.). 1980. reprint ed. lib. bdg. 37.95 (*0-405-12319-1*) Ayer.

American Business Manual, 3 vols., 2. Edward M. Carney, Jr. et al. Ed. by Alfred D. Chandler. LC 79-7536. (History of Management Thought & Practice Ser.). 1980. reprint ed. lib. bdg. 37.95 (*0-405-12320-5*) Ayer.

American Business Manual, 3 vols., 3. Edward M. Carney, Jr. et al. Ed. by Alfred D. Chandler. LC 79-7536. (History of Management Thought & Practice Ser.). 1980. reprint ed. lib. bdg. 37.95 (*0-405-12321-3*) Ayer.

American Business Manual, 3 vols., Set. Edward M. Carney, Jr. et al. Ed. by Alfred D. Chandler. LC 79-7536. (History of Management Thought & Practice Ser.). 1980. reprint ed. lib. bdg. 113.95 (*0-405-12318-3*) Ayer.

***American Business Travel Planner.** (Illus.). 300p. (Orig.). 1995. pap. 295.00 (*0-7605-1973-0*) Rector Pr.

American Business Values. 3rd ed. Gerald F. Cavanagh. 256p. (C). 1989. pap. text ed. write for info. (*0-13-025529-7*) P-H.

American Bypaths: Essays in Honor of E. Hudson Long. Ed. by Robert G. Collmer & Jack W. Herring. LC 80-82061. 250p. 1980. 19.50 (*0-918954-22-3*) Baylor Univ Pr.

***American Cabinetmakers: Marked American Furniture 1640 - 1940.** William C. Ketchum, Jr. & Museum of American Folk Art Staff. LC 94-40639. 1995. write for info. (*0-517-59562-1*, Crown) Crown Pub Group.

American Caesar: Douglas MacArthur, 1880-1964. William Manchester. 1058p. (gr. 7 up). 1983. mass mkt. 6.95 (*0-440-30424-5*, LE) Dell.

American Caesar: Douglas MacArthur 1880-1964. William Manchester. LC 78-8004. (Illus.). 1978. 35.00 (*0-316-54498-1*) Little.

American Calendar Customs, Vol. I. Catherine H. Ainsworth. LC 79-52827. 112p. (Orig.). (J). (ps-12). 1979. 12.00 (*0-933190-06-9*) Clyde Pr.

American Calendar Customs, Vol. II. Catherine H. Ainsworth. LC 79-55784. 110p. (Orig.). (J). (ps-12). 1980. 12.00 (*0-933190-07-7*) Clyde Pr.

American Campaigns of Rochambeau's Army, 1780-1783: The Journals of Clermont-Crevecoeur, Verger & Berthier, 2 vols., Vol. I, The Journals; Vol. II, Maps & Views. Ed. by Howard C. Rice & Anne S. Brown. LC 71-166388. 1972. 275.00x (*0-691-04610-7*) Princeton U Pr.

American Cancer Society Cookbook. Anne Lindsay. 1990. 9.98 (*0-671-07484-9*) S&S Trade.

American Cancer Society Cookbook: A Menu for Good Health. Anne Lindsay & Diane J. Fine. LC 87-28230. (Illus.). 256p. 1988. 25.00 (*0-688-07484-7*) Hearst Bks.

***American Cancer Society Textbook of Clinical Oncology.** 2nd ed. Ed. by Gerald P. Murphy et al. LC 95-132. 1995. write for info. (*0-944235-10-7*) Am Cancer NY.

American Cancer Society's "Freshstart" 21 Days to Stop Smoking. Dee Burton. 1986. mass mkt. 4.99 (*0-671-62086-X*) PB.

American Candy Market: An Analysis of Current Markets & Prospects for Future Growth. 400p. 1992. 1,150.00 (*0-317-55215-5*) Busn Trend.

American Canoe Association River Safety Report, 1986-1988. Charles C. Walbridge. 94p. 1989. pap. 2.95 (*0-943117-01-1*) Am Canoe Assn.

***American Canoe Association River Safety Report, 1989-1991.** Charles C. Walbridge. 1992. pap. 5.95 (*0-943117-03-8*) Am Canoe Assn.

American Canvas: Art, Eye & Spirit of Pioneer Artists. Ron Tyler. 208p. 1990. 15.99 (*0-517-01736-9*) Random Hse Value.

American Capital Market, Eighteen Forty-Six to Nineteen Fourteen: A Study of the Effects of Public Policy on Economic Development. Richard E. Sylla. LC 75-2599. (Dissertations in American Economic History Ser.). (Illus.). 1979. 40.95 (*0-405-07220-1*) Ayer.

American Capitalism. John Kenneth Galbraith. pap. 3.25 (*0-395-08367-2*, 18, SenEd) HM.

American Capitalism. Louis M. Hacker. LC 78-11581. (Anvil Ser.). 190p. 1979. reprint ed. pap. text ed. 9.50 (*0-88275-750-4*) Krieger.

American Capitalism: A Macro View. David Ramsett. 208p. (C). 1992. pap. text ed. 32.95 (*0-8403-8150-6*) Kendall-Hunt.

American Capitalism: The Concept of Countervailing Power. rev. ed. John Kenneth Galbraith. 221p. (C). 1993. pap. text ed. 19.95 (*1-56000-674-9*) Transaction Pubs.

American Capitols: An Encyclopedia of the State, National & Territorial Capitol Edifices of the United States. Eldon Hauck. LC 90-53609. (Illus.). 320p. 1991. lib. bdg. 43.50x (*0-89950-551-1*) McFarland & Co.

American Carbon Manual; Or, the Production of Photographic Prints in Permanent Pigments. Edward L. Wilson. LC 72-9246. (Literature of Photography Ser.). 1980. reprint ed. 11.95 (*0-405-04950-1*) Ayer.

American Carousel, The. Sally A. Denno. LC 90-64384. (Illus.). 54p. 1991. pap. text ed. 8.95 (*0-916809-48-X*) Scott Pubns MI.

***American Carpatho-Russian Orthodox Greek Catholic Diocese: A History & Chronology.** Lawrence Barriger. Ed. by Karl Pruter. LC 95-3867. (Autocephalous Orthodox Churches Ser.: No. 4). 1995. lib. bdg. write for info. (*0-912134-20-8*, St Willibrords Pr); pap. write for info. (*0-912134-21-6*, St Willibrords Pr) Borgo Pr.

American Carriages, Sleighs, Sulkies & Carts. Ed. by Don H. Berkebile. LC 76-17222. (Pictorial Archive Ser.). (Illus.). 1977. pap. 7.95 (*0-486-23328-6*) Dover.

American Carriages, Sleighs, Sulkies & Carts: 168 Illustrations from Victorian Sources. Ed. by Don H. Berkebile. (Illus.). 20.75 (*0-8446-5556-2*) Peter Smith.

American Cars. L. Mandel. 1984. 24.95 (*0-517-44767-3*) Random Hse Value.

American Cartridge. Suydam. 1960. 18.00 (*0-87505-106-5*) Borden.

American Case Furniture in the Mabel Brady Garvan & Other Collections at Yale University. Gerald W. Ward. (C). 1988. text ed. 60.00 (*0-300-03357-5*) Yale U Pr.

American Cassandra: The Life of Dorothy Thompson. Peter Kurth. 1991. pap. 12.95 (*0-316-50724-5*) Little.

American Cassiinae. Howard S. Irwin & Rupert C. Barneby. LC 82-8282. (Memoirs Ser.: Vol. 35, 2 Pts.). (Illus.). 918p. 1982. pap. 100.00 (*0-89327-241-8*) NY Botanical.

American Caste & the Negro College. Buell G. Gallagher. LC 66-29471. 478p. 1966. reprint ed. 75.00 (*0-87752-041-0*) Gordian.

An Asterisk (*) at the beginning of an entry indicates that the title is appearing in BIP for the first time.

An Asterisk (*) at the beginning of an entry indicates that the title is appearing in BIP for the first time.

American Civil War. Peter Parish. LC 74-84660. 728p. 1975. reprint ed. 55.00 (*0-8419-0176-7*) Holmes & Meier.

***American Civil War: A Multicultural Encyclopedia, 7 vols.** Civil War Society. (Illus.). 1994. write for info. (*0-7172-7348-2*) Grolier Inc.

American Civil War: Recreated in Colour Photographs. David Schiller. (Europa Militaria Special Ser.). (Illus.). 96p. 1990. pap. 19.95 (*1-872004-40-7*) Motorbooks Intl.

American Civil War & the Origins of Modern Warfare: Ideas, Organization, & Field Command. Edward Hagerman. LC 87-46015. (Illus.). 384p. 1992. 37.50 (*0-253-30546-2*); pap. 12.95 (*0-253-20715-0*, MB-715) Ind U Pr.

American Civil War Armies, Vol. 1: Confederate Artillery, Cavalry, & Infantry. Philip Katcher. (Men-at-Arms Ser.: No. 170). (Illus.). 48p. pap. 11.95 (*0-85045-679-7*, 9102, Pub. by Osprey UK) Stackpole.

American Civil War Armies, Vol. 2: Union Troops. Philip Katcher. (Men-at-Arms Ser.: No. 177). (Illus.). 48p. 1989. pap. 11.95 (*0-85045-690-8*, 9109, Pub. by Osprey Pubng Ltd UK) Stackpole.

American Civil War Armies, Vol. 3: Specialist Troops. Philip Katcher. (Men-at-Arms Ser.: No. 179). (Illus.). 48p. 1989. pap. 11.95 (*0-85045-722-X*, 9111, Pub. by Osprey Pubng Ltd UK) Stackpole.

American Civil War Armies, Vol. 4: State Troops. Philip Katcher. (Men-at-Arms Ser.: No. 190). (Illus.). 48p. 1987. pap. 11.95 (*0-85045-747-5*, 9123, Pub. by Osprey Pubng Ltd UK) Stackpole.

American Civil War Armies, Vol. 5: Volunteer Militia. Philip Katcher. (Men-at-Arms Ser.: No. 207). (Illus.). 48p. 1989. pap. 11.95 (*0-85045-853-6*, 9140, Pub. by Osprey Pubng Ltd UK) Stackpole.

American Civil War Medical Series, 12 vols., Set. reprint ed. 595.00 (*0-930405-45-5*) Norman SF.

American Civil War Surgery Series, 11 vols., Set. reprint ed. 495.00 (*0-930405-46-3*) Norman SF.

American Civilization. C. L. James. Ed. by Anna Grimshaw & Keith Hart. LC 93-27470. 360p. (Orig.). (C). 1993. text ed. 49.95 (*0-631-18908-4*); pap. text ed. 19.95 (*0-631-18909-2*) Blackwell Pubs.

***American Civilization: An Introduction.** David Mauk & John Oakland. LC 95-13129. 1995. write for info. (*0-415-10171-9*, Routledge NY) Routledge.

American Civilization: An Introduction to Research & Bibliography. Lionel D. Wyld & Edwards Everett. LC 75-89568. 1975. 14.00 (*0-685-46267-6*) CSNY.

American Civilization & the Negro. Charles V. Roman. LC 74-37316. (Black Heritage Library Collection). 1977. reprint ed. 39.95 (*0-8369-8953-8*) Ayer.

American Civilization in the Nineteenth Century: A Book of Primary Source Readings. Lawrence Kohl. 480p. (C). 1990. per., pap. text ed. 26.95 (*0-8403-6117-3*) Kendall-Hunt.

American Civilization on Trial: Black Masses As Vanguard. 4th ed. National Editorial Board, New & Letters Staff. (Illus.). 48p. 1983. pap. 2.00 (*0-914441-03-5*) News & Letters.

American Claimant. Samuel L. Clemens. (Works of Mark Twain). 1988. reprint ed. lib. bdg. 79.00 (*0-7812-1126-3*) Rprt Serv.

American Claimant. Samuel L. Clemens. 1981. reprint ed. lib. bdg. 59.00 (*0-685-38421-7*) Scholarly.

American Claimant. Mark Twain. LC 72-144588. (Illus.). reprint ed. 36.00 (*0-404-01576-X*) AMS Pr.

American Claimant Manuscripts: The "Ancestral Footstep", "Etherege" & "Grimshawe" Nathaniel Hawthorne. Ed. by William Charvat et al. LC 77-75175. (Centenary Edition of the Works of Nathaniel Hawthorne: Vol. 12). 666p. 1977. 72.50 (*0-8142-0251-9*) Ohio St U Pr.

American Class Society in Numbers. enl. rev. ed. Beth Belton. Ed. by Bob Howard & John Logue. LC 79-121955. (Illus.). 112p. 1981. pap. 2.95 (*0-933522-07-X*) Kent Popular.

American Class Structure. Joseph A. Kahl. LC 57-6451. 1957. 29.50 (*0-03-008815-1*) Irvington.

American Class Structure: A New Synthesis. 4th ed. Dennis Gilbert & Joseph A. Kahl. LC 92-14141. 356p. (C). 1993. pap. 25.95 (*0-534-16374-2*) Intl Thomson.

***American Class System: Divide & Rule.** Paul Kalra. LC 95-77609. 348p. 1995. 23.45 (*0-9647173-5-2*) Antenna Pub.

American Classic: Car Poems. Ed. by Mary Swope & Walter Kerr. LC 85-14061. (SCOP Ser.: No. VIII). 1985. pap. 8.95 (*0-930526-07-4*) SCOP Pubns.

***American Classic: The Durango & Silverton Narrow Gauge Railroad.** Robert T. Royem. (Illus.). 152p. 1995. 39.95 (*0-9643430-0-2*); pap. 24.95 (*0-9643430-1-0*) Limelight Pr.

American Classic Organ: A History in Letters. Charles Callahan. (Illus.). xxv, 531p. 1990. 34.00 (*0-913499-05-6*) Organ Hist Soc.

American Classical Music. Ed. by Kenneth Cooper. (Three Centuries of Music in Score Ser.: vol.13). 225p. 1988. lib. bdg. 25.00 (*0-8240-0940-1*) Garland.

American Classicist: The Architecture of Philip Trammell Shutze. Elizabeth M. Dowling. LC 88-43452. (Illus.). 256p. 1989. 50.00 (*0-8478-1035-6*); pap. 35.00 (*0-8478-1036-4*) Rizzoli Intl.

American Classrooms: Photographs by Catherine Wagner. Ed. by Willie Morris. (Illus.). 96p. (Orig.). 1988. pap. 25.00 (*0-89381-338-9*) Aperture.

American Clipper Ships, 2 vols., Set. Octavius T. Howe & Frederick C. Matthews. 37.50 (*0-8446-6260-7*) Peter Smith.

American Clipper Ships, Eighteen Thirty-Three to Eighteen Fifty-Eight, 2 vols., 1. Octavius T. Howe & Frederick C. Matthews. 928p. 1986. reprint ed. pap. 8.95 (*0-486-25115-2*) Dover.

American Clipper Ships, Eighteen Thirty-Three to Eighteen Fifty-Eight, 2 vols., 2. Octavius T. Howe & Frederick C. Matthews. 928p. 1986. reprint ed. pap. 8.95 (*0-486-25116-0*) Dover.

American Clock. Arthur Miller. 1981. pap. 4.75 (*0-8222-0027-9*) Dramatists Play.

American Clock & Archbishop's Ceiling. Arthur Miller. 176p. 1989. pap. 8.95 (*0-8021-3127-1*) Grove-Atltic.

American Clocks: Highlights from the Collections of the National Museum of American History. Otto Mayr & Carlene Stephens. (Illus.). 48p. (Orig.). 1989. pap. 6.95 (*0-929847-03-2*) Natl Mus Am.

American Clocks: Price Guide Up-Date, 1995, Vol. 1. Tran D. Ly. 16p. 1995. pap. 5.00 (*0-930163-52-4*) Arlington Bk.

American Clocks & Clockmakers. Harriett Swedberg. LC 88-51500. 1989. 16.95 (*0-8019-5258-1*) Chilton.

American Clocks & Clockmakers. Robert W. Swedberg & Harriett Swedberg. LC 88-51500. 192p. 1989. pap. 16.95 (*0-87069-525-8*, Wallace-Hmestead) Chilton.

American Clocks, Vol. 1: A Guide to Identification & Prices. Tran D. Ly. (Illus.). 320p. 1989. pap. 39.50 (*0-930163-39-7*) Arlington Bk.

American Clocks, Vol. 2: Price Guide Up-Date, 1993. Tran D. Ly. 12p. 1993. pap. 5.00 (*0-930163-54-0*) Arlington Bk.

American Clocks, Vol. 2: With a Special Section on Self-Winding Clocks. Tran D. Ly. (Illus.). 336p. 1991. 39.50 (*0-930163-44-3*); pap. 30.00 (*0-685-60151-X*) Arlington Bk.

American Clockwork Toys. Blair Whitton. LC 81-51443. (Illus.). 224p. 1981. 25.00 (*0-916838-55-2*) Schiffer.

American Clyde: A History of Iron & Steel Shipbuilding on the Delaware from 1840 to World War I. David B. Tyler. 132p. 20.00 (*0-87413-101-4*) U Delaware Pr.

American Coaching Effectiveness Program, Level: 1: Self-Study Manual. American Coaching Effectiveness Program Staff. 1987. pap. text ed. 17.00x (*0-87322-095-1*, ACEP5700) Human Kinetics.

American Coaching Effectiveness Program Level 2, Master Level: Sport Injuries Study Guide. J. David Bergeron & Holly Greene. (Illus.). 1989. ring bd. 32.00 (*0-87322-227-X*, ACEP0203) Human Kinetics.

***American Cocker Book.** Michael Allen. (Illus.). 528p. 1989. text ed. 24.95 (*0-9623515-0-4*) Amer Cocker Mag.

American Cocker Spaniel. Alvin Grossman. Ed. by Beverly Black & Nancy Bridge. LC 87-73056. (Pure Breds Ser.). (Illus.). 682p. 1988. 26.95 (*0-944875-00-9*) Doral Pub.

American Codification Movement: A Study of Antebellum Legal Reform. Charles M. Cook. LC 80-662. (Contributions in Legal Studies: No. 14). xi, 234p. 1981. text ed. 59.95 (*0-313-21314-3*, CAC/, Greenwood Pr) Greenwood.

American Collectibles As Advertised, 1860-1899. Comp. by Ada Fitzsimmons. (Illus.). 210p. 1982. 10.00 (*0-915195-00-3*) Paper Pile.

American Collections, Columbus Museum of Art. Nannette V. Maciejunes et al. Ed. by Norma J. Roberts. LC 88-23774. (Illus.). 288p. (Orig.). 1988. 35.00 (*0-8109-1811-0*); pap. 22.50 (*0-918881-20-X*) Columbus Mus Art.

American Collector Dolls Price Guide Book One: 1891 to 1931. Sherry L. Ehrhardt & Dorothy F. Westbrook. (Illus.). 1975. ring bd. 9.00 (*0-913902-14-4*) Heart Am Pr.

American College: A Criticism. Abraham Flexner. LC 73-89179. (American Education: Its Men, Institutions & Ideas, Ser.). 1975. reprint ed. 21.95 (*0-405-01417-1*) Ayer.

American College & the Culture of Aspiration, 1915-1940. David O. Levine. LC 86-4169. 288p. 1986. 42.50 (*0-8014-1884-4*); pap. 15.95 (*0-8014-9498-2*) Cornell U Pr.

American College & University: A History. Frederick Rudolph. LC 90-40967. 616p. 1991. 35.00 (*0-8203-1285-1*); pap. 15.00 (*0-8203-1284-3*) U of Ga Pr.

American College Golf Guide: 1989-90 Edition. Dean W. Frischknecht. 295p. (Orig.). (gr. 9-12). 1989. pap. 9.95 (*0-685-29187-1*) D Frischknecht.

American College of Cardiology Guide to CPT-4, 1994. 161p. (Orig.). (C). 1993. pap. text ed. write for info. (*1-882764-07-2*) Am Coll Cardiology.

American College of Legal Medicine Foundation Medicolegal Primer, 1991 Edition. 400p. 1991. write for info. (*0-9629575-0-X*) Amer Coll Legal.

American College of Physicians Ethics Manual. 2nd ed. 35p. 1989. pap. 7.50 (*0-943126-14-2*, ETM89) Amer Coll Phys.

American College of Physicians Ethics Manual. 3rd ed. American College of Physicians. Ad Hoc Committee on Medical Ethics. LC 92-48551. 1993. 12.00 (*0-943126-26-6*) Amer Coll Phys.

American College of Physicians Home Care Guide for Cancer: How to Care for Family & Friends at Home. Ed. by Peter S. Houts. LC 94-5995. (American College of Physicians Homecare Guides Ser.). 1994. 19.00 (*0-943126-30-4*) Amer Coll Phys.

American College of Sports Medicine 40th Anniversary Lectures. aniversary limited ed. American College of Sports Medicine Staff. (Illus.). 120p. (Orig.). 1994. pap. 20.00 (*1-885377-00-2*) Am Coll Sports Med.

American College President, 1636-1989: A Critical Review & Bibliography. Ann H. Sontz. LC 90-23419. (Bibliographies & Indexes in Education Ser.: No. 10). 224p. 1991. text ed. 55.00 (*0-313-27325-1*, SZC/, Greenwood Pr) Greenwood.

American College Regalia: A Handbook. Ed. by Bruce Emerton. LC 88-188. 392p. 1988. text ed. 49.95 (*0-313-26266-7*, SKR/, Greenwood Pr) Greenwood.

American College Student, 1988: National Norms for 1984 & 1986. Alexander W. Astin et al. (American College Student, 1985, 1987 & 1988 Ser.). 210p. (Orig.). 1990. pap. 8.00 (*1-878477-02-1*) UCLA Higher Educ Rsch Inst.

American College Student, 1989: National Norms for 1985 & 1987 College Freshman. Tamara Wingard et al. (Illus.). 213p. (Orig.). 1991. pap. 15.00 (*1-878477-08-0*) UCLA Higher Educ Rsch Inst.

American College Student, 1990: National Forms for 1986 & 1988 College Freshman. Tamara Wingard et al. (Illus.). 196p. (Orig.). 1991. pap. 15.00 (*1-878477-09-9*) UCLA Higher Educ Rsch Inst.

American College Student, 1991: National Norms for 1987 & 1989 College Freshman. Higher Education Research Institute Staff. (Illus.). 215p. (Orig.). 1992. pap. 15.00 (*1-878477-11-0*) UCLA Higher Educ Rsch Inst.

American College Teacher: National Norms for the HERI Faculty Survey, 1989-90. Alexander W. Astin & William S. Korn. 104p. (Orig.). 1990. pap. 12.00 (*1-878477-04-8*) UCLA Higher Educ Rsch Inst.

American College Teacher: National Norms for the 1992-93 HERI Faculty Survey. E. L. Dey et al. 109p. (Orig.). 1993. pap. 20.00 (*1-878477-13-7*) UCLA Higher Educ Rsch Inst.

American College Testing Program: Official Guide to the ACT Assessment. pap. 12.95 (*0-685-48955-8*) HarBrace.

American Colleges & the American Public. Noah Porter. LC 78-89219. (American Education: Its Men, Institutions & Ideas, Ser.). 1978. reprint ed. 17.95 (*0-405-01458-9*) Ayer.

***American Colonial: Puritan Simplicity to Georgian Grace.** Wendell Garrett. Ed. by David Larlan. (Illus.). 300p. 1995. 65.00 (*1-885254-05-9*) Monacelli Pr.

American Colonial Brides Paper Dolls. Peggy J. Rosamond. 32p. 1981. pap. 4.95 (*0-87588-239-0*, 49) Hobby Hse.

American Colonial Charter. Louise P. Kellogg. LC 71-75291. (Era of the American Revolution Ser.). 1971. reprint ed. lib. bdg. 19.50 (*0-306-71292-X*) Da Capo.

American Colonial Furniture in Scaled Drawings. Alvan C. Nye. 1983. 12.75 (*0-8446-6009-4*) Peter Smith.

American Colonial Furniture in Scaled Drawings. Alvan C. Nye. (Crafts Ser.). (Illus.). 64p. 1982. reprint ed. pap. 3.95 (*0-486-21560-1*) Dover.

American Colonial Life. Mavis Elrod. (Social Studies Ser.). 24p. (gr. 5-9). 1979. student ed 5.00 (*0-8209-0248-9*, SS-15) ESP.

American Colonial Life: Eyewitness Accounts. Intro. by Albert B. Hart. (American History As Told By Contemporaries Ser.). (Illus.). 128p. (Orig.). (C). 1992. pap. text ed. 2.00 (*1-877891-26-6*) Paperbook Pr Inc.

American Colonial Mind & the Classical Tradition: Essays in Comparative Culture. Richard M. Gummere. LC 85-24783. xiii, 241p. 1986. reprint ed. text ed. 59.75 (*0-313-23890-1*, GUAM, Greenwood Pr) Greenwood.

American Colonial Painting: Materials for a History. Waldron P. Belknap, Jr. Ed. by Charles C. Sellers. LC 59-10313. (Illus.). 398p. 1960. text ed. 37.50 (*0-674-02250-5*) Belknap Pr.

American Colonial Portraits, 1700-1776. Ellen G. Miles & Richard H. Saunders. LC 87-600059. (Illus.). 356p. (C). 1987. pap. 37.50 (*0-87474-695-7*) Smithsonian.

American Colonial Press & the Townshend Crisis, 1766-1770: A Study in Political Imagery. Carol L. Knight. LC 89-13774. (Studies in Colonial America: Vol. 1). 296p. 1990. lib. bdg. 89.95 (*0-88946-841-9*) E Mellen.

American Colonial Wealth: Documentary Evidence & Methodology. Alice H. Jones. LC 73-17851. 950p. 1974. 40.00 (*0-405-05695-8*) Ayer.

American Colonial Wealth: Documents & Methods, 3 vols., 1. Alice H. Jones. LC 76-39706. (Individual Publications). 1978. 36.95 (*0-405-05547-1*) Ayer.

American Colonial Wealth: Documents & Methods, 3 vols., 2. Alice H. Jones. LC 76-39706. (Individual Publications). 1978. 36.95 (*0-405-05548-X*) Ayer.

American Colonial Wealth: Documents & Methods, 3 vols., 3. Alice H. Jones. LC 76-39706. (Individual Publications). 1978. 36.95 (*0-405-05549-8*) Ayer.

American Colonial Wealth: Documents & Methods, 3 vols., Set. Alice H. Jones. LC 76-39706. (Individual Publications). 1978. lib. bdg. 108.95 (*0-405-05546-3*) Ayer.

American Colonial Wine Industry: An Economic Interpretation, 2 vols., 1. David J. Mishkin. (Dissertations in American Economic History Ser.). (Illus.). 1975. 26.95 (*0-405-07209-0*) Ayer.

American Colonial Wine Industry: An Economic Interpretation, 2 vols., 2. David J. Mishkin. (Dissertations in American Economic History Ser.). (Illus.). 1975. 60.95 (*0-405-07210-4*) Ayer.

American Colonial Wine Industry: An Economic Interpretation, 2 vols., Set. David J. Mishkin. (Dissertations in American Economic History Ser.). (Illus.). 1975. 87.95 (*0-405-07208-2*) Ayer.

American Colonial Writers, 1735-1781, Vol. 31. Ed. by Emory Elliott. (Dictionary of Literary Biography Ser.: Vol. 31). 300p. 1984. 128.00 (*0-8103-1709-5*) Gale.

American Colonies & the British Empire, 1607-1763. 2nd ed. Carl Ubbelohde. Ed. by John H. Franklin & A. S. Eisenstadt. LC 75-17525. (American History Ser.). (C). 1975. pap. text ed. write for info. (*0-88295-767-8*) Harlan Davidson.

American Colonies from Settlement to Independence. Richard C. Simmons. 448p. 1981. reprint ed. pap. 12.95 (*0-393-00999-8*) Norton.

American Colonies in the Eighteenth Century, 1689-1763. Jack P. Greene. LC 73-79166. (Goldentree Bibliographies Series in American History). (C). 1969. pap. text ed. write for info. (*0-88295-514-4*) Harlan Davidson.

American Colonization Society & Emigration: Solutions to "The Negro Problem" Ed. by John D. Smith. LC 92-32110. (Anti-Black Thought, 1863-1925 Ser.: Vol. 10). 296p. 1993. 46.00 (*0-8153-0982-1*) Garland.

American Colonization Society & the Creation of the Liberian State: A Historical Perspective, 1822-1900. Amos J. Beyan. 224p. (Orig.). (C). 1991. lib. bdg. 49.50 (*0-8191-7991-4*); pap. text ed. 24.00 (*0-8191-7992-2*) U Pr of Amer.

American Colonization Society, 1817-1840. Early L. Fox. reprint ed. 32.50 (*0-404-00159-9*) AMS Pr.

American Colonization Society, 1817-1840. Early L. Fox. (History - United States Ser.). 231p. 1992. reprint ed. lib. bdg. 79.00 (*0-7812-6158-9*) Rprt Serv.

***American Color.** Photos by Constantine Manos. (Illus.). 96p. 1995. 29.95 (*0-393-03912-9*) Norton.

American Color Woodcuts: Bounty from the Block, 1890s-1990s. Ed. by Patricia Powell. LC 92-90494. (Illus.). 135p. 1993. pap. 29.95 (*0-932900-32-1*) Elvejhem Mus.

American Combat Vehicle Handbook. Loren K. Wiseman. (Twilight: Two Thousand Ser.). (Illus.). 104p. (Orig.). (YA). (gr. 9-12). 1990. pap. 12.00 (*1-55878-061-0*) Game Designers.

American Comedy. Harold C. Lloyd & Wesley W. Stout. LC 75-91907. (Illus.). 1972. 20.95 (*0-405-08749-7*, Pub. by Blom Pubns UK) Ayer.

American Comedy & Other Plays. Richard Nelson. 1984. pap. 12.95 (*0-933826-70-2*) PAJ Pubns.

American Comic Strip Collections, 1884-1939: The Evolutionary Phase. Denis Gifford. (Monograph Ser.). 240p. (C). 1990. text ed. 50.00 (*0-8161-7270-6*, Hall Reference) Macmillan.

American Commander in Spain: Robert Hale Merriman & the Abraham Lincoln Brigade. Marion Merriman & Warren Lerude. LC 86-1360. (Wilbur S. Shepperson Series in History & Humanities: No. 21). (Illus.). 272p. 1986. 29.95 (*0-87417-106-7*) U of Nev Pr.

American Commanders & the Use of Signal Intelligence. Ed. by Arthur L. Funk. 93p. 1984. pap. 19.95 (*0-89126-157-5*) MA-AH Pub.

***American Commentary.** Dennis L. Cuddy. 100p. (Orig.). 1993. pap. 5.95 (*1-879366-40-1*) Hearthstone OK.

American Commerce As Affected by the Wars of the French Revolution & Napoleon. Amelia C. Clauder. LC 68-55509. (Reprints of Economic Classics Ser.). 1972. reprint ed. 37.50 (*0-678-00905-8*) Kelley.

American Commercial Banking: A History. Benjamin J. Klebaner. (Twayne's Evolution of American Business Ser.: No. 5). 304p. 1990. text ed. 26.95 (*0-8057-9804-8*, Twayne); pap. 14.95 (*0-8057-9815-3*, Twayne) Macmillan.

American "Commercial Invasion" of Europe. Frank A. Vanderlip. Ed. by Stuart Bruchey & Eleanor Bruchey. LC 76-5046. (American Business Abroad Ser.). (Illus.). 1976. reprint ed. 19.95 (*0-405-09312-8*) Ayer.

American Committee on the History of the Second World War: Newsletter, Spring 1968-Fall 1992, Nos. 1-43. 930p. pap. 138.00 (*0-89126-060-9*) MA-AH Pub.

American Common Law & the Principle Nullum Crimen Sine Lege. 2nd rev. ed. Stanislaw Pomorski. Tr. by Elzbieta Chodakowska. x, 219p. 1975. pap. 10.00 (*0-8377-1051-0*) Rothman.

American Common-Place Book of Poetry. George B. Cheever. LC 74-15734. (Popular Culture in America Ser.). 406p. 1975. reprint ed. 35.95 (*0-405-06369-5*) Ayer.

American Commonplace: Essays on the Popular Culture of the United States. Bruce A. Lohof. LC 82-73977. 1983. 16.95 (*0-87972-221-5*); pap. 8.95 (*0-87972-222-3*) Bowling Green Univ.

American Commonwealth, 3 vols, 1. James B. Bryce. LC 73-39551. reprint ed. write for info. (*0-404-03771-2*) AMS Pr.

American Commonwealth, 3 vols, 2. James B. Bryce. LC 73-39551. reprint ed. write for info. (*0-404-03772-0*) AMS Pr.

American Commonwealth, 3 vols, 3. James B. Bryce. LC 73-39551. reprint ed. write for info. (*0-404-03773-9*) AMS Pr.

American Commonwealth, 3 vols, Set. James B. Bryce. LC 73-39551. reprint ed. 345.00 (*0-404-03770-4*) AMS Pr.

American Commonwealths, 20 vols., Set. Horace E. Scudder. 1908. lib. bdg. 846.50 (*0-404-57200-6*) AMS Pr.

American Communes to Eighteen Sixty: A Bibliography. Philip N. Dare. LC 89-16930. (Sects & Cults in America Ser.: Vol. 12). 212p. 1989. 32.00 (*0-8240-8572-8*, SS348) Garland.

American Communes, 1860-1960. Timothy Miller. LC 89-27481. (Sects & Cults in America Ser.). 624p. 1990. 44.00 (*0-8240-8470-5*, SS402) Garland.

American Communication in a Global Society. rev. ed. Glen Fisher. Ed. by Melvin J. Voigt. LC 86-32132. (Communication & Information Science Ser.). 192p. (C). 1987. text ed. 39.50 (*0-89391-353-7*) Ablex Pub.

***American Communication Research: The Remembered History.** Ed. by Everette E Dennis & Ellen Wartella. (LEA's Communication Ser.). 350p. 1996. text ed. 70.00 (*0-8058-1743-3*); pap. 35.00 (*0-8058-1744-1*) L Erlbaum Assocs.

American Communism & Black Americans, Vol. 2: A Documentary History, 1930-1934. Ed. by Philip S. Foner & Herbert Shapiro. 416p. 1991. 49.95 (*0-87722-761-6*) Temple U Pr.

American Communism & Soviet Russia. Theodore Drape. pap. write for info. (*0-318-60883-9*) Random.

American Communism in Crisis, 1943-1957. Joseph R. Starobin. LC 79-172326. 352p. 1972. 34.50 (*0-674-02275-0*) HUP.

An Asterisk (*) at the beginning of an entry indicates that the title is appearing in BIP for the first time.

An Asterisk (*) at the beginning of an entry indicates that the title is appearing in BIP for the first time.

American Corporate Identity, No. 8. Ed. by David E. Carter. LC 85-72864. 256p. 1992. text ed. 44.95 (*0-88108-106-X*) Art Dir.

American Corporate Identity, No. 10. David E. Carter. LC 94-72169. (Illus.). 1994. text ed. 49.95 (*0-88108-149-3*) Art Dir.

American Corporate Identity 2. David E. Carter. 1987. 39. 95 (*0-88108-039-X*) Art Dir.

American Corrections. 2nd ed. Todd R. Clear & George F. Cole. LC 89-38335. 594p. (C). 1990. text ed. 50.95 (*0-534-12018-0*) Intl Thomson.

American Corrections. 3rd ed. Todd R. Clear & George F. Cole. 551p. 1994. text ed. 52.95 (*0-534-18972-5*) Intl Thomson.

American Corys: Their Settlement & Dispersion in the United States & Canada. Vernon Cory & Michael R. Cory. (Illus.). 98p. (Orig.). 1991. pap. 17.00 (*1-55613-464-9*) Heritage Bk.

American Cossack. Pennsylvania State Federation of Labor Staff. LC 76-154583. (Police in America Ser.). (Illus.). 1978. reprint ed. 22.95 (*0-405-03380-X*) Ayer.

American Cost of Living Survey. Ed. by Arsen Darnay. 800p. 1993. 149.00 (*0-8103-6400-X*) Gale.

American Costume, 1915-1970: A Source Book for the Stage Costumer. Shirley M. O'Donnol. LC 81-48390. (Illus.). 286p. (C). 1982. 35.00 (*0-253-30589-6*); pap. 15. 00 (*0-253-20543-3*, MB-543) Ind U Pr.

American Cottage Gardens. Ed. by Ruth R. Haskell. (Plants & Gardens Ser.). (Illus.). 1990. per., pap. 6.95 (*0-945352-56-5*) Bklyn Botanic.

American Council on Pharmaceutical Education Accreditation Standards & Guidelines. 8th ed. 30p. 1988. pap. 4.00 (*0-318-12486-6*) Am Council Pharmaceutical Educ.

American Counterpoint: Slavery & Racism in the North-South Dialogue. C. Vann Woodward. (C). 1983. pap. 9.95 (*0-19-503269-1*) OUP.

American Counters, Pt. 1: Double Eagle & Eagle Gold. L. B. Fauver. (Illus.). 100p. 1983. 16.95 (*0-9607162-1-1*) Oak Grove Pubns.

American Counters, Pt. 1: Double Eagle & Eagle Gold. 2nd ed. L. B. Fauver. (Illus.). 106p. 1990. pap. 16.95 (*0-9607162-7-0*) Oak Grove Pubns.

American Counters, Pt. 2: Half Eagle Gold. L. B. Fauver. (Illus.). 100p. 1989. pap. 16.95 (*0-9607162-3-8*) Oak Grove Pubns.

American Counters, Pt. 3: Three Dollar & Quarter Eagle Gold. L. B. Fauver. 100p. 1989. pap. 16.95 (*0-9607162-4-6*) Oak Grove Pubns.

American Counters, Pt. 4: One Dollar Gold & One Dollar Silver. L. B. Fauver. (Illus.). 100p. (Orig.). 1990. pap. 16.95 (*0-9607162-5-4*) Oak Grove Pubns.

American Counters, Pt. 5: Less-Than One Dollar & Miscellaneous. L. B. Fauer. (Illus.). 100p. 1990. pap. 16.95 (*0-9607162-6-2*) Oak Grove Pubns.

American Counters, Pt. 6: Latin America & Canada. L. B. Fauver. (Illus.). 100p. 1990. pap. text ed. 16.95 (*0-9607162-8-9*) Oak Grove Pubns.

American Counties: Origins of County Names, Dates of Creation & Organization, Area, Population Including 1980 Census Figures, Historical Data & Published Sources. 4th ed. Joseph N. Kane. LC 82-5982. 546p. 1983. 52.50 (*0-8108-1558-3*) Scarecrow.

American Country: A Style & Source Book. Mary E. Emmerling. 1980. 40.00 (*0-517-53846-6*, C P Pubs) Crown Pub Group.

American Country Cheese. Laura Chenel. 1990. pap. 12.45 (*0-201-52337-X*) Addison-Wesley.

American Country Cheese: Cooking with America's Speciality & Farmstead Cheeses. Laura Chenel & Linda Siegfried. 1989. 18.22 (*0-201-19662-X*) Addison-Wesley.

American Country Christmas. Mary E. Emmerling & Chris Mead. 1989. 14.95 (*0-517-57386-5*, C P Pubs) Crown Pub Group.

***American Country Christmas Bk. 2.** Oxmoor Staff. 1994. pap. 14.95 (*0-8487-1186-6*) Oxmoor Hse.

American Country Christmas, 1993. LC 89-61909. 160p. 1993. pap. 14.95 (*0-8487-1174-2*) Oxmoor Hse.

American Country Companion. Judith Miller & Martin Miller. LC 93-28954. (Country Companion Ser.). 1994. 12.95 (*0-00-255367-8*) Collins SF.

American Country Folk Crafts: Fifty Country Craft Projects for Decorating Your Home. Carol E. Sterbenz. (Illus.). 176p. 1987. 29.95 (*0-8109-1857-9*) Abrams.

American Country Furniture: Projects from the Workshops of David T. Smith. Nick Engler & Mary J. Favorite. LC 90-8573. 1990. 29.95 (*0-87857-916-8*, 14-104-0) Rodale Pr Inc.

American Country Furniture, 1780-1875. Ralph M. Kovel & Terry H. Kovel. (Illus.). 256p. 1965. pap. 14.95 (*0-517-54668-X*, Crown) Crown Pub Group.

American Country Girl. Martha F. Crow. LC 74-3936. (Women in America Ser.). (Illus.). 398p. 1974. reprint ed. 34.95 (*0-405-06083-1*) Ayer.

American Country House. Clive Aslet. (Illus.). 320p. (C). 1990. 50.00x (*0-300-04757-6*) Yale U Pr.

American Country Houses of the Gilded Age: Sheldon's "Artistic Country-Seats" Arnold Lewis. (Illus.). 128p. (C). 1983. pap. 9.95 (*0-486-24301-X*) Dover.

American Country Inn & Bed & Breakfast Cookbook, Vol. I. Kitty Maynard & Lucian Maynard. LC 87-10105. (Illus.). 528p. 1987. 24.95 (*0-934395-50-0*) Rutledge Hill Pr.

American Country Inn & Bed & Breakfast Cookbook, Vol. I. 2nd ed. Kitty Maynard & Lucian Maynard. Ed. by Julie M. Pitkin. LC 87-10105. (Illus.). 511p. (C). 1990. reprint ed. pap. 17.95 (*1-55853-064-9*) Rutledge Hill Pr.

American Country Inn & Bed & Breakfast Cookbook, Vol. II. Kitty Maynard & Lucian Maynard. LC 87-10105. (Illus.). 628p. 1990. 24.95 (*1-55853-059-2*) Rutledge Hill Pr.

American Country Inn & Bed & Breakfast Cookbook, Vol. II. Kitty Maynard & Lucian Maynard. LC 87-10105. (Illus.). 640p. 1993. pap. 16.95 (*1-55853-218-8*) Rutledge Hill Pr.

***American Country Kitchen.** Marion Ham. (Brownstone Library). Orig. Title: Gifts from a Country Kitchen. (Illus.). 168p. 1995. 24.95 (*0-8317-3886-3*) A D Bragdon.

American Country Living: The Ultimate Lifestyle Compendium - Cooking, Design, & Gardening. 1992. 24.99 (*0-517-07277-7*) Random Hse Value.

American Country Pottery: Yellowware & Spongeware. William C. Ketchum, Jr. LC 87-45132. 160p. 1987. pap. 19.95 (*0-394-75244-9*) Knopf.

American Country Store: A Wallace-Homestead Price Guide. Don Raycraft. 1994. pap. 14.95 (*0-87069-723-4*) Chilton.

American Country Stores. Bruce Roberts & Ray Jones. LC 91-12279. (Illus.). 128p. 1991. 19.95 (*0-87106-228-3*) Globe Pequot.

American Country Woodworker: Fifty Country Accents You Can Build in a Weekend. Michael Dunbar. LC 92-30997. 1993. 26.95 (*0-87596-568-7*) Rodale Pr Inc.

***American Countryside: Rural People & Places.** Ed. by Emery N. Castle. LC 95-8076. (Rural America Ser.). 512p. (C). 1995. 45.00x (*0-7006-0724-2*) U Pr of KS.

***American Countryside: Rural People & Places.** Frwd. by Cliff Warden. LC 95-8076. (Rural America Ser.). (C). 1995. pap. 25.00x (*0-7006-0725-0*) U Pr of KS.

American Court Management: Theories & Practices. David J. Saari. LC 82-371. (Illus.). xviii, 163p. 1982. text ed. 49.95 (*0-89930-006-5*, SCR/, Quorum Bks) Greenwood.

American Courthouse: Planning & Design for the Judicial Process. 320p. 1983. reprint ed. 79.50 (*1-57073-001-6*, 523-0013) Amer Bar Assn.

American Courts. Daniel J. Meador. 113p. 1992. reprint ed. pap. text ed. 9.50 (*0-314-86717-1*) West Pub.

American Courts: A Critical Assessment. John B. Gates & Charles A. Johnson. 534p. 1990. 32.95 (*0-87187-541-1*) Congr Quarterly.

***American Cousin.** Dawn Lindsey. (Regency Romance Ser.). 224p. 1995. 3.99 (*0-451-17946-3*, Sig) NAL-Dutton.

American Covenant: The Untold Story. rev. ed. Marshall E. Foster & Mary E. Swanson. (Illus.). 186p. (Orig.). 1982. pap. text ed. 11.00 (*0-941370-00-3*) Mayflower Inst.

American Covered Bridges: A Pictorial History. Jill Caravan. (Illus.). 80p. 1994. 12.98 (*1-56138-472-0*) Running Pr.

American Cowboy: The Myth & the Reality. Joe B. Frantz & Julian E. Choate, Jr. LC 81-6580. (Illus.). xiii, 232p. 1981. reprint ed. text ed. 49.50 (*0-313-23109-5*, FRAMC, Greenwood Pr) Greenwood.

American Crafts: Easy-to-Make Projects from Traditional Folk Crafts. Madeline H. Guyon. LC 92-4789. (Illus.). 56p. (J). (ps-3). 1992. 18.95 (*0-8478-1579-X*) Rizzoli Intl.

American Cranberry. Paul Eck. (Illus.). 450p. (C). 1990. text ed. 50.00 (*0-8135-1491-6*) Rutgers U Pr.

American Credo: A Contribution Toward Interpretation of the National Mind. enl. rev. ed. George J. Nathan. (BCL1 - U. S. History Ser.). 266p. 1991. reprint ed. lib. bdg. 79.00 (*0-7812-6016-7*) Rprt Serv.

American Crime & Punishment: The Religious Origins of American Criminology. William Burger. 176p. (C). 1994. text ed. 39.95 (*1-883218-08-X*); pap. text ed. 24. 95 (*1-883218-09-8*) Vande Vere.

American Crime Fiction: Studies in the Genre. Brian Docherty. LC 87-30759. 192p. 1988. text ed. 29.95 (*0-312-01685-9*) St Martin.

American Criminal: An Anthropological Study. Earnest A. Hooton. LC 69-13935. (Illus.). 1969. reprint ed. text ed. 99.50 (*0-8371-0481-5*, HOAC, Greenwood Pr) Greenwood.

American Criminal Justice Process. 1992. lib. bdg. 79.95 (*0-8490-5267-X*) Gordon Pr.

American Criminal Justice Process: Habeas Corpus, Appellate Procedure, Evidence, Federal Statutes, State Provisions, Sentencing Guidelines. 1991. lib. bdg. 79.95 (*0-87700-964-3*) Revisionist Pr.

American Criminal Law Review: 1962-1989, 30 vols. mic. film write for info. (*0-318-57399-7*) Rothman.

American Criminal Law Review: 1962-1989, 30 vols., Set. 1,322.50 (*0-685-42624-6*) Rothman.

American Criminal Procedure, Cases & Commentary. 4th ed. Stephen A. Saltzburg & Daniel J. Capra. (American Casebook Ser.). 1434p. 1993. reprint ed. text ed. 50.00 (*0-314-00351-7*) West Pub.

***American Criminal Procedure, Cases & Commentary: 1994 Supplement.** 4th ed. Stephen Saltzburg & Daniel J. Capra. (American Casebook Ser.). 265p. 1994. pap. text ed. 13.50 (*0-314-04404-3*) West Pub.

American Criminal Procedure, Cases & Commentary, Teacher's Manual to Accompany. Stephen A. Saltzburg & Daniel J. Capra. (American Casebook Ser.). 390p. (C). 1992. pap. text ed. write for info. (*0-314-01112-9*) West Pub.

American Criminal Trials, 2 Vols, Set. Peleg W. Chandler. LC 77-109618. (Select Bibliographies Reprint Ser.). 1977. 66.95 (*0-8369-5227-8*) Ayer.

American Criminal Trials, 2 vols., Set. Peleg W. Chandler. LC 71-113576. reprint ed. 87.50 (*0-404-01445-3*) AMS Pr.

American Criticism: A Study in Literary Theory from Poe to the Present. Norman Foerster. (BCL1-PS American Literature Ser.). 273p. 1992. reprint ed. lib. bdg. 79.00 (*0-7812-6602-5*) Rprt Serv.

American Criticism in the Post-Structuralist Age. Ed. by Ira Konigsberg & Ladislav Matejka. (Michigan Studies in the Humanities: No. 4). (C). 1981. pap. 10.00 (*0-936534-03-6*) Mich Studies Human.

American Criticism, Nineteen Twenty-Six. Ed. by William A. Drake. LC 67-28734. (Essay Index Reprint Ser.). 1977. 23.95 (*0-8369-0389-7*) Ayer.

American Critics at Work: Examinations of Contemporary Literary Theory. Ed. by Victor A. Kramer. LC 83-50327. 450p. (C). 1985. 30.00 (*0-87875-279-X*) Whitston Pub.

American Crow & the Common Raven. Lawrence Kilham. LC 88-10174. (W. L. Moody, Jr. Natural History Ser.: No. 10). (Illus.). 272p. 1989. 32.50 (*0-89096-377-0*) Tex A&M Univ Pr.

American Crow & the Common Raven. Lawrence Kilham. LC 88-10174. (W. L. Moody, Jr. Natural History Ser.: No. 10). (Illus.). 272p. 1991. pap. 18.95 (*0-89096-466-1*) Tex A&M Univ Pr.

American Cruisers of WW II. Steve Ewing. LC 84-61620. (Pictorial Encylopedia Ser.). (Illus.). 152p. (Orig.). 1984. pap. 9.95 (*0-933126-51-4*) Pictorial Hist.

American Cultural Dialogue & Its Transmission. Ed. by George D. Spindler et al. 224p. 1990. 49.00 (*1-85000-773-X*, Falmer Pr); pap. 27.00 (*1-85000-774-8*, Falmer Pr) Taylor & Francis.

American Cultural History, Sixteen Seven to Eighteen Twenty-Nine. Samuel L Knapp. LC 60-6514. 1977. reprint ed. 50.00 (*0-8201-1257-7*) Schol Facsimiles.

American Cultural Leaders: From Colonial Times to Present. Bill McGuire & Leslie Wheeler. Ed. by Richard Ludwig et al. 550p. 1993. lib. bdg. 65.00 (*0-87436-673-9*) ABC-CLIO.

American Cultural Patterns: A Cross-Cultural Perspective. rev. ed. Edward C. Stewart & Milton J. Bennett. LC 91-4256. 206p. 1991. pap. text ed. 16.95 (*1-877864-01-3*) Intercult Pr.

American Cultural Pluralism & the Law. Jill Norgren & Serena Nanda. LC 88-42540. 265p. 1988. text ed. 55.00 (*0-275-92695-8*, C2695, Praeger Pubs); pap. text ed. 19. 95 (*0-275-92696-6*, B2696, Praeger Pubs) Greenwood.

American Culture: Essays on the Familiar & Unfamiliar. Ed. by Leonard Plotnicov. LC 89-16638. 320p. 1990. 49. 95 (*0-8229-1157-4*); pap. 19.95 (*0-8229-6092-3*) U of Pittsburgh Pr.

American Culture & the Marketplace: R.R. Donnelley's Four American Books Campaign, 1926-1930. Claire Badaracco. LC 91-45120. 67p. 1992. 15.00 (*0-8444-0724-0*) Lib Congress.

American Culture Between the Wars: Revisionary Modernism & Postmodern Critique. Walter Kalaidjian. LC 93-15213. 1993. 55.00 (*0-231-08278-9*); pap. write for info. (*0-231-08279-7*) Col U Pr.

American Culture, 1776-1815. Ed. by Peter Onuf. LC 91-15465. (New American Nation, 1775-1820 Ser.: Vol. 12). 508p. 1991. 80.00 (*0-8153-0447-1*) Garland.

American Cultures. (Illus.). 32p. (J). (gr. 6-12). 1980. pap. 1.85 (*0-8395-3388-8*, 33399) BSA.

***American Cultures: Assimilation & Multiculturalism.** Ed. by Elzibieta Oleksy. 1995. pap. 39.95 (*1-57309-012-3*) Intl Scholars.

***American Cultures: Assimilation & Multiculturalism.** Ed. by Elzibieta Oleksy. 264p. 1995. 64.95 (*1-57309-013-1*) Intl Scholars.

American Curriculum: A Documentary History. Ed. by George Willis et al. LC 92-29468. (Documentary Reference Collections). 448p. 1992. text ed. 65.00 (*0-313-26730-8*, WAB, Greenwood Pr) Greenwood.

American Customs & Traditions. Terry Tomscha. (American Background Readers Ser.). (Illus.). 31p. (Orig.) (YA). 1990. pap. text ed. 5.25 (*0-582-03641-0*, 78662) Longman.

American Cut & Engraved Glass. Albert C. Revi. LC 65-22016. (Illus.). 498p. 1982. reprint ed. 35.00 (*0-916838-57-9*) Schiffer.

American Cut & Engraved Glass of the Brilliant Period. Martha L. Swan. LC 84-52053. (Illus.). 328p. 1986. pap. 2.95 (*0-87069-447-2*, Wallace-Hmestead) Chilton.

American Cut & Engraved Glass of the Brilliant Period. Martha L. Swan. 1994. 45.00 (*0-87069-713-7*) Chilton.

American Cut Glass Price Guide: Book 1. rev. ed. Alpha L. Ehrhardt. (Illus.). 1977. ring bd. 7.00 (*0-913902-04-7*) Heart Am Pr.

***American Cyanamid Company: A Report on the Company's Environment Policies & Practices.** (Illus.). 30p. (C). 1994. reprint ed. pap. text ed. 200.00x (*0-7881-0915-4*, Coun on Econ) Diane Pub.

American Dad. Tama Janowitz. 256p. 1987. pap. 10.00 (*0-517-56573-0*, Crown) Crown Pub Group.

American Daguerreotypes from the Matthew R. Isenburg Collection. Richard S. Field & Robin J. Frank. LC 89-51508. (Illus.). 128p. (C). 1989. 35.00 (*0-89467-053-0*) Yale Art Gallery.

American Dame. Philip C. Lewis. 1963. pap. 4.75 (*0-8222-0028-7*) Dramatists Play.

American Dance Festival. Jack Anderson. LC 86-23942. (Illus.). x, 324p. 1987. lib. bdg. 31.95 (*0-8223-0683-2*) Duke.

American Darters. Robert A. Kuehne & Roger W. Barbour. LC 83-5934. (Illus.). 208p. 1983. 45.00 (*0-8131-1452-7*) U Pr of Ky.

American Darts Organization Book of Darts. Chris Carey. (Illus.). 128p. 1994. pap. 9.95 (*1-55821-247-7*) Lyons & Burford.

American Datelines: One Hundred Forty Major News Stories from Colonial Times to the Present. Ed Cray et al. (Illus.). 400p. (C). 1990. 24.95 (*0-8160-2033-7*) Facts on File.

American Daughter. Era B. Thompson. LC 86-12786. (Illus.). 296p. 1986. reprint ed. pap. 9.95 (*0-87351-201-4*, Borealis Book) Minn Hist.

American Daughter Gone to War: On the Front Lines with an Army Nurse in Vietnam. Winnie Smith. (Illus.). 296p. 1992. 22.00 (*0-688-11188-2*) Morrow.

American Daughter Gone to War: On the Front Lines with an Army Nurse in Vietnam. Winnie Smith. Ed. by Julie Rubenstein. LC 93-27366. 352p. 1994. reprint ed. pap. 12.00 (*0-671-87048-3*) PB.

American Days Cookbook. Phillip S. Schulz. 1994. 25.00 (*0-671-70189-4*) S&S Trade.

American Deaf Culture. Ed. by Sherman Wilcox. 1989. pap. text ed. 15.95 (*0-685-34612-9*) Linstok Pr.

American Death Orbit. Ryder Stacy. (Doomsday Warrior Ser.: No. 14). 256p. 1988. pap. 2.50 (*0-8217-2458-4*) Zebra.

***American Decades 1940-1949, Vol. 8.** 1995. 75.00 (*0-8103-5726-7*) Gale.

American Decades 1950-1959, Vol. 9. (American Decades 1900-2000 Ser.). 490p. 1994. 75.00 (*0-8103-5727-5*) Gale.

American Decades 1960-1969, Vol. 3. Matthew J. Bruccoli & Richard Layman. (American Decades 1900-2000 Ser.). 500p. 1994. 75.00 (*0-8103-8883-9*, 021002) Gale.

American Decades 1980-1989. Ed. by Matthew J. Bruccoli & Richard Layman. (American Decades 1900-2000 Ser.). 500p. 1996. 75.00 (*0-8103-8881-2*, 021000) Gale.

***American Decades 1980-1989, Vol. 2.** Ed. by Matthew J. Bruccoli & Richard Layman. (American Decades 1900-2000 Ser.). 500p. 1995. 75.00 (*0-8103-8882-0*, 021001) Gale.

American Declarations of Love. Ed. by Ann Massa. LC 89-6106. 192p. 1990. text ed. 39.95 (*0-312-03190-4*) St Martin.

American Decorative Tiles: 1870-1930. Intro. by Thomas P. Bruhn. (Illus.). 48p. 1979. write for info. (*0-918386-23-3*) W Benton Mus.

American Defender of Bataan & Corregidor. Turner Publishing Co. Staff. LC 91-75226. 240p. 1991. 48.00 (*1-56311-037-7*) Turner Pub KY.

American Defense & Foreign Policy Institutions: Toward a Sound Foundation. Duncan L. Clarke. LC 92-15660. 268p. (C). 1992. reprint ed. pap. text ed. 28.50 (*0-8191-8732-1*) U Pr of Amer.

American Defense Annual, 1988-1989. Ed. by Joseph J. Kruzel. 352p. (Orig.). 1988. text ed. 45.00 (*0-669-17837-3*); pap. 24.95 (*0-669-17838-1*) Free Pr.

American Defense Annual, 1989-1990. Ed. by Joseph J. Kruzel. 352p. 1989. text ed. 49.95 (*0-669-21118-4*); pap. 24.95 (*0-669-21119-2*) Free Pr.

American Defense Annual, 1990-1991. Ed. by Joseph J. Kruzel. 352p. 1990. text ed. 49.95 (*0-669-24543-7*); pap. 24.95 (*0-669-24542-9*) Free Pr.

American Defense Annual, 1991-1992. Ed. by Joseph J. Kruzel. 352p. 1991. text ed. 49.95 (*0-669-27971-4*); pap. 22.95 (*0-669-27970-6*) Free Pr.

American Defense Annual 1993. Ed. by Joseph J. Kruzel. 1993. text ed. 49.95 (*0-02-917671-9*); pap. 19.95 (*0-02-917672-7*) Free Pr.

American Defense Policy. rev. ed. Ed. by Schuyler Foerster & Edward N. Wright. LC 89-48186. 890p. 1990. pap. text ed. 24.95 (*0-8018-3868-1*) Johns Hopkins.

American Defense Policy. 4th ed. Ed. by John E. Endicott et al. LC 77-23161. 640p. reprint ed. pap. 180.00 (*0-8357-5360-3*, 2017569) Bks Demand.

American Defense Policy. 5th ed. Ed. by John F. Reichart & Steven R. Sturm. LC 81-48186. 874p. reprint ed. pap. 180.00 (*0-8357-6906-2*, 2037964) Bks Demand.

American Defense Policy. 6th rev. ed. Ed. by Schuyler Foerster & Edward N. Wright. LC 89-48186. 890p. 1990. text ed. 65.00 (*0-8018-3867-3*) Johns Hopkins.

American Defense Policy & Liberal Democracy. Ed. by Fred E. Baumann & Kenneth M. Jensen. LC 88-34899. 170p. reprint ed. pap. 48.50 (*0-7837-3562-6*, 2043418) Bks Demand.

American Defiance. Ryder Stacy. (Doomsday Warrior Ser.: No. 7). 1986. pap. 2.50 (*0-8217-1745-6*) Zebra.

American Deficit-Fulfillment of a Prophecy? "America Will Spend Herself Out of Existence" (Lenin 1917) Helen P. Rogers. LC 85-52235. 244p. 1988. 17.95 (*0-915915-07-3*) Wellington Pubns.

American Deists: Voices of Reason & Dissent in the Early Republic. Kerry S. Walters. LC 92-2827. x, 394p. 1992. 35.00 (*0-7006-0540-1*) U Pr of KS.

American Delinquency: Its Meaning & Construction. 3rd ed. LaMar T. Empey & Mark C. Stafford. 536p. (C). 1991. text ed. 48.95 (*0-534-14100-5*) Intl Thomson.

***American Demand for Household Furniture & Anticipated Trends.** 2nd ed. Thomas W. McCormack. 70p. (Orig.). 1994. pap. 280.00 (*0-921577-46-X*) AKTRIN.

American Demand for Office Furniture & Anticipated Trends. 2nd ed. Thomas W. McCormack. LC 94-20733. 72p. 1994. pap. text ed. 280.00 (*0-921577-44-3*) AKTRIN.

American Democracy. 2nd ed. Thomas E. Patterson. LC 92-17429. 1993. text ed. write for info. (*0-07-048835-5*) McGraw.

American Democracy. 3rd ed. Lewis Lipsitz & David M. Speak. LC 92-50017. (Illus.). 736p. (C). 1993. pap. text ed. 30.50 (*0-312-06663-5*) St Martin.

American Democracy. 3rd ed. Lewis Lipsitz & David M. Speak. LC 92-50017. (Illus.). 736p. (C). 1993. pap. text ed. 13.00 (*0-312-08080-8*) St Martin.

American Democracy. 10th ed. Michael N. Danielson & Walter F. Murphy. LC 83-4313. (Illus.). 590p. 1983. text ed. 26.95 (*0-8419-0839-7*) Holmes & Meier.

American Democracy: A Commentary & an Interpretation. Harold J. Laski. LC 74-122066. 1974. reprint ed. 57.50 (*0-678-03165-7*) Kelley.

American Democracy: Aspects of Practical Liberlism. Gottfried Dietze. 304p. 1993. text ed. 39.95 (*0-8018-4507-6*) Johns Hopkins.

American Democracy: Institutions, Politics, & Policies. 3rd ed. William J. Keefe et al. 672p. (C). 1990. text ed. 59. 50 (*0-06-043582-8*) HarpCollege.

An Asterisk (*) at the beginning of an entry indicates that the title is appearing in BIP for the first time.

An Asterisk (*) at the beginning of an entry indicates that the title is appearing in BIP for the first time.

237

American Drama, 1940-1960. (Critical History of American Drama Ser.). 1994. lib. bdg. 25.95 (*0-8057-8959-6*, Twayne) Macmillan.

American Drama, 1940-1960. Thomas P. Adler. LC 93-33791. (Critical History of American Drama Ser.). 272p. 1994. text ed. 25.95 (*0-8057-8957-X*, Twayne) Macmillan.

American Dramatist. rev. ed. Montrose J. Moses. LC 64-14706. (Illus.). 1972. reprint ed. 24.95 (*0-405-08800-0*, Pub. by Blom Pubns UK) Ayer.

American Drawing: A Guide to Information Sources. Ed. by Lamia Doumato. LC 79-63743. (Art & Architecture Information Guide Ser.: Vol. 11). 256p. 1979. 68.00 (*0-8103-1441-X*) Gale.

American Drawings & Watercolors. Carol Clark. (Robert Lehman Collection: Vol. 8). (Illus.). 272p. 1992. pap. 45.00 (*0-87099-640-1*) Metro Mus Art.

American Drawings & Watercolors from the Huntington Collections. Susan Danly. LC 87-38073. 44p. (Orig.). 1988. pap. 10.00 (*0-87328-094-6*) Huntington Lib.

American Drawings & Watercolors from the Kansas City Region. Henry Adams et al. LC 92-20319. (Illus.). 495p. (Orig.). (C). 1993. pap. 35.00 (*0-942614-19-4*) Nelson-Atkins.

American Drawings & Watercolors from the Wadsworth Atheneum. Judith A. Barter. LC 87-72426. (Illus.). 96p. 1988. pap. 19.95 (*0-917418-85-9*) Am Fed Arts.

American Drawings & Watercolors from the Wadsworth Atheneum. Judith A. Barter. LC 87-72426. (Illus.). 96p. 1988. 35.00 (*0-933920-99-7*) Hudson Hills.

American Drawings & Watercolors in the Museum of Art, Carnegie Institute. Henry Adams et al. LC 85-2984. (Illus.). 320p. (Orig.). 1985. pap. 15.95 (*0-88039-009-3*) Mus Art Carnegie.

American Drawings in the Art Museum, Princeton University: 130 Selected Examples. Barbara T. Ross. LC 76-27117. (Illus.). 144p. 1977. 45.00x (*0-691-03921-6*) Princeton U Pr.

American Dream. Lily Liu. Ed. by H. L. Peng. 240p. (Orig.). Date not set. pap. 14.98 (*0-9639426-0-3*) Think Big Pubng.

American Dream. Norman Mailer. LC 64-20280. 288p. 1987. pap. 12.95 (*0-8050-0349-5*, Owl) H Holt & Co.

American Dream. Ed. by Jim Villani. (Pig Iron Ser.: No. 19). (Illus.). 128p. 1993. pap. 10.95 (*0-917530-33-0*) Pig Iron Pr.

American Dream, 6 bks., Set. (Illus.). (YA). (gr. 7-10). 1989. lib. bdg. 54.75 (*0-382-09933-8*) Silver Burdett Pr.

***American Dream: A Damien Lords Story.** Damien Lords. Ed. by Andrew Loraditch. 198p. (Orig.). 1995. pap. write for info. (*1-885591-89-6*) Morris Pubng.

American Dream: Advanced Readings on the U. S. A. G. Hocmard et al. Ed. by Joanne Dresner. (English As a Second Language Bk.). 144p. (Orig.). (C). 1982. pap. text ed. 14.00 (*0-582-79799-3*, 75053) Longman.

***American Dream: American Popular Music.** rev. ed. Margaret M. Mayer & Claude Castagner. (Illus.). 218p. (C). 1994. pap. text ed. write for info. (*0-9640120-3-0*) Front Desk LLC.

American Dream: Florida Cattle Baron & Land Developer. Joe B. Hendry, Jr. 1990. 9.95 (*0-9627174-1-X*); pap. write for info. (*0-9627174-0-1*) Jo Bee Pr.

American Dream: From Reconstruction to Reagan, Vol. 1. Edmond Wright. (History of the United States of America Ser.). (Illus.). 352p. (C). 1995. 26.95 (*1-55786-588-4*) Blackwell Pubs.

American Dream: The Ten Power Principles for Financial Freedom. J. W. Dicks & James L. Paris. LC 92-25907. 1992. write for info. (*1-881209-00-8*) Crown Oak Pub.

American Dream: Waking Up. Swami Param. LC 93-91691. 182p. (Orig.). 1994. pap. 14.95 (*0-9637659-0-6*) Dawn Pubns MD.

American Dream, American Burnout: How to Cope When It All Gets to Be Too Much. Gerald L. Fishkin. 201p. (Orig.). 1994. pap. 16.95 (*0-9638371-0-9*) Loren Pubns.

American Dream & the Impact of Class: Teaching Poor Kids to Labor. Larry Van Sickle. 400p. 1985. pap. text ed. 19.95 (*0-8290-1382-2*) Irvington.

American Dream & the Popular Novel. Elizabeth Long. 224p. 1985. 32.50 (*0-7100-9934-7*, RKP) Routledge.

American Dream & Zoo Story. Edward Albee. 1963. pap. 4.99 (*0-451-16643-4*, Sig) NAL-Dutton.

American Dream Business Park. Kathleen Barrett. (Money Is Fun Ser.). (Illus.). 40p. (J). (gr. 1-4). 1995. pap. 14.98 (*1-883579-02-3*) Nordic Goddess. "I loved it-- & I learned from it. A great little book!"...Heather Hughes-Colero, "Winged Wolf", author. "Wow! This is very good stuff...The graphics are super, theme on target. Everything is right & tight...This is a very professional piece.".. Michael Cowden, technical advisor. AMERICAN DREAM BUSINESS PARK by Kathleen Barrett, with illustrations by Oscar Solis, Jr. is a beginner's book that highlights the investments & finance steps needed to help a company start its business. The finance pieces are interlocked for the fledgling business's growth & merger. The author, Kathleen Barrett brings private limited partnership investment, bonds, & stocks into focus for her young readers with a touch of enthusiasm that makes her writing a treat to read. Her personal experience in both finance & small business gives her that special skill of writing from experience. The book is a finance beginner's delight! Fanciful illustrations by Oscar Solis, Jr., brings out the best in each child's imagination. Mr. Solis combines fanciful imagination with thoughts of finance & investment to bring us his most unique & playful style. He engages the reader interactively! Excellent for classroom use, as well as casual reading between parent & child. This is a unique book for grandparent gift selections. Mothers & aunts find themselves reading it to learn finance for themselves, before giving it to the children in their lives. Recommended by the publisher for home education programs on money, business, & creative art. Bonus offer of collector's actual (cancelled) stock certificate available on request. To order contact: Nordic Goddess Press, 2175 Kingsley Ave., Suite 110, Orange Park, FL 32073. Or call 1-(800)-544-2132. *Publisher Provided Annotation.*

American Dream Foreclosed: Strategies for an Affordable Housing Revival. Peter Dreier. (Orig.). 1993. pap. 14.95 (*0-9628504-2-X*) Bywood.

American Dream in the Great Depression. Charles R. Hearn. LC 76-56623. (Contributions in American Studies: No. 28). 222p. 1977. text ed. 55.00 (*0-8371-9478-4*, HAD/, Greenwood Pr) Greenwood.

American Dream Machine. Ryder Stacey. (Doomsday Warrior Ser.: No. 18). 1990. pap. 2.95 (*0-8217-3074-6*) Zebra.

American Dream of Captain John Smith. J. A. Lemay. 1991. text ed. 32.50 (*0-8139-1321-7*) U Pr of Va.

American Dream; The Death of Bessie Smith; Fam & Yam: Three Plays. Edward Albee. 1962. pap. 4.75 (*0-8222-0030-9*) Dramatists Play.

American Dream Visions: Chaucer's Surprising Influence on F. Scott Fitzgerald. Deborah D. Schlacks. LC 93-14219. (Studies on Themes & Motifs in Literature: Vol. 5). 248p. (C). 1994. text ed. 44.95 (*0-8204-2246-0*) P Lang Pubs.

American Dreamer: A Psychoanalytic Study of the Fiction of Norman Mailer. Andrew Gordon. LC 77-79778. 240p. 1978. 32.50 (*0-8386-2158-9*); pap. 14.95 (*0-8386-3066-9*) Fairleigh Dickinson.

***American Dreaming: Immigrant Life on the Margins.** Sarah J. Mahler. LC 95-13473. 1995. write for info. (*0-691-03783-3*); pap. write for info. (*0-691-03782-5*) Princeton U Pr.

American Dreams. Lisa Banim. LC 93-22573. (Stories of the States Ser.). 80p. (J). (gr. 4-6). 1993. lib. bdg. 12.95 (*1-881889-34-3*) Silver Moon.

***American Dreams.** Lisa Banim. (Stories of the States Ser.). 108p. (Orig.). (J). (gr. 4-6). 1995. pap. 4.95 (*1-881889-68-8*) Silver Moon.

American Dreams. Peter Frisch. 1987. pap. 4.75 (*0-8222-0029-5*) Dramatists Play.

American Dreams. Bruce Price. LC 83-63241. 266p. 1985. 22.00 (*0-932966-37-3*); pap. 16.00 (*0-932966-62-4*) Permanent Pr.

American Dreams. Sapphire. 128p. (Orig.). 1994. pap. 10.99 (*1-85242-327-7*) Serpents Tail.

American Dreams: Australian Movies. Peter Hamilton & Sue Mathews. (C). 1990. 65.00 (*0-86819-141-8*, Pub. by Currency Pr AT) St Mut.

American Dreams: Lost & Found. Studs Terkel. 1985. mass mkt. 6.99 (*0-345-32993-7*) Ballantine.

American Dreams: Meditations on Life in the United States. John K. Roth. LC 76-26877. 194p. 1976. pap. 8.95 (*0-88316-527-9*) Chandler & Sharp.

American Dreams: One Hundred Years of Business Ideas & Innovation from The Wall Street Journal. Kenneth Morris et al. (Illus.). 224p. 1991. 35.00 (*0-8109-3656-9*) Abrams.

American Dreams: The Imagination of Sam Shepard. Ed. by Bonnie Marranca. LC 80-85438. 223p. 1981. pap. 14.95 (*0-933826-13-3*) PAJ Pubns.

***American Dreams: The Story of a Jewish Immigrant Family.** Sidney R. Lewitter. Ed. by Sarah Lehman. LC 94-70749. (YA). Date not set. write for info. (*1-56062-262-8*); pap. write for info. (*1-56062-263-6*) CIS Comm.

American Dreams, American Nightmares. Ed. by David Madden. LC 72-5512. (Arcturus Books Paperbacks). 271p. 1972. pap. 9.95 (*0-8093-0600-X*) S Ill U Pr.

American Dreams, Rural Realities: Family Farms in Crisis. Peggy F. Barlett. LC 92-18027. (Rural Culture Ser.). xviii, 328p. (C). 1993. 45.00 (*0-8078-2067-9*); pap. 18.95 (*0-8078-4399-7*) U of NC Pr.

American Dress Pattern Catalogs, 1873-1909: Four Complete Reprints. Nancy V. Bryk. (Illus.). 160p. 1988. reprint ed. pap. 7.95 (*0-486-25654-5*) Dover.

American Dressage. 2nd ed. Chuck Grant. (Illus.). 116p. 1986. 16.00 (*0-917231-04-X*) Ferguson Comns Pubs.

American Drinking Practices. Don Cahalan et al. 1969. 19.95 (*0-8084-0412-1*) NCUP.

American Drinking Practices: A National Study of Drinking Behavior & Attitudes. Don Cahalan et al. LC 70-626701. (Monograph Ser.: No. 6). 1969. pap. 10.95 (*0-911290-37-0*) Rutgers Ctr Alcohol.

American Drive-In. Michael K. Witzel. (Illus.). 192p. 1994. 29.95 (*0-87938-919-2*) Motorbooks Intl.

American Drop-Shippers Directory. 15th ed. George F. Lucas. 32p. 1986. pap. text ed. 7.00 (*0-911652-00-0*) Wrld Wide Trade.

American Dropshippers Directory. 1987. lib. bdg. 79.95 (*0-8490-3872-3*) Gordon Pr.

American Drug Index, 1993. 37th ed. Norman A. Billups. Ed. by Bernie R. Olin. 776p. 1992. 37.95 (*0-932686-30-3*) Facts & Comparisons.

***American Drug Index, 1995.** Lippincott. 1994. 45.00 (*0-932686-32-X*) Facts & Comparisons.

American Drug Reference. Ed. by M. A. Malik. 550p. 1992. 85.00 (*0-9633782-0-1*) Am Drug Ref.

American Drug Scene: An Anthology. Ed. by James A. Inciardi & Karen McElrath. (Illus.). 367p. (Orig.). (C). 1994. pap. text ed. 22.95 (*0-935732-61-6*) Roxbury Pub Co.

***American Druggist Complete Family Guide to Prescriptions, Pills & Drugs.** John J. Fried & Sharon Petska. Ed. by Gerard Cooney et al. LC 94-39831. 1995. 17.95 (*0-688-12385-6*) Hearst Bks.

American Duchess. large type ed. Rosamond Fitzroy. 432p. 1983. 15.95 (*0-7089-1000-9*) Ulverscroft.

American Duck Shooting. George B. Grinnell. LC 91-8789. (Classics of American Sport Ser.). (Illus.). 640p. 1991. reprint ed. pap. 17.95 (*0-8117-2427-1*) Stackpole.

American Dulcimer. Jerry Rockwell. LC 85-754651. (Illus.). 52p. (Orig.). 1985. pap. text ed. 5.95 (*0-9614939-2-5*) Backyard Music.

American Dynasty: Story of the MacCormicks, Medills & Pattersons. John W. Tebbel. LC 68-10162. (Illus.). 363p. 1968. reprint ed. text ed. 65.00 (*0-8371-0246-4*, TEAD, Greenwood Pr) Greenwood.

American Eagle. Tom Leeson & Pat Leeson. Ed. by Cynthia Black. (Earthsong Collection Ser.). (Illus.). 128p. (C). 1990. 39.95 (*0-941831-30-2*); pap. 22.95 (*0-941831-51-5*) Beyond Words Pub.

American Eagle. Lynda Sorensen. LC 94-7051. (American Symbols Ser.). (J). 1994. write for info. (*1-55916-045-4*) Rourke Bk Co.

American Eagle: Spirit & Symbol, 1782-1882. Joseph T. Butler. (Illus.). 16p. 1988. 5.00 (*0-915171-11-2*) Katonah Gal.

American Eagle: The Ascent of Bob Crandall & American Airlines. Dan Reed. LC 92-44216. (Thomas Dunne Book Ser.). (Illus.). 302p. 1993. 23.95 (*0-312-08696-2*) St Martin.

American Eagle: The Story of a Navajo Vietnam Veteran. Larry Lee. (C). 1977. pap. text ed. 6.00 (*0-686-12227-5*) Packrat Pr.

American Eagle in Art & Design. Clarence P. Hornung. LC 77-15711. (Pictorial Archive Ser.). (Illus.). 1978. pap. 8.95 (*0-486-23604-8*) Dover.

American Eagle Pommel Sword: The Early Years 1794-1830. E. Andrew Mowbray. LC 88-61132. (Illus.). 244p. 1988. 45.00 (*0-917218-36-1*) A Mowbray.

***American Earlier Black English: Morphological & Syntactic.** Edgar W. Schneider. LC 88-29611. (Illus.). 330p. 1989. pap. 94.10 (*0-7837-8402-3*, 2059213) Bks Demand.

American Earthquakes. Constance Urdang. LC 88-11890. 136p. (Orig.). 1988. pap. 9.95 (*0-918273-42-0*) Coffee Hse.

American-East Asian Relations: A Survey. Ed. by Ernest R. May & James C. Thomson, Jr. LC 70-188970. (Harvard Studies in American-East Asian Relations: No. 1). 440p. reprint ed. pap. 125.40 (*0-7837-4141-3*, 2057964) Bks Demand.

American Economic Development in Historical Perspective. Ed. by Thomas Joseph Weiss & Donald Schaefer. LC 92-47404. 344p. 1993. 45.00 (*0-8047-2084-3*) Stanford U Pr.

American Economic Enterprises in Korea, 1895-1939. Dean A. Arnold. Ed. by Stuart Bruchey & Eleanor Bruchey. (American Business Abroad Ser.). (Illus.). 1976. 47.95 (*0-405-09264-4*) Ayer.

American Economic Growth. Ed. by William F. Donnelly. LC 73-10339. 1973. 28.50 (*0-8422-5110-3*) Irvington.

American Economic Growth & Standards of Living Before the Civil War. Ed. by Robert E. Gallman & John J. Wallis. (National Bureau of Economic Research Conference Report Ser.). (Illus.). 464p. 1992. 70.00 (*0-226-27945-6*) U Ch Pr.

American Economic History. 3rd ed. Robert C. Puth. LC 92-72940. 732p. (C). 1993. text ed. 56.00 (*0-03-096905-0*) Dryden Pr.

American Economic History. 4th ed. Hughes & Cain. (C). 1993. text ed. 67.50 (*0-673-46868-2*) HarpCollege.

American Economic History: From Abundance to Constraint. 2nd ed. John O'Sullivan & Edward F. Keuchel. LC 80-25339. (History Texts Ser.). 300p. (Orig.). (C). 1989. reprint ed. 29.95 (*1-55876-009-1*); reprint ed. pap. text ed. 16.95 (*1-55876-010-5*) Wiener Pubs Inc.

American Economic History Before 1860. George R. Taylor. LC 70-79173. (Goldentree Bibliographies Series in American History). (C). 1969. pap. text ed. write for info. (*0-88295-526-8*) Harlan Davidson.

American Economic History since 1860. Edward C. Kirkland. LC 74-158954. (Goldentree Bibliographies Series in American History). (C). 1971. pap. text ed. write for info. (*0-88295-519-5*) Harlan Davidson.

American Economic Impact of Canada. Duke University Commonwealth Studies Center Staff. LC 81-4163. xviii, 176p. 1981. reprint ed. text ed. 52.50 (*0-313-23056-0*, AIAI, Greenwood Pr) Greenwood.

American Economic Policy & National Security. Theodore H. Moran. (Pew Project Ser.). 96p. 1992. pap. 10.95 (*0-87609-137-0*) Coun Foreign.

American Economic Policy in the 1980s. Ed. by Martin Feldstein. LC 93-27972. (C). 1993. 75.00 (*0-226-24093-2*) U Ch Pr.

***American Economic Policy in the 1980s.** Ed. & Intro. by Martin Feldstein. (National Bureau of Economic Research Conference Reports Ser.). (Illus.). 840p. 1995. pap. 35.00x (*0-226-24096-7*) U Ch Pr.

American Economic Pre-Eminence: Goals for the 1990s. Anthony Harrigan & William R. Hawkins. LC 88-51556. (Illus.). 140p. (Orig.). (C). 1989. 33.00 (*0-944468-02-0*); pap. 18.25 (*0-944468-01-2*) USIC Ed Found.

American Economy. Roy J. Sampson. 1982. text ed. 46.88 (*0-395-31776-2*); pap. 14.76 (*0-395-31777-0*) HM.

American Economy: Contemporary Problems & Analysis. Robert B. Carson & Wade L. Thomas. LC 92-10897. (Illus.). 576p. (C). 1992. student ed, pap. write for info. (*0-02-319515-0*) Macmillan.

American Economy: Contemporary Problems & Analysis. Robert B. Carson & Wade L. Thomas. LC 92-10897. (Illus.). 576p. (C). 1993. pap. write for info. (*0-02-319516-9*) Macmillan.

***American Economy: Government's Role, Citizen's Choice.** Close Up Foundation Staff. (Illus.). (YA). 1994. teacher ed 9.95 (*0-614-04070-1*, 977-920) Close Up.

***American Economy: Government's Role, Citizen's Choice.** 2nd ed. Close Up Foundation Staff. LC 94-19525. (Illus.). 61p. (YA). 1994. pap. text ed. 9.95 (*0-932765-55-6*, 956-920) Close Up.

American Economy: Income, Wealth, & Want. Stanley Lebergott. LC 75-4661. 364p. 1975. 60.00x (*0-691-04210-1*) Princeton U Pr.

***American Economy: Income, Wealth, & Want.** Stanley Lebergott. LC 75-4461. reprint ed. pap. 111.50 (*0-7837-9371-5*, 2060115) Bks Demand.

American Economy: Its Problems & Prospects. Sumner H. Slichter. LC 78-12055. 214p. 1979. reprint ed. text ed. 55.00 (*0-313-21083-7*, SLAE, Greenwood Pr) Greenwood.

***American Economy: The Struggle for Supremacy in the 21st Century.** Nicolas Spulber. (Cambridge Studies in Economic Policies & Institutions: 3). (Illus.). 288p. (C). 1995. 34.95 (*0-521-48013-2*) Cambridge U Pr.

American Economy During the Great Depression: Selected Articles. Ed. by Melvyn Dubofsky & Stephen Burwood. LC 89-25952. (Outstanding Articles on the Great Depression & the New Deal Ser.). 320p. 1990. reprint ed. 58.00 (*0-8240-0895-2*) Garland.

American Economy from the Great Crash to the Third Industrial Revolution. Joseph Finkelstein. (Illus.). 340p. (C). 1992. pap. text ed. write for info. (*0-88295-873-9*) Harlan Davidson.

American Economy in Perspective. 2nd ed. Lloyd G. Reynolds. 512p. (C). 1987. pap. text ed. write for info. (*0-07-052056-9*) McGraw.

American Economy in the Twentieth Century. Smiley. (C). 1994. text ed. 49.95 (*0-538-83238-X*, HJ60AA) S-W Pub.

American Economy in Transition. Martin Feldstein. LC 80-17450. (National Bureau of Economic Research Ser.). 1982. 17.95 (*0-226-24081-9*); pap. text ed. 17.95 (*0-226-24082-7*, PHOEN) U Ch Pr.

American Economy, Nineteen Sixty to Two Thousand. Richard M. Cyert. LC 82-48600. (Charles C. Moskowitz Memorial Lectures: Vol. XXXII). (C). 1983. 19.95 (*0-02-923100-0*) Free Pr.

American Eden. Ryder Stacy. (Doomsday Warrior Ser.: No. 11). 256p. 1987. pap. 2.50 (*0-8217-2098-8*) Zebra.

American Edge: Leveraging the Nation's Unique Core Competencies. Ed. by Janice A. Klein & Jeffrey G. Miller. 240p. 1993. text ed. 24.95 (*0-07-035040-X*) McGraw.

American Education. James R. Angell. LC 72-106403. (Essay Index Reprint Ser.). 1977. 26.95 (*0-8369-1440-6*) Ayer.

American Education. 6th ed. Joel Spring. LC 93-8342. 1994. pap. text ed. write for info. (*0-07-060551-3*) McGraw.

***American Education.** 7th ed. Joel Spring. LC 95-11726. 1995. write for info. (*0-07-060557-2*) McGraw.

American Education. 9th ed. Richard Wynn & Joanne L. Wynn. 476p. (C). 1990. text ed. 50.00 (*0-06-047293-6*) HarpCollege.

American Education: A Guide to Information Sources. Ed. by Richard G. Durnin. LC 73-17553. (American Studies Information Guide: Vol. 14). 264p. 1982. 68.00 (*0-8103-1265-4*) Gale.

American Education: An Introduction to Teaching. 7th ed. John H. Johansen et al. 480p. (C). 1993. pap. text ed. write for info. (*0-697-12578-5*) Brown & Benchmark.

American Education: Challenges & Images. Frank R. Paulsen. LC 66-28787. 124p. reprint ed. pap. 35.40 (*0-8357-5363-8*, 2056212) Bks Demand.

American Education: Its Men, Ideas, & Institutions, Series 1-2, 92 vols., Set. Ed. by Lawrence A. Cremin & Frederick A. Barnard. 1972. 984.00 (*0-405-01497-X*) Ayer.

American Education: Making It Work. William J. Bennett. (Illus.). 66p. (Orig.). 1988. pap. 3.25 (*0-16-006726-X*, S/N 065-000-00330-9) USGPO.

American Education & the Dynamics of Choice. James R. Rinehart & Jackson F. Lee. LC 90-21312. 184p. 1991. text ed. 49.95 (*0-275-93823-9*, C3823, Praeger Pubs) Greenwood.

American Education & the European Immigrant: 1840-1940. Ed. by Bernard J. Weiss. LC 81-1773. 248p. 1982. pap. 11.95 (*0-252-00907-X*) U of Ill Pr.

***American Education & Vocationalism: A Documentary History, 1870-1970.** Ed. by Marvin Lazerson & W. Norton Grubb. LC 73-87511. (Classics in Education Ser.: Vol. 48). 189p. 1974. pap. 53.90 (*0-7837-8951-3*, 2049663) Bks Demand.

An Asterisk (*) at the beginning of an entry indicates that the title is appearing in BIP for the first time.

American Education in a Global Society: Internationalizing Teacher Education. Gerald L. Gutek. 240p. (C). 1993. pap. text ed. 24.95 (0-8013-0530-6, 78413) Longman.

American Education in International Development. Robert F. Butts. LC 73-117763. (Essay Index Reprint Ser.). 1977. 19.95 (0-8369-1786-3) Ayer.

American Education in the Electric Age: New Perspectives on Media & Learning. Ed. by Peter L. Klinge. LC 74-1220. 222p. 1974. pap. 21.95 (0-87778-069-2) Educ Tech Pubns.

American Education in the Twentieth Century: A Documentary History. Ed. by Marvin Lazerson. (Classics in Education Ser.). 224p. (C). 1987. pap. text ed. 6.00 (0-8077-2851-9) Tchrs Coll.

American Education 1870-1991: A Statistical Handbook. LC 93-36450. 1993. 25.00 (0-935061-56-8) Contemp Res.

American Educators' Encyclopedia. rev. ed. Edward L. Dejnozka et al. LC 90-41510. 752p. 1991. text ed. 105.00 (0-313-25269-6, DAY/, Greenwood Pr) Greenwood.

American Effects on Hungarian Imagination & Political Thought, 1559-1848. Geza Zavodszky. (Atlantic Studies on Society in Change: No. 79). 300p. 1993. 42.00 (0-88033-272-7, 375) East Eur Quarterly.

American Egypt: A Record of Travel in the Yucatan. Channing Arnold & F. J. Frost. (Yucatan Ser.). 1979. lib. bdg. 69.95 (0-8490-2863-9) Gordon Pr.

American Eight: Nov. 15-Dec. 30, 1979. Intro. by Jon W. Kowalek. (Illus.). 64p. (Orig.). 1979. pap. 1.00 (0-924335-00-9) Tacoma Art Mus.

American Elections of Nineteen Eighty-Four. Ed. by Austin Ranney. LC 85-24573. (At the Polls Ser.). (Illus.). xii, 368p. 1985. 41.95 (0-8223-0230-6); pap. 18.95 (0-8223-0697-2) Duke.

American Elections of Nineteen Eighty-Two. Ed. by Thomas E. Mann & Norman J. Ornstein. LC 83-11843. (AEI Studies: No. 389). (Illus.). 223p. reprint ed. pap. 63.60 (0-7837-1079-8, 2041609) Bks Demand.

American Elections of 1980. Austin Ranney. LC 81-7907. (AEI Studies: No. 327). 408p. reprint ed. pap. 116.30 (0-8357-4433-7, 2037267) Bks Demand.

American Elections of 1984. Austin Ranney. LC 85-24573. (Illus.). 382p. reprint ed. pap. 108.90 (0-8357-4434-5, 2037268) Bks Demand.

American Electoral Behavior: Change & Stability. Ed. by Samuel A. Kirkpatrick. LC 75-32374. (Sage Contemporary Social Science Issues Ser.: No. 24). 144p. reprint ed. pap. 41.10 (0-8357-5364-6, 2021918) Bks Demand.

American Electoral Behavior: 1952-1992. Norman R. Luttbeg & Michael M. Gant. LC 94-66866. 248p. 1994. pap. text ed. 28.00 (0-87581-386-0) Peacock Pubs.

American Electoral Mosaics. J. Clark Archer & Fred M. Shelley. LC 85-26810. (Resource Publications in Geography). (Orig.). 1986. pap. text ed. 10.00 (0-89291-195-6) Assn Am Geographers.

American Electric. Edward J. Whetmore. 1992. pap. text ed. write for info. (0-07-069998-4) McGraw.

American Electricians' Handbook. 12th ed. Croft Terrell & Wilford I. Summers. (Illus.). 1728p. 1992. text ed. 74.50 (0-07-013933-4) McGraw.

American Elegance: Classic & Contemporary Menus from Celebrated Hosts & Hostesses. Henry Francis du Pont Winterthur Museum Staff. (Illus.). 248p. 1988. 55.00 (0-89659-886-1) Abbeville Pr.

American Elegy: The Airs & Graces of Corporate Life. Richard E. Petitti. (Self Realization Bks.: Bk. IV). (Illus.). 100p. 1986. pap. 10.00 (0-938582-08-9) Sensitive Man.

*American Elves: An Encyclopedia of Little People from the Lore of 340 Ethnic Groups of the Western Hemisphere. John E. Roth. 528p. 1995. lib. bdg. 68.50 (0-89950-944-4) McFarland & Co.

American Elves - the Yankoos: The Yankoos & the Oak-Hickory Forest Ecology, Bk. Two. Robert Frieders. LC 93-61530. (Illus.). 96p. (J). (gr. 3). 1994. pap. 7.95 (0-9639284-1-4) Yankoo Pubng.

*American Elves - the Yankoos Bk. 3: The Yankoos & the Oak-Hickory Forest Ecology, Bk. 3. Robert Frieders. (Illus.). 96p. (J). (gr. 3-3). 1995. pap. 7.95 (0-9639284-2-2) Yankoo Pubng.

American Elves - the Yankoos, Bk. 1: The Yankoos & the Oak-Hickory Forest Ecology. Robert Frieders. LC 93-61530. (Illus.). 64p. (J). (gr. 3). 1993. pap. 7.95 (0-9639284-0-6) Yankoo Pubng.

American Emergency. Robert Briggs. LC 88-38176. 1989. 18.95 (0-89087-552-9); pap. 8.95 (0-89087-546-4) Celestial Arts.

American Empire: A Study of the Outlying Territories of the United States. Ed. by William H. Haas. LC 75-156656. (Essay Index Reprint Ser.). 1977. reprint ed. 31.95 (0-8369-2319-7) Ayer.

American Empirical Movement in Theology. Delores J. Rogers. LC 89-77291. (American University Studies: Theology & Religion: Ser. VII, Vol. 70). 254p. (C). 1990. text ed. 47.50 (0-8204-1218-X) P Lang Pubs.

*American Empress: The Life & Times of Marjorie Merriweather Post. Nancy Rubin. LC 94-27664. 1995. 27.50 (0-679-41347-2, Villard Bks) Random.

American Encounter with Buddhism, 1844-1912: Victorian Culture & the Limits of Dissent. Thomas A. Tweed. LC 91-17949. (Religion in North America Ser.). (Illus.). 276p. 1992. text ed. 29.95 (0-253-36099-4) Ind U Pr.

American Encounters. Howard Morrison. (Illus.). 80p. (Orig.). 1992. pap. write for info. (0-929847-05-9) Natl Mus Am.

American Encounters: Lewis & Clark, the People, & the Land. Gary Moulton. (Illus.). 32p. (Orig.). 1991. pap. text ed. 10.00 (0-938932-03-9) U Nebr CFGPS.

American Engineer in Stalin's Russia: The Memoirs of Zara Witkin, 1932-1934. Intro. by Michael Gelb. (Illus.). 352p. 1991. 30.00 (0-520-07134-4) U CA Pr.

American Engineers' & Surveyors' Instruments: W. & L. E. Gurley 1874 Manual & Catalog. Ed. by David C. Garcelon. (Illus.). 225p. 1993. reprint ed. pap. 19.95 (1-879335-34-4) Astragal Pr.

American Engineers' Contributions to Cost Accounting: An Original Anthology. Ed. by Murry C. Wells & Richard P. Brief. LC 77-87320. (Development of Contemporary Accounting Thought Ser.). 1978. lib. bdg. 37.95 (0-405-10932-6) Ayer.

American English: A Bibliography. Comp. by Vito J. Brenni. LC 81-13412. 221p. 1981. reprint ed. text ed. 35.00 (0-313-23344-6, BRAE, Greenwood Pr) Greenwood.

American English & German Banking Dictionary: Englisch-Amerikanische Fachausdruecke im Bank-Geschaeft. rev. ed. Hans Klaus. 220p. (ENG & GER.). 1990. lib. bdg. 59.95 (0-8288-3886-0, M8242) Fr & Eur.

American English Dialects in Literature. Eva M. Burkett. LC 78-17742. 222p. 1978. 22.50 (0-8108-1151-0) Scarecrow.

American English-French Management Dictionary: Dictionnaire Americain-Anglais-Francais du Management. Maud Tixier. 381p. (ENG & FRE.). 1985. 85.00 (0-8288-0808-2, F56100) Fr & Eur.

American English Grammar. Charles C. Fries. 1940. 32.50 (0-89197-010-X); pap. text ed. 9.95 (0-89197-011-8) Irvington.

American English One, Bk. 1. Edwin T. Cornelius, Jr. (American English One Video Ser.). (Illus.). 150p. 1987. pap. text ed. 8.00 (0-89209-700-0) Pace Intl Res.

American English One, Bk. 2. Edwin T. Cornelius, Jr. (American English One Video Ser.). (Illus.). 169p. 1987. pap. text ed. 8.00 (0-89209-701-9) Pace Intl Res.

American English One, Bk. 3. Edwin T. Cornelius, Jr. (American English One Video Ser.). (Illus.). 171p. 1987. pap. text ed. 8.00 (0-89209-702-7) Pace Intl Res.

American English One, Bk. 4. Edwin T. Cornelius, Jr. (American English One Video Ser.). (Illus.). 185p. 1987. pap. text ed. 8.00 (0-89209-703-5) Pace Intl Res.

American English One, No. 1. Edwin T. Cornelius, Jr. (American English One Video Ser.). (Illus.). 150p. 1987. audio 12.00 (0-89209-709-4) Pace Intl Res.

American English One, No. 1A. Edwin T. Cornelius, Jr. (American English One Video Ser.). (Illus.). 150p. 1987. vhs 60.00 (0-89209-725-6) Pace Intl Res.

American English One, No. 2. Edwin T. Cornelius, Jr. (American English One Video Ser.). (Illus.). 150p. 1987. audio 12.00 (0-89209-710-8) Pace Intl Res.

American English One, No. 2A. Edwin T. Cornelius, Jr. (American English One Video Ser.). (Illus.). 169p. 1987. vhs 60.00 (0-89209-727-2) Pace Intl Res.

American English One, No. 2B. Edwin T. Cornelius, Jr. (American English One Video Ser.). (Illus.). 150p. 1987. vhs 60.00 (0-89209-726-4); vhs 60.00 (0-89209-728-0) Pace Intl Res.

American English One, No. 3. Edwin T. Cornelius, Jr. (American English One Video Ser.). (Illus.). 150p. 1987. audio 12.00 (0-89209-711-6) Pace Intl Res.

American English One, No. 3A. Edwin T. Cornelius, Jr. (American English One Video Ser.). (Illus.). 171p. 1987. vhs 60.00 (0-89209-729-9) Pace Intl Res.

American English One, No. 3B. Edwin T. Cornelius, Jr. (American English One Video Ser.). (Illus.). 171p. 1987. vhs 60.00 (0-89209-730-2) Pace Intl Res.

American English One, No. 4. Edwin T. Cornelius, Jr. (American English One Video Ser.). (Illus.). 150p. 1987. audio 12.00 (0-89209-712-4) Pace Intl Res.

American English One, No. 4A. Edwin T. Cornelius, Jr. (American English One Video Ser.). (Illus.). 185p. 1987. vhs 60.00 (0-89209-731-0) Pace Intl Res.

American English One, No. 4B. Edwin T. Cornelius, Jr. (American English One Video Ser.). (Illus.). 185p. 1987. vhs 60.00 (0-89209-732-9) Pace Intl Res.

American English One, No. 5. Edwin T. Cornelius, Jr. (American English One Video Ser.). (Illus.). 169p. 1987. audio 12.00 (0-89209-713-2) Pace Intl Res.

American English One, No. 6. Edwin T. Cornelius, Jr. (American English One Video Ser.). (Illus.). 169p. 1987. audio 12.00 (0-89209-714-0) Pace Intl Res.

American English One, No. 7. Edwin T. Cornelius, Jr. (American English One Video Ser.). (Illus.). 169p. 1987. audio 12.00 (0-89209-715-9) Pace Intl Res.

American English One, No. 8. Edwin T. Cornelius, Jr. (American English One Video Ser.). (Illus.). 169p. 1987. audio 12.00 (0-89209-716-7) Pace Intl Res.

American English One, No. 9. Edwin T. Cornelius, Jr. (American English One Video Ser.). (Illus.). 171p. 1987. audio 12.00 (0-89209-717-5) Pace Intl Res.

American English One, No. 10. Edwin T. Cornelius, Jr. (American English One Video Ser.). (Illus.). 171p. 1987. audio 12.00 (0-89209-718-3) Pace Intl Res.

American English One, No. 11. Edwin T. Cornelius, Jr. (American English One Video Ser.). (Illus.). 171p. 1987. audio 12.00 (0-89209-719-1) Pace Intl Res.

American English One, No. 12. Edwin T. Cornelius, Jr. (American English One Video Ser.). (Illus.). 171p. 1987. audio 12.00 (0-89209-720-5) Pace Intl Res.

American English One, No. 13. Edwin T. Cornelius, Jr. (American English One Video Ser.). (Illus.). 185p. 1987. audio 12.00 (0-89209-721-3) Pace Intl Res.

American English One, No. 14. Edwin T. Cornelius, Jr. (American English One Video Ser.). (Illus.). 185p. 1987. audio 12.00 (0-89209-722-1) Pace Intl Res.

American English One, No. 15. Edwin T. Cornelius, Jr. (American English One Video Ser.). (Illus.). 185p. 1987. audio 12.00 (0-89209-723-X) Pace Intl Res.

American English One, No. 16. Edwin T. Cornelius, Jr. (American English One Video Ser.). (Illus.). 185p. 1987. audio 12.00 (0-89209-724-8) Pace Intl Res.

American English Pronounciation: Exercises for Accent Reduction, 2 vols. Dorothy M. Taguchi. LC 91-90741. 507p. 1991. Set. pap. text ed. 159.95 (1-880822-00-8) Linguistic Edge.

American English Pronounciation: Exercises for Accent Reduction, 2 vols., I. Dorothy M. Taguchi. LC 91-90741. 507p. 1991. write for info. (1-880822-01-6) Linguistic Edge.

American English Pronounciation: Exercises for Accent Reduction, 2 vols., II. Dorothy M. Taguchi. LC 91-90741. 507p. 1991. write for info. (1-880822-02-4) Linguistic Edge.

American English Pronounciation: Exercises for Accent Reduction, 2 vols. rev. ed. Dorothy M. Taguchi. (Illus.). 191p. (C). 1993. reprint ed. Set. text ed., ring bd. 27.71 (1-880822-04-0) Linguistic Edge.

American English Pronounciation: Exercises for Accent Reduction, 2 vols., I. rev. ed. Dorothy M. Taguchi. (Illus.). 191p. (C). 1993. reprint ed. write for info. (1-880822-05-9) Linguistic Edge.

American English Pronounciation: Exercises for Accent Reduction, 2 vols., II. rev. ed. Dorothy M. Taguchi. (Illus.). 191p. (C). 1993. reprint ed. write for info. (1-880822-06-7) Linguistic Edge.

American English Reader. Grant Taylor. (Saxon Series in English As a Second Language). 1960. text ed. 4.50 (0-07-062944-7) McGraw.

American English Rhetoric. 3rd ed. Robert G. Bander. 370p. (C). 1983. pap. text ed. 21.75 (0-03-061066-4) HB Coll Pubs.

American English Spelling: An Informal Description. D. W. Cummings. LC 86-30537. 608p. 1988. text ed. 65.00 (0-8018-3443-0) Johns Hopkins.

American English Today: Exploring English. 3rd ed. Hans P. Guth. (gr. 7). 1980. text ed. 22.36 (0-07-025017-0) McGraw.

American English Today: Our Changing Language. 3rd ed. Hans P. Guth. (Illus.). (gr. 12). 1980. text ed. 22.36 (0-07-025022-7) McGraw.

American English Today: The Tools of English. 3rd ed. Hans P. Guth & Edgar H. Schuster. LC 79-4066. (American English Today Ser.). (gr. 9). 1980. text ed. 22.36 (0-07-025019-7) McGraw.

American English Today: The Uses of Language. 3rd ed. Hans P. Guth. (American English Today Ser.). (gr. 11). 1980. text ed. 22.36 (0-07-025021-9) McGraw.

American English Today: The World of English. 3rd ed. Hans P. Guth. (American English Today Ser.). (Illus.). (gr. 10). 1980. text ed. 22.36 (0-07-025020-0) McGraw.

American English Today, Bk. 10: The World of English. 2nd ed. Hans P. Guth & Edgar H. Schuster. (gr. 10). 1977. text ed. 23.00 (0-07-025336-6) McGraw.

American English Today, Bk. 11: The Uses of Language. 2nd rev. ed. Hans P. Guth & Edgar H. Schuster. LC 75-4772. (gr. 11). 1977. text ed. 23.24 (0-07-025337-4) McGraw.

American English Today, Bk. 12: The Growth of English. 2nd rev. ed. Hans P. Guth & Edgar H. Schuster. LC 75-4948. (Illus.). 1977. text ed. 23.24 (0-07-025338-2) McGraw.

*American Engravers upon Copper & Steel, 3 vols., Set. David M. Stauffer et al. (Illus.). 1520p. 1994. 175.00 (0-938768-47-6, Pub. by St Pauls Bibliog UK) Oak Knoll Pr.

American Enlightenment. Ed. by Frank Shuffleton. (Library of the History of Western Music). 416p. (C). 1993. text ed. 67.50 (1-878822-24-1) Boydell & Brewer.

American Enterprise. Jeffrey Sweet. 62p. 1992. pap. 5.95 (1-56850-012-2) Chicago Plays.

American Enterprise in Foreign Markets: Singer & International Harvester in Imperial Russia. Fred V. Carstensen. LC 83-17069. vi, 289p. 1984. 39.95 (0-8078-1585-3) U of NC Pr.

American Enterprise in Japan. Tomoko Hamada. LC 90-38186. (Anthropology of Work Ser.). 294p. (C). 1991. 59.50 (0-7914-0638-5); pap. 19.95 (0-7914-0639-3) State U NY Pr.

American Enterprise in South Africa. Richard Hull. 436p. 1990. 50.00 (0-8147-3462-6); pap. 25.00 (0-8147-3468-5) NYU Pr.

American Entrepreneurial & Small-Business Culture. John E. Jackson. 42p. 1986. pap. 6.00 (0-940791-03-X) NFIB Found.

American Environment: Historical Geographic Interpretations of Impact & Policy. Ed. by Lary M. Dilsaver & Craig E. Colten. LC 92-12812. (Geographical Perspectives on the Human Past Ser.). 288p. (C). 1992. text ed. 60.00 (0-8476-7753-2); pap. 22.95 (0-8476-7754-0) Rowman.

American Environment: Perceptions & Policies. Ed. by J. Wreford Watson & Timothy O'Riordan. LC 74-32224. 352p. reprint ed. pap. 100.40 (0-8357-5365-4, 2024287) Bks Demand.

American Environment: Readings in the History of Conservation. Roderick Nash. 398p. (C). 1987. text ed. 12.00 (0-394-37398-7, KnopfC) Knopf.

American Environmental History. 2nd ed. Joseph M. Petulla. 464p. (C). 1988. pap. write for info. (0-675-20885-8, Merrill Pub Co) Macmillan.

*American Environmental Liability Risks. James T. O'Reilly. (International Environmental Law & Policy Ser.). 256p. (C). 1995. lib. bdg. 90.00 (1-85966-093-2, Pub. by Graham & Trotman UK) Kluwer Ac.

American Environmental Studies, 42 Vols, Set. 1971. reprint ed. 994.00 (0-405-02650-1) Ayer.

American Environmentalism: Reading in Conservation History. 3rd ed. Roderick Nash. 398p. (C). 1990. pap. text ed. write for info. (0-07-046059-0) McGraw.

American Environmentalism: The U. S. Environmental Movement, 1970-1990. Ed. by Riley E. Dunlap & Angela G. Mertig. 115p. 1992. pap. 13.95 (0-8448-1730-9, Crane Russak) Taylor & Francis.

American Ephemeris: 1901 to 1930. Neil F. Michelsen. (American Ephemeris Ser.). 368p. 1980. pap. 14.95 (0-917086-12-0) ACS Pubns.

American Ephemeris: 1931 to 1980 & Book of Tables. 2nd ed. Neil F. Michelsen. LC 76-11919. 740p. 1982. 29.95 (0-917086-01-5) ACS Pubns.

American Ephemeris: 1981 to 1990. Neil F. Michelsen. (American Ephemeris Ser.). 128p. 1977. pap. 9.95 (0-917086-10-4) ACS Pubns.

American Ephemeris: 1991 to 2000. Neil F. Michelsen. (American Ephemeris Ser.). 128p. 1980. pap. 9.95 (0-917086-21-X) ACS Pubns.

American Ephemeris for the Twentieth Century Revised 1900 to 2000 At: Midnight. 5th rev. ed. Comp. by Neil F. Michelsen. (American Ephemeris Ser.). 608p. 1994. pap. 19.95 (0-935127-19-4) ACS Pubns.

American Ephemeris for the Twentieth Century Revised 1900 to 2000 At: Noon. 5th rev. ed. Neil F. Michelsen. (American Ephemeris Ser.). 608p. 1992. pap. 19.95 (0-935127-20-8) ACS Pubns.

American Ephemeris for the Twenty-First Century: 2001 to 2050 At: Midnight Only. 2nd ed. Comp. by Neil F. Michelsen. (American Ephemeris Ser.). 304p. (Orig.). 1992. pap. 16.95 (0-935127-00-3) ACS Pubns.

American Epic: Transformations of a Genre 1770-1860. John P. McWilliams, Jr. (Cambridge Studies in American Literature & Culture: No. 36). 304p. (C). 1989. 54.95 (0-521-37322-0) Cambridge U Pr.

American Epoch: A History of the United States since the 1890's, 3 Vols., 2. 5th ed. Arthur S. Link & William B. Catton. (Illus.). 1980. 12.00 (0-394-32358-0) Knopf.

American Epoch: A History of the United States since 1900. 7th ed. William A. Link & Arthur S. Link. LC 92-16975. 1992. pap. text ed. write for info. (0-07-037951-3) McGraw.

American Epoch: Southern Portraiture in the National Picture. Howard W. Odum. (BCL1 - United States Local History Ser.). 379p. 1991. reprint ed. lib. bdg. 89.00 (0-7812-6292-5) Rprt Serv.

American Epoch - A History of the United States since 1900: Affluence & Anxiety, 1940-1992, Vol. 2. 7th ed. William A. Link & Arthur S. Link. 1992. pap. text ed. write for info. (0-07-037952-1) McGraw.

American Eskimo. Nancy J. Hofman & Cathy J. Flamholtz. (Illus.). 128p. (Orig.). 1989. pap. 9.95 (0-940269-04-X) OTR Pubns.

*American Eskimo Dogs: Everything about Purchase, Care, Nutrition, Breeding, Behavior, & Training. D. Caroline Coile. LC 95-7319. (Complete Pet Owner's Manual Ser.). (Illus.). 1995. write for info. (0-8120-1981-4) Barron.

American Eskimos. Monica Sellers. (Illus.). 160p. 1990. 11.95 (0-86622-566-8); lib. bdg. 9.95 (0-86622-505-6, KW160) TFH Pubns.

American Essay Serials from Franklin to Irving. Bruce I. Granger. LC 78-4120. 285p. reprint ed. 81.30 (0-8357-5366-2, 2027565) Bks Demand.

American Essays for the Newman Centennial. Ed. by John K. Ryan & Edmond Benard. LC 47-30528. 258p. reprint ed. pap. 73.60 (0-8357-5367-0, 2005379) Bks Demand.

American Essays of Henry James. Frwd. by Leon Edel. 323p. (C). 1990. 45.00 (0-691-06822-4); pap. 14.95 (0-691-01471-X) Princeton U Pr.

American Establishment & Other Reports, Opinions, & Speculations. Richard H. Rovere. LC 80-22247. x, 308p. 1981. reprint ed. text ed. 59.75 (0-313-22646-6, ROAE, Greenwood Pr) Greenwood.

American Etching: The Eighteen Eighties. Thomas P. Bruhn. (Illus.). 134p. 1985. write for info. (0-918386-36-5) W Benton Mus.

American Etchings. S. R. Koehler. Bd. with American Art. LC 75-28876. LC 75-28876. (Art Experience in Late 19th Century America Ser.: Vol. 12). (Illus.). 1978. reprint ed. Set lib. bdg. 88.00 (0-8240-2236-X) Garland.

*American Ethic: A Philosophy of Freedom Applied to Contemporary Issues. Gerken. (C). 1995. text ed. 35.00 (0-391-03936-9) Humanities.

American Ethics & Public Policy. Abraham D. Kaplan. LC 80-12151. 110p. 1980. reprint ed. text ed. 35.00 (0-313-22354-8, KAAE, Greenwood Pr) Greenwood.

American Ethnic Groups. Ed. by Thomas Sowell. LC 77-89996. (Illus.). 254p. (Orig.). 1978. pap. text ed. 24.00 (0-87766-210-X) Urban Inst.

American Ethnic Groups, 47 bks., Set. Ed. by Francesco Cordasco. (European Heritage Ser.). 1981. lib. bdg. 1,580.00 (0-405-13400-2) Ayer.

American Ethnic Groups: The European Heritage. Francesco Cordasco & David N. Alloway. LC 80-28775. 376p. 1981. 27.50 (0-8108-1405-6) Scarecrow.

*American Ethnic Literatures. David R. Peck. (Magill Bibliographies Ser.). 218p. 1992. 40.00 (0-8108-2792-1) Scarecrow.

American Ethnicity. 2nd ed. Joseph Hraba. LC 92-61958. 636p. (C). 1994. boxed 40.00 (0-87581-370-4) Peacock Pubs.

American Ethnological Society Monographs, 1940-1972. American Ethnological Society Staff. 1988. write for info. (0-404-62900-8) AMS Pr.

American Ethnological Society Proceedings, 1957-1972, 16 vols. American Ethnological Society Staff. 1988. write for info. (0-404-62650-5) AMS Pr.

American Ethos: Public Attitudes Toward Capitalism & Democracy. Herbert McClosky & John R. Zaller. LC 84-12793. (Twentieth Century Fund Study). 360p. 1988. pap. 17.50 (0-674-02331-5) HUP.

An Asterisk (*) at the beginning of an entry indicates that the title is appearing in BIP for the first time.

American Evangelical Missionaries in France, 1945-1975. Allen V. Koop. (Illus.). 220p. (Orig.). (C). 1986. lib. bdg. 50.50 (*0-8191-5204-8*); pap. text ed. 23.00 (*0-8191-5205-6*) U Pr of Amer.

American Evangelicalism: An Annotated Bibliography. Norris A. Magnuson & William G. Travis. LC 90-33989. 495p. (C). 1990. lib. bdg. 45.00 (*0-933951-27-2*) Locust Hill Pr.

American Evangelicalism: Conservative Religion & the Quandary of Modernity. James D. Hunter. LC 82-317. 166p. 1983. pap. 15.00 (*0-8135-0985-8*) Rutgers U Pr.

American Evangelicals, 1800-1900: An Anthology. William G. McLoughlin. 12.00 (*0-8446-0793-2*) Peter Smith.

American Evasion of Philosophy: A Genealogy of Pragmatism. Cornel West. LC 88-40446. (Wisconsin Project on American Writers Ser.). 400p. (Orig.). (C). 1989. pap. text ed. 16.95 (*0-299-11964-5*) U of Wis Pr.

***American Ex Pow III.** Turner Publishing Company Staff. LC 89-157506. 184p. 1995. 48.00 (*1-56311-173-X*) Turner Pub KY.

American Ex-Prisoners of War. Turner Publishing Company Staff. LC 88-50048. 184p. 1988. 48.00 (*0-938021-60-5*) Turner Pub KY.

American Ex-Prisoners of War 50 Year Commemorative History. Turner Publishing Co. Staff. LC 91-67158. 300p. 1992. 48.00 (*1-56311-066-0*) Turner Pub KY.

***American Executive: Observations of a Poet.** Tony Frame. 65p. (Orig.). 1994. pap. 7.95 (*0-9644240-7-X*) T Frame.

American Executive & Executive Methods. John H. Finley & John F. Sanderson. LC 91-55450. (American State Ser.). 352p. 1991. reprint ed. lib. bdg. 61.00 (*0-912004-99-1*) W W Gaunt.

American Exodus: A Record of Human Erosion. Dorothea Lange & Paul S. Taylor. LC 74-30641. (American Farmers & the Rise of Agribusiness Ser.). (Illus.). 1979. reprint ed. 23.95 (*0-405-06811-5*) Ayer.

American Exodus: The Dust Bowl Migration & Okie Culture in California. James N. Gregory. (Illus.). 368p. 1991. reprint ed. pap. 12.95 (*0-19-507136-0*) OUP.

American Expansion: A Book of Maps. Randall D. Sale & Edwin D. Karn. LC 78-24508. (Illus.). ii, 28p. 1979. reprint ed. pap. 8.95x (*0-8032-9104-3*, Bison Books) U of Nebr Pr.

American Expansion in the Late Nineteenth Century: Colonialist or Anticolonialist? Ed. by J. R. Hollingsworth. LC 82-10008. 128p. (C). 1983. reprint ed. pap. text ed. 8.50 (*0-89874-531-4*) Krieger.

American Expedition to Idalion, Cyprus: 1973-1980. Ed. by L. E. Stager & A. M. Walker. LC 87-60773. (Oriental Institute Communications Ser.: No. 24). (Illus.). xxiv, 516p. 1989. pap. 48.00 (*0-918986-52-4*) Orientl Inst Pr IT.

American Expedition to Idalion, Cyprus, First Preliminary Report: Seasons of 1971 & 1972. Ed. by Lawrence E. Stager et al. (American Schools of Oriental Research, Supplement Ser.: Vol. 18). 178p. (Orig.). 1974. pap. text ed. 12.50 (*0-89757-318-8*) Am Sch Orient Res.

American Experience: A Foreign Student Guide. Ed. by Karen M. Holgerson. 172p. (C). 1990. pap. text ed. 17.95 (*0-89863-122-X*) Star Pub CA.

American Experience: A Writer's Sourcebook. Laurence Behrens & Annabel Nelson. 560p. (C). 1991. pap. text ed. 23.00 (*0-205-13088-7*) Allyn.

American Experience: An Interpretation of the History & Civilization of the American People. Henry B. Parkes. LC 82-15518. xii, 355p. 1982. text ed. 65.00 (*0-313-22574-5*, PAAE, Greenwood Pr) Greenwood.

American Experience & China's Urban Choices. Melvin R. Levin. (Working Paper Ser.: No. 8). 54p. 1987. 5.00 (*0-913749-18-4*) U MD Urban Stud.

American Experience in Vietnam. Boston Publishing Co. Editors. Ed. by Robert Manning. (Illus.). 352p. 1988. 39.95 (*0-939526-39-5*) Boston Pub Co.

American Experience in Vietnam: A Reader. Grace Sevy. LC 89-40222. 505p. 1991. pap. 14.95 (*0-8061-2390-7*) U of Okla Pr.

American Experience of God: The Spirituality of Isaac Hecker. John Farina. LC 81-80875. 240p. 1981. 11.95 (*0-8091-0321-4*) Paulist Pr.

American Experience with Alcohol: Contrasting Cultural Perspectives. Ed. by Linda A. Bennett & Genevieve M. Ames. LC 85-9302. 514p. 1985. 85.00 (*0-306-41945-9*, Plenum Pr) Plenum.

American Experiences, 2 vols., I. 3rd ed. Roberts & Charles L. Olson. (C). 1993. text ed. 28.50 (*0-673-46736-8*) HarpCollege.

American Experiences, 2 vols., II. 3rd ed. Roberts & Charles L. Olson. (C). 1993. text ed. 28.50 (*0-673-46737-6*) HarpCollege.

American Experiences: Readings in Social & Political History. Robbins & Stevens. 17.75 (*0-536-58310-2*) Ginn Pr.

American Experiment: The Theory & Practice of Liberty. Ed. by Peter A. Lawler & Robert M. Schaefer. 420p. (C). 1994. lib. bdg. 58.50 (*0-8476-7903-9*); pap. text ed. 24.95 (*0-8476-7904-7*) Rowman.

American Experiment I: Vineyard of Liberty. James M. Burns. LC 81-47510. 864p. 1982. 39.95 (*0-394-50546-8*) Knopf.

American Experimental Music 1890-1940. David Nicholls. (Illus.). (C). 1990. 64.95 (*0-521-34578-2*) Cambridge U Pr.

American Experimental Music, 1890-1940. David Nicholls. (Illus.). 300p. (C). 1991. pap. 21.95 (*0-521-42464-X*) Cambridge U Pr.

American Explorer Series, 10 titles in 17 vols., Set. Ed. by John B. McMaster. reprint ed. 565.00 (*0-404-54900-4*) AMS Pr.

American Export Register, 2 vols., I. Orig. Title: American Register of Exporters & Importers. (Illus.). 2910p. 1987. write for info. (*0-937200-39-5*) Thomas Intl Pub.

American Export Register, 2 vols., II. Orig. Title: American Register of Exporters & Importers. (Illus.). 2910p. 1987. write for info. (*0-937200-40-9*) Thomas Intl Pub.

American Export Register, 2 vols., Set. Orig. Title: American Register of Exporters & Importers. (Illus.). 2910p. 1987. 120.00 (*0-937200-38-7*) Thomas Intl Pub.

American Export Register, 1989 Edition, 2 vols., I. (Illus.). 3110p. 1988. write for info. (*0-937200-49-2*) Thomas Intl Pub.

American Export Register, 1989 Edition, 2 vols., II. (Illus.). 3110p. 1988. write for info. (*0-937200-50-6*) Thomas Intl Pub.

American Export Register, 1989 Edition, 2 vols., Set. (Illus.). 3110p. 1988. 120.00 (*0-937200-48-4*) Thomas Intl Pub.

American Export Register, 1992 Edition, 2 vols. (Illus.). 3000p. 1991. Set. 120.00 (*0-937200-74-3*) Thomas Intl Pub.

American Export Register, 1992 Edition, 2 vols., I. (Illus.). 3000p. 1991. write for info. (*0-937200-72-7*) Thomas Intl Pub.

American Export Register, 1992 Edition, 2 vols., II. (Illus.). 3000p. 1991. write for info. (*0-937200-73-5*) Thomas Intl Pub.

American Exports During Business Cycles, 1879-1958. Ilse Mintz. (Occasional Papers: No. 76). 106p. 1961. reprint ed. 27.60 (*0-87014-390-5*) Natl Bur Econ Res.

American Express: An Unauthorized History. Peter Z. Grossman. (Illus.). 384p. 1987. 0.99 (*0-517-56238-3*) Random Hse Value.

American Express Business Traveler's City Guide: International Edition. Paul B. Finney. Ed. by Susan Crandell. (Illus.). 216p. 1988. pap. 8.95 (*0-916103-07-2*) Am Express Food.

American Express Guide to Corporate Travel Management. Jeffery Lang. 196p. 1993. 29.95 (*0-8144-0204-6*) AMACOM.

American Express Guide to Corporate Travel Management. Jeffrey B. Lang. 1993. 29.95 (*0-8100-0204-3*) Northwest Pub.

American Express Guide to Europe: The Discerning Traveler's Guide to the Best of Europe. (Illus.). 480p. 1992. pap. 24.95 (*0-13-025263-8*) P-H.

American Express International Traveler's Pocket Dictionaries & Phrase Books. American Express Staff. 240p. 1984. pap. write for info. (*0-318-57599-X*) S&S Trade.

American Express Pocket Travel Guides: Spain. rev. ed. 1988. pap. 9.95 (*0-13-025131-3*) P-H.

American Express Travel Guide Amsterdam, Rotterdam & the Hague. 2nd ed. (American Express Pocket Travel Guides Ser.). (Illus.). 352p. 1992. pap. 15.00 (*0-13-028713-X*, P-H Travel) P-H Gen Ref & Trav.

American Express Travel Guide Australia's Major Cities. (American Express Pocket Travel Guides Ser.). (Illus.). 320p. 1992. pap. 15.00 (*0-13-028739-3*, P-H Travel) P-H Gen Ref & Trav.

American Express Travel Guide Florence & Tuscany. 4th ed. (American Express Pocket Travel Guides Ser.). (Illus.). 320p. 1992. pap. 15.00 (*0-13-029653-8*, P-H Travel) P-H Gen Ref & Trav.

American Express Travel Guide Hong Kong & Taiwan. (American Express Pocket Travel Guides Ser.). (Illus.). 288p. 1992. pap. 13.00 (*0-13-028762-8*, P-H Travel) P-H Gen Ref & Trav.

American Express Travel Guide Rome. (American Express Pocket Travel Guides Ser.). (Illus.). 304p. 1992. pap. 15.00 (*0-13-029034-3*, P-H Travel) P-H Gen Ref & Trav.

American Express Travel Guide San Francisco & the Wine Regions. (American Express Pocket Travel Guides Ser.). (Illus.). 192p. 1992. pap. 13.00 (*0-13-029026-2*, P-H Travel) P-H Gen Ref & Trav.

American Express Travel Guide to Florida. Eve P. Steinberg. (American Express Pocket Travel Guides Ser.). 1994. pap. 13.00 (*0-671-88165-5*, P-H Travel) P-H Gen Ref & Trav.

American Express Travel Guide to Rome. (American Express Pocket Travel Guides Ser.). 1994. pap. 13.00 (*0-671-88167-1*, P-H Travel) P-H Gen Ref & Trav.

American Express Travel Guide Vienna & Budapest. (American Express Pocket Travel Guides Ser.). (Illus.). 304p. 1992. pap. 13.00 (*0-13-032558-9*, P-H Travel) P-H Gen Ref & Trav.

American Express Travel Guide Washington, D. C. (American Express Pocket Travel Guides Ser.). (Illus.). 224p. 1992. pap. 13.00 (*0-13-028804-7*, P-H Travel) P-H Gen Ref & Trav.

***American Eye: Eleven Artists of the 20th Century.** Jan Greenberg & Sandra Jordan. LC 94-30625. (J). (gr. 1-8). 1995. write for info. (*0-385-32173-2*) Delacorte.

***American Eyes: New Asian-American Short Stories for Young Adults.** Ed. by Lori M. Carlson. 160p. (YA). (gr. 7 up). 1994. 14.95 (*0-8050-3544-3*) H Holt & Co.

American Ezra Pound. Wendy S. Flory. LC 88-27528. 272p. (C). 1989. text ed. 35.00 (*0-300-04236-1*) Yale U Pr.

***American Face of Edgar Allen Poe.** Ed. by Shawn Rosenheim & Stephen Rachman. LC 95-10302. 408p. 1995. text ed. 55.00x (*0-8018-5024-X*); pap. text ed. 19.95x (*0-8018-5025-8*) Johns Hopkins.

American Factory Decoys. Henry A. Fleckenstein, Jr. LC 81-51466. (Illus.). 240p. 1981. 37.50 (*0-916838-53-6*) Schiffer.

American Fairy Tales. L. Frank Baum. (Illus.). xxi, 224p. 1978. pap. 4.95 (*0-486-23643-9*) Dover.

American Falls. Greg Keeler. LC 87-47733. (Illus.). 136p. (Orig.). 1987. 14.95 (*0-917652-63-0*) Confluence Pr.

American Families: A Research Guide & Historical Handbook. Ed. by Joseph M. Hawes & Elizabeth I. Nybakken. LC 90-25221. 448p. 1991. text ed. 79.50 (*0-313-26233-0*, HWF/, Greenwood Pr) Greenwood.

American Families: Twenty-Eight Short Stories. Ed. by Barbara H. Solomon. 448p. 1989. pap. 5.99 (*0-451-62736-9*, 029) NAL-Dutton.

American Families & Households. James A. Sweet & Larry Bumpass. LC 87-43097. (Census Monograph Ser.). 416p. 1990. text ed. 45.00 (*0-87154-148-3*); pap. text ed. 16.95 (*0-87154-149-1*) Russell Sage.

American Families & the Economy: The High Cost of Living. Conference on Families & the Economy Staff. Ed. by Richard R. Nelson & Felicity Skidmore. LC 83-12134. 317p. reprint ed. pap. 90.40 (*0-8357-3449-8*, 2039709) Bks Demand.

American Families & the Future: Analyses of Possible Destinies. Ed. by Barbara H. Settles et al. LC 93-26749. (Marriage & Family Review Ser.: Vol. 18, Nos. 3-4). (Illus.). 364p. 1993. lib. bdg. 49.95 (*1-56024-468-2*) Haworth Pr.

American Families in Trouble. Bruce Haas & Maureen Wahl. 40p. 1991. pap. 5.00 (*0-87304-257-3*) Families Intl.

American Family. Faith Baldwin. 390p. reprint ed. lib. bdg. 21.95 (*0-88411-629-8*, Aeonian Pr) Amereon Ltd.

American Family: A Compendium of Data & Sources. Ed. by Josefina J. Card. LC 93-24328. (Reference Library of Social Science: Vol. 925). 560p. 1994. 72.00 (*0-8153-1492-2*, SS925) Garland.

***American Family: A Pictorial Celebration of America.** Eastman Kodak Company Staff & Parade Magazine Staff. LC 95-12038. (Illus.). 1995. write for info. (*0-8264-0826-5*) Continuum.

American Family: Can It Survive? Karen Bornemann Spies. (Issues of Our Time Ser.). (Illus.). 64p. (J). (gr. 5-8). 1993. lib. bdg. 15.98 (*0-8050-2568-5*) TFC Bks NY.

American Family: Historical Perspectives. Ed. by Jean E. Hunter & Paul T. Mason. LC 90-21135. 240p. 1991. text ed. 44.50 (*0-8207-0219-6*) Duquesne.

American Family: Life & Health. Ed. by Rob D. Patton. LC 84-50757. 664p. 1986. text ed. 22.95 (*0-89914-014-9*) Third Party Pub.

American Family Album. Illus. by Norman Rockwell. 40p. 1993. 6.95 (*0-8362-4711-6*) Andrews & McMeel.

***American Family Albums, 5 vols., Set.** Dorothy Hoobler & Thomas Hoobler. (Illus.). 128p. (YA). (gr. 6 up). 1995. 114.75 (*0-19-509768-8*) OUP.

American Family & the State. Ed. by Joseph R. Peden & Fred R. Glahe. LC 85-63547. (Illus.). 488p. 1984. 34.95 (*0-936488-12-3*); pap. 14.95 (*0-936488-05-0*) PRIPP.

American Family Farm. George Anderson. (J). (gr. 3 up). 1989. 18.95 (*0-15-203025-5*) HarBrace.

American Family Farm Antiques. Terri Clemens. LC 94-13886. 1994. 17.95 (*0-87069-690-4*, Wallace-Hmestead) Chilton.

American Family Home, 1800-1960. Clifford E. Clark, Jr. LC 85-24496. (Illus.). xvi, 281p. 1986. 37.50 (*0-8078-1675-2*); pap. 18.95 (*0-8078-4151-X*) U of NC Pr.

American Family in World War Two. Ed. by Ray H. Abrams. LC 79-169365. (Family in America Ser.). 196p. 1977. reprint ed. 21.95 (*0-405-03842-9*) Ayer.

American Family Life Films. Judith Trojan. LC 80-14748. 508p. 1981. 39.50 (*0-8108-1313-0*) Scarecrow.

American Family Menu Planner. LC 93-70601. (Illus.). 312p. 1993. 19.98 (*1-56138-342-2*) Courage Bks.

American Family of the Civil War Era Paper Dolls in Full Color. Tom Tierney. (J). 1985. pap. 4.95 (*0-486-24833-X*) Dover.

American Family of the Colonial Era Paper Dolls in Full Color. Tom Tierney. (J). 1982. pap. 3.95 (*0-486-24394-X*) Dover.

American Family of the Pilgrim Period Paper Dolls. Tom Tierney. (Illus.). (J). (gr. k-3). 1987. pap. 3.95 (*0-486-25335-X*) Dover.

American Family of the 1940s Paper Dolls. Tom Tierney. (Illus.). (J). (gr. k-3). 1992. pap. 3.95 (*0-486-27336-9*) Dover.

American Family on the African Frontier: The Burnham Family Letters, 1893-1896. Mary E. Bradford & Richard H. Bradford. LC 93-85472. (Illus.). 300p. 1993. 24.95 (*1-879373-66-1*) R Rinehart.

American Family Style. Mary R. Carter. LC 87-18959. (Illus.). 280p. 1994. 24.95 (*0-670-81806-2*) Studio Bks.

American Family Style: Decorating, Cooking, Gardening, Entertaining. Mary R. Carter. (Illus.). 288p. 1990. reprint ed. pap. 18.95 (*0-14-014489-7*, Viking Studio) Studio Bks.

American Family Treasury. Ed. by Ideals Editorial Staff. (Illus.). 160p. 1993. 22.95 (*0-8249-4049-0*) Ideals.

American Family Versus American Art. Eli Siegel. 17p. 1964. pap. 3.00 (*0-911492-02-X*) Aesthetic Realism.

American Fantasies: Collected Poems 1945-1980. James Schevill. LC 82-3584. 203p. 1983. lib. bdg. 24.95x (*0-8040-0393-9*); pap. 12.95 (*0-8040-0394-7*) Swallow.

American Fantasy & Science Fiction. Marshall B. Tymn. LC 76-55151. xiii, 228p. 1979. lib. bdg. 33.00x (*0-913960-23-3*); pap. 23.00x (*0-913960-15-2*) Borgo Pr.

American Far Eastern Policy & the Sino-Japanese War. Miriam S. Farley. LC 75-30122. (Institute of Pacific Relations Ser.). reprint ed. 29.50 (*0-404-59521-9*) AMS Pr.

American Farm Crisis: An Annotated Bibliography. Earl M. Rogers & Susan H. Rogers. LC 89-31667. 162p. 1989. 26.00 (*0-8240-7243-X*) Garland.

American Farm Crisis: An Annotated Bibliography with Analytical Introductions. Harold D. Guither & Harold G. Halcrow. LC 87-32846. (Resources on Contemporary Issues Ser.: No. 1). 164p. 1988. pap. 40.00 (*0-87650-240-0*) Pierian.

American Farm Policy, 1948-1973. Willard W. Cochrane & Mary E. Ryan. LC 75-32671. 445p. reprint ed. pap. 126.90 (*0-7837-2969-3*, 2057485) Bks Demand.

American Farm School: A Family Album, 1904-1944. Charlotte W. Draper. (Illus.). 144p. (Orig.). 1994. pap. 30.00 (*0-9640411-0-3*) Am Farm Schl.

American Farm Tools: From Hand-Power to Steam-Power. R. Douglas Hurt. (Illus.). 121p. 1989. reprint ed. pap. 15.00 (*0-89745-026-4*) Sunflower U Pr.

American Farm Tractor. Randy Leffingwell. (Illus.). 176p. 1991. 29.95 (*0-87938-532-4*) Motorbooks Intl.

American Farm Tractor Trademarks. C. H. Wendel. (Illus.). 128p. 1994. pap. 19.95 (*0-87938-931-1*) Motorbooks Intl.

American Farmer. Ethel Cole. (Social Studies Ser.). 24p. (gr. 5-9). 1976. student ed. 5.00 (*0-8209-0245-4*, SS-12) ESP.

American Farmer. A. M. Simons. LC 74-30652. (American Farmers & the Rise of Agribusiness Ser.). 1975. reprint ed. 21.95 (*0-405-06828-X*) Ayer.

American Farmer Battles for Survival: An Overview on Protecting the Farm Family's Pride & Health. Del Witherspoon. (Illus.). 93p. (Orig.). 1987. pap. 6.00 (*0-929254-00-7*) Spoons Pub.

American Farmers & the Rise of Agribusiness: Seeds of Struggle, 46 bks., Set. Ed. by Dan C. McCurry & Richard E. Rubenstein. 1975. 1,674.00 (*0-405-06760-7*) Ayer.

American Farmhouse. Henry J. Kauffman. 1988. 12.99 (*0-517-29598-9*) Random Hse Value.

American Farming & Food. Finlay Dunn. 1980. lib. bdg. 75.00 (*0-8490-3185-0*) Gordon Pr.

***American Farms 1996.** Hurt. 1996. write for info. (*0-89464-891-8*) Krieger.

American Favorite Ballads. Pete Seeger. (Illus.). 144p. pap. 9.95 (*0-8256-0028-6*, Oak) Music Sales.

American Federal Government. 14th ed. John H. Ferguson & Dean E. McHenry. Ed. by Eric M. Munson. 592p. (C). 1981. text ed. write for info. (*0-07-020527-2*) McGraw.

American Federal Government. 14th ed. John H. Ferguson & Dean E. McHenry. 1981. pap. text ed. write for info. (*0-07-020529-9*) McGraw.

***American Federal-State-Local Relations in 1990s.** Walker. (Political Pamphleteer Ser.). (C). 1994. text ed. 3.00 (*0-673-99780-4*) HarpCollege.

American Federal Tax Reports. ring bd. write for info. (*0-318-57352-0*) P-H.

American Federalism: A New Partnership for the Republic. Ed. by Robert B. Hawkins, Jr. LC 82-80329. 200p. 1982. pap. text ed. 21.95 (*0-917616-50-2*) Transaction Pubs.

American Federalism: Competition among Governments. Thomas R. Dye. 240p. 1989. pap. 17.95 (*0-669-21474-4*) Free Pr.

American Federalism & Public Policy: How the System Works. Thomas J. Anton. 320p. (C). 1989. pap. text ed. write for info. (*0-07-553789-3*) McGraw.

American Federalism in the 1980s: Changes & Consequences: Conference Summary & Papers May 19-20, 1981. Lincoln Institute of Land Policy Staff. (Lincoln Institute Monograph Ser.: No. 81-7). 86p. reprint ed. pap. 25.00 (*0-7837-2171-4*, 2042494) Bks Demand.

American Federalism Series: The Urban Dimension, 37 vols. Ed. by Robert M. Fogelson et al. 1978. lib. bdg. 1,092.50 (*0-405-10474-X*) Ayer.

American Federation of Labor. Lewis L. Lorwin & Jean A. Flexner. LC 70-126699. 1970. reprint ed. 15.00 (*0-404-04027-6*) AMS Pr.

American Federation of Labor. Lewis L. Lorwin. LC 70-174559. (Library of American Labor History). 1972. reprint ed. 49.50 (*0-678-00880-9*) Kelley.

American Federation of Labor: History, Encyclopedia, Reference Book, 3 vols., 1. American Federation of Labor Staff. Ed. by William C. Roberts & Mary Erb. LC 77-3562. 1977. text ed. 55.00 (*0-8371-9569-1*, AFLI) Greenwood.

American Federation of Labor: History, Encyclopedia, Reference Book, 3 vols., Set. American Federation of Labor Staff. Ed. by William C. Roberts & Mary Erb. LC 77-3562. 1977. text ed. 295.00 (*0-8371-9568-3*, AFLH) Greenwood.

American Federation of Labor: History, Encyclopedia, Reference Book, 3 vols., Vol. 2. American Federation of Labor Staff. Ed. by William C. Roberts & Mary Erb. LC 77-3562. 1977. text ed. 55.00 (*0-8371-9570-5*, AFLJ) Greenwood.

American Federation of Labor: History, Encyclopedia, Reference Book, 3 vols., Vol. 3. American Federation of Labor Staff. Ed. by William C. Roberts & Mary Erb. LC 77-3562. 1977. text ed. 75.00 (*0-8371-9571-3*, AFLK) Greenwood.

American Federation of Labor: History, Encyclopedia, Reference Book, 3 vols., Vol. 4. American Federation of Labor Staff. Ed. by William C. Roberts & Mary Erb. LC 77-3562. 1977. Vol. 3, Pt. 2. text ed. 85.00 (*0-8371-9572-1*, AFLL) Greenwood.

American Federation of Labor: History, Encyclopedia, Reference Book, 3 vols., Vol. 5. American Federation of Labor Staff. Ed. by William C. Roberts & Mary Erb. LC 77-3562. 1977. Vol. 3, Pt. 3. text ed. 65.00 (*0-8371-9598-5*, AFLM) Greenwood.

American Federation of Labor Records: The Samuel Gompers Era, 1877-1937. Ed. by Peter J. Albert & Harold L. Miller. 67p. 1991. pap. 69.00 (*0-87020-190-5*) Chadwyck-Healey.

American Federation of Teachers Bibliography. Wayne State University, Archives of Labor History & Urban Affairs Staff. LC 80-13142. 240p. 1980. 29.95 (*0-8143-1659-X*); pap. 17.95 (*0-8143-1660-3*) Wayne St U Pr.

An Asterisk (*) at the beginning of an entry indicates that the title is appearing in BIP for the first time.

A

An Asterisk (*) at the beginning of an entry indicates that the title is appearing in BIP for the first time.

241

American Foreign Policy: Changing Perspectives on National Security. rev. ed. Henry T. Nash. LC 77-91308. (Dorsey Series in Political Science). 395p. reprint ed. pap. 112.60 (*0-8357-5370-0*, 2024232) Bks Demand.

American Foreign Policy: Current Documents. United States Department of State, Historical Office. 1971. 72.95 (*0-405-01793-6*, 13573); 36.95 (*0-405-01794-4*, 13574); 54.95 (*0-405-01795-2*, 13575); 60.95 (*0-405-01792-8*, 13572); 60.95 (*0-405-01791-X*, 13571); 54.95 (*0-405-01790-1*, 13570) Ayer.

American Foreign Policy: Current Documents. United States Department of State, Historical Office Staff. 1971. 60.95 (*0-405-01796-0*, 13576) Ayer.

American Foreign Policy: Current Documents, 1963. United States Department of State, Historical Office. 1971. 54.95 (*0-405-01797-9*, 13577) Ayer.

American Foreign Policy: Current Documents, 1984. (State Department Publications: No. 9462). 1230p. 1986. 37.00 (*0-16-004414-6*, S/N 044-000-02087-4) USGPO.

American Foreign Policy: Current Documents, 1985. Ed. by David S. Patterson. (Department of State Publication Ser.: No. 9485). 1179p. 1986. text ed. 31.00 (*0-16-004431-6*, S/N 044-000-02136-6) USGPO.

American Foreign Policy: Opposing Viewpoints. Ed. by Carol Wekesser. LC 92-40707. (Opposing Viewpoints Ser.). (Illus.). 264p. (YA). (gr. 10 up). 1993. lib. bdg. 19.95 (*0-89908-199-1*); pap. text ed. 11.55 (*0-89908-174-6*) Greenhaven.

American Foreign Policy: Pattern & Process. 4th ed. Charles W. Kegley, Jr. & Eugene R. Wittkopf. LC 89-63944. 704p. (C). 1991. pap. text ed. 26.00 (*0-312-03656-6*) St Martin.

American Foreign Policy: Theoretical Essays. G. John Ikenberry. (C). 1989. pap. text ed. 28.50 (*0-673-39815-3*) HarpCollege.

American Foreign Policy & Moral Rhetoric: The Example of Vietnam. David Little. LC 74-77373. (Special Studies Ser.). 1969. pap. 2.00 (*0-87641-206-1*) Carnegie Ethics & Intl Affairs.

American Foreign Policy & Process. 2nd ed. James M. McCormick. LC 91-67848. 584p. 1992. pap. 35.00 (*0-87581-360-7*) Peacock Pubs.

American Foreign Policy & the Blessings of Liberty, & Other Essays. Samuel F. Bemis. LC 75-11972. 423p. 1975. reprint ed. text ed. 35.00 (*0-8371-8132-1*, BEAF, Greenwood Pr) Greenwood.

American Foreign Policy & the Cold War. Herbert Aptheker. 1962. 32.00 (*0-527-02771-5*) Periodicals Srv.

American Foreign Policy Current Documents, 1986. Ed. by David S. Patterson et al. (State Department Publications: No. 9620). 887p. 1987. 26.00 (*0-16-004464-2*, S/N 044-000-02194-3) USGPO.

American Foreign Policy During the French Revolution-Napoleonic Period, 1789-1815: Napoleonic Periods, 1789-1815. James A. Carr. LC 94-2422. (Reference Library of Social Science: Vol. 593). 192p. 1994. 27.00 (*0-8240-5697-3*, SS593) Garland.

American Foreign Policy in an Uncertain World. Ed. by David P. Forsythe. LC 83-27370. 593p. reprint ed. pap. 169.10 (*0-7837-1820-9*, 2042020) Bks Demand.

American Foreign Policy in Canadian Relations. James M. Callahan. 1937. 20.00 (*0-686-33257-1*) R S Barnes.

American Foreign Policy in Canadian Relations. James M. Callahan. LC 66-30786. 1970. reprint ed. 71.00 (*0-8154-0044-6*) Cooper Sq.

American Foreign Policy in Canadian Relations. James M. Callahan. (History - United States Ser.). 576p. 1993. reprint ed. lib. bdg. 99.00 (*0-7812-4929-5*) Rprt Serv.

American Foreign Policy in Mexican Relations. James M. Callahan. LC 66-30787. 1970. reprint ed. 73.50 (*0-8154-0045-4*) Cooper Sq.

American Foreign Policy in the Nuclear Age. 5th ed. Cecil V. Crabb, Jr. 512p. (C). 1990. pap. text ed. 36.50 (*0-06-041383-2*) HarpCollege.

American Foreign Policy in the Post-War Years. Frank H. Simonds. 1979. 18.95 (*0-405-10627-0*) Ayer.

*__American Foreign Policy Index 1993, 2 vols.__ Ed. by Congressional Information Service, Inc., Staff. write for info. (*0-88692-280-1*) Cong Info.

*__American Foreign Policy Index 1993: Abstracts Volume.__ Ed. by Congressional Information Service, Inc., Staff. write for info. (*0-88692-281-X*) Cong Info.

*__American Foreign Policy Index 1993: Index Volume.__ Ed. by Congressional Information Service, Inc., Staff. write for info. (*0-88692-282-8*) Cong Info.

*__American Foreign Policy Index, 1994, 2 vols.__ Ed. by Congressional Information Service, Inc., Staff. 1178p. 1995. write for info. (*0-88692-313-1*) Cong Info.

*__American Foreign Policy Index, 1994 Abstracts Volume.__ Ed. by Congressional Information Service, Inc., Staff. 1995. write for info. (*0-88692-314-X*) Cong Info.

*__American Foreign Policy Index, 1994 Index Volume.__ Ed. by Congressional Information Service, Inc., Staff. 1995. write for info. (*0-88692-315-8*) Cong Info.

American Foreign Policy Making & the Democratic Dilemmas. 5th ed. John Spanier & Eric M. Uslaner. 397p. (C). 1989. pap. 25.95 (*0-534-11087-8*) Intl Thomson.

American Foreign Policy Making & the Democratic Dilemmas. 6th ed. John W. Spanier & Eric M. Uslaner. 416p. (C). 1994. pap. write for info. (*0-02-414201-8*) Macmillan.

American Foreign Policy, Nineteen Forty-One to Nineteen Sixty-Three: Basic Documents 1941-1949; Current Documents 1950-1963. United States Department of State, Historical Office. 1971. 575.00 (*0-405-01788-X*, 13) Ayer.

American Foreign Policy since World War II. 12th rev. ed. John Spanier. 448p. 1992. 30.95 (*0-87187-727-9*) Congr Quarterly.

*__American Foreign Policy Since World War II.__ 13th ed. John Spanier & Steven W. Hook. 375p. 1995. pap. 31.95 (*0-87187-819-4*) Congr Quarterly.

American Foreign Policy Towards Latin America in the Eighties & Nineties: Issues & Controversies from Reagan to Bush. Howard J. Wiarda. 384p. (C). 1993. text ed. 50.00 (*0-8147-9250-2*); pap. 17.50 (*0-8147-9257-X*) NYU Pr.

American Foreign Policy, Vol. 2: A History since 1900. 3rd rev. ed. Thomas G. Paterson & J. Garry Clifford. LC 90-82956. 502p. (C). 1991. pap. text ed. write for info. (*0-669-24678-6*) Heath.

American Foreign Relations: A Historiographical Review. Ed. by Gerald K. Haines & J. Samuel Walker. LC 80-545. (Contributions in American History Ser.: No. 90). (Illus.). xiii, 369p. 1981. text ed. 65.00 (*0-313-21061-6*, HAF/, Greenwood Pr) Greenwood.

*__American Foreign Relations Vol. I: A History: To 1920.__ 4th ed. Thomas G. Paterson et al. 352p. (C). 1995. pap. text ed. write for info. (*0-669-35155-5*) Heath.

*__American Foreign Relations Vol. II: A History: Since 1895.__ 4th ed. Thomas G. Paterson et al. 554p. (C). 1995. pap. text ed. write for info. (*0-669-35156-3*) Heath.

American Foreign Relations Reconsidered, 1890-1993. Ed. by Gordon Martel. LC 93-36339. 280p. 1994. 59.95x (*0-415-10476-9*, B3803, Routledge NY); pap. 16.95 (*0-415-10477-7*, B3807, Routledge NY) Routledge.

American Foreign Service Officer. 2nd ed. E. P. Steinberg & Arva C. Floyd. 192p. 1992. pap. 18.00 (*0-13-037250-1*, Arco Test) P-H Gen Ref & Trav.

American Forest Magazine. 2.50 (*0-317-59260-2*) Am Forests.

American Forest Policy in Development. Stephen H. Spurr. LC 76-16648. (George S. Long Publication Ser.). 96p. 1976. text ed. 15.00 (*0-295-95532-5*) U of Wash Pr.

American Forestry: A History of National, State, & Private Cooperation. William G. Robbins. LC 84-28122. xvi, 344p. 1985. 35.00 (*0-8032-3872-X*) U of Nebr Pr.

*__American Forests: A History of Resiliency & Recovery.__ Douglas MacCleery. (Illus.). 58p. (Orig.). (C). (gr. 12 up). 1994. pap. text ed. 40.00 (*0-7881-0858-1*) Diane Pub.

American Forests: A History of Resiliency & Recovery. Douglas W. MacCleery. LC 92-29771. (Issues Ser.). (Illus.). 58p. (C). 1993. pap. 6.95 (*0-89030-048-8*) Forest Hist Soc.

*__American Forests Famous & Historic Trees: Make History. Plant a Tree.__ (Illus.). 44p. (Orig.). 1994. pap. text ed. 2.00 (*0-9642811-0-4*) Famous & Hist.

American Formalism & the Problem of Interpretation. J. Timothy Bagwell. LC 85-30096. 160p. 1986. 14.95 (*0-89263-260-7*) Rice Univ.

American Forts: Architectural Form & Function. Willard B. Robinson. LC 76-25130. (Illus.). 244p. reprint ed. 69.60 (*0-8357-9662-0*, 2011138) Bks Demand.

American Forty-Five & Seventy-Eight RPM Record Dating Guide, 1940-1959. William R. Daniels. LC 84-22420. (Discographies Ser.: No. 16). xi, 157p. 1985. text ed. 49.95 (*0-313-24232-1*, DRP/, Greenwood Pr) Greenwood.

American Founders of Modern Japan: The Occupation As New Deal. Theodore Cohen. Ed. by Herbert Passin. 791p. 1987. 39.95 (*0-02-906050-8*) Free Pr.

American Founding: Essays on the Federalist Papers. Ed. by Charles R. Kesler. 300p. 1987. text ed. 40.00 (*0-02-919730-9*) Free Pr.

American Founding: Essays on the Formation of the Constitution. Ed. by J. Jackson Barlow et al. LC 87-29558. (Contributions in Political Science Ser.: No. 205). 368p. 1988. text ed. 59.95 (*0-313-25610-1*, LMS/, Greenwood Pr) Greenwood.

American Founding Experience: Political Community & Republican Government. Charles S. Hyneman. Ed. by Charles E. Gilbert. LC 93-4095. 304p. (C). 1994. 34.95 (*0-252-02053-7*); pap. 17.95 (*0-252-06348-1*) U of Ill Pr.

American Foxhound Champions, English Foxhound Champions, Harrier Champions, 1952-1992. Camino E. E. & B. Co. Staff. (Illus.). 150p. 1995. pap. 36.95 (*1-55893-010-8*) Camino E E & Bk.

American Free Verse: The Modern Revolution in Poetry. Walter Sutton. LC 72-93980. 256p. 1973. pap. 3.95 (*0-8112-0473-1*, NDP351) New Directions.

*__American Freedom: Why the Colonists Risked Their Lives, Their Fortunes & Their Sacred Honor.__ Frank Manak. LC 95-60858. (Illus.). 250p. (Orig.). 1995. pap. 12.95 (*0-9634940-7-4*) York Pub.

American Freedom & Catholic Power. Paul Blanshard. LC 84-19141. xii, 402p. 1984. reprint ed. text ed. 79.50 (*0-313-24620-3*, BLAF, Greenwood Pr) Greenwood.

American Freedom & the Social Sciences. James Deese. LC 84-23683. 232p. 1985. text ed. 42.00 (*0-231-05914-0*) Col U Pr.

American Freedoms: A Bicentennial Essay on the Bill of Rights. rev. ed. Gray L. Dorsey. LC 74-20856. x, 54p. 1987. pap. 17.50 (*0-89941-539-3*, 300290) W S Hein.

American Freestyle Karate. Dan Anderson. LC 81-50512. (Illus.). 200p. 1981. pap. 9.95 (*0-86568-021-3*, 303) Unique Pubns.

American Freethought, 1860-1914. Sidney Warren. LC 66-20711. 257p. 1966. reprint ed. 50.00 (*0-87752-116-6*) Gordian.

American-French - French-American Dictionary of Police Force & Underworld Language. J. P. Brunet. (Illus.). 1000p. (ENG & FRE.). 1990. 112.50 (*2-85608-037-5*) IBD Ltd.

American Freshman: National Norms for Fall 1990. Alexander W. Astin et al. 172p. (Orig.). 1990. pap. 19.00 (*1-878477-06-4*) UCLA Higher Educ Rsch Inst.

American Freshman: National Norms for Fall, 1991. Alexander W. Astin et al. 168p. (Orig.). 1991. pap. 20.00 (*1-878477-10-2*) UCLA Higher Educ Rsch Inst.

American Freshman: National Norms for Fall, 1992. E. L. Dey et al. (Illus.). 162p. (Orig.). Date not set. pap. 20.00 (*1-878477-12-9*) UCLA Higher Educ Rsch Inst.

American Freshman: National Norms for Fall 1993. A. W. Astin et al. (Illus.). 169p. (Orig.). 1993. pap. 20.00 (*1-878477-14-5*) UCLA Higher Educ Rsch Inst.

American Freshman: Twenty-Five Year Trends. rev. ed. Alexander W. Astin et al. 220p. 1991. pap. 27.50 (*1-878477-07-2*) UCLA Higher Educ Rsch Inst.

American Friends' Handbook. 1989. 2.95 (*0-317-04075-8*) Intl Students Inc.

American Friends Service Committee, Philadelphia, 2 vols. Ed. by Jack Sutters. LC 89-19615. (Archives of the Holocaust Ser.: Vol. 2). 1327p. 1990. reprint ed. 295.00 (*0-8240-5484-9*) Garland.

American from Sweden: The Story of A. V. Swanson. Betty S. Cain. LC 86-33029. 99p. 1987. text ed. 15.95 (*0-8093-1362-6*) S Ill U Pr.

American Frontier. Roger Barr. (World History Ser.). (Illus.). 128p. (J). (gr. 5-9). 1995. lib. bdg. 16.95 (*1-56006-282-7*, 2827) Lucent Bks.

American Frontier: An Archaeological Study of Settlement Pattern & Process. Kenneth E. Lewis. LC 83-19725. (Studies in Historical Archaeology). 1984. text ed. 68.00 (*0-12-446560-9*) Acad Pr.

American Frontier: Opposing Viewpoints. Ed. by Mary E. Jones. LC 93-29898. (American History Ser.). 1994. lib. bdg. 19.95 (*1-56006-086-7*); pap. 11.55 (*1-56006-085-9*) Greenhaven.

American Frontier: Pioneers, Settlers, & Cowboys, 1800-1890. William C. Davis. Ed. by Carole Clements. (Illus.). 256p. 1995. 24.98 (*0-8317-1825-0*) Smithmark.

American Frontier Activities in Asia: U. S.-Asian Relations in the Twentieth Century. Young H. Kim. LC 81-3989. 384p. (C). 1981. text ed. 33.95 (*0-88229-707-4*) Nelson-Hall.

American Frontier & Western Issues: A Historiographical Review. Ed. by Roger L. Nichols. LC 85-30181. (Contributions in American History Ser.: No. 118). 312p. 1986. text ed. 49.95 (*0-313-24356-5*, NAF/, Greenwood Pr) Greenwood.

American Frontier Photography. Robyn G. Peterson. (Illus.). 36p. 1993. pap. 5.00 (*0-9622038-4-X*) Rockwell NY.

American Frontiers: The Photographs of Timothy H. O'Sullivan, 1867-1874. deluxe limited ed. Joel Snyder. (Illus.). 120p. 1981. 400.00 (*0-89381-094-0*) Aperture.

American Frugal Housewife. Lydia M. Child. (Illus.). 130p. 1971. 7.00 (*0-88215-022-7*) Friends Ohio St U Lib.

American Frugal Housewife. Lydia M. Child. 140p. 1985. reprint ed. 9.95 (*0-918222-98-2*) Applewood.

American Fuguing-Tunes, 1770-1820: A Descriptive Catalog. Karl Kroeger. LC 93-30774. (Music Reference Collection Ser.: No. 41). 240p. 1993. text ed. 65.00 (*0-313-29000-8*, Greenwood Pr) Greenwood.

American Fuhrer: Lyndon LaRouche & the Politics of Paranoia. Paul Roberts. 208p. 1988. 16.95 (*0-312-02161-5*, Pub. by Thomas Dunne Bks) St Martin.

American Funeral: A Study in Guilt, Extravagance & Sublimity. LeRoy Bowman. viii, 181p. 1990. reprint ed. lib. bdg. 23.00 (*1-55888-884-5*) Omnigraphics Inc.

American Fur Seal Diplomacy: The Alaskan Fur Seal Controversy. James T. Gay. (American University Studies: History: Ser. IX, Vol. 31). 180p. (C). 1987. text ed. 28.00 (*0-8204-0482-9*) P Lang Pubs.

American Fur Trade: A Bibliography of Sources in English. M. Louise Reynells et al. (Stokvis Studies in Historical Chronology & Thought). 191p. Date not set. lib. bdg. write for info. (*0-89370-333-8*) Borgo Pr.

American Fur Trade: A Bibliography of Sources in English. M. Louise Reynells et al. (Stokvis Studies in Historical Chronology & Thought: No. 9). 191p. Date not set. pap. write for info. (*0-89370-433-4*) Borgo Pr.

American Fur Trade of the Far West, 3 vols. Hiram M. Chittenden. 1992. reprint ed. lib. bdg. 225.00 (*0-7812-5013-7*) Rprt Serv.

American Fur Trade of the Far West, Vol. 1. Hiram M. Chittenden. LC 86-11227. (Illus.). xliv, 584p. 1986. reprint ed. pap. 12.95 (*0-8032-6320-1*, Bison Books) U of Nebr Pr.

American Fur Trade of the Far West, Vol. 2. Hiram M. Chittenden. LC 86-11227. (Illus.). xxiv, 457p. 1986. reprint ed. pap. 11.95 (*0-8032-6321-X*, Bison Books) U of Nebr Pr.

American Furniture. Luke Beckerdite. (Chipstone Foundation Ser.). (Illus.). 312p. 1993. pap. 45.00 (*0-87451-648-X*) U Pr of New Eng.

*__American Furniture.__ John S. Bowman. 1995. 17.99 (*0-517-12024-0*, Crown) Crown Pub Group.

American Furniture: From the Kaufman Collection. LC 86-27844. (Illus.). 1986. 29.95 (*0-89468-099-4*) Natl Gallery Art.

American Furniture: Seventeenth, Eighteenth & Nineteenth Century Styles. Helen Comstock. LC 62-18074. (Illus.). 336p. 1980. reprint ed. 44.95 (*0-916838-28-5*) Schiffer.

American Furniture at Chipstone. Oswaldo Rodriguez-Roque. LC 83-40270. (Illus.). 480p. 1984. 50.00 (*0-299-09760-9*) U of Wis Pr.

American Furniture Craftsmen Working Prior to 1920: An Annotated Bibliography. Comp. by Charles J. Semowich. LC 84-4459. (Art Reference Collection Ser.: No. 7). x, 381p. 1984. text ed. 59.95 (*0-313-23275-X*, SEF/, Greenwood Pr) Greenwood.

American Furniture in Pendleton House. Christopher P. Monkhouse. (Illus.). 228p. (C). 1986. pap. 25.00 (*0-685-18008-5*) Mus of Art RI.

American Furniture in the Bybee Collection. Charles L. Venable. (Illus.). 212p. 1989. 45.00 (*0-292-70774-6*) U of Tex Pr.

American Furniture in The Metropolitan Museum of Art: Late Colonial Period - the Queen Anne & Chippendale Styles, 3 vols., Vol. 2. Morrison H. Heckscher. (Illus.). 384p. 1985. 39.50 (*0-87099-427-1*) Metro Mus Art.

American Furniture in the Metropolitan Museum of Art: Late Colonial Period: Queen Anne & Ch... Morrison H. Heckscher. 1994. 39.50 (*0-8109-6438-4*) Abrams.

American Furniture in the Museum of Fine Arts, Boston. Richard H. Randall, Jr. LC 65-24149. 278p. 1965. reprint ed. pap. 29.95 (*0-87846-003-9*) Mus Fine Arts Boston.

American Furniture of the 19th Century, 1840-1880. Richard Dubrow & Eileen Dubrow. LC 82-50615. (Illus.). 248p. 1983. 30.00 (*0-916838-68-4*) Schiffer.

American Furniture with Related Decorative Arts, 1660-1830: The Milwaukee Art Museum & the Layton Art Collection. Brock W. Jobe et al. Ed. by Gerald W. R. Ward. LC 91-71554. (Illus.). 316p. 1992. 85.00 (*1-55595-068-X*) Hudson Hills.

American Furniture, 1680-1880: From the Collection of the Baltimore Museum of Art. William V. Elder, III & Jayne E. Stokes. LC 86-26518. (Illus.). 184p. 1987. pap. 20.00 (*0-912298-62-6*) Baltimore Mus.

American Furniture 1994. Ed. by Luke Beckerdite. (Illus.). 288p. 1994. pap. 45.00 (*0-87451-681-1*) U Pr of New Eng.

American Future: New Visions Beyond Old Frontiers. Tom Hayden. LC 80-52244. 325p. 1980. 30.00 (*0-89608-030-7*); pap. 8.00 (*0-89608-029-3*) South End Pr.

American Future (What Would George & Tom Do Now?) William Van Dusen Wishard. 122p. 1992. pap. 12.95 (*0-9633057-0-0*) Congress Inst.

American Game Cooking: A Contemporary Guide to Preparing Farm-Raised Game Birds & Meats. John Ash & Sid Goldstein. (Illus.). 304p. 1993. pap. 16.30 (*0-201-62468-0*) Addison-Wesley.

American Game Mammals & Birds: A Catalogue of Books. John C. Phillips. Ed. by Keir B. Sterling. LC 77-83129. (Biologists & Their World Ser.). (Illus.). 1978. reprint ed. lib. bdg. 54.95 (*0-405-10744-7*) Ayer.

American Garden City & the New Towns Movement. Carol A. Christensen. Ed. by Stephen Foster. LC 85-20866. (Architecture & Urban Design Ser.: No. 13). 216p. reprint ed. 61.30 (*0-8357-1684-8*, 2070450) Bks Demand.

American Garden Design. McGuire. 1994. 22.00 (*0-671-79921-5*, P-H Gen Ref & Trav.

American Garden Guidebook: West. Everitt L. Miller & Jay S. Cohen. LC 89-37897. 294p. 1989. pap. 9.95 (*0-87131-580-7*) M Evans.

American Garden Guidebook East. Everitt L. Miller & Jay S. Cohen. LC 87-6857. 294p. 1987. pap. 8.95 (*0-87131-499-1*) M Evans.

American Garden Guides: Herb Gardening. Cornell Plantations Staff et al. LC 93-11362. 1994. 25.00 (*0-679-41432-0*) Pantheon.

*__American Garden Guides: Rose Gardening.__ American Garden Guides Staff. 1995. pap. 25.00 (*0-679-75830-5*) Pantheon.

American Garden Guides: Shrubs & Vines. Holden Arboretum Staff. LC 93-11359. 1994. 25.00 (*0-679-41433-9*) Pantheon.

American Garden Guides: Perennial Gardening. New York Botanical Garden Staff. 224p. 1994. 25.00 (*0-679-41431-2*) Pantheon.

American Garden Guides: Vegetable Gardening. Callaway Gardens Staff. 224p. 1994. 25.00 (*0-679-41434-7*) Pantheon.

American Garden Writing: Gleanings from Garden Lives Then & Now. Ed. by Bonnie Marranca. LC 87-73280. 325p. 23.95 (*1-55554-029-5*) PAJ Pubns.

American Gardener. Allen Lacy. 1990. pap. 10.95 (*0-374-52217-0*, Noonday) FS&G.

American Gardener: A Sampler. Ed. by Allen Lacy. LC 87-37965. 324p. 1988. 18.95 (*0-374-10404-2*) FS&G.

American Gardener's Calendar: Adapted to the Climates & Seasons of the United States. Bernard M'Mahon. 1977. reprint ed. 25.00 (*0-913728-25-X*) Theophrastus.

American Gardener's World of Bulbs. Judy Glattstein. LC 93-38714. 1994. 24.95 (*0-316-31593-1*) Little.

*__American Gardens: A Tour of the Nation's Finest Private Gardens.__ Peter Loewer. LC 95-7409. 1995. 19.99 (*0-517-14712-2*, Pub. by Wings Bks) Random.

American Gardens: A Traveler's Guide. Ed. by Claire E. Sawyers. (Plants & Gardens Ser.). (Illus.). 1989. per., pap. 5.95 (*0-945352-44-1*) Bklyn Botanic.

American Gardens in the Eighteenth Century: "For Use or for Delight" Ann Leighton. LC 86-6975. (Illus.). 544p. 1986. reprint ed. pap. 20.95 (*0-87023-531-1*) U of Mass Pr.

American Gardens of the Nineteenth Century: "For Comfort & Affluence" Ann Leighton. LC 86-11330. (Illus.). 424p. 1987. 37.50 (*0-87023-532-X*); pap. 18.95 (*0-87023-533-8*) U of Mass Pr.

American Gargoyles: Flannery O'Connor & the Medieval Grotesque. Anthony Di Renzo. LC 92-32128. 312p. (C). 1993. 34.95 (*0-8093-1848-2*) S Ill U Pr.

*__American Gargoyles: Flannery O'Connor & the Medieval Grotesque.__ Anthony Di Renzo. LC 95-11478. (Illus.). 272p. (C). 1995. reprint ed. pap. 14.95x (*0-8093-2030-4*) S Ill U Pr.

American Garland. C. H. Firth. 1976. 59.95 (*0-87968-601-4*) Gordon Pr.

*__American Gas & Oil Company Logos.__ Wayne Henderson. (Illus.). 128p. 1995. pap. 19.95 (*0-7603-0008-9*) Motorbooks Intl.

American Gas Association Gas Industry Training Directory. 11th ed. 80p. 1980. pap. 15.00 (*0-318-12582-X*, C02980) Am Gas Assn.

An Asterisk (*) at the beginning of an entry indicates that the title is appearing in BIP for the first time.

An Asterisk (*) at the beginning of an entry indicates that the title is appearing in BIP for the first time.

***American Greetings: A Report on the Company's Environmental Policies & Practices.** (Illus.). 22p. (C). 1994. reprint ed. pap. text ed. 200.00x (*0-7881-0950-2*, Coun on Econ) Diane Pub.

American Gridmark: Why You've Always Suspected That Measuring Up Doesn't Count. James M. Mannon. LC 90-39598. 208p. (Orig.). 1990. pap. 9.95 (*0-943173-55-8*) Harbinger AZ.

American Grill. David Barich & Thomas Ingalls. (Illus.). 72p. 1994. 12.95 (*0-8118-0699-5*) Chronicle Bks.

American Grocery Store: The Business Evolution of an Architectural Space. James M. Mayo. LC 92-45072. (Contributions in American History Ser.: No. 150). 304p. 1993. text ed. 59.95 (*0-313-26520-8*, MGS, Greenwood Pr) Greenwood.

American Ground: Vistas, Visions & Revisions. Ed. by Robert H. Fossum & John K. Roth. LC 87-20180. 426p. 1988. pap. 14.95 (*1-55778-114-1*) Paragon Hse.

American Ground Zero: The Secret Nuclear War. Carole Gallagher. (Illus.). 355p. 1993. 55.00x (*0-262-07146-0*) MIT Pr.

American Ground Zero: The Secret Nuclear War. Carole Gallagher. 1994. pap. 30.00 (*0-679-75432-6*) Random.

American Guerrilla: My War Behind Japanese Lines. Roger Hilsman. (Brassey's WWII Commemorative Ser.). (Illus.). 328p. 1991. pap. 12.95 (*0-08-040580-0*) Brasseys Inc.

American Guidance for Seniors. braille ed. Ken Skala. Orig. Title: American Guidance for Those over Sixty. 1240p. (Orig.). 1992. vinyl bd. 99.20 (*1-56956-034-X*, BR8566) W A T Braille.

American Guidance for Seniors. 3rd ed. Ken Skala. LC 89-124309. Orig. Title: American Guidance for Those over Sixty. 556p. (Orig.). 1991. pap. 15.95 (*0-944873-01-4*) Am Guide Inc.

American Guidance for Seniors. 4th ed. Ken Skala. Orig. Title: American Guidance for Those over Sixty. 560p. (Orig.). 1992. pap. 17.95 (*0-944873-02-2*, Career Pr Inc) Am Guide Inc.

American Guidance for Seniors. 5th ed. Ken Skala. Orig. Title: American Guidance for Those over Sixty. (Orig.). 1993. pap. 17.95 (*0-944873-03-0*) Am Guide Inc.

American Guidance for Seniors...And Their Caregivers: An Indispensable Guide to Social Security, Medicare & Other Vital Benefits, Services & Financial Assistance for Senior Americans. 5th ed. Ken Skala. 564p. 1994. pap. 17.95 (*0-944873-04-9*) Key Comm Grp.

American Guidance for Those over Sixty. Ken Skala. 550p. (Orig.). 1990. pap. 15.95 (*0-944873-00-6*) Am Guide Inc.

American Guidance for Those over Sixty see American Guidance for Seniors

American Guide to Doing Business in Australia. 66p. 1992. pap. 26.50 (*0-9626617-1-6*, DU80) PacRim Pub.

American Guide to Hotels, Motels, Resorts & Inns. Millard Morgan. (Western Edition Ser.). 180p. (Orig.). 1989. pap. 6.95 (*0-685-29015-8*) Guide Pr CA.

American Guide to Hotels, Motels, Resorts & Inns: Central Edition. Millard Morgan. 180p. 1989. pap. 6.95 (*0-685-29018-2*) Guide Pr CA.

American Guide to Hotels, Motels, Resorts & Inns: Eastern Edition. Millard Morgan. 180p. (Orig.). 1989. pap. 6.95 (*0-685-29017-4*) Guide Pr CA.

American Guide to Hotels, Motels, Resorts & Inns: Southern Edition. Millard Morgan. 180p. (Orig.). 1989. pap. 6.95 (*0-685-29016-6*) Guide Pr CA.

American Guide to U. S. Coins, 1985. rev. ed. Charles F. French. 1984. pap. 4.95 (*0-317-05145-8*, Fireside) S&S Trade.

American Guide to U. S. Coins, 1994. Charles French. 1993. pap. 6.99 (*0-671-78124-3*, Fireside) S&S Trade.

American Guide to U. S. Coins, 1995. Charles French. 1994. pap. 6.99 (*0-671-78125-1*, Fireside) S&S Trade.

***American Guide to U. S. Coins 1996.** Charles F. French. 1995. pap. 6.99 (*0-684-80333-X*, Fireside) S&S Trade.

American Guitars: An Illustrated History. Tom Wheeler. LC 91-58288. (Illus.). 384p. 1992. pap. 27.50 (*0-06-273154-8*, Harper Ref) HarpC.

American Gunboat Diplomacy & the Old Navy. Kenneth J. Hagan. LC 75-176288. (Contributions in Military History Ser.: No. 4). 262p. 1973. text ed. 59.95 (*0-8371-6274-2*, HCN/, Greenwood Pr) Greenwood.

American Gunsmiths: A Source Book. Frank M. Sellers. 1983. 39.95 (*0-88227-018-4*) Gun Room.

American Half-Century: Postwar Culture & Politics in the U. S. A. Ed. by Michael Klein. (C). 1994. text ed. 59.95 (*0-7453-0500-8*, Pub. by Pluto Pr UK); pap. text ed. 19.95 (*0-7453-0501-6*, Pub. by Pluto Pr UK) Westview.

American Handbook of the Daguerreotype. 5th ed. S. D. Humphrey. LC 72-9211. (Literature of Photography Ser.). 1978. reprint ed. 16.95 (*0-405-04919-6*) Ayer.

American Harvest: Readings in American History, 2 vols., Vol. 1. Joseph R. Conlin & C. H. Peterson. 208p. (C). 1986. pap. text ed. 16.00 (*0-15-502304-7*) HB Coll Pubs.

American Harvest: Readings in American History, 2 vols., Vol. 2. Joseph R. Conlin & C. H. Peterson. 254p. (C). 1986. pap. text ed. 16.00 (*0-15-502305-5*) HB Coll Pubs.

American Harvest: Regional Recipes for the Vegetarian Kitchen. 2nd ed. Nava Atlas. (Illus.). 191p. 1991. reprint ed. pap. 11.95 (*0-9630243-0-2*) Amberwood Pr.

American Harvest: The Story of Weil Brothers-Cotton. George S. Bush. LC 82-9797. 495p. 25.00 (*0-13-027458-5*, Busn) P-H.

American Health Care: Realities, Rights, & Reforms. Charles J. Dougherty. 288p. 1988. 35.00 (*0-19-505271-4*); pap. 19.95 (*0-19-505272-2*) OUP.

American Health Care: Rebirth or Suicide? Benjamin F. Fuller. LC 94-9868. 112p. (C). 1994. text ed. 31.95 (*0-398-05914-4*) C C Thomas.

***American Health Care: Rebirth or Suicide.** Benjamin F. Fuller. LC 94-9868. 112p. (C). 1994. pap. text ed. 16.95 (*0-398-06465-2*) C C Thomas.

American Health Care System: Its Genesis & Trajectory. John G. Freymann. LC 77-11759. (Medcom Medical Update Ser.). 431p. reprint ed. pap. 122.90 (*0-7837-3746-7*, AU00434) Bks Demand.

American Health Care System - Betrayed by Greed. Esmond H. Coleman. 1993. 17.95 (*0-533-10494-7*) Vantage.

American Health Empire. 279p. 2.45 (*0-394-41484-5*) Health PAC.

American Health Food Book: Nutrition News for the 90s - Plus More Than 250 Fabulous Recipes. Ed. by American Health Staff & Robert A. Barnett. (Illus.). 416p. 1991. 29.95 (*0-525-24908-7*, Dutton) NAL-Dutton.

American Health Law. Law & Business Inc. Staff & Annas. 1990. 51.00 (*0-316-04309-5*) Little.

American Health Policy: Critical Issues for Reform. Intro. by Robert Helms. LC 92-22281. 433p. 1993. 39.75 (*0-8447-3818-2*) Am Enterprise.

American Health Quackery: Collected Essays of James Harvey Young. James H. Young. (Illus.). 288p. 1992. text ed. 29.95 (*0-691-04782-0*) Princeton U Pr.

American Heart Association Brand Name Fat & Cholesterol Counter. American Heart Association Staff. LC 94-14293. 1994. pap. 4.99 (*0-8129-2366-9*, Times Bks) Random.

***American Heart Association Cookbook.** American Heart Association Staff. 1994. pap. 6.99 (*0-345-80165-2*) Ballantine.

American Heart Association Cookbook. 5th ed. American Heart Association Staff. 1991. 25.00 (*0-8129-1895-9*) Random.

American Heart Association Cookbook. 5th ed. American Heart Association Staff. (Illus.). 1993. pap. 14.00 (*0-8129-2282-4*, Times Bks) Random.

American Heart Association Cookbook. 5th large type ed. American Heart Association Staff. 1993. pap. 29.95 (*0-679-42920-4*) Random.

American Heart Association Cookbook. 5th rev. ed. American Heart Association Staff. (Illus.). 1994. mass mkt. 6.99 (*0-345-38889-5*) Ballantine.

***American Heart Association Cookbook No. 5.** American Heart Association Staff. (Heart Care Titles Ser.). 1994. mass mkt. 6.99 (*0-345-39488-7*) Ballantine.

American Heart Association Family Guide to Stroke: Treatment, Recovery, & Prevention. Louis R. Caplan. 1994. 23.00 (*0-8129-2011-2*, Times Bks) Random.

American Heart Association Fat & Cholesterol Counter. American Heart Association Staff. 1991. pap. 3.99 (*0-8129-1885-1*) Random.

American Heart Association Kids' Cookbook. American Heart Association Staff. LC 92-56800. 128p. (J). (gr. 4 up). 1993. pap. 15.00 (*0-8129-1930-0*, Times Bks) Random.

American Heart Association Low-Fat, Low-Cholesterol Cookbook. Ed. by Scott Grundy & Mary Winston. 1989. 23.00 (*0-8129-1783-9*, Times Bks) Random.

American Heart Association Low-Fat, Low-Cholesterol Cookbook. Ed. by Scott Grundy & Mary Winston. 1991. pap. 13.00 (*0-8129-1982-3*, Times Bks) Random.

***American Heart Association Low-Fat, Low-Cholesterol Cookbook: More Than 200 Delicious.** Scott Grundy. 1994. pap. 5.99 (*0-8129-2475-4*, Times Bks) Random.

***American Heart Association Low-Salt Cookbook: A Complete Guide to Reducing Sodium & Fat.** Rodman D. Starke. 1994. pap. 5.99 (*0-8129-2476-2*, Times Bks) Random.

American Heart Association Low Salt Cookbook: A Complete Guide to Reducing Sodium & Fat in the Diet. Rodman D. Starke. Ed. by Mary Winston. (Illus.). 368p. 1990. 20.00 (*0-8129-1852-5*, Times Bks) Random.

American Heart Association Quick & Easy Cookbook. American Heart Association Staff. LC 94-19973. (Illus.). 1995. 25.00 (*0-8129-2251-4*) Random.

***American Heart Association's Your Heart: An Owner's Manual.** American Heart Association Staff. LC 94-45518. 1995. text ed. 27.95 (*0-13-359324-X*) P-H.

***American Heart Association's Your Heart! An Owner's manual.** American Heart Association Staff. 1995. mass mkt. 5.99 (*0-671-53081-X*) PB.

American-Hebrew Baby Name Book. Smadar S. Sidi. LC 88-45679. 192p. 1989. pap. 11.00 (*0-06-254850-6*) Harper SF.

American Hegemony: Political Morality in a One-Superpower World. Lea Brilmayer. LC 94-11807. 1994. 30.00 (*0-300-06033-5*) Yale U Pr.

American Hegemony & the Trilateral Commission. Stephen Gill. (Cambridge Studies in International Relations: No. 5). (Illus.). 317p. (C). 1992. pap. 19.95 (*0-521-42433-X*) Cambridge U Pr.

American Hegemony & World Oil: The Industry, the State System & the World Economy. Simon Bromley. 300p. 1991. 45.00 (*0-271-00746-X*) Pa St U Pr.

American Heliocentric Ephemeris for 1901-2000. Neil F. Michelsen. (American Ephemeris Ser.). 608p. (Orig.). 1982. pap. 24.95 (*0-917086-36-8*) ACS Pubns.

***American Hellenic Who's Who 1994-1995.** Date not set. write for info. (*0-941882-02-0*) Amer Hellenic Inst.

American Heralds of the Spirit: Emerson, Whitman, Melville. John F. Gardner. 320p. (Orig.). 1991. pap. 16.95 (*0-940262-44-4*) Lindisfarne Pr.

American Herbalism: Essays on Herbs & Herbalism by Members of the American Herbalist Guild. Ed. by Michael Tierra. 270p. (Orig.). 1992. pap. 15.95 (*0-89594-540-1*) Crossing Pr.

American Heritage. (Illus.). 48p. (gr. 6-12). 1976. pap. 1.85 (*0-8395-3398-5*, 33398) BSA.

American Heritage. Ed. by P. J. Larkin. 64p. (C). 1988. 30.00 (*0-685-33812-6*, Pub. by S Thornes Pubs UK) St Mut.

American Heritage: Selected Readings. Ralph Hancock. 144p. (C). 1989. pap. text ed. 9.75 (*0-8403-5640-4*) Kendall-Hunt.

American Heritage Battlemaps Civil War. Richard O'Shea. 176p. 1994. 19.98 (*0-8317-1372-0*) Smithmark.

American Heritage Book of Indians. William Brandon. 1988. 24.99 (*0-517-39180-5*) Random Hse Value.

American Heritage Children's Dictionary. (Illus.). 864p. (J). (gr. 3-5). 1994. 14.95 (*0-395-69191-5*) HM.

American Heritage College Dictionary. 3rd deluxe ed. LC 92-42124. 1664p. 1993. 24.95 (*0-395-66918-9*) HM.

American Heritage College Dictionary. 3rd ed. LC 92-42124. 1664p. 1993. 21.95 (*0-395-44638-4*) HM.

American Heritage College Dictionary. 3rd ed. Heritage Staff American. 1993. 21.95 (*0-395-67161-2*) HM.

American Heritage College Dictionary: Print & Floppy Disk Edition. 3rd ed. 1664p. 1994. 35.00 (*0-395-70682-3*) HM.

American Heritage Concise Dictionary. 3rd rev. ed. LC 93-34989. 1994. 10.95 (*0-395-69187-7*, AHD & Ref) HM.

American Heritage Desk Dictionary. 1981. 14.95 (*0-395-31256-6*) HM.

American Heritage Dictionary. Incl. Roget's II the New Thesaurus. (*0-318-57744-5*); 1984. 29.95 (*0-685-08361-6*); Incl. (*0-318-57744-5*); Set pap. 4.95 (*0-395-35605-9*) HM.

American Heritage Dictionary. 3rd ed. Heritage Staff American. 1994. pap. 12.95 (*0-385-31254-7*, Delta) Dell.

American Heritage Dictionary. 3rd ed. Dell Publishing Staff. 1994. mass mkt. 4.99 (*0-440-21861-6*) Dell.

***American Heritage Dictionary: College Edition.** 3rd ed. Heritage Staff American. (C). 1994. pap. 4.95 (*0-395-69956-8*) HM.

American Heritage Dictionary of the English Language. 3rd ed. (Illus.). 2184p. 1992. 45.00 (*0-395-44895-6*) HM.

American Heritage Dictionary of the English Language: New College Edition. LC 76-86995. (gr. 9 up). 1982. Thumb-indexed. 7.00 (*0-395-32944-2*) HM.

American Heritage Dictionary of the English Language: Print & CD-Rom Edition. 3rd ed. 2184p. 1994. 75.00 (*0-395-71146-0*) HM.

American Heritage Electronic Dictionary(Mac) Ed. by American Heritage Staff. 1991. pap. 12.95 (*0-395-57707-1*, AHD & Ref) HM.

***American Heritage Essential Reference Set, 3 Vols.** 1994. pap. 13.95 (*0-395-71811-2*) HM.

American Heritage First Dictionary. (Illus.). 368p. (J). (gr. 1-2). 1994. 13.95 (*0-395-67289-9*) HM.

American Heritage Haggadah. deluxe ed. Ed. by David Geffen. Tr. by Moshe Kohn. (Illus.). 120p. (ENG & HEB.). 1992. 35.00 (*965-229-083-1*, Pub. by Gefen Pub Hse IS) Gefen Bks.

American Heritage High School Dictionary. LC 93-20479. 1993. 21.95 (*0-395-67148-5*) HM.

American Heritage History of Railroads in America. Oliver Jensen. 1993. reprint ed. 19.99 (*0-517-36236-8*) Random Hse Value.

American Heritage History of the American Revolution: The History of America's Struggle for Independence. Lancaster. 384p. 1984. 17.95 (*0-517-44736-3*) Random Hse Value.

American Heritage History of the Bill of Rights, 10 vols. Joan C. Hawxhurst et al. (Illus.). (YA). (gr. 7 up). 1991. Set, 128-184p. ea. lib. bdg. 199.00 (*0-382-24190-8*) Silver Burdett Pr.

American Heritage History of World War I. S. L. Marshall. 1988. 19.99 (*0-517-38555-4*) Random Hse Value.

American Heritage Junior Library, 20 vols. American Heritage Magazine Editorial Staff. (J). (gr. 5-12). 1989. 14.95 (*0-8167-1536-X*) Troll Assocs.

American Heritage Larousse Spanish Dictionary. Ed. by Houghton Mifflin Company Staff & Librairie Larousse Staff. LC 86-7207. 1152p. 1986. 22.95 (*0-395-32429-7*); pap. text ed. 3.95 (*0-317-65694-5*) HM.

American Heritage Larousse Spanish Dictionary. abr. ed. Ed. by Houghton Mifflin Company Staff. 640p. 1989. 15.95 (*0-395-43412-2*) HM.

American Heritage Leverguns. Paco Kelly. (Illus.). 230p. (Orig.). 1985. 17.95 (*0-935737-57-X*); lib. bdg. 9.95 (*0-935737-58-8*); pap. 12.95 (*0-685-13543-8*) Tarantula Pr.

American Heritage of James Norman Hall: The Woodshed Poet of Iowa & Co-Author of Mutiny on the Bounty. Robert L. Johnson. LC 70-83702. 175p. reprint ed. pap. 49.90 (*0-8357-6290-4*, AU00389) Bks Demand.

American Heritage Picture Dictionary. (Illus.). 144p. (J). (gr. k-1). 1994. 10.95 (*0-395-69585-6*) HM.

American Heritage Picture History of the Civil War. Bruce Catton. 630p. 1988. 19.99 (*0-517-38556-2*) Random Hse Value.

American Heritage Picture History of World War II. C. L. Sulzberger. Ed. by David G. McCullough. LC 66-24214. (Illus.). 610p. 1987. 19.99 (*0-517-10523-3*); Vol. 1, 303 Pgs., Vol 2, 345 Pgs. 15.00 (*0-8281-0332-1*) Random Hse Value.

American Heritage Picture History of World War Two see World War Two

American Heritage Spanish Dictionary: Spanish - English, English - Spanish. (ENG & SPA.). 1992. write for info. (*0-318-69293-7*) HM.

***American Heritage Stedman's Medical Dictionary.** LC 95-10806. 1995. 24.95 (*0-395-69955-X*) HM.

American Heritage Student Dictionary. LC 93-32433. (Illus.). (J). 1994. 16.95 (*0-395-55857-3*, AHD & Ref) HM.

American Heritage Student Thesaurus. LC 93-33755. (J). 1994. pap. 6.95 (*0-395-68177-4*) HM.

American Heritage View of Washington, DC. Nita Scoggan. LC 86-60219. 32p. 1989. pap. 2.50 (*0-910487-07-3*) Royalty Pub.

American Hero. Larry Beinhart. 1994. reprint ed. mass mkt. 5.99 (*0-345-36663-8*) Ballantine.

American Hero: A Novel. Larry Beinhart. 1993. 23.00 (*0-679-47276-2*) Pantheon.

American Hero: A Sapphick Ode. Nathaniel Niles. 1975. 3.00 (*0-89073-039-3*) Boston Public Lib.

American Hero: The Red Adair Story. large type ed. Philip Singerman. LC 90-23165. 554p. 1991. reprint ed. lib. bdg. 19.95 (*1-56054-083-4*) Thorndike Pr.

American Hero Myths. D. G. Brinton. 1971. 59.95 (*0-87968-602-2*) Gordon Pr.

American Heroes: Their Lives, Their Values, Their Beliefs. Robert B. Pamplin, Jr. & Gary K. Eisler. LC 95-76884. 256p. 1995. 18.95 (*1-57101-010-6*) MasterMedia Ltd. WHAT DOES IT TAKE TO BE AN AMERICAN HERO? "It can be done! Check small things. Share credit. Have a vision. Be demanding. Perpetual optimism is a force multiplier."--General Colin Powell. "My faith means a lot to me. I can face challenging situations & feel that it's not all just on my shoulders."--Elizabeth Dole. In a world of turmoil, what qualities do our inspirational leaders & heroes of the twentieth century possess? Author & businessman Dr. Robert B. Pamplin, Jr., profiles American men & women of outstanding achievement. They share their stories of courage, integrity & compassion. Billy Graham, Colin Powell, Elie Wiesel, Oprah Winfrey, Johnny Cash, Jackie Joyner-Kersee, Chris Burke, Elizabeth Dole, Bill Cosby & others discuss the inner values that guide their lives & make possible their incredible achievements. ABOUT THE AUTHORS: Dr. Robert B. Pamplin, Jr, has experienced incredible financial success. As an undergraduate in the 1960s, he caught the rise of the stock market, making his first million. He later invested those profits in timber & farmlands just before they shot up in value. And his $30,000 investment in an unproven "cutting" horse led to $2million in stud fees, & the horse's eventual sale for $850,000. Dr. Pamplin & his father R.B. Pamplin, run a corporation that owns 19 textile facilities & a concrete & asphalt company, with annual revenues of approximately $800 million. He has written 12 books & been awarded many honorary degrees. Gary K. Eisler is a writer, published in The Wall Street Journal & Forbes.** ***Publisher Provided Annotation.

American Heroes in a Media Age. Susan J. Drucker & Robert S. Cathcart. Ed. by Lee Becker. (Communication Series: Mass Communications & Journalism). 368p. (C). 1994. text ed. 68.50 (*1-881303-19-5*); pap. text ed. 26.50 (*1-881303-20-9*) Hampton Pr NJ.

American Heroes, Myth & Reality. Marshall W. Fishwick. LC 72-10695. 242p. 1975. reprint ed. text ed. 35.00 (*0-8371-6610-1*, FIAH, Greenwood Pr) Greenwood.

***American Heroes of Exploration & Flight.** Anne Schraff. LC 95-13466. (Collective Bibliographies Ser.). (J). 1995. write for info. (*0-89490-619-4*) Enslow Pubs.

American Heroine: The Life & Legend of Jane Addams. Allen F. Davis. LC 73-82664. (Illus.). (C). 1975. pap. 10.95 (*0-19-501897-4*) OUP.

American Hieroglyphics: The Symbol of the Egyptian Hieroglyphics in the American Renaissance. John T. Irwin. LC 83-6153. 384p. 1983. pap. 15.95x (*0-8018-2908-9*) Johns Hopkins.

American Hieroglyphics: The Symbol of the Egyptian Hieroglyphics in the American Renaissance. John T. Irwin. LC 80-130. (Illus.). 384p. 1980. 45.00x (*0-300-02471-1*) Yale U Pr.

American High: The Years of Confidence, 1945-1960. William L. O'Neil. 1987. 27.95 (*0-02-923680-0*) Free Pr.

American High: The Years of Confidence, 1945-1960. William L. O'Neill. 336p. 1989. pap. 12.95 (*0-02-923679-7*) Free Pr.

American High School: Time for Reform. Bruce O. Boston. 33p. (C). 1982. pap. 3.00 (*0-317-20289-8*) Coun Basic Educ.

American High School Adolescent Life & Ethos: An Ethnography. Heewon Chang. 170p. 1992. 80.00 (*1-85000-865-5*, Falmer Pr); pap. 27.00 (*1-85000-866-3*, Falmer Pr) Taylor & Francis.

American Higher Education: A Guide to Reference Sources. Peter P. Olevnik. LC 93-25015. (Bibliographies & Indexes in Education Ser.: No. 12). 232p. 1993. text ed. 55.00 (*0-313-27749-4*, OHU/, Greenwood Pr) Greenwood.

An Asterisk (*) at the beginning of an entry indicates that the title is appearing in BIP for the first time.

An Asterisk (*) at the beginning of an entry indicates that the title is appearing in BIP for the first time.

American Humorists, 1800-1950, 2 vols., Set. Stanley Truchtenberg. (Dictionary of Literary Biography Ser.: Vol. 11). 736p. 1982. 238.00 (*0-8103-1147-X*) Gale.

American Humourists. H. R. Hawaeis. 1972. 59.95 (*0-87968-603-0*) Gordon Pr.

American-Hungarian Relations, Nineteen Eighteen-Nineteen Forty-Four. Mark Major. LC 74-80001. 288p. 1974. 10.00 (*0-87934-036-3*) Danubian.

American Hunger. Richard Wright. LC 76-47248. 160p. 1983. pap. 11.00 (*0-06-090991-9*, CN 991, PL) HarpC.

American Hunger. Richard Wright. 147p. 1991. reprint ed. lib. bdg. 27.00x (*0-8095-9067-0*) Borgo Pr.

American Hunting & Fishing Guide. Timothy E. Manion. 292p. (Orig.). pap. 9.95 (*0-9612936-1-6*) Manion Outdoors Co.

American Hunting Myth. Ron Baker. LC 84-90300. 287p. 1989. 15.95 (*0-533-06344-2*) Vantage.

***American Hunting Rifles: Their Application in the Field for Practical Shooting.** C. Boddington. (Illus.). 300p. 1995. 35.00 (*1-57157-016-0*) Safari Pr.

***American Hunting Rifles: Their Application in the Field for Practical Shooting.** C. Boddington. (Illus.). 1995. boxed 85.00 (*1-57157-030-6*) Safari Pr.

American Hurrah: Three Views of the U. S. A. Jean-Claude Van Itallie. 1968. pap. 4.75 (*0-8222-0024-4*) Dramatists Play.

American Husbands & Other Alternatives. Alexander Black. LC 68-57305. (Essay Index Reprint Ser.). 1977. 18.95 (*0-8369-1021-4*) Ayer.

American Hymns Old & New. Christ-Janer. 1980. text ed. 65.00 (*0-231-03458-X*) Col U Pr.

American Hymns Old & New: Notes on the Hymns & Biographies of the Authors & Composers. Charles W. Hughes. LC 79-4630. 633p. reprint ed. pap. 180.00 (*0-8357-6867-8*, 2035565) Bks Demand.

American Ice Boxes. Joseph C. Jones, Jr. LC 81-85407. (Illus.). 106p. (Orig.). 1981. pap. 7.95 (*0-9607572-0-1*) Jobeco Bks.

American Icon: Brother Jonathan & American Identity. Winifred Morgan. LC 86-40597. (Illus.). 224p. 1988. 32.50 (*0-87413-307-6*) U Delaware Pr.

American Iconology: New Approaches to Nineteenth-Century Art & Literature. Ed. by David C. Miller. LC 92-46082. (Illus.). 360p. 1993. 40.00 (*0-300-05478-5*) Yale U Pr.

American Icons: Transatlantic Perspectives on Eighteenth- & Nineteenth-Century American Art. Ed. by Thomas W. Gaehtgens & Heinz Ickstadt. LC 92-22423. (Issues & Debates Ser.). (Illus.). 372p. (C). 1993. 55.00 (*0-89236-246-4*); pap. 29.95 (*0-89236-247-2*) J P Getty Trust.

American Idea. Eugene T. Adams et al. LC 73-117747. (Essay Index Reprint Ser.). 1977. 21.95 (*0-8369-1820-7*) Ayer.

American Idea. Ed. by Joseph B. Gilder. LC 74-109139. (Granger Index Reprint Ser.). 1977. 20.95 (*0-8369-6123-4*) Ayer.

American Idea. Lydia K. Commander. LC 77-169378. (Family in America Ser.). 352p. 1972. reprint ed. 20.95 (*0-405-03855-0*) Ayer.

American Idea: The Literary Response to American Optimism. Everett Carter. LC 76-13867. 286p. reprint ed. pap. 81.60 (*0-8357-4409-4*, 2037229) Bks Demand.

American Idea of Industrial Democracy, 1865-1965. Milton Derber. LC 70-100376. 569p. reprint ed. pap. 162.20 (*0-8357-5371-9*, 2020216) Bks Demand.

American Idea of Success. Richard Huber. 475p. 1987. pap. 19.95 (*0-916366-43-X*) Pushcart Pr.

American Ideal. Arthur Bryant. LC 77-90617. (Essay Index Reprint Ser.). 1977. 21.95 (*0-8369-1251-9*) Ayer.

American Ideal: Literary History as a Worldly Activity. Peter Carafiol. 224p. 1991. 45.00 (*0-19-506765-7*) OUP.

American Ideals. Ed. by Norman Foerster & William W. Pierson. LC 70-128243. (Essay Index Reprint Ser.). 1977. 23.95 (*0-8369-1925-4*) Ayer.

American Ideals & Other Essays, Social & Political. Theodore Roosevelt. LC 70-106519. reprint ed. 34.50 (*0-404-05398-X*) AMS Pr.

American Ideals & Other Essays, Social & Political. Theodore Roosevelt. 1971. reprint ed. 15.00 (*0-403-00195-1*) Scholarly.

American Ideals, Character & Life. Hamilton W. Mabie. LC 74-157965. (Essay Index Reprint Ser.). 1977. reprint ed. 23.95 (*0-8369-2240-9*) Ayer.

American Ideals Versus the New Deal. Herbert Hoover. 1988. reprint ed. lib. bdg. 59.00 (*0-7812-0550-6*) Rprt Serv.

American Ideals Vs. the New Deal. Herbert Hoover. LC 78-131746. 1971. reprint ed. 29.00 (*0-403-00633-3*) Scholarly.

American Ideals vs the New Deal. Herbert C. Hoover. (History - United States Ser.). 96p. 1993. reprint ed. lib. bdg. 59.00 (*0-7812-4918-X*) Rprt Serv.

American Identities: Contemporary Multicultural Voices. Ed. by Robert Pack & Jay Parini. LC 94-8809. (Bread Loaf Anthology Ser.). 1994. 29.95 (*0-87451-641-2*) U Pr of New Eng.

American Ideologies: The Competing Political Beliefs of the 1970s. 3rd ed. Kenneth M. Dolbeare & Patricia Dolbeare. 232p. (C). 1988. reprint ed. pap. text ed. 14.95 (*0-88133-339-5*) Waveland Pr.

American Ideologies Today: From Neopolitics to New Ideas. Kenneth M. Dolbeare & Linda J. Medcalf. 1988. pap. text ed. write for info. (*0-07-553540-8*) McGraw.

American Ideologies Today: Shaping the New Politics of the 1990s. 2nd ed. Kenneth M. Dolbeare & Linda J. Medcalf. LC 92-16441. 1992. pap. text ed. write for info. (*0-07-017411-3*) McGraw.

***American Ideology: An Exploration of the Origins, Meaning, & Role of American Political Ideas.** 80p. 1994. pap. 9.95 (*0-614-04959-8*) Roper Ctr User.

***American Ideology: An Exploration of the Origins, Meaning, & Role of American Political Ideas.** Everett C. Ladd. (Occasional Papers & Monographs Ser.: No. 1). (Illus.). 90p. (Orig.). (C). 1994. pap. text ed. 9.95 (*1-887415-00-9*) RCPOR.

American Ideology of National Science, 1919-1930. Ronald C. Tobey. LC 70-151507. 277p. reprint ed. pap. 79.00 (*0-8357-5372-7*, 2020621) Bks Demand.

American Idiom: A Correspondence. William Carlos Williams & Harold Norse. (Illus.). 176p. (Orig.). (C). 1991. 21.95 (*0-944378-80-3*); pap. 10.95 (*0-944378-79-X*) Bright Tyger Pr.

***American Idioms: Idiomy Amerykanskie.** Jan Kaluza. Ed. by Polish Book Fair Staff. (Illus.). 220p. 1995. pap. 12.00 (*1-885889-56-9*) Home Tutor.

American Idioms Dictionary & American Slang & Colloquial Expressions Dictionary. Richard A. Spears. 1990. 33.95 (*0-8442-5441-X*, Natl Textbk) NTC Pub Grp.

American Idol: Emerson & the "Jewish Idea" Robert J. Loewenberg. LC 84-7206. 148p. (Orig.). (C). 1984. lib. bdg. 40.00 (*0-8191-3955-6*); pap. text ed. 19.50 (*0-8191-3956-4*) U Pr of Amer.

American Iliad: The Story of the Civil War. Charles P. Roland. 1991. pap. text ed. write for info. (*0-07-053594-9*) McGraw.

American Iliad: The Story of the Civil War. Charles P. Roland. LC 90-38392. (Illus.). 304p. 1991. text ed. 32.00 (*0-8131-1737-2*) U Pr of Ky.

American Illustrated Book in the Nineteenth Century. Gerald W. Ward. LC 87-26255. (Illus.). 270p. 1988. lib. bdg. 35.00 (*0-912724-17-X*, Winterthur Museum) U Pr of Va.

American Illustration, No. 12. Clibborn E. Booth. (Illus.). 1994. 65.00 (*0-8478-5752-2*) Rizzoli Intl.

American Illustration Eleven. 11th ed. Ed. by Edward Booth-Clibborn. (Illus.). 200p. 1992. 60.00 (*0-8478-5640-2*) Rizzoli Intl.

American Illustration Showcase, 2 vols., No. 15. Ed. by American Showcase Staff. (Illus.). 1264p. Set. pap. 75.00 (*0-931144-71-X*) Am Showcase.

American Illustration Showcase, No. 16. 392p. 1993. pap. 45.00 (*0-931144-77-9*); pap. 75.00 (*0-931144-78-7*) Am Showcase.

***American Illustration Thirteen: AI13.** 368p. 1994. 65.00 (*1-886212-01-5*) Amilus.

***American Illustration 14.** (Illus.). 332p. Date not set. 60.00 (*1-886212-03-1*) Amilus.

American Images: Selections from the James & Mari Michener Collection of 20th Century American Art. 2nd ed. Susan M. Mayer & Becky D. Reese. (Illus.). 28p. 1981. pap. 12.95 (*0-935213-06-6*) A M Huntington Art.

American Imaginations. Richard Kostelanetz. (GER.). 1983. 5.00 (*0-932360-56-4*) Archae Edns.

American Immigrant Leaders, Eighteen Hundred to Nineteen Ten: Marginality & Identity. Victor R. Greene. LC 86-20942. 208p. 1987. text ed. 30.00x (*0-8018-3355-8*) Johns Hopkins.

American Immigrants & Their Generations: Studies & Commentaries on the Hansen Thesis after Fifty Years. Ed. by Peter Kivisto & Dag Blanck. 232p. 1990. 21.95 (*0-252-01689-0*) U of Ill Pr.

American Immigrants in Israel: A Select Annotated Bibliography, 1948-85. Shoshana Kaufmann. LC 87-70997. 70p. 1987. pap. 7.50 (*0-87495-090-2*) Am Jewish Comm.

American Immigrants in Israel: Social Identities & Change. Kevin Avruch. LC 81-1291. (Illus.). (C). 1981. 25.00 (*0-226-03241-8*) U Ch Pr.

American Immigration. 2nd ed. Maldwyn A. Jones. (Chicago History of American Civilization Ser.). 392p. 1992. lib. bdg. 35.00 (*0-226-40634-2*); pap. text ed. 17.95 (*0-226-40633-4*) U Ch Pr.

***American Immigration: Should the Open Door Be Closed?** Gerald Leinwand. (Impact Bks.). (Illus.). 154p. (YA). (gr. 9-12). 1995. lib. bdg. 14.56 (*0-531-13038-X*) Watts.

American Immigration & Ethnicity, 20 vols. Ed. by George E. Pozzetta. Set. 1,365.00 (*0-8240-7400-9*) Garland.

American Immigration Collection: Series 1, 42 vols. Ed. by Oscar Handlin. 1969. reprint ed. 1,493.00 (*0-405-00500-8*) Ayer.

American Immigration Collection: Series 2, 33 Vols. Ed. by Victor Greene et al. 1970. reprint ed. 568.50 (*0-405-00543-1*) Ayer.

American Immigration Policy Nineteen Twenty-Four to Nineteen Fifty-Two. Robert A. Divine. LC 70-166323. (Civil Liberties in American History Ser.). 200p. 1972. reprint ed. lib. bdg. 27.50 (*0-306-70244-4*) Da Capo.

American Impact on Postwar Germany, 1945-1965. Reiner Pommerin. LC 94-27019. 208p. (C). 1995. text ed. 32.00 (*1-57181-004-8*) Berghahn Bks.

American Imperative: Higher Expectations for Higher Education. Wingspread Group on Higher Education Staff. 160p. 1993. pap. text ed. 14.95 (*0-9639160-0-9*) Johnson Fnd.

American Imperialism: A Speculative Essay. Ernest R. May. 1991. 14.95 (*1-879176-03-3*) Imprint Pubns.

American Imperialism: Viewpoints of United States Foreign Policy, 1898-1941, 53 Bks. 1970. reprint ed. 1,123.50 (*0-405-02000-7*) Ayer.

American Imperialism in the Image of Peer Gynt: Memoirs of a Professor-Bureaucrat. Edgar A. Johnson. LC 79-152300. 370p. reprint ed. pap. 105.50 (*0-8357-5373-5*, 2055884) Bks Demand.

American Impressionism. (Gallery of Art Ser.). 1990. 19.98 (*0-8317-0291-5*) Smithmark.

American Impressionism. William H. Gerdts. LC 84-6365. (Illus.). 336p. 1990. 39.98 (*0-89660-001-7*, Artabras) Abbeville Pr.

American Impressionism. William H. Gerdts. LC 93-46621. (Tiny Folios Ser.). (Illus.). 320p. 1994. pap. 10.95 (*1-55859-801-4*) Abbeville Pr.

American Impressionism. H. Barbara Weinberg. LC 93-43142. (Rizzoli Art Ser.). 24p. 1994. pap. 7.95 (*0-8478-1790-3*) Rizzoli Intl.

American Impressionism. limited ed. William H. Gerdts. LC 84-6365. (Illus.). 336p. 1990. Special Collector's Edition. ring bd. 70.00 (*0-89659-507-2*, Artabras) Abbeville Pr.

American Impressionism: A California Collage. Jean Stern. Ed. by Donna Fleischer & Kathy Verplank. (Illus.). 39p. (Orig.). 1991. pap. 10.00 (*0-685-75301-8*) FFCA Pub.

American Impressionism & Realism: The Painting of Modern Life, 1885-1915. H. Barbara Weinberg. (Illus.). 400p. 1994. 75.00 (*0-87099-700-9*, Abrams); pap. 45.00 (*0-87099-701-7*, Abrams) Metro Mus Art.

***American Impressionism & Realism: The Painting of Modern Life, 1885-1915.** H. Barbara Weinberg et al. LC 94-2762. 384p. 1994. 75.00 (*0-8109-6437-6*) Abrams.

American Impressionism in Georgia Collections. Donald D. Keyes. LC 93-34846. (Illus.). 129p. 1993. 30.00 (*0-915977-13-3*) Georgia Museum of Art.

***American Impressionist.** Dennis M. Bunker. Date not set. 45.00 (*0-87846-422-0*) Antique Collect.

American Impressionist & Realist Paintings & Drawings from the William Marshall Fuller Collection. Carol Clark. LC 78-54779. (Illus.). 56p. 1978. pap. 8.95 (*0-88360-029-3*) Amon Carter.

American Impressionists. (American Artists Ser.). (Illus.). 112p. 1991. 15.99 (*0-517-06514-2*, Crescent) Random Hse Value.

American Imprints Inventory No. Five: Check List of Kentucky Imprints, 1787-1810. D. C. McMurtrie & A. H. Allen. (Historical Records Survey Monographs). 1972. reprint ed. pap. 20.00 (*0-527-01902-X*) Periodicals Srv.

American Imprints on Art Through 1865: An Annotated Bibliography of Books & Pamphlets on Drawing, Painting, Sculpture, Aesthetics, Art Criticism & Instruction. Janice G. Schimmelman. (Monograph Ser.). 450p. (C). 1990. lib. bdg. 65.00 (*0-8161-7261-7*, Hall Reference) Macmillan.

American in California: The Biography of William Heath Davis 1822-1909. Andrew F. Rolle. LC 56-10064. (Illus.). 155p. 1981. reprint ed. pap. 9.95 (*0-87328-120-9*) Huntington Lib.

American in England During the First Half Century of Independence. Robert E. Spiller. LC 76-8454. (Perspectives in American History Ser.: No. 36). (Illus.). xiv, 416p. 1976. reprint ed. lib. bdg. 45.00 (*0-87991-360-6*) Porcupine Pr.

American in Exile: The Story of Arthur Rudolph. Thomas Franklin. Ed. by Michael R. Kaylor. LC 87-71503. 280p. 1987. 16.95 (*0-916039-04-8*) Kaylor Christ Co.

American in Japan, 1945-1948: A Civilian View of the Occupation. Staavern Jacob Van. LC 94-5717. 304p. 1994. text ed. 35.00x (*0-295-97363-3*) U of Wash Pr.

American in Jeopardy. Joseph G. Panozzo. LC 85-90478. 215p. (Orig.). 1986. text ed. 14.95 (*0-9615974-0-2*); pap. text ed. 9.95 (*0-9615974-1-0*) J G Panozzo.

American in Paris. LeRoy Neiman. LC 94-263. 1994. write for info. (*0-8109-1950-8*) Abrams.

American in Poland. Anne J. Pawelek. 1967. 3.75 (*0-685-09282-8*) Endurance.

American in Regency England: The Journal of a Tour in 1810-1811. Louis Simond. Ed. by Christopher Hibbert. reprint ed. 22.50 (*0-89979-001-1*) British Am Bks.

American in the Great War: The Rise of the War Welfare State. Ronald Schaffer. 256p. 1994. reprint ed. pap. 12.95 (*0-19-504904-7*) OUP.

American Incarnation. Myra Jehlen. 288p. 1986. 32.00 (*0-674-02426-5*) HUP.

American Incarnation: The Individual, the Nation, & the Continent. Myra Jehlen. 288p. 1989. pap. 15.95 (*0-674-02427-3*) HUP.

American Independent Business: Formation, Operations & Philosophy for the 1980's. Phillip B. Chute. (Illus.). (Orig.). 1985. pap. text ed. 19.95 (*0-930981-00-6*) Chute Corp.

American Independent Business Instructor Workbook. Phillip B. Chute. Ed. by Alice Wakefield. (American Independent Business Ser.). 225p. (C). 1986. teacher ed 19.95 (*0-930981-02-2*); student ed 19.95 (*0-930981-03-0*); student ed 9.95 (*0-930981-01-4*) Chute Corp.

American Independent Business Workbook for Entrepreneurs. Phillip B. Chute. Ed. by Alice Wakefield. (American Independent Business Ser.). (Illus.). 225p. (Orig.). 1986. pap. 19.95 (*0-930981-04-9*) Chute Corp.

American Independents: Eighteen Color Photographers. Sally Eauclaire. LC 86-28789. (Illus.). 248p. 1987. 29.98 (*0-89659-666-4*) Abbeville Pr.

American Indian. Ed. by Raymond F. Locke. (Great Adventures of History Ser.). 1976. 1.75 (*0-87687-003-5*, BM003) Mankind Pub.

American Indian. 3rd ed. Clark Wissler. 11.25 (*0-8446-1482-3*) Peter Smith.

American Indian, 2 vols. Ed. by Lee F. Harkins. LC 77-131270. 1970. reprint ed. 99.99 (*0-87140-523-7*) Liveright.

American Indian: A Dictionary. 1991. lib. bdg. 87.75 (*0-8490-4987-3*) Gordon Pr.

American Indian: Language & Literature. Jack W. Marken. LC 76-4624. (Goldentree Bibliographies Series in Language & Literature). (C). 1978. pap. text ed. write for info. (*0-88295-553-5*) Harlan Davidson.

American Indian: North, South & Central America. A. Hyatt Verrill. 1977. lib. bdg. 59.95 (*0-8490-1414-X*) Gordon Pr.

American Indian: Past & Present. 4th ed. Roger L. Nichols. 1992. pap. text ed. write for info. (*0-07-046499-5*) McGraw.

American Indian: Perspectives for the Study of Social Change. Fred Eggan. LC 80-67926. (Lewis Henry Morgan Lectures). 192p. 1981. 37.50 (*0-521-23752-1*) Cambridge U Pr.

American Indian: Prehistory to the Present. Arrell M. Gibson. 618p. (C). 1980. pap. text ed. 17.00 (*0-669-04493-8*) Heath.

American Indian Activity Book: Art, Crafts, Cooking. Linda Milliken. 40p. 1980. pap. text ed. 4.95 (*1-56472-000-4*) Edupress.

American Indian Alaska Native Resource Directory for the Puget Sound & Olympic Peninsula, 1994. Seattle Indian Services Commission Staff. Ed. by Jeannette Finley. 64p. Date not set. pap. text ed. write for info. (*0-9632138-1-4*) Seattle Indian.

American Indian & Alaska Native Higher Education Funding Guide. Gregory W. Frazier. 100p. 1991. 21.90 (*0-935151-24-9*) Arrowstar Pub.

American Indian & Alaska Native Newspapers & Periodicals, 1826-1924. Daniel F. Littlefield, Jr. & James W. Parins. LC 83-1483. (Historical Guides to the World's Periodicals & Newspapers Ser.). xxxv, 482p. 1984. text ed. 105.00 (*0-313-23426-4*, LNA/01) Greenwood.

American Indian & Alaska Native Newspapers & Periodicals, 1925-1970. Ed. by Daniel F. Littlefield, Jr. & James W. Parins. LC 83-1483. (Historical Guides to the World's Periodicals & Newspapers Ser.). 577p. 1986. text ed. 105.00 (*0-313-23427-2*, LNA/02) Greenwood.

American Indian & Alaska Native Newspapers & Periodicals, 1971-1985. Ed. by Daniel F. Littlefield, Jr. & James W. Parins. LC 83-1483. (Historical Guides to the World's Periodicals & Newspapers Ser.). 629p. 1986. text ed. 105.00 (*0-313-24834-6*, LNA/03/) Greenwood.

American Indian & Alaska Native Traders Directory. Gregory W. Frazier. 140p. 1990. lib. bdg. 21.45 (*0-935151-16-8*) Arrowstar Pub.

American Indian & Indoeuropean Studies: Papers in Honor of Madison S. Beeler. Margaret Langdon & Shirley Silver. Ed. by Kathryn Klar et al. (Trends in Linguistics, Studies & Monographs: No. 16). 495p. 1980. 103.85 (*90-279-7876-X*) Mouton.

American Indian & the End of the Confederacy, 1863-1866. Annie H. Abel. LC 93-17686. viii, 419p. 1993. pap. 12.95 (*0-8032-5921-2*, Bison Books) U of Nebr Pr.

American Indian & the Media. Ed. by Tim Giago et al. LC 91-67943. (Illus.). 84p. (Orig.). (C). 1991. pap. text ed. 17.50 (*0-9631926-0-4*) Natl Conf C&J.

American Indian & the Problem of History. Ed. by Calvin Martin. 320p. 1987. pap. 15.95 (*0-19-503856-8*) OUP.

American Indian Archery. Reginald Laubin & Gladys Laubin. LC 78-58108. (Civilization of the American Indian Ser.: Vol. 154). (Illus.). 192p. 1991. 27.95 (*0-8061-1467-3*); pap. 14.95 (*0-8061-2387-7*) U of Okla Pr.

American Indian Archival Material: A Guide to Holdings in the Southeast. Comp. by Ronald Chepesiuk & Arnold M. Shankman. LC 82-15447. xiii, 323p. 1982. text ed. 69.50 (*0-313-23731-X*, CAI/, Greenwood Pr) Greenwood.

***American Indian Art.** Norman Feder. LC 95-888. (Illus.). 1995. 29.98 (*0-8109-8132-7*) Abrams.

American Indian As Participant in the Civil War. Annie H. Abel. 1988. reprint ed. lib. bdg. 79.00 (*0-7812-0727-4*) Rprt Serv.

American Indian As Slaveholder & Secessionist. Annie H. Abel. 1988. reprint ed. lib. bdg. 79.00 (*0-7812-0728-2*) Rprt Serv.

American Indian as Slaveholder & Secessionist. Annie H. Abel. LC 92-13971. (Illus.). x, 394p. (C). 1992. reprint ed. pap. 12.95 (*0-8032-5920-4*, Bison Books) U of Nebr Pr.

American Indian Autobiography. H. David Brumble, III. (Illus.). 289p. 1988. pap. 13.00 (*0-520-07182-4*) U CA Pr.

American Indian Autobiography. H. David Brumble, III. 336p. (C). 1988. 45.00 (*0-520-06245-0*) U CA Pr.

American Indian Basketry. Tufton O. Mason. 800p. 1988. pap. 16.95 (*0-486-25777-0*) Dover.

American Indian Beadwork. B. Hunt. 64p. 1971. pap. 9.95 (*0-02-011700-0*, Collier S&S) S&S Trade.

American Indian Ceremonies: A Practical Workbook & Study Guide to the Medicine Path. Medicine Hawk & Grey Cat. (Illus.). 144p. 1992. reprint ed. 12.95 (*0-938294-72-5*) Glob Comm-Inner Lght.

American Indian Children at School, 1850-1930. Michael C. Coleman. LC 92-37760. 240p. 1993. 38.50 (*0-87805-616-5*) U Pr of Miss.

American Indian Coloring Book. Thomas B. Underwood. (Illus.). 20p. (J). (gr. k-2). 1969. 3.50 (*0-935741-02-X*) Cherokee Pubns.

American Indian Contributions to World Civilization: A Bibliogrpahy. 1993. lib. bdg. 250.95 (*0-8490-8936-0*) Gordon Pr.

American Indian Cooking & Herblore. Thomas B. Underwood & J. Edward Sharpe. (Illus.). 32p. 1973. 3.50 (*0-935741-05-4*) Cherokee Pubns.

American Indian Craft Book. Marz Minor & Nono Minor. LC 77-14075. (Illus.). 416p. 1978. pap. 10.95 (*0-8032-5891-7*) U of Nebr Pr.

American Indian Cut & Use Stencils. Ed Sibbett. (J). pap. 5.95 (*0-486-24183-1*) Dover.

American Indian Design & Decoration. Leroy H. Appleton. Orig. Title: Indian Art of the Americas. (Illus.). 21.50 (*0-8446-0007-5*) Peter Smith.

An Asterisk (*) at the beginning of an entry indicates that the title is appearing in BIP for the first time.

An Asterisk (*) at the beginning of an entry indicates that the title is appearing in BIP for the first time.

247

American Industry in International Competition: Government Policies & Corporate Strategies. Ed. by John Zysman & Laura Tyson. LC 82-22044. (Cornell Studies in Political Economy). 432p. 1983. pap. 21.00 (0-8014-9297-1) Cornell U Pr.

American Inequality: A Macroeconomic History. Jeffrey G. Williamson & Peter H. Lindert. (Institute for Research on Poverty Monograph). 1980. text ed. 44.00 (0-12-757160-4) Acad Pr.

American Influence in Canadian Mining. Elwood S. Moore. Ed. by Stuart Bruchey. LC 80-561. (Multinational Corporations Ser.). (Illus.). 1981. reprint ed. lib. bdg. 19.95 (0-405-13358-8) Ayer.

American Influence in Greece, 1917-1929. Louis P. Cassimatis. LC 88-3012. 320p. 1988. 25.00 (0-87338-357-5) Kent St U Pr.

American Influence on Higher Education in India. M. Shahnaz Suri. 88p. 1979. 8.95 (0-318-36819-6) Asia Bk Corp.

American Influence on Higher Education in India. M. Shahnaz Suri. 88p. 1979. 12.95 (0-86578-065-X) Ind-US Inc.

American Infrared Survey. Ed. by Stephen Paternite & David Paternite. LC 82-6160. (Illus.). 88p. (C). 1982. 21.95 (0-9609812-0-9) Photo Survey.

American Inquisition: Justice & Injustice in the Cold War. Stanley I. Kutler. (American Century Ser.). 285p. 1983. pap. 10.95 (0-8090-0157-8) Hill & Wang.

American Inquisitors. Walter Lippmann. LC 92-16068. 142p. (C). 1992. pap. 19.95 (1-56000-635-8) Transaction Pubs.

American Insects: A Handbook of the Insects of America North of Mexico. Ross H. Arnett. LC 92-41053. (Illus.). xiv, 850p. 1993. 79.95 (1-877743-19-4) Sandhill Crane.

American Institute of Biological Sciences: Membership Directory & Handbook, 1986-1987. American Institute of Biological Sciences. Ed. by Charles M. Chambers. 230p. (Orig.). 1986. pap. text ed. 5.00 (0-936829-00-1) Am Inst Bio Sci.

American Institute of Real Estate Appraisers Financial Tables, No. 373. Ed. by Financial Publishing Company Staff. 480p. 1981. 45.00 (0-87600-373-0) Finan Pub.

American Intellectual Histories & Historian. Robert A. Skotheim. LC 77-25991. 326p. 1978. reprint ed. text ed. 35.00 (0-313-20120-X, SKAI, Greenwood Pr) Greenwood.

American Intellectual Tradition: A Sourcebook, Vol. I: 1630-1865. Ed. by David A. Hollinger & Charles Capper. 488p. (C). 1993. pap. text ed. 19.95 (0-19-507779-2) OUP.

American Intellectual Tradition: A Sourcebook, Vol. I: 1630-1865. 2nd ed. Ed. by David A. Hollinger & Charles Capper. 488p. (C). 1993. text ed. 45.00 (0-19-507778-4) OUP.

American Intellectual Tradition: A Sourcebook, Vol. II: 1865 to the Present. Ed. by David A. Hollinger & Charles Capper. 448p. (C). 1993. pap. text ed. 19.95 (0-19-507781-4) OUP.

American Intellectual Tradition: A Sourcebook, Vol. II: 1865 to the Present. 2nd ed. Ed. by David A. Hollinger & Charles Capper. 448p. (C). 1993. text ed. 45.00 (0-19-507780-6) OUP.

American Intellectuals & African Nationalists, 1955-1970. Martin Staniland. 320p. (C). 1991. text ed. 35.00 (0-300-04838-6) Yale U Pr.

American Intelligence, 1775-1990: A Bibliographical Guide. Neal H. Petersen. LC 92-16324. (New War - Peace Bibliographical Ser.: Vol. 2). 1992. 49.95 (0-941690-45-8) Regina Bks.

American Inter-State Law. David Rorer. Ed. by Levy Mayer. lvii, 400p. 1983. reprint ed. lib. bdg. 35.00 (0-8377-1038-3) Rothman.

American Interests, American Purpose: Moral Reasoning & U. S. Foreign Policy. George Weigel. LC 89-3564. (Washington Papers: No. 139). 118p. 1989. text ed. 45.00 (0-275-93335-0, C3335, Praeger Pubs); pap. text ed. 11.95 (0-275-93336-9, B3336, Praeger Pubs) Greenwood.

American Interests & Policies in the Middle East, 1900-1939. John A. DeNovo. LC 63-21129. 459p. reprint ed. pap. 130.90 (0-8357-8795-8, 2033216) Bks Demand.

American Intergovernmental Relations: Foundations, Perspectives, & Issues. 2nd ed. Ed. by Laurence J. O'Toole, Jr. LC 92-30912. 311p. 1992. 25.95 (0-87187-718-X) Congr Quarterly.

American Interior Design: The Traditions & Development of Domestic Design from Colonial Times to the Present. Meyric R. Rogers. LC 75-22838. (America in Two Centuries Ser.). (Illus.). 1976. reprint ed. 34.95 (0-405-07709-2) Ayer.

American Interiors: New England & the South. Donald C. Peirce & Hope Alswang. (Illus.). 62p. pap. 4.87 (0-87273-095-6) Bklyn Mus.

American International Law Cases: Sources & Documents, 1979-1989, 7 vols. Ed. by Bernard D. Reams, Jr. LC 91-50825. (Second Series, 1979-1989). 1991. Set. lib. bdg. 420.00 (0-379-21059-2) Oceana.

American International Law Cases: 1783-1978, Set, incl. index & 2 binders (88 vols. to date) Incl. Vols. 21-31. F. Ruddy. LC 78-140621. 1980. (0-318-56894-2); Sources & Documents Section Bernard Reams. LC 78-140621. (0-318-56895-0); LC 78-140621. Set ring bd. 5,342.00 (0-379-20075-9) Oceana.

American International Law Cases, Second Series, 27 vols., Set. Bernard D. Reams. LC 86-33167. 1986. 1,540.00 (0-685-73851-5) Oceana.

American International Law Cases, 3rd Series, 24 vols. 3rd ed. Ed. by Bernard D. Reams, Jr. 1993. lib. bdg. 1,560.00 (0-379-21250-1) Oceana.

American Intervention in Greece: 1943-1949. Lawrence S. Wittner. LC 81-38521. (Contemporary American History Ser.). 432p. 1982. text ed. 39.50 (0-231-04196-9) Col U Pr.

American Invaders. Fred A. McKenzie. Ed. by Stuart Bruchey & Eleanor Bruchey. LC 76-5016. (American Business Abroad Ser.). 1976. reprint ed. 24.95 (0-405-09284-9) Ayer.

***American Inventors of the 20th Century.** Laura Jeffrey. LC 95-14628. (Collective Biographies Ser.). (Illus.). (J). 1995. write for info. (0-89490-632-1) Enslow Pubs.

American Investment in Australian Industry. Donald T. Brash. LC 66-31366. 381p. 1966. 37.00 (0-674-02500-8) HUP.

American Investment in British Manufacturing Industry. John H. Dunning. Ed. by Stuart Bruchey & Eleanor Bruchey. LC 76-5004. (American Business Abroad Ser.). (Illus.). 1976. 33.95 (0-405-09273-3) Ayer.

American Investment Trusts. John F. Fowler, Jr. LC 75-2633. (Wall Street & the Security Market Ser.). 1975. reprint ed. 39.95 (0-405-06958-8) Ayer.

American Irish: A Political & Social Portrait. 2nd ed. William V. Shannon. LC 89-33218. (Illus.). 504p. (Orig.). (C). 1989. reprint ed. pap. 19.95 (0-87023-689-X) U of Mass Pr.

American Iron Hand Presses. 2nd ed. Stephen O. Saxe. (Illus.). 128p. 1992. 35.00 (0-938768-35-2) Oak Knoll.

American Islam: Growing Up Muslim in America. Richard Wormser. LC 94-12335. 1994. 15.95 (0-8027-8343-0); 16.85 (0-8027-8344-9) Walker & Co.

American Island in Hitler's Reich: The Bad Nauheim Internment. Charles B. Burdick. (Illus.). 120p. (C). 1988. 32.95 (0-944109-01-2); pap. 18.95 (0-944109-00-4) Margraf Pubns Grp.

American Issue: The U. S. Postage Stamp, 1842-1869. Peter T. Rohrbach & Lowell S. Newman. LC 83-27146. (Illus.). 232p. 1984. text ed. 32.50 (0-87474-816-X, ROAI) Smithsonian.

American Issues: A Primary Source Reader in United States History, 2 vols., 1. Ed. by Irwin Unger. LC 93-10920. 1993. pap. text ed. 15.00 (0-13-031956-2) P-H Gen Ref & Trav.

American Issues: A Primary Source Reader in United States History, 2 vols., 2. Ed. by Irwin Unger. LC 93-10920. 1993. pap. text ed. write for info. (0-13-031964-3) P-H Gen Ref & Trav.

American, Italian, & Mexican Art 1979-1989: From the Collection of Francesco Pellizzi. Ed. by Gail Gelburd. (Illus.). 60p. 1990. pap. 17.95 (0-8122-1340-8, Hofstra U Hofstra Mus) U of Pa Pr.

American Jail: Its Development & Growth. J. M. Moynahan & Earle K. Stewart. LC 79-19372. (Illus.). 200p. 1980. text ed. 26.95 (0-88229-531-4) Nelson-Hall.

American Jails: Public Policy Issues. Ed. by Joel A. Thompson & G. Larry Mays. 288p. 1990. 31.95 (0-8304-1251-4); pap. text ed. 20.95 (0-8304-1262-X) Nelson-Hall.

American Jazz Mass: For Mixed Voices with Instrumental Ensemble (Trumpet, Saxophone, Baritone,Saxophone, String Bass, & Drums). Frank P. Tirro. 121p. reprint ed. pap. 34.50 (0-8357-5375-1, 2003559) Bks Demand.

American Jazz Music. Wilder Hobson. LC 76-22565. (Roots of Jazz Ser.). 1976. reprint ed. lib. bdg. 29.50 (0-306-70816-7) Da Capo.

American Jeremiad. Sacvan Bercovitch. LC 78-53283. 254p. 1978. 32.50 (0-299-07350-5) U of Wis Pr.

American Jeremiad. Sacvan Bercovitch. LC 78-53283. 254p. 1980. pap. 15.95 (0-299-07354-8) U of Wis Pr.

American Jesuit Spirituality: The Maryland Tradition, 1634-1900. Ed. by Robert E. Curan. (Sources of American Spirituality Ser.). 384p. 1988. 19.95 (0-8091-0381-8) Paulist Pr.

American Jesuits. James J. Walsh. LC 68-29251. (Essay Index Reprint Ser.). 1977. 20.95 (0-8369-0970-4) Ayer.

American Jesuits. James J. Walsh. 1976. 59.95 (0-87968-605-7) Gordon Pr.

American Jew. Michael Greenstein. 114p. 1992. pap. 9.95 (965-229-063-7, Pub. by Gefen Pub Hse IS) Gefen Bks.

American Jew. Ed. by Oscar I. Janowsky. LC 76-142647. (Essay Index Reprint Ser.). 1977. 20.95 (0-8369-2166-6) Ayer.

American Jew: A Zionistic Analysis. Ben Halpern. LC 82-16875. 196p. 1988. reprint ed. pap. 6.95 (0-8052-0742-2) Wiener Pubs Inc.

***American Jew: Voices from an American Jewish Community.** Dan Cohn-Sherbok & Lavinia Cohn-Sherbok. 357p. (Orig.). 1995. pap. 19.99 (0-8028-4138-4) Eerdmans.

American Jew As Patriot, Soldier, & Citizen. Simon Wolf. LC 72-8739. (American Revolutionary Ser.). 1979. reprint ed. lib. bdg. 47.00 (0-8398-2179-4) Irvington.

American Jewelry Manufacturers. Dorothy T. Rainwater. LC 87-63485. (Illus.). 280p. 1988. pap. 45.00 (0-88740-120-1) Schiffer.

American Jewish Archives, Cincinnati: The Papers of the World Jewish Congress, 1945-1950. Ed. by Abraham Peck. LC 89-16915. (Archives of the Holocaust Ser.: Vols. 8-9). 544p. 1991. Vol. 8, 544p. 135.00 (0-8240-5490-3); Vol. 9, 448p. 120.00 (0-8240-5491-1) Garland.

American Jewish Bibliography: Being a List of Books & Pamphlets by Jews, or Relating to Them, Printed in the United States from the Establishment of the Press in the Colonies until 1850. Abraham S. Rosenbach. (American Jewish Historical Society Publications: No. 30). (Illus.). 509p. reprint ed. pap. 145.10 (0-8357-5376-X, 2017816) Bks Demand.

American Jewish Business Enterprise. (American Jewish Historical Quarterly Ser.: Vol. 66, Pt.1). 1976. 8.00 (0-911934-03-0) Am Jewish Hist Soc.

American Jewish Committee, New York. Ed. by Frederick D. Bogin. LC 89-16915. (Archives of the Holocaust Ser.: Vol. 17). 464p. 1993. 113.00 (0-8240-5499-7) Garland.

American Jewish Community: Social Science Research & Policy Implications. Calvin Goldscheider. LC 86-26051. (Studies on Jews & Their Societies). 183p. 1986. 29.95 (1-55540-081-7, 14-50-03) Scholars Pr GA.

American Jewish Community: The Story of the Jews in Stamford, Connecticut (1889-1939) Samuel Koenig. LC 91-3998. 200p. 1991. pap. text ed. 18.00 (0-9629560-0-7) Stamford Jewish.

American Jewish Disunity. Intro. by David S. Wyman. (America & the Holocaust Ser.: Vol. 5). 384p. 1990. lib. bdg. 60.00 (0-8240-4537-8) Garland.

American Jewish Experience. Ed. by Jonathan D. Sarna. LC 86-7579. 336p. 1986. 37.95 (0-8419-0934-2); pap. 19.50 (0-8419-0935-0) Holmes & Meier.

American Jewish Fertility. Calvin Goldscheider. LC 85-18446. (Brown Studies on Jews & Their Societies). (C). 1986. text ed. 24.95 (0-89130-919-5, 14-50-01); pap. 19.95 (0-89130-920-9) Scholars Pr GA.

American-Jewish Filmmakers: Traditions & Trends. David Desser & Lester D. Friedman. LC 92-39669. 336p. (C). 1993. 44.95 (0-252-01564-9); pap. 19.95 (0-252-06301-5) U of Ill Pr.

American Jewish High School Students: A National Profile. James L. Peterson & Nicholas Zill. LC 84-72249. vi, 32p. (Orig.). 1984. pap. 2.50 (0-87495-065-1) Am Jewish Comm.

American Jewish History: A Bibligrahical Guide. Jeffrey S. Gurock. 1983. 6.95 (0-88464-037-X) ADL.

American Jewish Joint Distribution Committee, New York, 2 vols., Set. Ed. by Sybil Milton & Frederick D. Bogin. LC 94-40786. (Archives of the Holocaust Ser.: Vol. 10). 1200p. 1995. 250.00 (0-8240-5492-X) Garland.

American-Jewish Media Directory, 1989. Ray Kestenbaum. Ed. by Jeffrey A. Haveson. 212p. (Orig.). 1989. pap. text ed. 50.00 (0-9621905-0-0) RK Assocs.

American Jewish Organizations & Israel: Arabic Edition. Lee O'Brien. Tr. by Institute for Palestine Studies Staff. 393p. (Orig.). (C). 1987. pap. 10.00 (0-88728-198-2) Inst Palestine.

American Jewish Woman: A Documentary History. Jacob R. Marcus. 1981. 45.00 (0-87068-752-2) Ktav.

American Jewish Woman: 1654-1980. Ed. by Jacob R. Marcus. 1981. 19.95 (0-87068-751-4) Ktav.

American Jewish Year Book Index. Emily C. Cohen. 1968. 45.00 (0-87068-040-4) Ktav.

American Jewish Year Book 1986, Vol 86. Ed. by Milton Himmelfarb & David Singer. LC 99-4040. 516p. 1986. 25.95 (0-8276-0269-3) Am Jewish Comm.

American Jewry: The Formative Years. Bertram W. Korn. (Texts & Studies). (HEB.). 1971. 10.00 (0-911934-04-9) Am Jewish Hist Soc.

American Jewry & Conservative Politics: A New Direction. Alan J. Steinberg. LC 88-24027. (Illus.). 216p. 1989. 14.95 (0-933503-86-5) Sure Sellers.

American Jewry & the Holocaust: The American Jewish Joint Distribution Committee, 1939-1945. Yehuda Bauer. LC 80-26035. 522p. 1981. 40.00 (0-8143-1672-7) Wayne St U Pr.

American Jewry & United States Immigration Policy, 1881-1953. Sheldon M. Neuringer. Ed. by Francesco Cordasco. LC 80-883. (American Ethnic Groups Ser.). 1981. lib. bdg. 54.95 (0-405-13444-4) Ayer.

American Jewry During the Holocaust. Seymour M. Finger. 1984. pap. 35.00 (0-9613537-3-2) Am Jewish Holo.

American Jewry During the Holocaust. Seymour M. Finger. 412p. 1984. pap. text ed. 35.00 (0-8419-7506-X) Holmes & Meier.

American Jews. Arthur A. Goren. (Dimensions of Ethnicity Ser.). 128p. 1982. pap. 10.50 (0-674-02516-4) HUP.

American Jews. Ed. by Marshall Sklare. 352p. (C). 1983. pap. text ed. 14.95x (0-87441-348-6) Behrman.

American Jews: The Building of a Voluntary Community. Eli Ginzberg. (Texts & Studies). 1980. 15.00 (0-911934-06-5) Am Jewish Hist Soc.

American Jews: Their Story. Oscar Handlin. 48p. 2.50 (0-88464-011-6) ADL.

American Jews & the Labor Movement. (American Jewish Historical Quarterly Ser.: Vol. 65, Pt.3). 1976. 4.00 (0-911934-05-7) Am Jewish Hist Soc.

American Jews & the Separationist Faith: The New Debate on Religion in Public Life. David G. Dalin. 182p. 1992. 19.95 (0-89633-176-8) Ethics & Public Policy.

American Jews & the Zionist Idea. Naomi Cohen. pap. 9.95 (0-87068-272-5) Ktav.

American Jews into the 21st Century: A Leadership Challenge. Ed. by Earl Raab. 134p. 1991. 49.95 (1-55540-622-X, 14 50 88) Scholars Pr GA.

American Jihad. Steven Barboza. 1994. pap. 25.00 (0-385-47011-8) Doubleday.

American Jitters: A Year of the Slump. Edmund Wilson. LC 68-16989. (Essay Index Reprint Ser.). 1980. 18.95 (0-8369-1002-8) Ayer.

American Jobs Abroad. Ed. by Edward Knappman & Vicki Harlow. 550p. 1994. 55.00 (0-8103-8899-5, M89334-101560) Gale.

***American Jobs Abroad.** Edward W. Knappman & Victoria Harlow. 898p. 1994. pap. 19.95 (0-8103-5145-5) Visible Ink Pr.

American Journal. Robert Hayden. 1982. pap. 4.95 (0-87140-127-4) Liveright.

American Journal of Ambrose Serle, Secretary to Lord Howe 1776-1778. Ambrose Serle. Ed. by Edward H. Tatum, Jr. LC 72-76240. (Eyewitness Accounts of the American Revolution Ser., No. 1). (Illus.). 1969. reprint ed. 25.95 (0-405-01183-0) Ayer.

American Journal of Comparative Law: 1952-1988, 41 vols., Set. 1,947.50 (0-8377-9016-6) Rothman.

American Journal of International Law: 1907-1988, Set. 9,700.00 (0-8377-9017-4) Rothman.

American Journal of Legal History: 1957-1992, 37 vols., Set. 1,665.00 (0-8377-9018-2) Rothman.

American Journal of Numismatics, Vol. 2 - 1990. (AJN Sec Ser.). (Illus.). 215p. 1990. pap. 30.00 (0-89722-244-X) Am Numismatic.

American Journal of Numismatics, Vols. 3 & 4 - 1991 & 1992. (AJN Sec.). 270p. pap. 40.00 (0-89722-251-2) Am Numismatic.

American Journal of Nursing Question & Answer Book. 4th ed. American Journal of Nursing Company Staff et al. LC 93-31113. 365p. 1993. pap. 21.95 (0-8016-7780-7) Mosby Yr Bk.

American Journal of Sociology: Supplementary Index, Vols. 71-75. 1989. 5.00 (0-685-24921-2); pap. 3.50 (0-685-24922-0) U Ch Pr.

American Journal of Sociology: Supplementary Index, Vols. 76-80. 1989. 7.95 (0-685-24919-0); pap. 3.95 (0-685-24920-4) U Ch Pr.

American Journal of Trial Advocacy: 1977-1991, 16 vols., 1-2. 30.00 (0-318-57400-4) Rothman.

American Journal of Trial Advocacy: 1977-1991, 16 vols., 3-9. 32.50 (0-318-57401-2) Rothman.

American Journal of Trial Advocacy: 1977-1991, 16 vols., Set. 680.00 (0-8377-9019-0) Rothman.

American Journalism. Henry King. LC 79-125700. (American Journalists Ser.). 1971. reprint ed. 16.95 (0-405-01679-4) Ayer.

American Journalism History: An Annotated Bibliography. Comp. by W. David Sloan. LC 88-35800. (Bibliographies & Indexes in Mass Media & Communications Ser.: No. 1). 359p. 1989. text ed. 79.50 (0-313-26350-7, SLO/, Greenwood Pr) Greenwood.

American Journalist: A Portrait of U. S. News People & Their Work. 2nd ed. David H. Weaver & G. Cleveland Wilhoit. LC 91-62. (Illus.). 288p. 1991. 35.00 (0-253-36364-0); pap. 12.95 (0-253-20668-5, MB-668) Ind U Pr.

American Journalist: Paradox of the Press. Loren Ghiglione. LC 89-600392. 225p. 1990. 19.95 (0-8444-0701-1) Lib Congress.

American Journalists, 49 Vols, Set. 1971. reprint ed. 1,137.50 (0-405-01650-6) Ayer.

***American Journals.** Camus. 1995. pap. text ed. 12.95 (1-56924-823-0) Marlowe & Co.

American Journals of Lt. John Enys. Ed. by Elizabeth Cometti. (Illus.). 377p. 1976. 29.95 (0-8156-0121-2) Syracuse U Pr.

American Journey by Rail. Dudley Whitney. 1990. pap. 14.99 (0-517-05204-0) Random Hse Value.

***American Journey of Eric Sevareid.** Raymond A. Schroth. LC 94-44441. (Illus.). 462p. 1995. 28.00 (1-883642-12-4) Steerforth Pr.

American Jubilee: The Art of Jane Wooster Scott. (Illus.). 304p. Date not set. 75.00 (1-55859-763-8) Abbeville Pr.

American Judaism. 2nd rev. ed. Nathan Glazer. Ed. by Daniel J. Boorstin. (Chicago History of American Civilization Ser.). 236p. 1988. pap. 15.95 (0-226-29843-4) U Ch Pr.

American Judaism: A Pluralistic Religious Community. Abraham J. Karp. (Texts & Studies). (HEB.). 1984. 15.00 (0-318-41703-0) Am Jewish Hist Soc.

American Judaism: Adventure in Modernity. Jacob Neusner. reprint ed. pap. 9.95 (0-87068-681-X) Ktav.

American Judaism: The Religion & Religious Institutions of the Jewish People in the United States. Joseph Leiser. LC 78-26230. 1979. reprint ed. text ed. 69.50 (0-313-20879-4, LEAJ, Greenwood Pr) Greenwood.

American Judaism of Mordecai M. Kaplan. Emanuel S. Goldsmith et al. 352p. 1989. 50.00 (0-8147-3024-8) NYU Pr.

American Judaism of Mordecai M. Kaplan. Ed. by Emanuel S. Goldsmith et al. (Reappraisals in Jewish Social & Intellectual History Ser.). 460p. (C). 1993. pap. text ed. 20.00 (0-8147-3052-3) NYU Pr.

American Judicial Behavior. Ed. by Saul Brenner. LC 73-10235. 250p. 1974. text ed. 34.50 (0-8422-5116-2) Irvington.

American Judicial Politics. Harry P. Stumpf. 494p. (C). 1988. text ed. 36.00 (0-15-502340-3) HB Coll Pubs.

American Judicial Proceedings First Printed Before 1801: An Analytical Bibliography. Comp. by Wilfred J. Ritz. LC 83-18605. (Illus.). xlviii, 364p. 1984. text ed. 59.95 (0-313-24057-4, RAJ/, Greenwood Pr) Greenwood.

American Judicial Tradition: Profiles of Leading American Judges. G. Edward White. 576p. 1988. pap. 15.95 (0-19-505685-X) OUP.

American Judiciary. Simeon E. Baldwin. (American State Ser.). xiii, 403p. 1991. reprint ed. lib. bdg. 42.50 (0-8377-1922-4) Rothman.

American Judiciary. Simeon E. Baldwin. LC 91-55366. (American State Ser.). 416p. 1991. reprint ed. lib. bdg. 66.00 (0-912004-92-4) W W Gaunt.

American Judiciary: Critical Issues. Russell R. Wheeler. Ed. by A. Leo Levin. (Annals of the American Academy of Political & Social Science Ser.: Vol. 462). 224p. 1982. 26.00 (0-8039-1852-6); pap. 17.00 (0-8039-1853-4) Sage.

American Jukebox: The Classic Years. Vincent Lynch. (Illus.). 120p. (Orig.). 1990. 29.95 (0-87701-722-0); pap. 16.95 (0-87701-678-X) Chronicle Bks.

American Junk: How to Hunt for, Haggle over, Rescue, & Transform America's Forgotten Treasures (from Five Dollar Chairs to Five Cent Swizzle Sticks) from Flea Markets, Tag Sales, Trash Heaps, Thrift Shops, Auctions, & Attics for a One-of-a-Kind Look for Your House, Apartment, Getaway, Kitchen, Bedroom - Home! Mary R. Carter. (Illus.). 256p. 1994. 29.95 (0-670-84400-4) Studio Bks.

An Asterisk (*) at the beginning of an entry indicates that the title is appearing in BIP for the first time.

American Jurisprudence: Legal Forms 2d, 20 vols. suppl. ed. 1993. Suppl. 1993. write for info. (*0-318-57189-7*) Lawyers Cooperative.

American Jurisprudence: Pleading & Practice Forms, 25 vols. rev. suppl. ed. 1993. Suppl. 1993. write for info. (*0-318-57188-9*) Lawyers Cooperative.

American Jurisprudence: Proof of Facts, 30 vols. suppl. ed. 1993. Suppl. 1993. write for info. (*0-318-57176-5*) Lawyers Cooperative.

American Jurisprudence Proof of Facts, 50 vols. suppl. ed. 1993. Suppl. 1993. write for info. (*0-318-59412-9*); Suppl. 1993. write for info. (*0-318-64393-6*) Lawyers Cooperative.

American Jurisprudence Proof of Facts, 50 vols., Set. 1988. write for info. (*0-318-59411-0*) Lawyers Cooperative.

American Jurisprudence Trials, 48 vols. suppl. ed. 1993. Suppl. 1993. write for info. (*0-318-59410-2*) Lawyers Cooperative.

American Jurisprudence, 1870-1970: A History. James E. Herget. LC 90-52941. 320p. 1990. 35.00 (*0-89263-302-6*) Rice Univ.

American Jury on Trial: Psychological Perspectives. Saul M. Kassin & Lawrence S. Wrightsman. 232p. 1988. 52.00 (*0-89116-737-4*); pap. 27.00 (*0-89116-856-7*) Hemisp Pub.

***American Justice.** Paul Begg. 1994. 12.99 (*0-517-12017-8*) Random Hse Value.

American Justice: Research of the National Institute of Justice. Larry J. Siegel. Ed. by Schiller. 269p. (C). 1990. pap. text ed. 20.50 (*0-314-56565-5*) West Pub.

American Kaleidoscope: Race, Ethnicity, & the Civic Culture. Lawrence H. Fuchs. LC 89-21481. 637p. 1990. pap. 24.95 (*0-8195-6250-5*, Wesleyan Univ Pr) U Pr of New Eng.

American Kamikaze. James J. Hall. (Illus.). 345p. (Orig.). 1988. pap. 19.95 (*0-9621745-0-5*) J Bryant Ltd.

American Kasten: The Dutch-Style Cupboards of New York & New Jersey, 1650-1800. Peter M. Kenny. 1994. pap. 24.95 (*0-8109-6439-2*) Abrams.

American Kasten: The Dutch-Style Cupboards of New York & New Jersey, 1650-1800. Peter M. Kenny et al. (Illus.). 88p. 1990. 25.00 (*0-87099-605-3*) Metro Mus Art.

American Keiretsu: A Strategic Weapon for Global Competitiveness. David N. Burt & Michael F. Doyle. LC 92-46913. 251p. 1993. text ed. 25.00 (*1-55623-852-5*) Irwin Prof Pubng.

American Kennel Club Dog Care & Training. American Kennel Club Staff. (Illus.). 192p. 1991. pap. 11.50 (*0-87605-405-X*) Howell Bk.

American Kernel Lessons: Advanced Student Book. Robert O'Neill et al. (Illus.). 142p. (Orig.). 1981. pap. 12.95 (*0-582-79741-1*, 74995); audio 8.95 (*0-582-79764-0*, 75018) Longman.

American Kernel Lessons: Advanced Student Book, No. 1. Robert O'Neill et al. (Illus.). 142p. (Orig.). 1981. audio 39.95 (*0-582-79765-9*, 75019) Longman.

American Kernel Lessons: Advanced Student Book, No. 2. Robert O'Neill et al. (Illus.). 142p. (Orig.). 1981. audio write for info. (*0-582-79766-7*, 75020) Longman.

American Kernel Lessons: Advanced Student's Tests. Robert O'Neill & Linda Markstein. (Orig.). 1982. pap. text ed. 8.95 (*0-582-79807-8*, 75057) Longman.

American Kernel Lessons: Advanced Teacher's Edition. Penny LaPorte & Robert O'Neill. 101p. 1982. 18.95 (*0-582-79763-2*, 75017) Longman.

American Kernel Lessons: Beginning Level. Robert O'Neill et al. (English As a Second Language Bk.). 1981. teacher ed 18.95 (*0-582-79779-9*, 75033); student ed 8.95 (*0-582-79899-X*, 75132); student ed, pap. text ed. 12.95 (*0-582-79734-9*, 74990); audio 8.95 (*0-582-78342-9*, 74909); audio 8.95 (*0-582-78341-0*, 74908) Longman.

American Kernel Lessons: Beginning Level, No. 1. Robert O'Neill et al. (English As a Second Language Bk.). 1981. teacher ed, audio 39.95 (*0-582-79778-0*, 75032) Longman.

American Kernel Lessons: Beginning Level, No. 2. Robert O'Neill et al. (English As a Second Language Bk.). 1981. audio 69.95 (*0-582-79800-0*, 75054) Longman.

American Kernel Lessons: Intermediate Level. Robert O'Neill, Jr. et al. (English As a Second Language Bk.). (Illus.). 1978. teacher ed 18.95 (*0-582-79707-1*, 74974); student ed 8.95 (*0-582-90624-5*, 75196); student ed, pap. text ed. 12.95 (*0-582-79706-3*, 74973); teacher ed 8.95 (*0-582-79708-X*, 74975); audio 8.95 (*0-582-79709-8*, 74976) Longman.

American Kernel Lessons: Intermediate Level, Set 1. Robert O'Neill, Jr. et al. (English As a Second Language Bk.). (Illus.). 1978. audio 24.95 (*0-582-79715-2*, 74978) Longman.

American Kernel Lessons: Intermediate Level, Set 2. Robert O'Neill, Jr. et al. (English As a Second Language Bk.). (Illus.). 1978. audio 39.95 (*0-582-79716-0*, 74979) Longman.

American Kernel Lessons: Intermediate Level, Set 3. Robert O'Neill, Jr. et al. (English As a Second Language Bk.). (Illus.). 1978. audio 69.95 (*0-582-79710-1*, 74977) Longman.

American Key Personnel List; Advanced Composites Materials. 575.00 (*0-686-48251-4*, 0601) T-C Pubns CA.

American Kin Universe: A Genealogical Study. David M. Schneider & Calvert B. Cottrell. LC 75-37961. (Studies in Anthropology, Series in Social, Cultural, & Linguistic Anthropology: No. 3). 109p. 1975. pap. 6.00 (*0-916256-02-2*) U Chi Dept Anthro.

American Kinship: A Cultural Account. David M. Schneider. LC 79-18185. 1980. pap. text ed. 9.95 (*0-226-73930-9*) U Ch Pr.

***American Knees: A Novel.** Shawn Wong. 1995. 21.00 (*0-684-80304-6*) S&S Trade.

***American Knights.** (Endless Quest Ser.). 192p. (Orig.). (YA). Date not set. pap. 3.95 (*1-56076-899-1*) TSR Inc.

American Knitting Book. rev. ed. Taylor. 1985. pap. 12.95 (*0-684-13741-0*, Scribners) S&S Trade.

American Knives. Harold L. Peterson. 1980. 24.95 (*0-88227-016-8*) Gun Room.

American Knives & Weapons to 1900. Camille Page. (Illus.). 60p. (FRE.). 1993. reprint ed. 25.00 (*0-87556-181-0*) Saifer.

American Labor. Boy Scouts of America. (Illus.). 48p. (Orig.). (YA). (gr. 6-12). 1987. pap. 1.85 (*0-8395-3326-8*, 33326) BSA.

American Labor. Henry Pelling. LC 60-7247. (Chicago History of American Civilization Ser.). (Illus.). 1961. pap. text ed. 10.95 (*0-226-65393-5*, CHAC16) U Ch Pr.

American Labor: A Pictorial History. (Illus.). 1992. lib. bdg. 88.95 (*0-8490-5460-5*) Gordon Pr.

American Labor: From Conspiracy to Collective Bargaining, Ser. 1, 45 vols., Set. 1971. 796.00 (*0-405-02910-1*) Ayer.

American Labor: From Conspiracy to Collective Bargaining, Ser. 1, 60 vols., Set. 1969. reprint ed. 2,316.00 (*0-405-02100-3*) Ayer.

American Labor: The Twentieth Century. Ed. by Jerold S. Auerbach. LC 69-14822. (American Heritage Ser.). 1969. pap. 9.95 (*0-672-60128-1*, 78, Bobbs) Macmillan.

American Labor & American Democracy. William E. Walling. LC 75-89769. (American Labor Ser., No. 2: No. 2). 1971. reprint ed. 25.95 (*0-405-02947-0*) Ayer.

American Labor & Consensus Capitalism, 1935-1990. Patrick Renshaw. LC 91-13034. 258p. 1992. text ed. 38.50 (*0-87805-536-3*); pap. text ed. 16.95 (*0-87805-537-1*) U Pr of Miss.

American Labor & Postwar Italy, 1943-1953: A Study of Cold War Politics. Ronald L. Filippelli. LC 88-34262. 304p. 1989. 35.00 (*0-8047-1579-3*) Stanford U Pr.

American Labor & the Conservative Republicans, 1946-1948: A Study in Economic & Political Conflict. George S. Roukis. LC 88-10266. (Modern American History Ser.). 392p. 1988. 20.00 (*0-8240-4338-3*) Garland.

American Labor & the War. Samuel Gompers. LC 74-75239. (United States in World War I Ser.). 377p. 1974. reprint ed. lib. bdg. 38.95 (*0-89198-103-9*) Ozer.

American Labor Dynamics. Ed. by J. B. Hardman. LC 72-89736. (American Labor Ser.). 432p. 1970. reprint ed. 23.95 (*0-405-02125-9*) Ayer.

American Labor from Defense to Reconversion. Joel I. Seidman. (Midway Reprint Ser.). 319p. reprint ed. pap. 91.00 (*0-8357-5377-8*, 2026742) Bks Demand.

American Labor History. Leon Fink. (New American History Ser.). 30p. (C). 1991. reprint ed. 5.00 (*0-87229-061-1*) Am Hist Assn.

American Labor History & Comparative Labor Movements: A Selected Bibliography. James C. McBrearty. LC 78-190624. 272p. reprint ed. pap. 77.60 (*0-8357-5378-6*, 2022750) Bks Demand.

American Labor in a Changing World Economy. Carnegie Endowment for International Peace Staff. Ed. by Ward Morehouse. LC 78-15545. (Praeger Special Studies). 362p. 1980. text ed. 75.00 (*0-275-90460-1*, C0460, Praeger Pubs) Greenwood.

***American Labor in the Era of World War II.** Sally M. Miller & Daniela Cornford. LC 94-24570. (Contributions in Labor Studies Ser.: Vol. 45). 240p. 1995. text ed. 59.95 (*0-313-29074-1*) Greenwood.

***American Labor in the Era of World War II.** Ed. by Sally M. Miller. LC 94-24570. 240p. 1995. pap. text ed. 18.95 (*0-275-95185-5*, Praeger Pubs) Greenwood.

American Labor in the Southwest: The First 100 Years. Ed. by James C. Foster. LC 81-21819. 236p. (C). 1982. 27.50 (*0-8165-0741-4*); pap. 14.95 (*0-8165-0758-9*) U of Ariz Pr.

American Labor Movement. Mary R. Beard. LC 71-89717. (American Labor Ser., No. 1). 206p. 1971. reprint ed. 16.95 (*0-405-02103-8*) Ayer.

American Labor Movement. David Brody. LC 85-7482. 168p. 1985. reprint ed. pap. 15.00 (*0-8191-4667-6*) U Pr of Amer.

American Labor Movement, Student Syllabus. Charlotte Butsch. 30p. 1976. pap. text ed. 4.85 (*0-89420-078-X*, 330011); audio 24.60 (*0-89420-206-5*, 330000) Natl Book.

American Labor Policy: A Critical Appraisal of the NLRA. Ed. by Charles J. Morris. 484p. 1987. text ed. 62.00 (*0-87179-532-9*, 0532) BNA.

American Labor Songs of the Nineteenth Century. Philip S. Foner. LC 74-20968. (Music in American Life Ser.). (Illus.). 373p. 1975. 34.95 (*0-252-00187-7*) U of Ill Pr.

American Labor Struggles. Samuel Yellen. LC 70-89773. (American Labor Ser., No. 1). 398p. 1971. reprint ed. 38.95 (*0-405-02160-7*) Ayer.

American Labor Struggles. Samuel Yellen. LC 73-93633. (Illus.). 416p. 1988. reprint ed. pap. 21.95 (*0-913460-33-8*) Pathfinder NY.

American Labor Today. Victor Perlo. 1968. pap. 0.25 (*0-87898-029-6*) New Outlook.

American Labor Unions. Helen Marot. LC 70-89754. (American Labor, from Conspiracy to Collective Bargaining Ser., No. 1). 1974. reprint ed. 19.95 (*0-405-02141-0*) Ayer.

American Labor Unions: An Outline of Growth & Structure. 2nd ed. Reed C. Richardson. (ILR Bulletin Ser.: No. 30). 24p. 1970. pap. 3.00 (*0-87546-238-3*) ILR Pr.

American Land Planning Law, 8 vols., Set. Norman Williams & John Taylor. (Real Property-Zoning Ser.). 1974. 750.00 (*0-685-30631-3*) Clark Boardman Callaghan.

American Land Planning Law: Cases & Materials. Ed. by Norman Williams, Jr. 1978. text ed. 35.00 (*0-88285-041-5*) Ctr Urban Pol Res.

American Landmark Legislation: Primary Materials, 10 vols., Set. Irving J. Sloan. LC 75-42876. 1979. 750.00 (*0-379-10125-4*) Oceana.

American Landmark Legislation Labor Laws, 5 vols., Set. Irving J. Sloan. LC 83-11428. (Second Ser.). 1984. 375.00 (*0-379-10141-6*) Oceana.

American Landscape. Photos by David Muench. LC 86-83243. (Illus.). 208p. 1987. 42.50 (*0-932575-30-7*) Gr Arts Ctr Pub.

American Landscape: 1776-1976, Two Centuries of Change. 91p. 1976. 2.00 (*0-318-23135-2*) Wildlife Mgmt.

American Landscape & Genre Paintings in the New York Historical Society: A Catalog of the Collection Including Historical, Narrative & Marine Art, 3 vols., Set. New York Historical Society Staff. (Illus.). 1982. lib. bdg. 400.00 (*0-8161-0364-X*, Hall Library) G K Hall.

American Landscape Architecture: Designers & Places. Ed. by William H. Tishler. LC 88-19632. (Building Watchers Ser.). (Illus.). 240p. (Orig.). 1989. pap. 10.95 (*0-89133-145-X*) Preservation Pr.

American Landscape Video: The Electronic Grove. William D. Judson et al. LC 88-10931. (Illus.). 128p. (Orig.). 1988. pap. 12.95 (*0-88039-017-4*) Mus Art Carnegie.

American Landscapes. Neil A. Silberman. 1992. 45.00 (*0-13-026436-9*) P-H.

American Landscapes: Sources & Documents, 3 vol. set. Ed. by Graham Clarke. (Sources & Documents Ser.). (Illus.). 1400p. 1993. 375.00 (*1-873403-05-4*, A9755, Routledge NY) Routledge.

American Landscapes: 1968-1990. Enrico Natali & Mark Sandrof. (Illus.). 104p. (Orig.). 1991. pap. 29.00 (*0-945149-02-6*) Panopticon Pr.

American Landscapes in the Wake of French Impressionism. Frank A. Trapp. (Illus.). 17p. 1986. pap. 1.00 (*0-914337-09-2*) Mead Art Mus.

American Language. H. L. Mencken. 1977. pap. 22.95 (*0-394-73315-0*) Knopf.

American Language, 3 vols. 4th ed. Incl. Vol. 1. American Language. 1936. 40.00 (*0-394-40075-5*); Vol. 2. American Language, Supplement One. 1945. 50.00 (*0-394-40076-3*); Vol. 3. American Language, Supplement 2. 1948. 50.00 (*0-394-40077-1*); write for info. (*0-318-54003-7*) Knopf.

American Language: AMERCE Language. abr. ed. Luanna C. Blagrove. 250p. 1987. 24.95 (*0-939776-20-0*) Blagrove Pubns.

American Language Abridged. H. L. Mencken. Ed. by Raven I. McDavid, Jr. 1963. 35.00 (*0-394-40081-X*) Knopf.

***American Laughter: Immigrants, Ethnicity & 1930's Hollywood Film Comedy.** Mark Winokur. LC 95-12030. 1995. text ed. 29.95 (*0-312-12342-6*) St Martin.

American Law: An Introduction. Lawrence M. Friedman. (C). 1985. pap. text ed. 19.95 (*0-393-95251-7*) Norton.

American Law: The Formative Years, 28 bks., Set. Ed. by Morton J. Horwitz et al. 1972. reprint ed. 1,160.50 (*0-405-03990-5*) Ayer.

American Law - the Third Century: The Law Bicentennial Volume. Ed. by Bernard Schwartz. iv, 454p. 1976. text ed. 22.50 (*0-8377-0204-6*) Rothman.

American Law - the Third Century: The Law Bicentennial Volume. deluxe limited ed. Ed. by Bernard Schwartz. iv, 454p. 1976. boxed, text ed. 37.50 (*0-8377-0205-4*) Rothman.

American Law: An Introductory Survey of Some Principles: Cases & Text. Ed. by Samuel I. Shuman & Norbert D. West. LC 71-130427. 639p. reprint ed. pap. 180.00 (*0-8357-5379-4*, 2027655) Bks Demand.

American Law & Legal Systems. 2nd ed. James V. Calvi & Susan Coleman. 352p. (C). 1991. pap. text ed. 20.00 (*0-13-028853-5*, 680702) P-H.

American Law & the Constitutional Order: Historical Perspectives. enl. ed. Ed. by Lawrence M. Friedman & Harry N. Scheiber. 640p. 1988. 58.00 (*0-674-02528-8*); pap. 23.50 (*0-674-02527-X*) HUP.

American Law Dictionary. Peter G. Renstrom. (Clio Dictionaries in Political Science Ser.). 308p. 1990. lib. bdg. 52.00 (*0-87436-226-1*) ABC-CLIO.

American Law Enforcement: A History. David Johnson. LC 80-68814. 220p. 1981. pap. text ed. write for info. (*0-88273-270-6*) Forum Pr IL.

American Law Enforcement & Criminal Justice, Priciples of. Donald O. Schultz & Erik Beckman. LC 78-180804. (Orig.). (C). 1987. pap. text ed. 34.95 (*0-942728-27-0*) Copperhouse.

American Law Institute, Restatement of the Law, Second, Property - Donative Transfers, Vol. 4. 2nd ed. American Law Institute Ser. 500p. (C). 1992. text ed. write for info. (*0-314-94409-5*) West Pub.

American Law Institute, Restatement of the Law, Second, Torts 2d Appendix Volume 310-402 (July 1984-June 1991) American Law Institute Staff. 577p. (C). 1992. text ed. write for info. (*0-314-01271-0*) West Pub.

American Law Institute 50th Anniversary. 302p. 1973. 17.50 (*0-317-30867-X*, 5002) Am Law Inst.

American Law Journal: 1848-1852, Set. 120.00 (*0-8377-9203-7*) Rothman.

American Law Journal: 1848-1852, Vol. 1-4. mic. film write for info. (*0-318-57403-9*) Rothman.

American Law Magazine: 1843-1846, Set. 180.00 (*0-8377-9204-5*) Rothman.

American Law Magazine: 1843-1846, Vol. 1-6. mic. film write for info. (*0-318-57404-7*) Rothman.

American Law of Collision. John W. Griffin. (Illus.). xvi, 946p. 1988. reprint ed. lib. bdg. 65.00 (*0-8377-2209-8*) Rothman.

American Law of Landlord & Tenant. Robert S. Schoshinski. LC 80-81653. (Real Property-Zoning Ser.). 1980. Revised annually with supplement. 135.00 (*0-685-59794-6*) Clark Boardman Callaghan.

American Law of Medical Malpractice, 3 vols., Set. 2nd ed. Steven E. Pegalis & Harvey F. Wachsman. LC 92-90712. 1992. 365.00 (*0-685-59872-1*) Clark Boardman Callaghan.

American Law of Mining, 6 vols. 1960. write for info. (*0-8205-1010-6*) Bender.

American Law of Mining: The Rocky Mountain Mineral Law Foundation, 6 vols., Set. 2nd ed. 1984. write for info. (*0-318-67984-1*) Bender.

American Law of Products Liability, 15 vols. 3rd ed. LC 85-82984. 1987. ring bd. 1,900.00 (*0-685-59897-7*) Clark Boardman Callaghan.

American Law of Property, No. 1. A. James Casner. 1952. 135.00 (*0-316-13090-7*) Little.

American Law of Property, No. 2. A. James Casner. 1952. 135.00 (*0-316-13091-5*) Little.

American Law of Property, No. 3. A. James Casner. 1952. 135.00 (*0-316-13092-3*) Little.

American Law of Property, No. 4. A. James Casner. 1952. 135.00 (*0-316-13093-1*) Little.

American Law of Property, No. 5. A. James Casner. 1952. 135.00 (*0-316-13095-8*) Little.

American Law of Property, No. 6. A. James Casner. 1952. 135.00 (*0-316-13096-6*) Little.

American Law of Property, No. 6A. A. James Casner. 1954. 135.00 (*0-316-13099-0*) Little.

American Law of Property, No. 7. A. James Casner. 1952. 135.00 (*0-316-13097-4*) Little.

American Law of Property, 8 vols., Set. Ed. by A. James Casner. LC 52-10235. 1952. 550.00 (*0-316-13145-8*) Little.

American Law of Real Property, 3 vols. R. Gaudio. 1991. write for info. (*0-8205-1037-8*) Bender.

American Law of Torts, 10 vols. Stuart Speiser et al. LC 82-84380. 1983. Set. 1,000.00 (*0-685-59917-5*) Clark Boardman Callaghan.

American Law of Treason: Revolutionary & Early National Origins. Bradley Chapin. LC 64-11053. (Publications in History Ser.). 182p. 1964. 25.00 (*0-295-73705-0*, UWPH) U of Wash Pr.

American Law of Zoning, 5 vols. 3rd ed. Robert M. Anderson. LC 86-80879. (Real Property-Zoning Ser.). 1986. Set, revised annually with supplements. 550.00 (*0-685-59795-4*) Clark Boardman Callaghan.

American Law Publishing 1860-1900: Historical Readings & Bibliography. Betty W. Taylor & Robert J. Munro. LC 83-9049. 1984. Pt. 1: Historical Readings, 2 vols. 250.00 (*0-87802-061-6*) Glanville.

American Law Publishing 1860-1900: Historical Readings & Bibliography, 4 vols. in 2 pts., Set. Betty W. Taylor & Robert J. Munro. LC 83-9049. 1984. lib. bdg. 400.00 (*0-87802-058-6*) Glanville.

American Law Publishing 1860-1900 Pt. 1: Bibliographic Indexes, 2 vols., Pt. 2. Betty W. Taylor & Robert J. Munro. LC 83-9049. 1984. Pt. II: Bibliographic Indexes (author & subject), 2 vols. 250.00 (*0-87802-062-4*) Glanville.

American Law Reports (ALR) Digest of Decisions & Annotations: With Related Total Client-Service Library References: ALR 3rd, ALR 4th, ALR Fed., 9 vols. suppl. ed. 1993. Suppl. 1993. write for info. (*0-318-61827-3*) Lawyers Cooperative.

American Law School & the Rise of Administrative Government. William C. Chase. LC 81-69816. 192p. 1982. text ed. 23.50 (*0-299-09100-7*) U of Wis Pr.

American Law Source Book for the Classroom Teacher. 115p. 1989. pap. 15.00 (*0-89707-423-8*, 549-0090) Amer Bar Assn.

American Lawyer: A Summary of the Survey of the Legal Profession. Albert P. Blaustein & Charles O. Porter. LC 72-5452. 360p. 1972. reprint ed. text ed. 65.00 (*0-8371-6438-9*, BLAL, Greenwood Pr) Greenwood.

American Lawyer: As He Was - As He Is - As He Can Be. John R. Dos Passos. iv, 185p. 1986. reprint ed. lib. bdg. 25.00 (*0-8377-0524-X*) Rothman.

American Lawyer: When & How to Use One. American Bar Association, Public Education Staff. 36p. 1993. pap. 2.50 (*0-89707-848-9*, 235-0021) Amer Bar Assn.

American Lawyer Guide to Leading Law Firms, 5 vols., Vol. I. Intro. & Pref. by Joan Friedman. 1036p. 1991. 395.00 (*1-879590-01-8*) Amer Law Media.

American Lawyers. Richard L. Abel. 424p. 1989. 48.00 (*0-19-505140-8*) OUP.

American Lawyers. Richard L. Abel. 424p. 1991. reprint ed. pap. 19.95 (*0-19-507263-4*) OUP.

American Lawyers & Their Communities: Ethics in the Legal Profession. Thomas L. Shaffer. LC 90-50974. (Revisions: A Series of Books on Ethics: Vol. 10). (C). 1991. text ed. 29.95 (*0-268-00630-X*) U of Notre Dame Pr.

American Lawyers & Their Communities: Ethics in the Legal Profession. Thomas L. Shaffer. LC 90-50974. (Revisions: A Series of Books on Ethics: Vol. 10). (C). 1992. pap. text ed. 15.95 (*0-268-00640-7*) U of Notre Dame Pr.

American Lawyers in a Changing Society, 1776-1876. Maxwell Bloomfield. (Studies in Legal History). 425p. 1976. 40.00 (*0-674-02910-0*) HUP.

American Lawyers the Ultimate Insiders: Unseating the Lawyer Power Brokers. Steen-Olsen. LC 94-65902. 225p. (Orig.). 1994. 19.95 (*0-9639168-6-6*) Pro Se Pubs.

American Leader. Ken Lipke & Frank Swiatek. (Illus.). 250p. (C). 1989. write for info. (*0-318-65231-5*) Gibraltar LIF.

American Leaders 1789-1991. CQ Inc. Staff. 1991. 37.95 (*0-87187-594-2*) Congr Quarterly.

***American Leaders, 1789-1994: A Biographical Summary.** rev. ed. Congressional Quarterly Staff. LC 94-27169. 1994. 39.95 (*0-87187-841-0*) Congr Quarterly.

***American League.** Zoss & Bowman. (Illus.). 160p. 1995. 14.98 (*0-8317-0753-4*) Smithmark.

An Asterisk (*) at the beginning of an entry indicates that the title is appearing in BIP for the first time. 249

American League: A History. Joel Zoss & John S. Bowman. 192p. 1992. 24.95 (*1-56657-002-6*) NDM Pubns.

American League Baseball Card Classics. Bert R. Sugar. 1982. pap. 3.50 (*0-486-24286-2*) Dover.

***American League 1995 Red Book.** Sporting News Staff. 1995. pap. 12.95 (*0-89204-522-1*) Sporting News.

American Learned Societies in Transition: The Impact of Dissent & Recession. Harland G. Bloland & Sue M. Bloland. LC 74-1339. 150p. reprint ed. pap. 42.80 (*0-8357-5380-8*, 2029488) Bks Demand.

American Leaves: Familiar Notes of Thought & Life. Samuel Osgood. LC 72-374. (Essay Index Reprint Ser.). 1977. reprint ed. 24.95 (*0-8369-2814-8*) Ayer.

American Left 1955-1970: A National Union Catalog of Pamphlets Published in the United States & Canada. Ed. by Ned Kehde. LC 76-8002. 526p. (Orig.). 1976. text ed. 79.50 (*0-8371-8282-4*, KTA/, Greenwood Pr) Greenwood.

American Legal & Constitutional History: Cases & Materials. Clifford K. Dorne & Kenneth Gewerth. 350p. 1994. pap. 44.95 (*1-880921-13-8*) Austin & Winfield.

American Legal & Constitutional History: Cases & Materials. Herbert A. Johnson. 600p. 1994. pap. 64.95 (*1-880921-12-X*) Austin & Winfield.

American Legal & Social Environment of Business. Douglas Whitman & John W. Gergacz. 608p. (C). 1984. write for info. (*0-394-35225-4*, F05) Random.

American Legal Culture, 1908-1940. John W. Johnson. LC 80-1027. (Contributions in Legal Studies: No. 16). x, 185p. 1981. text ed. 49.95 (*0-313-22337-8*, JAM/, Greenwood Pr) Greenwood.

American Legal Environment: Individuals, Business Law & Government. William T. Schantz & Janice Jackson. (Illus.). 975p. (C). 1984. teacher ed, pap. text ed. write for info. (*0-314-77786-5*); student ed, pap. text ed. 22.75 (*0-314-89320-2*) West Pub.

American Legal Environment: Individuals, Business Law & Government. 2nd ed. William T. Schantz & Janice Jackson. (Illus.). 975p. (C). 1984. text ed. 65.75 (*0-314-72229-7*) West Pub.

American Legal Ethics: Text, Readings & Discussion Topics. Shaffer. 1985. write for info. (*0-8205-0016-X*, 025); teacher ed write for info. (*0-8205-0017-8*) Bender.

American Legal Processes. William P. McLauchlan. LC 76-26579. (Viewpoints on American Politics Ser.). 233p. reprint ed. pap. 66.50 (*0-7837-3497-2*, 2057830) Bks Demand.

American Legal Realism. Ed. by William W. Fisher, III et al. LC 92-33872. 344p. 1993. pap. 15.95 (*0-19-507123-9*) OUP.

American Legal Realism & Empirical Social Science. John H. Schlegel. LC 94-17950. (Studies in Legal History Ser.). 450p. 1995. text ed. 55.00x (*0-8078-2179-9*) U of NC Pr.

American Legal System. David E. Brody. 585p. 1978. text ed. 33.00 (*0-669-01439-7*); Instr.'s. teacher ed. 2.00 (*0-669-01840-6*) Heath.

American Legal System. 2nd ed. Blair J. Kolasa & Bernadine Meyer. LC 86-9418. 1986. text ed. write for info. (*0-13-027962-5*) P-H.

American Legal System: The Administration of Justice in the United States by Judicial, Administrative, Military, & Arbitral Tribunals. rev. ed. Lewis Mayers. xi, 594p. 1981. reprint ed. lib. bdg. 42.50 (*0-8377-0839-7*) Rothman.

American Legal Theory. Ed. by Robert S. Summers & Arthur L. Goodhart. (International Library of Essays in Law & Legal Theory). 550p. 1992. text ed. 150.00 (*0-8147-7951-4*) NYU Pr.

American Legends of the Wild West. Richard Mancini. LC 91-58653. (Illus.). 128p. 1992. 12.98 (*1-56138-119-5*) Courage Bks.

American Legion: An Official History, 1919-1989. Thomas A. Rumer. 732p. 1990. 24.95 (*0-87131-622-6*) M Evans.

American Legion & American Foreign Policy. Roscoe Baker. LC 74-39. (Illus.). 329p. 1974. reprint ed. text ed. 69.50 (*0-8371-7360-4*, BAAL, Greenwood Pr) Greenwood.

American Legislative Leaders, 1850-1910, Vol. 2. Charles Ritter & Jon L. Wakelyn. Ed. by James H. Broussard et al. LC 88-24734. 1156p. 1989. text ed. 155.00 (*0-313-23943-6*, BLL02, Greenwood Pr) Greenwood.

American Legislative Process: Congress & the States. 8th ed. William J. Keefe & Morris S. Ogul. LC 92-13574. 496p. (C). 1992. text ed. write for info. (*0-13-038290-6*) P-H.

American Legislatures & Legislative Methods. Paul S. Reinsch. LC 91-55447. (American State Ser.). 347p. 1991. reprint ed. lib. bdg. 61.00 (*0-912004-97-5*) W W Gaunt.

American Letters & the Historical Consciousness: Essays in Honor of Lewis P. Simpson. Ed. by J. Gerald Kennedy & Daniel M. Fogel. LC 87-13547. 288p. 1988. text ed. 35.00 (*0-8071-1416-2*) La State U Pr.

American Liberal Tradition: A Reinterpretation. James P. Young. 300p. 1995. 16.95 (*0-8133-0648-5*); pap. 34.95 (*0-8133-0647-7*) Westview.

American Liberalism: Laudable End, Controversial Means. rev. ed. William Gerber. LC 87-2180. 338p. (C). 1987. reprint ed. lib. bdg. 55.00 (*0-8191-6266-3*, N Amer Soc for Social Philosophy); reprint ed. pap. text ed. 29.50 (*0-8191-6267-1*, N Amer Soc for Social Philosophy) U Pr of Amer.

American Liberalism & World Politics, 1931-1941, 2 vol. set. James J. Martin. 1963. 35.00 (*0-8159-5005-5*) Devin.

American Liberties & American Slavery. S. B. Treadwell. LC 79-79016. (Black Heritage Library Collection). 1977. 23.95 (*0-8369-8669-5*) Ayer.

American Liberty & "Natural Law" Eugene C. Gerhart. xi, 212p. 1986. reprint ed. lib. bdg. 25.00 (*0-8377-2206-3*) Rothman.

American Library Association Best of the Best for Children: Software - Books - Magazines - Video. Denise P. Donavin. 1992. pap. 20.00 (*0-679-74250-6*, Random Ref) Random.

American Library Association Index to General Literature, 3 vols., Set. American Library Association Staff. Incl. Vol. 1. Basic Volume. LC 79-143240. 1977. 90.00 (*0-87650-017-3*); Vol. 2. Supplement. LC 79-143240. 1977. 39.50 (*0-87650-018-1*); Vol. 3. Author Index. LC 79-143240. 1971. 39.50 (*0-87650-019-X*); LC 79-143240. 1977. 155.00 (*0-685-24375-3*) Pierian.

American Library Association Research Handbook: An Information-Age Guide to Researching Facts & Topics. Ed. by Sandy Whitely. LC 94-10861. 1994. 35.00 (*0-679-43060-1*) Random.

American Library Directory 1994-95. Ed. by Bowker, R. R., Staff. 2200p. 1994. Set. 239.95 (*0-8352-3420-7*) Bowker.

American Library Directory 1994-95, 1. Ed. by Bowker, R. R., Staff. 2200p. 1994. write for info. (*0-8352-3421-5*) Bowker.

American Library Directory 1994-95, 2. Ed. by Bowker, R. R., Staff. 2200p. 1994. write for info. (*0-8352-3422-3*) Bowker.

***American Library Directory 1995-96, 2 vols. Ed. by Bowker, R. R., Staff. 2200p. 1995. 245.00 (*0-8352-3583-1*) Bowker.**

"Simply indispensable for librarians, patrons, researchers suppliers & anyone interested in locating libraries, library personnel, & library organizations."-- RESEARCH & REFERENCE BOOK NEWS. "Suffice it to say, ALD is as useful as ever."--REFERENCE QUARTERLY. Find information on more than 36,000 public, academic, special & government libraries & library related organizations in the U.S., Canada, & Mexico. This vital resource also includes a PERSONNEL INDEX, featuring the names of over 72, 000 library professionals; & OPAC & Internet information. Locate special collections...contact colleagues across the continent...compare your facilities, services, & expenditures with similar libraries in other locales. Libraries are listed alphabetically by state & city, & registries of library schools & library consortia are also included. ***Publisher Provided Annotation.***

***American Library Directory 1995-96, Vol. 1.** Ed. by Bowker, R. R., Staff. 1995. Not sold separately (*0-8352-3584-X*) Bowker.

***American Library Directory 1995-96, Vol. 2.** Ed. by Bowker, R. R., Staff. 1995. Not sold separately (*0-8352-3585-8*) Bowker.

***American Library Directory 1996-97, 2 vols.** Ed. by Bowker, R. R., Staff. Incl. Vol. 1. American Library Directory 1996-97. 1996. (*0-8352-3756-7*); Vol. 2. American Library Directory 1996-97. 1996. (*0-8352-3757-5*); write for info. (*0-8352-3755-9*) Bowker.

American Library History: A Bibliography of Dissertations & Theses. 3rd rev. ed. Arthur P. Young. LC 88-10072. 479p. 1988. 42.50 (*0-8108-2138-9*) Scarecrow.

American Library Laws. Ed. by Alex Ladenson. LC 83-21543. 2019p. reprint ed. pap. 180.00 (*0-7837-5915-0*, 2045714) Bks Demand.

American Life, American People, 2 vols., Vol. 1. Timothy J. Crimmins & Neil L. Shumsky. 298p. (C). 1988. pap. text ed. 17.50 (*0-15-502360-8*) HB Coll Pubs.

American Life, American People, 2 vols., Vol. 2. Timothy J. Crimmins & Neil L. Shumsky. 323p. (C). 1988. pap. text ed. 17.50 (*0-15-502361-6*) HB Coll Pubs.

American Life in Literature, 2 vols. Jay Hubbell. (BCL1-PS American Literature Ser.). 1993. reprint ed. Set. lib. bdg. 150.00 (*0-7812-6529-0*) Rprt Serv.

American Life in Literature, 1. rev. ed. Ed. by Jay B. Hubbell. (Play Anthology Reprint Ser.). 1977. reprint ed. 47.95 (*0-8369-8222-3*) Ayer.

American Life in Literature, 2. rev. ed. Ed. by Jay B. Hubbell. (Play Anthology Reprint Ser.). 1977. reprint ed. 46.95 (*0-8369-8223-1*) Ayer.

American Lifestyle Issues see Social Science Skills: Activities for the Secondary Classroom, Grades 9-12

American Light: The Luminist Movement, 1850-1875. Ed. by John Wilmerding. (Illus.). 330p. (C). 1990. 65.00 (*0-691-04074-5*) Princeton U Pr.

American Lighting: 1840-1940. Nadja Maril. LC 89-84163. (Illus.). 160p. 1989. 29.95 (*0-88740-177-5*) Schiffer.

***American Lighting 1840-1940.** Nadja Maril. (Illus.). 160p. 1995. 39.95 (*0-88740-879-6*) Schiffer.

American Line: One Hundred Years of American Drawing. Bartlett H. Hayes, Jr. 116p. (Orig.). 1959. pap. write for info. (*1-879886-13-8*) Addison Gallery.

American Line: One Hundred Years of American Drawing. Bartlett H. Hayes, Jr. 116p. (Orig.). 1961. write for info. (*1-879886-14-6*) Addison Gallery.

American Lit. Harold Witt. LC 93-74755. 156p. (Orig.). 1994. pap. 17.00 (*0-912592-35-4*) Ashland Poetry.

American Literacy. J. N. Conway. LC 93-2654. 1993. 18.00 (*0-688-11963-8*) Morrow.

***American Literacy: Five Books That Define Our Culture & Ourselves.** J. North Conway. 1995. pap. 12.00 (*0-688-14076-9*, Quill) Morrow.

American Literary Almanac: From 1608 to the Present. Ed. by Karen Rood. (Illus.). 448p. 1989. pap. 19.95 (*0-8160-1575-9*) Facts on File.

American Literary Anecdotes. Robert Hendrickson. 320p. 1990. 27.95 (*0-8160-1599-6*) Facts on File.

American Literary Autographs from Washington Irving to Henry James. Herbert Cahoon et al. LC 77-89415. (Illus.). (Orig.). 1977. pap. 14.95 (*0-486-23548-3*) Dover.

American Literary Autographs from Washington Irving to Henry James. Herbert Cahoon et al. (Orig.). 19.00 (*0-8446-5655-0*) Peter Smith.

American Literary Criticism. Ed. by William M. Payne. LC 68-26465. (Wampum Library of American Literature, Index Reprint Ser.). 1977. reprint ed. 23.95 (*0-8369-0779-5*) Ayer.

American Literary Criticism: Nineteen Hundred to Nineteen Fifty. Ed. by Charles I. Glicksberg. 584p. 1969. 12.95 (*0-87532-064-3*) Hendricks House.

American Literary Criticism from the Thirties to the Eighties. Vincent B. Leitch. 480p. 1989. text ed. 67.00 (*0-231-06426-8*); pap. text ed. 18.00 (*0-231-06427-6*) Col U Pr.

American Literary Critics & Scholars, 1800-1850, Vol. 59. Ed. by Ellen R. Kovner. (Dictionary of Literary Biography Ser.: Vol. 59). 428p. 1987. 128.00 (*0-8103-1737-0*) Gale.

American Literary Critics & Scholars, 1850-1880, Vol. 64. Ed. by John W. Rathbun & Monica M. Grecu. (Dictionary of Literary Biography Ser.: Vol. 64). 450p. 1987. 128.00 (*0-8103-1742-7*) Gale.

American Literary Critics & Scholars, 1880-1900, Vol. 71. (Dictionary of Literary Biography Ser.: Vol. 71). 1988. 128.00 (*0-8103-1749-4*) Gale.

***American Literary History Reader.** Gordon Hutner. 432p. 1995. pap. 22.00 (*0-19-509504-9*) OUP.

American Literary Landscapes: The Fiction & the Fact. Ed. by Ian F. Bell & D. K. Adams. LC 88-18173. (Critical Studies). 208p. 1989. text ed. 39.95 (*0-312-02421-5*) St Martin.

American Literary Magazines: The Eighteenth & Nineteenth Centuries. Ed. by Edward E. Chielens. LC 85-24793. (Historical Guides to the World's Periodicals & Newspapers Ser.). 519p. 1986. text ed. 75.00 (*0-313-23985-1*, CHA/, Greenwood Pr) Greenwood.

American Literary Magazines: The Twentieth Century. Ed. by Edward E. Chielens. LC 91-30603. (Historical Guides to the World's Periodicals & Newspapers Ser.). 488p. 1992. text ed. 95.00 (*0-313-23986-X*, CHT/, Greenwood Pr) Greenwood.

American Literary Manuscripts in the Boston Public Library: A Checklist. 1973. 3.00 (*0-89073-021-0*) Boston Public Lib.

American Literary Masters. Leon H. Vincent. LC 75-90689. (Essay Index Reprint Ser.). 1977. 25.95 (*0-8369-1216-0*) Ayer.

American Literary Naturalism, a Divided Stream. Charles C. Walcutt. LC 73-10584. 332p. 1974. text ed. 38.50 (*0-8371-7017-6*, WALN, Greenwood Pr) Greenwood.

American Literary Naturalism & Its Twentieth-Century Transformations: Frank Norris, Ernest Hemingway, Don DeLillo. Paul Civello. LC 93-41004. 208p. 1995. 35.00 (*0-8203-1649-0*) U of Ga Pr.

American Literary Publishing Houses 1638-1899, 2 vols., Set. Ed. by Peter Dzwonkoski. (Dictionary of Literary Biography Ser.: Vol. 49). 715p. 1986. 238.00 (*0-8103-1727-3*) Gale.

American Literary Publishing Houses 1900-1980, Vol. 46. Peter Dzwonkoski. (Dictionary of Literary Biography Ser.: Vol. 46). 400p. 1986. 128.00 (*0-8103-1724-9*) Gale.

***American Literary Publishing in the Mid-Nineteenth Century: The Business of Ticknor & Fields.** Michael Winship. (Cambridge Studies in Publishing & Printing History). (Illus.). 234p. (C). Date not set. write for info. (*0-521-45469-7*) Cambridge U Pr.

American Literary Scholarship: An Annual, 1963. Ed. by James L. Woodress. LC 65-19450. xi, 224p. 1965. 48.00 (*0-8223-0196-2*) Duke.

American Literary Scholarship: An Annual, 1964. Ed. by James L. Woodress. LC 65-19450. xi, 256p. 1966. 48.00 (*0-8223-0197-0*) Duke.

American Literary Scholarship: An Annual, 1965. Ed. by James L. Woodress. LC 65-19450. xi, 303p. 1967. 48.00 (*0-8223-0198-9*) Duke.

American Literary Scholarship: An Annual, 1966. Ed. by James L. Woodress. LC 65-19450. xiv, 284p. 1968. 48. 00 (*0-8223-0199-7*) Duke.

American Literary Scholarship: An Annual, 1967. Ed. by James L. Woodress. LC 65-19450. xii, 329p. 1969. 48.00 (*0-8223-0200-4*) Duke.

American Literary Scholarship: An Annual, 1968. Ed. by J. Albert Robbins. LC 65-19450. xiv, 335p. 1970. 48.00 (*0-8223-0235-7*) Duke.

American Literary Scholarship: An Annual, 1969. Ed. by J. Albert Robbins. LC 65-19450. xiv, 385p. 1971. 48.00 (*0-8223-0248-9*) Duke.

American Literary Scholarship: An Annual, 1970. Ed. by J. Albert Robbins. LC 65-19450. xii, 434p. 1972. 48.00 (*0-8223-0270-5*) Duke.

American Literary Scholarship: An Annual, 1971. Ed. by J. Albert Robbins. LC 65-19450. xiv, 418p. 1973. 48.00 (*0-8223-0293-4*) Duke.

American Literary Scholarship: An Annual, 1972. Ed. by J. Albert Robbins. LC 65-19450. xvi, 448p. 1974. 48.00 (*0-8223-0324-8*) Duke.

American Literary Scholarship: An Annual, 1973. annuals Ed. by James L. Woodress. LC 65-19450. xvi, 490p. 1975. 48.00 (*0-8223-0338-8*) Duke.

American Literary Scholarship: An Annual, 1974. annuals Ed. by James L. Woodress. LC 75-19450. xii, 492p. 1976. 48.00 (*0-8223-0362-0*) Duke.

American Literary Scholarship: An Annual, 1975. Ed. by James L. Woodress. LC 65-19450. xvi, 542p. 1977. 48. 00 (*0-8223-0384-1*) Duke.

American Literary Scholarship: An Annual, 1976. Ed. by J. Albert Robbins. LC 65-19450. xv, 490p. 1978. 48.00 (*0-8223-0406-6*) Duke.

American Literary Scholarship: An Annual, 1977. Ed. by James L. Woodress. LC 65-19450. xv, 554p. 1979. 48.00 (*0-8223-0423-6*) Duke.

American Literary Scholarship: An Annual, 1978. Ed. by J. Albert Robbins. LC 65-19450. xviii, 528p. 1980. 48.00 (*0-8223-0443-0*) Duke.

American Literary Scholarship: An Annual, 1979. Ed. by James L. Woodress. LC 65-19450. xviii, 574p. 1981. 48. 00 (*0-8223-0455-4*) Duke.

American Literary Scholarship: An Annual, 1983. Ed. by Warren G. French. LC 65-19450. xvi, 535p. 1985. 48.00 (*0-8223-0640-9*) Duke.

American Literary Scholarship: An Annual, 1985. Ed. by J. Albert Robbins. LC 65-19450. 536p. (C). 1987. 48.00 (*0-8223-0720-0*) Duke.

American Literary Scholarship: An Annual, 1987. Ed. by James L. Woodress. LC 65-19450. 575p. 1989. lib. bdg. 48.00 (*0-8223-0903-3*) Duke.

American Literary Scholarship: An Annual, 1988. Ed. by J. Albert Robbins. 616p. (C). 1990. lib. bdg. 48.00 (*0-8223-1033-3*) Duke.

American Literary Scholarship: An Annual, 1989. Ed. by David J. Nordloh. 523p. 1991. lib. bdg. 48.00 (*0-8223-1139-9*) Duke.

American Literary Scholarship: An Annual, 1990. Ed. by Louis Owens. 545p. 1992. lib. bdg. 50.00 (*0-8223-1234-4*) Duke.

American Literary Scholarship: An Annual, 1991. Ed. by David J. Nordloh. LC 65-19450. 540p. 1993. lib. bdg. 45.00 (*0-8223-1315-4*) Duke.

American Literary Scholarship: An Annual, 1992. Ed. by David J. Nordloh. 500p. 1994. lib. bdg. 48.00 (*0-8223-1480-0*) Duke.

***American Literary Scholarship: An Annual 1993.** Ed. by Gary Scharnhorst. 550p. 1995. 52.00 (*0-8223-1628-5*) Duke.

American Literary Scholarship, 1980. Ed. by J. Albert Robbins. LC 65-1950. xix, 625p. 1982. 48.00 (*0-8223-0464-3*) Duke.

American Literary Scholarship, 1981. annuals Ed. by James L. Woodress. LC 65-19450. (American Literary Scholarship Ser.). xviii, 549p. 1983. 48.00 (*0-8223-0552-6*) Duke.

American Literary Scholarship, 1984. Ed. by J. Albert Robbins. LC 65-19450. 613p. 1986. text ed. 48.00 (*0-8223-0666-2*) Duke.

American Literary Scholarship, 1986. Ed. by David J. Nordloh. LC 65-19450. xvii, 522p. (C). 1988. lib. bdg. 48.00 (*0-8223-0802-9*) Duke.

American Literary West. Ed. by Richard W. Etulain. (Illus.). 81p. 1980. pap. text ed. 15.00 (*0-89745-006-X*) Sunflower U Pr.

American Literary Yearbook, 1919. 1976. 59.95 (*0-87968-606-5*) Gordon Pr.

American Literature. Jack Rudman. (College Level Examination Ser.: CLEP-3). 1994. pap. 23.95 (*0-8373-5303-3*) Nat Learn.

American Literature. Jack Rudman. (College Proficiency Examination Ser.: CPEP-4). 1994. pap. 23.95 (*0-8373-5404-8*) Nat Learn.

American Literature, 2 vols. Charles F. Richardson. LC 79-122461. (American Literature Ser.: No. 49). 1970. reprint ed. lib. bdg. 89.95 (*0-8383-0901-1*) M S G Haskell Hse.

American Literature, 2 vols., Set. Harvard University Library Staff. Incl. Vol. 1. Classification Schedule, Classified Listing by Call Number, Chronological Listing. LC 69-11163. xxii, 631p. 1970. (*0-318-53004-X*); Vol. 2. Author & Title Listing. LC 69-11163. vi, 632p. 1970. (*0-318-53005-8*); LC 69-11163. (Widener Library Shelflist: No. 26-27). 1990. 100.00 (*0-674-02535-0*) HUP.

American Literature: A Chronological Approach. G. Robert Carlsen et al. 896p. 1985. text ed. 31.20 (*0-07-009844-1*) McGraw.

American Literature: A Prentice Hall Anthology, Vol. I. Emory Elliott et al. 2128p. (C). 1990. pap. text ed. write for info. (*0-13-027244-2*) P-H.

American Literature: A Prentice Hall Anthology, Vol. II. Emory Elliott et al. 2464p. (C). 1991. pap. text ed. 20.00 (*0-13-027269-8*, 640202) P-H.

American Literature: A Thematic Approach. 4th ed. G. Robert Carlsen et al. 1985. text ed. 31.20 (*0-07-009817-4*) McGraw.

American Literature: An Historical Sketch. John Nichol. 1972. 59.95 (*0-87968-607-3*) Gordon Pr.

American Literature: An Historical Sketch, 1620-1880. John Nichol. LC 77-39071. (Essay Index Reprint Ser.). 1977. reprint ed. 26.95 (*0-8369-2706-0*) Ayer.

American Literature: Civil War to the Present. Jack Rudman. (College Proficiency Examination Ser.: CPEP-27). 1994. pap. 23.95 (*0-8373-5427-7*) Nat Learn.

American Literature: E Z 101 Study Keys Ser. Francis E. Skipp. 144p. (Orig.). (C). 1992. pap. 5.95 (*0-8120-4694-3*) Barron.

An Asterisk (*) at the beginning of an entry indicates that the title is appearing in BIP for the first time.

An Asterisk (*) at the beginning of an entry indicates that the title is appearing in BIP for the first time.

251

A

American Medical Association Straight-Talk No-Nonsense Guide to Backcare. rev. ed. 1984. 8.95 (*0-394-73864-0*); pap. 8.95 (*0-685-08087-0*) Random.

American Medical Association Straight-Talk No-Nonsense Guide to Heartcare. rev. ed. 1984. pap. 8.95 (*0-394-73545-5*) Random.

American Medical Association Straight-Talk No-Nonsense Guide to Womancare. rev. ed. 1984. pap. 8.95 (*0-394-71576-4*) Random.

American Medical Biography, 2 vols. 2nd ed. James Thacher. LC 67-25447. (American Medicine Ser.). 1967. reprint ed. lib. bdg. 75.00 (*0-306-70944-9*) Da Capo.

American Medical Directory, 4 vols. 33th ed. American Medical Association Staff. 645.00 (*0-685-65164-9*, OP390890) AMA.

American Medical Education: The Formative Years, 1765-1910. Martin Kaufman. LC 75-35346. 224p. 1976. text ed. 55.00 (*0-8371-8590-4*, KME/, Greenwood Pr) Greenwood.

American Medical Imprints, 1820-1910: A Checklist of Publications Illustrating the History & Progress of Medical Science, Medical Education, & the Healing Arts in the United States: A Preliminary Contribution, 2 vols. Francesco Cordasco. 1654p. 1985. 275.00 (*0-940198-01-0*) Junius-Vaughn.

American Medical Research Past & Present. Richard H. Shryock. Ed. by I. Bernard Cohen. LC 79-7989. (Three Centuries of Science in America Ser.). 1980. reprint ed. lib. bdg. 34.95 (*0-405-12571-2*) Ayer.

American Medicinal Plants: An Illustrated & Descriptive Guide to Plants Indigenous to & Naturalized in the United States Which Are Used in Medicine. Charles F. Millspaugh. LC 73-91487. (Illus.). 450p. 1974. reprint ed. pap. 15.95 (*0-486-23034-1*) Dover.

American Medicine: The Power Shift. Eli Ginzberg. LC 85-8173. 224p. 1985. text ed. 56.00 (*0-8476-7439-8*) Rowman.

*__American Medicine: The Quest for Competence.__ Mary-Jo D. Good. LC 94-36162. 1995. 35.00 (*0-520-08896-4*) U CA Pr.

American Medicine & Statistical Thinking, 1800-1860. James H. Cassedy. LC 83-12831. (Illus.). 312p. 1984. 38.00 (*0-674-02560-1*) HUP.

American Medicine As Culture. Howard F. Stein. (C). 1993. pap. text ed. 24.50 (*0-8133-1910-2*) Westview.

American Medicine in Transition, 1840-1910. John S. Haller, Jr. LC 80-14546. (Illus.). 461p. 1981. 39.95 (*0-252-00806-5*) U of Ill Pr.

American Meditation & Beginning Yoga. Robert L. Peck. 1976. 6.00 (*0-917828-05-4*) Personal Dev Ctr.

American Mediterranean. Stephen Bonsal. 1977. lib. bdg. 69.95 (*0-8490-1415-8*) Gordon Pr.

American Melodrama. Ed. by Daniel Gerould. LC 82-62096. 1983. pap. 13.95 (*0-933826-21-4*) PAJ Pubns.

American Memories. Illus. by Norman Rockwell. 40p. 1993. 6.95 (*0-8362-4710-8*) Andrews & McMeel.

American Memory. Eric Larsen. 240p. 1988. 12.95 (*0-912697-68-7*) Algonquin Bks.

American Memory: A Report on the Humanities in the Nation's Public Schools. Lynne V. Cheney. 35p. (Orig.). 1988. pap. 2.00 (*0-16-004284-4*, S/N 036-000-00050-3) USGPO.

*__American Memory User Evaluation 1991-1993.__ Susan Veccia et al. (Illus.). 128p. (Orig.). (C). 1994. pap. text ed. 25.00x (*0-7881-1368-2*) Diane Pub.

American Men & Women of Science, 1995-96: A Biographical Directory of Today's Leaders in Physical, Biological & Related Sciences, 8 vols. 19th ed. Ed. by Bowker, R. R., Staff. 9441p. 1994. Set. 850.00 (*0-8352-3463-0*) Bowker. "Continues to be the standard reference tool in its field."-- BOOKLIST. "...the prime reference in the field."-- REFERENCE & RESEARCH BOOK NEWS. Your most authoritative resource for information on over 123, 000 leading U.S. & Canadian scientists & engineers, the new 19th edition of this prestigious multi-volume directory has been extensively updated with more than 65 percent new or substantially revised entries. Ranging across 10 major disciplines & 180 National Science Foundation subdisciplines, it identifies & profiles leading experts in all the physical, biological & related sciences - from Acoustics to Zoology. What's more, its Discipline Index makes it easy to locate the leading authorities in each field. All figures selected for inclusion have established exceptional scientific credentials - through experience & training, distinguished research, or attainment of a post of recognized responsibility. Their entries include such vital background details as birthplace & date, field of expertise, education, experience, concurrent positions, honors & awards, research focus, professional memberships, & mailing address. For over 85 years AMERICAN MEN & WOMEN OF SCIENCE has been indispensable to scientists, research administrators, consulting firms, government agencies, publishers, journalists, & college & university administrators researching North America's most accomplished scientific authorities. Now more than ever, the new 19th Edition continues that great tradition. Published triennially. *Publisher Provided Annotation.*

American Men & Women of Science, 1995-96: A Biographical Directory of Today's Leaders in Physical, Biological & Related Sciences Vol. 1: A - B. 19th ed. Ed. by Bowker, R. R., Staff. 1065p. 1994. Vol. 1 A-B. write for info. (*0-8352-3464-9*) Bowker.

American Men & Women of Science, 1995-96: A Biographical Directory of Today's Leaders in Physical, Biological & Related Sciences Vol. 2: C - F, 8 vols. 19th ed. Ed. by Bowker, R. R., Staff. 1523p. 1994. Vol. 2 C-F. write for info. (*0-8352-3465-7*) Bowker.

American Men & Women of Science, 1995-96: A Biographical Directory of Today's Leaders in Physical, Biological & Related Sciences Vol. 3: G - I, 8 vols. 19th ed. Ed. by Bowker, R. R., Staff. 1168p. 1994. Vol. 3 G-I. write for info. (*0-8352-3466-5*) Bowker.

American Men & Women of Science, 1995-96: A Biographical Directory of Today's Leaders in Physical, Biological & Related Sciences Vol. 4: J - L, 8 vols. 19th ed. Ed. by Bowker, R. R., Staff. 1136p. 1994. Vol. 4 J-L. write for info. (*0-8352-3467-3*) Bowker.

American Men & Women of Science, 1995-96: A Biographical Directory of Today's Leaders in Physical, Biological & Related Sciences Vol. 5: M - P, 8 vols. 19th ed. Ed. by Bowker, R. R., Staff. 1411p. 1994. Vol. 5 M-P. write for info. (*0-8352-3468-1*) Bowker.

American Men & Women of Science, 1995-96: A Biographical Directory of Today's Leaders in Physical, Biological & Related Sciences Vol. 6: Q - X, 8 vols. 19th ed. Ed. by Bowker, R. R., Staff. 1441p. 1994. Vol. 6 Q-S. write for info. (*0-8352-3469-X*) Bowker.

American Men & Women of Science, 1995-96: A Biographical Directory of Today's Leaders in Physical, Biological & Related Sciences Vol. 7: T - Z, 8 vols. 19th ed. Ed. by Bowker, R. R., Staff. 1101p. 1994. Vol. 7 T-Z. write for info. (*0-8352-3470-3*) Bowker.

American Men & Women of Science, 1995-96: A Biographical Directory of Today's Leaders in Physical, Biological & Related Sciences Vol. 8: Discipline Index, 8 vols. 19th ed. Ed. by Bowker, R. R., Staff. 596p. 1994. Vol. 8 Discipline Index. write for info. (*0-8352-3471-1*) Bowker.

American Men of Letters: Their Nature & Nurture. Edwin L. Clarke. LC 76-76714. (Columbia University. Studies in the Social Sciences: No. 168). reprint ed. 32.50 (*0-404-51168-6*) AMS Pr.

American Mennonites & Protestant Movements. Beulah S. Hostetler. LC 87-288. (Studies in Anabaptist & Mennonite History: No. 28). 384p. 1987. 29.95 (*0-8361-1288-1*) Herald Pr.

American Mennonites & the Great War, 1914-1918. Gerlof D. Homan. (Studies in Anabaptist & Mennonite History: No. 34). 240p. 1994. pap. 19.95x (*0-8361-3114-2*) Herald Pr.

American Merchant Seaman's Manual. 6th ed. F. M. Cornell & A. C. Hoffman. Ed. by William B. Hayler. LC 80-25488. (Illus.). 635p. 1981. text ed. 35.00 (*0-87033-267-8*) Cornell Maritime.

American Merchant Ships Eighteen Fifty to Nineteen Hundred, 2 Vols., I. Frederick Matthews. (Illus.). 960p. 1987. reprint ed. pap. 11.95 (*0-486-25538-7*) Dover.

American Merchant Ships Eighteen Fifty to Nineteen Hundred, 2 Vols., II. Frederick Matthews. (Illus.). 960p. 1987. reprint ed. pap. 11.95 (*0-486-25539-5*) Dover.

American Merchant Ships on the Yangtze. David H. Grover. LC 92-5841. 256p. 1992. text ed. 47.95 (*0-275-94337-2*, C4337, Praeger Pubs) Greenwood.

American Mercury: Facsimile Edition of Vol. One: The Original Issues of Jan., Feb., March & April, 1924. Ed. by George J. Nathan & H. L. Mencken. 600p. 1984. reprint ed. lib. bdg. 50.00 (*0-8334-1005-9*, Freedeeds Libr) Garber Comm.

American Mercury Reader. Ed. by Lawrence E. Spivak & Charles Angoff. 25.95 (*0-8488-0119-9*, Amereon Hse) Amereon Ltd.

American Mercury Reader. American Mercury Staff. (BCL1-PS American Literature Ser.). 378p. 1993. reprint ed. lib. bdg. 89.00 (*0-7812-6597-5*) Rprt Serv.

American Mercury Reader: A Selection of Distinguished Articles. American Mercury Staff. Ed. by Lawrence E. Spivak & Charles Angoff. LC 75-41009. (BCL Ser.: No. II). reprint ed. 24.50 (*0-404-14765-8*) AMS Pr.

American Metal Typefaces of the Twentieth Century. 2nd ed. Mac McGrew. (Illus.). 384p. 1993. 75.00 (*0-938768-34-4*); pap. 49.95 (*0-938768-39-5*) Oak Knoll.

American Method of Sprinting & Relay Racing. Ken Brauman & Ken Taylor. 64p. (Orig.). 1981. pap. 8.95 (*0-932741-96-7*) Championship Bks & Vid Prodns.

American Methodist Pioneer: The Life & Journals of the Rev. Freeborn Garrettson 1752-1827. Ed. by Robert D. Simpson. LC 83-72532. (Illus.). 444p. 1983. text ed. 25.00 (*0-914960-49-0*) Academy Bks.

American Midpoint Ephemeris: 1991-1995. Neil F. Michelsen. (American Ephemeris Ser.). 60p. 1991. pap. 9.95 (*0-935127-17-8*) ACS Pubns.

American Midwife Debate: A Sourcebook on Its Modern Origins. Judy B. Litoff. LC 85-17694. (Contributions in Medical Studies: No. 18). (Illus.). 251p. 1986. text ed. 55.00 (*0-313-24191-0*, LMD/, Greenwood Pr) Greenwood.

American Midwives: Eighteen Sixty to Present. Judy B. Litoff. LC 77-83893. (Contributions in Medical History Ser.: No. 1). 197p. 1978. text ed. 38.50 (*0-8371-9824-0*, LAM/) Greenwood.

American Migrational Patterns. Arlene H. Eakle. 78p. 1974. pap. 11.00 (*0-940764-07-5*) Genealog Inst.

American Militaria Sourcebook & Directory. Ed. by Terry Hannon. 147p. 1987. pap. 19.95 (*0-943345-00-6*) Phoenix Militaria.

American Militaria Sourcebook & Directory. 2nd ed. Ed. by Terry Hannon. 234p. 1992. pap. 29.95 (*0-943345-01-4*) Phoenix Militaria.

American Military. Ed. by Martin Oppenheimer. LC 73-78698. (Society Bks.). 180p. (C). 1971. reprint ed. 29.95 (*0-87855-056-9*); reprint ed. pap. text ed. 17.95 (*0-87855-549-8*) Transaction Pubs.

American Military Cartridge Belts & Related Equipment. Stephen Dorsey. 1984. 10.95 (*0-913150-49-5*) Pioneer Pr.

American Military Cemeteries: A Comprehensive Illustrated Guide to the Hallowed Grounds of the United States, Including Cemeteries Overseas. Dean W. Holt. LC 91-51215. 528p. 1992. lib. bdg. 62.50x (*0-89950-666-6*) McFarland & Co.

*__American Military Collectibles Price Guide.__ Manions International Auction Staff. 1995. pap. 16.95 (*0-930625-47-1*) Antique Trader.

American Military Equipage: Eighteen Fifty-One to Eighteen Seventy-Two, II. Incl. LC 74-83403. 1974. text ed. (*0-318-54410-5*); LC 74-83403. 1977. text ed. (*0-318-54411-3*); LC 74-83403. 1978. text ed. (*0-318-54412-1*); LC 74-83403. (Illus.). 1979. 20.00 (*0-917218-11-6*) A Mowbray.

American Military Ethic: A Meditation. James H. Toner. LC 91-28747. 288p. 1992. text ed. 59.95 (*0-275-94195-7*, C4195, Praeger Pubs) Greenwood.

American Military Experience Series, 43 bks., Vols. 1-32. Ed. by Richard H. Kohn. (Illus.). 1979. lib. bdg. 2,278.50 (*0-405-11850-3*) Ayer.

American Military Government: Its Organization & Policies. Hajo Holborn. LC 77-23165. 243p. 1977. reprint ed. text ed. 35.00 (*0-8371-9450-4*, HOAMG, Greenwood Pr) Greenwood.

American Military Government: Its Organization & Policies. Hajo Holborn. Ed. by Igor I. Kavass & Adolf Sprudz. LC 75-766. (International Military Law & History Ser.: Vol. 10). 243p. 1975. reprint ed. lib. bdg. 42.00 (*0-930342-47-X*, 300620) W S Hein.

American Military History. 1992. lib. bdg. 350.00 (*0-8490-8856-9*) Gordon Pr.

American Military History: A Guide to Reference & Information Sources. Daniel K. Blewett. (Reference Sources in the Social Sciences Ser.). 250p. 1995. lib. bdg. 52.00 (*1-56308-035-4*) Libs Unl.

American Military History: From Colonial Times to Vietnam. 1984. lib. bdg. 89.95 (*0-87700-618-0*) Revisionist Pr.

American Military in the Twenty-First Century. Barry L. Blechman et al. LC 93-33963. 530p. 1993. text ed. 49.95 (*0-312-10369-7*) St Martin.

American Military Leaders. Ed. by Roger J. Spiller & Joseph G. Dawson, III. LC 88-32344. 438p. 1989. pap. text ed. 24.95 (*0-275-93139-0*, B3139, Praeger Pubs) Greenwood.

American Military Movement Relating Sacred Dance. Ruth E. Neilan. Ed. & Intro. by Doug Adams. (Orig.). 1985. pap. 3.00 (*0-941500-37-3*) Sharing Co.

American Military Policy. C. Joseph Bernardo & Eugene H. Bacon. LC 74-9697. 548p. 1974. reprint ed. text ed. 75.00 (*0-8371-7615-8*, BEMP, Greenwood Pr) Greenwood.

American Military Shoulder Arms, Vol. II: From the 1790s to the End of the Flintlock Period. George D. Moller. (Illus.). 496p. 1993. 75.00 (*0-87081-308-0*) Univ Pr Colo.

American Military Shoulder Arms, 1492-1992, Vol. I. George D. Moller. (Illus.). 528p. 1993. 75.00 (*0-87081-286-6*) Univ Pr Colo.

American Military Space Policy: Information Systems, Weapon Systems & Arms Control. Colin S. Gray. 138p. 1984. reprint ed. lib. bdg. 58.50 (*0-8191-4076-7*) U Pr of Amer.

American Military Strategy. Samuel P. Huntington. LC 86-83045. (Policy Papers in International Affairs Ser.: No. 28). vii, 57p. 1986. pap. 4.95 (*0-87725-528-8*) U of Cal IAS.

American Military Tradition: From Colonial Times to the Present. Ed. by Colin F. Baxter. 1993. 40.00 (*0-8420-2381-X*); pap. text ed. 15.95 (*0-8420-2450-6*) Scholarly Res Inc.

American Militia in the Frontier Wars, 1790-1796. Murtie J. Clark. 394p. 1990. 30.00 (*0-685-54335-8*, 1001) Genealog Pub.

American Millionaire. Murray Schisgal. 1975. pap. 4.75 (*0-8222-0031-7*) Dramatists Play.

American Mind: An Interpretation of American Thought & Character Since the 1800s. Henry S. Commager. (C). 1959. pap. 17.00x (*0-300-00046-4*, Y7) Yale U Pr.

American Mind in the Mid-Nineteenth Century. 2nd ed. Irving H. Bartlett. Ed. by John H. Franklin & A. S. Eisenstadt. LC 81-14988. (American History Ser.). 160p. (C). 1982. pap. text ed. write for info. (*0-88295-809-7*) Harlan Davidson.

American Minds: A History of Ideas. rev. ed. Stow Persons. LC 74-12326. 540p. 1975. 49.00 (*0-88275-203-0*) Krieger.

American Miners' Carbide Lamps: A Collector's Guide to American Carbide Mine Lighting. Gregg S. Clemmer. LC 87-50676. (Illus.). 136p. 1987. 26.95 (*0-87026-064-2*) Westernlore.

American Mines Directory. (Illus.). 345p. (C). 1994. pap. 75.00 (*1-57205-011-X*) Rector Pr.

American Miniatures Seventeen Thirty to Eighteen Fifty: One Hundred & Seventy-Three Portraits. Harry B. Wehle. LC 71-87684. (Library of American Art Ser.). 1970. reprint ed. lib. bdg. 35.00 (*0-306-71708-5*) Da Capo.

American Minimal Music. Wim Mertens. (Illus.). 128p. reprint ed. pap. 12.50 (*0-912483-15-6*) Pro-Am Music.

American Mining Code: Embracing the United States, State, & Territorial Mining Laws, the Land Office Regulations, & a Digest of Federal & State Court & Land Department Decisions. Henry N. Copp. 160p. 1994. reprint ed. lib. bdg. 35.00 (*0-8377-2052-4*) Rothman.

American Minorities & Majorities: A Syllabus of United States History for Secondary Schools. William L. Katz & Warren J. Halliburton. LC 70-132694. 1970. 4.95 (*0-405-00283-1*); pap. 2.95 (*0-405-00282-3*) Ayer.

American Minority Relations. 4th ed. James V. Zanden. 576p. (C). 1983. text ed. write for info. (*0-07-554368-0*) McGraw.

American Mirror: Social, Ethical & Religious Aspects of American Literature, 1930-1940. Halford E. Luccock. LC 75-156806. 300p. 1971. reprint ed. lib. bdg. 60.50 (*0-8154-0385-2*) Cooper Sq.

American Mission in the Allied Control Commission for Bulgaria 1944-1947. Michael M. Boll. 1985. text ed. 48.00 (*0-88033-068-6*, 176) Col U Pr.

American Missionaries among the Bulgarians: 1858-1912. Tatyana Nestorova. 160p. 1987. text ed. 36.00 (*0-88033-114-3*, 218) East Eur Quarterly.

American Missionaries in China: Papers from Harvard Seminars. Ed. by Liu Kwang-Ching. LC 66-31226. (East Asian Monographs: No. 21). 316p. 1966. pap. 11.00 (*0-674-02600-4*) HUP.

American Missionary Community in China, 1895-1905. Sidney A. Forsythe. LC 70-178077. (East Asian Monographs: No. 43). 154p. 1971. pap. 11.00 (*0-674-02626-8*) HUP.

American Missions in Bicentennial Perspective. Ed. by R. Pierce Beaver. LC 77-7569. 438p. 1977. pap. 11.95 (*0-87808-153-4*) William Carey Lib.

American Missions in Syria. 2nd ed. Adnan Abu-Ghazaleh. 94p. (Orig.). 1990. pap. 12.50 (*0-915597-25-X*) Amana Bks.

American Mixed Border: Gardens for All Seasons. Ann Lovejoy. LC 92-27309. 240p. 1993. text ed. 35.00 (*0-02-575580-3*) Macmillan.

*__American Mixed Race: Exploring "Microdiversity"__ Naomi Zack. 420p. 1995. lib. bdg. 68.50 (*0-8476-8012-6*); pap. text ed. 26.95 (*0-8476-8013-4*) Rowman.

American Model of Revolutionary Leadership: George Washington & Other Founders. Ed. by Daniel J. Elazar & Ellis Katz. 264p. (C). 1991. lib. bdg. 55.00 (*0-8191-8350-4*); pap. text ed. 32.50 (*0-8191-8351-2*) U Pr of Amer.

American Model on the Scales of History. A. Kortunov & A. Nikitin. 232p. (C). 1985. 50.00 (*0-685-31596-7*, Pub. by Collets UK) Pro-Am Music.

American Modernity & Jewish Identity. Steven M. Cohen. 250p. 1983. pap. 14.95 (*0-422-77750-1*, NO.3495) Routledge Chapman & Hall.

*__American Mom: Motherhood, Politics & Humble Pie.__ Blakely. 1995. pap. 14.00 (*0-671-53520-X*) PB.

*__American Mom: Motherhood, Politics, & Humble Pie.__ Mary K. Blakely. LC 94-26098. 291p. 1994. 19.95 (*1-56512-052-3*) Algonquin Bks.

American Moment. Bill Harris. 1990. 12.99 (*0-517-02214-1*) Random Hse Value.

American Moment: American Poetry in the Mid-Century. Geoffrey Thurley. LC 77-91071. 1978. text ed. 35.00 (*0-312-02884-9*) St Martin.

American Monetary System: A Concise Survey of Its Evolution since 1896. Robert A. Degen. LC 86-46363. 256p. 1987. text ed. 35.00 (*0-669-15827-5*) Free Pr.

American Money & Banking. Maxwell J. Fry & Raburn M. Williams. LC 83-21619. (Illus.). 495p. reprint ed. pap. 141.10 (*0-8357-7520-8*, 2036015) Bks Demand.

American Money & the Weimar Republic: Economics & Politics on the Eve of the Great Depression. William C. McNeil. 320p. 1988. text ed. 50.50 (*0-231-06236-2*); pap. text ed. 16.00 (*0-231-06237-0*) Col U Pr.

American Monroe: The Making of a Body Politic. S. Paige Baty. LC 94-10258. 1995. 40.00 (*0-520-08805-0*); pap. 15.00 (*0-520-08806-9*) U CA Pr.

*__American Monument.__ Lee Friedlander. (Illus.). 77p. 1976. ring bd. 475.00 (*0-87130-043-5*) Res Art Media.

American Moralist: On Law, Ethics, & Government. George Anastaplo. 648p. (C). 1992. text ed. 110.00 (*0-8214-1001-6*) Ohio U Pr.

American Moralist: On Law, Ethics, & Government. George Anastaplo. LC 91-35715. 600p. (C). 1994. pap. text ed. 50.00x (*0-8214-1079-2*) Ohio U Pr.

American Mornings: Favorite Breakfast Recipes from Bed & Breakfast Inns. Tracy Winters & Phyllis Winters. LC 92-63198. (Illus.). 320p. (Orig.). 1993. pap. 12.95 (*0-9625329-6-7*) Winters IN.

*__American Mosaic: An In-Depth Report on the Advantage of Diversity in the U. S. Work Force.__ Anthony P. Carnevale & Susan C. Stone. LC 95-12618. 1995. 29.95 (*0-07-011377-7*) McGraw.

American Mosaic: Church Planting in Ethnic America. Oscar Romo. (Orig.). 1993. pap. 8.95 (*0-8054-6070-5*) Broadman.

An Asterisk (*) at the beginning of an entry indicates that the title is appearing in BIP for the first time.

An Asterisk (*) at the beginning of an entry indicates that the title is appearing in BIP for the first time.

253

A

American National Standard for Directories of Libraries & Information Centers, Z39.10. 1971. 6.00 (*0-686-01887-7*, R1977) ANSI.

American National Standard for Extended Latin Alphabet Coded Character Set for Bibliographic Use, Z39.47. 1985. 9.00 (*0-318-22734-7*) ANSI.

American National Standard for Format for Scientific & Technical Translations, Z39.31. 1976. 6.00 (*0-686-28237-X*) ANSI.

American National Standard for Guidelines for Organization, Preparation & Production of Scientific & Technical Reports, Z39.18-1987. 14.00 (*0-686-15226-3*) ANSI.

American National Standard for Guidelines for Thesaurus Structure, Construction & Use, Z39.19. 1980. 7.00 (*0-686-15227-1*) ANSI.

American National Standard for Identification Code for the Book Industry, Z39.43. 1980. 6.00 (*0-686-38030-4*, Z39.43) ANSI.

American National Standard for Information on Microfiche Headings, Z39.32. 1981. 6.00 (*0-686-40420-3*, 239.32) ANSI.

American National Standard for International Standard Serial Numbering, Z39.9. 1979. 6.00 (*0-686-01886-9*) ANSI.

American National Standard for Library Statistics, Z39.7. 1983. 13.00 (*0-686-01884-2*) ANSI.

American National Standard for Metric Practice: ANSI-IEEE Std. 268, 1992. Institute of Electrical & Electronics Engineers, Inc. Staff. (Illus.). 80p. (Orig.). 1992. pap. 35.00 (*1-55937-246-X*, SH15529) IEEE Standards.

American National Standard for Order Form for Single Titles of Library Materials in 3-Inch by 5-Inch Format, Z39.30. 1982. 7.00 (*0-686-38032-0*) ANSI.

American National Standard for Patent Documents-Identification of Bibliographic Data, Z39.46. Council of National Library & Information Associations (U.S.). Secretariat & American National Standards Committee on Library Work & information Science. 1983. 6.00 (*0-685-07730-6*) ANSI.

American National Standard for Periodicals: Format & Arrangement, Z39.1. 1977. 7.00 (*0-686-02641-1*) ANSI.

American National Standard for Permanence of Paper for Printed Library Materials, Z39.48. 1984. 6.00 (*0-685-18382-3*) ANSI.

American National Standard for Proof Corrections, Z39.22. 1981. 8.00 (*0-686-15230-1*) ANSI.

American National Standard for Romanization of Hebrew, Z39.25. 1975. 7.00 (*0-686-15232-8*) ANSI.

American National Standard for Serials Holding Statements, Z39.44. 1986. 14.00 (*0-318-22731-2*) ANSI.

American National Standard for Standard Address Number for the Publishing Industry. Niso. LC 93-149. (National Information Standards Ser.). 18p. (C). 1993. pap. 20.00 (*0-88738-933-3*) Transaction Pubs.

American National Standard for Standard Order Form for Multiple Titles of Library Materials Z39.52. 1987. 8.00 (*0-318-23470-X*) ANSI.

American National Standard for Standard Technical Report Number, (STRN), Z39.23. 1983. 6.00 (*0-686-15231-X*) ANSI.

American National Standard for Structure for the Representation of Names of Countries Dependencies & Areas of Special Sovereignty for Information Interchange , Z39.27. 1984. 6.00 (*0-686-16672-8*) ANSI.

American National Standard for Synoptics, Z39.34. 1977. 7.00 (*0-686-02642-X*) ANSI.

American National Standard for System for the Romanization of Arabic, Z39.12. 1972. 6.00 (*0-686-01889-3*) ANSI.

American National Standard for System for the Romanization of Japanese, Z39.11. 1972. 6.00 (*0-686-01888-5*) ANSI.

American National Standard for System for the Romanization of Lao, Khmer, & Pali, Z39.35. 1979. 7.00 (*0-686-28238-8*) ANSI.

American National Standard for System for the Romanization of Slavic Cyrillic Characters, Z39.24. 1976. 6.00 (*0-686-16673-6*) ANSI.

American National Standard for the Development of Identification Codes for Use by the Bibliographic Community: Z39.33. 1977. 6.00 (*0-686-10588-5*) ANSI.

American National Standard for the Preparation of Scientific Papers for Written or Oral Presentation, Z39.16. 1979. 7.00 (*0-686-05270-6*) ANSI.

American National Standard for Title Leaves of a Book, Z39.15. 1980. 6.00 (*0-686-01892-3*, Z39.15) ANSI.

American National Standard for Trade Catalogs, Z39.6. 1983. 6.00 (*0-686-01883-4*) ANSI.

American National Standard for Voltage or Current Reference Devices: Solid-State Devices. 1984. pap. 25.00 (*0-87664-840-5*, ANSI C100.6-3) Instru Soc.

American National Standard for Writing Abstracts, Z39.14. 1979. 7.00 (*0-686-01891-5*) ANSI.

American National Standard Guide for Electrostatic Discharge Test Methodologies & Criteria for Electronic Equipment: ANSI C63.16-1993. Institute of Electrical & Electronics Engineers, Inc. Staff. (Illus.). 64p. (Orig.). 1994. pap. 47.00 (*1-55937-403-9*, SH17111) IEEE Standards.

American National Standard Mathematical Signs & Symbols for Use in Physical Sciences & Technology. Institute of Electrical & Electronics Engineers, Inc. Staff. 36p. 1993. pap. write for info. (*1-55937-318-0*, SH 16207) IEEE Standards.

American National Standard Nomenclature & Definitions for Illuminating Engineering. rev. ed. Illuminating Engineering Society of North America, Nonmenclature Committee. (Illus.). 48p. 1986. pap. text ed. 30.00 (*0-87995-022-6*, RP-161-186) Illum Eng.

American National Standard Practice for Industrial Lighting. rev. ed. Ed. by John Kaufman. 50p. (C). 1991. pap. 28.00 (*0-87995-032-3*, RP-7-91) Illum Eng.

American National Standard Price for Roadway Lighting (Reaffirmed 1991) 60p. 1991. 25.00 (*0-87995-013-7*, RP-8-83) Illum Eng.

American National Standard Safety Requirements for Cleaning & Finishing Castings ANSI Z241.3. 35p. 1989. pap. 10.00 (*0-317-59832-5*, EC8021) Am Foundrymen.

American National Standard Safety Requirements for Melting & Pouring of Metals ANSI Z241.2. 40p. 1989. pap. 10.00 (*0-317-59831-7*, EC8200) Am Foundrymen.

American National Standard Safety Requirements for Sand Preparation, Mold & Coremaking in the Sand Foundry Industry ANSI Z241.1. 40p. 1989. pap. 10.00 (*0-317-59830-9*, EC8101) Am Foundrymen.

American National Standard System for the Romanization of Armenian, Z39.37. 1979. 6.00 (*0-686-28239-6*) ANSI.

American National Standards for Information System - Programming Languages - MUMPS. MUMPS Development Committee Staff. 1990. 30.00 (*0-918118-37-9*) M Technol.

American National Standards Practice for Tunnel Lighting. IES Subcommittee on Tunnels & Underpasses. (Recommended Practice Ser.). 16p. (Orig.). 1987. pap. text ed. 25.00 (*0-87995-026-9*, RP-22-1987) Illum Eng.

American Nations Past & Present. Incl. Barbados. 1976. pap. 1.00 (*0-8270-4630-8*); Bolivia. 1973. pap. 1.00 (*0-8270-4635-9*); Brazil. 1975. pap. 1.00 (*0-8270-4640-5*); Canada. 1974. pap. 1.00 (*0-8270-4645-6*); Chile. 1971. pap. 1.00 (*0-8270-4650-2*); Colombia. 1977. pap. 1.00 (*0-318-54714-7*); Costa Rica. 1973. pap. 1.00 (*0-8270-4660-X*); Dominican Republic. 1976. pap. 1.00 (*0-8270-4665-0*); Ecuador. 1972. pap. 1.00 (*0-318-54715-5*); Salvador. 1979. pap. 1.00 (*0-318-54716-3*); Guatemala. 1972. pap. 1.00 (*0-318-54717-1*); Haiti. 1979. pap. 1.00 (*0-8270-4685-5*); Jamaica. 1974. pap. 1.00 (*0-8270-4690-1*); Mexico. 1978. pap. 1.00 (*0-8270-4925-0*); Nicaragua. 1978. pap. 1.00 (*0-8270-4695-2*); Panama. 1971. pap. 1.00 (*0-8270-4700-2*); Paraguay. 1974. pap. 1.00 (*0-8270-4705-3*); Peru. 1971. pap. 1.00 (*0-8270-4710-X*); Trinidad & Tobago. 1974. pap. 1.00 (*0-8270-4715-0*); Venezuela. 1978. pap. 1.00 (*0-8270-4915-3*); (Image Ser.). (Illus.). Set pap. write for info. (*0-318-54713-9*) OAS.

American Native Paintings. Ed. by Deborah Chotner. (Collections of the National Gallery of Art Systematic Catalogue). (Illus.). 670p. (C). 1993. 165.00 (*0-521-44301-6*) Cambridge U Pr.

American Nativism, Eighteen Thirty to Eighteen Sixty. Ira M. Leonard & Robert D. Parmet. LC 71-156750. (Anvil Ser.). 192p. 1971. pap. 10.50 (*0-88275-901-9*) Krieger.

American Natural History: A Guide to the Microfilm Collection. 33p. 1978. 40.00 (*0-89235-052-0*) Res Pubns CT.

American Natural History: Mastogogy & Rambles of a Naturalist, Part 1, 3 vols. in one. John D. Godman. LC 73-17821. (Natural Sciences in America Ser.). (Illus.). 1079p. 1974. reprint ed. 81.95 (*0-405-05737-7*) Ayer.

American Natural History Studies: The Bairdian Period. Ed. by Keir B. Sterling. LC 73-17793. (Natural Sciences in America Ser.). (Illus.). 912p. 1974. reprint ed. 70.95 (*0-405-05703-2*) Ayer.

American Nature Guides: Shore Birds. 1991. 9.98 (*0-8317-6962-9*) Smithmark.

American Nature Writing, 1994. Ed. by John A. Murray. 288p. (Orig.). 1994. pap. 12.00 (*0-87156-479-3*) Sierra.

***American Nature Writing, 1994.** Ed. by John A. Murray. 1995. 21.00 (*0-8446-6858-3*) Peter Smith.

***American Nature Writing 1995.** Ed. by John Murray. 1995. pap. 12.00 (*0-87156-438-6*) Sierra.

American Naval Biography. John Frost. 1980. lib. bdg. 79.95 (*0-8490-3155-9*) Gordon Pr.

American Naval Diplomat in Revolutionary Russia: The Life & Times of Vice Admiral Newton A. McCully, 1867-1951. Charles J. Weeks, Jr. LC 92-19274. 348p. 1993. 39.95 (*1-55750-920-4*) Naval Inst Pr.

American Naval Heritage in Brief. 3rd ed. Paolo E. Coletta. 654p. (C). 1987. text ed. 66.50 (*0-8191-5596-9*); pap. 42.00 (*0-8191-5597-7*) U Pr of Amer.

American Naval History: An Illustrated Chronology of the U. S. Navy & Marine Corps, 1775 to Present. 2nd ed. Jack Sweetman. LC 90-29872. (Illus.). 384p. (YA). (gr. 7-12). 1991. 45.00 (*1-55750-785-6*) Naval Inst Pr.

American Navy, Seventeen Eighty-Nine to Eighteen Sixty: A Bibliography. Myron J. Smith, Jr. LC 73-18464. (American Naval Bibliography Ser.: Vol. 2). 489p. 1974. 35.00 (*0-8108-0659-2*) Scarecrow.

American Negro. William H. Thomas. LC 74-95449. (Studies in Black History & Culture: No. 54). 1970. reprint ed. lib. bdg. 75.00 (*0-8383-1206-3*) M S G Haskell Hse.

American Negro: A Study in Racial Crossing. Melville J. Herskovits. LC 85-7671. 112p. 1985. reprint ed. text ed. 49.75 (*0-313-24795-1*, HEAN, Greenwood Pr) Greenwood.

American Negro: A Study in Racial Crossing. Melville J. Herskovits. (BCL1 - U. S. History Ser.). 92p. 1991. reprint ed. lib. bdg. 59.00 (*0-7812-6081-7*) Rprt Serv.

American Negro: History & Literature, Ser. 1, 44 bks, Set. Ed. by William L. Katz. 1968. 2,448.00 (*0-405-01800-2*) Ayer.

American Negro: Old World Background & New World Experience. rev. ed. Rayford W. Logan & Irving S. Cohen. Ed. by Howard R. Anderson. (Illus.). (gr. 7-12). 1970. pap. 20.12 (*0-395-03157-5*) HM.

***American Negro Academy: Voice of the Talented Tenth.** fac. ed. Alfred A. Moss. LC 80-18026. 349p. 1981. reprint ed. pap. 99.50 (*0-7837-7806-6*, 2047562) Bks Demand.

American Negro Academy Occasional Papers Nos. 1-22. American Negro Academy Staff. LC 77-94134. (American Negro: His History & Literature, Ser. No. 3). 1970. 24.95 (*0-405-01913-0*) Ayer.

American Negro As Dependent, Defective & Delinquent. Charles H. McCord. 1973. 59.95 (*0-87968-609-X*) Gordon Pr.

American Negro Folksongs. Newman I. White. 501p. 1990. reprint ed. lib. bdg. 99.00 (*0-7812-9124-0*) Rprt Serv.

***American Negro Poetry: An Anthology.** Intro. by Arna Bontemps. 256p. Date not set. 10.00 (*0-8090-1564-1*) FS&G.

American Negro Revolution. Benjamin Muse. 1970. pap. 2.95 (*0-8065-0003-4*, Citadel Pr) Carol Pub Group.

American Negro Revolution: From Nonviolence to Black Power, 1963-1967. Benjamin Muse. LC 68-27350. 359p. reprint ed. 102.40 (*0-8357-9194-7*, 2015831) Bks Demand.

American Negro Slave Revolts. 50th aniversary ed. Herbert Aptheker. LC 83-7063. 428p. 1993. pap. 9.95 (*0-7178-0605-7*) Intl Pubs Co.

American Negro Slavery. Ulrich B. Phillips. 26.75 (*0-8446-1348-7*) Peter Smith.

American Negro Slavery. 3rd ed. Allen Weinstein et al. 1979. pap. text ed. 15.95 (*0-19-502470-2*) OUP.

American Negro Slavery. Ulrich B. Phillips. (History - United States Ser.). 529p. 1992. reprint ed. lib. bdg. 99.00 (*0-7812-6155-4*) Rprt Serv.

American Negro Slavery: A Survey of the Supply, Employment, & Control of Negro Labor As Determined by the Plantation Regime. Ulrich B. Phillips. LC 66-31730. (Illus.). xxvi, 530p. 1966. pap. text ed. 16.95 (*0-8071-0109-5*) La State U Pr.

American Negro Slavery & Abolition. W. Moore. LC 73-148362. 1971. 29.95 (*0-89388-000-0*); pap. 14.95 (*0-89388-001-9*) Okpaku Communications.

American Negro Slavery & Abolition: A Sociological Study. Wilbert E. Moore. Ed. by Harriet Zuckerman & Robert K. Merton. LC 79-9015. (Dissertations on Sociology Ser.). 1980. lib. bdg. 19.95 (*0-405-12982-3*) Ayer.

American Neighborhoods & Residential Differentiation. Michael J. White. LC 86-42951. (Population of the United States in the 1980s: A Census Monograph Ser.). 400p. 1988. text ed. 39.95 (*0-87154-922-0*) Russell Sage.

American Neighbors. rev. ed. Ed. by John P. Augelli. LC 85-81413. (World Cultures Ser.). (Illus.). (YA). (gr. 5 up). 1986. teacher ed 8.95 (*0-88296-355-4*); text ed. 12.95 (*0-88296-087-3*); 6.95 (*0-934291-49-7*); 9.95 (*0-934291-50-0*) Gateway Pr MI.

American Neo-Colonialism: Its Emergence in the Philippines & Asia. William J. Pomeroy. LC 71-108385. 255p. reprint ed. pap. 72.70 (*0-8357-5383-2*, 2020636) Bks Demand.

American Neptune Pictorial Supplements, Vol. 2. Antoine Roux. 1960. pap. 3.95 (*0-87577-091-6*, Peabody Museum) Peabody Essex Mus.

American Neptune Pictorial Supplements, Vol. 6. Steamships. 1964. pap. 3.95 (*0-87577-093-2*, Peabody Museum) Peabody Essex Mus.

American Neptune Pictorial Supplements, Vol. 7. Fitz Hugh Lane. 1965. pap. 3.95 (*0-87577-094-0*, Peabody Museum) Peabody Essex Mus.

American Neptune Pictorial Supplements, Vol. 8. American & Canadian Fishing Schooners. 1966. pap. 3.95 (*0-87577-095-9*, Peabody Museum) Peabody Essex Mus.

American Neptune Pictorial Supplements, Vol. 10. Penobscot Maine Museum Searsport, Maine. 1968. pap. 3.95 (*0-87577-097-5*, Peabody Museum) Peabody Essex Mus.

American Neptune Pictorial Supplements, Vol. 12. Yachting. 1970. pap. 3.95 (*0-87577-099-1*, Peabody Museum) Peabody Essex Mus.

American Neptune Pictorial Supplements, Vol. 13. Life Between Decks Under Sail. 1971. pap. 3.95 (*0-87577-100-9*, Peabody Museum) Peabody Essex Mus.

American Neptune Pictorial Supplements, Vol. 14. Michele F. Corne. pap. 3.95 (*0-87577-101-7*, Peabody Museum) Peabody Essex Mus.

American Neptune Pictorial Supplements, Vol. 15 Whaling Vessels. 1973. pap. 3.95 (*0-87577-102-5*, Peabody Museum) Peabody Essex Mus.

American Neptune Pictorial Supplements, Vol. 16 Antonio N. G. Jacobsen. 1974. pap. 3.95 (*0-87577-103-3*, Peabody Museum) Peabody Essex Mus.

American Neptune Pictorial Supplements, Vol. 1: Prints, Paintings, Photographs of American Clipper Ships. 1959. pap. 3.95 (*0-87577-090-8*, Peabody Museum) Peabody Essex Mus.

American Neptune Pictorial Supplements, Vol. 17: Instruments of Navigation. (Illus.). 1975. pap. 3.95 (*0-87577-104-1*, Peabody Museum) Peabody Essex Mus.

American Neptune Pictorial Supplements, Vol. 18: Marine Paintings of John Faunce Leavitt. 1976. pap. 3.95 (*0-87577-105-X*, Peabody Museum) Peabody Essex Mus.

American Neptune Pictorial Supplements, Vol. 19: The Art of the Shipcarvers at the Peabody Museum of Salem, Vol. 19. 1977. pap. 3.95 (*0-87577-106-8*, Peabody Museum) Peabody Essex Mus.

American Neptune Pictorial Supplements, Vol. 20: Marine Paintings of William Henry Luscomb & Benjamin Franklin West of Salem. 1978. pap. 3.95 (*0-87577-107-6*, Peabody Museum) Peabody Essex Mus.

American Nervousness, Its Causes & Consequences: A Supplement to Nervous Exhaustion. George M. Beard. LC 72-180552. (Medicine & Society in America Ser.). 382p. 1972. reprint ed. 24.95 (*0-405-03932-8*) Ayer.

American Nervousness, 1903: An Anecdotal History. Tom Lutz. LC 90-55737. (Illus.). 366p. 1991. 36.95 (*0-8014-2581-6*) Cornell U Pr.

American Nervousness, 1903: An Anecdotal History. Tom Lutz. LC 90-55737. (Illus.). 344p. 1993. pap. 14.95 (*0-8014-9901-1*) Cornell U Pr.

American Neutrality in 1793: A Study in Cabinet Government. Charles M. Thomas. LC 31-33753. (Columbia University. Studies in the Social Sciences: No. 350). reprint ed. 22.50 (*0-404-51350-6*) AMS Pr.

American Neutrality, Trial & Failure. Charles G. Fenwick. LC 78-138609. 190p. 1974. reprint ed. text ed. 49.75 (*0-8371-5719-6*, FEAN, Greenwood Pr) Greenwood.

American Newness: Culture & Politics in the Age of Emerson. Irving Howe. LC 85-24903. (William E. Massey Sr. Lectures in the History of American Civilization). 112p. 1986. 20.00 (*0-674-02640-3*) HUP.

American Newspaper Journalists, Eighteen Seventy-Three to Nineteen Hundred, Vol. 23. Ed. by Perry J. Ashley. (Dictionary of Literary Biography Ser.: Vol. 23). 432p. 1983. 128.00 (*0-8103-1145-3*) Gale.

American Newspaper Journalists, Nineteen One to Nineteen Twenty-Five, Vol. 25. Ed. by Perry J. Ashley. (Dictionary of Literary Biography Ser.: Vol. 25). (Illus.). 400p. 1984. 128.00 (*0-8103-1704-4*) Gale.

American Newspaper Journalists, Nineteen Twenty-Six to Nineteen Fifty, Vol. 29. Perry J. Ashley. (Dictionary of Literary Biography Ser.: Vol. 29). 424p. 1984. 128.00 (*0-8103-1707-9*) Gale.

American Newspaper Journalists, Sixteen Ninety to Eighteen Seventy-Two, Vol. 43. Ed. by Perry J. Ashley. (Dictionary of Literary Biography Ser.). 537p. 1985. 128.00 (*0-8103-1721-4*) Gale.

American Newspapers, 1821-1936: A Union List of Files Available in the United States & Canada. Ed. by W. Gregory. LC 37-12783. 1937. 198.00 (*0-527-02250-0*) Periodicals Srv.

American Nicknames. 2nd ed. George E. Shankle. LC 55-5038. 524p. 1955. 44.00 (*0-8242-0004-7*) Wilson.

American Night. Axel Crieger. (Illus.). 156p. 1991. 40.00 (*0-9627387-1-9*) Seven Wolves.

American Night. Jim Morrison. 1993. pap. 3.99 (*0-517-08683-2*) Random Hse Value.

American Night: The Writings of Jim Morrison. Jim Morrison. LC 90-50901. 224p. 1991. pap. 9.00 (*0-679-73462-7*, Vin) Random.

American Night Cry: A Trilogy. Phillip H. Dean. 1990. pap. 4.75 (*0-8222-0032-5*) Dramatists Play.

American Nightmare. Ryder Stacy. (Doomsday Warrior Ser.: No. 10). 272p. 1987. pap. 2.50 (*0-8217-2021-X*) Zebra.

American Nineteen Sixties: Imaginative Acts in a Decade of Change. Jerome Klinkowitz. LC 80-11943. 129p. reprint ed. pap. 36.80 (*0-8357-5384-0*, 2029779) Bks Demand.

American Ninja. James A. Johnson & John R. Ormsby, Jr. LC 84-46168. (Illus.). 112p. 1984. pap. 7.95 (*0-943736-03-X*) Ormsby.

American Noise. Campbell McGrath. LC 93-20698. 1994. 23.00 (*0-88001-335-4*) Ecco Pr.

***American Noise: Poems.** Campbell McGrath. 1994. pap. 11.00 (*0-88001-374-5*) Ecco Pr.

American Non-Fiction, 1900-1950. May Brodbeck et al. LC 70-106668. 198p. 1970. reprint ed. text ed. 49.75 (*0-8371-3420-X*, BRNF, Greenwood Pr) Greenwood.

American Nonpublic Schools: Patterns of Diversity. Otto F. Kraushaar. LC 75-186475. 403p. reprint ed. pap. 114.90 (*0-8357-5385-9*, 2024149) Bks Demand.

American Northwest: A History of Washington & Oregon. Gordon Dodds. LC 85-2072. (Illus.). 374p. (Orig.). (C). 1986. text ed. write for info. (*0-88273-239-0*); pap. text ed. write for info. (*0-88273-238-2*) Forum Pr IL.

American Nostalgia. Charlene Beeler. (Simulation Ser.). 62p. 1991. pap. 19.95 (*1-882664-01-9*) Prufrock Pr.

American Notebooks. Nathaniel Hawthorne. Ed. by Claude M. Simpson. LC 70-150222. (Centenary Edition of the Works of Nathaniel Hawthorne: Vol. 8). (Illus.). 849p. 1972. 85.00 (*0-8142-0159-8*) Ohio St U Pr.

American Notes. Len Jenkin. 1989. pap. 4.75 (*0-8222-0033-3*) Dramatists Play.

American Notes. James L. Roberts. (Orig.). 1965. pap. 4.50 (*0-8220-0164-0*) Cliffs.

American Notes. Charles Dickens. 92p. 1993. reprint ed. lib. bdg. 69.00 (*0-7812-5121-4*); reprint ed. lib. bdg. 89.00 (*0-7812-5356-X*) Rprt Serv.

American Notes. Rudyard Kipling. LC 73-13159. (Foreign Travelers in America, 1810-1935 Ser.). (Illus.). 142p. 1974. reprint ed. 16.95 (*0-405-05463-7*) Ayer.

American Notes. Rudyard Kipling. LC 72-5679. (Select Bibliographies Reprint Ser.). 1977. reprint ed. 20.95 (*0-8369-6917-0*) Ayer.

American Notes: Selected Essays. Daniel Aaron. 288p. 1994. text ed. 29.95 (*1-55553-195-4*) NE U Pr.

American Notes & Pictures from Italy **see Oxford Illustrated Dickens**

American Notes & Queries Supplement, Vol. 1. Ed. by John L. Cutler & Lawrence S. Thompson. LC 77-93778. (Studies in American & English Literature). 1978. 18.50 (*0-87875-139-4*) Whitston Pub.

American Notes & Queries Supplement, First Person Female American: A Selected & Annotated Bibliography of the Autobiographies of American Women Living after 1950, Vol. II. Ed. by Carolyn H. Rhodes. LC 77-93778. 453p. 1980. 28.50 (*0-87875-140-8*) Whitston Pub.

An Asterisk (*) at the beginning of an entry indicates that the title is appearing in BIP for the first time.

***American Paintings from the Parrish Art Museum.** Intro. by Ronald G. Pisano. LC 82-61450. (Illus.). 54p. (Orig.). (C). 1982. pap. 10.00 (*0-943526-27-2*) Parrish Art.

American Paintings in the Detroit Institute of Arts, Vol. 1: Works by Artists Born Before 1816. Mary Black et al. LC 90-85027. (Collections of the Detroit Institute of Arts). (Illus.). 368p. 1991. 75.00 (*1-55595-044-2*) Hudson Hills.

American Paintings in the Metropolitan Museum of Art: A Catalogue of Works by Artists Born Between 1846 & 1864, Vol. 3. Doreen B. Burke. LC 80-81074. 528p. 1980. 110.00 (*0-691-03961-5*) Princeton U Pr.

American Paintings in the Metropolitan Museum of Art, Vol. 2: A Catalogue of Works by Artists Born Between 1816 & 1845. Natalie Spassky et al. (Illus.). 496p. 1984. text ed. 110.00x (*0-691-04004-4*) Princeton U Pr.

American Paintings in the Pennsylvania Academy of the Fine Arts. Nancy Fresella-Lee. Ed. by Jacolyn A. Mott. LC 89-16205. (Illus.). 222p. 1989. pap. 22.95 (*0-295-96862-1*) U of Wash Pr.

American Paintings in the Pennsylvania Academy of the Fine Arts: An Illustrated Checklist. Ed. by Jacolyn A. Mott. (Illus.). 204p. (Orig.). 1989. pap. 22.95 (*0-943836-11-5*) Penn Acad Art.

American Paintings in the Rhode Island Historical Society. Frank Goodyear, Jr. LC 73-91890. (Illus.). 116p. 1974. 10.00 (*0-917012-33-X*) RI Hist Soc.

American Paintings in the Rhode Island Historical Society. Frank H. Goodyear, Jr. (Museum Treasures Ser.). (Illus.). 126p. 1974. lib. bdg. 14.50 (*0-685-21323-4*) RI Pubns Soc.

***American Paintings of the Eighteenth Century.** Ellen G. Miles. LC 94-37473. (Collection of the National Gallery of Art, Systematic Catalogue Ser.). 1994. write for info. (*0-89468-210-5*) Natl Gallery Art.

American Paintings, Seventeen Fifty to Nineteen Hundred: From the Collection of the Baltimore Museum of Art. Sona K. Johnston. LC 82-70391. (Illus.). 184p. 1983. pap. 9.98 (*0-912298-53-7*) Baltimore Mus.

American Paintings, Watercolors & Drawings from the Collection of Rita & Daniel Fraad. Linda Ayres & Jane Myers. LC 85-70941. (Illus.). 128p. 1985. pap. 12.95 (*0-88360-075-7*) Amon Carter.

American Panorama, East of the Mississippi. Holiday Magazine Editors. LC 72-4557. (Essay Index Reprint Ser.). 1977. reprint ed. 36.95 (*0-8369-2950-0*) Ayer.

American Paper Currency: Series One, Historical Sketches of the Paper Currency of the American Colonies Prior to the Adoption of the Federal Constitution: Series Two, Continental Paper Money, 2 Vols. in 1. Henry Phillips. LC 68-18223. (Library of Money & Banking History). 1972. reprint ed. lib. bdg. 49.50 (*0-678-00787-X*) Kelley.

American Papyrus. Stephen Sills. 64p. 1990. pap. 6.95 (*0-932616-33-X*) New Poets Chestnut Hills.

American Paradise. Ryder Stacy. (Doomsday Warrior Ser.: No. 13). 1988. pap. 2.95 (*0-8217-2338-3*) Zebra.

American Paradox: Censorship in a Nation of Speech. Patrick Garry. LC 92-31846. 200p. 1993. text ed. 22.95 (*0-275-94522-7*, C4522, Praeger Pubs) Greenwood.

American Parties in Decline. 2nd ed. William Crotty & Gary C. Jacobson. (C). 1987. pap. text ed. 14.25 (*0-673-39430-1*) HarpCollege.

American Party System & the American People. 3rd ed. Fred I. Greenstein & Frank B. Feigert. (Illus.). 190p. (C). 1985. text ed. write for info. (*0-318-58104-3*) P-H.

***American Passages.** William Bryans et al. 320p. (C). 1994. per., pap. text ed. 26.95 (*0-7872-0197-9*) Kendall-Hunt.

American Passenger Arrival Records: A Guide to the Records of Immigrants Arriving at American Ports by Sail & Steam. enl. ed. Michael Tepper. (Illus.). 144p. 1993. 19.95 (*0-8063-1380-3*, 5735) Genealog Pub.

American Passenger Ships: The Ocean Lines & Liners, 1875-1983. Frederick E. Emmons. LC 83-50652. (Illus.). 192p. 1985. 50.00 (*0-87413-248-7*) U Delaware Pr.

American Passport. R. D. Lakin. 60p. 1992. 30.00 (*0-930126-38-6*) Typographeum.

American Past: A Brief History. Joseph R. Conlin. 672p. (C). 1991. pap. text ed. 33.25 (*0-15-502382-9*) HB Coll Pubs.

American Past: A Survey of American History. Thomas H. Greer & Gavin Lewis. 1993. lib. bdg. write for info. (*0-15-500613-4*) HB Coll Pubs.

American Past: A Survey of American History. 3rd ed. Joseph R. Conlin. 964p. (C). 1990. text ed. 46.00 (*0-15-502376-4*); pap. text ed. 28.50 (*0-15-502381-0*); student ed write for info. (*0-318-67030-5*) HB Coll Pubs.

American Past: A Survey of American History since 1865, Chapters 26-51. 3rd ed. Joseph R. Conlin. 539p. (C). 1989. pap. text ed. 34.00 (*0-15-502378-0*) HB Coll Pubs.

American Past: A Survey of American History to 1877, Chapters 1-26. 3rd ed. Joseph R. Conlin. 489p. (C). 1989. pap. text ed. 34.00 (*0-15-502377-2*) HB Coll Pubs.

***American Past & Present.** 4th ed. Robert A. Divine et al. LC 94-39705. (C). 1994. text ed. write for info. (*0-673-99192-X*) HarpCollege.

***American Past & Present, Vol. 1.** 4th ed. Robert A. Divine et al. (C). 1994. text ed. write for info. (*0-673-99193-8*) HarpCollege.

***American Past & Present, Vol. 1.** 4th ed. Smith et al. (C). 1995. student ed, text ed. 14.25 (*0-673-99239-X*) HarpCollege.

***American Past & Present, Vol. 2.** Divine et al. (C). 1994. text ed. write for info. (*0-673-99194-6*) HarpCollege.

***American Past & Present, Vol. 2.** 4th ed. Smith et al. (C). 1995. student ed, text ed. 14.25 (*0-673-99240-3*) HarpCollege.

American Pastels in the Metropolitan Museum of Art. Doreen Bolger et al. 1989. 39.50 (*0-87099-547-2*, Abrams) Metro Mus Art.

American Patchwork Quilt Designs. Ondori Publishing Company Editors. (Illus.). 78p. (Orig.). 1987. pap. 13.95 (*0-87040-744-9*) Japan Pubns USA.

American Patented Brace, 1829-1924: An Illustrated Directory of Patents. Ronald W. Pearson. (Illus.). 192p. (Orig.). 1994. pap. 22.95 (*1-879335-48-4*) Astragal Pr.

American Patriotic Prose & Verse. Ed. by Ruth D. Stevens & David H. Stevens. LC 77-133074. (Granger Index Reprint Ser.). 1977. 15.95 (*0-8369-6204-4*) Ayer.

American Patriotism, & Other Social Studies. Hugo Munsterberg. LC 68-22934. (Essay Index Reprint Ser.). 1977. 19.95 (*0-8369-0726-4*) Ayer.

American Patriots & the Rituals of Revolution. Peter Shaw. LC 80-18657. 279p. reprint ed. pap. 79.60 (*0-7837-4124-3*, 2057947) Bks Demand.

American Peace Movement: Ideals & Activism. Charles Chatfield. (Social Movements Past & Present Ser.). 226p. 1992. text ed. 24.95 (*0-8057-3851-7*, Twayne); pap. 13.95 (*0-8057-3852-5*, Twayne) Macmillan.

American Peace Movement: References & Resources. Charles F. Howlett. 300p. 1991. text ed. 39.95 (*0-8161-1836-1*, Hall Reference) Macmillan.

American Peace Movement & Social Reform, 1898-1918. C. Roland Marchand. LC 70-166382. 360p. 1972. 67.50x (*0-691-04609-3*) Princeton U Pr.

***American Peace Movement & Social Reform, 1898-1918.** C. Roland Marchand. LC 70-166382. Date not set. reprint ed. pap. 131.40 (*0-7837-9379-0*, 2060123) Bks Demand.

American Peace Movement in the Twentieth Century. Christine A. Lunardini. (Clio Companions Ser.). 269p. 1994. lib. bdg. 55.00 (*0-87436-714-X*) ABC-CLIO.

American Peace Movements: History, Root Causes, & Future. David Adams. (Illus.). 46p. (Orig.). 1985. pap. 2.00 (*0-9619209-1-2*) D Adams.

American Peace Movements: History, Root Causes, & Future. David Adams. (Illus.). 46p. (Orig.). (C). 1985. pap. text ed. 1.20 (*0-9619209-0-4*) D Adams.

American Peace Society: A Centennial History. Edson L. Whitney. LC 77-137562. (Peace Movement in America Ser.). 360p. 1972. reprint ed. lib. bdg. 41.95 (*0-89198-092-X*) Ozer.

American Peace Writers, Editors, & Periodicals: A Dictionary. Nancy L. Roberts. LC 90-23169. 408p. 1991. text ed. 69.50 (*0-313-26842-8*, RPB, Greenwood Pr) Greenwood.

American Pediatric Urology. Frank Hinman. (Illus.). 287p. 1991. 75.00 (*0-930405-44-7*) Norman SF.

American Pediatrics: The Social Dynamics of Professionalism, 1880-1980. Sydney A. Halpern. 256p. (C). 1988. 37.50 (*0-520-05195-5*) U CA Pr.

American Penmanship Eighteen Hundred to Eighteen Fifty: A History of Writing & a Bibliography of Copybooks from Jenkins to Spencer. Ray Nash. LC 78-106556. 303p. 1969. 27.50 (*0-912296-10-0*, U Pr of Va) Am Antiquarian.

American Pentecostal Movement: A Bibliographic Essay. David W. Faupel. LC 76-361994. (Occasional Bibliographic Papers of the B. L. Fisher Library: No. 2). 56p. 1972. 3.00 (*0-914368-01-X*) Asbury Theological.

American People, 2 vols. Incl. Vol. I. To 1877. David Burner et al. 342p. 1980. pap. text ed. 11.95 (*0-9603726-2-8*); Vol. II. From 1860. David Burner et al. 440p. 1980. pap. text ed. 11.95 (*0-9603726-3-6*); (Illus.). (Orig.). (C). 1980. Combined Edition. Set pap. text ed. 16.95 (*0-9603726-0-1*) Brandywine Press.

American People. 3rd ed. Gary B. Nash et al. (C). 1993. Set. text ed. 58.00 (*0-06-501055-8*); Vol. I Study guide. 19.50 (*0-06-501058-2*); Vol. II Study guide. 19.50 (*0-06-501059-0*) HarpCollege.

American People, I. 3rd ed. Gary B. Nash et al. (C). 1993. text ed. 43.50 (*0-06-501056-6*) HarpCollege.

American People, II. 3rd ed. Gary B. Nash et al. (C). 1993. text ed. 43.50 (*0-06-501057-4*) HarpCollege.

American People: A History. Arthur S. Link et al. LC 80-69272. (Illus.). 1008p. (C). 1981. text ed. write for info. (*0-88295-804-6*) Harlan Davidson.

American People: A History, Vol. 1 to 1877. 2nd rev. ed. Arthur S. Link et al. LC 86-24261. (Illus.). 504p. (C). 1987. pap. text ed. write for info. (*0-88295-848-8*) Harlan Davidson.

American People: A History, Vol. 2 since 1865. 2nd rev. ed. Arthur S. Link et al. LC 86-24261. (Illus.). 582p. (C). 1987. pap. text ed. write for info. (*0-88295-849-6*) Harlan Davidson.

***American People: Creating a Nation & a Society, 2 vols.** 2nd abr. ed. Gary B. Nash et al. Incl. American People Vol. 1: Creating a Nation & a Society. 2nd abr. ed. LC 95-8877. (C). 1995. (*0-673-99527-5*); Vol. 2. American People Vol. 2: Creating a Nation & a Society. 2nd abr. ed. LC 95-8877. (C). 1995. (*0-673-99528-3*); LC 95-8877. write for info. (*0-673-99526-7*) HarpCollege.

American People & Foreign Policy. 2nd ed. Gabriel A. Almond. LC 77-7019. 269p. 1977. reprint ed. text ed. 35.00 (*0-8371-9617-5*, ALAM, Greenwood Pr) Greenwood.

American People Brief Edition, 2 vols., I. Gary B. Nash. (C). 1991. 12.50 (*0-06-500433-7*) HarpCollege.

American People Brief Edition, 2 vols., I. Gary B. Nash. (C). 1991. text ed. 22.00 (*0-06-500262-8*) HarpCollege.

American People Brief Edition, 2 vols., II. Gary B. Nash. (C). 1991. 12.50 (*0-06-500434-5*) HarpCollege.

American People Brief Edition, 2 vols., II. Gary B. Nash. (C). 1991. text ed. 22.00 (*0-06-500263-6*) HarpCollege.

American People Brief Edition, 2 vols., Vols. I-II. Gary B. Nash. (C). 1991. Set. text ed. 31.50 (*0-06-044748-6*) HarpCollege.

American People in the Twentieth Century. Oscar Handlin. LC 66-22368. (Library of Congress Series in American Civilization). 254p. reprint ed. pap. 72.40 (*0-7837-4106-5*, 2057929) Bks Demand.

American People's Money. Ignatius Donnelly. LC 75-311. (Radical Tradition in America Ser.). 186p. 1975. reprint ed. 18.70 (*0-88355-215-9*) Hyperion Conn.

American People's Money. Ignatius Donnelly. (Notable American Authors Ser.). 1992. reprint ed. lib. bdg. 75.00 (*0-7812-2671-6*) Rprt Serv.

American Perception of Class. Reeve Vanneman & Lynn W. Cannon. LC 86-14349. (Labor & Social Change Ser.). (Illus.). 368p. (C). 1988. pap. text ed. 18.95 (*0-87722-593-1*) Temple U Pr.

American Perceptions of Drug Addiction: Five Studies, 1872 to 1912. Ed. by Gerald N. Grob. LC 80-1209. (Addiction in America Ser.). 1981. lib. bdg. 33.95 (*0-405-13558-0*) Ayer.

American Period Interiors. Klavan. 1984. 35.00 (*0-684-18122-3*, Scribners) S&S Trade.

American Periodical Verse Index: 1989. Rafael Catala & James D. Anderson. LC 73-3060. 606p. 1991. 59.50 (*0-8108-2456-6*) Scarecrow.

American Periodicals Seventeen Forty-One to Nineteen Hundred: An Index to the Microfilm Collections. Jean Hoornstra. Ed. by Trudy Heath. 341p. 1979. 75.00 (*0-8357-0374-6*) Univ Microfilms.

American Personal Religious Accounts, 1600-1980: Toward an Inner History of America's Faiths. Jon Alexander. LC 83-21950. (Studies in American Religion: Vol. 8). 518p. 1984. lib. bdg. 119.95 (*0-88946-654-8*) E Mellen.

American Perspective: Paintings from the Maier Museum of Art, Randolph-Macon Woman's College. Nancy Mathews. LC 85-63217. (Illus.). 24p. (Orig.). 1985. pap. 4.00 (*0-88259-950-X*) NCMA.

American Perspectives: The National Self-Image in the Twentieth Century. American Studies Association Staff. Ed. by Robert E. Spiller & Eric Larrabee. LC 61-8841. (Library of Congress Series in American Civilization). 223p. reprint ed. pap. 65.00 (*0-7837-1727-X*, 2057257) Bks Demand.

American Perspectives on the Fifth International Congress on Mathematical Education. Ed. by Warren Page. 134p. 1984. pap. 5.00 (*0-88385-055-9*, NTE-05) Math Assn.

American Perspectives on the Seventh International Congress on Mathematical Education. Ed. by John A. Dossey. 73p. (Orig.). 1993. pap. 10.00 (*0-87353-360-7*) NCTM.

American Perspectives on the Sixth International Congress on Mathematical Education. Ed. by Thomas J. Cooney. LC 91-42282. (Illus.). 64p. 1989. pap. 8.00 (*0-87353-276-7*) NCTM.

American Pescadero. Sherman Welden. 1973. pap. 5.95 (*0-915572-49-4*) Panjandrum.

American Petroleum Industry, Vol. 1, 1. Incl. Vol. 1. Age of Illumination, 1859 to 1899. Harold F. Williamson et al. LC 80-22253. (Illus.). 1981. 195.00 (*0-318-52722-7*, WIAC01, Greenwood Pr); Vol. 2. Age of Energy, 1899 to 1959. Harold F. Williamson et al. LC 80-22253. (Illus.). 1981. 195.00 (*0-318-52723-5*, WIAC02, Greenwood Pr); LC 80-22253. (Northwestern University Studies in Business History). (Illus.). xxxvi, 1792p. 1981. Set text ed. 195.00 (*0-313-22789-6*, WIAC01, Greenwood Pr) Greenwood.

American Petroleum Industry, 2 vols., Set. Incl. Vol. 1. Age of Illumination, 1859 to 1899. Harold F. Williamson et al. LC 80-22253. (Illus.). 1981. 195.00 (*0-318-52722-7*, WIAC01, Greenwood Pr); Vol. 2. Age of Energy, 1899 to 1959. Harold F. Williamson et al. LC 80-22253. (Illus.). 1981. 195.00 (*0-318-52723-5*, WIAC02, Greenwood Pr); LC 80-22253. (Northwestern University Studies in Business History). (Illus.). xxxvi, 1792p. 1981. Set text ed. 245.00 (*0-313-22788-8*, WIAC, Greenwood Pr) Greenwood.

American Petroleum Industry, 2 vols., Vol. 2. Incl. Vol. 1. Age of Illumination, 1859 to 1899. Harold F. Williamson et al. LC 80-22253. (Illus.). 1981. 195.00 (*0-318-52722-7*, WIAC01, Greenwood Pr); Vol. 2. Age of Energy, 1899 to 1959. Harold F. Williamson et al. LC 80-22253. (Illus.). 1981. 195.00 (*0-318-52723-5*, WIAC02, Greenwood Pr); LC 80-22253. (Northwestern University Studies in Business History). (Illus.). xxxvi, 1792p. 1981. Set text ed. 195.00 (*0-313-22790-X*, WIAC02, Greenwood Pr) Greenwood.

American Petroleum Interests in Foreign Countries. U. S. Congress, Senate Staff. Ed. by Stuart Bruchey & Eleanor Bruchey. LC 76-5037. (American Business Abroad Ser.). (Illus.). 1976. reprint ed. 45.95 (*0-405-09303-9*) Ayer.

American Pewter in the Museum of Fine Arts Boston. Contrib by Daniel Farber. LC 74-78551. (Illus.). 122p. (Orig.). 1974. pap. 7.95 (*0-686-67134-1*) Mus Fine Arts Boston.

***American Pewterer: His Techniques & His Products.** Henry J. Kauffman. (Illus.). 132p. 1994. pap. 22.95 (*1-879335-53-0*) Astragal Pr.

American Phenomenology: Origins & Developments. Ed. by Eugene F. Kaelin & Calvin O. Schrag. (C). 1988. lib. bdg. 162.00 (*90-277-2690-6*) Kluwer Ac.

American Philanthropy. Robert H. Bremner. Ed. by Daniel J. Boor. (Chicago History of American Civilization Ser.). (Illus.). xii, 296p. 1988. pap. text ed. 14.95 (*0-226-07325-4*) U Ch Pr.

American Philanthropy: A Guide for South Africans. Michael Sinclair & Julia Weinstein. 122p. 1988. pap. 10.00 (*0-931035-72-4*) IRRC Inc DC.

American Philanthropy Abroad. Merle Curti. 656p. 1988. 49.95 (*0-88738-711-X*) Transaction Pubs.

American Philatelic Congress Book. 57th ed. Ed. by Michel Forand. (Illus.). 198p. 1991. 25.00 (*0-929333-17-9*) Am Philat Congr.

American Philatelic Congress Book. 58th ed. Ed. by Michel Forand. (Illus.). 198p. 1992. 27.50 (*0-929333-18-7*) Am Philat Congr.

American Philatelic Congress Book, 1993. 59th ed. Ed. by Michel Forand. (Illus.). 192p. 1993. 40.00 (*0-929333-19-5*) Am Philat Congr.

American Philosopher: Conversations with Quine, Davidson, Putnam, Nozick, Danto, Rorty, Cavell, MacIntyre, & Kuhn. Giovanna Borradori. Tr. by Rosanna Crocitto. LC 93-5294. 168p. 1993. pap. 13.95 (*0-226-06648-7*) U Ch Pr.

American Philosophic Naturalism in the Twentieth Century. Ed. by John Ryder. 566p. (C). 1994. 34.95x (*0-87975-894-5*) Prometheus Bks.

American Philosophy. Ed. by Marcus G. Singer. (Royal Institute of Philosophy Lecture Ser.: Vol. 19). 540p. 1986. pap. 21.95 (*0-521-31048-2*) Cambridge U Pr.

American Philosophy: An Historical Anthology. Barbara MacKinnon. LC 84-2458. (SUNY Series in Philosophy). 688p. 1985. 59.50 (*0-87395-922-1*); pap. 19.95 (*0-87395-923-X*) State U NY Pr.

American Philosophy & the Romantic Tradition. Russell B. Goodman. (Cambridge Studies in American Literature & Culture: No. 5). 208p. (C). 1991. 44.95 (*0-521-39443-0*) Cambridge U Pr.

American Philosophy of Social Security. J. Douglas Brown. LC 71-39781. 212p. 1972. 45.00x (*0-691-03092-8*) Princeton U Pr.

American Philosophy Today & Other Philosophical Studies. Nicholas Rescher. LC 94-16451. 188p. reprint ed. lib. bdg. 49.50 (*0-8476-7935-7*); reprint ed. pap. 19.95 (*0-8476-7936-5*) Rowman.

American Philosophy Today & Tomorrow. Ed. by Horace M. Kallen & Sidney Hook. LC 68-8474. (Essay Index Reprint Ser.). 1977. reprint ed. 23.95 (*0-8369-0583-0*) Ayer.

American Philosophy Today & Tomorrow. Ed. by Horace M. Kallen & Sidney Hook. (Essay Index Reprint Ser.). 525p. 1982. reprint ed. lib. bdg. 20.00 (*0-686-79689-6*) Irvington.

***American Photographers at the Turn of the Century: Art of the Human Form.** Five Corners Staff. 1995. 24.95 (*0-9627262-6-5*) Five Corners.

American Photographers at the Turn of the Century: People & Our World. Five Corners Publications Staff. 1993. 19.95 (*0-9627262-2-2*) Five Corners.

American Photographers of the Depression. Pantheon Photo Library. Incl. Eugene Atget. 1985. (*0-318-59515-X*); Henri Cartier-Bresson. 1985. (*0-318-59516-8*); Robert Frank. 1985. (*0-318-59517-6*); 1985. (*0-318-59518-4*); 1985. Set pap. 7.95 (*0-394-74086-6*) Pantheon.

***American Photographs in Europe.** Ed. by M. Gidley & D. E. Nye. (European Contributions to American Studies: Vol. 29). (Illus.). 286p. 1995. pap. 33.00 (*90-5383-304-8*, Pub. by VU Univ Pr NE) Paul & Co Pubs.

American Photography, No. 4. Edward Booth-Clibborn. (Illus.). 176p. 1989. 55.00 (*0-89659-948-5*) Abbeville Pr.

American Photography, No. 5. Ed. by Edward Booth-Clibborn. (American Illustration Annual Ser.). (Illus.). 176p. 1990. 60.00 (*0-8478-5540-6*) Rizzoli Intl.

American Photography, No. 9. Clibborn E. Booth. (Illus.). 1994. 65.00 (*0-8478-5753-0*) Rizzoli Intl.

American Photography: A Critical History 1945 to the Present. Jonathan Green. LC 83-15532. (Illus.). 248p. 1984. 39.95 (*0-8109-1814-5*) Abrams.

American Photography & the American Dream. James Guimond. LC 90-46730. (Cultural Studies of the United States). (Illus.). xvi, 341p. (C). 1991. 45.00 (*0-8078-1946-8*); pap. 18.95 (*0-8078-4308-3*) U of NC Pr.

American Photography Eight. Ed. by Edward Booth-Clibborn. (Illus.). 140p. 1992. 60.00 (*0-8478-5641-0*) Rizzoli Intl.

American Photography Showcase, No. 15. Ed. by American Showcase Staff. (Illus.). 448p. pap. 45.00 (*0-931144-72-8*) Am Showcase.

American Photography Six. (Illus.). 208p. 1991. 60.00 (*0-8478-5570-8*) Rizzoli Intl.

***American Photography Ten: AP10.** 332p. 1994. 65.00 (*1-886212-00-7*) Amilus.

***American Photography 11.** (Illus.). 224p. Date not set. 60.00 (*1-886212-02-3*) Amilus.

American Phrasebook for Poles. Jacek Galazka. (Illus.). 144p. (Orig.). 1991. pap. 7.95 (*0-87052-907-2*) Hippocrene Bks.

***American Phrasebook for Poles.** rev. ed. Dla Polakow. 1993. pap. 7.95 (*0-7818-0198-2*) Hippocrene Bks.

American Phrasebook for Russians. Blagowidow. (ENG & RUS.). 1992. pap. 8.95 (*0-7818-0054-4*) Hippocrene Bks.

American Physicians in the Nineteenth Century: From Sects to Science. William G. Rothstein. 256p. 1992. reprint ed. pap. text ed. 18.95 (*0-8018-4427-4*) Johns Hopkins.

American Piano Concertos: A Bibliography. William Phemister. LC 85-19746. (Bibliographies in American Music Ser.: No. 9). 323p. 1986. 35.00 (*0-89990-026-7*) Info Coord.

***American Pictographic Images: Historical Works on Paper by Plains Indians.** Contrib by Karen D. Petersen. (Illus.). 176p. 1988. 45.00 (*0-614-04592-4*) Morning Star Gal.

American Pictorial Quilts. Caron Mosey. (Illus.). 112p. 1986. 19.95 (*0-89145-910-3*, 1662) Collector Bks.

American Picture Show: A Cultural Reader. Elizabeth Mejia et al. 240p. (C). 1991. pap. text ed. 18.25 (*0-13-029687-2*) P-H.

American Pictures. rev. ed. Jacob Holdt. Ed. by Karen Duff. Tr. by Camilla Decarnin. (Illus.). 304p. (Orig.). 1986. 18.95 (*87-981702-4-4*); pap. 14.95 (*87-981702-0-1*) Amer Pictures.

American Pie. Teresa Kennedy. LC 84-40345. (Illus.). 96p. (Orig.). 1984. pap. 5.95 (*0-89480-808-7*, 808) Workman Pub.

An Asterisk (*) at the beginning of an entry indicates that the title is appearing in BIP for the first time.

American Piety: The Nature of Religious Commitment. Rodney Stark & Charles Y. Glock. 1968. pap. 10.00 (*0-520-01756-0*) U CA Pr.

American Pilgrimage. Frank A. Russell. LC 72-167408. (Essay Index Reprint Ser.). 1977. reprint ed. 25.95 (*0-8369-2715-X*) Ayer.

American Pilot in the Skies of France. David K. Vaugman. 1992. text ed. 22.95 (*0-685-50684-3*) U Pr of Amer.

American Pilot in the Skies of France: The Diaries & Letters of Lt. Percival T. Gates, 1917-1918. Ed. by David K. Vaughan. (Illus.). 222p. (C). 1992. lib. bdg. 22.95 (*1-882090-02-0*) Wright State Univ Pr.

American Pilots in the RAF: The WWII Eagle Squadrons. Philip D. Caine. (Brassey's WWII Commemorative Ser.). (Illus.). 429p. 1993. 25.00 (*0-02-881070-8*) Brasseys Inc.

American Pioneer. E. Dean Edwards. (Illus.). 36p. (Orig.). (J). (gr. 1 up). 1988. pap. 2.95 (*0-685-44554-2*) E D Edwards.

American Pioneer: Natural Fibers, Spinning Wheels-Weaving & Animals. E. D. Edwards. (Illus.). 36p. (Orig.). 1987. pap. 2.95 (*0-9615120-2-4*) E D Edwards.

American Pioneer Drama see California Gold-Rush Plays

***American Pioneers.** Alan Rich. (20th Century Composers Ser.). (Illus.). 240p. (Orig.). (C). 1995. pap. 19.95 (*0-7148-3173-5*, Pub. by Phaidon Press UK) Chronicle Bks.

American Pioneers & the Japanese Frontier: American Experts in Nineteenth Century Japan. Fumiko Fujita. LC 93-39346. (Contributions in Asian Studies: Vol. 4). 208p. 1994. text ed. 55.00 (*0-313-28788-0*, Greenwood Pr) Greenwood.

American Pioneers Classic. Date not set. 9.95 (*0-7866-0028-4*, 95203); audio 9.98 (*0-7866-0052-7*, 95203C) Mel Bay.

***American Pit Bull Terrier.** Jacqueline Fraser. (Owner's Guide to a Happy, Healthy Pet Ser.). 160p. Date not set. 12.95 (*0-87605-383-5*) Howell Bk.

American Pit Bull Terrier. Bill Sanford & Carl Green. LC 89-31072. (Top Dog Ser.). (Illus.). 48p. (J). (gr. 4-5). 1989. text ed. 12.95 (*0-89686-447-2*, Crstwood Hse) Silver Burdett Pr.

***American Pit Bull Terriers, American Staffordshire Terriers: Everything about Purchase, Care, Nutrition, Breeding, Behavior & Training.** Joe Stahlkuppe. LC 95-14955. (Complete Pet Owner's Manuals Ser.). (Illus.). 1995. write for info. (*0-8120-9200-7*) Barron.

***American Place.** Ronald G. Pisano. LC 81-81364. (Illus.). 40p. (Orig.). (C). 1981. pap. 5.00 (*0-943526-28-0*) Parrish Art.

American Place-Names: A Concise & Selective Dictionary for the Continental United States of America. George R. Stewart. LC 72-83018. 1970. 35.00 (*0-19-500121-4*) OUP.

American Places. Wallace & P. Stegner. 1993. 19.99 (*0-517-41361-2*) Random Hse Value.

American Places: A Writer's Pilgrimage to 15 of This Country's Most Visited & Cherished Sites. William K. Zinsser. LC 91-58381. 208p. 1993. pap. 11.00 (*0-06-092426-8*, PL) HarpC.

American Places Dictionary: A Guide to Populated Places, Natural Features, & Other United States Places, 4 vols. Ed. by Frank R. Abate. (Illus.). 1994. Set. lib. bdg. 350.00 (*1-55888-747-4*) Omnigraphics Inc.

American Places Dictionary, Vol. 1: Northeast, 4 vols., Vol. 1. Ed. by Frank R. Abate. (Illus.). 1994. lib. bdg. 100.00 (*1-55888-146-8*) Omnigraphics Inc.

American Places Dictionary, Vol. 2: South, 4 vols., Vol. 2. Ed. by Frank R. Abate. (Illus.). 1994. lib. bdg. 100.00 (*1-55888-147-6*) Omnigraphics Inc.

American Places Dictionary, Vol. 3: Midwest, 4 vols., Vol. 3. Ed. by Frank R. Abate. (Illus.). 1994. lib. bdg. 100.00 (*1-55888-148-4*) Omnigraphics Inc.

American Places Dictionary, Vol. 4: West Appendices & Index, 4 vols., Vol. 4. Ed. by Frank R. Abate. (Illus.). 1994. lib. bdg. 100.00 (*1-55888-149-2*) Omnigraphics Inc.

American Plains Indians. Jason Hook. (Men-at-Arms Ser.: No. 163). (Illus.). 48p. pap. 11.95 (*0-85045-608-8*, 9095, Pub. by Osprey UK) Stackpole.

American Plan. Richard Greenberg. 1991. pap. 4.75 (*0-8222-0034-1*) Dramatists Play.

American Planner: Biographies & Recollections. 2nd ed. Ed. by Donald A. Krueckeberg. LC 94-6087. (Illus.). 552p. (C). 1994. pap. text ed. 19.95 (*0-88285-148-9*) Ctr Urban Pol Res.

American Plant Ecology, Eighteen Ninety-Seven to Nineteen Seventeen: An Original Anthology. Ed. by Frank N. Egerton, 3rd. LC 77-74202. (History of Ecology Ser.). (Illus.). 1978. lib. bdg. 65.95 (*0-405-10372-7*) Ayer.

American Plant Migration, Vol.1: The Potato. Berthold Laufer. (Field Museum of Natural History Ser.: Vol. 28). (Illus.). 1938. 15.00 (*0-527-01888-0*) Periodicals Srv.

***American Plastic: A Cultural History.** Jeffrey L. Meikle. LC 95-15187. 1995. pap. write for info. (*0-8135-2235-8*) Rutgers U Pr.

***American Plastic: A Cultural History.** Jeffrey L. Meikle. LC 95-15187. (Illus.). 500p. (C). 1995. text ed. 49.95 (*0-8135-2234-X*) Rutgers U Pr.

American Plated Silver see Early American Plated Silver: Flat & Holloware

American Play & Other Works. Suzan-Lori Parks. 208p. 1995. pap. 14.95 (*1-55936-092-5*) Theatre Comm.

American Plays. Ed. by Allan G. Halline. LC 75-41125. reprint ed. 44.50 (*0-404-14763-1*) AMS Pr.

American Plays Printed from Seventeen Fourteen to Eighteen Thirty. Frank P. Hill. LC 68-20229. 1972. reprint ed. 21.95 (*0-405-08616-4*) Ayer.

***American Plays, 1900-1920.** Thomas et al. Ed. by Keith Newlin. (Masterworks of Literature Ser.). 1995. pap. 17.95x (*0-8084-0488-1*) NCUP.

American Playwrights: Nineteen Eighteen to Nineteen Thirty-Eight. Eleanor Flexner. LC 77-99634. (Essay Index Reprint Ser.). 1977. 35.95 (*0-8369-1412-0*) Ayer.

American Playwrights since 1945: A Guide to Scholarship, Criticism, & Performance. Ed. by Philip C. Kolin. LC 88-10245. 610p. 1989. text ed. 95.00 (*0-313-25543-1*, KPY/, Greenwood Pr) Greenwood.

American Playwrights, 1880-1945: A Research & Production Sourcebook. Ed. by William W. Demastes. LC 94-13690. 512p. 1994. text ed. 85.00 (*0-313-28638-8*, Greenwood Pr) Greenwood.

American Pluralism & the Jewish Community. Ed. by Seymour M. Lipset. 220p. 1989. 24.95 (*0-88738-286-X*) Transaction Pubs.

American Pocket & Wrist Watch Balance Staff Interchangeability List. George Townsend. Ed. by Roy Ehrhardt. 36p. (Orig.). 1984. pap. 10.00 (*0-913902-52-7*) Heart Am Pr.

American Pocket Dictionary. 1983. 5.00 (*0-394-52900-6*) Random.

American Pocket Watch: Serial Number Grade Book. Roy Ehrhardt & William Meggers. (Illus.). 324p. 1993. spiral bd. 35.00 (*0-913902-79-9*); spiral bd. 25.00 (*0-913902-78-0*) Heart Am Pr.

American Pocket Watch Identification & Price Guide, Book 2. rev. ed. Roy Ehrhardt. 1974. ring bd. 25.00 (*0-913902-09-8*) Heart Am Pr.

American Poems. Horace E. Scudder. LC 76-149116. (Granger Index Reprint Ser.). 1977. 24.95 (*0-8369-6241-9*) Ayer.

American Poems. Ed. by Elihu H. Smith. LC 66-60007. 352p. 1979. 60.00 (*0-8201-1042-6*) Schol Facsimiles.

American Poems. William M. Rossetti. LC 74-131501. reprint ed. 47.50 (*0-404-05419-6*) AMS Pr.

American Poet: A Role Investigation. Robert N. Wilson. LC 90-24222. (Harvard Studies in Sociology: Vol. 21). 288p. 1991. reprint ed. 20.00 (*0-8240-2566-0*) Garland.

***American Poet at the Movies: A Critical History.** Goldstein. 1995. pap. (*0-472-08318-X*) U of Mich Pr.

American Poet at the Movies: A Critical History. Laurence Goldstein. LC 93-48036. (Illus.). 272p. (C). 1994. text ed. 29.95 (*0-472-10508-6*) U of Mich Pr.

American Poet Exiled in America. rev. ed. Bruce Einsidler-Moore. LC 87-73556. 64p. 1988. pap. 4.95 (*0-9619369-0-8*) Cider Mill NH.

American Poetics of History: From Emerson to the Moderns. Joseph G. Kronick. LC 83-24827. xiii, 302p. 1984. text ed. 37.50 (*0-8071-1152-X*) La State U Pr.

American Poetry. Mutlu K. Blasing. LC 86-22395. 272p. 1987. 35.00x (*0-300-03793-7*) Yale U Pr.

American Poetry. Ed. by A. B. DeMille. LC 77-94805. (Granger Poetry Library). (Illus.). 1978. reprint ed. 38.50 (*0-89609-082-5*) Roth Pub Inc.

***American Poetry: The Modernist Ideal.** Clive Bloom & Brian Docherty. LC 94-3770. 1995. write for info. (*0-312-12388-4*) St Martin.

American Poetry: The Nineteenth Century, 2 vols. Ed. by John Hollander. 1993. Boxed Set. 70.00 (*1-883011-00-0*); Vol. 1: Freneau to Whitman, 1199p. 35.00 (*0-940450-60-7*); Vol. 2: Melville to Stickney, American Indian Poetry, Folk Songs & Spirituals, 1150p. 35.00 (*0-940450-78-X*) Library of America.

American Poetry: The Puritans Through Walt Whitman. Alan Shucard. (Critical History of Poetry Ser.). 208p. 1988. text ed. 23.95 (*0-8057-8450-0*, Twayne) Macmillan.

American Poetry: The Puritans through Walt Whitman. Alan Shucard. LC 89-49466. 224p. (C). 1990. reprint ed. pap. 15.95x (*0-87023-719-5*) U of Mass Pr.

American Poetry: The Rhetoric of Its Forms. Mutlu K. Blasing. 248p. (C). 1989. reprint ed. pap. 15.00x (*0-300-04607-3*) Yale U Pr.

American Poetry: Wildness & Domesticity. Robert Bly. LC 89-45628. 288p. 1991. reprint ed. pap. 12.00 (*0-06-092082-3*, PL) HarpC.

American Poetry & Culture, 1945-1980. Robert Von Hallberg. 320p. 1985. 32.00 (*0-674-03011-7*) HUP.

American Poetry & Culture, 1945-1980. Robert Von Hallberg. 288p. 1988. reprint ed. pap. 14.95x (*0-674-03012-5*) HUP.

American Poetry & Prose, 2 pts. 5th ed. Ed. by Norman Foerster et al. (C). 1972. write for info. (*0-318-53376-6*) HM.

American Poetry & Prose, 5 Vols., Set. 5th ed. Ed. by Norman Foerster et al. LC 70-137981. (C). 1970. text ed. 50.76 (*0-395-04456-1*) HM.

American Poetry Anthology. Ed. by Daniel Halpern. 1975. pap. 9.95 (*0-380-00399-6*, 84376) Avon.

American Poetry Archives Videotape Catalogue: 1974-1990. Ed. by Laura Moriarty. 120p. 1991. per., pap. 3.00 (*0-685-56990-X*) Poetry Ctr Pr.

American Poetry Confronts the 1990's. 2nd rev. ed. Ed. by Peter Gravis & Harry Burrus. LC 90-298. (Illus.). 216p. (Orig.). 1991. 12.50 (*0-941749-13-4*) Black Tie Pr.

American Poetry in the 1890's: A Study of American Verse, 1890-1899, Based upon the Volumes from that Period Contained in the Harris Collection of American Poetry & Plays in the Brown University Library. Carlin T. Kindilien. LC 56-12410. (Brown University Studies: No. 20). 241p. reprint ed. 68.70 (*0-8357-5388-3*, 2027509) Bks Demand.

American Poetry Index, Vol. 2: 1983. Granger Book Company, Editorial Board Staff. LC 83-81682. 1985. 52.00x (*0-89609-241-0*) Roth Pub Inc.

American Poetry Index, Vol. 4. Ed. by Roth Publishing Inc., Editorial Board. 400p. 1988. 52.00 (*0-89609-268-2*) Roth Pub Inc.

American Poetry Index, 1984, Vol. 3. Roth Publishing, Inc., Editorial Board Staff. 570p. 1987. 52.00 (*0-89609-262-3*) Roth Pub Inc.

American Poetry Observed: Poets on Their Work. Ed. by Joe D. Bellamy. LC 83-6961. (Illus.). 328p. 1984. 27.50 (*0-252-01042-6*) U of Ill Pr.

American Poetry Observed: Poets on Their Work. Ed. by Joe D. Bellamy. LC 83-6961. (Illus.). 328p. 1988. pap. 12.95 (*0-252-06010-5*) U of Ill Pr.

American Poetry of the Seventeenth Century. Ed. by Harrison T. Meserole. LC 85-21701. 576p. 1985. reprint ed. pap. text ed. 16.95 (*0-271-00418-5*) Pa St U Pr.

American Poetry of the Twentieth Century. Richard Gray. (Literature in English Ser.). 424p. (C). 1990. text ed. 37.95 (*0-582-49437-0*, 78290); pap. text ed. 25.95 (*0-582-49444-3*, 78290) Longman.

American Poetry since 1900. Louis Untermeyer. (BCL1-PS American Literature Ser.). 405p. 1992. reprint ed. lib. bdg. 99.00 (*0-7812-6632-7*) Rprt Serv.

American Poetry since 1950: Innovators & Outsiders. Intro. by Eliot Weinberger. LC 92-62373. 448p. (Orig.). 1993. 40.00 (*0-941419-91-6*); pap. 19.95 (*0-941419-92-4*) Marsilio Pubs.

American Poetry since 1970: Up Late. 2nd ed. Intro. by Andrei Codrescu. LC 89-16844. 624p. 1990. pap. 16.95 (*0-941423-26-3*) FWEW.

American Poetry Through Nineteen Fourteen. Ed. & Intro. by Harold Bloom. (Critical Cosmos Ser.). 576p. 1987. 69.95 (*0-87754-951-6*) Chelsea Hse.

American Poetry 1609-1870: A Guide to the Microfilm Collection. Ed. by Research Publications, Inc. Staff. LC 82-7641. 592p. 1982. 105.00 (*0-89235-039-3*) Res Pubns CT.

American Poetry, 1915-1945. Ed. & Intro. by Harold Bloom. (Critical Cosmos Ser.). 424p. 1987. 69.95 (*0-87754-952-4*) Chelsea Hse.

American Poetry 1946-1965. Ed. & Intro. by Harold Bloom. (Critical Cosmos Ser.). 1987. 69.95 (*0-87754-953-2*) Chelsea Hse.

American Poets, Vol. 2. Ed. by Ronald Baughman. (Contemporary Authors Bibliographical Ser.: Vol. 2). 392p. 1986. 122.00 (*0-8103-2226-9*) Gale.

American Poets: From the Puritans to the Present. rev. ed. Hyatt H. Waggoner. LC 83-19624. xxiv, 656p. 1984. pap. 17.95 (*0-8071-1163-5*) La State U Pr.

American Poets & Their Theology. Augustus H. Strong. LC 68-26477. (Essay Index Reprint Ser.). 1977. reprint ed. 23.95 (*0-8369-0910-0*) Ayer.

American Poets in 1976. William Heyen. LC 75-37522. (Illus.). 517p. 1976. 12.05 (*0-672-52174-1*, Bobbs); pap. 10.50 (*0-672-61349-2*, Bobbs) Macmillan.

American Poets since World War II, 2 Vols., Set. Ed. by Donald J. Greiner. (Dictionary of Literary Biography Ser.: Vol. 5). (Illus.). 904p. 1980. 245.00 (*0-8103-0924-6*) Gale.

American Poets since World War II, Vol. 120. Ed. by R. S. Gwynn. LC 92-25459. (Third Ser.). 425p. 1992. 128.00 (*0-8103-7597-4*) Gale.

American Poets, 1880 to 1945 First Series. Ed. by Peter Quartermain. (Dictionary of Literary Biography Ser.: Vol. 45). 514p. 1985. 128.00 (*0-8103-1723-0*) Gale.

American Poets 1880 to 1945 Second Series. Ed. by Peter Quartermain. (Dictionary of Literary Biography Ser.: Vol. 48). 350p. 1986. 128.00 (*0-8103-1726-5*) Gale.

American Poets 1880 to 1945 Third Series, 2 vols., Set. Ed. by Peter Quartermain. (Dictionary of Literary Biography Ser.: Vol. 54). (Illus.). 743p. 1986. 238.00 (*0-8103-1732-X*) Gale.

American Police Administration: A Handbook on Police Organization & Methods of Administration in American Cities. Elmer D. Graper. LC 69-14929. (Criminology, Law Enforcement, & Social Problems Ser.: No. 37). 1969. reprint ed. 24.00 (*0-87585-037-5*) Patterson Smith.

American Police Systems. Raymond B. Fosdick. LC 69-14925. (Criminology, Law Enforcement, & Social Problems Ser.: No. 53). (C). 1969. reprint ed. 25.00 (*0-87585-053-7*) Patterson Smith.

American Policy & African Famine: The Nigeria-Biafra War, 1966-1970. Joseph E. Thompson. LC 89-23353. (Contributions in Afro-American & African Studies: No. 130). 208p. 1990. text ed. 49.95 (*0-313-27218-2*, TAA/, Greenwood Pr) Greenwood.

American Policy & the Reconstruction of West Germany, 1945-1955. Ed. by Jeffry M. Diefendorf et al. (Publications of the German Historical Institute, Washington, D.C.). 300p. (C). 1994. 69.95 (*0-521-43120-4*) Cambridge U Pr.

American Policy for Peace in the Middle East, 1969-1971: Problems of Principle, Maneuver & Time. Robert J. Pranger. LC 70-188039. (Foreign Affairs Study Ser.: No. 1). 74p. reprint ed. pap. 25.00 (*0-8357-5389-1*, 2017131) Bks Demand.

American Policy in Nicaragua. Henry L. Stimson. LC 70-165511. reprint ed. 24.50 (*0-404-06269-5*) AMS Pr.

American Policy in Nicaragua. Henry L. Stimson. LC 76-111733. (American Imperialism: Viewpoints of United States Foreign Policy, 1898-1941 Ser.). 1970. reprint ed. 15.95 (*0-405-02051-1*) Ayer.

American Policy in Nicaragua. Henry L. Stimson. (BCL1 - U. S. History Ser.). 129p. 1991. reprint ed. lib. bdg. 69.00 (*0-7812-6076-0*) Rprt Serv.

American Policy in Southern Africa: The Stakes & the Stance. 2nd ed. Ed. by Rene Lemarchand. LC 80-6222. 513p. (C). 1981. lib. bdg. 57.00 (*0-8191-1436-7*) U Pr of Amer.

American Policy in the Far East, 1931-1941. Thomas A. Bisson. LC 75-30096. (Institute of Pacific Relations Ser.). reprint ed. 39.50 (*0-404-59505-7*) AMS Pr.

American Policy of Recognition Toward Mexico. Stuart A. MacCorkle. LC 72-131774. 1971. reprint ed. 9.00 (*0-403-00661-9*) Scholarly.

American Policy of Recognition Towards Mexico. Stuart A. MacCorkle. LC 70-155620. reprint ed. 11.50 (*0-404-04108-6*) AMS Pr.

American Policy Toward China. Wen-Hwan Ma. LC 73-111743. (American Imperialism: Viewpoints of United States Foreign Policy, 1898-1941 Ser.). 1977. reprint ed. 25.95 (*0-405-02037-6*) Ayer.

American Policy Toward Communist China, 1949-1969. Foster R. Dulles. LC 70-184974. (C). 1972. pap. text ed. write for info. (*0-88295-728-7*) Harlan Davidson.

American Policy Toward Communist Eastern Europe: The Choices Ahead. John C. Campbell. LC 65-15982. 150p. reprint ed. pap. 42.80 (*0-8357-5390-5*, 2055846) Bks Demand.

American Policy Toward Laos. Martin E. Goldstein. LC 72-416. (Illus.). 347p. 1973. 30.00 (*0-8386-1131-1*) Fairleigh Dickinson.

American Policy Toward Russia Since 1917: A Study of Diplomatic History, International Law & Public Opinion. Frederick L. Schuman. LC 75-39061. (Russian Studies: Perspectives on the Revolution). (Illus.). ix, 399p. 1977. reprint ed. 29.00 (*0-88355-441-0*) Hyperion Conn.

***American Politcal Thought: Four Hundred Years of Ideas & Ideologies.** Sue Davis. LC 94-41915. 1995. pap. text ed. write for info. (*0-13-280629-0*) P-H.

American Political & Economic Penetration of Mexico, 1877-1920. Jules David. Ed. by Stuart Bruchey & Eleanor Bruchey. LC 76-5001. (American Business Abroad Ser.). 1976. lib. bdg. 40.95 (*0-405-09269-5*) Ayer.

American Political Campaign Badges & Medaletes 1789-1892. 2nd ed. Edmund B. Sullivan. LC 80-54038. (Illus.). 648p. 1981. lib. bdg. 100.00 (*0-88000-067-8*) Quarterman.

American Political Cultures. Richard Ellis. LC 92-33873. 272p. 1993. 45.00 (*0-19-507900-0*) OUP.

American Political Dictionary. 8th ed. Jack C. Plano & Milton Greenberg. 700p. (C). 1989. pap. text ed. 22.00 (*0-03-022932-4*) HB Coll Pubs.

American Political Dictionary. 9th ed. Milton Greenberg & Jack Plano. LC 92-71199. 672p. (C). 1993. pap. text ed. 21.75 (*0-15-500281-3*) HB Coll Pubs.

American Political Economy: Macroeconomics & Electoral Politics in the United States. Douglas A. Hibbs, Jr. LC 87-155. 400p. 1987. 48.00 (*0-674-02735-3*) HUP.

American Political Economy: Macroeconomics & Electoral Politics in the United States. Douglas A. Hibbs, Jr. (Illus.). 400p. 1989. reprint ed. pap. 21.50 (*0-674-02736-1*) HUP.

American Political Experience: Introduction to Government. 4th ed. David V. Edwards. (Illus.). 704p. (C). 1987. text ed. write for info. (*0-13-028482-3*) P-H.

American Political Family. Ed. by Donn M. Kurtz, II. 176p. (Orig.). (C). 1993. lib. bdg. 46.50 (*0-8191-9001-2*); pap. text ed. 24.50 (*0-8191-9002-0*) U Pr of Amer.

American Political History, 2 vols. Alexander Johnston. Ed. by J. A. Woodburn. (Notable American Authors Ser.). 1992. reprint ed. lib. bdg. 75.00 (*0-7812-3506-5*) Rprt Serv.

American Political History As Social Analysis: Essays by Samuel P. Hays. Samuel P. Hays. LC 79-17567. (Twentieth-Century America Ser.). 468p. 1980. 45.00x (*0-87049-276-4*) U of Tenn Pr.

American Political Ideas. Charles E. Merriam. LC 70-97887. reprint ed. 20.00 (*0-404-04310-0*) AMS Pr.

American Political Ideas. Charles E. Merriam. LC 68-56259. 481p. 1969. reprint ed. 45.00 (*0-678-00511-7*) Kelley.

American Political Ideas: Traditions & Usages. Michael Foley. LC 90-25493. 224p. 1991. text ed. 35.00 (*0-7190-3293-8*, Pub. by Manchester Univ Pr UK) St Martin.

American Political Ideas: Traditions & Usages. Michael Foley. 224p. 1993. text ed. 19.95 (*0-7190-3294-6*, Pub. by Manchester Univ Pr UK) St Martin.

American Political Ideas Viewed from the Standpoint of Universal History. John Fiske. (Notable American Authors Ser.). 1992. reprint ed. lib. bdg. 75.00 (*0-7812-2846-8*) Rprt Serv.

American Political Leaders. Ed. by Steven O'Brien et al. 473p. 1991. lib. bdg. 65.00 (*0-87436-570-8*) ABC-CLIO.

American Political Movies: An Annotated Filmography. James Combs. LC 89-78251. (Filmographies Ser.). 198p. 1990. 32.00 (*0-8240-7847-0*) Garland.

American Political Nation, 1838-1893. Joel H. Silbey. LC 90-25813. (Studies in the New Political History). (Illus.). xiv, 348p. 1991. 35.00 (*0-8047-1878-4*) Stanford U Pr.

American Political Nation, 1838-1893. Joel H. Silbey. 1994. pap. 15.95 (*0-8047-2338-9*) Stanford U Pr.

American Political Novel. Gordon Milne. 1972. pap. 11.95 (*0-8061-1050-3*) U of Okla Pr.

American Political Parties: A Reader. Ed. by Eric M. Uslaner. LC 92-61955. 620p. (Orig.). (C). 1993. pap. 32.50 (*0-87581-367-4*) Peacock Pubs.

American Political Parties: The Formation, Decline & Reform of the American Party System. Dean McSweeney & John Zvesper. 288p. 1991. 75.00 (*0-415-01169-8*, A5500); pap. 17.95 (*0-415-01170-1*, A5504) Routledge.

American Political Parties & Constitutional Politics. Ed. by Peter W. Schramm & Bradford P. Wilson. (Ashbrook Series on Constitutional Politics). 264p. (Orig.). (C). 1993. lib. bdg. 58.50 (*0-8476-7819-9*); pap. text ed. 22.95 (*0-8476-7820-2*) Rowman.

American Political Prisoners: Prosecutions under the Espionage & Sedition Acts. Stephen M. Kohn. LC 93-37883. 248p. 1994. text ed. 49.95 (*0-275-94415-8*, Praeger Pubs) Greenwood.

American Political Process. 2nd ed. Richard A. Maidment & Anthony G. McGrew. (Illus.). 224p. 1991. text ed. 49.95 (*0-8039-8525-8*); pap. text ed. 19.95 (*0-8039-8434-0*) Sage.

An Asterisk (*) at the beginning of an entry indicates that the title is appearing in BIP for the first time.

257

American Political Process. 5th ed. Alan Grant. 356p. (C). 1994. text ed. 57.95 (*1-85521-505-5*, Pub. by Dartmth Pub UK); pap. text ed. 21.95 (*1-85521-495-4*, Pub. by Dartmth Pub UK) Ashgate Pub Co.

American Political Rhetoric: A Reader. 2nd ed. Peter Lawler. 180p. 1990. pap. text ed. 14.95 (*0-8476-7642-0*) Rowman.

***American Political Rhetoric: A Reader.** 3rd ed. Ed. by Peter A. Lawler & Robert M. Schaefer. 320p. (C). 1995. pap. text ed. 19.95 (*0-8476-8047-9*) Rowman.

American Political Ribbons & Ribbon Badges 1825-1981. Roger A. Fischer & Edmund B. Sullivan. LC 84-62281. (Illus.). 409p. 1985. lib. bdg. 75.00 (*0-88000-138-0*) Quarterman.

American Political Scandals Past & Present. Barbara S. Feinberg. LC 92-25485. (Illus.). 160p. (YA). (gr. 9-12). 1992. lib. bdg. 14.98 (*0-531-11126-1*) Watts.

American Political Scientists: A Dictionary. Ed. by Glenn H. Utter & Charles Lockhart. LC 92-35958. 400p. 1993. text ed. 89.50 (*0-313-27849-0*, UPS/) Greenwood.

American Political System. David P. Calleo. LC 69-17194. (Background Ser.). 1969. 16.95 (*0-8023-1210-1*) Dufour.

American Political System: A Radical Approach. 5th ed. Edward S. Greenberg. (C). 1988. pap. text ed. 39.50 (*0-673-39888-9*) HarpCollege.

American Political System: Readings. Frank Bryan. Ed. by Baxter. 513p. (C). 1991. pap. text ed. 26.75 (*0-314-85391-X*) West Pub.

American Political Theology: Historical Perspective & Theoretical Analysis. Charles W. Dunn. LC 84-13308. 208p. 1984. text ed. 55.00 (*0-275-91146-2*, C1146, Praeger Pubs); pap. text ed. 15.95 (*0-275-91603-0*, B1603, Praeger Pubs) Greenwood.

American Political Thinking: Readings from the Origins to the 21st Century. Robert A. Isaak. 850p. (Orig.). (C). 1994. pap. text ed. 32.00 (*0-15-500365-8*) HarBrace.

American Political Thought. 2nd ed. Kenneth M. Dolbeare. LC 89-22077. 576p. 1989. pap. text ed. 34.95x (*0-934540-78-0*) Chatham Hse Pubs.

American Political Thought: Readings. Ed. by Larry I. Peterman & Louis F. Weschler. LC 78-184069. (C). 1972. pap. text ed. 16.95 (*0-89197-015-0*) Irvington.

American Political Tradition. Richard Hofstadter. 1989. pap. 12.00 (*0-679-72315-3*, Vin) Random.

American Political Tradition & the Men Who Made It. 2nd ed. Richard Hofstadter. 1973. 24.95 (*0-394-48880-6*) Knopf.

American Political Trials. exp. rev. ed. Ed. by Michal R. Belknap. LC 93-30888. (Contributions in American History Ser.: No. 152). 352p. 1994. text ed. 69.50 (*0-313-28687-6*, Greenwood Pr); pap. text ed. 22.95 (*0-275-94437-9*, Greenwood Pr) Greenwood.

American Political Writing During the Founding Era: 1760-1805, 2 vols., Set. Charles S. Hyneman & Donald S. Lutz. LC 82-24884. 1983. 28.50 (*0-86597-038-6*); pap. 16.00 (*0-86597-041-6*) Liberty Fund.

American Politician. Francis M. Crawford. LC 32-33609. 1967. 8.00 (*0-403-00034-3*) Scholarly.

American Politician. Joyner Conrad. LC 70-160811. 247p. reprint ed. pap. 70.40 (*0-8357-5391-3*, 2024318) Bks Demand.

American Politician. Francis M. Crawford. LC 73-111088. (BCL Ser. I). reprint ed. 29.50 (*0-404-01828-9*) AMS Pr.

***American Politicians: Photographs 1840 to 1993.** Susan Kismaric. (Illus.). 1994. 39.95 (*0-8109-6135-0*) Abrams.

American Politicians Photographs 1843 to 1993. Peter Galassi. (Illus.). 256p. 1995. 60.00 (*0-87070-140-1*, 0-8109-6135-0); pap. 29.95 (*0-87070-141-X*) Mus of Modern Art.

American Politics. Kenneth M. Dolbeare et al. 572p. (C). 1985. teacher ed 2.00 (*0-685-45690-0*); pap. text ed. 23.00 (*0-685-45689-7*) Heath.

American Politics: A Study in Political Dynamics. Peter H. Odegard & E. Allen Helms. LC 73-19164. (Politics & People Ser.). 900p. 1974. reprint ed. 69.95 (*0-405-05886-1*) Ayer.

American Politics: Changing Expectations. 4th ed. Ronald Pynn. 480p. (C). 1993. pap. text ed. write for info. (*0-697-12893-8*) Brown & Benchmark.

American Politics: Classic & Contemporary Readings. Allen J. Cigler & Burdett A. Loomis. LC 88-81326. 1989. 2.76 (*0-318-36887-0*) HM.

American Politics: Directions of Change, Dynamics of Choice. 2nd ed. Richard E. Morgan et al. 672p. (C). 1982. student ed 5.75 (*0-394-34931-8*); text ed. 20.00 (*0-394-34930-X*) Random.

American Politics: How It Really Works. Milton Meltzer. LC 88-26635. (Illus.). 192p. (YA). (gr. 7 up). 1989. 12.95 (*0-688-07494-4*) Morrow Jr Bks.

American Politics: Policies, Power, & Change. 5th ed. Kenneth M. Dolbeare & Murray J. Edelman. LC 84-81190. 572p. (C). 1985. pap. text ed. 23.00 (*0-669-07323-7*); Instr.'s guide. teacher ed 2.00 (*0-669-07235-4*) Heath.

American Politics: The Pluralist Tradition. USMA Staff. 608p. (C). 1993. per., pap. text ed. 35.00 (*0-8403-8619-2*) Kendall-Hunt.

American Politics: The Promise of Disharmony. Samuel P. Huntington. 310p. (C). 1983. pap. text ed. 15.50 (*0-674-03021-4*) HUP.

American Politics & Everyday Life. 2nd ed. Robert D. Holsworth & J. Harry Wray. 399p. (C). 1987. pap. write for info. (*0-02-356800-3*) Macmillan.

American Politics & Foreign Economic Challenge. Hongsuk H. Park. LC 90-41583. (Foreign Economic Policy of the United States Ser.). 283p. 1990. reprint ed. 25.00 (*0-8240-7434-3*) Garland.

American Politics & Government. Richard M. Pious. 752p. 1986. text ed. 34.95 (*0-07-050121-1*) McGraw.

American Politics & Government: Structure, Processes, Institutions & Policies. Barbara Hinckley & Sheldon Goldman. (C). 1989. pap. text ed. 43.00 (*0-673-39813-7*) HarpCollege.

American Politics & Society. 3rd ed. David McKay. LC 93-7211. (Illus.). 340p. (YA). (gr. 10 up). 1993. pap. 19.95 (*0-631-18814-2*) Blackwell Pubs.

American Politics in a Bureaucratic Age: Citizens, Constituents, Clients & Victims. Eugene Lewis. 192p. (C). 1988. reprint ed. pap. text ed. 19.50 (*0-8191-7049-6*) U Pr of Amer.

American Politics in a Changing World. Janet A. Flammang et al. 750p. (C). 1990. text ed. 47.95 (*0-534-12342-2*); student ed, pap. 16.95 (*0-534-12344-9*) Intl Thomson.

American Politics in an Age of Failure (1963-1985) Lewis P. Fickett, Jr. LC 85-51988. 65p. (Orig.). 1985. pap. text ed. 14.95 (*0-932269-73-7*) Wyndhall Pr.

American Politics in the Early Republic: The New Nation in Crisis. James R. Sharp. LC 93-19179. 352p. 1993. 30.00 (*0-300-05530-7*) Yale U Pr.

American Politics in the Heartland. Madsen et al. 304p. (C). 1990. pap. text ed. 23.95 (*0-8403-5890-3*) Kendall-Hunt.

American Politics in the Media Age. 4th ed. Thomas R. Dye et al. LC 91-15973. 432p. (C). 1992. pap. 29.95 (*0-534-16776-4*) Intl Thomson.

American Politics, Policies & Priorities. 5th ed. Alan Shank. 540p. (Orig.). (C). 1988. pap. write for info. (*0-697-06810-2*) Brown & Benchmark.

American Politics, Policies, & Priorities. 6th ed. Alan Shank. 528p. (C). 1993. pap. text ed. write for info. (*0-697-11134-2*) Brown & Benchmark.

American Politics Today. J. D. Lees et al. LC 85-23145. 208p. (Orig.). 1988. text ed. 9.95 (*0-7190-1838-2*, Pub. by Manchester Univ Pr UK) St Martin.

American Politics Today. 4th ed. Richard Maidment. (Politics Today Ser.). 248p. 1994. text ed. write for info. (*0-7190-3939-8*, Pub. by Manchester Univ Pr UK); text ed. write for info. (*0-7190-3940-1*, Pub. by Manchester Univ Pr UK) St Martin.

American Polity. 3rd ed. Everett C. Ladd, Jr. (C). 1989. disk write for info. (*0-318-63777-4*) Norton.

American Polity. 3rd ed. Everett C. Ladd, Jr. (C). 1993. student ed, pap. text ed. 15.95 (*0-393-96352-7*) Norton.

American Polity. 5th ed. Everett C. Ladd, Jr. (C). 1993. pap. text ed. 37.95 (*0-393-96351-9*); teacher ed, pap. text ed. write for info. (*0-393-96353-5*) Norton.

American Polity Reader. Everett C. Ladd et al. Ed. by W. Wayne Shannon, Jr. & Everett C. Ladd, Jr. (C). 1993. pap. text ed. write for info. (*0-393-96306-3*) Norton.

American Polity Reader. 2nd ed. Everett C. Ladd et al. Ed. by W. Wayne Shannon, Jr. & Everett C. Ladd, Jr. (C). 1993. pap. text ed. 21.95 (*0-393-96305-5*) Norton.

***American Popular Ballad of the Golden Era, 1924-1950: A Study in Musical Design.** Allen Forte. LC 94-47249. 1995. write for info. (*0-691-04399-X*) Princeton U Pr.

American Popular Culture: A Guide to the Reference Literature. Frank W. Hoffman. (Reference Sources in the Humanities Ser.). 250p. 1994. lib. bdg. 37.50 (*1-56308-142-3*) Libs Unl.

American Popular Entertainment: Paper & Proceedings of the Conference on the History of American Popular Entertainment. Myron Matlaw. LC 78-74655. (Contributions in Drama & Theatre Studies: No. 1). (Illus.). 338p. 1979. text ed. 35.00 (*0-313-21072-1*, MEN/) Greenwood.

American Popular Entertainments: A Collection of Jokes, Monologues & Comedy Routines. Ed. by Brooks McNamara. LC 83-61192. 1983. 28.50 (*0-933826-36-2*); pap. 12.95 (*0-933826-37-0*) PAJ Pubns.

American Popular Illustration: A Reference Guide. James J. Best. LC 83-14150. (American Popular Culture Ser.). x, 121p. 1984. text ed. 49.95 (*0-313-23389-6*, BEI/, Greenwood Pr) Greenwood.

American Popular Music. David L. Joyner. 352p. (C). 1993. pap. text ed. write for info. (*0-697-11439-2*) Brown & Benchmark.

American Popular Music: A Reference Guide. Mark W. Booth. LC 82-21062. (American Popular Culture Ser.). xvi, 212p. 1983. text ed. 49.95 (*0-313-21305-4*, BPM/, Greenwood Pr) Greenwood.

American Popular Music & Its Business: The First Four Hundred Years, Vol. 1: Beginning to 1790. Russell Sanjek. (Illus.). 494p. 1988. Vol. I: The Beginning to 1790, 494 pgs. 60.00 (*0-19-504028-7*) OUP.

American Popular Music & Its Business: The First Four Hundred Years, Vol. 2: 1790-1909. abr. ed. Russell Sanjek. (Illus.). 494p. 1988. Vol. II: From 1790-1909, 494 pgs. 60.00 (*0-19-504310-3*) OUP.

American Popular Music & Its Business: The First Four Hundred Years, Vol. 3: 1900-1984. Russell Sanjek. (Illus.). 750p. 1988. Vol. III: From 1900-1984, 750 pgs. 69.00 (*0-19-504311-1*) OUP.

American Popular Music Business in the Twentieth Century. Russell Sanjek & David Sanjek. 368p. 1991. 30.00 (*0-19-505828-3*) OUP.

American Popular Music, Vol. 1: The Nineteenth Century Tin Pan Alley. Ed. by Timothy E. Scheurer. LC 89-62346. (Readings from the Popular Press Ser.). 181p. (C). 1990. lib. bdg. 37.95 (*0-87972-465-X*); pap. 17.95 (*0-87972-466-8*) Bowling Green Univ.

American Popular Music, Vol. 2: The Age of Rock. Ed. by Timothy E. Scheurer. LC 89-62346. (Readings from the Popular Press Ser.). 267p. (C). 1990. lib. bdg. 41.95 (*0-87972-467-6*); pap. 23.95 (*0-87972-468-4*) Bowling Green Univ.

***American Popular Psychology: An Interdisciplinary Research Guide.** Stephen B. Fried. LC 94-13412. 272p. 1994. 39.00 (*0-8153-0402-1*, SS785) Garland.

American Popular Song: The Great Innovators, 1900-1950. Alec Wilder. LC 70-159643. (Illus.). 576p. 1972. 35.00 (*0-19-501445-6*) OUP.

American Popular Song: The Great Innovators, 1900-1950. Alec Wilder. LC 70-159643. (Illus.). 576p. 1975. pap. 14.95 (*0-19-501925-3*) OUP.

American Popular Songs from the Revolutionary War to the Present. Ed. by David Ewen. 1966. 19.95 (*0-394-41705-4*) Random.

American Popular Stage Music, 1860-1880. Deane L. Root. LC 81-1512. (Studies in Musicology: No. 44). (Illus.). 294p. reprint ed. pap. 83.80 (*0-8357-1509-4*, 2070293) Bks Demand.

American Population Before the Federal Census of 1790. Evarts B. Greene & Virginia D. Harrington. 252p. 1993. reprint ed. 25.00 (*0-8063-1377-3*, 2345) Genealog Pub.

American Population Change Annual: A Between-the-Census-Years Guide to Local Area Population Data & Trends. (Illus.). 379p. (Orig.). 1994. pap. 42.00 (*1-884925-01-4*) Toucan Valley.

***American Populism.** Ed. & Intro. by William F. Holmes. (Problems in American Civilization Ser.). 222p. (C). 1994. pap. write for info. (*0-669-33495-2*) Heath.

American Populism. Robert McMath. 1992. pap. 10.95 (*0-374-52264-2*, Noonday) FS&G.

American Populism. Robert Mcmath. 1992. 30.00 (*0-8090-7796-5*) Hill & Wang.

American Porcelain, Seventeen Seventy to Nineteen Twenty. Alice C. Frelinghuysen. (Illus.). 320p. 1989. 60.00 (*0-8109-1887-0*) Abrams.

American Porcelain, Seventeen Seventy to Nineteen Twenty. Alice C. Frelinghuysen. (Illus.). 336p. 1989. 29.95 (*0-87099-540-5*, Abrams) Metro Mus Art.

American Porcelain Tradition. Norton, R. W., Art Gallery Staff. LC 72-82888. (Illus.). 1972. pap. 3.00 (*0-9600182-8-X*) Norton Art.

***American Portfolios: Three Wilderness Portfolios.** David Muench & Marc Muench. (Illus.). 168p. 1994. 39.95 (*1-56313-441-1*) BrownTrout Pubs Inc.

American Portrait Miniatures: In the Manney Collection. Dale T. Johnson. (Illus.). 272p. 1990. 39.50 (*0-8109-6401-5*, Abrams) Metro Mus Art.

American Portrait Miniatures: The Worcester Art Museum Collection. Susan E. Strickler. (Illus.). 160p. (Orig.). 1989. pap. 15.00 (*0-936042-44-3*) Worcest Art.

American Portraits Vol. 1 to 1877: History Through Biography. Donald W. Whisenhunt. 352p. (C). 1993. per., pap. text ed. 23.95 (*0-8403-8525-0*) Kendall-Hunt.

American Portraits, Vol. II: From 1865 - History Through Biography. Donald W. Whisenhunt. 368p. (C). 1993. per., pap. text ed. 23.95 (*0-8403-8530-7*) Kendall-Hunt.

American Portraits 1800-1850: A Catalogue of Early Portraits in the Collection of Union College. Rita Feigenbaum. LC 71-173916. (Illus.). 155p. (C). 1972. text ed. 10.95x (*0-912756-01-2*) Union Coll.

American Postcard Guide to Tuck. rev. ed. Sally S. Carver. (Illus.). 1980. pap. 7.95 (*0-686-18747-4*) Carves.

American Postcard Guide to Tuck. rev. ed. Sally S. Carver. (Illus.). 1982. pap. 10.95 (*0-686-38919-0*) Carves.

American Postcard Publishers, 1895-1945. James A. Maccaro. (Illus.). 52p. (Orig.). 1986. pap. write for info. (*0-930429-00-1*) Bibliographic Pr.

American Poster: Graphic Communications in the Twentieth Century. Edgar Breitenbach. Ed. by Margaret Cogswell. LC 66-18340. (Illus.). 1968. 17.50 (*0-8079-0002-8*); pap. 9.95 (*0-8079-0003-6*) October.

American Posters of the Nineties. Roberta Wong et al. (Illus.). 1974. 10.00 (*0-89073-037-7*) Boston Public Lib.

American Pot Lids. Barbara Jackson & Sonny Jackson. (Illus.). 150p. (Orig.). 1987. 39.95 (*0-9618987-0-4*) S & B Jackson.

American Potters: Mary & Edwin Scheier. Michael K. Komanecky. LC 93-72197. (Illus.). 110p. 1994. pap. 29.95 (*0-929710-12-6*) Currier Gal.

American Potters & Pottery. John Ramsay. LC 76-22944. (Illus.). 1976. reprint ed. 34.95 (*0-89344-006-X*) Ars Ceramica.

American Pottery & Porcelain: Identification & Price Guide. William C. Ketchum, Jr. LC 93-50203. (Illus.). 496p. (Orig.). 1994. pap. 18.00 (*0-380-77138-1*, Confident Collect) Avon.

American Poultry History 1823-1973. O. A. Hanke et al. 1974. 25.00 (*0-318-17814-1*) Am Poultry Soc.

American POW's. Samuel Kim. LC 77-90036. 1978. pap. 14.95 (*0-8283-1708-9*) Branden Pub Co.

American POWs of World War II: Forgotten Men Tell Their Stories. Tom Bird. LC 91-46991. 184p. 1992. text ed. 45.00 (*0-275-93707-0*, C3707, Praeger Pubs) Greenwood.

American Practical Navigator: Being an Epitome of Navigation, 2 vols., Set. Nathaniel Bowditch. 1977. reprint ed. 75.00 (*0-403-08994-8*, Regency) Scholarly.

American Practices in the Design of Prestressed Concrete Containment Structures. (PCI Journal Reprints Ser.). 24p. 1968. pap. 6.00 (*0-685-06890-0*, JR64) P-PCI.

American Pragmatism: Peirce, James & Dewey. Edward C. Moore. LC 84-25291. 285p. 1985. reprint ed. text ed. 52.50 (*0-313-24740-4*, MOOA, Greenwood Pr) Greenwood.

American Preachers of Today: Intimate Appraisals of Thirty-Two Leaders. Edgar D. Jones. LC 76-156667. (Essay Index Reprint Ser.). 1977. reprint ed. 21.95 (*0-8369-2279-4*) Ayer.

American Precedents in Australian Federation. Erling M. Hunt. LC 68-58591. (Columbia University. Studies in the Social Sciences: No. 326). reprint ed. 22.50 (*0-404-51326-3*) AMS Pr.

***American Prejudice: With Liberty & Justice for Some.** Richard H. Ropers & Daniel J. Pence. 290p. 1995. 27.95 (*0-306-44946-3*) Da Capo.

American Prejudice Against Color. William G. Allen. LC 75-82165. (Anti-Slavery Crusade in America Ser.). 1970. reprint ed. 21.95 (*0-405-00603-9*) Ayer.

American Prelude. Lars Eighner. (Orig.). 1994. pap. text ed. 4.95 (*1-56333-170-5*) Masquerade.

***American Premium Guide to Pocket Knives & Razors: Identification & Value Guide.** 4th rev. ed. Jim Sargent. (American Premium Guide to Pocket Knives & Razors Ser.). (Illus.). 504p. 1995. pap. 22.95 (*0-89689-110-0*) Bks Americana.

American Premium Record Guide. 1984. lib. bdg. 79.95 (*0-87700-497-8*) Revisionist Pr.

American Premium Record Guide (1915-1965) 4th ed. L. R. Docks. 400p. (Orig.). 1991. 22.95 (*0-89689-088-0*) Bks Americana.

American Presidency. Harold Laski. LC 80-50104. (Social Science Classics Ser.). 278p. 1980. 34.95 (*0-87855-390-8*); pap. 18.95 (*0-87855-821-7*) Transaction Pubs.

***American Presidency.** 2nd ed. James W. Davis. LC 95-7981. 1995. text ed. write for info. (*0-275-94874-9*, Praeger Pubs); pap. text ed. write for info. (*0-275-94875-7*, Praeger Pubs) Greenwood.

American Presidency. Clinton Rossiter. LC 87-2824. 304p. (Orig.). 1987. reprint ed. pap. 13.95 (*0-8018-3545-3*) Johns Hopkins.

American Presidency: A Bibliography. Fenton S. Martin & Robert U. Goehlert. 1987. 105.00 (*0-87187-415-6*) Congr Quarterly.

American Presidency: A Guide to Information Sources. Ed. by Kenneth E. Davison. LC 73-17552. (American Studies Information Guide Ser.: Vol. 11). 488p. (C). 1983. 68.00 (*0-8103-1261-1*) Gale.

American Presidency: A Policy Perspective from Readings & Documents. Ed. by David C. Kozak & Kenneth N. Ciboski. LC 84-16587. 632p. (Orig.). (C). 1985. pap. text ed. 24.95 (*0-8304-1053-8*) Nelson-Hall.

American Presidency: An Intellectual History. Forrest McDonald. LC 93-30235. 624p. (Orig.). (C). 1995. 29.95 (*0-7006-0652-1*) U Pr of KS.

***American Presidency: An Intellectual History.** Forrest McDonald. LC 93-30235. (Orig.). (C). 1995. pap. 17.95 (*0-7006-0749-8*) U Pr of KS.

American Presidency: Origins & Development, 1776-1993. Sidney M. Milkis & Michael Nelson. LC 93-43358. 1993. pap. 25.95 (*0-87187-766-X*) Congr Quarterly.

American Presidency: Origins & Development, 1776-1993. 2nd ed. Sidney M. Milkis & Michael Nelson. LC 93-43358. 1993. 37.95 (*0-87187-949-2*) Congr Quarterly.

American Presidency: Perspectives from Abroad. Ed. by Kenneth W. Thompson. (Miller Center Tenth Anniversary Commemorative Publication, 1975-1985). 140p. (Orig.). (C). 1986. pap. text ed. 14.50 (*0-8191-5487-3*, Pub. by White Miller Center) U Pr of Amer.

American Presidency: Perspectives from Abroad, Vol. II. Ed. by Kenneth W. Thompson. (Miller Center Bicentennial Commemorative Publication, 1986-1988). 148p. (Orig.). (C). 1989. lib. bdg. 37.00 (*0-8191-7257-X*, Pub. by White Miller Center); pap. text ed. 17.00 (*0-8191-7258-8*, Pub. by White Miller Center) U Pr of Amer.

American Presidency & Civil Rights Policy. Ed. by Donald Jackson & James Riddlesperger. (Orig.). 1993. pap. 12.00 (*0-944285-34-1*) Pol Studies.

American Presidency, Vol. III: Perspectives from Abroad. Ed. by Kenneth W. Thompson. 234p. (Orig.). (C). 1992. lib. bdg. 52.50 (*0-8191-8550-7*) U Pr of Amer.

***American President.** 4th ed. Robert E. DiClerico. LC 94-35158. 448p. 1994. pap. text ed. write for info. (*0-13-211004-0*) P-H.

American President. Sidney Hyman. LC 73-15166. 342p. 1974. reprint ed. text ed. 55.00 (*0-8371-7170-9*, HYAP, Greenwood Pr) Greenwood.

American Presidential Elections: Trust & the Rational Voter. Jeffrey A. Smith. LC 80-17228. 224p. 1980. text ed. 55.00 (*0-275-90553-5*, C0553, Praeger Pubs) Greenwood.

American Presidential Families. LC 93-32206. Orig. Title: Burke's Presidential Families of the United States of America. 792p. 1994. text ed. 95.00 (*0-02-897305-4*) Macmillan.

***American Presidents.** Norman S. Cohen. (Magill Bibliograhies Ser.). 175p. 1989. 40.00 (*0-8108-2815-4*) Scarecrow.

***American Presidents.** 8th ed. David C. Whitney & Robin V. Whitney. (Illus.). 624p. 1993. 17.50 (*1-56865-031-0*, GuildAmerica) Dblday Bk Music.

American Presidents: A Bibliography. Fenton S. Martin & Robert U. Goehlert. 756p. 1987. 155.00 (*0-87187-416-4*) Congr Quarterly.

American Presidents: The Office & the Men, 3 vols. rev. ed. Ed. by Frank N. Magill. LC 85-30338. (Illus.). 1989. Set: Vol. 1, 284p.; Vol. 2, 290p.; Vol. 3, 303p. 150.00 (*0-7172-7166-8*) Grolier Inc.

American Presidents: Their Individualities & Their Contributions to American Progress. Thomas F. Moran. (Essay Index Reprint Ser.). 1977. reprint ed. 21.95 (*0-518-10157-6*) Ayer.

American Presidents & Education. Maurice R. Berube. LC 90-24709. (Contributions to the Study of Education Ser.: No. 46). 184p. 1991. text ed. 49.95 (*0-313-27848-2*, BBQ/, Greenwood Pr) Greenwood.

American Presidents & the Middle East. George Lenczowski. LC 89-17056. 368p. (C). 1989. lib. bdg. 42.00 (*0-8223-0963-7*); pap. text ed. 21.95 (*0-8223-0972-6*) Duke.

American Presidents & the Presidency. Marcus Cunliffe. 1986. 19.95 (*0-317-40595-0*); pap. 9.95 (*0-317-40596-9*) HM.

An Asterisk (*) at the beginning of an entry indicates that the title is appearing in BIP for the first time.

American Presidents & Their Knowledge of Foreign Languages. John R. Krueger. 1980. pap. 2.00 (0-911706-22-4) Selbstverlag.

American Press Opinion, Washington to Coolidge: A Documentary Record of Editorial Leadership & Criticism, 1785-1927. Allen Nevins. (BCL1 - U. S. History Ser.). 598p. 1991. reprint ed. lib. bdg. 99.00 (0-7812-6023-X) Rprt Serv.

***American Pressed Glass & Bottles Price Guide.** Kyle Husfloen. 1994. pap. 15.95 (0-930625-50-1) Antique Trader.

American Primer. Ed. by Daniel J. Boorstin. 1968. pap. 17.95 (0-452-00922-7, Mer) NAL-Dutton.

American Primer. Walt Whitman. 1971. 59.95 (0-87968-610-3) Gordon Pr.

American Primer. rev. ed. Walt Whitman. Ed. by Horace Traubel. 64p. (C). 1987. reprint ed. 13.00 (0-930100-24-7); reprint ed. pap. 5.95 (0-930100-23-9) Holy Cow.

***American Primer: 1890-1910: Primary Sources in American History.** Daniel J. Boorstin. (PaperBook Series in History). (Illus.). 128p. (Orig.). 1995. pap. text ed. 2.25 (0-614-06681-6) Paperbook Pr Inc.

American Primitive. William Gibson. 1972. pap. 4.75 (0-8222-0035-X) Dramatists Play.

American Primitive: Discoveries in Folk Sculpture. Roger Ricco et al. LC 88-45341. (Illus.). 304p. 1988. 75.00 (0-394-54467-6) Knopf.

American Primitive Art. (Illus.). 1977. pap. 3.00 (0-910810-19-2) Johannes.

American Primitive Music, with Special Attention to Songs of the Highways. Frederick R. Burton. 1977. lib. bdg. 59.95 (0-8490-1416-6) Gordon Pr.

American Primitive Painting. Jean Lipman. LC 79-184124. (Illus.). 158p. 1972. reprint ed. pap. 9.95 (0-486-22815-0) Dover.

American Prince, American Pauper: The Contemporary Vice-Presidency in Perspective. Marie D. Natoli. LC 84-28965. (Contributions in Political Science Ser.: No. 134). xiv, 204p. 1985. text ed. 45.00 (0-313-24750-1, NAR/, Greenwood Pr) Greenwood.

American Printing. James M. Wells. 1985. 6.00 (0-912296-69-0, U Pr of Va) Am Antiquarian.

American Printmakers, 1880-1945: An Index to Reproductions & Biocritical Information. Lynn B. Williams. LC 93-41591. 1993. 52.50 (0-8108-2786-7) Scarecrow.

American Prints from the Sixties. (Illus.). 70p. 1992. pap. 25.00 (0-9629512-2-6) S Sheehan Gallery.

American Prints in the Library of Congress: A Catalog of the Collection. Library of Congress Staff. LC 73-106134. (Illus.). 590p. reprint ed. 168.20 (0-8357-9262-5, 2051253) Bks Demand.

American Prints in the Library of Congress: A Catalogue of the Collection. Karen Beall & Library of Congress Prints Division Staff. (Illus.). 592p. 1991. reprint ed. 125.00 (1-55660-088-7) A Wofsy Fine Arts.

American Prints, 1860-1950. Baltimore Museum of Art Staff. Ed. by Robert F. Johnson. LC 76-13195. 1977. fiche, lib. bdg. 15.00 (0-226-68824-0) U Ch Pr.

American Prints, 1860-1960: From the Collection of Matthew Marks. Intro. by Matthew Marks. LC 85-71125. (Illus.). 32p. 1985. pap. 5.90 (0-9614940-0-X) Bennington Coll.

American Prints 1870 to 1950: Whistler to Weidenaar. Deborah J. Johnson & Lora S. Urbanelli. LC 87-62345. (Illus.). 128p. 1987. pap. 19.95 (0-911517-47-2) Mus of Art RI.

American Prints 1960-1980. Verna P. Curtis. LC 81-85990. (Illus.). 28p. (Orig.). 1982. pap. 3.00 (0-944110-20-7) Milwauk Art Mus.

American Prison from the Beginning - a Pictorial History. LC 83-71616. (Illus.). 264p. 1983. 31.75 (0-942974-48-4, 212) Am Correctional.

American Prison Systems: Punishment & Justice. Richard Hawkins & Geoffrey Alpert. 464p. 1989. text ed. 66.00 (0-13-028572-2) P-H.

American Prisoners of the Revolution. Danske Dandridge. 504p. 1994. reprint ed. pap. 36.00 (0-685-75126-0, 1315) Clearfield Co.

American Prisoners of War, Vol. II. Turner Publishing Co. Staff. LC 90-71719. 244p. 1990. 48.00 (0-685-59051-8) Turner Pub KY.

American Prisons: A History of Good Intentions. 2nd rev. ed. Blake McKelvey. LC 75-14556. (Criminology, Law Enforcement, & Social Problems Ser.: No. 17). (Illus.). (C). 1977. 25.00 (0-87585-704-3) Patterson Smith.

American Problems: A Selection of Speeches & Prophecies. William E. Borah. Ed. by Horace Green. LC 77-111472. (BCL Ser.: I). reprint ed. 15.00 (0-404-00624-8) AMS Pr.

American Problems: A Selection of Speeches & Prophecies. William E. Borah. (History - United States Ser.). 329p. 1992. reprint ed. lib. bdg. 89.00 (0-7812-6214-3) Rprt Serv.

American Problems: A Selection of Speeches & Prophecies. William E. Borah. 1971. reprint ed. 13.00 (0-403-00874-3) Scholarly.

American Problems from the Point of View of a Psychologist. Hugo Munsterberg. LC 75-84328. (Essay Index Reprint Ser.). 1977. 19.95 (0-8369-1098-2) Ayer.

American Procession. Alfred Kazin. LC 83-48855. 394p. 1984. 18.95 (0-394-50378-3) Knopf.

American Procession, 1855-1914. William A. Croffut. LC 68-20293. (Essay Index Reprint Ser.). 1977. 23.95 (0-8369-0352-8) Ayer.

American Prodigals. Liam Rector. 1994. 19.95 (0-685-72739-4); pap. 11.95 (0-685-72740-8) Story Line.

American Profession of Arms: The Army Officer Corps, 1784-1861. William B. Skelton. LC 92-10089. (Modern War Studies). xviii, 486p. 1993. 45.00 (0-7006-0560-6) U Pr of KS.

American Professors: A National Resource Imperiled. Howard R. Bowen & Jack H. Schuster. (Illus.). 304p. 1986. 35.00 (0-19-503693-X) OUP.

American Profile: Attitude & Behaviors of the American People, 1972-1989. Wood. 1990. 89.50 (0-8103-7723-3) Gale.

American Profile: Opinions - Behavior 72-92. 1995. 89.50 (0-8103-8324-1) Gale.

American Profile, 1900-1909. Edward Wagenknecht. LC 81-16510. (Illus.). 384p. 1982. lib. bdg. 37.50x (0-87023-350-5); pap. 19.95x (0-87023-351-3) U of Mass Pr.

American Profiles. Ed. by Esmond Wright. LC 68-90664. (Selections from History Today Ser.: No. 7). (Illus.). 1969. 10.95 (0-8023-9021-8); pap. 8.95 (0-05-001534-6) Dufour.

American Profiles: Portraits of Somebodies & Nobodies Who Matter. Walt Harrington. LC 91-42712. (Illus.). 296p. (C). 1992. 24.95 (0-8262-0839-8) U of Mo Pr.

American Progressive History: An Experiment in Modernization. Ernst A. Breisach. LC 92-31012. 256p. (C). 1993. pap. text ed. 13.95 (0-226-07277-0) U Ch Pr.

American Progressive History: An Experiment in Modernization. Ernst A. Breisach. LC 92-31012. 256p. (C). 1993. lib. bdg. 35.95 (0-226-07276-2) U Ch Pr.

***American Promise.** James C. Crimmins. (Illus.). 224p. (Orig.). 1995. pap. 24.95 (0-912333-71-5) KQED.

American Promise: Equal Justice & Economic Opportunity. Ed. by Arthur I. Blaustein. LC 81-16313. 140p. (Orig.). 1982. pap. 14.95 (0-87855-905-1) Transaction Pubs.

American Pronghorn Antelope. Comp. by James D. Yoakum & Donald E. Spalinger. LC 79-89207. (Illus.). 244p. (Orig.). 1979. pap. 6.00 (0-933564-05-8) Wildlife Soc.

***American Pronunciation.** 12th enl. expanded ed. John S. Kenyon. Ed. by Stewart A. Kingsbury. 1994. write for info. (1-884739-08-3); pap. write for info. (0-911586-47-4) Wahr.

American Pronunciation see Society's Work

American Property Law Teacher's Manual to Accompany Cases & Materials On. 2nd ed. Sheldon F. Kurtz & Herbert Movenkamp. (American Casebook Ser.). 700p. (C). 1993. pap. text ed. write for info. (0-314-02521-9) West Pub.

American Property Records. Arlene H. Eakle. 77p. 1973. pap. 11.00 (0-940764-10-5) Genealog Inst.

American Prophet's Record: The Diaries & Journals of Joseph Smith. Ed. by Scott H. Faulring. 534p. 1989. pap. 9.95 (0-685-37394-0) Sisters New Covenant.

American Prophet's Record: The Diaries & Journals of Joseph Smith. 2nd ed. Joseph Smith. LC 89-6219. 518p. 1989. reprint ed. pap. 9.95 (0-941214-78-8) Signature Bks.

American Prose. Ed. by Walter C. Bronson. LC 71-121525. (Short Story Index Reprint Ser.). 1977. 35.95 (0-8369-3481-4) Ayer.

American Prose. Horace E. Scudder. LC 70-149117. (Granger Index Reprint Ser.). 1977. 24.95 (0-8369-6242-7) Ayer.

American Prose & Criticism, 1820-1900: A Guide to Information Sources. Ed. by Elinore H. Partridge. LC 74-11519. (American Literature, English Literature, & World Literatures in English Information Guide Ser.: Vol. 39). 592p. 1983. 68.00 (0-8103-1213-1) Gale.

American Prose to Eighteen Twenty: A Guide to Information Sources. Tr. by Donald Yannella & John Roch. LC 79-63741. (American Literature, English Literature, & World Literatures in English Information Guide Ser.: Vol. 21). 680p. 1979. 68.00 (0-8103-1361-8) Gale.

American Prosody. Gay Allen. (BCL1-PS American Literature Ser.). 342p. 1993. reprint ed. lib. bdg. 89.00 (0-7812-6582-7) Rprt Serv.

***American Prospect Reader in American Politics.** Ed. by Walter D. Burnham. LC 94-23157. 400p. (Orig.). (C). 1994. pap. text ed. 19.95x (1-56643-012-7) Chatham Hse Pubs.

American Prospector: Contemporary Issues in Prospect Research. American Prospect Researchers Association Staff. 176p. 1991. 26.95 (0-930807-19-7, 600229) Fund Raising.

American Prospects. Photos by Joel Sternfeld. (Illus.). 1987. 40.00 (0-8129-1659-X, Times Bks) Random.

American Prospects: Photographs. Joel Sternfeld. LC 93-35406. 128p. 1994. 24.95 (0-8118-0660-X) Chronicle Bks.

American Protestant Thought in the Liberal Era. Ed. by William R. Hutchison. LC 84-19614. 252p. 1985. reprint ed. pap. text ed. 24.00 (0-8191-4336-7) U Pr of Amer.

American Protestant Women in World Mission. R. Pierce Beaver. LC 80-14366. Orig. Title: All Loves Excelling. 237p. reprint ed. pap. 67.60 (0-8357-9122-X, 2019317) Bks Demand.

American Protestantism. Winthrop S. Hudson. LC 61-15936. (Chicago History of American Civilization Ser.). 1963. pap. text ed. 6.95 (0-226-35803-8, CHAC10) U Ch Pr.

American Protestantism & a Jewish State. Hertzel Fishman. LC 72-3746. 250p. reprint ed. pap. 71.30 (0-8357-5392-1, 2033174) Bks Demand.

American Protestantism & United States Indian Policy, 1869-82. Robert H. Keller, Jr. LC 82-8514. (Illus.). xvi, 383p. 1983. 35.00 (0-8032-2706-X) U of Nebr Pr.

American Protestantism's Response to Germany's Jews & Refugees, 1933-1941. William E. Nawyn. LC 81-7552. (Studies in American History & Culture: No. 30). 342p. reprint ed. pap. 97.50 (0-8357-1208-7, 2070108) Bks Demand.

American Proverbs, Maxims & Folk Sayings. (Americana Book Ser.). (Illus.). 1968. 3.00 (0-911410-19-8) Applied Arts.

American Psalmody. 2nd ed. Frank J. Metcalf. LC 68-13274. (Music Reprint Ser.). (Illus.). 1968. reprint ed. lib. bdg. 19.50 (0-306-71132-X) Da Capo.

American Psychiatric Association Annual Review, Vol. 4. Ed. by Robert E. Hales & Allen J. Frances. 1985. pap. text ed. 30.00 (0-88048-239-7, 8239); pap. text ed. 20.00 (0-88048-039-4, 8039) Am Psychiatric.

American Psychiatric Association Annual Review, Vol. 5. Ed. by Allen J. Frances & Robert E. Hales. 832p. 1986. 30.00 (0-88048-241-9, 8241); pap. 20.00 (0-88048-240-0, 8240) Am Psychiatric.

American Psychiatric Association Annual Review, Vol. 6. Ed. by Robert E. Hales & Allen J. Frances. (Illus.). 800p. 1987. text ed. 30.00 (0-88048-243-5, 48-243-5); pap. text ed. 20.00 (0-88048-242-7, 48-242-7) Am Psychiatric.

***American Psychiatric Association Appointment Book-1996.** American Psychiatric Association Staff. 240p. 1995. spiral bd. 12.00 (0-89042-172-2, 2172); boxed 18.00 (0-89042-171-4, 2171) Am Psychiatric.

***American Psychiatric Association Appointment Book-1996, 2 bks., Set.** American Psychiatric Association Staff. 1995. boxed, spiral bd. 26.00 (0-89042-173-0, 2173) Am Psychiatric.

American Psychiatric Association Auxiliary Cookbook: One Hundred Fifty Years of Cooking & Caring. Ed. by Venie Palasota. LC 94-11008. 1994. write for info. (0-89042-249-4) Am Psychiatric.

American Psychiatric Association's Psychiatric Glossary. American Psychiatric Association Staff. LC 84-473. 152p. reprint ed. pap. 43.40 (0-8357-7805-3, 2036175) Bks Demand.

American Psychiatric Glossary. 7th ed. Ed. by Jane E. Edgerton & Robert J. Campbell, III. 145p. 1994. text ed. write for info. (0-88048-526-4); pap. text ed. 16.70 (0-88048-508-6) Am Psychiatric.

American Psychiatric Press Review of Clinical Psychiatry & the Law. Ed. by Robert I. Simon. 500p. 1989. text ed. 42.50 (0-88048-375-X) Am Psychiatric.

American Psychiatric Press Review of Clinical Psychiatry & the Law, Vol. 2. Ed. by Robert I. Simon. 400p. 1990. text ed. 42.50 (0-88048-376-8) Am Psychiatric.

***American Psychiatric Press Review of Psychiatry, Vol. 14.** Ed. by John M. Oldham & Michelle B. Riba. 992p. 1995. boxed 59.95 (0-88048-441-1, 8441) Am Psychiatric.

American Psychiatric Press Review of Psychiatry, Vol. 7. Robert E. Hales & Allen J. Frances. 700p. 1988. text ed. 30.00 (0-88048-245-1) Am Psychiatric.

American Psychiatric Press Review of Psychiatry, Vol. 8. Ed. by Allan Tasman et al. 641p. 1989. 30.00 (0-88048-247-8, 8247) Am Psychiatric.

American Psychiatric Press Review of Psychiatry, Vol. 9. Ed. by Allan Tasman et al. 672p. 1990. 30.00 (0-88048-248-6, FCNA8248) Am Psychiatric.

American Psychiatric Press Review of Psychiatry, Vol. 10. Ed. by Allan Tasman & Stephen M. Goldfinger. 800p. 1991. 54.95 (0-88048-436-5, CG1A8436) Am Psychiatric.

American Psychiatric Press Review of Psychiatry, Vol. 11. Ed. by Allan Tasman & Michelle Riba. 1992. text ed. 54.95 (0-88048-437-3) Am Psychiatric.

American Psychiatric Press Review of Psychiatry, Vol. 12. Ed. by John M. Oldham et al. 1993. 59.95 (0-88048-439-X) Am Psychiatric.

***American Psychiatric Press Review of Psychiatry, Vol. 13.** Ed. by John M. Oldham & Michelle B. Riba. 1994. boxed 59.95 (0-88048-440-3, 8440) Am Psychiatric.

American Psychiatric Press Textbook of Geriatric Neuropsychiatry. Ed. by C. Edward Coffey & Jeffrey L. Cummings. 1994. text ed. 105.00 (0-88048-391-1, 8391) Am Psychiatric.

***American Psychiatric Press Textbook of Geriatric Psychiatry.** Ed. by Ewald W. Busse & Dan G. Blazer. 1995. boxed 89.95 (0-88048-713-5, 8713) Am Psychiatric.

American Psychiatric Press Textbook of Neuropsychiatry. 2nd ed. Ed. by Stuart C. Yudofsky & Robert E. Hales. 864p. 1992. text ed. 105.00 (0-88048-387-3, 8387) Am Psychiatric.

American Psychiatric Press Textbook of Neuropsychiatry. Ed. by Robert E. Hales & Stuart C. Yudofsky. LC 86-32238. (Illus.). 510p. reprint ed. pap. 145.40 (0-7837-2502-7, 2042602) Bks Demand.

American Psychiatric Press Textbook of Psychiatry. 2nd ed. Ed. by Robert E. Hales et al. LC 93-48305. 1600p. 1994. text ed. 150.00 (0-88048-388-1, 8388) Am Psychiatric.

***American Psychiatric Press Textbook of Psychopharmacology.** Ed. by Alan F. Schatzberg & Charles B. Nemeroff. 846p. 1995. boxed 120.00 (0-88048-389-X, 8389) Am Psychiatric.

American Psychiatric Press Textbook of Substance Abuse Treatment. Ed. by Marc Galanter & Herbert D. Kleber. LC 93-26826. 848p. 1994. text ed. 71.55 (0-88048-532-9, 8532) Am Psychiatric.

American Psychiatrist in Vienna, 1935-1937 & His Sigmund Freud. John M. Dorsey. 213p. 1976. 26.95 (0-8143-1644-1) Wayne St U Pr.

American Psychiatrists Abroad: An Original Anthology. Isaac Ray & Pliny Earle. LC 75-16679. (Classics in Psychiatry Ser.). 1976. 30.95 (0-405-07411-5) Ayer.

American Psycho. Bret E. Ellis. 416p. 1991. pap. 14.00 (0-679-73577-1, Vin) Random.

American Psycho. Bret E. Ellis. 400p. 1991. 19.95 (0-671-66397-6) S&S Trade.

American Psychological Association: A Historical Perspective. Ed. by Rand B. Evans et al. (Illus.). 431p. 1992. text ed. 40.00 (1-55798-136-1) Am Psychol.

American Psychologist Special Issue, Vol. 46, No. 11: Homelessness. Ed. by Allison A. Rosenberg et al. 156p. 1991. pap. 16.00 (1-55798-161-2) Am Psychol.

American Psychologist Special Issue, Vol. 47, No. 2: The History of American Psychology. Ed. by Ludy T. Benjamin, Jr. 263p. 1992. pap. 20.00 (1-55798-170-1) Am Psychol.

American Psychology in Historical Perspective: Addresses of the Presidents of the American Psychological Association, 1892-1977. Ed. by Ernest R. Hilgard. LC 78-15672. 568p. reprint ed. pap. 161.90 (0-7837-2678-3, 2043055) Bks Demand.

American Psychology in the Quest for Nuclear Peace. Marilyn S. Jacobs. LC 88-19028. 192p. 1989. text ed. 55.00 (0-275-92850-0, C2850, Praeger Pubs) Greenwood.

American Psychology since World War II: A Profile of the Discipline. Albert R. Gilgen. LC 81-23740. (Illus.). xiii, 272p. 1982. text ed. 59.95 (0-313-23027-7, GAM/, Greenwood Pr) Greenwood.

American Public Administration. Melvin J. Dubnick. 416p. (C). 1991. write for info. (0-02-330661-0) Macmillan.

American Public Administration: Concepts & Cases. 3rd ed. Carl E. Lutrin & Allen K. Settle. (Illus.). 544p. (C). 1985. text ed. write for info. (0-13-028705-9) P-H.

American Public Administration: Concepts & Cases. 4th ed. Carl E. Lutrin & Allen K. Settle. Ed. by Jucha. 522p. (C). 1992. text ed. 53.75 (0-314-91349-1) West Pub.

American Public Administration: Past, Present, Future. Ed. by Frederick C. Mosher. LC 74-17916. 312p. 1975. pap. 14.95 (0-8173-4829-8) U of Ala Pr.

American Public Administration: Patterns of the Past. Ed. by James W. Fesler. (PAR Classics Ser.: No. 4). 333p. reprint ed. pap. 95.00 (0-8357-4221-0, 2037006) Bks Demand.

American Public Architecture: European Roots & Native Expressions. Ed. by Craig Zabel & Susan S. Munshower. LC 89-42842. (Papers in Art History: Vol. V). (Illus.). 307p. 1989. pap. 22.00 (0-915773-04-X) Penn St Univ Dept Art Hist.

American Public Discourse: A Multicultural Perspective. Ronald K. Burke. LC 92-14800. 338p. (Orig.). (C). 1992. lib. bdg. 54.00 (0-8191-8752-6); pap. text ed. 34.00 (0-8191-8753-4) U Pr of Amer.

American Public Education: Let's Cut the Yarn. John J. Hunt. LC 85-13170. 1986. 19.95 (0-88280-113-9) ETC Pubns.

American Public Finance & Financial Services, 1700-1815. Edwin J. Perkins. LC 93-28736. (Historical Perspectives on Business Enterprise Ser.). 448p. 1994. 49.50 (0-8142-0619-0) Ohio St U Pr.

American Public Library & the Problem of Purpose. Patrick Williams. LC 88-16382. (Contributions in Librarianship & Information Science Ser.: No. 62). 144p. 1988. text ed. 39.95 (0-313-25590-3, WAL/, Greenwood Pr) Greenwood.

American Public Opinion. Michael Corbett. 381p. (Orig.). (C). 1991. pap. text ed. 33.95 (0-8013-0323-0, 78091) Longman.

American Public Opinion. 4th rev. ed. Robert S. Erikson et al. 400p. (C). 1991. pap. write for info. (0-02-334011-8) Macmillan.

***American Public Opinion: Its Origins, Content, & Impact.** 5th ed. Robert S. Erikson. LC 94-21993. 390p. 1994. pap. text ed. 29.00 (0-02-334042-8) Allyn.

American Public Opinion & U. S. Foreign Policy, 1982. 2nd ed. Chicago Council on Foreign Relations Staff. LC 84-81558. 1984. write for info. (0-89138-896-6) ICPSR.

American Public Opinion Data 1981. 1984. fiche 100.00 (0-913577-03-0) Opinion Res.

American Public Opinion Data 1982. 1984. fiche 100.00 (0-913577-04-9) Opinion Res.

American Public Opinion Data 1983. 1985. fiche 100.00 (0-913577-05-7) Opinion Res.

American Public Opinion Data, 1984. 1985. fiche 100.00 (0-913577-07-3) Opinion Res.

American Public Opinion Data, 1985. 1986. fiche 100.00 (0-913577-14-6) Opinion Res.

American Public Opinion Data, 1986. 1987. fiche 100.00 (0-913577-18-9) Opinion Res.

American Public Opinion Data, 1987. 1988. fiche 125.00 (0-913577-21-9) Opinion Res.

American Public Opinion Data, 1988. 1989. fiche 125.00 (0-913577-32-4) Opinion Res.

American Public Opinion Data, 1989. 1990. fiche 149.50 (0-913577-35-9) Opinion Res.

American Public Opinion Data, 1990. 1991. fiche 174.50 (0-913577-38-3) Opinion Res.

American Public Opinion Data, 1991. 1992. fiche 174.50 (0-913577-41-3) Opinion Res.

American Public Opinion Data, 1992. 1993. fiche 174.50 (0-913577-47-2) Opinion Res.

American Public Opinion Data, 1993. 1994. fiche 184.50 (0-913577-52-9) Opinion Res.

***American Public Opinion Data 1994.** 1995. fiche 184.50 (0-913577-55-3) Opinion Res.

American Public Opinion Index & Data, 1981. 1983. 225.00 (0-913577-22-7) Opinion Res.

American Public Opinion Index & Data, 1982. 1984. 225.00 (0-913577-23-5) Opinion Res.

American Public Opinion Index & Data, 1983. 1985. 225.00 (0-913577-24-3) Opinion Res.

American Public Opinion Index & Data, 1984. 900p. 1985. fiche 225.00 (0-913577-25-1) Opinion Res.

An Asterisk (*) at the beginning of an entry indicates that the title is appearing in BIP for the first time.

259

American Public Opinion Index & Data, 1985. 1300p. 1986. fiche 225.00 (*0-913577-26-X*) Opinion Res.

American Public Opinion Index & Data, 1986. 1000p. 1987. fiche 225.00 (*0-913577-27-8*) Opinion Res.

American Public Opinion Index & Data, 1987. 1200p. 1988. fiche 249.50 (*0-913577-28-6*) Opinion Res.

American Public Opinion Index & Data, 1988. 1550p. 1989. fiche 249.50 (*0-913577-29-4*) Opinion Res.

American Public Opinion Index & Data, 1989. 1990. fiche 274.50 (*0-913577-33-2*) Opinion Res.

American Public Opinion Index & Data, 1990. 1530p. 1991. fiche 299.00 (*0-913577-36-7*) Opinion Res.

American Public Opinion Index & Data, 1991. 1992. fiche 299.00 (*0-913577-39-1*) Opinion Res.

American Public Opinion Index & Data, 1992. 1740p. 1993. 299.00 (*0-913577-45-6*) Opinion Res.

American Public Opinion Index & Data, 1993. 1994. 314.00 (*0-913577-50-2*) Opinion Res.

***American Public Opinion Index & Data 1994.** 1995. 314.00 (*0-913577-53-7*) Opinion Res.

American Public Opinion Index, 1981. LC 83-646386. 600p. 1983. 125.00 (*0-913577-00-6*); fiche 125.00 (*0-913577-11-1*) Opinion Res.

American Public Opinion Index, 1982. LC 83-646386. 750p. 1984. 125.00 (*0-913577-01-4*); fiche 125.00 (*0-913577-10-3*) Opinion Res.

American Public Opinion Index, 1983. LC 83-646386. 800p. 1985. 125.00 (*0-913577-02-2*); fiche 125.00 (*0-913577-09-X*) Opinion Res.

American Public Opinion Index, 1984. LC 83-646386. 900p. 1985. 125.00 (*0-913577-06-5*); fiche 125.00 (*0-913577-08-1*) Opinion Res.

American Public Opinion Index, 1985. LC 83-646386. 1300p. 1986. 125.00 (*0-913577-12-X*); fiche 125.00 (*0-913577-13-8*) Opinion Res.

American Public Opinion Index, 1986. LC 83-646386. 1000p. 1987. 125.00 (*0-913577-16-2*); fiche 125.00 (*0-913577-17-0*) Opinion Res.

American Public Opinion Index, 1987. LC 83-646386. 1200p. 1988. 149.50 (*0-913577-19-7*); fiche 149.50 (*0-913577-20-0*) Opinion Res.

American Public Opinion Index, 1988. LC 83-646386. 1550p. 1989. 149.50 (*0-913577-30-8*) Opinion Res.

American Public Opinion Index, 1989. LC 83-646386. 162p. 1990. 149.50 (*0-913577-34-0*) Opinion Res.

American Public Opinion Index, 1990. LC 83-646386. 1530p. 1991. 174.50 (*0-913577-37-5*) Opinion Res.

American Public Opinion Index 1991. LC 83-646386. 1840p. 1992. 174.50 (*0-913577-40-5*) Opinion Res.

American Public Opinion Index, 1992. LC 83-64638. 1740p. 1993. 174.50 (*0-913577-46-4*) Opinion Res.

American Public Opinion Index, 1993. LC 83-64638. 2200p. 1994. 184.50 (*0-913577-51-0*) Opinion Res.

***American Public Opinion Index 1994.** LC 83-64638. 2200p. 1995. 184.50 (*0-913577-54-5*) Opinion Res.

American Public Opinion on NATO, Extended Deterrence, & Use of Nuclear Weapons: Future Fission? Thomas W. Graham. LC 88-36476. (Occasional Papers Ser.: No. 4). (Illus.). 158p. (Orig.). (C). 1989. lib. bdg. 32.00 (*0-8191-7373-8*, HU Ctr Sci); pap. text ed. 17.50 (*0-8191-7374-6*, HU Ctr Sci) U Pr of Amer.

American Public Opinion Toward Israel & the Arab-Israeli Conflict. Eytan Gilboa. 384p. 1986. text ed. 45.00 (*0-669-13426-0*) Free Pr.

***American Public Policy.** annuals Ed. by Bruce Stinebrickner. (Illus.). 256p. (C). 1995. pap. text ed. 12.95x (*1-56134-402-8*) Dushkin Pub.

American Public Policy: An Introduction. 4th ed. Clarke E. Cochran et al. LC 92-50014. (Illus.). 492p. (C). 1992. pap. text ed. 35.50 (*0-312-06190-0*) St Martin.

American Public Policy: Promise & Performance. 3rd ed. B. Guy Peters. LC 92-25245. 400p. (Orig.). 1993. pap. text ed. 33.95x (*0-934540-87-X*) Chatham Hse Pubs.

***American Public Policy: Promise & Performance.** 4th ed. B. Guy Peters. LC 95-13597. (Orig.). 1995. write for info. (*1-56643-024-0*) Chatham Hse Pubs.

American Public Policy in a Comparative Context. H. M. Leichter, Jr. & Harrell R. Rodgers. 1984. text ed. write for info. (*0-07-037067-2*) McGraw.

American Public School Law. 3rd ed. Kern Alexander & David Alexander. Ed. by Hannan. 880p. (C). 1992. text ed. 61.25 (*0-314-92952-5*) West Pub.

American Pueblo Indian Activity Book. Walter D. Yoder. (Illus.). 48p. (J). (gr. 3-9). 1994. pap. 7.95 (*0-86534-219-9*) Sunstone Pr.

American Pulp & Paper Industry, 1900-1940: Mill Survival, Firm Structure, & Industry Relocation. Nancy K. Ohanian. LC 92-18362. (Contributions in Economics & Economic History Ser.: No. 140). 240p. 1993. text ed. 52.95 (*0-313-27366-9*, KPJ, Greenwood Pr) Greenwood.

American Puritan Imagination: Essays in Revaluation. Ed. by Sacvan Bercovitch. LC 73-94136. 273p. reprint ed. pap. 77.90 (*0-8357-5393-X*, 2027269) Bks Demand.

American Puritan Studies: An Annotated Bibliography of Dissertations, 1882-1981. Comp. by Michael S. Montgomery. LC 84-6553. (Bibliographies & Indexes in American History Ser.: No. 1). xxii, 419p. 1984. text ed. 89.50 (*0-313-24237-2*, MON/) Greenwood.

American Puritanism & the Defense of Mourning: Religion, Grief, & Ethnology in Mary White Rowlandson's Captivity Narrative. Mitchell R. Breitwieser. LC 90-50080. (Wisconsin Project on American Writers Ser.). 224p. (Orig.). (C). 1990. text ed. 40.00 (*0-299-12650-1*); pap. text ed. 17.50 (*0-299-12654-4*) U of Wis Pr.

American Puritans: Their Prose & Poetry. Perry Miller. LC 81-10222. 360p. 1982. reprint ed. pap. text ed. 18.00 (*0-231-05419-X*) Col U Pr.

American Pursuit Pilot in France: Roland W. Richardson's Diaries & Letters, 1917-1919. Ed. by Carl M. Becker & Ritchie Thomas. (Illus.). 244p. (C). 1994. 24.95 (*0-942597-64-8*) White Mane Pub.

American Quaker in the British Isles: The Travel Journals of Jabez Maud Fisher, 1775-1779. Jabez M. Fisher. Ed. by Kenneth Morgan. (Records of Social & Economic History, New Series British Academy: No. 16). (Illus.). 300p. 1992. 79.00 (*0-19-726096-9*, 12189) OUP.

American Quality Legend: How Maytag Saved Our Moms, Vexed the Competition, & Presaged America's Quality Revolution. Robert Hoover & John Hoover. 240p. 1993. text ed. 21.95 (*0-07-030309-6*) McGraw.

***American Quarter Century: U. S. Politics from Vietnam to Clinton.** Ed. by Philip J. Davies. LC 95-3503. 1995. text ed. write for info. (*0-7190-4514-2*, Pub. by Manchester Univ Pr UK); text ed. write for info. (*0-7190-4515-0*) St Martin.

American Quarter Horse in Pictures. Margaret C. Self. 1979. pap. 5.00 (*0-87980-237-5*) Wilshire.

American Quest for a Supreme Fiction: Whitman's Legacy in the Personal Epic. James E. Miller, Jr. LC 78-15176. 1981. pap. text ed. 9.95 (*0-226-52612-7*) U Ch Pr.

American Quest for the City of God. Leland D. Baldwin. LC 81-14125. ix, 368p. (C). 1981. 18.95 (*0-86554-016-0*, H16) Mercer Univ Pr.

American Quest for the Primitive Church. Ed. by Richard T. Hughes. 272p. (C). 1995. pap. 14.95 (*0-252-06029-6*) U of Ill Pr.

American Quest for the Primitive Church. Ed. by Richard T. Hughes. LC 88-5437. 267p. reprint ed. pap. 76.10 (*0-7837-5738-7*, 2045399) Bks Demand.

American Question in Its National Aspect. Elias Peissner. LC 71-152928. (Black Heritage Library Collection). 1977. 17.95 (*0-8369-8772-1*) Ayer.

American Quilt: Cloth & Comfort, 1750-1950. Roderick Kiracofe. 1993. 60.00 (*0-517-57535-3*, C P Pubs) Crown Pub Group.

American Quilt Story: The How-to & Heritage of a Craft Tradition. Susan Jenkins & Linda Seward. LC 94-16741. 1995. 17.99 (*0-517-12000-3*, Pub. by Wings Bks) Random Hse Value.

American Quilt Story: The How-to & Heritage of a Craft Tradition. Susan Jenkins & Linda Seward. LC 91-20619. (Illus.). 256p. 1992. 26.95 (*0-87857-992-3*, 11-420-0) Rodale Pr Inc.

American Quilts & Coverlets in the Metropolitan Museum of Art. Amelia Peck. (Illus.). 264p. 1990. 35.00 (*0-87099-592-8*) Metro Mus Art.

American Quilts & Coverlets in the Metropolitan Museum of Art. Amelia Peck. 256p. 1990. 50.00 (*0-525-24912-5*, Dutton Studio) Studio Bks.

American Quiz Book. Robert Duffy. 134p. (YA). (gr. 7 up). 1993. pap. 6.95 (*1-85371-187-X*, Pub. by Poolbeg Pr IE) Dufour.

American Quotations. Ed. by Gorton Carruth. Orig. Title: Harper Book of American Quotations. 848p. 1992. reprint ed. 14.99 (*0-517-07361-7*, Pub. by Wings Bks) Random Hse Value.

American Rabbinate: A Century of Continuity & Change 1883-1983. Jacob R. Marcus & Abraham J. Peck. 300p. 1985. text ed. 25.00 (*0-88125-076-7*) Ktav.

American Race. Daniel G. Brinton. (Works of Daniel Garrison Brinton). 1989. reprint ed. lib. bdg. 79.00 (*0-7812-2057-2*) Rprt Serv.

American Race Theorists. Byram Campbell. 1984. lib. bdg. 250.00 (*0-87700-638-5*) Revisionist Pr.

American Racer Nineteen Forty to Nineteen Eighty. Stephen Wright. (Illus.). 240p. 1989. 39.95 (*0-87938-377-1*) Motorbooks Intl.

American Racer Nineteen Hundred to Nineteen Thirty-Nine. Stephen Wright. (Illus.). 276p. 1989. 39.95 (*0-87938-376-3*) Motorbooks Intl.

American Racing Motorcycles. Jerry Hatfield. (Illus.). 224p. 1989. pap. 17.95 (*0-87938-355-0*) Motorbooks Intl.

American Radical. Ed. by Mari J. Buhle et al. LC 93-41221. 1994. 55.00 (*0-415-90803-5*); pap. 18.95 (*0-415-90804-3*) Routledge.

American Radicalism, 1865-1901, Essays & Documents. Chester M. Destler. (History - United States Ser.). 276p. 1993. reprint ed. lib. bdg. 79.00 (*0-7812-4905-8*) Rprt Serv.

American Radio: A Report on the Broadcasting Industry in the United States from the Commission on Freedom of the Press. Llewellyn White. LC 70-161177. (History of Broadcasting: Radio to Television Ser.). 1977. reprint ed. 26.95 (*0-405-03583-7*) Ayer.

American Radio Industry & Its Latin American Activities, 1900-1939. James Schwoch. 200p. 1990. 29.95 (*0-252-01690-4*) U of Ill Pr.

American Railroad As Investments: A Handbook for Investors in American Railroad Securities. S. F. Van Oss. Ed. by Mira Wilkins. LC 76-29744. (European Business Ser.). (Illus.). 1977. reprint ed. lib. bdg. 63.95 (*0-405-09761-1*) Ayer.

American Railroad Builder: John Murray Forbes. Henry G. Pearson. LC 72-29. (Select Bibliographies Reprint Ser.). 1977. reprint ed. 18.95 (*0-8369-9968-1*) Ayer.

American Railroad Freight Car: From the Wood-Car Era to the Coming of Steel. John H. White, Jr. LC 92-24255. (Illus.). 665p. (C). 1993. 125.00 (*0-8018-4404-5*) Johns Hopkins.

***American Railroad Freight Car: From the Wood-Car Era to the Coming of Steel.** John H. White, Jr. (Illus.). 665p. 1995. reprint ed. pap. 49.95 (*0-8018-5236-6*) Johns Hopkins.

American Railroad Network, Eighteen Sixty-One to Eighteen Ninety. George Taylor & Irene D. Neu. Ed. by Stuart Bruchey. LC 80-1350. (Railroads Ser.). 1981. reprint ed. lib. bdg. 18.95 (*0-405-13819-9*) Ayer.

American Railroad Passenger Car, 2 pts., Pt. 1. John H. White, Jr. LC 84-26161. (Illus.). 730p. 1985. reprint ed. pap. 29.95 (*0-8018-2722-1*) Johns Hopkins.

American Railroad Passenger Car, 2 pts., Pt. 2. John H. White, Jr. LC 84-26161. (Illus.). 730p. 1985. reprint ed. pap. 29.95 (*0-8018-2747-7*) Johns Hopkins.

American Railroad Passenger Car, 2 pts., Set. John H. White, Jr. LC 84-26161. (Illus.). 730p. 1985. reprint ed. pap. 49.95 (*0-8018-2743-4*) Johns Hopkins.

American Railroad Watches: George Townsend 1977, with 1983 Price Guide. Roy Ehrardt. 1982. 25.00 (*0-913902-40-3*) Heart Am Pr.

American Railroads: The Case for Nationalization. Dick Roberts. LC 80-80795. (Illus.). 1980. lib. bdg. 35.00 (*0-87348-601-3*); pap. 11.95 (*0-87348-600-5*) Pathfinder NY.

American Railroads & the Transformation of the Ante-Bellum Economy. Albert Fishlow. LC 65-22068. (Economic Studies: No. 127). (Illus.). 467p. 1965. 27.50 (*0-674-02850-3*) HUP.

American Railway: Its Constructon, Development, Management, & Appliances. Thomas Clarke et al. LC 74-189048. (Illus.). reprint ed. 25.00 (*0-405-08364-5*, Pub. by Blom Pubns UK) Ayer.

American Rain. Jim Stempel. 364p. 1991. 18.95 (*0-9629340-9-7*); pap. 9.95 (*0-685-47981-1*) Monocacy River.

American Reader. D. Ravitch. 1992. 35.00 (*0-06-270065-0*, HarpT) HarpC.

American Reader: Words That Moved a Nation. Ed. by Diane Ravitch. LC 89-46553. 400p. 1991. reprint ed. pap. 14.00 (*0-06-272016-3*, Harper Ref) HarpC.

American Reading Instruction: Its Development & Its Significance in Gaining a Perspective on Current Practices in Reading. rev. ed. Nila B. Smith. 465p. reprint ed. pap. 132.60 (*0-8357-5394-8*, 2029726) Bks Demand.

American Reading Instruction: With a Prologue by Leonard Courtney & an Epilogue by H. Alan Robinson. Nila B. Smith. 536p. reprint ed. pap. 152.80 (*0-8357-2627-4*, 2040115) Bks Demand.

American Realism. Edward Lucie-Smith. LC 93-48535. 1994. write for info. (*0-8109-1941-9*) Abrams.

American Realism: New Essays. Ed. by Eric J. Sundquist. LC 82-3010. 311p. reprint ed. pap. 88.70 (*0-7837-6187-2*, 2045909) Bks Demand.

American Realism & American Drama: 1800-1940. Brenda Murphy. (Cambridge Studies in American Literature & Culture: No. 22). 272p. 1987. 54.95 (*0-521-32711-3*) Cambridge U Pr.

American Realism & the Canon. Ed. by Tom Quirk & Gary Scharnhorst. LC 94-11782. 1995. write for info. (*0-87413-524-9*) U Delaware Pr.

American Realism & the Industrial Age. Marianne Doezema. LC 80-67347. (Themes in Art Ser.). (Illus.). 144p. 1981. pap. 5.00 (*0-910386-61-7*) Cleveland Mus Art.

American Realist Painting, 1945-1980. John L. Ward. Ed. by Stephen Foster. (Studies in the Fine Arts: The Avant-Garde: No. 60). 450p. reprint ed. pap. 127.40 (*0-8357-2079-9*, 2070678) Bks Demand.

American Realists & Magic Realists. Ed. by Dorothy C. Miller & Alfred H. Barr, Jr. LC 77-86431. (Museum of Modern Art Publications in Reprint). (Illus.). 1969. reprint ed. 12.95 (*0-405-01539-9*) Ayer.

American Realists & Naturalists, Vol. 12. Ed. by Earl Harbert & Donald Pizer. (Dictionary of Literary Biography Ser.: Vol. 12). 486p. 1982. pap. 128.00 (*0-8103-1149-6*, 006390-M99348) Gale.

American Realities, 1. 3rd ed. J. William Youngs. (C). 1993. 28.50 (*0-673-52239-3*) HarpCollege.

American Realities, 2. 3rd ed. J. William Youngs. (C). 1993. 28.50 (*0-673-52240-7*) HarpCollege.

American Realities: Episodes in American History from Reconstruction to the Present, Vol. II. 2nd ed. J. William Youngs. (C). 1987. pap. text ed. 16.00 (*0-673-39362-3*) HarpCollege.

American Realities: Episodes in American History from the First Settlements to the Civil War, Vol. I. 2nd ed. J. William Youngs. (C). 1987. pap. text ed. 16.00 (*0-673-39361-5*) HarpCollege.

American Rebellion. Henry W. Beecher. LC 70-168510. (Black Heritage Library Collection). 1977. reprint ed. 22.95 (*0-8369-8863-9*) Ayer.

American Reconstruction, Eighteen Sixty-Five to Eighteen Seventy. 2nd ed. Georges Clemenceau. LC 68-16229. (American Scene Ser.). 1969. reprint ed. 35.00 (*0-306-71010-2*) Da Capo.

American Record, 1. William Graebner & Leonard Richards. LC 81-13748. (C). 1981. pap. text ed. 10.00 (*0-394-32216-9*, KnopfC) Knopf.

American Record, 2. William Graebner & Leonard Richards. LC 81-13748. (C). 1981. pap. text ed. 10.00 (*0-394-32665-2*, KnopfC) Knopf.

American Record: Images of the Nation's Past, 2 Vols. 2nd ed. William Graebner & Leonard Richards. 325p. 1988. pap. text ed. write for info. (*0-318-60655-0*) McGraw.

***American Record: Images of the Nation's Past.** 3rd ed. Ed. by William Graebner & Leonard Richards. LC 94-26793. 1995. pap. text ed. write for info. (*0-07-023987-8*) McGraw.

American Record: Images of the Nation's Past, 2 Vols., Vol. 1 to 1877. 2nd ed. William Graebner & Leonard Richards. 325p. 1988. Vol. 1 to, 1877. pap. text ed. write for info. (*0-07-553881-4*) McGraw.

American Record: Images of the Nation's Past, 2 Vols., Vol. 2, since 1865. 2nd ed. William Graebner & Leonard Richards. 325p. 1988. pap. text ed. write for info. (*0-07-553855-5*) McGraw.

American Record Label Book: From the Mid-19th Century Through 1942. Brian Rust. LC 83-18921. (Roots of Jazz Ser.). (Illus.). 336p. 1983. reprint ed. lib. bdg. 49.50 (*0-306-76211-0*) Da Capo.

***American Recreational Property Survey: 1993.** (Industry Issues Ser.). 17p. 1993. 65.00 (*0-614-04624-6*, 21300) ARDA.

American Recycling Market Directory "ARM" 8th ed. Robert Boulanger. 800p. 1992. lib. bdg. 125.00 (*1-880978-00-8*) Am Recycling Mkt.

American Red Cross. Patrick F. Gilbo. (Know Your Government Ser.). (Illus.). 96p. (YA). (gr. 5 up). 1987. lib. bdg. 14.95 (*0-87754-827-7*) Chelsea Hse.

American Red Cross, a History. Foster R. Dulles. LC 71-138110. 554p. (C). 1971. reprint ed. text ed. 38.50 (*0-8371-5686-6*, DUAR, Greenwood Pr) Greenwood.

American Red Cross Adult CPR. American Red Cross Staff. LC 92-583. 1993. pap. 8.75 (*0-8016-7062-4*) Mosby Yr Bk.

American Red Cross Adult CPR Workbook. American Red Cross Staff. 171p. (Orig.). 1990. pap. write for info. (*0-86536-075-8*, 329128) Am Red Cross.

American Red Cross Basic Water Safety & Emergency Water Safety Instructor's Manual. American Red Cross Staff. 182p. 1990. teacher ed write for info. (*0-86536-148-7*, 329314) Am Red Cross.

American Red Cross Basic Water Safety Textbook. American Red Cross Staff. (Illus.). 102p. (Orig.). 1990. student ed, pap. write for info. (*0-86536-141-X*, 329312) Am Red Cross.

American Red Cross Child Story Activity Book. American Red Cross Staff. (J). (ps-3). 1992. pap. 39.50 (*0-8016-6509-4*) Mosby Yr Bk.

American Red Cross Community CPR Workbook. American Red Cross Staff. 304p. (Orig.). 1990. pap. write for info. (*0-86536-083-9*, 329364) Am Red Cross.

American Red Cross Community First Aid & Safety. American Red Cross Staff. 31p. 1992. pap. 150.00 (*0-8016-7147-7*); pap. 12.00 (*0-8016-7064-0*) Mosby Yr Bk.

American Red Cross Community First Aid & Safety. American Red Cross Staff. 1993. 150.00 (*0-8016-7539-1*) Mosby Yr Bk.

American Red Cross Community First Aid & Safety. American Red Cross Staff. 1993. 12.00 (*0-8016-7538-3*) Mosby Yr Bk.

American Red Cross CPR: Basic Life Support for the Professional Rescuer Workbook. American Red Cross Staff. 137p. (Orig.). 1990. pap. write for info. (*0-86536-082-0*, 329365) Am Red Cross.

American Red Cross CPR for the Professional Rescue. Rescue American Red Cross Staff. 32p. 1993. 100.00 (*0-8016-7254-6*); pap. 11.00 (*0-8016-7067-5*) Mosby Yr Bk.

American Red Cross CPR: Infant Child: Infant Child - Workbook. American Red Cross Staff. 202p. (Orig.). 1990. pap. write for info. (*0-86536-135-5*, 329369) Am Red Cross.

American Red Cross CPR Instructor's Manual. American Red Cross Staff. 316p. (Orig.). 1990. teacher ed, pap. write for info. (*0-86536-133-9*, 329367) Am Red Cross.

American Red Cross CPR Instructor's Manual Supplement: Basic Life Support for the Professional Rescuer. American Red Cross Staff. 146p. 1990. teacher ed write for info. (*0-86536-130-4*, 329368) Am Red Cross.

American Red Cross Emergency Water Safety Textbook. American Red Cross Staff. (Illus.). 74p. (Orig.). 1990. student ed, pap. write for info. (*0-86536-142-8*, 329313) Am Red Cross.

American Red Cross First Aid & Safety Handbook. American Red Cross Staff & Kathleen A. Handal. 1992. 29.95 (*0-316-73645-7*); pap. 15.95 (*0-316-73646-5*) Little.

American Red Cross Infant & Preschool Aquatic Program Instructor's Manual. American Red Cross Staff. (Illus.). 150p. 1990. teacher ed write for info. (*0-86536-137-1*, 329321) Am Red Cross.

American Red Cross Infant & Preschool Aquatic Program Parent's Guide. American Red Cross Staff. 24p. (Orig.). 1990. pap. write for info. (*0-86536-136-3*, 329320) Am Red Cross.

American Red Cross Lifeguard Training Instructor's Manual. American Red Cross Staff. (Illus.). 200p. 1990. teacher ed write for info. (*0-86536-147-9*, 329447) Am Red Cross.

American Red Cross Lifeguard Training Supplement. American Red Cross Staff. 90p. (Orig.). 1990. student ed, pap. write for info. (*0-86536-145-2*, 329448) Am Red Cross.

American Red Cross Lifeguard Training Textbook. American Red Cross Staff. (Illus.). 1990. student ed write for info. (*0-86536-057-X*, 321119) Am Red Cross.

American Red Cross Oxygen Administration. American Red Cross Staff. 24p. 1993. pap. 62.50 (*0-8016-7276-7*) Mosby Yr Bk.

American Red Cross Preventing Disease Transmission. American Red Cross Staff. 24p. 1993. 30.00 (*0-8016-7273-2*); pap. 31.25 (*0-8016-7272-4*) Mosby Yr Bk.

American Red Cross Safety Training for Swim Coaches Instructor's Manual. American Red Cross Staff. 102p. (Orig.). 1990. teacher ed, pap. write for info. (*0-86536-146-0*, 329450) Am Red Cross.

American Red Cross Safety Training for Swim Coaches Manual. American Red Cross Staff. (Illus.). 88p. 1990. student ed write for info. (*0-86536-143-6*) Am Red Cross.

American Red Cross Standard First Aid. American Red Cross Staff. 231p. 1992. pap. 12.00 (*0-8016-7065-9*) Mosby Yr Bk.

American Red Cross Swimming & Diving. American Red Cross Staff. 356p. (J). 1992. pap. 20.00 (*0-8016-6506-X*) Mosby Yr Bk.

An Asterisk (*) at the beginning of an entry indicates that the title is appearing in BIP for the first time.

American Red Cross 'til Help Arrives. American Red Cross Staff. LC 92-39673. 16p. 1992. pap. 18.75 (*0-8016-7063-2*) Mosby Yr Bk.

American Reference Books Annual, 1989, Vol. 20. Ed. by Bohdan S. Wynar & Anna G. Patterson. 850p. 1989. lib. bdg. 75.00 (*0-87287-758-2*) Libs Unl.

American Reference Books Annual, 1990, Vol. 21. Ed. by Bohdan S. Wynar et al. 850p. 1990. lib. bdg. 85.00 (*0-87287-825-2*) Libs Unl.

American Reference Books Annual, 1991, Vol. 22. Ed. by Bohdan S. Wynar et al. 850p. 1991. lib. bdg. 85.00 (*0-87287-885-6*) Libs Unl.

American Reference Books Annual, 1992, Vol. 23. Ed. by Bohdan S. Wynar et al. 850p. 1992. lib. bdg. 85.00 (*0-87287-964-X*) Libs Unl.

American Reference Books Annual, 1993, Vol. 24. Ed. by Bohdan S. Wynar et al. xxvii, 837p. 1993. lib. bdg. 87.50 (*1-56308-076-1*) Libs Unl.

American Reference Books Annual, 1994, Vol. 25. Ed. by Bohdan S. Wynar & Anna G. Patterson. 850p. 1994. lib. bdg. 90.00 (*1-56308-177-6*) Libs Unl.

***American Reference Books Annual, 1995, Vol. 26.** Ed. by Bohdan S. Wynar. 825p. 1995. lib. bdg. 95.00 (*1-56308-178-4*) Libs Unl.

American Reflections: Paintings 1830-1940 from the Collections of Pomona College & Scripps College. Ed. by Kay Koeninger et al. (Illus.). 130p. 1984. 15.00 (*0-915478-52-8*) Galleries Coll.

***American Reform & Reformers: A Biographical Dictionary.** Ed. by Randall M. Miller & Paul A. Cimbala. LC 95-16048. 1996. text ed. write for info. (*0-313-28839-9*, Greenwood Pr) Greenwood.

American Reform Responsa. Ed. by Walter Jacob. LC 83-7565. 561p. 1983. pap. text ed. 20.00 (*0-916694-83-6*) Central Conf.

American Reformers. Ed. by Alden Whitman. LC 85-636. (Illus.). 944p. 1985. 89.00 (*0-8242-0705-X*) Wilson.

American Reformers Eighteen Fifteen to Eighteen Sixty. Ronald G. Walters. (American Century Ser.). 256p. 1978. pap. 9.95 (*0-8090-0130-6*) Hill & Wang.

American Refugee Poet. Laimons Juris G. 1970. pap. 4.00 (*0-9600288-0-3*) Poet Papers.

American Refugee Policy & European Jewry, 1933-1945. Richard Breitman & Alan M. Kraut. LC 86-42997. 320p. 1988. 29.95 (*0-253-30415-6*) Ind U Pr.

American Refugees. Jim Hubbard. (Illus.). 126p. 1991. text ed. 44.95 (*0-8166-1896-8*); pap. 19.95 (*0-8166-1927-1*) U of Minn Pr.

American Regional Cookery Index. Rhonda Kleiman. 221p. 1989. 59.95 (*1-55570-029-2*) Neal-Schuman.

American Regional Cooking for Eight or Fifty. George Karousos et al. LC 92-27316. 300p. 1993. text ed. 39.95 (*0-471-57085-0*) Wiley.

American Regional Dialects: A Word Geography. Craig M. Carver. (Illus.). 416p. 1987. pap. text ed. 18.95 (*0-472-08103-9*) U of Mich Pr.

***American Regional Favorites.** Knapp. 1994. 7.99 (*0-517-13604-X*) Random Hse Value.

American Regional Menus. LC 83-9321. (Great Meals in Minutes Ser.). (gr. 7 up). 1984. lib. bdg. 18.60 (*0-86706-163-4*) Time-Life.

American Regional Theatre History to 1900: A Bibliography. Comp. by Carl F. Larson. LC 79-11282. 200p. 1979. 22.00 (*0-8108-1216-9*) Scarecrow.

American Register of Exporters & Importers see American Export Register

American Registry of Professional Entomologists. 102p. 30.00 (*0-317-01121-9*) Am Reg Pro Entomologists.

American Regulatory Federalism & Telecommunications Infrastructure. Ed. by Paul Teske. (Telecommunications Ser.). 176p. 1995. text ed. 36.00 (*0-8058-1615-1*) L Erlbaum Assocs.

American Reinforcement in the World War. Thomas G. Frothingham. LC 70-152984. (Select Bibliographies Reprint Ser.). 1977. reprint ed. 30.95 (*0-8369-5736-9*) Ayer.

American Relations in the Caribbean. Charles P. Howland. LC 76-111717. (American Imperialism: Viewpoints of United States Foreign Policy, 1898-1941 Ser.). 1977. reprint ed. 25.95 (*0-405-02027-9*) Ayer.

American Religion: A Cultural Perspective. Mary F. Bednarowski. LC 83-22895. (Illus.). 182p. (C). 1984. pap. text ed. 19.00 (*0-13-029059-9*) P-H.

American Religion: The Emergence of the Post-Christian Nation. Harold Bloom. 288p. 1992. 22.00 (*0-671-67997-X*) S&S Trade.

American Religion: The Emergence of the Post-Christian Nation. Harold Bloom. 288p. 1993. pap. 12.00 (*0-671-86737-7*, Touchstone Bks) S&S Trade.

American Religious & Biblical Spectaculars. Gerald E. Forshey. LC 91-47578. (Media & Society Ser.). 224p. 1992. text ed. 45.00 (*0-275-93197-8*, C3197, Praeger Pubs) Greenwood.

American Religious Creeds, Vols. 1-3: An Essential Compendium of More Than 450 Statements of Belief & Doctrine, 3 vols. Ed. by J. Gordon Melton. LC 90-47872. 1992. reprint ed. Vol. 1, 349p. pap. 14.95 (*0-89243-487-2*, Triumph Books); reprint ed. Vol. 2, 323p. pap. 14.95 (*0-89243-488-0*, Triumph Books); reprint ed. Vol. 3, 201p. pap. 14.95 (*0-89243-489-9*, Triumph Books); reprint ed. Set. pap. 39.95 (*0-89243-490-2*, Triumph Books) Liguori Pubns.

American Religious Empiricism. William Dean. LC 85-27769. (SUNY Series in Religious Studies). 150p. 1986. 64.50 (*0-88706-280-6*); pap. 21.95 (*0-88706-281-4*) State U NY Pr.

American Religious Groups View Foreign Policy: Trends in Rank-&-File Opinion, 1937-1969. Alfred O. Hero. LC 72-81335. 566p. reprint ed. pap. 147.20 (*0-8357-5395-6*, 2052237) Bks Demand.

American Religious Thought: A History. William A. Clebsch. LC 73-82911. xii, 212p. 1985. reprint ed. pap. text ed. 13.95 (*0-226-10962-3*) U Ch Pr.

American Renaissance. Marvin Cetron. 1990. pap. 10.95 (*0-312-05050-X*) St Martin.

American Renaissance. Robert L. Duffus. LC 70-105679. reprint ed. 34.50 (*0-404-02214-6*) AMS Pr.

American Renaissance. Francis Matthiessen. (BCL1-PS American Literature Ser.). 678p. 1993. reprint ed. lib. bdg. 109.00 (*0-7812-6577-0*) Rprt Serv.

American Renaissance: Art & Expression in the Age of Emerson & Whitman. F. O. Matthiessen. (C). 1968. reprint ed. pap. 19.95 (*0-19-500759-X*) OUP.

American Renaissance: New Dimensions. Ed. by Harry R. Garvin. LC 82-45565. (Bucknell Review Ser.: Vol. 28, No.1). 176p. 1983. 22.00 (*0-8387-5054-0*) Bucknell U Pr.

American Renaissance & the Critics. Jeanetta Boswell. LC 90-5996. 526p. 1990. 55.00 (*0-89341-599-5*, Longwood Academic) Hollowbrook.

American Renaissance in New England. Ed. by Joel Myerson. LC 77-82803. (Dictionary of Literary Biography Ser.: Vol. 1). (Illus.). 240p. 1978. 128.00 (*0-8103-0913-0*) Gale.

American Renaissance Reconsidered. Ed. by Walter B. Michaels & Donald E. Pease. LC 84-47940. (Selected Papers from the English Institute; 1982-83, New Ser.: No. 9). 231p. reprint ed. pap. 65.90 (*0-8357-8020-1*, 2034118) Bks Demand.

American Renaissance Reconsidered. Ed. by Walter B. Michaels & Donald E. Pease. LC 84-47940. (Selected Papers from the English Institute; 1982-83, New Ser.: No. 9). 208p. 1989. reprint ed. pap. text ed. 12.95 (*0-8018-3937-8*) Johns Hopkins.

American "Reparations" to Germany, 1919-33: Implications for the Third-World Debt Crisis. Stephen A. Schuker. LC 88-12747. (Studies in International Finance: No. 61). 170p. 1988. pap. text ed. 11.00 (*0-88165-233-4*) Princeton U Int Finan Econ.

American Reporters on the Western Front, 1914 to 1918. Emmet Crozier. LC 80-19400. (Illus.). xii, 299p. 1980. reprint ed. text ed. 65.00 (*0-313-22655-5*, CRAR, Greenwood Pr) Greenwood.

American Republic. Orestes A. Brownson. Ed. by Americo D. Lapati. (Masterworks of Literature Ser.). 1972. 17.95x (*0-8084-0012-6*); pap. 13.95 (*0-8084-0013-4*) NCUP.

American Republic, Vol. 1, to 1877. John A. Schutz & Richard S. Kirkendall. LC 77-93846. (Illus.). 1978. pap. text ed. write for info. (*0-88273-250-1*) Forum Pr IL.

American Republic, Vol. 2, since 1877. John A. Schutz & Richard S. Kirkendall. LC 77-93846. (Illus.). 1978. pap. text ed. write for info. (*0-88273-252-8*) Forum Pr IL.

American Republic: Its Constitution, Tendencies, & Destiny. rev. ed. Orestes A. Brownson. LC 68-55493. 1972. reprint ed. lib. bdg. 49.50 (*0-678-00785-3*) Kelley.

American Republic: Its Constitution, Tendencies, & Destiny. Orestes A. Brownson. (Works of Orestes Augustus Brownson). 1989. reprint ed. lib. bdg. 79.00 (*0-7812-2111-0*) Rprt Serv.

American Republic: Politics, Institutions & Policies. Charles M. Redenius et al. LC 86-24695. (Illus.). 353p. (Orig.). (C). 1987. pap. text ed. 40.50 (*0-314-28509-1*); teacher ed. pap. text ed. write for info. (*0-314-35236-8*) West Pub.

American Republic & Ancient Israel. Abiel Abbot et al. 1977. 23.95 (*0-405-10231-3*, 14482) Ayer.

American Republicanism: Roman Ideology in the United States Constitution. M. N. Sellers. 288p. 1994. 45.00 (*0-8147-8005-9*) NYU Pr.

American Reputation & Influence of William Blake. R. E. Blois. 1971. 59.95 (*0-87968-611-1*) Gordon Pr.

American Research on Russia. Ed. by Harold H. Fisher. LC 88-10129. 240p. 1990. reprint ed. text ed. 59.75 (*0-313-24177-5*, FIAM, Greenwood Pr) Greenwood.

American Resources: Their Management & Conservation. J. Russell Whitaker & Edward A. Ackerman. LC 72-2874. (Use & Abuse of America's Natural Resources Ser.). 514p. 1972. reprint ed. 33.95 (*0-405-04542-5*) Ayer.

***American Response: The Last Laugh Must be Ours.** Mitchell Lawrence Morino. LC 93-85076. 224p. (Orig.). 1993. pap. 14.99 (*1-884176-01-1*) Thee Am Response.

American Response to Canada since 1776. Gordon T. Stewart. LC 92-53706. (Canadian Ser.: No. 3). 218p. (C). 1992. 35.00 (*0-87013-312-8*) Mich St U Pr.

American Response to Professional Crime, 1870-1917. Larry K. Hartsfield. LC 84-22549. (Contributions in Criminology & Penology Ser.: No. 8). x, 277p. 1985. text ed. 55.00 (*0-313-24503-7*, HRA/, Greenwood Pr) Greenwood.

***American Retrospectives.** Ed. by Stanley I. Kutler. 384p. 1995. text ed. 48.50x (*0-8018-5212-9*); pap. text ed. 16.95x (*0-8018-5213-7*) Johns Hopkins.

American Review of International Commercial Arbitration. Ed. by Columbia University, Parker School of Foreign & Comparative Law Staff. 1990. 120.00 (*0-929179-40-4*) Transnatl Juris Pubns.

American Revisionists: The Lessons of Intervention in World War I. Warren I. Cohen. LC 66-20594. 266p. reprint ed. pap. 75.90 (*0-8357-5397-2*, 2020046) Bks Demand.

***American Revolution.** (Voices in African American History Ser.). (YA). 1994. lib. bdg. 11.95 (*0-8136-4963-3*) Modern Curr.

***American Revolution.** (Voices in African American History Ser.). (YA). 1994. pap. 5.95 (*0-8136-4964-1*) Modern Curr.

American Revolution. Bruce Bliven, Jr. (Landmark Ser.: No. 83). (Illus.). (J). (gr. 4-6). 1963. lib. bdg. 9.99 (*0-394-90383-8*) Random Bks Yng Read.

American Revolution. Colin Bonwick. 315p. (C). 1991. text ed. 35.00 (*0-8139-1346-2*); pap. text ed. 14.95 (*0-8139-1347-0*) U Pr of Va.

American Revolution. Philip Clark. (Wars That Changed the World Ser.). (Illus.). 32p. (J). (gr. 3-9). 1988. lib. bdg. 10.95 (*0-86307-930-X*) Marshall Cavendish.

American Revolution. Edward Countryman. Ed. by Eric Foner. 288p. 1985. pap. 9.95 (*0-8090-0162-4*) Hill & Wang.

***American Revolution.** David W. Felder. 52p. 1995. pap. text ed. 5.00 (*0-910959-60-9*, B&G 25A) Felder Bks.

***American Revolution.** Rich G. Grant. (Revolution! Ser.). (Illus.). 48p. (J). (gr. 4-6). 1995. 15.95 (*1-56847-393-1*) Thomson Lrning.

American Revolution. Harry Knill. (J). (gr. 1-9). 1992. pap. 3.95 (*0-88388-021-0*) Bellerophon Bks.

American Revolution. Bruce Lancaster. LC 85-3982. (American Heritage Library). (Illus.). 334p. 1985. pap. 12.95 (*0-8281-0281-3*) HM.

American Revolution. Comp. by Elizabeth R. Miller. (Illus.). 146p. (Orig.). 1991. pap. 14.50 (*1-55613-466-5*) Heritage Bk.

American Revolution. Francene Sabin. LC 84-2582. (Illus.). 32p. (J). (gr. 3-6). 1985. lib. bdg. 9.49 (*0-8167-0136-9*); pap. text ed. 2.95 (*0-8167-0137-7*) Troll Assocs.

American Revolution. P. D. Thomas. LC 85-5955. (English Satirical Print Ser.). 276p. 1986. lib. bdg. 100.00 (*0-85964-172-4*) Chadwyck-Healey.

American Revolution. fac. ed. James Boggs. LC 63-20103. 93p. pap. 26.60 (*0-7837-6969-5*, 2056173) Bks Demand.

American Revolution. rev. ed. Richard B. Morris. LC 85-12878. (American History Topic Bks.). (Illus.). 72p. (J). (gr. 5-10). 1985. lib. bdg. 13.50 (*0-8225-1701-9*, Lerner Publctns) Lerner Group.

American Revolution. John Fiske. (Notable American Authors Ser.). 1992. reprint ed. lib. bdg. 75.00 (*0-7812-2852-2*) Rprt Serv.

American Revolution. John Guyatt. Ed. by Malcolm Yapp et al. (World History Ser.). (Illus.). 32p. (YA). (gr. 6-11). 1980. reprint ed. pap. text ed. 4.35 (*0-89908-110-X*) Greenhaven.

***American Revolution.** David Johnson. (Jackdaws Ser.). (Illus.). 1991. reprint ed. 24.95 (*1-56696-096-7*) Golden Owl NY.

***American Revolution.** David Johnson. (Jackdaws Ser.). (Illus.). 1995. reprint ed. student ed 32.00 (*0-614-03231-8*) Golden Owl NY.

American Revolution. Eric Robson. LC 74-171392. (Era of the American Revolution Ser.). 254p. 1971. reprint ed. lib. bdg. 29.50 (*0-306-70417-X*) Da Capo.

American Revolution, 4 vols., Set. rev. ed. George O. Trevelyan. (BCL1 - U. S. History Ser.). 1991. reprint ed. lib. bdg. 300.00 (*0-7812-6107-4*) Rprt Serv.

American Revolution: "Give Me Liberty, or Give Me Death!" Deborah Kent. LC 93-39046. (American War Ser.). (Illus.). 128p. (J). (gr. 5 up). 1994. lib. bdg. 17.95 (*0-89490-521-X*) Enslow Pubs.

American Revolution: A Constitutional Interpretation. Charles H. McIlwain. LC 74-166335. (Era of the American Revolution Ser.). 198p. 1973. reprint ed. lib. bdg. 27.50 (*0-306-70249-5*) Da Capo.

American Revolution: A Heritage of Change. Ed. by John Parker & Carol Urness. LC 75-24503. 1975. 10.00 (*0-685-00552-6*) Assocs James Bell.

American Revolution: A Heritage of Change. Ed. by John Parker & Carol Urness. 1975. 10.00 (*0-87018-078-9*) Ross.

American Revolution: A Picture Sourcebook. John Grafton. (Pictorial Archive Ser.). (Illus.). 160p. 1975. pap. 8.95 (*0-486-23226-3*) Dover.

American Revolution: A Selected Reading List. 1992. lib. bdg. 79.95 (*0-8490-8778-3*) Gordon Pr.

American Revolution: A Short History. Richard B. Morris. LC 78-24604. (Anvil Ser.). 192p. 1979. reprint ed. pap. text ed. 10.50 (*0-88275-812-8*) Krieger.

American Revolution: Crisis of Law & Change. James R. Giese & Mary E. Glade. (Public Issues Ser.). (Illus.). 68p. (Orig.). 1988. teacher ed 2.00 (*0-89994-334-9*); pap. 3.50 (*0-89994-331-4*) Soc Sci Ed.

American Revolution: Explorations in the History of American Radicalism. Ed. by Alfred F. Young. LC 75-45359. (Illus.). 481p. 1976. pap. 12.00 (*0-87580-519-1*) N Ill U Pr.

American Revolution: How Revolutionary Was It? 4th ed. George A. Billias. LC 89-34020. 256p. (C). 1990. pap. text ed. 17.50 (*0-03-031042-3*) HB Coll Pubs.

***American Revolution: How We Fought the War of Independence.** Edward F. Dolan. LC 94-44440. (Illus.). 112p. (J). (gr. 5-8). 1995. lib. bdg. 19.90 (*1-56294-521-1*) Millbrook Pr.

American Revolution: Its Character & Limits. Ed. by Jack P. Greene. 448p. 1988. pap. 20.00 (*0-8147-3020-5*) NYU Pr.

***American Revolution: Nationhood Achieved, 1763-1788.** Harry M. Ward. 448p. (C). 1994. pap. text ed. 14.50 (*0-312-07162-0*) St Martin.

***American Revolution: Nationhood Achieved, 1763-1788.** Harry M. Ward. 432p. 1994. 35.00 (*0-312-12259-4*) St Martin.

American Revolution: Opposing Viewpoints. Ed. by William Dudley. LC 92-21795. (American History Ser.). 288p. (YA). 1992. lib. bdg. 19.95 (*1-56510-011-5*); pap. 11.55 (*1-56510-010-7*) Greenhaven.

American Revolution: War for Independence. Alden R. Carter. LC 92-5586. (First Book Ser.). (Illus.). 64p. (J). (gr. 5-8). 1992. lib. bdg. 13.93 (*0-531-20082-5*) Watts.

American Revolution: War for Independence. Alden R. Carter. (First Bks.). (Illus.). 64p. (J). (gr. 5-8). 1993. pap. 5.95 (*0-531-15652-4*) Watts.

American Revolution: Whose Revolution? James K. Martin & Karen R. Stubaus. LC 76-18740. (American Problem Studies). 158p. 1981. reprint ed. pap. 10.50 (*0-88275-397-5*) Krieger.

American Revolution: a Continuing Commitment: Papers Presented at the Fifth Library of Congress Symposium on the American Revolution May 6 & 7, 1976. LC 76-608237. 88p. 1976. 1.50 (*0-8444-0196-X*) Lib Congress.

American Revolution Abroad. Ed. by Richard L. Park & Richard D. Lambert. LC 76-19935. (Annals Ser.: No. 428). 200p. 1976. 27.00 (*0-87761-206-4*); pap. 18.00 (*0-87761-207-2*) Am Acad Pol Soc Sci.

American Revolution & "A Candid World" Ed. by Lawrence S. Kaplan. LC 77-6671. 170p. 1977. 15.00 (*0-87338-205-6*) Kent St U Pr.

American Revolution & Eighteenth-Century Culture. Ed. by Paul J. Korshin. LC 83-45275. (Studies in the Eighteenth Century: No. 5). 1986. 42.50 (*0-404-61471-X*) AMS Pr.

American Revolution & the British Empire: The Sir George Watson Lectures for 1928, Delivered Before the University of London in the Winter of 1928-9. Ed. by Reginald Coupland. (BCL1 - U. S. History Ser.). 331p. 1991. reprint ed. lib. bdg. 89.00 (*0-7812-6104-X*) Rprt Serv.

American Revolution & the French Alliance. William C. Stinchcombe. LC 69-18862. (Illus.). 1969. 29.95x (*0-8156-2134-5*) Syracuse U Pr.

American Revolution & the Politics of Liberty. Robert H. Webking. LC 88-11777. xii, 181p. 1988. text ed. 30.00 (*0-8071-1438-3*) La State U Pr.

American Revolution Bicentennial: A Book of Readings. Ed. by Emma L. Fundaburk. 168p. 1991. reprint ed. 12.00 (*0-910642-05-2*) Am Bicent Mus.

American Revolution, Canadian Theater, French & Native American Life: Eyewitness Account by an Officer of the Prinz Friedrich Regiment, 1776-1783. Tr. by Helga Doblin & Mary C. Lynn. LC 92-42433. (Contributions in Military Studies: No. 144). 192p. 1993. text ed. 55.00 (*0-313-28887-9*, GM8887, Greenwood Pr) Greenwood.

American Revolution Considered As a Social Movement. J. Franklin Jameson. (YA). (gr. 9-12). 1940. pap. 12.95x (*0-691-00550-8*) Princeton U Pr.

American Revolution Considered As a Social Movement. John F. Jameson. (BCL1 - U. S. History Ser.). 105p. 1991. reprint ed. lib. bdg. 69.00 (*0-7812-6105-8*) Rprt Serv.

***American Revolution in Indian Country: Crisis & Diversity in Native American Communities.** Colin G. Calloway. (Cambridge Studies in North American Indian History). (Illus.). 352p. (C). 1995. 59.95 (*0-521-47149-4*); pap. 16.95 (*0-521-47569-4*) Cambridge U Pr.

American Revolution in New York. Alexander C. Flick. 371p. 1993. reprint ed. lib. bdg. 89.00 (*0-7812-5176-1*) Rprt Serv.

American Revolution in the Law: Anglo-American Jurisprudence Before John Marshall. Shannon C. Stimson. 240p. 1990. text ed. 32.50 (*0-691-07874-2*) Princeton U Pr.

American Revolution in the West. George M. Waller. LC 75-44471. (Illus.). 155p. 1976. 42.95 (*0-88229-279-X*) Nelson-Hall.

American Revolution Reconsidered. Richard B. Morris. LC 78-27608. 178p. 1979. reprint ed. text ed. 41.50 (*0-313-20909-X*, MOAM, Greenwood Pr) Greenwood.

American Revolution, 1760-1783. Bruce Bliven, Jr. 1981. pap. 4.99 (*0-394-84696-6*) Random.

American Revolution, 1763-1783. Herbert Aptheker. LC 60-9948. 340p. (C). 1960. pap. 4.95 (*0-7178-0005-9*) Intl Pubs Co.

American Revolution, 1775-1783. John R. Alden. (New American Nation Ser.). (Illus.). 1942. pap. text ed. 14.00 (*0-06-133011-6*, TB3011, Torch) HarpC.

American Revolution 1775-1783: An Encyclopedia, 2 vols. Ed. by Richard L. Blanco. LC 92-42541. (Military History of the U. S. Ser.: Vol. 1). (Illus.). 1896p. 1993. 175.00 (*0-8240-5623-X*, H926) Garland.

American Revolution, 1776-1783. Claude H. Van Tyne. LC 70-158212. (Illus.). reprint ed. 31.50 (*0-404-06753-0*) AMS Pr.

American Revolutionaries: A History in Their Own Words. Milton Meltzer. LC 86-47846. (Illus.). 256p. (YA). (gr. 7 up). 1987. lib. bdg. 14.89 (*0-690-04643-X*, Crowell Jr Bks) HarpC Child Bks.

American Revolutionaries: A History in Their Own Words 1750-1800. Milton Meltzer. LC 86-47846. (Trophy Bk.). (Illus.). 224p. (YA). (gr. 7 up). 1993. pap. 6.95 (*0-06-446145-9*, Trophy) HarpC Child Bks.

American Revolutionaries in the Making. Charles S. Sydnor. Orig. Title: Gentlemen Freeholders. 1965. pap. 14.95 (*0-02-932390-8*) Free Pr.

American Revolutionary: A Biography of General Alexander McDougall. William L. MacDougall. LC 76-15324. (Contributions in American History Ser.: No. 57). (Illus.). 186p. 1977. text ed. 45.00 (*0-8371-9035-5*, MAR/, Greenwood Pr) Greenwood.

American Rhetoric. 5th ed. William W. Watt. LC 79-19764. 416p. (C). 1980. pap. text ed. 23.50 (*0-03-044166-8*) HB Coll Pubs.

American Rhetoric: Context & Criticism. Ed. by Thomas W. Benson. LC 88-29689. 432p. (C). 1989. 39.95 (*0-8093-1509-2*) S Ill U Pr.

American Rhetoric & the Vietnam War. J. Justin Gustainis. LC 92-36553. (Series in Political Communication). 192p. 1993. text ed. 45.00 (*0-275-93361-X*, C3361, Praeger Pubs) Greenwood.

***American Rhetorical Discourse.** 2nd rev. ed. Ronald F. Reid. 841p. (C). 1995. pap. text ed. 25.95x (*0-88133-839-7*) Waveland Pr.

A

An Asterisk (*) at the beginning of an entry indicates that the title is appearing in BIP for the first time.

American Rhythm: Studies & Reexpression of Amer-Indian Songs. Mary Austin. LC 72-141890. 1971. reprint ed. lib. bdg. 40.00 (0-8154-0367-4) Cooper Sq.

American Ritual Dramas: Social Rules & Cultural Meanings. Mary Jo Deegan. LC 88-17772. (Contributions in Sociology Ser.: No. 76). 201p. 1989. text ed. 45.00 (0-313-26337-X, DAU, Greenwood Pr) Greenwood.

American River. Gary McCarthy. (RW Ser.: No. 7). 1992. mass mkt. 4.99 (0-553-29532-2, Bantam Domain) Bantam.

American Road to Culture: A Social Interpretation of Education in the United States. George S. Counts. LC 70-165736. (American Education Ser.: No.2).). 1978. reprint ed. 17.95 (0-405-03605-1) Ayer.

American Roads. Freya Manfred. LC 79-51029. 96p. 1984. pap. 8.95 (0-87951-958-4) Overlook Pr.

American Roads: A Book of Poems. Freya Manfred. LC 79-51029. 96p. 1980. 14.95 (0-87951-100-1); 50.00 (0-87951-103-6) Overlook Pr.

American Robin: A Backyard Institution. Len Eiserer. LC 76-25438. (Illus.). 187p. 1976. 37.95 (0-88229-228-5) Nelson-Hall.

American Rock 'n' Roll Tour. Dave Walker. (Illus.). 272p. 1992. pap. 13.95 (1-56025-041-0) Thunders Mouth.

American Rococo, 1750-1775: Elegance in Ornament. Morrison H. Heckscher & Leslie G. Bowman. (Illus.). 304p. 1992. 50.00 (0-8109-6412-0, Abrams); pap. 24.50 (0-87099-631-2, Abrams) Metro Mus Art.

American Rodeo: From Buffalo Bill to Big Business. Kristine Fredriksson. LC 83-40501. (Illus.). 270p. 1993. pap. 12.95 (0-89096-565-X) Tex A&M Univ Pr.

American Role in Vietnam & East Asia: Between Two Revolutions. Henry J. Kenny. LC 83-24792. (Vietnam in Contemporary Perspective Ser.). (Illus.). 128p. 1984. text ed. 55.00 (0-275-91616-2, C1616, Praeger Pubs) Greenwood.

American Roman Noir: Hammett, Cain, & Chandler. William Marling. LC 94-25550. 256p. 1995. 35.00 (0-8203-1658-X) U of Ga Pr.

American Romance. John Casey. 432p. 1990. reprint ed. pap. 12.00 (0-380-71240-7) Avon.

***American Romance Fiction: The 19th Century.** Budick. Date not set. 24.95 (0-8057-0960-6, Twayne) Macmillan.

American Romance, Tenth Anniversary. 1993. write for info. (0-373-15234-5, 1-15234-5) Harlequin Bks.

American Romantic-Realist Abroad: Templeton Strong & His Music. William C. Loring. LC 94-19028. (Composers of North America Ser.: No. 4). 1995. write for info. (0-8108-2766-2) Scarecrow.

American Romanticism, Vol. 2. David Morse. LC 85-13424. 144p. 1986. 52.00 (0-389-20587-7, N8145 3) B&N Imports.

American Romanticism & the Marketplace. Michael T. Gilmore. LC 84-23936. 192p. 1988. pap. text ed. 11.95 (0-226-29396-3) U Ch Pr.

American Roulette. Tom McCormack. 1969. pap. 2.75 (0-8222-0036-8) Dramatists Play.

American Rubber Workers & Organized Labor, 1900-1941. Daniel Nelson. (Illus.). 520p. 1988. text ed. 49.50 (0-691-04752-9) Princeton U Pr.

American-Russian Economic Relations, 1770s-1990s: A Survey of Issues & References, No. 4. James K. Libbey. (Guides to Historical Issues Ser.). 220p. 1989. 21.95 (0-941690-35-0); pap. text ed. 12.95 (0-941690-36-9) Regina Bks.

American-Russian Rivalry in the Far East. Edward H. Zabriskie. LC 72-11484. (Illus.). 226p. 1973. reprint ed. text ed. 65.00 (0-8371-6666-7, ZAAR, Greenwood Pr) Greenwood.

American-Russian Rivalry in the Far East, a Study in Diplomacy & Power Politics, 1895-1914. Edward H. Zabriskie. (History - United States Ser.). 226p. 1993. reprint ed. lib. bdg. 79.00 (0-7812-4866-3) Rprt Serv.

American Sacred Music Imprints, 1698-1810: A Bibliography. Allen Britton et al. 828p. 1990. 160.00 (0-912296-95-X, U Pr of Va) Am Antiquarian.

***American Sacred Space.** Ed. by David Chidester & Edward T. Linenthal. LC 95-3986. (Religion in North America Ser.). 1995. write for info. (0-253-32915-9) Ind U Pr.

***American Safari: Adventures on the North American Prairie.** Jim Brandenburg. LC 94-24654. (Illus.). 48p. (J). 1995. 16.95 (0-8027-8319-8) Walker & Co.

***American Safari: Adventures on the North American Prairie.** Jim Brandenburg. Ed. by JoAnn B. Guernsey. LC 94-24654. (Illus.). 48p. (J). 1995. lib. bdg. 17.85 (0-8027-8320-1) Walker & Co.

American Saga: Columbus, Cortes, Montezuma, Three Who Made History. Mark Graubard. (Illus.). 144p. (Orig.). (C). 1994. pap. 24.50 (0-685-71274-5) KABEL Pubs.

American Saga: Columbus, Cortes, Montezuma, Three Who Made History. Mark Grubard. (Illus.). 155p. (Orig.). (C). 1993. text ed. 29.50 (0-930329-63-5) KABEL Pubs.

American Saga: The Story of Helen Thomas & Simon Flexner. James T. Flexner. LC 93-12573. (Illus.). xvii, 494p. 1993. reprint ed. 35.00 (0-8232-1520-2); reprint ed. pap. 20.00 (0-8232-1521-0) Fordham.

***American Saga: Columbus, Cortes, Montezuma: Three Who Made History.** Mark Grubard. (Illus.). 155p. (C). 1993. pap. 19.95 (0-614-04353-0) KABEL Pubs.

American Saga; the History & Literature of the Promised Dream of a Better Life. Marjorie L. Greenbie. (History - United States Ser.). 682p. 1993. reprint ed. lib. bdg. 109.00 (0-7812-4851-5) Rprt Serv.

***American Saga William George Hughes (1859-1902) A Pioneer Texas Rancher: His Life, His Times, His Story.** Garland Perry. LC 95-75913. 250p. 1995. 24.95 (0-9646196-0-1) G Perry.

American Sailing Association's "Let's Go Sailing" Peter Isler. 1993. pap. 10.00 (0-688-12545-X) Hearst Bks.

American Sailing Association's Let's Go Windsurfing. Algis Steponaitis. LC 94-6818. 1994. 10.00 (0-688-13477-7, Hearst Marine Bks) Morrow.

American Sailing Ships. Charles G. Davis. (Antiques Series: Transportation). 240p. 1984. reprint ed. pap. 6.95 (0-486-24658-2) Dover.

American Sailing Ships: Their Plans & History. Charles Davis. 17.50 (0-8446-6136-8) Peter Smith.

American Sailor's Treasury. Frank Shay. 1991. 7.98 (0-8317-0288-5) Smithmark.

American Salaries & Wages Survey, 1993: Statistical Data Derived from More Than 300 Government, Business & News Sources. Ed. by Marlita A. Reddy. 1000p. 1993. 105.00 (0-8103-8591-0, 101401) Gale.

American Salons: Encounters with European Modernism, 1885-1917. Robert M. Crunden. 528p. 1993. 35.00 (0-19-506569-7) OUP.

American Salvage Yard Treasures. Eric Brockman et al. Ed. by Jim Cain. (Illus.). 235p. 1993. pap. text ed. 19.95 (1-880524-09-0) Cars & Parts.

American Salvage Yard Treasures II. Car Parts Magazine Editors. (Illus.). 288p. 1994. pap. text ed. 19.95 (0-685-70201-4, 1-800524-09-0) Motorbooks Intl.

American Samoa. William A. Setchell. LC 75-35210. (Carnegie Institution of Washington. Publications: No. 341). 1976. reprint ed. 57.50 (0-404-14233-8) AMS Pr.

American Samoa: Inadequate Management & Oversight Contribute to Financial Problems. (Illus.). 92p. (Orig.). (C). 1993. pap. text ed. 30.00 (1-56806-328-8) Diane Pub.

American Samoa Digest. 300p. 1982. 38.00 (0-88063-450-2, Equity Pub NH) Butterworth Legal Pubs.

American Samoa Reports, 4 vols. 3700p. 1977. 140.00 (0-88063-451-0, Equity Pub NH) Butterworth Legal Pubs.

American Samoa Reports, 4 vols., Vol. 1, 1900-1938. 1987. 33.00 (0-685-73912-0) Equity Pubng NH.

American Samoa Reports, 4 vols., Vol. 2, 1938-1951. 1987. 33.00 (0-685-73913-9) Equity Pubng NH.

American Samoa Reports, 4 vols., Vol. 3, 1951-1961. 1987. 33.00 (0-685-73914-7) Equity Pubng NH.

American Samoa Reports, 4 vols., Vol. 4, 1961-1975. 1987. 33.00 (0-685-73915-5) Equity Pubng NH.

American Sampler: Folk Art from the Shelburne Museum. David P. Curry et al. LC 87-24676. (Illus.). 211p. (Orig.). 1987. pap. 5.99 (0-89468-104-4) Natl Gallery Art.

American Sampler: Gifts of Nature. Meredith Press Staff. 1994. 22.95 (0-696-20036-8) Meredith Bks.

American Sampler Cookbook. Sel. by Linda Bauer. 296p. 1991. 5.99 (0-517-03216-3) Random Hse Value.

***American Sampler Designs.** Dolores Andrew. (International Design Library). (Illus.). 48p. (Orig.). 1995. pap. 5.95 (0-614-03633-X) Stemmer Hse.

American Samplers. Ethel S. Bolton & Eva J. Coe. xiv, 416p. 1987. reprint ed. pap. 13.95 (0-486-25418-6) Dover.

American Samurai. William Lareau. 1992. reprint ed. pap. 13.99 (0-446-39360-6) Warner Bks.

American Samurai: Blending American & Japanese Managerial Practice. Jon P. Alston. (Studies in Organization: No. 6). (Illus.). xii, 370p. 1985. 80.80 (0-89925-063-7); pap. 26.95 (3-11-012034-8) De Gruyter.

American Samurai: Captain L. L. Janes & Japan. F. G. Notehelfer. LC 84-42896. (Illus.). 381p. 1985. text ed. 55.00x (0-691-05443-6) Princeton U Pr.

American Samurai: Myth, Imagination, & the Conduct of Battle in the First Marine Division, 1941-1951. Craig M. Cameron. 320p. (C). 1994. 24.95 (0-521-44168-4) Cambridge U Pr.

American Samurai: Warrior for the Coming Dark Ages of American Business. William Lareau. 336p. 1991. 17.95 (0-8329-0458-9) New Win Pub.

American Sanctuary Movement. Robert Tomsho. LC 87-10228. (Illus.). 256p. 1987. 18.95 (0-87719-067-4, Lone Star Bks) Gulf Pub.

American Satan. Kirby Farrell. 192p. 1990. 18.95 (0-8027-5756-1) Walker & Co.

American-Scandinavian Foundation 1910-1960: A Brief History. E. J. Friis. 1961. 3.95 (0-89067-036-6) Am Scandinavian.

American Scandinavian Studies. A. B. Benson. 1952. 11.95 (0-89067-030-7) Am Scandinavian.

American Scenarios: The Uses of Film Genre. Joseph W. Reed. LC 88-27930. (Illus.). 376p. 1989. 30.00 (0-8195-5215-1, Wesleyan Univ Pr) U Pr of New Eng.

American Scene. James Henry. (BCL1 - United States Local History Ser.). 442p. 1991. reprint ed. lib. bdg. 99.00 (0-7812-6270-4) Rprt Serv.

American Scene: A Basic Reader for ESL. Mary Thurber. 164p. (C). 1986. pap. text ed. 14.75 (0-15-502587-2) HB Coll Pubs.

American Scene: A Reader. H. L. Mencken. Ed. by Huntington Cairns. 1965. 20.00 (0-394-43594-X) Knopf.

American Scene: Essays on Nineteenth-Century American Literature. Stuart Hutchinson. LC 90-28500. 160p. 1991. text ed. 45.00 (0-312-06134-X) St Martin.

American Scene: Reflections of a Small Town Columnist. Leo E. Schottland. 1990. 10.00 (0-940591-09-X) Basin Pub.

American Scene: Varieties of American History, 2 vols. Ed. by Robert D. Marcus & David Burner. LC 73-136426. (Orig.). (C). 1971. teacher ed write for info. (0-89197-020-7); Vol. 1 Colonial Period To 1877. pap. text ed. 11.95 (0-89197-018-5); Vol. 2 Since 1865. pap. text ed. 11.95 (0-8290-1409-8); pap. text ed. 9.95 (0-89197-019-3) Irvington.

American Scene Painting: California, 1930s & 1940s. Ed. by Ruth L. Westphal & Janet B. Dominik. (Illus.). 1991. 65.00 (0-9610520-3-1) Westphal Pub.

American Scenes & Christian Slavery. Ebenezer Davies. LC 70-123671. reprint ed. 39.50 (0-404-00026-6) AMS Pr.

American Scholar. Ralph Waldo Emerson. (Notable American Authors Ser.). 1992. reprint ed. lib. bdg. 75.00 (0-7812-2804-2) Rprt Serv.

American School & the Melting Pot: Minority Self-Esteem & Public Education. 2nd ed. Natalie Isser & Lita L. Schwartz. LC 85-51432. (Illus.). 271p. (Orig.). (C). 1989. text ed. 39.95 (1-55605-090-9); pap. text ed. 29.95 (0-685-29610-5) Wyndhall Pr.

American School Counselor: A Case Study in the Sociology of Professions. David J. Armor. LC 68-58127. 228p. 1969. 22.00 (0-87154-069-X) Russell Sage.

American School Language: Culturally Patterned Conflicts in a Suburban High School. Herve Varenne. 400p. 1983. text ed. 49.50 (0-8290-1337-7); pap. text ed. 19.95 (0-8290-1338-5) Irvington.

American School Reform: Progressive, Equity, & Excellence Movements, 1883-1993. Maurice R. Berube. LC 94-25043. 168p. 1994. text ed. 55.00 (0-275-95036-0, Praeger Pubs) Greenwood.

***American School Reform: Progressive, Equity & Excellence Movements, 1883-1993.** Maurice R. Berube. LC 94-25043. 168p. 1994. pap. text ed. 16.95 (0-275-95160-X, Praeger Pubs) Greenwood.

American School Superintendency, 1982. (Summary Report Ser.). 4.95 (0-318-01708-3, 021-00263) Am Assn Sch Admin.

American School Superintendency, 1982: A Full Report. 114p. (Orig.). 1983. pap. 12.95 (0-87652-082-4, 021-00259) Am Assn Sch Admin.

American School, 1642-1994. 3rd rev. ed. LC 93-1645. Orig. Title: The American School, 1642 - 1985. 1993. reprint ed. pap. text ed. write for info. (0-07-060539-4) McGraw.

American Science & Technology: A Bicentennial Bibliography. George W. Black, Jr. LC 78-15820. 172p. 1979. 15.95 (0-8093-0898-3) S Ill U Pr.

American Science in the Age of Jackson. George H. Daniels. LC 67-28710. 282p. 1968. text ed. 46.50 (0-231-03073-8) Col U Pr.

***American Science in the Age of Jackson.** George H. Daniels. (History of American Science & Technology Ser.). 304p. 1994. reprint ed. pap. 24.95 (0-8173-0740-0) U of Ala Pr.

American Science of Politics: Its Origin & Conditions. Bernard Crick. LC 82-15829. xv, 252p. 1982. text ed. 49.75 (0-313-23696-8, CRAS, Greenwood Pr) Greenwood.

American Science Policy since World War 2. Bruce Smith. 1990. 34.95 (0-8157-7998-4); pap. 14.95 (0-8157-7997-6) Brookings.

American Scientific Community, 1800 to 1860: A Statistical Historical Study. Donald D. Beaver. Ed. by Harriet Zuckerman & Robert K. Merton. LC 79-8973. (Dissertations on Sociology Ser.). 1980. lib. bdg. 36.95 (0-405-12950-5) Ayer.

American Scientist in Early Meiji Japan: The Autobiographical Notes of Thomas C. Mendenhall. Ed. by Richard Rubinger. LC 88-27833. (Asian Studies at Hawaii: No. 35). (Illus.). 112p. 1989. pap. text ed. 11.00 (0-8248-1177-1) UH Pr.

American Scientists & Nuclear Weapons Policy. Robert G. Gilpin, Jr. 1962. 55.00 (0-691-07501-8) Princeton U Pr.

American Screenwriters. Thomas L. Wright & Karl Schanzer. 288p. (Orig.). 1993. pap. 12.00 (0-380-76727-9) Avon.

American Screenwriters, Vol. 26. Ed. by Robert Morsberger & Stephen Lesser. (Dictionary of Literary Biography Ser.: Vol. 26). (Illus.). 400p. 1984. 128.00 (0-8103-0917-3) Gale.

American Screenwriters, Vol. 44. Ed. by Randall Clark. (Dictionary of Literary Biography Ser.: Vol. 44, Pt. 2). 350p. 1986. 128.00 (0-8103-1722-2) Gale.

American Sculptor on the Grand Tour: The Life & Works of William Couper (1853-1942) Greta E. Couper. Ed. by M. V. Calcott. LC 88-50666. (Illus.). 188p. 1988. 34.95 (0-9620635-4-1) TreCavalli Pr.

American Sculpture: A Tenth Anniversary Exhibition. Norton, R. W., Art Gallery Staff. LC 76-50425. (Illus.). 1976. pap. 3.50 (0-913060-11-9) Norton Art.

American Sea Power in the Old World: The United States Navy in European & Near Eastern Waters, 1865-1917. William N. Still, Jr. LC 79-6572. (Contributions in Military History Ser.: No. 24). (Illus.). xi, 291p. 1980. text ed. 55.00 (0-313-22120-0, STA/) Greenwood.

American Sea Songs & Chanteys. Ed. by Frank Shay. LC 77-84358. (Granger Index Reprint Ser.). 1977. 25.95 (0-8369-6061-0) Ayer.

American Seafarer in the Age of Sail: The Intimate Diaries of Philip C. Van Buskirk 1851-1870. B. R. Burg. LC 93-29923. 248p. 1994. 28.00 (0-300-05637-0) Yale U Pr.

American Search for Economic Justice. Peter D. McClelland. (Interpretive Economics Ser.). (Illus.). 400p. 1990. text ed. 42.95 (1-55786-068-8) Blackwell Pubs.

American Search for Mideast Peace: Prelude to Requiem. Daniel Tschirgi. LC 88-25481. 305p. 1989. text ed. 65.00 (0-275-92583-8, C2583, Praeger Pubs) Greenwood.

American Search for Peace: Moral Reasoning, Religious Hope & National Security. Ed. by George Weigel & John Langan. LC 90-25416. 281p. 1991. text ed. 30.00 (0-87840-507-0); pap. text ed. 15.00 (0-87840-519-4) Georgetown U Pr.

American Secretary of State. Alexander DeConde. LC 75-27680. 182p. 1976. reprint ed. text ed. 49.75 (0-8371-8453-3, DEAS, Greenwood Pr) Greenwood.

American Security: Dilemmas for a Modern Democracy. Bruce D. Berkowitz. LC 86-1700. 276p. 1988. pap. 15.00 (0-300-04266-3) Yale U Pr.

American Security in a Changing World: Issues & Choices. Joseph Goldman. LC 86-24588. 328p. (Orig.). (C). 1987. lib. bdg. 53.00 (0-8191-5706-6); pap. text ed. 28.00 (0-8191-5707-4) U Pr of Amer.

American Security in an Interdependent World. Zbigniew Brzezinski et al. 108p. (Orig.). (C). 1988. lib. bdg. 29.50 (0-8191-7084-4); pap. text ed. 15.00 (0-8191-7085-2) Atl Coun US.

American Selection of Lessons in Reading & Speaking. 5th ed. Noah Webster. LC 74-15752. (Popular Culture in America Ser.). 240p. 1975. reprint ed. 23.95 (0-405-06386-5) Ayer.

American Self-Dosage Medicines: An Historical Perspective. James H. Young. Ed. by Robert P. Hudson. (Logan Clendening Lectures Ser.: No. 1). 1974. 5.00 (0-87291-068-7) Coronado Pr.

American Self-Taught. Frank Maresca et al. LC 93-267. 1993. 75.00 (0-394-58212-8) Knopf.

***American Semi Trucks.** Stan Holtzman. (Enthusiast Color Ser.). (Illus.). 96p. 1995. pap. 12.95 (0-7603-0038-0) Motorbooks Intl.

American Senator. Anthony Trollope. Ed. & Intro. by John Halperin. (World's Classics Ser.). 592p. 1986. pap. 8.95 (0-19-281739-6) OUP.

American Senator. Anthony Trollope. 576p. 1994. 8.95 (0-14-043838-6, Penguin Classics) Viking Penguin.

American Senator, 3 vols. Anthony Trollope. Ed. by N. John Hall. LC 80-1895. (Selected Works of Anthony Trollope Ser.). 1981. reprint ed. lib. bdg. 115.95 (0-405-14164-5) Ayer.

American Senator. Anthony Trollope. 561p. 1979. reprint ed. pap. 8.95 (0-486-23801-6) Dover.

American Service Markings. 2nd ed. Reg Morris & Bob Payne. 102p. 1992. pap. 10.00 (1-880065-02-9) Machine Cancel Soc.

***American Service Stations: 1935-1943 Photo Archive.** Ed. by M. Kirn. (Photo Archive Ser.). (Illus.). 144p. 1995. pap. 24.95 (0-614-04502-9) Iconografix.

American Set Design. Arnold Aronson. LC 84-72626. (Illus.). 182p. 1985. 25.95 (0-930452-38-0); pap. 18.95 (0-930452-39-9) Theatre Comm.

American Set Design, 2. Ronn Smith. LC 91-4413. (Illus.). 192p. 1991. 29.95 (1-55936-017-8); pap. 18.95 (1-55936-018-6) Theatre Comm.

American Sexual Politics: Sex, Gender, & Race since the Civil War. Ed. by John C. Fout & Maura S. Tantillo. 412p. (C). 1993. lib. bdg. 39.95 (0-226-25784-3); pap. 17.95 (0-226-25785-1) U Ch Pr.

American Shakers & Their Furniture with Measured Drawings of Museum Classics see Making Authentic Shaker Furniture: With Measured Drawings of Museum Classics

American Shakespeare Theatre: Stratford, 1955-1985. Roberta K. Cooper. LC 85-45578. (Illus.). 352p. 1987. 48.50 (0-918016-88-6) Folger Bks.

American Shakespearean Criticism 1607-1865. Alfred R. Westfall. LC 68-21233. 1972. 26.95 (0-405-09060-9, Pub. by Blom Pubns UK) Ayer.

American Shelf & Wall Clocks: A Pictorial History for Collectors. Robert W. Ball. LC 92-60630. (Illus.). 288p. 1992. text ed. 69.95 (0-88740-427-8) Schiffer.

American Shelter: An Illustrated Encyclopedia of the American Home. Lester Walker. LC 81-47414. (Illus.). 320p. 1981. 40.00 (0-87951-131-1) Overlook Pr.

***American Sheriff.** David R. Struckhoff. (Illus.). 195p. (Orig.). (C). 1994. pap. text ed. 25.00 (1-884028-08-X) SL Pubs.

American Shore. Samuel R. Delany. 1978. 30.00 (0-911499-00-8, Dragon Pr) Ultramarine Pub.

American Shore. limited ed. Samuel R. Delany. 1978. 75.00 (0-911499-01-6, Dragon Pr) Ultramarine Pub.

American Short Fiction, Vol. 1. Laura Furman. 1991. pap. 9.95 (0-292-70430-5) U of Tex Pr.

American Short Fiction, Vol. 2. Laura Furman. 1991. pap. 9.95 (0-292-70431-3) U of Tex Pr.

American Short Fiction, Vol. 3. Laura Furman. 1991. pap. 9.95 (0-292-70432-1) U of Tex Pr.

American Short Fiction, Vol. 4. Laura Furman. 1991. pap. 9.95 (0-292-70436-4) U of Tex Pr.

American Short Fiction, Vol. 5. Laura Furman. 1992. pap. 9.95 (0-292-70439-9) U of Tex Pr.

American Short Fiction, No. 8: Winter 1992. Laura Furman. 1992. pap. 9.95 (0-292-70445-3) U of Tex Pr.

American Short Stories. Ed. by B. Taylor. (Bridge Ser.). (Illus.). 119p. (YA). 1964. pap. text ed. 5.95 (0-582-53026-1) Longman.

American Short Stories. 5th ed. Eugene Current-Garcia & Bert Hitchcock. (C). 1989. pap. text ed. 27.50 (0-673-38568-X) HarpCollege.

American Short Stories: Exercises in Reading & Writing. Greg Costa. 142p. (C). 1983. pap. text ed. 14.75 (0-15-502391-8) HB Coll Pubs.

American Short Stories Series: 1832-1936, 83 vols., Set. Ed. by Clarence Gohdes. 1,000.00 (0-8290-2352-6) Irvington.

American Short Story. Elias Lieberman. LC 71-128995. reprint ed. 31.50 (0-404-03986-3) AMS Pr.

American Short Story, Vol. I. Ed. by Calvin Skaggs. 400p. (J). (gr. 7 up). 1979. mass mkt. 5.99 (0-440-30294-3, LE) Dell.

American Short Story, Vol. 2. Ed. by Calvin Skaggs. (Illus.). 464p. 1980. mass mkt. 5.95 (0-440-30297-8, LE) Dell.

***American Short Story: A Collection of the Best-Known & Most Memorable Stories by the Great.** Thomas K. Parkes. 1994. 15.98 (0-88365-873-9) Galahad Bks.

American Short Story: A Critical Survey. Arthur Voss. LC 72-9264. 399p. 1980. pap. 16.95 (0-8061-1644-7) U of Okla Pr.

An Asterisk (*) at the beginning of an entry indicates that the title is appearing in BIP for the first time.

American Short Story: A Study of the Influence of Locality in Its Development. Elias Lieberman. (BCL1-PS American Literature Ser.). 183p. 1992. reprint ed. lib. bdg. 69.00 (*0-7812-6637-8*) Rprt Serv.

American Short Story Before Eighteen Fifty: A Critical History. Ed. by Eugene Current-Garcia. (Twayne Short Story Ser.). 1985. text ed. 23.95 (*0-8057-9359-3*, Twayne) Macmillan.

American Short Story Masterpieces. Ed. by Raymond Carver & Tom Jenks. 1989. mass mkt. 6.99 (*0-440-20423-2*, LE) Dell.

American Short Story Writers Before Eighteen Eighty, Vol. 74. Ed. by Bobby E. Kimbel. (Dictionary of Literary Biography Ser.: Vol. 74). 437p. 1988. pap. 128.00 (*0-8103-4552-8*, 006542-M99348) Gale.

American Short Story Writers, 1880-1910, Vol. 78. Ed. by Bobby E. Kimbel. (Dictionary of Literary Biography Ser.: Vol. 78). 402p. 1988. pap. 128.00 (*0-8103-4556-0*, 006546-M99348) Gale.

American Short Story, 1900-1945: A Critical History. Ed. by Philip Stevick. (Critical History of the Short Story Ser.). 224p. 1984. text ed. 23.95 (*0-8057-9353-4*, Twayne); pap. 14.95 (*0-8057-9356-9*, Twayne) Macmillan.

American Short Story, 1945-1980: A Critical History. Ed. by Gordon Weaver. (Critical History of the Modern Short Story Ser.). 176p. 1983. text ed. 23.95 (*0-8057-9350-X*, Twayne) Macmillan.

American Short Story, 1945-1980: A Critical History. Ed. by Gordon Weaver. (Critical History of the Modern Short Story Ser.). 1984. pap. 12.95 (*0-8057-9355-0*, Twayne) Macmillan.

American Shorthair Cat. Ingeborg Urcia. (Illus.). (Orig.). 1992. pap. 14.95 (*0-9634121-1-6*) Elias Holl Pr.

American Shortline Railway Guide. 4th ed. Edward Lewis. Ed. by Michael Emmerich. (Illus.). 264p. 1990. pap. 18.95 (*0-89024-109-0*) Kalmbach.

American Shotgun. Charles Askins. (Library Classics Ser.). (Illus.). 336p. 1987. reprint ed. 39.00 (*0-935632-45-X*) Wolfe Pub Co.

American Show Jumping Style: Modern Techniques of Successful Horsemanship. George H. Morris. LC 92-42850. 1993. 27.50 (*0-385-41082-4*) Doubleday.

American Siberia: Or, Fourteen Years Experience in a Southern Convict Camp. J. C. Powell. LC 70-90188. (Mass Violence in America Ser.). 1969. reprint ed. 15.95 (*0-405-01333-7*) Ayer.

American Siberia, or Fourteen Years' Experience in a Southern Convict Camp. J. C. Powell. LC 79-108222. (Criminology, Law Enforcement, & Social Problems Ser.: No. 105). (Illus.). 1970. reprint ed. 12.00 (*0-87585-105-3*) Patterson Smith.

American Siberia, or Fourteen Years' Experience in a Southern Convict Camp. J. C. Powell. LC 76-44514. (Floridiana Facsimile & Reprint Ser.). 1976. reprint ed. 22.95 (*0-8130-0372-5*) U Press Fla.

American Siberian Adventure. William S. Graves. 11.75 (*0-8446-1205-7*) Peter Smith.

American Sidereal Ephemeris, 1976-2000. Neil F. Michelsen. (American Ephemeris Ser.). 320p. (Orig.). 1981. pap. 19.50 (*0-917086-30-9*) ACS Pubns.

American Sign Language. Martin L. Sternberg. (Illus.). 1184p. (ENG, FRE, GER, ITA, JPN, RUS & SPA.). 1981. 95.00 (*0-8288-0192-4*, M9827) Fr & Eur.

American Sign Language: A Beginning Course. Catherine Kettrick. (Illus.). 199p. (Orig.). 1984. 17.95 (*0-913072-64-8*) Natl Assn Deaf.

American Sign Language: A Comprehensive Dictionary. Martin Sternberg. (Illus.). 1184p. 1981. 75.00 (*0-317-34986-4*, SL039) HarpC.

American Sign Language: A Comprehensive Dictionary. Martin L. Sternberg. 1993. 75.00 (*0-06-270052-9*, Harper Ref) HarpC.

American Sign Language: A Look at Its History, Structure & Community. Charlotte Baker & Carol Padden. 1978. pap. 2.50 (*0-932666-01-9*) T J Pubs.

American Sign Language: A Student Text, Units 1-9. Dennis Cokely & Charlotte Baker-Shenk. (Green Book Ser.). 178p. 1991. pap. 16.95 (*0-930323-86-6*, 008AP) Gallaudet Univ Pr.

American Sign Language: A Student Text, Units 10-18. Dennis Cokely & Charlotte Baker-Shenk. (Green Book Ser.). 169p. 1991. pap. 16.95 (*0-930323-87-4*, 008BP) Gallaudet Univ Pr.

American Sign Language: A Student Text, Units 19-27. Dennis Cokely & Charlotte Baker-Shenk. (Green Book Ser.). 167p. 1991. pap. 16.95 (*0-930323-88-2*, 008CP) Gallaudet Univ Pr.

American Sign Language Concise Dictionary. rev. ed. Martin L. Sternberg. (Illus.). 736p. (Orig.). 1994. pap. 9.00 (*0-06-274010-5*, Harper Ref) HarpC.

American Sign Language Dictionary. (Illus.). 96p. 1994. write for info. (*1-56288-462-X*) Checkerboard.

***American Sign Language Dictionary.** rev. ed. Ed. by Martin L. Sternberg. (Illus.). 576p. (Orig.). 1995. pap. 18.00 (*0-06-273275-7*, Harper Ref) HarpC.

American Sign Language Dictionary & Thesaurus. Ron Houston. 79p. (Orig.). 1992. pap. text ed. 10.00 (*0-9611704-7-6*) Soc Folk Dance.

American Sign Language Handshape Game Cards. rev. ed. Frank A. Paul & Ben Bahan. 16.95 (*0-915035-25-1*, 8110) Dawn Sign.

American Sign Language Phrase Book. Lou Fant. (Illus.). 256p. (Orig.). 1983. pap. 15.95 (*0-8092-5507-3*) Contemp Bks.

American Sign Language Phrase Book. Lou Fant. (Illus.). 352p. (Orig.). 1994. pap. 16.95 (*0-8092-3500-5*) Contemp Bks.

American Sign Language Syntax. Scott K. Liddell. (Approaches to Semiotics Ser.: No. 52). 194p. 1980. 50.00 (*90-279-3437-1*) Mouton.

American Signatures: Semiotic Inquiry & Method. Thomas A. Sebeok & Iris Smith. LC 90-50239. (Project for Discourse & Theory Ser.: Vol. 6). (Illus.). 272p. 1991. 27.95 (*0-8061-2310-9*) U of Okla Pr.

American Signatures: Semiotic Inquiry & Method. Thomas A. Sebeok & Iris Smith. LC 90-50239. (Project for Discourse & Theory Ser.: Vol. 6). (Illus.). 272p. (C). 1992. pap. text ed. 12.95 (*0-8061-2355-9*) U of Okla Pr.

American Signs for Children. M. Sternberg. Date not set. 30.00 (*0-06-270071-5*, HarpT) HarpC.

American Silences: The Realism of James Agee, Walker Evans, & Edward Hopper. J. A. Ward. LC 84-21765. (Illus.). 210p. 1985. text ed. 32.50 (*0-8071-1179-1*) La State U Pr.

***American Silent Film Comedies: An Illustrated Encyclopedia of Persons, Studios & Terminology.** Blair Miller. 288p. 1995. lib. bdg. 42.50x (*0-89950-929-0*) McFarland & Co.

American Silhouettes. Albert Furtwangler. LC 86-23424. 192p. 1987. 27.00 (*0-300-03798-8*) Yale U Pr.

American Silhouettes: Rhetorical Identities of the Founders. Albert Furtwangler. LC 86-23424. 176p. (C). 1989. reprint ed. 13.00x (*0-300-04501-8*) Yale U Pr.

American Silver: Garvan & Other Collections in the Yale University Art Gallery, 2 vols. Kathryn C. Buhler & Graham Hood. (Illus.). 1995. reprint ed. Set, Vol. 1, 368p. Vol. 2, 312p. 250.00 (*1-55660-176-X*) A Wofsy Fine Arts.

American Silver & Pressed Glass. Norton, R. W., Art Gallery Staff. LC 67-24712. (Illus.). 1967. pap. 3.50 (*0-9600182-0-4*) Norton Art.

***American Silver at Winterthur.** Ian M. Quimby. LC 95-14228. (Illus.). 512p. (C). 1995. text ed. 75.00 (*0-912724-32-3*) Winterthur.

American Silver from the Kossack Collection: A Checklist. David L. Barquist et al. (Illus.). 23p. (Orig.). 1988. pap. 1.00 (*0-89467-049-2*) Yale Art Gallery.

American Silver, Sixteen Seventy to Eighteen Thirty: The Cornelius C. Moore Collection at Providence College. Alice Hauck et al. (Illus.). 156p. 1980. 29.95 (*0-917012-18-6*) RI Pubns Soc.

American Silver Thimbles. Gay A. Rogers. LC 88-82066. (Illus.). 224p. 1989. 47.95 (*1-869812-03-4*) Needlewrk Unltd.

American Silverplate. enl. rev. ed. Dorothy T. Rainwater & H. Ivan Rainwater. LC 72-7998. (Illus.). 480p. 1988. 37.50 (*0-88740-128-7*) Schiffer.

American Silversmiths & Their Marks. rev. ed. Stephen G. Ensko. LC 88-82003. 496p. 1989. 65.00 (*0-87923-778-3*) Godine.

American Silversmiths & Their Marks: The Definitive Edition, 1948. 2nd ed. Stephen G. Ensko. (Illus.). 287p. 1983. reprint ed. pap. 6.95 (*0-486-24428-8*) Dover.

American Singers: Twenty-Seven Portraits in Song. Whitney Balliett. 256p. 1988. 27.95 (*0-19-504610-2*) OUP.

American Singers: Twenty-Seven Portraits in Song. Whitney Balliett. 256p. 1990. reprint ed. pap. 9.95 (*0-19-506573-5*) OUP.

American Singing Book. Simeon P. Cheney. LC 80-13923. (Earlier American Music Ser.: No. 17). (Illus.). 1980. reprint ed. lib. bdg. 37.50 (*0-306-77322-8*) Da Capo.

***American Singing Societies & Their Partsongs: Ten Prominent American Composers of the Genre (1860-1940) & the Seminall Singing Societies That Performed the Repertory.** William Osborne. (Monograph Ser.: No. 8). 112p. 1994. 15.00 (*0-614-05595-4*) Am Choral Dirs.

American Skeptic: Robert Altman's Genre-Commentary Films. Norman Kagan. LC 82-61033. (Illus.). 190p. 1982. 40.00 (*0-87650-144-7*) Popular Culture.

American Sketches. John Stewart. 1992. pap. write for info. (*1-880950-01-4*) Crow Pr.

American Skinheads: The Criminology & Control of Hate Crime. Mark S. Hamm. LC 92-23061. (Criminology & Crime Control Policy Ser.). 264p. 1993. text ed. 55.00 (*0-275-94355-0*, C4355, Praeger Pubs) Greenwood.

American Skinheads: The Criminology & Control of Hate Crime. Mark S. Hamm. LC 92-23061. 264p. 1994. pap. text ed. 17.95 (*0-275-94987-7*, Praeger Pubs) Greenwood.

***American Slang.** Robert L. Chapman. LC 87-45028. 499p. 1994. reprint ed. pap. 5.99 (*0-06-109284-3*, Harp PBks) HarpC.

***American Slanguage Phonetic Dictionary.** 250p. 1995. pap. 25.00 (*0-929350-50-2*) Spoken English Pubns.

American Slave: A Composite Autobiography, 19 vols., Set. Ed. by George P. Rawick. Incl. Vol. 1. LC 71-38591. 208p. 1971. text ed. 75.00 (*0-8371-6299-8*, RSM&, Greenwood Pr); Vol. 2. LC 71-38591. 1972. text ed. 75.00 (*0-8371-6300-5*, RSN&, Greenwood Pr); Vol. 3. LC 71-38591. 1972. text ed. 75.00 (*0-8371-6301-3*, RSO&, Greenwood Pr); Vol. 4. LC 71-38591. 1972. text ed. 75.00 (*0-8371-6302-1*, RSP&, Greenwood Pr); Vol. 5. LC 71-38591. 1972. text ed. 75.00 (*0-8371-6303-X*, RSQ&, Greenwood Pr); Vol. 6. LC 71-38591. 1972. text ed. 75.00 (*0-8371-6304-8*, RSR&, Greenwood Pr); Vol. 7. LC 71-38591. 1971. text ed. 75.00 (*0-8371-6305-6*, RSS&, Greenwood Pr); Vol. 8. LC 71-38591. 1972. text ed. 75.00 (*0-8371-6306-4*, RST&, Greenwood Pr); Vol. 2. LC 71-38591. 1972. text ed. 75.00 (*0-8371-6307-2*, RSU&, Greenwood Pr); Vol. 3. LC 71-38591. 1972. text ed. 75.00 (*0-8371-6308-0*, RSV&, Greenwood Pr); Vol. 4. LC 71-38591. 1972. text ed. 75.00 (*0-8371-6309-9*, RSW&, Greenwood Pr); Vol. 5. LC 71-38591. 1972. text ed. 75.00 (*0-8371-6310-2*, RSX&, Greenwood Pr); Vol. 6. LC 71-38591. 1972. text ed. 75.00 (*0-8371-6311-0*, RSY&, Greenwood Pr); Vol. 7. LC 71-38591. 1972. text ed. 75.00 (*0-8371-6312-9*, RSZ&, Greenwood Pr); Vol. 8. LC 71-38591. 1972. text ed. 75.00 (*0-8371-6313-7*, RSA&, Greenwood Pr); Vol. 9. LC 71-38591. 1972. text ed. 75.00 (*0-8371-6314-5*, RSB&, Greenwood Pr); Vol. 10. LC 71-38591. 1972. text ed. 75.00 (*0-8371-6315-3*, RSC&, Greenwood Pr); Vol. 11. LC 71-38591. 1972. text ed. 75.00 (*0-8371-6316-1*, RSD&, Greenwood Pr); Vol. 12. LC 71-38591. 1972. text ed. 75.00 (*0-8371-6317-X*, RSE&, Greenwood Pr); LC 71-38591. (Contributions in Afro-American & African Studies: No. 11). 1972. Set text ed. 495.00 (*0-8371-3314-9*, RSL & RSF, Greenwood Pr) Greenwood.

American Slave: A Composite Autobiography, Vols. 1-7, Vols. 1-7. Ed. by George P. Rawick. Incl. Vol. 1. LC 71-38591. 208p. 1971. text ed. 75.00 (*0-8371-6299-8*, RSM&, Greenwood Pr); Vol. 2. LC 71-38591. 1972. text ed. 75.00 (*0-8371-6300-5*, RSN&, Greenwood Pr); Vol. 3. LC 71-38591. 1972. text ed. 75.00 (*0-8371-6301-3*, RSO&, Greenwood Pr); Vol. 4. LC 71-38591. 1972. text ed. 75.00 (*0-8371-6302-1*, RSP&, Greenwood Pr); Vol. 5. LC 71-38591. 1972. text ed. 75.00 (*0-8371-6303-X*, RSQ&, Greenwood Pr); Vol. 6. LC 71-38591. 1972. text ed. 75.00 (*0-8371-6304-8*, RSR&, Greenwood Pr); Vol. 7. LC 71-38591. 1971. text ed. 75.00 (*0-8371-6305-6*, RSS&, Greenwood Pr); Vol. 8. LC 71-38591. 1972. text ed. 75.00 (*0-8371-6306-4*, RST&, Greenwood Pr); Vol. 2. LC 71-38591. 1972. text ed. 75.00 (*0-8371-6307-2*, RSU&, Greenwood Pr); Vol. 3. LC 71-38591. 1972. text ed. 75.00 (*0-8371-6308-0*, RSV&, Greenwood Pr); Vol. 4. LC 71-38591. 1972. text ed. 75.00 (*0-8371-6309-9*, RSW&, Greenwood Pr); Vol. 5. LC 71-38591. 1972. text ed. 75.00 (*0-8371-6310-2*, RSX&, Greenwood Pr); Vol. 6. LC 71-38591. 1972. text ed. 75.00 (*0-8371-6311-0*, RSY&, Greenwood Pr); Vol. 7. LC 71-38591. 1972. text ed. 75.00 (*0-8371-6312-9*, RSZ&, Greenwood Pr); Vol. 8. LC 71-38591. 1972. text ed. 75.00 (*0-8371-6313-7*, RSA&, Greenwood Pr); Vol. 9. LC 71-38591. 1972. text ed. 75.00 (*0-8371-6314-5*, RSB&, Greenwood Pr); Vol. 10. LC 71-38591. 1972. text ed. 75.00 (*0-8371-6315-3*, RSC&, Greenwood Pr); Vol. 11. LC 71-38591. 1972. text ed. 75.00 (*0-8371-6316-1*, RSD&, Greenwood Pr); Vol. 12. LC 71-38591. 1972. text ed. 75.00 (*0-8371-6317-X*, RSE&, Greenwood Pr); LC 71-38591. (Contributions in Afro-American & African Studies: No. 11). 1972. Set lib. bdg. 250.00 (*0-685-42146-5*, Greenwood Pr) Greenwood.

American Slave: A Composite Autobiography, Vols. 8-19, Vols. 8-19. Ed. by George P. Rawick. Incl. Vol. 1. LC 71-38591. 208p. 1971. text ed. 75.00 (*0-8371-6299-8*, RSM&, Greenwood Pr); Vol. 2. LC 71-38591. 1972. text ed. 75.00 (*0-8371-6300-5*, RSN&, Greenwood Pr); Vol. 3. LC 71-38591. 1972. text ed. 75.00 (*0-8371-6301-3*, RSO&, Greenwood Pr); Vol. 4. LC 71-38591. 1972. text ed. 75.00 (*0-8371-6302-1*, RSP&, Greenwood Pr); Vol. 5. LC 71-38591. 1972. text ed. 75.00 (*0-8371-6303-X*, RSQ&, Greenwood Pr); Vol. 6. LC 71-38591. 1972. text ed. 75.00 (*0-8371-6304-8*, RSR&, Greenwood Pr); Vol. 7. LC 71-38591. 1971. text ed. 75.00 (*0-8371-6305-6*, RSS&, Greenwood Pr); Vol. 8. LC 71-38591. 1972. text ed. 75.00 (*0-8371-6306-4*, RST&, Greenwood Pr); Vol. 2. LC 71-38591. 1972. text ed. 75.00 (*0-8371-6307-2*, RSU&, Greenwood Pr); Vol. 3. LC 71-38591. 1972. text ed. 75.00 (*0-8371-6308-0*, RSV&, Greenwood Pr); Vol. 4. LC 71-38591. 1972. text ed. 75.00 (*0-8371-6309-9*, RSW&, Greenwood Pr); Vol. 5. LC 71-38591. 1972. text ed. 75.00 (*0-8371-6310-2*, RSX&, Greenwood Pr); Vol. 6. LC 71-38591. 1972. text ed. 75.00 (*0-8371-6311-0*, RSY&, Greenwood Pr); Vol. 7. 1972. text ed. 75.00 (*0-8371-6312-9*, RSZ&, Greenwood Pr); Vol. 8. LC 71-38591. 1972. text ed. 75.00 (*0-8371-6313-7*, RSA&, Greenwood Pr); Vol. 9. LC 71-38591. 1972. text ed. 75.00 (*0-8371-6314-5*, RSB&, Greenwood Pr); Vol. 10. LC 71-38591. 1972. text ed. 75.00 (*0-8371-6315-3*, RSC&, Greenwood Pr); Vol. 11. LC 71-38591. 1972. text ed. 75.00 (*0-8371-6316-1*, RSD&, Greenwood Pr); Vol. 12. LC 71-38591. 1972. text ed. 75.00 (*0-8371-6317-X*, RSE&, Greenwood Pr); LC 71-38591. (Contributions in Afro-American & African Studies: No. 11). 1972. Set lib. bdg. 445.00 (*0-685-42147-3*, Greenwood Pr) Greenwood.

American Slave: A Composite Autobiography, Supplement Series 1, 12 vols., Set. Ed. by George P. Rawick. Incl. Vol. 1. Alabama Supplement. LC 77-88899. 1978. text ed. 69.50 (*0-8371-9761-9*, RAA/01, Greenwood Pr); Vol. 2. Arkansas Collected Supplement. LC 77-88899. 1978. text ed. 69.50 (*0-8371-9762-7*, RAA/02, Greenwood Pr); Vol. 3. Georgia, Supplement 1. LC 77-88899. 1978. text ed. 69.50 (*0-8371-9763-5*, RAA/03, Greenwood Pr); Vol. 4. Georgia, Supplement 2. LC 77-88899. 1978. text ed. 69.50 (*0-8371-9764-3*, RAA/04, Greenwood Pr); Vol. 5. Ind-Ohio Supplement. LC 77-88899. 1978. text ed. 69.50 (*0-8371-9765-1*, RAA/05, Greenwood Pr); Vol. 6. Mississippi, Supplement 1. LC 77-88899. 1978. text ed. 69.50 (*0-8371-9766-X*, RAA/06, Greenwood Pr); Vol. 7. Mississippi, Supplement 2. LC 77-88899. 1978. text ed. 69.50 (*0-8371-9767-8*, RAA/07, Greenwood Pr); Vol. 8. Mississippi, Supplement 3. LC 77-88899. 1978. text ed. 69.50 (*0-8371-9768-6*, RAA/08, Greenwood Pr); Vol. 9. Mississippi, Supplement 4. LC 77-88899. 1978. text ed. 69.50 (*0-8371-9769-4*, RAA/09, Greenwood Pr); Vol. 10. Mississippi, Supplement 5. LC 77-88899. 1978. text ed. 69.50 (*0-8371-9770-8*, RAA/10, Greenwood Pr); Vol. 11. North Carolina-South Carolina Supplement. LC 77-88899. 1978. text ed. 69.50 (*0-8371-9771-6*, RAA/11, Greenwood Pr); Vol. 12. Oklahoma Supplement. LC 77-88899. 1978. text ed. 69.50 (*0-8371-9772-4*, RAA/12, Greenwood Pr); LC 77-88899. (Contributions in Afro-American & African Studies: No. 35). 1978. Set text ed. 795.00 (*0-8371-9756-2*, RAA/, Greenwood Pr) Greenwood.

American Slave: A Composite Autobiography, Supplement Series 2, 10 vols., Set. Ed. by George P. Rawick. Incl. Vol. 1. LC 79-12456. 1979. text ed. 69.50 (*0-313-21979-6*, RAB/01, Greenwood Pr); Vol. 2. LC 79-12456. 1979. text ed. 69.50 (*0-313-21980-X*, RAB/02, Greenwood Pr); Vol. 3. LC 79-12456. 1979. text ed. 69.50 (*0-313-21981-8*, RAB/03, Greenwood Pr); Vol. 4. LC 79-12456. 1979. text ed. 69.50 (*0-313-21982-6*, RAB/04, Greenwood Pr); Vol. 5. LC 79-12456. 1979. text ed. 69.50 (*0-313-21983-4*, RAB/05, Greenwood Pr); Vol. 6. LC 79-12456. 1979. text ed. 69.50 (*0-313-21984-2*, RAB/06, Greenwood Pr); Vol. 7. LC 79-12456. 1979. text ed. 69.50 (*0-313-21985-0*, RAB/07, Greenwood Pr); Vol. 8. LC 79-12456. 1979. text ed. 69.50 (*0-313-21986-9*, RAB/08, Greenwood Pr); Vol. 9. LC 79-12456. 1979. text ed. 69.50 (*0-313-21987-7*, RAB/09, Greenwood Pr); Vol. 10. LC 79-12456. 1979. text ed. 69.50 (*0-313-21988-5*, RAB/10, Greenwood Pr); LC 79-12456. (Contributions in Afro-American & African Studies: No. 49). 1980. Set text ed. 675.00 (*0-313-21423-9*, RAB/, Greenwood Pr) Greenwood.

American Slave Code in Theory & Practice: Its Distinctive Features As Shown by Its Statutes, Judicial Decisions, & Illustrative Facts. William Goodell. LC 73-82194. (Anti-Slavery Crusade in America Ser.). 1970. reprint ed. 20.95 (*0-405-00633-0*) Ayer.

American Slave Code in Theory & Practice: Its Distinctive Features Shown by Its Statutes, Judicial Decisions, & Illustrative Facts. William Goodell. LC 68-55888. 431p. 1969. reprint ed. text ed. 52.50 (*0-8371-0450-5*, GOC&, Negro U Pr) Greenwood.

American Slave Trade. John R. Spears. (Illus.). 1970. 12.95 (*0-87651-135-3*); pap. 7.95 (*0-87651-211-2*) Southern U Pr.

American Slave Trade. John R. Spears. 232p. 1970. reprint ed. 22.50 (*0-87928-009-3*) Corner Hse.

American Slave-Trade: An Account of Its Origin, Growth, & Suppression. John R. Spears. (History - United States Ser.). 232p. 1992. reprint ed. lib. bdg. 79.00 (*0-7812-6156-2*) Rprt Serv.

American Slavers & the Federal Law, 1837-1862. Warren S. Howard. LC 75-5811. (Illus.). 336p. 1976. reprint ed. text ed. 59.75 (*0-8371-8796-6*, HOAF, Greenwood Pr) Greenwood.

American Slavery - American Freedom: The Ordeal of Colonial Virginia. Edmund S. Morgan. 454p. (C). 1976. pap. text ed. 10.95 (*0-393-09156-2*) Norton.

***American Slavery - American Freedom: The Ordeal of Colonial Virginia.** Edmund S. Morgan. 464p. 1995. pap. 14.95 (*0-393-31288-7*, Norton Paperbks) Norton.

American Slavery & the American Novel: 1852-1977. 2nd ed. Edward M. Jackson. LC 86-51367. 90p. (C). 1988. text ed. 24.95 (*1-55605-089-5*); pap. text ed. 14.95 (*0-932269-97-4*) Wyndhall Pr.

American Slavery As It Is: Testimony of a Thousand Witnesses. Ed. by Theodore D. Weld. LC 69-19635. (American Negro: His History & Literature, Ser. No. 1). 1969. reprint ed. 27.95 (*0-405-01843-6*) Ayer.

American Slavery Distinguished from the Slavery of English Theorists, & Justified by the Law of Nature. Samuel Seabury. LC 71-83878. (Black Heritage Library Collection). 1977. 24.95 (*0-8369-8650-4*) Ayer.

American Slavery, 1619-1877. Peter Kolchin. Ed. by Eric Foner. LC 92-46358. 1993. 25.00 (*0-8090-2568-X*) Hill & Wang.

American Slavery, 1619-1877. Peter Kolchin. 1994. pap. 10.95 (*0-8090-1554-4*) Hill & Wang.

American Small Businessman. John A. Bunzel. Ed. by Stuart Bruchey & Vincent P. Carosso. LC 78-18956. (Small Business Enterprise in America Ser.). (Illus.). 1979. reprint ed. lib. bdg. 28.95 (*0-405-11460-5*) Ayer.

American Small City Profiles. Comp. by Toucan Valley Publications Research Staff. LC 93-21929. (Illus.). 339p. 1993. pap. 35.00 (*0-9634017-6-9*) Toucan Valley.

American Small Sailing Craft. Howard I. Chapelle. (Illus.). 1951. 35.00 (*0-393-03143-8*) Norton.

American Social Attitudes Data Sourcebook: 1947-1978. Philip E. Converse et al. 441p. 1980. 37.00 (*0-674-02880-5*) HUP.

An Asterisk (*) at the beginning of an entry indicates that the title is appearing in BIP for the first time.

American Social Character: Modern Interpretations. Comment & Intro. by Rupert Wilkinson. LC 90-56402. 400p. 1992. pap. text ed. 17.00 (*0-06-430979-7*, HarpT) HarpC.

***American Social Classes in the 1950s: Selections from Vance Packard's The Status Seekers.** Ed. by Daniel Horowitz. (Bedford Series in History & Culture). 224p. 1995. 35.00 (*0-312-12247-0*) St Martin.

***American Social History - 1959, Vol. 19.** Eugen Rosenstock-Huessy. (Eugen Rosenstock-Huessy Lectures). 622p. Date not set. audio, pap. 275.00 (*0-614-05384-6*); pap. 135.00 (*0-912148-38-1*); audio 205.00 (*0-614-05383-8*) Argo Bks.

American Social History Before 1860. Gerald N. Grob. LC 72-102037. (Goldentree Bibliographies Series in American History). (C). 1970. pap. text ed. write for info. (*0-88295-515-2*) Harlan Davidson.

American Social History since 1860. Robert H. Bremner. LC 70-146848. (Goldentree Bibliographies Series in American History). (C). 1971. text ed. write for info. (*0-88295-504-7*); pap. text ed. write for info. (*0-88295-503-9*) Harlan Davidson.

American Social Leaders: From Colonial Times to Present. Bill McGuire & Leslie Wheeler. Ed. by Gary Gerstle & James MacPherson. 500p. 1993. lib. bdg. 65.00 (*0-87436-633-X*) ABC-CLIO.

American Social Problems. Howard W. Odum. LC 70-128283. (Essay Index Reprint Ser.). 1977. 44.95 (*0-8369-1839-8*) Ayer.

American Social Psychology: Its Origins, Development, & European Background. Fay B. Karpf. (Reprint Series in Sociology). 1971. reprint ed. lib. bdg. 36.00 (*0-697-00216-0*); reprint ed. pap. 9.95 (*0-89197-658-2*) Irvington.

American Social Reform Movements: Their Pattern Since 1865. Thomas H. Greer. LC 80-11282. ix, 313p. 1980. reprint ed. text ed. 59.75 (*0-313-22382-3*, GRAR, Greenwood Pr) Greenwood.

American Social Trends. Theodore Caplow. 250p. (C). 1990. pap. text ed. 16.00 (*0-15-502588-0*) HB Coll Pubs.

American Social Welfare Policy: A Pluralist Approach. 2nd ed. Howard J. Karger & David Stoesz. LC 93-2172. 400p. (C). 1994. boxed, text ed. 43.95 (*0-8013-1170-5*, 79664) Longman.

American Social Welfare Policy: A Structural Approach. Howard J. Karger & David Stoesz. 371p. (C). 1990. text ed. 44.95 (*0-8013-0193-9*, 75852) Longman.

American Social Worker in Italy. Jean Charnley. LC 61-7941. 331p. reprint ed. pap. 94.40 (*0-8357-5399-9*, 2055848) Bks Demand.

American Socialism & Black Americans: From the Age of Jackson to World War II. Philip S. Foner. LC 77-71858. (Contributions in Afro-American & African Studies: No. 33). 462p. 1977. text ed. 39.95 (*0-8371-9545-4*, FAS/, Greenwood Pr) Greenwood.

American Socialist Movement, 1897-1912. Ira Kipnis. LC 68-23304. 496p. 1968. reprint ed. text ed. 75.00 (*0-8371-0130-1*, KIAS, Greenwood Pr) Greenwood.

American Socialists & Evolutionary Thought, 1870-1920. Mark Pittenger. LC 92-28041. (History of American Thought & Culture Ser.). 320p. (Orig.). (C). 1993. 60.00 (*0-299-13600-0*); pap. 24.95 (*0-299-13604-3*) U of Wis Pr.

American Socialists & the War. Ed. by Alexander Trachtenberg et al. Bd. with Socialists & the Problems of War. LC 70-147533. LC 70-147533. (Library of War & Peace: Labor, Socialism & War). (C). 1973. reprint ed. Set lib. bdg. 46.00 (*0-8240-0314-4*) Garland.

American Society. Charles F. Thwing. LC 75-117856. (Essay Index Reprint Ser.). 1977. 18.95 (*0-8369-1729-4*) Ayer.

American Society: An Introduction to Macrosociology. Daniel W. Rossides. LC 91-75942. 550p. 1993. lib. bdg. 39.95 (*0-930390-16-4*) Gen Hall.

American Society: An Introduction to Macrosociology. Daniel W. Rossides. LC 92-75606. 695p. 1993. text ed. 64.95 (*1-882289-05-6*); pap. text ed. 39.95 (*1-882289-04-8*) Gen Hall.

American Society & Politics: Comparative Historical & Theoretical Perspectives. Theda Skocpol & John Campbell. 1994. pap. text ed. write for info. (*0-07-057915-6*) McGraw.

American Society for Composites: Proceedings of the 6th Technical Conference. Ed. by American Society for Composites Staff. LC 91-66307. 1100p. 1991. text ed. 175.00 (*0-87762-893-9*) Technomic.

American Society for Composites: Proceedings of 2nd Technical Conference. LC 87-50951. 600p. 1987. 55.00 (*0-87762-569-7*) Technomic.

American Society for Composites: Proceedings of 3rd Technical Conference. LC 88-71942. 751p. 1988. 95.00 (*0-87762-638-3*) Technomic.

American Society for Composites: Proceedings of 4th Technical Conference. LC 89-51358. 1005p. 1989. 125.00 (*0-87762-717-7*) Technomic.

American Society for Composites: Proceedings of 5th Technical Conference. LC 90-70522. 1045p. 1990. 165.00 (*0-87762-767-3*) Technomic.

American Society for Composites; Proceedings of the 7th Technical Conference: Composite Materials, Mechanics & Processing. American Society for Composites Staff. Ed. by H. Thomas Hahn. LC 92-61749. 1260p. 1992. text ed. 175.00 (*0-87762-997-8*) Technomic.

American Society for Professional Geographers: Papers Presented on the Occasion of the Fiftieth Anniversary of Its Founding. Shannon McCune et al. LC 93-18849. (Occasional Publications of the Association of American Geographers: No. 3). 1993. 5.00 (*0-89291-211-1*) Assn Am Geographers.

American Society for Stereotactic & Functional Neurosurgery. (Journal: Applied Neurophysiology: Vol. 43, Nos. 3-5, 1980). (Illus.). 184p. 1981. pap. 84.00 (*3-8055-3458-2*) S Karger.

American Society for Stereotactic & Functional Neurosurgery, Montreal, Quebec, June 1987: Journal: Applied Neurophysiology, Vol. 50, Nos. 1-6, 1987. Ed. by A. Olivier et al. xii, 512p. 1987. pap. 189.00 (*3-8055-4756-0*) S Karger.

American Society for Training & Development Directory of Academic Programs in Training & Development-Human Resource Development. 220p. 11.00 (*0-318-13262-1*); pap. 13.75 (*0-318-13261-3*, PDAPP) Am Soc Train & Devel.

American Society in the Buddhist Mirror, Vol. 24. Joseph B. Tamney. LC 91-39409. (Library of Sociology). 216p. 1992. 33.00 (*0-8153-0721-7*) Garland.

American Society in Wartime. Ed. by William F. Ogburn. LC 72-2380. (FDR & the Era of the New Deal Ser.). 237p. 1972. reprint ed. lib. bdg. 29.50 (*0-306-70484-6*) Da Capo.

American Society of Composers, Authors, & Publishers Copyright Law Symposium, No. 21. LC 40-8341. 1974. text ed. 40.00 (*0-231-03834-8*) Col U Pr.

American Society of Composers, Authors, & Publishers Copyright Law Symposium, No. 22. LC 40-8341. 1977. text ed. 40.00 (*0-231-04278-7*) Col U Pr.

American Society of Composers, Authors, & Publishers Copyright Law Symposium, No. 23. LC 40-8341. 1977. text ed. 40.00 (*0-231-04348-1*) Col U Pr.

American Society of Composers, Authors, & Publishers Copyright Law Symposium, No. 24. 1980. text ed. 40.00 (*0-231-04864-5*) Col U Pr.

American Society of Composers, Authors, & Publishers Copyright Law Symposium, No. 25. LC 40-8341. 1980. text ed. 40.00 (*0-231-04866-1*) Col U Pr.

American Society of Composers, Authors, & Publishers Copyright Law Symposium, No. 29. Ed. by ASCAP Staff. LC 40-8341. 250p. 1983. text ed. 40.00 (*0-231-05554-4*) Col U Pr.

American Society of Composers, Authors, & Publishers Copyright Law Symposium, No. 31. 1984. text ed. 40.00 (*0-231-05766-0*) Col U Pr.

American Society of Composers, Authors, & Publishers Copyright Law Symposium, No. 36. ASCAP Staff. 1991. text ed. 31.50 (*0-231-07308-9*) Col U Pr.

American Society of Ophthalmic Plastic & Reconstructive Surgery (ASOPRS): The First Twenty-Five Years 1969-1994: With a Brief History of Ophthalmic Plastic Surgery, 2500 BC-1995 AD. Ed. by David M. Reifler. LC 94-7908. (Illus.). 493p. 1994. 75.00 (*0-930405-64-1*) Norman SF.

American Society, 1776-1815. Ed. by Peter Onuf. LC 91-13745. (New American Nation, 1775-1820 Ser.: Vol. 11). 550p. 1991. 90.00 (*0-8153-0446-3*) Garland.

American Sociological Assn. Rose Monograph Ser. Orrin E. Klapp. LC 77-87382. (American Sociological Assn. Rose Monograph Ser.). (Illus.). 1978. pap. 12.95 (*0-521-29311-1*) Cambridge U Pr.

American Sociological Hegemony: Transnational Explorations. Dan A. Chekki. 184p. (Orig.). (C). 1987. lib. bdg. 45.00 (*0-8191-6611-1*); pap. text ed. 20.50 (*0-8191-6612-X*) U Pr of Amer.

American Sociological Theory: A Critical History. Robert Bierstedt. LC 81-10820. 1981. text ed. 61.00 (*0-12-097480-0*) Acad Pr.

American Sociological Theory: A Critical History. Robert Bierstedt. LC 81-10820. 1981. pap. text ed. 42.00 (*0-12-097482-7*) Acad Pr.

American Sociology: Worldly Rejections of Religion & Their Directions. Arthur J. Vidich & Stanford M. Lyman. LC 84-2268. 394p. reprint ed. pap. 112.30 (*0-7837-5302-0*, 2080313) Bks Demand.

American Sociology & Pragmatism: Mead, Chicago Sociology, & Symbolic Interaction. J. David Lewis & Richard L. Smith. LC 80-15489. (Illus.). 1981. 30.00 (*0-226-47697-9*) U Ch Pr.

American Socket Bayonets & Scabbards. Robert M. Reilly. LC 90-81582. (Illus.). 208p. 1990. 40.00 (*0-917218-45-0*) A Mowbray.

American Soldier: Adjustment During Army Life, Vol. 1. Samuel A. Stouffer et al. 600p. 1949. pap. text ed. 33.95 (*0-89126-034-X*) MA-AH Pub.

American Soldier: Combat & Its Aftermath, Vol. 2. Samuel A. Stouffer et al. 675p. 1949. pap. text ed. 35.95 (*0-89126-035-8*) MA-AH Pub.

American Soldier of the Revolutionary War: Illustrated Drill Manual & Regulations. A. N. Schultz. 1981. 4.00 (*0-913150-47-9*) Pioneer Pr.

American Soldiers: Adjustment During Army Life see Studies in Social Psychology in World War 2

American Soldiers: Combat & Its Aftermath see Studies in Social Psychology in World War 2

American Solution: Origins of the U. S. Constitution. Robert A. Rutland. LC 86-607919. 76p. 1987. 6.00 (*0-8444-0547-7*, 030-001-00118-1) Lib Congress.

***American Solution No. II.** Albert M. Juergens, Jr. LC 94-76201. 190p. 1994. 19.95 (*0-9635010-2-X*) Huntersfld Mtn.

American Song, a Book of Poems. Paul Engle. LC 76-11505. (BCL Ser.: II). reprint ed. 20.00 (*0-404-15285-6*) AMS Pr.

American Song Sheets, Slip Ballads, & Poetical Broadsides, 1850-1870. 2nd ed. Edwin Wolf, II. LC 82-204150. 205p. 1963. 18.00 (*0-527-70950-6*) Lib Co Phila.

American Song Treasury: One Hundred Favorites. Ed. by Theodore Raph. 416p. 1986. reprint ed. pap. 12.95 (*0-486-25222-1*) Dover.

American Song, Vol. 2: The Complete Musical Theatre Companion. Ken Bloom. LC 84-24728. 628p. reprint ed. pap. 179.00 (*0-8357-3499-4*, 2039760) Bks Demand.

American Songbag. Carl Sandburg. LC 28-681. 528p. 1990. reprint ed. pap. 16.95 (*0-15-605650-X*, Harvest Bks) HarBrace.

American Songwriters: One Hundred Forty-Six Biographies of America's Greatest Popular Composers & Lyricists. David Ewen. 489p. 1986. 68.00 (*0-8242-0744-0*) Wilson.

***American Sonnets.** Wanda Coleman. (Light & Dust Bks.). 62p. (Orig.). 1994. pap. 6.00 (*0-87924-069-5*) Membrane Pr.

American Soul. Franz Schurmann. LC 94-15727. 248p. (Orig.). 1995. pap. 14.95 (*1-56279-068-4*) Mercury Hse Inc.

American Source Delius' Style. Philip Jones. LC 89-30809. (British Music Theses Ser.). 576p. 1990. 50.00 (*0-8240-2014-6*) Garland.

American Sources of Modern Art. Holger Cahill. LC 78-86426. (Museum of Modern Art Publications in Reprint). (Illus.). 1969. reprint ed. 18.95 (*0-405-01532-1*) Ayer.

***American South.** Sybil Kein. (Lotus Poetry Ser.). 60p. 1995. pap. 10.00 (*0-87013-412-4*) Mich St U Pr.

American South. Ed. by Richard L. Nostrand & Sam B. Hilliard. LC 88-81746. (Geoscience & Man Ser.: Vol. 25). (Illus.). 174p. (Orig.). (C). 1988. pap. text ed. 25.00 (*0-938909-60-6*) Geosci Pubns LSU.

American South, 7 bks., Set. Ed. by C. Vann Woodward. 108.00 (*0-405-05058-5*) Ayer.

American South: A History. William J. Cooper, Jr. & Thomas E. Terrill. 1990. 50.00 (*0-394-58948-3*) Knopf.

American South - a History: Since 1860, Vol. 3. William J. Cooper & Thomas E. Terrill. 1991. text ed. write for info. (*0-07-063742-3*) McGraw.

American South - a History: To 1865, Vol. 2. William J. Cooper & Thomas E. Terrill. 1991. pap. text ed. write for info. (*0-07-063741-5*) McGraw.

American-South African Relations, 1784-1980: Review & Select Bibliography. C. Tsehloane Keto. LC 85-4937. 174p. 1985. pap. text ed. 11.00 (*0-89680-128-4*, Ohio U Ctr Intl) Ohio U Pr.

American South Comes of Age: Study Guide. Jack Bass et al. 54p. (C). 1986. student ed, pap. text ed. 6.50 (*0-685-14207-8*); pap. text ed. write for info. (*0-07-554205-6*) McGraw.

American-Southern African Relations: Bibliographic Essays. Ed. by Francis A. Kornegay. LC 75-25331. (African Bibliographic Ser.: No. 1). 188p. 1976. text ed. 42.95 (*0-8371-8398-7*, EA/A01, Greenwood Pr) Greenwood.

American Southwest. (Insight Guides, Windows on the World Ser.). 1993. pap. 21.95 (*0-395-66168-4*) HM.

American Southwest: A People & Their Landscape. Michael Grant. 192p. 1992. 29.98 (*0-934429-97-9*) Thunder Bay CA.

***American Southwest: The American Southwest.** (Travellers Guides Ser.). (Illus.). 736p. 1994. pap. 15.95 (*2-8315-1719-2*) Berlitz.

American Southwest & Mesoamerica: Systems of Prehistoric Exchange. Ed. by J. E. Ericson & T. G. Baugh. (Interdisciplinary Contributions to Archaeology Ser.). (Illus.). 290p. (C). 1992. 45.00 (*0-306-44178-0*, Plenum Pr) Plenum.

American Souvenir Teaspoon Handbook. Jonathan F. Caron. LC 90-92280. (Illus.). 247p. (Orig.). 1991. pap. 19.95 (*0-9628713-0-3*) J F Caron.

American-Soviet Playwrights Directory. Ed. by Phyllis J. Kaye & George C. White. (Illus.). 1988. 39.00 (*0-9605160-1-8*) E O'Neill.

American-Soviet Relations: From Nineteen Forty-Seven to the Nixon-Kissinger Grand Design. Dan Caldwell. LC 80-27333. (Contributions in Political Science Ser.: No. 69). (Illus.). 288p. 1981. text ed. 59.95 (*0-313-22538-9*, CCC/, Greenwood Pr) Greenwood.

American-Soviet Relations: From the Russian Revolution to the Fall of Communism. Peter G. Boyle. LC 92-21102. 304p. 1993. 59.95 (*0-415-02020-4*, B0155); pap. 18.95 (*0-415-09327-9*, B0159) Routledge.

American-Soviet Trade in the Cold War. Philip J. Funigiello. LC 87-35836. xiii, 289p. (C). 1988. 37.50 (*0-8078-1784-8*) U of NC Pr.

American-Soviet Walk: Taking Steps to End the Nuclear Arms Race. Fred Segal & Fred E. Basten. Tr. by Ljilja Grubisic. 144p. (Orig.). (ENG & RUS.). 1988. pap. write for info. (*0-9621677-0-3*) UWOTUF.

American Spanish Pronunciation. Ed. by Peter C. Bjarkman & Robert M. Hammond. LC 89-17189. 283p. (Orig.). 1989. pap. 18.95 (*0-87840-099-0*) Georgetown U Pr.

American Speaker. Ed. by Aram Bakshian, Jr. 400p. 1992. ring bd. 297.00 (*0-9634672-0-4*) Georgetwn Pub Hse.

American Speaker. John Frost. LC 74-15740. (Popular Culture in America Ser.). (Illus.). 454p. 1975. reprint ed. 36.95 (*0-405-06375-X*) Ayer.

American Speakership: The Office in Historical Perspective. Ronald M. Peters, Jr. LC 89-20025. 352p. 1990. text ed. 48.50x (*0-8018-3955-6*) Johns Hopkins.

American Species of Dacnusinae Hymenoptera-Braconidae. Garland T. Riegel. (Novitates Arthropodae Ser.). (Illus.). 200p. (Orig.). 1982. pap. 11.00 (*0-916170-19-5*) J-B Pub.

American Species of Marchantia. Alexander W. Evans. (Connecticut Academy of Arts & Sciences Ser., Trans.: Vol. 21). 1917. pap. 89.50 (*0-685-44364-7*) Elliots Bks.

American Species of Orthophragmina & Lepidocyclina. J. A. Cushman. 1971. reprint ed. 16.00 (*0-934454-06-X*) Lubrecht & Cramer.

American Species of Scutallaria. Carl C. Epling. LC 42-3897. (University of California Publications in Botany: Vol. 20, No. 1). (Illus.). 149p. reprint ed. pap. 42.50 (*0-8357-5400-6*, 2014726) Bks Demand.

American Spectacles & Other Cultivated Illusions. Deborah Shai. LC 92-6709. 251p. 1993. 18.95 (*0-913275-01-8*) New Haven Pr.

American Speech Sounds & Rhythm: Advanced. 2nd ed. Hazel P. Brown. (Speechphone Ser.). 64p. (Orig.). 1981. audio, pap. text ed. 39.50 (*0-88432-063-4*, S23709) Audio-Forum.

American Speech Sounds & Rhythm: Elementary. 2nd ed. Hazel P. Brown. (Speechphone Ser.). 64p. (Orig.). 1981. audio, pap. text ed. 39.50 (*0-88432-061-8*, S23701) Audio-Forum.

American Speech Sounds & Rhythm: Intermediate. 3rd ed. Hazel P. Brown. (Speechphone Ser.). 64p. 1981. audio, pap. text ed. 39.50 (*0-88432-062-6*, S23705) Audio-Forum.

American Speeches. Ed. by Wayland M. Parrish & Marie Hochmuth. LC 69-14028. 518p. 1969. reprint ed. text ed. 35.00 (*0-8371-1962-6*, PAAM, Greenwood Pr) Greenwood.

American Speeches of the Earl of Halifax. Edward F. Halifax. LC 73-121476. (Essay Index Reprint Ser.). 1977. reprint ed. 31.95 (*0-8369-1946-7*) Ayer.

American Spice Trade Association Analytical Methods. 68p. 35.00 (*0-318-13290-7*) Am Spice Trade.

American Spice Trade Association Microbiological Methods. 82p. 12.75 (*0-318-13291-5*) Am Spice Trade.

American Spirit. Oscar S. Straus. LC 68-8497. (Essay Index Reprint Ser.). 1977. 23.95 (*0-8369-0128-2*) Ayer.

American Spirit, I. 6th ed. Thomas A. Bailey & David M. Kennedy. LC 86-82149. 565p. 1987. pap. text ed. 15.00 (*0-669-12800-7*) Heath.

American Spirit, II. 6th ed. Thomas A. Bailey & David M. Kennedy. LC 86-82149. 565p. 1987. pap. text ed. 15.00 (*0-669-12801-5*) Heath.

***American Spirit: The Paintings of Mort Kunstler.** Mort Kuntsler et al. LC 94-29044. (Illus.). 1994. 39.95 (*1-55853-309-5*) Rutledge Hill Pr.

American Spirit: United States History as Seen by Contemporaries, 2 vols., Vol. I. 7th ed. Thomas A. Bailey & David M. Kennedy. LC 90-80758. 486p. (C). 1991. Vol. 1, 486 p. pap. text ed. 15.00 (*0-669-21472-8*) Heath.

American Spirit: United States History as Seen by Contemporaries, 2 vols., Vol. 2. 7th ed. Thomas A. Bailey & David M. Kennedy. LC 90-80758. 666p. (C). 1991. pap. text ed. 15.00 (*0-669-21473-6*) Heath.

American Spirit: Visions of a New Corporate Culture. Lawrence M. Miller. 256p. 1985. mass mkt. 3.95 (*0-446-32710-7*) Warner Bks.

***American Spirit Chapters 1-24: United States History as Seen by Contemporaries, 2 vols., Vol. 1.** 8th ed. Thomas A. Bailey & David M. Kennedy. 542p. (C). 1994. pap. text ed. write for info. (*0-669-34361-7*) Heath.

***American Spirit Chapters 24-45: United States History as Seen by Contemporaries, 2 vols., Vol. 2.** 8th ed. Thomas A. Bailey & David M. Kennedy. 718p. (C). 1994. pap. text ed. write for info. (*0-669-34362-5*) Heath.

American Spirit in Architecture. Talbot Hamlin. 353p. 1993. reprint ed. lib. bdg. 89.00 (*0-7812-5296-2*) Rprt Serv.

American Spirit in Europe, a Survey of Transatlantic Influences. Halvadan Koht. (History - United States Ser.). 289p. 1993. reprint ed. lib. bdg. 79.00 (*0-7812-4860-4*) Rprt Serv.

American Spirit in Letters. Stanley T. Williams. 1926. 79.50x (*0-686-83468-2*) Elliots Bks.

American Spirit in Literature: A Chronicle of Great Interpreters. Bliss Perry. (BCL1-PS American Literature Ser.). 281p. 1992. reprint ed. lib. bdg. 79.00 (*0-7812-6605-X*) Rprt Serv.

American Spiritualist Assembly Minister's Handbook & Service Manual 1987. A. S. A. Directors. 78p. 1987. pap. 21.00 (*0-939795-28-0*) Amer Spirit.

American Spiritualist Ministry. Arden Rizer, Jr. Ed. by American Spiritualist Assembly Directors. 240p. (Orig.). 1987. pap. 20.00 (*0-939795-30-2*) Amer Spirit.

American Spiritualist Psychology. Arden Rizer, Jr. 24p. 1987. pap. 9.00 (*0-939795-20-5*) Amer Spirit.

***American Spoken English: Introductory Basics, Urgent Survival - No Foreign Accent.** 260p. 1995. pap. 15.00 (*0-929350-24-3*); audio write for info. (*0-614-03142-7*) Spoken English Pubns.

***American Spoken English: Real Life Selections 1-41, Listening Comprehension Phonology.** 130p. 1995. pap. 10.00 (*0-929350-47-2*) Spoken English Pubns.

***American Spoken English: Real Life Selections 1-41, Listening Comprehension Phonology.** 1995. audio 10.00 (*0-614-03141-9*) Spoken English Pubns.

American Spoken English in Real Life - Fast Natural, Urgent Survival, Foreign Accent Begone! The Phonology of General American Colloquial, Vol. 1. D. G. Davis. 300p. (Orig.). 1994. pap. 25.00 (*0-929350-01-4*) Spoken English Pubns.

American Spoken English in Real Life, Basic Course: Learning to Understand Americans Talking Naturally & to Talk So They Readily Understand You, Vol. 2. D. G. Davis. 128p. (Orig.). Date not set. audio 10.00 (*0-685-74561-9*) Spoken English Pubns.

American Spoken English in Real Life, Basic Course: Learning to Understand Americans Talking Naturally & to Talk So They Readily Understand You, Vol. 2. D. G. Davis. 128p. (Orig.). 1994. pap. 10.00 (*0-929350-02-2*) Spoken English Pubns.

American Spoons: Souvenir & Historical. Donna H. Felger & Dorothy Rainwater. LC 90-61799. (Illus.). 368p. 1990. reprint ed. 45.00 (*0-88740-266-6*) Schiffer.

American Sport. Peter Levine. 224p. (C). 1989. pap. text ed. write for info. (*0-13-031378-5*) P-H.

American Sport Culture: The Humanist Dimensions. Wiley L. Umphlett. LC 83-45967. 320p. 1985. 34.50 (*0-8387-5070-2*) Bucknell U Pr.

264

An Asterisk (*) at the beginning of an entry indicates that the title is appearing in BIP for the first time.

An Asterisk (*) at the beginning of an entry indicates that the title is appearing in BIP for the first time.

American Still Life, 1945-1985. Text by Linda L. Cathcart. (Illus.). 144p. 1983. pap. 19.95 (0-936080-12-4) Cont Arts Museum.

***American Stock Exchange: A Guide to Information Resources.** Carol Z. Womack & Alice C. Littlejohn. LC 94-42750. (Research & Information Guides in Business, Industry, & Economic Institutions Ser.: Vol. 7). 240p. 1995. 35.00 (0-8153-0223-1, SS768) Garland.

American Stock Exchange, Inc. Constitution & Rules: Revised to May, 1992. 1040p. (Orig.). 1992. pap. 21.00 (0-318-33080-6, 4780) Commerce.

American Stock Exchange, Inc. Directory: Revised to May 1992. 240p. 1992. write for info. (0-685-57997-2, 4779) Commerce.

American Stoneware. William C. Ketchum, Jr. (Illus.). 192p. 1991. 50.00 (0-8050-1263-X) H Holt & Co.

***American Stoneware: A Wallace-Homestead Price Guide.** Don Raycraft & Carol Raycraft. 1995. pap. 16.95 (0-87069-714-5) Chilton.

***American Stoneware Bottles: A History & Study.** David Graci. (Illus.). 90p. (Orig.). 1995. pap. 24.95 (0-9616444-1-9) Calem Pub Co.

American Stonewares: The Art & Craft of Utilitarian Potters. Georgeanna H. Greer. LC 81-51449. (Illus.). 286p. 1981. 40.00 (0-916838-52-8) Schiffer.

***American Stories.** Pierre-Yves Pepin. (Prose Ser.: No. 28). 128p. 1995. 12.00 (0-920717-96-9) Guernica Editions.

American Stories: Case Studies in Politics & Government. James R. Bowers. LC 92-17211. 441p. 1993. pap. 22.95 (0-534-14502-7) Intl Thomson.

American Story. Jacques Godbout. Tr. by Yves Saint-Pierre. LC 88-4737. (Emergent Literatures Ser.). 161p. (Orig.). 1988. text ed. 19.95 (0-8166-1709-0); pap. 8.95 (0-8166-1710-4) U of Minn Pr.

American Story: Best of StoryQuarterly. Ed. by Diane Williams et al. LC 89-81157. 296p. (Orig.). 1990. pap. 8.95 (0-943433-05-3) Cane Hill Pr.

American Story: Photography from the Permanent Collection. Tom Bamberger. (Illus.). 32p. (Orig.). 1992. pap. 9.95 (0-944110-29-0) Milwauk Art Mus.

American Story: Pietro DiDonato's Christ in Concrete. Louise Napolitano. LC 93-36534. (Studies in Southern Italian & Italian-American Culture: Vol. 4). 1994. write for info. (0-8204-2094-8) P Lang Pubs.

American Story: The Rea Award for the Short Story. Michael Rea. 1993. 25.00 (0-88001-341-9) Ecco Pr.

American Story in Art: The Murals of Allyn Cox in the U. S. Capital. Robert Schwengel. Ed. by Paul Martin. LC 86-60792. 44p. (Orig.). 1986. pap. 4.50 (0-916200-07-8) US Capitol Hist.

American Storytelling. Claude Browning. 1993. 7.95 (0-8062-4733-9) Carlton.

American Strategic Theology. John A. Coleman. 1985. pap. 10.95 (0-8091-2469-6) Paulist Pr.

American Strategy in World War II: A Reconsideration. Kent R. Greenfield. LC 63-19554. 157p. reprint ed. 44.80 (0-8357-9263-3, 2001185) Bks Demand.

American Strategy in World War II: A Reconsideration. Kent R. Greenfield. LC 78-12870. 145p. 1979. reprint ed. text ed. 35.00 (0-313-21175-2, GRAW, Greenwood Pr) Greenwood.

American Strategy in World War II: A Reconsideration. Kent R. Greenfield. LC 82-14881. 158p. (C). 1982. reprint ed. pap. 10.50 (0-89874-557-8) Krieger.

American Streamline: A Handbook of Neon Advertising Design. Philip Lemme. LC 87-37650. (Illus.). 160p. 1988. reprint ed. pap. 12.95 (0-911380-80-9) ST Pubns.

American Streamline: Connections (Intermediate) Bernard Hartley & Peter Viney. 1984. Student's ed. student ed, pap. 9.75 (0-19-434115-1) OUP.

American Streamline: Connections (Intermediate) Bernard Hartley & Peter Viney. 1984. Tchr's. ed. teacher ed 15.95 (0-19-434116-X) OUP.

American Streamline: Connections (Intermediate) Bernard Hartley & Peter Viney. 1985. Tests. write for info. (0-19-434187-9) OUP.

American Streamline: Connections (Intermediate) Bernard Hartley & Peter Viney. 1987. Tchr's. Extra. write for info. (0-19-434256-5) OUP.

American Streamline: Connections (Intermediate), Set. Bernard Hartley & Peter Viney. 1984. audio 31.95 (0-19-434119-4) OUP.

American Streamline: Connections (Intermediate), Wkbk. A, Units 1-40. Bernard Hartley & Peter Viney. 1984. student ed 4.95 (0-19-434117-8) OUP.

American Streamline: Connections (Intermediate), Wkbk. B, Units 41-80. Bernard Hartley & Peter Viney. 1984. student ed 4.95 (0-19-434118-6) OUP.

American Streamline: Destinations (Advanced) Bernard Hartley & Peter Viney. 1985. student ed, pap. 9.75 (0-19-434120-8) OUP.

American Streamline: Destinations (Advanced) Bernard Hartley & Peter Viney. 1985. Tchr's. ed. teacher ed 15.95 (0-19-434121-6) OUP.

American Streamline: Destinations (Advanced) Bernard Hartley & Peter Viney. 1986. Tests. write for info. (0-19-434188-7) OUP.

American Streamline: Destinations (Advanced), Set. Bernard Hartley & Peter Viney. 1985. audio 42.95 (0-19-434124-0) OUP.

American Streamline: Destinations (Advanced), Wkbk. A, Units 1-40. Bernard Hartley & Peter Viney. 1985. student ed 4.95 (0-19-434122-4) OUP.

American Streamline: Destinations (Advanced), Wkbk. B, Units 41-80. Bernard Hartley & Peter Viney. 1985. student ed 4.95 (0-19-434123-2) OUP.

American Streamline: Departures: An Intensive American English Course for Beginners. Bernard Hartley & Peter Viney. (Illus.). (Orig.). 1983. student ed, pap. 9.75 (0-19-434110-0); audio 17.50 (0-19-434114-3) OUP.

American Streamline: Departures: An Intensive American English Course for Beginners. Bernard Hartley & Peter Viney. (Illus.). (Orig.). 1983. Tchr's. ed. teacher ed 15.95 (0-19-434111-9) OUP.

American Streamline: Departures: An Intensive American English Course for Beginners. Bernard Hartley & Peter Viney. (Illus.). (Orig.). 1985. Tests. write for info. (0-19-434186-0) OUP.

American Streamline: Departures: An Intensive American English Course for Beginners. Bernard Hartley & Peter Viney. (Illus.). (Orig.). 1987. Tchr's. Extra. write for info. (0-19-434222-0) OUP.

American Streamline: Departures: An Intensive American English Course for Beginners, Wkbk. A, Units 1-40. Bernard Hartley & Peter Viney. (Illus.). (Orig.). 1984. student ed 4.95 (0-19-434112-7) OUP.

American Streamline: Departures: An Intensive American English Course for Beginners, Wkbk. B, Units 41-80. Bernard Hartley & Peter Viney. (Illus.). (Orig.). 1984. student ed 4.95 (0-19-434113-5) OUP.

***American Street Gang: Its Nature, Prevalence, & Control.** Malcolm Klein. (Studies in Crime & Public Policy). (Illus.). 304p. 1995. 27.50 (0-19-509534-0) OUP.

American Streets. Laurence Schulz. (Illus.). 47p. (Orig.). Date not set. pap. 5.00 (1-882634-01-2) Poetry Sucks Pr.

American Streets. Lawrence Schulz. (Illus.). 48p. (Orig.). 1993. reprint ed. pap. 5.00 (1-885021-01-1) Orange Ocean.

American Structuralism. D. Hymes & J. G. Fought. (State-of-the-Art Reports). 1979. text ed. 55.40 (90-279-3228-X) Mouton.

American Struggle for the British West India Carrying-Trade 1815-1830. F. Lee Benns. LC 68-55479. (Reprints of Economic Classics Ser.). 1972. reprint ed. lib. bdg. 29.50 (0-678-00793-4) Kelley.

American Studies. Mark Merlis. LC 94-6593. 1994. 21.95 (0-395-68992-9) HM.

American Studies: An Annotated Bibliography, 3 Vols., Set. Ed. by Jack Salzman. 1500p. 1986. 250.00 (0-521-32555-2) Cambridge U Pr.

American Studies: An Annotated Bibliography: 1984-1988 Supplement, 4 Vols. Ed. by Jack Salzman. 1000p. (C). 1990. 99.95 (0-521-36559-7) Cambridge U Pr.

American Studies: Essays in Honour of Marcus Cunliffe. Ed. by Brian H. Reid & John White. 320p. 1991. text ed. 65.00 (0-312-05305-3) St Martin.

American Studies: Topics & Sources. Ed. by Robert H. Walker. LC 75-35675. (Illus.). 320p. (Orig.). 1976. text ed. 75.00 (0-8371-8559-9, WBE/, Greenwood Pr) Greenwood.

American Studies Abroad. Robert H. Walker. LC 75-16963. (Contributions in American Studies: No. 22). (Illus.). 160p. 1975. text ed. 45.00 (0-8371-7951-3, WAS/, Greenwood Pr) Greenwood.

American Studies & American Musicology: A Point of View & a Case in Point. Richard Crawford. LC 75-874. (I.S.A.M. Monographs: No. 4). 34p. 1975. pap. 4.00 (0-914678-03-5) Inst Am Music.

American Studies in Africa, Vol. I. Ed. by Andrew Horn & George E. Carter. LC 85-136710. 133p. 1984. pap. 8.00 (0-89410-490-X) Three Continents.

American Studies in Africa, Vol. II: Contacts & Divergences. Ed. by George E. Carter. 100p. (C). 1989. 22.00 (0-89410-494-2); pap. 12.00 (0-89410-495-0) Three Continents.

American Studies in Black & White: Selected Essays, 1949-1989. Sidney Kaplan. Ed. by Allan D. Austin. LC 90-47298. (Illus.). 278p. (C). 1991. lib. bdg. 40.00 (0-87023-469-2) U of Mass Pr.

American Studies in China: A Directory. George T. Yu et al. 182p. (Orig.). (C). 1993. lib. bdg. 49.50 (0-8191-8829-8); pap. text ed. 24.50 (0-8191-8830-1) U Pr of Amer.

American Studies in Honor of William Kenneth Boyd. Americana Club Staff. Ed. by D. K. Jackson. LC 68-20295. (Essay Index Reprint Ser.). 1977. 23.95 (0-8369-0395-1) Ayer.

American Studies in Sweden. S. B. Liljegren. (Essays & Studies on American Language & Literature: Vol. 14). (Orig.). 1962. pap. 18.00 (0-8115-0194-9) Periodicals Srv.

American Studies in the Anthropology of India. Ed. by Sylvia Vatuk. 1979. 11.50 (0-8364-0319-3) S Asia.

American Studies in Transition: Essays. Ed. by David E. Nye & Christen K. Thomsen. 234p. (Orig.). 1985. pap. text ed. 43.50 (87-7492-532-6) Coronet Bks.

American Studies of Contemporary China. Ed. by David Shambaugh. LC 93-5618. (Studies on Contemporary China). 382p. 1993. text ed. 57.95 (1-56324-266-4, East Gate Bk); pap. text ed. 23.95 (1-56324-267-2, East Gate Bk) M E Sharpe.

American Studio Ceramics, Nineteen Twenty to Nineteen Fifty. Ed. by Susan Brown. LC 88-51175. (Illus.). 100p. (Orig.). 1988. pap. text ed. 20.00 (0-938713-04-3) Univ MN Art Mus.

American Stuff. Federal Writer's Project Staff. (FDR & the Era of the New Deal Ser.). 1976. reprint ed. lib. bdg. 39.50 (0-306-70806-X) Da Capo.

American-Style Flower Arranging. Peter Pfahl & Elwood Kalin. (Illus.). 256p. (C). 1981. text ed. 71.00 (0-13-029538-8) P-H.

American Style of Foreign Policy: Cultural Politics & Foreign Affairs. Robert Dallek. LC 82-48877. 336p. 1983. 19.95 (0-394-51360-6) Knopf.

American Style of Foreign Policy: Cultural Politics & Foreign Affairs. Robert Dallek. (Illus.). 352p. 1990. pap. 10.95 (0-19-506205-1) OUP.

American Sublime. Ed. by Mary Arensberg. LC 85-31824. 218p. (C). 1986. 69.50 (0-88706-189-3); pap. 24.95 (0-88706-190-7) State U NY Pr.

American Sublime: Landscape & Scenery of the Lower Hudson Valley. Raymond J. O'Brien. LC 80-21827. (Illus.). 353p. 1981. text ed. 40.00 (0-231-04778-9) Col U Pr.

American Sublime: The Genealogy of a Poetic Genre. Rob Wilson. LC 90-50654. (Wisconsin Project on American Writers Ser.). 366p. 1991. 45.00 (0-299-12770-2); pap. text ed. 18.50 (0-299-12774-5) U of Wis Pr.

American Subsidiaries of German Firms 1992-1993 (Tochtergesellschaften Deutscher Unternehmen in Den U. S. A. 1992-1993) 20th ed. Ed. by Erwin Mueller & Oliver Nolte. 280p. (ENG & GER.). 1992. 100.00 (0-86640-042-7) Manhattan Pub Co.

American Suburbs Rating Guide & Fact Book. Alan Willis & Bennett Jacobstein. LC 93-4750. (Illus.). 846p. 1993. pap. text ed. 74.00 (0-9634017-5-0) Toucan Valley.

American Suicide: A Psychocultural Exploration. Howard I. Kushner. 284p. (Orig.). (C). 1991. pap. 14.95 (0-8135-1610-2) Rutgers U Pr.

American SuperCar. Roger Huntington. (Illus.). 176p. 1990. pap. 9.98 (0-87938-464-6) Motorbooks Intl.

American Support of Free Elections Abroad. Theodore P. Wright, Jr. LC 80-15872. 184p. 1980. reprint ed. text ed. 65.00 (0-313-22507-9, WRAM, Greenwood Pr) Greenwood.

American Supreme Court. Robert G. McCloskey. LC 60-14235. (Chicago History of American Civilization Ser.). 1961. pap. text ed. 10.95 (0-226-55675-1, CHAC13) U Ch Pr.

American Supreme Court. Robert G. McCloskey. Ed. by Sanford Levinson. LC 94-10905. 352p. 1994. pap. text ed. 12.95 (0-226-55678-6) U Ch Pr.

American Supreme Court. 2nd ed. Robert G. McCloskey. Ed. by Sanford Levinson. LC 94-10905. 352p. 1994. lib. bdg. 45.00 (0-226-55677-8) U Ch Pr.

American-Swedish Handbook. 11th rev. ed. Ed. by C. Olsson & R. McLaughlin. 200p. 1992. pap. 8.50 (0-9609620-2-6) Swedish Council.

American Swing. Earl Atkinson. (Ballroom Dance Ser.). 1986. lib. bdg. 250.00 (0-8490-3633-X) Gordon Pr.

American Sword. Ryder Stacy. (Doomsday Warrior Ser.: No. 17). 1990. pap. 2.95 (0-8217-2872-5) Zebra.

American Sword, Seventeen Seventy-Five to Nineteen Forty-Five. Harold L. Peterson. LC 65-25409. (Illus.). 1983. 35.00 (0-9603094-1-1) Ray Riling.

American Swords & Sword Makers. Richard H. Bezdek. (Illus.). 648p. 1994. text ed. 79.95 (0-87364-765-3) Paladin Pr.

American Symphony Orchestra: A Social History of Musical Taste. John H. Mueller. LC 76-8875. (Illus.). 437p. 1976. reprint ed. text ed. 79.50 (0-8371-8915-2, MUAS, Greenwood Pr) Greenwood.

American Synagogue: A Sanctuary Transformed. Ed. by Jack Wertheimer. (Illus.). 432p. 1988. 64.95 (0-521-33290-7) Cambridge U Pr.

***American Synagogue: A Sanctuary Transformed.** Ed. by Jack Wertheimer. (Brandeis Series in American Jewish History, Culture, & Life). (Illus.). 452p. 1995. pap. 19.95 (0-87451-709-5) U Pr of New Eng.

American Synagogue History: A Bibliography & State-of-the-Field Survey. Alexandra S. Korros & Jonathan D. Sarna. LC 88-31731. 224p. (C). 1988. 34.95 (0-910129-90-8) Wiener Pubs Inc.

American Syndicalism. John G. Brooks. LC 78-86170. reprint ed. 31.50 (0-404-01118-7) AMS Pr.

American Syndicalism. John G. Brooks. LC 70-89722. (American Labor, from Conspiracy to Collective Bargaining Ser., No. 1). 264p. 1970. reprint ed. 17.95 (0-405-02107-0) Ayer.

American Syndicalism: The I.W.W. John G. Brooks. LC 78-107407. (Civil Liberties in American History Ser.). 1970. reprint ed. lib. bdg. 32.50 (0-306-71887-1) Da Capo.

American System: A New View of Government in the United States. Morton Grodzins. Ed. by Daniel J. Elazar. LC 82-8449. (Political Theory Ser.). 404p. 1983. 24.95 (0-87855-916-7) Transaction Pubs.

American System of Criminal Justice. 6th ed. George F. Cole. LC 91-18701. 752p. (C). 1992. student ed, pap. 17.95 (0-534-14702-X) Intl Thomson.

American System of Criminal Justice. 6th ed. George F. Cole. LC 91-18701. 752p. (C). 1992. text ed. 53.95 (0-534-14700-3) Intl Thomson.

American System of Criminal Justice. 7th ed. George F. Cole. LC 94-11411. 686p. 1995. text ed. 53.95 (0-534-24048-8) Intl Thomson.

American System of Government. 6th ed. Ernest S. Griffith. LC 83-8226. 224p. 1984. 23.00 (0-685-07802-7); pap. 13.95 (0-416-35100-X, NO. 3962) Routledge Chapman & Hall.

American System of Practical Bookkeeping: Adopted to the Commerce of the United States, 2 vols. in 1. James A. Bennett & Benjamin Foster. LC 75-18457. (History of Accounting Ser.). (Illus.). 1978. reprint ed. 19.95 (0-405-07541-3) Ayer.

American T. S. Eliot: A Study of the Early Writings. Eric Sigg. (Cambridge Studies in American Literature & Culture). (C). 1989. 49.95 (0-521-36561-9) Cambridge U Pr.

***American Table: Traditional & Contemporary Regional Cooking Featuring Recipes from America's Most Celebrated Chefs.** Anthony Dias-Blue. LC 95-10800. (Illus.). 1995. 34.95 (1-57036-161-4) Turner Pub GA.

American Tables & Looking Glasses in the Mabel Brady Garvan & Other Collections at Yale University. David L. Barquist. (Illus.). 530p. (C). 1992. text ed. 70.00 (0-300-05240-5) Yale U Pr.

***American Tabloid: A Novel.** James Ellroy. 1995. 25.00 (0-679-40391-4) Knopf.

American Tail II. D. G. Chichester & George Wildman. (Illus.). 64p. 1991. 2.95 (0-87135-758-5) Marvel Entmnt.

American Talk Show Directory. Ed. by William T. Harrison. 200p. 1990. ring bd. 195.00 (0-685-33378-7) Bradley Comm.

American Tall Tales. Mary P. Osborne. LC 89-37235. (Illus.). 128p. (J). (gr. 1 up). 1991. 18.00 (0-679-80089-1); lib. bdg. 18.99 (0-679-90089-6) Knopf Bks Yng Read.

American Tall Tales. Adrien Stoutenburg. (Storybooks Ser.). (Illus.). (J). (gr. 3-7). 1976. pap. 3.99 (0-14-030928-4, Puffin) Puffin Bks.

American Tall Tales: Literature Mini-Unit. Joy Evans & Jo E. Moore. (Illus.). 16p. (J). (gr. 2-5). 1987. pap. 5.95 (1-55799-088-3, EMC509) Evan-Moor Corp.

American Tally: Statistics & Rankings for 3,165 U. S. Cities & Towns. Toucan Valley Publications Research Staff. LC 93-42443. 437p. (Orig.). 1993. pap. 38.00 (0-9634017-8-5) Toucan Valley.

American Tango Syllabus. (Ballroom Dance Ser.). 1986. lib. bdg. 250.00 (0-8490-3280-6) Gordon Pr.

American Tango Syllabus. (Ballroom Dance Ser.). 1985. lib. bdg. 250.00 (0-87700-776-4) Revisionist Pr.

American Tanks of WWII. Thomas Berhdt. (Enthusiast Color Ser.). (Illus.). 96p. 1994. pap. 12.95 (0-87938-930-3) Motorbooks Intl.

American Tapestry: Educating a Nation. 32p. 1991. 7.00 (0-317-05332-9) NASBE.

American Tapestry Today. Ed. by Jim Brown. (Illus.). 40p. (Orig.). 1990. pap. 12.95 (0-945858-02-7) Am Tapestry Alliance.

American Tarpan Studbook, Vol. 1. Comp. by Ellen Thrall. (Illus.). 1975. 12.50 (0-912830-32-8) Printed Horse.

American Task in Persia. A. C. Millspaugh. LC 73-6293. (Middle East Ser.). 1973. reprint ed. 25.95 (0-405-05350-9) Ayer.

American Teacher: Evolution of a Profession in a Democracy. Willard S. Elsbree. LC 74-104262. 566p. 1970. reprint ed. text ed. 65.00 (0-8371-3921-X, ELAT, Greenwood Pr) Greenwood.

American Teacher in China: Coping with Cultures. F. A. Kretschmer. LC 93-40163. 184p. 1994. text ed. 45.00 (0-89789-389-1, Bergin & Garvey) Greenwood.

American Teacher in Early Meiji Japan. Edward R. Beauchamp. LC 75-45222. (Asian Studies at Hawaii: No. 17). (Illus.). 173p. reprint ed. pap. 49.40 (0-8357-8529-7, 2034831) Bks Demand.

American Teachers: Histories of a Profession at Work. Ed. by Donald R. Warren. 520p. (C). 1989. text ed. write for info. (0-318-65227-7) Macmillan.

American Teaching about Russia. Ed. by Cyril E. Black & John M. Thompson. LC 59-15377. 189p. reprint ed. pap. 53.90 (0-8357-5402-2, 2005734) Bks Demand.

American Teaching System: Alpine Skiing. 2nd ed. Professional Ski Instructors of America, Inc. Staff. LC 92-61778. (Illus.). 1992. pap. 49.90 (1-882409-00-0); pap. 24.95 (0-685-61451-4) Prof Ski Instructors.

American Teaching System: Snowboard Skiing. Professional Ski Instructors of America, Inc. Staff. LC 92-61802. (Illus.). (Orig.). 1992. pap. 35.90 (1-882409-01-9); pap. 17.95 (0-685-61452-2) Prof Ski Instructors.

American Technological Sublime. David E. Nye. 440p. 1994. 35.00x (0-262-14056-X) MIT Pr.

American Technology: Are We Falling Behind? Ed. by Melinda Maidens. LC 82-15603. 191p. reprint ed. pap. 54.50 (0-8357-3493-5, 2039752) Bks Demand.

American Technology & the British Vehicle Industry. Wayne Lewchuk. 250p. 1987. 64.95 (0-521-30269-2) Cambridge U Pr.

***American Teddy Bear Encyclopedia.** Linda Mullins. 144p. 1995. 29.95 (0-87588-432-6) Hobby Hse.

American Tel & Tel; the Story of a Great Monopoly. Horace Coon. 1977. 24.95 (0-8369-5691-5) Ayer.

American Telegrapher: A Social History, 1860-1900. Edwin Gabler. (Class & Culture Ser.). (Illus.). 260p. (C). 1988. pap. text ed. 20.00 (0-8135-1285-9) Rutgers U Pr.

American Television: New Directions in History & Theory. Ed. by Nick Browne. 1994. pap. text ed. 18.00 (3-7186-0563-5) Gordon & Breach.

American Television Drama: The Experimental Years. William Hawes. LC 85-8549. (Illus.). 296p. 1986. 31.50 (0-8173-0276-X) U of Ala Pr.

American Television Genres. Stuart M. Kaminsky & Jeffrey H. Mahan. LC 84-1022. (Illus.). 250p. 1985. lib. bdg. 31.95 (0-8304-1084-8); pap. text ed. 19.95 (0-88229-828-3) Nelson-Hall.

American Temperance Movements: Cycles of Reform. Jack S. Blocker, Jr. (Social Movements Past & Present Ser.). 1988. pap. 12.95 (0-8057-9728-9, Twayne) Macmillan.

American Temperance Movements: Cycles of Reform. Jack S. Blocker, Jr. (Social Movements Past & Present Ser.). 264p. (C). 1988. text ed. 26.95 (0-8057-9727-0, Twayne) Macmillan.

American Testament. Peter T. Curto. LC 84-90220. 67p. 1984. 6.95 (0-533-06273-X) Vantage.

American Thanksgiving. Ed. by Nancy Skarmeas & Fran Morley. (Illus.). 160p. 1991. 22.95 (0-8249-4042-3) Ideals.

American Theater & Drama Research: An Annotated Guide to Information Sources, 1945-1990. Irene Shaland. LC 91-52741. 168p. 1991. lib. bdg. 29.95 (0-89950-626-7) McFarland & Co.

American Theater As Seen by Its Critics, 1752-1934. Montrose Moses. 391p. 1993. reprint ed. lib. bdg. 89.00 (0-7812-5279-2) Rprt Serv.

***American Theater History.** Thomas J. Taylor. (Magill Bibliographies Ser.). 162p. 1992. 40.00 (0-8108-2800-6) Scarecrow.

American Theater of the 1960s. Zoltan Szilassy. LC 85-8405. (Crosscurrents-Modern Critiques, Third Ser.). 126p. 1986. text ed. 15.95 (0-8093-1227-1) S Ill U Pr.

An Asterisk (*) at the beginning of an entry indicates that the title is appearing in BIP for the first time.

American Theatre: A Chronicle of Comedy & Drama, 1869-1914. Gerald Bordman. LC 92-16066. 808p. 1994. 95.00 (*0-19-503764-2*) OUP.

***American Theatre: A Chronicle of Comedy & Drama, 1914-1930.** Gerald Bordman. 832p. 1995. 49.95 (*0-19-509078-0*) OUP.

American Theatre: A Sum of Its Parts. Intro. by Henry B. Williams. 423p. 1972. 12.00 (*0-573-69002-2*) French.

American Theatre Companies, 1749-1887. Ed. by Weldon B. Durham. LC 84-27947. 606p. 1986. text ed. 115.00 (*0-313-20886-7*, DAT/, Greenwood Pr) Greenwood.

American Theatre Companies, 1888-1930. Ed. by Weldon B. Durham. LC 85-30213. 551p. 1987. text ed. 115.00 (*0-313-25359-5*, DHT/, Greenwood Pr) Greenwood.

American Theatre Companies, 1931-1986. Ed. by Weldon B. Durham. LC 88-32039. 605p. 1989. text ed. 105.00 (*0-313-25360-9*, DTP/, Quorum Bks) Greenwood.

American Theatrical Arts: A Guide to Manuscripts & Special Collections in the United States & Canada. William C. Young. LC 78-161234. 176p. reprint ed. pap. 50.20 (*0-8357-5403-0*, 2024190) Bks Demand.

American Theatrical Film: Stages in Development. John Tibbetts. LC 85-70427. 277p. 1986. 30.95 (*0-87972-289-4*); pap. 15.95 (*0-87972-290-8*) Bowling Green Univ.

American Theatrical Periodicals, 1798-1967: A Bibliographical Guide. LC 72-110577. 165p. reprint ed. pap. 47.10 (*0-8357-5404-9*, 2023456) Bks Demand.

American Theatrical Regulation, 1607-1900: Conspectus & Texts. George B. Bryan. LC 93-42485. 447p. 1993. 49.50 (*0-8108-2825-1*) Scarecrow.

American Themes. Ed. by Esmond Wright. LC 68-88949. (Selections from History Today Ser.: No. 1). (Illus.). 1969. 10.95 (*0-686-85911-1*); pap. 8.95 (*0-05-001529-X*) Dufour.

American Themes. Denis W. Brogan. (History - United States Ser.). 284p. 1993. reprint ed. lib. bdg. 79.00 (*0-7812-4847-7*) Rprt Serv.

American Theories of Federalism. Walter H. Bennett. LC 63-17399. reprint ed. 45.10 (*0-8357-9614-0*, 2051546) Bks Demand.

American Thought in Transition: The Impact of Evolutionary Naturalism, 1865-1900. Paul F. Boller, Jr. LC 80-6210. 285p. 1981. reprint ed. pap. text ed. 22.00 (*0-8191-1551-7*) U Pr of Amer.

American Threat, National Security & Foreign Policy. James L. Payne. 344p. (Orig.). 1981. pap. text ed. 19.95 (*0-915728-07-9*) Lytton Pub.

American Thunder: Thirty Photographs of Harley-Davidson Motorcycles. (Postcard Books Ser.). (Illus.). 64p. (Orig.). 1994. pap. 7.95 (*1-56138-487-9*) Running Pr.

American Topics. 2nd ed. Robert C. Lugton. (Illus.). 272p. (C). 1985. pap. text ed. 18.95 (*0-13-029588-4*) P-H.

American Topographer: The Working Years of George Stanley Druhot, 1914-1983. George S. Druhot. Ed. by Phyllis Levers et al. (Illus.). 238p. 1986. 39.00 (*0-910845-25-5*, 976) Landmark Ent.

American Tort Process. John G. Fleming. (Illus.). 288p. 1988. 59.00 (*0-19-825597-7*) OUP.

American Tort Process. John G. Fleming. 288p. 1991. reprint ed. pap. 29.95 (*0-19-825680-9*) OUP.

American Tory. William H. Nelson. 224p. 1992. reprint ed. pap. text ed. 12.95 (*1-55553-148-2*) NE U Pr.

American Tough: The Tough-Guy Tradition & American Character. Rupert Wilkinson. LC 83-10794. (Contributions in American Studies: No. 69). xii, 221p. 1984. text ed. 55.00 (*0-313-23797-2*, WCH/, Greenwood Pr) Greenwood.

American Tourist Manual Lhasa (Xizang) Tibet Sightseeing Guide. John E. Felber. LC 73-932101. (Illus.). 8p. 1985. pap. 2.95 (*0-317-28647-1*) Intl Intertrade.

American Town Plans: A Comparative Timeline. Keller Easterling. LC 93-9772. (Illus.). 120p. (Orig.). 1993. pap. 19.95 (*1-878271-69-5*) Princeton Arch.

American Tract Society Documents, Eighteen Twenty-Four to Nineteen Twenty-Five. American Tract Society Staff. LC 74-38434. (Religion in America, Ser. 2). 484p. 1972. reprint ed. 31.95 (*0-405-04055-5*) Ayer.

American Trade Adjustment: The Global Impact. William R. Cline. LC 89-2070. (Policy Analysis in International Economics Ser.: No. 26). 81p. 1989. pap. 12.95 (*0-88132-095-1*) Inst Intl Eco.

American Trade & Power in the 1960s. Thomas W. Zeiler. 357p. 1992. text ed. 45.00 (*0-231-07930-3*) Col U Pr.

American Trade Marks, 1930-1950, Vol. 1. Ed. by John Mendenhall. LC 83-7316. (Illus.). 160p. 1991. reprint ed. pap. text ed. 22.50 (*0-88108-095-0*) Art Dir.

***American Trade Policy: A Tragedy in the Making.** Anne O. Krueger. 1995. 29.95 (*0-8447-3888-3*); pap. 12.95 (*0-8447-3889-1*) Am Enterprise.

***American Trade Politics.** 3rd ed. I. M. Destler. LC 94-44644. 336p. (C). 1995. pap. text ed. 19.95 (*0-88132-215-6*) Inst Intl Eco.

American Trade Schools Directory, 1987. LC 54-5165. 1990. 54.95 (*0-87514-002-5*) Croner.

American Trade Strategy: Options for the 1990's. Ed. by Robert Z. Lawrence & Charles L. Schultze. 234p. 1990. pap. 12.95 (*0-8157-5179-6*) Brookings.

American Trade Union Democracy. William M. Leiserson. LC 75-40926. 354p. 1976. reprint ed. text ed. 65.00 (*0-8371-8688-9*, LEAT, Greenwood Pr) Greenwood.

American Trademark Designs: A Survey of 732 Marks, Logos & Corporate Identity Symbols. Barbara B. Capitman. 16.50 (*0-8446-5517-1*) Peter Smith.

American Trademark Designs: A Survey with 732 Marks, Logos, & Corporate-Identity Symbols. Barbara Capitman. 1976. pap. 7.95 (*0-486-23259-X*) Dover.

American Trademarks 1930-1950, Vol. 2. John Mendenhall. (Illus.). 160p. reprint ed. pap. text ed. 22.50 (*0-88108-112-4*) Art Dir.

American Trademarks 1930-1950, Vol. 3. Ed. by John Mendenhall. LC 86-81966. 160p. 1991. text ed. 24.95 (*0-88108-080-2*) Art Dir.

American Traders in European Ports. John S. Carter. LC 82-303. (Illus.). 56p. 1982. pap. 15.00 (*0-87577-068-1*, Peabody Museum) Peabody Essex Mus.

American Tradition. Clarence B. Carson. 306p. 1970. reprint ed. pap. 12.95 (*0-910614-17-2*) Foun Econ Ed.

American Tradition Handguns. Palo Kelly. (Illus.). 250p. (Orig.). 1986. lib. bdg. 12.95 (*0-935737-60-X*); pap. 9.95 (*0-935737-61-8*) Tarantula Pr.

American Tradition in Literature. 8th ed. Ed. by George Perkins & Barbara Perkins. LC 93-42292. 1994. text ed. write for info. (*0-07-049369-3*); pap. text ed. write for info. (*0-07-049370-7*) McGraw.

American Tradition in Literature, 2 vols., 1. 6th ed. George Perkins et al. (C). 1985. pap. text ed. 20.95 (*0-685-08386-1*) McGraw.

American Tradition in Literature, Vol. 1. 7th ed. George Perkins et al. 2000p. (C). 1990. pap. text ed. write for info. (*0-07-557208-7*) McGraw.

American Tradition in Literature, 2 vols., Vol. 2. 8th ed. Ed. by George Perkins & Barbara Perkins. LC 93-11009. 1993. text ed. write for info. (*0-07-049365-0*); pap. text ed. write for info. (*0-07-049366-9*) McGraw.

American Tradition in Literature, 2 vols., Vol. 3. 8th ed. Ed. by George Perkins & Barbara Perkins. LC 93-11009. 1993. text ed. write for info. (*0-07-049367-7*); pap. text ed. write for info. (*0-07-049368-5*) McGraw.

American Tradition of Liberty Eighteen Hundred to Eighteen Sixty: From Jefferson to Lincoln. J. W. Cooke. LC 86-18081. (Studies in Social & Political Theory: Vol. 1). 236p. 1986. lib. bdg. 89.95 (*0-88946-101-5*) E Mellen.

American Traditions: Art from the Collections of Culver Alumni. Marla K. Dankert et al. LC 93-61168. (Illus.). 356p. 1993. 50.00 (*0-936260-59-9*) Ind Mus Art.

American Traditions in Watercolor: The Worcester Art Museum Collection. Ed. by Susan E. Strickler et al. LC 86-14183. (Illus.). 236p. 1987. pap. 24.95 (*0-89659-680-X*) Abbeville Pr.

American Tragedy. Theodore Dreiser. 832p. 1964. pap. 4.95 (*0-451-52204-4*, Sig Classics) NAL-Dutton.

American Tragedy. Theodore Dreiser. 1990. reprint ed. lib. bdg. 39.95 (*0-89966-709-0*) Buccaneer Bks.

American Tragedy. Theodore Dreiser. LC 78-55741. 1978. reprint ed. lib. bdg. 32.00 (*0-8376-0424-9*) Bentley.

American Tragedy & Aliens. 1992. lib. bdg. 75.00 (*0-8490-5408-7*) Gordon Pr.

American Tragedy Notes. Martin Bucco. 75p. (Orig.). (C). 1974. pap. text ed. 3.95 (*0-8220-0169-1*) Cliffs.

***American Train Depot & Roundhouse.** Hans Halberstadt. (Illus.). 192p. 1995. 29.95 (*0-7603-0003-8*) Motorbooks Intl.

***American Train Letters.** rev. ed. Bob Arnold. Ed. by James Koller. LC 94-32001. 256p. (Orig.). 1995. pap. 10.00 (*0-940556-08-1*) Coyote.

American Trajectories: Authors & Readings, 1790-1970. Warner Berthoff. LC 92-41208. 200p. (C). 1994. 29.95 (*0-271-01051-7*) Pa St U Pr.

American Transcendentalism & Asian Religions. Arthur Versluis. LC 92-24770. (Religion in America Ser.). 368p. (C). 1993. 48.00 (*0-19-507658-3*) OUP.

American Transformations. Jan Lechan. 1959. 3.00 (*0-940962-00-4*) Polish Inst Art & Sci.

American Transportation: History & Museums. Allan Lee. 1993. pap. 17.95 (*0-943231-57-4*) Howell Pr VA.

American Transportation in Prosperity & Depression. Thor Hultgren. (Studies in Business Cycles: No. 3). 431p. 1948. reprint ed. 112.10 (*0-87014-086-8*); reprint ed. mic. film 56.10 (*0-685-61273-2*) Natl Bur Econ Res.

American Travel Narratives As a Literary Genre from 1542-1832: The Art of a Perpetual Journey. Sharon R. Brown. LC 93-19567. 152p. 1993. text ed. 69.95 (*0-7734-9304-2*) E Mellen.

American Traveler: Michigan. Nancy M. Davies. 1992. 7.98 (*0-8317-0504-3*) Smithmark.

American Traveler: North Carolina. 1991. 7.98 (*0-8317-0261-3*) Smithmark.

American Traveler: Ohio. Irene S. Korn. 1992. 7.98 (*0-8317-0510-8*) Smithmark.

American Traveler Cookbook: Stylish Cooking & Dining Almost Anywhere. Joyce Williams. 1991. pap. 12.95 (*1-883470-03-X*) Amer Traveler.

American Treasure: The Hudson River Valley. Jeffrey Simpson. (Illus.). 1987. 29.95 (*0-912882-70-0*); pap. 14.95 (*0-912882-62-X*) Sleepy Hollow.

American Treasure & the Price Revolution in Spain. Earl J. Hamilton. LC 83-45661. reprint ed. 48.50 (*0-404-19811-2*) AMS Pr.

American Treasure Hunt: The Legacy of Israel Sack. Harold Sack & Max Wilk. 1986. 24.95 (*0-316-76593-7*) Little.

***American Treasure Hunt: The Legacy of Israel Sack.** Harold Sack. 1994. pap. 15.00 (*0-9638464-0-X*) DKB Pubng.

American Treaty of Peaceful Settlement: Pact of Bogota. rev. ed. Organization of American States - Bogota Staff. (Treaty Ser.: No. 17). (ENG, FRE, POR & SPA.). 1978. pap. 1.00 (*0-8270-0355-2*) OAS.

American Tree Houses & Play Houses: Childhood Retreats from Yesteryear...Play Houses & Tree Houses of Today...& Six "Build-It-Yourself" Play House Plans. Kathy S. Anthenat. (Illus.). 176p. (Orig.). 1991. pap. 14.95 (*1-55870-204-0*) Betterway Bks.

***American Trilogy, 1900-1937: Norris, Drieser, Dos Passos & the History of Mammon.** John C. Waldmeir. (Literary Studies: No. 19). 172p. (C). 1995. lib. bdg. 24.00 (*0-933951-64-7*) Locust Hill Pr.

American Triptych: Anne Bradstreet, Emily Dickinson, & Adrienne Rich. Wendy Martin. LC 83-6864. x, 272p. 1983. pap. 11.95 (*0-8078-4112-9*) U of NC Pr.

American Trojan Horse: U. S. Television Confronts Canadian Economic & Cultural Nationalism. Berry Berlin. LC 90-3338. (Contributions to the Study of Mass Media & Communications Ser.: No. 22). 128p. 1990. text ed. 47.95 (*0-313-27508-4*, BAX, Greenwood Pr) Greenwood.

***American Trucking Trends.** American Trucking Assns. Statistics Dept. Staff. 38p. 1994. pap. text ed. 20.00 (*0-88711-227-7*) Am Trucking Assns.

American Twins of Eighteen Twelve. Lucy F. Perkins. 18.95 (*0-89190-473-5*, Am Repr) Amereon Ltd.

American Type Culture Collection - NIH Repository Catalogue of Human & Mouse DNA Probes & Libraries. 8th ed. Ed. by W. C. Nierman & D. R. Maglott. 200p. 1995. pap. text ed. write for info. (*0-930009-52-5*) ATCC.

American Type Culture Collection Catalogue of Animal Viruses & Antisera, Chlamydiae & Rickettsiae. 6th ed. Ed. by C. Buck & G. Paulino. 216p. 1990. pap. text ed. write for info. (*0-930009-32-0*) ATCC.

American Type Culture Collection Catalogue of Bacteria & Phages. 18th ed. Ed. by R. Gherna et al. 694p. 1992. pap. text ed. write for info. (*0-930009-44-4*) ATCC.

American Type Culture Collection Catalogue of Filamentous Fungi. 18th ed. Ed. by S. C. Jong & M. J. Edwards. 667p. 1991. pap. text ed. write for info. (*0-930009-39-8*) ATCC.

American Type Culture Collection Catalogue of Plant Viruses & Antisera. 7th ed. Ed. by L. L. McDaniel et al. 84p. 1993. pap. text ed. write for info. (*0-930009-48-7*) ATCC.

American Type Culture Collection Catalogue of Protists. 18th ed. Ed. by T. A. Nerad. 100p. 1993. pap. text ed. write for info. (*0-930009-50-9*) ATCC.

American Type Culture Collection Catalogue of Recombinant DNA Materials. 3rd ed. Ed. by D. R. Maglott & W. C. Nierman. 150p. 1993. pap. text ed. write for info. (*0-930009-51-7*) ATCC.

American Type Culture Collection Microbes & Cells at Work: An Index to ATCC Strains with Special Applications. 2nd ed. Ed. by M. J. Edwards. 305p. (Orig.). 1991. pap. text ed. write for info. (*0-930009-40-1*) ATCC.

American Type Culture Collection Names of Industrial Fungi. Shung-Chang Jong et al. 270p. (Orig.). 1994. pap. text ed. write for info. (*0-930009-53-3*) ATCC.

American Type Culture Collection Preservation Methods: Freezing & Freeze-Drying. 2nd ed. Ed. by F. P. Simione & E. M. Brown. (Illus.). 42p. 1991. pap. text ed. write for info. (*0-930009-41-X*) ATCC.

American Type Culture Collection Quality Control Methods for Cell Lines. Ed. by R. J. Hay et al. (Illus.). 132p. 1992. pap. text ed. write for info. (*0-930009-46-0*) ATCC.

American Typeplay. Steven Heller & Gail Anderson. LC 94-5872. 1994. 45.00 (*0-86636-194-4*) PBC Intl Inc.

American Typewriters: A Collector's Encyclopedia. Paul Lippman. 288p. 1992. 55.00 (*0-9633201-0-6*) Orig & Copy.

***American Typewriters: A Collector's Encyclopedia.** Paul Lippman. 288p. 1995. pap. 39.95 (*0-614-05026-X*) Orig & Copy.

American Typography Today. Rob Carter. 1993. pap. 29.95 (*0-442-01457-0*) Van Nos Reinhold.

American Ultimatum. Ryder Stacy. (Doomsday Warrior Ser.: No. 15). 224p. 1989. pap. 2.95 (*0-8217-2587-4*) Zebra.

American Ultraminiature Component Parts Data 1965-66. Geoffrey W. Dummer & J. M. Robertson. LC 65-27562. 1965. 203.00 (*0-08-011778-3*, Pub. by Pergamon Repr UK) Franklin.

American Unbound: World War II & the Making of a Superpower. Warren F. Kimball. LC 92-548. 224p. 1992. text ed. 39.95 (*0-312-07957-5*) St Martin.

American Understanding of English Education: A Manual for American Visitors to England. Mary L. Kansfield. LC 92-15882. x, 40p. (Orig.). 1992. pap. 8.00 (*1-55635-016-3*) Pickwick.

American Union in Federalist Political Thought. Clive S. Thomas. LC 91-11214. (Political Theory & Political Philosophy Ser.). 304p. 1991. 20.00 (*0-8153-0127-8*) Garland.

American Unionism: Fallacies & Follies. 164p. (Orig.). 1994. pap. write for info. (*0-910614-97-0*) Foun Econ Ed.

American Unitarianism, 1805-1865. Ed. by Conrad E. Wright. 272p. 1989. text ed. 40.00 (*1-55553-047-8*) NE U Pr.

American Unity & Asia. Pearl S. Buck. LC 72-107687. (Essay Index Reprint Ser.). 1977. 19.95 (*0-8369-1550-X*) Ayer.

American Universities & Colleges. 14th ed. 2200p. (C). 1992. lib. bdg. 149.95 (*0-89925-861-1*) De Gruyter.

American Universities & Colleges: A Dictionary of Name Changes. Alice H. Songe. LC 78-5497. 272p. 1978. lib. bdg. 27.50 (*0-8108-1137-5*) Scarecrow.

American University. Talcott Parsons & Gerald M. Platt. LC 73-77470. 477p. reprint ed. pap. 136.00 (*0-7837-1524-2*, 2041801) Bks Demand.

American University: How It Runs, Where It Is Going. Jacques Barzun. LC 92-28479. xxxvi, 320p. (C). 1992. pap. 14.95 (*0-226-03845-9*) U Ch Pr.

American University: Problems, Prospects & Trends. Ed. by Jan H. Blits. LC 84-62895. 150p. 1985. 30.95x (*0-87975-283-1*) Prometheus Bks.

American University in Cairo, 1919-1986. Lawrence R. Murphy. (Illus.). 256p. 1987. 50.00 (*977-424-156-8*, Pub. by Am Univ Cairo Pr UA) Col U Pr.

American University in Summer. Clay Schoenfeld & Donald N. Zillman. LC 67-25941. 243p. reprint ed. pap. 69.30 (*0-8357-5405-7*, 2023721) Bks Demand.

American University of Beirut Festival Book. Ed. by Fuad Sarruf & Suha Tamim. 1967. 22.95 (*0-8156-6003-0*, Am U Beirut) Syracuse U Pr.

American University Programs in Computer Science: Their Resources, Facilities & Course Offerings. 2nd ed. Ed. by William W. Lau. LC 85-70986. 220p. 1986. 26.00 (*0-915751-23-2*) GGL Educ Press.

American Urban Architecture: Catalysts in the Design of Cities. Wayne Attoe & Donn Logan. (Illus.). 1989. 48.00 (*0-520-06152-7*) U CA Pr.

American Urban Architecture: Catalysts in the Design of Cities. Wayne Attoe & Donn Logan. (Illus.). 1992. pap. 18.00 (*0-520-08105-6*) U CA Pr.

American Urban History: An Interpretive Reader with Commentaries. 3rd ed. Ed. by Alexander B. Callow, Jr. (Illus.). (C). 1982. pap. text ed. 21.00 (*0-19-502981-X*) OUP.

***American Urban Typologies: Key West, Florida.** Erick Valle. 114p. 1995. pap. 39.95 (*1-886993-00-9*) Village Pub.

American Urbanism: A Historiographical Review. Ed. by Howard Gillette, Jr. & Zane L. Miller. LC 86-29614. (Contributions in American History Ser.: No. 125). 334p. 1987. text ed. 65.00 (*0-313-24967-9*, GIU/, Greenwood Pr) Greenwood.

American Usage & Style: The Consensus. Roy H. Copperud. 1979. pap. 12.95 (*0-685-05217-6*) Van Nos Reinhold.

American Utilitarian: Richard Hildreth As a Philosopher. Richard Hildreth. LC 48-8960. reprint ed. 20.00 (*0-404-05054-9*) AMS Pr.

American Utopian Adventure: Series 1-2, 24 vols. 1974. 780.00 (*0-87991-048-8*) Porcupine Pr.

American Utopias. Charles Nordhoff. 1993. pap. 14.95 (*0-936399-53-8*) Berkshire Hse.

American Utopias: Selected Short Fiction. Ed. by Arthur O. Lewis. LC 77-154448. (Utopian Literature Ser.). 1973. reprint ed. 23.95 (*0-405-03530-6*) Ayer.

American Values: Continuity & Change. Ralph H. Gabriel. LC 74-24. (Contributions in American Studies: No. 15). 230p. 1974. text ed. 35.00 (*0-8371-7355-8*, GAV/, Greenwood Pr) Greenwood.

American Values: Opposing Viewpoints. rev. ed. (Opposing Viewpoints Ser.). (Illus.). 312p. 1995. lib. bdg. 19.95 (*1-56510-242-8*, 2428); pap. text ed. 11.55 (*1-56510-241-X*, 241X) Greenhaven.

American Values & Social Welfare. John E. Tropman. 256p. (C). 1988. text ed. write for info. (*0-13-031675-X*) P-H.

American Vampires: Fans, Victims, Practitioners. Norine Dresser. LC 90-50152. 256p. 1990. pap. 12.00 (*0-679-73041-9*, Vin) Random.

American Variations see Persian Words in English

American Vaudeville As Seen by Its Contemporaries. Ed. by Charles W. Stein. LC 85-13224. (Quality Paperbacks Ser.). (Illus.). 392p. 1985. reprint ed. pap. 11.95 (*0-306-80256-2*) Da Capo.

American Vegetable Cookbook: The Definitive Guide to America's Exotic & Traditional Vegetables. Georgeanne Brennan et al. LC 85-14766. (Illus.). 325p. (Orig.). 1985. 24.95 (*0-943186-24-2*); pap. 14.95 (*0-943186-25-0*) Aris Bks.

American Vegetarian Cookbook from the Fit for Life Kitchen. Marilyn Diamond. 1990. 26.95 (*0-446-51561-2*) Warner Bks.

American Vegetarian Resource Directory: Some Signposts on the Journey Towards a Healthier, More Ethically & Environmentally Balanced Lifestyle. Georgia Wheatley. 96p. (Orig.). 1993. pap. 8.95 (*0-9637499-1-9*) WheatSong Pr.

American Vernacular: Regional Influences in Architecture & Design. Jim Kemp. (Illus.). 256p. (Orig.). 1990. pap. 19.95 (*1-55835-074-8*) AIA Press.

American Vernacular Interior Architecture, 1870-1940. Jan Jennings & Herbert Gottfried. (Illus.). 464p. 1993. reprint ed. pap. 32.95 (*0-8138-1408-1*) Iowa St U Pr.

American Verse, Sixteen Twenty-Five to Eighteen Hundred Seven: A History. William B. Otis. 303p. (C). 1966. lib. bdg. 75.00 (*0-8383-0605-5*) M S G Haskell Hse.

American Victorian Architecture. Ed. by Arnold Lewis & Keith Morgan. LC 73-92261. Orig. Title: L' Architecture American. (Illus.). 160p. 1975. reprint ed. pap. 10.95 (*0-486-23177-1*) Dover.

American Victorian Costume in Early Photographs. Priscilla H. Dalrymple. 1990. pap. 12.95 (*0-486-26533-1*) Dover.

American Victorian Cottage Homes. Palliser Palliser & Co Staff. 1990. pap. 6.95 (*0-486-26506-4*) Dover.

American Victorian Woman: The Myth & the Reality. Mabel C. Donnelly. LC 86-358. (Contributions in Women's Studies: No. 71). 179p. 1986. text ed. 42.95 (*0-313-25327-7*, DVI/) Greenwood.

American-Vietnamese Negotiations: May 1977-October 1978. Helen Chauncey. (Pew Case Studies in International Affairs). 50p. (C). 1988. pap. text ed. 2.50 (*1-56927-446-0*) Geo U Inst Dplmcy.

American Views: Essays on American Art. John Wilmerding. (Illus.). 450p. 1991. 70.00 (*0-691-04090-7*) Princeton U Pr.

American Views: Essays on American Art. John Wilmerding. (Illus.). 398p. 1993. pap. text ed. 35.00 (*0-691-02491-X*) Princeton U Pr.

American Views: Prospects & Vistas. Gloria-Gilda Deak. LC 76-40041. (Illus.). 134p. 1976. 25.00 (*0-87104-263-0*) NY Pub Lib.

American Vignette. Jerry Gildemeister. LC 88-10485. (Illus.). 192p. 1988. boxed 29.50 (*0-936376-05-8*) Bear Wallow Pub.

An Asterisk (*) at the beginning of an entry indicates that the title is appearing in BIP for the first time.

267

American Vignola: A Guide to the Making of Classical Architecture. unabridged ed. William R. Ware et al. LC 94-20782. (Classical America Series in Art & Architecture). (Illus.). 160p. 1994. pap. text ed. 8.95 (*0-486-28310-0*) Dover.

American Vincentians. Ed. by John E. Rybold. (Illus.). 560p. (Orig.). 1988. pap. 35.00 (*0-911782-61-3*) New City.

American Vineyards. Barbara Ensrud. 1990. pap. 14.99 (*0-517-05278-4*) Random Hse Value.

***American Viola Society: A History & Reference.** 2nd ed. Dwight R. Pounds. 293p. 1994. write for info. (*1-886601-00-3*) Am Viola Soc.

American Violence & Public Policy. Ed. by Lynn A. Curtis. LC 84-40194. 288p. 1986. pap. 13.00 (*0-300-03631-0*) Yale U Pr.

American Visa. Ping Wang. 172p. (Orig.). 1994. pap. 11.95 (*1-56689-025-X*) Coffee Hse.

American Vision. James H. Duff. 1990. pap. 19.99 (*0-517-03703-3*) Random Hse Value.

American Vision: Actual & Ideal Society in 19th Century Fiction. A. N. Kaul. LC 80-13606. (Yale Publications in American Studies: No. 7). xi, 340p. 1980. reprint ed. text ed. 37.50 (*0-313-22427-7*, KAAV, Greenwood Pr) Greenwood.

American Vision: Far Western Landscape & National Culture 1820-1920. Anne F. Hyde. 1990. 45.00 (*0-8147-3466-9*); pap. 20.00 (*0-8147-3481-2*) NYU Pr.

American Vision: John G. Bullock & the Photo-Secession. Tom Beck. 160p. 1989. 29.95 (*0-89381-405-9*) Aperture.

American Vision: Policies for the '90s. Ed. by Edward H. Crane & David Boaz. LC 88-35280. 358p. 1989. pap. 15. 95 (*0-932790-73-9*) Cato Inst.

American Vision: Three Generations of Wyeth Art. James H. Duff et al. 1989. 24.95 (*0-318-41643-3*) Little.

American Vision of a Free Press: A Historical & Constitutional Vision of a Free Press As a Marketplace of Ideas. Patrick M. Garry. LC 90-36933. (Distinguished Studies in American Legal & Constitutional History). 215p. 1990. reprint ed. 53.00 (*0-8240-0022-6*) Garland.

American Vision of Robert Penn Warren. William B. Clark. LC 90-28299. 176p. 1991. text ed. 19.00 (*0-8131-1756-9*) U Pr of Ky.

American Visions: Multi-Cultural Literature for Writers. Dolores La Guardia & Hans P. Guth. LC 94-6444. 768p. (C). 1995. pap. 25.95 (*1-55934-322-2*) Mayfield Pub.

American Visions - Visiones de las Americas: Artistic & Cultural Identity in the Western Hemisphere. Mary J. Jacob. LC 93-38997. 1993. pap. 35.00 (*1-879903-14-8*) Am Council Arts.

American Visions of Europe: Franklin D. Roosevelt, George F. Kennan, & Dean G. Acheson. John L. Harper. (Illus.). 352p. (C). 1994. 27.95 (*0-521-45483-2*) Cambridge U Pr.

American Visions, the Films of Chaplin, Ford, Capra & Welles, 1936-1941. Charles J. Maland. 1977. 36.95 (*0-405-09892-8*, 11487) Ayer.

American Vistas: 1877 to the Present, Vol. 2. 7th ed. Ed. by Leonard Dinnerstein & Kenneth T. Jackson. 400p. (C). 1995. pap. text ed. 16.95 (*0-19-508784-4*) OUP.

American Vistas Vol. 1: 1607-1877. 7th ed. Ed. by Leonard Dinnerstein & Kenneth T. Jackson. 384p. (C). 1995. pap. text ed. 16.95 (*0-19-508783-6*) OUP.

American Vitruvius: An Architect's Handbook of Civic Art. Werner Hegemann & Elbert Peets. (Illus.). 324p. 1988. reprint ed. 65.00 (*0-910413-35-5*) Princeton Arch.

American Vocabulary Builder, 2 vols., 1. Bernard Seal. 1990. pap. text ed. 13.95 (*0-8013-0496-2*, 78349) Longman.

American Vocabulary Builder, 2 vols., 2. Bernard Seal. 1990. pap. text ed. 13.95 (*0-8013-0536-5*) Longman.

American Vocal Chamber Music, 1945-1980: An Annotated Bibliography. Comp. by Patricia Lust. LC 84-25212. (Music Reference Collection Ser.: No. 4). (Illus.). xvi, 273p. 1985. text ed. 49.95 (*0-313-24599-1*, LUC/, Greenwood Pr) Greenwood.

American Voices. Jackson & DiPietro. 1992. teacher ed, pap. 7.95 (*0-8384-3912-8*) Heinle & Heinle.

American Voices. Jackson & DiPietro. 1992. pap. 19.95 (*0-8384-3847-4*) Heinle & Heinle.

American Voices: A Thematic-Rhetorical Reader. Warren Rosenberg et al. 493p. (C). 1989. pap. text ed. 26.50 (*0-06-045763-5*) HarpCollege.

American Voices: Best Short Fiction by Contemporary Authors. Ed. by Jane Rosenman. LC 92-30087. 400p. 1993. pap. 12.00 (*0-671-78315-7*, WSP) PB.

American Voices: Five Contemporary Playwrights in Essays & Interviews. Esther Harriott. LC 88-42500. 206p. 1988. lib. bdg. 27.50x (*0-89950-283-0*) McFarland & Co.

American Voices: Multicultural Literacy & Critical Thinking. Delores LaGuardia & Hans P. Guth. LC 92-26825. 693p. 1992. pap. text ed. 24.95 (*1-55934-185-8*); teacher ed, pap. text ed. write for info. (*1-55934-186-6*) Mayfield Pub.

American Voices: Readings in History & Literature, 2 vols., Set. Ed. by Robert Marcus. (Illus.). (C). 1992. reprint ed. Net. pap. text ed. 10.36 (*0-685-61616-9*) Brandywine Press.

American Voices: Readings in History & Literature, Vol. I. Ed. by Robert Marcus. (Illus.). (C). 1992. reprint ed. Vol. 1, 385p. pap. write for info. (*1-881089-04-5*) Brandywine Press.

American Voices: Readings in History & Literature, Vol. 2. Ed. by Robert Marcus. (Illus.). (C). 1992. reprint ed. pap. write for info. (*1-881089-05-3*) Brandywine Press.

American Voices: Significant Speeches in American History, 1640-1945. James R. Andrews & David Zarefsky. 506p. (C). 1989. pap. text ed. 30.50 (*0-8013-0217-X*, 75875) Longman.

American Voices Series, 6 bks. (J). 1991. Set. 83.70 (*0-86593-134-8*) Rourke Corp.

American Volunteer Firetrucks. Don Wood & Wayne Sorensen. LC 92-74800. (Illus.). 300p. 1993. pap. 16.95 (*0-87341-236-2*) Krause Pubns.

American Voter. Angus Campbell et al. LC 76-21115. (Midway Reprint Ser.). 576p. 1980. pap. text ed. 28.00 (*0-226-09254-2*) U Ch Pr.

American Voting Behavior. Ed. by Eugene Burdick & Arthur J Brodbeck. LC 77-7237. (Illus.). 475p. 1977. text ed. 35.00 (*0-8371-9668-X*, BUAV, Greenwood Pr) Greenwood.

American Voting Behavior: Presidential Elections from 1952 to 1980. William H. Flanigan & Nancy H. Zingale. LC 82-83324. 1982. boxed write for info. (*0-89138-920-2*, ICPSR 7581) ICPSR.

American Voyage. Joe Ross. (New American Poetry Ser.: No. 12). 92p. (Orig.). 1993. pap. 9.95 (*1-55713-070-1*) Sun & Moon CA.

American Waltz. Earl Atkinson. (Ballroom Dance Ser.). 1986. lib. bdg. 250.00 (*0-8490-3635-6*) Gordon Pr.

American War Ballads & Lyrics, 2 vols. Ed. by George C. Eggleston. 1971. 250.00 (*0-87968-612-X*) Gordon Pr.

American War in Vietnam. Ed. by Jayne Werner & David Hunt. (Southeast Asia Program Ser.: No. 13). 132p. (Orig.). 1993. pap. text ed. 13.00 (*0-87727-131-3*) Cornell SE Asia.

American War in Vietnam: Lessons, Legacies, & Implications for Future Conflicts. Lawrence E. Grinter & Peter M. Dunn. LC 87-11856. 192p. 1987. text ed. 49.95 (*0-313-25759-0*, GWV/, Greenwood Pr) Greenwood.

American War Plans, 1919-1941, 5 vols. rev. ed. Ed. by Steven T. Ross. LC 92-20669. 1992. Set. 588.00 (*0-8153-0688-1*) Garland.

American War Series, 8 bks., Set. (Illus.). (YA). (gr. 5 up). 1994. lib. bdg. 143.60 (*0-89490-569-4*) Enslow Pubs.

American War, 1812-1814. Philip R. Katcher. (Men-at-Arms Ser.: No. 226). (Illus.). 48p. 1990. pap. 11.95 (*0-85045-197-3*, 9184, Pub. by Osprey UK) Stackpole.

American Warblers: An Ecological & Behavioral Perspective. Douglass H. Morse. LC 89-31622. (Illus.). 424p. 1989. 42.50 (*0-674-03035-4*) HUP.

American Warplanes, 1908-1988: A Bibliography. Myron J. Smith, Jr. LC 90-48967. (Bibliographies of Battles & Leaders Ser.: No. 3). 500p. 1990. text ed. 75.00 (*0-313-28139-4*, SXW/, Greenwood Pr) Greenwood.

American Warrior. Janet Morris & Chris Morris. 288p. 1992. 18.95 (*0-681-41401-4*) Longmeadow Pr.

***American Waste.** Everette Maddox. 92p. 1993. 10.00 (*0-614-05039-1*) Portals Pr.

American Watches: Beginning to End Identification & Price Guide 1780-1980. Roy Ehrhardt. (Orig.). 1987. pap. 15. 00 (*0-913902-53-5*) Heart Am Pr.

American Watchmaker & Jeweler. Henry G. Abbott. (Illus.). 354p. 1989. pap. 19.95 (*0-930163-42-7*) Arlington Bk.

American Water Resources, 2 vols. Yang-ch'eng Shih. 732p. write for info. (*0-318-53699-4*); write for info. (*0-318-53700-1*) Irvington.

American Water Resources, 2 vols., Set. Yang-ch'eng Shih. 732p. text ed. 48.00 (*0-8290-0390-8*) Irvington.

American Water Ski Association Official Instructor's Manual: Level I Instructor's Certification. Reg Barnes. 36p. 1985. pap. 4.50 (*0-318-19111-3*) Am Water Ski.

American Water Spaniel Champions, 1952-1992. Camino E. E. & B. Co. Staff. (Illus.). 70p. 1995. pap. 36.95 (*1-55893-018-3*) Camino E E & Bk.

American Watercolors. Christopher Finch. LC 86-1031. (Illus.). 312p. 1986. 49.98 (*0-89659-967-1*, Artabras) Abbeville Pr.

***American Watercolors.** Random. 1995. 16.99 (*0-517-12081-X*) Random Hse Value.

American Watercolors from the Metropolitan Museum of Art. John K. Howat et al. (Illus.). 204p. 1991. pap. 29. 00 (*0-917418-92-1*) Am Fed Arts.

American Way. David C. Coyle et al. LC 68-58781. (Essay Index Reprint Ser.). 1977. 19.95 (*0-8369-0107-X*) Ayer.

American Way. Dexter Perkins. LC 77-128285. (Essay Index Reprint Ser.). 1977. 19.95 (*0-8369-2011-2*) Ayer.

American Way: An Introduction to American Culture. Edward Kearny et al. (Illus.). 240p. (C). 1983. pap. text ed. 18.75 (*0-13-031682-2*) P-H.

American Way: More Than Skin Deep. Yelone Clagne. LC 92-85168. 132p. (Orig.). 1993. pap. 9.95 (*0-939644-92-4*, Midgrd Press) Media Pub.

***American Way in Taxation: Internal Revenue, 1862-1963.** Ed. by Lillian Doris. LC 94-76047. xvi, 302p. 1994. 45. 00 (*0-89941-877-5*, 308230) W S Hein.

American Way of Birth. Jessica Mitford. 320p. 1993. pap. 12.00 (*0-452-27068-5*, Dutton-W Abrahams Bk) NAL-Dutton.

American Way of Death. Jessica Mitford. 1987. pap. 3.95 (*0-449-21506-7*) Fawcett.

American Way of Death. Jessica Mitford. 1993. reprint ed. lib. bdg. 25.95x (*1-56849-159-X*) Buccaneer Bks.

American Way of Health: Why Medicine Costs So Much & How We Can Fix It. Janice Castro. 1994. 19.95 (*0-316-13272-1*); pap. 9.95 (*0-316-13275-6*) Little.

American Way of Life Need Not Be Hazardous to Your Health. John W. Farquhar. (Illus.). 208p. 1987. pap. 10. 53 (*0-201-12186-7*) Addison-Wesley.

American Way of Sex. Bradley Smith. LC 78-61204. (Illus.). 1978. 19.95 (*0-8467-0567-2*) Gemini Smith.

American Way of War: A History of United States Military Strategy & Policy. Russell F. Weigley. LC 77-74434. (Illus.). 602p. 1977. reprint ed. pap. 14.95 (*0-253-28029-X*) Ind U Pr.

American Way West. (Trade & Travel Routes Ser.). (Illus.). 128p. (YA). 1990. 17.95 (*0-8160-1880-4*) Facts on File.

American Ways: A Guide for Foreigners. Gary Althen. LC 87-46023. 192p. (Orig.). 1988. pap. text ed. 15.95 (*0-933662-68-8*) Intercult Pr.

American Weather Book. David Ludlum. (Illus.). 296p. 1989. reprint ed. pap. 20.00 (*0-933876-97-1*) Am Meteorological.

American Weekend Garden. Patricia Thorpe. LC 87-42671. 224p. 1988. 24.95 (*0-394-56025-6*) Random.

American West. Lucius Beebe. 512p. 1989. 17.99 (*0-517-68356-3*) Random Hse Value.

***American West.** Brown. 1995. pap. 14.00 (*0-684-80441-7*) Macmillan.

American West. Dee Brown. 1994. text ed. 22.00 (*0-02-517421-5*, Scribners) S&S Trade.

American West. Michael L. Tate. 100p. 1981. pap. 26.00 (*0-08-026758-0*, Pergamon Pr) Elsevier.

American West: A Historical Chronology. Keith Cochran. LC 91-78032. (Illus.). 464p. 1992. 30.00 (*0-936259-18-3*) Cochran Pub.

American West: A Narrative Bibliography & a Study in Regionalism. Charles F. Wilkinson. LC 89-9044. 144p. (Orig.). 1989. pap. 9.95 (*0-87081-181-9*) Univ Pr Colo.

American West: A Twentieth-Century History. Michael P. Malone & Richard W. Etulain. LC 88-26840. (Illus.). xii, 347p. 1989. pap. 14.95 (*0-8032-8167-6*) U of Nebr Pr.

***American West: Year by Year.** 17.99 (*0-517-12186-7*) Random Hse Value.

American West As Living Space. Wallace Stegner. 350p. 1987. pap. 13.95 (*0-472-06375-8*) U of Mich Pr.

American West Designs. C. B. Mordan. (International Design Library). (Illus.). 48p. (Orig.). 1994. pap. 5.95 (*0-88045-127-0*) Stemmer Hse.

American West from Fiction (1823-1976) into Film (1909-1986) Jim Hitt. LC 89-42723. 384p. 1990. lib. bdg. 38. 50x (*0-89950-378-0*) McFarland & Co.

American West in Film: Critical Approaches to the Western. Jon Tuska. LC 84-10812. (Contributions to the Study of Popular Culture Ser.: No. 11). (Illus.). xix, 303p. 1985. text ed. 59.95 (*0-313-24603-3*, TUA/, Greenwood Pr) Greenwood.

American West in the Nineteenth Century: 255 Illustrations from "Harper Weekly" & Other Contemporary Sources. Ed. by John Grafton. LC 92-15667. (Illus.). 1992. pap. write for info. (*0-486-27304-0*) Dover.

American West in the Twentieth-Century: A Bibliography. Ed. by Richard W. Etulain et al. LC 94-16520. 456p. 1994. text ed. 60.00 (*0-8061-2658-2*) U of Okla Pr.

American West of Frederic Remington. Ariel Books Staff. 1994. 4.95 (*0-8362-3060-4*) Andrews & McMeel.

American West Transformed: The Impact of the Second World War. Gerald D. Nash. LC 83-49524. (Illus.). 316p. 1985. 35.00 (*0-253-30649-3*) Ind U Pr.

American West Transformed: The Impact of the Second World War. Gerald D. Nash. LC 89-24957. xii, 320p. 1990. reprint ed. pap. 12.50 (*0-8032-8360-1*, Bison Books) U of Nebr Pr.

American West, 1840-1895. S. J. Styles & R. A. Rees. 1986. pap. text ed. 15.08 (*0-582-22397-0*, 70933) Longman.

American Western Art. Dorothy Harmsen. Ed. by Mildred Uhlig & Dick Hilker. LC 78-134925. (Illus.). 256p. 1978. write for info. (*0-87358-061-3*) Harmsen.

American Western Art. Intro. by Arthur C. Townsend. (Illus.). 84p. 1989. text ed. 25.00 (*0-9622038-0-7*); pap. text ed. 17.50 (*0-9622038-1-5*) Rockwell NY.

American West's Acid Rain Test. Philip Roth et al. LC 85-50619. 60p. (Orig.). 1985. pap. text ed. 10.00 (*0-915825-07-4*) World Resources Inst.

American Whaleman. Elmo P. Hohmann. 1977. lib. bdg. 59. 95 (*0-8490-1418-2*) Gordon Pr.

American Whalers in the Western Arctic: The Final Epoch of the Great American Sailing Whaling Fleet. William Gilkerson et al. (Illus.). 1983. ring bd. 1,500.00 (*0-9617194-1-9*) E J Lefkowicz.

American Whaling on the Chatham Grounds. Rhys Richards. (Illus.). 70p. 1971. 1.00 (*0-9607340-3-1*) Nantucket Hist Assn.

American Whig: William Livingston of New York. rev. ed. Milton M. Klein. LC 93-19024. (Outstanding Studies in Early American History). 648p. 1993. 95.00 (*0-8153-1475-2*) Garland.

American Who Couldn't Say Noh: Everything You Need to Know about Japan but Had No One to Ask. Charles Danziger. Ed. by Lancet. LC 93-23986. (Illus.). 160p. 1994. 20.00 (*4-7700-1681-6*) Kodansha.

American Wholefoods Cuisine. (Illus.). 580p. 1983. 17.95 (*0-453-00434-2*) Ceres Pr.

American Wholefoods Cuisine: 1300 Meatless, Wholesome Recipes from Short Order to Gourmet. Nikki Goldbeck & David Goldbeck. (Illus.). 580p. reprint ed. 22.95 (*0-9606138-5-4*) Ceres Pr.

***American Wholesalers & Distributors Directory.** 3rd ed. Ed. by Holly M. Selden. 2004p. 1994. 170.00 (*0-8103-5682-1*) Gale.

American Wicker: Woven Furniture from 1850 to 1930. Jeremy Adamson. LC 92-27817. (Illus.). 160p. 1993. 45. 00 (*0-8478-1670-2*); pap. 25.00 (*0-8478-1703-2*) Rizzoli Intl.

American Wild Life. Writers' Program, New York Staff. LC 73-3644. (American Guide Ser.). (Illus.). reprint ed. 57. 50 (*0-404-57943-4*) AMS Pr.

American Wild Turkey. Henry E. Davis. (Illus.). 328p. 1984. 29.95 (*0-685-62739-X*) Real Turkeys Pubs.

American Wilderness. Ansel Adams. Ed. by Andrea G. Stillman. (Illus.). 146p. 1990. 125.00 (*0-8212-1799-2*) Bulfinch Pr.

American Wilderness & Its Future: Conservation Versus Use. Edward F. Dolan. LC 91-33440. (Illus.). 160p. (YA). (gr. 9-12). 1992. lib. bdg. 15.33 (*0-531-11062-1*) Watts.

American Wildflower Florilegium. Jean Andrews. LC 92-22135. (Illus.). 125p. (C). 1992. text ed. 50.00 (*0-929398-43-2*) UNTX Pr.

American Wildflower Florilegium. limited ed. Jean Andrews. LC 92-22135. (Illus.). 125p. (C). 1992. 200.00 (*0-929398-45-9*) UNTX Pr.

American Wildlife & Plants: A Guide to Wildlife Food Habits. Alexander C. Martin et al. 1951. pap. 8.95 (*0-486-20793-5*) Dover.

American Wildlife in Symbol & Story. Ed. by Angus K. Gillespie & Jay Mechling. LC 86-19315. (Illus.). 262p. 1987. 30.00x (*0-87049-522-4*) U of Tenn Pr.

American Wildlife Law. Thomas A. Lund. LC 78-68829. 1980. 35.00 (*0-520-03883-5*) U CA Pr.

American Wills & Administrations in the Prerogative Court of Canterbury, 1610-1857. Peter W. Coldham. xii, 416p. 1989. 30.00 (*0-8063-1235-1*, 1108) Genealog Pub.

American Wills Proved in London, 1611-1775. Peter W. Coldham. 350p. 1992. 30.00 (*0-8063-1363-3*, 1116) Genealog Pub.

American Wind Symphony Commissioning Project: A Descriptive Catalog of Published Editions 1957-1991. Jeffrey H. Renshaw. LC 91-30220. (Music Reference Collection Ser.: No. 34). 408p. 1991. text ed. 65.00 (*0-313-28146-7*, RWY/, Greenwood Pr) Greenwood.

American Wine Society Presents "Growing Wine Grapes" J. R. McGrew et al. Ed. by Randall J. Reichwage. (Illus.). 96p. (Orig.). 1993. pap. 10.95 (*0-9619072-0-7*) G W Kent.

American Wine Society Presents the Complete Handbook of Winemaking. Moorhead et al. Ed. by Randall J. Reichwaye. (Illus.). 225p. (Orig.). 1993. pap. 15.95 (*0-9619072-2-3*) G W Kent.

***American Winemakers Cookbook.** Ken Parry. (Illus.). 200p. (Orig.). 1995. pap. 13.95 (*1-886026-03-3*) Wine Grape.

American Wines of the Northwest: A Guide to the Wines of Oregon, Washington & Idaho. Corbet Clark. LC 89-3050. 324p. 1989. 22.95 (*0-688-07556-8*) Morrow.

American Wines of the Northwest: A Guide to the Wines of Oregon, Washington, & Idaho. Corbet Clark. (Illus.). 400p. 1992. pap. 14.00 (*0-688-11276-5*, Quill) Morrow.

American Winners of the Nobel Literary Prize. Ed. by Warren G. French & Walter E. Kidd. LC 67-24622. 253p. reprint ed. 72.20 (*0-8357-9718-X*, 2016218) Bks Demand.

American Wire Service. Richard A. Schwarzlose. Ed. by Christopher H. Sterling. LC 78-21738. (Dissertations in Broadcasting Ser.). (Illus.). 1980. lib. bdg. 37.95 (*0-405-11774-4*) Ayer.

American Woman: Her Role in the Revolutionary War. Esther Perica. LC 80-28294. (Cameo Series of Notable Women). (Orig.). 1981. pap. 5.00 (*0-912526-28-9*) Lib Res.

American Woman: Hidden in History, Forging the Future. Roger A. Hammer. 18p. 1980. pap. 4.95 (*0-932991-02-5*) Place in the Woods.

American Woman: Hidden in History, Forging the Future. 2nd enl. ed. Roger A. Hammer. (Hidden America Ser.: Vol. 2). (Illus.). 80p. (YA). (gr. 7 up). 1993. pap. 19.95 (*0-932991-27-0*) Place in the Woods.

American Woman: The Feminine Side of a Masculine Civilization. Ernest R. Groves. LC 72-2605. (American Women Ser.: Images & Realities). 478p. 1974. reprint ed. 29.95 (*0-405-04460-7*) Ayer.

American Woman in Sport. Ellen W. Gerber et al. (C). 1974. text ed. write for info. (*0-201-02353-9*) Addison-Wesley.

American Woman in the Chinese Hat. Carole Maso. LC 93-36137. 200p. 1994. 19.95 (*1-56478-045-7*) Dalkey Arch.

***American Woman in the Chinese Hat.** Carole Maso. 201p. 1995. 10.95 (*0-452-27507-5*, Plume) NAL-Dutton.

American Woman in Transition: The Urban Influence, 1870-1920. Margaret G. Wilson. LC 78-67911. (Contributions in Women's Studies: No. 6). 252p. 1979. text ed. 59.95 (*0-313-20638-4*, WAM/, Greenwood Pr) Greenwood.

American Woman Today: Free or Frustrated. 2nd ed. E. Gould. 1977. pap. text ed. 11.84 (*0-13-032359-4*) P-H.

American Woman, 1990-91: A Status Report. Sara E. Rix. 1990. 10.95 (*0-393-02840-2*) Norton.

American Woman, 1990-91: A Status Report. Ed. by Sara E. Rix. 420p. 1990. 13.50 (*0-685-55242-X*) SLA.

American Woman, 1992-1993. Ed. by Paula Ries & Anne J. Stone. 560p. 1992. 24.95 (*0-393-03110-1*) Norton.

American Woman, 1992-1993. Ed. by Pauls Ries & Anne J. Stone. 560p. 1992. pap. 12.95 (*0-393-30871-5*) Norton.

American Woman 1994-95 CL. Stone Costello. 1994. 25.00 (*0-393-03625-1*) Norton.

American Woman's Garden. Rosemary Verey & Ellen Samuels. (Illus.). 192p. 1984. 50.00 (*0-8212-1580-9*) Bulfinch Pr.

American Woman's Home. Catharine E. Beecher & Harriet Beecher Stowe. LC 75-22526. (Illus.). 1975. pap. 12.95 (*0-917482-04-2*) Stowe-Day.

American Woman's Home: Or, Principles of Domestic Science. Catharine E. Beecher & Harriet Beecher Stowe. LC 77-165703. (American Education Ser.: No. 2). 1977. reprint ed. 27.95 (*0-405-03692-2*) Ayer.

American Women: A Story of Social Change. Robert E. Riegel. LC 78-99327. 376p. 1975. 35.00 (*0-8386-7615-4*) Fairleigh Dickinson.

American Women: Four Centuries of Progress. 2nd rev. ed. Polly Zane & John Zane. (Illus.). (YA). (gr. 7 up). 1989. write for info. (*0-935070-03-6*) Proof Pr.

American Women: Images & Realities, 44 bks, Set. Ed. by Annette K. Baxter & Leon Stein. 17788p. 1972. reprint ed. 1,088.00 (*0-405-04445-3*) Ayer.

An Asterisk (*) at the beginning of an entry indicates that the title is appearing in BIP for the first time.

American Women: Their Lives in Their Words. Ed. by Doreen Rappaport. LC 89-77621. (Illus.). 336p. (YA). (gr. 7 up). 1990. 18.00 (*0-690-04819-X*, Crowell Jr Bks); lib. bdg. 17.89 (*0-690-04817-3*, Crowell Jr Bks) HarpC Child Bks.

American Women: Their Lives in Their Words. Doreen Rappaport. LC 89-77621. (Trophy Nonfiction Bk.). (Illus.). 336p. (YA). (gr. 7 up). 1992. pap. 7.95 (*0-06-446127-0*, Trophy) HarpC Child Bks.

***American Women Afield: Writings by Pioneering Women Naturalists.** Ed. by Marcia M. Bonta. LC 94-3664. (Louise Lindsey Merrick Natural Environment Ser.: No. 20). (Illus.). 264p. (C). 1995. pap. 15.95x (*0-89096-634-6*) Tex A&M Univ Pr.

***American Women Afield: Writings by Pioneering Women Naturalists.** Ed. by Marcia M. Bonta. LC 94-3664. (Louise Lindsey Merrick Natural Environment Ser.: No. 20). (Illus.). 264p. (C). 1995. 35.00x (*0-89096-633-8*) Tex A&M Univ Pr.

American Women & Political Participation: The Impacts of Work, Generation & Feminism. Karen Beckwith. LC 85-27284. (Contributions in Women's Studies: No. 68). 199p. 1986. text ed. 49.95 (*0-313-24507-X*, BAW/, Greenwood Pr) Greenwood.

American Women & the Labor Movement, 1825-1974: An Annotated Bibliography. Martha J. Soltow & Mary K. Wery. LC 76-40169. 255p. 1976. 22.50 (*0-8108-0986-9*) Scarecrow.

***American Women & the Repeal of Prohibition.** Kenneth D. Rose. (American Social Experience Ser.). (Illus.). 230p. 1996. 40.00 (*0-8147-7464-4*) NYU Pr.

American Women & the U. S. Armed Forces: A Guide to the Records of Military Agencies in the National Archives Relating to American Women. rev. ed. Ed. by Robert Gruber. LC 91-40430. (Books from the National Archives Ser.). (Illus.). 360p. (C). 1992. text ed. 25.00 (*0-911333-90-8*) Smithsonian.

American Women & the World War. Ida C. Clarke. LC 74-75233. (United States in World War I Ser.). xix, 545p. 1974. reprint ed. lib. bdg. 53.95 (*0-89198-096-2*) Ozer.

American Women & World War Two. Doris Weatherford. (Illus.). 384p. (J). 1990. 29.95 (*0-8160-2038-8*) Facts on File.

***American Women Antebellum.** Hewitt. 1996. 26.95 (*0-8057-9915-X*, Twayne) Macmillan.

American Women Artists: From Early Indian Times to the Present. Charlotte S. Rubenstein. (Illus.). 608p. 1982. pap. 15.95 (*0-380-61101-5*) Avon.

American Women Artists: Works on Paper & an American Album. Cynthia Navaretta. LC 85-62160. (Illus.). 45p. 1985. pap. 7.00 (*0-9602476-5-3*) Midmarch Arts-WAN.

American Women Artists, Past Present, Vol. 2: A Selected Bibliographic Guide. Eleanor Tufts. LC 83-48201. (Illus.). 549p. 1989. 65.00 (*0-8240-1511-8*, H1123) Garland.

American Women Artists, 1830-1930. Eleanor Tufts et al. LC 86-83190. (Illus.). 256p. 1987. pap. 32.95 (*0-940979-02-0*) Natl Museum Women.

American Women Civil Rights Activists: Biobibliographies of 68 Leaders, 1825-1992. Gayle J. Hardy. LC 92-56649. 503p. 1993. lib. bdg. 45.00 (*0-89950-773-5*) McFarland & Co.

***American Women Colonial.** Treckel. 1995. 26.95 (*0-8057-9917-6*, Twayne) Macmillan.

***American Women Composers Before 1870.** Judith Tick. 264p. (C). 1995. reprint ed. text ed. 45.00 (*1-878822-58-6*); reprint ed. pap. text ed. 19.95 (*1-878822-59-4*) Univ Rochester Pr.

American Women Dramatists of the Twentieth Century: A Bibliography. Brenda Coven. LC 82-5942. 244p. 1982. 25.00 (*0-8108-1562-1*) Scarecrow.

American Women Humorists: Critical Essays. Ed. by Linda A. Morris. LC 93-21788. (Studies in Humor: Vol. 4). 480p. 1993. 72.00 (*0-8153-0622-9*, H1500) Garland.

American Women in Poverty. Paul E. Zopf, Jr. LC 88-21348. (Contributions in Women's Studies: No. 100). 226p. 1989. text ed. 45.00 (*0-313-25980-1*, ZFA/, Greenwood Pr) Greenwood.

American Women in Science: A Biographic Dictionary. Martha J. Bailey. 463p. 1994. lib. bdg. 60.00 (*0-87436-740-9*) ABC-CLIO.

American Women in Science & Engineering, 15 bks. Mary E. Verheyden-Hilliard. (Biographies). (Illus.). (J). (gr. 1-4). 1988. Set. pap. 75.00 (*0-932469-19-1*) Equity Inst.

American Women in Sport, Eighteen Eighty-Seven to Nineteen Eighty-Seven: A 100-Year Chronology. Ed. by Mary E. Leslie et al. LC 89-6150. (Illus.). 173p. 1989. 25.00 (*0-8108-2205-9*) Scarecrow.

American Women in the Nineteen Sixties: Changing the Future. Blanche Linden-Ward & Carol H. Green. LC 92-592. (American Women in the Twentieth Century Ser.). 608p. 1992. text ed. 55.00 (*0-8057-9905-2*, Twayne); pap. 19.95 (*0-8057-9913-3*, Twayne) Macmillan.

American Women in the Nineties: Today's Critical Issues. Ed. by Sherri Matteo. 288p. 1993. text ed. 37.50 (*1-55553-150-4*); pap. text ed. 14.95 (*1-55553-151-2*) NE U Pr.

American Women in the Progressive Era, 1900-1920. Carl Schneider & Dorothy Schneider. LC 92-22588. (Illus.). 256p. 1992. lib. bdg. 24.95 (*0-8160-2513-4*) Facts on File.

American Women in the Progressive Era, 1900-1920. Dorothy Schneider & Carl J. Schneider. LC 93-5890. 1994. 12.95 (*0-385-47283-8*, Anchor NY) Doubleday.

American Women in the Twentieth Century: A Festival of Life. Robert L. Daniel. 478p. (Orig.). (C). 1987. pap. text ed. 18.75 (*0-15-502590-2*) HB Coll Pubs.

American Women in the Twentieth Century: The Festival of Life. Angela G. Dorenkamp et al. 462p. (C). 1985. pap. text ed. 18.75 (*0-15-540600-0*) HB Coll Pubs.

American Women in Transition. Susanne M. Bianchi & Daphne Spain. LC 85-62809. (Population of the United States in the 1980s: A Census Monograph Ser.). 320p. (C). 1986. pap. text ed. 14.95 (*0-87154-112-2*) Russell Sage.

American Women Managers & Administrators: A Selective Biographical Dictionary of Twentieth Century Leaders in Business, Education, & Government. Judith A. Leavitt. LC 84-12814. xv, 317p. 1985. text ed. 69.50 (*0-313-23748-4*, LAO/, Greenwood Pr) Greenwood.

American Women Nineteen Thirty-Five to Nineteen Forty, 2 vols., Set. Ed. by Durwood Howes. LC 80-17368. (Composite Biographical Dictionary Ser.: No. 6). 1500p. 1981. 160.00 (*0-8103-0403-1*) Gale.

American Women of Achievement Series, 50 vols., Set. (Illus.). 5600p. 1987. lib. bdg. 897.50 (*1-55546-634-6*) Chelsea Hse.

American Women of Faith. Rawley Myers. LC 89-61665. (Orig.). 1989. pap. 4.95 (*0-87973-435-3*, 435) Our Sunday Visitor.

American Women of the Etching Revival. Phyllis Peet. Ed. by Kelly Morris & Amanda Woods. (Illus.). 72p. 1988. pap. 10.00 (*0-939802-45-7*) High Mus Art.

American Women Orators, 1830-1925: A Biographical Dictionary. Ed. by Karlyn K. Campbell. LC 92-14615. 544p. 1993. text ed. 75.00 (*0-313-27533-5*, CAG, Greenwood Pr) Greenwood.

American Women Painters of the 1930s & 1940s: The Lives & Work of Ten Artists. Robert Henkes. LC 90-53708. (Illus.). 252p. 1991. lib. bdg. 32.50x (*0-89950-474-4*) McFarland & Co.

American Women Philosophers, 1650-1930: Six Exemplary Thinkers. Ed. by Therese B. Dykeman. LC 93-9573. (Illus.). 404p. 1993. text ed. 109.95 (*0-7734-9266-6*) E Mellen.

American Women Playwrights, Nineteen Sixty-Four to Nineteen Eighty-Nine: A Research Guide and Annotated Bibliography, Vol. 879. Christy Gavin. LC 92-42768. (Reference Library of the Humanities). 504p. 1993. 75.00 (*0-8240-3046-X*, H879) Garland.

American Women Playwrights, 1900-1930: A Checklist. Comp. by Frances D. Bzowski. LC 92-12301. (Bibliographies & Indexes in Women's Studies Ser.: No. 15). 448p. 1992. text ed. 65.00 (*0-313-24238-0*, BZA/, Greenwood Pr) Greenwood.

American Women Poets. Ed. & Intro. by Harold Bloom. (Critical Cosmos Ser.). 362p. 1986. 59.95 (*0-87754-960-5*) Chelsea Hse.

American Women Poets. Ed. by Talat S. Halman. (Turkish Ser.). (Illus.). 80p. 1991. pap. 15.00 (*0-89304-072-X*) Cross-Cultrl NY.

***American Women Poets.** Talat S. Halman. (Turkish Ser.). (Illus.). 80p. 1991. 30.00 (*0-89304-071-1*) Cross-Cultrl NY.

American Women Poets of the Nineteenth-Century: An Anthology. Ed. by Cheryl Walker. LC 91-33080. (American Women Writers Ser.). 325p. 1992. text ed. 45.00 (*0-8135-1790-7*); pap. text ed. 15.00 (*0-8135-1791-5*) Rutgers U Pr.

***American Women Regionalists: A Norton Anthology.** Ed. by Judith Fetterley & Marjorie Pryse. 672p. 1995. reprint ed. pap. 17.95 (*0-393-31363-8*, Norton Paperbks) Norton.

American Women Regionalists, 1850-1930. Ed. by Judith Feterley & Majorie Pryse. (Orig.). (C). 1992. pap. text ed. 19.95 (*0-393-96137-0*) Norton.

American Women Sculptors: A History of Women Working in Three Dimensions. Charlotte S. Rubinstein. (Monograph Ser.). 600p. (C). 1990. lib. bdg. 49.95 (*0-685-38164-1*) G K Hall.

American Women Sculptures: A History of Women Working in Three Dimensions. Charlotte S. Rubinstein. (Monograph Ser.). (Illus.). 600p. (C). 1990. lib. bdg. 50.00 (*0-8161-8732-0*, Hall Reference) Macmillan.

American Women Short Story Writers Vol. 8: A Collection of Essays. Ed. by Julie Brown. LC 94-8739. (Wellesley Studies in Critical Theory: Vol. 8). 400p. 1995. 53.00 (*0-8153-1338-1*, H1737) Garland.

American Women since 1945. Rochelle Gatlin. LC 87-2139. 298p. 1987. 37.50 (*0-87805-318-2*); pap. 15.95 (*0-87805-319-0*) U Pr of Miss.

American Women Songwriters: A Biographical Dictionary. Virginia L. Grattan. LC 92-32211. 294p. 1993. text ed. 39.95 (*0-313-28510-1*) Greenwood.

American Women Writers. Ed. by Eileen Barrett & Mary Cullinan. LC 90-71610. 1280p. 1992. text ed. 49.95 (*0-312-06556-6*) St Martin.

American Women Writers. abr. ed. Ed. by Langdon L. Faust. 944p. 1982. 59.50 (*0-8044-3157-4*, F Ungar Bks) Continuum.

American Women Writers: A Critical Reference Guide, 4 vols., 4. Ed. by Lina Mainiero & Langdon L. Faust. LC 78-20945. 600p. 1982. 95.00 (*0-8044-3155-8*, F Ungar Bks) Continuum.

American Women Writers: A Critical Reference Guide, 4 vols., Set. Ed. by Lina Mainiero & Langdon L. Faust. LC 78-20945. 600p. 1982. 380.00 (*0-8044-3150-7*, F Ungar Bks) Continuum.

American Women Writers: A Critical Reference Guide, Vol. 2, F-Le. Ed. by Lina Mainiero. LC 78-20945. 600p. 1981. 75.00 (*0-8044-3152-3*, F Ungar Bks) Continuum.

American Women Writers: A Critical Reference Guide, Vol. 3, Li-R. Ed. by Lina Mainiero. LC 78-20945. 600p. 1981. 95.00 (*0-8044-3153-1*, F Ungar Bks) Continuum.

American Women Writers: A Critical Reference Guide, Vol. 1, A-E. Ed. by Lina Mainiero. LC 78-20945. 600p. 1979. 95.00 (*0-8044-3151-5*, F Ungar Bks) Continuum.

American Women Writers: Bibliographical Essays. Ed. by Maurice Duke et al. LC 82-6156. 464p. 1983. text ed. 49.95 (*0-313-22116-2*, DAW/, Greenwood Pr) Greenwood.

American Women Writers: Diverse Voices in Prose since 1845. Eileen Barrett & Mary Cullinan. LC 90-71610. 784p. (Orig.). (C). 1992. pap. text ed. 24.00 (*0-312-04121-7*) St Martin.

American Women Writers & the Work of History, 1790-1860. Nina Baum. LC 94-11283. 325p. (C). 1995. text ed. 48.00 (*0-8135-2142-4*); pap. text ed. 17.95 (*0-8135-2143-2*) Rutgers U Pr.

American Women Writers on Vietnam: Unheard Voices; A Selected Annotated Bibliography. Deborah A. Butler. LC 89-11963. (Reference Library of the Humanities: Vol. 1278). 336p. 1989. 40.00 (*0-8240-3528-3*, H1278) Garland.

***American Women Writers to 1800.** Sharon M. Harris. 496p. (C). 1995. pap. text ed. 19.95 (*0-19-508453-5*) OUP.

American Women Writers, Vol. 5, Supplement: From Colonial Times to the Present, a Critical Reference Guide. Ed. by Carol H. Green & Mary G. Mason. 672p. (C). 1994. lib. bdg. 95.00 (*0-8264-0603-3*) Continuum.

American Women Writing Fiction: Memory, Identity, Family, Space. Ed. by Mickey Pearlman. LC 88-18667. 248p. 1989. 27.00 (*0-8131-1657-0*); pap. 12.00 (*0-8131-0182-4*) U Pr of Ky.

American Women's Autobiography: Fea(s) ts of Memory. Ed. & Intro. by Margo Culley. LC 91-46700. (Studies in American Autobiography). 352p. (Orig.). (C). 1992. lib. bdg. 42.50 (*0-299-13290-0*); pap. 16.95 (*0-299-13294-3*) U of Wis Pr.

American Women's History. Weatherford. 1994. 30.00 (*0-671-85009-1*); pap. 18.00 (*0-671-85028-8*) P-H Gen Ref & Trav.

American Women's Novels, 19th-Century Interpretive Strategies. Susan K. Harris. (Cambridge Studies in American Literature & Culture: No. 42). 246p. (C). 1992. pap. 19.95 (*0-521-42870-X*) Cambridge U Pr.

American Wood Type, 1828-1900. Rob R. Kelly. (Quality Paperbacks Ser.). 1977. reprint ed. pap. 8.95 (*0-306-80059-4*) Da Capo.

American Wooden Bridges. 182p. 1976. pap. 27.00 (*0-87262-002-6*) Am Soc Civil Eng.

American Woodland Indians. Michael G. Johnson. (Men-at-Arms Ser.: No. 228). (Illus.). 48p. 1990. pap. 11.95 (*0-85045-999-0*, 9186, Pub. by Osprey UK) Stackpole.

American Work Force: Labor & Employment in the 1980s. Robert A. Ullrich. LC 84-21635. (ITT Key Issues Lecture Ser.). 138p. 1985. pap. 5.95 (*0-86569-125-8*, R125, Auburn Hse) Greenwood.

***American Work Force: 1992-2005.** 1995. lib. bdg. 259.95 (*0-8490-7444-4*) Gordon Pr.

***American Work Force: 1992-2005.** (Illus.). 141p. (Orig.). (C). 1995. pap. text ed. 40.00 (*0-7881-1623-1*) Diane Pub.

***American Work Force: 1992-2005.** (Illus.). 135p. (Orig.). (C). 1994. pap. text ed. 40.00x (*0-7881-1201-5*) Diane Pub.

American Work Trucks. John Gunnell. LC 93-80692. (Illus.). 304p. 1994. pap. text ed. 16.95 (*0-87341-290-7*) Krause Pubns.

American Worker. Paul Romano & Ria Stone. ix, 70p. 1972. reprint ed. pap. 3.00 (*0-935590-01-3*) Bewick Edns.

American Worker in the Twentieth Century. Eli Ginzberg & H. Berman. LC 63-10647. 1963. pap. 22.95 (*0-02-911730-5*) Free Pr.

American Workers, American Unions. Robert H. Zieger. (American Moment Ser.). 232p. 1994. pap. text ed. 12.95x (*0-8018-4944-6*) Johns Hopkins.

American Workers, American Unions. 2nd ed. Robert H. Zieger. (American Moment Ser.). 232p. 1994. text ed. 35.00x (*0-8018-4943-8*) Johns Hopkins.

American Working Class Culture: Explorations in American Labor & Social History. Ed. by Milton Cantor. LC 78-59260. (Contributions in Labor History Ser.: No. 7). 444p. 1979. text ed. 65.00 (*0-313-20611-2*, CAW/, Greenwood Pr) Greenwood.

American Working Class Today: Prospects for the 1980s. Ed. by Irving L. Horowitz et al. 312p. 1979. 34.95x (*0-87855-082-8*); pap. 21.95x (*0-87855-578-1*) Transaction Pubs.

American Workman. Emile Levasseur. Ed. by Leon Stein & Theodore Marburg. Tr. by Thomas S. Adams. LC 77-70510. (Work Ser.). 1977. lib. bdg. 47.95 (*0-405-10180-5*) Ayer.

American Works of Art in the Walters Art Gallery. Edward S. King. (Illus.). 1956. pap. 3.00 (*0-911886-00-1*) Walters Art.

American Worlds since Emerson. David Marr. LC 87-5989. 248p. (C). 1988. lib. bdg. 30.00x (*0-87023-588-5*) U of Mass Pr.

American Woven Coverlets. Carol Strickler. LC 87-80524. (Illus.). 200p. (Orig.). 1988. pap. 8.95 (*0-934026-30-0*) Interweave.

American Wristwatches. Edward Faber et al. LC 88-62691. (Illus.). 272p. 1988. 79.95 (*0-88740-146-5*) Schiffer.

American Writer & the Condition of England, 1815-1860. Phyllis Cole. Ed. by Stephen Orgel. (Harvard Dissertations in American & English Literature Ser.). 543p. 1987. lib. bdg. 15.00 (*0-8240-0056-0*) Garland.

American Writer & the University. Ed. by Ben Siegel. LC 87-40499. 200p. 1989. 32.50 (*0-87413-336-X*) U Delaware Pr.

***American Writers, 10 Vols.** Unger. 1992. 780.00 (*0-684-19594-1*) Macmillan.

American Writers, 4 vols. Ed. by A. Unger. 1974. text ed. 179.00 (*0-07-079378-6*) McGraw.

American Writers: A Collection of Literary Biographies, 8 vols. (4 base vols. plus 2 2-vol. suppl.), Set. Ed. by Leonard Unger. 1981. lib. bdg. 625.00 (*0-684-17322-0*, Scribners) S&S Trade.

American Writers: A Collection of Literary Biographies, 2 vols., Suppl. III. Ed. by Lea Baechler & A. Walton Litz. 800p. 1991. Pt. 1. 85.00 (*0-684-19356-6*, Scribners); Pt. 2. 85.00 (*0-684-19357-4*, Scribners) S&S Trade.

American Writers: A Collection of Literary Biographies, 2 vols., Vol. 2. Ed. by Lea Baechler & A. Walton Litz. 800p. 1991. Set. text ed. 180.00 (*0-684-19196-2*, Scribners) S&S Trade.

American Writers: Supplement I, 2 Vols. Ed. by A. Walton Litz. LC 73-1759. 1979. lib. bdg. 160.00 (*0-684-15797-7*, Scribners) S&S Trade.

American Writers & Radical Politics, 1900-39: Equivocal Commitments. Eric Homberger. 192p. 1987. text ed. 39.95 (*0-312-02792-3*) St Martin.

American Writers & the European Tradition. Ed. by Margaret M. Denny. LC 68-24936. 1970. reprint ed. 75.00 (*0-8383-0934-8*) M S G Haskell Hse.

American Writers Before Eighteen Hundred: A Biographical & Critical Reference Guide, 3 vols., 1. Ed. by James A. Levernier & Douglas R. Wilmes. LC 82-933. 1984. text ed. 125.00 (*0-313-23476-0*, LWB/01) Greenwood.

American Writers Before Eighteen Hundred: A Biographical & Critical Reference Guide, 3 vols., Set. Ed. by James A. Levernier & Douglas R. Wilmes. LC 82-933. 1764p. 1984. text ed. 295.00 (*0-313-22229-0*, LWB/) Greenwood.

American Writers Before Eighteen Hundred: A Biographical & Critical Reference Guide, 3 vols., Vol. 2. Ed. by James A. Levernier & Douglas R. Wilmes. LC 82-933. 1984. text ed. 125.00 (*0-313-23477-9*, LWB/02) Greenwood.

American Writers Before Eighteen Hundred: A Biographical & Critical Reference Guide, 3 vols., Vol. 3. Ed. by James A. Levernier & Douglas R. Wilmes. LC 82-933. 1984. text ed. 125.00 (*0-313-24096-5*, LWB/03) Greenwood.

American Writers for Children Before 1900, Vol. 42. Ed. by Glenn E. Estes. (Dictionary of Literary Biography Ser.: Vol.42). 460p. 1985. 128.00 (*0-8103-1720-6*) Gale.

American Writers for Children since 1960: Fiction, Vol. 52. (Dictionary of Literary Biography Ser.: Vol. 52). 488p. 1986. 128.00 (*0-8103-1730-3*) Gale.

American Writers for Children since 1960: Non-Fiction, Vol. 61. Ed. by Glenn E. Estes. LC 87-14352. (Dictionary of Literary Biography Ser.: Vol. 61). 430p. 1987. 128.00 (*0-8103-1739-7*) Gale.

American Writers for Children, 1900-1960, Vol. 22. Ed. by John Cech. LC 83-14199. (Dictionary of Literary Biography Ser.: Vol. 22). (Illus.). 432p. 1983. 128.00 (*0-8103-1146-1*) Gale.

American Writers in Paris, Nineteen Twenty to Nineteen Thirty-Nine, Vol. 4. Ed. by Karen L. Rood. LC 79-26101. (Dictionary of Literary Biography Ser.: Vol. 4). (Illus.). 448p. 1980. 128.00 (*0-8103-0916-5*) Gale.

American Writers of the Early Republic, Vol. 37. Ed. by Elliot Emony & Peter Quartermain. (Dictionary of Literary Biography Ser.: Vol. 37). 392p. 1985. 128.00 (*0-8103-1715-X*) Gale.

American Writers of Today. Henry C. Vedder. LC 72-8513. (Essay Index Reprint Ser.). 1977. reprint ed. 25.95 (*0-8369-7334-8*) Ayer.

American Writers Supplement II, 2 vols. Ed. by A. Walton Litz. LC 73-1759. 1981. lib. bdg. 160.00 (*0-684-16482-5*, Scribners) S&S Trade.

American Writing in the Twentieth Century. Willard Thorp. LC 59-14739. (Library of Congress Series in American Civilization). 367p. 104.60 (*0-8357-9151-3*, 2017751) Bks Demand.

American Writing since 1945: A Critical Survey. Robert F. Kiernan. 225p. 1983. 24.95 (*0-8044-2458-6*) Continuum.

American Writing since 1945: A Critical Survey. Robert F. Kiernan. 225p. 1983. pap. text ed. 7.95 (*0-8044-6359-X*) Continuum.

American Writing Today. London Times Staff. Ed. by Allan Angoff. LC 74-134144. (Essay Index Reprint Ser.). 1977. 30.95 (*0-8369-2030-9*) Ayer.

American Writing Today. rev. ed. Ed. by Richard Kostelanetz. LC 89-51492. (Illus.). 614p. 1991. 65.00 (*0-87875-379-6*) Whitston Pub.

American Writings on Popular Education: The 19th Century. Ed. by Rush Welter. LC 73-151611. (American Heritage Ser.). 1971. 13.50 (*0-672-51508-3*, AHS-81, Bobbs); pap. 7.95 (*0-672-60134-6*, Bobbs) Macmillan.

American Xenophobia & the Slav Immigrant: A Living Legacy of Mind & Spirit. Josephine Wtulich. LC 93-73469. (East European Monographs: No. CCCLXXXV). 203p. 1993. 25.00 (*0-88033-282-4*) East Eur Quarterly.

American Yearnings: Love, Money, & Endless Possibility. Richard L. Rapson. LC 88-17216. 282p. (Orig.). (C). 1988. pap. text ed. 25.00 (*0-8191-7089-5*) U Pr of Amer.

American Years. Harold Sinclair. LC 88-17424. (Prairie State Bks.). 464p. 1988. pap. 10.95 (*0-252-06037-7*) U of Ill Pr.

American Years of John Boyle O'Reilly. Francis G. McManamin. LC 76-6356. (Irish American Ser.). 1976. 29.95 (*0-405-09349-7*) Ayer.

American Yiddish Poetry: A Bilingual Anthology. 1987. lib. bdg. 90.00 (*0-8490-3926-6*) Gordon Pr.

American Yiddish Poetry: A Bilingual Anthology. Benjamin Harshav & Barbara Harshav. 1986. 60.00 (*0-520-04842-3*) U CA Pr.

American Yoga Association Beginner's Manual. Alice Christensen. 1987. pap. 15.00 (*0-671-61935-7*, Fireside) S&S Trade.

***American Young Adult Test: A Self-Help Adult Maturity Workbook.** Walter A. McCray. 48p. (Orig.). 1995. pap. 2.99 (*0-933176-18-X*) Black Light Fellow.

A

An Asterisk (*) at the beginning of an entry indicates that the title is appearing in BIP for the first time.

A

American Zimmer. Paul Zimmer. 24p. 1984. pap. 12.50 (*0-912960-15-9*) Nightowl.

American Zionism: A Documentary Series of American Jewish & Zionist History from the Nineteenth Century to 1968, 15 vols. Ed. by Adrian L. Kleiman. 1992. Set. 2,285.00 (*0-8240-6108-X*) Garland.

***American Zionism from Herzl to the Holocaust: From Herzl to the Holocaust.** Melvin Urofsky. LC 94-45691. xiv, 538p. 1995. pap. 15.00 (*0-8032-9559-6*, Bison Books) U of Nebr Pr.

American Zoom. Peter Golenbock. 1994. pap. 12.00 (*0-02-051050-0*) P-H.

American Zoom: An Inside Look at America's Love Affair with Stock Car Racing. Peter Golenbock. LC 92-38026. (Illus.). 416p. 1993. text ed. 23.00 (*0-02-544615-0*) Macmillan.

***American Zoom: Stock Car Racing from the Dirt Tracks to Daytona.** Peter Golenbock. 1994. pap. 12.00 (*0-02-032782-X*) Macmillan.

Americana. Don DeLillo. 388p. 1989. pap. 11.95 (*0-14-011948-5*, Penguin Bks) Viking Penguin.

Americana. Lee T. Rector. Ed. by Kathleen Tibbetts & Laurene Tibbetts. LC 81-90246. 168p. 1981. write for info. (*0-9606170-0-0*) Rector Pub.

Americana. Virginia Sale. 64p. 1952. 5.00 (*0-573-60062-7*) French.

Americana: A Basic Reader. Pamela McPartland. 171p. (C). 1983. pap. text ed. 14.75 (*0-15-502597-X*) HB Coll Pubs.

***Americana: Historical Sportlights in Story & Song.** Myrtis Mixon. (Illus.). 112p. (Orig.). 1995. pap. 12.95 (*0-943327-13-X*) JAG Pubns.

***Americana: Historical Spotlights in Story & Song.** Myrtis Mixon. (Illus.). 112p. (Orig.). 1995. audio, pap. 16.95 (*0-943327-15-6*) JAG Pubns.

Americana Anthology: Bicentennial Edition 1776-1976, Vol. 1. Ed. by Stanley H. Barkan et al. LC 76-47154. (New York Poetry Forum Ser.). (Illus.). 96p. 1976. 20.00 (*0-89304-011-8*, CCC107); pap. 10.00 (*0-89304-009-6*) Cross-Cultrl NY.

Americana Catalogues, 4 vols. deluxe ed. Charles Eberstadt et al. 1966. 500.00 (*0-87266-010-9*) Argosy.

***Americana Crafted: Jehu Camper, Delaware Whittler.** Robert D. Bethke. (Folk Art & Artists Ser.). (Illus.). 72p. 1995. text ed. 32.50 (*0-87805-762-5*); pap. 16.95 (*0-87805-763-3*) U Pr of Miss.

Americana for Autoharp. Brimhall. (Miscellaneous Ser.). 1990. 2.95 (*0-685-32016-2*, G076) Hansen Ed Mus.

***Americana Germanica: Paul Ben Baginsky's Bibliography of German Works Relating to America, 1493-1800.** Ed. & Intro. by Don H. Tolzman. 219p. (Orig.). 1995. reprint ed. pap. text ed. 17.00 (*0-7884-0151-3*) Heritage Bk.

Americana Library. 34.95 (*0-86545-165-6*) Spizzirri.

Americana on Foreign Stamps, No.I. 112p. 1967. 6.00 (*0-318-13294-X*) Am Topical Assn.

Americanisation of West German Industry, 1945-1973. Volker R. Berghahn. 360p. 1986. 49.95 (*0-521-32990-6*) Cambridge U Pr.

Americanisation Syndrome. Robert A. Carlson. LC 87-4804. 160p. 1987. text ed. 45.00 (*0-312-00855-4*) St Martin.

Americanism: Revolutionary Order & Societal Self-Interpretation in the American Republic. Jurgen Gebhardt. Tr. by Ruth Hein. LC 92-14094. 576p. (C). 1992. text ed. 45.00 (*0-8071-1514-2*) La State U Pr.

Americanism Betrayed. A. O. Tittman. 1984. lib. bdg. 79.95 (*0-87700-606-7*) Revisionist Pr.

Americanismo of Ruben Dario. M. Nunn. 1972. 150.00 (*0-87968-613-8*) Gordon Pr.

Americanizacion de Puerto Rico y el Sistema de Instruccion Publica. 2nd ed. Aida Negron De Montilla. LC 76-14880. 290p. (SPA.). 1977. reprint ed. pap. 9.95 (*0-8477-0101-8*) U of PR Pr.

Americanization, Acculturation, & Ethnic Identity: The Nisei Generation in Hawaii. Eileen H. Tamura. LC 93-18118. (Asian American Experience Ser.). 400p. 1993. 49.95 (*0-252-02031-6*); pap. 19.95 (*0-252-06358-9*) U of Ill Pr.

Americanization in Puerto Rico & the Public School System, 1900-1930. Aida Negron De Montilla. 282p. 1975. 5.00 (*0-8477-2727-0*) U of PR Pr.

Americanization of a Rural Immigrant Church: The General Conference Mennonites in Central Kansas, 1874-1939. Dennis D. Engbrecht. LC 90-41236. (European Immigrants & American Society Ser.). 344p. 1990. reprint ed. 25.00 (*0-8240-7424-6*) Garland.

Americanization of Alaska, 1867-1897. Ted C. Hinckley. LC 71-180900. (Illus.). 285p. 1994. pap. 12.95 (*0-87015-240-8*) Pacific Bks.

Americanization of Brazil: A Study of U. S. Cold War Diplomacy in the Third World, 1945-1954. Gerald K. Haines. LC 89-32065. (America in the Modern World: Studies in International History). 227p. 1989. 40.00 (*0-8420-2339-9*) Scholarly Res Inc.

Americanization of Carl Aaron Swensson. Daniel M. Pearson. LC 77-151736. (Augustana Historical Society Publication Ser.: No.25). 169p. 1977. 5.95 (*0-910184-25-9*) Augustana.

Americanization of Chinese New Year: A History of Traditional New Year Customs & of the Louisiana Chinese. Louis Illar. 128p. 1993. per., pap. text ed. 15.95 (*0-8403-8547-1*) Kendall-Hunt.

Americanization of Edward Bok. Edward Bok. 26.95 (*0-8488-0199-7*) Amereon Ltd.

Americanization of Edward Bok. Edward Bok. 1993. reprint ed. lib. bdg. 89.00 (*0-7812-5428-0*) Rprt Serv.

Americanization of Emily. William B. Huie. 18.95 (*0-89190-322-4*, Am Repr) Amereon Ltd.

Americanization of French Louisiana: A Study of the Process of Adjustment Between French & Anglo-American Population of Louisiana. Lewis W. Newton. Ed. by Francesco Cordasco. LC 80-884. (American Ethnic Groups Ser.). 1981. lib. bdg. 30.95 (*0-405-13445-2*) Ayer.

Americanization of Germany: Post-War Culture, 1945-1949. Ralph Willett. (Studies in Film, Television & the Media). 192p. 1989. 52.50 (*0-415-00287-7*) Routledge.

Americanization of Germany: Post-War Culture 1945-1949. Ralph Willett. (Studies in Film, Television & the Media). 192p. 1992. pap. 17.50 (*0-415-07710-9*, A7562) Routledge.

Americanization of Labor. Robert W. Dunn. LC 74-22740. (Labor Movement in Fiction & Non-Fiction Ser.). reprint ed. 41.50 (*0-404-58492-6*) AMS Pr.

Americanization of Odysseus. Nick Lambros. 189p. 1988. pap. 8.95 (*0-89697-286-0*) Intl Univ Pr.

Americanization of Sex. Edwin M. Schur. LC 87-17993. 256p. (C). 1988. pap. 16.95 (*0-87722-633-4*) Temple U Pr.

Americanization of the Common Law: The Impact of Legal Change of Massachusetts Society, 1760-1830. William E. Nelson. LC 74-21231. (Studies in Legal History). 288p. (C). 1975. pap. 13.95 (*0-674-02972-0*) HUP.

Americanization of the Common Law: The Impact of Legal Change on Massachusetts Society, 1760-1830. William E. Nelson. LC 74-21231. 288p. 1994. reprint ed. pap. 18.00 (*0-8203-1587-7*) U of Ga Pr.

Americanization of the Croats in St. Louis, Missouri During the Past Thirty Years. C. S. Mihanovich. LC 75-146895. 1971. reprint ed. pap. 8.00 (*0-88247-122-8*) Ragusan Pr.

Americanization of the Global Village: Essays in Comparative Popular Culture. Ed. by Roger Rollin. LC 89-83393. (Illus.). 154p. (C). 1990. lib. bdg. 26.95 (*0-87972-469-2*); pap. 13.95 (*0-87972-470-6*) Bowling Green Univ.

Americanization of the Jews. Ed. by Robert M. Seltzer & Norman J. Cohen. 400p. 1994. 50.00 (*0-8147-8000-8*); pap. 20.00 (*0-8147-8001-6*) NYU Pr.

Americanization of the Synagogue, 1820-1870. Leon A. Jick. LC 91-50817. (Brandeis Series in American Jewish History, Culture, & Life). 262p. 1992. pap. 18.00 (*0-87451-573-4*) U Pr of New Eng.

Americanization of the World: The Trend of the Twentieth Century. William T. Stead. 1972. 59.95 (*0-8490-1419-0*) Gordon Pr.

Americanization on the Gulf Coast, 1803-1850. (Gulf Coast History & Humanities Conference Publications Ser.). 1972. 15.00 (*0-940836-04-1*); pap. 10.00 (*0-940836-05-X*) U of W Fla.

Americanization, Social Control, & Philanthropy. George Pozzetta. LC 90-49267. (Immigration & Ethnicity Ser.: Vol. 14). 360p. 1991. reprint ed. 60.00 (*0-8240-7414-9*) Garland.

Americanization Studies: The Acculturation of Immigrant Groups into American Society, 10 vols., Set. Incl. New Homes for Old. S. P. Breckinridge. LC 73-108242. 1971. (*0-318-54960-3*); Immigrant's Day in Court. K. H. Claghorn. LC 73-108242. 1971. (*0-318-54961-1*); America Via the Neighborhood. J. Daniels. LC 73-108242. 1971. (*0-318-54962-X*); Immigrant Health & the Community. M. M. Davis. LC 73-108242. 1971. (*0-318-54963-8*); Americans by Choice. J. P. Gavit. LC 73-108242. 1971. (*0-318-54964-6*); Adjusting Immigrant & Industry. W. M. Leiserson. LC 73-108242. (*0-318-54965-4*); Immigrant Press & Its Control. R. E. Park. LC 73-108242. 1971. (*0-318-54966-2*); Stake in the Land. P. A. Speek. LC 73-108242. 1971. (*0-318-54967-0*); Old World Traits Transplanted. W. I. Thomas et al. LC 73-108242. 1971. (*0-318-54968-9*); Schooling of the Immigrant. F. V. Thompson. LC 73-108242. 1971. (*0-318-54969-7*); LC 73-108242. (Criminology, Law Enforcement, & Social Problems Ser.: No. 125). (Illus.). 1971. 200.00 (*0-685-03958-7*) Patterson Smith.

Americanizing the American Orchestra: Report of the National Task Force for the American Orchestra, an Initiative for Change. American Symphony Orchestra League Staff. 250p. 1993. student ed 20.00 (*1-883807-00-X*) Am Symphony Orch.

***Americanizing Your Communication Skills.** Thomas Wong. Ed. by Liz Miller. (Illus.). 120p. (Orig.). (C). 1996. write for info. (*0-9638349-3-2*); pap. write for info. (*0-9638349-4-0*) TransCore Strategies.

***Americanos.** Brigitte Balster. Tr. by Soledad San Miguel Carmona. (Illus.). 399p. 1993. 19.95 (*2-7005-0175-6*, Pub. by ASSIMIL FR) Distribks Inc.

***Americanos, Incl. 3 60-min. cassettes.** Brigitte Balster & Soledad San Miguel Carmona. 1993. audio 59.95 (*2-7005-1334-7*) Distribks Inc.

Americans. Henry James. 1976. 20.95 (*0-8488-0756-1*) Amereon Ltd.

Americans. Henry James. 1965. pap. 4.50 (*0-451-52241-9*, Sig Classics) NAL-Dutton.

Americans. Salvador De Madariaga. LC 68-29229. (Essay Index Reprint Ser.). 1977. reprint ed. 17.95 (*0-8369-0661-6*) Ayer.

Americans. Stuart P. Sherman. (BCL1-PS American Literature Ser.). 336p. 1992. reprint ed. lib. bdg. 89.00 (*0-7812-6613-0*) Rprt Serv.

Americans. Stuart P. Sherman. 1971. reprint ed. 29.00 (*0-403-01207-4*) Scholarly.

Americans, 3 vols., Set. Daniel J. Boorstin. Incl. Vol. 1. Colonial Experience. 1958. 40.00 (*0-394-41506-X*); Vol. 2. Democratic Experience. 1973. 39.95 (*0-394-48724-9*); Vol. 3. National Experience. 1965. 35.00 (*0-394-41453-5*); 1975. 114.95 (*0-394-49588-8*) Random.

Americans: An Economic Record. Stanley Lebergott. 526p. (C). 1984. pap. text ed. 14.95 (*0-393-95311-4*) Norton.

Americans: The Landscape. Text by Linda L. Cathcart. (Illus.). 44p. 1981. pap. 10.00 (*0-936080-03-5*) Cont Arts Museum.

Americans - A Nation of Dupes, Sheep, & Wimps?, Vol. B: The F.O.J. Syndrome in America: Brainwashing Americans into a Special Neurosis, the Fear of the Jews - A Psychosocial & Political Inquiry about the Real U. S. Rulers, the Pharisees-Zionists. Ratibor-Ray M. Jurjevich. (Demonic Maladies Ser.). 360p. 1988. text ed. 21.95 (*0-930711-34-3*); pap. 14.95 (*0-930711-33-5*) Ichthys Bks.

Americans - Mexicans Folk Wisdom. Juan Amaro & John Culpepper. (Illus.). 38p. (Orig.). (C). 1994. pap. write for info. (*0-9624186-2-5*) Warm Days Retirement.

Americans Abroad: A Comparative Study of Emigrants from the United States. A. Dashefsky et al. (Environment, Development, & Public Policy: Public Policy & Social Services Ser.). (Illus.). 176p. 1991. 27.50 (*0-306-43941-7*, 589, Plenum Pr) Plenum.

Americans Abroad: A Handbook for Living & Working Overseas. John Z. Kepler et al. LC 82-630. 588p. 1983. text ed. 65.00 (*0-275-91024-5*, C1024, Praeger Pubs) Greenwood.

Americans All: Race & Ethnic Relations in Historical, Structural & Comparative Perspectives. Peter Kivisto. LC 94-12581. 521p. 1995. text ed. 47.95 (*0-534-24366-5*) Intl Thomson.

Americans All: Stories of American Life Today. Ed. by Benjamin A. Heydrick. LC 74-160934. (Short Story Index Reprint Ser.). 1977. reprint ed. 23.95 (*0-8369-3913-1*) Ayer.

Americans & Chinese: A Historical Essay & a Bibliography. Kwang-Ching Liu. LC 63-19141. 223p. reprint ed. pap. 63.60 (*0-7837-1521-8*, 2041798) Bks Demand.

Americans & Chinese: Passage to Differences. 3rd ed. Francis L. Hsu. LC 81-10461. 562p. 1981. pap. text ed. 12.95 (*0-8248-0757-X*) UH Pr.

Americans & Drug Abuse: Report from the Aspen Conference. Christian Kryder & Stephen P. Strickland. 4.95 (*0-686-26004-X*) Aspen Inst Human.

Americans & German Scholarship, 1770-1870. Carl Diehl. LC 77-12931. (Yale Historical Publications: Miscellany: No. 115). 205p. reprint ed. pap. 58.50 (*0-7837-3292-9*, 2057694) Bks Demand.

Americans & Oil in the Middle East. Charles W. Hamilton. LC 62-18873. 319p. reprint ed. pap. 91.00 (*0-8357-5406-5*, 2052222) Bks Demand.

Americans & Others. Agnes Repplier. LC 70-121503. (Essay Index Reprint Ser.). 1977. 23.95 (*0-8369-2025-2*) Ayer.

Americans & Paris. Michael Marlais & Marianne Doezema. LC 90-1866. (Illus.). 62p. (Orig.). 1991. pap. 12.95 (*0-295-97102-9*) U of Wash Pr.

Americans & the Arts, No. Six: Nationwide Survey of Public Opinion. Louis Harris. 100p. (Orig.). 1992. pap. 16.00 (*1-879903-06-7*) Am Council Arts.

Americans & the Arts, No. V: Highlights. Ed. by National Research Center of the Arts Staff. 32p. (Orig.). 1988. pap. 2.00 (*0-915400-65-0*, ACA Bks) Am Council Arts.

Americans & the California Dream. Kevin Starr. (Illus.). 1973. 35.00 (*0-19-501644-0*) OUP.

Americans & the California Dream, 1850-1915. Kevin Starr. (Illus.). 494p. 1986. pap. 16.95 (*0-19-504233-6*) OUP.

Americans & the China Opium Trade in the Nineteenth Century. Charles C. Stelle. Ed. by Gerald N. Grob. LC 80-1248. (Addiction in America Ser.). 1981. lib. bdg. 18.95 (*0-405-13557-2*) Ayer.

Americans & the Soviet Experiment, 1917-1933. Peter G. Filene. LC 67-11669. (Illus.). 403p. reprint ed. pap. 114.90 (*0-7837-1512-9*, 2041789) Bks Demand.

Americans & Their Forests: A Historical Geography. Michael Williams. (Cambridge Studies in Environmental History). (Illus.). 736p. 1989. 69.95 (*0-521-33247-8*) Cambridge U Pr.

Americans & Their Forests: A Historical Geography. Michael Williams. (Cambridge Studies in Environmental History). (Illus.). 640p. (C). 1992. pap. 29.95 (*0-521-42837-8*) Cambridge U Pr.

Americans & Their Schools. Ed. by E. V. Johanningmeier. 328p. (C). 1985. reprint ed. pap. text ed. 21.95 (*0-88133-160-0*) Waveland Pr.

Americans Are Singing about Lady Liberty. Frank Di Silvestro. (Illus.). 74p. 1986. pap. 10.95 (*0-934591-01-6*) Songs & Stories.

Americans Assess Their Health: United States, 1987. (Series 10: Data from the National Health Interview Survey: No. 174). 63p. 1987. 3.50 (*0-685-40094-8*, 017-022-01105-1) Natl Ctr Health Stats.

Americans at Home. M. D. Elevitch. LC 75-36319. 128p. (Orig.). 1976. pap. 5.50 (*0-916452-01-8*) Foolscap.

Americans at Play: Recent Trends in Recreation & Leisure Time Activities. Jesse F. Steiner. LC 73-112574. (Rise of Urban America Ser.). 1974. reprint ed. 20.95 (*0-405-02476-2*) Ayer.

Americans at School. A. Mors & J. Williams. (American Background Readers Ser.). (YA). 1991. pap. text ed. 5.25 (*0-582-01714-9*) Longman.

Americans at War. John S. Morgan. 120p. (Orig.). 1991. pap. 13.76 (*0-685-48272-3*) Dayspring Pr.

Americans Before Columbus: Ice Age Origins. Ed. by Ronald C. Carlisle. LC 88-82770. (Ethnology Monographs: No. 12). 123p. (C). 1988. pap. 16.50 (*0-945428-01-4*) Ctr Study First Am.

Americans Betrayed: Politics & the Japanese Evacuation. Morton Grodzins. (Midway Reprint Ser.). 462p. pap. 131.70 (*0-8357-8796-6*, 2056749) Bks Demand.

Americans by Adoption. Joseph Husband. LC 70-86763. (Essay Index Reprint Ser.). 1977. 18.95 (*0-8369-1142-3*) Ayer.

Americans by Choice: Italians in Utica, New York. George Schiro. LC 74-17953. (Italian American Experience Ser.). (Illus.). 192p. 1975. reprint ed. 16.95 (*0-405-06422-5*) Ayer.

Americans by Choice see Americanization Studies: The Acculturation of Immigrant Groups into American Society

American's Chess Heritage. Walter Korn. pap. 6.95 (*0-317-63118-7*) McKay.

Americans Doing Business in Japan: A Resource Book. Cameron Northouse. LC 92-27061. 1992. 21.95 (*0-935061-48-7*) Contemp Res.

Americans for Democratic Action: Its Role in National Politics. Clifton Brock. LC 85-7976. 240p. 1985. reprint ed. text ed. 59.75 (*0-313-24284-4*, BRAD, Greenwood Pr) Greenwood.

Americans for Democratic Action Papers, 1932-1973: A Guide to the Microfilm Edition. Ed. by Jack T. Ericson. 121p. 1979. pap. 80.00 (*0-667-00540-4*) Chadwyck-Healey.

***Americans from Germany.** Gerard Wilk. (Illus.). xii, 83p. 1995. pap. 3.50 (*1-880788-06-3*) MKGAC & IGHS.

Americans from Hungary. Emil Lengyel. (History - United States Ser.). 319p. 1993. reprint ed. lib. bdg. 89.00 (*0-7812-4868-X*) Rprt Serv.

Americans from Yugoslavia. Gerald G. Govorchin. 1961. 15.00 (*0-686-61036-9*) Ragusan Pr.

Americans from Yugoslavia. Gerald G. Govorchin. LC 61-11312. 365p. reprint ed. pap. 104.10 (*0-7837-4985-6*, 2044652) Bks Demand.

American's Guide to English Parish Churches. John Betjeman. (Illus.). 1959. 20.00 (*0-8392-1004-3*) Astor-Honor.

Americans, I: The Colonial Experience. Daniel J. Boorstin. 1964. pap. 12.00 (*0-394-70513-0*, Vin) Random.

Americans, II: The National Experience. Daniel J. Boorstin. 1965. pap. 8.95 (*0-685-29461-7*, Vin) Random.

Americans in Agriculture, Portraits of Diversity: Yearbook of Agriculture, 1990. Ed. by Deborah T. Smith. (Illus.). 191p. 1990. text ed. 10.00 (*0-16-023990-7*) USGPO.

Americans in Canada: Migration & Settlement since 1840. David D. Harvey. LC 90-6048. (Canadian Studies: Vol. 10). 442p. 1991. lib. bdg. 109.95 (*0-88946-215-1*) E Mellen.

Americans in Denmark: Comparisons of the Two Cultures by Writers, Artists, & Teachers. Ed. by F. Richard Thomas. LC 88-38908. 224p. (C). 1990. 24.50 (*0-8093-1536-X*) S Ill U Pr.

Americans in England. Robert B. Mowat. LC 79-99642. (Essay Index Reprint Ser.). 1977. 28.95 (*0-8369-1423-6*) Ayer.

Americans in Japan: An Abridgment of the Government Narrative of the U. S. Expedition to Japan, under Commodore Perry. Robert Tomes. LC 72-82113. (Japan Library Ser.). 1973. reprint ed. lib. bdg. 35.00 (*0-8420-1406-3*) Scholarly Res Inc.

Americans in London: A Street-By-Street Guide. Brian N. Morton. LC 86-6621. (Illus.). 296p. 1986. pap. 12.95 (*0-688-06555-4*) Olivia & Hill.

Americans in Paris. George Wickes. LC 80-18371. (Quality Paperbacks Ser.). (Illus.). xvi, 302p. 1980. reprint ed. pap. 6.95 (*0-306-80127-2*) Da Capo.

Americans in Paris: An Anecdotal Street Guide. Brian N. Morton. (Illus.). 313p. 1986. 20.00 (*0-934034-06-0*); pap. 12.95 (*0-934034-05-2*) Olivia & Hill.

Americans in Paris in 1887. limited ed. 1983. pap. 15.00 (*0-318-00404-6*) K Starosciak.

Americans in Paris in 1887. limited ed. 1983. reprint ed. 25.00 (*0-318-00403-8*) K Starosciak.

Americans in Paris, 1900-1930: A Selected, Annotated Bibliography. Comp. by William G. Bailey. LC 89-1924. (Bibliographies & Indexes in World Literature Ser.: No. 19). 181p. 1989. text ed. 55.00 (*0-313-26442-2*, BAM, Greenwood Pr) Greenwood.

Americans in Persia. Arthur Millspaugh. LC 76-9837. (Politics & Strategy of World War II Ser.). 1976. reprint ed. lib. bdg. 37.50 (*0-306-70764-0*) Da Capo.

Americans in Process: A Settlement Study. Ed. by Robert A. Woods. LC 78-129419. (American Immigration Collection Ser. 2). (Illus.). 1970. reprint ed. 26.95 (*0-405-00573-3*) Ayer.

Americans in Process: A Study of Our Citizens of Oriental Ancestry. William C. Smith. LC 76-129413. (American Immigration Collection Ser. 2). 1976. reprint ed. 25.95 (*0-405-00567-9*) Ayer.

Americans in Santo Domingo. Melvin M. Knight. LC 75-111722. (American Imperialism: Viewpoints of United States Foreign Policy, 1898-1941 Ser.). 1970. reprint ed. 17.95 (*0-405-02032-5*) Ayer.

Americans in Southeast Asia: The POW-MIA Issue. William Homolka. LC 85-60054. 201p. 1986. pap. 9.95 (*0-917601-01-7*) New World NY.

Americans in Spain: Patriots, Expatriots & the Early American Hispanists 1780-1850. Norman P. Tucker. LC 80-84165. (Illus.). 24p. (Orig.). 1980. pap. 7.50 (*0-934552-35-5*) Boston Athenaeum.

Americans in the Arts, 1890-1920: Critiques by James Gibbons Huneker. James G. Huneker. Ed. by Arnold T. Schwab. LC 84-45357. (Studies in Modern Literature: No. 14). 1985. 57.50 (*0-404-61584-8*) AMS Pr.

Americans in the Making: The Natural History of the Assimilation of Immigrants. William C. Smith. LC 70-129414. (American Immigration Collection Ser. 2). 1970. reprint ed. 28.95 (*0-405-00568-7*) Ayer.

Americans in the Philippines, 2 Vols. James A. Le Roy. LC 73-126681. reprint ed. 125.00 (*0-404-03974-X*) AMS Pr.

Americans in the Spanish Civil War: The Odyssey of the Abraham Lincoln Brigade. Peter N. Carroll. LC 93-21131. (C). 1994. 45.00 (*0-8047-2276-5*); pap. 15.95 (*0-8047-2277-3*) Stanford U Pr.

An Asterisk (*) at the beginning of an entry indicates that the title is appearing in BIP for the first time.

An Asterisk (*) at the beginning of an entry indicates that the title is appearing in BIP for the first time.

271

*America's Automotive Love Affair: 75 Years of Snap. David K. Wright. (Illus.). 160p. 1995. 29.95 (0-7603-0036-4) Motorbooks Intl.

America's Bald Eagle. Hope Ryden. (Illus.). 64p. (J). 1992. pap. 9.95 (1-55821-141-1) Lyons & Burford.

*America's Best. Sinclair Browning. LC 95-77267. 500p. 1995. 24.00 (1-887037-00-4) AMC Pub.

America's Best: A National Community Cookbook to Benefit the U. S. Ski Team. LC 83-40037. (Illus.). 320p. 1983. pap. 13.95 (0-89480-593-2, 593) Workman Pub.

America's Best Appetizers. JoNett Butler & Bea Farwell. (Illus.). 220p. (Orig.). 1985. pap. 9.95 (0-9614834-0-7) Butler-Farwell.

*America's Best Beers Vol. 1: A Complete Guide to the More Than 350 Microbreweries & Brewpubs. Christopher Finch. 1994. pap. 14.95 (0-316-28204-9) Little.

America's Best Classrooms: How Award-Winning Teachers Are Shaping Our Children's Future. Daniel T. Seymour & Terrence J. Seymour. LC 91-40206. 155p. 1992. 17.95 (1-56079-076-8) Petersons Guides.

America's Best Classrooms: How Award-Winning Teachers Are Shaping Our Children's Future. rev. ed. Daniel Seymour & Terry Seymour. Ed. by Kitty Colton. 155p. 1993. pap. 9.95 (1-56079-326-0) Petersons Guides.

America's Best Harley-Davidson Customs. Timothy Remus. LC 92-29760. 160p. 1993. pap. 19.95 (0-87938-702-5) Motorbooks Intl.

America's Best Hoax: How Doctors Get Fat on Fitness. John LeMarr. LC 93-77223. (Illus.). 160p. (Orig.). 1993. pap. 12.95 (0-9632923-7-4) HealthMasters.

America's Best Indoor Plants & Plant People: Photography Contest Winners, 1991. Ed. by Patricia A. Hamilton. (Illus.). 80p. (Orig.). 1992. pap. 5.95 (1-877809-51-9) Park Pl Pubns.

America's Best Kept Secret. James L. Gagan & Robert L. Shock. 240p. 1991. 19.95 (0-8092-3976-0) Contemp Bks.

America's Best-Loved Community Recipes. Better Homes & Gardens Staff. 1994. 29.95 (0-696-20095-3) Meredith Bks.

America's Best Project Plans, No. A100. Ed. by National Plan Service, Inc. Staff. (Ucando Ser.). (Illus.). 64p. 1990. per., pap. 4.95 (0-934039-30-5) Natl Plan Serv.

America's Best Quilting Projects: Scrap Quilts, Vol. 2. Mariane Fons & Liz Porter. Ed. by Mary V. Green. LC 93-33166. (Illus.). 176p. 1994. 25.95 (0-87596-604-7) Rodale Pr Inc.

America's Best Quilting Projects: Special Feature: Holidays & Celebrations. Marianne Fons & Liz Porter. Ed. by Mary V. Green. LC 92-41508. 1993. 25.95 (0-87596-551-2) Rodale Pr Inc.

*America's Best Quilting Projects: Special Feature Star Quilts. Marianne Fons & Liz Porter. Ed. by Karen C. Soltys. LC 94-23049. 1994. 25.95 (0-87596-642-X) Rodale Pr Inc.

America's Best Recipes. 336p. 1993. pap. 17.99 (0-8487-1126-2) Oxmoor Hse.

America's Best Recipes 1992. Sunset Publishing Staff. 336p. 1992. pap. 17.99 (0-8487-1085-1) Oxmoor Hse.

America's Best State Fair Recipes. Catherine Hanley. (Illus.). 240p. 1993. 7.98 (0-8317-0310-5) Smithmark.

America's Biggest Cover-Up: Fifty More Things Everyone Should Know about the Chronic Fatigue Syndrome Epidemic & Its Link to AIDS. Neenyah Ostrom. 100p. 1993. 14.95 (0-9624142-3-9) That New Mag.

America's Bimodal Crisis: Black Intelligence in White Society. 3rd ed. Stanley Burnham. 160p. 1993. 10.00 (0-936396-06-7) Foun Human GA.

America's Black & Tribal Colleges: The Comprehensive Guide to Historically & Predominantly Black & Native American Colleges & Universities. Janet W. Bowman. LC 94-66573. 320p. (Orig.). (C). 1994. pap. 19.95 (1-883995-02-7) Sandcastle Pub.

America's Black Musical Heritage. Tilford Brooks. (Illus.). 384p. 1983. pap. text ed. 50.00 (0-13-024307-8) P-H.

America's Bread Book: Three Hundred Authentic Recipes for America's Favorite Homemade Breads. Mary Gubser. 1992. pap. 12.00 (0-688-11608-6, Quill) Morrow.

America's British Culture. Russell Kirk. LC 92-13217. (Library of Conservative Thought). 150p. (C). 1992. 29.95 (1-56000-066-X) Transaction Pubs.

America's Business. James O. Robertson. 288p. 1986. pap. 7.95 (0-8090-0164-0) Hill & Wang.

America's Business Climate & Economic Profiles. Priscilla C. Geahigan. 1993. 129.00 (0-8103-5545-0) Gale.

America's Capacity to Produce. Edwin G. Nourse et al. (Brookings Institution Reprint Ser.). (Illus.). reprint ed. lib. bdg. 36.00 (0-697-00176-8) Irvington.

America's Care of the Mentally Ill: A Photographic History. William E. Baxter & David W. Hathcox. LC 93-48732. 1994. text ed. write for info. (0-88048-539-6) Am Psychiatric.

America's Castle: The Evolution of the Smithsonian Building & Its Institution, 1840-1878. Kenneth Hafertepe. LC 83-600216. (Illus.). 208p. 1984. 27.50 (0-87474-500-4, HAAC) Smithsonian.

America's Centenarians: Data from the 1980 Census. (Current Population Reports Series P-23, Special Studies: No. 153). (Illus.). 127p. (Orig.). 1987. pap. 6.00 (0-16-013380-7, S/N 803-005-10006-5) USGPO.

America's Centennial Celebration. Floyd Rinhart & Marion Rinhart. LC 75-38859. (Illus.). 1976. pap. 4.95 (0-914042-08-4) Laura Bks.

America's Century: Perspectives on Twentieth-Century American History. Ed. by Iwan W. Morgan & Neil A. Wynn. LC 91-29508. 340p. (C). 1993. 45.00 (0-8419-1303-X); pap. 19.95 (0-8419-1304-8) Holmes & Meier.

America's Changing Families: A Guide for Educators. Karen W. Appel. LC 84-62989. (Fastback Ser.: No. 219). 50p. 1985. pap. 1.25 (0-87367-219-4) Phi Delta Kappa.

America's Changing Investment Market. Ed. by Ernest M. Patterson & Mira Wilkins. LC 76-29983. (European Business Ser.). (Illus.). 1977. reprint ed. lib. bdg. 31.95 (0-405-09748-4) Ayer.

America's Changing Role As a World Leader. James C. Charlesworth. Ed. by Richard D. Lambert. LC 76-85466. (Annals Ser.: 384). 1969. 27.00 (0-87761-118-1); pap. 18.00 (0-87761-117-3) Am Acad Pol Soc Sci.

America's Changing Role in the World System. Ed. by Terry Boswell & Albert Bergesen. LC 86-25245. 320p. 1987. text ed. 65.00 (0-275-92417-3, C2417, Praeger Pubs) Greenwood.

America's Changing Workforce: About You, Your Job & Your Changing Work Environment. Nuventures Consultants, Inc. Staff. Ed. by Ellen McNamara. 270p. (Orig.). 1990. pap. 12.95 (0-9625632-1-8) NUVENTURES Pub.

America's Chess Heritage. Walter Korn. pap. 6.95 (0-679-14104-9) McKay.

America's Children: New Generation, New Troubles. Ed. by Oliver Trager. (Editorials on File Bk.). 224p. 1991. 29.95 (0-8160-2663-7) Facts on File.

America's Children: Opposing Viewpoints. Ed. by Carol Wekesser. LC 90-24085. (Opposing Viewpoints Ser.). (Illus.). 240p. (YA). (gr. 10 up). 1991. lib. bdg. 19.95 (0-89908-486-9); pap. 11.55 (0-89908-461-3) Greenhaven.

America's Children: Resources from Family, Government, & the Economy. Donald J. Hernandez. LC 92-9368. (Population of the United States in the 1980s: A Census Monograph Ser.). (Illus.). 480p. 1993. 49.95 (0-87154-381-8) Russell Sage.

*America's Children: Resources from Family, Government, & the Economy. Donald J. Hernandez. LC 92-9368. (Population of the United States in the 1980s). (Illus.). 504p. 1995. pap. 22.50x (0-87154-382-6) Russell Sage.

America's Children: Stories, Poems, & Real-Life Adventures of Children Through Our Nation's History. Ed. by Bebe Willoughby. (Illus.). 96p. (J). (gr. 2-7). 1992. write for info. (0-307-15876-4, 15876, Golden Pr) Western Pub.

***America's Children: Triumph or Tragedy. Charles N. Oberg et al. 94p. 1994. pap. 22.50 (0-87553-218-7) Am Pub Health. America's children are in a state of crisis. Their representation among the poor & disadvantaged has grown at an unprecedented rate. This book delineates the dimensions of the problem by presenting tragic cases & aggregate data. To foster children's potential for autonomy, the authors propose a solution in the form of an Integrated Children's Network, which consists of six interlocking "gears" necessary for the health of our children: economic security, medical care, shelter, proper nutrition, child care, & early education. Nonmembers: $22.50 APHA Members: $15.75.** *Publisher Provided Annotation.*

America's Children: Who Cares? Growing Need & Declining Assistance in the Reagan Era. Madeleine H. Kimmich. LC 85-11114. (Changing Domestic Priorities Ser.). 130p. (Orig.). 1985. pap. text ed. 17.50 (0-87766-386-6) Urban Inst.

*America's Children & Youth in Crisis: Challenges & Options for Programs & Policies. Richard M. Lerner. 160p. 1994. 39.95 (0-8039-7068-4); pap. 18.95 (0-8039-7069-2) Sage.

America's China Trade in Historical Perspective: The Chinese & American Performance. Ed. by Ernest R. May & John K. Fairbank. (Studies in American-East Asian Relations: No. 11). 390p. 1986. 25.00 (0-674-03075-3) HUP.

America's Choice: The Elections of 1992. William Crotty. 208p. 1993. pap. text ed. 14.95 (1-56134-252-1) Dushkin Pub.

*America's Christian Heritage: Voices in the Wilderness, Vol. 1. George P. Hudson. (Illus.). 255p. (YA). (gr. 8 up). 1994. pap. text ed. 18.95 (1-879908-05-0) Milton Pub.

*America's Cities. Roger L. Kemp. 197p. (C). 1995. boxed, pap. text ed. 55.95 (1-85972-013-7, Pub. by Avebury Pub UK) Ashgate Pub Co.

America's Cities: Opposing Viewpoints. Ed. by Charles P. Cozic. LC 92-40708. (Opposing Viewpoints Ser.). (Illus.). 264p. (YA). (gr. 10 up). 1993. lib. bdg. 19.95 (0-89908-195-9); pap. text ed. 11.55 (0-89908-170-3) Greenhaven.

America's Cities: Strategic Planning for the Future. Roger L. Kemp. 270p. (Orig.). (C). 1988. pap. text ed. 16.95 (0-8134-2810-6) Interstate.

America's Collectible Cookbooks: The History, the Politics, the Recipes. Mary A. DuSablon. (Illus.). 272p. 1994. 24.95 (0-8214-1057-1); pap. 15.95 (0-8214-1077-6) Ohio U Pr.

America's Colorful Railroads. Don Ball. 1988. 17.99 (0-517-30488-0) Random Hse Value.

America's Coming-of-Age. Van Wyck Brooks. 18.95 (0-8488-0433-3) Amereon Ltd.

America's Coming Tax Revolt. Ed. by Matt S. Hellman et al. (Illus.). (Orig.). 1992. write for info. (1-882438-01-9); pap. write for info. (1-882438-00-0) Parrot Comm.

America's Commitment to Culture: Government & the Arts. Ed. by Kevin V. Mulcahy et al. 235p. 1994. text ed. 49.95 (0-8133-0692-2) Westview.

America's Commitment to South Korea: The First Decade of the Nixon Doctrine. Joo-Hong Nam. (London School of Economics Monographs in International Studies). (Illus.). 256p. 1986. 59.95 (0-521-26765-X) Cambridge U Pr.

*America's Competitive Secret: Women Managers. Judy B. Rosener. (Illus.). 288p. 1995. 25.00 (0-19-508079-3) OUP.

America's Constitutional Soul. Harvey C. Mansfield. LC 90-19210. (Series in Constitutional Thought). 224p. 1991. 35.00 (0-8018-4114-3) Johns Hopkins.

America's Constitutional Soul. Harvey C. Mansfield, Jr. (Series in Constitutional Thought). 224p. 1993. reprint ed. pap. 13.95 (0-8018-4634-X) Johns Hopkins.

America's Continuing Story: An Introduction to Serial Fiction, 1850-1900. Michael Lund. LC 92-18953. 228p. (C). 1992. text ed. 29.95 (0-8143-2401-0) Wayne St U Pr.

America's Corporate Families & International Affiliates, 1993. Dun & Bradstreet Information Services Staff. 1993. 470.00 (1-56203-267-4, 01222830) Dun & Bradstreet.

America's Corporate Families, 1993. Dun & Bradstreet Information Services Staff. 1993. 575.00 (1-56203-266-6, 01222834) Dun & Bradstreet.

America's Corporate Finance Directory 1994. National Register Publishing Staff. 2300p. 1994. 525.00 (0-87217-939-7) Natl Register.

***America's Corporate Finance Directory 1995. Ed. by National Register Press Editing Staff. LC 67-22770. 1600p. 1995. 479.00 (0-87217-940-0) Natl Register. AMERICA'S CORPORATE FINANCE DIRECTORY 1995 profiles 5,000 of America's leading companies including their 18,000 subsidiaries & 31,000 outside service firms. Entries provide vital corporate statistics, such as sales earnings, assets, liabilities, stock exchange ticker symbol, even details about the company's pension plan, contact information, & a listing of wholly-owned U.S. subsidiaries. Each entry also lists up to 23 financial service firms, including insurance brokers, insurers, pension managers, investment bankers, auditors, legal counsel & registrars. Hardbound format makes it easy to use!** *Publisher Provided Annotation.*

America's Correctional Crisis: Prison Populations & Public Policy. Ed. by Stephen D. Gottfredson & Sean McConville. LC 86-27143. (Contributions in Criminology & Penology Ser.). 266p. 1987. text ed. 55.00 (0-313-25487-7, MVC/, Greenwood Pr) Greenwood.

America's Cottage Gardens. Patricia Thorpe & Eve Sonneman. LC 89-42777. (Illus.). 192p. 1990. 29.95 (0-394-56989-X) Random.

*America's Country Schools. 3rd ed. Andrew Gulliford. (Illus.). 296p. (Orig.). 1996. pap. 19.95 (0-87081-413-3) Univ Pr Colo.

*America's Court & the Criminal Justice System. 5th ed. David W. Neubauer. LC 95-2518. 1996. text ed. 44.95 (0-534-23952-8) Intl Thomson.

America's Courts & the Criminal Justice System. 4th ed. David W. Neubauer. LC 91-32391. 489p. (C). 1992. text ed. 44.95 (0-534-15432-8) Intl Thomson.

America's Crisis Situation: AIDS via Fiat Money. Jerry L. Smith. LC 91-77180. 1991. pap. 24.95 (0-9631130-0-3) JLS Pub.

*America's Crossroads. (Illus.). 1993. write for info. (1-878097-12-1) Canisius Coll Pr.

America's Cube: Solving the Social Security Puzzle. Paul C. Light. 224p. (C). 1985. pap. text ed. write for info. (0-07-554485-7) McGraw.

*Americas Cumulative Twenty-Seven Year Index Vols. XXI-XLVII: 1964-1991. Contrib by Patsy H. Stann. 1991. pap. 15.00 (0-614-05571-7) AAFH.

America's Cup. Pat Ryan. (Great Moments in Sports Ser.). (J). (gr. 5 up). 1992. lib. bdg. 14.95 (0-88682-532-6) Creative Ed.

America's Cup. Intro. by Olin Stephens. (Beken of Cowes Maritime Ser.). (Illus.). 192p. Date not set. 60.00 (0-00-272077-9) T Reed Pubns.

America's Cup 1851-1992. Michael Levitt. (Illus.). 208p. 1992. 50.00 (1-55868-105-1) Gr Arts Ctr Pub.

America's Currency, 1789-1866. Intro. by Richard G. Doty. (Coinage of the Americas Conference at the American Numismatic Society, New York Ser.). (Illus.). 142p. 1986. 15.00 (0-89722-214-8) Am Numismatic.

America's Daughters. Suellen M. Fast. 100p. (Orig.). (J). (gr. k up). pap. 19.00 (0-935281-13-4) Daughter Cult.

America's Debt to John Peter Tetard, 1722-1787. William A. Tieck. LC 87-80017. (Illus.). 203p. 1987. 21.25 (0-9600398-2-1) W A Tieck.

*America's Declaration of Financial Independence. Robert H Schuller & Paul D. Dunn. 224p. 1995. reprint ed. 19.95 (1-55853-376-1) Rutledge Hill Pr.

America's Defense. Ed. by Michael Mandelbaum. LC 87-35705. 360p. 1989. 45.00 (0-8419-1156-8); pap. 24.95 (0-8419-1157-6) Holmes & Meier.

America's Defense: Opposing Viewpoints. Ed. by Carol Wekesser. LC 91-20163. (Opposing Viewpoints Ser.). (Illus.). 240p. (YA). (gr. 10 up). 1991. lib. bdg. 19.95 (0-89908-184-3); pap. 11.55 (0-89908-159-2) Greenhaven.

America's Democracy: The Ideal & the Reality. 3rd ed. Fred R. Harris. LC 85-14182. 751p. reprint ed. pap. 180.00 (0-7837-4510-9, 2044287) Bks Demand.

America's Detente Dilemma. Steve Spiegel. (Research Note Ser.: No. 18). 32p. (Orig.). Date not set. pap. 5.00 (0-86682-072-8) Ctr Intl Relations.

Americas Discovery Activities Kit: Ready-to-Use Worksheets for the Age of Exploration. Judie L. Strouf. 272p. 1991. spiral bd. 27.95 (0-87628-108-0) Ctr Appl Res.

America's Disposable Workforce. Charles P. Fetterman. (Illus.). 144p. 1994. 13.95 (0-8059-3544-4) Dorrance.

America's Downtowns: Growth, Politics & Preservation. Richard C. Collins et al. Ed. by Constance E. Beaumont. (Illus.). 162p. (Orig.). 1991. pap. 14.95 (0-89133-177-8) Preservation Pr.

America's Dream Team: The Nineteen Ninety-Two U. S. A. Basketball Team. Chuck Daly. 1992. pap. 19.95 (1-878685-29-5) Turner Pub GA.

*America's Dumbest Criminals. Daniel Butler et al. 224p. (Orig.). 1995. pap. 7.95 (1-55853-372-9) Rutledge Hill Pr.

America's Early Canals. Tim McNeese. LC 91-41353. (Americans on the Move Ser.). (Illus.). 48p. (J). (gr. 5). 1993. text ed. 11.95 (0-89686-730-7, Crstwood Hse) Silver Burdett Pr.

America's Early Taverns. (Americana Book Ser.). (Illus.). 1992. 4.50 (0-911410-51-1) Applied Arts.

America's Economic Growth. F. A. Shannon. 1990. lib. bdg. 75.00 (0-8490-4054-X) Gordon Pr.

America's Economic Heritage, 2 vols. Meyer Weinberg. LC 83-10877. (Documentary Reference Collections). (Illus.). 1136p. 1983. Vol. 1, From a Colonial to a Capitalist Economy 1634-1900. text ed. 100.00 (0-313-24135-X, WGE/01) Greenwood.

America's Economic Heritage, 2 vols., Set. Meyer Weinberg. LC 83-10877. (Documentary Reference Collections). (Illus.). 1136p. 1983. text ed. 195.00 (0-313-23751-4, WGE/) Greenwood.

America's Economic Heritage, 2 vols., Vol. 2. Meyer Weinberg. LC 83-10877. (Documentary Reference Collections). (Illus.). 1136p. 1983. text ed. 100.00 (0-313-24136-8, WGE/02) Greenwood.

America's Economic Supremacy. Brooks Adams. LC 77-152155. (Essay Index Reprint Ser.). 1977. reprint ed. 18.95 (0-8369-2477-0) Ayer.

America's Economic Supremacy. Brooks Adams. (Principle Works of Brooks Adams). 1989. reprint ed. lib. bdg. 79.00 (0-7812-2570-1) Rprt Serv.

America's Elderly: A Sourcebook. Ed. by Edward E. Duensing. LC 88-6132. 197p. 1988. 3.00 (0-88285-125-X) Ctr Urban Pol Res.

*America's Electric Utilities: Past, Present & Future. 5th ed. Leonard S. Hyman. (Illus.). 398p. 1994. pap. 50.00 (0-910325-51-0) Public Util.

America's Endangered Banks: Check the Safety of Your Savings. rev. ed. Kenneth Coleman. 36p. 1986. pap. 14.95 (0-942632-02-8) Seraphim Pr.

America's Energy Famine: Its Cause & Cure. Ruth S. Knowles. LC 80-8040. 352p. 1980. 26.95 (0-8061-1669-2) U of Okla Pr.

America's Ethnic Politics. Ed. by Joseph S. Roucek & Bernard Eisenberg. LC 81-986. (Contributions in Ethnic Studies: No. 5). (Illus.). x, 403p. 1982. text ed. 75.00 (0-313-22024-7, ROA/, Greenwood Pr) Greenwood.

*Americas Exhibition. Madeleine Grynsztejn. (Illus.). 96p. 1995. pap. 22.95 (0-614-07212-3) Art Inst Chi.

America's Fabrics: Origin & History, Manufacture, Characteristics & Uses. Zelma Bendure & Gladys Pfeiffer. LC 72-5260. (Technology & Society Ser.). (Illus.). 703p. 1972. reprint ed. 50.95 (0-405-04685-5) Ayer.

America's Fair Share: The Admission & Resettlement of Displaced Persons 1945-1952. Haim Genizi. 273p. 1994. text ed. 39.95 (0-8143-2460-6) Wayne St U Pr.

America's Family Crisis. Peter Popoff. Ed. by Don Tanner. LC 82-82843. 80p. 1982. pap. 2.00 (0-938544-15-2) Faith Messenger.

America's Family Support Programs: Perspectives & Prospects. Ed. by Sharon L. Kagan et al. 413p. (C). 1993. pap. 20.00 (0-300-05785-7) Yale U Pr.

America's Far Eastern Policy. Thomas A. Bisson. LC 75-30095. (Institute of Pacific Relations Ser.). reprint ed. 39.50 (0-404-59506-5) AMS Pr.

America's Fascinating Indian Heritage. Reader's Digest Editors. LC 78-55614. (Illus.). 416p. 1990. reprint ed. 30.00 (0-89577-372-4, Random) RD Assn.

America's Fastest Growing Employers: The Complete Guide to Finding Jobs with over 300 of America's Hottest Companies. 2nd ed. Carter Smith. LC 94-15472. 1994. 30.00 (1-55850-397-8); pap. 16.00 (1-55850-383-8) Adams Pubng.

America's Fastest Growing Jobs: A Complete Guide. 1992. lib. bdg. 250.95 (0-8490-5556-3) Gordon Pr.

America's Fastest Way to Become a Millionaire! The Magic Nine System. Mark J. Reynolds. 150p. 1986. 4.95 (0-915451-06-9) New Start Pubns.

America's Favorite Backyard Birds. Kit Harrison & George H. Harrison. 1989. pap. 12.00 (0-671-67341-6, Fireside) S&S Trade.

America's Favorite Backyard Wildlife. Kit Harrison & George H. Harrison. 1987. pap. 12.95 (0-671-63972-2, Fireside) S&S Trade.

America's Favorite Buildings: A Postcard Book. (Illus.). 20p. (Orig.). 1992. pap. 7.95 (0-89133-167-0) Preservation Pr.

An Asterisk (*) at the beginning of an entry indicates that the title is appearing in BIP for the first time.

A

An Asterisk (*) at the beginning of an entry indicates that the title is appearing in BIP for the first time.

America's Land & Its Uses. Marion Clawson. LC 70-167985. (Resources for the Future Ser.). (Illus.). 166p. 1972. pap. 8.95 (*0-8018-1330-1*) Johns Hopkins.

America's Land & Its Uses. Marion Clawson. LC 70-167985. (Illus.). 178p. reprint ed. pap. 50.80 (*0-8357-5407-3*, 2030194) Bks Demand.

America's Landfall: The Lighthouses of Cape Cod, Nantucket & Martha's Vineyard. Donald W. Davidson. LC 93-84725. (Illus.). 148p. 1993. pap. 9.95 (*1-883684-00-5*) Peninsula MA.

America's Last Declaration. Ryder Stacy. 1985. pap. 2.50 (*0-8217-1608-5*) Zebra.

America's Last Wild Horses. rev. ed. Hope Ryden. 1990. pap. 14.95 (*1-55821-081-4*) Lyons & Burford.

America's Leading Daily Newspapers. Michael Emery. 36p. (Orig.). 1983. pap. 6.00 (*0-89730-114-5*) Blue-Rib Grp.

America's Leading Lawyers. 160p. 1992. 165.00 (*0-685-60665-1*) Blue Bk CA.

America's Least Competent Criminals: True Tales of Would-Be Outlaws Who Have Botched, Bungled, & Otherwise Haplessly but Hilariously Fumbled Their Crimes. Chuck Shepherd. LC 92-56271. (Illus.). 224p. (Orig.). 1993. pap. 9.00 (*0-06-095002-1*, PL) HarpC.

America's Light Trucks. Motor Vehicle Manufacturers Association of the U. S. Staff. Ed. by Sheridan Brinley. 36p. 1986. write for info. (*0-943350-13-1*) Motor Veh Man.

America's Lighthouses: An Illustrated History. Francis R. Holland, Jr. (Illus.). 240p. 1988. reprint ed. pap. 10.95 (*0-486-25576-X*) Dover.

America's Literary Revolt. Michael Yatron. LC 70-99653. (Essay Index Reprint Ser.). 1977. 20.95 (*0-8369-1437-6*) Ayer.

America's Living Past. 1990. 19.99 (*0-517-69475-1*) Random Hse Value.

America's Longest War: Rethinking Our Tragic Crusade Against Drugs. Steven B. Duke & Albert C. Gross. 352p. 1994. 25.95 (*0-87477-541-8*, J P T-Putnam) Putnam Pub Group.

America's Longest War: Rethinking Our Tragic Crusade Against Drugs. Steven B. Duke & Albert C. Gross. 356p. 1994. reprint ed. pap. 13.95 (*0-87477-788-7*, J P T-Putnam) Putnam Pub Group.

America's Longest War: The United States & Vietnam, 1950-1975. George C. Herring. 298p. (C). 1979. pap. text ed. write for info. (*0-394-34185-6*) Random.

America's Longest War: The United States & Vietnam, 1950-1975. 2nd ed. George C. Herring. (C). 1986. pap. text ed. write for info. (*0-07-554795-3*) McGraw.

America's Longest War: The United States & Vietnam, 1950-1975. 2nd ed. George C. Herring. LC 85-30295. 296p. 1986. 39.95 (*0-87722-419-6*) Temple U Pr.

***America's Longest War: The United States & Vietnam, 1950-1975.** 3rd ed. George C. Herring. LC 95-16062. (America in Crisis Ser.). 1996. write for info. (*0-07-028393-1*) McGraw.

Americas Lost: The First Encounter, 1492-1713. Ed. by Daniel Levine. 192p. 1992. pap. 39.95 (*2-04-014499-4*, GC4994, Pub. by Grp De La Cite FR) UNIPUB.

America's Lowest Cost Colleges. Nicholas A. Roes. 256p. (Orig.). 1985. 12.95 (*0-88191-026-0*) Freundlich.

America's Lowest Cost Colleges. 6th rev. ed. Nicholas A. Roes. 128p. (Orig.). 1989. pap. 8.95 (*0-89780-010-9*) NAR Pubns.

***America's Lowest Cost Colleges.** 9th rev. ed. Nicholas A. Roes. 156p. (Orig.). 1995. pap. 9.95 (*0-89780-041-9*) NAR Pubns.

America's Lowest Cost Colleges: A Comprehensive Directory of More Than 1,000 Fully Accredited Colleges & Universities with Low or No Tuition. rev. ed. Nicholas A. Roes. 144p. 1991. pap. 9.95 (*0-89780-012-5*) NAR Pubns.

America's Lowest Cost Colleges: A Comprehensive Directory of More Than 1,000 Fully Accredited Colleges & Universities with Low or No Tuition. 8th rev. ed. Nicholas A. Roes. 1993. pap. 9.95 (*0-89780-014-1*) NAR Pubns.

America's Majestic Canyons. Ed. by Donald J. Crump. LC 78-61263. (Special Publications Series 14: No. 1). (Illus.). 1979. 16.00 (*0-87044-271-6*) Natl Geog.

America's March Toward Communism. Mark W. Hendrickson. 102p. (Orig.). 1987. pap. 5.95 (*0-910884-19-6*) Libertarian Press.

***America's Mass Media Merchants.** William H. Read. LC 76-17231. 222p. 1976. pap. 63.30 (*0-7837-7457-5*, 2049179) Bks Demand.

America's Medal of Honor Recipients. Government Printing Office Staff. LC 85-152004. 1110p. 1980. 18.95 (*0-9615009-0-5*) Highland Pub.

America's Military Revolution: Strategy & Structure after the Cold War. William E. Odom. LC 93-9704. 186p. (C). 1993. lib. bdg. 22.95 (*1-879383-15-2*) Am Univ Pr.

America's Minorities & the Multicultural Debate. Oliver Trager. 1992. 29.95 (*0-8160-2815-X*) Facts on File.

America's Mission: The United States & the Worldwide Struggle for Democracy in the Twentieth Century. Tony Smith. LC 94-11314. (Studies in International History & Politics). 1994. 24.95 (*0-691-03784-1*) Princeton U Pr.

America's Misunderstood Welfare State: Persistent Myths, Enduring Realities. Theodore R. Marmor et al. LC 90-80240. 268p. 1992. reprint ed. pap. 14.00 (*0-465-00123-8*) Basic.

***America's Modernisms: Revaluing the Canon Essays in Honor of Joseph N. Riddel.** Ed. by Kathryne V. Lindberg & Joseph G. Kronick. (Horizons in Theory & American Culture Ser.). (Illus.). 256p. (C). 1995. text ed. 35.00 (*0-8071-2018-9*) La State U Pr.

America's Money Trauma: How Washington Blunders Crippled the U. S. Financial System. William B. O'Connell. 176p. (Orig.). 1992. pap. 14.95 (*0-9634395-0-2*) Conversation Pr.

America's Most Admired Corporations Research Report 1994. Fortune Magazine Staff et al. 270p. 1994. pap. 995.00 (*0-9640489-0-6*) Occam Res.

America's Most Challenging Objectives. Ed. by Richard D. Lambert. LC 76-160739. (Annals Ser.: 396). 1971. 27.00 (*0-87761-140-8*); pap. 18.00 (*0-87761-139-4*) Am Acad Pol Soc Sci.

America's Most Charming Towns & Villages: A Traveller's Guide to the 200 Most Enchanting. Larry Brown. 400p. 1994. pap. 14.95 (*1-883323-09-6*) Open Rd Pub.

America's Most Haunted Places. Nancy Roberts. (Illus.). 95p. (J). (gr. 4 up). 1987. reprint ed. pap. 8.95 (*0-87844-074-7*) Sandlapper Pub Co.

America's Most Influential First Ladies. Carl S. Anthony. LC 92-18444. (Profiles Ser.). (Illus.). 160p. (YA). (gr. 5-12). 1992. lib. bdg. 14.95 (*1-881508-00-5*) Oliver Pr MN.

America's Most Wanted. Jack Breslin. 1990. mass mkt. 4.95 (*0-06-100025-6*, Harp PBks) HarpC.

America's Mount Olympus: What's Really Gone Wrong in Corporate America & How Its Shareholders Can Fix It. Edwin M. Bartee. (Illus.). 256p. (Orig.). 1993. pap. 16.00 (*0-9635771-0-7*) Henderson Grp.

America's Mountain. 2nd ed. Ed. by Pearl Richard & Mignon W. Pearl. (Illus.). 36p. 1990. reprint ed. pap. 3.50 (*0-936564-38-5*) Little London.

America's Mountains. Clark Hubler. (Illus.). 272p. 1994. 35.00 (*0-8160-2661-0*) Facts on File.

America's Music: From the Pilgrims to the Present. 3rd ed. Gilbert Chase. LC 86-30795. (Music in American Life Ser.). 744p. 1987. 34.95 (*0-252-00454-X*) U of Ill Pr.

***America's Music: From the Pilgrims to the Present.** 3rd fac. rev. ed. Gilbert Chase. LC 86-30795. (Music in American Life Ser.). (Illus.). 742p. 1994. pap. 180.00 (*0-7837-7613-6*, 2047365) Bks Demand.

America's Music: From the Pilgrims to the Present. 3rd rev. ed. Gilbert Chase. 1992. pap. 24.95 (*0-252-06275-2*) U of Ill Pr.

America's Musical Landscape. Jean Ferris. 320p. (C). 1990. pap. write for info. (*0-697-03055-5*) Brown & Benchmark.

America's Musical Landscape. 2nd ed. Jean Ferris. 352p. (C). 1993. pap. text ed. write for info. (*0-697-12516-5*); audio, pap. text ed. 39.87 (*0-697-16946-4*); audio write for info. (*0-697-12518-1*) Brown & Benchmark.

America's Musical Pulse: Popular Music in Twentieth-Century Society. Ed. by Kenneth J. Bindas. LC 92-1122. (Contributions to the Study of Popular Culture Ser.: No. 33). 328p. 1992. text ed. 55.00 (*0-313-27465-7*, BIZ/, Greenwood Pr); pap. text ed. 17.95 (*0-275-94306-2*, B4306, Praeger Pubs) Greenwood.

America's Musical Stage: Two Hundred Years of Musical Theatre. Julian Mates. LC 85-935. (Contributions in Drama & Theatre Studies: No. 18). (Illus.). xii, 252p. 1985. text ed. 55.00 (*0-313-23948-7*, MLY/, Greenwood Pr) Greenwood.

America's Musical Stage: Two Hundred Years of Musical Theatre. Julian Mates. (Illus.). 264p. 1987. pap. text ed. 15.95 (*0-275-92714-8*, B2714, Praeger Pubs) Greenwood.

America's Mysterious Places. Hans Holzer. LC 92-15894. (Illus.). 192p. 1992. 14.98 (*0-681-41571-1*) Longmeadow Pr.

America's Nation-Time: 1607-1789. Benjamin W. Labaree. 272p. 1976. reprint ed. pap. 9.95 (*0-393-00821-5*) Norton.

America's National Battlefield Parks: A Guide. Joseph E. Stevens. LC 89-40739. (Illus.). 352p. 1990. 32.95 (*0-8061-2268-4*) U of Okla Pr.

America's National Battlefield Parks: A Guide. Joseph E. Stevens. LC 89-40739. (Illus.). 352p. 1991. pap. 19.95 (*0-8061-2319-2*) U of Okla Pr.

America's National Gallery of Art: A Gift to the Nation. Philip Kopper. (Illus.). 320p. 1991. 60.00 (*0-8109-3658-5*) Abrams.

America's National Gallery of Art: A Gift to the Nation. Philip Kopper & George Bush. LC 90-28788. (Illus.). 338p. 1991. 47.50 (*0-89468-159-1*) Natl Gallery Art.

America's National Game. A. G. Spaulding. 542p. 1991. 35.00 (*0-941567-19-2*) J C & A L Fawcett.

America's National Game. Albert G. Spalding. LC 91-43078. (Illus.). xxviii, 550p. 1992. reprint ed. 45.00 (*0-8032-4220-4*); reprint ed. pap. 19.95 (*0-8032-9207-4*) U of Nebr Pr.

America's National Game of Chance: Video Poker. Lenny Frome. Ed. by Maryann Guberman. LC 97-71652. (Illus.). 200p. (Orig.). 1992. pap. 19.95 (*0-9623766-8-X*) Compu-Flyers.

America's National Interest in a Post-Cold War World: Issues & Dilemmas. Ed. by Alvin Z. Rubinstein. LC 93-33417. 1993. pap. text ed. write for info. (*0-07-054162-0*) McGraw.

America's National Monuments: The Politics of Preservation. Hal Rothman. (Illus.). 280p. 1994. pap. 14.95 (*0-7006-0672-6*) U Pr of KS.

America's National Park. James P. Delgado. 1991. 24.99 (*0-517-03170-1*) Random Hse Value.

America's National Park System: The Critical Document. Ed. by Larry M. Dilsaver. 400p. (C). 1994. lib. bdg. 75.00 (*0-8476-7922-5*) Rowman.

America's National Parks. 1985. 14.99 (*0-517-40552-0*) Random Hse Value.

America's National Parks. 1991. 29.98 (*0-8317-0319-9*) Smithmark.

America's National Parks. Outlet Staff. 1993. 14.99 (*0-517-06044-2*) Random Hse Value.

America's National Parks: National Park Service 75th Anniversary. (Illus.). 256p. 1993. 29.95 (*0-88176-959-2*, 3300200) Pubns Intl Ltd.

America's National Parks: Photographic Journey. Outlet Book Company Staff. (Illus.). 1993. 14.99 (*0-517-07257-2*) Random Hse Value.

America's National Parks & Their Keepers. Ronald A. Foresta. LC 83-43262. 382p. 1984. lib. bdg. 45.00 (*0-915707-02-0*); pap. text ed. 18.95 (*0-915707-03-9*) Resources Future.

***America's National Pastime: A Study of Race & Merit in Professional Baseball.** Bret L. Billet & Lance J. Formwalt. LC 95-3331. 184p. 1995. text ed. 49.95 (*0-275-95193-6*, Praeger Pubs) Greenwood.

America's Natural Beauty. Ed. by Ideals Editorial Staff. (Illus.). 160p. 1993. 22.95 (*0-8249-4048-2*) Ideals.

America's Natural Beauty. P. N. Steele. 1993. 12.99 (*0-517-49640-2*) Random Hse Value.

America's Natural Resources. Ed. by Charles H. Callison. LC 67-14482. 229p. reprint ed. pap. 65.30 (*0-8357-5408-1*, 2055092) Bks Demand.

America's Nazis: A Democratic Dilemma. Susan Canedy. LC 88-63604. (Illus.). 240p. (C). 1990. 28.95 (*0-944109-07-1*); pap. 18.95 (*0-944109-06-3*) Margraf Pubns Grp.

America's Neighborhood Bats: Understanding & Learning to Live in Harmony with Them. Merlin D. Tuttle. (Illus.). 104p. (YA). (gr. 10-12). 1988. 19.95 (*0-292-70403-8*); pap. 9.95 (*0-292-70406-2*) U of Tex Pr.

***America's Network Directory 1995.** Ed. by America's Network Magazine Staff. 200p. 1994. pap. 125.00 (*0-929870-30-1*) Advanstar Commns.

America's New Blue Chips: An Investment Guide to the Hottest Growth Stocks. Gene Walden. LC 92-45078. 288p. 1993. 24.95 (*0-681-41641-6*) Longmeadow Pr.

America's New Foundation 1997. Bohdan R. Romaniuk. Date not set. 150.00 (*1-56995-001-6*) Taft Group.

America's New Foundations 1996, Vol. 1. Bohdan R. Romaniuk. 1995. 170.00 (*1-56995-000-8*) Taft Group.

America's New Immigration Law: Origins, Rationales, & Potential Consequences. Wayne A. Cornelius & Ricardo Anzaldua. (Monograph Ser.: No. 11). 182p. (C). 1983. ring bd. 10.95 (*0-935391-49-5*, MN-11) UCSD Ctr US-Mex.

***America's New War on Poverty: A Reader for Action.** Ed. by Blackside, Inc. Staff & Robert Lavelle. LC 94-40666. (Illus.). 288p. (Orig.). 1994. pap. 12.95 (*0-912333-37-5*) KQED.

America's New Wolf. Gene Letourneau. (Illus.). 116p. 1984. pap. 8.95 (*0-930096-34-7*) G Gannett.

***America's Newcomers: A State & Local Policymakers' Guide to Immigration Immigrant Policy.** Jonathan C. Dunlap. 32p. 1993. 10.00 (*1-55516-930-9*, 9353) Natl Conf State Legis.

***America's Newcomers: An Immigrant Policy Handbook.** Ed. by Ann Morse. 108p. 1994. 35.00 (*1-55516-996-1*, 9366) Natl Conf State Legis.

***America's Newcomers: Community Relations & Ethnic Diversity.** Ann Morse & Jonathan C. Dunlap. 20p. 1994. 10.00 (*1-55516-995-3*, 9365) Natl Conf State Legis.

***America's Newcomers: Employment & Training Programs for Refugees & Immigrants.** Ann Morse. 18p. 1993. 10.00 (*1-55516-927-9*, 9360) Natl Conf State Legis.

***America's Newcomers: Health Care Issues for New Americans.** Jonathan C. Dunlap. 18p. 1993. 10.00 (*1-55516-928-7*, 9359) Natl Conf State Legis.

America's Next Twenty Years. Peter F. Drucker. LC 72-6759. (Essay Index Reprint Ser.). 1980. reprint ed. 18.95 (*0-8369-7267-8*) Ayer.

America's Nonprofit Sector: A Primer. Lester M. Salamon. LC 92-11083. 120p. (Orig.). (C). 1992. pap. 14.95 (*0-87954-451-1*) Foundation Ctr.

America's North Coast Gateway: Minneapolis-St. Paul International Airport. Karl D. Bremer. (Illus.). 208p. 1993. 34.95 (*1-882933-00-1*) Cherbo Pub Grp.

America's Northern Heartland. John R. Borchert. LC 86-4317. (Illus.). 264p. (Orig.). 1988. pap. text ed. 24.95 (*0-8166-1499-7*) U of Minn Pr.

America's Oak Furniture. Nancy Schiffer. LC 88-64078. (Illus.). 128p. 1989. pap. 19.95 (*0-88740-158-9*) Schiffer.

America's Obsession: Sports & Society since 1945. Richard O. Davies. Ed. by Gerald D. Nash & Richard W. Etulain. (Books on America since 1945 Ser.). 192p. (C). 1994. pap. text ed. 18.75 (*0-03-073332-4*) HB Coll Pubs.

America's Old Masters: Benjamin West, John Singleton Copley, Charles Willson Peale & Gilbert Stuart. James T. Flexner. (Illus.). 448p. 1994. reprint ed. pap. 12.95 (*0-486-27957-X*) Dover.

America's Older Population. Paul E. Zopf, Jr. LC 84-71505. 344p. (C). 1986. text ed. 34.95 (*0-88105-055-5*); pap. text ed. 26.95 (*0-88105-056-3*) Cap & Gown.

America's Only Hope: Impacting Society in the '90s. Anthony T. Evans. pap. 8.99 (*0-8024-0742-0*) Moody.

America's Original Sin: A Study Guide on White Racism. Sojourners Editors. 180p. 1994. pap. 10.00 (*0-9641109-0-3*) Sojrners.

America's Other Voice: The Story of Radio Free Europe & Radio Liberty. Sig Mickelson. LC 83-13659. 288p. 1983. text ed. 55.00 (*0-275-91722-3*, C1722, Praeger Pubs) Greenwood.

America's Outdoor Wonders: State Parks & Sanctuaries. Ed. by Donald J. Crump. LC 87-11001. (Special Publications Series 22: No. 1). (Illus.). 200p. 1987. 16.00 (*0-87044-624-X*) Natl Geog.

America's Painted Ladies: The Ultimate Celebration of Our Victorians. Elizabeth Pomada & Michael Larsen. LC 92-52872. (Illus.). 304p. 1992. 40.00 (*0-525-93440-5*, Dutton Studio) Studio Bks.

America's Painted Ladies: The Ultimate Celebration of Our Victorians. Elizabeth Pomada & Michael Larsen. LC 92-52872. (Illus.). 304p. 1994. 24.95 (*0-14-023857-3*, Viking Studio) Studio Bks.

America's Patriotic Poems & Prose. George Shea. 100p. 1991. pap. 12.00 (*0-9630113-0-8*) G&C.

America's Paul Revere. Esther Forbes. (Illus.). 48p. (J). (gr. 3-5). 1990. pap. 5.95 (*0-395-24907-4*) HM.

America's Paul Revere. Esther Forbes. LC 90-48984. (American Cavalcade Ser.). (Illus.). 88p. (J). (gr. 6-10). 1991. lib. bdg. 9.95 (*1-55905-093-4*) Marshall Cavendish.

America's Pay-Per-Call Directory: A Billion Dollar Baby. Barry W. Winton. 200p. 1991. pap. 5.95 (*0-9630041-1-5*) Infoman Pub.

America's Philosophical Vision. John E. Smith. LC 91-22376. 200p. 1992. lib. bdg. 39.95 (*0-226-76367-6*); pap. text ed. 15.95 (*0-226-76368-4*) U Ch Pr.

America's Phone Book. Comp. by General Information, Inc. Staff. 800p. 1989. pap. 12.95 (*0-318-41874-6*) P-H.

America's Phunniest Phellow - Josh Billings. Ed. by James E. Myers. 275p. 1985. 14.95 (*0-942936-05-1*); pap. 7.95 (*0-942936-07-8*) Lincoln-Herndon Pr.

America's Planetariums & Observatories: A Sampling. R. L. Beck & Daryl Schrader. (Illus.). 230p. 1991. pap. 16.95 (*0-9630565-0-6*) Sunwest Space.

America's Poisoned Playground: Children & Toxic Chemicals. 55p. 1983. 9.95 (*0-685-09945-8*) CPA Washington.

America's Polish Heritage: A Social History of the Poles in America. Joseph A. Wytrwal. (Illus.). 1961. 7.50 (*0-685-09283-6*) Endurance.

America's Political Dilemma: From Limited to Unlimited Democracy. Gottfried Dietze. LC 85-13338. 310p. 1985. reprint ed. pap. text ed. 22.50 (*0-8191-4788-5*) U Pr of Amer.

America's Political System. 4th ed. Peter Woll & Robert H. Binstock. (C). 1984. student ed 8.95 (*0-685-07246-0*) McGraw.

America's Political System: A Text with Cases, Fifth Edition. 5th ed. Peter Woll & Robert Binstock. 1991. pap. text ed. write for info. (*0-07-071584-X*) McGraw.

America's Power Brokers. Ed. by Christopher Bandouveris. 450p. 1987. pap. write for info. (*0-941105-00-8*) Power Pubns.

America's Prairies. Frank Staub. LC 93-7841. (J). 1993. 19.95 (*0-87614-781-3*, Carolrhoda) Lerner Group.

America's Presidents Activity & Fun Book. Elvira Gamiello. (Illus.). (Orig.). (J). (gr. 4-6). 1989. pap. 1.95 (*0-942025-51-2*) Kidsbks.

America's Prisoner of War 1943-1946. William Oberdieck. 1995. 9.95 (*0-8062-4981-1*) Carlton.

America's Prisons. rev. ed. Stacey Tipp. LC 91-12661. (Opposing Viewpoints Ser.). (Illus.). 264p. (YA). (gr. 10 up). 1991. lib. bdg. 19.95 (*0-89908-178-9*); pap. text ed. 11.55 (*0-89908-153-3*) Greenhaven.

America's Private Carriers. Transportation Technical Services Staff. (Illus.). 82p. student ed 60.00 (*1-880701-03-0*) Trans Tech Srvs.

America's Problems: Social Issues & Public Policy. 2nd ed. Elliott Currie & Jerome H. Skolnick. (C). 1988. text ed. 57.50 (*0-673-39714-9*) HarpCollege.

America's Productivity Slump: Are We Working Hard Enough? William G. Belding & Roger W. Widness. (Illus.). 216p. (Orig.). 1989. pap. 11.95 (*0-685-29366-1*) PTV Pubns.

***America's Providential History.** Mark A. Beliles & Stephen K. McDowell. 300p. 1989. pap. 14.95 (*1-887456-00-7*) Providence Found.

***America's Psychic Malignancy: The Problem of Crime, Substance Abuse, Poverty & Welfare - Identifying Causes with Possible Remedies.** Norman Q. Brill. (American Series Psychiatry & Law). 150p. 1993. pap. 16.95 (*0-398-06031-2*) C C Thomas.

America's Psychic Malignancy: The Problem of Crime, Substance Abuse, Poverty & Welfare - Identifying Causes with Possible Remedies. Norman Q. Brill. (American Series Psychiatry & Law). 150p. (C). 1993. text ed. 31.95x (*0-398-05831-8*) C C Thomas.

America's Purpose: Toward a New Foreign Policy. Ed. by Owen Harries. 190p. (C). 1991. 19.95 (*1-55815-131-1*) ICS Pr.

***America's Pursuit of Precision Bombing.** Stephen L. McFarland. LC 94-21955. (History of Aviation Ser.). 368p. 1995. 29.95 (*1-56098-407-4*) Smithsonian.

America's Quest for Supremacy in the Third World: An Essay in Gramscian Analysis. Enrico Augelli & Craig Murphy. 200p. 1989. text ed. 49.00 (*0-86187-930-9*, Pub. by Pinter Pubs UK) St Martin.

America's Quest for the Ideal Self: Dissent & Fulfillment in the 60s & 70s. Peter Clecak. 1985. pap. 18.95 (*0-19-503544-5*) OUP.

America's Quilts. Jacqueline M. Atkins & Merikay Waldvogel. (Illus.). 192p. 1993. 19.98 (*0-88176-960-6*, 3300100) Pubns Intl Ltd.

America's Quilts & Coverlets. C. L. Safford & R. Bishop. 1985. 15.95 (*0-517-14391-7*) Random Hse Value.

America's Race Heritage: An Account of the Diffusion of Ancestral Stocks in the United States. Clinton S. Burr. LC 76-46069. (Anti-Movements in America Ser.). 1977. reprint ed. lib. bdg. 37.95 (*0-405-09943-6*) Ayer.

America's Race Problems. American Academy of Political & Social Science Staff. LC 72-95419. (Studies in Black History & Culture: No. 54). 1970. reprint ed. lib. bdg. 58.95 (*0-8383-0959-3*) M S G Haskell Hse.

America's Radical Right, 1962. Raymond Wolfinger et al. 1974. write for info. (*0-89138-069-8*) ICPSR.

America's Railroads: The Second Generation. Don Ball, Jr. (Illus.). 224p. 1980. 55.00 (*0-393-01416-9*) Norton.

America's Rain Forests. Karen Kane. 160p. 1991. 45.00 (*1-55971-129-9*) NorthWord.

An Asterisk (*) at the beginning of an entry indicates that the title is appearing in BIP for the first time.

America's Real Religion: Separation Between Religion & Government in the U.S.A. Gene Garman. LC 91-70374. 128p. (Orig.). 1991. pap. 5.00 (*0-9629306-0-1*) Amer Real Relgn.

Americas Reconstruction. Eric Foner. Date not set. 30.00 (*0-685-69291-4*, HarpT) HarpC.

America's Reconstruction. Eric Foner. 1995. pap. 17.50 (*0-06-096989-X*) HarpC.

America's Recovery Program. A. A. Berle, Jr. et al. Ed. by Clair Wilcox et al. LC 76-104990. (Essay Index Reprint Ser.). 1977. 23.95 (*0-8369-1591-7*) Ayer.

America's Religions: Traditions & Cultures. Peter W. Williams. 496p. (C). 1989. pap. write for info. (*0-02-427880-7*) Macmillan.

America's Renewable Resources: Historical Trends & Current Challenges. Ed. by Kenneth D. Frederick & Roger A. Sedjo. LC 91-23102. (Illus.). (C). 1991. text ed. 34.95 (*0-915707-60-8*); pap. text ed. 19.95 (*0-915707-61-6*) Resources Future.

America's Response to China: A History of Sino-American Relations. 3rd ed. Warren I. Cohen. 256p. 1989. text ed. 47.50 (*0-231-06804-2*); pap. text ed. 14.00 (*0-231-06805-0*) Col U Pr.

America's Restless Ghosts. Hans Holzer. 192p. 1993. 14.98 (*0-681-45231-5*) Longmeadow Pr.

America's Revolutionary Heritage. rev. ed. Ed. & Intro. by George Novack. LC 76-12292. 1993. reprint ed. lib. bdg. 60.00 (*0-87348-464-9*); reprint ed. pap. 21.96 (*0-87348-465-7*) Pathfinder NY.

America's Right Turn: From Nixon to Bush. William C. Berman. LC 93-38003. (American Moment Ser.). 1994. text ed. 38.95 (*0-8018-4825-3*); pap. 12.95 (*0-8018-4826-1*) Johns Hopkins.

***America's Rising Star Chefs: At the Robert Mondavi Great Chefs Cooking School in Napa Valley.** Robert Mondavi. 1994. pap. 19.95 (*0-9641403-0-6*) Santa Fe Ventures.

America's Road to Empire: The War with Spain & Overseas Expansion. H. Wayne Morgan. 124p. (C). 1965. pap. text ed. write for info. (*0-07-554680-9*) McGraw.

America's Road to Socialism. James P. Cannon. LC 74-26234. 128p. 1978. reprint ed. pap. 11.95 (*0-87348-417-7*) Pathfinder NY.

America's Robert E. Lee. Henry S. Commager. LC 90-48983. (American Cavalcade Ser.). (Illus.). 128p. (J). (gr. 6-10). 1991. lib. bdg. 13.95 (*1-55905-088-8*) Marshall Cavendish.

America's Role in International Social Welfare. Alva Myrdal et al. 11.25 (*0-8446-1320-7*) Peter Smith.

America's Role in the World. National Issues Forum Staff. 32p. 1991. 2.95 (*0-8403-6925-5*) Kendall-Hunt.

America's Rome, Vol. 2: Catholic & Contemporary Rome. William Vance. LC 88-20737. 544p. (C). 1989. text ed. 40.00 (*0-300-04453-4*) Yale U Pr.

***America's Royalty: All the Presidents' Children.** expanded rev. ed. Sandra L. Quinn & Sanford Kanter. LC 95-7545. 304p. 1995. text ed. 59.95 (*0-313-29535-2*, Greenwood Pr) Greenwood.

America's Rural Hub: Railroading in Central Illinois in the Late Twentieth Century. Stanley A. Changnon. (Illus.). 220p. 1991. pap. 39.95 (*1-878044-04-4*) Mayhaven Pub.

America's Saints: The Rise of Mormon Power. Robert Gottlieb & Peter Wiley. LC 85-24879. 288p. 1986. pap. 5.95 (*0-15-605658-5*, Harvest Bks) HarBrace.

America's Schools: Passing the Test of the '80s? Ed. by Carol C. Collins & Tracey Dewart. LC 85-20412. (Editorials on File Book Ser.). (Illus.). 239p. reprint ed. pap. 68.20 (*0-8357-4240-7*, 2037028) Bks Demand.

America's Schools & Churches. David W. Beggs. LC 65-12279. 253p. reprint ed. pap. 72.20 (*0-8357-5409-X*, 2055190) Bks Demand.

America's Schools & the Mass Media. Ed. by Everette E. Dennis & Craig L. LaMay. 155p. (C). 1992. pap. 18.95 (*1-56000-652-8*) Transaction Pubs.

America's Science Museums. Victor J. Danilov. LC 90-33627. 496p. 1990. text ed. 65.00 (*0-313-25865-1*, DVS, Greenwood Pr) Greenwood.

***America's Seal: It's End-Time Connection: How the Great Seal of the United States, the New Age Movement, & Biblical End-Time Prophecy Merge.** James J. Jefferies. 300p. (Orig.). 1994. pap. text ed. 13.95 (*0-9642275-0-9*) Battleline Pubns.

America's Search for Economic Stability: Monetary & Fiscal Policy since 1913. Kenneth Weiher. (Twayne's Evolution of American Business Ser.: No. 9). 250p. (C). 1992. text ed. 26.95 (*0-8057-9813-7*, Twayne) Macmillan.

America's Search for Economic Stability: Monetary & Fiscal Policy since 1913. Kenneth Weiher. (Twayne's Evolution of American Business Ser.: No. 9). 250p. (C). 1992. pap. 14.95 (*0-8057-9819-6*, Twayne) Macmillan.

America's Seashore Wonderlands. Ed. by Donald J. Crump. LC 85-25848. (Special Publications Series 20: No. 2). (Illus.). 1985. 16.00 (*0-87044-543-X*) Natl Geog.

America's Second Crusade. William H. Chamberlin. 1962. pap. 2.00 (*0-87926-000-9*) R Myles.

America's Secret Aristocracy. Stephen Birmingham. 1990. pap. 4.95 (*0-425-11912-2*) Berkley Pub.

America's Secret Aristocracy. Stephen Birmingham. (Illus.). 334p. 1991. 4.99 (*0-517-67616-8*) Random Hse Value.

America's Secret Destiny: Spiritual Vision & the Founding of a Nation. Robert R. Hieronimus. 224p. 1989. pap. 10.95 (*0-89281-255-9*, Destiny Bks) Inner Tradit.

America's Secret Government. 1992. lib. bdg. 75.00 (*0-8490-5437-0*) Gordon Pr.

America's Secret Power: The CIA in a Democratic Society. Loch K. Johnson. (Illus.). 368p. 1989. 30.00 (*0-19-505490-3*) OUP.

America's Secret Power: The CIA in a Democratic Society. Loch K. Johnson. (Illus.). 368p. 1991. pap. 12.95 (*0-19-506944-7*) OUP.

***America's Secret Recreation Area: Your Recreation Guide to the Bureau of Land Management's Wild Lands of the West.** 2nd ed. Michael Hodgson. 640p. 1995. pap. 17.95 (*0-935701-61-3*) Foghorn Pr.

America's Secret Recreation Areas: Your Guide to the Forgotten Wild Lands of the Bureau of Land Management. Michael Hodgson. (Illus.). 557p. (Orig.). 1993. pap. 15.95 (*0-935701-60-5*) Foghorn Pr.

***America's Secret War Against Bolshevism: United States Intervention in the Russian Civil War, 1917-1920.** David S. Foglesong. LC 94-49528. 1995. write for info. (*0-8078-2228-0*) U of NC Pr.

America's Security in the Nineteen Eighties. Christopher Bertram. LC 82-16814. 200p. 1983. text ed. 32.50 (*0-312-02199-2*) St Martin.

***America's Sexual Crisis: And Its Resolution.** Anne S. Hastings. 1995. 21.00 (*0-9637891-5-5*) Atrium Pubs.

***America's Sexual Crisis: And Its Resolution.** Anne S. Hastings. 336p. 1995. pap. 15.00 (*0-9637891-6-3*) Printed Voice.

***America's Shasta Dam: A History of Construction, 1936-1945.** Al M. Rocca & J. Paul Capener. (Illus.). 165p. (Orig.). 1994. pap. 15.95 (*0-9643378-0-0*) Renown Pubng.

America's Siberian Adventure. William. Graves. 1972. 59.95 (*0-87968-615-4*) Gordon Pr.

America's Siberian Adventure, 1918-1920. William S. Graves. LC 76-150951. (Russia Observed Ser.). (Illus.). 1971. reprint ed. 21.95 (*0-405-03083-5*) Ayer.

America's Siberian Expedition, 1918-1920: A Study of National Policy. Betty M. Unterberger. LC 69-14128. 271p. 1969. reprint ed. text ed. 59.75 (*0-8371-0726-1*, UNSE, Greenwood Pr) Greenwood.

America's Silver Coinage, 1794-1891: Coinage of the Americas Conference at the American Numismatic Society, New York, Proceedings, No. 3. Intro. by Richard G. Doty. 210p. 1987. 15.00 (*0-89722-219-9*) Am Numismatic.

America's Silver Coinage, 1794-1891, No. 6: Handbook. John W. McCloskey. 38p. 1986. 6.00 (*0-685-72023-3*); boxed, sl. 25.00 (*0-685-72024-1*) Am Numismatic.

America's Soapbox: Seventy-Five Years of Free Speaking at Cleveland's City Club Forum. Mark Gottlieb & Diana Tittle. LC 87-14684. (Illus.). 256p. 1987. 17.95 (*0-940601-03-6*, Citizens Pr) Octavia Ohio.

America's Soccer Heritage: A History of the Game. Sam Foulds & Paul Harris. LC 79-63981. (Illus.). 1979. pap. 8.95 (*0-916802-14-0*) Soccer for Am.

America's Society of Separated & Divorced Men, Inc. 97p. write for info. (*0-318-59904-X*) Am Soc Separated.

America's South: The Atlantic States. Tom Weil. (U. S. A. Guides Ser.). (Illus.). 400p. (Orig.). 1993. pap. 14.95 (*0-7818-0139-7*) Hippocrene Bks.

***America's Spelling & Reading with Riggs Series.** Myrna McCullough. (Illus.). 1993. pap. write for info. (*0-924277-10-6*) K & M Pub.

America's Spelling & Reading with Riggs Series: Supplements to The Writing Road to Reading. Myrna T. McCulloch. Ed. by R. J. Huneger. (Illus.). 1993. write for info. (*0-318-66814-9*); Self-study course with audio cass. 17.50 (*0-924277-08-4*); Orton phonogram cards with handwriting instructions, boxed set of 70. 20.00 (*0-924277-06-8*); Orton phonogram tape with visual aids & spelling rules. 6.50 (*0-924277-07-6*); Spelling & Usage Vocabulary Builder, 478p. 26.50 (*0-685-74194-X*); Tchr.'s ed. teacher ed, pap. 43.50 (*0-924277-02-5*); Lesson plans, study guide, syllabus, 25p. pap. 12.95 (*0-924277-09-2*) K & M Pub.

America's Stake in European Telecommunication Policies. Alfred L. Thimm. LC 91-44111. 272p. 1992. text ed. 55.00 (*0-89930-544-X*, TGE/, Quorum Bks) Greenwood.

America's Stake in International Investments. Cleona Lewis & Karl T. Schlotterbeck. Ed. by Stuart Bruchey & Eleanor Bruchey. LC 76-5015. (Essay Index Reprint Ser.). 1976. reprint ed. 62.95 (*0-405-09283-0*) Ayer.

America's State Church: Will It Be the Dominant Religion in the Twenty First Century? Jay Liechty. 197p. (Orig.). 1994. pap. 11.95 (*0-9624576-1-2*) Calder Pr.

America's States: Building a Progressive Future. Ed. by Linda Tarr-Whelan & Jeffrey Tryens. 350p. 1986. 14.95 (*0-89788-096-X*) CPA Washington.

America's Stealth Fighters & Bombers. James C. Goodall. LC 92-10964. (Illus.). 128p. 1992. pap. 19.95 (*0-87938-609-6*) Motorbooks Intl.

America's Story As Told in Postage Stamps. E. M. Allen. 1975. 250.00 (*0-87968-381-3*) Gordon Pr.

America's Strategy in a Changing World. Ed. by Sean M. Lynn-Jones & Steven E. Miller. (International Security Reader Ser.). (Illus.). 410p. 1993. 18.00x (*0-262-62085-5*) MIT Pr.

America's Struggle Against Poverty, 1900-1985. rev. ed. James T. Patterson. 320p. 1986. pap. 15.95 (*0-674-03122-9*) HUP.

***America's Struggle Against Poverty, 1900-1994.** James T. Patterson. LC 94-22736. 323p. 1995. pap. text ed. 16.95 (*0-674-03123-7*, PATAMZ) HUP.

America's Struggle for Leadership in Technology. Jean-Claude Derian. Tr. by Severen Schaeffer. 336p. 1990. 32.50x (*0-262-04102-2*) MIT Pr.

America's Struggle for Leadership in Technology. Jean-Claude Derian. Tr. by Severen Schaeffer. (Illus.). 324p. 1992. pap. 15.00 (*0-262-54070-3*) MIT Pr.

Americas Study Guide. Barbara Cruz. (Illus.). 200p. (C). 1993. pap. text ed. 18.95 (*0-19-507793-8*) OUP.

America's Suburban Centers. Robert Cervero. 256p. 1989. text ed. 49.95 (*0-04-445333-7*) Routledge Chapman & Hall.

America's Suburban Gangs see Wannabe

America's Taj Mahal: The Singing Tower of Florida. 2nd ed. Edward W. Bok. 48p. 1989. reprint ed. 14.95 (*0-9623313-0-9*) Bok Tower.

America's Teacher Quality Problem: Alternatives for Reform. Timothy Weaver. LC 83-13804. 286p. 1984. text ed. 49.95 (*0-275-91289-2*, C1289, Praeger Pubs) Greenwood.

America's Teachers: An Introduction to Education. 2nd ed. Joseph W. Newman. LC 93-16924. 355p. (Orig.). (C). 1994. teacher ed write for info. (*0-8013-1424-0*, 76491); pap. text ed. 31.95 (*0-8013-0843-7*, 78910) Longman.

America's Teachers: Profile of a Profession. Susan P. Choy et al. (Illus.). 189p. (Orig.). (C). 1994. pap. text ed. 45.00 (*0-7881-0682-1*) Diane Pub.

America's Teachers: Profiles of a Profession. 1994. lib. bdg. 250.00 (*0-8490-8522-5*) Gordon Pr.

America's Technology Slip. Simon Ramo. LC 80-21525. 304p. reprint ed. pap. 86.70 (*0-8357-5410-3*, 2021503) Bks Demand.

America's Theologian: A Recommendation of Jonathan Edwards. Robert W. Jenson. 240p. 1988. 45.00 (*0-19-504941-1*) OUP.

America's Theologian: A Recommendation of Jonathan Edwards. Robert W. Jenson. 238p. 1992. pap. 17.95 (*0-19-507786-5*) OUP.

***America's Third-Party Presidential Candidates.** Nathan Aaseng. LC 94-22102. (Profiles Ser.). (Illus.). 160p. (YA). (gr. 5-12). 1995. 14.95 (*1-881508-19-6*) Oliver Pr MN.

America's Thousand Bishops: From 1513 to 1974, from Abramowicz to Zuroweste. Clarence A. Liederbach. LC 73-94081. 80p. 1974. pap. 3.50 (*0-913228-09-5*) R J Liederbach.

America's Throwaway Children: The Foster-Care Dilemma. Joy M. Garland. LC 90-91822. (Illus.). 127p. (Orig.). 1990. pap. text ed. 6.00 (*0-9627325-0-8*) J Russell Pub.

America's Top Jobs for College Graduates. Ed. by J. Michael Farr. (America Ser.). 300p. (Orig.). 1994. pap. 14.95 (*1-56370-140-5*, ATCG) JIST Works.

***America's Top Medical & Human Service Jobs.** 3rd ed. J. Michael Farr & U. S. Department of Labor Staff. (America's Ser.). (Orig.). 1995. pap. 14.95 (*1-56370-238-X*) JIST Works.

America's Top Medical & Human Services Jobs. 2nd ed. Comp. by J. Michael Farr. (America Ser.). 192p. 1994. pap. 11.95 (*1-56370-118-9*, ATM) JIST Works.

America's Top Military Careers: The Official Guide to Occupations in the Armed Forces. JIST Editorial Staff. (America Ser.). 488p. 1993. pap. 19.95 (*1-56370-124-3*, ATMC) JIST Works.

America's Top Office, Management & Sales Jobs. 2nd ed. Comp. by J. Michael Farr. (America Ser.). 224p. 1994. pap. 11.95 (*1-56370-117-0*, ATO) JIST Works.

***America's Top-Rated Cities: A Statistical Handbook, 5 vols., Set.** Ed. by Rhoda Garoogian & Andrew Garoogian. 1500p. 1996. pap. 139.95 (*1-881220-20-6*) Univ Ref Pubns.

***America's Top-Rated Cities: A Statistical Handbook, 5 vols., Set.** rev. ed. Ed. by Rhoda Garoogian & Andrew Garoogian. 1470p. 1995. pap. 139.95 (*1-881220-14-1*) Univ Ref Pubns.

***America's Top-Rated Cities: A Statistical Handbook: Central Region, Vol. 3.** 310p. 1996. pap. 31.95 (*1-881220-23-0*) Univ Ref Pubns.

***America's Top-Rated Cities: A Statistical Handbook Central Region, Vol. 3.** rev. ed. Ed. by Rhoda Garoogian & Andrew Garoogian. 310p. 1995. pap. 31.95 (*1-881220-17-6*) Univ Ref Pubns.

***America's Top-Rated Cities: A Statistical Handbook: Eastern Region, Vol. 4.** 270p. 1996. pap. 31.95 (*1-881220-24-9*) Univ Ref Pubns.

***America's Top-Rated Cities: A Statistical Handbook Eastern Region, Vol. 4.** rev. ed. Ed. by Rhoda Garoogian & Andrew Garoogian. 270p. 1995. pap. 31.95 (*1-881220-18-4*) Univ Ref Pubns.

***America's Top-Rated Cities: A Statistical Handbook: Northeastern Region, Vol. 5.** 270p. 1996. pap. 31.95 (*1-881220-25-7*) Univ Ref Pubns.

***America's Top-Rated Cities: A Statistical Handbook Northeastern Region, Vol. 5.** rev. ed. Ed. by Rhoda Garoogian & Andrew Garoogian. 270p. 1995. pap. 31.95 (*1-881220-19-2*) Univ Ref Pubns.

***America's Top-Rated Cities: A Statistical Handbook: Southern Region, Vol. 1.** 310p. 1996. pap. 31.95 (*1-881220-21-4*) Univ Ref Pubns.

***America's Top-Rated Cities: A Statistical Handbook Southern Region, Vol. 1.** rev. ed. Ed. by Rhoda Garoogian & Andrew Garoogian. 310p. 1995. pap. 31.95 (*1-881220-15-X*) Univ Ref Pubns.

***America's Top-Rated Cities: A Statistical Handbook: Western Region, Vol. 2.** 310p. 1996. pap. 31.95 (*1-881220-22-2*) Univ Ref Pubns.

***America's Top-Rated Cities: A Statistical Handbook Western Region, Vol. 2.** rev. ed. Ed. by Rhoda Garoogian & Andrew Garoogian. 310p. 1995. pap. 31.95 (*1-881220-16-8*) Univ Ref Pubns.

America's Top-Rated Cities, a Statistical Handbook, 5 vols. 2nd rev. ed. Ed. by Rhoda Garoogian et al. 1516p. 1993. Set. pap. 134.95 (*1-881220-06-0*) Univ Ref Pubns.

America's Top-Rated Cities, a Statistical Handbook, Vol. 1: Southern Region. 2nd rev. ed. Ed. by Rhoda Garoogian et al. (Illus.). 358p. 1993. pap. 31.95 (*1-881220-07-9*) Univ Ref Pubns.

America's Top-Rated Cities, a Statistical Handbook, Vol. 2: Western Region. 2nd rev. ed. Ed. by Rhoda Garoogian et al. 306p. 1993. pap. 31.95 (*1-881220-08-7*) Univ Ref Pubns.

America's Top-Rated Cities, a Statistical Handbook, Vol. 3: Central Region. 2nd rev. ed. Ed. by Rhoda Garoogian et al. 302p. 1993. pap. 31.95 (*1-881220-09-5*) Univ Ref Pubns.

America's Top-Rated Cities, a Statistical Handbook, Vol. 4: Eastern Region. 2nd rev. ed. Ed. by Rhoda Garoogian et al. 294p. 1993. pap. 31.95 (*1-881220-10-9*) Univ Ref Pubns.

America's Top-Rated Cities, a Statistical Handbook, Vol. 5: Northeastern Region. 2nd rev. ed. Ed. by Rhoda Garoogian et al. 256p. 1993. pap. 31.95 (*1-881220-11-7*) Univ Ref Pubns.

America's Top-Rated Small Cities: A Statistical Profile. Ed. by Rhoda Garoogian & Andrew Garoogian. 750p. (Orig.). 1994. pap. 65.00 (*1-881220-13-3*) Univ Ref Pubns.

***America's Top-Rated Smaller Cities: A Statistical Profile.** Ed. by Rhoda Garoogian & Andrew Garoogian. 730p. 1996. pap. 69.95 (*1-881220-26-5*) Univ Ref Pubns.

America's Top Technical & Trade Jobs. 2nd ed. Comp. by J. Michael Farr. (America Ser.). 180p. 1994. pap. 11.95 (*1-56370-116-2*, ATT) JIST Works.

America's Top Three Hundred Jobs: A Complete Career Handbook. 4th ed. Ed. by U. S. Dept. of Labor Staff. (America Ser.). 473p. 1994. pap. 17.95 (*1-56370-163-4*, T300) JIST Works.

***America's Top Trial Lawyers: Who They Are & Why They Win.** Donald E. Vinson. 1994. write for info. (*0-13-356635-8*) Aspen Law.

America's Traditional Crafts. Robert Shaw. (Illus.). 320p. 1993. 95.00 (*0-88363-693-X*) H L Levin.

America's Transition: Blueprints for the 1990's. Ed. by Mark Green & Mark Pinsky. LC 89-22489. 616p. (C). 1990. reprint ed. lib. bdg. 66.00 (*0-8191-7591-9*); reprint ed. pap. text ed. 49.00 (*0-8191-7592-7*) U Pr of Amer.

America's Triumph: Stories of American Jewish Heroes. Dorothy Alofsin. LC 72-148205. (Biography Index Reprint Ser.). 1977. 24.95 (*0-8369-8052-2*) Ayer.

America's Triumph at Panama. R. Avery. 1976. lib. bdg. 59.95 (*0-8490-1420-4*) Gordon Pr.

America's Troubled Children. Ed. by Jeanne Burr & Melinda Maidens. LC 80-20541. 192p. reprint ed. pap. 54.80 (*0-8357-5412-X*, 2022894) Bks Demand.

America's Twelve Great Women Leaders During the Past Hundred Years As Chosen by the Women of America. Ladies Home Journal Editors & Christian Science Monitor Editors. LC 74-90600. (Essay Index Reprint Ser.). 1977. 17.95 (*0-8369-1202-0*) Ayer.

America's Tyrant: The CIA & Mobutu of Zaire. Sean Kelly. 302p. 1993. 22.95 (*1-879383-17-9*) Am Univ Pr.

America's Unfairest Taxes: Tariffs & Quotas. James Bovard. (C). 1992. pap. 10.00 (*0-943802-74-1*, 171) Natl Ctr Pol.

***America's Untapped Oil.** Interstate Oil & Gas Compact Commission Staff. 7p. (Orig.). 1995. pap. text ed. write for info. (*1-879386-14-3*) IOGCC.

***America's Unwritten Constitution: Science, Religion, & Political Responsibility.** Don K. Price. LC 83-5439. (Miller Center Series on the American Presidency). 220p. 1983. pap. 62.70 (*0-7837-8468-6*, 2049273) Bks Demand.

America's Unwritten Constitution: Science, Religion & Political Responsibility. Don K. Price. 224p. 1985. pap. 13.50 (*0-674-03142-3*) HUP.

America's Utopian Experiments: Communal Havens from Long-Wave Crises. Brian J. Berry. LC 92-10001. (Nelson A. Rockefeller Series in Social Science & Public Policy). (Illus.). 293p. 1992. text ed. 40.00 (*0-87451-589-0*); pap. 18.95 (*0-87451-590-4*) U Pr of New Eng.

America's Vietnam War: A Narrative History. Elizabeth Becker. 160p. (J). (gr. 7 up). 1992. 15.95 (*0-395-59094-9*, Clarion Bks) HM.

America's Voluntary Spirit. Brian O'Connell. 460p. 1983. 14.95 (*0-87954-081-8*) Ind Sector.

America's Voluntary Spirit: A Book of Readings. Brian O'Connell. LC 83-81223. 461p. 1983. 19.95 (*0-87954-079-6*) Foundation Ctr.

America's Volunteer Military: Progress and Prospects. Martin Binkin. LC 84-14943. (Studies in Defence Policy). 63p. 1984. pap. 8.95 (*0-8157-0975-7*) Brookings.

America's War of Independence: A Concise Illustrated History of the American Revolution. David Rubel. (Illus.). 48p. (Orig.). 1993. pap. 6.95 (*1-881889-39-4*) Silver Moon.

America's Wars & Military Encounters: From Colonial Times to the Present. Edwin P. Hoyt. (Quality Paperbacks Ser.). (Illus.). 535p. 1988. reprint ed. pap. 14.95 (*0-306-80338-0*) Da Capo.

America's Water: Federal Roles & Responsibilities. Peter P. Rogers. LC 93-1740. (Illus.). 285p. 1993. 29.95x (*0-262-18156-8*) MIT Pr.

America's Wealthiest People: Their Philanthropic & Nonprofit Affiliations. Benjamin Lord. 78p. 1984. pap. 57.50 (*0-914756-57-5*) Taft Group.

America's Wealthy & the Future of Foundations: A Study of Private Philanthropy in America. Ed. by Teresa Odendahl. LC 87-7397. 325p. 1987. 34.95 (*0-87954-197-0*); pap. 24.95 (*0-87954-194-6*) Foundation Ctr.

America's Weapons of Psychological Warfare. Ed. by Robert E. Summers. LC 72-4679. (International Propaganda & Communications Ser.). 206p. 1972. reprint ed. 18.95 (*0-405-04763-0*) Ayer.

America's Weather Warriors, 1814-1985. Charles C. Bates & John F. Fuller. LC 85-40746. (Illus.). 384p. 1986. 29.95 (*0-89096-240-5*) Tex A&M Univ Pr.

America's Welfare State: From Roosevelt to Reagan. Edward D. Berkowitz. LC 90-46424. (American Moment Ser.). 224p. 1991. text ed. 38.95 (*0-8018-4127-5*); pap. text ed. 12.95 (*0-8018-4128-3*) Johns Hopkins.

America's Wetlands. Frank Staub. LC 94-3872. (J). (gr. 1-4). 1994. 19.95 (*0-87614-827-5*, Carolrhoda) Lerner Group.

A

An Asterisk (*) at the beginning of an entry indicates that the title is appearing in BIP for the first time.

275

America's Wild & Scenic Rivers. Ed. by Donald J. Crump. LC 83-47843. (Special Publications Series 18: No. 2). 200p. 1983. 12.95 (0-87044-440-9) Natl Geog.

America's Wild Woodlands. W. Howarth et al. Ed. by Donald J. Crump. LC 85-355. (Special Publications Series 20: No. 1). (Illus.). 200p. 1985. lib. bdg. 16.00 (0-87044-547-2) Natl Geog.

America's Wildlife Hideaways. deluxe ed. Bob Devine et al. Ed. by Elaine Furlow. LC 89-8290. (Illus.). 240p. 1989. 40.00 (0-945051-12-3, 19739) Natl Wildlife.

America's Wit. William Gibson et al. (Illus.). 864p. 1992. Gift box. 34.95 (0-936023-05-8, 34586) Interp Mktg Prods.

America's Witness for Jesus Christ. Comp. by Arthur Wallace. 70p. 1978. pap. 1.95 (0-937892-04-1) LL Co.

America's Wonderful Little Hotels & Inns: New England. 14th ed. Sandra W. Soule. 512p. 1994. pap. 16.99 (0-312-11483-4) St Martin.

America's Wonderful Little Hotels & Inns: The South. 14th ed. Sandra W. Soule. 336p. 1994. pap. 15.99 (0-312-11484-2) St Martin.

America's Wonderful Little Hotels & Inns: The West Coast. 14th ed. Sandra W. Soule. 448p. 1994. pap. 15.99 (0-312-11238-6) St Martin.

America's Wonderful Little Hotels & Inns, 1981-1982. Barbara Crossette. (Illus.). 400p. 1989. pap. 3.95 (0-312-92016-4) St Martin.

America's Wonderful Little Hotels & Inns, 1993-1994: New England. 12th ed. Sandra W. Soule. (Illus.). 512p. 1992. pap. 16.95 (0-312-08130-8) St Martin.

America's Wonderful Little Hotels & Inns, 1993-1994: The South. 12th ed. Sandra W. Soule. (Illus.). 336p. 1992. pap. 14.95 (0-312-08131-6) St Martin.

America's Wonderful Little Hotels & Inns, 1993-1994: The West Coast. 12th ed. Sandra W. Soule. (Illus.). 464p. 1992. pap. 15.95 (0-312-08132-4) St Martin.

America's Wonderful Little Hotels & Inns, 1994-1995: The Middle Atlantic. 13th ed. Sandra W. Soule. (Illus.). 432p. (Orig.). 1993. pap. 14.99 (0-312-10096-5) St Martin.

America's Wonderful Little Hotels & Inns, 1994-1995: The Midwest. 13th ed. Sandra W. Soule. (Illus.). 320p. (Orig.). 1993. pap. 13.99 (0-312-09737-9) St Martin.

America's Wonderful Little Hotels & Inns, 1994-1995: The Rocky Mountains & the Southwest. 13th ed. Sandra W. Soule. (Illus.). 336p. (Orig.). 1993. pap. 13.99 (0-312-09738-7) St Martin.

America's Wonderful Little Hotels & Inns, 1994-1995: U. S. A. & Canada. 13th ed. Sandra W. Soule. (Illus.). 864p. (Orig.). 1993. pap. 19.99 (0-312-09739-5) St Martin.

America's Wonderful Little Hotels & Inns, 1995: U. S. A. & Canada. Sandra W. Soule. 848p. 1994. pap. 19.99 (0-312-11239-4) St Martin.

America's Wooden Age: Aspects of Its Early Technology. Ed. by Brooke Hindle. LC 74-7842. (Illus.). 224p. 1985. reprint ed. pap. 14.95 (0-912882-60-3) Sleepy Hollow.

America's Work Force Is Coming of Age: What Every Business Needs to Know to Recruit, Train, Manage & Retain an Aging Work Force. Catherine D. Fyock. 224p. 1990. text ed. 36.95 (0-669-21884-7) Free Pr.

***America's Workhorse Locomotive: The 2-8-2.** Robert LeMassena. 1993. pap. 14.95 (0-915276-54-2) Quadrant Pr.

America's Working Man: Work, Home, & Politics among Blue-Collar Property Owners. David Halle. LC 84-2566. (Illus.). xviii, 360p. 1984. 24.95 (0-226-31365-4) U Ch Pr.

America's Working Man: Work, Home, & Politics among Blue-Collar Property Owners. David Halle. LC 84-2566. (Illus.). xviii, 360p. 1987. pap. text ed. 14.95 (0-226-31366-2) U Ch Pr.

***America's Working Poor.** Ed. by Thomas R. Swartz & Kathleen M. Weigert. LC 95-9128. (C). 1996. text ed. 29.95 (0-268-00648-2); pap. text ed. 15.95 (0-268-00649-0) U of Notre Dame Pr.

America's Working Women. Rosalyn Baxandall. 430p. 1995. 27.50 (0-393-03653-7); pap. 12.95 (0-393-31262-3) Norton.

America's Youth: 1977-1988. Robert Bezilla. (Illus.). 320p. 1988. 99.00 (0-685-24657-4) Gallup NJ.

America's Zero Hour. Ryder Stacy. (Doomsday Warrior Ser.: No. 9). 256p. 1986. pap. 2.50 (0-8217-1929-7) Zebra.

***America's 365 Best Festivals.** Comp. by Paul Obis. 240p. (Orig.). 1995. pap. 12.95 (1-57067-014-5) Book Pub Co.

Americium & Curium Chemistry & Technology. Ed. by Norman M. Edelstein et al. 1985. lib. bdg. 110.00 (90-277-2097-5) Kluwer Ac.

Americo Castro & the Meaning of Spanish Civilization. Ed. by Jose R. Barcia & Selma Margaretten. LC 74-27282. 1977. 52.00 (0-520-02920-8) U CA Pr.

Americo Castro: The Impact of His Thought: Essays to Mark the Centenary of His Birth. Ed. by Ronald E. Surtz. Tr. by Jaime Ferran & Daniel P. Testa. 284p. (ENG & SPA.). 1988. 25.00 (0-940639-21-1) Hispanic Seminary.

Americruiser. F. A. Nettelbeck. 64p. (Orig.). 1984. pap. 8.95 (0-317-11782-3) Illuminati.

Americruiser. deluxe limited ed. F. A. Nettelbeck. 64p. (Orig.). 1984. 20.00 (0-317-13028-5) Illuminati.

Amerigo: The Amerigo Vespucci Story. Frances S. Nilsen & James L. Salter. LC 92-93878. (Illus.). 253p. (YA). (gr. 10-12). 1992. 14.95 (0-9633937-6-6) Shamrock TN.

Amerika. Franz Kafka. Tr. by Edwin Muir. LC 62-10411. (Illus.). (C). 1962. pap. 10.95 (0-8112-0075-2, NDP117) New Directions.

Amerika. Franz Kafka. 1990. pap. 13.00 (0-8052-0944-1) Schocken.

Amerika: Bilderbuch Tines Architekten. Erich Mendelsohn. LC 76-40319. (Architecture & Decorative Art Ser.). (GER.). 1977. reprint ed. lib. bdg. 55.00 (0-306-70830-2) Da Capo.

Amerika, Rossiia I Ia. Diana Vin'kovetskaia. LC 93-31468. (Illus.). 490p. (Orig.). (RUS.). 1993. pap. 12.00 (1-55779-066-3) Hermitage.

Amerika Samoa. J. A. Gray. LC 79-6109. (Navies & Men Ser.). (Illus.). 1980. reprint ed. lib. bdg. 31.95 (0-405-13038-4) Ayer.

Amerika Samoa: An Anthropological Photo Essay. Frederic K. Sutter. LC 84-51832. (Illus.). 136p. 1984. 24.95 (0-8248-0990-4) UH Pr.

Amerikan Journeys: Jornadas Americanas. Ricardo Sanchez. 76p. 1994. pap. 8.50 (0-9640662-0-3) R Lewis Pub.

Amerikanische Sicherheitssystem, 1945-1949: Studie zur Aussenpolitik der buergerlichen Gesellschaft. Ernst O. Czempiel. (Beitraege zur Auswaertigen und Internationalen Politik Ser.: Vol. 1). (C). 1966. 100.00 (3-11-000527-1) De Gruyter.

Amerikanische Verfassung & Deutsch-Amerikanisches Verfassungsdenken: Krefelder Historische Symposien: Deutschland & America. Ed. by Hermann Wellenreuther et al. LC 90-39572. 464p. 1991. 75.00 (0-85496-713-3) Berg Pubs.

Amerikanische Zivilprozess. William Schurtman & Otto L. Walter. 122p. 1978. pap. 14.00 (90-200-0545-6) Kluwer Ac.

***Amerikanskaia Azbuka.** Aleksandr Genis. LC 94-35498. 104p. (Orig.). (RUS.). 1994. pap. 9.00 (1-55779-072-8) Hermitage.

Amerikanuak: Basques in the New World. William A. Douglass & Jon Bilbao. LC 75-30830. (Basque Ser.). (Illus.). 536p. 1975. 35.00 (0-87417-043-5) U of Nev Pr.

Amerikos Lietuviu Gydytoju Vardynas: Lithuanian-American Medical Directory (1884-1984) Milda Budrys. LC 90-64053. 139p. 1991. 15.00 (0-929700-06-6) Lith Res & Studies.

AmeriModern. Poems. Don Paul. LC 75-785. 82p. 1982. 5.00 (0-943096-02-2); pap. 2.50 (0-943096-03-0) Harts Spring Wks.

Amerindian Coastline Poem. deluxe ed. Fanny Howe. Ed. by Maureen Owen. LC 75-45247. (Illus.). (Orig.). 1976. 10.00 (0-685-04872-1) Telephone Bks.

Amerindian Images & the Legacy of Columbus. Ed. by Rene Jara & Nicholas Spadaccini. (Hispanic Issues Ser.: Vol. 9). (Illus.). 736p. (C). 1992. text ed. 49.95 (0-8166-2166-7); pap. text ed. 24.95 (0-8166-2167-5) U of Minn Pr.

Amerindian Rebirth: Reincarnation Belief among North American Indians & Inuit. Ed. by Antonia Mills & Richard Slobodin. (Illus.). 240p. 1994. 60.00 (0-8020-2829-2); pap. 19.95 (0-8020-7703-X) U of Toronto Pr.

Amerindians in Guyana, 1803-1873: A Documentary History. Ed. by Mary N. Menezes. 314p. 1979. 40.00 (0-7146-3054-3, Pub. by F Cass Pubs UK) Intl Spec Bk.

Amerindians of South America. Lewis B. Sckolnick. (Civil Rights Reporter Ser.). (Illus.). 60p. (Orig.). (C). 1994. pap. 45.00 (1-57205-101-9) Rector Pr.

AmerInds & Their Paleoenvironments in Northeastern North America, Vol. 288. Ed. by Walter S. Newman & Bert S. Salwen. 1977. 37.00 (0-89072-034-7) NY Acad Sci.

Amerique. Franz Kafka. 366p. (FRE.). 1976. pap. 11.95 (0-7859-2370-5, 2070368033) Fr & Eur.

Amerique Latine: Philosophie De la Conquete. S. Zavala. 1977. 28.50 (90-279-7624-4) Mouton.

Amerique Latine-Latin America: Catalogues et Inventaires. Ed. by Anne-Marie Metailie. (Maison des Sciences de l'Homme, Service d'Echange d'Information Scientifiques Publications: No. 5). 1974. pap. 21.25 (0-686-21808-6) Mouton.

Amerique Meridionale: An "Antique" Map of South America in the Form of a Commemorative Reconstruction. limited ed. Nicolas Sanson. (Illus.). 1988. 125.00 (0-943435-01-3) Cartographer Ink.

Ameritech-Bell Operating Company Relationship: A Regulatory Perspective. 84p. 1986. 12.00 (0-317-01641-5) NARUC.

Ameritech Corporate Expense Allocations. 205p. 1987. 17.00 (0-317-01642-3) NARUC.

Amers see Oeuvre Poetique

Amers & Oiseaux. Saint-John Perse. (Poesie Ser.). 256p. (FRE.). 1970. 9.95 (2-07-030248-2) Schoenhof.

Amers, Oiseaux, Poesie. Saint-John Perse. (FRE.). 1970. pap. 12.95 (0-8288-3873-9, F123891) Fr & Eur.

***Ameru.** Esther Wangari. LC 94-30208. (Heritage Library of African Peoples). 1994. pap. 15.95 (0-8239-1766-5) Rosen Group.

Ameryka Dla Kazdego: Czyli Poradnik Dla Polakow W U. S. A. Elzbieta Baumgartner. 360p. 1992. pap. text ed. 25.00 (0-9633932-0-0) Polpress Servs.

Ameryka Dla Kazdego: Czyli Poradnik Dlo Polakow w Ujn, Vol. 2. Elzbieta Baumgartner. 420p. (Orig.). (POL.). 1993. pap. text ed. 25.00 (0-9633932-1-9) Polpress Servs.

Ames Ancestry-Europe to Maine. enl. ed. Agnes Ames. LC 79-91192. 210p. 1982. reprint ed. pap. 20.00 (0-941216-05-5) Cay-Bel.

Ames du Purgatoire. Prosper Merimee. 192p. (FRE.). 1973. 10.95 (0-7859-0078-0, M2466) Fr & Eur.

Ames Fortes. Jean Giono. 384p. (FRE.). 1972. pap. 10.95 (0-7859-2290-3, 2070362493) Fr & Eur.

Ames Fortes. Jean Giono. (Folio Ser.: No. 249). 384p. (FRE.). 1972. 8.95 (2-07-036249-3) Schoenhof.

Ames Mortes. Nicolas Gogol. (FRE.). 1973. pap. 11.95 (0-7859-2315-2, 2070364259) Fr & Eur.

Ames Research Center (NASA) Conference on Geometric Control Theory, 1976. Ed. by Clyde F. Martin & Robert Hermann. (Lie Groups: History, Frontiers & Applications Ser.: Vol. 7). 1977. 60.00 (0-915692-21-X) Math Sci Pr.

Ames Research Center (NASA) Conference on Geometric Nonlinear Wave Theory, 1976. Ed. by Robert Hermann. (Lie Groups; History, Frontiers & Applications Ser.: Vol. 6). 1977. pap. 25.00 (0-915692-19-8) Math Sci Pr.

Ames Sword Company, 1829-1935. John D. Hamilton. LC 81-85194. (Illus.). 255p. 1995. 45.00 (0-917218-18-3) A Mowbray.

Ameslan - An Introduction to American Sign Language. Louie J. Fant, Jr. LC 72-90793. 11.95 (0-917002-37-7) Joyce Media.

Amethyst & Lampblack. Leilah Wendell. (Illus.). 90p. (Orig.). 1985. pap. 5.00 (0-09-913136-6) Westgate Pr.

Amethyst Crown. Katherine Deauxville. 448p. 1994. mass mkt. 5.99 (0-8217-4555-7) Zebra.

Amethyst Mining Inscriptions of Wadi El-Hudi, Vol. 2: Additional Text & Plates. Sadek. 1985. pap. 99.00 (0-85668-264-0, Pub. by Aris & Phillips UK) David Brown.

Amethyst Mining Inscriptions of Wadi El-Hudi, Vol. 1: Text. Sadek. 1981. pap. 55.00 (0-85668-162-8, Pub. by Aris & Phillips UK) David Brown.

***Amethyst Moon.** Janice Bennett. 384p. 1995. pap. 4.99 (0-7860-0170-4) Windsor NY.

Amfiparnaso: A New Edition of the Music with Historical & Analytical Essays. Orazio Vecchi. Ed. by Cecil Adkins. LC 76-15183. (Early Musical Masterworks Ser.). 117p. reprint ed. pap. 33.40 (0-8357-3882-5, 2036614) Bks Demand.

Amharic. 529p. 1964. Incl. 26 cassettes. 245.00 (0-88432-154-1, AFAM10); 49.50 (0-88432-796-5, AFAM98) Audio-Forum.

Amharic-English English-Amharic Dictionary. (AMH & ENG.). 1992. 40.00 (0-7818-0115-X) Hippocrene Bks.

Amharic Newspaper Reader. Mulugeta Kebede. LC 84-72434. iv, 371p. 1984. text ed. 44.00 (0-931745-01-2); audio 20.00 (0-931745-11-X) Dunwoody Pr.

***Amherst County: Virginia Publick Claims.** Janice L. Abercrombie & Richard Slatten. (Virginia Publick Claims Ser.). ix, 50p. 1991. pap. 7.00 (0-8095-8507-3) Borgo Pr.

Amherst County: Virginia Publick Claims. Janice L. Abercrombie & Richard Slatten. (Virginia Publick Claims Ser.). ix, 50p. (C). 1991. reprint ed. lib. bdg. 20.00x (0-8095-8303-8) Borgo Pr.

Amherst County, Virginia, Wills, 1761-1865. Bailey F. Davis. 472p. 1985. 37.50 (0-89308-302-X) Southern Hist Pr.

Amherst, New Hampshire: 1881-1982. Historical Society of Amherst, New Hampshire. LC 83-17371. 272p. 1983. 15.00 (0-914659-00-6) Phoenix Pub.

Ami. Joe Aved. LC 81-51961. 192p. 1981. 12.95 (0-88400-077-X) Shengold.

Ami Commun: Le Mystere d'Edwin Drood. Charles Dickens. Ed. by Sylvere Monod. (FRE.). 1991. lib. bdg. 135.00 (0-7859-3891-5) Fr & Eur.

AMI Complete Listing of Remote Control, Wall Boxes, Accessories & Service Bulletins, for the Model K, Lyric, Continental I & II. rev. ed. Ed. by Frank Adams. (Illus.). 60p. reprint ed. 24.50 (1-56642-107-1, R-531) AMR Pub Co.

Ami d'Enfance de Maigret. Georges Simenon. pap. 10.95 (0-8288-6099-8, F126480) Fr & Eur.

AMI Forty Selection Wall Boxes & Steppers As Used on the A, B & C Models Service Manual. 18p. 1983. reprint ed. spiral bd. 12.50 (0-913698-77-6, R-93) AMR Pub Co.

Ami Maupassant. Guy De Maupassant. (FRE.). 1992. pap. 10.95 (0-7859-3277-1, 2277220477) Fr & Eur.

AMI Model "A" & Model "B" Service Manual, 1946-49 Models. (Illus.). 22p. 1983. reprint ed. spiral bd. 19.50 (0-913698-71-7, R-185) AMR Pub Co.

AMI Model "C" Service, Parts Manual & Trouble Shooting. 76p. 1983. reprint ed. spiral bd. 32.50 (0-913698-72-5, R-216) AMR Pub Co.

AMI Model CD II Phonograph, 1971: Owners Manual. rev. ed. Ed. by Frank Adams. (Illus.). 64p. reprint ed. spiral bd. 30.00 (1-56642-135-7, R-430) AMR Pub Co.

AMI Model CD II Phonograph, 1971: Parts Catalog. rev. ed. Ed. by Frank Adams. (Illus.). 62p. reprint ed. spiral bd. 25.00 (1-56642-136-5, R-431) AMR Pub Co.

AMI Model CMM-1 "Cadette" of 1967-68 Parts Catalog. rev. ed. Ed. by Frank Adams. (Illus.). 58p. reprint ed. 25.00 (1-56642-055-5, R-380) AMR Pub Co.

AMI Model CMM-1 "Cadette" of 1967-68 Service Manual. rev. ed. Ed. by Frank Adams. (Illus.). 126p. reprint ed. 35.00 (1-56642-054-7, R-379) AMR Pub Co.

AMI Model Continental II of 1962 Parts Catalog. Rowe Ami. Ed. by Frank Adams. 92p. 1986. reprint ed. 29.50 (0-939971-15-1, R-373) AMR Pub Co.

AMI Model Continental II of 1962 Service Manual. rev. ed. Ed. by Frank Adams. (Illus.). 126p. reprint ed. 37.50 (1-56642-050-4, R-375) AMR Pub Co.

AMI Model CTI-1 "Crestwood" of 1974 Parts Catalog. rev. ed. Ed. by Frank Adams. (Illus.). 62p. reprint ed. 24.50 (1-56642-015-6, R-45) AMR Pub Co.

AMI Model CTI-1 "Crestwood" of 1974 Service Manual. rev. ed. Ed. by Frank Adams. (Illus.). 104p. reprint ed. 35.00 (1-56642-014-8, R-44) AMR Pub Co.

AMI Model CTI-1SC "Camelot" of 1978 Furniture Style Service Manual. rev. ed. Ed. by Frank Adams. (Illus.). 132p. reprint ed. 35.00 (1-56642-008-3, R-26) AMR Pub Co.

AMI Model CT1-1SC Camelot, 1978: Parts Catalog. rev. ed. Ed. by Frank Adams. (Illus.). 34p. reprint ed. spiral bd. 24.50 (1-56642-009-1, R-27) AMR Pub Co.

AMI Model D-40 Service Manual & Parts List of 1951. AMI Company Staff. Ed. by Frank Adams. 88p. 1984. reprint ed. spiral bd. 32.50 (0-913599-20-4, R-270) AMR Pub Co.

AMI Model D-80 of 1952 Service & Parts Manual: Including Parts List. AMI Company Staff. Ed. by Frank Adams. 94p. 1985. reprint ed. spiral bd. 32.50 (0-913599-18-2, R-264) AMR Pub Co.

AMI Model "E-80" & "E-120" Service & Parts Manual. 90p. 1983. reprint ed. spiral bd. 29.50 (0-913698-73-3, R-160) AMR Pub Co.

AMI Model "F" Service & Parts Manual. 122p. 1983. reprint ed. spiral bd. 29.50 (0-913698-74-1, R-183) AMR Pub Co.

AMI Model F, 1954: Quick Reference Guide & Operators Manual. rev. ed. Ed. by Frank Adams. (Illus.). 24p. reprint ed. spiral bd. 12.50 (1-56642-132-2, R-302) AMR Pub Co.

AMI Model G, H, & I Service Bulletins. rev. ed. Ed. by Frank Adams. (Illus.). 51p. reprint ed. spiral bd. 25.00 (1-56642-133-0, R-16) AMR Pub Co.

AMI Model G of 1955 Service Manual. rev. ed. Ed. by Frank Adams. (Illus.). 128p. reprint ed. 35.00 (1-56642-026-1, R-195) AMR Pub Co.

AMI Model "G" Operator's Guide of 1955: 78 & 45 rpm. 30p. 1983. reprint ed. pap. 9.95 (0-913698-75-X, R-227) AMR Pub Co.

AMI Model "G-200" of 1956 Service Manual. rev. ed. Ed. by Frank Adams. (Illus.). 104p. reprint ed. 35.00 (1-56642-051-2, R-376) AMR Pub Co.

AMI Model G-200 Operator's Guide of 1956: Part No. F-5124. 28p. 1983. reprint ed. spiral bd. 9.95 (0-913698-76-8, R-228) AMR Pub Co.

AMI Model "H" & "I" of 1957-58: Credit & Selection System Service Manual. rev. ed. Ed. by Frank Adams. (Illus.). 18p. reprint ed. 12.50 (1-56642-068-7, R-397) AMR Pub Co.

AMI Model "H" Series of 1957: Service Manual. rev. ed. Ed. by Frank Adams. (Illus.). 118p. reprint ed. 37.50 (1-56642-067-9, R-396) AMR Pub Co.

AMI Model I PF, 1958: Parts Catalog. rev. ed. Ed. by Frank Adams. (Illus.). 100p. reprint ed. 35.00 (1-56642-106-3, R-529) AMR Pub Co.

AMI Model I, 1958: Service Manual. rev. ed. Ed. by Frank Adams. (Illus.). 140p. reprint ed. 37.50 (1-56642-105-5, R-528) AMR Pub Co.

AMI Model "J" Series of 1959 Service Manual. rev. ed. Ed. by Frank Adams. (Illus.). 142p. reprint ed. 35.00 (1-56642-061-X, R-389) AMR Pub Co.

AMI Model "K" of 1960 Parts Catalog & R-1865 & R- 2358 Automatic Selectors Service Manual. rev. ed. Ed. by Frank Adams. (Illus.). 108p. reprint ed. 33.50 (1-56642-069-5, R-399) AMR Pub Co.

AMI Model K, Record Changer & R-1473 Credit Unit & Pricing System, 1960: Service Manuals. rev. ed. Ed. by Frank Adams. (Illus.). 48p. reprint ed. 24.50 (1-56642-111-X, R-537) AMR Pub Co.

AMI Model "L" Series "JAL" & "JEL" of 1963 Parts Catalog. rev. ed. Ed. by Frank Adams. (Illus.). 144p. reprint ed. 32.50 (1-56642-060-1, R-388) AMR Pub Co.

AMI Model "L" Series "JAL" & "JEL" of 1963 Service Manual. rev. ed. Ed. by Frank Adams. (Illus.). 164p. reprint ed. 39.50 (1-56642-059-8, R-387) AMR Pub Co.

AMI Model Lyric & Continental, No. 1: Cabinets & Components Parts Catalog. rev. ed. Ed. by Frank Adams. (Illus.). 33p. reprint ed. 22.50 (1-56642-175-6, R-63) AMR Pub Co.

AMI Model "M" Series "Tropicana," "JBM" of 1964-65: Parts Catalog. rev. ed. Ed. by Frank Adams. (Illus.). 98p. reprint ed. 29.50 (1-56642-066-0, R-394) AMR Pub Co.

AMI Model "M" Series "Tropicana," "JBM," 1964-65: Service Manual. rev. ed. Ed. by Frank Adams. (Illus.). 140p. reprint ed. spiral bd. 37.50 (1-56642-134-9, R-393) AMR Pub Co.

AMI Model MM-1 "Music Merchant" of 1967: Parts Catalog. rev. ed. Ed. by Frank Adams. (Illus.). 84p. reprint ed. 29.50 (1-56642-072-5, R-413) AMR Pub Co.

AMI Model MM-1 "Music Merchant" of 1967: Service Manual. rev. ed. Ed. by Frank Adams. (Illus.). 186p. reprint ed. 39.95 (1-56642-071-7, R-410) AMR Pub Co.

AMI Model MM-2 "Music Master" of 1968: Parts Catalog. rev. ed. Ed. by Frank Adams. (Illus.). 80p. reprint ed. 29.50 (1-56642-065-2, R-392) AMR Pub Co.

AMI Model MM-2 "Music Master" of 1968: Service Manual. rev. ed. Ed. by Frank Adams. (Illus.). 170p. reprint ed. 39.95 (1-56642-064-4, R-391) AMR Pub Co.

AMI Model MM-3 "Music Miracle" & "MM4 "Trimount" Combined Service Manual of 1969-70. rev. ed. Ami Rowe. Ed. by Frank Adams. 164p. 1986. reprint ed. 39.95 (0-939971-12-7, R-370) AMR Pub Co.

AMI Model MM-3 "Music Miracle" & MM4 "Trimount" Parts Catalog of 1969-70. rev. ed. Ami Rowe. Ed. by Frank Adams. 126p. 1986. reprint ed. 32.95 (0-939971-13-5, R-371) AMR Pub Co.

AMI Model MM-5 "Presidential Line" of 1970-71 Parts Catalog. rev. ed. Seeburg Company Staff. Ed. by Frank Adams. 70p. 1986. reprint ed. 25.00 (0-939971-05-4, R-365) AMR Pub Co.

AMI Model MM-5 "Presidential" of 1970-71 Service Manual. rev. ed. Seeburg Company Staff. Ed. by Frank Adams. 124p. 1986. reprint ed. 35.00 (0-939971-06-2, R-364) AMR Pub Co.

AMI Model MM6 "Super Star" of 1971-72 Service & Parts Manual Supplement. rev. ed. Rowe Ami. Ed. by Frank Adams. 66p. 1986. 25.00 (0-939971-14-3, R-372) AMR Pub Co.

AMI Model "N" Series "JAN" Diplomat & the "O" Series "JAO" Bandstand of 1965-66 Parts Catalog. rev. ed. Ed. by Frank Adams. (Illus.). 142p. reprint ed. 35.00 (1-56642-053-9, R-378) AMR Pub Co.

An Asterisk (*) at the beginning of an entry indicates that the title is appearing in BIP for the first time.

AMI Model "N" Series "JAN" Diplomat & the "O" Series "JAO" Bandstand of 1965-66 Service Manual. rev. ed. Ed. by Frank Adams. (Illus.). 182p. reprint ed. 39.50 (*1-56642-052-0*, R-377) AMR Pub Co.

AMI Model R-74 "Arlington" & "Classic" of 1975: Parts Catalog. rev. ed. Ed. by Frank Adams. (Illus.). 50p. reprint ed. 25.00 (*1-56642-085-7*, R-448) AMR Pub Co.

AMI Model R-74 "Arlington" & "Classic" of 1975: Service Manual. rev. ed. Ed. by Frank Adams. (Illus.). 118p. reprint ed. 35.00 (*1-56642-084-9*, R447) AMR Pub Co.

AMI Model R-80 Imperial & Fleetwood, 1976: Parts Catalog. rev. ed. Ed. by Frank Adams. (Illus.). 50p. reprint ed. 25.00 (*1-56642-088-1*, R-466) AMR Pub Co.

AMI Model R-80 Imperial & Fleetwood, 1976: Service Manual. rev. ed. Ed. by Frank Adams. (Illus.). 128p. reprint ed. 35.00 (*1-56642-087-3*, R-465) AMR Pub Co.

AMI Model R-80S Imperial, 1976: Parts Catalog. rev. ed. Ed. by Frank Adams. (Illus.). 40p. reprint ed. 25.00 (*1-56642-100-4*, R-478) AMR Pub Co.

AMI Model R-80S Imperial, 1976: Service Manual. rev. ed. Ed. by Frank Adams. (Illus.). 108p. reprint ed. 37.50 (*1-56642-099-7*, R-477) AMR Pub Co.

AMI Model R-81 Laser Blue, Pulsar Orange, Constellation, & Moondrops, 1977: Parts Catalog. rev. ed. Ed. by Frank Adams. (Illus.). 40p. reprint ed. 25.00 (*1-56642-090-3*, R-468) AMR Pub Co.

AMI Model R-81 Laser Blue, Pulsar Orange, Constellation, & Moondrops, 1977: Service Manual. rev. ed. Ed. by Frank Adams. (Illus.). 116p. reprint ed. 35.00 (*1-56642-089-X*, R-467) AMR Pub Co.

AMI Model R-82 Woodhue & Black Magic, 1978: Parts Catalog. rev. ed. Ed. by Frank Adams. (Illus.). 34p. reprint ed. 25.00 (*1-56642-092-X*, R-470) AMR Pub Co.

AMI Model R-82 Woodhue & Black Magic, 1978: Service Manual. rev. ed. Ed. by Frank Adams. (Illus.). 114p. reprint ed. 35.00 (*1-56642-091-1*, R-469) AMR Pub Co.

AMI Model R-83 Claremont, Disco, & Fiesta, 1979: Parts Catalog. rev. ed. Ed. by Frank Adams. (Illus.). 34p. reprint ed. 25.00 (*1-56642-094-6*, R-472) AMR Pub Co.

AMI Model R-83 Claremont, Disco, & Fiesta, 1979: Service Manual. rev. ed. Ed. by Frank Adams. (Illus.). 126p. reprint ed. 37.50 (*1-56642-093-8*, R-471) AMR Pub Co.

AMI Model R-84 Tempo, Tempo-Disco, & Prelude, 1980: Parts Catalog. rev. ed. Ed. by Frank Adams. (Illus.). 50p. reprint ed. 25.00 (*1-56642-096-2*, R-474) AMR Pub Co.

AMI Model R-84 Tempo, Tempo-Disco & Prelude, 1980: Service Manual. rev. ed. Ed. by Frank Adams. (Illus.). 76p. reprint ed. 32.50 (*1-56642-095-4*, R-473) AMR Pub Co.

AMI Model R-85 Starlight, Starburst & Starwood, 1981: Parts Catalog. rev. ed. Ed. by Frank Adams. (Illus.). 48p. reprint ed. 25.00 (*1-56642-098-9*, R-476) AMR Pub Co.

AMI Model R-85 Starlight, Starburst, & Starwood, 1981: Service Manual. rev. ed. Ed. by Frank Adams. (Illus.). 98p. reprint ed. 32.50 (*1-56642-097-0*, R-475) AMR Pub Co.

AMI Model R-86 Blue Magic & Gold Magic, 1982: Field Service Manual. rev. ed. Ed. by Frank Adams. (Illus.). 76p. reprint ed. spiral bd. 32.50 (*1-56642-139-X*, R-459) AMR Pub Co.

AMI Model R-86 Blue Magic & Gold Magic, 1982: Parts Catalog. rev. ed. Ed. by Frank Adams. (Illus.). 50p. reprint ed. spiral bd. 22.50 (*1-56642-140-3*, R-24) AMR Pub Co.

AMI Model RI-1 Heritage, 1973: Service & Parts Catalog. rev. ed. Ed. by Frank Adams. (Illus.). 90p. reprint ed. 35.00 (*1-56642-109-8*, R-535) AMR Pub Co.

AMI Model RI-1G Heritage, 1974: Service & Parts Manual. rev. ed. Ed. by Frank Adams. (Illus.). 102p. reprint ed. 35.00 (*1-56642-110-1*, R-536) AMR Pub Co.

AMI Model RI-2 "Fantasia" & "Canterbury" of 1977 Service & Parts Manual. rev. ed. Ed. by Frank Adams. (Illus.). 180p. reprint ed. 35.00 (*1-56642-012-1*, R35) AMR Pub Co.

AMI Model RI-3 Jewel, 1980: Field Service Manual. rev. ed. Ed. by Frank Adams. (Illus.). 72p. reprint ed. spiral bd. 32.50 (*1-56642-137-3*, R-154) AMR Pub Co.

AMI Model RI-3 Jewel, 1980: Parts Catalog. rev. ed. Ed. by Frank Adams. (Illus.). 44p. reprint ed. spiral bd. 22.50 (*1-56642-138-1*, R-28) AMR Pub Co.

AMI Model RI-4 & RI-5, 1982: Parts Catalog. rev. ed. Ed. by Frank Adams. (Illus.). 44p. reprint ed. spiral bd. 22.50 (*1-56642-142-X*, R-25) AMR Pub Co.

AMI Model RI-4 Jewel & RI-5 Romantica, 1982: Field Service Manual. rev. ed. Ed. by Frank Adams. (Illus.). 72p. reprint ed. spiral bd. 32.50 (*1-56642-141-1*, R-405) AMR Pub Co.

AMI Model TI-1 "Seville," "Monte Carlo" & "Deauville" of 1973 Parts Catalog. rev. ed. Ed. by Frank Adams. (Illus.). 70p. reprint ed. 25.00 (*1-56642-057-1*, R-385) AMR Pub Co.

AMI Model TI-1 "Seville," "Monte Carlo" & "Deauville" of 1973 Service Manual. rev. ed. Ed. by Frank Adams. (Illus.). 122p. reprint ed. 35.00 (*1-56642-056-3*, R-384) AMR Pub Co.

AMI Model TI-2 "Woodridge," "Rhapsody," & "Caprice" of 1974: Parts Catalog. rev. ed. Ed. by Frank Adams. (Illus.). 64p. reprint ed. 25.00 (*1-56642-083-0*, R-446) AMR Pub Co.

AMI Model TI-2 "Woodridge," "Rhapsody" & "Caprice" of 1974: Service Manual. rev. ed. Ed. by Frank Adams. (Illus.). 118p. reprint ed. 35.00 (*1-56642-082-2*, R-445) AMR Pub Co.

AMI Models CTI-2, CTI-3, R-84, R-85, R-86, R-87, RI-4, RI-5 & HML Hideaway: Shop Service Manual. rev. ed. Ed. by Frank Adams. (Illus.). 99p. reprint ed. 37.50 (*1-56642-108-X*, R-534) AMR Pub Co.

Ami Pro: The Visual Learning Guide. David C. Gardner & Grace J. Beatty. (Illus.). 300p. (Orig.). 1993. pap. 19.95 (*1-55958-407-6*) Prima Pub.

Ami Pro for Dummies. Jim Meade. 356p. 1993. pap. 19.95 (*1-56884-049-7*) IDG Bks.

AMI Pro for Windows 3.0. DDC Publishing Staff. 1993. disk, pap. 19.95 (*1-56243-172-2*) DDC Pub.

Ami Pro for Windows 3.0 Quick Reference Guide. Pam Toliver. Ed. by Kathy Berkemeyer. (DDC Quick Reference Guides Ser.). (Illus.). 215p. (Orig.). 1993. spiral bd., pap. 8.95 (*1-56243-121-8*, Z-18) DDC Pub.

AMI Pro Made Easy. Daniel J. Fingerman. 1992. pap. text ed. 19.95 (*0-07-881019-1*) Osborne-McGraw.

***Ami Pro X for Dummies.** 2nd ed. Jim Meade. 1995. pap. 19.99 (*1-56884-232-5*) IDG Bks.

Ami Pro 3 Made Easy. 2nd ed. Daniel J. Fingerman. 1992. pap. text ed. 19.95 (*0-07-881857-5*) Osborne-McGraw.

Ami Pro 3 Quick Reference. Trudi Reisner. (Illus.). 192p. (Orig.). 1992. pap. 9.95 (*1-56529-113-1*) Que.

***Ami Pro 3 QuickStart, Corporate Edition.** 1994. pap. (*1-56529-732-6*) Que.

Ami Pro 3.0 for Windows Step by Step. Moira Stephen. (Illus.). 248p. 1993. pap. 21.95 (*0-7506-1698-9*) Buttrwrth-Heinemann.

Ami Pro 3.0 Quickstart. Que Development Group Staff. 1994. pap. 21.95 (*1-56529-683-4*) Que.

AMI Prof Two for Windows: Self Teaching Guide. Pamela S. Beason & Stephen Guild. (Self-Teaching Guides Ser.). 448p. 1992. pap. text ed. 19.95 (*0-471-55217-8*) Wiley.

AMI Singing Towers Series "100" of 1941-42: Service Manual. rev. ed. Ed. by Frank Adams. (Illus.). 50p. reprint ed. 32.50 (*1-56642-070-9*, R-409) AMR Pub Co.

AMI WALL BOX Models W-40, W-80 & W-120 Service Manual. rev. ed. Ed. by Frank Adams. (Illus.). 48p. reprint ed. 19.50 (*1-56642-019-9*, R-92) AMR Pub Co.

Amiable Arrangement. Barbara Allister. (Signet Regency Romance Ser.). 224p. (Orig.). 1994. pap. 3.99 (*0-451-17942-0*, Sig) NAL-Dutton.

Amiable Baltimoreans. Francis F. Beirne. LC 84-47953. (Maryland Paperback Bookshelf Ser.). 1984. reprint ed. pap. 10.95 (*0-8018-2513-X*) Johns Hopkins.

Amiable Renegade: The Memoirs of Captain Peter Drake, 1671-1753. Peter Drake. (Illus.). xiii, 410p. 1960. 52.50 (*0-8047-0022-2*) Stanford U Pr.

***Amicable Agreement vs. Majority Rule: Conflict Resolution in Switzerland.** enl. rev. ed. Jurg Steiner. LC 73-4688. reprint ed. pap. 93.00 (*0-7837-9040-6*, 2049791) Bks Demand.

Amicable Parting. George S. Kaufman & Leueen McGrath. 1957. pap. 2.75 (*0-8222-0038-4*) Dramatists Play.

Amicalement: Advanced Beginning Through Intermediate. Ross Steele & Patricia Marechal-Ross. 170p. (FRE.). 1993. teacher ed 5.25 (*0-8442-1514-7*, Natl Textbk); pap. 15.95 (*0-8442-1513-9*, Natl Textbk) NTC Pub Grp.

Amicus Dei: Essays on Faith & Friendship. Philip J. Anderson. 1988. pap. 4.95 (*0-910452-67-9*) Covenant.

***Amid These Empty Years.** Brendan Tripp. 52p. 1989. pap. 5.00 (*1-57353-016-6*) Eschaton Prods.

***Amidon: A Record of the Descendants of Roger Amadowne of Rehobeth, MA.** Frank E. Best. 165p. 1994. reprint ed. lib. bdg. 36.00 (*0-8328-4291-5*); reprint ed. pap. 26.00 (*0-8328-4292-3*) Higginson Bk Co.

Amidst a Nightmare of Crime: Manuscripts of Prisoners in Crematorium Squads Found at Auschwitz. Ed. by J. Bezwinska & Danuta Czech. Tr. by K. Michalik. LC 91-24978. 207p. 1992. reprint ed. lib. bdg. 35.00 (*0-86527-404-5*) Fertig.

Amidst Babel, Speak the Truth: Reflections on the Southern Baptist Convention Struggle. Ed. by Robert U. Ferguson, Jr. LC 93-14912. 198p. 1993. pap. 10.95 (*1-880837-17-X*) Smyth & Helwys.

Amidst Cultivated & Pleasant Fields: A Bicentennial History of North Haven, Connecticut. Lucy M. Brusic. LC 86-18721. (Illus.). 352p. 1986. 10.00 (*0-914659-20-0*) Phoenix Pub.

Amidst Peril & Pain: The Mental Health & Well-Being of the World's Refugees. Ed. by Anthony J. Marsella et al. 410p. 1994. text ed. 45.00 (*1-55798-223-6*) Am Psychol.

Amie de Madame Maigret. Georges Simenon. pap. 10.95 (*0-8288-6156-0*, F126404) Fr & Eur.

Amiel. Gregorio Maranon. (Nueva Austral Ser.: Vol. 23). (SPA.). 1991. pap. text ed. 24.95x (*84-239-1823-8*) Elliots Bks.

Amiel's Journal. Henri F. Amiel. 1976. lib. bdg. 250.00 (*0-8490-1421-2*) Gordon Pr.

Amiens & Munich. Ernst L. Presseisen. (Comparisons in Appeasement Ser.). 1978. lib. bdg. 62.00 (*90-247-2067-2*) Kluwer Ac.

Amiga Assembly Language Programming. Jake Commander. (Illus.). 240p. 1987. 19.95 (*0-8306-0711-0*, 2711) TAB Bks.

Amiga Companion. Robert A. Peck. 256p. 1988. pap. 19.95 (*0-928579-00-X*) IDG NH.

Amiga Companion. 2nd rev. ed. Robert A. Peck. 306p. 1989. pap. 19.95 (*0-928579-01-8*) IDG NH.

Amiga Desktop Video Workbook. Jay Gross. (Illus.). 279p. 1990. pap. 34.95 (*1-879211-00-9*) Amigadget Pr.

Amiga Desktop Videography. R. Shamms Mortier. (Illus.). (Orig.). 1991. pap. 39.95 (*0-944500-62-5*) MichTron.

Amiga Developers Reference Guide, Edition 1.3. 3rd ed. David Lai. LC 88-92561. 228p. (C). 1988. pap. 19.95 (*0-945119-02-X*) Pacific Pr CA.

Amiga DOS Manual. 3rd ed. Commodore Amiga Staff. 1991. pap. 24.95 (*0-679-79074-8*) Random.

Amiga Multimedia Workbook. Jay Gross. (Workbook Amiga Ser.). 200p. 1991. pap. 29.95 (*1-879211-07-6*) Amigadget Pr.

Amiga Rom Kernel Reference Manual: Devices. 3rd ed. 512p. 1991. pap. 28.95 (*0-201-56775-X*) Addison-Wesley.

Amiga Rom Kernel Reference Manual: Exec. Commodore Business Machines, Inc. Staff. write for info. (*0-318-60215-6*) Addison-Wesley.

Amiga Rom Kernel Reference Manual: Includes & Autodocs. 3rd ed. Commodore-Amiga, Inc. Staff. (Illus.). 1000p. 1991. pap. 38.95 (*0-201-56773-3*) Addison-Wesley.

Amiga Rom Kernel Reference Manual: Libraries. 3rd ed. Commodore-Amiga, Inc. Staff. (Illus.). 960p. 1992. pap. 39.95 (*0-201-56774-1*) Addison-Wesley.

Amiga User Interface Style Guide. Commodore-Amiga, Inc. Staff. 1991. pap. 21.95 (*0-201-57757-7*) Addison-Wesley.

Amigo. Bertha D. Rodriguez et al. (ENG & SPA.). 1989. 93.25 (*0-8442-7674-X*, Passport Bks) NTC Pub Grp.

Amigo. 2nd ed. Byrd Baylor. (Illus.). 48p. (J). (gr. 1-3). 1989. reprint ed. pap. 4.95 (*0-689-71299-5*, Aladdin Paperbacks) S&S Childrens.

Amigo Means Friend. Louise Everett. LC 87-11274. (Illus.). 32p. (J). (gr. k-2). 1988. lib. bdg. 7.89 (*0-8167-1000-7*); pap. text ed. 1.95 (*0-8167-1001-5*) Troll Assocs.

***Amigo Nuevo.** Maria Puncel. (Illus.). 32p. (Orig.). (J). (gr. 3-5). Date not set. pap. text ed. 7.50 (*1-56492-108-5*) Laredo.

Amigo, the Friendly Gray Whale. Artie K. Lay & Gayle S. Runnels. LC 91-65227. (Blubber Buddy Adventure Ser.). (Illus.). 140p. (J). (gr. 2-6). 1991. audio 24.95 (*0-9628626-0-6*) Blubber Budd.

Amigos de Becky. Rolando Hinojosa. LC 90-39166. 128p. (SPA.). 1991. pap. 9.50 (*1-55885-021-X*) Arte Publico.

Amigos de Dios. Mig Holder. Orig. Title: Friends of God. 20p. (SPA.). 1994. pap. 5.99 (*0-8254-1320-6*) Kregel.

Amigos de Dios. Sylvia Mandeville. Tr. by Edna L. Gutierrez. (Serie Apunta Con Tu Dedo). 24p. 1980. pap. 7.50 (*0-311-38532-X*, Edit Mundo) Casa Bautista.

Amigos de Jesus (The Friends of Jesus) Christian Focus Staff. (SPA.). Date not set. 1.29 (*1-56063-388-3*, 494013) Editorial Unilit.

Amigos de Snoopy. Charles M. Schulz. (Peanuts Ser.). 64p. (SPA.). (J). 1971. 1.50 (*0-8288-4507-7*) Fr & Eur.

Amigos en el Hospital. 1979. pap. 1.10 (*0-685-30745-X*) Centering Corp.

Amigos Especiales de Jesus (Jesus's Special Friends) P. Frank. (SPA.). Date not set. 1.50 (*0-8423-6308-4*, 490334) Editorial Unilit.

Amigos y Enemigos de Jesucristo-bL-Alumno. Daniel Roeda. (SPA.). 1993. 0.20 (*1-55955-154-2*) CITE MI.

Amigos y Enemigos de Jesucristo-bL-Maestro. Jeff Stam. (SPA.). 1993. 0.40 (*1-55955-155-0*) CITE MI.

Amigos y Enemigos de Jesucristo-C-Alumno. Daniel Roeda. (SPA.). 1993. 0.20 (*1-55955-150-X*) CITE MI.

Amigos y Enemigos de Jesucristo-C-Maestro. Jeff Stam. (SPA.). 1993. 0.40 (*1-55955-151-8*) CITE MI.

Amigos y Enemigos de Jesucristo-Db-Alumno. Daniel Roeda. (SPA.). 1993. 0.20 (*1-55955-152-6*) CITE MI.

Amigos y Enemigos de Jesucristo-Db-Maestro. Jeff Stam. (SPA.). 1993. 0.40 (*1-55955-153-4*) CITE MI.

Amik! A Pioneer Fur Trader's Adventures. Ione M. Thompson. (Illus.). 218p. (Orig.). 1991. pap. text ed. 11.95x (*0-9643687-2-2*) Cloud Nine.

Amilcar Cabral's Revolutionary Theory & Practice: A Critical Guide. Ronald H. Chilcote. LC 91-11829. 292p. 1991. lib. bdg. 48.00 (*1-55587-058-9*) Lynne Rienner.

Amillenialism Today. William E. Cox. LC 66-28450. 1972. pap. 5.99 (*0-87552-151-7*) Presby & Reformed.

Amiloride & Its Analogs: Unique Cation Transport Inhibitors. Ed. by Edward J. Cragoe, Jr. et al. LC 92-24492. 1992. 115.00 (*1-56081-056-4*) VCH Pubs.

Amin & Sastri's Law of Easements. rev. ed. Justice G. Mathur. 839p. 1984. 360.00 (*0-317-54827-1*) St Mut.

***Aminal.** Lorna Balian. (Illus.). 48p. (J). (ps-3). 1994. 12.95 (*1-881772-19-5*) Humbug Bks.

Amindra Gamble. John Sherlock & David Westheimer. 1983. pap. 3.50 (*0-8217-1228-4*) Zebra.

Amine Oxidases & Their Impact on Neurobiology. Ed. by P. Riederer & M. B. Youdim. (Journal of Neural Transmission Ser.: Suppl. 32). xii, 491p. 1990. pap. 155.00 (*0-387-82239-9*) Spr-Verlag.

Amine Oxidases: Function & Dysfunction: Proceedings of the Fifth INternational Amine Oxidase Workshop, Galway, Ireland, August 22-25, 1992. Ed. by K. F. Tipton et al. (Journal of Neural Transmission Ser.: Vol. 41). (Illus.). 1994. pap. 129.00 (*0-387-82521-5*) Spr-Verlag.

Aminergic & Peptidergic Receptors: Satellite Symposium of the Third Congress of the Hungarian Pharmacological Society, Szeged, 1979. Ed. by E. S. Vizi & Marie Wollemann. LC 80-41281. (Advances in Pharmacological Research & Practice Ser.: Vol. VII). 220p. 1980. 99.00 (*0-08-026839-0*, Pub. by Pergamon Repr UK) Franklin.

Amines & Schizophrenia. H. Himwich & Seymour S. Kety. LC 66-23046. 1967. 128.00 (*0-08-012039-3*, Pub. by Pergamon Repr UK) Franklin.

Amino Acid Analysis by Gas Chromatography, 3 vol. Zumwalt. 1987. Set. 192.00 (*0-8493-4328-3*, QD431) CRC Pr.

Amino Acid & Peptide Synthesis. John H. Jones. (Oxford Chemistry Primers Ser.: No. 7). (Illus.). 96p. (C). 1992. 29.95 (*0-19-855669-1*); pap. 9.95 (*0-19-855668-3*) OUP.

Amino Acid & Peptides, Vol. 24. J. S. Davies. 286p. 1993. 190.00 (*0-85186-224-1*, R6224) CRC Pr.

Amino Acid Availability & Brain Function in Health & Disease. Ed. by G. Huether. (NATO ASI Series H: Vol. 20). (Illus.). 487p. 1988. 173.00 (*0-387-18563-1*) Spr-Verlag.

Amino-Acid Biosynthesis & Genetic Regulation. Klaus Herrmann & Ronald Somerville. (Biotechnology Ser.: No. 3). (Illus.). 330p. (C). 1983. text ed. write for info. (*0-201-10520-9*) Addison-Wesley.

Amino Acid Composition & Biological Value of Cereal Proteins. Ed. by Radomir Laszity & Mate Hidvegi. 1985. lib. bdg. 164.50 (*90-277-1937-3*) Kluwer Ac.

Amino Acid Determination: Methods & Techniques. 2nd ed. Ed. by S. Blackburn. 384p. 1978. 160.00 (*0-8247-6349-1*) Dekker.

Amino Acid Metabolism. 2nd ed. David A. Bender. LC 84-26941. (Illus.). 275p. reprint ed. pap. 78.40 (*0-8357-2885-4*, 2039121) Bks Demand.

Amino Acid Metabolism. 2nd ed. David A. Bender. LC 84-26941. 263p. 1985. text ed. 105.00 (*0-471-90668-9*, Wiley-Interscience) Wiley.

***Amino Acid Metabolism & Therapy in Health & Nutritional Disease.** Ed. by Luc A. Cynober. LC 94-37722. 1995. write for info. (*0-8493-8962-3*) CRC Pr.

Amino Acid Products & Technology. Business Communications Co., Inc. Staff. 120p. 1991. pap. 1,750.00 (*0-89336-448-7*, C-056R) BCC.

Amino Acids & Other Ergogenic Aids. Health for Life Staff. 32p. 1988. pap. 9.95 (*0-685-72100-0*) Health Life.

Amino Acids & Peptides, Vol. 20. J. H. Jones. 350p. 1989. 158.00 (*0-85186-184-9*, CRC Reprint) Franklin.

***Amino Acids & Proteins.** Cold Spring Harbor Symposia on Quantitative Biology Staff. LC 34-8174. (Cold Spring Harbor Symposia on Quantitative Biology Ser.: Vol. 14). (Illus.). 247p. 1950. pap. 70.40 (*0-7837-8972-6*, 2049753) Bks Demand.

***Amino Acids & Their Derivatives in Higher Plants.** Ed. by R. M. Wallsgrove. (Society for Experimental Biology Seminar Ser.: No. 56). (Illus.). 278p. (C). 1995. 64.95 (*0-521-45453-0*) Cambridge U Pr.

Amino Acids for Health. 1992. lib. bdg. 88.95 (*0-8490-5520-2*) Gordon Pr.

Amino Acids in Critical Care & Cancer. Ed. by Rifat Latifi. 118p. 1994. 89.95 (*1-57059-027-3*, LN9027) CRC Pr.

***Amino Acids in Farm Animal Nutrition.** Ed. by J. P. D'Mello. 400p. 1994. 99.00 (*0-85198-881-4*) CAB Intl.

Amino Acids in Psychiatric Disease. Ed. by Mary A. Richardson. LC 89-18455. (Progress in Psychiatry Ser.). 250p. 1990. text ed. 25.00 (*0-88048-186-2*) Am Psychiatric.

Amino Acids in Therapy: A Guide to the Therapeutic Application of Protein Constituents. Leon Chaitow. 96p. (Orig.). 1985. pap. 12.95 (*0-89281-287-7*, Heal Arts VT) Inner Tradit.

Amino-Acids, Peptides, & Proteins, Vols. 1-9. Ed. by R. C. Sheppard. Incl. 1968 LiteratureLC 72-92548. 1970. 32.00 (*0-85186-004-4*); 1969 LiteratureLC 79-67610. 1971. 32.00 (*0-85186-014-1*); 1970 LiteratureLC 72-23822. 1972. 32.00 (*0-85186-024-9*); 1971 LiteratureLC 72-83459. 1973. 38.00 (*0-85186-034-6*); 1972 LiteratureLC 72-92548. 1974. 41.00 (*0-85186-044-3*); 1973 LiteratureLC 72-83459. 1975. 49.00 (*0-85186-054-0*); 1974 LiteratureLC 72-92548. 1976. 54.00 (*0-85186-064-8*); 1975 LiteratureLC 72-92548. 1977. 70.00 (*0-85186-074-5*); 1976 LiteratureLC 72-92548. 1978. 80.00 (*0-85186-084-2*); LC 72-92548. write for info. (*0-318-50461-8*) Am Chemical.

***Amino Acids, Peptides, & Proteins Vol. 25.** J. S. Davies. 424p. 1994. 195.00 (*0-85186-234-9*, R6234) CRC Pr.

Amino Acids Technology-Recent Developments. J. . C. Johnson. LC 78-54000. (Chemical Technology Review Ser.: No. 108). 1978. 42.00 (*0-8155-0703-8*) Noyes.

Amino-Carbonyl Reactions in Food & Biological Systems: Proceedings of the Third International Symposium on the Maillard Reaction, Susono, Shizuoka, Japan, 1-5 July 1985. Ed. by M. Fujimaki et al. (Developments in Food Science Ser.: Vol. 13). 600p. 1986. 192.50 (*0-444-99510-2*) Elsevier.

Amino Revolution: The Breakthrough Program That Will Change the Way You Feel. Robert Erdmann & Meirion Jones. 1989. pap. 10.00 (*0-671-67359-9*, Fireside) S&S Trade.

Aminoacidopathies, Immunoglobinopathies Neuro-Genetics & Neuro-Ophthalmology: Proceedings of the International Congress on Neuro-Genetics & Neuro-Ophthalmology, 3rd, Brussels, 1970. International Congress on Neuro-Genetics & Neuro-Ophthalmology Staff. Ed. by J. Francois. (Monographs in Human Genetics: Vol. 6). (Illus.). 1972. 52.00 (*3-8055-1280-5*) S Karger.

Aminoglycoside Antibiotics: Guide to Therapy. W. Barnes & G. Hodges. LC 83-2558. 1984. 134.00 (*0-8493-5426-9*, CRC Reprint) Franklin.

Aminoglycosides, Microbiology, Clinical Use, & Toxicology. Ed. by Andrew Welton & Harold C. Neu. LC 81-15202. (Kidney Disease Ser.: No. 2). (Illus.). 656p. reprint ed. pap. 180.00 (*0-7837-0789-4*, 2041103) Bks Demand.

Aminopyridines & Similarly Acting Drugs: Effects on Nerves, Muscles & Synapses. Ed. by P. Lechat et al. LC 82-533. (Advances in the Biosciences Ser.: Vol. 35). (Illus.). 352p. 1982. 151.00 (*0-08-028000-5*, Pub. by Pergamon Repr UK) Franklin.

Amiodarone & Arrhythmias: Based on the Scientific Symposium Sponsored by the International Society & Federation of Cardiology. Ed. by D. M. Krikler et al. (Illus.). 100p. 1983. 48.00 (*0-08-029798-6*, Pub. by Pergamon Repr UK) Franklin.

Amiodarone Profile: Report XIII of the Senate Commission for Clinical-Toxicological Analysis. Ed. by David W. Holt et al. (DFG Ser.). 44p. 1990. pap. 25.00 (*0-89573-963-1*) VCH Pubs.

Amion Transport Protein of the Red Blood Cell Membrane. N. Hamasaki & M. L. Jennings. 1990. 92.50 (*0-444-81119-2*) Elsevier.

Amipaque Vascular. Ed. by J. Valk & F. L. Peeters. (Journal: Diagnostic Imaging in Clinical Medicine: Vol. 48, No. 4, 1979). (Illus.). 1979. pap. 18.50 (*3-8055-0196-X*) S Karger.

AMIPM Guide to Northern California. 11th ed. Ed. by Donnali Fifield & Maia Madden. (Illus.). 288p. Date not set. pap. 9.95 (*1-883232-00-7*) AM-PM Pub.

Amiri Baraka (Le Roi Jones) Bob Bernotas. (Black Americans of Achievement Ser.). (Illus.). 112p. (YA). (gr. 5 up). 1991. lib. bdg. 17.95 (*0-7910-1117-8*) Chelsea Hse.

***Amis De la Ferme.** Ed. by Editors of ELI Staff. (Raconte et Chante Ser.). (Illus.). 27p. (Orig.). (FRE.). (J). (gr. k-2). 1992. pap. 19.95 (*88-85148-64-6*, Pub. by Europ Lang Inst IT) Midwest European Pubns.

***Amis De la Ferme Petite Fille: Cahier D'Activites.** Ed. by Editors of ELI Staff. (Raconte et Chante Ser.). (Illus.). 27p. (Orig.). (FRE.). (J). (gr. k-2). 1992. pap. 3.95 (*0-614-07143-7*, Pub. by Europ Lang Inst IT) Midwest European Pubns.

Amis Inconnus. Jules Supervielle. 152p. (FRE.). 1934. pap. 10.95 (*0-7859-1326-2*, 2070261395) Fr & Eur.

Amish. Fred L. Israel. (Peoples of North America Ser.). (Illus.). 112p. (J). 1986. lib. bdg. 17.95 (*0-87754-853-6*) Chelsea Hse.

Amish. rev. ed. John A. Hostetler. LC 94-20202. (Illus.). 40p. (YA). 1995. pap. 4.95 (*0-8361-3692-6*) Herald Pr.

Amish. John A. Hostetler. (Illus.). 40p. 1982. reprint ed. pap. 3.95 (*0-8361-3317-X*) Herald Pr.

Amish: An Illustrated Essay. (Pennsylvania Dutch Bks.). 1966. 3.00 (*0-911410-14-7*) Applied Arts.

***Amish: Images of a Tradition.** Jan Folsom. LC 94-43064. (Illus.). 160p. 1995. pap. 19.95 (*0-8117-2558-8*) Stackpole.

Amish: The Art of the Quilt. Julie Silber. 1993. pap. 30.00 (*0-679-75142-4*) Knopf.

Amish: The Art of the Quilt. Julie Silber. (Illus.). 1990. 99.50 (*0-394-58781-2*) Random.

Amish: The Art of the Quilt Address Book. Callaway Editions Staff. 1991. pap. 18.95 (*0-02-079862-8*) Macmillan.

Amish: The Enduring Spirit. Leslie A. Haslein. 1990. 7.99 (*0-517-03047-0*) Random Hse Value.

Amish: Two Perceptions Two. James A. Perkins & Nelson Oestreich. (Illus.). 24p. (Orig.). 1981. pap. 4.00 (*0-936014-10-5*) Dawn Valley.

Amish Adventure. Barbara Smucker. LC 83-80892. (Illus.). 144p. (Orig.). (J). (gr. 6-9). 1983. pap. 6.95 (*0-8361-3339-0*) Herald Pr.

Amish Adventure: A Workbook for Color in Quilts. Roberta M. Horton. (Illus.). 80p. (Orig.). 1983. pap. 16.95 (*0-914881-01-9*) C & T Pub.

Amish Agriculture in Iowa: Indigenous Knowledge for Sustainable Small Farm Systems. Rhonda L. Yoder. (Studies in Technology & Social Change: No. 15). 73p. (Orig.). (C). 1990. pap. 8.00 (*0-945271-24-7*) ISU-TSCP.

***Amish Americans.** Israel. 1995. (*0-7910-3368-6*) Chelsea Hse.

Amish & the State. Ed. by Donald B. Kraybill. LC 92-31568. (Illus.). 328p. 1993. text ed. 45.00 (*0-8018-4468-1*); pap. text ed. 14.95 (*0-8018-4469-X*) Johns Hopkins.

***Amish Barnraising.** Merle Good. (Illus.). 48p. 1995. 9.95 (*1-56148-150-5*) Good Bks PA.

Amish Barns Across America. John M. Zielinski. (Amish Across America Ser.). 136p. (Orig.). 1988. 17.95 (*0-910381-12-7*, Amish Heritage); pap. 10.95 (*0-910381-13-5*, Amish Heritage) Iowa Heritage Pubns.

Amish Children: Education in the Family, School, & Community. 2nd ed. John A. Hostetler & Gertrude E. Huntington. Ed. by Louise Spindler. LC 91-31733. (Spindler Ser.). (Illus.). 130p. (C). 1992. pap. text ed. 13.50 (*0-03-031592-1*) HB Coll Pubs.

Amish Children Across America. John M. Zielinski. (Amish Across America Ser.). 48p. (Orig.). 1987. pap. 4.95 (*0-910381-16-X*, Amish Heritage) Iowa Heritage Pubns.

Amish Cook Cookbook. Elizabeth Coblentz. Ed. by Kevin Williams. (Illus.). 192p. 1993. pap. 15.95 (*0-9638775-1-8*) Oasis Newsfeatures.

Amish Cookbook. Alvin K. Lapp et al. (Illus.). 433p. 1992. 11.25 (*0-9637275-0-8*) A K Lapp.

Amish Cooking. 96p. 1989. 10.99 (*0-517-68911-1*) Random Hse Value.

Amish Cooking. Sallie Y. Lapp. 48p. 1982. 1.69 (*0-9637275-2-4*) A K Lapp.

Amish Cooking: Flatboard Edition. rev. ed. Committee of Amish Women Staff. 320p. 1992. spiral bd. 16.95 (*0-8361-3626-8*); spiral bd. 15.95 (*0-8361-3600-4*) Herald Pr.

***Amish Cooking: More Than Fifty Authentic Recipes, Enriched with History & Tradition.** Stewart. 1995. 12.98 (*1-56138-562-X*) Courage Bks.

Amish Cooking for Kids: For Six to Twelve Year-Old Cooks. Phyllis P. Good et al. (Illus.). 96p. (Orig.). 1994. pap. 9.95 (*1-56148-131-9*) Good Bks PA.

Amish Country. 1991. 12.99 (*0-517-62365-X*, Crown) Random Hse Value.

Amish Country: Land of Buggies, Beards, Barns, Bridges, Bonnets & Barefeet. Marshall A. Dussinger. (Illus.). 1980. pap. 3.95 (*0-935456-00-7*) Stel-Mar.

***Amish Country: 1996 Calendar.** (Illus.). 26p. 1996. 12.95 (*1-886154-05-8*) Phoenix IL.

Amish Country Address Book. Marshall A. Dussinger. (Illus.). 28p. 1987. pap. 4.95 (*0-935456-02-3*) Stel-Mar.

Amish Country Cookbook. Bob Miller & Sue Miller. (Illus.). 296p. (Orig.). 1981. pap. 11.99 (*0-934998-00-0*) Bethel Pub.

Amish-Country Cookbook, Vol. 2. Bob Miller & Sue Miller. 320p. 1986. spiral bd. 11.99 (*0-934998-23-X*) Bethel Pub.

Amish Country Cookbook, Vol. 3. Bob Miller & Sue Miller. 320p. (Orig.). 1993. spiral bd., pap. 11.99 (*0-934998-49-3*) Bethel Pub.

Amish Country Cooking. Judith Ferguson. 1991. 17.99 (*0-517-06597-5*) Random Hse Value.

Amish Crib Quilts. deluxe ed. Rachel T. Pellman & Kenneth Pellman. LC 85-70281. (Illus.). 96p. (Orig.). 1985. pap. 15.95 (*0-934672-29-6*) Good Bks PA.

Amish Doll Quilts, Dolls & Other Playthings. Rachel Pellman & Kenneth Pellman. LC 86-81060. (Illus.). 96p. (Orig.). 1986. pap. 15.95 (*0-934672-35-0*) Good Bks PA.

Amish Drawings of Florence Starr Taylor. Illus. by Florence S. Taylor. LC 87-20895. 96p. 1987. 12.95 (*0-934672-55-5*) Good Bks PA.

***Amish Enterprise: From Plow to Profits.** Donald B. Kraybill & Steven M. Nolt. LC 95-1433. (Illus.). 240p. 1995. text ed. 45.00x (*0-8018-5062-2*); pap. text ed. 14.95x (*0-8018-5063-0*) Johns Hopkins.

Amish Family. Phyllis R. Naylor. 18.95 (*0-8488-0109-1*, Amereon Hse) Amereon Ltd.

Amish Folk Remedies for Plain & Fancy Ailments. Ed. by William R. McGrath. 104p. 1988. pap. 6.99 (*0-9617405-8-2*) S Schupp.

Amish Guide Book. 1990. 4.49 (*0-942618-27-0*) Penrod-Hiawatha.

Amish Home. Raymond Bial. (Illus.). 40p. (J). (gr. 4-7). 1993. 14.95 (*0-395-59504-5*) HM.

***Amish Home.** Raymond Bial. LC 92-4406. (J). (gr. 4-7). 1995. pap. 5.95 (*0-395-72021-4*) HM.

Amish Horsefarming Across America. John M. Zielinski. (Amish Across America Ser.). (Illus.). 48p. (Orig.). 1988. pap. 4.95 (*0-910381-18-6*, Amish Heritage) Iowa Heritage Pubns.

Amish Houses & Barns. Stephen Scott. LC 92-28090. (People's Place Book Ser.: No. 11). (Illus.). 158p. 1991. pap. 6.95 (*1-56148-052-5*) Good Bks PA.

Amish in Switzerland & Other European Countries. Betty Miller. 1978. pap. 1.50 (*0-685-46025-8*) O R Miller.

Amish Life. John V. Wasilchick. 1991. 19.99 (*0-517-06584-3*) Random Hse Value.

Amish Life. 2nd ed. John A. Hostetler. LC 82-83964. (Illus.). 48p. (Orig.). 1983. pap. 5.95 (*0-8361-3326-9*) Herald Pr.

Amish Life Style Illustrated. Terry L. Troyer. LC 82-90105. (Illus.). 96p. (J). (gr. 6-12). 1982. 19.95 (*0-943314-00-3*) TLT.

Amish Literacy: What & How It Means. Andrea Fishman. LC 87-34487. xiii, 225p. (Orig.). 1988. pap. 18.50 (*0-435-08455-0*) Heinemann.

Amish of Canada. Orland Gingerich. LC 72-94800. 244p. reprint ed. pap. 69.60 (*0-8357-2654-1*, 2040189) Bks Demand.

***Amish of Harmony.** Drucilla Milne. Ed. by Martha King & Paula Michel. (Illus.). 134p. (Orig.). 1993. pap. 10.00 (*0-9638637-0-3*) D Milne.

Amish Patchwork: Full-Size Patterns for 46 Authentic Designs. Suzy Lawson. (Illus.). 144p. 1988. reprint ed. pap. 5.95 (*0-486-25701-0*) Dover.

Amish Pioneers of the Walnut Creek Valley. Betty Miller. 1978. pap. 2.50 (*0-685-87375-7*) O R Miller.

Amish Portrait: Song of a People. Merle Good. LC 93-30733. (Illus.). 48p. 1993. 9.95 (*1-56148-095-9*) Good Bks PA.

***Amish Potpourri Cookbook.** Adrienne F. Lund. (Illus.). 170p. (Orig.). 1991. pap. 12.95 (*1-886645-02-7*) Jupiter Press.

Amish Quilt. Eve W. Granick. LC 89-39987. (Illus.). 192p. 1989. 45.00 (*0-934672-74-1*) Good Bks PA.

Amish Quilt. Eve W. Granick. LC 89-39987. (Illus.). 192p. 1994. pap. 24.95 (*1-56148-109-2*) Good Bks PA.

Amish Quilt Designs. Doreen L. Saunders. 1990. pap. 3.95 (*0-486-26519-6*) Dover.

Amish Quilt in a Day, Variations of Roman Stripe. Eleanor Burns. (Illus.). 46p. 1986. 7.95 (*0-922705-05-4*) Quilt Day.

Amish Quilt Patterns. Rachel T. Pellman. LC 84-80652. (Illus.). 128p. 1984. pap. 12.95 (*0-934672-23-7*) Good Bks PA.

Amish Quilting Patterns: Fifty-Six Full-Size Ready-to-Use Designs & Complete Instructions. Gwen Marston & Joe Cunningham. 96p. (Orig.). 1987. pap. 4.95 (*0-486-25326-0*) Dover.

Amish Quiltmaker: From Small Projects to Full-Sized Quilts. Bettina Havig. LC 92-17121. (Illus.). 160p. 1991. pap. 15.95 (*0-8069-8524-0*, Sterling-Main St) Sterling.

Amish Quilts: With Plastic Templates. Mary C. Waldrep. LC 94-6007. 1994. write for info. (*0-486-28141-8*) Dover.

***Amish Recipe Sampler.** Adrienne F. Lund. 65p. (Orig.). 1982. pap. 4.95 (*1-886645-00-0*) Jupiter Press.

Amish Roots: A Treasury of History, Wisdom, & Lore. Ed. by John A. Hostetler. LC 88-31688. (Illus.). 344p. 1989. 35.00 (*0-8018-3769-3*) Johns Hopkins.

Amish Roots: A Treasury of History, Wisdom, & Lore. Ed. by John A. Hostetler. (Illus.). 336p. 1992. reprint ed. pap. 16.95 (*0-8018-4402-9*) Johns Hopkins.

Amish School. Sara E. Fisher & Rachel K. Stahl. LC 84-81142. (People's Place Book Ser.: No. 6). (Illus.). 96p. 1986. pap. 5.95 (*0-934672-17-2*) Good Bks PA.

Amish Society. rev. ed. John A. Hostetler. (Illus.). 448p. (C). 1993. pap. 14.95 (*0-8018-4442-8*) Johns Hopkins.

Amish Society. 4th rev. ed. John A. Hostetler. (Illus.). 448p. (C). 1993. text ed. 45.00 (*0-8018-4441-X*) Johns Hopkins.

Amish Struggle with Modernity. Ed. by Donald B. Kraybill & Marc A. Olshan. LC 94-13668. (Illus.). 256p. 1994. text ed. 40.00x (*0-87451-683-8*); pap. 17.95 (*0-87451-684-6*) U Pr of New Eng.

Amish Style: Clothing, Home Furnishing, Toys, Dolls, & Quilts. Kathleen McLary. LC 92-43967. (C). 1993. 39.95 (*0-253-33622-8*); pap. 24.95 (*0-253-20820-3*) Ind U Pr.

Amish Table. Phyllis P. Good. LC 94-33292. (Illus.). 48p. 1994. 9.95 (*1-56148-130-0*) Good Bks PA.

Amish Taste Cooking Step by Step. Alma Hershberger. (Illus.). 104p. 1992. pap. 4.95 (*1-881061-01-9*) Art of Amish.

***Amish, the Art of the Quilt.** Robert Hughes. LC 95-13536. (Illus.). 1995. 49.99 (*0-517-14751-3*, Pub. by Wings Bks) Random.

Amish Treats from My Kitchen. Sallie Y. Lapp. (Illus.). 47p. (Orig.). 1981. 3.29 (*0-9637275-1-6*) A K Lapp.

Amish Ways. Ruth H. Seitz. LC 90-63838. (Illus.). 120p. 1991. 24.95 (*1-879441-77-2*) RB Bks.

Amish Wedding & Other Special Occasions of the Old Order Communities. Stephen Scott. LC 87-38310. (People's Place Book Ser.: No. 8). (Illus.). 128p. 1988. pap. 5.95 (*0-934672-19-9*) Good Bks PA.

Amish Women. Alma Hershberger. (Illus.). (Orig.). 1992. pap. 5.95 (*1-881061-00-0*) Art of Amish.

Amish Women: Lives & Stories. Louise Stoltzfus. LC 94-34166. (Illus.). 123p. 1994. 14.95 (*1-56148-129-7*) Good Bks PA.

Amishman Travels Around the World: The Life of Jonathan B. Fisher. H. Harold Hartzler. 33p. 1991. pap. 4.50 (*1-883294-09-6*) Olde Sprgfld.

***Amistad E Intimidad.** Gloria Ricardo. 28p. 1992. pap. 1.00 (*1-885630-17-4*) HLM Producciones.

Amistad e Intimidad (Friendship & Intimacy) G. Ricardo. (SPA.). Date not set. 1.79 (*0-945792-70-0*, 498108) Editorial Unilit.

Amistad Factor Decisivo. Alan L. McGinnis. Orig. Title: The Friendship Factor. 204p. (SPA.). 1986. reprint ed. pap. 5.95 (*0-311-46093-3*, Edit Mundo) Casa Bautista.

***Amistad International Dictionary of Black Quotations.** Vastiana Belfon. 480p. 1994. 34.95 (*1-56743-066-X*) Amistad Pr.

Amistad Intima con Dios. Joy Dawson. 112p. (Orig.). (SPA.). 1990. pap. 3.95 (*0-88113-019-2*) Edit Betania.

***Amistad Pictorial History of the African-American Athlete: Collegiate & Professional, Vols. 1 & 2.** Francis C. Harris & Charles F. Harris, Jr. (Illus.). 512p. 1994. boxed 50.00 (*1-56743-068-6*) Amistad Pr.

***Amistad Pictorial History of the African-American Athlete: Professional, Vol. 2.** Francis C. Harris & Charles F. Harris, Jr. (Illus.). 256p. 1994. 25.00 (*1-56743-067-8*) Amistad Pr.

Amistad Pictorial History of the African-American Athlete Vol. 1: Collegiate. Francis C. Harris & Charles F. Harris, Jr. (Illus.). 256p. 1994. 25.00 (*1-56743-048-1*) Amistad Pr.

Amitabha: A Story of Buddhist Theology. Paul Carus. 1988. reprint ed. lib. bdg. 49.00 (*0-317-90092-7*) Rprt Serv.

Amitabha: A Story of Buddhist Theology. Paul Carus. 1977. reprint ed. 49.00 (*0-403-07255-7*) Scholarly.

Amitie Antique D'apres les Moeurs Populaires & les Theories Des Philosophes. Ludovic Dugas. LC 75-13263. (History of Ideas in Ancient Greece Ser.). (FRE.). 1976. reprint ed. 35.95 (*0-405-07305-4*) Ayer.

Amitie Exemplaire: Villiers De L'isle-Adam et Stephane Mallarme. Georges Jean-Aubry. LC 80-205. (Symbolists Ser.). (Illus.). (FRE.). reprint ed. 39.50 (*0-404-16300-9*) AMS Pr.

Amitie Francaise: Avec: Correspondance entre Charles Peguy et Romain Rolland. Romain Rolland & Charles Peguy. 360p. (FRE.). 1955. pap. 8.95 (*0-7859-5438-4*) Fr & Eur.

Amitie-Friendship: An Investigation into Cross-Cultural Styles in the United States & Canada. J. Barry Gurdin. LC 93-6060. 325p. 1995. 64.95 (*1-880921-52-9*); pap. 54.95 (*1-880921-51-0*) Austin & Winfield.

Amities et Rencontres. Jules Romains. 231p. (FRE.). 1970. pap. 17.95 (*0-7859-1412-9*, 2080604899) Fr & Eur.

Amity Cemetery Family Plot Map, 1938. Orange County Genealogical Society Staff. 1986. pap. text ed. 0.50 (*0-937135-01-1*) Orange County Genealog.

Amityville: The Nightmare Continues. Robin Karl. 336p. (Orig.). 1991. pap. 4.50 (*0-8439-3079-9*) Dorchester Pub Co.

Amityville Horror. Deborah Crisfield. LC 91-4528. (Tales of Terror Ser.). (Illus.). 48p. (J). (gr. 5-6). 1991. text ed. 13.95 (*0-89686-576-2*, Crstwood Hse) Silver Burdett Pr.

AMJ Graffica's Cartons for Kids I: Adventures in Creating Carton Toys, Games, Gifts, & Crafts. Elaine Gross & Randal Kochenderfer. LC 85-72414. (Illus.). 73p. (Orig.). 1985. pap. 6.95 (*0-935575-00-6*) AMJ Graffica.

Amka's Story. Nick Wyche. (Illus.). (C). 1990. 35.00 (*0-7223-2508-8*, Pub. by A H S Ltd UK) St Mut.

Amkoullel, L'Enfant Peul, Memoires. Amadou H. Ba. 534p. (FRE.). 1992. pap. 24.95 (*0-7859-3307-7*, 2868699065) Fr & Eur.

AML Workbook (ARC Macro Language) rev. ed. Environmental Systems Research Institute Staff. (Illus.). 794p. Date not set. pap. text ed. 50.00 (*1-879102-18-8*) ERS Inst.

***Amler's Precedent of Pleadings.** 4th ed. L. T. Harms. 420p. 1993. boxed 150.00 (*0-409-01103-7*, SA) Butterworth Legal Pubs.

Amleth. Mark Dunster. 1979. pap. 4.00 (*0-89642-056-6*) Linden Pubs.

Amlodipine. W. G. Nayler. LC 93-23381. (Illus.). 325p. 1993. pap. 125.00 (*0-387-56698-8*) Spr-Verlag.

Amma: The Life & Words of Amy Carmichael. Elizabeth Skoglund. LC 94-28212. 260p. 1994. 16.99 (*0-8010-8383-4*) Baker Bk.

Amma Section. 72p. 1987. pap. 35.00 (*1-85077-012-3*, Darf Pubs Ltd) St Mut.

Ammachi: A Biography of Mata Amritanandamayi. 2nd ed. Swami Amritaswarupananda. 317p. (Orig.). 1991. 13.00 (*1-879410-50-8*) M A Ctr.

Ammar Yasir: The Distinguished Companion of the Holy Prophet. rev. ed. Sadruddin Sharafuddin. Tr. by M. Fazal Haq. Orig. Title: Halif al-Makhzum. 264p. (YA). reprint ed. pap. 7.00 (*0-941724-40-9*) Islamic Seminary.

Ammassalick Eskimo: Contributions to the Ethnology of the East Greenland Natives, 2 vols. Ed. by William C. Thalbitzer. LC 74-5881. reprint ed. Set. 245.00 (*0-404-11689-2*) AMS Pr.

Ammianstudien. Hans Drexler. (Spudasmata Ser.: Bd. 31). 207p. (GER.). 1974. write for info. (*3-487-05289-X*, Pub. by Georg Olms GW) Lubrecht & Cramer.

Ammianus Marcellinus: A Selection. R. C. Blockley. 168p. 1981. 16.95 (*0-906515-07-6*, Pub. by Brstl Class Pr UK) Focus Info Gr.

Ammianus Marcellinus - Ammiani Marcellini Rerum Gestarum Lexicon, 2 vols. (Alpha-Omega, Reihe A Ser.: Bd. LXXIX). xxi, 1621p. (GER.). 1985. Set. write for info. (*3-487-07710-8*, Pub. by Georg Olms GW) Lubrecht & Cramer.

Ammianus Marcellinus - Index Verborum Ammiani Marcellini, 2 vols. Ed. by Maria Chiabo. (Alpha-Omega, Reihe A Ser.: Bd. XLIV). xii, 903p. (GER.). 1983. Set. write for info. (*3-487-07353-6*, Pub. by Georg Olms GW) Lubrecht & Cramer.

Ammie, Come Home. Barbara Michaels. 256p. 1987. mass mkt. 5.99 (*0-425-09949-0*) Berkley Pub.

Ammie, Come Home. Barbara Michaels. 1979. pap. 1.95 (*0-449-23926-8*, Crest) Fawcett.

Ammie, Come Home. large type ed. Barbara Michaels. LC 93-13246. 1993. 18.95 (*0-7927-1672-8*, Eagle Lrg Print); pap. 17.95 (*0-7927-1671-X*, Eagle Lrg Print) Chivers N Amer.

***Ammo Forever: The Complete What to Shoot & How Manual for Rifles & Shotguns.** Don Paul & David B. Smith. LC 94-69563. (Illus.). 192p. (Orig.). 1995. pap. 14.95 (*0-938263-15-3*) Path Finder.

***Ammo Forever II: The Complete What to Shoot & How Manual for Handguns.** Don Paul & David B. Smith. (Illus.). 160p. (Orig.). 1995. pap. 14.95 (*0-938263-19-6*) Path Finder.

Ammon & the King. Sherrie Johnson. 1994. pap. 4.95 (*0-87579-812-8*) Deseret Bk.

Ammonia. (Environmental Health Criteria Ser.: No. 54). 210p. 1986. pap. 10.80 (*92-4-154194-6*) World Health.

Ammonia, Pts. 1. Ed. by Archie V. Slack & G. Russell James. LC 72-97482. (Fertilizer Science & Technology Ser.: No. 2). 432p. reprint ed. Pt. 1. pap. 123.20 (*0-8357-5413-8*, 2030861); reprint ed. Pt. 3. pap. 136.60 (*0-8357-5414-6*, 2030861) Bks Demand.

***Ammonia: Catalysis & Manufacture.** K. Aika. Ed. by Anders Nielsen. LC 94-36677. 1995. write for info. (*0-387-58335-1*) Spr-Verlag.

***Ammonia Pt. 4.** fac. ed. Ed. by Archie V. Slack & G. Russell James. LC 72-97482. (Fertilizer Science & Technology Ser.: No. 2). (Illus.). 207p. 1994. pap. 59.00 (*0-7837-7303-X*, 2030861) Bks Demand.

***Ammonia Absorption Refrigeration in Industrial Processes.** fac. ed. Marcel Bogart. LC 81-197. (Illus.). 493p. Date not set. pap. 140.60 (*0-7837-7424-9*, 2047219) Bks Demand.

Ammonia Plant Safety, Vol. 30. Ammonia Plant Safety Committee Staff. LC 72-625346. 253p. 1990. pap. 80.00 (*0-8169-0489-8*, T-84) Am Inst Chem Eng.

Ammonia Plant Safety, Vol. 31. Comp. by AIChE Ammonia Plant Safety Committee Staff. LC 72-625346. 262p. 1991. pap. 150.00 (*0-8169-0551-7*) Am Inst Chem Eng.

Ammonia Volitilization from Urea Fertilizer. Ed. by B. R. Bock & D. E. Kissel. (Illus.). 189p. 1988. 15.00 (*0-87077-003-9*) TVA.

Ammonite. Nicola Griffith. (Orig.). 1992. mass mkt. 3.99 (*0-345-37891-1*, Del Rey Discovery) Ballantine.

***Ammonite.** Nicola Griffith. 1995. pap. 3.99 (*0-345-90351-X*, Del Rey) Ballantine.

Ammonite Language of the Iron Age. Kent P. Jackson. LC 82-16813. (Harvard Semitic Monographs). 134p. (C). 1984. 24.75 (*0-89130-592-0*, 040027) Scholars Pr GA.

Ammonium Nitrate, Storage of, Code. (Forty Ser.). 1993. pap. 16.75 (*0-685-58152-7*, 490) Natl Fire Prot.

***Ammonius Saccus & His "Eclectic Philosophy" As Presented by Alexander Wilder.** Jean-Louis Siemons. Ed. & Frwd. by James A. Santucci. (Theosophical History Occasional Papers: Vol. III). (Illus.). 31p. (Orig.). 1994. pap. text ed. 15.00 (*1-883279-03-8*) J Santucci.

Ammonoidea. Ed. by M. R. Howse & J. R. Senior. 584p. 1981. text ed. 190.00 (*0-12-356780-7*) Acad Pr.

Ammonoidea: Environment, Ecology, & Evolutionary Change. Ed. by M. R. House. LC 92-23357. (Systematics Association Special Volume Ser.: Vol. 47). (Illus.). 352p. 1993. 83.00 (*0-19-857765-6*, Clarendon Pr) OUP.

Ammunition & Explosive Standards. 1991. lib. bdg. 79.95 (*0-8490-4089-2*) Gordon Pr.

Ammunition for the Land Battle. P. R. Courtney-Green. Ed. by R. G. Lee & Frank Hartley. (Brassey's Battlefield Weapons Systems & Technology Ser.: Vol. 4). 300p. 1991. 40.00 (*0-08-035821-7*, Pub. by Brasseys UK); 25.00 (*0-08-035807-1*, Pub. by Brasseys UK) Brasseys Inc.

Ammunition, Grenades & Mines. K. J. Goad & D. H. Halsey. LC 81-23411. (Brassey's Battlefield Weapons Systems & Technology Ser.: Vol. 3). 160p. 1982. 39.00 (*0-08-028326-8*, T120, Pergamon Pr); pap. 21.00 (*0-08-028327-6*, Pergamon Pr) Elsevier.

Ammunition Handbook. 1991. lib. bdg. 250.00 (*0-8490-4075-2*) Gordon Pr.

Ammunition Handbook. 1990. lib. bdg. 79.95 (*0-87700-896-5*) Revisionist Pr.

Amnesia. Douglas Cooper. 240p. 1994. 19.95 (*1-56282-748-0*) Hyperion.

***Amnesia Moon.** Jonathan Lethem. LC 95-4127. 256p. 1995. 20.00 (*0-15-100091-3*) HarBrace.

An Asterisk (*) at the beginning of an entry indicates that the title is appearing in BIP for the first time.

An Asterisk (*) at the beginning of an entry indicates that the title is appearing in BIP for the first time.

279

Amor en los Tiempos de Colera. 9th ed. Gabriel G. Marquez. 360p. (SPA.). 1989. pap. 24.95 (*0-7859-4987-9*) Fr & Eur.

Amor en Peligro: Love in Danger. Nancy Fernandez. (SPA.). 3.25 (*84-7228-335-6*, 220023, Pub. by Edit Clie SP) TSELF.

Amor Es Cosa Seria: Love Is Serious Business. Pablo A. Deiros. 64p. (SPA.). 1988. pap. 2.50 (*0-311-12339-2*) Casa Bautista.

Amor es una Decision. Gary Smalley & John Trent. 224p. (Orig.). (SPA.). 1990. pap. 4.95 (*0-88113-025-7*) Edit Betania.

Amor et Amicitia. Patricia E. Bell. (C). 1989. pap. 9.50 (*0-521-37736-6*) Cambridge U Pr.

Amor, Fe y Esperanza, No. 1. Adolfo Robleto. 96p. 1987. reprint ed. pap. 3.25 (*0-311-08755-8*) Casa Bautista.

Amor, Fe y Esperanza, No. 2. Adolfo Robleto. (No. 2). 96p. 1990. reprint ed. pap. 3.25 (*0-311-08757-4*) Casa Bautista.

Amor Gemelo. Jorge E. Florian. (Romance Real Ser.). 189p. 1981. pap. 1.50 (*0-88025-002-X*) Roca Pub.

Amor Hasta Lo Sumo: Love on the Highest Plain. F. B. Meyer. (SPA.). 7.95 (*84-7228-800-5*, 220025, Pub. by Edit Clie SP) TSELF.

Amor, Honor y Obesidad: Love, Honor & Obesity. Allison Hugues. (SPA.). 4.95 (*84-7228-365-8*, 220024, Pub. by Edit Clie SP) TSELF.

Amor Maravilloso: Wondrous Love. D. L. Moody. (SPA.). 4.95 (*84-7228-969-9*, 223021, Pub. by Edit Clie SP) TSELF.

Amor Nunca Deja de Ser. Kenneth E. Hagin. (SPA.). 1992. pap. 0.75 (*0-89276-164-4*) Hagin Ministries.

Amor Para Toda la Vida. James C. Dobson. 128p. (Orig.). (SPA.). 1990. pap. 3.95 (*0-88113-021-4*) Edit Betania.

Amor que No Se Apaga. Ed Wheat. 224p. 1984. 4.95 (*0-88113-010-9*) Edit Betania.

Amor Resucitado y Amor y Filosofia. Herminia D. Ibaceta. 48p. (Orig.). (SPA.). 1992. pap. 6.00 (*0-9623552-8-3*) Ed Arcas.

Amor Sin Fronteras. Tirso R. Herrera. LC 86-80887. (Coleccion Espejo de Paciencia Ser.). 112p. (Orig.). (SPA.). 1986. pap. 7.00 (*0-89729-399-1*) Ediciones.

Amor Sin Limites: Love Unlimited. Festo Kivengere. (SPA.). 3.95 (*84-7228-282-1*, 220026, Pub. by Edit Clie SP) TSELF.

Amor Vincitore. Ernest Warburton. (Johann Christian Bach Ser.). 275p. 1987. lib. bdg. 72.00 (*0-8240-6064-4*) Garland.

Amor y Anarquia: Los Escritos de Luisa Capetillo. Ed. by Julio Ramos. LC 91-78121. (Clasicos Huracan Ser.). 222p. (SPA.). 1992. pap. 7.95 (*0-929157-15-X*) Ediciones Huracan.

Amor y la Juventud. Joan Goetz. Tr. by Lidia D. Montero. (Illus.). 96p. 1987. reprint ed. pap. 2.95 (*0-311-46058-5*) Casa Bautista.

Amor y Pasion (Love & Passion) I. Palau. (SPA.). Date not set. 1.79 (*1-56063-180-5*, 498014) Editorial Unilit.

Amor y Pedagogia. Miguel Unamuno. Ed. by Ana Caballe. (Nueva Austral Ser.: Vol. 263). (SPA.). 1991. pap. text ed. 24.95x (*84-239-7263-1*) Elliots Bks.

Amor y Sexo: Lo Que Ud. Debe Saber: Love & Sex: What It's All About. Wilson Grant. (SPA.). 5.50 (*84-7228-204-X*, 220029, Pub. by Edit Clie SP) TSELF.

Amorak. Tim Jessell. LC 93-48622. 32p. (J). 1994. 16.95 (*0-88682-662-4*) Creative Ed.

Amorak. Tim Jessell. (Illus.). 32p. (J). (gr. 1-7). 1994. 14.95 (*1-56846-092-9*) Creative Ed.

Amoral America. rev. ed. George C. Benson & Thomas S. Engeman. LC 81-70432. 317p. 1982. lib. bdg. 22.75 (*0-89089-208-3*); pap. 9.95 (*0-89089-209-1*) Carolina Acad Pr.

Amoral Politics: The Persistent Truth of Machiavellism. Ben-Ami Scharfstein. LC 94-8609. 320p. (C). 1995. text ed. 59.50x (*0-7914-2279-8*); pap. text ed. 19.95 (*0-7914-2280-1*) State U NY Pr.

Amoralists. Tom Mooney. pap. 3.00 (*0-317-28509-2*) Mooney.

Amorelle. Grace L. Hill. 320p. reprint ed. lib. bdg. 19.95 (*0-89190-055-1*, Rivercity Pr) Amereon Ltd.

Amorelle, No. 4. Grace L. Hill. 224p. 1989. pap. 4.99 (*0-8423-0310-3*) Tyndale.

Amores. Ovid. Ed. by Edwin J. Kenney. Incl. Medicamina Faciei Femineae. 1961. (*0-318-54803-8*); Ars Amatoria. 1961. (*0-318-54804-6*); Remedia Amoria. 1961. (*0-318-54805-4*); (Oxford Classical Texts Ser.). 1961. 21.00 (*0-19-814642-6*) OUP.

Amores II. Ovid. Ed. by Booth. (Classical Texts Ser.). 49.85 (*0-85668-174-1*, Pub. by Aris & Phillips UK); pap. 24.95 (*0-85668-175-X*, Pub. by Aris & Phillips UK) David Brown.

Amores, Medicamina Faciei Femineae, Ars Amatoria, Remedia Amoris. 2nd ed. Ovid. Ed. by E. J. Kenney. (Classical Texts). (Illus.). 280p. 1994. 17.50 (*0-19-814969-7*) OUP.

Amorite Personal Names in the Mari Texts: A Structural & Lexical Study. Herbert B. Huffmon. LC 64-24346. 320p. reprint ed. pap. 91.20 (*0-8357-8021-X*, 2034128) Bks Demand.

Amorolfine, A Breakthrough in Topical Antimyocotic Therapy. Ed. by R. J. Hay. (Journal: Dermatologica: Vol. 184, Suppl. 1, 1992). (Illus.). vi, 30p. 1992. pap. 14.50 (*3-8055-5573-3*) S Karger.

Amorosa Ero. Ed. & Tr. by Harry B. Lincoln. LC 66-64729. 134p. 1968. 49.50 (*0-87395-030-5*) State U NY Pr.

***Amorosa Visione.** Giovanni Boccaccio. Tr. by Robert Hollander et al. LC 85-40488. 285p. (ENG & ITA.). 1986. reprint ed. pap. 81.30 (*0-7837-8194-6*, 2047899) Bks Demand.

Amoroscopo. Indira Shankar. 168p. (Orig.). (SPA.). 1985. pap. 3.50 (*0-939193-05-1*) Edit Concepts.

Amoroscopo, 1990. Ed. by Creative Publishing Concepts Staff. (Illus.). 208p. (Orig.). (SPA.). 1990. pap. 1.95 (*0-944499-73-2*) Editorial Amer.

Amoroscopo, 1991. Ed. by Frank Calderon. (Illus.). 226p. Date not set. pap. 2.95 (*0-944499-98-8*) Editorial Amer.

Amoroscopo, 1992. Ed. by Frank Calderon. (Illus.). 226p. Date not set. pap. 2.95 (*1-56259-006-5*) Editorial Amer.

Amoroscopo, 1993. Ed. by Frank Calderon. (SPA.). Date not set. pap. 3.95 (*1-56259-023-5*) Editorial Amer.

Amoroscopo, 1994. Indira Shankar & Zellagro. Ed. by Mirtha Forest. 272p. (SPA.). 1993. pap. 3.95 (*1-56259-029-4*) Editorial Amer.

Amoroso Creador (The Caring Creator) C. MacKenzie. (SPA.). Date not set. 9.99 (*1-56063-305-0*, 490445) Editorial Unilit.

Amorous Adventures. 1991. pap. 4.50 (*0-8216-5091-2*, Univ Books) Carol Pub Group.

Amorous Cannibal. Chris Wallace-Crabbe. LC 84-29481. 64p. 1985. pap. 7.95 (*0-19-211968-0*) OUP.

***Amorous Exploits of a Young Rakehill.** Guillaume Apollinaire. (Orig.). 1994. pap. 9.95 (*1-56201-083-2*, North Star Line) Blue Moon Bks.

Amorous Fiammetta. Giovanni Boccaccio. LC 76-98821. 356p. 1970. reprint ed. text ed. 65.00 (*0-8371-3026-3*, BOAF, Greenwood Pr) Greenwood.

Amorous Initiation: A Novel of Sacred & Profane Love. O. V. Milosz. 256p. 1993. 22.95 (*0-89281-418-7*) Inner Tradit.

Amorous Professor. (Red Stripe Ser.). 1988. pap. 4.50 (*0-8216-5053-X*, Univ Books) Carol Pub Group.

Amorphic Brain Jans. Franklin H. Stover. 30p. 1989. pap. 6.00 (*0-685-32642-X*) Oneiric Pr.

Amorphic Brain Jars. Franklin H. Stover. 30p. (Orig.). 1989. pap. 6.00 (*0-931553-07-5*) Oneiric Pr.

Amorphismes Ypocras De Martin De Saint-Gille. Hippocrates. Ed. by Germaine Lafeuille. (Harvard Studies in Romance Languages: Vol. 24 & 25). 1954. 64.00 (*0-527-01123-1*) Periodicals Srv.

Amorphous & Crystalline Silicon Carbide II. Ed. by M. M. Rahman et al. (Proceedings in Physics Ser.: Vol. 43). (Illus.). x, 232p. 1989. 65.00 (*0-387-51656-5*, 3515) Spr-Verlag.

Amorphous & Crystalline Silicon Carbide III & Other Group IV-IV Materials: Proceedings of the 3rd International Conference Howard University, Washington, DC, April 11-13, 1990. Ed. by G. L. Harris et al. (Proceedings in Physics Ser.: Vol. 56). (Illus.). 224p. 1992. 69.00 (*0-387-53603-5*) Spr-Verlag.

Amorphous & Crystalline Silicon Carbide IV: Proceedings of the 4th International Conference, Santa Clara, CA, October 9-11, 1991. Ed. by C. Y. Yang et al. LC 92-26760. (Proceedings in Physics Ser.: Vol. 71). 1992. 109.00 (*0-387-55687-7*) Spr-Verlag.

Amorphous & Liquid Materials. Ed. by E. Luscher et al. 1987. lib. bdg. 154.50 (*90-247-3411-8*) Kluwer Ac.

Amorphous & Microcrystalline Semiconductor Devices: Optoelectronic Devices. Ed. by Jerzy Kanicki. (Optoelectronics Library). 504p. 1991. text ed. 98.00 (*0-89006-490-3*) Artech Hse.

Amorphous & Microcrystalline Semiconductor Devices, Vol. II: Materials & Device Physics. Ed. by Jerzy Kanicki. LC 92-19374. (Materials Ser.). 687p. 1992. text ed. 125.00 (*0-89006-379-6*) Artech Hse.

Amorphous Inorganic Materials & Glasses. A. Feltz. LC 93-4088. 1993. 132.00 (*1-56081-212-5*) VCH Pubs.

Amorphous Insulating Thin Films. Ed. by J. Kanicki et al. (Materials Research Society Symposium Proceedings Ser.: Vol. 284). 1993. text ed. 69.00 (*1-55899-179-4*) Materials Res.

Amorphous Magnetism. Takahito Kaneyoski. 200p. 1984. 129.95 (*0-8493-5796-9*, QC766, CRC Reprint) Franklin.

Amorphous Magnetism & Metallic Magnetic Materials Digest. A. R. Ferchmin & S. Kobe. (Selected Topics in Solid State Physics Ser.: Vol. 17). 345p. 1984. 92.50 (*0-444-86532-2*, North Holland) Elsevier.

Amorphous Materials: Modeling of Structure & Properties: Proceedings of Symposium Held at the Fall Meeting of the Metallurgical Society of AIME, St. Louis, Missouri, October 25-26, 1982. Metallurgical Society of AIME Staff. Ed. by V. Vitek. LC 83-61432. 355p. reprint ed. pap. 101.20 (*0-8357-2596-0*, 2052376) Bks Demand.

Amorphous Materials: Papers Presented to the Third International Conference on the Physics of Non-Crystalline Solids, Sheffield University, September 1970. Ed. by R. W. Douglas & Bryan Ellis. LC 77-162326. 568p. reprint ed. pap. 161.90 (*0-317-08992-7*, 2016152) Bks Demand.

Amorphous Metallic Materials. 2nd ed. Ed. by P. Duhaj et al. 480p. 1990. text ed. 128.00 (*0-87849-601-7*, Pub. by Trans Tech GW) LPS Dist Ctr.

Amorphous Metallic Materials 3. Ed. by P. Duhaj et al. 686p. (C). 1993. text ed. 204.00 (*0-87849-655-6*, Pub. by Trans Tech SZ) LPS Dist Ctr.

Amorphous Metals & Semiconductors: Proceedings of the Acta-Scripta Workshop, Coronada, CA, U. S. A., 12-18 May 1985. Ed. by Peter Haasen & R. I. Jaffee. (Acta-Scripta Metallurgica Proceedings Ser.: Vol. 3). 1986. 201.00 (*0-08-034334-1*, A145) Franklin.

Amorphous Polymers & Non-Newtonian Fluids. C. M. Dafermos et al. (IMA Ser.: Vol. 6). (Illus.). 215p. 1987. 36.00 (*0-387-96556-4*) Spr-Verlag.

Amorphous Semiconductor Technologies & Devices. Y. Hamakawa. (Japan Annual Reviews in Electronics, Computers & Telecommunications Ser.: Vol. 22). 1988. 141.00 (*0-444-87977-3*) Elsevier.

Amorphous Semiconductor Technologies & Devices, 1984. Y. Hamakawa. (Japan Annual Reviews Ser.: Vol. 16). 1985. 136.00 (*0-444-87584-0*) Elsevier.

Amorphous Semiconductor Technologies & Devices 1982 see **Japan Annual Reviews in Electronics, Computers & Telecommunications, 1982**

Amorphous Semiconductors. 2nd ed. Ed. by M. Brodsky. (Topics in Applied Physics Ser.: Vol. 36). (Illus.). 370p. 1986. pap. 43.00 (*0-387-16008-6*) Spr-Verlag.

Amorphous Semiconductors: Proceedings of the International Workshop on Amorphous Semiconductors, Bejing, China, October 13-18, 1986. Ed. by H. Fritzsche et al. 356p. 1987. pap. 47.00 (*9971-5-0334-4*) World Scientific Pub.

***Amorphous Semiconductors '76: Proceedings of the International Conference Balatonfured, Hungary, 20-25 Sept. 1976.** I. kosa-Somogyi. 565p. (C). 1977. 99.00x (*963-05-1272-6*, Pub. by Akad Kiado HU) St Mut.

Amorphous Silicon & Related Materials, 2 vols. Ed. by H. Fritzsche. (Advanced Series on Amorphous Semiconductors). 1152p. 1989. pap. 90.00 (*9971-5-0619-X*) World Scientific Pub.

Amorphous Silicon Materials & Solar Cells. Bryon L. Stafford. LC 91-55575. (AIP Conference Proceedings Ser.: No. 234). (Illus.). 344p. 1991. lib. bdg. 90.00 (*0-88318-831-7*) Am Inst Physics.

Amorphous Silicon Pin Diodes - Their Fabrication & Application to Thin Film Devices: Their Fabrication & Application to Thin Film Devices. H. Sakai & Y. Ichikawa. 250p. (C). 1996. text ed. 61.00 (*9971-5-0889-3*) World Scientific Pub.

Amorphous Silicon Semiconductors Pure & Hydrogenated. Ed. by A. Madan et al. (MRS Symposium Proceedings Ser.: Vol. 95). 1987. text ed. 52.00 (*0-931837-62-6*) Materials Res.

Amorphous Silicon Technology. Ed. by A. Madan et al. (Symposium Proceedings Ser.: Vol. 118). 1988. text ed. 45.00 (*0-931837-88-X*) Materials Res.

Amorphous Silicon Technology - 1989: Materials Research Society Symposium Proceedings, Vol. 149. Ed. by A. Madan et al. 1989. text ed. 54.00 (*1-55899-022-4*) Materials Res.

Amorphous Silicon Technology - 1990: Symposium Proceedings Ser., Vol. 192. Ed. by P. C. Taylor et al. 1990. text ed. 50.00 (*1-55899-081-X*) Materials Res.

Amorphous Silicon Technology - 1991: Materials Research Society Symposium Proceedings, Vol. 219. Ed. by A. Madan et al. 1991. text ed. 72.00 (*1-55899-113-1*) Materials Res.

***Amorphous Silicon Technology - 1995.** Ed. by M. Hack et al. (Symposium Proceedings Ser.: Vol. 377). 1995. text ed. 75.00 (*1-55899-280-4*) Materials Res.

Amorphous Silicon Technology 1992. Ed. by M. J. Thompson et al. (Materials Research Society Symposium Proceedings Ser.: Vol. 258). 1992. text ed. 66.00 (*1-55899-153-0*) Materials Res.

Amorphous Silicon Technology, 1993. Ed. by E. A. Schiff et al. (Symposium Proceedings Ser.: Vol. 297). 1993. text ed. 75.00 (*1-55899-193-X*) Materials Res.

Amorphous Silicon Technology, 1994: Materials Research Society Symposium Proceedings, Vol. 336. Ed. by E. A. Schiff et al. 1994. text ed. 74.00 (*1-55899-236-7*) Materials Res.

Amorphous Solids. Ed. by W. A. Phillips. (Topics in Current Physics Ser.: Vol. 24). (Illus.). 167p. 1981. 53.00 (*0-387-10330-9*) Spr-Verlag.

Amorphous Solids & the Liquid State. Ed. by Norman H. March et al. LC 85-12031. (Physics of Solids & Liquids Ser.). 560p. 1985. 135.00 (*0-306-41947-5*, Plenum Pr) Plenum.

Amortization Book. Bob H. Workman. 172p. 1989. pap. 3.95 (*0-943605-01-6*) United Fin Pubs.

Amortization Handbook: Complete Monthly Mortgage Payment Tables. 244p. 1986. pap. 5.50 (*0-681-40053-6*) Longmeadow Pr.

***Amorum Emblemata.** Otto Vaenius. (Emblem Book Facsimile Ser.). 260p. 1995. 68.95 (*1-85928-001-3*) Ashgate Pub Co.

Amorum Emblemata. Otto Van Veen. Ed. by D. Tschizewskij. xiii, 247p. 1970. reprint ed. write for info. (*0-318-71285-7*, Pub. by Georg Olms GW) Lubrecht & Cramer.

Amorum Libri: The Lyric Poems of Matteo Maria Boiardo. Tr. by Andrea Di Tommaso. (Medieval & Renaissance Texts & Studies: Vol. 101). 320p. 1993. 25.00 (*0-86698-117-9*) MRTS.

Amorum Libri Tres. Ed. by Paul Brandt. 239p. 1977. reprint ed. write for info. (*3-487-00370-8*, Pub. by Georg Olms GW) Lubrecht & Cramer.

Amos. Shalom Paul. LC 90-45137. (Hermeneia Ser.). 440p. (Orig.). 1991. text ed. 46.00 (*0-8006-6023-4*, 1-6023, Fortress Pr) Augsburg Fortress.

Amos: A Commentary. James L. Mays. LC 79-76885. (Old Testament Library). 176p. 1969. 20.00 (*0-664-20863-0*, Westminster) Westminster John Knox.

Amos: A New Translation. Ed. & Comment by David N. Freedman. 1989. 30.00 (*0-385-00773-6*, Anchor Bible) Doubleday.

***Amos: A Study Guide.** Robert Baker. 128p. 1995. pap. write for info. (*1-57312-020-0*) Smyth & Helwys.

Amos: Our Ancestry (Amos, Beverly, Goodale, Graham, Keeney, Miller, Walton) Hazel C. Amos. (Illus.). 202p. 1994. reprint ed. lib. bdg. 42.00 (*0-8328-4166-8*); reprint ed. pap. 32.00 (*0-8328-4167-6*) Higginson Bk Co.

Amos: The Story of an Old Dog & His Couch. Howie Schneider & Susan Seligson. LC 87-2813. (Illus.). 32p. (J). (ps-3). 1987. 14.95 (*0-316-77404-9*) Little.

Amos: The Story of an Old Dog & His Couch. Susan Seligson. (J). (ps-3). 1992. reprint ed. mass mkt. 4.95 (*0-316-78034-0*, Joy St Bks) Little.

Amos - Abdias: Comentario Biblico Hispanoamericano. Washington Padilla. 244p. 1991. 18.95 (*0-89922-375-3*) Edit Caribe.

Amos & Abraham. Sharyn Bellafiore. LC 94-33000. (Illus.). 32p. (J). (gr. k-4). 1994. lib. bdg. 14.95 (*1-56148-139-4*) Good Bks PA.

Amos & Hosea: Critical & Exegetical Commentary. William R. Harper. Ed. by Samuel R. Driver et al. LC 05-7893. (International Critical Commentary Ser.). 608p. 1905. 39.95 (*0-567-05018-1*, Pub. by T & T Clark UK) Bks Intl VA.

Amos & Susie: An Amish Story. Merle Good. LC 93-11483. (Illus.). 24p. (J). (ps-3). 1993. 12.95 (*1-56148-088-6*); pap. 4.95 (*0-934672-46-6*) Good Bks PA.

Amos & the Alien. Gary Paulsen. (Culpepper Adventures Ser.: No. 19). (J). (gr. 4-7). 1994. 3.50 (*0-440-40990-X*) Dell.

Amos & the Davidic Empire: A Socio-Historical Approach. Max E. Polley. (Illus.). 256p. 1989. 45.00 (*0-19-505478-4*) OUP.

Amos Benevolos. 2nd ed. Enrique Laguerre. LC 76-21797. 258p. 1990. pap. 7.95 (*0-8477-3523-0*) U of PR Pr.

Amos Bronson Alcott: An Intellectual Biography. Frederick C. Dahlstrand. LC 80-65282. (Illus.). 500p. 1982. 48.50 (*0-8386-3016-2*) Fairleigh Dickinson.

Amos Camps Out: A Couch Adventure in the Woods. Howie Schneider. (J). (ps-3). 1992. 14.95 (*0-316-77402-2*, Joy St Bks) Little.

***Amos for Windows: Analysis of Moment Structures Version 3.5 (Program & Manual)** James L. Arbuckle. (Illus.). iv, 557p. 1995. disk 465.00 (*1-886744-00-9*); 45.00 (*1-886744-01-7*) SmallWaters.

Amos Fortune, Free Man. Elizabeth Yates. (Illus.). (J). (gr. 7 up). 1967. 15.00 (*0-525-25570-2*, DCB) Dutton Child Bks.

Amos Fortune, Free Man. Elizabeth Yates. (Illus.). 192p. (J). (gr. 3-7). 1989. pap. 3.99 (*0-14-034158-7*, Puffin) Puffin Bks.

Amos Fortune, Free Man: L-I-T Guide. Charlotte Jaffe & Barbara Roberts. (L-I-T Guides: Literature in Teaching Ser.). 1991. Grades 4-8. teacher ed 8.95 (*0-910857-99-7*) Educ Impress.

Amos Gets Famous. Gary Paulsen. (Culpepper Adventures Ser.: No. 8). (J). (gr. 4-7). 1993. pap. 3.25 (*0-440-40749-4*) Dell.

***Amos Gets Married.** Gary Paulsen. (Culpepper Adventure Special Ser.: No. 23). (J). (gr. 4-7). 1995. pap. 3.50 (*0-440-40933-0*) Dell.

***Amos Goes Bananas.** Paulsen. (Culpepper Adventures Ser.: No. 24). (J). 1995. pap. 3.50 (*0-440-41008-8*) Dell.

Amos, Hosea, Micah: An Archaeological Commentary. Philip J. King. LC 87-29539. (Illus.). 176p. (Orig.). 1988. pap. 15.99 (*0-664-24077-1*, Westminster) Westminster John Knox.

Amos, Hosea, Micah, Nahum, Zephaniah, Habakkuk. Carroll Stuhlmueller. (Collegeville Bible Commentary - Old Testament Ser.: No. 15). 120p. 1986. pap. 3.95 (*0-8146-1422-1*) Liturgical Pr.

Amos Kilbright: His Adscititious Experiences; with Other Stories. Frank R. Stockton. LC 72-2024. (Black Heritage Library Collection). 1977. reprint ed. 22.95 (*0-8369-9067-6*) Ayer.

Amos of Israel: A New Interpretation. Stanley N. Rosenbaum. LC 89-39065. xii, 129p. (C). 1990. 25.00 (*0-86554-355-0*, MUP/H296) Mercer Univ Pr.

Amos Starr Cooke & Juliette Montague Cooke, Their Autobiographies Gleaned from their Journals & Letters. rev. ed. Mary A. Richards. (Illus.). text ed. 19.95 (*0-938851-03-9*) Daughters of HI.

Amos' Theory of Evolutionary Creation. Russell W. Smith, Jr. 168p. 1993. pap. 10.49 (*0-9636354-6-8*) R W Smith Pub.

Amos y Boris: Amos & Boris. William Steig. (J). (ps-3). 1992. 17.00 (*0-374-30279-0*) FS&G.

***Amoskeag: Life & Work in an American Factory-City.** Tamara K. Hareven & Randolph Langenbach. (Library of New England). (Illus.). 416p. (C). 1996. pap. 16.95 (*0-87451-736-2*) U Pr of New Eng.

Amoskeag Steam Fire Engines. Ed Hass. write for info. (*0-318-62389-7*) E Hass.

***Amos's Killer Concert Caper.** Gary Paulsen. (Culpepper Adventures Ser.: No. 22). (J). (gr. 4-7). 1995. pap. 3.50 (*0-440-40989-6*) Dell.

Amos's Last Stand. Gary Paulsen. (Culpepper Adventures Ser.: No. 11). (J). (gr. 4-7). 1993. pap. 3.25 (*0-440-40775-3*) Dell.

Amos's Sweater. Janet Lunn. (J). (ps-3). 1991. 12.95 (*0-88899-074-X*, Pub. by Groundwood-Douglas & McIntyre CN) Firefly Bks Ltd.

Amostra de Salmos. Henry Morris. Orig. Title: Sampling the Psalms. 180p. (POR.). 1986. 7.95 (*0-8297-0698-4*) Life Pubs Intl.

Amour. Marguerite Duras. (Folio Ser.: No. 2918). (FRE.). 8.95 (*2-07-038553-1*) Schoenhof.

Amour see **Encyclopedic Poetique: Anthologie Thematique de la Poesie Francaise Contemporaine**

Amour Absolu: Avec: La Vieux de la Montagne, L'Autre Alceste. Albert Jarry. 224p. (FRE.). 1964. 22.95 (*0-7859-5347-7*) Fr & Eur.

Amour Comble les Fosses. Paul E. Billheimer. 176p. (FRE.). 1990. pap. 4.95 (*0-8297-1424-3*) Life Pubs Intl.

Amour Conjugal. Alberto Moravia. (FRE.). 1972. pap. 10.95 (*0-7859-3988-1*) Fr & Eur.

Amour de Charlie Brown. Charles M. Schulz. (Peanuts Ser.). (FRE.). (J). 1985. 4.95 (*0-8288-4514-X*) Fr & Eur.

Amour de Ma Vie. Guy Des Cars. 320p. (FRE.). 1973. pap. 10.95 (*0-7859-4789-2*); pap. 6.95 (*0-686-55606-2*) Fr & Eur.

Amour de Swann. Marcel Proust. (FRE.). 1976. pap. 10.95 (*0-8288-3760-0*, F119603) Fr & Eur.

Amour de Swann. Marcel Proust. Ed. by Albert Sonnenfeld. 278p. (ENG & FRE.). 1986. 3.95 (*0-88332-466-0*) Schoenhof.

An Asterisk (*) at the beginning of an entry indicates that the title is appearing in BIP for the first time.

Amour de Swann. Marcel Proust. (Folio Ser.: No. 780). 254p. (FRE.). 1987. 8.95 (*2-07-036780-0*) Schoenhof.

Amour Durable. Jacques De Bourbon Busset. (Journal Ser.: Vol. III). 448p. (FRE.). 1973. pap. 10.95 (*0-7859-1752-7*, 2070364275) Fr & Eur.

Amour en Face. Georges Conchon. 256p. (FRE.). 1987. pap. 11.95 (*0-7859-2077-3*, 2070378969) Fr & Eur.

Amour en Visites. Alfred Jarry. 112p. (FRE.). 1972. pap. 10.95 (*0-7859-1339-4*, 2070282813) Fr & Eur.

Amour et la Rose: Le Grand Dessein de Jean de Meun. Per Nykrog. LC 85-73552. (Harvard Studies in Romance Languages: No. 41). 100p. (Orig.). (FRE.). 1986. pap. 10.00 (*0-940940-41-8*) Harvard U Romance Lang & Lit.

Amour et Vieillesse: Avec: Etude sur Chateaubriand Romanesque et Amoreaux. Rene de Chateaubriand & Victor Giraud. 43p. 1922. 50.00 (*0-686-54359-9*) Fr & Eur.

Amour Flou. Maurice Denuziere. 338p. (FRE.). 1991. pap. 10.95 (*0-7859-2163-X*, 2070383725) Fr & Eur.

Amour Fou. Andre Breton. (FRE.). 1976. pap. 10.95 (*0-8288-3659-0*, M11012); pap. 10.95 (*0-7859-1813-2*, 2070367231) Fr & Eur.

Amour Fou. Andre Breton. (Folio Ser.: No. 723). (FRE.). 8.95 (*2-07-036723-1*) Schoenhof.

Amour, la Reve et la Mort. Gustave W. Andrian & Jane D. Davies. (C). 1980. pap. text ed. write for info. (*0-13-718669-X*) P-H.

Amour, L'Amitie et la Fourberie: Une Etude Des Premieres Comedies de Corneille. Cynthia B. Kerr. (Stanford French & Italian Studies: Vol. 20). viii, 139p. (FRE.). 1980. pap. 46.50 (*0-915838-19-2*) Anma Libri.

Amour les Yeux Fermes. Michel Henry. 352p. (FRE.). 1982. pap. 12.95 (*0-7859-2463-9*, 2070374017) Fr & Eur.

Amour Medecin. Moliere. 128p. (FRE.). 1992. reprint ed. pap. 8.95 (*0-685-73252-5*) Fr & Eur.

Amour pour Rien. Jean D'Ormesson. (FRE.). 1978. pap. 10. 95 (*0-7859-4099-5*) Fr & Eur.

Amour Profane. Alfred Kern. 224p. (FRE.). 1974. pap. 10. 95 (*0-7859-2346-2*, 2070366103) Fr & Eur.

***Amour Rebelle.** Patricia Wilson. (Azur Ser.). (FRE.). 1994. pap. 3.50 (*0-373-34435-X*, 1-34435-7) Harlequin Bks.

Amour s'en va-t-en Guerre. Guy Des Cars. (FRE.). 1978. pap. 6.95 (*0-8288-9548-1*, M4669) Fr & Eur.

Amour Triste. Bernard Pingaud. (FRE.). 1973. pap. 8.95 (*0-7859-4020-0*) Fr & Eur.

Amouretta Landscape & Other Stories. Adeline V. Adams. LC 79-103486. (Short Story Index Reprint Ser.). 1977. 19.95 (*0-8369-3192-0*) Ayer.

Amours. Pierre De Ronsard. 480p. (FRE.). 1981. pap. 13.95 (*0-7859-4641-1*) Fr & Eur.

Amours. Pierre De Ronsard. (Poesie Ser.). 448p. (FRE.). 1974. pap. 13.95 (*2-07-032134-7*) Schoenhof.

Amours. Paul Leautaud. (FRE.). 1973. pap. 8.95 (*0-7859-4019-7*) Fr & Eur.

Amours: Amours de Cassandre; Amours de Marie. Pierre De Ronsard. (FRE.). 1974. pap. 17.95 (*0-7859-2777-8*) Fr & Eur.

Amours see Moments of Love

Amours Blessees. Jeanne Bourin. (Folio Ser.: No. 2031). (FRE.). 1989. pap. 10.95 (*2-07-038119-6*) Schoenhof.

Amours Blessees. Jeanne Bourin. 415p. (FRE.). 1989. pap. 11.95 (*0-7859-2114-1*, 2070381196) Fr & Eur.

Amours of Zeokinizal King of the Kofiranis, 1749 see Zadie; or, the Book of Fate, 1749

AMP Book. Donald Brosnac. (Illus.). 64p. (C). 1987. reprint ed. pap. 9.95 (*0-933224-05-2*) Bold Strummer Ltd.

Ampere-Neumann Electrodynamics of Metals. Ed. by Peter Graneau. 311p. 1985. pap. 60.00 (*0-911767-37-1*) Hadronic Pr Inc.

***Ampere Neumann Electrodynamics of Metals.** 2nd ed. Peter Graneau. 330p. (C). 1993. pap. text ed. 80.00 (*0-911767-75-4*) Hadronic Pr Inc.

Ampersandia: This & That & Other Things. Vera C. Erickson. (Illus.). 200p. (Orig.). 1988. pap. 8.95 (*0-9621008-0-3*) Sharples Pubs.

Amphetamine & Its Analogs: Psychopharmacology, Toxicology, & Abuse. Ed. by Arthur Cho & David S. Segal. (Illus.). 503p. 1994. text ed. 120.00 (*0-12-173375-0*) Acad Pr.

Amphetamines: Danger in the Fast Lane. Scott E. Lukas. (Encyclopedia of Psychoactive Drugs - Compact Paperback Library). (Illus.). 32p. (YA). (gr. 5 up). 1991. pap. 4.49 (*0-7910-0003-6*) Chelsea Hse.

Amphetamines: Danger in the Fast Lane. Scott E. Lukas. (Encyclopedia of Psychoactive Drugs Ser.: No. 1). (Illus.). (YA). (gr. 5 up). 1992. lib. bdg. 19.95 (*0-685-54573-3*) Chelsea Hse.

Amphetamines: Toxicity & Addiction. Oriana J. Kalant. LC 74-373452. (Brookside Monograph Ser.: No. 5). (Illus.). 163p. reprint ed. pap. 46.50 (*0-8357-8022-8*, 2034039) Bks Demand.

Amphetamines & Other Stimulants. Lawrence Clayton. Ed. by Ruth Rosen. (Drug Abuse Prevention Library). (YA). (gr. 7-12). 1994. 15.95 (*0-8239-1534-4*) Rosen Group.

Amphetamines & PH-Shift Agents for Brain Imaging: Basic Research & Clinical Results. Ed. by H. J. Biersack & C. Winkler. (Illus.). 208p. 1986. 119.25 (*0-89925-156-0*) De Gruyter.

Amphetamines & Related Stimulants, Vol. 1. John Caldwell. 216p. 1981. 144.00 (*0-8493-5347-5*, RM666, CRC Reprint) Franklin.

Amphibamidae (Amphibia: Temnospondyli), with a Description of a New Genus from the Upper Pennsylvanian of Kansas. Eleanor Daly. Ed. by Robert M. Mengel et al. (Miscellaneous Publications: No. 85). (Illus.). 61p. (Orig.). (C). Date not set. pap. text ed. write for info. (*0-89338-046-6*) U of KS Mus Nat Hist.

Amphibia. Max King. (Animal Cytogenetics Ser.: Vol. 4: Chordata 2). (Illus.). 241p. 1990. pap. 138.60 (*3-443-36013-0*, Pub. by Gebrueder Borntraeger GW) Lubrecht & Cramer.

Amphibian. Barry Clarke et al. LC 92-1589. (Eyewitness Bks.). 64p. (J). (gr. 5 up). 1993. 16.00 (*0-679-83879-1*); lib. bdg. 16.99 (*0-679-93879-6*) Knopf Bks Yng Read.

Amphibian Biology. Ed. by Harold Heatwole. 1993. 150.00 (*0-949324-54-X*, Pub. by Surrey Beatty & Sons AT) St Mut.

Amphibian Cytogenetics & Evolution. Ed. by David M. Green & Stanley K. Sessions. (Illus.). 456p. 1991. text ed. 110.00 (*0-12-297880-3*) Acad Pr.

Amphibian Ear. Ernest G. Wever. LC 84-17767. (Illus.). 520p. 1985. text ed. 95.00x (*0-691-08365-7*) Princeton U Pr.

Amphibian in Transplantation Immunity. Ed. by E. P. Volpe. (Monographs in Developmental Biology: Vol. 14). (Illus.). x, 150p. 1980. pap. 99.25 (*3-8055-1087-X*) S Karger.

***Amphibian Medicine & Captive Husbandry.** Kevin M. Wright & Brent R. Whitaker. 1997. write for info. (*0-89464-917-5*) Krieger.

Amphibian Morphogenesis. Harold Fox. LC 83-26526. (Bioscience Ser.). 320p. 1984. 79.50 (*0-89603-043-1*) Humana.

Amphibian Species of the World: Additions & Corrections. William E. Duellman. Ed. by Linda Trueb. (Special Publication Ser.: No. 21). 372p. Date not set. pap. text ed. 35.00 (*0-89338-045-8*) U of KS Mus Nat Hist.

Amphibians. Ray E. Ashton, Jr. & Patricia S. Ashton. Ed. by Sandra Romashko. LC 81-51066. (Handbook of Reptiles & Amphibians of Florida Ser.: Bk. 3). (Illus.). 192p. 1988. pap. 16.95 (*0-89317-037-2*) Windward Pub.

Amphibians. J. F. Frazer & O. H. Frazer. (Wykeham Science Ser.: No. 25). 128p. (C). 1972. 18.00 (*0-8448-1152-1*, Crane Russak) Taylor & Francis.

Amphibians. Giuseppe Minelli. (History of Life on Earth Ser.). (Illus.). 64p. (YA). 1987. 15.95 (*0-8160-1557-0*) Facts on File.

Amphibians. Edward Ricciuti. (Our Living World Ser.). (Illus.). 64p. (J). (gr. 4-8). 1993. lib. bdg. 16.95 (*1-56711-045-2*) Blackbirch.

Amphibians: Creatures of the Land & Water. Edward J. Maruska. LC 93-29843. (Cincinnati Zoo Book Ser.). (Illus.). 56p. (J). (gr. 5-7). 1994. lib. bdg. 15.47 (*0-531-11158-X*); pap. 9.95 (*0-531-15714-8*) Watts.

Amphibians: Look & Learn. Will P. Mara. (Illus.). 64p. 7.95 (*0-7938-0067-6*, KD006) TFH Pubns.

Amphibians & Reptiles. Royce E. Ballinger et al. 240p. (C). 1983. spiral bd. write for info. (*0-697-04786-5*) Wm C Brown Pubs.

Amphibians & Reptiles. Henry Berkowitz. (Illus.). 32p. (Orig.). (J). (gr. 1-9). 1985. pap. 2.50 (*0-317-66182-5*) Banyan Bks.

***Amphibians & Reptiles: Science Nature Guides.** Gunzi. 1995. 12.95 (*1-57145-020-3*) Thunder Bay CA.

Amphibians & Reptiles in Kansas. rev. ed. Joseph T. Collins. LC 93-18564. (PE Ser.: No. 13). (Illus.). 1993. pap. text ed. 19.95 (*0-89338-043-1*) U Pr of KS.

Amphibians & Reptiles in Kansas. 2nd ed. Joseph T. Collins. (Public Education Ser.: No. 8). (Illus.). 356p. 1982. 17.95 (*0-89338-013-X*); pap. 12.95 (*0-89338-012-1*) U of KS Mus Nat Hist.

Amphibians & Reptiles in Kansas. 3rd rev. ed. Joseph T. Collins. LC 93-18564. (PE Ser.: No. 13). (Illus.). 1993. text ed. 29.95 (*0-89338-044-X*) U Pr of KS.

Amphibians & Reptiles in West Virginia. N. Bayard Green & Thomas K. Pauley. LC 86-190291. (Illus.). 284p. 1987. 29.95 (*0-8229-3819-7*); pap. 19.95 (*0-8229-5802-3*) U of Pittsburgh Pr.

Amphibians & Reptiles Native to Minnesota. Barney Oldfield & John J. Moriarty. LC 93-45018. (C). 1994. 25.95 (*0-8166-2384-8*) U of Minn Pr.

Amphibians & Reptiles of Connecticut & Adjacent Regions. Michael W. Klemens. (Bulletin Ser.: No. 112). (Illus.). 368p. 1993. 39.95 (*0-942081-04-8*) CT DEP CGNHS.

Amphibians & Reptiles of Great Smoky Mountains National Park. James E Huheey & Arthur Stupke. LC 67-21108. (Illus.). 134p. reprint ed. pap. 38.20 (*0-317-55794-7*, 2029375) Bks Demand.

Amphibians & Reptiles of New England: Habitats & Natural History. Richard M. DeGraaf & Deborah D. Rudis. LC 83-5125. (Illus.). 96p. 1983. pap. 10.95 (*0-87023-400-5*) U of Mass Pr.

Amphibians & Reptiles of the Carolinas & Virginia. Bernard S. Martof et al. LC 79-11790. (Illus.). 264p. (C). 1989. reprint ed. pap. 16.95 (*0-8078-4252-4*) U of NC Pr.

Amphibians & Reptiles of the Pacific Northwest. Ronald A. Nussbaum et al. LC 82-60202. (Illus.). 332p. 1983. pap. 24.95 (*0-89301-086-3*) U of Idaho Pr.

Amphibians & Reptiles of the West Indies: Descriptions, Distributions, & Natural History. Albert Schwartz & Robert W. Henderson. 736p. 1991. lib. bdg. 75.00 (*0-8130-1049-7*) U Press Fla.

***Amphibians & Reptiles of the Yucatan Peninsula.** Julian C. Lee. (Comstock Book Ser.). (Illus.). 512p. 1996. 175. 00 (*0-8014-2450-X*) Cornell U Pr.

***Amphibians & Reptiles of Yellowstone & Grand Teton National Parks.** Edward D. Koch & Charles R. Peterson. (Illus.). 236p. (Orig.). Date not set. pap. 12.95 (*0-87480-472-8*) U of Utah Pr.

Amphibians of Illinois. Paul W. Parmalee. (Story of Illinois Ser.: No. 10). (Illus.). 38p. 1954. pap. 1.00 (*0-89792-011-2*) Ill St Museum.

Amphibians of Missouri. Tom R. Johnson. (Public Education Ser.: No. 6). (Illus.). 134p. (Orig.). 1977. pap. 7.95 (*0-89338-005-9*) U of KS Mus Nat Hist.

Amphibious Campaign for West Florida & Louisiana, 1814-1815: A Critical Review of Strategy & Tactics at New Orleans. Wilburt S. Brown. LC 68-10992. (Illus.). reprint ed. 61.30 (*0-8357-9615-9*, 2050448) Bks Demand.

Amphibious Embarkation & Loading. (Military Science Ser.). 1991. lib. bdg. 79.95 (*0-8490-4314-X*) Gordon Pr.

Amphibious Operations: The Projection of Sea Power Ashore. M. H. Evans. Ed. by Geoffrey Till. (Naval Vessels, Weapons Systems & Technology Ser.: Vol. 4). 219p. 1990. pap. 25.00 (*0-08-034736-3*, Pub. by Brasseys UK) Brasseys Inc.

Amphibious Operations: The Projection of Sea Power Ashore. M. H. Evans. Ed. by Geoffrey Till. (Naval Vessels, Weapons Systems & Technology Ser.: Vol. 4). 219p. 1990. 40.00 (*0-08-034737-1*, Pub. by Brasseys UK) Brasseys Inc.

Amphibious Techniques. James D. Ladd. LC 84-10003. (Modern Military Techniques Ser.). (Illus.). 48p. (J). (gr. 5 up). 1985. pap. 4.95 (*0-8225-9505-2*, Lerner Publctns) Lerner Group.

Amphibious Techniques. James D. Ladd. LC 84-10003. (Modern Military Techniques Ser.). (Illus.). 48p. (YA). (gr. 5 up). 1985. lib. bdg. 14.95 (*0-8225-1379-X*, Lerner Publctns) Lerner Group.

Amphibious Warfare in the Eighteenth Century: The British Expedition to the West Indies, 1740-42. Richard Harding. (Royal Historical Society: Studies in History: No. 62). (Illus.). 256p. 1991. 71.00 (*0-86193-218-8*) Boydell & Brewer.

Amphiboles: Petrology & Experimental Phase Relations. Ed. by D. R. Veblen & P. H. Ribbe. (Reviews in Mineralogy Ser.: Vol. 9B). 390p. 1982. per. 17.00 (*0-939950-11-1*) Mineralogical Soc.

Amphiboles & Other Hydrous Pyriboles Mineralogy. Ed. by D. R. Veblen. (Reviews in Mineralogy Ser.: Vol. 9A). 372p. 1981. per. 10.00 (*0-939950-10-3*) Mineralogical Soc.

Amphigorey Also. Edward Gorey. 1993. 29.95 (*0-15-106443-1*); pap. 14.95 (*0-15-605672-0*) HarBrace.

Amphion see Poesies

Amphion Anglicus see Monuments of Music & Music Literature in Facsimile: Series One

Amphipathic Helix. Ed. by Richard M. Epand. 1993. 189. 95 (*0-8493-4926-5*, QP551) CRC Pr.

Amphipolis: The Civic Coinage in Silver & Gold. Catharine C. Lorber. 196p. 1990. 87.50 (*0-9626987-0-9*) Numismatic Fine Arts.

***Amphitheatres & Circuses: A History from Their Earliest Date to 1861, with Sketches of Some of the Principal Performers.** T. Allston Brown. Ed. by William L. Slout. LC 94-22302. (Clipper Studies in the Theatre: No. 9). (Illus.). xiv, 87p. 1994. lib. bdg. 25.00x (*0-913960-32-2*); pap. 15.00x (*0-913960-33-0*) Borgo Pr.

Amphitryon. Mark Dunster. 11p. (Orig.). 1993. pap. 4.00 (*0-89642-223-2*) Linden Pubs.

Amphitryon. Jean Giraudoux. 1967. 10.95 (*0-685-10998-4*, F104300) Fr & Eur.

***Amphitryon.** Moliere. Tr. by Richard Wilbur. 1995. pap. 4.75 (*0-8222-1439-3*) Dramatists Play.

Amphitryon. Moliere. (FRE.). 1973. 7.95 (*0-8288-9933-9*, F39870) Fr & Eur.

***Amphitryon.** Richard Wilbur. 160p. 1995. 20.00 (*0-15-100156-1*); pap. 12.00 (*0-15-600211-6*) HarBrace.

Amphitryon, Vol I. Plautus. Bd. with Comedy of Asses.; Pot of Gold.; Two Bacchises.; Captives. (Loeb Classical Library: No. 60). 15.50 (*0-674-99067-6*) HUP.

Amphitryon: George Dandin. L'Avare. Moliere. (Folio Ser.: No. 333). (FRE.). 1973. pap. 9.95 (*2-07-036333-3*) Schoenhof.

Amphitryon: Index Verborum, Lexiques Inersese, Releves Lexicaux et Grammaticaux. Plautus. Ed. by Albert Maniet & Annette Paquot. Bd. XIX. vii, 217p. (GER.). 1970. write for info. (*0-318-70439-0*, Pub. by Georg Olms GW) Lubrecht & Cramer.

Amphitryon & Two Other Plays. Plautus. Ed. by Lionel Casson. 1971. pap. 8.95 (*0-393-00601-8*) Norton.

Amphitryon; George Dandin; L'Avare. Moliere. (FRE.). 1973. pap. 12.95 (*0-7859-2873-1*) Fr & Eur.

Amphitryon Thirty-Eight. Jean Giraudoux. 1952. pap. 4.75 (*0-8222-0039-2*) Dramatists Play.

Amphizoic Amoebae: Human Pathology. E. G. Rondanelli. (Infectious Diseases Color Atlas Monographs: No. 1). 276p. 1988. text ed. 32.00 (*1-57235-028-8*) Piccin NY.

Amphora. Aleister Crowley. 1993. reprint ed. 25.00 (*1-55818-218-7*, First Impress) Holmes Pub.

Amphora: Festschrift fur Hans Wussing Zu Seinem 65. Geburtstag - Festschrift for Hans Wussing on the Occasion of His 65th Birthday. Sergei S. Demidov et al. LC 92-30657. xi, 782p. (ENG, FRE, GER & ITA.). 1992. 140.00 (*0-8176-2815-0*) Birkhauser.

Amphora for Metaphors. Richard McKane. LC 92-42540. 198p. (Orig.). 1993. pap. 12.00 (*0-922792-56-9*) Gnosis Pr.

Amphorae: Metaphoric Techniques for Understanding, Enhancing, & Improving Your Self-Image. E. Gene Rooney. 244p. (Orig.). 1993. student ed 19.95 (*1-881596-03-6*) L E A D Cnslts.

Amphorae & Roman Economy. D. P. Peacock & D. F. Williams. (Archaeology Ser.). 304p. 1986. text ed. 53.95 (*0-582-49304-8*) Longman.

Amphoras & the Ancient Wine Trade. Virginia R. Grace. (Excavations of the Athenian Agora Picture Bks.: No. 6). (Illus.). 32p. 1979. pap. 3.00 (*0-87661-619-8*) Am Sch Athens.

Amphoteric Surfactants. Ed. by Bernard R. Bluestein & Clifford Hilton. LC 82-12999. (Surfactant Science Ser.: No. 12). 351p. reprint ed. pap. 100.10 (*0-8357-4257-1*, 2037046) Bks Demand.

Amphoto Black & White Data Guide: The Complete Listing of Films, Papers, & Chemicals for Black & White Photography. George Schaub. LC 92-31998. (Illus.). 160p. 1993. pap. 16.95 (*0-8174-3475-5*, Amphoto) Watsn-Guptill.

Amphoto Guide to Photography: The Essentials of Successful Photography...from Cameras to Image. Michael Freeman. (Illus.). 176p. 1993. pap. 22.50 (*0-8174-5451-9*, Amphoto) Watsn-Guptill.

Amphytrion. Moliere. Tr. by Oscar Mandel. LC 76-41934. (Illus.). 1977. 7.50 (*0-914502-03-4*) Spectrum Prods.

Ampico Catalog, 1920. 148p. 1973. pap. 14.95 (*1-56642-170-5*, R-2) AMR Pub Co.

Ampico Roll Bulletins: August 1928 Through July 1929, 12 Vols. (Illus.). 76p. 1976. reprint ed. pap. 24.50 (*1-56642-171-3*, R-23) AMR Pub Co.

AMPL: A Modeling Language for Mathematical Programming. Robert Fourer et al. 351p. 1992. 5.25 hd 52.50 (*0-89426-233-5*); 3.5 hd 52.50 (*0-89426-232-7*) Boyd & Fraser.

Ample Food for Stupid Thought. Robert Filliou. LC 65-19530. 1965. 75.00 (*0-89366-052-3*) Ultramarine Pub.

Ample Subvarieties of Algebraic Varieties. R. Hartshorne. (Lecture Notes in Mathematics Ser.: Vol. 156). (C). 1986. pap. 37.40 (*0-387-05184-8*) Spr-Verlag.

Amplenomics Ample for All Can Be Created: Workable Solutions & Practical Insights into the Problems of Our Time. Wesley E. Arnold. 224p. (Orig.). 1984. pap. 6.00 (*0-915935-00-7*) W Arnold.

Ampliacion y Reposo: Espanol. 2nd ed. Carlos A. Sole, Jr. & Yolanda R. Sole. 352p. (SPA.). (C). 1992. Wkbk. pap. text ed. write for info. (*0-13-034067-7*) P-H.

Amplification in Education. Ed. by Fred H. Bess et al. LC 81-68721. (Illus.). 400p. (Orig.). (C). pap. 12.95 (*0-88200-146-9*, F3002) Alexander Graham.

Amplification of Medical Certification of Cause of Death: Inquiries to Certifiers Concerning Incomplete or Vague Statements. 44p. (ENG & FRE.). 1953. pap. 1.20 (*92-4-156008-8*) World Health.

***Amplified Bible.** 1995. mass mkt. 5.99 (*0-310-95185-2*) Zondervan.

Amplified Bible. enl. ed. 1987. 26.99 (*0-310-95168-2*) Zondervan.

Amplified Harmonica Playing...Made Possible. Kevin D. Hagerty. Ed. by Marilyn Nulman. 64p. (Orig.). 1991. pap. 7.95 (*0-9632537-0-0*, 3-063-032) Potential Pubns.

Amplifier Applications Guide. Analog Devices, Applications Engineering Staff. (Analog Devices Technical Reference Bks.). (Illus.). 680p. 1992. pap. 20.00 (*0-916550-10-9*) Analog Devices.

Amplifiers, Waveform Generators, & Other Low-Cost IC Projects. Delton T. Horn. LC 93-30161. 1994. pap. text ed. 19.95 (*0-07-030415-7*) McGraw.

Amplitude: New & Selected Poems. Tess Gallagher. LC 87-81375. 216p. 1987. 15.00 (*1-55597-099-0*) Graywolf.

Amplitude: New & Selected Poems. Tess Gallagher. LC 87-81375. 216p. 1988. pap. 10.95 (*1-55597-110-5*) Graywolf.

Amplitude & Intensity Spatial Interferometry. Ed. by J. Breckinridge. 1990. 86.00 (*0-8194-0281-8*, VOL. 1237) SPIE.

Amplitude-Phase Patterns in Dynamic Scintigraphic Imaging. A. Bossuyt & F. Deconinck. (Developments in Nuclear Medicine Ser.). 1984. lib. bdg. 94.00 (*0-89838-641-1*) Kluwer Ac.

Amplitude Variation with Offset: Gulf Coast Case Studies. James L. Allen & Carolyn P. Peddy. LC 93-6249. (Geophysical Developments Ser.: No. 4). 111p. 1993. 66.00 (*1-56080-063-1*) Soc Expl Geophys.

Amps! The Other Half of Rock 'n' Roll. Ritchie Fliegler. Ed. by Jon Eiche. (Illus.). 120p. (Orig.). 1993. pap. 24.95 (*0-7935-2411-3*, 00330057) H Leonard.

***Amputation: Surgical Practice & Patient Management.** Murdoch. 1995. text ed. write for info. (*0-7506-0843-9*, Focal) Buttrwrth-Heinemann.

Amputation Surgery & Rehabilitation: The Toronto Experience. Ed. by John P. Kostuik & Robert Gillespie. LC 81-9998. (Illus.). 464p. reprint ed. pap. 132.30 (*0-7837-2553-1*, 2042712) Bks Demand.

Amputation Surgery of the Lower Extremity. Thomas J. Moore. 400p. 1994. 115.00 (*0-8016-6926-X*) Mosby Yr Bk.

Amputations see Immediate & Early Prosthetic Management: Rehabilitation Aspects

Amputees & Devotees. Grant Riddle. 1989. 29.95 (*0-8290-1824-7*) Irvington.

AMRA Medical Record Administrator National Registration Examination (RRA) Jack Rudman. (Admission Test Ser.: ATS-84). 1994. pap. 23.95 (*0-8373-5084-0*) Nat Learn.

AMRA Medical Record Technician National Registration Examination (ART) Jack Rudman. (Admission Test Ser.: ATS-85). 1994. pap. 23.95 (*0-8373-5085-9*) Nat Learn.

Amritanubhava: Ambrosial Experience. Sri Jnanadeva. Tr. by R. K. Bhagwat. 149p. 1989. pap. 12.95 (*0-910261-02-4*, Pub. by Samata Bks II) Lotus Light.

Amritsar. Beryl Dhanjal. LC 93-31445. (Holy Cities Ser.). (Illus.). 48p. (J). (gr. 5 up). 1994. text ed. 13.95 (*0-87518-571-1*, Dillon Silver Burdett) Silver Burdett Pr.

Amritsar: Mrs. Gandhi's Last Battle. Mark Tully & Satish Jacob. (C). 1991. pap. 6.00 (*0-8364-2826-9*, Pub. by Rupa II) S Asia.

Amritsar Legacy: The Dyer Massacre of 1919 & the Effect on Subsequent History. Picton Publishing (Chippenham) Ltd. Staff. (C). 1987. 75.00 (*0-948251-44-1*, Pub. by Picton UK) St Mut.

AMS Ancient & Classical Studies, Vol. 1. Date not set. write for info. (*0-404-64300-0*) AMS Pr.

AMS Ars Poetica, 5 vols. write for info. (*0-404-62500-2*) AMS Pr.

A

An Asterisk (*) at the beginning of an entry indicates that the title is appearing in BIP for the first time.

AMS Asian Studies, 3 vols. write for info. (0-404-61550-3) AMS Pr.

AMS Henry James Studies, 2 vols., Vols. 1-2. Date not set. Set. write for info. (0-404-62460-X) AMS Pr.

AMS International Studies, Vol. 1. Date not set. write for info. (0-404-63150-9) AMS Pr.

AMS Studies in Anthropology, 11 vols. write for info. (0-404-62600-9) AMS Pr.

AMS Studies in Criminal Justice, 3 vols. Set. write for info. (0-404-61640-2) AMS Pr.

AMS Studies in Cultural History, 3 vols. 1991. write for info. (0-404-64250-0) AMS Pr.

AMS Studies in Education, 9 vols. write for info. (0-404-61670-4) AMS Pr.

AMS Studies in German Literature & Culture, 4 vols., Vols. 1-4. Date not set. Set. write for info. (0-404-64050-8) AMS Pr.

AMS Studies in Library & Information Science, 3 vols. 1991. write for info. (0-404-64000-1) AMS Pr.

AMS Studies in Modern Literature, 21 vols. write for info. (0-404-61570-8) AMS Pr.

AMS Studies in Modern Society: Political & Social Issues, 24 vols. write for info. (0-404-61620-8) AMS Pr.

AMS Studies in Religious Tradition, 2 vols., Vols. 1-2. Date not set. Set. write for info. (0-404-62530-4) AMS Pr.

AMS Studies in Social History, 12 vols. write for info. (0-404-61600-3) AMS Pr.

AMS Studies in the Eighteenth Century, 27 vols. write for info. (0-404-61470-1) AMS Pr.

AMS Studies in the Emblem, 12 vols. Ed. by Peter M. Daly & Daniel Russell. (Numbered Monographic Ser.). 1993. write for info. (0-404-63700-0) AMS Pr.

AMS Studies in the Middle Ages, 24 vols. write for info. (0-404-61430-2) AMS Pr.

AMS Studies in the Nineteenth Century, 14 vols. write for info. (0-404-61480-9) AMS Pr.

AMS Studies in the Renaissance, 34 vols. write for info. (0-404-61460-4) AMS Pr.

AMS Studies in the Seventeenth Century, 5 vols. write for info. (0-404-61720-4) AMS Pr.

Amsterdam. (Insight Guides Ser.). 1993. pap. 21.95 (0-395-66186-2) HM.

Amsterdam. (Baedeker's Ser.). (Illus.). 1991. 16.95 (0-13-094707-5, P-H Travel) P-H Gen Ref & Trav.

***Amsterdam.** (Eyewitness Travel Guides Ser.). 312p. 1995. 22.95 (0-7894-0186-X, 6-70500) Dorling Kindersley.

Amsterdam. Rod Bolt. (Cadogan City Guides Ser.). (Illus.). 256p. (Orig.). 1992. pap. 13.95 (1-56440-001-8) Globe Pequot.

Amsterdam. Charles Ford. (Blue Guides Ser.). (Illus.). 192p. 1993. pap. 19.95 (0-393-31041-8) Norton.

Amsterdam. Victoria Sherrow. LC 91-31627. (Cities at War Ser.). (Illus.). 96p. (J). (gr. 6 up). 1992. text ed. 14.95 (0-02-782465-9, Mac Bks Young Read) S&S Childrens.

***Amsterdam, Vol. 1.** Butler. (City Breaks Travel Ser.). 1995. pap. 5.95 (1-872876-22-6) Atrium Pubs.

Amsterdam Affair. large type ed. Nerina Thorne. 256p. 1992. pap. 14.95 (0-7089-7138-5, Linford) Ulverscroft.

***Amsterdam Growth Study: A Longitudinal Analysis of Health, Fitness & Lifestyle.** Ed. by Han C. Kemper. (Illus.). 240p. (Orig.). 1994. pap. text ed. write for info. (0-614-00508-6) Human Kinetics.

***Amsterdam Growth Study: A Longitudinal Analysis of Health, Fitness, & Lifestyle.** Ed. by Han C. Kemper. LC 94-33964. (Sport Science Monograph). (Illus.). 240p. (Orig.). 1995. pap. text ed. write for info. (0-87322-507-4, BKEM0507) Human Kinetics.

Amsterdam in the Age of Rembrandt. John J. Murray. (Centers of Civilization Ser.: No. 21). 203p. reprint ed. 57.90 (0-8357-9719-8, 2016242) Bks Demand.

Amsterdam Mahzor: History, Liturgy, Illumination. Ed. by A. Van der Heide & E. Van Voolen. LC 89-22180. (Litterae Textuales Ser.). (Illus.). 83p. (C). 1989. pap. 36.75 (90-04-08971-3) E J Brill.

Amsterdam Passover Haggadah. Haggadah. 1984. 80.00 (0-915361-06-X) Modan-Adama Bks.

Amsterdam Pocket Guide. Berlitz Editors. (Travellers Guides Ser.). (Illus.). 144p. 1993. pap. 7.95 (2-8315-0653-0) Berlitz.

Amsterdam up Close. Fiona Duncan. 1993. pap. 12.95 (0-8442-9453-5) NTC Pub Grp.

Amstrad PC 1512-1640 Owners Handbook. 2nd ed. 1987. 47.95 (0-434-91376-6) Buttrwrth-Heinemann.

Amstrad PC1512-1640 ADV Users Guide. Reid. 1989. pap. 64.95 (0-434-91998-5) Buttrwrth-Heinemann.

Amstrad PPC Companion: Personal Computing. Ian Sinclair. (Illus.). 208p. (C). 1988. pap. 38.95 (0-8464-1507-0) Beekman Pubs.

Amstrad Programmer's Guide. Clive Gifford & Tim Hartnell. (C). 1985. pap. text ed. 70.00 (0-273-02447-7, Pub. by Pitman Pubng UK) St Mut.

***Amtracs in Action.** Jim Mesko. (Armor in Action Ser.). (Illus.). 50p. Date not set. pap. 8.95 (0-89747-298-5) Squad Sig Pubns.

Amtrak: The National Railroad Passenger Corporation. George W. Hilton. LC 79-25118. (AEI Studies: No. 266). 86p. reprint ed. pap. 25.00 (0-7837-1080-1, 2041610) Bks Demand.

AMTRAKing: A Guide to Enjoyable Train Travel. Mauris L. Emeka. LC 93-90727. (Illus.). 136p. 1994. pap. 8.95 (0-9640125-0-2) Apollo Pubng.

Amukah - The Hidden Valley. Menachem M. Reich. 150p. 1992. write for info. (1-56062-129-X) CIS Comm.

Amulet. Carl Rakosi. 88p. 1967. pap. 1.50 (0-87685-248-7) Black Sparrow.

Amulet & Alphabet: Magical Amulets in the First Book of Cyranides. Maryse Waegeman. (Illus.). 231p. (C). 1987. 55.00 (90-70265-80-X, Pub. by Gieben NE) Benjamins North Am.

Amulet of the Salkti. David S. Moscowitz. (Illus.). 1984. 6.95 (0-940244-20-9) Flying Buffalo.

Amulets Against the Dragon Forces. Paul Zindel. 1989. pap. 4.75 (0-8222-0040-6) Dramatists Play.

Amulets & Magic Bowls: Aramaic Incantations of Late Antiquity. 2nd ed. Joseph Naveh & S. Shaked. (Illus.). 340p. 1987. text ed. 28.00 (0-685-74254-7, Pub. by Magnes Press IS) Eisenbrauns.

Amulets & Superstitions. E. Wallis Budge. LC 77-86708. (Illus.). 1978. reprint ed. pap. 10.95 (0-486-23573-4) Dover.

Amulets & Talismans. Wallis Budge. (Illus.). 592p. 1992. pap. 14.95 (0-8065-1323-3, Citadel Pr) Carol Pub Group.

Amulets of Ancient Egypt. Carol Andrews. (Illus.). 128p. (Orig.). (C). 1994. pap. 17.95 (0-292-70464-X) U of Tex Pr.

Amulets of the Goddess: Oracle of Ancient Wisdom. Nancy Blair. LC 92-35945. (Illus.). 1993. pap. 32.95 (0-914728-80-6) Wingbow Pr.

***Amulets, Talismans & Charms.** C. J. Thompson. 1994. pap. 3.95 (1-55818-294-2, Sure Fire) Holmes Pub.

Amur, Monggol-un Tobci Teuke. (Mongolia Society Special Papers: No. 9). 30.00 (0-910980-29-2) Mongolia.

Amurru Akkadian, Vol. 1: A Linguistic Study. Shlomo Izre'el. 394p. 1991. 39.95 (1-55540-633-5, 04 04 40) Scholars Pr GA.

Amurru Akkadian, Vol. 2: A Linguistic Study. Shlomo Izre'el. 258p. 1991. 29.95 (1-55540-634-3, 04 04 41) Scholars Pr GA.

***Amusement & Theme Parks Industry Market.** 141p. (Orig.). 1995. pap. 1,195.00 (0-7605-2111-5) Rector Pr.

Amusement Business. Freddie Greenfield. 1976. pap. 3.00 (0-915480-07-7) Good Gay.

Amusement Facilities. (Illus.). 188p. 1994. 95.00 (4-7858-0029-1, Pub. by Shotenkenchiku-Sha JA) Bks Nippan.

Amusement for Your Bible Hour. J. G. Malphurs. 1961. pap. 0.60 (0-88027-100-0) Firm Foun Pub.

***Amusement Machines.** Lynn F. Pearson. (C). 1989. pap. 25.00x (0-7478-0179-7, Pub. by Shire UK) St Mut.

Amusement Machines: Your Route to Success. Dick McNicholas. 48p. (Orig.). 1981. pap. 6.95 (0-943592-00-3, TX 773-174) Publishers Pr.

Amusement Park Guide: Fun for the Whole Family at More Than 250 Amusement Parks from Coast to Coast. Tim O'Brien. LC 91-7421. (Illus.). 320p. (Orig.). 1991. pap. 12.95 (0-87106-300-X) Globe Pequot.

Amusement Park Mystery. Created by Gertrude C. Warner. (Boxcar Children Mysteries Ser.: No. 25). (Illus.). (J). (gr. 2-7). 1992. 10.95 (0-8075-0320-7); pap. 3.50 (0-8075-0319-3) A Whitman.

Amusement Parks: An American Guidebook. 2nd ed. John Norris & Joann Norris. LC 93-27805. 168p. 1994. pap. 24.95 (0-89950-789-1) McFarland & Co.

Amusement Tokens of the United States & Canada. Stephen P. Alpert & Kenneth E. Smith. LC 79-88433. (Illus.). 136p. (Orig.). 1979. pap. 24.95 (0-934422-20-6) Mead Pub Corp.

Amusements & Sports in American Life. Robert B. Weaver. LC 68-57644. (Illus.). 195p. 1969. reprint ed. text ed. 52.50 (0-8371-0742-3, WEAM, Greenwood Pr) Greenwood.

Amusements Developing Algebra Skills, 1. Alice Clack & Carol Leitch. 1975. pap. 7.95 (0-910974-76-4) Crit Think Soft.

Amusements Developing Algebra Skills, 2. Alice Clack & Carol Leitch. 1975. pap. 7.95 (0-910974-77-2) Crit Think Soft.

Amusements in Mathematics. Henry E. Dudeney. 1917. pap. 6.95 (0-486-20473-1) Dover.

Amusements of Old London, 2 Vols. in 1. William B. Boulton. LC 75-82820. (Illus.). 1972. 36.95 (0-405-08295-9, Pub. by Blom Pubns UK) Ayer.

***Amusing Alliterations.** Sherry Felty. 28p. (J). (ps-6). 1995. pap. 1.00 (1-884801-08-0) Fun Enter.

Amusing Anecdotes: Humorous Stories with a Moral. Logan M. Brady. xx, 299p. 1993. write for info. (0-932364-21-7) Ann Arbor Bk.

Amusing Arrangements. Leigh Rubin. LC 84-90632. (Notable Quotes Ser.: Vol. III). (Illus.). 80p. (Orig.). 1985. pap. text ed. 5.95 (0-943384-04-4) Rubes Pubns.

Amusing Glance at Life & Leaders in Early Colorado. Michael Yates. 111p. 1992. pap. 8.95 (0-9635793-0-4) Green Hse Pr.

***Amusing Grace.** Ed Koehler. LC 88-13056. (Illus.). 104p. (Orig.). 1994. pap. text ed. 6.99 (0-8308-1821-9, 1821) InterVarsity.

Amusing Grace: Humor to Heal Mind, Soul, & Body. King Duncan & Angela Akers. 320p. 1993. 19.95 (0-936497-09-2) Seven Worlds Pr.

Amusing Ourselves to Death: Public Discourse in the Age of Show Business. Neil Postman. 192p. 1986. pap. 11.95 (0-14-009438-5, Penguin Bks) Viking Penguin.

Amusing the Million: Coney Island at the Turn of the Century. John F. Kasson. (American Century Ser.). (Illus.). 128p. 1978. pap. 9.95 (0-8090-0133-0) Hill & Wang.

***AMVETS: Fifty Years of Proud Service to America's Veterans. Richard W. Flanagan & Patrick McCaffrey. LC 94-72575. (Illus.). 120p. 1994. 19.95 (0-9642526-0-0) AMVETS.**
While World War II was still raging, thousands of young Americans returned home with battle wounds...& before long, the idea of a national veterans organization began to take shape. Here, in one comprehensive volume, is the story of those formative years...the struggle for recognition & members... later, the triumphs in national & international arenas. This fascinating history traces the events that had people calling AMVETS "the most successful of the new veterans' organizations"...& how it became one of the most influential. The book features a large 8 1/2" by 11" format & comes bound in a handsome cloth hardcover. It also carries more than 90 pages of photographs - many in full color - together with lively anecdotes & a chronology of key events. To order, contact: AMVETS National Headquarters, ATTN: Public Relations Dept., 4647 Forbes Blvd., Lanham, MD 20706-4380; 301-459-9600; FAX: 301-459-7924. ***Publisher Provided Annotation.***

Amway: The Cult of Free Enterprise. Stephen Butterfield. LC 85-2133. 187p. 1985. 30.00 (0-89608-254-7); pap. 14.00 (0-89608-253-9) South End Pr.

***AMX & Javelin: Muscle Portfolio 1968-1974.** R. M. Clarke. (Illus.). 140p. 1994. pap. 18.95 (1-85520-248-4, Pub. by Brooklands Bks UK) Motorbooks Intl.

***AMX & Javelin History & Restoration.** James E. Bresnahan. (Illus.). 192p. 1995. pap. 24.95 (0-7603-0007-0) Motorbooks Intl.

Amy. Amy Chesley. 285p. (Orig.). 1986. pap. 9.95 (0-931703-00-X) Wellman Pub.

Amy. Randy J. Landon. LC 85-63064. (Illus.). 44p. 1986. 12.00 (0-936563-07-9); pap. 4.50 (0-936563-08-7) Signpost.

***Amy.** Abbey Strauss. LC 93-93766. 184p. (Orig.). 1994. pap. 10.00 (1-56002-302-3) Aegina Pr.

Amy: A Search for the Treasure Within. Evarts G. Loomis. LC 85-73540. (Illus.). 144p. (Orig.). 1986. pap. 5.50 (0-87516-564-8) DeVorss.

Amy Alcott's Guide to Women's Golf. Amy Alcott & Don Wade. (Illus.). 240p. 1991. 19.95 (0-525-24957-5, Dutton) NAL-Dutton.

Amy Alcott's Guide to Women's Golf. Amy Alcott & Don Wade. (Illus.). 240p. 1993. pap. 12.95 (0-452-26853-2, Plume) NAL-Dutton.

Amy & Gully in Rainbowland. W. W. Rowe. LC 92-9075. (Illus.). 84p. (Orig.). (J). (gr. k-4). 1992. pap. 5.95 (1-55939-003-4) Snow Lion Pubns.

Amy & Nathaniel. Welleran Poltarnees. (Illus.). 32p. (J). 1991. 11.95 (0-88138-118-7, Green Tiger S&S) S&S Childrens.

Amy Armadillo. Dave Sargent & Pat Sargent. (Animal Pride Ser.). (Illus.). 48p. (Orig.). (J). (gr. k-8). 1993. text ed. 11.95 (1-56763-046-4); pap. text ed. 5.95 (1-56763-047-2) Ozark Pub.

Amy Ashwood Garvey: Pan-Africanist, Feminist, & Wife, No. 1. Tony Martin. (New Marcus Garvey Library: No. 4). (Illus.). (Orig.). Date not set. text ed. write for info. (0-912469-06-4); pap. text ed. write for info. (0-912469-07-2) Majority Pr.

Amy Avocet. Joan E. Pizzo. LC 83-70739. (Tales of the Back Bay Ser.). (Illus.). (J). (gr. k-6). 1983. 8.95 (0-939126-06-0) Back Bay.

Amy Beach & Her Chamber Music: Biography, Documents, Style. Jeanell W. Brown. LC 94-9689. (Composers of North America Ser.: Vol. 16). (Illus.). 439p. 1994. 49.50 (0-8108-2884-7) Scarecrow.

Amy, Ben, & Catalpa the Cat: A Fanciful Story of This & That. Alma S. Coon. (Illus.). 40p. (J). (ps-2). 1990. 8.95 (0-87935-079-2) Colonial Williamsburg.

Amy Carmichael. Kathleen White. (Women of Faith Ser.). 96p. (Orig.). 1992. pap. 4.99 (1-55661-302-4) Bethany Hse.

Amy Carmichael: Let the Little Children Come. Lois H. Dick. (Orig.). 1984. pap. 4.25 (0-8024-0433-2) Moody.

Amy Carmichael of Dohnavur. Frank Houghton. 1991. pap. 7.95 (0-87508-084-7) Chr Lit.

Amy Clampitt. Amy Clampitt. write for info. (0-944521-10-X) Dia Ctr Arts.

Amy Dunn Quits School. Susan Shreve. LC 92-41772. (Illus.). 96p. (J). (gr. 3 up). 1993. 13.00 (0-688-10320-0, Tambourine Bks) Morrow.

Amy Elizabeth Explores Bloomingdale's. E. L. Konigsburg. LC 91-40132. (Illus.). 32p. (J). (ps-3). 1992. text ed. 14.95 (0-689-31766-2, Atheneum Bks Young) S&S Childrens.

Amy Emm's Story of Durham Quilting. Amy Emms. 1991. pap. 19.95 (0-85532-669-7, Pub. by Search Pr UK) A Schwartz & Co.

***Amy Fay: Pioneering American Woman Musician.** Margaret W. McCarthy. LC 95-10196. (Detroit Monographs in Musicology/Studies in Music: No. 17). 1995. write for info. (0-89990-074-7) Info Coord.

Amy Grant. Bob Italia. Ed. by Rosemary Wallner. LC 92-16692. (Reaching for the Stars Ser.). (J). 1992. lib. bdg. 12.94 (1-56239-145-3) Abdo & Dghtrs.

Amy Grant - Heart in Motion. (Piano-Vocal-Guitar Ser.). 64p. (Orig.). 1991. pap. 12.95 (0-7935-0834-7, 00308106) H Leonard.

Amy Grant - Home for Christmas. (Piano-Vocal-Guitar Ser.). (Illus.). 64p. (Orig.). 1993. pap. 12.95 (0-7935-2825-9, HL00308208) H Leonard.

Amy Jean. Lorinda Hagen. 256p. 1983. pap. 2.95 (0-8439-2001-7) Dorchester Pub Co.

Amy Johnson. Eva Bailey. (Profiles Ser.). (Illus.). 64p. (J). (gr. 5-9). 1991. 11.95 (0-237-60032-3, Pub. by Evans Bros Ltd UK) Trafalgar.

Amy Lowell. Richard Benvenuto. (Twayne's United States Authors Ser.). 189p. 1985. text ed. 22.95 (0-8057-7436-X, Twayne) Macmillan.

Amy Lowell. Horace Gregory. LC 69-16855. (Select Bibliographies Reprint Ser.). 1977. 27.95 (0-8369-5008-9) Ayer.

Amy Lowell. F. Cudworth Flint. LC 70-628285. (University of Minnesota Pamphlets on American Writers Ser.: No. 82). 48p. (Orig.). reprint ed. pap. 25.00 (0-7837-2889-1, 2057566) Bks Demand.

Amy Moves In. Francine Pascal. (Sweet Valley Twins Ser.: No. 44). (J). (gr. 4-7). 1991. 3.50 (0-553-15837-6) Bantam.

***Amy Rose.** Noel Peattie. 250p. (Orig.). 1995. pap. 19.95 (0-916147-62-2) Regent Pr.

Amy Spangler's Breastfeeding: A Parent's Guide. 4th rev. ed. Amy Spangler. (Illus.). 70p. 1990. 5.75 (0-9627450-9-X) A Spangler.

Amy the Dancing Bear. Carly Simon. (Illus.). (J). (ps-3). 1989. 15.00 (0-385-26637-5) Doubleday.

Amy Vanderbilt's Complete Book of Etiquette. Nancy Tuckerman & Nancy Dunnan. LC 93-44452. 1995. 32.00 (0-385-41342-4) Doubleday.

Amy Vanderbilt's Everyday Etiquette. rev. ed. Amy Vanderbilt. 304p. 1983. mass mkt. 5.99 (0-553-27754-5) Bantam.

Amy, Wendy & Beth: Learning Language in South Baltimore. Peggy J. Miller. LC 81-11656. 208p. (C). 1982. text ed. 22.95x (0-292-70357-0) U of Tex Pr.

Amycus. Bernard Evslin. (Monsters of Mythology Ser.). (Illus.). 85p. 1989. lib. bdg. 19.95 (1-55546-240-5) Chelsea Hse.

Amygdala. John P. Aggleton. 628p. 1992. text ed. 159.95 (0-471-56129-0, Wiley-Liss) Wiley.

***Amygdale: Neurobiological Aspects of Emotion, Memory, & Mental Dysfunction.** Ed. by John P. Aggleton. 1993. pap. text ed. 74.95 (0-471-30825-0) Wiley.

Amygdaloid Complex. M. Ben-Ari. (INSERM Symposia Ser.: Vol. 20). 516p. 1982. 149.75 (0-444-80397-1) Elsevier.

Amylograph Handbook. Ed. by W. Shuey & K. Tipples. LC 80-65382. 37p. 1982. 59.00x (0-913250-15-5) Am Assn Cereal Chem.

Amyloid & Amyloidosis. Ed. by T. Isobe et al. LC 88-22425. (Illus.). 906p. 1988. 165.00 (0-306-42997-7, Plenum Pr) Plenum.

Amyloid & Amyloidosis 1991. Ed. by Jacob B. Natvig et al. (C). 1991. lib. bdg. 270.00 (0-7923-1089-6) Kluwer Ac.

Amyloid Protein Precursor in Development, Aging, & Alzheimer's Disease. C. L. Masters. LC 94-4461. (Research & Perspectives in Alzheimer's Disease Ser.). 1994. 100.00 (0-387-57788-2) Spr-Verlag.

Amyloidosis. Ed. by George G. Glenner et al. LC 86-4889. 876p. 1986. 145.00 (0-306-42261-1, Plenum Pr) Plenum.

Amyloids, Part II. Ed. by S. Battaglia. (Journal: Applied Pathology: Vol. 3, Nos. 1-2). (Illus.). 116p. 1986. pap. 51.25 (3-8055-4458-8) S Karger.

Amyloids, Pt. 1. Ed. by S. Battaglia. (Journal: Applied Pathology: Vol. 2, No. 6, 1984). (Illus.). vi, 86p. 1986. pap. 38.50 (3-8055-4351-4) S Karger.

Amyntas. Andre Gide. Tr. by Richard Howard. (Ecco Travel Ser.). 158p. 1988. 17.00 (0-88001-165-3); pap. 7.50 (0-88001-166-1) Ecco Pr.

Amyotrophic Lateral Sclerosis. F. Clifford Rose. (Illus.). 275p. 1990. 69.95 (0-939957-23-X) Demos Vermande.

Amyotrophic Lateral Sclerosis. Ed. by A. C. Williams. LC 93-32613. 1993. write for info. (0-412-54780-5, Chap & Hall NY) Chapman & Hall.

Amyotrophic Lateral Sclerosis: A Comprehensive Guide to Management. Mitsumoto. 1994. 39.95 (0-939957-58-2) Demos Vermande.

Amyotrophic Lateral Sclerosis: Recent Advances in Research & Treatment. Ed. by T. Tsubaki & Y. Yase. (International Congress Ser.: No. 769). 394p. 1988. 115.50 (0-444-80979-1, Excerpta Medica) Elsevier.

Amyotrophic Lateral Sclerosis: Therapeutic, Psychological & Research Aspects. Ed. by V. Cosi et al. LC 87-1748. (Advances in Experimental Medicine & Biology Ser.: Vol. 209). 372p. 1987. 75.00 (0-306-42546-7, Plenum Pr) Plenum.

Amyotrophic Lateral Sclerosis (ALS) Current Clinical & Pathophysiological Evidence for Differences in Etiology. Ed. by Arthur J. Hudson. 304p. 1990. pap. 75.00 (0-8020-3446-2) U of Toronto Pr.

Amyotrophic Lateral Sclerosis (& Other Motor Neuron Diseases) Lewis P. Rowland. (Advances in Neurology Ser.: Vol. 56). 1991. 149.50 (0-88167-748-5) Raven.

Amy's Eyes. Richard Kennedy. LC 82-48841. (Illus.). 448p. (J). (ps up). 1985. 15.00 (0-06-023219-6) HarpC Child Bks.

Amy's Gold. Robert O. Burgess. LC 85-62546. (Illus.). 234p. 1985. 17.95 (0-9615504-0-6) Sweetwater Pr.

Amy's (Not So) Great Camp-Out. Jane O'Connor. LC 92-45881. (Here Come the Brownies, Brownie Girl Scout Bks.: No. 4). (Illus.). 64p. (J). (gr. 1-4). 1993. 7.99 (0-448-40167-3, G&D); pap. 3.95 (0-448-40166-5, G&D) Putnam Pub Group.

Amy's Pen Pal. Francine Pascal. (Sweet Valley Twins Ser.: No. 35). (J). 1990. pap. 3.25 (0-553-15772-8) Bantam.

Amy's Secret Sister. Francine Pascal. (Sweet Valley Twins & Friends Ser.: No. 83). (J). (gr. 4-7). 1994. 3.50 (0-553-48101-0) Bantam.

Amy's True Love. Francine Pascal. (Sweet Valley High Ser.: No. 75). (YA). 1991. pap. 2.99 (0-553-28963-2) Bantam.

Amythia: Crisis in the Natural History of Western Culture. Loyal D. Rue. LC 88-27846. (Illus.). 232p. 1989. 29.95 (0-8173-0428-2) U of Ala Pr.

Amzat & His Brothers: Three Italian Tales. Paula Fox. LC 92-19494. (Illus.). 80p. (J). (gr. 3-5). 1993. lib. bdg. 16.99 (0-531-08612-7) Orchard Bks Watts.

282

An Asterisk (*) at the beginning of an entry indicates that the title is appearing in BIP for the first time.

Anahulu: The Anthropology of History in the Kingdom of Hawaii, Vol. I: Historical Ethnography. Patrick V. Kirch & Marshall D. Sahlins. LC 91-33830. (Illus.). 272p. 1992. 50.00 (*0-226-73363-7*) U Ch Pr.

Anahulu: The Anthropology of History in the Kingdom of Hawaii, Vol. II: The Archaeology of History. Patrick V. Kirch & Marshall D. Sahlins. LC 91-33830. (Illus.). 264p. 1992. 50.00 (*0-226-73364-5*) U Ch Pr.

Anahulu: The Anthropology of History in the Kingdom of Hawaii, Vol. II: The Archaeology of History. Patrick V. Kirch. (C). 1994. pap. text ed. 24.95 (*0-226-73366-1*) U Ch Pr.

Anais: An International Journal, Vol. 1. Ed. by Gunther Stuhlmann. (Illus.). 136p. (Orig.). 1983. pap. 7.00 (*0-9611238-0-X*) Anais Nin Found.

Anais: An International Journal, Vol. 2. Ed. by Gunther Stuhlmann. (Illus.). 136p. (Orig.). 1984. pap. 7.00 (*0-9611238-1-8*) Anais Nin Found.

Anais: An International Journal, Vol. 3. Ed. by Gunther Stuhlmann. (Illus.). 136p. (Orig.). 1985. pap. 7.00 (*0-9611238-2-6*) Anais Nin Found.

Anais: An International Journal, Vol. 4. Ed. by Gunther Stuhlmann. (Illus.). 136p. (Orig.). 1986. pap. 7.00 (*0-9611238-3-4*) Anais Nin Found.

Anais: An International Journal, Vol. 5. Ed. by Gunther Stuhlmann. (Illus.). 136p. (Orig.). 1987. pap. 7.00 (*0-9611238-4-2*) Anais Nin Found.

Anais: An International Journal, Vol. 6. Ed. by Gunther Stuhlmann. (Illus.). 136p. (Orig.). 1988. pap. 7.00 (*0-9611238-5-0*) Anais Nin Found.

Anais: An International Journal, Vol. 7. Ed. by Gunther Stuhlmann. (Illus.). 128p. (Orig.). 1989. pap. 7.00 (*0-9611238-6-9*) Anais Nin Found.

Anais: An International Journal, Vol. 8. Ed. by Gunther Stuhlmann. (Illus.). 128p. (Orig.). 1990. pap. 7.00 (*0-9611238-7-7*) Anais Nin Found.

Anais: An International Journal, Vol. 9. Ed. by Gunther Stuhlmann. (Illus.). 128p. (Orig.). 1991. pap. 7.50 (*0-9611238-8-5*) Anais Nin Found.

Anais: The Erotic Life of Anais Nin. Noel R. Fitch. LC 93-7029. 1993. 24.95 (*0-316-28428-9*) Little.

***Anais: The Erotic Life of Anais Nin.** Noel R. Fitch. 1994. pap. 14.95 (*0-316-28431-9*) Little.

Anais Nin. Bettina L. Knapp. LC 78-57692. (Literature & Life Ser.). 177p. (C). 1978. 19.95 (*0-8044-2481-0*, F Ungar Bks) Continuum.

Anais Nin: A Bibliography. Benjamin Franklin. LC 72-619701. (Serif Series: Bibliographies & Checklists: No. 29). 125p. reprint ed. pap. 35.70 (*0-317-10335-0*, 2051212) Bks Demand.

Anais Nin: A Biography. Deidre Bair. 672p. 1994. 35.00 (*0-399-13988-5*) Putnam Pub Group.

Anais Nin: An Introduction. Benjamin Franklin & Duane Schneider. LC 79-10635. 1980. 20.00 (*0-8214-0395-8*) Ohio U Pr.

Anais Nin & Her Critics. Philip K. Jason. x, 121p. 1993. 45.95 (*1-879751-41-0*) Camden Hse.

Anais Nin, Art & Artists: A Collection of Essays. Ed. by Sharon Spencer. (Modern Literatures Annual Ser.: Vol. II). (Illus.). 208p. 1987. 20.00 (*0-913283-11-8*) Penkevill.

Anais, Vol. 10: An International Journal. Ed. by Gunther Stuhlmann. (Illus.). 136p. (Orig.). 1992. pap. 7.50 (*0-9611238-9-3*) Anais Nin Found.

Anais, 1994, No. 12: An International Journal. Ed. by Gunther Stuhlmann. (Illus.). 136p. (Orig.). 1994. pap. 7.50 (*0-685-71950-2*) Anais Nin Found.

Anakah: Little Ferret of Galilee. Pat A. Meaden. 1993. 9.95 (*0-8062-4077-6*) Carlton.

Anal Pleasure & Health: A Guide for Men & Women. 2nd rev. ed. Jack Morin. LC 81-9789. (Illus.). 278p. (Orig.). 1986. reprint ed. pap. 12.50 (*0-940208-08-3*, Yes Pr) Down There Pr.

Analecta, 4 Vols. Robert Wodrow. LC 74-178318. (Maitland Club, Glasgow. Publications: No. 60). reprint ed. Set. 175.00 (*0-404-53051-6*) AMS Pr.

Analecta Alexandrina. August Meineke. vii, 440p. 1964. reprint ed. write for info. (*0-318-70975-9*, Pub. by Georg Olms GW) Lubrecht & Cramer.

Analecta Biographica: A Handful of New England Portraits. Walter M. Whitehill. reprint ed. 7.95 (*0-87577-048-7*, Peabody Museum) Peabody Essex Mus.

Analecta Dublinensia: Three Mediaeval Latin Texts in the Library of Trinity College Dublin. Ed. by Marvin L. Colker. LC 75-1954. (Medieval Academy Bks.: No. 82). 1975. 30.00 (*0-910956-56-1*) Medieval Acad.

Analecta Euripidea. Ulrich Von Wilamowitz-Moellendorff. iv, 256p. 1963. reprint ed. write for info. (*0-318-71062-5*, Pub. by Georg Olms GW) Lubrecht & Cramer.

Analecta Frankliana. Ed. by Sandra A. Wawrytko. 362p. (Orig.). 1982. write for info. (*0-89407-075-4*); pap. 12.95 (*0-89407-052-5*) Inst Logo.

Analecta Hafniensia: Southeast Asian Studies in Copenhagen. Littrup. (C). 1988. text ed. 60.00 (*0-7007-0199-0*, Pub. by Curzon Pr UK) Humanities.

Analecta Husserliana: The Yearbook of Phenomenological Research, Vol. 1. Ed. by Anna-Teresa Tymieniecka. LC 70-135105. 207p. 1970. lib. bdg. 65.50 (*90-277-0171-7*) Kluwer Ac.

Analecta Husserliana, the Later Husserl & the Idea of Phenomenology, Idealism-Realism, Historicity & Nature: Proceedings of the International Phenomenology Conference, University of Waterloo, 1969, Vol. 2. International Phenomenology Conference Staff. Ed. by Anna-Teresa Tymieniecka & L. Hayworth. LC 78-25369. 374p. 1972. lib. bdg. 94.00 (*90-277-0223-3*) Kluwer Ac.

Analecta Orientalia Ad Poeticam Aristoteleam. David S. Margoliouth. vi, 243p. reprint ed. write for info. (*0-318-71531-7*, Pub. by Georg Olms GW) Lubrecht & Cramer.

Analects. Confucius. Tr. by D. C. Lau. 1979. pap. 8.95 (*0-14-044348-7*, Penguin Classics) Viking Penguin.

Analects. Tr. & Intro. by Raymond Dawson. LC 92-46274. (World's Classics Ser.). 160p. (C). 1993. 7.95 (*0-19-283091-0*) OUP.

***Analects.** unabridged ed. Confucius. Tr. by William E. Soothill. LC 94-24742. (Thrift Editions Ser.). 144p. 1995. pap. text ed. 2.00 (*0-486-28484-0*) Dover.

Analects Confucius. Confucius. 1960. pap. 4.95 (*0-394-70173-9*) Random.

Analects of Confucius. Tr. by Arthur Waley. 1989. pap. 9.00 (*0-679-72296-3*, Vin) Random.

Analects of Self-Contempt: Sweet Cheat of Freedom. Ursule Molinaro. 24p. (Orig.). 1983. pap. 3.00 (*0-917061-16-0*) Top Stories.

Analgesic & NSAID-Induced Kidney Disease. Ed. by J. H. Stewart. LC 92-22709. (Oxford Monographs on Clinical Nephrology: Vol. 2). 160p. 1993. 65.00 (*0-19-261956-X*) OUP.

Analgesic Drugs. (Medical Ser.). 1986. lib. bdg. 79.95 (*0-8490-3803-0*) Gordon Pr.

***Analgesics: Neurochemical, Behavioral, & Clinical.** Ed. by Michael J. Kuhar & Gavril W. Pasternak. LC 84-3437. (Central Nervous System Pharmacology Ser.). (Illus.). Date not set. reprint ed. pap. 100.10 (*0-7837-9518-1*, 2060267) Bks Demand.

Analise. Candace Camp. 1991. mass mkt. 4.50 (*0-06-104045-2*, Harp PBks) HarpC.

Analisis Arquetipico, Mitico y Simbolico de Pedro Paramo. Nicolas E. Alvarez. LC 83-80471. (Coleccion Polymita Ser.). 139p. (Orig.). (SPA.). 1983. pap. 12.00 (*0-89729-330-4*) Ediciones.

Analisis de Costos Marginales y Diseno de Tarifas de Electricidad y Agua: Estudios de Caso. Ed. by Yves Albouy. 276p. 1983. write for info. (*0-940602-11-3*) IADB.

Analisis de Costos Marginales y Diseno de Tarifas de Electricidad y Agua: Notas de Metodologia. Ed. by Yves Albouy. 230p. 1983. write for info. (*0-940602-09-1*) IADB.

Analisis e Interpretacion de Don Juan De Castro de Lope de Vega. Antonio Gonzalez. LC 79-54185. (Coleccion Polymita Ser.). 241p. (Orig.). (SPA.). (C). 1981. pap. 10.00 (*0-89729-235-9*) Ediciones.

Analisis Existencial de Abaddon, el Exterminador de Ernesto Sabato. Ed. by Gemma Roberts. 98p. 1990. pap. 15.00 (*0-89295-061-7*) Society Sp & Sp-Am.

Analisis General Libros de la Biblia: Bible Book Outlines. B. C. Taylor. (SPA.). 4.25 (*84-7645-059-1*, 223125, Pub. by Edit Clie SP) TSELF.

Analisis Historico De la Violencia en Puerto Rico see Violencia y Criminalidad En Puerto Rico, 1898-1973: Apuntes para un Estudio De Historia Social

Analiz Energeticheskogo Sovershenstva Tekhnologicheskikh Protesssov - Analysis of Energy Efficiency of Industrial Processes. Vladimir S. Stepanov. LC 92-33780. (Illus.). 250p. (ENG & RUS.). 1993. 89.00 (*0-387-54908-0*) Spr-Verlag.

***Analog: The Best of Science Fiction.** Analog Magazine Staff. 1994. 11.98 (*0-88365-637-X*) Galahad Bks.

Analog & Computer Electronics for Scientists. 4th ed. Basil H. Vassos & Galen W. Ewing. 1993. text ed. 69.95 (*0-471-54559-7*) Wiley.

Analog & Digital Circuits Theory & Experimentation, Vol. 1. Mansour Eslami. LC 86-15260. 376p. (C). 1986. pap. 32.50 (*0-89874-959-X*) Krieger.

Analog & Digital Circuits Theory & Experimentation, Vol. 2. Mansour Eslami. LC 86-15260. 408p. 1986. pap. 34.50 (*0-89874-983-2*) Krieger.

Analog & Digital Communication Systems. 3rd ed. Martin S. Roden. 1990. text ed. 76.00 (*0-13-033325-5*) P-H.

***Analog & Digital Communication Systems.** 4th ed. Martin S. Roden. LC 95-11659. 1995. text ed. 75.00 (*0-13-372046-2*) P-H.

Analog & Digital Communications. Hwei P. Hsu. LC 92-38804. (Schaum's Outline Ser.). 416p. 1993. pap. text ed. 12.95 (*0-07-030636-2*) McGraw.

Analog & Digital Electronics. 2nd ed. Peter H. Beards. 560p. 1990. text ed. 84.00 (*0-13-035320-5*, 420201) P-H.

Analog & Digital Filters: Design & Realization. H. Ying-Fai Lam. (Electrical & Computer Engineering Ser.). 1979. text ed. 71.00 (*0-13-032755-7*) P-H.

***Analog & Digital Signal Processing.** Ashok Ambardar. (Electrical Engineering Ser.). 656p. 1995. disk, pap. 64.95 (*0-534-94086-2*) Intl Thomson.

Analog & Digital Signal Transmission: Student Text. Lawrence M. Thompson. LC 85-135658. (Instructional Resource Package Ser.). (Illus.). 170p. reprint ed. pap. 48.50 (*0-7837-5152-4*, 2044881) Bks Demand.

Analog & Hybrid Computing. D. E. Hyndman. LC 75-120691. (C). 1970. 100.00 (*0-08-015573-1*, Pub. by Pergamon Repr UK) Franklin.

***Analog & Switching Circuit Design: Using Integrated & Discrete Devices.** fac. ed. Joseph Watson. LC 83-238570. (Illus.). 618p. 1984. reprint ed. pap. 176.20 (*0-7837-8017-6*, 2047773) Bks Demand.

Analog & Switching Circuit Design: Using Integrated & Discrete Devices. 2nd ed. J. Watson. 1989. text ed. 134.00 (*0-471-50862-4*) Wiley.

Analog Automatic Control Loops in Radar & EW. Richard S. Hughes. (Radar Library). 252p. 1988. text ed. 29.00 (*0-89006-321-4*) Artech Hse.

***Analog Board User's Manual.** Christopher E. Strangio. (Illus.). 72p. (Orig.). (C). 1989. pap. text ed. 15.00 (*0-929955-04-8*) CAMI Research.

Analog Circuit Design. Vincent F. Leonard, Jr. Ed. by Jim Fry. LC 84-21727. (Circuit Design Ser.). (Illus.). 750p. 1984. ring bd. 69.95 (*0-87119-102-4*, EE-1003) Heathkit-Zenith Ed.

Analog Circuit Design: Art Science & Personalities. Ed. by Jim Williams. (Illus.). 222p. 1991. text ed. 47.95 (*0-7506-9166-2*) Buttrwrth-Heinemann.

***Analog Circuit Design: Art, Science & Personalities.** Ed. by Jim Williams. 368p. 1994. pap. 29.95 (*0-7506-9640-0*) Buttrwrth-Heinemann.

***Analog Circuit Design: Low-Power Low-Voltage, Integrated Filters & Smart Power.** Rudy J. Van de Plassche. 392p. (C). 1994. lib. bdg. 110.00 (*0-7923-9513-1*) Kluwer Ac.

Analog Circuit Design - Mixed AD Circuit Design, Sensor Interface Circuits & Communication Circuits: Proceedings of the Workshop, April 6-8, 1993, Faculty Club Leuven. Ed. by Willy Sansen et al. LC 93-47515. 328p. (C). 1994. lib. bdg. 98.00 (*0-7923-9408-9*) Kluwer Ac.

***Analog Circuits Cookbook.** Ian Hickman. (Illus.). 240p. 1995. pap. 29.95 (*0-7506-2002-1*) Buttrwrth-Heinemann.

Analog CMOS Filters for Very High Frequencies. Bram Nauta. LC 92-27778. (International Series in Engineering & Computer Science, VLSI, Computer Architecture, & Digital Screen Processing). (C). 1992. lib. bdg. 73.00 (*0-7923-9272-8*) Kluwer Ac.

Analog Communications for Technology. Thomas S. Laverghetta. 600p. (C). 1991. text ed. 51.00 (*0-03-029403-7*) SCP.

Analog Computation Applied to the Study of Chemical Processes. R. Vichnevetsky. 172p. 1970. text ed. 171.00 (*0-677-00860-0*) Gordon & Breach.

Analog Computer Simulation of the Runoff Characteristics of an Urban Watershed. Dhruva Narayana et al. LC 77-141023. 88p. 1969. 19.00 (*0-403-04522-3*) Scholarly.

Analog Device-Level Layout Automation. John M. Cohn et al. LC 93-42917. (International Series in Engineering & Computer Science, VLSI, Computer Architecture, & Digital Screen Processing). 304p. (C). 1994. lib. bdg. 88.00 (*0-7923-9431-3*) Kluwer Ac.

***Analog-Digital & Digital-Analog Conversion.** fac. ed. Bernard Loriferne. 206p. 1983. reprint ed. pap. 58.80 (*0-7837-8287-X*, 2049069) Bks Demand.

Analog-Digital ASIC Design. Janez Trontelj. 1990. pap. text ed. 50.00 (*0-07-707300-2*) McGraw.

Analog-Digital Conversion Handbook. 3rd ed. Ed. by Analog Devices, Inc. Staff. (Illus.). 720p. 1985. text ed. 65.00 (*0-13-032848-0*) P-H.

Analog Electronic Circuits: Analysis & Applications. Robert B. Northrop. (Electrical & Computer Engineering Ser.). (Illus.). 512p. (C). 1990. text ed. 69.95 (*0-201-11656-1*) Addison-Wesley.

Analog Electronic Design. Jonathon Scott. 550p. 1991. pap. text ed. 71.00 (*0-13-033192-9*) P-H.

Analog Electronic Handbook. T. H. Collins. 320p. 1989. reprint ed. boxed, text ed. 48.00 (*0-318-37807-8*) P-H.

Analog Electronics. Hickman. 1990. 51.95 (*0-8493-7147-3*, TK7867) CRC Pr.

***Analog Electronics: Devices, Circuits & Technique.** Gerald E. Williams. 700p. 1995. text ed. write for info. (*0-314-04553-8*) West Pub.

Analog Electronics for Scientific Application. Dennis Barnaal. (Illus.). 366p. (C). 1989. reprint ed. pap. text ed. 21.95 (*0-88133-422-7*) Waveland Pr.

Analog Electronics with Op Amps: A Source Book of Practical Circuits. A. J. Peyton & Y. Walsh. LC 92-22691. (Illus.). 300p. (C). 1993. 94.95 (*0-521-33305-9*); pap. 37.95 (*0-521-33604-X*) Cambridge U Pr.

Analog Estimation Methods in Econometrics. Charles F. Manski. (Monographs in Statistics & Applied Probability). 250p. 1988. text ed. 45.00 (*0-412-01141-7*, 9961, Chap & Hall NY) Chapman & Hall.

Analog Filter Design. M. E. Van Valkenberg. 608p. (C). 1982. text ed. 73.25 (*0-03-059246-1*); Solutions manual. write for info. (*0-03-063826-7*) SCP.

Analog I-O Design: Acquisition, Conversion, Recovery. Patrick H. Garrett. (Illus.). 1981. text ed. 58.40 (*0-8359-0208-0*, Reston) P-H.

Analog IC. Walter H. Buchsbaum. (Vestpocket Handbook Ser.). (Illus.). 1986. 8.95 (*0-13-032748-4*, Busn) P-H.

Analog Integrated Circuit Design. Alan B. Grebene. LC 78-15389. 416p. 1979. reprint ed. lib. bdg. 36.50 (*0-88275-710-5*) Krieger.

Analog Integrated Circuits. E. Greeneich. 1992. text ed. 69.95 (*0-442-01333-7*) Van Nos Reinhold.

Analog Integrated Circuits. Sidney Soclof. (Illus.). 720p. (C). 1984. text ed. 79.00 (*0-13-032772-7*) P-H.

Analog Integrated Circuits for Communications: Principles, Simulation & Design. Donald O. Pederson & Kartikeya Mayaram. 592p. (C). 1990. lib. bdg. 114.50 (*0-7923-9089-X*) Kluwer Ac.

Analog Interface & DSP Sourcebook. Alan Clements. LC 92-36743. 1000p. 1993. text ed. 80.00i (*0-07-707694-X*) McGraw.

Analog Methods for Computer-Aided Circuit Analysis & Diagnosis. Ozawa. (Electrical Engineering & Electronics Ser.: No. 48). 440p. 1988. 135.00 (*0-8247-7843-X*) Dekker.

Analog MOS Integrated Circuits. Ed. by P. R. Gray et al. LC 80-22116. 415p. 1980. 39.95 (*0-87942-142-8*, PC01354) Inst Electrical.

Analog MOS Integrated Circuits for Signal Processing. Roubik Gregorian & Gabor C. Temes. LC 85-31493. (Filters: Design, Manufacturing & Applications Ser.). 598p. 1986. text ed. 99.00 (*0-471-09797-7*) Wiley.

Analog MOS Integrated Circuits, II. P. R. Gray. 512p. 1988. 59.95 (*0-87942-247-5*, PC02394) Inst Electrical.

***Analog Signal Generation for Built-in-Self-Test of Mixed-Signal Integrated Circuits.** Gordon W. Roberts & Albert K. Lu. LC 95-989. (International Engineering & Computer Science Ser., Vol. 312; Analog Circuits & Signal Processing: 312). 136p. (C). 1995. lib. bdg. 75.00 (*0-7923-9564-6*) Kluwer Ac.

***Analog Signal Processing.** Ed. by Peter B. Aronhime & F. W. Stephenson. LC 94-33388. 104p. (C). 1994. lib. bdg. 75.00 (*0-7923-9510-7*) Kluwer Ac.

Analog Signal Processing & Instrumentation. Arie F. Arbel. LC 79-13461. (Illus.). 1980. 120.00 (*0-521-22469-1*) Cambridge U Pr.

Analog Signal Processing & Instrumentation. Arie F. Arbel. (Illus.). 246p. 1984. pap. 39.95 (*0-521-31866-1*) Cambridge U Pr.

Analog Switches: Applications & Projects. Delton T. Horn. 1990. text ed. 21.95 (*0-07-156989-8*); pap. text ed. 12.95 (*0-07-156995-2*) McGraw.

Analog Switches: Applications & Projects. Delton T. Horn. (Illus.). 160p. 1990. 21.95 (*0-8306-8445-X*, 3445); pap. 12.95 (*0-8306-3445-2*) TAB Bks.

Analog-to-Digital & Digital-to-Analog Conversion Techniques. 2nd ed. David F. Hoeschele, Jr. LC 93-11417. 397p. 1994. text ed. 74.95 (*0-471-57147-4*) Wiley.

***Analog to Digital Conversion: A Practical Approach.** Kevin M. Daugherty. LC 94-5266. 1994. write for info. (*0-07-015675-1*) McGraw.

Analog VLSI: Signal & Information Processing. Mahammed Ismail. 1994. text ed. write for info. (*0-07-032386-0*) McGraw.

Analog VLSI & Neural Systems. Carver Mead. (Computation & Neural Systems Ser.). (Illus.). 384p. (C). 1989. text ed. 49.50 (*0-201-05992-4*, Adv Bk Prog) Addison-Wesley.

Analog VLSI Implementation of Neural Systems. Ed. by Carver Mead & Mohammed I. Ismail. (C). 1989. lib. bdg. 67.00 (*0-7923-9040-7*) Kluwer Ac.

Analog VLSI System for Stereoscopic Vision. Misha Mahowald. LC 93-49498. (International Series in Engineering & Computer Science, VLSI, Computer Architecture, & Digital Screen Processing). 232p. (C). 1994. lib. bdg. 95.00 (*0-7923-9444-5*) Kluwer Ac.

Analogica. Armand E. Prieditis. LC 86-33749. (Research Notes in Artificial Intelligence Ser.). (Illus.). 176p. (Orig.). 1988. pap. text ed. 29.95 (*0-934613-37-0*) Morgan Kaufmann.

Analogica: Proceedings of the First Workshop on Analogical Reasoning. Ed. by Armand Prieditis. 160p. (C). 1988. pap. text ed. 180.00 (*0-273-08780-0*, Pub. by Pitman Pubng UK) St Mut.

Analogical & Inductive Inference. Ed. by K. P. Jantke. (Lecture Notes in Computer Science Ser.: Vol. 265). 233p. 1987. pap. 33.00 (*0-387-18081-8*) Spr-Verlag.

Analogical & Inductive Inference. Ed. by K. P. Jantke. (Lecture Notes in Artificial Intelligence Ser.: Vol. 397). ix, 338p. 1989. pap. 40.00 (*0-387-51734-0*, 3565) Spr-Verlag.

Analogical & Inductive Inference: Proceedings of International Workshop AII, 1992, Dagstuhl Castle, Germany, October 1992. Ed. by K. P. Jantke. LC 92-31741. 1992. 52.00 (*0-387-56004-1*) Spr-Verlag.

***Analogical Connections.** Ed. by Keith J. Holyoak & John A. Barnden. (Advances in Connectionist & Neural Computation Theory Ser.: Vol. 2). 501p. 1994. 69.50 (*1-56750-039-0*) Ablex Pub.

Analogical Imagination. David Tracy. 496p. 1985. pap. 19.95 (*0-8245-0694-4*) Crossroad NY.

Analogical Modeling of Language. Royal Skousen. (C). 1989. lib. bdg. 80.50 (*0-7923-0517-5*) Kluwer Ac.

***Analogical Natural Language Processing.** Daniel Jones. (Studies in Computational Linguistics). 160p. 1995. 59.95 (*1-85728-218-3*, Pub. by UCL Pr UK) Taylor & Francis.

Analogical Possibilities: How Words Refer to God. Philip A. Rolnick. LC 92-46630. (American Academy of Religion Academy Ser.: No. 81). 328p. 1993. 29.95 (*1-55540-824-9*, 010181); pap. 19.95 (*1-55540-825-7*, 010181) Scholars Pr GA.

Analogical Reasoning. Ed. by David H. Helman. 1988. lib. bdg. 150.00 (*90-277-2711-2*) Kluwer Ac.

Analogical Reasoning in Islamic Jurisprudence. Ahmad Hassan. 24.50 (*0-935782-35-4*) Kazi Pubns.

Analogies at War. Yuen Foong Khong. (Korea, Munich, Dien Bien Phu, & the Vietnam Decisions of 1965). (Illus.). 272p. 1992. text ed. 42.50 (*0-691-07846-7*); pap. text ed. 16.95 (*0-691-02535-5*) Princeton U Pr.

Analogies Between Analogies: The Mathematical Reports of S. M. Ulam & His Los Alamos Collaborators. S. M. Ulam. Ed. by A. R. Bednarek & Francoise Ulam. 1990. 65.00 (*0-520-05290-0*) U CA Pr.

Analogies in Isaiah, 2 vols., Set. Archibald Van Wieringen. 985p. 1994. pap. 90.00 (*90-5383-210-6*, Pub. by VU Univ Pr NE) Paul & Co Pubs.

Analogies in Optics & Micro Electronics: Selected Contributions on Recent Developments. Ed. by Willem Van Haeringen & Daan Lenstra. (C). 1990. lib. bdg. 102.50 (*0-7923-0708-9*) Kluwer Ac.

Analogue & Digital Signal Processing. Hussein Baher. 1990. pap. text ed. 54.95 (*0-471-92342-7*) Wiley.

***Analogue Electric Circuits.** Michael Soderstrand & Gary Ford. 128p. (C). 1994. per., pap. text ed. 29.94 (*0-7872-0503-6*) Kendall-Hunt.

Analogue Electronic Circuits & Systems. A. Basak. (Electronics Texts for Engineers & Scientists Ser.). (Illus.). 256p. (C). 1991. 99.95 (*0-521-36046-3*); pap. 42.95 (*0-521-36913-4*) Cambridge U Pr.

Analogue Electronics. John C. Morris. 256p. 1991. pap. 25.00 (*0-340-54461-9*, A6450, Pub. by E Arnold UK) Routledge Chapman & Hall.

Analogue Electronics Circuit Analysis. Richardson & Reader. 200p. 1992. boxed 30.00 (*0-13-026311-7*) P-H.

Analogue IC Design: The Current Mode Approach. Toumazou. 1990. 105.00 (*0-86341-215-7*, CS002) Inst Elect Eng.

An Asterisk (*) at the beginning of an entry indicates that the title is appearing in BIP for the first time.

An Asterisk (*) at the beginning of an entry indicates that the title is appearing in BIP for the first time.

Analysis & Evaluation of Nursing Theories. Jacqueline Fawcett. (Illus.). 268p. (C). 1993. text ed. 29.95 (*0-8036-3413-7*) Davis Co.

Analysis & Fate of Pollutants: Selected Papers from the 16th Annual Symposium on the Analytical Chemistry of Pollutants & from the 3rd Workshop on the Chemistry & Analysis of Hydrocarbons, Lausanne, Switzerland, 17- 21 March, 1986. J. Tarradellas et al. (Current Topics In Environmental & Toxicological Chemistry Ser.: Vol. 13). 564p. 1988. text ed. 171.00 (*2-88124-652-4*) Gordon & Breach.

Analysis & History of Inflation. Don Paarlberg. LC 92-17815. 208p. 1992. text ed. 49.95 (*0-275-94416-6*, C4416, Praeger Pubs) Greenwood.

Analysis & Idealogy. Kenneth Lawson. (C). 1982. 90.00 (*0-902031-77-5*, Pub. by Univ Nottingham UK) St Mut.

Analysis & Ideology: Conceptual Essays on the Education of Adults. K. H. Lawson. 100p. (C). 1983. text ed. 75.00 (*0-685-22156-3*, Pub. by Univ Nottingham UK) St Mut.

Analysis & Improvement of Plant Cold Hardiness. Charles R. Olien & Myrtle N. Smith. 224p. 1981. 132.00 (*0-8493-5397-1*, SB781, CRC Reprint) Franklin.

Analysis & Integration of Behavioral Units. Travis Thompson & Michael Zeiler. 392p. (C). 1986. text ed. 79.95 (*0-89859-577-0*) L Erlbaum Assocs.

***Analysis & Interpretation of Financial Statements.** 3rd ed. B. Popoff & T. K. Cowan. 451p. 1989. pap. 54.00 (*0-409-49588-3*, Austral) Butterworth Legal Pubs.

***Analysis & Interpretation of Financial Statements.** 3rd ed. B. Popoff & T. Cowan. 464p. 1989. pap. 51.00 (*0-614-05475-3*, Austral) Butterworth Legal Pubs.

***Analysis & Interpretation of Literature.** Research & Education Association Staff. (CLEP Ser.). 368p. 1995. pap. text ed. 16.95 (*0-87891-897-3*) Res & Educ.

Analysis & Interpretation of Literature. Jack Rudman. (College-Level Examination Ser.: CLEP-4). 1994. 39.95 (*0-8373-5354-8*); pap. 23.95 (*0-8373-5304-1*) Nat Learn.

Analysis & Interpretation of Range Images. Ed. by R. C. Jain & A. K. Jain. (Perception Engineering Ser.). (Illus.). xiii, 387p. 1989. 72.00 (*0-387-97200-5*) Spr-Verlag.

Analysis & Management of Petroleum Investments: Risks, Taxes, & Time. 2nd ed. John M. Campbell, Jr. 490p. 1991. 68.00 (*0-685-54777-9*, P7287) PennWell Bks.

Analysis & Management of Uncertainty: Theory & Applications. Ed. by Bilal M. Ayyub & Madan M. Gupta. LC 92-8502. (Machine Intelligence & Pattern Recognition Ser.: Vol. 13). 1992. write for info. (*0-444-88901-9*, North Holland) Elsevier.

Analysis & Mathematical Physics. Hans Triebel. 1987. lib. bdg. 154.50 (*90-277-2077-0*) Kluwer Ac.

Analysis & Metaphysics: An Introduction to Philosophy. P. F. Strawson. 160p. 1992. pap. 13.95 (*0-19-875118-4*) OUP.

Analysis & Metaphysics: Essays in Honor of R. M. Chisholm. Ed. by Keith Lehrer. LC 75-5500. (Philosophical Studies: No. 4). 316p. 1975. lib. bdg. 117.00 (*90-277-0571-2*) Kluwer Ac.

Analysis & Modeling of Neural Systems. Ed. by Frank H. Eeckman. 432p. (C). 1991. lib. bdg. 95.50 (*0-7923-9217-5*) Kluwer Ac.

Analysis & Optimization of Stochastic Systems. Ed. by O. L. Jacobs et al. (IMA Conference Ser.). 1980. text ed. 137.00 (*0-12-378680-0*) Acad Pr.

Analysis & Optimization of Systems. Ed. by Alain Benoussan & J. L. Lions. (Lecture Notes in Control & Information Sciences Ser.: Vol. 111). (Illus.). 1175p. 1988. pap. 146.00 (*0-387-19237-9*) Spr-Verlag.

Analysis & Optimization of Systems. Ed. by A. Bensoussan & J. L. Lions. (Lecture Notes in Control & Information Sciences Ser.: Vol. 83). xiv, 901p. 1986. pap. 106.00 (*0-387-16729-3*) Spr-Verlag.

Analysis & Optimization of Systems: State & Frequency Domain Approaches for Infinite-Dimensional Systems: Proceedings of the 10th International Conference, Sophia-Antipolis, France, June 9-12, 1992. Ed. by R. F. Curtain et al. LC 92-37327. (Lecture Notes in Control & Information Sciences Ser.: Vol. 185). 1993. 162.00 (*0-387-56155-2*) Spr-Verlag.

Analysis & Optimization of Systems, Versailles, France, 1982: Proceedings. Ed. by Alain Benoussan & J. L. Lions. (Lecture Notes in Control & Information Sciences Ser.: Vol. 44). (Illus.). 987p. 1982. pap. 83.00 (*0-387-12089-0*) Spr-Verlag.

Analysis & Partial Differential Equations: A Collection of Papers Dedicated to Mischa Cotlar. Sadosky. (Lecture Notes in Pure & Applied Mathematics Ser.: Vol. 122). 784p. 1990. 165.00 (*0-8247-8302-6*) Dekker.

Analysis & Performance of Fiber Composites. 2nd ed. Bhagwan D. Agarwal & L. J. Broutman. (Society of Plastics Engineers Monographs). 1990. text ed. 79.95 (*0-471-51152-8*); 20.00 (*0-471-53994-5*) Wiley.

Analysis & Performance of Fibre Composites. B. D. Agarwal & L. J. Broutman. (SPE Monograph). (Illus.). 350p. 1980. 53.00 (*0-686-48244-1*, 0801) T-C Pubns CA.

Analysis & Prediction. Noel Tyl. LC 73-19928. (Principles & Practice of Astrology Ser.: Vol. 8). 190p. 1974. pap. 3.95 (*0-87542-807-X*) Llewellyn Pubns.

Analysis & Recommendations on Employee Classification & Pay: Orleans Parish Juvenile Court. Gerald Kaban. 49p. 1986. 3.00 (*0-685-15205-7*, SERO-015) Natl Ctr St Courts.

Analysis & Representation of Fatigue Data. J. B. Conway & L. H. Sjodahl. (Illus.). 300p. 1991. 93.00 (*0-87170-427-7*) ASM.

Analysis & Simulation of Chaotic Systems. Frank C. Hoppensteadt. Ed. by F. John et al. LC 92-33590. (Applied Mathematical Sciences Ser.: Vol. 94). (Illus.). 360p. 1993. 49.00 (*0-387-97916-6*) Spr-Verlag.

Analysis & Simulation of Semiconductor Devices. S. Selberherr. (Illus.). 300p. 1985. 99.50 (*0-387-81800-6*) Spr-Verlag.

Analysis & Simulation of the Cardiac System Ischemia. Ed. by Samuel Sideman & Rafael Beyar. 464p. 1989. 144.00 (*0-8493-5355-6*, RC685) CRC Pr.

Analysis & Simulations Fortran Programs: Applications in Process Design. Sami Matar & Lewis F. Hatch. LC 93-43441. 850p. 1994. 75.00 (*0-88415-198-0*) Gulf Pub.

***Analysis & Software of Cylindrical Members.** Wai-Fah Chen & Shouji Toma. 336p. 1995. 89.95 (*0-8493-8282-3*, 8282) CRC Pr.

Analysis & Summary of the Institutes of Roman Law. T. Whitcombe Greene. LC 93-79693. 122p. 1994. reprint ed. 45.00 (*1-56169-051-1*) W W Gaunt.

Analysis & Synthesis of Chemical Process Systems. Ed. by K. Hartmann & K. Kaplick. (Computer Aided Chemical Engineering Ser.: No. 4). 240p. 1991. 157.25 (*0-444-98745-2*) Elsevier.

Analysis & Synthesis of Computer Systems. Erol Gelenbe & I. Mitrani. LC 80-49992. (Computer Science & Applied Mathematics Ser.). 1980. text ed. 119.00 (*0-12-279350-1*) Acad Pr.

Analysis & Synthesis of Logic Systems. Daniel Mange. 700p. (C). 1986. text ed. 29.00 (*0-89006-188-2*) Artech Hse.

Analysis & Synthesis of MOS Translinear Circuits. Remco J. Wiegerink. LC 93-26664. (International Series in Engineering & Computer Science, VLSI, Computer Architecture, & Digital Screen Processing). 176p. (C). 1993. lib. bdg. 75.00 (*0-7923-9390-2*) Kluwer Ac.

Analysis & Synthesis of Speech: Strategic Research Towards High-Quality Text-to-Speech Generation. Ed. by Vincent J. Van Heuven & Louis C. Pols. (Speech Research Ser.: No. 1). (Illus.). xxii, 420p. (C). 1993. lib. bdg. 152.35 (*3-11-013588-4*) Mouton.

Analysis & Synthesis of Time Delay Systems. Henryk Gorecki et al. LC 79-40508. 369p. 1989. text ed. 98.00 (*0-471-27622-7*) Wiley.

Analysis & Synthesis of Translinear Integrated Circuits. E. Seevinck. (Studies in Electrical & Electronic Engineering: Vol. 31). 238p. 1987. 95.00 (*0-444-42888-7*) Elsevier.

Analysis & Synthesis of Wire-Antennas. Branko D. Popovic et al. LC 82-11078. (Electronic & Electrical Engineering Research Ser.: No. 2). (Illus.). 320p. reprint ed. pap. 91.20 (*0-8357-6011-1*, 2034233) Bks Demand.

***Analysis & Technique: For the Chiropractic Professional.** J. Clay Thompson. Ed. by Jacquelyn O'Keefe. (Life J. Clay Thompson Technique Ser.). (Illus.). 72p. (C). 1995. text ed. 24.95 (*1-886011-02-8*) Life College.

Analysis & Testing in Production of Circuit Boards & Plated Plastics. A. F. Bogenschutz & V. George. 210p. 1991. 250.00 (*0-904477-08-8*, Pub. by FMJ Intl UK) St Mut.

Analysis & Testing of Pipe Response to Buried Explosive Detonations. 73p. 1978. pap. 12.00 (*0-318-12583-8*, L51378) Am Gas Assn.

Analysis & Use of Financial Statements. Gerald I. White et al. 896p. (C). 1993. text ed. write for info. (*0-471-58470-3*) Wiley.

***Analysis & Use of Financial Statements.** Gerald I. White et al. 1993. pap. text ed. write for info. (*0-471-02419-8*) Wiley.

Analysis at Urbana, Vol. 1: Analysis in Function Spaces. Ed. by E. Berkson et al. (London Mathematical Society Lecture Note Ser.: No. 137). (C). 1989. pap. 54.95 (*0-521-36436-1*) Cambridge U Pr.

Analysis at Urbana, Vol. 2: Analysis in Abstract Spaces. Ed. by E. Berkson et al. (London Mathematical Society Lecture Note Ser.: No. 138). (C). 1989. pap. 47.95 (*0-521-36437-X*) Cambridge U Pr.

Analysis Bar Charting. John Mulvaney. LC 77-670112. 100p. (Orig.). 1980. 10.00 (*0-317-17178-X*, Mgmt Planning & Control) Kumarian Pr.

Analysis, Communication, & Perception of Risk. Ed. by B. J. Garrick & W. C. Gekler. LC 91-10372. (Advances in Risk Analysis Ser.: Vol. 9). (Illus.). 724p. 1991. 145.00 (*0-306-43833-X*, Plenum Pr) Plenum.

Analysis, Computation, Presentation of Engineering Information. Robert M. Barnett. 8.50 (*0-89741-000-9*); pap. 7.95 (*0-686-96874-3*) Roadrunner Tech.

Analysis, Design & Applications of Fin Lines. Bharathi Bhat & Shiban K. Koul. (Microwave Library). 550p. (C). 1987. text ed. 29.00 (*0-89006-195-5*) Artech Hse.

Analysis, Design & Behavior of Underground Culverts. (Transportation Research Record Ser.: No. 1231). 104p. 1989. 15.50 (*0-309-04824-9*) Transport Res Bd.

Analysis, Design & Construction of Braced Barrel Vaults. Ed. by Z. S. Makowski. 416p. 1986. 162.00 (*0-85334-377-2*, Pub. by Elsevier Applied Sci UK) Elsevier.

Analysis, Design, & Evaluation of Man-Machine Systems: Proceedings of the IFAC-IFIP-IEA-IFORS Symposium, Baden-Baden, Brd, Sept., 1982. IFAC-IFIP-IEA-IFORS Symposium Staff & G. Johannsen. Ed. by J. E. Rijnsdorp. (IFAC Proceedings Ser.). 434p. 1983. 185.00 (*0-08-029348-4*, Pub. by Pergamon Repr UK) Franklin.

Analysis, Design & Evaluation of Man-Machine Systems, 1988: Selected Papers from the Third IFAC-IFIP-IEA-IFORS Conference, Oulu, Finland, 14-16 June, 1988. Ed. by J. Ranta. (IFAC Proceedings Ser.). 442p. 1989. 235.00 (*0-08-036226-5*, Pergamon Pr) Elsevier.

Analysis, Design & Evaluation of Man-Machine Systems, 1989. Ed. by Baosheng Hu. LC 89-72170. (IFAC Proceedings Ser.: No. 9011). (Illus.). 192p. 1990. 110.00 (*0-08-035743-1*, Pergamon Pr) Elsevier.

Analysis, Design & Implementation of Information Systems. 4th ed. Henry C. Lucas, Jr. 1992. text ed. write for info. (*0-07-038933-0*) McGraw.

Analysis, Design, & Measurement of Small & Low-Profile Antennas. Ed. by Kazuhiro Hirasawa & Misao Haneishi. (Antenna Library). 304p. 1991. text ed. 75.00 (*0-89006-486-5*) Artech Hse.

Analysis, et Cetera: Research Papers Published in Honor of Jurgen Moser's 60th Birthday. Ed. by Paul H. Rabinowitz & Eduard Zehnder. 694p. 1990. text ed. 109.00 (*0-12-574249-5*) Acad Pr.

Analysis for Decision Making: (Complete Program), 10 notebks. Howard Raiffa. 821p. (C). 1987. reprint ed. Set. audio, ring bd. 795.00 (*1-55678-012-5*) Learn Inc.

Analysis for Decision Making, Module 1: Decision Trees. Howard Raiffa. 83p. (C). 1987. reprint ed. audio, ring bd. 70.00 (*1-55678-013-3*) Learn Inc.

Analysis for Decision Making, Module 10: Case Analysis: Caroline Development & the Stephen Douglas. Howard Raiffa. 104p. (C). 1987. reprint ed. audio, ring bd. 70.00 (*1-55678-022-2*) Learn Inc.

Analysis for Decision Making, Module 2: New Information: Effect on Uncertainties. Howard Raiffa. 73p. (C). 1987. reprint ed. audio, ring bd. 70.00 (*1-55678-014-1*) Learn Inc.

Analysis for Decision Making, Module 3: Strategies & the Value of Information. Howard Raiffa. 79p. (C). 1987. reprint ed. audio, ring bd. 70.00 (*1-55678-015-X*) Learn Inc.

Analysis for Decision Making, Module 4: Case Analysis: The Rositex Company. Howard Raiffa. 89p. (C). 1987. reprint ed. audio, ring bd. 70.00 (*1-55678-016-8*) Learn Inc.

Analysis for Decision Making, Module 5: Utility Theory: Basic Concepts. Howard Raiffa. 81p. (C). 1987. reprint ed. audio, ring bd. 70.00 (*1-55678-017-6*) Learn Inc.

Analysis for Decision Making, Module 6: Utility Theory: The Assessment Problem. Howard Raiffa. 80p. (C). 1987. reprint ed. audio, ring bd. 70.00 (*1-55678-018-4*) Learn Inc.

Analysis for Decision Making, Module 7: Case Analysis: Edgartown Fisheries & J. B. Robinson. Howard Raiffa. 55p. (C). 1987. reprint ed. audio, ring bd. 70.00 (*1-55678-019-2*) Learn Inc.

Analysis for Decision Making, Module 8: Subjective Probability. Howard Raiffa. 60p. (C). 1987. reprint ed. audio, ring bd. 70.00 (*1-55678-020-6*) Learn Inc.

Analysis for Decision Making, Module 9: The Atr & Science of Probability Assessment. Howard Raiffa. 117p. (C). 1987. reprint ed. audio, ring bd. 70.00 (*1-55678-021-4*) Learn Inc.

Analysis for Design of Fiber Reinforced Plastic Vessels & Pipings. S. V. Hoa. LC 91-65982. 580p. 1991. text ed. 125.00 (*0-87762-872-6*) Technomic.

Analysis for Financial Management. 2nd ed. Robert C. Higgins. 320p. 1988. text ed. 37.50 (*1-55623-142-3*) Irwin Prof Pubng.

Analysis for Financial Management. 3rd ed. Robert Higgins. 368p. (C). 1992. pap. text ed. write for info. (*0-318-69106-X*, 06-1666-03) Irwin.

Analysis for Financial Management. 3rd ed. Robert C. Higgins. 350p. 1991. text ed. 50.00 (*1-55623-549-6*) Irwin Prof Pubng.

Analysis for Financial Management. 3rd ed. Robert C. Higgins. 380p. (C). 1991. pap. text ed. 39.95 (*0-256-09234-6*) Irwin.

***Analysis for Financial Management.** 4th ed. Robert C. Higgins. LC 94-35658. 432p. (C). 1994. 39.95 (*0-256-13568-1*) Irwin.

Analysis for Improving Performance: Tools for Diagnosing Organizations & Documenting Workplace Expertise. Richard A. Swanson. LC 94-13445. 300p. 1994. 32.95 (*1-881052-48-6*) Berrett-Koehler.

Analysis for Marketing Planning. 2nd ed. Ronald R. Lehmann & Russell S. Winer. 200p. (C). 1990. text ed. 33.95 (*0-256-08681-8*) Irwin.

Analysis for Marketing Planning. 3rd ed. Donald R. Lehmann & Russell S. Winer. LC 93-12894. 208p. (C). 1993. text ed. 33.95 (*0-256-12276-8*) Irwin.

Analysis for Public Decisions. 3rd ed. E. S. Quade & G. M. Carter. 410p. 1989. 42.75 (*0-444-01471-3*) P-H.

Analysis for Residuals-Environmental Quality Management: Case Study of the Ljubljana Area of Yugoslavia. Daniel J. Basta et al. LC 77-17250. (Resources for the Future Ser.). 258p. reprint ed. pap. 73.60 (*0-317-26216-5*, 2052112) Bks Demand.

Analysis for Strategic Market Decisions. George S. Day. LC 85-13917. (Illus.). 259p. (C). 1986. pap. text ed. 32.75 (*0-314-85227-1*); Course design guide. pap. text ed. 20.50 (*0-314-96039-2*) West Pub.

Analysis for Well Completion. Mark Longley. Ed. by Jodie Leecraft. (Oil & Gas Production Ser.). (Illus.). 108p. (Orig.). (C). 1984. pap. text ed. 15.00 (*0-88698-084-4*, 3.31110) PETEX.

***Analysis, Geometry & Groups: A Riemann Legacy Volume.** Ed. by H. M. Srivastava & T. M. Rassias. 712p. 1993. text ed. 180.00 (*0-911767-85-1*); pap. text ed. 120.00 (*0-911767-59-2*) Hadronic Pr Inc.

Analysis, Geometry & Probability: Proceedings of the First Chilean Symposium of Mathematics. Rolando Chuaqui. (Lecture Notes in Pure & Applied Mathematics Ser.: Vol. 96). 288p. 1985. 110.00 (*0-8247-7419-1*) Dekker.

Analysis I. Ed. by R. V. Gamkrelidze. (Encyclopaedia of Mathematical Sciences Ser.: Vol. 13). 265p. 1989. 69.00 (*0-387-17008-1*, 1052) Spr-Verlag.

Analysis II. Ed. by R. V. Gamkrelidze. (Encyclopaedia of Mathematical Sciences Ser.: Vol. 14). (Illus.). 264p. 1990. 69.00 (*0-387-18179-2*, 3031) Spr-Verlag.

Analysis Instrumentation, Vol. 24. 180p. 1990. pap. text ed. 30.00 (*1-55617-248-6*, A248-6) Instru Soc.

Analysis Instrumentation, Vol. 25. 250p. 1991. 30.00 (*1-55617-311-3*, A311-3) Instru Soc.

Analysis IV: Linear & Boundary Integral Equations. V. G. Maz'ya & S. M. Nikol'skij. Ed. by G. V. Gamkrelidze. Tr. by A. Bottcher & S. Prossdorf. (Encyclopaedia of Mathematical Sciences Ser.: Vol. 27). (Illus.). 248p. 1991. 65.00 (*0-387-51997-1*) Spr-Verlag.

Analysis, Manifolds & Physics. rev. ed. Y. Choquet-Bruhat et al. 630p. 1982. 55.00 (*0-444-86017-7*, North Holland) Elsevier.

Analysis, Manifolds & Physics, Part II: Ninety-Two Applications. Y. Choquet-Bruhat & C. Dewitt-Morette. 452p. 1989. 40.00 (*0-444-87071-7*, North Holland) Elsevier.

Analysis Manual for Hospital Information Systems. Owen Doyle et al. LC 80-13875. (Illus.). 472p. (Orig.). 1980. pap. text ed. 46.00 (*0-914904-41-8*, 0636) Health Admin Pr.

Analysis mit und fur Kinder (7, tatsachlich 7 Jahre alt und alter) Donald Cohen. Tr. by Gudrun Reimerth. (Illus.). 179p. (GER.). 1991. spiral bd. write for info. (*0-9621674-6-0*) D Cohen Mathman.

Analysis, Networks, Peptides. (Advances in Polymer Science Ser.: Vol. 65). (Illus.). 230p. 1984. 79.00 (*0-387-13656-8*) Spr-Verlag.

Analysis Now. G. Pedersen. (Graduate Texts in Mathematics Ser.: Vol. 118). xiv, 277p. 1988. 49.90 (*0-387-96788-5*) Spr-Verlag.

Analysis of a Dedicated Experiment in TFTR. W. M. Stacey. (Illus.). 88p. (Orig.). (C). 1994. pap. text ed. 60.00 (*0-7881-0346-6*) Diane Pub.

***Analysis of a Hydrogen Peroxide Solution.** George Deekey. Ed. by H. A. Neidig. (Modular Laboratory Program in Chemistry Ser.). 12p. (C). 1987. pap. text ed. 1.25x (*0-87540-335-2*) Chem Educ Res.

***Analysis of a Log-Periodic Folded Slot Antenna Array on Planar & Cylindrical Platforms.** fac. ed. M. W. Nurnberger et al. (University of Michigan Report: No. 031169-1-T). 61p. 1994. pap. 25.00 (*0-7837-7697-7*, 2047454) Bks Demand.

Analysis of a Middle Mississippian House in Butler County, Missouri. James E. Price. LC 70-628940. (Museum Briefs Ser.: No. 1). (Illus.). iv, 31p. 1969. pap. 1.70 (*0-913134-00-7*) Mus Anthro MO.

***Analysis of a Mixture of Sodium Hydrogen Carbonate & Sodium Chloride.** John T. Yoke. Ed. by H. A. Neidig. (Modular Laboratory Program in Chemistry Ser.). 8p. (C). 1987. pap. text ed. 1.25x (*0-87540-330-1*) Chem Educ Res.

Analysis of a Slot Coupled & Stripline Fed Patch Antenna. Jui-Ching Cheng & Linda P. Katehi. (University of Michigan Report Ser.: No. 390442-2-T). 22p. reprint ed. pap. 25.00 (*0-7837-6287-9*, 2046002) Bks Demand.

Analysis of Access to Bank Credit. Faith H. Ando. (Minority Economic Development Ser.: No. 4). 55p. 1988. pap. 5.95 (*0-318-39972-5*) UCLA CAAS.

Analysis of Actual Versus Perceived Risks. Ed. by Vincent T. Covello et al. LC 83-11071. (Advances in Risk Analysis Ser.: Vol. 1). 388p. 1983. 105.00 (*0-306-41397-3*, Plenum Pr) Plenum.

***Analysis of Addictive & Misused Drugs.** John A. Adamovics. LC 94-22885. 800p. 1995. 195.00 (*0-8247-9238-6*) Dekker.

Analysis of Air Pollutants. W. Leithe. 304p. 1970. text ed. 77.50 (*0-317-46403-5*, Pub. by Keter Pub IS) Coronet Bks.

Analysis of Air Pollutants. Peter O. Warner. LC 75-26685. (Environmental Science & Technology Ser.). 340p. reprint ed. pap. 96.90 (*0-317-11251-1*, 2055094) Bks Demand.

Analysis of Aircraft Structures: An Introduction. Bruce K. Donaldson. 1992. text ed. write for info. (*0-07-017539-X*) McGraw.

Analysis of Algorithms. Paul S. Purdom & Cynthia A. Brown. 448p. (C). 1985. text ed. 52.00 (*0-03-072044-3*) SCP.

***Analysis of Algorithms: Computational Methods & Mathematical Tools.** Micha Hofri. (Illus.). 600p. 1995. 65.00 (*0-19-509954-0*) OUP.

Analysis of Algorithms & Data & Structures. Lesek Banachowski. 1991. text ed. 36.75 (*0-201-41693-X*) Addison-Wesley.

Analysis of Amino Acids, Proteins & Nucleic Acids. BIOTOL Project Members. (Illus.). 255p. 1992. pap. 32.95 (*0-7506-1502-8*) Buttrwrth-Heinemann.

Analysis of Ancient Metals. E. Caley & R. Belcher. LC 64-13498. (International Series of Monographs on Analytical Chemistry: Vol. 19). 1964. 84.00 (*0-08-010666-8*, Pub. by Pergamon Repr UK) Franklin.

Analysis of & on Uniformly Rectifiable Sets. Guy David & Stephen Semmes. LC 93-36311. (Mathematical Surveys & Monographs: Vol. 38). 1993. 111.00 (*0-8218-1537-7*) Am Math.

Analysis of Animal Bones from Archeological Sites. Richard G. Klein & Kathryn Cruz-Uribe. LC 84-247. (Prehistoric Archeology & Ecology Ser.). (Illus.). (C). 1984. pap. text ed. 15.00 (*0-226-43958-5*) U Ch Pr.

Analysis of Antibiotic - Drug Residues in Food Products. Ed. by V. K. Agarwal. (Illus.). 264p. (C). 1992. 79.50 (*0-306-44199-3*, Plenum Pr) Plenum.

Analysis of Aperture Antennas in Inhomogeneous Media. Dikran Damiamayan. LC 77-141023. 93p. 1969. 17.50 (*0-403-04493-6*) Scholarly.

Analysis of Appraisive Characterization. Karl Aschenbrenner. 1983. lib. bdg. 103.00 (*90-277-1452-5*) Kluwer Ac.

Analysis of Approximation Methods for Differential & Integral Equations. H. J. Reinhardt. (Applied Mathematical Sciences Ser.: Vol. 57). (Illus.). xi, 398p. 1985. pap. 76.00 (*0-387-96214-X*) Spr-Verlag.

Analysis of Arithmetic for Mathematics Teaching. Gaea Leinhardt et al. 464p. 1991. text ed. 89.95 (*0-8058-0929-5*) L Erlbaum Assocs.

An Asterisk (*) at the beginning of an entry indicates that the title is appearing in BIP for the first time.

Analysis of Art. De Witt Parker. LC 75-3304. reprint ed. 39.50 (*0-404-59289-9*) AMS Pr.

Analysis of Autobody Stamping Technology: SAE International Congress & Exposition 1994, 19 papers. (Special Publications). 1994. pap. 61.00 (*1-56091-473-4*, SP-1021) Soc Auto Engineers.

Analysis of Axisymmetric Shells by a Mixed Variational Principle. Z. M. Elias. 60p. (C). 1972. pap. text ed. 10.00 (*0-8156-6037-5*, Am U Beirut) Syracuse U Pr.

Analysis of Bank Marketing Expenditures. Incl. 1982 1983. 65.00 (*0-318-18258-0*); 19831984. 70.00 (*0-318-18259-9*); 1982 1983. 65.00 (*0-318-18258-0*); write for info. (*0-318-59548-6*, ABME) Bank Mktg Assn.

Analysis of Behavior: A Program for Self-Instruction. James G. Holland & B. F. Skinner. 1961. pap. text ed. write for info. (*0-07-029565-4*) McGraw.

Analysis of Behavior in Planning Instruction. James G. Holland et al. LC 75-28722. (Illus.). 512p. 1976. text ed. write for info. (*0-201-02912-X*) Addison-Wesley.

Analysis of Binary Data. 2nd ed. David R. Cox & E. Joyce Snell. 200p. 1989. 39.95 (*0-412-30620-4*, A2799) Chapman & Hall.

Analysis of Biogeochemical Cycling Process in Walker Branch Watershed. Ed. by D. W. Johnson & R. I. Van Hook. (Illus.). 1988. 96.00 (*0-387-96745-1*) Spr-Verlag.

***Analysis of Biological Development.** Klaus Kalthoff. LC 95-896. 1995. text ed. write for info. (*0-07-033308-4*) McGraw.

Analysis of Biological Material for Trace Elements Using X-Ray Spectroscopy. Vlado Valkovic. 256p. 1980. 129.00 (*0-8493-5723-3*, QP534, CRC Reprint) Franklin.

Analysis of Biological Materials: Proceedings of a Conference Held in Pretoria, South Africa, October 1977. Ed. by L. R. Butler. (Illus.). 1979. 50.00 (*0-08-022853-4*, Pub. by Pergamon Repr UK) Franklin.

Analysis of Bulk Flow of Materials under Gravity Caving Process: Pt. 1: Sublevel Caving in Relation to Flow in Bins & Bunkers. Li Itunda Yenge. Ed. by Jon W. Raese. LC 81-129. (Colorado School of Mines Quarterly Ser.: Vol. 75, No. 4). (Illus.). 45p. 1981. pap. 8.00 (*0-686-74853-0*) Colo Sch Mines.

Analysis of Bulk Flow of Materials Under Gravity Caving Process: Pt. 2: Theoretical and Physical Modelling of Gravity Flow of Broken Rock. Li I. Yenge. Ed. by Jon W. Raese. LC 81-129. (Colorado School of Mines Quarterly Ser.: Vol. 76, No. 3). (Illus.). 67p. 1981. pap. text ed. 8.00 (*0-686-46968-2*) Colo Sch Mines.

Analysis of Cache Performance for Operating Systems & Multiprogramming. Anant Agarwal. (C). 1989. lib. bdg. 61.00 (*0-7923-9005-9*) Kluwer Ac.

Analysis of Carbohydrates by GLC & MS. Ed. by Christopher J. Biermann & Gary D. McGinnis. 288p. 1988. text ed. 216.00 (*0-8493-6851-0*, QP701) CRC Pr.

Analysis of Casting Defects. 140p. 30.00 (*0-317-32554-X*); 50.00 (*0-87433-004-1*, GM7409) Am Foundrymen.

Analysis of Casting Defects. 4th ed. 140p. 60.00 (*0-317-32553-1*, GM7409) Am Foundrymen.

Analysis of Categorical Data: Dual Scaling & Its Applications. Shizuhiko Nishisato. LC 81-116307. (Mathematical Expositions Ser.: No. 24). 290p. reprint ed. pap. 82.70 (*0-8357-8023-6*, 2034012) Bks Demand.

Analysis of Causes & Determination of Possible Means of Prevention of External Damage to Pipelines. Kenneth F. Connell & Robert B. Smith. 100p. 1968. 2.50 (*0-318-12584-6*, U78173) Am Gas Assn.

Analysis of Certain Traits of Selected High School Seniors Interested in Teaching. Tressa C. Yeager. LC 70-177613. (Columbia University. Teachers College. Contributions to Education Ser.: No. 660). reprint ed. 37.50 (*0-404-55660-4*) AMS Pr.

Analysis of Change. Ed. by John M. Gottman. 544p. 1995. 99.95 (*0-8058-1356-X*); pap. 49.95 (*0-8058-1357-8*) L Erlbaum Assocs.

Analysis of Chemically Reacting Systems: A Stochastic Approach. Ed. by L. K. Doraiswamy & B. D. Kulkarni. (Topics in Chemical Engineering Ser.: Vol. 4). 488p. 1987. text ed. 200.00 (*0-677-21670-X*) Gordon & Breach.

Analysis of Chinese Characters. G. Wilder. 1972. lib. bdg. 79.95 (*0-87968-567-0*) Krishna Pr.

Analysis of Chinese Characters. 2nd ed. G. D. Wilder & J. H. Ingram. LC 74-75626. 384p. 1974. reprint ed. pap. 9.95 (*0-486-23045-7*) Dover.

Analysis of Citrus Fruits & Their Products. Ting & Rouseff. (Food Science & Technology Ser.: No. 18). 312p. 1986. 125.00 (*0-8247-8492-8*) Dekker.

Analysis of Classis of Discontinuous Functions & Equations of Mathematical Physics. A. I. Vol'pert & S. I. Hudjaev. (Mechanics: Analysis Ser.). 1985. lib. bdg. 275.00 (*90-247-3109-7*) Kluwer Ac.

***Analysis of Climate Variability: Applications of Statistical Techniques: Proceedings of an Autumn School Organized by the Commission of the European Community on Elba from October 30 to November 6, 1993.** Commission of the European Communities Staff. Ed. by Hans Von Storch & Antonio Navarra. LC 95-10071. 1995. write for info. (*3-540-58918-X*) Spr-Verlag.

Analysis of Coastal Algonquin Culture. Regina Flannery. LC 76-43705. (Catholic University of America Anthropological Ser.: No. 7). 1983. reprint ed. 37.50 (*0-404-15537-5*) AMS Pr.

Analysis of Coeur d'Alene Indian Myths. Gladys A. Reichard. LC 48-2411. (AFS Memoirs Ser.). 1972. reprint ed. 25.00 (*0-527-01093-6*) Periodicals Srv.

Analysis of Completion Sentences & Arithmetical Problems As Items for Intelligence Tests. Henry D. Rinsland. LC 73-177192. (Columbia University. Teachers College. Contributions to Education Ser.: No. 666). reprint ed. 37.50 (*0-404-55666-3*) AMS Pr.

Analysis of Complex Surveys. Ed. by C. J. Skinner et al. 1989. text ed. 79.95 (*0-471-92377-X*) Wiley.

Analysis of Concurrent Systems. Ed. by B. T. Denwit et al. (Lecture Notes in Computer Science Ser.: Vol. 207). vii, 398p. 1985. pap. 42.00 (*0-387-16047-7*) Spr-Verlag.

Analysis of Contaminants in Edible Aquatic Resources: General Considerations, Metals, Organometallics, Tainting & Organics. Ed. by J. W. Kiceniuk & S. Ray. LC 94-678. (Food Science & Technology Ser.). 1994. pap. write for info. (*1-56081-528-0*) VCH Pubs.

Analysis of Content of Student-Teaching Courses. Esther M. Nelson. LC 70-177100. (Columbia University. Teachers College. Contributions to Education Ser.: No. 723). reprint ed. 37.50 (*0-404-55723-6*) AMS Pr.

Analysis of Contingency Tables. 2nd ed. B. S. Everitt. (Monographs on Statistics & Applied Probability: No. 8). (Illus.). 144p. (C). 1992. text ed. 39.95 (*0-412-39850-8*, A6888) Chapman & Hall.

Analysis of Controlled Dynamical Systems: Proceedings of a Conference in Lyon, France, July 1990, Vol. 8. Ed. by B. Bonnard et al. (Progress in Systems & Control Theory Ser.). viii, 403p. 1991. 105.00 (*0-8176-3576-9*) Spr-Verlag.

Analysis of Copper & Its Alloys. W. T. Elwell & I. Scholes. LC 66-28406. 1967. 82.00 (*0-08-012160-8*, Pub. by Pergamon Repr UK) Franklin.

Analysis of Covariance. Albert R. Wildt & Olli Vahtola. LC 78-64331. (Quantitative Applications in the Social Sciences Ser.: Vol. 12). 93p. 1978. pap. 9.95 (*0-8039-1164-5*) Sage.

Analysis of Credit & Equilibrium Credit Rationing. Ying Wu. LC 93-47525. (Financial Sector of the American Economy Ser.). 192p. 1994. pap. 45.00 (*0-8153-1683-6*) Garland.

Analysis of Criminal Liability. E. C. Clark. xii, 115p. 1983. reprint ed. lib. bdg. 20.00 (*0-8377-0446-4*) Rothman.

Analysis of Cross-Classified Categorical Data. 2nd ed. Stephen E. Fienberg. 1980. 28.50x (*0-262-06071-X*) MIT Pr.

Analysis of Cross-Classified Data Having Ordered Categories. Leo A. Goodman. 432p. 1984. 37.00 (*0-674-03145-8*) HUP.

Analysis of Cross-Tabulated Data. Graham J. Upton. LC 78-4210. (Wiley Series in Probability & Mathematical Statistics). (Illus.). 160p. reprint ed. pap. 45.60 (*0-8357-8647-1*, 2035071) Bks Demand.

Analysis of Decisions under Uncertainty. Robert Schlaifer. LC 77-5729. (Illus.). 746p. 1978. reprint ed. 59.50 (*0-88275-560-9*) Krieger.

Analysis of Defense: The Ego & the Mechanisms of Defense Revisited. Joseph Sandler & Anna Freud. LC 84-12980. 560p. (C). 1985. text ed. 65.00 (*0-8236-0141-2*) Intl Univs Pr.

Analysis of Delinquency & Aggression. Ed. by E. Ribes-Inesta & A. Bandura. 256p. 1976. text ed. 49.95 (*0-89859-360-3*) L Erlbaum Assocs.

Analysis of Design of Swirl Augmented Heat Exchanges. Ievlev. 1990. 131.00 (*0-89116-701-3*) Hemisp Pub.

Analysis of Detergents & Detergent Products. George F. Longman. LC 74-4649. (Illus.). 649p. reprint ed. pap. 180.00 (*0-8357-8797-4*, 2033619) Bks Demand.

Analysis of Dietary Associations of Vitamin A with Cancer. Ritenbaugh & Meyskens, Jr. 1989. pap. 4.95 (*0-87983-456-0*) Keats.

Analysis of Dietary Fiber in Food. James & Theander. (Basic & Clinical Nutrition Ser.: Vol. 3). 288p. 1981. 140.00 (*0-8247-1192-0*) Dekker.

Analysis of Dimensional Accuracy for Building Structures. M. Vorlicek & M. Holicky. (Developments in Civil Engineering Ser.: Vol. 26). 1990. 115.50 (*0-444-98875-0*, DCE 26) Elsevier.

Analysis of Directional Time Series. J. Breckling. (Lecture Notes in Statistics Ser.: Vol. 61). viii, 238p. 1989. pap. 29.00 (*0-387-97182-3*, 3627) Spr-Verlag.

Analysis of Discretization Methods for Ordinary Differential Equations. H. J. Stetter. LC 72-90188. (Tracts in Natural Philosophy Ser.: Vol. 23). (Illus.). 390p. 1973. 75.00 (*0-387-06008-1*) Spr-Verlag.

Analysis of Distance Protection. Vivian Cook. LC 85-2060. (Lines & Cables for Power Transmission Research Ser.). 188p. 1985. text ed. 120.00 (*0-471-90749-9*) Wiley.

Analysis of Drapery & the Upholsterers' Accelerator: A Reprint of Two Rare 19th Century Drapery Manuals in the Winterthur Library 19th Century: Landmarks in Design. Ed. by James Arrowsmith. (Nineteenth Century: Landmarks in Design Ser.: Vol. 1). (Illus.). 166p. 1993. reprint ed. 27.50 (*0-926494-03-1*) Acanthus Pr.

Analysis of Drugs & Metabolites by Gas Chromatography: Mass Spectrometry. Benjamin J. Gudzinowicz et al. LC 76-56481. 507p. Vol. 2, 507p. pap. 144.50 (*0-7837-0032-6*, 2034536); Vol. 4, 472p. pap. 134.60 (*0-7837-0033-4*); Vol. 5, 555p. pap. 158.20 (*0-7837-0034-2*); Vol. 6, 460p. pap. 131.10 (*0-7837-0035-0*) Bks Demand.

Analysis of Drugs & Metabolites by Gas Chromatography: Mass Spectrometry, 2 vols. Benjamin J. Gudzinowicz & Michael J. Gudzinowicz. LC 76-56481. (Illus.). 237p. reprint ed. Vol. 1, 237p. pap. 67.60 (*0-8357-6013-8*, 2034536) Bks Demand.

Analysis of Drugs & Metabolites by Gas Chromatography: Mass Spectrometry, 2 vols., 7. Benjamin J. Gudzinowicz & Michael J. Gudzinowicz. LC 76-56481. (Illus.). 571p. reprint ed. pap. 162.80 (*0-8357-6014-6*, 2034536) Bks Demand.

Analysis of Drugs & Metabolites by Gas Chromatography - Mass Spectrometry, Vol. 3: Antipsychotic, Antiemetic & Antidepressant Drugs. Benjamin J. Gudzinowicz & Michael J. Gudzinowicz. LC 76-56481. (Illus.). 280p. reprint ed. pap. 79.80 (*0-8357-6012-X*, 2052301) Bks Demand.

Analysis of Drugs in Biological Fluids. Joseph Chamberlain. 320p. 1985. 161.00 (*0-8493-5144-8*, RB52) CRC Pr.

***Analysis of Drugs in Biological Fluids.** 2nd ed. Joseph Chamberlain. 352p. 1995. 95.00 (*0-8493-2492-0*, 2492) CRC Pr.

Analysis of Drugs of Abuse. M. Cole & B. Caddy. 1994. 65.00 (*0-13-035098-2*) P-H.

Analysis of Drugs of Abuse. Ed. by T. A. Gough. (Separation Science Ser.). 628p. 1991. text ed. 295.00 (*0-471-92267-6*) Wiley.

Analysis of Dynamic Effects on Engineering Structures. M. Bata & V. Plachy. (Developments in Civil Engineering Ser.: No. 16). 290p. 1987. 102.75 (*0-444-98980-3*) Elsevier.

Analysis of Dynamic Psychological Systems, Vol. 1: Basic Approaches to General Systems, Dynamic Systems, & Cybernetics. Ed. by R. L. Levine & H. E. Fitgerald. (Illus.). 265p. 1992. 50.00 (*0-306-43745-7*, Plenum Pr) Plenum.

Analysis of Dynamic Psychological Systems, Vol. 2: Methods & Applications. Ed. by R. L. Levine & Hiram E. Fitzgerald. (Illus.). 370p. 1992. 60.00 (*0-306-43746-5*, Plenum Pr) Plenum.

***Analysis of Dynamical & Cognitive Systems: Proceedings of Advanced Course, Stockholm, Sweden, August 1993.** Ed. by Stig I. Andersson. LC 95-14541. (Lecture Notes in Computer Science: Vol. 888). 1995. write for info. (*0-387-58843-4*) Spr-Verlag.

Analysis of Earnings & Profits with Recommendations, Taxation of Corporate Distribution & Adjustments Subcommittee, Earnings & Profits Task Force. American Institute of Certified Public Accountants. LC 78-109540. 210p. reprint ed. pap. 59.90 (*0-685-16084-X*, 2027573) Bks Demand.

Analysis of Ecological Systems: State-of-the-Art in Ecological Modelling. W. K. Lauenroth et al. (Developments in Environmental Modelling Ser.: Vol. 5). 1983. 182.00 (*0-444-42179-3*) Elsevier.

Analysis of Economic Time Series: A Synthesis. Marc Nerlove et al. LC 78-26059. (Economic Theory, Econometrics & Mathematical Economics Ser.). 1979. text ed. 75.00 (*0-12-515750-9*) Acad Pr.

***Analysis of Economic Time Series: A Synthesis.** rev. ed. Marc Nerlove et al. (Economic Theory, Econometrics, & Mathematical Economics Ser.). (Illus.). 486p. 1995. boxed write for info. (*0-12-515751-7*) Acad Pr.

Analysis of Effective Property Tax Rates in the City of Omaha. Ralph H. Todd. 18p. (Orig.). 1972. pap. 2.00 (*1-55719-049-6*) U NE CPAR.

Analysis of Effigy Mound Complexes in Wisconsin. William M. Hurley. LC 75-622026. (Anthropological Papers: No. 59). (Illus.). 480p. reprint ed. pap. 136.80 (*0-7837-0551-4*, 2040885) Bks Demand.

Analysis of Electric Circuits. Ed. by G. Zeueke et al. Tr. by MIR Publishers. (Illus.). 690p. (C). 1969. text ed. 30.00 (*0-8464-0129-0*) Beekman Pubs.

Analysis of Electric Machinery. Paul C. Krause et al. LC 94-20083. 1994. reprint ed. 49.95 (*0-7803-1101-9*) Inst Electrical.

Analysis of Electromechanical Motion Devices. P. C. Krause & Oleg Wasynczuk. (Illus.). 544p. 1989. text ed. write for info. (*0-07-035494-4*) McGraw.

Analysis of Electronic Wire & Cable: Markets & Opportunities. Amadee Bender. (Illus.). 196p. 1988. pap. text ed. 1,800.00 (*1-878218-02-6*) World Info Tech.

Analysis of Elemental Boron. Morris W. Lerner. LC 74-607964. (AEC Critical Review Ser.). 137p. 1970. pap. 11.25 (*0-87079-134-6*, TID-25190); fiche 9.00 (*0-87079-135-4*, TID-25190) DOE.

Analysis of Emergency Medical Services in Austin, Texas, 2 Vols. Ed. by David Eaton. Incl. Vol. 1. Results. 164p. 1980. 8.50 (*0-89940-641-6*); Vol. II. Analytical Methods. 96p. 1980. 7.95 (*0-89940-642-4*); (Policy Research Project Report Ser.: No. 41). 1980. Set. 16.45 (*0-89940-643-2*) LBJ Sch Pub Aff.

***Analysis of Emission Lines.** Ed. by Robert E. Williams & Mario Livio. (Space Telescope Science Institute Symposium Ser.: No. 8). (Illus.). 304p. (C). 1995. write for info. (*0-521-48081-7*) Cambridge U Pr.

Analysis of Engineering Cycles. 3rd ed. R. W. Haywood. LC 79-41225. (Illus.). 320p. 1980. text ed. 86.00 (*0-08-025441-1*, Pergamon Pr); pap. text ed. 27.00 (*0-08-025440-3*, Pergamon Pr) Elsevier.

Analysis of Engineering Cycles: Power, Refrigeration & Gas Liquefaction Plant. rev. ed. R. W. Haywood. (Thermodynamics & Fluid Mechanics for Mechanical Engineers Ser.). (Illus.). 348p. 1991. pap. text ed. 33.00 (*0-08-040738-2*, Pergamon Pr) Elsevier.

Analysis of Engineering Cycles: Worked Problems: Power, Refrigerating & Gas Liquefaction Plant. R. W. Haywood. (Thermodynamics & Fluid Mechanics for Mechanical Engineers Ser.). (Illus.). 192p. 1986. pap. text ed. 34.00 (*0-08-032571-8*, Pergamon Pr) Elsevier.

***Analysis of Enzyme Kinetic Data.** Athel Cornish-Bowden. (Illus.). 256p. 1995. 89.00 (*0-19-854878-8*); pap. 39.95 (*0-19-854877-X*) OUP.

Analysis of Essential Nuclear Reactor Materials. AEC Technical Information Center Staff. Ed. by C. J. Rodden. LC 64-60035. 1291p. 1964. 40.00 (*0-87079-393-4*, TID-21384); fiche 9.00 (*0-87079-136-2*, TID-21384) DOE.

Analysis of Evidence. Anderson. 1991. 30.00 (*0-316-03963-2*) Little.

Analysis of Experiments with Missing Data. Yadolah Dodge. LC 85-5296. (Probability & Mathematical Statistics Ser.). 499p. 1985. text ed. 74.95 (*0-471-88736-6*) Wiley.

Analysis of Exploration & Mining Technology for Manganese Nodules. (Seabed Minerals Ser.: Vol. 2). 1984. lib. bdg. 48.00 (*0-86010-348-X*) G & T Inc.

Analysis of Factors Determining the Location of New Firms & Plants in Texas Counties. Ardeshir Anjomani et al. 291p. (Orig.). 1986. pap. text ed. 15.00 (*0-936440-70-8*) U TX SUPA.

Analysis of Fantasy: The Thematic Technique in the Study of Personality. William E. Henry. LC 56-7157. 292p. 1973. 21.50 (*0-88275-114-X*) Krieger.

Analysis of Fats & Oils. Ed. by R. J. Hamilton & B. A. Rossell. 456p. 1986. 119.00 (*0-85334-385-3*, Pub. by Elsevier Applied Sci UK) Elsevier.

Analysis of Fatty Acids & Their Esters by Chromatographic Methods. Ed. by R. G. Ackman & L. D. Metcalfe. 1976. 35.00 (*0-912474-07-6*) Preston Pubns.

***Analysis of Faulted Power Systems.** Paul M. Anderson. LC 95-15246. (Power System Engineering Ser.). 1995. reprint ed. write for info. (*0-7803-1145-0*) Inst Electrical.

Analysis of Financial Statements. 3rd ed. Leopold A. Berstein. 432p. 1990. text ed. 60.00 (*1-55623-292-6*) Irwin Prof Pubng.

Analysis of Financial Statements. 4th ed. Leopold A. Bernstein. LC 93-1209. 432p. 1993. 60.00 (*1-55623-930-0*) Irwin Prof Pubng.

Analysis of Financial Statements: Financial Accounting & the Capital Market. Gonedes & Dopuch. (Studies in Accounting Research: No. 30). 421p. 1988. 25.00 (*0-86539-069-X*) Am Accounting.

Analysis of Fire Test Methods for Foam Plastic Insulation Materials. Joel S Stahl. 1978. 4.00 (*0-686-12078-7*, TR 78-4) Society Fire Protect.

Analysis of Fiscal Policy Alternatives for Serving Special Populations in Vocational Education. L. Allen Phelps. 45p. 1984. 4.95 (*0-318-22026-1*, IN278) Ctr Educ Trng Employ.

Analysis of Five-Nitrofuran Derivatives. V. Egerts et al. 180p. 1971. text ed. 51.00 (*0-7065-0765-7*, Pub. by Keter Pub IS) Coronet Bks.

Analysis of Flow in Pipe Networks. Roland W. Jeppson. LC 75-36280. 1976. 52.95 (*0-250-40119-3*) Buttrwrth-Heinemann.

Analysis of Flow in Water Distribution Networks. Pramod R. Bhave. LC 91-52908. 460p. 1991. pap. text ed. 65.00 (*0-87762-732-0*) Technomic.

Analysis of Fluoroscopic Principles, Image Intensification, & Television Systems: Workbook & Laboratory Manual. Robert J. Parelli. 115p. (C). 1991. text ed. 35.00 (*1-880359-00-6*) Par Rad.

Analysis of Food Carbohydrate. Gordon G. Birch. 288p. 1985. 95.50 (*0-85334-354-3*, Pub. by Elsevier Applied Sci UK) Elsevier.

Analysis of Food Contaminants. Ed. by J. Gilbert. (Illus.). 400p. 1984. 106.25 (*0-85334-255-5*, I-168-84, Pub. by Elsevier Applied Sci UK) Elsevier.

Analysis of Foods & Beverages: Modern Techniques. George Charalambous. LC 83-11783. (Food Science & Technology Ser.). 1984. text ed. 174.00 (*0-12-169160-8*) Acad Pr.

Analysis of Franz Grillparzer's Dramas: Fate, Guilt, & Tragedy. Eva Wagner. LC 91-47728. (Studies in German Language & Literature: Vol. 10). 264p. 1992. lib. bdg. 89.95 (*0-7734-9459-6*) E Mellen.

Analysis of Fuzzy Information: Applications in Engineering & Science, Vol. III. James C. Bezdek. 304p. 1987. 228.00 (*0-8493-6298-9*, QA248) CRC Pr.

Analysis of Fuzzy Information: Artificial Intelligence & Decision Systems, Vol. II. James C. Bezdek. 272p. 1987. 149.00 (*0-8493-6297-0*, CRC Reprint) Franklin.

Analysis of Fuzzy Information: Mathematics & Logic, Vol. I. James C. Bezdek. 304p. 1987. 228.00 (*0-8493-6296-2*, QA248) CRC Pr.

Analysis of Gases by Chromatography. C. J. Cowper & A. J. Derose. LC 83-6207. (Pergamon Series on Analytical Chemistry: Vol. 7). (Illus.). 159p. 1983. text ed. 71.00 (*0-08-024027-5*, Pub. by Pergamon Repr UK) Franklin.

Analysis of Geologic Structures. John M. Dennison. (Illus.). (C). 1968. pap. text ed. 14.95 (*0-393-09801-X*) Norton.

Analysis of Geological Materials. Riddle. 480p. 1993. 165.00 (*0-8247-9132-0*) Dekker.

Analysis of Geological Structures. Neville J. Price & John W. Cosgrove. (Illus.). 560p. 1990. pap. 49.95 (*0-521-31958-7*) Cambridge U Pr.

***Analysis of Geometrically Non-Linear Structures.** Robert Levy & William R. Spillers. LC 94-38086. 1995. 49.95 (*0-412-99601-4*) Chapman & Hall.

Analysis of Global Expansion Methods: Weakly Asymptotically Diagonal Systems. L. M. Delves & T. L. Freeman. LC 80-42084. (Computational Mathematics & Applications Ser.). 1981. text ed. 134.00 (*0-12-208880-8*) Acad Pr.

Analysis of Groups: Contributions to Theory, Research, & Practice. Ed. by Graham S. Gibbard et al. LC 73-10941. (Social & Behavioral Science Ser.). 468p. 1974. 41.95x (*0-87589-205-1*) Jossey-Bass.

Analysis of Growth: The Responses of Cells & Tissues in Culture see Plant Physiology: A Treatise

Analysis of Happiness. Wladislow Tatarkiewicz. (Melbourne International Philosophy Ser.: No. 3). 1976. lib. bdg. 94.00 (*90-247-1807-4*) Kluwer Ac.

Analysis of Heat & Mass Transfer. Ernest R. Eckert. Ed. by Robert M. Drake, Jr. LC 66-41146. 806p. 1986. 99.50 (*0-89116-553-3*) Hemisp Pub.

Analysis of High Purity Materials. Ed. by I. P. Alimarin. 608p. 1968. text ed. 132.00 (*0-7065-0596-4*, Pub. by Keter Pub IS) Coronet Bks.

Analysis of High Temperature Materials. O. Van der Biest. (Illus.). 261p. 1983. 74.00 (*0-85334-172-9*, I-464-82, Pub. by Elsevier Applied Sci UK) Elsevier.

Analysis of Hispanic Texts: Current Trends in Methodology. Ed. by Mary Ann Beck et al. LC 76-5741. (First York College Colloquium). 1976. pap. 18.00 (*0-916950-00-X*) Biling Rev-Pr.

Analysis of Hispanic Texts: Current Trends in Methodology. Ed. by Lisa E. Davis & Isabel C. Taran. LC 76-45294. (Second York College Colloquium). 1976. lib. bdg. 26.00 (*0-916950-03-4*); pap. 18.00 (*0-916950-17-4*) Biling Rev-Pr.

Analysis of Historical Ceramics from the Central Salt River Valley of Northeast Missouri. T. Majewski & M. J. O'Brien. (Illus.). viii, 121p. 1984. 15.00 (*0-917111-02-8*) Mus Anthro MO.

Analysis of Human Behavior: A Psychological Laboratory Manual. Sonja Grover. 130p. 1985. pap. text ed. 8.95 (*0-8290-0725-3*) Irvington.

Analysis of Human Genetic Linkage. 2nd rev. ed. Jurg Ott. LC 91-7048. (Series in Contemporary Medicine & Public Health). (Illus.). 320p. 1991. text ed. 47.50 (*0-8018-4257-3*) Johns Hopkins.

Analysis of Human Mandibular Movement. J. M. Goodson & E. L. Johansen. (Monographs in Oral Science: Vol. 5). 1975. 47.25 (*3-8055-1416-6*) S Karger.

Analysis of Human Motion: A Textbook in Kinesiology. 2nd ed. M. Gladys Scott. LC 63-13839. (Illus.). 1963. 19.95 (*0-89197-023-1*); pap. text ed. 9.50 (*0-89197-024-X*) Irvington.

Analysis of Ice Age Art: Its Psychology & Belief System. Noel W. Smith. LC 91-17245. (American University Studies: Fine Arts: Ser. XX, Vol. 15). (Illus.). 242p. (C). 1992. text ed. 47.95 (*0-8204-1557-X*) P Lang Pubs.

Analysis of Ideology. Raymond Boudon. Tr. by Malcolm Slater. LC 89-4930. 250p. 1989. 39.95 (*0-226-06730-0*) U Ch Pr.

Analysis of Income Differentials among Self-Employed Minorities. Timothy Bates. (Minority Economic Development Ser.: No. 1). 57p. 1988. pap. 5.95 (*0-318-39975-X*) UCLA CAAS.

Analysis of Industrial Air Pollutants. Paul R. Harrison et al. (Air Pollution Ser.: Vol. 3). 185p. (C). 1974. text ed. 29.00 (*0-8422-7154-6*) Irvington.

Analysis of Infectious Disease Data. N . G. Becker. 224p. 1989. 39.95 (*0-412-30990-4*, A2802) Chapman & Hall.

Analysis of Inflation, 1965-1974. Conference on Price Behavior (1974, Bethesda, Md). LC 77-581. (Studies in Income & Wealth: No. 42). 519p. reprint ed. pap. 148.00 (*0-317-55569-3*, 2056364) Bks Demand.

Analysis of International Relations. 3rd ed. Karl W. Deutsch. (Illus.). 320p. (C). 1988. pap. text ed. write for info. (*0-13-033010-8*) P-H.

***Analysis of Interpanetary Dust NASA - LPI Workshop: Papers Presented at the... Workshop.** Ed. by M. E. Zolensky et al. LC 94-71292. (AIP Conference Proceedings Ser.: No. 310). 357p. 1994. text ed. 95.00x (*1-56396-341-8*) Am Inst Physics.

Analysis of Investment in Electric Power. Henry D. Jacoby. Ed. by Stuart Bruchey. LC 78-22688. (Energy in the American Economy Ser.). (Illus.). 1979. lib. bdg. 25.95 (*0-405-11991-7*) Ayer.

Analysis of Janitor Service in Elementary Schools. Charles E. Reeves. LC 77-177185. (Columbia University. Teachers College. Contributions to Education Ser.: No. 167). reprint ed. 37.50 (*0-404-55167-X*) AMS Pr.

Analysis of Japanese Patent Law: Translated from the Original Treatise. Masami Hanabusa. LC 91-37113. 384p. 1992. text ed. 140.00 (*1-55618-099-3*) Brunswick Pub.

Analysis of Key SEC No-Action Letters: 1992-1993 Edition. Robert J. Haft. (Securities Law Ser.). (Orig.). 1992. pap. 97.50 (*0-87632-880-X*) Clark Boardman Callaghan.

Analysis of Knowing: A Decade of Research. Robert K. Shope. LC 82-15099. 377p. 1983. 45.00x (*0-691-07275-2*); pap. 14.95x (*0-691-02025-6*) Princeton U Pr.

Analysis of Landscape Characteristics Relevant to Preference. Carla B. Rabinowitz & Robert E. Coughlin. (Discussion Paper Ser.: No. 38). 1970. pap. 10.00 (*1-55869-009-3*) Regional Sci Res Inst.

Analysis of Leadership & How to Be a Better Leader. Leon Bly. 117p. (Orig.). (YA). (gr. 9). 1988. student ed. text ed. 24.95 (*0-9621505-0-9*) Schwarz Pauper.

Analysis of Leadership & How to Be a Better Leader: A Textbook. Leon Bly. 60p. (Orig.). 1989. student ed 12.95 (*0-9621505-2-5*); pap. text ed. 12.95 (*0-9621505-1-7*) Schwarz Pauper.

Analysis of Least-Squares Velocity Inversion. Fadil Santosa & William W. Symes. Ed. by Raymon L. Brown. (Geophysical Monograph Ser.: No. 4). 168p. 1989. pap. 32.00 (*0-931830-78-8*, 484) Soc Expl Geophys.

Analysis of Linear Circuits. Clayton R. Paul. 896p. 1988. text ed. 49.95 (*0-07-045919-3*) McGraw.

Analysis of Linear Circuits. Clayton R. Paul. 1989. text ed. write for info. (*0-07-909340-X*) McGraw.

Analysis of Linear Dynamic Systems. John B. Lewis. (Illus.). 880p. 1977. 59.95 (*0-916460-20-7*, Matrix Pubs Inc) Weber Systems.

Analysis of Linear Models. Ronald R. Hocking. LC 84-14606. (Statistics Ser.). 385p. (C). 1985. text ed. 68.00 (*0-534-03618-X*) Brooks-Cole.

Analysis of Linear Partial Differential Operators I: Distribution Theory & Fourier Analysis. L. Hoermander. (Grundlehren der Mathematischen Wissenschaften Ser.: Vol. 256). (Illus.). 380p. 1983. 79.00 (*0-387-12104-8*) Spr-Verlag.

Analysis of Linear Partial Differential Operators I: Distribution Theory & Fourier Analysis. L. Hormander. (Grundlehren der Mathematischen Wissenschaften Ser.: Vol. 256). (Illus.). 391p. 1990. student ed, pap. 39.50 (*0-387-52343-X*) Spr-Verlag.

Analysis of Linear Partial Differential Operators II: Differential Operators with Constant Coefficients. L. Hoermander. (Grundlehren der Mathematischen Wissenschaften Ser.: Vol. 257). (Illus.). 380p. 1990. 107.00 (*0-387-12139-0*) Spr-Verlag.

***Analysis of Linear Partial Differential Operators III No. 274, Vol. 274.** L. Hormander. 525p. 1995. 98.00 (*0-387-13828-5*) Spr-Verlag.

Analysis of Linear Partial Differential Operators IV. L. Hormander. (Grundlehren der Mathematischen Wissenschaften Ser.: Vol. 275). 360p. 1985. 98.00 (*0-387-13829-3*) Spr-Verlag.

Analysis of Linear Systems. D. G. Cheng. (C). 1959. text ed. 73.25 (*0-201-01020-8*) Addison-Wesley.

Analysis of Literary Texts: Current Trends in Methodology (Third & Fourth York College Colloquia) Ed. by Randolph D. Pope. LC 79-54144. (Studies in Literary Analysis). 330p. 1980. lib. bdg. 26.00 (*0-916950-14-X*); pap. text ed. 18.00 (*0-916950-13-1*) Biling Rev-Pr.

Analysis of Lithic Workshop Debris from Iron Mountain, Union County, Illinois. Deborah A. Billings. LC 87-71130. (Center for Archaeological Investigations Research Paper Ser.: No. 47). (Illus.). ix, 63p. (Orig.). 1984. pap. 7.50 (*0-88104-023-1*) Center Archaeo.

Analysis of Longitudinal Data. Peter J. Diggle et al. (Oxford Statistical Science Ser.: Vol. 13). (Illus.). 272p. 1994. 45.00 (*0-19-852284-3*) OUP.

Analysis of Management Consulting Business in the U. S. Today. Ed. by James H. Kennedy. 1992. 35.00 (*0-916654-77-X*) Kennedy Pubns.

Analysis of Marine Insurance Clauses, Bk. 1: The Institute Cargo Clauses. R. H. Brown. 59p. 1983. pap. 80.00 (*0-900886-84-6*, Pub. by Witherby & Co UK) St Mut.

Analysis of Marine Insurance Clauses, Bk. 2: The Institute Time Clauses Hulls. R. H. Brown. 50p. 1984. pap. 80.00 (*0-900886-89-7*, Pub. by Witherby & Co UK) St Mut.

Analysis of Material Removal Processes. W. R. DeVries. Ed. by Frederick F. Ling. (Texts in Mechanical Engineering Ser.). (Illus.). xvii, 254p. 1991. 54.00 (*0-387-97728-7*) Spr-Verlag.

***Analysis of Medical Savings Accounts: Do Two Wrongs Make a Right?** Mark V. Pauly. 32p. 1994. pap. 9.95 (*0-8447-7027-2*) Am Enterprise.

Analysis of Mendelssohn's Organ Works. Joseph W. Hathaway. LC 74-24107. reprint ed. 30.00 (*0-404-12956-0*) AMS Pr.

Analysis of Men's Selected Summer Clothing Items & How to Promote Them. 8p. 1957. 7.00 (*0-318-19673-5*) Clothing Mfrs.

Analysis of Mental Functions see Two Studies in Mental Tests

Analysis of Messy Data, Vol. 1. George A. Milliken. 1992. pap. 39.95 (*0-442-01309-4*) Chapman & Hall.

Analysis of Messy Data II: Nonreplicated Experiments. Dallas E. Johnson & George A. Milliken. 356p. 1988. text ed. 64.95 (*0-442-24408-8*) Chapman & Hall.

Analysis of Messy Data, Vol. 1: Designing Experiment. George A. Milliken. 1987. 47.95 (*0-317-63765-7*) Chapman & Hall.

Analysis of Metal - Nonmetal Underground Mining Accidents Involving Mobile Mining Equipment. P. A. Hendricks et al. 1994. write for info. (*0-318-72928-8*) US Interior.

***Analysis of Metallic Antennas & Scatterers.** B. D. Popovic & B. M. Kolundzija. (Electromagnetic Waves Ser.: 38). 208p. 1994. 79.00 (*0-85296-807-8*) Inst Elect Eng.

Analysis of Metallurgical Failures. 2nd ed. Vito J. Colangelo & F. A. Heiser. LC 86-22406. 360p. 1987. text ed. 97.95 (*0-471-89168-1*) Wiley.

Analysis of Metals: Overview & Selected Methods. F. E. Beamish & Jon C. Van Loon. 1977. text ed. 106.00 (*0-12-083950-4*) Acad Pr.

Analysis of Metaphor in the Light of W. M. Urban's Theories. Warren Shibles. LC 78-159471. (C). 1971. pap. 10.00 (*0-912386-12-6*) Language Pr.

Analysis of Microelectronic Materials & Devices. Ed. by M. Grasserbauer & H. W. Werner. 934p. 1991. text ed. 275.00 (*0-471-91713-3*) Wiley.

Analysis of Mineral Number Four. Moses Goldberg. (Orig.). (J). (gr. 4 up). 1982. 5.00 (*0-87602-234-4*) Anchorage.

Analysis of Mississippi Industrial Location Factors. William F. Davidge & Kenneth W. Hollman. 1978. 4.00 (*0-938004-02-6*) U MS Bus Econ.

Analysis of Mortality & Other Acturial Statistics. B. Benjamin & J. H. Pollard. (C). 1980. 200.00 (*0-685-33797-9*, Pub. by Witherby & Co UK) St Mut.

Analysis of Mortgage Lending Patterns in Omaha. Jack Ruff. 84p. (Orig.). 1983. pap. 4.50 (*1-55719-095-X*) U NE CPAR.

Analysis of Motion Pictures About War Released by American Film Industry, 1939-1970. Russell E. Shain. Ed. by Garth S. Lowett. LC 75-21435. (Dissertations on Film Ser.). 1976. lib. bdg. 30.95 (*0-405-07536-7*) Ayer.

Analysis of Multiconductor Transmission Lines. Clayton R. Paul. LC 94-5704. (Microwave & Optical Engineering Ser.). 1994. text ed. 79.95 (*0-471-02080-X*) Wiley.

Analysis of Multistep Scenarios in the Natural History of Human or Animal Cancer. Ed. by George Klein. (Advances in Viral Oncology Ser.: Vol. 7). 232p. 1987. text ed. 114.50 (*0-88167-191-6*) Raven.

Analysis of Natural Waters Vol. 1: Complex-Formation Preconcentration Techniques, 2 vols., Vol. 1. T. R. Crompton. LC 92-23860. (Illus.). 232p. 1993. 52.50 (*0-19-855395-1*) OUP.

Analysis of Natural Waters Vol. 2: Direct Preconcentration Techniques, 2 vols., Vol. 2. T. R. Crompton. (Illus.). 264p. 1993. 60.00 (*0-19-855394-3*) OUP.

Analysis of Navajo Temporality. Douglas R. Givens. 1977. pap. text ed. 15.00 (*0-8191-0213-X*) U Pr of Amer.

Analysis of Neural Networks. U. Heiden. (Lecture Notes in Biomathematics Ser.: Vol. 35). 159p. 1980. pap. text ed. 25.00 (*0-387-09966-2*) Spr-Verlag.

Analysis of Neuronal Microcircuits & Synaptic Interactions, No. 8: Handbook of Chemical Neuroanatomy. Ed. by Anders T. Bjorklund et al. 528p. 1990. 289.50 (*0-444-81231-8*) Elsevier.

Analysis of Neuropeptides by Liquid Chromatography & Mass Spectrometry. D. M. Desiderio. (Techniques & Instrumentation in Analytical Chemistry Ser.: No. 6). 236p. 1984. 100.00 (*0-444-42418-0*) Elsevier.

***Analysis of New Diesel Engine & Component Design: 1995 International Congress & Exposition Meeting.** 1995. pap. 36.00 (*1-56091-641-9*, SP1091) Soc Auto Engineers.

Analysis of Nominal Data. 2nd ed. H. T. Reynolds. (Quantitative Applications in the Social Sciences Ser.: Vol. 7). 82p. 1984. 9.95 (*0-8039-0653-6*) Sage.

Analysis of Non-Alcoholic Beverages. Ed. by H. F. Linskens & J. F. Jackson. (Modern Methods of Plant Analysis Ser.: Vol. 8). (Illus.). 450p. 1988. 224.00 (*0-387-18820-7*) Spr-Verlag.

Analysis of Normal & Abnormal Cell Growth: Model-System Formulations & Analog Computer Studies. Ferdinand Heinmets. LC 66-11882. 301p. reprint ed. pap. 85.80 (*0-685-15816-0*, 2056105) Bks Demand.

Analysis of Numberical Methods. Eugene Isaacson & Herbert B. Keller. LC 94-7740. (Illus.). 560p. 1994. reprint ed. pap. 13.95 (*0-486-68029-0*) Dover.

Analysis of Nutrients in Foods. D. R. Osborne & P. Voogt. (Food Science & Technology Ser.). 1978. text ed. 121.00 (*0-12-529150-7*) Acad Pr.

Analysis of Omaha's Comprehensive Manpower Program. David W. Hinton. 88p. (Orig.). 1975. pap. 7.00 (*1-55719-067-4*) U NE CPAR.

Analysis of Optical Structures. D. C. O'Shea. 1992. 53.00 (*0-8194-0660-0*, 1532) SPIE.

Analysis of Ordinal Categorical Data. Alan Agresti. LC 83-23535. (Probability & Mathematical Statistics: Applied Probability & Statistics Section Ser.: No 1-287). 287p. 1984. text ed. 94.95 (*0-471-89055-3*, Wiley-Interscience) Wiley.

Analysis of Ordinal Data. David K. Hildebrand et al. (Quantitative Applications in the Social Sciences Ser.: Vol. 8). 1977. 9.95 (*0-8039-0795-8*) Sage.

Analysis of Organic Micropollutants in Water. Ed. by G. Angeletti & A. Bjorseth. 1984. lib. bdg. 132.00 (*90-277-1726-5*) Kluwer Ac.

Analysis of Organic Micropollutants in Water. Ed. by A. Bjorseth & G. Angeletti. 1982. lib. bdg. 112.50 (*90-277-1398-7*) Kluwer Ac.

Analysis of Paints & Related Materials: Current Techniques for Solving Coatings Problems. (ASTM Special Technical Publication Ser.: No. 1119). (Illus.). 215p. 1992. text ed. 51.00 (*0-8031-1465-6*, 04-011190-14) ASTM.

Analysis of Panel Data. Cheng Hsiao. (Econometric Society Monographs: No. 11). (Illus.). 288p. 1986. 69.95 (*0-521-25150-8*) Cambridge U Pr.

Analysis of Panel Data. Cheng Hsiao. (Econometric Society Monographs: No. 11). (Illus.). 246p. (C). 1989. pap. 19.95 (*0-521-38933-X*) Cambridge U Pr.

Analysis of Pascal Programs. Lynn R. Carter. LC 82-4925. (Computer Science: Systems Programming Ser.: No. 6). 203p. reprint ed. pap. 57.90 (*0-685-20858-3*, 2070113) Bks Demand.

Analysis of Peptides & Proteins by Mass Spectrometry: Proceedings of the Fourth Texas Symposium on Mass Spectrometry. Ed. by Catherine J. McNeal. 322p. 1988. text ed. 270.00 (*0-471-92062-2*) Wiley.

Analysis of Periodically Time-Varying Systems. J. A. Richards. (Communications & Control Engineering Ser.). (Illus.). 173p. 1983. 89.00 (*0-387-11689-3*) Spr-Verlag.

Analysis of Personnel Classification, Organizational Structure, & Financial Record Keeping Practices of the Circuit Court of Eau Claire County, Wisconsin. National Center for State Courts Staff. 52p. 1980. 3.12 (*0-685-15207-3*, DPO, T/A-504) Natl Ctr St Courts.

Analysis of Personnel Rules, Policies, & Procedures for the General, Juvenile, & Domestic Relations Divisions of the Cuyahoga County, Ohio, Court of Common Pleas: Final Report. Gerald Kaban. 22p. 1985. 2.00 (*0-685-15212-X*, NERO-172) Natl Ctr St Courts.

Analysis of Pesticide Residues. H. Anson Moye. LC 90-33710. 478p. (C). 1990. reprint ed. 89.50 (*0-89464-330-4*) Krieger.

***Analysis of Pesticides in Ground & Surface Water II.** Ed. by H. Borner et al. (Chemistry of Plant Protection Ser.: Vol. 12). 221p. 1995. 164.00 (*3-540-59053-6*) Spr-Verlag.

Analysis of Pesticides in Water: Analysis Chlorine & Phosphorus-Containing Pesticides, Vol. II, Vol. II. Ed. by Alfred S. Chau & B. K. Afghan. 256p. 1982. 134.00 (*0-8493-5211-8*, TP248, CRC Reprint) Franklin.

Analysis of Pesticides in Water: Analysis Nitrogen-Containing Pesticides, Vol. III, Vol. III. A. S. Chau & B. K. Afghan. 264p. 1982. 139.00 (*0-8493-5212-6*, TP248, CRC Reprint) Franklin.

Analysis of Pesticides in Water: Significance, Principles, Techniques, & Chemistry of Pesticides, Vol. I. B. K. Afghan. Ed. by S. Y. Chau. 216p. 1982. 144.00 (*0-8493-5210-X*, TP248) CRC Pr.

Analysis of Petroleum for Trace Elements. O. Milner & R. Belcher. LC 63-19331. (International Series Mono on Analytical Chemistry: Vol. 14). 1963. 55.00 (*0-08-010448-7*, Pub. by Pergamon Repr UK) Franklin.

Analysis of Petroleum for Trace Metals. Ed. by Robert A. Hofstader et al. LC 76-46297. (Advances in Chemistry Ser.: No. 156). 189p. 1976. 38.95 (*0-8412-0349-0*) Am Chemical.

Analysis of Petroleum Products & Lubricants. Ed. by R. A. Nadkarni. LC 91-10488. (Special Technical Publication Ser.: No. STP 1109). (Illus.). 165p. 1991. text ed. 55.00 (*0-8031-1416-8*, 04-011090-12) ASTM.

Analysis of Phenolic Plant Metabolites. P. Waterman & S. Mole. (Methods in Ecology). (Illus.). 256p. 1994. pap. 35.00 (*0-632-02969-2*) Blackwell Sci.

Analysis of Plastics. T. R. Crompton. (Series in Analytical Chemistry: Vol. 8). (Illus.). 452p. 1984. text ed. 140.00 (*0-08-026251-1*, Pergamon Pr) Elsevier.

Analysis of Poetic Thinking. Max Rieser. Tr. by Herbert M. Schueller. LC 69-11535. (Criticism Monograph Ser.: No. 1). 170p. reprint ed. pap. 48.50 (*0-7837-3641-X*, 2043509) Bks Demand.

Analysis of Policy Arguments. Ralph S. Hambrick, Jr. & William P. Snyder. (Learning Packages in the Policy Sciences Ser.: No. 13). 72p. (C). 1979. pap. text ed. 10.50 (*0-936826-02-9*) PS Assocs Croton.

Analysis of Policy Impact. Ed. by John Grumm & Stephen Wasby. (C). 1980. pap. 12.00 (*0-918592-39-9*) Pol Studies.

Analysis of Political Structure. David Easton. 304p. 1990. 37.50 (*0-415-90310-6*, A4794, Routledge NY) Routledge.

Analysis of Polling Systems. Hideaki Takagi. (Computer Systems Ser.). (Illus.). 175p. (Orig.). 1986. 25.00 (*0-262-20057-0*) MIT Pr.

Analysis of Polymer Systems. L. S. Bark & N. S. Allen. (Illus.). 311p. 1982. 88.25 (*0-85334-122-2*, Pub. by Elsevier Applied Sci UK) Elsevier.

Analysis of Polymers: An Introduction. T. R. Crompton. LC 88-19696. (Illus.). 375p. 1989. pap. 48.00 (*0-08-033936-0*, Pergamon Pr) Elsevier.

Analysis of Power: Core Elements & Structure. Geoffrey Debnam. LC 83-4556. 150p. 1984. text ed. 29.95 (*0-312-03284-6*) St Martin.

Analysis of Prehistoric Artifacts from Lassen National Forest, California. Lonnie Pippin & Eugene Hattori. (Social Sciences Center Technical Report Ser.: No. 15). (Illus.). 140p. (C). 1980. spiral bd. 15.00 (*0-945920-15-6*) Desert Rsch Inst.

Analysis of Prehistoric Coprolites from Utah. Gary F. Fry. (Anthropological Papers: No. 97). (Illus.). 1978. pap. text ed. 10.00 (*0-87480-142-7*) U of Utah Pr.

Analysis of Prehistoric Diets. Robert I. Gilbert, Jr. & James H. Mielke. (Studies in Archaeology). 1984. text ed. 81.00 (*0-12-283260-4*) Acad Pr.

Analysis of Prescribing in General Practice: A Guide to Audit & Research. C. M. Harris & P. L. Heywood. 155p. 1990. pap. 17.00 (*0-11-321287-9*, HM8279) UNIPUB.

Analysis of Processes of Role Change. Samuel N. Eisenstadt et al. 46p. 1967. pap. 18.95x (*0-87855-626-5*) Transaction Pubs.

Analysis of Productivity Levels & Economic Efficiency in Agriculture. Suryanarayana S. Raju. 1987. 41.00 (*81-85076-12-X*, Pub. by Chugh Pubns II) S Asia.

Analysis of Psychological Theory: Meta-Psychological Perspectives. Ed. by Henderikus J. Stam. 300p. 1987. 68.00 (*0-89116-597-5*) Hemisp Pub.

Analysis of Public Output. Ed. by Julius Margolis. (Universities-National Bureau Conference Ser.: No. 23). 425p. 1970. text ed. 111.10 (*0-87014-220-8*) Natl Bur Econ Res.

Analysis of Public Output: A Conference of the Universities - National Bureau Committee for Economic Research. Ed. by Julius Margolis. LC 78-119997. (Universities-National Bureau Conference Ser.: No. 23). (Illus.). 427p. reprint ed. pap. 121.70 (*0-8357-7565-8*, 2056886) Bks Demand.

Analysis of Public Policy: A Bibliography of Dissertations, 1977-1982. Ed. by John S. Robey. LC 83-22556. x, 225p. 1984. text ed. 47.95 (*0-313-23957-6*, RPU/, Greenwood Pr) Greenwood.

Analysis of Qualitative Data: Vol. I - Introductory Topics (TXX) Shelby J. Haberman. LC 77-25731. 1978. text ed. 70.00 (*0-12-312501-4*) Acad Pr.

Analysis of Qualitative Data: Vol. 2 - New Developments. Shelby J. Haberman. LC 77-25731. 1979. text ed. 65.00 (*0-12-312502-2*) Acad Pr.

Analysis of Quality of Care for Patients Who Are Black or Poor in Rural & Urban Settings. Katherine L. Kahn et al. LC 93-29147. 1993. write for info. (*0-8330-1433-1*, MR-292-HCFA) Rand Corp.

Analysis of Quatal Response Data. B. J. Morgan. (Monographs on Statistics & Applied Probability: No. 44). 250p. 1991. 49.95 (*0-412-31750-8*, A4554) Chapman & Hall.

***Analysis of Radiographic Quality.** 3rd ed. Daniel P. Donohue. 300p. 1995. pap. 49.00 (*0-8342-0678-1*) Aspen Pub.

Analysis of Random Walks. Ed. by Jacob W. Cohen. LC 92-52688. 382p. 1992. 98.00 (*90-5199-086-3*, Pub. by IOS Pr NE) IOS Press.

Analysis of Reactor Vessel Radiation Effects Surveillance Programs - STP 481. 275p. 1970. 26.00 (*0-8031-0276-3*, 04-481000-35) ASTM.

Analysis of Real & Complex Manifolds. 2nd rev. ed. Raghavan Narasimhan. (North-Holland Mathematical Library: Vol. 25). 246p. 1986. 79.50 (*0-444-87776-2*, North Holland) Elsevier.

***Analysis of Relationships Between Lightning, Precipitation, & Runoff.** James R. Gosz et al. (Illus.). 52p. (Orig.). (C). 1994. pap. text ed. 30.00 (*0-7881-1467-0*) Diane Pub.

***Analysis of Religious Assortative Marriage: An Application of Design Techniques for Categorical Models.** John Hendrickx. 312p. 1994. pap. 30.00 (*90-5170-263-9*, Pub. by Thesis Pubs NE) IBD Ltd.

Analysis of Religious Belief. John R. Amberley. 1974. 59.95 (*0-87968-619-7*) Gordon Pr.

Analysis of Religious Belief. John R. Amberley. LC 76-161318. (Atheist Viewpoint Ser.). 745p. 1972. reprint ed. 45.95 (*0-405-03621-3*) Ayer.

An Asterisk (*) at the beginning of an entry indicates that the title is appearing in BIP for the first time.

An Asterisk (*) at the beginning of an entry indicates that the title is appearing in BIP for the first time.

A

Analysis of the University Village Complex: With a Reappraisal of Central California Archaeology. Bert A. Gerow & Roland W. Force. (Illus.). ix, 209p. 1968. reprint ed. pap. text ed. 15.65 (*1-55567-030-X*) Coyote Press.

Analysis of the Uses & Limitations of Information in the Iringa Nutrition Program, Tanzania. David L. Pelletier. (Working Paper Ser.). (C). 1991. pap. text ed. 7.00 (*1-56401-105-4*) Cornell Food.

Analysis of the Work of General Clerical Employees. Thelma M. Potter. LC 78-177161. (Columbia University. Teachers College. Contributions to Education Ser.: No. 903). reprint ed. 37.50 (*0-404-55903-4*) AMS Pr.

***Analysis of Thin-Walled Structures.** I. E. Mileikovskii & S. I. Trushin. (Russian Translations Ser.: No. 108). (Illus.). 196p. (ENG.). (C). 1994. text ed. 85.00 (*90-5410-250-0*, Pub. by A A Balkema NE) Ashgate Pub Co.

***Analysis of Thinking & Research about Qualitative Methods.** W. James Potter. (LEA's Communication Ser.). 400p. 1996. text ed. 80.00 (*0-8058-1750-6*); pap. 40.00 (*0-8058-1751-4*) L Erlbaum Assocs.

Analysis of Three Hundred & Thirty-Three Necro-Kidney-Allografts. G. K. Uhlschmid. (European Surgical Research Journal: Vol. 11, Suppl. 1). (Illus.). 1979. pap. 20.00 (*3-8055-3004-8*) S Karger.

Analysis of Thyristor Power-Conditioned Motors. S. K. Pillai. 1993. text ed. 25.00 (*0-86311-188-2*, Pub. by Universities Pr II) Apt Bks.

Analysis of Tides. Gabriel Godin. LC 77-151367. 285p. reprint ed. pap. 81.30 (*0-8357-5441-3*, 2056115) Bks Demand.

Analysis of Time Series: An Introduction. 4th ed. Christopher Chatfield. 288p. 1989. pap. 25.00 (*0-412-31820-2*) Chapman & Hall.

Analysis of Toeplitz Operators. A. Bottcher & B. Silbermann. 496p. 1990. 79.00 (*0-387-52147-X*) Spr-Verlag.

Analysis of Trace Metals in Biological Materials. Pleban. 1981. write for info. (*0-85501-624-8*) Wiley.

Analysis of Trace Organics in the Aquatic Environment. Ed. by B. K. Afghan & Alfred S. Chau. 384p. 1989. 242.00 (*0-8493-4626-6*, TD427) CRC Pr.

Analysis of Transference: Theory & Technique, Vol. 1. Merton M. Gill. LC 81-23654. (Psychological Issues Monograph: No. 53). 200p. 1981. text ed. 32.50 (*0-8236-0139-0*) Intl Univs Pr.

Analysis of Transference, Vol. 2: Studies of Seven Audio-Recorded Psychoanalytic Sessions. Merton M. Gill & Irwin Z. Hoffman. LC 81-23654. (Psychological Issues Monograph: No. 54). 240p. 1982. 35.00 (*0-8236-0140-4*) Intl Univs Pr.

***Analysis of Transient Electromagnetic Fields in an Electrical Utility Substation Environment.** B. J. Kooij. 224p. (Orig.). 1994. pap. 52.50x (*90-6275-969-6*, Pub. by Delft U Pr NE) Coronet Bks.

Analysis of Turbulent Boundary Layers. Tuncer Cebeci & A. M. Smith. 1974. text ed. 151.00 (*0-12-164650-5*) Acad Pr.

***Analysis of Two-Way Layouts.** Mandel. 1994. (*0-412-98611-6*) Chapman & Hall.

Analysis of Two-Way Layouts. John Mandel. LC 93-48326. 1994. 69.95 (*0-442-01212-8*) Chapman & Hall.

***Analysis of U. S. Army RDT & E Funding FY 1980-FY 1995.** Elmer Engstrom et al. 90p. 1995. 20.00 (*0-614-04672-6*) Inst Def & Dis.

Analysis of Usury. Jeffrey P. Mark. 1980. lib. bdg. 250.00 (*0-8490-3085-4*) Gordon Pr.

Analysis of Variance. Lisa Custer et al. LC 92-33531. (Six Sigma Research Institute Ser.). 1993. write for info. (*0-201-63402-3*) Addison-Wesley.

Analysis of Variance. Gudmund R. Iversen & Helmut Norpoth. (Quantitative Applications in the Social Sciences Ser.: Vol. 1). 95p. 1987. 9.95 (*0-8039-3001-1*) Sage.

Analysis of Variance. P. R. Krishnaiah. (Handbook of Statistics Ser.: Vol. 1). 1002p. 1981. 105.00 (*0-444-85335-9*, North Holland) Elsevier.

Analysis of Variance. Henry Scheffe. LC 59-14994. (Probability & Mathematical Statistics Ser.). (Illus.). 477p. 1959. text ed. 119.00 (*0-471-75834-5*) Wiley.

Analysis of Variance: A Basic Course. A. Huitson. (Griffin's Statistical Monographs: No. 18). 91p. 1980. pap. 17.95 (*0-85264-174-5*) Lubrecht & Cramer.

Analysis of Variance: The Basic Designs. Charles E. Collyer & James T. Enns. LC 86-872. 310p. 1986. spiral bd. 25.95 (*0-8304-1170-4*) Nelson-Hall.

Analysis of Variance in Experimental Designs. H. R. Lindman. (Texts in Statistics Ser.). (Illus.). ix, 531p. 1991. 49.95 (*0-387-97571-3*) Spr-Verlag.

Analysis of Variance Primer. Richard J. Harris. LC 93-71269. 540p. (C). 1994. boxed 48.00 (*0-87581-373-9*) Peacock Pubs.

Analysis of Vatican 30. Lewis M. Barth. (Monographs of the Hebrew Union College: No. 1). 342p. 1973. 25.00 (*0-87820-400-8*) Hebrew Union Coll Pr.

Analysis of Vehicle Aerodynamics: SAE International Congress & Exposition 1994, 11 papers. (Special Publications). 1994. pap. 31.00 (*1-56091-488-2*, SP-1036) Soc Auto Engineers.

Analysis of Vertebrate Pest Control. Jim Hone. LC 93-49727. (Cambridge Studies in Applied Ecology & Resource Management). (Illus.). 300p. (C). 1995. 59.95 (*0-521-41528-4*) Cambridge U Pr.

Analysis of Vertebrate Populations. Graeme Caughley. LC 76-913. 244p. reprint ed. pap. 69.60 (*0-8357-5442-1*, 2031467) Bks Demand.

Analysis of Vertebrate Structure. 3rd ed. Milton Hildebrand. LC 87-21545. 701p. 1988. Net. text ed. write for info. (*0-471-82568-9*) Wiley.

Analysis of Vertebrate Structure. 4th ed. Milton Hildebrand. LC 94-4652. (Illus.). 1994. text ed. 46.00 (*0-471-30823-4*) Wiley.

Analysis of Visual Behavior. Ed. by David J. Ingle et al. (Illus.). 1982. 95.00 (*0-262-09022-8*) MIT Pr.

Analysis of Volatiles. Methods-Applications: Proceedings-International Workshop. Ed. by Peter Schreier. LC 84-1721. xi, 469p. 1984. 153.85 (*3-11-009805-9*) De Gruyter.

Analysis of Water Distribution Systems. Thomas M. Walski. LC 91-3777. 288p. (C). 1992. reprint ed. lib. bdg. 53.95 (*0-89464-624-9*) Krieger.

Analysis of Water Resource Systems: Developments in Water Science, 32, 1988. Ed. by L. Votruba. 440p. 1988. 141.00 (*0-444-98944-7*) Elsevier.

Analysis of Water Surge. J. Pickford. 214p. 1969. text ed. 169.00 (*0-677-61670-8*) Gordon & Breach.

Analysis of Water Transport in Plants. Ed. by M. Borghetti et al. (Illus.). 300p. (C). 1993. 59.95 (*0-521-44219-2*) Cambridge U Pr.

Analysis of Waters Associated with Alternative Fuel Production - STP 720. Ed. by Jackson & Wright. 205p. 1981. 23.00 (*0-8031-0763-3*, 04-720000-16) ASTM.

Analysis of Weapon System Cost Growth. Jeffrey Drezner et al. LC 93-26135. 1993. write for info. (*0-8330-1432-3*, MR-291-AF) Rand Corp.

Analysis of Wildlife Radio-Tracking Data. Gary C. White & Robert A. Garrott. 383p. 1990. text ed. 49.95 (*0-12-746725-4*) Acad Pr.

Analysis of Wisconsin Income. Frank A. Hanna et al. (Studies in Income & Wealth: No. 9). 284p. 1948. reprint ed. 73.90 (*0-87014-164-3*) Natl Bur Econ Res.

Analysis of Workers Compensation Laws, 1990. Ed. by Carol B. Meyer. 64p. 1990. pap. 25.00 (*0-685-32871-6*) Natl Chamber Foun.

Analysis of Workers' Compensation Laws, 1993, No. 0338. U. S. Chamber of Commerce Staff. Ed. by Noelle C. Fahey. 55p. 1993. 15.00 (*0-89834-127-2*) Chamber Comm US.

Analysis of Workers' Compensation Laws, 1994, No. 0366. U. S. Chamber of Commerce Staff. Ed. by Noelle C. Sotack. 64p. 1994. 15.00 (*0-89834-079-9*) Chamber Comm US.

***Analysis of Worker's Compensation Laws, 1995.** U. S. Chamber of Commerce Staff. 61p. 1995. 25.00 (*0-89834-080-2*) Chamber Comm US.

Analysis of Working Capital Decisions. Daniel E. McCarty & Jerome S. Osteryoung. write for info. (*0-318-57698-8*, Reston) P-H.

Analysis of Zionism. L. Fry. 1982. lib. bdg. 59.00 (*0-87700-416-1*) Revisionist Pr.

Analysis on Lie Groups. Nicholas T. Varopoulos et al. (Tracts in Mathematics Ser.: No. 100). 200p. (C). 1993. 47.95 (*0-521-35382-3*) Cambridge U Pr.

Analysis on Lie Groups & Homogeneous Spaces. Sigurdur Helgason. LC 72-10153. (CBMS Regional Conference Series in Mathematics: No. 14). 64p. 1990. reprint ed. pap. text ed. 22.00 (*0-8218-1664-0*, CBMS-14) Am Math.

Analysis on Manifolds. James R. Munkres. (Illus.). 384p. (C). 1991. 49.95 (*0-201-51035-9*, Adv Bk Prog) Addison-Wesley.

Analysis on Non-Riemannian Symmetric Spaces. M. Flensted-Jensen. LC 85-30694. (CBMS Regional Conference Series in Mathematics: No. 61). 77p. 1986. pap. text ed. 19.00 (*0-8218-0711-0*, CBMS-61) Am Math.

***Analysis on Symmetric Cones.** Jacques Faraut & Adam Koranyi. (Oxford Mathematical Monographs). 400p. 1995. text ed. 79.95 (*0-19-853477-9*) OUP.

Analysis, Part 1: Elements. Krzysztof Maurin. Tr. by Eugene Lepa. LC 74-80525. 672p. 1976. lib. bdg. 117.00 (*90-277-0484-8*) Kluwer Ac.

Analysis, Perception & Processing of Spoken Language. Ed. by K. Hirose. 1993. 157.25 (*0-444-81777-8*, North Holland) Elsevier.

Analysis Philogica Novi Testamenti Graeci: Editio Tertia. Max Zerwick. (Scripta Pontificci Instituti Biblica Ser.: Vol.107). (LAT.). 1966. pap. 20.00 (*88-7653-551-9*) Loyola Univ Pr.

Analysis-Reactions-Morphology. Ed. by H. J. Cantow et al. (Advances in Polymer Science Ser.: Vol. 71). (Illus.). 220p. 1985. 102.00 (*0-387-15482-5*) Spr-Verlag.

Analysis Synthesis & Design Hydraulic Servosystem & Pipelines. T. J. Viersma. (Studies in Mechanical Engineering: Vol. 1). 280p. 1980. 95.00 (*0-444-41869-5*) Elsevier.

Analysis Three: Spaces of Differentiable Functions. Ed. by S. M. Nikol'skij & R. V. Gamkrelidze. Tr. by J. Peetre. (Encyclopaedia of Mathematical Sciences Ser.: Vol. 26). (Illus.). 232p. (RUS.). 1990. 65.00 (*0-387-51866-5*) Spr-Verlag.

***Analysis Through Composition: Principles of the Classical Style.** Nicholas Cook. (Illus.). 200p. 1995. spiral bd. 29.95 (*0-19-879013-9*) OUP.

Analysis to Synthesis: The Development of Complex Verb Morphology in the Dravidian Language. Sanford B. Steever. LC 92-39431. 272p. (C). 1993. 55.00 (*0-19-506446-1*) OUP.

Analysis und Zahlentheorie: Vorlesung Hamburg 1920. Erich Hecke. (Dokumente zur Geschichte der Mathematik Ser.: Vol. 3). xxviii, 234p. (GER.). (C). 1987. 34.00 (*3-528-08997-0*, Pub. by Vieweg & Sohn GW) Ballen Bkslr.

Analysis, Understanding, & Presentation of Cases Involving Traumatic Brain Injury. Ed. by Charles N. Simkins. LC 93-44705. 1994. 200.00 (*0-927093-01-4*) Natl Head Injury.

Analysis Using Glass Electrodes. P. W. Linder et al. 160p. 1984. 65.00 (*0-335-10420-7*, Open Univ Pr) Taylor & Francis.

Analysis with an Introduction to Proof. 2nd ed. Steven R. Lay. 304p. (C). 1990. Casebound. text ed. write for info. (*0-13-033267-4*) P-H.

Analysis with Ion-Selective Electrodes. 2nd ed. Peter L. Bailey. LC 80-49971. (Heyden International Topics in Science Ser.). 263p. reprint ed. pap. 75.00 (*0-8357-5443-X*, 2025976) Bks Demand.

Analysis with Local Census Data: Portraits of Change. Dowell Myers. (Illus.). 369p. 1992. pap. text ed. 44.95 (*0-12-512308-6*) Acad Pr.

Analysis with Standard Contagious Distributions. J. B. Douglas. (Statistical Distributions in Scientific Work Ser.: Vol. 4). 530p. 1980. 35.00 (*0-89974-012-X*) Intl Co-Op.

Analysis with Supercritical Fluids: Extraction & Chromatography. Bernd Wenclawiak. LC 92-18355. (Laboratory Ser.). (Illus.). 250p. 1992. 99.00 (*0-387-55420-3*) Spr-Verlag.

Analysis Within the Systems Development Life-Cycle: Activity Analysis - the Deliverables. Rosemary Rock-Evans. (RRES Ser.: No. 3). (Illus.). 600p. 1987. pap. 59.95 (*0-08-034107-1*, Pergamon Pr) Elsevier.

Analysis Within the Systems Development Life-Cycle: Data Analysis - the Deliverables, Bk. 1. Ed. by Rosemary Rock-Evans. (RRES Ser.: No. 1). (Illus.). 300p. 1987. pap. 59.95 (*0-08-034105-5*, Pergamon Pr) Elsevier.

Analysis Within the Systems Development Life-Cycle: Data Analysis - the Methods. Rosemary Rock-Evans. (RRES Ser.: No. 2). (Illus.). 360p. 1987. pap. 59.95 (*0-08-034106-3*, Pergamon Pr) Elsevier.

Analyst & the Mystic: Psychoanalytic Reflections on Religion & Mysticism. Sudhir Kakar. LC 90-29159. 112p. 1992. 15.95 (*0-226-42283-6*) U Ch Pr.

***Analyst-Patient Interaction: Collected Papers on Technique.** Michael Fordham. Ed. by Sonu Shamdasani. LC 95-8618. Date not set. write for info. (*0-415-12184-1*) Routledge.

***Analysts at Work: Practice, Principles, & Techniques.** Ed. by Joseph Reppen. LC 94-36490. 268p. 1995. pap. text ed. 30.00 (*1-56821-423-5*) Aronson.

Analysts at Work: Practice, Principles & Techniques. Ed. by Joseph Reppen. LC 84-28207. (Advances in Psychoanalysis Ser.). 264p. reprint ed. pap. 75.30 (*0-8357-2739-4*, 2039848) Bks Demand.

Analyst's Guide to TRIM2: The Transfer Income Model, Version 2. Linda Giannarelli. (Illus.). 268p. (Orig.). (C). 1992. pap. text ed. 39.95 (*0-87766-561-3*) Urban Inst.

Analytic Aesthetics. Ed. by Richard Shusterman. 240p. 1989. text ed. 46.95 (*0-631-16253-4*) Blackwell Pubs.

Analytic Ambition: An Introduction to Philosophy. William Charlton. 256p. 1991. pap. text ed. 21.95x (*0-631-16935-0*) Blackwell Pubs.

Analytic & Combinatorial Generalizations of the Rogers-Ramanujan Identities. David M. Bressoud. LC 79-27622. (Memoirs Ser.: Vol. 24/227). 54p. 1980. pap. 16.00 (*0-8218-2227-6*, MEMO 24/227) Am Math.

Analytic & Probabilistic Methods in Number Theory. Ed. by E. Manstavicius & F. Schweiger. (New Trends in Probability & Statistics Ser.: No. 2). 400p. 1992. 225.00 (*90-6764-094-8*) Coronet Bks.

Analytic Approaches to Human Cognition. Ed. by Jesus Alegria et al. LC 92-22089. 1992. write for info. (*0-444-89220-6*, North Holland) Elsevier.

***Analytic Architecture for Joint Staff Decision Support.** Leslie Lewis et al. LC 95-1950. (MR-511-JS Ser.). (Illus.). 68p. 1995. pap. text ed. 13.00 (*0-8330-1623-7*) Rand Corp.

Analytic Arithmetic in Algebraic Number Fields. B. Z. Moroz. (Lecture Notes in Mathematics Ser.: Vol. 1205). vii, 177p. 1986. pap. 31.30 (*0-387-16784-6*) Spr-Verlag.

Analytic Arithmetic of Algebraic Function Fields. Knopfmacher. (Lecture Notes in Pure & Applied Mathematics Ser.: Vol. 50). 144p. 1979. 95.00 (*0-8247-6907-4*) Dekker.

Analytic Art: Nine Studies in Algebra, Geometry, & Trigonometry from the Opus Restitutae Mathematicae Analyseos, Seu, Algebra Nova. Francois Viete. Tr. by T. Richard Witmer. LC 82-21381. 456p. reprint ed. pap. 130.00 (*0-7837-0344-9*, 2040663) Bks Demand.

Analytic Attitude. Roy Schafer. LC 82-16245. 316p. 1983. text ed. 35.00 (*0-465-00268-4*) Basic.

Analytic Chemistry of the Condensed Phosphates. S. Greenfield & S. Clift. LC 74-32261. (C). 1975. 94.00 (*0-08-018174-0*, Pub. by Pergamon Repr UK) Franklin.

Analytic Continuation of Group Representatives. Elias M. Stein. LC 73-151591. (Yale Mathematical Monographs: No. 2). 40p. (C). reprint ed. 25.00 (*0-8357-5444-8*, 2016791) Bks Demand.

Analytic Continuation of the Irreducible Unitary Representations of the Universal Covering Group of SL(2,R) Paul J. Sally, Jr. LC 52-42839. (Memoirs Ser.: No. 1/69). 94p. 1967. pap. 16.00 (*0-8218-1269-6*, MEMO 1/69) Am Math.

Analytic D-Modules & Applications. Jan-Erik Bjork. LC 92-44826. (Mathematics & Its Applications Ser.: Vol. 239). 1993. lib. bdg. 245.00 (*0-7923-2114-6*) Kluwer Ac.

Analytic Dictionary of Chinese & Sino-Japanese. Bernhard Karlgren. 448p. reprint ed. pap. 12.95 (*0-486-26887-X*) Dover.

***Analytic Element Modeling of Groundwater Flow.** H. M. Haitjema. (Illus.). 416p. 1995. boxed write for info. (*0-12-316550-4*) Acad Pr.

***Analytic Encounter.** Jacoby. 1995. pap. 15.00 (*0-919123-14-7*) Atrium Pubs.

Analytic Essays in Folklore. Alan Dundes. (Studies in Folklore: No. 2). 1975. pap. text ed. 41.55 (*90-279-3231-X*) Mouton.

Analytic Function Methods in Probability Theory. Bela Gyires. (Colloquia Mathematics Societatis Janos Bolyoi Ser.: Vol. 21). 379p. 1979. 115.50 (*0-444-85333-2*, North Holland) Elsevier.

Analytic Function Theory, 2 vols., 1. 2nd ed. Einar Hille. LC 73-647. 308p. 1973. 25.00 (*0-8284-0269-8*) Chelsea Pub.

Analytic Function Theory, 2 vols., 2. 2nd ed. Einar Hille. LC 73-647. 308p. 1973. 29.50 (*0-8284-0270-1*) Chelsea Pub.

Analytic Functions. M. A. Evgrafov. (C). 1978. reprint ed. pap. text ed. 7.95 (*0-486-63648-8*) Dover.

Analytic Functions & Classical Orthogonal Polynomials. P. Rusev. 1984. 28.00 (*0-317-52902-1*, Pub. by Collets UK) Pro-Am Music.

Analytic Functions, Blazejewko 1982. Ed. by Julian Lawrynowicz & J. Lodz. (Lecture Notes in Mathematics Ser.: Vol. 1039). 494p. (ENG & FRE.). 1984. pap. 52.60 (*0-387-12712-7*) Spr-Verlag.

Analytic Functions of One Complex Variable. Ed. by C. Chuang & C. Yang. LC 85-23004. (Contemporary Mathematics Ser.: Vol. 48). 254p. 1986. pap. text ed. 35.00 (*0-8218-5050-4*, CONM-48) Am Math.

Analytic Functions Smooth up to the Boundary. N. A. Shirokov. (Lecture Notes in Mathematics Ser.: Vol. 1312). 213p. 1988. pap. 36.20 (*0-387-19255-7*) Spr-Verlag.

Analytic Functions with Mathematical Philosophy. Li-Chung Wang. LC 89-90388. 104p. (Orig.). (C). 1989. pap. text ed. 9.95 (*0-9624242-1-8*) L C Wang Pr.

Analytic Geometry. Joseph H. Kindle. (Orig.). 1950. pap. text ed. 9.95 (*0-07-034575-9*) McGraw.

Analytic Geometry. Peter Selby. LC 84-22542. (College Outline Ser.). 249p. (C). 1986. pap. text ed. 10.50 (*0-15-601525-0*) HB Coll Pubs.

Analytic Geometry. Smith. (One-Unit Series in Precalculus Mathematics). (C). 1991. pap. 13.95 (*0-534-14928-6*) Brooks-Cole.

Analytic Geometry. 5th ed. Gordon Fuller. LC 78-55820. 1979. text ed. write for info. (*0-201-02414-4*) Addison-Wesley.

Analytic Geometry. 5th ed. Douglas F. Riddle. 445p. (C). 1992. text ed. 55.95 (*0-534-17274-1*) PWS Pubs.

Analytic Geometry. 6th ed. George G. Fuller. LC 84-28218. (C). 1986. pap. text ed. 47.95 (*0-201-10861-5*) Addison-Wesley.

Analytic Geometry. 7th ed. Gordon Fuller & Dalton J. Tarwater. (Illus.). 432p. (C). 1992. text ed. 51.75 (*0-201-13484-5*) Addison-Wesley.

Analytic Geometry: School Edition. 7th ed. Gordon Fuller. (Illus.). 432p. (C). 1994. text ed. 51.75 (*0-201-52914-9*) Addison-Wesley.

Analytic Geometry & Calculus. Herbert Federer & Bjarni Jonsson. LC 61-6325. 677p. reprint ed. pap. 180.00 (*0-8357-5445-6*, 2012452) Bks Demand.

Analytic Geometry & Calculus. William R. Longley et al. LC 60-3940. 616p. reprint ed. pap. 175.60 (*0-8357-5446-4*, 2055267) Bks Demand.

Analytic Hierarchy Process. Ed. by B. I. Golden et al. (Illus.). vi, 265p. 1989. 69.00 (*0-387-51440-6*, 3303) Spr-Verlag.

Analytic Juror Rater. Walter F. Abbott. 142p. 1987. 31.00 (*0-8318-0588-9*, B588) Am Law Inst.

Analytic Life: Personal & Professional Aspects of Being a Jungian Analyst. Ed. by New England Society of Jungian Analysts Staff. 78p. 1988. pap. 11.95 (*0-938434-28-4*) Sigo Pr.

Analytic Mapping & Geographic Databases. G. David Garson. (Quantitative Applications in the Social Sciences Ser.: Vol. 87). 96p. (C). 1992. text ed. 9.95 (*0-8039-4752-6*) Sage.

Analytic Methods in Commutative Algebra. Draper. (Lecture Notes in Pure & Applied Mathematics Ser.: Vol. 68). 308p. 1982. 115.00 (*0-8247-1282-X*) Dekker.

Analytic Methods in Mathematical Physics. Robert P. Gilbert & Roger G. Newton. 590p. (C). 1970. text ed. 339.00 (*0-677-13560-2*) Gordon & Breach.

Analytic Methods in the Analysis & Design of Number Theoretic Algorithms. Eric Bach. (ACM Distinguished Dissertation Award Ser.). 50p. 1985. 17.50 (*0-262-02219-2*) MIT Pr.

Analytic Methods of Probability Theory. Ed. by Collet's Holdings, Ltd. Staff. 1985. 125.00 (*0-317-46572-4*, Pub. by Collets UK) Pro-Am Music.

Analytic Movement in Rabbinic Jurisprudence. Norman Solomon. (USF Studies in the History of Judaism). 271p. 1993. 64.95 (*1-55540-764-1*, 240058) Scholars Pr GA.

Analytic Number Theory. Bruce C. Berndt et al. (Progress in Mathematics Ser.: Vol. 85). 558p. 1990. 54.50 (*0-8176-3481-9*) Birkhauser.

Analytic Number Theory. Pure Mathematics Symposium Staff. Ed. by H. G. Diamond. LC 72-10198. (Proceedings of Symposia in Pure Mathematics Ser., Humboldt State University, Arcata, CA, July 29-August 16, 1974: Vol. 24). 344p. 1990. 67.00 (*0-8218-1424-9*, PSPUM-24) Am Math.

Analytic Number Theory: Proceedings of the Japanese-French Symposium Held in Tokyo, Japan, October 10-13, 1988. Ed. by E. Fouvry et al. (Lecture Notes in Mathematics Ser.: Vol. 1434). (Illus.). vi, 218p. 1990. pap. 30.00 (*0-387-52787-7*) Spr-Verlag.

Analytic Number Theory & Diophantine Problems. Ed. by A. Adolphson et al. (Progress in Mathematics Ser.: No. 70). 346p. 1987. 47.50 (*0-8176-3361-8*) Birkhauser.

Analytic Number Theory & Related Topics: Proceedings of the Conference. Kenji Nagasaka. 190p. 1993. text ed. 53.00 (*981-02-1499-5*) World Scientific Pub.

Analytic Number Theory, Mathematical Analysis & Their Applications. N. N. Bogolyubov et al. LC 84-265. (Trudy Steklov Ser.: No.158). 247p. 1984. pap. 101.00 (*0-8218-3077-5*, STEKLO-158) Am Math.

An Asterisk (*) at the beginning of an entry indicates that the title is appearing in BIP for the first time.

An Asterisk (*) at the beginning of an entry indicates that the title is appearing in BIP for the first time.

A

A

Analytical Chemistry Refresher Manual. Kenkel. 1992. 65.00 (0-87371-398-2, QD75) Lewis Pubs.

Analytical Comparison of the Sanskrit, Greek, Latin, & Teutonic Languages. 2nd rev. ed. Franz Bopp & E. F. Koerner. LC 74-84628. (Amsterdam Classics in Linguistics Ser.: No. 3). xxxviii, 68p. 1989. 33.00x (90-272-0874-3) Benjamins North Am.

Analytical Concordance of the Greek New Testament: Grammatical Focus, Vol. 2. Philip S. Clapp et al. LC 91-21204. (Baker's Greek NT Library). 2000p. 1990. text ed. 95.00 (0-8010-2549-4) Baker Bk.

Analytical Concordance of the Greek New Testament, Vol. 1: Lexical Focus. Ed. by Philip S. Clapp et al. LC 91-21204. (Greek New Testament Library). 2000p. 1990. text ed. 95.00 (0-8010-2548-6) Baker Bk.

Analytical Concordance to the Revised Standard Version of the New Testament. Clinton Morrison. LC 77-26210. 800p. 1979. 20.00 (0-664-20773-1, Westminster) Westminster John Knox.

Analytical Contribution Accounting: The Interface of Cost Accounting & Pricing Policy. Walter Georges & Robert W. McGee. LC 86-16973. 266p. 1987. text ed. 65.00 (0-89930-209-2, GSL/, Quorum Bks) Greenwood.

***Analytical Decision-Making.** David Targett. 384p. 1995. pap. 72.50 (0-273-60453-8, Pub. by Pitman Pub Ltd UK) Trans-Atl Phila.

Analytical Description of CHILL, the CCITT High Level Language. P. Branquart et al. (Lecture Notes in Computer Science Ser.: Vol. 128). 277p. 1982. pap. 28.00 (0-387-11196-4) Spr-Verlag.

***Analytical Design Techniques.** T. A. Stolarski. LC 95-6101. (Advances in Industrial Engineering Ser.: No. 21). 1995. write for info. (0-444-89487-X) Elsevier.

Analytical Dictionary of Nahuatl. Frances Karttunen. LC 91-50855. 374p. (C). 1992. reprint ed. pap. 17.95 (0-8061-2421-0) U of Okla Pr.

***Analytical Dynamics: A New Approach.** Firdaus E. Udwadia & Robert E. Kalaba. (Illus.). 275p. (C). 1995. write for info. (0-521-48217-8) Cambridge U Pr.

Analytical Dynamics - Course N. Samuel D. Lindenbaum. 316p. 1994. text ed. 74.00 (981-02-1467-7) World Scientific Pub.

***Analytical Electrochemistry.** Joseph Wang. LC 94-29760. 1994. 59.95 (1-56081-575-2) VCH Pubs.

Analytical Electron Microscopy. (Illus.). 1944. 40.00 (0-685-45467-3) San Francisco Pr.

Analytical Electron Microscopy. (Illus.). 1981. 25.00 (0-685-45466-5) San Francisco Pr.

Analytical Electron Microscopy. (Illus.). 1987. 50.00 (0-685-45468-1) San Francisco Pr.

Analytical Emission Spectroscopy, Pt. 2. Ed. by E. L. Grove. LC 79-134783. (Analytical Spectroscopy Ser.: No. 1). (Illus.). 584p. reprint ed. pap. 166.50 (0-7837-0759-2, 2041073) Bks Demand.

Analytical Emission Spectroscopy: Fundamentals. enl. rev. ed. Jozsef Mika & Tibor Torok. Ed. by P. A. Floyd. Tr. by Laszlo Nemes. LC 74-196239. (Illus.). 533p. reprint ed. pap. 152.00 (0-8357-5455-3, 2025724) Bks Demand.

Analytical Emission Spectroscopy, Part 1. Ed. by E. L. Grove. LC 79-134783. (Analytical Spectroscopy Ser.: Vol.1). 417p. reprint ed. pap. 118.90 (0-8357-5454-5, 2055079) Bks Demand.

Analytical Engine: An Introduction to Computer Science Using HyperCard. Richard Decker & Stuart Hirshfield. 160p. (C). 1990. Incl. 2 disks. pap. 45.95 (0-534-12540-9) PWS Pubs.

Analytical Engine: An Introduction to Computer Science Using HyperCard. 2nd ed. Rick Decker & Stuart Hirschfield. LC 93-25430. 1994. pap. 48.95 (0-534-93696-2) PWS Pubs.

Analytical Engine: An Introduction to Computer Science Using ToolBook. Richard Decker & Stuart Hirshfield. 380p. (C). 1992. pap. 48.95 (0-534-14046-7) PWS Pubs.

Analytical Experimental Physics. 3rd rev. ed. Michael Ference et al. LC 55-5124. (Illus.). 622p. reprint ed. pap. 180.00 (0-8357-8800-8, 2056774) Bks Demand.

Analytical Fleet Maintenance Management. John E. Dolce. 1994. 59.00 (1-56091-379-7, R-126) Soc Auto Engineers.

Analytical Fluid Dynamics. George Emanuel. 1993. 59.95 (0-8493-8687-X, QA911) CRC Pr.

Analytical Foundations of Marxian Economic Theory. John E. Roemer. LC 80-22646. (Illus.). 224p. 1989. pap. 17.95 (0-521-34775-0) Cambridge U Pr.

Analytical Foundations of Physical Statistics. A. I. Khinchin. 64p. 1961. text ed. 62.00 (0-677-20140-0) Gordon & Breach.

***Analytical Fracture Mechanics.** David J. Unger. (Illus.). 340p. 1995. text ed. write for info. (0-12-709120-3) Acad Pr.

Analytical Framework for Accounting Theory. Stanley C. Salvary. LC 88-39870. (McQueen Accounting Monograph Ser.: Vol. 5). xiv, 121p. (Orig.). 1989. pap. text ed. 10.00 (0-935951-04-0) U AR Acc Dept.

Analytical Franco-Jewish Gazetteer, 1939-1945. Soza Szajkowski. 1966. 50.00 (0-87068-112-5) Ktav.

Analytical Gas Chromatography. Walter Jennings. 239p. 1987. text ed. 59.00 (0-12-384355-3) Acad Pr.

Analytical Greek New Testament. Ed. by Timothy Friberg & Barbara Friberg. 1000p. (C). 1981. 34.99 (0-8010-3496-5) Baker Bk.

Analytical Groundwater Modeling: Flow & Contaminant Migration. William C. Walton. (Illus.). 170p. 1988. 99.95 (0-87371-178-5, GB1197) Lewis Pubs.

Analytical Guide & Indexes to The Crisis: 1910-1960, 3 vols. George Washington University, American Studies Program, Rose Bibliography Staff. LC 73-15078. 1975. text ed. 350.00 (0-8371-7175-X, RBCRR, Greenwood Pr) Greenwood.

Analytical Hebrew & Chaldee Lexicon. Benjamin Davidson. 784p. (ENG & HEB.). 1981. 27.95 (0-913573-03-5) Hendrickson MA.

Analytical Hebrew & Chaldee Lexicon. Benjamin Davidson. 896p. (ENG & HEB.). 1993. reprint ed. pap. 24.99 (0-310-39891-6) Zondervan.

Analytical History of World War II, 1. Edward N. Peterson. LC 93-46254. (AUS IX: Vol. 154). 480p. (C). 1995. pap. text ed. 29.95 (0-8204-2395-5) P Lang Pubs.

Analytical History of World War II, 2. Edward N. Peterson. LC 93-46254. (AUS IX: Vol. 155). 400p. (C). 1995. pap. text ed. 29.95 (0-8204-2396-3) P Lang Pubs.

Analytical History of World War II, 2 vols., Set. Edward N. Peterson. LC 93-46254. (AUS IX: Vols. 154 & 155). 880p. (C). 1995. pap. text ed. write for info. (0-8204-2500-1) P Lang Pubs.

Analytical Hypnotherapy: Principles & Practice. E. A. Barnett. 510p. 1989. reprint ed. 37.50 (0-930298-30-6) Westwood Pub Co.

Analytical Index of Presence Africaine (1948-1972) Femi Ojo-Ade. LC 77-71232. (Illus.). 1977. boxed 22.00 (0-914478-92-3) Three Continents.

Analytical Index to American Literature: Vols. I-XXX, Mar. 1929-Jan. 1959, Vols. 1-30, Mar. 1929-Jan. 1959. Thomas F. Marshall. LC 30-20216. ix, 253p. 1963. 31.95 (0-8223-0114-8) Duke.

Analytical Index to Publications of the Texas Folklore Society, Vols. 1-36. James T. Bratcher. LC 72-97597. (Illus.). 348p. 1973. 15.95 (0-87074-135-7) UNTX Pr.

Analytical Index to the Journal International d'Archeologie Numismatique: Numismatic Literature Supplement, No. 1. J. R. Jones. 49p. 1967. pap. 2.50 (0-89722-054-4) Am Numismatic.

Analytical Index to the Laws of Texas, 1823-1905 (Both Dates Inclusive) Cadwell W. Raines. 559p. 1987. reprint ed. lib. bdg. 47.50 (0-8377-2534-8) Rothman.

Analytical Infrared Spectroscopy: Fundamentals, Techniques & Analytical Problem-Solving, Vol. 54. A. Lee Smith. LC 78-27198. (Chemical Analysis: a Series of Monographs on Analytical Chemistry & Its Applications). 322p. 1979. text ed. 130.00 (0-471-04378-8) Wiley.

Analytical Instrument Markets for Biological Testing. (Market Research Reports: No. 380). 171p. 1992. 795.00 (0-317-04975-5) Theta Corp.

Analytical Instrumentation. Bela G. Liptak. LC 93-48731. 496p. 1994. pap. 44.95 (0-8019-8397-5) Chilton.

Analytical Instrumentation: A Laboratory Guide for Chemical Analysis. Galen W. Ewing. LC 66-5557. (Illus.). 171p. reprint ed. pap. 48.80 (0-8357-5456-1, 2019392) Bks Demand.

Analytical Instrumentation for the Water Industry. T. R. Crompton. (Illus.). 264p. 1991. 95.00 (0-7506-1139-1) Buttrwrth-Heinemann.

Analytical Instrumentation Handbook. Ewing. 1088p. 1990. 250.00 (0-8247-8184-8) Dekker.

Analytical Instrumentation Markets: Product Sophistication Meets Tough Environmental Regulations & Biotech Research Demands. Market Intelligence Staff. 255p. (Orig.). 1992. 2,295.00 (1-56753-059-1) Frost & Sullivan.

Analytical Instruments Market. 300p. 1988. pap. 1,295.00 (0-941285-22-7) FIND-SVP.

Analytical Isotachophoresis. Ed. by P. Bocek et al. LC 87-23041. (Electrophoresis Library). 237p. 1988. lib. bdg. 170.00 (0-89573-477-X) VCH Pubs.

Analytical Isotachophoresis. Ed. by F. M. Everaerts et al. (Analytical Chemistry Symposia Ser.: Vol. 6). 234p. 1981. 100.00 (0-444-41957-8) Elsevier.

Analytical Issues in Debt. Ed. by Jacob A. Frenkel et al. v, 415p. 1989. pap. 26.50 (1-55775-041-6) Intl Monetary.

Analytical Key to the Old Testament, 4 vols. John J. Owens. LC 89-437. Set. 189.95 (0-8010-6754-5) Baker Bk.

Analytical Key to the Old Testament, Vol. 1: Genesis-Joshua. Ed. by John J. Owens. LC 89-437. 1032p. 1990. text ed. 49.99 (0-8010-6714-6) Baker Bk.

Analytical Key to the Old Testament, Vol. 2: Judges - 2 Chronicles. John J. Owens. LC 89-437. 960p. 1992. 49.99 (0-8010-6753-7) Baker Bk.

Analytical Key to the Old Testament, Vol. 3: Ezra-Song of Solomon. John J. Owens. LC 89-437. 656p. 1991. text ed. 49.99 (0-8010-6715-4) Baker Bk.

Analytical Key to the Old Testament, Vol. 4: Isaiah-Malachi. John J. Owens. LC 89-437. 960p. 1989. 49.99 (0-8010-6713-8) Baker Bk.

Analytical Kinematics: Analysis & Synthesis of Planar Mechanisms. Roger F. Gans. 256p. 1991. text ed. 49.95 (0-7506-9011-9) Buttrwrth-Heinemann.

Analytical Legislative History of the Medical Device Amendments of 1976: An Amendment to the Federal Food, Drug, & Cosmetic Act. Daniel O'Keefe, Jr. & Robert A. Spiegel. (Food & Drug Law Institute Ser.). 323p. 1976. pap. write for info. (1-885259-03-4) Food & Drug Law.

Analytical Lexicon of Navajo. Robert W. Young et al. LC 91-34431. 1469p. 1988. 55.00x (0-8263-1356-6) U of NM Pr.

Analytical Lexicon to the Greek New Testament. William D. Mounce. 608p. 1993. 34.99 (0-310-54210-3) Zondervan.

Analytical Lexicon to the Septuagint: A Complete Parsing Guide. Bernard A. Taylor. 608p. 1994. 39.99 (0-310-53540-9) Regency Ref Lib.

Analytical Linguistic Concordance to the Book of Isaiah. Yehuda T. Radday. (Computer Bible Ser.: Vol. II). 1975. 20.00 (0-935106-15-4) Biblical Res Assocs.

Analytical Linguistic Key-Word-in-Context Concordance to the Book of Exodus. Yehuda Radday & Yaakov Levi. Ed. by Arthur J. Baird & David Freedman. (Computer Bible Ser.: Vol. 28). (Orig.). 1985. 45.00 (0-935106-23-5) Biblical Res Assocs.

Analytical, Linguistic Key-Word-in-Context Concordance to the Book of Judges. Yehuda T. Radday. (Computer Bible Ser.: Vol. XI). 1977. pap. 20.00 (0-935106-10-3) Biblical Res Assocs.

Analytical Lung Pathology. Klaus Kayser. LC 92-2154. (Illus.). xiii, 404p. 1992. 133.00 (0-387-54263-9) Spr-Verlag.

Analytical Marxism. Thomas F. Mayer. LC 94-4601. (Contemporary Social Theory Ser.). 1994. 48.00 (0-8039-4680-5); pap. 24.95 (0-8039-4681-3) Sage.

Analytical Marxism. Ed. by John E. Roemer. (Studies in Marxism & Social Theory). 280p. 1986. pap. 21.95 (0-521-31731-2) Cambridge U Pr.

***Analytical Mathematics, No. 11.** Anthony Nicolaides. (C). 1990. pap. 39.95x (1-872684-14-9, Pub. by P A S S Pubns UK) St Mut.

Analytical Mechanics. 4th ed. Grant R. Fowles. 320p. (C). 1986. text ed. 60.00 (0-03-004124-4) SCP.

Analytical Mechanics of Gears. LC 63-21681. 546p. 1978. pap. 15.00 (0-317-00956-7) Buckingham Assoc.

Analytical Mechanics of Gears. Earle Buckingham. (Illus.). 546p. 1988. reprint ed. pap. text ed. 14.95 (0-486-65712-4) Dover.

Analytical Metabolic Chemistry of Drugs. Jean L. Hirtz. Ed. by Edward R. Garrett. LC 75-157838. (Medicinal Research Ser.: Vol. 4). 415p. reprint ed. pap. 118.30 (0-8357-5457-X, 2055027) Bks Demand.

Analytical Methods Developed for Application to Lunar Sample Analysis - STP 539. 156p. 1973. 15.00 (0-8031-0791-9, 04-539000-38) ASTM.

Analytical Methods for a Textile Laboratory. 3rd ed. Ed. by J. William Weaver. LC 84-70596. (Illus.). x, 403p. 1984. 56.00 (0-9613350-0-9) AATCC.

Analytical Methods for Electromagnetic Wave Problems. Ed. by Eikichi Yamashita. (Microwave Library). 350p. 1990. 89.00 (0-89006-364-8) Artech Hse.

Analytical Methods for Geochemical Exploration. Jon C. Van Loon & R. R. Barefoot. 366p. 1988. text ed. 79.00 (0-12-714170-7) Acad Pr.

Analytical Methods for Materials Investigation. George A. Kirkendale. (Illus.). 274p. 1971. text ed. 215.00 (0-677-14500-4) Gordon & Breach.

Analytical Methods for Organic Cyano Groups. M. F. Ashworth. 1971. 69.00 (0-08-016191-X, Pub. by Pergamon Repr UK) Franklin.

Analytical Methods for Pesticides & Plant Growth Regulators, Vol. 14. Ed. by Gunter Zweig & Joseph Sherma. 265p. 1986. text ed. 91.00 (0-12-784314-0) Acad Pr.

Analytical Methods for Pesticides & Plant Growth Regulators, Vol. 15. Ed. by Gunter Zweig & Joseph Sherma. 286p. 1986. text ed. 99.00 (0-12-784315-9) Acad Pr.

Analytical Methods for Pesticides & Plant Growth Regulators, Vol. 17. Ed. by Joseph Sherma. 272p. 1989. text ed. 104.00 (0-12-784317-5) Acad Pr.

Analytical Methods for Pesticides & Plant Growth Regulators: Specific Applications, Vol. 16. Ed. by Joseph Sherma. 333p. 1988. text ed. 99.00 (0-12-784316-7) Acad Pr.

Analytical Methods for Pesticides & Plant Growth Regulators: Synthetic Pyrethroids & Other Pesticides, Vol. 13. Ed. by Gunter Zweig & Joseph Sherma. 312p. 1984. text ed. 138.00 (0-12-784313-2) Acad Pr.

Analytical Methods for Pesticides, Plant Growth Regulators & Food Additives, 11 vols., Vols. 1-8, 10-11. Incl. Vol. 1. Principles, Methods & General Applications. Ed. by Gunter Zweig. 1963. text ed. 182.00 (0-12-784301-9); Vol. 2. Insecticides. Ed. by Gunter Zweig. 1964. text ed. 182.00 (0-12-784302-7); Vol. 3. Fungicides, Nematocides & Soil Fumigants, Rodenticides, & Food & Feed Additives. Ed. by Gunter Zweig. 1964. text ed. 121.00 (0-12-784303-5); Vol. 4. Herbicides (Plant Growth Regulators) Ed. by Gunter Zweig. 1964. text ed. 121.00 (0-12-784304-3); Vol. 5. Ed. by Gunter Zweig. 1967. text ed. 182.00 (0-12-784305-1); Vol. 8. Government Regulations, Pheromone Analyses, Additional Pesticides. Ed. by Gunter Zweig & Joseph Sharma. 1976. text ed. 182.00 (0-12-784308-6); Vol. 10. Newer & Updated Methods. Ed. by Gunter Zweig & Joseph Sharma. 1978. text ed. 156.00 (0-12-784310-8); Vol. 11. Ed. by Gunter Zweig. 1980. text ed. 139.00 (0-12-784311-6); write for info. (0-318-50226-7) Acad Pr.

Analytical Methods for Successful Speculation: The Complete Book of Trading Systems. James E. Schildgen. LC 86-71700. (Illus.). 273p. (C). 1986. pap. 49.95 (0-939397-00-5) Capital Futures Assocs.

Analytical Methods in Bin-Load Analysis. A. Drescher. (Developments in Civil Engineering Ser.: No. 36). 256p. 1991. 111.50 (0-444-88368-1) Elsevier.

Analytical Methods in Clinical Chemistry. Ed. by Larry J. Kricka. (Illus.). 96p. 1984. pap. 28.00 (0-08-031453-8, Pergamon Pr) Elsevier.

Analytical Methods in Conduction Heat Transfer. Glen E. Myers. LC 87-8790. (Illus.). 508p. 1987. reprint ed. text ed. 55.00 (0-931690-24-2) Genium Pub.

Analytical Methods in Economics. Akira Takayama. 706p. (C). 1993. text ed. 54.50 (0-472-10162-5); pap. text ed. 24.95 (0-472-08135-7) U of Mich Pr.

Analytical Methods in Geochemical Prospecting. W. K. Fletcher. (Handbook of Exploration Geochemistry Ser.: Vol. 1). 256p. 1981. 89.75 (0-444-41930-6) Elsevier.

Analytical Methods in Human Toxicology, Pt. 1. Ed. & Intro. by A. S. Curry. LC 85-147165. (Illus.). 319p. 1985. 115.00 (0-89573-416-8) VCH Pubs.

Analytical Methods in Human Toxicology, Pt. 2. Ed. by A. S. Curry. LC 85-147165. 354p. 1986. 145.00 (0-89573-417-6) VCH Pubs.

Analytical Methods in Oceanography. Ed. by Thomas R. Gibb, Jr. LC 75-41463. (Advances in Chemistry Ser.: No. 147). 238p. 1975. 43.95 (0-8412-0245-1) Am Chemical.

Analytical Methods in Probability Theory: Proceedings. Ed. by D. Dugue. (Lecture Notes in Mathematics Ser.: Vol. 861). 183p. 1981. pap. 24.00 (0-387-10823-8) Spr-Verlag.

Analytical Methods in Rotor Dynamics. A. D. Dimaragonas et al. (Illus.). 217p. 1983. 79.25 (0-85334-199-0, Pub. by Elsevier Applied Sci UK) Elsevier.

Analytical Methods in Software Engineering Economics. Ed. by Thomas R Gulledge, Jr. & William P Hutzler. LC 92-43808. 1993. 89.00 (0-387-55950-7) Spr-Verlag.

Analytical Methods in the Food Industry: A Collection of the Papers of the Symposium, San Francisco, 1949. American Chemical Society, Analytical Methods in the Food Industry Symposium Staff. LC 50-12845. (American Chemical Society Advances in Chemistry Ser.: No. 3). (Illus.). 77p. reprint ed. pap. 25.00 (0-8357-5458-8, 2011562) Bks Demand.

Analytical Methods in Toxicology. H. M. Stahr. 368p. 1991. text ed. 95.00 (0-471-85136-1) Wiley.

Analytical Methods in Vibrations. Leonard Meirovitch. 576p. (C). 1967. write for info. (0-02-380140-9) Macmillan.

Analytical Microbiology Methods: Gas Chromatography & Mass Spectrometry. Ed. by A. Fox et al. LC 90-34252. (Illus.). 290p. 1990. 79.50 (0-306-43536-5, Plenum Pr) Plenum.

Analytical Modeling & Occupant Protection Technologies. 184p. 1992. pap. 65.00 (1-56091-223-5, SP-906) Soc Auto Engineers.

Analytical Modelling Structural Systems. MacLeod. 1990. pap. write for info. (0-318-68283-4) P-H.

Analytical NMR. L. S. Sternhel. 1989. text ed. 167.00 (0-471-91714-1) Wiley.

Analytical, Numerical, & Computational Methods for Science & Engineering. Gene H. Hostetter et al. 512p. 1990. text ed. 76.00 (0-13-026055-X) P-H.

Analytical Perspectives on Shan Agriculture & Village Economics. Paul Durrenberger & Nicola Tannenbaum. (Monograph Ser.: No. 37). 112p. 1990. 25.00 (0-938692-45-3); pap. 15.00 (0-685-57339-7) Yale U SE Asia.

Analytical Philosophy in Comparative Perspective. Ed. by Bimal K. Matilal & Jaysankar L. Shaw. 1984. lib. bdg. 119.00 (90-277-1870-9) Kluwer Ac.

Analytical Philosophy of Technology. Friedrich Rapp. xiv, 199p. 1981. lib. bdg. 62.00 (90-277-1221-2) Kluwer Ac.

Analytical Photochemistry & Photochemical Analysis: Solids, Solutions, & Polymers. Ed. by J. M. Fitzgerald. LC 78-142894. (Illus.). 376p. reprint ed. pap. 107.20 (0-7837-0950-1, 2041255) Bks Demand.

Analytical Photogrammetry. 2nd ed. Sanjib K. Ghosh. (Illus.). 338p. 1987. 74.00 (0-08-036103-X, Pergamon Pr) Elsevier.

Analytical Planning, Thomas L. Saaty & Kevin P. Kearns. 208p. 1991. pap. write for info. (0-9620317-4-7) RWS Pubns.

***Analytical Polymer Rheology: Structure - Processing - Property Relationships.** Charles L. Rohn. 320p. (C). 1995. text ed. write for info. (1-56990-149-X) Hanser-Gardner.

Analytical Population Dynamics. T. Royama. (Population & Community Biology Ser.: No. 10). 352p. (C). 1992. 79.95 (0-412-24320-2, A6700) Chapman & Hall.

Analytical Profile of the Resin Spot Test Method. Ed. by Vladimir Grdinic et al. 336p. 1989. 220.00 (0-8493-4708-4, QD98, CRC Reprint) Franklin.

Analytical Profiles of Drug Substances, Vol. 10. Ed. by Klaus Florey et al. 1981. text ed. 149.00 (0-12-260810-0) Acad Pr.

Analytical Profiles of Drug Substances, Vol. 11. Ed. by Klaus Florey et al. LC 70-187259. 1982. text ed. 128.00 (0-12-260811-9) Acad Pr.

Analytical Profiles of Drug Substances, Vol. 12. Ed. by Klaus Florey et al. 1983. text ed. 128.00 (0-12-260812-7) Acad Pr.

Analytical Profiles of Drug Substances, Vol. 14. Ed. by Klaus Florey et al. 621p. 1985. text ed. 119.00 (0-12-260814-3) Acad Pr.

Analytical Profiles of Drug Substances, Vol. 15. Ed. by Klaus Florey et al. 796p. 1986. text ed. 125.00 (0-12-260815-1) Acad Pr.

Analytical Profiles of Drug Substances, Vol. 17. Ed. by Klaus Florey et al. 802p. 1988. text ed. 119.00 (0-12-260817-8) Acad Pr.

Analytical Profiles of Drug Substances, Vol. 20. Ed. by Klaus Florey et al. (Illus.). 770p. 1991. text ed. 94.00 (0-12-260820-8) Acad Pr.

Analytical Profiles of Drug Substances & Excipients Vol. 23. Ed. by Harry G. Brittain. (Illus.). 611p. 1994. text ed. 95.00 (0-12-260823-2) Acad Pr.

Analytical Profiles of Drug Substances & Excipients Vol. 23, Vol. 21. Ed. by Harry Brittain. (Illus.). 696p. 1992. text ed. 99.00 (0-12-260821-6) Acad Pr.

Analytical Profiles of Drug Substances & Excipients Vol. 23, Vol. 22. Ed. by Harry Brittain. (Illus.). 691p. 1993. text ed. 99.00 (0-12-260822-4) Acad Pr.

Analytical Properties & Bounds of Scattering Amplitudes. A. Martin & F. Cheung. 142p. 1970. text ed. 152.00 (0-677-02290-5) Gordon & Breach.

Analytical Properties of Automorphic L-Functions. Ed. by Stephen Gelbart & Freydoon Shahidi. 131p. 1988. text ed. 44.00 (0-12-279175-4) Acad Pr.

An Asterisk (*) at the beginning of an entry indicates that the title is appearing in BIP for the first time.

An Asterisk (*) at the beginning of an entry indicates that the title is appearing in BIP for the first time.

293

Analyzing Qualitative Data: Log-Linear Analysis for Behavioral Research. 2nd ed. John J. Kennedy. LC 91-4936. 320p. 1992. text ed. 57.95 (*0-275-93446-2*, C3446, Praeger Pubs) Greenwood.

Analyzing Quantitative Behavioral Observation Data. H. K. Suen & D. Ary. 376p. 1989. 75.00 (*0-89859-945-8*) L Erlbaum Assocs.

Analyzing Ratios: A Perceptive Approach. Jerry A. Viscione. Ed. by James J. Andover. LC 82-19000. 123p. 1983. 16.50 (*0-934914-46-X*) NACM.

Analyzing Real Estate Decisions Using Lotus 1-2-3. Austin J. Jaffe. (C). 1985. disk 135.75 (*0-8359-9193-8*, Reston) P-H.

Analyzing Real Estate Decisions Using Visicalc. Austin J. Jaffe. (C). 1985. pap. text ed. 23.00 (*0-8359-9189-X*, Reston); disk 69.95 (*0-685-09773-0*, Reston) P-H.

Analyzing Real Estate Investment Opportunities. Gaylon E. Greer et al. Ed. by Doris Stokes. (Correspondence Course Ser.). (Illus.). 126p. (C). Date not set. pap. text ed. write for info. (*0-945359-24-1*) Mortgage Bankers.

Analyzing Redistribution Policies: A Study Using Australian Data. Nanak Kakwani. (Illus.). 320p. 1986. 69.95 (*0-521-30838-0*) Cambridge U Pr.

Analyzing Safety Performance. Dan Petersen. LC 83-26610. 328p. 1984. reprint ed. 28.50 (*0-913690-08-2*) Aloray.

Analyzing Sales Promotion. John C. Totten. 1990. pap. 24.95 (*0-913247-06-5*) Commerce Comns.

Analyzing Sales Promotion. 2nd ed. John Totten & Martin Block. 1994. pap. 34.95 (*0-85013-229-0*) Dartnell Corp.

Analyzing Sales Promotion Text & Cases. John C. Totten & Martin P. Block. LC 86-73148. (Illus.). 140p. (Orig.). (C). 1987. pap. text ed. 19.95 (*0-317-60665-4*) Commerce Comns.

Analyzing Sentences: An Introduction to English Syntax. Noel Burton-Roberts. (Learning about Language Ser.). 272p. (C). 1986. pap. text ed. 19.95 (*0-582-29136-4*, 71761) Longman.

Analyzing Shakespeare's Action: Scene Versus Sequence. Charles Hallett & Elaine Hallett. 264p. (C). 1991. 54.95 (*0-521-39203-9*) Cambridge U Pr.

Analyzing Short Stories. 2nd ed. Lostracco & Wilkerson. 208p. (C). 1992. pap. text ed. 11.96 (*0-8403-8012-7*) Kendall-Hunt.

Analyzing Social Behavior: Behavior Analysis & the Social Sciences. Bernard Guerin. (Illus.). 399p. (C). 1994. text ed. 51.95 (*1-878978-14-4*); pap. text ed. 39.95 (*1-878978-13-6*) Context Pr.

Analyzing Social Interaction: Advances in Affect Control Theory. Ed. by Lynn Smith-Lovin & David R. Heise. 192p. 1988. text ed. 46.00 (*0-677-21780-3*) Gordon & Breach.

Analyzing Social Settings: A Guide to Qualitative Observation & Analysis. 2nd ed. John Lofland & Lyn H. Lofland. 186p. (C). 1984. pap. 18.95 (*0-534-02814-4*) Intl Thomson.

***Analyzing Social Settings: A Guide to Qualitative Observation & Analysis.** 3rd ed. John Lofland & Lyn H. Lofland. LC 94-25337. 267p. 1995. pap. 17.95 (*0-534-24780-6*) Intl Thomson.

Analyzing Social Work Practice by Fields. rev. ed. Harriett M. Bartlett. LC 88-29152. 68p. 1988. reprint ed. 8.95 (*0-87101-167-0*) Natl Assn Soc Wkrs.

Analyzing Strategic Nuclear P... Charles Glaser. 1991. pap. 16.95 (*0-691-02312-3*) Princeton U Pr.

Analyzing Strategic Nuclear Policy. Charles L. Glazer. 372p. 1991. text ed. 49.50 (*0-691-07828-9*) Princeton U Pr.

***Analyzing Superfund: Economics, Science, & Law.** Ed. by Richard L. Revesz & Richard B. Stewart. 260p. 1995. text ed. 39.00 (*0-915707-75-6*) Resources Future.

***Analyzing Survival Data from Clinical Trials & Observational Studies.** Ettore Marubini & Marai Grazia. LC 94-30632. (Statistics in Practice Ser.). 1994. text ed. 63.95 (*0-471-93987-0*) Wiley.

Analyzing Syntax & Semantics. Virginia A. Heidinger. LC 84-10296. 248p. (C). 1984. pap. 29.95 (*0-913580-91-0*, Clerc Bks); student ed, pap. 19.95 (*0-913580-92-9*, Clerc Bks) Gallaudet Univ Pr.

Analyzing Tabular Data: Loglinear & Logistic Models for Social Researchers. Nigel Gilbert. (Social Research Today Ser.: No. 1). 224p. 1993. 75.00 (*1-85728-090-3*, Pub. by UCL Pr UK); pap. 25.00 (*1-85728-091-1*, Pub. by UCL Pr UK) Taylor & Francis.

Analyzing Taxes on Business Income with the Marginal Effective Tax Rate Model, No. 79. David Dunn & Anthony Pellechio. 122p. 1990. pap. 7.95 (*0-8213-1521-8*, 11521) World Bank.

Analyzing the Curriculum. George J. Posner. 1992. pap. text ed. write for info. (*0-07-050620-5*) McGraw.

***Analyzing the Curriculum.** 2nd ed. George J. Posner. LC 94-33750. 1995. pap. text ed. write for info. (*0-07-050705-8*) McGraw.

Analyzing the Grammar of English: A Brief Undergraduate Textbook. Richard V. Teschner & Eston Evans. LC 93-13729. 320p. (C). 1993. pap. text ed. 23.95 (*0-87840-242-X*) Georgetown U Pr.

Analyzing the Hazard Evaluation Process. Ed. by K. L. Dickson et al. 159p. 1979. pap. 15.50 (*0-913235-24-5*) Am Fisheries Soc.

Analyzing the Instructional Setting: Environmental Analysis. Martin Tessmer & Duncan Harris. 192p. 1992. 63.00 (*0-7494-0371-3*, Pub. by Kogan Page Educ UK) Taylor & Francis.

Analyzing the Physical Universe. Michael H. Suckley. 1991. spiral bd. 25.00 (*0-88252-140-3*) Paladin Hse.

Analyzing the Presidency. 2nd ed. Robert E. DiClerico. LC 85-71298. (Illus.). 276p. 1990. pap. text ed. 14.95 (*0-87967-815-1*) Dushkin Pub.

Analyzing the Third World: Essays from "Comparative Politics" Ed. by Norman W. Provizer. 510p. 1978. pap. 21.95 (*0-87073-943-3*) Transaction Pubs.

Analyzing the Third World: Essays from Comparative Politics. Ed. by Norman W. Provizer. LC 77-13286. 509p. reprint ed. pap. 145.10 (*0-8357-5430-8*, 2056583) Bks Demand.

Analyzing Total Cost Claims. John A. Smith. Ed. by Anne M. Rankin. (National Contract Management Association Workshop Ser.). 66p. (Orig.). 1993. pap. 10.95 (*0-940343-44-4*) Natl Contract Mgmt.

Analyzing U. S. Relations with South Africa: Past, Present & Future. Y. G-M. Lulat. LC 90-38974. 1024p. (C). 1996. lib. bdg. write for info. (*0-944265-08-1*); pap. text ed. write for info. (*0-944265-07-3*) Librosmondiale.

Analyzing Visual Data. Michael S. Ball & Gregory W. Smith. (Qualitative Research Methods Ser.: Vol. 24). 96p. (C). 1992. text ed. 21.50 (*0-8039-3434-3*); pap. text ed. 9.50 (*0-8039-3435-1*) Sage.

Anamnese en Lichamelijk Onderzoek bij Gezelschapsdieren see Medical History & Physical Examination in Companion Animals

Anamnesis. Eric Voegelin. Ed. & Tr. by Gerhart Niemeyer. LC 89-27990. 239p. (Orig.). (C). 1990. pap. text ed. 14.95 (*0-8262-0737-5*) U of Mo Pr.

Anamorphic Art. Jurgis Baltrusaitis. Tr. by W. J. Strachan. (Illus.). 182p. 1977. 75.00 (*0-85964-029-9*) Chadwyck-Healey.

***Ananak's Berries.** Betty Huffmon & Teri Sloat. LC 94-46640. (Illus.). 1996. write for info. (*0-688-12535-2*); lib. bdg. write for info. (*0-688-12536-0*) Lothrop.

Anancy & Mister Dry-Bone. Fiona French. (Illus.). (J). (ps-3). 1991. 14.95 (*0-316-29298-2*) Little.

Anancy in the Great House: Ways of Reading West Indian Fiction. Joyce Jonas. LC 89-25880. (Contributions in Afro-American & African Studies: No. 136). 168p. 1990. text ed. 49.95 (*0-313-27344-8*, JGH/, Greenwood Pr) Greenwood.

Ananda: Where Yoga Lives. John Ball. LC 82-82100. 240p. 1982. 16.95 (*0-87972-207-X*) Bowling Green Univ.

Ananda: Where Yoga Lives. John Ball. LC 82-82100. (Illus.). 232p. 1982. pap. 8.95 (*0-87972-208-8*, DS1) Crystal Clarity.

Ananda K. Coomaraswamy. P. S. Sastri. Ed. by C. D. Narasimhaiah. (Indian Writers Ser.). 203p. 1975. 8.50 (*0-88253-700-8*) Ind-US Inc.

Ananda Vacanamrtam: The Writings of Shrii Shrii Anandamurti. Incl. Vol. I. 56p. 1978. pap. 1.50 (*0-686-95440-8*); Vol. II. 116p. 1978. pap. 3.00 (*0-686-95441-6*); Set pap. write for info. (*0-318-56741-5*) Ananda Marga.

Anandamath: A Novel. Bankim C. Chatterji. (C). 1991. 14.00 (*81-7094-091-5*, Pub. by Vision) S Asia.

Anandibai & Other Stories. Parashuram. Tr. by Swapna Dutta. (C). 1992. pap. text ed. 6.00 (*81-7201-263-2*, Pub. by National Sahitya Akademi) S Asia.

Ananse & the Stories: West African Story Pak. Ret. by K. Hollenbeck. (Graphic Learning Literature Program Series: Folk Tales). (Illus.). (ENG & SPA.). 1992. 39.00 (*0-87746-261-5*) Graphic Learning.

Anansi. Brian Gleeson. LC 91-40671. (We All Have Tales Ser.). (Illus.). 36p. (J). (gr. k up). 1992. audio 19.95 (*0-88708-231-9*, Rabbit); pap. 14.95 (*0-88708-230-0*, Rabbit) S&S Childrens.

***Anansi & the Moss Covered Rock.** Eric A. Kimmel. (Illus.). (J). (gr. k-3). 1991. audio, pap. 14.95 (*0-87499-170-6*); audio, pap. 22.95 (*0-87499-171-4*) Live Oak Media.

Anansi & the Moss-Covered Rock. Eric A. Kimmel. LC 87-31766. (Illus.). 32p. (J). (ps-3). 1988. reprint ed. lib. bdg. 15.95 (*0-8234-0689-X*); reprint ed. pap. 6.95 (*0-8234-0798-5*) Holiday.

***Anansi & the Moss Covered Rock, 4 bks., Set.** Eric A. Kimmel. (Illus.). (J). (gr. k-3). 1991. audio, pap. 33.95 (*0-87499-172-2*) Live Oak Media.

***Anansi & the Rubber Man.** Kath Lock. 32p. (J). 1995. 12.95 (*1-86374-073-2*, Pub. by ERA Pubns AT) Pubs Dist MI.

Anansi & the Talking Melon. Ret. by Eric A. Kimmel. LC 03-4239. (Illus.). 32p. (J). (ps-3). 1994. lib. bdg. 15.95 (*0-8234-1104-4*) Holiday.

***Anansi & the Talking Melon.** Eric A. Kimmel. (Illus.). (J). (ps-3). 1995. pap. 6.95 (*0-8234-1167-2*) Holiday.

***Anansi & the Talking Melon.** Eric A. Kimmel. (Illus.). (J). (gr. k-3). 1995. audio, pap. 14.95 (*0-87499-339-3*) Live Oak Media.

***Anansi & the Talking Melon.** Eric A. Kimmel. (Illus.). (J). (gr. k-3). 1995. audio 22.95 (*0-87499-340-7*) Live Oak Media.

***Anansi & the Talking Melon, 4 bks., Set.** Eric A. Kimmel. (Illus.). (J). (gr. k-3). 1995. audio, pap. 36.95 (*0-87499-341-5*) Live Oak Media.

Anansi Finds a Fool. Verna Aardema. LC 91-21127. (Illus.). 32p. (J). (ps-3). 1992. 14.99 (*0-8037-1164-6*); lib. bdg. 13.89 (*0-8037-1165-4*) Dial Bks Young.

Anansi Goes Fishing. Illus. by Janet Stevens. LC 91-17813. 32p. (J). (ps-3). 1992. lib. bdg. 15.95 (*0-8234-0918-X*) Holiday.

Anansi Goes Fishing. Illus. by Janet Stevens. (J). (ps-3). 1993. reprint ed. pap. 5.95 (*0-8234-1022-6*) Holiday.

***Anansi Goes Fishing, 4 bks., Set.** Eric A. Kimmel. (Illus.). (J). (gr. k-3). 1993. audio, pap. 33.95 (*0-87499-190-0*) Live Oak Media.

***Anansi the Spider.** Garrett Christopher. Ed. by J. Friedland & R. Kessler. (Novel-Ties Ser.). (J). (gr. k-1). 1994. student ed, pap. text ed. 14.95 (*1-56982-076-7*) Lrn Links.

Anansi the Spider: A Tale from the Ashanti. Illus. & Ret. by Gerald McDermott. LC 76-150028. 48p. (J). (ps-2). 1972. 15.95 (*0-8050-0310-X*, Bks Young Read) H Holt & Co.

Anansi the Spider: A Tale from the Ashanti. Illus. & Ret. by Gerald McDermott. LC 76-150028. 48p. (J). (ps-2). 1987. pap. 5.95 (*0-8050-0311-8*, Bks Young Read) H Holt & Co.

Anansi's Narrow Waist. 2nd ed. Len Cabral. (Let Me Read Ser.). 16p. (J). (ps-2). 1994. text ed. 2.95 (*0-673-36200-0*) GdYrBks.

Anaphilosophia. Martino Oberto. Tr. by Rosa Maria Salamone & Peter Carravetta. LC 78-58984. (Illus.). 1984. pap. 17.95 (*0-915570-10-6*) Oolp Pr.

Anaphora & Definite Descriptions: Two Applications of Game-Theoretical Semantics. Jaakko Hintikka & Jack Kulas. LC 85-10770. 1985. lib. bdg. 89.00 (*90-277-2055-X*) Kluwer Ac.

Anaphora & Quantification in Situation Semantics. Jean M. Gawron & Stanley Peters. LC 90-1583. (CSLI Lecture Notes Ser.: No. 19). 352p. (C). 1990. 37.50 (*0-937073-49-0*); pap. 15.95 (*0-937073-48-2*) Ctr Study Language.

Anaphora in Celtic & Universal Grammar. Randall Hendrick. (C). 1988. lib. bdg. 107.50 (*1-55608-066-2*) Kluwer Ac.

Anaphora in Norwegian & the Theory of Grammar. Lars Hellan. (Studies in Generative Grammar: No. 32). xiv, 310p. 1988. 91.45 (*90-6765-336-5*); pap. 67.70 (*90-6765-335-7*) Mouton.

Anaphoric Relation in Hindi & English. Madhu Gurtu. (C). 1992. text ed. 11.00 (*81-215-0541-0*, Pub. by Munshiram Manoharial II) S Asia.

Anaphoric Relations in English & French: A Discourse Perspective. Francis Cornish. 256p. 1986. 49.95 (*0-7099-3437-8*, Pub. by Croom Helm UK) Routledge Chapman & Hall.

Anaphylactic Reactions in Anesthesia & Intensive Care. 2nd ed. Jerrold H. Levy. 1992. 50.00 (*0-7506-9064-X*) Buttrwrth-Heinemann.

Anaphylactoid Edema. Hans Selye. LC 67-26017. (Illus.). 344p. 1968. 22.50 (*0-87527-071-9*) Green.

Anaplus Bospori. Dionysius Byzantius. Ed. by Rudolf Gungerich. xlvi, 45p. (GER.). 1958. write for info. (*3-296-12400-4*, Pub. by Georg Olms GW) Lubrecht & Cramer.

***Anapolis, MD.** Historical Briefs, Inc. Ed. by Thomas Antonucci & Michael Antonucci. 176p. 1991. pap. 11.95 (*0-89677-009-5*) Hist Briefs.

Anarcadium Pan. Carl Watson. (Illus.). 116p. (Orig.). 1985. pap. 4.95 (*0-942582-08-X*) Erie St Pr.

Anarch Cookbook. (Vampire Ser.). per., pap. 15.00 (*1-56504-048-1*, 2207) White Wolf.

Anarchi. Cesare Lombroso. (History of Political Violence Ser.). (ITA.). 1985. reprint ed. lib. bdg. 35.00 (*0-527-41196-5*) Periodicals Srv.

Anarchiad: A New England Poem 1786-1787. LC 67-18713. 1967. 50.00x (*0-8201-1027-2*) Schol Facsimiles.

Anarchic Harmony. William J. Murray. LC 91-78422. 144p. (Orig.). 1992. pap. 11.95 (*1-55950-082-4*, 94187) Loompanics.

Anarchical Society: A Study of Order in World Politics. Hedley Bull. LC 76-21786. 335p. 1979. pap. text ed. 17.00 (*0-231-04133-0*) Col U Pr.

***Anarchical Society: A Study of Order in World Politics.** 2nd ed. Hedley Bull. 1995. write for info. (*0-231-10296-8*); pap. write for info. (*0-231-10297-6*) Col U Pr.

Anarchism. P. Eltzbacher. 272p. 1970. 22.50 (*0-912378-01-8*) Chips.

Anarchism. Ed. by Robert L. Hoffman. LC 71-105604. (Controversy Ser.). 165p. (C). 1970. text ed. 12.95 (*0-88311-001-6*) Lieber-Atherton.

Anarchism. Joseph A. Labadie. 1976. 250.00 (*0-87700-231-2*) Revisionist Pr.

Anarchism. Richard D. Sonn. LC 92-16954. (Studies in Intellectual & Cultural History: No. 4). 200p. 1992. text ed. 24.95 (*0-8057-8611-2*, Twayne); pap. 12.95 (*0-8057-8636-8*, Twayne) Macmillan.

Anarchism. E. Zenker. 1975. 250.00 (*0-87968-370-8*) Gordon Pr.

Anarchism: Exponents of the Anarchist Philosophy. Paul Eltzbacher. Ed. by James J. Martin. Tr. by Steven T. Byington. LC 72-8550. (Essay Index Reprint Ser.). 1977. reprint ed. 23.95 (*0-8369-7311-9*) Ayer.

Anarchism: From Theory to Practice. Daniel Guerin. Tr. by Mary Klopper. LC 71-105316. 1970. pap. 9.00 (*0-85345-175-3*) Monthly Rev.

Anarchism: Left Right & Green. Ulrike Heider. Tr. by Danny Lewis & Ulrike Bode. LC 94-162. 256p. (Orig.). 1994. pap. 12.95 (*0-87286-289-5*) City Lights.

Anarchism: There's Nothing More Revolutionary Than Marxism-Lenisim, Mao Tsetung Thoughts. Bob Anarchism. 32p. 1982. 2.25 (*0-89851-060-0*) RCP Pubns.

Anarchism see Leadership

Anarchism & Anarchist Communism: Its Basis & Principles. rev. ed. Peter Kropotkin. Ed. by Nicolas Walter. (Anarchist Classics Ser.). 64p. 1987. reprint ed. pap. 4.50 (*0-900348-34-8*) Left Bank.

***Anarchism & Anarchists.** Woodcock. Date not set. per. 14.95 (*1-55082-018-4*, Pub. by Quarry Pr CN) InBook.

Anarchism & Anarcho-Syndicalism. Karl Marx et al. 387p. 1973. 25.00 (*0-8464-0130-4*) Beekman Pubs.

Anarchism & Anarcho-Syndicalism. Karl Marx et al. 414p. 1983. 23.00 (*0-685-17083-7*, Pub. by Collets UK) Pro-Am Music.

Anarchism & Anarcho-Syndicalism. rev. ed. Rudolf Rocker. (Anarchist Classics Ser.). 48p. 1988. reprint ed. pap. 3.50 (*0-900384-45-X*) Left Bank.

***Anarchism & Cultural Politics in Fin de Siecle France.** Richard D. Sonn. LC 88-10622. (Illus.). 375p. 1989. reprint ed. pap. 106.90 (*0-7837-8914-9*, 2049625) Bks Demand.

Anarchism & Environmental Survival. Graham Purchase. 160p. (Orig.). 1994. reprint ed. pap. 9.95 (*0-9613289-8-3*) See Sharp Pr.

Anarchism & Libertarian Socialism in Israel: A Study of Anti-Statist Movements. Joseph E. Cohen. 1979. lib. bdg. 42.95 (*0-686-24784-1*) M Buber Pr.

Anarchism, & Other Essays. Emma Goldman. 1972. 250.00 (*0-87968-621-9*) Gordon Pr.

Anarchism & Other Essays. Emma Goldman. (Illus.). 1970. reprint ed. pap. 4.95 (*0-486-22484-8*) Dover.

Anarchism & Socialism. George Plechanoff. Tr. by Eleanor M. Aveling. LC 79-2921. 148p. 1990. reprint ed. 21.00 (*0-88350-090-6*) Hyperion Conn.

Anarchism & the Mexican Revolution: The Political Trials of Ricardo Flores Magon in the United States. Colin M. MacLachlan. LC 90-42212. 201p. 1991. 38.00 (*0-520-06928-5*); pap. 13.00 (*0-520-07117-4*) U CA Pr.

Anarchism & the Mexican Working Class, 1860-1931. John M. Hart. (Illus.). 259p. 1987. reprint ed. pap. 12.95 (*0-292-70400-3*) U of Tex Pr.

Anarchism in England One Hundred Years Ago. Max Nettlau. 1971. 59.95 (*0-8490-1422-0*) Gordon Pr.

Anarchism in Japan: A Study of the Great Treason Affair, 1910-1911. Ira L. Plotkin. LC 90-24281. (Japanese Studies: Vol. 1). 180p. 1991. lib. bdg. 79.95 (*0-88946-729-3*) E Mellen.

Anarchism in Socialistic Evolution. Peter Kropotkin. 1971. 250.00 (*0-87968-050-4*) Gordon Pr.

Anarchism in the Chinese Revolution. Arif Dirlik. LC 90-21407. 336p. 1991. 40.00 (*0-520-07297-9*); pap. 15.00 (*0-520-08264-8*) U CA Pr.

Anarchisme, Vol. 2. 300p. 1993. lib. bdg. 70.00 (*3-598-11134-7*) K G Saur.

Anarchist AIDS Medical Formulary: A Guide to Guerrilla Immunology. Charles R. Caulfield & Billi Goldberg. LC 93-43598. (Illus.). 155p. (Orig.). (C). 1994. pap. 9.95 (*1-55643-175-9*) North Atlantic.

Anarchist Arsenal: Incendiary & Explosives Techniques. (Illus.). 112p. 1990. pap. 12.00 (*0-87364-580-4*) Paladin Pr.

Anarchist Arsenal for Explosive & Incendiary Techniques, 2 vols. 1992. Set. lib. bdg. 600.95 (*0-8490-8751-1*) Gordon Pr.

Anarchist Book of Bombs & Explosives: A Guide to Homemade Mayhem & Pyrotechnics for the Amateur James Bond. 1989. lib. bdg. 250.00 (*0-8490-3964-9*) Gordon Pr.

Anarchist Cinema. A. Lovell. 1974. 250.00 (*0-87968-189-6*) Gordon Pr.

Anarchist Constitution; or, Let's Get Big Government off Our Backs! D. K. Sturber. (Borgo Political Scenarios Ser.: No. 2). 192p. Date not set. lib. bdg. write for info. (*0-8095-2700-6*); pap. write for info. (*0-8095-3700-1*) Borgo Pr.

Anarchist Cookbook. William Powell. 19.95 (*0-8488-1130-5*) Amereon Ltd.

Anarchist Cookbook. William Powell. LC 71-127797. (Illus.). 160p. 1990. reprint ed. pap. 25.00 (*0-9623032-0-8*) Barricade Bks.

Anarchist Critique of the Politics of AIDS. 1991. lib. bdg. 69.00 (*0-8490-4609-2*) Gordon Pr.

Anarchist Handbook. Robert Wells. Ed. by E. Flores. (Illus.). 72p. 1985. pap. 10.00 (*0-918751-02-0*) J O Flores.

Anarchist Handbook, Vol. 2. Robert Wells. (Illus.). 64p. (Orig.). 1991. pap. 10.00 (*0-918751-18-7*, 18) J O Flores.

Anarchist Handbook, Vol. 3. Robert Wells. (Illus.). 64p. (Orig.). 1991. pap. 10.00 (*0-918751-24-1*) J O Flores.

Anarchist Heart. Bill Tremblay. 1977. 2.50 (*0-912284-87-0*) New Rivers Pr.

Anarchist Passion: Class Conflict in Southern Spain 1810-1965. James Corbin. (Studies in Spanish Anthropology). 224p. 1993. 59.95 (*1-85628-431-X*, Pub. by Avebury Pub UK) Ashgate Pub Co.

Anarchist Perspectives Against Post-Industrial Capitalism. 1991. lib. bdg. 76.95 (*0-8490-4624-6*) Gordon Pr.

Anarchist Portraits. Paul Avrich. (Illus.). 344p. (Orig.). 1990. 49.50 (*0-691-04753-7*); pap. text ed. 14.95 (*0-691-00609-1*) Princeton U Pr.

Anarchist Thinkers & Thought: An Annotated Bibliography. Paul Nursey-Bray et al. LC 91-33407. (Bibliographies & Indexes in Law & Political Science Ser.: No. 17). 320p. 1992. text ed. 59.95 (*0-313-27592-0*, NBR, Greenwood Pr) Greenwood.

Anarchist Voices: An Oral History of Anarchism in America. Paul Avrich. LC 94-16620. 1994. 75.00 (*0-691-03412-5*) Princeton U Pr.

Anarchist Writings of William Godwin. William Godwin. Ed. by Peter Marshall. 182p. (Orig.). 1986. pap. 9.00 (*0-900384-29-8*) Left Bank.

Anarchists. John H. Mackay. LC 77-185840. 1972. reprint ed. lib. bdg. 250.00 (*0-87700-059-X*) Revisionist Pr.

Anarchists: A Biographical Encyclopedia. V. Munoz. Tr. by Scott Johnson. (History of Anarchism Ser.). 1980. lib. bdg. 300.00 (*0-8490-3101-X*) Gordon Pr.

Anarchists in the Spanish Revolution. Jose Peirats. Tr. by Ann Slocombe & Paul Hollow. (Illus.). 388p. (Orig.). (C). 1990. pap. 15.00 (*0-900384-53-0*) Left Bank.

Anarchists of Casas Viejas. Jerome R. Mintz. LC 93-2425. 1994. pap. 14.95 (*0-253-20854-8*) Ind U Pr.

Anarcho-Syndicalism. Rudolf Rocker. 1972. 250.00 (*0-87968-038-5*) Gordon Pr.

Anarcho-Syndicalism. Rudolf Rocker. 93p. (Orig.). (C). 1993. pap. 5.95 (*0-948984-05-8*, Pub. by Phoenix Pr UK) AK Pr Dist.

Anarcho-Syndicalism. Rudolph Rocker. 166p. (C). 1989. pap. text ed. 19.00 (*0-85305-077-5*, Pub. by Pluto Pr UK); pap. text ed. 16.95 (*0-685-68138-6*, Pub. by Pluto Pr UK) Westview.

An Asterisk (*) at the beginning of an entry indicates that the title is appearing in BIP for the first time.

An Asterisk (*) at the beginning of an entry indicates that the title is appearing in BIP for the first time.

295

A

*Anatomy: Embryology, Gross Anatomy, Neuroanatomy, Microanatomy. Ed. & Contrib by Raymond E. Papka. LC 94-45449. (Oklahoma Notes Ser.). 1995. write for info. (0-387-94395-1) Spr-Verlag.

Anatomy: MedCharts. Thomas P. Gest. 1994. 14.95 (1-882531-01-9) ILOC.

Anatomy: Medical Exam Review. 9th ed. Jack Wilson. 1991. pap. text ed. 19.95 (0-8385-0095-1, A0095-8, Medical Exam) Appleton & Lange.

Anatomy: Palpation & Surface Markings. Derek Field. (Illus.). 480p. 1994. pap. 39.95 (0-7506-0062-4) Buttrwrth-Heinemann.

*Anatomy: PreTest Self-Assessment & Review. Ernest April. (PreTest Basic Science Ser.). (Illus.). 240p. 1995. pap. 16.95 (0-07-052090-9) Hlth Prof Div.

*Anatomy: PreTest Self-Assessment & Review. 8th ed. Ed. by Ernest W. April. LC 95-3635. 1995. pap. write for info. (0-07-050520-9) Hlth Prof Div.

Anatomy: PSAAR. 7th ed. Ernest W. April. (Basic Sciences PreTest Ser.). (Illus.). 240p. 1993. pap. text ed. 16.95 (0-07-052002-X) Hlth Prof Div.

Anatomy: Review for New National Boards. Kurt E. Johnson & Frank J. Slaby. LC 92-81332. (Illus.). 217p. 1992. pap. text ed. 25.00 (0-9632873-0-3) J & S Pub VA.

Anatomy & Ballet. 5th ed. Celia Sparger. LC 76-146051. (Illus.). 1970. 22.50 (0-87830-006-6, Theatre Arts Bks) Routledge Chapman & Hall.

Anatomy & Biology of the Human Skeleton. D. Gentry Steele & Claud A. Bramblett. LC 86-14394. (Illus.). 304p. 1988. 29.50 (0-89096-300-2); pap. text ed. 32.50x (0-89096-326-6) Tex A&M Univ Pr.

Anatomy & Consequences of Exchange Control Regimes. Jagdish N. Bhagwati. LC 78-18799. (National Bureau of Economic Research Ser.). 252p. reprint ed. pap. 71.90 (0-8357-5460-X, 2026237); reprint ed. Vol. 11, Foreign Trade Regimes & Economic Development. write for info. (0-318-61243-7) Bks Demand.

Anatomy & Development of Formula Ford Race Cars. Steve Nickless. 1993. pap. 29.95 (0-87938-807-2) Motorbooks Intl.

Anatomy & Development of the Formula One Racing Car from 1975. 3rd ed. Sal Incandela. (Illus.). 336p. 1990. 34.95 (0-85429-714-6, Pub. by G T Foulis Ltd) Haynes Pubns.

*Anatomy & Development of the Grand Prix Motorcycle. Tony Sakkis. (Illus.). 160p. 1995. pap. 21.95 (0-87938-978-8) Motorbooks Intl.

Anatomy & Development of the Indy Race Car. Tony Sakkis. (Illus.). 160p. 1994. pap. 21.95 (0-87938-874-9) Motorbooks Intl.

Anatomy & Development of the Sports Prototype. 3rd ed. Ian Bamsey. (Illus.). 232p. 1991. 32.95 (0-87938-586-3) Motorbooks Intl.

Anatomy & Development of the Stock Car. John Craft. (Anatomy & Development Ser.). (Illus.). 160p. 1993. pap. 21.95 (0-87938-800-5) Motorbooks Intl.

Anatomy & Dissection of the Fetal Pig. 4th ed. Warren F. Walker, Jr. 116p. (C). 1988. 1.25 (0-685-19624-0) W H Freeman.

Anatomy & Dissection of the Fetal Pig. 4th ed. Warren F. Walker, Jr. 116p. (C). 1995. pap. text ed. write for info. (0-7167-1943-6) W H Freeman.

Anatomy & Drawing. Victor Perard. 1989. 5.99 (0-517-68018-1) Random Hse Value.

Anatomy & Function. W. Rall. 1990. 75.00 (0-8176-3502-5) Birkhauser.

Anatomy & Health Sciences: Medical Analysis Index with Research Bibliography. Rocco Z. De Forto. LC 85-47861. 150p. 1988. 39.50 (0-88164-264-9); pap. 34.50 (0-88164-265-7) ABBE Pubs Assn.

Anatomy & Human Movement. Palastanga. (Illus.). 891p. 1989. pap. 60.00 (0-7506-0134-5) Buttrwrth-Heinemann.

*Anatomy & Human Movement: Structure & Function. 2nd ed. Nigel Palastanga et al. LC 94-24695. 1994. write for info. (0-7506-0970-2) Buttrwrth-Heinemann.

Anatomy & Imaging of the Cranial Nerves: Investigative Technique for the Imaging by Magnetic Resonance Imaging (MRI) & Computed Tomography (CT) A. Leblanc. (Illus.). xv, 277p. 1992. 248.00 (0-387-18240-3) Spr-Verlag.

Anatomy & Imaging of the Cranial Nerves see Cranial Nerves: Anatomy, Imaging, Vascularisation

Anatomy & MRI of the Joints: A Multiplanar Atlas. Ed. by William D. Middleton & Thomas L. Lawson. (Illus.). 316p. 1989. text ed. 153.50 (0-88167-455-9) Raven.

Anatomy & Physiology, 4 bks. B. J. Melloni et al. 1971. 100.00 (0-07-076420-4); Bk. 1. text ed. 100.00 (0-07-076421-2); Bk. 2. text ed. 100.00 (0-07-076422-0); Bk. 3. text ed. 100.00 (0-07-076423-9); Bk. 4. text ed. 100.00 (0-07-076424-7) McGraw.

Anatomy & Physiology. Jack Rudman. (College Proficiency Examination Ser.: CPEP-37). 1994. pap. 23.95 (0-8373-5437-4) Nat Learn.

Anatomy & Physiology. Jack Rudman. (ACT Proficiency Examination Program Ser.: PEP-4). 1994. 39.95 (0-8373-5554-0); pap. 23.95 (0-8373-5504-4) Nat Learn.

Anatomy & Physiology. Eva L. Weinreb. 896p. (C). 1982. teacher ed write for info. (0-201-08854-1); text ed. write for info. (0-201-08852-5); trans. write for info. (0-201-08857-6); write for info. (0-201-08856-8) Addison-Wesley.

Anatomy & Physiology, 2 vols. 2nd ed. Edwin B. Steen & Ashley Montagu. 1985. Vol. I- Cells, Tissues, Integument, Skeletal, Muscular & Digestive Systems, Blood, Lymph, Circulator. 8.95 (0-317-57094-3, CO 190) HarpC.

Anatomy & Physiology. 2nd ed. Thibodeau. 1992. 30.00 (0-8016-7691-6) Mosby Yr Bk.

Anatomy & Physiology, No. 2. Seeley & McMinn. 1992. 93.95 (0-8016-7234-1) Mosby Yr Bk.

Anatomy & Physiology, No. 2. Rod R. Seeley et al. 1080p. 1991. 56.95 (0-8016-4832-7) Mosby Yr Bk.

Anatomy & Physiology, No. 2. Gary A. Thibodeau et al. 992p. 1992. 56.95 (0-8016-5005-4) Mosby Yr Bk.

Anatomy & Physiology: A Dynamic Approach. 4th ed. Anthony N. Chee. (Illus.). 344p. 1991. pap. text ed. 33.95x (0-89641-198-2) American Pr.

Anatomy & Physiology: A Laboratory Manual. James E. Crouch & Micheline H. Carr. LC 76-56507. (Illus.). 369p. (C). 1989. reprint ed. 18.00 (0-87484-356-1) Circle Pr CA.

Anatomy & Physiology: A Programmed Approach, 15 bks. Brady, Robert J., & Co. Staff. Incl. Cell. 1972. pap. 6.95 (0-87618-031-4); Cardiovascular System. 1970. pap. 6.95 (0-87618-037-3); Digestive System. 1972. pap. 6.95 (0-87618-040-3); Muscular System. 1972. pap. 6.95 (0-87618-034-9); Respiratory System. 1972. pap. 6.95 (0-87618-039-X); Special Senses. 1972. pap. 6.95 (0-87618-036-5); (Illus.). Set. Set pap. 89.95 (0-87618-635-5) P-H.

Anatomy & Physiology: A Text-Workbook. Stanley E. Gunstream. 560p. (C). 1992. pap. text ed. write for info. (0-697-10052-9) Wm C Brown Pubs.

Anatomy & Physiology: An Easy Learner. Ethel Sloane. LC 93-44843. 544p. 1994. pap. text ed. 25.00 (0-86720-832-5) Jones & Bartlett.

Anatomy & Physiology: Complete Version, Lab Manual. 6th ed. Harold J. Benson et al. 664p. (C). 1994. spiral bd. write for info. (0-697-16016-5) Wm C Brown Pubs.

Anatomy & Physiology No. 2: Clinic. Springhouse Staff. 1991. pap. 14.95 (0-87434-443-3) Springhouse Pub.

Anatomy & Physiology Applied to Obstetrics. 3rd ed. Sylvia Verralls. LC 92-20055. 240p. 1993. pap. 36.00 (0-443-04211-X) Churchill.

Anatomy & Physiology Clinical. Springhouse Staff. 1990. pap. 14.95 (0-87434-351-8) Springhouse Pub.

Anatomy & Physiology Essentials. Seeley. (Illus.). 640p. (C). 1990. 43.95 (0-8016-0227-0) Mosby Yr Bk.

Anatomy & Physiology Essentials Lab Manual. Patton & Seeley. 320p. 1991. spiral bd. 24.95 (0-685-65100-2) Mosby Yr Bk.

Anatomy & Physiology Essentials Study Guide. Kennedy & Seeley. 336p. 1990. pap. 16.95 (0-8016-4419-4) Mosby Yr Bk.

Anatomy & Physiology Lab Manual. 2nd ed. Thibodeau & Patton. 1993. write for info. (0-318-70161-8) Mosby Yr Bk.

Anatomy & Physiology Lab Manual. 4th ed. Gerard J. Tortora. (Illus.). 608p. (C). 1994. pap. write for info. (0-02-421191-5) Macmillan.

Anatomy & Physiology Lab Manual: Pig Version. Donnelly & George A. Wistreich. (C). 1993. 47.00 (0-06-500905-3) HarpCollege.

Anatomy & Physiology Laboratory Manual. rev. ed. Carolyn Robertson et al. 256p. (C). 1994. pap. text ed., spiral bd. 24.95 (0-8403-9466-7) Kendall-Hunt.

Anatomy & Physiology Laboratory Manual. 2nd ed. Carolyn C. Robertson et al. 256p. 1991. spiral bd. 23.95 (0-8403-6755-4) Kendall-Hunt.

Anatomy & Physiology Laboratory Textbook: Intermediate Version (Cat) 3rd ed. Harold J. Benson et al. 528p. (C). 1992. spiral bd. write for info. (0-697-15017-8) Wm C Brown Pubs.

Anatomy & Physiology Laboratory Textbook, Complete Version. 5th ed. Harold J. Benson et al. 640p. (C). 1991. spiral bd. write for info. (0-697-08691-7) Wm C Brown Pubs.

Anatomy & Physiology Laboratory Textbook, Complete Version. 5th ed. Harold J. Benson et al. 640p. (C). 1992. Short Version. spiral bd. write for info. (0-697-08689-5) Wm C Brown Pubs.

Anatomy & Physiology Laboratory Textbook Essentials Version. Stanley E. Gunstream et al. 312p. (C). 1989. spiral bd. write for info. (0-697-03153-5) Wm C Brown Pubs.

*Anatomy & Physiology Laboratory Textbook (Essentials Version) 2nd ed. Stanley E. Gunstream et al. 320p. (C). 1995. spiral bd. write for info. (0-697-11311-6) Wm C Brown Pubs.

*Anatomy & Physiology Laboratory Textbook, Intermediate Version, Cat. 4th ed. Harold J. Benson et al. 552p. (C). 1995. spiral bd. write for info. (0-697-21932-1) Wm C Brown Pubs.

*Anatomy & Physiology Laboratory Textbook, Intermediate Version, Fetal Pig. 3rd ed. Harold Benson et al. 552p. (C). 1995. spiral bd. write for info. (0-697-21930-5) Wm C Brown Pubs.

Anatomy & Physiology Laboratory Textbook, Short Version. 6th ed. Harold J. Benson et al. 512p. (C). 1994. text ed., spiral bd. write for info. (0-697-16014-9) Wm C Brown Pubs.

Anatomy & Physiology Learning System: Textbook. Edith J. Applegate. LC 93-44258. 1994. write for info. (0-7216-6835-6) Saunders.

Anatomy & Physiology Lecture Outline. 2nd ed. William G. Klopfenstein & Betty A. Huffman. 267p. (C). 1986. pap. text ed. 16.95 (0-89917-480-9) Tichenor Pub.

Anatomy & Physiology, No. 2: Lab Manual. Thibodeau & Patton. 1992. pap. 28.95 (0-8016-7268-6) Mosby Yr Bk.

Anatomy & Physiology, No. 2: Pig Supplement. Templin. 1992. 6.95 (0-8016-7294-5) Mosby Yr Bk.

Anatomy & Physiology, No. 2: Study Guide. Thibodeau & Patton. 1992. 18.95 (0-8016-7269-4) Mosby Yr Bk.

Anatomy & Physiology Notebook. Eugene P. Rutheny. 272p. (C). 1993. spiral bd. write for info. (0-697-20349-2) Wm C Brown Pubs.

Anatomy & Physiology of Capillaries. August Krogh. 1929. 100.00 (0-685-89734-6) Elliots Bks.

Anatomy & Physiology of Diseased Plants. Ed. by Sutic. 1990. 167.00 (0-8493-4806-4, SB381) CRC Pr.

Anatomy & Physiology of Farm Animals. Banks. 1994. 32.50 (0-8016-6395-4) Mosby Yr Bk.

Anatomy & Physiology of Farm Animals. 5th ed. R. D. Frandson & T. L. Spurgeon. (Illus.). 572p. 1992. text ed. 49.50 (0-8121-1435-3) Williams & Wilkins.

Anatomy & Physiology of Speech: Laboratory Textbook. Harold M. Kaplan. LC 80-82927. (Illus.). 180p. 1981. text ed. 42.95 (0-932126-04-9); pap. text ed. 37.95 (0-932126-05-7) Graceway.

*Anatomy & Physiology of the Mammalian Larynx. D. F. Harrison. (Illus.). 325p. (C). Date not set. write for info. (0-521-45321-6) Cambridge U Pr.

Anatomy & Physiology of the Peripheral Hearing Mechanism. J. Donald Harris. LC 73-12474. (Studies in Communicative Disorders). (C). 1974. pap. text ed. write for info. (0-672-61304-2, Bobbs) Macmillan.

Anatomy & Physiology of the Speech Mechanism. Joel C. Kahane. Ed. by Harvey Halpern. LC 86-17004. (Studies in Communicative Disorders). 136p. (Orig.). 1986. pap. text ed. 9.00 (0-89079-086-8, 1375) PRO-ED.

Anatomy & Physiology of the Speech Mechanism. Boyd Sheets. LC 72-81499. (Studies in Communicative Disorders). (C). 1973. pap. text ed. write for info. (0-672-61275-5, Bobbs) Macmillan.

Anatomy & Physiology Quiz Art. Thibodeau & Patton. 1993. 12.95 (0-8016-7531-6) Mosby Yr Bk.

Anatomy & Physiology Study Guide: Biology 233. Edwin J. Krol. 260p. 1992. spiral bd. 23.95 (0-8403-8106-9) Kendall-Hunt.

Anatomy & Physiology Study Guide - Biology 234. Edwin J. Krol. 220p. 1993. spiral bd. 17.95 (0-8403-8336-3) Kendall-Hunt.

Anatomy & Physiology Text Plus. 2nd ed. Thibodeau & Patton. 1993. 63.95 (0-8016-7709-2) Mosby Yr Bk.

Anatomy & Physiology Text Plus. 2nd ed. Thibodeau & Patton. 1993. 72.95 (0-8016-7710-6) Mosby Yr Bk.

Anatomy & Physiology with Catalog: Lab Manual. 3rd ed. Donnelly. (C). 1990. pap. text ed. 27.25 (0-06-041708-0) HarpCollege.

*Anatomy & Physiology 120 & 121. Wayne Seifert. 130p. (C). 1994. 12.10 (1-56870-158-6) RonJon Pub.

Anatomy & Positioning, Nos. 1-18. 2nd ed. Bontrager. 1995. student ed write for info. (0-8016-6283-4) Mosby Yr Bk.

Anatomy & Positioning, Nos. 19-25. 2nd ed. Bontrager. 1995. student ed write for info. (0-8016-6282-6) Mosby Yr Bk.

Anatomy & Surgery of the Cavernous Sinus. V. V. Dolenc. (Illus.). 360p. 1989. 200.00 (0-387-82155-4, 3503) Spr-Verlag.

Anatomy & Systematics of Bagridae (Teleostei), & Siluroid Phylogeny. Tianpei Mo. Ed. by Ronald Fricke. (Theses Zoologicae Ser.: Vol. 17). (Illus.). vii, 216p. 1991. 135.00 (1-878762-27-3) Koeltz Sci Bks.

Anatomy As a Basis for Clinical Medicine. 2nd enl. rev. ed. E. C. Hall-Craggs. (Illus.). 616p. 1990. text ed. 48.00 (0-683-03831-1) Williams & Wilkins.

Anatomy Charts for Reflexology. Sandra B. Rogers. Ed. by Christine Issel. (Illus.). 21p. 1994. student ed write for info. (0-9638862-0-7) B J Scott.

Anatomy Charts for Reflexology: Student Edition. Sandra B. Rogers. Ed. by Christine Issel. (Illus.). 55p. 1994. write for info. (0-9638862-1-5) B J Scott.

Anatomy Charts for Reflexology: Teacher's Edition. Sandra B. Rogers. Ed. by Christine Issel. (Illus.). 56p. 1994. write for info. (0-9638862-2-3) B J Scott.

Anatomy Coloring Book. Wynn Kapit & Lawrence M. Elson. (C). 1977. pap. 13.95 (0-06-453914-8) HarpCollege.

Anatomy Coloring Book. 2nd ed. Wynn Kapit & Lawrence M. Elson. (Illus.). 352p. (C). 1993. reprint ed. pap. 16.00 (0-06-455016-8, Harper Ref) HarpC.

Anatomy for Anaesthetists. 6th ed. H. Ellis & S. Feldman. (Illus.). 368p. 1993. 99.95 (0-632-03304-5) Blackwell Sci.

Anatomy for Artists. Reginald Marsh. LC 75-129078. (Illus.). 1970. reprint ed. pap. 7.95 (0-486-22613-1) Dover.

Anatomy for Dental Students. 2nd ed. D. R. Johnson & W. J. Moore. (Illus.). xviii, 262p. 1990. 110.00 (0-19-261846-6); pap. 50.00 (0-19-261845-8) OUP.

Anatomy for Speech & Hearing. 4th ed. John M. Palmer. (Illus.). 304p. 1993. pap. 29.00 (0-683-06737-0) Williams & Wilkins.

Anatomy for Surgeons, Vol. 1: The Head & Neck. 3rd ed. W. Henry Hollinshead. (Illus.). 624p. 1982. text ed. 98.00 (0-06-141264-3, 14-12642, Harper Medical) Lippincott.

Anatomy for the Artist. Jeno Barcsay. LC 73-1885. (Illus.). 320p. 1973. reprint ed. 19.95 (0-8148-0010-6) L Amiel Pub.

Anatomy for the Medical Record Librarian. Thompson & Hayden. 1969. 12.75 (0-917036-09-3) Physicians Rec.

*Anatomy for Trial Lawyers. Mikel A. Rothenberg. LC 94-40261. (Personal Injury Library). 1995. text ed. 105.00 (0-471-09056-5) Wiley.

Anatomy in Diagnostic Imaging. Fleckenstein & Jensen. 350p. 1993. 65.00 (87-16-10907-4) Mosby Yr Bk.

Anatomy in Surgery. 3rd ed. P. Thorek. (Illus.). 900p. 1985. 264.00 (0-387-90978-8) Spr-Verlag.

Anatomy Lesson. Marshall Goldberg. 1976. 20.95 (0-8488-0802-9) Amereon Ltd.

Anatomy Lesson. deluxe limited ed. Philip Roth. LC 83-11645. 291p. 1983. boxed 60.00 (0-374-10492-1) FS&G.

Anatomy Lesson. Marshall Goldberg. 3rd ed. 352p. 1985. reprint ed. pap. 3.95 (0-8439-2344-X) Dorchester Pub Co.

Anatomy Lesson, & Other Stories. Evan S. Connell. LC 79-38719. (Short Story Index Reprint Ser.). 1977. reprint ed. 18.95 (0-8369-4132-2) Ayer.

Anatomy Lessons from the Great Masters. Robert B. Hale & Terence Coyle. (Illus.). 272p. 1977. 27.95 (0-8230-0222-5, Watsn-Guptill) Watsn-Guptill.

Anatomy, Mechanics & Human Motion. 2nd ed. James G. Hay & J. Gavin Reid. (Illus.). 496p. (C). 1988. text ed. 55.33 (0-13-035213-6) P-H.

Anatomy of a Business Plan. Linda Pinson & Jerry Jinnet. 176p. 1993. pap. 17.95 (0-7931-0618-4, 561408, Enter-Dearbrn) Dearborn Finan.

Anatomy of a Business Strategy: Bell, Western Electric, & the Origins of the American Telephone Industry. George D. Smith. LC 84-23419. (AT&T Series in Telephone History). (Illus.). 264p. 1985. 38.50x (0-8018-2710-8) Johns Hopkins.

Anatomy of a Chaotic Inquiry: SKEETS & Other Thought Experiments by Artemis Smith, a Course Outline in Epistemological Aesthetics. Artemis Smith, pseud. (Unification of Science Ser.). (Illus.). (C). 1997. cd-rom 25.00 (1-878998-17-X) Savant Garde.

Anatomy of a Church: Greek Orthodoxy Today. Mario Rinvolucri. LC 66-30071. 192p. reprint ed. pap. 54.80 (0-7837-0468-2, 2040791) Bks Demand.

Anatomy of a Competition: Urban Design for Milwaukee's Lakefront. Lawrence P. Witzling & W. Paul Farmer. (Publications in Architecture & Urban Planning: No. R82-5). (Illus.). 40p. 1985. reprint ed. 2.00 (0-938744-23-2) U of Wis Ctr Arch-Urban.

Anatomy of a Confrontation: Ayodha & the Rise of Communal Politics in India. Ed. by Sarvepalli Gopal. 240p. 1993. pap. 15.95 (1-85649-050-5, Pub. by Zed Books UK) Humanities.

Anatomy of a Confrontation: Ayodha & the Rise of Communal Politics in India. Ed. by Sarvepalli Gopal. 240p. (C). 1993. text ed. 49.95 (1-85649-049-1, Pub. by Zed Books UK) Humanities.

Anatomy of a Constitutional Law Case. Alan Westin. 1990. text ed. 37.00 (0-231-07334-8); pap. text ed. 15.00 (0-231-07335-6) Col U Pr.

Anatomy of a Controversy: The Debate over "Essays & Reviews" Josef L. Altholz. 208p. 1994. 59.95 (1-85928-040-4, Pub. by Scolar Pr UK) Ashgate Pub Co.

Anatomy of a Controversy: The Question of a "Language" among Bees. Adrian Wenner & Patrick Wells. 1990. text ed. 55.00 (0-231-06552-3) Col U Pr.

Anatomy of a Crash: Nineteen Twenty-Nine. Comp. by J. R. Levien. (Illus.). 1989. reprint ed. 11.00 (0-87034-037-9) Fraser Pub Co.

Anatomy of a Crusade, 1213-1221. James M. Powell. LC 86-11403. (Middle Ages Ser.). (Illus.). 310p. (C). 1986. pap. text ed. 17.95 (0-8122-1323-8) U of Pa Pr.

*Anatomy of a Dictatorship: Inside the GDR. Mary Fulbrook. (Illus.). 280p. 1995. 29.95 (0-19-820312-8) OUP.

*Anatomy of a Diet: How to Evaluate Weight-Loss Plans. L. G. Foster. LC 95-76367. (Illus.). 120p. (Orig.). 1995. pap. 8.95 (0-942691-04-0) Beta Bks.

Anatomy of a Food Addiction: The Brain Chemistry of Overeating. Anne Katherine. 243p. (Orig.). 1991. pap. 9.95 (0-942421-32-9) Hazelden.

Anatomy of a Fraud: Inside the Finance of the PTL Ministries. Gary Tidwell & James McKee. 1993. text ed. 24.95 (0-471-57110-5) Wiley.

Anatomy of a Game: Football, the Rules, & the Men Who Made the Game. David M. Nelson. LC 91-51009. 1994. Alk. paper. 25.00 (0-87413-455-2) U Delaware Pr.

Anatomy of a Golf Course. Tom Doak. 228p. 1992. 22.95 (1-55821-146-2) Lyons & Burford.

Anatomy of a Great Executive. John Wareham. LC 91-58532. (Illus.). 272p. 1992. reprint ed. pap. 11.00 (0-06-098300-0, PL) HarpC.

Anatomy of a Guitar Player. Tommy Tedesco. 1993. 15.00 (1-56222-352-6, 94199); audio 9.98 (1-56222-639-8, 94199) Mel Bay.

Anatomy of a Hospital. Julian Ashley. (Illus.). 176p. 1988. 24.95 (0-19-261578-5) OUP.

Anatomy of a House: A Picture Dictionary of Architectural & Design Elements. Fayal Greene. 1991. 9.95 (0-385-41242-8) Doubleday.

Anatomy of a Jury: The System on Trial. Seymour Wishman. LC 86-25327. 336p. 1987. pap. 10.95 (0-14-009851-8, Penguin Bks) Viking Penguin.

*Anatomy of a Little War: A Diplomatic & Military History of the Gundovald Affair (568-586) Bernard S. Bachrach. LC 94-23140. 276p. 1995. text ed. 49.85 (0-8133-1492-5) Westview.

Anatomy of a Lynching: The Killing of Claude Neal. James R. McGovern. LC 81-17140. (Illus.). 170p. (C). 1992. pap. 9.95 (0-8071-1766-8) La State U Pr.

Anatomy of a Male Slut: PO Box 61564. Bill Shields. (Illus.). 16p. (Orig.). (YA). (gr. 10 up). 1988. pap. 2.00 (0-929611-02-0) Plutonium Pr.

Anatomy of a Massacre. Elinor Karpf & Jason Karpf. (Illus.). 240p. 1994. 19.95 (1-56796-040-5) WRS Group.

Anatomy of a Merger: Strategies & Techniques for Negotiating Corporate Acquisitions. James C. Freund. 559p. 1975. 80.00 (0-317-01346-7, 00526) NY Law Pub.

Anatomy of a Merger: The Causes & Effects of Mergers & Acquisitions. Alexandra Post. LC 93-16695. 1993. text ed. 62.00 (0-13-179243-1); pap. text ed. 34.00 (0-13-179235-0) P-H Gen Ref & Trav.

Anatomy of a Mortgage Loan Department. 68p. 1988. 12.50 (0-685-69763-0) Sav & Comm Bank.

Anatomy of a Murder. Robert Traver. 21.95 (0-8488-1491-6) Amereon Ltd.

Anatomy of a Murder. Robert Traver. 448p. 1983. pap. 9.95 (0-312-03356-7) St Martin.

Anatomy of a Murder. Robert Traver. 1988. mass mkt. 4.95 (0-312-91278-1) St Martin.

Anatomy of a Murder. Robert Traver. 300p. 1991. reprint ed. lib. bdg. 22.95 (0-89966-859-3) Buccaneer Bks.

An Asterisk (*) at the beginning of an entry indicates that the title is appearing in BIP for the first time.

An Asterisk (*) at the beginning of an entry indicates that the title is appearing in BIP for the first time.

***Anatomy of Public Policy Implementation: The Case of Decentralization Policies in Ghana.** Joseph R. Ayee. (Making of Modern Africa Ser.). 256p. 1994. 63.95 (*1-85628-957-5*, Pub. by Avebury Pub UK) Ashgate Pub Co.

Anatomy of Puck: An Examination of Fairy Beliefs among Shakespeare's Contemporaries & Successors. Katherine M. Briggs. Ed. by Richard M. Dorson. LC 77-70581. (International Folklore Ser.). 1977. reprint ed. lib. bdg. 24.95 (*0-405-10082-5*) Ayer.

Anatomy of Racism. Ed. by David Goldberg. (Illus.). 384p. (Orig.). (C). 1990. pap. text ed. 16.95x (*0-8166-1804-6*) U of Minn Pr.

Anatomy of Reality: Merging of Intuition & Reason. Jonas Salk. LC 82-17828. (Convergence Ser.). 168p. 1983. text ed. 34.00 (*0-231-05328-2*) Col U Pr.

Anatomy of Religious Philosophy: Comparative Answers to Life's Most Perplexing Questions. Ronald Spatz. LC 93-31509. 172p. (Orig.). 1994. pap. 14.95 (*1-56825-013-4*) Rainbow Books.

Anatomy of Revolution. Crane Brinton. 19.50 (*0-8446-1740-7*) Peter Smith.

Anatomy of Revolution. rev. ed. Crane Brinton. 1965. pap. 8.00 (*0-394-70044-9*, V44, Vin) Random.

Anatomy of Riding. Heinrich Schusdziarra & Volker Schusdziarra. Tr. by Sandra L. Newkirk. LC 85-62431. Orig. Title: Gymnasium des Reiters. (Illus.). 128p. 1985. 19.95 (*0-914327-08-9*) Breakthrgh NY.

Anatomy of Risk. rev. ed. William D. Rowe. LC 84-14431. 504p. (C). 1988. reprint ed. lib. bdg. 54.50 (*0-89874-784-8*) Krieger.

Anatomy of Rural Poverty in Assam. A. Ahmed. (C). 1987. 32.00 (*0-317-66956-7*, Pub. by Mittal II) S Asia.

Anatomy of Science. Gilbert N. Lewis. LC 75-156680. (Essay Index Reprint Ser.). 1977. reprint ed. 20.95 (*0-8369-2408-8*) Ayer.

***Anatomy of Secret Sins.** rev. ed. Obadiah Sedgwick. Ed. by Don Kistler. 396p. 1995. 24.95 (*1-877611-78-6*) Soli Deo Gloria.

Anatomy of Seed Plants. 2nd ed. Katherine Esau. LC 76-41191. 550p. 1977. Net. text ed. write for info. (*0-471-24520-8*) Wiley.

Anatomy of Seismograms. O. Kulhanek. (Developments in Solid Earth Geophysics Ser.: No. 18). 188p. 1990. 87.25 (*0-444-88375-4*) Elsevier.

Anatomy of Self: The Individual vs. Society. Takeo Doi. LC 88-80300. 168p. 1988. pap. 9.00 (*0-87011-902-8*) Kodansha.

Anatomy of Skiing. rev. ed. R. J. Sanders. LC 79-11421. (Illus.). 1979. pap. 11.00 (*0-394-72975-7*, Vin) Random.

Anatomy of Solitude: Towards a New Interpretation of the Sources of Creative Inspiration. Agnes E. Mackay. 235p. 1982. 35.00 (*0-85335-229-1*, Pub. by Stuart Titles Ltd UK) St Mut.

Anatomy of South African Misery. Cornelius W. De Kiewiet. LC 83-5635. (Whidden Lectures Ser., 1956). viii, 88p. (C). 1983. reprint ed. text ed. 49.75 (*0-313-23960-6*, DEAN, Greenwood Pr) Greenwood.

Anatomy of Speech Notions. R. E. Longacre. v, 394p. (Orig.). (C). 1986. pap. text ed. 82.00 (*3-11-013322-9*) Mouton.

Anatomy of Spirituality, 10 vols. Barbara M. Muhl. Set. pap. write for info. (*1-880863-00-6*) Christus Pub.

Anatomy of Supervision: Developing Learning & Professional Competence for Social Work Students. Derek Gardiner. 192p. 1989. 95.00 (*0-335-09573-9*, Open Univ Pr); pap. 39.00 (*0-335-09572-0*, Open Univ Pr) Taylor & Francis.

Anatomy of Teacher Institutes: A Design for Professional Development. James M. Banner. 30p. (C). 1985. pap. 4.95 (*0-931989-25-6*) Coun Basic Educ.

Anatomy of Telecommunications. rev. ed. Tom Smith. LC 73-85629. (Specialized Ser.). (Illus.). 164p. (C). 1987. pap. text ed. 23.95 (*1-56016-022-5*) ABC TeleTraining.

Anatomy of Terror. Nikita S. Khrushchev. LC 78-23884. 73p. 1979. reprint ed. text ed. 35.00 (*0-313-21218-X*, KHAT, Greenwood Pr) Greenwood.

Anatomy of Terrorism. David E. Long. 1990. text ed. 27.95 (*0-02-919345-1*) Free Pr.

Anatomy of Thatcherism. Shirley R. Letwin. 377p. (C). 1993. text ed. 32.95 (*1-56000-106-2*) Transaction Pubs.

Anatomy of the Abuses in England. Philip Stubbs. Ed. by F. J. Furnival. (New Shakespeare Society, London, Ser.: 6, Nos. 5 & 8). 1972. reprint ed. pap. 90.00 (*0-8115-0245-7*) Periodicals Srv.

Anatomy of the Amazon Gold Rush. David Cleary. LC 89-50857. (Illus.). 287p. (Orig.). 1990. pap. 18.95 (*0-87745-262-8*) U of Iowa Pr.

Anatomy of the Auschwitz Death Camp. Ed. by Yisrael Gutman et al. LC 93-45729. (Illus.). 528p. 1994. 39.95 (*0-253-32684-2*) Ind U Pr.

Anatomy of the Body of God: Being the Supreme Revelation of Cosmic Consciousness. Frater Achad. 120p. 1992. pap. 17.95 (*1-56459-140-9*) Kessinger Pub.

Anatomy of the Car. Jeff Daniels. write for info. (*0-318-59660-1*) S&S Trade.

Anatomy of the Chordates. 4th ed. Charles K. Weichert. LC 70-121668. (C). 1970. text ed. write for info. (*0-07-069007-3*) McGraw.

***Anatomy of the Commercial Motor Vehicle.** Les Geary. LC 94-22817. 1995. write for info. (*0-88734-912-9*) Players Pr.

Anatomy of the Common Lemon Butterfly, Papilio Demoleus Demoleus. Shobha Goyle. (Illus.). 150p. 1990. 125.00 (*1-55528-189-3*, Messers Today & Tomorrow) Scholarly Pubns.

Anatomy of the Common Marmoset. J. Beattie. LC 78-72711. reprint ed. 27.50 (*0-404-18281-X*) AMS Pr.

Anatomy of the Confederate Congress: A Study of the Influences of Member Characteristics on Legislative Voting Behavior, 1861-1865. Thomas B. Alexander & Richard E. Beringer. LC 76-138985. 447p. reprint ed. pap. 127.40 (*0-8357-3199-5*, 2039470) Bks Demand.

Anatomy of the Cortex: Statistics & Geometry. V. Braitenberg & A. Schuz. Ed. by H. B. Barlow et al. (Studies of Brain Function: Vol. 18). (Illus.). ix, 249p. 1991. pap. 39.00 (*0-387-53233-1*) Spr-Verlag.

Anatomy of the Dicotyledons, Vol. I: Systematic Anatomy of the Leaf & Stem, with a Brief History of the Subject. 2nd ed. Ed. by C. R. Metcalfe & L. Chalk. (Illus.). 304p. 1988. reprint ed. pap. 49.95 (*0-19-854253-4*) OUP.

Anatomy of the Dicotyledons, Vol. II: Wood Structure & Conclusion of the General Introduction. 2nd ed. Ed. by C. R. Metcalfe & L. Chalk. (Illus.). 324p. 1989. reprint ed. pap. 55.00 (*0-19-854594-0*) OUP.

Anatomy of the Dicotyledons, Vol. III: Magnoliales, Illiciales, & Laurales, Sensu Armen Takhtainan. 2nd ed. C. R. Metcalfe. (Illus.). 240p. 1987. 85.00 (*0-19-854593-2*) OUP.

Anatomy of the Domestic Birds. R. Nickel et al. 1977. 71.00 (*0-387-91134-0*) Spr-Verlag.

Anatomy of the Dromedary. Malie M. Smuts & R. J. Bezuidenhout. (Illus.). 244p. 1987. 175.00 (*0-19-857188-7*) OUP.

Anatomy of the Economic Crisis. Sam Marcy. 120p. 1982. pap. 3.25 (*0-89567-077-1*) World View Forum.

Anatomy of the Film: An Illustrated Guide to Film Appreciation. H. H. Wollenberg. LC 71-169355. (Arno Press Cinema Program Ser.). (Illus.). 108p. 1977. reprint ed. 15.95 (*0-405-03926-3*) Ayer.

Anatomy of the Foot & Ankle: Descriptive, Topographic, Functional. 2nd ed. Sarrafian. (Illus.). 1993. text ed. 160.00 (*0-397-51042-X*) Lippincott.

Anatomy of the Fourth Gospel: A Study in Literary Design. R. Alan Culpepper. LC 82-16302. 256p. 1987. text ed. 17.00 (*0-8006-2068-2*, 1-2068, Fortress Pr) Augsburg Fortress.

Anatomy of the Frog. Ecker. Tr. by G. Haslam. 1971. 67.50 (*90-6123-240-6*) Lubrecht & Cramer.

Anatomy of the Guinea Pig. Gale Cooper & Alan L. Schiller. LC 74-81866. (Commonwealth Fund Publications). (Illus.). 392p. 1975. 59.00 (*0-674-03159-8*) HUP.

Anatomy of the Head, Neck, Face & Jaws. Lawrence A. Fried. LC 80-16800. (Illus.). 310p. reprint ed. pap. 88.40 (*0-8357-5464-2*, 2056682) Bks Demand.

Anatomy of the Honey Bee. Robert E. Snodgrass. (Comstock Ser.). (Illus.). 358p. 1956. 42.50 (*0-8014-0400-2*); Paperback Ser. pap. 14.95 (*0-8014-9302-1*) Cornell U Pr.

Anatomy of the Horse. Ed. by William E. Jones. (Horse Health & Care Ser.). (Illus.). 1973. pap. 9.95 (*0-912830-07-7*) Printed Horse.

Anatomy of the Horse. George Stubbs. Ed. by J. C. McCunn & C. W. Ottaway. LC 76-17945. (Illus.). 128p. 1977. pap. 11.95 (*0-486-23402-9*) Dover.

Anatomy of the Horse. George Stubbs. 1990. 2.00 (*0-517-03302-X*) Random Hse Value.

Anatomy of the Horse. Robert F. Way & Donald G. Lee. (Illus.). 241p. 1983. reprint ed. pap. 14.95 (*0-914327-03-8*) Breakthrgh NY.

Anatomy of the Human Orbit & Accessory Organs of Vision. Ernest S. Whitnall. LC 78-27070. 480p. 1979. lib. bdg. 37.50 (*0-88275-840-3*) Krieger.

Anatomy of the Human Skeleton: A Question & Answer Tutorial Text. Eric E. Denman. (Illus.). 240p. (Orig.). 1991. pap. text ed. 31.00 (*0-443-04498-8*) Churchill.

Anatomy of the Hypothalmus. Ed. by P. Morgane & J. Panksepp. (Handbook of the Hypothalamus Ser.: Vol. 1). 756p. 250.00 (*0-8247-6834-5*) Dekker.

Anatomy of the Infant Head. James F. Bosma. LC 84-20099. (Contemporary Medicine & Public Health Ser.). (Illus.). 480p. 1986. text ed. 165.00x (*0-8018-2936-4*) Johns Hopkins.

Anatomy of the Law. Lon L. Fuller. LC 75-36095. v, 122p. 1977. reprint ed. text ed. 55.00 (*0-8371-8622-6*, FUAL, Greenwood Pr) Greenwood.

Anatomy of the Law: A Logical Presentation of the Parts of the Body of the Law. Adolph J. Rodenbeck. xi, 292p. 1992. reprint ed. 37.50 (*0-8377-2546-1*) Rothman.

Anatomy of the Monocotyledons: Helobiae Alismatidae, Vol. 7. P. B. Tomlinson. Ed. by C. R. Metcalfe. (Illus.). 576p. 1982. 105.00 (*0-19-854502-9*) OUP.

***Anatomy of the Monocotyledons Vol. 8: Iridaceae.** Paula Rudall. (Illus.). 500p. 1995. 118.00 (*0-19-854504-5*) OUP.

Anatomy of the Nectaurus: Text & Dissection Guide. Lionel Rosenzweig. 112p. (C). 1988. spiral bd. write for info. (*0-697-03025-3*) Wm C Brown Pubs.

Anatomy of the New Testament: A Guide to Its Structure & Meaning. 4th ed. Robert A. Spivey & D. Moody Smith. 528p. (C). 1988. text ed. write for info. (*0-02-415330-3*) Macmillan.

Anatomy of the New Testament: A Guide to Its Structure & Meaning. 5th ed. Robert Spivey & D. Moody Smith. LC 93-46079. (Illus.). 528p. (C). 1995. pap. write for info. (*0-02-415322-2*) Macmillan.

Anatomy of the Nuremberg Trials: A Personal Memoir. Telford Taylor. 1993. pap. 17.95 (*0-316-83400-9*) Little.

Anatomy of the Orchestra. Norman Del Mar. LC 81-11559. 512p. 1982. 55.00 (*0-520-04500-9*); pap. 18.00 (*0-520-05062-2*) U CA Pr.

Anatomy of the Psyche: Alchemical Symbolism in Psychotherapy. Edward F. Edinger. LC 85-11546. 278p. (C). 1986. pap. 18.95 (*0-8126-9009-5*) Open Court.

Anatomy of the Sacred: An Introduction to Religion. 2nd ed. James C. Livingston. LC 92-32308. (Illus.). 480p. (C). 1993. pap. write for info. (*0-02-371401-8*) Macmillan.

Anatomy of the Screaming Man: A Comic Strip Collection. Bob Therrien, Jr. (Illus.). 1993. 7.95 (*0-942986-22-9*) LongRiver Bks.

***Anatomy of the Senses: Natural Symbols in Medieval & Early Modern Italy.** Piero Camporesi. Tr. by Allan Cameron. 230p. 1995. 49.95 (*0-7456-0506-0*, Pub. by Polity Pr UK) Blackwell Pubs.

Anatomy of the Sexes: Candid Questions & Answers Regarding Man-Woman Relationships (Individual Profiles - Male & Female) Sue Thompson. LC 91-72947. 214p. 1992. pap. 10.95 (*0-9603672-1-7*) Crossrds CA.

Anatomy of the Shark: Text & Dissection Guide. Lionel Rosenzweig. 128p. (C). 1988. Wire Coil. write for info. (*0-697-01542-4*) Wm C Brown Pubs.

***Anatomy of the Ship the Naval Cutter Alert.** Peter Goodwin. (Illus.). 128p. (C). 1992. 32.95 (*0-9615021-8-5*) Phoen Pubns.

***Anatomy of the Ship the 24-Gun Ship Pandora.** John McKay. (Illus.). 128p. (C). 1992. 32.95 (*0-9615021-9-3*) Phoen Pubns.

Anatomy of the Ship the 32-Gun Frigate Essex. Portia Takakjian. (Illus.). 128p. (C). 1990. 32.95 (*0-9615021-6-9*) Phoen Pubns.

Anatomy of the Temporal Bone with Surgical Implications. 2nd ed. A. Julianna Gulya & Harold F. Schuknecht. 350p. 1994. 89.95 (*1-85070-586-0*) Prthnon Pub.

Anatomy of the Trunk: A Review. Barbara E. Kent. 1974. pap. 5.00 (*0-912452-02-1*) Am Phys Therapy Assn.

Anatomy of the Turn of the Screw. Thomas M. Cranfill & Robert L. Clark, Jr. LC 78-159037. 195p. (C). 1971. reprint ed. 50.00 (*0-87752-151-4*) Gordian.

Anatomy of the Verb: The Gothic Verb As a Model for a Unified Theory of Aspect, Actional Types, & Verbal Velocity. Albert L. Lloyd. (Studies in Language Companion: No. 4). x, 351p. 1979. 71.00x (*90-272-3003-X*, 4) Benjamins North Am.

Anatomy of the Vertebrates: A Lab Guide. Kent. Date not set. pap. write for info. (*0-8016-2645-5*) Mosby Yr Bk.

Anatomy of the Vertebrates: A Laboratory Guide. Donn D. Martin et al. 112p. (C). 1988. spiral bd. write for info. (*0-697-03159-4*) Wm C Brown Pubs.

Anatomy of the Visual System see System of Ophthalmology Series

***Anatomy of the Zulu Army: From Shaka to Cetshwayo 1818-1879.** Ian Knight. (Illus.). 272p. 1995. 44.95 (*1-85367-213-0*, Pub. by Greenhill Bks UK) Stackpole.

Anatomy of Thought: Maimomian Skepticism & the Relation Between Thoughts & Objects. Jan Bransen. (Nijhoff International Philosophy Ser.). 216p. 1991. lib. bdg. 87.00 (*0-7923-1383-6*) Kluwer Ac.

Anatomy of Treason. V. Cherednychenko. 278p. 1984. 40.00 (*0-317-42763-6*, Pub. by Collets UK) St Mut.

Anatomy of Two Traitors: Story of the Defection of Two Americans to the Soviet Union. Wayne G. Barker & Rodney E. Coffman. LC 81-69674. 131p. 1981. lib. bdg. 14.45 (*0-89412-079-4*); pap. 4.95 (*0-89412-041-7*) Aegean Park Pr.

Anatomy of Values: Problems of Personal & Social Choice. Charles Fried. LC 78-111483. 276p. reprint ed. pap. 79.60 (*0-7837-1698-2*, 2057227) Bks Demand.

Anatomy of Victory: Battle Tactics, 1689-1763. Brent Nosworthy. (Illus.). 395p. 1991. pap. 16.95 (*0-87052-014-8*) Hippocrene Bks.

Anatomy of Voice: An Illustrated Manual of Vocal Training. 7th ed. Regnier Winsel. (Illus.). 1984. pap. 4.95 (*0-317-00265-1*) R Talbert.

Anatomy of Wonder: A Critical Guide to Science Fiction. 4th rev. ed. Ed. by Neil Barron. 1000p. 1994. 52.00 (*0-8352-3288-3*) Bowker. "Indispensable to any public/school/academic collection, even if the previous editions are owned."--VOICE OF YOUTH ADVOCATES. "Admirably meets its objectives...highly recommended to high school, academic, & public libraries."--BOOKLIST. Fully revised & updated, the 4th edition of this Bowker classic continues to provide both a rich historical survey of the science fiction genre & an incomparable annotated science fiction bibliography. Divided into two parts: primary literature & secondary literature & research aids, this volume is invaluable for acquisition, course development, & research, as well as for browsing. It features: * concise summaries & evaluations of approximately 3,000 adult & juvenile science fiction titles published from SF's beginning through today--hundreds of titles appear for the first time. * discussion of science fiction poetry, comic books/strips & graphic novels. * "best book" indicators * detailed coverage of science fiction awards & organizations * a chapter on classroom aids with detailed guidance for junior/senior high school & college instructors * listings of films based on SF novels & short stories & guidance to books on tape & similar audio materials * a chapter on SF magazines * a tabulation of sources of information on authors * a comprehensive theme index, encouraging readers to explore works with similar themes * extensive cross-referencing & series information. ***Publisher Provided Annotation.***

***Anatomy of Wonder 1995.** 4th ed. Ed. by Neil Barron. 1995. pap. write for info. (*0-8352-3684-6*) Bowker.

Anatomy of Word Class: A Chapter of Polish Grammar. A. A. Fokker & Emilia Smolikowska. (Slavistic Printings & Reprintings Ser.: No. 254). 108p. 1971. text ed. 29.25 (*90-279-2049-4*) Mouton.

Anatomy of Work: Labor, Leisure, & the Implications of Automation. Georges Friedmann & Donald C. King. 222p. (C). 1992. pap. 21.95 (*1-56000-615-3*) Transaction Pubs.

Anatomy of Work: Labor, Leisure & the Implications of Automation. Georges Friedmann. LC 78-6171. 203p. 1978. reprint ed. text ed. 59.75 (*0-313-20464-0*, FRAW, Greenwood Pr) Greenwood.

Anatomy of Xerography: Its Invention & Evolution. J. Mort. LC 89-42739. 240p. 1989. lib. bdg. 32.50x (*0-89950-442-6*) McFarland & Co.

Anatomy, Physiology & Hygiene. 4th ed. Janet K. Raeburn & H. A. Raeburn. 1975. pap. text ed. 7.95 (*0-7195-3213-2*) Transatl Arts.

Anatomy, Physiology & Microbiology. Jack Rudman. (College Level Examination Ser.: CLEP-38). 1994. pap. 23.95 (*0-8373-5338-6*) Nat Learn.

Anatomy, Physiology & Psychology of Erosion. Ernest G. Hallsworth. LC 86-15688. 176p. 1987. text ed. 149.95 (*0-471-91212-3*, Wiley-Interscience) Wiley.

***Anatomy, Physiology, & Psychology of Erosion.** fac. ed. Ernest G. Hallsworth. LC 86-15688. (IFIAS Monograph: No. 1). (Illus.). 190p. 1994. pap. 54.20 (*0-7837-7655-1*, 2047408) Bks Demand.

Anatomy, Radiology, & Kinesiology of Hand-Unit. 8th ed. Hosein A. Motamed. LC 81-90206. (Illus.). 344p. 1995. reprint ed. 150.00 (*0-910161-06-2*) Motamed Med Pub.

Anatomy to Color & Study. Ray Poritsky. (Illus.). 544p. (Orig.). 1989. student ed 26.95 (*0-932883-18-4*) Hanley & Belfus.

Anatomy Workbook: Coloring Book of Human Regional & Sectional Anatomy. Sandra L. Hagen-Ansert. (Illus.). 304p. 1986. text ed. 19.50 (*0-397-50694-5*, Lippincott Medical) Lippincott.

Anatosaurus. Janet Riehecky. (Dinosaurs Bks.). (Illus.). 32p. (ENG & SPA.). (J). (ps-2). 1989. lib. bdg. 21.36 (*0-89565-545-4*) Childs World.

Anatosaurus. D. White. (Dinosaur Library). (Illus.). 24p. (J). (gr. 3 up). 1989. lib. bdg. 14.60 (*0-86592-520-8*) Rourke Corp.

Anauroch. Ed Greenwood. (Advanced Dungeons & Dragons Ser.). (Illus.). 1991. FR13. pap. 10.95 (*1-56076-126-1*) TSR Inc.

Anax: Novel. Joaquin J. Delgado. Ed. by Olimpo Staff. (Illus.). 98p. (Orig.). 1986. pap. write for info. (*0-938873-00-8*) Olimpo Pub.

Anaximander & the Origins of Greek Cosmology. Charles H. Kahn. LC 94-18778. 272p. (C). 1994. reprint ed. lib. bdg. 37.95 (*0-87220-256-9*); reprint ed. pap. text ed. 19.95 (*0-87220-255-0*) Hackett Pub.

Anaya Reader. Rudolfo Anaya. 592p. (Orig.). 1995. pap. 11.99 (*0-446-67077-4*) Warner Bks.

Anazazi Woman. Karla Andersdutter. (Fastbook 1985 Ser.). 20p. 1985. 6.00 (*0-685-10809-0*) Plain View.

ANC & Black Workers in South Africa, 1912-1992: An Annotated Bibliography. Peter Limb. LC 93-26607. 394p. 1993. 95.00 (*1-873836-95-3*, Pub. by H Zell Pubs UK) Bowker-Saur.

ANCA Associated Vasculitides: Immunological & Clinical Aspects. Ed. by W. L. Gross. (Advances in Experimental Medicine & Biology Ser.: Vol. 336). (Illus.). 590p. (C). 1993. 135.00 (*0-306-44573-5*, Plenum Pr) Plenum.

Ancestor Charts, Vol. I. Ed. by James M. Templeton, Jr. 154p. 1986. pap. write for info. (*0-318-65847-X*) EAG & HS.

Ancestor Charts, Vol. II. Ed. by James M. Templeton, Jr. 110p. 1989. pap. write for info. (*0-318-65846-1*) EAG & HS.

Ancestor Game. Alex Miller. 320p. 1994. 24.00 (*1-55597-217-9*) Graywolf.

Ancestor Hunting. M. S. Watkins. 1969. 25.00 (*0-87511-131-9*) Claitors.

Ancestor Spirits. Ed. by M. J. Charlesworth et al. 92p. (C). 1991. 59.00 (*0-685-57280-3*, Pub. by Deakin Univ AT) St Mut.

***Ancestor Spirits: Aspects of Australian Aboriginal Life & Spirituality.** M. J. Charlesworth et al. 92p. 1991. pap. 60.00 (*0-948823-14-3*, Pub. by Deakin Univ AT) St Mut.

Ancestor Trail in Ireland. (C). 1987. 40.00 (*0-317-89832-9*, Pub. by Birmingham Midland Soc UK) St Mut.

Ancestor Trail in Ireland. Donal F. Begley. (Illus.). 32p. (Orig.). 1982. pap. 3.95 (*0-9502455-8-5*, Heraldic Art) Irish Bks Media.

Ancestor Tree. T. Obinkaram Echewa. (Illus.). 32p. (J). (gr. k-3). 1994. 13.99 (*0-525-67467-5*, Lodestar Bks) Dutton Child Bks.

Ancestor Worship & Christianity in Korea. Ed. by Jung Y. Lee. LC 88-39988. (Studies in Asian Thought & Religion). 112p. 1989. lib. bdg. 59.95 (*0-88946-059-0*) E Mellen.

An Asterisk (*) at the beginning of an entry indicates that the title is appearing in BIP for the first time.

An Asterisk (*) at the beginning of an entry indicates that the title is appearing in BIP for the first time.

299

*Anchored Nowhere: A Navy Wife's Story. Barbara K. Bennett. 288p. (Orig.). 1995. pap. text ed. 9.95 (0-9644870-0-4) Messmer & Waters.

*Anchored Within the Vail: A Pictorial History of the Seamen's Church Institute. Leah R. Rousmaniere & Peter Larom. (Illus.). 135p. (Orig.). 1995. pap. 18.00 (0-9643657-0-7) Seamens Church.

*Anchored Within the Vail: A Pictorial History of the Seamen's Church Institute. deluxe ed. Leah R. Rousmaniere & Peter Larom. (Illus.). 135p. (Orig.). 1995. 75.00 (0-9643657-1-5) Seamens Church.

Anchoring. Steven Hull. 1992. 29.95 (0-87827-151-1) Ency Brit Ed.

Anchoring. 2nd ed. Steven Holl. (Illus.). 172p. (Orig.). 1991. 29.95 (1-878271-51-2) Princeton Arch.

Anchoring: All Techniques for All Bottoms. Don Bamford. write for info. (0-318-59657-1) S&S Trade.

Anchoring & Mooring Techniques Illustrated. Alain Gree. Tr. by Mark Brackenbury. (Illus.). 176p. 1991. pap. 24.95 (0-924486-19-8) Sheridan.

Anchoring in Rock & Soil. L. Hobst & J. Zajic. (Developments in Geotechnical Engineering Ser.: Vol. 33). 570p. 1983. 133.50 (0-444-99689-3, I-478-82) Elsevier.

*Anchoring of Floating Structures: Design Guides for Offshore Structures. (Design Guides for Offshore Structures Ser.: Vol. 2). 248p. (C). 1990. text ed. 84.00 (2-7108-0572-3) Technip.

Anchoring Systems. Ed. by Michael E. McCormick. 1979. 36.00 (0-08-022694-9, Pergamon Pr) Elsevier.

Anchoring Systems & Procedures for Large Tankers. OCIMF Staff. (C). 1988. 80.00 (0-900886-73-0, Pub. by Witherby & Co UK) St Mut.

Anchoritic Spirituality: Ancrene Wisse & Associated Works. Tr. by Nicholas Watson. (Classics of Western Spirituality Ser.). 1991. 27.95 (0-8091-0449-0); pap. 22.95 (0-8091-3257-5) Paulist Pr.

Anchors: Brokaw, Jennings, Rather & the Evening News. Robert Goldberg & Gerald J. Goldberg. (Illus.). 399p. 1990. 19.95 (1-55972-019-0, Birch Ln Pr) Carol Pub Group.

Anchors for the Asking: Rediscovering a Secure Faith in a Shifting World. Harold Hazelip & Ken Durham. 144p. (Orig.). 1989. pap. 5.99 (0-8010-4341-7) Baker Bk.

Anchors for the Innocent: Inner Power for Today's Single Mothers & Fathers. Gail C. Christopher. 350p. (Orig.). 1993. pap. 12.95 (1-883811-00-7) Human Capacity.

Anchors for the Soul. Dennis L. Largey. 9.95 (0-88494-692-4) Bookcraft Inc.

***Anchors Health Network Resource Book. American Health Network Staff. 100p. (Orig.). 1995. pap. 10.50 (0-9634399-9-5) Funmakers.**

This is a collection of information, for local & national resources, provided by Anchors Health Network (a nonprofit group). It contains listings of speakers, consultants, nonprofit & profit groups providing health (social, emotional, physical & spiritual) resources, hobbies & humor. Some of the information is free & some may cost a fee. There will be 100 pages & it costs $10.50. Members receive an 18% discount. Profits at the end of each year are put in a fund for ANimals, CHildren OR Seniors. *Publisher Provided Annotation.*

Anchors in Concrete - Design & Behavior. 281p. 1992. 78.75 (0-685-60177-3, SP-130) ACI.

*Anchors in the Sky-12.95. Date not set. 7.98 (0-89141-034-1) Presidio Pr.

Anchors of Hope. Dick Bolks. 1988. 5.25 (0-685-74869-3, MB-595) Lillenas.

Anchovy Breath to Zoo Food: One Hundred Seventy-Five Names I Call My Brother When I'm Mad. Jenny Davis. (Illus.). 80p. (Orig.). (YA). 1994. pap. 3.50 (0-380-77135-7, Camelot) Avon.

Ancien Regime. C. B. Behrens. (Library of World Civilization). (Illus.). 216p. (C). 1989. pap. text ed. 9.95 (0-393-95801-9) Norton.

Ancien Regime. William Doyle. LC 86-376. (Studies in European History). 72p. (C). 1986. pap. 10.95 (0-391-03412-X) Humanities.

Ancien Regime et la Revolution. Alexis De Tocqueville. (Folio-Histoire Ser.: No. 5). 384p. (FRE.). 1985. pap. 12.95 (2-07-032299-8) Schoenhof.

Ancien Regime in France. Peter R. Campbell. (Historical Association Studies). 96p. 1989. pap. 10.95 (0-631-15107-9) Blackwell Pubs.

Ancienne Medecine. Hippocrates. Ed. by W. R. Connor. LC 78-18573. (Greek Texts & Commentaries Ser.). (Illus.). 1979. reprint ed. lib. bdg. 22.95 (0-405-11417-6) Ayer.

Anciens Systemes de Poids et Mesures en Occident. Jean-Claude Hocquet. (Collected Studies: Vol. CS388). 320p. 1992. 99.50 (0-86078-346-4, Pub. by Variorum UK) Ashgate Pub Co.

Ancient - Modern Witch: The Halloween Lecture. Marion Weinstein. LC 91-77634. (Illus.). 95p. (Orig.). 1993. pap. 6.95 (0-9604128-4-0) Earth Magic.

*Ancient Acid Flashing Back: Poems of the Sixties. Adrian C. Louis. LC 94-32912. 1994. 12.95 (0-9636829-3-8); pap. 9.95 (0-9636829-4-6) Mother Road.

Ancient Affections: Ethnic Groups & Foreign Policy. Laurence Halley. LC 84-18328. 192p. 1985. text ed. 49.95 (0-275-90116-5, C0116, Praeger Pubs) Greenwood.

Ancient Africa. F. A. Chijioke. LC 75-80850. (Illus.). 48p. (J). (gr. 5-8). 1969. pap. 5.50 (0-8419-0013-2, Africana) Holmes & Meier.

*Ancient Africa. Eyewitness Staff. (J). Date not set. 19.00 (0-679-87334-1) Random.

*Ancient Africa. Eyewitness Staff. (J). Date not set. lib. bdg. 20.99 (0-679-97334-6) Random.

Ancient Africa, Vol. I. Bellerophon Staff. (J). (gr. 1-9). 1992. pap. 2.50 (0-88388-090-3) Bellerophon Bks.

Ancient Africa, Vol. II. Harry Knill. (J). (gr. 1-9). 1993. pap. 2.50 (0-88388-174-8) Bellerophon Bks.

Ancient Africa see UNESCO General History of Africa

*Ancient Africa & the Atlantic Slave Trade. (Voices in African American History Ser.). (YA). 1994. lib. bdg. 11.95 (0-8136-4955-2) Modern Curr.

*Ancient Africa & the Atlantic Slave Trade. (Voices in African American History Ser.). (YA). 1994. pap. 5.95 (0-8136-4956-0) Modern Curr.

Ancient African Religion & the African American Church. Ulysses D. Jenkins. LC 78-65794. (Illus.). 1978. 12.95 (0-933184-00-X); pap. 6.95 (0-933184-01-8) Flame Intl.

Ancient Air: A Biography of John Stringfellow of Chard. Harald Penrose. LC 88-60696. (Illus.). 176p. 1988. 35.00 (0-87474-752-X) Smithsonian.

Ancient Amber Routes & the Discovery of the Eastern Baltic. Arnolds Spekke. (Illus.). 1976. 20.00 (0-89005-178-X) Ares.

Ancient America. Marian Wood. (Cultural Atlas for Young People Ser.). (J). 1990. 17.95 (0-8160-2210-0) Facts on File.

Ancient America. John Guyatt. Ed. by Margaret Killingray et al. (World History Ser.). (Illus.). 32p. (YA). (gr. 6-11). 1980. reprint ed. pap. text ed. 4.35 (0-89908-008-1) Greenhaven.

Ancient America: Contributions to New World Archaeology. Ed. by Nicholas J. Saunders. (Oxbow Monographs in Archaeology: No. 24). (Illus.). 289p. 1992. pap. 48.00 (0-946897-48-4, Pub. by Oxbow Bks UK) David Brown.

Ancient America: Paradise Lost. Edmond B. Szekely. (Illus.). 96p. 1974. pap. 5.95 (0-89564-025-2) IBS Intl.

Ancient America, In Notes on America Archaeology. John D. Baldwin. 301p. 1974. reprint ed. spiral bd. 11.05 (0-7873-0065-9) Mokelumne.

Ancient American Indians: Their Origins, Civilizations & Old World Connections. Paul R. Cheesman. 288p. 1991. 18.98 (0-88290-416-7) Horizon Utah.

Ancient American Inscriptions: Plowmarks or History? William R. McGlone et al. (Illus.). 415p. (Orig.). (C). 1993. pap. 19.95 (1-884810-00-4) Early Sites.

Ancient American Setting for the Book of Mormon. John L. Sorenson. LC 84-43240. xxi, 415p. 1985. 21.00 (0-87747-608-X) Deseret Bk.

Ancient Americas: Art from Sacred Landscapes. Ed. by Richard F. Townsend. LC 92-21869. (Illus.). 400p. 1992. pap. 39.95 (0-86559-104-0) Art Inst Chi.

Ancient Americas: Art from Sacred Landscapes. Ed. by Richard F. Townsend. (Illus.). 400p. 1992. 60.00 (3-7913-1188-3, Pub. by Prestel) TeNeues.

Ancient Anatolia: Aspects of Change & Cultural Development. Ed. by Brunilde Ridgway et al. LC 86-40059. (Studies in Classics). (Illus.). 144p. 1986. text ed. 35.00 (0-299-10620-9) U of Wis Pr.

Ancient & Accepted Scottish Rite of Freemasonry. Charles S. Lobingier. 170p. 1992. pap. 19.95 (1-56459-289-8) Kessinger Pub.

*Ancient & Classicising Finger-Rings & Gems - La Collection des Antiquities Greco-Romaines de l'Universite McGill. Eunice A. Tees. (McGill University Monographs in Classical Archaeology & History: No. 4.2). (Illus.). xvi, 84p. 1993. lib. bdg. 50.00x (90-5063-186-X, Pub. by Gieben NE) Benjamins North Am.

Ancient & Historic Metals: Conservation & Scientific Research: Proceedings of a Symposium Organized by the J Paul Getty Museum & the Getty Conservation Institute, November 1991. David A. Scott et al. LC 92-28095. (Illus.). 304p. (Orig.). 1995. pap. 50.00 (0-89236-231-6) J P Getty Trust.

Ancient & Medieval Architecture of India. E. B. Havell. 260p. 1988. pap. text ed. 100.00 (0-317-52130-6, Pub. by S Chand II) St Mut.

Ancient & Medieval England: Beginnings to 1509 see Harbrace History of England

Ancient & Medieval History of Andhra Pradesh. P. R. Rao. 1993. 15.95 (81-207-1495-4, Pub. by Sterling Pubs II) Apt Bks.

*Ancient & Medieval Legacies. Ed. by Reinhard Ulrich & Barbara B. Zikmund. LC 95-12480. (The Living Theological Heritage of the United Church of Christ Ser.: Vol. 1). 576p. 1995. 50.00 (0-8298-1064-1) Pilgrim OH.

Ancient & Medieval Memories. Janet Coleman. (Studies in the Reconstruction of the Past). 648p. (C). 1992. 89.95 (0-521-41144-0) Cambridge U Pr.

Ancient & Medieval Nepal. S. Rishikesh. (C). 1990. 65.00 (0-89771-058-4, Pub. by Ratna Pustak Bhandar) St Mut.

Ancient & Medieval Nepal. Rishikesh Shah. 1990. 69.00 (0-7855-0252-1, Pub. by Ratna Pustak Bhandar) St Mut.

Ancient & Medieval Theatre: A Historiographical Handbook. Ronald W. Vince. LC 83-18330. xi, 156p. 1984. text ed. 55.00 (0-313-24107-4, VAT/, Greenwood Pr) Greenwood.

Ancient & Medieval Warfare. Ed. by Thomas Griess. (West Point Military History Ser.). 152p. 1986. pap. 19.95 (0-89529-262-9) Avery Pub.

Ancient & Medival Nepal. Rishikesh Shah. (C). 1991. text ed. 75.00 (0-7855-0128-2, Pub. by Ratna Pustak Bhandar) St Mut.

Ancient & Modern: Essays in Honor of Gerald F. Else. Ed. by John H. D'Arms & John W. Eadie. LC 77-76612. 234p. (Orig.). 1977. pap. 10.00 (0-915932-04-0) Trillium Pr.

Ancient & Modern Israel: An Exploration of Political Parallels. Ira Sharkansky. LC 90-35226. (SUNY Series in Israeli Studies). 206p. (C). 1991. 59.50 (0-7914-0548-6); pap. 19.95 (0-7914-0549-4) State U NY Pr.

Ancient & Modern Liberty Stated & Compar'd. Hervey John. LC 92-24237. (Augustan Reprints Ser.: Nos. 255-256 (1989)). reprint ed. 18.50 (0-404-70255-4) AMS Pr.

Ancient & Modern Songs of Ireland for Piano. Gail Smith. 1993. 10.95 (1-56222-659-2, 94883); audio 9.98 (1-56222-909-5, 94883) Mel Bay.

Ancient & Oriental Music see New Oxford History of Music

Ancient & Shining Ones: World Myth, Magick & Religion. D. J. Conway. LC 93-29628. (Illus.). 448p. 1993. pap. 17.95 (0-87542-170-9) Llewellyn Pubns.

Ancient Andean Arts: In the Collection of the Krannert Art Museum. Alan R. Sawyer. LC 75-13962. (Illus.). 189p. 1975. 20.00 (0-8139-0944-9) U Pr of Va.

Ancient Andean Life. Edgar L. Hewett. LC 67-29547. (Illus.). (C). 1968. reprint ed. 25.00 (0-8196-0204-3) Biblo.

Ancient Andean Political Economy. Charles Stanish. LC 91-14442. (Illus.). 207p. 1992. text ed. 37.50 (0-292-76526-6) U of Tex Pr.

Ancient Answers to Modern Gay Problems: The Canticles Manuscript. Paul R. Johnson. (Illus.). 244p. (Orig.). 1990. pap. 5.95 (0-685-45865-2) Paul R Johnson.

Ancient Arabs: Nomads on the Borders of the Fertile Crescent 9th-5th Centuries B.C. rev. ed. Israel Eph'al. viii, 265p. 1984. 25.00 (0-685-74243-1, Pub. by Magnes Press IS) Eisenbrauns.

Ancient Aramaic & Hebrew Letters. James M. Lindenberger. LC 93-6657. (SB Writings from the Ancient World Ser.: No. 4). 172p. 1994. 44.95 (1-55540-839-7, 061504) Scholars Pr GA.

Ancient Aramaic & Hebrew Letters. Ed. by James M. Lindenberger. LC 93-6657. (Writings from the Ancient World Ser.: No. 4). 1994. pap. 29.95 (1-55540-840-0) Scholars Pr GA.

Ancient Aramaic Prayer of Jesus. Rocco A. Errico. (Illus.). 96p. 1978. reprint ed. pap. 5.95 (0-911336-69-9) Sci of Mind.

Ancient Architecture: Mesopotamia, Egypt, Crete. Seton Lloyd & Hans W. Muller. LC 85-30006. (History of World Architecture Ser.). (Illus.). 220p. 1986. pap. 29.95 (0-8478-0692-8) Rizzoli Intl.

Ancient Architecture of the Southwest. William N. Morgan. LC 93-21256. (Illus.). 320p. (C). 1994. 55.00 (0-292-75159-1) U of Tex Pr.

Ancient Armenian Translations. Levon T. Petrosian. Tr. by Krikor Maksoudian & Nubar Kupelian. LC 92-39098. (ARM & ENG.). 1992. write for info. (0-934728-24-0) D O A C.

Ancient Armies of the Middle East. Terence Wise. (Men-at-Arms Ser.: No. 109). (Illus.). 48p. pap. 11.95 (0-85045-384-4, 9042, Pub. by Osprey UK) Stackpole.

Ancient Art. Jillian Powell. LC 94-6079. (Arts & Artists Ser.). (Illus.). 48p. (J). (gr. 6-10). 1994. 16.95 (1-56847-216-1) Thomson Lrning.

Ancient Art: The Challenge to Modern Thought. Lloyd Laing & Jennifer Laing. (Illus.). 256p. (C). 1993. text ed. 45.00 (0-7165-2473-2, Pub. by Irish Acad Pr IE) Intl Spec Bk.

Ancient Art from Afghanistan: Treasures of the Kabul Museum. Benjamin Rowland, Jr. LC 74-27419. (Asia Society Ser.). (Illus.). 1976. reprint ed. lib. bdg. 33.95 (0-405-06567-1) Ayer.

Ancient Art from the Barbier-Mueller Museum. Jean-Louis Zimmermann. (Illus.). 184p. 1991. 65.00 (0-8109-1904-4) Abrams.

Ancient Art in Seals: Essays in Pierre Amiet, Nimet Ozguc, & John Boardman. Edith Porada. LC 79-19462. (Franklin Jasper Walls Lectures). (Illus.). 153p. reprint ed. pap. 43.70 (0-8357-4035-8, 2036727) Bks Demand.

Ancient Art of Colima, Mexico. Richard D. Reynolds. LC 88-92600. (Illus.). 96p. (Orig.). 1993. 18.95 (0-9618577-1-4) Squibob Pr.

Ancient Art of Northern Asia. Anatoly I. Martynov. Ed. by Demitri Shimkin & Edith Shimkin. Tr. by Edith Shimkin. (Illus.). 320p. 1991. 39.95 (0-252-01219-4) U of Ill Pr.

Ancient Art of Skating. Robert L. Merriam. (Illus.). 25p. 1957. pap. 1.50 (0-686-33162-1) R L Merriam.

Ancient Art of the Andes. Wendell C. Bennett & Rene D'Harnoncourt. LC 54-6135. (Museum of Modern Art Publications in Reprint). (Illus.). reprint ed. 18.00 (0-405-01521-6) Ayer.

Ancient Arts of Western & Central Asia: A Guide to the Literature. Bernard Goldman. LC 91-16944. 314p. 1991. text ed. 41.95 (0-8138-0597-X) Iowa St U Pr.

Ancient Assyrians. Mark Healy. (Elite Ser.: No. 39). (Illus.). 64p. pap. 12.95 (1-85532-163-7, 9454, Pub. by Osprey UK) Stackpole.

Ancient Astrology. Tamsyn Barton. LC 93-32441. (Sciences of Antiquity Ser.). (Illus.). 264p. 1994. 59.95x (0-415-08066-5, B3714, Routledge NY); pap. 16.95 (0-415-11029-7, B3718, Routledge NY) Routledge.

Ancient Astronauts, Cosmic Collisions & Other Popular Theories about Man's Past. William H. Stiebing, Jr. LC 84-42792. (Science & the Paranormal Ser.). (Illus.). 217p. 1984. pap. 17.95 (0-87975-285-8) Prometheus Bks.

Ancient Astronomers. Anthony F. Aveni. LC 93-38463. (Exploring the Ancient World Ser.). 1993. write for info. (0-89599-037-7) Smithsonian Bks.

Ancient Astronomical Observations & the Accelerations of the Earth & Moon. Robert R. Newton. LC 70-122011. (Illus.). 329p. reprint ed. 93.80 (0-8357-9264-1, 2013730) Bks Demand.

Ancient Astronomy. rev. ed. Isaac Asimov et al. (Library of the Universe). (Illus.). (J). (gr. 3 up). 1995. lib. bdg. 18.60 (0-8368-1191-7) Gareth Stevens Inc.

Ancient Astronomy & Civilization. Norriss S. Hetherington. (History of Astronomy Ser.: Vol. 6). (Illus.). 187p. 1987. pap. 26.00 (0-88126-225-0) Pachart Pub Hse.

Ancient Athenian Building Methods. John M. Camp, II & William B. Dinsmoor, Jr. (Excavations of the Athenian Agora Picture Bks.: No. 21). (Illus.). 32p. 1984. pap. 3.00 (0-87661-626-0) Am Sch Athens.

Ancient Athens. Ernest A. Gardner. LC 68-25236. (World History Ser.: No. 48). (Illus.). 1969. reprint ed. lib. bdg. 75.00 (0-8383-0945-3) M S G Haskell Hse.

Ancient Athens, Piraeus & Phaleron: Schriftquellen Zur Topographie Von Athen. A. Milchhoefer. 156p. 1977. 20.00 (0-89005-215-8) Ares.

Ancient Aztlan. Samuel A. Barrett. LC 70-11394. 1970. reprint ed. text ed. 85.00 (0-8371-4624-0, BAAA, Greenwood Pr) Greenwood.

Ancient Ballads & Legends of Hindustan. Toru Dutt. 1975. pap. text ed. 6.75 (0-88253-495-5) Ind-US Inc.

Ancient Bangladesh: A Study of the Archaeological Sources. Dilip K. Chakrabarti. (Illus.). 224p. 1993. 24.95 (0-19-562879-9) OUP.

Ancient Black Youth & Elders Reborn. Ed. by Linda Cousins. LC 84-50898. (Illus.). 252p. (Orig.). 1985. pap. 10.00 (0-930569-00-8) Univ Black Pr.

Ancient Boeotians & the Coins of Ancient Boeotia. Barclay V. Head & W. R. Roberts. xii, 92p. 1974. 20.00 (0-89005-488-6) Ares.

Ancient Book of Formulas. Lewis De Claremont. 9.95 (0-685-05341-5) Wehman.

Ancient Boys see Gay Plays: An International Anthology

Ancient Bristlecone Pine Forest. rev. ed. Anne Johnson & Russ Johnson. LC 70-126317. 1978. pap. 7.00 (0-912494-03-4) Chalfant Pr.

Ancient Britain & the Invasions of Julius Caesar. Thomas R. Holmes. LC 71-175701. (Select Bibliographies Reprint Ser.). 1977. reprint ed. 66.95 (0-8369-6616-3) Ayer.

Ancient Britons & Antiquarian Imagination. Stuart Piggott. LC 89-50547. (Illus.). 1989. 19.95 (0-500-01470-1) Thames Hudson.

Ancient Building in Cyprus, 2 vols. G. R. Wright. LC 92-14171. (Handbuch der Orientalistik Ser.: Vols. 1 & 2). (Illus.). 1992. Vol. 1: Text, xxvii, 556p. write for info. (90-04-09545-4); Vol. 2: Illustrations, xviii, 343p. write for info. (90-04-09546-2) E J Brill.

Ancient Building in Cyprus, 2 vols., Set. G. R. Wright. LC 92-14171. (Handbuch der Orientalistik Ser.: Vols. 1 & 2). (Illus.). 1992. 325.75 (90-04-09547-0) E J Brill.

Ancient Buildings. Bellerophon Books Staff. (J). (gr. 4-7). 1992. pap. 3.95 (0-88388-121-7) Bellerophon Bks.

Ancient Buildings of Rome. Antoine Desgodetz. (Printed Sources of Western Art Ser.). (Illus.). 324p. (FRE.). 1981. reprint ed. pap. 135.00 (0-915346-49-4) A Wofsy Fine Arts.

Ancient Bundelkhand. K. K. Shah. (C). 1987. 50.00 (0-8364-2141-8, Pub. by Gian Publng Hse II) S Asia.

Ancient Canada. Robert McGhee. (Canadian Museum of Civilization Mercury Ser.). (Illus.). 175p. 1992. 29.95 (0-660-10795-3) U Ch Pr.

Ancient Caribbean. John M. Weeksk & Peter J. Ferbel. LC 94-22798. (Research Guides to Ancient Civilizations Ser.: Vol. 4). (Illus.). 400p. 1994. 60.00 (0-8153-1303-9, H1705) Garland.

Ancient Castle. Robert Graves. LC 81-17204. (Illus.). 72p. (YA). (gr. 7 up). 1981. 13.95 (0-935576-06-1); pap. 8.95 (0-935576-33-9) Kesend Pub Ltd.

Ancient Cataclysms Which Changed Earth's Surface. Karl H. Isselstein. 9p. 1965. reprint ed. spiral bd. 4.40 (0-7873-0465-4) Mokelumne.

*Ancient Caves of the Great Salt Lake. Julian H. Steward. (Bureau of American Ethnology Bulletins Ser.). 131p. 1995. lib. bdg. 79.00 (0-7812-4116-2) Rprt Serv.

Ancient Celts: Stencils. Mira Bartok & Christine Ronan. (Ancient & Living Cultures Ser.). (Illus.). 32p. (Orig.). (J). (gr. 3 up). 1993. pap. 9.95 (0-673-36101-2) GdYrBks.

Ancient Ceylon. H. Parker. (Illus.). 696p. 1986. reprint ed. 32.00 (0-8364-1742-9, Pub. by Manohar II) S Asia.

Ancient Chalcatzingo. Ed. by David C. Grove. LC 85-22673. (Texas Pan American Ser.). (Illus.). 581p. 1987. text ed. 75.00 (0-292-70372-4) U of Tex Pr.

Ancient Chamorro Society. Lawrence J. Cunningham. LC 91-78031. (Illus.). 240p. (Orig.). 1992. student ed 10.95 (1-880188-07-4); text ed. 34.95 (1-880188-05-8) Bess Pr.

Ancient Chiefdoms of the Tombigbee. John H. Blitz. LC 92-28876. 232p. (Orig.). (C). 1993. pap. 24.95 (0-8173-0672-2) U of Ala Pr.

Ancient Child: A Novel. N. Scott Momaday. LC 89-46497. 336p. 1990. reprint ed. pap. 12.00 (0-06-097345-5, PL) HarpC.

Ancient Child: Poetry about Incest. Marcella Bryant. 1990. pap. 10.00 (0-911051-47-3) Plain View.

Ancient China. Mira Bartok & Christine Ronan. (Ancient & Living Cultures Ser.). (Illus.). 32p. (J). (gr. 3 up). 1994. pap. 9.95 (0-673-36180-2) GdYrBks.

Ancient China. Bellerophon Staff. (J). (gr. 1-9). 1992. pap. 3.95 (0-88388-077-6) Bellerophon Bks.

Ancient China. Arthur Cotterell. (Eyewitness Bks.). (Illus.). 64p. (YA). (gr. 5 up). 1994. 16.00 (0-679-86167-X); lib. bdg. 17.99 (0-679-96167-4) Knopf Bks Yng Read.

*Ancient China. Robert Nicholson. (Journey into Civilization Ser.). (Illus.). 32p. (J). (gr. 3-7). 1994. lib. bdg. 14.95 (0-7910-2702-3) Chelsea Hse.

An Asterisk (*) at the beginning of an entry indicates that the title is appearing in BIP for the first time.

An Asterisk (*) at the beginning of an entry indicates that the title is appearing in BIP for the first time.

301

Ancient Egyptian Literature, a Book of Readings, Vol. 1: The Old & the Middle Kingdoms. Miriam Lichtheim. LC 75-189225. (Near Eastern Center Series, UCLA: No. 12). 1973. pap. 13.00 (*0-520-02899-6*) U CA Pr.

Ancient Egyptian Literature: A Book of Readings, Vol. 2: The New Kingdom. Miriam Lichtheim. LC 75-189225. (Near Eastern Center Series, UCLA: No. 12). 1976. pap. 13.00 (*0-520-03615-8*) U CA Pr.

Ancient Egyptian Magic. Bob Brier. LC 80-15608. (Illus.). 322p. 1981. reprint ed. pap. 13.45 (*0-688-00796-1*, Quill) Morrow.

Ancient Egyptian Medicine: The Papyrus Ebers. Cyril Bryan. 208p. 1991. 25.00 (*0-89005-004-X*) Ares.

Ancient Egyptian Myths & Legends. Lewis Spence. 1990. pap. 8.95 (*0-486-26525-0*) Dover.

Ancient Egyptian Myths & Legends. Lewis Spence. 1992. 19.75 (*0-8446-6541-X*) Peter Smith.

***Ancient Egyptian Poetry & Prose.** Adolf Erman. Tr. by Aylward M. Blackman. LC 95-15857. Orig. Title: The Literature of the Ancient Egyptians. 1995. pap. write for info. (*0-486-28767-X*) Dover.

Ancient Egyptian Pyramid Texts. Faulkner. 1993. pap. 37.50 (*0-85668-297-7*, Pub. by Aris & Phillips UK) David Brown.

Ancient Egyptian Religion. Stephen Quirke. 1993. pap. 14.95 (*0-486-27427-6*) Dover.

Ancient Egyptian Religion. Jaroslav Cerny. LC 78-9931. 159p. 1979. reprint ed. text ed. 55.50 (*0-313-21104-3*, CEAE, Greenwood Pr) Greenwood.

Ancient Egyptian Religion: An Interpretation. Henri Frankfort. 20.25 (*0-8446-2084-X*) Peter Smith.

Ancient Egyptian Scarabs. P. E. Newberry. 278p. pap. 25.00 (*0-89005-092-9*) Ares.

Ancient Egyptian Science, Vol. 1. Marshall Clagett. LC 89-84668. (Memoirs Ser.: Vol. 184). (Illus.). 863p. (C). 1992. pap. 50.00 (*0-87169-184-1*, M184-PAP) Am Philos.

***Ancient Egyptian Science, Vol. 2.** Marshall Clagett. (Memoirs Ser.: Vol. 214). (Illus.). 518p. (C). 1994. 65.00 (*0-87169-214-7*, M124-clm); pap. 50.00 (*0-614-03014-5*, M214-pap) Am Philos.

Ancient Egyptian Society. David O'Connor. LC 89-85824. (Illus.). 48p. (Orig.). (C). 1990. pap. text ed. 7.95 (*0-911239-17-0*) Carnegie Mus.

Ancient Egyptian "Tale of Two Brothers" The Oldest Fairy Tale in the World. Susan T. Hollis. LC 90-50236. (Oklahoma Series in Classical Culture: Vol. 7). (Illus.). 288p. 1990. 37.50 (*0-8061-2269-2*) U of Okla Pr.

***Ancient Egyptian Tarot.** Clive Barrett. 1995. pap. 29.00 (*0-85030-968-9*, Pub. by Aquarian Pr UK) Thorsons SF.

Ancient Egyptian Theology. E. A. Budge. 1985. pap. 6.95 (*0-916411-91-5*) Holmes Pub.

Ancient Egyptians. Anne Boyd. (YA). 1981. pap. 6.25 (*0-521-28233-0*) Cambridge U Pr.

Ancient Egyptians. Fiona MacDonald. (Insights Ser.). (Illus.). 60p. (J). (gr. 4 up). 1993. 15.95 (*0-8120-6378-3*) Barron.

Ancient Egyptians. Lise Manniche. (British Museum Activity Bks.). (Illus.). 16p. (J). 1995. pap. 5.95 (*0-500-27787-7*) Thames Hudson.

***Ancient Egyptians.** Elsa Marston. (Cultures of the Past Ser.). 80p. (J). (gr. 5-8). 1995. lib. bdg. write for info. (*0-7614-0073-7*, Benchmark NY) Marshall Cavendish.

Ancient Egyptians. J. Gardner Wilkinson. 1988. 9.99 (*0-517-67193-X*) Random Hse Value.

Ancient Egyptians: A Popular Introduction to Life in the Pyramid Age. Jill Kamil. 152p. 1986. pap. 18.50 (*977-424-051-0*, Pub. by Am Univ Cairo Pr UA) Col U Pr.

Ancient Egyptians: Life in the Nile Valley. Viviane Koenig. Tr. by Mary K. LaRose. LC 91-25772. (Peoples of the Past Ser.). (Illus.). 64p. (J). (gr. 4-6). 1992. lib. bdg. 15.90 (*1-56294-161-5*) Millbrook Pr.

Ancient Egyptians: Religious Beliefs & Practices. A. Rosalie David. (Religious Beliefs & Practices Ser.). 250p. 1982. pap. 19.95 (*0-7100-0878-3*, RKP) Routledge.

Ancient Egyptians: The Philosophy of Structuralism & Post-Structuralism. A. Rosalie David. 1982. pap. 19.95 (*0-415-04536-3*) Routledge.

Ancient Egyptians & the Origin of Civilization. Grafton E. Smith. LC 79-133534. (Select Bibliographies Reprint Ser.). 1977. 19.95 (*0-8369-5566-8*) Ayer.

Ancient Elections & Politics: Mini-Lessons. Ed. by Gregory A. Staley. 17p. (Orig.). 1991. 1.40 (*0-939507-02-1*, B316) Amer Classical.

Ancient Empires & Mighty People. Richard Sanchez. LC 94-15860. (J). 1994. lib. bdg. 14.96 (*1-56239-331-6*) Abdo & Dghtrs.

Ancient Empires of the New Age. Paul DeParrie & Mary Pride. LC 89-50335. 228p. 1989. pap. 9.99 (*0-89107-530-5*) Crossway Bks.

***Ancient Enchantresses.** Ed. by Kathleen M. Massie-Ferch et al. 352p. (Orig.). 1995. mass mkt. 5.50 (*0-88677-677-5*) DAW Bks.

Ancient Enemies. Elizabeth North. 240p. 1986. reprint ed. pap. 7.95 (*0-89733-214-8*) Academy Chi Pubs.

Ancient Engineers. L. Sprague De Camp. 1987. mass mkt. 4.95 (*0-345-32029-8*) Ballantine.

Ancient Engineers: Technology & Invention from the Earliest Times to the Renaissance. L. Sprague De Camp. (Illus.). 408p. 1990. 19.95 (*0-88029-456-6*) Marboro Bks.

Ancient English Houses. Christopher S. Sykes. 1989. 42.00 (*0-7011-3176-4*) Random.

Ancient Environments. 2nd ed. Leo F. Laporte. (Foundations of the Earth Ser.). (Illus.). 1979. pap. text ed. write for info. (*0-13-036384-7*) P-H.

Ancient Environments. 3rd ed. Cathryn Newton & Leo F. Laporte. 208p. (C). 1989. pap. text ed. write for info. (*0-13-036476-2*) P-H.

Ancient Environments & the Interpretation of Geologic History. Lynn Fichter & David J. Poche. (Illus.). 224p. (C). 1992. teacher ed write for info. (*0-318-69917-6*) Macmillan.

Ancient Environments & the Interpretation of Geologic History. 2nd ed. Lynn Fichter & David J. Poche. (Illus.). 224p. (C). 1993. pap. write for info. (*0-02-337145-5*) Macmillan.

Ancient Epic Poetry: Homer, Apollonius, Virgil. Charles R. Beye. LC 92-28920. 296p. 1993. 37.95 (*0-8014-2673-1*); pap. 13.95 (*0-8014-9964-X*) Cornell U Pr.

Ancient Epistolary Theorists. Abraham J. Malherbe. LC 87-9565. (Society of Biblical Literature Ser.). 98p. 1988. pap. 18.95 (*1-55540-247-X*, 06 03 19) Scholars Pr GA.

Ancient Eugenics. Allen G. Roper. 1982. reprint ed. 15.00 (*0-941694-05-4*) Cliveden Pr.

Ancient Europe. Charles Frazee & Hallie K. Yopp. (Illus.). (J). (gr. 6). 1990. pap. text ed. write for info. (*0-318-66701-0*) Delos Pubns.

Ancient Europe & the Mediterranean. Markotic. 1977. 65.00 (*0-85668-083-4*, Pub. by Aris & Phillips UK) David Brown.

Ancient Evenings. Norman Mailer. 864p. 1988. mass mkt. 7.99 (*0-446-35769-3*) Warner Bks.

Ancient Evil. Christopher Pike. Ed. by Patricia MacDonald. (Chain Letter Ser.: No. 2). 240p. (Orig.). (YA). 1992. mass mkt. 3.99 (*0-671-74506-9*, Archway) PB.

***Ancient Evil: The Knight's Tale of Mystery & Murder As He Goes on Pilgrimage from London to Canterbury.** P. C. Doherty. LC 94-46267. 1995. 21.00 (*0-312-11740-X*) St Martin.

Ancient Faces. Anderson. pap. 5.95 (*0-88388-080-6*) Bellerophon Bks.

Ancient Faiths & Modern (1876) Thomas Inman. 550p. 1993. reprint ed. pap. 50.00 (*1-56459-411-4*) Kessinger Pub.

Ancient Fathers of the Desert, No. 2. Tr. by Archimandrite Chrysostomos. 90p. (C). Date not set. pap. text ed. 3.00 (*0-917653-25-4*) Hellenic Coll Pr.

Ancient Fathers of the Desert, Vol. 2. Archimandrite Chrysostomos. 90p. 1986. pap. 5.95 (*0-917653-22-X*) Holy Cross Orthodox.

Ancient Fathers of the Desert: Translated Narratives from the Evergetinos on Passions & Perfection in Christ. Archimandrite Chrysostomos. (Illus.). 118p. 1980. 7.95 (*0-916586-77-4*); pap. 4.95 (*0-686-69869-X*) Hellenic Coll Pr.

Ancient Fiction: The Novel in the Graeco-Roman World. Graham Anderson. LC 84-12319. 256p. (C). 1984. 57.50 (*0-389-20516-8*, N8078) B&N Imports.

Ancient Fighting Secrets of the Yin-Yang: Martial Arts Combative Hand Sciences. Sid Campbell. (Audio Cassette Book Ser.). 1988. 29.95 (*0-318-37594-X*) Gong Prods.

Ancient Finger Rings & Dress Brooches 1891-1990. F. W. Fairholt. (Illus.). 150p. 1991. pap. 25.00 (*0-87556-805-X*) Saifer.

Ancient Forest. Guy Spencer. LC 87-3487. (Let's Take a Trip Ser.). (Illus.). 32p. (J). (gr. 3-6). 1988. lib. bdg. 10.79 (*0-8167-1167-4*); pap. text ed. 2.95 (*0-8167-1168-2*) Troll Assocs.

Ancient Forests. Margaret Anderson et al. (Illus.). 40p. (Orig.). (J). (gr. 3-8). 1994. pap. 4.95 (*0-941042-14-6*) Dog Eared Pubns.

Ancient Forests. Alexandra Siy. LC 91-15422. (Circle of Life Ser.). (Illus.). 72p. (J). (gr. 5 up). 1991. text ed. 14.95 (*0-87518-466-9*, Dillon Silver Burdett) Silver Burdett Pr.

Ancient Forests: A Celebration of North America's Old-Growth Wilderness. David Middleton. (Illus.). 108p. (Orig.). 1992. pap. 16.95 (*0-87701-814-6*) Chronicle Bks.

Ancient Forests & Western Man: A Pictorial History of the West Coast. Ann Amato. (Illus.). 96p. (Orig.). 1993. pap. 14.95 (*1-878175-29-7*) F Amato Pubns.

Ancient Forests of the Pacific Northwest. Elliott A. Norse. LC 89-20029. (Illus.). 325p. (C). 1989. 34.95 (*1-55963-017-5*); pap. 19.95 (*1-55963-016-7*) Island Pr.

Ancient France: Neolithic Societies & Their Landscapes. Christopher Scarre. 400p. 1989. pap. 22.50 (*0-7486-0107-4*, Pub. by Edinburgh U Pr UK) Col U Pr.

Ancient Freemasonry: An Introduction to Masonic Archaeology. Frank C. Higgins. 470p. 1993. pap. 27.95 (*1-56459-339-8*) Kessinger Pub.

Ancient Funeral Monuments Within the United Monarchie of Great Britaine, Ireland & the Islands Adjacent. John Weever. LC 79-84145. (English Experience Ser.). 910p. 1979. reprint ed. lib. bdg. 125.00 (*90-221-0961-5*) Walter J Johnson.

Ancient Funerary Lamps, 3 vols. Pietro S. Bartoli & Giovanni P. Bellori. (Printed Sources of Western Art Ser.). (Illus.). 324p. (ITA.). 1972. reprint ed. pap. 60.00 (*0-915346-70-2*) A Wofsy Fine Arts.

Ancient Future of the Itza: The Book of Chilam Balam of Tizimin. Tr. by Munro S. Edmonson. LC 82-216667. (Texas Pan American Ser.). (Illus.). 240p. (C). 1982. text ed. 37.50 (*0-292-70353-8*) U of Tex Pr.

Ancient Futures: Learning from Ladakh. Helena Norberg-Hodge. LC 91-13868. (Illus.). 224p. 1992. reprint ed. pap. 12.00 (*0-87156-643-5*) Sierra.

Ancient Futures - Learning from Ladakh. Helena Norberg-Hodge. LC 91-13868. (Illus.). 192p. 1991. 25.00 (*0-87156-559-5*) Sierra.

Ancient Gems & Finger Rings: Catalogue of the Collections of the J. Paul Getty Museum. Jeffrey Spier. LC 91-44150. (Illus.). 248p. 1993. 60.00 (*0-89236-215-4*) J P Getty Trust.

Ancient Geography of India. Alexander Cunningham. 1990. reprint ed. 16.50 (*81-85395-47-0*) S Asia.

***Ancient Ghana: The Land of Gold.** Philip Koslow. LC 94-26192. (Kingdoms of Africa). (J). 1995. pap. write for info. (*0-7910-2941-7*) Chelsea Hse.

***Ancient Ghana: The Land of Gold.** Philip Koslow. LC 94-26192. (Kingdoms of Africa). (YA). (gr. 10 up). 1995. write for info. (*0-7910-3126-8*) Chelsea Hse.

Ancient Ghana & Mali. Nehemia Levtzion. LC 79-27281. 290p. (C). 1980. reprint ed. 29.50 (*0-8419-0431-6*, Africana) Holmes & Meier.

Ancient Ghosts & Modern Spectres: Eastern & Western World Contrast. Rudolf Steiner. 8p. 1969. reprint ed. spiral bd. 2.20 (*0-7873-0841-2*) Mokelumne.

Ancient Glass at the Newark Museum. Susan H. Auth. LC 76-47222. 1977. 15.95 (*0-932828-02-7*); pap. 9.95 (*0-932828-08-6*) Newark Mus.

Ancient Glass in the Yale University Art Gallery. Susan B. Matheson. 1980. pap. 13.00 (*0-89467-010-7*) Yale Art Gallery.

Ancient Gold of Kazakhstan. Comp. by K. Akishev. 262p. 1983. 65.00 (*0-317-40854-2*, Pub. by Collets UK) Pro-Am Music.

Ancient Grace: Inside the Cedar Sanctuary of Yakushima Island. Hiroaki Yamashita. Ed. by Seiji Horibuchi. 124p. 1992. 34.95 (*0-929279-79-4*, Cadence Bks) Viz Commns Inc.

Ancient Greece. John Artman. (Gifted Learning Ser.). 64p. (J). (gr. 4-8). 1991. 8.95 (*0-86653-583-7*, GA1310) Good Apple.

Ancient Greece. Rae Bains. LC 84-2685. (Illus.). 32p. (J). (gr. 3-6). 1985. lib. bdg. 9.49 (*0-8167-0244-6*); pap. text ed. 2.95 (*0-8167-0245-4*) Troll Assocs.

***Ancient Greece.** Mira Bartok & Christine Ronan. (Ancient & Living Cultures Ser.). 28p. (Orig.). (YA). (gr. 3 up). 1995. pap. 9.95 (*0-673-36255-8*) GdYrBks.

Ancient Greece. Bellerophon Staff. (J). (gr. 1-9). 1992. pap. 3.95 (*0-88388-000-8*) Bellerophon Bks.

Ancient Greece. Ed. by John D. Clare. LC 93-6267. (J). 1994. 16.95 (*0-15-200516-1*, Gulliver Bks) HarBrace.

Ancient Greece. Rowena Loverance. (See Through History Ser.). (Illus.). 48p. (J). (gr. 3-7). 1993. 14.99 (*0-670-84754-2*) Viking Child Bks.

Ancient Greece. Don Nardo. LC 93-6904. (World History Ser.). (J). (gr. 6-9). 1994. 16.95 (*1-56006-229-0*) Lucent Bks.

Ancient Greece. Robert Nicholson. LC 93-29442. (Journey into Civilization Ser.). (Illus.). 32p. (J). (gr. 3-7). 1994. 7.95 (*0-7910-2727-9*); lib. bdg. 14.95 (*0-7910-2703-1*) Chelsea Hse.

Ancient Greece. Anne Pearson. LC 92-4713. (Eyewitness Bks.). (Illus.). 64p. (J). (gr. 5 up). 1992. 16.00 (*0-679-81682-8*); lib. bdg. 16.99 (*0-679-91682-2*) Knopf Bks Yng Read.

Ancient Greece. Anton Powell. (Cultural Atlas for Young People Ser.). (Illus.). 96p. (YA). 1989. 17.95 (*0-8160-1972-X*) Facts on File.

Ancient Greece. Marinella Terzi. LC 92-7508. (World Heritage Ser.). (Illus.). 36p. (J). (gr. 3 up). 1992. lib. bdg. 15.00 (*0-516-08376-7*) Childrens.

Ancient Greece. Marinella Terzi. LC 92-7508. (World Heritage Ser.). (Illus.). 36p. (J). (gr. 3 up). 1993. pap. 6.95 (*0-516-48376-5*) Childrens.

Ancient Greece. Margaret Killingray. Ed. by Malcolm Yapp & Edmund O'Connor. (World History Ser.). Orig. Title: The Mediterranean. (Illus.). 32p. (YA). (gr. 6-11). 1980. reprint ed. pap. text ed. 4.35 (*0-89908-001-4*) Greenhaven.

Ancient Greece: A Thematic Unit. David Jefferies. (Thematic Units Ser.). (Illus.). 80p. (Orig.). (J). (gr. 6-8). 1993. student ed, pap. 8.95 (*1-55734-297-0*) Tchr Create Mat.

Ancient Greece: An Illustrated History. Peter Green. (Illus.). 1979. pap. 15.95 (*0-500-27161-5*) Thames Hudson.

Ancient Greece: Art, Culture, History. Kallas. (C). 1989. The Trojan War, IBM. 29.99 (*0-89824-607-5*); Greek Mythology, Apple. disk, pap. 29.99 (*0-89824-602-4*); Greek Mythology, IBM. pap. 29.99 (*0-89824-603-2*); Greek History & Culture, Apple. pap. 29.99 (*0-89824-604-0*); Greek History & Culture, IBM. pap. 29.99 (*0-89824-605-9*); The Trojan War, Apple. pap. 29.99 (*0-89824-606-7*); Odyssey, Apple. pap. 29.99 (*0-89824-608-3*); The Odyssey, IBM. pap. 29.99 (*0-89824-609-1*) Trillium Pr.

Ancient Greece: Documentary Perspectives. Stylianos Spyridakis & Bradley Nystrom. 320p. (C). 1993. per. 22.95 (*0-8403-8520-X*) Kendall-Hunt.

***Ancient Greece: Drawing History.** Raphael. (Illus.). 1995. pap. (*0-590-22729-7*) Scholastic Inc.

Ancient Greece: Social & Historical Documents from Archaic Times to the Death of Socrates. Matthew Dillon & Lynda Garland. LC 94-20490. (Classical Studies Ser.). 496p. 1995. 65.00x (*0-415-11366-0*, C0372); pap. 22.95 (*0-415-11367-9*, C0373) Routledge.

Ancient Greece: Using Evidence. Pamela Bradley. Ed. by David Patterson. (Illus.). 356p. (C). 1992. pap. text ed. 36.00 (*0-7131-8327-6*, Pub. by Hodder & Stoughton Ltd UK) Lubrecht & Cramer.

Ancient Greece & Rome. (Ultimate Sticker Bks.). (Illus.). 20p. (J). 1994. 6.95 (*1-56458-716-9*) Dorling Kindersley.

Ancient Greece at Work: An Economic History of Greece from the Homeric Period to the Roman Conquest. Gustave Glotz. (Illus.). xii, 402p. 1987. reprint ed. lib. bdg. 89.70 (*3-487-07928-3*, Pub. by Georg Olms GW) Lubrecht & Cramer.

Ancient Greece Resource Book. James Mason. (Sense of History Ser.). 1991. pap. text ed. 13.32 (*0-582-06819-3*) Longman.

Ancient Greek: A New Approach. 2nd ed. Carl A. Ruck. 1979. pap. 27.50 (*0-262-68031-9*) MIT Pr.

Ancient Greek Agriculture: An Introduction. Signe Isager & Jens E. Skydsgaard. LC 91-40139. (Illus.). 288p. 1992. 82.95 (*0-415-00164-1*, A7561) Routledge.

***Ancient Greek Agriculture: An Introduction.** Signe Isager & Jens E. Skydsgaard. (Illus.). 256p. 1995. pap. 18.95 (*0-415-11671-6*, C0201) Routledge.

Ancient Greek Architects at Work: Problems of Structure & Design. J. J. Coulton. 208p. 1982. pap. 15.95 (*0-8014-9234-3*) Cornell U Pr.

Ancient Greek Art & Iconography. Ed. by Warren G. Moon. LC 83-47765. (Illus.). 368p. 1983. 50.00 (*0-299-09250-X*) U of Wis Pr.

Ancient Greek Coins. 2nd rev. ed. Kenneth Jenkins. (Illus.). 181p. 1990. 75.00 (*1-85264-014-6*, Pub. by Seaby UK) Trafalgar.

Ancient Greek History. G. Polyzoides. (Illus.). (GRE.). (J). (gr. 4-6). 4.00 (*0-686-79636-5*) Divry.

Ancient Greek Literature. Kenneth J. Dover. (Oxford Paperbacks University Ser.). 1980. pap. 16.95 (*0-19-289124-3*) OUP.

Ancient Greek Literature. Harvard University Library Staff. (Widener Library Shelflist: No. 58). 638p. 1979. text ed. 55.00 (*0-674-03310-8*) HUP.

Ancient Greek Literature & Society. rev. ed. Charles R. Beye. LC 86-47979. (Illus.). 376p. 1987. pap. 14.95 (*0-8014-9444-3*) Cornell U Pr.

Ancient Greek Literature & Society. 2nd rev. ed. Charles R. Beye. LC 86-47979. (Illus.). 376p. 1987. 44.95 (*0-8014-1874-7*) Cornell U Pr.

Ancient Greek Military Practices, Part 1. William Kendrick Pritchett. LC 71-633960. (University of California Publications: Classical Studies: Vol. 7). 177p. reprint ed. pap. 50.50 (*0-8357-5465-0*, 2011037) Bks Demand.

Ancient Greek Monuments to Make: The Parthenon & the Theatre of Dionysos. Stephen Savage. (Great Architectural Replica Ser.). (Illus.). 48p. (Orig.). (YA). (gr. 7 up). 1990. pap. 7.95 (*0-88045-096-7*) Stemmer Hse.

Ancient Greek Music. M. L. West. (Illus.). 440p. 1994. reprint ed. pap. 24.00 (*0-19-814975-1*) OUP.

Ancient Greek Novels - The Fragments: Introduction, Text, Translation, & Commentary. Ed. by Susan A. Stephens & John J. Winkler. LC 92-23526. 472p. (C). 1993. 59.50 (*0-691-06941-7*) Princeton U Pr.

***Ancient Greek Philosophy: Its Development & Relevance to Our Time.** Robert C. Trundle. (Philosophy Ser.). 344p. 1994. 68.95 (*1-85628-978-8*, Pub. by Avebury Pub UK) Ashgate Pub Co.

Ancient Greek Psychology and the Modern Mind-Body Debate. Erik Ostenfeld. 109p. (Orig.). 1986. pap. 20.00 (*87-7288-010-4*) Coronet Bks.

Ancient Greek Terracottas. C. F. Vafopoulou-Richardson. (Illus.). 56p. 1995. pap. 12.95 (*1-85444-009-8*, 0098, Pub. by Ashmolean Mus UK) A Schwartz & Co.

Ancient Greek Theophoric Proper Names. E. Sittig. 167p. 1912. 20.00 (*0-89005-369-3*) Ares.

Ancient Greek Theophoric Toponyms. Busso Loewe. 128p. 1980. 15.00 (*0-89005-333-2*) Ares.

Ancient Greeks. Jenny Chattington & Mary Firman. (Illus.). (J). (gr. 2-6). pap. 4.95 (*0-7141-1283-6*, Pub. by Brit Mus UK) Parkwest Pubns.

Ancient Greeks. Jenny Chattington. (British Museum Activity Bks.). (Illus.). 16p. (J). (gr. 2 up). 1995. pap. 5.95 (*0-500-27788-5*) Thames Hudson.

Ancient Greeks. Moses I. Finley. 1987. pap. 9.95 (*0-14-055223-5*, Penguin Bks) Viking Penguin.

***Ancient Greeks.** Virginia Schomp. (Cultures of the Past Ser.). 80p. (J). (gr. 5-8). 1995. lib. bdg. write for info. (*0-7614-0070-2*, Benchmark NY) Marshall Cavendish.

Ancient Greeks. Nick Secunda. (Elite Ser.: No. 7). (Illus.). 64p. pap. 12.95 (*0-85045-686-X*, 9406, Pub. by Osprey Pubng Ltd UK) Stackpole.

Ancient Greeks. Morton Smith. (Development of Western Civilization Ser.). (Illus.). 144p. 1960. 8.95 (*0-8014-9852-X*) Cornell U Pr.

Ancient Greeks: A Critical History. John V. Fine. 744p. 1985. pap. text ed. 24.50 (*0-674-03314-0*) Belknap Pr.

Ancient Greeks: In the Land of the Gods. Sophie Descamps-Lequime & Denise Vernerey. Tr. by Mary K. LaRose. LC 91-35941. (Peoples of the Past Ser.). (Illus.). 64p. (J). (gr. 4-6). 1992. lib. bdg. 15.90 (*1-56294-069-4*) Millbrook Pr.

Ancient Grimoire of Dark Magick. Robert Blanchard. Ed. by Thorguard Templar. 105p. (Orig.). 1993. 25.00 (*1-883147-57-3*) Intern Guild ASRS.

Ancient Haunting: An Orginal Anthology. Ed. by R. Reginald & Douglas Menville. LC 75-46269. (Supernatural & Occult Fiction Ser.). (Illus.). 1976. lib. bdg. 39.95 (*0-405-08163-4*) Ayer.

Ancient Hawaii. Bellerophon Staff. (J). (gr. 1-9). 1992. pap. 2.95 (*0-88388-091-1*) Bellerophon Bks.

Ancient Hawaiian Music. Helen H. Roberts. (BMB Ser.). 1972. reprint ed. pap. 60.00 (*0-527-02132-6*) Periodicals Srv.

Ancient Hearts Whisper: Egyptian Love Poetry. Kathleen L. Mendel. Ed. & Pref. by Candy K. Brethauer. LC 92-97166. 36p. (Orig.). (C). 1992. pap. 5.20 (*1-878142-28-3*) Telstar TX.

Ancient Heavens. Robert E. Vardeman. 256p. (Orig.). 1989. pap. 3.50 (*0-380-75439-8*) Avon.

Ancient Hebrew Inscriptions: Corpus & Concordance. Ed. by G. I. Davies. 596p. (C). 1991. 130.00 (*0-521-40248-4*) Cambridge U Pr.

Ancient Hebrew Social Life & Custom As Indicated in Law, Narrative & Metaphor. R. H. Kennett. (British Academy, London, Schweich Lectures on Biblical Archaeology Series, 1930). 1972. reprint ed. pap. 20.00 (*0-8115-1273-8*) Periodicals Srv.

Ancient Herbs in the J. Paul Getty Museum. Jeanne D'Andrea. LC 82-81306. (Illus.). 96p. 1989. reprint ed. pap. 7.95 (*0-89236-035-6*) J P Getty Trust.

An Asterisk (*) at the beginning of an entry indicates that the title is appearing in BIP for the first time.

An Asterisk (*) at the beginning of an entry indicates that the title is appearing in BIP for the first time.

303

Ancient Logic & Its Modern Interpretations: Proceedings of the Buffalo Symposium on Modernist Interpretation of Ancient Logic, April 21 & 22, 1972. Buffalo Symposium on Modernist Interpretation of Ancient Logic Staff. Ed. by J. Corcoran. LC 73-88589. (Synthese Historical Library: No. 9). 1974. lib. bdg. 94.00 (*90-277-0395-7*) Kluwer Ac.

Ancient Machine & Contrivances, Greek & Roman. William Smith. (Illus.). 68p. 1972. pap. 5.00x (*0-87291-035-0*) Coronado Pr.

Ancient Magicks for a New Age. Alan Richardson & Geoff Hughes. LC 88-45185. (High Magick Ser.). (Illus.). 320p. (Orig.). 1989. pap. 12.95 (*0-87542-671-9*) Llewellyn Pubns.

Ancient Man: A Handbook of Puzzling Artifacts. William R. Corliss & John C. Holden. LC 77-99243. (Illus.). 1978. 21.95 (*0-915554-03-8*) Sourcebook.

***Ancient Mariner One Hundred-Two Hour Cruise Specialist Series.** rev. ed. Pat Cashman. (Illus.). 1995. 1,500.00 (*0-614-04773-0*) Eclectic Trvl.

Ancient Mariners: Seafarers & Sea Fighters of the Mediterranean in Ancient Times. 2nd ed. Lionel Casson. (Illus.). 299p. 1991. text ed. 44.50 (*0-691-06836-4*); pap. text ed. 14.95 (*0-691-01477-9*) Princeton U Pr.

Ancient Mariners of Samuel Taylor Coleridge: The Texts of 1798-1828. Comment by Martin Wallen. LC 92-37977. (Clinamen Studies). 1993. 34.95 (*0-88268-123-0*); pap. 16.95 (*0-88268-148-6*) Station Hill Pr.

***Ancient Masonry: The Spiritual Meaning of Masonic Degrees, Rituals & Symbols.** C. C. Zain. (Brotherhood of Light Ser.: Course 4). 344p. 1994. pap. 14.95 (*0-87887-374-0*) Church of Light.

Ancient Maya. 4th rev. ed. Sylvanus G. Morley & George W. Brainerd. LC 81-85451. (Illus.). xx, 708p. 1983. 45.00 (*0-8047-1137-2*); pap. 19.95 (*0-8047-1288-3*) Stanford U Pr.

Ancient Maya. 5th ed. Ed. by Robert J. Sharer. LC 93-13566. 1994. 45.00 (*0-8047-2130-0*) Stanford U Pr.

Ancient Maya. 5th ed. Robert J. Sharer. 1994. pap. 24.95 (*0-8047-2310-9*) Stanford U Pr.

Ancient Maya City of Sayil: The Mapping of a Puuc Region Center. Jeremy A. Sabloff & Gair Tourtellot. LC 90-44402. (Publication Ser.: No. 60). 1991. 37.50 (*0-939238-88-8*) Tulane MARI.

Ancient Maya Civilization. Norman Hammond. (Illus.). 337p. (C). 1982. 15.00 (*0-8135-0906-8*) Rutgers U Pr.

Ancient Maya Temples to Make. Stephen A. Savage. (Great Architectural Replica Ser.). (Illus.). 32p. (Orig.). 1987. pap. 7.95 (*0-88045-091-6*) Stemmer Hse.

Ancient Medicine. Ludwig Edelstein. Ed. by Owsei Temkin & C. Lilian Temkin. Tr. by C. Lilian Temkin. LC 67-12425. 448p. 1987. reprint ed. pap. text ed. 18.95 (*0-8018-3491-0*) Johns Hopkins.

Ancient Medicine: Selected Papers of Ludwig Edelstein. Ludwig Edelstein. Ed. by Owsei Temkin & C. Lilian Temkin. LC 67-12425. 510p. reprint ed. pap. 145.40 (*0-8357-5466-9*, 2020329) Bks Demand.

Ancient Mediterranean. Michael Grant. 384p. 1988. pap. 9.95 (*0-452-00949-9*, Mer) NAL-Dutton.

Ancient Mediterranean. Michael Grant. 1988. pap. 13.95 (*0-452-01037-3*, Plume) NAL-Dutton.

Ancient Memories. Ronald Way. 1991. 21.95 (*1-880004-05-4*) Masterworks.

Ancient Memory & Other Stories. John G. Neihardt. LC 91-2603. xiv, 230p. 1991. 19.95 (*0-8032-3327-2*) U of Nebr Pr.

Ancient Menippean Satire. Joel C. Relihan. LC 92-36271. 344p. (C). 1993. text ed. 47.50 (*0-8018-4524-6*) Johns Hopkins.

Ancient Mesoamerica: A Comparison of Change in Three Regions. 2nd ed. Richard E. Blanton et al. (New Studies in Archaeology). (Illus.). 300p. (C). 1993. pap. 19.95 (*0-521-44606-6*) Cambridge U Pr.

Ancient Mesoamerica: A Comparison of Change in Three Regions. 2nd ed. Richard E. Blanton et al. (New Studies in Archaeology). (Illus.). 300p. (C). 1993. 79.95 (*0-521-44053-X*) Cambridge U Pr.

Ancient Mesoamerica: Selections from the University Gallery Collection. John F. Scott. (Illus.). 1987. pap. 9.95 (*0-8130-0882-4*) U Press Fla.

Ancient Mesopotamia: Portrait of a Dead Civilization. 2nd rev. ed. A. Leo Oppenheim. LC 64-19847. (Illus.). 1977. pap. text ed. 16.95 (*0-226-63187-7*) U Ch Pr.

Ancient Mesopotamian Materials & Industries: The Archaeological Evidence. P. R. Moorey. (Illus.). 448p. 1994. 105.00 (*0-19-814921-2*) OUP.

Ancient Metal Axes & Other Tools in the Royal Ontario Museum: European & Mediterranean Types. John W. Hayes. (Illus.). 120p. 1994. pap. 50.00 (*0-88854-393-X*, Pub. by Royal Ont Mus CN) U of Toronto Pr.

Ancient Metallurgy in the U. S. S. R. The Early Metal Age. E. N. Chernykh. (New Studies in Archaeology). (Illus.). 416p. (C). 1993. 94.95 (*0-521-25257-1*) Cambridge U Pr.

Ancient Metrology. Donald L. Lenzen. (Illus.). 108p. 1989. 14.95 (*0-9625309-0-5*) D L Lenzen.

Ancient Mexico: Aztec, Mixtec, & Mayo Landscapes. George E. Stuart & Winfield Swanson. LC 92-9985. (Touring North America Ser.). (Illus.). 150p. 1992. 25.00 (*0-8135-1892-X*); pap. 9.95 (*0-8135-1893-8*) Rutgers U Pr.

Ancient Mexico: Cultural Traditions in the Land of the Feathered Serpent. 4th ed. Jacqueline P. Lathrop. 208p. (C). 1994. per., pap. text ed. 21.95 (*0-8403-6426-1*) Kendall-Hunt.

Ancient Mexico: Stencils. Mira Bartok & Christine Ronan. (Ancient & Living Cultures Ser.). (Illus.). 32p. (Orig.). (J). (gr. 3 up). 1992. pap. 9.95 (*0-673-36055-5*) GdYrBks.

Ancient Mind: Elements of Cognitive Archaeology. Ed. by Colin Renfrew & Ezra B. Zubrow. (New Directions in Archaeology Ser.). (Illus.). 208p. (C). 1994. pap. 19.95 (*0-521-45620-7*) Cambridge U Pr.

Ancient Mind: Elements of Cognitive Archaeology. Ed. by Colin Renfrew & Ezra B. Zubrow. (New Directions in Archaeology Ser.). (Illus.). 208p. (C). 1994. 59.95 (*0-521-43488-2*) Cambridge U Pr.

Ancient Mineralogy: An Inquiry Respecting Mineral Substances Mentioned by the Ancients. Nathaniel F. Moore. Ed. by Claude C. Albritton, Jr. LC 77-6532. (History of Geology Ser.). 1978. reprint ed. lib. bdg. 23.95 (*0-405-10452-9*) Ayer.

Ancient Mining. Robert Shepherd. LC 92-43982. 1993. write for info. (*1-85861-011-7*) Elsevier.

Ancient Mirrors of Womanhood: A Treasury of Goddess & Heroine Lore from Around the World. Merlin Stone. LC 83-73164. (Illus.). 425p. 1984. pap. 14.00 (*0-8070-6751-2*, BP676) Beacon Pr.

Ancient Modocs of California & Oregon. Carrol B. Howe & Patricia J. Easterla. LC 79-1870. (Illus.). 264p. 1994. pap. 14.95 (*0-8323-0338-0*) Binford Mort.

Ancient Monuments of Shetland. Noel Fojut & Denys Pringle. 64p. 1993. pap. 7.95 (*0-11-494200-5*, HM42005, Pub. by HMSO UK) UNIPUB.

Ancient Monuments of the Mississippi Valley. Ephraim G. Squier & E. H. Davis. LC 72-4998. (Harvard University. Peabody Museum of Archaeology & Ethnology. Antiquities of the New World Ser.: No. 2). (Illus.). reprint ed. 105.00 (*0-404-57302-9*) AMS Pr.

Ancient Monuments of the Mississippi Valley: Complete 48 Plate Collection. E. G. Squier & E. H. Davis. (Archaeology, Ohio History, Prehistoric Indians Ser.). (Illus.). 48p. 1992. reprint ed. pap. 12.90 (*1-56651-063-5*); reprint ed. pap. 6.00 (*1-56651-073-2*) A W McGraw.

Ancient Monuments of the Mississippi Valley: Comprising the Results of Extensive Original Surveys & Explorations. E. G. Squier & E. H. Davis. (Archaeology, Ohio History, Prehistoric Indians Ser.). (Illus.). 444p. 1992. reprint ed. lib. bdg. 66.80 (*1-56651-061-9*); reprint ed. pap. 49.65 (*1-56651-060-0*) A W McGraw.

Ancient Monuments of the Western Isles. 72p. 1994. pap. 7.95 (*0-11-495201-9*, HM52019, Pub. by HMSO UK) UNIPUB.

Ancient Mortuary Traditions of China: Papers on Chinese Ceramic Funerary Sculptures. Ed. by George Kuwayama. (Illus.). 106p. (C). 1991. pap. text ed. 20.00 (*0-87587-157-7*) LA Co Art Mus.

Ancient Murrelet: A Natural History in the Queen Charlotte Islands. Anthony J. Gaston. (Poyser Popular Bird Bks.). (Illus.). 249p. 1992. text ed. 34.95 (*0-85661-070-4*, 784670) Acad Pr.

***Ancient Musics: A Poetry Sequence.** Albert Goldbarth. Ed. by Gloria V. Hickok. 24p. (Orig.). 1995. pap. 5.00 (*1-884235-08-5*) Helicon Nine Eds.

Ancient Mysteries. Rupert Furneaux. 240p. 1987. mass mkt. 4.95 (*0-345-34528-2*) Ballantine.

Ancient Mysteries: A Sourcebook. Ed. by Marvin Meyer. LC 86-45022. (Illus.). 256p. (Orig.). 1987. pap. 16.00 (*0-06-065576-3*) Harper SF.

Ancient Mysteries & Modern Masonry. C. H. Vail. 214p. 1992. reprint ed. pap. 24.95 (*1-56459-061-5*) Kessinger Pub.

Ancient Mysteries & Modern Masonry. Charles H. Vail. (African Studies). reprint ed. 25.00 (*0-938818-77-5*) ECA Assoc.

Ancient Mysteries & Modern Revelations. W. J. Colville. 366p. 1993. reprint ed. pap. 24.95 (*1-56459-400-9*) Kessinger Pub.

Ancient Mysteries Described. William Hone. 1972. 59.95 (*0-8490-1426-3*) Gordon Pr.

Ancient Mysteries Described. William Hone. 300p. 1973. spiral bd. 10.45 (*0-7873-0418-2*) Mokelumne.

Ancient Mystery & Modern Revelation. W. J. Colville. 366p. 1994. pap. 30.00 (*0-89540-122-3*, SB-122) Sun Pub.

Ancient Mystery Cults. Walter Burkert. (Carl Newell Jackson Lectures). 176p. 1989. pap. 12.95 (*0-674-03387-6*) HUP.

Ancient Mystic Oriental Masonry. R. Swinburne Clymer. 193p. 1969. reprint ed. spiral bd. 8.25 (*0-7873-0183-3*) Mokelumne.

Ancient Mystic Rites. Charles W. Leadbeater. LC 86-40125. Orig. Title: Glimpses of Masonic History. (Illus.). 270p. 1986. reprint ed. pap. 9.75 (*0-8356-0609-0*, Quest) Theos Pub Hse.

Ancient Mystical White Brotherhood. Frater Achad. pap. 4.95 (*0-87707-068-7*) CSA Pr.

Ancient Mystical White Brotherhood. 4th rev. ed. Frater Achad. Ed. by Constance Roggo. 186p. (Orig.). 1991. pap. text ed. 10.95 (*0-926872-02-8*) Great Seal Pr.

Ancient Myth & Modern Life. rev. ed. Gerald A. Larue. (Illus.). 304p. 1988. pap. 16.95 (*0-913111-24-4*) Centerline.

Ancient Myths. Norma L. Goodrich. 256p. (gr. 9). 1960. pap. 3.95 (*0-451-62361-4*, Ment) NAL-Dutton.

Ancient Myths. Norma L. Goodrich. (Illus.). 256p. 1994. pap. 10.95 (*0-452-01129-9*, Mer) NAL-Dutton.

Ancient Myths & the New Isis Mystery. Rudolf Steiner. (Illus.). 160p. (Orig.). 1994. pap. 14.95 (*0-88010-377-9*) Anthroposophic.

Ancient Nahuatl Poetry. Ed. by Daniel G. Brinton. LC 70-83462. (Library of Aboriginal American Literature: No. 7). reprint ed. 30.00 (*0-404-52187-8*) AMS Pr.

Ancient Names: Etymologies. Ed. by K. A. Girvilas. LC 86-82212. (Illus.). 126p. 1986. 10.00 (*0-936694-57-2*) Lith Inst Educ.

Ancient Names of Localities. Edward Burgess & Ellis Brewster. (Pilgrim Society Notes Ser.: No. 20). 1970. 2.00 (*0-940628-07-4*) Pilgrim Soc.

Ancient Natural History: Histories of Nature. Roger French. LC 94-5131. (Sciences of Antiquity Ser.). 368p. 1994. 65.00x (*0-415-08880-1*, B4511); pap. 19.95 (*0-415-11545-0*, B4515) Routledge.

Ancient Near East. Bellerophon Staff. (J). (gr. 1-9). 1992. pap. 3.95 (*0-88388-002-4*) Bellerophon Bks.

***Ancient Near East.** Amelie Kurht. LC 94-41951. (Routledge History of the Ancient World Ser.). 1995. write for info. (*0-415-01352-6*) Routledge.

***Ancient Near East.** Amelie Kurht. LC 94-41951. (History of the Ancient World Ser.). (C). 1995. write for info. (*0-415-12872-2*) Routledge.

Ancient Near East. P. R. Moorey. (Illus.). 58p. 1995. pap. 12.95 (*0-907849-58-X*, 58-X, Pub. by Ashmolean Mus UK) A Schwartz & Co.

***Ancient Near East.** Clarice Swisher. LC 94-37173. (J). 1995. 16.95 (*1-56006-284-3*) Lucent Bks.

Ancient Near East. Malcolm Yapp. Ed. by Margaret Killingray et al. (World History Ser.). (Illus.). 32p. (YA). (gr. 6-11). 1980. reprint ed. pap. text ed. 4.35 (*0-89908-000-6*) Greenhaven.

***Ancient Near East, Vol. 1.** Amelie Kurht. LC 94-41951. (History of the Ancient World Ser.). (C). 1995. write for info. (*0-415-01353-4*) Routledge.

Ancient Near East: A History. William W. Hallo & William K. Simpson. LC 71-155560. 319p. (C). 1971. pap. text ed. 20.00 (*0-15-502755-7*) HB Coll Pubs.

Ancient Near East in Pictures. 2nd ed. Ed. by James B. Pritchard. Incl. , 2 vols. 1969. Set. 99.50 (*0-691-03502-4*); An Anthology of Texts & Pictures1969. pap. 14.95 (*0-691-00209-6*); An Anthology of Texts & Pictures1969. pap. 16.95 (*0-691-00200-2*); Pictures1969. (*0-691-03610-1*); 1969. Set pap. write for info. (*0-318-70291-6*) Princeton U Pr.

Ancient Near East in the Walters Art Gallery. Jeanny Canby. LC 75-310215. (Illus.). 1974. pap. 1.50 (*0-911886-01-X*) Walters Art.

***Ancient Near Eastern Art.** Dominique Collon. 1995. write for info. (*0-520-20307-0*) U CA Pr.

Ancient Near Eastern Cylinder Seals from the Marcopoli Collection. Beatrice Teissier. 1984. 77.50 (*0-317-01206-1*) Numismatic Fine Arts.

Ancient Near Eastern Cylinder Seals from the Marcopoli Collection. Beatrice Teissier. LC 83-3628. (Illus.). 420p. 1984. 90.00 (*0-520-04927-6*) U CA Pr.

Ancient Near Eastern Texts: Relating to the Old Testament. 3rd ed. Ed. by James B. Pritchard. LC 78-76499. 734p. reprint ed. pap. 180.00 (*0-8357-8801-6*, 2052276) Bks Demand.

Ancient Near Eastern Texts Relating to the Old Testament, Set. 3rd ed. Ed. by James B. Pritchard. 1969. 89.50 (*0-691-03503-2*) Princeton U Pr.

Ancient North America: The Archaeology of a Continent. Brian M. Fagan. LC 90-70290. (Illus.). 480p. (C). 1991. pap. text ed. 34.95 (*0-500-27606-4*) Thames Hudson.

***Ancient North America: The Archaeology of a Continent.** rev. ed. Brian Fagan. LC 94-61064. (Illus.). 480p. 1995. 45.00 (*0-500-05075-9*) Thames Hudson.

***Ancient North America: The Archaeology of a Continent.** rev. ed. Brian Fagan. LC 94-61064. (Illus.). 480p. (C). 1995. per., pap. text ed. 34.95 (*0-500-27817-2*) Thames Hudson.

Ancient Novel: An Introduction. Niklas Holzberg. Tr. by Christine Jackson-Holzberg. LC 94-16557. 140p. 1995. 39.95 (*0-415-10752-0*, B4844) Routledge.

***Ancient Novel: An Introduction.** Niklas Holzberg. Tr. by Christine Jackson-Holzberg. 140p. 1995. pap. 13.95 (*0-415-10753-9*, B4848) Routledge.

Ancient Novgorod: Applied Art & Archaeology. B. Kilchin. 168p. 1985. 158.00 (*0-317-61207-7*, Pub. by Collets UK) Pro-Am Music.

***Ancient Nubia.** P. L. Shinnie. LC 95-15878. 1995. write for info. (*0-7103-0517-6*, Pub. by Kegan Paul Intl UK) Routledge Chapman & Hall.

Ancient Oaxaca: Discoveries in Mexican Archeology & History. Ed. by John Paddock. (Illus.). xvi, 416p. 1966. 42.50 (*0-8047-0170-9*) Stanford U Pr.

Ancient of Days. Michael Bishop. LC 84-28324. 384p. 1995. pap. 13.95 (*0-312-89027-3*) Orb NYC.

Ancient Olympic Games. Judith Swaddling. LC 83-51502. (Illus.). 80p. (C). 1984. pap. 9.95 (*0-292-70373-2*) U of Tex Pr.

Ancient One. T. A. Barron. 352p. 1994. mass mkt. 4.99 (*0-8125-3654-1*) Tor Bks.

Ancient One. Tom Barron. (Illus.). 368p. (YA). (gr. 6 up). 1992. 17.95 (*0-399-21899-8*, Philomel Bks) Putnam Pub Group.

Ancient One: A Disciple's Memoirs of Meher Baba. Ed. by Anzar Naosherwan. (Illus.). 280p. (Orig.). 1985. 16.95 (*0-685-10268-8*); pap. 12.00 (*0-685-10269-6*) Beloved Bks.

Ancient Ones: Sacred Monuments of the Inca, Maya & Cliffdwellers. Hans Li. 1994. 35.00 (*0-9639556-0-8*) City of Light.

Ancient Ones: The World of the Old-Growth Douglas Fir. Barbara Bash. (Illus.). 32p. (J). (gr. 1-5). 1994. 16.95 (*0-87156-561-7*) Sierra.

Ancient Operative Masonry. S. R. Parchment. 209p. 1975. reprint ed. spiral bd. 8.25 (*0-7873-1114-6*) Mokelumne.

Ancient Ophthamological Agents. Harald Nielsen. (Acta Historica Scientarium Ser.: No. 31). 117p. (Orig.). 1974. pap. 24.00 (*87-7492-108-8*, Pub. by Odense Universitets Forlag DK) Coronet Bks.

Ancient Orkney Melodies. David Balfour. (C). 1986. 60.00 (*0-907618-12-X*, Pub. by Orkney Pr UK) St Mut.

Ancient, Pagan & Modern Christian Symbolism. Thomas Inman. 147p. 1978. reprint ed. 20.00 (*0-87928-101-4*) Corner Hse.

Ancient Pagan & Modern Christian Symbolism: With an Essay on Baal Worship, on the Assyrian Sacred "Grove," & Other Allied Symbols (1915) Thomas Inman. (Illus.). 190p. 1993. pap. 17.95 (*1-56459-408-4*) Kessinger Pub.

Ancient Pagan Symbols. Elizabeth E. Goldsmith. (Illus.). reprint ed. 17.00 (*0-404-02861-6*) AMS Pr.

Ancient Painted Images of the Columbia Gorge. John Woodward. (Illus.). 100p. (Orig.). 1982. pap. 19.95 (*0-916552-28-4*) Acoma Bks.

Ancient Painting from the Earliest Times to the Period of Christian Art. Mary H. Swindler. LC 75-41269. (Illus.). reprint ed. 87.50 (*0-404-14808-5*) AMS Pr.

Ancient Path. Edward M. Matthews. 56p. 1989. reprint ed. pap. 1.75 (*0-935461-23-X*) St Alban Pr CA.

Ancient Paths. Craig Hill. 111p. (Orig.). 1992. pap. 8.99 (*1-881189-01-5*) Harv Bks & Pub.

Ancient Patterns in Modern Prayer. Thomas A. Krosnicki. LC 74-172790. (Cahtolic University of America Studies in Christian Antiquity: Vol. 19). 317p. reprint ed. pap. 90.40 (*0-8357-5467-7*, 2029516) Bks Demand.

***Ancient Peoples & Landscapes.** Pat Shipman et al. Ed. by Eileen Johnson. (Illus.). 350p. (Orig.). (C). Date not set. pap. text ed. 29.95 (*0-9640188-1-0*) Mus TX Tech.

Ancient Persia. John Curtis. (British Museum Paperbacks Ser.). (Illus.). 72p. 1990. pap. 13.50 (*0-674-03415-5*) HUP.

Ancient Persia: The Art of an Empire. Ed. by Denise Schmandt-Besserat. LC 79-67267. (Invited Lectures on the Middle East at the University of Texas at Austin Ser.: Vol. 4). (Illus.). 141p. 1980. pap. 21.25 (*0-89003-040-5*) Undena Pubns.

Ancient Persia & Iranian Civilization. Clement Huart. 1976. lib. bdg. 59.95 (*0-8490-1427-1*) Gordon Pr.

Ancient Persian Numismatics: Elymais. De Morgan. (Illus.). 62p. 1975. 12.50 (*0-915018-15-2*) Attic Bks.

Ancient Peruvian Textiles. Judith C. Riley. (Illus.). 15p. 1980. pap. 3.50 (*0-940744-28-7*) Chrysler Museum.

Ancient Philosophy & Grammar: The Syntax of Appolonius Dyscolus. David Blank. LC 82-5751. (American Philological Association, American Classical Studies). 136p. 1983. pap. 15.95 (*0-89130-580-7*, 40 04 10) Scholars Pr GA.

***Ancient Philosophy, Mystery, & Magic: Empedocles & Pythagorean.** Peter Kingsley. (Illus.). 375p. 1995. 60.00 (*0-19-814988-3*) OUP.

Ancient Phoenicia & Ancient Israel. A. S. Wilkins. 220p. 1980. reprint ed. 25.00 (*0-89005-361-8*) Ares.

Ancient Planetary Observations & the Validity of Ephemeris Time. Robert R. Newton. LC 75-44392. 768p. 1976. 65.00 (*0-8018-1842-7*) Johns Hopkins.

Ancient Plants. M. C. Stopes. 197p. (C). 1984. reprint ed. 110.00 (*81-7089-021-7*, Pub. by Intl Bk Distr II) St Mut.

Ancient Polynesian Society. Irving Goldman. LC 74-116028. 657p. reprint ed. pap. 180.00 (*0-8357-5468-5*, 2026735) Bks Demand.

Ancient Population of Siberia & Its Cultures. Aleksei P. Okladnikov. Tr. by Vladimir M. Maurin. LC 76-38729. (Harvard University. Peabody Museum of Archaeology & Ethnology. Antiquities of the New World Ser.: Vol. 1, No. 1). reprint ed. 47.50 (*0-404-52641-1*) AMS Pr.

Ancient Portraits from the Athenian Agora. Evelyn B. Harrison. (Excavations of the Athenian Agora Picture Bks.: No. 5). (Illus.). 32p. 1960. pap. 3.00 (*0-87661-605-8*) Am Sch Athens.

Ancient Portraits in the J. Paul Getty Museum 1. Ed. by Jiri Frel & Marion True. LC 87-5647. (Occasional Papers on Antiquities: No. 4). (Illus.). 142p. (Orig.). 1987. pap. 37.50 (*0-89236-071-2*) J P Getty Trust.

Ancient Prophets & Modern Problems. Samuel L. Brengle. 1978. reprint ed. pap. 4.95 (*0-86544-000-X*) Salv Army Suppl South.

Ancient Proverbs & Maxims from Burmese Sources: The Niti Literature of Burma. Ed. by James Gray. LC 77-87014. reprint ed. 17.50 (*0-404-16822-1*) AMS Pr.

Ancient Province of Tusayan see Hopi Villages (the Ancient Province of Tusayan)

Ancient Pueblo Peoples. Linda Cordell. LC 94-2308. (Exploring the Ancient World Ser.). 1994. write for info. (*0-89599-038-5*) Smithsonian Bks.

Ancient Pueblos Ruins see West on Wood: Antique Wood Engravings of the Old West

Ancient Puzzles: Classic Brainteasers & Other Timeless Mathematical Games of the Last Ten Centuries. Dominic Olivastro. LC 93-1985. 1993. pap. 12.95 (*0-553-37297-1*) Bantam.

Ancient Quarrel Between Poetry & Philosophy. Thomas Gould. 340p. 1991. text ed. 45.00 (*0-691-07375-9*) Princeton U Pr.

***Ancient Quarry in Indian Territory.** William H. Holmes. (Bureau of American Ethnology Bulletins Ser.). 99p. 1995. lib. bdg. 69.00 (*0-7812-4021-2*) Rprt Serv.

Ancient Quarry in Indian Territory. William H. Holmes. 1988. reprint ed. lib. bdg. 49.00 (*0-7812-0027-X*) Rprt Serv.

Ancient Quotes & Anecdotes: From Crib to Crypt. Ed. by Vernon K. Robbins. LC 88-12583. (Foundations & Facets: Reference Ser.). 512p. 1989. 29.95 (*0-944344-02-X*); pap. 21.95 (*0-944344-03-8*) Polebridge Pr.

***Ancient Rage.** May L. Wile. 144p. 1995. 16.00 (*0-943914-70-1*) Larson Pubns.

Ancient Rain: Poems Nineteen Fifty-Six to Nineteen Seventy-Eight. Bob Kaufman. Ed. by Raymond Foye. LC 81-1250. 96p. (C). 1981. 5.95 (*0-8112-0790-0*) New Directions.

Ancient Records from North Arabia. Frederick V. Winnett & W. L. Reed. LC 73-472676. (Near & Middle East Ser.: No. 6). (Illus.). 263p. reprint ed. pap. 75.00 (*0-8357-5470-7*, 2020535) Bks Demand.

An Asterisk (*) at the beginning of an entry indicates that the title is appearing in BIP for the first time.

An Asterisk (*) at the beginning of an entry indicates that the title is appearing in BIP for the first time.

Ancient Wisdom: Nyingma Teachings on Dream Yoga, Meditation & Transformation. Gyatrul Rinpoche. Tr. by B. Alan Wallace & Sangye Khandro. LC 93-13992. 1993. pap. 14.95 (*1-55939-018-2*) Snow Lion Pubns.

Ancient Wisdom & Modern Science. Ed. by Stanislav Grof. LC 83-17877. 285p. 1984. 44.50 (*0-87395-848-9*); pap. 14.95 (*0-87395-849-7*) State U NY Pr.

Ancient Wisdom & Secret Sects. (Mysteries of the Unknown Ser.). (Illus.). 160p. 1989. 17.27 (*0-8094-6348-2*); lib. bdg. 23.27 (*0-8094-6349-0*) Time-Life.

***Ancient Wisdom for Modern Ignorance.** Swami B. Tripurari. (Illus.). 174p. (Orig.). 1994. pap. 11.95 (*1-886069-11-5*) Clarion Call.

Ancient Wisdom for Today's World: A Commentary on the Book of Proverbs. Daniel L. Segraves. LC 89-29358. 352p. (Orig.). (C). 1990. pap. 8.99 (*0-932581-60-9*) Word Aflame.

Ancient Wisdom, New Spirit: Investigations into Being Alive. Peter Ralston. LC 94-25348. 238p. 1994. pap. 12.95 (*1-883319-21-8*) Frog CA.

Ancient Wisdom, New Spirit: Investigations into Being Alive. Peter Ralston. 300p. (C). 1994. pap. 12.95 (*0-685-72179-5*) North Atlantic.

Ancient Wisdom of Origin. John C. Smith. LC 90-53315. 376p. 1992. 49.50 (*0-8387-5204-7*) Bucknell U Pr.

Ancient Wizdom Stories. Roberta S. Herzog. Ed. by Julia Wright. (Illus.). 144p. (Orig.). 1994. pap. 12.95 (*1-884695-08-6*) Wrds of Wizdom.

***Ancient Women: The Making of Lucy.** J. R. Whittaker. 1995. 11.95 (*0-8062-5077-1*) Carlton.

***Ancient World.** (J). (gr. 5-8). 1991. teacher ed 54.00 (*0-382-24273-4*) Silver Burdett Pr.

Ancient World. Mike Corbishley. (Timelink Ser.). (Illus.). 60p. (YA). (gr. 5 up). 1993. 17.95 (*0-87226-354-1*) P Bedrick Bks.

Ancient World. Helen Howe & Robert T. Howe. (Illus.). 304p. (C). 1988. pap. text ed. 23.95 (*0-8013-0226-9*, 75884) Longman.

Ancient World. Helen Howe & Robert T. Howe. (Illus.). 304p. 1992. pap. text ed. 23.92 (*0-582-36761-1*, 72537) Longman.

Ancient World. P. J. Larkin. 64p. (C). 1988. 35.00 (*0-685-33810-X*, Pub. by S Thornes Pubs UK) St Mut.

Ancient World. A. Millard et al. (Illustrated World History Ser.). (Illus.). 288p. (YA). (gr. 7-12). 1992. pap. 24.95 (*0-7460-1233-0*) EDC.

Ancient World. 2nd ed. R. J. Cootes & L. E. Snellgrove. (Longman Secondary Histories Ser.). (Illus.). 208p. (YA). (gr. 6-12). 1991. student ed 11.72 (*0-582-36690-9*, 72482); pap. text ed. 23.00 (*0-582-31785-1*, 79165) Longman.

Ancient World. 2nd ed. D. Brendan Nagle. 464p. (C). 1989. pap. text ed. write for info. (*0-13-036419-3*) P-H.

Ancient World. P. J. Larkin. (Illus.). 64p. 1971. reprint ed. pap. 10.95 (*0-7175-0588-X*) Dufour.

Ancient World, 12 bks., Set. Pamela Odijk. (Illus.). 48p. (J). (gr. 5-8). 1991. lib. bdg. 179.40 (*0-382-09883-8*) Silver Burdett Pr.

***Ancient World, 12 bks., Set, 48pg. ea.** Pamela Odijk. (Illus.). (J). (gr. 5-8). 1991. pap. 95.40 (*0-382-24258-0*) Silver Burdett Pr.

Ancient World: A Beginning. Terrot R. Glover. LC 79-11456. 350p. 1980. reprint ed. text ed. 35.00 (*0-313-21459-X*, GLAW, Greenwood Pr) Greenwood.

Ancient World: A Reading & Writing Approach. Ralph Sawyer. (Illus.). 196p. 1993. teacher ed 6.60 (*0-8442-5626-9*, Natl Textbk); pap. text ed. 12.95 (*0-8442-5625-0*, Natl Textbk) NTC Pub Grp.

***Ancient World: A Social & Cultural History.** 3rd ed. D. Brendan Nagle. LC 95-6482. 1995. pap. text ed. write for info. (*0-13-310806-6*) P-H.

Ancient World: Readings in Social & Cultural History. Ed. by D. B. Nagle & Stanley M. Burstein. LC 94-18200. 323p. 1994. pap. text ed. write for info. (*0-13-756222-5*) P-H.

Ancient World: The Pagan Background of Early Christianity. W. R. Haliday. 1991. lib. bdg. 79.95 (*0-8490-4302-6*) Gordon Pr.

***Ancient World Lists & Numbers: Numerical Phrases & Rosters in Greco-Roman & Near Eastern Civilizations.** David Matz. 320p. 1995. lib. bdg. 44.50x (*0-7864-0039-0*) McFarland & Co.

Ancient World of the Bible. Malcolm Day. (Illus.). 80p. (J). (gr. 2 up). 1994. 19.99 (*0-670-85607-X*) Viking Child Bks.

Ancient Worlds: Gender Representation: Northeast Region National Collegiate Honor Society Symposium, February 11-13, 1994. LC 94-13696. 1994. write for info. (*0-933699-33-6*) Hillwood Art Galry.

Ancient Writers: Greece & Rome, 2 Vols., Vol. 2. Ed. by T. James Luce. LC 82-50612. 1184p. 1982. text ed. 180.00 (*0-684-16595-3*, Scribners) S&S Trade.

Ancient Writers on Greek Sculpture. H. Stuart Jones. 313p. 1966. 25.00 (*0-89005-194-1*) Ares.

Ancient Writing & Its Influence. Berthold L. Ullman. (Medieval Academy Reprints for Teaching Ser.). 260p. 1981. pap. 12.95 (*0-8020-6435-3*) U of Toronto Pr.

Ancient Writing & Its Influence. Berthold L. Ullman. LC 81-166366. (Medieval Academy Reprints for Teaching Ser.: No. 10). (Illus.). 274p. reprint ed. pap. 78.10 (*0-8357-6370-6*, 2035724) Bks Demand.

Ancient Writing on Metal Plates: Archaeological Findings Support Mormon Claims. Paul R. Cheesman. LC 85-80542. 93p. 1985. 9.98 (*0-88290-303-9*, 1002) Horizon Utah.

***Ancient Yemen: Some General Trends of the Evolution of the Sabaic Language & Sabaean Culture.** Andrey Korotayev. (Journal of Semitic Studies Supplement: No. 5). (Illus.). 142p. 1995. 49.95 (*0-19-922237-1*) OUP.

Ancient Zionism. Victor Erlich. 1994. text ed. 23.00 (*0-02-902352-1*) Free Pr.

Ancients & Axioms: Secondary Education in Eighteenth-Century New England. Robert Middlekauff. LC 79-165725. (American Education Ser, No. 2). 1979. reprint ed. 23.95 (*0-405-03713-9*) Ayer.

Ancients & Moderns: A Study of the Rise of the Scientific Movement in Seventeenth Century England. 2nd ed. Richard F. Jones. 1961. 12.75 (*0-8446-2340-7*) Peter Smith.

Ancients & Moderns: A Study of the Rise of the Scientific Movement in Seventeenth Century England. Richard F. Jones. 384p. 1982. reprint ed. pap. 7.95 (*0-486-24414-8*) Dover.

Ancients & the Moderns: Rethinking Modernity. Stanley Rosen. 246p. (C). 1991. reprint ed. pap. text ed. 14.00 (*0-300-05030-5*) Yale U Pr.

Anciet Jaffna. C. Rasanayagam Madaliyar. (Illus.). 478p. 1986. reprint ed. 22.00 (*0-8364-1744-5*, Pub. by Manohar II) S Asia.

Ancilla to Classical Reading. Moses Hadas. LC 54-6132. 397p. 1961. pap. text ed. 17.00 (*0-231-08517-6*) Col U Pr.

Ancilla to the Pre-Socratic Philosophers. Kathleen Freeman. 172p. 1983. pap. 11.95 (*0-674-03501-1*) HUP.

Ancillary (Bedside) Blood Glucose Testing in Acute & Chronic Care Facilities. (Tentative Guideline Ser.: Vol. 9). 1991. 40.00 (*1-56238-126-1*, C30-T) Natl Comm Clin Lab Stds.

Ancillary Literature of the Atharva-Veda: A Study with Special Reference to the Parisistas. B. R. Modak. 570p. 1993. 53.50 (*81-215-0607-7*, Pub. by M Manoharial II) Coronet Bks.

Ancilla's Share: An Indictment of Sex Antagonism. Elizabeth Robins. LC 75-21815. (Pioneers of the Woman's Movement an International Perspective Ser.). 1976. reprint ed. 23.65 (*0-88355-272-8*) Hyperion Conn.

Ancren Riwle, a Treatise on the Rules & Duties of Monastic Life from a Semi-Saxon MS. of the Thirteenth Century. Ed. by James Morton. LC 72-158250. (Camden Society, London. Publications, First Ser.: No. 1). reprint ed. 115.00 (*0-404-50157-5*) AMS Pr.

Ancrene Riwle: Introduction & Part One. Ed. by Robert W. Ackerman & Roger Dahood. LC 83-21987. (Medieval & Renaissance Texts & Studies: Vol. 31). 128p. 1984. 16.00 (*0-86698-055-5*) MRTS.

Ancrene Wisse: Guide for Anchoresses. Tr. & Intro. by Hugh White. 256p. 1994. pap. 10.95 (*0-14-044585-4*, Penguin Classics) Viking Penguin.

And. Debora Greger. LC 85-42670. (Contemporary Poets Ser.). 88p. 1985. 21.95 (*0-691-06646-9*); pap. 9.95 (*0-691-01423-X*) Princeton U Pr.

And a Deer's Ear, Eagle's Song & Bear's Grace: Animals & Women. Ed. by Theresa Corrigan & Stephanie Hoppe. 234p. (Orig.). 1990. 24.95 (*0-939416-38-7*); pap. 9.95 (*0-939416-39-5*) Cleis Pr.

***And a Happy New Year! More Seasonal Stories.** Alison Campbell. 1994. pap. 10.95 (*0-7043-4386-X*) Interlink Pub.

And a Hard Rain Fell: A GI's True Story of the War in Vietnam. John Ketwig. Ed. by Paul McCarthy. 352p. 1988. mass mkt. 4.99 (*0-671-68054-4*) PB.

And a Little Child: Stories of Anyone. Patricia Meyerowitz. Tr. by Peter Strobel. LC 81-52891. 52p. (ENG & GER.). 1982. pap. 5.00 (*0-9607034-0-3*) RRP Pub.

***And a Time to Die.** Frances B. Greaser. 160p. (Orig.). 1995. pap. 9.95 (*0-8361-9028-9*) Herald Pr.

And a Time to Die. Mark Pelgrin. Ed. by Sheila Moon & Elizabeth Howes. LC 75-26836. 159p. 1976. reprint ed. pap. 5.25 (*0-8356-0305-9*, Quest) Theos Pub Hse.

And a Woodstock in a Birch Tree. Charles M. Schulz. LC 79-1926. (Peanuts Classics Ser.). 128p. 1991. pap. 6.95 (*0-8050-1865-4*, Owl) H Holt & Co.

And a Year Went By. Richard Madden & Stephen Clark. (Illus.). 128p. 1994. pap. 22.00 (*0-7509-0540-9*) A Sutton Pub.

***And Adam Knew Eve: A Dictionary of Sex in the Bible.** Ronald L. Ecker. LC 94-78430. (Illus.). 208p. 1995. 35.00 (*0-9636512-4-2*) Hodge & Braddock.

And after the Journey. Georgette W. Amowitz. 1990. pap. 20.00 (*1-878084-03-8*) Danscores.

And Afterward, the Dark. Basil Copper. LC 77-78594. 1977. 8.95 (*0-87054-079-3*) Arkham.

And Again? Sean O'Faolain. Ed. by Stewart Richardson. 290p. 1989. 16.95 (*1-55972-003-4*, Birch Ln Pr) Carol Pub Group.

And All Between. Zilpha K. Snyder. 224p. (J). (gr. 5 up). 1992. pap. 3.50 (*0-440-21265-0*, LFL) Dell.

And All My War Is Done. Stephen Abbott. 154p. (C). 1989. text ed. 59.00 (*0-946270-99-6*, Pub. by Pentland Pr UK) St Mut.

And All Our Wounds Forgiven. Julius Lester. 256p. 1994. 19.95 (*1-55970-258-3*) Arcade Pub Inc.

And All Points West! William S. Hart & Mary E. Hart. LC 70-144156. (Short Story Index Reprint Ser.). 1977. reprint ed. 20.95 (*0-8369-3771-6*) Ayer.

And All That Piano. Anita S. Smith. 54p. 1984. pap. 5.00 (*1-880649-16-0*) Writ Ctr Pr.

And All Through the House. Ed McBain. 48p. 1994. 12.95 (*0-446-51845-X*) Warner Bks.

"And All Your Children Shall Be Learned" Women & the Study of Torah in Jewish Law & History. Shoshana P. Zolty. LC 93-1229. 360p. 1993. 30.00 (*1-56821-029-9*) Aronson.

And Also Teach Them to Read. Sheryl L. Hirshon & Judy Butler. LC 83-18370. 240p. 1984. 17.95 (*0-88208-170-5*); pap. 9.95 (*0-88208-171-3*) L Hill Bks.

And Also with You - Year B: Worship Resources Based on the Revised Common Lectionary. Timothy J. Crouch et al. (And Also with You Ser.). (Illus.). 158p. 1993. ring bd. 24.95 (*1-878009-15-X*, OSL Pubns); spiral bd. 24.95 (*1-878009-14-1*, OSL Pubns) Order St Luke Pubns.

And Also with You - Year C: Worship Resources Based on the Revised Common Lectionary. Timothy J. Crouch et al. (And Also with You Ser.). (Illus.). 168p. 1994. ring bd. 24.95 (*1-878009-18-4*); spiral bd. 24.95 (*1-878009-17-6*, OSL Pubns) Order St Luke Pubns.

And Another Collection of Works of Phil King. Phil King. LC 79-92822. (Orig.). 1979. pap. 5.00 (*0-9601900-2-3*) Phil King.

And Are We Yet Alive? Richard B. Wilke. 1986. VHS Video: 60 min. vhs 29.95 (*0-687-01377-1*); Beta Video. bmax write for info. (*0-687-01376-3*) Abingdon.

And As for Darkness: Poems. Michael Burns et al. Ed. by Craig Goad. 28p. 1987. pap. 3.50 (*0-9616467-1-3*) GreenTower Pr.

And As I Rode Out on the Morning. Buck Ramsey. 64p. (Orig.). 1993. pap. 9.95 (*0-89672-310-0*); audio, pap. 18.95 (*0-89672-313-5*); audio 9.95 (*0-89672-312-7*) Tex Tech Univ Pr.

And at the Last. Ed. by Blair G. Meeks. (Liturgy Ser.). (Illus.). 90p. (Orig.). 1992. pap. 10.95 (*0-918208-60-2*) Liturgical Conf.

And Autumn Came. Rod McKuen. 1969. 50.00 (*0-318-00971-4*) Cheval Bks.

And Baby & Kitty & Mommy & Daddy. Jane D. Smith. (J). (ps). 1994. 9.95 (*1-56305-668-2*) Workman Pub.

And Baby Makes Four. Karen L. Nutt. 172p. 1994. pap. 7.95 (*1-56901-278-4*) NW Pub.

And Baby Makes None. Stephen Lewis. 208p. 1991. 18.95 (*0-8027-5789-8*) Walker & Co.

***And Baby Makes Three: Wise & Witty Observations on the Joys of Parenthood.** Comp. by Maxine Reed. 144p. 1995. 7.95 (*0-8092-3496-3*) Contemp Bks.

And Be a Villain. Rex Stout. 1994. mass mkt. 4.99 (*0-553-23931-7*) Bantam.

And Be My Love. Joyce C. Ware. 512p. 1993. mass mkt. 4.50 (*0-8217-4291-4*) Zebra.

And Bid Him Sing. Vernon A. February. 200p. 1988. text ed. 55.00 (*0-7103-0278-9*, Pub. by Kegan Paul Intl UK) Routledge Chapman & Hall.

And Blessed Is She: Sermons by Women. Ed. by David Farmer & Edwina Hunter. 256p. 1994. pap. 15.00 (*0-8170-1216-8*) Judson.

And Both Were Young. Madeleine L'Engle. (Young Love Romance Ser.). (Orig.). (YA). (gr. 7 up). 1983. mass mkt. 3.99 (*0-440-90229-0*, LFL) Dell.

And Bring Them Closer to Torah: The Life & Works of Rabbi Aaron H. Blumenthal. Ed. by David R. Blumenthal. 235p. 1986. text ed. 9.95 (*0-88125-082-1*) Ktav.

And Carry a Big Stick. J. Garrison. 256p. (Orig.). 1991. pap. 3.95 (*0-87067-371-8*) Holloway.

And Condors Danced. Zilpha K. Snyder. 224p. (J). (gr. k-6). 1989. reprint ed. pap. 3.50 (*0-440-40153-4*, YB) Dell.

***And Death Shall Have No Dominion.** Sheila Yarbrough. 200p. Date not set. pap. 8.95 (*0-7610-0326-6*) NW Pub.

And Deliver Us from Evil: A Trilogy of Millionaires, Ministers, & Murder. Mike Cochran. Ed. by John Lumpkin. (Illus.). 1989. 17.95 (*0-87719-159-X*, Lone Star Bks) Gulf Pub.

And Did Murder Him. large type ed. Peter Turnbull. (Mystery Ser.). 320p. 1993. 21.95 (*0-7089-2922-2*) Ulverscroft.

And Disregards the Rest. Paul Voermans. 256p. 1994. pap. 9.95 (*0-575-05282-1*, Pub. by V Gollancz UK) Trafalgar.

And Do Remember Me. Marita Golden. 208p. 1994. reprint ed. pap. 10.00 (*0-345-38271-4*, One World) Ballantine.

***And Do You Have Anything Else? Audition Pieces from Canadian Plays.** Ed. by Margaret Bard et al. 106p. 1991. pap. text ed. 15.00 (*0-88924-217-8*, Pub. by Simon & Pierre Pub CN) Empire Pub Srvs.

And down Will Come Baby. Bonnie Faber. 352p. 1994. mass mkt. 4.50 (*1-55817-791-4*, Pinnacle NY) Windsor NY.

And Eagles Sweep Across the Sky: Indian Textiles of the North American West. Dena S. Katzenberg. LC 77-83121. (Illus.). 1977. 6.98 (*0-912298-45-6*) Baltimore Mus.

And Education for All: Public Policy & Handicapped Children. 2nd ed. Roberta Weiner & Maggie Hume. LC 87-6049. 217p. 1987. pap. 29.95 (*0-937925-31-4*, AEFA) Capitol Publns.

And Education for All: Public Policy & Handicapped Children. 2nd ed. Roberta Weiner & Maggie Hume. LC 87-6049. 217p. 1987. 53.00 (*0-937925-26-8*, EFAH) Capitol VA.

And Eternity. Piers Anthony. (Incarnations of Immortality Ser.). 384p. 1991. mass mkt. 4.99 (*0-380-75286-7*) Avon.

***And Everywhere, Children: An International Story Festival.** Association for Childhood Education International. LC 78-25932. 282p. 1979. reprint ed. pap. 80.40 (*0-7837-8942-4*, 2049652) Bks Demand.

***And Father Makes Three.** Laurie Campbell. 1995. mass mkt. 3.75 (*0-373-09990-8*, 1-09990-2) Silhouette.

And Finding No Mouse There. Vivian Smallwood. (Illus.). 64p. 1983. 8.95 (*0-942544-04-8*); pap. 4.95 (*0-942544-03-X*) Negative Capability Pr.

***And Flights of Angels.** William Shakespeare. 1994. 5.00 (*0-87129-474-5*, A55) Dramatic Pub.

And, for Example: Poems. Ann Lauterbach. LC 94-5814. (Poets Ser.). 1994. 25.95 (*0-670-85883-8*, Penguin Classics); pap. 14.95 (*0-14-058715-2*, Penguin Classics) Viking Penguin.

And Forgive Us Our Debts: A Guide to Ending Financial Stress in Your Life - Permanently! George B. Moore. 160p. 1992. pap. 9.95 (*0-9632783-3-9*) Cleveland Bk.

And from That Hour... Pope John Paul, II. 1989. 0.50 (*0-911988-77-7*) AMI Pr.

And from Their Breath Came Ashes. M. S. Wilson. 240p. (Orig.). 1990. pap. 7.95 (*1-879210-06-1*) B Lee Pub CA.

And Garnish with Memories. Patty S. Fulton. (Illus.). 290p. 1985. 14.95 (*0-932807-13-5*) Overmountain Pr.

And Gently He Shall Lead Them: Robert Parris Moses & Civil Rights in Mississippi. Eric R. Burner. (Illus.). 272p. 1994. 35.00 (*0-8147-1209-6*) NYU Pr.

***And Gently He Shall Lead Them: Robert Parris Moses & Civil Rights in Mississippi.** Eric R. Burner. (Illus.). 272p. 1996. pap. 17.95 (*0-8147-1250-9*) NYU Pr.

And Gladly Teach: Reminiscences. Bliss Perry. (BCL1-PS American Literature Ser.). 315p. 1993. reprint ed. lib. bdg. 89.00 (*0-7812-6998-9*) Rprt Serv.

And God Came In: An Extraordinary Love Story; Joy Davidman, Her Life & Marriage to C.S. Lewis. Lyle W. Dorsett. LC 91-16149. 192p. (Orig.). 1991. reprint ed. pap. 9.99 (*0-89107-636-0*) Crossway Bks.

And God Changed His Mind...Because His People Dared to Ask. Brother Andrew. LC 90-44749. 192p. 1991. reprint ed. pap. 8.99 (*0-8007-9193-2*) Chosen Bks.

And God Created... David Webster. (Illus.). 52p. (J). (gr. k-6). 1992. 3.95 (*0-9633597-0-3*) doodle-bug.

And God Created Laughter: The Bible as Divine Comedy. Conrad Hyers. LC 86-46037. 132p. (Orig.). 1987. pap. 10.99 (*0-8042-1653-3*, John Knox) Westminster John Knox.

And God Created Squash: How the World Began. Martha W. Hickman. Ed. by Abby Levine. LC 92-22654. (Illus.). 32p. (J). (ps-3). 1993. lib. bdg. 14.95 (*0-8075-0340-1*) A Whitman.

***And God Cried.** Charles Lawliss. 175p. 1994. write for info. (*1-57215-036-X*) World Pubns.

***And God Said, Let There Be Light! Vol. I.** W. H. Powell. 84p. (Orig.). Date not set. pap. text ed. 9.95 (*0-9643370-0-2*) W H R Powell.

And God Said What? An Introduction to Biblical Literary Forms for Bible Lovers. Margaret N. Ralph. 1986. pap. 10.95 (*0-8091-2780-6*) Paulist Pr.

And God Saw That It Was Good. Board of St. Paul Editorial Staff. (C). 1989. 35.00 (*0-85439-296-3*, Pub. by St Paul Pubns UK) St Mut.

And God Saw That It Was Good. Carlo Carretto. 1990. pap. 9.95 (*0-88344-654-5*) Orbis Bks.

And, God, What About...? James T. Cumming & Hans G. Moll. (J). 1980. 5.99 (*0-570-03806-5*, 12-2915) Concordia.

And Gold Was Ours. Rebecca Brandewyne. 512p. (Orig.). 1994. reprint ed. 22.00 (*0-7278-4554-3*) Severn Hse.

***And Grace Will Lead Me Home: A Spiritual Journey.** John Powers. LC 94-31498. 208p. 1994. 9.95 (*1-56977-635-0*) McCracken Pr.

And Grandpa Sat on Friday. Val Marshall & Bronwyn Tester. LC 92-34159. (Voyages Ser.). (Illus.). (J). 1993. 4.25 (*0-383-03610-0*) SRA Schl Grp.

And Hannah Wept. Michael Gold. 252p. 1988. text ed. 29.95 (*0-8276-0306-1*) JPS Phila.

And Hannah Wept: Infertility, Adoption, & the Jewish Couple. Michael Gold. 252p. 1993. pap. 17.95 (*0-8276-0442-4*) JPS Phila.

And He Gave Pastors. Ed. by Thomas F. Zimmerman et al. LC 78-50485. 500p. (YA). (gr. 12). 1979. 15.95 (*0-88243-460-8*, 02-0460) Gospel Pub.

And He Gave Some Pastors Teachers. Ed. by James Stone. 324p. (Orig.). 1986. pap. text ed. 9.95 (*0-934942-61-7*, 4052) White Wing Pub.

And He Had Compassion: The Miracles of Jesus. William Barclay. 2725p. 1994. pap. 13.00 (*0-8170-0686-9*) Judson.

And He Had Compassion: The Miracles of Jesus. William Barclay. 272p. (C). 1992. pap. 35.00 (*0-685-60697-X*, Pub. by St Andrew UK) St Mut.

And He Had Compassion: The Miracles of Jesus. William Barclay. 272p. 1993. pap. 21.00 (*0-7152-0667-2*) St Mut.

And He Loved Her. Carolyn Hobbs. 185p. (Orig.). 1979. pap. 5.95 (*0-89084-113-6*) Bob Jones Univ Pr.

And He Said..."Come One, Come All" Rita M. Smith. 80p. 1994. pap. text ed. 5.95 (*1-885718-05-5*) Lagniappe Pub.

***And He Sent Them Forth.** Pearl B. Jenkins. 74p. (Orig.). (C). 1991. pap. text ed. 5.95 (*0-929263-04-9*) Great Love Church Intl.

And He Sought for a Man. Jonathan Berman. 250p. (Orig.). 1989. pap. write for info. (*0-318-64791-5*) JMPS Pubs.

And He Tells the Little Horse the Whole Story. Steve Barthelme. LC 87-45477. (Poetry & Fiction Ser.). 160p. 1987. 16.95 (*0-8018-3543-7*) Johns Hopkins.

***And He Thought She Was Single.** Karen Carr. 170p. 1995. pap. 7.95 (*1-56901-911-8*) NW Pub.

And Heaven Cried. Lawrence J. Babin. 1971. 3.00 (*0-685-02597-7*); pap. 1.00 (*0-912492-01-5*) Pyquag.

And Heaven Too. Julie Tetel. 1990. mass mkt. 4.50 (*0-445-21039-7*) Warner Bks.

And Here the World Ends: The Life of an Argentine Village. Kristin H. Ruggiero. LC 87-20311. 248p. 1988. 35.00 (*0-8047-1379-0*) Stanford U Pr.

And Him Crucified. Bettie Scott. 1994. pap. 3.75 (*1-55673-701-7*) CSS OH.

***And His Love Shone Down.** Elizabeth Barrett & Victoria Borard. 290p. Date not set. pap. 8.95 (*0-7610-0350-9*) NW Pub.

And Holy Is His Name. Robert Flynn. 1983. pap. 8.95 (*0-87193-197-4*) Dimension Bks.

And Horns on the Toads. Ed. by Mody C. Boatright et al. LC 59-15694. (Texas Folklore Society Publications: No. 29). 248p. 1959. 12.95 (*0-87074-013-X*) UNTX Pr.

And How Are We Feeling Today? The Impatient Patient's Hospital Survival Guide. Kathryn Hammer. LC 92-38382. 128p. 1993. pap. 8.95 (*0-8092-3834-9*) Contemp Bks.

An Asterisk (*) at the beginning of an entry indicates that the title is appearing in BIP for the first time.

And How Are We Today? June L. La Point. (Illus.). 96p. 1984. pap. 4.95 (*0-930422-32-5*) Dennis-Landman.

And I Alone. Fox Lyal. 150p. 1985. 12.00 (*0-88107-025-4*) Curtis Media.

And I Am Afraid of My Dreams. Wanda Poltawska. Tr. by Mary Craig. 192p. 1989. 16.95 (*0-87052-745-2*) Hippocrene Bks.

And I Cry. Christine L. Giannini. (Illus.). 56p. (Orig.). 1992. pap. 8.95 (*1-55618-117-5*) Brunswick Pub.

And I Don't Want to Live This Life. Deborah Spungen. 448p. 1984. mass mkt. 5.99 (*0-449-20543-6*, Crest) Fawcett.

***And I Loved Them Madly.** Matthew Parkhill. 296p. Date not set. pap. 9.95 (*0-7490-0261-1*, London Bridge) Genl Dist Srvs.

And I Mean It, Stanley. Crosby N. Bonsall. (I Can Read Bk. & Cassette). 32p. (J). (ps-2). 1990. pap. 6.95 (*1-55994-265-7*, Caedmon) HarperAudio.

And I Mean It, Stanley. Crosby N. Bonsall. LC 73-14324. (Early I Can Read Bk.). (Illus.). 32p. (J). (gr. k-3). 1974. lib. bdg. 14.89 (*0-06-020568-7*) HarpC Child Bks.

And I Mean It, Stanley. Crosby N. Bonsall. LC 73-14324. (Trophy Early I Can Read Bk.). (Illus.). 32p. (J). (ps-1). 1984. pap. 3.50 (*0-06-444046-X*, Trophy) HarpC Child Bks.

***And I Never Learned to Yodel: Growing up on "Old" Cape Cod.** Anne N. Harmon. (Illus.). 132p. (Orig.). 1995. pap. text ed. 10.00 (*0-9636949-1-X*) North Bay Pr.

And I Quote: The Definitive Collecton of Quotes, Sayings, & Jokes for the Contemporary Speechmaker. Ashton Applewhite et al. 544p. 1992. 24.95 (*0-312-06897-2*, Pub. by Thomas Dunne Bks) St Martin.

And I Remember. Woodson Reynolds. LC 87-90716. (Illus.). 59p. 1987. pap. text ed. 12.50 (*0-318-23782-2*) Midnight Pubns.

And I Saw the Mountain: A Daily Devotional Guide. Kenneth E. Sullivan. 374p. 1990. pap. 12.95 (*0-8341-1344-9*) Beacon Hill.

And I Shall Be Your Ancestor. Mary E. Peterson. (Illus.). 48p. (Orig.). 1980. pap. 3.00 (*0-912701-02-1*) Balance Beam Pr.

***And I Shall Dwell Among Them: Historic Synagogues of the World.** Neil Folberg. 176p. Date not set. 50.00 (*0-89381-640-X*) FS&G.

***And I the Wind.** Charlie Mehrhoff. 36p. 1994. pap. 4.00 (*0-9629902-2-1*) Hummngbrd WI.

And I Thought I Knew How to Communicate. Josiah Dilley. Ed. by Don L. Sorenson. (Illus.). 168p. (Orig.). 1985. pap. text ed. 8.95x (*0-932796-17-6*) Ed Media Corp.

And I Travel by Rhythms & Words: New & Selected Poems. Naomi F. Faust. LC 89-63039. 318p. (YA). (gr. 7-12). 1990. per., pap. 18.00 (*0-916418-77-4*) Lotus.

And I Was There: Pearl Harbor & Midway--Breaking the Secrets. Edwin T. Layton et al. LC 86-21199. (Illus.). 596p. 1987. reprint ed. pap. 15.00 (*0-688-06968-1*, Quill) Morrow.

***And I Will Never Be the Same: Collaboration & Change in Psychoanalysis & Psychoanalytic Psychotherapy.** Steven A. Frankel. 1995. 40.00 (*1-56821-590-8*) Aronson.

***And If Defeated Allege Fraud: Stories.** fac. ed. Paul Friedman. LC 77-141520. 154p. 1994. pap. 43.90 (*0-7837-7623-3*, 2047375) Bks Demand.

And If You Play Golf You're My Friend. Harvey Penick. 1993. 20.00 (*0-671-87188-9*) S&S Trade.

And in Creating Live: The Early Life of Nikola Tesla. Benjamin H. Johnston. LC 83-81332. (Illus.). 175p. (Orig.). 1990. pap. 8.95 (*0-910077-02-9*) Hart Bro Pub.

And in the Beginning... Sheron Williams. LC 90-43094. (Illus.). 40p. (J). (gr. 1-5). 1992. text ed. 13.95 (*0-689-31650-X*, Atheneum Bks Young) S&S Childrens.

And in the Seventh Day. Guy L. Robbins. (American University Studies: Ser. VII, Vol. 36). 242p. (C). 1995. pap. text ed. 32.95 (*0-8204-0504-3*) P Lang Pubs.

And It Came to Pass: An Old Testament, Reader for Children. Rudolf Steiner. (J). 1973. lib. bdg. 79.95 (*0-87968-556-5*) Krishna Pr.

And It Is Still That Way. Byrd Baylor. (Illus.). 96p. (J). (gr. k-8). 1987. reprint ed. pap. 6.95 (*0-939729-06-7*) Trails West Pub.

And It Tastes Just Like Chicken: Endless Retail Sales & Management Success. Gregory L. Will. LC 93-5930. 240p. 1993. text ed. 20.00 (*0-7863-0194-5*) Irwin Prof Pubng.

And It Was Good. Illus. by Harold H. Nofziger. 36p. (J). (ps up). 1993. 12.95 (*0-8361-3634-9*) Herald Pr.

And It Was Good: Reflections on Beginnings. Madeleine L'Engle. LC 83-8518. (Wheaton Literary Ser.). 219p. 1983. 14.99 (*0-87788-046-8*) Shaw Pubs.

And It Was So: Words from the Scripture. 2nd rev. ed. Illus. by Tasha Tudor. LC 87-16130. 48p. (J). (ps up). 1988. 12.00 (*0-664-32724-9*, Westminster) Westminster John Knox.

And It Was Told of a Certain Potter. Walter C. Lanyon. LC 78-163038. (Short Story Index Reprint Ser.). 1977. reprint ed. 13.95 (*0-8369-3952-2*) Ayer.

And It's All Over. David Francey & Phil McEntee. 130p. (C). 1989. pap. 21.00 (*0-85976-221-1*, Pub. by J Donald) St Mut.

And Its Supplement: Neuer Bildungskatalog, 5 Vols. H. W. Singer. 1972. 420.00 (*0-685-13240-4*); pap. 400.00 (*0-8115-3503-7*) Periodicals Srv.

And Jesus Said: A Handbook on the Parables of Jesus. William Barclay. LC 77-120410. 224p. 1970. reprint ed. pap. 9.99 (*0-664-24898-5*, Westminster) Westminster John Knox.

And Jesus Said: The Parables of Jesus. Ed. by William Barclay. 208p. (C). 1992. pap. 35.00 (*0-685-60696-1*, Pub. by St Andrew UK) St Mut.

And Jesus Said: The Parables of Jesus. William Barclay. 208p. 1993. pap. 22.00 (*0-7152-0666-4*) St Mut.

And Jesus Said...Through Tom Barnes. T. W. Barnes & Nona Freeman. Ed. by Nell Perry. LC 90-84929. 170p. 1990. 8.50 (*1-878366-03-3*) Nonas Bk Sales.

And Justice for All. Stan Proper. 24p. (Orig.). (C). 1988. pap. 2.00 (*0-9619992-1-7*) Walden Sudbury.

And Justice for All? A Dissenting Opinion of the American Legal System. John C. Sullivan. LC 89-80382. 248p. 1989. 17.98 (*0-88290-330-6*) Horizon Utah.

And Justice for All: An Oral History of the Japanese American Interment Camps. John Tateishi. LC 82-42823. 288p. 1984. 18.95 (*0-394-52955-3*) Random.

And Justice for All: New Introductory Essays in Ethics & Public Policy. Ed. by Tom Regan & Donald Van DeVeer. LC 81-23446. (Philosophy & Society Ser.). 320p. 1982. 52.25 (*0-8476-7059-7*); pap. 21.00 (*0-8476-7060-0*) Rowman.

***And Justice for All: Understanding & Controlling Police Abuse of Force.** Ed. by William A. Geller & Hans Toch. 372p. 1995. pap. 29.95 (*1-878734-37-7*) Police Exec Res.

And Justice for One. John Clarkson. 320p. 1992. 20.00 (*0-517-58274-0*, Crown) Crown Pub Group.

And Justice for One. John Clarkson. 368p. 1993. mass mkt. 5.99 (*0-515-11055-8*) Jove Pubns.

And Justice for Some: Judge Jack Hampton & the Richard Lee Bednarski Gang. Arthur F. Ide. LC 89-29157. (Illus.). 100p. (Orig.). 1990. pap. 7.00 (*0-930383-16-8*) Monument Pr.

***...And Justice for Some: The Story of Stephen G. James. Hugh N. Griffith. (Illus.). 170p. (Orig.). 1995. pap. 11.95 (*0-9644819-0-1*) Alxndr Pub.**
The story of Stephen G. James, a young (age 28) African-American attorney specializing in criminal law. It unfolds via two interwoven strands. The first is an autobiography of Stephen G. James, from birth to the present. The second strand takes you into the courtroom during high-profile cases such as the Korean grocery store boycott of 1990 & the Sunrise Theatre "Godfather III" shootout. The autobiography describes the Horatio Alger-like rise of Mr. James from his beginnings in an overcrowded Brooklyn project apartment, capturing the work ethic that is the foundation of his success. Establishing a contracting business at the age of nine was but one of a series of self-created opportunities. He is the quintessential role model for African-Americans--indeed, ALL American youth. The cases selected provide insights to the Criminal Justice System & that System's disparate effect on African- Americans. His clients are alleged perpetrators of violent crimes, victims of equally violent crimes, challengers of the law through civil disobedience & parents fighting to save their children from the System. In every instance, the intervention of this skilled attorney ensured a more equitable treatment of his clients by that System. All Americans should know that attorney's story. To order: ALEXANDER Publishing, P.O. Box 110769, Cambria Heights, NY 11411-0769; 718-525-7315. ***Publisher Provided Annotation.***

And Keep Your Powder Dry: An Anthropologist Looks at America. Margaret Mead. LC 77-156694. (Essay Index Reprint Ser.). 1977. reprint ed. 20.95 (*0-8369-2416-9*) Ayer.

And Kyroot Said: Contemporary Commentaries from a Sanguinary Cosmic Sage. Jan, pseud. 324p. 1981. 20.00 (*0-936380-04-7*) Chan Shal Imi.

And Ladies of the Club. Helen H. Santmyer. LC 81-22401. 1348p. 1982. 62.50 (*0-8142-0323-X*) Ohio St U Pr.

...And Ladies of the Club. Helen H. Santmyer. 1440p. 1986. pap. 7.95 (*0-425-10243-2*) Berkley Pub.

And Lead Us Not into Temptation: Educators & Interscholastic Football. J. C. Bennett. LC 92-62376. xvi, 125p. 1993. 18.00 (*0-9634751-3-4*) Mencken Mem.

And Left for Dead. Frances Lockridge & Richard Lockridge. (Mr. & Mrs. North Mystery Ser.). 18.95 (*0-89190-912-5*, Am Repr) Amereon Ltd.

And Love Survived. R. Chetwynd-Hayes. 1990. pap. 3.95 (*0-89083-531-4*); pap. 3.95 (*0-8217-3051-7*) Zebra.

And Maggie Makes Three. Joan L. Nixon. LC 85-16389. 112p. (J). (gr. 3-7). 1986. 12.95 (*0-15-250355-2*, HB Juv Bks) HarBrace.

And Mao Makes Five: Mao Tsetung's Last Great Battle. Ed. by Raymond Lotta. LC 78-70431. (Illus.). 1978. 15.00 (*0-916650-09-X*); pap. 5.95 (*0-916650-08-1*) Banner Pr.

And Marries Another: Divorce & Remarriage in the Teaching of the New Testament. Craig S. Keener. LC 91-47185. 276p. 1991. pap. 9.95 (*0-943575-46-X*) Hendrickson MA.

And Mary Could Really Cook. J. Clifton Williams. 400p. 1991. write for info. (*0-9627505-0-6*) Grand Amer Enter.

And Merely Teach: Irreverent Essays on the Mythology of Education. 2nd ed. Arthur E. Lean. LC 75-42233. (Illus.). 143p. 1976. 8.95 (*0-8093-0744-8*); pap. 4.95 (*0-8093-0745-6*) S Ill U Pr.

And Miss Reardon Drinks a Little. Paul Zindel. 1971. pap. 4.75 (*0-8222-0043-0*) Dramatists Play.

And More by Andy Rooney. Andrew A. Rooney. 256p. 1991. reprint ed. pap. 9.95 (*0-02-010202-X*, Collier S&S) S&S Trade.

And More Celebrating the Seasons with Children. Philip E. Johnson. LC 86-12387. 120p. (Orig.). 1986. pap. 9.95 (*0-8298-0735-7*) Pilgrim OH.

And More Phil King. Phil King. 50p. 1994. pap. 5.00 (*0-685-71543-4*) Phil King.

And More Stories. Leslie W. Hedley. 120p. (Orig.). 1992. pap. 13.95 (*0-933515-14-6*) Exile Pr.

And Morning in His Eyes. Philip Henderson. LC 75-39861. (English Literature Ser.: No. 33). 1972. reprint ed. lib. bdg. 75.00 (*0-8383-1406-6*) M S G Haskell Hse.

And Muhammad Is His Messenger: The Veneration of the Prophet in Islamic Piety. Annemarie Schimmel. LC 84-17374. (Studies in Religion). (Illus.). xii, 377p. 1985. 39.95 (*0-8078-1639-6*); pap. 14.95 (*0-8078-4128-5*) U of NC Pr.

And Murder Won. large type ed. Howard C. Davis. (Linford Mystery Library). 320p. 1989. pap. 11.95 (*0-7089-6733-7*, Linford) Ulverscroft.

And My Mean Old Mother Will Be Sorry, Blackboard Bear. Martha Alexander. LC 72-707. (Pied Piper Bks.). (Illus.). (J). (gr. k-2). 1977. reprint ed. pap. 3.50 (*0-8037-0126-8*) Dial Bks Young.

And Never Said a Word. Heinrich Boll. Tr. by Leila Vennewitz. (European Classics Ser.). 204p. (C). 1994. 29.95 (*0-8101-1153-5*); pap. text ed. 10.95 (*0-8101-1147-0*) Northwestern U Pr.

And Never the Twain Shall Meet: Cross-Cultural Conflict in the Administrative Process - U. S. Military Procurement in Korea. 56p. 1983. 2.00 (*0-89249-034-9*) Intl Development.

And Night Fell: Memoirs of a Political Prisoner in South Africa. Molefe Pheto. LC 84-234158. (African Writers Ser.). 218p. (C). 1985. reprint ed. pap. 9.95 (*0-435-90258-X*) Heinemann.

And No Birds Sang. Farley Mowat. 19.95 (*0-89190-821-8*, Am Repr) Amereon Ltd.

And No Birds Sang. Farley Mowat. 208p. 1982. mass mkt. 5.99 (*0-7704-2237-3*) Bantam.

And No Birds Sing: The Story of an Ecological Disaster in a Tropical Paradise. Mark Jaffe. 1994. 23.00 (*0-671-75107-7*) S&S Trade.

And None of It Was Nonsense: The Power of Storytelling in School. Betty Rosen. LC 87-35272. 176p. 1988. pap. text ed. 16.00 (*0-435-08464-X*) Heinemann.

And Not Alone the Aspiring Trees: Collections of Poems by Writers in Delaware, Maryland, Virginia, & the District of Columbia. Comp. & Pref. by Joseph D. Adams. (Poet's Domain Ser.: Vol. 8). xiv, 98p. (Orig.). 1993. pap. 6.95 (*1-880016-13-3*) Road Pubs.

And Notes on the Folklore of the Raven & Owl see Birds of Omen in Shetland

And Nothing but the Truth: Insights, Anecdotes & Stories from Rabbi Menachem Mendel of Kotzk. Ephraim Oratz. 1989. 13.95 (*0-910818-81-9*) Judaica Pr.

And Now a Word from Our Creator. Thomas G. Savage. LC 72-1370. (Illus.). 299p. reprint ed. pap. 85.30 (*0-8357-8025-2*, 2033969) Bks Demand.

And Now a Word from Our Sponsor. Dorothy Hoobler & Thomas Hoobler. (Her Story Ser.). (Illus.). 64p. (J). (gr. 4-6). 1992. 6.95 (*0-382-24153-3*); lib. bdg. 9.95 (*0-382-24146-0*); pap. 3.95 (*0-382-24350-1*) Silver Burdett Pr.

And Now, about God's Word: A Layman's Handbook Designed to Aid & Enrich Personal Bible Study. Lee White. (Illus.). 400p. 1989. pap. 9.95 (*0-9622195-0-9*) CalmSeas Pub.

And Now, about God's Word: A Simplified Commentary Designed to Aid & Enrich Personal Bible Study. Lee V. White. (Has One Only Ser.). (Illus.). 400p. 1989. pap. 9.95 (*0-685-27815-8*) CalmSeas Pub.

And Now, & Here, Vol. I. Osho Rajneesh. Ed. by Swami Satya Mahasattva. LC 84-42798. (Early Discourses & Writings Ser.). 320p. (Orig.). 1984. pap. 4.95 (*0-88050-709-8*) Osho Chidvilas.

And Now, & Here, Vol. II. Osho Rajneesh. Ed. by Swami S. Vedant. LC 84-42798. (Early Writings & Discourses Ser.). 384p. (Orig.). 1985. pap. 4.95 (*0-88050-712-8*) Osho Chidvilas.

And Now for Something Completely Trivial: The Monty Python Trivia & Quiz Book. Kim H. Johnson. 192p. (Orig.). 1991. pap. 8.95 (*0-312-06289-3*, Pub. by Thomas Dunne Bks) St Martin.

And Now I Know. Ed. by Judy Gilley. (Illus.). 96p. 1986. pap. 8.00 (*0-9616013-7-X*) Midwest Media.

And Now I See. Clyde Bolton. LC 88-35625. (Orig.). 1989. pap. 7.00 (*0-915541-42-4*) Star Bks Inc.

And Now Infanticide. 2nd ed. Effie A. Quay. 64p. 1980. pap. 1.25 (*0-937930-01-6*) Sun Life.

And Now Miguel. Joseph Krumgold. LC 53-8415. (Illus.). 245p. (J). (gr. 5 up). 1953. 16.00 (*0-690-09118-4*, Crowell Jr Bks) HarpC Child Bks.

And Now Miguel. Joseph Krumgold. LC 53-8415. (Trophy Bk.). (Illus.). 245p. (J). (gr. 5 up). 1984. pap. 3.95 (*0-06-440143-X*, Trophy) HarpC Child Bks.

And Now Miguel. Joseph Krumgold. LC 53-8415. (Illus.). 245p. (J). (gr. 5 up). 1987. lib. bdg. 15.89 (*0-690-04696-0*, Crowell Jr Bks) HarpC Child Bks.

And Now Miguel. braille ed. Joseph Krumgold. 289p. (J). 1993. 23.12 (*1-56956-396-9*, BR9200) W A T Braille.

And Now My Soul Is Hardened: Abandoned Children in Soviet Russia, 1918-1930. Alan M. Ball. LC 92-46236. 1994. 55.00 (*0-520-08010-6*) U CA Pr.

And Now We'll Play a Man's Game: Montana Stories. Dean Phelps. LC 76-1979. (Illus.). 132p. (Orig.). 1976. pap. 5.95 (*0-914974-10-6*) Holmgangers.

***And Now, Your Chicago Bulls: A 30-Year Celebration.** Roland Lazenby. 240p. 1995. 39.95 (*0-87833-113-1*) Taylor Pub.

***And Now, Your Chicago Bulls: A 30-Year Celebration.** limited ed. Roland Lazenby. 1995. 75.00 (*0-87833-114-X*) Taylor Pub.

And Now...the Weather. Anita Ganeri. LC 91-26682. (Aladdin Basics Ser.). (Illus.). 32p. (J). (ps-2). 1992. pap. 5.95 (*0-689-71583-8*, Aladdin Paperbacks) S&S Childrens.

And of Course Another Collection of Works by Phil King. Phil King. 50p. (Orig.). pap. 5.00 (*0-9601900-9-0*) Phil King.

And on the Eighth Day. Ellery Queen. (Ellery Queen Mystery Ser.). 192p. 1994. pap. 8.00 (*0-06-097603-9*, PL) HarpC.

And on the Seventh Day: Faculty Consulting & Supplemental Income. Carol M. Boyer & Darrell R. Lewis. Ed. by Jonathan D. Fife. LC 85-72834. (ASHE-ERIC Higher Education Report Ser.: No. 3, 1985). 89p. (Orig.). (C). 1985. pap. 10.00 (*0-913317-22-5*) GWU Schl E&HD.

And on the Sixth Day God Made Man...Honest! Humorous Reflections of James Kavanaugh. James Kavanaugh. LC 93-84525. (Illus.). 128p. 1993. 15.95 (*1-878995-22-7*) S J Nash Pub.

And Once Again Abu Dharr. Ali Shariati. Tr. by Laleh Bakhtiar. 76p. (Orig.). (C). 1989. pap. 7.50 (*1-871031-06-0*) Abjad Bk.

And One for All. Theresa Nelson. (J). (gr. 4-7). 1991. pap. 3.50 (*0-440-40456-8*) Dell.

And One for All. Theresa Nelson. LC 88-22490. 192p. (J). (gr. 6-8). 1989. 15.95 (*0-531-05804-2*); lib. bdg. 15.99 (*0-531-08404-3*) Orchard Bks Watts.

And One Rode West. Heather X. Graham. 1992. mass mkt. 5.99 (*0-440-21148-4*) Dell.

***And One Rode West.** Heather Graham. 1994. reprint ed. 22.00 (*0-614-07216-6*) Severn Hse.

And One Slice with Anchovies! Tom Batiuk & Chuck Ayers. (Crankshaft Collection Ser.). (Illus.). 128p. 1993. pap. 8.95 (*0-8362-1707-1*) Andrews & McMeel.

***And One to Die On.** Jane Haddam. LC 94-46007. 1996. write for info. (*0-553-09975-2*) Bantam.

***And One to Grow On.** John Gould. (American Autobiography Ser.). 253p. 1995. reprint ed. lib. bdg. 79.00 (*0-7812-8534-8*) Rprt Serv.

And One Wore Gray. Heather X. Graham. 1992. mass mkt. 5.99 (*0-440-21147-6*) Dell.

And One Wore Grey. Heather Graham. 1993. 22.00 (*0-7278-4416-4*) Severn Hse.

And Other Neighborly Names: Social Process & Cultural Image in Texas Folklore. Ed. by Richard Bauman & Roger D. Abrahams. (Illus.). 332p. (C). 1981. text ed. 25.00 (*0-292-70352-X*) U of Tex Pr.

And Other Poems. Rudi Holzapfel. 56p. (Orig.). 1988. pap. write for info. (*0-9620265-0-6*) Syntony.

And Our Faces, My Heart, Brief As Photos. John Berger. 92p. 1984. pap. 7.95 (*0-394-72427-5*) Pantheon.

And Our Faces, My Heart, Brief As Photos. John Berger. LC 91-50221. (Vintage International Ser.). 112p. 1991. pap. 9.00 (*0-679-73656-5*, Vin) Random.

And Part of Which I Was - Recollections of a Research Engineer. George H. Brown. LC 82-72256. (Illus.). 342p. 1982. 20.00 (*0-9612524-0-5*) Angus Cupar.

And People All Around. George Sklar. 1968. pap. 4.75 (*0-8222-0044-9*) Dramatists Play.

And Peter Said Goodbye. Liz Farrington & Jennifer C. Weil. LC 92-35977. (Illus.). 40p. (J). (gr. k-4). 1993. 14.95 (*1-56844-000-6*) Enchante Pub.

And Promenade Home. Agnes De Mille. LC 79-28690. (Series in Dance). 1980. reprint ed. lib. bdg. 27.50 (*0-306-79614-7*) Da Capo.

And Promises to Keep: The Southern Conference for Human Welfare, 1938-1948. Thomas A. Krueger. LC 67-13996. 1967. 14.95 (*0-8265-1093-0*) Vanderbilt U Pr.

And Quiet Flows the Don. Mikhail Sholokhov. 1965. pap. 9.95 (*0-394-70330-8*) Random.

And Quiet Flows the Don. Mikhail Sholokhov. Tr. by Stephen Garry. (Vintage International Ser.). 1989. pap. 15.00 (*0-679-72521-0*, Vin) Random.

And Rachel Was His Wife. Marsi Tabak. 1990. 16.95 (*0-87306-488-7*) Feldheim.

And Sadly Teach: Teacher Education & Professionalization in American Culture. Jurgen Herbst. LC 89-4775. 246p. (Orig.). (C). 1991. text ed. 30.00 (*0-299-12180-1*); pap. text ed. 14.95 (*0-299-12184-4*) U of Wis Pr.

***And Say Hi to Joyce: America's First Gay Column Comes Out.** Deb Price & Joyce Murdoch. LC 94-24067. 368p. 1995. 22.50 (*0-385-47365-6*) Doubleday.

And Say What He Is: The Life of a Special Child. J. B. Murray & Emily Murray. LC 75-5810. 304p. 1975. pap. 5.95 (*0-262-63069-9*) MIT Pr.

And Send the Sun Tomorrow: A Journal of My Father's Last Days. Maura Bremer. 1979. pap. 2.95 (*0-03-049396-X*) Harper SF.

And Serve It with Love. Brownlow. 1991. 16.99 (*1-877719-28-5*) Brownlow Pub Co.

And Serve It with Love: Favorite Family Recipes. 1989. 16.99 (*0-915720-39-6*) Brownlow Pub Co.

And Set Aglow a Sacred Flame. Margaret T. Neal. (Illus.). 1983. 8.50 (*0-317-00833-1*) Puddingstone.

And Sew On... Alida Macor. LC 82-91121. (Illus.). 56p. 1983. pap. 3.95 (*0-9610632-0-3*) Alida Macor.

And Shira Imagined. Giora Carmi. 32p. 1988. 14.95 (*0-8276-0288-X*) JPS Phila.

An Asterisk (*) at the beginning of an entry indicates that the title is appearing in BIP for the first time.

And Should She Die. Blaine M. Yorgason. (Gospel Power Ser.). Orig. Title: The Courage Covenant. 183p. (Orig.). 1991. pap. write for info. (0-929985-56-7) Jackman Pubng.

And Sin No More: Social Policy & Unwed Mothers in Cleveland, 1855-1990. Marian J. Morton. LC 92-39087. (Women & Health Ser.). (Illus.). 216p. 1993. 39.50 (0-8142-0602-6) Ohio St U Pr.

And So Forth. Richard Kostelanetz. LC 79-52317. 1979. pap. text ed. 20.00 (0-918406-10-2) Future Pr.

And So Forth. deluxe limited ed. Richard Kostelanetz. LC 79-52317. 1979. 100.00 (0-918406-11-0) Future Pr.

And So I Sing: African-American Divas of Opera & Concert. Rosalyn M. Story. 1990. 24.95 (0-446-71016-4) Warner Bks.

And So I Sing: African-American Divas of Opera & Concert. Rosalyn M. Story. (Illus.). 256p. 1993. reprint ed. pap. 12.95 (1-56743-011-2) Amistad Pr.

And So It Goes: Adventures in Television. Linda Ellerbee. 1987. mass mkt. 4.99 (0-425-10237-8) Berkley Pub.

And So It Happened. Gordon S. Ziegler. 400p. 1992. 18.95 (0-9630632-1-9) Abbott-Sterling.

And So Man Dreams. Bruce Kaduk. 60p. 1991. 15.95 (0-9621914-5-0); pap. 8.95 (0-9621914-4-2) Morn Star Bks.

***And So On: New Designs for Teaching Mathematics.** John V. Trivett. (Illus.). 192p. (Orig.). (C). 1980. pap. text ed. 13.95x (0-920490-10-7) Temeron Bks.

***And So They Build.** Kitchen. LC 92-54403. 1995. pap. text ed. 5.99 (1-56402-502-0) Candlewick Pr.

And So They Build. Bert Kitchen. LC 92-54403. (Illus.). 32p. (J). (ps up). 1993. 15.95 (1-56402-217-X) Candlewick Pr.

And So to Bed: A Bibliography of Diaries Published in English. Patricia P. Havlice. LC 86-13738. 706p. 1987. 62.50 (0-8108-1923-6) Scarecrow.

And So to God. Hubert Van Zeller. LC 92-18971. 1992. pap. 9.95 (0-932506-60-7) St Bedes Pubns.

And So to Murder. Carter Dickson. 1988. pap. 3.50 (0-8217-2536-X) Zebra.

And So to Murder. large type ed. Carter Dickson. 18.95 (0-7451-6426-9, Scarlet Dagger Lrg Print) Chivers N Amer.

And So to Murder. large type ed. Carter Dickson. 1993. pap. 16.95 (0-7451-6432-3, Scarlet Dagger Lrg Print) Chivers N Amer.

And So You Want to Go Cross-Country Skiing? Jim Houldsworth. (Illus.). 46p. (Orig.). (J). (gr. 5 up). 1981. pap. 3.95 (0-936198-06-0) Hollow Spring Pr.

And Some Are Walked Home: Stories of Grace. Linda Quanstrom. 68p. 1994. pap. 4.95 (0-8341-1478-X) Beacon Hill.

***And Some Believed.** Arthur Glasser. (American Autobiography Ser.). 208p. 1995. reprint ed. lib. bdg. 79.00 (0-7812-8531-3) Rprt Serv.

And Somebody Gives a Damn! Paul L. Ashton. (Illus.). 439p. 1990. text ed. 35.00 (0-9627164-2-1); pap. 30.00 (0-9627164-1-3) Ashton Pubns.

And Soon I'll Come to Kill You. Susan B. Kelly. LC 90-28833. 224p. 1991. 18.00 (0-394-58415-5, Villard Bks) Random.

And Star Maker see Last & First Men

And Still Drink More! Jakob Arjouni. Tr. by Anselm Hollu. LC 94-32004. 156p. 1994. 16.95 (0-88064-161-4) Fromm Intl Pub.

And Still, I Cry. Barbara A. Robinson. LC 90-86221. 220p. (Orig.). 1992. 17.95 (1-878647-06-7); pap. 13.95 (1-878647-01-6) Duncan & Duncan.

And Still I Rise. Maya Angelou. 1978. 15.00 (0-394-50252-3) Random.

And Still More Addenda to Belknap's Oregon Imprints, 1845-1870. George N. Belknap. 35p. 1986. pap. 5.95 (0-912296-86-0, Am Antiquarian) Am Antiquarian.

And Still More Meatmen: An Anthology of Gay Male Comics, Vol. 3. 2nd ed. Ed. by Winston Leyland. (Illus.). 160p. 1990. reprint ed. pap. 14.95 (0-943595-10-X) Leyland Pubns.

And Still the Turtle Watched. Sheila MacGill-Callahan. (J). (ps-3). 1991. 15.99 (0-8037-0931-5); lib. bdg. 14.89 (0-8037-0932-3) Dial Bks Young.

And Still the Waters Run: The Betrayal of the Five Civilized Tribes. Angie Debo. 417p. (Orig.). (C). 1990. pap. text ed. 15.95 (0-691-00578-8) Princeton U Pr.

***And Still They Come: Immigrants & American Society, 1920 to the 1990s.** Elliott R. Barkan. Ed. by John H. Franklin & A. S. Eisenstadt. (The American History Ser.). (Illus.). 175p. (C). 1996. pap. text ed. 11.95 (0-88295-928-X) Harlan Davidson.

And Still They Dance: Women, Destabilization, & the Struggle for Change in Mozambique. Stephanie Urdang. 320p. (C). 1988. 28.00 (0-85345-772-7); pap. 14.00 (0-85345-773-5) Monthly Rev.

And Still We Rise. Barbara Reynolds. 1988. 14.95 (0-944347-02-9) USA Today Bks.

And Suddenly Spring. Ed. by Stanley H. Barkan. Tr. by Adam Szyper. (Review Chapbook Ser.: No. 26: Polish Poetry). 48p. (ENG & POL.). 1991. 15.00 (0-89304-859-3); 15.00 (0-89304-861-5); pap. 5.00 (0-89304-860-7); pap. 5.00 (0-89304-862-3); audio 10.00 (0-685-26550-1) Cross-Cultrl NY.

And Suddenly They're Gone: What Parents Need to Know about the Empty Nest. Patricia S. Olson. LC 92-61770. 237p. (Orig.). 1993. pap. 14.00 (0-9634523-0-4) Tiffany Pr CO.

And Sunday Makes Seven. Robert Baden. Ed. by Judith Mathews. LC 89-37823. (Illus.). 40p. (J). (ps-3). 1990. 13.95 (0-8075-0356-8) A Whitman.

And Tears No More: A Misty Rose Collection. Ed. by Zenaida Artacho-Kintziger. Tr. by Margaret E. Glasgwyn & Mario Del Rosso. LC 92-91014. (Illus.). 64p. (Orig.). 1992. pap. 5.95 (0-9633485-0-7) M R Arts & Poetry.

And Tell of Time. Laura Krey. 1993. reprint ed. lib. bdg. 75.00 (0-7812-5889-8) Rprt Serv.

And That's the Way It Isn't: A Reference Guide to Media Bias. rev. ed. Ed. by L. Brent Bozell, III & Brent H. Baker. (Illus.). 360p. 1990. pap. 14.95 (0-9627348-0-2) Media Res Ctr.

And the Angels Sing. Museum of Fine Arts Staff. 1991. 19.95 (0-8478-1408-4) Rizzoli Intl.

And the Angels Sing: A Songbook of Classic Christmas Carols. Ed. by Museum of Fine Arts Staff. LC 91-17327. 80p. 1991. 19.99 (0-8010-0224-9) Baker Bk.

And the Angels Were Silent: The Final Week of Jesus. Max Lucado. LC 92-20146. 261p. 1992. 16.99 (0-88070-487-X, Multnomah Bks) Questar Pubs.

***And the Angels Were Silent: The Final Week of Jesus.** Max Lucado. LC 92-20146. 1995. pap. 11.99 (0-88070-727-5) Questar Pubs.

And the Angels Were Silent: The Final Weeks of Jesus. large type ed. Max Lucado. LC 93-24027. (EasyRead Type Ser.). 286p. 1993. reprint ed. pap. 11.95 (0-8027-2675-5) Walker & Co.

And the Ass Saw the Angel. Nick Cave. 1992. mass mkt. 5.50 (0-06-109091-3, Harp PBks) HarpC.

And the Band Played On: Politics, People, & the AIDS Epidemic. Randy Shilts. 672p. 1993. pap. 15.00 (0-14-023221-4, Penguin Bks) Viking Penguin.

And the Beagles & the Bunnies Shall Lie Down Together: The Theology in PEANUTS. Charles M. Schulz. LC 83-83150. 80p. 1984. pap. 6.95 (0-8050-1066-1, Owl) H Holt & Co.

And the Beat Goes On. Campbell. 1996. pap. 29.95 (0-02-870165-8) Schirmer Bks.

And the Birds Appeared. Julie S. Williams. (Illus.). 32p. (J). (ps-3). 1988. 8.95 (0-8248-1194-1, Kolowalu Bk) UH Pr.

***And the Bride Wore Black.** Helen Brooks. (Romance Ser.). 1995. pap. 2.99 (0-373-03350-8, 1-03350-5) Harlequin Bks.

And the Bridge Is Love: Life Stories. Faye Moskowitz. LC 91-14217. 160p. 1993. pap. 12.00 (0-8070-6327-4) Beacon Pr.

***And the Cat Peed on the Toaster.** Carol A. Friges. (Illus.). 1994. pap. 6.95 (0-9630237-1-3) Carol Ann Ent.

And the Cheat Goes On: An Expose on How Students Are Cheating in School. Howard Baker. Ed. by David Schiller. LC 89-84658. (Illus.). 202p. (Orig.). 1989. pap. 12.95 (0-9623660-0-5) Forum Pr Intl.

***And the Children Played.** Blaire Smith. 300p. 1995. pap. 8.95 (1-56901-776-X) NW Pub.

And the Children Pray: A Practical Book for Prayerful Catechists. Janaan Manternach & Carl J. Pfeifer. LC 89-85064. 192p. (Orig.). 1989. spiral bd. 9.95 (0-87793-412-6) Ave Maria.

***And the Clock Struck Ten.** Clarence Ferguson. 1995. 16.50 (0-614-06085-0) Texian.

And the Crooked Places Made Straight: The Struggle for Social Change in the 1960s. David Chalmers. LC 91-11021. (American Moment Ser.). (Illus.). 272p. 1991. text ed. 38.95 (0-8018-4173-9); pap. text ed. 12.95 (0-8018-4174-7) Johns Hopkins.

And the Desert Shall Blossom. Phyllis Barber. LC 90-42363. 285p. reprint ed. pap. 81.30 (0-7837-3965-6, 2043794) Bks Demand.

And the Desert Shall Blossom. Phyllis Barber. LC 93-13570. 281p. 1993. reprint ed. pap. 14.95 (1-56085-036-1) Signature Bks.

And the Desert Shall Rejoice: Conflict, Growth, & Justice in Arid Environments. Arthur Maass & Raymond L. Anderson. LC 85-24157. 456p. (C). 1986. reprint ed. lib. bdg. 38.50 (0-89874-908-5) Krieger.

And the Desert Shall Rejoice, Part 2: A Simulation of Irrigation Systems. Arthur Maass & Raymond L. Anderson. LC 86-20027. 56p. 1987. reprint ed. pap. 10.50 (0-89874-978-6) Krieger.

And the Devil Will Drag You Under. Jack L. Chalker. 1984. mass mkt. 4.95 (0-345-32334-3, Del Rey) Ballantine.

And the Earth Cried. Bettydean Harrington. 463p. (Orig.). 1993. pap. 6.95 (0-9636833-0-6) Piros Pr.

And the Fires Not Green. Dewey Whetsell. (Illus.). 87p. (Orig.). 1981. pap. text ed. 6.95 (0-9607358-0-1) Fathom Pub.

***And the Flag Was Still There: Straight People, Gay People & Sexuality in the Military.** Lois Shawver. LC 94-31507. 254p. 1994. lib. bdg. 34.95 (1-56024-909-9) Harrington Pk.

***And the Flag Was Still There: Straight People, Gay People & Sexuality in the Military.** Lois Shawver. LC 94-31507. 1995. pap. 14.95 (1-56023-851-8) Haworth Pr.

And the Flowers Showered: Discourses on Zen. Osho. Ed. by Ma A. Nirgun. (Zen Ser.). 256p. 1992. 14.95 (81-7261-002-5, Pub. by Rebel Hse GW) Osho Chidvilas.

And the Girls Saw Europe! Ann O. Thomson. LC 85-51131. (Senda Biografica Ser.). (Illus.). 112p. (Orig.). 1985. 14.95 (0-918454-54-9); pap. 10.95 (0-918454-51-4) Senda Nueva.

And the Gods Laughed. Fredric Brown. 1987. 19.00 (0-932096-47-6) Phantasia Pr.

And the Gods Spoke. 369p. 1993. pap. 12.95 (0-9640518-0-X) Vortex Pr NH.

And the Greatest of These. William B. Moody. 112p. Date not set. 10.00 (0-9616499-1-7) Good Soldier.

And the Green Grass Grew All Around: Folk Poetry from Everyone. Alvin Schwartz. LC 89-26722. (Illus.). 208p. (J). (gr. 1-7). 1992. 15.00 (0-06-022757-5); lib. bdg. 14.89 (0-06-022758-3) HarpC Child Bks.

And the Hits Just Keep on Comin' Peter E. Berry. LC 76-48921. 1977. 24.95 (0-8156-0134-4); pap. 17.95 (0-8156-0135-2) Syracuse U Pr.

And the Horse's Name Was... A Dictionary of Famous Horses from History, Literature, Mythology, Television, & Movies. Terri A. Wear. LC 92-37724. 217p. 1993. 27.50 (0-8108-2599-6) Scarecrow.

And the Kansas Wind Blows: Poems about the People, the Land. Raymond S. Nelson. (Illus.). 96p. (Orig.). 1991. pap. 7.95 (0-9627947-1-6) Hearth KS.

And the Laugh Shall Be First: A Treasury of Religious Humor. Ed. by William H. Willimon. 1988. pap. 10.95 (0-687-01384-4) Abingdon.

And the Laugh Shall Be First: A Treasury of Religious Humor. braille ed. Comp. by William H. Willimon. 292p. 1991. vinyl bd. 23.26 (1-56956-183-4, BR7655) W A T Braille.

And the Lord Added to the Church. Dan Beller. 1989. pap. 6.95 (0-911866-08-6) LifeSprings Res.

And the Lord Said... Triumph Over Tragedy. Patricia Berardi. 214p. (Orig.). 1991. pap. 5.95 (1-879946-77-7) Key Pub & Print.

And the Lurid Glare of the Comet. Brian W. Aldiss. 128p. 1986. 13.50 (0-934933-01-4) Serconia Pr.

And the Man Who Was Travelling Never Got Home. H. L. Van Brunt. LC 80-65698. (Poetry Ser.). 1980. 16.95 (0-915604-35-3); pap. 9.95 (0-915604-36-1) Carnegie-Mellon.

And the Meek. Anthony Pascarella. 218p. 1994. pap. 8.95 (1-56901-288-1) NW Pub.

And the Miracle Is... John F. Campoli. 66p. (Orig.). 1990. pap. text ed. 4.95 (0-9625676-0-4) His Love Pr.

And the Miracle Is: Finding God in the Present Moment. John F. Campoli. LC 93-19327. 64p. 1993. pap. 3.95 (0-8091-3386-5) Paulist Pr.

And the Mountains Will Move: The Story of the Building of the Panama Canal. Miles P. Du Val. LC 69-10086. (Illus.). 374p. 1969. reprint ed. text ed. 49.50 (0-8371-0400-9, DUBP, Greenwood Pr) Greenwood.

And the New Nation, 1783-1793 see George Washington: A Biography

And the Night Rambles Past. Raymond Dotson. 45p. (Orig.). 1992. pap. 5.00 (0-9627087-8-X) Mt Olive Coll Pr.

And the Night Shall Be No More: Spiritual Healing For. Glenn Sanderfur. 176p. 1993. pap. 9.95 (0-87604-303-1, 380) ARE Pr.

And the Poor Get Children: Radical Perspectives on Population Dynamics. Ed. by Karen L. Michaelson. LC 81-38389. 272p. 1981. 16.00 (0-85345-552-X); pap. 8.50 (0-85345-553-8) Monthly Rev.

And the Poor Get Children: Sex, Contraception, & Family Planning in the Working Class. Lee Rainwater. LC 84-12770. xiv, 202p. 1984. reprint ed. text ed. 55.00 (0-313-24452-9, RAPG, Greenwood Pr) Greenwood.

And the Poor Get Welfare: The Ethics of Poverty in the U. S. Warren R. Copeland. Ed. by Rex Matthews. LC 94-9873. (Churches Center for Theology & Public Policy Ser.). 224p. (Orig.). 1994. pap. 13.95 (0-687-01386-0) Abingdon.

And the Race Goes On. Gail Blanton. 1986. 8.50 (0-8341-9174-1, MP-637) Lillenas.

And the Sea Will Tell. Vincent Bugliosi & Bruce B. Henderson. 1992. mass mkt. 5.99 (0-8041-0917-6) Ivy Books.

And the Shots Rang Out! A Musical Play about Harvey Milk. 2nd rev. ed. Ray L. Caley. (Illus.). 65p. 1990. reprint ed. spiral bd. 14.95 (0-910987-06-8) Dragon's Lair.

And the Show Goes On: Broadway & Hollywood Adventures. Sheldon Leonard. LC 94-40934. (Illus.). 256p. 1995. 25.00 (0-87910-184-9) Limelight Edns.

***And the Song Goes On: Older Adults in Music Ministry.** Linda B. Hansen. 96p. (Orig.). 1995. pap. 9.95 (0-687-01147-7) Abingdon.

And the Stars Were Shining. John Ashbery. LC 93-14255. 1994. 18.00 (0-374-10500-6) FS&G.

And the Sun Is Up: Kundalini Rises in the West. W. Thomas Wolfe. (Illus.). 1978. per., pap. 4.95 (0-932312-00-4) Academy Hill.

And the Sun Is Up: Kundalini Rises in the West. W. Thomas Wolfe. 183p. 1987. pap. 15.00 (0-89540-166-5, SB-166) Sun Pub.

And the Sun Kept Shining. Bertha Ferderber-Salz. LC 80-81684. (Illus.). 240p. (Orig.). 1980. 12.95 (0-89604-015-1); pap. 5.95 (0-89604-017-8) Holocaust Pubns.

And the Talons of Weng-Chiang. Terrance Dicks. (Dr. Who Ser.: No. 7). 1989. pap. 3.50 (1-55817-209-2, Pinnacle NY) Windsor NY.

And the Tide Shall Cover the Earth. Norma Cole. (YA). 1994. 5.00 (0-87602-328-6) Anchorage.

***And the Trees Clapped Their Hands: Stories of Bahai Pioneers.** Comp. by Claire Vreeland. 408p. 1994. pap. 19.95 (0-85398-378-X) G Ronald Pub.

***And the Two Became One Plus: An Upfront Look at Today's Blended Family.** Sharon Anderson. LC 94-96253. 175p. 1994. pap. text ed. 11.95 (0-9642838-0-8) Bridges of Hope.

And the Two Shall Become One Wedding Book. 1990. 9.95 (0-685-51753-5, D1025) Warner Pr.

And the View from the Shore: Literary Traditions of Hawaii. Stephen H. Sumida. LC 90-46127. (Samuel & Althea Stroum Book Ser.). 330p. (C). 1991. text ed. 30.00 (0-295-97078-2) U of Wash Pr.

And the War Came: The North & the Secession Crisis, 1860-1861. Kenneth M. Stampp. LC 50-9835. (Illus.). 332p. 1950. pap. text ed. 12.95 (0-8071-0101-X) La State U Pr.

And the War Came: The North & the Secession Crisis, 1860-1861. Kenneth M. Stampp. LC 80-15742. (Illus.). xvii, 331p. 1980. reprint ed. text ed. 35.00 (0-313-22566-4, STAN, Greenwood Pr) Greenwood.

And the War Is Over. Novel. Ismail Marahimin. Tr. by John H. McGlynn. LC 86-10625. 173p. 1987. 16.95 (0-8071-1340-9) La State U Pr.

And the Winner Is.... Janet H. McHenry. Ed. by Sue Reck. LC 94-6636. (Golden Rule Duo Ser.). 48p. (J). (gr. 2-4). 1994. pap. 2.99 (0-7814-0170-4, Chariot Bks) Chariot Family.

And the Winner Is . . . Stephen Roos. LC 88-27519. (Illus.). 128p. (J). (gr. 3-7). 1989. text ed. 13.95 (0-689-31300-4, Atheneum Bks Young) S&S Childrens.

And the Wolf Finally Came: The Decline of the American Steel Industry. John P. Hoerr. LC 87-24932. (Social & Labor History Ser.). (Illus.). 736p. (C). 1988. 49.95 (0-8229-3572-4); pap. 22.50 (0-8229-5398-6) U of Pittsburgh Pr.

And the Word. Cid Corman. LC 87-18182. 135p. (Orig.). 1987. pap. 8.95 (0-918273-34-X) Coffee Hse.

And the Word Became History: Messages Forged in the Fires of Central American Conflict. Medardo E. Gomez. LC 91-23448. 112p. (Orig.). 1992. pap. 8.99 (0-8066-2574-0, 9-2574, Augsburg) Augsburg Fortress.

***And the Word Became Poem.** Kaissar A. Afif. Ed. by Barbara De Graff Ajami. Tr. & Intro. by Mansour Ajami. LC 94-73623. (Illus.). 137p. (Orig.). (ARA & ENG.). (C). 1995. pap. 12.00 (0-9626898-3-1) Grindstone Pr.

And the Word Came with Power How God Met & Changed a People Forever. Jo Shetler & Patricia Purvis. Ed. by Liz Heaney. 1992. pap. 8.99 (0-88070-475-6, Multnomah Bks) Questar Pubs.

And the World Stood Silent: Sephardic Poetry of the Holocaust. Tr. by Isaac J. Levy. LC 88-19932. 248p. 1989. 22.50 (0-252-01580-0) U of Ill Pr.

And Their Children after Them. Dale Maharidge. 1990. pap. 14.95 (0-679-72878-3) Pantheon.

And Their Children after Them: The Legacy of Let Us Now Praise Famous Men: James Agee, Walker Evans, & the Rise & Fall of the Cotton in the South. Dale Maharidge & Michael Williamson. 1989. 24.95 (0-394-57766-3) Pantheon.

And Then a Harvest Feast. George Dennison. (J). (gr. 4-7). 1992. pap. 4.50 (0-374-40377-5) FS&G.

And Then a Rainbow. Mili Shimonishi-Lamb. LC 90-3634. (Illus.). 192p. (Orig.). 1990. pap. 9.95 (0-931832-61-6) Fithian Pr.

And Then Arnie Told Chi-Chi... More Than 200 of the Best True Golf Stories Ever Told. Don Wade. 224p. 1993. 16.95 (0-8092-3852-7) Contemp Bks.

And Then Arnie Told Chi Chi... More Than 200 of the Best True Golf Stories Ever Told. Don Wade. (Illus.). 256p. 1994. pap. 9.95 (0-8092-3549-8) Contemp Bks.

And Then Came Morning: Year Down Under. Daphne Clair. (Presents Ser.). 1993. mass mkt. 2.99 (0-373-11586-5, 1-11586-4) Harlequin Bks.

And Then Came the Darkness. Ellen Jamison. 1992. mass mkt. 4.50 (0-8217-3736-8) Zebra.

***And Then Chi Chi Told Fuzzy... More Than 250 of the Greatest True Golf Stories Ever Told.** Don Wade. (Illus.). 256p. 1995. 18.95 (0-8092-3545-5) Contemp Bks.

And Then Comes the End. David Ewert. LC 79-28410. 200p. reprint ed. pap. 57.00 (0-7837-1189-1, 2041719) Bks Demand.

And Then Forgot to Tell Us Why: A Look at the Campaign Against River Blindness in West Africa. David Wigg. LC 93-22321. 56p. 1993. write for info. (0-8213-2382-2, 12382) World Bank.

And Then I Had Kids. Susan Yates. 209p. 1992. pap. 9.99 (0-8499-3456-7) Word Inc.

And Then I Met This Woman: Previously Married Women's Journeys into Lesbianism. Barbee J. Cassingham & Sally M. O'Neil. LC 93-77709. 192p. 1993. pap. 9.95 (0-941300-25-0) Mother Courage.

And Then Jack Said to Arnie... A Collection of the Greatest True Golf Stories of All Time. Don Wade. (Illus.). 240p. 1992. pap. 10.95 (0-8092-3936-1) Contemp Bks.

And Then Shall the End Come. Robert J. Pruitt. 1979. pap. 2.25 (0-934942-20-X) White Wing Pub.

And Then She Said: More Quotations by Women for Every Occasion. Comp. by J. D. Zahniser. 75p. (Orig.). 1990. pap. 6.95 (0-9624836-2-1) Caillech Pr.

And Then She Said: Quotations by Women for Every Occasion. Comp. by J. D. Zahniser. 75p. (Orig.). 1990. pap. 6.95 (0-9624836-1-3) Caillech Pr.

And Then She Said: Quotations by Women for Every Occasion & More Quotations by Women for Every Occasion, 2 vols., Set. Comp. by J. D. Zahniser. 150p. 1990. pap. 12.95 (0-9624836-4-8) Caillech Pr.

***And Then She Said: Quotations from Women Around the World.** Ed. & Comp. by J. D. Zahniser. 150p. (Orig.). 1995. pap. text ed. 10.95 (0-9624836-7-2) Caillech Pr.

And Then the End Shall Come. Dale Rumble. 154p. (Orig.). 1991. pap. 7.99 (1-56043-063-X) Destiny Image.

And Then the Feather Fell. Wade Blevins. (Cherokee Indian Legend Ser.). (Illus.). 48p. (Orig.). (J). (gr. k-8). 1993. text ed. 11.95 (1-56763-060-X); pap. text ed. 5.95 (0-685-67465-7) Ozark Pub.

And Then the Harvest: Three T.V. Plays. Regina O'Neal. 1975. 6.00 (0-910296-90-1) Broadside Pr.

And Then the Sun. Pradip Sen. 8.00 (0-89253-734-5); 4.80 (0-89253-735-3) Ind-US Inc.

An Asterisk (*) at the beginning of an entry indicates that the title is appearing in BIP for the first time.

And Then the Vulture Eats You. James E. Shapiro et al. Ed. by John L. Parker. 163p. (Orig.). 1990. pap. 9.95 (*0-915297-07-8*, VUL) Cedarwinds.

And Then There Was... William Hawes. (Illus.). 27p. (Orig.). 1990. pap. 7.00 (*0-910147-84-1*) World Poetry Pr.

And Then There Was Now. Robert F. Reid, III. LC 80-82920. (Illus.). (Orig.). 1980. pap. 4.25 (*0-9603490-5-7*) Noble Hse.

***And Then There Was One.** P. J. O'Keefe. Ed. by DHP, Inc. Staff. 160p. 1994. write for info. (*1-885531-54-0*) Doghouse Pubng.

And Then There Was One. John W. Wright. 111p. (Orig.). 1985. pap. 4.95 (*0-8341-1057-1*) Beacon Hill.

And Then There Was One, Vol. 1. Margery Facklam. (J). (gr. 4-7). 1990. 14.95 (*0-316-25984-5*, Joy St Bks) Little.

And Then There Was One: A History of the Hotels of the Summit & the West Side of Mount Washington. George E. McAvoy. 356p. 1988. 34.95 (*0-9630647-0-3*) Crawford Pr.

And Then There Was One: A History of the Hotels of the Summit & the West Side of Mount Washington. limited ed. George E. McAvoy. 356p. 1988. 100.00 (*0-9630647-1-1*) Crawford Pr.

And Then There Was One: The Mysteries of Extinction. Margery Facklam. (Illus.). 56p. (J). (gr. 3-6). 1993. pap. 5.95 (*0-316-25982-9*) Little.

And Then There Was Peace. Dennis M. Jones. LC 88-5903. (Orig.). 1988. pap. 5.25 (*0-941992-08-X*) Los Arboles Pub.

And Then There Were Dinosaurs. Sari Steinberg. (J). (ps-3). 1993. 14.95 (*0-943706-19-X*) Pitspopany.

***And Then There Were Nine.** Ann E. Weeks. 186p. 1994. pap. 12.95 (*1-886036-00-4*) Passages Pbg.

And Then There Were Nine: More Women of Mystery. Ed. by Jane S. Bakerman. (Illus.). 219p. 1985. 20.95 (*0-87972-319-X*); pap. 10.95 (*0-87972-320-3*) Bowling Green Univ.

And Then There Were None. Agatha Christie. 208p. 1991. pap. text ed. 4.99 (*0-425-12958-6*) Berkley Pub.

And Then There Were None. Agatha Christie. (Agatha Christie Ser.). 218p. 1985. 14.95 (*0-399-15018-8*, Putnam) Putnam Pub Group.

***And Then There Were Ten: A Stokes Moran Mystery.** Neil McGaughey. LC 94-44395. 1995. 20.00 (*0-684-19760-X*, Scribners) S&S Trade.

And Then There Were Two. Piper. 109p. 1993. pap. text ed. 14.50 (*0-88751-060-4*) Heinemann.

And Then There Were Two: Empty Nesting after Your Kids Fly the Coop. Cliff Schimmels. LC 89-31988. 144p. (Orig.). 1989. pap. 6.99 (*0-87788-050-6*) Shaw Pubs.

And Then We Heard the Thunder. John O. Killens. LC 83-6174. (Howard University Press Library of Contemporary Literature). 485p. 1984. pap. 9.95 (*0-88258-115-5*) Howard U Pr.

And Then We Heard the Thunder. braille ed. John O. Killens. 1059p. 1991. vinyl bd. 84.72 (*1-56956-184-2*, BR7486) W A T Braille.

And Then We Went Fishing: A Story of Fatherhood, Fate & Forgiveness. Dirk Benedict. LC 93-15107. 196p. 1993. pap. 9.95 (*0-89529-559-8*) Avery Pub.

And Then We Were Women. Dee Brestin. 192p. (Orig.). 1994. pap. 8.99 (*1-56476-343-9*, Victor Books) SP Pubns.

And Then What? Jake Wolf. LC 90-24644. (Illus.). 32p. (J). (ps up). 1993. 14.00 (*0-688-10285-9*); lib. bdg. 13.93 (*0-688-10286-7*) Greenwillow.

And Then What Happened, Paul Revere? Jean Fritz. (Illus.). 48p. (J). (gr. 2-6). 1973. 13.95 (*0-698-20274-0*, Coward); pap. 6.95 (*0-698-20541-3*, Coward) Putnam Pub Group.

And Then You Die. James E. Martin. 224p. 1993. mass mkt. 4.99 (*0-380-71696-8*) Avon.

And Then You Die: A Novel. James E. Martin. 1992. 18.00 (*0-688-11198-X*) Morrow.

***And There Shall Be Signs . . .** (Illus.). 80p. 1995. 9.95 (*1-57036-234-3*) Turner Pub GA.

And There Was Light. Irene Rowcliffe. 1993. 15.00 (*0-533-10482-3*) Vantage.

And There Was Light. Jacques Lusseyran. Tr. by Elizabeth R. Cameron. 320p. 1987. reprint ed. pap. text ed. 10.95 (*0-930407-03-2*) Parabola Bks.

***And There Was Light! The 120 Year History of Knoxville College, Knoxville, Tennessee, 1875-1995.** Robert J. Booker. LC 94-28493. 1994. write for info. (*0-89865-907-8*) Donning Co.

And There Was Television. Ellis Cashmore. LC 93-33670. (Illus.). 240p. 1994. 59.95x (*0-415-09130-6*, B3521, Routledge NY); pap. 17.95 (*0-415-09131-4*, B3525, Routledge NY) Routledge.

***And There You Have It.** Teddy Allen. 224p. (Orig.). 1995. pap. 12.95 (*1-885033-12-5*) Blue Acorn Pr.

And They All Sang Hallelujah: Plain-Folk Camp-Meeting Religion, 1800-1845. Dickson D. Bruce, Jr. LC 74-11344. (Illus.). 1974. 21.00x (*0-87049-157-1*); pap. 11.00x (*0-87049-310-8*) U of Tenn Pr.

And They Blessed Rebecca. Pat Molloy. 352p. (C). 1987. pap. text ed. 55.00 (*0-86383-187-7*, Pub. by Gomer Pr UK) St Mut.

And They Built a Crooked House: An (Unlucky) Homeowner's Account of One of the Largest Residential Construction Cases Ever Tried in Court. Ruth S. Martin. LC 91-90070. (Illus.). 257p. (Orig.). 1991. pap. 12.95 (*1-879653-02-8*) Lakeside Pr.

And They Call It Help: The Psychiatric Policing of America's Children. Louise Armstrong. LC 92-34929. (Illus.). 320p. 1993. 22.07 (*0-201-57794-1*) Addison-Wesley.

And They Called His Name Immanuel: I Am Sananda. Sananda & Judas Iscarioth. (Phoenix Journals). (Illus.). 141p. (Orig.). (C). 1990. pap. 10.00 (*0-922356-06-8*) Amer West Pubs.

And They Called His Name Immanuel: I Am Sananda. Sananda & Judas Iscarioth. (Phoenix Journals). 224p. (Orig.). 1993. pap. 6.00 (*1-56935-014-0*) Phoenix Source.

And They Dance Real Slow in Jackson. Jim Leonard, Jr. 91p. 1986. pap. 4.75 (*0-8222-0045-7*) Dramatists Play.

And They Danced On. Waltraud G. Karkar. Ed. by Michael Kronenwetter & Deirdre Towers. (Illus.). 221p. 1989. 24.95 (*0-9624609-0-7*) J & W Karkar.

And They Didn't Die. Lauretta Ngcobo. 246p. 1991. 17.50 (*0-8076-1263-4*) Braziller.

***And They Said I Was Guilty.** Donald Skillin. 250p. 1996. pap. 8.95 (*0-7610-0500-5*) NW Pub.

***And They Shall Be My People: An American Rabbi & His Congregation.** Paul Wilkes. 368p. 1995. pap. 12.00 (*0-345-39434-8*) Ballantine.

And They Shall Be My People: An American Rabbi & His People. Paul Wilkes. 1994. 23.00 (*0-87113-561-2*) Grove-Atltic.

And They Shall Walk. Elizabeth Kenny. Ed. by William R. Phillips & Janet Rosenberg. LC 79-6907. (Physically Handicapped in Society Ser.). (Illus.). 1980. reprint ed. lib. bdg. 30.95 (*0-405-13117-8*) Ayer.

And Things That Go Bump in the Night. Terrence McNally. 1969. pap. 4.75 (*0-8222-0046-5*) Dramatists Play.

And This I Know. 2nd ed. Barbara S. Cambridge. (Illus.). 24p. (J). 1987. pap. write for info. (*0-9621018-1-8*) CBridge Pubns.

And This I Know: Affirmations for Children. rev. ed. Barbara S. Cambridge. (Illus.). 28p. (J). 1987. reprint ed. pap. 6.95 (*0-317-91380-8*) CBridge Pubns.

And This Is How It Is. Earl Partin. LC 77-81768. 1977. 10.00 (*0-8187-0028-9*) Harlo Press.

And This Is Laura. Ellen Conford. (Illus.). 192p. (J). (gr. 3-7). 1992. mass mkt. 4.95 (*0-316-15354-0*) Little.

And This Is the Bathroom! How to Really Sell Real Estate. Andy Kane. (Illus.). 208p. 1989. pap. 15.95 (*0-87364-524-3*) Paladin Pr.

And This Is What They Said. Stan Proper. (Illus.). 24p. (Orig.). (C). 1988. pap. 2.00 (*0-9619992-0-9*) Walden Sudbury.

And Thus Became Man & World. John A. Z'graggen. 143p. (C). 1989. text ed. 60.00 (*1-872795-54-4*, Pub. by Pentland Pr UK) St Mut.

And Thy House. Diana Liptak. 123p. (Orig.). 1985. pap. 3.00 (*0-9615057-0-2*) D Liptak.

And Time Began. Eugene J. McCarthy. (Illus.). 1993. 10.00 (*0-9627860-6-3*) Lone Oak MN.

***And Time Stood Still.** 260p. 1994. pap. 39.99 (*1-886352-03-8*) Crow Feather.

***And to Every Beast--** Pier C. Decembrio. LC 94-31018. (Treasures of the Vatican Library). (Illus.). 1994. pap. 9.95 (*1-57036-101-0*) Turner Pub GA.

And to Think That I Saw It on Mulberry Street. Dr. Seuss. LC 88-38411. (Illus.). 32p. (J). (ps-3). 1989. reprint ed. 13.00 (*0-394-84494-7*); reprint ed. lib. bdg. 11.99 (*0-394-94494-1*) Random Bks Yng Read.

And to Y'all a Good Night: A Guide to Alabama's Bed & Breakfasts. Lynn Edge. (Illus.). 128p. (Orig.). 1992. pap. 8.00 (*1-878561-04-9*) Seacoast AL.

AND U. S. Pro-IPO-100 1993: Initial Graphics Exchange Specification Version 5.2. IGES-PDES Organization Staff. (IGES Ser.). 658p. 1993. pap. 300.00 (*1-885389-00-0*) US Prod Data.

***AND U. S. Pro-IPO-100 1993: Initial Graphics Exchange Specification Version 5.2.** IGES-PDES Organization Staff. (IGES Ser.). 1993. cd-rom write for info. (*1-885389-02-7*) US Prod Data.

And We Are Not Saved: The Elusive Quest for Racial Justice. Derrick Bell. 304p. 1989. pap. 13.00 (*0-465-00329-X*) Basic.

And We Have Danced: The History of the Sacred Dance Guild, 1958-1978. Carlynn Reed. Ed. by Doug Adams. 1978. 5.95 (*0-941500-00-4*) Sharing Co.

And We Have Touched. Theta Burke. LC 78-67725. (Orig.). 1978. pap. 5.95 (*0-916872-05-X*) Delafield Pr.

And We Sold the Rain: Contemporary Fiction from Central America. Ed. by Rosario Santos. LC 88-21299. 215p. 1988. 18.95 (*0-941423-16-6*); pap. 9.95 (*0-941423-17-4*) FWEW.

And Weapons for All. William D. Hartung. 341p. 1994. 25.50 (*0-06-019014-0*) World Policy.

***And Weapons for All.** William D. Hartung. 1995. pap. 12.00 (*0-06-092641-4*, PL) HarpC.

And We're Off! Stephen McNamee. LC 86-42963. 165p. 1987. 13.75 (*0-930950-01-1*); pap. 8.75 (*0-930950-02-X*) Nopoly Pr.

And West Is West: The Wests of Winston County, Alabama, Their Kin & Kith. Charles E. Wilson et al. (Way West Ser.: Vol. 2). (Illus.). 1992. pap. 9.95 (*0-945301-07-3*) Druid Pr.

And What about You? Illustrations for Guided & Free Conversation. 2nd ed. Ralph West. (Illus.). (Orig.). (C). 1992. pap. text ed. 14.30 (*1-880596-08-3*) Allegan Educ.

***And What Are You Going to Do for Us? Audition Pieces from Canadian Plays.** Ed. by Margaret Bard et al. 111p. 1984. pap. text ed. 15.00 (*0-88924-144-9*, Pub. by Simon & Pierre Pub CN) Empire Pub Srvs.

And What Do You Do? Biblical Perspectives on Vocation & Work. Bruce Nelson & Dwight Nelson. 1984. pap. 1.95 (*0-910452-54-7*) Covenant.

***And When Did You Last See Your Father? A Son's Memoir of Love & Loss.** Blake Morrison. 224p. 1995. 21.00 (*0-312-13023-6*) St Martin.

And When I Need to Dream. Margoe Jane. (Illus.). 54p. 1975. 4.00 (*0-9602330-2-4*) Margoe Jane.

And When You Pray. large type ed. Norma Kramin & Lucille Roehrkasse. spiral bd. write for info. (*0-318-66322-8*) LBW.

And Where Were You, Adam? Heinrich Boll. Tr. by Leila Vennewitz. (European Classics Ser.). 156p. 1994. reprint ed. 35.00 (*0-8101-1179-9*); reprint ed. pap. 10.95 (*0-8101-1164-0*) Northwestern U Pr.

And Where Were You, Dr. Spock? Mary P. Riedley. 1990. pap. 9.95 (*0-925928-08-9*) Tiny Thought.

And Who Is My Neighbor? Poverty, Privilege & the Gospel of Christ. Gerald W. Schlabach. 212p. (Orig.). 1990. pap. 10.95 (*0-8361-3525-3*) Herald Pr.

And Why Did You Come to the Emergency Room? John Beneck. LC 80-20360. 1983. pap. 13.95 (*0-87949-192-2*) Ashley Bks.

And Why Not Every Man? Helene C. Phelan. LC 86-90667. (Illus.). 248p. (Orig.). 1987. pap. 12.95 (*0-317-56096-4*) Phelan.

And with a Light Touch: Learning about Reading, Writing, & Teaching with First Graders. Carol Avery. LC 92-42680. 480p. (YA). 1993. pap. text ed. 25.00 (*0-435-08787-8*, 08787) Heinemann.

And Without End. Cid Corman. 1968. 4.00 (*0-685-00992-0*) Elizabeth Pr.

And Ye Shall Be Baptized: Into the Body of Christ, into a Body of Water, into the Holy Spirit. Marvin L. Smith. LC 93-71936. 84p. (Orig.). 1993. pap. 5.00 (*1-882581-02-4*) Campbell Rd Pr.

And Yet Another Collection of Works. Phil King. LC 81-90710. 51p. 1982. pap. 5.00 (*0-9601900-3-1*) Phil King.

And Yet It Moves: Dream & Reality in the Ecumenical Movement. Ernst Lange. Tr. by Edwin Robertson. 181p. reprint ed. pap. 51.60 (*0-7837-5993-2*, 2045803) Bks Demand.

And Yet It Moves: Strange Systems & Subtle Questions in Physics. Mark P. Silverman. (Illus.). 250p. (C). 1993. 54.95 (*0-521-39173-3*); pap. 24.95 (*0-521-44631-7*) Cambridge U Pr.

And Yet We Are Human & Kierkegaard: The Cripple, 2 vols. in 1. Finn Carling & Theodor Haecker. Ed. by William R. Phillips & Janet Rosenberg. Tr. by C. V. Bruyn. LC 79-6897. (Physically Handicapped in Society Ser.). (Illus.). 1980. reprint ed. lib. bdg. 25.95 (*0-405-13108-9*) Ayer.

And You Are Christ's: The Charism of Virginity & the Celibate Life. Thomas Dubay. LC 87-80793. 149p. (Orig.). 1987. pap. 9.95 (*0-89870-161-9*) Ignatius Pr.

And You Can Be the Cat. Hazel Hutchins. (Illus.). 24p. (J). (ps-3). 1992. lib. bdg. 14.95 (*1-55037-219-X*, Pub. by Annick CN); pap. 4.95 (*1-55037-216-5*, Pub. by Annick CN) Firefly Bks Ltd.

And You Didn't Think You Had a Prayer. William D. Murray. 1993. pap. write for info. (*1-878287-03-6*) Type & Temperament.

And You Give Me a Pain, Elaine. Stella Pevsner. (J). (gr. 7-9). 1989. pap. 2.99 (*0-671-68838-3*, Archway) PB.

And You Shall Be a Blessing: An Unfolding of the Six Words That Begin Every Brakhah. Joel L. Grishaver. LC 92-28681. 208p. 1993. 25.00 (*0-87668-464-9*) Aronson.

And You Shall Be My Witnesses! An Introduction to a Life in the Spirit. Angeline Bukowiecki & Brigid Meierotto. (Evangelizer's Handbook, Evangelistic Series Sisters of the New Covenant). 98p. (Orig.). (C). 1981. pap. text ed. 10.00 (*0-317-92539-3*) Sisters New Covenant.

***And You Shall Tell Your Son: The Concept of the Exodus in the Bible.** Y. Zakovitch. 144p. 1991. text ed. 10.00x (*965-223-780-9*, Pub. by Magnes Press IS) Eisenbrauns.

And You Shall Tell Your Son: The Concept of the Exodus in the Bible. Yair Zakovitch. 144p. 1991. text ed. 10.00 (*0-317-05836-3*, Pub. by Magnes Press IS) Gefen Bks.

And You Think You Have Problems: Teen Dilemmas. Patricia McClure. Ed. by Tate Bird. LC 90-70582. (Illus.). 150p. (J). (gr. 8-9). 1990. 14.27 (*0-914127-73-X*) Univ Class.

And You Thought It Was All Over: Mothers & Their Adult Children. Zenith H. Gross. 1989. pap. 4.95 (*0-318-43147-5*) St Martin.

And You Visited Me: Sacramental Ministry to the Sick & the Dying. Charles W. Gusmer. 224p. 1992. pap. 14.95 (*0-8146-6061-4*, Pueblo Bks) Liturgical Pr.

And You, Who Do You Say I Am? 3.50 (*0-318-02212-5*) Chrstphrs NY.

And You Wonder Why Your Life Isn't Working? Waking Up to the Realities of Childhood & Society. Barry A. Ellsworth. LC 90-81802. (Illus.). 274p. (Orig.). 1990. pap. 9.95 (*0-929175-02-6*) Brkthrough Pub UT.

Anda Sobre las Aguas Pedro: Walk on Water Peter. Luis Palau. (SPA.). 3.25 (*84-7228-160-4*, 220032, Pub. by Edit Clie SP) TSELF.

Andalousie Du Quotidien Au Sacre (XIe-XIIIe Siecles) Lucie Bolens. (Collected Studies: No. CS 337). 320p. 1991. text ed. 89.95 (*0-86078-290-5*, Pub. by Variorum UK) Ashgate Pub Co.

***Andaluces en America.** A. Dominguez Ortiz. (Gran Enciclopedia de Espana y America Ser.). (Illus.). (SPA.). 1989. 200.00x (*84-87053-15-7*) Elliots Bks.

Andalucia. Passport Staff. 120p. 1993. pap. 17.95 (*0-8442-9970-7*, Passport Bks) NTC Pub Grp.

Andalusia. Robin Totton. (Crowood Travel Guides Ser.). (Illus.). 336p. 1991. pap. 24.95 (*1-85223-446-6*, Pub. by Crowood Pr UK) Trafalgar.

Andalusia: The Land of the Blessed Virgin. W. Somerset Maugham. LC 75-25381. (Works of W. Somerset Maugham Ser.). 1977. reprint ed. 23.95 (*0-405-07833-1*) Ayer.

Andalusian Ceramics in Spain & New Spain: A Cultural Register from the Third Century B.C. to 1700. Florence C. Lister & Robert H. Lister. LC 87-23781. 411p. 1988. 70.00 (*0-8165-0974-3*) U of Ariz Pr.

Andalusian Whore. Rafael Alberti. Ed. by Stanley H. Barken. Tr. by Linda Scheer & Brian Swann. (Review Chapbook Ser.: No. 29: Spanish Poetry 1). 48p. (ENG & SPA.). 1992. 15.00 (*0-89304-967-0*); 15.00 (*0-685-26547-1*); pap. 5.00 (*0-89304-968-9*); pap. 5.00 (*0-685-26548-X*) Cross-Cultrl NY.

Andaman & Nicobar Islands. Imperial Gazetteer Staff. 1986. reprint ed. 14.00 (*0-8364-1644-9*, Pub. by Usha II) S Asia.

***Andaman & Nicobar Islands: Challenges of Development.** Ed. by V. Suryanarayan & V. Sudarsen. (C). 1994. text ed. 18.50 (*81-220-0338-9*, Pub. by Konark Pubs II) S Asia.

Andaman Islands. F. A. Dass. (C). 1988. reprint ed. 15.00 (*81-206-0408-3*, Pub. by Asian Educ Servs II) S Asia.

Andaman, Nicobar & Laksha-Deep Islands. Cecil J. Saldanha. (C). 1988. 28.00 (*81-204-0390-8*, Pub. by Oxford IBH II) S Asia.

Andando en el Espiritu: Walking in the Spirit. A. B. Simpson. (SPA.). 4.95 (*84-7228-855-2*, 220033, Pub. by Edit Clie SP) TSELF.

Andando Entre Lo Invisible: Walking among the Unseen. Hanna Hurnard. (SPA.). 4.95 (*84-7228-575-8*, 220019, Pub. by Edit Clie SP) TSELF.

Andaraeon Theory. . . of the Physical-NonPhysical Universe System. Robert D. Gidel & Kathryn B. Bostwick. LC 89-85247. (Illus.). 560p. (Orig.). (C). 1990. pap. 12.95 (*0-9623887-0-X*) Andaraeon.

Andariega de Dios: Tiempo de Exilio. Mercedes Garcia-Tuduri. LC 83-50874. (Senda Poetica Ser.). (Illus.). 73p. (Orig.). 1983. pap. 6.95 (*0-918454-39-5*) Senda Nueva.

Andean & Caribbean Basin Financing Directory. (Illus.). 146p. (Orig.). (C). 1994. pap. text ed. 75.00 (*0-7881-0250-8*) Diane Pub.

Andean Archaeology: Papers in Memory of Clifford Evans. Ed. by Ramiro Matos et al. LC 85-11854. (Monograph: No. 27). (Illus.). 238p. (Orig.). 1986. pap. text ed. 18.25 (*0-917956-52-4*) UCLA Arch.

***Andean Art: Visual Expression & Its Relation to Andean Beliefs & Values.** Ed. by Penny Dransart. 325p. 1995. 51.95 (*1-85628-712-2*, Pub. by Avebury Pub UK) Ashgate Pub Co.

Andean City at Mid-Century: A Traditional Urban Society. Andrew H. Whiteford. LC 76-20923. (Latin American Studies Center Monograph: No. 14). (Illus.). 366p. reprint ed. pap. 104.40 (*0-8357-4335-7*, 2037136) Bks Demand.

Andean Cosmologies Through Time: Persistence & Emergence. Ed. by Robert V. Dover et al. LC 91-22250. (Caribbean & Latin American Studies). (Illus.). 288p. 1992. text ed. 29.95 (*0-253-31815-7*) Ind U Pr.

Andean Ecology: Adaptive Dynamics in Ecuador, Vol. 27. Gregory Knapp. 220p. (C). 1991. pap. text ed. 44.00 (*0-8133-8189-4*) Westview.

Andean Folk Knitting. 2nd ed. Cynthia G. Le Count. LC 87-72565. 1990. pap. 29.95 (*0-685-66216-0*) Dos Tejedoras.

Andean Kinship & Marriage. Ed. by R. Bolton & E. Mayer. (Special Publication: No. 7). 1977. 7.50 (*0-686-36559-3*); 5.00 (*0-685-06017-9*) Am Anthro Assn.

Andean Magmatism & Its Tectonic Setting. R. S. Harmon & C. W. Rapela. (Special Paper Ser.: No. 265). (Illus.). 1992. pap. 62.00 (*0-8137-2265-9*) Geol Soc.

Andean Past: Land, Societies & Conflicts. Magnus Morner. LC 83-23136. 316p. reprint ed. pap. 90.10 (*0-7837-0421-6*, 2040744) Bks Demand.

AndeLear Nail Care. Anna A. Leary. LC 86-73045. (Illus.). 78p. 1987. 9.95 (*0-9617600-0-1*) AndeLear Pub.

Andere: Studien Zur Sozialontologie der Gegenwart. Michael Theunissen. (C). 1983. 63.10 (*3-11-006780-3*) De Gruyter.

***Andere der Vernunft Als Ihr Prinzip: Grundzuege der Philosophischen Entwicklung Schellings Mit Einem Ausblick Auf Die Nachidealistischen Philosophiekonzeptionen Heideggers und Adornos.** Christian Iber. 425p. (GER.). (C). 1994. lib. bdg. 175.40 (*3-11-014400-X*) De Gruyter.

Andere und das Denken der Verschiedenheit: Akten eines Internationalen Kolloquiums. Ed. by Heinz Kimmerle. (Schriften Zur Philosophie der Differenz Ser.: Vol. 1). 391p. (FRE & GER.). (C). 1987. 50.00x (*90-6032-296-7*, Pub. by B R Gruener NE) Benjamins North Am.

Anders Knutsson: Lightscapes - Ljusskap. Barnaby Ruhe et al. Tr. by Kjersti Board Staff & Swedish Information Service Staff. (Illus.). 40p. (SWE.). (C). 1990. pap. text ed. 10.00 (*0-9627455-0-2*) U ME Museum Art.

Anders Lernen im Fremdsprachenunterricht. 160p. 1988. 24.50 (*3-468-49436-X*) Langenscheidt.

Andersen's Classic Fairy Tales. Illus. by Michael Adams. (Gateway Classic Ser.). 48p. (J). (gr. k-5). 1993. 5.95 (*0-88101-276-9*) Unicorn Pub.

Andersen's Fables & Fairy Tales. Illus. by Michael Adams. (Gateway Classic Ser.). 48p. (J). (gr. k-5). 1993. 5.95 (*0-685-63134-6*) Unicorn Pub.

Andersen's Fairy Tales. Hans Christian Andersen. (J). 1991. lib. bdg. 250.00 (*0-8490-4569-X*) Gordon Pr.

Andersen's Fairy Tales. Hans Christian Andersen. (Children's Classics Ser.). (Illus.). (J). 1992. write for info. (*0-89434-122-7*) Ferguson.

Andersen's Fairy Tales. Hans Christian Andersen. 1987. pap. 4.95 (*0-451-52107-2*, Sig Classics) NAL-Dutton.

Andersen's Fairy Tales. Hans Christian Andersen. (Children's Classics Ser.). 1988. 12.99 (*0-517-66718-5*) Random Hse Value.

Andersen's Fairy Tales. Ed. by Sheila Black. LC 90-55649. (Children's Classics Ser.). (Illus.). 56p. (J). (gr. 1-4). 1991. 9.98 (*0-89471-981-5*) Courage Bks.

Andersen's Fairy Tales. Hans Christian Andersen. LC 58-6191. (Illustrated Junior Library). (Illus.). 352p. (J). (gr. 3-9). 1981. reprint ed. 13.95 (*0-448-06005-1*, G&D) Putnam Pub Group.

An Asterisk (*) at the beginning of an entry indicates that the title is appearing in BIP for the first time.

***Anderson: A Pictorial History.** Esther Dittlinger. (Indiana Pictorial History Ser.). (Illus.). 1991. write for info. (0-943963-16-8) G Bradley.

Anderson: European Economic Interest Groupings. Margaret Anderson. 1990. pap. 180.00 (0-406-04567-4) Butterworth Legal Pubs.

Anderson - Krogh Genealogy: Ancestral Lines & Descendants. L. W. Hansen. (Illus.). 323p. 1991. reprint ed. lib. bdg. 61.50 (0-8328-1695-7); reprint ed. pap. 51.50 (0-8328-1696-5) Higginson Bk Co.

Anderson - Overton Genealogy: A Continuation of Anderson Family Records (1936) & Early Descendants of William Overton & Elizabeth Waters of VA (1938) W. P. Anderson. (Illus.). 376p. 1991. reprint ed. lib. bdg. 69.59 (0-8328-1773-2); reprint ed. pap. 59.50 (0-8328-1774-0) Higginson Bk Co.

***Anderson: A Genealogy: The Legacy.** Burton F. Anderson. 500p. (Orig.). Date not set. pap. write for info. (0-9643110-1-1) Tracy Pubng.

Anderson County Kentucky 1830-1850 Censuses. Lawson Rowena. iii, 78p. (Orig.). 1987. pap. 11.50 (1-55613-075-9) Heritage Bk.

Anderson County Tennessee: A Pictorial History. James Overholt. (Illus.). 1989. 29.95 (0-89865-770-9) Donning Co.

Anderson House Cookbook. Jeanne M. Hall & John Hall. LC 85-31040. 389p. 1986. 17.95 (0-88289-475-7) Pelican.

Anderson Island Poetry. Gale T. Richardson. 14p. 1989. 5.00 (0-9614337-3-6) Poetry Unltd.

Anderson Localization. Ed. by T. Ando & H. Fukuyama. (Proceedings in Physics Ser.: Vol. 28). (Illus.). 376p. 1988. 77.00 (0-387-19122-4) Spr-Verlag.

Anderson Localization, Kyoto, Japan, 1981: Proceedings. Ed. by Y. Nagaoka & H. Fukuyama. (Solid-State Sciences Ser.: Vol. 39). (Illus.). 225p. 1982. 61.00 (0-387-11518-8) Spr-Verlag.

Anderson Tapes. Lawrence Sanders. 20.95 (0-89190-854-4, Am Repr) Amereon Ltd.

Anderson Tapes. Lawrence Sanders. 336p. 1987. mass mkt. 5.99 (0-425-10364-1) Berkley Pub.

Anderson Tapes. Lawrence Sanders. 1994. reprint ed. lib. bdg. 32.95 (1-56849-331-2) Buccaneer Bks.

***Anderson's American Law of Zoning, 5 vols., Set.** Kenneth Young. (Real Property - Zoning Ser.). 1995. write for info. (0-614-06262-4) Clark Boardman Callaghan.

Anderson's Campground Directory. Skip Deegans & Judy Deegans. 335p. pap. 6.25 (1-881774-00-7) Meadow Bluff.

Anderson's Complete Guide to Revenue Rulings on Qualified Plans. 3rd ed. Arthur W. Anderson. 185p. (C). 1993. pap. 35.00 (1-56698-080-1) Actex Pubns.

Anderson's Directory of Criminal Justice Education, 1990-91. Charles P. Nemeth. LC 87-654284. 800p. (C). 1990. pap. text ed. 59.95 (0-87084-195-5) Anderson Pub Co.

Anderson's Estate Planning Forms & Clauses. rev. ed. 1991. 75.00 (0-685-55313-2) Anderson Pub Co.

Anderson's Manual for Notaries Public. Anderson Publishing Co. Staff. 698p. 1991. pap. 19.95 (0-87084-040-1) Anderson Pub Co.

Anderson's Ohio Civil Practice with Forms, 7 vols., 8 bks., Set. John W. McCormac et al. 1991. ring bd. 475.00 (0-87084-594-2) Anderson Pub Co.

Anderson's Ohio Civil Practice with Forms, 1972-1989, 7 vols. 4409p. 1983. 475.00 (0-317-99868-4) Anderson Pub Co.

Anderson's Ohio Civil Practice with Forms, 1972-1989, 7 vols. suppl. ed. 4409p. 1989. 50.00 (0-317-99869-2) Anderson Pub Co.

Anderson's Ohio Civil Practice with Forms, 1972-1989, 7 vols. suppl. ed. 4409p. 1990. 125.00 (0-685-45381-2) Anderson Pub Co.

Anderson's Ohio Civil Practice with Forms, 1972-1989, 7 vols. suppl. ed. 4409p. 1991. 100.00 (0-685-54056-1) Anderson Pub Co.

Anderson's Ohio Civil Practice with Forms, 1972-1989, 7 vols., No. 1. suppl. ed. 4409p. 1989. 125.00 (0-317-99870-6) Anderson Pub Co.

Anderson's Ohio Criminal Practice & Procedure, 2 vols. 2nd ed. Robert Gorman et al. 1989. pap. write for info. (0-87084-620-5); Incl. handbk. ring bd. 250.00 (0-87084-029-0) Anderson Pub Co.

Anderson's Ohio Evidence 1980-1985, 2 vols. Josiah H. Blackmore & Glen Weissenberger. LC 82-238692. 1025p. 1984. ring bd. 150.00 (0-685-42573-8) Anderson Pub Co.

Anderson's Ohio Evidence 1980-1985, 2 vols., No. 3. suppl. ed. Josiah H. Blackmore & Glen Weissenberger. LC 82-238692. 1025p. 1988. 40.00 (0-685-42574-6) Anderson Pub Co.

Anderson's Ohio Evidence, 1980-1990, 2 vols. Josiah H. Blackmore & Glen Weissenberger. LC 82-238692. 1025p. 1984. ring bd. 250.00 (0-317-99871-4) Anderson Pub Co.

Anderson's Ohio Evidence, 1980-1990, 2 vols. suppl. ed. Josiah H. Blackmore & Glen Weissenberger. LC 82-238692. 1025p. 1991. 60.00 (0-685-45384-7) Anderson Pub Co.

Anderson's Ohio Evidence, 1980-1990, 2 vols., No. 1. suppl. ed. Josiah H. Blackmore & Glen Weissenberger. LC 82-238692. 1025p. 1989. 55.00 (0-317-99872-2) Anderson Pub Co.

Anderson's Ohio Evidence, 1980-1990, 2 vols., No. 1. suppl. ed. Josiah H. Blackmore & Glen Weissenberger. LC 82-238692. 1025p. 1990. 60.00 (0-317-99875-7) Anderson Pub Co.

Anderson's Ohio Evidence, 1980-1990, 2 vols., No. 1. suppl. ed. Josiah H. Blackmore & Glen Weissenberger. LC 82-238692. 1025p. 1992. 61.50 (0-685-45382-0) Anderson Pub Co.

Anderson's Ohio Evidence, 1980-1990, 2 vols., No. 2. suppl. ed. Josiah H. Blackmore & Glen Weissenberger. LC 82-238692. 1025p. 1989. 50.00 (0-317-99873-0) Anderson Pub Co.

Anderson's Ohio Evidence, 1980-1990, 2 vols., No. 2. suppl. ed. Josiah H. Blackmore & Glen Weissenberger. LC 82-238692. 1025p. 1991. 65.00 (0-685-45385-5) Anderson Pub Co.

Anderson's Ohio Evidence, 1980-1990, 2 vols., No. 3. suppl. ed. Josiah H. Blackmore & Glen Weissenberger. LC 82-238692. 1025p. 1989. 50.00 (0-317-99874-9) Anderson Pub Co.

Anderson's Ohio Evidence, 1980-1990, 2 vols., No. 3. suppl. ed. Josiah H. Blackmore & Glen Weissenberger. LC 82-238692. 1025p. 1990. 97.50 (0-685-45383-9) Anderson Pub Co.

Anderson's Ohio Family Law, 2 vols., Set. 2nd ed. John Gilchrist et al. 1989. 225.00 (0-87084-027-4) Anderson Pub Co.

Anderson's Ohio Probate Practice & Procedure, 3 vols., Set. Marilyn Maag et al. 2074p. 1990. text ed. 350.00 (0-87084-019-3) Anderson Pub Co.

Anderson's Pathology. 10th ed. Damjanov & Linder. 2150p. 1995. 199.00 (0-8016-7236-8) Mosby Yr Bk.

***Anderson's Travel Companion: A Guide to the Best Fiction & Non-Fiction.** Sarah Anderson. 500p. 1995. 76.95 (1-85928-013-7, Pub. by Scolar Pr UK) Ashgate Pub Co.

Andersonville. MacKinlay Kantor. 768p. 1993. pap. 14.95 (0-452-26956-3, Plume) NAL-Dutton.

Andersonville. MacKinley Kantor. 1993. 22.75 (0-8446-6682-3) Peter Smith.

Andersonville. Mackinlay Kantor. 1994. reprint ed. lib. bdg. 39.95 (1-56849-297-9) Buccaneer Bks.

Andersonville: A Civil War Tragedy. Linda R. Wade. LC 90-46576. (Doors to America's Past Ser.). 48p. (J). (gr. 4-7). 1991. 11.95 (0-86592-472-4) Rourke Enter.

Andersonville: A Story of Rebel Military Prisons. John McElroy. (Illus.). 664p. 1993. reprint ed. pap. text ed. 38.00 (1-55613-851-2) Heritage Bk.

Andersonville: The Last Depot. William Marvel. LC 93-40101. (Civil War America Ser.). (Illus.). xii, 338p. 1994. 29.95 (0-8078-2152-7) U of NC Pr.

***Andersonville: The Southern Perspective.** Ed. by J. H. Segars. (Journal of Confederate History Ser.: Vol. XIII). (Illus.). 200p. (Orig.). 1995. pap. 15.00 (0-614-06042-7) So Herit Pr.

Andersonville Diary. John L. Ransom. LC 73-21807. (American History & Americana Ser.: No. 47). 1974. lib. bdg. 75.00 (0-8383-1783-9) M S G Haskell Hse.

Andersonville Diary & Memoirs of Charles Hopkins, 1st New Jersey Infantry. Charles Hopkins & William Styple. Ed. by John J. Fitzpatrick. 221p. 1988. 21.95 (0-9622053-0-3) Belle Grv Pub.

***Andersonville National Cemetery.** G. Michael Strack. (Illus.). 16p. (Orig.). 1983. pap. 4.25 (0-915992-79-5) Eastern Acorn.

Andersonville Prison: Lessons in Organizational Failure. Ed. by Joseph P. Cangemi & Casimir J. Kowalski. LC 92-16723. 134p. (C). 1992. 35.00 (0-8191-8758-5) U Pr of Amer.

Andersonville Trial. Saul Levitt. 1961. pap. 4.75 (0-8222-0042-2) Dramatists Play.

Andes. Stephen Lee. (Illus.). 144p. 1992. 39.95 (0-7134-6595-6, Pub. by Batsford UK) Trafalgar.

Andes: A Geological Review, Vol. 13. W. Zeil. (Illus.). 1979. lib. bdg. 89.95 (3-443-11013-4) Lubrecht & Cramer.

Andes: A Quest for Justice. Neil MacDonald. 128p. (C). 1993. pap. text ed. 24.00 (0-85598-200-4, Pub. by Oxfam Pubns UK) St Mut.

Andes Mountains. Rose Blue & Corinne Naden. LC 94-3028. (Wonders of the World Ser.). (Illus.). 64p. (J). (gr. 5-8). 1994. lib. bdg. 24.36 (0-8114-6363-X) Raintree Steck-V.

Andes of Southern Peru. Isaiah Bowman. LC 68-23277. (Illus.). 336p. 1968. reprint ed. text ed. 35.00 (0-8371-0025-9, B0AP, Greenwood Pr) Greenwood.

Andes Viewed from the City: Literary & Political Discourse on the Indian in Peru, 1848-1930. Efrain Kristal. (American University Studies: General Literature: Ser. XIX, Vol. 6). 249p. (C). 1987. text ed. 41.00 (0-8204-0437-3) P Lang Pubs.

Andesites: Orogenic Andesites & Related Rocks. Ed. by Richard S. Thorpe. LC 80-42307. 237p. 1982. text ed. 415.00 (0-471-28034-8, Wiley-Interscience) Wiley.

***Andesites: Orogenic Andesites & Related Rocks.** fac. ed. Ed. by R. S. Thorpe. LC 80-42307. (Illus.). 738p. 1994. pap. 180.00 (0-7837-7658-6, 2047411) Bks Demand.

***And...Howe! The Authorized Autobiography of Gordie & Colleen Howe.** Gordon Howe & Colleen Howe. 512p. 1995. write for info. (0-9647149-0-6); pap. write for info. (0-9647149-1-4) Power Play.

Andiamo Avanti: Attualita e Racconti. Franca C. Merlonghi & Ferdianando Merlonghi. 200p. (C). 1991. pap. text ed. write for info. (0-13-036542-4) P-H.

Andiamo Avanti! Lingua e Cultura. Franca C. Merlonghi & Ferdinando Merlonghi. 352p. (C). 1992. pap. text ed. write for info. (0-13-031451-X) P-H.

Andie MacDowell. Bob Italia. LC 92-13690. (Cover Girls Ser.). (J). 1992. lib. bdg. 12.94 (1-56239-111-9) Abdo & Dghtrs.

Andie Out of Control. Alison Hart. LC 93-86084. (Riding Academy Ser.: No. 2). 132p. (Orig.). (J). (gr. 3-7). 1994. pap. 3.50 (0-679-85693-5) Random Bks Yng Read.

Andie Shows Off. Alison Hart. (Riding Academy Ser.). 132p. (Orig.). (J). (gr. 3-7). 1994. pap. 3.50 (0-679-85697-8, Bullseye Bks) Random Bks Yng Read.

***Andie's Risky Business.** Hart. 1995. 3.50 (0-679-87141-1) Random.

Ando Shoeki: Selected Writings. Ando Shoeki. Tr. by Yasunaga Toshinobu. (Illus.). 240p. (C). 1992. 35.00 (0-8348-0232-5) Weatherhill.

Ando Shoeki & the Anatomy of Japanese Feudalism. E. Herbert Norman. LC 79-52922. 340p. 1979. reprint ed. text ed. 75.00 (0-313-27034-1, U7034, Greenwood Pr) Greenwood.

Andor Weininger. (Illus.). 168p. 1990. 55.00 (3-89322-192-1, Pub. by Edition Cantz GW) Dist Art Pubs.

Andorff the Energy Ant's Coloring Book. abr. ed. Ed. by Michael P. Jones. (Illus.). 34p. (J). 1984. text ed. 11.00 (0-89904-071-3); pap. text ed. 6.00 (0-89904-072-1) Crumb Elbow Pub.

Andorra. Barry Taylor. (World Bibliographical Ser.). 1993. lib. bdg. 60.00 (1-85109-211-0) ABC-CLIO.

***Andorra & Gibraltar Handbook.** 240p. (C). 1994. 225.00 (0-7605-0880-1) Rector Pr.

***Andover: A Century of Change.** Eleanor M. Richardson. LC 95-7906. 1995. write for info. (0-89865-938-8) Donning Co.

Andover Cookbook II: Passport Edition. (Illus.). 240p. (Orig.). 1993. pap. 19.95 (0-9637368-3-3) Ladies Benevolent.

Andovers: Portrait of Two New England Towns. Illus. by Thea Wheelwright. LC 80-50887. 96p. (Orig.). 1980. pap. 9.95 (0-931474-10-8) Kennebec River.

Andra. Louise Lawrence. LC 90-38595. 240p. (YA). (gr. 7 up). 1991. lib. bdg. 14.89 (0-06-023705-8) HarpC Child Bks.

Andragogy in Action: Applying Modern Principles of Adult Learning. Knowles, Malcolm S., & Associates. LC 84-47989. (Management Ser.). 468p. 1984. 39.95 (0-87589-621-9) Jossey-Bass.

Andrasil. Carl A. Faber. 30p. (Orig.). 1989. pap. write for info. (0-318-66439-9) Perseus Pr.

***Andre Agassi.** Richard Rambeck. (Sports Superstars Ser.). (Illus.). 24p. (J). (gr. 2-6). 1995. lib. bdg. 21.36 (1-56766-202-1) Childs World.

Andre Antoine. Jean Chothia. (Directors in Perspective Ser.). (Illus.). 232p. (C). 1991. 69.95 (0-521-25219-9) Cambridge U Pr.

Andre Bazin. Dudley Andrew & Francois Truffaut. (Illus.). 304p. 1990. text ed. 39.50 (0-231-07398-4); pap. text ed. 16.50 (0-231-07399-2) Col U Pr.

Andre Breton. J. F. Matthews. LC 67-16892. (Columbia Essays on Modern Writers Ser.: No. 26). 48p. (Orig.). (C). 1967. pap. text ed. 7.50 (0-231-02910-1) Col U Pr.

***Andre Breton.** rev. ed. Caws. 1996. 22.95 (0-8057-4623-4, Twayne) Macmillan.

Andre Breton: Magus of Surrealism. Anna Balakian. LC 78-83006. 1971. 20.00 (0-19-501298-4) Hawkshead Bk.

Andre Breton: Sketch for an Early Portrait. J. H. Matthews. LC 86-20741. (Purdue University Monographs in Romance Languages: No. 22). xii, 176p. (Orig.). 1986. pap. 46.00x (0-915027-71-2) Benjamins North Am.

Andre Breton, Arbiter of Surrealism. Brodwer. 29.95 (0-7859-0637-1, F89730) Fr & Eur.

Andre Breton, Quelques Aspects de l'Ecrivain. Michel De Ghelderode. 190p. (FRE.). 1986. 29.95 (0-7859-1201-0, 2871320284) Fr & Eur.

Andre Breton Today. Ed. by Rudolf E. Kuenzli. LC 89-2482. (Illus.). (Orig.). 1989. 18.95 (0-930279-16-6); pap. 9.95 (0-930279-15-8) Willis Locker & Owens.

Andre Breton's Selected Writings. Andre Breton. 1992. lib. bdg. 88.00 (0-8490-5459-1) Gordon Pr.

Andre Campra (Sixteen Sixty to Seventeen Forty-Four) Book 1 (1708) & Book 2 (1714) Comment by David Tunley. LC 90-752276. (Eighteenth-Century French Cantata Ser.: Vol. 2). 320p. 1990. 160.00 (0-8240-9651-7) Garland.

Andre Chenier. Richard A. Smernoff. LC 76-50038. (Twayne's World Authors Ser.). 168p. (C). 1977. lib. bdg. 17.95 (0-8057-6258-2) Irvington.

Andre Dawson. Andre Dawson & Tom Bird. (Today's Heroes Ser.). 112p. 1994. pap. 4.99 (0-310-41181-5) Zondervan.

Andre Dubus: A Study of the Short Fiction. Thomas E. Kennedy. 208p. 1988. text ed. 22.95 (0-8057-8305-9, Twayne) Macmillan.

Andre Gide. Vinio Rossi. LC 68-54458. (Columbia Essays on Modern Writers Ser.: No. 35). (Orig.). (C). 1968. pap. text ed. 7.50 (0-231-02960-8) Col U Pr.

Andre Gide: An Annotated Bibliography, 1973-1988. Catherine S. Brosman. LC 89-16846. 368p. 1989. 48.00 (0-8240-7973-6, H959) Garland.

Andre Gide: And the Codes of Homotextuality. Emily S. Apter. (Stanford French & Italian Studies: Vol. 48). 174p. 1987. pap. 46.50 (0-915838-64-8) Anma Libri.

Andre Gide: The Homosexual Moralist. Patrick Pollard. (Illus.). 448p. (C). 1992. text ed. 47.50 (0-300-04998-6) Yale U Pr.

Andre Gide: The Theism of an Atheist. H. J. Nersoyan. LC 69-17717. 1969. 39.95x (0-8156-2135-3) Syracuse U Pr.

***Andre Gide dans le Labyrinthe de la Mythotextualite.** Pamela A. Genova. LC 95-3684. (Purdue Studies in Romance Literatures: Vol. 8). 200p. (FRE.). 1995. 30.00x (1-55753-067-X) Purdue U Pr.

Andre Gide, Eighteen Sixty-Nine to Nineteen Fifty-One. (Yale French Studies: No. 7). 1972. reprint ed. pap. 15.00 (0-527-01715-9) Periodicals Srv.

Andre Gide Revisited. Thomas Cordle. (Twayne's World Authors Ser.). 160p. 1992. text ed. 22.95 (0-8057-8283-4, Twayne) Macmillan.

***Andre Gorz: A Critical Reader.** Jeremy Tatman. (C). 1996. pap. text ed. 15.95 (0-7453-0787-6) Westview.

***Andre Gorz: A Critical Reader.** Ed. by Jeremy Tatman. (Modern European Thinkers Ser.). (C). 1996. text ed. 49.95 (0-7453-0786-8, Pub. by Pluto Pr UK) Westview.

Andre Kertesz: A Lifetime of Perception. Ed. by Jane Corkin. 162p. 1993. write for info. (0-9637867-0-9) Andalusian.

***Andre Kertesz: His Life & Work.** Ed. by Pierre Borhan. (Illus.). 368p. 1994. 65.00 (0-8212-2140-X) Bulfinch Pr.

Andre Kertesz - A Stranger to Paris. Ed. by Jane Corkin. (Illus.). 96p. 1992. pap. 24.95 (0-969350-2-4) Firefly Bks Ltd.

Andre Laurendeau: French Canadian Nationalist 1912-1968. Donald J. Horton. 280p. (C). 1993. 35.00 (0-19-540917-5, 14471) OUP.

Andre Levinson on Dance: Writings from Paris in the Twenties. Andre Levinson. Ed. by Lynn Garafola. LC 90-50911. (Illus.). 174p. 1991. 25.00 (0-8195-5227-5, Wesleyan Univ Pr) U Pr of New Eng.

Andre Malraux. Wilbur M. Frohock. LC 74-1198. (Columbia Essays on Modern Writers Ser.: No. 71). 48p. 1974. pap. text ed. 7.50 (0-231-03441-5) Col U Pr.

Andre Malraux. James R. Hewitt. LC 70-15661. (Literature & Life Ser.). 160p. (C). 1978. 19.95 (0-8044-2379-2, F Ungar Bks) Continuum.

Andre Malraux: A Reference Guide, 1940-1990. John B. Romeiser. LC 93-46322. (Reference Publications in Literature). 384p. 1994. text ed. 45.00 (0-8161-9071-2) G K Hall.

Andre Malraux: Man's Fate, Man's Hope. Kenneth Murphy. 680p. 1993. 29.95 (0-02-922319-9) Free Pr.

***Andre Malraux: Politics & the Temptation of Myth.** Gino Raymond. 210p. 1995. 59.95 (1-85972-132-X, Pub. by Avebury Pub UK) Ashgate Pub Co.

Andre Malraux: The "Farfelu" As Expression of the Feminine & the Erotic. Domnica Radulescu. LC 93-23079. (American University Studies, II, Romance Language & Literature: Vol. 209). 216p. (C). 1994. text ed. 55.95 (0-8204-2296-7) P Lang Pubs.

Andre Malraux: Towards the Expression of Transcendence. David Bevan. 128p. 1986. 42.95 (0-7735-0552-0, Pub. by McGill CN) U of Toronto Pr.

Andre Malraux & the Metamorphosis of Death. Thomas J. Kline. 197p. 1973. text ed. 40.50 (0-231-03608-6) Col U Pr.

Andre Malraux & the Tragic Imagination. Wilbur M. Frohock. xvi, 175p. 1952. 29.50 (0-8047-0441-4); pap. 10.95 (0-8047-0442-2) Stanford U Pr.

Andre Malraux's Espoir: The Propaganda-Art Film & the Spanish Civil War. John J. Michalczyk. LC 77-7308. (Romance Monographs: No. 27). 1977. 25.00 (84-399-6811-6) Romance.

***Andre-Marie Ampere (1775-1836)** James R. Hofmann. LC 94-5248. (Science Biographies Ser.). 380p. 1995. 44.95 (0-631-17849-X) Blackwell Pubs.

Andre Masson. Dawn Ades. (Illus.). 128p. 1994. 24.95 (0-8478-1799-7) Rizzoli Intl.

Andre Maurois: Avec des Remarques d'Andre Maurois. Suffel. 208p. (FRE.). 1963. pap. 11.95 (0-7859-1407-2, 2080506609) Fr & Eur.

Andre Messager: A Bio-Bibliography. John Wagstaff. LC 90-22928. (Bio-Bibliographies in Music Ser.: No. 33). 208p. 1991. text ed. 47.95 (0-313-25736-1, WFD, Greenwood Pr) Greenwood.

Andre Michaux's Travels into Kentucky, 1792-96. Francois Andre Michaux's Travels West of the Allegheny Mountains, 1802. Thaddeus Mason Harris's Journal of a Tour Northwest of the Allegheny Mountains, 1803 see Early Western Travels, 1748-1846

Andre Minaux. George Besson. (Illus.). 72p. 1967. pap. 175.00 (1-55660-135-2) A Wofsy Fine Arts.

Andre Morellet (1727-1819) in the Republic of Letters & the French Revolution. Ed. by Jeffrey W. Merrick & Dorothy Medlin. LC 94-12273. (Eighteenth Century French Intellectual History Ser.: Vol. 2). 272p. (C). 1995. text ed. 57.95 (0-8204-2494-3) P Lang Pubs.

***Andre Motion Picture Soundtrack Songbook.** Ed. by Milton Okun. (Illus.). 55p. (YA). 1994. pap. 14.95 (0-89524-876-X, 02502155) Cherry Lane.

***Andre Norton: A Primary & Secondary Bibliography.** 2nd rev. ed. Roger C. Schlobin & Irene R. Harrison. LC 94-69292. xxvii, 92p. 1995. pap. 12.50 (0-915368-64-1) New Eng SF Assoc.

Andre Norton: Fables & Futures. Ed. by Anne Braude. 52p. (C). 1989. reprint ed. lib. bdg. 23.00x (0-8095-6854-3) Borgo Pr.

Andre Norton: Grand Master of the Witch World. Gordon Benson, Jr. & Phil Stephensen-Payne. (Galactic Central Bibliographies Ser.: No. 41). ix, 74p. (C). 1992. lib. bdg. 23.00x (0-8095-4739-2) Borgo Pr.

Andre Ostier: Masques et Bergamasques. Intro. by Thomas M. Gunther. LC 88-11225. (Illus.). 45p. (Orig.). 1988. pap. 5.00 (0-933444-46-X) French Inst.

Andre Thevet's North America: A Sixteenth-Century View. Ed. by Roger Schlesinger & Arthur Stabler. 352p. 1986. 49.95 (0-7735-0587-3, Pub. by McGill CN) U of Toronto Pr.

***Andrea.** Gloria Chisholm. (Springsong Bks.). 176p. (Orig.). 1995. mass mkt. 3.99 (1-55661-622-8) Bethany Hse.

Andrea. Ellen West. LC 91-67751. 161p. (Orig.). 1993. pap. 6.95 (1-56002-159-4, Univ Edtns) Aegina Pr.

Andrea Alciato & the Emblem Tradition. Ed. by Peter M. Daly. LC 88-39895. (AMS Studies in the Emblem: No. 4). 1989. 57.50 (0-404-63704-3) AMS Pr.

Andrea at the Center. J. P. Kansas. (Orig.). 1994. pap. text ed. 4.95 (1-56333-206-X) Masquerade.

***Andrea at the Center.** 2nd ed. J. P. Kansas. (Orig.). 1995. pap. text ed. 5.95 (1-56333-324-4) Masquerade.

Andrea Barbarigo, Merchant of Venice, 1418-1449. Frederic C. Lane. LC 78-64194. (Johns Hopkins University. Studies in the Social Sciences. Thirtieth Ser. 1912: 1). reprint ed. 37.50 (0-404-61300-4) AMS Pr.

Andrea Branzi. Intro. by Germano Celant. LC 91-50875. (Illus.). 224p. (Orig.). 1992. pap. 35.00 (0-8478-1504-8) Rizzoli Intl.

Andrea del Castagno & His Patrons. John R. Spencer. LC 91-11748. (Illus.). 195p. 1991. text ed. 36.95 (0-8223-1150-X) Duke.

An Asterisk (*) at the beginning of an entry indicates that the title is appearing in BIP for the first time.

An Asterisk (*) at the beginning of an entry indicates that the title is appearing in BIP for the first time.

Andrew Young: Freedom Fighter. rev. ed. Naurice Roberts. LC 83-7633. (Picture-Story Biographies Ser.). (Illus.). 32p. (J). (gr. 2-5). 1990. lib. bdg. 11.85 (0-516-03450-2); pap. 3.95 (0-516-43450-0) Childrens.

Andrew Young - Remembrance & Homage. Illus. by Charles E. Wadsworth. LC 78-575150. 1978. 10.00 (0-930954-09-2); boxed 75.00 (0-930954-10-6) Tidal Pr.

Andrew's Amazing Monsters. Kathryn H. Berlan. LC 91-39131. (Illus.). 32p. (J). (ps-2). 1993. text ed. 13.95 (0-689-31739-5, Atheneum Bks Young) S&S Childrens.

*Andrew's Angry Words. Dorothea Lachner. (Illus.). 32p. (J). (gr. k-3). 1995. 14.95 (1-55858-435-8); lib. bdg. 14. 88 (1-55858-436-6) North-South Bks NYC.

Andrews Collection: Personal Treasures. Anne D. Smith. Ed. by Deanna Hacker. (Illus.). 104p. 1989. 34.95 (0-938685-04-X); pap. 19.95 (0-938685-05-8) Dees Delights.

Andrews' Diseases of the Skin: Clinical Dermatology. 8th ed. Harry L. Arnold, Jr. et al. (Illus.). 1058p. 1990. text ed. 135.00 (0-7216-2424-3) Saunders.

Andrews Field: First United States World War Two Airbase in Europe, with a Brief History of Great Saling. Rodney J. Pope. (Illus.). 80p. (Orig.). 1991. pap. 15.00 (0-86025-428-3, Pub. by Ian Henry Pubns UK) Empire Pub Srvs.

Andrews Memorial: Genealogy of the Andrews of Taunton & Stoughton, Mass., Descendants of John & Hannah Andrews of Boston, Mass., 1656-1886. George Andrews. 86p. 1988. reprint ed. lib. bdg. 27.00 (0-8328-0122-4); reprint ed. pap. 17.00 (0-8328-0123-2) Higginson Bk Co.

Andrew's Own Place. Nancy Riecken. LC 92-22953. (Illus.). (J). 1993. 14.95 (0-395-64723-1) HM.

Andrew's Secret. Arleta Richardson. Ed. by Peggy Payne & Tamra Yoder. (Illus.). 30p. (Orig.). (J). (gr. 1-3). 1989. pap. 3.00 (0-89367-143-6) Light & Life.

Andrey Bely: A Critical Review. Ed. by Gerald Janecek. LC 77-75449. 232p. 1978. 25.00 (0-8131-1368-7) U Pr of Ky.

Andrey Bely: A Critical Study of the Novels. John D. Elsworth. LC 83-1793. (Cambridge Studies in Russian Literature). 220p. 1984. 69.95 (0-521-24724-1) Cambridge U Pr.

Andrey Bely: Spirit of Symbolism. John E. Malmstad. (Illus.). 352p. 1987. 52.50 (0-8014-1984-0); pap. 22.95 (0-8014-9445-1) Cornell U Pr.

Andreyev, Leonid-Photographs by a Russian Writer: An Undiscovered Portrait of Pre-Revolutionary Russia. C. Davies. (C). 1990. 170.00 (0-685-34324-3, Pub. by Collets) St Mut.

Andro, This Is Crazy. Jack Lawson. 96p. (Orig.). (J). 1991. pap. 2.95 (0-380-76234-X, Camelot) Avon.

Androcles & the Lion. Emory H. Michael. LC 87-51492. (Illus.). 44p. (J). (gr. k-4). 1988. 6.95 (1-55523-132-2) Winston-Derek.

Androcles & the Lion. Bernard Shaw. (Orig.). 1988. mass mkt. 6.00 (0-14-045013-0, Penguin Bks) Viking Penguin.

Androcles & the Lion. George Bernard Shaw. LC 91-51226. 60p. (Orig.). 1992. pap. 6.00 (0-88734-247-7) Players Pr.

Androcles & the Lion. George Bernard Shaw. Ed. by Catherine Storr. LC 86-6665. (Legends & Folktales Ser.). (Illus.). 32p. (Orig.). (J). (gr. 2-5). 1986. lib. bdg. 19.97 (0-8172-2625-7) Raintree Steck-V.

Androcles & the Lion. George Bernard Shaw. (Penguin Plays Ser.). (Orig.). (YA). (gr. 9 up). 1963. pap. 3.95 (0-14-048010-2, PL5) Viking Child Bks.

*Androcles & the Lion. Smithmark Staff. Date not set. pap. 4.98 (0-8317-0816-6) Smithmark.

Androcles & the Lion. Illus. & Ret. by Janet Stevens. LC 89-1953. 32p. (J). (ps-3). 1989. lib. bdg. 14.95 (0-8234-0768-3); pap. 5.95 (0-8234-0906-6) Holiday.

Androcles & the Lion: And Other Aesop's Fables. Illus. by Robert Rayevsky. LC 90-19173. 40p. (J). (ps up). 1991. 13.95 (0-688-09682-4); lib. bdg. 13.88 (0-688-09683-2) Morrow Jr Bks.

Androcles & the Lion: Musical. Aurand Harris. (J). 1964. 5.00 (0-87602-105-4) Anchorage.

Androcles & the Lion see St. Joan, Major Barbara, Androcles

Androcles & the Lion; Overruled; Pygmalion. George Bernard Shaw. (BCL1-PR English Literature Ser.). 224p. 1992. reprint ed. lib. bdg. 79.00 (0-7812-7645-4) Rprt Serv.

*Androgenic Disorders. Geoffrey P. Redmond. 356p. 1995. 89.00 (0-7817-0274-7) Raven.

*Androgenization in Women: Pathophysiology & Clinical Aspects. fac. ed. Ed. by Gian M. Molinatti et al. LC 81-48338. (Illus.). 216p. Date not set. pap. 61.60 (0-7837-7216-5, 2047082) Bks Demand.

Androgens: Pathophysiological & Behavioural Aspects. Ed. by T. Lemarchand-Beraud & P. Fossati. (Journal: Hormone Research: Vol. 18, No. 1-3). (Illus.). 152p. 1983. pap. 65.75 (3-8055-3728-X) S Karger.

Androgens & Anti-Androgen Therapy. Ed. by S. L. Jeffcoate. LC 81-19712. (Current Topics in Reproductive Endocrinology Ser.: No. 1). (Illus.). 198p. reprint ed. pap. 56.50 (0-8357-8639-0, 2035063) Bks Demand.

Androgens & Antiandrogens. International Symposium on Androgens & Antiandrogens Staff. Ed. by Luciano Martini & Marcella Motta. LC 76-19853. (Illus.). 395p. reprint ed. pap. 112.60 (0-7837-7112-6, 2046941) Bks Demand.

Androgens & Prostate Cancer. Labrie. Date not set. write for info. (0-8493-5824-8) CRC Pr.

Androgens in Childhood: Biological, Physiological, Clinical & Therapeutic Aspects. Ed. by M. G. Forest. (Pediatric & Adolescent Endocrinology Ser.: Vol. 19). (Illus.). viii, 282p. 1989. 179.25 (3-8055-4850-8) S Karger.

Androgens of the Testis. Ed. by Kristen B. Eik-Nes. LC 70-98064. 260p. reprint ed. pap. 74.10 (0-8357-5474-X, 2055037) Bks Demand.

Androgens 11 & Antiandrogens. R. K. Wagner et al. (Handbook of Experimental Pharmacology Ser.: Vol. 35, Pt. 2). (Illus.). x, 625p. 1974. 266.00 (0-387-06883-X) Spr-Verlag.

Androgyne: The Creative Tension of Male & Female. Elemire Zolla. Ed. by Jill Purce. LC 81-67701. (Illustrated Library of Sacred Imagination). (Illus.). 96p. 1981. 9.95 (0-8245-0065-2) Crossroad NY.

Androgyne Journal. James Broughton. LC 90-86381. 96p. (Orig.). 1991. pap. 10.00 (0-913089-22-2) Broken Moon.

Androgyne, Mon Amour. Tennessee Williams. LC 76-52956. 1977. 8.50 (0-8112-0648-3) New Directions.

Androgynous Judaism: Masculine & Feminine in the Dual Torah. Jacob Neusner. LC 93-32291. 216p. 1993. 30.00 (0-86554-428-X, MUP/H342) Mercer Univ Pr.

Androgyny: The Opposites Within. June Singer. 273p. 1989. pap. 16.95 (0-938434-30-6) Sigo Pr.

Androgyny: The Opposites Within. June Singer. 273p. 1991. 27.50 (0-938434-29-2) Sigo Pr.

Androgyny & the Denial of Difference. Kari Weil. LC 92-16774. (Feminist Issues: Practice, Politics, Theory Ser.). 224p. (C). 1992. text ed. 35.00 (0-8139-1404-3); pap. text ed. 12.95 (0-8139-1405-1) U Pr of Va.

*Android Epistemology. Ed. by Ken Ford et al. (AAAI Press Ser.). (Illus.). 350p. 1995. 25.00x (0-614-07258-1) MIT Pr.

*Android Epistemology. Ed. by Ken Ford et al. (Illus.). 350p. (C). 1995. 25.00 (0-262-06184-8) MIT Pr.

Android Invasion. Terrance Dicks. (Dr. Who Ser.: No. 9). 1989. pap. 3.50 (1-55817-287-4, Pinnacle NY) Windsor NY.

Androids at Arms. Andre Norton. 240p. 1987. pap. text ed. 2.95 (0-345-34282-8, Del Rey) Ballantine.

Androids, Humanoids, & Other Folklore Monsters: Science & Soul in Science Fiction Films. Schelde Per. LC 93-274. (Illus.). 288p. (C). 1993. text ed. 40.00 (0-8147-7930-1) NYU Pr.

Androids, Humanoids & Other Science Fiction Monsters: Science & Soul in Science Fiction. Per Schelde. 288p. 1994. pap. 17.95 (0-8147-7995-6) NYU Pr.

Andrology: Basic & Clinical Aspects of Male Reproduction & Infertility. Ed. by J. Bain et al. (Progress in Reproductive Biology & Medicine Ser.: Vol. 3). (Illus.). 1978. 78.50 (3-8055-2807-8) S Karger.

Andromache. Jean Racine. Tr. by Eric Korn. (Old Vic Theatre Collection Ser.: Vol. 1). 116p. 1988. pap. 7.95 (1-55783-021-5) Applause Theatre Bk Pubs.

Andromache. Jean Racine. Tr. by Richard Wilbur. 1982. pap. 4.75 (0-8222-0048-1) Dramatists Play.

Andromache. Jean B. Racine. Tr. by Richard Wilbur. 1984. pap. 6.95 (0-15-607510-5, Harvest Bks) HarBrace.

Andromache & Other Plays. Jean B. Racine. Tr. by John Cairncross. (Classics Ser.). 288p. 1976. pap. 8.95 (0-14-044195-6, Penguin Classics) Viking Penguin.

Andromache Beneath the Load of Life. Richard M. Byers. LC 89-84139. (Illus.). 240p. 1989. 15.00x (0-9602048-4-9) Fairfield Hse.

Andromache-Szenen in der Ilias. Dieter Lohmann. (Spudasmata Ser.: Bd. 42). iv, 82p. (GER.). 1988. write for info. (3-487-09009-0, Pub. by Georg Olms GW) Lubrecht & Cramer.

Andromache's Hector & Helenus. Richard M. Byers. LC 89-83539. (Illus.). 279p. 1989. 16.00x (0-9602048-3-0) Fairfield Hse.

Andromaque. Jean B. Racine. (Illus.). 1965. pap. 4.95 (0-685-10999-2, F41504) Fr & Eur.

Andromaque. Jean B. Racine. Ed. by R. C. Knight & H. T. Barnwell. 210p. 1977. 33.95 (0-686-54708-X, FC1729) Fr & Eur.

Andromaque, Racine: Critical Monographs in English. Peter France. 64p. 1993. pap. 32.00 (0-85261-284-2, Pub. by Univ of Glasgow UK) St Mut.

Andromeda Galaxy. Paul W. Hodge. LC 92-13215. (Astrophysics & Space Science Library: Vol. 176). 368p. (C). 1992. lib. bdg. 100.00 (0-7923-1654-1) Kluwer Ac.

*Andromeda Strain. Crichton. 1992. mass mkt. 6.99 (0-345-37848-2) Ballantine.

Andromeda Strain. Michael Crichton. 1992. mass mkt. 5.99 (0-345-90225-4) Ballantine.

Andromeda Strain. Michael Crichton. 1969. 25.00 (0-394-41525-6) Knopf.

Andromeda Strain. large type ed. Michael Crichton. LC 93-33304. 1994. 21.95 (0-7927-1882-8, Eagle Lrg Print) Chivers N Amer.

Andromeda Strain. large type ed. Michael Crichton. 1994. pap. 19.95 (0-7927-1881-X, Paragon Lrg Print) Chivers N Amer.

Andromeda Strain. Michael Crichton. 1991. reprint ed. lib. bdg. 21.95 (1-56849-066-6) Buccaneer Bks.

Andromeda's Chains: Gender & Interpretation in Victorian Literature & Art. Adrienne Munich. (Illus.). 222p. (C). 1993. text ed. 35.50 (0-231-06872-7); pap. 14.00 (0-231-06873-5) Col U Pr.

Andros Papers, Sixteen Seventy-Nine to Sixteen Eighty. Ed. by Peter R. Christoph & Florence A. Christoph. Tr. by Charles T. Gehring. (New York Historical Manuscripts Ser.). 584p. 1991. text ed. 75.00 (0-8156-2520-0) Syracuse U Pr.

Andros Papers, 1674-1676. Ed. by Florence A. Christoph & Peter R. Christoph. Tr. by Charles T. Gehring. (New York Historical Manuscripts). 664p. 1989. text ed. 75.00 (0-8156-2457-3) Syracuse U Pr.

Andros Papers, 1677-1678. Ed. by Peter R. Christoph. (New York Historical Manuscripts). (Illus.). 450p. 1990. text ed. 75.00 (0-8156-2496-4) Syracuse U Pr.

Androtion & the Atthis: The Fragments Translated with Introduction & Commentary. Phillip Harding. LC 93-16135. (Ancient History Ser.). 1993. 49.95 (0-19-872148-X, Clarendon Pr) OUP.

Andy. Mary C. Borntrager. (Ellie's People Ser.: Bk. 6). 144p. (Orig.). 1993. pap. 6.95 (0-8361-3633-0) Herald Pr.

Andy. Robert Gluck. 1973. 6.00 (0-915572-05-2) Panjandrum.

Andy. large type ed. Mary C. Borntrager. (Ellie's People Ser.: Bk. 6). 144p. (Orig.). 1993. pap. 8.95 (0-8361-3641-1) Herald Pr.

Andy: An Alaskan Tale. Susan Welsh-Smith. (Illus.). 24p. (J). 1988. 14.95 (0-521-35535-4) Cambridge U Pr.

Andy: That's My Name. Tomie De Paola. 32p. (J). (ps-2). 1991. 10.95 (0-13-036731-1, S&S Bks Young Read); pap. 6.00 (0-671-66465-4, S&S Bks Young Read) S&S Childrens.

Andy Adams' Campfire Tales. Andy Adams. Ed. by Wilson M. Hudson. LC 75-29131. (Illus.). xxxii, 296p. 1976. reprint ed. pap. 12.95 (0-8032-5835-6) U of Nebr Pr.

Andy Adams, His Life & Writings. Wilson M. Hudson. LC 64-16632. 292p. reprint ed. pap. 83.30 (0-8357-8802-4, 2033425) Bks Demand.

*Andy & His Daddy. Aline D. Wolf. (Illus.). 48p. 1994. 18. 95 (0-939195-14-3); pap. 12.95 (0-939195-06-2) Parent-Child Pr.

Andy & the Lion. James Daugherty. (Illus.). 72p. (J). (ps-3). 1989. pap. 4.99 (0-14-050277-7, Puffin) Puffin Bks.

Andy & the Lion. James Daugherty. LC 38-27390. (Illus.). 80p. (J). (gr. 1-4). 1938. pap. 14.99 (0-670-12433-8) Viking Child Bks.

Andy Capp Sounds Off. Reginald Smythe. 1983. pap. 1.95 (0-449-12626-9, GM) Fawcett.

Andy Capp Strikes Back. Reginald Smythe. 1979. pap. 1.25 (0-449-13788-0, GM) Fawcett.

Andy Capp, the One & Only. Reginald Smythe. 1979. pap. 1.25 (0-449-13684-1, GM) Fawcett.

Andy Finds a Turtle. Nan Holcomb. (Illus.). 32p. (Orig.). (J). (ps-2). 1988. pap. 6.95 (0-944727-02-6) Jason & Nordic Pubs.

Andy Finds a Turtle. Nan Holcomb. (Illus.). 32p. (Orig.). (J). (ps-2). 1992. reprint ed. 13.95 (0-944727-13-1) Jason & Nordic Pubs.

Andy Finds a Way. rev. ed. Jesse Stuart. Ed. & Aft. by Jerry A. Herndon. LC 91-41495. (Jesse Stuart Foundation Juvenile Ser.). (Illus.). 96p. (J). (gr. 3-6). 1992. reprint ed. 12.00 (0-945084-25-0); reprint ed. pap. 6.00 (0-945084-26-9) J Stuart Found.

Andy Goes to the Zoo. Melinda Leeka. LC 89-51092. 44p. (J). (gr. k-3). 1990. 5.95 (1-55523-247-7) Winston-Derek.

Andy Goldsworthy: Collaboration with Nature. Andy Goldsworthy. (Illus.). 120p. 1990. 45.00 (0-8109-3351-9) Abrams.

Andy Goldsworthy: Touching North. (Illus.). 48p. 1989. 75. 00 (0-948274-06-9, Pub. by Graeme Murray UK) Dist Art Pubs.

Andy Grant's Pluck. Horatio Alger, Jr. (Works of Horatio Alger Jr.). 1989. reprint ed. lib. bdg. 79.00 (0-7812-3553-7) Rprt Serv.

Andy Griffith Show. exp. rev. ed. Richard Kelly. LC 81-10268. (Illus.). 286p. 1985. pap. 9.95 (0-89587-043-6) Blair.

*Andy Griffith Show Book. 35th anniversary ed. Ken Beck & Jim Clark. LC 94-46271. (Illus.). 1995. pap. 13.95 (0-312-11741-8) St Martin.

Andy Griffith Show Book: From Miracle Slave to Kerosene Cucumbers, the Complete Guide to One of Television's Best-Loved Shows. Ken Beck & Jim Clark. (Illus.). 160p. 1985. pap. 13.95 (0-312-03654-X) St Martin.

Andy Little: Idaho Sheep King. Louise Shadduck. LC 90-1818. (Illus.). 298p. 1990. 22.95 (0-87004-340-4) Caxton.

Andy Opens Wide. Nan Holcomb. (Illus.). 32p. (J). (ps-2). 1990. pap. 6.95 (0-944727-06-9) Jason & Nordic Pubs.

Andy Opens Wide. Nan Holcomb. (Illus.). 32p. (J). (ps-2). 1992. reprint ed. 13.95 (0-944727-17-4) Jason & Nordic Pubs.

Andy Toots His Horn. Harriet Ziefert. (Illus.). (Orig.). (J). (ps-3). 1988. pap. 3.50 (0-14-050813-9, Puffin) Puffin Bks.

Andy Warhol. (Parkett Art Magazine Ser.: No. 12). (Illus.). 200p. 1986. 19.50 (3-907509-62-5, Pub. by Parkett Pubs SZ) Dist Art Pubs.

Andy Warhol. Jonathan Katz. LC 93-10441. (Rizzoli Art Ser.). (Illus.). 24p. 1993. pap. 7.95 (0-8478-1752-0) Rizzoli Intl.

*Andy Warhol. Melissa McDaniel. (Pop Culture Legends Ser.). (J). 1995. 18.95 (0-7910-2347-8) Chelsea Hse.

Andy Warhol. Carter Ratcliff. LC 83-3835. (Modern Masters Ser.). (Illus.). 128p. 1986. 29.95 (0-89659-385-1); pap. 19.95 (1-55859-257-1) Abbeville Pr.

Andy Warhol. Eric Shanes. (Masterworks Ser.). 1991. 15.99 (0-517-05376-4) Random Hse Value.

Andy Warhol: A Retrospective. Ed. by Kynaston McShine. (Illus.). 480p. 1991. pap. 35.00 (0-87070-681-0, 0-8109-6082-6) Mus of Modern Art.

Andy Warhol: Films & Paintings: The Factory Years. Peter Gidal. (Quality Paperbacks Ser.). (Illus.). 159p. 1991. reprint ed. pap. 14.95 (0-306-80456-5) Da Capo.

Andy Warhol: Polaroids. Andy Grundberg & Vincent Freemont. (Illus.). 112p. 1992. pap. 24.95 (0-685-57558-6) Pace-MacGill.

*Andy Warhol: Retrospektiv. Zdenek Felix & Tilman Osterwold. (Illus.). 214p. Date not set. 45.00 (3-7757-0458-2) Dist Art Pubs.

Andy Warhol: The Film Factory. Ed. by Michael O'Pray. (Illus.). 196p. 1990. 45.00 (0-85170-250-3, Pub. by British Film Inst UK); pap. 19.95 (0-85170-243-0, Pub. by British Film Inst UK) Ind U Pr.

Andy Warhol Abstracts. Ed. by Thomas Kellein. (Illus.). 84p. 1993. pap. 24.95 (3-7913-1328-2, Pub. by Prestel) TeNeues.

*Andy Warhol Art from Art. Laszlo Glozer. Ed. by Jorg Schellmann. 96p. 1995. 35.00 (3-88814-725-5) Dist Art Pubs.

Andy Warhol, Cars: Werner Spies. (Illus.). 139p. 1988. pap. 29.95 (3-7757-0271-7) S R Guggenheim.

Andy Warhol Collection, Set. (Illus.). 1988. 95.00 (0-8109-1793-9) Abrams.

Andy Warhol Death & Disasters. Walter Hopps et al. LC 88-13657. (Illus.). 135p. (C). 1988. pap. 24.95 (0-939594-19-6) Menil Found.

Andy Warhol Diaries. Pat Hackett. 1991. pap. 19.95 (0-446-39138-7) Warner Bks.

Andy Warhol Diaries. Andy Warhol. Ed. by Pat Hackett. LC 88-40565. 1989. 29.95 (0-446-51426-8) Warner Bks.

Andy Warhol Et Al: The FBI File on Andy Warhol. Margia Kramer. 64p. 1988. pap. 15.00 (0-318-35416-0) UnSub Pr.

Andy Warhol: Heaven & Hell are Just One Breath Away! Late Paintings & Related Works, 1984-86. Charles Stuckey. LC 92-14299. 1992. pap. 40.00 (0-8478-1620-6) Gagosian Gallery.

Andy Warhol Museum: The Inaugural Publication. Contrib by Callie Angell et al. LC 94-7351. 1994. 40.00 (0-88039-026-3) Mus Art Carnegie.

*Andy Warhol Museum: The Inaugural Publication. Callie Angell. (Illus.). 188p. 1994. 40.00 (1-881616-34-7) Dist Art Pubs.

Andy Warhol Portraits. Henry Geldzahler & Robert Rosenblum. LC 93-60560. (Illus.). 250p. 1993. 45.00 (0-500-09237-0) Thames Hudson.

Andy Warhol Prints. Ed. by Frayda Feldman & Jorg Schellmann. 160p. 1989. 55.00 (1-55859-050-1) Abbeville Pr.

Andy Warhol Prints, Nineteen Sixty-Two to Nineteen Eighty-Five. Frayda Feldman & Jorg Schellmann. (Illus.). 128p. 1985. 75.00 (1-55660-059-3) A Wofsy Fine Arts.

Andy Warhol, 1928-1987: Paintings from the Collection of Jose Mugrabi & an Isle of Man Company. Ed. by Jacob Baal-Teshuva. (Illus.). 144p. (Orig.). 1993. pap. 24. 95 (3-7913-1277-4, Pub. by Prestel) TeNeues.

Andy Warhol's Art & Films. Patrick S. Smith. Ed. by Stephen Foster. LC 86-11400. (Studies in the Fine Arts: The Avant-Garde: No. 54). (Illus.). 613p. reprint ed. pap. 178.20 (0-8357-1733-X, 2070770) Bks Demand.

Andy's Headache. Leslie T. Hallam. (J). 1990. 6.95 (0-533-08821-6) Vantage.

Andy's Pirate Ship. Philippe Dupasquier. 32p. (J). 1994. 11. 95 (0-8050-3154-5) H Holt & Co.

Ane. Victor Hugo. 370p. (FRE.). 1970. 35.00 (0-7859-1173-1, 2082103080) Fr & Eur.

Ane Breif Descriptioun of the Well of the Woman-Hill Besyde Abirdene. Gilbert Skeyne. LC 72-233. (English Experience Ser.: No. 104). 1969. reprint ed. 7.00 (90-221-0104-5) Walter J Johnson.

Ane Breve Descriptioun of the Pest. John Skene. LC 72-38109. (English Experience Ser.: No. 415). 1971. reprint ed. 20.00 (90-221-0415-X) Walter J Johnson.

Ane Culotte. Henri Bosco. (FRE.). 1973. pap. 10.95 (0-7859-1735-7, 2070363376) Fr & Eur.

Ane d'Or Ou les Metamorphoses. Apulee. 320p. (FRE.). 1975. pap. 10.95 (0-7859-1794-2, 2070366294) Fr & Eur.

Ane Resonyng of Ane Scottis & Inglis Merchand Betuix Rowand & Lionis: William Lamb (c. 1494 - c. 1550) Ane Resonyng. R. J. Lyall. 250p. 1985. text ed. 35.00 (0-08-030386-2, Pergamon Pr); pap. text ed. 18.50 (0-08-028485-X, Pergamon Pr) Elsevier.

Ane Satyre of the Thrie Estaits. David Lindsay. LC 75-26333. (English Experience Ser.: No. 137). 156p. 1969. reprint ed. 45.00 (90-221-0137-1) Walter J Johnson.

Ane Verie Excellent & Delectabill Tratise. Intitulit Philotus Quhairin We May Persave the Greit Inconveineences That Fallis Out in the Marriage Betwene Age & Youth. Philotus. LC 75-26325. (English Experience Ser.: No. 121). 48p. 1969. reprint ed. 8.00 (90-221-0121-5) Walter J Johnson.

Anecdota Graeca. Jean F. Boissonade. lxii, 2881p. 1962. reprint ed. write for info. (0-318-70879-5, Pub. by Georg Olms GW) Lubrecht & Cramer.

Anecdota Graeca. Ed. by Petrus Matranga. 799p. 1971. reprint ed. write for info. (3-487-04163-4, Pub. by Georg Olms GW) Lubrecht & Cramer.

Anecdota Graeca e Codicibus Manuscriptis Bibliothecae Regiae Parisiensis, 2 vols., Set. Ludwig Bachmann. xii, 978p. 1965. reprint ed. write for info. (0-318-70871-X, Pub. by Georg Olms GW); reprint ed. write for info. (0-318-71733-6, Pub. by Georg Olms GW) Lubrecht & Cramer.

Anecdota Graeca e Codicibus Manuscriptis Bibliothecae Regiae Parisiensis, 4 vols., Set. J. A. Cramer. vi, 1802p. 1967. reprint ed. write for info. (0-318-70903-1, Pub. by Georg Olms GW) Lubrecht & Cramer.

Anecdota Oxoniensia, Vols. 1-15 Set. (Medieval & Modern Ser.). 1989. Set. 933.50 (0-404-63950-X) AMS Pr.

Anecdota Varia Graeca et Latina, 2 vols. in 1. Ed. by R. Schoell & G. Studemund. vi, 551p. 1989. write for info. (3-615-00050-1, Pub. by Georg Olms GW) Lubrecht & Cramer.

*Anecdotage. Gregor Von Rezzori. Tr. by Susan Bernofsky. 288p. Date not set. 25.00 (0-374-22295-9) FS&G.

Anecdotal Sculpture of Ancient West Mexico. Hasso von Winning. (Illus.). 96p. 1972. 17.50 (0-938644-15-7) Nat Hist Mus.

*Anecdotas Casi Veridicas de Cardenas. Frank Villafana. LC 94-61139. (Coleccion Caniqui). 92p. (Orig.). (SPA.). 1994. pap. 9.95 (0-89729-755-5) Ediciones.

Anecdotas, Sonrisas y Poemas: Anectdotes, Smiles & Poems. Rodolfo Loyola. (SPA.). 5.00 (84-7645-476-7, 223572, Pub. by Edit Clie SP) TSELF.

An Asterisk (*) at the beginning of an entry indicates that the title is appearing in BIP for the first time.

An Asterisk (*) at the beginning of an entry indicates that the title is appearing in BIP for the first time.

313

Angel. Ruth Langan. 1994. mass mkt. 3.99 (0-373-28845-X, 1-28845-5) Harlequin Bks.

Angel. Johanna Lindsey. 416p. (Orig.). 1992. mass mkt. 5.99 (0-380-75628-5) Avon.

Angel. Mindlanguage Industries Staff. 80p. 1989. pap. text ed. 10.95 (0-8403-5542-4) Kendall-Hunt.

Angel. Ruth Padel. 80p. 1994. pap. 14.95 (1-85224-278-7, Pub. by Bloodaxe Bks UK) Dufour.

Angel. large type ed. Barbara Taylor Bradford. LC 93-20385. 1993. pap. 21.00 (0-679-74726-5) Random.

Angel. large type ed. Johanna Lindsey. (Romance Ser.). (Orig.). 1993. 22.95 (0-8161-5760-X) Hall.

Angel. large type ed. Johanna Lindsey. 362p. (Orig.). 1994. pap. 16.95 (0-8161-5761-8) Thorndike Pr.

Angel. Barbara Taylor Bradford. 1995. reprint ed. mass mkt., pap. 6.99 (0-345-38859-3) Ballantine.

Angel. Merle Collins. LC 88-18373. 294p. 1988. reprint ed. pap. 9.95 (0-931188-64-4) Seal Pr Feminist.

Angel: The Complete Quintet. 5th ed. John Patrick. LC 90-7008. (Illus.). 640p. 1991. pap. 14.95 (1-877978-08-6, STARbks Pr) Woldt.

***Angel a Day.** Ann Splanger. LC 94-28206. 1994. 12.99 (0-310-48720-X) Zondervan.

Angel a Week. Ed. by David Laskin. 1992. mass mkt. 4.00 (0-345-38075-4) Ballantine.

***Angel Academy: A Collection of Angel Tales.** Misty Taggart. LC 94-21206. (Angel Bedtime Ser.). (Illus.). (J). 1994. 14.99 (0-8499-1161-3) Word Pub.

Angel among Witches. large type ed. Adela Gale. LC 94-475. 1994. 18.95 (0-7927-2070-9, Curley Lrg Print); pap. 17.95 (0-7927-2069-5, Curley Lrg Print) Chivers N Amer.

Angel & Me. Mary J. Auch. (J). 1989. 9.95 (0-316-05914-5) Little.

Angel & Me & the Bayside Bombers. Mary J. Auch. (Illus.). (J). (gr. 2-4). 1991. pap. 2.95 (0-316-05915-3) Little.

Angel & the Ants: Bringing Heaven Closer to Your Daily Life. Peter Kreeft. 220p. 1994. pap. 9.99 (0-89283-881-7, Charis) Servant.

Angel & the Beehive: The Mormon Struggle with Assimilation. Armand L. Mauss. LC 93-11328. 296p. 1994. 29.95 (0-252-02071-5) U of Ill Pr.

***Angel & the Child: An Incidental Incident in Twelve Scenes.** Dominique Falda. Tr. by J. Alison James. LC 95-13134. (J). 1995. write for info. (1-55858-488-9); lib. bdg. write for info. (1-55858-489-7) North-South Bks NYC.

***Angel & the Donkey.** Illus. by Alexander Koshkin. LC 94-22430. (J). 1996. write for info. (0-395-68969-4, Clarion Bks) HM.

Angel & the Machine: Nathaniel Hawthorne's Rational Psychology. E. Michael Jones. 210p. (Orig.). 1991. pap. 10.95 (0-89385-195-7) Sugden.

***Angel & the Renegade.** Cathryn Clare. (Intimate Moments Ser.: No. 599). 1994. pap. 3.50 (0-373-07599-5) Silhouette.

Angel & the Serpent: The Story of New Harmony. William E. Wilson. LC 64-10827. (Illus.). 256p. 1984. 19.95 (0-253-10360-6); pap. 9.95 (0-253-20326-0, MB-326) Ind U Pr.

Angel & the Soldier Boy. Peter Collington. Ed. by Janet Schulman. LC 86-20169. (Illus.). 32p. (J). (ps-3). 1994. 13.00 (0-394-88626-7); lib. bdg. 10.99 (0-394-98626-1) Knopf Bks Yng Read.

Angel Angel. April Stevens. LC 94-20137. 1995. 19.95 (0-670-85839-0, Viking) Viking Penguin.

***Angel Answers: A Joyful Guide to Creating Heaven on Earth.** Andrew Ramer. Ed. by Emily Bestler. 192p. (Orig.). 1995. pap. 10.00 (0-671-52589-1) PB.

Angel, Archangel. Nick Cook. 1993. mass mkt. 4.99 (0-312-95094-2) St Martin.

Angel at Large. Peggy Webb. (Silhouette Romance Ser.: No. 867). 1992. pap. 2.69 (0-373-08867-1, 5-08867-9) Silhouette.

***Angel at My Side.** Bob Hoyt. 160p. 1994. per. 8.95 (0-945383-86-X) Teach Servs.

***Angel at Risk.** Leann Harris. (Intimate Moments Ser.). 1995. pap. 3.50 (0-373-07618-5, 1-07618-1) Silhouette.

***Angel Babies: You Are Special.** Mike Berry. (J). 1995. 3.99 (0-7814-0208-5) Cook.

***Angel Babies: Your Family Is Special.** Mike Berry. (J). 1995. 3.99 (0-7814-0209-3) Cook.

***Angel Baby.** Leandra Logan. 1995. mass mkt. 3.25 (0-373-25664-7) Harlequin Bks.

Angel Baskets: A Little Story about the Shakers. Mary L. Ray. LC 87-50789. (Illus.). 32p. (Orig.). (J). 1987. pap. write for info. (0-9609384-3-5) M Wetherbee.

Angel Blue. Naomi Albright. 99p. 1993. pap. 10.00 (1-882218-00-0) Blue Star Pubs.

Angel Book: A Handbook for Aspiring Angels. Karen Goldman. LC 92-20362. 1993. 18.00 (0-671-79699-2) S&S Trade.

Angel Bride. Diane Haeger. Ed. by Linda Marrow. 480p. (Orig.). 1994. mass mkt. 5.99 (0-671-86481-5) PB.

Angel by My Side. Pearl M. Grant. Ed. by G. Gail Gesell. 137p. 1987. lib. bdg. 10.50 (0-942078-13-6) R Tanner Assocs Inc.

***Angel by My Side: Amelia's Story.** Erin Flanagan. 128p. (Orig.). (J). (gr. 4-5). 1995. pap. 3.50 (0-380-78215-4, Camelot) Avon.

***Angel by My Side: Lily's Story.** Erin Flanagan. 144p. (Orig.). (J). (gr. 4-5). 1995. pap. 3.50 (0-380-78254-5, Camelot) Avon.

Angel Came. Richard Schultz. LC 93-84084. 176p. (Orig.). 1993. pap. 11.00 (0-9634897-1-2) Outback Insides.

Angel Cards. Joy Drake & Kathy Tyler. (Illus.). (SPA.). Date not set. pap. text ed. write for info. (0-934245-28-2); pap. text ed. write for info. (0-934245-27-4); pap. text ed. write for info. (0-934245-25-8); pap. text ed. write for info. (0-934245-26-6) Narada Prodns.

Angel Carver. Rosanne D. Thomas. LC 92-37032. 208p. 1993. 20.00 (0-679-42363-X) Random.

Angel Carver. Rosanne D. Thomas. 272p. 1995. pap. 11.99 (0-446-67054-5) Warner Bks.

Angel Carving. Ron Ransom. LC 88-64157. (Illus.). 80p. 1989. pap. text ed. 9.95 (0-88740-147-3) Schiffer.

Angel Chairs: New Work by Wendell Castle. Arthur C. Danto et al. LC 91-60156. (Illus.). 112p. (Orig.). 1991. pap. text ed. 40.00 (0-9628849-0-1) P J Gallery.

Angel Child, Dragon Child. Michele M. Surat. LC 83-8606. (Heritage Bks.). (Illus.). 32p. (J). (gr. 3-6). 1983. lib. bdg. 12.96 (0-940742-12-8) Raintree Steck-V.

Angel Child, Dragon Child. Michele M. Surat. (J). (gr. 3-6). 1989. pap. 3.95 (0-590-42271-5) Scholastic Inc.

Angel Children: Those Who Die Before Accountability. Mary V. Hill. LC 73-75397. (Illus.). 70p. (Orig.). 1973. pap. 6.98 (0-88290-017-X) Horizon Utah.

***Angel City.** Mike Ripley. 1995. 18.95 (0-312-11742-6) St Martin.

Angel City. Patrick D. Smith. LC 78-55491. (Illus.). 190p. 1978. 23.00 (0-912760-71-0) Valkyrie Pub Hse.

***Angel Cookbook: Heavenly Light Cuisine.** Diane Pfeifer. Ed. by Gail Poulton. LC 94-92351. (Illus.). 160p. (Orig.). 1994. pap. 9.95 (0-9618306-6-2) Strawberry GA.

***Angel Crafts.** Gary Puglisi. 1995. 15.00 (0-517-70093-X) Random.

Angel Creek. Linda Howard. 352p. (Orig.). 1991. mass mkt. 5.99 (0-671-66081-0) PB.

Angel Cuadra: The Poet in Socialist Cuba. Intro. by Warren Hampton. LC 93-34678. (Illus.). 168p. (C). 1994. bds. 19.95 (0-8130-1261-9) U Press Fla.

***Angel Days: A Journal & Daybook for Everyone Who Walks with Angels.** Terry L. Taylor. 192p. 1995. 20.00 (0-345-39160-8) Ballantine.

Angel de la Bondad: Angel of Kindness. J. F. Rodriguez. (SPA.). 2.95 (84-7228-017-9, 220035, Pub. by Edit Clie SP) TSELF.

Angel Death. Patricia Moyes. LC 80-1396. 240p. (Orig.). 1982. pap. 4.95 (0-8050-0505-6, Owl) H Holt & Co.

Angel del Hogar: Galdos & the Ideology of Domesticity in Spain. Bridget A. Aldaraca. LC 91-30892. (Studies in the Romance Languages & Literatures). 260p. 1992. pap. 30.00x (0-8078-9243-2) U of NC Pr.

Angel, Devils, Mermaids, & Monsters. Karen Duffy & Judith Lokenvitz. (Illus.). (J). 1989. pap. 4.95 (0-89013-187-2) Museum NM Pr.

Angel Drank Diet Soda: Eleven Plays & Sketches for Performance & Praise. Terry Pagoota. 1989. 8.50 (0-8341-9049-4, BCMP-654) Lillenas.

***Angel Dreams.** Van. Date not set. pap. write for info. (0-345-39541-7) Ballantine.

Angel Dust: Facts about PCP. rev. ed. 1993. pap. 0.25 (0-89230-165-1) Do It Now.

Angel Dust: What Everyone Should Know about PCP. Stuart J. Faber et al. 1982. pap. 7.95 (0-89074-066-6) Lega Bks.

Angel en el Circo. Alfredo Villanueva-Collado. LC 88-80880. (Arte y Poesia Ser.). (Illus.). 50p. (Orig.). (SPA.). 1988. pap. 6.00 (0-685-20048-5) Ichali.

***Angel Encounters: Real Stories of Angelic Intervention.** Karen Goldman. 1995. 20.00 (0-684-80184-1) S&S Trade.

***Angel Energy: How to Harness the Power of Angels in Your Everyday Life.** John R. Price. 240p. 1995. pap. 12.00 (0-449-90983-2) Fawcett.

Angel Eyes. Suzannah Davis. 416p. (Orig.). 1993. mass mkt. 4.50 (0-380-76822-4) Avon.

Angel Eyes. Thea Devine. 1991. mass mkt. 4.50 (0-8217-3467-9) Zebra.

Angel Eyes. Eric V. Lustbader. 1992. mass mkt. 5.99 (0-449-21852-X, Crest) Fawcett.

***Angel Falls.** Martin Jordan. LC 94-30243. (Illus.). (J). 1995. 15.95 (1-85697-541-X, Kingfisher LKC) LKC.

***Angel Fingerprints: The Little Book of Joyous Thoughts.** Sharon Warren. LC 94-96699. (Illus.). 192p. (Orig.). 1995. pap. 4.95 (0-9636074-4-8) Imagic Unltd.

Angel Fire. Andrew Greeley. 336p. 1989. mass mkt. 4.95 (0-8125-8341-8) Tor Bks.

Angel Fire. Deborah Satinwood. 384p. 1992. mass mkt. 4.25 (0-8217-3949-2) Zebra.

Angel Fishes. (Colorguide Ser.). 1982. pap. 6.95 (0-940842-08-4) South Group.

Angel Flame. Eugenia Riley. 1990. mass mkt. 4.95 (0-446-34938-0) Warner Bks.

***Angel Flight Vol. I: A Poetic Journey, 3 vol. set, Vol. I.** LaVonne Sullivan. (Flight Ser.). (Illus.). 16p. 1994. pap. 3.00 (1-885800-04-5) PineTree Pr.

Angel Food. John L. Martin. LC 88-7978. 248p. 1989. 16.95 (0-89407-092-4) Strawberry Hill.

Angel Food. Sacred Heart Program Staff. LC 92-32006. 1992. write for info. (0-87197-354-5) Favorite Recipes.

Angel for a Martyr: Jacob Epstein's Tomb for Oscar Wilde. Michael Pennington. 96p. 1987. pap. 15.00 (0-7049-0113-7, WK3, Whiteknights) MRTS.

***Angel for Hire.** large type ed. Justine Davis. (Desire Ser.). 1994. 17.95 (0-373-58869-0, Silhouette Lrg Print) Chivers N Amer.

***Angel for May.** Melvin Burgess. LC 94-25740. (J). 1995. 15.00 (0-671-89004-2, S&S Bks Young Read) S&S Childrens.

Angel for May. large type ed. Melvyn Burgess. (J). (gr. 1-8). 1994. 16.95 (0-7451-2086-5, Galaxy Child Lrg Print) Chivers N Amer.

Angel for Solomon Singer. Cynthia Rylant. LC 91-15957. (Illus.). 32p. (J). 1992. 15.95 (0-531-05978-2); lib. bdg. 15.99 (0-531-08578-3) Orchard Bks Watts.

***Angel from Heaven.** James Q. Neidner. (Illus.). 120p. (Orig.). 1995. pap. 9.95 (0-9642737-0-5) J Q Neidner.

Angel Gang. Ken Kuhlken. 288p. 1994. 20.95 (0-312-10930-X, Pub. by Thomas Dunne Bks) St Martin.

Angel Ganivet. Judith Ginsberg. (Serie A: Monagrafias, LXIII). 124p. 1985. 35.00 (0-7293-0203-2, Pub. by Tamesis Bks Ltd UK) Boydell & Brewer.

Angel Guerra. Benito P. Galdos. Tr. by Karen O. Austin. LC 90-48172. (Hispanic Literature Ser.: Vol. 10). 744p. 1990. lib. bdg. 139.95 (0-88946-373-5) E Mellen.

Angel Heart. Victoria Thompson. 512p. 1988. pap. 3.95 (0-8217-2426-6) Zebra.

Angel Hunter. Ana Leigh. 448p. (Orig.). 1992. pap. 4.99 (0-8439-3365-8) Dorchester Pub Co.

Angel in Blue Jeans. Lynda S. Landers. 192p. 1992. 13.95 (0-8034-8975-7, Avalon Bks) Bouregy.

Angel in Charge. Judy Delton. LC 84-27862. (Illus.). 152p. (J). (gr. 2-5). 1985. 14.95 (0-395-37488-X) HM.

Angel in Disguise. Ann Wiley. 224p. (Orig.). 1993. pap. 2.95 (1-56597-037-3, Kismet) Meteor Pub.

Angel in Marble. Elaine Coffman. 1991. mass mkt. 4.95 (0-440-20530-1) Dell.

Angel in My Attic. Mary L. Carney. (Herbie the Angel Ser.). 128p. 1988. pap. 6.99 (0-310-28611-5, 11343P) Zondervan.

Angel in My Backpack. Mary L. Carney. (Herbie the Angel Ser.). 128p. (J). (gr. 7-9). 1987. pap. 6.99 (0-310-28501-1, 11342P) Zondervan.

***Angel in My House.** Tobias Palmer. 1994. 12.00 (0-06-251194-7) Harper SF.

Angel in My Stocking. Diane Richards. 100p. 1992. pap. 7.50 (1-56770-254-6) S Scheewe Pubns.

Angel in Paradise. large type ed. Lindsay Hicks. (Linford Romance Library). 366p. 1993. pap. 14.95 (0-7089-7334-5, Linford) Ulverscroft.

Angel in Scarlet. Jennifer Wilde. 608p. 1986. mass mkt. 4.95 (0-380-89782-2) Avon.

***Angel in Tesuque.** Michael Glasco. 160p. (Orig.). 1995. text ed. 18.95 (0-86534-103-6); pap. 14.95 (0-86534-071-4) Sunstone Pr.

Angel in the Bowl: Family & Collected Recipes. Stalker. 1991. 12.95 (0-533-08677-9) Vantage.

Angel in the Deluge. Rosario Murillo. Tr. by Alejandro Murguia. (Pocket Poets Ser.: No. 50). 120p. (Orig.). 1993. pap. 6.95 (0-87286-274-7) City Lights.

Angel in the Fire. Frances J. Roberts. 1979. pap. 4.25 (0-932814-31-X) Kings Farspan.

Angel in the Forest: A Fairy Tale of Two Utopias. 2nd ed. Marguerite Young. LC 94-8748. 331p. 1994. reprint ed. pap. 13.95 (1-56478-054-6) Dalkey Arch.

Angel in the House. Norris. 1976. 15.95 (0-89190-301-1) Amereon Ltd.

Angel in the Midst "the Science of Healing in the Human Garden" Sylvia J. Michaelson. 1988. pap. 4.95 (0-317-91059-0) Ministering Angel.

***Angel in the Night.** Joanna H. Kraus. Date not set. 5.00 (0-87129-587-3, A61) Dramatic Pub.

Angel in the Park. Maxine Minson. 1983. pap. 1.75 (0-686-38379-6) Eldridge Pub.

Angel in the Rock. limited ed. Bernard Grebanier. LC 79-176132. (Living Poets' Library Ser.). pap. 2.50 (0-686-01281-X) Dragons Teeth.

***Angel Is...** Ariel Books Staff. (Illus.). 80p. 1995. 4.95 (0-8362-3133-3) Andrews & McMeel.

Angel Island. Inez H. Gillmore. Ed. by R. Reginald & Douglas Melville. LC 77-84229. (Lost Race & Adult Fantasy Ser.). (Illus.). 1978. reprint ed. lib. bdg. 36.95 (0-405-10979-2) Ayer.

Angel Island Prisoner. Helen Chetin. Tr. by Catherine Harvey. LC 82-51170. (Illus.). (CHI & ENG.). (J). (gr. 3 up). 1982. pap. 7.95 (0-938678-09-4) New Seed.

Angel Kingdom see Galaxy Gate

Angel Landing. Alice Hoffman. 1993. mass mkt. 6.50 (0-425-13952-2) Berkley Pub.

***Angel Letters.** Sophy Burnham. Date not set. pap. write for info. (0-345-37866-0) Ballantine.

***Angel Letters.** Sophy Burnham. Date not set. write for info. (0-345-39508-5) Ballantine.

Angel Letters: What You Wrote to Me. Sophy Burnham. LC 91-91880. 192p. 1991. 15.00 (0-345-37342-1, Ballantine Trade) Ballantine.

***Angel Love.** Bonnie Altenhein. LC 94-33168. (Illus.). 1994. 5.99 (0-517-12238-3) Random Hse Value.

Angel Mae: A Tale of Trotter Street. Shirley Hughes. LC 89-45288. (Illus.). 32p. (J). (ps-1). 1989. 12.95 (0-688-08538-5); lib. bdg. 12.88 (0-688-08539-3) Lothrop.

Angel Mae: A Tale of Trotter Street. Shirley Hughes. Ed. by ALC Staff. LC 89-45288. (Illus.). 32p. (J). (ps up). 1992. pap. 4.95 (0-688-11847-X, Mulberry) Morrow.

***Angel Magic: The Ancient Art of Summoning & Communicating with Angelic Beings.** Geoffrey James. (Llewellyn's World Religion & Magic Ser.). (Illus.). 224p. 1995. pap. 12.95 (1-56718-368-9) Llewellyn Pubns.

Angel Maker. Ridley Pearson. 1994. mass mkt. 5.99 (0-440-21632-X) Dell.

Angel Maker: A Novel. large type ed. Ridley Pearson. LC 93-19761. 614p. 1993. reprint ed. 22.95 (1-56054-606-9); reprint ed. pap. 14.95 (1-56054-890-8) Thorndike Pr.

***Angel Messages from Above: Stories, Poems, Essays & Loving Words from John, My Guardian Angel.** Fran Lenzo. Ed. by Jerry Lenzo. (Illus.). 224p. (Orig.). 1995. pap. 14.95 (0-9644821-0-X) Angel Guidance.

***Angel Numero Doce - The Twelfth Angel.** Og Mandino. Tr. by Maria De La Luz Broissin F. 192p. (SPA.). 1995. pap. 10.00 (0-449-91016-4) Fawcett.

Angel Oak Story. Ruth M. Miller & Linda A. Lennor. (Illus.). 1989. 5.00 (0-937684-26-0) Tradd St Pr.

Angel of Apocalypse: Blake's Idea of Milton. Joseph A. Wittreich, Jr. LC 74-27316. 358p. 1975. 37.50 (0-299-06800-5) U of Wis Pr.

Angel of Armageddon. Robert Marcum. 1992. pap. 9.95 (0-88494-854-4) Bookcraft Inc.

Angel of Attack. Robin A. White. 1992. mass mkt. 5.99 (0-449-14870-X, GM) Fawcett.

Angel of Bethesda. Cotton Mather. Ed. by Gordon W. Jones. LC 72-185323. 384p. 1972. 30.00 (0-8271-7220-6, U Pr of Va) Am Antiquarian.

***Angel of Darkness.** Lynne Graham. (Presents Ser.). 1995. pap. 2.99 (0-373-11712-4, 1-11712-6) Harlequin Bks.

Angel of Darkness. Dennis McDougal. 1991. 19.95 (0-446-51538-8) Warner Bks.

Angel of Darkness. Dennis McDougal. (Illus.). 416p. 1992. mass mkt. 6.99 (0-446-36302-2) Warner Bks.

***Angel of Darkness.** large type ed. Lynne Graham. Date not set. 18.95 (0-263-14039-3) Thorndike Pr.

Angel of Death. David Alexander. 288p. (Orig.). 1990. pap. 3.50 (0-8439-2922-7) Dorchester Pub Co.

***Angel of Death.** Jack Higgins. LC 94-46855. 1995. write for info. (0-399-14042-5, Putnam) Putnam Pub Group.

Angel of Death. Rochelle M. Krich. 384p. 1994. 18.95 (0-89296-508-8) Mysterious Pr.

***Angel of Death.** Rochelle M. Krich. 352p. 1996. mass mkt. 5.99 (0-446-40311-3, Mysterious Paperbk) Warner Bks.

***Angel of Death.** large type ed. Jack Higgins. LC 95-14157. 423p. 1995. 25.95 (0-7862-0466-4) Thorndike Pr.

***Angel of Death.** large type ed. Jack Higgins. LC 95-14157. 1995. pap. write for info. (0-7862-0465-6) Thorndike Pr.

Angel of Death: The Romance of Margaret Pollard & James Lockert. Ed. by C. W. Tazewell & Peggy A. Haile. LC 91-76296. 60p. (Orig.). 1992. pap. 8.00 (1-878515-88-8) W S Dawson.

***Angel of Death in the Adonis Lounge.** Almond. Date not set. per. 7.95 (0-85449-079-5, Pub. by Gay Mens Pr UK) InBook.

Angel of Democracy. A. R. Towner. 1981. 14.95 (0-87012-402-1) McClain.

Angel of Desire. Joann Ross. (Temptation Ser.). 1994. mass mkt. 2.99 (0-373-25582-9, 1-25582-7) Harlequin Bks.

Angel of Fire. Tanya A. Crosby. 384p. (Orig.). 1992. mass mkt. 4.50 (0-380-76773-2) Avon.

Angel of God. Piera Paltro. Tr. by Daughters of St. Paul Staff. (Illus.). 14p. (Orig.). (J). (ps-1). 1981. pap. 2.50 (0-8198-0739-7, CH0031P) Pauline Bks.

***Angel of His Presence.** Grace L. Hill. (Grace Livingston Hill Ser.: No. 94). 107p. 1994. pap. 3.99 (0-8423-1680-9) Tyndale.

Angel of His Presence. Mary R. Stott. 1990. 9.95 (0-89697-417-0) Intl Univ Pr.

Angel of His Presence. Grace L. Hill. reprint ed. lib. bdg. 15.95 (0-89190-032-2, Rivercity Pr) Amereon Ltd.

Angel of His Presence. Grace L. Hill. 1990. reprint ed. lib. bdg. 13.95 (0-89968-519-6) Buccaneer Bks.

Angel of History. Carolyn Forche. 80p. 1994. 20.00 (0-06-017078-6, HarpT) HarpC.

***Angel of History.** Carolyn Forche. 96p. 1995. pap. 10.00 (0-06-092584-1, PL) HarpC.

***Angel of Marye's Heights: Sergeant Richard Kirkland's Extraordinary Deed at the Battle of Fredericksburg.** Les Carroll. (Illus.). 87p. (YA). (gr. 10-12). 1994. 15.00 (0-9623065-7-6) Palmetto Bookworks.

Angel of Mercy. Andrew Neiderman. LC 93-31259. 256p. 1994. 22.95 (0-399-13926-5, Putnam) Putnam Pub Group.

***Angel of Mercy.** Heather G. Pozzessere. 1995. 4.99 (1-55166-069-5, 1-66069-5, Mira Bks) Harlequin Bks.

Angel of Midnight. Power. 1995. mass mkt. 5.99 (0-671-89705-5) PB.

Angel of My Heart. abr. ed. Jeffrey K. Mayo. 180p. 1995. pap. 7.95 (1-56901-348-9) NW Pub.

Angel of Obsession. Julie Suk. LC 91-37208. 88p. 1992. 14.95 (1-55728-246-3); pap. 8.95 (1-55728-247-1) U of Ark Pr.

Angel of Passage. Joan Avery. 1993. mass mkt. 4.50 (0-06-108095-0, Harp PBks) HarpC.

Angel of Rainbow Gulch. Helen M. Swanson. 128p. (Orig.). (J). (gr. 3-6). 1992. pap. 6.95 (1-880188-08-2) Bess Pr.

Angel of Solitude. Marie-Claire Blais. Tr. by Laura Hodes. 168p. 1994. pap. 12.95 (0-88922-337-8, Pub. by Talonbooks CN) InBook.

Angel of the Battlefield. Nellie McCaslin. LC 93-2604. 20p. (J). 1993. pap. 4.00 (0-88734-430-5) Players Pr.

Angel of the Evening. large type ed. Rowena Summers. 279p. 1994. 18.95 (0-7505-0538-9, Pub. by Magna Print Bks) Ulverscroft.

Angel of the Evening. Rowena Summers. 224p. 1992. reprint ed. 17.95 (0-7278-4345-1) Severn Hse.

Angel of the Lake. Ana Seymour. (Historical Ser.). 1993. mass mkt. 3.99 (0-373-28773-9, 1-28773-9) Harlequin Bks.

Angel of the Lord. Laurence M. Vance. LC 94-90190. 128p. (Orig.). 1994. pap. 5.95 (0-9628898-2-2) Vance FL.

Angel of the Opera: Sherlock Holmes Meets the Phantom of the Opera. Sam Siciliano. 272p. 1994. 21.95 (1-883402-46-8) S&S Trade.

Angel of the Presence. Elise N. Morgan. (Meditation Ser.). 1922. 6.95 (0-87516-327-0) DeVorss.

Angel of the Revolution. George Griffith. LC 73-13254. (Classics of Science Fiction Ser.). (Illus.). 410p. 1986. reprint ed. 25.00 (0-88355-109-8); reprint ed. pap. 10.00 (0-88355-138-1) Hyperion Conn.

***Angel of the Sea B & B Cookbook. Sherry Girton & John Girton. (Illus.). 112p. 1994. spiral bd. 14.95 (0-9642924-0-8) Angel of Cape May.**

An Asterisk (*) at the beginning of an entry indicates that the title is appearing in BIP for the first time.

This cookbook has been written by the Girton Family who restored & now own & operate the Inn. The Angel of the Sea Bed & Breakfast has been rated as one of the top 10 B & B's in the U.S. for the past 6 years. She has been featured in dozens of national & regional magazines & hundreds of national & regional newspapers. She has received numerous prestigious awards such as "The Most Recognized Victorian Structure in the U.S." & "The Restoration of the Year" awarded by the National Trust for Historic Preservation. She has been featured on NBC, CBS, & ABC, Public TV, The Learning Channel, Discovery, Great Country Inns of the World, Good Morning America & Oprah Winfrey's "The Best Vacations in the World." Over the years all members of the Girton Family have shared in the cooking at the Angel & have gathered a collection of the 100 most loved & requested recipes by her guests. The recipes are divided into 4 categories: "Breakfast Entrees," "Baked Fruit," "Bread, Muffins & Coffee Cakes" & "Tea Time Goodies." All our recipes are prepared at the Inn with natural ingredients & loving care, making tasty meals & desserts you will want to serve your family. Order from The Angel of Cape May, Inc., 34 Tuckahoe Rd. #361, Marmora, NJ 08223-1206; 609-898-1517. ***Publisher Provided Annotation.***

Angel of the West Window. Gustav Meyrink. Tr. & Intro. by Mike Mitchell. (Studies in Austrian Literature, Culture, & Thought. Translation Ser.). 421p. 1991. pap. 17.00 (*0-929497-44-9*) Ariadne CA.

Angel of Torremolinos. large type ed. David Serafin. 1990. 21.95 (*0-7089-2245-7*) Ulverscroft.

Angel on His Wing. Tay Thomas. LC 89-32523. (Illus.). 296p. 1989. 22.95 (*0-8192-1481-7*) Morehouse Pub.

***Angel on My Shoulder: Remembrances at 80.** Christopher G. Janus. LC 93-91421. 1993. pap. 12.95 (*0-87012-500-1*) Sheffield Bks.

Angel on My Shoulder & Other Stories see Stories of Misbegotten Love

Angel on Our Wing. Robert H. Armstrong & Leroy W. Newby. (Illus.). 360p. Date not set. 24.95 (*0-9632257-0-7*) R H Armstrong.

Angel on Skis. Betty Cavanna. (J). (gr. 4-7). 1992. pap. 2.50 (*0-8167-1268-9*) Troll Assocs.

Angel on the Bridge. Kitty M. Kiser. LC 86-83409. 320p. (Orig.). 1994. pap. 19.95 (*0-89896-320-6*) Larksdale.

Angel on the Yardarm: The Beginnings of Fleet Radar Defense & the Kamikaze Threat. John Monsarrat. LC 85-13850. (Historical Monograph: No. 6). (Illus.). 188p. (C). 1985. pap. 4.25 (*0-9637973-7-9*) Naval War Coll.

Angel on the Yardarm: The Beginnings of Fleet Radar Defense & the Kamikaze Threat. John Monsarrat. LC 85-13850. (Naval War College Historical Monograph: No. 6). (Illus.). 196p. 1985. pap. 4.25 (*0-16-002043-3*, S/N 008-046-001) USGPO.

***Angel on the Yardarm: The Beginnings of Fleet Radar Defense & the Kamikaze Threat.** John Monsarrat. (Illus.). 188p. 1994. reprint ed. pap. text ed. 29.95x (*0-7881-1453-0*) Diane Pub.

***Angel Parade Pileup.** Misty Taggart. LC 94-25673. (Angel Academy Ser.). (Illus.). (J). 1994. 3.99 (*0-8499-5016-3*) Word Pub.

***Angel Park Series.** Dean Hughes. Date not set. 37.92 (*0-679-87020-2*) Random.

***Angel Party.** Misty Taggart. LC 94-45102. (Angel Academy Ser.: Vol. 4). (Illus.). (J). 1995. pap. 4.99 (*0-8499-5083-X*) Word Pub.

Angel Passes: How the Sexes Became Undivided. Stuart Schneiderman. 384p. 1988. pap. 18.50 (*0-8147-7920-4*) NYU Pr.

***Angel Pop-up Book.** Ives. (J). 1995. 4.95 (*0-689-80333-8*, Litl Simon S&S) S&S Childrens.

***Angel Pop-up Book, Bk. 1.** Ives. (J). 1995. 4.95 (*0-689-80332-X*, Aladdin Paperbacks) S&S Childrens.

***Angel Pop-up Book, Bk. 3.** Ives. (J). 1995. pap. 4.95 (*0-689-80334-6*, Aladdin Paperbacks) S&S Childrens.

***Angel Pop-up Book, Bk. 4.** Ives. (J). 1995. pap. 4.95 (*0-689-80335-4*, Aladdin Paperbacks) S&S Childrens.

***Angel Postcards.** Ho Phi Le. 30p. 1995. pap. 6.95 (*0-87588-434-2*) Hobby Hse.

***Angel Power.** Janice T. Connell. 288p. (Orig.). 1995. pap. 12.00 (*0-345-39123-3*) Ballantine.

Angel Prayers. Diana L. Michael. 208p. 1993. pap. 12.95 (*0-9634910-4-0*) Trust Pub MN.

Angel Prayers. Sally Sharp. (Illus.). 112p. 1994. 18.00 (*0-9634910-5-9*) Trust Pub MN.

Angel Prophet. Ward Andrews. 1992. 16.95 (*0-533-10258-8*) Vantage.

***Angel Reflections: A Personal Journal of Awareness.** Nora Monaco & Juliet Hubbs. (Illus.). 112p. 1995. pap. write for info. (*0-9631714-3-7*) AngelStar.

Angel Riding Shotgun. Juanita Yates. (Illus.). 1992. pap. 8.95 (*0-9627655-2-X*) J Yates.

***Angel Rogue.** Mary J. Putney. 384p. (Orig.). 1995. mass mkt., pap. 5.99 (*0-451-40598-6*, Topaz) NAL-Dutton.

Angel-Seaxisc Grammaticcraeft. Richard L. Groff, Jr. (Beginning Anglo-Saxon Wordsmid Ser.). (Illus.). 66p. (Orig.). (ANG & ENG.). (C). 1992. audio 15.98 (*0-9630718-3-1*) New Dawn NY.

Angel Site: An Archaeological, Historical, & Ethnological Study, Vols. I & II. Glenn A. Black. LC 79-19508. (Illus.). 616p. 1967. 20.00 (*0-253-30700-7*) Ind Hist Soc.

Angel Songbook. 3rd ed. 1982. spiral bd. 11.95 (*0-89556-032-1*) Gateways Bks & Tapes.

***Angel Souls & Devil Hearts.** Christopher Golden. 416p. (Orig.). 1995. pap. text ed. 5.99 (*0-425-14831-9*) Berkley Pub.

Angel Square. Brian Doyle. 128p. (J). (gr. 4-7). 1991. pap. 4.95 (*0-88899-070-7*, Pub. by Groundwood-Douglas & McIntyre CN) Firefly Bks Ltd.

Angel Station. Walter J. Williams. 1990. mass mkt. 4.95 (*0-8125-5787-5*) Tor Bks.

Angel Stories. Dianthus. (Illus.). 48p. (Orig.). 1990. pap. 8.75 (*0-9622160-1-1*) Dianthus.

***Angel Strings.** Gary Eberle. 300p. (Orig.). 1995. pap. 12.95 (*1-56689-034-9*) Coffee Hse.

***Angel Talk.** Ruth C. Bancone. (Illus.). 128p. 1995. 15.00 (*1-887010-01-7*) Edin Bks.

Angel Tarot. Stuart R. Kaplan. 56p. 1980. 15.00 (*0-913866-98-9*) US Games Syst.

Angel Tech: A Modern Shaman's Guide to Reality Selection. 2nd ed. Antero Alli. LC 86-82908. 292p. (Orig.). 1991. pap. 12.95 (*1-56184-009-2*) New Falcon Pubns.

Angel the Pig. Arnold Clapman. LC 94-20302. (Illus.). (J). 1994. pap. 5.95 (*0-382-24662-4*) Silver Burdett Pr.

***Angel Thoughts: A Journal of Faith & Reflection.** 160p. (Orig.). 1995. pap. 7.95 (*1-57071-059-7*) Sourcebks.

Angel to Watch over Me: True Stories of Children's Encounters with Angels. Joan W. Anderson. LC 94-15722. 160p. 1994. 19.00 (*0-345-38815-1*) Ballantine.

Angel Told Me to Tell You Good-Bye. Leia A. Greene. (Little Angel Books Ser.). (Illus.). 24p. (J). (gr. k-12). 1991. pap. text ed. 4.95 (*1-880737-06-X*) Crystal Jrns.

Angel Tree: A Christmas Celebration: The Loretta Hines Howard Collection of Eighteenth-Century Neapolitan Creche Figures at the Metropolitan Museum of Art. Linn Howard & Mary J. Pool. LC 93-25365. (Illus.). 1994. 24.95 (*0-8109-1934-6*) Abrams.

Angel Unaware. Clara Wimberly. 512p. 1994. mass mkt. 4.99 (*0-8217-4719-3*) Zebra.

Angel Unaware. Dale E. Rogers. 64p. (Orig.). 1991. reprint ed. lib. bdg. 10.95 (*0-89966-811-9*) Buccaneer Bks.

***Angel Voices: A Book of Postcards.** Karen Goldman. (Illus.). 30p. 1995. pap. 8.95 (*0-8362-3200-3*) Andrews & McMeel.

Angel Voices: The Advanced Handbook for Aspirint Angels. Karen Goldman. 1993. 18.00 (*0-671-88079-9*) S&S Trade.

***Angel Watching.** J. Michael Ross. 32p. 1995. 14.95 (*0-9643748-1-1*) Side Door.

***Angel Whispers.** Rik McGuire. 1995. 11.95 (*0-8062-5245-6*) Carlton.

***Angel Whispers: A Personal Journal of Reflection.** Nora Monaco & Juliet J. Hubbs. (Universal Angels Ser.). (Illus.). 112p. 1994. pap. 9.95 (*0-9631714-2-9*) AngelStar.

Angel Who Forgot. Elisa Bartone. LC 91-34233. (Illus.). 48p. (Orig.). (J). (ps up). 1992. 10.00 (*0-671-76037-8*, Green Tiger S&S) S&S Childrens.

Angel-Wind: A Collection of Poems. Rick L. Wright. (Illus.). 65p. 1989. pap. 4.00 (*0-685-30086-2*) R L Wright.

Angel Wisdom: Three Sixty-Five Meditations & Insights from the Heavens. Terry L. Taylor & Mary Beth Crain. 400p. 1994. pap. 12.00 (*0-06-251067-3*) Harper SF.

Angel with a Bushy Beard. Dudley Gardner. 1980. pap. 8.95 (*0-7152-0425-4*) Outlook.

Angel with Bush-Baby Eyes & the Love Song of Achilles. Bahman Sholevar. LC 82-73947. (Literature-Poetry Ser.). (Illus.). 60p. (Orig.). 1982. pap. 5.95 (*0-911323-04-X*) Concourse Pr.

Angel with Horns: Fifteen Lectures on Shakespeare. A. P. Rossiter. 316p. (Orig.). (C). 1989. pap. text ed. 22.75 (*0-582-01499-9*, 78287) Longman.

Angel with the Sword. C. J. Cherryh. (Merovingen Nights Ser.). 304p. 1987. pap. 3.50 (*0-88677-143-9*) DAW Bks.

***Angel Within Us: The Gift of Giving.** John P. Beilenson & Diane J. Johnson. (Keepsakes Ser.). (Illus.). 56p. 1995. 7.99 (*0-88088-887-3*) Peter Pauper.

Angela. 192p. (Orig.). 1991. pap. 4.95 (*1-878320-76-9*) Masquerade.

Angela & the Broken Heart. Nancy K. Robinson. (J). 1991. 12.95 (*0-590-43212-5*, Scholastic Hardcover) Scholastic Inc.

Angela & the King-Size Crusade. Susan Smith. (Best Friends Ser.). (J). (gr. 3-7). 1988. pap. 2.50 (*0-317-69592-4*) PB.

Angela Carter. Lorna Sage. 1990. 39.00 (*0-7463-0722-5*, Pub. by Northcote UK); pap. 21.00 (*0-7463-0727-6*, Pub. by Northcote UK) St Mut.

Angela Davis: An Autobiography. Angela Y. Davis. LC 88-8232. (Illus.). 408p. 1988. reprint ed. pap. 12.95 (*0-7178-0667-7*) Intl Pubs Co.

Angela Davis: Traitor or Martyr of the Freedom of Expression? Blythe F. Finke. Ed. by D. Steve Rahmas. LC 77-190246. (Outstanding Personalities Ser.: No. 28). 32p. (Orig.). (J). (gr. 7-12). 1972. lib. bdg. 4.95 (*0-87157-528-0*) SamHar Pr.

Angela de Hoyos: A Critical Look. Ed. by Luis A. Ramos & Jose Armas. (Illus.). 53p. 1979. pap. 3.50 (*0-918358-08-6*) Pajarito Pubns.

***Angela Goes to Daycare.** Wendy Tisdell & Jodi Takhar. 14p. (J). (ps-3). Date not set. 19.95 (*1-886000-01-8*) J Takhars.

***Angela Grauerholz: Recent Photographs.** Helaine Posner. LC 93-79813. (Illus.). 32p. (Orig.). 1993. pap. 8.00 (*0-938437-45-3*) MIT List Visual Arts.

Angela Lansbury's Positive Moves. large type ed. Angela Lansbury. 160p. 1991. reprint ed. lib. bdg. 21.95 (*1-56054-124-5*) Thorndike Pr.

Angela Lansbury's Positive Moves. large type ed. Angela Lansbury. 160p. 1991. pap. 14.95 (*1-56054-990-4*) Thorndike Pr.

Angela of Foligno: Complete Works. Angela of Foligno. Tr. & Intro. by Paul Lachance. LC 92-38830. (Classics of Western Spirituality Ser.). 448p. 1993. 26.95 (*0-8091-0460-1*); pap. 18.95 (*0-8091-3366-0*) Paulist Pr.

***Angela Weaves a Dream.** Michele Sola. LC 94-35488. (Illus.). (J). 1996. write for info. (*0-7868-0073-9*); lib. bdg. write for info. (*0-7868-2060-8*) Hyprn Child.

Angela's Airplane. Robert Munsch. (Annikin Ser.: Series 3). (Illus.). 24p. (J). (ps-1). 1986. pap. 0.99 (*0-920236-75-8*, Pub. by Annick CN) Firefly Bks Ltd.

Angela's Airplane. Robert Munsch. 24p. (J). (gr. k-3). 1988. lib. bdg. 14.95 (*1-55037-027-8*, Pub. by Annick CN); pap. 4.95 (*1-55037-026-X*, Pub. by Annick CN) Firefly Bks Ltd.

Angela's Heart: (An Original Story for Reading & Language Arts Education in Grades 3-12) Flora Joy. (Storytelling in Education Funbooks Ser.). (Illus.). 48p. 1994. pap. text ed. 7.00 (*1-884624-02-2*) Intl Storytelling.

***Angela's Wings.** Eric J. Nones. LC 94-30321. (Illus.). 32p. (J). 1995. 16.00 (*0-374-30331-2*) FS&G.

Angele. Marcel Pagnol. pap. 9.95 (*0-685-23894-6*, F117230) Fr & Eur.

Angele. Marcel Pagnol. 216p. (FRE.). 1976. pap. 10.95 (*0-8288-9889-8*, F117420) Fr & Eur.

Angeles de Dios: Angels of God. Arno C. Gaebelein. (SPA.). 4.25 (*84-7645-000-1*, 223075, Pub. by Edit Clie SP) TSELF.

Angeles-Diablo-Dios-Jesucristo y Mas Alla (Angels-Devil-God-Christ & the Life After) D. Fernandez. (SPA.). Date not set. 1.99 (*1-56063-644-0*, 498179) Editorial Unilit.

Angeles en Campos Concentracion: Angels in the Camp. Jan Markell. (SPA.). 4.95 (*84-7228-785-8*, 220038, Pub. by Edit Clie SP) TSELF.

Angeles en el Infierno: Angels in Hell. Erinno Dapozzo. (SPA.). 2.95 (*84-7228-106-X*, 220037, Pub. by Edit Clie SP) TSELF.

Angeles en Misiones Especiales: Angels on Assignment. Roland Buck. (SPA.). 6.95 (*84-7228-559-6*, 360023, Pub. by Edit Clie SP) TSELF.

Angeles National Forest. Murphy et al. (Illus.). 80p. (Orig.). 1991. pap. 9.95 (*0-9615421-4-4*) Big Santa Hist.

Angelettes & Cosmic Sex. Pusser. LC 88-81436. 120p. (Orig.). 1988. pap. 9.95 (*0-941404-86-2*) New Falcon Pubns.

Angelfire. Linda L. Miller. Ed. by Linda Marrow. 352p. 1991. mass mkt. 5.99 (*0-671-73765-1*) PB.

Angeli Politiani Opera, 3 vols. in 2. Angelo A. Poliziano. xviii, 1406p. reprint ed. write for info. (*0-318-71606-2*, Pub. by Georg Olms GW) Lubrecht & Cramer.

Angelic Avengers. Isak Dinesen. LC 94-60156. 304p. Date not set. pap. 12.95 (*0-9627987-8-9*) Turtle Point Pr.

Angelic Doctor: The Life & World of St. Thomas Aquinas. Matthew E. Bunson. LC 93-87517. 168p. (Orig.). 1994. pap. 9.95 (*0-87973-552-X*, 552) Our Sunday Visitor.

Angelic Healing: Working with Your Angels to Heal Your Life. Eileen E. Freeman. 240p. 1994. 16.95 (*0-446-51846-8*) Warner Bks.

***Angelic Healing: Working with Your Angels to Heal Your Life.** Eileen E. Freeman. 240p. 1995. pap. 9.99 (*0-446-67146-0*) Warner Bks.

Angelic Messenger Cards: A Divination System for Spiritual Self-Discovery. Meredith L. Young-Sowers. (Illus.). 224p. 1993. 29.95 (*0-913299-95-2*) Stillpoint.

Angelic Monks & Earthly Men: Monasticism & Its Meaning in Medieval Society. Ludo Milis. (Illus.). 192p. (C). 1992. text ed. 50.00 (*0-85115-303-8*) Boydell & Brewer.

Angelic Mysteries. James D. Sanderson. 240p. (Orig.). 1994. pap. 12.95 (*1-884787-00-2*) Colonia Bks.

Angelic Orders. Poems. T. R. Hummer. LC 81-19357. 62p. 1982. pap. 6.95 (*0-8071-1000-0*) La State U Pr.

Angelic Revelations of Divine Truth, 2 vols., Set. James E. Padgett & Daniel G. Samuels. 437p. 1992. Vol. I, 437p. pap. 17.00 (*0-317-04950-X*); pap. 17.00 (*0-317-05505-4*) Found Ch Divine Truth.

***Angelic Wisdom: The Cherubim & the Grace of Contemplation in Richard of St. Victor.** Steven Chase. LC 94-47439. (Studies in Spirituality & Theology: Vol. 2). (C). 1995. text ed. 32.95x (*0-268-00644-X*) U of Notre Dame Pr.

Angelica Kauffman: A Continental Artist in Georgian England. Ed. by Wendy W. Roworth. (Illus.). 208p. 1993. pap. 22.50 (*0-948462-41-8*) U of Wash Pr.

Angelica Kauffmann R. A. 1741-1807. Dorothy M. Mayer. 192p. 1972. 50.00 (*0-900675-68-3*, Pub. by Colin Smythe Ltd UK) Dufour.

Angelical Conjunction: The Preacher-Physicians of Colonial New England. Patricia A. Watson. LC 90-22214. 200p. (C). text ed. 29.95 (*0-87049-696-4*) U of Tenn Pr.

Angelina & Alice. Katharine Holabird. (J). (ps-2). 1988. 15.00 (*0-517-56074-7*, Clarkson Potter) Crown Bks Yng Read.

Angelina & the Princess. Katharine Holabird. LC 84-6818. (Illus.). 24p. (J). (ps-2). 1988. 15.00 (*0-517-55273-6*, Clarkson Potter) Crown Bks Yng Read.

Angelina at the Fair. Katharine Holabird. LC 84-28931. (Illus.). 24p. (J). (ps-2). 1988. 15.00 (*0-517-55744-4*, Clarkson Potter) Crown Bks Yng Read.

Angelina Ballerina. Katharine Holabird. LC 83-8233. (Illus.). (J). (ps-2). 1988. 15.00 (*0-517-55083-0*, Clarkson Potter) Crown Bks Yng Read.

Angelina Ballerina. Katharine Holabird. (Illus.). 24p. (J). (ps-2). 1990. 4.99 (*0-517-57668-6*, Clarkson Potter) Crown Bks Yng Read.

Angelina Book & Doll Package. Katharine Holabird. LC 83-8233. (Illus.). 32p. (J). (ps-2). 1989. 25.00 (*0-517-57089-0*, Clarkson Potter) Crown Bks Yng Read.

Angelina Dances. Katharine Holabird. LC 92-80524. (Angelina Board Bks.). (Illus.). 6p. (J). (ps-00). 1992. bds. 5.99 (*0-679-83484-2*) Random Bks Yng Read.

Angelina Ice Skates. Katharine Holabird. (Illus.). 32p. (J). (ps-2). 1993. 15.00 (*0-517-59619-9*, Clarkson Potter) Crown Bks Yng Read.

Angelina Ice Skates. Katharine Holabird. (Illus.). 32p. (J). (ps-2). 1994. 4.99 (*0-517-59982-1*, Clarkson Potter) Crown Bks Yng Read.

Angelina on Stage. Katharine Holabird. (Illus.). 24p. (J). (ps-2). 1988. 15.00 (*0-517-56073-9*, Clarkson Potter) Crown Bks Yng Read.

Angelina Trueheart & the Fox. Margaret Card. LC 93-26224. (Illus.). (J). 1994. 4.25 (*0-383-03732-8*) SRA Schl Grp.

Angelina's Baby Sister. Katharine Holabird. (J). (ps-2). 1991. 14.00 (*0-517-58600-2*, Clarkson Potter) Crown Bks Yng Read.

Angelina's Birthday Surprise. Katharine Holabird. LC 89-3513. (Illus.). 32p. (J). (ps-2). 1989. 15.00 (*0-517-57325-3*, Clarkson Potter) Crown Bks Yng Read.

Angelina's Christmas. Katharine Holabird. LC 85-12389. (Illus.). 32p. (J). (gr. 1 up). 1986. 15.00 (*0-517-55823-8*, Clarkson Potter) Crown Bks Yng Read.

Angelina's Christmas. Katharine Holabird. 1988. 4.99 (*0-517-57188-9*) Random Hse Value.

Angelina's Favorite Recipes: A Personal Collection of Sicilian Style Italian Recipes. Angelina M. Mitchell. (Illus.). 104p. (Orig.). 1988. pap. text ed. 8.95 (*0-9619750-0-8*) A Mitchell.

Angeline de Montbrun. Laure Conan. LC 73-82585. (Literature of Canada, Poetry & Prose in Reprint Ser.: No. 14). 202p. reprint ed. pap. 57.60 (*0-8357-5475-8*, 2023605) Bks Demand.

Angelique. Alain Robbe-Grillet. 1994. pap. 13.95 (*0-7145-4197-4*) Riverrun NY.

Angelita's Magic Yarn. Doris Lecher. (Illus.). 32p. (J). (ps-3). 1992. 14.00 (*0-374-30332-0*) FS&G.

Angell & Sons. Pamela Hill. 400p. 1994. 22.95 (*0-7089-3077-8*) Ulverscroft.

***Angelle & the Comet.** Dolores Comeaux. 20p. 1994. 8.95 (*0-9642936-9-2*) Clothes For You.

Angelo. Jean Giono. (FRE.). 1983. pap. 10.95 (*0-7859-2472-8*, 2070374572) Fr & Eur.

Angelo. Jean Giono. (Folio Ser.: No. 1457). 8.95 (*2-07-037457-2*) Schoenhof.

Angelo Beolco (Il Ruzante) Linda L. Carroll. (Twayne's World Authors Ser.: No. 815). 168p. (C). 1990. text ed. 29.95 (*0-8057-8255-9*, Twayne) Macmillan.

Angelo Herndon Case & Southern Justice. Charles H. Martin. LC 73-91777. 256p. reprint ed. pap. 73.00 (*0-8357-5476-6*, 2051653) Bks Demand.

Angelo Poliziano "Lamia", Praelectio in Priora Aristotelis Analytica: Critical Edition, Introduction & Commentary. Ari Wesseling. (Studies in Medieval & Reformation Thought: No. 38). xxxx, 128p. 1986. 29.75 (*90-04-07738-3*) E J Brill.

Angelo Savelli: White on White Paintings. Howard D. Spencer. LC 88-50531. (Illus.). 16p. 1988. pap. 5.00 (*0-939324-35-0*) Wichita Art Mus.

Angelos Sikelianos & the Delphic Idea. Theofanis G. Stavrou. Bd. with Life with Angelos Sikelianos. Anna Sikelianos.; Sibyl. Angelos Sikelianos. (Modern Greek History & Culture Ser.). write for info. (*0-318-59121-9*) Nostos Bks.

***Angels.** (Postcard Bks.). (Illus.). 18p. 1994. 8.95 (*3-7913-1409-2*) TeNeues.

Angels. Ariel Books Staff. (Illus.). 80p. 1993. 4.95 (*0-8362-3042-6*) Andrews & McMeel.

Angels. Walton J. Brown & Raymond H. Woolsey. 177p. (Orig.). 1987. pap. 7.95 (*0-8280-0409-9*) Review & Herald.

Angels. Charles Capps. 224p. (Orig.). 1984. pap. 4.95 (*0-89274-308-5*, HH-308) Harrison Hse.

***Angels!** Jack Dann & Gardner Dozois. 240p. (Orig.). 1995. pap. text ed. 4.99 (*0-441-00220-X*) Ace Bks.

Angels. Billy Graham. 1991. pap. 4.99 (*0-8499-3299-8*) Word Inc.

Angels. Denis Johnson. (Contemporaries Ser.). 1989. pap. 11.00 (*0-394-75987-7*, Vin) Random.

Angels. James R. Peebles & Betty P. Peebles. 21p. (Orig.). 1989. pap. 5.00 (*0-918925-25-8*) Jericho Chr Trng.

***Angels.** Hope Price. 240p. (Orig.). 1994. mass mkt. 4.99 (*0-380-72331-X*) Avon.

***Angels.** George J. Seidel. LC 94-22414. (Revisioning Philosophy Ser.: 19). 1995. write for info. (*0-8204-2602-4*) P Lang Pubs.

***Angels.** James Underhill. 1995. pap. 15.95 (*1-85230-750-1*) Element MA.

Angels. Nicholai Velimirovich. 1988. pap. 0.75 (*0-89981-201-5*) Eastern Orthodox.

Angels. Peter L. Wilson. LC 93-61374. (Illus.). 96p. 1994. pap. 15.95 (*0-500-81044-3*) Thames Hudson.

***Angels.** Vinita H. Wright. 64p. 1995. pap. 4.99 (*0-87788-013-1*) Shaw Pubs.

Angels. Joseph F. Rutherford. 64p. 1987. reprint ed. pap. 2.95 (*1-883858-31-3*) Witness CA.

***Angels: A Book of Ornaments; Five Ornaments to Press Out.** Metropolitan Museum of Art Staff. 1994. 9.95 (*0-8118-0813-0*) Chronicle Bks.

***Angels: A Book of Poems.** Joan W. Anglund. LC 95-6309. 1995. write for info. (*0-679-40902-5*) Random.

An Asterisk (*) at the beginning of an entry indicates that the title is appearing in BIP for the first time.

A

Angels: A History of the 11th Airborne Division, 1943-46. Edward Flanagan. (Airborne Ser.). (Illus.). 192p. 1988. reprint ed. 29.95 (*0-89839-117-2*) Battery Pr.

***Angels: A Journal.** (Illus.). 128p. 1995. 17.95 (*0-87654-361-1*) Pomegranate Calif.

Angels: Anything Book. 1993. 7.99 (*0-517-10001-0*) Random Hse Value.

Angels: God's Messengers & Our Helpers. Lawrence G. Lovasik. (Saint Joseph Picture Bks.). (Illus.). 1978. 0.95 (*0-89942-281-0*, 281) Catholic Bk Pub.

Angels: God's Secret Agents. Billy Graham. LC 93-34808. 1994. 4.99 (*0-8499-5074-0*) Word Pub.

Angels: Gods Secret Agents. Billy Graham. 1994. 15.99 (*0-8499-1167-2*) Word Inc.

***Angels: Guardians of the Light.** Karen Haughey. Ed. by Jill Kramer. (Illus.). 112p. 1995. 35.00 (*1-56170-316-8*) Hay House.

Angels: Messengers From. Ed. by Nancy C. Akmon. (Illus.). 24p. 1994. text ed. 3.95 (*1-884807-09-7*) Blushing Rose.

Angels: Ministers of Grace. Geddes MacGregor. LC 87-11243. (Illus.). 230p. 1987. pap. 12.95 (*1-55778-001-3*) Paragon Hse.

Angels: Spiritual & Exegetical Notes. Maria P. Giudici. Tr. by Edmund C. Lane. LC 93-30849. 152p. 1993. pap. 7.95 (*0-8189-0636-7*) Alba.

***Angels: The Entities Trilogy.** Larry Dossey et al. Ed. by Robert Sardello. 273p. (Orig.). 1994. pap. 20.00 (*0-911005-27-7*) Dallas Inst Pubns.

Angels: The Messengers of God. Lester Sumrall. 88p. (C). 1987. pap. text ed. 10.00 (*0-937580-52-X*) LeSEA Pub Co.

***Angels: The Mysterious Messengers.** Ed. by Rex Hauck. LC 94-29248. 1994. 25.00 (*0-345-39301-5*) Ballantine.

Angels: The Role of Celestial Guardians & Beings of Light. Paola Giovetti. (Illus.). 264p. (Orig.). 1993. pap. 20.00 (*0-87728-779-1*) Weiser.

Angels - An Endangered Species. Malcolm Godwin. 1990. 22.50 (*0-671-70650-0*) S&S Trade.

***Angels - Musical.** Phillip DePoy. 1995. write for info. (*0-87129-480-X*, A09) Dramatic Pub.

***Angels A to Z.** Date not set. 17.95 (*0-7876-0652-9*) Jossey-Bass.

***Angels All About.** Judith G. Sherrouse. LC 94-60831. 71p. 1995. 6.95 (*1-55523-713-4*) Winston-Derek.

Angels All Around. write for info. (*1-56441-000-5*) M Hickey Min.

***Angels All Around Me.** Sarah Hornsby. (Illus.). 92p. 1995. 12.99 (*0-8007-9225-4*) Chosen Bks.

***Angels Among Us.** Ron Rhodes. LC 94-22294. (Orig.). 1994. pap. 9.99 (*1-56507-271-5*) Harvest Hse.

Angels among Us. Don Fearheiley. 272p. 1993. reprint ed. mass mkt. 4.99 (*0-380-77377-5*) Avon.

Angels among Us: A Celestial Sourcebook for Beginning Your Journey. David Connolly. LC 93-26752. (Illus.). 160p. (Orig.). 1994. pap. 8.95 (*0-399-51851-7*, Perigree Bks) Berkley Pub.

***Angels among Us & Other Hot Country Singles.** Ed. by Carol Cuellar. 64p. (Orig.). (YA). 1995. pap. text ed. 9.95 (*0-89724-611-X*) Warner Brothers.

Angels & Aliens. Keith Thompson. 256p. 1991. 19.18 (*0-201-55084-9*) Addison-Wesley.

Angels & Aliens. Keith Thompson. 304p. 1993. pap. 12.00 (*0-449-90837-2*, Columbine) Fawcett.

Angels & Aliens: UFO's & the Mythic Imagination. Keith Thompson. 1992. pap. 9.95 (*0-201-63227-6*) Addison-Wesley.

Angels & Amazons: A Hundred Years of American Women. Inez H. Irwin. LC 74-3956. (Women in America Ser.). 542p. 1974. reprint ed. 37.95 (*0-405-06104-8*) Ayer.

Angels & Awakenings: Stories of the Miraculous. Ed. by M. C. Grey. LC 94-11447. 1994. 20.00 (*0-385-15311-2*) Doubleday.

***Angels & Awakenings: Stories of the Miraculous by Great Modern Writers.** large type ed. Ed. by M. Cameron Grey. LC 95-5416. (Large Print Book Ser.). 1995. 22.95 (*1-56895-207-4*) Wheeler Pub.

Angels & Citizens: British Women As Military Nurses, 1854-1914. Anne R. Summers. (Illus.). 320p. 1988. text ed. 35.00 (*0-7102-1479-0*, RKP) Routledge.

Angels & Cupids. Sylvia Lawrence. LC 93-85149. (Illus.). 1993. 12.95 (*0-8478-1774-1*) Rizzoli Intl.

Angels & Demons According to Lactantius. Emil Schneweis. LC 79-8121. (Satanism Ser.). 192p. reprint ed. 31.50 (*0-404-18433-2*) AMS Pr.

***Angels & Dreams.** Susan E. Martinez. Ed. by Sherokee Ilse. (Gifts from the Universe Ser.). 116p. (Orig.). 1995. pap. 7.95 (*0-9625379-4-2*) Safe & Sound Prodns.

***Angels & Elves (Man of the Month, Baby Bet)** Joan E. Pickart. 1995. mass mkt. 3.25 (*0-373-05961-2*, 1-05961-7) Silhouette.

Angels & Franciscans: Innovative Architecture from Los Angeles & San Francisco. Frank O. Gehry et al. LC 92-19583. (Illus.). 128p. 1992. pap. 29.95 (*0-8478-1630-3*) Rizzoli Intl.

Angels & Friends Favorite Recipes. Angels of Easter Seal, Youngstown, Ohio Staff. (Illus.). 436p. 1981. 9.50 (*0-9613501-0-5*) Angels Easter.

***Angels & Goddesses.** Michael Howard. Date not set. pap. 19.95 (*1-898307-03-2*, Pub. by Capall Bann Pubng UK) Holmes Pub.

Angels & Gods. Gabriel Chufu. Tr. by Victor Olaru. 20p. 1992. pap. 4.00 (*1-881489-00-0*) Poetry Miscellany.

Angels & Insects: Two Novellas. A. S. Byatt. LC 92-56806. 1993. 21.00 (*0-679-40512-7*) Random.

Angels & Insects: Two Novellas. A. S. Byatt. 1994. pap. 12.00 (*0-679-75134-3*, Vin) Random.

Angels & Man. Nada-Yolanda. LC 73-90881. 138p. 1974. 15.00 (*0-912322-03-9*) Mark-Age.

Angels & Me. Carolyn Nystrom. (Children's Bible Basics Ser.). (Illus.). (J). (ps-2). 1984. pap. 4.99 (*0-8024-6150-6*) Moody.

Angels & Me: Children's Bible Basics. Carolyn Nystrom. (J). (ps-3). 1994. 5.99 (*0-8024-7863-8*) Moody.

Angels & Men. Ladislaus Boros. 128p. 1990. pap. text ed. 24.00 (*0-85532-375-2*, Pub. by Srch Pr UK) St Mut.

Angels & Mermaids. Gemma Alphie. 88p. 1992. pap. 8.95 (*0-8059-3280-1*) Dorrance.

Angels & Mortals: Their Co-Creative Power. Comp. by Maria Parisen. LC 90-50205. (Illus.). 307p. (Orig.). 1990. pap. 14.95 (*0-8356-0665-1*, Quest) Theos Pub Hse.

Angels & Other Strangers: Family Christmas Stories. Katherine Paterson. LC 79-63797. 128p. (J). (gr. 1 up). 1979. 14.00 (*0-690-03992-1*, Crowell Jr Bks) HarpC Child Bks.

Angels & Other Strangers: Family Christmas Stories. Katherine Paterson. LC 79-63797. 128p. (YA). (gr. 7 up). 1991. lib. bdg. 13.89 (*0-690-04911-0*, Crowell Jr Bks) HarpC Child Bks.

Angels & Other Strangers: Family Christmas Stories. Katherine Paterson. LC 79-63797. (Trophy Bk.). 128p. (YA). (gr. 7 up). 1988. reprint ed. pap. 3.95 (*0-06-440283-5*, Trophy) HarpC Child Bks.

Angels & Others. Ken Smith. LC 91-77162. 146p. (Orig.). 1992. pap. 9.95 (*0-917652-94-0*) Confluence Pr.

Angels & Outcasts: An Anthology of Deaf Characters in Literature. 3rd ed. Ed. by Trent Batson & Eugene Bergman. LC 85-20669. 349p. 1985. pap. text ed. 16.95 (*0-930323-17-3*) Gallaudet Univ Pr.

Angels & the Bible. Bill Haberman. 55p. (Orig.). 1993. pap. 4.95 (*1-56794-048-X*, C2307) Star Bible.

***Angels & the New Spirituality.** Duane A. Garrett. LC 95-12467. 1995. write for info. (*0-8054-6176-0*) Broadman.

Angels & the Other Heavenly Bodiless Powers. Dimitry of Rostov. pap. 0.25 (*0-89981-003-9*) Eastern Orthodox.

***Angels & the Perverts.** Lucie Delarue-Mardrus. Tr. by Anna Livia. (Cutting Edge). 184p. (FRE.). 1995. 45.00 (*0-8147-5080-X*); pap. 14.95 (*0-8147-5098-2*) NYU Pr.

Angels & Their Mission. Jean Danielou. LC 56-11414. 118p. (C). 1987. reprint ed. pap. 7.50 (*0-87061-056-2*, 6914) Chr Classics.

Angels & Us. Mortimer J. Adler. 1988. pap. 7.95 (*0-02-016021-6*, Collier S&S) S&S Trade.

Angels & Us. Mortimer J. Adler. 224p. 1993. pap. 9.00 (*0-02-030065-4*, Collier S&S) S&S Trade.

Angels & Us. Mortimer J. Adler. 1982. 11.95 (*0-02-500550-2*) Macmillan.

Angels & Visitations: A Miscellany. Neil Gaiman. (Illus.). 166p. 1993. 20.00 (*0-9630944-2-4*); write for info. (*0-9630944-3-2*) Dreamhaven.

Angels & Wild Things: The Archetypal Poetics of Maurice Sendak. John Cech. LC 92-39709. (Illus.). 296p. 1995. 29.95 (*0-271-00949-7*) Pa St U Pr.

Angels, Angels All Around. Bob Hartman. (Illus.). 96p. (J). (gr. 1-5). 1993. 15.95 (*0-7459-2623-1*) Lion USA.

Angels, Angels, Angels. Landrum P. Leavell. LC 73-75627. 96p. 1973. pap. 6.99 (*0-8054-2222-6*) Broadman.

Angels, Angels, Angels. Andy Warhol. LC 94-14069. (Illus.). 76p. 1994. 9.95 (*0-8212-2131-0*) Bulfinch Pr.

***Angels, Angels, Angels - Embraced by the Light...or... Embraced by the Darkness?** Phil Phillips. 320p. 1995. pap. 10.95 (*0-914984-65-9*) Starburst.

***Angels, Angels Everywhere.** Dawn Myers. 128p. (Orig.). (J). 1994. pap. 3.99 (*0-380-77935-8*, Camelot) Avon.

Angels, Apes & Men. Stanley L. Jaki. 128p. (Orig.). 1983. pap. 7.95 (*0-89385-017-9*) Sugden.

***Angels, Archangels & All the Company of Heaven.** Gottfried Knapp. (Illus.). 112p. 1995. 29.95 (*3-7913-1482-3*, Pub. by Prestel) TeNeues.

***Angels, Archangels, & All the Company of Heaven.** Gottfried Knapp. (Illus.). 112p. Date not set. text ed. 29.95 (*0-614-07420-7*) Pegasus.

***Angels Are for Real: Real Angels Through Time & Space.** Harold Snyder. 300p. (C). 1995. pap. text ed. write for info. (*1-885591-64-0*) Morris Pubng.

Angels Are Forever. Illus. by Jenny Faw. (Petites Ser.). 80p. 1994. 4.95 (*0-88088-787-7*) Peter Pauper.

Angels Are My Friends. Annetta E. Dellinger. LC 85-7858. 32p. (J). (gr. 5-9). 1985. 5.99 (*0-570-04120-1*, 56-1531) Concordia.

***Angels Around the World.** B. Steiger. Date not set. pap. write for info. (*0-449-98369-2*) Fawcett.

Angels Around Us: What the Bible Really Says. Douglas Connelly. LC 94-3574. 168p. (Orig.). 1994. pap. 9.99 (*0-8308-1695-X*, 1695) InterVarsity.

Angels Ascending & Descending. Angeln Ray. 176p. 1984. 12.95 (*0-915763-00-1*) Starseed Pubns.

Angels at Qumren: A Comparative Study of 1 Enoch 1-36, 72-108 & Sectarion Writings from Qumran. Davidson. (JSPS Ser.: No. 11). 390p. (C). 1992. 40.00 (*1-85075-332-6*, Pub. by Sheffield Acad UK) CUP Services.

Angels at the Arno. Photos by Eric Lindbloom. LC 93-50142. (Illus.). 1994. 35.00 (*0-87923-974-3*) Godine.

Angels at the Arno: Photographs by Eric Lindbloom. Photos by Eric Lindbloom. (Illus.). 84p. 1995. pap. 19.95 (*0-87923-994-8*) Godine.

***Angel's Aura.** Jernigan. 1995. mass mkt. 4.50 (*0-06-104323-0*, Harp PBks) HarpC.

***Angels Beside You.** James Pruitt. 224p. (Orig.). 1994. mass mkt. 4.99 (*0-380-77766-5*) Avon.

Angel's Bidding. Sharon G. Short. (Midwest Mysteries Ser.). (Orig.). 1993. mass mkt. 4.99 (*0-449-14873-4*, GM) Fawcett.

***Angels Blind Spot.** Barbara L. Elmore. 160p. 1995. pap. 7.95 (*1-56901-799-9*) NW Pub.

Angel's Bride. Beverly H. Watson. Ed. by Kay L. Barrett. (Illus.). 50p. (Orig.). (J). (gr. 4-7). 1993. pap. 4.95 (*0-9623647-3-8*) B H Watson.

Angels, Bulldogs & Dragons: 355th Fighter Group in World War 2. Bill Marshall. 192p. 1985. pap. 14.95 (*0-685-10425-7*) Champlin Museum.

Angels Burning; "Ocian" in View. Thomas Sanchez & Lawrence C. Powell. (Capra Back-to-Back Ser.: No. 10). 110p. (C). 1988. reprint ed. lib. bdg. 25.00x (*0-8095-4109-2*) Borgo Pr.

Angels Can Fly Because They Take Themselves Lightly. Richard Bimler. LC 92-8586. 1992. 8.99 (*0-570-04577-0*) Concordia.

Angels Can Light up Your Life. Helen M. Alexander. 1992. 13.95 (*0-533-10131-X*) Vantage.

Angel's Caress. Deana James. 448p. 1989. mass mkt. 4.50 (*0-8217-2675-7*) Zebra.

Angel's Cry: Beyond the Pleasure Principle in Opera. Michel Poizat. Tr. by Arthur Denner. LC 91-55532. 240p. 1992. 25.00 (*0-8014-2388-0*) Cornell U Pr.

Angels Dark & Light. Gary D. Kinnaman. 220p. 1994. pap. 9.99 (*0-89283-846-9*, Vine Bks) Servant.

Angels, Demons, Miracles & Prayer. Group Publishing, Inc. Editors. (Active Bible Curriculum Ser.). (Illus.). 48p. (YA). (gr. 9-12). 1993. pap. 9.99 (*1-55945-235-8*) Group Pub.

Angels Do Not Forget. Raymond C. Morgan. (Illus.). (Orig.). 1979. pap. text ed. 7.95 (*0-9602718-0-5*) Law & Justice.

***Angels Don't Die.** Patti Davis. 1995. 12.50 (*0-06-017324-6*) HarpC.

***Angels Don't Knock.** Dan Yates. LC 94-22438. 1994. 7.95 (*1-55503-711-9*) Covenant Comms.

***Angels Don't Knock!** Dan Yates. 1994. pap. 8.95 (*1-55503-723-2*) Covenant Comms.

Angel's Ecstasy. Joyce Myrus. 512p. 1988. pap. 3.95 (*0-8217-2347-2*) Zebra.

Angels, Elect & Evil. C. Fred Dickason. 256p. (C). 1975. pap. 9.99 (*0-8024-0222-4*) Moody.

Angels Fall. Lanford Wilson. 102p. 1983. pap. 9.95 (*0-374-52231-6*, Noonday) FS&G.

Angel's Flight, 1993. rev. ed. Walt Wheelock. 1993. pap. 4.95 (*0-87505-401-3*) Borden.

***Angels from the Heart.** Ho P. Le. 64p. 1995. 14.95 (*0-87588-431-8*, 4828) Hobby Hse.

***Angels from the Louvre.** 24p. 1995. pap. 18.00 (*0-345-39539-5*) Ballantine.

***Angel's Gate.** Gary Crew. LC 95-4047. (J). 1995. 15.00 (*0-689-80166-1*, S&S Bks Young Read) S&S Childrens.

Angels Gift Pack. LC 94-35497. (Illus.). 192p. (J). 1994. 9.95 (*1-56458-709-6*) Dorling Kindersley.

Angels: God's Secret Agents. Billy Graham. 1986. lib. bdg. 11.00 (*0-394-29860-8*) Random.

***Angels Guide Her Life. Bonnie Ireland. (Illus.). 175p. 1995. pap. text ed. 19.95 (*0-9645217-0-9*) B Ireland.**

An autobiography filled with adventure & hope. An amazing pact with an Angel who saved her life at age 13, is the beginning of many life-saving incidents including a death experience. A re-awakening love from her father 3 weeks after he passed from this life, & the extraordinary gifts he gave her to show his true love, which helped her survive. Now, fulfilling her promise to the Angel & Higher Beings through many spiritual writings which were given through desktop publishing, she has written ANGELS GUIDE HER LIFE. It is a gripping story of true facts, inciting an amazing force of Love & Hope for all. This is a book to be read by all ages, creating a new awakening experience. The beautiful magenta & gold jacket portrays Glenda Green's (Ft. Worth, TX) famous painting, ANGEL OF THE RAINFOREST, in full colour inset. Lettering in gold, both on jacket & magenta hard cover of book, printed in Taipei. It is 6-1/4 X 8-1/2. Voice & FAX 214-840-2260, or write to order Bonnie Ireland, Publisher, 2027 Court Place, Garland, TX 75041. ***Publisher Provided Annotation.***

Angel's Guide to Heaven on Earth. Susan Gossett. Ed. by Barbara Wuest. (Illus.). 200p. 1992. pap. 14.95 (*0-9632029-0-1*) Angelic Mission.

Angels Have Gizzards: A Child's-Eye View of Religion. Lois B. Eades. (Illus.). 88p. 1987. pap. 4.95 (*0-8341-1150-0*) Beacon Hill.

Angel's Head: A Novel of Suspense. John Smolens. 240p. 1994. 19.00 (*0-88150-297-9*, Foul Play) Countryman.

***Angels in Action: What Swedenborg Saw & Heard.** Robert H. Kirven. 111, xiiip. 1994. pap. 8.95 (*0-87785-147-6*) Swedenborg.

Angels in Africa: A Memoir of Colonial Nursing. Bridget M. Robertson. 200p. 1993. text ed. 39.50 (*1-85043-527-8*, Pub. by I B Tauris UK) St Martin.

***Angels in America, Pts. 1-2.** Tony Kushner. 352p. 1995. boxed 35.00 (*1-55936-107-7*) Theatre Comm.

***Angels in America Parts 1 & 2.** Tony Kushner. 312p. 1995. boxed, per. 21.95 (*1-55936-098-4*) Theatre Comm.

Angels in America, Pt. 1: Millennium Approaches: A Gay Fantasia on National Themes. Tony Kushner. LC 92-44011. 136p. 1993. 19.95 (*1-55936-060-7*); pap. 9.95 (*1-55936-061-5*) Theatre Comm.

Angels in America, Pt. 2: Perestroika: A Gay Fantasia on National Themes. Tony Kushner. 176p. 1993. 21.95 (*1-55936-072-0*); pap. 10.95 (*1-55936-073-9*) Theatre Comm.

Angels in Blue Jackets: The Navy at Messina, 1908. J. W. Wilson & R. Perkins. 108p. (C). 1987. 105.00 (*0-948251-01-8*, Pub. by Picton UK) St Mut.

Angels in Heaven. David M. Pierce. 240p. 1992. 17.95 (*0-89296-483-9*) Mysterious Pr.

Angels in Heaven. David M. Pierce. 208p. 1993. mass mkt. 4.99 (*0-446-40163-3*, Mysterious Paperbk) Warner Bks.

Angels in Marble: Working Class Conservatives in Urban England. Robert McKenzie & Allan Silver. LC 67-30555. (Studies in Contemporary Sociology). 307p. reprint ed. pap. 87.50 (*0-8357-5477-4*, 2024057) Bks Demand.

***Angels in Our Midst.** Guideposts Editors. LC 94-30045. 1994. 15.00 (*0-385-47536-5*) Doubleday.

Angels in Our Midst. Ed. by Liesl Vazquez. (Keepsakes Ser.). (Illus.). 56p. 1994. 7.99 (*0-88088-857-1*) Peter Pauper.

***Angels in Red Hats: Paratroopers of the Second Indochina War.** Michael N. Martin. Ed. by William Strode. (Illus.). 168p. 1995. 39.95 (*1-56469-025-3*) Harmony Hse Pub LO.

Angels in Religion & Art. Valentine Long. LC 77-117712. 1971. reprint ed. pap. 9.95 (*0-8199-0430-9*, Frncscn Herld) Franciscan Pr.

Angels in the Air. Ed. by Ania Mochlinska. 1994. pap. 14.95 (*0-671-51013-4*, Fireside) S&S Trade.

***Angels in the Dust.** Margot Raven. LC 95-3627. (Illus.). 32p. (J). (gr. k-3). 1996. lib. bdg. 13.95 (*0-8167-3806-8*) BrdgeWater.

Angels in the House: Poems by Jerred Metz. deluxe ed. Jerred Metz. (Illus.). 1978. 75.00 (*0-685-27838-7*) Heron Pr.

Angels in the Kitchen. Patricia Corrigan. 1994. 10.00 (*0-671-51711-2*) PB.

Angels in the Light. Margot Dalton. (Superromance Ser.). 1993. mass mkt. 3.50 (*0-373-70576-X*, 1-70576-3) Harlequin Bks.

Angels in the Outfield. Adapt. by Jordan Horowitz. (Junior Novel Ser.). (Illus.). (J). (gr. 3-7). 1994. pap. 3.95 (*0-685-74708-5*) Disney Pr.

Angels in the Trees: A Poetry Collection. Wanda Lee. (Spiritual Growth & Awareness Ser.). 96p. (Orig.). Date not set. pap. 7.95 (*1-883855-03-9*) St Georges Pr.

Angels in Traditional Design. Silvia Crockett. (International Design Library). (Illus.). 48p. (Orig.). 1987. pap. 5.95 (*0-88045-086-X*) Stemmer Hse.

Angel's Kiss. Judith Steel. 448p. 1994. mass mkt. 4.50 (*0-8217-4653-7*) Zebra.

Angel's Kite. Alberto Blanco. Tr. by Dan Bellm. LC 93-42285. (Illus.). (ENG & SPA.). (J). 1994. 13.95 (*0-89239-121-9*) Childrens Book Pr.

***Angels Laughed: The Promotion of a Dunghill Beggar. Samuel Marrs. Ed. by Jeanne Mel. (Illus.). 200p. (Orig.). 1995. pap. 12.95 (*0-9645387-0-9*) Yeshurun Pub.**

EARTH: A.D. 2000 - The evil empire has arrived. In one final, calculated power-grab, the secret brotherhood has united the earth in one global government. It is the culmination of a plan set in motion & nurtured for thousands of years. Their purpose for global unification is to repel a long-anticipated invasion of the planet Earth from outer space. This invasion will be led by a former Jewish carpenter from Nazareth, who will be carrying out another plan, which was set in motion from before the beginning of time. The prelude to this final drama has already begun. A modern-day prophet recounts his life before & after his call from God, revelations & dreams he received for the times ahead, & visions he was shown while out-of-body. His revelations include: the identity of "THE ANTICHRIST," "THE 666 BEAST," & "THE FALSE PROPHET," the truth about "THE GREAT APOSTASY" & "THE ABOMINATION OF DESOLATION" - & the proclaiming of "THE DAY OF THE LORD." The Dunghill Beggar's promotion to the office of prophet was so unlikely - so totally unexpected - that when it was announced, THE ANGELS LAUGHED! Order from: Yeshurun Publishing, P.O. Box 720849, Dallas, TX 75372-0849; 214-823-6421. ***Publisher Provided Annotation.***

Angels' Little Instruction. Eileen E. Freeman. 160p. 1994. pap. 5.99 (*0-446-67121-5*) Warner Bks.

Angel's Mother's Baby. Judy Delton. (Illus.). 144p. (J). (gr. 2-5). 1989. 13.95 (*0-395-50926-2*) HM.

Angel's Mother's Boyfriend. Judy Delton. LC 82-27054. (Illus.). 176p. (J). (gr. 2-5). 1986. 14.95 (*0-395-39968-8*) HM.

An Asterisk (*) at the beginning of an entry indicates that the title is appearing in BIP for the first time.

*Angels Proclaim Radiant Living. Juanita O. Keith. LC 94-96870. 192p. 1995. pap. 12.50 (0-9628351-2-9) Archer Creat Pr. Public awareness is tuning into metaphysical enlightenment through Angel Guidance. A powerful network of communication is developing between the Angel Realm & Earth people. It is a crucial network of cooperation. Metamorphosis is taking place. The veil is lifting from the fog which stymied Earth people through the years of wandering. From their vantage point in the Angel Realm, Angels can see our dire need today & they welcome the use of human energies to work through. Yet they never interfere. You remain in charge of your own life. Sections of THE ANGELS PROCLAIM RADIANT LIVING BOOK are written from visions & direct channeling. The forerunner of this newly published book, is RADIANT LIVING, THE CHALLENGE OF CHANGE published in 1990. It deals with cleansing your angel antenna by dispelling anger & fear which lead to excessive worry. Instead, trust. Angel Guidance heals the

individual so that the individual contributes to healing the world. Finally, what is RADIANT LIVING? Attracting & radiating Unconditional Love, in energy explained through Divine Wisdom. Order direct from Archer Creative Press, Box 7087, Grand Station, Des Moines, IA 50309. Call 515-279-7769. Discounts available. *Publisher Provided Annotation.*

A

A

Angiotensin & the Heart. Ed. by H. Grobecker et al. (Illus.). viii, 224p. 1993. 47.00 (*0-387-91432-3*) Spr-Verlag.

Angiotensin-Converting-Enzym-Hemmer Bei Hypertonie, Teil 1 - Angiotensin Converting Inhibitors in Treatment of Hypertension, Pt. I: Schwerpunkt auf Cilazapril - Emphasis on Cilazapril. Ed. by J. Rosenthal & K. O. Stumpe. (Journal: Cardiology: Vol. 82, Suppl. 1, 1993). (Illus.). iv, 80p. 1993. pap. 32.00 (*3-8055-5764-7*) S Karger.

*__Angiotensin Converting Enzyme Inhibitors.__ 2nd ed. Lionel H. Opie. Date not set. pap. text ed. 34.95 (*0-471-11195-3*) Wiley.

*__Angiotensin II Receptors: Medicinal Chemistry, Vol. II.__ Ed. by Robert R. Ruffolo, Jr. 256p. 1994. 99.50 (*0-8493-8545-8*) CRC Pr.

Angiotensin-Konversionsenzyme-Hemmer Bei Hypertonie, Teil 2 (Angiotensin Converting Inhibitors in Treatment of Hypertension, Pt. 2) Schwerpunkt auf Cilazapril (Emphasis on Cilazapril) Ed. by J. Rosenthal & K. O. Stumpe. (Journal: Cardiology: Vol. 82, Suppl. 2, 1993). (Illus.). iv, 84p. 1993. pap. 32.00 (*3-8055-5772-8*) S Karger.

Angiotensin Receptors. Ed. by Juan M. Saavedra & Pieter B. Timmermans. LC 94-5810. 438p. (C). 1994. 95.00 (*0-306-44691-X*, Plenum Pr) Plenum.

Angiotension - Converting Enzyme Inhibitors: Scientific Basis for Clinical Use. Lionel H. Opie. 320p. (Orig.). 1992. text ed. 37.95 (*0-471-58836-9*) Wiley.

Angiporto, Inc. Story & Cookbook. rev. ed. Deedee Borland & Barbara McCormack. 193p. 1991. pap. text ed. 10.80 (*0-9630876-0-6*) Angiporto.

Angkor. Photos by Marc Riboud. LC 93-60222. (Illus.). 160p. 1993. 65.00 (*0-500-54182-5*) Thames Hudson.

*__Angkor: Heart of an Asian Empire.__ Bruno Dagens. Tr. by Ruth Sharman. (Discoveries Ser.). 192p. 1995. pap. 12.95 (*0-8109-2801-9*) Abrams.

Angkor: Temples of Cambodia's Kings. Dawn Rooney. 1993. pap. 15.95 (*0-8442-9888-3*, Passport Bks) NTC Pub Grp.

*__Anglada-Camarasa.__ Francesc Fontbona & Francesc Miralles. (Grandes Monografias). (Illus.). 340p. (SPA.). 1993. 250.00 (*84-343-0335-3*) Elliots Bks.

*__Anglais: Guide de Conversation et Dictionnaire.__ Larousse Staff. 175p. (ENG & FRE.). 1991. pap. 16.95 (*0-7859-7655-8*, 2034035011) Fr & Eur.

Anglais Banque. Nathan Staff. 141p. (ENG & FRE.). 1992. 18.95 (*0-7859-0971-0*, 2098866011) Fr & Eur.

Anglais dans la Terminologie de la Construction et du Batiment dans le Monde. 64p. (FRE.). 1992. reprint ed. write for info. (*0-7859-4564-4*) Fr & Eur.

Anglais Dans le Batiment: Text in English with an Illustrated Glossary. Gunter Wallnig & Harry Evered. 192p. (ENG, FRE & GER.). 1976. pap. 75.00 (*0-8288-5574-9*, M6565) Fr & Eur.

Anglais de l'Expert-Comptable. Patrick Lafond & Richard Vaughan. 159p. (FRE.). 1993. pap. 69.95 (*0-7859-1661-X*, 2906471054) Fr & Eur.

Anglais Des Affaires: Business English for French Speakers. Assimil Staff. (ENG & FRE.). 1989. 28.95 (*0-8288-4481-X*, M5808); audio 125.00 (*0-685-53066-3*) Fr & Eur.

Anglais Hotellerie. Nathan Staff. 125p. (ENG & FRE.). 1992. 18.95 (*0-7859-0972-9*, 2098866046) Fr & Eur.

Anglais Medical: Medical English. Mireille Mandelbrojt-Sweeney. 168p. (ENG & FRE.). 1992. 49.95 (*0-8288-6918-9*, 2225827028) Fr & Eur.

Anglais Medical: Spoken & Written Medical English. C. Coude et al. 272p. (ENG & FRE.). 1983. pap. 79.95 (*0-8288-0561-X*, M14533) Fr & Eur.

*__Anglais Medical Pratique.__ Peter Gross. 217p. (ENG & FRE.). 1993. pap. 4,995.00 (*0-614-00401-2*, 2711412717) Fr & Eur.

Anglais Restauration. Nathan Staff. 125p. (ENG & FRE.). 1992. 18.95 (*0-7859-0973-7*, 2098866070) Fr & Eur.

Anglais Simplifie: English for French Students. (Hugo's Language Courses Ser.). 224p. (Orig.). (ENG & FRE.). 1988. pap. text ed. 7.95 (*0-85285-110-3*); audio, pap. text ed. 39.95 (*0-85285-120-0*) Hunter NJ.

Anglais Touristique - English for French Speakers. (Hugo's Phrasebks.). 128p. (Orig.). 1988. pap. 4.95 (*0-85285-106-5*) Hunter NJ.

Angle Antics. Mary Hickey. Ed. by Liz McGehee. LC 90-24773. 1991. pap. 18.95 (*0-943574-76-5*) That Patchwork.

Angle-Closure Glaucoma. Stanley Hyams. LC 90-4179. (Illus.). 186p. 1990. lib. bdg. 45.00 (*90-6299-059-2*, Pub. by Kugler NE) Kugler Pubns.

Angle Iron: Basketball. J. Grubbs. 20p. (Orig.). (YA). 1992. pap. 15.00 (*1-56611-008-4*) Jonas.

Angle Iron: The Junior High Team. J. Grubbs. Ed. by J. Abell. 50p. (J). (gr. 6-8). 1988. lib. bdg. 25.00 (*1-56611-003-3*) Jonas.

Angle Modulation: The Theory of System Assessment. J. H. Roberts. LC 78-317398. (IEE Telecommunications Ser.: Vol. 5). (Illus.). 294p. reprint ed. pap. 83.80 (*0-8357-5478-2*, 2032253) Bks Demand.

Angle of Attack. Robin A. White. 352p. 1992. 20.00 (*0-517-57809-3*, Crown) Crown Pub Group.

Angle of Attack: Harrison Storms & the Race to the Moon. Mike Gray. 304p. 1994. pap. 11.95 (*0-14-023280-X*, Penguin Bks) Viking Penguin.

Angle of Attack: Harrison Storms & the Race to the Moon. Mike Gray. 384p. 1992. 22.95 (*0-393-01892-X*) Norton.

Angle of Repose. Ed. by Nancy Peskin. 100p. (Orig.). 1986. pap. 5.95 (*0-936739-01-0*) Hallwalls Inc.

Angle of Repose. Wallace Stegner. (Contemporary American Fiction Ser.). 512p. 1992. pap. 12.95 (*0-14-016930-X*, Penguin Bks) Viking Penguin.

*__Angle of the Sun.__ Brad Schaedler. LC 94-25349. 1995. pap. 12.95 (*0-7734-2730-9*, Mellen Poetry Pr) E Mellen.

Angle of Vision: Christians & the Middle East. Charles A. Kimball. (Orig.). 1992. pap. 7.95 (*0-377-00240-2*) Friendship Pr.

Angle-Resolved Photoemission: Theory & Current Applications. Ed. by S. D. Kevan. LC 92-14461. (Studies in Surface Science & Catalysis: Vol. 74). 1992. write for info. (*0-444-88183-2*) Elsevier.

Angler Survey Methods & Their Applications in Fisheries Management. K. H. Pollock et al. LC 94-70490. (Special Publication Ser.: No. 25). 371p. 1994. text ed. 88.00 (*0-913235-88-1*) Am Fisheries Soc.

Anglers Astoria. Dave Hughes. (Illus.). 177p. (Orig.). 1982. pap. 9.95 (*0-936608-07-2*) F Amato Pubns.

Angler's Coast. 2nd ed. Russell Chatham. LC 88-63678. (Illus.). 184p. 1991. 34.95 (*0-944439-12-8*) Clark City Pr.

*__Angler's Guide & Calendar '96.__ Mountain Lion, Inc., Staff. Date not set. pap. write for info. (*0-679-76117-9*) Random.

Angler's Guide to Alaska. Evan Swenson & Margaret Swenson. Ed. by Malcolm Bates. (Falcon Guidebook Ser.). (Illus.). 216p. (Orig.). 1993. pap. 12.95 (*1-56044-107-0*) Falcon Pr MT.

*__Angler's Guide to Aquatic Insects & Their Imitations.__ rev. ed. Rick Hafele & Scott Roederer. (Illus.). 192p. 1995. pap. 15.95 (*1-55566-161-0*) Johnson Bks.

Angler's Guide to Baja California. Tom Miller. (Illus.). 1987. pap. 7.95 (*0-914622-04-8*) Baja Trail.

Angler's Guide to Bass Patterns: Productive Methods, Places & Times. Larry Larsen. LC 89-92685. (Bass Series Library). (Illus.). 160p. (Orig.). 1990. pap. 9.95 (*0-936513-07-1*, BSL8) Larsens Outdoor.

Anglers Guide to Florida. Kris Thoenike. (Falcon Guides Ser.). (Illus.). 300p. (Orig.). 1994. pap. 16.95 (*1-56044-231-X*) Falcon Pr MT.

Angler's Guide to Jigs & Jigging. Kenn Oberrecht. (Illus.). 342p. 1991. pap. 14.95 (*0-88317-161-9*) Stoeger Pub Co.

Angler's Guide to Michigan's Great Lakes. 80p. 1979. pap. 6.95 (*0-941912-23-X*) Mich Nat Res.

Angler's Guide to Montana. rev. ed. Michael S. Sample. (Illus.). 272p. 1992. pap. 12.95 (*1-56044-147-X*) Falcon Pr MT.

Angler's Guide to San Pablo Dam Reservoir. Jack Spinali. (Illus.). 50p. (Orig.). 1986. pap. 2.95 (*0-9616975-0-4*) Fishing with Jack Pubns.

*__Angler's Guide to Twelve Classic Trout Streams in Michigan.__ rev. ed. Gerth E. Hendrickson. LC 94-26044. (Illus.). 290p. 1994. pap. text ed. 16.95x (*0-472-08272-8*) U of Mich Pr.

Angler's Handbook for India. E. Cretin. 332p. 1984. 150.00 (*81-7089-095-0*, Pub. by Intl Bk Distr II); 175.00 (*81-7089-950-8*, Pub. by Intl Bk Distr II) St Mut.

Angler's Handbook for India. E. Cretin. 332p. (C). 1984. 250.00 (*0-685-61475-1*, Pub. by Intl Bk Distr II) St Mut.

Angler's Handbook for India. E. Cretin. 332p. 1984. reprint ed. 175.00 (*0-685-54030-8*, Pub. by Intl Bk Distr II) St Mut.

Angler's Journal: For Freshwater Fishing. Virgil Lungstrom. 120p. 1993. pap. 7.95 (*1-883607-02-7*) Prairie Ldr.

Angler's Journal: For Ice Fishing. Virgil Lungstrom. 120p. 1993. pap. 7.95 (*1-883607-03-5*) Prairie Ldr.

Angles. Marion Smoothey. LC 92-26322. (J). 1993. 16.95 (*1-85435-466-3*) Marshall Cavendish.

Angles see Key to Geometry Series

Angles & Chambers. Arthur Dobrin. (Review Long Island Writers Chapbook Ser.: No. 2). 48p. 1991. 15.00 (*0-89304-257-9*); 15.00 (*0-89304-255-2*); pap. 5.00 (*0-89304-258-7*); pap. 5.00 (*0-89304-256-0*); audio 10.00 (*0-89304-259-5*) Cross-Cultrl NY.

Angles of Incidence. Mark Robbins. LC 92-29640. (Illus.). 80p. (Orig.). 1992. pap. 19.95 (*1-878271-67-9*) Princeton Arch.

Angles of Vision: A Memoir of My Lives. Philip M. Klutznick & Sidney Hyman. (Illus.). 416p. 1991. 27.50 (*0-929587-64-2*) I R Dee.

Angles of Vision: Conversations on Philippine Literature. Roger J. Bresnahan. 185p. (Orig.). 1992. pap. 9.00 (*971-10-0420-8*, Pub. by New Day Pub PH) Cellar.

Angles of Vision: French Art Today, 1986 Exxon International Exhibition. Lisa Dennison. (Illus.). 156p. 1986. 15.00 (*0-89207-058-7*) S R Guggenheim.

Angles of Vision: Poetry. Roy P. Fairfield. LC 93-90773. 120p. (Orig.). 1993. pap. 8.95 (*0-9621921-4-7*) Bastille Bks.

Angles to Grow By. John G. Bruhn. 107p. (Orig.). 1986. pap. 11.95 (*0-9616570-1-4*) J G Bruhn.

Anglesey & Lleyn Shipwrecks. Ian Skidmore. 168p. (C). 1992. 39.00 (*0-7154-0704-X*, Pub. by C Davies Pubs) St Mut.

Anglesey, Wales a Research Reference. William A. Rowlands. LC 91-90538. 285p. 1991. pap. 25.00 (*0-9630454-0-7*) MBR Co.

Anglesko-Slovenski Moderni Slovar. Dasa Komac & Skerlj Ruzena. 788p. (ENG & SLA.). 1987. 49.95 (*0-8288-0550-4*, F130180) Fr & Eur.

Angleterre au XVIIIE Siecle, 2 vols. in one. Charles F. De Remusat. Ed. by J. P. Mayer. LC 78-67378. (Angleterre au XVIIIe siecle Ser.). (FRE.). 1980. reprint ed. lib. bdg. 78.95 (*0-405-11728-0*) Ayer.

Anglian Images. Richard Tames. (Illus.). 192p. 1991. 30.00 (*0-86299-746-1*) A Sutton Pub.

Anglican - Orthodox Pilgrimage. Ed. by Franklin Billerbeck. LC 93-23496. 1993. 4.50 (*0-9622713-5-7*) Conciliar Pr.

Anglican & Puritan: The Basis of Their Opposition, 1558-1640. John F. New. 140p. 1964. 22.50 (*0-8047-0066-4*) Stanford U Pr.

Anglican Church in Nineteenth Century Britain: Hyms Ancient & Modern 1860-1875. Susan Drain. LC 89-34070. (Texts & Studies in Religion: Vol. 40). 552p. 1989. lib. bdg. 119.95 (*0-88946-829-X*) E Mellen.

Anglican Church Today & Tomorrow. Michael E. Marshall. LC 83-62178. 176p. (Orig.). 1984. pap. 7.95 (*0-8192-1341-1*) Morehouse Pub.

Anglican Clergy in Maryland, 1692-1776. Carol Van Voorst. (Outstanding Studies in Early American History). 344p. 1989. reprint ed. 20.00 (*0-8240-6293-0*) Garland.

Anglican Cycle of Prayer, 1995. Ed. by Robert B. Horine. (Illus.). 144p. (Orig.). 1995. pap. 1.95 (*0-88028-148-0*, 1245) Forward Movement.

*__Anglican Cycle of Prayer 1996.__ Ed. by Robert B. Horine. (Illus.). 144p. (Orig.). 1995. pap. 1.95 (*0-88028-162-6*, 1314) Forward Movement.

Anglican Humanitarianism in Colonial New York. Frank J. Klingberg. LC 71-164612. (Select Bibliographies Reprint Ser.). 1977. reprint ed. 22.95 (*0-8369-5896-9*) Ayer.

Anglican Left: Radical Social Reformers in the Church of England & the Protestant Episcopal Church, 1846-1954. Bernard K. Markwell. LC 91-28031. (Chicago Studies in the History of American Religion Ser.: Vol. 13). 325p. 1991. 60.00 (*0-926019-26-0*) Carlson Pub.

Anglican Maryland, 1692-1792. Arthur P. Middleton. LC 92-13669. 1992. write for info. (*0-89865-841-1*) Donning Co.

Anglican Mind: A Theological Compendium of the Classic Statements (from the 17th Century) Intro. by John H. Morgan. LC 90-50109. 500p. (C). 1990. text ed. 37.95 (*1-55605-148-4*); pap. text ed. 27.95 (*1-55605-147-6*) Wyndhall Pr.

Anglican Ministry in Virginia, 1723-1776: A Study of Social Class. Joan R. Gunderson. (Outstanding Studies in Early American History). 368p. 1989. reprint ed. 25.00 (*0-8240-6183-7*) Garland.

Anglican Moral Choice. Ed. by Paul Elmen. LC 82-62391. (Anglican Studies Ser.). 274p. (Orig.). 1983. pap. 11.95 (*0-8192-1322-5*) Morehouse Pub.

Anglican-Orthodox Dialogue. LC 85-1766. 73p. 1986. pap. text ed. 5.95 (*0-88141-047-0*) St Vladimirs.

Anglican-Orthodox Intercommunion. Bishop Raphael. pap. 0.25 (*0-89981-004-7*) Eastern Orthodox.

Anglican Religious Orders & Communities: A Directory. Intro. by James Francis. 120p. (Orig.). 1991. pap. 4.00 (*0-88028-126-X*, 1150) Forward Movement.

Anglican Service Book: A Traditional Language Adaptation of the 1979 Book of Common Prayer Together with the Psalter or Psalms of David & Additional Devotions. 734p. 1991. 14.00 (*0-9629955-0-9*) Church Good Shepherd.

*__Anglican Shakespeare: Elizabethan Orthodoxy in the Great Histories.__ Daniel Wright. 278p. 1993. pap. 24.95 (*1-880365-94-4*) Prof Pr NC.

Anglican Spirit. Michael Ramsey & Dale Coleman. LC 91-6599. 175p. (Orig.). 1991. pap. 11.95 (*1-56101-027-8*) Cowley Pubns.

Anglican Spiritual Tradition. John R. Moorman. LC 82-229111. 240p. 1985. pap. text ed. 14.95 (*0-87243-139-8*) Templegate.

Anglican Spirituality. Ed. by William J. Wolf. LC 81-84717. (Anglican Studies Ser.). 176p. (Orig.). (C). 1982. pap. 10.95 (*0-8192-1297-0*) Morehouse Pub.

Anglican Theology & Pastoral Care. Ed. by James Griffiss. LC 84-62463. (Anglican Studies Ser.). 160p. (Orig.). 1985. pap. 10.95 (*0-8192-1364-0*) Morehouse Pub.

Anglican Tradition. Ed. by Richard Holloway. LC 83-62541. 132p. (Orig.). 1984. pap. 6.95 (*0-8192-1338-1*) Morehouse Pub.

Anglican Tradition: A Handbook of Sources. Ed. by G. R. Evans & J. Robert Wright. LC 90-27180. 640p. (Orig.). 1991. pap. 32.00 (*0-8006-2483-1*, 1-2483, Fortress Pr) Augsburg Fortress.

Anglican Tradition in Eighteenth Century Verse. H. Grant Sampson. (De Proprietatibus Litterarum, Ser. Practica: No. 33). 1971. pap. text ed. 52.35 (*90-279-1907-0*) Mouton.

Anglicanism. 4th ed. Stephen Neill. 1978. pap. 23.00 (*0-19-520033-0*) OUP.

Anglicanism & the Bible. Ed. by Frederick H. Borsch. LC 83-62717. (Anglican Studies Ser.). (Orig.). 1984. pap. 10.95 (*0-8192-1337-3*) Morehouse Pub.

Anglicanism & the Christian Church: Theological Resources in Historical Perspective. Paul Avis. LC 89-11785. 370p. 1989. 29.00 (*0-8006-2416-5*, 1-2416) Augsburg Fortress.

Anglicimos Profesionales De Puerto Rico. Elena Mellado De Hunter. LC 80-17935. (Coleccion Mente y Palabra). 204p. (SPA.). 1981. 6.00 (*0-8477-0578-1*); pap. 5.20 (*0-8477-0579-X*) U of PR Pr.

Anglicising the Government of Ireland: The Irish Privy Council & the Expansion of Tudor Rule, 1556-78. Jon Crawford. (Illus.). 352p. 1993. text ed. 49.50 (*0-7165-2498-8*, Pub. by Irish Acad Pr IE) Intl Spec Bk.

Anglicisms, Americanisms. T. Magay & I. L. Lang. 320p. (ENG & HUN.). 1991. 14.95 (*0-8288-7190-6*, F88860) Fr & Eur.

*__Anglicisms, Americanisms.__ T. Magay & I. L. Lang. 320p. (C). 1993. 24.00x (*963-05-6043-7*, Pub. by Akad Kiado HU) St Mut.

Anglicisms of Quebec. Gilles Colpron. 247p. (FRE.). 1979. 59.95 (*0-8288-9167-2*, M6080) Fr & Eur.

Angling for Words. Carolyn C. Bowen. 1972. student ed 18.00 (*0-87879-047-0*); student ed 10.00 (*0-87879-048-9*) Acad Therapy.

Angling for Words: The Teacher's Line. Dorothy B. Montgomery. 1975. pap. 10.00 (*0-87879-105-1*) Acad Therapy.

Angling for Words-Memory Foundations for Reading: MFR Manual. Regina Richards & Jeralee A. Smith. (Angling for Words Ser.). 64p. 1983. 8.00 (*0-87879-369-0*); 8.00 (*0-685-53923-7*); 6.00 (*0-87879-371-2*); 6.00 (*0-87879-372-0*) Acad Therapy.

Angling into Light. Carl Lindner. LC 94-83572. 72p. (Orig.). 1994. pap. 7.95 (*0-943512-15-8*) Linwood Pub.

Angling Success, by Leading Outdoor Writers. Ed. by Mortimer Norton. LC 67-30224. (Essay Index Reprint Ser.). 1977. 23.95 (*0-8369-0747-7*) Ayer.

Anglish-Yinglish: Yiddish in American Life & Literature. Gene Bluestein. LC 88-10922. 152p. 1989. pap. 11.95 (*0-8203-1084-0*) U of Ga Pr.

Anglo-African Magazine, Vol. 1. Eighteen Fifty-Nine. LC 68-28984. (American Negro: His History & Literature, Ser. No. 1). 1969. 25.95 (*0-405-01803-7*) Ayer.

Anglo-American Advance into Texas, 1810-1830. W. H. Timmons. (Texas History Ser.). (Illus.). 46p. 1982. pap. text ed. 3.95 (*0-89641-103-6*) American Pr.

Anglo-American & German Abbreviations in Data-Processing. Peter Wennrich. 736p. (ENG & GER.). 1984. 325.00 (*0-8288-0004-9*, M14181) Fr & Eur.

Anglo American & the Rise of Modern South Africa. Duncan Innes. LC 83-42523. 352p. 1984. pap. 14.00 (*0-85345-629-1*) Monthly Rev.

Anglo-American Anti-Military Tracts, Sixteen Ninety-Seven to Eighteen Thirty: An Original Anthology. Ed. by Richard H. Kohn. LC 78-22412. (American Military Experience Ser.). 1980. lib. bdg. 31.95 (*0-405-11886-4*) Ayer.

Anglo-American Antiphony: The Late Romanticism of Tennyson & Emerson. Richard E. Brantley. LC 93-30648. 360p. (C). 1994. lib. bdg. 39.95 (*0-8130-1247-3*) U Press Fla.

Anglo American Artist in Italy: 1750-1820. Corlette R. Walker. (Illus.). 156p. 1982. 10.00 (*0-942006-01-1*) U of CA Art.

*__Anglo-American Ballad: A Folklore Casebook.__ Ed. by Dianne Dugaw. LC 94-24348. (Folklore Casebks.: Vol. 8). 360p. 1995. 54.00 (*0-8153-1747-6*, H1858) Garland.

Anglo-American Cataloguing Rules. rev. ed. Ed. by Michael Gorman & Paul Winkler. LC 88-19349. 656p. 1988. text ed. 52.00 (*0-8389-3346-7*); pap. text ed. 45.00 (*0-8389-3360-2*) ALA.

Anglo-American Cataloguing Rules. 2nd rev. ed. Ed. by Michael Gorman & Paul Winkler. LC 88-19349. 656p. 1988. ring bd. 72.00 (*0-8389-3361-0*) ALA.

Anglo-American Cataloguing Rules: Amendments, 1993. 2nd rev. ed. Joint Steering Committee for Revision of Anglo-American Cataloguing Rules Staff. LC 93-21165. 160p. 1993. pap. text ed. 12.00 (*0-8389-3431-5*) ALA.

Anglo-American Contributions to Basque Studies: Essays in Honor of Jon Bilbao. Ed. by William A. Douglass et al. (Publications in the Social Sciences Ser.: No. 13). (Illus.). 221p. (Orig.). (C). 1977. 6.75 (*0-945920-93-8*); pap. 7.00 (*0-945920-94-6*) Desert Rsch Inst.

Anglo-American Croatian Rapprochement. Ivo Omrcanin. 650p. 1989. 25.00 (*0-9613814-6-9*) Ivor Pr.

Anglo-American Establishment. 1991. lib. bdg. 79.95 (*0-8490-4408-1*) Gordon Pr.

Anglo American Establishment. Quigley Carroll. 354p. 1949. 10.00 (*0-913022-45-4*) Angriff Pr.

Anglo-American Establishment. Carroll Quigley. 354p. reprint ed. pap. 12.95 (*0-945001-01-0*) GSG & Assocs.

*__Anglo-American Feminist Challenges to the Rhetorical Traditions: Virginia Woolf, Mary Daly, & Adrienne Rich.__ Krista Ratcliffe. LC 94-40053. 248p. (C). 1995. 29.95x (*0-8093-1934-9*) S Ill U Pr.

Anglo-American Folksong Scholarship since 1898. Donald K. Wilgus. LC 81-23741. xx, 466p. 1982. reprint ed. text ed. 75.00 (*0-313-22622-9*, WIAN, Greenwood Pr) Greenwood.

Anglo-American Innovation. Peter A. Clark. (Studies in Organization: No. 9). 404p. (C). 1987. lib. bdg. 74.95 (*3-11-010572-1*) De Gruyter.

*__Anglo-American Interplay in Recent Drama.__ Ruby Cohn. (Illus.). 225p. (C). 1995. 39.95 (*0-521-47267-9*) Cambridge U Pr.

Anglo-American Isthmian Diplomacy, 1815-1915. Mary W. Williams. (Illus.). 1965. 11.75 (*0-8446-1479-3*) Peter Smith.

Anglo-American Jury: Keystone of Human Rights. 1992. lib. bdg. 75.00 (*0-8490-8726-0*) Gordon Pr.

Anglo-American Landscapes: A Study of Nineteenth-Century Anglo-American Travel Literature. Christopher Mulvey. LC 82-4380. (Illus.). 300p. 1983. 49.95 (*0-521-23755-6*) Cambridge U Pr.

Anglo-American Law of the Frontier: Thomas Rodney & His Territorial Cases. Ed. by William Hamilton. LC 53-8265. 510p. reprint ed. pap. 145.40 (*0-8357-5479-0*, 2023762) Bks Demand.

Anglo-American Legal Bibliographies: An Annotated Guide. William L. Friend. LC 78-168085. reprint ed. 24.50 (*0-404-02599-4*) AMS Pr.

Anglo-American Legal System: Introduction, Readings & Cases. 2nd ed. Edgar Bodenheimer et al. (American Casebook Ser.). 166p. (C). 1992. reprint ed. pap. text ed. 20.00 (*0-314-36662-8*) West Pub.

Anglo-American Liberalism: A Collection of Readings in Political Economy. Ed. by Conrad Waligorski & Thomas Hone. LC 81-4008. 330p. (C). 1981. text ed. 32.95 (*0-88229-617-5*) Nelson-Hall.

Anglo American Literary Relations. George Gordon. (BCL1-PS American Literature Ser.). 116p. 1993. reprint ed. lib. bdg. 69.00 (*0-7812-6568-1*) Rprt Serv.

Anglo-American Literary Relations: The Watson Chair Foundation Lectures of the Sulgrave Manor Board. George S. Gordon. LC 76-167346. (Essay Index Reprint Ser.). 1977. reprint ed. 16.95 (*0-8369-2649-8*) Ayer.

An Asterisk (*) at the beginning of an entry indicates that the title is appearing in BIP for the first time.

An Asterisk (*) at the beginning of an entry indicates that the title is appearing in BIP for the first time.

A

Anglo-Saxon History: An Annotated Bibliography: 450-1066. Joel T. Rosenthal. LC 84-45279. (Studies in the Middle Ages: No. 7). vii, 178p. 1985. 39.50 (*0-404-61437-X*) AMS Pr.

Anglo-Saxon Leechcraft. abr. ed. Henry S. Wellcome. (Illus.). 100p. (C). 1992. reprint ed. pap. 6.95 (*1-877934-04-6*) Rose & Nefr Pr.

Anglo-Saxon Litanies of the Saints. Michael Lapidge. (Henry Bradshaw Society Ser.: No. CVI). 352p. (C). 1991. text ed. 50.00 (*1-870252-01-2*) Boydell & Brewer.

Anglo-Saxon Literature. John Earle. (BCL1-PR English Literature Ser.). 262p. 1992. reprint ed. lib. bdg. 79.00 (*0-7812-7030-8*) Rprt Serv.

Anglo-Saxon Literature. John Earle. LC 79-131694. 1970. reprint ed. 7.00 (*0-403-00581-7*) Scholarly.

Anglo-Saxon Magic. Godfried Storms. 1973. 300.00 (*0-87968-074-1*) Gordon Pr.

Anglo-Saxon Manner: The English Contribution to Civilization. Edith Simon. 1972. 25.00 (*0-8464-0136-3*) Beekman Pubs.

Anglo-Saxon Manuscripts. Michelle P. Brown. (Illus.). 80p. (Orig.). 1992. pap. 18.95 (*0-8020-7728-5*) U of Toronto Pr.

Anglo-Saxon Manuscripts: Basic Readings. Ed. by Mary P. Richards. LC 94-12990. (Basic Readings in Anglo-Saxon England Ser.: Vol. 2). 424p. 1994. 62.00 (*0-8153-0100-6*, H1434) Garland.

***Anglo-Saxon Manuscripts in Microfiche Facsimile Vol. 1: Books of Prayer & Healing.** Ed. by A. N. Doane. LC 94-37257. (Medieval & Renaissance Texts & Studies: Vol. 136). 64p. 1994. mic. film, pap. 90.00 (*0-86698-141-1*, MR136) MRTS.

***Anglo-Saxon Manuscripts in Microfiche Facsimile Vol. 2: Psalters I.** Ed. by Phillip Pulsiano. 68p. 1994. mic. film, pap. 90.00 (*0-86698-146-2*, MR137) MRTS.

Anglo-Saxon Medicine. M. L. Cameron. LC 92-29974. (Studies in Anglo-Saxon England: No. 7). 240p. (C). 1993. 64.95 (*0-521-40521-1*) Cambridge U Pr.

Anglo-Saxon Minor Poems. Ed. by Elliot V. Dobbie. LC 43-1513. (Anglo-Saxon Poetic Records Ser.). 220p. 1942. text ed. 41.00 (*0-231-08770-5*) Col U Pr.

Anglo-Saxon Northumbria. Peter H. Blair. Ed. by Michael Lapidge & Pauline H. Blair. (Collected Studies: No. CS192). (Illus.). 338p. (C). 1984. reprint ed. lib. bdg. 95.00 (*0-86078-140-2*, Pub. by Variorum UK) Ashgate Pub Co.

Anglo-Saxon Oral Poetry: A Study of the Traditions. Jeff Opland. LC 79-24202. 301p. reprint ed. pap. 85.80 (*0-8357-3754-3*, 2036480) Bks Demand.

Anglo-Saxon Oxfordshire. John Blair. LC 94-4453. (Illus.). 224p. 1994. 50.00 (*0-7509-0147-0*) A Sutton Pub.

Anglo-Saxon Paganism. David Wilson. LC 92-9366. 208p. 1993. 59.95 (*0-415-01897-8*, A9767) Routledge.

Anglo-Saxon Poetry. Gavin D. Bone. LC 75-128874. (Select Bibliographies Reprint Ser.). 1977. 12.95 (*0-8369-5494-7*) Ayer.

Anglo-Saxon Poetry. Gavin Bone. LC 79-161951. 1950. reprint ed. 39.00 (*0-403-01347-X*) Scholarly.

Anglo-Saxon Poetry: Essays in Appreciation. Lewis Nicholson & Dolores Frese. LC 74-27893. 400p. 1977. pap. 14.95 (*0-268-00576-1*) U of Notre Dame Pr.

Anglo-Saxon Pottery. David H. Kennett. 1989. pap. 25.00 (*0-7478-0006-5*, Pub. by Shire UK) St Mut.

Anglo-Saxon Primer. 9th ed. Henry Sweet. Ed. by Norman Davis. 1982. pap. 14.95 (*0-19-811178-9*) OUP.

Anglo-Saxon Prose. Ed. & Tr. by Michael Swanton. 266p. 1993. pap. 7.95 (*0-460-87341-5*, Everyman's Classic Lib) C E Tuttle.

Anglo-Saxon Reader in Prose & Verse. 15th ed. Henry Sweet. Ed. by Dorothy Whitelock. 1975. pap. 16.95 (*0-19-811169-X*) OUP.

***Anglo-Saxon Riddles.** Tr. by John Porter. 112p. 1995. pap. 8.95 (*1-898281-13-0*) Paul & Co Pubs.

Anglo-Saxon Runes. John M. Kemble. 80p. 1992. pap. text ed. 14.95 (*0-9516209-1-6*, Pub. by Anglo-Saxon Bks UK) Paul & Co Pubs.

Anglo-Saxon Sagas: An Examination of Their Value As Aids to History. Daniel H. Haigh. 1976. lib. bdg. 59.95 (*0-8490-1431-X*) Gordon Pr.

Anglo-Saxon Saints & Heroes. Ed. by Clinton Albertson. LC 67-16652. 375p. reprint ed. pap. 106.90 (*0-7837-0437-2*, 2040760) Bks Demand.

Anglo-Saxon Sculpture. James Lnag. 1989. pap. 25.00 (*0-85263-927-9*, Pub. by Shire UK) St Mut.

Anglo-Saxon Settlements. Ed. by Della Hooke. (Illus.). 320p. 1988. text ed. 82.95 (*0-631-15454-X*) Blackwell Pubs.

Anglo-Saxon Superiority. Edmond Demolins. (Select Bibliographies Reprint Ser.). 1977. reprint ed. 24.95 (*0-8369-6875-1*) Ayer.

Anglo-Saxon Textual Illustration: Photographs of Sixteen Manuscripts with Description & Index. Ed. by Thomas Ohlgren. (Illus.). 1992. boxed 75.00 (*1-879288-10-9*) Medieval Inst.

Anglo-Saxon Verse Charms, Maxims & Heroic Legends. Louis J. Rodrigues. 176p. (Orig.). 1993. pap. text ed. 14.95 (*0-317-05875-4*, Pub. by Anglo-Saxon Bks UK) Paul & Co Pubs.

Anglo-Saxon Wills. Dorothy Whitelock. LC 85-82256. (Cambridge Studies in English Legal History). 290p. 1986. reprint ed. 69.00 (*0-912004-54-1*) W W Gaunt.

Anglo-Saxon Women & the Early Church: Sharing a Common Fate. Stephanie Hollis. 288p. (C). 1992. text ed. 79.00 (*0-85115-317-8*) Boydell & Brewer.

***Anglo-Saxon World.** Ed. by Kevin Crossley-Holland. (Illus.). 288p. (C). 1994. text ed. 45.00 (*0-85115-169-8*, Boydell Pr) Boydell & Brewer.

Anglo-Saxon World: An Anthology. Ed. by Kevin Crossley-Holland. (World's Classics Paperback Ser.). 1984. pap. 9.95 (*0-19-281632-2*) OUP.

Anglo-Saxon Writs. Florence E. Harmer. LC 80-2225. reprint ed. 74.50 (*0-404-18762-5*) AMS Pr.

Anglo-Saxons. Ed. by James Campbell. (Illus.). 272p. 1991. pap. 24.95 (*0-14-014395-5*, Penguin Bks) Viking Penguin.

Anglo-Saxons. Roger Coote. LC 93-34486. (Look into the Past Ser.). (Illus.). 32p. (J). (gr. 4-6). 1994. 14.95 (*1-56847-062-2*) Thomson Lrning.

Anglo-Saxons. Rowena Loverance. (Fact Finders Ser.). (Illus.). 48p. (Orig.). (YA). (gr. 7 up). 1992. pap. 7.50 (*0-563-35001-6*, BBC-Parkwest) Parkwest Pubns.

Anglo-Saxons. John Reeve et al. (Illus.). (J). (gr. 2-6). pap. 4.95 (*0-7141-0537-6*, Pub. by Brit Mus UK) Parkwest Pubns.

Anglo-Saxons: Synthesis & Achievement. Ed. by J. D. Woods & David A. Pelteret. 176p. (C). 1985. pap. 18.50 (*0-88920-166-8*, Pub. by Wilfrid Laurier CN) Humanities.

Anglo-Saxons Activity Book. John Reeve & Jenny Chattington. (British Museum Activity Bks.). (Illus.). 16p. (J). 1994. pap. 5.95 (*0-500-27762-1*) Thames Hudson.

Anglo-Saxons in England During the Early Centuries after the Invasion. Nils F. Aberg. 235p. 1975. reprint ed. 32.37 (*3-487-05723-9*, Pub. by Georg Olms GW) Lubrecht & Cramer.

Anglo-Saxons Resource Book. (Sense of History Ser.). 1991. pap. text ed. 13.32 (*0-582-07312-X*) Longman.

Anglo-Scandinavian England: Norse-English Relations in the Period Before Conquest. Ed. by John D. Niles & Mark Amodio. LC 88-31728. (Old English Colloquium Ser.: No. 4). 94p. (Orig.). (C). 1989. lib. bdg. 29.00 (*0-8191-7267-7*, Old English Colloquium); pap. text ed. 17.00 (*0-8191-7268-5*, Old English Colloquium) U Pr of Amer.

Anglo-Scottish Literary Relations, 1430-1550. Gregory C. Kratzmann. LC 78-74537. 294p. reprint ed. pap. 83.80 (*0-8357-5482-0*, 2031679) Bks Demand.

Anglo-Soviet Accord see Anglo-Soviet Relations, 1917-1921

Anglo-Soviet Relations, 1917-1921, 3 vols., Set. Richard H. Ullman. Incl. Vol. 1. Intervention & the War. LC 61-6290. 1961. pap. 15.95 (*0-691-01065-X*); Vol. 3. Anglo-Soviet Accord. LC 61-6290. 536p. 1973. pap. 27.50 (*0-691-10012-8*); LC 61-6290. (Illus.). 88.50 (*0-686-64844-7*) Princeton U Pr.

Anglo-Spanish Confrontation on the Gulf Coast During the American Revolution: Proceedings of the Gulf Coast History & Humanities Conference, Vol IX. Ed. by William S. Coker & Rober R. Rea. 1983. 15.00 (*0-940836-16-5*); pap. 10.00 (*0-940836-17-3*) U of W Fla.

Anglo-Spanish Relations in Tudor Literature. Gustav Ungerer. LC 73-138944. reprint ed. 39.50 (*0-404-06704-2*) AMS Pr.

Anglo-Ukrainian Studies in the Analysis of Scientific Discourse: Reason & Rhetoric. Ed. by Rom Harre. LC 93-16626. 148p. 1993. text ed. 69.95 (*0-7734-9284-4*) E Mellen.

Anglo-Welsh Literature: An Illustrated History. Roland Mathias. LC 86-63547. (Illus.). 142p. 1987. pap. 16.95 (*0-907476-64-3*, Pub. by Poetry Wales Pr UK) Dufour.

Anglo-Welsh Poetry, 1480-1980. Ed. by Raymond Garlick & Roland Mathias. LC 84-72667. (Illus.). 377p. 1985. 35.00 (*0-907476-21-X*, Pub. by Poetry Wales Pr UK) Dufour.

Anglo-Welsh Poetry 1480-1990. 2nd ed. Ed. by Raymond Garlick & Roland Mathias. 377p. 1994. pap. 17.95 (*1-85411-082-9*, Pub. by Seren Bks UK) Dufour.

Anglomaniacs. Constance C. Harrison. Ed. by Elizabeth Hardwick. LC 76-51669. (Rediscovered Fiction by American Women Ser.). 1977. reprint ed. lib. bdg. 33.95 (*0-405-10048-5*) Ayer.

Anglos & Mexicans in the Making of Texas, 1836-1986. David Montejano. (Illus.). 397p. 1987. pap. 14.95 (*0-292-77596-2*) U of Tex Pr.

Angoisse de Roi Salomon. Romain Gary. 350p. (FRE.). 1990. pap. 11.95 (*0-7859-2525-2*, 2070377970) Fr & Eur.

Angoisse du Gardien de But au Moment du Penalty. Peter Handke. 160p. (FRE.). 1982. pap. 10.95 (*0-7859-2464-7*, 2070374076) Fr & Eur.

Angoisse du Roi Solomon. Romain Gary. (Folio Ser.: No. 1797). (FRE.). pap. 9.95 (*2-07-037797-0*) Schoenhof.

Angol-Magyar Szotar English-Hungarian Dictionary. L. Orszagn. 791p. (ENG & HUN.). 42.50 (*0-685-04460-2*, 043-7) Saphrograph.

Angol Nyelvkonyv: English Language Book for Self-Learners & Student with Teachers. Latzko Hugo. 180p. (ENG & HUN.). pap. 19.50 (*0-87557-093-3*, 093-3) Saphrograph.

Angola. R. Black. (World Bibliographical Ser.). 1993. lib. bdg. 69.00 (*1-85109-143-2*) ABC-CLIO.

Angola. Jason Laure. LC 90-2143. (Enchantment of the World Ser.). (Illus.). 128p. (J). (gr. 5-9). 1990. lib. bdg. 20.55 (*0-516-02721-2*) Childrens.

Angola. Somerville. (Marxist Regimes Ser.). 228p. 1986. text ed. 49.00 (*0-86187-394-7*, Pub. by Pinter Pubs UK); pap. text ed. 17.50 (*0-86187-395-5*, Pub. by Pinter Pubs UK) St Martin.

Angola. Douglas L. Wheeler & Rene Pelissier. LC 77-20095. (Praeger Library of African Affairs). (Illus.). 296p. 1978. reprint ed. text ed. 38.50 (*0-313-20011-4*, WHAN, Greenwood Pr) Greenwood.

Angola: An Introductory Economic Review. (Country Study Ser.). 426p. 1990. 25.95 (*0-8213-1748-2*, 11748) World Bank.

Angola: Business Risk Overview. Ed. by Lewis B. Sckolnick. 125p. (Orig.). (C). 1994. pap. text ed. 495.00 (*1-57205-528-6*) Rector Pr.

Angola: Five Centuries of Conflict. Lawrence W. Henderson. LC 79-5089. (Africa in the Modern World Ser.). 272p. reprint ed. pap. 77.60 (*0-8357-5483-9*, 2032048) Bks Demand.

Angola: Louisiana State Penitentiary, a Half-Century of Rage & Reform. Anne Butler & C. Murray Henderson. LC 90-82517. 180p. 1990. 19.95 (*0-940984-61-X*) U of SW LA Ctr LA Studies.

Angola: Military Technical Atlas Scale: 1: 200000. Ed. by Lewis B. Sckolnick. 125p. (Orig.). (RUS.). (C). 1994. pap. text ed. 3,000.00 (*1-57205-457-3*) Rector Pr.

Angola: Violations of the Laws of War by Both Sides. Africa Watch Staff. 160p. 1989. pap. 10.00 (*0-929692-19-5*, Africa Watch) Hum Rts Watch.

Angola & the Politics of Intervention: From Local Bush War to Chronic Crisis in Southern Africa. Daniel Spikes. LC 92-51088. (Illus.). 400p. 1993. lib. bdg. 45.00 (*0-89950-888-X*) McFarland & Co.

Angola & the River Congo, 2 vols., Set. J. J. Monteiro. 1968. reprint ed. 85.00 (*0-7146-1838-1*, BHA-01838, Pub. by F Cass Pubs UK) Intl Spec Bk.

Angola Beloved. Ernest T. Wilson. LC 67-31008. 1967. pap. 4.50 (*0-87213-961-1*) Loizeaux.

***Angola Business Executive Outlook.** 70p. (Orig.). 1994. pap. 295.00 (*0-7605-1366-X*) Rector Pr.

Angola Business Forecaster. Ed. by Lewis B. Sckolnick. 70p. (Orig.). (C). 1994. pap. 675.00 (*1-57205-399-2*) Rector Pr.

***Angola Business Intelligence Handbook.** (Illus.). 70p. (Orig.). 1994. pap. 295.00 (*0-7605-1094-6*) Rector Pr.

Angola in Ferment: The Background & Prospects of Angolan Nationalism. Thomas M. Okuma. LC 73-17929. (Illus.). 137p. 1974. reprint ed. text ed. 49.75 (*0-8371-7272-1*, OKAF, Greenwood Pr) Greenwood.

Angola, Mozambique, & the West. Ed. by Helen Kitchen. LC 87-21818. (Washington Papers: No. 130). 168p. 1987. text ed. 45.00 (*0-275-92879-9*, C2879, Praeger Pubs); pap. text ed. 11.95 (*0-275-92880-2*, B2880, Praeger Pubs) Greenwood.

***Angola Since the 1992 Elections.** 200p. (Orig.). 1994. pap. 65.00 (*0-7605-0970-0*) Rector Pr.

***Angola Tax Law.** 150p. (C). 1994. pap. 295.00 (*0-7605-0066-5*) Rector Pr.

Angola under the Portuguese: The Myth & the Reality. Gerald J. Bender. LC 76-7751. (Perspectives on Southern Africa Ser.: No. 23). 1978. 50.00 (*0-520-03221-7*); pap. 14.00 (*0-520-04274-3*) U CA Pr.

Angolan Economy: Prospects for Growth in a Postwar Economy. Shawn H. McCormick. LC 94-11211. (Significant Issues Ser.). 88p. (Orig.). (C). (gr. 13). 1994. pap. 8.95 (*0-89206-187-1*) CSI Studies.

Angolan Revolution: The Anatomy of an Explosion, 1950-1962, Vol. 1. John A. Marcum. (Studies in Communism, Revisionism & Revolution). 1969. 45.00 (*0-262-13048-3*) MIT Pr.

Angora: A Handbook for Spinners. Erica Lynne. LC 92-367. (Illus.). 120p. (Orig.). 1992. pap. 14.95 (*0-934026-75-0*) Interweave.

Angora Goat & Mohair Production. Maurice Shelton. (Illus.). 233p. 1993. 18.95 (*0-943639-18-2*) Anchor Pub Co.

Angorwat & Cultural Ties with India. K. Srivastava. xiv, 146p. (C). 1987. 64.00 (*81-85016-19-4*, Pub. by Bks & Bks IA) S Asia.

Angriffe Gegen Descartes und Malebranche Im Journal De Trevoux 1701-1715. Emmy Allard. (Abhandlungen Zur Philosophie und Ihrer Geschichte Ser.: No. 43). viii, 58p. 1985. reprint ed. write for info. (*3-487-07611-X*, Pub. by Georg Olms GW) Lubrecht & Cramer.

Angry. Janine Amos. LC 90-46540. (Feelings Ser.). (Illus.). 32p. (J). (ps-3). 1991. 19.97 (*0-8172-3776-3*); pap. 4.95 (*0-8114-6909-3*) Raintree Steck-V.

Angry. Sue Riley. LC 77-16791. (What Does It Mean? Ser.). (Illus.). (J). (ps-2). 1978. lib. bdg. 18.50 (*0-89565-014-2*) Childs World.

***Angry All the Time: An Emergency Guide to Anger Control.** Ron Potter-Efron. LC 94-67046. 160p. (Orig.). Date not set. text ed. 19.95 (*1-879237-97-0*) New Harbinger.

***Angry All the Time: An Emergency Guide to Anger Control.** Ron Potter-Efron. LC 94-67046. (Orig.). Date not set. pap. 12.95 (*1-879237-98-9*) New Harbinger.

Angry at Death & Other Poems. Jennifer Loucks. 1993. 8.95 (*0-533-10392-4*) Vantage.

Angry Book. Theodore I. Rubin. 224p. 1993. pap. 8.00 (*0-02-036565-9*, Collier S&S) S&S Trade.

Angry Candy. Harlan Ellison. 372p. 1989. pap. 11.95 (*0-452-26335-2*, Dutton) NAL-Dutton.

Angry Candy. John Pauker. (Poetry Ser.). 48p. 1976. pap. 5.95 (*0-917530-01-2*) Pig Iron Pr.

Angry Child: Sleeping Giant or Paper Tiger? Kim J. Masters. 144p. (Orig.). 1991. pap. 8.95 (*0-929162-49-8*) PIA Pr.

***Angry Christian: How to Control, & Use, Your Anger.** Bert Ghezzi. LC 95-192. (Orig.). 1995. pap. 7.50 (*0-8198-0761-3*) Pauline Bks.

Angry Classrooms, Vacant Minds: What's Happened to Our High Schools? Martin M. Wooster. LC 93-34168. 1993. 19.95 (*0-936488-74-3*) PRIPP.

Angry Days. Sesshu Foster. 80p. (Orig.). 1987. pap. 5.95 (*0-931122-46-5*) West End.

Angry Days in Mindanao. Peter Schreurs. (San Carlos Humanities Ser.: No. 17). (Illus.). vi, 146p. (Orig.). (C). 1987. pap. 13.75 (*971-10-0052-0*, Pub. by San Carlos Univ PH) Cellar.

Angry? Do You Mind If I Scream? Devon Hansen. 99p. reprint ed. pap. text ed. 8.95 (*1-885714-00-9*) Inner Dynamics.

Angry Dust. Clement R. Hoopes. 1967. 4.95 (*0-8159-5008-X*) Devin.

Angry Goddess. Jai Ratan. 8.00 (*0-89253-634-9*) Ind-US Inc.

Angry Gut: Coping with Colitis & Crohn's Disease. W. G. Thompson. (Illus.). 364p. 1993. 26.95 (*0-306-44470-4*, Plenum Pr) Plenum.

Angry Gymnast. Jerry Jenkins. (Dallas O'Neil & the Baker Street Sports Club Ser.). (Orig.). (YA). (gr. 7-12). 1986. pap. text ed. 4.99 (*0-8024-8235-X*) Moody.

Angry Mammoth. Jack London. (Illus.). 40p. 1984. pap. 1.95 (*0-932458-21-1*) Star Rover.

Angry Man. Stephen Arterburn & David Stoop. 1992. pap. 9.99 (*0-8499-3420-6*) Word Inc.

***Angry Man.** James Lardner. Date not set. 25.00 (*0-394-57648-9*) Random.

Angry Man. David Stoop & Steve Arterburn. 1991. 12.99 (*0-8499-0779-9*) Word Inc.

Angry Marriage: Overcoming the Rage, Reclaiming the Love. Bonnie Maslin. LC 93-19272. 288p. 1994. 19.95 (*1-56282-806-1*) Hyperion.

Angry Marriage: Overcoming the Rage, Reclaiming the Love. Bonnie Maslin. 288p. 1995. pap. 12.95 (*0-7868-8069-4*) Hyperion.

Angry Men, Passive Men: Understanding the Roots of Men's Anger & How to Move Beyond It. Marvin Allen & Jo Robinson. Orig. Title: In the Company of Men. 256p. 1994. reprint ed. pap. 10.00 (*0-449-90811-9*, Columbine) Fawcett.

Angry Mountain. large type ed. Hammond Innes. 1967. 21.95 (*0-85456-583-3*) Ulverscroft.

***Angry Nights.** Larry Fondation. 1994. pap. 8.95 (*0-932511-94-5*) Fiction Coll.

Angry Saints. George Knight. Ed. by Gerald Wheeler. 190p. 1989. 13.95 (*0-8280-0536-2*) Review & Herald.

Angry Scar: The Story of Reconstruction. Hodding Carter, III. LC 73-10751. 425p. 1974. reprint ed. text ed. 49.75 (*0-8371-7022-2*, CAAS, Greenwood Pr) Greenwood.

Angry Summer: A Poem of Nineteen Twenty-Six. Idris Davies. xxxii, 74p. 1993. 29.00 (*0-7083-1090-7*, Pub. by U of Wales UK) Bks Intl VA.

Angry Waters. Walt Morey. (Walt Morey Adventure Library). (YA). (gr. 5-9). 1990. reprint ed. 7.95 (*0-936085-10-X*) Blue Heron OR.

Angry Women. Ed. by V. Vale & Andrea Juno. (Illus.). 260p. (Orig.). 1992. pap. 18.99 (*0-940642-24-7*) Re Search Pubns.

***Angry Women in Rock Vol. 1.** Ed. by A. Juno & V. Vale. 1995. pap. 18.99 (*0-940642-31-X*) Re Search Pubns.

Angry Young Men of the Thirties. Elton E. Smith. LC 74-20731. (Crosscurrents-Modern Critiques Ser.). 186p. 1975. 6.95 (*0-8093-0698-0*) S Ill U Pr.

Angst: Cartography. Balch Baratloo & Clifton C. Moji. 1990. pap. 9.95 (*0-930829-10-7*) Lumen Inc.

Angst: Cartography. Mojdeh Baratloo & Clifton J. Balch. 1989. pap. 9.95 (*0-685-30868-5*) SITES.

Angst & the Abyss: The Hermeneutics of Nothingness. David K. Coe. (American Academy of Religion, Academic Ser.). 1985. pap. 18.95 (*0-89130-863-6*) Scholars Pr GA.

Angst-Ridden Executive. Manuel V. Montalban. Tr. by Ed Emery. (Mask Noir Ser.). 240p. (Orig.). 1990. pap. 9.95 (*1-85242-159-2*) Serpents Tail.

Anguilla: Consolidated Index of Statutes & Subsidiary Legislation. C. J. Hammett. (West Indian Legislation Indexing Project Ser.). viii, 74p. (Orig.). 1991. pap. text ed. 25.00 (*0-317-58004-3*, Pub. by UWI Fac Law BB) W W Gaunt.

Anguilla, St. Martin & St. Barthelemy. Wilson Ltd. Staff & Imray L. Norie. (C). 1989. 75.00 (*0-685-40402-1*, Pub. by Imray Laurie Norie & Wilson UK) St Mut.

Anguilla to Guadeloupe. Wilson Ltd. Staff & Imray L. Norie. (C). 1990. 75.00 (*0-685-40394-7*, Pub. by Imray Laurie Norie & Wilson UK) St Mut.

Anguish: A Case History of a Dying Trajectory. Anselm Strauss & Barney G. Glaser. 193p. 1970. pap. 22.00 (*1-884156-03-7*) Sociology Pr.

Anguish: The Case History of a Dying Trajectory. Anselm Strauss & Barney Glaser. (Orig.). 1977. pap. 12.75 (*0-686-24890-2*) Sociology Pr.

***Anguish Among Pearls.** Pearl Atchenson-Becker. 260p. Date not set. pap. 8.95 (*0-7610-0411-4*) NW Pub.

Anguish & Farewell, 1793-1799 see George Washington: A Biography

Anguish & the Word: Preaching That Touches Pain. David N. Duke & Paul D. Duke. 112p. (Orig.). 1992. pap. 10.95 (*0-9628455-9-0*) Smyth & Helwys.

Anguish of Central Banking. Arthur F. Burns et al. LC 81-482170. (Per Jacobsson Lectures: 1979). 55p. reprint ed. pap. 25.00 (*0-8357-5484-7*, 2019262) Bks Demand.

Anguish of Earth's Tribulation. William W. Orr. (Prophecy Ser.). 48p. reprint ed. pap. 3.50 (*0-944412-01-7*) Glad Tid.

Anguish of Hell & Peace of Soul: A 1623 collection of Sixteen Motets on Psalm 116. Christopher Wolff. (Harvard Publications in Music: Vol. 17). 313p. 1994. pap. 49.95x (*0-674-03675-1*) HUP.

Anguish of Loss. Sherokee Ilse & Julie Fritsch. 56p. 1988. pap. 10.95 (*0-9609456-5-2*) Wntergrn.

Anguish of Love. Edith Witmer. 1986. 6.70 (*0-318-22865-3*) Rod & Staff.

Anguish of the Earth. Franklin D. Richardson. LC 89-50183. 181p. (Orig.). 1990. pap. 5.95 (*0-916383-92-X*) Aegina Pr.

Anguish of the Jews: Twenty-Three Centuries of Antisemitism. rev. ed. Edward Flannery. LC 85-60298. (Stimulus Book Ser.). 384p. 1985. reprint ed. pap. 14.95 (*0-8091-2702-4*) Paulist Pr.

Anguish of Third World Independence: The Sierra Leone Experience. George O. Roberts. LC 81-48679. (Illus.). (Orig.). 1982. pap. text ed. 34.50 (*0-8191-2396-X*) U Pr of Amer.

An Asterisk (*) at the beginning of an entry indicates that the title is appearing in BIP for the first time.

Anguish of Tibet. Petra K. Kelly. LC 91-2964. (Illus.). 382p. 1991. pap. 17.00 (*0-938077-47-3*) Parallax Pr.

Anguished English. Richard Lederer. 1989. mass mkt. 5.99 (*0-440-20352-X*, LFL) Dell.

Anguished English: An Anthology of Accidental Assaults upon Our Language. Richard Lederer. LC 87-40532. (Illus.). 128p. 1987. pap. 7.95 (*0-941711-04-8*) Wyrick & Co.

***Angular Equivalencies & Nightmare Concentricities.** Brendan Tripp. 24p. 1976. pap. 5.00 (*1-57353-001-8*) Eschaton Prods.

Angular Light Scattering Maxima & Minima in Monodisperse & Heterodisperse Systems of Spheres. Werner Bergman & Wilfried Heller. LC 77-6931. (Illus.). 362p. reprint ed. pap. 103.20 (*0-8357-9828-3*, 2013660) Bks Demand.

Angular Momentum. D. M. Brink & G. R. Satchler. LC 93-32190. (Orig.). 1994. pap. 24.95 (*0-19-851759-9*, Clarendon Pr) OUP.

Angular Momentum: An Illustrated Guide to Rotational Symmetries for Physical Systems. William J. Thompson. LC 93-44636. 1994. text ed. 64.95 (*0-471-55264-X*, Wiley-Interscience) Wiley.

Angular Momentum: Understanding Spatial Aspects in Chemistry & Physics. Richard Zare. LC 87-16204. (Baker Lecture Ser.). 349p. 1988. text ed. 64.95 (*0-471-85892-7*) Wiley.

Angular Momentum & Mass Loss for Hot Stars. Ed. by L. A. Willson & R. Stalio. (C). 1990. lib. bdg. 129.50 (*0-7923-0881-6*) Kluwer Ac.

Angular Momentum Calculus in Quantum Physics. M. Danos & V. Gillet. 176p. 1990. text ed. 36.00 (*981-02-0412-4*) World Scientific Pub.

Angular Momentum Evolution of Young Stars. Ed. by S. Catalano & J. R. Stauffer. (C). 1991. lib. bdg. 154.50 (*0-7923-1316-X*) Kluwer Ac.

Angular Momentum in Quantum Mechanics. rev. ed. A. R. Edmonds. (Investigations in Physics Ser.: No. 4). 1968. 32.50x (*0-691-07912-9*) Princeton U Pr.

Angular Scattering Functions for Spheres. Harry H. Denman et al. LC 66-14228. 315p. reprint ed. pap. 89.80 (*0-8357-5485-5*, 2027656) Bks Demand.

Angular Scattering Functions for Spherical Particles. William J. Pangonis & Wilfried Heller. LC 60-8930. 227p. reprint ed. pap. 64.70 (*0-7837-3828-5*, 2043649) Bks Demand.

Angular Scattering Functions for Spheroids. Wilfried Heller et al. LC 77-156067. 119p. reprint ed. pap. 34.00 (*0-7837-3635-5*, 2043502) Bks Demand.

Angus & the Cat. Marjorie Flack. 40p. (J). (ps-00). 1989. reprint ed. lib. bdg. 13.99 (*0-685-01488-6*); reprint ed. pap. 12.95 (*0-685-01489-4*) Doubleday.

Angus MacIntyre's Ceilidii Collection. Picton Publishing Staff & Angus MacIntyre. (C). 1987. 22.00 (*0-317-90412-4*, Pub. by Picton UK) St Mut.

Angus' Mull. rev. ed. Picton Publishing Staff. 1987. 30.00 (*0-317-90396-9*, Pub. by Picton UK) St Mut.

Angus Thought He Was Big-Small Book. A. Graham & W. Wood. 8p. (J). 1987. 2.95 (*0-88679-545-1*) Educ Insights.

Angus Thought He Was Big-Tall Book. A. Graham & W. Wood. 8p. (J). 1987. 17.95 (*0-88679-544-3*) Educ Insights.

Angus Wilson: A Bibliography. J. H. Stape & A. N. Thomas. 343p. 1988. text ed. 100.00 (*0-7201-1872-7*, Mansell Pub) Cassell.

Angustia, Depresion y Esperanza: Anguish, Depression & Hope. Juan A. Monroy. (SPA.). 3.95 (*84-7645-389-2*, 223516, Pub. by Edit Clie SP) TSELF.

Anh-Viet Viet-Anh Tu Dien Ke Toan: English-Vietnamese Vietnamese-English Accounting Dictionary. Ed. by Francis M. Albin. Tr. by Cecile P. Thomson et al. LC 92-80731. 342p. (Orig.). 1992. pap. 24.95 (*0-9626407-1-9*) Paper Tig Pr.

Anhedonia & Affect Deficit States. Ed. by David C. Clark & Jan Fawcett. LC 87-2476. 1987. text ed. 35.00 (*0-89335-236-5*) PMA Pub Corp.

Anhelli. Juliusz Slowacki. Ed. by George R. Noyes. Tr. by Dorothea Radin. LC 78-21548. 118p. 1979. reprint ed. text ed. 35.00 (*0-313-20828-X*, SLAN, Greenwood Pr) Greenwood.

***Anheuser Busch Companies Report.** 60p. (Orig.). 1995. pap. text ed. 595.00 (*0-7605-2177-8*) Rector Pr.

Anhydrous Ammonia Safety. Don Brooks. LC 81-730680. 1982. student ed 7.00 (*0-8064-0031-5*, 266); audio 99.00 (*0-8064-0032-3*) Bergwall.

Anicet ou le Panorama, Vol. 3. Louis Aragon. 288p. (FRE.). 1972. pap. 10.95 (*0-7859-2865-0*, F82562) Fr & Eur.

Anika. Anne-Marie Hilgarth. 1981. 18.00 (*0-7223-1391-8*, Pub. by A H S Ltd UK) St Mut.

Anika's Mountain. Karen Rispin. LC 93-31345. (Anika Scott Ser.: No. 3). (Illus.). (J). 1994. pap. 4.99 (*0-8423-1219-6*) Tyndale.

Anima. Mary Chadwick et al. (Illus.). 96p. (Orig.). 1988. pap. 5.00 (*1-880306-00-X*) SF Women Writs.

Anima. Dick Lourie. 1977. pap. 5.00 (*0-914610-09-0*) Hanging Loose.

Anima: An Anatomy of a Personified Notion. James Hillman. LC 85-18320. (Illus.). 188p. (Orig.). 1985. pap. 16.00 (*0-88214-316-6*) Spring Pubns.

Anima: Photographs & Text by James Balog. LC 93-90168. (Illus.). 64p. 1993. 29.95 (*0-9636266-0-4*) Arts Alternat.

Anima Mundi. Ed. by Richard Grossinger & Lindy Hough. (Earth Geography Booklet Ser.: No. 4). (Illus.). 256p. (Orig.). 1973. pap. 4.00 (*0-913028-17-7*) North Atlantic.

Anima Mundi: Still Life in Britain. Canadian Museum of Contemporary Photography Staff. (Illus.). 68p. 1992. pap. 29.95 (*0-88884-555-3*) U Ch Pr.

***Anima Speaking.** Virginia Davis. 120p. 1994. pap. 8.95 (*1-882550-04-8*) Quiet Lion Pr.

Animacy in Russian: A New Interpretation. Emily R. Klenin. (UCLA Slavic Studies: Vol. 6). 139p. 1983. 19.95 (*0-89357-115-6*) Slavica.

Animadversions upon M. Seldens History of Tithes & His Review Thereof. Richard Tillesley. LC 77-7435. (English Experience Ser.: No. 896). 1977. reprint ed. lib. bdg. 26.50 (*90-221-0896-1*) Walter J Johnson.

Animae. Sam Hamill. 70p. 1980. pap. 6.00 (*0-914742-53-1*) Copper Canyon.

Animal. (Ultimate Sticker Ser.). (Illus.). 20p. (J). (gr. k-6). 1994. pap. 6.95 (*1-56458-481-X*) Dorling Kindersley.

Animal: Find the Difference. (J). 1992. pap. 2.99 (*0-517-06726-9*) Random Hse Value.

Animal ABC. Jean Edades. (Illus.). (J). (gr. 3-5). 1979. pap. 3.50 (*0-686-25221-7*, Pub. by New Day Pub PH) Cellar.

Animal ABC. Illus. by Patricia Wynne. LC 77-74470. (Board Bks.). 14p. (J). (ps-00). 1977. bds. 3.95 (*0-394-83589-1*) Random Bks Yng Read.

Animal ABC Stickers. Cathy Beylon. (Illus.). (J). (gr. k-3). 1994. pap. 1.00 (*0-486-27936-7*) Dover.

***Animal ABCs.** Susan Hood. LC 94-41642. (Illus.). 32p. (J). (gr. k-3). 1995. pap. text ed. 2.95 (*0-8167-3572-7*, Whistlstop) Troll Assocs.

Animal ABC's. Denise Lewis-Patrick. (My First Golden Board Bks.). (J). (ps). 1990. bds. write for info. (*0-307-06127-2*) Western Pub.

Animal Acrobats; Secret Treasures, 2 vols., Set. Illus. by Robert Cremins. LC 93-9768. (National Geographic Action Book Ser.). (J). 1993. 21.95 (*0-87044-955-9*) Natl Geog.

Animal Activist's Handbook. 103p. 3.00 (*0-318-13342-3*) Animal Prot Inst.

Animal Activities, 4 vols., Set. Jane Burton. (Illus.). 128p. (J). (gr. 2-3). 1989. lib. bdg. 69.07 (*0-8368-0184-9*) Gareth Stevens Inc.

Animal Acts. Rhoda Lerman. 272p. 1994. 22.50 (*0-8050-1418-7*) H Holt & Co.

Animal Acts. Cris Mazza. 163p. (Orig.). 1989. 18.95 (*0-932511-15-5*); pap. 8.95 (*0-932511-16-3*) Fiction Coll.

Animal Adaption to Cold. Ed. by L. C. Wang. (Advances in Comparative & Environmental Physiology Ser.: Vol. 4). (Illus.). 450p. 1989. 143.00 (*0-387-50301-3*, 2543) Spr-Verlag.

***Animal Affections.** Illus. by Diane Ackerman. LC 94-35232. 1995. write for info. (*0-8109-1959-1*) Abrams.

Animal Aggregations, A Study in General Sociology. Warder C. Allee. LC 75-41007. reprint ed. 37.50 (*0-404-14501-9*) AMS Pr.

Animal Agriculture: The Biology, Husbandry, & Use of Domestic Animals. 2nd ed. Ed. by H. H. Cole & W. N. Garrett. LC 79-18984. (Animal Science Ser.). (Illus.). 739p. (C). 1995. text ed. write for info. (*0-7167-1099-4*) W H Freeman.

***Animal Agriculture Impacts on Water Quality in California.** Ed. by Ray Coppock & Stephanie Weber. 87p. (Orig.). Date not set. pap. text ed. 15.00 (*1-885976-00-3*, AA-1) U CA Agricult Issues.

***Animal Alphabet.** 1995. 7.98 (*1-85854-181-6*) Brimax Bks.

Animal Alphabet. Bert Kitchen. LC 83-23929. (Pied Piper Paperback Ser.). (Illus.). 32p. (J). (ps up). 1988. pap. 4.95 (*0-8037-0431-3*, Puff Pied Piper) Puffin Bks.

Animal Alphabet. Bert Kitchen. (J). 1992. pap. 5.99 (*0-14-054601-4*) Viking Child Bks.

Animal Alphabet. 2nd ed. Doris Ehrlich. (Illus.). 36p. (J). (ps-00). 1988. teacher ed 4.50 (*0-932957-91-9*); student ed 3.90 (*0-932957-89-7*); pap. text ed. 80.00 (*0-932957-90-0*); 17.50 (*0-932957-96-X*) Natl School.

Animal Alphabet: An Educational Coloring Book. Spizzirri Publishing Co. Staff. Ed. by Linda Spizzirri. (Illus.). 32p. (J). (gr. 1-8). 1982. pap. 1.75 (*0-86545-042-0*) Spizzirri.

Animal Alphabet Book. (World Wildlife Ser.: No. S864-1). (Illus.). (J). (gr. k-3). 3.95 (*0-7214-9532-X*) Ladybird Bks.

Animal Alphabet Coloring Book. Nina Barbaresi. (Illus.). (J). (gr. k-3). 1991. pap. 2.50 (*0-486-26698-2*) Dover.

Animal Analogy in Shakespeare's Character Portrayal. Audrey E. Yoder. LC 70-178381. reprint ed. 15.45 (*0-404-07067-1*) AMS Pr.

***Animal Anatomy: An Illustrated Reference to Drawing Animals.** Gottfried Bammes. 1994. 14.98 (*0-7858-0055-7*) Bk Sales Inc.

Animal Anatomy & Physiology. 2nd ed. Jesse F. Bone. (C). 1981. text ed. 38.00 (*0-8359-0216-1*, Reston) P-H.

Animal Anatomy & Physiology. 3rd ed. Jesse F. Bone. (Illus.). 560p. (C). 1988. text ed. 25.00 (*0-685-19514-7*) P-H.

Animal Anatomy on File. Diagram Group Staff. (On File Ser.). (Illus.). 300p. 1990. ring bd. 155.00 (*0-8160-2244-5*) Facts on File.

Animal & Clinical Pharmacologic Techniques in Drug Evaluation. Ed. by John H. Nodine & Peter E. Siegler. LC 64-19787. 680p. reprint ed. pap. 180.00 (*0-8357-5486-3*, 2051708) Bks Demand.

Animal & Human Biology Exercises. rev. ed. Earl G. Zimmerman et al. 240p. (C). 1993. spiral bd. 19.96 (*0-8403-8855-1*) Kendall-Hunt.

Animal & Human Calorimetry. J. A. McLean & G. Tobin. (Illus.). 352p. 1988. 94.95 (*0-521-30905-0*) Cambridge U Pr.

Animal & Plant Lore, Collected from the Oral Tradition of English Speaking Folk. Ed. by Fanny D. Bergen. LC 99-4363. (AFS Memoirs Ser.). 1972. reprint ed. 25.00 (*0-527-01059-6*) Periodicals Srv.

Animal Antics. (Snapshot Big Picture Paperbacks Ser.). (Illus.). 32p. (Orig.). (J). (gr. 1-3). 1994. pap. 4.95 (*1-56458-547-6*) Dorling Kindersley.

Animal Antics. (Harmonica Fun! Ser.). (Illus.). 24p. (Orig.). 1993. pap. 9.95 (*0-7935-2300-1*, 00821018) H Leonard.

Animal Antics ABC's. Chatham River. (Fun with Words Ser.). 48p. (J). 1990. 4.99 (*0-517-68881-6*) Random Hse Value.

Animal Applications of Research in Mammalian Development. Ed. by Roger A. Pedersen et al. (Current Communications in Cell & Molecular Biology Ser.: No. 4). (Illus.). 334p. (C). 1991. pap. text ed. 44.00 (*0-87969-333-9*) Cold Spring Harbor.

Animal Architects. Ed. by Donald J. Crump. LC 87-12198. (Books for World Explorers Series 8: No. 4). (Illus.). 104p. (J). (gr. 3-8). 1987. lib. bdg. 12.50 (*0-87044-617-7*) Natl Geog.

Animal Architects. National Geographic Society Staff. Ed. by Donald J. Crump. LC 87-12198. (Books for World Explorers Series 8: No. 4). (Illus.). 104p. (J). (gr. 3-8). 1994. 12.50 (*0-87044-612-6*) Natl Geog.

Animal Architects: How Animals Weave, Tunnel, & Build Their Remarkable Homes. Wanda Shipman. (Illus.). 160p. 1994. pap. 16.95 (*0-8117-2404-2*) Stackpole.

Animal Architecture. Jennifer O. Dewey. LC 90-43010. (Illus.). 72p. (J). (gr. 3-6). 1991. 16.95 (*0-531-05930-8*); lib. bdg. 16.99 (*0-531-08530-9*) Orchard Bks Watts.

***Animal Athletes.** (Snap Pops Ser.). (J). Date not set. write for info. (*0-7894-0301-3*, 5-70661) Dorling Kindersley.

Animal Atlas. Barbara Taylor. LC 91-53142. (Illus.). 64p. (J). (gr. 3-7). 1992. 20.00 (*0-679-80501-X*) Knopf Bks Yng Read.

***Animal Babies.** (Animal Friends Ser.). 8p. (J). 1994. bds. 1.49 (*0-86112-518-5*) Brimax Bks.

Animal Babies. Rebecca Dickinson. LC 87-81765. (Golden Sturdy Bks.). (Illus.). 22p. (J). (ps). 1988. write for info. (*0-307-12116-X*, Golden Bks) Western Pub.

Animal Babies. Anita Ganeri. (Questions & Answers about Animals Ser.). (Illus.). 32p. (J). (ps-1). 1991. 6.95 (*0-8120-6241-8*) Barron.

***Animal Babies.** Golden Staff. (J). 1995. 3.25 (*0-307-12728-1*, Golden Pr) Western Pub.

Animal Babies. Bobbie Hamsa. LC 84-27459. (Rookie Reader Ser.). (Illus.). 32p. (J). (ps-2). 1985. lib. bdg. 10.35 (*0-516-02066-8*); pap. 2.95 (*0-516-42066-6*) Childrens.

Animal Babies. Bobbie Kalman. (North American Wildlife Ser.). (Illus.). 56p. (J). (gr. 3-4). 1987. 15.95 (*0-86505-166-6*); pap. 7.95 (*0-86505-186-0*) Crabtree Pub Co.

Animal Babies. Harry McNaught. LC 76-24175. (Pictureback Bks.). (Illus.). (J). (ps-1). 1977. 2.25 (*0-394-83570-0*) Random Bks Yng Read.

Animal Babies. Joyce Pope. LC 91-45381. (Nature Club Ser.). (Illus.). 32p. (J). (gr. 3-6). 1993. lib. bdg. 11.59 (*0-8167-2773-2*); pap. text ed. 3.95 (*0-8167-2774-0*) Troll Assocs.

Animal Babies: A Habitat-by-Habitat Guide to How Young Animals Grow. Steve Parker. LC 93-28287. (Illus.). 176p. 1994. 30.00 (*0-87596-595-4*) Rodale Pr Inc.

Animal Babies One Two Three. Eve Spencer. (Ready-Set-Read Ser.). (Illus.). 24p. (J). (ps-2). 1990. lib. bdg. 17.84 (*0-8172-3581-7*); pap. 4.95 (*0-8114-6738-4*) Raintree Steck-V.

Animal Bandits. Robert Henno. LC 93-31750. (Illus.). (J). 1993. 14.95 (*0-88106-672-9*); lib. bdg. 15.88 (*0-88106-692-3*) Charlesbridge Pub.

Animal Behavior. Anita Ganeri. (Questions & Answers about Animals Ser.). (Illus.). 32p. (J). (ps-1). 1992. 6.95 (*0-8120-6301-5*) Barron.

Animal Behavior. Ed. by Tim Halliday. LC 93-42912. (Illus.). 144p. (C). 1994. 25.95 (*0-8061-2647-7*) U of Okla Pr.

Animal Behavior. C. Stockley. (Science & Nature Ser.). (Illus.). 64p. (J). (gr. 4-12). 1992. lib. bdg. 13.96 (*0-88110-513-9*, Usborne); pap. 7.95 (*0-7460-0639-X*, Usborne) EDC.

Animal Behavior. Ed. by Time-Life Books Staff. (Understanding Science & Nature Ser.). 144p. (J). 1992. write for info. (*0-8094-9658-5*); lib. bdg. write for info. (*0-8094-9659-3*) Time-Life.

Animal Behavior. Dava J. Walker. (Science Fair Projects Ser.). (Illus.). 48p. (J). (gr. 3-6). Date not set. lib. bdg. 12.95 (*1-56065-116-4*) Capstone Pr.

Animal Behavior. 2nd ed. M. Ridley. 1994. pap. write for info. (*0-632-03833-0*) Blackwell Sci.

Animal Behavior. 2nd rev. ed. John P. Scott. LC 76-188823. 328p. 1972. pap. text ed. 6.95 (*0-226-74337-3*, P480) U Ch Pr.

Animal Behavior: A Course for Everyone. Erika K. Honore & Peter H. Klopfer. (Illus.). 186p. 1990. pap. text ed. 42.00 (*0-12-355065-3*) Acad Pr.

Animal Behavior: An Evolutionary Approach. 5th rev. ed. John Alcock. LC 92-39692. (Illus.). 640p. (C). 1993. text ed. 48.95 (*0-87893-017-5*) Sinauer Assocs.

***Animal Behavior: An Introduction to Behavioral Mechanisms, Development, & Ecology.** 2nd ed. Mark Ridley. (Illus.). 223p. 1994. pap. (*0-86542-390-3*) Blackwell Sci.

Animal Behavior: Index of New Information with Authors, Subjects & Bibliography. rev. ed. R. C. Mahoney. 1994. 49.50 (*0-7883-0170-5*); pap. 45.50 (*0-7883-0171-3*) ABBE Pubs Assn.

Animal Behavior: Mechanisms, Ecology, & Evolution. 3rd ed. Lee C. Drickamer & Stephen H. Vessey. 496p. (C). 1991. text ed. write for info. (*0-697-07471-4*) Wm C Brown Pubs.

***Animal Behavior: Mechanisms, Ecology, & Evolution.** 4th ed. Lee C. Drickamer et al. 496p. (C). 1995. text ed. write for info. (*0-697-13642-6*) Wm C Brown Pubs.

Animal Behavior: Psychobiology, Ethology & Evolution. David J. McFarland. 576p. 1985. text ed. 43.25 (*0-8053-6790-X*) Benjamin-Cummings.

Animal Behavior & Thanatology. Ed. by Peter Borchelt et al. LC 86-82709. (Current Thanatology Ser.). 105p. 1988. pap. 14.95 (*0-930194-37-3*) Ctr Thanatology.

***Animal Behavior Science Projects.** Nancy W. Cain. (Best Science Projects for Young Adults Ser.). (YA). 1995. pap. text ed. 12.95 (*0-471-02636-0*) Wiley.

Animal Behaviour. M. Ridley. 1986. pap. 29.95 (*0-632-01416-4*) Blackwell Sci.

Animal Behaviour. 2nd ed. David J. McFarland. 585p. 1993. pap. text ed. 52.95 (*0-470-22047-3*) Halsted Pr.

Animal Behaviour: A Systems Approach. Frederick M. Toates. LC 79-41485. (Illus.). 311p. reprint ed. pap. 88.70 (*0-8357-5487-1*, 2027887) Bks Demand.

Animal Behaviour: Psychobiology, Ethology, & Evolution. 2nd ed. David J. McFarland. LC 92-16276. 1993. write for info. (*0-582-06721-9*) Longman.

Animal Biology Lab Manual. Montgomery. 96p. (C). 1992. spiral bd. 9.95 (*0-8403-8178-6*) Kendall-Hunt.

Animal Biomarkers As Pollution Indicators. D. B. Peakall. (Ecotoxicology Ser.: No. 1). (Illus.). 336p. (C). 1992. text ed. 77.50 (*0-412-40200-9*, A6762) Chapman & Hall.

Animal Biotechnology: Comprehensive Biotechnology, No. 1. Ed. by L. A. Babiuk et al. (Comprehensive Biotechnology Supplement Ser.: No. 1). (Illus.). 250p. 1989. 125.00 (*0-08-034730-4*, Pergamon Pr) Elsevier.

Animal Biotechnology & the Quality of Meat Production: Proceedings of the Organization for Economic Cooperation & Development (OECD) Workshop, Melle, Belgium 7-9 Nov., 1990. Ed. by L. O. Fiems et al. (Developments in Animal & Veterinary Science Ser.: No. 25). 230p. 1991. 100.00 (*0-444-88930-2*) Elsevier.

Animal, Bird & Myth in African Art: April 12 Through October 13, 1985, Primitive Art Gallery, the Heard Museum. Robert G. Breunig. LC 85-61030. (Illus.). 48p. (Orig.). 1985. pap. 5.00 (*0-934351-06-6*) Heard Mus.

Animal Body Fluids & Their Regulation. Antony P. Lockwood. LC 64-9913. (Illus.). 184p. 1963. 21.50 (*0-674-03700-6*) HUP.

Animal Bone Archeology: From Objectives to Analysis. Brian Hesse & Paula Wapnish. LC 83-51521. (Manuals on Archeology Ser.: No. 5). (Illus.). xii, 132p. (C). 1985. 18.00 (*0-9602822-3-8*) Taraxacum.

Animal Bones. James Rackham. LC 93-45789. 1994. pap. 10.00 (*0-520-08833-6*) U CA Pr.

Animal Book. Eric Felderman. LC 77-5512. 1978. pap. 4.95 (*0-914974-15-7*) Holmgangers.

***Animal Book.** Ann Morris. LC 95-13804. (World's Family Ser.). (J). 1995. write for info. (*0-382-24701-9*); lib. bdg. write for info. (*0-382-24702-7*); pap. write for info. (*0-382-24703-5*) Silver Burdett Pr.

Animal Breeding & Production: An Outline. E. Sasimowski. (Developments in Animal & Veterinary Science Ser.: No. 19). 840p. 1987. 179.50 (*0-444-99504-8*) Elsevier.

Animal Breeding Plans. Jay L. Lush. 451p. reprint ed. pap. 128.60 (*0-7837-1249-9*, 2041386) Bks Demand.

Animal Bride: Poems by Paulann Petersen. Paulann Petersen. 35p. (Orig.). pap. 7.00 (*0-932264-05-0*) Trask Hse Bks.

Animal Brigade Three Thousand. Ed. by Charles J. Waugh & Martin H. Greenberg. 288p. (Orig.). 1994. mass mkt. 4.99 (*0-441-00014-2*) Ace Bks.

Animal Brucellosis. Ed. by Klaus Nielsen & J. Robert Duncan. 464p. 1990. 240.00 (*0-8493-5878-7*, SF809) CRC Pr.

Animal Builders. Jim Flegg. (Wild World Ser.). (Illus.). 32p. (J). (gr. 4-6). 1991. lib. bdg. 12.40 (*1-878137-05-0*) Newington.

Animal Cafe. John Stadler. LC 85-26789. (Illus.). 32p. (J). (ps-2). 1986. reprint ed. pap. 3.95 (*0-689-71063-1*, Aladdin Paperbacks) S&S Childrens.

Animal Camouflage. Anita Ganeri. (Questions & Answers about Animals Ser.). (Illus.). 32p. (J). (ps-1). 1991. 6.95 (*0-8120-6236-1*) Barron.

Animal Camouflage: A Closer Look. Joyce Powzyk. LC 89-9848. (Illus.). 40p. (J). (gr. 2-9). 1990. text ed. 15.95 (*0-02-774980-0*, Bradbury S&S) S&S Childrens.

***Animal Camouflage: Fun Facts for Curious Kids.** Donati. (J). 1995. 4.95 (*0-307-11328-0*, Golden Pr) Western Pub.

Animal Camouflage: Hide & Seek Animals. Janet McDonnell. LC 89-28083. (Discovery World Ser.). (Illus.). 32p. (J). (ps-2). 1990. lib. bdg. 21.36 (*0-89565-562-4*) Childs World.

Animal Capers. Roger Pare. (Illus.). 24p. (J). 1992. lib. bdg. 14.95 (*1-55037-243-2*, Pub. by Annick CN); pap. 4.95 (*1-55037-244-0*, Pub. by Annick CN) Firefly Bks Ltd.

Animal Car. Joanne Barkan. (Circus Train Come Aboard Bks.). (Illus.). 12p. (J). (ps). 1993. bds. 3.50 (*0-689-71676-1*, Aladdin Paperbacks) S&S Childrens.

Animal Care. Earl Ganz. LC 90-39576. (Contemporary Short Fiction Ser.). 100p. (Orig.). 1990. 15.95 (*0-89924-069-0*); pap. 8.50 (*0-89924-068-2*) Lynx Hse.

Animal Care & Control in Connecticut: Including Fisheries & Game. 350p. 1994. ring bd. 15.95 (*0-930137-75-2*) Looseleaf Law.

Animal Caretaker. Jack Rudman. (Career Examination Ser.: C-1091). 1994. pap. 23.95 (*0-8373-1091-1*) Nat Learn.

Animal Carton Craft. Hideharu Naitoh. (Illus.). 70p. (Orig.). 1993. pap. 12.00 (*0-87040-919-0*) Japan Pubns USA.

Animal Cartoons. Ed Nofziger. (How to Draw & Paint Ser.). (Illus.). 32p. (Orig.). 1989. pap. 5.95 (*0-929261-53-4*, HT134) W Foster Pub.

Animal Cell. John G. Moner. Ed. by J. J. Head. LC 83-70597. (Carolina Biology Readers Ser.: No. 147). (Illus.). 32p. (YA). (gr. 10 up). 1987. pap. text ed. 3.00 (*0-89278-347-8*, 45-9747) Carolina Biological.

Animal Cell Bioreactors. Ed. by Chester S. Ho & Daniel I. Wang. (Biotechnology Ser.). 494p. 1991. text ed. 46.00 (*0-409-90123-7*) Buttrwrth-Heinemann.

Animal Cell Biotechnology, Vol. 3. Ed. by Raymond E. Spier & J. B. Griffiths. 450p. 1988. text ed. 139.00 (*0-12-657553-3*) Acad Pr.

Animal Cell Biotechnology, Vol. 4. Ed. by Raymond E. Spier & J. B. Griffiths. 502p. 1990. 125.00 (*0-685-28490-5*) Acad Pr.

An Asterisk (*) at the beginning of an entry indicates that the title is appearing in BIP for the first time.

Animal Cell Biotechnology, Vol. 5. Ed. by Raymond E. Spier & J. B. Griffiths. (Illus.). 313p. 1992. text ed. 129.00 (*0-12-657555-X*) Acad Pr.

Animal Cell Biotechnology, Vol. 6. Ed. by R. E. Spier & J. B. Griffiths. (Illus.). 416p. 1994. text ed. 105.00 (*0-12-657556-8*) Acad Pr.

Animal Cell Biotechnology: Edited Treatise, 1. Ed. by Raymond E. Spier & J. B. Griffiths. 1985. text ed. 143.00 (*0-12-657551-7*) Acad Pr.

Animal Cell Biotechnology: Edited Treatise, 2. Ed. by Raymond E. Spier & J. B. Griffiths. 1985. text ed. 143.00 (*0-12-657552-5*) Acad Pr.

Animal Cell Culture: A Practical Approach. Ed. by R. Ian Freshney. (Practical Approach Ser.: Vol. 104). (Illus.). 352p. 1992. pap. 39.00 (*0-19-963213-8*) OUP.

Animal Cell Culture: A Practical Approach. 2nd ed. Ed. by R. Ian Freshney. (Practical Approach Ser.: Vol. 104). (Illus.). 352p. 1992. 70.00 (*0-19-963212-X*) OUP.

Animal Cell Culture & Production of Biologicals. Ed. by R. Sasaki & K. Ikura. (C). 1991. lib. bdg. 193.50 (*0-7923-1326-7*) Kluwer Ac.

Animal Cell DNA Polymerases. Michael Fry & Lawrence A. Loeb. 240p. 1986. 191.00 (*0-8493-6507-4*, QP606, CRC Reprint) Franklin.

Animal Cell Structure. S. J. Morgan & D. C. Darling. (Introduction to Biotechniques Ser.). 176p. (Orig.). 1993. pap. 47.50x (*1-872748-16-3*, Pub. by Bios Scientific UK) Coronet Bks.

Animal Cell Technology. Ed. by R. E. Spier et al. LC 92-15733. (BIOTOL Ser.). 756p. 1992. 130.00 (*0-7506-0421-2*) Buttrwrth-Heinemann.

Animal Cell Technology: Basic & Applied Aspects: Proceedings of the Fourth Annual Meeting of the Japanese Association for Animal Cell Technology, Fukuoka, Japan, 13-15 November 1991. Ed. by H. Murakami & S. Shirahata. LC 92-23657. 600p. (C). 1992. lib. bdg. 225.00 (*0-7923-1882-X*) Kluwer Ac.

Animal Cell Technology: Products of Today, Prospects for Tomorrow. Ed. by R. E. Spier et al. LC 93-48085. 860p. 1994. 175.00 (*0-7506-1845-0*) Buttrwrth-Heinemann.

*__Animal Cell Technology: Basic & Applied Aspects Vol. 6: Proceedings of the Sixth International Meeting of the Japanese Association for Animal Cell Technology, Nagoya, Japan, November 9-12, 1993.__ Ed. by T. Kobayashi. 631p. (C). 1994. lib. bdg. 262.50 (*0-7923-3156-7*) Kluwer Ac.

Animal Cell Technology: Basic & Applied Aspects, Vol. 5: Proceedings of the Fifth International Meeting of the Japanese Association, Omiyaa, Japan, November 30-December 4, 1992. S. Kaminogawa. 688p. (C). 1993. lib. bdg. 260.00 (*0-7923-2477-3*) Kluwer Ac.

Animal Cells. Ed. by A. E. Doyle et al. (Living Resources for Biotechnology Ser.). (Illus.). 200p. (C). 1991. 42.95 (*0-521-35223-1*) Cambridge U Pr.

*__Animal Cells: Culture & Media.__ D. C. Darling & S. J. Morgan. (Bios Essential Data Ser.). 1995. pap. text ed. 19.95 (*0-471-94300-2*) Wiley.

Animal Cells As Bioreactors. Terence Cartwright. LC 93-33980. (Studies in Biotechnology: No. 11). (Illus.). 250p. (C). 1994. 44.95 (*0-521-41258-7*) Cambridge U Pr.

Animal Champions. (Zoobooks Ser.). (J). 1991. lib. bdg. 14.95 (*0-88682-409-5*) Creative Ed.

Animal Champions. Wildlife Education, Ltd. Staff. (Zoobooks Ser.). 1983. pap. 2.75 (*0-937934-19-4*) Wildlife Educ.

Animal Champions, Vol. 1. Ed. by Wildlife Education, Ltd. Staff. (Illus.). 20p. (J). 1992. 13.95 (*0-937934-73-9*) Wildlife Educ.

Animal Champions Two. Wildlife Education, Ltd. Staff. (Zoobooks Ser.). (Illus.). 20p. (Orig.). (J). 1990. pap. 2.75 (*0-937934-64-X*) Wildlife Educ.

*__Animal Chatter.__ YES! Entertainment Corporation Staff. (Interactive Books - Listen to This Ser.). 12p. (J). (ps-2). 1994. write for info. (*1-57234-040-1*) YES Ent.

Animal Church. Jim Spillman. 156p. (Orig.). 1988. pap. 5.95 (*0-86694-107-X*) Omega Pubns OR.

Animal Clinical Biochemistry: The Future. Ed. by D. J. Blackmore et al. 400p. (C). 1988. 99.95 (*0-521-35518-4*) Cambridge U Pr.

*__Animal Clowns.__ 1995. 8.00 (*0-87044-772-6*) Natl Geog.

Animal Cognition. Charles Flaherty. 450p. (C). 1985. pap. text ed. write for info. (*0-07-554410-5*) McGraw.

Animal Cognition. Ed. by Charles R. Gallistel. (Bradford-Special Issue of Cognition Ser.). (Illus.). 203p. 1991. pap. 21.00 (*0-262-57089-0*, Bradford Bks) MIT Pr.

Animal Cognition. Ed. by H. L. Roitblat et al. (Comparative Cognition & Neuroscience Ser.). 696p. 1984. pap. text ed. 99.95 (*0-89859-334-4*) L Erlbaum Assocs.

Animal Cognition: A Tribute to Donald A. Riley. Ed. by Thomas R. Zentall & William S. Maki. (Comparative Cognition & Neuroscience Ser.). 376p. 1993. text ed. 79.95 (*0-8058-1183-4*); pap. 34.50 (*0-8058-1184-2*) L Erlbaum Assocs.

Animal Cognition & Behavior. Ed. by R. L. Mellgren. (Advances in Psychology Ser.: Vol. 13). 514p. 1983. 92.50 (*0-444-86627-2*, I-122-83, North Holland) Elsevier.

Animal Colors. Vanessa Bailey. (Animal Concept Ser.). (Illus.). 16p. (J). (ps). 1991. 5.95 (*0-8120-6245-0*) Barron.

Animal Communication. Jim Flegg. (Wild World Ser.). (Illus.). 32p. (J). (gr. 4-6). 1991. lib. bdg. 12.40 (*1-878137-23-9*) Newington.

Animal Communication. J. E. Goodenough. Ed. by John J. Head. LC 83-70598. (Carolina Biology Readers Ser.: No. 143). (Illus.). 16p. (YA). (gr. 10 up). 1984. pap. 2.75 (*0-89278-343-5*, 45-9743) Carolina Biological.

Animal Communication: Opposing Viewpoints. Jacci Cole. LC 88-24401. (Great Mysteries Ser.). (Illus.). 112p. (J). (gr. 5-8). 1989. lib. bdg. 16.95 (*0-89908-062-6*) Greenhaven.

Animal Communications: Index of New Information with Authors, Subjects & Bibliography. Ruth C. Mahoney. 180p. 1993. 49.50 (*1-55914-792-X*); pap. 39.50 (*1-55914-793-8*) ABBE Pubs Assn.

Animal Communicators. Jeremy Cherfas. (How Animals Behave Ser.). (Illus.). 32p. (J). (gr. 4-6). 1991. lib. bdg. 15.95 (*0-8225-2252-7*, Lerner Publctns) Lerner Group.

Animal Communities in Temperate America: Illustrated in the Chicago Region, Study in Animal Ecology. Victor E. Shelford. Ed. by Frank N. Egerton, 3rd. LC 77-74252. (History of Ecology Ser.). (Illus.). 1978. reprint ed. lib. bdg. 35.95 (*0-405-10421-9*) Ayer.

Animal Conflict. Felicity A. Huntingford & Angela K. Hunter. 460p. 1987. text ed. 59.95 (*0-412-25920-6*); pap. text ed. 27.50 (*0-412-28750-1*) Chapman & Hall.

Animal Connection: Link Between Cancer & Other Diseases from Animals & Foods of Animal Origin. Agatha M. Thrash & Calvin L. Thrash, Jr. 126p. (Orig.). 1983. pap. 4.95 (*0-942658-04-3*) NewLife Bks.

Animal Connection: The Confessions of an Ex-Wild Animal Trafficker. Jean-Yves Domalain. Tr. by Marguerite Barnett. (Illus.). 250p. 1978. 25.00 (*0-8464-1181-4*) Beekman Pubs.

Animal Consciousness. Daisie Radner & Michael Radner. 253p. 1989. lib. bdg. 46.95 (*0-87975-459-1*) Prometheus Bks.

Animal Control Law for North Carolina Local Governments, 1986. 2nd ed. Ben F. Loeb & L. Poindexter Watts. LC 86-225342. 69p. 1986. 12.00 (*1-56011-003-1*) Institute Government.

Animal Control Law Supplement, 1988: Civil Liability for the Misdeeds of Animals. Ben F. Loeb, Jr. & John I. Lazar. 43p. (Orig.). (C). 1989. pap. text ed. 5.00 (*1-56011-004-X*, 86.10A) Institute Government.

Animal Cookbook. Mary Buckman. (One in a Series of Cook & Learn Books). (Illus.). (J). (gr. k-2). 1982. pap. text ed. 9.95 (*1-879414-01-5*) Mary Bee Creat.

Animal Count. Susan Bonagurio. Ed. by Gary Tunmore. (Illus.). 22p. (J). (ps). 1991. 12.95 (*0-924649-09-7*); lib. bdg. 15.95 (*0-924649-08-9*); pap. text ed. 9.95 (*0-685-48844-6*) Scribblers Pub.

Animal Count. Harriet Ziefert. (Illus.). 20p. (J). (ps-1). 1989. pap. 4.95 (*0-14-054174-8*, Puffin) Puffin Bks.

Animal Court: A Political Fable from Old Japan. Ando Shoeki. Tr. by Jeffrey Hunter. LC 92-19902. (Illus.). 136p. 1992. pap. 12.95 (*0-8348-0268-6*) Weatherhill.

Animal Crackers. Tom Porter. (Illus.). 64p. (Orig.). 1994. pap. 5.95 (*0-941711-09-9*) Wyrick & Co.

Animal Craft Fun: Indoor & Outdoor Animal Crafts Projects. Ed. by Beth Murray. (Illus.). 32p. (J). (gr. k-5). 1994. pap. 3.95 (*1-56397-314-6*) Boyds Mills Pr.

Animal Crafts. Chris Deshpande & Iain Macleod-Brudenell. (Worldwide Crafts). (Illus.). 32p. 1994. lib. bdg. 18.60 (*0-8368-1151-8*) Gareth Stevens Inc.

Animal Cytogenetics, Vol. 1: Playhelminthes. Mario Benazzi & B. L. Giuseppina. (Illus.). 187p. 1976. text ed. 77.50 (*3-443-26006-3*, Pub. by Gebruder Borntraeger GW) Lubrecht & Cramer.

Animal Cytogenetics, Vol. 3: Insecta, Pt. 1, Orthoptera: Grasshoppers & Crickets. Godfrey Hewitt. (Illus.). 175p. 1979. text ed. 68.50 (*0-685-18996-1*, Pub. by Gebruder Borntraeger GW) Lubrecht & Cramer.

Animal Cytogenetics, Vol. 3: Insecta, Pt. 3: Diptera I -- Cecidomyiidae. Bohdan Matuszewski. (Illus.). 144p. 1982. text ed. 54.00 (*3-443-26011-X*, Pub. by Gebruder Borntraeger GW) Lubrecht & Cramer.

Animal Cytogenetics, Vol. 3: Insecta, Pt. 5: Coleoptera. Stanley G. Smith & Nilo Virkki. (Illus.). 376p. 1978. text ed. 135.00 (*3-443-26007-1*, Pub. by Gebruder Borntraeger GW) Lubrecht & Cramer.

Animal Cytogenetics, Vol. 3: Insecta, Pt. 6: Hemiptera II - Heteroptera. Norihiro Ueshima. (Illus.). 122p. 1979. text ed. 54.00 (*0-685-18999-6*, Pub. by Gebruder Borntraeger GW) Lubrecht & Cramer.

Animal Cytogenetics, Vol. 3: Insecta, Pt. 7: Hymenoptera. R. H. Crozier. (Illus.). 100p. 1975. text ed. 56.50 (*3-443-26004-7*, Pub. by Gebruder Borntraeger GW) Lubrecht & Cramer.

Animal Cytogenetics, Vol. 4: Chordata, Pt. 1: Protochordata, Cyclostomata, & Pisces. Susumu Ohno. (Illus.). 100p. 1974. text ed. 33.50 (*3-443-26001-2*, Pub. by Gebruder Borntraeger GW) Lubrecht & Cramer.

Animal Cytogenetics, Vol. 4: Chordata, Pt. 3: Reptilia. Ettore Olmo. (Illus.). 104p. 1986. text ed. 62.50 (*0-685-55889-4*, Pub. by Gebrueder Borntraeger GW) Lubrecht & Cramer.

Animal Defenses. Jeremy Cherfas. (How Animals Behave Ser.). (Illus.). 32p. (J). (gr. 4-6). 1991. lib. bdg. 15.95 (*0-8225-2253-5*, Lerner Publctns) Lerner Group.

Animal Defenses. Jean C. Echols. Ed. by Lincoln Bergman & Kay Fairwell. (Great Explorations in Math & Science (GEMS) Ser.). (Illus.). 27p. (Orig.). (J). (ps-2). 1987. pap. 8.50 (*0-912511-09-5*) Lawrence Science.

Animal Designs. Anne Hershenburgh. (Classic Coloring Ser.). (Illus.). 48p. (Orig.). (J). (ps-3). 1987. pap. 2.95 (*0-8431-1931-4*) Price Stern.

Animal Disease Control: Regional Programs. Robert P. Hanson & Martha G. Hanson. LC 83-226. (Illus.). 332p. 1983. pap. text ed. 29.95 (*0-8138-0121-4*) Iowa St U Pr.

Animal Diseases in Archaeology. John R. Baker & Don R. Brothwell. LC 79-42813. (Studies in Archaeology Science). 1980. text ed. 101.00 (*0-12-074150-4*) Acad Pr.

Animal Dispersal: Small Mammals As a Model. Ed. by Nils C. Stenseth & W. Z. Lidicker. (Population & Community Biology Ser.). (Illus.). 288p. (C). 1992. text ed. 77.50 (*0-412-29330-7*, A2354) Chapman & Hall.

Animal Diversity. Cleveland P. Hickman, Jr. & Larry S. Roberts. 408p. (C). 1994. pap. text ed. write for info. (*0-697-24228-5*) Wm C Brown Pubs.

Animal Diversity. Cleveland P. Hickman, Jr. & Larry S. Roberts. 320p. (C). 1994. student ed, spiral bd. write for info. (*0-697-25373-2*) Wm C Brown Pubs.

Animal Diversity: A Textbook of Invertebrate Zoology. Eylers. 1991. 38.95 (*0-8016-8793-0*) Mosby Yr Bk.

Animal Doctor. Betsy Imershein. LC 87-20266. (Illus.). 32p. (J). (gr. 1-5). 1988. lib. bdg. 4.95 (*0-671-65862-X*, Julian Messner) Silver Burdett Pr.

Animal Doctor. P. C. Jersild. Tr. by David M. Paul & Margareta Paul. LC 88-14323. iv, 267p. 1988. 25.00 (*0-8032-2573-3*); pap. 8.95 (*0-8032-7569-2*) U of Nebr Pr.

Animal Doctor's Answer Book see New Animal Doctor's Answer Book

Animal Drawing: Animal Anatomy & Psychology for Artists & Laymen. Charles R. Knight. (Illus.). 20.00 (*0-8446-0742-8*) Peter Smith.

Animal Drawing - Anatomy & Action for Artists. Charles R. Knight. 149p. (Orig.). 1959. pap. text ed. 5.95 (*0-486-20426-X*) Dover.

Animal Drawing & Painting. Walter J. Wilwerding. (Illus.). 1966. pap. 6.95 (*0-486-21716-7*) Dover.

Animal-Drawn Wheeled Toolcarriers - Perfected Yet Rejected: A Cautionary Tale of Development. Paul Starkey. Ed. by Deutsches Zentrum fur Entwicklungstechnolgien-GATE. (GATE Ser.). 161p. 1988. pap. 17.50 (*3-528-02034-2*, Pub. by Vieweg & Sohn GW) Ballen Bkslr.

Animal Dreams. large type ed. Barbara Kingsolver. (General Ser.). 490p. 1991. text ed. 22.95 (*0-8161-5159-8*, Large Print Bks) Hall.

Animal Dreams: A Novel. Barbara Kingsolver. LC 89-46571. 352p. 1991. reprint ed. pap. 13.00 (*0-06-092114-5*, PL) HarpC.

Animal Drugs & Human Health. Ed. by Lester M. Crawford & Donald A. Franco. LC 93-61759. 345p. 1994. pap. text ed. 65.00 (*1-56676-102-6*) Technomic.

*__Animal Eating Habits.__ Kyle Carter. LC 94-46846. (Things Animals Do Ser.). (J). 1995. write for info. (*1-55916-111-6*) Rourke Bk Co.

Animal Ecology: Special Reference to Insects. Royal N. Chapman. Ed. by Frank N. Egerton, 3rd. LC 77-74208. (History of Ecology Ser.). 1978. reprint ed. lib. bdg. 40.95 (*0-405-10379-4*) Ayer.

Animal Ecology in Tropical Africa. 2nd ed. Denis F. Owen. LC 75-46586. (Tropical Ecology Ser.). (Illus.). 140p. reprint ed. pap. 39.90 (*0-8357-6016-2*, 2034502) Bks Demand.

Animal Energetics, Vol. 1: Protozoa Through Insects. Ed. by T. J. Pandian & F. John Vernberg. 523p. 1987. text ed. 178.00 (*0-12-544791-4*) Acad Pr.

Animal Energetics, Vol. 2: Bivalvia Through Reptilia. Ed. by T. J. Pandian & F. John Vernberg. 631p. 1987. text ed. 174.00 (*0-12-544792-2*) Acad Pr.

Animal Estate: The English & Other Creatures in the Victorian Age. Harriet Ritvo. LC 87-11848. (Illus.). 368p. 1987. text ed. 38.00 (*0-674-03706-5*) HUP.

Animal Estate: The English & Other Creatures in the Victorian Age. Harriet Ritvo. (Illus.). 368p. 1989. reprint ed. pap. text ed. 12.95 (*0-674-03707-3*) HUP.

*__Animal Evolution: Interrelationships of the Living Phyla.__ Claus Nielsen. (Illus.). 528p. 1995. 85.00 (*0-19-854868-0*); pap. 40.00 (*0-19-854867-2*) OUP.

Animal Evolution in Changing Environments: With Special Reference to Abnormal Metamorphosis. Ryuichi Matsuda. LC 86-15942. 355p. 1987. text ed. 74.95 (*0-471-87856-1*, Wiley-Interscience) Wiley.

Animal Experimentation: Cruelty or Science? Nancy Day. LC 93-46996. (Issues in Focus Ser.). (Illus.). 128p. (YA). (gr. 6 up). 1994. lib. bdg. 17.95 (*0-89490-578-3*) Enslow Pubs.

Animal Experimentation: The Moral Issues. Ed. by Robert M. Baird & Stuart E. Rosenbaum. (Contemporary Issues Ser.). 182p. (Orig.). (C). 1991. pap. 15.95 (*0-87975-667-5*) Prometheus Bks.

*__Animal Experimentation & Human Health.__ Al Frazza. 52p. 1994. pap. 2.95 (*1-886605-00-9*) People for Reason.

Animal Experimentation & the Future of Medical Research. Ed. by Jack Botting. (Proceedings Ser.: No. 3). 97p. 1993. pap. 30.00 (*1-85578-038-0*, Pub. by Portland Pr Ltd UK) Ashgate Pub Co.

Animal Expressions. Walter J. Wilwerding. (How to Draw & Paint Ser.). (Illus.). 32p. (Orig.). 1989. pap. 5.95 (*0-929261-80-1*, HT99) W Foster Pub.

Animal Extinctions: What Everyone Should Know. Ed. by R. J. Hoage. LC 85-8342. (National Zoological Park Symposia for the Public Ser.). (Illus.). 206p. (Orig.). 1985. pap. 13.95 (*0-87474-521-7*, HOAEP) Smithsonian.

Animal Fables. Ed. by Ogawa & Katayama. (Nihongo Folktales Ser.). (Illus.). 32p. (J). 1994. pap. 7.00 (*4-7700-1794-4*) Kodansha.

Animal Fables & Other Tales Retold: Africa in the New World. Enid F. D'yley. LC 87-73226. 40p. (Orig.). (J). (gr. 1-7). 1989. 12.95 (*0-86543-075-6*); pap. 5.95 (*0-86543-076-4*) Africa World.

Animal Fables from Aesop. Barbara McClintock. 1991. 18.95 (*0-87923-913-1*) Godine.

Animal Fables of India. Narayana. Tr. & Aft. by F. G. Hutchins. LC 85-71820. (Illus.). 269p. 1985. 26.00 (*0-935100-03-2*); pap. 12.00 (*0-935100-04-0*) Amarta Pr.

Animal Faces: Fifteen Punch-Out Masks. Pierre-Marie Valat. (Illus.). 32p. (J). (ps up). 1988. pap. 17.99 (*0-525-44440-8*, DCB) Dutton Child Bks.

Animal Fact: Animal Fable. Seymour Simon. LC 78-14866. (Illus.). (J). (gr. k-3). 1986. pap. 7.99 (*0-517-53794-X*) Crown Bks Yng Read.

Animal Fact - Animal Fable. Seymour Simon. LC 78-14866. (Illus.). 48p. (J). (gr. 1-5). 1992. lib. bdg. 12.99 (*0-517-58846-3*) Crown Bks Yng Read.

Animal Factories Update. Jim Mason. 1990. pap. 12.95 (*0-517-57751-8*, Harmony) Crown Pub Group.

Animal Facts. A. Ganeri. (Facts & Lists Ser.). (Illus.). 48p. (J). (gr. 3-7). 1988. lib. bdg. 12.96 (*0-88110-317-9*); pap. 5.95 (*0-86020-971-7*) EDC.

Animal Faith & Spiritual Life: Previously Unpublished & Uncollected Writings by George Santayana with Critical Essays on His Thought. Ed. by John Lachs. LC 67-20665. (Century Philosophy Ser.). 1967. 39.50 (*0-89197-607-8*) Irvington.

Animal Families, 12 vols. 48p. (J). (gr. 4 up). lib. bdg. 223.20 (*0-8368-1095-3*) Gareth Stevens Inc.

Animal Families. (Animal Board Bks.). (Illus.). 8p. (J). (ps). 1991. bds. 1.99 (*0-517-66919-6*) Random Hse Value.

*__Animal Families.__ (Animal Friends Ser.). 8p. (J). 1994. bds. 1.49 (*0-86112-516-9*) Brimax Bks.

*__Animal Families.__ (Sticker Puzzle Bks.). 16p. (J). 1995. 4.95 (*0-7894-0002-2*) Dorling Kindersley.

Animal Families. Ed. by Chicago Zoological Society Staff. (Brookfield Zoo Connections Ser.). (Orig.). (J). (gr. k-2). 1986. pap. text ed. 30.00 (*0-913934-04-6*) Chicago Zoo.

Animal Families. Jim Flegg. (Wild World Ser.). (Illus.). 32p. (J). (gr. 4-6). 1991. lib. bdg. 12.40 (*1-878137-20-4*) Newington.

Animal Families. Anita Ganeri. (Questions & Answers about Animals Ser.). (Illus.). 32p. (J). (ps-1). 1992. 6.95 (*0-8120-6274-4*) Barron.

Animal Families, 4 vols., Set. 74.40 (*0-8368-0844-4*) Gareth Stevens Inc.

Animal Families, 4 vols., Set. (Illus.). 32p. (J). (gr. 4-6). 1991. lib. bdg. 74.40 (*0-8368-0683-2*) Gareth Stevens Inc.

Animal Families, Set. Gene S. Stuart & National Geographic Society Staff. (Books for Young Explorers Ser.: Set 17, No. 2). (Illus.). (J). (gr. k-4). 1994. pap. 8.00 (*0-87044-819-6*) Natl Geog.

Animal Families of the Forest. Stacie Strong. (Illus.). 12p. (J). (gr. 1 up). 1993. 14.99 (*0-8431-3391-0*) Price Stern.

*__Animal Family.__ Randall Jarrell. LC 94-76270. (Illus.). 192p. (J). (gr. 3 up). 1995. 15.00 (*0-06-205088-5*); lib. bdg. 14.89 (*0-06-205089-3*); pap. 5.95 (*0-06-205904-1*, Trophy) HarpC Child Bks.

Animal Family. braille ed. Randall Jarrell. 93p. (J). 1992. vinyl bd. 7.44 (*1-56956-107-9*, BR7865) W A T Braille.

Animal Family: (Familia Animal) Randall Jarrell. (SPA.). (J). 6.95 (*84-204-4105-8*) Santillana.

Animal Family Calendar: An Educational Coloring Book. Spizzirri Publishing Co. Staff & Linda Spizzirri. (Illus.). 32p. (J). (gr. k-5). 1983. pap. 2.25 (*0-86545-048-X*) Spizzirri.

Animal Fare: Zoological Nonsense Poems. Jane Yolen. LC 92-44931. (Illus.). (J). (gr. 4 up). 1994. 14.95 (*0-15-203550-8*) HarBrace.

Animal Farm. George Orwell. LC 92-54299. 1993. 15.00 (*0-679-42039-8*, Everymans Lib) Knopf.

Animal Farm. George Orwell. 15.95 (*0-8488-0120-2*) Amereon Ltd.

Animal Farm. George Orwell. LC 54-11330. (Illus.). 160p. 1954. 12.95 (*0-15-107252-3*) HarBrace.

Animal Farm. George Orwell. 132p. 1990. 15.95 (*0-15-107255-8*) HarBrace.

Animal Farm. George Orwell. (Bridge Ser.). 122p. (YA). 1945. pap. text ed. 5.95 (*0-582-53008-3*) Longman.

Animal Farm. George Orwell. 1983. mass mkt. 6.95 (*0-452-26277-1*, Plume); mass mkt. 8.95 (*0-452-26490-1*, Plume) NAL-Dutton.

Animal Farm. George Orwell. 128p. (YA). (gr. 10). 1986. pap. 4.95 (*0-451-52466-7*, Sig Classics) NAL-Dutton.

*__Animal Farm.__ Scalia. (Max Notes Ser.). 96p. 1995. pap. text ed. 3.95 (*0-87891-988-0*) Res & Educ.

Animal Farm. large type ed. George Orwell. (Classics Ser.). 144p. 1984. 23.95 (*0-7089-8200-X*, Charnwood) Ulverscroft.

Animal Farm. George Orwell. 1982. reprint ed. lib. bdg. 21.95 (*0-89966-369-9*) Buccaneer Bks.

Animal Farm: A Study Guide. Lynne Manovrier. (Novel-Ties Ser.). (J). (gr. 6-10). 1983. student ed, teacher ed 15.95 (*0-88122-021-3*) Lrn Links.

Animal Farm: Pastoralism & Politics. Richard I. Smyer. (Masterwork Studies: No. 19). 176p. 1988. text ed. 21.95 (*0-8057-7980-9*, Twayne); pap. 12.95 (*0-8057-8030-0*, Twayne) Macmillan.

Animal Farm: The Next Generation. Adel Murad. LC 93-73346. x, 135p. 1994. 19.95 (*0-9638643-7-8*); pap. 7.00 (*0-9638643-9-4*) Child War Trust.

Animal Farm & Nineteen Eighty-Four. Jenni Calder. (Open Guides to Literature Ser.). 112p. 1987. 75.00 (*0-335-15266-X*, Open Univ Pr); pap. 22.00 (*0-335-15265-1*, Open Univ Pr) Taylor & Francis.

Animal Farm Notes. L. David Allen. 1981. pap. 3.95 (*0-8220-0174-8*) Cliffs.

Animal Farm (Orwell) Ball. (Book Notes Ser.). (C). 1984. pap. 2.95 (*0-8120-3402-3*) Barron.

Animal Fashions. Wendy Rotton & Nelson A. Ossorio. (Illus.). 48p. (J). (gr. 3-5). 1994. pap. 6.95 (*1-56721-069-4*) Twnty-Fifth Cent Pr.

Animal Fathers. Judy Cutchins & Ginny Johnston. LC 93-27014. (Illus.). 40p. (J). (gr. 2 up). 1994. 15.00 (*0-688-12255-8*) Morrow Jr Bks.

Animal Fathers. Photos by Ginny Johnston & Judy Atchins. LC 93-27014. (Illus.). 40p. (YA). (gr. 7 up). 1994. lib. bdg. 14.93 (*0-688-12256-6*) Morrow Jr Bks.

*__Animal Feed Additives.__ BCC Staff. 1995. 26.50 (*0-614-03448-5*, GA086) BCC.

Animal Feeding & Nutrition. 7th ed. Marshall H. Jurgens. 656p. 1993. 54.95 (*0-8403-8213-8*) Kendall-Hunt.

Animal Figures. Mike Schneider. LC 90-61511. (Illus.). 256p. (Orig.). 1990. pap. 29.95 (*0-88740-275-5*) Schiffer.

Animal Figures in the Maya Codices. Alfred M. Tozzer & G. M. Allen. 1910. 23.00 (*0-527-01203-3*) Periodicals Srv.

An Asterisk (*) at the beginning of an entry indicates that the title is appearing in BIP for the first time.

An Asterisk (*) at the beginning of an entry indicates that the title is appearing in BIP for the first time.

Animal Mania. YES! Entertainment Corporation Staff. (Where Is It? Ser.). 12p. (J). (ps-2). 1994. write for info. (*1-883366-52-6*) YES Ent.

Animal Manure on Grassland & Fodder Crops: Fertilizer or Waste? Ed. by H. G. Van der Meer et al. (Developments in Plant & Soil Sciences Ser.). (C). 1987. lib. bdg. 177.00 (*90-247-3568-8*) Kluwer Ac.

Animal Market. Joyce R. Wilkins & Edeltraud Hawkins. LC 93-25202. (J). 1993. 8.95 (*1-880373-06-8*) Pictorial Herit.

Animal Mas Grande del Mundo - The Biggest Animal Ever. Allan Fowler. LC 92-9410. (Rookie Read-about Science - Spanish Ser.). (Illus.). 32p. (SPA.). (J). (ps-2). 1993. 23.48 (*0-516-59628-4*); lib. bdg. 11.10 (*0-516-36001-9*); pap. 3.95 (*0-516-56001-8*) Childrens.

***Animal Math.** Ellen Keller. 72p. 1995. pap. text ed. 8.95 (*0-938587-81-1*) Cuisenaire.

Animal Mazes. Kim Blundell & Jenny Tyler. (Maze Puzzles Ser.). (Illus.). 24p. (J). (gr. k-2). 1993. pap. 3.95 (*0-7460-1323-X*, Usborne) EDC.

Animal Mazes. Dave Phillips. (Illus.). 48p. (J). 1991. pap. 2.95 (*0-486-26707-5*) Dover.

Animal Mechanics. R. McNeill Alexander. (Illus.). 312p. (C). 1983. text ed. 60.00 (*0-632-00956-X*) Blackwell Sci.

Animal Migration, Orientation & Navigation. Ed. by S. A. Gathreaux, Jr. 1981. text ed. 59.95 (*0-12-277750-6*) Acad Pr.

Animal Mind. James L. Gould & Carol G. Gould. LC 93-48197. 1995. text ed. 32.95 (*0-7167-5046-5*) W H Freeman.

Animal Minds. Donald R. Griffin. LC 92-6538. 320p. 1992. 24.95 (*0-226-30863-4*) U Ch Pr.

Animal Minds. Donald R. Griffin. LC 92-6538. x, 310p. (C). 1994. pap. 14.95 (*0-226-30864-2*) U Ch Pr.

Animal Minds & Human Morals: The Origins of the Western Debate. Richard Sorabji. LC 93-25811. (Cornell Studies in Classical Philology - The Townsend Lecture Ser.: No. 54). 1993. 39.95 (*0-8014-2948-X*) Cornell U Pr.

***Animal Minds & Human Morals: The Origins of the Western Debate.** Richard Sorabji. (Studies in Classical Philology - Townsend Lectures). 280p. 1995. pap. 15.95 (*0-8014-8298-4*) Cornell U Pr.

Animal Mobiles. Anne Wild. (Illus.). 32p. (Orig.). (J). (gr. 3-5). 1993. pap. 5.95 (*0-906212-11-1*, Pub. by Tarquin UK) Parkwest Pubns.

Animal Models: Assessing the Scope of Their Use in Biomedical Research, Proceedings of the Sixth Charles River International Symposium on Laboratory Animals, Held in Kyoto, Japan, October 8-9, 1985. Charles River International Symposium on Laboratory Animals Staff. Ed. by Junichi Kawamata & Edward C. Melby, Jr. LC 86-27718. (Progress in Clinical & Biological Research Ser.: No. 229). 400p. reprint ed. pap. 114.00 (*0-7837-2821-2*, 2057651) Bks Demand.

Animal Models & Hypoxia: Proceedings of an International Symposium on Animal Models & Hypoxia, Held at Weisbaden, FRG, 19 November 1979. V. Stefanovich. (Advances in Biosciences Ser.: Vol. 30). (Illus.). 138p. 1981. 54.00 (*0-08-025911-1*, Pub. by Pergamon Repr UK) Franklin.

Animal Models for Cystic Fibrosis: The Reserpine-Treated Rat. Ed. by J. R. Martinez & B. J. Barbero. (Illus.). 1985. 20.00 (*0-911302-54-9*) San Francisco Pr.

***Animal Models for Human Related Calcium Metabolic Disorders.** Asher Ornoy. 240p. 1995. 149.95 (*0-8493-6024-2*, 6024) CRC Pr.

Animal Models for Intestinal Disease. Ed. by Carl J. Pfeiffer. 320p. 1985. 191.00 (*0-8493-6215-6*, RC860, CRC Reprint) Franklin.

Animal Models for Psychiatry. J. D. Keehn. (Illus.). 237p. (C). 1986. 45.00 (*0-7102-0562-7*, 05627, RKP) Routledge.

Animal Models in AIDS: International TNO Meeting, Maastricht, The Netherlands, 23-26 Oct., 1989. Ed. by H. Schellekens & M. Horzinek. 400p. 1991. 138.25 (*0-444-81264-4*) Elsevier.

Animal Models in Biomedical Research: Poultry. 80p. (Orig.). (C). 1993. pap. text ed. 40.00 (*1-56806-924-3*) Diane Pub.

***Animal Models in Biomedical Research: Swine-A Bibliography.** Ed. by Cynthia P. Smith. 118p. (Orig.). (C). 1994. pap. text ed. 45.00x (*0-7881-1075-6*) Diane Pub.

Animal Models in Cardiovascular Research. David R. Gross. LC 93-50932. (Developments in Cardiovascular Medicine Ser.: Vol. 153). 560p. (C). 1994. lib. bdg. 169.00 (*0-7923-2712-8*) Kluwer Ac.

Animal Models in Chronic Renal Failure. Ed. by N. Gretz & M. Strauch. (Contributions to Nephrology Ser.: Vol. 60). (Illus.). viii, 268p. 1988. 191.25 (*3-8055-4619-X*) S Karger.

Animal Models in Dermatology, Relevance to Human Dermatopharmacology & Dermatotoxicology: Proceedings of a Symposium, University of California Medical School, San Francisco. Ed. by Howard I. Maibach. LC 75-16283. 288p. reprint ed. pap. 82.10 (*0-8357-5489-8*, 2056327) Bks Demand.

Animal Models in Fetal Medicine (I) Ed. by P. W. Nathanielsz. LC 80-17292. (Monographs in Fetal Physiology). (Illus.). 368p. 1985. reprint ed. 80.00 (*0-916859-14-2*) Perinatology.

Animal Models in Fetal Medicine (II) Ed. by P. W. Nathanielsz. (Monographs in Fetal Physiology). (Illus.). 339p. 1982. 80.00 (*0-444-80425-0*) Perinatology.

Animal Models in Fetal Medicine (III) Ed. by P. W. Nathanielsz. (Monographs in Fetal Physiology). (Illus.). 226p. 1984. 70.00 (*0-916859-00-2*) Perinatology.

Animal Models in Fetal Medicine (IV) Intrauterine Growth. Ed. by P. W. Nathanielsz. (Monographs in Fetal Physiology). (Illus.). 222p. 1984. 70.00 (*0-916859-01-0*) Perinatology.

Animal Models in Fetal Medicine (V) Parturition. Ed. by P. W. Nathanielsz. (Monographs in Fetal Physiology). (Illus.). 330p. 1986. 80.00 (*0-916859-09-6*) Perinatology.

Animal Models in Fetal Medicine (VI) Metabolism. Ed. by P. W. Nathanielsz. (Monographs in Fetal Physiology). 1987. 80.00 (*0-916859-15-0*) Perinatology.

Animal Models in Human Reproduction. Ed. by Mario Serio & Luciano Martini. 500p. 1980. text ed. 115.00 (*0-89004-522-4*) Raven.

Animal Models in Medical Mycology. Ed. by Miyaji. 1987. 99.00 (*0-8493-5844-2*, RC117, CRC Reprint) Franklin.

Animal Models in Psychiatry & Neurology. Israel Hanin & Earl Usdin. LC 77-30306. 1977. 212.00 (*0-08-021556-4*, Pub. by Pergamon Repr UK) Franklin.

Animal Models in Psychopharmacology. Ed. by B. Olivier et al. (Advances in Pharmacological Sciences Ser.). 476p. 1991. 112.00 (*0-8176-2503-8*) Spr-Verlag.

Animal Models in the Evaluation of Chemotherapeutic Agents Against HIV: Journal: Intervirology, Vol. 30, Suppl. 1. Ed. by H. D. Schlumberger & E. Schrinner. (Illus.). iv, 72p. 1989. pap. 21.75 (*3-8055-4982-2*) S Karger.

Animal Models in Toxicology. Ed. by Chengelis & Gad. (Drug & Chemical Toxicology Ser.: Vol. 8). 928p. 1992. 250.00 (*0-8247-8456-1*) Dekker.

Animal Models of Depression. George Koob et al. 304p. 1989. 74.50 (*0-8176-3407-X*) Birkhauser.

Animal Models of Drug Addiction. Ed. by Alan A. Boulton et al. LC 92-49180. (Neuromethods Ser.: Vol. 24). (Illus.). 460p. 1992. 99.50 (*0-89603-217-5*) Humana.

Animal Models of HIV & Other Retroviral Infections. Ed. by P. Racz et al. (Illus.). viii, 200p. 1993. 58.50 (*3-8055-5677-2*) S Karger.

Animal Models of Human Behavior: Conceptual, Evolutionary & Neurobiological Perspectives. Ed. by Graham C. Davey. 371p. 1983. text ed. 165.00 (*0-471-90038-9*) Wiley.

***Animal Models of Human Behavior: Conceptual, Evolutionary, & Neurobiological Perspectives.** fac. ed. Ed. by Graham C. Davey. LC 82-13714. (Illus.). 383p. Date not set. pap. 109.20 (*0-7837-7362-5*, 2047171) Bks Demand.

Animal Models of Human Pathology: A Bibliography of a Quarter Century of Behavioral Research, 1967-1992. Ed. by J. Bruce Overmier & Patricia D. Burke. 336p. 1992. pap. 27.50 (*1-55798-184-1*) Am Psychol.

Animal Models of Immunological Processes. Ed. by J. B. Hay. 1982. text ed. 139.00 (*0-12-333520-5*) Acad Pr.

***Animal Models of Mucosal Inflammation.** Timothy S. Gaginella. 160p. 1995. 125.00 (*0-8493-7816-8*, 7816) CRC Pr.

Animal Models of Neurological Disease, No. 1: Neurodegenerative Diseases. Ed. by Alan A. Boulton et al. LC 91-35401. (Neuromethods Ser.: Vol. 21). (Illus.). 388p. 1992. 94.50 (*0-89603-208-6*) Humana.

Animal Models of Neurological Disease, No. 2: Metabolic Encephalopathies & the Epilepsies. Ed. by Alan A. Boulton et al. LC 91-35401. (Neuromethods Ser.: Vol. 22). (Illus.). 380p. 1992. 94.50 (*0-89603-211-6*) Humana.

Animal Motivation. Patrick Colgan. (Chapman & Hall Animal Behavior Ser.). (Illus.). 160p. 1989. 55.00 (*0-412-31850-4*); pap. 19.95 (*0-412-31860-1*) Chapman & Hall.

Animal Movement. R. McNeill Alexander. Ed. by J. J. Head. LC 84-45834. (Carolina Biology Readers Ser.: No. 164). (Illus.). 16p. (Orig.). (YA). (gr. 10 up). 1985. pap. text ed. 2.75 (*0-89278-364-8*, 45-9764) Carolina Biological.

Animal Movement. Jill Bailey & Tony Seddon. (Nature Watch Ser.). (Illus.). 64p. (YA). 1988. 15.95 (*0-8160-1656-9*) Facts on File.

Animal Movement. Jim Flegg. (Wild World Ser.). (Illus.). 32p. (J). (gr. 4-6). 1991. lib. bdg. 12.40 (*1-878137-22-0*) Newington.

Animal Movements. Anita Ganeri. (Questions & Answers about Animals Ser.). (Illus.). 32p. (J). (ps-1). 1991. 6.95 (*0-8120-6238-8*) Barron.

Animal Mysteries. Lise Winer. Ed. by Jean McConochie. 96p. 1987. pap. text ed. write for info. (*0-13-037169-6*, 21042) Prentice ESL.

Animal Myths & Metaphors in South America. Ed. by Gary Urton. LC 84-26345. (Illus.). 288p. (Orig.). 1985. pap. 20.00 (*0-87480-205-9*) U of Utah Pr.

Animal Navigation. Talbot H. Waterman. LC 88-15811. (Scientific American Library). (Illus.). 256p. 1995. text ed. write for info. (*0-7167-5024-4*) W H Freeman.

Animal Navigators. Jeremy Cherfas. (How Animals Behave Ser.). (Illus.). 32p. (J). (gr. 4-6). 1991. lib. bdg. 15.95 (*0-8225-2250-0*, Lerner Publctns) Lerner Group.

Animal Numbers. Bert Kitchen. LC 87-5365. (Illus.). 24p. (J). (ps up). 1987. 12.95 (*0-8037-0459-3*) Dial Bks Young.

Animal Numbers. Bert Kitchen. LC 87-5365. (Illus.). 24p. (J). (gr. k up). 1991. pap. 4.95 (*0-8037-0910-2*, Puff Pied Piper) Puffin Bks.

Animal Numbers. Bert Kitchen. (J). 1993. pap. 5.99 (*0-14-054602-2*, Puff Pied Piper) Puffin Bks.

***Animal Nursery Rhymes.** (Nursery Rhymes Ser.). 12p. (J). Date not set. bds. 4.98 (*0-86112-958-X*) Brimax Bks.

***Animal Nursery Rhymes.** 7.99 (*0-517-12175-1*) Random Hse Value.

Animal Nursery Rhymes. Comp. by Angela Wilkes. LC 92-52818. (Illus.). 32p. (J). (ps-00). 1992. 13.95 (*1-56458-122-5*) Dorling Kindersley.

Animal Nutrition. J. W. Lassiter & Hardy M. Edwards. (C). 1982. teacher ed write for info. (*0-8359-0223-4*, Reston) P-H.

Animal Nutrition. 4th ed. P. McDonald et al. LC 86-28723. 543p. 1988. pap. text ed. 58.95 (*0-470-20791-4*) Halsted Pr.

***Animal Nutrition.** 5th ed. McDonald et al. Date not set. pap. text ed. 49.95 (*0-470-23488-1*) Wiley.

***Animal Nutrition.** 5th rev. ed. P. McDonald. LC 95-53. 1995. write for info. (*0-470-23988-3*) Wiley.

Animal Nutrition. 7th ed. Leonard A. Maynard et al. (Illus.). 1979. text ed. write for info. (*0-07-041049-6*) McGraw.

Animal Nutrition: In Partial Collaboration with David Drori. Aron A. Bondi. LC 85-26376. 568p. reprint ed. pap. 161.90 (*0-8357-6935-6*, 2037994) Bks Demand.

Animal Nutrition & Feeding. James R. Gillespie. LC 86-8982. 576p. (C). 1986. teacher ed 12.00 (*0-8273-2355-7*); text ed. 36.50 (*0-8273-2354-9*) Delmar.

Animal Nutrition & Feeding Practices. 4th ed. S. K. Ranjhan. Date not set. 40.00 (*0-7069-7101-9*, Pub. by Vikas II) S Asia.

Animal Nutrition & Transport Processes, Set, Vol. 5 & 6. (Comparartive Physiology Ser.: Vol. 5-6). (Illus.). xvi, 478p. 1990. 309.00 (*3-8055-5170-3*) S Karger.

Animal Nutrition & Transport Processes, No. 1: Nutrition in Wild & Domestic Animals. Ed. by J. Mellinger. (Comparative Physiology Ser.: Vol. 5). viii, 288p. 1990. 204.00 (*3-8055-5157-6*) S Karger.

Animal Nutrition & Transport Processes, No. 2: Transport, Respiration & Excretion: Comparative & Environmental Aspects. Ed. by J. Truchot & B. Lahlou. (Comparative Physiology Ser.: Vol. 6). viii, 188p. 1990. 139.25 (*3-8055-5158-4*) S Karger.

Animal Nutrition in Tropics. S. K. Ranjhan. 446p. 1980. 19.95 (*0-7069-1005-2*) Asia Bk Corp.

Animal Observations. Ray Broekel. LC 89-25363. (New True Bks.). (Illus.). 48p. (J). (gr. k-4). 1990. lib. bdg. 13.50 (*0-516-01182-0*) Childrens.

Animal Olympians. Thane Maynard. LC 93-30769. (Cincinnati Zoo Ser.). (Illus.). (J). (gr. 5-7). 1994. lib. bdg. 15.47 (*0-531-11159-8*); pap. 9.95 (*0-531-15715-6*) Watts.

Animal Opposites. Vanessa Bailey. (Animal Concept Ser.). (J). (ps). 1991. 5.95 (*0-8120-6244-2*) Barron.

Animal Origami for the Enthusiast: Step-by-Step Instructions in over 900 Diagrams. John Montroll. 1985. pap. 6.95 (*0-486-24792-9*) Dover.

Animal Origion Drugs Used in Unani Medicine. S. B. Vohra. 137p. 1979. 19.95 (*0-7069-0768-X*) Asia Bk Corp.

Animal Pain: Perception & Alleviation. Ed. by Ralph L. Kitchell & Howard H. Erickson. (Animal Welfare Ser.). (Illus.). 231p. 1988. 39.95 (*0-19-520695-9*) OUP.

Animal Painting & Anatomy. W. Frank Calderon. LC 72-75583. (Illus.). 352p. 1975. reprint ed. pap. 7.95 (*0-486-22523-2*) Dover.

Animal Parade. Dick King-Smith. LC 91-30332. (Illus.). 96p. (J). (gr. 1-8). 1992. 16.00 (*0-688-11375-3*, Tambourine Bks) Morrow.

Animal Parade. Jakki Wood. LC 92-22826. (Illus.). 32p. (J). (ps-k). 1993. text ed. 14.95 (*0-02-793394-6*, Bradbury S&S) S&S Childrens.

Animal Parasite Control Utilizing Biotechnology. Yong. 1992. 196.00 (*0-8493-6843-X*, QH547) CRC Pr.

Animal Parasites: Their Life Cycles & Ecology. O. Wilford Olsen. xii, 564p. 1986. reprint ed. pap. text ed. 19.95 (*0-486-65126-6*) Dover.

Animal Parenting. Jill Bailey & Tony Seddon. (Nature Watch Ser.). (Illus.). 64p. (YA). 1989. 15.95 (*0-8160-1654-2*) Facts on File.

Animal Parents. Jeremy Cherfas. (How Animals Behave Ser.). (Illus.). 32p. (J). (gr. 4-6). 1991. lib. bdg. 15.95 (*0-8225-2251-9*, Lerner Publctns) Lerner Group.

Animal Patents. W. Lesser. 380p. 1990. 100.00 (*0-935859-63-2*, Stockton Pr) Groves Dictionaries.

***Animal Patterns.** (Mix & Match Pattern Ser.). (Illus.). 240p. (J). 1995. teacher ed 16.95 (*0-614-06828-2*, WPH 1301) Totline Bks.

Animal Patterns. Jean Warren. Ed. by Gayle Bittinger. (Mix & Match Ser.). (Illus.). 240p. (Orig.). (J). (ps-1). 1990. pap. text ed. 16.95 (*0-911019-31-6*) Warren Pub Hse.

Animal Pests & How to Get the Upper Hand on 'Em. S. Meyer. (Illus.). 175p. 1993. pap. 9.95 (*1-878488-91-0*) Quixote Pr IA.

Animal Physiology. 2nd ed. Richard Hill & Gordon Wyse. 736p. (C). 1989. text ed. 70.50 (*0-06-042826-0*) HarpCollege.

Animal Physiology: Adaptation & Environment. 4th ed. Knut Schmidt-Nielsen. (Illus.). 620p. (C). 1990. 44.95 (*0-521-38196-7*) Cambridge U Pr.

Animal Physiology: Adaptations in Function. F. Reed Hainsworth. (Life Sciences Ser.). (Illus.). 600p. 1981. text ed. write for info. (*0-201-03401-8*) Addison-Wesley.

Animal Physiology: Index of New Information with Authors, Subjects & Bibliography. rev. ed. O. O. Ottoson. 1994. 49.50 (*0-7883-0166-7*); pap. 45.50 (*0-7883-0167-5*) ABBE Pubs Assn.

Animal Physiology: Mechanisms & Adaptations. 3rd ed. Roger Eckert et al. 816p. (C). 1995. text ed. 50.95 (*0-7167-1828-6*) W H Freeman.

Animal Picture-English. Zeff. (Picture Word Bks.). (Illus.). (J). (gr. 1-9). 1980. English ed. pap. 8.95 (*0-7460-0395-1*, Usborne) EDC.

Animal Piggyback Songs. Ed. by Gayle Bittinger. LC 89-51957. (Piggyback Song Ser.). (Illus.). 96p. (Orig.). 1990. pap. text ed. 8.95 (*0-911019-29-4*) Warren Pub Hse.

***Animal Piggyback Songs.** Illus. by Marion H. Ekberg. (Piggyback Songs Ser.). 96p. (J). 1995. 8.95 (*0-614-06875-4*, WPH 0207) Totline Bks.

***Animal Place: Where Magical Things Happen.** Kim Sturla. 48p. (J). (gr. 1-2). 1994. pap. 8.95 (*0-9644062-0-9*) Animal Place.

Animal Plant & Microbial Toxins. Ed. by Y. Sawai. 1975. pap. 19.75 (*0-08-019965-8*, Pergamon Pr) Elsevier.

Animal Play Behavior. Robert M. Fagen. (Illus.). (C). 1981. text ed. 39.95 (*0-19-502760-4*); pap. text ed. 22.50 (*0-19-502761-2*) OUP.

Animal Playmates. Ernest Nister. (Illus.). 10p. (J). 1990. 5.95 (*0-399-21957-9*, Philomel Bks) Putnam Pub Group.

***Animal Poems.** (Jarrold Poets Ser.). 146p. 1994. pap. 5.95 (*0-7117-0676-X*) Seven Hills Bk.

Animal Poems. Comp. by H. Amery. (Poetry Bks.). (Illus.). 32p. (J). (gr. 2-6). 1990. pap. 5.95 (*0-7460-0442-7*, Usborne) EDC.

Animal Poems. John Hollander. 1994. 10.95 (*0-679-43631-6*, Everymans Lib) Knopf.

Animal Poems. Polly Richardson. (J). (ps-3). 1992. 12.95 (*0-8120-6283-3*) Barron.

Animal Power in Farming Systems: West Animal Traction Networkshop Held Freetown, September 19-25, 1986: Proceedings. Ed. by Paul Starkey et al. (GATE Ser.). (Illus.). 363p. 1988. pap. 34.00 (*3-528-02047-4*, Pub. by Vieweg & Sohn GW) Ballen Bkslr.

***Animal Powered Machines.** J. Kenneth Major. (C). 1989. pap. 25.00x (*0-85263-710-1*, Pub. by Shire UK) St Mut.

Animal Powered Systems: An Alternative Approach to Agricultural Mechanization. Peter Lowe. (GATE Ser.). (Illus.). 60p. 1986. pap. 12.00 (*3-528-02023-7*, Pub. by Vieweg & Sohn GW) Ballen Bkslr.

***Animal Pride Series, 20 vols.** Dave Sargent & Pat Sargent. (Illus.). (J). (gr. 1-5). 1992. boxed, lib. bdg. 199.95 (*1-56763-157-6*); pap. 99.95 (*1-56763-158-4*) Ozark Pub.

***Animal Pride Series, 10 vols.** Dave Sargent & Pat Sargent. Set 1. (Illus.). (J). (gr. 1-5). 1992. boxed, lib. bdg. 107.55 (*1-56763-153-3*) Ozark Pub.

***Animal Pride Series, 10 vols.** Dave Sargent & Pat Sargent. Set 2. (Illus.). (J). (gr. 1-5). 1992. boxed, lib. bdg. 107.55 (*1-56763-155-X*) Ozark Pub.

***Animal Pride Series Set 1, 10 vols.** Dave Sargent & Pat Sargent. (Illus.). (J). (gr. 1-5). 1992. pap. 53.55 (*1-56763-154-1*) Ozark Pub.

***Animal Pride Series Set 2, 10 vols.** Dave Sargent & Pat Sargent. (Illus.). (J). (gr. 1-5). 1992. pap. 53.55 (*1-56763-156-8*) Ozark Pub.

Animal Production & Environmental Health. Ed. by F. J. Smulders. 338p. 1987. 161.75 (*0-444-42731-7*) Elsevier.

Animal Production & Management. R. K. Barrick & H. Harmon. 416p. 1988. text ed. 19.96 (*0-07-003852-X*) McGraw.

Animal Production in Australia: Proceedings of the Australian Society of Animal Production, 14th Biennial Conference, Brisbane, Queensland, May 1982. Australian Society of Animal Production Staff. (Illus.). 708p. 1982. pap. 40.00 (*0-08-024837-3*, Pergamon Pr) Elsevier.

Animal Production in Australia: Proceedings of the Australian Society of Animal Production, 14th Biennial Conference, Brisbane, Queensland, May 1982. Australian Society of Animal Production Staff. (Illus.). 708p. 1982. 72.00 (*0-08-024836-5*, Pergamon Pr) Elsevier.

Animal Production in Australia: Proceedings of the Australian Society of Animal Production, 14th Biennial Conference, Brisbane, Queensland, May 1982. Australian Society of Animal Production Staff. 521p. 1988. pap. 40.00 (*0-08-034439-9*, PPA) Elsevier.

Animal Production in Australia: Proceedings of the Australian Society of Animal Production, 15th Biennial Conference, Armidale, New South Wales February 1984. 804p. 1985. pap. 60.00 (*0-08-029853-2*) Elsevier.

Animal Production Quarterly Statistics 1-1991. European Communities Staff. 116p. 1991. pap. 25.00 (*0-685-49254-0*, CA-BF-91-001-3A-C) UNIPUB.

Animal Productivity. H. C. Srivastava et al. (C). 1988. 48.00 (*81-204-0381-9*, Pub. by Oxford IBH II) S Asia.

***Animal Puppet Plays.** Elaine Cole & David Cole. 32p. (Orig.). (J). (gr. 1-6). 1994. pap. 4.50 (*1-883426-17-0*) Chldrns Outrch.

***Animal Puppets.** Joy Evans et al. (Illus.). 48p. (J). (gr. 1-6). 1989. teacher ed, pap. 5.95 (*1-55799-136-7*, EMC 227) Evan-Moor Corp.

***Animal Puppets on Stage, Bk. 1.** Elaine Cole & David Cole. 16p. (Orig.). (J). (gr. 1-6). 1994. pap. 9.95 (*1-883426-15-4*) Chldrns Outrch.

***Animal Puppets on Stage, Bk. 2.** Elaine Cole & David Cole. 16p. (Orig.). (J). (gr. 1-6). 1994. pap. 9.95 (*1-883426-16-2*) Chldrns Outrch.

Animal Quality & Models in Biomedical Research: 7th Symposium of the Internt'l Council for Laboratory Animal Science, Utrecht 1979. Ed. by A. Spiegel et al. (Illus.). 397p. 1980. pap. 92.00 (*3-437-30316-3*, Pub. by G Fischer Verlag GW) Lubrecht & Cramer.

***Animal Quarantine in Asia & the Pacific.** Animal Production Organization Staff. 309p. 1994. pap. 15.00 (*92-833-2145-6*, APO321456, Pub. by Asian Prod Organ) UNIPUB.

Animal Quizbook. M. Claridge & P. Downswell. (Quizbooks Ser.). (Illus.). 32p. (J). (gr. 4 up). 1993. lib. bdg. 13.96 (*0-88110-536-8*, Usborne); pap. 6.95 (*0-7460-0720-5*, Usborne) EDC.

Animal Rap! Robert Crowther. LC 92-54586. (Illus.). 10p. (J). (ps). 1993. 9.95 (*1-56402-207-2*) Candlewick Pr.

Animal Records. Anita Ganeri. (Questions & Answers about Animals Ser.). (Illus.). 32p. (J). (ps-1). 1992. 6.95 (*0-8120-6300-7*) Barron.

Animal Reintroductions: The Arabian Oryx in Oman. Mark R. Price. (Cambridge Studies in Applied Ecology & Resource Management). (Illus.). 250p. (C). 1989. 42.95 (*0-521-34411-5*) Cambridge U Pr.

Animal Remains in Archaeology. Rosemary M. Luff. 1989. pap. 25.00 (*0-85263-633-4*, Pub. by Shire UK) St Mut.

An Asterisk (*) at the beginning of an entry indicates that the title is appearing in BIP for the first time.

An Asterisk (*) at the beginning of an entry indicates that the title is appearing in BIP for the first time.

325

A

Animal Vision. Jill Bailey & Tony Seddon. (Nature Watch Ser.). (Illus.). 64p. (YA). 1988. 15.95 (0-8160-1652-6) Facts on File.

Animal Warden. Jack Rudman. (Career Examination Ser.: C-1844). 1994. pap. 23.95 (0-8373-1844-0) Nat Learn.

Animal Wastes. Ed. by E. P. Taiganides. (Illus.). 429p. 1977. 117.00 (0-85334-721-2, Pub. by Elsevier Applied Sci UK) Elsevier.

*Animal Watching. Desmond Morris. 1992. pap. 17.99 (0-517-08338-8) Random.

Animal Way to Love. Sena J. Naslund. LC 92-75262. 1993. pap. 12.00 (0-935331-14-X) Ampersand RI.

Animal Welfare. Julie Catalano. LC 93-26841. (Earth at Risk Ser.). (J). 1994. write for info. (0-7910-1591-2); pap. write for info. (0-7910-1616-1) Chelsea Hse.

Animal Welfare: Index of Modern Information. Michael R. Freeman. LC 88-47539. 150p. 1990. 39.50 (0-88164-826-4); pap. 34.50 (1-55914-187-5) ABBE Pubs Assn.

Animal Welfare & Human Values. Rod Preece & Lorna Chamberlain. 280p. (C). 1993. text ed. 45.00 (0-88920-227-3, Pub. by Wilfrid Laurier CN) Humanities.

*Animal Welfare & Human Values. Rod Preece & Lorna Chamberlain. 334p. 1995. pap. 19.95 (0-88920-256-7, Pub. by Wilfrid Laurier CN) Humanities.

Animal Wife. Elizabeth M. Thomas. 336p. 1991. reprint ed. mass mkt. 5.99 (0-671-73323-0, Pocket Star Bks) PB.

*Animal Wisecracks. YES! Entertainment Corporation Staff. (Interactive Books - Listen to This Ser.). 12p. (J). (ps-2). 1994. write for info. (1-57234-041-X) YES Ent.

Animal Wonders. (Zoobooks Ser.). (J). 1991. lib. bdg. 14.95 (0-88682-407-9) Creative Ed.

Animal Wonders. Wildlife Education, Ltd. Staff. (Zoobooks Ser.). (Illus.). 20p. (Orig.). 1983. pap. 2.75 (0-937934-12-7) Wildlife Educ.

Animal Wonders. Wildlife Education, Ltd. Staff. (Zoobooks Ser.). (Illus.). 20p. (Orig.). (J). 1992. 13.95 (0-937934-74-7) Wildlife Educ.

Animal Wonders, 6 vols., Set. 111.60 (0-8368-0853-3) Gareth Stevens Inc.

Animal Word Puzzles Coloring Book. Nina Barbaresi. (Illus.). (J). (gr. k-3). 1991. pap. 2.50 (0-486-26848-9) Dover.

Animal World. Ingrid Cranfield. (Young Readers' Nature Library). (Illus.). 64p. (J). (gr. 4-6). 1991. lib. bdg. 15.40 (1-56294-008-2) Millbrook Pr.

*Animal World. Cecilia Fitzsimons. LC 95-5999. (Hidden World Ser.). (Illus.). (J). 1996. write for info. (0-8172-3969-3) Raintree Steck-V.

Animal World. Goaman. (Mysteries & Marvels Ser.). (Illus.). 32p. (J). (gr. 6-p). 1984. 13.96 (0-88110-168-0); lib. bdg. 5.95 (0-86020-751-X) EDC.

Animal World: From Single-Cell Creatures to Giants of the Land & Sea. Donald M. Silver. LC 86-3894. (Library of Knowledge). (Illus.). 112p. (J). (gr. 5 up). 1987. lib. bdg. 9.99 (0-394-96650-3) Random Bks Yng Read.

Animal Worlds. Bobbie Kalman. (In My World Ser.). (Illus.). 32p. (J). (gr. 2-3). 1986. 15.95 (0-86505-071-6); pap. 6.95 (0-86505-093-7) Crabtree Pub Co.

Animaland Cookbook, Vol. 2. Animaland Staff. LC 93-71222. 1993. write for info. (0-87197-372-3) Favorite Recipes.

Animalcular & Cryptogamic Theories on the Origins of Fevers: An Original Anthology. Ed. by Barbara G. Rosenkrantz. LC 76-40658. (Public Health in America Ser.). 1977. reprint ed. 23.95 (0-405-09839-1) Ayer.

Animales - Animals. Ed. by Maria Puncel. Tr. by Maria Del Carmen Blazquez. (Diccionarios Visuales Altea Ser. - Visual Dictionary Ser.). (Illus.). 64p. (SPA.). (YA). (gr. 5-12). 1992. write for info. (84-372-4525-7) Santillana.

Animales - Animals: Spanish-English Activity Workbook. Micha Archer & Esha Baupus. 48p. 1992. write for info. (0-318-71690-9) Amherst Educ.

Animales Bebes: Spanish Take-Home Parent Pack, Set. (Take-Home Parent Packs Ser.). (Illus.). (Orig.). (SPA.). 1993. pap. 11.95 (1-56334-385-1) Hampton-Brown.

Animales Bebes: Teacher's Theme Guide. (Que Maravilla! Ser.). (Illus.). (Orig.). (SPA.). 1992. pap. 29.95 (1-56334-159-X) Hampton-Brown.

Animales Del Arca. Patricia Shely. Tr. by Nola Cranberry. (Libros Para Colorear Ser.). (Illus.). 16p. (SPA.). (J). (gr. 1-3). 1987. pap. 1.99 (0-311-38561-3) Casa Bautista.

Animales del Parque. Arcadia Lopez. (Illus.). (J). (gr. k-2). 1973. pap. 2.00 (0-913632-06-6) All Things Pr.

Animales Domesticos: Como Seleccionarlos y Como Cuidarlos. Editorial America, S. A. Staff. Ed. by Maria E. Del Real. (Illus.). 352p. (Orig.). (SPA.). 1990. pap. write for info. (0-944499-89-9) Editorial Amer.

Animales en el Folklore y la Magia de Cuba. Lydia Cabrera. LC 86-83333. (Coleccion del Chichereku). 213p. (Orig.). (SPA.). 1988. pap. 16.00 (0-89729-434-3) Ediciones.

*Animales No Se Visten. Judi Barrett. (Illus.). (SPA.). (J). (gr. k-3). 1991. audio, pap. 14.95 (0-87499-227-3) Live Oak Media.

*Animales No Se Visten, 4 bks., Set. Judi Barrett. (Illus.). (J). (gr. k-3). 1991. audio, pap. 36.95 (0-87499-229-X) Live Oak Media.

Animales Polares. Norman S. Barrett. LC 90-70882. (Picture Library). (Illus.). 32p. (SPA.). (J). (gr. k-4). 1990. lib. bdg. 12.60 (0-531-07900-7) Watts.

Animales Que Dios Creo. Guillermo Woggon. Tr. by Nola Cranberry. (Libros Para Colorear Ser.). (Illus.). 16p. (SPA.). (J). (gr. 1-3). 1987. reprint ed. pap. 1.99 (0-311-38560-5) Casa Bautista.

Animales y Sus Crias. Lada J. Kratky. (Que Maravilla! Ser.). (Illus.). 24p. (Orig.). (SPA.). (J). (gr. 1-3). 1991. pap. text ed. 29.95 (1-56334-020-8); pap. text ed. 6.00 (1-56334-034-8) Hampton-Brown.

Animalia. Graeme Base. (Illus.). 32p. (J). (ps up). 1987. 17.95 (0-8109-1868-4) Abrams.

Animalia. Graeme Base. (Illus.). 32p. (J). 1993. 11.95 (0-8109-1939-7) Abrams.

Animalia. Barbara Berger. LC 82-9521. (Illus.). 64p. 1987. pap. 12.95 (0-89087-508-1) Celestial Arts.

Animalia Wall Frieze. Graeme Base. (Illus.). 26p. 1991. pap. 24.95 (0-8109-2475-7) Abrams.

Animalimericks. Raymond Driver. (J). 1994. pap. 5.95 (0-671-87232-X, Half Moon Paper) S&S Childrens.

Animalitos Amistosos (Furry Friends) Scandinavia. (SPA.). Date not set. 4.50 (0-685-74902-9, 491397) Editorial Unilit.

*Animalogies: A Fine Kettle of Fish & 150 Other Animal Expressions. Michael Macrone. LC 95-6739. (Illus.). 1995. write for info. (0-385-47587-X) Doubleday.

AnimAlphabet Encyclopedia. Keith McConnell. (NaturEncyclopedia Library). (Illus.). 48p. (J). (gr. 4 up). 1982. pap. 5.95 (0-916144-97-6) Stemmer Hse.

Animals. (Blank Bks.). 32p. (J). 1986. 2.95 (0-88682-115-0, 95166-098) Creative Ed.

Animals. LC 91-60901. (Eyewitness Visual Dictionaries Ser.). (Illus.). 64p. (J). (gr. 6 up). 1991. 14.95 (1-879431-19-X); lib. bdg. 15.99 (1-879431-34-3) Dorling Kindersley.

Animals. (Talkabouts Ser.: No. 735-1). (Illus.). (J). (ps). 3.50 (0-7214-1096-0) Ladybird Bks.

Animals. (World Wildlife Ser.: No. S864-4). (Illus.). (J). (gr. k-3). 1989. 3.95 (0-7214-5215-9) Ladybird Bks.

Animals. (Ladybird Learners Ser.: No. 8911-4). (J). (gr. 1-4). 1991. pap. 3.95 (0-7214-5323-6) Ladybird Bks.

Animals. (Huggable Book Ser.). (Illus.). 5p. (J). (ps). 1991. 3.95 (0-681-41091-4) Longmeadow Pr.

Animals. (Little Book of Questions & Answers Ser.). (Illus.). 32p. (J). 1993. 4.98 (1-56173-470-5); 8.98 (1-56173-316-4) Pubns Intl Ltd.

Animals. (Classic Natural History Prints Ser.). (Illus.). 128p. 1990. 9.99 (0-517-02731-3) Random Hse Value.

Animals. 1990. pap. 1.95 (0-8167-1642-0) Troll Assocs.

*Animals. (Learners Ser.). 48p. (J). Date not set. 3.50 (0-7214-1705-1) Ladybird Bks.

Animals. R. McNeill Alexander. (Illus.). 500p. (C). 1990. pap. 42.95 (0-521-34865-X) Cambridge U Pr.

Animals. Roma Bishop. (Nursery Board Mini Pop Bks.). (Illus.). 14p. (J). (ps-00). 1991. ring bd. 2.95 (0-671-74833-5, Litl Simon S&S) S&S Childrens.

Animals. David A. Burnie. LC 92-15434. (Picture Pockets Ser.). (J). 1993. pap. 13.00 (0-671-79130-3, S&S Bks Young Read); pap. 8.00 (0-671-79135-4, S&S Bks Young Read) S&S Childrens.

Animals. (Feelings & Growth Development Coloring Bks.). (Illus.). (J). (ps). 1986. pap. 0.75 (0-8091-6542-2) Paulist Pr.

Animals. Christopher Carrie. (Crayola Kinder Art BKs.). (Illus.). 12p. (Orig.). (J). (gr. 3-6). 1987. pap. 4.70 (0-86696-201-8) Binney & Smith.

*Animals. Brad Caudle & Richard Caudle. (Illus.). (J). 1995. audio, pap. 9.95 (1-878489-49-6) Rock & Learn Educ Prod.

Animals. Lorraine Conway. 64p. (J). (gr. 5 up). 1980. 7.95 (0-916456-68-4, GA 177) Good Apple.

*Animals. Zoe Davenport. LC 94-20821. (Words for Everyday Ser.). (Illus.). 16p. (J). 1995. 5.95 (0-395-71537-7) Ticknor & Flds Bks Yng Read.

Animals. Kay Davis & Wendy Oldsfield. LC 91-23413. (Starting Science Ser.). (Illus.). 32p. (J). (gr. 2-5). 1991. lib. bdg. 19.97 (0-8114-3002-2); pap. 4.95 (0-8114-1528-7) Raintree Steck-V.

Animals. Derrydale. (Stencil Playbooks Ser.). (J). 1989. 2.49 (0-517-67588-9) Random Hse Value.

Animals. Michael Evans. (Little Surprises Ser.). (Illus.). 24p. (J). (ps). 1992. bds. 2.95 (0-8249-8525-7, Ideals Child) Hambleton-Hill.

Animals. Walter Foster. (How to Draw & Paint Ser.). (Illus.). 32p. (Orig.). 1989. pap. 5.95 (0-929261-73-9, HT12) W Foster Pub.

Animals. Carla Grillis. (Illus.). (J). (ps). 1988. bds. 5.50 (0-86315-072-1, 20232) Gryphon Hse.

Animals. Richard Grossman. 500p. (C). 1990. pap. 15.00 (1-55597-142-3) Graywolf.

*Animals. Sally Hewitt. (Now I Know Ser.). (Illus.). 48p. (J). (gr. 3-6). 1995. 15.95 (1-56847-265-X) Thomson Lrning.

Animals. Eric Hill. (Spot Cloth Ser.). (Illus.). 8p. (J). (ps). 1993. 4.95 (0-399-22524-2, Putnam) Putnam Pub Group.

Animals. Ellen V. Mahoney. (Ringtales Ser.). (Illus.). 8p. (J). (ps). 1994. vinyl bd. 3.95 (0-8431-3545-X) Price Stern.

Animals. Deborah Manley. (It's Fun Finding out about Ser.). 48p. 1990. 4.99 (0-517-69617-7) Random Hse Value.

Animals. Burton Marks. LC 91-3656. (Read-a-Picture Ser.). (Illus.). 24p. (J). (gr. k-2). 1992. lib. bdg. 9.89 (0-8167-2415-6); pap. text ed. 2.95 (0-8167-2416-4) Troll Assocs.

Animals. Alice Mattison. LC 79-54884. 72p. 1979. pap. 9.95 (0-914086-29-4) Alicejamesbooks.

Animals. Christopher McHugh. LC 93-43265. (Discovering Art Ser.). (Illus.). 32p. (J). (gr. 4-6). 1993. 14.95 (1-56847-025-8) Thomson Lrning.

Animals. Illus. by Lyn Mitchell. (Baby Bumper Bks.). 10p. (J). (ps). 1992. 4.95 (0-448-40304-8, G&D) Putnam Pub Group.

Animals. Ting Morris & Neil Morris. LC 93-20415. (Sticky Fingers Ser.). (Illus.). 32p. (J). (gr. 2-4). 1993. lib. bdg. 13.23 (0-531-14268-X) Watts.

Animals. Kaye Quinn. (Science Crossword Puzzles Ser.). (Illus.). 48p. (Orig.). (J). (gr. 2-6). 1990. pap. 2.95 (0-8431-2293-5) Price Stern.

Animals. Raintree Publishers Staff. LC 87-28712. (Science & Its Secrets Ser.). (Illus.). 64p. (Orig.). (J). (gr. 5-9). 1988. lib. bdg. 11.95 (0-8172-3083-1) Raintree Steck-V.

*Animals. Illus. by Tony Ross. LC 94-49432. (First Discovery Art Bk.). (ENG & FRE.). (J). 1995. write for info. (0-590-55202-3, Cartwheel) Scholastic Inc.

*Animals. Ernest T. Seton. (Illus.). 295p. 1995. pap. 17.95 (1-885529-07-4) Stevens Pub.

*Animals. Sterling Staff. (Bip Quiz Ser.). (J). (gr. 4-7). 1995. pap. 2.95 (0-8069-0933-1) Sterling.

Animals. rev. ed. Marlene J. McCracken & Robert A. McCracken. (Themes Ser.). (Illus.). 83p. (J). (gr. k-4). 1985. pap. 11.95 (0-920541-12-7) Peguis Pubs Ltd.

Animals, Set. (Children's Encyclopedia Ser.: Vol. 2). (Illus.). 96p. (J). (gr. 3-8). 1987. lib. bdg. 240.00 (0-685-18918-X) Raintree Steck-V.

Animals: A Thematic Unit. Janet Hale. (Thematic Units Ser.). (Illus.). 80p. (ps-1). 1990. student ed 8.95 (1-55734-250-4) Tchr Create Mat.

Animals: An Integrated Unit. Kathy Rogers. (Primary Thematic Units Ser.). (Illus.). 96p. (Orig.). 1993. pap. 12.95 (0-944459-75-7) ECS Lrn Systs.

Animals: How They Work. David Burnie. LC 93-43404. (Illus.). 48p. (J). 1994. 14.95 (0-8069-0742-8) Sterling.

Animals: How to Draw Them. Hugh Laidman. LC 75-11930. (Illus.). 160p. (YA). (gr. 7 up). 1979. pap. 12.95 (0-685-46950-6, Dutton) NAL-Dutton.

Animals: Illustrations of Mammals, Birds, Fish, Insects, Etc. A Pictorial Archive from Nineteenth-Century Sources. Ed. by Jim Harter. LC 78-73302. (Pictorial Archive Ser.). (Illus.). 1979. pap. 9.95 (0-486-23766-4) Dover.

Animals: Males, Females & Babies. Fred Justus. (Early Education Ser.). 24p. (ps-1). 1981. student ed 5.00 (0-8209-0226-8, K-28) ESP.

Animals: Origin & Evolution. Cristiano Dal Sasso. Tr. by Rocco Serini. LC 94-2541. (Beginnings Ser.). (Illus.). 48p. (J). (gr. 6-8). 1994. lib. bdg. 22.80 (0-8114-3333-1) Raintree Steck-V.

Animals: Selected Poems. Michio Mado. Tr. by HRM the Empress of Japan. LC 92-10356. (Illus.). 48p. (ENG & JPN.). (J). (ps up). 1992. text ed. 16.95 (0-689-50574-4, McElderry) S&S Childrens.

Animals: Sixty Things I Can Draw. Kay Quinn. (J). 1990. 4.99 (0-517-03564-2) Random Hse Value.

Animals: Stories for under Fives. Joan Stimson. (Series 922). (Illus.). 44p. (J). (ps-00). 1992. 3.50 (0-7214-1484-2) Ladybird Bks.

Animals: Through the Eyes of Artists. Wendy Richardson & Jack Richardson. LC 90-34276. (Artists of the World Ser.). (Illus.). 48p. (J). (gr. 4 up). 1991. pap. 7.95 (0-516-49281-0) Childrens.

Animals: Unique Moments. Miriam Austerman. LC 77-11699. 1977. lib. bdg. 10.00 (0-916004-06-6); pap. 4.95 (0-916004-05-8) Theorex.

Animals' ABC's. (Pop-Up Bks.). (Illus.). (J). (ps-3). 1988. 9.95 (0-8167-1443-6) Troll Assocs.

Animals' Advent. Illus. by Lisa McCue. (Lift-&-Peek-a-Board Bks.). 14p. (J). (ps-00). 1994. bds. 4.50 (0-679-86015-0) Random Bks Yng Read.

Animals, Aging, & the Aged. Leo K. Bustad. LC 80-24415. (Wesley W. Spink Lectures on Comparative Medicine: No. 5). 245p. reprint ed. pap. 69.90 (0-8357-2589-8, 2052369) Bks Demand.

Animals Alive! An Ecological Guide to Animal Activities. Dennis Holley. (Illus.). 300p. (YA). (gr. 5-12). 1993. pap. text ed. 29.95 (1-879373-58-0) R Rinehart.

Animals All Around. (Look - Find - Listen Ser.). (Illus.). 24p. (J). 1993. 16.98 (0-7853-0138-0) Pubns Intl Ltd.

*Animals All Around Us. Sara Corbett. LC 95-7024. (World of Difference Ser.). (Illus.). (J). 1995. write for info. (0-516-08177-2) Childrens.

Animals All the Way. Dorrie Draper. 72p. (C). 1988. 35.00 (0-7212-0721-9, Pub. by Regency Press) St Mut.

*Animals & Alternatives in Testing: History, Science & Ethics. J. Zurlo et al. (Illus.). 86p. 1994. pap. 43.00 (0-913113-67-0) M Liebert.

Animals & Alternatives in Toxicity Testing. Michael Balls et al. 1983. text ed. 84.00 (0-12-077480-1) Acad Pr.

Animals & Alternatives in Toxicology: Present Status & Future Prospects. Michael Balls. 390p. 1991. lib. bdg. 95.00 (1-56081-511-6) VCH Pubs.

Animals & Babies. Martha McFerron. (Science Ser.). 24p. (gr. 2-3). 1980. student ed 5.00 (0-8209-0160-1, S-22) ESP.

Animals & Birds of the Bible. Willard Smith. (Ichthus Ser.). 1989. pap. 3.95 (0-687-18298-0) Abingdon.

Animals & Birds of the Desert. Illus. by Mary Clutterbuck. (Butterfly Bks.). 32p. (J). (gr. 3-5). 1985. 7.95 (0-86685-445-2) Intl Bk Ctr.

Animals & Birds Text & Prints. (Illus.). 16p. 1992. pap. text ed. 52.50 (0-935493-64-6) Modern Learn Pr.

Animals & Christianity. Andrew Linzey & Tom Regan. 360p. (Orig.). 1988. pap. 14.95 (0-8245-0902-1) Crossroad NY.

Animals & Christianity. Ed. by Andrew Linzey & Tom Regan. (Orig.). 1992. 23.00 (0-8446-6531-2) Peter Smith.

Animals & Disease: An Introduction to the History of Comparative Medicine. Lise Wilkinson. (Illus.). 256p. (C). 1992. 79.95 (0-521-37573-8) Cambridge U Pr.

Animals & Environment Fitness; Physiological & Biochemical Aspects of Adaptations & Ecology: Proceedings of the European Society for Comparative Physiology & Biochemistry, 1st Conference, Liege, Belgium, 1979, 2 vols., 1. European Society for Comparative Physiology & Biochemistry Staff. Ed. by R. Gilles. (Illus.). 638p. 1980. 260.00 (0-08-024938-8, Pub. by Pergamon Repr UK) Franklin.

Animals & Environment Fitness; Physiological & Biochemical Aspects of Adaptations & Ecology: Proceedings of the European Society for Comparative Physiology & Biochemistry, 1st Conference, Liege, Belgium, 1979, 2 vols., 2. European Society for Comparative Physiology & Biochemistry Staff. Ed. by R. Gilles. (Illus.). 638p. 1980. 87.00 (0-08-024939-6, Pub. by Pergamon Repr UK) Franklin.

Animals & Man. J. Stefanatos. 1992. pap. 12.95 (0-937032-90-5) Light&Life Pub Co MN.

Animals & Man: The Romane Lecture for 1984-5. Miriam Rothschild. 108p. 1987. pap. 13.95 (0-19-854210-0) OUP.

*Animals & Nature. Ed. by Scholastic Encyclopedia Staff. LC 94-28587. (First Encyclopedia Ser.). (J). 1995. 12.95 (0-590-47524-X, Scholastic Ref) Scholastic Inc.

*Animals & Nature Pack. Sterling Staff. (Bip Quiz Ser.). (J). (gr. 4-7). 1995. pap. 10.95 (0-8069-0938-2) Sterling.

*Animals & People: 3D Studio Tips & Tricks. Michele Bousquet. (3D Studio Tips & Tricks Ser.). 240p. 1994. pap. text ed. 24.95 (0-8273-7016-4) Delmar.

Animals & People Sharing the World. Ed. by Andrew N. Rowan. LC 88-40114. (Illus.). 206p. 1988. text ed. 30.00 (0-87451-449-5); pap. 13.95 (0-87451-465-7) U Pr of New Eng.

Animals & Pets in Pastel. (Leisure Arts Ser.: No. 24). (Illus.). 32p. pap. 4.95 (0-85532-534-8, Pub. by Search Pr UK) A Schwartz & Co.

Animals & Society: Changing Perspectives. Ed. by Audrey Manning & James Serpell. LC 93-10557. 1994. write for info. (0-415-09155-1) Routledge.

Animals & Society: The Humanity of Animal Rights. Keith Tester. 208p. 1991. 65.00 (0-415-04731-5, A5260); pap. 16.95 (0-415-04732-3, A5264) Routledge.

Animals & the New Zoos. Patricia Curtis. (Illus.). 64p. (J). (gr. 3-8). 1991. 15.95 (0-525-67347-4, Lodestar Bks) Dutton Child Bks.

Animals & Their Babies. Melvin Berger. (Early Science Big Bks.). (Illus.). 16p. (J). (ps-2). 1993. pap. text ed. 14.95 (1-56784-005-1) Newbridge Comms.

Animals & Their Babies. Walt Disney Productions Staff. (Walt Disney's Fun-to-Learn Library Ser.: Vol. 5). (Illus.). 44p. (J). (gr. 1-6). reprint ed. 2.99 (0-9619525-6-3) Advance Pubs.

Animals & Their Babies: Mini Books. Melvin Berger. Ed. by Natalie Lunis. (Early Science Big Bks.). (Illus.). 16p. (J). (ps-2). 1993. pap. text ed. 2.95 (1-56784-030-2) Newbridge Comms.

Animals & Their Hiding Places see Books for Young Explorers

Animals & Their Homes. Pat Lauber. LC 92-13129. (J). 1994. 16.95 (0-590-45071-9) Scholastic Inc.

Animals & Their Homes Series, Set. (Illus.). (J). (gr. k-6). 1987. 10.95 (0-685-74138-9); lib. bdg. 95.94 (0-8172-3110-2) Raintree Steck-V.

*Animals & Their Young. 1995. 5.99 (0-88705-754-3) Joshua Morris.

Animals & Their Young. Lada J. Kratky. (Wonders! Ser.). (Illus.). 24p. (Orig.). (J). (gr. 1-3). 1991. pap. text ed. 29.95 (1-56334-048-8); pap. text ed. 6.00 (1-56334-054-2) Hampton-Brown.

Animals & Where They Live. LC 91-58202. (See & Explore Library). (Illus.). 64p. (J). (gr. 3 up). 1992. 11.95 (1-879431-99-8); lib. bdg. 12.99 (1-56458-000-8) Dorling Kindersley.

Animals & Why They Matter. Mary Midgley. LC 83-17933. 160p. (C). 1984. 18.00 (0-8203-0704-1); pap. 10.00 (0-8203-0756-4) U of Ga Pr.

Animals, Animals, Animals: At Home - In the Circus - At the Zoo. Bank Street College of Education Editors. (Bunny Bks.). (Illus.). 64p. (J). (ps-00). 1985. pap. 2.95 (0-8120-3610-7) Barron.

Animals! Animals! Animals! see Guided Research Discovery Units: Six Project Books

Animals Are Innocent: The Search for Julie's Killers. John Ward. (Illus.). 512p. 1993. pap. 13.95 (0-7472-3763-8, Pub. by Headline UK) Trafalgar.

Animals Arrival. Elizabeth Jennings. LC 69-19124. 1969. 13.95 (0-8023-1207-1) Dufour.

Animals As Companions: Demographic, Motivational & Ethical Aspects of Companion Animal Ownership. N. Endenburg. 144p. 1991. pap. 25.00 (90-5170-101-2, Pub. by Thesis Pubs NE) IBD Ltd.

Animals as Sentinels of Environmental Health Hazards. Committee on Animals As Sentinels of Environmental Health Hazards Staff. 176p. 1991. 17.50 (0-309-04046-9) Natl Acad Pr.

Animals at Colonial Williamsburg. Colonial Williamsburg Foundation Staff. (Illus.). 8p. (J). (ps). 1993. bds. 3.95 (0-87935-092-X) Colonial Williamsburg.

Animals at Home. Jane Burton. (Animal Ways Ser.). (Illus.). 24p. (J). (gr. k-4). 1991. lib. bdg. 10.40 (1-878137-12-3) Newington.

Animals at Night. Jane Burton. (Animal Ways Ser.). (Illus.). 24p. (J). (gr. k-4). 1991. lib. bdg. 10.40 (1-878137-13-1) Newington.

Animals at Night. Sharon Peters. LC 82-19226. (Now I Know Ser.). (Illus.). 32p. (J). (gr. k-2). 1983. lib. bdg. 11.59 (0-89375-903-1); pap. 2.95 (0-8167-1477-0) Troll Assocs.

Animals at Play, Set. Ed. by Donald J. Crump. (Books for Young Explorers Ser.: Set 15, No. 2). (Illus.). (J). (gr. k-4). 1988. lib. bdg. 16.95 (0-87044-744-0) Natl Geog.

Animals at Play, Set. National Geographic Society Staff. Ed. by Donald J. Crump. (Books for Young Explorers Ser.: Set 15, No. 2). (Illus.). (J). (gr. k-4). 1994. pap. 8.00 (0-87044-739-4) Natl Geog.

Animals at Rest. Jane Burton. (Animal Ways Ser.). (Illus.). 24p. (J). (gr. k-4). 1991. lib. bdg. 10.40 (1-878137-14-X) Newington.

An Asterisk (*) at the beginning of an entry indicates that the title is appearing in BIP for the first time.

An Asterisk (*) at the beginning of an entry indicates that the title is appearing in BIP for the first time.

Animals Should Definitely Not Wear Clothing. 2nd ed. Judi Barrett. (Illus.). 32p. (J). (ps-1). 1988. reprint ed. pap. 3.95 (*0-689-70807-6*, Aladdin Paperbacks) S&S Childrens.

Animals Should Definitely Not Wear Clothing. Judi Barrett. (Illus.). 32p. (J). (gr. k-3). 1990. reprint ed. audio 22.95 (*0-87499-147-1*); reprint ed. audio, pap. 14.95 (*0-87488-146-3*) Live Oak Media.

Animals Should Definitely Not Wear Clothing, 4 vols., Set. Judi Barrett. (Illus.). 32p. (J). (gr. k-3). 1990. reprint ed. audio, pap. 29.95 (*0-87499-148-X*) Live Oak Media.

Animals Sticker Jigsaw Book. (Illus.). (J). (gr. 3-6). 1992. pap. 3.95 (*1-56680-510-4*) Mad Hatter Pub.

Animals Talk to One Another: A Christmas Folktale Retold & Illustrated by Fran Stake, Set. Fran Stake. (Illus.). 20p. (J). (ps). 1993. 1,100.00 (*0-9619075-0-9*) Stake Studio.

Animals Talking. Jane Burton. (Animal Ways Ser.). (Illus.). 24p. (J). (gr. k-4). 1991. lib. bdg. 10.40 (*1-878137-02-6*) Newington.

***Animals That Build Homes.** Kyle Carter. LC 94-46845. (Things Animals Do Ser.). (J). 1995. write for info. (*1-55916-112-4*) Rourke Bk Co.

Animals That Burrow. rev. ed. Dean Morris. LC 87-16694. (Read about Animals Ser.). (Illus.). 48p. (J). (gr. 2-6). 1987. lib. bdg. 10.95 (*0-8172-3201-X*) Raintree Steck-V.

***Animals That Change: Metamorphsis.** Illus. by Ruth Lindsay. LC 95-4062. (J). 1995. 15.99 (*0-525-67496-9*, Lodestar Bks) Dutton Child Bks.

***Animals That Fight.** Kyle Carter. LC 94-46854. (Things Animals Do Ser.). (J). 1995. write for info. (*1-55916-113-2*) Rourke Bk Co.

Animals That Glow. Judith J. Presnall. LC 92-25529. (First Bks.). (J). 1993. lib. bdg. 13.93 (*0-531-20071-X*) Watts.

Animals That Glow. Judith J. Presnall. (First Bks.). (Illus.). 64p. (J). (gr. 5-8). 1993. pap. 5.95 (*0-531-15672-9*) Watts.

Animals That Hibernate. Larry D. Brimner. LC 90-13116. (First Book Ser.). (Illus.). 64p. (J). (gr. 3-6). 1991. lib. bdg. 13.93 (*0-531-20018-3*) Watts.

Animals That Live in Shells. rev. ed. Dean Morris. LC 87-20556. (Read about Animals Ser.). (Illus.). 48p. (J). (gr. 2-6). 1987. lib. bdg. 10.95 (*0-8172-3202-8*) Raintree Steck-V.

Animals That Live in the Sea see Books for Young Explorers

Animals That Live in Trees see Books for Young Explorers

Animals That Show & Tell. William Coleman. LC 85-15122. 144p. (J). (gr. 2-7). 1985. pap. 6.99 (*0-87123-807-1*) Bethany Hse.

Animals That Stand in Dreams. Harley Elliott. 1977. pap. 5.00 (*0-914610-08-2*) Hanging Loose.

***Animals That Survive.** Kyle Carter. LC 94-46847. (Things Animals Do Ser.). (J). 1995. write for info. (*1-55916-114-0*) Rourke Bk Co.

***Animals That Talk.** Kyle Carter. LC 94-47362. (Things Animals Do Ser.). (J). 1995. write for info. (*1-55916-115-9*) Rourke Bk Co.

***Animals That Travel.** Kyle Carter. LC 94-47360. (Things Animals Do Ser.). (J). 1995. write for info. (*1-55916-110-8*) Rourke Bk Co.

***Animals to Look At.** (Country Friends Ser.). 8p. (J). 1994. bds. 1.98 (*0-86112-850-8*) Brimax Bks.

***Animals to Love.** (Country Friends Ser.). 8p. (J). 1994. bds. 1.98 (*0-86112-848-6*) Brimax Bks.

Animals to Protect: Fifteen Paper Animal Models to Make. Dominique Simon & Olivier Massina. (Illus.). (J). (gr. 4 up). 1995. pap. text ed. 9.95 (*0-7167-6540-3*) W H Freeman.

Animals to Wear. Barry Greller. (Illus.). 90p. 1990. 9.95 (*0-937769-78-9*) Mark Inc CA.

***Animals Together.** (Animal Friends Ser.). 8p. (J). 1994. bds. 1.49 (*0-86112-514-2*) Brimax Bks.

Animals Two by Two. (J). (ps-1). 1990. bds. 6.99 (*0-7459-1839-5*) Lion USA.

Animals Undercover. Stephen Savage. (J). 1994. 10.95 (*0-671-89133-2*, Litl Simon S&S) S&S Childrens.

Animals Underground. Charlotte Ruffault. Tr. by Sarah Matthews. LC 87-34616. (Young Discovery Library). (Illus.). 38p. (J). (gr. k-5). 1988. 5.95 (*0-944589-03-0*, 030) Young Discovery Lib.

Animals Utilized by Woodland Peoples Occupying the Apple Creek Site, Illinois. Paul W. Parmalee et al. (Reports of Investigations Ser.: No. 23). (Illus.). 62p. 1972. pap. 3.00 (*0-89792-048-1*) Ill St Museum.

***Animals We Know.** (Country Friends Ser.). 8p. (J). 1994. bds. 1.98 (*0-86112-849-4*) Brimax Bks.

Animals We Love, Bk. 1. Illus. by Mirko Hanak. LC 72-89571. 32p. (J). (gr. k-4). 1973. 9.95 (*0-87592-005-5*) Scroll Pr.

Animals We Love, Bk. 2. Illus. by Mirko Hanak. LC 72-89571. 32p. (J). (gr. k-4). 1973. 9.95 (*0-87592-006-3*) Scroll Pr.

Animals Who Have Won Our Hearts. Jean C. George. LC 92-28326. (Illus.). 64p. (J). (gr. 3-7). 1994. 15.00 (*0-06-021543-7*) HarpC Child Bks.

Animals Who Have Won Our Hearts. Jean C. George. LC 92-28326. (Illus.). 64p. (J). (gr. 3-7). 1994. lib. bdg. 14.89 (*0-06-021544-5*) HarpC Child Bks.

Animals with Novel Genes. Ed. by Norman MacLean. LC 94-11728. (Illus.). 295p. (C). 1995. 49.95 (*0-521-43256-1*) Cambridge U Pr.

Animals Within. David Day. 1984. 6.95 (*0-920806-61-9*, Pub. by Penumbra Pr CN) U of Toronto Pr.

Animals Without Backbones. Ralph Buchsbaum et al. LC 86-7046. (Illus.). x, 572p. (C). 1987. pap. text ed. 20.00 (*0-226-07874-4*) U Ch Pr.

Animals Without Backbones. 3rd ed. Ralph Buchsbaum et al. LC 86-7046. (Illus.). x, 572p. (C). 1987. lib. bdg. 35.00 (*0-226-07873-6*) U Ch Pr.

Animalscam: The Beastly Abuse of Human Rights. Kathleen Marquardt. LC 93-24500. 221p. 1993. 24.00 (*0-89526-498-6*) Regnery Pub.

Animals...Our Return to Wholeness: Our Return to Wholeness. Penelope Smith. LC 93-84568. (Illus.). 357p. 1993. pap. 19.95 (*0-936552-10-7*) Pegasus Pubns.

Animalwatching: A Field Guide to Animal Behavior. Desmond Morris. (Illus.). 1990. 35.00 (*0-517-57859-X*, Crown) Crown Pub Group.

Animani see Hanimals

Animas Quilts. Jackie Robinson. Ed. by Ursula Reikes. LC 93-25007. (Quilt Shop Ser.). (Illus.). 88p. (Orig.). 1993. pap. 19.95 (*1-56477-037-0*, B160) That Patchwork.

Animate Illusions: Explorations of Narrative Structure. Harold Toliver. LC 72-97975. x, 412p. 1974. 31.95 (*0-8032-0831-6*) U of Nebr Pr.

Animated Algorithms: A Hypermedia Learning Environment for Introduction to Algorithms. Peter Gloor et al. (Illus.). 250p. 1993. text ed. 49.95x (*0-262-57096-3*) MIT Pr.

Animated Animal Alphabet & Make up Your Own Book. Todd Tarbox. (Illus.). 1976. pap. 2.00 (*0-89297-001-4*) Todd Tarbox.

Animated Art of Ralph Bakshi. Ralph Bakshi. 1989. pap. 12.95 (*0-89865-786-5*) Donning Co.

Animated Cartoons. E. G. Lutz. 1976. lib. bdg. 150.00 (*0-8490-1433-6*) Gordon Pr.

Animated Christmas Dough Art. Jeanne Earnhart. (Advanced Dough Art Made Easy Ser.: Vol. 1). (Illus.). 52p. 1986. pap. text ed. 9.95 (*0-9615406-0-5*) G B Pr.

Animated Earth: The Whistling Jugs of Pre-Columbian Peru. Daniel Statnekov. (Illus.). 200p. (Orig.). 1987. text ed. 20.00 (*1-55643-001-9*); pap. 9.95 (*1-55643-000-0*) North Atlantic.

Animated Film: Concepts, Methods, Uses. Roy P. Madsen. 1976. 24.95 (*0-8488-0830-4*) Amereon Ltd.

Animated Films. Rhoda Nottridge. LC 91-36041. (Films Ser.). (Illus.). 32p. (J). (gr. 5). 1992. text ed. 13.95 (*0-89686-717-X*, Crstwood Hse) Silver Burdett Pr.

Animated Films of Don Bluth. John Cawley. (Illus.). 200p. (Orig.). 1991. pap. 14.95 (*0-685-50334-8*) Image NY.

Animated Haggadah Activity Book. Janet Zwebner. 48p. (J). (ps-8). 1990. pap. 5.95 (*0-944007-46-5*) Sure Sellers.

Animated Haggadah (1990 Edition) Rony Oren. (Illus.). 54p. (J). 1990. 14.95 (*0-944007-43-0*) Sure Sellers.

Animated Israel. Sidon et al. 54p. (J). 1987. 14.95 (*0-8246-0326-5*) Jonathan David.

Animated Megillah. Ephraim Sidon. (Animated Holydays Ser.). 54p. (J). (gr. 1-5). 1987. 14.95 (*0-8246-0324-9*) Jonathan David.

Animated Menorah. Ephraim Sidon. 54p. 1987. 14.95 (*0-8246-0327-3*) Jonathan David.

Animated Menorah. Janet Zwebner. (Illus.). 48p. (J). (gr. 1-4). 1989. 9.95 (*0-685-28790-4*) Sure Sellers.

Animated Menorah Chanukah Activity. Janet Zwebner. (J). (gr. 4-7). 1991. pap. 5.95 (*0-944007-61-9*) Sure Sellers.

Animated Paper Crafts. Pat Karch. Ed. by Shirley Beegle. (Illus.). 64p. (J). (gr. 1-6). 1991. Grades 1-6. teacher ed, per. 5.99 (*0-87403-810-3*, 14-02110) Standard Pub.

Animated Photography: The ABC of the Cinematograph. Cecil M. Hepworth. LC 73-124009. (Literature of Cinema Ser.). reprint ed. 7.50 (*0-405-01615-8*) Ayer.

Animated Pictures. C. Francis Jenkins. LC 79-124013. (Literature of Cinema Ser.). 1979. reprint ed. 12.95 (*0-405-01619-0*) Ayer.

Animated Teddy Bears. Jeanne Earnhart. (Advanced Dough Art Made Easy Ser.: Vol. 2). (Illus.). 52p. 1986. pap. text ed. 9.95 (*0-9615406-1-3*) G B Pr.

Animated TV Specials: The Complete Directory to the First Twenty-Five Years, 1962-1987. George W. Woolery. LC 89-5856. (Illus.). 570p. 1989. 59.50 (*0-8108-2198-2*) Scarecrow.

Animating Calculus: Mathematica Notebooks for the Laboratory. Ed Packel & Stan Wagon. LC 93-21054. (C). 1995. pap. text ed. write for info. (*0-7167-2428-6*) W H Freeman.

Animating Culture: Hollywood Cartoons from the Sound Era. Eric Smoodin. LC 92-32891. (Media, Culture, & Communication Ser.). (Illus.). 232p. (C). 1993. text ed. 40.00 (*0-8135-1948-9*); pap. 15.95 (*0-8135-1949-7*) Rutgers U Pr.

Animating Maria. large type ed. Marion Chesney. (Nightingale Ser.). 232p. 1991. pap. 14.95 (*0-8161-5099-0*) G K Hall.

Animating Pursuits of Speculation. Elgin Williams. LC 68-58641. (Columbia University. Studies in the Social Sciences: No. 547). reprint ed. 20.00 (*0-404-51547-9*) AMS Pr.

Animation. Patrick Jenkins. (J). (gr. 2-7). 1991. pap. 9.57 (*0-201-56757-1*) Addison-Wesley.

Animation: A Reference Guide. Thomas W. Hoffer. LC 81-67. (American Popular Culture Ser.). (Illus.). 448p. 1981. text ed. 59.95 (*0-313-21095-0*, HAG, Greenwood Pr) Greenwood.

Animation: Drawings Spring to Life. Don Nardo. LC 92-5151. (Encyclopedia of Discovery & Invention Ser.). (Illus.). 96p. (J). (gr. 5-8). 1992. lib. bdg. 17.95 (*1-56006-218-5*) Lucent Bks.

Animation: The Art of Friz Freleng. Friz Freleng & David Weber. 1993. 1,200.00 (*1-880538-06-7*) Donovan Pub.

Animation & Scientific Visualization. Ed. by R. A. Earnshaw & D. Watson. (Illus.). 336p. 1993. text ed. 44.95 (*0-12-227745-7*) Acad Pr.

Animation Art: Buyers Guide & Price Guide. 1,992th ed. Jim Korkis. 1992. pap. 9.95 (*1-56398-025-8*) Malibu Graphics.

***Animation Art: Illustrated Guide to Animation Art at Auction.** Jeff Lotman. (Illus.). 420p. 1995. 125.00 (*0-88740-763-3*) Schiffer.

Animation Art Buyer's Guide & Price Guide, 1993: 1993 Edition. John Cawley & Jim Korkis. 1993. pap. 14.95 (*1-56398-047-9*) Malibu Graphics.

Animation Book. Kit Laybourne. 1988. pap. 20.00 (*0-517-52946-7*, Crown) Crown Pub Group.

Animation Book. Peter Viska. (J). (gr. 4-7). 1994. pap. 5.95 (*0-590-47573-8*) Scholastic Inc.

Animation, Caricature & Gag & Political Cartoons in the United States: An International Bibliography. Ed. by John Lent. LC 94-14433. (Bibliographies & Indexes in Popular Culture Ser.: No. 3). 440p. 1994. text ed. 75.00 (*0-313-28681-7*, Greenwood Pr) Greenwood.

Animation from Script to Screen. Shamus Culhane. 1990. 13.95 (*0-312-05052-6*) St Martin.

Animation, Games, & Sound for the VIC-20. Tony Fabbri. (Personal Computing Ser.). (Illus.). 224p. 1984. disk 32.95 (*0-685-07962-7*); pap. 19.50 (*0-685-07961-9*) P-H.

Animation How-to CD. Jeff Bowermaster. (Illus.). 480p. (Orig.). 1993. cd-rom, pap. 34.95 (*1-878739-54-9*) Waite Group Pr.

Animation Rurale: Education for Rural Development. Jeanne M. Moulton. 249p. (Orig.). (C). 1977. pap. 6.00 (*0-932288-48-0*) Ctr Intl Ed U of MA.

Animation Rurale & Rural Development: The Experience of Upper Volta. Robert B. Charlick et al. (Special Series on Animation Rurale: No. 3). 133p. (Orig.). (C). 1982. pap. text ed. 6.65 (*0-86731-043-X*) Cornell CIS RDC.

Animation Rurale Revisited: Participatory Techniques for Improving Agriculture & Social Services in 5 Francophone Nations. Robert B. Charlick. (Special Series on Animation Rurale: No. 1). 243p. (Orig.). (C). 1984. pap. text ed. 10.00 (*0-86731-041-3*) Cornell CIS RDC.

Animation Techniques. Christopher D. Watkins & Stephen R. Marenka. (Illus.). 300p. 1995. disk, pap. text ed. 44.95 (*0-12-737870-7*) Acad Pr.

***Animation Techniques in Win32: A C++ Programmer's Guide to DIBs, Palettes & Sprites.** Nigel Thompson. 261p. 1994. cd-rom, pap. 34.95 (*1-55615-669-3*) Microsoft.

Animation, the Whole Story. Howard Beckerman. 29.95 (*0-8488-0867-3*) Amereon Ltd.

Animations. Adam Cornford. (Pocket Poets Ser.: No. 45). 128p. (Orig.). 1987. pap. 5.95 (*0-87286-208-9*) City Lights.

Animator's Workbook. Tony White. (Illus.). 160p. 1988. pap. 18.95 (*0-8230-0229-2*, Watsn-Guptill) Watsn-Guptill.

Animator's Workbook: Step-by-Step Techniques of Drawn Animation. Tony White. LC 86-1346. (Illus.). 160p. 1986. 29.95 (*0-86729-177-X*) Knowledge Indus.

Animaux Denatures: Avec: La Marche a l'Etoile. Jean Vercors. 317p. (FRE.). 1984. pap. 10.95 (*0-7859-1466-8*, 2253010235) Fr & Eur.

Animaze! A Collection of Amazing Nature Mazes. Wendy Madgwick. LC 91-46892. (Illus.). 40p. (J). (ps-3). 1992. 13.00 (*0-679-82665-3*) Knopf Bks Yng Read.

Animism: Primitive Myth & Religion. Edward Clodd. 100p. reprint ed. pap. 11.95 (*1-872736-41-6*, Pub. by Mandrake Pr UK) Holmes Pub.

Animoa: A Social History of the Western Igbo People. Don C. Ohadike. LC 93-31029. (Illus.). 272p. (C). 1994. text ed. 39.95 (*0-8214-1072-5*); pap. text ed. 17.95 (*0-8214-1073-3*) Ohio U Pr.

Animus. Ed Kelleher & Harriette Vidal. 304p. (Orig.). 1993. pap. 4.50 (*0-8439-3473-5*) Dorchester Pub Co.

***Animus Aeternus.** McNeely. 1995. pap. 18.00 (*0-919123-50-3*) Atrium Pubs.

Animus & Anima. Emma Jung. Tr. by Cary F. Baynes & Hildegard Nagel. LC 85-18299. 94p. 1985. reprint ed. pap. 9.00 (*0-88214-301-8*) Spring Pubns.

Anioma's Attainment of Humanity. rev. ed. Osodi E. Echezonam. 1993. 8.95 (*0-8062-4648-0*) Carlton.

Anion & Proton Transport, Vol. 341. Ed. by William A. Brodsky. LC 80-15917. (Annals Ser.). 570p. 1980. 109.00 (*0-89766-070-6*); pap. 109.00 (*0-89766-071-4*) NY Acad Sci.

Anion Carries of Mitochondrial Membranes. Ed. by A. Azzi et al. (Illus.). xii, 381p. 1989. 83.00 (*0-387-50853-8*) Spr-Verlag.

Anionic Polymerization. L. J. Fetters et al. (Advances in Polymer Science Ser.: Vol. 56). (Illus.). 1984. 68.00 (*0-387-12792-5*) Spr-Verlag.

Anionic Polymerization. Ed. by James E. McGrath. LC 81-14911. (Symposium Ser.: No. 166). 594p. 1981. 63.95 (*0-8412-0643-0*) Am Chemical.

Anionic Polymerization. Ed. by Maurice Morton. LC 82-11627. 268p. 1983. text ed. 95.00 (*0-12-508080-8*) Acad Pr.

***Anionic Surfactants.** Stache. (Surfactant Science Ser.). 1076p. 1995. write for info. (*0-8247-9394-3*) Dekker.

Anionic Surfactants, Pt. 1. Ed. by Warner A. Linfield. LC 75-22777. (Surfactant Science Ser.: No. 7). (Illus.). 328p. reprint ed. pap. 93.50 (*0-8357-5490-1*, 2032990) Bks Demand.

Anionic Surfactants: Biochemistry, Toxicology, Dermatology. Christian Gloxhuber. LC 80-24317. (Surfactant Science Ser.: No. 10). (Illus.). 472p. reprint ed. pap. 134.60 (*0-8357-6017-0*, 2034534) Bks Demand.

Anionic Surfactants: Chemical Analysis. Ed. by John Cross. LC 77-21835. (Surfactant Science Ser.: No. 8). (Illus.). 273p. reprint ed. pap. 77.90 (*0-8357-4703-4*, 2052358) Bks Demand.

Anish Kapoor. Pier L. Tazzi. Ed. by Julie Dunn. Tr. by Marguerite Shore. LC 91-67707. 57p. 1992. 35.00 (*0-934418-38-1*); pap. 20.00 (*0-685-61427-1*) Mus Contemp Art.

Anish Kapoor, No. 28. Ed. by Kyoichi Tsuzuki. (Art Random Ser.). (Illus.). 48p. 1991. 32.95 (*4-7636-8530-9*, Pub. by Kyoto Shoin JA) Bks Nippan.

Anisotropic Analysis Using Boundary Elements. LC 94-70618. (Topics in Engineering Ser.: No. 20). 168p. 1994. text ed. 79.00 (*1-56252-257-4*) Computational Mech MA.

Anisotropic & Nonlinear Optical Waveguides. Ed. by Carlo G. Someda & George Stegeman. LC 92-17900. (Optical Wave Sciences & Technology Ser.: Vol. 2). 1992. write for info. (*0-444-88489-0*) Elsevier.

***Anisotropic Elasticity.** Thomas C. Ting. (Oxford Engineering Science Ser.: No. 45). (Illus.). 592p. 1995. 85.00 (*0-19-507447-5*) OUP.

Anisotropic Plates. 2nd ed. S. G. Lekhnitskii. 550p. 1968. text ed. 210.00 (*0-677-20670-4*) Gordon & Breach.

Anisotropy & Inhomogeneity in Elasticity & Plasticity. Ed. by Y. C. Angel. LC 93-71572. (AMD Ser.: Vol. 158). 61p. 1993. pap. 30.00 (*0-7918-1137-9*, G00781) ASME.

Anisotropy & Localization of Plastic Deformation: Proc. of the Third Internat. Symp. on Plasticity & Its Current Applications, Plasticity '91, 12-16 Aug. 1991, Grenoble, France. Ed. by J. P. Boehler & Akhtar S. Khan. 702p. 1991. 153.00 (*1-85166-688-5*) Elsevier.

Anisotropy in Geoelectromagnetism. J. G. Negi & P. D. Saraf. (Methods in Geochemistry & Geophysics Ser.: Vol. 28). 1989. 133.50 (*0-444-87495-X*) Elsevier.

Anita. Keith Roberts. (Illus.). 195p. 1990. reprint ed. 20.25 (*0-913896-27-6*) Owlswick Pr.

Anita, Vol. 1. Guido Crepax. Tr. by S. Gaudiano. 48p. 1991. pap. 11.95 (*1-56163-031-4*, Eurotica) NBM.

Anita, Vol. 2. Guido Crepax. Tr. by S. Gaudiano. 48p. 1992. pap. 11.95 (*1-56163-044-6*, Eurotica) NBM.

Anita & Franco Columbu's Firm-Up Your Thighs in 15 Minutes a Day. Anita Columbu & Franco Columbu. 1980. pap. 1.95 (*0-8092-7078-1*) Contemp Bks.

Anita, Anita. Dorothy Bryant. LC 93-72365. 300p. 1994. 20.00 (*0-931688-17-5*); pap. 12.95 (*0-931688-18-3*) Ata Bks.

Anita Brookner. Lynn V. Sadler. (English Authors Ser.: No. 473). 192p. 1990. text ed. 21.95 (*0-8057-6991-9*, Twayne) Macmillan.

Anita, Enemy of the People: Let's Take the Communism Out of Womynism. Mary J. Rachner. 102p. (Orig.). 1991. pap. 9.95 (*0-9623133-3-5*) Oxner Inst.

Anita Hill. Bob Italia. LC 93-4615. (Everyone Contributes Ser.). 40p. (J). 1993. lib. bdg. 12.94 (*1-56239-259-X*) Abdo & Dghtrs.

Anita Mills Falling Stars. Anita Mills. 384p. 1993. pap. 4.99 (*0-451-40365-7*, Topaz) NAL-Dutton.

Anita Niesz: Photographs. Anita Niesz. (Illus.). 152p. 1989. pap. 35.00 (*3-7165-0672-9*, Pub. by Benteli Verlag SZ) Dist Art Pubs.

Anita of Rancho del Mar. Elaine F. O'Brien. LC 90-19711. (Illus.). 176p. (Orig.). (YA). (gr. 4-8). 1991. pap. 8.95 (*0-931832-79-9*) Fithian Pr.

Anitya. Paul Twitchell. 89p. 1987. 12.00 (*1-57043-027-6*) ECKANKAR.

Anitya. Paul Twitchell. (Illus.). 1969. 12.00 (*0-914766-01-5*) Illum Way Pub.

Aniversario de Larga Duracion & el "Long Playing" de Nuestra Historia. Antonio G. Del Toro. (Biblioteca de Autores de Puerto Rico Ser.). 92p. (SPA.). 1992. pap. text ed. 5.00 (*1-56328-021-3*) Edit Plaza Mayor.

***Aniyunwiya, Real Human Beings: Contemporary Cherokee Indian Fiction.** Ed. by Joseph Bruchac. 1995. pap. 14.95 (*0-912678-92-5*) Greenfld Rev Lit.

Anjea. Infanticide, Abortion & Contraception in Savage Society. Herbert Aptekar. LC 79-2929. 192p. 1981. reprint ed. 19.25 (*0-8305-0097-9*) Hyperion Conn.

Anjuna: Profile of a Village in Goa. Teresa Albuquerque. (C). 1987. 27.00 (*81-85002-06-1*, Pub. by Promilla) S Asia.

Ankh - Eternal Light: Eternal Light. Kathleen L. Mendel. LC 94-60587. (Illus.). 40p. (Orig.). (C). 1994. pap. 6.10 (*1-878142-38-0*) Telstar TX.

Ankle & Foot. Jason H. Calhoun. (Current Opinion in Orthopedics Ser.). (Illus.). 99p. (Orig.). 1994. pap. text ed. 59.95 (*1-85922-650-7*) Current Science.

Ankle & Foot. Ferkel. Ed. by Terry L. Whipple. (Arthroscopic Surgery Ser.). (Illus.). 220p. 1995. write for info. (*0-397-51093-4*) Lippincott.

Ankoku Buto: The Premodern & Postmodern Influences on the Dance of Utter Darkness. Susan B. Klein. (Cornell East Asia Ser.: No. 49). 112p. 1989. 9.00 (*0-939657-49-X*) Cornell East Asia Pgm.

Anky Techua-Te: Classical Khamitic Afrikan Medicine. Cwolde Kyte. 181p. (Orig.). 1986. pap. 19.41 (*0-936901-00-4*) Ctr Sacred Healing.

Ankylosaurus. Oliver. (Dinosaur Library: Set II). (Illus.). 24p. (J). 1984. lib. bdg. 14.00 (*0-86592-212-8*) Rourke Enter.

***Ankylosaurus.** Janet Riehecky. (Dinosaur Bks.). (Illus.). 32p. (ENG & SPA.). (J). (ps-2). 1990. lib. bdg. 21.36 (*1-56766-126-2*) Childs World.

Ankylosaurus. Janet Riehecky. (Dinosaur Bks.). (Illus.). 32p. (ENG & SPA.). (J). (ps-2). 1990. lib. bdg. 21.36 (*0-89565-621-3*) Childs World.

Ankylosaurus: The Armored Dinosaur. Elizabeth Sandell. Ed. by Marjorie Oelerich & Harlan S. Hansen. LC 88-39806. (Dinosaur Discovery Era Ser.). (Illus.). 32p. (J). (gr. k-5). 1989. lib. bdg. 12.95 (*0-944280-16-1*); pap. text ed. 5.95 (*0-944280-22-6*) Bancroft-Sage.

Ankylosing Spondylitis. Ed. by John J. Calabro & W. Carson Dick. (New Clinical Applications Rheumatology Ser.). 1987. lib. bdg. 78.00 (*0-85200-994-1*) Kluwer Ac.

Anleitung Zu der Naturlichsten und Leichtesten Art Pferde Abzurichten. Ludwig Hunersdorf. (Documenta Hippologica Ser.). xxxviii, 579p. (GER.). 1992. reprint ed. write for info. (*3-487-08058-3*, Pub. by Georg Olms GW) Lubrecht & Cramer.

***Anleitung Zum HACCP-Konzept.** Europe Scientific Committee on Microbiology Staff. 13p. 1994. pap. text ed. 12.50 (*0-944398-40-5*) ILSI.

An Asterisk (*) at the beginning of an entry indicates that the title is appearing in BIP for the first time.

An Asterisk (*) at the beginning of an entry indicates that the title is appearing in BIP for the first time.

329

Annabel. Janice Boland. LC 91-46490. (Illus.). 32p. (J). (ps-2). 1993. 12.99 (0-8037-1254-5); lib. bdg. 12.89 (0-8037-1255-3) Dial Bks Young.

Annabel Again. Janice Boland. LC 94-189. (J). (gr. 2 up). 1995. 13.99 (0-8037-1756-3); pap. 13.89 (0-8037-1757-1) Dial Bks Young.

Annabel Lee. Edgar Allan Poe. 24p. 1987. 19.95 (0-88776-200-X); pap. 7.95 (0-88776-230-1) Tundra Bks.

Annabelle. Ruby J. Jensen. 320p. 1987. pap. 3.95 (0-8217-2011-2) Zebra.

Annabelle. Beverlee Ross. (Historical Ser.). 1993. mass mkt. 3.99 (0-373-28778-X, 1-28778-8) Harlequin Bks.

***Annabelle Bk. 2: Celebrating the American Woman.** Meredith B. McMath. 350p. 1995. pap. 10.99 (0-89283-895-7, Vine Bks) Servant.

Annabelle & the Big Slide. Rita Pocock. 28p. (J). (ps-00). 1989. 10.95 (0-15-200407-6, Gulliver Bks) HarBrace.

Annabelle Swift, Kindergartner. Amy Schwartz. LC 87-15403. (Illus.). 32p. (J). (ps-2). 1988. 15.95 (0-531-05737-2); lib. bdg. 15.99 (0-531-08337-3) Orchard Bks Watts.

Annabelle Swift, Kindergartner. Amy Schwartz. LC 87-15403. (Illus.). 32p. (J). (ps-2). 1991. pap. 5.95 (0-531-07027-1) Orchard Bks Watts.

***Annabelle's Awful Waffle.** Tracey E. Dils. (Illus.). 24p. (J). (gr. k-3). 1995. pap. 2.99 (0-87406-721-9) Willowisp Pr.

Annabel's House. Norman Messenger. LC 88-60089. (Illus.). 28p. (J). 1989. 18.95 (0-531-05764-X) Orchard Bks Watts.

Annable's Treasury of Literary Teasers. H. D. Annable. 216p. 1989. pap. 10.95 (0-89879-368-8) Writers Digest.

Annadel State Park - The First Twenty Years. Bill Krumbein. 195p. 1993. pap. 6.95 (0-9639822-0-6) Valley of the Moon.

***Annaeherungen: Zur Urchristlichen Theologiegeschichte und zum Umgang mit Ihren Quellen.** Juergen Becker. (Beihefte Zur Zeitschrift Fuer die Neutestamentliche Wissenschaft Ser.: Bd. 76). 508p. (GER.). (C). 1994. lib. bdg. 136.95 (3-11-014551-0) De Gruyter.

Annal Begins with Ezekiel & Margaret (Watkins) Phelps. Geneva M. Phelps. 179p. 1988. 25.75 (0-9620925-0-9) G Phelps.

Annalee Price Index & Collector's Information Guide, Vol. II: Annalee Animals. Rosemary Turner. 160p. (Orig.). 1989. pap. 12.95 (0-317-91167-8) Whiteface Pub.

Annalen der Alteren Deutschen Literatur, 3 vols., Set. Georg W. Panzer. 1961. reprint ed. write for info. (0-318-71851-0, Pub. by Georg Olms GW) Lubrecht & Cramer.

Annalen der Poetischen Nationalliteratur der Deutschen Im XVI und XVII Jahrhundert. Emil Weller. xvi, 1041p. 1963. reprint ed. write for info. (0-318-71874-X, Pub. by Georg Olms GW) Lubrecht & Cramer.

Annales Cambriae (444-1288) Ed. by John Williams. (Rolls Ser.: No. 20). 1972. reprint ed. 45.00 (0-8115-1026-3) Periodicals Srv.

Annales de l'Imprimere des Alde, Ou Histoire des Trois Manuce et de Leurs Editions. Antoine-Augustin Renouard. 680p. (FRE.). 1991. reprint ed. 80.00 (0-938768-27-1) Oak Knoll.

Annales des Mines: Lexique Technique Allemand-Francais. J. Armanet & A. Becquer. 344p. (FRE & GER.). 1951. 19.95 (0-8288-6881-6, M6011) Fr & Eur.

Annales Historiography & Theory: A Selective & Annotated Bibliography. Ed. by Jean-Pierre Herubel. LC 94-16073. (Bibliographies & Incexes in World History: No. 34). 192p. 1994. text ed. 59.95 (0-313-29125-X, Greenwood Pr) Greenwood.

Annales, I-VI, XI-XVI. Tacitus. Ed. by C. D. Fisher. (Oxford Classical Texts Ser.). 1922. 24.95 (0-19-814633-7) OUP.

Annales Monastici, 5 vols., Set. Ed. by Henry R. Luard. Incl. Vol. 1. De Margam. 1972. (0-8115-1088-3); Vol. 2. De Wintonia. 1972. (0-8115-1085-9); Vol. 3. De Dunstaplia. 1972. (0-8115-1086-7); Vol. 4. De Oseneia. 1972. (0-8115-1087-5); Vol. 5. Index & Glossary. 1972. (0-318-58898-6); (Rolls Ser.: No. 36). 1972. reprint ed. 225.00 (0-8115-1084-0) Periodicals Srv.

Annales School & Archaeology. Ed. by John Bintliff. 132p. 1991. text ed. 40.00x (0-8147-1168-5) NYU Pr.

Annales Sex Regum Angliae: Qui a Comitibus Andergavensibus Originem Traxerunt, A. D. 1136-1307. Nicholas Trivet. (English Historical Society Publications Ser.: Vol. 13). 1972. reprint ed. 45.00 (0-8115-1543-5) Periodicals Srv.

Annales Typographici, 11 vols., Set. Georg W. Panzer. 1964. reprint ed. write for info. (0-318-71852-9, Pub. by Georg Olms GW) Lubrecht & Cramer.

Annali Dell' Islam, 10 vols. (Illus.). 1972. reprint ed. write for info. (3-487-04404-8, Pub. by Georg Olms GW) Lubrecht & Cramer.

Annalium in Islandia Farrago, & De Mirabilibus Islandiae. Gisli Oddsson. Ed. by Halldor Hermannsson. (Islandica Ser.: Vol. 10). 1917. 15.00 (0-527-00340-9) Periodicals Srv.

Annals, Bk. IV. Tacitus. Ed. by R. H. Martin & A. J. Woodman. (Cambridge Greek & Latin Classics Ser.). (Illus.). 280p. (C). 1990. 59.95 (0-521-30504-7); pap. 21.95 (0-521-31543-3) Cambridge U Pr.

Annals: Southeast Conference Association for Asian Studies. Ed. by Kenneth W. Berger. pap. 10.00 (0-317-91076-0) SE Conf Assn Asian Studies.

Annals & Antiquities of Rajasthan, 3 vols. James Tod. (C). 1990. reprint ed. text ed. 38.00 (81-85395-68-3, Pub. by Low Price II) S Asia.

Annals & Antiquities of Rajasthan, 3 vols., Set. James Tod. Ed. by William Crooke. 1987. reprint ed. 60.00 (81-208-0380-9, Pub. by Motilal Banarsidass II) S Asia.

Annals & Antiquities of Rajasthan, or the Central & Western Rajpoot States of India, 2 vols., Set. James Tod. 1267p. 1829. reprint ed. text ed. 87.50 (0-685-43636-5) Coronet Bks.

Annals & Antiquities of the Counties & County Families of Wales, 2 vols., I. Thomas Nicholas. (Illus.). 964p. 1991. write for info. (0-8063-1316-1, 4103) Genealog Pub.

Annals & Antiquities of the Counties & County Families of Wales, 2 vols., II. Thomas Nicholas. (Illus.). 964p. 1991. write for info. (0-8063-1315-3, 4103) Genealog Pub.

Annals & Family Records of Winchester, Connecticut. John Boyd. (Illus.). 632p. 1988. reprint ed. lib. bdg. 63.50 (0-8328-0019-8, CT0028) Higginson Bk Co.

Annals & Memorials of the Handys & Their Kindred: The Handy Annals. Isaac W. Handy. Ed. by Mildred H. Ritchie & Sarah R. Mallon. LC 92-64116. (Illus.). 800p. 1992. write for info. (1-881606-00-7) W L Clements.

Annals & Parish Register of St. Thomas & St. Denis Parish, in South Carolina, from 1680 to 1884. Robert F. Clute. 111p. 1989. reprint ed. 12.95 (0-685-60445-4, 1070) Clearfield Co.

Annals & Recollections of Oneida County, N.Y. Pomroy Jones. 893p. 1993. reprint ed. lib. bdg. 89.50 (0-8328-3073-9) Higginson Bk Co.

Annals, Comprising Memoirs, Incidents, & Statistics of Harrisburg, from the Period of Its First Settlement (Pennsylvania) George H. Morgan. 446p. (Orig.). reprint ed. pap. text ed. 29.00 (1-55613-931-4) Heritage Bk.

Annals Index. Ed. by Bill Boland et al. (Annals Ser.: Vol. 391). 154p. 1982. lib. bdg. 30.00 (0-89766-172-9); pap. 30.00 (0-89766-173-7) NY Acad Sci.

Annals Index, 1960-1974, Vol. 289. Ed. by Bill Boland. (Annals Ser.). 581p. 1977. 47.00 (0-89072-035-5) NY Acad Sci.

Annals Index 1975-1977. Ed. by Bill M. Boland & Justine Cullinan. (Annals Ser.: Vol. 331). 226p. 1979. 41.00 (0-89766-041-2) NY Acad Sci.

Annals Index, 1978-1979, Vol. 351. (Annals Ser.). 90p. 1980. 23.00 (0-89766-091-9); pap. 23.00 (0-89766-092-7) NY Acad Sci.

Annals Index, 1988-1989. Vance Weaver. 577p. 1992. 40.00 (0-89766-627-5) NY Acad Sci.

Annals IV. Tacitus. Ed. by Shotter. (Classical Texts Ser.). 1989. 49.95 (0-85668-403-1, Pub. by Aris & Phillips UK); pap. 24.95 (0-85668-404-X, Pub. by Aris & Phillips UK) David Brown.

Annals Ninetieth Anniversary Index: 1976-1980. Ed. by Richard D. Lambert & Alan W. Heston. 192p. 1981. 26.00 (0-8039-1762-7); pap. 17.00 (0-8039-1763-5) Sage.

Annals of a Publishing House: William Blackwood & His Son, Their Magazine & Friends, 3 Vols, 1. Margaret O. Oliphant. LC 70-148282. reprint ed. write for info. (0-404-07731-5) AMS Pr.

Annals of a Publishing House: William Blackwood & His Son, Their Magazine & Friends, 3 Vols, 2. Margaret O. Oliphant. LC 70-148282. reprint ed. write for info. (0-404-07732-3) AMS Pr.

Annals of a Publishing House: William Blackwood & His Son, Their Magazine & Friends, 3 Vols, 3. Margaret O. Oliphant. LC 70-148282. reprint ed. write for info. (0-404-07733-1) AMS Pr.

Annals of a Publishing House: William Blackwood & His Son, Their Magazine & Friends, 3 Vols, Set. Margaret O. Oliphant. LC 70-148282. reprint ed. 205.00 (0-404-07730-7) AMS Pr.

Annals of a Quiet Neighbourhood. deluxe ed. George MacDonald. 1992. 37.50 (0-940652-60-9) Sunrise Bks.

***Annals of a Quiet Neighbourhood.** George MacDonald. (George MacDonald Original Works: Series V). 600p. 1995. reprint ed. 20.00 (1-881084-29-9) Johannesen.

Annals of America, 24 vols. 549.00 (0-87827-199-6) Ency Brit Ed.

Annals of American Bookselling, 1638-1850. Henry W. Boynton. (History of the Book Ser.: Vol. 5). 248p. 1991. reprint ed. 35.00 (0-938768-25-5) Oak Knoll.

Annals of American Literature, 1602-1983. Ed. by Richard M. Ludwig & Clifford A. Nault, Jr. (Oxford Paperback Reference Ser.). (Illus.). 352p. 1989. pap. 14.95 (0-19-505919-0) OUP.

Annals of an Ancient Cornish Town: Redruth. Frank Michell. (C). 1989. 65.00 (0-907566-85-5, Pub. by Dyllansow Truran UK) St Mut.

Annals of Arid Zone: Annotated Index, Vol. 1-25, 1962-1986. Scientific Publishers Staff. 368p. (C). 1989. 135.00 (81-85046-79-4, Scientific) St Mut.

Annals of Assurance Sciences: Vol. 8: Assurance Technologies in Action. 598p. 1969. text ed. 273.00 (0-677-13690-0) Gordon & Breach.

Annals of Australian Literature. 2nd ed. Ed. by Joy Hooton & Harry Heseltine. 376p. 1993. 52.00 (0-19-553475-1) OUP.

Annals of Bath County, Virginia. Oren F. Morton. 208p. 1990. reprint ed. 21.00 (0-685-60473-X, 9260) Clearfield Co.

Annals of Blackwater & the Land of Canaan, 1746-1880. Stuart E. Brown, Jr. LC 59-10184. (Illus.). 42p. 1959. reprint ed. pap. 3.00 (0-685-05214-1); reprint ed. write for info. (0-685-65060-X) VA Bk.

Annals of British & Commonwealth Air Transport, 1919-1960. John Stroud. LC 82-72839. (Airlines History Project Ser.). (Illus.). 1983. reprint ed. 110.00 (0-404-19237-4) AMS Pr.

Annals of Britons of Court Pedigree of Hywel the Good see Nennius's "History of the Brittons"

Annals of Brookfield, Fairfield County, Ct. Emily C. Hawley. (Illus.). 656p. 1993. reprint ed. lib. bdg. 66.00 (0-8328-2852-1) Higginson Bk Co.

Annals of Buffalo Valley, Pennsylvania, 1755-1855. John B. Linn. (Illus.). 630p. 1989. reprint ed. pap. 30.00 (1-55613-206-9) Heritage Bk.

Annals of Child Development, Vol. 7. Ed. by Ross Vasta. 300p. 1990. 75.00 (1-85302-081-8, Pub. by J Kingsley Pubs UK) Taylor & Francis.

Annals of Child Development, Vol. 8. Ed. by Ross Vasta. 300p. 1992. 79.00 (1-85302-114-8, Pub. by J Kingsley Pubs UK) Taylor & Francis.

Annals of Child Development, Vol. 9. Ed. by Ross Vasta. 240p. 1993. 75.00 (1-85302-219-5, Pub. by J Kingsley Pubs UK) Taylor & Francis.

***Annals of Child Development Vol. 10.** Ed. by Ross Vasta. 300p. 1995. 75.00 (1-85302-238-1, Pub. by J Kingsley Pubs UK) Taylor & Francis.

***Annals of Child Development Vol. 11.** Ross Vasta. 300p. 1995. 79.00 (1-85302-239-X, Pub. by J Kingsley Pubs UK) Taylor & Francis.

***Annals of Chile.** Paul Muldoon. 191p. Date not set. 10.00 (0-374-52456-4) FS&G.

Annals of Chile. Paul Muldoon. LC 94-10874. 1994. 21.00 (0-374-10518-9) FS&G.

Annals of Clarke County, Virginia: Old Homes, Families, Etcetera of the Southern (South of U. S. Route 50) Section, Vol. 1. Stuart E. Brown, Jr. (Illus.). 425p. 1983. 42.50 (0-317-05706-5) VA Bk.

Annals of Clarke County, Virginia, Vol. 2: Biographical & Genealogical Records of Persons Buried at Old Chapel. Stuart E. Brown, Jr et al. (Illus.). iv, 210p. 1987. Indexed. 32.50 (0-685-34653-6); Indexed. pap. 22.50 (0-685-34654-4) VA Bk.

Annals of Dublin Fair City. E. E. O'Donnell. (Illus.). 237p. 1987. 32.00 (0-86327-149-9, Pub. by Wolfhound Pr IE) Dufour.

Annals of Dyslexia. Ed. by Rosemary F. Bowler. 1983. 9.75 (0-685-08474-4) Orton Dyslexia.

Annals of European Civilization, 1501-1900. Comp. by Alfred Mayer. LC 83-45811. reprint ed. 42.00 (0-404-20172-5) AMS Pr.

Annals of Fort Mackinac. rev. ed. Dwight H. Kelton. (Illus.). 143p. 1992. reprint ed. pap. 7.95 (0-911872-61-2) Mackinac Island.

Annals of Fulda. Tr. & Anno. by Timothy Reuter. LC 92-8388. (Ninth-Century Histories Ser.: Vol. 2). (ENG & LAT.). 1993. text ed. 59.95 (0-7190-3457-4); text ed. 19.95 (0-7190-3458-2) St Martin.

Annals of Imperial Rome. Tacitus. (Illus.). 455p. 1985. 16.95 (0-88029-024-2) Dorset Pr.

Annals of Imperial Rome. Tacitus. Tr. by Michael Grant. (Classics Ser.). 1956. pap. 9.95 (0-14-044060-7, Penguin Classics) Viking Penguin.

Annals of Innocence & Experience. Herbert E. Read. LC 74-7019. (English Literature Ser.: No. 33). 1974. lib. bdg. 75.00 (0-8383-1993-9) M S G Haskell Hse.

Annals of Insanity: Comprising a Selection of Curious & Interesting Cases in the Different Species of Lunacy, Melancholy, or Madness. William Perfect. LC 75-16726. (Classics in Psychiatry Ser.). 1976. reprint ed. 28.95 (0-405-07449-2) Ayer.

Annals of Jamaica, 2 vols., Set. G. Wilson Bridges. 1968. reprint ed. 95.00 (0-7146-1931-0, Pub. by F Cass Pubs UK) Intl Spec Bk.

Annals of Kansas: 1541-1885. Daniel W. Wilder. LC 75-130. (Mid-American Frontier Ser.). 1975. reprint ed. 95.95 (0-405-06895-6) Ayer.

Annals of Kansas, 1886-1925, 2 vols., Set. Jennie S. Owen. Ed. by Kirke Mechem. Incl. Vol. 1. LC 55-62029. 526p. 1954. 4.00 (0-87726-009-5); Vol. 2. LC 55-62029. 551p. 1956. 7.00 (0-87726-010-9); LC 55-62029. (Illus.). 12.50 (0-87726-008-7) Kansas St Hist.

Annals of Kokonor. Ho-Chin Yang. (Uralic & Altaic Ser.: Vol. 106). 1969. pap. text ed. 11.00 (0-87750-084-3) Res Inst Inner Asian Studies.

Annals of Life Insurance Medicine: Proceedings of the International Congress of Life Insurance, 13th, Madrid, 1979, Vol. 6. International Congress of Life Insurance Staff. Ed. by E. Tanner & M. L. Hefti. (Illus.). 270p. 1980. 48.80 (0-387-10050-4) Spr-Verlag.

Annals of Loch Ce: A Chronicle of Irish Affairs from 1014-1590, 2 vols., Set. Ed. by William Hennessy. (Rolls Ser.: No. 54). 1972. reprint ed. 120.00 (0-8115-1113-8) Periodicals Srv.

Annals of Music in America. Henry C. Lahee. LC 72-107810. (Select Bibliographies Reprint Ser.). 1977. 23.95 (0-8369-5185-9) Ayer.

Annals of Music in America. Henry C. Lahee. LC 78-97889. reprint ed. 32.50 (0-404-03801-8) AMS Pr.

Annals of Music in America: A Chronological Record of Significant Musical Events. Henry C. Lahee. 298p. 1990. reprint ed. lib. bdg. 69.00 (0-7812-9031-7) Rprt Serv.

Annals of Music in Philadelphia & History of the Musical Fund Society. Comp. by Louis C. Madeira. LC 78-169650. (Music Reprint Ser.). (Illus.). 234p. 1973. reprint ed. lib. bdg. 29.50 (0-306-70260-6) Da Capo.

Annals of Natural History. Donnell Hunter. 28p. (Orig.). 1989. pap. 5.00 (0-917005-25-2) Honeybrook Pr.

Annals of New York Stage. G. C. Odel. 1993. reprint ed. lib. bdg. 89.00 (0-7812-5282-2) Rprt Serv.

Annals of Newberry, South Carolina, Historical Biographical & Anecodotal: Also Religious Medical & Literary, 2 vols., Set. John B. O'Neall & John A. Chapman. iii, 890p. 1993. reprint ed. pap. text ed. 51.00 (1-55613-772-9) Heritage Bk.

Annals of Newtown, of Queens County, New York, Containing Its History from Its Settlement, Together with Many Interesting Facts Concerning the Adjacent Towns, with Genealogies. James Riker. (Illus.). 437p. 1992. reprint ed. lib. bdg. write for info. (0-8328-2341-4) Higginson Bk Co.

Annals of Nyingma Lineage in America, Vol. III. Ed. by Michael Dow & Elizabeth Cook. 255p. (Orig.). 1985. pap. 14.95 (0-913546-99-2) Dharma Pub.

Annals of Oman. Sirhan Sirhan. Tr. by E. C. Ross. (Arabia Past & Present Ser.: Vol. 16). 136p. 1985. 35.00 (0-900891-46-7) Oleander Pr.

Annals of Opera, Fifteen Ninety-Seven to Nineteen Forty, 2 vols., Set. Alfred Loewenberg. 1988. reprint ed. lib. bdg. 149.00 (0-7812-0999-4) Rprt Serv.

Annals of Oxford, Maine, from its Incorporation, February 27, 1829 to 1850; Prefaced by a Brief Account of the Settlement of Shepardsfield Plantation, Now Hebron & Oxford, with Genealogical Notes from the Earliest Records of Both Towns. Marquis F. King. LC 86-62444. (Illus.). 322p. 1987. reprint ed. 45.00 (0-89725-064-8) Picton Pr.

***Annals of Oxford, Me., from Its Incorporation...in 1829 to 1850, with a Brief Account of the Settlement of Shepardsfield Plantation, Now Hebron & Oxford, & Genealogical Notes from...Both Towns.** Marquis F. King. (Illus.). 298p. 1995. reprint ed. lib. bdg. 35.00 (0-8328-4464-0) Higginson Bk Co.

Annals of Oxford, New York, with Illustrations & Biographical Sketches of Some of Its Prominent Men & Early Pioneers. Henry J. Galpin. (Illus.). 568p. 1992. reprint ed. lib. bdg. 57.00 (0-8328-2340-6) Higginson Bk Co.

Annals of Pennsylvania, from the Discovery of the Delaware, 1609-1682. Samuel Hazard. 672p. 1993. reprint ed. pap. text ed. 38.00 (1-55613-862-8) Heritage Bk.

Annals of Philadelphia & Pennsylvania in the Olden Time, 3 vols., Set. John F. Watson. 1993. reprint ed. lib. bdg. 225.00 (0-7812-5853-7) Rprt Serv.

Annals of Platte County, Missouri, from Its Exploration down to June 1, 1897: With Genealogies of Its Noted Families, & Sketches of Its Pioneers & Distinguished People. W. M. Paxton. 1188p. 1992. reprint ed. pap. 70.00 (1-55613-520-3) Heritage Bk.

***Annals of Polk County, Iowa.** Will Porter. (Illus.). 1064p. 1993. lib. bdg. 105.00 (0-8328-3531-5) Higginson Bk Co.

Annals of Portsmouth. Nathaniel Adams. 400p. 1992. reprint ed. lib. bdg. 39.00 (0-8328-2238-8) Higginson Bk Co.

Annals of Portsmouth, New Hampshire: Comprising a Period of Two Hundred Years from the First Settlement of the Town with Biographical Sketches... Nathaniel Adams. 412p. 1989. reprint ed. pap. 25.00 (1-55613-225-5) Heritage Bk.

Annals of Progress: The Story of Lenoir County & Kinston, North Carolina. William S. Powell. (Illus.). x, 107p. 1963. pap. 5.00 (0-86526-124-5) NC Archives.

Annals of Quintus Ennius. Ethel M. Steuart. ix, 246p. 1976. reprint ed. 44.20 (3-487-05881-2, Pub. by Georg Olms GW) Lubrecht & Cramer.

Annals of Roger De Hoveden, 2 Vols, 1. Roger De Hoveden. Tr. by H. T. Riley. LC 68-57865. (Bohn's Antiquarian Library). reprint ed. write for info. (0-404-50061-7) AMS Pr.

Annals of Roger De Hoveden, 2 Vols, 2. Roger De Hoveden. Tr. by H. T. Riley. LC 68-57865. (Bohn's Antiquarian Library). reprint ed. write for info. (0-404-50062-5) AMS Pr.

Annals of Roger De Hoveden, 2 Vols, Set. Roger De Hoveden. Tr. by H. T. Riley. LC 68-57865. (Bohn's Antiquarian Library). reprint ed. 87.50 (0-404-50060-9) AMS Pr.

Annals of Rutherford County, Vol I of 2. John C. Spence. 250p. 1991. write for info. (0-9621673-3-9) C B Arnette.

Annals of Rutherford County, Vol. II of 2. John C. Spence. 250p. 1991. write for info. (0-9621673-4-7) C B Arnette.

Annals of San Francisco. Frank Soule. 1992. reprint ed. lib. bdg. 75.00 (0-7812-5090-0) Rprt Serv.

Annals of San Francisco & History of California. Frank Soule et al. (Illus.). 824p. 1993. reprint ed. lib. bdg. 84.00 (0-8328-3493-9) Higginson Bk Co.

Annals of Scotland: From the Accession of Malcolm III to the Accession of Robert I to the Accession of the House of Stewart, 2 vols. in 1. David D. Hailes. LC 78-67523. (Scottish Enlightenment Ser.). reprint ed. 195.00 (0-404-17204-0) AMS Pr.

Annals of Sennacherib. Daniel D. Luckenbill. LC 78-72760. (Ancient Mesopotamian Texts & Studies). reprint ed. 37.50 (0-404-18206-2) AMS Pr.

Annals of Shawnee Methodist Mission & Indian Manual Labor School. 2nd ed. Martha B. Caldwell. LC 39-28738. (Illus.). 120p. 1977. pap. 3.00 (0-87726-005-2) Kansas St Hist.

Annals of Southwest Virginia 1769-1811, Set. Lewis P. Summers. (Illus.). 1764p. 1992. reprint ed. 59.95 (0-932807-80-1) Overmountain Pr.

Annals of St-Bertin: Ninth-Century Histories, Vol. 1. Ed. by Janet L. Nelson. LC 91-4030. 256p. 1992. text ed. 69.95 (0-7190-3425-6, Pub. by Manchester Univ Pr UK); text ed. 24.95 (0-7190-3426-4, Pub. by Manchester Univ Pr UK) St Martin.

Annals of St. Louis in Its Early Days under the French & Spanish Dominations. Frederic L. Billon. LC 72-146373. (First American Frontier Ser.). (Illus.). 1971. reprint ed. 41.95 (0-405-02824-5) Ayer.

Annals of St. Louis in Its Territorial Days from 1804 to 1821: Being a Continuation of the Author's Previous Work, the Annals of the French & Spanish Period. Frederic L. Billon. LC 76-146374. (First American Frontier Ser.). (Illus.). 1971. reprint ed. 41.95 (0-405-02825-3) Ayer.

Annals of Staten Island, from Its Discovery to the Present Time. J. J. Clute. LC 86-11962. (Illus.). 516p. 1986. reprint ed. lib. bdg. 35.00 (0-932334-79-2, NY43025) Hrt of the Lakes.

An Asterisk (*) at the beginning of an entry indicates that the title is appearing in BIP for the first time.

An Asterisk (*) at the beginning of an entry indicates that the title is appearing in BIP for the first time.

Anne Hebert: Selected Poems. Anne Hebert. 1987. 25.00 (*0-918526-56-6*); pap. 12.50 (*0-918526-57-4*) BOA Edns.

Anne Hooper's Kama Sutra. Anne Hooper. LC 94-21871. (Illus.). 160p. 1994. 22.95 (*1-56458-649-9*) Dorling Kindersley.

Anne Hooper's Pocket Sex Guide. Anne Hooper. LC 93-45836. (Illus.). 96p. 1994. 9.95 (*1-56458-509-3*) Dorling Kindersley.

Anne Hutchinson. Elizabeth IlgenFritz. (American Women of Achievement Ser.). (Illus.). 112p. (J). (gr. 5 up). 1991. lib. bdg. 17.95 (*1-55546-660-5*) Chelsea Hse.

Anne Hutchinson: Fighter for Religious Freedom. Dennis B. Fradin. LC 88-31329. (Colonial Profiles Ser.). (Illus.). 48p. (J). (gr. 3-6). 1990. lib. bdg. 14.95 (*0-89490-229-6*) Enslow Pubs.

***Anne Hutchinson: The Life of America's First Feminist, Female Minister, & Martyr, 1591-1643.** Winnifred K. Rugg. LC 95-3439. 1996. pap. 14.95 (*0-930852-30-3*) Tree Life Pubns.

Anne Hutchinson: Troubler of the Puritan Zion. Ed. by Francis J. Bremer. LC 80-13218. 180p. (Orig.). 1981. pap. text ed. 11.50 (*0-89874-063-0*) Krieger.

Anne Hutchinson & the Puritans: An Early American Tragedy. William Dunlea. 288p. (Orig.). 1993. pap. 10.95 (*0-8059-3434-0*) Dorrance.

Anne Hutchinson, Guilty or Not? A Closer Look at Her Trials. Jean Cameron. LC 93-17290. (American University Studies: History: Ser. IX, Vol. 146). 248p. (C). 1994. text ed. 45.95 (*0-8204-2227-4*) P Lang Pubs.

Anne Is Elegant. Mary L. Cuneo. LC 92-42417. 176p. (J). (gr. 4 up). 1993. lib. bdg. 14.89 (*0-06-022993-4*) HarpC Child Bks.

***Anne Kursinski's Riding & Jumping Clinic: A Step-by-Step Guide to Winning in the Hunter & Jumper Rings.** Anne Kursinski & Miranda Lorraine. LC 94-40229. 1995. 27.95 (*0-385-47405-9*) Doubleday.

Anne McCaffrey. Mary T. Brizzi. LC 85-17160. (Starmont Reader's Guide Ser.: Vol. 30). (Illus.). viii, 95p. 1986. lib. bdg. 25.00x (*0-930261-30-5*); pap. 15.00x (*0-930261-29-1*) Borgo Pr.

Anne McCaffrey: Dragonlady & More: A Working Bibliography. 3rd ed. Phil Stephensen-Payne & Gordon Benson, Jr. (Galactic Central Bibliographies Ser.: No. 13). ix, 30p. (C). 1990. lib. bdg. 15.00x (*0-8095-4712-0*) Borgo Pr.

Anne Morrow Lindbergh. David K. Vaughan. (United States Authors Ser.: No. 939). 136p. 1988. text ed. 20.95 (*0-8057-7520-X*, TUSAS 539, Twayne) Macmillan.

Anne Morrow Lindbergh: A Gift for Life. Dorothy Herrmann. (Illus.). 400p. 1993. reprint ed. pap. 12.50 (*0-14-023238-9*, Penguin Bks) Viking Penguin.

Anne of Austria: Queen of France, 1601-1666. Ruth Kleinman. LC 85-15453. 350p. 1985. pap. 21.50 (*0-8142-0429-5*) Ohio St U Pr.

Anne of Avonlea. L. M. Montgomery. (Airmont Classics Ser.). (YA). (gr. 8 up). 1984. pap. 0.75 (*0-8049-0219-4*) Airmont.

***Anne of Avonlea.** L. M. Montgomery. 304p. (YA). 1995. mass mkt. 2.99 (*0-8125-5196-6*) Tor Bks.

Anne of Avonlea. Lacy M. Montgomery. 1976. 20.95 (*0-89190-155-8*, Am Repr) Amereon Ltd.

Anne of Avonlea. Lucy M. Montgomery. (J). 1992. pap. 3.25 (*0-553-15114-2*) Bantam.

Anne of Avonlea. Lucy M. Montgomery. LC 93-85541. (Courage Literary Classics Ser.). 256p. 1994. 5.98 (*1-56138-368-6*) Courage Bks.

Anne of Avonlea. Lucy M. Montgomery. 288p. 1987. pap. 3.95 (*0-451-52113-7*, Sig Classics) NAL-Dutton.

Anne of Avonlea. Lucy M. Montgomery. LC 92-10199. (Children's Classics Ser.). (Illus.). (YA). 1992. 12.99 (*0-517-08127-X*, Child Classics) Random Hse Value.

Anne of Avonlea. Lucy M. Montgomery. (J). (gr. 4-7). 1991. pap. 3.25 (*0-590-44556-1*, Apple Classics) Scholastic Inc.

Anne of Avonlea. large type ed. Lucy M. Montgomery. (Large Print Ser.). 435p. 1993. reprint ed. lib. bdg. 22.00 (*0-939495-26-0*) North Bks.

Anne of Avonlea. large type ed. Lucy M. Montgomery. LC 93-22574. (YA). 1993. 15.95 (*1-56054-780-4*) Thorndike Pr.

Anne of Avonlea, No. 2. Lucy M. Montgomery. 1984. pap. 2.95 (*0-553-21314-8*) Bantam.

Anne of Avonlea: An Anne of Green Gables Story. Lucy M. Montgomery. (Illustrated Junior Library). (Illus.). 320p. (YA). 1990. 13.95 (*0-448-40063-4*, G&D) Putnam Pub Group.

Anne of Green Gables. L. M. Montgomery. (Airmont Classics Ser.). (YA). (gr. 7 up). 1984. pap. 1.95 (*0-8049-0218-6*) Airmont.

Anne of Green Gables. L. M. Montgomery. (J). (gr. 1-7). 1994. pap. 12.95 (*0-7704-2589-5*, Little Rooster) Bantam.

Anne of Green Gables. L. M. Montgomery. 1989. 4.95 (*0-87129-242-4*, A41) Dramatic Pub.

Anne of Green Gables. L. M. Montgomery. (Illustrated Junior Library). (Illus.). (J). (gr. 4 up). 1983. 13.95 (*0-448-06030-2*, G&D) Putnam Pub Group.

Anne of Green Gables. L. M. Montgomery. LC 93-36331. (Bullseye Step into Classics Ser.). 108p. (J). (gr. 2-6). 1994. pap. 2.99 (*0-679-85467-3*) Random Bks Yng Read.

Anne of Green Gables. L. M. Montgomery. (YA). 1995. pap. 2.99 (*0-8125-5152-4*) Tor Bks.

***Anne of Green Gables.** L. M. Montgomery. (Dover Children's Thrift Classics Ser.). (Illus.). 96p. (J). 1994. pap. text ed. 1.00 (*0-486-28366-6*) Dover.

Anne of Green Gables. Lacy M. Montgomery. 1976. 21.95 (*0-8488-0584-4*) Amereon Ltd.

Anne of Green Gables. Lucy M. Montgomery. (J). 1982. 2.95 (*0-553-21313-X*, Bantam Classics) Bantam.

Anne of Green Gables. Lucy M. Montgomery. (J). 1987. Boxed set. boxed 8.95 (*0-553-33306-2*) Bantam.

Anne of Green Gables, 3 vols. Lucy M. Montgomery. (YA). (gr. 7-12). 1987. Boxed Set. boxed 8.85 (*0-553-33307-0*) Bantam.

Anne of Green Gables. Lucy M. Montgomery. LC 93-70551. (Literary Classics Ser.). 240p. (J). (gr. 4 up). 1993. 5.98 (*1-56138-324-4*) Courage Bks.

Anne of Green Gables. Lucy M. Montgomery. 338p. (YA). 1993. pap. 4.95 (*0-7710-9883-9*) Firefly Bks Ltd.

Anne of Green Gables. Lucy M. Montgomery. (Illus.). 256p. (J). 1994. 25.00 (*0-88363-994-7*) H L Levin.

Anne of Green Gables. Lucy M. Montgomery. 320p. 1987. pap. 3.95 (*0-451-52112-9*, Sig Classics) NAL-Dutton.

Anne of Green Gables. Lucy M. Montgomery. 256p. (J). (gr. 5 up). 1994. pap. 2.99 (*0-14-035148-5*) Puffin Bks.

Anne of Green Gables, 3 vols. in 1. Lucy M. Montgomery. 1988. 11.99 (*0-517-60517-1*) Random Hse Value.

Anne of Green Gables. Lucy M. Montgomery. LC 87-31868. (Children's Classics Ser.). (J). 1988. 12.99 (*0-517-65958-1*) Random Hse Value.

Anne of Green Gables. Lucy M. Montgomery. 384p. (J). (gr. 4-7). 1989. pap. 2.95 (*0-590-42243-X*, Apple Classics) Scholastic Inc.

Anne of Green Gables. Lucy M. Montgomery. Ed. by Joanne Mattern. LC 92-12703. (Illustrated Classics Ser.). (Illus.). 48p. (J). (gr. 3-6). 1992. lib. bdg. 12.89 (*0-8167-2866-6*); pap. text ed. 3.95 (*0-8167-2867-4*) Troll Assocs.

Anne of Green Gables. large type ed. Lucy M. Montgomery. 448p. 1993. reprint ed. lib. bdg. 22.00 (*0-939495-25-2*) North Bks.

Anne of Green Gables. large type ed. Lucy M. Montgomery. LC 92-43772. 484p. (YA). 1993. reprint ed. lib. bdg. 15.95 (*1-56054-643-3*) Thorndike Pr.

Anne of Green Gables. L. M. Montgomery. 429p. 1977. reprint ed. lib. bdg. 21.95 (*0-89966-262-5*) Buccaneer Bks.

Anne of Green Gables. Lucy M. Montgomery. 352p. (J). 1992. reprint ed. 16.95 (*1-55109-013-9*, Pub. by Nimbus Publishing Ltd CN) Chelsea Green Pub.

Anne of Green Gables, Vol. 1. Lucy M. Montgomery. (J). (gr. 4-7). 1984. pap. 3.50 (*0-553-15327-7*) Bantam.

Anne of Green Gables: A Literature Unit. Betty Burke. Ed. by Janet Cain. (Illus.). 48p. 1994. student ed 6.95 (*1-55734-438-8*) Tchr Create Mat.

Anne of Green Gables: A Study Guide. Gloria Levine. (Novel-Ties Ser.). (J). (gr. 6-8). 1989. student ed, teacher ed 15.95 (*0-88122-056-6*) Lrn Links.

***Anne of Green Gables: Pop-up Dollhouse.** Richard Row. (Illus.). (J). (ps-3). 1994. 18.00 (*0-679-86391-5*) Random Bks Yng Read.

Anne of Green Gables Birthday Book. Lucy M. Montgomery. (Illus.). (J). 1990. 8.95 (*0-7704-2362-0*) Bantam.

Anne of Green Gables Cookbook. Kate Macdonald. (Illus.). 48p. (J). 1987. 12.95 (*0-19-540496-3*) OUP.

Anne of Green Gables Cookbook. Kate Macdonald. 1988. mass mkt. 4.95 (*0-7704-2258-6*) Bantam.

Anne of Green Gables Storybook. Lucy M. Montgomery. (Illus.). 80p. (J). (gr. 3 up). 1987. 16.95 (*0-920668-43-7*); pap. 9.95 (*0-920668-42-9*) Firefly Bks Ltd.

Anne of Green Gables Treasury. Carolyn S. Collins & Christina W. Eriksson. LC 91-65448. (Illus.). 168p. 1991. 24.95 (*0-670-82591-3*, Viking) Viking Penguin.

Anne of Green Gables Treasury of Days. Carolyn S. Collins & Christina W. Eriksson. (Illus.). 128p. 1994. 15.95 (*0-670-85508-1*, Viking) Viking Penguin.

Anne of Ingleside. 21.95 (*0-8488-0890-8*) Amereon Ltd.

Anne of Ingleside. Lacy M. Montgomery. 1976. 21.95 (*0-8488-1101-1*) Amereon Ltd.

Anne of Ingleside, No. 6. Lucy M. Montgomery. (J). 1984. 2.95 (*0-553-21315-6*, Bantam Classics) Bantam.

Anne of the Island. Lacy M. Montgomery. 1976. 20.95 (*0-8488-0585-2*) Amereon Ltd.

Anne of the Island. Lucy M. Montgomery. (J). 1983. pap. 2.95 (*0-553-21317-2*, Bantam Classics) Bantam.

Anne of the Island. Lucy M. Montgomery. (J). (gr. 3-7). 1992. pap. 3.50 (*0-553-48066-9*) Bantam.

Anne of the Island. Lucy M. Montgomery. LC 93-85542. (Courage Literary Classics Ser.). 240p. 1994. 5.98 (*1-56138-369-4*) Courage Bks.

Anne of the Island. Lucy M. Montgomery. (Illustrated Junior Library). (Illus.). 288p. (J). (gr. 4 up). 1992. 14.95 (*0-448-40311-0*, G&D) Putnam Pub Group.

Anne of the Island. Lucy M. Montgomery. (J). (gr. 4-7). 1993. pap. 3.25 (*0-590-46163-X*) Scholastic Inc.

Anne of the Island. large type ed. L. M. Montgomery. LC 94-1765. 377p. (J). 1994. pap. 17.95 (*0-7862-0205-X*) Thorndike Pr.

Anne of the Island. large type ed. Lucy M. Montgomery. 1991. pap. 2.95 (*0-451-52534-5*, Sig Classics) NAL-Dutton.

Anne of the Island & Other Tales of Avonlea. Lucy M. Montgomery. (J). 1991. 10.99 (*0-517-03705-X*) Random Hse Value.

Anne of the Thousand Days. Maxwell Anderson. 1950. pap. 4.75 (*0-8222-0049-X*) Dramatists Play.

Anne of Windy Poplars. Lacy M. Montgomery. 1976. 20.95 (*0-8488-0586-0*) Amereon Ltd.

Anne of Windy Poplars. Lucy M. Montgomery. (J). (gr. 3-7). 1992. pap. 3.50 (*0-553-48065-0*) Bantam.

Anne of Windy Poplars, No. 4. Lucy M. Montgomery. (J). 1984. pap. 2.95 (*0-553-21316-4*, Bantam Classics) Bantam.

Anne Orr's Afghans to Crochet & Knit. Anne Orr. (Illus.). 32p. 1987. reprint ed. pap. 2.95 (*0-486-25440-2*) Dover.

Anne Orr's Charted Designs. Anne Orr. (Needlework Ser.). (Illus.). 1979. pap. 3.50 (*0-486-23704-4*) Dover.

Anne Orr's Classic Tatting Patterns. Anne Orr. LC 85-4523. 32p. 1985. reprint ed. pap. 2.95 (*0-486-24897-6*) Dover.

Anne Orr's Filet Crochet Designs. Anne Orr. 48p. (Orig.). 1986. pap. 2.95 (*0-486-25103-9*) Dover.

Anne Orr's Treasury of Charted Designs, 3 bks. Anne Orr. (Illus.). 112p. 1985. Set. pap. 11.50 (*0-486-25011-3*) Dover.

Anne Predaille. Henri Troyat. (FRE.). 1990. pap. 10.95 (*0-7859-3274-7*, 2277126195) Fr & Eur.

***Anne Radcliffe: The Great Enchantress.** Robert Miles. 208p. 1995. text ed. 49.95 (*0-7190-3828-6*, Pub. by Manchester Univ Pr UK); text ed. 19.95 (*0-7190-3829-4*, Pub. by Manchester Univ Pr UK) St Martin.

Anne Rice. Bette B. Roberts. LC 93-40509. (Twayne's United States Author Ser.: No. 644). 192p. 1994. text ed. 22.95x (*0-8057-3961-0*, Twayne) Macmillan.

***Anne Rice Trivia Book.** Katherine Ramsland. (Orig.). 1994. mass mkt. 5.99 (*0-345-39251-5*) Ballantine.

Anne Rice's The Vampire Lestat: The Graphic Novel. Illus. by Daerick Gross. 384p. (Orig.). 1991. pap. 25.00 (*0-345-37394-4*, Ballantine Trade) Ballantine.

Anne Scott Plummer. Ed. by William S. Bartman. (Exploring the Work of Artists in Mid-Career Ser.). (Illus.). 32p. (Orig.). 1989. pap. text ed. 14.95 (*0-923183-02-7*) ART Pr CA.

Anne Sexton. Caroline H. Barnard-King. (United States Authors Ser.). 208p. 1989. text ed. 22.95 (*0-8057-7538-2*, Twayne) Macmillan.

Anne Sexton. Diane W. Middlebrook. LC 92-50093. 1992. pap. 14.00 (*0-679-74182-8*, Vin) Random.

Anne Sexton: A Biography. Diane W. Middlebrook. (Illus.). 448p. 1991. 24.95 (*0-395-35362-9*, P Davison Bk) HM.

Anne Sexton: A Self-Portrait in Letters. Ed. by Linda Sexton & Lois Ames. (Illus.). 1992. reprint ed. pap. 12.95 (*0-395-62880-6*) HM.

Anne Sexton: Telling the Tale. Ed. by Steven E. Colburn. 1988. 39.50 (*0-472-09379-7*) U of Mich Pr.

Anne Sexton's Poetry. Richard Morton. LC 88-39019. (Studies in Art & Religious Interpretation: Vol. 11). 150p. 1988. lib. bdg. 69.95 (*0-88946-563-0*) E Mellen.

***Anne Smith's Journal: 1933-1939: A.A.'s Principles of Success.** rev. ed. Dick B. LC 94-68062. 176p. 1995. reprint ed. pap. text ed. 14.00 (*1-885803-01-X*, 942) Paradise Res.

Anne Smith's Spiritual Workbook: An AA-Good Book Connection. 3rd ed. B. Dick. LC 92-90140. (Good Book Connection of A. A. Ser.). 200p. 1995. reprint ed. pap. text ed. 16.95 (*1-881212-01-7*, 0944) Good Bk Pub.

Anne Thackeray Ritchie: Journals & Letters. Ed. by Abigail B. Bloom & John Maynard. (Studies in Victorian Life & Literature). 370p. 1995. 62.50 (*0-8142-0638-7*) Ohio St U Pr.

Anne, the White Woman in Contemporary African-American Fiction: Archetypes, Stereotypes, & Characterizations. Anna M. Chupa. LC 89-25919. (Contributions in Afro-American & African Studies: No. 133). 176p. 1990. text ed. 49.95 (*0-313-25447-8*, PWW/, Greenwood Pr) Greenwood.

Anne Tyler. Elizabeth Evans. LC 92-44339. (Twayne's United States Authors Ser.). 192p. 1993. text ed. 21.95 (*0-8057-3985-8*, Twayne) Macmillan.

***Anne Tyler: A Bio-Bibliography.** Robert W. Croft. LC 94-42115. (Bio-Bibliographies in American Literature Ser.: No. 5). 192p. 1995. text ed. 45.00 (*0-313-28952-2*, Greenwood Pr) Greenwood.

Anne Tyler: Four Complete Novels. Anne Tyler. 1990. 11.99 (*0-517-03204-X*) Random Hse Value.

Anne Tyler: A New Collection: Two Complete Novels. Anne Tyler. 704p. 1991. reprint ed. 12.99 (*0-517-06459-6*, Pub. by Wings Bks) Random Hse Value.

Anne Tyler as Novelist. Ed. by Dale Salwak. LC 94-17014. 240p. 1994. 29.95x (*0-87745-479-5*); pap. 14.95 (*0-87745-487-6*) U of Iowa Pr.

Anne Wilkinson & Her Works. Christopher Armitage. (Canadian Author Studies). 40p. (C). 1989. pap. text ed. 9.95 (*1-55022-012-8*, Pub. by ECW Press CN) Genl Dist Srvs.

Anne Wilson Schaef in Conversation with Michael Toms. Michael Toms. Ed. by Hal Z. Bennett. (New Dimensions Bks.). 112p. (Orig.). 1995. pap. 8.95 (*0-944031-54-4*) Aslan Pub.

Annealing Algorithm. R. H. Otten & L. P. Van Ginneken. (International Series in Engineering & Computer Science, VLSI, Computer Architecture, & Digital Screen Processing). 224p. (C). 1989. lib. bdg. 81.00 (*0-7923-9022-9*) Kluwer Ac.

Annealing & Strengthening in the Glass Industry. 2nd ed. Ed. by Alexis G. Pincus & Thomas R. Holmes. LC 87-70822. (Processing in the Glass Industry Ser.). (Illus.). 1988. text ed. 39.95 (*0-911993-24-X*) Ashlee Pub Co.

Anneau d'Amethyste. Anatole France. (FRE.). 1965. pap. 10.95 (*0-8288-9755-7*, F101141) Fr & Eur.

Anneau d'Amethyste see Romans et Contes

Annee dans le Monde, 1990. Edouard Masurel. (FRE.). 1991. pap. 11.95 (*0-7859-3974-1*) Fr & Eur.

Annee Derniere a Marienbad: Cine-roman. Alain Robbe-Grillet. 176p. (FRE.). 1961. pap. 19.95 (*0-7859-1512-5*, 2707303119) Fr & Eur.

Annee Terrible. Victor Hugo. (Poesie Ser.). 320p. (FRE.). 1984. pap. 13.95 (*2-07-032277-7*) Schoenhof.

Annee Terrible. Victor Hugo. (FRE.). 1984. pap. 16.95 (*0-7859-2791-3*) Fr & Eur.

Annees d'Apprentissage d'Alphonse Daudet. Jacques-Henry Bornecque. 538p. (FRE.). 1951. pap. 29.95 (*0-7859-5306-X*) Fr & Eur.

Annees Louisiane. Jacqueline Denuziere & Maurice Denuziere. 442p. (FRE.). 1989. pap. 12.95 (*0-7859-2127-3*, 2070381897) Fr & Eur.

Annees Vingt: Les Ecrivains Americains a Paris et Leurs Amis, 1920-1930. Centre Culturel Americain, Paris Staff. (Illus.). (FRE.). 1959. pap. 9.50 (*0-910664-09-9*) Gotham.

Anneese Courtes. Felicien Marceau. (FRE.). 1973. pap. 10.95 (*0-7859-4016-2*) Fr & Eur.

Anneke Jans-Bogardus & Adam Brouwer Research Aid Bibliography. William B. Bogardus. vi, 46p. (C). 1989. 10.00 (*0-9621897-0-7*) W B Bogardus.

Annelida. Bent Christensen. (Animal Cytogenetics Ser.: Vol. 2). (Illus.). 81p. 1980. pap. text ed. 47.50 (*3-443-26010-1*, Pub. by Gebrueder Borntraeger GW) Lubrecht & Cramer.

Annelida, Vol. 7. Frederick W. Harrison & Edward E. Ruppert. (Microscopic Anatomy of Invertebrates Ser.: Vol. 7). 428p. 1992. text ed. 225.00 (*0-471-56114-2*, Wiley-Liss) Wiley.

Annemann's Card Magic. Ted Annemann. LC 77-75234. (Illus.). 1977. reprint ed. pap. 4.95 (*0-486-23522-X*) Dover.

***Annemarie Roeper: Selected Writings & Speeches.** Annemarie Roeper. Ed. by Richard Medeiros & Linda Silverman. 136p. (Orig.). 1995. pap. 15.95 (*0-915793-93-8*) Free Spirit Pub.

Anne's Back Door Cookbook: With Helpful Hints for the Hypersensitive. Anne Browning. (Illus.). vii, 70p. (Orig.). 1985. pap. 6.99 (*0-933145-00-4*) Stoneground Pub.

Anne's House of Dreams. Lacy M. Montgomery. 1976. 18.95 (*0-8488-0587-9*) Amereon Ltd.

Anne's House of Dreams. Lucy M. Montgomery. (J). 1983. 2.95 (*0-553-21318-0*, Bantam Classics) Bantam.

Anne's House of Dreams. Lucy M. Montgomery. (Courage Literary Classics Ser.). 304p. 1994. 5.98 (*1-56138-430-5*) Running Pr.

***Anness: Beauty & the Beast.** Madame De Villeneuve. (Illus.). 48p. (J). 1995. 7.98 (*0-8317-1718-1*) Smithmark.

***Anness: Red Riding Hood.** Charles Perrault. (Illus.). 48p. (J). 1995. 7.98 (*0-8317-0746-1*) Smithmark.

***Anness: Sleeping Beauty.** Charles Perrault. (Illus.). 48p. (J). 1995. 7.98 (*0-8317-1719-X*) Smithmark.

***Anness: Snow White.** Jacob Grimm & Wilhelm K. Grimm. (Illus.). 48p. (J). 1995. 7.98 (*0-8317-1148-5*) Smithmark.

Annette Covington: Paintings & Drawings. Sterling Cook et al. LC 82-82113. (Illus.). 50p. (Orig.). 1982. pap. 5.00 (*0-940784-02-5*) Miami Univ Art.

***Annette et le Criminel, ou Suite du Vicaire des Ardennes.** Honore D. Balzac. 446p. (FRE.). 1982. pap. 10.95 (*0-7859-3479-0*, F118145) Fr & Eur.

Annette et le Criminel, ou Suite du Vicaire des Ardennes. Honore De Balzac. 10.95 (*0-8288-9325-X*, 2080703919) Fr & Eur.

Annette Lemieux. Kyoichi Tsuzuki. (Art Random Ser.: No. 92). (Illus.). 48p. 1991. 32.95 (*4-7636-8593-7*, Pub. by Kyoto Shoin JA) Bks Nippan.

Annette von Droste-Huelshoff: A Biography. Mary E. Morgan. LC 83-48746. (American University Studies: Germanic Languages & Literature: Ser. I, Vol. 23). 221p. (Orig.). (C). 1984. text ed. 26.10 (*0-8204-0036-X*) P Lang Pubs.

Annette von Droste-Hulshoff: A Re-Assessment of Her Life & Writings. John Guthrie. (Women's Ser.). (Illus.). 128p. 1989. 35.00 (*0-85496-174-7*) Berg Pubs.

Annex to Unified Theory of Ether, Field & Matter. R. B. Driscoll. 83p. 1985. pap. 5.00 (*0-317-19556-5*) R B Driscoll.

Annexation: A Solution to the Metropolitan Area Problem. Frank S. Sengstock. LC 61-62622. (Michigan Legal Publications). vi, 120p. 1985. reprint ed. lib. bdg. 37.50 (*0-89941-386-2*, 303560) W S Hein.

***Annexation of Assam.** R. M. Lahiri. (C). 1994. text ed. 16.00 (*81-7102-008-9*, Pub. by Firma KLM) S Asia.

Annexation of Burma. Anil C. Banerjee. LC 77-87007. reprint ed. 25.00 (*0-404-16793-4*) AMS Pr.

Annexation of Texas. Justin H. Smith. LC 77-175984. 506p. 1972. reprint ed. 49.50 (*0-404-06125-7*) AMS Pr.

Annexation of Texas. Justin H. Smith. (BCL1 - United States Local History Ser.). 496p. 1991. reprint ed. lib. bdg. 99.00 (*0-7812-6311-5*) Rprt Serv.

Annexation of the Baltic States & Its Effect on the Development of Law Prohibiting Forcible Seizure of Territory. William J. Hough, III. (New York Law School Journal of International & Comparative Law: Winter 1985). 533p. 5.00 (*0-317-61419-3*) World Fed Free Latvians.

Annexation Practices in Michigan: The City Perspective, Pt. I. 1988. pap. 5.00 (*0-317-04599-7*) MI Municipal.

Annexation Practices in Michigan: The City Perspective, Pt. II. 1989. pap. 5.00 (*0-317-04600-4*) MI Municipal.

Annexation, Preferential Trade & Reciprocity: An Outline of the Canadian Annexation Movement of 1849-50, with Special Reference to the Questions of Preferential Trade & Reciprocity. Cephas D. Allin. (BCL1 - History - Canada Ser.). 398p. 1991. reprint ed. text ed. 89.00 (*0-7812-6356-5*) Rprt Serv.

Annexation Procedures in Michigan in General Law Villages. (Technical Topics Ser.: No. 34). 1987. pap. 5.00 (*0-317-03716-1*) MI Municipal.

Annexation to Home Rule Cities. (Technical Topics Ser.: No. 37). 1987. pap. 5.00 (*0-317-04598-9*) MI Municipal.

Annexins. Ed. by S. E. Moss. (Monograph Ser.: Vol. 2). 173p. 1992. 70.00 (*1-85578-008-9*, Pub. by Portland Pr Ltd UK) Ashgate Pub Co.

Annibal Caro: The Scruffy Scoundrels. Tr. by Massimo Ciavolella & D. A. Beecher. 125p. 1989. pap. 6.00 (*0-88920-103-X*, DH45, Pub. by Dovehouse CN) MRTS.

***Annibale Carracci: The Farnese Palace, Rome.** Charles Dempsey. (Great Fresco Cyles of the Renaissance Ser.). (Illus.). 96p. 1995. 25.00 (*0-8076-1316-9*) Braziller.

Annibale Carracci & the Beginnings of Baroque Style. Charles Dempsey. 1977. 22.00 (*0-686-92334-0*) J J Augustin.

An Asterisk (*) at the beginning of an entry indicates that the title is appearing in BIP for the first time.

Annibale Padovano: Il Primo Libro de Ricercari a Quattro Voci, Venice, 1556. Ed. by James Ladewig. LC 93-48854. (Italian Instrumental Music of the Sixteenth & Early Seventeenth Centuries Ser.: Vol. 4). 208p. 1994. 69.00 (0-8240-4503-3) Garland.

Annick ABC. Roger Pare. (Annick Press Ser.: Series 6). (Illus.). 24p. (J). (ps-2). 1989. pap. 0.99 (0-920303-78-1, Pub. by Annick CN) Firefly Bks Ltd.

Annick Baby Diary. (Illus.). 32p. 1987. 7.95 (0-920303-82-X, Pub. by Annick CN) Firefly Bks Ltd.

Annie. (Vocal Score Ser.). 1982. pap. 35.00 (0-88188-001-9, 00383054) H Leonard.

***Annie.** (Best of Broadway Ser.). Date not set. 13.95 (0-614-03930-4, XW1653) Astor Bks.

***Annie.** Luanne Armstrong. 200p. (Orig.). 1995. pap. 12.95 (1-896095-00-3) Orca Bk Pubs.

Annie. rev. ed. Rape & Abuse Crisis Center Staff. (Illus.). 21p. (J). (ps up). 1985. pap. text ed. 2.50 (0-914633-03-1) Rape Abuse Crisis.

Annie ... Anya: A Month in Moscow. Irene Trivas. LC 91-46433. (Illus.). 32p. (J). (gr. k-2). 1992. 14.95 (0-531-05452-7); lib. bdg. 14.99 (0-531-08602-X) Orchard Bks Watts.

Annie Adams Fields: The Spirit of Charles Street. Judith A. Roman. LC 89-46328. (Illus.). 204p. 1991. 27.95 (0-253-35022-0) Ind U Pr.

Annie & Co. David McPhail. LC 90-34119. 40p. (J). (gr. 2-4). 1991. 13.95 (0-8050-1596-5, Bks Young Read) H Holt & Co.

Annie & Company II. David McPhail. 40p. (J). 1997. 13.95 (0-8050-2819-6) H Holt & Co.

Annie & Cousin Precious. Kay Chorao. LC 93-32611. (J). 1994. 14.99 (0-525-45238-9, DCB) Dutton Child Bks.

Annie & Moon. Miriam Smith. Ed. by Rhoda Sherwood. Tr. by A. T. Mahuika. LC 88-42909. (Illus.). 32p. (J). (gr. 3-4). 1988. lib. bdg. 18.60 (1-55532-928-4) Gareth Stevens Inc.

Annie & the Old One. Miska Miles. (Illus.). (J). (gr. 1-3). 1972. lib. bdg. 14.95i (0-316-57117-2, Joy St Bks) Little.

Annie & the Old One. Miska Miles. (Illus.). (J). (gr. 1-3). 1985. reprint ed. mass mkt. 7.95 (0-316-57120-2) Little.

Annie & the Old One: A Study Guide. Garrett Christopher. Ed. by Joyce Friedland & Rikki Kessler. (Novel-Ties Ser.). (J). (gr. 1-4). 1991. pap. text ed. 15.95 (0-88122-564-9) Lrn Links.

Annie & the Old One Literature Mini-Unit. Janet Lovelady. (Illus.). 32p. (J). (gr. 3-5). 1990. student ed 4.95 (1-56096-018-3) Mari.

Annie & the Outlaw. Sharon Sala. 1994. mass mkt. 3.50 (0-373-07597-9, 1-07597-7) Harlequin Bks.

***Annie & the Outlaw.** large type ed. Sharon Sala. LC 95-13708. 305p. 1995. 19.95 (0-7838-1350-3, Large Print Bks) Hall.

Annie & the Wild Animals. Jan Brett. LC 84-19818. (Illus.). 32p. (J). (gr. k-3). 1985. 14.95 (0-395-37800-1) HM.

Annie & the Wild Animals. Jan Brett. (Illus.). (J). (ps-3). 1989. pap. 4.95 (0-395-51006-6, Sandpiper) HM.

Annie & the Wild Animals. Jan Brett. LC 84-19818. (Illus.). 32p. (J). (gr. k-3). 1990. pap. 7.95 (0-395-53962-5) HM.

Annie & the Wise Men: Under the Mistletoe. Lindsay Longford. (Silhouette Romance Ser.). 1993. pap. 2.75 (0-373-08977-5, 5-08977-6) Silhouette.

Annie Armstrong: Dreamer in Action. Bobbie Sorrill. LC 83-70842. 1984. 10.99 (0-8054-6333-X) Broadman.

Annie Bananie. Leah Komaiko. LC 86-45767. (Trophy Picture Bk.). (Illus.). 32p. (J). (gr. k-3). 1989. pap. 4.95 (0-06-443198-3, Trophy) HarpC Child Bks.

Annie, Bea, & Chi Chi Dolores: A School Day Alphabet. Donna Maurer. LC 92-25104. (Illus.). 32p. (J). (ps-k). 1993. 14.95 (0-531-05467-5); lib. bdg. 14.99 (0-531-08617-8) Orchard Bks Watts.

Annie Besant. Olivia Bennett. (In Her Time Ser.). (Illus.). 64p. (YA). (gr. 6-10). 1991. 13.95 (0-237-60038-2, Pub. by Evans Bros Ltd UK) Trafalgar.

Annie Besant. Ed. by Verinder Grover. (Great Women of Modern India Ser.: No. 1). (C). 1993. 34.00 (81-7100-455-5, Pub. by Deep) S Asia.

Annie Besant: A Biography. Anne Taylor. (Illus.). 384p. 1992. 59.00 (0-19-211796-3) OUP.

Annie Besant: An Autobiography. Annie Besant. 1939. 19.50 (0-8356-7568-8) Theos Pub Hse.

Annie Besant: Founder of Home Rule Movement. S. R. Bakshi. 1990. 42.00 (81-7041-259-5, Pub. by Anmol II) S Asia.

Annie Besant, an Autobiography. Annie W. Besant. 1988. reprint ed. lib. bdg. 59.00 (0-7812-0569-7) Rprt Serv.

Annie Besant, an Autobiography. Annie W. Besant. 1976. reprint ed. 29.00 (0-403-06689-1, Regency) Scholarly.

Annie (Broadway) (Illus.). 64p. 1984. pap. 9.95 (0-88188-057-4, 00383056) H Leonard.

Annie Chambers. Lenore Carroll. 215p. 1990. pap. 8.50 (0-922820-07-4) Watermark Pr.

Annie Dillard. Linda Smith. (Twayne's United States Authors Ser.). 170p. (C). 1991. text ed. 22.95 (0-8057-7637-0, Twayne) Macmillan.

Annie Dillard Reader. Annie Dillard. LC 94-19482. 1994. 25.00 (0-06-017158-8, HarpT) HarpC.

Annie Flies the Birthday Bike. Crescent Dragonwagon. LC 90-42861. (Illus.). 32p. (J). (gr. k-3). 1993. text ed. 14.95 (0-02-733155-5, Mac Bks Young Read) S&S Childrens.

Annie Graham: Or, The Young Lawyer's Fee & The Uncle's Return. Horatio Alger, Jr. (Gold Signature Ser.). (Illus.). 118p. 1987. 20.00 (0-317-62761-9) G K Westgard.

Annie Gwen Lilly Pam & Tulip. Jamaica Kincaid. 1989. 25.00 (0-394-58035-4) Knopf.

***Annie Henry & the Birth of Liberty.** Susan Olasky. LC 94-45739. (Adventures of the American Revolution Ser.: Vol. 2). 128p. (Orig.). (J). (gr. 4-6). 1995. pap. 4.99 (0-89107-842-8) Crossway Bks.

***Annie Henry & the Secret Mission.** Susan Olasky. LC 94-38671. (Adventures of the American Revolution Ser.). 128p. (Orig.). (J). (gr. 3-7). 1995. pap. 4.99 (0-89107-830-4) Crossway Bks.

Annie Horniman: A Pioneer in the Theatre. Sheila Gooddie. 216p. 1991. pap. 34.95 (0-413-17330-5, A0009, Pub. by Methuen UK) Heinemann.

Annie John. Jamaica Kincaid. LC 84-28630. 160p. 1985. 18.95 (0-374-10521-9) FS&G.

Annie John. Jamaica Kincaid. 1986. pap. 8.95 (0-452-26356-5, Plume); mass mkt. 6.95 (0-452-26016-7, Plume) NAL-Dutton.

Annie Kilburn. William Dean Howells. (Notable American Authors Ser.). 1992. reprint ed. lib. bdg. 75.00 (0-7812-3241-4) Rprt Serv.

Annie Kilburn: A Novel. William Dean Howells. LC 72-145096. 331p. 1972. reprint ed. 29.00 (0-403-01033-0) Scholarly.

Annie Lash. Dorothy Garlock. 400p. (Orig.). 1985. mass mkt. 5.99 (0-445-20037-5) Warner Bks.

***Annie Lash.** Dorothy Garlock. 400p. (Orig.). 1995. mass mkt. 5.99 (0-446-60303-1) Warner Bks.

***Annie Lash.** large type ed. Dorothy Garlock. LC 94-47822. 464p. 1995. 21.95 (0-7862-0393-5) Thorndike Pr.

Annie Learns to Ride. Jennifer Bell. (C). 1990. 32.00 (0-85131-508-9, Pub. by J A Allen & Co UK); pap. 24.00 (0-85131-492-9, Pub. by J A Allen & Co UK) St Mut.

Annie Leibovitz, Photographs, 1970-1990. (Illus.). 1992. 250.00 (0-06-016725-4, HarpT) HarpC.

Annie Leibovitz, Photographs, 1970-1990: Including a Conversation with Ingrid Sischy. LC 90-56384. 232p. 1991. 85.00 (0-06-016608-8, HarpT) HarpC.

Annie Lennox: Sweet Dreams Are Made of This. Lucy O'Brien. (Illus.). 224p. (Orig.). 1993. pap. 13.95 (0-312-09740-9) St Martin.

Annie McCune: Shreveport Madam. Goodloe Stuck. Ed. by Doug Woolfolk. (Illus.). 120p. 1981. 9.95 (0-86518-022-9); pap. 7.95 (0-686-78168-6) Moran Pub Corp.

Annie (Motion Picture) (Illus.). 1982. 9.95 (0-88188-617-3, 00383058) H Leonard.

Annie Nelles. Annie H. Dumond. Ed. by Annette K. Baxter. LC 79-8788. (Signal Lives Ser.). 1980. reprint ed. lib. bdg. 42.95 (0-405-12836-3) Ayer.

Annie Oakley. (Story Clippers Ser.). (Illus.). (J). (gr. 2-5). 1989. 29.28 (0-8172-2955-8) Raintree Steck-V.

Annie Oakley. Jan Gleiter & Kathleen Thompson. (Biographical Stories Ser.). (Illus.). 32p. (J). (gr. 2-5). 1986. lib. bdg. 19.97 (0-8172-2641-9) Raintree Steck-V.

***Annie Oakley.** Jan Gleiter & Kathleen Thompson. LC 94-24007. (First Biographies Ser.). (J). 1995. 19.97 (0-8114-8451-3) Raintree Steck-V.

Annie Oakley. Shirl Kasper. LC 91-50864. (Illus.). 352p. (C). 1992. 22.95 (0-8061-2418-0) U of Okla Pr.

Annie Oakley. James H. Kunstler. LC 93-19246. (Illus.). (J). 1993. 14.95 (0-88708-338-2, Rabbit); audio, pap. 19.95 (0-88708-337-4, Rabbit) S&S Childrens.

Annie Oakley. Ellen Wilson. (Childhood of Famous Americans Ser.). (Illus.). 192p. (J). (gr. 2-6). 1989. reprint ed. pap. 3.95 (0-689-71346-0, Aladdin Paperbacks) S&S Childrens.

Annie Oakley: The Shooting Star. Charles P. Graves. (Discovery Biographies Ser.). (Illus.). 80p. (J). (gr. 2-6). 1991. reprint ed. lib. bdg. 12.95 (0-7910-1448-7) Chelsea Hse.

Annie Oakley & Buffalo Bill's Wild West: One Hundred Two Illustrations. Isabelle S. Sayers. (Illus.). 96p. (Orig.). 1981. pap. 6.95 (0-486-24120-3) Dover.

Annie Oakley in the Wild West Extravaganza! Ron Fontes & Justine Korman. LC 93-70937. (American Frontier Ser.: Bk. 9). (Illus.). 80p. (J). (gr. 1-4). 1993. lib. bdg. 12.89 (1-56282-492-9); pap. 3.50 (1-56282-491-0) Disney Pr.

Annie Oakley of the Wild West. Walter Havighurst. LC 91-41864. (Illus.). xx, 254p. 1992. reprint ed. pap. 10.95 (0-8032-7253-7, Bison Books) U of Nebr Pr.

Annie Oakley's Girl. Rebecca Brown. 160p. (Orig.). 1993. pap. 8.95 (0-87286-279-8) City Lights.

Annie of Oak Hill. Prudence Scott. LC 90-81152. (Illus.). 240p. (Orig.). 1990. pap. 14.95 (0-938991-56-6) Colonial Pr AL.

Annie on My Mind. Nancy Garden. (YA). 1992. pap. 3.95 (0-374-40414-3) FS&G.

Annie Owns a Pony. Jennifer Bell. (C). 1990. 32.00 (0-85131-524-0, Pub. by J A Allen & Co UK); pap. 24.00 (0-85131-523-2, Pub. by J A Allen & Co UK) St Mut.

Annie Parsons. large type ed. Sarah Shears. 363p. 1993. 21.95 (0-7505-0511-7, Pub. by Magna Print Bks) Ulverscroft.

Annie Pitts, Artichoke. Diane Degroat. LC 91-759108. (J). (gr. 4-7). 1992. pap. 13.00 (0-671-75910-8, S&S Bks Young Read) S&S Childrens.

Annie Pitts, Swamp Monster. Diane DeGroat. LC 93-2474. (J). 1994. pap. 13.00 (0-671-87004-1, S&S Bks Young Read) S&S Childrens.

***Annie Salem.** Wellman. 1995. pap. text ed. 12.95 (1-55713-207-0) Sun & Moon CA.

***Annie Says I Do.** Carole Buck. (Desire Ser.). 1995. mass mkt. 3.25 (0-373-05934-5, 1-05934-4) Silhouette.

***Annie Sprinkle's Post-Modern Pin-Ups: Pleasure Activist Playing Cards.** Annie Sprinkle. Ed. by Katharine Gates. (Illus.). 64p. (Orig.). 1995. pap. 19.95 (0-9638129-3-9) Gates of Heck.

Annie Stories. Doris Brett. LC 87-42744. 228p. 1988. pap. 5.95 (0-89480-528-2, 1528) Workman Pub.

Annie Wilkins Mystery Series, 5 novels, Set. AnnaMaria Sands. (Illus.). 240p. (Orig.). (J). (gr. 2-7). 1988. pap. 17.00 (0-87879-571-5) High Noon Bks.

Annie's Attic: Surviving Sexual Abuse: A Journey from Realization to Recovery. Sarah A. Stevens. LC 94-96605. (Illus.). 333p. (Orig.). 1995. pap. 16.95 (0-9641177-0-3) Hubbard Pubng.

Annie's Body Paint Academy. Annie Kubler. (J). (ps-3). 1993. pap. 13.95 (0-85953-527-4) Childs Play.

Annie's Choice. Clara G. Clark. (Illus.). 196p. (J). (gr. 5 up). 1993. 14.95 (1-56397-053-8) Boyds Mills Pr.

Annie's City Adventures. Marek Mann. Ed. by Jill Max. Tr. by Mangold Verlag. LC 91-21302. (Magic Mountain Fables Ser.). (Illus.). 24p. (J). (gr. k-3). 1991. lib. bdg. 14.60 (1-56074-031-0) Garrett Ed Corp.

Annie's Cottage Crafts. Anne Mayne. (Illus.). 56p. 1993. pap. 7.95 (0-86417-406-3, Pub. by Kangaroo Pr AT) Seven Hills Bk.

Annie's Country Crafts. Anne Mayne. (Illus.). 48p. 1993. reprint ed. pap. 7.95 (0-86417-307-5, Pub. by Kangaroo Pr AT) Seven Hills Bk.

Annie's Creative Crafts. Anne Mayne. (Illus.). 56p. (Orig.). 1993. pap. 7.95 (0-86417-537-X, Pub. by Kangaroo Pr AT) Seven Hills Bk.

***Annie's Easy Crafts.** Anne Mayne. (Annie's Ser.). (Illus.). 72p. (Orig.). 1995. pap. 10.95 (0-86417-583-3) Seven Hills Bk.

***Annie's Easy Treats.** Anne Mayne & Diane Simmonds. (Annie's Ser.). (Illus.). 64p. (Orig.). 1995. pap. 10.95 (0-86417-618-X) Seven Hills Bk.

Annie's Gifts. Angela S. Medearis. LC 92-71998. (Feeling Good Ser.). (Illus.). 32p. (J). (gr. 1-4). 1994. 14.95 (0-940975-30-0); pap. 6.95 (0-940975-31-9) Just Us Bks.

Annie's High Sea Adventure. Marek Mann. Ed. by Jill Max & Elizabeth Bradford. Tr. by Mangold Verlag. LC 91-21305. (Magic Mountain Fables Ser.). (Illus.). 24p. (J). (gr. k-3). 1991. lib. bdg. 14.60 (1-56074-027-2) Garrett Ed Corp.

Annie's Kingdom. large type ed. Sarah A. Shears. 249p. 1993. 21.95 (0-7505-0513-3, Pub. by Magna Print Bks) Ulverscroft.

Annie's Monster. Barbara Corcoran. LC 89-28121. 192p. (J). (gr. 3-7). 1990. text ed. 14.95 (0-689-31632-1, Atheneum Bks Young) S&S Childrens.

Annie's Night Out. Carole Murphy. Ed. by Roy Zarucci & Carolyn Page. (Chapbook Ser.). 28p. (Orig.). 1990. pap. 5.00 (0-9623862-5-1) Nightshade Pr.

Annie's Pet: Level 2. Barbara A. Brenner. (J). (ps-3). 1989. 3.99 (0-553-34693-8) Bantam.

Annie's Promise. Sonia Levitin. LC 92-16819. 192p. (J). (gr. 5 up). 1993. text ed. 14.95 (0-689-31752-2, Atheneum Bks Young) S&S Childrens.

Annie's Rainbow. Diana Oliver. (McCracken's Class Ser.). 120p. (Orig.). (J). (gr. 3-7). 1993. pap. 3.50 (0-679-85006-6, Bullseye Bks) Random Bks Yng Read.

Annihilation. Piotr Szewc. Tr. by Ewa Hryniewicz-Yarbrough. LC 93-18996. 107p. 1993. 16.95 (1-56478-034-1) Dalkey Arch.

Annihilation of the Cathares: Thirteenth Century Holocaust. Daisy Aldan. 1989. pap. 4.95 (0-318-42002-3) Folder Edns.

Annihilator: All Must Die. Pete Billac. Ed. by Sharon K. Davis. LC 80-85318. 176p. (Orig.). (YA). (gr. 12 up). 1987. pap. 1.95 (0-317-67266-5) Swan Pub.

Annihilator...All Must Die. Pete Billac. Ed. by Roger Arnhart. LC 80-85318. 176p. 1987. pap. 1.95 (0-685-43871-6) Swan Pub.

Annikadel: The History of the Universe As Told by the Achumawi Indians of California. Istet Woiche. Ed. by C. Hart Merriam. LC 91-19895. 166p. 1992. reprint ed. pap. 11.95 (0-8165-1283-3) U of Ariz Pr.

Annikin Series, 3 bks., Set. (Illus.). (J). (ps-1). 1992. write for info. (1-55037-251-3, Pub. by Annick CN) Firefly Bks Ltd.

Anniranni & Mollymishi the Wild-Haired Doll. C. Drew Lamm. (Illus.). 24p. (J). (ps-2). 1990. 14.95 (1-55037-105-3, Pub. by Annick CN); pap. 5.95 (1-55037-106-1, Pub. by Annick CN) Firefly Bks Ltd.

Anni's Diary of France. Anni Axworthy. LC 93-27278. (Illus.). 32p. (J). (gr. 1-5). 1994. 14.95 (1-879085-58-5) Whsprng Coyote Pr.

Anni's India Diary. Anni Axworthy. LC 92-17524. (Illus.). 32p. (YA). (gr. 1-5). 1992. 14.95 (1-879085-59-3) Whsprng Coyote Pr.

***Anniversaire a la Ferme.** Ed. by Editors of ELI Staff. (Raconte et Chante Ser.). (Illus.). 27p. (Orig.). (FRE.). (J). (gr. k-2). 1992. pap. 19.95 (88-85148-65-4, Pub. by Europ Lang Inst IT) Midwest European Pubns.

***Anniversaire a la Ferme: Cahier D'Activites.** Ed. by Editors of ELI Staff. (Raconte et Chante Ser.). (Illus.). 27p. (Orig.). (FRE.). (J). (gr. k-2). 1992. pap. 3.95 (0-614-07146-1, Pub. by Europ Lang Inst IT) Midwest European Pubns.

Anniversaire de Babar. Laurent de Brunhoff. 28p. (J). 1975. 17.95 (0-7859-0677-0, M11806) Fr & Eur.

Anniversaries: From the Life of Gesine Cresspahl. Uwe Johnson. Tr. by Leila Vennewitz. LC 74-20942. (Helen & Kurt Wolff Bk.). 504p. 1975. 10.00 (0-15-107561-1) HarBrace.

Anniversaries & Epicedes & Obserquies, Vol. 6. John Donne. Ed. by Donald R. Dickson et al. LC 93-11800. (Variorum Edition of the Poetry of John Donne Ser.). 736p. 1995. text ed. 49.95 (0-253-31811-4) Ind U Pr.

Anniversaries & Holidays. 4th ed. Ruth W. Gregory. LC 83-3784. 260p. 1983. 35.00 (0-8389-0389-4) ALA.

Anniversaries II. Uwe Johnson. Tr. by Leila Vennewitz & Walter Arndt. 1987. 29.95 (0-15-107562-X) HarBrace.

Anniversary. Anton Chekhov. Ed. by William-Alan Landes. Tr. by Sergius Ponomarov. LC 92-53530. 60p. (Orig.). 1992. pap. 5.00 (0-88734-334-1) Players Pr.

Anniversary. Alan Feldman. LC 92-72077. (Illus.). 77p. (Orig.). 1992. pap. 20.00 (0-9633860-0-X) Chekhov & Co.

Anniversary Address on the Progress of the Natural Sciences of the United States. James E. DeKay. LC 76-125737. (American Environmental Studies). 1977. reprint ed. 14.95 (0-405-02662-5) Ayer.

Anniversary Essays in Mediaeval History, by Students of Charles Homer Haskins: Presented on His Completion of Forty Years of Teaching. Ed. by Charles H. Taylor. LC 67-30194. (Essay Index Reprint Ser.). 1977. 24.95 (0-8369-0155-X) Ayer.

Anniversary Issue, 50 Years of 'Cardiology' Ed. by J. J. Kellermann. (Journal: Cardiology: Vol. 74, No. 4, 1987). (Illus.). 88p. 1987. pap. 33.75 (3-8055-4638-6) S Karger.

Anniversary of the Air. Michael Waters. LC 84-72995. (Poetry Ser.). 60p. 1985. 16.95 (0-88748-011-X); pap. 9.95 (0-88748-012-8) Carnegie-Mellon.

***Anniversary Promise.** Pearle M. Pearson. 290p. Date not set. pap. 8.95 (0-7610-0302-9) NW Pub.

Anniversary to Remember: Years One to Seventy-Five. Cynthia L. Sowden. LC 92-7570. 159p. 1992. pap. 9.95 (0-918420-17-2) Brighton Pubns.

Anniversary Waltz. Jerome Chodorov & Joseph Fields. 1957. pap. 4.75 (0-8222-0050-3) Dramatists Play.

Anniversary Waltz. Anne M. Duquette. (Great Escapes Ser.). 1994. pap. 1.99 (0-373-83272-9, 1-83272-4) Harlequin Bks.

Anno Domini, 4 Vols. Hal M. Helms. Incl. Vol. 1. LC 82-62569. 240p. 1982. (0-941478-10-6); Vol. 2. LC 82-62569. 240p. 1982. (0-941478-21-1); Vol. 3. LC 82-62569. 240p. 1983. (0-941478-22-X); Vol. 4. LC 82-62569. 240p. 1983. (0-941478-23-8); LC 82-62569. (Anno Domini Ser.). (Orig.). Set pap. 14.95 (0-685-57847-X) Paraclete MA.

Anno Domini. George Steiner. LC 80-15345. 208p. 1986. pap. 9.95 (0-87951-252-0) Overlook Pr.

Anno Domini: Three Stories. George Steiner. LC 80-15345. 206p. 1980. reprint ed. 22.50 (0-87951-113-3) Overlook Pr.

Anno-Dracula. Kim Newman. 400p. 1993. 21.00 (0-88184-967-7) Carroll & Graf.

Anno Dracula. Kim Newman. 416p. 1994. mass mkt. 5.99 (0-380-72345-X) Avon.

Annoatated Bibliography of Serials on Migration. Silvano M. Tomasi. 14p. 1978. 3.00 (0-913256-33-1) Ctr Migration.

Annonce Faite a Marie. Paul Claudel. (FRE.). 1972. pap. 10.95 (0-8288-3628-0, F93892); 1959. pap. 10.95 (0-7859-1687-3, 2070360261) Fr & Eur.

Annonce Faite a Marie: Theatre. Paul Claudel. (Folio Ser.: No. 26). (FRE.). 1959. 8.95 (2-07-036026-1) Schoenhof.

Annonciade. Elizabeth Spires. 64p. 1989. pap. 12.50 (0-14-058638-5, Penguin Bks) Viking Penguin.

Anno's Aesop: A Book of Fables by Aesop & Mr. Fox. Illus. & Ret. by Mitsumasa Anno. LC 88-60087. 64p. (J). (ps-2). 1989. 19.95 (0-531-05774-7); lib. bdg. 19.99 (0-531-08374-8) Orchard Bks Watts.

Anno's Alphabet: An Adventure in Imagination. Mitsumasa Anno. LC 73-21652. (Illus.). 64p. (J). (gr. k up). 1975. 16.00 (0-690-00540-7, Crowell Jr Bks); lib. bdg. 15.89 (0-690-00541-5, Crowell Jr Bks) HarpC Child Bks.

Anno's Alphabet: An Adventure in Imagination. Mitsumasa Anno. LC 73-21652. (Trophy Picture Bk.). (Illus.). 64p. (J). (ps up). 1988. reprint ed. pap. 7.95 (0-06-443190-8, Trophy) HarpC Child Bks.

Anno's Counting Book. Mitsumasa Anno. LC 76-28977. (Illus.). 32p. (J). (ps-3). 1977. 16.00 (0-690-01287-X, Crowell Jr Bks) HarpC Child Bks.

Anno's Counting Book. Mitsumasa Anno. LC 76-28977. (Illus.). 32p. (J). (ps-3). 1977. lib. bdg. 15.89 (0-690-01288-8, Crowell Jr Bks) HarpC Child Bks.

Anno's Counting Book. Mitsumasa Anno. LC 76-28977. (Trophy Picture Bk.). (Illus.). 32p. (J). (ps-3). 1986. reprint ed. pap. 5.95 (0-06-443123-1, Trophy) HarpC Child Bks.

Anno's Counting Book Big Book. Mitsumasa Anno. LC 65-28977. (Trophy Picture Bk.). (Illus.). 32p. (J). (ps-3). 1992. pap. 19.95 (0-06-443315-3, Trophy) HarpC Child Bks.

Anno's Counting House. Mitsumasa Anno. (Illus.). 48p. (J). (ps-3). 1982. 16.95 (0-399-20896-8, Philomel Bks) Putnam Pub Group.

Anno's Hat Tricks. Akihiro Nozaki & Mitsumasa Anno. LC 84-18900. (Illus.). 44p. (J). (gr. 3 up). 1985. 15.95 (0-399-21212-4, Philomel Bks) Putnam Pub Group.

Anno's Journey. Mitsumasa Anno. 48p. (J). (gr. 4 up). 1981. 15.95 (0-399-20762-7, Philomel Bks) Putnam Pub Group.

Anno's Magic Seed. Mitsumasa Anno. LC 92-39309. (J). 1994. write for info. (0-399-22538-2, Philomel Bks) Putnam Pub Group.

Anno's Math Games. Mitsumasa Anno. 104p. (J). (ps-3). 1987. 19.95 (0-399-21151-9, Philomel Bks) Putnam Pub Group.

Anno's Math Games, No. III. Mitsumasa Anno. (Illus.). 112p. (J). (ps-3). 1991. 19.95 (0-399-22274-X, Philomel Bks) Putnam Pub Group.

Anno's Math Games II. Mitsumasa Anno. (Illus.). 104p. (J). (gr. 1-4). 1989. 19.95 (0-399-21615-4, Philomel Bks) Putnam Pub Group.

Anno's Medieval World. Mitsumasa Anno. LC 79-28367. (Illus.). 56p. (J). (gr. 3 up). 1990. 16.95 (0-399-20742-2, Philomel Bks) Putnam Pub Group.

Anno's Mysterious Multiplying Jar. Mitsumasa Anno. LC 82-22413. (Illus.). 48p. (J). (gr. 3 up). 1983. 16.95 (0-399-20951-4, Philomel Bks) Putnam Pub Group.

Anno's Peekaboo. Mitsumasa Anno. (Illus.). 32p. (J). (ps-00). 1988. 10.95 (0-399-21520-4, Philomel Bks) Putnam Pub Group.

Anno's Twice Told Tales: The Fisherman & His Wife & The Four Clever Brothers. Jacob Grimm et al. LC 92-25307. (Illus.). 64p. (J). (ps up). 1993. lib. bdg. 17.95 (0-399-22005-4, Philomel Bks) Putnam Pub Group.

An Asterisk (*) at the beginning of an entry indicates that the title is appearing in BIP for the first time.

333

Anno's U. S. A. Mitsumasa Anno. (Sandcastle Ser.). 48p. (J). (ps-8). 1992. 16.95 (*0-399-20974-3*, Philomel Bks); pap. 7.95 (*0-399-21595-6*, Philomel Bks) Putnam Pub Group.

Annotated Admiralty Legislation. Stuart Hetherington. xxvi, 183p. 1989. 62.50 (*0-455-20810-7*, Pub. by Law Bk Co) W W Gaunt.

Annotated Alice. Lewis Carroll. LC 93-10983. 1993. reprint ed. 19.99 (*0-517-02962-6*, Pub. by Wings Bks) Random Hse Value.

Annotated & Classified Bibliography of Indian Demography. R. B. Desai & R. P. Tyagi. 1986. 27.50 (*0-8364-1604-X*, Pub. by Popular Prakashan II) S Asia.

Annotated & Classified Bibliography on Parenting: Current Literature 1980-1990. Rama K. Rao. (Social Science Resource Guides Ser.: No. 1). 31p. (C). 1991. pap. text ed. 9.95 (*0-9628998-0-1*) Ramdil.

Annotated & Extended Bibliography of Higher Education Marketing. Ed. by Karen K. Constantine. LC 86-17356. (Bibliography Ser.). 71p. (Orig.). 1986. pap. 17.00 (*0-87757-184-8*) Am Mktg.

Annotated ANSI C Standard. ANSI C Standard Committee. 1993. pap. text ed. 39.95 (*0-07-881952-0*) Osborne-McGraw.

Annotated Archaeological Bibliography of Selected Works on Northern & Central Asia. Don Y. Lee. LC 83-81570. 94p. (C). 1983. 33.00 (*0-939758-05-9*) Eastern Pr.

*__Annotated Art.__ Robert Cumming. LC 94-31843. (Illus.). 104p. 1995. 22.95 (*1-56458-848-3*) Dorling Kindersley.

Annotated Bankers Blanket Bond with First Supplement. 348p. 1987. ring bd. 80.00 (*0-685-29703-9*, 519-0032-01) Amer Bar Assn.

*__Annotated Baseball Stories of Ring W. Lardner, 1914-1919.__ Ed. by George W. Hilton. LC 94-28020. 1995. 35.00 (*0-8047-2405-9*) Stanford U Pr.

Annotated Bibliographies of Mineral Deposits in Africa Asia (Exclusive of the U. S. S. R.) & Australasia. J. D. Ridge. 545p. 1976. 223.00 (*0-08-020459-7*, Pub. by Pergamon Repr UK) Franklin.

Annotated Bibliographies of Mineral Deposits in the Western Hemisphere: Includes 1974 Supplementary References. John D. Ridge. LC 72-178773. (Geological Society of America, Memoir Ser.: No. 131). 705p. reprint ed. pap. 180.00 (*0-8357-5491-X*, 2025459) Bks Demand.

Annotated Bibliographies of Simulation. Oren. 132p. 1976. 36.00 (*0-685-66776-6*, SS04-1) Soc Computer Sim.

Annotated Bibliography: World's Columbian Exposition, Chicago 1893. G. L. Dybwad & Joy V. Bliss. LC 91-77456. (Illus.). 459p. (Orig.). 1992. pap. 39.95 (*0-9631612-0-2*) Bk Stops Here.

*__Annotated Bibliography Bk. IV.__ John Langstaff. (Music Makes a Difference Ser.). 12p. 1994. pap. 1.95 (*1-886380-03-1*) Langstaff Vid.

Annotated Bibliography see Creativity in the Life Cycle

Annotated Bibliography, & Index, of Conodonts. S. P. Ellison, Jr. (Publication Ser.: 6210). (Illus.). 128p. 1962. 2.25 (*0-318-03316-X*) Bur Econ Geology.

Annotated Bibliography & Study of the Contemporary Criticism of Tennyson's Idylls of the King, 1859-1886. Aletha Andrew. LC 93-469. (American University Studies: English Language & Literature: Ser. IV, Vol. 163). 243p. (C). 1993. text ed. 43.95 (*0-8204-2084-0*) P Lang Pubs.

Annotated Bibliography for Marketing to an Older Population. Ed. by Anne L. Balazs et al. LC 89-18278. 89p. 1989. pap. text ed. 25.00 (*0-87757-202-X*) Am Mktg.

Annotated Bibliography for Transportation Planning in Small & Medium-Sized Communities. (Bibliography Ser.: No. 62). 22p. 1984. 8.20 (*0-309-03767-0*) Transport Res Bd.

Annotated Bibliography for Underground Storage Tanks. NWWA Staff. 207p. 1988. 18.75 (*1-56034-063-0*, K441) Natl Water Well.

*__Annotated Bibliography of Adventure Therapy & Related Programs: 1980-1992.__ Comp. by Lee Gillis & April Babb. 1995. 7.50 (*0-614-02597-4*) Assn Exper Ed.

Annotated Bibliography of Afghanistan. 4th ed. Mohammed J. Hanifi. LC 82-82467. 561p. reprint ed. pap. 159.90 (*0-8357-5609-2*, 2027171) Bks Demand.

Annotated Bibliography of American Doctoral Dissertations on Arabic Language, Literature, & Culture, 1967-1987. Dona S. Straley. Ed. by Frederic J. Cadora. (Al-Carabiyya: AATA Monographs in Arabic Studies). 163p. (Orig.). (C). 1988. pap. text ed. 15.00 (*0-9621530-0-1*) AM Assn Teach.

Annotated Bibliography of American Indian & Eskimo Autobiographies. H. David Brumble, III. LC 80-23449. xii, 170p. 1981. 25.00 (*0-8032-1175-9*) U of Nebr Pr.

Annotated Bibliography of Bibliographies of Statutory Materials of the United States. Lawrence Keitt. xvii, 191p. 1934. 25.00 (*0-678-08035-6*) Kelley.

Annotated Bibliography of Bibliographies of Statutory Materials of the United States. Lawrence Keitt. xvii, 191p. 1934. 6.50 (*0-8377-2325-6*) Rothman.

Annotated Bibliography of Books & Short Stories on Childhood & Youth. 1968. 2.00 (*0-685-35076-2*) Coun Soc Wk Ed.

Annotated Bibliography of Books for Writers. 2nd ed. Ann Adams. 12p. 1989. pap. 1.95 (*0-915433-17-6*) Packrat WA.

Annotated Bibliography of Canada's Major Authors, Vol. I. Ed. by Robert Lecker & Jack David. 263p. (C). 1979. text ed. 45.00 (*0-920802-02-8*) Genl Dist Srvs.

Annotated Bibliography of Canada's Major Authors, Vol. 2. Ed. by Robert Lecker & Jack David. 277p. (C). 1980. text ed. 45.00 (*0-920802-38-9*); pap. text ed. 28.00 (*0-920802-40-0*) Genl Dist Srvs.

Annotated Bibliography of Canada's Major Authors, Vol. 3. Ed. by Robert Lecker & Jack David. 395p. (C). 1981. text ed. 45.00 (*0-920802-23-0*) Genl Dist Srvs.

Annotated Bibliography of Canada's Major Authors, Vol. 4. Ed. by Robert Lecker & Jack David. 370p. (C). 1983. text ed. 45.00 (*0-920802-52-4*); pap. text ed. 28.00 (*0-920802-54-0*) Genl Dist Srvs.

Annotated Bibliography of Canada's Major Authors, Vol. 5. Ed. by Robert Lecker & Jack David. 480p. (C). 1984. text ed. 45.00 (*0-920802-68-0*) Genl Dist Srvs.

Annotated Bibliography of Canada's Major Authors, Vol. 6. Ed. by Robert Lecker & Jack David. 448p. (C). 1985. text ed. 45.00 (*0-920802-93-1*); pap. text ed. 28.00 (*0-920802-95-8*) Genl Dist Srvs.

Annotated Bibliography of Canada's Major Authors, Vol. 7. Ed. by Robert Lecker & Jack David. 477p. (C). 1987. text ed. 45.00 (*0-920763-11-1*); pap. text ed. 28.00 (*0-920763-12-X*) Genl Dist Srvs.

Annotated Bibliography of Canada's Major Authors, Vol. 8. Ed. by Robert Lecker & Jack David. (C). 1993. pap. text ed. 28.00 (*1-55022-043-8*) Genl Dist Srvs.

Annotated Bibliography of Canada's Major Authors: Marian Engel, Anne Hebert, Robert Kroetsch, Stephen Leacock & Thomas Raddall, Vol. 7. Ed. by Robert Lecker & Jack David. (G. K. Hall Reference Bks.). 450p. 1988. text ed. 50.00 (*0-8161-8796-7*, Hall Reference) Macmillan.

Annotated Bibliography of Canada's Major Authors Vol. 8, Vol. 8. Ed. by Robert Lecker & Jack David. (C). 1993. text ed. 50.00 (*1-55022-044-6*, Pub. by ECW Press CN) Genl Dist Srvs.

Annotated Bibliography of Cultural Resources Literature for the Nevada Nuclear Waste Storage Investigations. Lonnie C. Pippin & Donald L. Zerga. (Social Sciences Center Technical Report Ser.: No. 30). (Illus.). 142p. (C). 1981. spiral bd. 14.00 (*0-945920-30-X*) Desert Rsch Inst.

Annotated Bibliography of Dance - Movement Therapy: 1940-1990. Heidi Fledderjohn & Judith Sewickley. LC 93-80089. 95p. (Orig.). 1993. pap. 10.00 (*1-881766-03-9*) M Chace Mem Fund.

Annotated Bibliography of DSM-III. Andrew E. Skodol & Robert L. Spitzer. 496p. 1987. text ed. 45.00 (*0-88048-257-5*) Am Psychiatric.

Annotated Bibliography of ERIC Bibliographies, 1966-1980. Comp. by Joseph G. Drazan. LC 82-6151. (Illus.). xiv, 520p. 1982. text ed. 59.95 (*0-313-22688-1*, DRE/, Greenwood Pr) Greenwood.

Annotated Bibliography of Faculty Status in Library & Information Science. Karl E. Johnson. (Occasional Papers: No. 193). 1992. pap. 8.00 (*0-685-56566-1*) U of Ill Lib Info Sci.

Annotated Bibliography of Florida Fiction, 1801-1980. limited ed. Janette C. Gardner. LC 82-83598. 238p. 1983. 25.00 (*0-9609804-0-7*) Little Bayou.

Annotated Bibliography of Gabriel Miro. Ricardo Landeira. LC 78-70765. 200p. 1978. pap. 12.00 (*0-89295-005-6*) Society Sp & Sp-Am.

Annotated Bibliography of Genetic Variation in Eucalyptus Camaldulensis. K. G. Eldridge. 1975. 50.00 (*0-85074-023-1*) St Mut.

Annotated Bibliography of Geology & Land Use Planning, No. 1230. F. V. Kieffer. 1977. 6.00 (*0-686-19687-2*) CPL Biblios.

Annotated Bibliography of Gilpinia Hercyniae (Hartig) European Spruce. P. H. Adams & P. F. Entwistle. 1981. 30.00 (*0-85074-051-7*) St Mut.

Annotated Bibliography of Health Economics: English Language Sources. Ed. by A. J. Culyer et al. LC 77-79018. 1977. text ed. 49.95 (*0-312-03873-9*) St Martin.

Annotated Bibliography of Historical Fiction for the Social Studies. National Council for the Social Studies Staff. 112p. 1992. pap. text ed. 14.95 (*0-8403-7516-6*) Kendall-Hunt.

Annotated Bibliography of Jane Austen Studies, 1973-83. Barry Roth. LC 84-20814. 359p. 1985. 35.00 (*0-8139-1054-4*) U Pr of Va.

Annotated Bibliography of John Bunyan Studies. Comp. by Richard L. Greaves. LC 72-177693. (Bibliographia Tripotamopolitana Ser.: No. 5). 1972. 7.00 (*0-931222-04-4*) Pitts Theolog.

Annotated Bibliography of Juniper (Juniperus) of the Western United States. M. A. Smith & J. L. Schuster. 37p. 1975. 0.50 (*0-317-03295-X*) Intl Ctr Arid & Semi-Arid.

Annotated Bibliography of Korean Music. Bang-Song Song. LC 75-163013. (Bibliographies Ser.: No. 2). xiv, 251p. (Orig.). 1971. pap. text ed. 11.25 (*0-913360-04-X*) Asian Music Pub.

Annotated Bibliography of Latin American Sport: Pre-Conquest to the Present. Comp. by Joseph L. Arbena. LC 89-37527. (Bibliographies & Indexes in World History Ser.: No. 17). 337p. 1989. text ed. 79.50 (*0-313-25495-8*, ABS, Greenwood Pr) Greenwood.

Annotated Bibliography of Mascarene Plant Life: Including the Useful & Ornamental Plants of the Region, Covering the Period 1609-1990. David H. Lorence & Reginald E. Vaughan. 280p. (C). 1992. 29.95 (*0-915809-15-X*) Natl Trop Bot.

*__Annotated Bibliography of Metallogenic Maps (1960-1987)__ Comp. by M. P. Foose & Karen Bryant. 91p. (Orig.). (C). 1994. pap. text ed. 50.00x (*0-7881-1249-X*) Diane Pub.

Annotated Bibliography of Mineral Deposits in Trans-Pecos Texas. J. G. Price et al. (Mineral Resource Circular Ser.: MRC 73). (Illus.). 108p. 1983. 5.00 (*0-318-17363-8*) Bur Econ Geology.

Annotated Bibliography of Modern Anglo-Irish Drama. E. H. Mikhail. LC 80-51874. 306p. 1981. 20.00 (*0-87875-201-3*) Whitston Pub.

Annotated Bibliography of New Indonesian Literature on the History of Indonesia. Holk H. Dengel. (BASF Ser.: No. 113). 120p. (Orig.). 1987. pap. 28.50 (*3-515-04988-6*) Coronet Bks.

Annotated Bibliography of North American Doctoral Dissertations on Old English Language & Literature. Phillip Pulsiano. LC 87-51125. (Medieval Texts & Studies: No. 3). 332p. 1988. 48.00 (*0-937191-06-X*) Colleagues Pr Inc.

*__Annotated Bibliography of Oceanic Music & Dance.__ 2nd enl. rev. ed. Mervyn McLean. LC 95-9755. (Detroit Studies in Music Bibliography: No. 74). 1995. write for info. (*0-89990-073-9*) Info Coord.

*__Annotated Bibliography of Papers Using the General Social Surveys.__ 10th ed. Tom W. Smith et al. 779p. 1995. pap. text ed. 36.00 (*0-932132-52-9*) NORC.

Annotated Bibliography of Pathology in Invertebrates Other Than Insects. Phyllis T. Johnson. LC 68-29453. 338p. reprint ed. pap. 96.40 (*0-8357-5610-6*, 2003467) Bks Demand.

Annotated Bibliography of Pediatric Cardiology. American Academy of Pediatrics Staff. 188p. 1994. pap. 29.95 (*0-910761-55-8*) Am Acad Pediat.

Annotated Bibliography of Philippine Bibliographies, 1965-1974. Donn V. Hart. (Occasional Paper Ser.: No. 4). 158p. 1974. 10.00 (*0-685-62386-6*) North Ill U Ctr SE Asian.

*__Annotated Bibliography of Printed Materials on Australian Law (1788-1900)__ Alex Castles. 464p. 1994. 120.00 (*0-455-21299-6*, Pub. by Law Bk Co) W W Gaunt.

Annotated Bibliography of Puerto Rican Bibliographies. Comp. by Fay Fowlie-Flores. LC 89-28610. (Bibliographies & Indexes in Ethnic Studies). 186p. 1990. text ed. 49.95 (*0-313-26124-5*, FFC, Greenwood Pr) Greenwood.

Annotated Bibliography of Quarternary Shorelines (Supplement, 1965-1969) Horace G. Richards et al. (Special Publication: No. 10). 240p. 1970. lib. bdg. 9.00 (*0-910006-37-7*); pap. 7.00 (*0-910006-44-X*) Acad Nat Sci Phila.

Annotated Bibliography of Quaternary Shorelines (Second Supplement, 1970-1973) Horace G. Richards. (Special Publication: No. 11). 214p. 1974. pap. 10.00 (*0-910006-45-8*) Acad Nat Sci Phila.

Annotated Bibliography of Quaternary Shorelines (1945-1964) Horace G. Richards & Rhodes W. Fairbridge. (Special Publication: No. 6). 280p. (Orig.). 1965. pap. 7.00 (*0-910006-34-2*) Acad Nat Sci Phila.

Annotated Bibliography of Recursive Science Fiction. Anthony R. Lewis. 56p. 1990. pap. 6.00 (*0-915368-47-1*) New Eng SF Assoc.

Annotated Bibliography of Russian Language Publications on Accounting, 1736-1917, 2 vols. W. Motyka. 848p. 1993. Vol. I, 1736-1900. write for info. (*0-318-70046-8*); Vol. II, 1901-1917. write for info. (*0-318-70047-6*) Garland.

Annotated Bibliography of Russian Language Publications on Accounting, 1736-1917, 2 vols., Set. W. Motyka. LC 93-2711. (New Works in Accounting History). 848p. 1993. 132.00 (*0-8153-1247-4*) Garland.

Annotated Bibliography of Scientific Articles on AIDS for Policymakers, 2 vols., Set. (AIDS Ser.). 1991. lib. bdg. 500.00 (*0-8490-4218-6*) Gordon Pr.

Annotated Bibliography of Selected Chinese Reference Works. 3rd ed. Ed. by Teng Ssu-Yu & Knight Biggerstaff. LC 77-150012. (Harvard-Yenching Institute Studies: No. 2). 262p. 1971. pap. 14.00 (*0-674-03851-7*) HUP.

Annotated Bibliography of Selected Works on China. Don Y. Lee. LC 81-67771. 270p. (C). 1990. reprint ed. 46.50 (*0-939758-02-4*) Eastern Pr.

*__Annotated Bibliography of Shakespeare Studies: Love's Labor Lost, A Midsummer Night's Dreams, & the Merchant of Venice.__ Ed. by Clifford C. Huffman. LC 95-8285. (Pegasus Paperbks.). 80p. 1995. pap. 6.00 (*0-86698-177-2*, P28) MRTS.

Annotated Bibliography of Slipmouths: Pisces: Leiognathidae. Daniel Pauly & Sandra Wade-Pauly. (Bibliographies Ser.: No. 2). 62p. (Orig.). 1983. pap. 7.00 (*0-89955-374-5*, Pub. by ICLARM PH) Intl Spec Bk.

Annotated Bibliography of Solar Energy Research & Technology Applicable to Community Buildings & Other Non-Residential Construction. Nan C. Burg. 1977. 3.00 (*0-686-19118-8*, 1263) CPL Biblios.

Annotated Bibliography of Southern American English. James B. McMillan & Michael B. Montgomery. LC 88-36856. 464p. (C). 1989. 34.95 (*0-8173-0448-7*) U of Ala Pr.

Annotated Bibliography of Southern American English. James B. McMillan. LC 70-129666. 1971. 10.95 (*0-87024-183-4*) U of Miami Pr.

Annotated Bibliography of Soviet & CIS Studies on Nuclear Nonproliferation. 16p. 1992. pap. write for info. (*0-9633859-0-9*) Ctr Rus & Eura Stud.

Annotated Bibliography of Spanish Folklore in New Mexico & Southern Colorado. Marjorie F. Tully & Juan B. Rael. Ed. by Richard M. Dorson. LC 77-70628. (International Folklore Ser.). 1977. reprint ed. lib. bdg. 19.95 (*0-405-10132-5*) Ayer.

Annotated Bibliography of Spanish Folklore in New Mexico & Southern Colorado. Marjorie F. Tully & Juan B. Rael. LC 50-63083. 124p. 1982. reprint ed. lib. bdg. 43.00x (*0-89370-705-8*) Borgo Pr.

Annotated Bibliography of Taxonomic Botany of Peninsula India 1959-1978. S. Karthikeyan et al. 201p. 1981. pap. text ed. 15.00 (*0-945345-49-6*, Pub. by Mahendra Pal Singh II) Lubrecht & Cramer.

Annotated Bibliography of Teaching-Learning Materials for Schools of Nursing & Midwifery. (Offset Publication Ser.: No. 19). 1975. pap. 20.40 (*92-4-052005-8*) World Health.

Annotated Bibliography of Technical & Specialized Dictionaries. Marisa Luz E. Elerick. Tr. by Charles Elerick & Richard V. Teschner. LC 82-50416. 109p. 1982. 20.00 (*0-87875-234-X*) Whitston Pub.

Annotated Bibliography of the College Union, No. 7, Vol. 5. Ed. by Robin Brown. 110p. 1987. pap. 40.00 (*0-317-93266-7*) Assn Coll Unions Intl.

Annotated Bibliography of the College Union: 1915-1966, No. 7, Vol. 1. 1989. fiche 8.00 (*0-317-93252-7*) Assn Coll Unions Intl.

Annotated Bibliography of the College Union: 1967-1970, No. 7, Vol. 2. 148p. 1974. pap. 10.00 (*0-317-93253-5*) Assn Coll Unions Intl.

Annotated Bibliography of the College Union: 1971-1977, No. 7, Vol. 3. 176p. 1978. pap. 14.00 (*0-317-93254-3*) Assn Coll Unions Intl.

Annotated Bibliography of the College Union: 1978-1983, No. 7, Vol. 4. 155p. 1984. pap. 30.00 (*0-317-93255-1*) Assn Coll Unions Intl.

Annotated Bibliography of the Holy Roman Empire. Comp. by Jonathan W. Zophy. LC 85-30210. (Bibliographies & Indexes in World History Ser.: No. 3). 411p. 1986. text ed. 85.00 (*0-313-24028-0*, ZBR/, Greenwood Pr) Greenwood.

Annotated Bibliography of the Literature on Livability: With an Introduction & an Analysis of the Literature, No. 853. Linda Brown. 1975. 6.00 (*0-686-20366-6*) CPL Biblios.

Annotated Bibliography of the Napoleonic Era: Recent Publications, 1945-1985. Comp. by Jack A. Meyer. LC 87-7605. (Bibliographies & Indexes in World History Ser.: No. 8). 305p. 1987. text ed. 69.50 (*0-313-24901-6*, MNF, Greenwood Pr) Greenwood.

Annotated Bibliography of the Novels of the Mexican Revolution of 1910-1917. John Rutherford. LC 73-150334. 180p. (ENG & SPA.). 1972. 10.00 (*0-87875-015-0*) Whitston Pub.

Annotated Bibliography of the Peshitta of the Old Testament. P. B. Dirksen. LC 88-31530. (Monographs of the Peshitta Institute Leiden: Vol. V). xiv, 119p. 1989. text ed. 36.75 (*90-04-09017-7*) E J Brill.

Annotated Bibliography of the Published Writings of W. E. B. Du Bois. Herbert Aptheker. LC 73-13805. 626p. 1973. 54.00 (*0-527-02750-2*) Kraus Intl.

Annotated Bibliography of the Reproduction & Propagation of the Unionoidea (Primarily of North America) G. Thomas Watters. Ed. by Veda M. Cafazzo. LC 94-66175. (Miscellaneous Contributions Ser.: No. 1). vi, 162p. 1994. pap. 20.00 (*0-86727-112-4*) Ohio Bio Survey.

Annotated Bibliography of the Visual Arts of East Africa. Eugene C. Burt. LC 80-7805. (Traditional Arts of Africa Ser.). 392p. 1980. 25.00 (*0-253-17225-X*) Ind U Pr.

Annotated Bibliography of the Work of the Canon Law Society of America 1965-1980. Richard G. Cunningham. 121p. (Orig.). 1982. pap. 4.50 (*0-943616-06-9*) Canon Law Soc.

Annotated Bibliography of Tree Growth & Growth Rings, 1950-1962. Sharlene R. Agerter & Waldo S. Glock. LC 64-17274. 188p. reprint ed. pap. 53.60 (*0-8357-5611-4*, 2055332) Bks Demand.

Annotated Bibliography of West Indian Plant Ecology. Philip W. Rundel. (Illus.). 72p. 1974. 10.00 (*0-318-14610-X*) Isl Resources.

Annotated Bibliography of Western Manuscripts in the Merrill Library at Utah State University, Logan, Utah. Mary Washington. (Western Text Society Ser.: Vol. 1, No. 3). 180p. (Orig.). 1971. pap. 6.95 (*0-87421-046-1*) Utah St U Pr.

Annotated Bibliography on Carlos Fuentes: 1949-69. Richard M. Reeve. 56p. 1970. 2.00 (*0-318-12189-1*) AATSP.

Annotated Bibliography on Clandestine Employment. (International Labour Bibliography Ser.: No. 2). iii, 132p. (Orig.). 1987. pap. 14.00 (*92-2-105726-7*) Intl Labour Office.

Annotated Bibliography on Inner Asia. Don Y. Lee. LC 83-80529. 183p. (C). 1983. 45.50 (*0-939758-04-0*) Eastern Pr.

Annotated Bibliography on Laboratory Animal Welfare. Ed. by R. A. Murphy et al. LC 91-67379. 91p. 1991. 15.00 (*0-685-59679-6*) Scientists Ctr.

Annotated Bibliography on Lifeline Earthquake Engineering. 247p. 1980. pap. 28.00 (*0-87262-326-2*) Am Soc Civil Eng.

Annotated Bibliography on Noise. 369p. 1955. 33.00 (*0-911890-02-5*) Indus Health Inc.

Annotated Bibliography on Puerto Rican Materials & Other Sundry Matters. Luis A. Cardona. LC 83-50536. (Illus.). 154p. (Orig.). (C). 1983. text ed. 36.95 (*0-914199-00-5*) Carreta Pr.

Annotated Bibliography on Soil Micromorphology, 1968-1986. Ed. by Rienk Miedema & Ahmed R. Mermut. 250p. (Orig.). 1990. pap. text ed. 50.00 (*0-85198-681-1*) CAB Intl.

*__Annotated Bibliography on South Asia: Research.__ Ed. by Don Lee et al. LC 94-78180. 200p. (C). 1995. 57.00x (*0-939758-29-6*) Eastern Pr.

Annotated Bibliography on the History of Data Processing. Comp. by James W. Cortada. LC 83-8539. xiii, 216p. 1983. text ed. 69.50 (*0-313-24001-9*, CDP, Greenwood Pr) Greenwood.

Annotated Bibliography on Urban Design Storms. 47p. 1983. pap. 10.00 (*0-87262-372-6*) Am Soc Civil Eng.

Annotated Bibliography, 1971-1977. 84p. 1978. pap. write for info. (*0-318-61962-8*, F-001) Natl Ctr St Courts.

An Asterisk (*) at the beginning of an entry indicates that the title is appearing in BIP for the first time.

Annotated Black Beauty. Anna Sewell. 500p. 1990. 140.00 (*0-85131-438-4*, Pub. by J A Allen & Co UK) St Mut.

Annotated C Plus Plus Reference Manual. Margaret A. Ellis & Bjarne Stroustrup. (Illus.). 400p. (C). 1990. text ed. 49.50 (*0-201-51459-1*) Addison-Wesley.

Annotated Calendar of the Letters of Charles Darwin in the Library of the American Philosophical Society. Ed. by P. Thomas Carroll. LC 75-29739. 233p. 1976. reprint ed. 50.00 (*0-8420-2077-2*) Scholarly Res Inc.

Annotated Canada Shipping Act. Fernandes & Burke. 472p. 1988. 97.00 (*0-409-81145-9*) Butterworth Legal Pubs.

***Annotated Casey at the Bat: A Collection of Ballads about the Mighty Casey.** Ed. by Martin Gardner. (Illus.). 256p. 1995. pap. text ed. 6.95 (*0-486-28598-7*) Dover.

Annotated Catalog of Louisiana Railroads. William F. Rapp. (Railway History Monograph). (Illus.). 34p. 1990. pap. 8.00 (*0-916170-37-3*) J-B Pub.

Annotated Catalog of Primary Types of Siphonaptera in the National Museum of Natural History, Smithsonian Istitution. Nancy E. Adams & Robert E. Lewis. No. 560. 1994. write for info. (*0-318-72787-0*) Smithsonian.

Annotated Catalog of the Pyrenomycetes Described by Charles H. Peck. Margaret E. Barr et al. (Bulletin Ser.: No. 459). (Illus.). 74p. (Orig.). 1986. pap. 7.00 (*1-55557-005-4*) NYS Museum.

***Annotated Catalog South Texas College of Law.** Christopher Anglim. LC 94-30980. xxx, 434p. 1995. 65.00 (*0-89941-902-X*, 308340) W S Hein.

Annotated Catalogue of New Zealand Hymenoptera. Errol W. Valentine & Annette K. Walker. 84p. 1991. 140.00 (*0-477-02560-9*, Horticult & Food Res) St Mut.

Annotated Catalogue of Scenedesmus & Nomenclaturally Related Genera Including Original Descriptions & Figures. E. Hegewald & P. C. Silva. (Bibliotheca Phycologica Ser.: Vol. 80). 588p. 1988. lib. bdg. 120.00 (*3-443-60007-7*) Lubrecht & Cramer.

Annotated Catalogue of the Butterflies Named by Roger Verity. Otakar Kudrna. LC 83-80952. 106p. (C). 1983. pap. text ed. 8.00 (*0-9611464-0-0*) Lepidoptera.

Annotated Catalogue of the Plants of Baja California Sur, Mexico. Lee W. Lenz. 128p. 1993. pap. 16.50 (*0-9634595-0-3*) Cape Pr.

Annotated Charlotte's Web. E. B. White. LC 92-37470. (Illus.). 330p. (J). 1994. 35.00 (*0-06-024387-2*) HarpC Child Bks.

Annotated Checklist & Distribution Maps of the Royal Moths & Giant Silkworm Moths (Lepidoptera: Saturniidae) in Ohio. Eric H. Metzler. (Biological Notes Ser.). 1980. 3.00 (*0-86727-088-8*) Ohio Bio Survey.

Annotated Checklist of Birds of the U. S. Virgin Islands. Robert L. Norton & Charles F. Leck. (Illus.). 35p. 1986. pap. text ed. 6.95 (*0-916611-01-9*) Antilles Pr.

Annotated Checklist of Ornamental Plants of Coastal Southern California. Elizabeth McClintock et al. LC 82-71105. 172p. (Orig.). 1982. pap. text ed. 12.00 (*0-931876-58-3*, 3276) ANR Pubns CA.

Annotated Checklist of Peruvian Birds. Theodore A. Parker, III et al. LC 81-66046. (Illus.). 104p. (Orig.). 1982. pap. 20.00 (*0-931130-07-7*) Harrell Bks.

Annotated Checklist of the Birds of Arizona. 2nd rev. ed. Gale Monson & Allan Phillips. LC 81-11687. 240p. 1981. pap. 12.95 (*0-8165-0753-8*) U of Ariz Pr.

Annotated Checklist of the Birds of Ontario. 2nd ed. Ross D. James. 1994. pap. 13.95 (*0-88854-394-8*, Pub. by Royal Ont Mus CN) U of Toronto Pr.

Annotated Checklist of the Birds of Organ Pipe Cactus National Monument. Brian Brown et al. Ed. by Carolyn Dodson. LC 87-63354. 52p. 1988. pap. 4.95 (*0-911408-74-6*) SW Pks Mnmts.

Annotated Checklist of the Birds of Tennessee. John C. Robinson. LC 89-77251. 288p. 1990. 29.95 (*0-87049-642-5*) U of Tenn Pr.

Annotated Checklist of the Freshwater Fishes of Peru. Hernan Ortega & Richard P. Vari. LC 86-600237. (Smithsonian Contributions to Zoology Ser.: No. 437). 29p. reprint ed. pap. 25.00 (*0-8357-5612-2*, 2029554) Bks Demand.

Annotated Checklist of the Weevils (Curculionidae Sensu Lato) of South America (Coleoptera: Curculionoidea) Guillermo J. Wibmer & Charles W. O'Brien. (Memoir Ser.: No. 39). 561p. 1986. 55.00 (*1-56665-037-2*) Assoc Pubs FL.

Annotated Checklist of the Weevils of North America, Central America, & the West Indies (Coleoptera: Curculionoidea) Charles O'Brien & Guillermo Wibmer. (Memoir Ser.: No. 34). 382p. 1982. 45.00 (*1-56665-032-1*) Assoc Pubs FL.

Annotated Checklist of Vascular Plants of Grand Canyon National Park 1986. Barbara G. Phillips et al. (Monographs: No. 7). (Illus.). 96p. (Orig.). 1987. pap. 15.00 (*0-938216-30-9*) GCNHA.

Annotated Checklist of Woody Ornamental Plants of California, Oregon, & Washington. Elizabeth McClintock & Andrew T. Leiser. LC 78-73983. 134p. 1979. pap. 6.00 (*0-931876-28-1*, 4091) ANR Pubns CA.

Annotated Civil Code of Japan, 1. Tr. by Joseph E. De Becker. LC 79-65471. (Studies in Japanese Law & Government). 197p. 1979. text ed. 65.00 (*0-313-27115-1*, U7115) Greenwood.

Annotated Civil Code of Japan, Vol. 2. Tr. by Joseph E. De Becker. LC 79-65471. (Studies in Japanese Law & Government). 197p. 1979. text ed. 65.00 (*0-313-27116-X*, U7116) Greenwood.

Annotated Civil Code of Japan, Vol. 3. Tr. by Joseph E. De Becker. LC 79-65471. (Studies in Japanese Law & Government). 197p. 1979. text ed. 45.00 (*0-313-27117-8*, U7117) Greenwood.

Annotated Civil Code of Japan, Vol. 4. Tr. by Joseph E. De Becker. LC 79-65471. (Studies in Japanese Law & Government). 181p. 1979. text ed. 50.00 (*0-313-27118-6*, U7118) Greenwood.

Annotated Commonwealth Employees' Rehabilitation & Compensation Act, 1988. John Ballard. 260p. 1991. pap. 48.00 (*1-86287-069-1*, Pub. by Federation Pr AU) W W Gaunt.

Annotated Communist Manifesto. 2nd ed. Hal Draper. 300p. (C). 1988. pap. 20.00 (*0-916695-06-9*) Ctr Social Hist.

Annotated Compilation of Cercospora Names. Flora G. Pollack. (Mycologia Memoirs Ser.: No. 12). 210p. 1987. lib. bdg. 55.50 (*3-443-76002-3*) Lubrecht & Cramer.

***Annotated Corporate Voluntary Administration Law.** Philip Crutchfield. 280p. 1994. pap. 70.00 (*0-455-21262-7*, Pub. by Law Bk Co) W W Gaunt.

Annotated Critical Bibliography of Augustan Literature. Ed. by David Nokes & Janet Barron. 256p. 1989. text ed. 39.95 (*0-312-01961-0*) St Martin.

Annotated Critical Bibliography of Feminist Criticism. Maggie Humm. LC 87-9078. 256p. 1987. text ed. 40.00 (*0-8161-8937-4*, Hall Reference) Macmillan.

Annotated Critical Bibliography of George Eliot. Ed. by George L. Levine. LC 88-3044. 256p. 1988. text ed. 39.95 (*0-312-01959-9*) St Martin.

Annotated Critical Bibliography of Henry James. Nicola Bradbury. LC 86-27971. 1987. text ed. 39.95 (*0-312-00481-8*) St Martin.

Annotated Critical Bibliography of James Joyce. Ed. by Thomas F. Staley. 256p. 1989. text ed. 39.95 (*0-312-01963-7*) St Martin.

Annotated Critical Bibliography of Langland. Ed. by Derek Pearsall. LC 90-50103. 240p. 1990. reprint ed. text ed. 44.50 (*0-472-10185-4*) U of Mich Pr.

Annotated Critical Bibliography of Milton. C. A. Patrides. 190p. 1987. text ed. 39.95 (*0-312-00480-X*) St Martin.

Annotated Critical Bibliography of Modernism, No. 1. Ed. by Alastair Davies. LC 82-13864. (Harvester-Barnes & Noble Annotated Critical Bibliographies Ser.). 276p. (C). 1982. text ed. 53.50 (*0-389-20303-3*, N7138) B&N Imports.

Annotated Critical Bibliography of Tennyson. Ed. by Marion Shaw. 256p. 1989. text ed. 39.95 (*0-312-01962-9*) St Martin.

Annotated Critical Bibliography of William Morris. David Latham & Sheila Latham. LC 90-47281. 220p. 1991. text ed. 49.95 (*0-312-05656-7*) St Martin.

***Annotated Dictionary of Technical, Historical, & Stylistic Terms Relating to Theatre & Drama: A Handbook of Dramaturgy.** R. Kerry White. LC 95-7. 264p. 1995. spiral bd. 29.95 (*0-7734-8989-4*) E Mellen.

Annotated Directory of Hispanic Organizations of the Washington Area, Vol. O9. Tia A. Murchie-Beyma. 1991. 6.50 (*0-317-04775-2*) GWU CWAS.

Annotated Discography of Music in Spain Before 1650. 2nd ed. Comp. by Roger D. Tinnell. (Bibliographical Ser.: No. 8). xlviii, 248p. 1990. 25.00 (*0-940639-53-X*) Hispanic Seminary.

Annotated Edition of Lectures on Moral Philosophy. John Witherspoon. Ed. by Jack Scott. LC 80-24404. 213p. 1982. 32.50 (*0-87413-164-2*) U Delaware Pr.

Annotated Exploratory Bibliography on New Towns, No. 956. Robert V. Kemper et al. 1976. 5.50 (*0-686-20384-4*) CPL Biblios.

Annotated FAA Practical Test Standards-Single-Engine & Multi-Engine Land. Albert J. Taylor. (Illus.). 400p. (Orig.). 1987. 21.95 (*0-8306-0701-3*) TAB Bks.

Annotated Fiduciary: Materials on Fiduciary Responsibility & Prohibited Transactions under ERISA. Marc Gertner & Vivian C. Folk. Ed. by Mary E. Brennan. LC 89-84459. 592p. (Orig.). 1989. pap. 45.00 (*0-89154-382-1*) Intl Found Employ.

Annotated General Chemistry. Atkins. (C). 1995. text ed. write for info. (*0-7167-2284-4*) W H Freeman.

Annotated Gilbert & Sullivan. Ed. by Ian Bradley. 448p. 1983. pap. 10.95 (*0-14-070848-0*, Penguin Bks) Viking Penguin.

Annotated Glossary of Arabic Musical Terms. Ed. by Lois I. Al Faruqi. LC 81-4129. 536p. (ARA & ENG.). 1981. text ed. 125.00 (*0-313-20554-X*, AFM/, Greenwood Pr) Greenwood.

***Annotated Glossary of Terms Used in the Economic Analysis of Agricultural Projects: Taken from J. Price Gittinger, 1982, Economic Analysis of Agricultural Projects, Johns Hopkins University Press, Baltimore.** LC 94-21185. (ENG & SPA.). 1994. write for info. (*0-8213-2954-5*) World Bank.

Annotated Guide to Bass Trombone Literature. 2nd ed. Thomas G. Everett. write for info. (*0-318-61405-7*) Brass Pr.

Annotated Guide to Bass Trombone Literature. 3rd ed. Thomas G. Everett. Ed. by Stephen L. Glover. LC 85-11129. (Brass Research Ser.: No. 6). 1985. pap. 16.00 (*0-914282-80-8*) Brass Pr.

Annotated Guide to Bass Trombone Literature. 3rd enl. rev. ed. Thomas G. Everett. 1985. pap. text ed. 16.00 (*0-914282-03-4*) Brass Pr.

Annotated Guide to Current National Bibliographies. Comp. by Barbara Bell. (Government Documents Bibliographies Ser.). 1986. 149.00 (*0-85964-123-6*) Chadwyck-Healey.

Annotated Guide to Fantastic Adventures. Edward J. Gallagher. LC 84-16228. (Starmont Reference Guide Ser.: Vol. 2). xxii, 170p. 1985. reprint ed. lib. bdg. 29.00x (*0-916732-71-1*); reprint ed. pap. 19.00x (*0-916732-70-3*) Borgo Pr.

Annotated Guide to Global Development: Capacity-Building for Effective Social Change. Guy Gran. LC 87-60006. (Illus.). xi, 154p. (Orig.). 1987. pap. 7.95 (*0-9618388-0-9*) Resc Devel Demo.

Annotated Guide to Models & Algorithms for Energy Calculations Relating to HVAC Equipment. Ed. by M. Geshwiler. (C). 1990. pap. 37.00 (*0-910110-73-5*) Am Heat Ref & Air Eng.

Annotated Guide to Philippine Serials. Frank H. Golay & Marianne H. Hauswedell. LC 76-380136. (Cornell University, Southeast Asia Program, Data Paper Ser.: No. 101). 153p. reprint ed. pap. 43.70 (*0-8357-3680-6*, 2036404) Bks Demand.

Annotated Guide to Startling Stories. Leon Gammell. LC 86-6012. (Starmont Reference Guide Ser.: No. 3). iv, 90p. 1986. lib. bdg. 25.00x (*0-930261-51-8*); pap. 15.00x (*0-930261-50-X*) Borgo Pr.

Annotated Guide to Stephen King: A Primary & Secondary Bibliography of the Works of America's Premier Horror Writer. Michael R. Collings. LC 86-1854. (Starmont Reference Guide Ser.: No. 8). vi, 176p. (Orig.). 1986. lib. bdg. 29.00x (*0-930261-81-X*) Borgo Pr.

Annotated Guide to Unknown & Unknown Worlds. Stefan R. Dziemianowicz. LC 93-202547. (Starmont Studies in Literary Criticism: No. 13). 212p. 1991. lib. bdg. 31.00x (*1-55742-141-2*); pap. 21.00x (*1-55742-140-4*) Borgo Pr.

Annotated Hessian Chaplaincy Record of the American Revolution, 1776-1784: Christenings, Marriages, Deaths. Clifford N. Smith. (German-American Genealogical Research Monograph: No. 30). i, 29p. (Orig.). 1994. pap. 15.00 (*0-915162-72-5*) Westland Pubns.

Annotated ICD-9-CM Code Books, 3 vols., Set. 79.00 (*0-685-66044-3*); pap. 69.00 (*0-685-66045-1*) HCIA.

Annotated ICD-9-CM Code Books, Set, Vols. 1 & 2. pap. 39.00 (*0-685-74595-3*) HCIA.

Annotated ICD-9-CM Code Books: Diseases, Index, Vol. 2. pap. 39.00 (*1-880678-58-6*) HCIA.

Annotated ICD-9-CM Code Books, Vol. 1: Diseases, Tabular. pap. 32.00 (*1-880678-57-8*) HCIA.

Annotated ICD-9-CM Code Books, Vol. 3: Procedures. pap. 39.00 (*0-685-66050-8*) HCIA.

Annotated Index of Medieval Women. Anne Echols & Marty Williams. 700p. (C). 1992. text ed. 69.95 (*0-910129-27-4*) Wiener Pubs Inc.

Annotated Index of Occupational Therapy Evaluation Tools. Ina E. Asher. 205p. (Orig.). (C). 1989. pap. 24.00 (*0-910317-50-X*) Am Occup Therapy.

Annotated Index to Species & Infraspecific Taxa of Agaricales & Boletales Described by William A. Murrill. Roy E. Halling. LC 86-23777. (Memoirs Ser.: Vol. 40). 120p. 1986. pap. text ed. 19.25 (*0-89327-306-6*) NY Botanical.

Annotated Index to the Commentary on John Gower's "Confessio Amantis" Peter Nicholson. (Medieval & Renaissance Texts & Studies: Vol. 62). 608p. 1989. 36.00 (*0-86698-046-6*) MRTS.

Annotated Index to the "Syrian World," 1926-1932. John G. Moses & Eugene P. Nassar. Ed. by Judith Rosenblatt. LC 93-80115. (Illus.). xiii, 129p. 1994. spiral bd. 18.00 (*0-932833-13-6*) Immig His Res.

Annotated Index to The Thrill Book: Complete Indexes to & Descriptions of Everything Published in Street & Smith's the Thrill Book. Richard J. Bleiler. (Starmont Reference Guide Ser.: Vol. 18). vii, 256p. (Orig.). 1991. lib. bdg. 35.00x (*1-55742-206-0*); pap. 25.00x (*1-55742-205-2*) Borgo Pr.

***Annotated Insurance Contracts Act.** Peter Mann & Candace Lewis. 300p. 1994. pap. 65.00 (*0-455-21255-4*, Pub. by Law Bk Co) W W Gaunt.

Annotated International Accounting Bibliography 1972-1981. Agami & Kollaritsch. 175p. 1983. 7.00 (*0-86539-043-6*) Am Accounting.

Annotated International Bibliography of Nutrition Education: Materials, Resource Personnel, & Agencies. Clara Mae Taylor & Katharine P. Riddle. LC 71-132937. 200p. reprint ed. pap. 57.00 (*0-8357-5613-0*, 2026074) Bks Demand.

Annotated Inventory of Distinctive Choral Literature for Performance at the High School Level. (Monograph Ser.: No. 2). 70p. 1976. 3.50 (*0-318-17583-5*) Am Choral Dirs.

***Annotated Inventory of Distinctive Choral Literature for Performance at the High School Level.** Margaret B. Hawkins. (Monograph Ser.: No. 2). 69p. 1976. 5.00 (*0-614-05589-X*) Am Choral Dirs.

Annotated Key to the Long-Tailed Shrews (Genus Sorex) of the United States & Canada: With Notes on Middle American Sorex. Jane A. Junge & Robert S. Hoffman. (Occasional Papers: No. 94). 48p. 1981. pap. 1.00 (*0-317-04860-0*) U of KS Mus Nat Hist.

Annotated Laws of Massachusetts, 75 vols., Set. suppl. ed. 1991. write for info. (*0-318-57155-2*) Lawyers Cooperative.

Annotated Letters of Christopher Smart. Ed. by Betty Rizzo & Robert Mahony. 144p. (C). 1991. 24.50 (*0-8093-1609-9*) S Ill U Pr.

Annotated List & Indexes of the New York State Legislative Document Series, 1919-1976, 7 vols., Set. Robert A. Carter. 559p. 1986. 35.00 (*0-318-22978-1*) NYS Library.

Annotated List of "Chicago Tribune" Editorials on Elementary & Secondary Education in the U. S. 1852-1971. Ed. by Peter P. DeBoer. LC 92-26145. 324p. 1992. text ed. 99.95 (*0-7734-9595-9*) E Mellen.

Annotated List of Corticiaceae, Sensu Lato (Aphyllophorales, Basidiomycotina) for Peninsular Spain & Balearic Islands. M. T. Telleria. (Bibliotheca Mycologica Ser.: Vol. 135). 152p. 1990. pap. 50.00 (*3-443-59036-5*, Pub. by Cramer-Borntraeger GW) Lubrecht & Cramer.

Annotated List of Indexes & Reports of New York State Governors Committees & Task Forces, 1925-1985. Robert A. Carter. 33p. 1986. 5.00 (*0-318-22977-3*) NYS Library.

Annotated List of Ontario Lepidoptera. J. C. Riotte. 1994. pap. 19.95 (*0-88854-397-2*, Pub. by Royal Ont Mus CN) U of Toronto Pr.

Annotated List of the Birds of Bolivia. J. V. Remsen, Jr. & Melvin A. Traylor, Jr. LC 89-61415. (Illus.). 1989. 15.00 (*0-931130-16-6*) Harrell Bks.

Annotated List of the Published Names in Mycosphaerella & Sphaerella. M. Corlett & R. M. McGregor. (Mycologia Memoirs Ser.: No. 18). 250p. 1991. text ed. 85.00 (*0-945345-35-6*, Pub. by Cramer-Borntraeger GW) Lubrecht & Cramer.

Annotated Listing of Resources for the Study of the History of Medicine & Health Care in Nevada. Ed. by Michael L. Ezell. (Great Basin History of Medicine Ser.). 84p. 1991. lib. bdg. 22.00 (*1-56475-004-3*) U NV Oral Hist.

Annotated Lists & Indexes of the NYS Assembly & Senate Document Series, 1831-1918, 3 vols., Set. New York State Library Staff. 1992. 50.00 (*0-317-05247-0*) NYS Library.

Annotated Lolita. Vladimir Nabokov. LC 90-50264. 544p. 1991. pap. 19.00 (*0-679-72729-9*, Vin) Random.

Annotated Mahabharata Bibliography. P. Lal. 31p. 1973. 10.00 (*0-88253-306-1*) Ind-US Inc.

Annotated Manifesto. Hal Draper. (Orig.). (C). 1984. pap. 24.00 (*0-916695-01-8*) Ctr Social Hist.

Annotated Mergers & Acquisitions Law of Australia. 3rd ed. D. McDonough. 470p. 1993. pap. 70.00 (*0-455-21182-5*, Pub. by Law Bk Co) W W Gaunt.

Annotated Model Rules of Professional Conduct. 2nd ed. Center for Professional Responsibility Staff. 633p. 1992. pap. 74.95 (*0-89707-736-9*, 561-0102) Amer Bar Assn.

Annotated Mona Lisa: A Crash Course in Art History from Prehistoric to Post-Modern. Carol Strickland & John Boswell. LC 92-27904. (Illus.). 208p. (Orig.). 1992. 29.95 (*0-8362-8009-1*); French flaps. pap. 22.50 (*0-8362-8005-9*) Andrews & McMeel.

Annotated Narrative of Joe Blackburn's a Clown's Log. Joe Blackburn. Ed. by William Slout. LC 92-44479. (Clipper Studies in the Theatre: No. 6). (Illus.). x, 138p. 1993. lib. bdg. 27.00x (*0-8095-6250-2*, 27173336, Emeritus Ent); pap. 17.00x (*0-8095-6251-0*, 27173336, Emeritus Ent) Borgo Pr.

Annotated Opening Statements. rev. ed. Peter Perlman. Ed. by ATLA Press Staff. LC 94-15354. (Illus.). 165p. 1994. pap. 42.00 (*0-941916-69-3*) ATLA Pr.

***Annotated Prehistoric Bibliography on South Asia.** Don Y. Lee. 170p. (C). 1995. 47.50 (*0-939758-32-6*) Eastern Pr.

***Annotated Queensland Building Services Authority Act.** Stephen J. Pyman. 138p. 1993. pap. 39.00 (*0-455-21218-X*, Pub. by Law Bk Co) W W Gaunt.

Annotated Quotations from Chairman Mao. John DeFrancis. LC 74-20080. 326p. 1975. reprint ed. pap. 93.00 (*0-7837-3317-8*, 2057721) Bks Demand.

Annotated Ramona. Antoinette May. LC 88-27696. 256p. (Orig.). 1989. pap. 14.95 (*0-933174-52-7*) Wide World-Tetra.

Annotated Reader in Environmental Planning & Management. Ed. by Timothy O'Riordan & K. Turner. LC 82-7569. (Urban & Regional Planning Ser.: Vol. 30). (Illus.). 484p. 1983. 196.00 (*0-08-024669-9*, Pub. by Pergamon Repr UK) Franklin.

Annotated Rules of North Carolina. Michie Company Editorial Staff. 1116p. 1992. 35.00 (*0-87473-866-0*) Michie Butterworth.

Annotated Selected Bibliography of Bibliographies on Women. Margaret Eichler. 1976. pap. 3.50 (*0-912786-38-8*) Know Inc.

Annotated Shakespeare: The Comedies, Histories, Sonnets & Other Poems, Tragedies & Romances; Complete, 3 vols. in one. Ed. by A. L. Rowse. 2464p. 1984. 29.95 (*0-517-43603-5*) Random Hse Value.

Annotated "She" A Critical Edition of H. Rider Haggard's Victorian Romance. H. Rider Haggard. LC 90-43751. (Visions Ser.). (Illus.). 288p. 1991. 37.50 (*0-253-32072-0*) Ind U Pr.

Annotated Sherlock Holmes, 2 vols. in 1. Arthur Conan Doyle. 1992. 29.99 (*0-517-48102-2*) Random Hse Value.

Annotated Sherlock Holmes: The Four Novels & the Fifty-Six Short Stories Complete. Arthur Conan Doyle. Ed. by William S. Baromg-Gould. LC 92-14297. 1992. 29.99 (*0-685-57417-2*, Pub. by Wings Bks) Random Hse Value.

Annotated Social Security Act. 5th ed. Peter Johnson. 500p. 1989. pap. 55.00 (*1-86287-015-2*, Pub. by Federation Pr AU) W W Gaunt.

Annotated St. John's College Book List. St. John's College Staff. pap. 4.00 (*0-88411-348-5*) Amereon Ltd.

***Annotated Statutes of Malaysia.** Vincent Powell-Smith & Tan Hashim. 1100p. 1994. write for info. (*0-409-99718-8*) Butterworth Legal Pubs.

Annotated Statutes of the Indian Territory, 1 vol. in 2, Set. Indian Territory Staff. LC 74-15117. reprint ed. 98.50 (*0-404-12000-8*) AMS Pr.

Annotated Summary Offences Act: (South Australia) Kelvyn Prescott. 157p. 1992. pap. 93.00 (*0-455-21156-6*, Pub. by Law Bk Co) W W Gaunt.

Annotated Synopsis of the Genera & Subgenera of Lejeuneacea, 1: Introduction, Annotated Keys to Subfamilies & Genera. R. M. Schuster. 1963. 36.00 (*3-7682-5409-7*) Lubrecht & Cramer.

Annotated Tax Forms. Sidney I. Roberts et al. write for info. (*0-318-57361-X*) P-H.

Annotated Texts for Translation: French-English. Beverly J. Adab. LC 93-11423. (Topics in Translation Ser.: Vol. 3). 180p. 1993. 69.00 (*1-85359-206-4*, Pub. by Multilingual Matters UK); pap. 24.95 (*1-85359-205-6*, Pub. by Multilingual Matters UK) Taylor & Francis.

Annotated Topical Guide to U. S. Income Tax Treaties: A Service, 6 vols. J. Ross Macdonald. 6618p. 1988. ring bd. 790.00 (*0-13-103037-X*) Aspen Law.

An Asterisk (*) at the beginning of an entry indicates that the title is appearing in BIP for the first time.

335

Annotated Trade Practices Act. 14th ed. Russell V. Miller. 770p. 1993. pap. 45.00 (*0-455-21186-8*, Pub. by Law Bk Co) W W Gaunt.

Annotated Trade Practices Act 1991. 12th ed. Russell V. Miller. liv, 520p. 1991. pap. 39.00 (*0-455-21042-X*, Pub. by Law Bk Co) W W Gaunt.

***Annotated Trade Practices Act 1994.** 15th ed. Russell V. Miller. 678p. 1994. pap. 45.00 (*0-455-21239-2*, Pub. by Sweet & Maxwll) W W Gaunt.

***Annotated Trade Practices Act, 1995.** 16th ed. Russell V. Miller. 680p. 1995. pap. 45.00 (*0-455-21312-7*, Pub. by Law Bk Co) W W Gaunt.

***Annotated Workers Compensation & Rehabilitation Act 1981 (WA)** R. Guthrie. 1995. write for info. (*0-409-30737-8*, Austral) Butterworth Legal Pubs.

Annotated World List of Selected Current Geographical Serials. 4th rev. ed. Chauncy D. Harris. LC 80-17561. (Research Papers Ser.: No. 194). 165p. 1980. pap. 12.00 (*0-89065-101-9*) U Chicago Comm Geo.

Annotated Writer's Guide to Professional Educational Journals. Elizabeth S. Manera et al. 188p. 1982. pap. 9.95 (*0-9609782-0-8*) Bobets.

Annotation of the Singapore Companies (Amendment) Act, 1987. N. Subramaniam & Dorothy Chan. 212p. 1987. pap. 50.00 (*0-409-99550-9*) Butterworth Legal Pubs.

***Annotations.** John Keene. 64p. (Orig.). 1995. pap. 8.95 (*0-8112-1304-8*, NDP809) New Directions.

Annotations for the Selected Works of William Makepeace Thackeray, Vol. 1 & 2: The Complete Novels, the Major Non-Fictional Prose, & Selected Shorter Pieces, 2 vols., Set. Edgar F. Harden. LC 89-16913. 1990. 171.00 (*0-8240-3140-7*, H1000) Garland.

Annotations on the Pentateuch, Psalms & Song of Solomon, 2 vols., Set. Henry Ainsworth. 1991. reprint ed. 70.00 (*1-877611-35-2*) Soli Deo Gloria.

Annotations on the Pentateuch, Psalms & Song of Solomon, 2 vols., Vol. 1. Henry Ainsworth. 785p. 1991. reprint ed. 35.00 (*1-877611-33-6*) Soli Deo Gloria.

Annotations on the Pentateuch, Psalms & Song of Solomon, 2 vols., Vol. 2. Henry Ainsworth. 748p. 1991. reprint ed. 35.00 (*1-877611-34-4*) Soli Deo Gloria.

Annotations to Finnegans Wake. rev. ed. Roland McHugh. LC 90-23512. 640p. 1991. pap. text ed. 26.50 (*0-8018-4190-9*) Johns Hopkins.

Annotations to Finnegans Wake. 2nd rev. ed. Roland McHugh. LC 90-23512. 640p. 1991. 75.00 (*0-8018-4226-3*) Johns Hopkins.

Annotations to Finnegans Wake. Roland McHugh. LC 79-18419. 640p. reprint ed. pap. 180.00 (*0-8357-7881-9*, 2036299) Bks Demand.

Annotations to Surplus Lines Statutes. LC 89-82256. 1038p. 1990. ring bd. 124.00 (*0-89707-519-6*, 519-0153) Amer Bar Assn.

Annotations to the Acts & Regulations of the Australian Parliament. Ed. by J. Malor et al. 227.00 (*0-409-49007-5*) Butterworth Legal Pubs.

Annotations to the Homeowners' Policy. 2nd ed. LC 90-85034. 464p. 1990. 89.95 (*0-89707-627-3*, 519-0132) Amer Bar Assn.

Annotations to the Model Procurement Code for State & Local Governments. American Bar Association, Urban, State & Local Government Staff. LC 92-80969. 144p. 1992. pap. 79.95 (*0-89707-780-6*, 533-0046) Amer Bar Assn.

***Annotations to the Social Security Act, 1991.** 2nd ed. Peter Sutherland & Allan Anforth. 720p. 1994. pap. 64.00 (*1-86287-141-8*, Pub. by Federation Pr AU) W W Gaunt.

Annotations to Vanity Fair. 2nd ed. John Sutherland & Oscar Mandel. LC 88-20883. (Illus.). 130p. (C). 1989. pap. text ed. 15.00 (*0-8191-7187-5*) U Pr of Amer.

Annotator. Alan Keen & Roger Lubbock. LC 76-153334. (Illus.). reprint ed. 32.50 (*0-404-03641-4*) AMS Pr.

Annoted Bibliography of U. S. Scholarship on the History of the Family. Elizabeth Benson-von der Ohe & Valmari M. Mason. LC 85-48008. (Studies in Social History: No. 6). 1986. 45.00 (*0-404-61606-2*) AMS Pr.

Annotirovannyi Ukazatel' Rukopisnykh Fondov Gosudarstvennoi Publichnoi Biblioteki Im. M. E. Saltykova-Shchedrina - Annotated Index of the Manuscript Collections of the State Public Library, M. E. Saltykov-Shchedrin: Fondy Russkikh Deiatelei XVIII-XX vv. (Leningrad, 1981 ff.) - Manuscript Collections of Russian Public Figures of the 18th-20th Centuries, 4 vols., Set. Ed. by I. G. Iakovleva. 1995. reprint ed. 390.00 (*0-685-67419-3*) N Ross.

Annotirovannyi Ukazatel' Rukopisnykh Fondov Gosudarstvennoi Publichnoi Biblioteki Im. M. E. Saltykova-Shchedrina - Annotated Index of the Manuscript Collections of the State Public Library, M. E. Saltykov-Shchedrin: Fondy Russkikh Deiatelei XVIII-XX vv. (Leningrad, 1981 ff.) - Manuscript Collections of Russian Public Figures of the 18th-20th Centuries, Vol. 1. Ed. by I. G. Iakovleva. 258p. 1995. reprint ed. write for info. (*0-88354-115-7*) N Ross.

Annotirovannyi Ukazatel' Rukopisnykh Fondov Gosudarstvennoi Publichnoi Biblioteki Im. M. E. Saltykova-Shchedrina - Annotated Index of the Manuscript Collections of the State Public Library, M. E. Saltykov-Shchedrin: Fondy Russkikh Deiatelei XVIII-XX vv. (Leningrad, 1981 ff.) - Manuscript Collections of Russian Public Figures of the 18th-20th Centuries, Vol. 2. Ed. by I. G. Iakovleva. 390p. 1995. reprint ed. write for info. (*0-88354-116-5*) N Ross.

Annotirovannyi Ukazatel' Rukopisnykh Fondov Gosudarstvennoi Publichnoi Biblioteki Im. M. E. Saltykova-Shchedrina - Annotated Index of the Manuscript Collections of the State Public Library, M. E. Saltykov-Shchedrin: Fondy Russkikh Deiatelei XVIII-XX vv. (Leningrad, 1981 ff.) - Manuscript Collections of Russian Public Figures of the 18th-20th Centuries, Vol. 3. Ed. by I. G. Iakovleva. 397p. 1995. reprint ed. write for info. (*0-88354-117-3*) N Ross.

Annotirovannyi Ukazatel' Rukopisnykh Fondov Gosudarstvennoi Publichnoi Biblioteki Im. M. E. Saltykova-Shchedrina - Annotated Index of the Manuscript Collections of the State Public Library, M. E. Saltykov-Shchedrin: Fondy Russkikh Deiatelei XVIII-XX vv. (Leningrad, 1981 ff.) - Manuscript Collections of Russian Public Figures of the 18th-20th Centuries, Vol. 4. Ed. by I. G. Iakovleva. 352p. 1995. reprint ed. write for info. (*0-88354-118-1*) N Ross.

Announcement Borders. (Photocopier Bks.). (Orig.). 1984. pap. 19.95 (*0-87280-017-2*, 714, Asher-Gallant) Caddylak Systs.

Announcer. Jack Rudman. (Career Examination Ser.: C-14). 1994. pap. 29.95 (*0-8373-0014-2*) Nat Learn.

Announcing: Broadcast Communicating Today. 2nd ed. Lewis B. O'Donnell et al. 437p. (C). 1992. text ed. 46.95 (*0-534-14958-8*) Intl Thomson.

Announcing the Reign of God: Evangelization & the Subversive Memory of Jesus. Mortimer Arias. LC 83-5696. 176p. 1984. pap. 13.00 (*0-8006-1712-6*, 1-1712, Fortress Pr) Augsburg Fortress.

Annoying Monologue Book. Mary Booker. 54p. 1992. pap. 7.95 (*1-56850-026-2*) Chicago Plays.

Annoying the Victorians. James R. Kincaid. LC 93-42943. 1994. 49.95 (*0-415-90728-4*, Routledge NY); pap. 15.95 (*0-415-90729-2*, Routledge NY) Routledge.

Ann's Pans & Cans. Francis H. Wise & Joyce M. Wise. (Phonetic Readers Ser.: No. 6). (Illus.). 20p. (J). (ps-1). 1974. pap. text ed. 1.50 (*0-915766-28-0*) Wise Pub.

***Annuaire de la Recherche Bio-Medicale: The Directory of Biomedical Research in France.** 4th ed. 608p. 1994. 127.00 (*2-906077-48-8*) Elsevier.

Annuaire des Cotes - Art Price Annual: Art Auction Guide-1992. 1992. write for info. (*0-8288-7590-1*) Fr & Eur.

Annuaire Europeen 1988 - European Yearbook 1988, Vol. XXXVI. Ed. by P. Drillien. (C). 1990. lib. bdg. 338.50 (*0-7923-0417-9*) Kluwer Ac.

Annuaire Europeen 1989 - European Yearbook 1989, Vol. XXXVII. Ed. by P. Drillien. (C). 1991. lib. bdg. 338.50 (*0-7923-0839-5*) Kluwer Ac.

Annuaire Europeen 1990 - European Handbook 1990, Vol. XXXVIII. Ed. by G. Adinolfi. 1016p. (C). 1992. lib. bdg. 328.50 (*0-7923-1395-X*) Kluwer Ac.

Annuaire Europeen 1991 - European Yearbook 1991, Vol. XXXIX. Ed. by G. Adinolfi. 1256p. (C). 1993. lib. bdg. 364.00 (*0-7923-1959-1*) Kluwer Ac.

Annual: Art in General, 1992-1993. Art in General Staff. (Illus.). 112p. (Orig.). 1993. pap. write for info. (*1-883967-00-7*) Art in General.

Annual Abstract of Statistics, 1991. 340p. 1991. pap. 50.00 (*0-11-620446-X*, HM644X) UNIPUB.

Annual Abstract of Statistics, 1994. HMSO. 1994. pap. 45.00 (*0-11-620605-5*, HMO6055, Pub. by HMSO UK) UNIPUB.

Annual American Engineering Model Society Seminar, 1970-1988: Proceedings. (Illus.). 177p. pap. text ed. 20.00 (*0-318-17303-4*) Am Eng Model Soc.

Annual & Biennial Exhibition Record of the Whitney Museum of American Art: 1918-1989. Peter H. Falk. 468p. (C). 1991. text ed. 64.00 (*0-932087-12-4*) Sound View Pr.

Annual & Semiannual Promotion, with Special Reference to the Elementary School. James A. Lindsay. LC 72-176996. (Columbia University. Teachers College. Contributions to Education Ser.: No. 570). reprint ed. 22.50 (*0-404-55570-5*) AMS Pr.

Annual Bibliography of European Ethnomusicolgy, Bratislava, Vols. 1-10, 1966-1975, Vol. 1-10, Index. 1981. Index I-X (1966-75). 8.00 (*0-318-23311-8*) Intl Coun Trad.

Annual Bibliography of European Ethnomusicolgy, Bratislava, Vols. 1-10, 1966-1975, Vols. I-X: 1966-75. 1975. Vol. I-X (1966-75). write for info. (*0-318-23310-X*) Intl Coun Trad.

Annual Bibliography of Indian Archaeology. Ed. by Kern Institute Staff. 1984. lib. bdg. 167.00 (*90-277-1642-0*) Kluwer Ac.

Annual Bibliography of Modern Art: Nineteen-Hundred Ninety-One. Museum of Modern Art Library Staff. 600p. 1992. text ed. 225.00 (*0-8161-0557-X*) G K Hall.

Annual Bibliography of Modern Art: 1992. Museum of Modern Art Library Staff. 700p. 1993. lib. bdg. 225.00 (*0-8161-0597-9*, Hall Reference) Macmillan.

Annual Bibliography of Modern Art, Nineteen Eighty-Seven: The Museum of Modern Art Library, New York. 700p. 1988. lib. bdg. 190.00 (*0-8161-0475-1*, Hall Library) G K Hall.

Annual Bibliography of Modern Art, 1986: The Museum of Modern Art Library, New York. (Library Catalogs). 450p. 1987. lib. bdg. 165.00 (*0-8161-0461-1*, Hall Library) G K Hall.

Annual Bibliography of Modern Art, 1989: The Museum of Modern Art Library, New York. Museum of Modern Art Library Staff. (Monograph Ser.). 700p. (C). 1990. lib. bdg. 215.00 (*0-8161-0508-1*) G K Hall.

Annual Bibliography of Modern Art: 1990: The Museum of Modern Art, New York. annuals Museum of Modern Art Library Staff. 700p. 1991. text ed. 225.00 (*0-8161-0517-0*) G K Hall.

Annual Bibliography of the History of the Printed Book & Libraries. Ed. by Hendrik D. Verliet. 1983. lib. bdg. 196.00 (*90-247-2853-3*) Kluwer Ac.

Annual Bibliography of the History of the Printed Book & Libraries. Ed. by Hendrik D. Vervliet. 1984. lib. bdg. 179.00 (*90-247-2970-X*) Kluwer Ac.

Annual Bibliography of the History of the Printed Book & Libraries. Ed. by Hendrik D. Vervliet. 1984. lib. bdg. 186.50 (*90-247-2995-5*) Kluwer Ac.

Annual Bibliography of the History of the Printed Book & Libraries. Ed. by Hendrik D. Vervliet. 1985. lib. bdg. 194.00 (*90-247-3191-7*) Kluwer Ac.

Annual Bibliography of the History of the Printed Book & Libraries. Ed. by Hendrik D. Vervliet. 1986. lib. bdg. 202.50 (*90-247-3382-0*) Kluwer Ac.

Annual Bibliography of the History of the Printed Book & Libraries. Ed. by Hendrik D. Vervliet. (C). 1987. lib. bdg. 202.50 (*90-247-3640-4*) Kluwer Ac.

Annual Bibliography of the History of the Printed Book & Libraries. Ed. by Hendrik D. Vervliet. (C). 1988. lib. bdg. 205.00 (*90-247-3680-3*) Kluwer Ac.

Annual Bibliography of the History of the Printed Book & Libraries. Ed. by Hendrik D. Vervliet. (C). 1989. lib. bdg. 193.50 (*0-7923-0385-7*) Kluwer Ac.

Annual Bibliography of the History of the Printed Book & Libraries. Incl. Publications of 1973. 1975. pap. text ed. 154.50 (*90-247-1758-2*); Publications of 1974. 1976. pap. text ed. 136.50 (*90-247-1753-1*); Publications of 1975. 1977. pap. text ed. 154.50 (*90-247-1963-1*); Set pap. write for info. (*0-318-53995-0*) Kluwer Ac.

Annual Bibliography of the History of the Printed Book & Libraries: Cumulated Subject Index Vol. 1 (1970) - Vol. 17 (1986) Ed. by Hendrik D. Vervliet. (C). 1988. lib. bdg. 133.00 (*0-7923-0039-4*) Kluwer Ac.

Annual Bibliography of the History of the Printed Book & Libraries: Publications of 1976. Ed. by Hendrik D. Vervliet. 1978. pap. text ed. 177.50 (*90-247-2062-1*) Kluwer Ac.

Annual Bibliography of the History of the Printed Book & Libraries (ABHB) Ed. by Hendrik D. Vervliet. (C). 1990. lib. bdg. 194.50 (*0-7923-0749-6*) Kluwer Ac.

Annual Bibliography of the Museum of Modern Art Library, 1988 Edition. Museum of Modern Art Library Staff. (Library Catalogs Ser.). 525p. 1989. lib. bdg. 190.00 (*0-8161-0487-5*) G K Hall.

Annual Book of ASTM Standards, 48 vols. Incl. Pt. 1. Steel Piping, Tubing & Fittings (108 Standards) 1975. 26.00 (*0-8031-0140-6*, 01-001075-02); Pt. 2. Ferrous Castings, Ferroalloys (80 Standards) 1975. 16.00 (*0-8031-0141-4*, 01-002075-01); Pt. 3. Steel Plate, Sheet, Strip & Wire; Metallic Coated Products (120 Standards) 1975. 24.00 (*0-8031-0142-2*, 01-003075-02); Pt. 4. Structural Steel, Concrete Reinforcing Steel, Pressure Vessel Plate, Steel Rails, Wheels & Tires (117 Standards) 1975. 21.00 (*0-8031-0143-0*, 01-004075-02); Pt. 5. Steel Bars, Chain & Springs; Bearing Steel; Steel Forgings (117 Standards) 868p. 1975. 26.00 (*0-8031-0144-9*, 01-005075-02); Pt. 6. Copper & Copper Alloys Including Electrical Conductors (180 Standards) 1975. 28.00 (*0-8031-0145-7*, 01-006075-03); Pt. 7. Die-Cast Metals, Light Metals & Alloys Including Electrical Conductors (97 Standards) 1975. 24.00 (*0-8031-0146-5*, 01-007075-04); Pt. 8. Nonferrous Metals-Nickel, Lead & Tin Alloys, Precious Metals, Primary Metals; Reactive Metals (130 Standards) 1975. 25.00 (*0-8031-0147-3*, 01-008075-05); Pt. 9. Electrodeposited Metallic Coatings; Metal Powders; Sintered P-M Structural Parts (108 Standards) 1975. 16.00 (*0-8031-0148-1*, 01-009075-05); Pt. 12. Chemical Analysis of Metals; Sampling & Analysis of Metal Bearing Ores (83 Standards) 1975. 26.00 (*0-8031-0149-X*, 01-012075-24); Pt. 15. Bituminous Materials for Highway Construction, Waterproofing & Roofing, & Pipe; Skid Resistance (223 Standards) 1975. 28.00 (*0-8031-0150-3*, 01-015075-08); Pt. 16. Chemical-Resistant Nonmetallic Materials; Clay & Concrete Pipe & Tile; Masonry Mortars & Units; Asbestos-Cement Products (106 Standards) 1975. 16.00 (*0-8031-0151-1*, 01-016075-10); Pt. 17. Refractories, Glass & Other Ceramic Materials; Manufactured Carbon & Graphite Products (193 Standards) 1975. 28.00 (*0-8031-0152-X*, 01-016075-10); Pt. 19. Natural Building Stones; Soil & Rock; Peats, Mossses & Humus (117 Standards) 1975. 15.00 (*0-8031-0153-8*, 01-019075-38); Pt. 20. Paper; Packaging; Business Copy Products (175 Standards) 1975. 23.00 (*0-8031-0154-6*, 01-020075-11); Pt. 21. Cellulose; Leather; Flexible Barrier Materials, (91 Standards) 1975. 13.00 (*0-8031-0155-4*); Pt. 27. Paint-Tests for Formulated Products & Applied Coatings (199 Standards) 1975. 26.00 (*0-8031-0156-2*, 01-027075-14); Pt. 28. Paint-Pigments, Resins & Polymers (141 Standards) 1975. 17.00 (*0-8031-0157-0*, 01-028075-14); Pt. 29. Paint-Fatty Oils & Acids, Solvents, Miscellaneous; Aromatic Hydrocarbons; Naval Stores (244 Standards) 1975. 26.00 (*0-8031-0158-9*, 01-029075-14); Pt. 33. Textile Materials-Fibers, Zippers; High Modulus Fibers (116 Standards) Date not set. 24.00 (*0-8031-0159-7*, 01-033075-18); Pt. 34. Plastic Pipe (90 Standards) 1975. 18.00 (*0-8031-0160-0*, 01-034075-19); Pt. 35. Plastics-General Test Methods; Nomenclature, (158 Standards) 1975. 31.00 (*0-8031-0161-9*, 01-035075-19); Pt. 36. Plastics-Materials, Film, Reinforced & Cellular. 1975. 24.00 (*0-8031-0162-7*, 01-036075-19); Pt. 37. Rubber-Test Methods (107 Standards) 1975. 22.00 (*0-8031-0163-5*, 01-037075-20); Pt. 38. Rubber-Specifications; Carbon Black; Gaskets; Tires (147 Standards) 1975. 25.00 (*0-8031-0164-3*, 01-038075-20); Pt. 39. Rubber-Products; Specifications & Related Test Methods. 1975. 24.00 (*0-8031-0165-1*, 01-039075-21); Pt. 40. Electrical Insulating Materials-Specifications; Electrical Insulating Liquids & Gases (144 Standards) 1975. 24.00 (*0-8031-0166-X*, 01-040075-21); Pt. 41. General Test Methods (Non-Metal); Statistical Methods; Space Simulation; Particle Size Measurement; Deterioration of Non-Metallic Materials (115 Standards) 1975. 25.00 (*0-8031-0167-8*, 01-041075-41); Emission, Molecular, & Mass Spectroscopy; Chromatography; Resinography; Microscopy (59 Standards) 104pt. 42. 1975. 14.00 (*0-8031-0168-6*, 01-042075-39); 1,070.00 (*0-8031-0139-2*) ASTM.

Annual Book of ASTM Standards, Section 1, 1992, Vols. 01.01-01.07. 5206p. 1992. 474.00 (*0-8031-1669-1*, 01-010092-02); fiche write for info. (*0-318-69816-1*, 25-010092-02) ASTM.

Annual Book of ASTM Standards, Section 10, 1992, Vols. 10.01-10.05. 3222p. 308.00 (*0-8031-1721-3*, 01-100092-21); fiche write for info. (*0-318-69032-2*, 25-100092-21) ASTM.

Annual Book of ASTM Standards, Section 11, 1992, Vols. 11.01-11.04. 3854p. 334.00 (*0-8031-1727-2*, 01-110092-16); fiche write for info. (*0-318-69033-0*, 25-110092-16) ASTM.

Annual Book of ASTM Standards, Section 12, 1992, Vols. 12.01-12.02. 1904p. 166.00 (*0-8031-1732-9*, 01-120092-35); fiche write for info. (*0-318-69034-9*, 25-120092-35) ASTM.

Annual Book of ASTM Standards, Section 14, 1992, Vols. 14.01-14.03. 2616p. 221.00 (*0-8031-1736-1*, 01-140092-32); fiche write for info. (*0-318-69035-7*, 25-140092-32) ASTM.

Annual Book of ASTM Standards, Section 15, 1992, Vols. 15.01-15.09. 6210p. 594.00 (*0-8031-1740-X*, 01-150092-44); fiche write for info. (*0-318-69036-5*, 25-150092-44) ASTM.

Annual Book of ASTM Standards, Section 2, 1992, Vols. 02.01-02.05. 4332p. 361.00 (*0-8031-1677-2*, 01-020092-04); fiche write for info. (*0-318-69024-1*, 25-020092-04) ASTM.

Annual Book of ASTM Standards, Section 3, 1992, Vols. 03.01-03.06. 4228p. 383.00 (*0-8031-1683-7*, 01-030092-23); fiche write for info. (*0-318-69025-X*, 25-030092-23) ASTM.

Annual Book of ASTM Standards, Section 4, Vols. 04.01-04.09. 7392p. 676.00 (*0-8031-1607-1*, 01-040091-10); fiche write for info. (*0-318-69026-8*, 25-040091-10) ASTM.

An Asterisk (*) at the beginning of an entry indicates that the title is appearing in BIP for the first time.

An Asterisk (*) at the beginning of an entry indicates that the title is appearing in BIP for the first time.

Annual Book of ASTM Standards, 1993, Vol. 03.02: Wear & Erosion; Metal Corrosion. 550p. 1993. 63.00 (*0-8031-1916-X*, 01-030293-27); fiche write for info. (*0-318-69845-5*, 25-030293-27) ASTM.

Annual Book of ASTM Standards, 1993, Vol. 03.03: Nondestructive Testing. 808p. 1993. 75.00 (*0-8031-1917-8*, 01-030393-22); fiche write for info. (*0-318-69846-3*, 25-030393-22) ASTM.

Annual Book of ASTM Standards, 1993, Vol. 03.04: Magnetic Properties; Metallic Materials for Thermostats, Electrical Resistance, Heating, Contacts. 562p. 1993. 63.00 (*0-8031-1918-6*, 01-030493-06); fiche write for info. (*0-318-69847-1*, 25-030493-06) ASTM.

Annual Book of ASTM Standards, 1993, Vol. 03.05: Analytical Chemistry for Metals, Ores, & Related Materials (I) 754p. 1993. 79.00 (*0-8031-1919-4*, 01-030593-50); fiche write for info. (*0-318-69848-X*, 25-030593-50) ASTM.

Annual Book of ASTM Standards, 1993, Vol. 03.06: Analytical Chemistry for Metals, Ores, & Related Materials (II) 638p. 1993. 70.00 (*0-8031-1920-8*, 01-030693-50); fiche write for info. (*0-318-69849-8*, 25-030693-50) ASTM.

Annual Book of ASTM Standards, 1993, Vol. 04.01: Cement; Lime; Gypsum. 588p. 1993. 69.00 (*0-8031-1922-4*, 01-040193-07); fiche write for info. (*0-318-69859-5*, 25-040193-07) ASTM.

Annual Book of ASTM Standards, 1993, Vol. 04.02: Concrete & Aggregates. 848p. 1993. 83.00 (*0-8031-1923-2*, 01-040293-07); fiche write for info. (*0-318-69860-9*, 25-040293-07) ASTM.

Annual Book of ASTM Standards, 1993, Vol. 04.03: Road & Paving Materials; Pavement Management Technologies. 828p. 1993. 83.00 (*0-8031-1924-0*, 01-040393-08); fiche write for info. (*0-318-69861-7*, 25-040393-08) ASTM.

Annual Book of ASTM Standards, 1993, Vol. 04.04: Roofing, Waterproofing, & Bituminous Materials. 462p. 1993. 56.00 (*0-8031-1925-9*, 01-040493-57); fiche write for info. (*0-318-69862-5*, 25-040493-57) ASTM.

Annual Book of ASTM Standards, 1993, Vol. 04.05: Chemical-Resistant Materials; Vitrified Clay, Concrete, Fiber-Cement Products; Mortars; Masonry. 924p. 1993. 85.00 (*0-8031-1926-7*, 01-040593-60); fiche write for info. (*0-318-69863-3*, 25-040593-60) ASTM.

Annual Book of ASTM Standards, 1993, Vol. 04.06: Thermal Insulation; Environmental Acoustics. 956p. 1993. 99.00 (*0-8031-1927-5*, 01-040693-61); fiche write for info. (*0-318-69864-1*, 25-040693-61) ASTM.

Annual Book of ASTM Standards, 1993, Vol. 04.07: Building Seals & Sealants; Fire Standards; Building Constructions. 1222p. 1993. 115.00 (*0-8031-1928-3*, 01-040793-10); fiche write for info. (*0-318-69865-X*, 25-040793-10) ASTM.

Annual Book of ASTM Standards, 1993, Vol. 04.08: Soil & Rock; Dimension Stone; Geosynthetics. 1464p. 1993. 129.00 (*0-8031-1929-1*, 01-040893-38); fiche write for info. (*0-318-69866-8*, 25-040893-38) ASTM.

Annual Book of ASTM Standards, 1993, Vol. 04.09: Wood. 650p. 1993. 72.00 (*0-8031-1930-5*, 01-040993-45); fiche write for info. (*0-318-69867-6*, 25-040993-45) ASTM.

Annual Book of ASTM Standards, 1993, Vol. 05.01: Petroleum Products & Lubricants (I) 1066p. 1993. 119.00 (*0-8031-1932-1*, 01-050193-12); fiche write for info. (*0-318-69868-4*, 25-050193-12) ASTM.

Annual Book of ASTM Standards, 1993, Vol. 05.02: Petroleum Products & Lubricants (II) 1070p. 1993. 119.00 (*0-8031-1933-X*, 01-050293-12); fiche write for info. (*0-318-69869-2*, 25-050293-12) ASTM.

Annual Book of ASTM Standards, 1993, Vol. 05.03: Petroleum Products & Lubricants (III) 890p. 1993. 108.00 (*0-8031-1934-8*, 01-050393-12); fiche write for info. (*0-318-69870-6*, 25-050393-12) ASTM.

Annual Book of ASTM Standards, 1993, Vol. 05.04: Test Methods for Rating Motor, Diesel, & Aviation Fuels. 312p. 1993. 62.00 (*0-8031-1935-6*, 01-050493-12); fiche write for info. (*0-318-69871-4*, 25-050493-12) ASTM.

Annual Book of ASTM Standards, 1993, Vol. 05.05: Gaseous Fuels; Coal & Coke. 546p. 1993. 61.00 (*0-8031-1936-4*, 01-050593-13); fiche write for info. (*0-318-69872-2*, 25-050593-13) ASTM.

Annual Book of ASTM Standards, 1993, Vol. 06.01: Paint - Tests for Chemical, Physical, & Optical Properties; Appearance. 1110p. 1993. 104.00 (*0-8031-1938-0*, 01-060193-14); fiche write for info. (*0-318-69892-7*, 25-060193-25) ASTM.

Annual Book of ASTM Standards, 1993, Vol. 06.02: Paint - Products & Applications; Protective Coatings; Pipeline Coatings. 792p. 1993. 77.00 (*0-8031-1939-9*, 01-060293-14); fiche write for info. (*0-318-69893-5*, 25-060293-14) ASTM.

Annual Book of ASTM Standards, 1993, Vol. 06.03: Paint - Pigments, Drying Oils, Polymers, Resins, Naval Stores, Cellulosic Esters, & Ink Vehicles. 700p. 1993. 70.00 (*0-8031-1940-2*, 01-060393-14); fiche write for info. (*0-318-69894-3*, 25-060393-14) ASTM.

Annual Book of ASTM Standards, 1993, Vol. 06.04: Paint - Solvents; Aromatic Hydrocarbons. 736p. 1993. 73.00 (*0-8031-1941-0*, 01-060493-14); fiche write for info. (*0-318-69895-1*, 25-060493-14) ASTM.

Annual Book of ASTM Standards, 1993, Vol. 07.01: Textiles (I) 962p. 1993. 99.00 (*0-8031-1943-7*, 01-070193-18); fiche write for info. (*0-318-69896-X*, 25-070193-18) ASTM.

Annual Book of ASTM Standards, 1993, Vol. 07.02: Textiles (II) 904p. 1993. 94.00 (*0-8031-1944-5*, 01-070293-17); fiche write for info. (*0-318-69897-8*, 25-070293-18) ASTM.

Annual Book of ASTM Standards, 1993, Vol. 08.01: Plastics (I) 828p. 1993. 85.00 (*0-8031-1946-1*, 01-080193-19); fiche write for info. (*0-318-69937-0*, 25-080193-19) ASTM.

Annual Book of ASTM Standards, 1993, Vol. 08.02: Plastics (II) 826p. 1993. 85.00 (*0-8031-1947-X*, 01-080293-19); fiche write for info. (*0-318-69938-9*, 25-080293-19) ASTM.

Annual Book of ASTM Standards, 1993, Vol. 08.03: Plastics (III) 662p. 1993. 70.00 (*0-8031-1948-8*, 01-080393-19); fiche write for info. (*0-318-69939-7*, 25-080393-19) ASTM.

Annual Book of ASTM Standards, 1993, Vol. 08.04: Plastic Pipe & Building Products. 1208p. 1993. 112.00 (*0-8031-1949-6*, 01-080493-58); fiche write for info. (*0-318-69940-0*, 25-080493-58) ASTM.

Annual Book of ASTM Standards, 1993, Vol. 09.01: Rubber, Natural & Synthetic - General Test Methods; Carbon Black. 932p. 1993. 89.00 (*0-8031-1951-8*, 01-090193-20); fiche write for info. (*0-318-69941-9*, 25-090193-20) ASTM.

Annual Book of ASTM Standards, 1993, Vol. 09.02: Rubber Products, Industrial - Specifications & Related Test Methods; Gaskets; Tires. 736p. 1993. 78.00 (*0-8031-1952-6*, 01-090293-20); fiche write for info. (*0-318-69942-7*, 25-090293-20) ASTM.

Annual Book of ASTM Standards, 1993, Vol. 10.01: Electrical Insulation (I) 622p. 1993. 68.00 (*0-8031-1954-2*, 01-100193-21); fiche write for info. (*0-318-69943-5*, 25-100193-21) ASTM.

Annual Book of ASTM Standards, 1993, Vol. 10.02: Electrical Insulation (II) 554p. 1993. 63.00 (*0-8031-1955-0*, 01-100293-21); fiche write for info. (*0-318-69944-3*, 25-100293-21) ASTM.

Annual Book of ASTM Standards, 1993, Vol. 10.03: Electrical Insulating Liquids & Gases; Electrical Protective Equipment. 532p. 1993. 63.00 (*0-8031-1956-9*, 01-100393-21); fiche write for info. (*0-318-69945-1*, 25-100393-21) ASTM.

Annual Book of ASTM Standards, 1993, Vol. 10.04: Electronics (I) 760p. 1993. 79.00 (*0-8031-1957-7*, 01-100493-46); fiche write for info. (*0-318-69955-9*, 25-100493-46) ASTM.

Annual Book of ASTM Standards, 1993, Vol. 10.05: Electronics(II) 872p. 1993. 90.00 (*0-8031-1958-5*, 01-100593-46); fiche write for info. (*0-318-69956-7*, 25-100593-45) ASTM.

Annual Book of ASTM Standards, 1993, Vol. 11.01: Water (I) 750p. 1993. 72.00 (*0-8031-1960-7*, 01-110193-16); fiche write for info. (*0-318-69957-5*, 25-110193-16) ASTM.

Annual Book of ASTM Standards, 1993, Vol. 11.02: Water (II) 1008p. 1993. 110.00 (*0-8031-1961-5*, 01-110293-16); fiche write for info. (*0-318-69958-3*, 25-110293-16) ASTM.

Annual Book of ASTM Standards, 1993, Vol. 11.03: Atmospheric Analysis; Occupational Health & Safety; Protective Clothing. 858p. 1993. 85.00 (*0-8031-1962-3*, 01-110393-17); fiche write for info. (*0-318-69959-1*, 25-110393-17) ASTM.

Annual Book of ASTM Standards, 1993, Vol. 11.04: Pesticides; Resource Recovery; Hazardous Substances & Oil Spill Responses; Waste Management; Biological Effects. 1598p. 1993. 132.00 (*0-8031-1963-1*, 01-110493-48); fiche write for info. (*0-318-69960-5*, 25-110493-48) ASTM.

Annual Book of ASTM Standards, 1993, Vol. 12.01: Nuclear Energy (I) 928p. 1993. 96.00 (*0-8031-1965-8*, 01-120193-35); fiche write for info. (*0-318-69961-3*, 25-120193-35) ASTM.

Annual Book of ASTM Standards, 1993, Vol. 12.02: Nuclear (II), Solar, & Geothermal Energy. 950p. 1993. 97.00 (*0-8031-1966-6*, 01-120293-35); fiche write for info. (*0-318-69962-1*, 25-120293-35) ASTM.

Annual Book of ASTM Standards, 1993, Vol. 13.01: Medical Devices; Emergency Medical Services. 932p. 1993. 89.00 (*0-8031-1967-4*, 01-130193-54); fiche write for info. (*0-318-69963-X*, 25-130193-54) ASTM.

Annual Book of ASTM Standards, 1993, Vol. 14.01: Analytical Methods - Spectroscopy; Chromatography; Computerized Systems. 810p. 1993. 81.00 (*0-8031-1969-0*, 01-140193-32); fiche write for info. (*0-318-69964-8*, 25-140193-32) ASTM.

Annual Book of ASTM Standards, 1993, Vol. 14.02: General Test Methods, Non-Metal; Laboratory Apparatus; Statistical Methods; Forensic Sciences. 1282p. 1993. 112.00 (*0-8031-1970-4*, 01-140293-32); fiche write for info. (*0-318-69965-6*, 25-140293-32) ASTM.

Annual Book of ASTM Standards, 1993, Vol. 14.03: Temperature Measurement. 502p. 1993. 54.00 (*0-8031-1971-2*, 01-140393-40); fiche write for info. (*0-318-69970-2*, 25-140393-40) ASTM.

Annual Book of ASTM Standards, 1993, Vol. 15.01: Refractories; Carbon & Graphite Products; Activated Carbon. 538p. 1993. 61.00 (*0-8031-1973-9*, 01-150193-60); fiche write for info. (*0-318-69971-0*, 25-150193-60) ASTM.

Annual Book of ASTM Standards, 1993, Vol. 15.02: Glass; Ceramic Whitewares. 482p. 1993. 56.00 (*0-8031-1974-7*, 01-150293-09); fiche write for info. (*0-318-69972-9*, 25-150293-09) ASTM.

Annual Book of ASTM Standards, 1993, Vol. 15.03: Space Simulation; Aerospace & Aircraft; High Modulus Fibers & Composites. 734p. 1993. 73.00 (*0-8031-1975-5*, 01-150393-26); fiche write for info. (*0-318-69973-7*, 25-150393-26) ASTM.

Annual Book of ASTM Standards, 1993, Vol. 15.04: Soap; Polishes; Leather; Resilient Floor Coverings. 678p. 1993. 70.00 (*0-8031-1976-3*, 01-150493-44); fiche write for info. (*0-318-69974-5*, 25-150493-44) ASTM.

Annual Book of ASTM Standards, 1993, Vol. 15.05: Engine Coolants; Halogenated Organic Solvents; Industrial Chemicals. 598p. 1993. 66.00 (*0-8031-1977-1*, 01-150593-15); fiche write for info. (*0-318-69975-3*, 25-150593-15) ASTM.

Annual Book of ASTM Standards, 1993, Vol. 15.06: Adhesives. 504p. 1993. 55.00 (*0-8031-1978-X*, 01-150693-25); fiche write for info. (*0-318-69976-1*, 25-150693-25) ASTM.

Annual Book of ASTM Standards, 1993, Vol. 15.07: End Use Products. 956p. 1993. 109.00 (*0-8031-1979-8*, 01-150793-47); fiche write for info. (*0-318-69977-X*, 25-150793-47) ASTM.

Annual Book of ASTM Standards, 1993, Vol. 15.08: Fasteners. 474p. 1993. 62.00 (*0-8031-1980-1*, 01-150893-59); fiche write for info. (*0-318-69978-8*, 25-150893-59) ASTM.

Annual Book of ASTM Standards, 1993, Vol. 15.09: Paper; Packaging; Flexible Barrier Materials; Business Imaging Products. 1398p. 1993. 130.00 (*0-8031-1981-X*, 01-150993-11); fiche write for info. (*0-318-69979-6*, 25-150993-11) ASTM.

Annual Bulletin of Coal Statistics for Europe, Vol. XXIII, 1988. 105p. 25.00 (*92-1-016227-7*, EFR.89.II.E.4) UN.

Annual Bulletin of Coal Statistics for Europe, 1989, Vol. XXIV. 86p. 1991. 25.00 (*92-1-016240-4*, 90.II.E.15); 25.00 (*92-1-016260-9*, 90.II.E.15) UN.

Annual Bulletin of Electric Energy Statistics for Europe, Vol. 23. (Energy, Environment, Metals & Natural Resources Ser.). 130p. 1987. 22.00 (*92-1-016213-7*, EFR.88.II.E.8) UN.

Annual Bulletin of Electric Energy Statistics for Europe, Vol. XXXIV, 1988. 129p. 25.00 (*92-1-016235-8*, EFR. 89.II.E.11) UN.

Annual Bulletin of Electric Energy Statistics for Europe, Vol. XXXVI. 1991. 25.00 (*92-1-016255-2*, 91.II.E.10) UN.

Annual Bulletin of Electric Energy Statistics for Europe, 1989, Vol. XXXV. 84p. 1989. 25.00 (*92-1-016244-7*, 90. II.E.19) UN.

Annual Bulletin of Gas Statistics for Europe, Vol. XXXV. 84p. 1991. 25.00 (*92-1-016239-0*, 90.II.E.14) UN.

Annual Bulletin of Gas Statistics for Europe: 1987, Vol. XXXIII. (ENG, FRE & RUS.). 1988. 23.00 (*92-1-016212-9*, EFR.88.II.E.7) UN.

Annual Bulletin of Gas Statistics for Europe, 1990, Vol. XXXIV. 78p. 1990. 25.00 (*92-1-016232-3*, 89.II.E.9) UN.

Annual Bulletin of Gas Statistics for Europe, 1992, Vol. XXXVI. 1992. 25.00 (*92-1-016253-6*, 91.II.E.8) UN.

Annual Bulletin of General Energy Statistics for Europe, Vol. XX, 1987. 160p. 25.00 (*92-1-016233-1*, EFR.89.II. E.10) UN.

Annual Bulletin of General Energy Statistics for Europe, 1986, Vol. 19. 134p. 1988. pap. 25.00 (*92-1-016210-2*, 88.II.E.5) UN.

Annual Bulletin of General Energy Statistics for Europe, 1988, Vol. XXI. 161p. 1988. 30.00 (*92-1-016238-2*, 90. II.E.12) UN.

Annual Bulletin of General Energy Statistics for Europe, 1991, Vol. XXII. 1991. 30.00 (*92-1-016259-5*, 91.II.E. 14) UN.

Annual Bulletin of Housing & Building Statistics for Europe, Vol. XXXII, 1988. 127p. 25.00 (*92-1-016236-6*, EFR.89.II.E.12) UN.

Annual Bulletin of Housing & Building Statistics for Europe, Vol. XXXIV. 1990. 25.00 (*92-1-016256-0*, 91. II.E.11) UN.

Annual Bulletin of Housing & Building Statistics for Europe, 1987, Vol. 231. 126p. (ENG, FRE & RUS.). 1988. pap. 22.00 (*92-1-016214-5*, 88.II.E.9) UN.

Annual Bulletin of Housing & Building Statistics for Europe, 1989, Vol. XXXIII. 63p. 1991. 25.00 (*92-1-016243-9*, 90.II.E.18) UN.

Annual Bulletin of Steel Statistics for Europe, Vol. XV, 1987. 87p. (ENG, FRE & RUS.). 1988. 16.00 (*92-1-016216-1*, EFR. 88. II.E.11) UN.

Annual Bulletin of Steel Statistics for Europe, Vol. XVII. 80p. 1989. 25.00 (*92-1-016241-2*) UN.

Annual Bulletin of Steel Statistics for Europe, 1990, Vol. XVIII. 1991. write for info. (*92-1-016258-7*, 91.II.E.13) UN.

Annual Bulletin of Steel Statistics for Europe, 1988, Vol. XVI. 179p. 1988. 25.00 (*92-1-016230-7*, 89.II.E.7) UN.

Annual Bulletin of Trade in Chemical Products, Vol. XV. 286p. 1988. 40.00 (*92-1-016249-8*) UN.

Annual Bulletin oF Trade in Chemical Products: 1987, Vol. XIV. (ENG, FRE & RUS.). 1988. 40.00 (*92-1-016223-4*, 88.II.E.35) UN.

Annual Bulletin of Trade in Chemical Products, Vol. 13, 1986. 286p. (ENG, FRE & RUS.). 1988. 39.00 (*92-1-016209-9*, EFR.88.II.E.3) UN.

Annual Bulletin of Transport Statistics for Europe, Vol. XXXIX, 1987. 281p. 36.00 (*92-1-016218-8*, EFR.88.II. E.12) UN.

Annual Bulletin of Transport Statistics for Europe, 1988, Vol. XL. 281p. 1990. 55.00 (*92-1-016228-5*, 89.II.E.6) UN.

Annual Bulletin of Transport Statistics for Europe, 1989, Vol. XLI. 1990. 55.00 (*92-1-016246-3*, 90.II.E.21); 55. 00 (*92-1-016252-8*, 91.II.E.7) UN.

Annual California-Alaska Oil & Gas Review, 1993. 1994. 50.00 (*0-318-39821-4*) Munger Oil.

Annual Chipping Potato Seminar Proceedings. Ed. by Mary Humann. (Illus.). 82p. 30.00 (*0-318-19544-5*) Natl Potato Coun.

***Annual Condominium Act & Administrative Rule Update.** Florida Bar Legal Education Staff. 142p. 1994. pap. text ed. 15.00 (*0-945979-63-0*, 255) FL Bar Legal Ed.

Annual Conference Abstracts, 10th, Boston see Annual Conference Abstracts, 11th, Philadelphia

Annual Conference Abstracts, 11th, Philadelphia. Incl. Annual Conference Abstracts, 12th, Cleveland. 56p. 1984. 3.50 (*0-317-36388-3*); Annual Conference Abstracts, 13th, Los Angeles. 84p. 1985. 5.00 (*0-317-36389-1*); Annual Conference Abstracts, 14th, New York. 72p. 1986. 5.00 (*0-685-11708-1*); Annual Conference Abstracts, 10th, Boston. 48p. 1983. 3.50 (*0-685-11710-3*); Annual Conference Abstracts, 15th, Washington D. C. 64p. 1987. 5.00 (*0-685-11711-1*); Annual Conference Abstracts, 16th, Dallas. 48p. 1988. 7.00 (*0-685-11712-X*); 56p. 1983. 3.50 (*0-317-36387-5*) Art Libs Soc.

Annual Conference Abstracts, 12th, Cleveland see Annual Conference Abstracts, 11th, Philadelphia

Annual Conference Abstracts, 13th, Los Angeles see Annual Conference Abstracts, 11th, Philadelphia

Annual Conference Abstracts, 14th, New York see Annual Conference Abstracts, 11th, Philadelphia

Annual Conference Abstracts, 15th, Washington D. C. see Annual Conference Abstracts, 11th, Philadelphia

Annual Conference Abstracts, 16th, Dallas see Annual Conference Abstracts, 11th, Philadelphia

Annual Conference of the American Academy of Advertising: Proceedings. Ed. by James E. Haefner. 1980. pap. 25.00 (*0-931030-03-X*) Am Acad Advert.

Annual Conference Proceedings of the Society for Technical Communication, 41st. Ed. by Avon J. Murphy. Date not set. per., pap. text ed. 50.00 (*0-914548-79-4*); ring bd. 50.00 (*0-914548-80-8*) Soc Tech Comm.

Annual Conference, 35th: Advanced Printing of Paper Summaries. Society of Photographic Scientists & Engineers Staff. 132p. reprint ed. pap. 37.70 (*0-8357-5615-7*, 2017860) Bks Demand.

Annual Cropping Systems in the Tropics: An Introduction. Michael J. Norman. LC 79-10625. (Illus.). 288p. reprint ed. pap. 82.10 (*0-7837-4924-4*, 2044590) Bks Demand.

Annual Customs & Festivals in Peking. Tun Li Ch'en. Tr. by Derk Bodde. 182p. (Orig.). (C). 1987. pap. text ed. 42.00 (*0-685-65780-9*, Pub. by Hong Kong U Pr HK) St Mut.

Annual Customs & Festivals in Peking. 3rd ed. Tun Li Ch'en. Tr. by Derk Bodde. (Illus.). 182p. (Orig.). (C). 1987. pap. text ed. 33.50 (*962-209-195-4*, Pub. by Hong Kong Univ Pr HK) Coronet Bks.

Annual Cycles of Diving Behavior & Ecology of the Weddell Seal. Michael A. Castellini et al. LC 92-21717. (Bulletin of the Scripps Institute of Oceanography Ser.: Vol. 28). 1992. pap. 10.00 (*0-520-09779-3*) U CA Pr.

Annual Diagram. Reinheld Ebestin. 160p. 1980. reprint ed. pap. 10.00 (*0-88231-122-0*) ASI Pubs Inc.

Annual Diagram As an Aid to Life. Reinhold Ebertin. 151p. 1973. 7.00 (*0-86690-085-3*, E1087-014) Am Fed Astrologers.

***Annual Directory of American & Canadian Bed & Breakfasts, 1996 Edition.** Ed. by Tracey Menges. (Illus.). 1502p. (Orig.). 1995. pap. 19.95 (*1-55853-367-2*) Rutledge Hill Pr.

Annual Directory of Graduate Law Programs in the United States, 2nd. 1992. 27.50 (*0-685-45336-7*) Graduate Group.

Annual Directory of Vegetarian Restaurants see Guide to Natural Food Restaurants

Annual Directory of World Leaders, 1988-89. Ed. by Thomas S. Garrison. 170p. (Orig.). 1989. pap. 39.95 (*0-9610590-2-8*) IASB Enviro.

Annual Directory of World Leaders, 1991, Vol. 3. Ed. by Thomas S. Garrison. 200p. (Orig.). (YA). (gr. 9-12). 1991. pap. 39.95 (*0-9610590-5-2*) IASB Enviro.

***Annual Directory, 1994-1995.** Ed. by S. Oehme. 290p. (GER.). 1994. 80.00 (*0-86640-051-6*) German Am Chamber.

***Annual Editions: Aging.** annuals 10th rev. ed. Harold Cox. (Annual Ser.). (Illus.). 256p. (C). 1995. pap. text ed. 12. 95x (*1-56134-342-0*) Dushkin Pub.

***Annual Editions: American Foreign Policy, 95-96.** annuals 2nd rev. ed. Glenn P. Hastedt. (Illus.). 288p. (C). 1995. pap. text ed. 12.95x (*1-56134-385-4*) Dushkin Pub.

***Annual Editions: American Government, 95-96.** 25th rev. ed. Ed. by Bruce Stinebrickner. (Illus.). 256p. (C). 1995. pap. text ed. 12.95x (*1-56134-343-9*) Dushkin Pub.

***Annual Editions: American History, Vol. 1.** annuals 13th rev. ed. Robert J. Maddox. (Illus.). 256p. (C). 1995. pap. text ed. 12.95x (*1-56134-344-7*) Dushkin Pub.

***Annual Editions: American History, Vol. 2.** annuals 13th rev. ed. Robert Maddox. (Illus.). 256p. (C). 1995. pap. text ed. 12.95x (*1-56134-345-5*) Dushkin Pub.

***Annual Editions: Anthropology, 95-96.** 18th rev. ed. Ed. by Elvio Angeloni. (Illus.). 256p. (C). 1995. pap. text ed. 12.95x (*1-56134-346-3*) Dushkin Pub.

Annual Editions: Archaeology 95-96. Linda Hasten. (Illus.). 256p. 1995. pap. text ed. 12.95 (*1-56134-335-8*) Dushkin Pub.

Annual Editions: Biology. 6th ed. LC 74-30680. 256p. 1992. pap. text ed. 12.95x (*1-56134-069-3*) Dushkin Pub.

Annual Editions: Biopsychology 95-96. Boyce Jubilan. (Illus.). 256p. 1995. pap. text ed. 12.95 (*1-56134-336-6*) Dushkin Pub.

***Annual Editions: Business Ethics, 95-96.** 7th rev. ed. Ed. by John E. Richardson. (Illus.). 256p. (C). 1995. pap. text ed. 12.95x (*1-56134-347-1*) Dushkin Pub.

Annual Editions: Canadian Politics 93-94. 3rd ed. Roman March & Greg Mahler. 256p. 1993. pap. text ed. 12.95 (*1-56134-191-6*) Dushkin Pub.

Annual Editions: Child Growth & Development. 2nd ed. Ellen Junn & Chris Boyatzis. 256p. 1995. pap. text ed. 12.95 (*1-56134-337-4*) Dushkin Pub.

***Annual Editions: Comparative Politics, 95-96.** 13th rev. ed. Ed. by Christian Soe. (Illus.). 288p. (C). 1995. pap. text ed. 12.95x (*1-56134-348-X*) Dushkin Pub.

An Asterisk (*) at the beginning of an entry indicates that the title is appearing in BIP for the first time.

A

An Asterisk (*) at the beginning of an entry indicates that the title is appearing in BIP for the first time.

339

A

Annual Meeting, 39th, 1986, New Orleans: Proceedings. 1987. 15.00 (*0-913447-33-1*) Indus Relations Res.

Annual Meeting, 41st, 1988, New York: Proceedings. 1989. 20.00 (*0-913447-42-0*) Indus Relations Res.

Annual Meeting, 42nd, 1989, Atlanta: Proceedings. 1990. 20.00 (*0-913447-45-5*) Indus Relations Res.

Annual Meeting, 43rd, 1990, Washington, D. C. Proceedings. 1990. 20.00 (*0-913447-51-X*) Indus Relations Res.

Annual Meeting, 44th, 1992, New Orleans: Proceedings. 1992. 22.50 (*0-913447-54-4*) Indus Relations Res.

***Annual Meeting, 45th, 1993, Anaheim: Proceedings.** 1993. 20.00 (*0-913447-57-9*) Indus Relations Res.

***Annual Meeting, 46th, 1994, Boston: Proceedings.** 1994. 20.00 (*0-913447-59-5*) Indus Relations Res.

Annual Message of the Governor of Washington Territory, Delivered December 17th, 1862. William Pickering. 12p. 1972. pap. 1.00 (*0-87770-098-2*) Ye Galleon.

Annual Metropolitan Directory, 1994: Women's, Misses & Junior Ready to Wear Buyers. Ed. by Edgar Adcock et al. 135p. (Orig.). 1993. pap. 50.00 (*0-87228-046-2*) Salesmans.

Annual National Conference Proceedings. 43th ed. 364p. 1991. pap. 35.00 (*0-685-56807-5*, P144-K) Soc Human Resc Mgmt.

Annual, Nineteen Ninety-Four: Developing Human Resources. Ed. by J. W. Pfeiffer. LC 86-643030. 320p. 1994. pap. text ed. 39.95 (*0-88390-413-6*); ring bd. 89.95 (*0-88390-412-8*) Pfeiffer & Co.

Annual North American Seed Potato Seminar Proceedings. Ed. by Mary Humann. (Illus.). 82p. 30.00 (*0-318-17875-3*) Natl Potato Coun.

Annual Obituary 1980. Ed. by Roland Turner. 1981. 95.00 (*0-912289-50-3*); Standing Order. write for info. (*0-318-59343-2*) St James Pr.

Annual Obituary 1981. Ed. by Janet Podell. 1982. 95.00 (*0-912289-51-1*) St James Pr.

Annual Obituary 1982. Ed. by Janet Podell. 1983. 85.00 (*0-912289-01-5*) St James Pr.

Annual Obituary 1983. Ed. by Elizabeth Devine. 1984. 95. 00 (*0-912289-07-4*) St James Pr.

Annual Obituary 1984. Ed. by Margot Levy. 1986. 95.00 (*0-912289-53-8*) St James Pr.

Annual Obituary, 1986. Ed. by Trish Burgess. 1989. 95.00 (*1-55862-013-3*) St James Pr.

Annual Obituary, 1987. Ed. by Trish Burgess. 1990. 95.00 (*1-55862-021-4*) St James Pr.

Annual Obituary, 1988. Ed. by Trish Burgess. 760p. 1990. lib. bdg. 95.00 (*1-55862-050-8*) St James Pr.

Annual Obituary, 1989. Ed. by Deborah Andrews. 913p. 1990. lib. bdg. 95.00 (*1-55862-056-7*) St James Pr.

Annual Obituary, 1990. Ed. by Deborah Andrews. 875p. 1991. lib. bdg. 95.00 (*1-55862-092-3*, 200152) St James Pr.

Annual Obituary, 1991. Ed. by Deborah Andrews. 850p. 1992. 95.00 (*1-55862-175-X*, 200153) St James Pr.

Annual Obituary, 1995. Ed. by Louise Mooney. 850p. 1993. 92.00 (*1-55862-339-6*, 200267) St James Pr.

Annual of Auction Prices for Posters. Alain Weill. Orig. Title: Affiches et Art Publicitaire. (Illus.). (FRE.). 1987. 120.00 (*0-318-37090-5*) Edns Publisol.

Annual of Bernard Shaw Studies, Vol. 8. Stanley Weintraub. 180p. 1988. lib. bdg. 35.00 (*0-271-00613-7*) Pa St U Pr.

Annual of Bernard Shaw Studies, Vol. 10. Ed. by Stanley Weintraub & Fred D. Crawford. (Illus.). 176p. 1990. lib. bdg. 35.00 (*0-271-00694-3*) Pa St U Pr.

Annual of Light & Architecture, 1993. Ed. by Ingeborg Flagge. (Illus.). 180p. 1994. pap. 45.00 (*1-85490-900-2*, Academy Edits) St Martin.

Annual of Ophthalmic Laser Surgery. Ed. by William E. Benson et al. LC 92-71636. (Illus.). 132p. 1992. text ed. 125.00 (*1-878132-10-5*) Current Med.

Annual of Psychoanalysis, Vol. I. Chicago Institute for Psychoanalysis Staff. LC 72-91376. 395p. (C). 1973. text ed. 60.00 (*0-8236-0361-X*) Intl Univs Pr.

Annual of Psychoanalysis, Vol. IX. Ed. by Chicago Institute for Psychoanalysis Staff. 1981. 60.00 (*0-8236-0370-9*) Intl Univs Pr.

Annual of Psychoanalysis, Vol. X. Ed. by Chicago Institute for Psychoanalysis Staff. 1982. 60.00 (*0-8236-0371-7*) Intl Univs Pr.

Annual of Psychoanalysis, Vol. XIV. Chicago Institute for Psychoanalysis Staff. LC 72-91376. 375p. (C). 1987. text ed. 60.00 (*0-8236-0374-1*) Intl Univs Pr.

Annual of Psychoanalysis, Vol. XV. George H. Pollock. (Chicago Institute for Psychoanalysis Ser.). 1987. lib. bdg. 60.00 (*0-8236-0375-X*) Intl Univs Pr.

Annual of Psychoanalysis, Vol. XVI. Ed. by Chicago Institute of Psychoanalysis Staff. 391p. 1988. 60.00 (*0-8236-0376-8*) Intl Univs Pr.

Annual of Psychoanalysis, Vol. 17. Ed. by Chicago Institute for Psychoanalysis Staff. 376p. 1989. text ed. 36.00 (*0-88163-092-6*) Analytic Pr.

Annual of Psychoanalysis, Vol. 18. Ed. by Chicago Institute of Psychoanalysis Staff. (Annual Ser.). 296p. 1990. text ed. 29.95 (*0-88163-093-4*) Analytic Pr.

Annual of Psychoanalysis, Vol. 19. Ed. by Chicago Inst. for Psychoanalysis Staff. 280p. 1991. text ed. 32.50 (*0-88163-094-2*) Analytic Pr.

Annual of Psychoanalysis, Vol. 20. Ed. by Chicago Institute for Psychoanalysis Staff. 336p. 1992. 34.50 (*0-88163-133-7*) Analytic Pr.

Annual of Psychoanalysis, Vol. 21. Ed. by Jerome A. Winer. 384p. 1993. text ed. 36.00 (*0-88163-134-5*) Analytic Pr.

Annual of Psychoanalysis, Vol. 22. Ed. by Jerome A. Winer. 384p. 1994. text ed. 36.00 (*0-88163-135-3*) Analytic Pr.

***Annual of Psychoanalysis, Vol. 23.** Ed. by Jerome A. Winer. 330p. 1995. text ed. write for info. (*0-88163-187-6*) Analytic Pr.

***Annual of Psychoanalysis, Vol. 24.** Ed. by Jerome A. Winer. 1996. write for info. (*0-88163-188-4*) Analytic Pr.

***Annual of Psychoanalysis, Vol. 25.** Ed. by Jerome A. Winer. 1997. write for info. (*0-88163-189-2*) Analytic Pr.

Annual of Psychoanalysis, 1974, Vol. II. Ed. by Chicago Institute for Psychoanalysis Staff. LC 72-91376. (Illus.). x, 420p. (C). 1975. text ed. 60.00 (*0-8236-0362-8*) Intl Univs Pr.

Annual of Psychoanalysis, 1975, Vol. III. Ed. by Chicago Institute for Psychoanalysis Staff. LC 72-91376. viii, 441p. (C). 1976. text ed. 60.00 (*0-8236-0363-6*) Intl Univs Pr.

Annual of Psychoanalysis, 1976, Vol. IV. Ed. by Chicago Institute for Psychoanalysis Staff. LC 72-91376. (Illus.). xi, 508p. (C). 1977. text ed. 60.00 (*0-8236-0364-4*) Intl Univs Pr.

Annual of Psychoanalysis, 1977, Vol. V. Ed. by Chicago Institute for Psychoanalysis Staff. LC 72-91376. (Illus.). ix, 443p. (C). 1978. text ed. 60.00 (*0-8236-0366-0*) Intl Univs Pr.

Annual of Psychoanalysis, 1978, Vol. VI. Ed. by Chicago Institute for Psychoanalysis Staff. LC 72-91376. (Illus.). x, 489p. (C). 1979. text ed. 60.00 (*0-8236-0367-9*) Intl Univs Pr.

Annual of Psychoanalysis, 1979, Vol. VII. Ed. by Chicago Institute for Psychoanalysis Staff. LC 72-91376. (Illus.). x, 416p. (C). 1980. pap. text ed. 60.00 (*0-8236-0368-7*) Intl Univs Pr.

Annual of Psychoanalysis, 1980, Vol. VIII. Ed. by Chicago Institute for Psychoanalysis Staff. LC 72-91376. (Illus.). xiii, 359p. (C). 1981. text ed. 60.00 (*0-8236-0369-5*) Intl Univs Pr.

Annual of Psychoanalysis, 1983, Vol. XI. Ed. by Chicago Institute for Psychoanalysis Staff. LC 72-91376. xii, 365p. (C). 1984. text ed. 60.00 (*0-8236-0372-5*) Intl Univs Pr.

Annual of Psychoanalysis, 1985, Vol. XII-XIII. Ed. by Chicago Institute for Psychoanalysis Staff. LC 72-91376. 452p. 1985. text ed. 60.00 (*0-8236-0373-3*, 00373) Intl Univs Pr.

Annual of Report of the Tennessee Valley Authority. TVA Staff. 1969. 15.95 (*0-405-00147-9*, 18795) Ayer.

Annual of the Attorney General, 1984-1985. 1985. pap. 8.00 (*0-318-20362-6*) VA Atty Genl.

Annual of the Society of Christian Ethics. Ed. by Harlan Beckley. 300p. (Orig.). 1993. pap. 15.00 (*0-685-66864-9*) Georgetown U Pr.

Annual of the Society of Christian Ethics, 1987. Society of Christian Ethics Staff. Ed. by D. M. Yeager et al. LC 82-642723. 268p. reprint ed. pap. 76.40 (*0-7837-6833-8*, 2046662) Bks Demand.

Annual of Victorian Literature & Cultural History, Vol. 19: Victorian Literature & Culture, Vol. 19. Ed. by John Maynard & Adrienne A. Munich. (Browning Institute Studies Ser.). 1991. 57.50 (*0-404-64219-5*) AMS Pr.

Annual on Terrorism, 1986. Ed. by Yonah Alexander. 1987. pap. text ed. 128.00 (*90-247-3608-0*) Kluwer Ac.

Annual on Terrorism, 1987. Ed. by Yonah Alexander. (C). 1989. lib. bdg. 175.50 (*90-247-3801-6*) Kluwer Ac.

Annual on Terrorism, 1988-1989. Ed. by Yonah Alexander & Abraham H. Foxman. (C). 1990. lib. bdg. 120.00 (*0-7923-0757-7*) Kluwer Ac.

Annual Orthodox Conference, Seventh: Proceedings. limited ed. Ed. by St. Nectarios Press Staff & Holy Transfiguration Monastery Staff. 186p. (Orig.). 1987. pap. 10.00 (*0-913026-64-6*) St Nectarios.

Annual Papers of Winchester, Virginia, Vol. 1. 248p. 1931. write for info. (*0-318-64322-7*) Winchester-Frederick Cty Hist Soc.

***Annual Poetry Contest 1986: Imagery Poetry.** Ed. by Brigitta Geltrich. (Poetry Contest Ser.). 15p. (Orig.). 1986. pap. text ed. 3.00 (*0-936945-12-5*) Creat with Wds.

Annual Potato Statistical Yearbook. Ed. by Mary R. Humann. (Illus.). 52p. 10.00 (*0-318-19543-7*) Natl Potato Coun.

Annual Proceedings, No. 3. Incl. No. 4. Annual Proceedings. 383p. 1964. 25.00 (*0-318-16482-5*); No. 7. Annual Proceedings. 287p. 1966. 25.00 (*0-318-16483-3*); No. 8. Annual Proceedings. 290p. 1967. 25.00 (*0-318-16484-1*); No. 9. Annual Proceedings. 207p. 1968. 25.00 (*0-318-16485-X*); 299p. 1964. 25.00 (*0-318-16481-7*) SID.

Annual Proceedings of the Fordham Corporate Law Institute: Index & Tables of Cases, 1981-1990. Ed. by Barry Hawk. 1992. 95.00 (*1-56425-006-7*) Transnatl Juris Pubns.

***Annual Proceedings, 47th, 1995, Washington D.C. Proceedings.** 1995. 22.00 (*0-614-06237-3*) Indus Relations Res.

Annual Progress in Child & Adolescent Psychiatry & Child Development, 1994. Ed. by Margaret E. Hertzig & Ellen A. Farber. LC 68-23452. 600p. 1994. 64.95 (*0-87630-744-6*) Brunner-Mazel.

Annual Progress in Child Psychiatry & Child Development, Vols. 1-12. Ed. by Stella Chess & Alexander Thomas. Incl. Vol. 1. LC 68-23452. 1968. 52.95 (*0-318-51244-0*); Vol. 3. LC 68-23452. 1970. 52.95 (*0-87630-003-4*); Vol. 4. LC 68-23452. 1971. 52.95 (*0-87630-004-2*); Vol. 6. LC 68-23452. 1973. 52.95 (*0-87630-080-8*); Vol. 10. LC 68-23452. 1977. 52.95 (*0-87630-155-3*); Vol. 11. LC 68-23452. 1978. 52.95 (*0-87630-180-4*); Vol. 12. LC 68-23452. 1979. 52.95 (*0-87630-216-9*); LC 68-23452. (Illus.). write for info. (*0-318-51243-2*) Brunner-Mazel.

Annual Progress in Child Psychiatry & Child Development, 1980. Ed. by Stella Chess & Alexander Thomas. LC 68-23452. 624p. 1980. 52.95 (*0-87630-248-7*) Brunner-Mazel.

Annual Progress in Child Psychiatry & Child Development, 1981. Ed. by Stella Chess & Alexander Thomas. LC 68-23452. 670p. 1981. 52.95 (*0-87630-284-3*) Brunner-Mazel.

Annual Progress in Child Psychiatry & Child Development, 1982. Ed. by Stella Chess & Alexander Thomas. LC 68-23452. 696p. 1982. 52.95 (*0-87630-317-3*) Brunner-Mazel.

Annual Progress in Child Psychiatry & Child Development, 1983. Ed. by Stella Chess & Alexander Thomas. LC 68-23452. 562p. 1983. 52.95 (*0-87630-343-2*) Brunner-Mazel.

Annual Progress in Child Psychiatry & Child Development, 1984. Ed. by Stella Chess & Alexander Thomas. LC 68-23452. 514p. 1984. 52.95 (*0-87630-375-0*) Brunner-Mazel.

Annual Progress in Child Psychiatry & Child Development, 1985. Ed. by Stella Chess & Alexander Thomas. LC 68-23452. 664p. 1985. 52.95 (*0-87630-402-1*) Brunner-Mazel.

Annual Progress in Child Psychiatry & Child Development, 1986. Ed. by Stella Chess et al. LC 68-23452. 704p. 1986. 52.95 (*0-87630-437-4*) Brunner-Mazel.

Annual Progress in Child Psychiatry & Child Development, 1987. Ed. by Stella Chess et al. LC 68-23452. 650p. 1987. 52.95 (*0-87630-476-5*) Brunner-Mazel.

Annual Progress in Child Psychiatry & Child Development, 1988. Ed. by Stella Chess et al. LC 68-23452. 704p. 1988. 52.95 (*0-87630-538-9*) Brunner-Mazel.

Annual Progress in Child Psychiatry & Child Development, 1989. Ed. by Stella Chess & Margaret Hertzig. LC 68-23452. 576p. 1989. 52.95 (*0-87630-569-9*) Brunner-Mazel.

Annual Progress in Child Psychiatry & Child Development, 1990. Ed. by Stella Chess & Margaret Hertzig. LC 68-23452. (Illus.). 624p. 1990. 62.95 (*0-87630-602-4*) Brunner-Mazel.

Annual Progress in Child Psychiatry & Child Development, 1991. Ed. by Stella Chess & Margaret E. Hertzig. LC 68-23452. 656p. 1991. 62.95 (*0-87630-651-2*) Brunner-Mazel.

Annual Progress in Child Psychiatry & Child Development, 1992. Ed. by Margaret E. Hertzig & Ellen A. Farber. LC 68-23452. 653p. 1992. 62.95 (*0-87630-692-X*) Brunner-Mazel.

Annual Progress in Child Psychiatry & Child Development, 1993. Ed. by Margaret Hertzig & Ellen A. Farber. LC 68-23452. 580p. 1993. 62.95 (*0-87630-729-2*) Brunner-Mazel.

***Annual Progress in Child Psychiatry & Child Development, 1995.** Ed. by Hertzig & Farber. 600p. 1995. 64.95 (*0-87630-793-4*) Brunner-Mazel.

Annual Progress in Reproductive Medicine. R. Asch & J. Studd. (Illus.). 250p. 1993. 55.00 (*1-85070-376-0*) Prthnon Pub.

Annual Register of Grant Support 1995. 28th ed. Ed. by Bowker, R. R., Staff. 1275p. 1994. 185.00 (*0-8352-3522-X*) Bowker.

Annual Register of Grant Support 1996. Ed. by Bowker, R. R., Staff. 1275p. 1995. 189.95 (*0-8352-3671-4*) Bowker. "A literal 'gold mine' for any organization that depends upon non-repayable support for the continuation of its programs."--ART TIMES. "...(a) comprehensive standard reference source on non-repayable financial support..."--REFERENCE & RESEARCH BOOK NEWS. This guide to over 3,000 programs offering billions of dollars in non-repayable support shows how to unlock the funding potential of these sources. Organized by 11 major subject areas--with 61 specific subcategories--it is the definitive resource for all types of funding: nontraditional, such as educational associations & unions; & traditional corporate private, & public funding. There is no comparable resource available!** ***Publisher Provided Annotation.

Annual Register of Indian Political Parties: 1972-1987, 8 vols., Set. A. M. Zaidi. 1986. 1,200.00 (*0-317-52131-4*, Pub. by S Chand II) St Mut.

Annual Register of the Baptist Denomination in North America to 1790. John Asplund. 1979. reprint ed. 10.00 (*0-317-01254-1*) Church History.

Annual Register Pharm Chemist, 1993. 1993. pap. 170.00 (*0-85369-298-X*, Pub. by Pharmaceutical Pr UK) Rittenhouse.

Annual Register, 1980: A Record of World Events. 80th ed. Ed. by H. V. Hodson. (Illus.). 550p. (C). 1981. 75.00 (*0-8103-2026-6*, Pub. by Longman Grp UK) Gale.

Annual Register 1983: A Record of World Events. Ed. by H. V. Hodson. 550p. 1984. 90.00 (*0-8103-2033-9*) Gale.

Annual Register 1984: A Record of World Events. Ed. by H. V. Hodson. 550p. 1985. 90.00 (*0-8103-2039-8*) Gale.

Annual Register 1985: A Record of World Events. Ed. by H. V. Hodson. 550p. 1986. 95.00 (*0-8103-2043-6*) Gale.

Annual Register 1986: A Record of World Events. Ed. by H. V. Hodson. 550p. 1987. 100.00 (*0-8103-2053-3*) Gale.

Annual Register, 1988: A Record of World Events. H. V. Hodson. 550p. 1989. 110.00 (*0-8103-5325-3*, Pub. by Longman Grp UK) Gale.

Annual Register 1990. H. V. Hodson. 1991. 147.00 (*0-582-07926-8*) Longman.

Annual Register, 1991. 1992. 500.00 (*0-8103-9667-X*, 071018, Pub. by Longman Grp UK); 157.00 (*0-582-09585-9*, 071018, Pub. by Longman Grp UK) Gale.

Annual Register, 1992. 650p. 1993. 165.00 (*0-582-21787-3*, 071070, Pub. by Longman Grp UK) Gale.

***Annual Register, 1993: A Record of World Events.** Ed. by Alan J. Day & Verena Hoffman. LC 94-17979. 635p. 1994. 170.00 (*0-582-23449-2*, Pub. by Longman UK) Longman.

***Annual Register 1994.** 628p. 1995. 195.00 (*1-56159-138-6*, Stockton Pr) Groves Dictionaries.

Annual Report: A Guide to Planning, Producing & Promoting Company Reports. Jasper G. Grinling. 144p. 1986. text ed. 69.95 (*0-566-02600-7*) Ashgate Pub Co.

Annual Report: 1848-1851, 3 vols. in 1. Oneida Community Staff. LC 78-72358. (Free Love in America Ser.). reprint ed. 18.50 (*0-404-60982-1*) AMS Pr.

Annual Report & Proxy Rules of the SEC. 7th ed. Charles C. Zall. 235p. 25.00 (*0-685-71082-3*) Packard Pr Fin.

Annual Report & Proxy Rules of the Securities & Exchange Commission, 1992. 1992. pap. text ed. 25.00 (*0-936093-30-7*) Packard Pr Fin.

Annual Report, European Foundation for the Improvement of Living & Working, 1990. 84p. 1991. pap. 11.00 (*92-826-2846-9*, SY-71-91-130-EN-C) UNIPUB.

Annual Report-Federal Communications Commission. United States Federal Communications Commission. 1971. 58.95 (*0-405-03590-X*, 11256); 52.95 (*0-405-03589-6*, 11255); 58.95 (*0-405-03588-8*, 11254) Ayer.

Annual Report Glossary: An Easy-to-Understand Guidebook for Shareholders. Richard B. Loth. LC 89-155320. 174p. 1988. ring bd. 26.00 (*0-924399-00-7*) FIPS Partners Inc.

Annual Report of Activities of the National Advisory Council on International Monetary & Financial Policies 1965-1982, 7 bks., Set. 1984. reprint ed. lib. bdg. 350. 00 (*0-89941-337-4*, 201670) W S Hein.

Annual Report of Communications, Vol. 47: 1993-94. 1050p. 1994. 195.00 (*0-933217-09-9*) Prof Educ Intl.

Annual Report of the ACP-EEC Council of Ministers: 1989. 186p. 1990. pap. 17.00 (*92-824-0787-X*, BX-59-90-516-EN-C) UNIPUB.

Annual Report of the ACP-EEC Council of Ministers 1991. 186p. 1992. pap. 25.00 (*92-824-0986-4*, BX-75-92-211-EN-C, Pub. by Europ Com) UNIPUB.

Annual Report of the Administrator for 1984. 288p. 1984. 23.00 (*92-1-126000-0*) UN.

***Annual Report of the American Civil Liberties Union for 1988.** American Civil Liberties Union Staff. 12p. (Orig.). 1989. pap. write for info. (*0-914031-13-9*) Amer Civil Lib.

Annual Report of the American Numismatic Society 1993. (Illus.). 160p. pap. 1.50 (*0-685-72020-9*) Am Numismatic.

Annual Report of the Attorney General, 1980-1981. 1981. pap. 6.50 (*0-317-46927-4*) VA Atty Genl.

Annual Report of the Attorney General, 1981-1982. 1982. pap. 7.00 (*0-318-20359-6*) VA Atty Genl.

Annual Report of the Attorney General, 1982-1983, 2 vols. 1983. pap. 9.00 (*0-318-20360-X*) VA Atty Genl.

Annual Report of the Attorney General, 1983-1984. 1984. pap. 7.00 (*0-318-20361-8*) VA Atty Genl.

Annual Report of the Board of Regents of the Smithsonian Institution Showing the Operation, Expenditures & Condition of the Institution for the Year Ending June 30, 1897: A Memorial of George Brown Goode Together with a Selection of His Papers on Museums & on the History of Science in America, 55th Congress, 2nd Session, Doc. No. 575. U. S. House of Representatives Staff. Ed. by I. Bernard Cohen. LC 79-7964. (Three Centuries of Science in America Ser.: Pt. 3). (Illus.). 1980. reprint ed. lib. bdg. 69.95 (*0-405-12545-3*) Ayer.

Annual Report of the Council on Tribunals, 1988-89. 68p. 1990. pap. 20.00 (*0-10-211490-0*, HM0049) UNIPUB.

Annual Report of the Council on Tribunals 1992-93. 68p. 1993. pap. 30.00 (*0-10-207894-7*, HM78947, Pub. by HMSO UK) UNIPUB.

Annual Report of the Director General of Fair Trading for January to December, 1988, to the Secretary of State for Trade & Industry. 102p. 1989. pap. 25.00 (*0-10-244089-1*, HM5123, Pub. by HMSO UK) UNIPUB.

Annual Report of the Director General of Fair Trading, 1987. (Illus.). 84p. 1988. pap. 18.00 (*0-10-254488-3*, HM3774, Pub. by HMSO UK) UNIPUB.

Annual Report of the Federal Reserve Board, 1923 **see Credit Policies of the Federal Reserve System**

Annual Report of the Former Secretaries of State, 1983. LC 85-50888. (Papers on International Issues). 9p. (Orig.). teacher ed 5.00 (*0-935082-07-7*) Southern Ctr Intl Stud.

Annual Report of the Industrial Commissioner. 1993. reprint ed. lib. bdg. 89.00 (*0-7812-5242-3*) Rprt Serv.

Annual Report of the Inter-American Commission on Human Rights 1979-1980. OAS, General Secretariat, Inter-American Commission of Human Rights. Tr. by OAS Staff. (Inter-American Commission on Human Rights Ser.). 153p. (C). 1980. lib. bdg. 6.00 (*0-8270-1285-3*) OAS.

Annual Report of the Inter-American Commission on Human Rights, 1980-1981. OAS, General Secretariat, Inter-American Commission of Human Rights. (OEA Ser.: L/V/II.53 Doc. 9, Rev. 1). 130p. (SPA.). (C). 1981. pap. 5.00 (*0-686-81338-3*) OAS.

 An Asterisk (*) at the beginning of an entry indicates that the title is appearing in BIP for the first time.

Annual Report of the Keeper of Public Records on the Work of the P.R.O. 34th, 1992. 64p. 1993. pap. 35.00 (*0-10-022093-2*, HM20932, Pub. by HMSO UK) UNIPUB.

Annual Report of the Librarian of Congress: For the Fiscal Year Ending September 30, 1991. Comp. by James W. McLung. 93p. 1992. 3.50 (*0-16-037931-8*) Lib Congress.

Annual Report of the Secretary of State to the Governor of Ohio: Jail Reports 1854 & 1855. 138p. 1988. reprint ed. pap. 12.00 (*1-55613-103-8*) Heritage Bk.

Annual Report of the Secretary of State to the Governor of Ohio, Appendix B: Return of the Number of Deaf & Dumb, Blind, Insane & Idiotic Persons, May, 1856. 211p. 1987. reprint ed. pap. 15.00 (*1-55613-089-9*) Heritage Bk.

Annual Report of the Tennessee Valley Authority. TVA Staff. 1969. 12.95 (*0-405-00131-2*, 18749) Ayer.

Annual Report of the Tennessee Valley Authority. Tennessee Valley Authority Staff. 1969. 14.95 (*0-405-00151-7*, 18799); 12.95 (*0-405-00150-9*, 18798) Ayer.

Annual Report of the Tennessee Valley Authority. TVA Staff. 1934. 5.00 (*0-405-00121-5*, 18770) Ayer.

Annual Report of the Tennessee Valley Authority. TVA Staff. 1969. 14.95 (*0-405-00143-6*, 18791); 12.95 (*0-405-00142-8*, 18790); 12.95 (*0-405-00141-X*, 18789); 15.95 (*0-405-00146-0*, 18794); 15.95 (*0-405-00145-2*, 18793); 15.95 (*0-405-00144-4*, 18792); 15.95 (*0-405-00149-5*, 18797); 15.95 (*0-405-00148-7*, 18796); 15.95 (*0-405-00134-7*, 18782); 16.95 (*0-405-00135-5*, 18783); 12.95 (*0-405-00138-X*, 18786); 12.95 (*0-405-00139-8*, 18787); 12.95 (*0-405-00137-1*, 18785); 20.95 (*0-405-00127-4*, 18776); 22.95 (*0-405-00126-6*, 18775); 12.95 (*0-405-00140-1*, 18788); 20.95 (*0-405-00128-2*, 18777); 16.95 (*0-405-00130-4*, 18778); 15.95 (*0-405-00133-9*, 18781); 14.95 (*0-405-00132-0*, 18780); 20.95 (*0-405-00124-X*, 18773); 19.95 (*0-405-00123-1*, 18772); 17.95 (*0-405-00122-3*, 18771) Ayer.

Annual Report of The Tennessee Valley Authority. TVA Staff. 1969. 15.95 (*0-405-00136-3*, 18784) Ayer.

Annual Report of the Tennessee Valley Authority: 1934-67, 33 vols. Tennessee Valley Authority Staff. 415.00 (*0-405-19021-2*, 18803) Ayer.

Annual Report on Alaska's Mineral Resources, 1990: U. S. Geological Survey Circular. Ed. by Jill L. Schneider. (Illus.). 67p. (Orig.). (C). 1993. pap. text ed. 35.00 (*1-56806-698-8*) Diane Pub.

Annual Report on Exchange Arrangements & Exchange Restrictions. 570p. 1992. 39.50 (*1-55775-308-3*) Intl Monetary.

Annual Report on Mining Activities: 1983. Pennsylvania Bureau of Mining & Reclamation Staff & Bureau of Deep Mine Safety Staff. Ed. by Patsie Nichols. 420p. (C). 1983. 8.10 (*0-8182-0060-X*) Commonweal PA.

Annual Report on Mining Activities, 1984. Bureau of Deep Mine Safety, Mining & Reclamation Staff. Ed. by Patsie Nichols. 400p. (C). 1984. 6.90 (*0-8182-0068-5*) Commonweal PA.

Annual Report on Mining Activities, 1986. 117th ed. Bureau of Deep Mine Safety & Mining & Reclamation Staff. Ed. by Patsie Nichols. 536p. 1986. pap. text ed. 8.10 (*0-8182-0096-0*) Commonweal PA.

Annual Report on the Implementation of the Reform of the Structural Funds, 2nd, 1990. European Communities Staff. 146p. 1992. pap. 25.00 (*92-826-3786-7*, C2-72-91-439-EN-C, Pub. by Europ Com) UNIPUB.

Annual Report on Wood Protection, 1955. Ed. by G. Becker & G. Theden. viii, 170p. 1956. 31.00 (*0-387-02057-8*) Spr-Verlag.

Annual Report on Wood Protection, 1959-1960. Ed. by G. Becker & G. Theden. v, 481p. 1969. 77.00 (*0-387-04576-7*) Spr-Verlag.

Annual Report on Wood Protection, 1961-62. Ed. by G. Becker & G. Theden. 1972. 66.00 (*0-387-05827-3*) Spr-Verlag.

***Annual Report Production.** 120p. (Orig.). 1994. pap. 125.00 (*0-7605-0803-8*) Rector Pr.

Annual Report Report, 1992. 150p. 1991. spiral bd. 150.00 (*0-942454-28-6*) Black Bk.

Annual Report Section of Public Utility Law. 432p. 1990. pap. 10.00 (*0-685-19035-8*, 541-0019-01) Amer Bar Assn.

Annual Report (YR) European Foundation for the Improvement of Living & Working 1991. 84p. 1992. pap. 13.00 (*92-826-4484-7*, SY-75-92-485-EN-C, Pub. by Europ Com) UNIPUB.

***Annual Report (Yr.) European Foundation for the Improvement of Living & Working 1993.** 84p. 1994. pap. 10.00 (*92-826-8731-7*, SY85-94-244ENC, Pub. by Europ Com) UNIPUB.

Annual Report, 1988. (Illus.). 1989. pap. 1.50 (*0-89468-134-6*) Natl Gallery Art.

Annual Report, 1989. (Illus.). 124p. (Orig.). 1990. 1.50 (*0-89468-146-X*) Natl Gallery Art.

***Annual Report 1992-1993: American Civil Liberties Union.** ACLU Staff. 12p. (Orig.). 1993. pap. text ed. 2.00 (*0-914031-22-8*) Amer Civil Lib.

Annual Report 1993. 75p. Date not set. spiral bd. 150.00 (*0-942454-43-X*) Black Bk.

Annual Reporting under the Federal Securities Laws. Stephen Middlebrook. LC 83-7484. (Corporate Practice Ser.: No. 33). 1983. 92.00 (*1-55871-243-7*) BNA.

Annual Reports. (Human Rights Ser.). 180p. 1978. 7.00 (*0-685-43394-3*) OAS.

Annual Reports. 1993. reprint ed. lib. bdg. 89.00 (*0-7812-5138-9*) Rprt Serv.

Annual Reports: March 11, 1942 to June 30, 1943; for the Fiscal Year Ending June 30, 1944; for the Fiscal Year Ending June 30, 1945; for the Fiscal Year Ending June 30, 1946., 4 vols. in 1. U. S. Office of the Alien Property Custodian Staff. Ed. by Mira Wilkins. LC 76-29749. (European Business Ser.). (Illus.). 1977. reprint ed. lib. bdg. 76.95 (*0-405-09765-4*) Ayer.

Annual Reports for College Libraries. Comp. by Kenneth Oberembt. (CLIP Note Ser.: No. 10). 135p. 1988. 21.95 (*0-8389-7219-5*); 18.75 (*0-685-67652-8*) Assn Coll & Res Libs.

Annual Reports in Fermentation Processes, Vol. 6. Ed. by D. Perlman. (Serial Publication Ser.). 1983. pap. text ed. 116.00 (*0-12-040306-4*) Acad Pr.

Annual Reports in Medicinal Chemistry, Vol. 1. Ed. by Cornelius K. Cain. (Serial Publication Ser.). 1966. pap. text ed. 116.00 (*0-12-040501-6*) Acad Pr.

Annual Reports in Medicinal Chemistry, Vol. 2. Ed. by Cornelius K. Cain. (Serial Publication Ser.). 1967. pap. text ed. 116.00 (*0-12-040502-4*) Acad Pr.

Annual Reports in Medicinal Chemistry, Vol. 3. Ed. by Cornelius K. Cain. (Serial Publication Ser.). 1968. pap. text ed. 116.00 (*0-12-040503-2*) Acad Pr.

Annual Reports in Medicinal Chemistry, Vol. 4. Ed. by Cornelius K. Cain. (Serial Publication Ser.). 1969. pap. text ed. 116.00 (*0-12-040504-0*) Acad Pr.

Annual Reports in Medicinal Chemistry, Vol. 5. Ed. by Cornelius K. Cain. (Serial Publication Ser.). 1970. pap. text ed. 116.00 (*0-12-040505-9*) Acad Pr.

Annual Reports in Medicinal Chemistry, Vol. 6. Ed. by Cornelius K. Cain. (Serial Publication Ser.). 1971. pap. text ed. 116.00 (*0-12-040506-7*) Acad Pr.

Annual Reports in Medicinal Chemistry, Vol. 7. Ed. by Cornelius K. Cain. (Serial Publication Ser.). 1972. pap. text ed. 116.00 (*0-12-040507-5*) Acad Pr.

Annual Reports in Medicinal Chemistry, Vol. 8. Ed. by Cornelius K. Cain. (Serial Publication Ser.). 1973. pap. text ed. 116.00 (*0-12-040508-3*) Acad Pr.

Annual Reports in Medicinal Chemistry, Vol. 9. Ed. by Cornelius K. Cain. (Serial Publication Ser.). 1974. pap. text ed. 116.00 (*0-12-040509-1*) Acad Pr.

Annual Reports in Medicinal Chemistry, Vol. 10. Ed. by Cornelius K. Cain. (Serial Publication Ser.). 1975. pap. text ed. 116.00 (*0-12-040510-5*) Acad Pr.

Annual Reports in Medicinal Chemistry, Vol. 11. Ed. by Cornelius K. Cain. (Serial Publication Ser.). 1976. pap. text ed. 116.00 (*0-12-040511-3*) Acad Pr.

Annual Reports in Medicinal Chemistry, Vol. 17. Ed. by Cornelius K. Cain. (Serial Publication Ser.). 400p. 1982. pap. text ed. 116.00 (*0-12-040517-2*) Acad Pr.

Annual Reports in Medicinal Chemistry, Vol. 18. Ed. by Cornelius K. Cain. (Serial Publication Ser.). 1983. pap. text ed. 116.00 (*0-12-040518-0*) Acad Pr.

Annual Reports in Medicinal Chemistry, Vol. 19. Denis M. Bailey. Ed. by Cornelius K. Cain. (Serial Publication Ser.). 1984. pap. text ed. 116.00 (*0-12-040519-9*) Acad Pr.

Annual Reports in Medicinal Chemistry, Vol. 21. Ed. by Denis M. Baily. (Serial Publication Ser.). 366p. 1986. pap. text ed. 97.00 (*0-12-040521-0*) Acad Pr.

Annual Reports in Medicinal Chemistry, Vol. 22. Ed. by Denis M. Bailey et al. (Serial Publication Ser.). 384p. 1987. pap. text ed. 97.00 (*0-12-040522-9*) Acad Pr.

Annual Reports in Medicinal Chemistry, Vol. 23. Ed. by Richard C. Allen. (Serial Publication Ser.). 390p. 1988. pap. text ed. 92.00 (*0-12-040523-7*) Acad Pr.

Annual Reports in Medicinal Chemistry, Vol. 24. Ed. by Richard C. Allen. (Serial Publication Ser.). 363p. 1989. pap. text ed. 92.00 (*0-12-040524-5*) Acad Pr.

Annual Reports in Medicinal Chemistry, Vol. 25. Ed. by James A. Bristol. (Illus.). 388p. 1990. pap. text ed. 83.00 (*0-12-040525-3*) Acad Pr.

Annual Reports in Medicinal Chemistry, Vol. 26. Ed. by James A. Bristol. (Illus.). 369p. 1991. pap. text ed. 77.00 (*0-12-040526-1*) Acad Pr.

Annual Reports in Medicinal Chemistry, Vol. 27. Ed. by James A. Bristol. (Illus.). 373p. 1992. pap. text ed. 75.00 (*0-12-040527-X*) Acad Pr.

Annual Reports in Medicinal Chemistry, Vol. 28. Ed. by James A. Bristol. (Illus.). 388p. 1993. pap. text ed. 75.00 (*0-12-040528-8*) Acad Pr.

***Annual Reports in Medicinal Chemistry, Vol. 29.** Ed. by James A. Bristol. (Illus.). 397p. 1994. pap. text ed. 70.00 (*0-12-040529-6*) Acad Pr.

Annual Reports in NMR Spectroscopy, Vol. 17. Ed. by Graham A. Webb. 368p. 1986. text ed. 208.00 (*0-12-505317-7*) Acad Pr.

Annual Reports in NMR Spectroscopy, Vol. 18. Ed. by Graham A. Webb. 371p. 1987. text ed. 274.00 (*0-12-505318-5*) Acad Pr.

Annual Reports in NMR Spectroscopy, Vol. 19. Ed. by Graham A. Webb. 325p. 1987. text ed. 184.00 (*0-12-505319-3*) Acad Pr.

Annual Reports in NMR Spectroscopy, Vol. 27. Ed. by G. A. Webb. (Illus.). 352p. 1993. text ed. 125.00 (*0-12-505327-4*) Acad Pr.

Annual Reports in Organic Synthesis, Vol. 3. Ed. by John McMurry & R. Bryan Miller. (Serial Publication Ser.). 1973. pap. text ed. 106.00 (*0-12-040803-1*) Acad Pr.

Annual Reports in Organic Synthesis, Vol. 11. Martin J. O'Donnell. Ed. by L. G. Wade, Jr. (Serial Publication Ser.). 1981. pap. text ed. 106.00 (*0-12-040811-2*) Acad Pr.

Annual Reports in Organic Synthesis, Vol. 12. Ed. by John McMurrary et al. (Serial Publication Ser.). 1982. pap. text ed. 106.00 (*0-12-040812-0*) Acad Pr.

Annual Reports in Organic Synthesis, Vol. 13. Ed. by L. G. Wade, Jr. & Martin J. O'Donnell. (Serial Publication Ser.). 1983. pap. text ed. 106.00 (*0-12-040813-9*) Acad Pr.

Annual Reports in Organic Synthesis, Vol. 14. Ed. by John McMurray & R. Bryan Miller. (Serial Publication Ser.). 1984. pap. text ed. 92.00 (*0-12-040814-7*) Acad Pr.

Annual Reports in Organic Synthesis 1976, Vol. 7. Ed. by R. Bryan Miller & L. G. Wade, Jr. 1977. pap. text ed. 106.00 (*0-12-040807-4*) Acad Pr.

Annual Reports in Organic Synthesis, 1985. Ed. by Martin J. O'Donnell & F. V. Scriven. 513p. 1986. pap. text ed. 92.00 (*0-12-040816-3*) Acad Pr.

Annual Reports in Organic Synthesis, 1987. Ed. by Eric F. Scriven & Kenneth Turnbull. 473p. 1988. pap. text ed. 72.00 (*0-12-040818-X*) Acad Pr.

Annual Reports in Organic Synthesis, 1989. Ed. by Kenneth Turnbull. 493p. 1989. pap. text ed. 68.00 (*0-12-040819-8*) Acad Pr.

Annual Reports in Organic Synthesis, 1990. Ed. by Kenneth Turnbull et al. (Illus.). 472p. 1990. pap. text ed. 61.00 (*0-12-040820-1*) Acad Pr.

Annual Reports in Organic Synthesis, 1991. Ed. by Philip M. Weintraub & Kenneth Turnbull. (Illus.). 475p. 1991. pap. text ed. 55.00 (*0-12-040821-X*) Acad Pr.

Annual Reports in Organic Synthesis 1992. Ed. by Philip M. Weintraub et al. (Illus.). 485p. 1992. pap. text ed. 55.00 (*0-12-040822-8*) Acad Pr.

Annual Reports in Organic Synthesis, 1993. Ed. by Philip M. Weintraub et al. (Illus.). 546p. 1993. pap. text ed. 69.00 (*0-12-040823-6*) Acad Pr.

***Annual Reports in Organic Synthesis, 1994.** Ed. by Philip M. Weintraub et al. (Illus.). 461p. 1994. pap. text ed. 59.95 (*0-12-040824-4*) Acad Pr.

Annual Reports of the Federal Communications Commission, 1935-1955. Federal Communications Commission. LC 72-161167. (History of Broadcasting: Radio to Television Ser.). 1971. reprint ed. 158.95 (*0-405-03577-2*) Ayer.

Annual Reports of the Federal Radio Commission, 1927-1933. Federal Radio Commission. LC 70-161169. (History of Broadcasting: Radio to Television Ser.). 1979. reprint ed. 56.95 (*0-405-03578-0*) Ayer.

Annual Reports of the National Labor Relations Board, 1936-1965, 10 Vols, Set. National Labor Relations Board Staff. LC 79-136753. 1971. reprint ed. 18.95 (*0-405-01715-4*) Ayer.

Annual Reports on Fermentation Processes, Vol. 2. Ed. by D. Perlman & G. T. Tsao. (Serial Publication Ser.). 1978. pap. text ed. 116.00 (*0-12-040302-1*) Acad Pr.

Annual Reports on Fermentation Processes, Vol. 3. Ed. by D. Perlman & G. T. Tsao. (Serial Publication Ser.). 1979. pap. text ed. 116.00 (*0-12-040303-X*) Acad Pr.

Annual Reports on Fermentation Processes, Vol. 5. Ed. by D. Perlman. (Serial Publication Ser.). 1982. pap. text ed. 116.00 (*0-12-040305-6*) Acad Pr.

Annual Reports on Fermentation Processes, Vol. 7. Ed. by D. Perlman & G. T. Tsao. (Serial Publication Ser.). 1984. pap. text ed. 116.00 (*0-12-040307-2*) Acad Pr.

Annual Reports on NMR Spectroscopy. Ed. by Webb. 1985. text ed. 208.00 (*0-12-505316-9*) Acad Pr.

Annual Reports on NMR Spectroscopy, 2 Vols., 13. Ed. by E. F. Mooney & Graham A. Webb. 1983. text ed. 222.00 (*0-12-505313-4*) Acad Pr.

Annual Reports on NMR Spectroscopy, Vol. 10A. Ed. by E. F. Mooney & Graham A. Webb. 1980. text ed. 203.00 (*0-12-505310-X*) Acad Pr.

Annual Reports on NMR Spectroscopy, Vol. 10B. Ed. by E. F. Mooney & Graham A. Webb. 1980. text ed. 222.00 (*0-12-505348-7*) Acad Pr.

Annual Reports on NMR Spectroscopy, Vol. 11A. Ed. by E. F. Mooney & Graham A. Webb. 1981. text ed. 203.00 (*0-12-505311-8*) Acad Pr.

Annual Reports on NMR Spectroscopy, Vol. 12. Ed. by E. F. Mooney & Graham A. Webb. 1982. text ed. 203.00 (*0-12-505312-6*) Acad Pr.

Annual Reports on NMR Spectroscopy, Vol. 15. E. F. Mooney & Graham A. Webb. 1984. text ed. 203.00 (*0-12-505315-0*) Acad Pr.

Annual Reports on NMR Spectroscopy, Vol. 20. Ed. by Graham A. Webb. 375p. 1988. text ed. 230.00 (*0-12-505320-7*) Acad Pr.

Annual Reports on NMR Spectroscopy, Vol. 21. Ed. by Graham A. Webb. 304p. 1989. text ed. 134.00 (*0-12-505321-5*) Acad Pr.

Annual Reports on NMR Spectroscopy, Vol. 22. Ed. by Graham A. Webb. 429p. 1990. text ed. 154.00 (*0-12-505322-3*) Acad Pr.

Annual Reports on NMR Spectroscopy, Vol. 23. Ed. by Graham A. Webb. 425p. 1991. text ed. 165.00 (*0-12-505323-1*) Acad Pr.

Annual Reports on NMR Spectroscopy, Vol. 24. Ed. by Graham A. Webb. (Illus.). 384p. 1992. text ed. 149.00 (*0-12-505324-X*) Acad Pr.

Annual Reports on NMR Spectroscopy, Vol. 25. Ed. by Graham A. Webb. (Illus.). 480p. 1993. text ed. 129.00 (*0-12-505325-8*) Acad Pr.

Annual Reports on NMR Spectroscopy, Vol. 26. Ed. by Graham A. Webb. 304p. 1993. text ed. 118.00 (*0-12-505326-6*) Acad Pr.

Annual Reports on NMR Spectroscopy, Vol. 28. Ed. by A. H. Webb. 368p. 1994. text ed. 125.00 (*0-12-505328-2*) Acad Pr.

Annual Reports on NMR Spectroscopy, Vols. 1, 5B, 6-9. Incl. Vol. 8. 1978. text ed. 203.00 (*0-12-505308-8*); Vol. 9. 1979. text ed. 203.00 (*0-12-505309-6*); write for info. (*0-318-50227-5*) Acad Pr.

***Annual Reports on NMR Spectroscopy Vol. 29.** Ed. by G. A. Webb. (Illus.). 432p. 1994. text ed. 105.00 (*0-12-505329-0*) Acad Pr.

***Annual Reports on NMR Spectroscopy Vol. 30, Vol. 30.** Ed. by G. A. Webb. (Illus.). 488p. 1995. boxed 105.00 (*0-12-505330-4*) Acad Pr.

***Annual Reports on NMR Spectroscopy Vol. 31: Special Edition "Food Science", Vol. 31.** Ed. by G. A. Webb et al. (Illus.). 448p. 1995. boxed 105.00 (*0-12-505331-2*) Acad Pr.

Annual Reports on NMR Spectroscopy, 1982, Vol. 11B. E. F. Mooney. 1982. text ed. 222.00 (*0-12-505349-5*) Acad Pr.

Annual Reports on Organic Synthesis 1986. Ed. by Eric F. Scriven & Kenneth Turnbull. 456p. 1987. pap. text ed. 80.00 (*0-12-040817-1*) Acad Pr.

Annual Reports That Pay Their Way: Selling the Corporate Message. F. N. Arfin. (Financial Times Management Ser.). 224p. 1993. 105.00x (*0-273-60100-8*, Pub. by Pitman Pubng UK) St Mut.

Annual Review in Automatic Programming. Incl. Vol. 5, Pt. 2. Generalized File Processing. W. C. McGee. Ed. by M. I. Halpern et al. LC 60-12884. 1969. 68.00 (*0-08-012964-1*); Vol. 6, Pt. 1. Some Studies in Machine Learning Using the Game of Checkers 2. A. L. Samuel. Ed. by M. I. Halpern et al. LC 60-12884. 1969. pap. 24.00 (*0-08-006575-9*); Vol. 6, Pt. 2. Survey of Macro Processors: A Machine-Independent Assembly Language for Systems Programs. P. J. Brown & G. F. Colouris. Ed. by M. I. Halpern et al. LC 60-12884. 1969. pap. 24.00 (*0-08-006586-4*); Vol. 6, Pt. 3. On the Formal Description of PL-1. P. Lucas & K. Walk. Ed. by M. I. Halpern et al. LC 60-12884. 1970. pap. 24.00 (*0-08-006689-5*); Vol. 6, Pt. 4. Joss Two: Design Philosophy. J. W. Smith. Ed. by M. I. Halpern et al. LC 60-12884. 1970. pap. 24.00 (*0-08-006694-1*); Vol. 6, Pt. 5. New Approach to Optimization of Sequencing Decisions. R. M. Shapiro & H. Saint. Ed. by M. I. Halpern et al. LC 60-12884. 1970. pap. 24.00 (*0-08-016336-X*); Vol. 7, Pt. 1. Tutorial on Data-Base Organization. J. W. Smith. Ed. by M. I. Halpern et al. LC 60-12884. 1972. pap. 24.00 (*0-08-016947-3*); Vol. 7, Pt. 2. Incremental Complication & Conversational Interpretation. M. Bertrand & M. M. Griffiths. Ed. by M. I. Halpern et al. LC 60-12884. 1973. pap. 24.00 (*0-08-017049-8*); Vol. 7, Pt. 3. Introduction to Algol 68: Automatic Theorem Proving Based on Resolution. A. Bekis. Ed. by M. I. Halpern et al. LC 60-12884. 1973. pap. 24.00 (*0-08-017128-1*); Vol. 7, Pt. 4. Survey of Extensible Programming Language. N. Solnsteff & A. Yezerski. Ed. by M. I. Halpern et al. LC 60-12884. 1973. pap. 24.00 (*0-08-017145-1*); Vol. 7, Pt. 5. Ed. by M. I. Halpern et al. LC 60-12884. 1974. pap. 24.00 (*0-08-017881-2*); Vol. 7 Complete. Ed. by M. I. Halpern et al. LC 60-12884. 1974. 68.00 (*0-08-017806-5*); LC 60-12884. Set pap. write for info. (*0-318-55133-0*, Pergamon Pr) Elsevier.

Annual Review in Automatic Programming. M. I. Halpern & C. Shaw. LC 60-12884. 1971. 140.00 (*0-08-016007-7*, Pub. by Pergamon Repr UK) Franklin.

Annual Review in Automatic Programming, Vol. 9C. Ed. by M. I. Halpern. (Illus.). 222p. 1981. 68.00 (*0-08-020242-X*, Pergamon Pr) Elsevier.

Annual Review in Automatic Programming, Vols. 1, 4. Ed. by R. E. Goodman. Incl. Vol. 1. 1960. 130.00 (*0-08-009217-9*); Vol. 2. 1961. 161.00 (*0-08-009333-7*); Vol. 3. 1963. 150.00 (*0-08-009763-4*); Vol. 4. rev. ed. 1964. 118.00 (*0-08-010857-1*); write for info. (*0-318-55132-2*, Pub. by Pergamon Repr UK) Franklin.

Annual Review in Political Science, Vol. III. Ed. by Samuel Long. 256p. (C). 1990. text ed. 65.00 (*0-89391-501-7*) Ablex Pub.

Annual Review of Agriculture see Agriculture in the United Kingdom 1992

Annual Review of Anthropology, Vol. 1. Ed. by Bernard J. Siegel et al. (Illus.). 1972. text ed. 41.00 (*0-8243-1901-X*) Annual Reviews.

Annual Review of Anthropology, Vol. 2. Ed. by Bernard J. Siegel et al. LC 72-82136. (Illus.). 1973. 41.00 (*0-8243-1902-8*) Annual Reviews.

Annual Review of Anthropology, Vol. 3. Ed. by Bernard J. Siegel et al. LC 72-82136. (Illus.). 1974. text ed. 41.00 (*0-8243-1903-6*) Annual Reviews.

Annual Review of Anthropology, Vol. 4. Ed. by Bernard J. Siegel et al. LC 72-82136. (Illus.). 1975. text ed. 41.00 (*0-8243-1904-4*) Annual Reviews.

Annual Review of Anthropology, Vol. 5. Ed. by Bernard J. Siegel et al. LC 72-82136. (Illus.). 1976. text ed. 41.00 (*0-8243-1905-2*) Annual Reviews.

Annual Review of Anthropology, Vol. 6. Ed. by Bernard J. Siegel et al. LC 72-82136. (Illus.). 1977. text ed. 41.00 (*0-8243-1906-0*) Annual Reviews.

Annual Review of Anthropology, Vol. 7. Ed. by Bernard J. Siegel et al. LC 72-82136. (Illus.). 1978. text ed. 41.00 (*0-8243-1907-9*) Annual Reviews.

Annual Review of Anthropology, Vol. 8. Ed. by Bernard J. Siegel et al. LC 72-82136. (Illus.). 1979. text ed. 41.00 (*0-8243-1908-7*) Annual Reviews.

Annual Review of Anthropology, Vol. 9. Ed. by Bernard J. Siegel et al. LC 72-82136. (Illus.). 1980. 41.00 (*0-8243-1909-5*) Annual Reviews.

Annual Review of Anthropology, Vol. 10. Ed. by Bernard J. Siegel et al. LC 72-82136. (Illus.). 1981. 41.00 (*0-8243-1910-9*) Annual Reviews.

Annual Review of Anthropology, Vol. 11. Ed. by Bernard J. Siegel et al. LC 72-82136. (Illus.). 1982. 41.00 (*0-8243-1911-7*) Annual Reviews.

Annual Review of Anthropology, Vol. 12. Ed. by Bernard J. Siegel et al. LC 72-82136. (Illus.). 1983. 41.00 (*0-8243-1912-5*) Annual Reviews.

Annual Review of Anthropology, Vol. 13. Ed. by Bernard J. Siegel et al. LC 72-82136. (Illus.). 1984. 41.00 (*0-8243-1913-3*) Annual Reviews.

Annual Review of Anthropology, Vol. 14. Ed. by Bernard J. Siegel et al. LC 72-82136. (Illus.). 1985. 41.00 (*0-8243-1914-1*) Annual Reviews.

An Asterisk (*) at the beginning of an entry indicates that the title is appearing in BIP for the first time.

Annual Review of Anthropology, Vol. 15. Ed. by Bernard J. Siegel et al. LC 72-82136. (Illus.). 1986. text ed. 41.00 (*0-8243-1915-X*) Annual Reviews.

Annual Review of Anthropology, Vol. 16. Ed. by Bernard J. Siegel et al. LC 72-82136. (Illus.). 1987. text ed. 41.00 (*0-8243-1916-8*) Annual Reviews.

Annual Review of Anthropology, Vol. 17. Ed. by Bernard J. Siegel et al. LC 72-82136. (Illus.). 1988. text ed. 41.00 (*0-8243-1917-6*) Annual Reviews.

Annual Review of Anthropology, Vol. 18. Ed. by Bernard J. Siegel et al. LC 72-82136. (Illus.). 1989. text ed. 41.00 (*0-8243-1918-4*) Annual Reviews.

Annual Review of Anthropology, Vol. 19. Ed. by Bernard J. Siegel et al. 1990. text ed. 41.00 (*0-8243-1919-2*) Annual Reviews.

Annual Review of Anthropology, Vol. 20. Ed. by Bernard J. Siegel et al. 1991. text ed. 41.00 (*0-8243-1920-6*) Annual Reviews.

Annual Review of Anthropology, Vol. 21. Ed. by Bernard J. Siegel et al. 1992. text ed. 44.00 (*0-8243-1921-4*) Annual Reviews.

Annual Review of Anthropology, Vol. 22. Ed. by William H. Durham et al. 1993. text ed. 44.00 (*0-8243-1922-2*) Annual Reviews.

Annual Review of Anthropology, Vol. 23. Ed. by William H. Durham et al. 1994. text ed. 47.00 (*0-8243-1923-0*) Annual Reviews.

***Annual Review of Anthropology, Vol. 24.** Ed. by William H. Durham. 1995. lib. bdg. 47.00 (*0-8243-1924-9*) Annual Reviews.

Annual Review of Astronomy & Astrophysics, Vol. 1. Ed. by L. Goldberg et al. LC 63-8846. (Illus.). 1963. 53.00 (*0-8243-0901-4*) Annual Reviews.

Annual Review of Astronomy & Astrophysics, Vol. 5. Ed. by L. Goldberg et al. LC 63-8846. (Illus.). 1967. 53.00 (*0-8243-0905-7*) Annual Reviews.

Annual Review of Astronomy & Astrophysics, Vol. 6. Ed. by L. Goldberg et al. LC 63-8846. (Illus.). 1968. 53.00 (*0-8243-0906-5*) Annual Reviews.

Annual Review of Astronomy & Astrophysics, Vol. 7. Ed. by L. Goldberg et al. LC 63-8846. (Illus.). 1969. 53.00 (*0-8243-0907-3*) Annual Reviews.

Annual Review of Astronomy & Astrophysics, Vol. 8. Ed. by L. Goldberg et al. LC 63-8846. (Illus.). 1970. 53.00 (*0-8243-0908-1*) Annual Reviews.

Annual Review of Astronomy & Astrophysics, Vol. 9. Ed. by L. Goldberg et al. LC 63-8846. (Illus.). 1971. 53.00 (*0-8243-0909-X*) Annual Reviews.

Annual Review of Astronomy & Astrophysics, Vol. 10. Ed. by L. Goldberg et al. LC 63-8846. (Illus.). 1972. 53.00 (*0-8243-0910-3*) Annual Reviews.

Annual Review of Astronomy & Astrophysics, Vol. 11. Ed. by L. Goldberg et al. LC 63-8846. (Illus.). 1973. 53.00 (*0-8243-0911-1*) Annual Reviews.

Annual Review of Astronomy & Astrophysics, Vol. 12. Ed. by Geoffrey R. Burbidge et al. LC 63-8846. (Illus.). 1974. 53.00 (*0-8243-0912-X*) Annual Reviews.

Annual Review of Astronomy & Astrophysics, Vol. 13. Ed. by Geoffrey R. Burbidge et al. LC 63-8846. (Illus.). 1975. 53.00 (*0-8243-0913-8*) Annual Reviews.

Annual Review of Astronomy & Astrophysics, Vol. 14. Ed. by Geoffrey R. Burbidge et al. LC 63-8846. (Illus.). 1976. 53.00 (*0-8243-0914-6*) Annual Reviews.

Annual Review of Astronomy & Astrophysics, Vol. 16. Ed. by Geoffrey R. Burbidge et al. LC 63-8846. (Illus.). 1978. 53.00 (*0-8243-0916-2*) Annual Reviews.

Annual Review of Astronomy & Astrophysics, Vol. 17. Ed. by Geoffrey R. Burbidge et al. LC 63-8846. (Illus.). 1979. 53.00 (*0-8243-0917-0*) Annual Reviews.

Annual Review of Astronomy & Astrophysics, Vol. 18. Ed. by Geoffrey R. Burbidge et al. LC 63-8846. (Illus.). 1980. 53.00 (*0-8243-0918-9*) Annual Reviews.

Annual Review of Astronomy & Astrophysics, Vol. 19. Ed. by Geoffrey R. Burbidge et al. LC 63-8846. (Illus.). 1981. 53.00 (*0-8243-0919-7*) Annual Reviews.

Annual Review of Astronomy & Astrophysics, Vol. 20. Ed. by Geoffrey R. Burbidge et al. LC 63-8846. (Illus.). 1982. 53.00 (*0-8243-0920-0*) Annual Reviews.

Annual Review of Astronomy & Astrophysics, Vol. 21. Ed. by Geoffrey R. Burbidge et al. LC 63-8846. (Illus.). 1983. 53.00 (*0-8243-0921-9*) Annual Reviews.

Annual Review of Astronomy & Astrophysics, Vol. 22. Ed. by Geoffrey R. Burbidge et al. LC 63-8846. (Illus.). 1984. 53.00 (*0-8243-0922-7*) Annual Reviews.

Annual Review of Astronomy & Astrophysics, Vol. 23. Ed. by Geoffrey R. Burbidge et al. LC 63-8846. (Illus.). 1985. 53.00 (*0-8243-0923-5*) Annual Reviews.

Annual Review of Astronomy & Astrophysics, Vol. 24. Ed. by Geoffrey R. Burbidge et al. LC 63-8846. (Illus.). 1986. text ed. 53.00 (*0-8243-0924-3*) Annual Reviews.

Annual Review of Astronomy & Astrophysics, Vol. 25. Ed. by Geoffrey R. Burbidge et al. LC 63-8846. (Illus.). 1987. text ed. 53.00 (*0-8243-0925-1*) Annual Reviews.

Annual Review of Astronomy & Astrophysics, Vol. 26. Ed. by Geoffrey R. Burbidge et al. LC 63-8846. (Illus.). 700p. 1988. text ed. 53.00 (*0-8243-0926-X*) Annual Reviews.

Annual Review of Astronomy & Astrophysics, Vol. 27. Ed. by Geoffrey R. Burbidge et al. 1989. text ed. 53.00 (*0-8243-0927-8*) Annual Reviews.

Annual Review of Astronomy & Astrophysics, Vol. 28. Ed. by Geoffrey R. Burbidge et al. 1990. 53.00 (*0-8243-0928-6*) Annual Reviews.

Annual Review of Astronomy & Astrophysics, Vol. 29. Ed. by Geoffrey R. Burbidge et al. 1991. text ed. 53.00 (*0-8243-0929-4*) Annual Reviews.

Annual Review of Astronomy & Astrophysics, Vol. 30. Ed. by Geoffrey R. Burbidge et al. 1992. text ed. 57.00 (*0-8243-0930-8*) Annual Reviews.

Annual Review of Astronomy & Astrophysics, Vol. 31. Ed. by Geoffrey Burbidge et al. (Illus.). 1993. 57.00 (*0-8243-0931-6*) Annual Reviews.

Annual Review of Astronomy & Astrophysics, Vol. 32. Ed. by Geoffrey Burbidge et al. (Illus.). 1994. text ed. 60.00 (*0-8243-0932-4*) Annual Reviews.

***Annual Review of Astronomy & Astrophysics, Vol. 33.** Ed. by Geoffrey E. Burbidge. 1995. lib. bdg. 60.00 (*0-8243-0933-2*) Annual Reviews.

***Annual Review of Banking Law.** Morin Center for Banking Law Studies Staff. 1987. boxed 400.00 (*0-614-05779-5*) Michie Butterworth.

Annual Review of Banking Law, Vols. 6-13, Set. Morin Center for Banking Law Studies Staff. 1992. text ed. 400.00 (*0-88063-162-7*) Butterworth Legal Pubs.

Annual Review of Banking Law, Vol. 6. Morin Center for Banking Law Studies Staff. 500p. 1987. 50.00 (*0-88063-168-6*) Butterworth Legal Pubs.

Annual Review of Banking Law, Vol. 7. Morin Center for Banking Law Studies Staff. 600p. 1988. 50.00 (*0-88063-224-0*) Butterworth Legal Pubs.

Annual Review of Banking Law, Vol. 8. Morin Center for Banking Law Studies Staff. 700p. 1989. 50.00 (*0-88063-273-9*) Butterworth Legal Pubs.

Annual Review of Banking Law, Vol. 9. Morin Center for Banking Law Studies Staff. 700p. 1990. 50.00 (*0-88063-394-8*) Butterworth Legal Pubs.

Annual Review of Banking Law, Vol. 10. Morin Center for Banking Law Studies. 270p. 1991. boxed 80.00 (*0-88063-782-X*) Butterworth Legal Pubs.

Annual Review of Banking Law, Vol. 11. 620p. 1992. boxed 100.00 (*1-56257-208-3*) Butterworth Legal Pubs.

Annual Review of Banking Law, Vol. 12. 600p. 1993. boxed 125.00 (*1-56257-209-1*) Butterworth Legal Pubs.

Annual Review of Banking Law, Vol. 13. 515p. 1994. boxed 125.00 (*1-56257-210-5*) Butterworth Legal Pubs.

Annual Review of Behavior Therapy Vol. 2: Theory & Practise. Ed. by Cyril M. Franks et al. 317p. 1994. lib. bdg. 36.95 (*0-89862-569-6*) Guilford Pr.

Annual Review of Behavior Therapy, Vol. 10: Theory & Practice. Cyril M. Franks et al. 389p. 1985. lib. bdg. 50.00 (*0-89862-750-8*) Guilford Pr.

Annual Review of Behavior Therapy, Vol. 9: Theory & Practice. G. Terence Wilson et al. LC 76-126864. 437p. 1984. lib. bdg. 50.00 (*0-89862-618-8*, 2618) Guilford Pr.

Annual Review of Biochemistry, Vol. 31. Ed. by P. D. Boyer et al. 1962. text ed. 41.00 (*0-8243-0831-X*) Annual Reviews.

Annual Review of Biochemistry, Vol. 32. Ed. by P. D. Boyer et al. 1963. text ed. 41.00 (*0-8243-0832-8*) Annual Reviews.

Annual Review of Biochemistry, Vol. 33. Ed. by P. D. Boyer et al. 1964. text ed. 41.00 (*0-8243-0833-6*) Annual Reviews.

Annual Review of Biochemistry, Vol. 34. Ed. by P. D. Boyer et al. 1965. text ed. 41.00 (*0-8243-0834-4*) Annual Reviews.

Annual Review of Biochemistry, Vol. 36. Ed. by P. D. Boyer et al. 1967. text ed. 41.00 (*0-8243-0836-0*) Annual Reviews.

Annual Review of Biochemistry, Vol. 37. Ed. by P. D. Boyer et al. 1968. text ed. 41.00 (*0-8243-0837-9*) Annual Reviews.

Annual Review of Biochemistry, Vol. 38. Ed. by Edmund E. Snell et al. 1969. text ed. 41.00 (*0-8243-0838-7*) Annual Reviews.

Annual Review of Biochemistry, Vol. 39. Ed. by Edmund E. Snell et al. 1970. text ed. 41.00 (*0-8243-0839-5*) Annual Reviews.

Annual Review of Biochemistry, Vol. 40. Ed. by Edmund E. Snell et al. 1971. text ed. 41.00 (*0-8243-0840-9*) Annual Reviews.

Annual Review of Biochemistry, Vol. 41. Ed. by E. E. Snell et al. LC 32-25093. (Illus.). 1972. 41.00 (*0-8243-0841-7*) Annual Reviews.

Annual Review of Biochemistry, Vol. 42. Ed. by E. E. Snell et al. LC 32-25093. (Illus.). 1973. 41.00 (*0-8243-0842-5*) Annual Reviews.

Annual Review of Biochemistry, Vol. 43. Ed. by E. E. Snell et al. LC 32-25093. (Illus.). 1974. 41.00 (*0-8243-0843-3*) Annual Reviews.

Annual Review of Biochemistry, Vol. 44. Ed. by E. E. Snell et al. LC 32-25093. (Illus.). 1975. 41.00 (*0-8243-0844-1*) Annual Reviews.

Annual Review of Biochemistry, Vol. 45. Ed. by E. E. Snell et al. LC 32-25093. (Illus.). 1976. 41.00 (*0-8243-0845-X*) Annual Reviews.

Annual Review of Biochemistry, Vol. 46. Ed. by E. E. Snell et al. LC 32-25093. (Illus.). 1977. 41.00 (*0-8243-0846-8*) Annual Reviews.

Annual Review of Biochemistry, Vol. 47. Ed. by E. E. Snell et al. LC 32-25093. (Illus.). 1978. 41.00 (*0-8243-0847-6*) Annual Reviews.

Annual Review of Biochemistry, Vol. 48. Ed. by E. E. Snell et al. LC 32-25093. (Illus.). 1979. 41.00 (*0-8243-0848-4*) Annual Reviews.

Annual Review of Biochemistry, Vol. 49. Ed. by E. E. Snell et al. LC 32-25093. (Illus.). 1980. 41.00 (*0-8243-0849-2*) Annual Reviews.

Annual Review of Biochemistry, Vol. 50. Ed. by E. E. Snell et al. LC 32-25093. (Illus.). 1981. 41.00 (*0-8243-0850-6*) Annual Reviews.

Annual Review of Biochemistry, Vol. 51. Ed. by E. E. Snell et al. LC 32-25093. (Illus.). 1982. 41.00 (*0-8243-0851-4*) Annual Reviews.

Annual Review of Biochemistry, Vol. 52. Ed. by E. E. Snell et al. LC 32-25093. (Illus.). 1983. 41.00 (*0-8243-0852-2*) Annual Reviews.

Annual Review of Biochemistry, Vol. 53. Ed. by Charles C. Richardson et al. LC 32-25093. (Illus.). 1984. text ed. 41.00 (*0-8243-0853-0*) Annual Reviews.

Annual Review of Biochemistry, Vol. 54. Ed. by Charles C. Richardson et al. LC 32-25093. (Illus.). (C). 1985. text ed. 41.00 (*0-8243-0854-9*) Annual Reviews.

Annual Review of Biochemistry, Vol. 55. Ed. by Charles C. Richardson et al. LC 32-25093. (Illus.). 1986. text ed. 41.00 (*0-8243-0855-7*) Annual Reviews.

Annual Review of Biochemistry, Vol. 56. Ed. by Charles C. Richardson et al. LC 32-25093. (Illus.). 1987. text ed. 41.00 (*0-8243-0856-5*) Annual Reviews.

Annual Review of Biochemistry, Vol. 57. Ed. by Charles C. Richardson et al. LC 32-25093. (Illus.). 1988. text ed. 41.00 (*0-8243-0857-3*) Annual Reviews.

Annual Review of Biochemistry, Vol. 58. Ed. by Charles C. Richardson et al. 1989. text ed. 41.00 (*0-8243-0858-1*) Annual Reviews.

Annual Review of Biochemistry, Vol. 59. Ed. by Charles C. Richardson et al. 1990. 41.00 (*0-8243-0859-X*) Annual Reviews.

Annual Review of Biochemistry, Vol. 60. Ed. by Charles C. Richardson et al. 1991. text ed. 41.00 (*0-8243-0860-3*) Annual Reviews.

Annual Review of Biochemistry, Vol. 61. Ed. by Charles C. Richardson et al. 1992. text ed. 46.00 (*0-8243-0861-1*) Annual Reviews.

Annual Review of Biochemistry, Vol. 62. Ed. by Charles C. Richardson et al. (Illus.). 1993. text ed. 46.00 (*0-8243-0862-X*) Annual Reviews.

Annual Review of Biochemistry, Vol. 63. Ed. by Charles C. Richardson et al. (Illus.). 1994. text ed. 49.00 (*0-8243-0863-8*) Annual Reviews.

***Annual Review of Biochemistry, Vol. 64.** Ed. by Charles C. Richardson. 1995. lib. bdg. 49.00 (*0-8243-0864-6*) Annual Reviews.

Annual Review of Biophysics & Bioengineering, Vol. 1. Ed. by M. F. Morales et al. LC 79-188446. (Illus.). 1972. 55.00 (*0-8243-1801-3*) Annual Reviews.

Annual Review of Biophysics & Bioengineering, Vol. 2. Ed. by L. J. Mullins et al. LC 79-188446. (Illus.). 1973. 55.00 (*0-8243-1802-1*) Annual Reviews.

Annual Review of Biophysics & Bioengineering, Vol. 3. Ed. by L. J. Mullins et al. LC 79-188446. (Illus.). 1974. 55.00 (*0-8243-1803-X*) Annual Reviews.

Annual Review of Biophysics & Bioengineering, Vol. 4. Ed. by L. J. Mullins et al. LC 79-188446. (Illus.). 1975. 55.00 (*0-8243-1804-8*) Annual Reviews.

Annual Review of Biophysics & Bioengineering, Vol. 5. Ed. by L. J. Mullins et al. LC 79-188446. (Illus.). 1976. 55.00 (*0-8243-1805-6*) Annual Reviews.

Annual Review of Biophysics & Bioengineering, Vol. 6. Ed. by L. J. Mullins et al. LC 79-188446. (Illus.). 1977. 55.00 (*0-8243-1806-4*) Annual Reviews.

Annual Review of Biophysics & Bioengineering, Vol. 7. Ed. by L. J. Mullins et al. LC 79-188446. (Illus.). 1978. 55.00 (*0-8243-1807-2*) Annual Reviews.

Annual Review of Biophysics & Bioengineering, Vol. 8. Ed. by L. J. Mullins et al. LC 79-188446. (Illus.). 1979. 55.00 (*0-8243-1808-0*) Annual Reviews.

Annual Review of Biophysics & Bioengineering, Vol. 9. Ed. by L. J. Mullins et al. LC 79-188446. (Illus.). 1980. 55.00 (*0-8243-1809-9*) Annual Reviews.

Annual Review of Biophysics & Bioengineering, Vol. 10. Ed. by L. J. Mullins et al. LC 79-188446. (Illus.). 1981. 55.00 (*0-8243-1810-2*) Annual Reviews.

Annual Review of Biophysics & Bioengineering, Vol. 11. Ed. by L. J. Mullins et al. LC 79-188446. (Illus.). 1982. 55.00 (*0-8243-1811-0*) Annual Reviews.

Annual Review of Biophysics & Bioengineering, Vol. 12. Ed. by L. J. Mullins et al. LC 79-188446. (Illus.). 1983. 55.00 (*0-8243-1812-9*) Annual Reviews.

Annual Review of Biophysics & Bioengineering, Vol. 13. Ed. by Donald M. Engelman et al. LC 79-188446. (Illus.). 1984. 55.00 (*0-8243-1813-7*) Annual Reviews.

Annual Review of Biophysics & Biomolecular Structure, Vol. 22. Ed. by Donald M. Engelman et al. (Illus.). 1993. 59.00 (*0-8243-1822-6*) Annual Reviews.

Annual Review of Biophysics & Biomolecular Structure, Vol. 23. Ed. by Robert M. Stroud et al. (Illus.). 1994. text ed. 62.00 (*0-8243-1823-4*) Annual Reviews.

***Annual Review of Biophysics & Biomolecular Structure, Vol. 24.** Ed. by Robert M. Stroud. 1995. lib. bdg. 62.00 (*0-8243-1824-2*) Annual Reviews.

Annual Review of Biophysics & Biomolecular Structure (Formerly Annual Review of Biophysics & Biophysical Chemistry), Vol. 21. Ed. by Donald M. Engelman et al. 1992. text ed. 59.00 (*0-8243-1821-8*) Annual Reviews.

Annual Review of Biophysics & Biophysical Chemistry, Vol. 14. Ed. by Donald M. Engelman et al. LC 79-188446. (Illus.). 1985. text ed. 55.00 (*0-8243-1814-5*) Annual Reviews.

Annual Review of Biophysics & Biophysical Chemistry, Vol. 15. Ed. by Donald M. Engelman et al. LC 79-188446. (Illus.). 1986. text ed. 55.00 (*0-8243-1815-3*) Annual Reviews.

Annual Review of Biophysics & Biophysical Chemistry, Vol. 16. Ed. by Donald M. Engelman et al. LC 79-188446. (Illus.). 450p. 1987. text ed. 55.00 (*0-8243-1816-1*) Annual Reviews.

Annual Review of Biophysics & Biophysical Chemistry, Vol. 17. Ed. by Donald M. Engelman et al. LC 79-188446. (Illus.). 1988. text ed. 55.00 (*0-8243-1817-X*) Annual Reviews.

Annual Review of Biophysics & Biophysical Chemistry, Vol. 18. Ed. by Donald M. Engelman et al. LC 79-188446. (Illus.). 1989. text ed. 55.00 (*0-8243-1818-8*) Annual Reviews.

Annual Review of Biophysics & Biophysical Chemistry, Vol. 19. Ed. by Donald M. Engelman et al. 1990. text ed. 55.00 (*0-8243-1819-6*) Annual Reviews.

Annual Review of Biophysics & Biophysical Chemistry, Vol. 20. Ed. by Donald M. Engelman et al. 1991. text ed. 55.00 (*0-8243-1820-X*) Annual Reviews.

Annual Review of Birth Defects, 1977: Proceedings of the Birth Defects Annual Conference, 10th, Memphis, Tenn., June, 1977, 3 vols. Birth Defects Annual Conference Staff. Ed. by Robert L. Summitt & Daniel Bergsma. Incl. Vol. XIV, No. 6A. Cell Surface Factors, Immune Deficiencies, Twin Studies. 240p. 1978. 41.00 (*0-8451-1020-9*); Vol. XIV, No. 6B. Recent Advances & New Syndromes. 400p. 1978. 68.00 (*0-8451-1021-7*); Vol. XIV, No. 6C. Sex Differentiation & Chromosomal Abnormalities. 440p. 1978. 74.00 (*0-8451-1022-5*); (Birth Defects Original Article Ser.: Vol. 14, No. 6). (Illus.). 1978. write for info. (*0-318-50125-2*) A R Liss.

***Annual Review of Cell & Developmental Biology, Vol. 11.** Ed. by James A. Spudich. 1995. lib. bdg. 49.00 (*0-8243-3111-7*) Annual Reviews.

Annual Review of Cell Biology, Vol. 1. Ed. by George E. Palade et al. (Illus.). (C). 1985. text ed. 41.00 (*0-8243-3101-X*) Annual Reviews.

Annual Review of Cell Biology, Vol. 2. Ed. by George E. Palade et al. (Illus.). 1986. text ed. 41.00 (*0-8243-3102-8*) Annual Reviews.

Annual Review of Cell Biology, Vol. 3. Ed. by George E. Palade et al. (Illus.). 1987. text ed. 41.00 (*0-8243-3103-6*) Annual Reviews.

Annual Review of Cell Biology, Vol. 4. Ed. by George E. Palade et al. (Illus.). 1988. text ed. 41.00 (*0-8243-3104-4*) Annual Reviews.

Annual Review of Cell Biology, Vol. 5. Ed. by George E. Palade et al. 1989. text ed. 41.00 (*0-8243-3105-2*) Annual Reviews.

Annual Review of Cell Biology, Vol. 6. Ed. by George E. Palade et al. 1990. 41.00 (*0-8243-3106-0*) Annual Reviews.

Annual Review of Cell Biology, Vol. 7. Ed. by George E. Palade et al. 1991. text ed. 41.00 (*0-8243-3107-9*) Annual Reviews.

Annual Review of Cell Biology, Vol. 8. Ed. by George E. Palade et al. 1992. text ed. 46.00 (*0-8243-3108-7*) Annual Reviews.

Annual Review of Cell Biology, Vol. 9. Ed. by George E. Palade et al. (Illus.). 1993. text ed. 46.00 (*0-8243-3109-5*) Annual Reviews.

Annual Review of Cell Biology, 1994, Vol. 10. Ed. by James A. Spudich et al. (Illus.). 1994. text ed. 49.00 (*0-8243-3110-9*) Annual Reviews.

Annual Review of Chronopharmacology, Vol. 2. Ed. by Alain Reinberg et al. (Illus.). 334p. 1986. 108.00 (*0-08-034135-7*, Pub. by PPL UK) Elsevier.

Annual Review of Communications: National Engineering Consortium, Vol. XXXXVI. Intro. by John J. Pappas. (Illus.). 1108p. 1992. 139.00 (*0-933217-08-0*) Prof Educ Intl.

***Annual Review of Communications Vol. 46.** fac. ed. National Engineering Consortium Staff. LC 86-642827. 1132p. 1992. pap. 180.00 (*0-7837-8644-1*, 2047852) Bks Demand.

Annual Review of Computer Science, 4 vols., Set. Ed. by J. F. Traub et al. (Illus.). text ed. 100.00 (*0-685-61686-X*) Annual Reviews.

Annual Review of Computer Science, Vol. 1. Ed. by J. F. Traub et al. (Illus.). 1986. text ed. 41.00 (*0-8243-3201-6*) Annual Reviews.

Annual Review of Computer Science, Vol. 2. Ed. by J. F. Traub et al. (Illus.). 1987. text ed. 41.00 (*0-8243-3202-4*) Annual Reviews.

Annual Review of Computer Science, Vol. 3. Ed. by J. F. Traub et al. (Illus.). 1988. text ed. 47.00 (*0-8243-3203-2*) Annual Reviews.

Annual Review of Computer Science, Vol. 4. Ed. by J. F. Traub et al. (Illus.). 1990. text ed. 47.00 (*0-8243-3204-0*) Annual Reviews.

Annual Review of Conflict Knowledge & Conflict Resolution, Vol. 2. Ed. by Joseph B. Gittler. 314p. 1991. 42.00 (*0-8153-0064-6*, SS0754) Garland.

Annual Review of Conflict Knowledge & Conflict Resolution, Vol. 3: The Role of Formal Education in Conflict Resolution. Ed. by Larry S. Bowen & Joseph B. Gittler. LC 10-478671. 256p. 1993. 45.00 (*0-8153-1306-3*, SS902) Garland.

Annual Review of Conflict Knowledge & Conflict Resolution, 1989, Vol. 1. Ed. by Joseph B. Gittler. LC 10-478671. 274p. 1990. 34.00 (*0-8240-3645-X*, SS509) Garland.

Annual Review of Earth & Planetary Sciences, Vol. 1. Ed. by Fred A. Donath et al. LC 72-82137. (Illus.). 1973. 55.00 (*0-8243-2001-8*) Annual Reviews.

Annual Review of Earth & Planetary Sciences, Vol. 2. Ed. by Fred A. Donath et al. LC 72-82137. (Illus.). 1974. 55.00 (*0-8243-2002-6*) Annual Reviews.

Annual Review of Earth & Planetary Sciences, Vol. 3. Ed. by Fred A. Donath et al. LC 72-82137. (Illus.). 1975. 55.00 (*0-8243-2003-4*) Annual Reviews.

Annual Review of Earth & Planetary Sciences, Vol. 4. Ed. by Fred A. Donath et al. LC 72-82137. (Illus.). 1976. 55.00 (*0-8243-2004-2*) Annual Reviews.

Annual Review of Earth & Planetary Sciences, Vol. 5. Ed. by Fred A. Donath et al. LC 72-82137. (Illus.). 1977. 55.00 (*0-8243-2005-0*) Annual Reviews.

Annual Review of Earth & Planetary Sciences, Vol. 6. Ed. by Fred A. Donath et al. LC 72-82137. (Illus.). 1978. 55.00 (*0-8243-2006-9*) Annual Reviews.

Annual Review of Earth & Planetary Sciences, Vol. 8. Ed. by Fred A. Donath et al. LC 72-82137. (Illus.). 1980. 55.00 (*0-8243-2008-5*) Annual Reviews.

Annual Review of Earth & Planetary Sciences, Vol. 9. Ed. by George W. Wetherill et al. LC 72-82137. (Illus.). 1981. 55.00 (*0-8243-2009-3*) Annual Reviews.

Annual Review of Earth & Planetary Sciences, Vol. 10. Ed. by George W. Wetherill et al. LC 72-82137. (Illus.). 1982. 55.00 (*0-8243-2010-7*) Annual Reviews.

An Asterisk (*) at the beginning of an entry indicates that the title is appearing in BIP for the first time.

An Asterisk (*) at the beginning of an entry indicates that the title is appearing in BIP for the first time.

343

Annual Review of Gerontology & Geriatrics, Vol. 3. Ed. by Carl Eisdorfer. 448p. 1982. 43.00 (*0-8261-3082-8*) Springer Pub.

Annual Review of Gerontology & Geriatrics, Vol. 5. M. Powell Lawton & George L. Maddox. 352p. 1985. 39.00 (*0-8261-3084-4*) Springer Pub.

Annual Review of Gerontology & Geriatrics, Vol. 6. Carl Eisdorfer. 304p. 1986. 39.95 (*0-8261-3085-2*) Springer Pub.

Annual Review of Gerontology & Geriatrics, Vol. 7. Ed. by K. Warner Schaie. 352p. 1987. 39.00 (*0-8261-3086-0*) Springer Pub.

Annual Review of Gerontology & Geriatrics, Vol. 8. Ed. by George L. Maddox & M. Powell Lawton. 320p. 1988. 36.95 (*0-8261-6490-0*) Springer Pub.

Annual Review of Gerontology & Geriatrics, Vol 9, 1989. Ed. by M. Powell Lawton. 416p. 1989. 43.00 (*0-8261-6491-9*) Springer Pub.

***Annual Review of Gerontology & Geriatrics Vol. 14.** Ed. by M. Powell Lawton & Jeanne Teresi. (Illus.). 416p. 1994. 54.00 (*0-8261-6496-X*) Springer Pub.

Annual Review of Gerontology & Geriatrics, 1984, Vol. 4. Carl Eisdorfer. 304p. 1984. 39.95 (*0-8261-3083-6*) Springer Pub.

Annual Review of Gerontology & Geriatrics, 1990, Vol. 10. Ed. by Vincent J. Cristofalo. 240p. (C). 1990. 36.95 (*0-8261-6492-7*) Springer Pub.

Annual Review of Gerontology & Geriatrics 1991, Vol. 11. K. Warner Schaie. 384p. 1991. 43.00 (*0-8261-6493-5*) Springer Pub.

Annual Review of Gerontology & Geriatrics 1992, Vol. 12: With Focus on Medications. Ed. by John W. Rowe & Judith C. Ahronheim. 180p. 1992. 46.00 (*0-8261-6494-3*) Springer Pub.

Annual Review of Gerontology & Geriatrics, 1993. Ed. by George L. Maddox & M. Powell Lawton. (Annual Review of Gerontology Ser.: Vol. 13). 280p. 1993. text ed. 46.00 (*0-8261-6495-1*) Springer Pub.

Annual Review of Government Funded Research & Development, 1993. 210p. 1993. pap. 55.00 (*0-11-430083-6*, HM00836, Pub. by HMSO UK) UNIPUB.

Annual Review of Heat Transfer, Vol. 4. Ed. by Chang L. Tien. 385p. 1992. 170.00 (*1-56032-176-8*) Hemisp Pub.

Annual Review of Heat Transfer, Vol. 5. Tien. 1993. 179.95 (*0-8493-9905-X*) CRC Pr.

Annual Review of Hydrocephalus, 1988, Vol. 6. Ed. by Shoichi Matsumoto et al. (Illus.). xvi, 171p. 1990. 104.00 (*0-387-52204-2*) Spr-Verlag.

Annual Review of Hydrocephalus, 1989, Vol. 7. Ed. by Shoichi Matsumoto et al. 176p. 1990. 104.00 (*0-387-52937-3*) Spr-Verlag.

Annual Review of Hydrocephalus, 1990, Vol. 8. Ed. by Shoichi Matsumoto et al. 192p. 1992. 125.00 (*0-387-54846-7*) Spr-Verlag.

Annual Review of Immunology, Vol. 1. Ed. by William E. Paul et al. (Illus.). 1983. text ed. 41.00 (*0-8243-3001-3*) Annual Reviews.

Annual Review of Immunology, Vol. 2. Ed. by William E. Paul et al. (Illus.). 1984. text ed. 41.00 (*0-8243-3002-1*) Annual Reviews.

Annual Review of Immunology, Vol. 3. Ed. by William E. Paul et al. (Illus.). 1985. text ed. 41.00 (*0-8243-3003-X*) Annual Reviews.

Annual Review of Immunology, Vol. 4. Ed. by William E. Paul et al. (Illus.). 1986. text ed. 41.00 (*0-8243-3004-8*) Annual Reviews.

Annual Review of Immunology, Vol. 5. Ed. by William E. Paul et al. (Illus.). 1987. text ed. 41.00 (*0-8243-3005-6*) Annual Reviews.

Annual Review of Immunology, Vol. 6. Ed. by William E. Paul et al. 1988. text ed. 41.00 (*0-8243-3006-4*) Annual Reviews.

Annual Review of Immunology, Vol. 7. Ed. by William E. Paul et al. (Illus.). 1989. text ed. 41.00 (*0-8243-3007-2*) Annual Reviews.

Annual Review of Immunology, Vol. 8. Ed. by William E. Paul et al. 1990. text ed. 41.00 (*0-8243-3008-0*) Annual Reviews.

Annual Review of Immunology, Vol. 9. Ed. by William E. Paul et al. 1991. text ed. 41.00 (*0-8243-3009-9*) Annual Reviews.

Annual Review of Immunology, Vol. 10. Ed. by William E. Paul et al. (Illus.). 1992. text ed. 45.00 (*0-8243-3010-2*) Annual Reviews.

Annual Review of Immunology, Vol. 11. Ed. by William E. Paul et al. (Illus.). 1993. text ed. 45.00 (*0-8243-3011-0*) Annual Reviews.

Annual Review of Immunology, Vol. 12. Ed. by William E. Paul. (Illus.). 1994. text ed. 48.00 (*0-8243-3012-9*) Annual Reviews.

Annual Review of Information Science & Technology, Vol. 10. Ed. by Carlos Cuadra et al. LC 66-25096. 1975. 27.50 (*0-87715-210-1*) Am Soc Info Sci.

Annual Review of Information Science & Technology, Vol. 11. Ed. by Martha E. Williams. LC 66-25096. 1976. 35.00 (*0-87715-212-8*) Am Soc Info Sci.

Annual Review of Information Science & Technology, Vol. 22. Ed. by M. E. Williams. 440p. 1987. 73.00 (*0-444-70302-0*) Elsevier.

Annual Review of Information Science & Technology, Vol. 23. M. E. Williams. 380p. 1988. 79.50 (*0-444-70543-0*) Elsevier.

Annual Review of Information Science & Technology, Vol. 24. Ed. by M. E. Williams. 458p. 1989. 91.00 (*0-444-87418-6*) Elsevier.

Annual Review of Information Science & Technology, Vol. 25. Ed. by M. E. Williams. 492p. 1990. 104.50 (*0-444-88531-5*) Elsevier.

Annual Review of Irish Law. Raymond Byrne & William Binchy. 1989. 95.00 (*0-947686-61-4*, Pub. by Round Hall) Intl Spec Bk.

Annual Review of Irish Law, 1992. Raymond Byrne & William Binchy. 528p. 1994. text ed. 95.00 (*0-947686-78-9*, Pub. by Round Hall) Intl Spec Bk.

Annual Review of Jazz Studies, Vol. 5: 1991. Ed. by Edward Berger et al. LC 82-644466. (Illus.). 274p. 1991. 29.50 (*0-8108-2478-7*) Scarecrow.

Annual Review of Jazz Studies, 1993, Vol. 6. Ed. by Edward Berger et al. (Illus.). 308p. 1993. 39.50 (*0-8108-2727-1*) Scarecrow.

Annual Review of Materials Science, Vol. 1. Ed. by Robert A. Huggins et al. LC 75-172108. (Illus.). 1971. text ed. 68.00 (*0-8243-1701-7*) Annual Reviews.

Annual Review of Materials Science, Vol. 3. Ed. by Robert A. Huggins et al. LC 75-172108. (Illus.). 1973. text ed. 68.00 (*0-8243-1703-3*) Annual Reviews.

Annual Review of Materials Science, Vol. 4. Ed. by Robert A. Huggins et al. LC 75-172108. (Illus.). 1974. text ed. 68.00 (*0-8243-1704-1*) Annual Reviews.

Annual Review of Materials Science, Vol. 5. Ed. by Robert A. Huggins et al. LC 75-172108. (Illus.). 1975. text ed. 68.00 (*0-8243-1705-X*) Annual Reviews.

Annual Review of Materials Science, Vol. 6. Ed. by Robert A. Huggins et al. LC 75-172108. (Illus.). 1976. text ed. 68.00 (*0-8243-1706-8*) Annual Reviews.

Annual Review of Materials Science, Vol. 7. Ed. by Robert A. Huggins et al. LC 75-172108. (Illus.). 1977. text ed. 68.00 (*0-8243-1707-6*) Annual Reviews.

Annual Review of Materials Science, Vol. 8. Ed. by Robert A. Huggins et al. LC 75-172108. (Illus.). 1978. text ed. 68.00 (*0-8243-1708-4*) Annual Reviews.

Annual Review of Materials Science, Vol. 9. Ed. by Robert A. Huggins et al. LC 75-172108. (Illus.). 1979. text ed. 68.00 (*0-8243-1709-2*) Annual Reviews.

Annual Review of Materials Science, Vol. 10. Ed. by Robert A. Huggins et al. LC 75-172108. (Illus.). 1980. text ed. 68.00 (*0-8243-1710-6*) Annual Reviews.

Annual Review of Materials Science, Vol. 11. Ed. by Robert A. Huggins et al. LC 75-172108. (Illus.). 1981. text ed. 68.00 (*0-8243-1711-4*) Annual Reviews.

Annual Review of Materials Science, Vol. 12. Ed. by Robert A. Huggins et al. LC 75-172108. (Illus.). 1982. text ed. 68.00 (*0-8243-1712-2*) Annual Reviews.

Annual Review of Materials Science, Vol. 13. Ed. by Robert A. Huggins et al. LC 75-172108. (Illus.). 1983. text ed. 68.00 (*0-8243-1713-0*) Annual Reviews.

Annual Review of Materials Science, Vol. 14. Ed. by Robert A. Huggins et al. (Illus.). 1984. text ed. 68.00 (*0-8243-1714-9*) Annual Reviews.

Annual Review of Materials Science, Vol. 15. Ed. by Robert A. Huggins et al. (Illus.). (C). 1985. text ed. 68.00 (*0-8243-1715-7*) Annual Reviews.

Annual Review of Materials Science, Vol. 16. Ed. by Robert A. Huggins et al. LC 75-172108. (Illus.). 1986. text ed. 68.00 (*0-8243-1716-5*) Annual Reviews.

Annual Review of Materials Science, Vol. 17. Ed. by Robert A. Huggins et al. LC 75-172108. (Illus.). 1987. text ed. 68.00 (*0-8243-1717-3*) Annual Reviews.

Annual Review of Materials Science, Vol. 18. Ed. by Robert A. Huggins et al. LC 75-172108. 1988. text ed. 68.00 (*0-8243-1718-1*) Annual Reviews.

Annual Review of Materials Science, Vol. 19. Ed. by Robert A. Huggins et al. 1989. text ed. 68.00 (*0-8243-1719-X*) Annual Reviews.

Annual Review of Materials Science, Vol. 20. Ed. by Robert A. Huggins et al. 1990. 72.00 (*0-8243-1720-3*) Annual Reviews.

Annual Review of Materials Science, Vol. 21. Ed. by Robert A. Huggins et al. 1991. text ed. 72.00 (*0-8243-1721-1*) Annual Reviews.

Annual Review of Materials Science, Vol. 22. Ed. by Robert A. Huggins et al. 1992. text ed. 72.00 (*0-8243-1722-X*) Annual Reviews.

Annual Review of Materials Science, Vol. 23. Ed. by Robert A. Huggins et al. (Illus.). 1993. text ed. 72.00 (*0-8243-1723-8*) Annual Reviews.

Annual Review of Materials Science, Vol. 24. Ed. by Elton N. Kaufmann et al. (Illus.). 1994. text ed. 75.00 (*0-8243-1724-6*) Annual Reviews.

Annual Review of Medicine, Vol. 45. Ed. by C. H. Coggins. (Illus.). 1994. 47.00 (*0-8243-0545-0*) Annual Reviews.

Annual Review of Medicine: Selected Topics in the Clinical Sciences, Vol. 9. Ed. by William P. Creger et al. 1958. text ed. 40.00 (*0-8243-0509-4*) Annual Reviews.

Annual Review of Medicine: Selected Topics in the Clinical Sciences, Vol. 11. Ed. by William P. Creger et al. 1960. text ed. 40.00 (*0-8243-0511-6*) Annual Reviews.

Annual Review of Medicine: Selected Topics in the Clinical Sciences, Vol. 12. Ed. by William P. Creger et al. 1961. text ed. 40.00 (*0-8243-0512-4*) Annual Reviews.

Annual Review of Medicine: Selected Topics in the Clinical Sciences, Vol. 13. Ed. by William P. Creger et al. 1962. text ed. 40.00 (*0-8243-0513-2*) Annual Reviews.

Annual Review of Medicine: Selected Topics in the Clinical Sciences, Vol. 14. Ed. by William P. Creger et al. 1963. text ed. 40.00 (*0-8243-0514-0*) Annual Reviews.

Annual Review of Medicine: Selected Topics in the Clinical Sciences, Vol. 15. Ed. by William P. Creger et al. 1964. text ed. 40.00 (*0-8243-0515-9*) Annual Reviews.

Annual Review of Medicine: Selected Topics in the Clinical Sciences, Vol. 17. Ed. by William P. Creger et al. 1966. text ed. 40.00 (*0-8243-0517-5*) Annual Reviews.

Annual Review of Medicine: Selected Topics in the Clinical Sciences, Vol. 18. Ed. by William P. Creger et al. 1967. text ed. 40.00 (*0-8243-0518-3*) Annual Reviews.

Annual Review of Medicine: Selected Topics in the Clinical Sciences, Vol. 19. Ed. by William P. Creger et al. 1968. text ed. 40.00 (*0-8243-0519-1*) Annual Reviews.

Annual Review of Medicine: Selected Topics in the Clinical Sciences, Vol. 20. Ed. by William P. Creger et al. 1969. text ed. 40.00 (*0-8243-0520-5*) Annual Reviews.

Annual Review of Medicine: Selected Topics in the Clinical Sciences, Vol. 21. Ed. by William P. Creger et al. 1970. text ed. 40.00 (*0-8243-0521-3*) Annual Reviews.

Annual Review of Medicine: Selected Topics in the Clinical Sciences, Vol. 22. Ed. by William P. Creger et al. 1971. text ed. 40.00 (*0-8243-0522-1*) Annual Reviews.

Annual Review of Medicine: Selected Topics in the Clinical Sciences, Vol. 23. Ed. by William P. Creger et al. LC 51-1659. (Illus.). 1972. text ed. 40.00 (*0-8243-0523-X*) Annual Reviews.

Annual Review of Medicine: Selected Topics in the Clinical Sciences, Vol. 24. Ed. by William P. Creger et al. LC 51-1659. (Illus.). 1973. text ed. 40.00 (*0-8243-0524-8*) Annual Reviews.

Annual Review of Medicine: Selected Topics in the Clinical Sciences, Vol. 25. Ed. by William P. Creger et al. LC 51-1659. (Illus.). 1974. text ed. 40.00 (*0-8243-0525-6*) Annual Reviews.

Annual Review of Medicine: Selected Topics in the Clinical Sciences, Vol. 26. Ed. by William P. Creger et al. LC 51-1659. (Illus.). 1975. text ed. 40.00 (*0-8243-0526-4*) Annual Reviews.

Annual Review of Medicine: Selected Topics in the Clinical Sciences, Vol. 27. Ed. by William P. Creger et al. LC 51-1659. (Illus.). 1976. text ed. 40.00 (*0-8243-0527-2*) Annual Reviews.

Annual Review of Medicine: Selected Topics in the Clinical Sciences, Vol. 28. Ed. by William P. Creger et al. LC 51-1659. (Illus.). 1977. text ed. 40.00 (*0-8243-0528-0*) Annual Reviews.

Annual Review of Medicine: Selected Topics in the Clinical Sciences, Vol. 29. Ed. by William P. Creger et al. LC 51-1659. (Illus.). 1978. text ed. 40.00 (*0-8243-0529-9*) Annual Reviews.

Annual Review of Medicine: Selected Topics in the Clinical Sciences, Vol. 30. Ed. by William P. Creger et al. LC 51-1659. (Illus.). 1979. text ed. 40.00 (*0-8243-0530-2*) Annual Reviews.

Annual Review of Medicine: Selected Topics in the Clinical Sciences, Vol. 31. Ed. by William P. Creger et al. LC 51-1659. (Illus.). 1980. text ed. 40.00 (*0-8243-0531-0*) Annual Reviews.

Annual Review of Medicine: Selected Topics in the Clinical Sciences, Vol. 32. Ed. by William P. Creger et al. LC 51-1659. (Illus.). 1981. text ed. 40.00 (*0-8243-0532-9*) Annual Reviews.

Annual Review of Medicine: Selected Topics in the Clinical Sciences, Vol. 33. Ed. by William P. Creger et al. LC 51-1659. (Illus.). 1982. text ed. 40.00 (*0-8243-0533-7*) Annual Reviews.

Annual Review of Medicine: Selected Topics in the Clinical Sciences, Vol. 34. Ed. by William P. Creger et al. LC 51-1659. (Illus.). 1983. text ed. 40.00 (*0-8243-0534-5*) Annual Reviews.

Annual Review of Medicine: Selected Topics in the Clinical Sciences, Vol. 35. Ed. by William P. Creger et al. LC 51-1659. (Illus.). 1984. text ed. 40.00 (*0-8243-0535-3*) Annual Reviews.

Annual Review of Medicine: Selected Topics in the Clinical Sciences, Vol. 36. Ed. by William P. Creger et al. LC 51-1659. (Illus.). 1985. text ed. 40.00 (*0-8243-0536-1*) Annual Reviews.

Annual Review of Medicine: Selected Topics in the Clinical Sciences, Vol. 37. Ed. by William P. Creger et al. LC 51-1659. (Illus.). 1986. text ed. 40.00 (*0-8243-0537-X*) Annual Reviews.

Annual Review of Medicine: Selected Topics in the Clinical Sciences, Vol. 38. Ed. by William P. Creger et al. LC 51-1659. (Illus.). 1987. text ed. 40.00 (*0-8243-0538-8*) Annual Reviews.

Annual Review of Medicine: Selected Topics in the Clinical Sciences, Vol. 39. Ed. by William P. Creger et al. 1988. text ed. 40.00 (*0-8243-0539-6*) Annual Reviews.

Annual Review of Medicine: Selected Topics in the Clinical Sciences, Vol. 40. Ed. by William P. Creger et al. (Illus.). 1989. text ed. 40.00 (*0-8243-0540-X*) Annual Reviews.

Annual Review of Medicine: Selected Topics in the Clinical Sciences, Vol. 41. Ed. by William P. Creger et al. 1990. text ed. 40.00 (*0-8243-0541-8*) Annual Reviews.

Annual Review of Medicine: Selected Topics in the Clinical Sciences, Vol. 42. Ed. by William P. Creger et al. 1991. text ed. 40.00 (*0-8243-0542-6*) Annual Reviews.

Annual Review of Medicine: Selected Topics in the Clinical Sciences, Vol. 43. Ed. by William P. Creger et al. 1992. text ed. 44.00 (*0-8243-0543-4*) Annual Reviews.

Annual Review of Medicine: Selected Topics in the Clinical Sciences, Vol. 44. Ed. by William P. Creger et al. (Illus.). 1993. text ed. 44.00 (*0-8243-0544-2*) Annual Reviews.

***Annual Review of Medicine Vol. 46 (1995)** Ed. by C. H. Coggins. (Illus.). 590p. 1995. text ed. 47.00 (*0-8243-0546-9*) Annual Reviews.

Annual Review of Microbiology, Vol. 21. Ed. by C. E. Clifton et al. 1967. text ed. 41.00 (*0-8243-1121-3*) Annual Reviews.

Annual Review of Microbiology, Vol. 22. Ed. by C. E. Clifton et al. 1968. text ed. 41.00 (*0-8243-1122-1*) Annual Reviews.

Annual Review of Microbiology, Vol. 23. Ed. by C. E. Clifton et al. 1969. text ed. 41.00 (*0-8243-1123-X*) Annual Reviews.

Annual Review of Microbiology, Vol. 24. Ed. by C. E. Clifton et al. 1970. text ed. 41.00 (*0-8243-1124-8*) Annual Reviews.

Annual Review of Microbiology, Vol. 26. Ed. by C. E. Clifton et al. LC 49-432. (Illus.). 1972. text ed. 41.00 (*0-8243-1126-4*) Annual Reviews.

Annual Review of Microbiology, Vol. 27. Ed. by Mortimer P. Starr et al. LC 49-432. (Illus.). 1973. text ed. 41.00 (*0-8243-1127-2*) Annual Reviews.

Annual Review of Microbiology, Vol. 28. Ed. by Mortimer P. Starr et al. LC 49-432. (Illus.). 1974. text ed. 41.00 (*0-8243-1128-0*) Annual Reviews.

Annual Review of Microbiology, Vol. 29. Ed. by Mortimer P. Starr et al. LC 49-432. (Illus.). 1975. text ed. 41.00 (*0-8243-1129-9*) Annual Reviews.

Annual Review of Microbiology, Vol. 30. Ed. by Mortimer P. Starr et al. LC 49-432. (Illus.). 1976. text ed. 41.00 (*0-8243-1130-2*) Annual Reviews.

Annual Review of Microbiology, Vol. 31. Ed. by Mortimer P. Starr et al. LC 49-432. (Illus.). 1977. text ed. 41.00 (*0-8243-1131-0*) Annual Reviews.

Annual Review of Microbiology, Vol. 32. Ed. by Mortimer P. Starr et al. LC 49-432. (Illus.). 1978. text ed. 41.00 (*0-8243-1132-9*) Annual Reviews.

Annual Review of Microbiology, Vol. 33. Ed. by Mortimer P. Starr et al. LC 49-432. (Illus.). 1979. text ed. 41.00 (*0-8243-1133-7*) Annual Reviews.

Annual Review of Microbiology, Vol. 34. Ed. by Mortimer P. Starr et al. LC 49-432. (Illus.). 1980. text ed. 41.00 (*0-8243-1134-5*) Annual Reviews.

Annual Review of Microbiology, Vol. 35. Ed. by Mortimer P. Starr et al. LC 49-432. (Illus.). 1981. text ed. 41.00 (*0-8243-1135-3*) Annual Reviews.

Annual Review of Microbiology, Vol. 36. Ed. by Mortimer P. Starr et al. LC 49-432. (Illus.). 1982. text ed. 41.00 (*0-8243-1136-1*) Annual Reviews.

Annual Review of Microbiology, Vol. 37. Ed. by L. Nicholas Ornston et al. LC 49-432. (Illus.). 1983. text ed. 41.00 (*0-8243-1137-X*) Annual Reviews.

Annual Review of Microbiology, Vol. 38. Ed. by L. Nicholas Ornston et al. LC 49-432. (Illus.). 1984. text ed. 41.00 (*0-8243-1138-8*) Annual Reviews.

Annual Review of Microbiology, Vol. 39. Ed. by L. Nicholas Ornston et al. LC 49-432. (Illus.). (C). 1985. text ed. 41.00 (*0-8243-1139-6*) Annual Reviews.

Annual Review of Microbiology, Vol. 40. Ed. by L. Nicholas Ornston et al. LC 49-432. (Illus.). 1986. text ed. 41.00 (*0-8243-1140-X*) Annual Reviews.

Annual Review of Microbiology, Vol. 41. Ed. by L. Nicholas Ornston et al. LC 49-432. (Illus.). 1987. text ed. 41.00 (*0-8243-1141-8*) Annual Reviews.

Annual Review of Microbiology, Vol. 42. Ed. by L. Nicholas Ornston et al. LC 49-432. (Illus.). 1988. text ed. 41.00 (*0-8243-1142-6*) Annual Reviews.

Annual Review of Microbiology, Vol. 43. Ed. by L. Nicholas Ornston et al. 1989. text ed. 41.00 (*0-8243-1143-4*) Annual Reviews.

Annual Review of Microbiology, Vol. 44. Ed. by L. Nicholas Ornston et al. 1990. 41.00 (*0-8243-1144-2*) Annual Reviews.

Annual Review of Microbiology, Vol. 45. Ed. by L. N. Ornston et al. 1991. text ed. 41.00 (*0-8243-1145-0*) Annual Reviews.

Annual Review of Microbiology, Vol. 46. Ed. by L. Nicholas Ornston et al. 1992. text ed. 45.00 (*0-8243-1146-9*) Annual Reviews.

Annual Review of Microbiology, Vol. 47. Ed. by L. Nicholas Ornston et al. (Illus.). 1993. text ed. 45.00 (*0-8243-1147-7*) Annual Reviews.

Annual Review of Microbiology, Vol. 48. Ed. by L. Nicholas Ornston et al. (Illus.). 1994. text ed. 60.00 (*0-8243-1148-5*) Annual Reviews.

***Annual Review of Microbiology, Vol. 49.** L. Nicholas Ornston. 1995. lib. bdg. 48.00 (*0-8243-1149-3*) Annual Reviews.

Annual Review of Military Research & Development, 1982. Kosta Tsipis & Sheena Phillips. LC 83-7287. 186p. 1983. text ed. 45.00 (*0-275-91093-8*, C1093, Praeger Pubs) Greenwood.

Annual Review of Nations: Year, 1988. Ed. by Louise Haberman & Paul M. Sacks. 610p. 1989. text ed. 110.00 (*0-8448-1586-1*) Taylor & Francis.

Annual Review of Neuroscience, Vol. 1. Ed. by W. Maxwell Cowan et al. (Illus.). 1978. text ed. 40.00 (*0-8243-2401-3*) Annual Reviews.

Annual Review of Neuroscience, Vol. 2. Ed. by W. Maxwell Cowan et al. (Illus.). 1979. text ed. 40.00 (*0-8243-2402-1*) Annual Reviews.

Annual Review of Neuroscience, Vol. 3. Ed. by W. Maxwell Cowan et al. (Illus.). 1980. text ed. 40.00 (*0-8243-2403-X*) Annual Reviews.

Annual Review of Neuroscience, Vol. 4. Ed. by W. Maxwell Cowan et al. (Illus.). 1981. text ed. 40.00 (*0-8243-2404-8*) Annual Reviews.

Annual Review of Neuroscience, Vol. 5. Ed. by W. Maxwell Cowan et al. (Illus.). 1982. text ed. 40.00 (*0-8243-2405-6*) Annual Reviews.

Annual Review of Neuroscience, Vol. 6. Ed. by W. Maxwell Cowan et al. (Illus.). 1983. text ed. 40.00 (*0-8243-2406-4*) Annual Reviews.

Annual Review of Neuroscience, Vol. 7. Ed. by W. Maxwell Cowan et al. (Illus.). 1984. text ed. 40.00 (*0-8243-2407-2*) Annual Reviews.

Annual Review of Neuroscience, Vol. 8. Ed. by Maxwell W. Cowan et al. 500p. 1985. 24.00 (*0-318-18123-1*); 21.50 (*0-318-18124-X*) Soc Neuroscience.

Annual Review of Neuroscience, Vol. 8. Ed. by W. Maxwell Cowan et al. (Illus.). 1985. text ed. 40.00 (*0-8243-2408-0*) Annual Reviews.

Annual Review of Neuroscience, Vol. 9. Ed. by W. Maxwell Cowan et al. (Illus.). 1986. text ed. 40.00 (*0-8243-2409-9*) Annual Reviews.

Annual Review of Neuroscience, Vol. 10. Ed. by W. Maxwell Cowan. (Illus.). 1987. text ed. 40.00 (*0-8243-2410-2*) Annual Reviews.

An Asterisk (*) at the beginning of an entry indicates that the title is appearing in BIP for the first time.

Annual Review of Sociology, Vol. 15. Ed. by W. R. Scott et al. 1989. text ed. 45.00 (*0-8243-2215-0*) Annual Reviews.

Annual Review of Sociology, Vol. 16. Ed. by W. R. Scott et al. 1990. 45.00 (*0-8243-2216-9*) Annual Reviews.

Annual Review of Sociology, Vol. 17. Ed. by W. R. Scott et al. 1991. text ed. 45.00 (*0-8243-2217-7*) Annual Reviews.

Annual Review of Sociology, Vol. 18. Ed. by Judith Blake et al. 1992. text ed. 49.00 (*0-8243-2218-5*) Annual Reviews.

Annual Review of Sociology, Vol. 19. Ed. by Judith Blake et al. (Illus.). 1993. text ed. 49.00 (*0-8243-2219-3*) Annual Reviews.

Annual Review of Sociology, Vol. 20. Ed. by Elton N. Kaufmann et al. (Illus.). 1994. text ed. 52.00 (*0-8243-2220-7*) Annual Reviews.

***Annual Review of Sociology, Vol. 21.** Ed. by John Hagan. 1995. lib. bdg. 52.00 (*0-8243-2221-5*) Annual Reviews.

Annual Review of the Chemical Industry, 1986. 210p. (ENG & FRE.). 1988. pap. 36.00 (*0-685-44277-2*); write for info. (*92-1-116421-4*, 88.II.E.17) UN.

Annual Review of the Chemical Industry, 1987. 209p. 36.00 (*92-1-116443-5*, E.89.II.E.2) UN.

Annual Review of the Chemical Industry, 1988. 300p. 1988. 40.00 (*92-1-116472-9*, 90.II.E.7) UN.

Annual Review of United Nations Affairs: Covering Years from 1949 Thru 1993, 40 vols., Set. annuals Kumiko Matsuura et al. LC 50-548. 1949. lib. bdg. 1,995.00 (*0-379-12300-2*) Oceana.

Annual Review of United Nations Affairs: Covering Years from 1980 Thru 1993, 22 vols., Set. annuals Kumiko Matsuura et al. LC 50-548. 1949. 1,095.00 (*0-685-73396-3*) Oceana.

Annual Review of Women in World Religions, Vol. 1. Ed. by Arvind Sharma & Katherine K. Young. 180p. 1991. 39.50 (*0-7914-0865-5*); pap. 12.95 (*0-7914-0866-3*) State U NY Pr.

Annual Review of Women in World Religions, Vol. III. Ed. by Arvind Sharma & Katherine K. Young. 192p. (C). 1993. 39.50 (*0-7914-2031-0*); pap. 12.95 (*0-7914-2032-9*) State U NY Pr.

Annual Review of Women in World Religions, Vol. II: Heroic Women. Ed. by Arvind Sharma & Katherine K. Young. 168p. (C). 1992. 39.50 (*0-7914-1611-9*); pap. 12.95 (*0-7914-1612-7*) State U NY Pr.

***Annual Review of Women's Health, Vol. I.** Ed. by Beverly J. McElmurry & Randy S. Parker. 1993. pap. 37.95 (*0-88737-598-7*) Natl League Nurse.

***Annual Review of Women's Health, Vol. II.** Ed. by Beverly J. McElmurry & Randy S. Parker. 1995. pap. 37.95 (*0-88737-636-3*) Natl League Nurse.

Annual Review, 1992-1993. Her Majesty's Stationery Office Staff. 84p. 1993. pap. 10.00 (*0-11-887535-3*, HM75353, Pub. by HMSO UK) UNIPUB.

Annual Reviews of Computational Physics, Vol. 1. Deitrich Stauffer. 356p. 1995. text ed. 86.00 (*981-02-1881-8*) World Scientific Pub.

***Annual Reviews of Immunology Vol. 13, 1995.** Ed. by William E. Paul. (Illus.). 825p. 1995. lib. bdg. 48.00 (*0-8243-3013-7*) Annual Reviews.

***Annual Reviews of Physical Chemistry, Vol. 46.** Herbert L. Strauss. 1995. lib. bdg. 51.00 (*0-8243-1046-2*) Annual Reviews.

Annual Series of European Research in Behavior Therapy: Topics in Behavioral Medicine, Vol. 1. Ed. by J. Vinck. 1986. 30.00 (*90-265-0762-3*, Pub. by Swets Pub Serv NE) Taylor & Francis.

Annual Seventy-Nine: Bologna Book Fair. 5.00 (*0-686-70265-4*) Boston Public Lib.

Annual Shareholders' Meeting. 3rd ed. Bertram T. Ebzery. (Corporate Practice Ser.: No. 12). 1991. 95.00 (*1-55871-234-8*) BNA.

Annual State-of-the-Child Indicators for New York City, 1985-1992. 26p. (Orig.). 1993. pap. 5.00 (*0-88156-157-6*) Comm Serv Soc NY.

Annual Statement Diskette Filing Specifications: Fraternal. 344p. (C). 1992. ring bd. 100.00 (*0-89382-206-X*) Nat Assn Insu Comm.

Annual Statement Diskette Filing Specifications: Health Maintenance Organization. 90p. (C). 1992. ring bd. 100.00 (*0-89382-207-8*) Nat Assn Insu Comm.

Annual Statement Diskette Filing Specifications: Life - Health. 430p. (C). 1992. ring bd. 100.00 (*0-89382-204-3*) Nat Assn Insu Comm.

Annual Statement Diskette Filing Specifications: Property - Casualty. 454p. (C). 1992. ring bd. 100.00 (*0-89382-205-1*) Nat Assn Insu Comm.

***Annual Statement Diskette Filing Specifications - Fraternal Insurance Companies.** 400p. (C). 1994. 100.00 (*0-89382-285-X*) Nat Assn Insu Comm.

***Annual Statement Diskette Filing Specifications - Health Maintenance Organizations.** 136p. (C). 1994. 100.00 (*0-89382-286-8*) Nat Assn Insu Comm.

***Annual Statement Diskette Filing Specifications - Hospital, Medical, Dental Service & Indemnity Corporation.** 286p. (C). 1994. 100.00 (*0-89382-287-6*) Nat Assn Insu Comm.

Annual Statement Diskette Filing Specifications- Life - Health. 1993. ring bd. 100.00 (*0-89382-232-9*) Nat Assn Insu Comm.

***Annual Statement Diskette Filing Specifications - Life & Health Insurance Companies.** 848p. (C). 1994. 100.00 (*0-89382-284-1*) Nat Assn Insu Comm.

***Annual Statement Diskette Filing Specifications - Property Casualty Insurance Companies.** 628p. (C). 1994. 100.00 (*0-89382-283-3*) Nat Assn Insu Comm.

Annual Statement Diskette Filing Specifications- Property - Casualty. 352p. 1993. ring bd. 100.00 (*0-89382-233-7*) Nat Assn Insu Comm.

Annual Statement Diskette Filing Specifications-Fraternal. 320p. 1993. ring bd. 100.00 (*0-89382-234-5*) Nat Assn Insu Comm.

Annual Statement Diskette Filing Specifications Fraternal, 1991. 244p. (C). 1991. ring bd. 100.00 (*0-89382-179-9*) Nat Assn Insu Comm.

***Annual Statement Diskette Filing Specifications-HMO, 1993.** annuals 138p. (C). 1993. ring bd. 100.00 (*0-89382-235-3*) Nat Assn Insu Comm.

Annual Statement Diskette Filing Specifications (1991) Life-Health & Property-Casualty. 610p. (C). 1991. ring bd. 200.00 (*0-89382-178-0*) Nat Assn Insu Comm.

Annual Statement Instructions - Fraternal. 186p. (C). 1992. ring bd. 150.00 (*0-89382-202-7*) Nat Assn Insu Comm.

***Annual Statement Instructions - Fraternal Insurers.** 256p. (C). 1994. 150.00 (*0-89382-278-7*) Nat Assn Insu Comm.

***Annual Statement Instructions - Health Maintenance Organizations.** 77p. (C). 1994. 150.00 (*0-89382-279-5*) Nat Assn Insu Comm.

***Annual Statement Instructions - Hospital, Medical, Dental Service or Indemnity Corporations.** 157p. (C). 1994. 50.00 (*0-89382-280-9*) Nat Assn Insu Comm.

Annual Statement Instructions - Life, Accident & Health. 265p. (C). 1992. ring bd. 150.00 (*0-89382-201-9*) Nat Assn Insu Comm.

***Annual Statement Instructions - Life & Health Insurance.** 317p. (C). 1994. 150.00 (*0-89382-276-0*) Nat Assn Insu Comm.

***Annual Statement Instructions - Limited Health Services Organization.** 58p. (C). 1994. 50.00 (*0-89382-281-7*) Nat Assn Insu Comm.

Annual Statement Instructions - Property & Casualty. 217p. (C). 1992. ring bd. 150.00 (*0-89382-200-0*) Nat Assn Insu Comm.

***Annual Statement Instructions - Property & Casualty Insurance.** 409p. (C). 1994. 150.00 (*0-89382-277-9*) Nat Assn Insu Comm.

***Annual Statement Instructions - Title Insurance Companies.** 163p. (C). 1994. 50.00 (*0-89382-282-5*) Nat Assn Insu Comm.

Annual Statement Instructions for Life-Accident & Health, 1991. 260p. (C). 1991. ring bd. 150.00 (*0-89382-175-6*) Nat Assn Insu Comm.

***Annual Statement Instructions for Limited Health Services Organizations.** annuals (C). 1994. ring bd. 50.00 (*0-89382-288-4*) Nat Assn Insu Comm.

***Annual Statement Instructions for Title Insurance Companies.** annuals 163p. (C). 1994. ring bd. 50.00 (*0-89382-289-2*) Nat Assn Insu Comm.

Annual Statement Instructions Fraternal. 203p. 1993. ring bd. 150.00 (*0-89382-238-8*) Nat Assn Insu Comm.

Annual Statement Instructions Health Maintenance Organizations. 57p. (C). 1992. ring bd. 50.00 (*0-89382-195-0*) Nat Assn Insu Comm.

Annual Statement Instructions Health Maintenance Organizations. 69p. 1993. ring bd. 150.00 (*0-89382-239-6*) Nat Assn Insu Comm.

***Annual Statement Instructions-Hospital, Medical & Dental Service Or Indemnity Corporations.** 125p. (C). 1993. ring bd. 50.00 (*0-89382-240-X*) Nat Assn Insu Comm.

Annual Statement Instructions Life, Accident & Health. 291p. 1993. ring bd. 150.00 (*0-89382-236-1*) Nat Assn Insu Comm.

Annual Statement Instructions Limited Health Service Organizations. 53p. (C). 1992. ring bd. 50.00 (*0-89382-193-4*) Nat Assn Insu Comm.

Annual Statement Instructions Limited Health Service Organizations. 58p. 1993. ring bd. 50.00 (*0-89382-241-8*) Nat Assn Insu Comm.

Annual Statement Instructions Property & Casualty. 238p. 1993. ring bd. 150.00 (*0-89382-237-X*) Nat Assn Insu Comm.

Annual Statement Instructions Title Insurance. 107p. (C). 1992. ring bd. 50.00 (*0-89382-194-2*) Nat Assn Insu Comm.

***Annual Statement Instructions-Title, 1993.** 123p. (C). 1993. ring bd. 50.00 (*0-89382-242-6*) Nat Assn Insu Comm.

Annual Statement Studies. Ed. by Susan M. Kelsay. 900p. 1994. 110.00 (*0-936742-56-9*) Robt Morris Assocs.

Annual Statistical Report on Profit, Sales & Production Trends in the Mens' & Boys' Tailored Clothing Industry. 23p. 25.00 (*0-685-71054-8*) Clothing Mfrs.

***Annual Summary of Births, Marriages, Divorces, & Deaths Vol. 42, No. 13: United States, 1993.** National Center for Health Statistics Staff. (Monthly Vital Statistics Report Ser.). 36p. Date not set. write for info. (*0-614-02947-3*) Natl Ctr Health Stats.

Annual Summary of Investigations Relating to Reading July 1, 1988 to June 30, 1989. Ed. by Sam Weintraub. LC 91-662321. 272p. reprint ed. pap. 77.60 (*0-7837-6148-1*, 2045800) Bks Demand.

Annual Summary of Investigations Relating to Reading, July 1, 1989 to June 30, 1990. Ed. by Sam Weintraub. 232p. 1991. pap. 23.00 (*0-87207-363-7*) Intl Reading.

Annual Summary of Investigations Relating to Reading, July 1, 1990 to June 30, 1991. Ed. by Sam Weintraub. 242p. 1992. pap. 23.00 (*0-87207-372-6*) Intl Reading.

Annual Summary of Investigations Relating to Reading, July 1, 1991 to June 30, 1992. Ed. by Sam Weintraub. 222p. 1993. pap. 23.00 (*0-87207-384-X*) Intl Reading.

Annual Summary of Investigations Relating to Reading, July 1, 1992 to June 30, 1993. Ed. by Sam Weintraub. 228p. 1994. pap. 23.00 (*0-87207-396-3*) Intl Reading.

Annual Survey of African Law, Vol. 3: 1969. Ed. by N. N. Rubin & E. Cotran. 416p. 1973. 45.00 (*0-7146-2948-0*, Pub. by F Cass Pubs UK) Intl Spec Bk.

Annual Survey of American Law, 1942-1991, 56 vols., Set. Ed. by New York University School of Law Staff. LC 46-30523. 1942. lib. bdg. 2,057.50 (*0-379-12200-6*) Oceana.

***Annual Survey of American Law, 1980-1991, 22 vols., Set.** Ed. by New York University School of Law Staff. 807.50 (*0-614-02966-X*) Oceana.

Annual Survey of American Poetry, 1985. Ed. by Roth Publishing, Inc., Staff. LC 86-62135. 300p. 1987. 34.95 (*0-89609-266-6*) Roth Pub Inc.

Annual Survey of American Poetry, 1986. Ed. by Roth Publishing, Inc Staff. LC 86-62135. 279p. 1987. 34.95 (*0-89609-272-0*) Roth Pub Inc.

Annual Survey of Australian Law, 1976-1990, 15 vols., Set. 1993. 1,125.00 (*0-685-70250-2*, Pub. by Law Bk Co) W W Gaunt.

Annual Survey of Australian Law 1990. Ed. by R. Baxt & G. Kewley. xxxii, 499p. 1991. 110.00 (*0-685-50928-1*, Pub. by Law Bk Co) W W Gaunt.

Annual Survey of Bankruptcy. William L. Norton, Jr. et al. LC 93-71459. 1979. 145.00 (*0-685-59826-8*) Clark Boardman Callaghan.

Annual Survey of Communication Services. (Illus.). 65p. (Orig.). (C). 1993. pap. text ed. 30.00 (*1-56806-463-2*) Diane Pub.

Annual Survey of English Law, 1928-1940, 13 vols., Set. London School of Economics & Political Science Department of Law Staff. LC 87-83497. 5000p. 1988. reprint ed. Price per volume $82.50. lib. bdg. 1,024.00 (*0-912004-63-0*) W W Gaunt.

Annual Survey of Massachusetts Law: 1954-1983, 33 vols., Set. 1,155.00 (*0-8377-9020-4*) Rothman.

Annual Survey of South African Law, 45 vols., Set. University of Witwatersrand School of Law Staff. 1991. reprint ed. 2,545.00 (*0-685-68182-3*, Pub. by Juta SA) W W Gaunt.

Annual Survey of South African Law 1991. Ed. by C. Lewis et al. 781p. 1992. write for info. (*0-7021-2939-9*, Pub. by Juta SA) W W Gaunt.

Annual Symposium on Microlithography, 10th: September 1990, Sunnyvale, CA. Ed. by J. N. Wiley. 1991. 62.00 (*0-8194-0605-8*, VOL. 1496) SPIE.

Annual Symposium on Principles of Programming Languages, No. 15. (Illus.). 329p. 1988. pap. text ed. 28.00 (*0-89791-252-7*) Assn Compu Machinery.

***Annual Tax Planning Guide for S Corporations, Partnerships & LLCs.** M. Kevin Bryant. 500p. 1994. per. 85.00 (*1-886035-00-8*) Pro Tax & Business.

Annual Technical Conference, 43rd: Proceedings of the Society of Plastics Engineers, Sheraton Washington Hotel, Washington, D. C., April 29-May 2, 1985. Society of Plastics Engineers Staff. 1379p. reprint ed. pap. 180.00 (*0-8357-5618-1*, 2025358) Bks Demand.

Annual Technical Meeting of the Institute of Environmental Sciences Staff: Proceedings of the Annual Technical Meeting of the Institute of Environmental Sciences, Fort Worth, Texas, April 1978. Annual Technical Meeting of the Institute of Environmental Sciences Staff. LC 62-38584. (Illus.). 511p. 1978. pap. text ed. 75.00 (*0-915414-18-X*) Inst Environ Sci.

Annual Technical Meeting of the Institute of Environmental Sciences Staff: Proceedings of the Annual Technical Meeting of the Institute of Environmental Sciences, Fort Worth, Texas, April 1978. Annual Technical Meeting of the Institute of Environmental Sciences Staff. LC 62-38584. (Illus.). 456p. 1980. pap. text ed. 75.00 (*0-915414-20-1*) Inst Environ Sci.

Annual Technical Session Proceedings, 1991: Inelastic Behavior & Design of Frames. Multi Conference Attendees Staff. Ed. by Yixian Gu. 500p. (Orig.). 1991. pap. text ed. 55.00 (*1-879749-51-3*) Structural Stability.

Annual Technical Session Proceedings 1992: Earthquake Stability Problems in Eastern North America. Ed. by Yixian Gu. 420p. 1992. pap. text ed. 55.00 (*1-879749-52-1*) Structural Stability.

Annual Technical Session Proceedings, 1993. Ed. by James M. Ricles. 434p. (Orig.). 1993. pap. 50.00 (*1-879749-54-8*) Structural Stability.

Annual Update Program Workbook. Van K. Tharp. 1989. pap. 145.00 (*0-935219-06-4*) Invest Psych Consult.

Annual Uranium Seminar: Proceedings, No. 5. LC 81-71601. (Illus.). 187p. 1982. text ed. 5.00 (*0-89520-291-3*) SMM&E Inc.

Annual Uranium Seminar, 3rd: Proceedings. LC 79-48044. (Illus.). 177p. 1980. pap. 20.00 (*0-89520-260-3*) SMM&E Inc.

Annual Workshop on Formal Approaches to Slavic Linguistics. Ed. by Sergey Avrutin et al. (Michigan Slavic Materials Ser.: Vol. 36). 1994. pap. 26.00 (*0-930042-74-3*) Mich Slavic Pubns.

Annual World's Best Science Fiction, 1988. Ed. by Donald A. Wollheim. 1988. pap. 3.50 (*0-318-33026-1*) DAW Bks.

Annual, 1984: Developing Human Resources. Ed. by J. William Pfeiffer & Leonard D. Goodstein. LC 73-92841. (Illus.). 292p. (Orig.). 1984. pap. 39.95 (*0-88390-010-6*); ring bd. 89.95 (*0-88390-009-2*) Pfeiffer & Co.

Annual, 1985: Developing Human Resources. Ed. by Leonard D. Goodstein & J. William Pfeiffer. LC 73-92841. (Human Resource Development Ser.). (Illus.). 294p. (Orig.). 1985. pap. 39.95 (*0-88390-012-2*); ring bd. 89.95 (*0-88390-011-4*) Pfeiffer & Co.

Annual, 1986: Developing Human Resources. Ed. by J. William Pfeiffer & Leonard D. Goodstein. LC 73-92841. (Human Resource Development Ser.). (Illus.). 294p. (Orig.). 1986. pap. text ed. 39.95 (*0-88390-014-9*); ring bd. 89.95 (*0-88390-013-0*) Pfeiffer & Co.

Annual 1987: Developing Human Resources. Ed. by J. William Pfeiffer. LC 86-643030. (Human Resource Development Ser.). (Illus.). 294p. (Orig.). 1987. pap. 39.95 (*0-88390-016-5*); ring bd. 89.95 (*0-88390-015-7*) Pfeiffer & Co.

Annual 1988: Developing Human Resources. Ed. by J. William Pfeiffer. LC 86-643030. (Human Resource Development Ser.). (Illus.). 293p. (Orig.). 1988. pap. 39.95 (*0-88390-018-1*); ring bd. 89.95 (*0-88390-017-3*) Pfeiffer & Co.

Annual, 1989: Developing Human Resources. Ed. by J. William Pfeiffer. LC 86-643030. (Human Resource Development Ser.). (Illus.). 291p. (Orig.). 1989. pap. 39.95 (*0-88390-020-3*); ring bd. 89.95 (*0-88390-019-X*) Pfeiffer & Co.

Annual, 1990: Developing Human Resources. Ed. by J. William Pfeiffer. LC 86-643030. (Human Resource Development Ser.). (Illus.). 294p. (Orig.). 1990. pap. 39.95 (*0-88390-022-X*); ring bd. 89.95 (*0-88390-021-1*) Pfeiffer & Co.

Annual 1990, Illustrators of Children's Books. 1991. pap. 34.95 (*0-88708-135-5*, Picture Book Studio) S&S Childrens.

Annual, 1991: Developing Human Resources. Ed. by J. William Pfeiffer. LC 86-643030. (Human Resource Development Ser.). (Illus.). 309p. 1991. pap. text ed. 39.95 (*0-88390-289-3*); ring bd. 89.95 (*0-88390-288-5*) Pfeiffer & Co.

Annual, 1992: Developing Human Resources. Ed. by J. William Pfeiffer. LC 86-643030. (Human Resource Development Ser.). (Illus.). 294p. (Orig.). 1992. pap. 39.95 (*0-88390-305-9*); ring bd. 89.95 (*0-88390-304-0*) Pfeiffer & Co.

Annual, 1993: Developing Human Resources. Ed. by J. William Pfeiffer. LC 86-643030. (Human Resource Development Ser.). (Illus.). 294p. (Orig.). 1993. pap. 39.95 (*0-88390-353-9*); ring bd. 89.95 (*0-88390-352-0*) Pfeiffer & Co.

Annual '91: Illustrators of Children's Books - Bologna International Children's Book Fair. (Illus.). 196p. 1991. pap. 34.95 (*0-88708-164-9*, Picture Book Studio) S&S Childrens.

Annuals. Derek Fell. (American Garden Association's Garden Guides Ser.). (Illus.). 192p. 1993. 9.98 (*0-8317-6936-X*) Smithmark.

***Annuals.** Marston. 1994. pap. text ed. 12.99 (*0-517-13453-5*) Random Hse Value.

Annuals. Ed. by Sunset Staff. LC 91-66252. 96p. 1992. pap. text ed. 9.99 (*0-376-03064-X*) Sunset Menlo Pk.

Annuals: A Beginner's Guide to a Colorful Garden. (Illus.). 64p. 1993. spiral bd. 5.98 (*1-56173-753-4*, 3615500) Pubns Intl Ltd.

Annuals: A Gardeners's Guide. (Illus.). 96p. 1993. per., pap. 6.95 (*0-945352-76-X*) Bklyn Botanic.

Annuals: How to Select, Grow & Enjoy. Derek Fell. LC 83-82466. (Illus.). 160p. 1983. pap. 12.95 (*0-89586-240-9*) Price Stern.

***Annuals & Bedding Plants.** Nigel Colborn. (Illus.). 96p. 1995. 22.95 (*1-57076-010-1*, Trafalgar Sq Pub) Trafalgar.

***Annuals & Bulbs.** Text by Rob Proctor. LC 95-13796. (Successful Organic Gardening Ser.). 1995. write for info. (*0-87596-669-1*) Rodale Pr Inc.

***Annuals & Bulbs.** Text by Rob Proctor. LC 95-13796. (Successful Organic Gardening Ser.). 1995. pap. write for info. (*0-87596-670-5*) Rodale Pr Inc.

Annuals & Perennials. Sunset Books Staff. 216p. 1993. pap. 15.99 (*0-376-03066-6*) Sunset Menlo Pk.

Annuals & Surveys Appearing in Legal Periodicals: An Annotated Listing. Comp. by Eleanor DeLashmitt. 1987. ring bd. write for info. (*0-8377-2033-8*) Rothman.

Annuals for Connoisseurs: Classics & Novelties from Abelmoschus to Zinnia. Wayne Winterrowd. (Illus.). 224p. 1993. 25.00 (*0-13-038175-6*, Horticulture Bk) P-H Gen Ref & Trav.

Annuities. David Shapiro & Thomas F. Streiff. LC 92-19521. 125p. 1992. pap. 24.95 (*0-7931-0379-7*, 540410) Dearborn Finan.

Annuities, Mutual Funds & Life Insurance As Investment Products. Institute of Financial Education Staff. 1988. pap. 32.95 (*0-912857-46-3*) Inst Finan Educ.

Annulenes, Benzo-Hetero-, Homoderivatives & Their Valence Isomers, 3 Vols. Alexandru T. Balaban. 1987. Vol. I 304 p. 149.00 (*0-8493-6880-4*, CRC Reprint); Vol. III 208 p. 131.00 (*0-8493-6882-0*, CRC Reprint) Franklin.

Annulenes, Benzo-Hetero-, Homoderivatives & Their Valence Isomers, 3 Vols., Set. Alexandru T. Balaban. 1987. 156.00 (*0-8493-6879-0*, QD341) CRC Pr.

Annulenes, Benzo-Hetero-, Homoderivatives & Their Valence Isomers, 3 Vols., Vol. 2. Alexandru T. Balaban. 1987. Vol. II 232 p. Apple II 139.00 (*0-8493-6881-2*, CRC Reprint) Franklin.

Annulet of Gilt. Phoebe A. Taylor. (Asey Mayo Cape Cod Ser.). 288p. 1986. reprint ed. pap. 6.00 (*0-88150-078-X*, Foul Play) Countryman.

Annulment. Joseph P. Zwack. 5.95 (*0-317-52389-9*, BN 3004) Harper SF.

Annulment: Do You Have a Case? 2nd rev. ed. Terence E. Tierney & Joseph J. Campo. LC 93-7090. 152p. 1993. pap. 9.95 (*0-8189-0667-7*) Alba.

Annulment-Your Chance to Remarry Within the Catholic Church: A Step-by-Step Guide Using the New Code of Canon Law. Joseph P. Zwack. LC 83-47739. (Using the New Code of Canon Law Ser.). 144p. (Orig.). 1983. pap. 11.00 (*0-06-250990-X*, BN-3004) Harper SF.

Annulments. 5th rev. ed. Lawrence G. Wrenn. 145p. (Orig.). 1988. pap. 10.00 (*0-943616-42-5*) Canon Law Soc.

Annunciation. Ellen Gilchrist. 1985. 14.95 (*0-316-31302-5*); pap. 12.95 (*0-316-31308-4*) Little.

An Asterisk (*) at the beginning of an entry indicates that the title is appearing in BIP for the first time.

347

A

Annunciation. David Plante. LC 93-44724. 1994. 21.95 (*0-395-68091-3*) Ticknor & Fields.

***Annunciation of the Theotokos, Vol. 10.** Monks of New Skete Staff. Tr. by Laurence Mancuso. (Liturgical Music Ser.: Vol. I). 35p. (Orig.). 1995. pap. 15.00 (*0-935129-33-2*) Monks of New Skete.

Annunciations. Charles Tomlinson. (Oxford Poets Ser.). 64p. 1989. pap. 10.95 (*0-19-282680-8*) OUP.

Annunciations to Anyone: The Disclosure of Authority in Writing & Painting. John W. Erwin. LC 90-34175. (Literature & the Visual Arts: New Foundations Ser.: Vol. 5). 314p. (C). 1991. text ed. 62.50 (*0-8204-1300-3*) P Lang Pubs.

Annunciator Sequences & Specifications. 1992. reprint ed. pap. 40.00 (*0-87664-346-2*, S18.1) Instru Soc.

Annus Mirabilis: A Bibliography of Medieval Times. Jill Phillips. (Bibliographies for Librarians Ser.). 1980. lib. bdg. 250.00 (*0-8490-1398-4*) Gordon Pr.

Annus Mirabilis of Sir Isaac Newton: An Exhibit of Books & Manuscripts from the History of Science Collection. George Basalla & Robert Palter. (Illus.). 32p. 1966. 5.00 (*0-87959-121-8*) U of Tex H Ransom Ctr.

Ano' Ano: The Seed. Kristin Zambucka. 25.00 (*0-935038-01-9*); pap. 17.00 (*0-935038-00-0*) Mana Pub.

Ano de Gato Galano (Calico Cat's Year) Donald Charles. Tr. by Lada Kratky. (Spanish Calico Cat Storybooks Ser.). (Illus.). 32p. (SPA.). (J). (ps-3). 1984. lib. bdg. 12.23 (*0-516-33461-1*); pap. 3.95 (*0-516-53461-0*) Childrens.

Ano del Ras de Mar. Manuel C. Diaz. LC 93-72253. (Coleccion Caniqui Ser.). 79p. (Orig.). (SPA.). 1993. pap. 9.95 (*0-89729-699-0*) Ediciones.

Ano Lani: The Hawaiian Monarchy Years. Linda Ching & Malcolm N. Chun. (Illus.). 168p. 1993. 21.00 (*0-9619891-3-0*) Hawaiian Goddesses.

Ano Nuevo: A Children's Guide. rev. ed. Judy Beach-Balthis. Ed. by Frank S. Balthis. (Children's Guides on the National Parks Ser.). (Illus.). 24p. (Orig.). (J). (gr. k-8). 1994. pap. 3.95 (*0-918355-02-8*) Firehole Pr.

Ano 501: La Conquista Continua. (SPA.). (C). 1994. pap. 18.00 (*0-89608-488-4*) South End Pr.

Anobiidae of Ohio. Richard E. White. (Bulletin New Ser.: Vol. I, No. 4). 1962. 3.00 (*0-86727-046-2*) Ohio Bio Survey.

Anode Resistance Fundamentals & Applications - Classic Papers & Reviews. Ed. by R. L. Benedict. LC 86-63053. (Illus.). 201p. 1986. 53.00 (*0-915567-25-3*) NACE Intl.

Anodes for Electrowinning: Proceedings of the Sessions. Ed. by Douglas J. Robinson & Stephen E. James. LC 84-60151. (Illus.). 119p. reprint ed. pap. 34.00 (*0-8357-5619-X*, 2032592) Bks Demand.

Anodic Oxidation of Aluminum & Its Alloys. V. F. Henley. (Materials Engineering Practice Ser.). (Illus.). 150p. 1982. text ed. 80.00 (*0-08-026726-2*, A145, A115, Pub. by Pergamon Repr UK) Franklin.

Anodic Protection: Theory & Practice in the Prevention of Corrosion. Olen L. Riggs, Jr. & Carl E. Locke. LC 80-20412. 298p. 1981. 85.00 (*0-306-40597-0*, Plenum Pr) Plenum.

***Anodized Aluminum: Building Well...the Architectural Uses of the New Anodized Aluminum.** (Illus.). v, 200p. (Orig.). 1995. pap. 195.00 (*0-7605-1891-2*) Rector Pr.

***Anodized Aluminum Electrolytic Two Step Color Standards for Architectural Applications.** (Illus.). 60p. (Orig.). 1995. pap. 130.00 (*0-7605-1892-0*) Rector Pr.

***Anodizing Aluminum: The Finish of Choixe.** (Illus.). 60p. (Orig.). 1995. pap. 120.00 (*0-7605-1893-9*) Rector Pr.

Anodizing, Plating & Other Inorganic Processes. LC 82-60312. 153p. 1992. pap. text ed. 32.00 (*0-87263-422-1*) SME.

Anodyne Necklace. Martha Grimes. 256p. 1990. reprint ed. mass mkt. 5.99 (*0-440-10280-4*) Dell.

Anointed. Ann-Ree Colton & Jonathan Murro. LC 87-70497. (Illus.). 480p. 1987. 21.95 (*0-917189-06-X*) Colton Found.

Anointed Community: The Holy Spirit in the Johannine Tradition. Gary M. Burge. LC 86-29226. 287p. (Orig.). reprint ed. pap. 81.80 (*0-8357-4357-8*, 2037185) Bks Demand.

***Anointed One: Messiah.** W. Stan McKibbon. 215p. (Orig.). 1994. pap. write for info. (*0-9642975-0-7*) S McKibbon Min.

Anointed Praise: The Ministry of Music in the Church Today. Curtis Redmon. (Practical Church Ser.). 54p. 1992. pap. text ed. 4.95 (*1-881685-00-4*) LUA Stand Minist.

Anointed to Fly. Gloria Gayles. 148p. (Orig.). 1991. 25.00 (*0-86316-304-1*); pap. 12.00 (*0-86316-309-2*) Writers & Readers.

Anointed to Serve: The Story of the Assemblies of God. William W. Menzies. LC 79-146707. (Illus.). 440p. 1971. 15.95 (*0-88243-465-9*, 02-0465) Gospel Pub.

Anointing. large type ed. Benny Hinn. 1993. 20.95 (*0-8161-5639-5*) Hall.

Anointing of His Spirit. Smith Wigglesworth. 220p. 1994. pap. 9.99 (*0-89283-863-9*, Vine Bks) Servant.

Anointing of Joy. Sally Glenn. 80p. (Orig.). 1989. pap. write for info. (*0-318-65036-3*) S Glenn NC.

Anointing of Peace. Sally Glenn. 96p. (Orig.). 1989. pap. write for info. (*0-318-65037-1*) S Glenn NC.

Anointing of the Sick. Karl Rahner. 1979. pap. 4.95 (*0-87193-108-7*) Dimension Bks.

Anointing of the Sick: A Theological & Canonical Study. Andrew Cuschieri. 198p. (Orig.). (C). 1993. lib. bdg. 39.50 (*0-8191-8832-8*) U Pr of Amer.

Anointing the Sick. Maria Roccapriore. LC 80-65722. (Illus.). 144p. (Orig.). 1980. pap. 2.95 (*0-8189-1160-3*, 160, Pub. by Alba Bks AT) Alba.

Anointing the Unsanctified. Mark Hanby. 196p. (Orig.). 1993. pap. 8.99 (*1-56043-071-0*) Destiny Image.

Anointing with the Spirit: The Rite of Confirmation: The Use of Oil & Chrism. Gerard Austin. 178p. 1992. pap. 12.95 (*0-8146-6070-3*, Pueblo Bks) Liturgical Pr.

***Anolis Lizards of the Caribbean: Ecology, Evolution, & Plate Tectonics.** Jonathan Roughgarden. (Oxford Series in Ecology & Evolution). (Illus.). 224p. 1995. 59.95 (*0-19-506731-2*); pap. 29.95 (*0-19-509605-3*) OUP.

Anomalies & Curiosities of Medicine. George M. Gould & Walter L. Pyle. Date not set. reprint ed. write for info. (*0-930405-58-7*) Norman SF.

Anomalies, Geometry & Topology: Proceedings of the Symposium, Argonne, Illnois March 28-30, 1985. Ed. by W. A. Bardeen & A. R. White. 558p. 1985. 104.00 (*9971-978-69-5*); pap. 55.00 (*9971-978-72-5*) World Scientific Pub.

Anomalies in Geology: Physical, Chemical, Biological. LC 89-90680. (Catalog of Geological Anomalies Ser.). (Illus.). 335p. 1989. 18.95 (*0-915554-23-2*) Sourcebook.

Anomalies of Binocular Vision: Diagnosis & Management. Rutstein & Daum. 400p. 1995. 54.95 (*0-8016-6916-2*) Mosby Yr Bk.

Anomalies of Geomagnetic Variations in the Southwestern United States. Ulrich Schmucker. LC 74-627675. (University of California, Scripps Institution of Oceanography, Bulletin: Vol. 13). 178p. reprint ed. pap. 50.80 (*0-8357-5620-3*, 2021289) Bks Demand.

Anomalies of the English Law. Samuel B. Chester. 287p. 1980. reprint ed. lib. bdg. 22.50 (*0-8377-0426-X*) Rothman.

Anomalies of the Fetal Head, Neck & Neural Axis: Ultrasound Diagnosis & Management. Frank A. Chervenak et al. (Illus.). 192p. 1988. text ed. 83.95 (*0-7216-1957-6*) Saunders.

Anomalistic Psychology: A Study of Magical Thinking. 2nd ed. Ed. by Leonard Zusne & Warren Jones. 328p. (C). 1989. text ed. 69.95 (*0-8058-0507-9*); pap. 36.00 (*0-8058-0508-7*) L Erlbaum Assocs.

Anomalous Dispersion Techniques & Calculations Tutorial, Philadelphia, 1988. (American Crystallographic Association Lecture Notes Ser.: No. 8). 1991. pap. 15.00 (*0-685-51613-X*) Polycrystal Bk Serv.

Anomalous Magnetic Field of the World Ocean. Gorodnitsky. 1994. write for info. (*0-8493-8937-2*) CRC Pr.

Anomalous Nuclear Effects in Deuterium - Solid Systems, No. 228: AIP Conference Proceedings. Ed. by Steven E. Jones et al. LC 91-55245. (Illus.). 344p. 1991. text ed. 95.00 (*0-88318-833-3*) Am Inst Physics.

Anomalous Photoconductivity. M. I. Korsunskii. 180p. 1973. text ed. 55.50 (*0-7065-1369-X*, Pub. by Keter Pub IS) Coronet Bks.

Anomalous States: Irish Writing & the Post-Colonial Moment. David Lloyd. LC 93-3105. (Post-Contemporary Interventions Ser.). 184p. 1993. lib. bdg. 42.95 (*0-8223-1326-X*); pap. text ed. 14.95 (*0-8223-1344-8*) Duke.

Anomalouschool. 2nd ed. Paul E. Johnson. (Why Ser.: Sect. 1, Vol. 1; Pubn. 18, Vol. 1). 107p. 1981. pap. 10.00 (*0-685-28931-1*) P E Johnson.

***Anomeric Effect.** Eusebio Juaristi. (New Directions in Organic & Biological Chemistry Ser.). 256p. 1994. 59.95 (*0-8493-8941-0*, 8941) CRC Pr.

Anomeric Effect & Associated Stereoelectronic Effects. Ed. by Gregory R. J. Thatcher. LC 93-34423. 305p. 1994. 74.95 (*0-8412-2729-2*) Am Chemical.

Anomie: History & Meanings. Marco Orru. LC 86-32144. 288p. (C). 1987. text ed. 65.00 (*0-04-301267-1*) Routledge Chapman & Hall.

Anomie & Aspirations: A Reinterpretation of Durkheim's Theory. Ralph B. Ginsberg. Ed. by Harriet Zuckerman & Robert K. Merton. LC 79-8999. (Dissertations on Sociology Ser.). 1980. lib. bdg. 33.95 (*0-405-12969-6*) Ayer.

Anomie & Social Change in India. Satyendra Tripathi. 1986. 27.00 (*0-685-14208-6*, Pub. by Rawat II) S Asia.

Anomodontia. Gillian M. King. (Encyclopedia of Paleoherpetology Ser.: Pt. 17 C). 174p. 1988. pap. text ed. 195.00 (*0-89574-250-0*, Pub. by Gustav Fischer Verlag) VCH Pubs.

Anomodontia: Encyclopedia of Paleoherpetology 17 C. Gillian M. King. (Illus.). 174p. 1988. pap. text ed. 119.95 (*3-437-30483-6*) Lubrecht & Cramer.

Anon. Walter G. Perz. 176p. 1992. 7.95 (*1-55523-513-1*) Winston-Derek.

Anonimo: Notes on Pictures & Works of Art in Italy Made by an Anonymous Writer in the Sixteenth Century. 1972. reprint ed. lib. bdg. 16.95 (*0-405-08208-8*, Pub. by Blom Pubns UK) Ayer.

***Anonym.** Serge Bramley. 128p. Date not set. 45.00 (*3-929078-32-5*) Dist Art Pubs.

Anonyme. Ralph Gibson. (Illus.). 88p. 1986. 19.95 (*0-912810-53-X*) Lustrum Pr.

Anonymer Kommentar Zu Platons Theaetet. Plato. xxxvii, 62p. (GER.). 1905. write for info. (*0-318-70540-0*, Pub. by Georg Olms GW) Lubrecht & Cramer.

Anonymity. Susan Bergman. LC 93-27136. 1994. 20.00 (*0-374-25407-9*) FS&G.

Anonymity: A Study in the Philosophy of Alfred Schutz. Maurice Natanson. LC 85-45989. (Studies in Phenomenology & Existential Philosophy). 192p. 1986. 25.00 (*0-253-30746-5*) Ind U Pr.

Anonymity: The Secret Life of an American Family. Susan Bergman. 208p. 1995. pap. 10.99 (*0-446-67119-3*) Warner Bks.

Anonymity & Identity. Leslie A. Brothers et al. (Illus.). 40p. 1993. 8.00 (*0-935519-15-7*) Anderson Gal.

Anonymous & Pseudononymous Publications of Twentieth Century Authors. M. C. Dobelis. Date not set. 16.95 (*0-918230-06-3*) Barnstable.

Anonymous Client. J. P. Hailey. 300p. 1989. 16.95 (*1-55611-124-X*) D I Fine.

Anonymous Dinner Guest. Scott Neuman. 1988. 3.00 (*0-685-25016-4*) Windless Orchard.

***Anonymous Dutch Manuscript on West Africa in the Mid-Seventeenth Century: An Anonymous Dutch Manuscript.** Ed. by Adam Jones. LC 94-43758. (African Historical Sources Ser.: No. 10). 1995. 29.00 (*0-918456-73-8*) African Studies Assn.

Anonymous Letters. Robert Saudek. LC 75-38671. (Foundations of Criminal Justice Ser.). (Illus.). reprint ed. 37.50 (*0-404-09182-2*) AMS Pr.

Anonymous Life of William Cecil, Lord Burghley. Ed. by Alan G. Smith. LC 89-13815. (Studies in British History: Vol. 20). 160p. 1990. lib. bdg. 69.95 (*0-88946-481-2*) E Mellen.

Anonymous Lover. John Logan. 1973. 5.95 (*0-87140-564-4*) Liveright.

Anonymous Miss Addams. Kasey Michaels. 192p. (Orig.). 1989. pap. 2.95 (*0-380-75668-4*) Avon.

Anonymous Miss Addams. braille ed. Kasey Michael. 322p. 1992. vinyl bd. 25.76 (*1-56956-038-2*, BR8670) W A T Braille.

Anonymous Miss Addams. large type ed. Leigh Michaels. (Orig.). 1991. pap. 17.95 (*0-7927-0748-6*, Curley Lrg Print) Chivers N Amer.

Anonymous Old French Translation of the Pseudo-Turpin "Chronicle" Ronald N. Walpole. LC 78-70246. (Medieval Academy Bks.: No. 89). 1979. 25.00 (*0-910956-68-5*) Medieval Acad.

Anonymous Parts of the Old English Hexateuch: Latin-Old English, Old-English Latin Glossary. Ed. by Andrea B. Smith. 471p. 1985. 81.00 (*0-85991-197-7*) Boydell & Brewer.

Anonymous Toil: A Reevaluation of the American Radical Novel in the Twentieth Century. Alan A. Block. 152p. (Orig.). (C). 1992. lib. bdg. 46.00 (*0-8191-8558-2*); pap. text ed. 23.50 (*0-8191-8559-0*) U Pr of Amer.

Anonymous Was a Woman. Mirra Bank. 1979. pap. 12.95 (*0-312-04186-1*) St Martin.

Anonymous Woman Her Work Wrought in the Seventeenth Century. Kathleen A. Epstein. LC 92-90280. (Illus.). 52p. (Orig.). 1992. pap. 19.95 (*0-9633331-1-9*) Curious Works.

Anonymously Yours. Richard Peck. (J). 1991. 12.95 (*0-671-74162-4*, Julian Messner) Silver Burdett Pr.

Anonyms: A Dictionary of Revealed Authorship. William Cushing. 1968. reprint ed. 230.00 (*3-487-02714-3*) Adlers Foreign Bks.

Anonyms: A Dictionary of Revealed Authorship. William Cushing. iv, 829p. 1969. reprint ed. 154.70 (*0-685-67778-8*, 05102516, Pub. by Georg Olms GW) Lubrecht & Cramer.

***Anopheline Names - Their Derivations & Histories.** J. Kitzmiller. (Thomas Say Monographs: Vol. 8). 632p. 1982. 75.00 (*0-614-05663-2*) Entomol Soc.

Anophthalmic Socket. Stephen L. Bosniak. 1990. text ed. 85.00 (*0-07-105251-8*) Hlth Prof Div.

Anophthalmic Socket. Stephen L. Bosniak & Byron C. Smith. (Advances in Ophthalmic Plastic & Reconstructive Surgery Ser.: No. 8). (Illus.). 304p. 1990. 82.50 (*0-08-040292-5*, Pub. by PPI UK) McGraw.

Anoqcou: Ceremony Is Life Itself. Gkisedtanamoogk & Frances Hancock. (Illus.). 60p. 1993. per. 6.50 (*0-9624626-6-7*) Astarte Shell Pr.

Anorectal Malformations: A Surgeon's Experience. Subir K. Chatterjee. LC 93-5318. 228p. 1993. 45.00 (*0-19-262453-9*) OUP.

Anorectal, Presacral & Sacral Tumors: Anatomy, Physiology, Pathogenesis & Management. S. Arthur Localio et al. (Illus.). 378p. 1987. text ed. 115.00 (*0-7216-1982-7*) Saunders.

Anorectic Agents: Mechanisms of Action & Tolerance. Ed. by Silvio Garattini & Rosario Samanin. LC 80-6089. (Monographs of Mario Negri Institute for Pharmacological Research, Milan). (Illus.). 256p. reprint ed. pap. 73.00 (*0-7837-7114-2*, 2046943) Bks Demand.

Anorectic Bodies: A Feminist & Sociological Perspective On Anorexia Nervosa. Morag MacSween. LC 93-7246. 1993. write for info. (*0-415-02846-9*) Routledge.

Anorexia. Joan Mallick. Ed. by J. J. Head. LC 86-72198. (Carolina Biology Readers Ser.: No. 173). (Illus.). 16p. (Orig.). (YA). (gr. 10 up). 1987. pap. text ed. 2.75 (*0-89278-373-7*, 45-9773) Carolina Biological.

Anorexia. Jann Mitchell. 28p. (Orig.). 1985. pap. 1.55 (*0-89486-337-1*, 5232B) Hazelden.

***Anorexia & Bulimia.** Rita Milios. 87p. (YA). (gr. 7-12). 1993. pap. write for info. (*1-57515-030-1*) PPI Pubng.

Anorexia & Bulimia. Dayna Wolhart. LC 88-21553. (Facts About Ser.). (Illus.). 48p. (J). (gr. 5-6). 1988. text ed. 12.95 (*0-89686-416-2*, Crstwood Hse) Silver Burdett Pr.

Anorexia & Bulimia: Anatomy of a Social Epidemic. Richard A. Gordon. 1990. pap. 18.95 (*0-631-15928-2*) Blackwell Pubs.

Anorexia & Bulimia: Anatomy of a Social Epidemic. Richard A. Gordon. 1990. 27.95 (*0-631-14851-5*) Blackwell Pubs.

Anorexia & Bulimia Nervosa: How to Help. Marilyn Duker & Roger Slade. 256p. 1988. 85.00 (*0-335-09836-3*, Open Univ Pr); pap. 29.00 (*0-335-09832-0*, Open Univ Pr) Taylor & Francis.

Anorexia & Bulimia Nervosa: Practical Approaches. Ed. by Derek W. Scott. (Psychoanalytic Crosscurrents Ser.). 240p. 1988. 45.00x (*0-8147-7884-4*) NYU Pr.

Anorexia Nervosa. Crisp. 1990. 33.00 (*0-685-49102-1*) Saunders.

Anorexia Nervosa. Cheryl G. Mercier & Waln K. Brown. 20p. 1989. 2.95 (*1-56456-023-6*, 223) W Gladden Found.

Anorexia Nervosa. R. L. Palmer. 160p. 1981. mass mkt. 4.95 (*0-14-022065-8*, Penguin Bks) Viking Penguin.

Anorexia Nervosa. Ed. by H. Remschmidt & M. H. Schmidt. LC 90-4848. (Child & Youth Psychiatry: European Perspectives Ser.: Vol. 1). (Illus.). 270p. 1990. text ed. 64.00 (*0-88937-041-9*) Hogrefe & Huber Pubs.

Anorexia Nervosa. Helmut Thoma. LC 67-27020. 342p. 1967. text ed. 50.00 (*0-8236-0360-1*) Intl Univs Pr.

Anorexia Nervosa: A Clinician's Guide to Treatment. Walter Vandereycken & Rolf Meermann. LC 84-72039. xiv, 252p. 1984. 79.25x (*3-11-009531-9*) De Gruyter.

Anorexia Nervosa: A Guide for Sufferers & Their Families. R. L. Palmer. 144p. 1989. pap. 11.95 (*0-14-010034-2*, Penguin Bks) Viking Penguin.

***Anorexia Nervosa: The Historical & Cultural Specificity.** S. E. van't Hof. 282p. 1995. 44.50x (*90-265-1424-7*, Pub. by Swets Pub Serv NE) Taylor & Francis.

Anorexia Nervosa - Bulimia: A Source Guide. 1991. lib. bdg. 250.00 (*0-8490-4886-9*) Gordon Pr.

Anorexia Nervosa & Bulimia: An Annotated Bibliography. Izabella Taler. LC 85-14963. (CompuBibs Ser.: No. 13). 65p. 1985. pap. 15.00 (*0-914791-12-5*) Vantage Info.

Anorexia Nervosa & Bulimia: Diagnosis & Treatment. James E. Mitchell. LC 84-26933. (Continuing Medical Education Ser.: Vol. 3). 222p. 1985. text ed. 29.95 (*0-8166-1388-5*) U of Minn Pr.

Anorexia Nervosa & Bulimic Disorders: Current Perspectives: Proceedings of the Conference on Anorexia Nervosa & Related Disorders Held at University College, Swansea, Wales, on 3-7 September 1984. Ed. by G. I. Szmukler et al. 458p. 1986. 185.00 (*0-08-032704-4*) Franklin.

Anorexia Nervosa & Recovery: A Hunger for Meaning. Karen Way. LC 91-22225. 146p. 1993. pap. 14.95 (*0-918393-95-7*) Harrington Pk.

Anorexia Nervosa & Recovery: A Hunger for Meaning. Karen Way. LC 91-23995. 150p. 1992. lib. bdg. 26.95 (*1-56024-130-6*) Haworth Pr.

***Anorexic Bodies: A Feminist & Sociological Perspective on Anorexia Nervosa.** Morag MacSween. LC 95-9185. 1996. write for info. (*0-415-02847-7*) Routledge.

Anorganisch-Chemische Praparate: Darstellung und Charakterisierung Ausgewahlter Vernindungen. Alfred Golloch et al. (Illus.). xvi, 324p. (GER.). 1985. 60.00 (*3-11-004821-3*) De Gruyter.

Anorthosites. Lewis D. Ashwal. LC 93-9391. (Minerals & Rocks Ser.: Vol. 21). 1993. 119.00 (*0-387-55361-4*) Spr-Verlag.

Anos de Matrimonio en la Novela de Galdos. Robert Kirsner. 1983. pap. 9.95 (*0-88303-037-3*) E Torres & Sons.

Anos De Ofun: Recuerdos, Relatos y Anotaciones. Mercedes Muriedas. LC 92-75279. (Coleccion Caniqui Ser.). (Illus.). 85p. (Orig.). (SPA.). 1993. pap. 9.95 (*0-89729-667-2*) Ediciones.

Anos Muchos y Buenos: "Good Years & Many More" Turkey's Sephardim: 1492-1992. Ayse Gursan-Salzmann. 80p. 1992. write for info. (*0-9603924-2-4*); pap. write for info. (*0-9603924-1-6*) Blue Flower.

Anos Sorprendentes: Como Comprender los Cambios en Su Adolescente. Cliff Schimmels & Hank Resnik. Ed. by Juan Callejas et al. Tr. by Judith Ferdinandi. (Destrezas para la Adolescencia Ser.). (Illus.). 132p. (Orig.). (SPA.). 1987. pap. text ed. 6.85 (*0-933419-20-1*) Quest Intl.

Another Account of the Incidents, from Which the Title, & a Part of the Story of Shakspeare's Tempest Were Derived. George Chalmers. LC 72-1051. reprint ed. 29.50 (*0-404-01442-9*) AMS Pr.

Another America: Otra America. Barbara Kingsolver. Tr. by Rebecca Cartes. LC 91-38056. 103p. 1994. pap. 10.95 (*1-878067-57-5*) Seal Pr Feminist.

***Another American: The Politics of Race & Blame.** Kofi B. Hadjor. Date not set. pap. text ed. 15.00 (*0-89608-515-5*) South End Pr.

***Another American: The Politics of Race & Blame.** abr. ed. Kofi B. Hadjor. 256p. Date not set. text ed. 40.00 (*0-89608-516-3*) South End Pr.

Another Antigone. A. R. Gurney. 1988. pap. 4.75 (*0-8222-0051-1*) Dramatists Play.

Another Auntie La La Children's Story: The Clumsy Tooth Fairy. Lucille D. Zegers. LC 92-91121. (Illus.). 64p. (J). 1994. pap. 8.00 (*1-56002-260-4*) Aegina Pr.

Another Birthday? Mary Engelbreit. (Illus.). 32p. 1992. 6.95 (*0-8362-4603-9*) Andrews & McMeel.

Another Birthday. Doris L. Seger. (Illus.). 18p. (J). (gr. k-6). 1988. pap. text ed. 4.25 (*1-55976-134-2*) CEF Press.

Another Black Voice: A Different Drummer. Leonard A. Slade, Jr. LC 87-51041. 65p. 1988. pap. 7.95 (*1-55523-124-1*) Winston-Derek.

Another Blue Strawberry: More Brilliant Cooking Without Recipes. James Haller. LC 83-12727. (Illus.). 110p. 1983. 14.95 (*0-916782-47-6*); pap. 8.95 (*0-916782-46-8*) Harvard Common Pr.

Another Body. Stephen Tapscott. LC 89-61230. (CSU Poetry Ser.: No. XXVII). 83p. (Orig.). 1989. 14.00 (*0-914946-75-7*); pap. 7.00 (*0-914946-76-5*) Cleveland St Univ Poetry Ctr.

Another Book of Verses for Children. Edward V. Lucas. LC 73-37017. (Granger Index Reprint Ser.). (Illus.). 1977. reprint ed. 29.95 (*0-8369-6316-4*) Ayer.

Another Bridge. Brigitte Barrell & Brent Filson. 128p. 1992. 14.95 (*0-9631422-7-5*) Far Hills Pubns.

Another Bridge over the Pacific. Naoshi Koriyama. 1993. 14.95 (*0-533-10385-1*) Vantage.

Another Brown Bag. Jerry M. Jordan. LC 80-36849. (Illus.). 120p. 1980. pap. 9.95 (*0-8298-0406-4*) Pilgrim OH.

Another Celebrated Dancing Bear. Gladys Scheffrin-Falk. LC 89-13152. (Illus.). 32p. (J). (gr. k-2). 1991. text ed. 13.95 (*0-684-19164-4*, C Scribner Sons Young) S&S Childrens.

An Asterisk (*) at the beginning of an entry indicates that the title is appearing in BIP for the first time.

An Asterisk (*) at the beginning of an entry indicates that the title is appearing in BIP for the first time.

Another Wave of Revival. rev. ed. Frank Bartleman. Ed. by John Meyers. Orig. Title: Another Wave Rolls In. 176p. 1982. reprint ed. pap. text ed. 4.99 (0-88368-111-0) Whitaker Hse.

Another Wave Rolls In see Another Wave of Revival

Another Way: A Directory of Accredited Home Study Schools. Sandra K. Donelson. 104p. (Orig.). 1988. pap. 12.95 (0-9616851-1-5) Ed Data Res.

Another Way: An Alternative Path to Health & Personal Growth. Diana Davies. Ed. by Audrey Brinkerhoff. LC 85-73905. (Illus.). 320p. (Orig.). 1986. pap. 9.95 (0-937251-00-3) Another Way.

Another Way: The Tao of Lao Tzu. Gerald Kaminski. LC 93-26269. 86p. 1993. pap. 9.95 (0-931896-15-0) Cove View.

***Another Way of Living.** Jeannine Margolin & Malcolm Margolin. 1995. 37.00 (0-8095-4988-3) Borgo Pr.

Another Way of Putting It: Twenty Short Plays with a Point. Tim Jones & Jim Butterworth. 128p. (YA). (gr. 7-12). 1991. pap. 7.99 (0-87403-854-5, 14-03354) Standard Pub.

***Another Way of Telling.** John Berger. 1995. pap. 17.00 (0-679-73724-3, Vin) Random.

Another Way to Be: Selected Works of Rosario Castellanos. Rosario Castellanos. Ed. & Intro. by Myralyn F. Allgood. LC 89-20530. 192p. 1990. 27.50 (0-8203-1222-3); pap. 13.95 (0-8203-1240-1) U of Ga Pr.

Another Way to Live: Experiencing Intentional Community. James Best. LC 78-51384. 32p. (Orig.). 1978. pap. 3.00 (0-87574-218-1) Pendle Hill.

Another Way's Guide to Growing Your Blue Ribbon Body. Diana Davies. Ed. by Audrey Brinkerhoff. (Illus.). 128p. (Orig.). 1986. pap. 6.95 (0-937251-01-1) Another Way.

Another Wilderness: New Outdoor Writing by Women. Ed. by Susan F. Rogers. 288p. (Orig.). 1994. pap. 14.95 (1-878067-54-0) Seal Pr Feminist.

Another Will Gird You: A Message to the Society of Friends. Mildred B. Young. (C). 1960. pap. 3.00 (0-87574-109-6) Pendle Hill.

Another Woman. Margot Dalton. (Harlequin Promo Ser.). 1994. mass mkt. 3.99 (0-373-83306-7, 1-83306-0) Harlequin Bks.

Another Woman: Women Who Dare. Margot Dalton. (Superromance Ser.). 1993. mass mkt. 3.50 (0-373-70558-1, 1-70558-1) Harlequin Bks.

Another Woman's House. large type ed. Mignon Eberhart. 352p. 1993. reprint ed. lib. bdg. 20.95 (1-56054-557-7) Thorndike Pr.

Another World. Jan Myrdal. LC 93-41239. 1994. 19.95 (1-884468-00-4) Ravenswood Bks.

Another World. Chad Oliver. 1993. reprint ed. lib. bdg. 18.95 (0-89968-356-8, Lghtyr Pr) Buccaneer Bks.

Another World: Wolfi, Aloise, Muller. 56p. 1979. 30.00 (0-906474-00-0, Pub. by Third Eye Centre UK) St Mut.

Another Year in Africa. Rose Zwi. 172p. 1988. reprint ed. pap. 14.95 (0-86975-316-9, Pub. by Ravan Pr ZA) Ohio U Pr.

Another You. Paul Vangelisti. (Illus.). 64p. (Orig.). 1981. pap. 4.00 (0-88031-058-8) Invisible-Red Hill.

Another's Fandango. Lennon. Date not set. 5.95 (0-685-75000-0, 93987) Mel Bay.

Anouilh. Eurydice & Medee. Ed. by Freeman. (Bristol French Texts Ser.). (FRE.). 1992. 18.95 (0-685-49967-7, Pub. by Brstl Class Pr UK) Focus Info Gr.

Anouilh: Five Plays. Jean Anouilh. Tr. by Christopher Fry et al. (Methuen World Dramatists Ser.). 424p. (Orig.). 1986. pap. 9.95 (0-413-14030-X, Pub. by Methuen UK) Heinemann.

Anouilh: Five Plays, Vol. 1. Jean Anouilh. Incl. Romeo & Jeannette. 1987. (0-318-53301-4); Rehearsal. 1987. (0-318-53302-2); Ermine. 1987. (0-318-53303-0); Antigone. 1987. (0-318-53304-9); Eurydice. 1987. (0-318-53305-7); (Mermaid Dramabook Ser.). 340p. (Orig.). 1987. Set pap. 8.95 (0-8090-0710-X) Hill & Wang.

Anouilh: Plays Two. Jean Anouilh. Tr. by Jeremy Sams & Peter Meyer. 1995. pap. 13.95 (0-413-66600-X, A0656, Pub. by Methuen UK) Heinemann.

Anoush: An Opera by Armen Tigranian. Gerald E. Papasian. 59p. 1982. pap. 5.95 (0-8143-1708-1) Wayne St U Pr.

ANOVA: Repeated Measures. Ellen R. Girden. (Quantitative Applications in the Social Sciences Ser.: Vol. 84). (Illus.). 96p. 1992. pap. 9.95 (0-8039-4257-5) Sage.

ANOVA 45: A Flexible Computer Program for the Analysis of Variance-Instructions for Use. Roger J. Weldon & Alan B. Humphrey. LC 70-163009. 80p. reprint ed. pap. 25.00 (0-8357-5621-1, 2022751) Bks Demand.

ANPAO: An American Indian Odyssey. Jamake Highwater. LC 77-9264. (Trophy Bk.). (Illus.). 256p. (J). (gr. 7 up). 1992. pap. 6.95 (0-06-440437-4, Trophy) HarpC Child Bks.

ANPAO: An American Indian Odyssey. Jamake Highwater. LC 77-9264. (Illus.). 256p. (YA). (gr. 7 up). 1993. lib. bdg. 14.89 (0-06-022878-4) HarpC Child Bks.

Anpassung an die Inflation - The Adaption to Inflation. Ed. by Gerald D. Feldman et al. (Veroeffentlichungen der Historischen Kommission zu Berlin, Band 67, Beitraege zu Inflation und Wiederaufbau in Deutschland und Europa 1914-1924: Vol. 8). xvi, 513p. 1986. lib. bdg. 97.70 (0-89925-287-7) De Gruyter.

***Anpassung an Die Inflation - The Adaption to Inflation.** Ed. by Gerald D. Feldman et al. (Veroeffentlichungen der Historischen Kommision Zu Berlin Ser.: Vol. 8). xvi, 513p. 1986. lib. bdg. 97.70 (3-11-009935-7) De Gruyter.

Anphilex '71 Anniversary Philatelic Exhibition Commemorating the 75th Year of the Collectors Club of New York. John J. Boker, Jr. et al. (Illus.). 1971. 12.50 (0-912574-28-3) Collectors.

ANS - ASME Nuclear Energy Conference Proceedings, San Diego, CA, Aug, 23-26, 1992. 384p. 60.00 (0-89448-169-X, 700170) Am Nuclear Soc.

ANS First Regional Conference, Pittsburgh, PA, Sept. 22-23, 1986. 282p. 1986. 30.00 (0-89448-130-4, 700123) Am Nuclear Soc.

ANS US PRO-IPO-110: Three-D Piping IGES Application Protocol Version 1.2. IGES-PDES Organization Staff. 268p. 1994. pap. 200.00 (1-885389-01-9) US Prod Data.

Ansa PAL Tutorial: Programming with the Paradox Application Language. Ansa Software Staff. 224p. 1986. pap. write for info. (0-201-03944-3) Addison-Wesley.

Ansaar Cult Rebuttal to the Slanderers: The Truth about the Ansaarullaii Community in America, Truth Is Truth. Isa Al Haadi Al Mahdi. (Illus.). 624p. (Orig.). 1989. pap. write for info. (0-318-66295-7) Al Mahdi.

Ansata Tarot. B. A. Mertz. 36p. 1985. 15.00 (0-88079-296-5) US Games Syst.

***Anschluss Movement, 1931-1938.** Alfred D. Low. 512p. 1985. 43.50 (0-88033-078-3) East Eur Quarterly.

Anschluss Question in the Weimar Era: A Study of Nationalism in Germany & Austria, 1918-1932. Stanley Suval. LC 73-17174. 264p. reprint ed. pap. 75.30 (0-8357-8026-0, 2034120) Bks Demand.

Anse de Benodet to Presqu'ile De Quiberon. Imray Laurie Norie & Wilson Ltd. Staff. (Illus.). (C). 1989. text ed. 60.00 (0-685-40218-5, Pub. by Imray Laurie Norie & Wilson UK) St Mut.

Ansel Adams. (American Photographers Ser.). 1991. 15.99 (0-517-06034-5, Crescent) Random Hse Value.

Ansel Adams. Photos by Ansel Adams. (Miniature Art Bks.). (Illus.). 64p. 1992. 4.99 (0-517-07763-9, Pub. by Wings Bks) Random Hse Value.

Ansel Adams: An Autobiography. Ansel Adams & Mary S. Alinder. (Illus.). 1990. pap. 39.95 (0-8212-1787-9) Bulfinch Pr.

***Ansel Adams: An Autobiography.** Ansel Adams & Mary S. Alinder. 312p. 1996. 13.95 (0-8212-2241-4) Bulfinch Pr.

Ansel Adams: Classic Images. Photos by Ansel Adams. (Illus.). 1986. 35.00 (0-8212-1629-5) Bulfinch Pr.

Ansel Adams: Images of the American West. Richard Wrigley. (Illus.). 48p. 1995. 7.98 (0-8317-0518-3) Smithmark.

Ansel Adams: Letters & Images, 1916-1984. Mary S. Alinder & Andrea G. Stillman. (Illus.). 1990. pap. 29.95 (0-8212-1788-7) Bulfinch Pr.

Ansel Adams: Our National Parks. Ed. by William A. Turnage & Andrea G. Stillman. (Illus.). 128p. 1992. pap. 17.95 (0-8212-1910-3) Bulfinch Pr.

***Ansel Adams: The National Park Service Photographs.** Intro. by Alice Gray. LC 94-42782. 1995. write for info. (0-89660-056-4, Artabras) Abbeville Pr.

***Ansel Adams & the American Landscape.** Jonathan Spaulding. LC 95-1601. (Illus.). 524p. 1995. 34.95 (0-520-08992-8) U CA Pr.

Ansel Adams Guide: Basic Techniques of Photography. John P. Schaefer. (Illus.). 432p. 1992. 50.00 (0-8212-1801-8); pap. 29.95 (0-8212-1882-4) Bulfinch Pr.

Ansel Adams in Color. Ed. by Harry M. Callahan. LC 92-46502. (Illus.). 132p. 1993. 55.00 (0-8212-1980-4) Bulfinch Pr.

Ansel Adam's National Parks. Abbeville Press Staff. (Tiny Folios Ser.). (Illus.). 304p. 1994. pap. 10.95 (1-55859-817-0) Abbeville Pr.

Ansel Adams, New Light: Essays on His Legacy & Legend. Robert Dawson. LC 92-74384. (Untitled Ser.: No. 55). (Illus.). 96p. 1993. pap. 16.95 (0-933286-61-9) Frnds Photography.

Anselm. Gillian R. Evans. (Outstanding Christian Thinkers Ser.). 122p. 1989. pap. 8.95 (0-8192-1483-3) Morehouse Pub.

Anselm: Fides Quaerens Intellectum. Karl Barth. Tr. by Ian W. Robertson. LC 76-10795. (Pittsburgh Reprint Ser.: No. 2). 1995. text ed. 15.00 (0-915138-75-1) Pickwick.

Anselm & Luther on the Atonement: Was It "Necessary"? Burnell F. Eckardt, Jr. LC 92-27796. 248p. 1992. text ed. 89.95 (0-7734-9825-7) E Mellen.

Anselm Kiefer. Mark Rosenthal. LC 87-29007. (Illus.). 216p. (Orig.). 1987. pap. 35.00 (0-87633-071-5) Phila Mus Art.

Anselm Kiefer. Mark Rosenthal. (Illus.). 216p. (Orig.). 1988. pap. 55.00 (3-7913-0847-5, Pub. by Prestel) TeNeues.

Anselm Kiefer: Lilith. Anselm Kiefer. LC 91-65065. (Illus.). 1992. pap. text ed. 45.00 (0-944219-10-1) M Goodman Gallery.

Anselm of Bec & Robert of Meulan: The Innocence of the Dove & the Wisdom of the Serpent. Sally N. Vaughn. LC 86-891. (Illus.). 392p. 1987. 60.00 (0-520-05674-4) U CA Pr.

Anselm of Canterbury: Vol. I, Monologion, Proslogion, Debate with Gaunilo, & a Meditation on Human Redemption. Anselm of Canterbury. Ed. by Jasper Hopkins. Tr. by Herbert Richardson. LC 74-19840. 161p. 1974. lib. bdg. 79.95 (0-88946-000-0) E Mellen.

Anselm of Canterbury: Vol. II, Philosophical Fragments; De Grammatico; on Truth; Freedom of Choice; the Fall of the Devil; the Harmony of the Foreknowledge, the Predestination, & the Grace of God with Free Choice. Anselm Of Canterbury. Tr. by Jasper Hopkins & Herbert Richardson. LC 74-19840. 237p. 1976. lib. bdg. 109.95 (0-88946-250-X) E Mellen.

Anselm of Canterbury: Vol. III, Two Letters Concerning Roscelin; the Incarnation of the Word; Why God Became a Man; the Virgin Conception & Original Sin; the Procession of the Holy Spirit; Three Letters on the Sacraments. Anselm of Canterbury. Tr. by Jasper Hopkins & Herbert Richardson. LC 74-19840. 265p. 1976. lib. bdg. 109.95 (0-88946-350-6) E Mellen.

Anselm of Canterbury: Vol. IV, Hermeneutical & Textual Problems in the Complete Treatises of St. Anselm. Jasper Hopkins. LC 74-19840. 202p. 1976. lib. bdg. 89.95 (0-88946-551-7) E Mellen.

Anselm of Canterbury: Why God Became Man. Anselm Of Canterbury. Ed. by Jasper Hopkins & Herbert Richardson. 105p. (C). 1980. pap. 39.95 (0-88946-009-4) E Mellen.

Anselm of Canterbury Complete Treatises: Anselm History, 4 vols., Set. Ed. by Jasper Hopkins. Tr. by Herbert Richardson. LC 74-19840. 1974. lib. bdg. 124.95 (0-88946-977-6) E Mellen.

Anselm Weber, O.F.M. Missionary to the Navaho. Robert L. Wilken. 1955. 12.50 (0-686-32658-X, 55-1235) St Michaels.

Anselmian Explorations: Essays in Philosophical Theology. Thomas V. Morris. LC 86-40239. 264p. (C). 1989. text ed. 29.95 (0-268-00616-4); pap. text ed. 12.95 (0-268-00621-0) U of Notre Dame Pr.

Anselmic Shift: Christology & Method in Karl Barth's Theology. Jeffrey C. Pugh. LC 90-34802. (American University Studies: Theology & Religion: Ser. VII, Vol. 68). 179p. (C). 1990. text ed. 42.95 (0-8204-1121-3) P Lang Pubs.

Anselmo Lorenzo: A Chronology. V. Munoz. Tr. by W. Scott Johnson. (Libertarian & Anarchist Chronology Ser.). 1979. lib. bdg. 59.95 (0-8490-3052-8) Gordon Pr.

Anselm's Argument: The Logic of Divine Existence. Robert Brecher. 200p. 1985. 63.95 (0-566-05022-6) Ashgate Pub Co.

Anselm's Discovery: A Re-Examination of the Ontological Proof for God's Existence. Charles Hartshorne. LC 65-20278. 349p. 1973. pap. 14.95 (0-87548-217-1) Open Court.

Anselm's Doctrine of Freedom & the Will. G. Stanley Kane. LC 81-16939. (Texts & Studies in Religion: Vol. 10). 240p. (C). 1982. lib. bdg. 89.95 (0-88946-914-8) E Mellen.

ANSI - AIHA Z9.5 Standard for Laboratory Ventilation. Ed. by Louis J. DiBerardinis. (C). 1993. pap. 30.00 (0-932627-50-1, 143-EQ-93) Am Indus Hygiene.

ANSI - ASQC Q90-1S0 9000 Guidelines for Use by the Chemical & Process Industries. 112p. 1992. 20.50 (0-87389-196-1) ASQC Qual Pr.

ANSI - IEEE Std 770X3.160-1989, An American National Standard IEEE Standard for the Programming Language Extended Pascal. Institute of Electrical & Electronics Engineers, Inc. Staff. (Illus.). 229p. (Orig.). 1990. pap. 55.00 (1-55937-031-9, SH13243) IEEE Standards.

ANSI-ASCE 2-84 Measurement of Oxygen Transfer in Clear Water: ASCE Subcommittee on Oxygen Transfer Standards. 40p. 1984. 16.00 (0-87262-430-7) Am Soc Civil Eng.

ANSI-ASCE 3-84 Specifications for the Design & Construction of Composite Slabs & Commentary on Specifications for the Design & Construction of Composite Slabs. ASCE Composite Steel Deck Slabs Standards Committee. 56p. 1985. 14.00 (0-87262-470-6) Am Soc Civil Eng.

ANSI C: A Lexical Guide. Mark Williams Company Staff. 522p. 1988. pap. text ed. 57.00 (0-13-037814-3) P-H.

ANSI C: A User's Guide. Alan C. Elliott. pap. 26.67 (0-13-037806-2) P-H.

ANSI C: Problem Solving & Programming. Kenneth Barclay. 500p. 1991. pap. text ed. 53.00 (0-13-037326-5) P-H.

ANSI C Card. rev. ed. Specialized Systems Consultants, Inc. Staff. 16p. (Orig.). (C). 1991. reprint ed. pap. text ed. 3.00 (0-916151-48-4) Specialized Sys.

ANSI C Programming. Steven C. Lawlor. LC 94-189251. 550p. 1995. pap. text ed. 46.50 (0-314-02830-7) West Pub.

ANSI C12.1-1988, American National Standard Code for Electricity Metering. rev. ed. Accredited Standards Committee C12 on Electricity Metering. LC 88-46182. (Illus.). 200p. 1989. 51.50 (1-55937-004-1, SH12252) IEEE Standards.

ANSI C63.4-1991, American National Standard for Methods of Measurement of Radio-Noise Emissions from Low-Voltage Electrical & Electronic Equipment in the Range of 9 kHz to 40 GHz. Accredited Standards Committee on Electromagnetic Compatibility, C63 Staff. (Illus.). 64p. (Orig.). 1991. pap. 49.00 (1-55937-086-6, SH13896) IEEE Standards.

ANSI-IEEE Pascal Standard: The American Pascal Standard. Henry Ledgard. 1984. 39.00 (0-387-91248-7) Spr-Verlag.

ANSI-RIA Robot Safety Standard. 2nd rev. ed. Robotic Industries Association, Robot Safety Subcommittee. 12p. (Orig.). 1986. pap. 8.00 (0-317-39388-X) Robot Inst Am.

ANSI-SPARC DBMS Model: Proceedings of the Share Working Conference on Data Base Management Systems, 2nd, Canada, 1977. Share Working Conference Staff. Ed. by D. A. Jardine. 226p. 1977. 77.00 (0-7204-0719-2, North Holland) Elsevier.

ANSI Z136.2 Safe Use of Optical Fiber Communications Systems Utilizing Laser Diode & LED Sources, No. 112. 46p. 1988. 35.00 (0-685-30507-4) Laser Inst.

ANSI Z136.3 Safe Use of Lasers in Health Care Facilities, No. 113. 50p. 1988. 50.00 (0-685-30508-2) Laser Inst.

Ansias de Infinito en la Avellaneda. Florinda Alzaga. LC 79-51297. (Coleccion Polymita Ser.). (Illus.). 1979. pap. 9.00 (0-89729-169-7) Ediciones.

Ansiotensin in Receptors. Ruffolo. 1994. 159.95 (0-8493-8380-3) CRC Pr.

Anson County, North Carolina Deed Abstracts, 1749 to 1766: Abstracts of Wills & Estates, 1749 to 1795. Brent H. Holcomb. LC 79-67870. 170p. 1991. reprint ed. 20.00 (0-8063-0871-0) Genealog Pub.

Anson Dickinson: The Celebrated Miniature Painter 1779-1852. Mona L. Dearborn. LC 83-70635. 224p. 1983. pap. text ed. 7.95 (0-940748-86-X) Conn Hist Soc.

Anson-Donaldson Surgical Anatomy of the Temporal Bone. 4th ed. James A. Donaldson et al. 576p. 1992. 147.00 (0-88167-915-1, 2393) Raven.

Anson, Hudson, Suderland: In Australian Service. Stewart Wilson. (Illus.). 216p. 1993. pap. 22.95 (1-875671-02-1, Pub. by Australian Aviation AT) Motorbooks Intl.

Anson Jones: The Last President of Texas. Herbert Gambrell. (Illus.). 544p. 1988. reprint ed. pap. 14.95 (0-292-70405-4) U of Tex Pr.

Anson to Zuber: Iowa Boys in the Major Leagues. Jerry E. Clark. vi, 228p. 1992. pap. 20.00 (0-9631699-1-2) Making Hist.

Ansonia Clock Company: 1906-1907 Catalogue. (Illus.). 213p. 1988. reprint ed. pap. 14.95 (0-930163-04-4) Arlington Bk.

Ansonia Clock Company Catalogue, 1894-1895. (Illus.). 168p. 1988. pap. 14.95 (0-930163-27-3) Arlington Bk.

Ansonia Clock Company Catalogue, 1901. (Illus.). 228p. 1988. pap. 14.95 (0-930163-11-7) Arlington Bk.

Ansonia Clock Company, 1880. 1991. write for info. (0-930476-04-2) Am Clock & Watch.

Ansonia Clock Company 1895 Supplementary Catalogue. (Illus.). 40p. 1988. reprint ed. pap. 6.00 (0-930163-07-9) Arlington Bk.

Ansonia Clock Company 1920 Catalogue. (Illus.). 58p. 1988. reprint ed. pap. 7.95 (0-930163-03-6) Arlington Bk.

Ansonia Clocks: History, Identification & Price Guide. Tran D. Ly. (Illus.). 304p. 1989. 35.00 (0-930163-32-X); pap. 25.00 (0-685-25237-X) Arlington Bk.

Ansonia Clocks: Price Guide Up-Date 1992. Tran D. Ly. (Illus.). 16p. pap. 5.00 (0-930163-56-7) Arlington Bk.

Ansonia Clocks: Price Guide Up-Date, 1992. Tran Duy Ly. (Illus.). 16p. 1992. pap. 5.00 (0-685-60152-8) Arlington Bk.

Anstey's Abbeys. John Anstey. 120p. (C). 1987. text ed. 60.00 (0-85406-336-4, Pub. by Surveyors Pubns) St Mut.

***Answer: Israel Through the Eyes of Mexican-Jewish Photographer: Leopoldo Kram.** (Illus.). 16p. Date not set. pap. text ed. write for info. (1-881456-15-3) B B K Natl Jew Mus.

Answer - La Respuesta. Sor J. De la Cruz. Tr. by Electa Arenal & Amanda Powell. 208p. (C). 1994. 35.00 (1-55861-076-6); pap. 12.95 (1-55861-077-4) Feminist Pr.

Answer As a Man. Taylor Caldwell. 1976. 27.95 (0-88411-143-1, Aeonian Pr) Amereon Ltd.

Answer As a Man. Taylor Caldwell. 1982. mass mkt. 4.95 (0-449-20050-7) Fawcett.

Answer Back. Donald Finkel. LC 68-17382. (C). 1968. pap. 1.95 (0-689-10087-6, Atheneum S&S) S&S Trade.

Answer Book: A Reference Manual for Office Personnel. 2nd rev. ed. Jean Dorrell. LC 92-61272. (Illus.). 358p. (C). 1993. pap. text ed., spiral bd. write for info. (0-935732-43-8) Roxbury Pub Co.

Answer Book: For Writers & Storytellers. Robert J. Hastings. LC 91-91758. 168p. (Orig.). 1991. pap. 10.95 (0-9600706-0-5) R J Hastings.

Answer Book for the First Hebrew Primer. 3rd ed. Ethelyn Simon & Dorey Brandt-Finell. 100p. (Orig.). (C). 1992. pap. text ed. 8.95 (0-939144-16-6) EKS Pub Co.

***Answer Book Student Workbook: A Reference Manual for Office Workers.** 2nd ed. Jean Dorrell. (Illus.). 130p. 1994. pap. write for info. (0-935732-56-X) Roxbury Pub Co.

Answer Book to Calculus. 2nd ed. Michael Spivak. 412p. 1984. text ed. 25.00x (0-914098-78-0) Publish or Perish.

***Answer Book to Calculus.** 3rd ed. Michael Spivak. (Illus.). ii, 418p. (C). 1994. text ed. 25.00x (0-914098-90-X) Publish or Perish.

***Answer Cancer, Answers for Living: A Mind Model for Healing.** Stephen C. Parkhill. LC 94-49127. 200p. (Orig.). 1995. pap. 9.95 (1-55874-333-2, 332) Health Comm.

Answer for Oppression. Kenneth Hagin, Jr. 1983. pap. 0.75 (0-89276-717-0) Hagin Ministries.

Answer in the Affirmative & The Oldest Man. deluxe ed. Mary F. Fisher. (Canto Bello Ser.: No. 3). (Illus.). 72p. 1989. 225.00 (0-685-58449-6) Engdahl Typo.

Answer in the Affirmative & The Oldest Man. Mary F. Fisher. (Canto Bello Ser.: No. 3). (Illus.). 72p. 1989. reprint ed. 75.00 (0-939489-07-4) Engdahl Typo.

***Answer in the Heart.** Hazelden. 1995. pap. text ed. 9.95 (0-89486-568-4) Hazelden.

***Answer in the Sky, Almost: Confessions of an Astrologer.** Sydney Omarr. 240p. (Orig.). 1995. pap. 10.95 (1-57174-028-7) Hampton Roads Pub Co.

Answer in the Tide. Elisabeth Ogilvie. 1976. 21.95 (0-8488-1117-8) Amereon Ltd.

Answer in the Tide. Elisabeth Ogilvie. 288p. 1991. reprint ed. pap. 12.95 (0-89272-311-4) Down East.

Answer Is at School: Bringing Health Care to Our Students. Illus. by Linda Bleck. 36p. (Orig.). 1993. pap. write for info. (0-942054-07-5) R W Johnson Found.

Answer Is Baseball. Luke Salisbury. LC 89-40588. 256p. 1990. pap. 8.95 (0-679-72642-X, Vin) Random.

Answer Is Baseball: An Inquisitive Guide to the Great Game. Luke Salisbury. 256p. 1989. 15.95 (0-8129-1601-8, Times Bks) Random.

Answer Is No: Saying It & Sticking to It. Cynthia Whitham. LC 93-87726. (Illus.). 224p. (Orig.). 1994. pap. 12.95 (0-9622036-4-5) Prspctive Pub.

Answer Is Within You, Women's Connections Psychology, & Breast Cancer. Lauren Ayers. 240p. 1994. 21.95 (0-8245-1431-9) Crossroad NY.

Answer Me. Ruth Edwards. LC 83-61453. (Illus.). 64p. (Orig.). 1983. pap. 7.95 (0-89390-041-9) Resource Pubns.

An Asterisk (*) at the beginning of an entry indicates that the title is appearing in BIP for the first time.

An Asterisk (*) at the beginning of an entry indicates that the title is appearing in BIP for the first time.

Ant & Bee & the Rainbow. Angela Banner. (Illus.). 96p. (J). (ps-1). 1992. 6.95 (*0-434-92972-7*, Pub. by W Heinemann Ltd) Trafalgar.

Ant & Bee & the Secret. Angela Banner. (Illus.). 96p. (J). (ps-1). 1989. 6.95 (*0-434-92959-X*, Pub. by W Heinemann Ltd) Trafalgar.

Ant & Bee Go Shopping. Angela Banner. (Illus.). 96p. (J). (ps-1). 1992. 6.95 (*0-434-92970-0*, Pub. by W Heinemann Ltd) Trafalgar.

Ant & Bee Time. Angela Banner. (Ant & Bee Ser.). (Illus.). 94p. (J). (ps-3). 1988. 6.95 (*0-434-92961-1*, Pub. by W Heinemann Ltd) Trafalgar.

Ant & the Cricket: Story Pak. Ret. by K. Hollenbeck. (Graphic Learning Literature Program Series: Folk Tales). (Illus.). (ENG & SPA.). 1992. 39.00 (*0-87746-237-2*) Graphic Learning.

Ant & the Dove. Jane P. Resnick. (Aesop's Fables Ser.). (Illus.). (J). 1992. bds. 3.25 (*0-8378-2523-7*) Gibson.

Ant & the Dove. Mary L. Wang. LC 89-34414. (Start-Off Stories Ser.). (Illus.). 32p. (J). (ps-2). 1989. lib. bdg. 10.35 (*0-516-02367-5*); pap. 3.95 (*0-516-42367-3*) Childrens.

Ant & the Duck. Alice H. Garside. (Garside Readers Ser.). (Illus.). 16p. (Orig.). (J). (gr. k-2). 1990. pap. 2.10 (*1-882063-07-4*) Cottage Pr MA.

Ant & the Elephant. Bill Peet. LC 74-179918. (Illus.). 48p. (J). (gr. k-3). 1980. 14.95 (*0-395-16963-1*); pap. 5.95 (*0-395-29205-0*) HM.

Ant & the Grasshopper: A Love Story. Sushiela. LC 89-92067. (Illus.). 129p. (Orig.). (J). (gr. 5 up). 1990. pap. 15.95 (*0-9623363-1-9*) Running Water.

Ant & the Peacock: Altruism & Sexual Selection from Darwin to Today. Helena Cronin. (Illus.). 400p. (C). 1992. 44.95 (*0-521-32937-X*) Cambridge U Pr.

Ant & the Peacock: Altruism & Sexual Selection from Darwin to Today. Helena Cronin. (Illus.). 506p. (C). 1993. pap. 19.95 (*0-521-45765-3*) Cambridge U Pr.

***Ant Book & See-Through Model.** Luann Colombo. (J). (gr. 1-4). 1994. 14.95 (*0-8362-4229-7*) Andrews & McMeel.

Ant Books. Laura C. Busch. (Little Readers Ser.). 180p. (J). (ps-1). 1990. 13.95 (*1-880642-01-8*) Little Read.

Ant Cities. Arthur Dorros. LC 85-48244. (Let's-Read-&-Find-Out Science Bk.). (Illus.). 32p. (J). (ps-3). 1987. lib. bdg. 14.89 (*0-690-04570-0*, Crowell Jr Bks) HarpC Child Bks.

Ant Cities. Arthur Dorros. LC 85-48244. (Trophy Let's-Read-&-Find-Out Bk.). (Illus.). 32p. (J). (gr. k-3). 1988. reprint ed. pap. 4.95 (*0-06-445079-1*, Trophy) HarpC Child Bks.

Ant Colony. Heiderose Fischer-Nagel & Andreas Fischer-Nagel. (Nature Watch Bks.). (Illus.). 48p. (J). (gr. 2-5). 1989. lib. bdg. 19.95 (*0-87614-333-8*, Carolrhoda); pap. 6.95 (*0-87614-519-5*, Carolrhoda) Lerner Group.

Ant Generator. Elizabeth Harris. LC 91-17231. (John Simmons Short Fiction Award Winner Ser.). 169p. 1991. 22.95 (*0-87745-342-X*) U of Iowa Pr.

Ant Heap. V. G. Dethier. LC 79-52701. (Illus.). 151p. 1979. 7.95 (*0-87850-034-0*) Darwin Pr.

Ant Heap. Margitt Kaffka. Tr. by Charlotte Franklin. LC 94-12706. 176p. 1995. 22.95 (*0-7145-2989-3*) M Boyars Pubs.

***Ant Hill Odyssey.** William Mann. (American Autobiography Ser.). 338p. 1995. reprint ed. lib. bdg. 89.00 (*0-7812-8585-2*) Rprt Serv.

Ant Nest. Stephen Ray & Kathleen Murdoch. LC 92-34254. (Voyages Ser.). (Illus.). (J). 1993. 4.25 (*0-383-03614-3*) SRA Schl Grp.

Ant on the Ground. Linda Losito. LC 89-4460. (Animal Habitats Ser.). (Illus.). 32p. (J). (gr. 4-6). 1989. lib. bdg. 17.27 (*0-8368-0111-3*) Gareth Stevens Inc.

Ant-Plant Interactions. Ed. by Camilla R. Huxley & David F. Cutler. (Illus.). 624p. 1991. 75.00 (*0-19-854639-4*) OUP.

Ant-Plant Interactions in Australia. R. Buckley. 1982. lib. bdg. 117.00 (*90-6193-684-5*) Kluwer Ac.

Antacids & Anti-Reflux Agents. Ed. by Neena Washington. 1991. 156.00 (*0-8493-5444-7*, RM365) CRC Pr.

Antacids & Other Drugs in Gastrointestinal Diseases. W. A. Ritschel. LC 84-6049. (Illus.). 189p. 1984. pap. text ed. 24.50 (*0-914768-42-5*) Drug Intell Pubns.

Antaeus, No. 44. Ed. by Daniel Halpern. 1982. pap. 7.00 (*0-912946-90-3*) Ecco Pr.

Antaeus, No. 62. Ed. by Daniel Halpern. 288p. 1989. pap. 10.00 (*0-88001-223-4*) Ecco Pr.

Antaeus: Contemporary Fiction, Vol. I, No. 48. Ed. by Daniel Halpern. 1982. pap. 8.00 (*0-88001-020-7*) Ecco Pr.

Antaeus: Contemporary Fiction, Vol. II & III, No. 49-50. Ed. by Daniel Halpern. 1983. pap. 8.00 (*0-88001-026-6*) Ecco Pr.

Antaeus: Essays on Ford Madox Ford, No. 56. Ed. by Sondra Stang. 400p. 1986. pap. 10.00 (*0-88001-097-5*) Ecco Pr.

Antaeus No. 42: The Prolific & the Devourer, W. H. Auden. Ed. by Daniel Halpern. LC 70-612646. 93p. (Orig.). (C). 1981. 12.00 (*0-912946-94-6*); pap. 6.00 (*0-912946-80-6*) Ecco Pr.

Antaeus No. 45-46: The Autobiographical Eye. Ed. by Daniel Halpern. LC 70-612646. (Illus.). 320p. 1982. 12.95 (*0-88001-003-7*); pap. 8.00 (*0-88001-002-9*) Ecco Pr.

Antaeus No. 51: Contemporary Fiction Vol. IV. Ed. by Daniel Halpern. LC 70-612646. 198p. (Orig.). (C). 1983. pap. 7.00 (*0-88001-027-4*) Ecco Pr.

Antaeus No. 52. Ed. by Daniel Halpern. LC 70-612646. 215p. (Orig.). (C). 1984. pap. 7.00 (*0-88001-042-8*) Ecco Pr.

Antaeus No. 53. Ed. by Daniel Halpern. LC 70-612646. 285p. (Orig.). (C). 1984. pap. 10.00 (*0-88001-066-5*) Ecco Pr.

Antaeus No. 57: On Nature. Ed. by Daniel Halpern. LC 70-612646. 344p. (Orig.). (C). 1986. pap. 10.00 (*0-88001-121-1*) Ecco Pr.

Antaeus No. 58. Ed. by Daniel Halpern. 1987. pap. 10.00 (*0-88001-143-2*) Ecco Pr.

Antaeus No. 59: Literature As Pleasure. Ed. by Daniel Halpern. 1987. pap. 10.00 (*0-88001-144-0*) Ecco Pr.

Antaeus No. 60: Spring 1988. Ed. by Daniel Halpern. 1988. pap. 10.00 (*0-88001-163-7*) Ecco Pr.

Antaeus No. 61: Journals, Notebooks, & Diaries. Ed. by Daniel Halpern. 300p. (Orig.). (C). 1988. pap. 15.00 (*0-88001-202-1*) Ecco Pr.

Antaeus No. 63: Essays. Ed. by Daniel Halpern. 1989. pap. 10.00 (*0-88001-226-9*) Ecco Pr.

Antaeus No. 66: Plays in One Act. Ed. by Daniel Halpern. 240p. (Orig.). 1991. pap. 15.00 (*0-88001-268-4*) Ecco Pr.

Antaeus No. 67: Fall 1991. Daniel Halpern. 1991. pap. 10.00 (*0-88001-318-4*) Ecco Pr.

Antaeus No. 69: Fall 1992. Daniel Halpern. 1992. pap. 10.00 (*0-88001-292-7*) Ecco Pr.

Antaeus No. 70: Special Fiction Issue. Daniel Halpern. 1993. pap. 10.00 (*0-88001-326-5*) Ecco Pr.

Antaeus No. 71: On Music. Daniel Halpern. 1993. pap. 15.00 (*0-88001-337-0*) Ecco Pr.

Antaeus No. 73-74. Daniel Halpern. 1994. pap. 13.00 (*0-88001-361-3*) Ecco Pr.

Antaeus Nos. 40 & 41: Tenth Anniversary Issue. Ed. by Daniel Halpern. LC 70-612646. 552p. 1981. 25.00 (*0-912946-81-4*) Ecco Pr.

Antaeus Nos. 64 & 65: Twentieth Anniversary Issue. Ed. by Daniel Halpern. 352p. 1990. pap. 15.00 (*0-88001-252-8*) Ecco Pr.

Antaeus 68: Writers on Food & Wine. 240p. 1992. pap. 15.00 (*0-88001-276-5*) Ecco Pr.

***Antagonists.** Jennifer Albrights. (Mind's Eye Theatre Ser.). 128p. 1995. per., pap. 15.00 (*1-56504-502-5*, 5020) White Wolf.

Antagonists: A Comparative Combat Assessment of the Soviet & American Soldier. Richard A. Gabriel. LC 83-1645. (Contributions in Military History Ser.: No. 34). (Illus.). xi, 208p. 1984. text ed. 49.95 (*0-313-23127-3*, GTA/, Greenwood Pr) Greenwood.

Antagonists: A Complete Microworld Adventure for the IBM-PC. Hal Renko et al. 128p. 1985. pap. write for info. (*0-201-16492-2*) Addison-Wesley.

Antagonists in the Church: How to Identify & Deal with Destructive Conflict. Kenneth C. Haugk. LC 88-6354. 192p. (Orig.). 1988. pap. 11.99 (*0-8066-2310-1*, 10-0372, Augsburg); student ed 4.99 (*0-8066-2373-X*, 10-0373, Augsburg) Augsburg Fortress.

Antal & Her Path of Love: Poems of a Woman Saint from South India. Vidya Dehejia. LC 89-48505. (SUNY Series in Hindu Studies). 183p. 1990. 59.50 (*0-7914-0395-5*); pap. 19.95 (*0-7914-0396-3*) State U NY Pr.

Antalo the Antelope, B-era the Bear, C-esto the Cheetah, D-opicooko the Deer. Frank Nwabugwu. (Bed Time Stories Ser.). 18p. (J). 1992. write for info. (*1-881687-04-X*); teacher ed write for info. (*1-881687-07-4*); lib. bdg. write for info. (*1-881687-05-8*); pap. write for info. (*1-881687-06-6*) F Nwabugwu.

Antar: A Bedoueen Romance. LC 81-21401. 320p. 1983. reprint ed. 50.00 (*0-8201-1375-1*) Schol Facsimiles.

Antarctic. Janice Meadows. (World Bibliographical Ser.). 1994. lib. bdg. 87.50 (*1-85109-121-1*) ABC-CLIO.

Antarctic Ascidiacea. Ed. by P. Kott. LC 77-601086. (Antarctic Research Ser.: Vol. 13). (Illus.). 239p. 1969. 18.00 (*0-87590-113-1*) Am Geophysical.

Antarctic Bibliography, Vol. 19, 1991. Ed. by Stuart G. Hibben. 559p. 1992. 36.00 (*0-16-036186-9*) Lib Congress.

Antarctic Bird Studies. Ed. by O. L. Austin. LC 68-61438. (Antarctic Research Ser.: Vol. 12). (Illus.). 262p. 1968. 21.00 (*0-87590-112-3*) Am Geophysical.

Antarctic Birds: An Ecological & Behavioral Approach (Exploration of Palmer Archipelago by an Artist-Ornithologist. David F. Parmelee. (Illus.). 221p. (C). 1992. 39.95 (*0-8166-2000-8*) U of Minn Pr.

Antarctic Birds & Seals: A Pocket Guide. Sharon Chester. LC 93-94946. (Illus.). 80p. (Orig.). 1993. pap. text ed. 15.00 (*0-9638511-2-8*) Wander Albatross.

Antarctic Circumpolar Ocean. George Deacon. LC 83-26332. (Studies in Polar Research). (Illus.). 170p. 1985. 39.95 (*0-521-25410-8*) Cambridge U Pr.

Antarctic Cirripedia. Ed. by William A. Newman & Arnold Ross. LC 74-129339. (Antarctic Research Ser.: Vol. 14). (Illus.). 257p. 1971. 32.00 (*0-87590-114-X*) Am Geophysical.

Antarctic Comrades: An American with the Russians in Antarctica. Gilbert Dewart. (Illus.). 192p. 1989. 36.50 (*0-8142-0490-2*) Ohio St U Pr.

Antarctic Continental Margin: Geology & Geophysics of Offshore Wilkes Land. Ed. by Stephen L. Eittreim & Monty A. Hampton. (Earth Science Ser.: Vol. 5A). (Illus.). 221p. 1987. pap. 24.00 (*0-933687-04-4*) Circum-Pacific.

Antarctic Continental Margin: Geology & Geophysics of the Western Ross Sea. Ed. by Alan K. Cooper & Frederick Davey. (Earth Science Ser.: Vol. 5B). (Illus.). 253p. 1987. pap. 24.00 (*0-933687-05-2*) Circum-Pacific.

***Antarctic Conventions.** Kenneth R. Simmonds. 325p. 1993. 85.00 (*1-898029-00-8*, Pub. by Simmonds & Hill Pubng UK) W W Gaunt.

Antarctic Diary. Maria Buxton. (C). 1988. 40.00 (*0-86138-024-X*, Pub. by T Dalton UK) St Mut.

Antarctic Diary. Trish Hart. LC 93-110. (J). 1994. pap. write for info. (*0-383-03675-5*) SRA Schl Grp.

Antarctic Ecology, 1. Ed. by Richard M. Laws. 1984. text ed. 137.00 (*0-12-439501-5*) Acad Pr.

Antarctic Environment & International Law. Ed. by Philippe Sands. (International Environmental Law & Policy Ser.). 288p. (C). 1992. lib. bdg. 115.00 (*1-85333-630-0*, Pub. by Graham & Trotman UK) Kluwer Ac.

Antarctic Fish & Fisheries. Karl-Hermann Kock. (Studies in Polar Research). (Illus.). 375p. (C). 1992. 115.00 (*0-521-36250-4*) Cambridge U Pr.

Antarctic Fish Biology: Evolution in a Unique Environment. Joseph T. Eastman. (Illus.). 322p. 1993. text ed. 74.95 (*0-12-228140-3*) Acad Pr.

Antarctic Geoscience: Proceedings of 1977 Symposium. Ed. by Campbell Craddock. (International Union of Geological Sciences Series B: No. 4). (Illus.). 1204p. 1982. 61.50 (*0-299-08410-8*) U of Wis Pr.

Antarctic Glacial History & World Palaeoenvironments: Proceedings of a Symposium Held on 17th August 1977 During the Xth INQUA Congress at Birmingham, UK. Ed. by E. M. Van Zinderen Bakker. 180p. (C). 1978. text ed. 130.00 (*90-6191-027-7*, Pub. by A A Balkema NE) Ashgate Pub Co.

Antarctic Legal Regime. Ed. by Christopher C. Joyner & Sudhir Chopra. 1988. lib. bdg. 117.50 (*90-247-3618-8*) Kluwer Ac.

Antarctic Meteorology & Climatology: Studies Based on Automatic Weather Stations. Ed. by David H. Bromwich & Charles R. Stearns. LC 94-3154. (Antarctic Research Ser.: Vol. 61). 207p. 1994. 70.00 (*0-87590-839-X*) Am Geophysical.

Antarctic Microbiology. E. Imre Friedmann. Ed. by Anne B. Thistle. (Series in Ecological & Applied Microbiology). 644p. 1993. text ed. 199.95 (*0-471-50776-8*, Wiley-Liss) Wiley.

Antarctic Mineral Exploitation: The Emerging Legal Framework. Francisco Orrego-Vicuna. LC 86-28392. (Studies in Polar Research). (Illus.). 450p. 1988. 125.00 (*0-521-32383-5*) Cambridge U Pr.

Antarctic Navigation. Elizabeth Arthur. LC 93-23075. 1995. 25.00 (*0-679-41895-4*) Knopf.

Antarctic Obsession. Clements Markham. Ed. & Intro. by Clive Holland. (Antarctic Classics Ser.). (Illus.). 208p. (C). 1989. pap. 51.00 (*0-948285-09-5*, Pub. by Archival Facs UK) St Mut.

***Antarctic Ocean.** Lynn M. Stone. LC 95-5984. (Antarctica Ser.). (J). 1995. write for info. (*1-55916-138-8*) Rourke Bk Co.

Antarctic Ocean & Resources Variability. Ed. by D. Sahrhage. (Illus.). 320p. 1988. 139.00 (*0-387-19294-8*) Spr-Verlag.

Antarctic Oceanology One. Ed. by Joseph L. Reid. LC 78-151300. (Antarctic Research Ser.: Vol. 15). (Illus.). 343p. 1971. 28.50 (*0-87590-115-8*) Am Geophysical.

Antarctic Oceanology Two: The Australian-New Zealand Sector. Ed. by D. E. Hayes. (Antarctic Research Ser.: Vol. 19). (Illus.). 364p. 1972. 41.00 (*0-685-55229-2*) Am Geophysical.

Antarctic Oceanology Two: The Australian-New Zealand Sector. Ed. by Dennis E. Hayes. LC 78-151300. (Antarctic Research Ser.: Vol. 19). (Illus.). 364p. 1972. 41.00 (*0-87590-119-0*) Am Geophysical.

Antarctic Paleobiology. Ed. by T. N. Taylor & Edith L. Taylor. (Illus.). x, 261p. 1989. 149.00 (*0-387-97006-1*, 2870) Spr-Verlag.

Antarctic Paleoenvironment: A Perspective on Global Change, Pt. 1. Ed. by James P. Kennett & Detlef A. Warnke. LC 92-37312. (Antarctic Research Ser.: Vol. 56, Pt. 1). 400p. 1992. 58.00 (*0-87590-823-3*) Am Geophysical.

Antarctic Paleoenvironment Pt. 2: A Perspective on Global Change. Ed. by J. P. Kennett & D. A. Warnke. (Antarctic Research Ser.: Vol. 60). 273p. 1993. 57.00 (*0-87590-838-1*) Am Geophysical.

Antarctic Pinnipedia. Ed. by William H. Burt. LC 76-182566. (Antarctic Research Ser.: Vol. 18). (Illus.). 226p. 1971. 32.00 (*0-87590-118-2*) Am Geophysical.

Antarctic Research: The Matthew Fontaine Maury Memorial Symposium. Ed. by H. Wexler et al. (Geophysical Monograph Ser.: Vol. 7). (Illus.). 228p. 1962. 10.00 (*0-87590-007-0*, GM0700) Am Geophysical.

Antarctic Resources Policy: Scientifc, Legal & Political Issues. Ed. by Francisco Orrego-Vicuna. LC 83-7871. (Studies in Polar Research). 300p. 1984. 105.00 (*0-521-25952-5*) Cambridge U Pr.

Antarctic Science. David Walton. (Illus.). 288p. 1987. 54.95 (*0-521-26233-X*) Cambridge U Pr.

Antarctic Science: Global Concerns. G. Hempel. (Illus.). 315p. 1994. pap. 26.00 (*0-387-57559-6*) Spr-Verlag.

Antarctic Seals: Research Methods & Techniques. Richard M. Laws. LC 92-47467. (Illus.). 350p. (C). 1993. 84.95 (*0-521-44302-4*) Cambridge U Pr.

Antarctic Sector of the Pacific. Ed. by G. P. Glasby. (Oceanography Ser.: No. 51). 396p. 1990. 97.50 (*0-444-88510-2*) Elsevier.

Antarctic Serolidae & Cirolanidae (Crustacea, Isopoda) New Genera, Species, & Redescriptions. Angelika Brandt. (Theses Zoologicae Ser.: Vol. 10). (Illus.). 172p. 1988. text ed. 80.00 (*3-87429-288-6*) Koeltz Sci Bks.

Antarctic Sinphnophores from Plankton Samples of the United States Antarctic Research Program: Biology of the Antarctic Seas, Vol. XX. Ed. by L. S. Kornicker. (Antarctic Research Ser.: Vol. 49). 487p. 1990. 69.00 (*0-87590-173-5*) Am Geophysical.

Antarctic Snow & Ice Studies, I & II, 2 Vols., Vol. 2. LC 64-60078. (Antarctic Research Ser.: Vols. 2 & 16). (Illus.). 277p. 1964. 15.00 (*0-87590-102-6*) Am Geophysical.

Antarctic Snow & Ice Studies, I & II, 2 Vols., Vol. 16. LC 64-60078. (Antarctic Research Ser.: Vols. 2 & 16). (Illus.). 412p. 1971. 32.00 (*0-87590-116-6*) Am Geophysical.

Antarctic Terrestrial Biology. Ed. by George A. Llano. LC 72-92709. (Antarctic Research Ser.: Vol. 20). (Illus.). 322p. 1972. 39.00 (*0-87590-120-4*) Am Geophysical.

Antarctic Traveller. Katha Pollitt. LC 81-47521. 1982. pap. 9.95 (*0-394-74895-6*) Knopf.

Antarctic Treaty System: An Assessment. National Research Council. 456p. (Orig.). 1986. text ed. 45.95 (*0-309-03640-2*) Natl Acad Pr.

Antarctic Treaty System in World Politics. Ed. by Arnfinn Jorgensen-Dahl & Willy Ostreng. LC 91-9080. 400p. 1991. text ed. 79.95 (*0-312-06206-0*) St Martin.

Antarctic Valviferans (Crustacea, Isopoda, Valvifera) New Genera, New Species & Redescriptions. Angelika Brandt. LC 89-49705. (Illus.). 176p. 1990. pap. 43.00 (*90-04-09238-2*) E J Brill.

***Antarctic Voyage of HMAS Wyatt Earp.** Phillp Law. (Illus.). 158p. 1995. pap. 29.95 (*1-86373-803-7*) Paul & Co Pubs.

Antarctica. Henry Billings. LC 94-9142. (Enchantment of the World Ser.). (Illus.). 128p. (J). (gr. 5-9). 1994. lib. bdg. 21.53 (*0-516-02624-0*) Childrens.

***Antarctica.** Jean F. Blashfield. LC 94-40911. (Wonders of the World Ser.). (J). 1995. 24.26 (*0-8114-6366-4*) Raintree Steck-V.

Antarctica. Helen Cowcher. (Illus.). 1990. 15.00 (*0-374-30368-1*) FS&G.

Antarctica. Helen Cowcher. (Illus.). 1991. pap. 4.95 (*0-374-40371-6*) FS&G.

Antarctica. Helen Cowcher. (Illus.). 32p. (J). (gr. k-3). 1990. audio 19.95 (*0-924483-24-5*); audio 44.95 (*0-924483-65-2*) Soundprints.

Antarctica. Michael George. LC 93-18281. (J). 1994. lib. bdg. 16.95 (*0-88682-600-4*) Creative Ed.

Antarctica. Jo E. Moore. (Illus.). 16p. 1993. pap. 5.95 (*1-55799-246-0*) Evan-Moor Corp.

Antarctica. Ron Naveen. (Carolina Biology Readers Ser.). (Illus.). 16p. (Orig.). (YA). (gr. 10 up). 1992. pap. text ed. 2.75 (*0-89278-124-6*, 45-9624) Carolina Biological.

Antarctica. Eliot Porter. (Illus.). 168p. 1988. 22.99 (*0-517-66571-9*) Random Hse Value.

Antarctica. Laurence Pringle. 64p. (J). 1992. pap. 16.00 (*0-671-73850-X*, S&S Bks Young Read) S&S Childrens.

Antarctica. Roy Siegfried & Creina Bond. (Illus.). 176p. (C). 1988. 110.00 (*1-85368-027-3*, Pub. by New Holland Pubs UK) St Mut.

***Antarctica.** Tony Soper. (Bradt Guides Ser.). (Illus.). 144p. 1994. 19.95 (*1-56440-533-8*) Globe Pequot.

Antarctica. Gail B. Stewart. LC 91-8523. (Places in the News Ser.). (Illus.). 48p. (J). (gr. 6-7). 1991. text ed. 12.95 (*0-89686-656-4*, Crstwood Hse) Silver Burdett Pr.

Antarctica. Lynn M. Stone. (New True Bks.). 48p. (J). (gr. k-4). 1985. lib. bdg. 12.90 (*0-516-01265-7*) Childrens.

Antarctica: Accounts from Journals of Numerous Explorers. Richard E. Byrd et al. (Dorset Reprints Ser.). 460p. 1990. 24.95 (*0-88029-506-6*) Marboro Bks.

Antarctica: An Encyclopedia, 2 vols. John Stewart. LC 89-43631. 1220p. 1990. lib. bdg. 135.00 (*0-89950-470-1*) McFarland & Co.

Antarctica: Both Heaven & Hell. Reinhold Messner. (Illus.). 400p. 1991. text ed. 35.00 (*0-89886-305-8*) Mountaineers.

Antarctica: Chile's Claim. Luis H. Mericq. LC 86-23570. (Illus.). 137p. (Orig.). 1987. pap. 3.50 (*0-16-001657-6*, S/N 008-020-01103-7) USGPO.

Antarctica: Exploration, Perception & Metaphor. Paul Simpson-Housley. LC 91-43903. (Illus.). 192p. 1992. 55.00 (*0-415-08225-0*, A7381) Routledge.

Antarctica: Geopolitics & Resources. Ishwar C. Sharma. (C). 1992. text ed. 33.00 (*81-210-0285-0*, Pub. by Inter-India Pubns) S Asia.

Antarctica: Private Property or Public Heritage? Keith D. Suter. LC 89-35867. 160p. (C). 1991. text ed. 49.95 (*0-86232-846-2*, Pub. by Zed Books UK); pap. 17.50 (*0-86232-847-0*, Pub. by Zed Books UK) Humanities.

Antarctica: Recent Advances in the Understanding of the Continental Shelf. Karl Hinz & Y. Krisoffersen. (Geologisches Jahrbuch Reihe E Ser.: Heft 37). (Illus.). 54p. 1987. pap. text ed. 35.00 (*0-685-19269-5*) Lubrecht & Cramer.

Antarctica: Soils, Weathering , Processes & Environment. I. B. Campbell & G. G. Claridge. (Developments in Soil Science Ser.: No. 16). 406p. 1987. 118.00 (*0-444-42784-8*) Elsevier.

Antarctica: The Continuing Experiment. Philip W. Quigg. LC 85-81558. (Headline Ser.: No. 273). (Illus.). 64p. (Orig.). 1985. pap. 5.95 (*0-87124-100-5*) Foreign Policy.

Antarctica: The Extraordinary History of Man's Conquest of the Frozen Continent. 2nd ed. Reader's Digest Editors. (Illus.). 320p. 1990. 32.95 (*0-86438-167-0*, Random) RD Assn.

***Antarctica: The Land.** Lynn M. Stone. LC 95-5992. (J). 1995. write for info. (*1-55916-139-6*) Rourke Bk Co.

Antarctica: The Next Decade. Ed. by Anthony Parsons. (Studies in Polar Research). (Illus.). 176p. 1987. 59.95 (*0-521-33181-1*) Cambridge U Pr.

Antarctica & Environmental Change. Ed. by D. J. Drewry et al. (Illus.). 152p. (C). 1994. 55.00 (*0-19-854068-X*, 4001) OUP.

Antarctica & International Law, 1982-1988: A Collection of Inter-State & National Documents, 4 vols. including index vol. W. M. Bush. LC 82-12408. 1983. ring bd. 175.00 (*0-379-01255-3*) Oceana.

Antarctica & International Law, 1982-1988: A Collection of Inter-State & National Documents, 4 vols. including index vol., Set. W. M. Bush. LC 82-12408. 1983. lib. bdg. 200.00 (*0-379-20320-0*) Oceana.

Antarctica & South American Geopolitics: Frozen Lebensraum. Jack Child. LC 87-29948. 256p. 1988. text ed. 55.00 (*0-275-92886-1*, C2886, Praeger Pubs) Greenwood.

An Asterisk (*) at the beginning of an entry indicates that the title is appearing in BIP for the first time.

An Asterisk (*) at the beginning of an entry indicates that the title is appearing in BIP for the first time.

353

Anthem. Ayn Rand. 1961. pap. 4.99 (0-451-16683-3, Sig) NAL-Dutton.

***Anthem.** aniversary ed. Ayn Rand. LC 95-9854. 1995. 22.95 (0-525-94015-4, Dutton) NAL-Dutton.

***Anthem: 50th Anniversay Edition.** Ayn Rand. 128p. 1995. mass mkt. 5.99 (0-451-18532-3, Sig) NAL-Dutton.

Anthem in New England before Eighteen Hundred. Ralph T. Daniel. LC 78-31121. (Music Reprint Ser.). 1979. reprint ed. 39.50 (0-306-79511-6) Da Capo.

Anthems & Anthem Composers. Myles B. Foster. LC 76-125047. (Music Ser.). 1970. reprint ed. lib. bdg. 32.50 (0-306-70012-3) Da Capo.

Anthems & Anthem Composers: An Essay upon the Development of the Anthem from the Time of the Reformation to the End of the Nineteenth Century. Myles B. Foster. (Illus.). 225p. 1980. reprint ed. 44.20 (3-487-06952-0, Pub. by Georg Olms GW) Lubrecht & Cramer.

Anthems for Choirs Four. Ed. by Christopher Morris. 1976. pap. 16.95 (0-19-353018-X) OUP.

Anthems for Choirs One: Fifty Anthems for Mixed Voices. Ed. by Francis Jackson. 1973. pap. 12.95 (0-19-353214-X) OUP.

Anthems for Choirs Three: Twenty-Four Anthems for Sopranos & Altos, Three or More Parts. Ed. by Philip Ledger. 1974. pap. text ed. 16.95 (0-19-353242-5) OUP.

Anthems for Choirs Two: Twenty-Four Anthems for Sopranos & Altos, Unison & Two-Part. Ed. by Philip Ledger. 1974. pap. text ed. 16.95 (0-19-353240-9) OUP.

Anthems for Men's Voices, 2 vols. Peter Le Huray et al. Incl. Vol. 1. Altos, Tenors & Basses. 1985. 21.95 (0-19-353234-4); 1965. write for info. (0-318-54806-2) OUP.

Anthems of Defeat: Crackdown in Human Province 1989-1992. Ed. by Human Rights Watch Staff. 272p. (Orig.). 1992. pap. 15.00 (1-56432-074-X) Hum Rts Watch.

Anthenium. Ernest L. Norman. 1964. 8.95 (0-932642-13-6) Unarius Acad Sci.

***Anther: Form, Function & Phylogeny.** Ed. by William G. D'Arcy & Richard C. Keating. (Illus.). 360p. (C). 1995. write for info. (0-521-48063-9) Cambridge U Pr.

Anthills of the Savannah. Chinua Achebe. 224p. 1989. mass mkt. 8.95 (0-385-26045-8, Anchor NY) Doubleday.

Anthisthenes Sokratikos. H. D. Rankin. vi, 210p. 1986. 44.00 (90-256-0896-5, Pub. by A M Hakkert NE) Benjamins North Am.

Anthocyanins As Flower Pigments: Feasibilities for Flower Colour Modification. T. Mulder-Krieger & R. Verpoorte. LC 93-11838. 164p. (C). 1993. pap. text ed. 0.01 (0-7923-2465-X) Kluwer Ac.

Anthocyanins As Food Colors. Ed. by Pericles Markakis. LC 81-22902. (Food Science & Technology Ser.). 1982. text ed. 85.00 (0-12-472550-3) Acad Pr.

Anthocyanins of Food Crops. Mazza. 1992. 188.95 (0-8493-0172-6, QK898) CRC Pr.

Anthologia Anthropologica: The Native Races of Africa & Madagascar: a Copious Selection of Passages for the Study of Social Anthropology. James G. Frazer. Ed. by Robert A. Downie. LC 73-21266. reprint ed. 97.50 (0-404-11422-9) AMS Pr.

Anthologia Anthropologica: The Native Races of America. James G. Frazer. LC 73-21267. reprint ed. 71.00 (0-404-11423-7) AMS Pr.

Anthologia Anthropologica: The Native Races of Asia & Europe. James G. Frazer. LC 73-21268. reprint ed. 71.00 (0-404-11424-5) AMS Pr.

Anthologia Anthropologica: The Native Races of Australasia. James G. Frazer. LC 73-21269. reprint ed. 71.00 (0-404-11425-3) AMS Pr.

Anthologia Graeca Carminum Christianorum. Wilhelm Von Christ & Matthaios K. Paranikas. cxliv, 268p. 1974. reprint ed. write for info. (3-487-05370-5, Pub. by Georg Olms GW) Lubrecht & Cramer.

Anthologie: Des Prefaces de Romans Francais. Herbert Gershman & Kernan Whitworth. 366p. 1964. 9.95 (0-8288-7426-3) Fr & Eur.

Anthologie aus der Suaheli-Literatur (Gedichte und Geschichten der Suaheli) Carl G. Buttner. (B. E. Ser.: No. 44). (GER.). 1894. 33.00 (0-8115-2995-9) Periodicals Srv.

Anthologie de la Litterature Francaise Tome I: Des Origines a la Fin du Dix-Huitieme Siecle. 4th ed. Ed. by Robert Leggewie. (Illus.). 432p. (C). Date not set. pap. text ed. 27.95 (0-19-508585-X) OUP.

Anthologie de la Litterature Francaise Tome II: Dix-Neuvieme et Vingtieme Siecles. 4th ed. Ed. by Robert Leggewie. (Illus.). 480p. (C). Date not set. pap. 27.95 (0-19-508586-8) OUP.

Anthologie de la Litterature Francaise, Tome 1: Des Origines a la fin du Dix-Huitieme Siecle. 3rd ed. Robert Leggewie. (Illus.). 464p. (C). 1990. pap. text ed. 29.95 (0-19-506276-0) OUP.

Anthologie de la Litterature Francaise, Tome 2: Dix-Neuvieme et Vinqtieme Siecles. 3rd ed. Robert Leggewie. (Illus.). 480p. (C). 1990. pap. text ed. 29.95 (0-19-506277-9) OUP.

Anthologie de la Nouvelle Poesie Negre et Malgache de Langue Francaise: Avec: Sartre, Jean-Paul. Orphee Noir. 4th ed. Leopold S. Senghor. (FRE.). 1985. pap. 17.95 (0-7859-1442-0, 2130387152) Fr & Eur.

Anthologie de la Poesie Francaise. Andre Gide. 848p. (FRE.). 1987. lib. bdg. 95.00 (0-7859-3739-0, 2070100103) Fr & Eur.

Anthologie de la Poesie Francaise. Ed. by Andre Gide. (Pleiade Ser.). (FRE.). 1954. 63.95 (2-07-010010-3) Schoenhof.

Anthologie de la Poesie Francaise du Seizieme Siecle. Ed. by Floyd Gray. LC 67-10343. (FRE.). 1977. reprint ed. 46.50 (0-89197-026-6); reprint ed. pap. text ed. 24.95 (0-89197-659-0) Irvington.

Anthologie de la Poesie Francaise du XIX Siecle, de Chateaubriand a Baudelaire. Ed. by B. Leuilliot. (Poesie Ser.). (FRE.). pap. 18.95 (2-07-032258-0) Schoenhof.

Anthologie de la Poesie Francaise du XVIIe Siecle. Ed. by Jean-Pierre Chaveau. (Poesie Ser.). 501p. (FRE.). 1987. pap. 17.95 (2-07-032437-0) Schoenhof.

Anthologie de la Poesie Francaise du XXe Siecle, de Paul Claudel a Rene Char. Ed. by M. Decaudin. (Poesie Ser.). (FRE.). 1992. pap. 16.95 (2-07-032231-9) Schoenhof.

Anthologie de la Poesie Lyrique Francaise des XIIe et XIIIe Siecles. Ed. by Jean Dufournet. (Poesie Ser.). (FRE.). 1987. pap. 16.95 (2-07-032462-1) Schoenhof.

Anthologie de l'Humour Noir. Andre Breton. pap. 14.95 (0-7859-0784-X, F89450) Fr & Eur.

Anthologie des Ecrits Sur l'Art. Paul Eluard. (Illus.). 328p. 1972. 80.00 (0-7859-0047-0, FA888) Fr & Eur.

Anthologie Des Maitres Religieux Primitifs des 15th, 16th & 17th Siecles, 6 vols., Set. Ed. by Charles Bordes. (Music Ser.). 1981. reprint ed. lib. bdg. 250.00 (0-306-76089-4) Da Capo.

Anthologie Des Maitres Religieux Primitifs des 15th, 16th & 17th Siecles, 6 vols., Vol. 1; IV. Ed. by Charles Bordes. (Music Ser.). 184p. 1981. reprint ed. lib. bdg. 47.50 (0-306-76114-9) Da Capo.

Anthologie Des Maitres Religieux Primitifs des 15th, 16th & 17th Siecles, 6 vols., Vol. 2; VIII. Ed. by Charles Bordes. (Music Ser.). 194p. 1981. reprint ed. lib. bdg. 47.50 (0-306-76115-7) Da Capo.

Anthologie Des Maitres Religieux Primitifs des 15th, 16th & 17th Siecles, 6 vols., Vol. 3; IV. Ed. by Charles Bordes. (Music Ser.). 184p. 1981. reprint ed. lib. bdg. 47.50 (0-306-76116-5) Da Capo.

Anthologie Des Maitres Religieux Primitifs des 15th, 16th & 17th Siecles, 6 vols., Vol. 4; IV. Ed. by Charles Bordes. (Music Ser.). 190p. 1981. reprint ed. lib. bdg. 47.50 (0-306-76117-3) Da Capo.

Anthologie Des Maitres Religieux Primitifs des 15th, 16th & 17th Siecles, 6 vols., Vol. 5; II. Ed. by Charles Bordes. (Music Ser.). 190p. 1981. reprint ed. lib. bdg. 47.50 (0-306-76118-1) Da Capo.

Anthologie Des Maitres Religieux Primitifs des 15th, 16th & 17th Siecles, 6 vols., Vol. 6; II. Ed. by Charles Bordes. (Music Ser.). 202p. 1981. reprint ed. lib. bdg. 47.50 (0-306-76119-X) Da Capo.

Anthologie d'un Siecle de Poesie Haitienne, 1817-1925, avec une Etude sur la Muse Haitienne d'Expression Franciase et une Etude sur la Muse Haitienne d'Expression Creole. Louis Morpeau. (B. E. Ser.: No. 10). (FRE.). 1925. 30.00 (0-8115-2961-4) Periodicals Srv.

Anthologie Grammaticale Arabe. Antoine I. Silvestre De Sacy. LC 73-12742. reprint ed. 32.50 (0-404-11237-4) AMS Pr.

Anthologie Negre. Blaise Cendrars. (FRE.). 1985. pap. 12.95 (0-7859-3105-8) Fr & Eur.

Anthologies by & about Women: An Analytical Index. Comp. by Susan Cardinale. LC 81-13423. xxvii, 922p. 1982. text ed. 105.00 (0-313-22180-4, CAB/, Greenwood Pr) Greenwood.

Anthologies of Music: An Annotated Index. 2nd ed. Sterling E. Murray. LC 92-34086. (Detroit Studies in Music Bibliography: No. 68). 1992. 35.00 (0-89990-061-5) Info Coord.

Anthologium Vol. I: Libri Duo Priores, Librum Primum Continens. Stobaeus. Ed. by Kurt Wachsmuth & Otto Hense. xl, 502p. 1974. write for info. (3-296-15701-8, Pub. by Georg Olms GW) Lubrecht & Cramer.

Anthologium Vol. II: Libri Duo Priores, Librum Alterum Continens. Stobaeus. Ed. by Kurt Wachsmuth & Otto Hense. iv, 332p. 1974. write for info. (3-296-15702-6, Pub. by Georg Olms GW) Lubrecht & Cramer.

Anthologium Vol. III: Anthologii Librum Tertium Continens. Stobaeus. Ed. by Kurt Wachsmuth & Otto Hense. lxxx, 769p. 1974. write for info. (3-296-15703-4, Pub. by Georg Olms GW) Lubrecht & Cramer.

Anthologium Vol. IV: Anthologii Libri Quarti Partem Priorem Continens. Stobaeus. Ed. by Kurt Wachsmuth & Otto Hense. xiii, 675p. 1974. write for info. (3-296-15704-2, Pub. by Georg Olms GW) Lubrecht & Cramer.

Anthologium Vol. V: Anthologii Libri Quarti Partem Alteram Continens. Stobaeus. Ed. by Kurt Wachsmuth & Otto Hense. xxxviii, 480p. 1974. write for info. (3-296-15705-0, Pub. by Georg Olms GW) Lubrecht & Cramer.

Anthology. Elbert Hubbard. 1974. 59.95 (0-87968-643-X) Gordon Pr.

Anthology. William Shakespeare. Ed. by Levi Fox. (Shakespeare Collection). 160p. 1993. 4.95 (0-85306-949-2, Pub. by Jarrold Pub UK); 5.95 (0-85306-948-4, Pub. by Jarrold Pub UK) Seven Hills Bk.

Anthology. 2nd rev. ed. Antonin Artaud. Ed. by Jack Hirschman. LC 65-12730. 1965. pap. 10.95 (0-87286-000-0) City Lights.

Anthology: A Collection of Poems. B. Doutt et al. Ed. by David Shephard. LC 74-25359. 1974. 3.50 (0-915176-04-1) Woods Hole Pr.

Anthology: The Writings of Josef Marx. Comp. by Gloria Ziegler. LC 83-19893. 1983. 10.00 (0-941084-09-4) McGinnis & Marx.

Anthology Vol. 3: Universal K Postal Markings. 225p. (C). 1993. pap. text ed. 12.50 (1-880065-06-1) Machine Cancel Soc.

Anthology Vol. 4: Machine Postal Markings. 1993. pap. text ed. 10.00 (1-880065-07-X) Machine Cancel Soc.

Anthology & Handbook for Music Analysis. Gene J. Cho. 176p. (C). 1992. spiral bd. 24.95 (0-8403-7327-9) Kendall-Hunt.

Anthology by Women Poets: Tracing the Tradition. Ed. by Linda Hall. (Women on Women Ser.). 224p. 1994. 55.00 (0-304-32415-9, Pub. by Cassell Pubng UK); pap. 14.95 (0-304-32434-5, Pub. by Cassell Pubng UK) InBook.

Anthology Eight: Poetry. Ed. by Madelyn Eastlund & Sybella B. Snyder. (Illus.). 136p. (Orig.). 1990. pap. 8.50 (0-9620219-2-X) Verdure Pubns.

Anthology for Musical Analysis. 4th ed. Charles Burkhart. 602p. (C). 1986. pap. text ed. 38.75 (0-03-001289-9) HB Coll Pubs.

Anthology for Musical Analysis. 5th ed. Charles Burkhart. 640p. (C). 1993. pap. text ed. write for info. (0-03-055318-0) HB Coll Pubs.

Anthology for the Fretted Dulcimer. Lois Hornbostel. 1993. 12.95 (0-87166-507-7, 93850) Mel Bay.

Anthology in Print. Rebecca Wooley. (Orig.). 1978. reprint ed. pap. write for info. (0-685-59506-4) R S Wooley.

Anthology of Absurdist Theatre. Ed. by John Calder. 450p. (Orig.). 1997. pap. 18.95 (0-7145-4222-9) Riverrun NY.

Anthology of Advanced Placement French Literature: For the 1992-95 Exam. Ed. by David P. Greuel. 408p. (Orig.). (FRE.). (YA). (gr. 11-12). 1991. pap. text ed. 18.60 (1-877653-14-4) Wayside Pub.

Anthology of American Literature, Vol. 1: Colonial Through Romantic. 5th ed. Ed. by George McMichael. 2384p. (C). 1993. pap. write for info. (0-02-379601-4) Macmillan.

Anthology of American Literature, Vol. 2: Realism to the Present, Vol. 2. 5th ed. Ed. by George McMichael et al. LC 92-11568. 2432p. (C). 1993. pap. write for info. (0-02-379604-9) Macmillan.

***Anthology of American Poetry.** George Gesner. 1994. pap. 12.99 (0-517-11890-4) Random Hse Value.

Anthology of Another Town. E. W. Howe. (Collected Works of E. W. Howe). 1988. reprint ed. lib. bdg. 79.00 (0-7812-1298-7) Rprt Serv.

Anthology of Another Town see Collected Works of E. W. Howe

Anthology of Armenian Poetry. Ed. by Diana Der Hovanessian & Marzbed Margossian. LC 78-8048. 1978. text ed. 50.00 (0-231-04564-6) Col U Pr.

Anthology of Atheism & Rationalism. Ed. by Gordon Stein. LC 80-81326. (Skeptic's Bookshelf Ser.). 354p. 1984. reprint ed. pap. 22.95 (0-87975-256-4) Prometheus Bks.

Anthology of Atheism & Rationality. Gordon Stein. 1984. pap. 21.95 (0-87975-267-X) Prometheus Bks.

Anthology of Australian Gay & Lesbian Writing. Ed. by Robert Dessaix. 392p. 1994. 35.00 (0-19-553457-3) OUP.

Anthology of Austrian Drama. Ed. & Intro. by Douglas A. Russell. LC 76-19836. 450p. 1982. 49.50 (0-8386-2003-5) Fairleigh Dickinson.

Anthology of Belgian Symbolist Poets. Ed. by James J. Wilhelm. Tr. by Donald F. Friedman. LC 90-3052. (Library of World Literature in Translation: Vol. 2). (Illus.). 320p. 1992. 70.00 (0-8240-2988-7) Garland.

Anthology of Beloved Hymns for Guitar. Ronald Purcell. 1993. 7.95 (0-685-64339-5, 94065) Mel Bay.

Anthology of Beowulf Criticism. Ed. by Lewis E. Nicholson. 1963. pap. 14.95 (0-268-00006-9) U of Notre Dame Pr.

Anthology of Black Folk Wit, Wisdom, & Sayings. Ariel Books Staff. 1994. 4.95 (0-8362-3064-7) Andrews & McMeel.

Anthology of Blues Guitar. Woody Mann. (Illus.). 160p. 1993. pap. 19.95 (0-8256-0315-3, Oak) Music Sales.

Anthology of Brazilian Modernist Poetry. G. Pontiero. 1969. 110.00 (0-08-013327-4, Pub. by Pergamon Repr UK); pap. 110.00 (0-08-013326-6, Pub. by Pergamon Repr UK) Franklin.

Anthology of Byzantine Poetry. Barry Baldwin. (London Studies in Classical Philology: Vol. 14). xiii, 371p. 1985. lib. bdg. 49.00 (90-70265-27-3, Pub. by Gieben NE) Benjamins North Am.

Anthology of Byzantine Prose. Nigel G. Wilson. (Kleine Texte fuer Vorlesungen und Uebungen Ser.: Vol. 189). (C). 1971. 18.50 (3-11-001898-5) De Gruyter.

Anthology of Caribbean Short Stories. E. Bertram Baisden et al. 125p. (Orig.). (J). (gr. 7-12). 1989. pap. text ed. write for info. (0-318-66545-X) Caribbean Rsch Ctr.

Anthology of Catalan Folktales. Ed. & Tr. by Edward J. Neugaard. LC 94-16323. (Catalan Studies: Vol. 16). 1994. write for info. (0-8204-2530-3) P Lang Pubs.

Anthology of Chancery English 1417-1455. John H. Fisher et al. LC 84-3516. 440p. 1984. text ed. 49.50 (0-87049-433-3) U of Tenn Pr.

Anthology of Chartist Poetry: Poetry of the British Working Class, 1830s-1850s. Ed. by Peter Scheckner. LC 88-45722. 352p. 1989. 47.50 (0-8386-3345-5) Fairleigh Dickinson.

***Anthology of Children's Poetry.** Ed. & Intro. by Claire Ottenstein. (Illus.). 36p. (Orig.). (J). (gr. 1-5). 1993. pap. 4.00 (1-878149-23-7) Counterpoint Pub.

Anthology of Children's Poetry, 1992. Ed. by Claire Ottenstein. (Illus.). 36p. (Orig.). 1992. pap. 4.00 (1-878149-15-6) Counterpoint Pub.

***Anthology of Children's Poetry, 1994.** Ed. by Claire Ottenstein. (Illus.). 36p. (Orig.). (J). (gr. 1-5). 1994. pap. 4.00 (1-878149-30-X) Counterpoint Pub.

***Anthology of Chinese Literature: Beginnings to 1911.** Ed. & Tr. by Stephen Owen. LC 95-11409. 1996. write for info. (0-393-03823-8) Norton.

Anthology of Chinese Literature, Vol. 1: From the Earliest Times to the Fourteenth Century. Ed. by Cyril Birch & Donald Keene. (Illus.). 528p. 1987. pap. 15.95 (0-8021-5038-1, E417) Grove-Atltic.

Anthology of Chinese Literature, Vol. 2. From the Fourteenth Century to the Present Day. Ed. & Tr. by Cyril Birch. (Illus.). 512p. 1987. pap. 14.95 (0-8021-5090-X) Grove-Atltic.

Anthology of Christian Mysticism. Ed. by Paul De Jaegher. 1977. 12.95 (0-87243-073-1) Templegate.

Anthology of Christian Mysticism. Harvey Egan. 705p. (Orig.). 1991. pap. 34.95 (0-8146-6012-6) Liturgical Pr.

Anthology of Chuvash Poetry. Ed. by Gennady Aygi. Tr. by Peter France. (UNESCO Library of World Poetry). 220p. (Orig.). 1991. pap. 27.00 (1-85610-003-0, Pub. by Forest Bks UK) Dufour.

Anthology of Classic Anonymous Erotic Writing. Ed. by Michael Perkins. (Orig.). 1993. pap. text ed. 6.95 (1-56333-140-3) Masquerade.

Anthology of Classical Music. Ed. by Philip G. Downs. (C). 1992. pap. text ed. 29.95 (0-393-95209-6) Norton.

Anthology of Concrete Poetry. Emmett Williams. Ed. by Williams Emmett. LC 67-24980. 1967. 75.00 (0-87110-030-4) Ultramarine Pub.

Anthology of Contemporary Austrian Folk Plays. Veza Canetti et al. Tr. & Aft. by Richard Dixon. LC 93-18742. (Studies in Austrian Literature, Culture, & Thought. Translation Ser.). 397p. 1993. pap. 28.50 (0-929497-67-8) Ariadne CA.

Anthology of Contemporary Chinese Literature, 2 vols., Set. Chi Pang-Yuan et al. 1976. 50.00 (0-295-95504-X) U of Wash Pr.

Anthology of Contemporary Japanese Poetry. Ed. & Tr. by Leith Morton. LC 93-19734. (World Literature in Translation Ser.: Vol. 25). (Illus.). 486p. 1993. 75.00 (0-8240-0037-4) Garland.

Anthology of Contemporary Latin American Literature: 1960 to 1984. Ed. by Barry J. Luby & Wayne H. Finke. 320p. 1986. 48.50 (0-8386-3255-6) Fairleigh Dickinson.

Anthology of Contemporary Latin American Poetry. Ed. by Dudley Fitts. LC 76-17656. 677p. 1976. reprint ed. text ed. 52.50 (0-8371-8905-5, FIAC, Greenwood Pr) Greenwood.

Anthology of Contemporary Poetry. Ed. by Gregory N. Cameron. (Illus.). 208p. 1988. 24.95 (0-944653-00-6) Silver State Pub.

Anthology of Contemporary Romanian Poetry. Ed. by Andrea Deletant & B. Walker. LC 84-81308. 1990. pap. 16.95 (0-9509487-4-8) Dufour.

Anthology of Contemporary Romanian Poetry. Ed. by Roy MacGregor-Hastie. 1969. 25.00 (0-7206-0280-7) Dufour.

Anthology of Correspondence. Umberto Benedetti. 232p. 1991. 30.00 (0-9630506-0-5) U Benedetti.

Anthology of Country Blues CD. Cpp Belwin Staff. 1993. pap. 18.95 (0-89898-693-1) CPP Belwin.

Anthology of Creative Ojo Books. Diane Thomas. LC 79-89670. (Illus.). 1980. pap. 15.95 (0-918126-07-X) Hunter Ariz.

Anthology of Dalit Literature. Ed. by Mulk R. Anand & Eleanor Zelliot. (C). 1992. 14.00 (81-212-0419-4, Pub. by Gian Publng Hse II) S Asia.

Anthology of Danish Literature: Middle Ages to Romanticism. Ed. by F. J. Billeskov-Jansen & P. M. Mitchell. LC 72-5610. (Arcturus Books Paperbacks). 272p. (DAN & ENG.). 1972. pap. 16.95 (0-8093-0596-8) S Ill U Pr.

Anthology of Danish Literature: Realism to the Present. Ed. by F. J. Billeskov-Jansen & P. M. Mitchell. LC 72-5610. (Arcturus Books Paperbacks). 349p. (DAN & ENG.). 1972. pap. 16.95 (0-8093-0597-6) S Ill U Pr.

Anthology of Delaware Papermaking. Barbara E. Benson et al. (Illus.). 96p. 1991. 195.00 (0-938768-26-3) Oak Knoll.

Anthology of Early Renaissance Music. Ed. by Noah Greenberg & Paul Maynard. (Illus.). 304p. (C). 1975. text ed. 20.00 (0-393-02182-3) Norton.

***Anthology of Eighteenth-Century Satire: Grub-Street.** Ed. by Peter Heaney. LC 94-26075. 244p. 1994. text ed. 89.95 (0-7734-9026-4) E Mellen.

Anthology of Elizabethan Poetry. Ed. by Sukanta Chaudhuri. 180p. 1993. pap. 7.95 (0-19-563204-4) OUP.

Anthology of Elizabethan Prose Fiction. Paul Salzman. (World's Classics Ser.). 464p. 1987. pap. 10.95 (0-19-281744-2) OUP.

Anthology of English Poetry: Dryden to Blake. Ed. by Kathleen Campbell. LC 75-168777. (Granger Index Reprint Ser.). 1977. reprint ed. 23.95 (0-8369-6297-4) Ayer.

Anthology of Fingerstyle Guitar. Tommy Flint. 1993. 9.95 (0-87166-517-4, 93446); audio 18.95 (0-87166-519-0, 93446); audio 9.98 (0-87166-518-2, 93446) Mel Bay.

Anthology of Five String Banjo Styles. Neil Griffin. 1993. 7.95 (0-87166-925-0, 93663) Mel Bay.

Anthology of French Horn Music. Richard C. Moore & Eugene Ettore. 1993. 15.00 (1-56222-191-4, 93801) Mel Bay.

Anthology of French Poetry. Ed. by Henry Carrington. (Granger Poetry Library). 318p. 1985. reprint ed. 27.50 (0-89609-247-X) Roth Pub Inc.

Anthology of Galician Short Stories: Asi Vai o Conto. Ed. by Kathleen March. LC 91-25884. (Hispanic Literature Ser.: Vol. 13). 248p. 1991. lib. bdg. 89.95 (0-7734-9749-8) E Mellen.

Anthology of Georgian Folk Poetry. Ed. & Tr. by Kevin Tuite. LC 92-55124. 1994. write for info. (0-8386-3527-X) Fairleigh Dickinson.

Anthology of German Expressionist Drama. Ed. by Walter Sokel. LC 84-45197. 336p. 1984. pap. 14.95 (0-8014-9296-3) Cornell U Pr.

Anthology of German Literature of the Romantic Era & Age of Goethe. Ed. by Klaus-Peter Hinze & Leonard M. Trawick. LC 93-30394. 280p. 1993. pap. 69.95 (0-7734-1974-8) E Mellen.

***Anthology of Great U. S. Women Poets 1850-1990: Temples & Palaces.** Ed. by Glenn R. Ruihley. LC 95-19529. (Illus.). 604p. 1996. text ed. 129.95 (0-7734-8903-7) E Mellen.

Anthology of Greek Prose. Comp. by D. A. Russell. 328p. 1991. pap. 22.95 (0-19-872122-6) OUP.

An Asterisk (*) at the beginning of an entry indicates that the title is appearing in BIP for the first time.

An Asterisk (*) at the beginning of an entry indicates that the title is appearing in BIP for the first time.

355

Anthology of War Poetry, 1914-1918. Robert Nichols. 1973. 200.00 (0-87968-646-4) Gordon Pr.

Anthology of Western Armenian Literature. Ed. by James Etmekjian. LC 80-10608. 500p. 1980. 35.00 (0-88206-026-0) Caravan Bks.

Anthology of Western Marxism: From Lukacs & Gramsci to Socialist-Feminism. Ed. by Roger S. Gottlieb. 400p. (C). 1989. pap. text ed. 17.95 (0-19-505569-1) OUP.

Anthology of Western Reserve Literature. Ed. by David R. Anderson & Gladys Haddad. LC 92-4313. 328p. (Orig.). 1992. pap. 23.00 (0-87338-461-X) Kent St U Pr.

***Anthology of Wisconsin Writers.** 275p. 1995. pap. 13.95 (0-9647347-0-2) Crowbar Pr.

Anthology of World Poetry. Mark Van Doren. LC 29-26038. 1476p. 1936. 49.95 (0-15-107665-0) HarBrace.

Anthology of World Scriptures. Robert E. Van Voorst. 344p. 1994. pap. 23.95 (0-534-19176-2) Intl Thomson.

***Anthology of Yiddish Folksongs, Vol. 4.** Vinkovetzky. 1983. 32.50 (965-223-447-8, Pub. by Magnes Pr IS) Gefen Bks.

Anthology on Armed Jewish Resistance 1939-1945, Vol. 1. Isaac Kowalski. (Illus.). 648p. 1984. reprint ed. 30.00 (0-685-08344-6) Jewish Com Pub.

Anthology on Armed Jewish Resistance 1939-1945, Vol. 2. Isaac Kowalski. 648p. 1985. reprint ed. 30.00 (0-317-46999-1) Jewish Com Pub.

Anthology on Armed Jewish Resistance 1939-1945, Vol. 3. Isaac Kowalski. 648p. 1986. reprint ed. 30.00 (0-317-47002-7) Jewish Com Pub.

Anthology on Caring. Ed. by Peggy Chinn. 352p. 1991. 32.95 (0-88737-516-2) Natl League Nurse.

Anthology Seven. Ed. by Earl A. Monaghan. LC 89-91096. 128p. (Orig.). 1989. pap. text ed. 7.50 (0-9622840-0-9) NEB Pr.

Anthology with Comments. Elizabeth J. Gray. (C). 1942. pap. 3.00 (0-87574-018-9) Pendle Hill.

Anthology, 1934-1944. Jewish Frontier (Periodical) Staff. LC 76-167370. (Essay Index Reprint Ser.). 1977. reprint ed. 34.95 (0-8369-2459-2) Ayer.

Anthon Genealogy. S. Fish. xl, 214p. 1993. reprint ed. lib. bdg. 49.50 (0-8328-2774-6); reprint ed. pap. 39.50 (0-8328-2775-4) Higginson Bk Co.

Anthonisen: Woodmere Art Museum Exhibit. Photos by Stephen Perloff & Charles Callaghan. (Illus.). 36p. (Orig.). 1992. pap. 12.00 (0-9634109-0-3) Anthonisen.

Anthony. Kally. 1993. 12.95 (0-533-10488-2) Vantage.

Anthony. Teddy Milne. LC 86-62446. 197p. (Orig.). (J). (gr. 5 up). 1986. pap. 5.00 (0-938875-01-9) Pittenbruach Pr.

Anthony: Anatomy & Physiology Lab Manual, No. 13 SE. Thibodeau. 304p. 1989. pap. 15.95 (0-8016-6235-4) Mosby Yr Bk.

***Anthony & Berryman's Magistrates' Court Guide.** Ed. by T. G. Moore. 510p. 1994. pap. 59.00 (0-406-02873-7) Butterworth Legal Pubs.

Anthony & Cleopatra. William Shakespeare. Ed. by Michael Hall. (Oxford Shakespeare Ser.). (Illus.). 400p. 1994. 65.00 (0-19-812909-2) OUP.

Anthony & Cleopatra. rev. ed. William Shakespeare. 1964. pap. 3.95 (0-451-52264-8, Sig Classics) NAL-Dutton.

Anthony & Cleopatra. William Shakespeare. LC 94-9777. (Shakespeare Ser.). (Illus.). 384p. 1994. reprint ed. pap. 6.95 (0-19-281447-8) OUP.

***Anthony & Cleopatra: Granville Barkers Prefaces to Shakespeare.** Granville Barker. 160p. 1995. pap. 6.95 (0-435-08645-6) Heinemann.

Anthony & Cleopatra: Modern Text with Introduction. Ed. by A. L. Rowse. LC 86-11034. (Contemporary Shakespeare Ser.). 152p. (C). 1986. pap. text ed. 3.45 (0-8191-3931-9) U Pr of Amer.

Anthony & the Aardvark. Lesley Sloss. LC 90-6528. (Illus.). 32p. (J). (ps up). 1991. 13.95 (0-688-10302-2); lib. bdg. 13.88 (0-688-10303-0) Lothrop.

***Anthony Ant Pop-up, No. 1.** Lorna Philpot & Graham Philpot. (Illus.). (J). Date not set. 5.99 (0-679-87445-3) Random.

***Anthony Ant Pop-up, No. 2.** Lorna Philpot & Graham Philpot. (Illus.). (J). Date not set. 5.99 (0-679-87446-1) Random.

***Anthony Ant Pop-up, No. 3.** Lorna Philpot & Graham Philpot. (Illus.). (J). Date not set. 5.99 (0-679-87447-X) Random.

***Anthony Ant's Creepy Crawly Party.** Philpot. LC 94-67150. 1995. 7.99 (0-679-87056-3) Random.

Anthony Ashley Cooper, Earl of Shaftesbury & 'Le Refuge Francais' Correspondence. Rex A. Barrell. LC 88-13823. (Studies in British History: Vol. 15). (Illus.). 264p. 1989. lib. bdg. 89.95 (0-88946-466-9) E Mellen.

Anthony Asquith. Peter Noble. (Film Ser.). 1979. lib. bdg. 6.95 (0-8490-2866-3) Gordon Pr.

Anthony Benezet. Anthony Benezet. LC 77-152916. (Black Heritage Library Collection). 1977. 18.95 (0-8369-8760-8) Ayer.

Anthony Burgess. Intro. by Harold Bloom. (Modern Critical Views Ser.). 183p. 1987. 29.95 (0-87754-676-2) Chelsea Hse.

Anthony Burgess: A Bibiliography. Jeutonne Brewer. LC 80-413. (Author Bibliographies Ser.: No. 47). 193p. 1980. lib. bdg. 22.50 (0-8108-1286-X) Scarecrow.

***Anthony Burgess: The Artist as Novelist.** fac. ed. Geoffrey Aggeler. LC 78-12200. 253p. 1979. pap. 72.20 (0-7837-8361-2, 2059170) Bks Demand.

Anthony Burgess Revisited. John J. Stinson. (Twayne's English Authors Ser.: No. 482). 184p. (C). 1991. text ed. 22.95 (0-8057-7000-3, Twayne) Macmillan.

Anthony Burns: A History. Charles E. Stevens. 232p. 1973. reprint ed. 22.50 (0-87928-027-1) Corner Hse.

Anthony Burns: The Defeat & Triumph of a Fugitive Slave. Virginia Hamilton. LC 87-38063. 192p. (J). (gr. 5 up). 1988. lib. bdg. 12.99 (0-394-98185-5) Knopf Bks Yng Read.

Anthony Burns: The Defeat & Triumph of a Fugitive Slave. Virginia Hamilton. LC 87-38063. 192p. (J). (gr. 5 up). 1992. pap. 4.99 (0-679-83997-6) Knopf Bks Yng Read.

Anthony Burns, a History. Charles E. Stevens. LC 74-82225. (Anti-Slavery Crusade in America Ser.). 1970. reprint ed. 17.95 (0-405-00664-0) Ayer.

Anthony Burns, a History. Charles E. Stevens. LC 79-97439. 295p. 1969. reprint ed. text ed. 52.50 (0-8371-2724-6, SBU&, Greenwood Pr) Greenwood.

Anthony Caro: Explorations in Sculpture. Ed. by Karen Wilkin. (Illus.). 160p. 1991. 65.00 (3-7913-1137-9, Pub. by Prestel) TeNeues.

Anthony Comstock: His Career of Cruelty & Crime. De Robigne M. Bennett. LC 73-121102. (Civil Liberties in American History Ser.). 1971. reprint ed. lib. bdg. 22.50 (0-306-71968-1) Da Capo.

Anthony Eden at the Foreign Office, 1931-1938. Anthony R. Peters. LC 85-24994. 410p. 1987. text ed. 45.00 (0-312-04236-1) St Martin.

***Anthony Eden, 1897-1977: A Bibliography.** Alan Lawrance & Peter Dodd. LC 95-7480. (Bibliographies of British Statesmen Ser.). 240p. 1995. text ed. 75.00 (0-313-28286-2, Greenwood Pr) Greenwood.

Anthony Evans of Colonial Southside Virginia: Lines of Banks, Blackwell, Bugg, Burnett, Davis, Evans, Fox, Ingram, Mathews, Smith, Walker, & a Sourcebook for Related Materials. June B. Evans. LC 83-70347. (Illus.). 182p. 1983. 25.50 (0-9611114-0-2) Bryn Ffyliaid.

Anthony Gets Ready for Church. Mary Landis. (Jewel Bks.). (J). 1990. pap. 2.15 (0-317-02906-1) Rod & Staff.

Anthony Giddens. Clark & Celia Modgil. 1990. 90.00 (1-85000-548-6, Falmer Pr) Taylor & Francis.

Anthony Giddens. Ian Craib. 240p. 1992. 49.95 (0-415-07072-4, A6510) Routledge.

Anthony Giddens: Consensus & Controversy. Ed. by Jon Clark et al. 362p. 1990. pap. 60.00 (1-85000-983-X, Falmer Pr) Taylor & Francis.

Anthony Gross. Peter Gross. 144p. 1992. 69.95 (0-85967-889-X, Pub. by Scolar Pr UK) Ashgate Pub Co.

Anthony Hecht. Norman German. (American University Studies: American Literature: Ser. XXIV, Vol. 7). 230p. (C). 1989. text ed. 36.60 (0-8204-0840-9) P Lang Pubs.

Anthony Hopkins: A Biography. Michael F. Callan. LC 93-40256. 288p. 1994. text ed. 20.00 (0-684-19679-4, Scribners) S&S Trade.

Anthony Hopkins: The Authorized Biography. Quentin Falk. LC 93-4277. (Illus.). 232p. 1993. 22.95 (1-56656-125-6) Interlink Pub.

Anthony Hopkins: The Authorized Biography. Quentin Falk. 1994. pap. 12.95 (1-56656-145-0) Interlink Pub.

Anthony Hopkins: Too Good to Waste. large type ed. Quentin Fack. 272p. 1990. 10.97 (1-85089-421-3, Pub. by ISIS UK) Transaction Pubs.

Anthony Kennedy. Bob Italia. Ed. by Paul Deegan. LC 92-13710. (Supreme Court Justices Ser.). 40p. (J). 1992. lib. bdg. 13.99 (1-56239-094-5) Abdo & Dghtrs.

Anthony Milner: A Bio-Bibliography. James Siddons. LC 88-32822. (Bio-Bibliographies in Music Ser.: No. 20). (Illus.). 180p. 1989. text ed. 47.95 (0-313-25732-9, SYM, Greenwood Pr) Greenwood.

Anthony Mouse Goes Swimming. Elizabeth C. Powhida. (Illus.). 40p. (J). (ps-5). 1995. pap. write for info. (0-9625842-1-5, TXU538146) Kinderhook Pubs.

Anthony Philip Heinrich: A Nineteenth Century Composer in America. William T. Upton. LC 39-2473. reprint ed. 37.50 (0-404-06706-9) AMS Pr.

Anthony Powell. Neil McEwan. Ed. by Norman Page. LC 90-43271. (Modern Novelists Ser.). 160p. 1991. text ed. 35.00 (0-312-05571-4) St Martin.

***Anthony Powell.** rev. ed. Neil Brennan. LC 94-49326. (English Authors Ser.: Vol. TEAS 158). 1995. write for info. (0-8057-4545-9, Twayne) Macmillan.

Anthony Powell: A Bibliography. George Lilley. (Illus.). 320p. 1993. 78.00 (0-938768-46-8) Oak Knoll.

Anthony Quinn. (Hispanics of Achievement Ser.). (Illus.). 112p. (J). (gr. 6-12). 1993. lib. bdg. 17.95 (0-7910-1251-4); pap. write for info. (0-7910-1278-6) Chelsea Hse.

Anthony Rose: Manuscript Edition. Jules Feiffer. 1990. pap. 13.00 (0-8222-0057-0) Dramatists Play.

Anthony Salvin: Pioneer of Gothic Revival Architecture, 1799-1881. Jill Allibone. LC 86-16477. 224p. 1987. text ed. 38.00 (0-8262-0629-8, 83-36273) U of Mo Pr.

Anthony T. Rossi. Sanna B. Rossi. LC 86-27651. 199p. 1986. pap. 9.99 (0-8308-4999-8, 4999) InterVarsity.

Anthony, the Man, the Company, the Cameras. William Marder & Estelle Marder. Ed. by Robert G. Duncan. LC 81-90597. 384p. 1982. 135.00 (0-9607480-0-8) Marder.

Anthony, the Man, the Company, the Cameras. limited ed. William Marder & Estelle Marder. Ed. by Robert G. Duncan. LC 81-90597. 384p. 1982. 200.00 (0-685-05986-3) Marder.

***Anthony, the Perfect Monster.** LC 94-26105. (Step into Reading Ser.). 1995. 3.99 (0-679-86845-3) Random.

***Anthony, the Perfect Monster.** Angelo DeCesare. LC 94-26105. (Step into Reading Ser.: Step 3). (J). (gr. 2-5). 1995. 9.99 (0-679-96845-8) Random Bks Yng Read.

Anthony Trollope. Alice Fredman. LC 74-136496. (Columbia Essays on Modern Writers Ser.: No. 56). 48p. 1971. pap. text ed. 7.50 (0-231-03081-9) Col U Pr.

Anthony Trollope. Victoria Glendinning. (Illus.). 576p. 1994. pap. 15.00 (0-14-023512-4, Penguin Bks) Viking Penguin.

Anthony Trollope. Susan P. MacDonald. (Twayne's English Authors Ser.: No. 441). 167p. 1987. text ed. 21.95 (0-8057-6945-5, TEAS 441, Twayne) Macmillan.

Anthony Trollope. Victoria Glendinning. LC 92-54275. 1993. reprint ed. 30.00 (0-394-58268-3) Knopf.

Anthony Trollope. Hugh Walpole. LC 75-161000. (Select Bibliographies Reprint Ser.). 1977. reprint ed. 20.95 (0-8369-5868-3) Ayer.

Anthony Trollope. Hugh Walpole. (BCL1-PR English Literature Ser.). 206p. 1992. reprint ed. lib. bdg. 79.00 (0-7812-7530-X) Rprt Serv.

Anthony Trollope: A Victorian in His World. Richard Mullen. LC 91-16912. 767p. 1991. 45.00 (0-913720-77-1) Beil.

Anthony Trollope: An Annotated Bibliography of Periodical Works by & about Him in the United States & Great Britain to 1900. Anne K. Lyons. 175p. 1985. 25.00 (0-913283-04-5) Penkevill.

Anthony Trollope: Dream & Art. Andrew Wright. LC 82-50171. x, 174p. 1983. 20.00 (0-226-90806-2) U Ch Pr.

***Anthony Trollope: The Complete Short Stories, Vol. 3, Tourists & Colonials.** Anthony Trollope. Ed. by Betty J. Breyer. reprint ed. pap. 77.90 (0-7837-9014-7, 2043376) Bks Demand.

Anthony Trollope: The Complete Short Stories - Editors & Writers, Vol. II. Anthony Trollope. Ed. by Betty J. Breyer. LC 79-19986. 238p. 1979. 17.50 (0-912646-57-8) Tex Christian.

Anthony Trollope: The Complete Short Stories-Courtship & Marriage, Vol. IV. Anthony Trollope. Ed. by Betty J. Breyer. LC 79-15519. 282p. 1982. 17.50 (0-912646-75-6) Tex Christian.

Anthony Trollope: The Complete Short Stories, Vol. 1: The Christmas Stories. Anthony Trollope. LC 79-15520. 261p. reprint ed. pap. 74.40 (0-7837-3409-3, 2043376) Bks Demand.

Anthony Trollope: The Complete Shorter Fiction. Ed. by Julian Thompson. 996p. 1992. 38.00 (0-88184-854-9) Carroll & Graf.

Anthony Trollope: The Complete Shorter Fiction. Ed. by Julian Thompson. 972p. 1993. pap. 16.95 (0-7867-0021-1) Carroll & Graf.

Anthony Trollope: The Critical Heritage. Ed. by Donald Smalley. 1978. 65.00 (0-7100-6153-6, RKP) Routledge.

Anthony Trollope see Benjamin Disraeli

Anthony Van Dyck. LC 75-99493. (Illus.). 384p. 1990. pap. 29.95 (0-89468-155-9) Natl Gallery Art.

Anthony Van Dyck. Natalia Gritsai. 1982. 50.00 (0-317-61200-X, Pub. by Collets) St Mut.

Anthony Van Dyck. Text by Alfred Moir. LC 94-8419. 1994. write for info. (0-8109-3917-7) Abrams.

***Anthony Van Dyck: The Earl of Arundel.** Christopher White et al. LC 94-42442. (Museum Studies on Art). 1995. write for info. (0-89236-227-8, J P Getty Museum) J P Getty Trust.

Anthony Wayne: Soldier of the Early Republic. Paul D. Nelson. LC 84-48543. (Illus.). 380p. 1985. 29.95 (0-253-30751-1) Ind U Pr.

Anthony's Text of Anatomy & Physiology. Thibodeau & Patton. 1993. 35.95 (0-8016-7671-1) Mosby Yr Bk.

Anthracite: An Instance of Natural Resource Monopoly. Scott Nearing. LC 78-169772. (Select Bibliographies Reprint Ser.). 1977. reprint ed. 20.95 (0-8369-5992-2) Ayer.

Anthracite & Slackwater: The North Branch Canal 1828-1901. Charles Petrillo. LC 86-26872. (Orig.). 1987. 28.75 (0-930973-03-8); pap. 16.25 (0-930973-04-6) Canal Hist Tech.

Anthracite Aristocracy: Leadership & Social Change in the Hard Coal Regions of Northeastern Pennsylvania, 1800-1930. Edward Davies, II. LC 85-2947. 277p. 1985. 27.00 (0-87580-107-2) N Ill U Pr.

Anthracite Basins of Eastern Pennsylvania: Field Trip Guide Book. J. R. Levine & J. R. Eggleston. (Illus.). 54p. (Orig.). (C). 1994. pap. text ed. 40.00 (1-56806-478-0) Diane Pub.

Anthracite Coal: A Study in Advanced Industrial Decline. Theodore Bakerman. Ed. by Stuart Bruchey. LC 78-22656. (Energy in the American Economy Ser.). (Illus.). 1979. lib. bdg. 25.95 (0-405-11960-7) Ayer.

Anthracite Coal Communities: A Study of the Demography, the Social, Educational & Moral Life of the Anthracite Regions. Peter Roberts. LC 75-129410. (American Immigration Collection Ser. 2). (Illus.). 1970. reprint ed. 26.95 (0-405-00564-4) Ayer.

***Anthracite Ghosts.** Ed. by Walter Dinteman. (Illus.). 1995. 35.00 (0-940866-44-7) Fordham.

Anthracite Iron Industry of the Lehigh Valley. Craig L. Bartholomew & Lance E. Metz. Ed. by Ann Bartholomew. LC 88-25719. 1988. pap. 17.95 (0-930973-08-9) Canal Hist Tech.

Anthracite Miner: The Photographs of George Harvan. Ed. by David L. Salay. (Illus.). 36p. pap. 4.00 (0-917445-02-3) Anthracite.

Anthracite People: Families, Unions & Work, 1900-1940. John Bodnar. (Illus.). 100p. 1983. pap. text ed. 6.95 (0-89271-023-3) Pa Hist & Mus.

***Anthracite Trust.** Aileen S. Freeman. LC 94-61931. (Illus.). 329p. (Orig.). 1994. pap. 14.95 (0-9644199-0-4) Freeman Open Syst.

Anthracycline & Anthracenedione-Based Anticancer Agents. Ed. by J. W. Lown. (Bioactive Molecules Ser.: No. 6). 738p. 1989. 225.75 (0-444-87275-2) Elsevier.

***Anthracycline Antibiotics: New Analogues, Methods of Delivery, & Mechanisms of Action.** American Chemical Society Division of Carbohydrate Chemistry Staff. Ed. by Waldemar Priebe. LC 94-38929. (Symposium Ser.: No. 574). (Illus.). 380p. 1994. 99.95 (0-8412-3040-4) Am Chemical.

Anthracycline Antibiotics in Cancer Therapy. Franco M. Muggia et al. 1982. text ed. 69.50 (0-686-37594-7) Kluwer Ac.

Anthraquinone Laxatives: Proceedings of the Symposium, Bissone (Lugano), Switzerland, Sept. 1975. Symposium, Bissone (Lugano) Switzerland Staff. Ed. by J. W. Fairbairn. (Pharmacology Journal: Vol. 14, Suppl. 1). (Illus.). 1976. pap. 36.00 (3-8055-2426-9) S Karger.

Anthrax: State of Euphoria. Date not set. pap. 11.95 (0-685-68978-6) Music Sales.

Anthrax - Fistful of Metal: Guitar - Vocal. Ed. by Mark Phillips. (Illus.). 63p. (Orig.). 1990. pap. text ed. 16.95 (0-89524-493-4) Cherry Lane.

***Anthromorphic Stelae of the Ukraine: The Early Iconography of the Indo-Europeans.** D. Ya Telegin & J. P. Mallory. (Journal of Indo-European Monograph Ser.: No. 11). (Illus.). 136p. 1994. lib. bdg. 55.00x (0-941694-45-3) Inst Study Man.

Anthrophysical Form: Two Families & Their Neighborhood Environments. Robert L. Vickery. LC 73-183896. (Illus.). 95p. reprint ed. pap. 27.10 (0-7837-4373-4, 2044084) Bks Demand.

Anthropic Cosmological Principle. John D. Barrow & Frank J. Tipler. LC 85-4824. (Illus.). 728p. 1986. 39.95 (0-19-851949-4) OUP.

Anthropic Cosmological Principle. John D. Barrow & Frank J. Tipler. 736p. 1988. pap. 17.95 (0-19-282147-4) OUP.

Anthropic Principle: Man As the Focal Point of Nature. Reinhard Breuer. 218p. 1990. 34.50 (0-8176-3482-7) Birkhauser.

Anthropic Principle: The Conditions for the Existence of Mankind in the Universe. Ed. by F. Bertola & U. Curi. (Illus.). 222p. (C). 1993. 59.95 (0-521-38203-3) Cambridge U Pr.

Anthropocentric Approach to Computing & Reactive Machines. Stoyan O. Kableshkov. LC 82-24836. (Electronic & Electrical Engineering Research Ser.: No. 2). (Illus.). 142p. reprint ed. pap. 40.50 (0-8357-6019-7, 2034227) Bks Demand.

Anthropogenic Climatic Change. M. I. Budyko & Y. A. Izrael. LC 91-3722. 485p. 1990. 60.00 (0-8165-1122-5) U of Ariz Pr.

Anthropogenic Compounds. (Handbook of Environmental Chemistry Ser.: Vol. 3, Pt. A). (Illus.). 290p. 1980. 91.00 (0-387-09690-6) Spr-Verlag.

Anthropogenic Compounds. (Handbook of Environmental Chemistry Ser.: Vol. 3, Part C). (Illus.). 250p. 1984. 139.00 (0-387-13019-5) Spr-Verlag.

Anthropogenic Compounds. Ed. by O. Hutzinger. (Handbook of Environmental Chemistry Ser.: Vol. 3, Pt. D). (Illus.). 260p. 1986. 155.00 (0-387-15555-4) Spr-Verlag.

Anthropogenic Compounds. Ed. by O. Hutzinger. (Handbook of Environmental Chemistry Ser.: Vol. 3, Pt. E). (Illus.). 190p. 1990. 83.00 (0-387-51423-6, 3373) Spr-Verlag.

Anthropogenic Compounds. Ed. by O. Hutzinger. (Handbook of Environmental Chemistry Ser.: Vol. 3, Pt. G). (Illus.). 248p. 1991. 110.00 (0-387-53198-X) Spr-Verlag.

Anthropogenic Compounds: Detergents. Ed. by N. T. De Oude & O. Hutzinger. (Handbook of Environmental Chemistry Ser.: Vol. 3, Pt. F). (Illus.). 456p. 1992. 175.00 (0-387-53797-X) Spr-Verlag.

Anthropogenic Indicators in Pollen Diagrams. Ed. by K. E. Behre. 245p. (C). 1986. text ed. 95.00 (90-6191-673-9, Pub. by A A Balkema NE) Ashgate Pub Co.

Anthropogeny: The Esoteric History of Man's Origin. Douglas Baker. (Illus.). (C). 1987. 90.00 (0-906006-03-1, Pub. by Claregate Coll UK) St Mut.

***Anthropoid Origins.** Ed. by J. G. Fleagle & R. F. Kay. (Advances in Primatology Ser.). (Illus.). 724p. 1994. 139.50 (0-306-44791-6, Plenum Pr) Plenum.

Anthropolis: A Tale of Two Cities. Daniel P. Fischer. LC 92-23847. 1992. 12.95 (0-86554-417-4, P100) Mercer Univ Pr.

Anthropological Analysis of Chinese Geomancy. Stephan D. Feuchtwang. 264p. 1985. reprint ed. 25.00 (0-89986-361-2) Oriental Bk Store.

Anthropological & Cross-Cultural Themes in Mental Health: An Annotated Bibliography, 1925-1974. Armando R. Favazza & Mary Oman. LC 76-48620. (University of Missouri Studies: Vol. 65). 392p. 1977. 40.00 (0-8262-0215-2) U of Mo Pr.

Anthropological Approaches to Diabetes: A Special Issue to the Journal of Medical Anthropology. Ed. by M. L. Urdaneta & R. Krehbiel. 130p. 1989. pap. text ed. 27.00 (2-88124-346-0) Gordon & Breach.

Anthropological Approaches to Political Behavior: Contributions from Ethnology. Frank McGlynn & Arthur Tuden. LC 90-50916. 352p. (C). 1991. 49.95 (0-8229-1162-0); pap. 19.95 (0-8229-6094-X) U of Pittsburgh Pr.

Anthropological Approaches to Resettlement: Policy, Practice, & Theory. Ed. by Michael M. Cernea & Scott E. Guggenheim. 406p. (C). 1993. pap. text ed. 47.50 (0-8133-8102-9) Westview.

Anthropological Approaches to the Study of Ethnomedicine. Ed. by Mark Nichter. LC 92-20369. 1992. text ed. 58.00 (2-88124-530-7); pap. text ed. 24.00 (2-88124-529-3) Gordon & Breach.

Anthropological Approaches to the Study of Religion. Ed. by Michael P. Banton. 1968. pap. 15.95 (0-422-72510-2, NO.2068, Pub. by Tavistock UK) Routledge Chapman & Hall.

Anthropological Archaeology. Guy Gibbon. LC 84-4321. 432p. 1984. text ed. 41.50 (0-231-05662-1) Col U Pr.

Anthropological Bibliography of South Asia Together with a Directory of Recent Anthropological Field Work, 3 vols. E. V. Fuehrer-Haimendorf. Incl. Vol. 1. Up to 1964. 1958. pap. 112.00 (90-279-7741-0); Vol. 2. 1955-1959. 1964. pap. text ed. 78.75 (90-279-6206-5); Vol. 3. 1960-1964. 1970. pap. 102.00 (90-279-6302-9); Set pap. write for info. (0-318-54398-2) Mouton.

An Asterisk (*) at the beginning of an entry indicates that the title is appearing in BIP for the first time.

An Asterisk (*) at the beginning of an entry indicates that the title is appearing in BIP for the first time.

Anthropology & the Greeks. S. C. Humphreys. (International Library of Anthropology). 357p. 1984. pap. 15.95 (*0-7102-0016-1*, 00161, RKP) Routledge.

Anthropology & the Human Experience. 5th ed. Edward A. Hoebel & Thomas Weaver. (Illus.). 1979. text ed. write for info. (*0-07-029140-3*) McGraw.

Anthropology & the Peace Corps: Case Studies in Career Preparation. Ed. by Brian E. Schwimmer & Dennis M. Warren. LC 90-20352. (Illus.). 272p. 1993. text ed. 32. 95 (*0-8138-0493-0*) Iowa St U Pr.

Anthropology & the Riddle of the Sphinx: Paradoxes of Change in the Life Course. Ed. by Paul Spencer. (ASA Monographs). 240p. 1990. 29.95 (*0-415-04089-2*, A4673) Routledge.

Anthropology & the Western Tradition: Toward An Authentic Anthropology. Jacob Pandian. 135p. (Orig.). 1985. pap. text ed. 9.50 (*0-88133-127-9*) Waveland Pr.

***Anthropology & Third World Issues.** Bill Geddes et al. 317p. (C). 1993. 49.00x (*0-949823-42-2*, Pub. by Deakin Univ AT) St Mut.

Anthropology, Art, & Aesthetics. Ed. by Jeremy Coote & Anthony Shelton. (Oxford Studies in the Anthropology of Cultural Forms). (Illus.). 304p. 1994. reprint ed. pap. 19.95 (*0-19-827945-0*) OUP.

Anthropology As Cultural Critique: An Experimental Moment in the Human Sciences. George E. Marcus & Michael M. Fischer. LC 85-20686. xiv, 206p. (Orig.). 1986. pap. 11.95 (*0-226-50449-2*) U Ch Pr.

Anthropology at Home. Anthony Jackson. 1987. pap. text ed. 22.50 (*0-422-60560-3*, 1084, Pub. by Tavistock UK) Routledge Chapman & Hall.

Anthropology Development & Nation Building. A. K. Kalla & K. S. Singh. (C). 1987. 39.00 (*81-7022-001-7*, Pub. by Concept II) S Asia.

Anthropology for Archaeologists. Bryony Orme. LC 80-69817. (Illus.). 293p. 1981. 45.00 (*0-8014-1398-2*) Cornell U Pr.

Anthropology for the Nineties: Introductory Readings. Ed. by Johnnetta B. Cole. 592p. 1988. pap. 19.95 (*0-02-906441-4*) Free Pr.

Anthropology for the People: A Refutation of the Theory of the Adamic Origin of All Races. William H. Campbell. LC 72-6467. (Black Heritage Library Collection). 1977. reprint ed. 29.95 (*0-8369-9154-0*) Ayer.

Anthropology for Tomorrow: Creating Practitioner-Oriented Applied Anthropology Programs. Ed. by Robert T. Trotter. (Special Publication: No. 24). 1988. 20.00 (*0-913167-25-8*) Am Anthro Assn.

Anthropology Goes to War: Professional Ethics & Counterinsurgency in Thailand. Eric Wakin. LC 91-74029. 319p. (Orig.). (C). 1992. lib. bdg. 27.95 (*1-881261-02-6*); pap. 14.95 (*1-881261-03-4*) U Wisc Ctr SE Asian.

Anthropology in China: Defining the Discipline. Ed. by Gregory E. Guldin. LC 90-21710. (Chinese Studies on China). 232p. 1991. reprint ed. 51.95 (*0-87332-833-7*) M E Sharpe.

Anthropology in Indian Context. Ed. by I. J. Bansal. 278p. 1983. 59.00 (*1-55528-069-2*, Pub. by Today & Tomorrows P & P II) Scholarly Pubns.

Anthropology in the High Valleys. Ed. by L. L. Langness & Terence E. Hays. LC 86-26415. (Publications in Anthropology & Related Fields). 384p. 1987. 24.95 (*0-88316-555-4*) Chandler & Sharp.

Anthropology in Use: A Source Book on Anthropological Practice. John Van Willigen. (C). 1991. pap. text ed. 43.50 (*0-8133-8250-5*) Westview.

Anthropology Journals & Serials: An Analytical Guide. Comp. by John T. Williams. LC 86-19574. 301p. 1986. text ed. 69.50 (*0-313-23834-0*, WAN/, Greenwood Pr) Greenwood.

Anthropology of Aging: A Partially Annotated Bibliography. Ed. by Marjorie M. Schweitzer. LC 91-9707. (Bibliographies & Indexes in Gerontology Ser.: No. 13). 360p. 1991. text ed. 69.50 (*0-313-26119-9*, SWZ/, Greenwood Pr) Greenwood.

Anthropology of Ancient Greece. Louis Gernet. LC 81-47598. 395p. reprint ed. pap. 112.60 (*0-8357-7884-3*, 2036302) Bks Demand.

Anthropology of Art. 2nd ed. Robert Layton. (Illus.). 264p. (C). 1991. 64.95 (*0-521-36367-5*); pap. 17.95 (*0-521-36894-4*) Cambridge U Pr.

Anthropology of Breast-Feeding. Ed. by Vanessa A. Maher. 176p. 1993. 49.95 (*0-85496-721-4*) Berg Pubs.

Anthropology of Breast-Feeding. Ed. by Vanessa A. Maher. 224p. 1993. pap. 15.95 (*0-85496-814-8*) Berg Pubs.

Anthropology of Curing in Multiethnic Thailand. Louis Golomb. LC 84-8649. (Illinois Studies in Anthropology Ser.: No. 15). (Illus.). 328p. 1985. 23.95 (*0-252-01170-8*) U of Ill Pr.

Anthropology of Development: Commemoration Volume in Honour of Professor I. P. Singh. Ed. by R. Malhotra. (C). 1992. text ed. 37.50 (*81-7099-328-8*, Pub. by Mittal II) S Asia.

Anthropology of Development: Demystification & Relevance. Jaganath Pathy. 214p. 1987. 13.00 (*81-212-0081-4*, Pub. by Gian Publng Hse II) S Asia.

Anthropology of Eastern China & Kwantung Province. Sergei M. Shirokogorov. LC 73-18081. (China Classic & Contemporary Works in Reprint Ser.). reprint ed. 34.50 (*0-404-56945-5*) AMS Pr.

***Anthropology of Europe: Identities & Boundaries in Conflict.** Ed. by Victoria A. Goddard et al. (Explorations in Anthropology Ser.). 256p. 1994. 49.95 (*0-85496-901-2*) Berg Pubs.

***Anthropology of Europe: Identities & Boundaries in Conflict.** Ed. by Victoria A. Goddard et al. (Explorations in Anthropology Ser.). 256p. 1994. pap. 19.95 (*0-85496-904-7*) Berg Pubs.

Anthropology of Everyday Life: An Autobiography. Edward T. Hall. LC 92-39059. 1993. pap. 14.50 (*0-385-23743-X*, Anchor NY) Doubleday.

Anthropology of Evil. Ed. by David Parkin. 288p. 1987. pap. 21.95 (*0-631-15432-9*) Blackwell Pubs.

Anthropology of Experience. Ed. by Victor W. Turner & Edward M. Bruner. LC 85-1200. (Illus.). 406p. 1986. pap. 15.95 (*0-252-01249-6*) U of Ill Pr.

Anthropology of Florida. Ales Hrdlicka. LC 76-43750. (Publications of the Florida State Historical Society: No. 1). reprint ed. 55.00 (*0-404-15590-1*) AMS Pr.

Anthropology of Human Birth. Margarita A. Kay. LC 81-9776. (Illus.). 445p. 1982. text ed. 30.00 (*0-8036-5240-2*) Davis Co.

***Anthropology of Iceland.** Ed. by E. P. Durrenberger & Gisli Palsson. LC 89-4657. (Illus.). 286p. 1995. pap. text ed. 14.95x (*0-87745-499-X*) U of Iowa Pr.

Anthropology of Iraq, Pt. 1. Henry Field. (HU PMP Ser.). (Illus.). 1940. 47.00 (*0-527-01321-8*) Periodicals Srv.

Anthropology of Johannes Scottus Eriugena. Willemien Otten. LC 90-42391. (Brill's Studies in Intellectual History: Vol. 20). viii, 242p. 1990. 51.50 (*90-04-09302-8*) E J Brill.

Anthropology of Justice: Law As Culture in Islamic Society. Lawrence Rosen. (Lewis Henry Morgan Lectures). (Illus.). 134p. (C). 1989. pap. 16.95 (*0-521-36740-9*) Cambridge U Pr.

Anthropology of Kodiak Island. Ales Hrdlicka. LC 74-5848. reprint ed. 60.50 (*0-404-11653-1*) AMS Pr.

***Anthropology of Landscape: Perspectives on Place & Space.** Ed. by Eric Hirsch & Michael O'Hanlon. (Oxford Studies in Social & Cultural Anthropology). (Illus.). 320p. 1995. 55.00 (*0-19-827880-2*) OUP.

***Anthropology of Landscape: Perspectives on Place & Space.** Ed. by Eric Hirsch & Michael O'Hanlon. (Oxford Studies in Social & Cultural Anthropology). (Illus.). 320p. 1995. pap. 19.95 (*0-19-828010-6*) OUP.

Anthropology of Learning. Ed. by Harry F. Wolcott. (Special Issues of the Anthropology & Education Quarterly Ser.: Vol. 13, No. 2). 1982. 7.50 (*0-317-66340-2*) Am Anthro Assn.

***Anthropology of Lower Income Urban Enclaves: The Case of East Harlem.** Ed. by Judith Freidenberg. LC 95-5500. (Annals of Sciences Ser.). 1995. write for info. (*0-89766-891-X*); pap. text ed. write for info. (*0-89766-892-8*) NY Acad Sci.

Anthropology of Medicine: From Culture to Method. Ed. by Lola Romanucci-Ross et al. (Illus.). 416p. (C). 1985. text ed. 44.95 (*0-03-062192-5*, Bergin & Garvey) Greenwood.

Anthropology of Medicine: From Culture to Method. Ed. by Lola Romanucci-Ross et al. LC 91-21999. 464p. 1991. pap. text ed. 22.95 (*0-89789-263-1*, G263, Bergin & Garvey) Greenwood.

Anthropology of Medicine: From Culture to Method. 2nd ed. Ed. by Lola Romanucci-Ross et al. LC 91-21999. 464p. 1991. text ed. 75.00 (*0-89789-262-3*, H262, Bergin & Garvey) Greenwood.

***Anthropology of Minority Groups: Index of New Information with Authors & Subjects.** rev. ed. American Health Research Institute Staff. LC 94-24771. 151p. 1994. 44.50 (*0-7883-0268-X*); pap. 39.50 (*0-7883-0269-8*) ABBE Pubs Assn.

Anthropology of Music. Alan P. Merriam. 358p. 1964. pap. 16.95 (*0-8101-0607-8*) Northwestern U Pr.

Anthropology of Numbers. Thomas Crump. (Cambridge Studies in Social & Cultural Anthropology: No. 70). (Illus.). 240p. (C). 1990. 69.95 (*0-521-38045-6*) Cambridge U Pr.

Anthropology of Numbers. Thomas Crump. (Cambridge Studies in Social & Cultural Anthropology: No. 70). (Illus.). 210p. (C). 1992. pap. 17.95 (*0-521-43807-1*) Cambridge U Pr.

Anthropology of Organizations. Ed. by Susan Wright. LC 93-47627. 208p. 1994. 59.95x (*0-415-08748-1*, B3932, Routledge NY); pap. 16.95 (*0-415-08747-3*, B3936, Routledge NY) Routledge.

Anthropology of Peace & Nonviolence. Ed. by Leslie E. Sponsel & Thomas A. Gregor. LC 93-40822. 300p. 1994. lib. bdg. 45.00 (*1-55587-424-X*); pap. text ed. 18. 95 (*1-55587-450-9*) Lynne Rienner.

Anthropology of Performance. Victor Turner. 188p. 1986. pap. 12.95 (*1-55554-001-5*) PAJ Pubns.

***Anthropology of Reading.** Eric Livingston. LC 94-39577. 1995. write for info. (*0-253-33509-4*) Ind U Pr.

Anthropology of Self & Behavior. Gerald M. Erchak. LC 91-19666. 200p. (C). 1992. text ed. 34.00 (*0-8135-1761-3*); pap. text ed. 15.00 (*0-8135-1762-1*) Rutgers U Pr.

Anthropology of Slavery: The Womb of Iron & Gold. Claude Meillassoux. Tr. by Alide Dasnois. 1991. lib. bdg. 49.95 (*0-226-51911-2*); pap. text ed. 18.95 (*0-226-51912-0*) U Ch Pr.

Anthropology of Space: Explorations into the Natural Philosophy & Semantics of the Navajo. Rik Pinxten et al. LC 82-23703. 252p. reprint ed. pap. 71.90 (*0-7837-3005-5*, 2042936) Bks Demand.

***Anthropology of Sport: An Introduction.** rev. ed. Kendall Blanchard. LC 95-6948. 1995. text ed. write for info. (*0-89789-329-8*, Bergin & Garvey); pap. text ed. write for info. (*0-89789-330-1*, Bergin & Garvey) Greenwood.

Anthropology of St. John of Damascus. Constantine N. Tsirpanlis. 64p. 1980. pap. 6.00 (*0-317-36320-4*) EO Pr.

Anthropology of Taiwanese Society. Ed. by Emily M. Ahern & Hill Gates. LC 79-64212. xvi, 491p. 1981. 52. 50 (*0-8047-1043-0*) Stanford U Pr.

Anthropology of the Desert West: Essays in Honor of Jesse D. Jennings. Ed. by Carol J. Condie & Don D. Fowler. LC 85-15810. 339p. reprint ed. pap. 96.70 (*0-8357-5628-9*, 2031915) Bks Demand.

Anthropology of the Desert West: Essays in Honor of Jesse D. Jennings. Ed. by Carol J. Condie & Don D. Fowler. (Anthropological Papers: No. 110). (Illus.). 336p. (C). 1993. reprint ed. pap. 27.50 (*0-87480-248-2*) U of Utah Pr.

Anthropology of the North Pacific Rim. Ed. by William W. Fitzhugh & Valerie Chaussonnet. LC 92-38689. (Illus.). (C). 1993. text ed. 49.00 (*1-56098-202-0*) Smithsonian.

***Anthropology of the Self.** Brian Morris. (Anthropology, Culture & Society Ser.). (C). 1994. pap. text ed. 19.95 (*0-7453-0858-9*) Westview.

Anthropology of the Self: The Individual in Cultural Perspective. Brian Morris. LC 94-9670. (Anthropology, Culture, & Society Ser.). (C). 1994. text ed. 69.95 (*0-7453-0857-0*, Pub. by Pluto Pr UK) Westview.

Anthropology of Time: Cultural Constructions of Temporal Maps & Images. Alfred Gell. LC 92-12417. (Explorations in Anthropology Ser.). 350p. 1992. 69.95 (*0-85496-717-6*); pap. 22.95 (*0-85496-890-3*) Berg Pubs.

Anthropology of War. Ed. by Jonathan Haas. (School of American Research Advanced Seminar Ser.). (Illus.). 272p. (C). 1990. 69.95 (*0-521-38042-1*) Cambridge U Pr.

Anthropology of War & Peace: Perspectives on the Nuclear Age. Paul R. Turner et al. LC 89-6925. 224p. 1988. text ed. 50.95 (*0-89789-142-2*, Bergin & Garvey); pap. text ed. 18.95 (*0-89789-143-0*, Bergin & Garvey) Greenwood.

Anthropology of World's Fairs: San Francisco's Panama Pacific International Exposition of 1915. Burton Benedict. 175p. 1983. 65.00 (*0-85967-676-5*, Pub. by Scolar Pr UK); pap. 39.95 (*0-85967-677-3*, Pub. by Scolar Pr UK) Ashgate Pub Co.

Anthropology on the Great Plains. Ed. by W. Raymond Wood & Margot Liberty. LC 79-28369. 314p. reprint ed. pap. 89.50 (*0-7837-6469-3*, 2046473) Bks Demand.

Anthropology, Public Policy, & Native Peoples in Canada. Ed. by Noel Dyck & James B. Waldram. 368p. 1993. 49. 95 (*0-7735-0961-5*, Pub. by McGill CN); pap. 19.95 (*0-7735-0978-X*, Pub. by McGill CN) U of Toronto Pr.

Anthropology Through the Looking-Glass: Critical Enthnography in the Margins of Europe. Michael Herzfeld. (Illus.). 288p. (C). 1989. pap. 19.95 (*0-521-38908-9*) Cambridge U Pr.

Anthropology Through the Looking-Glass: Critical Ethnography in the Margins of Europe. Michael Herzfeld. 288p. 1988. 64.95 (*0-521-34003-9*) Cambridge U Pr.

Anthropology, Vol. 27: International Bibliography of the Social Sciences. Ed. by International Committee for Social Science Information & Documentation. 560p. 1984. lib. bdg. 110.00 (*0-422-80960-8*, 4054, Pub. by Tavistock UK) Routledge Chapman & Hall.

Anthropology 1980. Ed. by International Committee for Social Science Information & Documentation. 500p. 1983. 110.00 (*0-422-80950-0*, NO. 3973) Routledge Chapman & Hall.

Anthropometric Assessment of Nutritional Status. John H. Himes. 1991. text ed. 115.00 (*0-471-56876-7*) Wiley.

Anthropometric Data: Background & Illustrated Guidlines for Survey Managers. Kees Kostermans. LC 93-47898. (Living Standards Measurement Study (LSMS) Paper Ser.: No. 101). (Illus.). 62p. 1994. 7.95 (*0-8213-2755-0*, 12755) World Bank.

Anthropometric Data & Prevalence of Overweight for Hispanics, 1982-84. Tr. by Matthew F. Najjar & Robert J. Kuczmarski. (DHHS Publication PHS Ser., No. 89-1689: Vital & Health Statistics, Ser. 11: No. 239). (Illus.). 110p. (Orig.). 1989. pap. 5.50 (*0-16-002379-3*, S/N 017-022-01070-4) USGPO.

Anthropometric Facial Proportions in Medicine. Leslie G. Farkas & Ian R. Munro. (Illus.). 368p. (C). 1987. 89.95 (*0-398-05261-1*) C C Thomas.

Anthropometric Methods: Designing to Fit the Human Body. John A. Roebuck, Jr. LC 93-16975. 200p. 1995. pap. 20.00 (*0-945289-01-4*) Human Factors.

Anthropometric Standardization Reference Manual. Ed. by Timothy G. Lohman et al. LC 87-8623. (Illus.). 184p. 1988. text ed. 44.00x (*0-87322-121-4*, BLOH0121) Human Kinetics.

Anthropometric Standardization Reference Manual. abr. ed. Timothy G. Lohman et al. LC 90-29003. (Illus.). 96p. 1991. text ed. 19.00x (*0-87322-331-4*, BLOH0331) Human Kinetics.

Anthropometric Standards for the Assessment of Growth & Nutritional Status. A. Roberto Frisancho. LC 89-20695. 130p. 1990. text ed. 75.00 (*0-472-10146-3*) U of Mich Pr.

Anthropometric Study of Hawaiians of Pure & Mixed Blood. L. C. Dunn. Ed. by A. M. Tozzer. (HU PMP Ser.). 1928. pap. 15.00 (*0-527-01220-3*) Periodicals Srv.

Anthropometry: The Individual & the Population. Ed. by S. J. Ulijaszek & C. G. Mascie-Taylor. (Studies in Biological Anthropology: No. 13). (Illus.). 236p. (C). 1994. 54.95 (*0-521-41798-8*) Cambridge U Pr.

Anthropometry of the American Negro. Melville Herskovits. LC 73-121370. (Studies in Black History & Culture: No. 54). 1970. reprint ed. lib. bdg. 62.95 (*0-8383-1116-4*) M S G Haskell Hse.

Anthropometry of the American Negro. Melville J. Herskovits. LC 76-82369. (Columbia University. Contributions to Anthropology Ser.: No. 11). reprint ed. 32.50 (*0-404-50561-9*) AMS Pr.

Anthropometry of the Head & Face. 2nd ed. Ed. by Leslie G. Farkas. LC 94-991. 432p. 1994. 145.00 (*0-7817-0519-3*) Raven.

***Anthropometry of the Head & Face.** 2nd ed. Ed. by Leslie G. Farkas. 405p. 1994. 145.00 (*0-7817-0159-7*) Raven.

Anthropometry of the Natives of Arnhem Land & the Australian Race Problem. W. W. Howells. (HU PMP Ser.). 1937. pap. 13.00 (*0-527-01236-X*) Periodicals Srv.

Anthropometry of the Ovimbundu, Angola see Skeletal Material from San Jose Ruin, British Honduras

Anthropomorphism & Physics. T. Percy Nunn. 1977. lib. bdg. 59.95 (*0-8490-1438-7*) Gordon Pr.

Anthroponymie et Anthropologie De Nuzi: Les Anthroponymes, Vol. 1. Elena Cassin & Jean-Jacques Glassner. 187p. (FRE.). 1977. 50.00 (*0-89003-024-3*) Undena Pubns.

Anthropopolis: City for Human Development. C. A. Doxiadis. (Illus.). 398p. (C). 1975. pap. text ed. 5.95 (*0-393-08737-9*) Norton.

Anthropos & Son of Man. Carl H. Kraeling. LC 27-23162. (Columbia University. Oriental Studies: No. 25). reprint ed. 18.50 (*0-404-50515-5*) AMS Pr.

Anthropos-Specter-Beast. Tadeusz Konwicki. Tr. by George Korwin-Rodziszewski & Audrey Korwin-Rodziszewski. LC 77-13500. 320p. (J). (gr. 9 up). 1977. 22.95 (*0-87599-218-8*) S G Phillips.

Anthroposophia Theomagica. Thomas Vaughn. reprint ed. pap. 6.95 (*0-916411-76-1*, Sure Fire) Holmes Pub.

Anthroposophic Medicine Today. Richard Leviton. 40p. 1988. pap. 3.95 (*0-88010-265-9*) Anthroposophic.

Anthroposophical Approach to Cancer. Rita Leroi. 45p. (Orig.). 1982. pap. 5.00 (*0-936132-21-3*) Merc Pr NY.

Anthroposophical Approach to Medicine, Vol. 1. Friedrich Husemann et al. (Illus.). 411p. 1983. 39.95 (*0-88010-031-1*) Anthroposophic.

Anthroposophical Approach to Medicine, Vol. 2. Ed. by Otto Wolff. Tr. by G. Karnow. 1987. 39.95 (*0-88010-174-1*) Anthroposophic.

Anthroposophical Approach to Medicine, Vol. 3. Otto Wolff et al. Ed. & Tr. by Brian Kelly. Tr. by Peter Luborsky. (Illus.). 450p. 1989. 50.00 (*0-88010-273-X*) Anthroposophic.

Anthroposophical Leading Thoughts. Rudolf Steiner. Tr. by George Adams & Mary Adams. 220p. 1985. reprint ed. 24.95 (*0-85440-268-3*, Steinerbks) Anthroposophic.

Anthroposophical Medicine: Spiritual Science & the Art of Healing. Victor Bott. 208p. (Orig.). 1984. pap. 8.95 (*0-89281-327-X*, Heal Arts VT) Inner Tradit.

Anthroposophical Understanding of the Soul. F. W. Emmichoven. Tr. by Friedemann Schwarzkopf. 170p. (Orig.). 1983. pap. 10.95 (*0-88010-019-2*) Anthroposophic.

Anthroposophy & Christianity. Rudolf Steiner. 26p. (Orig.). 1985. pap. 3.95 (*0-88010-149-0*) Anthroposophic.

Anthroposophy As a Healing Force. L. Francis Edmunds. 14p. reprint ed. pap. 3.50 (*0-88010-037-0*) Anthroposophic.

Anti-Abolition Tracts & Anti-Black Stereotypes: General Statements of "the Negro Problem" Ed. by John D. Smith. LC 92-27186. (Anti-Black Thought, 1863-1925 Ser.: Vol. 1). 472p. 1993. 71.00 (*0-8153-0973-2*) Garland.

Anti-Abortion Movement. Dallas A. Blanchard. (Social Movements Past & Present Ser.). 200p. 1994. text ed. 26.95 (*0-8057-3872-X*, Twayne); pap. 15.95 (*0-8057-3871-1*, Twayne) Macmillan.

Anti-Achitophel: Three Verse Replies to Absalom & Achitophel by John Dryden. Ed. by Harold W. Jones. LC 60-6430. 1978. reprint ed. 50.00 (*0-8201-1256-9*) Schol Facsimiles.

Anti-Aesthetic: Essays on Postmodern Culture. Ed. by Hal Foster. LC 83-70650. (Illus.). 176p. (Orig.). 1983. pap. 9.95 (*0-941920-01-1*) Bay Pr.

Anti-Aging Diet. Lisa Walford & Roy Walford. 300p. 1994. 19.95 (*1-56858-010-X*) FWEW.

Anti-Aging Pills, I. Q. & Memory Boosters: Life Extension Innovations for a Healthier Longer Life. A. Glenn Braswell. 335p. 1993. 29.95 (*1-883201-00-4*) Hlth Quest.

***Anti-Aging Secrets & Strategies.** 176p. (Orig.). 1993. pap. 14.95 (*1-57327-015-6*, M Pr CA) Busn Concepts.

Anti-Aircraft Artillery, 1914-55: A History of the Royal Regiment of Artillery. N. W. Routledge. (Illus.). 460p. 1994. 66.00 (*1-85753-099-3*, Pub. by Brasseys UK) Brasseys Inc.

Anti-American Generation. Ed. by Edgar Z. Friedenberg. LC 83-4956. (Society Bks.). 277p. 1971. reprint ed. pap. text ed. 19.95x (*0-87855-566-8*) Transaction Pubs.

Anti-American Myths: Their Causes & Consequences. Arnold Beichman. 358p. (C). 1992. pap. 21.95 (*1-56000-590-4*) Transaction Pubs.

Anti-Americanism: Critiques at Home & Abroad, 1965-1990. Paul Hollander. 544p. 1992. 35.00 (*0-19-503824-X*) OUP.

***Anti-Americanism: Irrational & Rational.** rev. ed. Paul Hollander. LC 94-26253. 530p. (C). 1994. pap. 24.95 (*1-56000-774-5*) Transaction Pubs.

Anti-Americanism: Origins & Context. Ed. by Thomas P. Thornton. (Annals Ser.: Vol. 497). 1988. 26.00 (*0-8039-3100-X*); pap. 17.00 (*0-8039-3101-8*) Sage.

Anti-Americanism: Steps on a Dangerous Path. Stephen Haseler. (C). 1990. 60.00 (*0-907967-74-4*, Pub. by Inst Euro Def & Strat UK) St Mut.

Anti-Americanism in the Third World: Implications for U. S. Foreign Policy. Ed. by Alvin Z. Rubinstein & Donald E. Smith. (Foreign Policy Research Institute Ser.). 284p. 1984. text ed. 65.00 (*0-275-91257-4*, C1257, Praeger Pubs) Greenwood.

Anti-Anxiety Agents. G. D. Burrows et al. Ed. by T. R. Norman & B. Davies. (Drugs in Psychiatry Ser.: No. 2). 1984. 54.00 (*0-444-80555-9*, I-271-84) Elsevier.

Anti-Apartheid: Transnational Conflict & Western Policy in the Liberation of South Africa. George W. Shepherd, Jr. LC 77-71868. (Studies in Human Rights: No. 3). 246p. 1977. text ed. 55.00 (*0-8371-9537-3*, SHA/, Greenwood Pr) Greenwood.

Anti-Apocalypse: Exercises in Genealogical Criticism. Lee Quinby. LC 93-28600. 1994. text ed. 44.95 (*0-8166-2278-7*); pap. 17.95 (*0-8166-2279-5*) U of Minn Pr.

An Asterisk (*) at the beginning of an entry indicates that the title is appearing in BIP for the first time.

An Asterisk (*) at the beginning of an entry indicates that the title is appearing in BIP for the first time.

359

***Anti-Racist Science Teaching.** Ed. by Dawn Gill & Les Levidow. 324p. 1987. 55.00 (*0-946960-63-1*); pap. 20.00 (*0-946960-64-X*) NYU Pr.

Anti-Rationalists. Ed. by J. M. Richards & Nikolaus Pevsner. LC 72-95812. (Illus.). 216p. reprint ed. pap. 61. 60 (*0-8357-5630-0*, 2014339) Bks Demand.

Anti-Realism & Logic: Truth As Eternal. Neil Tennant. (Clarendon Library of Logic & Philosophy). 338p. 1987. 69.00 (*0-19-824925-X*) OUP.

Anti-Rebel: The Civil War Letters of Wilbur Fisk. Wilbur Fisk. LC 83-17774. 380p. 1983. 25.95 (*0-9610060-1-3*) E Rosenblatt.

Anti-Redeemers: Hill-Country Political Dissenters in the Lower South from Redemption to Populism. Michael R. Hyman. LC 90-35887. 304p. 1990. text ed. 39.95 (*0-8071-1594-0*); pap. text ed. 16.95 (*0-8071-1656-4*) La State U Pr.

Anti-Redlining Rules: An Analysis of the Federal Home Loan Bank Board's Proposed Nondiscrimination Requirements. George J. Benston. (LEC Occasional Paper). 1978. pap. text ed. 2.50 (*0-916770-06-0*) Law & Econ U Miami.

Anti-Rent Agitation in the State of New York, 1839-1846. Edward P. Cheyney. 64p. 1993. reprint ed. lib. bdg. 69. 00 (*0-7812-5170-2*) Rprt Serv.

Anti-Representational Response: Gertrude Stein's Lucy Church Amiably. V. M. Rose. 232p. (Orig.). 1985. pap. text ed. 33.00x (*91-554-1751-5*) Coronet Bks.

Anti-Rheumatic Drugs, Vol. 2. E. C. Huskisson. (Clinical Pharmacology & Therapeutics Ser.). 776p. 1983. text ed. 125.00 (*0-275-91397-X*, C1397, Praeger Pubs) Greenwood.

Anti-Rock: The Opposition to Rock 'n' Roll. Linda Martin & Kerry Segrave. 382p. 1993. reprint ed. pap. 14.95 (*0-306-80502-2*) Da Capo.

Anti-Sartre: With an Essay on Camus. Colin Wilson. LC 80-24098. (Milford Series: Popular Writers of Today: Vol. 34). 63p. (Orig.). 1981. lib. bdg. 20.00x (*0-89370-149-1*) Borgo Pr.

Anti-Satellite Weapons & U. S. Military Space Policy: An Aspen Strategy Group Report. Aspen Strategy Group Staff. 54p. (Orig.). (C). 1986. lib. bdg. 29.00 (*0-8191-5476-8*, Aspen Inst for Humanistic Studies); pap. text ed. 11.00 (*0-8191-5477-6*, Aspen Inst for Humanistic Studies) U Pr of Amer.

Anti-Scepticism: or Notes upon Each Chapter of Mr. Lock's Essay Concerning Human Understanding. Henry Lee. (Anglistica & Americana Ser.: No. 115). xxx, 342p. 1973. reprint ed. 115.70 (*3-487-04753-5*, Pub. by Georg Olms GW) Lubrecht & Cramer.

***Anti-Semite & Jew: An Exploration of the Etiology of Hate.** Jean-Paul Sartre. 160p. 1995. pap. 12.00 (*0-8052-1047-4*) Schocken.

***Anti-Semitic Stereotypes: A Paradigm of Otherness in English Popular Culture, 1660-1830.** Frank Felsenstein. Ed. by Sander Gilman & Steven T. Katz. LC 94-22411. (Jewish Studies). (Illus.). 376p. 1994. text ed. 39.95x (*0-8018-4903-9*) Johns Hopkins.

Anti-Semitic Stereotypes Without Jews: Images of the Jews in England, 1290-1700. Bernard Glassman. LC 75-16391. 190p. reprint ed. pap. 54.20 (*0-8357-5631-9*, 2032016) Bks Demand.

***Anti-Semitism.** Maurianne Adams. 60p. (C). 1994. 15.00 (*0-7872-0036-0*) Kendall-Hunt.

Anti-Semitism: A Case Study in Prejudice & Discrimination. J. Milton Yinger. 80p. pap. 2.50 (*0-88464-046-9*) ADL.

Anti-Semitism: A Disease of the Mind. Lawler & Theodor I. Rubin. 144p. 1993. reprint ed. 10.95 (*0-8245-1238-3*) Crossroad NY.

Anti-Semitism: Causes & Effects of a Prejudice. Paul E. Grosser & Edwin G. Halpern. 1979. pap. 5.95 (*0-8065-0703-9*, Citadel Pr) Carol Pub Group.

Anti-Semitism: Its History & Causes. Bernard Lazare. 1982. lib. bdg. 300.00 (*0-87700-426-9*) Revisionist Pr.

***Anti-Semitism: The Guilt of Jews & Christians.** Arthur Blech. 1994. 29.50 (*0-533-11090-4*) Vantage.

Anti-Semitism: The Jewish Response. Derek J. Penslar. Ed. by Adam Siegel. (Illus.). 62p. (Orig.). 1989. pap. text ed. 4.95 (*0-87441-494-6*) Behrman.

Anti-Semitism: The Road to the Holocaust & Beyond. Charles Patterson. 160p. (J). (gr. 8). 1989. pap. 9.95 (*0-8027-7318-4*) Walker & Co.

Anti-Semitism & Early Christianity: Issues of Polemic & Faith. Ed. by Craig A. Evans & Donald A. Hagner. LC 92-44701. 304p. 1993. pap. 16.00 (*0-8006-2748-2*, 1-2748, Fortress Pr) Augsburg Fortress.

Anti-Semitism & the Babylonian Connection. Des Griffin. 69p. (Orig.). 1988. pap. 5.00 (*0-941380-05-X*) Emissary Pubns.

Anti-Semitism & the Beirut Program. Fredy Perlman. 16p. (Orig.). 1983. pap. 1.75 (*0-939306-07-7*) Left Bank.

***Anti-Semitism & the Treatment of the Holocaust in Postcommunist Eastern Europe.** Ed. by Randolph L. Braham. 224p. 1994. 32.00 (*0-88033-301-4*) East Eur Quarterly.

Anti-Semitism & Zionism: Selected Marxist Writings. Daniel Rubin et al. LC 87-3123. 252p. (Orig.). (C). 1987. pap. 5.95 (*0-7178-0663-4*) Intl Pubs Co.

Anti-Semitism In America. Harold E. Quinley & Charles Y. Glock. LC 83-4956. 259p. 1983. reprint ed. pap. 21.95 (*0-87855-940-X*) Transaction Pubs.

Anti-Semitism in America, 1878-1939. An Original Anthology. LC 76-46110. (Anti-Movements in America Ser.). (Illus.). 1977. lib. bdg. 51.95 (*0-405-09981-9*) Ayer.

Anti-Semitism in American History. Ed. by David A. Gerber. LC 85-24488. 440p. 1986. 34.95 (*0-252-01214-3*) U of Ill Pr.

Anti-Semitism in American History. Ed. by David A. Gerber. LC 85-24488. 440p. 1987. pap. 13.95 (*0-252-01477-4*) U of Ill Pr.

Anti-Semitism in British Society Eighteen Seventy-Six to Nineteen Thirty-Nine. Colin Holmes. LC 78-21023. 328p. 1979. 49.50 (*0-8419-0459-6*) Holmes & Meier.

Anti-Semitism in France: A History from 1789 to the Present. Pierre Birnbaum. Tr. by Miriam Kochan. (Studies in Social Discontinuity). 384p. 1992. 59.95 (*1-55786-047-5*) Blackwell Pubs.

Anti-Semitism in the Soviet Union: Its Roots & Consequences. 664p. 1984. 35.00 (*0-88464-051-5*); pap. 16.95 (*0-88464-052-3*) ADL.

Anti-Semitism in Times of Crisis. Steven T. Katz. Ed. by Sander L. Gilman. 408p. 1991. text ed. 50.00 (*0-8147-3044-2*); pap. 18.50 (*0-8147-3056-6*) NYU Pr.

Anti-Semitism Through the Ages. H. Coudenhove-Kalergi. 59.95 (*0-87968-649-9*) Gordon Pr.

Anti-Slavery & Reform Papers. Henry David Thoreau. Ed. by H. S. Salt. LC 70-83883. (Black Heritage Library Collection). 1977. 24.95 (*0-8369-8665-2*) Ayer.

Anti-Slavery & Reform Papers. Henry David Thoreau. (Emulation Book Ser.). 167p. reprint ed. pap. 47.60 (*0-8357-6437-0*, 2035808) Bks Demand.

Anti-Slavery Crusade: A Chronicle of the Gathering Storm. Jesse Macy. (History - United States Ser.). 245p. 1992. reprint ed. lib. bdg. 79.00 (*0-7812-6154-6*) Rprt Serv.

Anti-Slavery Crusade in America, 70 vols., Set. Ed. by James M. McPherson & William L. Katz. 1970. 1,102.00 (*0-405-00600-4*) Ayer.

Anti-Slavery Days: A Sketch of the Struggle Which Ended in the Abolition of Slavery in the United States. James F. Clarke. LC 72-1050. reprint ed. 29.50 (*0-404-00252-8*) AMS Pr.

Anti-Slavery History of the John Brown Year: Being the Twenty-Seventh Report of the American Anti-Slavery Society. American Anti-Slavery Society Staff. LC 70-82169. (Anti-Slavery Crusade in America Ser.). 1974. reprint ed. 18.95 (*0-405-00604-7*) Ayer.

Anti-Slavery Impulse, 1830-1844. Gilbert Barnes. 298p. 1993. reprint ed. lib. bdg. 79.00 (*0-7812-5307-1*) Rprt Serv.

Anti-Slavery in America from the Introduction of African Slaves to the Prohibition of the Slave Trade (1619-1808) May S. Locke. 1988. 11.25 (*0-8446-1284-7*) Peter Smith.

Anti-Slavery in the Southwest. Lawrence R. Murphy. Ed. by E. H. Antone. (Southwestern Studies: No. 54). (Illus.). 55p. 1978. pap. text ed. 10.00 (*0-87404-112-0*) Tex Western.

Anti-Slavery Leaders of North Carolina. John S. Bassett. LC 78-63864. (Johns Hopkins University. Studies in the Social Sciences. Thirtieth Ser. 1912: 6). reprint ed. 37.50 (*0-404-61120-6*) AMS Pr.

Anti-Slavery Manual. La Roy Sunderland. LC 70-92443. 1837. 13.00 (*0-403-00174-9*) Scholarly.

Anti-Slavery Manual, Being an Examination, in the Light of the Bible, & of Facts, into the Moral & Social Wrongs of American Slavery. John G. Fee. LC 74-82189. (Anti-Slavery Crusade in America Ser.). 1978. reprint ed. 19. 95 (*0-405-00627-6*) Ayer.

Anti-Slavery Opinions Before the Year 1800. William F. Poole. LC 79-110001. reprint ed. 22.50 (*0-8371-4144-3*, POO&, Negro U Pr) Greenwood.

Anti-Slavery Poems. John Pierpont. LC 71-104544. reprint ed. lib. bdg. 37.50 (*0-8398-1570-0*) Irvington.

Anti-Slavery Poems: Songs of Labor & Reform. John Greenleaf Whittier. LC 73-82230. (Anti-Slavery Crusade in America Ser.). 1974. reprint ed. 31.95 (*0-405-00669-1*) Ayer.

Anti-Social Contract. Y. N. Kly. 108p. (Orig.). 1989. pap. 8.95 (*0-932863-09-4*) Clarity Pr.

Anti-Social Family. Michele Barrett & Mary McIntosh. 164p. 1991. 54.95 (*0-86091-330-9*, A5614, Pub. by Verso UK); pap. 16.95 (*0-86091-545-X*, A5618, Pub. by Verso UK) Routledge Chapman & Hall.

Anti-Story: An Anthology of Experimental Fiction. Philip Stevick. LC 78-131596. 1971. pap. text ed. 14.95 (*0-02-931500-X*) Free Pr.

Anti-Stress Workbook. Barbara North & Penelope Crittenden. (Illus.). 79p. (Orig.). 1980. pap. 4.95 (*0-938480-00-6*) Healthworks.

Anti-Stress Workbook see Cave Time: How to Survive in a Civilized World

***Anti-Submarine Handbook.** (Illus.). 240p. (Orig.). 1994. pap. 395.00 (*0-7605-1158-6*) Rector Pr.

Anti-Submarine Warfare. David Baker. (Military Aircraft Library). 48p. (J). (gr. 3-8). 1989. lib. bdg. 18.60 (*0-86592-532-1*) Rourke Corp.

Anti-Submarine Warfare. 2nd ed. J. R. Hill. LC 89-60936. 120p. 1989. 29.95 (*0-87021-998-7*) Naval Inst Pr.

Anti-Submarine Warfare: The Threat, the Strategy, the Solution. T. A. Heppenheimer. 284p. 1989. 247.00 (*0-935453-28-8*) Pasha Pubns.

Anti-Submarine Warfare & Superpower Strategic Stability. Donald C. Daniel. LC 85-14158. 240p. 1986. 32.50 (*0-252-01272-0*) U of Ill Pr.

Anti-Tank Helicopters. Steven Zaloga. (Vanguard Ser.: No. 44). (Illus.). 48p. pap. 10.95 (*0-85045-697-5*, 9333, Pub. by Osprey UK) Stackpole.

Anti-Tank Rifle. LC 83-6156. (Small Arms Training Ser.: Vol. 1, pamphlet no. 5). (Illus.). 12p. 1983. pap. text ed. 2.00 (*0-86663-989-6*) Ide Hse.

Anti-Terrorism Defense Tactics. Frank Bolz et al. 1989. write for info. (*0-318-66282-5*) Elsevier.

Anti-Terrorism Handbook. Karl A. Seger. (C). 1990. 24.00 (*81-7062-132-1*, Pub. by Lancer II) S Asia.

Anti-Theory in Ethics & Moral Conservatism. Ed. by Stanley G. Clarke & Evan Simpson. LC 88-12660. (SUNY Series in Ethical Theory). 308p. (C). 1989. 59.50 (*0-88706-912-6*); pap. 21.95 (*0-88706-913-4*) State U NY Pr.

Anti-Trust Act & the Supreme Court. William H. Taft. 133p. 1993. reprint ed. lib. bdg. 27.50 (*0-8377-2638-7*) Rothman.

Anti-Trust Law: A Guide for the Healthcare Professional. Jonathan P. Tomes. LC 92-35486. 90p. (Orig.). 1993. pap. 24.95 (*1-882198-02-6*) Hlthcare Fin Mgmt.

Anti-Trust Law Institute: Thirty-Third Annual, 2 vols., Set. 2056p. 1992. pap. 80.00 (*0-685-69379-1*) PLI.

Anti-Tussive Agents, 3 vols, Set. H. Salem & D. M. Aviado. 1970. 376.00 (*0-08-013340-1*, Pub. by Pergamon Repr UK) Franklin.

Anti-Viral Agents in Chronic Hepatitis B Virus Infection: Proceedings of an International Symposium, the Royal Society, London, UK, 11-12 Nov., 1985. Ed. by G. J. Alexander et al. 317p. 1987. 82.00 (*0-444-80901-5*) Elsevier.

***Anti-Virus Tools & Techniques for Computer Systems.** W. Timothy Polk et al. LC 94-31166. (Advanced Computing & Telecommunications Ser.). (Illus.). 79p. 1995. 24.00 (*0-8155-1364-X*) Noyes.

Anti-Warhol Museum Proposals for the Socially Responsible Disposal of Warholia. Bonnie O'Connell. (Illus.). 1993. 15.00 (*0-932526-48-9*) Nexus Pr.

Anti-Warrior: A Memoir. Milt Felsen. LC 88-30301. (Singular Lives: The Iowa Series in North American Autobiography). (Illus.). 271p. 1989. 32.95x (*0-87745-222-9*); pap. 13.95 (*0-87745-241-5*) U of Iowa Pr.

Anti-Wrinkle Plan. Anita Guyton. (Illus.). 192p. 1994. pap. 14.00 (*0-7225-2847-7*) Thorsons SF.

Anti-Zionism: Analytical Reflections. Ed. by Roselle Tekiner et al. (C). 1988. 19.95 (*0-915597-73-X*) Amana Bks.

Antiachievement: Perspectives on School Dropouts. Ed. by Emanuel F. Hammer. LC 76-136597. 104p. 1970. pap. 14.50 (*0-87424-045-X*, W-45) Western Psych.

Antiandrogen-Estrogen Therapy in Signs of Androgenization. Ed. by A. E. Schindler. (New Developments in Biosciences Ser.: No. 3). 244p. (C). 1987. pap. text ed. 79.25 (*0-89925-304-0*) De Gruyter.

***Antiandrogen-Estrogen Therapy in Signs of Androgenization.** Ed. by A. E. Schindler. (New Developments in Biosciences Ser.: No. 3). 244p. (C). 1987. pap. text ed. 79.25 (*3-11-011402-X*) De Gruyter.

Antiarrhythmic Drugs. Ed. by E. M. Williams & T. J. Campbell. (Handbook of Experimental Pharmacology Ser.: Vol. 89). (Illus.). 680p. 1988. 336.00 (*0-387-19239-5*) Spr-Verlag.

Antiarrhythmic Therapy: A Pathophysiologic Approach. Sicilian Gambit Staff. LC 94-13905. (Illus.). 352p. 1994. 65.00 (*0-87993-596-0*) Futura Pub.

***Antibacterial Effect of the Penicillium Mold: Billroth - 1874, Fleming - 1929.** Karel B. Absolon. (Illus.). 110p. (C). 1994. pap. 24.50 (*0-614-04348-4*) KABEL Pubs.

Antibacterial Effect of the Penicillium Mold: Billroth-1874 Fleming-1929. Karel B. Absolon & J. Lee Sedwitz. 111p. (Orig.). 1994. pap. 29.50 (*0-685-71277-X*) KABEL Pubs.

Antibacterial Effect of the Penicillium Mold: Billroth-1874 Fleming-1929. Karel B. Absolon & J. Lee Sedwitz. (Illus.). 110p. (Orig.). (C). 1994. text ed. 34.50 (*0-930329-71-6*) KABEL Pubs.

Antiballistic Missile Defense in the 1980s. Ed. by Ian Bellany & Coit D. Blacker. 100p. 1983. text ed. 32.50 (*0-7146-3207-4*, Pub. by F Cass Pubs UK) Intl Spec Bk.

Antibarbarus der Lateinischen Sprache, 2 vols., Set. 9th ed. Johann Krebs. 1587p. (GER & LAT.). 1984. 210.00 (*0-8288-1025-7*, M8028) Fr & Eur.

Antibiosis & Host Immunity. Ed. by Andor Szentivanyi et al. LC 87-18514. (Illus.). 324p. 1987. 75.00 (*0-306-42600-5*, Plenum Pr) Plenum.

Antibiotic - Antimicrobial Use in Dental Practice. Michael G. Newman & Kenneth G. Kornman. (Illus.). 1990. pap. text ed. 30.00 (*0-86715-172-2*) Quint Pub Co.

Antibiotic & Chemotherapy. 6th ed. Ed. by Harold P. Lambert & Francis O'Grady. (Illus.). 561p. 1991. text ed. 149.95 (*0-443-03203-3*) Churchill.

Antibiotic Associated Diarrhoea & Colitis. Ed. by S. P. Borriello. (Developments in Gastroenterology Ser.). 188p. 1984. lib. bdg. 80.50 (*0-89838-623-3*) Kluwer Ac.

Antibiotic Choice: The Importance of Colonisation Resistance. Dirk Van der Waaij. (Antimicrobial Chemotherapy Ser.: No. 5). (Illus.). 146p. reprint ed. pap. 41.70 (*0-8357-6020-0*, 2034242) Bks Demand.

Antibiotic-Impregnated Vascular Grafts. Wesley Moore & H. A. Gelabert. (Medical Intelligence Unit Ser.). 125p. 1992. 89.95 (*1-879702-25-8*) R G Landes.

Antibiotic Inhibition of Bacterial Cell Surface Assembly & Function. Ed. by Paul Actor et al. (Illus.). 657p. 1988. text ed. 49.00 (*0-914826-98-0*) Am Soc Microbio.

Antibiotic Inhibitors of Bacterial Cell Wall Biosynthesis. 2nd ed. D. J. Tipper. LC 87-21572. (International Encyclopedia of Pharmacology & Therapeutics Ser.: No. 127). (Illus.). 277p. 1988. 200.00 (*0-08-036130-7*, Pergamon Pr) Elsevier.

Antibiotic Paradox: How Miracle Drugs Are Destorying the Miracle. S. B. Levy. (Illus.). 280p. (C). 1992. 24.95 (*0-306-44331-7*, Plenum Pr) Plenum.

Antibiotic Resistance: Proceedings. Ed. by S. Mitsuhashi et al. (Illus.). 410p. 1981. 69.00 (*0-387-10322-8*) Spr-Verlag.

Antibiotic Resistance Genes: Ecology, Transfer, & Expression. Ed. by Stuart B. Levy & Richard Novick. LC 86-24361. (Banbury Report Ser.: No. 24). 436p. 1986. text ed. 68.00 (*0-87969-224-3*) Cold Spring Harbor.

Antibiotic Therapy in Clinical Practice. 2nd ed. Claus Simon et al. 623p. 1993. pap. text ed. 99.95 (*0-471-59825-9*) Wiley.

Antibiotic Therapy in Head & Neck Surgery. Johnson. (Science & Practice of Surgery Ser.: Vol. 11). 312p. 1987. 125.00 (*0-8247-7671-2*) Dekker.

Antibiotics: An Integrated View. G. Lancini & F. Parenti. (Microbiology Ser.). (Illus.). 250p. 1982. 84.00 (*0-387-90630-4*) Spr-Verlag.

Antibiotics: Origin Nature & Properties, 2 vols., Set. T. Koryzybski & Z. Gindifer. LC 64-21220. 1967. 683.00 (*0-08-010878-4*, Pub. by Pergamon Repr UK) Franklin.

Antibiotics see Methods in Enzymology

***Antibiotics - A Multidisciplinary Approach.** Giancarlo Lancini et al. 275p. 1995. 59.50 (*0-306-44924-2*) Plenum.

Antibiotics & Adverse Effects: Medical Subject Analysis & Research Guidebook with Bibliography. Katie L. Holt. LC 84-45865. 150p. 1987. 39.50 (*0-88164-290-8*); pap. 34.50 (*0-88164-291-6*) ABBE Pubs Assn.

Antibiotics & Antiviral Compounds: Chemical Synthesis & Modification. Ed. by Karsten Krohn et al. LC 93-8473. 1993. 85.00 (*1-56081-745-3*) VCH Pubs.

Antibiotics & Microbial Transformations. Ed. by Lamba. 1987. 87.00 (*0-8493-6408-6*, QR88) CRC Pr.

Antibiotics & Other Secondary Metabolites: Biosynthesis & Production. Ed. by R. Hutter et al. 1979. text ed. 129. 00 (*0-12-363250-1*) Acad Pr.

Antibiotics Containing the Beta-Lactam Structure One. Ed. by A. L. Damain & N. A. Solomon. (Handbook of Experimental Pharmacology Ser.: Vol. 67-I). (Illus.). 362p. 1983. 207.00 (*0-387-12107-2*) Spr-Verlag.

Antibiotics Containing the Beta-Lactam Structure Two. Ed. by A. L. Demain & N. A. Solomon. (Handbook of Experimental Pharmacology Ser.: Vol. 67, II). (Illus.). 500p. 1983. 261.00 (*0-387-12131-5*) Spr-Verlag.

Antibiotics for Surgical Infections. P. J. Sanderson. LC 82-21751. (Antimicrobial Chemotherapy Ser.: No. 4). 272p. reprint ed. pap. 77.60 (*0-8357-8803-2*, 2033353) Bks Demand.

Antibiotics, Hosts & Host Defences in Nosocomial Infections. Ed. by T. R. Beam. 35.00 (*0-915340-07-0*) PJD Pubns.

Antibiotics I: Beta-Lactams. Ed. by E. Tomlinson & A. Regosz. (Solubility Data Ser.: Vol. 16-17). 750p. 1985. 310.00 (*0-08-029235-6*, Pergamon Pr) Elsevier.

Antibiotics I: Lactams & Other Antimicrobial Agents. Isao Kawamoto. 1992. pap. text ed. 50.00 (*2-88124-855-1*) Gordon & Breach.

Antibiotics II: Antibiotics by Fermentation. Sadao Teshiba. (Japanese Technology Reviews, Section E. Ser.). 1993. pap. text ed. 45.00 (*2-88124-889-6*) Gordon & Breach.

Antibiotics in Animal Feeds. (Reports Ser.: No. 88). 79p. 1981. 4.50 (*0-318-13832-8*) CAST.

Antibiotics in Historical Perspective. David L. Cowen & Alvin B. Segelman. 238p. 1981. write for info. (*0-911910-71-9*) Merck-Sharp-Dohme.

Antibiotics in Laboratory Medicine. 3rd ed. Victor Lorian. (Illus.). 1268p. 1991. 185.00 (*0-683-05168-7*) Williams & Wilkins.

Antibiotics in Obstetrics & Gynecology: Developments in Perinatal Medicine, No. 2. William J. Ledger. 320p. 1982. lib. bdg. 112.50 (*90-247-2529-1*) Kluwer Ac.

Antibiotics in the Tropics. S. Enenkel & Wolfgang Stille. (Illus.). 340p. 1988. pap. 75.00 (*0-387-18683-2*) Spr-Verlag.

***Antibiotics May Be Hazardous to Your Health.** Walter Driver. (Illus.). 120p. (Orig.). 1995. pap. 7.95 (*1-886276-06-4*) Mammoth Pubns.

Antibiotics of the Beta-Lactam Group. David Greenwood. LC 82-6889. (Antimicrobial Chemotherapy Research Studies: No. 2). (Illus.). 94p. reprint ed. pap. 26.80 (*0-8357-6021-9*, 2034225) Bks Demand.

Antibiotics (Phenazines) to Bleaching Agents see Encyclopedia of Chemical Technology

Antibodies. Cold Spring Harbor Symposia on Quantitative Biology Staff. LC 34-8174. (Cold Spring Harbor Symposia on Quantitative Biology Ser.: No. 32). 639p. reprint ed. pap. 180.00 (*0-7837-2015-7*, 2042290) Bks Demand.

Antibodies: A Laboratory Manual. Ed Harlow & David Lane. (Illus.). 726p. (C). 1988. lib. bdg. 150.00 (*0-87969-374-6*) Cold Spring Harbor.

Antibodies: A Laboratory Manual. Ed. by Ed Harlow & David Lane. (Illus.). 726p. 1988. pap. text ed. 70.00 (*0-87969-314-2*) Cold Spring Harbor.

Antibodies: A Practical Approach, 2 vols. Ed. by D. Catty. (Practical Approach Ser.). 500p. 1989. pap. 70.00 (*0-19-963063-1*, IRL Pr) OUP.

Antibodies: A Practical Approach, Vol. 1. Ed. by D. Catty. (Practical Approach Ser.). 220p. 1988. 58.00 (*0-947946-86-1*, IRL Pr); pap. 39.00 (*0-947946-85-3*, IRL Pr) OUP.

Antibodies: A Practical Approach, Vol. 2. Ed. by D. Catty. (Practical Approach Ser.). (Illus.). 280p. 1989. 58.00 (*0-19-963018-6*, IRL Pr); pap. 39.00 (*0-19-963019-4*, IRL Pr) OUP.

Antibodies: Structure, Synthesis, Function, & Immunologic Intervention in Disease. Ed. by Andor Szentivanyi et al. LC 87-2457. (University of South Florida International Biomedical Symposia Ser.). 224p. 1987. 65. 00 (*0-306-42559-9*, Plenum Pr) Plenum.

Antibodies As Carriers of Cytotoxicity. H. H. Sedlacek et al. Ed. by J. Czech et al. (Beitraege zur Onkologie, Contributions to Oncology Ser.: Vol. 43). (Illus.). viii, 208p. 1992. 65.75 (*3-8055-5599-7*) S Karger.

Antibodies in Human Diagnosis & Therapy. Ed. by Edgar Haber & Richard M. Krause. LC 75-32089. (Royal Society of Medicine Foundation Ser.). 431p. 1977. 83.00 (*0-89004-089-3*) Raven.

360

An Asterisk (*) at the beginning of an entry indicates that the title is appearing in BIP for the first time.

An Asterisk (*) at the beginning of an entry indicates that the title is appearing in BIP for the first time.

*Antiepileptic Drugs: Mechanisms of Action. fac. ed. Ed. by Gilbert H. Glaser et al. LC 79-5215. (Advances in Neurology Ser.: No. 27). (Illus.). 750p. Date not set. pap. 180.00 (0-7837-7175-4, 2047124) Bks Demand.

*Antiepileptic Drugs: Quantitative Analysis & Interpretation. fac. ed. Ed. by C. E. Pippenger et al. LC 76-58055. 383p. Date not set. pap. 109.20 (0-7837-7503-2, 2047003) Bks Demand.

Antiepileptic Drugs & Pregnancy. Ed. by T. Sato & S. Shinagawa. (Current Clinical Practice Ser.: Vol. 9). 1985. 83.00 (4-900392-18-9) Elsevier.

Antiepileptic Drugs in Psychiatry. Ed. by J. Walden et al. (Journal: Neuropsychobiology: Vol. 27, No. 3, 1993). (Illus.). 76p. 1993. pap. 53.75 (3-8055-5839-2) S Karger.

*Antiepileptic Therapy: Advances in Drug Monitoring. fac. ed. Workshop on the Determination of Anti-Epileptic Drugs in Body Fluids Staff. Ed. by S. I. Johannessen et al. LC 79-66729. (Illus.). 451p. Date not set. pap. 128.60 (0-7837-7258-0, 2047047) Bks Demand.

Antietam: Essays on the 1862 Maryland Campaign. Ed. by Gary W. Gallagher. LC 89-33453. (Illus.). 113p. 1989. pap. 10.95 (0-87338-400-8) Kent St U Pr.

Antietam: The Photographic Legacy of America's Bloodiest Day. William A. Frassanito. LC 78-2336. (Encore Edition Ser.). (Illus.). 304p. 1982. pap. 18.00 (0-684-17645-9, Scribners) S&S Trade.

Antietam: The Soldiers Battle. John M. Priest. LC 89-5557. (Illus.). 463p. (C). 1989. 34.95 (0-942597-09-5) White Mane Pub.

Antietam: The Soldiers' Battle. John M. Priest. LC 92-46293. 424p. 1994. 15.95 (0-19-508466-7) OUP.

Antietam & the Maryland & Virginia Campaigns of 1862. Issac Heysinger. 322p. 1988. reprint ed. 28.00 (0-942211-55-3) Olde Soldier Bks.

Antietam Campaign: August-September 1862. rev. ed. John Cannan. (Illus.). 256p. 1994. 22.95 (0-938289-36-5, 7327) Combined Bks.

Antietam Hospitals. John W. Schildt. (Illus.). 64p. (Orig.). 1987. pap. 6.50 (0-936772-04-2) Antietam.

Antietam National Battlefield, Maryland. Frederick Tilberg. (National Park Service Handbook Ser.: No. 31). (Illus.). 60p. 1960. reprint ed. pap. 2.25 (0-16-003477-9, S/N 024-005-00892-6) USGPO.

*Antievolution Pamphlets of Harry Rimmer. Ed. & Intro. by Edward B. Davis. LC 94-42616. (Creationism in Twentieth-Century America: Vol. 6). (Illus.). 520p. 1995. 84.00 (0-8153-1807-3) Garland.

*Antievolution Pamphlets of William Bell Riley. William B. Riley. Ed. & Intro. by William V. Trollinger, Jr. LC 94-43258. (Creationism in Twentieth-Century America Ser.: Vol. 4). 1995. write for info. (0-8153-1801-4) Garland.

*Antievolution Pamphlets of William Bell Riley. Ed. by William Trollinger. LC 94-43258. (Creationism in Twentieth-Century America: Vol. 4). 248p. 1995. 55.00 (0-8153-1805-7) Garland.

*Antievolution Works of Arthur I. Brown. Ed. by Ronald L. Numbers. LC 94-45074. (Creationism in Twentieth-Century America Ser.: Vol. 3). 224p. 1995. 55.00 (0-8153-1804-9) Garland.

*Antievolutionism Before World War I. Alexander Patterson et al. Ed. & Intro. by Ronald L. Numbers. LC 94-45044. (Creationism in Twentieth-Century America Ser.: Vol. 1). 424p. 1995. 72.00 (0-8153-1802-2) Garland.

Antifaschistische Lyrik in Frankreich: 1930-1945. Petra Voigt-Langenberger. (European University Studies: Ser. 13, Vol. 84). 258p. (GER.). 1983. 46.15 (3-8204-7735-7) P Lang Pubs.

Antifascism in American Art. Cecile M. Whiting. LC 88-17184. 272p. (C). 1989. text ed. 37.00 (0-300-04259-0) Yale U Pr.

Antifederalism: The Legacy of George Mason. Ed. by Josephine F. Pacheco. LC 92-9206. (George Mason Lectures). 144p. (C). 1992. 42.50 (0-913969-47-8, G Mason Univ Pr) Univ Pub Assocs.

Antifederalist Papers. Ralph Ketcham. 1986. pap. 6.99 (0-451-62525-0, Ment) NAL-Dutton.

Antifederalists. Ed. by Cecelia M. Kenyon. LC 65-23008. (Orig.). 1966. pap. 9.10 (0-672-60052-8, AHS38, Bobbs) Macmillan.

Antifederalists. Ed. by Cecelia M. Kenyon. 578p. (Orig.). 1985. reprint ed. text ed. 45.00 (0-930350-75-8); reprint ed. pap. text ed. 16.95 (0-930350-74-X) NE U Pr.

Antifeminism in America: An Annotated Bibliography. Cynthia D. Kinnard. (Reference Bks.). 388p. 1986. text ed. 35.00 (0-8161-8122-5, Hall Reference) Macmillan.

Antifibrinolytic Drugs: Chemistry, Pharmacology, & Clinical Usage. Derek Ogston. LC 84-13099. (Wiley-Medical Publication Ser.). (Illus.). 194p. reprint ed. pap. 55.30 (0-8357-8642-0, 2035066) Bks Demand.

Antifouling Coatings: Marine Applications, 1970-Jan. 1987. 150p. 1985. pap. 85.00 (0-686-48282-4, LS110) T-C Pubns CA.

Antifoundationalism Old & New. Ed. by Tom Rockmore & Beth J. Singer. (C). 1991. 44.95 (0-87722-881-7) Temple U Pr.

Antifraternal Tradition in Medieval Literature. Penn R. Szittya. LC 85-43316. (Illus.). 320p. 1986. text ed. 52.50x (0-691-06680-9) Princeton U Pr.

Antifriction Bearings Industry: An Analysis of Current Markets & Prospects for Future Growth. 330p. 1993. 1,150.00 (0-317-55209-0) Busn Trend.

Antifungal Chemotherapy. Ed. by D. C. Speller. LC 79-40524. (Illus.). 458p. reprint ed. pap. 130.60 (0-8357-8621-8, 2035044) Bks Demand.

Antifungal Compounds, Vol. 1: Discovery, Development, & Uses. Ed. by Malcolm R. Siegel & Hugh D. Sisler. LC 76-46827. (Illus.). 616p. reprint ed. pap. 175.60 (0-7837-0971-4, 2041277) Bks Demand.

Antifungal Compounds, Vol. 2: Interactions in Biological & Ecological Systems. Ed. by Malcolm R. Siegel & Hugh D. Sisler. LC 76-46827. (Illus.). 688p. reprint ed. pap. 180.00 (0-7837-4722-5, 2041277) Bks Demand.

Antifungal Drug Therapy: A Complete Guide for the Practitioner. Paul H. Jacobs & Lexie Nall. 352p. 1990. 120.00 (0-8247-8353-0) Dekker.

Antifungal Susceptibility Testing: Committee Report, Vol. 5. National Committee for Clinical Laboratory Standards. 1985. 40.00 (1-56238-083-4, M20-CR) Natl Comm Clin Lab Stds.

Antifungals in Gynecology: Focus on Terconazole. Ed. by R. Y. Cartwright & H. A. Hirsch. (Journal: Gynaekologische Rundschau: Vol. 25, Suppl. 1). (Illus.). iv, 120p. 1985. pap. 30.50 (3-8055-4041-8) S Karger.

Antigen & Antibody Molecular Engineering in Breast Cancer: Diagnosis & Treatment. Ed. by R. L. Ceriani. (Advances in Experimental Medicine & Biology Ser.: Vol. 353). (Illus.). (C). 1994. text ed. 75.00 (0-306-44720-7, Plenum Pr) Plenum.

*Antigen-Antibody Complexes. E. A. Padlan. (Molecular Biology Intelligence Unit Ser.). 100p. 1994. 89.95 (1-57059-181-4) R G Landes.

Antigen Detection to Diagnose Bacterial Infections: Applications, I. 1987. 168.00 (0-8493-6698-4) Franklin.

Antigen Detection to Diagnose Bacterial Infections: Applications, II. 1987. 150.00 (0-8493-6699-2) Franklin.

Antigen Detection to Diagnose Bacterial Infections: Applications, Set. 1987. 384.00 (0-8493-6697-6, QR186) Franklin.

Antigen Processing - Recognition. Ed. by McCluskey. 248p. 1991. 167.00 (0-8493-6932-0, RB52) CRC Pr.

Antigen Processing & Presentation. Robert E. Humphreys & Susan K. Pierce. (Illus.). 326p. 1994. text ed. 59.95 (0-12-361555-0) Acad Pr.

Antigen Specific T Cell Receptors & Factors, 2 vols., Set. John J. Marchalonis. 336p. 1987. 305.00 (0-8493-6169-9, QR185) CRC Pr.

Antigenic Changes Associated with Complement Activation: Journal: Complement & Inflammation, Vol. 6, No. 3, 1989. Ed. by T. E. Mollnes. (Illus.). 120p. 1989. pap. 33.75 (3-8055-5048-0) S Karger.

Antigenic Determinants & Immune Regulation. Ed. by E. Sercarz. (Chemical Immunology Ser.: Vol. 46). (Illus.). viii, 190p. 1989. 119.25 (3-8055-4960-1) S Karger.

Antigenic Variation: Molecular & Genetic Mechanisms of Relapsing Disease. Ed. by J. M. Cruse & R. E. Lewis. (Contributions to Microbiology & Immunology Ser.: Vol. 8). (Illus.). vi, 246p. 1987. 156.00 (3-8055-4343-3) S Karger.

Antigenic Variations in Infectious Diseases. Ed. by T. H. Birkbeck & C. W. Penn. (Society for General Microbiology Special Publications: Vol. 19). 180p. 1986. 64.00 (1-85221-000-1, IRL Pr); pap. 40.00 (0-947946-99-3, IRL Pr) OUP.

Antigens, Vol. 1. Ed. by Michael Sela. 1974. text ed. 165.00 (0-12-635501-0) Acad Pr.

Antigens, Vol. 4. Ed. by Michael Sela. 1977. text ed. 158.00 (0-12-635504-5) Acad Pr.

Antigens, Vol. 5. Ed. by Michael Sela. 1979. text ed. 118.00 (0-12-635505-3) Acad Pr.

Antigens, Vol. 6. Ed. by Michael Sela. LC 73-799. 1982. text ed. 138.00 (0-12-635506-1) Acad Pr.

Antigens, Vol. 7. Ed. by Michael Sela. 341p. 1987. text ed. 149.00 (0-12-635507-X) Acad Pr.

Antiglobulins, Cryoglobulins & Glomerulonephritis. Ed. by C. Ponticelli et al. (Development in Nephrology Ser.). 1986. lib. bdg. 150.00 (0-89838-810-4) Kluwer Ac.

Antigone. Jean Anouilh. 136p. (FRE.). 1975. pap. 13.95 (0-8288-9016-1, F81800) Fr & Eur.

Antigone. Jean Anouilh. (Table Ronde Ser.). 1975. pap. 10.95 (2-7103-0025-7) Schoenhof.

Antigone. Sophokles. Ed. by Ernst Pilch. 138p. 1949. write for info. (3-296-70600-3, Pub. by Georg Olms GW) Lubrecht & Cramer.

Antigone. Timberlake Wertenbaker. 1993. 5.45 (0-87129-205-X, A51) Dramatic Pub.

Antigone: And Other Portraits of Women. Paul C. Bourget. Tr. by William Marchant. LC 71-150469. (Short Story Index Reprint Ser.). 1977. reprint ed. 20.95 (0-8369-3809-7) Ayer.

Antigone: With Selections from Brecht's Model Book. Bertolt Brecht. Tr. by Judith Malina. (Illus.). 96p. 1989. pap. 7.95 (0-936839-25-2) Applause Theatre Bk Pubs.

Antigone see Sophocles One

Antigone & les Maries de la Tour Eiffel. Jean Cocteau. (Folio Ser.: No. 908). 6.95 (2-07-036908-0) Schoenhof.

Antigone, Oedipus the King, Electra. Sophocles. Ed. by Edith Hall. Tr. by H. D. Kitto. (World's Classics Ser.). 224p. 1994. pap. 6.95 (0-19-282922-X) OUP.

Antigone Suivi De les Maries De la Tour Eiffel. Jean Cocteau. (FRE.). 1977. pap. 10.95 (0-7859-1841-8, 2070369080) Fr & Eur.

Antigonos the One-Eyed & the Creation of the Hellenistic State. Richard A. Billows. LC 89-4677. (Hellenistic Culture & Society Ser.: No. 4). 544p. 1990. 55.00 (0-520-06378-3) U CA Pr.

Antigrav Unlimited. Duncan Long. 176p. 1988. pap. 2.95 (0-380-75357-X) Avon.

Antigua. Wilson Ltd. Staff & Imray L. Norie. (C). 1988. 75.00 (0-685-40399-8, Pub. by Imray Laurie Norie & Wilson UK) St Mut.

*Antigua: Commercial Law. 300p. (Orig.). 1994. pap. 295.00 (0-7605-1222-1) Rector Pr.

Antigua see Monumental Cities

Antigua & Barbuda. (Let's Visit Places & Peoples of the World Ser.). (Illus.). (J). (gr. 5 up). 1988. 14.95 (0-7910-0151-2) Chelsea Hse.

Antigua & Barbuda. Dyde. (Caribbean Guides Ser.). (Illus.). 160p. (Orig.). 1990. pap. 11.95 (0-333-56930-X) Hunter NJ.

Antigua & Barbuda: Consolidated Index of Statutes & Subsidiary Legislation. Ed. by C. J. Hammett. (West Indian Legislation Indexing Project Ser.). vi, 100p. (Orig.). 1991. pap. text ed. 25.00 (0-317-60528-3, Pub. by UWI Fac Law BB) W W Gaunt.

Antigua California: Mission & Colony on the Peninsular Frontier, 1697-1768. Harry W. Crosby. LC 93-38946. (University of Arizona Southwest Center Ser.). 573p. 1994. 39.95 (0-8263-1495-3) U of NM Pr.

Antigua China: Hechos, Historias, Actividades. Robert Nicholson & Claire Watts. Tr. by Jose R. Araluce. (Raices Ser.). (Illus.). 32p. (SPA.). (YA). (gr. 6-10). 1993. 14.95 (1-56492-093-3) Laredo.

*Antigua Commercial Law. 150p. (C). 1994. pap. 295.00 (0-7605-0075-4) Rector Pr.

Antigue Kiss. Anne Weale. 512p. 1983. pap. 2.95 (0-373-97001-3) Harlequin Bks.

Antiguedad Y Actualidad de Luis Velez de Guevara: Estudios Criticos. George C. Peale et al. xii, 298p. 1983. 71.00x (90-272-1720-3) Benjamins North Am.

Antiguedades de los Judios: Antiquities of the Jews, Vol. 1. Flavio Josefo. (SPA.). 7.95 (84-7645-129-6, 223170, Pub. by Edit Clie SP) TSELF.

Antiguedades de los Judios: Antiquities of the Jews, Vol. 2. Flavio Josefo. (SPA.). 8.95 (84-7645-130-X, 223171, Pub. by Edit Clie SP) TSELF.

Antiguedades de los Judios: Antiquities of the Jews, Vol. 3. Flavio Josefo. (SPA.). 7.95 (84-7645-131-8, 223172, Pub. by Edit Clie SP) TSELF.

Antiguo Egipto: Hechos - Histoias - Actividades. Robert Nicholson & Claire Watts. Tr. by Jose R. Araluce. (Raices Ser.). (Illus.). 32p. (SPA.). (J). (gr. 6-10). 1993. 14.95 (1-56492-094-1) Laredo.

Antiguo Evangelio Para Una Nueva Era: The Old Gospel for a New Age. H. C. Moule. (SPA.). 5.50 (84-7645-015-X, 223092, Pub. by Edit Clie SP) TSELF.

Antiguo Testamento Interlineal: Interlinear Hebrew - Sp. O. T., Vol. 1. (SPA.). 25.95 (84-7645-397-3, 223518, Pub. by Edit Clie SP) TSELF.

Antiguo Testamento y la Mujer: The Woman in the Old Testament. Clapp Welles. (SPA.). 4.95 (84-7228-961-3, 223024, Pub. by Edit Clie SP) TSELF.

Antiheroine's Voice: Narrative Discourse & Transformations of the Picaresque. Edward H. Friedman. LC 86-30870. 280p. 1987. text ed. 32.50 (0-8262-0641-7) U of Mo Pr.

Antihormones. Ed. by M. K. Agarwal. 458p. 1979. 94.50 (0-444-80119-7) Elsevier.

Antihormones in Health & Disease. Ed. by M. K. Agarawal. (Frontiers of Hormone Research Ser.: Vol. 19). (Illus.). viii, 200p. 1991. 164.00 (3-8055-5297-1) S Karger.

Antiinflammatory Steroid Action: Basic & Clinical Aspects. Robert P. Schleimer et al. 400p. 1989. text ed. 164.00 (0-12-625145-2) Acad Pr.

Antike Mnemotechnik. Herwig Blum. Bd. 15. 219p. (GER.). 1970. write for info. (0-318-70620-2, Pub. by Georg Olms GW) Lubrecht & Cramer.

Antike Mysterienwesen in Seinem Einflubauf das Christentum. Gustav Anrich. viii, 238p. (GER.). 1990. reprint ed. write for info. (3-487-09283-2, Pub. by Georg Olms GW) Lubrecht & Cramer.

Antike Rhetorik und Kommunikative Aufsatzdidaktik. Lonni Bahmer. (Germanistische Texte und Studien Ser.: Bd. 37). 299p. 1991. write for info. (3-487-09454-1, Pub. by Georg Olms GW) Lubrecht & Cramer.

Antike Roman: Power Symbology & the Roman Play in Early Modern England, 1585-1635. Clifford Ronan. LC 94-7604. 240p. 1995. 50.00 (0-8203-1672-5) U of Ga Pr.

Antike Theorie der "Varietas" Henri L. Drijepondt. (Spudasmata Ser.: Bd. XXXVII). xiii, 256p. (GER.). 1979. write for info. (3-487-06947-4, Pub. by Georg Olms GW) Lubrecht & Cramer.

Antike Tierwelt, 2 vols. Otto Keller. xxvii, 1098p. 1980. reprint ed. Bd. I: Saugetiere. write for info. (0-318-70769-1, Pub. by Georg Olms GW) Lubrecht & Cramer.

Antike Tierwelt, 2 vols., Set. Otto Keller. xxvii, 1098p. 1980. reprint ed. write for info. (3-487-00557-3, Pub. by Georg Olms GW) Lubrecht & Cramer.

Antike Tierwelt, 2 vols., Vol. II. Otto Keller. xxvii, 1098p. 1980. reprint ed. Vogel, Reptilien, Fische, Insekten. write for info. (0-318-70770-5, Pub. by Georg Olms GW) Lubrecht & Cramer.

Antike und Orient im Mittelalter: Vortraege der Koelner Mediaevistentagungen 1956-1959. 2nd ed. Ed. by P. Wilpert. (Miscellanea Mediaevalia Ser.: Vol. 1). 274p. (C). 1971. 89.25x (3-11-002395-4) De Gruyter.

Antiken Grundlagen der Fruhmittelalterlichen Privaturkunden. Harold Steinacker. (Grundrib der Geschichtswissenschaft. Erg. Ser.: Bd. 1). x, 171p. 1975. reprint ed. write for info. (3-487-05827-8, Pub. by Georg Olms GW) Lubrecht & Cramer.

Antikhrist. Archpriest Boris Molchanov. 24p. 1976. pap. 1.00 (0-317-29128-9) Holy Trinity.

*Antilles. Dennis C. Smith. 1995. 17.95 (0-533-11446-2) Vantage.

Antilles: Fragments of Epic Memory. Derek Walcott. 1993. 7.00 (0-374-10530-8) FS&G.

Antilock Systems for Air-Braked Vehicles. 1989. 20.00 (0-89883-446-5, SP789) Soc Auto Engineers.

Antimacassars. C. A. De Lomellini. 64p. (C). 1988. 25.00 (0-947612-03-3, Pub. by Rivelin Grapheme Pr) St Mut.

Antimalarial Drugs. Ed. by W. Peters & W. H. Richards. (Handbook of Experimental Pharmacology Ser.: Vol. 68, Pt. 1). (Illus.). 540p. 1984. 247.00 (0-387-12616-3) Spr-Verlag.

Antimalarial Drugs II: Current Antimalarials & New Drug Developments. Ed. by W. Peters & W. H. Richards. (Handbook of Experimental Pharmacology Ser.: Vol. 68). (Illus.). xxiii, 520p. 1984. 261.00 (0-387-12617-1) Spr-Verlag.

Antimanics, Anticonvulsants & Other Drugs in Psychiatry. Ed. by G. D. Burrows et al. (Drugs in Psychiatry Ser.: Vol. 4). 460p. 1987. 133.25 (0-317-61529-7) Elsevier.

Antimasonic Party in the United States, 1826-1843. William P. Vaughn. LC 82-40180. 256p. 1982. 28.00 (0-8131-1474-8) U Pr of Ky.

Antimatter. John Vornholt. Ed. by John Ordover. (Star Trek: Deep Space Ser.: No. 8). 288p. (Orig.). 1994. mass mkt. 5.50 (0-671-88560-X) PB.

Antimatter Universe. Kate Mueller. (Young Readers Ser.: No. 147). (J). (gr. 6 up). 1994. pap. 3.50 (0-553-56391-2) Bantam.

Antimemoires: Miroir des Limbes. Andre Malraux. (Folio Ser.: No. 23). 1972. 14.95 (2-07-036023-7) Schoenhof.

Antimemoires see Oeuvres

Antimetabolites in Biochemistry, Biology & Medicine: Proceedings, Prague, 1978. Ed. by J. Skoda & P. Langen. (Federation of European Biochemical Societies Ser.: Vol. 57). (Illus.). 1979. 154.00 (0-08-024384-3, Pub. by Pergamon Repr UK) Franklin.

Antimetabolites of Nucleic Acid Metabolism. P. Langen. 286p. 1975. text ed. 190.00 (0-677-30760-8) Gordon & Breach.

Antimicrobial Agents & Intracellular Pathogens. Didier Raoult. LC 93-2668. 1993. 189.95 (0-8493-4924-9, RM409) CRC Pr.

Antimicrobial Chemotherapy. Ed. by David Greenwood. (Illus.). 300p. 1983. pap. text ed. 24.50 (0-7216-0805-1, Bailliere-Tindall) Saunders.

Antimicrobial Chemotherapy. 2nd ed. Ed. by David Greenwood. (Illus.). 392p. 1989. pap. 24.95 (0-19-261894-6) OUP.

*Antimicrobial Chemotherapy. 3rd ed. Ed. by David Greenwood. (Illus.). 422p. 1995. pap. 49.95 (0-19-854944-X) OUP.

Antimicrobial Drug Action: The Chemical Treatment of Infectious Diseases. R. A. Williams. (Medical Perspectives Ser.). 160p. (Orig.). 1995. pap. 42.50x (1-872748-81-3, Pub. by Bios Scientific UK) Coronet Bks.

Antimicrobial Drugs. William B. Pratt & Robert Fekety. LC 84-29603. (Illus.). 640p. 1986. text ed. 49.95 (0-19-503560-7); pap. text ed. 35.00 (0-19-503561-5) OUP.

Antimicrobial Food Additives: Characteristics, Uses, Effects. E. Lueck. (Illus.). 280p. 1980. 62.00 (0-387-10056-3) Spr-Verlag.

*Antimicrobial Peptides. Ed. by Hans G. Boman et al. LC 94-21647. (Ciba Foundation Symposium Ser.: 186). 1995. text ed. 76.00 (0-471-95025-4) Wiley.

*Antimicrobial Peptides: Powerful Weapons Against Resistant Bacteria. 118p. 1995. spiral bd., vinyl bd. 1,750.00 (1-56217-014-7) Tech Insights.

Antimicrobial Pocket Book. Gerald Bodey et al. 270p. (C). 1991. pap. text ed. 19.50 (3-528-07838-3, Pub. by Vieweg & Sohn GW) Ballen Bkslr.

*Antimicrobial Prescribing. 10th ed. Burt R. Meyers. 1995. write for info. (1-884065-06-6) Assocs in Med.

Antimicrobial Prophylaxis in Urology with Special Reference to the Quinolones. Ed. by T. C. Gasser. (Fortune West Ser.: Vol. 27). 88p. 1992. pap. 29.00 (0-387-91441-2) Spr-Verlag.

Antimicrobial Susceptibility Testing: Critical Issues for the 90s. Ed. by J. A. Poupard et al. (Advances in Experimental Medicine & Biology Ser.: Vol. 349). (Illus.). 200p. 1994. 69.50 (0-306-44673-1) Plenum.

Antimicrobial Susceptibility Testing (SC2) 3rd ed. NCCLS Staff. 200p. 1991. text ed. 160.00 (1-56238-113-X) Natl Comm Clin Lab Stds.

Antimicrobial Therapy. Ed. by Angela M. Ristuccia & Burke A. Cunha. (Handbook of Therapeutic Drug Monitoring Ser.). 636p. 1984. text ed. 159.00 (0-89004-826-6) Raven.

Antimicrobial Therapy - Abdominal Surgery: Precepts & Practices. Haragopal Thadepalli & Ashis K. Mandal. 120p. 1991. 85.00 (0-8493-4269-4, RD540) CRC Pr.

Antimicrobial Therapy for Newborns: Practical Application. 2nd ed. Ed. by George H. McCracken & John D. Nelson. 234p. 1983. text ed. 43.00 (0-8089-1565-7, 792831, Grune) Saunders.

*Antimicrobial Therapy Guide. 10th ed. Burt R. Meyers. 1995. write for info. (1-884065-00-7) Assocs in Med.

Antimicrobial Therapy in Infants & Children. Koren et al. (Clinical Pediatrics Ser.: Vol. 4). 848p. 1988. 199.00 (0-8247-7745-X) Dekker.

Antimicrobial Therapy in the Elderly Patient. Ed. by Yoshikawa & Norman. 584p. 1994. 165.00 (0-8247-9163-0) Dekker.

Antimicrobial Therapy in Veterinary Medicine. John Prescott & Desmond Bagget. LC 93-13907. (Illus.). 528p. (C). 1993. text ed. 64.95 (0-8138-0889-8) Iowa St U Pr.

Antimicrobials in Foods. Ed. by Alfred L. Branen & P. Michael Davidson. LC 93-16639. (Food Science & Technology Ser.). 195.00 (0-8247-8906-7) Dekker.

*Antimicrobials in Foods. fac. ed. Ed. by Alfred L. Branen & P. Michael Davidson. LC 83-18829. (Food Science Ser.: No. 10). 479p. Date not set. pap. 136.60 (0-7837-7397-8, 2047191) Bks Demand.

Antimicrobic Susceptibility Test: Principles & Practices. Arthur L. Barry. LC 76-18846. 248p. reprint ed. pap. 70.70 (0-8357-5633-5, 2055996) Bks Demand.

Antimodernism of Joyce's "Portrait of the Artist As a Young Man" Weldon Thornton. LC 93-5484. (Irish Studies). 352p. 1994. 45.00 (0-8156-2587-1); pap. text ed. 22.50 (0-8156-2613-4) Syracuse U Pr.

An Asterisk (*) at the beginning of an entry indicates that the title is appearing in BIP for the first time.

*Antimonopoly Laws & Policies of Japan. Hiroshi Iyori & Akinori Uesugi. LC 94-70047. 604p. 1994. 85.00x (0-87945-076-2); pap. 34.95x (0-87945-077-0) Fed Legal Pubn.

Antimonopoly Laws of Japan. 2nd ed. Hiroshi Iyori & Akinori Uesugi. 380p. 1983. 55.00 (0-87945-039-8) Fed Legal Pubn.

Antimony. (Metals & Minerals Ser.). 1994. lib. bdg. 200.95 (0-8490-5685-3) Gordon Pr.

Antimutagenesis & Anticarcinogenesis Mechanisms. Ed. by Delbert M. Shankel et al. LC 86-15070. (Basic Life Sciences Ser.: Vol. 39). 618p. 1986. 125.00 (0-306-42375-8, Plenum Pr) Plenum.

Antimutagenesis & Anticarcinogenesis Mechanisms, No. II. Ed. by Y. Kuroda et al. (Basic Life Sciences Ser.: Vol. 52). (Illus.). 498p. 1990. 110.00 (0-306-43403-2, Plenum Pr) Plenum.

Antimutagenesis & Anticarcinogenesis Mechanisms III. Ed. by G. Bronzetti et al. (Basic Life Sciences Ser.: Vol. 61). 494p. 1993. 125.00 (0-306-44577-8, Plenum Pr) Plenum.

Antimutagens in Anticarcinogens. T. Hughes & B. Casto. 1993. pap. text ed. 74.00 (2-88124-605-2) Gordon & Breach.

Antimycobacterial Susceptibility Testing: Proposed Standard. 1990. 40.00 (1-56238-100-8, M24-P) Natl Comm Clin Lab Stds.

Antineoplastic Agents. Ed. by William A. Remers. LC 83-12411. 286p. 1990. reprint ed. lib. bdg. 75.00 (0-471-08080-2) Krieger.

Antineoplastic, Immunogenic & Other Effects of the Tetrapeptide Tuftsin, Vol. 419. Ed. by Victor A. Najjar & Mati Fridkin. 55.00 (0-89766-232-6); pap. 55.00 (0-89766-233-4) NY Acad Sci.

Anting-Anting Stories, & Other Strange Tales of the Filipinos. Sargent Kayme. LC 71-81270. (Short Story Index Reprint Ser.). 1977. 19.95 (0-8369-3022-3) Ayer.

Antinomian Controversy. Charles F. Adams. LC 74-164507. 1976. reprint ed. lib. bdg. 25.00 (0-306-70290-8) Da Capo.

Antinomian Controversy, 1636-1638: A Documentary History. 2nd ed. Ed. by David D. Hall. LC 90-3237. 476p. (C). 1990. reprint ed. lib. bdg. 39.50 (0-8223-1083-X) Duke.

Antinomian Controversy, 1636-1638: A Documentary History. Ed. by David D. Hall. LC 90-3237. 476p. (C). 1990. reprint ed. pap. text ed. 16.95 (0-8223-1091-0) Duke.

*Antinomie: Italian Poetry. Gianni Diecidue. 90p. 1981. pap. 10.00 (0-89304-659-0) Cross-Cultrl NY.

Antinomies of Interdependence. Ed. by John G. Ruggie. LC 82-2123. (Political Economy of International Change Ser.). 392p. 1983. text ed. 59.50 (0-231-05724-5); pap. text ed. 19.50 (0-231-05725-3) Col U Pr.

Antinostalgia. Robert Anbian. (Oro Madre Ser.: Vol. 5, Nos. 1-4, 1992). (Illus.). 80p. (Orig.). 1992. pap. 12.00 (0-910697-08-6) Ruddy Duck Pr.

Antinous: A Romance of Ancient Rome. George Taylor & Adolf Hausrath. LC 78-63988. (Gay Experience Ser.). reprint ed. 28.50 (0-404-61507-4) AMS Pr.

Antinuclear Antibodies: Characterization of a Reference Preparation for Standardization of the IF-ANA Test. (Proposed Guideline Ser.: Vol. 6). 1986. 40.00 (1-56238-068-0, I LA2-P) Natl Comm Clin Lab Stds.

*Antinuclear Movement. Price. 1995. text ed. 40.00 (0-8161-7268-4) G K Hall.

Antinuclear Movement. Jerome B. Price. (Social Movements Past & Present Ser.). 224p. 1982. lib. bdg. 20.95 (0-8057-9705-X, Twayne) Macmillan.

Antinuclear Movement. Jerome B. Price. (Social Movements Past & Present Ser.). 224p. 1987. pap. 12.95 (0-8057-9720-3, Twayne) Macmillan.

Antinuclear Movement. rev. ed. Jerome B. Price. (Social Movements Past & Present Ser.). 240p. 1989. text ed. 14.95 (0-8057-9735-1, Twayne) Macmillan.

Antinuclear Movement. rev. ed. Jerome B. Price. (Social Movements Past & Present Ser.). 240p. 1990. pap. 14.95 (0-8057-9736-X, Twayne) Macmillan.

Antinucleon Nucleon Interactions: Proceedings 3rd European Symposium Wenner Gren Center, Stockholm 7-76. Gosta Ekspong & S. Nilsson. LC 76-52469. (Wenner Gren Center International Symposium Ser.: Vol. 29). 1977. 252.00 (0-08-021515-7, Pub. by Pergamon Repr UK) Franklin.

Antinutrients & Natural Toxicants in Foods. R. L. Ory. 378p. 1981. 74.00 (0-917678-15-X) Food & Nut Pr.

Antioch: A Place of Christians. Harriett Arnold. LC 93-60521. (Illus.). 132p. (Orig.). 1993. 18.95 (0-936029-29-3); pap. 12.95 (0-936029-30-7) Western Bk Journ.

Antioch: The Dixon Era, 1959-1975. Ed. by Edla Dixon & James Dixon. LC 91-70339. xii, 232p. (Orig.). 1991. pap. 9.95 (0-9621921-3-9) Bastille Bks.

Antioch & Rome: New Testament Cradles of Catholic Christianity. Raymond E. Brown & John Meier. 256p. 1983. pap. 11.95 (0-8091-2532-3) Paulist Pr.

*Antioch Career: The Memoirs of J. Dudley Dawson. J. Dudley Dawson. Ed. by Dan Hotaling & Dorothy O. Soctt. LC 95-75943. (Orig.). 1995. pap. text ed. 15.95 (0-9646148-4-7) Antioch Univ.

Antioch Effect: Eight Characteristics of Highly Effective Churches. Ken Hemphill. LC 93-40622. 240p. 1994. 17.99 (0-8054-3016-4, 4230-16) Broadman.

Antioch in the Age of Theodosius the Great. Glanville Downey. LC 62-16481. (Centers of Civilization Ser.: No. 6). 176p. reprint ed. pap. 50.20 (0-8357-5634-3, 2010090) Bks Demand.

*Antioch-on-the-Orontes Vol. 5: Les Portiques D'Antioche. Jean Lassus. LC 35-1197. (Publications of the Committee for the Excavation of Antioch & Its Vicinity). pap. 64.50 (0-7837-9368-5, 2060111) Bks Demand.

Antioch Review Anthology. Antioch Review Staff. Ed. by Paul Bixler. LC 79-117752. (Essay Index Reprint Ser.). 1977. 27.95 (0-8369-1782-0) Ayer.

Antioch Review Anthology. Ed. by Paul Bixler. (Essay Index Reprint Ser.). 480p. reprint ed. lib. bdg. 24.00 (0-8290-0793-8) Irvington.

Antioch Suite-Jazz. Abba Elethea, pseud. 36p. 1980. pap. 3.00 (0-916418-25-1) Lotus.

Antioqueno Colonization in Western Colombia. 2nd rev. ed. James J. Parsons. LC 68-58002. (University of California Publications in Social Welfare: No. 32). (Illus.). 260p. reprint ed. pap. 74.10 (0-8357-5635-1, 2029959) Bks Demand.

Antioquia's Corridor to the Sea: An Historical Geography of the Settlement of Uraba. James J. Parsons. LC 68-1378. 132p. 1983. reprint ed. lib. bdg. 25.00x (0-89370-766-X) Borgo Pr.

Antioxidant Health Plan: How to Beat the Effects of Free Radicals. Robert Youngson. (Illus.). 128p. 1994. pap. 8.00 (0-7225-2968-6) Thorsons SF.

Antioxidant Nutrients & Immune Functions. Ed. by A. Bendich et al. LC 89-26570. (Advances in Experimental Medicine & Biology Ser.: No. 262). (Illus.). 184p. 1990. 65.00 (0-306-43396-6, Plenum Pr) Plenum.

Antioxidant Pocket Counter: A Guide to the Essential Nutrients That Can Help Fight Cancer. Gail Becker. 1994. pap. 3.99 (0-8129-2403-7, Times Bks) Random.

Antioxidants. Richard A. Passwater. (Good Health Guide Ser.). (Orig.). 1985. pap. 2.50 (0-87983-404-8) Keats.

*Antioxidants: Chemical, Physiological, Nutritional & Toxicological Aspects. Ed. by Gary M. Williams et al. (Toxicology & Industrial Health Ser.: Vol. 9, Nos. 1-2). (Illus.). 390p. 1993. 70.00 (0-911131-49-3) Princeton Sci Pubs.

*Antioxidants: Free Radicals in Nutrition, Health & Disease. John M. Gutteridge & Barry Halliwell. (Illus.). 160p. 1995. 28.95 (0-19-854902-4) OUP.

Antioxidants: Markets, Materials, Trends. 137p. 1991. 2,150.00 (0-89336-863-6, C-020BR) BCC.

Antioxidants: Your Complete Guide. Carolyn Reuben. LC 93-49709. 1994. pap. write for info. (1-55958-522-6) Prima Pub.

Antioxidants & Stabilizers for Polymers. James R. Critser, Jr. (Ser. 3-72). 185p. 1973. 115.00 (0-914428-12-8) Lexington Data.

Antioxidants & Stabilizers for Polymers. James R. Critser, Jr. (Ser. 3-73). 136p. 1974. 115.00 (0-914428-19-5) Lexington Data.

Antioxidants & Stabilizers for Polymers. James R. Critser, Jr. (Ser. 3-74). 1975. 120.00 (0-914428-24-1) Lexington Data.

Antioxidants & Stabilizers for Polymers. James R. Critser, Jr. (Ser. 3-75). 1976. 120.00 (0-914428-34-9) Lexington Data.

Antioxidants & Stabilizers for Polymers. James R. Critser, Jr. (Ser. 3-76). 1977. 125.00 (0-914428-50-0) Lexington Data.

Antioxidants & Stabilizers for Polymers. James R. Critser, Jr. Incl. Indexes & Abstracts 1967-1971315.00 (0-914428-06-3, 3-6771B); 1972. write for info. (0-318-54072-X) Lexington Data.

Antioxidants in Higher Plants. Alscher. 1993. 144.00 (0-8493-6328-4, QK898) CRC Pr.

Antioxidants in Therapy & Preventive Medicine. Ed. by Ingrid Emerit et al. (Advances in Experimental Medicine & Biology Ser.: Vol. 264). (Illus.). 608p. 1990. 125.00 (0-306-43407-5, Plenum Pr) Plenum.

Antioxidative Stabilization of Polymers. Yu Shlyapnikov. 246p. 1995. text ed. 75.00 (0-13-106071-6) P-H.

Antiparasitic Chemotherapy. Ed. by H. Schoenfeld. (Antibiotics & Chemotherapy Ser.: Vol. 30). (Illus.). viii, 288p. 1981. 182.50 (3-8055-2160-X) S Karger.

Antipasti: Antipasti & Other Appetizers. Anna Del Conte. LC 93-13389. (Anna del Conte's Italian Kitchen Ser.). (Illus.). 1994. 14.00 (0-671-87029-7) S&S Trade.

*Antipasto. Harper Collins Staff. (Little Appetiser Library). 1994. 9.00 (0-207-18604-9, Pub. by Angus & Robertson AT) HarpC.

Antipasto Table. Michele Scicolone. 224p. 1991. 20.00 (0-688-10124-0) Morrow.

Antipeople. Sony L. Tansi. Tr. by J. A. Underwood. 170p. 1990. reprint ed. pap. 9.95 (0-7145-2901-X) M Boyars Pubs.

Antiperspirants & Deodorants. Laden & Felger. (Cosmetic Science & Technology Ser.: Vol. 7). 440p. 1988. 160.00 (0-8247-7893-6) Dekker.

Antiphon. Paula Aguilar. LC 90-71951. 1991. pap. 6.95 (1-55523-415-1) Winston-Derek.

Antiphon & Psalm in the Ambrosian Office. Terence Bailey. (Wissenschaftliche Abhandlungen-Musicological Studies: No. 50/3). 320p. 1994. 78.00 (0-685-74992-4) Inst Mediaeval Mus.

Antiphonal Swing: Selected Prose 1962-1987. Clayton Eshleman. Ed. by Caryl Eshleman. LC 88-1550. 296p. 1989. 25.00 (0-914232-94-0) McPherson & Co.

Antiphonale Monasticum: (Monastic Antiphonale) Abbey of St. Peter of Solesmes Monks. 1300p. (LAT.). (C). 1934. 56.95 (1-55725-073-1, 3003, Pub. by Abbey St Peter Solesmes FR) Paraclete MA.

Antiphonary. Hubert Aquin. Tr. by Alan Brown. 196p. 1973. reprint ed. 9.95 (0-88784-426-X, Pub. by Hse of Anansi Pr CN) Genl Dist Srvs.

Antiphons of the Ambrosian Office. Terence Bailey & Paul Merkley. (Wissenschaftliche Abhandlungen-Musicological Studies: Vol. 50, Pt. 1). 271p. (ENG.). 1989. 70.00 (0-931902-60-6) Inst Mediaeval Mus.

Antiphons, Responsories & Other Chants from the Mozarabic Rite. C. W. Brockett. (Wissenschaftliche Abhandlungen-Musicological Studies: Vol. 15). 300p. 1968. lib. bdg. 80.00 (0-912024-85-2) Inst Mediaeval Mus.

Antiphonstudien. Friedrich Solmsen. Heft 8. 78p. 1931. write for info. (0-318-71029-3, Pub. by Georg Olms GW) Lubrecht & Cramer.

Antiphony. Hubert Alquin. 196p. 1983. pap. 3.95 (0-7736-7053-X, Pub. by Stoddart Pubng CN) Genl Dist Srvs.

Antiphony of Bells. Alexis K. Rotella. 20p. 1988. 6.00 (0-917951-02-6) Jade Mtn.

Antiphospholipid Antibodies. Ed. by J. Monasterio et al. (Journal: Haemostasis Ser.: Vol. 24, No. 3, 1994). (Illus.). iv, 56p. 1994. pap. 18.50 (3-8055-6027-3) S Karger.

Antiplatelet Therapy: Twenty Years Experience. Ed. by G. V. Born & G. G. Neri Serneri. (Current Clinical Practice Ser.: Vol. 44). 282p. 1988. 107.75 (0-444-90499-9, Excerpta Medica) Elsevier.

*Antipodes. Richard Brome. Ed. by Ann Haaker. LC 66-13403. (Regents Renaissance Drama Ser.). 160p. 1966. pap. 45.60 (0-7837-8444-9, 2049248) Bks Demand.

Antipodes. Maria-Antonia Oliver. Tr. by Kathleen McNerney. LC 89-10199. (International Women's Crime Ser.). 224p. (Orig.). 1989. reprint ed. pap. 8.95 (0-931188-82-2) Seal Pr Feminist.

Antipoems: New & Selected. Nicanor Parra. Ed. by David Unger. Tr. by Lawrence Ferlinghetti et al. LC 85-11507. 224p. 1985. 19.95 (0-8112-0959-8); pap. 8.95 (0-8112-0960-1, NDP603) New Directions.

Antipolitics. George Konrad. Tr. by Richard E. Allen. LC 83-22718. 224p. 1984. 12.95 (0-15-107820-3) HarBrace.

Antipolitics: An Essay. George Konrad. Tr. by Richard E. Allen. 243p. 1984. 12.95 (0-317-53187-5) HarBrace.

Antipoverty Housekeeping: The Administration of the Economic Opportunity Act. Roger H. Davidson & Sar A. Levitan. LC 68-65876. (Policy Papers in Human Resources & Industrial Relations Ser.: No. 9). (Orig.). 1968. pap. 5.00 (0-87736-109-6) U of Mich Inst Labor.

Antipoverty Work & Training Efforts: Goals & Reality. 2nd ed. Sar A. Levitan. (Policy Papers in Human Resources & Industrial Relations Ser.: No. 3). (Orig.). 1970. pap. 5.00 (0-87736-103-7) U of Mich Inst Labor.

Antiprogestin Steroid RU 486 & Human Fertility Control. Ed. by Etienne-Emile Baulieu & Sheldon J. Segal. LC 85-19815. (Reproductive Biology Ser.). 364p. 1985. 95.00 (0-306-42103-8, Plenum Pr) Plenum.

Antiproton-Nucleon & Antiproton - Nucleus Interactions. Ed. by F. Bradamante et al. LC 90-6767. (Ettore Majorana International Science Series, Life Sciences: Vol. 47). (Illus.). 340p. 1990. 89.50 (0-306-43501-2, Plenum Pr) Plenum.

Antipsychotic Drugs: Pharmacodynamics & Pharmacokinetics. Ed. by G. Sedvall et al. 286p. 1976. 196.00 (0-08-019688-8, Pub. by Pergamon Repr UK) Franklin.

Antipsychotic Drugs & Their Side Effects. Ed. by T. R. Barnes. (Neuroscience Perspectives Ser.). (Illus.). 287p. 1994. text ed. 69.95 (0-12-079035-1) Acad Pr.

Antipsychotics: Drugs in Psychiatry, Vol. 3. Ed. by G. D. Burrows et al. 288p. 1985. 119.00 (0-444-80635-0) Elsevier.

Antiquaire. Henri Bosco. 538p. (FRE.). 1979. pap. 14.95 (0-7859-1884-1, 2070370828) Fr & Eur.

Antiquarian & the Myth of Antiquity: The Origins of Rome in Renaissance Thought. Philip Jacks. LC 92-35326. (Illus.). 368p. (C). 1993. 65.00 (0-521-44152-8) Cambridge U Pr.

Antiquarian Book Fair & Paper Show Directory, 1990: Including Antiquarian Booksellers & Collectors' Association Calendar & Directory for the U. S. & Canada. rev. ed. Ed. by James A. Visbeck. 151p. 1989. pap. 8.50 (0-685-30406-X) Isaiah Thomas Bks.

Antiquarian Book Fair & Paper Show Directory 1987-1988. Marjorie P. Adams. 120p. (Orig.). 1987. pap. 8.75 (0-317-62611-6) Parrott Pr.

Antiquarian Books: A Companion for Booksellers, Librarians & Collectors. Ed. by Leo Bernard & Angus O'Neill. LC 94-2436. (Illus.). 480p. (C). 1994. text ed. 79.95 (0-8122-3268-2) U of Pa Pr.

Antiquarian Bookselling in the United States: A History from the Origins to the 1940s. Madeleine B. Stern. LC 84-19273. xviii, 246p. 1985. text ed. 55.00 (0-313-24729-3, SAQ/, Greenwood Pr) Greenwood.

Antiquarian Catalogues of Musical Interest. J. Coover. 406p. 1988. text ed. 100.00 (0-7201-1979-0, Mansell Pub) Cassell.

Antiquarian Music Dealer's Education. Theodore Front. LC 81-159949. (Front Music Publications: No. 3). 10p. (Orig.). 1981. pap. 5.00 (0-934082-03-0) Theodore Front.

*Antiquarian Pursuits. Estill C. Pennington. LC 92-71543. (Illus.). 88p. (Orig.). 1992. pap. 20.00 (0-9632836-0-X) R M Hicklin.

Antiquarian, Specialty, & Used Book Sellers: A Subject Guide & Directory. Ed. by Karen Ethridge & James M. Ethridge. LC 93-9133. 1993. lib. bdg. 64.00 (1-55888-766-0) Omnigraphics Inc.

*Antiquarian, Specialty, & Used Book Sellers Directory. 2nd enl. ed. Ed. by James M. Ethridge. 1995. lib. bdg. 72.00x (0-7808-0024-9) Omnigraphics Inc.

Antiquated American. J. DuHadway Craig. 1976. pap. 4.50 (0-9602042-0-2) J D Craig.

Antiquated Subdivisions: Beyond Lot Mergers & Vested Rights Conference Proceedings. Ed. by Madelyn Glickfeld. 184p. reprint ed. pap. 52.50 (0-7837-5756-5, 2045418) Bks Demand.

Antique Advertising Encyclopedia, Vol. 2. Ray Klug. LC 88-61480. (Illus.). 240p. 1988. 39.95 (0-88740-141-4) Schiffer.

Antique Advertising Paper Dolls. Ed. by Barbara W. Jendrick. (Illus.). 64p. (Orig.). 1981. pap. 3.95 (0-486-24045-2) Dover.

Antique Airplanes. Sorenson. 1978. 30.00 (0-684-15817-5, Scribners) S&S Trade.

Antique American Country Furniture: A Field Guide. Thomas M. Voss. LC 77-15898. (Illus.). 1978. pap. 7.95 (0-685-42238-0, HarpT) HarpC.

*Antique American Frames: Identification & Price Guide. Mervyn Kaufman & Eli Wilner. LC 94-48748. (Illus.). 320p. (Orig.). 1995. pap. 15.00 (0-380-77011-3, Confident Collect) Avon.

Antique American Sewing Machines: A Value Guide. James W. Slaten. (Illus.). 258p. (Orig.). 1992. pap. 24.95 (0-9632287-0-6) Sing Deal Mus.

Antique & Classic Cars: Their Maintenance & Operation. Richard C. Wheatley & Brian Morgan. LC 75-37230. (Illus.). 168p. 1976. 12.50 (0-8376-0203-3) Bentley.

Antique & Collectible Marbles. 3rd ed. Everett Grist. (Illus.). 94p. 1992. pap. 9.95 (0-89145-488-8, 1846) Collector Bks.

Antique & Collectible Stanley Tools: A Guide to Identity & Value. John Walter. (Illus.). 455p. (Orig.). (C). 1990. pap. 24.95 (1-878911-00-7) Tool Merchant.

Antique & Deadly. Lucine H. Flynn. 1988. 16.95 (0-8027-5702-2) Walker & Co.

Antique & 20th Century Jewellery. Vivian Becker. (Illus.). 319p. 1989. 69.50 (0-7198-0171-0, Pub. by NAG Press UK) Antique Collect.

Antique Art on the Northern Black Sea Coast. G. Sokolov. (Illus.). 1974. 55.00 (0-8464-1455-4) Beekman Pubs.

Antique Art on the Northern Black Sea Coast. G. Sokolov. (Illus.). 1974. 90.00 (0-685-86581-9, 56911544) St Mut.

Antique Auto Body Accessories for the Restorer. Ed. by Alfred S. Lewerenz. (Vintage Craft Ser.: No. 7). (Illus.). 1970. pap. 6.95 (0-911160-07-8) Post Group.

Antique Auto Body Brass Work for the Restorer. Alfred S. Lewerenz. (Vintage Craft Ser.: No. 5). (Illus.). 1970. pap. 6.95 (0-911160-05-1) Post Group.

Antique Auto Body Leather Work for the Restorer. Ed. by Herbert J. Butler. LC 82-62713. (Vintage Craft Ser.: No. 3). (Illus.). 1969. pap. 6.95 (0-911160-03-5) Post Group.

Antique Auto Body Metal Work for the Restorer. Ed. by William Neubecker. LC 82-62579. (Vintage Craft Ser.: No. 1). (Illus.). 1969. pap. 6.95 (0-911160-01-9) Post Group.

Antique Auto Body Wood Work for the Restorer. C. W. Terry. LC 77-74129. (Vintage Craft Ser.: No. 2). (Illus.). 1969. pap. 6.95 (0-911160-02-7) Post Group.

Antique Bird Decoys. 2nd ed. Carl Luckey. 224p. 1992. 22.95 (0-89689-078-3) Bks Americana.

Antique Bottle Finds in New England. Virginia T. Bates & Beverly Chamberlain. LC 68-9146. 80p. reprint ed. pap. 25.00 (0-8357-5636-X, 2020941) Bks Demand.

Antique Brass & Copper Collectibles. Gaston. 1991. pap. 16.95 (0-89145-478-0) Collector Bks.

*Antique British Clocks: A Buyer's Guide. Brian Loomes. (Illus.). 224p. Date not set. 35.00 (0-7090-4611-1, Pub. by R Hale Ltd UK) Antique Collect.

Antique Builders Hardware: Knobs & Accessories. Maud L. Eastwood. (Illus.). 224p. (Orig.). 1982. ring bd. 19.50 (0-9610800-2-7) Ant Doorknob Pub.

Antique Builders' Hardware, Suppl. 1: Knobs & Accessories. rev. ed. Maud L. Eastwood. (Illus.). iv, 36p. 1992. pap. 4.75 (0-9610800-4-3) Ant Doorknob Pub.

Antique Car Wrecks. John Gunnell. LC 90-60581. (Illus.). 224p. 1990. pap. 14.95 (0-87341-139-0) Krause Pubns.

Antique Chains. Carmen Guappone. 1978. pap. 9.95 (0-686-22994-0) Guappones Pubs.

Antique Children's Fashions. Hazel Ulseth & Helen Shannon. 126p. 1982. pap. 14.95 (0-87588-192-0, 75) Hobby Hse.

Antique Clocks. Carmen Guappone. 1978. pap. 9.95 (0-686-22995-9) Guappones Pubs.

Antique Clothing, French Sewing by Machine. Martha C. Pullen. LC 90-91872. (Illus.). 352p. (Orig.). 1990. 29.00 (1-878048-00-7) M Pullen.

Antique Collecting for Pleasure. Ed. by David Coombs. 192p. 1981. 75.00 (0-85223-136-9, Pub. by Ebury Pr UK) Trafalgar.

Antique Collector Dolls, Vol. 2. Patricia Smith. pap. 17.95 (0-89145-476-4) Collector Bks.

Antique Collector's Handbook: How to Recognize, Collect & Enjoy Antiques. Anne Stone. 204p. 1989. 75.00 (0-85223-199-7, Pub. by Ebury Pr UK) Trafalgar.

Antique Collector's Picture Guide to Prices. David Coombs. 192p. 1989. 90.00 (0-85223-161-X, Pub. by Ebury Pr UK) Trafalgar.

Antique Combs & Purses. Evelyn M. Haertig. LC 81-90128. (Illus.). 325p. (C). 1983. 59.95 (0-943294-00-2) Gallery Graphics.

Antique Dealer. large type ed. R. P. Way. 1974. 15.95 (0-85456-257-5) Ulverscroft.

Antique Dental Instruments. Elisabeth Bennion. LC 86-50085. (Illus.). 176p. 1986. text ed. 45.00 (0-85667-310-2, Pub. by P Wilson Pubs) Sothebys Pubns.

Antique Dolls Go to a Paper Doll Wedding. 8p. (J). (gr. 8-12). 1978. pap. 4.00 (0-914510-09-6) Evergreen.

Antique Drums of War. James H. McRandle. LC 93-41325. (Military History Ser.: No. 33). (Illus.). 256p. 1994. 39.50 (0-89096-591-9); pap. 15.95 (0-89096-611-7) Tex A&M Univ Pr.

Antique Dust. large type ed. Robert Westfall. 320p. 1990. 9.97 (0-685-56330-8, Pub. by ISIS UK) Transaction Pubs.

An Asterisk (*) at the beginning of an entry indicates that the title is appearing in BIP for the first time.

363

Antique Enamels for Collectors. Joachim F. Richter. LC 90-61804. (Illus.). 176p. 1990. 59.95 (*0-88740-261-5*) Schiffer.

Antique European & American Firearms at the Hermitage Museum. L. Tarassuk. 1973. 150.00 (*0-685-86582-7*, 569080981) St Mut.

Antique Fashion Paper Dolls of the 1890s in Full Color. Illus. by Boston Children's Museum Staff. (Paper Dolls Ser.). 32p. 1984. pap. 3.95 (*0-486-24622-1*) Dover.

Antique Flower. (World Textile Collection Ser.: No. 7). (Illus.). 84p. 1993. pap. 42.95 (*4-7636-8102-8*, Pub. by Kyoto Shoin JA) Bks Nippan.

Antique Flowers: A Guide to Listing Old-Fashioned Species in Contemporary Gardens. Katherine Whiteside. LC 88-40217. (Illus.). 1988. 29.95 (*0-394-57339-0*, Villard Bks) Random.

Antique French Doll Paper Dolls: An Armenian-American Memoir. Peggy J. Rosamond. 8p. (J). (gr. 8-12). 1976. pap. 4.00 (*0-914510-07-X*) Evergreen.

Antique Furniture on a Budget. Graham Shearing. 160p. 1981. 39.00 (*0-85223-149-0*, Pub. by Ebury Pr UK) Trafalgar.

Antique Furniture Trail. V. J. Taylor. (Illus.). 192p. 1993. pap. 19.95 (*0-7153-0097-0*, Pub. by D & C Pub UK) Sterling.

Antique Gambling Chips. Dale Seymour. (Illus.). 285p. (Orig.). 1985. pap. 16.95 (*0-9614273-0-2*) Past Pleasures.

Antique Garden Ornament. John Davis. (Illus.). 389p. 1991. 79.50 (*1-85149-098-1*) Antique Collect.

Antique Gems & Rings, 2 vols. C. W. King. 1977. 250.00 (*0-8490-1440-9*) Gordon Pr.

Antique Guns: The Collector's Guide. John E. Traister. (Illus.). 288p. (Orig.). 1989. pap. 16.95 (*0-88317-144-9*) Stoeger Pub Co.

Antique Guns: The Collector's Guide. 2nd ed. John Traister. (Illus.). 32p. (Orig.). 1994. pap. 19.95 (*0-88317-175-9*) Stoeger Pub Co.

Antique Iron. Kathryn McNerney. (Illus.). 224p. 1989. pap. 9.95 (*0-89145-238-9*) Collector Bks.

Antique Iron, English & American: 15th Century Through 1850. Peter Schiffer et al. LC 79-88255. (Illus.). 320p. 1979. 59.95 (*0-88740-558-4*) Schiffer.

Antique Jewelry. Ada Darling. (Illus.). 200p. 1953. 20.00 (*0-87282-022-X*) Am Life Foun.

Antique Jewelry with Prices. rev. ed. Doris J. Snell. LC 81-52173. (Illus.). 128p. 1991. pap. 15.95 (*0-87069-628-9*) Chilton.

Antique Lace Patterns. Frances Bradbury. (International Design Library). (Illus.). 48p. 1985. pap. 5.95 (*0-88045-070-3*) Stemmer Hse.

Antique Map Price Record & Handbook for 1993, Vol. 11. Jon K. Rosenthal. (Illus.). viii, 344p. 1993. lib. bdg. 36.00 (*0-9638100-0-6*) Kimmel Pubns.

***Antique Map Price Record & Handbook for 1994 Vol. 12.** Jon K. Rosenthal. 360p. 1994. lib. bdg. 36.00 (*0-9638100-1-4*) Kimmel Pubns.

Antique Maps. 3rd ed. Carl Moreland & David Bannister. (Illus.). 314p. (C). 1993. reprint ed. pap. 24.95 (*0-7148-2954-4*, Pub. by Phaidon Press UK) Chronicle Bks.

Antique Maps of the Nineteenth Century World. Robert M. Martin. 1989. 29.99 (*0-517-67881-0*) Random Hse Value.

Antique Mechanical Fans. 2nd rev. ed. Kurt D. House. LC 85-51902. (Illus.). 154p. (Orig.). reprint ed. 26.95 (*0-318-18534-2*) Trade Rte Antiq.

Antique Medical Instruments. C. Keith Wilbur. LC 87-60204. (Illus.). 156p. (Orig.). 1987. pap. 12.95 (*0-88740-094-9*) Schiffer.

Antique Medical Instruments. rev. ed. Keith Wilbur. LC 87-60204. (Illus.). 156p. (Orig.). 1993. pap. 12.95 (*0-88740-506-1*) Schiffer.

Antique Musical Instruments & Their Players. rev. ed. Filippo Bonanni. (Illus.). 1923. pap. 7.95 (*0-486-21179-7*) Dover.

Antique Painted Pottery. N. A. Sidorova et al. 1985. 100.00 (*0-317-42746-6*, Pub. by Collets UK) St Mut.

Antique Paper Dolls, 1915-1920. Arnold Arnold. (J). 1976. pap. 3.95 (*0-486-23176-3*) Dover.

Antique Paperdolls of the Edwardian Era. Epinal. (J). 1983. pap. 3.95 (*0-486-23175-5*) Dover.

Antique Photo Printing Processes. 1989. 4.95 (*0-89816-030-8*) Embee Pr.

Antique Pocket Watches. Carmen Guappone. 1978. pap. 9.95 (*0-686-22993-2*) Guappones Pubs.

Antique Postcards of Rose O'Neill. Janet A. Banneck & Susan B. Nicholson. 100p. 1992. pap. text ed. 25.00 (*1-882207-00-9*) Greater Chicago Prods.

Antique Purses. 2nd rev. ed. Richard Holiner. (Illus.). 208p. 1990. 19.95 (*0-89145-334-2*, 1748) Collector Bks.

Antique Radio Boys & the Garrulous Grebe. Stan Dryer. 64p. 1992. 4.95 (*1-882452-00-3*) Antique Radio.

Antique Radio Restoration Guide. David Johnson. LC 92-50193. (Illus.). 160p. 1992. pap. 14.95 (*0-87069-638-6*, Wallace-Hmestead) Chilton.

Antique Roads of America: Bicycle Guide for Route 66. Dan Mahnke. (Illus.). 102p. (Orig.). 1992. pap. 9.95 (*0-9633853-0-5*, TX 3 345 672) D Mahnke.

Antique Roses for the South. William C. Welch. LC 90-34640. 216p. 1990. 29.95 (*0-87833-723-7*) Taylor Pub.

Antique Rugs from the Near East. 4th ed. Wilhelm Von Bode & Ernst Kuhnel. Tr. by Charles G. Ellis. LC 83-70866. (Illus.). 192p. 1984. 36.95 (*0-8014-1652-3*) Cornell U Pr.

Antique Santa Post Cards, Vol. III. Beverly Port. (Illus.). 12p. (Orig.). 1991. spiral bd. 4.95 (*0-87588-366-4*) Hobby Hse.

Antique Santa Postcards, Vol. II. Beverly Port. 12p. (Orig.). 1987. spiral bd. 4.95 (*0-87588-314-1*, 3596) Hobby Hse.

Antique Sewing Tools & Tales. Barbara D. Gullers. (Illus.). 118p. 1992. 45.00 (*0-941250-02-4*) Gullers Pict.

Antique Steins: A Collector's Guide. James R. Stevenson. LC 80-70730. (Illus.). 192p. 1982. 40.00 (*0-8453-4708-X*, Cornwall Bks) Assoc Univ Prs.

Antique Steins: A Collectors' Guide. 2nd rev. ed. James R. Stevenson. LC 86-47999. (Illus.). 224p. 1989. 45.00 (*0-8453-4806-X*, Cornwall Bks) Assoc Univ Prs.

Antique Store Cat. Leslie Baker. 32p. (J). (ps-3). 1992. 14.95 (*0-316-07837-9*) Little.

Antique Teddy Bear Postcards, Vol. II. Beverly Port. 12p. (Orig.). 1987. spiral bd. 4.95 (*0-87588-315-X*) Hobby Hse.

Antique Thorn. Horatio Colony. LC 73-93388. 100p. 1974. 15.95 (*0-8283-1534-5*) Branden Pub Co.

Antique Tins. Fred Dodge. 1994. 24.95 (*0-89145-604-X*) Collector Bks.

Antique Tool Collector's Guide to Value: 1750-1950. 3rd rev. ed. Ronald S. Barlow. LC 84-50055. (Illus.). 236p. 1991. pap. 12.95 (*0-933846-01-0*) Windmill Pub Co.

Antique Tools: Our American Heritage. Kathryn McNerney. (Illus.). 153p. 1991. pap. 9.95 (*0-89145-125-0*) Collector Bks.

Antique Trader Antiques & Collectibles Price Guide. 9th ed. Kyle Husfloen. 1992. pap. 12.95 (*0-930625-08-0*) Antique Trader.

Antique Trader Antiques & Collectibles Price Guide: 1994 Edition. Ed. by Kyle Husfloen. (Illus.). 908p. 1993. pap. 12.95 (*0-930625-09-9*) Antique Trader.

Antique Trader, Antiques & Collectibles Price Guide, 1995: A Comprehensive Price Guide to the Entire Field of Antiques & Collectibles. 11th ed. Intro. by Kyle Husfloen. (Illus.). 908p. 1994. pap. 12.95 (*0-930625-10-2*) Antique Trader.

***Antique Trader Books 1996 Antiques & Collectibles Price Guide: A Comprehensive Price Guide to the Entire Field of Antiques & Collectibles.** 12th ed. Ed. by Kyle Husfloen. (Illus.). 908p. 1995. pap. 13.95 (*0-614-06253-5*) Antique Trader.

Antique Views of Boston. rev. ed. Henry Stark. Ed. by Theodore Thomte. LC 67-30488. (Illus.). 1967. 10.00 (*0-910306-02-8*); 14.00 (*0-910306-03-6*) Burdette.

Antique Wicker from the Heywood-Wakefield Catalog. Bob Meschi. LC 94-65608. (Illus.). 160p. (Orig.). 1994. pap. 19.95 (*0-88740-618-1*) Schiffer.

Antique Woodstoves: Artistry in Iron. Will Curtis & Jane Curtis. (Illus.). 64p. 1975. pap. 12.95 (*0-89166-000-3*) Cobblesmith.

Antique Works of Art from Benin. Augustus H. Pitt-Rivers. LC 68-9011. (Illus.). 1971. 25.00 (*0-87817-017-0*) Hacker.

Antique Works of Art from Benin, West Africa. Augustus H. Pitt-Rivers. LC 74-138344. (Black Heritage Library Collection). 1977. 23.95 (*0-8369-8736-5*) Ayer.

Antiques: A Buyers' Guide to London. rev. ed. Irene E. Paige. (Illus.). 160p. 1987. pap. 6.95 (*0-938699-01-6*) Paige Pubns.

Antiques: A Buyer's Guide to London. 3rd ed. Ed. by Irene Paige. (Illus.). 160p. 1989. pap. 7.95 (*0-938699-03-2*) Paige Pubns.

Antiques: Guide to Wisconsin Antique Stores. Chris Boyce. Ed. by Barbara McCaig. 100p. (Orig.). pap. 4.95 (*0-935201-20-3*) Affordable Adven.

Antiques & Collectible Thimbles & Accessories. Averil Mathis. (Illus.). 184p. 1989. 19.95 (*0-89145-322-9*) Collector Bks.

Antiques & Their Values. Comp. by Anthony Curtis. Incl. China. pap. 9.95 (*0-698-11121-4*); Furniture. 1982. pap. 9.95 (*0-698-11159-1*); Glass. 1982. pap. 9.95 (*0-698-11158-3*); Silver. 1982. pap. 9.95 (*0-698-11160-5*); 1982. write for info. (*0-318-56554-4*, Coward) Putnam Pub Group.

Antiques & Their Values. Anthony C. Lyle. Incl. Americana. 1983. 5.95 (*0-698-11239-3*); Clocks & Watches. 1983. 5.95 (*0-698-11238-5*); Kitchenware. 1983. 5.95 (*0-698-11237-7*); Militaria. 1983. 5.95 (*0-698-11236-9*); 1983. write for info. (*0-318-56979-5*, Coward) Putnam Pub Group.

***Antiques & Treasures Lost & Found: With Some Small Observations.** Bill Guyton. Ed. by Linda Becht. (Illus.). 150p. 1995. text ed. 20.00 (*0-9642460-0-7*) Guytons Barn.

Antiques at Home. Barbara M. Ohrbach. 1989. 27.50 (*0-517-56986-8*, C P Pubs) Crown Pub Group.

Antiques Directory: Furniture. Judith Miller. 1988. 29.99 (*0-517-66190-X*) Random Hse Value.

Antiques for the Table: A Complete Guide to Dining Room Accessories for Collecting & Entertaining. Sheila Chefetz. LC 92-50728. (Illus.). 240p. 1993. 27.50 (*0-670-84057-2*, Viking Studio) Studio Bks.

Antiques in Pennsylvania Dutchland. (Pennsylvania Dutch Bks.). (Illus.). 1967. 3.00 (*0-911410-07-4*) Applied Arts.

Antiques Road Show: Tiaras, Tallboys & Teddy Bears: A Selection from Radio Times Antiques Roadshow Column. Ed. by Christopher Lewis. (Illus.). 93p. 1992. pap. 9.95 (*0-563-36179-4*, BBC-Parkwest) Parkwest Pubns.

Antiques, the Amateur's Questions. Hampden Gordon. (Illus.). 1951. 8.95 (*0-7195-0511-9*) Transatl Arts.

Antiques, the Best of the Best. Marjorie Glass. (Illus.). 176p. 1983. 19.95 (*0-913765-01-5*); pap. 14.95 (*0-913765-03-1*) Krantz Co.

Antiqui und Moderni: Traditionsbewusstsein und Fortschrittsbewusstsein Im spaeten Mittelalter. LC 73-82432. (Miscellanea Mediaevalia Ser.: Vol. 9). 545p. (C). 1974. 184.60 (*3-11-004538-9*) De Gruyter.

***Antiquing in Arizona: Where to Buy & Sell Your Treasures.** Kathy Finnegan. (Illus.). 134p. (Orig.). 1994. pap. 4.95 (*0-9642299-0-0*) KLF Pubng.

***Antiquing New York: The Guide to the Antique Dealers of New York.** John L. Michel & Barbara N. Michel. 1995. pap. write for info. (*0-231-10013-2*) Col U Pr.

***Antiquitates Curiosae: The Etymology of Many Remarkable Old Sayings, Proverbs & Singular Customs.** Joseph Taylor. Ed. & Pref. by Prudence Priest. 156p. (C). 1995. pap. write for info. (*0-9623780-8-9*) Ars Obscura.

Antiquitates Vulgaries: Or, the Antiquities of the Common People. Henry Bourne. 1977. 24.95 (*0-405-10081-7*, 14706) Ayer.

Antiquites Celtiques et Antediluviennes, 3 vols., Set. Jacques Boucher De Crevecoeur De Perthes. LC 77-86420. reprint ed. 135.00 (*0-404-16620-2*) AMS Pr.

Antiquitez de Rome Plus un Songe ou Vision sur le Mesme Subiect see Regrets et autres oeuvres poetiques

Antiquitie Triumphing over Noveltie. John Favour. LC 76-171757. (English Experience Ser.: No. 325). 602p. 1971. reprint ed. 95.00 (*90-221-0325-0*) Walter J Johnson.

***Antiquities from Europe & the Near East - Collection of the Lord McAlpine.** Ed. by Arthur MacGregor. (Illus.). 142p. 1995. pap. 29.95 (*0-907849-70-9*, 709, Pub. by Ashmolean Mus UK) A Schwartz & Co.

Antiquities from the City of Benin & from Other Parts of West Africa in the British Museum. Charles H. Read & Ormonde M. Dalton. LC 71-143360. (Illus.). 1973. reprint ed. 90.00 (*0-87817-079-0*) Hacker.

Antiquities of Asia: A Translation, with Commentary, of the Library of History, Book II, by Diodorus Siculus. Edwin W. Murphy. 117p. 1989. 39.95 (*0-88738-272-X*) Transaction Pubs.

Antiquities of Athens, 3 Vols, 1. James Stuart & Nicholas Revett. LC 68-21230. (Illus.). 1972. reprint ed. 35.95 (*0-405-09013-7*) Ayer.

Antiquities of Athens, 3 Vols, 2. James Stuart & Nicholas Revett. LC 68-21230. (Illus.). 1972. reprint ed. 35.95 (*0-405-09014-5*) Ayer.

Antiquities of Athens, 3 Vols, 3. James Stuart & Nicholas Revett. LC 68-21230. (Illus.). 1972. reprint ed. 35.95 (*0-405-09015-3*) Ayer.

Antiquities of Athens, 3 Vols, Set. James Stuart & Nicholas Revett. LC 68-21230. (Illus.). 1972. reprint ed. 138.95 (*0-405-09012-9*) Ayer.

Antiquities of Bail: Origin & Historical Development in Criminal Cases to the Year 1275. Elsa De Haas. LC 72-163693. reprint ed. 20.00 (*0-404-02067-4*) AMS Pr.

***Antiquities of Central & Southeastern Missouri.** Gerard Fowke. (Bureau of American Ethnology Bulletins Ser.). 116p. 1995. lib. bdg. 79.00 (*0-7812-4037-9*) Rprt Serv.

Antiquities of Constantinople. rev. ed. Peter Gilles. Tr. by John Ball. LC 86-82697. (Historical Travel Ser.). (Illus.). 300p. 1988. pap. 14.50 (*0-934977-01-1*) Italica Pr.

Antiquities of Constantinople. 2nd rev. ed. Peter Gilles. Tr. by John Ball. LC 86-82697. (Historical Travel Ser.). (Illus.). 300p. 1988. 30.00 (*0-934977-09-7*) Italica Pr.

Antiquities of Egypt: A Translation, with Notes, of Book I of the Library of History of Diodorus Siculus. Edwin Murphy. 178p. 1989. 39.95 (*0-88738-303-3*) Transaction Pubs.

Antiquities of Freemasonry Comprising Illustrations of the Five Grand Periods of Masonry from the Creation of the World to the Dedication of King Solomon's Temple. George Oliver. 250p. 1993. reprint ed. pap. 16.95 (*1-56459-398-3*) Kessinger Pub.

Antiquities of Himachal. Michel Postel. (C). 1992. 100.00 (*0-8364-2869-2*, Pub. by Franco-Indian II) S Asia.

Antiquities of India: An Account of the History & Culture of Ancient Hindustan. Lionel D. Barnett. (C). 1994. 36.00 (*81-206-0530-6*, Pub. by Asian Educ Servs II) S Asia.

***Antiquities of Indian Tibet, 2 vols.** Incl. Personal Narrative. A. H. France. (C). 1992. (*0-318-69692-4*, Pub. by Asian Educ Servs II); Chronicles of Ladakh & Minor Chronicles, 2 vols. A. H. Francke. (C). 1992. (*0-318-69693-2*, Pub. by Asian Educ Servs II); 84.00x (*81-206-0771-6*, Pub. by Asian Educ Servs II) S Asia.

Antiquities of Jordan. rev. ed. G. Lankester Harding. LC 67-15938. 247p. reprint ed. pap. 70.40 (*0-8357-5637-8*, 2051112) Bks Demand.

Antiquities of Long Island. Gabriel Furman. 17.50 (*0-911660-15-1*) Yankee Peddler.

Antiquities of Mexico, 9 Vols, Set. Edward K. Kingsborough. LC 74-171542. reprint ed. 950.00 (*0-404-03680-5*) AMS Pr.

Antiquities of Orissa, 2 vols., Set. Rajendralal L. Mitra. (Illus.). 600p. 1990. reprint ed. 27.50 (*1-55528-203-2*, Messers Today & Tomorrow) Scholarly Pubns.

Antiquities of Orissa, Vol. 2. Rajendra L. Mitra. 269p. 1984. 27.50 (*1-55528-086-2*, Pub. by Today & Tomorrows P & P II) Scholarly Pubns.

Antiquities of Tennessee & the Adjacent States & the State of the Aboriginal Society in the Scale of Civilization Represented by Them. Gates P. Thruston. Bd. with Ancient Society in Tennessee: The Mound Builders Were Indians, from the "Magazine of American History," May, 1888. LC 72-5005. LC 72-5005. (Illus.). reprint ed. 82.50 (*0-404-57311-8*) AMS Pr.

Antiquities of the Country of Kerry. John O'Donovan. 1983. pap. 39.95 (*0-946645-01-9*) Dufour.

***Antiquities of the Jemez Plateau, New Mexico.** Edgar Hewett. (Bureau of American Ethnology Bulletins Ser.). 99p. 1995. lib. bdg. 79.00 (*0-7812-4032-8*) Rprt Serv.

Antiquities of the Mesa Verde National Park. Jesse W. Fewkes. 1988. reprint ed. lib. bdg. 69.00 (*0-685-23001-5*) Rprt Serv.

***Antiquities of the Mesa Verde National Park, Cliff Palace: Bureau of American Ethnology Bulletins.** Jesse W. Fewkes. (Bureau of American Ethnology Bulletins Ser.). 82p. 1995. lib. bdg. 79.00 (*0-7812-4051-4*) Rprt Serv.

***Antiquities of the Mesa Verde National Park; Spruce-Tree House.** Jesse W. Fewkes. (Bureau of American Ethnology Bulletins Ser.). 99p. 1995. lib. bdg. 79.00 (*0-7812-4041-7*) Rprt Serv.

Antiquities of the New England Indians. Charles C. Willoughby. LC 72-5012. (Harvard University. Peabody Museum of Archaeology & Ethnology. Antiquities of the New World Ser.: No. 17). (Illus.). reprint ed. 43.50 (*0-404-57317-7*) AMS Pr.

Antiquities of the New World: Early Explorations in Archaeology, 18 titles in 19 vols. Harvard University, Peabody Museum of Archaeology & Ethnology Staff. reprint ed. write for info. (*0-404-57300-2*) AMS Pr.

Antiquities of the Southern Indians Particularly of the Georgia Tribes. Charles C. Jones, Jr. LC 72-5001. (Harvard University. Peabody Museum of Archaeology & Ethnology. Antiquities of the New World Ser.: No. 6). (Illus.). reprint ed. 57.50 (*0-404-57306-1*) AMS Pr.

Antiquities of the State of New York. Ephraim G. Squier. LC 76-43858. reprint ed. 24.50 (*0-404-15712-2*) AMS Pr.

***Antiquities of the Upper Gila & Salt River Valleys in Arizona & New Mexico.** Walter Hough. (Bureau of American Ethnology Bulletins Ser.). 96p. 1995. lib. bdg. 79.00 (*0-7812-4035-2*) Rprt Serv.

Antiquities of Wisconsin As Surveyed & Described. Increase A. Lapham. LC 72-5000. (Antiquities of the New World Ser.: Vol. 4). (Illus.). reprint ed. 42.50 (*0-404-57304-5*) AMS Pr.

***Antiquity & Anachronism in Japanese History.** Jeffrey P. Mass. 232p. 1995. pap. 14.95 (*0-8047-2592-6*) Stanford U Pr.

Antiquity & Anachronism in Japanese History. Jeffrey P. Mass. 232p. (C). 1995. 37.50x (*0-8047-1974-8*) Stanford U Pr.

Antiquity & Capitalism: Max Weber & the Sociological Foundations of Roman Civilization. John R. Love. 352p. (C). 1991. text ed. 49.95 (*0-415-04750-1*, A5188) Routledge.

Antiquity & the Middle Ages: From Ancient Greece to the Middle Ages. James McKinnon. 400p. (C). 1990. pap. text ed. write for info. (*0-13-036161-5*) P-H.

Antiquity Depicted: Aspects of Archaeological Illustration. Stuart Piggott. (Ancient Peoples & Places Ser.). (Illus.). 1979. 9.95 (*0-500-55010-7*) Thames Hudson.

Antiquity Forgot. Howard B. White. (Archives Internationales d'Histoire des Idees (International Archives of the History of Ideas) Ser.: Vol. 90). 1978. lib. bdg. 65.50 (*90-247-1971-2*) Kluwer Ac.

Antiquity of Disease. Roy L. Moodie. LC 75-23743. reprint ed. 29.50 (*0-404-13298-7*) AMS Pr.

Antiquity of Iraq. Svend A. Pallis. LC 78-72755. (Ancient Mesopotamian Texts & Studies). reprint ed. 37.50 (*0-404-18199-6*) AMS Pr.

Antiquity of Man, 2 vols., Set. Arthur Keith. 1976. 500.00 (*0-87968-159-4*) Gordon Pr.

Antiquity of Man in East Anglia. James R. Moir. LC 76-44762. reprint ed. 17.00 (*0-404-15953-2*) AMS Pr.

Antiquity of the Internal Combustion Engine: 1509-1688. 179p. 1993. 24.00 (*1-56091-373-8*, SP-977) Soc Auto Engineers.

Antiquity Street. Sonia Rami. 224p. 1992. 20.00 (*0-374-10534-0*) FS&G.

Antiquity Unveiled: Ancient Voices from the Spirit Realms. Jonathan M. Roberts. reprint ed. spiral bd. 27.50 (*0-7873-0729-7*) Mokelumne.

Antiquity Unveiled: The Heathen Origins of Christianity. J. M. Roberts. 1992. lib. bdg. 89.00 (*0-8490-8747-3*) Gordon Pr.

Antiqvarivm Forense. Old Vicarage Publications Staff. (C). 1982. pap. text ed. 34.00 (*0-685-22058-3*, Pub. by Old Vicarage UK) St Mut.

Antiracist Education: Theory, Policy & Practice. Andrew Johnson & Stuart Ainsworth. (C). 1989. 95.00 (*1-85098-375-5*, Pub. by Jordanhill College UK) St Mut.

Antiracist Strategies. Stephan Feuchtwang. 176p. 1990. text ed. 50.00 (*0-566-07065-0*, Pub. by Avebury Pub UK) Ashgate Pub Co.

Antiracist Teacher Education, No. 123. (C). 1989. 45.00 (*1-85098-185-X*, Pub. by Jordanhill College UK) St Mut.

Antirreflexiones. Juan Alborna-Salado. LC 92-73337. (Coleccion Cuba y Sus Jueces Ser.). 102p. (Orig.). (SPA.). 1992. pap. 12.00 (*0-89729-652-4*) Ediciones.

Antisemitism. Hannah Arendt. LC 66-22273. Orig. Title: Origins of Totalitarianism, Pt. 1. 136p. 1968. reprint ed. pap. 4.95 (*0-15-607810-4*, HB131, Harvest Bks) HarBrace.

Antisemitism: An Annotated Bibliography, Vol. 1. Vidal Sassoon International Center for the Study of Antisemitism. Ed. by Susan S. Cohen. LC 87-11842. (Reference Library of Social Science: No. 366). 392p. 1987. 56.00 (*0-8240-8532-9*) Garland.

Antisemitism: An Annotated Bibliography, Vol. II: 1986-87. Sasson, Vidal, International Center for the Study of Antisemitism Staff. Ed. by Susan Cohen. LC 87-11842. 592p. 1991. 70.00 (*0-8240-5846-1*, 462) Garland.

Antisemitism: Historically & Critically Examined. Hugo Valentin. Tr. by A. G. Chater. LC 79-164630. (Select Bibliographies Reprint Ser.). 1977. reprint ed. 24.95 (*0-8369-5914-0*) Ayer.

Antisemitism: The Longest Hatred. Robert S. Wistrich. LC 91-53083. (Illus.). 368p. 1992. 25.00 (*0-679-40946-7*) Pantheon.

Antisemitism: The Longest Hatred. Robert S. Wistrich. LC 93-38440. 1994. pap. 15.00 (*0-8052-1014-8*) Schocken.

Antisemitism During the French Second Empire. Natalie Isser. LC 90-21535. (American University Studies: History: Ser. IX, Vol. 100). 170p. (C). 1991. text ed. 33.95 (*0-8204-1454-9*) P Lang Pubs.

***Antisemitism in America.** Leonard Dinnerstein. 400p. 1995. pap. 13.95 (*0-19-510112-X*) OUP.

An Asterisk (*) at the beginning of an entry indicates that the title is appearing in BIP for the first time.

An Asterisk (*) at the beginning of an entry indicates that the title is appearing in BIP for the first time.

Antitrust Laws: A Basis for Economic Freedom. United States Congress, House Committee on the Judiciary. LC 78-11628. x, 109p. 1979. reprint ed. text ed. 49.75 (*0-313-20693-7*, USAN, Greenwood Pr) Greenwood.

Antitrust Laws: A Primer. John H. Shenefield & Irwin M. Stelzer. LC 93-17994. 129p. (Orig.). 1993. 19.95 (*0-8447-3808-5*, AEI Pr) Am Enterprise.

Antitrust Laws & Employee Relations: An Analysis of Their Impact on Management & Union Policies. Edward B. Miller. LC 84-48294. (Labor Relations & Public Policy Ser.: No. 26). 144p. 1984. pap. 20.00 (*0-89546-046-7*) U PA Wharton Ctr Human Resc.

Antitrust Laws & Trade Regulation, 16 vols. Julian O. Von Kalinowski et al. Ed. by Bender's Editorial Staff. 1969. Updates available. ring bd. write for info. (*0-8205-1762-3*) Bender.

Antitrust Laws & Trade Regulation: Desk Edition, 2 vols. Julian O. Von Kalinowski. 1981. ring bd. write for info. (*0-8205-1763-1*) Bender.

Antitrust Paradox: A Policy at War with Itself. Robert H. Bork. LC 92-39587. 1993. text ed. 35.00 (*0-02-904455-3*); pap. 18.95 (*0-02-904456-1*) Free Pr.

Antitrust Penalties: A Study in Law & Economics. Kenneth G. Elzinga & William Breit. LC 75-43316. 172p. reprint ed. pap. 49.10 (*0-8357-8028-7*, 2033717) Bks Demand.

Antitrust Perspectives & Issues. Roger Sherman. (Perspectives on Economics Ser.). (Illus.). 1978. pap. text ed. write for info. (*0-201-08363-9*) Addison-Wesley.

Antitrust Policy: An Economic & Legal Analysis. Carl Kaysen & Donald F. Turner. LC 59-12973. (Harvard University Series on Competition in American Industry: No. 7). 369p. reprint ed. pap. 105.20 (*0-7837-1518-8*, 2041795) Bks Demand.

Antitrust Policy: The Case for Repeal. D. T. Armentano. 78p. 1986. pap. 3.00 (*0-932790-58-5*) Cato Inst.

Antitrust Policy & Interest-Group Politics. William F. Shughart. LC 89-24336. (Illus.). 232p. 1990. text ed. 55.00 (*0-89930-517-2*, SAY/, Quorum Bks) Greenwood.

Antitrust Policy in Transition: The Covergence of Law & Economics. 483p. 1984. pap. 35.00 (*0-89707-147-6*, 503-0056) Amer Bar Assn.

Antitrust Problems In. Louis B. Schwartz et al. (University Casebook Ser.). 81p. 1983. pap. text ed. 6.00 (*0-88277-133-7*) Foundation Pr.

Antitrust Questions & Answers. Edwin S. Rockefeller. LC 73-93042. 703p. reprint ed. pap. 180.00 (*0-8357-5643-2*, 2024302) Bks Demand.

Antitrust Revolution. 2nd ed. John E. Kwoka, Jr. & White. (C). 1993. text ed. 23.50 (*0-673-46880-1*) HarpCollege.

Antitrust Teacher's Manual to Accompany Cases & Materials. Eleanor M. Fox. Ed. by Lawrence A. Sullivan. (American Casebook Ser.). 95p. 1993. pap. text ed. write for info. (*0-314-02165-5*) West Pub.

Antitrust, the Market, & the State: The Contributions of Walter Adams. Ed. by James W. Brock & Kenneth G. Elzinga. LC 90-32017. 320p. (C). 1991. 57.95 (*0-87332-854-X*); pap. text ed. 25.95 (*0-87332-855-8*) M E Sharpe.

Antitumor Compounds of Natural Origin, 2 vols., Vol. 1. Ed. by Adorjan Aszalos. 256p. 1981. 155.00 (*0-8493-5520-6*, RC271, CRC Reprint) Franklin.

Antitumor Compounds of Natural Origin, 2 vols., Vol. 2. Ed. by Adorjan Aszalos. 224p. 1981. 115.00 (*0-8493-5521-4*, RC271, CRC Reprint) Franklin.

Antitumor Drug-Radiation Interactions. Ed. by Bridget T. Hill & Angela S. Bellamy. 304p. 1989. 179.00 (*0-8493-4620-7*, RC271) CRC Pr.

Antitumor Natural Products: Basic & Clinical Research. Ed. by Tomio Takeuchi et al. (Gann Monograph on Cancer Research Ser.: No. 36). 230p. 1990. 125.00 (*0-85066-854-9*) Taylor & Francis.

Antitumor Steroids. Ed. by Robert Blickenstaff. (Illus.). 352p. 1992. text ed. 45.00 (*0-12-105952-9*) Acad Pr.

Antiviral Agents: The Development & Assessment of Antiviral Chemotherapy, 2 vols., Vol. I: Successful Selective Inhibitors of Viruses. Ed. by H. J. Field. 192p. 1988. Vol. I, Successful Selective Inhibitors of Viruses, 192 pgs. 174.00 (*0-8493-6684-4*, RM411) CRC Pr.

Antiviral Agents: The Development & Assessment of Antiviral Chemotherapy, 2 vols., Vol. II: Chemotherapy of Herpes Simplex Encephalit. Ed. by H. J. Field. 160p. 1988. Vol. II, Chemotherapy of Herpes Simplex Encephalitis, 160 pgs. 174.00 (*0-8493-6685-2*, RM411) CRC Pr.

Antiviral Agents & Viral Diseases of Man. 3rd ed. George J. Galasso et al. 784p. 1990. 174.00 (*0-88167-588-1*, 1948) Raven.

***Antiviral Chemotherapy.** Ed. by Erik DeClercq. LC 94-30007. 1994. text ed. 175.00 (*0-471-93040-7*) Wiley.

Antiviral Chemotherapy: New Directions for Clinical Applications & Research, Vol. 3. Ed. by John Mills & Lawrence Corey. LC 93-19985. (Illus.). 464p. (C). 1993. Alk. paper. text ed. 155.00 (*0-13-050717-2*) P-H.

Antiviral Chemotherapy, Interferons & Vaccines. D. O. White. (Monographs in Virology: Vol. 16). (Illus.). viii, 112p. 1984. 51.50 (*3-8055-3825-1*) S Karger.

Antiviral Compounds from Plants. J. B. Hudson. 200p. 1989. 144.00 (*0-8493-6541-4*, RS431) CRC Pr.

Antiviral Drug Development: A Multidisciplinary Approach. Ed. by Erik De Clercq & R. T. Walker. (NATO ASI Series A, Life Sciences: Vol. 143). (Illus.). 314p. 1988. 85.00 (*0-306-42796-6*, Plenum Pr) Plenum.

Antiviral Drugs. I. Becker. Ed. by J. L. Melnick. (Monographs in Virology: Vol. 11). (Illus.). 1976. 61.75 (*3-8055-2248-7*) S Karger.

Antiviral Drugs & Interferon: The Molecular Basis of Their Activity. Yechiel Becker. (Developments in Molecular Virology Ser.). 464p. 1984. lib. bdg. 106.00 (*0-89838-643-8*) Kluwer Ac.

Antiviral Proteins in Higher Plants. Chessin. 1994. write for info. (*0-8493-6989-4*) CRC Pr.

***Antiviral Therapy.** E. Littler et al. (Medical Perspectives Ser.). 160p. 1995. pap. 52.50 (*1-85996-070-7*, Pub. by Bios Scientific UK) Coronet Bks.

Antivoyage. Muriel Cerf. 224p. (FRE.). 1978. pap. 11.95 (*0-7859-1888-4*, 2070371069) Fr & Eur.

Antizionism & Antisemitism in the Contemporary World. R. S. Wistrich. 1990. 45.00 (*0-8147-9237-5*) NYU Pr.

Anti026327200 Bd. II: Die Klassische Kunst Griechenlands. Ludwig Curtius. 466p. 1959. write for info. (*0-318-70734-9*, Pub. by Georg Olms GW) Lubrecht & Cramer.

Antlantische Brucke. Lias Kahn. LC 92-32472. 84p. (GER.). 1992. pap. 12.95 (*0-7734-9569-X*) E Mellen.

Antler, Bear, Canoe: A Northwoods Alphabet Year. Betsy Bowen. (Illus.). 32p. (J). (ps-3). 1991. 15.95 (*0-316-10376-4*, Joy St Bks) Little.

Antler Development in Cervidae. Ed. by Robert D. Brown. LC 82-74285. (Illus.). 400p. 1983. 15.00 (*0-912229-04-7*); pap. 10.00 (*0-912229-05-5*) CK Wildlife Res.

Antlers: Nature's Magnificent Crown. Erwin A. Bauer & Peggy Bauer. LC 94-9033. 1994. 35.00 (*0-89658-253-1*) Voyageur Pr.

***Antoeus: The Final Issue.** Dan Halpern. 410p. (Orig.). 1994. pap. 17.00 (*0-88001-392-3*) Ecco Pr.

Antoine & the Theatre Libre. Samuel M. Waxman. LC 63-23192. 1972. reprint ed. 24.95 (*0-405-09056-0*) Ayer.

Antoine Arnauld: On True & False Ideas. Antoine Arnauld. (Classics of Philosophy & Science Ser.). 1990. text ed. 59.95 (*0-7190-3203-2*, Pub. by Manchester Univ Pr UK) St Martin.

Antoine Bloye: A Novel. Paul Nizan. LC 72-92034. 255p. reprint ed. pap. 72.70 (*0-7837-3897-8*, 2043745) Bks Demand.

***Antoine de Fevin: Lamentations Magnificals Motets & Chansons.** Ed. by Edward Clinkscale. (Collected Works: Vol. 3). 182p. 1994. lib. bdg. 88.00 (*0-931902-89-4*) Inst Mediaeval Mus.

Antoine de Montchrestien: Haman & New Tragedy of the Perfidy of Haman. Antoine De Montchrestien. Tr. by Perry Gethner. 124p. 1985. 8.00 (*0-919473-70-9*, DH57, Pub. by Dovehouse CN) MRTS.

Antoine de Saint-Exupery. Joy M. Robinson. (World Authors Ser.: No. 705). 200p. 1984. text ed. 22.95 (*0-8057-6552-2*, Twayne) Macmillan.

Antoine Lavoisier. Douglas McKie. (Series in Science). (Illus.). 448p. 1990. reprint ed. pap. 14.95 (*0-306-80408-5*) Da Capo.

Antoine Lavoisier: Science Administration & Revolution. Arthur Donovan. (Science Biographies Ser.). (Illus.). 368p. 1994. 29.95 (*0-631-17887-2*) Blackwell Pubs.

Antoine Plante: Mountain Man, Rancher, Miner, Guide, Hosteler & Ferryman. Jerome Peltier. 1983. 7.50 (*0-87770-286-1*); pap. 4.95 (*0-685-07495-1*) Ye Galleon.

Antoine Predock, Architect. Brad Collins & Juliette Robbins. (Illus.). 224p. 1994. 60.00 (*0-8478-1697-4*); pap. 35.00 (*0-8478-1698-2*) Rizzoli Intl.

Antoine Watteau: Paintings & Drawings from Soviet Museums. Yu Zolotov. 116p. (C). 1988. 150.00 (*0-569-51726-5*, Pub. by Collets) St Mut.

Antoine's Restaurant Cookbook. Roy F. Guste, Jr. (Illus.). 1989. 29.95 (*0-393-02666-3*) Norton.

Antoinette Brown Blackwell: A Biography. Elizabeth Cazden. LC 82-4986. (Illus.). 328p. (C). 1983. 29.95 (*0-935312-00-5*); pap. 12.95 (*0-935312-04-8*) Feminist Pr.

Antoinette Sibley. Illus. by Mary Clarke & Frederick Ashton. 128p. (J). (gr. 8-12). 1981. 29.95 (*0-903102-64-1*, Pub. by Dance Bks UK) Princeton Bk Co.

Antologia. Homero Aridjis. 107p. 1976. 9.95 (*0-8288-7484-0*) Fr & Eur.

Antologia. Ruben Dario. Ed. by Carmen Ruiz Barrionuevo. (Nueva Austral Ser.: Vol. 269). (SPA.). 1991. pap. text ed. 24.95x (*84-239-7269-0*) Elliots Bks.

Antologia. M. Hernandez. 199p. (SPA.). 1977. 8.50 (*0-8288-7136-1*, S8059) Fr & Eur.

***Antologia.** 11th ed. Manuel Machado. 152p. 1979. pap. 8.95 (*0-7859-5189-X*) Fr & Eur.

Antologia da Poesia Negra de Expressao Portuguese, Precedida de Cultura Negro-Africana e Assimilacao. Mario De Andrade. (B. E. Ser.: No. 30). (POR.). 1958. 18.00 (*0-8115-2981-9*) Periodicals Srv.

Antologia de Autores Espanoles, Vol. 1: Antiguos. A. Sanchez-Romeralo & F. Ibarra. (C). 1972. text ed. write for info. (*0-13-033838-9*) P-H.

Antologia de Cuentos Hispanoamericanos. Alberto M. Vazquez. (C). (gr. 12). 1976. pap. text ed. 7.50 (*0-88345-264-2*, 18421) Prentice ESL.

Antologia de Filosofia Griega. 6th rev. ed. Comp. by Pedro A. Badillo. (Illus.). 253p. (C). 1987. pap. 9.50 (*0-8477-2800-5*) U of PR Pr.

Antologia de Homilias Biblicas, Vol. I. Ed. by Hiram Almirudus. 159p. (SPA.). 1977. 7.95 (*0-87148-022-0*) Pathway Pr.

Antologia de Homilias Biblicas, Vol. II. Ed. by Hiram Almirudus. 159p. (SPA.). 1979. 6.95 (*0-87148-023-9*) Pathway Pr.

Antologia de Homilias Biblicas, Vol. III. Ed. by Hiram Almirudus. 148p. (SPA.). 1980. 7.95 (*0-87148-024-7*) Pathway Pr.

Antologia de Homilias Biblicas, Vol. IV. Ed. by Hiram Almirudus. 162p. (SPA.). 1981. 7.95 (*0-87148-025-5*) Pathway Pr.

Antologia de Homilias Biblicas, Vol. V. Ed. by Hiram Almirudus. 158p. (SPA.). 1982. 7.95 (*0-87148-026-3*) Pathway Pr.

Antologia de Homilias Biblicas, Vol. VI. Ed. by Hiram Almirudus. 158p. (SPA.). 1982. 7.95 (*0-87148-027-1*) Pathway Pr.

Antologia de Instantaneas II: Un Periodismo Local, Cotidiano y Vivo. Octavio R. Costa & Aurelio De La Vega. (Coleccion Cuba y Sus Jueces Ser.). 587p. (Orig.). (SPA.). 1990. pap. 25.00 (*0-89729-598-6*) Ediciones.

Antologia de la Literatura Espanola: Edad Media. Barbara Mujica. 260p. 1991. Net. text ed. write for info. (*0-471-53693-8*) Wiley.

Antologia de la Literatura Espanola: Renacimiento y Siglo de Oro, Vol. 2. Barbara Mujica. 640p. 1991. Net. text ed. write for info. (*0-471-53694-6*) Wiley.

***Antologia de la Literatura Espanola, from Seventeen Hundred Siglos Eighteen & Nineteen 2 Vol. Set.** Mujica. Date not set. pap. text ed. write for info. (*0-471-54535-X*) Wiley.

Antologia de la Literature Espanola - to 1681, 2 vols., 2. Barbara Mujica. 864p. 1991. text ed. 56.96 (*0-471-89027-8*) Wiley.

Antologia de la Literature Espanola - to 1681, 2 vols., Vol 1. Barbara Mujica. 864p. 1991. text ed. write for info. (*0-471-89028-6*) Wiley.

Antologia de la Poesia Cristiana: Anthology of Christian Poetry. Clie Staff. (SPA.). 20.95 (*84-7645-047-8*, 223107, Pub. by Edit Clie SP) TSELF.

Antologia de la Poesia del Romanticismo Hispanoamericano: (1820-1890) Catharina V. De Vallejo. LC 93-70446. (Coleccion Textos Ser.). (Illus.). 406p. (Orig.). (SPA.). 1993. pap. 25.00 (*0-89729-675-3*) Ediciones.

Antologia de la Poesia Latinoamericana, 2 vols., Set. Ed. by Stefan Baciu. LC 73-37514. 577p. 1974. pap. 44.95 (*0-87395-077-1*) State U NY Pr.

Antologia de la Poesia Mexicana Moderna. Ed. by Andrew P. Debicki. (Serie B: Textos, XX). 305p. (SPA.). (C). 1977. 35.00 (*0-7293-0028-5*, Pub. by Tamesis Bks Ltd UK) Boydell & Brewer.

Antologia de la Poesia Negra Americana. Ed. by Ildefonso Pereda Valdes. (B. E. Ser.: No. 9). (POR.). 1953. 29.00 (*0-8115-2960-6*) Periodicals Srv.

Antologia de Lecturas: Curso de Espanol, Primer Semestre, 2 tomes, Tome 1. 3rd rev. ed. (C). 1987. 11.95 (*0-8477-3512-5*) U of PR Pr.

Antologia de Lecturas: Curso de Espanol, Primer Semestre, 2 tomes, Tome 2. 3rd rev. ed. (C). 1987. 10.25 (*0-8477-3199-5*) U of PR Pr.

Antologia de Literatura Hispanica Contemporanea: Espanol 3101-3102, 2 vols. Matilde Colon et al. LC 84-20849. 362p. (SPA.). (C). 1991. Set. write for info. (*0-8477-3515-X*) U of PR Pr.

Antologia de Literatura Hispanica Contemporanea: Espanol 3101-3102, 2 vols., 2. Matilde Colon et al. LC 84-20849. 362p. (SPA.). (C). 1991. pap. 9.95 (*0-8477-3514-1*) U of PR Pr.

Antologia de Literatura Hispanica Contemporanea: Espanol 3101-3102, 2 vols., Vol. 1. Matilde Colon et al. LC 84-20849. 240p. (SPA.). (C). 1991. pap. 5.75 (*0-8477-3511-7*) U of PR Pr.

Antologia De los Poetas Del Veinte Siete. Intro. & Sel. by Jose L. Cano. (Nueva Austral Ser.: No. 8). (SPA.). 1991. pap. text ed. 34.95x (*84-239-1808-4*) Elliots Bks.

Antologia de Poesia Espanola, 1984. Ed. by Luis T. Gonzalez-del-Valle. LC 84-50645. 130p. 1984. pap. text ed. 20.00 (*0-89295-036-6*) Society Sp & Sp-Am.

Antologia de Poesia Infantil. Ana R. Nunez. LC 85-81795. (Coleccion Antologias Ser.). 180p. (Orig.). (SPA.). (J). (gr. 3-12). 1985. pap. 9.95 (*0-89729-369-X*) Ediciones.

Antologia de Poesia-Primavera: Anthology of Poetry-Spring. (SPA.). (J). (gr. k-6). 1990. 6.95 (*0-935303-02-2*) Victory Pub.

Antologia de Prosistas Espanoles, No. 110. Ramon Menendez Pidal. 261p. (SPA.). 1978. 10.95 (*0-8288-8556-7*, S2322) Fr & Eur.

Antologia de Textos Literarios. University of PR College of General Studies, Spanish Department Staff. 1994. text ed. 24.95 (*0-8477-0181-6*) U of PR Pr.

Antologia del Cuento Espanol, 1985. Ed. by Ramon Hernandez & Luis T. Gonzalez-del-Valle. LC 85-61850. 295p. 1986. pap. 40.00 (*0-89295-040-4*) Society Sp & Sp-Am.

Antologia del Cuento Guatemalteco. Ruth S. Lamb. 1958. pap. 5.00 (*0-912434-00-7*) Ocelot Pr.

Antologia del Pensamiento Puertorriqueno: 1900-1970, 2 vols., 1. Ed. by Eugenio Fernandez Mendez. (SPA.). 1976. 8.00 (*0-8477-0843-8*) U of PR Pr.

Antologia del Pensamiento Puertorriqueno: 1900-1970, 2 vols., 2. Ed. by Eugenio Fernandez Mendez. (SPA.). 1976. 8.00 (*0-8477-0844-6*) U of PR Pr.

Antologia del Pensamiento Puertorriqueno: 1900-1970, 2 vols., Set. Ed. by Eugenio Fernandez Mendez. (SPA.). 1976. 16.00 (*0-8477-0842-X*) U of PR Pr.

Antologia Essencial. Pablo Neruda. (SPA.). 1971. 14.95 (*0-8288-2542-4*, S20078) Fr & Eur.

Antologia General de La Literatura Espanola. Angel Del Rio & Amelia A. Del Rio. (SPA.). 1982. 29.95 (*0-86515-001-X*) Edit Mensaje.

Antologia Nueva De Nemesio Canales, 4 bks., Set. Nemesio Canales. Ed. by Servando Montana Palaez. Incl. Bk. 21. Glosario. 1.50 (*0-8477-0021-6*); Bk. 22. Meditaciones Acres. 1.50 (*0-8477-0022-4*); Bk. 23. Boberias. 1.50 (*0-8477-0023-2*); Bk. 24. Hacia un Lejano Sol. 1.50 (*0-8477-0024-0*); (UPREX, Puerto Rico Ayer Ser.). (C). 6.00 (*0-8447-0000-2*) U of PR Pr.

***Antologia Para Ninos.** Juan R. Jimenez. 125p. 1986. pap. 12.95 (*0-7859-5195-4*) Fr & Eur.

Antologia Personal. Jose L. Gonzalez. LC 90-43241. 376p. (SPA.). 1990. pap. 10.90 (*0-8477-3623-7*) U of PR Pr.

***Antologia Poetica.** Francisco De Quevedo Y Villegas. 290p. 1989. pap. 16.95 (*0-7859-5193-8*) Fr & Eur.

Antologia Poetica. Luis Hernandez Aquino & Jose E. Gonzales. i, 162p. (C). 1974. pap. 3.00 (*0-8477-3205-3*) U of PR Pr.

Antologia Poetica. Violeta Lopez Suria. 262p. (C). 1970. 3.50 (*0-8477-3207-X*) U of PR Pr.

Antologia Poetica. Pablo Neruda. 509p. (SPA.). 1982. 9.95 (*0-685-60725-9*, S39023) Fr & Eur.

Antologia Poetica. Carlos M. Passalacqua. LC 84-7594. (Illus.). 143p. (SPA.). 1985. pap. 5.00 (*0-8477-3234-7*) U of PR Pr.

Antologia Poetica. Francisco de Quevedo. Ed. by Pablo Jauralde Pou. (Nueva Austral Ser.: Vol. 186). (SPA.). 1991. pap. text ed. 15.95 (*84-239-1986-2*) Elliots Bks.

Antologia Poetica. Unamuno. 152p. (SPA.). 1975. 9.95 (*0-8288-7095-0*, S29738) Fr & Eur.

Antologia Poetica. 4th ed. Rafael Alberti. 264p. (SPA.). 1989. pap. 11.95 (*0-7859-5138-5*, S19845) Fr & Eur.

Antologia Poetica. 5th ed. Miguel De Unamuno. 112p. (SPA.). 1991. pap. 7.95 (*0-7859-5006-0*) Fr & Eur.

***Antologia Poetica.** 5th ed. Juan R. Jimenez. 416p. 1989. pap. 14.95 (*0-7859-5194-6*) Fr & Eur.

Antologia Poetica. 7th ed. Rafael Alberti. 160p. 1991. pap. 8.95 (*0-7859-5147-4*) Fr & Eur.

Antologia Poetica. El Poeta es un Fingidor. Fernando Pessoa. Ed. & Tr. by Angel Crespo. (Nueva Austral Ser.: Vol. 67). (SPA.). 1991. pap. text ed. 24.95x (*84-239-1867-X*) Elliots Bks.

***Antologia Poetica Familiar.** Alma R. Gil. Ed. by Lucia Garcia & Maggie Ghazi. 300p. (Orig.). Date not set. pap. text ed. 14.95 (*0-9641506-2-X*) Edit Interamerica.

***Antologia Poetica 1.** 43th ed. Pablo Neruda. 304p. 1990. pap. 12.95 (*0-7859-5197-0*) Fr & Eur.

***Antologia Poetica 2.** 3rd ed. Pablo Neruda. 256p. 1988. pap. write for info. (*0-7859-5198-9*) Fr & Eur.

Anton Bruckner: A Discography. Lee T. Lovallo. LC 86-46229. (Reference Books in Music: No. 6). xviii, 200p. 1991. 33.00 (*0-914913-05-0*) Fallen Leaf.

Anton Cexov As a Master of Story-Writing: Essays in Modern Soviet Literary Criticism. Ed. by Leo Hulanicke & D. Savignac. (Slavistic Printings & Reprintings Textbook Ser.: No. 6). 1976. pap. text ed. 50.00 (*90-279-3014-7*) Mouton.

Anton Chekhov. Irina Kirk. (World Authors Ser.: No. 568). 168p. 1981. text ed. 22.95 (*0-8057-6410-0*, Twayne) Macmillan.

Anton Chekhov. Lawrence Senelik. Ed. by Bruce King & Adele King. (Modern Dramatists Ser.). 183p. 1990. pap. 11.95 (*0-333-30882-4*) St Martin.

Anton Chekhov: A Study of the Short Fiction. Ronald L. Johnson. (Twayne's Studies in Short Fiction). 180p. 1993. text ed. 22.95 (*0-8057-8349-0*, Twayne) Macmillan.

Anton Chekhov: Four Plays. Anton Chekhov. Tr. by David Magarshack. Incl. Seagull. 1969. (*0-318-53306-5*); Uncle Vanya. 1969. (*0-318-53307-3*); Three Sisters. 1969. (*0-318-53308-1*); Cherry Orchard. 1969. (*0-318-53309-X*); (Mermaid Dramabook Ser.). 254p. (Orig.). 1969. Set pap. 8.95 (*0-8090-0743-6*) Hill & Wang.

Anton Chekhov: Great Short Stories from Around the World I. Illus. by James McConnell. LC 94-75341. (Classic Short Stories Ser.). 80p. 1994. pap. 4.50 (*1-56103-040-6*) Lake Pub Co.

Anton Chekhov: Literary & Theatrical Reminiscences. Anton P. Chekhov. Tr. by Samuel S. Koteliansky. LC 65-16231. 1927. 20.00 (*0-685-06946-X*, Pub. by Blom Pubns UK) Ayer.

Anton Chekhov: Literary & Theatrical Reminiscences. Ed. & Tr. by S. S. Koteliansky. LC 74-30166. (Studies in Russian Literature & Life: No. 100). 1974. lib. bdg. 49.95 (*0-8383-1871-1*) M S G Haskell Hse.

Anton Chekhov: Literary & Theatrical Reminiscences. Samuel S. Koteliansky & Anton P. Chekhov. 1972. 29.95 (*0-405-08353-X*, 832) Ayer.

***Anton Chekhov & His Times.** Tr. by Cynthia Carlile & Sharon McKee. LC 95-5839. 1995. write for info. (*1-55728-391-5*); pap. write for info. (*1-55728-390-7*) U of Ark Pr.

Anton Chekhov Collected Works, 5 vols. Tr. by A. Miller & I. Litvinov. 2266p. 1990. 59.95 (*0-8285-5000-X*) Firebird NY.

Anton Chekhov the Iconoclast. Lee J. Williames. LC 89-50848. 1990. pap. 21.50 (*0-940866-09-9*) U Scranton Pr.

Anton Chekhov's Letters on the Short Story. Anton P. Chekhov. Ed. by Louis S. Friedland. LC 64-14695. 1972. 29.95 (*0-405-08352-1*, Pub. by Blom Pubns UK) Ayer.

Anton Chekhov's Life & Thought: Selected Letters & Commentary. Ed. by Simon Karlinsky. Tr. by Michael H. Heim. LC 73-91678. 1976. reprint ed. pap. 12.00 (*0-520-02684-5*) U CA Pr.

Anton Chekhov's Plays. Anton P. Chekhov. Ed. by Eugene K. Bristow. (Critical Editions Ser.). (C). 1977. pap. text ed. 12.95 (*0-393-09163-5*) Norton.

Anton Chekhov's Short Stories. Anton P. Chekhov. Ed. by Ralph E. Matlaw. Tr. by Constance Garnett et al. (Critical Editions Ser.). (C). 1979. pap. text ed. 9.95 (*0-393-09002-7*) Norton.

Anton Dohrn: A Life for Science. T. Heuss et al. Tr. by L. Dieckmann. (Illus.). 440p. (GER.). 1991. 51.00 (*0-387-53561-6*) Spr-Verlag.

Anton Dvorak. Paul Stefan. LC 79-146147. (Music Reprint Ser.). 336p. 1971. reprint ed. lib. bdg. 42.50 (*0-306-70105-7*) Da Capo.

Anton Mosimann's Fish Cuisine. Anton Mosimann. (Illus.). 256p. 1993. 24.95 (*0-89815-543-6*) Ten Speed Pr.

Anton Pannekoek & the Socialism of Workers' Self Emancipation, 1873-1960. John P. Gerber. (C). 1990. lib. bdg. 89.00 (*0-7923-0274-5*) Kluwer Ac.

An Asterisk (*) at the beginning of an entry indicates that the title is appearing in BIP for the first time.

Anton Raphael Mengs. Nikolai Nikulin. (Masters of World Painting Ser.). 1984. pap. 55.00 (*0-317-57255-5*, Pub. by Collets UK) St Mut.

Anton Raphael Mengs: Anton Raphael Mengs: And His British Patrons. Steffi Roettgen. 1993. 50.00 (*0-302-00623-0*, Pub. by Zwemmer Bks UK) Sothebys Pubns.

Anton Reiser: A Psychological Novel. Karl P. Moritz. Tr. by P. E. Matheson. LC 76-48443. (Library of World Literature Ser.). 1986. reprint ed. 37.00 (*0-88355-582-4*) Hyperion Conn.

Anton Rubinstein. A. MacArthur. 1971. 35.00 (*0-87968-650-2*) Gordon Pr.

Anton Seidl: A Memorial by His Friends. (Music Ser.). (Illus.). 280p. 1982. reprint ed. lib. bdg. 39.50 (*0-306-76144-0*) Da Capo.

Anton Stankowski. (Illus.). 84p. 1989. pap. 35.00 (*3-89322-217-0*, Pub. by Edition Cantz GW) Dist Art Pubs.

Anton the Dove Fancier & Other Stories. Bernard Gotfryd. Ed. by Jane Rosenman. 192p. (Orig.). 1990. pap. 7.95 (*0-671-69137-6*) PB.

Anton Ulrich & Aramena: The Genesis & Development of a Baroque Novel. Blake L. Spahr. LC 66-64904. (University of California Publications in Social Welfare: Vol. 76). 223p. reprint ed. pap. 63.60 (*0-8357-5644-0*, 2013813) Bks Demand.

Anton Van Dalen - "The Memory Cabinet" Carlo McCormick. (Illus.). 32p. (Orig.). 1988. pap. 15.00 (*0-913263-24-9*) Exit Art.

***Anton von Webern.** Malcolm Hayes. (20th Century Composers Ser.). (Illus.). 240p. 1995. pap. 19.95 (*0-7148-3157-3*, Pub. by Phaidon Press UK) Chronicle Bks.

Anton Von Webern: Perspectives. Comp. by Hans Moldenhauer & Demar Irvine. LC 77-9523. (Music Reprint Ser.: 1978). (Illus.). 1978. reprint ed. lib. bdg. 32.50 (*0-306-77518-2*) Da Capo.

Anton Webern. Ed. by Herbert Eimert & Karlheinz Stockhausen. Tr. by Leo Black & Eric Smith. (Reihe Ser.: No. 2). 1958. pap. 14.95 (*3-7024-0151-2*, UE26102) Eur-Am Music.

Anton Webern. Friedrick Wildgans. 1967. 9.95 (*0-8079-0007-9*) October.

Anton Webern: An Introduction to His Works. Walter Kolneder. Tr. by Humphrey Searle. LC 81-20134. (Illus.). 232p. 1982. reprint ed. text ed. 38.50 (*0-313-23342-X*, KOAW, Greenwood Pr) Greenwood.

Anton Wilson's Cinema Workshop. Anton Wilson. LC 83-71274. (Illus.). 300p. (Orig.). (C). 1983. pap. 14.95 (*0-935578-02-1*) ASC Holding.

Antona Garcia. De Molina. Ed. by M. Wilson. (Spanish Texts Ser.). 136p. (SPA.). (C). 1988. text ed. 12.95 (*0-7190-0208-7*, Pub. by Manchester Univ Pr UK) St Martin.

Antonfrancesco Grazzini, Poet, Dramatist, & Novelliere, 1503-1584. Robert J. Rodini. LC 71-106041. (Illus.). 262p. reprint ed. pap. 74.70 (*0-8357-6780-9*, 2035457) Bks Demand.

Antoni Tapies. Ed. by Andreas Franzke. (Illus.). 364p. 1992. 100.00 (*3-7913-1231-6*, Pub. by Prestel) TeNeues.

Antoni Tapies. Robert S. Lubar. LC 93-83249. (Illus.). 64p. (Orig.). 1993. pap. write for info. (*1-878283-28-6*) PaceWildenstein.

***Antoni Tapies.** Roland Penrose. (Grandes Monografias). (Illus.). 280p. (SPA.). 1993. 75.00 (*84-343-0257-8*) Elliots Bks.

Antoni Tapies: Graphic Work 1947-1987. Steven S. High. (Orig.). 1988. 7.50 (*0-939799-03-0*) Portland Schl Baxter.

***Antoni Tapies: Materia, Signo, Espiritu.** Jose Corredor-Matheos. (Grandes Monografias). (Illus.). 128p. (SPA.). 1993. 100.00 (*84-343-0681-6*) Elliots Bks.

Antoni Tapies in Print. Deborah Wye. (Illus.). 128p. 1992. 37.50 (*0-87070-602-0*, 0-8109-6102-4); pap. 19.95 (*0-87070-603-9*, 0-8109-6136-9) Mus of Modern Art.

Antonia. Ed. by Harold Bloom. (Major Literary Characters Ser.). 224p. 1991. lib. bdg. 29.95 (*0-7910-0950-5*) Chelsea Hse.

Antonia Augusta: Portrait of a Great Roman Lady. Nikos Kokkinos. LC 91-48154. (Illus.). 224p. 1993. 39.95 (*0-415-08029-0*, A7929) Routledge.

Antonia Merce - la Argentina. Ensayos De Federico de Onis et al. 50p. 0.80 (*0-318-14238-4*) Hispanic Inst.

Antonia Novello. (J). (ps-3). 1993. 18.95 (*0-7910-1557-2*) Chelsea Hse.

Antonia Novello: U. S. Surgeon General. Joan C. Hawxhurst. LC 92-19564. (Hispanic Heritage Ser.). (Illus.). 32p. (J). (gr. 2-4). 1993. lib. bdg. 13.40 (*1-56294-299-9*) Millbrook Pr.

***Antonia Novello: U. S. Surgeon General.** Joan C. Hawxhurst. (Hispanic Heritage Ser.). (Illus.). 32p. (J). (gr. 2-4). 1993. pap. 4.95 (*1-56294-862-8*) Millbrook Pr.

***Antonia Novello, Doctor.** Mayra Fernandez. (Illus.). (J). (gr. 1-4). 1994. lib. bdg. 9.95 (*0-8136-5268-5*); pap. 4.95 (*0-8136-5274-X*) Modern Curr.

***Antonia Novello, Doctora.** Mayra Fernandez. (Illus.). (SPA.). (J). (gr. 1-4). 1994. lib. bdg. 9.95 (*0-8136-5296-0*); pap. 4.95 (*0-8136-5302-9*) Modern Curr.

Antonia Saw the Oryx First. Maria Thomas. LC 86-31570. 296p. 1987. 17.95 (*0-939149-02-8*) Soho Press.

Antonia Saw the Oryx First. Maria Thomas. LC 86-31570. 298p. 1993. pap. 12.00 (*0-939149-90-7*) Soho Press.

Antoine-Louis Barye: Sculptor of Romantic Realism. Glenn F. Benge. (Illus.). 210p. 1984. 75.00 (*0-271-00362-6*) A Wofsy Fine Arts.

Antonietta. John Hersey. LC 92-50626. 1993. pap. 11.00 (*0-679-74181-X*, Vin) Random.

Antonin Artaud. Martin Esslin. 1996. pap. 11.95 (*0-7145-4204-0*) Riverrun NY.

Antonin Artaud: Blows & Bombs. Stephen Barber. (Illus.). 176p. 1993. 19.95 (*0-571-16556-7*) Faber & Faber.

Antonin Artaud: Blows & Bombs. Stephen Barber. (Illus.). 176p. 1994. pap. 10.95 (*0-571-17252-0*) Faber & Faber.

Antonin Artaud: Man of Vision. Bettina L. Knapp. LC 79-9637. 233p. 1980. pap. 14.95 (*0-8040-0809-4*) Swallow.

Antonin Artaud: Selected Writings. Antonin Artaud. 720p. (Orig.). (C). 1988. pap. 17.00 (*0-520-06443-7*) U CA Pr.

Antonin Artaud & the Modern Theater. Ed. by Gene A. Plunka. LC 93-40087. 1994. write for info. (*0-8386-3550-4*) Fairleigh Dickinson.

Antonin Dvorak. Karel Hoffmeister. 132p. 1990. reprint ed. lib. bdg. 59.00 (*0-7812-0264-7*) Rprt Serv.

Antonin Dvorak: Letters & Reminiscences. Otakar Sourek. Tr. by Roberta F. Samsour. LC 84-1698. (Music Reprint Ser.). 234p. 1984. reprint ed. lib. bdg. 27.50 (*0-306-76201-3*) Da Capo.

Antonin Dvorak, His Achievement. Viktor Fischl. (Music Book Index Ser.). 297p. 1992. reprint ed. lib. bdg. 79.00 (*0-7812-9463-0*) Rprt Serv.

Antonin Dvorak, My Father. Otakar Dvorak. Ed. by Paul J. Polansky. 192p. 1993. 25.00 (*0-9636734-0-8*) Czech Hist.

Antonin Dvorak on Records. Comp. by John H. Yoell. LC 91-24038. (Discographies Ser.: No. 46). 176p. 1991. text ed. 45.00 (*0-313-27367-7*, YAD, Greenwood Pr) Greenwood.

Antonin Laube (1718-1784), One Symphony Symphony B - XIII - Austria. Ed. by Barry S. Brook. LC 84-758877. (Symphony, 1720-1840 Ser.: Vol. 52). 363p. 1984. 25.00 (*0-8240-3851-7*) Garland.

Antonin Nechodoma, Architect, 1877-1928: The Prairie School in the Caribbean. Thomas S. Marvel & H. Allen Brooks. LC 93-32486. (Illus.). 256p. (C). 1994. lib. bdg. 44.95 (*0-8130-1269-4*) U Press Fla.

Antonin Scalia. Bob Italia. Ed. by Paul Deegan. LC 92-13712. (Supreme Court Justices Ser.). 40p. (J). 1992. lib. bdg. 13.99 (*1-56239-093-7*) Abdo & Dghtrs.

Antonine Literature. Ed. by D. A. Russell. 256p. 1990. 55.00 (*0-19-814057-6*) OUP.

Antonine Monarchy. Mason Hammond. (American Academy in Rome. Papers & Monographs: Vol. 19). 537p. reprint ed. pap. 153.10 (*0-8357-5645-9*, 2026731) Bks Demand.

Antonines: The Roman Empire in Transition. Michael Grant. LC 94-597. 1994. 25.00 (*0-415-10754-7*, B4614) Routledge.

Antoninus Pius. Willy Huttl. LC 75-7326. (Roman History Ser.). (GER.). 1975. reprint ed. 62.95 (*0-405-07089-6*) Ayer.

Antonio & Clara. David Giannini. (Orig.). 1992. pap. 6.00 (*0-938566-53-9*) Adastra Pr.

***Antonio & His Enchanted Watering Can.** Frances R. Robinson. 48p. (J). (gr. 3-4). 1994. pap. text ed. 6.95 (*1-886114-01-3*) Arrow Pubns.

Antonio & Mellida. John Marston. Ed. by W. Reavley Gair et al. LC 90-13557. (Revels Plays Ser.). 192p. 1992. text ed. 49.95 (*0-7190-1547-2*, Pub. by Manchester Univ Pr UK) St Martin.

Antonio & Mellida: The First Part. John Marston. Ed. by G. K. Hunter. LC 64-17229. xxii, 88p. 1965. 12.95 (*0-8032-0272-5*) U of Nebr Pr.

***Antonio & Mellida: The First Part.** John Marston. Ed. by G. K. Hunter. LC 64-17229. (Regents Renaissance Drama Ser.). 110p. 1965. reprint ed. pap. 31.40 (*0-7837-8896-7*, 2049607) Bks Demand.

Antonio Buero Vallejo: The First Fifteen Years. Joelyn Ruple. 1971. 12.95 (*0-88303-006-3*); pap. 8.95 (*0-685-73210-X*) E Torres & Sons.

***Antonio Buero-Vallejo: The Music Window (Musica Cercana)** Ed. by Martha T. Halsey. Tr. by Marion P. Holt. xiv, 66p. 1993. 6.00 (*0-9631212-4-3*) Estreno.

Antonio Caladara Sixteen Seventy to Seventeen Thirty-Six. Ed. by Brian Pritchard. 400p. 1987. text ed. 93.95 (*0-85967-720-6*, Pub. by Scolar Pr UK) Ashgate Pub Co.

Antonio Canova. G. C. Argan et al. LC 92-82649. (Illus.). 400p. 1992. 65.00 (*0-941419-72-X*) Marsilio Pubs.

***Antonio Carlos Jobim Anthology.** Hal Leonard Publishing Staff. 1994. pap. 12.95 (*0-7935-1677-3*, HL00312477) H Leonard.

Antonio Caso: Philosopher of Mexico. John H. Haddox. LC 70-635001. (Texas Pan-American Ser.). 142p. reprint ed. pap. 40.50 (*0-8357-7742-1*, 2036099) Bks Demand.

Antonio de Cabezon Gestamtausgabe 1969-1975, Pt. 2. Cabezon. Ed. by Charles Jacobs. (Gesamtausgaben - Collected Works Ser.: Vol. IV). 80p. (ENG & GER.). lib. bdg. 43.00 (*0-912024-61-5*) Inst Mediaeval Mus.

Antonio de Cabezon Gestamtausgabe 1969-1975, Pt. 3. Cabezon. Ed. by Charles Jacobs. (Gesamtausgaben - Collected Works Ser.: Vol. IV). 80p. (ENG & GER.). lib. bdg. 43.00 (*0-912024-62-3*) Inst Mediaeval Mus.

Antonio de Cabezon Gestamtausgabe 1969-1975, Pt. 5. Cabezon. Ed. by Charles Jacobs. (Gesamtausgaben - Collected Works Ser.: Vol. IV). 80p. (ENG & GER.). lib. bdg. 43.00 (*0-912024-64-X*) Inst Mediaeval Mus.

Antonio de Cabezon Gestamtausgabe 1969-1975, Pts. 1-5. Cabezon. Ed. by Charles Jacobs. (Gesamtausgaben - Collected Works Ser.: Vol. IV). (ENG & GER.). Pt. 4, 116p. lib. bdg. 43.00 (*0-912024-63-1*) Inst Mediaeval Mus.

Antonio de Villegas' "El Abencerraje" Francisco Lopez Estrada & John E. Keller. (Studies in Comparative Literature: No. 33). (C). 1964. pap. 5.95 (*0-8078-7033-1*) U of NC Pr.

Antonio Enriquez Gomez: Literatura y Sociedad en el Siglo Pitagorico y Vida de Don Gregorio Guadana. Nechama Kramer-Hellinx. LC 92-12056. (American University Studies: Romance Languages & Literature: Ser. II, Vol. 193). 368p. (C). 1993. text ed. 55.95 (*0-8204-1868-4*) P Lang Pubs.

Antonio Era: Liber Memorialis. 231p. (GER.). 1963. 27.80 (*0-685-06609-6*) P Lang Pubs.

Antonio Ferreira: The Comedy of Bristo or the Pimp. Tr. by John R. Martyn. 120p. 1985. 8.00 (*0-919473-72-5*, DH58, Pub. by Dovehouse CN) MRTS.

Antonio Frasconi at the Library of Congress: A Lecture Presented May 18, 1989, for International Children's Book Day by Antonio Frasconi. Ed. by Sybille A. Jagusch. LC 93-16662. 1993. 3.00 (*0-8444-0783-6*) Lib Congress.

Antonio Frasconi's World. Antonio Frasconi. 1974. pap. write for info. (*0-685-42855-9*) Macmillan.

***Antonio Gala: The Bells of Orleans (Los Buenos Dias Perdidos)** Ed. by Martha T. Halsey. Tr. by Edward Borsoi. xiv, 64p. 1993. 6.00 (*0-9631212-3-5*) Estreno.

Antonio Gardano, Venetian Music Printer, 1538-1569: A Descriptive Bibliography & Historical Study, Vol. 1, 1538-1549. Mary S. Lewis. LC 87-21202. (Illus.). 964p. 1988. lib. bdg. 137.00 (*0-8240-8454-3*) Garland.

Antonio Gaudi. (Architecture & Urbanism Extra Edition Ser.). (Illus.). 284p. (Orig.). (ENG & JPN.). (C). pap. text ed. 75.00 (*4-900211-01-X*, Pub. by Japan Architect JA) Gingko Press.

Antonio Gramsci. Robert S. Dombrowski. (World Authors Ser.). 176p. (C). 1989. text ed. 26.95 (*0-8057-8245-1*, TWAS 808, Twayne) Macmillan.

Antonio Gramsci. Ed. by Joan Nordquist. (Social Theory: A Bibliographic Ser.: No. 7). 50p. (Orig.). 1987. pap. 15.00 (*0-937855-12-X*) Ref Rsch Serv.

Antonio Gramsci: Architect of a New Politics. Dante Germino. LC 89-49081. (Political Traditions in Foreign Policy Ser.). 296p. 1990. pap. text ed. 16.95 (*0-8071-1655-6*) La State U Pr.

Antonio Gramsci: Beyond Marxism & Postmodernism. Renata Nolub. 1992. pap. 16.95 (*0-415-07510-6*, A6855) Routledge.

***Antonio Gramsci: Further Selections from the Prison Notebooks.** Ed. & Tr. by Derek Boothman. 704p. 1995. write for info. (*0-85315-796-0*, Pub. by Lawrence & Wishart UK) Humanities.

Antonio Gramsci: Life of a Revolutionary. Giuseppe Fiori. 304p. 1990. pap. 17.95 (*0-86091-533-6*, A5071, Pub. by Verso UK) Routledge Chapman & Hall.

Antonio Gramsci: Selections from Political Writings, 1910-1920, with Additional Texts by Bordiga & Tasca. Antonio Gramsci. Tr. by John Mathews. LC 76-54252. 415p. reprint ed. pap. 118.30 (*0-8357-5646-7*, 2030044) Bks Demand.

Antonio Gramsci: Selections from Political Writings, 1921-1926, with Additional Texts by Other Italian Communist Leaders. Antonio Gramsci. Ed. & Tr. by Quintin Hoare. LC 78-6715. 528p. reprint ed. pap. 150.50 (*0-8357-5647-5*, 2030045) Bks Demand.

Antonio Gramsci & the Origins of Italian Communism. John M. Cammett. LC 66-22983. xiv, 306p. 1967. 39.50 (*0-8047-0141-5*) Stanford U Pr.

Antonio Gramsci & the Party: The Prison Years. Spriano. (C). 1979. pap. 15.00 (*0-85315-532-1*, Pub. by Lawrence & Wishart UK) Humanities.

Antonio Gramsci & the Revolution That Failed. Martin Clark. LC 76-49754. 267p. reprint ed. pap. 76.10 (*0-7837-3289-9*, 2057691) Bks Demand.

Antonio Lopez de Santa Anna. (Hispanics of Achievement Ser.). (Illus.). 112p. (J). (gr. 6-12). 1993. lib. bdg. 17.95 (*0-7910-1245-X*) Chelsea Hse.

Antonio Lopez Garcia. Francisco C. Serraller & Edward J. Sullivan. LC 90-52699. (Illus.). 350p. 1990. 150.00 (*0-8478-1249-9*) Rizzoli Intl.

Antonio Maceo: The "Bronze Titan" of Cuba's Struggle for Independence. Philip S. Foner. LC 77-76163. 340p. 1978. 15.00 (*0-85345-423-X*); pap. 5.95 (*0-85345-480-9*) Monthly Rev.

Antonio Machado. Alice J. McVan. (Illus.). 1959. 10.00 (*0-87535-095-X*) Hispanic Soc.

Antonio Machado. Alice J. McVan. (Illus.). 256p. 1959. 6.00 (*0-685-07664-4*) Interbk Inc.

Antonio Machado: Selected Poems. Alan S. Trueblood. LC 81-13481. 332p. 1982. 37.00 (*0-674-04065-1*) HUP.

Antonio Machado: Selected Poems. Antonio Machado. Ed. & Tr. by Alan S. Trueblood. LC 81-13481. 332p. 1988. reprint ed. pap. 16.95 (*0-674-04066-X*) HUP.

Antonio Martorell: A House for Us All. Susana T. Leval et al. (Illus.). 56p. (Orig.). (ENG & SPA.). 1992. pap. 20.00 (*1-882454-00-6*) El Museo Barrio.

Antonio Mira de Amescua: The Devil's Slave (El esclavo del demonio) Tr. by Michael D. McGaha. 114p. 1985. reprint ed. pap. 8.00 (*0-919473-46-6*, DH55, Pub. by Dovehouse CN) MRTS.

Antonio Mortaro, Primo De Canzoni Da Sonare a Quattra Voci. James Ladewig. LC 88-754002. (Italian Instrumental Music of the Sixteenth & Early Seventeenth Centuries Ser.: Vol. 13). 168p. 1989. 76.00 (*0-8240-4512-2*) Garland.

Antonio Pellegrini, 1675-1741. George Knox. (Clarendon Studies in the History of Art: Vol. 14). (Illus.). 336p. 1995. 120.00 (*0-19-817512-4*, Clarendon Pr) OUP.

Antonio Perez. Julia Fitzmaurice-Kelly. 1922. pap. 10.00 (*0-87535-011-9*) Hispanic Soc.

Antonio Pucci: Le Noie. Ed. by K. McKenzie. (Elliott Monographs: Vol. 26). 1931. 30.00 (*0-527-02629-8*) Periodicals Srv.

Antonio Royo Marin, O. P. A Master on the Spiritual Life, a Brilliant Preacher, & a Famous Writer. Joao S. Cla Dias. (Illus.). 62p. (Orig.). (ENG & SPA.). (C). 1987. pap. 5.00 (*1-877905-05-4*) Am Soc Defense TFP.

Antonio S. Pedreira. Fernando S. Berdicea. (Puerto Rico Ser.). 1979. lib. bdg. 59.95 (*0-8490-2867-1*) Gordon Pr.

Antonio S. Pedreira: Vida y Obra. Candida Maldonado de Ortiz. 192p. (C). 1974. 5.00 (*0-8477-0512-9*); pap. 4.00 (*0-8477-0513-7*) U of PR Pr.

Antonio Salazar Is Dead. James L. McManus. (Illus.). 56p. (Orig.). 1980. pap. 3.00 (*0-9603794-0-1*) Syncline.

***Antonio Saura-Elegia.** Antonio Saura et al. (Grandes Monografias). (Illus.). 272p. (SPA.). 1993. 250.00 (*84-343-0544-5*) Elliots Bks.

Antonio Saw the Oryx First. braille ed. Maria Thomas. 572p. 1991. vinyl bd. 45.76 (*1-56956-185-0*, BR8503) W A T Braille.

Antonio Stradivari, His Life & Work (1644-1739) 2nd ed. William H. Hill et al. (Illus.). 1909. pap. 6.95 (*0-486-20425-1*) Dover.

Antonio Torres - Guitar Maker: His Life & His Work. rev. ed. Jose L. Romanilos. (Illus.). 1995. 62.50 (*0-933224-26-5*) Bold Strummer Ltd.

Antonio Triana & the Spanish Dance: A Personal Recollection. Rita Vega de Triana. LC 93-19472. (Choreography & Dance Studies: Vol. 6). 1994. text ed. 39.00 (*3-7186-5407-5*); pap. text ed. 20.00 (*3-7186-5408-3*) Gordon & Breach.

Antonioni. Sam Rohdie. (Illus.). 224p. 1990. 49.95 (*0-85170-273-2*, Pub. by British Film Inst UK); pap. 19.95 (*0-85170-274-0*, Pub. by British Film Inst UK) Ind U Pr.

Antonioni: A Critical Study. William Arrowsmith. 224p. 1995. 25.00 (*0-19-509270-8*) OUP.

Antonioni, or, the Surface of the World. Seymour Chatman. LC 85-1025. 384p. 1985. 45.00 (*0-520-05205-6*); pap. 17.00 (*0-520-05341-9*) U CA Pr.

Antonio's Rain Forest. Anna Lewington. (Carolrhoda Picture Bks.). (Illus.). 48p. (J). (ps-5). 1993. 21.50 (*0-87614-749-X*, Carolrhoda) Lerner Group.

Antonius see St. Anthony: Doctor of the Church

Antonius de Carlenis O. P. Four Questions on the Subalternation of the Sciences. Steven J. Livesey. LC 94-72415. (Transactions Ser.: Vol. 84, Pt. 4). 125p. (C). 1994. pap. 20.00 (*0-87169-844-7*, T844-LIS) Am Philos.

Antonoio Buero Vallejo & Alfonso Sastre: An Annotated Bibliography. Marsha Forys. LC 87-32385. (Author Bibliographies Ser.: No. 81). 227p. 1988. 22.50 (*0-8108-2100-1*) Scarecrow.

Anton's Collected Drek. Anton Drek. (Eros Graphic Novel Ser.: No. 2). 104p. 1992. pap. 14.95 (*1-56097-201-7*) Fantagraph Bks.

Antony & Cleopatra. Arden. Ed. by Maynard. 1985. pap. 8.95 (*0-415-02680-6*) Routledge.

Antony & Cleopatra. Shakespeare. (BBC Television Plays Ser.). 1981. pap. 4.95 (*0-563-17853-1*, Pub. by BBC UK) Parkwest Pubns.

Antony & Cleopatra. William Shakespeare. (Airmont Shakespeare Ser.). (J). (gr. 10 up). 1966. pap. 0.60 (*0-8049-1011-1*, S-11) Airmont.

Antony & Cleopatra. William Shakespeare. (Classics Ser.). 1988. pap. 2.95 (*0-553-21289-3*, Bantam Classics) Bantam.

Antony & Cleopatra. William Shakespeare. Ed. by David Bevington. (New Cambridge Shakespeare Ser.). (Illus.). 220p. (C). 1990. 39.95 (*0-521-25256-3*); pap. 9.95 (*0-521-27250-5*) Cambridge U Pr.

Antony & Cleopatra. William Shakespeare. Ed. by Mary Berry & Michael Clamp. (School Shakespeare Ser.). (Illus.). 240p. (C). 1994. pap. 7.95 (*0-521-44584-1*) Cambridge U Pr.

Antony & Cleopatra. William Shakespeare. Ed. by John F. Andrews. (Everyman Shakespeare Ser.). 288p. 1993. pap. 3.95 (*0-460-87181-1*, Everyman's Classic Lib) C E Tuttle.

Antony & Cleopatra. William Shakespeare. (New Swan Shakespeare Ser.). 1990. pap. 9.95 (*0-582-52743-0*) Longman.

Antony & Cleopatra. William Shakespeare. Ed. by Barbara Everett. pap. 2.95 (*0-451-51956-6*, CE1859, Sig Classics) NAL-Dutton.

Antony & Cleopatra. William Shakespeare. Ed. by R. E. Houghton. (New Clarendon Shakespeare Ser.). 1976. 6.95 (*0-19-831929-0*) OUP.

Antony & Cleopatra. William Shakespeare. 336p. (gr. 10 up). 1988. mass mkt. 3.99 (*0-671-47711-0*, WSP) PB.

Antony & Cleopatra. William Shakespeare. Ed. by M. R. Ridley. (Arden Shakespeare Ser.). 278p. 1954. 49.95 (*0-416-47290-7*, NO.2442); pap. 8.95 (*0-416-47630-9*, NO.2443) Routledge Chapman & Hall.

Antony & Cleopatra. William Shakespeare. Ed. by Maynard Mack. (Pelican Shakespeare Ser.). 1960. mass mkt. 4.95 (*0-14-071420-0*, Pelican Bks) Viking Penguin.

Antony & Cleopatra. William Shakespeare. Ed. by E. Jones. (New Penguin Shakespeare Ser.). 1981. mass mkt. 5.50 (*0-14-070731-X*, Penguin Classics) Viking Penguin.

Antony & Cleopatra. Ed. by Marvin Spevack. LC 89-13691. (New Variorum Edition of Shakespeare Ser.: No. 30). xxxviii, 885p. 1990. text ed. 50.00 (*0-87352-286-9*, Z371C) Modern Lang.

***Antony & Cleopatra.** 3rd ed. Ed. by John Wilders. (Arden Shakespeare Ser.). (Illus.). 300p. 1995. 45.00 (*0-415-01102-7*, B4868) Routledge.

***Antony & Cleopatra.** 3rd ed. Ed. by John Wilders. (Arden Shakespeare Ser.). (Illus.). 300p. 1995. pap. 9.95 (*0-415-01103-5*, B4872) Routledge.

Antony & Cleopatra Notes. James Bellman & Kathryn Bellman. 1981. pap. 3.75 (*0-8220-0002-4*) Cliffs.

Antony & Cleopatra on the English Stage. Margaret Lamb. LC 78-66803. 248p. 1970. 32.50 (*0-8386-2198-8*) Fairleigh Dickinson.

Antony & Cleopatra, William Shakespeare. Ed. by John Drakakis. LC 93-36999. (New Casebooks Ser.). 1994. text ed. 39.95 (*0-312-12045-1*) St Martin.

Antony Begins. Mark Dunster. (Antony Ser.: Pt. 4). 26p. (Orig.). 1994. pap. 5.00 (*0-89642-229-1*) Linden Pubs.

***Antony Gormley.** John Hutchinson. (Contemporary Artists Ser.). (Illus.). 160p. (Orig.). 1995. pap. 29.95 (*0-7148-3383-5*, Pub. by Phaidon Press UK) Chronicle Bks.

An Asterisk (*) at the beginning of an entry indicates that the title is appearing in BIP for the first time. 367

Antony Tudor: The American Years. Ed. by M. Topaz. (Choreography & Dance Studies). 116p. 1989. pap. text ed. 17.00 (*3-7186-4955-1*) Gordon & Breach.

Antonyms: Individual Sets. Marion W. Stuart. Date not set. text ed. write for info. (*0-943343-07-0*) Lrn Wrap-Ups.

***Antonyms (Opposites)** (General Aptitude & Abilities Ser.: Series 2). Date not set. 17.95 (*0-8373-6753-0*) Nat Learn.

Antrim & Billy. Don Cline. LC 90-1598. (Early West Ser.). (Illus.). 170p. (YA). 1990. 21.95 (*0-932702-48-1*) Creative Texas.

Antrim Is My Stepfather's Name: The Boyhood of Billy the Kid. Jerry Weddle. LC 93-22925. (Historical Monograph: Vol. 9). (Illus.). xx, 96p. (Orig.). 1993. pap. 16.95 (*0-910037-31-0*) AZ Hist Soc.

Antrobus Complete. Lawrence Durrell. LC 85-6995. (Illus.). 202p. 1985. pap. 10.95 (*0-571-13603-6*) Faber & Faber.

***Ants.** Ruth Berman. LC 95-15123. (Early Bird Nature Bks.). (Illus.). (J). 1995. write for info. (*0-8225-3012-0*, Lerner Publctns) Lerner Group.

Ants. Patricia B. Demuth. LC 93-1769. (Illus.). 32p. (J). 1994. text ed. 14.95 (*0-02-728467-0*, Mac Bks Young Read) S&S Childrens.

Ants. Bert Holldobler & Edward O. Wilson. (Illus.). 752p. 1990. text ed. 75.00 (*0-674-04075-9*) Belknap Pr.

Ants. Cynthia Overbeck. LC 81-17216. (Natural Science Bks.). (Illus.). 48p. (J). (gr. 4 up). 1982. lib. bdg. 19.95 (*0-8225-1468-0*, Lerner Publctns); pap. 5.95 (*0-8225-9525-7*, Lerner Publctns) Lerner Group.

Ants. Edward S. Ross. LC 92-44257. (J). (gr. 2-6). 1993. lib. bdg. 22.79 (*1-56766-056-8*) Childs World.

Ants: Their Structure, Development, & Behavior. rev. ed. William M. Wheeler. LC 10-8253. (Columbia Biological Ser.: No. 9). (Illus.). 1960. text ed. 97.00 (*0-231-00121-5*) Col U Pr.

Ants, Alligators, Astronauts. Debbie DePauw. (Illus.). 48p. 1994. pap. text ed. 5.95 (*1-55799-275-4*) Evan-Moor Corp.

Ants & More Ants: An Integrated Activity Unit. Bev McKay. (Illus.). 32p. 1993. pap. text ed. 4.95 (*0-86530-225-1*) Incentive Pubns.

***Ants Dissolve in Moonlight.** W. B. Keckler. LC 95-60132. 80p. (C). 1995. pap. 7.00 (*1-879193-04-3*) Fugue State.

Ants Go Marching One by One. (Sing - with - Me Ser.). (Illus.). 24p. (J). 1993. 7.98 (*0-7853-0045-7*) Pubns Intl Ltd.

Ants (Hymenoptera, Formicidae) of Western Texas: Part I - Subfamily Myrmicinae. J. V. Moody & O. F. Francke. (Graduate Studes: No. 27). 80p. (Orig.). 1982. pap. 12.00 (*0-89672-107-8*) Tex Tech Univ Pr.

Ants (Hymenoptera, Formicidea) of Western Texas, Parts II & III: Subfamilies Ecitoninae, Ponerine, Psuedomyrmecinae, Dolichoderinae, & Formicinae, Additions & Corrections. James Cokendolpher & Oscar F. Francke. (Special Publications: Nos. 30 & 31). (C). 1990. pap. 14.00 (*0-89672-175-2*) Tex Tech Univ Pr.

***Ants in My Pants.** Denell Hilgendorf. LC 93-94129. (Illus.). 64p. (Orig.). (J). 1994. pap. 8.00 (*1-56002-388-0*, Univ Edtns) Aegina Pr.

Ants in the Sugar Bowl. Karren Boehr. 165p. (J). (gr. 4 up). 1986. 3.99 (*0-570-03638-0*, 39-1122) Concordia.

Ants' Nest. Muriel D. Daly. LC 79-37265. (Short Story Index Reprint Ser.). 1977. reprint ed. 20.95 (*0-8369-4076-8*) Ayer.

Ants of California. Thomas W. Cook. (Illus.). 1953. 29.95 (*0-87015-036-7*) Pacific Bks.

Ants of Deep Canyon. G. C. Wheeler. LC 73-88149. 1973. pap. 3.95 (*0-942290-01-1*) Boyd Deep Canyon.

Ants of Nevada. George C. Wheeler & Jeanette N. Wheeler. LC 86-60542. (Illus.). viii, 138p. (Orig.). 1986. pap. text ed. 40.00 (*0-938644-22-X*) Nat Hist Mus.

Ants of Southern Australia: A Guide to the Bassian Fauna. A. N. Anderson. (Illus.). 96p. 1991. pap. 20.00 (*0-643-05152-X*, Pub. by CSIRO AT) Intl Spec Bk.

Ants of the British Isles. G. J. Skinner. (Shire Natural History Ser.: No. 21). (Illus.). 24p. 1987. pap. text ed. 5.25 (*0-85263-896-5*, Pub. by Shire Pubns UK) Lubrecht & Cramer.

Antwerp: An Historical Descourse, or Rather a Teragicall Historie of Antwerpe since the Departure of King Phillip of Spaine Out of Netherland. LC 79-84083. (English Experience Ser.: No. 903). 56p. 1979. reprint ed. lib. bdg. 15.00 (*90-221-0903-8*) Walter J Johnson.

***Antwerp in the Age of Reformation: Underground Protestantism in a Commercial Metropolis, 1550-1577.** Guido Marnef. (Studies in Historical & Political Science, 112th Series (1994)). (Illus.). 360p. 1995. text ed. 48.50x (*0-8018-5169-6*) Johns Hopkins.

Antwerp's Golden Age: The Metropolis of the West in the 16th & 17th Centuries. 222p. 1986. pap. 5.00 (*0-318-22670-7*) Menil Collect.

Antwort der Reformatoren auf die Zehtenfrage. Gunter Zimmermann. (European University Studies: History & Allied Studies: Ser. 3, Vol. 164). 175p. 1982. 30.75 (*3-8204-5745-3*) P Lang Pubs.

Antysemityzm a Robotnicy. J. B. Marchlewski. 94p. reprint ed. 20.00 (*0-318-23360-6*) Szwede Slavic.

Anuario de Temas, Parte A: Alumno. (SPA.). 1992. 2.50 (*1-55955-163-1*) CITE MI.

Anuario de Temas, Parte A: Maestro. (SPA.). 1992. 5.00 (*1-55955-160-7*) CITE MI.

Anuario de Temas, Parte B: Maestro. (SPA.). 1992. 2.75 (*1-55955-162-3*) CITE MI.

Anuario de Termas, Parte B: Alumno. (SPA.). 1992. 2.50 (*1-55955-164-X*) CITE MI.

Anuario Estadistico de America Latina y el Caribe, 1989. 950p. 1990. 65.00 (*92-1-021027-1*, 90.II.G.1) UN.

Anuario Juridico Interamericano, 1949; 1952-1954; 1955-1957, 3 vols. (ENG, FRE, POR & SPA.). 3.00 (*0-8270-5205-7*) OAS.

Anuario Juridico Interamericano, 1980. OAS, General Secretariat for Juridical Affairs. 339p. 1981. text ed. 50.00 (*0-8270-1399-X*) OAS.

Anubis Gates. Tim Powers. 416p. 1984. pap. 4.95 (*0-441-02382-7*) Ace Bks.

Anubis Gates. limited ed. Tim Powers. (Illus.). 396p. 1990. reprint ed. 65.00 (*0-929480-11-2*) Mark Ziesing.

Anubis Gates. Tim Powers. (Illus.). 396p. 1990. reprint ed. 25.00 (*0-929480-10-4*) Mark Ziesing.

Anugita. Tr. by K. T. Telang. LC 81-50202. (Secret Doctrine Reference Ser.). 176p. 1981. reprint ed. 14.00 (*0-913510-40-8*) Wizards.

Anumanacintaman, 2 vols., Set. Ed. by Kamakhyanatha Tarkavagisa. (C). 1988. 25.00 (*81-7013-065-4*, Pub. by Navrang) S Asia.

Anvare Gholoube Salekin: Truth of Virtues. Jalaleddin-Ali M. Angha. 456p. (Orig.). (PER.). 1978. 75.00 (*0-910735-14-X*) MTO Printing & Pubn Ctr.

Anvari's Divan: A Pocket Book for Akbar. Annemarie Schimmel et al. (Illus.). 144p. 1983. 4.95 (*0-87099-331-3*) Metro Mus Art.

Anvari's Divan: A Pocket Book for Akbar. Annmarie Schimmel. 1994. 19.95 (*0-8109-6443-0*) Abrams.

Anvil. David Drake & S. M. Stirling. (General Ser.: Bk. 3). 320p. 1993. mass mkt. 4.99 (*0-671-72171-2*, PB) Baen Bks.

Anvil Chorus. Shane Stevens. 384p. 1993. 4.95 (*0-7867-0049-1*) Carroll & Graf.

Anvil of Ice Vol. I. Michael S. Rohan. (The Winter of the World). 368p. 1989. mass mkt. 4.99 (*0-380-70547-8*, AvoNova) Avon.

Anvil of Roses. 3rd ed. Thomas H. Ferril. Ed. by Orvis C. Burmaster. LC 82-73829. (Ahsahta Press Modern & Contemporary Poets of the West Ser.). 50p. 1983. pap. 6.95 (*0-916272-20-6*) Ahsahta Pr.

Anvil of Sinai. Fendel Zechariah. 1980. 16.95 (*0-686-76479-X*) Feldheim.

Anvil of Stars. Greg Bear. 448p. 1992. 19.95 (*0-446-51601-5*) Warner Bks.

Anvil of Stars. Greg Bear. 480p. 1993. mass mkt. 5.99 (*0-446-36403-7*) Warner Bks.

Anvil of the Heart. Bruce T. Holmes. 312p. 1983. 14.95 (*0-911361-00-6*) Haven Corp.

Anvil of Victory: The Communist Revolution in Manchuria. Steven I. Levine. LC 86-19821. (Illus.). 384p. 1987. text ed. 44.00 (*0-231-06436-5*) Col U Pr.

Anvil of War: German Generalship on the Eastern Front. Erhard Rauss & Oldwig Natzmer. Ed. by Peter G. Tsouras. 320p. 1994. 34.95 (*1-85367-181-9*, 5403) Stackpole.

***Anvils of Destiny. Howard Robb. 191p. 1991. 20.50 (*0-9630648-1-9*) Cyberdynamic.**
THIS BOOK COVERS MAJOR NEW DEVELOPMENTS THAT FOR THE FIRST TIME GIVE A CLEAR UNDERSTANDING OF THE ACTUAL FORCES THAT CONTROL THE RISE & DECLINE OF CIVILIZATIONS. It shows step-by-step how these forces, not kings or battles, controlled the entire path of ascent & decline of every major & minor civilization of our planet. And, though they are all of equal intellect, why only a few select races, ethnicities & societies of our planet made great cultural, intellectual, economic & technical progress. After each case, why all the others did not despite their equal intellects. The book shows how these forces alone precisely shaped every aspect & set the ultimate level of attainment of the culture & history of each race, ethnicity & society of our planet. It also shows how the same forces of decline that have collapsed every previous civilization are now rapidly converging to collapse the present global economy & civilization. Order directly from your bookstore or the Cyberdynamics Press, P.O. Box 105B, Monrovia, MD 21770. ANVILS OF DESTINY, $20.50, 191 pages, hard bound, acid free paper, ISBN 0-9630648-1-9, 1991. YOUR TOTAL SATISFACTION OR A PROMPT REFUND. ***Publisher Provided Annotation.***

Anwar Sadat. Patricia Aufderheide. (World Leaders - Past & Present Ser.). (Illus.). 112p. (YA). (gr. 5 up). 1985. lib. bdg. 17.95 (*0-87754-560-X*) Chelsea Hse.

Anwar Sadat. Arthur Diamond. LC 93-17096. (Importance of Ser.). (J). (gr. 5-8). 1994. 16.95 (*1-56006-020-4*) Lucent Bks.

***Anwar Sadat: Visionary Who Dared.** Joseph Finklestone. LC 95-6980. 1995. write for info. (*0-7146-3487-5*, Pub. by F Cass Pubs UK) Intl Spec Bk.

Anwar Sadat, Egyptian Ruler & Peace Maker. Blythe F. Finke. (Outstanding Personalities Ser.: No. 96). 32p. (YA). (gr. 7-12). 1986. lib. bdg. 4.95 (*0-87157-596-5*) SamHar Pr.

Anwendngen der Linearen Parametrischen Optimierung. Klaus Lommatzsch. (Mathematische Reihe Ser.: No. 69). 200p. (GER.). 1980. reprint ed. 44.50 (*0-8176-1058-8*) Birkhauser.

Anxiety. Donald W. Goodwin. LC 85-7179. 288p. 1985. 25.00 (*0-19-503665-4*) OUP.

Anxiety. Ed. by D. F. Klein. (Modern Problems of Pharmacopsychiatry Ser.: Vol. 22). (Illus.). viii, 196p. 1987. 78.50 (*3-8055-4488-X*) S Karger.

Anxiety: Current Trends in Theory & Research, 2 vols. Ed. by Charles D. Spielberger. 1972. write for info. (*0-318-50228-3*) Acad Pr.

Anxiety: Medical Subject Analysis & Research Directory with Bibliography. American Health Research Institute Staff. Ed. by John C. Bartone et al. LC 81-71807. 120p. 1982. 39.50 (*0-941864-28-6*); pap. 34.50 (*0-941864-29-4*) ABBE Pubs Assn.

Anxiety: New Findings for the Clinician. Peter Roy-Byrne. LC 88-26209. (Clinical Practice Ser.: No. 5). 224p. 1988. text ed. 25.00 (*0-88048-177-3*) Am Psychiatric.

Anxiety: Psychobiological & Clinical Perspectives. Norman Sartorius et al. (Series in Health Psychology & Behavioral Medicine). 300p. 1990. 68.00 (*1-56032-064-8*) Hemisp Pub.

Anxiety: Psychological Perspectives on Panic & Agoraphobia. Richard S. Hallam. 1985. text ed. 94.00 (*0-12-319620-5*) Acad Pr.

Anxiety: Recent Developments in Cognitive, Psychophysiological & Health Research. Ed. by Donald G. Forgays et al. (Series in Health Psychology & Behavioral Medicine). 275p. 1992. 59.50 (*1-56032-265-9*, Hemisp Pub) Taylor & Francis.

***Anxiety: Symptom & Signal.** Ed. by Steven P. Roose & Robert A. Glick. 200p. 1995. text ed. write for info. (*0-88163-118-3*) Analytic Pr.

Anxiety: Theory, Research & Intervention in Clinical & Health Psychology. Robert J. Edelmann. (Clinical Psychology Ser.). 349p. 1992. text ed. 59.95 (*0-471-92389-3*) Wiley.

Anxiety - Prevention & Control: Index of New Information with Authors & Subjects. Dean A. Jobber. 180p. 1993. 49.50 (*1-55914-914-0*); pap. 39.50 (*1-55914-915-9*) ABBE Pubs Assn.

Anxiety Across the Life Span: A Developmental Perspective. Ed. by Cynthia G. Last. LC 92-49675. (Behavior Therapy & Behavioral Medicine Ser.: Vol. 26). 232p. 1993. 37.95 (*0-8261-6460-9*) Springer Pub.

Anxiety & Ashes. deluxe ed. Laura Jensen. 1976. 45.00 (*0-686-16128-9*) Penumbra Press.

Anxiety & Defensive Strategies in Childhood & Adolescence. Gudmund Smith & Anna Danielsson. LC 81-23633. (Psychological Issues Monograph: No. 52, Vol. 13, No. 3). 212p. 1981. text ed. 30.00 (*0-8236-0389-X*) Intl Univs Pr.

Anxiety & Depression: Distinctive & Overlapping Features. Ed. by Philip C. Kendall & David H. Watson. (Personality, Psychopathology & Psychotherapy Ser.). 811p. 1989. text ed. 80.00 (*0-12-404170-1*) Acad Pr.

Anxiety & Depression: The Adaptive Emotions. Charles G. Costello. LC 76-382042. 159p. reprint ed. pap. 45.40 (*0-7837-1036-4*, 2041347) Bks Demand.

***Anxiety & Depression in Adults & Children.** Ed. by Kenneth D. Craig & Keith S. Dobson. (Banff International Conference Ser.: Vol. 1). 304p. 1994. pap. 22.50 (*0-8039-7021-8*) Sage.

***Anxiety & Depression in Adults & Children.** Ed. by Kenneth D. Craig & Keith S. Dobson. (Banff International Conference Ser.: Vol. 1). 304p. 1994. 46.00 (*0-8039-7020-X*) Sage.

Anxiety & Depressive Disorders in the Medical Patient. Ed. by Leonard R. Derogatis & Thomas N. Wise. LC 87-31940. (Clinical Practice Ser.: No. 4). 250p. 1988. pap. text ed. 27.50 (*0-88048-159-5*) Am Psychiatric.

Anxiety & Ego Formation in Infancy. Sylvia Brody & Sidney Axelrad. 432p. (C). 1993. reprint ed. pap. text ed. 24.95 (*0-8236-8003-7*) Intl Univs Pr.

Anxiety & Its Disorders: The Nature & Treatment of Anxiety & Panic. David H. Barlow. LC 87-24842. 698p. 1988. lib. bdg. 65.00 (*0-89862-720-6*) Guilford Pr.

Anxiety & Its Treatment. John H. Greist et al. 304p. 1988. mass mkt. 6.99 (*0-446-35362-0*) Warner Bks.

Anxiety & Its Treatment: Help Is Available. John H. Greist et al. LC 85-26874. 216p. 1986. boxed 18.50 (*0-88048-212-5*, 48-212-5) Am Psychiatric.

Anxiety & Magic Thinking: The Psychogenetic Analysis of Phobia & the Neurosis of Abandonment. Charles Odier. Tr. by Marie-Louise Schoelly & Mary J. Sherfey. LC 56-9335. 316p. 1956. text ed. 38.00 (*0-8236-0400-4*) Intl Univs Pr.

Anxiety & Musical Performance. Dale Reubart. LC 84-21422. (Music Ser.). 250p. 1985. 35.00 (*0-306-76253-6*) Da Capo.

Anxiety & Neurosis. Charles Rycroft. 184p. 1990. reprint ed. pap. 21.95 (*0-946439-52-4*, Pub. by Karnac Bks UK) Brunner-Mazel.

Anxiety & Panic Attacks: Their Cause & Cure. Robert W. Handly. 1987. mass mkt. 5.95 (*0-449-21331-5*, Crest) Fawcett.

Anxiety & Phobia Workbook. Ed Bourne. 368p. (Orig.). 1990. 26.95 (*0-934986-86-X*); pap. 13.95 (*0-934986-85-1*) New Harbinger.

***Anxiety & Phobia Workbook.** 2nd ed. Bourne. 1995. pap. text ed. 15.95 (*1-57224-003-2*) New Harbinger.

***Anxiety & Phobia Workbook.** 2nd ed. Bourne. 370p. 1995. 29.95 (*1-57224-004-0*) New Harbinger.

***Anxiety & Phobia Workbook.** Edmund J. Bourne. 355p. 1995. reprint ed. 12.98 (*1-56731-074-5*, MJF Bks) Fine Comms.

Anxiety & Phobias. Don Nardo. (Psychological Disorders & Their Treatment Ser.). (Illus.). 112p. (YA). (gr. 6-12). 1992. 18.95 (*0-7910-0041-9*) Chelsea Hse.

Anxiety & Related Disorders: A Handbook. Ed. by Benjamin B. Wolman & George Stricker. LC 93-925. (Series on Personality Processes). 462p. 1993. text ed. 70.00 (*0-471-54773-5*) Wiley.

Anxiety & Ritual: The Theories of Malinowski & Radcliffe-Brown. George C. Homans. (Reprint Series in Social Sciences). (C). 1993. reprint ed. pap. text ed. 1.00 (*0-8290-2725-4*, S-121) Irvington.

Anxiety & Stress: A Self-Help Program. Susan M. Lark. (Women's Health Ser.). 284p. 1993. pap. 12.95 (*0-917010-55-8*, Wstchstr Pub Co) Natl Nursing.

Anxiety & Stress Disorders: Cognitive-Behavioral Assessment & Treatment. Ed. by Larry Michelson & Michael L. Ascher. LC 86-29585. 624p. 1987. lib. bdg. 62.00 (*0-89862-693-5*) Guilford Pr.

Anxiety & Stress Management. Trevor Powell & Simon Enright. 176p. 1990. pap. 17.95 (*0-415-01069-1*, A3368) Routledge.

Anxiety & the Anxiety Disorders. Ed. by Hussain A. Tuma & Jack D. Maser. 1172p. 1985. text ed. 160.00 (*0-89859-532-0*) L Erlbaum Assocs.

Anxiety & the Dynamics of Collaboration. Paul Pengelly & Douglas Woodhouse. (Aberdeen University Press Bks.). 176p. (C). 1991. pap. text ed. 25.00 (*0-08-040912-1*, Pub. by Aberdeen U Pr) Macmillan.

Anxiety & the Heart. Ed. by D. G. Byrne & Ray H. Rosenman. (Series in Health Psychology & Behavioral Medicine). 325p. 1990. 68.00 (*0-89116-860-5*) Hemisp Pub.

Anxiety Attack. Lorrie Sprecher. 50p. 1992. 5.00 (*0-9631656-0-7*) Violet Ink.

Anxiety Attacked. John MacArthur, Jr. LC 93-3721. (MacArthur Study Ser.). (Illus.). 192p. (Orig.). 1993. pap. 9.99 (*1-56476-128-2*, Victor Books) SP Pubns.

Anxiety Attacks. Karen Randau. 66p. 1991. pap. 2.99 (*0-945276-25-7*) Rapha Pub.

Anxiety, Depression, & Mania. Ed. by P. Soubrie. (Animal Models of Psychiatric Disorders Ser.: Vol. 3). (Illus.). 134p. 1991. 118.50 (*3-8055-5247-5*) S Karger.

Anxiety Disease. David V. Sheehan. 1986. mass mkt. 5.99 (*0-553-27245-4*) Bantam.

Anxiety Disorders. Carl S. Warren. (Practitioner Guidebook Ser.). (C). 1991. 39.95 (*0-205-14498-5*, H4498, Longwood Div); pap. 25.95 (*0-205-14497-7*, H4497, Longwood Div) Allyn.

Anxiety Disorders: A Practitioner's Guide. Paul M. Emmelkamp et al. LC 92-18107. 202p. 1992. text ed. 46.95 (*0-471-93112-8*) Wiley.

Anxiety Disorders: A Scientific Approach for Selecting the Most Effective Treatment. Samuel Knapp & Leon VandeCreek. LC 94-7201. (Practitioner's Resource Ser.). 114p. 1994. pap. 14.70 (*1-56887-000-0*, ADBP) Pro Resource.

Anxiety Disorders: Medical Subject Analysis with Bibliography. Alexander D. Farrell. LC 87-47568. 150p. 1987. 39.50 (*0-88164-612-1*); pap. 34.50 (*0-88164-613-X*) ABBE Pubs Assn.

Anxiety Disorders: Proceedings Medical Symposium on Buspirone, Dusseldorf, Germany, April 18-19, 1985. 99p. (Orig.). 1985. write for info. (*0-934205-01-9*) Academy Prof Inform.

Anxiety Disorders: Psychological & Biological Perspectives. Ed. by Brian F. Shaw et al. LC 87-6998. 268p. 1987. 79.50 (*0-306-42485-1*, Plenum Pr) Plenum.

Anxiety Disorders & Phobias: A Cognitive Perspective. Aaron T. Beck & Gary Emery. LC 84-42849. 416p. 1985. pap. 14.95 (*0-685-09854-0*) Basic.

Anxiety Disorders & Phobias: A Cognitive Perspective. Aaron T. Beck. 368p. 1990. pap. 17.00 (*0-465-00385-0*) Basic.

Anxiety Disorders in African Americans. Ed. by Steven Friedman. 248p. 1994. 41.95 (*0-8261-8540-1*) Springer Pub.

Anxiety Disorders in Children. Rachel G. Klein & Cynthia G. Last. (Developmental Clinical Psychology & Psychiatry Ser.: Vol. 20). 146p. (C). 1989. text ed. 37.00 (*0-8039-3220-0*); pap. text ed. 16.95 (*0-8039-3221-9*) Sage.

Anxiety Disorders in Children & Adolescents. Ed. by Syed A. Husain & Javad Kashani. LC 91-22233. (Clinical Practice Ser.: No. 22). 250p. 1991. text ed. 30.00 (*0-88048-467-5*) Am Psychiatric.

***Anxiety Disorders in Children & Adolescents.** John S. March. 448p. 1995. lib. bdg. 40.00 (*0-89862-834-2*) Guilford Pr.

Anxiety Disorders Interview Schedule: ADIS-R. rev. ed. Peter A. Di Nardo & David H. Barlow. 57p. 1989. student ed 4.00 (*1-880659-03-4*) Graywind Pubns.

***Anxiety Epidemic.** 2nd ed. Billie J Sahley. (Illus.). 120p. 1995. pap. text ed. 9.95 (*0-9625914-4-0*) Pain & Stress.

Anxiety, Guilt & Freedom: Essays in Honor of Donald Gard. Ed. by Benjamin J. Hubbard & Bradley E. Starr. (Religious Studies Perspectives). 288p. (C). 1990. lib. bdg. 54.00 (*0-8191-7683-4*); pap. text ed. 39.95 (*0-8191-7684-2*) U Pr of Amer.

Anxiety in Childhood & Adolescence: Encouraging Self-Help Through Relaxation Training. Frank Carter & Peter Cheesman. 144p. 1988. text ed. 49.50 (*0-7099-4806-9*, A1479) Routledge Chapman & Hall.

Anxiety in Children. Ved P. Varma. 228p. (C). 1984. 35.00 (*0-416-01031-8*, 9206) Routledge Chapman & Hall.

Anxiety in Clinical Practice. A. C. Sims. 1988. pap. text ed. 82.00 (*0-471-92055-X*) Wiley.

Anxiety in Eden: A Kierkegaardian Reading of Paradise Lost. John S. Tanner. (Illus.). 224p. 1992. 39.95 (*0-19-507204-9*) OUP.

Anxiety in Elementary School Children. Seymour B. Sarason et al. LC 77-26021. (Illus.). 351p. 1978. reprint ed. text ed. 35.00 (*0-313-20075-0*, SAAE, Greenwood Pr) Greenwood.

An Asterisk (*) at the beginning of an entry indicates that the title is appearing in BIP for the first time.

An Asterisk (*) at the beginning of an entry indicates that the title is appearing in BIP for the first time.

369

***Anything Can Happen.** Fredy Perlman. 128p. (Orig.). Date not set. pap. 9.95 (0-948984-22-8, Pub. by Phoenix Pr UK) AK Pr Dist.

Anything Can Happen in High School: And It Usually Does. William D. McCants. LC 92-32982. (YA). 1993. 10.95 (0-15-276604-9); pap. 3.95 (0-15-276605-7) HarBrace.

***Anything Considered.** Peter Mayle. Date not set. pap. write for info. (0-679-44123-9) Random.

Anything Cuddly Will Do! Mick Inkpen. (Illus.). 12p. (J). (gr. 4-7). 1993. 4.99 (1-878685-71-6, Bedrock Press) Turner Pub GA.

Anything for a Dream: Original Manuscript. Regina Chaney. LC 90-63437. 157p. (C). 1991. text ed. 17.95 (0-9628246-0-7) Morgan Randolph & Assocs.

Anything for a Quiet Life. Michael Gilbert. 224p. 1991. pap. 3.95 (0-88184-715-1) Carroll & Graf.

Anything for Billy. Larry McMurtry. Ed. by Bill Grose. 416p. 1991. mass mkt. 5.99 (0-671-74605-7) PB.

Anything for Danny: (Fabulous Father, under the Mistletoe) Carla Cassidy. (Sil Romance Ser.). 1994. pap. 2.75 (0-373-19048-4, 1-19048-7) Silhouette.

Anything for Love. Connie Brockway. 384p. (Orig.). 1994. mass mkt. 4.50 (0-380-77754-1) Avon.

Anything for Love. Francine Pascal. (Sweet Valley Ser.: No. 4). (YA). 1994. pap. 3.50 (0-553-56311-4) Bantam.

Anything for Love. Sheila Rann. 288p. 1995. 21.95 (0-446-51830-1) Warner Bks.

***Anything for Love.** Janelle Taylor. 1995. mass mkt. 5.99 (0-8217-4992-7) Zebra.

Anything for You. large type ed. Rosemary Hammond. 288p. 1991. reprint ed. lib. bdg. 18.95 (0-263-12692-7, Pub. by Mills & Boon UK) Thorndike Pr.

Anything Goes. 1994. pap. 14.95 (0-943351-60-X, XW1620) Astor Bks.

Anything Goes: Practical Karate for the Streets. Loren W. Christensen. (Illus.). 176p. 1990. pap. 16.00 (0-87364-568-5) Paladin Pr.

Anything Goes: The Jazz-Age Adventures of Neysa McMein & Her Extravagant Circle of Friends. Brian Gallagher. LC 87-9954. (Illus.). 256p. 1987. 18.95 (0-8129-1215-2, Times Bks) Random.

Anything He Can Fix, I Can Fix Better. Lyn Herrick. (Illus.). 176p. (Orig.). 1990. pap. text ed. 9.95 (0-927494-01-9) Quality Living.

Anything I Can Play, You Can Play Better. Val Call. (Illus.). 105p. (Orig.). 1986. pap. 8.95 (0-940076-03-9) Fiesta City.

Anything Is Possible. Leo Dickinson. (Illus.). 224p. 1990. 34.95 (0-224-02826-X, Pub. by Jonathan Cape UK) Trafalgar.

***Anything Is Possible: A Selection of 11 Women Poets.** Ed. by Mary Di Mechele. 190p. 1995. lib. bdg. 33.00 (0-8095-4853-4) Borgo Pr.

***Anything New in Your Life, Teach? And Other Tales Told Out of School.** Gerald D. Sullivan. LC 91-61750. (Illus.). 72p. (Orig.). 1991. pap. 9.95 (0-9644573-2-6) Shamrock Sky Bks.

Anything on Its Side. Larry Eigner. 1974. 16.00 (0-685-40881-7); pap. 8.00 (0-685-40882-5) Elizabeth Pr.

Anything Out of Place Is Dirt. Michael C. Daniels. (Writers Workshop Ser.). 106p. 1975. 9.00 (0-88253-498-X); pap. text ed. 4.80 (0-88253-497-1) Ind-US Inc.

Anything to Win. Rosemary Joyce. (Dream Girls Ser.: No. 1). 160p. (YA). 1994. pap. 4.50 (1-56171-304-X, S P I Bks) Sure Sellers.

Anything to Win. Gloria D. Miklowitz. 1990. reprint ed. pap. 3.50 (0-440-20732-0, LFL) Dell.

Anything Toy. Susan Kern & Phil Kern. (Illus.). 125p. (J). (gr. 1-6). 1991. pap. 69.95 (1-56516-009-6) Houston IN.

Anything You Can Do. Sara Garrett. 224p. (Orig.). 1993. pap. 2.95 (1-56597-063-2) Meteor Pub.

Anything You Don't See. Enid Dame. 51p. (Orig.). 1992. pap. 6.95 (0-931122-67-8) West End.

***Anything's Possible!** Judith McWilliams. (Desire Ser.). 1995. mass mkt. 3.25 (0-373-05911-6, 1-05911-2) Silhouette.

Anything's Possible. Cathy G. Thacker. (American Romance Ser.: No. 452). 1992. mass mkt. 3.39 (0-373-16452-1) Harlequin Bks.

Anytime Parties for Children. Mary Reid. (Illus.). 80p. (J). (gr. 1-5). 1987. student ed 5.99 (0-87403-290-3, 2802) Standard Pub.

Anytime Prayers. Madeleine L'Engle. LC 93-46429. (Illus.). 64p. (J). (gr. 1-6). 1994. 14.99 (0-87788-055-7) Shaw Pubs.

Anytime Stories. Leo Sawicki. (Illus.). 64p. (J). (ps-8). 1988. 7.95 (0-920806-78-3, Pub. by Penumbra Pr CN) U of Toronto Pr.

Anyway. Cynthia Davidson. (Illus.). 1994. pap. 45.00 (0-8478-1766-0) Rizzoli Intl.

Anyway, We Won: A Civilian Soldier in World War II. John Brawley. (Illus.). 332p. 1988. 17.95 (0-929628-00-4) Scotch Pub.

Anywhere. Cynthia Davidson. (Illus.). 272p. 1992. 45.00 (0-8478-1617-6) Rizzoli Intl.

***Anywhere - Anytime.** John E. Olson. (Illus.). 238p. Date not set. 13.50 (0-9644432-2-8) J E Olson.

Anywhere but Here. Mona Simpson. 1986. 18.95 (0-394-55283-0) Knopf.

Anywhere but Here. Mona Simpson. LC 87-40088. 416p. 1987. pap. 9.95 (0-394-75559-6, Vin) Random.

Anywhere but Here. Mona Simpson. 1992. 12.00 (0-679-73738-3, Vin) Random.

Anywhere Else But Here. Bruce Clements. 1989. pap. 3.50 (0-374-40420-8) FS&G.

***Anywhere Ring: Miracle Island, No. 1.** Louise Ladd. 176p. (Orig.). 1995. pap. text ed. 3.99 (0-425-14879-3) Berkley Pub.

Anywhere with You! Vernell K. Miller. 208p. (Orig.). 1989. pap. 8.95 (0-8361-3505-9) Herald Pr.

Anza & the Northwest Frontier of New Spain. J. N. Bowman & Robert F. Heizer. 182p. 1967. 12.50 (0-916561-04-6) Southwest Mus.

***Anza-Borrego Desert Region.** 4th ed. Ed. by Lowell Lindsay & Diana Lindsay. LC 84-52660. (Illus.). 175p. 1996. pap. 13.95 (0-89997-187-3) Wilderness Pr.

Anza-Borrego Desert State Park. Harry Daniel & Mark C. Jorgensen. Ed. by Rose Houk. LC 82-73296. (Illus.). 74p. 1982. 24.95 (0-910805-00-8); pap. 12.50 (0-910805-01-6) Anza-Borrego.

Anzac Illusion: Anglo-Australian Relations During World War I. E. M. Andrews. (Illus.). 288p. (C). 1994. 49.95 (0-521-41914-X) Cambridge U Pr.

Anzac Memories: Living with the Legend. Alistair Thomson. (Illus.). 304p. 1994. 45.00 (0-19-553491-3) OUP.

Anzac Sonata: New & Selected Poems. Jon Stallworthy. 1987. 15.95 (0-393-02449-0) Norton.

Anzacs over England. David Goodland & Alan Vaughan. (Pocket Classic Ser.). (Illus.). 1993. 40.00 (0-7509-0277-9) A Sutton Pub.

Anza's California Expeditions, 5 vols., Set. Herbert E. Bolton. (BCL1 - United States Local History Ser.). 1991. reprint ed. lib. bdg. 375.00 (0-7812-6337-9) Rprt Serv.

Anzeiger fur Bibliographie und Bibliothekswissenschaft, 6 vols. Ed. by Julius Petzoldt. Set incl. 28 microfiches. write for info. (0-318-71730-1, Pub. by Georg Olms GW) Lubrecht & Cramer.

Anzeiger fur Bibliothekswissenschaft, 3 vols. Ed. by Julius Petzoldt. reprint ed. Set incl. 17 microfiches. write for info. (0-318-71729-8, Pub. by Georg Olms GW) Lubrecht & Cramer.

Anzeiger fur Literature der Bibliothekswissenschaft, 40 vols. Ed. by Julius Petzoldt. Set incl. 200 microfiches. write for info. (0-318-71728-X, Pub. by Georg Olms GW) Lubrecht & Cramer.

Anzia Yezierska: A Writer's Life. Louise L. Henriksen. LC 87-9588. 305p. (C). 1991. pap. 14.95 (0-8135-1664-1) Rutgers U Pr.

Anzin Coal Company, 1800-1833: Big Business in the Early Stages of the French Industrial Revolution. Reed G. Geiger. LC 74-77774. 345p. 35.00 (0-87413-108-1) U Delaware Pr.

Anzio: Epic of Bravery. Fred Sheehan. LC 94-11745. (Illus.). 256p. (Orig.). 1994. pap. 14.95 (0-8061-2678-7) U of Okla Pr.

Anzio: The Gamble That Failed. Martin Blumenson. LC 77-26027. (Great Battles of History). (Illus.). 212p. 1978. reprint ed. text ed. 35.00 (0-313-20093-9, BLAN, Greenwood Pr) Greenwood.

Anzio - Song of Destiny. Phillip Messina. 316p. 1992. pap. 5.95 (0-935648-38-0) Halldin Pub.

***Anzio Annie, She Was No Lady.** Richard J. O'Rourke. (Illus.). 256p. (Orig.). 1995. pap. text ed. 17.95 (0-9645084-0-0) ORourke Servs.

Anzio Beachhead, 22 January-25 May 1944. (Armed Forces in Action Ser.: No. 14). (Illus.). 132p. reprint ed. per., pap. 11.00 (0-16-002001-8, S/N 008-029-001) USGPO.

Anzuelo de Fenisa - Fenisa's Hook: Or Fenisa the Hooker. Lope De Vega. Tr. by David M. Gitlitz. 187p. 25.00 (0-939980-19-3) Trinity U Pr.

Anzus Crisis, Nuclear Visiting & Deterrence. Michael Pugh. (Cambridge Studies in International Relations: No. 4). (Illus.). (C). 1989. 64.95 (0-521-34355-0) Cambridge U Pr.

ANZUS Economics: Economic Trends & Relations among Australia, New Zealand & the United States. Ed. by Richard W. Baker & Gary R. Hawke. LC 92-16558. 276p. 1992. text ed. 55.00 (0-275-94381-X, C4381, Praeger Pubs) Greenwood.

ANZUS in Crisis: Alliance Management in International Affairs. Ed. by Jacob Bercovitch. LC 87-26856. 240p. 1988. text ed. 55.00 (0-312-01223-3) St Martin.

ANZUS States & Their Region: Regional Policies of Australia, New Zealand, & the United States. Ed. by Richard W. Baker. LC 93-14121. 228p. 1994. text ed. 57.95 (0-275-94693-2, C4693, Praeger Pubs) Greenwood.

ANZUS, the United States & Pacific Security. Henry S. Albinski. LC 87-10548. (Asian Agenda Report Ser.: No. 17). 76p. (Orig.). (C). 1987. lib. bdg. 27.00 (0-8191-6373-2); pap. text ed. 8.50 (0-8191-6374-0) U Pr of Amer.

AO - ASIF Instruments & Implants: A Technical Manual. 2nd rev. ed. R. Texhammar & C. Colton. LC 93-21299. 1993. 98.00 (0-387-56895-6) Spr-Verlag.

AO-ASIF Instrumentation: Manual of Use & Care. F. Sequin & R. Texhammar. (Illus.). 330p. 1981. 60.00 (0-387-10337-6) Spr-Verlag.

Ao Nagas. Surendra N. Majumdar. LC 77-87507. reprint ed. 12.00 (0-404-16841-8) AMS Pr.

Aofas Foot & Ankle Manual. G. James Sammarco. LC 90-13349. (Illus.). 390p. 1991. text ed. 49.50 (0-8121-1368-3) Williams & Wilkins.

AON, Vol. 19, 1986. 1990. 39.50 (0-316-06126-3) Little.

AON, Vol. 21, 1987. 1990. 39.50 (0-316-06129-8) Little.

AON, Vol. 22, 1987. 1990. 39.50 (0-316-06130-1) Little.

AON, Vol. 23, 1988. 1990. 39.50 (0-316-06132-8) Little.

AON, Vol. 25, 1989. 1990. 39.50 (0-316-06134-4) Little.

AON, Vol. 27, 1990. 1990. 39.50 (0-316-06281-2) Little.

AON, Vol. 28, 1990. 1991. 39.50 (0-316-04803-8) Little.

Aonian Hours, & Other Poems see Poems by Three Friends. (Thomas Raffles, Baldwin Brown, & J. H. Wiffen)

Aorist Participle of Antecedent Action. Earnell Sams, Jr. LC 81-67641. (C). 1982. pap. write for info. (0-940068-01-X) Doctrine Christ.

AORN Directory of Perioperative Nursing Courses. rev. ed. Association of Operating Room Nurses, Inc., Staff. 102p. 1994. 12.50 (0-939583-75-5) Assn Oper Rm Nurses.

***AORN Patient Classification Instrument for Perioperative Nursing.** rev. ed. AORN Staff. Ed. by Carol Applegeet. 50p. (Orig.). 1993. pap. text ed. 25.00 (0-939583-83-6) Assn Oper Rm Nurses.

AORN Standards & Recommended Practices for Perioperative Nursing. 242p. 1995. pap. text ed. 43.75 (0-939583-80-1) Assn Oper Rm Nurses.

Aortic Alterations in Rabbits Following Sheathing with Silastic & Polyethylene Tubes, Vol. 60. Incl. Radioactively Labeled Iododeoxyuridine in the Study of Experimental Liver Regeneration. K. Buerki et al. 1975. (0-318-55760-6); Human Placental Villitides: A Review of Chronic Intrauterine Infection. G. Altshuler & P. Russel. 1975. (0-318-55761-4); Ultrastructural Pathology of the Adrenal Glands Incushing's Syndrome. H. Mitschke & W. Saeger. 1975. (0-318-55762-2); DNA in Human Tumors: A Cytophotometric Study. N. Boehm & W. Sandritter. 1975. (0-318-55763-0); (Current Topics in Pathology Ser.). (Illus.). 260p. 1975. 93.30 (0-387-07434-1) Spr-Verlag.

Aortic Aneurysms: Surgical Therapy. Ed. by Charles D. Campbell. LC 81-69572. (Illus.). 108p. 1981. 25.00 (0-87993-162-0) Futura Pub.

Aortic Valve. Ed. by Kit V. Arom. LC 90-83246. (Illus.). 332p. 1991. text ed. 69.00 (0-932883-97-4) Hanley & Belfus.

Aortic Valve. Mano J. Thubrikar. 240p. 1989. 119.00 (0-8493-4771-8, QP114) CRC Pr.

Aortitis: Clinical, Pathologic, & Radiographic Aspects. Ed. by Adam Lande et al. (Illus.). 288p. 1986. text ed. 83.00 (0-88167-141-X) Raven.

Aorto-Coronary Bypass Surgery. B. Buis. 1974. pap. text ed. 47.00 (90-207-0474-5) Kluwer Ac.

AOTA Self Study Series: Classroom Applications for School-Based Practice. American Occupational Therapy Association, Inc. Staff. Ed. by Charlotte B. Royeen. (C). Date not set. pap. text ed. write for info. (0-910317-91-7) Am Occup Therapy.

AOTA Self Study Series: Neuroscience Foundations of Human Performance. American Occupational Therapy Association Staff. Ed. by Charlotte B. Royeen. (C). 1992. pap. text ed. write for info. (0-910317-82-8) Am Occup Therapy.

AOTA Self Study Series - Assessing Function: What's Working in Occupational Therapy. American Occupational Therapy Association Staff. Ed. by Charlotte B. Royeen. (C). 1992. pap. text ed. write for info. (0-910317-81-X) Am Occup Therapy.

AOTCB Study Guide for the COTA Certification Examination. Ed. by Susan M. Lang. 72p. (Orig.). (C). 1994. pap. text ed. 20.00 (0-9639373-0-8) Am Occupat Ther.

AOTCB Study Guide for the OTR Certification Examination. Ed. by Susan M. Lang. 76p. (Orig.). (C). 1994. pap. text ed. 20.00 (0-9639373-1-6) Am Occupat Ther.

Aotus: The Owl Monkey. Ed. by Ibulaimu Kakoma. (Illus.). 380p. 1994. text ed. 74.95 (0-12-072405-7) Acad Pr.

A.O.U. Checklist of North American Birds. 6th ed. 1983. write for info. (0-943610-32-X) Am Ornithologists.

AP American History. 3rd ed. John W. Crum. (AP Exam Guides Ser.). (Illus.). 352p. 1993. pap. 12.00 (0-671-84776-7, Arco Test) P-H Gen Ref & Trav.

AP American History. 4th ed. John W. Crum. (AP Exam Guides Ser.). 1994. pap. 12.00 (0-671-88824-2, Arco Test) P-H Gen Ref & Trav.

AP Biology. Phillip Pack. (Illus.). 555p. 1994. pap. 14.95 (0-8220-2301-6) Cliffs.

AP Biology. 2nd ed. Richard P. Heller & Rachael F. Heller. (AP Exam Guides Ser.). (Illus.). 288p. 1990. pap. 13.00 (0-671-86582-X, Arco Test) P-H Gen Ref & Trav.

AP Calculus AB. Kerry King. (Cliffs Test Preparation Guides Ser.). Date not set. Study Guide. student ed, pap. text ed. 12.95 (0-8220-2302-4) Cliffs.

AP Chemistry. Gary S. Thorpe & Cliff Staff. (Cliffs Test Preparation Guides Ser.). (Illus.). 404p. 1994. pap. text ed. 12.95 (0-8220-2303-2) Cliffs.

AP Chemistry. 2nd ed. Frederick J. Rowe. LC 93-18320. 1993. 14.00 (0-671-84778-3, Arco Test) P-H Gen Ref & Trav.

AP English Language & Composition. Barbara Swovelin. 1993. pap. 10.95 (0-8220-2304-0) Cliffs.

AP English Literature & Composition. Allen Casson & Abraham Hoffman. 1993. pap. 10.95 (0-8220-2305-9) Cliffs.

AP English Literature & Composition. 3rd ed. Laurie Rozakis. (AP Exam Guides Ser.). 320p. 1993. pap. 13.00 (0-671-84784-8, Arco Test) P-H Gen Ref & Trav.

AP Exam: American Government. Patton L. Feichter & Robert Schultz. 288p. 1991. pap. 12.95 (0-13-019043-8, Arco Test) P-H Gen Ref & Trav.

AP Exam in American History. 2nd ed. John W. Crum. (AP Exam Guides Ser.). 320p. (YA). (gr. 9-12). 1990. pap. 10.95 (0-685-31171-6, Arco Test) P-H Gen Ref & Trav.

AP Examination in English Language & Composition. (Illus.). 270p. 1994. pap. text ed. 14.95 (0-87891-923-6) Res & Educ.

AP Examination in English Literature & Composition. rev. ed. Research & Education Association Staff. (Illus.). 368p. 1994. pap. text ed. 14.95 (0-87891-843-4) Res & Educ.

AP Examination in European History. rev. ed. Research & Education Association Staff. (Illus.). 640p. 1994. pap. text ed. 17.95 (0-87891-863-9) Res & Educ.

AP Examination in Government & Politics. rev. ed. Robert F. Gorman et al. 400p. 1994. 16.95 (0-87891-884-1) Res & Educ.

***AP Examination in Spanish.** G. Braun et al. 400p. 1995. pap. text ed. 16.95 (0-87891-699-7) Res & Educ.

AP Examination in U. S. History. rev. ed. Research & Education Association Staff. (Illus.). 672p. 1994. pap. text ed. 17.95 (0-87891-844-2) Res & Educ.

AP French: A Guide for the Language Course. Richard Ladd & Colette Girard. 154p. 1992. 18.45 (0-8013-0640-X, 78580); teacher ed 11.95 (0-8013-0641-8, 78581) Longman.

AP French: A Guide for the Language Course, Set. Richard Ladd & Colette Girard. 154p. 1992. audio 39.95 (0-8013-0642-6, 78582) Longman.

A.P. Hill: Lee's Forgotten General. William W. Hassler. LC 57-13027. xv, 249p. 1957. 22.50 (0-8078-0973-X) U of NC Pr.

Ap Huw Manuscript. Claire Polin. (Wissenschaftliche Abhandlungen-Musicological Studies: Vol. 34). 1982. lib. bdg. 80.00 (0-931902-13-4) Inst Mediaeval Mus.

AP-PF Scoring Guidelines: Quality Assurance & Monitoring Functions. 1988. pap. 35.00 (0-86688-158-1) Joint Comm Hlthcare.

AP Spanish: A Guide for the Language Course. Jose Diaz et al. 1989. teacher ed 11.95 (0-8013-0168-8, 78002); pap. text ed. 18.45 (0-8013-0167-X, 78001) Longman.

AP Spanish: A Guide for the Language Course, Set. Jose Diaz et al. 1989. audio 39.95 (0-8013-0169-6, 78003) Longman.

AP United States History. Paul Soifer & Abraham Hoffman. 1993. pap. 10.95 (0-8220-2300-8) Cliffs.

Apache. Barbara McCall. (Native American People Ser.). (Illus.). 32p. (J). (gr. 5-8). 1990. lib. bdg. 15.94 (0-86625-384-X); lib. bdg. 11.95 (0-685-36387-2) Rourke Corp.

Apache. Barbara A. McCall. Tr. by Aida E. Marcuse. LC 92-12177. (J). 1992. 17.26 (0-86625-454-4); 12.95 (0-685-59386-X) Rourke Pubns.

Apache. Patricia McKissack. LC 84-7803. (New True Bks.). (Illus.). 48p. (J). (gr. k-4). 1984. lib. bdg. 12.90 (0-516-01925-2); pap. 4.95 (0-516-41925-0) Childrens.

Apache. Michael E. Melody. (Indians of North America Ser.). (Illus.). 112p. (J). (gr. 5 up). 1989. 17.95 (1-55546-689-3); pap. 9.95 (0-7910-0352-3) Chelsea Hse.

Apache. Will L. Comfort. 1976. reprint ed. lib. bdg. 21.95 (0-89190-851-X, Rivercity Pr) Amereon Ltd.

Apache. Will L. Comfort. LC 85-29021. 274p. 1986. reprint ed. pap. 9.95 (0-8032-6319-8, Bison Books) U of Nebr Pr.

Apache: The Long Ride Home. Grant Gall. LC 87-10137. 112p. (Orig.). 1988. pap. 9.95 (0-86534-105-2) Sunstone Pr.

Apache Agent: The Story of John P. Clum. W. Clum. 1977. lib. bdg. 59.95 (0-8490-1441-7) Gordon Pr.

Apache Agent: The Story of John P. Clum. Woodworth Clum. LC 77-14135. (Illus.). 313p. reprint ed. pap. 89.30 (0-8357-5649-1, 2027913) Bks Demand.

Apache Arrows. Jory Sherman. (Gunn Ser.: No. 8). 1981. pap. 2.25 (0-89083-791-0) Zebra.

Apache Autumn. Robert Skimin. 1994. mass mkt. 4.99 (0-312-95195-7) St Martin.

Apache Blanco. Jack Ballas. 208p. (Orig.). 1994. pap. text ed. 4.50 (0-515-11452-9) Jove Pubns.

***Apache Blessing: A Modern Tale of Texas Indians.** Kimberly A. Shope. 24p. (J). (gr. 3-8). 1992. pap. 5.00 (1-886210-03-9) Tyketoon Yng Author.

Apache Blood. David Thompson. (Wilderness Ser.: No. 12). 176p. (Orig.). 1992. pap. 3.50 (0-8439-3374-7) Dorchester Pub Co.

Apache Butte. large type ed. Gordon D. Shirreffs. (Linford Western Library). 186p. 1989. pap. 11.95 (0-7089-6719-1, Linford) Ulverscroft.

Apache Campaign in the Sierra Madre. John G. Bourke. LC 87-5940. (Illus.). xxiv, 134p. 1987. reprint ed. pap. 7.95 (0-8032-6085-7, Bison Books) U of Nebr Pr.

Apache Captive. Betty Brooks. 1990. mass mkt. 4.25 (0-8217-3132-7) Zebra.

Apache Caress. Georgina Gentry. 1991. mass mkt. 4.50 (0-8217-3560-8) Zebra.

Apache Coffin. John Legg. 1991. pap. 3.50 (0-8217-3476-8) Zebra.

Apache Conquest. Theresa Scott. 448p. (Orig.). 1993. pap. 4.99 (0-8439-3471-9) Dorchester Pub Co.

Apache Creek Ambush. Doyle Trent. 224p. 1991. pap. 3.50 (0-8217-3318-4) Zebra.

Apache Days & After. Thomas Cruse. Ed. by Eugene Cunningham. LC 87-10840. (Illus.). 364p. 1987. pap. 9.95 (0-8032-6327-9) U of Nebr Pr.

Apache Devil. Edgar Rice Burroughs. 15.95 (0-8488-1254-9) Amereon Ltd.

Apache Devil. Edgar Rice Burroughs. 1976. reprint ed. lib. bdg. 16.20 (0-89966-043-6) Buccaneer Bks.

Apache Dick: From the Pages of The Trouble with Girls. Will Jacobs & Gerard Jones. (Illus.). 99p. 1990. pap. 9.95 (0-944735-78-9) Malibu Graphics.

Apache Fire. Judith Steel. 1991. mass mkt. 4.50 (0-8217-3571-3) Zebra.

Apache Gold. Mark K. Roberts & Patrick Andrews. 336p. 1986. pap. 2.95 (0-8217-1899-1) Zebra.

Apache Gold. Joseph Altsheler. 1990. reprint ed. lib. bdg. 22.95 (0-89968-455-6) Buccaneer Bks.

Apache Gold. Joseph A. Altsheler. 1976. reprint ed. lib. bdg. 24.95 (0-88411-941-6, Aeonian Pr) Amereon Ltd.

Apache Gold & Yaqui Silver. J. Frank Dobie. (Illus.). 380p. 1985. reprint ed. pap. 12.95 (0-292-70381-3) U of Tex Pr.

Apache Half-Breed. large type ed. Glen A. Blackburn. (Linford Western Library). 288p. 1992. pap. 14.95 (0-7089-7170-9, Linford) Ulverscroft.

An Asterisk (*) at the beginning of an entry indicates that the title is appearing in BIP for the first time.

Apache Heartbeat. Judith Steel. 1989. pap. 3.75 (*0-8217-2641-2*) Zebra.

***Apache Heartsong.** Janis R. Hudson. 384p. 1995. mass mkt. 4.99 (*0-8217-4898-X*) Zebra.

Apache Hunter. Gordon D. Shirreffs. 1988. pap. 2.95 (*0-449-13479-2*) Fawcett.

***Apache Hunter; The Marauders, 2 vols. in 1.** Gordon D. Shirreffs. (Manhunter Ser.). 448p. 1995. mass mkt., pap. 4.99 (*0-8439-3872-2*) Dorchester Pub Co.

Apache Indian Baskets. Clara L. Tanner. LC 82-6920. (Illus.). 204p. 1982. 39.95 (*0-8165-0778-3*) U of Ariz Pr.

Apache Indian Coloring Book. O. T. Branson. 32p. (J). (gr. 1-6). 1983. pap. 2.95 (*0-918080-13-4*) Treas Chest Bks.

Apache Indians. Nicole Claro. (Junior Library of American Indians). (Illus.). 80p. (J). (gr. 3-7). 1993. lib. bdg. 14.95 (*0-7910-1656-0*) Chelsea Hse.

Apache Indians. Nicole Claro. (Junior Library of American Indians). (Illus.). 80p. (J). (gr. 3-7). 1993. pap. 6.95 (*0-7910-1946-2*) Chelsea Hse.

Apache Indians. Frank C. Lockwood. LC 86-25103. (Illus.). xxxii, 388p. 1987. reprint ed. pap. 11.95 (*0-8032-7925-6*) U of Nebr Pr.

Apache Indians, Vol. III. Incl. Aboriginal Use & Occupation of Certain Lands by Tigua, Manso & Suma Indians. Rex E. Gerald. 1974. (*0-318-52396-5*); History & Administration of the Tigua Indians of Ysleta Del Sur During the Spanish Colonial Period. Myra E. Jenkins. 1974. (*0-318-52397-3*); Apache Ethnohistory: Government, Land & Indian Policies Relative to Lipan, Mescalero & Tigua Indians. Kenneth F. Neighbours. 1974. (*0-318-52398-1*); (American Indian Ethnohistory Series: Indians of the Southwest). (Illus.). 1974. Set lib. bdg. 51.00 (*0-8240-0717-4*) Garland.

Apache Kill. large type ed. Matt Chisholm. (Linford Western Library). 352p. 1993. pap. 14.95 (*0-7089-7306-X*, Linford) Ulverscroft.

Apache Knight. Carol Finch. 448p. 1994. mass mkt. 5.99 (*0-8217-4712-6*) Zebra.

Apache Legacy. Janis R. Hudson. 448p. 1994. mass mkt. 4.50 (*0-8217-4589-1*) Zebra.

Apache Legends: Songs of the Wind Dancer. Lou Cuevas. Ed. by Keven Brown. (Illus.). 128p. (Orig.). (YA). 1991. pap. text ed. 8.95 (*0-87961-219-3*) Naturegraph.

Apache Life-Way. Morris E. Opler. LC 65-23533. 500p. reprint ed. 47.25 (*0-8154-0168-X*) Cooper Sq.

Apache Magic. Janis R. Hudson. 1991. mass mkt. 4.25 (*0-8217-3610-8*) Zebra.

Apache Medicine-Men. John G. Bourke. LC 93-36083. (Illus.). 176p. 1994. reprint ed. pap. text ed. 7.95 (*0-486-27842-5*) Dover.

Apache Moon. Jack Bodine. (Pecos Kid Ser.: No. 3). 1993. mass mkt. 3.50 (*0-06-100620-3*, Harp PBks) HarpC.

Apache Mother & Daughters: Four Generations of a Family. Ruth M. Boyer & Narcissus D. Gayton. LC 92-54149. (Illus.). 416p. 1992. 24.95 (*0-8061-2447-4*) U of Okla Pr.

***Apache, Navaho, & Spaniard.** 2nd ed. Jack D. Forbes. LC 94-17589. (Illus.). 323p. 1994. pap. 14.95 (*0-8061-2686-8*) U of Okla Pr.

Apache, Navaho, & Spaniard. Jack D. Forbes. LC 79-17069. (Illus.). 304p. 1980. reprint ed. text ed. 38.50 (*0-313-22021-2*, FOAN, Greenwood Pr) Greenwood.

Apache Odyssey: A Journey Between Two Worlds. Morris E. Opler. Ed. by George Spindler & Louise Spindler. LC 82-23355. (Case Studies in Cultural Anthropology). (Illus.). 320p. 1983. reprint ed. pap. text ed. 16.95 (*0-8290-1267-2*) Irvington.

Apache Promise. Janis R. Hudson. 384p. 1992. mass mkt. 4.25 (*0-8217-4005-9*) Zebra.

Apache Reservation: Indigenous Peoples & the American State. Richard J. Perry. LC 92-37253. (Illus.). 276p. (C). 1993. text ed. 37.50 (*0-292-76542-8*); pap. 15.95 (*0-292-76543-6*) U of Tex Pr.

Apache Rifles. Kit Dalton. (Buckskin Ser.: No. 28). 176p. (Orig.). 1990. pap. 2.95 (*0-8439-2943-X*) Dorchester Pub Co.

***Apache Rodeo.** Diane Hoyt-Goldsmith. LC 94-26583. (Illus.). (J). (gr. 3 up). 1995. lib. bdg. 15.95 (*0-8234-1164-8*) Holiday.

***Apache Runaway.** Madeline Baker. 448p. (Orig.). 1995. mass mkt. 5.99 (*0-8439-3742-4*) Dorchester Pub Co.

Apache Shadows. Albert R. Booky. LC 85-30435. 144p. (Orig.). 1986. pap. 10.95 (*0-86534-084-6*) Sunstone Pr.

***Apache Springs.** Lynn Erickson. (Superromance Ser.). 1995. mass mkt. 3.75 (*0-373-70656-1*, 1-70656-3) Harlequin Bks.

***Apache Sunrise.** Jerome M. Boyle. (Orig.). 1994. mass mkt. 4.99 (*0-8041-1069-7*) Ivy Books.

Apache Sunset. Betty Brooks. 1988. pap. 3.75 (*0-8217-2418-5*) Zebra.

Apache Temptation. Janis R. Hudson. 448p. 1993. mass mkt. 4.50 (*0-8217-4289-2*) Zebra.

Apache Thunder. Dan Mason. (Ranger Ser.: No. 6). (Orig.). 1992. mass mkt. 3.50 (*0-06-100415-4*, Harp PBks) HarpC.

Apache Tigress. Veronica Blake. 1990. mass mkt. 4.25 (*0-8217-3084-3*) Zebra.

Apache Trick. Buck Gentry. (Scout Ser.: No. 27). 224p. 1988. pap. 2.95 (*0-8217-2416-9*) Zebra.

Apache Warrior. Steve Mensing. 1981. pap. 2.25 (*0-89083-836-4*) Zebra.

Apache Wars: An Illustrated Battle History. E. Lisle Reedstrom. LC 90-38971. (Illus.). 272p. (YA). (gr. 10-12). 1992. pap. 19.95 (*0-8069-7255-6*) Sterling.

Apache Wells. Robert Steelman. 160p. 1980. pap. 1.75 (*0-345-29067-4*) Ballantine.

Apache Wind. Carol Finch. 448p. 1993. mass mkt. 4.99 (*0-8217-4361-9*) Zebra.

Apachean Culture: History & Ethnology. Ed. by Keith H. Basso & Morris E. Opler. LC 70-140453. (Anthropological Papers of the University of Arizona: No. 21). (Illus.). 176p. reprint ed. pap. 50.20 (*0-8357-5650-5*, 2029648) Bks Demand.

Apaches. Jason Hook. (Men-at-Arms Ser.: No. 186). (Illus.). 48p. 1987. pap. 11.95 (*0-85045-738-6*, 9118, Pub. by Osprey UK) Stackpole.

Apaches: Eagles of the Southwest. Donald E. Worcester. LC 78-21377. (Civilization of the American Indian Ser.: Vol. 149). (Illus.). 408p. (Orig.). (C). 1992. pap. 14.95 (*0-8061-2397-4*) U of Okla Pr.

Apaches & Longhorns: The Reminiscences of Will C. Barnes. Will C. Barnes. Ed. by Frank C. Lockwood. LC 82-7043. (Illus.). 254p. reprint ed. pap. 72.40 (*0-8357-8584-X*, 2034955) Bks Demand.

Apaches & Navajos. Craig A. Doherty & Katherine M. Doherty. LC 89-9079. (Full-Color First Bks.). (Illus.). 64p. (J). (gr. 3-5). 1989. lib. bdg. 13.93 (*0-531-10743-4*) Watts.

Apaches & Navajos. Craig A. Doherty & Katherine M. Doherty. (Full-Color First Bks.). (Illus.). 64p. (J). (gr. 5-8). 1991. pap. 5.95 (*0-531-15602-8*) Watts.

Apache's Angel. Karen A. Bale. 448p. 1992. mass mkt. 4.50 (*0-8217-3900-X*) Zebra.

Apaches at War & Peace: The Janos Presidio, 1750-1858. William B. Griffen. LC 88-20518. 316p. reprint ed. pap. 90.10 (*0-7837-5855-3*, 2045574) Bks Demand.

Apache's Desire. Karen A. Bale. 448p. 1993. mass mkt. 4.50 (*0-8217-4120-9*) Zebra.

Apaches of New York. Alfred H. Lewis. LC 73-37277. (Short Story Index Reprint Ser.). 1977. reprint ed. 23.95 (*0-8369-4088-1*) Ayer.

Apacible Vida Provinciana. Eulalia Donoso. LC 93-79289. 190p. (Orig.). (SPA.). 1993. pap. 16.00 (*0-9637939-1-8*) Edic Rio Claro.

Apah - The Sacred Waters: An Analysis of a Primordial Symbol in Hindu Myths. Frans Baartmans. 1990. 54.00 (*81-7018-582-3*, Pub. by BR Pub II) S Asia.

Apalachee: The Land Between the Rivers. John H. Hann. LC 87-2163. (Ripley P. Bullen Monographs in Anthropology & History: No. 7). (Illus.). 464p. 1988. 42.95 (*0-8130-0854-9*) U Press Fla.

Apamea in Syria: The Winter Quarters of Legio II Parthica, Roman Gravestones from the Military Cemetery. Wilfried Van Rengen & Jean C. Balty. (Illus.). 55p. 1994. pap. 14.95 (*90-5487-008-7*, Pub. by Mus Tusculanum DK) Paul & Co Pubs.

***Apariciones.** limited ed. Antoni Tapies. Ed. by Pere Gimgerrer. (Ediciones Especiales y de Bibliofilo Ser.). (Illus.). (CAT.). 1993. 3,750.00 (*84-343-0345-0*) Elliots Bks.

Aparoksanubhuti (Self-Realization) Shankara. Tr. by Swami Vimuktananda. 1938. Bilingual ed. pap. 2.50 (*0-87481-065-5*, Pub. by Advaita Ashrama II) Vedanta Pr.

Apart & Together: Mennonites in Oregon & Neighboring States, 1876-1976. Hope K. Lind. (Studies in Anabaptist & Mennonite History). (Illus.). 416p. 1990. 26.95 (*0-8361-3106-1*) Herald Pr.

Apart at the Seams. Sheri C. Sinykin. (Destination Ser.). 120p. (YA). (gr. 6-12). 1991. per., pap. 3.95 (*0-89486-733-4*, 5138A) Hazelden.

Apart from a Little Dampness, Herman, How's Everything Else? Jim Unger. 96p. 1984. pap. 1.95 (*0-451-12781-1*, Sig) NAL-Dutton.

Apart or A Part: Integration & the Growth of British Education. Ted Cole. 160p. 1989. 90.00 (*0-335-09226-8*, Open Univ Pr); pap. 32.00 (*0-335-09225-X*, Open Univ Pr) Taylor & Francis.

Aparte: Conceptions & Deaths of Soren Kierkegaard. Sylviane Agacinski. LC 87-24072. 1988. pap. 29.95 (*0-8130-0887-5*) U Press Fla.

Apartheid: A Collection of Writings on South African Racism. Ed. by Alex La Guma. 239p. (Orig.). reprint ed. pap. 68.20 (*0-7837-0584-0*, 2040928) Bks Demand.

Apartheid: Calibrations of Color. Ed. by Patra McSharry & Roger Rosen. (World Issues Ser.: Vol. 2). (Illus.). 176p. (YA). (gr. 7-12). 1991. lib. bdg. 16.95 (*0-8239-1330-9*); pap. 8.95 (*0-8239-1331-7*) Rosen Group.

Apartheid: The Story of a Dispossessed People. Ed. by Motsoko Pheko. LC 94-65533. 196p. 1994. 20.00 (*1-884921-02-7*) Pheko & Assocs.

Apartheid: The United Nations & Peaceful Change in South Africa. Ozdemir A. Ozgur. LC 83-23972. 240p. (Orig.). 1982. lib. bdg. 35.00 (*0-941320-01-4*) Transnatl Pubs.

Apartheid & Education: The Education of Black South Africans. Ed. by Peter Kallaway. 496p. (C). 1984. text ed. 24.95 (*0-86975-256-1*, Pub. by Ravan Pr ZA) Ohio U Pr.

Apartheid Axis: The United States & South Africa. William J. Pomeroy. LC 79-150661. 96p. reprint ed. pap. 27.40 (*0-8357-5652-1*, 2022868) Bks Demand.

Apartheid City & Beyond: Urbanization & Social Change in South Africa. Ed. by David M. Smith. 288p. 1992. 87.50 (*0-415-07601-3*, A7563); pap. 17.95 (*0-415-07602-1*, A7567) Routledge.

Apartheid Education & Popular Struggles. Ed. by Elaine Unterhalter et al. 272p. (C). 1991. text ed. 59.95 (*1-85649-026-2*, Pub. by Zed Books UK) Humanities.

Apartheid, Imperialism & African Freedom. William J. Pomeroy. Ed. by Betty Smith. LC 86-10488. 276p. (C). 1986. 14.00 (*0-7178-0640-5*); pap. 6.95 (*0-7178-0632-4*) Intl Pubs Co.

Apartheid in a South African Town, 1968-1985. Martin E. West. LC 87-3741. (Research Ser.: No. 67). (Illus.). xiv, 151p. (C). 1987. pap. 9.50 (*0-87725-167-3*) U of Cal IAS.

Apartheid in Fiction. Gurleena Mehta & Harish Narang. 1990. 33.00 (*81-7169-052-1*, Commonwealth) S Asia.

Apartheid in Our Living Rooms: U. S. Foreign Policy & South Africa. Prexy Nesbitt. (Midwest Research Monograph Ser.: No. 3). 58p. 1986. pap. 5.50 (*0-915987-02-3*) Political Rsch Assocs.

Apartheid in South Africa. 3rd ed. David M. Smith. (Update Ser.). (Illus.). 96p. (Orig.). (C). 1990. pap. 13.95 (*0-521-39720-0*) Cambridge U Pr.

Apartheid in Theory & Practice: An Economic Analysis. Mats Lundahl. 375p. (C). 1992. pap. text ed. 34.85 (*0-8133-8447-8*) Westview.

Apartheid Is a Heresy. Ed. by John W. De Gruchy & Charles Villa-Vincencio. LC 83-8935. 204p. (Orig.). reprint ed. pap. 58.20 (*0-8357-4361-6*, 2037189) Bks Demand.

Apartheid Is Wrong: A Curriculum for Young People. Paula R. Bower. (Illus.). 280p. (J). (gr. 1-12). 1989. ring bd. 15.00 (*1-878537-00-8*) Educ Racism & Apart.

Apartheid Is Wrong: A Curriculum for Young People. 2nd ed. Paula R. Bower. 1990. write for info. (*1-878537-03-2*) Educ Racism & Apart.

Apartheid, Militarism & the U. S. Southeast. Ann Seidman. LC 90-81486. 280p. (C). 1990. 29.95 (*0-86543-151-5*); pap. 9.95 (*0-86543-152-3*) Africa World.

***Apartheid of Sex: A Manifesto on the Freedom of Gender.** Martine A. Rothblatt. LC 94-20941. 1995. 21.00 (*0-517-59997-X*) Crown Pub Group.

Apartheid Reader. Ed. by Gary E. McCuen. (Ideas in Conflict Ser.). (Illus.). 173p. 1986. lib. bdg. 12.95 (*0-86596-057-7*) G E M.

Apartheid Regime: Political Power & Racial Domination. Ed. by Robert M. Price & Carl G. Rosberg. LC 79-27269. (Research Ser.: No. 43). (Illus.). 1980. pap. 12.50 (*0-87725-143-6*) U of Cal IAS.

Apartheid Terrorism. Phyllis Johnson & David Martin. (Illus.). 190p. 1990. 29.95 (*0-253-33133-1*) Ind U Pr.

Apartheid U. S. A. & Our Common Enemy, Our Common Cause: Freedom Organizing in the Eighties. Audre Lorde & Merle Woo. (Freedom Organizing Pamphlet Ser.). 28p. (Orig.). (C). 1986. pap. 3.50 (*0-913175-06-4*) Kitchen Table.

Apartheid Unravels. Ed. by R. Hunt Davis, Jr. (Carter Lecture Series, Center for African Studies). 264p. (C). 1991. lib. bdg. 36.95 (*0-8130-1069-1*) U Press Fla.

Apartheid Whitewash: South Africa Propaganda in the United States. Richard Leonard. 64p. 1989. pap. 5.00 (*0-685-39026-8*) Africa Fund.

Apartheid, 1979-1988: A Selected Annotated Bibliography. Sherman Pyatt. LC 89-7710. 190p. 1989. 29.00 (*0-8240-7637-0*, 55587) Garland.

Apartheid's Contras: An Inquiry into the Roots of War in Angola & Mozambique. William Minter. LC 95-41587. 320p. (C). 1994. text ed. 69.95 (*1-85649-265-6*, Pub. by Zed Books UK); pap. 29.95 (*1-85649-266-4*, Pub. by Zed Books UK) Humanities.

Apartheid's Environmental Toll. Alan B. Durning. (Orig.). (C). 1990. pap. 5.00 (*0-916468-96-8*) Worldwatch Inst.

Apartheid's Genesis, 1935-1962. Ed. by Philip Bonner et al. 465p. (Orig.). (C). 1994. pap. text ed. 24.95 (*0-86975-440-8*, Pub. by Ravan Pr ZA) Ohio U Pr.

Apartheid's Great Land Theft: The Struggle for the Right to Farm in South Africa. Ernest Harsch. 50p. 1986. 3.50 (*0-87348-487-8*) Pathfinder NY.

***Apartheid's Last Stand: The Rise & Fall of the South African Security State, 1978-90.** Chris Alden. LC 95-14916. 1995. write for info. (*0-312-12666-2*) St Martin.

Apartheid's Reluctant Uncle: The United States & Southern Africa in the Early Cold War. Thomas Borstelmann. LC 92-29686. 320p. 1993. 35.00 (*0-19-507942-6*) OUP.

Aparthied: The Untold Story. Corbin Seavers. 59p. (Orig.). Date not set. pap. 5.95 (*1-56411-029-X*) Untd Bros & Sis.

Apartment. Debbie Macomber. (To Mother with Love Ser.). 1993. pap. 4.99 (*0-685-61545-6*) Silhouette.

Apartment. Quin-Harkin. 1994. mass mkt. 3.50 (*0-06-106153-0*, Harp PBks) HarpC.

Apartment: An Original Screenplay, Directed by Billy Wilder. Billy Wilder et al. Ed. by George P. Garrett et al. LC 71-135273. (Film Scripts Ser.). (Illus.). 1989. pap. 19.95 (*0-89197-660-4*) Irvington.

***Apartment Book.** 32p. (J). 1995. 14.95 (*0-7894-0197-5*) Dorling Kindersley.

Apartment Building Exterior Inspection Form. 3.00 (*0-944298-43-5*, 981) Inst Real Estate.

Apartment Communities: The Next Big Market; A Survey of Who Rents & Why. Carl Norcross & John Hyson. LC 68-57114. (Urban Land Institute, Technical Bulletin Ser.: 61). 83p. reprint ed. pap. 25.00 (*0-8357-5653-X*, 2023244) Bks Demand.

Apartment Complex Recycling Guide. John P. Allison. 26p. (Orig.). (C). 1992. pap. 7.95 (*0-9632789-7-5*) RMC Pub Grp.

Apartment Development: A Strategy for Successful Decision Making. James R. McKeever. LC 74-79436. (Urban Land Institute Special Report Ser.). 64p. reprint ed. pap. 25.00 (*0-8357-5654-8*, 2023493) Bks Demand.

Apartment for Rent. Lionel Koechlin. (Child's World Library). (Illus.). 32p. (J). (ps-2). 1991. lib. bdg. 18.50 (*0-89565-742-2*) Childs World.

Apartment House Tree. Bette Killion. LC 88-35700. (Illus.). 32p. (J). (ps-2). 1989. lib. bdg. 14.89 (*0-06-023274-9*) HarpC Child Bks.

***Apartment Hunter's Guide: Boston: How to Find Your Perfect Apartment for No Money.** Edward Parks. LC 95-60224. (Illus.). 96p. (Orig.). 1995. pap. 7.95 (*0-9645575-0-9*) Tri Light Pub Grp.

Apartment Management: How to Maximize Your Profits. Rod Delson & Jeffrey Price. (Illus.). 150p. (Orig.). 1991. pap. 19.95 (*0-945909-02-0*) Idlewood Pub.

Apartment Management Contract. Ad Wittemann. 26p. (Orig.). 1984. pap. 65.00 (*0-938481-28-2*) Camelot Consult.

Apartment Three. Ezra J. Keats. LC 85-26791. (Illus.). 32p. (J). (gr. 1-5). 1986. reprint ed. pap. 3.95 (*0-689-71059-3*, Aladdin Paperbacks) S&S Childrens.

Apartment Unit Interior Inspection Form. 3.00 (*0-944298-44-3*, 982) Inst Real Estate.

Apata. Harold Bascom. (Caribbean Writers Ser.). 279p. (Orig.). 1986. pap. 8.95 (*0-435-98828-X*) Heinemann.

Apathy in America, Nineteen Sixty-Six to Nineteen Eighty-Four: Causes & Consequences of Citizen Political Indifference. Stephen E. Bennett. 202p. (C). 1986. text ed. 39.50 (*0-941320-39-1*) Transnatl Pubs.

Apathy in the Pew. Don M. Aycock. LC 87-71394. 130p. (Orig.). 1988. pap. 6.95 (*0-88270-636-5*) Bridge Pub.

Apatosaurus. David Petersen. LC 88-37654. (New True Bks.). (Illus.). 48p. (J). (gr. k-4). 1989. pap. 4.95 (*0-516-41159-4*) Childrens.

***Apatosaurus.** Janet Riehecky. LC 88-1694. (Dinosaur Bks.). (Illus.). 32p. (ENG & SPA.). (J). (ps-2). 1988. lib. bdg. 21.36 (*1-56766-131-9*) Childs World.

Apatosaurus. Janet Riehecky. LC 88-1694. (Dinosaurs Bks.). (Illus.). 32p. (ENG & SPA.). (J). (ps-2). 1988. lib. bdg. 21.36 (*0-89565-423-7*) Childs World.

Apatosaurus: The Deceptive Dinosaur. Elizabeth Sandell. Ed. by Marjorie Oelerich & Harlan S. Hansen. LC 88-39805. (Dinosaur Discovery Era Ser.). (Illus.). 32p. (J). (gr. k-5). 1989. lib. bdg. 12.95 (*0-944280-12-9*); pap. text ed. 5.95 (*0-944280-18-8*) Bancroft-Sage.

***Apatosaurus-Brontosaurus.** Graham Coleman. (Illus.). 1995. 12.95 (*0-614-01253-8*) Gareth Stevens Inc.

Apauk: Caller of Buffalo. James W. Schultz. (Native American Voices Ser.). (Illus.). 227p. 1993. reprint ed. 21.99 (*0-7835-1766-1*) Time-Life.

Apayao Life & Legends. Laurence L. Wilson. LC 77-86958. reprint ed. 18.00 (*0-404-16787-X*) AMS Pr.

APCO Legal Forms. 1988. write for info. (*0-318-57329-6*) Anderson Pub Co.

Ape & Essence. Aldous Huxley. 216p. 1992. reprint ed. pap. 9.95 (*0-929587-78-2*, Elephant Paperbacks) I R Dee.

Ape & the Whale: An Interplay Between Charles Darwin & Herman Melville in Their Own Words. Barbara Novak. LC 94-77616. (Illus.). 96p. (Orig.). 1994. pap. 12.95 (*0-943972-33-7*) Homestead WY.

Ape Ears & Beaky. Nancy J. Hopper. 112p. 1987. pap. 2.50 (*0-380-70270-3*, Camelot) Avon.

Ape Escape. Bob Reese. (Going Ape Ser.). (Illus.). (J). 1983. 7.95 (*0-89868-147-2*); pap. 2.95 (*0-89868-146-4*) ARO Pub.

Ape in a Cape: An Alphabet of Odd Animals. Fritz Eichenberg. LC 52-6908. (Illus.). 26p. (J). (ps-3). 1952. 15.95 (*0-15-203722-5*, HB Juv Bks) HarBrace.

Ape in a Cape: An Alphabet of Odd Animals. Fritz Eichenberg. LC 52-6908. (Illus.). 32p. (J). (ps-3). 1988. reprint ed. pap. 4.95 (*0-15-607830-9*, Voyager Bks) HarBrace.

Ape in Velvet see Velvet Web

Ape Man: The Story of Human Evolution. Rod Caird. Ed. by Robert Foley. LC 94-14090. 1994. 30.00 (*0-671-50146-1*) S&S Trade.

***Ape-Man Within.** L. Sprague De Camp. LC 95-6341. 250p. 1995. 25.95 (*0-87975-951-8*) Prometheus Bks.

Ape of Gods: The Art & Thought of Lafcadio Hearn. Beongcheon Yu. LC 64-10090. 361p. reprint ed. pap. 102.90 (*0-7837-3612-6*, 2043478) Bks Demand.

***Ape or Adam? Our Roots According to the Book of Genesis.** William Van der Zee. 120p. 1995. pap. 19.50 (*1-886670-03-X*) Genesis Publ.

Ape Team. Bob Reese. (Going Ape Ser.). (Illus.). (J). 1983. 7.95 (*0-89868-145-6*); pap. 2.95 (*0-89868-144-8*) ARO Pub.

Ape That Spoke. John McCrone. 288p. 1992. pap. 10.00 (*0-380-71399-3*) Avon.

Ape Woman Story. Nancy Harris. LC 89-62108. 68p. (Orig.). 1989. pap. 8.00 (*0-944100-03-1*) Pirogue Pub.

***APEC Challenges & Opportunities.** Ed. by Chai Siow Yue. (APEC Ser.). 196p. 1994. pap. text ed. 31.95 (*981-3016-92-2*, Pub. by Inst SE Asian Studies SI) Ashgate Pub Co.

***APEC Report.** 60p. (Orig.). 1995. pap. 165.00 (*0-7605-2381-9*) Rector Pr.

***APEC 1995 Tenth Annual Applied Power Electronics Conference & Exposition.** IEEE (Power Electronics Society, Industry Applications Society) Staff. Ed. by IEEE (Institute of Electrical & Electronics Engineers, Inc.) Staff. 1000p. 1995. lib. bdg. write for info. (*0-7803-2483-8*, 95CH35748); pap. text ed. write for info. (*0-7803-2482-X*, 95CH35748); fiche write for info. (*0-7803-2484-6*, 95CH35748) Inst Electrical.

Apedemak Lion God of Meroe: A Study in Meroitic Syncretism. Zabkar. 1975. 44.00 (*0-85668-027-3*, Pub. by Aris & Phillips UK) David Brown.

Apenas un Bolero: Novela. Omar Torres. LC 81-65511. (Coleccion Caniqui Ser.). 95p. (Orig.). (SPA.). 1981. pap. 6.95 (*0-89729-292-8*) Ediciones.

Apercus Statisques Internationaux. G. Sundbarg. (Demographic Monographs). 412p. 1968. text ed. 169.00 (*0-677-01590-9*) Gordon & Breach.

Apercus Sur Les-Utopies see Cahiers de l'Institut de Science Economique Appliquee: Bibliographie Marxologique. Liste Complementaire

***Aperiodic 1994, an International Conference on Aperiodic Crystals.** G. Chapuis. 648p. 1995. text ed. 162.00 (*981-02-2080-4*) World Scientific Pub.

Aperiodicity & Order: Icosahedral Structures, Vol. 3. Ed. by Marko V. Jaric & Denis Gratias. 225p. 1989. text ed. 92.00 (*0-12-040603-9*) Acad Pr.

Aperiodicity & Order: Introduction to Quasicrystals, Vol. 1. Ed. by Marko A. Jaric. 285p. 1988. text ed. 91.00 (*0-12-040601-2*) Acad Pr.

An Asterisk (*) at the beginning of an entry indicates that the title is appearing in BIP for the first time.

371

Aperiodicity & Order: Introduction to the Mathematics of Quasicrystals, Vol. 2. Ed. by Marko V. Jaric. 223p. 1989. text ed. 92.00 (*0-12-040602-0*) Acad Pr.

Aperture, Issue 78. Disfarmer et al. (Fine Photography Ser.). 1977. bds. 18.50 (*0-89381-014-2*) Aperture.

Aperture, Issue 82. (Fine Photography Ser.). 1978. 18.50 (*0-89381-030-4*) Aperture.

Aperture, Issue 88. Illus. by Nina Raginsky et al. (Fine Photography Ser.). 80p. 1982. pap. 18.50 (*0-89381-099-1*) Aperture.

Aperture, Issue 91. Carter Ratcliff et al. (Fine Photography Ser.). (Illus.). 80p. 1983. pap. 18.50 (*0-89381-127-0*) Aperture.

Aperture, Issue 92. Marketa Luskacovas et al. (Fine Photography Ser.). (Illus.). 80p. 1983. pap. 18.50 (*0-89381-128-9*) Aperture.

Aperture, Issue 94. Paul Bowles. (Fine Photography Ser.). (Illus.). 80p. 1984. pap. 18.50 (*0-89381-137-8*) Aperture.

Aperture, Issue 96. Illus. by William Eggleston et al. (Fine Photography Ser.). 80p. 1984. pap. 18.50 (*0-89381-151-3*) Aperture.

Aperture, Issue 97. Illus. by Gilles Peress et al. (Fine Photography Ser.). 80p. pap. 18.50 (*0-89381-155-6*) Aperture.

Aperture: Poems 1972-79. Taylor Graham. 28p. (Orig.). 1991. pap. 3.00 (*1-880575-05-1*) Hot Pepper.

Aperture: Western Spaces, Issue 98. Ed. by Mark Holborn. (Fine Photography Ser.). (Illus.). 80p. 1985. pap. 18.50 (*0-89381-168-8*) Aperture.

***Aperture Issue 138: On Location II.** LC 94-79648. (Illus.). 80p. 1995. 14.95 (*0-89381-609-4*) Aperture.

***Aperture Issue 139: Native North American Photography.** (Illus.). 80p. 1995. 18.50 (*0-89381-610-8*) Aperture.

Aperture No. 132: Immagini Italiane. 80p. 1993. pap. 18.50 (*0-89381-547-0*) Aperture.

Aperture No. 133: On Location. 80p. 1993. pap. 18.50 (*0-89381-548-9*) Aperture.

Aperture Antennas & Diffraction Theory. E. V. Jull. (Electromagnetic Waves Ser.: No. 10). 192p. 1981. boxed 109.00 (*0-906048-52-4*, EW010, Pub. by Peregrinus UK) Inst Elect Eng.

Aperture, Issue 101: The Human Street, Issue 101. Richard Avedon et al. (Illus.). 80p. 1985. 18.50 (*0-89381-183-1*) Aperture.

Aperture, Issue 102: Black Sun, The Eyes of Four, Issue 102. 88p. 1986. pap. 18.50 (*0-89381-193-9*) Aperture.

Aperture, Issue 103: Fiction & Metaphor. Illus. by Nan Goldin et al. 80p. (Orig.). 1986. pap. 18.50 (*0-89381-218-8*) Aperture.

Aperture, Issue 104: Alvin Langdon Coburn: Symbolist Photographer. Mike Weaver. (Illus.). 90p. 1986. pap. 18.50 (*0-89381-222-6*) Aperture.

Aperture, Issue 108: Witness to Crisis, Issue 108. (Illus.). 80p. 1987. pap. 18.50 (*0-89381-275-7*) Aperture.

Aperture, Issue 109: Latin American Photography, Issue 109. (Illus.). 80p. 1987. pap. 18.50 (*0-89381-276-5*) Aperture.

Aperture, Issue 110: Return of the Hero, Issue 110. 80p. 1988. pap. 18.50 (*0-89381-285-4*) Aperture.

Aperture, Issue 111: Swimmers, Issue 111. Pref. by Hans C. Adam. (Illus.). 96p. 1988. pap. 18.50 (*0-89381-332-X*) Aperture.

Aperture, Issue 112: The Storyteller, Issue 112. (Illus.). 1988. pap. 18.50 (*0-89381-286-2*) Aperture.

Aperture, Issue 113: British Photography, Issue 113. Text by Mark Haworth-Booth. (Illus.). 80p. 1989. pap. 18.50 (*0-89381-340-0*) Aperture.

Aperture, Issue 126: Haiti - Feeding the Spirit. (Illus.). 80p. 1992. pap. 18.50 (*0-89381-502-0*) Aperture.

Aperture, Issue 129: Fortieth Anniversary. (Illus.). 108p. 1992. pap. 18.50 (*0-89381-522-5*) Aperture.

Aperture, Issue 130: Explorations. (Illus.). 80p. 1993. pap. 18.50 (*0-89381-529-2*) Aperture.

Aperture, Issue 99: Bill Brandt, Behind the Camera, Issue 99. 100p. 1985. pap. 18.50 (*0-89381-181-5*) Aperture.

Aperture, No. 124: Connoisseurs & Collections. (Illus.). 80p. 1991. pap. 18.50 (*0-89381-486-5*) Aperture.

Aperture, No. 125: The Encompassing Eye: Photography As Drawing. (Illus.). 80p. 1991. pap. 18.50 (*0-89381-488-1*) Aperture.

Aperture, No. 131: Albert Renger-Patzsch. (Fine Photography Periodical Ser.). (Illus.). 80p. 1993. pap. 18. 50 (*0-89381-537-3*) Aperture.

Apertures: A Study of the Writings of Brian W. Aldiss. Brian Griffin & David Wingrove. LC 83-5514. (Contributions to the Study of Science Fiction & Fantasy Ser.: No. 8). xvi, 261p. 1984. text ed. 59.95 (*0-313-23428-0*, GRA/, Greenwood Pr) Greenwood.

Apertures to Anywhere. Phyllis Ford et al. LC 79-84675. (Salon Ser: No. 1). (Illus.). 1979. 10.00 (*0-933908-06-7*); pap. 3.95 (*0-933908-07-5*) Harper Sq Pr.

***Apes.** Eric S. Grace. Ed. by R. D. Lawrence. LC 95-2167. (Wildlife Library). (Illus.). 64p. (J). (gr. 3-6). 1995. 15.95 (*0-87156-365-7*) Sierra.

***Apes.** Casey Horton. (Endangered! Ser.). 32p. (J). (gr. 3-5). 1995. lib. bdg. write for info. (*0-7614-0212-8*, Benchmark NY) Marshall Cavendish.

Apes. Tess Lemmon. LC 92-37693. (Illus.). 32p. (J). (gr. 2-4). 1993. 15.95 (*0-395-66901-4*) Ticknor & Flds Bks Yng Read.

Apes. Annemarie Schmidt & Christian R. Schmidt. LC 92-10659. (Animal Families Ser.). (J). 1992. lib. bdg. 18.60 (*0-8368-0840-1*) Gareth Stevens Inc.

Apes. John B. Wexo. (Zoobooks Ser.). 24p. (J). (gr. 4). 1989. lib. bdg. 14.95 (*0-88682-265-3*) Creative Ed.

Apes. Wildlife Education, Ltd. Staff. (Zoobooks Ser.). (Illus.). 20p. (Orig.). (YA). (gr. 5 up). 1981. pap. 2.75 (*0-937934-03-8*) Wildlife Educ.

***Apes: They're Like Us.** Milton. 7.99 (*0-679-97284-6*) Random.

Apes & Angels. Richard E. Connell. LC 73-106272. (Short Story Index Reprint Ser.). 1977. 20.95 (*0-8369-3309-5*) Ayer.

Apes & Husbands. Frank Klock. 1970. 8.95 (*0-87505-212-6*) Borden.

Apes & Men see Corridors of Time: New Haven & London, 1927-1956

Apes & Peacocks. Rosalind Marshall. LC 91-4232. (Orig.). 1990. pap. 7.00 (*0-915541-79-3*) Star Bks Inc.

***Apes Find Shapes.** Jane B. Moncure. LC 87-11747. (Magic Castle Readers Ser.). (Illus.). 32p. (ENG & SPA.). (J). (ps-2). 1987. lib. bdg. 14.95 (*0-89565-917-4*) Childs World.

Apes Find Shapes. Jane B. Moncure. LC 87-11747. (Magic Castle Readers Ser.). (Illus.). 32p. (ENG & SPA.). (J). (ps-2). 1987. lib. bdg. 21.36 (*0-89565-364-8*) Childs World.

***Apes Find Shapes: Magic Castle Reader.** Moncure. (Magic Castle Ser.). 1993. pap. text ed. 3.95 (*1-56189-347-1*) Amer Educ Pub.

Apes, Men & Morons. Earnest A. Hooton. LC 76-134095. (Essay Index Reprint Ser). 1977. 23.95 (*0-8369-1956-4*) Ayer.

Apes of God. Wyndham Lewis. LC 81-7659. (Illus.). 642p. 1992. reprint ed. 25.00 (*0-87685-513-3*); reprint ed. pap. 15.00 (*0-87685-512-5*) Black Sparrow.

Apes of the World: Their Social Behavior, Communication, Mentality & Ecology. Russell H. Tuttle. LC 86-17960. (Illus.). 421p. 1987. 55.00 (*0-8155-1104-3*) Noyes.

Apex Treasury of Underground Comics: The Best of Bijou Funnies. (Illus.). 352p. 1991. reprint ed. pap. 14.95 (*0-685-39508-1*) Kitchen Sink.

***APhA Patient Counseling Handbook.** 1994. write for info. (*0-614-06362-0*) USPC.

Aphasia. Frederick L. Darley. (Illus.). 285p. 1982. text ed. 54.50 (*0-7216-2879-6*) Saunders.

Aphasia: A Clinical Approach. John C. Rosenbek et al. LC 90-52763. 311p. (C). 1989. pap. text ed. 36.00 (*0-89079-270-4*, 1781) PRO-ED.

***Aphasia: A Pathophysiological Key to Memory & Volitional Naming.** Cohn. 137p. 1995. lib. bdg. 67.00 (*1-56072-234-7*) Nova Sci Pubs.

***Aphasia: What Is It?** Barbara J. Lecomte. 16p. 1995. 14. 95 (*0-614-07072-4*, 1550) Speech Bin.

Aphasia, Alexia, & Agraphia. D. Frank Benson. (Clinical Neurology & Neurosurgery Monographs: Vol. 1). (Illus.). 320p. 1979. text ed. 36.00 (*0-443-08041-0*) Churchill.

Aphasia, Alexia, & Agraphia. David F. Benson. LC 79-17205. (Clinical Neurology & Neurosurgery Monographs: No. 1). (Illus.). 223p. 1979. reprint ed. pap. 63.60 (*0-7837-6266-6*, 2045978) Bks Demand.

Aphasia & Brain Organization. Ivar Reinvang. LC 85-9545. (Applied Psycholinguistics & Communication Disorders Ser.). 208p. 1985. 49.50 (*0-306-41975-0*, Plenum Pr) Plenum.

Aphasia & Other Neurogenic Language Disorders: A Coursebook. M. N. Hedge. (Illus.). 320p. (Orig.). (C). 1993. pap. text ed. 32.50x (*1-56593-263-3*, 0585) Singular Publishing.

Aphasia & Related Neurogenic Language Disorders. Leonard LaPointe. (Illus.). 256p. 1990. text ed. 46.00 (*0-86577-314-9*) Thieme Med Pubs.

Aphasia & Sensory-Perceptual Deficits in Adults. Ralph M. Retian. 173p. (Orig.). 1984. pap. text ed. 34.00 (*0-934515-00-X*) Neuropsych Pr.

Aphasia & Sensory-Perceptual Deficits in Children. Ralph M. Reitan. 208p. (Orig.). 1985. pap. text ed. 32.00 (*0-934515-01-8*) Neuropsych Pr.

Aphasia, Apraxia of Speech, & Dysarthria Samples. David E. Hartman & James P. Dworkin. (Illus.). 12p. (Orig.). (C). 1993. pap. text ed. 24.50x (*1-56593-309-5*, 0601) Singular Publishing.

Aphasia, My World Alone. rev. ed. Helen H. Wulf. LC 79-11334. 144p. 1986. pap. 12.95 (*0-8143-1823-1*) Wayne St U Pr.

Aphasia Rehabilitation: An Auditory & Verbal Task Hierarchy. Deborah Ross & Sara H. Spencer. (Illus.). 272p. 1980. 38.95 (*0-398-04031-1*) C C Thomas.

***Aphasia Rehabilitation: An Auditory & Verbal Task Hierarchy.** Deborah Ross & Sara H. Spencer. (Illus.). 272p. 1980. pap. 24.95 (*0-398-06409-1*) C C Thomas.

***Aphasia Screening Test (AST)** 2nd ed. Renata Whurr. 1995. 380.00 (*1-56593-513-6*, 1184) Singular Publishing.

***Aphasia Therapy.** 2nd ed. Code. 1991. 45.00 (*1-879105-14-4*, A012) Singular Publishing.

Aphasia Therapy. 2nd ed. Chris Code & Dave J. Muller. (Illus.). 236p. (C). 1991. pap. text ed. 39.50 (*1-879105-53-5*, A012) Singular Publishing.

Aphasia Treatment: World Perspectives. Ed. by Audrey L. Holland & Margaret M. Forbes. LC 93-18644. (Illus.). 391p. (Orig.). (C). 1993. pap. text ed. 55.00x (*1-879105-64-0*) Singular Publishing.

Aphasiology. Andre R. Lecours et al. (Illus.). 464p. 1983. text ed. 60.95 (*0-7020-1014-6*, Bailliere-Tindall) Saunders.

Aphelenchida, Longidoridae & Trichodoridae: Their Systematics & Bionomics. D. Hunt. 352p. 1993. 99.50 (*0-85198-758-3*) CAB Intl.

Aphid Parasites of the Central Asian Area. Ed. by P. Stary. (Illus.). 1979. pap. text ed. 56.50 (*90-6193-599-7*) Kluwer Ac.

Aphid-Plant Genotype Interactions. Ed. by R. K. Campbell & R. D. Eikenbary. 378p. 1990. 97.50 (*0-444-88257-X*) Elsevier.

Aphidoidea (Hemiptera) of Fennoscandia & Denmark III, Family Aphididae: Subfamily Pterocommatinae & Tribe Aphidini of Subfamily Aphidinae. Ole E. Heie. (Fauna Entomologica Scandinavica Ser.: No. 17). (Illus.). 314p. 1986. 52.50 (*90-04-08088-0*) E J Brill.

Aphidoidea (Hemiptera) of Fennoscandia & Denmark, Pt. 1: General Part. The Families Mindaridae, Hormaphididae, Thelaxidae, Anoeciidae, & Pemphigidae. O. E. Heie. (Fauna Entomologica Scandinavica Ser.: No. 9). (Illus.). 236p. 1980. pap. 48.00 (*87-87491-34-6*) Lubrecht & Cramer.

Aphidoidea (Hemiptera) of Fennoscandia & Denmark, Pt. 2: The Family Drepanosiphidae. Ole E. Heie. (Fauna Entomologica Sandinavica Ser.: No. 11). (Illus.). 176p. 1986. pap. 48.00 (*87-87491-44-3*) Lubrecht & Cramer.

Aphidoidea (Hemiptera) of Fennoscandia & Denmark, Pt. 3: Family Aphididae; Subfamily Pterocommatinae & Tribe of Subfamily Aphidinae. Ole E. Heie. (Fauna Entomologica Scandinavica Ser.: No. 17). (Illus.). 314p. 1986. text ed. 70.00 (*0-685-25031-8*) Lubrecht & Cramer.

Aphidoidea (Hemiptera of Fennoscandia & Denmark IV) Family Aphididae: Part 1 of Tribe Macrosiphini of Subfamily Aphidinae. Ole E. Heie. LC 82-231807. (Fauna Entomologica Scandinavica Ser.: No. 25). 189p. 1991. 54.50 (*90-04-09514-4*) E J Brill.

Aphids. Adapt. by Georgianne Heymann. (Nature Close-Ups Ser.). (Illus.). 32p. (J). (gr. 3-7). 1986. lib. bdg. 10. 95 (*0-8172-2717-2*) Raintree Steck-V.

Aphids: Their Biology, Natural Enemies & Control. Ed. by A. K. Minks & P. Harrewijn. (World Crop Pests Ser.: Vol. 2A). 472p. 1987. 172.00 (*0-444-42630-2*) Elsevier.

Aphids: Their Biology, Natural Enemies & Control, Vol. B. Ed. by A. K. Minks & P. Harrewijn. (World Crop Pests Ser.: Vol. 2B). 382p. 1988. 164.00 (*0-444-42798-8*) Elsevier.

Aphids: Their Biology, Natural Enemies & Control, Vol. C. Ed. by A. K. Minks & P. Harrewijn. (World Crop Pests Ser.). 322p. 1990. 141.00 (*0-444-42799-6*) Elsevier.

Aphids on the World's Crops: An Identificaton & Information Guide. R. L. Blackman & V. F. Eastop. 470p. 1984. text ed. 275.00 (*0-471-90426-0*) Wiley.

Aphids on the World's Trees. R. L. Blackman & V. F. Eastop. 1004p. 1994. 180.00x (*0-85198-877-6*) CAB Intl.

Aphorismes Civil & Militarie: A Briefe Inference upon Guicciardines Digression, 2 pts. Robert Dallington. LC 77-6869. (English Experience Ser.: No. 864). 1977. reprint ed. lib. bdg. 75.00 (*90-221-0864-3*) Walter J Johnson.

Aphorisms. Keith N. Ferreira. 1994. 13.95 (*0-533-10917-5*) Vantage.

Aphorisms. Ramon Gomez de la Serna. Ed. by Yvette E. Miller. Tr. & Intro. by Miguel Gonzalez-Gerth. LC 89-12823. (Discoveries Ser.). 214p. 1989. 26.95 (*0-935480-46-3*); pap. 13.50 (*0-935480-42-0*) Lat Am Lit Rev Pr.

Aphorisms. Georg C. Lichtenberg. 208p. 1990. pap. 7.95 (*0-14-044519-6*, Penguin Classics) Viking Penguin.

Aphorisms. Marie Von Ebner-Eschenbach. Tr. by David Scrase & Wolfgang Mieder. LC 94-14. (Studies in Austrian Literature, Culture & Thought). 88p. (Orig.). 1994. pap. 10.95 (*0-929497-86-4*) Ariadne CA.

Aphorisms: (Or Life with God the Father) Edouard Roditi. 16p. 1991. 5.00 (*0-88031-068-5*) Invisible-Red Hill.

Aphorisms & Other Observations. Joseph Prescott. 1985. 7.95 (*0-318-18396-X*) J Prescott.

Aphorisms of Orazio Rinaldi, Robert Greene, & Lucas Gracian Dantisco. Charles Speroni. LC 68-66092. (U. C. Publ. in Modern Philology Ser.: Vol. 88). 309p. reprint ed. 88.10 (*0-8357-9625-6*, 2013800) Bks Demand.

Aphorisms of Orazio Rinaldi, Robert Greene, & Lucas Gracian Dantisco. Charles Speroni. LC 68-66092. 280p. 1983. reprint ed. lib. bdg. 35.00x (*0-89370-790-2*) Borgo Pr.

Aphorisms of Siva: The Siva Sutra with Bhaskara's Commentary, the Varttika. Tr. by Mark S. Dyczkowski. LC 91-36927. (SUNY Series in Tantric Studies). 247p. (C). 1992. 39.50 (*0-7914-1263-6*); pap. 12.95 (*0-7914-1264-4*) State U NY Pr.

Aphorisms on Man. J. C. Lavater. LC 79-23298. 1980. reprint ed. 50.00 (*0-8201-1336-0*) Schol Facsimiles.

Aphorisms on Spiritual Method. J. H. Whiteman. 1993. 29. 00 (*0-86140-354-1*) Dufour.

Aphra Behn: Oroonoko or, the Royal Slave a Critical Edition. Intro. by Adelaide P. Amore. (Illus.). 130p. (Orig.). 1987. lib. bdg. 43.50 (*0-8191-6529-8*) U Pr of Amer.

Aphra Behn, the Incomparable Astrea. Victoria M. Sackville-West. (BCL1-PR English Literature Ser.). 92p. 1992. reprint ed. lib. bdg. 59.00 (*0-7812-7321-8*) Rprt Serv.

Aphraates & the Jews. Frank S. Gavin. LC 77-168102. (Columbia University. Contributions to Oriental History & Philology Ser.: No. 9). reprint ed. 20.00 (*0-404-50539-2*) AMS Pr.

Aphrodisiac Cooking. B. Carlson. (Illus.). 242p. 1993. 11.95 (*1-878488-83-X*) Quixote Pr IA.

Aphrodisiac Cooking. B. Carlson. (Illus.). 160p. 1994. 5.95 (*1-57166-007-0*) Quixote Pr IA.

Aphrodisiacs for Men: Effective Virilizing Foods & Herbs. Gary M. Griffin. (Illus.). 80p. (Orig.). 1991. pap. 9.95 (*1-879967-03-0*) Added Dimensns.

***Aphrodite: The Goddess of Love.** Manuela Dunn-Mascetti. LC 95-8281. 1996. write for info. (*0-8118-0918-8*) Chronicle Bks.

Aphrodite: The Psychology of Consciousness. Akhter Ahsen. LC 88-61344. 185p. 1988. pap. 14.95 (*0-913412-25-2*) Brandon Hse.

Aphrodite Cargo. large type ed. Alexander Fullerton. 448p. 1985. 23.95 (*0-7089-8295-6*, Charnwood) Ulverscroft.

Aphrodite, Moeurs Antiques. Pierre Louys. LC 75-41182. (FRE.). reprint ed. 30.00 (*0-404-14795-X*) AMS Pr.

***Aphrodite of Knidos & Her Successors: A Historical Review of the Female Nude in Greek Art.** Christine M. Havelock. LC 94-39539. 1995. 44.50 (*0-472-10585-X*) U of Mich Pr.

Aphrodite Rising. Steve Richmond. 66p. 1990. pap. 6.50 (*0-9625349-2-7*) Guerilla Poetics.

Api & the Boy Stranger: A Village Creation Tale. Patricia Roddy. LC 93-8359. (Illus.). (J). 1994. 14.99 (*0-8037-1221-9*); lib. bdg. 14.89 (*0-8037-1222-7*) Dial Bks Young.

API Clearinghouse Index. 3rd ed. 1988. 12.50 (*0-318-39983-0*) Am Prepaid.

API Newsbriefs. 50.00 (*0-317-46498-1*, 2-004) Am Prepaid.

***API to Directory Services (XDS) Issue 2.** X-Open Staff. (Illus.). 166p. (C). 1994. pap. text ed. 50.00 (*0-13-353509-6*) P-H.

***API to Electronic Mail (X.400) Issue 2.** X-Open Staff. (Illus.). 196p. (C). 1994. pap. text ed. 50.00 (*0-13-353517-7*) P-H.

APIC Curriculum for Infection Control Practice SD 19, Vol. III. APIC Staff. 480p. 1991. spiral bd. 70.00 (*0-8403-6493-8*) Kendall-Hunt.

Apic Membership Directory, 1992. APIC Staff. 288p. 1993. per., pap. text ed. 8.00 (*0-8403-8334-7*) Kendall-Hunt.

Apicius: Cookery & Dining in Imperial Rome. J. D. Vehling. 20.25 (*0-8446-5686-0*) Peter Smith.

Apicius - Concordantia et Index in Apicium. Ed. by Iliona Striegan-Keuntje. (Alpha-Omega, Reihe A Ser.: Bd. CXXIX). 265p. (GER.). 1993. write for info. (*3-487-09542-4*, Pub. by Georg Olms GW) Lubrecht & Cramer.

Apicius De Re Coquinaria see Cookery & Dining in Imperial Rome

APICS Dictionary 1992. 7th ed. Ed. by Cox, Blackstone & Spencer. 54p. 7.50 (*1-55822-087-9*) Am Prod & Inventory.

***Apigenin, Apigenin-7-Glucosid und Acylderivate aus Matricaria Recutita L Analytic, 14C-Markierung und Beitraege zur Pharmakokinetik.** Katharina Vogelsang-Tschiersch. (Dissertationes Botanicae Ser.: Vol. 214). (Illus.). 175p. 1994. pap. 55.95 (*3-443-64126-1*) Lubrecht & Cramer.

Aping Language. Joel Wallman. (Themes in the Social Sciences Ser.). 216p. (C). 1992. 47.95 (*0-521-40487-8*); pap. 15.95 (*0-521-40666-8*) Cambridge U Pr.

Apis: The Congenial Conspirator. David Mackenzie. (East European Monographs: No. 265). 320p. 1989. text ed. 54.00 (*0-88033-162-3*) East Eur Quarterly.

Apkritya Vidhi. S. L. Agarwal. 361p. (HIN.). 1979. 65.00 (*0-317-54829-8*) St Mut.

Apkritya Vidhi: (Law of Torts in Hindi) 2nd ed. S. L. Agarwal. (HIN.). (C). 1979. 25.00 (*0-685-39541-3*) St Mut.

APL: A Short Course. Sandra Pakin & Computer Innovations Staff. (Illus.). 176p. 1973. pap. text ed. 25.00 (*0-13-038877-7*) P-H.

APL: An Interactive Approach. 3rd ed. Leonard Gilman & Allen J. Rose. LC 91-258895. 380p. (C). 1992. reprint ed. text ed. 41.50 (*0-89464-657-5*) Krieger.

APL: An Introduction. Howard A. Peelle. 512p. (C). 1986. pap. text ed. 38.75 (*0-03-004953-9*) SCP.

APL: Developing More Flexible Colleges. Michael Field. LC 93-7216. (Further Education: the Assessment & Accreditation of Prior Learning Ser.). 160p. 1993. pap. 19.95 (*0-415-09015-6*, B0102) Routledge.

APL: The Language & Its Actuarial Applications. D. Stiers et al. (Insurance Ser.: No. 2). 240p. 1987. 92.50 (*0-444-70155-9*, North Holland) Elsevier.

APL, a Design Handbook for Commercial Systems. Adrian Smith. LC 81-16010. (Wiley Series in Information Processing). 198p. reprint ed. pap. 56.50 (*0-8357-5655-6*, 2032697) Bks Demand.

***APL Advisers.** IPM Staff. (Assessment of NVQs & SVQs Ser.). (C). 1994. 62.25x (*0-08-042122-9*, Pub. by IPM Hse UK) St Mut.

APL & Insight. Berry et al. (Orig.). 1978. pap. 6.50 (*0-917326-08-3*) APL Pr.

APL & the Bilingual Learner. Meena Wood. LC 94-13285. (Further Education: the Assessment & Accreditation of Prior Learning Ser.). 256p. 1994. pap. 22.95x (*0-415-10421-1*, B3971, Routledge NY) Routledge.

APL Compiler. Timothy A. Budd. (Illus.). 170p. 1988. pap. 31.00 (*0-387-96643-9*) Spr-Verlag.

APL Eighty-Four. (APL Quote Quad Ser.: Vol. 14, No. 4). (Illus.). 391p. 1984. pap. text ed. 32.00 (*0-89791-137-1*, 554840) Assn Compu Machinery.

APL Eighty-Six. (APL Quote Quad Ser.: Vol. 16, No. 4). (Illus.). 358p. 1986. pap. text ed. 30.00 (*0-901865-35-4*, 554860) Assn Compu Machinery.

APL Eighty-Two. (APL Quote Quad Ser.: Vol. 13, No. 1). (Illus.). 400p. 1982. pap. text ed. 32.00 (*0-89791-078-8*, 554820) Assn Compu Machinery.

APL-Fifty Years of Service to the Nation: History of the Johns Hopkins University Applied Physics Laboratory. William K. Klingaman. LC 93-77391. (Illus.). 283p. 1993. 10.00 (*0-912025-04-2*) JHU Applied Physics.

APL for the Future: Conference Proceedings of APL '90 Held in Copenhagen, Denmark, July '90. Frwd. by Per Gjerlov & Gitte Christenson. (APL Quote Quad Ser.: Vol. 20, No. 4). 435p. 1990. pap. text ed. 32.00 (*0-89791-371-X*, 554900) Assn Compu Machinery.

APL in Exposition. K. E. Iverson. (Orig.). 1976. pap. text ed. 3.50 (*0-917326-02-4*) APL Pr.

APL, Management Problems with Answers & "Kit of Tools" B. Legrand. Tr. by Julian G. Matthews. LC 83-25908. 167p. reprint ed. pap. 47.60 (*0-8357-5656-4*, 2032660) Bks Demand.

APL Programs for the Mathematics Classroom. N. D. Thomson. (Illus.). 200p. 1989. pap. 29.00 (*0-387-97002-9*) Spr-Verlag.

An Asterisk (*) at the beginning of an entry indicates that the title is appearing in BIP for the first time.

An Asterisk (*) at the beginning of an entry indicates that the title is appearing in BIP for the first time.

373

Apocalypticism in the Mediterranean & the Near East. 2nd ed. Ed. by David Hellhoim. 900p. 1988. lib. bdg. 217.50 (*3-16-145386-7*, Pub. by J C B Mohr GW) Coronet Bks.

Apocolocyntosis see Satyricon

Apocraphasis. Ray Buttigieg. pap. 5.50 (*0-932436-07-2*) Cykx.

Apocrine Glands & the Breast. Marshall B. Craigmyle. LC 84-7567. (Wiley Medical Publication). (Illus.). 92p. reprint ed. pap. 26.30 (*0-8357-4547-3*, 2037446) Bks Demand.

Apocrypha. Edgar J. Goodspeed. 1959. pap. 5.95 (*0-394-70163-1*) Random.

Apocrypha. Edgar J. Goodspeed. 1989. pap. 14.00 (*0-679-72452-4*, Vin) Random.

Apocrypha. Valerie Jones. (Miracleman Ser.). 1993. pap. 15.95 (*1-56060-180-9*) Eclipse Bks.

Apocrypha. Eric Pankey. 1993. pap. 12.00 (*0-679-74732-X*) Knopf.

Apocrypha. Robert Pinget. Tr. by Barbara Wright. LC 86-61607. 143p. 1987. 12.95 (*0-87376-050-6*) Red Dust.

Apocrypha see Oxford Illustrated Old Testament: With Drawings by Contemporary Artists

Apocrypha of Limbo. Ralph R. Toledano. LC 94-6559. 72p. 1994. 13.95 (*1-56554-066-2*) Pelican.

Apocryphal Acts of the Apostles I-II, 2 vols. in 1. William Wright. xx, 632p. 1990. reprint ed. 128.70 (*3-487-09342-1*, Pub. by Georg Olms GW) Lubrecht & Cramer.

Apocryphal Birth Stories, 2 vols., 1. Tr. by I. B. Horner & P. S. Jaini. (C). 1985. write for info. (*0-86013-151-3*, Pub. by Pali Text) Wisdom MA.

Apocryphal Birth Stories, 2 vols., 2. Tr. by I. B. Horner & P. S. Jaini. (C). 1985. write for info. (*0-86013-152-1*, Pub. by Pali Text) Wisdom MA.

Apocryphal Birth Stories, 2 vols., Set. Tr. by I. B. Horner & P. S. Jaini. (C). 1985. 100.00 (*0-86013-233-1*, Pub. by Pali Text) Wisdom MA.

Apocryphal New Testament. William Wake & Nathaniel Lardner. 340p. (Orig.). 1970. spiral bd. 13.75 (*0-7873-0923-0*) Mokelumne.

Apocryphal New Testament: A Collection of Apocryphal Christian Literature in an English Translation. rev. ed. J. K. Elliott. Tr. by Montague R. James. LC 92-38129. 1994. 49.95 (*0-19-826182-9*, Clarendon Pr) OUP.

Apocryphal Old Testament. H. F. Sparks. 990p. 1985. pap. 45.00 (*0-19-826177-2*) OUP.

Apocryphal Subject: Masochism, Identification, & Paranoia in Salvador Dali's Autobiographical Writing. David Vilaseca. LC 94-13003. (Catalan Studies: Vol. 17). 1995. write for info. (*0-8204-2581-8*) P Lang Pubs.

Apocryphon of Jannes & Jambres the Magicians: Papyrus Chester Beatty XVI (with New Editions of Papyrus Vindobonensis Greek Inv. 29456-29828 Verso & British Library Cotton Tiberius B. v f. 87) Tr. by Albert Pietersma. LC 94-4473. (Religions in the Graeco-Roman World Ser.: Vol. 119). (ENG, GEC & LAT.). 1994. 97.25 (*90-04-09938-7*) E J Brill.

Apocryphon of John & Other Coptic Translations. Howard N. Bream. 260p. (Orig.). 1987. pap. 18.00 (*0-9613805-3-5*) Halgo Inc.

Apogee. Lee Gibson. LC 91-66405. 147p. (Orig.). 1992. pap. 8.95 (*1-56002-099-7*, Univ Edtns) Aegina Pr.

Apokalupsis 1: Avatar of the Temple. Robert D. Buss. 334p. 1993. pap. 5.95 (*0-9638259-0-9*) Douglas Pubng.

Apokalupsis 2: The Beast at Bay. Robert D. Buss. 322p. 1993. pap. 5.95 (*0-9638259-1-7*) Douglas Pubng.

Apokalupsis 3: The Wrath of God. Robert D. Buss. 402p. 1993. pap. 5.95 (*0-9638259-2-5*) Douglas Pubng.

Apolcalypticism in the Western Tradition. Bernard McGinn. (Collected Studies). 336p. 1994. 89.95 (*0-86078-396-0*, Pub. by Variorum UK) Ashgate Pub Co.

Apolipoprotein Immunoassays: Development & Recommended Performance Characteristics: Proposed Guideline. 1991. 40.00 (*1-56238-117-2*, ILA15-P) Natl Comm Clin Lab Stds.

Apollinaire: Catalyst for Primitivism, Picabia, & Duchamp. Katia Samaltanos. Ed. by Stephen Foster. LC 84-2571. (Studies in the Fine Arts: The Avant-Garde: No. 45). 244p. reprint ed. 69.60 (*0-8357-1568-X*, 2070444) Bks Demand.

Apollinaire: Poet among the Painters. Francis Steegmuller. LC 78-179742. (Biography Index Reprint Ser.). 1977. reprint ed. 27.95 (*0-8369-8110-3*) Ayer.

Apollinaire & the Faceless Man: The Creation & Evolution of a Modern Motif. Willard Bohn. LC 90-55161. (Illus.). 176p. 1991. 32.50 (*0-8386-3416-8*) Fairleigh Dickinson.

Apollinaire on Art: Essays & Reviews 1902-1918. Guillaume Apollinaire & LeRoy C. Breunig. Tr. by Susan Suleiman. (Quality Paperbacks Ser.). (Illus.). 592p. 1988. reprint ed. pap. 13.95 (*0-306-80312-7*) Da Capo.

Apollinaire, Visual Poetry, & Art Criticism. Willard Bohn. LC 91-59059. (Illus.). 272p. 1993. 42.50 (*0-8387-5226-8*) Bucknell U Pr.

Apollinarianism: An Essay on the Christology of the Early Church. Charles Raven. LC 77-84706. reprint ed. 38.00 (*0-404-16113-8*) AMS Pr.

Apollinaris Sidonius, Carm. 22: Bvrgvs Pontii Leontii: Einleitung, Text und Kommentar. Norbert Delhey. (Untersuchungen zur Antiken Literatur und Geschichte Ser.: Vol. 40). x, 225p. (GER.). 1993. lib. bdg. 90.80 (*3-11-013631-7*) De Gruyter.

Apollinaris Von Laodicea und Seine Schule. Hans Lietzmann. xvi, 323p. 1970. reprint ed. write for info. (*0-318-70966-X*, Pub. by Georg Olms GW) Lubrecht & Cramer.

Apollinaris von Laodicea und seine Schule: Texte und Untersuchungen. Hans Lietzman. LC 82-45817. (Orthodoxies & Heresies in the Early Church Ser.). reprint ed. 37.50 (*0-404-62390-5*) AMS Pr.

Apollo: Origins & Influence. Ed. by Jon Solomon. 230p. 1994. 45.00 (*0-8165-1389-9*) U of Ariz Pr.

***Apollo - Saturn Launch Vehicles: A Technological History.** (Illus.). 525p. (Orig.). 1995. pap. 295.00 (*0-7605-1996-X*) Rector Pr.

Apollo & the Moon Landing. Gregory Vogt. (Missions in Space Ser.). (Illus.). 112p. (J). (gr. 4-6). 1991. lib. bdg. 15.90 (*1-878841-31-9*); pap. 4.95 (*1-878841-37-8*) Millbrook Pr.

Apollo 11. 2nd ed. R. Conrad Stein. LC 91-33220. (Cornerstones of Freedom Ser.). 32p. (J). (gr. 3-6). 1992. lib. bdg. 12.30 (*0-516-06651-X*) Childrens.

Apollo Eleven Lunar Science Conference, Jan., 1970: Proceedings, 3 vols, Set. Ed. by A. A. Levinson. Incl. Vol. 1. Minerology & Petrology. LC 72-119485. 1970. (*0-318-55135-7*); Vol. 2. Chemical & Isotope Analysis. LC 72-119485. 1970. (*0-318-55136-5*); Vol. 3. Physical Properties. LC 72-119485. 1970. (*0-318-55137-3*); LC 72-119485. c, 2000p. 1970. 1,032.00 (*0-08-016392-0*, Pub. by Pergamon Repr UK) Franklin.

***Apollo Expeditions to the Moon.** 1994. lib. bdg. 250.95 (*0-8490-6404-X*) Gordon Pr.

Apollo Expeditions to the Moon. Ed. by Edgar M. Cortright. LC 75-600071. (Illus.). 313p. 1985. reprint ed. boxed 13.00 (*0-16-004125-2*, S/N 033-000-00630-6) USGPO.

Apollo Heads for Alien Waters. O. Ignatiev. 212p. (C). 1988. 30.00 (*0-685-31595-9*, Pub. by Collets UK) Pro-Am Music.

Apollo Helmet. James Scully. LC 83-7269. (Illus.). 88p. (Orig.). 1983. 17.95 (*0-915306-39-5*); pap. 9.95 (*0-915306-38-7*) Curbstone.

Apollo in Snow: Selected Poems. Aleksandr Kushner. Tr. by Paul Graves & Carol Ueland. 1991. 19.95 (*0-374-10549-9*) FS&G.

Apollo in the Snow: Selected Poems. Aleksandr Kushner. 112p. 1992. pap. 10.00 (*0-374-52321-5*, Noonday) FS&G.

Apollo Larousse French-English, English-French Dictionary: Dictionnaire Larousse Apollo Francais-Anglais-Francais. Jean Mergault. 1028p. (ENG & FRE.). 1993. 23.95 (*0-7859-4734-5*) Fr & Eur.

Apollo Larousse French-German, German-French Dictionary: Dictionnaire Larousse Apollo Francais-Allemand-Francais. J. Clediere & D. Rocher. 1120p. (FRE & GER.). 1981. 24.95 (*0-8288-0339-0*, M14160) Fr & Eur.

Apollo Reservations & Ticketing. Philip Davidoff et al. LC 93-39910. (C). 1994. text ed. 35.95 (*0-256-15638-7*) Irwin.

Apollo Soyuz Mission Report. Ed. by Chester M. Lee. LC 57-43769. (Advances in the Astronautical Sciences Ser.: Vol. 34). (Illus.). 1977. lib. bdg. 35.00 (*0-87703-089-8*, Univelt Inc) Univelt Inc.

Apollo the Wolf-God. Daniel Gershenson. (Journal of Indo-European Studies Monograph: No. 8). 156p. (C). 1992. text ed. 25.00 (*0-941694-38-0*) Inst Study Man.

Apollo to the Moon. Gregory P. Kennedy. (World Explorers Ser.). (Illus.). 112p. (YA). (gr. 5 up). 1992. lib. bdg. 18.95 (*0-7910-1322-7*) Chelsea Hse.

Apollo Versus the Echomaker: A Langian Approach to Psychotherapy Dreams & Shamanism. Anthony Lunt. 1990. pap. 12.95 (*1-85230-153-8*, Pub. by Element Bks UK) Element MA.

***Apollo 13: Life in Space.** S. A. Kramer. LC 95-13069. (J). 1995. lib. bdg. write for info. (*0-448-41122-9*, G&D); pap. write for info. (*0-448-41121-0*, G&D) Putnam Pub Group.

***Apollo 13: Space Race.** Gail Herman. LC 95-13070. (All Aboard Reading Ser.). (Illus.). (J). (gr. 2-3). 1995. write for info. (*0-448-41117-2*, G&D) Putnam Pub Group.

***Apollo 13: The Junior Novelization.** Adapt. by Dina Anastasio. LC 95-14173. (J). 1995. write for info. (*0-448-41120-2*, G&D) Putnam Pub Group.

***Apollo 13: The Movie Storybook.** Adapt. by Jane B. Mason. LC 95-13068. (J). 1995. write for info. (*0-448-41119-9*, G&D) Putnam Pub Group.

Apollodori Atheniensis Biliothecae Libri Tres et Fragmenta. Apollodorus Atheniensis. (Illus.). lvi, 468p. 1972. reprint ed. write for info. (*3-487-04299-1*, Pub. by Georg Olms GW) Lubrecht & Cramer.

Apollodoros the Son of Pasion. Jeremy Trevett. (Classical Monographs). (Illus.). 232p. 1992. 52.00 (*0-19-814790-2*) OUP.

Apollodors Chronik: Eine Sammlung der Fragmente. Felix Jacoby. LC 72-7896. (Greek History Ser.). (GER.). 1973. reprint ed. 37.95 (*0-405-04795-9*) Ayer.

Apollodorus: The Library of Greek Mythology. Tr. by Keith Aldrich. 298p. 1975. 15.00 (*0-87291-072-5*) Coronado Pr.

Apollon de Bellac. Jean Giraudoux. 1962. pap. 27.95 (*0-685-11010-9*, F103935) Fr & Eur.

***Apollon de Bellac: Avec: L'Impromptu de Paris.** Jean Giraudoux. 120p. 1947. 28.95 (*0-7859-5262-4*) Fr & Eur.

Apollonii Rhodii Argonautica. Rhodius Apollonius. Ed. by Herman Frankel. 292p. 1986. 24.95 (*0-19-814559-4*) OUP.

***Apollonius' Argonautica: A Callimachean Epic.** Mary M. DeForest. LC 94-35522. (Supplements to Mnemosyne Ser.: Vol. 142). 1994. write for info. (*90-04-10017-2*) E J Brill.

Apollonius: Conics Books Five to Seven: The Arabic Translation of the Lost Greek Original in the Version of the Banu Musa. Ed. by G. J. Toomer. (Sources in the History of Mathematics & Physical Sciences Ser.: Vol. 9). (Illus.). xcv, 549p. 1990. 129.00 (*0-387-97216-1*) Spr-Verlag.

Apollonius Dyscole. Emile Egger. (Documenta Semiotica, Serie 1). vi, 350p. 1987. reprint ed. write for info. (*3-487-07926-7*, Pub. by Georg Olms GW) Lubrecht & Cramer.

Apollonius of Tyana. H. C. LaFontaine. (Orig.). 1993. pap. 5.95 (*1-55818-234-9*) Holmes Pub.

Apollonius of Tyana. G. R. Mead. 196p. 1980. 15.00 (*0-89005-350-2*) Ares.

Apollonius of Tyana. G. R. Mead. 170p. 1992. pap. 13.95 (*1-56459-131-X*) Kessinger Pub.

Apollonius of Tyana: A Sketch of the Life of Tyana Or the First Ten Decades of Our Era. Daniel M. Tredwell. 360p. 1992. pap. 30.00 (*1-56459-138-7*) Kessinger Pub.

Apollonius of Tyana the Philosopher - Reformer of the First Century A.D. (African Studies). reprint ed. 20.00 (*0-938818-71-6*) ECA Assoc.

Apollonius of Tyana, the Philosopher-Reformer of the First Century A.D. B. A. Mead. 159p. 1964. spiral bd. 8.25 (*0-7873-0600-2*) Mokelumne.

Apollonius of Tyre: Medieval & Renaissance Themes & Variations. Elizabeth Archibald. 288p. (C). 1991. text ed. 71.00 (*0-85991-316-3*) Boydell & Brewer.

Apollonius Rhodius - Index Verborum of Apollonius Rhodius. Ed. by Malcolm Campbell. (Alpha-Omega, Reihe A Ser.: Bd. LXII). viii, 292p. (GER.). 1983. write for info. (*3-487-07342-0*, Pub. by Georg Olms GW) Lubrecht & Cramer.

Apollonius Rhodius, Argonautica: Index Verborum. August Wellauer. 117p. 1970. reprint ed. write for info. (*0-318-72086-8*, Pub. by Georg Olms GW) Lubrecht & Cramer.

Apollonius Rhodius, Argonautica - Index Verborum. August Wellauer. 117p. (GER.). 1970. reprint ed. write for info. (*0-318-70484-6*, Pub. by Georg Olms GW); reprint ed. write for info. (*0-318-71060-9*, Pub. by Georg Olms GW) Lubrecht & Cramer.

Apollonius the Nazarene: Mystery Man of the Bible. Raymond W. Bernard. (Essene-Jesus-Apollonius Ser.: Vol. 3). 57p. 1956. reprint ed. spiral bd. 6.60 (*0-7873-1211-8*) Mokelumne.

Apollonius Von Tyros. Samuel Singer. vi, 228p. 1974. reprint ed. write for info. (*3-487-05304-7*, Pub. by Georg Olms GW) Lubrecht & Cramer.

Apollo's Day: Seventeenth Century Songs. Ed. by Richard O'Connell. 1969. pap. 10.00 (*0-685-62618-0*) Atlantis Edns.

Apollo's Seed. large type ed. Anne Mather. 278p. (Orig.). 1992. 21.95 (*0-7505-0385-8*, Pub. by Magna Print Bks) Ulverscroft.

Apollyon. Robert Stein. LC 85-13723. 237p. (Orig.). 1985. pap. 7.95 (*0-87414-037-4*) U IA Pubns Dept.

Apolo Milton Obote & His Times. G. A. Gingyera-Pinycwa. LC 73-91414. (Studies in East African Society & History). (Illus.). 1977. text ed. 21.50 (*0-88357-034-3*); pap. text ed. 7.95 (*0-88357-035-1*) NOK Pubs.

Apologetica Cristiana. William Dyrness. Tr. by Alirio E. Vilaire. 224p. (Orig.). 1989. pap. 5.95 (*0-311-05043-3*) Casa Bautista.

Apologetical Reply to a Book Called: An Answer to the Unjust Complaint of W.B. John Davenport. (English Experience Ser.: No. 792). 1977. reprint ed. lib. bdg. 50.00 (*90-221-0792-2*) Walter J Johnson.

Apologetics. Paul J. Glenn. LC 80-51330. 303p. 1980. reprint ed. pap. 9.00 (*0-89555-157-8*) TAN Bks Pubs.

Apologetics in the New Age: A Christian Critique of Pantheism. David K. Clark & Norman L. Geisler. LC 90-32058. 256p. (Orig.). 1990. pap. 15.99 (*0-8010-2544-3*) Baker Bk.

Apologetics to the Glory of God: An Introduction. John M. Frame. 280p. (Orig.). 1994. pap. 14.99 (*0-87552-243-2*) Presby & Reformed.

Apologia: Contextualization, Globalization, & Mission in Theological Education. Max L. Stackhouse et al. LC 87-33080. 253p. reprint ed. pap. 72.20 (*0-7837-6571-1*, 2046136) Bks Demand.

Apologia & Florida of Apuleius of Madaura. Madaurensis Apuleius. Tr. by H. E. Butler. LC 72-95084. 238p. 1970. reprint ed. text ed. 39.75 (*0-8371-3066-2*, APAF, Greenwood Pr) Greenwood.

Apologia & Two Folk Plays: The Crownbride, & Swanwhite. August Strindberg. Tr. by Walter Johnson. LC 80-51072. (Illus.). 244p. 1981. 30.00 (*0-295-95760-3*) U of Wash Pr.

Apologia de Socrates. Criton. Carta VII. Platon. Ed. & Tr. by Enrique Lopez Castellon. (Nueva Austral Ser.: Vol. 164). (SPA.). 1991. pap. text ed. 24.95x (*84-239-1964-1*) Elliots Bks.

Apologia Franchini Gafurii. Franchinus Gafurius. (Monuments of Music & Music Literature in Facsimile: Series II, Vol. 96). 1979. reprint ed. lib. bdg. 35.00 (*0-8450-2296-2*) Broude.

Apologia of Plato. Plato. Ed. by James Riddell. 244p. (GER.). 1974. reprint ed. 50.70 (*3-487-05225-3*, Pub. by Georg Olms GW) Lubrecht & Cramer.

Apologia of Robert Keayne: The Self-Portrait of a Puritan Merchant. Bernard Bailyn. 11.25 (*0-8446-0470-4*) Peter Smith.

Apologia Pro Marcel Lefebvre, Vol. 1. 3rd ed. Michael Davies. 461p. 1992. reprint ed. pap. text ed. 13.95 (*0-935952-00-4*) Angelus Pr.

Apologia Pro Marcel Lefebvre, Vol. 2. Michael Davies. 393p. 1983. pap. text ed. 10.00 (*0-935952-11-X*) Angelus Pr.

Apologia Pro Marcel Lefebvre, Vol. 3. Michael Davies. 468p. 1988. pap. text ed. 10.00 (*0-935952-19-5*) Angelus Pr.

Apologia Pro Vita Sua. John H. Newman. 432p. 1993. pap. 8.50 (*0-460-87232-X*, Everyman's Classic Lib) C E Tuttle.

Apologia Pro Vita Sua. John H. Newman. 1989. mass mkt. 9.95 (*0-385-12646-8*, Image Bks) Doubleday.

Apologia Pro Vita Sua. John H. Newman. Ed. by Arthur D. Culler. (C). 1956. pap. 9.96 (*0-395-05109-6*) Norton.

Apologia Pro Vita Sua. John H. Newman. (C). 1968. pap. text ed. 12.95 (*0-393-09766-8*) Norton.

***Apologia pro Vita Sua.** John H. Newman. Ed. & Intro. by Ian Ker. 608p. 1995. 12.95 (*0-14-043374-0*, Penguin Classics) Viking Penguin.

Apologia Pro Vita Sua: Being a History of His Religious Opinions. John H. Newman. Ed. & Intro. by Martin J. Svaglic. (Oxford English Texts Ser.). 664p. 1991. 140.00 (*0-19-811840-6*) OUP.

Apologia Sive Pro Se de Magia Liber. Apuleius. (Illus.). lxvi, 208p. 1983. reprint ed. 57.20 (*3-487-01463-7*, Pub. by Georg Olms GW) Lubrecht & Cramer.

Apologie de Jerome Contre Rufin: Un Commentaire. Pierre Lardet. LC 93-13086. (Supplements to Vigiliae Christianae Ser.: Vol. 15). xxxii, 564p. (FRE.). 1993. 140.00 (*90-04-09457-1*) E J Brill.

Apologie for Bartholmew Fayre. Freda L. Townsend. (MLA Rev. Fund Ser.). 1947. pap. 10.00 (*0-527-90680-8*) Periodicals Srv.

Apologie for Poetrie. Philip Sidney. LC 70-171790. (English Experience Ser.: No. 413). 88p. 1971. reprint ed. 25.00 (*90-221-0413-3*) Walter J Johnson.

Apologie for Women or an Opposition to Mr. Dr. G. His Assertion. William Heale. LC 74-80185. (English Experience Ser.: No. 665). 66p. 1974. reprint ed. 25.00 (*90-221-0665-9*) Walter J Johnson.

Apologie or Answer in Defence of the Church of England. John Jewel. Tr. by Ann Bacon. LC 72-38204. (English Experience Ser.: No. 470). 140p. 1972. reprint ed. 30.00 (*90-221-0470-2*) Walter J Johnson.

Apologie or Defence of Such True Christians As Are Commonly Called Brownists. Henry Ainsworth & Francis Johnson. LC 70-25742. (English Experience Ser.: No. 217). 1970. reprint ed. 45.00 (*0-685-05280-X*) Walter J Johnson.

Apologies. Brian Kral. 42p. (Orig.). (YA). (gr. 9-12). 1988. 5.50 (*0-87602-278-6*) Anchorage.

Apologies & Remedial Interchanges: A Study of Language Use in Social Interaction. Marion Owen. LC 83-13375. (Linguistic Supplementary Studies). x, 192p. 1983. 70.00 (*90-279-3360-X*); pap. 21.55 (*90-279-3370-7*) Mouton.

Apologies to the Iroquois: The Iroquois & Their Neighbors. Edmund Wilson. (Iroquois Studies). (Illus.). 356p. 1992. reprint ed. pap. 15.95 (*0-8156-2564-2*) Syracuse U Pr.

Apologies to Women. Jill Mann. (C). 1991. pap. 9.95 (*0-521-42376-7*) Cambridge U Pr.

Apologists. Ford L. Battles. (Study Outline Ser.: No. 1). 1991. pap. 8.00 (*1-55635-013-9*) Pickwick.

Apology. Thomas More. Ed. by J. B. Trapp. LC 75-7949. (Complete Works of St. Thomas More: Vol. 9). (Illus.). 1979. text ed. 75.00 (*0-300-02067-8*) Yale U Pr.

Apology. Plato. Ed. by Stokes. (Classical Texts Ser.). 1992. write for info. (*0-85668-371-X*, Pub. by Aris & Phillips UK); pap. write for info. (*0-85668-372-8*, Pub. by Aris & Phillips UK) David Brown.

Apology. Tertullian. Bd. with De Spectaculis. Tertullian.; Octavius. Felix Minucius & Tertullian. (Loeb Classical Library: No. 250). 15.50 (*0-674-99276-8*) HUP.

Apology & Crito of Plato & the Apology & Symposium of Xenophon. Intro. by Raymond Larson. 122p. (C). 1980. pap. 9.00 (*0-87291-141-1*) Coronado Pr.

Apology for Actors. Thomas Heywood. Bd. with Refutation of the Apology for Actors. LC 42-8174. LC 42-8174. 1978. 50.00 (*0-8201-1198-8*) Schol Facsimiles.

Apology for Actors. Thomas Heywood. Bd. with Refutation of the 'Apology for Actors' LC 74-170415. LC 74-170415. (English Stage Ser.: Vol. 12). 1973. Set lib. bdg. 61.00 (*0-8240-0595-3*) Garland.

Apology for Apologetics: A Study in the Logic of Interreligious Dialogue. Paul J. Griffiths. LC 91-15134. (Faith Meets Faith Ser.). 128p. (Orig.). 1991. 39.95 (*0-88344-762-2*); pap. 16.95 (*0-88344-761-4*) Orbis Bks.

Apology for Christianity in a Series of Letters Addressed to Edward Gibbon. Richard Watson. Ed. by Rene Wellek. Bd. with Apology for the Bible Addressed to Thomas Paine. LC 75-25132. LC 75-25132. (British Philosophers & Theologians of the 17th & 18th Centuries Ser.). 452p. 1978. Set lib. bdg. 20.00 (*0-8240-1765-X*) Garland.

Apology for Heroism. Mulk R. Anand. (Mayfair Paperbacks Ser.). 203p. 1975. pap. 3.60 (*0-86578-074-9*) Ind-US Inc.

Apology for Lollard Doctrines, Attributed to Wycliffe. John Wycliffe. LC 80-312858. (Camden Society, London, Publications: No. 20). reprint ed. 75.00 (*0-404-50120-6*) AMS Pr.

Apology for Loving Old Hymns. Jordan Smith. LC 82-476155. (Contemporary Poets Ser.). 90p. 1982. pap. 9.95 (*0-691-01399-3*) Princeton U Pr.

Apology for Old Maids, & Other Essays. Henry D. Sedgwick. LC 68-8492. (Essay Index Reprint Ser.). 1977. 19.95 (*0-8369-0860-0*) Ayer.

Apology for Perfection. Cecil F. Hinshaw. LC 64-22766. (Orig.). 1964. pap. 3.00 (*0-87574-138-X*) Pendle Hill.

Apology for Poetry: Sidney. Ed. by Forrest G. Robinson. 128p. (C). 1970. pap. write for info. (*0-02-402560-7*) Macmillan.

Apology for Printers. Benjamin Franklin. Ed. by Randolph Goodman. LC 72-12396. (Illus.). 40p. 1973. reprint ed. pap. 3.95 (*0-87491-146-X*) Acropolis.

Apology for Raymond Sebond. Michel E. De Montaigne. 240p. 1988. pap. 9.95 (*0-14-044493-9*, Penguin Classics) Viking Penguin.

Apology for Schoole-Masters. Thomas Morrice. LC 76-57401. (English Experience Ser.: No. 817). 1977. reprint ed. lib. bdg. 20.00 (*90-221-0817-1*) Walter J Johnson.

An Asterisk (*) at the beginning of an entry indicates that the title is appearing in BIP for the first time.

Apology for Sir James Dalrymple of Stair. James D. Stair. LC 70-176008. (Bannatyne Club, Edinburgh. Publications: No. 12). reprint ed. 18.50 (*0-404-52712-4*) AMS Pr.

Apology for the Believers in the Shakespeare Papers Which Were Exhibited in Norfolk Street. George Chalmers. 628p. 1971. reprint ed. 45.00 (*0-7146-2531-0*, Pub. by F Cass Pubs UK) Intl Spec Bk.

Apology for the Bible Addressed to Thomas Paine see Apology for Christianity in a Series of Letters Addressed to Edward Gibbon

Apology for the Life of Colley Cibber Written by Himself, 2 Vols. rev. ed. Colley Cibber. Ed. by R. W. Lowe. LC 25-7679. reprint ed. 125.00 (*0-404-01544-1*) AMS Pr.

Apology for the Life of James Fennell. James Fennell. LC 77-82826. 1972. reprint ed. 30.95 (*0-405-08499-4*, Pub. by Blom Pubns UK) Ayer.

Apology of Appeale: Also, an Epistle to the True Hearted Nobility. Henry Burton. LC 76-57364. (English Experience Ser.: No. 782). 1977. reprint ed. lib. bdg. 20.00 (*90-221-0782-5*) Walter J Johnson.

Apology of Plato. Plato. LC 72-9300. (Philosophy of Plato & Aristotle Ser.). (ENG & GRE.). 1977. reprint ed. 19.95 (*0-405-04855-6*) Ayer.

Apology of Socrates see Euthyphro

Apology of Socrates & Crito. rev. ed. Plato. Ed. by A. S. Ash. Tr. by Benjamin Jowett. LC 86-64057. (Humanist Classics Ser.). 48p. 1990. pap. 4.00 (*0-942208-05-6*) Bandanna Bks.

Apology of Socrates & Crito. Plato. Ed. by Louis Dyer. (College Classical Ser.). 246p. (C). 1992. reprint ed. lib. bdg. 32.50 (*0-89241-000-0*); reprint ed. pap. 17.50 (*0-89241-345-X*) Caratzas.

Apology to Apostrophe: Autobiography & the Rhetoric of Self-Representation in Spain. James D. Fernandez. LC 92-4879. 192p. 1992. 24.95 (*0-8223-1254-9*) Duke.

***Apology to Native Hawaiians: On Behalf of the U. S. for the Overthrow of the Kingdom of Hawaii.** U. S. Congress Staff. 48p. (Orig.). 1994. pap. 5.95 (*0-9643829-0-3*) Blue-Green Delta.

Apology to Women: Christian Images of the Female Sex. Ann Brown. (Illus.). 224p. 1991. pap. 13.99 (*0-8308-5470-3*, 5470, Pub. by IVP UK) InterVarsity.

Apologye of Syr Thomas More. Ed. by A. I. Taft. (EETS, OS Ser.: No. 180). 1972. reprint ed. 56.00 (*0-527-00177-5*) Periodicals Srv.

Apolonius Von Tyrus, Griseldis, Lucidarius. (Deutsche Volksbucher in Faksimiledrucken, Reihe A Ser.: Bd. 2). 1975. reprint ed. write for info. (*3-487-05089-7*, Pub. by Georg Olms GW) Lubrecht & Cramer.

Apolyge of Syr Thomas More. Thomas More. LC 72-221. (English Experience Ser.: No. 228). 1970. reprint ed. 65.00 (*90-221-0228-9*) Walter J Johnson.

Apomixis & Its Role in Evolution & Breeding. Ed. by D. F. Petrov. Tr. by B. R. Sharma. 275p. (C). 1984. text ed. 55.00 (*90-6191-437-X*, Pub. by A A Balkema NE) Ashgate Pub Co.

Apomixis in Angiosperms: Nucellar & Integumentary Embryony. T. N. Naumova. Tr. by I. Mershchikova. 1992. 130.95 (*0-8493-4570-7*, QK826) CRC Pr.

Apomixis in Plants. Asker. 1992. 173.00 (*0-8493-4545-6*, QK826) CRC Pr.

Apophthegmata Patrum. E. A. Budge. 150p. 1975. pap. 5.95 (*0-89981-008-X*) Eastern Orthodox.

Apophthegmes New & Old. Francis Bacon. LC 73-38144. (English Experience Ser.: No. 424). 310p. 1972. reprint ed. 45.00 (*90-221-0424-9*) Walter J Johnson.

Apophthegmes, That Is to Saie, Prompte Saiynges. Desiderius Erasmus. Tr. by Nicholas Udall. LC 76-6160. (English Experience Ser.: No. 99). 1969. reprint ed. 125.00 (*90-221-0099-5*) Walter J Johnson.

Apoptosis. Ed. by E. Mihich & R. T. Schimke. (Pezcoller Symposium Ser.: Vol. 5). (Illus.). 283p. (C). 1994. text ed. 89.50 (*0-306-44733-9*, Plenum Pr) Plenum.

Apoptosis: The Molecular Basis of Cell Death. Ed. by L. David Tomei & Frederick O. Cope. (Current Communications in Cell & Molecular Biology Ser.: No. 3). (Illus.). 336p. (C). 1991. pap. text ed. 44.00 (*0-87969-366-5*) Cold Spring Harbor.

***Apoptosis & Cell Cycle Control in Cancer: Basic Mechanisms & Implications for Treating Malignant Disease.** Ed. by N. S. Thomas. (UCL Molecular Pathology Ser.). 300p. 1995. 157.50 (*1-872748-89-9*, Pub. by Bios Scientific UK) Coronet Bks.

Apoptosis & Oncology. Christopher A. Smith. (Molecular Biology Intelligence Unit Ser.). 115p. 1994. 89.95 (*1-57059-099-0*, LN9099) R G Landes.

***Apoptosis & the Immune System.** Ed. by Christopher D. Gregory. LC 94-41047. 1995. text ed. 89.95 (*0-471-01251-3*) Wiley.

***Apoptosis in Hormone Dependent Cancers.** Ed. by Martin Tenniswood & Horst Michna. LC 95-952. (Ernst Schering Research Foundation Workshop Ser.: Vol. 14). 1995. write for info. (*3-540-58840-X*); write for info. (*0-387-58840-X*) Spr-Verlag.

***Apoptosis in Immunology.** Ed. by G. Kroemer & C. Martinez-A. (Current Topics in Microbiology & Immunology Ser.: Vol. 200). (Illus.). 260p. 1995. text ed. 128.00 (*3-540-58756-X*) Spr-Verlag.

Apoptosis Two: The Molecular Basis of Apoptosis in Disease. Ed. by L. David Tomei & Fred O. Cope. (Current Communications in Cell & Molecular Biology Ser.: No. 8). (Illus.). 300p. (C). 1994. pap. text ed. 65.00 (*0-87969-395-9*) Cold Spring Harbor.

Aporias. Jacques Derrida. Tr. by Thomas Dutoit. 104p. (C). 1994. 29.50 (*0-8047-2233-1*); pap. 12.95 (*0-8047-2252-8*) Stanford U Pr.

Apostasy: A Study in the Epistle to the Hebrews & in Baptist History. Dale Moody. 84p. (Orig.). 1991. pap. text ed. 6.95 (*0-9628455-3-1*) Smyth & Helwys.

Apostasy & Reform in the Revelations of St. Birgitta. Ingvar Fogelqvist. (Bibliotheca Theologiae Practicae Kyrkov Studier Ser.: No. 51). 262p. (Orig.). 1993. pap. 43.00x (*91-22-01572-8*, Pub. by Almqv & Wiksell SW) Coronet Bks.

Apostasy & the Antichrist. 46p. (Orig.). 1978. pap. 3.00 (*0-317-30297-3*) Holy Trinity.

Apostasy from the Gospel. John Owen. 184p. 1992. reprint ed. pap. 6.95 (*0-85151-609-2*) Banner of Truth.

Apostasy of the Last Days. James A. Stewart. 1964. pap. 1.99 (*1-56632-034-8*) Revival Lit.

Apostasy Within: The Demonic in the (Catholic) American Church. Paul Trinchard. LC 87-72185. 1989. pap. 14.95 (*0-8158-0447-4*) Chris Mass.

***Apostasy Within: The Demonic in the Catholic American Church.** Paul Trinchard. Date not set. pap. 14.95 (*0-8158-4447-6*) Chris Mass.

***Apostates: A Biblical Study for Local Churches.** Ed J. MacWilliams. 1995. ring bd. 12.95 (*1-878897-03-9*) Blueprint Revival.

Apostelspiel: Knaben Spiegel see Saemtliche Werke

Apostle. John Pollock. 312p. (Orig.). 1994. pap. 5.99 (*1-56476-242-4*, Victor Books) SP Pubns.

Apostle Arnold: The Life & Death of Arnold Toynbee (1852-1883) Alon Kadish. LC 85-25265. xiv, 286p. 1986. 48.00 (*0-8223-0489-9*) Duke.

Apostle Bas-Relief at Saint-Denis. Sumner M. Crosby. LC 71-179471. (Yale Publications in the History of Art: No. 21). (Illus.). 224p. reprint ed. pap. 63.90 (*0-8357-5657-2*, 2021993) Bks Demand.

Apostle Islands. National Park Service Staff & Mobium Corporation Staff. LC 87-600289. (Handbook Ser.: No. 141). (Illus.). 64p. (Orig.). 1988. pap. 2.25 (*0-912627-35-2*) Natl Park Serv.

Apostle Islands: A Guide to Apostle Islands National Lakeshore, Wisconsin. (Illus.). 64p. (Orig.). 1987. pap. 2.25 (*0-16-003545-7*, S/N 024-005-01023-8) USGPO.

Apostle Islands National Lakeshore. Kate Crowley & Mike Link. (Voyageur Wilderness Ser.). (Illus.). 96p. (Orig.). 1988. pap. 16.95 (*0-89658-084-9*) Voyageur Pr.

Apostle Islands National Lakeshore, WI. (Illus.). 1993. 8.99 (*1-56695-008-2*) Trails Illustrated.

Apostle John: His Life & Writings. W. Griffith Thomas. LC 84-785. 376p. (C). 1984. reprint ed. pap. 12.99 (*0-8254-3822-5*) Kregel.

Apostle of Life. Paul Marx. (Illus.). 204p. 1991. 12.95 (*1-55922-028-7*); pap. 6.95 (*1-55922-029-5*) Human Life Intl.

Apostle of Peace: Memoir of William Ladd. John Hemmenway. LC 70-137544. 272p. 1972. reprint ed. lib. bdg. 32.95 (*0-89198-072-5*) Ozer.

Apostle Paul: A History of the Development of the Doctrine of St. Paul. A. Sabatier. 1977. lib. bdg. 59.95 (*0-8490-1442-5*) Gordon Pr.

Apostle Paul: An Introduction to His Writings & Teaching. Marion L. Soards. 224p. (Orig.). 1987. pap. 11.95 (*0-8091-2864-0*) Paulist Pr.

Apostle Paul: Male Chauvinist or Proponent of Equality? Philip A. Cunningham. 24p. (Orig.). 1986. pap. 4.25 (*0-937997-03-X*) Hi-Time Pub.

Apostle Paul, Christian Jew: Faithfulness & Law. Edwin D. Freed. LC 93-43078. 272p. (Orig.). 1994. lib. bdg. 49.50 (*0-8191-9425-5*); pap. text ed. 32.50 (*0-8191-9426-3*) U Pr of Amer.

***Apostle Paul, His Life & His Testimony: The 23rd Annual Sidney B. Sperry Symposium.** Sperry Symposium Staff. LC 94-38322. 1994. 5.45 (*0-87579-887-X*) Deseret Bk.

Apostle Paul Pressing on to Greece. Fred B. Cook, Jr. 111p. (Orig.). 1987. pap. 9.95 (*0-9614001-1-0*) Cook MO.

Apostle Paul's Letter from Prison. Ed. by Bennie Goodwin. 64p. (Orig.). 1993. teacher ed 5.50 (*0-940955-24-5*); pap. text ed. 6.50 (*0-685-63573-2*) Urban Ministries.

Apostle Peter: His Life & Writings. W. Griffith Thomas. LC 84-1493. 304p. (C). 1984. reprint ed. pap. 10.99 (*0-8254-3823-3*) Kregel.

Apostle to the Nations. T. W. Buckley. 1981. 15.00 (*0-8198-0710-9*); 14.00 (*0-8198-0711-7*) Pauline Bks.

Apostles. Donald Guthrie. 422p. 1981. pap. 19.99 (*0-310-25421-3*) Zondervan.

Apostles' Creed. Inos Biffi. LC 93-39151. (My First Catechism Ser.). (Illus.). 48p. (J). 1994. pap. 9.99 (*0-8028-3756-5*) Eerdmans.

Apostles' Creed: A Faith to Live By. C. E. Cranfield. 72p. (Orig.). 1993. pap. text ed. 7.99 (*0-8028-0709-7*) Eerdmans.

Apostles' Creed: Beliefs That Matter. Stuart Briscoe. LC 93-41884. 250p. 1994. pap. 8.99 (*0-87788-052-2*) Shaw Pubs.

Apostles' Creed: Fresh Water from An Ancient Spring. James O. Speed, Jr. Ed. by Alexa Selph. LC 87-15772. 160p. 1987. 13.95 (*0-87797-144-7*) Cherokee.

Apostles' Doctrine of the Atonement. George Smeaton. 568p. 1991. text ed. 23.95 (*0-85151-599-1*) Banner of Truth.

Apostles Extraordinary: A Celebration of Saints & Sinners. Geddes MacGregor. LC 85-22118. (Illus.). 168p. (Orig.). 1986. pap. 8.95 (*0-89407-065-7*) Strawberry Hill.

Apostles Inner Life. Andrew Murray. 1989. pap. 5.99 (*0-310-56132-9*) Zondervan.

Apostles of Jesus. J. D. Jones. LC 91-22663. 192p. 1992. pap. 8.99 (*0-8254-2971-4*) Kregel.

Apostles of Light. Ellen Douglas. (Banner Book Ser.). 320p. 1994. reprint ed. lib. bdg. 37.50 (*0-87805-737-4*); reprint ed. pap. 16.95 (*0-87805-738-2*) U Pr of Miss.

Apostles of Mediaeval Europe. George F. Maclear. LC 72-624. (Essay Index Reprint Ser.). 1977. reprint ed. 23.95 (*0-8369-2803-2*) Ayer.

Apostles of Ramakrishna. Ed. by Swami Gambhirananda. (Illus.). 1966. pap. 5.95 (*0-87481-098-1*, Pub. by Advaita Ashrama II) Vedanta Pr.

Apostles of Silence: The Modern French Mimes. Mira Felner. LC 83-48682. (Illus.). 216p. 1985. 35.00 (*0-8386-3196-7*) Fairleigh Dickinson.

Apostles of the Last Days: The Fruits of Medjugorje. Thomas Rutkoski. (Illus.). 285p. (Orig.). 1992. pap. 20.00 (*0-9633667-7-7*) Gospa Missions.

Apostles of the Self-Made Man. John G. Cawelti. 296p. 1988. pap. text ed. 14.95 (*0-226-09870-2*, Midway Reprint) U Ch Pr.

Apostles, Prophets & Administrators. Gordon Lindsay. 1960. per. 2.95 (*0-89985-121-5*) Christ for the Nations.

Apostol. John Pollock. 336p. (SPA.). 1990. pap. 9.95 (*0-8297-0467-1*) Life Pubs Intl.

Apostol Extraterrestre: Apostle from Space. Gordon Harris. (SPA.). 4.95 (*84-7228-474-3*, 360025, Pub. by Edit Clie SP) TSELF.

Apostol Pedro: Peter the Apostle. W. Griffith Thomas. (SPA.). 7.95 (*84-7228-930-3*, 220998, Pub. by Edit Clie SP) TSELF.

Apostolate of Holy Motherhood. Ed. by Mark I. Miravalle. LC 91-62526. 144p. (Orig.). 1991. pap. 3.00 (*1-877678-18-X*) Riehle Found.

Apostolic Catechism. D. Rayford Bell. LC 84-90806. 60p. 1984. 1.50 (*0-317-39381-2*) D R Bell.

Apostolic Ceremony of Marriage: Victory Collection. Robert H. Prince. Ed. by Dorothy Koger. 1992. pap. text ed. write for info. (*1-882821-10-6*) DPK Pubns.

Apostolic Christianity see History of the Christian Church

Apostolic Church. Everett F. Harrison. LC 84-26061. 263p. (Orig.). reprint ed. pap. 75.00 (*0-8357-8561-0*, 2034917) Bks Demand.

***Apostolic Digest.** abr. ed. Michael Malone. 190p. Date not set. pap. 9.95 (*1-885692-00-5*) Cath Treas.

Apostolic Faith: Protestants & Roman Catholics. Frederick W. Norris. 206p. (Orig.). 1992. pap. text ed. 14.95 (*0-8146-5029-5*) Liturgical Pr.

Apostolic Faith in America. Ed. by Thaddeus D. Horgan. (Faith & Order Ser.). 1988. pap. 5.99 (*0-8028-0415-2*) Eerdmans.

Apostolic Fathers. Tr. by Francis X. Grimm et al. LC 47-31345. (Fathers of the Church Ser.: Vol. 1). 412p. 1947. 21.95 (*0-8132-0001-6*) Cath U Pr.

Apostolic Fathers. Simon Tugwell. LC 89-28406. (Outstanding Christian Thinkers Ser.). 160p. 1990. pap. 9.95 (*0-8192-1491-4*) Morehouse Pub.

Apostolic Fathers, 5 vols., Set. J. B. Lightfoot. 3024p. 1989. 99.95 (*0-943575-27-3*) Hendrickson MA.

Apostolic Fathers - Patres Apostolici, 5 vols. Tr. & Intro. by Joseph B. Lightfoot. lv, 2940p. (GER.). 1973. reprint ed. Vol. I, I & 2: S. Clement of Rome. write for info. (*0-318-70114-6*, Pub. by Georg Olms GW); reprint ed. Vol. II, 2 & 3: S. Ignatius, S. Polycarp. write for info. (*0-318-70116-2*, Pub. by Georg Olms GW) Lubrecht & Cramer.

Apostolic Fathers - Patres Apostolici, 5 vols., Set. Tr. & Intro. by Joseph B. Lightfoot. lv, 2940p. (GER.). 1973. reprint ed. 518.70 (*3-487-04687-3*, Pub. by Georg Olms GW) Lubrecht & Cramer.

Apostolic Fathers - Patres Apostolici, 5 vols., Vol. II. Tr. & Intro. by Joseph B. Lightfoot. lv, 2940p. (GER.). 1973. reprint ed. write for info. (*0-318-70115-4*, Pub. by Georg Olms GW) Lubrecht & Cramer.

Apostolic Origins of Priestly Celibacy. Christian Cochini. Tr. by Nelly Marans. LC 89-81430. 491p. (Orig.). 1990. 39.95 (*0-89870-280-1*) Ignatius Pr.

Apostolic Preaching of the Cross. Leon Morris. 1955. pap. 12.99 (*0-8028-1512-X*) Eerdmans.

***Apostolic See in the New Eastern Code of Canon Law.** Jobe Abbass. 216p. 1995. text ed. 89.95 (*0-7734-8976-2*, Mellen Univ Pr) E Mellen.

Apostolic Service Activities for Catholic Elementary School Students. Ed. by Robert J. Kealey. (Illus.). 48p. (Orig.). 1988. pap. text ed. 5.00 (*1-55833-010-0*) Natl Cath Educ.

Apostolic Succession in the Liberal Catholic Church. 2nd ed. Allan W. Cockerham. (Illus.). 1980. pap. text ed. 3.25 (*0-918980-09-7*) St Alban Pr.

Apostolic Tradition of St. Hippolytus. 2nd ed. Ed. by Gregory Dix & Henry Chadwick. LC 91-7205. 176p. 1991. reprint ed. pap. 12.95 (*0-8192-1572-4*) Morehouse Pub.

Apostolike Obedience: A Sermon. Robert Sibthorpe. LC 76-57418. (English Experience Ser.: No. 831). 1977. reprint ed. lib. bdg. 10.00 (*90-221-0831-7*) Walter J Johnson.

Apostolische Symbol, Bd. I: Die Grundgestalt Des Taufsymbols. Ferdinand Kattenbusch. xxii, 1471p. 1962. reprint ed. write for info. (*0-318-70768-3*, Pub. by Georg Olms GW) Lubrecht & Cramer.

Apostolos: The Acts & Letters of the Holy Apostles Read in the Orthodox Church Throughout the Year. Ed. by Nomikos M. Vaporis. 420p. 1980. pap. 35.00 (*0-916586-39-1*) Holy Cross Orthodox.

Apostolos Makrakis--An Evaluation of Half a Century. Constantine Andronis. 369p. (Orig.). 1966. pap. 6.95 (*0-938366-33-5*) Orthodox Chr.

Apostrophe, Colon, Hyphen. Barbara Gregorich. (Horizons II Ser.). (Illus.). 24p. (J). (gr. 3-4). 1980. student ed 3.50 (*0-89403-593-2*) EDC.

***Apostrophe Thief.** Date not set. (*0-8317-5828-7*) Smithmark.

Apostrophe Thief: A Mystery with Marian Larch. Barbara Paul. LC 93-16109. 256p. 1993. text ed. 20.00 (*0-684-19553-4*, Scribners) S&S Trade.

Apostrophe to the Skylark: The Bells of San Gabriel: Joe of Lahaina: Father Damien among His Lepers. Charles W. Stoddard. (BCL1-PS American Literature Ser.). 61p. 1992. reprint ed. lib. bdg. 59.00 (*0-7812-6867-2*) Rprt Serv.

Apostrophic Moment in Nineteenth & Twentieth Century German Lyric Poetry. Hugo Walter. (American University Studies: Germanic Languages & Literature: Ser. I, Vol. 67). (C). 1988. text ed. 36.90 (*0-8204-0690-2*) P Lang Pubs.

Apothecary. Lisa Robertson. 1991. pap. 4.00 (*0-921331-16-9*) SPD-Small Pr Dist.

Apothecary in Eighteenth-Century Williamsburg. Colonial Williamsburg Foundation Staff. (Historic Trades Ser.). (Illus.). 37p. (Orig.). 1965. pap. 2.95 (*0-910412-16-2*) Colonial Williamsburg.

Apothecary on the Street of Dreams: Little Shop of Poisons & Potions Two. Bob Liddil. (Illus.). (Orig.). pap. 12.00 (*0-926895-00-1*) B Liddil.

***Apothecary Rose Vol. 1.** Candace M. Robb. 1994. pap. 4.50 (*0-312-95360-7*) St Martin.

Apotheosis & after Life. Eugenia Strong. LC 78-103668. (Select Bibliographies Reprint Ser.). 1977. 25.95 (*0-8369-5168-9*) Ayer.

Apotheosis in Ancient Portraiture. H. P. L'Orange. (Illus.). 156p. 1982. reprint ed. lib. bdg. 55.00 (*0-89241-149-X*) Caratzas.

Apotheosis of Captain Cook: European Myth-Making in the Pacific. Gananath Obeyesekere. (Illus.). 272p. 1992. text ed. 39.50 (*0-691-05680-3*) Princeton U Pr.

Apotheosis of Captain Cook: European Mythmaking in the Pacific. Gananath Obeyesekere. (C). 1994. pap. 12.95 (*0-691-03621-7*) Princeton U Pr.

***Apotheosis of Democracy, 1908-1916: The Pediment for the House Wing of the United States Capitol.** Thomas P. Somma. (Illus.). 152p. 1995. 65.00 (*0-87413-528-1*) U Delaware Pr.

Appalachee Red. Illus. by Benny Andrews. LC 87-5901. (Brown Thrasher Bks.). 298p. 1987. reprint ed. pap. 10.95 (*0-8203-0961-3*) U of Ga Pr.

***Appalachia: A Meditation.** Albert J. Fritsch. LC 86-10457. (Illus.). 159p. (C). 1986. pap. 6.35 (*0-8294-0536-4*, Campion Bks) Loyola Univ Pr.

Appalachia: The Voices of Sleeping Birds. Cynthia Rylant. (Illus.). 32p. (J). (gr. k up). 1991. 14.95 (*0-15-201605-8*) HarBrace.

Appalachia in an International Context. Ed. by Phillip J. Obermiller & William W. Philliber. LC 94-6380. 256p. 1994. text ed. 55.00 (*0-275-94835-8*, Praeger Pubs) Greenwood.

Appalachia in the Sixties: Decade of Reawakening. Ed. by David S. Walls & John B. Stephenson. LC 78-160052. 273p. reprint ed. pap. 77.90 (*0-7837-5783-2*, 2045449) Bks Demand.

***Appalachia Inside Out: Conflict & Change.** Ed. by Robert J. Higgs et al. LC 94-18718. (Illus.). 376p. (C). 1995. lib. bdg. 35.00x (*0-87049-873-8*); pap. text ed. 17.00x (*0-87049-874-6*) U of Tenn Pr.

***Appalachia Inside Out: Culture & Custom.** Ed. by Robert J. Higgs et al. LC 94-18718. (Illus.). 432p. (C). 1995. pap. 35.00x (*0-87049-875-4*); pap. text ed. 17.00x (*0-87049-876-2*) U of Tenn Pr.

Appalachia on Our Mind: The Southern Mountains & Mountaineers in the American Consciousness, 1870-1920. Henry D. Shapiro. LC 77-2301. xvi, 376p. 1986. pap. 14.95 (*0-8078-4158-7*) U of NC Pr.

Appalachian - Ouachita Orogen in the United States. Ed. by R. D. Hatcher, Jr. et al. (DNAG, Geology of North America Ser.: Vol. F2). (Illus.). 781p. 1990. 75.00 (*0-8137-5209-4*) Geol Soc.

***Appalachian Adventure.** (Illus.). 200p. 1995. 25.00 (*1-56352-234-9*) Longstreet Pr Inc.

Appalachian Authors: A Selective Bibliography. Jefferson D. Caskey. LC 90-30744. 191p. (C). 1990. lib. bdg. 25.00 (*0-933951-35-3*) Locust Hill Pr.

Appalachian Autumn. Marcia Bonta. (Nature & Natural History Ser.). 256p. (C). 1994. 34.95 (*0-8229-3784-0*); pap. 15.95 (*0-8229-5534-2*) U of Pittsburgh Pr.

Appalachian Christmas. Date not set. 7.95 (*1-56222-885-4*, 95057) Mel Bay.

Appalachian Clogging & Flatfooting Steps. Ira Bernstein. (Illus.). 170p. 1992. student ed 19.95 (*1-880160-00-5*) I Bernstein.

Appalachian Crossing - The Pocahontas Roads. Eugene L. Huddleston. 64p. (Orig.). 1989. pap. write for info. (*0-9622003-0-1*) TLC VA.

Appalachian Dulcimer Book. Michael Murphy. LC 75-35427. (Illus.). 110p. 1976. pap. 8.95 (*0-916454-01-0*) Folksay Pr.

Appalachian Dulcimer Book. Michael Murphy. (Illus.). 102p. 1987. pap. 14.95 (*0-8256-2677-3*, AM41278) Music Sales.

Appalachian Elders: A Warm Hearth Sampler. Ed. by Nikki Giovanni & Cathee Dennison. LC 91-39638. 140p. 1992. 9.50 (*0-936015-32-2*) Pocahontas Pr.

Appalachian Fiddle. Miles Krassen. (Illus.). 88p. 1973. pap. 11.95 (*0-8256-0141-X*, OK62596, Oak) Music Sales.

Appalachian Folk Songs for Recorder. Ralph W. Zeitlin. (Illus.). 24p. 1986. pap. 7.95 (*0-8256-9966-5*, AM36560) Music Sales.

Appalachian Frontiers: Settlement, Society, & Development in the Pre-Industrial Era. Ed. by Robert D. Mitchell. LC 90-42857. 360p. 1991. text ed. 43.00 (*0-8131-1733-X*) U Pr of Ky.

Appalachian Geomorphology. Ed. by T. W. Gardner & W. D. Sevon. 318p. 1989. reprint ed. 102.75 (*0-444-88326-6*) Elsevier.

Appalachian Ghost Stories. 4th ed. James G. Jones. 112p. 1992. reprint ed. pap. 8.00 (*0-87012-203-7*) McClain.

Appalachian Gold. William P. Campbell. (Illus.). 52p. 1976. 3.95 (*0-932807-04-6*) Overmountain Pr.

Appalachian Haven. Robert L. Breeding. LC 81-2312. (Tennessee History Ser.). 280p. 1981. per., pap. 10.95 (*1-880258-00-5*) Thriftecon.

An Asterisk (*) at the beginning of an entry indicates that the title is appearing in BIP for the first time.

375

Appalachian Heritage Cookbook. 2nd ed. Steelesburg Homemakers Club Staff. (Illus.). 260p. 1994. spiral bd. 19.95 (*0-936015-55-1*) Pocahontas Pr.

Appalachian Hiker, II. rev. ed. Edward B. Garvey. Ed. by Estelle Mallinoff. LC 70-146063. (Illus.). 1978. pap. 5.95 (*0-912660-15-5*) Appalachian Bks.

Appalachian Homestead: By Marge Lawsin. Anthony Giancola. 50p. 1992. pap. text ed. 4.95 (*1-881692-02-7*) Trillium WV.

Appalachian Images in Folk & Popular Culture. 2nd ed. Ed. by W. K. Mcneil. LC 94-18229. 368p. (C). 1995. pap. text ed. 23.00x (*0-87049-866-5*) U of Tenn Pr.

Appalachian Indian Frontier: The Edmond Atkin Report & Plan of 1755. Edmond Atkin. Ed. by Wilbur R. Jacobs. LC 54-12059. (Illus.). xxxviii, 108p. 1967. pap. 6.95 (*0-8032-5011-8*, Bison Books) U of Nebr Pr.

***Appalachian Karst.** Ed. by Ernst H. Kastning & Karen M. Kastning. (Illus.). 239p. 1991. pap. 15.00 (*0-9615093-5-X*) Natl Speleological.

Appalachian Legacy: Mannington Life & Spirit. Arthur C. Prichard. (Illus.). 330p. 1983. 18.00 (*0-9612788-0-3*) McClain.

Appalachian Mental Health. Ed. by Susan E. Keefe. LC 88-20557. 264p. 1988. 29.00 (*0-8131-1614-7*) U Pr of Ky.

Appalachian Mountain Homespun. Frances L. Goodrich. (Illus.). 96p. 1988. reprint ed. pap. 7.95 (*1-55709-117-X*) Applewood.

Appalachian Mountain Religion: A History. Deborah V. McCauley. LC 94-18247. Date not set. write for info. (*0-252-02129-0*); pap. write for info. (*0-252-06414-3*) U of Ill Pr.

Appalachian National Scenic Trail: A Time to Be Bold. Charles H. Foster. 232p. 1987. pap. 12.95 (*0-917953-20-7*) Appalachian Trail.

Appalachian Passage. Helen B. Hiscoe. LC 90-22168. (Illus.). 336p. 1991. 29.95 (*0-8203-1354-8*) U of Ga Pr.

Appalachian Photographs of Doris Ulmann. Intro. by J. J. Niles. LC 70-137213. 1971. pap. 12.50 (*0-912330-00-7*, Inland Bk) Jargon Soc.

Appalachian Photographs of Earl Palmer. Jean H. Speer. LC 89-24772. (Illus.). 176p. 1990. 29.00 (*0-8131-1695-3*) U Pr of Ky.

Appalachian Portraits. Photos by Shelby L. Adams. LC 93-4688. (Author & Artist Ser.). (Illus.). 108p. 1993. 45.00 (*0-87805-646-7*); pap. 25.00 (*0-87805-667-X*) U Pr of Miss.

Appalachian Regional Commission: Twenty-Five Years of Government Policy. Michael Bradshaw. LC 91-26942. (Illus.). 184p. 1992. text ed. 21.00 (*0-8131-1761-5*) U Pr of Ky.

Appalachian Speech. Walt Wolfram & Donna Christian. LC 76-15079. 198p. reprint ed. pap. 56.50 (*0-8357-3351-3*, 2039585) Bks Demand.

Appalachian Spring. Marcia Bonta. LC 90-12478. 198p. (C). 1991. 34.95 (*0-8229-3658-5*); pap. 15.95 (*0-8229-5442-7*) U of Pittsburgh Pr.

Appalachian Studies Teacher's Manual. (Illus.). 283p. 1981. pap. 7.50 (*0-9606832-1-6*) Chldrns Mus.

***Appalachian Summer.** Robert Harvey. 140p. 1995. pap. 7.95 (*1-56901-755-7*) NW Pub.

Appalachian Tale: The Adventures of the Poetry Man. Don Hirsohn. LC 86-72569. (Illus.). 128p. (Orig.). 1986. pap. 5.00 (*0-942568-14-1*) Canyon Pub Co.

***Appalachian Trail: How to Prepare for It & How to Hike It.** Jan D. Curran. (Illus.). (Orig.). 1995. pap. 14.95 (*1-56825-050-9*) Rainbow Books.

Appalachian Trail: Journey of Discovery. Jan D. Curran. LC 91-21920. 330p. (Orig.). 1991. pap. 12.95 (*0-935834-66-4*) Rainbow Books.

***Appalachian Trail Data Book, 1995.** 7th ed. Ed. by Daniel Chazin. 88p. 1994. pap. 3.95 (*0-917953-81-9*) Appalachian Trail.

Appalachian Trail Fieldbook: A Self-Help Guide for Trail Maintainers. William Birchard, Jr. & Robert D. Proudman. (Illus.). 51p. 1982. pap. 2.95 (*0-917953-08-8*) Appalachian Trail.

Appalachian Trail Fun Book. Frank Logue & Victoria Logue. (J). (ps-3). 1993. pap. 6.95 (*0-917953-60-6*) Appalachian Trail.

Appalachian Trail Guide: Maryland & Northern Virginia, with Side Trails, No. 6. 14th ed. Michael T. Shoemaker. 180p. 1993. 6.00 (*0-915746-48-4*) Potomac Appalach.

***Appalachian Trail Guide: Shenandoah National Park, with Side Trails, No. 7.** 11th ed. Jean Golightly. LC 86-61071. 352p. 1994. 7.00 (*0-915746-75-1*) Potomac Appalach.

***Appalachian Trail Guide to Central Virginia.** (Illus.). 301p. 1994. pap. 17.95 (*0-917953-64-9*) Appalachian Trail.

Appalachian Trail Guide to New Hampshire - Vermont. 7th ed. 255p. 1992. pap. 16.95 (*0-917953-51-7*) Appalachian Trail.

***Appalachian Trail Guide to Southwest Virginia.** (Illus.). 148p. 1994. pap. 15.95 (*0-917953-63-0*) Appalachian Trail.

Appalachian Trail Guide to Tennessee - North Carolina. 10th ed. 254p. 1992. pap. 16.95 (*0-917953-52-5*) Appalachian Trail.

Appalachian Trail in Bits & Pieces. Mary Sands. (Illus.). 176p. 1992. 15.95 (*0-8059-3274-7*) Dorrance.

Appalachian Trail Thru-Hiker's Companion. 2nd ed. Ed. by Joe Cook & Monica Cook. (Illus.). 144p. 1994. Spiral bdg. spiral bd. 7.95 (*0-917953-77-0*) Appalachian Trail. More than 1,200 men & women each year set out to "thru-hike" the 2,155 mile Appalachian Trail, usually from Maine to Georgia but sometimes the other way. The backcountry will be their home for the next four to six months- if they don't drop out (80% do) from discouragement, poor planning, the wrong expectations, etc. Those who stay need groceries & a post office every few days, occasionally want a restaurant meal & a real bed, or might need a doctor or an automated teller machine. The APPALACHIAN TRAIL THRU HIKER'S COMPANION, focusing on the ADVENTURE of this journey of a lifetime, provides all the basic information the thru-hiker needs about the services available in towns along the trail through 14 eastern states. Designed for on-the-trail use, it's spiral bound & 4"-by-9"in size, easy to slip in & out of a pocket or backpack. The nonprofit managers of the trail (Appalachian Trail Conference), who know of all the last-minute route changes, joined forces with volunteers from the only organized thru-hikers "alumni" group (Appalachian Long Distance Hikers Association) to produce the COMPANION for the 1995 season. Users & managers plan to update it each fall. To order contact: Appalachian Trail Conference, P.O. Box 807, Harpers Ferry, WV 25425. Ph. (304) 535-6331; FAX: (304) 535-2665. ***Publisher Provided Annotation.***

***Appalachian Trail Workbook for Planning Thru-Hikes.** 2nd ed. Christopher Whalen. (Illus.). 72p. 1993. pap. 6.00 (*0-917953-62-2*) Appalachian Trail.

Appalachian Valley. rev. ed. George Hicks. (Illus.). 118p. (C). 1992. reprint ed. pap. text ed. 8.50 (*0-88133-639-4*) Waveland Pr.

Appalachian Values. Loyal Jones. LC 94-4372. (Illus.). 144p. (YA). (gr. 8 up). 1994. 19.95 (*0-945084-43-9*) J Stuart Found.

Appalachian Waters, 1: The Delaware River & Its Tributaries. Walter F. Burmeister. LC 74-80983. 1974. 6.95 (*0-912660-19-8*); pap. 6.95 (*0-686-96660-0*) Appalachian Bks.

Appalachian Waters 2: The Hudson River & Its Tributaries. Walter F. Burmeister. LC 74-80983. 1974. pap. 6.95 (*0-912660-20-1*) Appalachian Bks.

Appalachian Waters 3: The Susquehanna River & Its Tributaries. Walter F. Burmeister. LC 74-983. 1975. pap. 8.50 (*0-912660-21-X*) Appalachian Bks.

Appalachian Waters 4: Southeastern U. S. Rivers. Walter F. Burmeister. LC 74-80983. 1975. pap. 9.95 (*0-912660-22-8*) Appalachian Bks.

Appalachian Waters 5: The Upper Ohio & Its Tributaries. Walter F. Burmeister. Ed. by Estelle Mallinoff. 600p. 1978. pap. 9.95 (*0-912660-23-6*) Appalachian Bks.

Appalachian White Oak Basketmaking: Handing down the Basket. Rachel N. Law & Cynthia W. Taylor. LC 90-12043. 328p. 1990. 4.00 (*0-87049-668-9*); pap. 18.95 (*0-87049-672-7*) U of Tenn Pr.

Appalachian Whitewater, Vol. I: The Southern Mountains. Bob Sehlinger et al. LC 85-29762. (Illus.). 232p. (Orig.). 1986. pap. 14.95 (*0-89732-129-4*) Menasha Ridge.

Appalachian Whitewater, Vol. II: The Central Mountains. Ed Grove et al. LC 85-29762. (Appalachian Whitewater Ser.). (Illus.). 216p. (Orig.). 1987. pap. 13.95 (*0-89732-130-8*) Menasha Ridge.

Appalachian Wilderness. Eliot Porter. 1988. 19.98 (*0-88486-012-4*) Arrowood Pr.

Appalachian Winter. Betsy Sholl. LC 77-93267. 72p. 1978. pap. 9.95 (*0-914086-21-9*) Alicejamesbooks.

***Appalachian Women: An Annotated Bibliography.** Sydney S. Farr. LC 80-5174. reprint ed. pap. 57.90 (*0-7837-9582-3*, 2060331) Bks Demand.

Appalachians. Maurice Brooks. LC 75-3897. (Illus.). 346p. 1995. pap. 18.95 (*0-89092-005-2*) Seneca Bks.

Appalachia's Path to Dependency: Rethinking a Region's Economic History, 1730-1940. Paul Salstrom. LC 93-39818. 240p. 1994. 30.00 (*0-8131-1860-3*) U Pr of Ky.

Appalacia. Bruce Ergood & Bruce E. Kuhre. 448p. 1993. per. 37.95 (*0-8403-8913-2*) Kendall-Hunt.

Appaloosa. Ann Hyland. 140p. 1990. 44.00 (*0-85131-506-2*, Pub. by J A Allen & Co UK) St Mut.

Appaloosa. Robert MacLeod. 144p. 1980. pap. 1.95 (*0-449-13971-9*, GM) Fawcett.

Appaloosa: The Spotted Horse in Art & History. 2nd ed. Francis Haines. (Illus.). 1972. 17.95 (*0-912830-21-2*) Printed Horse.

Appaloosa Horse. Bill Richardson & Dana Richardson. 1979. pap. 7.00 (*0-87980-182-4*) Wilshire.

***Appaloosa Horse.** Stewart. (J). 1995. pap. 5.95 (*0-516-40243-9*) Childrens.

***Appaloosa Horse.** Gail B. Stewart. (Learning about Horses Ser.). 48p. (J). (gr. 3-4). 1994. lib. bdg. 13.35 (*1-56065-243-8*) Capstone Pr.

Appaloosa Horses. Dorothy H. Patent. LC 88-4470. (Illus.). 80p. (J). (gr. 3-7). 1988. lib. bdg. 15.95 (*0-8234-0706-3*) Holiday.

Appaloosa Rising: The Legend of the Cowboy Buddha. Gino Sky. 284p. 1984. reprint ed. pap. 12.95 (*0-938190-38-5*) North Atlantic.

Apparatus & Experiments on Sound Intensity see Voluntary Isolation of Control in a Natural Muscle Group

Apparatus of Death. Time-Life Books Editors. (Third Reich Ser.). 1991. write for info. (*0-8094-7004-7*); lib. bdg. write for info. (*0-8094-7005-5*) Time-Life.

Apparatus of Empire: Appointments & Titles in the Mughal Empire, 1574-1658. M. Athar Ali. 1985. 59.00 (*0-19-561500-X*) OUP.

Apparel & Accessories. Marilyn Mathisen. Ed. by Richard L. Lynch. (Career Competencies in Marketing Ser.). (Illus.). 1979. text ed. 12.04 (*0-07-040905-6*) McGraw.

Apparel & Accessories. 2nd ed. Marilyn G. Winn. 1989. pap. 12.64 (*0-07-040908-0*) McGraw.

Apparel Manufacturing: Sewn Product Analysis. Ruth E. Glock & Grace I. Kunz. (Illus.). 817p. (C). 1990. text ed. write for info. (*0-02-344131-3*) Macmillan.

Apparel Manufacturing: Sewn Product Analysis. 2nd ed. Ruth E. Glock & Grace I. Kunz. 576p. (C). 1995. text ed. write for info. (*0-02-344142-9*) Macmillan.

Apparel Manufacturing Handbook: Analysis, Principles & Practice. 2nd ed. Jacob Solinger. (Illus.). 872p. (C). reprint ed. pap. text ed. 70.00 (*1-879570-00-9*) Bobbin Blenheim.

Apparel Manufacturing Management Systems: A Computer-Oriented Approach. Ed. by Edwin M. McPherson. LC 87-12239. (Illus.). 392p. 1988. 48.00 (*0-8155-1141-8*) Noyes.

Apparent Resistivity Observations & the Use of Square Array Techniques. G. M. Habberjam. (Geoexploration Monographs: No. 1-9). (Illus.). 1979. lib. bdg. 51.95 (*3-443-13013-5*) Lubrecht & Cramer.

Apparent Wind. Dallas Murphy. Ed. by Jane Chelias. 320p. (Orig.). 1991. mass mkt. 4.99 (*0-671-68554-6*) PB.

Apparently Incongruous Parts: The Worlds of Malcolm Lowry. Ed. by Paul Tiessen. LC 89-29719. (Illus.). 242p. 1990. 27.50 (*0-8108-2283-0*) Scarecrow.

Apparition de l'Homme. Pierre Teilhard De Chardin. (FRE.). 1956. pap. 24.95 (*0-7859-1585-0*, 202002859X) Fr & Eur.

Apparition et Autre Contes d'Angoisse. Guy De Maupassant. (FRE.). 1987. pap. 10.95 (*0-7859-2985-1*) Fr & Eur.

Apparition in April. K. N. Daruwalla. 8.00 (*0-89253-454-0*); 4.80 (*0-89253-455-9*) Ind-US Inc.

Apparition in the Glass: Charles Brockden Brown's American Gothic. Bill Christophersen. LC 92-39711. 208p. 1994. 35.00 (*0-8203-1530-3*) U of Ga Pr.

Apparitional Lesbian: Female Homosexuality & Modern Culture. Terry Castle. LC 93-13830. (Gender & Culture Ser.). 307p. 1993. 29.95 (*0-231-07652-5*) Col U Pr.

***Apparitions.** Peter Heintz. 300p. Date not set. pap. 8.95 (*1-882972-50-3*) Queenship Pub.

Apparitions. John Warner & Margaret Warner. (Illus.). 160p. (J). (gr. 6 up). 1987. pap. text ed. 7.75 (*0-89061-465-2*) Jamestown Pubs.

Apparitions. deluxe limited ed. John Ashbery et al. 60p. 1981. 50.00 (*0-935716-10-6*) Lord John.

***Apparitions: An Autobiographical Study in Parapsychology.** Kate Christie. 1965. 49.50x (*0-614-01803-X*) Elliots Bks.

Apparitions & Survival of Death. Raymond Bayless. 1989. pap. 6.95 (*0-8065-1134-6*, Citadel Pr) Carol Pub Group.

***Apparitions at Medjugorje: Divine or Demonic?** Russell K. Tardo. 140p. 1989. pap. 3.95 (*1-881210-03-0*) Faithful Wrd.

Apparitions in Late Medieval & Renaissance Spain. William A. Christian, Jr. LC 80-8541. (Illus.). 304p. 1989. 55.00 (*0-691-05326-X*); pap. text ed. 16.95 (*0-691-00826-4*) Princeton U Pr.

Apparitions of a Black Pauper's Suit. Paul Mariah. 1988. 2.00 (*0-318-41323-X*) Man-Root.

Apparitions of a Black Pauper's Suit. deluxe ed. Paul Mariah. 1988. write for info. (*0-318-64675-7*) Man-Root.

Apparitions of a Black Pauper's Suit: Thirteen Eulogies. Paul Mariah. 1975. pap. 2.00 (*0-686-18839-X*) Man-Root.

Apparitions of Our Lady. Rene Laurentin. 163p. (Orig.). 1990. pap. 13.95 (*1-85390-054-0*, Pub. by Veritas Publns IE) Ignatius Pr.

Apparitions of Our Lady at Medugorje: An Historical Account with Interviews. Svetozar Kraljevic. Ed. by Michael Scanlan. LC 84-5983. 217p. 1984. 9.50 (*0-8199-0878-9*, Frncscn Herld) Franciscan Pr.

Apparitions of Things to Come: Edward Bellamy's Tales of Mystery & Imagination. Ed. by Franklin Rosemont. 160p. 1990. 25.95 (*0-88286-164-6*); pap. 9.95 (*0-88286-165-4*) C H Kerr.

Appartement de Beistegni, Cite Universitaire: Pavillion Suisse, Ville Radieuse, & Other Buildings & Projects, 1930, Vol. VIII. Le Corbusier. Ed. by H. Allen Brooks. LC 82-15492. (Le Corbusier Archive Ser.). 576p. 1982. lib. bdg. 260.00 (*0-8240-5057-6*) Garland.

Appassionata: Poems in Praise of Love. Jose G. Villa. 83p. (C). 1993. 20.00 (*1-884861-01-6*); pap. 10.00 (*1-884861-02-4*) Bravo Edit.

Appassionata Doctrines. David Citino. 97p. (Orig.). 1986. 12.00 (*0-914946-57-9*); pap. 6.00 (*0-914946-56-0*) Cleveland St Univ Poetry Ctr.

Appeal & Writ Handbook, Civil & Criminal: With Forms. Stuart J. Faber. write for info. (*0-318-63652-2*) Lega Bks.

Appeal from Mary in Argentina: The Apparitions of San Nicolas. Rene Laurentin. Ed. by Faith Publishing Company Staff. Tr. by Juan Gonzalez, Jr. LC 90-85751. (Illus.). 160p. (Orig.). 1990. pap. 6.00 (*0-9625975-5-4*) Faith Pub OH.

***Appeal in Favor of That Class of Americans Called Africans.** Lydia M. Child. Ed. & Intro. by Carolyn L. Karcher. 288p. (C). 1996. 40.00 (*1-55849-006-X*); pap. 14.95 (*1-55849-007-8*) U of Mass Pr.

Appeal in Favor of That Class of Americans Called Africans. Lydia M. Child. LC 68-28988. (American Negro: His History & Literature, Ser. No. 1). 1969. reprint ed. 25.95 (*0-405-01808-8*) Ayer.

***Appeal International Securities Laws Handbook: International Securities Laws Handbook.** (C). 1994. 625.50 (*1-886100-00-4*) Bowne Pubng.

Appeal of Adam to Lazarus in Hell. Donald R. Hitchcock. (Slavistic Printings & Reprintings Ser.: No. 302). 1979. text ed. 62.00 (*90-279-7856-5*) Mouton.

Appeal of Civil Law: A Political-Economic Analysis of Litigation. Wayne V. McIntosh. LC 88-29592. 240p. 1990. 26.95 (*0-252-01628-9*) U of Ill Pr.

Appeal of Fascism. Alistair Hamilton. 1976. pap. 2.25 (*0-380-01025-9*, Discus) Avon.

Appeal to Arms, 1861-63. James K. Hosmer. (Notable American Authors Ser.). 1992. reprint ed. lib. bdg. 75.00 (*0-7812-3181-7*) Rprt Serv.

Appeal to Conscience: America's Code of Caste, a Disgrace to Democracy. Kelly Miller. LC 71-89390. (Black Heritage Library Collection). 1977. 11.95 (*0-8369-8633-4*) Ayer.

Appeal to Conscience: America's Code of Caste a Disgrace to Democracy. Kelly Miller. LC 69-18553. (American Negro: His History & Literature, Ser. No. 2). 1968. reprint ed. 11.95 (*0-405-01881-9*) Ayer.

Appeal to Immediate Experience. Robert D. Mack. LC 68-58803. (Essay Index Reprint Ser.). 1977. 17.95 (*0-8369-0085-5*) Ayer.

Appeal to Impartial Posterity. Jeanne M. Roland de la Platiere. LC 90-36680. 364p. 1990. reprint ed. 55.00 (*1-85477-054-3*, Pub. by Woodstock Bks UK) Cassell.

Appeal to Impartial Posterity, 2 vols., Set. Marie J. Roland de la Platiere. LC 74-37718. reprint ed. 125.00 (*0-404-56826-2*) AMS Pr.

Appeal to Justice: Litigated Reform of Texas Prisons. Ben M. Crouch & James W. Marquart. (Illus.). 304p. 1989. 30.00 (*0-292-70407-0*) U of Tex Pr.

Appeal to the American Republic. Aleister Crowley. 1993. reprint ed. pap. 5.95 (*1-55818-250-0*) Holmes Pub.

Appeal to the Christian Women of the South. Angelina E. Grimke. LC 77-82195. (Anti-Slavery Crusade in America Ser.). 1974. reprint ed. 11.95 (*0-405-00635-7*) Ayer.

Appeal to the Women of the Nominally Free States. LC 79-154068. (Black Heritage Library Collection). 1977. 18.95 (*0-8369-8779-9*) Ayer.

Appeal to the Young. Peter Kropotkin. Tr. by H. M. Hyndman. (Revolutionary Classics Ser.). 32p. 1984. pap. 5.00 (*0-88286-081-X*) C H Kerr.

Appeal Your Property Taxes -- And Win! Ed Salzman. LC 93-6671. 1993. 9.95 (*1-882877-01-2*) Panoply Pr.

Appeals. Marshall Houts & Walter Rogosheske. (Art of Advocacy Ser.). 1981. Looseleaf updates available. ring bd. write for info. (*0-8205-1049-1*) Bender.

Appeals. David Price. 439p. 1982. 104.00 (*0-906840-42-2*, Pub. by Fourmat Pub UK) St Mut.

Appeals & Writs in Criminal Cases. Dennis A. Fischer & Russel I. Lynn. (California Criminal Law Practice Ser.). 743p. 1982. 110.00 (*0-88124-093-1*, CR-33480) Cont Ed Bar-CA.

Appeals in Scottish Criminal Cases. Lord McCluskey. 1991. U.K. pap. 47.00 (*0-406-12135-4*) Butterworth Legal Pubs.

Appeals Procedure. David Price. 1981. 100.00 (*0-686-97087-X*, Pub. by Fourmat Pub UK) St Mut.

Appeals Procedure Deskbook. Mississippi Judicial College Staff. 1980. write for info. (*0-318-57054-8*) U MS Law Ctr.

Appeals to the Eleventh Circuit, 1984-1994, 3 vols. suppl. ed. George K. Rahdert & Larry M. Roth. 1000p. 1994. 42.50 (*0-685-43647-0*, D & S Pub) Butterworth Legal Pubs.

***Appeals to the Eleventh Circuit, 1984-1994.** suppl. ed. George K. Rahdert & Larry M. Roth. 1994. ring bd. 47.00 (*0-614-03174-5*) Butterworth Legal Pubs.

Appeals to the Eleventh Circuit, 1984-1994, 3 vols., Set. George K. Rahdent & Larry M. Roth. 1000p. 1994. ring bd. 180.00 (*0-409-26067-3*) Michie Butterworth.

Appeals to the Fifth Circuit, 1977-1994, 2 vols. George K. Rahdert & Larry M. Roth. 1000p. 1994. ring bd. 175.00 (*0-409-26070-3*) Michie Butterworth.

Appeals to the Fifth Circuit, 1977-1994, 2 vols. suppl. ed. George K. Rahdert & Larry M. Roth. 1000p. 1994. 50.00 (*0-685-73809-4*) Butterworth Legal Pubs.

***Appeals to the Illinois Supreme & Appellate Courts.** rev. ed. Edward J. Kionka. 104p. 1994. pap. 35.00 (*1-884146-02-3*) Illinois Bar.

Appeals to the Second Circuit: Rules of the 2nd Circuit & Federal Rules of Appellate Procedure. 6th ed. 196p. 1988. 15.00 (*0-318-41578-X*) Fed Legal Pubn.

Appeals to the Third Circuit: 1986-1990, 2 vols. Ellen Wertheimer. 770p. 1990. ring bd. 130.00 (*0-88063-081-7*) Butterworth Legal Pubs.

Appeals to the Third Circuit: 1986-1990, 2 vols. suppl. ed. Ellen Wertheimer. 770p. 1990. Latest supp. 7/90. 65.00 (*0-88063-437-5*) Butterworth Legal Pubs.

Appearance & Aesthetics in Dental Practice. D. J. Lamb. (Dental Practitioners' Handbook Ser.: No. 37). (Illus.). 128p. 1988. pap. 24.95 (*0-7236-0753-2*, Pub. by John Wright UK) Buttrwrth-Heinemann.

Appearance & Reality: A Philosophical Investigation into Perception & Perceptual Qualities. P. M. Hacker. 1991. pap. 24.95 (*0-631-18053-2*) Blackwell Pubs.

Appearance & Sense: Phenomenology As the Fundamental Science & Its Problems. Gustav Shpet. (Phaenomenologica Ser.). (C). 1991. lib. bdg. 94.00 (*0-7923-1098-5*) Kluwer Ac.

Appearance Inspection of Finished Surfaces. Thomas G. Cleaver et al. (Illus.). 80p. 1991. pap. 23.95 (*0-87389-100-7*) ASQC Qual Pr.

An Asterisk (*) at the beginning of an entry indicates that the title is appearing in BIP for the first time.

An Asterisk (*) at the beginning of an entry indicates that the title is appearing in BIP for the first time.

377

Apple Cellar. Ruth Blackett & Bonnie Millhollin. Ed. by Kathey Shreves. (Illus.). 102p. (C). 1981. 5.95 (*0-940158-05-1*) Zucchini Patch.

***Apple Companion.** Jill Vorbeck. LC 94-78780. (Traditional Country Life Recipe Ser.). (Illus.). 110p. 1994. pap. 9.95 (*1-883283-05-1*) Brick Tower.

Apple Computer Program Writing Workbook. Fred White. 96p. 1983. 4.95 (*0-86668-813-7*) ARCsoft.

Apple Computer Programs for Beginners. Fred White. 96p. 1984. 8.95 (*0-86668-035-7*) ARCsoft.

Apple Connection. Beatrice R. Buszek. 1991. pap. 11.95 (*0-920852-48-3*, Pub. by Nimbus Publishing Ltd CN) Chelsea Green Pub.

***Apple Cookbook.** Hill. 1995. 7.98 (*1-56138-494-1*) Courage Bks.

Apple Cookbook. Olwen Woodier. LC 83-48976. (Illus.). 160p. (Orig.). 1984. pap. 10.95 (*0-88266-367-4*, Garden Way Pub) Storey Comm Inc.

Apple Country Cooking. 3rd ed. Patricia B. Mitchell. 1991. pap. 4.00 (*0-925117-47-1*) Mitchells.

Apple Dining & Entertainment Club. rev. ed. Martin Lieberman. (Illus.). 54p. 1988. pap. 6.95 (*0-943711-01-0*) Apple Dining.

Apple Fall. Helen Dunmore. 1983. pap. 12.95 (*0-906427-43-6*, Pub. by Bloodaxe Bks UK) Dufour.

Apple for My Teacher: Twelve Writers Tell All about Teachers Who Made the Difference. Ed. by Louis D. Rubin, Jr. (Illus.). 186p. 1987. 19.95 (*0-912697-34-2*); pap. 10.95 (*0-912697-57-1*) Algonquin Bks.

Apple Found in the Plowing. Robert Bly. (Illus.). 28p. (Orig.). 1989. pap. 12.00 (*0-9621666-4-2*) Haw River Bk.

Apple Graphics: Tools & Techniques. Roberta Schwartz & Michael Callery. (Illus.). 288p. 1986. 23.95 (*0-13-039512-9*) P-H.

Apple-Green Triumph & Other Stories. Martha L. Hall. LC 90-5658. 152p. 1990. 17.95 (*0-8071-1608-4*) La State U Pr.

***Apple Guide Complete: Designing & Developing Onscreen Assistance.** Apple Computer Staff. 1995. cd-rom, pap. 39.95 (*0-201-48334-3*) Addison-Wesley.

Apple II & Apple IIc Technical Reference Manual. 2nd ed. 1987. 24.95 (*0-201-17752-8*) Addison-Wesley.

Apple II BASIC. David C. Goodfellow. (Illus.). 240p. (Orig.). 1983. 19.95 (*0-8306-0113-9*) TAB Bks.

Apple II BASIC. David C. Goodfellow. (Orig.). 1991. 24.95 (*0-8306-6224-3*) TAB Bks.

Apple II Instant Pascal Language Reference Manual. Apple Computer, Inc. Staff. 288p. 1985. spiral bd. 22.95 (*0-201-17740-4*) Addison-Wesley.

Apple IIe: Step-by-Step Programming Guides, 2 Vols., I. Phil Robinson. 64p. 1984. 19.95 (*0-685-08723-9*) P-H.

Apple IIe BASIC Programming with Technical Applications. Vincent Kassab. LC 84-17821. (Illus.). 256p. 1985. 19.50 (*0-13-039421-1*) P-H.

Apple IIe Technical Reference Manual. 2nd ed. Apple Computer, Inc. Staff. 408p. 1987. 24.95 (*0-201-17750-1*) Addison-Wesley.

Apple IIgs Firmware Reference. Apple Computer, Inc. Staff. 304p. 1987. 24.95 (*0-201-17744-7*) Addison-Wesley.

Apple IIgs Hardware Reference. Apple Computer, Inc. Staff. 256p. 1987. 24.95 (*0-201-17743-9*) Addison-Wesley.

Apple IIgs Hardware Reference. 2nd ed. Apple Computer, Inc. Staff. 1989. pap. 26.95 (*0-201-52389-2*) Addison-Wesley.

Apple IIgs ProDOS 16 Reference: Includes System Loader. Apple Computer, Inc. Staff. 208p. 1987. 29.95 (*0-201-17754-4*) Addison-Wesley.

Apple IIgs Toolbox Reference, II. Apple Computer, Inc. Staff. 832p. 1988. 28.95 (*0-201-17747-1*) Addison-Wesley.

Apple Imagewriter II Technical Reference Manual. Apple Computer, Inc. Staff. 1987. 19.95 (*0-201-17766-8*) Addison-Wesley.

Apple in the Dark. Clarice Lispector. Tr. by Gregory Rabassa. (Texas Pan American Ser.). 378p. 1986. reprint ed. pap. 14.95 (*0-292-70392-9*) U of Tex Pr.

Apple in Your Hand. Ekkehard Floegel. 220p. 12.95 (*3-88963-178-9*) Blue Cat.

Apple Is My Sign. Mary Riskind. 160p. (J). (gr. 5-9). 1993. pap. 4.95 (*0-395-65747-4*) HM.

Apple Jack & the Big Storm: A Brave Horse to the Rescue. Zeno Zeplin & Judy Jones. Ed. by Margy Ebersapacher. (Apple Jack Ser.). (Illus.). 48p. (J). (gr. k-3). 1991. lib. bdg. 11.95 (*1-877740-10-1*); pap. text ed. 6.95 (*1-877740-11-X*) Nel-Mar Pub.

Apple Juice Tea. Martha Weston. LC 93-17437. (J). 1994. 14.95 (*0-395-65480-7*, Clarion Bks) HM.

Apple LOGO: A Complete, Illustrated Handbook. Drew Berentes. (Illus.). 406p. (Orig.). 1984. 18.95 (*0-8306-0751-X*) TAB Bks.

Apple LOGO: Programming & Problem Solving. Rick Billstein et al. 416p. (C). 1986. pap. text ed. 32.25 (*0-8053-0866-0*) Addison-Wesley.

Apple Logo for Teachers. Earl Babbie. 335p. (C). 1984. pap. 36.95 (*0-534-03392-X*) Intl Thomson.

Apple Logo for Teachers. Earl Babbie. 335p. (C). 1984. disk 21.95 (*0-534-03393-8*) Intl Thomson.

Apple LOGO Primer. Gary G. Bitter & Nancy R. Watson. 1983. pap. 19.50 (*0-8359-0314-1*, Reston) P-H.

Apple-Lovers' Cook Book. Shirley Munson & Jo Nelson. LC 89-23639. 120p. (Orig.). 1989. spiral bd. 6.95 (*0-914846-43-4*) Golden West Pub.

Apple Machine Language. Don Inman & Kurt Inman. 224p. 1986. text ed. 21.95 (*0-8359-0231-5*, Reston) P-H.

Apple Macintosh Book. 4th ed. Cary Lu. 528p. 1992. pap. 24.95 (*1-55615-278-7*) Microsoft.

Apple Macintosh Primer: (Datamost) William Sanders. 1984. 9.95 (*0-685-08117-6*) P-H.

Apple Maggot in the West. Robert Dowell. 104p. 1991. pap. 5.50 (*0-931876-95-8*, 3341) ANR Pubns CA.

Apple Magic. Ed. by Martina Boudreau. LC 84-50105. 56p. (Orig.). 1984. pap. 3.49 (*0-942320-09-3*) Am Cooking.

Apple Market in OECD Countries. OECD Staff. (Orig.). Date not set. pap. text ed. 30.00 (*92-64-13590-1*, 51-91-05-1) OECD.

Apple Megabook. William J. Birnes. 1985. pap. 12.95 (*0-671-54386-5*) S&S Trade.

Apple Numerics Manual. Apple Computer, Inc. Staff. 1986. 29.95 (*0-201-17741-2*) Addison-Wesley.

Apple Numerics Manual. 2nd ed. Apple Computer, Inc. Staff. 1988. 29.95 (*0-201-17738-2*) Addison-Wesley.

Apple of Discord: A Survey of Recent Greek Politics. C. M. Woodhouse. LC 84-62796. 320p. (C). 1985. reprint ed. 30.00 (*0-9615243-0-8*) Wm B ONeill.

Apple of Earthly Love Vol. 1: Female Development in Esther Tusquet's Fiction. Barbara F. Ichiishi. LC 93-23523. (Nuestra Voz Ser.: Vol. 1). 251p. (C). 1994. text ed. 49.95 (*0-8204-2302-5*) P Lang Pubs.

Apple of God: Constitutionalism in Israel & the United States. Gary J. Jacobsohn. LC 92-15743. 334p. (C). 1993. text ed. 39.50 (*0-691-08622-2*) Princeton U Pr.

***Apple of Gold: Constitutionalism in Israel & the United States.** Gary J. Jacobson. 1994. pap. 14.95 (*0-691-02953-9*) Princeton U Pr.

Apple of His Eye. Keith Intrater. 96p. 1990. 7.99 (*1-56043-414-7*) Destiny Image.

***Apple of Knowledge: An Inquiry about God & Science.** Stephen A. Foglein. 162p. 1981. pap. 5.00 (*1-884722-03-2*) Two Hrts Bks.

Apple of My Eye. Helene Hanff. 144p. (Orig.). 1989. 16.95 (*0-918825-88-1*); pap. 8.95 (*0-918825-73-3*) Moyer Bell.

Apple of the Automatic Zebra's Eye. 2nd ed. Franklin Rosemont. (Surrealist Research & Development Monographs). (Illus.). 1971. pap. 9.00 (*0-941194-03-5*) Black Swan Pr.

Apple Orchard Cookbook. 2nd ed. Janet Christensen & Betty B. Levin. 1992. pap. 9.95 (*0-936399-32-5*) Berkshire Hse.

Apple Pascal: A Problem-Solving Approach. Terry L. Dennis. (Illus.). 456p. 1985. pap. text ed. 39.00 (*0-314-85228-X*); Instr's. manual. teacher ed, pap. text ed. write for info. (*0-314-87191-8*) West Pub.

Apple Pickers' Children. Rick Lott. (Texas Review Southern & Southwestern Poets Breakthrough Ser.). 64p. 1993. pap. 6.95 (*1-881515-02-8*) TX Review Pr.

Apple Picking Time. Michele B. Slawson. LC 92-23400. (Illus.). 32p. (J). (ps-2). 1994. 15.00 (*0-517-58971-0*); lib. bdg. 15.99 (*0-517-58976-1*) Crown Bks Yng Read.

Apple Pie. Kate Greenaway. (J). 1993. 4.99 (*0-517-09302-2*) Random Hse Value.

***Apple Pie: Delta's Beginning ESL Program, Bk. 1A.** rev. ed. Jean Owensby et al. Ed. by Adae Iwataki. (Illus.). 222p. 1995. student ed, pap. text ed. 7.95 (*0-937354-56-2*); teacher ed, pap. text ed. 12.95 (*0-937354-60-0*); audio 10.95 (*0-937354-99-6*) Delta Systems.

***Apple Pie: Delta's Beginning ESL Program, Bk. 1A Visuals.** rev. ed. Jean Owensby et al. Ed. by Adae Iwataki. (Illus.). 123p. 1995. pap. text ed. 24.95 (*0-937354-64-3*) Delta Systems.

***Apple Pie: Delta's Beginning ESL Program, Bk. 1B.** rev. ed. Jean Owensby et al. Ed. by Sadae Iwataki. (Illus.). 238p. 1995. student ed, pap. text ed. 7.95 (*0-937354-57-0*); teacher ed, pap. text ed. 12.95 (*0-937354-61-9*); audio 10.95 (*0-937354-50-3*) Delta Systems.

***Apple Pie: Delta's Beginning ESL Program, Bk. 1B Visuals.** rev. ed. Jean Owensby et al. Ed. by Sadae Iwataki. (Illus.). 133p. 1995. pap. text ed. 24.95 (*0-937354-65-1*) Delta Systems.

***Apple Pie: Delta's Beginning ESL Program, Bk. 2A.** rev. ed. Jean Owensby et al. Ed. by Sadae Iwataki. (Illus.). 248p. 1995. student ed, pap. text ed. 7.95 (*0-937354-58-9*) Delta Systems.

***Apple Pie: Delta's Beginning ESL Program, Bk. 2A.** rev. ed. Jean Owensby et al. Ed. by Sadae Iwataki. (Illus.). 120p. 1995. teacher ed, pap. text ed. 12.95 (*0-937354-62-7*) Delta Systems.

***Apple Pie: Delta's Beginning ESL Program, Bk. 2A.** rev. ed. Jean Owensby et al. Ed. by Sadae Iwataki. (Illus.). 1995. audio 10.95 (*0-937354-51-1*) Delta Systems.

***Apple Pie: Delta's Beginning ESL Program, Bk. 2A Visuals.** rev. ed. Jean Owensby et al. Ed. by Sadae Iwataki. (Illus.). 187p. 1995. pap. text ed. 24.95 (*0-937354-66-X*) Delta Systems.

***Apple Pie: Delta's Beginning ESL Program, Bk. 2B.** rev. ed. Jean Owensby et al. Ed. by Sadae Iwataki. (Illus.). 240p. 1995. student ed, pap. text ed. 7.95 (*0-937354-59-7*) Delta Systems.

***Apple Pie: Delta's Beginning ESL Program, Bk. 2B.** rev. ed. Jean Owensby et al. Ed. by Sadae Iwataki. (Illus.). 136p. 1995. teacher ed, pap. text ed. 12.95 (*0-937354-63-5*) Delta Systems.

***Apple Pie: Delta's Beginning ESL Program, Bk. 2B.** rev. ed. Jean Owensby et al. Ed. by Sadae Iwataki. (Illus.). 1995. audio 10.95 (*0-937354-52-X*) Delta Systems.

***Apple Pie: Delta's Beginning ESL Program, Bk. 2B Visuals.** rev. ed. Jean Owensby et al. Ed. by Sadae Iwataki. (Illus.). 141p. 1995. pap. text ed. 24.95 (*0-937354-67-8*) Delta Systems.

Apple Pie: Three One Act Plays. Terrence McNally. 1968. pap. 4.75 (*0-8222-0061-9*) Dramatists Play.

Apple Pie & Onions. Judith Caseley. LC 86-9804. (Illus.). 32p. (J). (gr. 1-4). 1987. 15.00 (*0-688-06762-X*); lib. bdg. 14.93 (*0-688-06763-8*) Greenwillow.

Apple Pie Savings System. Christopher S. Browning. (Illus.). 96p. (Orig.). 1991. pap. 8.95 (*0-9626640-0-6*) Apple GA.

Apple ProDOS Data Files: A Basic Tutorial. David Miller. (Illus.). 232p. 18.95 (*0-8359-0134-3*, Reston) P-H.

Apple Programmer's Challenge. Steven Chen. (Illus.). 240p. (Orig.). 1987. pap. 14.95 (*0-8306-2827-4*, 2827) TAB Bks.

Apple Programming for Learning & Teaching: Over 50 Application Programs. Frederick Bell. (Illus.). 1984. text ed. 32.00 (*0-685-08091-9*, Reston) P-H.

Apple Programming Secrets "They Didn't Want You to Know" Wayne Dyrness. (Illus.). 256p. 1986. 27.95 (*0-13-039215-4*) P-H.

***Apple QuickTake 100 (H175)** John Larish. (Magic Lantern Guide Ser.). (Illus.). 174p. (Orig.). 1994. pap. 19.95 (*1-883403-14-6*) Saunders Photo.

Apple Recipes. Jeanne Amero. 36p. (Orig.). 1983. pap. 2.75 (*0-940844-14-1*) Wellspring.

Apple Sampler. Jan Siegrist. (Illus.). 48p. (Orig.). 1986. pap. 3.95 (*0-933050-38-0*) New Eng Pr VT.

Apple Sliced: Sociological Studies of New York City. Vernon W. Boggs et al. LC 82-22763. (Illus.). 352p. 1983. text ed. 49.95 (*0-275-91716-9*, C1716, Praeger Pubs) Greenwood.

Apple Technic Control One Technology Pack. Tom Barrowman et al. Ed. by Cathy Helgoe & Tom Lough. (Illus.). 416p. (YA). (gr. 6-12). 1991. 575.00 (*0-914831-75-5*, 958) Lego Dacta.

Apple That Astonished Paris. Billy Collins. LC 87-24191. 71p. 1988. 12.95 (*1-55728-023-1*); pap. 8.95 (*1-55728-024-X*) U of Ark Pr.

Apple That Wanted to Be Famous. Rhonda Kaplan. 1976. pap. 2.95 (*0-912284-81-1*) New Rivers Pr.

Apple Tree. Lynley Dodd. LC 85-9774. (Gold Star First Readers Ser.). (Illus.). 26p. (J). (gr. 1-2). 1985. lib. bdg. 17.27 (*0-918831-08-3*) Gareth Stevens Inc.

Apple Tree. Pref. by Edward Morgan. 24p. 1982. 30.00 (*0-906474-25-6*, Pub. by Third Eye Centre UK) St Mut.

Apple Tree. Tr. by Edwin Morgan. 1989. 50.00 (*0-906474-24-8*, Pub. by Third Eye Centre UK) St Mut.

Apple Tree. Peter Parnall. LC 86-23730. (Illus.). 32p. (J). (gr. k-3). 1988. lib. bdg. 14.95 (*0-02-770160-3*, Mac Bks Young Read) S&S Childrens.

Apple Tree. Barrie Watts. (Stopwatch Ser.). (Illus.). 24p. (J). (gr. k-4). 1991. lib. bdg. 9.95 (*0-382-09436-0*); pap. 3.95 (*0-382-24339-0*) Silver Burdett Pr.

Apple Tree! Apple Tree! Mary Blocksma. LC 82-19852. (Easy Reading Picture Bks.). (Illus.). 24p. (J). (ps-2). 1983. lib. bdg. 9.75 (*0-516-01584-2*); pap. 4.50 (*0-516-41584-0*) Childrens.

Apple Tree! Apple Tree! Big Book. Mary Blocksma. (Just One More Big Bks.). 24p. (J). (ps-2). 1990. pap. text ed. 23.48 (*0-516-49514-3*) Childrens.

Apple-Tree Canoe. Marie-Helene Delval. (I Love to Read Collection). (Illus.). 48p. (J). (gr. 3-8). 1990. 19.93 (*0-89565-805-4*) Childs World.

Apple Tree Christmas. Trinka H. Noble. LC 84-1901. (Illus.). 32p. (J). (ps-2). 1984. 14.99 (*0-8037-0102-0*) Dial Bks Young.

Apple Tree Leader's Guide. Helen Wessel & Kathy Nesper. 160p. 1983. 4.95 (*0-933082-06-1*); student ed 3.95 (*0-933082-07-X*) Bookmates Intl.

***Apple Tree Mystery.** Nancy Keats. (Illus.). 71p. (Orig.). (J). (gr. 4-7). 1995. pap. 3.99 (*0-9633740-1-X*) Purple Finch.

Apple Tree Poems. J. Azrael. LC 83-72019. 1983. pap. 4.00 (*0-917652-33-9*) Confluence Pr.

Apple Tree Table: And Other Sketches. Herman Melville. (BCL1-PS American Literature Ser.). 329p. 1992. reprint ed. lib. bdg. 89.00 (*0-7812-6793-5*) Rprt Serv.

Apple-Tree Table & Other Sketches. Herman Melville. LC 70-88907. 329p. 1969. reprint ed. text ed. 35.00 (*0-8371-2245-7*, MEAT, Greenwood Pr) Greenwood.

Apple Tree That Would Not Let Go of Its Apples. Sarai. (Illus.). 28p. (Orig.). (J). 1993. pap. 11.50 (*0-938837-13-3*) Behav Sci Ctr Pubs.

Apple Tree Through the Year. Claudia Schnieper. (Nature Watch Bks.). (Illus.). 48p. (J). (gr. 2-5). 1987. lib. bdg. 19.95 (*0-87614-248-X*, Carolrhoda); pap. 6.95 (*0-87614-483-0*, Carolrhoda) Lerner Group.

Apple Tree, Vol. 9: Pasitos English Language Development Books. Darlyne F. Schott. (Pasitos Hacia la Lectura Ser.). 16p. (J). (gr. k-1). 1990. pap. text ed. 11.00 (*1-56537-068-6*) D F Schott Educ.

Apple Trees. Sylvia A. Johnson. LC 83-16230. (Lerner Natural Science Bks.). (Illus.). 48p. (J). (gr. 4 up). 1983. lib. bdg. 19.95 (*0-8225-1479-6*, Lerner Publctns) Lerner Group.

Apple Trees to Zinnias. Nancy Polette. (Illus.). 48p. (J). 1992. pap. 5.95 (*1-879287-14-5*) Bk Lures.

Apple Turnover Treasure. Nancy S. Levene. Ed. by Sue Reck. LC 91-45922. (Alex Ser.). 128p. (J). (gr. 3-6). Date not set. pap. 4.99 (*1-55513-894-2*, Chariot Bks) Chariot Family.

***Apple Valley: Destiny.** Nancy C. Smith. (Apple Valley Ser.: Vol. 4). 160p. (Orig.). (YA). (gr. 6). 1995. pap. 3.50 (*0-380-78091-7*, Flare) Avon.

***Apple Valley: The Dare.** Nancy C. Smith. (Apple Valley Ser.). 160p. (Orig.). (YA). (gr. 6 up). 1994. pap. 3.50 (*0-380-77390-2*, Flare) Avon.

***Apple Valley: The Journey.** Nancy C. Smith. (Apple Valley Ser.). 144p. (Orig.). (YA). (gr. 6 up). 1994. pap. 3.50 (*0-380-77392-9*, Flare) Avon.

***Apple Valley: The Proposal.** Nancy C. Smith. (Apple Valley Ser.). 176p. (Orig.). (YA). (gr. 6 up). 1994. pap. 3.50 (*0-380-77391-0*, Flare) Avon.

Apple Valley Year. Ann Turner. LC 90-37733. (Illus.). 32p. (J). (gr. k-3). 1993. text ed. 14.95 (*0-02-789281-6*, Mac Bks Young Read) S&S Childrens.

***Apple World: Core & Periphery in a Transnational Organizational Culture. A Study of Apple Computer Inc.** Christina Garsten. (Stockholm Studies in Social Anthropology: No. 33). 250p. (Orig.). 1994. pap. 61.00x (*91-7153-211-0*, Pub. by Almqv & Wiksell SW) Coronet Bks.

Apple 16: A Comprehensive Guide to 16 Bit Apple IIGS Computing. Hank Harrison. (Illus.). 240p. 1987. pap. 19.95 (*0-918501-36-9*) Archives Pr.

Applebaum's Garage. Karen L. Williams. LC 92-31336. (J). 1993. 13.95 (*0-395-65227-8*, Clarion Bks) HM.

Applebet: An ABC. Clyde Watson. (Sunburst Ser.). (Illus.). 32p. (J). (ps up). 1987. pap. 3.95 (*0-374-40427-5*) FS&G.

Appleblossom. Shulamith L. Oppenheim. Ed. by Jane Yolen. (Illus.). 28p. (J). (gr. 1-7). 1991. 14.95 (*0-15-203750-0*, HB Juv Bks) HarBrace.

Applebroog. Ida Applebroog et al. (Illus.). 63p. 1987. pap. 20.00 (*0-914661-05-1*) Feldman Fine Arts.

Appleby File. large type ed. Michael Innes. 1978. 21.95 (*0-7089-0224-3*) Ulverscroft.

Appleby on Ararat. John I. Stewart. LC 70-106676. 254p. 1971. reprint ed. text ed. 55.00 (*0-8371-3377-7*, STAO, Greenwood Pr) Greenwood.

Appleby Talks Again. John I. Stewart. LC 77-81277. (Short Story Index Reprint Ser.). 1977. 19.95 (*0-8369-3029-0*) Ayer.

Appleby's End. John I. Stewart. LC 74-106677. 211p. 1970. reprint ed. text ed. 55.00 (*0-8371-3376-9*, STAE, Greenwood Pr) Greenwood.

Appleby's Other Story: A Sir John Appleby Mystery. Michael Innes. 208p. 1993. mass mkt. 6.00 (*0-14-014679-2*, Penguin Bks) Viking Penguin.

Applegate. Ray Cruzan. LC 88-84113. 582p. 1989. 19.95 (*0-925774-00-6*) Ashton Woods.

Applehood & Motherpie. Ed. by Tracy K. Kessler. 320p. 1981. 16.95 (*0-9605612-0-X*) Jr League Rochester.

Appler Family History. Charles R. Appler. 280p. 1994. reprint ed. lib. bdg. 54.00 (*0-8328-4047-5*); reprint ed. pap. 44.00 (*0-8328-4048-3*) Higginson Bk Co.

***Apples.** Kleinman. Date not set. 19.95 (*0-00-255454-2*, HarpT) HarpC.

Apples. Rhoda Nottridge. (Foods We Eat Ser.). (Illus.). 32p. (J). (gr. 1-4). 1991. lib. bdg. 14.96 (*0-87614-655-8*, Carolrhoda) Lerner Group.

Apples. Roger Yepsen. 224p. 1994. 17.95 (*0-393-03690-1*) Norton.

Apples: A Cookbook. Robert Berkley. 1991. pap. 16.95 (*0-671-72902-0*, Fireside) S&S Trade.

Apples: A Country Garden Cookbook. Christopher Idone. LC 93-7417. (Illus.). 1993. 14.95 (*0-00-255225-6*) Collins SF.

Apples: A Thematic Unit. Mary E. Sterling. (Thematic Units Ser.). (Illus.). 80p. (gr. 1-3). 1990. student ed 8.95 (*1-55734-266-0*) Tchr Create Mat.

Apples, Alligators, & Also Alphabets. Odette Johnson & Bruce H. Johnson. (Illus.). 32p. (J). (ps-1). 1991. 13.95 (*0-19-540757-1*) OUP.

Apples & Ashes: Culture, Metaphor & Morality in the American Dream. Ann-Janine Morey-Gaines. LC 81-14346. (American Academy of Religion Academy Ser.). 1982. 19.95 (*0-89130-535-1*, 01-01-38) Scholars Pr GA.

Apples & Oranges. Paul Marion. LC 86-81721. 28p. (Orig.). 1986. pap. 4.00 (*0-931507-02-2*) Loom Pr.

Apples & Pumpkins. Anne Rockwell. LC 88-22628. (Illus.). 24p. (J). (ps-1). 1989. text ed. 13.95 (*0-02-777270-5*, Mac Bks Young Read) S&S Childrens.

Apples & Pumpkins. Anne Rockwell. LC 94-629. (Illus.). 24p. (J). (ps-1). 1994. pap. 3.95 (*0-689-71861-6*, Aladdin Paperbacks) S&S Childrens.

***Apples, Apples.** Judy Mullican. (HRL Little Book Ser.). (Illus.). 8p. (J). (ps-k). 1995. pap. 10.95 (*1-57332-020-X*) HighReach Lrning.

Apples, Apples, Apples. Ann Clark & Johnie E. Clark. 112p. 1991. pap. 7.00 (*0-9632073-0-X*) Apples.

Apples, Bunnies & Bears. Kathy Christenson. (Illus.). 28p. 1984. pap. 5.95 (*0-9605904-8-X*) Hot off Pr.

Apples for Teachers Series, 5 bks. Cynthia Muller et al. (J). (ps). 1988. Letters A-Z. pap. write for info. (*0-8224-0456-7*); Numbers 0-10. pap. write for info. (*0-8224-0457-5*); Time. pap. write for info. (*0-8224-0458-3*); Colors & Shapes. pap. write for info. (*0-8224-0459-1*) Fearon Teach Aids.

Apples for Teachers Series, 5 bks. Cynthia Muller et al. (J). (ps-00). 1988. pap. 10.95 (*0-685-18080-8*) Fearon Teach Aids.

Apples for Teachers Series: Kindergarten Homework Packet. Diane C. Burkle et al. 1990. pap. 6.99 (*0-8224-4150-0*) Fearon Teach Aids.

Apples for the Missionaries. Barbara Wilkinson. (Illus.). 32p. (Orig.). (J). (gr. 1-3). 1989. pap. text ed. 2.95 (*0-936625-67-8*) Womans Mission Union.

***Apples from Heaven: Multicultural Folktales about Stories & Storytellers.** Naomi Baltuck. xvi, 144p. 1995. lib. bdg. write for info. (*0-208-02424-7*); pap. write for info. (*0-208-02434-4*) Shoe String.

Apples, How They Grow. Bruce McMillan. (Illus.). 48p. (J). (ps-3). 1979. 17.95 (*0-395-27806-6*) HM.

Apples in a Seed. Lloyd Mattson. 80p. 1983. pap. 3.50 (*0-942684-04-4*) Camp Guidepts.

Apples in the Sky. Christina McDade. LC 89-84590. 108p. (Orig.). 1989. pap. 3.95 (*0-939810-12-3*) Jordan Valley.

Apples of Gold. Illus. by Gordon Brown. 1962. boxed 9.50 (*0-8378-1793-5*) Gibson.

Apples of Gold. Ken Robaer, pseud. (Orig.). 1985. pap. text ed. 14.95 (*0-937957-00-3*) B Roberts.

Apples of Gold. large type ed. Jo Petty. 1985. pap. 8.95 (*0-8027-2502-3*) Walker & Co.

An Asterisk (*) at the beginning of an entry indicates that the title is appearing in BIP for the first time.

An Asterisk (*) at the beginning of an entry indicates that the title is appearing in BIP for the first time.

379

A

Application Guide for Ceramic Suspension Insulators. 1984. 6.50 (*0-318-18021-9*, HV 2-1984) Natl Elec Mfrs.

Application Guide to Optical Engineering. Blackwell & Thornton. 1995. text ed. 30.00 (*0-07-707756-3*) McGraw.

Application in Macintosh: Using Microsoft Works. Glenn T. Smith & Richard T. Christoph. 208p. (C). 1991. pap. 13.00 (*0-13-041633-9*, 220111) P-H.

Application Junction: A Catalog of dBase II Software Applications. Ashton-Tate Staff. pap. 29.95 (*0-07-912649-9*) McGraw.

***Application Manual for the Revised Niosh Lifting Equation.** (Illus.). 147p. (Orig.). (C). 1995. pap. text ed. 55.00x (*0-7881-1604-5*) Diane Pub.

Application Migration: IBM to VAX. Alan R. Simon. (Illus.). 300p. 1992. text ed. 44.95 (*0-442-00146-0*) Van Nos Reinhold.

Application Neuroleptanalgesia Anaesthetic & Other Practice: Proceedings of the 1st British Symposium Edinburgh 6-64. N. Shephard. LC 65-19097. 1965. 51.00 (*0-08-011194-7*, Pub. by Pergamon Repr UK) Franklin.

Application of a Screening Matrix for Industrial Development to Omaha, Nebraska. Michael Eskey et al. 74p. (Orig.). 1981. pap. 6.00 (*1-55719-002-X*) U NE CPAR.

Application of a Theoretical Learning Model to a Remote Handling Control System. Amos Freedy et al. LC 73-141073. 104p. 1970. 19.00 (*0-403-04501-0*) Scholarly.

Application of a Theory of Games to the Transitional Eskimo Culture. Robert G. Glassford. LC 75-35070. (Studies in Play & Games). 1976. 25.95 (*0-405-07920-6*) Ayer.

Application of Accelerated Corrosion Tests to Service Life Prediction of Materials, No. 1194. Ed. by Gustavo Cragnolino & Narasu Sribhar. LC 93-47376. (Special Technical Publication: No. 1194). (Illus.). 405p. 1994. 61.00 (*0-8031-1853-8*, 0401194027) ASTM.

***Application of Admixtures in Concrete.** A. M. Paillere. (Rilem Report Ser.: No. 10). 131p. 1994. 67.00 (*0-419-19960-8*, E & FN Spon) Routledge Chapman & Hall.

Application of Advanced & Nuclear Physics to Testing Materials. American Society for Testing & Materials Staff. LC 65-19687. (American Society for Testing & Materials Special Technical Publication Ser.: Special Technical Publication, No. 373). 141p. reprint ed. pap. 40.20 (*0-8357-5658-0*, 2000739) Bks Demand.

Application of Advanced Information Technologies: Effective Management of Natural Resources. LC 93-71586. 500p. 1993. pap. 46.00 (*0-929355-39-3*, P0493) Am Soc Ag Eng.

Application of Agricultural Analysis in Environmental Studies. Ed. by Keith B. Hoddinott & Tracey A. O'Shay. LC 92-36416. (Special Technical Publication Ser.: Vol. 1162). (Illus.). 178p. 1993. text ed. 53.00 (*0-8031-1475-3*, 04-011620-38) ASTM.

Application of Analytical Chemistry to Oceanic Carbon Studies. National Research Council, Commission on Geosciences, Environment, & Resources Staff. 96p. (Orig.). (C). 1993. pap. text ed. 26.00 (*0-309-04928-8*) Natl Acad Pr.

Application of Analytical Methods to Mining Geomechanics: Proceedings of the 7th Plenary Scientific Session of the International Bureau of Rock Mechanics, World Mining Congress, Katowice, 24-26 June 1981. Ed. by M. Borecki & M. Kwasniewski. 168p. (C). 1982. text ed. 160.00 (*90-6191-260-1*, Pub. by A A Balkema NE) Ashgate Pub Co.

Application of Artificial Intelligence in Process Control: Lecture Notes Erasmus Intensive Course. Ed. by L. Boullart et al. LC 92-26606. 1993. 155.00 (*0-08-042016-8*, Pergamon Pr); pap. 63.00 (*0-08-042017-6*, Pergamon Pr) Elsevier.

Application of Artificial Intelligence Techniques to Civil & Structural Engineering. Civil Comp Editors. 152p. 1987. pap. 102.00 (*0-948749-06-7*, Pub. by Civil-Comp UK) St Mut.

Application of Basic Neuroscience to Child Psychiatry. Ed. by S. I. Deutsch et al. LC 90-7203. (Illus.). 420p. 1990. 65.00 (*0-306-43357-5*, Plenum Pr) Plenum.

Application of Basic Science to Hematopoiesis & Treatment of Disease. Ed. by E. Donnall Thomas. LC 92-48858. (Bristol-Myers - Squibb Cancer Symposia Ser.: Vol. 15). 272p. 1993. 94.50 (*0-88167-999-2*) Raven.

***Application of Behavioral Pharmacology in Toxicology.** Ed. by Gerhard Zbinden et al. LC 82-42587. (Illus.). Date not set. reprint ed. pap. 116.60 (*0-7837-9549-1*, 2060298) Bks Demand.

***Application of Botany in Horticulture.** Andre Genin. 222p. 1994. text ed. 39.50 (*1-886106-00-2*) Science Pubs.

Application of BS Fifty Seven Fifty Quality Systems to Building Services. A. Foster. (C). 1985. 105.00 (*0-86022-137-7*, Pub. by Build Servs Info Assn UK) St Mut.

Application of Cancer Chemotherapy: Proceedings of the 10th International Congress, Zurich, September 1977. Anticancer-Symposium Staff et al. Ed. by H. Schoenfeld. (Antibiotics & Chemotherapy Ser.: Vol. 24). (Illus.). 1978. 59.25 (*3-8055-2831-0*) S Karger.

Application of Charge Density Research to Chemistry & Drug Design. Ed. by G. A. Jeffrey & J. F. Piniella. (NATO ASI Series B, Physics: Vol. 250). (Illus.). 426p. 1991. 120.00 (*0-306-43880-1*, Plenum Pr) Plenum.

***Application of Chess Theory.** Yefim Geller. 272p. 1995. 19.95 (*1-85744-067-6*, Pub. by Cadogan Books UK) Macmillan.

Application of Classification Techniques in Business, Banking & Finance. Edward I. Altman et al. Ed. by Ingo Walter. LC 76-5759. (Contemporary Studies in Economic & Financial Analysis: Vol. 3). 325p. 1981. lib. bdg. 73.25 (*0-89232-004-4*) Jai Pr.

Application of Climatic Data to House Design. U. S. Housing & Home Finance Agency. LC 77-10240. 1977. reprint ed. 45.00 (*0-404-16218-5*) AMS Pr.

Application of Cognitive Psychology: Problem Solving, Education & Computing. Ed. by Dale E. Berger et al. 264p. (C). 1986. text ed. 49.95 (*0-89859-710-2*) L Erlbaum Assocs.

Application of Composite Materials - STP 524. 191p. 1973. 16.75 (*0-8031-0115-5*, 04-524000-33) ASTM.

Application of Computer Techniques in Chemical Research. Institute of Petroleum Staff & P. Hepple. (Illus.). 282p. 1972. 68.50 (*0-85334-488-4*, Pub. by Elsevier Applied Sci UK) Elsevier.

Application of Computers & Operations Research in the Mineral Industry. International Symposium on the Application of Computers & Operations Research in the Mineral Industries Staff. Ed. by R. V. Ramani. (Illus.). 928p. reprint ed. pap. 180.00 (*0-8357-5659-9*, 2031592) Bks Demand.

Application of Computers & Operations Research in the Mineral Industry: 16th International Symposium. Ed. by Thomas J. O'Neil. LC 79-52273. (Illus.). 651p. 1979. text ed. 10.00 (*0-89520-261-1*) SMM&E Inc.

***Application of Computers & Operations Research in the Minerals Industry: 17th International Symposium.** Application of Computers & Operations Research in the Minerals Industry Staff. Ed. by Thys B. Johnson & Randal J. Barnes. LC 82-70116. (Illus.). reprint ed. pap. 180.00 (*0-7837-9181-X*, 2049880) Bks Demand.

Application of Conjugate Gradient Method to Electromagnetics & Signal Analysis. T. K. Sarkar & Jin A. Kong. (Progress in Electromagnetics Research (PIER) Ser.: No. 5). 656p. 1991. 82.00 (*0-444-01604-X*) Elsevier.

Application of Control Theory in Ecology: Lecture Notes in Biomathematics, Vol. 73. Ed. by Y. Cohn. vii, 101p. 1987. pap. 28.00 (*0-387-18104-0*) Spr-Verlag.

Application of Cryogenic Technology: Proceedings, Vol. 5. Conference of the Cryogenic Society of America, 5th, 1972. Ed. by Robert H. Carr. LC 68-57815. 352p. 1973. text ed. 30.00 (*0-87936-001-1*) Scholium Intl.

Application of Customary Law in Southern Africa. T. W. Bennett. 287p. 1985. pap. 30.00 (*0-7021-1601-7*, Pub. by Juta SA) W W Gaunt.

Application of Directional Blasting in Mining & Civil Engineering. 2nd enl. rev. ed. Ed. by A. A. Chernigovskii. 340p. (C). 1986. text ed. 130.00 (*90-6191-573-2*, Pub. by A A Balkema NE) Ashgate Pub Co.

Application of Disaggregate Travel Demand Models. (National Cooperative Highway Research Program Report Ser.: No. 253). 205p. 1982. 12.40 (*0-309-03423-X*) Transport Res Bd.

Application of Distributions to the Theory of Elementary Particles in Quantum Mechanics. Laurent Schwartz. LC 68-17535. (Illus.). 144p. 1969. text ed. 125.00 (*0-677-30090-5*) Gordon & Breach.

Application of Drainage. Ed. by George Leonov. 228p. text ed. 70.50 (*0-317-46401-9*, Pub. by Keter Pub IS) Coronet Bks.

Application of Ecological Modelling in Environmental Management. Sven E. Jorgensen. (Developments in Environmental Modelling Ser.: Vol. 4A). 736p. 1983. 166.75 (*0-444-42155-6*, I-530-82) Elsevier.

Application of Ecological Modelling in Environmental Management, Pt. B. Ed. by Sven E. Jorgensen & W. J. Mitsch. (Developments in Environmental Modelling Ser.: Vol. 4B). 700p. 1984. 102.75 (*0-444-42247-1*) Elsevier.

Application of Economic Techniques in Environmental Impact Assessment. David James. LC 94-349. (Environment & Management Ser.: Vol. 4). 320p. (C). 1994. lib. bdg. 110.00 (*0-7923-2721-7*) Kluwer Ac.

Application of Electro-Ultrafiltration (EUF) in Agricultural Production. K. Nemeth. 1982. pap. text ed. 47.00 (*90-247-2641-7*) Kluwer Ac.

Application of Expert Systems in Library & Information Centres. Ed. by Anne Morris. 247p. 1992. 65.00 (*0-86291-276-8*) Bowker-Saur.

Application of Feolites in Catalysis. G. K. Boreskov & Minachev. 180p. 1979. 74.00 (*0-569-08576-4*, Pub. by Collets UK) Pro-Am Music.

Application of Finite Difference Equations to Shell Analysis. M. Soare. 1967. 196.00 (*0-08-010214-X*, Pub. by Pergamon Repr UK) Franklin.

Application of Forcing in Analysis. H. G. Dales & Hugh Woodin. (London Mathematical Society Lecture Note Ser.: No. 115). 200p. 1987. pap. 44.95 (*0-521-33996-0*) Cambridge U Pr.

Application of Fracture Mechanics for Selection of Metallic Structural Materials. Ed. by James E. Campbell et al. LC 82-71791. (Illus.). 384p. reprint ed. pap. 109.50 (*0-7837-1859-4*, 2042060) Bks Demand.

Application of Fracture Mechanics to Cementitious Composites. Ed. by Surendra P. Shah. 1985. lib. bdg. 223.50 (*90-247-3176-3*) Kluwer Ac.

Application of Fracture Mechanics to Composite Materials. Ed. by Klaus Friedrich. (Composite Materials Ser.: No. 6). 672p. 1990. 179.50 (*0-444-87286-8*) Elsevier.

Application of Fracture Mechanics to Materials & Structures. Ed. by G. C. Sih et al. 1984. lib. bdg. 284.50 (*90-247-2958-0*) Kluwer Ac.

Application of Freqeuncy & Risk in Water Resources, Vol. 2. Ed. by Vijay P. Singh. (C). 1987. lib. bdg. 147.00 (*90-277-2573-X*) Kluwer Ac.

Application of Fuzzy Theory. K. Hirota. Tr. by H. Solomon. 290p. 1994. 65.00 (*0-387-70109-5*) Spr-Verlag.

Application of GaAs MESFETs. Ed. by Robert Soares et al. LC 83-71124. (Illus.). 578p. reprint ed. pap. 164.80 (*0-8357-5660-2*, 2033117) Bks Demand.

Application of Geology to Engineering Practice: Berkey Volume, Papers by John L. Savage. Geological Society of America Staff. LC 51-5562. 389p. reprint ed. pap. 110.90 (*0-8357-5661-0*, 2027374) Bks Demand.

Application of Gnotobiotics to Transplantation & Microbial Translocation. Ed. by Geza Bruckner. 1992. 49.95 (*0-915340-18-6*) PJD Pubns.

Application of Gold on Japanese Sword Fittings. Hawley. 1991. pap. 4.95 (*0-910704-24-4*) Hawley.

Application of Government Audit Standards in Developing Countries. 127p. 1990. 15.50 (*92-1-123114-0*, 90.II.H.1) UN.

Application of Group Theory in Physics. G. Lyubarskii & S. Dedijer. LC 59-15292. 1960. 157.00 (*0-08-009335-3*, Pub. by Pergamon Repr UK) Franklin.

Application of HAZOP & What-If Safety Reviews to the Petroleum, Petro-Chemical & Chemical Industries. Dennis P. Nolan. LC 94-4889. (Illus.). 127p. 1994. 45.00 (*0-8155-1353-4*) Noyes.

Application of High Magnetic Fields in Semiconductor Physics: Proceedings, Grenoble, France, 1982. Ed. by G. Landwehr. (Lecture Notes in Physics Ser.: Vol. 177). 552p. 1983. pap. 49.00 (*0-387-11996-5*) Spr-Verlag.

Application of Holography & Hologram Interferometry to Photoelasticity. 2nd ed. V. Brcic. (CISM International Centre for Mechanical Sciences Ser.: Vol. 14). (Illus.). 58p. 1975. pap. 14.00 (*0-387-81163-X*) Spr-Verlag.

Application of Hyperthermia in the Treatment of Cancer. Ed. by R. D. Issels & W. Wilmanns. (Recent Results in Cancer Research Ser.: Vol. 107). (Illus.). 290p. 1988. 101.00 (*0-387-18486-4*) Spr-Verlag.

Application of Ion-Selective Microelectrodes. Ed. by T. Zeuthen. (Research Monographs in Cell Tissue Pathology: Vol. 4). 284p. 1981. 155.50 (*0-444-80268-1*) Elsevier.

Application of Isotope Systems to Geological Problems. (Illus.). 366p. (Orig.). (C). 1993. pap. text ed. 95.00 (*1-56806-403-9*) Diane Pub.

Application of Item Response Theory to Language Testing. Inn-Chull Choi. LC 91-16472. (Theoretical Studies in Second Language Acquisition: Vol. 2). 202p. (C). 1992. text ed. 41.95 (*0-8204-1573-1*) P Lang Pubs.

Application of Learning Theory to Adult Teaching. K. Mackie. (C). 1988. text ed. 40.00 (*0-685-22143-1*, Pub. by Univ Nottingham UK) St Mut.

Application of Learning Theory to Adult Teaching. Karl Mackie. (C). 1981. 35.00 (*0-902031-88-0*, Pub. by Univ Nottingham UK) St Mut.

Application of Learning Theory to ESP Performance. Charles T. Tart. LC 75-14709. (Parapsychological Monograph Ser.: No. 15). 1975. pap. 8.00 (*0-912328-25-8*) Parapsych Foun.

Application of Math Statistics to Chemical Analysis. V. Nalilmov & Prabir Basu. LC 61-11161. 1963. 124.00 (*0-08-009916-5*, Pub. by Pergamon Repr UK) Franklin.

Application of Mathematical Modelling to Process Development & Design. L. M. Rose. (Illus.). 364p. 1974. 93.75 (*0-85334-584-8*, Pub. by Elsevier Applied Sci UK) Elsevier.

Application of Mechanics to Engineering & Technology. Frolov. 1993. write for info. (*0-8493-9326-4*) CRC Pr.

Application of Mental Health Statistics: Uses in Mental Health Programmes of Statistics Derived from Psychiatric Service & Selected Vital & Morbidity Records. M. Kramer. (Illus.). 112p. 1969. pap. 4.80 (*92-4-156013-4*, 1141) World Health.

Application of Metal Cutting. Fryderyk E. Gorczyca. LC 87-3882. (Illus.). 275p. 1987. 32.95 (*0-8311-1176-3*) Indus Pr.

Application of Metrological Laser Methods in Machines & Systems. Ed. by Gottfried Frankowski et al. (Physical Research Ser.: Vol. 15). 384p. 1991. text ed. 72.00 (*3-05-500789-1*, Pub. by Akademie GW) VCH Pubs.

Application of Micro-Computers in Information, Documentation, & Libraries: Proceedings of the International Conference, 2nd, Baden-Baden, West Germany, March 17-21, 1986. International Conference Staff. (Contemporary Topics in Information Transfer Ser.: No. 4). 814p. 1987. 143.75 (*0-444-70135-4*, North Holland) Elsevier.

***Application of Microfabrication to Fluid Mechanics: 1994 International Mechanical Engineering Congress & Exposition, Chicago, Illinois - November 6-11, 1994.** (FED Ser.: Vol. 197). 96p. 1994. 48.00 (*0-7918-1391-6*, G00886) ASME.

Application of Miner's Rule to Industrial Gear Drives. Donald R. McVittie & Robert L. Errichello. (Fall Technical Meeting Papers 99FTM9). (Illus.). 22p. 1988. pap. text ed. 30.00 (*1-55589-514-X*) AGMA.

Application of Modern Systematic Management: An Original Anthology. Ed. by Alfred D. Chandler, Jr. LC 79-7522. (History of Management Thought & Practice Ser.). (Illus.). 1980. lib. bdg. 19.95 (*0-405-12307-8*) Ayer.

Application of Multiple Scattering Theory to Materials Science. Ed. by W. H. Butler et al. (Symposium Proceedings Ser.: Vol. 253). 1992. text ed. 64.00 (*1-55899-147-6*) Materials Res.

Application of Multivariable System Techniques: AMST, 90. Ed. by R. Whalley. 408p. 1990. 90.00 (*1-85166-481-5*) Elsevier.

Application of Neural Networks to Modelling & Control. Ed. by G. F. Page et al. LC 93-14878. 1993. Alk. paper. write for info. (*0-412-54760-0*) Chapman & Hall.

Application of New Concepts of Physical-Chemical Waste Water Treatment see Progress in Water Technology

Application of NMR Spectroscopy to Cement Science. Ed. by Pierre Colombet & Arnd R. Grimmer. 1994. write for info. (*0-318-72613-0*) Gordon & Breach.

Application of NMR Techniques on the Body Composition of Live Animals: A Seminar Organized by the Commission of the European Communities in the Framework of the Community Programme for the Coordination of Agricultural Research & held at the Institut fur Tierzucht & Tierverhaven, Mariensee (FRG), 14-15 June 1988. Ed. by E. Kallweit et al. 176p. 1989. 39.75 (*1-85166-404-1*) Elsevier.

Application of Non-Animal Models to Biomedical & Behavioral Research. Kapis. 1993. 69.95 (*0-87371-504-7*, R852) Lewis Pubs.

Application of Non Linear Analysis to Structural Problems. Ed. by A. B. Pijco. (PVP Ser.: Vol. 76). 141p. 1983. pap. text ed. 30.00 (*0-317-02552-X*, H00262) ASME.

Application of Nonclonal Antibodies in Tumor Pathology. Ed. by Dirk J. Ruiter et al. (Developments in Oncology Ser.). 1987. lib. bdg. 180.00 (*0-89838-853-8*) Kluwer Ac.

Application of Nuclear Magnetic Resonance Spectroscopes to Quality-Control Measurements of Asphalt & Asphalt-Aggregate Mixes. Robert M. Pearson. 42p. (Orig.). (C). 1994. pap. text ed. 10.00 (*0-309-05760-4*, SHRP-A-382) SHRP.

Application of Nuclear Techniques in Geothermal Investigations. Ed. by E. Barbier. 192p. 1983. pap. 61.00 (*0-08-030269-6*, 2304, 1506, 1901, Pergamon Pr) Elsevier.

Application of Nuclear Techniques to Geothermal Studies: Proceedings. Ed. by E. Barbier. 1978. pap. 94.00 (*0-08-021670-6*, Pergamon Pr) Elsevier.

***Application of Nursing Process & Nursing Diagnosis: An Interactive Text for Diagnostic Reasoning.** 2nd ed. Marilyn E. Doenges et al. (Illus.). 311p. (Orig.). (C). 1995. pap. text ed. 22.95 (*0-8036-2676-2*) Davis Co.

Application of Operations Research to Court Delay. John H. Reed. LC 72-89647. (Special Studies in U. S. Economic, Social & Political Issues). 1973. 39.50 (*0-275-06690-8*) Irvington.

Application of Optimal Control Theory to Enhanced Oil Recovery. W. F. Ramirez. (Developments in Petrolem Science Ser.: No. 21). 244p. 1987. 79.50 (*0-444-42835-6*) Elsevier.

Application of Pade's Approximation Theory in Fluid: Advances in Mathematics for Applied Sciences Ser. A. Pozzi. 252p. 1994. text ed. 61.00 (*981-02-1414-6*) World Scientific Pub.

***Application of Particle & Laser Beams in Materials Technology.** Ed. by P. Misaelides. LC 94-46545. (NATO ASI Ser.: Series E, Applied Sciences: Vol. 283). 1995. lib. bdg. 280.00 (*0-7923-3324-1*) Kluwer Ac.

Application of Pattern Recognition to Catalytic Research. I. I. Ioffe. LC 87-36927. (Chemometrics Research Studies). 185p. 1988. text ed. 170.00 (*0-471-91907-1*) Wiley.

Application of Personnel Assessment Concepts & Methods in Job Evaluation Procedures see IPMA Assessment Council Monograph Series

Application of Plasmas to Chemical Processing. R. Baddour & R. Timmins. LC 67-17494. 1967. 92.00 (*0-08-012735-5*, Pub. by Pergamon Repr UK) Franklin.

Application of Polarization Measurements in the Control of Metal Deposition. Ed. by I. H. Warren. (Process Metallurgy Ser.: Vol. 3). 314p. 1984. 113.00 (*0-444-42345-1*, I-229-84) Elsevier.

Application of Polymeric Reinforcement in Soil Retaining Structures. Ed. by Peter M. Jarrett & Alan McGown. (C). 1988. lib. bdg. 197.00 (*90-247-3716-8*) Kluwer Ac.

***Application of Positron Spectroscopy to Materials Science.** Ed. by L. D. Hulett et al. (Advanced Materials Research Ser.: Vol. 3). (Illus.). 80p. (C). 1995. 62.00 (*3-908450-06-3*) LPS Dist Ctr.

Application of Probability in Decision Making. Shabir H. Banday. 200p. 1992. 80.00 (*81-7041-590-X*, Pub. by Scientific Pubs II) St Mut.

Application of Psychiatric Insights to Cross-Cultural Communicationn. Group for the Advancement of Psychiatry Staff. (Group for the Advancement of Psychiatry, Symposium Ser.: No. 7). 52p. reprint ed. pap. 25.00 (*0-8357-5662-9*, 2021836) Bks Demand.

***Application of Quality to Risk Management Practices.** Willis Corroon. 1994. pap. 60.00 (*0-88711-272-2*) Am Trucking Assns.

Application of Queueing Theory. 2nd ed. C. F. Newell. (Monographs on Statistics & Applied Probability). 220p. 1982. 42.50 (*0-412-24500-0*, 6620) Chapman & Hall.

Application of Radioiodinated Rose Bengal & Colloidal Radiogold in the Detection of Hepatobiliary Disease. Leonard Rosenthall. LC 68-59353. (Illus.). 98p. 1969. 8.00 (*0-87527-068-9*) Green.

Application of Redemption, by the Effectual Work of the Word, & the Spirit of Christ, for the Bringing Home of Lost Sinners to God. Thomas Hooker. LC 70-141111. (Research Library of Colonial Americana). 1972. reprint ed. 41.95 (*0-405-03324-9*) Ayer.

Application of Regression Analysis. Wittink. 336p. (C). 1988. teacher ed write for info. (*0-318-62187-8*, H12537) Allyn.

Application of Remote Sensing to Agricultural. J. G. Clevers. (C). 1981. text ed. 460.00 (*0-89771-587-X*, Pub. by Intl Bk Distr II) St Mut.

Application of Remote Sensing to Agricultural Field Trials. J. G. Clevers. 227p. (Orig.). 1992. 288.00 (*81-7089-122-1*, Pub. by Intl Bk Distr II) St Mut.

Application of Remote Sensing to Agricultural Production Forecasting: Proceedings of a Seminar Held at the Joint Research Centre of the Commission of the European Communities, Ispra, Italy. Ed. by A. Berg. 272p. (C). 1981. text ed. 120.00 (*90-6191-089-7*, Pub. by A A Balkema NE) Ashgate Pub Co.

An Asterisk (*) at the beginning of an entry indicates that the title is appearing in BIP for the first time.

***Application of RFLP & RAPD Molecular Technologies to Plant Breeding: A Project Listing & Bibliography.** Ed. by Andrew Kalinski. 166p. (Orig.). (C). 1994. pap. text ed. 50.00x (*0-7881-1495-6*) Diane Pub.

Application of Rock Characterization Techniques in Mine Design: International Symposium: Proceedings of the Symposium Held at the SME-AIME Annual Meeting, March, 1986, New Orleans, Louisiana. International Symposium on Application of Rock Characterization Techniques in Mine Design Staff. Ed. by Michael Karmis. LC 85-63026. 272p. pap. 77.60 (*0-8357-2567-7*, 2040257) Bks Demand.

Application of Rock Mechanics to Planning & Design Prior Mining: Proceedings of the Plenary Scientific Session of the International Bureau of Strata Mechanics, World Mining Congress, Essen, 8th, 22-24 June 1983. Ed. by A. Kidybinsky & M. Kwasniewski. 288p. (C). 1984. text ed. 160.00 (*90-6191-537-6*, Pub. by A A Balkema NE) Ashgate Pub Co.

Application of Rules in New Situations: A Hermeneutic Study. Bo Hanson. (Studia Philosophiae Religionis: Vol. 3). 1977. pap. 40.00x (*91-40-04537-4*) Coronet Bks.

Application of Scattering Methods to the Dynamics of Polymer Systems. Ed. by B. Ewen et al. (Progress in Colloid & Polymer Science Ser.: Vol. 91). viii, 173p. 1993. 83.00 (*0-387-91444-7*) Spr-Verlag.

Application of Science in Examination of Works of Art. Pamela England & Lambertus Van Zelst. Ed. by Cynthia Purvis. LC 85-61682. 264p. 1986. write for info. (*0-87846-255-4*) Mus Fine Arts Boston.

Application of Self-Adjoint Extensions in Quantum Physics. Ed. by P. Exner & P. Seba. (Lecture Notes in Physics Ser.: Vol. 324). 273p. 1989. 41.00 (*0-387-50883-X*) Spr-Verlag.

Application of Six Sigma Concepts to a Facilities Organization. Antoine D. Alldredge. LC 92-25880. (Six Sigma Research Institute Ser.). 1992. pap. write for info. (*0-201-63435-X*) Addison-Wesley.

Application of Solidification-Stabilization to Waste Materials. Jeffrey L. Means et al. 200p. 1994. 69.95 (*1-56670-080-9*, L1080) Lewis Pubs.

Application of Statewide Freight Demand Forecasting Techniques. (National Cooperative Highway Research Program Report Ser.: No. 260). 210p. 1983. 12.80 (*0-309-03601-1*) Transport Res Bd.

Application of Statistics in Behavioral Research. Richard B. May et al. 618p. (C). 1990. text ed. 49.00 (*0-06-044311-1*) HarpCollege.

Application of Stress-Wave Theory on Piles: Proceedings of the International Seminar, Stockholm, 4-5 June 1980. Ed. by H. Bredenberg. 350p. (C). 1980. text ed. 150.00 (*90-6191-095-1*, Pub. by A A Balkema NE) Ashgate Pub Co.

Application of Stress-Wave Theory on Piles: Second International Conference: Proceedings, 27-30 May 1984. Ed. by G. Holm et al. 462p. (C). 1985. text ed. 150.00 (*90-6191-547-3*, Pub. by A A Balkema NE) Ashgate Pub Co.

Application of Stress Wave Theory to Piles: Proceedings of the Fourth International Conference on the Application of Stress-Wave Theory to Piles The Hague - The Netherlands 21-24 September 1992. Ed. by Frans J. Barends. (Illus.). 726p. (C). 1992. text ed. 115.00 (*90-5410-082-6*, Pub. by A A Balkema NE) Ashgate Pub Co.

Application of Structural Systems: Reliability Theory. P. Thoft-Christensen & Y. Murotsu. (Illus.). 350p. 1986. 124.00 (*0-387-16362-X*) Spr-Verlag.

Application of Surface-Geophysical Methods to Investigations of Sand & Gravel Acquifers in the Glaciated Northeastern United States. F. P. Haeni. 1994. write for info. (*0-318-70185-5*) US Geol Survey.

Application of Synchrotron Radiation X-Rays in Materials Science. D. K. Bowen et al. 1984. write for info. (*0-318-57813-1*) Elsevier.

Application of System Identification in Engineering. Ed. by H. G. Natke. (CISM International Centre for Mechanical Sciences Ser.: Vol. 296). (Illus.). 583p. 1988. pap. 70.00 (*0-387-82052-3*) Spr-Verlag.

Application of Systems Analysis Irrigation, Drainage & Flood Control: A Manual for Engineers & Water Technologists. Ed. by International Commission on Irrigation & Drainage, New Delhi, India. (Water Development, Supply & Management Ser.: Vol. 11). (Illus.). 1980. 93.00 (*0-08-023425-9*, Pub. by Pergamon Repr UK) Franklin.

Application of Technology to Improve Productivity in the Service Sector of the National Economy: Summary Report & Recommendations Based on a Symposium & Workshops Held on the Occasion of the Eighth Annual Meeting, November 1 & 2, 1971, at the National Academy of Engineering. National Academy of Engineering Staff. LC 72-83855. 376p. reprint ed. pap. 107.20 (*0-8357-7695-6*, 2036047) Bks Demand.

Application of the Biosphere Reserve Concept to Coastal Marine Areas: Papers Presented at the UNESCO-IUCN San Francisco Workshop, 14-20 August 1989. Ed. by Andrew Price & Sarah Humphrey. 114p. (C). 1993. pap. text ed. 10.00 (*2-8317-0135-X*, Pub. by IUCN SZ) Island Pr.

Application of the European Convention on Human Rights. 2nd ed. J. E. Fawcett & Convention for the Protection of Human Rights & Fundamental Freedoms, 1950. LC 86-23774. 436p. 1987. 89.00 (*0-19-825510-1*) OUP.

Application of the European Convention on Human Rights. 2nd ed. J. E. Fawcett & Convention for the Protection of Human Rights & Fundamental Freedoms, 1950. LC 86-23774. 436p. 1987. pap. 32.50 (*0-19-825509-8*) OUP.

Application of the International Classification of Diseases to Dentistry & Stomatology (ICD-DA) 1973. pap. 6.40 (*92-4-154029-X*) World Health.

Application of the Kernel Function in Interpreting Geoelectrical Resistivity Measurements. O. Koefoed. (Geoexploration Monographs: No. 2). (Illus.). 111p. 1968. text ed. 25.25 (*3-443-13002-X*) Lubrecht & Cramer.

Application of the Makewhole Remedy under California's Labor Relations Act: Litigious Refusals to Bargain. Walter Fogel. (Monograph & Research Ser.: No. 50). 137p. (Orig.). 1989. pap. 11.00 (*0-89215-157-9*) U Cal LA Indus Rel.

Application of the Microcomputer in Schools: How School Administrators & Teachers Can Master the Microcomputer. Thomas C. Valesky & Eugene Connors. 250p. 1988. 25.95 (*0-915253-12-7*) Wilkerson Pub Co.

Application of the Principles for Limiting Releases of Radioactive Effluents in the Case of the Mining & Milling of Radioactive Ores. (Safety Ser.: No. 90). (Illus.). 78p. 1989. pap. 45.00 (*92-0-123089-3*, ISP779) UNIPUB.

Application of the Random Vibration Approach in the Seismic Analysis. A. Preumont et al. 89p. 1992. pap. 15.00 (*92-826-4287-9*, CD-NA-14153-EN-C, Pub. by Europ Com) UNIPUB.

Application of the Rorschach Test to Young Children, Vol. 23. Mary Ford. LC 70-141545. (University of Minnesota Institute of Child Welfare Monographs: No. 23). (Illus.). 114p. 1975. reprint ed. text ed. 45.00 (*0-8371-5892-3*, CWFR, Greenwood Pr) Greenwood.

Application of the Rule of Exhaustion of Local Remedies in International Law: Its Rationale in the International Protection of Individual Rights. A. Cancado Trindade. LC 82-4393. (Cambridge Studies in International & Comparative Law). 1983. 89.95 (*0-521-22947-2*) Cambridge U Pr.

Application of the Scriptures: A Refutation of Dispensationalism. Arthur W. Pink. pap. 2.99 (*0-87377-071-4*) GAM Pubns.

Application of Traffic Simulation Models. (Special Report Ser.: No. 194). 114p. 1981. 14.00 (*0-309-03262-8*) Transport Res Bd.

Application of Transition State Theory to Unimolecular Reactions: An Introduction. John H. Beynon & J. R. Gilbert. LC 83-17016. (Illus.). 93p. reprint ed. pap. 26.60 (*0-8357-3048-4*, 2039304) Bks Demand.

Application of Two & One Quarter Cr-1Mo Steel for Thick-Wall Pressure Vessels-STP 755. Ed. by Sangdahl & Semchyshen. 473p. 1982. 45.00 (*0-8031-0741-2*, 04-755000-02) ASTM.

Application of Ultrafiltration in the Dairy Industry. Ed. by E. Renner & M. H. El-Salam. 378p. 1991. 114.00 (*1-85166-531-5*) Elsevier.

Application of Variable Speed Drives. David W. Spitzer. LC 87-3585. 196p. reprint ed. pap. 55.90 (*0-8357-4425-6*, 2037256) Bks Demand.

Application of Vegetation Science to Grassland Husbandry. Ed. by W. Krause. (Handbook of Vegetation Science Ser.: No. 13). (Illus.). 1977. lib. bdg. 154.50 (*90-6193-194-0*) Kluwer Ac.

Application of Walls to Landslide Control Problems. Ed. by R. B. Reeves. LC 82-70668. 133p. 1982. pap. 17.00 (*0-87262-302-5*) Am Soc Civil Eng.

Application of Welded Botled & Riveted Connections in HSLA Steel in Structures, No. EUR 13626. J. L. Overbeeke. 174p. 1991. pap. 19.00 (*92-826-2819-1*, CD-NA-13626-EN-C) UNIPUB.

***Application Partitioning & Integration with SSADM.** 158p. 1994. pap. 80.00 (*0-11-330622-9*, HM06229, Pub. by HMSO UK) UNIPUB.

***Application Portability Profile (APP) Guide: The U. S. Government's Open System Environmental Profile OSE 1, Version 2.0.** (Illus.). 110p. (Orig.). (C). 1994. pap. text ed. 45.00x (*0-7881-1122-1*) Diane Pub.

Application Programming & File Processing in COBOL: Concepts, Techniques, & Applications. Yuksel Uckan. 1059p. (C). 1992. pap. text ed. write for info. (*0-669-16570-0*); Instr.'s guide with transparency masters. teacher ed, trans. write for info. (*0-669-16571-9*); Test item file. teacher ed write for info. (*0-669-28210-3*); Program/data disk 5-1/4". write for info. (*0-669-29721-6*); Program/data disk 3-1/2". write for info. (*0-669-29722-4*) Heath.

Application Programming & File Processing in COBOL: Concepts, Techniques, & Applications, Vol. I. Yuksel Uckan. 689p. (C). 1992. pap. text ed. write for info. (*0-669-28207-3*) Heath.

Application Programming & File Processing in COBOL: Concepts, Techniques, & Applications, Vol. II. Yuksel Uckan. 541p. (C). 1992. pap. text ed. write for info. (*0-669-28208-1*) Heath.

Application Programming for Windows NT. William H. Murray, III. 1993. text ed. 39.95 (*0-07-881933-4*) Osborne-McGraw.

Application Programming in CTOS. William O. Limkemann. 300p. 1993. pap. text ed. 38.00 (*0-13-041872-2*) P-H.

Application Prototyping: A Requirements Definition Strategy for the '80's. Bernard H. Boar. LC 83-16934. 210p. 1984. text ed. 55.00 (*0-471-89317-X*, Wiley-Interscience) Wiley.

Application Refused: Employment Vetting by the State. Ian Linn. 96p. (C). 1991. pap. text ed. 25.00 (*0-900137-33-9*, Pub. by NCCL UK) St Mut.

Application Software: Version A. 3rd ed. Dennis P. Curtin. LC 92-14812. (Computer Application Software Ser.). 816p. 1993. pap. text ed. 53.00 (*0-13-041971-0*) P-H.

Application Software on the IBM PC. 2nd ed. James Shuman. 1988. Incl. diskette. pap. write for info. (*0-07-556420-3*); Incl. diskettes. pap. write for info. (*0-07-556426-2*) McGraw.

Application Software Programming: With Fourth Generation Languages. W. Gregory Wojtkowski. 688p. (C). 1989. pap. text ed. write for info. (*0-538-91097-6*, BF3380) S-W Pub.

Application Software Tutorial. Keiko Pitter. 1987. pap. write for info. (*0-07-556490-4*) McGraw.

Application Software, Version B. 3rd ed. Dennis P. Curtin. 1993. pap. text ed. 53.00 (*0-13-096223-6*) P-H.

Application Software WordPerfect 5.1 Edition. Dennis P. Curtin. 1991. pap. text ed. 29.00 (*0-13-040312-1*, 220101) P-H.

Application Software, 3-E, Version C. 3rd ed. Dennis Curtis et al. 1994. pap. text ed. 36.75 (*0-13-057878-9*) P-H.

***Application Specific Array Processors: Proceedings of the International Conference on Application Specific Array Processors.** Ed. by Peter Cappello et al. 452p. 1994. text ed. 120.00 (*0-8186-6517-3*) IEEE Comp Soc.

Application Specific Array Processors (ASAP '92) International Conference. LC 92-71724. 712p. 1992. 98.00 (*0-8186-2967-3*, 2967) IEEE Comp Soc.

Application Specific Array Processors (ASAP '93) International Conference. 608p. 1993. text ed. 90.00 (*0-8186-3492-8*, 3492) IEEE Comp Soc.

Application Specific Integrated Circuits. Malcolm R. Haskard. 160p. 1990. boxed 30.80 (*0-13-471376-1*) P-H.

Application Specific Integrated Circuits. Michael J. Smith. LC 93-32538. 1994. write for info. (*0-02-015002-4*) Addison-Wesley.

Application Specific Integrated Circuits. Michael J. S. Smith. (VLSI Systems Ser.). (Illus.). 608p. (C). 1995. text ed. 49.50 (*0-201-50022-1*) Addison-Wesley.

Application Specifications for the UCC-128 Serial Shipping Container Code. 1989. 30.00 (*0-318-50028-0*) Uniform Code.

Application Technology for Crop Protection. Ed. by G. A. Matthews & E. C. Hislop. 359p. 1993. 99.50 (*0-85198-834-2*) CAB Intl.

Applications. Ed. by J. L. Goffin & J. M. Rousseau. (Mathematical Programming Studies: Vol. 20). 218p. 1982. pap. 51.50 (*0-444-86478-4*, I-341-82, North Holland) Elsevier.

Applications: A Guide to Filling Out All Kinds of Forms. Jeffrey Shniderman & Sue Hurwitz. LC 93-7911. (Life Skills Library). (YA). 1993. 13.95 (*0-8239-1609-X*) Rosen Group.

Applications: Issues for Reading & Writing. Audrey T. Edwards & R. Allan Dermott. LC 85-24851. 324p. (C). 1986. pap. text ed. 21.50 (*0-03-071838-4*) HB Coll Pubs.

Applications & Design with Analog Integrated Circuits. Jacob. (C). 1982. teacher ed write for info. (*0-8359-0246-3*, Reston) P-H.

Applications & Design with Analog Integrated Circuits. 2nd ed. J. Michael Jacob. 544p. (C). 1993. text ed. write for info. (*0-13-032145-1*) P-H.

***Applications & Developments in New Engine Design & Components: 1995 International Congress & Exposition Meeting.** 1995. pap. 99.00 (*1-56091-621-4*, SP1071) Soc Auto Engineers.

Applications & Efficiency of Heat Pump Systems in Environmentally Sensitive Times: Proceedings of the 4th International Conference, Munich, Germany, 1-3 October 1990. Ed. by I. E. Smith. 260p. 1991. 148.00 (*0-387-53624-8*) Spr-Verlag.

Applications & Implementation of Finite Element Methods. J. Ed Akin. 1984. pap. text ed. 47.00 (*0-12-047652-5*) Acad Pr.

Applications & Investigations in Earth Science. Edward J. Tarbuck. 336p. (C). 1994. pap. write for info. (*0-02-419011-X*) Macmillan.

Applications & Techiques. H. Ehringer et al. 1983. lib. bdg. 112.50 (*90-277-1580-7*) Kluwer Ac.

Applications des Inequations Variationnelles en Controle Stochastique see Applications of Variational Inequalities in Stochastic Control

Applications Exercises Using Lotus 1-2-3, dBASE III-III Plus & Wordstar. Alex Neely et al. 150p. (C). 1987. pap. write for info. (*0-675-20902-1*, Merrill Pub Co) Macmillan.

Applications Exercises Using VP-Planner, dBASE III-III Plus & Wordstar with VP-Planner, dBASE III-III Plus & Wordstar Student Software Disks. Alex Neely. 150p. (C). 1987. pap. write for info. (*0-675-20844-0*, Merrill Pub Co) Macmillan.

Applications Exercises Using VP-Planner with Student Software Disk. Alex Neely. 100p. (C). 1987. pap. write for info. (*0-675-20921-8*, Merrill Pub Co) Macmillan.

Applications for Computer Aided Drafting. Jeff Allen et al. 209p. (C). 1991. 21.80 (*1-56870-005-9*) RonJon Pub.

***Applications for Computer Concepts.** Sally A. Hanson. 96p. (C). 1994. ring bd. 26.95 (*0-8403-9600-7*) Kendall-Hunt.

Applications for Computers & Information Systems. 4th ed. William M. Fuori & Louis V. Gioia. LC 93-42133. 1994. pap. text ed. 15.00 (*0-13-300237-3*) P-H.

Applications for Distributed Systems & Network Management. Kornel Terplan & Jill Huntington-Lee. LC 94-19593. 350p. 1994. text ed. 44.95 (*0-442-01873-8*) Van Nos Reinhold.

***Applications for Judicial Review: Law & Practice of the Crown.** 2nd ed. Grahame L. Aldous & John Alder. 230p. 1993. pap. 70.00 (*0-406-00576-1*, U.K.) Butterworth Legal Pubs.

Applications for Voice Processing Technology. William W. Creitz. 126p. 1991. pap. text ed. 60.00 (*0-9631712-0-8*) Stoneridge Tech Srvs.

Applications HPLC in Biochemistry PPR. A. Fallon. (Laboratory Technology in Biochemistry & Molecular Biology Ser.: Vol. 17). 1987. pap. 37.00 (*0-444-80863-9*) Elsevier.

Applications in Basic Marketing: Clippings from the Popular Business Press, 1991-1992. 2nd ed. Ed. by E. Jerome McCarthy & William D. Perreault. 208p. (C). 1991. pap. text ed. 14.95 (*0-256-10116-7*) Irwin Prof Pubng.

Applications in Behavioral Medicine & Health Psychology: A Clinician's Source Book. Ed. by James A. Blumenthal & Daphne C. McKee. LC 86-62715. 616p. 1987. 33.20 (*0-943158-18-4*, ABMBP) Pro Resource.

Applications in Biology - Chemistry: "Air & Other Gases" Center for Occupational Research & Development Staff. (Illus.). 1991. teacher ed write for info. (*1-55502-405-X*); pap. text ed. write for info. (*1-55502-404-1*) CORD Commns.

Applications in Biology - Chemistry: "Animal Life Processes" Center for Occupational Research & Development Staff. (Illus.). 1993. teacher ed write for info. (*1-55502-478-5*); pap. text ed. write for info. (*1-55502-477-7*) CORD Commns.

Applications in Biology - Chemistry: "Continuity of Life" Center for Occupational Research & Development Staff. (Illus.). 1990. teacher ed write for info. (*1-55502-391-6*); pap. text ed. write for info. (*1-55502-390-8*) CORD Commns.

Applications in Biology - Chemistry: "Disease & Wellness" Center for Occupational Research & Development Staff. (Illus.). 260p. 1990. teacher ed write for info. (*1-55502-389-4*); pap. text ed. write for info. (*1-55502-388-6*) CORD Commns.

Applications in Biology - Chemistry: "Microorganisms" Center for Occupational Research & Development Staff. (Illus.). 1993. teacher ed write for info. (*1-55502-476-9*); pap. text ed. write for info. (*1-55502-472-6*) CORD Commns.

Applications in Biology - Chemistry: "Natural Resources" Center for Occupational Research & Development Staff. (Illus.). 160p. 1990. teacher ed write for info. (*1-55502-365-7*); pap. text ed. write for info. (*1-55502-364-9*) CORD Commns.

Applications in Biology - Chemistry: "Nutrition. Center for Occupational Research & Development Staff. (Illus.). 1990. teacher ed write for info. (*1-55502-401-7*); pap. text ed. write for info. (*1-55502-400-9*) CORD Commns.

Applications in Biology - Chemistry: "Plant Growth & Reproduction" Center for Occupational Research & Development Staff. (Illus.). 1991. teacher ed write for info. (*1-55502-407-6*); pap. text ed. write for info. (*1-55502-406-8*) CORD Commns.

Applications in Biology - Chemistry: "Water" Center for Occupational Research & Development Staff. (Illus.). 1991. teacher ed write for info. (*1-55502-403-3*); pap. text ed. write for info. (*1-55502-402-5*) CORD Commns.

Applications in Biology - Chemistry: A Workshop Presenter's Guide for Teacher Training. Center for Occupational Research & Development Staff. (Illus.). 1993. pap. text ed. write for info. (*1-55502-483-1*) CORD Commns.

Applications in Biology - Chemistry Series. Center for Occupational Research & Development Staff. (Illus.). 1992. pap. text ed. write for info. (*1-55502-363-0*) CORD Commns.

Applications in Biology-Chemistry: "Synthetic Materials" Center for Occupational Research & Development Staff. (Illus.). 1994. teacher ed write for info. (*1-55502-480-7*); pap. text ed. write for info. (*1-55502-479-3*) CORD Commns.

Applications in Coastal Modeling. Ed. by V. C. Lakhan & Alan S. Trenhaile. (Elsevier Oceanography Ser.: No. 49). 388p. 1989. 113.00 (*0-444-87452-6*) Elsevier.

Applications in Computing for Social Anthropologists. Michael D. Fischer. LC 93-10306. (ASA Research Methods in Social Anthropology Ser.). 1994. write for info. (*0-415-01818-8*); pap. write for info. (*0-415-01819-6*) Routledge.

Applications in Criminal Analysis: A Sourcebook. Marilyn B. Peterson. LC 94-11219. 336p. 1994. text ed. 79.50 (*0-313-28577-2*, Greenwood Pr) Greenwood.

Applications in General Microbiology: A Laboratory Manual. 4th ed. Kerr. 344p. 1990. text ed., spiral bd. 22.95 (*0-88725-134-X*) Hunter Textbks.

Applications in General Microbiology: Fundamental Exercises. Kerr. 160p. 1990. text ed., spiral bd. 16.95 (*0-88725-133-1*) Hunter Textbks.

Applications in Geomechanics. Ed. by C. A. Brebbia. (Topics in Boundary Elements Ser.: Vol. 4). 183p. 1987. 57.00 (*1-56252-144-6*) Computational Mech MA.

Applications in Health Psychology. Ed. by Marie Johnston & Theresa Marteau. 220p. 1988. 39.95x (*0-88738-254-1*) Transaction Pubs.

Applications in Human Resource Management. 2nd ed. Stella M. Nkomo et al. 256p. (C). 1992. pap. 30.95 (*0-534-92959-1*) Intl Thomson.

Applications in Lotus 1-2-3 Release 2.2. Robert Krumm. (Software Application Ser.). 1991. pap. 10.00 (*0-685-40577-X*, 220109) P-H.

Applications in Macintosh. Alan L. Eliason & Lorilee Sadler. 512p. (C). 1992. pap. text ed. write for info. (*0-13-041740-8*) P-H.

Applications in Macintosh: Using Hypercard. Alan L. Eliason & Lorilee Sadler. 160p. (C). 1991. pap. text ed. 13.00 (*0-13-041658-4*, 220103) P-H.

Applications in Mechanical Engineering Technology. K. V. Frolov et al. 1991. 150.00 (*0-89116-727-7*) CRC Pr.

Applications in Parallel & Distributed Computing. Ed. by C. Girault. LC 94-3095. (IFIP Transactions A: Computer Science & Technology Ser.: Vol. A-44). 1994. write for info. (*0-444-81870-7*, North Holland) Elsevier.

Applications in School & Home. R. Vance Hall. (Managing Behavior Ser.: Part 3). 63p. (C). 1971. pap. 10.00 (*0-89079-003-5*, 1047) PRO-ED.

An Asterisk (*) at the beginning of an entry indicates that the title is appearing in BIP for the first time.

Applications in School Mathematics: 1979 Yearbook. Ed. by Sidney Sharron. LC 79-1137. (Illus.). 248p. 1979. 20.00 (0-87353-139-6) NCTM.

Applications in Windows: Windows - Word for Windows - Excel for Windows. Bennett Dear. Date not set. pap. write for info. (0-13-088485-5) P-H.

Applications in Windows: Windows - WordPerfect for Windows - Lotus for Windows. Bennett Dear. Date not set. pap. write for info. (0-13-088477-4) P-H.

Applications of Absorption Spectroscopy of Organic Compounds. James A. Dyer. 1965. pap. text ed. 37.00 (0-13-038802-5) P-H.

Applications of Adaptive Control. Ed. by Kumpati S. Narendra & Richard Monopoli. 1980. text ed. 114.00 (0-12-514060-6) Acad Pr.

Applications of Advanced Technologies in Transportation Engineering. Ed. by Yargos I. Stephanedes & Kumares C. Sinha. LC 91-24882. 481p. 1991. pap. text ed. 47.00 (0-87262-818-3) Am Soc Civil Eng.

Applications of AI in Manufacturing. Steve M. Kim & Dana Nau. Ed. by A. Famili et al. (AAAI Press Ser.). (Illus.). 400p. 1992. pap. 39.95 (0-262-56066-6) MIT Pr.

Applications of Algebraic K-Theory to Algebraic Geometry & Number Theory, 2 pts., Pt. 1. S. J. Bloch et al. LC 86-7904. (Contemporary Mathematics Ser.: Vol. 55). 406p. 1986. pap. text ed. 45.00 (0-8218-5055-5, CONM-55.1) Am Math.

Applications of Algebraic K-Theory to Algebraic Geometry & Number Theory, 2 pts., Pt. 2. S. J. Bloch et al. LC 86-7904. (Contemporary Mathematics Ser.: Vol. 55). 818p. 1986. pap. text ed. 46.00 (0-8218-5056-3, CONM-55.2) Am Math.

Applications of Algebraic K-Theory to Algebraic Geometry & Number Theory, 2 pts., Set. S. J. Bloch et al. LC 86-7904. (Contemporary Mathematics Ser.: Vol. 55). 856p. 1986. pap. text ed. 79.00 (0-8218-5054-7, CONM55) Am Math.

Applications of Alternative Energy Sources: Selected Experiences. 271p. 1986. pap. 18.50 (0-685-49813-1, 0015, Pub. by APO JA) Qual Resc.

Applications of Analog Integrated Circuits. Sidney Soclof. (Illus.). 496p. (C). 1984. text ed. 82.00 (0-13-039173-5) P-H.

Applications of Analytic & Geometric Methods to Nonlinear Differential Equations. Ed. by Peter A. Clarkson. LC 93-11843. (NATO Advanced Study Institutes Series C, Mathematical & Physical Sciences: No. 413). 1993. lib. bdg. 197.00 (0-7923-2457-9) Kluwer Ac.

Applications of Analytical Techniques to the Characteristics. D. L. Perry. (Illus.). 190p. (C). 1992. 75.00 (0-306-44189-6, Plenum Pr) Plenum.

Applications of Artificial Intelligence, No. V. Ed. by Gilmore. 624p. 1987. 79.00 (0-89252-821-4, 786) SPIE.

Applications of Artificial Intelligence, No. VII. Ed. by M. M. Trivedi. 1167p. 1989. 132.00 (0-8194-0131-5, VOL. 1095) SPIE.

Applications of Artificial Intelligence in Chemistry. Hugh M. Cartwright. (Oxford Chemistry Primers Ser.: No. 11). (Illus.). 96p. (C). 1994. text ed. 29.95 (0-19-855737-X); pap. text ed. 9.95 (0-19-855736-1) OUP.

Applications of Artificial Intelligence in Engineering. Ed. by J. S. Gero & G. Rzevski. 1000p. 1989. 251.00 (0-387-51344-2, 3252) Spr-Verlag.

*__Applications of Artificial Intelligence in Engineering, 2 vols.__ Ed. by G. Rzevski & J. S. Gero. (AIENG Ser.: Vol. 4). 1040p. 1989. 193.50 (1-85312-039-1) Computational Mech MA.

Applications of Artificial Intelligence in Engineering: Proceedings of the Fifth International Conference, Boston, U. S. A., 17-20 July 1990, 2 vols., Set. Ed. by J. S. Gero & G. Rzevsky. 956p. 1990. 225.00 (0-387-52920-9) Spr-Verlag.

Applications of Artificial Intelligence in Engineering: Proceedings of the Fifth International Conference, Boston, U. S. A., 17-20 July 1990, 2 vols., Vol. 1: Design. Ed. by J. S. Gero & G. Rzevsky. vii, 319p. 1990. 94.00 (0-387-52918-7) Spr-Verlag.

Applications of Artificial Intelligence in Engineering: Proceedings of the Fifth International Conference, Boston, U. S. A., 17-20 July 1990, 2 vols., Vol. 2: Manufacture & Planning. Ed. by J. S. Gero & G. Rzevsky. x, 612p. 1990. 176.00 (0-387-52919-5) Spr-Verlag.

Applications of Artificial Intelligence in Engineering, IV: Proc. of the Sixth Internat. Conf., 2-4 July 1991, Oxford, UK. Ed. by G. Rzevski. 1064p. 1991. 255.00 (1-85166-678-8) Elsevier.

Applications of Artificial Intelligence in Engineering VI. Ed. by G. Rzevski & R. A. Adey. LC 91-72244. (AIENG Ser.: Vol. 6). 1064p. 1991. 275.00 (1-56252-069-5) Computational Mech MA.

Applications of Artificial Intelligence in Engineering VII: Proceedings of the Seventh International Conference on Applications of Artificial Intelligence in Engineering (AIENG 92) Held in Waterloo, Ontario, Canada, July 1992. Ed. by D. E. Grierson et al. LC 92-70440. (AIENG Ser.: Vol. 7). 1254p. 1992. 435.00 (1-56252-102-0) Computational Mech MA.

Applications of Artificial Intelligence in Engineering VIII: Vol. 1: Methods & Techniques - Vol. 2: Applications & Techniques, 1. Ed. by G. Rzevski et al. 1472p. 1993. write for info. (1-85166-838-1, Pub. by Elsevier Applied Sci UK) Elsevier.

Applications of Artificial Intelligence in Engineering VIII: Vol. 1: Methods & Techniques - Vol. 2: Applications & Techniques, 2. Ed. by G. Rzevski et al. 1472p. 1993. write for info. (1-85166-839-X, Pub. by Elsevier Applied Sci UK) Elsevier.

Applications of Artificial Intelligence in Engineering VIII: Vol. 1: Methods & Techniques - Vol. 2: Applications & Techniques, Set. Ed. by G. Rzevski et al. 1472p. 1993. 480.00 (1-85166-840-3, Pub. by Elsevier Applied Sci UK) Elsevier.

Applications of Artificial Intelligence in Engineering XI. Ed. by G. Rzevski et al. LC 94-70403. (AIENG Ser.: Vol. 9). 632p. 1994. text ed. 260.00 (1-56252-208-6) Computational Mech MA.

Applications of Artificial Intelligence IX, Vol. 1468. M. M. Trivedi. 1991. 117.00 (0-8194-0577-9) SPIE.

Applications of Artificial Intelligence to Engineering Problems, 2 vols. Ed. by Robert A. Adey & Duvvuru Sriram. 1226p. 1986. 266.00 (0-387-16349-2) Spr-Verlag.

Applications of Artificial Intelligence to Engineering Problems: First International Conference, 2 vol., Set. Ed. by D. Sriram & R. Adey. (AIENG Ser.: Vol. 1). 1986. 208.00 (0-931215-12-9) Computational Mech MA.

Applications of Artificial Intelligence to Real-World Autonomous Mobile Robots: Papers from the 1992 Fall Symposium. Ed. by Erann Gat. (Technical Reports). 207p. (Orig.). (C). 1993. spiral bd. 25.00 (0-929280-35-0) Amer Artificial.

Applications of Artificial Intelligence VIII. Ed. by M. M. Trivedi. 1990. 126.00 (0-8194-0344-X, VOL. 1293) SPIE.

Applications of Artificial Neural Networks. Ed. by S. Rogers. 1990. 86.00 (0-8194-0345-8, VOL. 1294) SPIE.

Applications of Artificial Neural Networks, Vol. 1469. S. K. Rogers. 1991. 109.00 (0-8194-0578-7) SPIE.

Applications of Automation to Fatigue & Fracture Testing. A. A. Braun et al. LC 90-43922. (Special Technical Publication Ser.: No. 1092). (Illus.). 306p. 1990. text ed. 73.00 (0-8031-1401-X, 04-010920-30) ASTM.

Applications of Biological Anthropology to Human Affairs. Ed. by C. G. Mascie-Taylor & Gabriel W. Lasker. (Cambridge Studies in Biological Anthropology: No. 8). (Illus.). 240p. (C). 1991. 69.95 (0-521-38112-6) Cambridge U Pr.

Applications of Biomaterials in Facial Plastic Surgery. Frederick H. Silver. Ed. by Alvin I. Glasgold. 1991. 199.00 (0-8493-5251-7, RD523, CRC Reprint) Franklin.

Applications of Biotechnology. Paul N. Cheremisinoff & Robert P. Quellette. LC 85-51485. 259p. 1985. pap. 29.50 (0-87762-438-0) Technomic.

Applications of Biotechnology in Forestry & Horticulture. Ed. by V. Dhawan. (Illus.). 398p. 1989. 110.00 (0-306-43375-3, Plenum Pr) Plenum.

Applications of Biotechnology in Traditional Fermented Foods. Panel on the Applications of Biotechnology to Traditional Fermented Foods. 208p. (C). 1992. pap. text ed. 19.00 (0-309-04685-8) Natl Acad Pr.

Applications of Calculus. Ed. by Philip Straffin. LC 92-62281. (Resources for Calculus, Vol. 3; MAA Notes Ser.: Vol. 29). 280p. 1993. pap. 26.00 (0-88385-085-0) Math Assn.

Applications of Case Study Research. Robert K. Yin. (Applied Social Research Methods Ser.: Vol. 34). (Illus.). 160p. (C). 1993. text ed. 37.00 (0-8039-5118-3); pap. text ed. 16.95 (0-8039-5119-1) Sage.

Applications of Categorical Algebra. Pure Mathematics Staff. Ed. by A. Heller. LC 72-89866. (Proceedings of Symposia in Pure Mathematics Ser., Humboldt State University, Arcata, CA, July 29-August 16, 1974: Vol. 17). 231p. 1970. 45.00 (0-8218-1417-6, PSPUM-17) Am Math.

Applications of Categories in Computer Science. Ed. by M. P. Fourman et al. (London Mathematical Society Lecture Note Ser.: No. 177). (Illus.). 350p. (C). 1992. pap. 47.95 (0-521-42726-6) Cambridge U Pr.

Applications of Category Theory to Fuzzy Subsets. Ed. by Stephen E. Rodabaugh. (Theory & Decision Library Series B). 412p. (C). 1991. lib. bdg. 115.50 (0-7923-1511-1) Kluwer Ac.

Applications of Centre Manifold Theory. J. Carr. (Applied Mathematical Sciences Ser.: Vol. 35). 160p. 1981. pap. 41.00 (0-387-90577-4) Spr-Verlag.

Applications of Charateristics Functions. E. Lukacs & R. G. Laha. (J). 1964. 17.95 (0-85264-086-2) Lubrecht & Cramer.

Applications of Chess Theory. Efim P. Geller. (Russian Chess Ser.). (Illus.). 300p. 1984. 39.90 (0-08-026914-1, Pergamon Pr); pap. 25.90 (0-08-029738-2, Pergamon Pr) Elsevier.

Applications of Chlorophyll Fluorescence: In Photosynthesis Research, Stress Physiology, Hydrobiology & Remote Sensing. Ed. by Hartmut L. Lichtenthaler. (C). 1988. lib. bdg. 122.00 (90-247-3787-7) Kluwer Ac.

Applications of Circulant Matrices to Functional, Diophantine, & Differential Equations. Alan C. Wilde. 1995. write for info. (0-911586-93-8) Wahr.

Applications of Clinical Nutrition. Frances J. Zeman & Denise M. Ney. (Illus.). 448p. (C). 1987. pap. text ed. 57.00 (0-13-039538-2) P-H.

Applications of Combinatorics & Graph Theory to the Biological & Social Sciences. Ed. by Fred S. Roberts. (IMA Volumes in Mathematics & Its Applications Ser.: Vol. 17). (Illus.). ix, 345p. 1989. 42.00 (0-387-97046-0, 2990) Spr-Verlag.

Applications of Computational Mechanics in Geotechnical Engineering: Proceedings of the International Workshop, Rio de Janeiro, Brazil, July 1991. Ed. by E. A. Vargas et al. (Illus.). 480p. (C). 1994. text ed. 115.00 (90-5410-348-5, Pub. by A A Balkema NE) Ashgate Pub Co.

Applications of Computer-Aided Engineering in Injection Molding. Louis T. Manzione. 1988. 83.00 (0-685-22187-3) T-C Pubns CA.

Applications of Computer Aided Engineering in Injection Molding. Louis T. Manzione. 302p. (C). 1987. text ed. 94.50 (1-56990-057-4) Hanser-Gardner.

*__Applications of Computer Card Technology.__ 1994. lib. bdg. 260.95 (0-8490-6429-5) Gordon Pr.

Applications of Computer Graphics in the Transportation-Land Use Field: A Review & Forecast for the Eighties. Ed. by Jerry B. Schneider. (CPL Bibliographies Ser.: No. 126). 35p. 1983. 8.00 (0-86602-126-4) Coun Plan Librarians.

Applications of Computer Techniques in Chemical Research: Proceedings, Manchester, 15-17 November, 1971. Ed. by Peter Hepple. LC 73-151797. 286p. reprint ed. pap. 81.60 (0-8357-5663-7, 2023687) Bks Demand.

*__Applications of Computer Vision in Medical Image Processing: Papers from the 1994 Spring Symposium.__ Ed. by William Wells, 3rd. (Technical Reports). (Illus.). 246p. (Orig.). 1994. pap. 25.00x (0-929280-69-5) Amer Artificial.

Applications of Computer Vision, 1992 IEEE Workshop on. LC 92-70738. 350p. 1992. 72.00 (0-8186-2840-5, 2840) IEEE Comp Soc.

*__Applications of Computers & Operations Research in the Mineral Industry: 23rd International Symposium.__ Applications of Computers & Operations Research in the Mineral Industry Staff. Ed. by Y. C. Kim. LC 91-68323. (Illus.). reprint ed. pap. 180.00 (0-7837-9182-8, 2049881) Bks Demand.

Applications of Computers in Cardiology: State of the Art & New Perspectives. G. Martin Quetglas et al. 1984. 82.00 (0-444-86824-0, I-029-84) Elsevier.

Applications of Computers to Engineering Design, Manufacturing & Management: Proceedings of the TC5 Conference on CAD-CAM Technology Transfer, Mexico City, Mexico 22-26 August, 1988. Ed. by G. L. Lastra et al. 338p. 1989. 82.00 (0-444-87314-7, North Holland) Elsevier.

*__Applications of Contingent Claims Theory to Microeconomic Problems.__ David A. Hennessy. LC 95-67774. (CARD Monograph Ser.: No. 95-M7). (Illus.). 120p. 1995. pap. text ed. 20.00 (0-936911-07-7) Ctr Agri & Rural Dev.

Applications of Continuous & Steady-State Methods to Root Biology. Ed. by John G. Torrey & Lawrence J. Winship. (Developments in Plant & Soil Sciences Ser.). (C). 1989. lib. bdg. 94.50 (0-7923-0024-6) Kluwer Ac.

Applications of Cryogenic Technology, Vol. 7. Ed. by James R. Missig & Robert W. Vance. LC 68-57815. (Cryogenic Society of America Applications of Cryogenic Technology Ser.). (Illus.). 1978. text ed. 35.00 (0-87936-009-7) Scholium Intl.

Applications of Cryogenic Technology, Vol. 8. Ed. by Sterling Booth & Robert W. Vance. LC 68-57815. (Cryogenic Society of America Applications of Cryogenic Technology Ser.). (Illus.). 1976. text ed. 30.00 (0-87936-010-0) Scholium Intl.

Applications of Cryogenic Technology, Vol. 10. Ed. by J. P. Kelley. (Illus.). 326p. 1991. 89.50 (0-306-43892-5, Plenum Pr) Plenum.

Applications of Cryogenic Technology: Proceedings, Vol. 6. Conference of the Cryogenic Society of America, 1973. Ed. by Robert H. Vance & Sterling H. Booth. LC 68-57815. (Illus.). 290p. 1974. text ed. 30.00 (0-87936-003-8) Scholium Intl.

Applications of Cryogenic Technology: Proceedings, Vol. 9. Cryogenic Society of America, LNG Terminals & Safety Symposium. Ed. by Robert E. Petsinger & Robert W. Vance. LC 68-57815. 1979. 45.00 (0-87936-014-3) Scholium Intl.

Applications of Databases: First International Conference, ADB-94, Vadstena, Sweden, June 1994, Proceedings. Ed. by Witold Litwin & Tore Risch. LC 94-21761. (Lecture Notes in Computer Science: Vol. 819). 1994. 62.00 (0-387-58183-9) Spr-Verlag.

Applications of Decision-Aiding Software. Ed. by Stuart S. Nagel. LC 91-25429. 280p. 1992. text ed. 59.95 (0-312-06811-5) St Martin.

Applications of Diamond Films & Related Materials. Y. Tzeng et al. (Materials Science Monographs: Vol. 73). 1991. 218.00 (0-444-89162-5) Elsevier.

Applications of Diffusion Theory to Cancer Care in the United States 1972-1981. Elinor R. Schoenfeld. (Studies in Historical Demography). 200p. 1990. reprint ed. 15.00 (0-8240-5198-X) Garland.

Applications of Digital Image Processing, No. 10. Ed. by Tescher. 382p. 1987. 59.00 (0-89252-864-8, 829) SPIE.

Applications of Digital Image Processing, No. 11. Ed. by A. G. Tescher. 1988. 59.00 (0-8194-0009-2, 974) SPIE.

Applications of Digital Image Processing XII. Ed. by Andrew G. Tescher. 666p. 1990. 86.00 (0-8194-0189-7, VOL. 1153) SPIE.

Applications of Digital Image Processing XIII, Vol. 1349. A. G. Tescher. 1990. 86.00 (0-8194-0410-1) SPIE.

Applications of Digital Image Processing XIV. A. G. Tescher. 1992. 92.00 (0-8194-0695-3, 1567) SPIE.

Applications of Digital Signal Processing. Alan V. Oppenheim. LC 77-8547. 1977. text ed. 94.00 (0-13-039115-8) P-H.

Applications of Direct Costing. 15.95 (0-86641-017-1, 6129) Inst Mgmt Account.

Applications of Discrete & Continuous Fourier Analysis. H. Joseph Weaver. LC 92-6540. 390p. (C). 1992. reprint ed. lib. bdg. 59.95 (0-89464-735-0) Krieger.

Applications of Discrete Functional Analysis to the Finite Difference Method. Zhou Yulin. (International Academic Publishers Ser.). 260p. 1991. 75.00 (0-08-037946-X, Pub. by IAP UK) Elsevier.

Applications of Discrete Mathematics. John G. Michaels & Kenneth H. Rosen. 1991. pap. text ed. write for info. (0-07-041823-3) McGraw.

Applications of Discrete Mathematics. Ed. by Fred S. Roberts et al. LC 87-51542. (Proceedings in Applied Mathematics Ser.: No. 33). x, 230p. 1988. 40.75 (0-89871-219-X) Soc Indus-Appl Math.

Applications of Dynamic NMR Spectroscopy to Organic Chemistry. Michinori Oki. LC 84-20844. (Methods in Stereochemical Analysis Ser.: Vol. 4). 423p. 1985. lib. bdg. 140.00 (0-89573-120-7) VCH Pubs.

Applications of Dynamic Programming to Agricultural Decision Problems. Ed. by C. Robert Taylor. LC 93-8532. (C). 1993. text ed. 58.00 (0-8133-8641-1) Westview.

*__Applications of Early Astronomical Records.__ fac. ed. Francis R. Stephenson & David H. Clark. LC 79-305856. (Monographs on Astronomical Subjects: No. 4). (Illus.). 124p. 1978. reprint ed. pap. 35.40 (0-7837-8015-X, 2047771) Bks Demand.

Applications of Economics: Contemporary Issues. Hassan Pirasteh. 1993. pap. text ed. 28.30 (1-56226-137-1) CT Pub.

Applications of Electrical Engineering with Mathematica. Alfy Riddle. (C). 1995. text ed. 39.75 (0-201-53477-0) Addison-Wesley.

Applications of Electro-Dynamics in Theoretical Physics & Astrophysics. 2nd rev. ed. V. L. Ginzburg. viii, 476p. 1989. pap. text ed. 109.00 (2-88124-719-9) Gordon & Breach.

Applications of Electroactive Polymers. Ed. by Bruno Scrosati. LC 92-44030. 354p. 1993. 74.05 (0-412-41430-9) Chapman & Hall.

Applications of Electroencephalography in Psychiatry: A Symposium. Ed. by William P. Wilson. LC 65-19449. 280p. reprint ed. pap. 79.80 (0-8357-5664-5, 2023471) Bks Demand.

Applications of Electron Microfractography to Materials Research. Symposium on Applications of Electron Microfractography to Materials Research Staff. LC 70-55959. (ASTM Special Technical Publication Ser.: No. 493). (Illus.). 96p. reprint ed. pap. 27.40 (0-8357-6880-5, 2056885) Bks Demand.

Applications of Electron Microfractography to Materials Research - STP 493. 96p. 1971. pap. 8.25 (0-8031-0746-3, 04-493000-30) ASTM.

Applications of Electronic Imaging. Ed. by John C. Urbach. (Critical Reviews of Optical Science & Technology Ser.). 199p. 1989. pap. 53.00 (0-8194-0117-X, VOL. 1082) SPIE.

Applications of Electronic Structure Theory. Ed. by Henry F. Schaefer, III. LC 77-349. (Modern Theoretical Chemistry Ser.: Vol. 4). (Illus.). 462p. 1977. 120.00 (0-306-33504-2, Plenum Pr) Plenum.

Applications of Entropy Minimax. Ed. by R. Christensen. LC 81-202346. (Entropy Minimax Sourcebook Ser.: Vol. IV). xxii, 787p. 1981. 59.50 (0-938876-07-4) Entropy Ltd.

Applications of Environment-Behavior Research: Case Studies & Analysis. Paul D. Cherulnik. (Cambridge Series in Envirinment & Behavior: No. 9). (C). 1993. 64.95 (0-521-33189-7); pap. 24.95 (0-521-33770-4) Cambridge U Pr.

Applications of Enzyme Biotechnology. Ed. by J. W. Kelly & T. O. Baldwin. (Industry-University Cooperative Chemistry Program Symposia Ser.). (Illus.). 326p. 1992. 85.00 (0-306-44095-4, Plenum Pr) Plenum.

Applications of Expert Systems, Vol. 1. J. Ross Quinlan. 224p. (C). 1987. text ed. 26.95 (0-201-17449-9) Addison-Wesley.

Applications of Expert Systems, Vol. 2. J. Ross Quinlan. 1989. text ed. 36.75 (0-201-41655-7) Addison-Wesley.

Applications of Fiber Optic Sensors in Engineering Mechanics: A Collection of State-of-the-Art Papers in the Application of Fiber Optic Technologies to Civil Structures. Ed. by Farhad Ansari. LC 93-604. 336p. 1993. 27.00 (0-87262-895-7) Am Soc Civil Eng.

Applications of Fibonacci Numbers, Vol. 3. Ed. by Gerald E. Bergum et al. (C). 1989. lib. bdg. 137.00 (0-7923-0523-X) Kluwer Ac.

Applications of Fibonacci Numbers, Vol. 4. Ed. by Gerald E. Bergum et al. (C). 1991. lib. bdg. 115.50 (0-7923-1309-7) Kluwer Ac.

Applications of Fibonacci Numbers: Proceedings of the Fifth International Conference on Fibonacci Numbers & Their Applications, Held at the University of St. Andrews, Scotland, July 20-24, 1992, Vol. 5. Ed. by G. E. Bergum. (DIVS-Diverse Ser.). 660p. (C). 1993. lib. bdg. 180.00 (0-7923-2491-9) Kluwer Ac.

Applications of Finite Fields. XuHong Gao & Ronald C. Mullin. Ed. by Alfred J. Menezes et al. LC 92-32895. (Kluwer International Series in Engineering & Computer Science: SECS 0199). 1992. lib. bdg. 75.00 (0-7923-9282-5) Kluwer Ac.

Applications of Finite Groups. unabridged ed. J. S. Lomont. LC 92-34875. (Illus.). 346p. 1993. reprint ed. pap. text ed. 9.95 (0-486-67376-6) Dover.

Applications of Fluid Mechanics to Wind Engineering: Presented at the Winter Annual Meeting of ASME, New York, N. Y. November 17-21, 1974. Jack E. Cermak. 36p. reprint ed. pap. 25.00 (0-8357-5665-3, 2016871) Bks Demand.

Applications of Fluorescence in Immunoassays. Ilkka Hemmila. (Chemical Analysis: a Series of Monographs on Analytical Chemistry & Its Applications). 360p. 1991. text ed. 99.95 (0-471-51091-2) Wiley.

Applications of Fractals & Chaos. Ed. by A. J. Crilly et al. LC 93-8105. 1993. 69.00 (0-387-56492-6) Spr-Verlag.

Applications of Fractals & Chaos: The Shape of Things. Ed. by A. J. Crilly et al. (Illus.). vii, 311p. 1993. write for info. (3-540-56492-6) Spr-Verlag.

An Asterisk (*) at the beginning of an entry indicates that the title is appearing in BIP for the first time.

An Asterisk (*) at the beginning of an entry indicates that the title is appearing in BIP for the first time.

Applications of Quality Control to the Service Industry. Rosander. (Quality & Reliability Ser.: Vol. 5). 432p. 1985. 69.75 (*0-8247-7466-3*) Dekker.

Applications of Radiation Thermometry- STP 895. Ed. by J. C. Richmond & D. P. DeWitt. LC 85-26709. (Illus.). 173p. 1985. text ed. 28.00 (*0-8031-0445-6*, 04-895000-40) ASTM.

Applications of Radio-Frequency Power to Plasmas: Seventh Topical Conference. Ed. by S. Bernabei & R. W. Bernabei. LC 87-71812. (Conference Proceeding Ser.: No. 159). 496p. 1987. lib. bdg. 70.00 (*0-88318-359-5*) Am Inst Physics.

***Applications of Random Vibrations.** N. C. Nigam. 557p. 1994. 114.00 (*0-387-19861-X*) Spr-Verlag.

Applications of Reflective Practice. Hart et al. Ed. by Frederick C. Wendel. 102p. (Orig.). (C). 1992. pap. text ed. 7.00 (*1-55996-150-3*) Univ Council Educ Admin.

Applications of Remote Sensing for Rice Production. Ed. by Adarsh Deepak & K. R. Rao. LC 85-1677. (Illus.). 449p. (C). 1985. 74.00 (*0-937194-03-4*) A Deepak Pub.

Applications of Remote Sensing in Agriculture. 1990. 165.00 (*0-408-04767-4*) Buttrwrth-Heinemann.

Applications of Remote Sensing to Agrometeorology: Proceedings of a Course Held at the Joint Research Centre of the Commission of the European Communities in the Framework of the Ispra-Courses, Ispra Varese, Italy, 6-10, April, 1987. Ed. by F. Toselli. (C). 1988. lib. bdg. 144.00 (*0-7923-0020-3*) Kluwer Ac.

Applications of Rock Mechanics: Proceedings - 15th Symposium on Rock Mechanics Held at the State Game Lodge, Custer State Park, South Dakota, Sept. 17-19, 1973. Rock Mechanics Symposium Staff. LC 78-307544. (Symposium on Rock Mechanics Proceedings Ser.: Vol. 15). (Illus.). 670p. reprint ed. pap. 180.00 (*0-8357-5672-6*, 2019534) Bks Demand.

Applications of Science in Examination of Works of Art: Proceedings of the Museum of Fine Arts, Research Laboratory Seminar, Boston, 1958. Museum of Fine Arts, Research Laboratory Staff. LC 78-99280. 1960. 19.95 (*0-405-00070-7*) Ayer.

Applications of Secondary School Mathematics: Readings from the "Mathematics Teacher" Ed. by Joe D. Austin. LC 91-5044. (Illus.). 339p. (Orig.). 1991. pap. 22.50 (*0-87353-336-4*) NCTM.

Applications of Small Computers in Construction: Proceedings of a Session Sponsored by the Construction Division (A Follow-Up of a Symposium on Small Computers in Construction) Ed. by Wayne C. Moore. 62p. 1984. 16.00 (*0-87262-416-1*) Am Soc Civil Eng.

Applications of Social Science to Clinical Medicine & Health Policy. Ed. by Linda H. Aiken & David Mechanic. 500p. (C). 1986. pap. text ed. 16.00 (*0-8135-1149-6*) Rutgers U Pr.

Applications of Soil Physics. Daniel J. Hillel. LC 80-535. 1980. text ed. 69.00 (*0-12-348580-0*) Acad Pr.

Applications of Space Developments II: Selected Papers of the International Astronautical Congress, Tokyo, Japan, September 22-27, 1980. International Astronautical Congress Staff & L. G. Napolitano. 310p. 1981. pap. 77.00 (*0-08-028676-3*, Pergamon Pr) Elsevier.

Applications of Spatial Data Structures: Computer Graphics, Image Processing, & Other Areas. Hanan Samet. (Computer Science Ser.). (Illus.). 480p. (C). 1990. text ed. 46.25 (*0-201-50300-X*) Addison-Wesley.

Applications of Statistical & Field Theory Methods to Condensed Matter. Ed. by D. Baeriswyl et al. LC 90-7153. (NATO ASI Series B, Physics: Vol. 218). (Illus.). 418p. 1990. 120.00 (*0-306-43526-8*, Plenum Pr) Plenum.

Applications of Statistical Sampling to Auditing. Alvin A. Arens & James K. Loebbecke. (Illus.). 400p. (C). 1981. text ed. write for info. (*0-13-039156-5*) P-H.

Applications of Statistics to Industrial Experimentation. Cuthbert Daniel. LC 76-2012. (Probability & Mathematical Statistics Ser.). 294p. 1976. text ed. 110.00 (*0-471-19469-7*) Wiley.

Applications of Stay-in-Place Prestressed Bridge Deck Panels. (PCI Journal Reprints Ser.). 8p. 1979. pap. 5.00 (*0-686-40119-0*, JR211) P-PCI.

Applications of Stochastic Processes to Sediment Transport. H. Kikkawa. Ed. by H. W. Shen. LC 79-67693. 1979. 38.00 (*0-918334-31-4*) WRP.

Applications of Subsea Systems. Goodfellow Associates Ltd. Staff. 254p. 1991. 79.95 (*0-87814-334-3*, P4459) PennWell Bks.

Applications of Supercomputers in Engineering, 2 vols., Set. Ed. by C. A. Brebbia & A. Peters. LC 89-62253. (ASE Ser.: Vol. 1). 1989. 182.00 (*0-945824-29-7*) Computational Mech MA.

Applications of Supercomputers in Engineering, Set. Carlos A. Brebbia & Alan A. Peters. 1989. 192.50 (*0-444-88112-3*) Elsevier.

Applications of Supercomputers in Engineering, 2 vols., Vol. 1: Algorithms, Computer Systems & User Experi. Ed. by C. A. Brebbia & A. Peters. LC 89-62253. (ASE Ser.: Vol. 1). 211p. 1989. 95.00 (*0-945824-27-0*) Computational Mech MA.

Applications of Supercomputers in Engineering, 2 vols., Vol. 2: Fluid Flow & Stress Applications. Ed. by C. A. Brebbia & A. Peters. LC 89-62253. (ASE Ser.). 311p. 1989. 107.00 (*0-945824-28-9*) Computational Mech MA.

Applications of Supercomputers in Engineering II. Ed. by C. A. Brebbia et al. LC 91-72946. (ASE Ser.: Vol. 2). 572p. 1991. 165.00 (*1-56252-052-0*) Computational Mech MA.

Applications of Supercomputers in Engineering II: Proc. of the Second Internat. Conf., ASE - 91, Aug. 1991, Cambridge, MA. Carlos A. Brebbia et al. Ed. by D. Howard & Alan A. Peters. 572p. 1991. 153.00 (*1-85166-695-8*) Elsevier.

Applications of Supercomputers in Engineering III. Ed. by C. A. Brebbia & A. Peters. LC 93-71024. (ASE Ser.: Vol. 3). 576p. 1993. 240.00 (*1-56252-160-8*) Computational Mech MA.

Applications of Supercomputers in Engineering III. Ed. by C. A. Brebbia & H. Power. 572p. 1993. 240.00 (*1-85166-845-4*, Pub. by Elsevier Applied Sci UK) Elsevier.

Applications of Supercomputers in Engineering, Vol. A: Algorithms, Computer Systems & Their User Experience. Carlos A. Brebbia & Alan A. Peters. 1989. 100.00 (*0-444-88110-7*) Elsevier.

Applications of Supercomputers in Engineering, Vol. B: Fluid Flow & Stress Analysis Applications. Carlos A. Brebbia & Alan A. Peters. 1989. 113.00 (*0-444-88111-5*) Elsevier.

Applications of Supercritical Fluids in Industrial Analysis. Ed. by J. R. Dean & S. Hitchen. 1993. 96.50 (*0-8493-7108-2*, TP156) CRC Pr.

Applications of Synchroton Radiation. Ed. by C. R. Catlow & G. N. Greaves. 388p. 1991. 145.00 (*0-412-02001-7*, A3597, Blackie & Son-Chapman NY) Routledge Chapman & Hall.

Applications of Synchrotron Radiation: High-Resolution Studies of Molecules & Molelcular Adsorbates on Surfaces. W. W. Eberhardt. LC 94-12947. 1994. 69.00 (*0-387-58031-X*) Spr-Verlag.

Applications of Synchrotron Radiation: Proceedings of the CCAST Symposium, June 1988, Beijing, China. Ed. by H. Winick et al. xxii, 626p. 1989. text ed. 54.00 (*2-88124-698-2*) Gordon & Breach.

Applications of Synchrotron Radiation Techniques to Materials Science. Ed. by D. L. Perry et al. (Symposium Proceedings Ser.: Vol. 307). 1993. text ed. 72.00 (*1-55899-203-0*) Materials Res.

***Applications of Synchrotron Radiation Techniques to Materials Science: 1994 MRS Fall Meeting, Boston, MA, Vol. II.** Ed. by Louis J. Terminello et al. (MRS Symposium Proceedings Ser.: Vol. 375). 335p. 1995. 69.00 (*1-55899-277-4*, 375N) Materials Res.

Applications of Tensor Analysis. A. J. McConnell. pap. 7.50 (*0-486-60373-3*) Dover.

Applications of the Conjugate Gradient FFT Method in Scattering & Radiation Including Simulations with Impedance Boundary Conditions. Kasra Barkeshli & John L. Volakis. (University of Michigan Report Ser.: No. 025921-21-T). 287p. reprint ed. pap. 81.80 (*0-7837-1389-4*, 2041567) Bks Demand.

Applications of the Electromagnetic Reciprocity Principle. C. D. Monteath. 1973. 72.00 (*0-08-016895-7*, Pub. by Pergamon Repr UK) Franklin.

Applications of the Expansion Method. Ed. by John P. Jones, III & Emilio Casetti. (Illus.). 304p. 1991. 74.50 (*0-415-03494-9*, A6534) Routledge.

Applications of the Interaction of Microwaves with the Natural Snow Cover. C. Matzler. Ed. by F. Becker. (Remote Sensing Reviews Ser.: Vol. 2, No. 2). ii, 132p. 1987. pap. text ed. 113.00 (*3-7186-0416-7*) Gordon & Breach.

Applications of the Laser. Leon Goldman. LC 82-7834. 332p. 1982. reprint ed. 54.00 (*0-89874-481-4*) Krieger.

Applications of the Mathematical Theory of Linguistics. Richard T. Daly. (Janua Linguarum, Series Minor: No. 185). 1974. pap. text ed. 71.55 (*90-279-2684-0*) Mouton.

Applications of the MBTI in Higher Education. Ed. by Judith A. Provost & Scott Anchors. 296p. 1987. pap. 21.95 (*0-89106-032-4*, 6869) Consulting Psychol.

Applications of the Monte Carlo Method in Statistical Physics. 2nd ed. Ed. by K. Binder. (Topics in Current Physics Ser.: Vol. 36). (Illus.). 360p. 1987. pap. 51.00 (*0-387-17650-0*) Spr-Verlag.

Applications of the Mossbauer Effect, 5 Vols., Vol. 5. Ed. by Yu M. Kagan & I. S. Lyubutin. 115p. 1985. Set. text ed. 1,036.00 (*2-88124-030-5*) Gordon & Breach.

Applications of the Mossbauer Effect, Vol. 1: Invited Papers. Yu. M. Kagan & I. S. Lyubutin. 464p. 1985. text ed. 242.00 (*2-88124-021-6*) Gordon & Breach.

Applications of the Mossbauer Effect, Vol. 2: Spectroscopy & Magnetism, Vol. 2. Yu. M. Kagan & I. S. Lyubutin. 458p. 1985. text ed. 254.00 (*2-88124-028-3*) Gordon & Breach.

Applications of the Mossbauer Effect, Vol. 3: Chemistry, Vol. 3. Yu. M. Kagan & I. S. Lyubutin. 444p. 1985. text ed. 254.00 (*2-88124-029-1*) Gordon & Breach.

Applications of the Mossbauer Effect, Vol. 4: Materials Science, Vol. 4. Yu. M. Kagan & I. S. Lyubutin. 334p. 1985. text ed. 254.00 (*2-88124-059-3*) Gordon & Breach.

Applications of the Mossbauer Effect, Vol. 5: Applications in Other Fields, Vol. 5. Yu. M. Kagan & I. S. Lyubutin. 415p. 1985. text ed. 205.00 (*2-88124-060-7*) Gordon & Breach.

Applications of the Theory of Distributions. Romulus Cristescu & Gheorgha Marinescu. Tr. by Silviu Teleman. LC 72-9080. 227p. reprint ed. pap. 64.70 (*0-8357-5673-4*, 2016146) Bks Demand.

Applications of the Tk! Solver Plus in Chemical Equilibrium & Chemical Analysis. Allan L. Smith. 1990. pap. text ed. write for info. (*0-07-058651-9*) McGraw.

Applications of Thermal Imaging. S. G. Burnay et al. (Illus.). 272p. 1988. 123.00 (*0-85274-421-8*) IOP Pub.

Applications of Thermodynamics. 2nd ed. B. D. Wood. 1982. text ed. 39.96 (*0-201-08741-3*); write for info. (*0-201-08789-8*) Addison-Wesley.

Applications of Thermodynamics. 2nd ed. Bernard D. Wood. (Illus.). 634p. (C). 1991. reprint ed. text ed. 51.95 (*0-88133-544-4*) Waveland Pr.

Applications of Time-Resolved Optical Spectroscopy. V. Bruckner et al. (Studies in Physical & Theoretical Chemistry: No. 66). 244p. 1990. 113.00 (*0-444-98812-2*) Elsevier.

Applications of Transputers One: Proceedings of the 1st International Conference on Applications of Transputers, Liverpool, U. K. August 23-25, 1989. Ed. by L. Freeman & C. Phillips. (Transputer & Occam Engineering Ser.). 332p. 1990. 95.00 (*90-5199-025-1*, Pub. by IOS Pr NE) IOS Press.

Applications of Transputers Three. Ed. by Tariq S. Durrani et al. (Transputer & Occam Engineering Ser.). 900p. 1991. 145.00 (*90-5199-064-2*, Pub. by IOS Pr NE) IOS Press.

Applications of Transputers Two: Proceedings of the 2nd International Conference on Applications of Transputers, Southampton, U. K. July 11-13, 1990. Ed. by D. J. Pritchard & C. J. Scott. (Transputer & Occam Engineering Ser.). 587p. 1990. 110.00 (*90-5199-035-9*, Pub. by IOS Pr NE) IOS Press.

Applications of Tributyl Phosphate in Nuclear Fuel Reprocessing, Vol. III. Ed. by Wallace W. Schulz et al. (Science & Technology of Tributyl Phosphate Ser.). 256p. 1989. 354.00 (*0-8493-6389-6*, QD305) CRC Pr.

Applications of Ultrashort Laser Pulses in Science & Technology. Ed. by A. Antonetti. 1990. 53.00 (*0-8194-0315-6*, VOL. 1268) SPIE.

Applications of Ultrasonics to Molecular Physics. V. F. Nozdrev. (Illus.). 542p. 1963. 232.00 (*0-685-01944-6*) Gordon & Breach.

Applications of UV-VIS Spectroscopy in Pharmaceutical Analysis. Ed. by Sandor Gorog. 416p. 1995. 125.00 (*0-8493-8691-8*, 8691) CRC Pr.

Applications of Variational Inequalities in Stochastic Control. Alain Benoussan & J. L. Lions. (Studies in Mathematics & Its Applications: Vol. 12). Orig. Title: Applications des Inequations Variationnelles en Controle Stochastique. 564p. 1982. 107.75 (*0-444-86358-3*, North Holland) Elsevier.

Applications of Walsh & Related Functions. Kenneth G. Beauchamp. (Microelectronics & Signal Processing Ser.). 1984. text ed. 118.00 (*0-12-084180-0*) Acad Pr.

Applications of Welding see Welding Handbook

Applications of Zeeman Graphite Furnace Atomic Absorption Spectroscopy in the Chemical Laboratory & in Toxicology. Ed. by C. Minoia & S. Caroli. LC 92-20198. 1992. 285.00 (*0-08-041019-7*, Pergamon Pr) Elsevier.

Applications on Management Science & Operations Research Methods. Ed. by William D. Whisler. 249p. 1974. pap. text ed. 14.95 (*0-8422-0376-1*) Irvington.

Applications Oriented Approach to Artificial Intelligence. Daniel Schutzer. (Illus.). 300p. 1987. text ed. 59.95 (*0-442-28034-3*) Van Nos Reinhold.

Applications Programming in ANSI-C. 2nd ed. Richard Johnsonbaugh & Martin Kalin. (Illus.). 850p. (C). 1993. pap. write for info. (*0-02-361131-6*) Macmillan.

Applications Programming in C. Richard Johnsonbaugh & Martin Kalin. 849p. (C). 1989. pap. write for info. (*0-02-359730-5*) Macmillan.

Applications Reference Manual. Ed. by Steve Guinta. (Analog Devices Technical Reference Bks.). (Illus.). 1344p. (Orig.). 1993. pap. 10.00 (*0-916550-12-5*) Analog Devices.

Applications Related Phenomena in Titanium Alloys - STP 432. 298p. 1968. 20.00 (*0-8031-0748-X*, 04-432000-05) ASTM.

Applications Software Programming with Fourth-Generation Languages. W. Gregory & Wita Wojtkowski. 626p. 1990. 38.00 (*0-87835-338-0*) Boyd & Fraser.

Applications Software Supplement. Pitter. 1987. pap. text ed. write for info. (*0-07-555298-1*) McGraw.

Applications Software Tutorials: A Computer Lab Manual Using WordPerfect 5.1, Lotus 1-2-3, dBase III PLUS & dBase IV. Patrick G. McKeown & Ravija Badarinathi. 300p. (C). 1993. pap. text ed. 21.00 (*0-03-097504-2*) Dryden Pr.

Applications to Wind up Companies. Derek French. 404p. 1993. 74.00 (*1-85431-290-1*, Pub. by Blackstone Pr UK) W W Gaunt.

Applications '85: Selected Proceedings of Closing The Gap's 1985 National Conference. Ed. by Michael Gergen. LC 85-73898. (Illus.). 338p. 1986. pap. text ed. 21.95 (*0-932719-01-5*) Closing Gap.

Applicative High-Order Programming. Stefan Sokolowski. 246p. (C). 1991. 38.95 (*0-442-30838-8*) Chapman & Hall.

Applicative Programming. Antony J. Davie. (Cambridge Computer Science Texts Ser.). 250p. (C). 1992. 74.95 (*0-521-25830-8*); pap. 29.95 (*0-521-27724-8*) Cambridge U Pr.

Applied Abstract Algebra. R. Lidl & G. Pilz. LC 84-10576. (Undergraduate Texts in Mathematics Ser.). (Illus.). 450p. 1984. 49.00 (*0-387-96035-X*) Spr-Verlag.

Applied Acoustics. G. Porges. 180p. 1987. reprint ed. 30.95 (*0-932146-18-X*) Peninsula CA.

Applied Aerospace & Defense Expert Systems. John Keller et al. (Illus.). 246p. (Orig.). (C). 1987. pap. text ed. 260.50 (*0-935453-15-6*) Pasha Pubns.

Applied Agricultural Entomology. L. K. Jha. (C). 1989. 55.00 (*0-89771-423-7*, Current Dist) St Mut.

Applied Agricultural Geography. B. L. Sharma. 1991. 44.00 (*0-685-48704-0*, Pub. by Rawat II) S Asia.

Applied Agricultural Research: Foundations & Methods. Chris O. Andrew. (C). 1993. pap. text ed. 37.00 (*0-8133-8781-7*) Westview.

Applied Air Conditioning & Refrigeration. 2nd ed. C. T. Gosling. (Illus.). xii, 410p. 1980. 79.25 (*0-85334-877-4*, Pub. by Elsevier Applied Sci UK) Elsevier.

Applied Algebra, Algebraic Algorithms & Error-Correcting Codes: Proceedings of International Conference, 8th, AAECC-8, Tokyo, Japan, August 20-24, 1990. Ed. by S. Sakata. (Lecture Notes in Computer Science Ser.: Vol. 508). ix, 390p. 1991. pap. 37.00 (*0-387-54195-0*) Spr-Verlag.

Applied Algebra, Algebraic Algorithms & Error-Correcting Codes: 9th International Symposium, AAECC-9 New Orleans, LA, U. S. A., October 7-11, 1991 Proceedings. Ed. by Harold F. Mattson et al. (Lecture Notes in Computer Science Ser.: Vol. 539). xi, 489p. 1991. pap. 44.00 (*0-387-54522-0*) Spr-Verlag.

Applied Algebra, Algorithmics & Error-Correcting Codes. A. Poli. (Lecture Notes in Computer Science Ser.: Vol. 228). (Illus.). vi, 265p. 1986. pap. 36.00 (*0-387-16767-6*) Spr-Verlag.

Applied Algebra & Functional Analysis. Anthony M. Michel & Charles J. Herget. LC 93-15006. Orig. Title: Mathematical Foundations in Engineering & Science. (Illus.). 496p. 1993. reprint ed. pap. 10.95 (*0-486-67598-X*) Dover.

Applied Algebra I. Thomas J. McHale & Paul T. Witzke. (C). 1979. pap. text ed. 46.25 (*0-201-04767-5*) Addison-Wesley.

Applied Algebra II. Thomas J. McHale & Paul T. Witzke. (C). 1980. pap. text ed. 50.50 (*0-201-04775-6*) Addison-Wesley.

Applied Analysis. Allan M. Krall. 1986. lib. bdg. 147.00 (*90-277-2328-1*) Kluwer Ac.

Applied Analysis. Cornelius Lanczos. (Illus.). 559p. 1988. reprint ed. pap. text ed. 12.95 (*0-486-65656-X*) Dover.

Applied Analysis by the Hilbert Space Method. Samuel Holland, Jr. (Pure & Applied Mathematics Ser.: Vol. 137). 584p. 1990. 65.00 (*0-8247-8259-3*) Dekker.

Applied Analysis of the Navier-Stokes Equations. Charles R. Doering & J. D. Gibbon. (Cambridge Texts in Applied Mathematics Ser.: No. 12). (Illus.). 250p. (C). 1995. 59.95 (*0-521-44557-4*); pap. 24.95 (*0-521-44568-X*) Cambridge U Pr.

Applied Analysis of Variance in Behavioral Science. Edwards. (Statistics Ser.: Vol. 137). 640p. 1993. 180.00 (*0-8247-8896-6*) Dekker.

***Applied Anatomy & Biomechanics in Sport.** John Bloomfield et al. (Illus.). 392p. (Orig.). 1994. pap. text ed. 35.00 (*0-86793-305-4*, BBLO0305) Blackwell Sci.

Applied Anatomy & Physiology: A Laboratory Manual & Workbook for Health Careers. Dawn K. Holtzmeier. 320p. (C). 1994. spiral bd. 23.96 (*0-8403-9160-9*) Kendall-Hunt.

Applied Anatomy of the Back. J. Rickenbacher et al. Tr. by R. R. Wilson & D. P. Winstanley. LC 85-9937. (Illus.). 425p. 1985. 587.00 (*0-387-15132-X*) Spr-Verlag.

Applied Anatomy of the Lymphatics. D. O. Millard. 278p. 1964. reprint ed. spiral bd. 19.25 (*0-7873-0615-0*) Mokelumne.

Applied Anatomy of the Pelvis. W. Lierse. (Illus.). 350p. 1987. 454.00 (*0-387-16750-1*) Spr-Verlag.

Applied & Computational Complex Analysis: Discrete Fourier Analysis - Cauchy Integrals - Construction of Conformal Maps - Univalent Functions, Vol. 3. Peter Henrici & William R. Kenan. (Classics Library). 656p. (Orig.). 1993. pap. text ed. 49.95 (*0-471-58986-1*) Wiley.

Applied & Computational Complex Analysis: Power Series, Integration, Conformal Mapping, Location of Zeros, 3 vols., Vol. 2. Peter Henrici & William R. Kenan. (Classics Library). 682p. 1991. pap. text ed. 59.95 (*0-471-54289-X*) Wiley.

Applied & Computational Complex Analysis: Power Series, Integration, Conformal Mapping, Location of Zeros, 3 vols., Vol. 2: 1991. Peter Henrici & William R. Kenan. (Classics Library). 682p. 1988. Vol. 2, 1991. pap. text ed. 59.95 (*0-471-60841-6*) Wiley.

Applied & Decorative Arts: A Bibliographic Guide. 2nd annot. ed. Donald L. Ehresmann. 500p. 1993. lib. bdg. 75.00 (*0-87287-906-2*) Libs Unl.

Applied & Engineering Physics at Cornell: A History of the School, with Various Asides & a Brief Look at the Department from Which It Came. Paul L. Hartman. (Engineering Histories Ser.). (Illus.). 128p. (Orig.). 1994. pap. write for info. (*0-918531-04-7*) Cornell Coll Eng.

Applied & Fundamental Aspects of Plant Cell, Tissue, & Organ Culture. Ed. by J. Reinert & Y. P. Bajaj. (Illus.). xviii, 803p. 1989. reprint ed. 148.00 (*0-387-07677-8*) Spr-Verlag.

Applied & Industrial Mathematics: Venice - 1, 1989. Ed. by Renato Spigler. (Mathematics & Its Applications Ser.). 392p. (C). 1990. lib. bdg. 150.00 (*0-7923-0521-3*) Kluwer Ac.

Applied Angiography for Radiographers. Paul Laudicina & Douglas Wean. LC 93-27002. 1994. text ed. 45.00 (*0-7216-3283-1*) Saunders.

Applied Animal Nutrition: Feeds & Feeding. Peter R. Cheeke. 528p. (C). 1991. write for info. (*0-02-322115-1*) Macmillan.

Applied Animal Reproduction. H. Joe Bearden & John W. Fuquay. (C). 1984. teacher ed write for info. (*0-8359-0107-6*, Reston) P-H.

Applied Animal Reproduction. 3rd ed. Joe H. Bearden & John H. Fuquay. 384p. 1991. text ed. 75.00 (*0-13-040346-6*) P-H.

Applied Anthropologist & Public Servant: The Life & Work of Philleo Nash. Ed. by Ruth Landman & Katherine S. Halpern. 1989. 7.50 (*0-913167-28-2*) Am Anthro Assn.

Applied Anthropology: A Practical Guide. rev. ed. Erve Chambers. 258p. (C). 1989. reprint ed. pap. text ed. 13.95x (*0-88133-449-9*) Waveland Pr.

Applied Anthropology: An Introduction. rev. ed. John Van Willigen. LC 92-31722. 296p. 1993. text ed. 65.00 (*0-89789-298-4*, H298, Bergin & Garvey); pap. text ed. 22.95 (*0-89789-303-4*, G303, Bergin & Garvey) Greenwood.

An Asterisk (*) at the beginning of an entry indicates that the title is appearing in BIP for the first time.

An Asterisk (*) at the beginning of an entry indicates that the title is appearing in BIP for the first time.

Applied Cross-Cultural Psychology. Ed. by Richard W. Brislin. (Cross-Cultural Research & Methodology Ser.: Vol. 14). (Illus.). 368p. (C). 1990. text ed. 49.95 (0-8039-3785-7); pap. text ed. 24.00 (0-8039-3786-5) Sage.

Applied Cryptography: Protocols, Algorithms, & Source Code in C. Bruce Schneier. 1993. pap. text ed. 44.95 (0-471-59756-2) Wiley.

***Applied Cryptography: Protocols, Algorithms & Source Code in C.** 2nd ed. Bruce Schneier. LC 95-12398. 1995. text ed. 69.95 (0-471-12845-7); pap. text ed. 49.95 (0-471-11709-9) Wiley.

Applied Cryptology, Cryptographic Protocols, & Computer Security Models. Ed. by Richard DeMillo et al. LC 83-15548. (Proceedings of Symposia in Applied Mathematics Ser.: Vol. 29). 192p. 1985. reprint ed. pap. 34.00 (0-8218-0041-8, PSAPM-29) Am Math.

Applied Crystal Chemistry & Physics. Ed. by Robert E. Newnham. (Transactions of the American Crystallographic Association Ser.: Vol. 11). 117p. 1975. pap. 25.00 (0-686-47114-8) Polycrystal Bk Serv.

Applied Crystallography: Proceedings of the Fifteenth International Conference. 296p. 1993. text ed. 109.00 (981-02-1362-X) World Scientific Pub.

Applied Cybernetics: Its Relevance to Operations Research. Amitava Ghosal. (Studies in Operations Research). 176p. 1978. text ed. 96.00 (0-677-05410-6) Gordon & Breach.

Applied Data Communications: A Business-Oriented Approach. James E. Goldman. LC 94-9354. 643p. 1994. text ed. 61.95 (0-471-59217-X) Wiley.

Applied Data Structures Using Pascal. Guy J. Hale & Richard J. Easton. LC 85-81813. 524p. (C). 1987. text ed. 38.00 (0-669-07579-5); Instr.'s guide. teacher ed 2.00 (0-669-11236-4) Heath.

Applied Decision Analysis & Economic Behavior. Ed. by A. J. Hallett. 1984. lib. bdg. 111.50 (90-247-2968-8) Kluwer Ac.

Applied Demography: An Introduction to Basic Concepts, Methods, & Data. Steve H. Murdock & David Ellis. 299p. (C). 1991. pap. text ed. 37.00 (0-8133-8372-2) Westview.

Applied Demography for Biologists: With Special Emphasis on Insects. James R. Carey. (Illus.). 592p. 1993. 39.95 (0-19-506687-1) OUP.

Applied Dental Materials. 7th ed. J. McCabe. 1990. pap. 55.00 (0-632-02826-2) Blackwell Sci.

Applied Depth of Field. Alfred A. Blaker. LC 84-28771. (Illus.). 302p. 1985. spiral bd. 40.00 (0-240-51730-X, Focal) Buttrwrth-Heinemann.

Applied Descriptive Geometry. Susan A. Stewart. 416p. 1986. teacher ed 15.00 (0-8273-2378-6); pap. text ed. 49.95 (0-8273-2377-8) Delmar.

Applied Developmental Psychology. Ed. by Celia B. Fisher & Richard M. Lerner. LC 93-43168. 1993. text ed. write for info. (0-07-021172-8) McGraw.

Applied Developmental Psychology, Vol. 1. Frederick J. Morrison. (Serial Publication Ser.). 1984. text ed. 91.00 (0-12-041201-2) Acad Pr.

Applied Developmental Psychology, Vol. 2. Ed. by Frederick J. Morrison & Daniel P. Keating. (Serial Publication Ser.). 1985. text ed. 91.00 (0-12-041202-0) Acad Pr.

Applied Developmental Psychology: Psychological Development in Infancy, Vol. 3. Ed. by Frederick J. Morrison et al. 267p. 1989. text ed. 92.00 (0-12-041203-9) Acad Pr.

***Applied Developmental Science Vol. 13: Graduate Training for Diverse Disciplines & Educational Settings.** Ed. by Celia B. Fisher et al. (Advances in Applied Developmental Psychology Ser.). 1995. write for info. (1-56750-130-3) Ablex Pub.

Applied Differential Equations. 3rd ed. Murray R. Spiegal. 1980. text ed. write for info. (0-13-040097-1) P-H.

Applied Differential Equations for Scientists & Engineers, 2 vols., Set. M. Rahman. LC 91-76270. 1991. 210.00 (1-56252-056-3) Computational Mech MA.

Applied Differential Equations for Scientists & Engineers, 2 vols., Vol. 1: Ordinary Differential Equations. Matiur Rahman. LC 91-76270. 656p. 1991. 170.00 (1-56252-057-1) Computational Mech MA.

Applied Differential Equations for Scientists & Engineers, 2 vols., Vol. 2: Partial Differential Equations. M. Rahman. LC 91-76270. 356p. 1991. 73.00 (1-56252-058-X) Computational Mech MA.

Applied Differential Games. A. Mehlmann. LC 88-15248. (Illus.). 208p. 1988. 55.00 (0-306-42897-0, Plenum Pr) Plenum.

Applied Differential Geometry. William L. Burke. LC 84-14952. (Illus.). 400p. 1985. pap. 42.95 (0-521-26929-6) Cambridge U Pr.

Applied Digital Control. Ed. by Spyros G. Tzafestas. (Systems & Control Ser.: Vol. 7). 306p. 1986. 100.00 (0-444-87882-3, North Holland) Elsevier.

Applied Digital Control. 2nd ed. Ron Leigh. 480p. 1992. pap. text ed. 48.00 (0-13-044249-6) P-H.

Applied Digital Filtering, Adaptive & Non-Adaptive: Proceedings, IASTED Symposium, Paris, France, June 19-21, 1985. Ed. by M. H. Hamza. 175p. 1985. 65.00 (0-88986-084-X, 086B) Acta Pr.

Applied Discrete Structures. K. D. Joshi. 600p. 1995. text ed. 34.95 (0-470-21333-7) Halsted Pr.

Applied Discriminant Analysis. Carl J. Huberty. LC 93-39710. (Probability & Mathematical Statistics: Applied Probability & Statistics Section Ser.). 466p. 1994. text ed. 74.95 (0-471-31145-6) Wiley.

Applied Dream Analysis: A Jungian Approach see Understanding Dreams

Applied Drilling Engineering. A. T. Bourgoyne, Jr. et al. 510p. 1986. 58.00 (1-55563-001-4, 31803) Soc Petrol Engineers.

Applied Dynamics of Manipulation Robots. M. Vukobratovic. (Illus.). 491p. 1989. 97.00 (0-387-51468-6, 3350) Spr-Verlag.

Applied Dynamics of Ocean Surface Waves. C. C. Mei. (Advanced Series in Ocean Engineering: Vol. 1). 764p. 1989. text ed. 76.00 (9971-5-0773-0, E-B752); pap. text ed. 38.00 (9971-5-0789-7) World Scientific Pub.

Applied ECM, Vol. 1. LeRoy B. Van Brunt. Ed. by EW Engineering Staff. LC 78-50538. (Illus.). 973p. 1978. 81.95 (0-931728-00-2) EW Eng.

Applied ECM, Vol. 2. Leroy B. Van Brunt. Ed. by EW Engineering Staff. LC 78-50538. (Illus.). 635p. 1982. 71.95 (0-931728-01-0) EW Eng.

***Applied ECM, Vol. 3.** LeRoy B. Van Brunt. Ed. by Engineering Staff. LC 78-50538. (Illus.). 558p. 1995. 76.95 (0-931728-03-7) Bunting.

Applied Econometric Techniques. Keith Cuthbertson et al. LC 91-25946. 250p. (C). 1991. text ed. 45.00 (0-472-10328-8) U of Mich Pr.

***Applied Econometric Time Series: A User's Guide.** Ed. by Walter Enders. LC 94-27849. 1994. text ed. 55.95 (0-471-03941-1) Wiley.

***Applied Econometrics.** K. P. Kalirajan. 222p. 1995. text ed. 29.95 (1-886106-36-3) Science Pubs.

Applied Econometrics. Lardaro. (C). 1992. text ed. 72.00 (0-06-043847-9) HarpCollege.

Applied Econometrics. Lardaro. (C). 1993. student ed 18.75 (0-06-501610-6) HarpCollege.

Applied Econometrics. William F. Lott & Subhash C. Ray. 450p. (C). 1992. pap. text ed. 27.00 (0-15-502907-X) Dryden Pr.

Applied Economic Forecasting Techniques. Stephen Hall. 274p. 1994. pap. text ed. 39.95 (0-13-302647-7) P-H.

Applied Economics. A. Griffiths & S. Hall. 526p. (C). 1986. 60.00 (0-685-29264-9, Inst Pur & Supply) St Mut.

Applied Economics. A. Griffiths & S. Hall. 526p. (C). 1989. 145.00 (0-685-36145-4, Inst Pur & Supply) St Mut.

Applied Economics: An Introductory Course. 5th ed. Ed. by Alan Griffiths & Stuart Wall. LC 92-45779. 1993. write for info. (0-582-21430-0, Pub. by Longman UK) Longman.

Applied Economics in Banking & Finance. H. C. Carter & I. Partington. (C). 1989. 600.00 (0-685-33796-0, Pub. by Witherby & Co UK) St Mut.

***Applied Ecotoxicology.** Ed. by Johann F. Moltmann & Jorg Rombke. 272p. 1995. 59.95 (1-56670-070-1, L1070) Lewis Pubs.

Applied Elasticity. Zhilun Xu. (Esther Booth Wiley Ser.). 373p. 1992. text ed. 47.95 (0-470-21868-1) Wiley.

Applied Elasto-Plasticity of Solids. T. Z. Blazynski. (Illus.). 272p. (C). 1984. text ed. 60.00 (0-333-34544-4) Scholium Intl.

Applied Electricity. Tel-A-Train, Inc. Staff. 1987. student ed 17.50 (1-56355-072-5) Tel-A-Train.

Applied Electro-Acupoint Therapy Workshop Manual. rev. ed. Carolyn W. Greenlee et al. (Illus.). 152p. 1982. 45.00 (0-9607836-0-1) See Do Pr.

Applied Electromagnetics. 2nd ed. J. E. Parton et al. 300p. 1986. 42.00 (0-387-91279-7) Spr-Verlag.

Applied Electromagnetics. 2nd ed. Martin Plonus. (Illus.). 1978. text ed. write for info. (0-07-050345-1) McGraw.

Applied Electromagnetism. P. Hammond. 396p. (C). 1971. pap. text ed. 30.00 (0-08-016382-3, Pergamon Pr) Elsevier.

Applied Electromagnetism. 2nd ed. Shen & Kong. (C). 1987. text ed. 69.95 (0-534-07620-3) PWS Pubs.

***Applied Electromagnetism.** 3rd ed. Liang C. Shen & Jin A. Kong. LC 95-47. 1995. text ed. 72.95 (0-534-94722-0) PWS Pubs.

Applied Electromyography. Alberto A. Marinacci. LC 68-25208. 308p. reprint ed. pap. 87.80 (0-8357-5676-9, 2003766) Bks Demand.

Applied Electron Spectroscopy for Chemical Analysis. Ed. by Hassan Windawi & Floyd F. Ho. LC 82-4781. (Chemical Analysis Ser.: No. 63). 223p. reprint ed. pap. 63.60 (0-7837-2800-X, 2057673) Bks Demand.

Applied Electronic Devices & Analog Integrated Circuits. J. Michael McMenamin. LC 94-59. (Illus.). 800p. 1995. 59.95 (0-8273-5416-9) Delmar.

Applied Electronics. J. F. Pierce & T. J. Paulus. 688p. (C). Date not set. 55.00 (1-878907-42-5) TechBooks.

***Applied Electronics Technology.** Joseph G. Sloop. (Technology Application Ser.). (Illus.). 125p. (C). 1990. write for info. (0-89704-046-5) E&L Instru.

Applied Electronics Technology: Instructor's Guide. Joseph G. Sloop. (Technology Application Ser.). (Illus.). 125p. (Orig.). 1990. ring bd. write for info. (0-89704-055-4) E&L Instru.

Applied Energy Research: Proceedings of the Institute of Energy Conference Held in Swansea, U. K., 5-7 September 1989. Institute of Energy, Great Britain, Conference Staff. LC 90-125967. 379p. reprint ed. pap. 108.10 (0-7837-3258-9, 2043277) Bks Demand.

Applied Engineering Mechanics. 4th ed. Alfred E. Jensen & Harry H. Chenoweth. 464p. 1983. text ed. 39.95 (0-07-032492-1) McGraw.

Applied Engineering Mechanics: Statics & Dynamics. Boothroyd & Poli. (Mechanical Engineering Ser.: Vol. 5). 368p. 1980. 60.00 (0-8247-6945-7) Dekker.

Applied Engineering Statistics. Robert M. Bethea & Russell Rhinehart. (Statistics Ser.: Vol. 121). 416p. 1991. 65.00 (0-8247-8503-7) Dekker.

Applied English Grammar. Byrd & Benson. 1992. pap. 20.95 (0-8384-2281-0) Heinle & Heinle.

Applied English Grammar. Byrd & Benson. 1992. teacher ed, pap. 7.95 (0-8384-2282-9) Heinle & Heinle.

Applied Enhanced Oil Recovery. Aurel Carcoana. 352p. 1991. text ed. 84.00 (0-13-044272-0) P-H.

Applied Enlightenment: Nineteenth Century Liberalism, 1800-1839, Set. Incl. Livingston Codes & the Guatemalan Crisis of 1837-1838. Mario Rodriguez. 1955. 3.00 (0-685-19985-1); Luces & la Civilization: The Social Reforms of Mariano Galvez. Miriam Williford. 1969. 1.00 (0-685-19986-X); Social Revolution in Guatemala: The Carrera Revolt. Ralph L. Woodward, Jr. 1971. 3.50 (0-685-19987-8); Attitudes Toward Foreign Colonization: The Evolution of Nineteenth-Century Guatemalan Immigration Policy. William J. Griffith. 1972. 3.50 (0-685-19988-6); (Publication Ser.: No. 23). 110p. 1972. 10.00 (0-939238-25-X) Tulane MARI.

Applied Environmental Geochemistry. Ed. by Iain Thornton. (Academic Press Geology Ser.). 1984. text ed. 143.00 (0-12-690640-8) Acad Pr.

***Applied Environmetrics: Hydrological Tables.** T. Beer. (Environmental Software Ser.). 1991. 195.00 (1-56252-228-0) Computational Mech MA.

***Applied Environmetrics: Meteorological Tables.** T. Beer. (Environmental Software Ser.). 1990. disk 195.00 (1-56252-229-9) Computational Mech MA.

***Applied Environmetrics: Oceanographic Tables.** T. Beer. (Environmental Software Ser.). 1989. disk 195.00 (1-56252-230-2) Computational Mech MA.

***Applied Environmetrics Set of 3 Tables.** T. Beer. (Environmental Software Ser.). 1993. disk 585.00 (1-56252-231-0) Computational Mech MA.

Applied Ergonomics Handbook. Mike Burke. 240p. 1991. 59.95 (0-87371-367-2, TA166) Lewis Pubs.

Applied Ergonomics Handbook. 2nd ed. Ed. by Ian A. Galer. (Illus.). 216p. 1987. pap. text ed. 62.95 (0-408-00880-6) Buttrwrth-Heinemann.

Applied Ethics. Ed. by Peter Singer. (Oxford Readings in Philosophy Ser.). 192p. (C). 1986. pap. 14.95 (0-19-875067-6) OUP.

Applied Ethics: A Multicultural Approach. Ed. by Larry May & Shari C. Sharratt. LC 93-5395. 1993. pap. text ed. write for info. (0-13-068842-8) P-H.

Applied Ethics: A Reader. Ed. by Earl Winkler & Jerrold R. Coombs. LC 92-36936. 1993. 49.95 (0-631-18832-0); pap. 19.95 (0-631-18833-9) Blackwell Pubs.

Applied Ethics & Ethical Theory. Ed. by David M. Rosenthal & Fadlou Shehadi. LC 88-14304. (Ethics in a Changing World Ser.: Vol. 1). 320p. 1988. 30.00 (0-87480-289-X) U of Utah Pr.

Applied Ethics in Student Services. Ed. by Harry J. Canon & Robert D. Brown. LC 84-82379. (New Directions for Student Services Ser.: No. 30). (Orig.). 1985. pap. 16.95x (0-87589-768-1) Jossey-Bass.

Applied Excel: Creating Spreadsheets Systems for Others. Tim Nguyen & Joseph R. Little. 420p. 1989. pap. 22.95 (0-13-039652-4) P-H.

Applied Exercise Physiology. Richard A. Berger. LC 81-2322. 301p. reprint ed. pap. 85.80 (0-8357-5677-7, 2056567) Bks Demand.

Applied Exercises for Fundamentals of Public Speaking. 2nd ed. Larry Lowe. 160p. (C). 1994. per., pap. text ed. 20.95 (0-8403-9246-X) Kendall-Hunt.

Applied Exercises for Fundamentals of Public Speaking. 2nd ed. Larry V. Lowe. 160p. 1992. 19.95 (0-8403-8186-7) Kendall-Hunt.

Applied Expert Systems. Efraim Turban & P. R. Watkins. (Studies in Management Science & Systems: No. 17). 270p. 1988. 97.50 (0-444-70489-2, North Holland) Elsevier.

Applied Extreme Value Statistics. Robert R. Kinnison. LC 84-24206. 160p. 1985. pap. 37.50 (0-02-947630-5) Battelle.

Applied Extreme Value Statistics. Robert R. Kinnison. 1985. text ed. 35.00 (0-07-034732-8) McGraw.

Applied Factor Analysis. Rudolph J. Rummel. 617p. 1970. pap. 28.95 (0-8101-0824-0) Northwestern U Pr.

Applied Factor Analysis in the Natural Sciences. 2nd ed. Richard A. Reyment & K. G. Joreskog. (Illus.). 250p. (C). 1993. 79.95 (0-521-41242-0) Cambridge U Pr.

Applied Factorial & Fractional Designs. Robert A. McLean & Virgil L. Anderson. LC 84-7015. (Statistics, Textbooks & Monographs: Vol. 55). 389p. reprint ed. pap. 110.90 (0-7837-0271-X, 2040580) Bks Demand.

Applied Finance for Natural Resources: United Nations Interregional Seminar, Bangkok, 1991. Ed. by Jon Rau. (Illus.). 373p. (Orig.). (C). 1993. pap. text ed. write for info. (0-9633833-1-0) UN Dept Econ & Soc Dev.

Applied Finite Element Analysis. 2nd ed. Larry J. Segerlind. LC 84-7455. 427p. 1984. Net. text ed. write for info. (0-471-80662-5) Wiley.

Applied Finite Element Analysis for Engineers. Francis L. Stasa. LC 85-742. 672p. (C). 1986. text ed. 63.00 (0-03-062737-0) SCP.

Applied Finite Mathematics. Richard J. Coppins & Paul M. Umberger. LC 85-1228. (C). 1986. teacher ed write for info. (0-201-10214-5); text ed. write for info. (0-201-10312-5); write for info. (0-201-10215-3) Addison-Wesley.

Applied Finite Mathematics. Alan Hoenig. 610p. (C). 1990. teacher ed write for info. (0-318-65054-1) McGraw.

Applied Finite Mathematics. 2nd ed. Laurence D. Hoffman & Gerald L. Bradley. LC 94-13393. 1995. text ed. write for info. (0-07-029354-6) McGraw.

Applied Finite Mathematics. 3rd ed. S. T. Tan. 688p. (C). 1990. text ed. 58.95 (0-534-92140-X) PWS Pubs.

Applied Finite Mathematics. 4th ed. Howard Anton et al. 600p. (C). 1988. Instr's manual avail. teacher ed, text ed. 46.75 (0-15-502940-1) HB Coll Pubs.

Applied Finite Mathematics. 4th ed. Soo T. Tan. LC 93-4401. 1993. write for info. (0-534-93515-X) PWS Pubs.

Applied Finite Mathematics. 5th ed. Howard Anton et al. 624p. (C). 1991. text ed. 53.25 (0-15-502942-8) SCP.

Applied Finite Mathematics & Calculus. George J. Kertz. (Illus.). 710p. (C). 1985. text ed. 43.25 (0-314-85317-0) West Pub.

Applied Finite Mathematics for Business & the Social & Natural Sciences. Chester Piascik. Ed. by Pullins. 795p. (C). 1992. text ed. 63.25 (0-314-88432-7) West Pub.

Applied Fluid Dynamics Handbook. Robert D. Blevins. LC 92-4247. 570p. 1992. reprint ed. lib. bdg. 83.50 (0-89464-717-2) Krieger.

Applied Fluid Flow Measurement: Fundamentals & Technology. Nicholas Cheremisinoff. (Engineering Measurement & Instrumentation Ser.: Vol. 1). 216p. 1979. 110.00 (0-8247-6871-X) Dekker.

Applied Fluid Mechanics. Tasos C. Papanastasiou. 500p. 1994. text ed. 74.00 (0-13-060799-1) P-H.

Applied Fluid Mechanics. 4th ed. Robert L. Mott. 704p. (C). 1994. text ed. write for info. (0-02-384231-8) Macmillan.

Applied Fluid Rheology. J. Ferguson. 324p. 1991. 110.50 (1-85166-588-9) Elsevier.

***Applied Food Microbiology.** G. Roland Vela. (Illus.). 520p. (C). 1995. pap. text ed. 36.95 (0-89863-185-8) Star Pub CA.

***Applied Food Microbiology Laboratory Manual.** G. Roland Vela. (Illus.). 520p. (C). 1995. 19.95 (0-89863-186-6) Star Pub CA.

Applied FoodService Sanitation: A Certification Coursebook. 4th ed. Education Foundation of the NRA Staff. 432p. 1993. per., pap. text ed. 36.00 (0-8403-8558-7) Kendall-Hunt.

Applied Foodservice Sanitation: Coursebook. 4th ed. Educational Foundation of the National Restaurant Association Staff. 410p. (Orig.). 1993. pap. 50.00 (0-915452-17-0) Educ Found.

Applied Foodservice Sanitation: Coursebook - Korean Translation. 4th ed. Educational Foundation of the National Restaurant Association Staff. 300p. (Orig.). 1993. pap. 50.00 (0-915452-18-9) Educ Found.

Applied Foodservice Sanitation: Instructor Guide. 4th ed. Educational Foundation of the National Restaurant Association Staff. 214p. (Orig.). 1993. pap. 15.00 (0-915452-71-5) Educ Found.

Applied Foodservice Sanitation: Textbook. 4th ed. Educ. Fdtn. of NRA Staff. 368p. 1993. boxed 32.95 (0-8403-8557-9) Kendall-Hunt.

Applied Foodservice Sanitation: Textbook. 4th ed. Educational Foundation of the National Restaurant Association Staff. 360p. (Orig.). 1993. pap. 34.95 (0-915452-16-2) Educ Found.

Applied Forest Tree Improvement. Bruce Zobel & John Talbert. (Illus.). 505p. (C). 1991. reprint ed. text ed. 42.95x (0-88133-604-1) Waveland Pr.

Applied Forms: A Sequel to Musical Form. 3rd ed. Ebenezer Prout. LC 71-155615. reprint ed. 34.50 (0-404-05138-3) AMS Pr.

Applied Forms: A Sequel to Musical Form. Ebenezer Prout. LC 77-10853. 1971. reprint ed. 7.00 (0-403-00329-6) Scholarly.

Applied Forms: A Sequel to "Musical Form" Ebenezer Prout. 307p. 1990. reprint ed. lib. bdg. 79.00 (0-7812-0784-3) Rprt Serv.

Applied Fourier Analysis. Kenneth J. Hsu. LC 83-22732. (College Outline Ser.). 223p. (C). 1984. pap. text ed. 13.50 (0-15-601609-5) HB Coll Pubs.

Applied Fourier Transforms. Ed. by K. Morita. LC 94-76401. 433p. 1995. 93.00 (90-5199-166-5) IOS Press.

Applied Fourth Generation Languages. John Watt. 156p. 1987. 21.95 (1-85058-061-8, Pub. by Sigma Pr UK) Bk Clearing Hse.

Applied Functional Analysis. D. H. Griffel. LC 81-6598. (Mathematics & Its Applications Ser.). 386p. 1984. 89.95 (0-470-27196-5) P-H.

***Applied Functional Analysis: Applications of Mathematical Physics.** Eberhard Zeidler. LC 94-43219. (Applied Mathematical Sciences Ser.: Vol. 108). 456p. 1995. 65.00 (0-387-94442-7) Spr-Verlag.

***Applied Functional Analysis: Main Principles & Their Applications.** Eberhard Zeidler. LC 94-41480. (Applied Mathematical Sciences Ser.: Vol. 109). (Illus.). 304p. 1995. 59.00 (0-387-94422-2) Spr-Verlag.

Applied Functional Analysis & Variational Methods in Engineering. J. N. Reddy. 560p. (C). 1991. reprint ed. lib. bdg. 59.50 (0-89464-585-4) Krieger.

Applied Fuzzy Systems. Toshiro Terano et al. (Illus.). 302p. 1994. 39.95 (0-12-685242-1, AP Prof) Acad Pr.

Applied Gamma-Ray Spectrometry. 2nd rev. ed. F. Adams & R. Dams. LC 79-114847. 1970. 317.00 (0-08-006888-X, Pub. by Pergamon Repr UK) Franklin.

Applied General Equilibrium. Ed. by J. Piggott & J. Whalley. (Studies in Empirical Economics). (Illus.). 160p. 1991. 35.00 (0-387-91397-1) Spr-Verlag.

Applied General Equilibrium & Economic Development. Ed. by Jean Mercenier & T. N. Srinivasan. 376p. 1993. text ed. 59.50 (0-472-10382-2) U of Mich Pr.

Applied General Equilibrium Modeling: Imperfect Competition & European Integration. Dirk Willenbockel. LC 94-2440. (Series in Financial Economics & Quantitative Analysis). 1994. text ed. 65.00 (0-471-95038-6) Wiley.

Applied General Equilibrium Modelling. Ed. by Henk Don et al. 188p. 1991. lib. bdg. 77.50 (0-7923-1376-3) Kluwer Ac.

Applied General Equilibrium Modelling: Applications, Limitations & Future Developments. D. Greenaway et al. 160p. 1993. pap. 50.00 (0-11-560049-3, HM00493, Pub. by HMSO UK) UNIPUB.

Applied General Mathematics. Robert Smith. LC 79-51586. (General Mathematics Ser.). (Illus.). 349p. (C). 1982. teacher ed 10.00 (0-8273-1675-5); text ed. 30.95 (0-8273-1674-7) Delmar.

Applied Geochemistry. Frederic R. Siegel. LC 74-13486. (Illus.). 361p. reprint ed. pap. 102.90 (0-7837-3471-9, 2057802) Bks Demand.

An Asterisk (*) at the beginning of an entry indicates that the title is appearing in BIP for the first time.

Applied Geochemistry in the 1980's. Ed. by Iain Thornton & R. Howarth. (Illus.). 1986. lib. bdg. 91.50 (*0-86010-796-5*) G & T Inc.

Applied Geodesy: Lecture Notes in Earth Sciences, Vol. 12. Ed. by S. Turner. viii, 393p. 1987. text ed. 51.00 (*0-387-18219-5*) Spr-Verlag.

Applied Geography: Issues, Questions, & Concerns. Ed. by Martin S. Kenzer. (C). 1990. lib. bdg. 99.50 (*0-7923-0438-1*) Kluwer Ac.

***Applied Geomechanics in Drilling.** V. S. Voitenko. (Russian Translation Ser.). 266p. 1995. 95.00 (*90-5410-217-9*, Pub. by A A Balkema NE) Ashgate Pub Co.

Applied Geometric Tolerancing II: (AGT II) Samuel J. Levy. 720p. 1993. pap. 59.00 (*1-883467-00-4*) Intl Geometric.

Applied Geometry & Discrete Mathematics: The "Victor Klee Festschrift" P. Gritzmann et al. LC 91-26934. (DIMACS Ser.: Vol. 4). 608p. 1991. 118.00 (*0-8218-6593-5*, DIMACS-4) Am Math.

Applied Geomorphological Mapping: Methodology by Example. Ed. by C. Embleton. (Annals of Geomorphology Ser.: Suppl. 68). (Illus.). 239p. 1988. pap. text ed. 95.00 (*0-685-53196-1*, Pub. by Gebrueder Borntraeger GW) Lubrecht & Cramer.

Applied Geomorphology. Ed. by John Gerrard. (Zeitschrift fuer Geomorphologie Supplement Ser.: Suppl. 51). (Illus.). 140p. 1984. pap. text ed. 46.95 (*3-443-21051-1*, Pub. by Gebruder Borntraeger GW) Lubrecht & Cramer.

Applied Geomorphology: Geomorphological Surveys for Environmental Development. H. Verstappen. 1983. 128.25 (*0-444-42181-5*, I-198-83) Elsevier.

Applied Geomorphology in the Tropics. Ed. by Ian Douglas & Tom Spencer. (Annals of Gemorphology Supplement Ser.: No. 44). (Illus.). 132p. 1982. text ed. 58.50 (*0-317-63481-X*, Pub. by Gebrueder Borntraeger GW) Lubrecht & Cramer.

Applied Geophysics. Chinese Geophysical Society Staff. 300p. 1989. 36.00 (*0-931830-28-1*, 651) Soc Expl Geophys.

Applied Geophysics. W. M. Telford & L. P. Goldart. (C). 1988. 30.00 (*81-204-0333-9*, Pub. by Oxford IBH II) S Asia.

Applied Geophysics. 2nd ed. W. M. Telford et al. (Illus.). (C). 1990. pap. 44.95 (*0-521-33938-3*) Cambridge U Pr.

Applied Geophysics. 2nd ed. W. M. Telford et al. (Illus.). (C). 1990. 110.00 (*0-521-32693-1*) Cambridge U Pr.

Applied Geophysics in Hydrogeological & Engineering Practice. Milos Karous et al. Ed. by William E. Kelly & Stanislav Mares. LC 92-45007. (Developments in Water Science Ser.: Vol. 44). 1993. write for info. (*0-444-88936-1*) Elsevier.

Applied Geophysics U. S. S. R. N. Rast. LC 60-53385. 1962. 176.00 (*0-08-009662-X*, Pub. by Pergamon Repr UK) Franklin.

Applied Geotechnology: A Text for Students & Engineers on Rock Excavation & Related Topics. A. B. Roberts. (Illus.). 416p. 1981. text ed. 138.00 (*0-08-024015-1*, Pub. by Pergamon Repr UK) Franklin.

Applied Geothermics. Ed. by M. Economides & P. Ungemach. LC 86-15696. 237p. 1987. text ed. 235.00 (*0-471-91179-8*) Wiley.

Applied Geothermics. Ed. by M. Economides & P. Ungemach. LC 86-15696. 252p. reprint ed. pap. 71.90 (*0-7837-6375-1*, 2046087) Bks Demand.

Applied Grammatology: Post(e)-Pedagogy from Jacques Derrida to Joseph Beuys. Gregory L. Ulmer. LC 84-47941. 352p. (C). 1984. text ed. 48.50 (*0-8018-3256-X*); pap. text ed. 15.95x (*0-8018-3257-8*) Johns Hopkins.

Applied Groundwater Hydrology: A British Perspective. Ed. by R. A. Downing & W. B. Wilkinson. (Illus.). 352p. 1992. 160.00 (*0-19-852139-1*) OUP.

Applied Groundwater Modeling: Simulation of Flow & Advective Transport. Mary P. Anderson & William W. Woessner. 381p. 1991. text ed. 79.95 (*0-12-059485-4*) Acad Pr.

Applied Group Theory. A. Cracknell & D. Ter Haar. LC 67-18948. (Selected Readings in Physics Ser.). 1968. 179.00 (*0-08-203190-8*, Pub. by Pergamon Repr UK) Franklin.

Applied Group Theory. George G. Hall. LC 67-73110. (Mathematical Physics Ser.). 136p. reprint ed. pap. 38.80 (*0-8357-5678-5*, 2004946) Bks Demand.

Applied Harmony, 2 bks., Bk. 1. George A. Wedge. 176p. 1930. pap. 15.00 (*0-02-872760-6*) Schirmer Bks.

Applied Harmony, 2 bks., Bk. 2. George A. Wedge. 128p. 1931. pap. 15.00 (*0-02-872770-3*) Schirmer Bks.

Applied Heterogeneous Catalysis: Design, Manufacture & Use of Solid Catalysts. Jean-Francois Le Page. (Illus.). 516p. 1988. 175.00 (*0-87201-146-1*) Gulf Pub.

***Applied Heterogeneous Catalysis: Design, Manufacture, Use of Solid Catalysts.** Jean-Franois Le Page. (Illus.). 552p. (C). 1987. text ed. 192.00 (*2-7108-0531-6*) Technip.

Applied High-Resolution Geophysical Methods. Trabant. 279p. 1988. text ed. 55.00 (*0-13-040841-7*) P-H.

Applied High-Resolution Geophysical Methods: Offshore Geoengineering Hazards. Peter K. Trabant. LC 83-26662. (Illus.). 265p. 1984. 40.00 (*0-934634-85-8*) Intl Human Res.

Applied Human Factors in Power Plant Design & Operation, 2 vols., Set. (Illus.). 418p. 1980. ring bd. 150.00 (*0-87683-141-2*) GP Pub.

***Applied Human Geography.** D. Gordon Bennett & Charles Hayes. 264p. (C). 1994. per., pap. text ed. 25.31 (*0-7872-0517-6*) Kendall-Hunt.

Applied Human Geography. 3rd ed. D. Gordon Bennett & Charles R. Hayes. 272p. (C). 1993. pap. text ed. 24.95 (*0-8403-8344-4*) Kendall-Hunt.

Applied Human Relations: An Organizational Approach. 4th ed. Douglas A. Benton & Jack Halloran. 576p. (C). 1990. text ed. write for info. (*0-13-040981-2*) P-H.

***Applied Human Relations: An Organizational Approach.** 5th ed. Douglas Benton. LC 94-31007. 576p. 1994. pap. text ed. 51.00 (*0-13-293564-3*) P-H.

Applied Humanities: Integrated Curricular Structures for Developmental Communication. Rajni Tandon. vii, 151p. 1989. text ed. 25.00 (*81-207-0916-0*, Pub. by Sterling Pubs II) Apt Bks.

Applied Hydraulics in Engineering. 2nd ed. Henry M. Morris & James M. Wiggert. 629p. 1972. Net. text ed. write for info. (*0-471-06669-9*); 3.00 (*0-471-07503-5*) Wiley.

Applied Hydro- & Aeromechanics. Ludwig Prandtl & O. G. Tietjens. Ed. by Jacob P. Den Hartog. (Illus.). 1934. pap. text ed. 8.95 (*0-486-60375-X*) Dover.

Applied Hydrocarbon Thermodynamics, Vol. 1. 2nd ed. Wayne C. Edmister & Byung Ik Lee. LC 83-22654. 234p. 1984. 75.00 (*0-87201-855-5*) Gulf Pub.

Applied Hydrocarbon Thermodynamics, Vol. 2. 2nd ed. Wayne C. Edmister. 240p. 1988. 77.00 (*0-87201-858-X*) Gulf Pub.

Applied Hydrodynamics in Petroleum Exploration. E. C. Dahlberg. (Illus.). 161p. 1982. pap. 36.50 (*0-387-90677-0*) Spr-Verlag.

Applied Hydrodynamics in Petroleum Exploration. Eric C. Dahlberg. LC 93-50624. 1994. 59.50 (*0-387-97880-1*) Spr-Verlag.

Applied Hydrogeology. 3rd ed. Charles W. Fetter, Jr. 691p. (C). 1994. text ed. write for info. (*0-02-336490-4*) Macmillan.

***Applied Hydrogeology for Scientists & Engineers.** Sekai Sen. 1995. write for info. (*1-56670-091-4*) Lewis Pubs.

Applied Hydrology. Chow Ven Te et al. 608p. 1988. text ed. write for info. (*0-07-010810-2*) McGraw.

Applied Hyperfunction Theory. Isao Imai. (Mathematics & Its Applications, Japan Ser.). 460p. (C). 1992. lib. bdg. 225.00 (*0-7923-1507-3*) Kluwer Ac.

Applied Hypertalk: The Scripting Process Revealed. Jerry Daniels & Mary J. Mara. 450p. 1989. disk 49.95 (*0-13-040882-4*) P-H.

Applied Hypnosis: An Overview. Benjamin Wallace. LC 79-65. 144p. 1979. 33.95 (*0-88229-415-6*) Nelson-Hall.

Applied Identification, Modelling & Simulation - AIMS '84: Proceedings, IASTED Symposium, New Orleans, U. S. A., November 12-14, 1984. Ed. by M. H. Hamza. 258p. 1984. 80.00 (*0-88986-070-X*, 080) Acta Pr.

Applied Identification, Modelling & Simulation: AIMS '87: Proceedings IASTED Symposium, New Orleans, Louisiana, U. S. A., November 10-13, 1987. Ed. by R. E. Trahan. 166p. 1988. 65.00 (*0-88986-134-X*, 112) Acta Pr.

Applied Illumination Engineering. Fairmont Press Staff & Jack L. Lindsey. 376p. 1991. text ed. 69.00 (*0-13-040726-7*) P-H.

Applied Illumination Engineering. Jack Lindsey. LC 88-45787. 500p. 1990. text ed. 69.00 (*0-88173-060-2*) Fairmont Pr.

Applied Image Processing. Thomas Awcock. 1995. text ed. 29.95 (*0-07-001470-1*) McGraw.

Applied Imagination. 3rd rev. ed. Alex F. Osborn. 1993. reprint ed. 25.95 (*0-930222-73-3*) Creative Ed.

Applied Immunodermatology. Marilyn C. Ray. LC 91-20900. (Topics in Clinical Dermatology Ser.). (Illus.). 232p. 1992. 80.00 (*0-89640-191-X*) Igaku-Shoin.

Applied Impression Management: How Image-Making Affects Managerial Decisions. Ed. by Robert A. Giacalone & Paul Rosenfeld. (Focus Editions Ser.). 320p. (C). 1991. 49.95 (*0-8039-3994-9*); pap. 24.95 (*0-8039-3995-7*) Sage.

***Applied Industrial Control.** Joseph G. Sloop. (Technology Application Ser.). (Illus.). 75p. 1990. write for info. (*0-89704-047-3*) E&L Instru.

Applied Industrial Control--an Introduction. Madan G. Singh et al. (International Series on Systems & Control: Vol. 1). (Illus.). 450p. 1980. pap. text ed. 47.00 (*0-08-024765-2*, Pergamon Pr) Elsevier.

Applied Industrial Controls Instructor's Guide. Joseph G. Sloop. (Technology Application Ser.). (Illus.). 75p. (Orig.). 1990. ring bd. write for info. (*0-89704-054-6*) E&L Instru.

***Applied Industrial Organization: Towards a Theory Based Empirical Industrial Organization.** Ed. by Karl Aiginger & Jorg Finsinger. LC 94-29539. 1994. lib. bdg. 84.00 (*0-7923-3050-1*) Kluwer Ac.

***Applied Industrial Organization: Towards a Theory Based Empirical Industrial Organization.** Ed. by Karl Aiginger. 250p. (C). 1995. lib. bdg. 93.00 (*0-7923-3051-X*) Kluwer Ac.

Applied Industrial-Organizational Psychology. Michael G. Aamodt. 529p. (C). 1991. text ed. 50.95 (*0-534-13770-9*) Brooks-Cole.

Applied Industrial Statistics see SPC Primer: Programmed Introduction to Statistical Process Control Techniques

Applied Informatics: Proceedings of IASTED Symposium, Innsbruck, Austria, February 19-21, 1990. Ed. by M. H. Hamza. 491p. 1990. 120.00 (*0-88986-142-0*) Acta Pr.

Applied Informatics - AI '84: Proceedings, IASTED Symposium, Innsbruck, Austria, February 14-17, 1984. Ed. by M. H. Hamza. 178p. 1984. 60.00 (*0-88986-057-2*, 064) Acta Pr.

Applied Informatics - AI '85: Proceedings, IASTED Symposium, Grindelwald, Switzerland, February 19-22, 1985. Ed. by M. H. Hamza. 194p. 1985. 65.00 (*0-88986-073-4*, 084) Acta Pr.

Applied Informatics - AI '88: Proceedings IASTED Symposium, Grindelwald, Switzerland, February 16-18, 1988. Ed. by M. H. Hamza. 222p. 1988. 98.00 (*0-88986-097-1*) Acta Pr.

Applied Informatics '86: Proceedings, IASTED Symposium, Innsbruck, Austria, February 18-21, 1986. Ed. by M. H. Hamza. 112p. 1986. 35.00 (*0-88986-086-6*, 102) Acta Pr.

Applied Informatics '87: Proceedings IASTED Symposium, Grindelwald, Switzerland, February 17-19, 1987. Ed. by M. H. Hamza. 215p. 1987. 77.00 (*0-88986-108-0*, 111) Acta Pr.

Applied Informatics '89: Proceedings of IASTED Symposium, Grindewald, Switzerland, February 8-10, 1989. Ed. by M. H. Hamza. 288p. 1989. 92.00 (*0-88986-117-X*, 133) Acta Pr.

Applied Information Theory. I. M. Kogan. 466p. 1988. text ed. 270.00 (*2-88124-064-X*) Gordon & Breach.

Applied Instrumentation in the Process Industries: Engineering Data & Resource Material. 3rd ed. William G. Andrew & H. B. Williams. (Illus.). 680p. 1993. 79.00 (*0-87201-047-3*) Gulf Pub.

Applied Instrumentation in the Process Industries, Vol. 1: A Survey. 2nd ed. William G. Andrew & H. B. Williams. LC 79-9418. 408p. 1979. 57.00 (*0-87201-382-0*) Gulf Pub.

Applied Instrumentation in the Process Industries, Vol. 2: Practical Guidelines. 2nd ed. William G. Andrew & H. B. Williams. LC 79-9418. 312p. 1980. 57.00 (*0-87201-383-9*) Gulf Pub.

Applied Instrumentation in the Process Industries, Vol. 4: Control Systems: Theory, Troubleshooting & Design. Leslie M. Zoss. LC 72-94067. 180p. 1979. 47.00 (*0-87201-391-X*) Gulf Pub.

Applied Integral Transforms. M. Ya. Antimirov et al. LC 92-38114. (CRM Monograph Ser.: No. 2). 265p. 1993. 66.00 (*0-8218-6998-1*) Am Math.

Applied Interactive Methods. L. A. Hageman & D. M. Young. LC 80-29546. (Computer Science & Applied Mathematics Ser.). 1981. text ed. 84.00 (*0-12-313340-8*) Acad Pr.

Applied Inverse Problems: Lectures Presented at the RCP 264 in Montpellier. Ed. by P. C. Sabatier. (Lecture Notes in Physics Ser.: Vol. 85). 1978. pap. 31.00 (*0-387-09094-0*) Spr-Verlag.

Applied Iridology & Herbology. Donald Bamer. (Illus.). 98p. 1982. pap. 12.95 (*0-913923-74-5*) Woodland UT.

Applied Isotope Hydrogeology: A Case Study in Northern Switzerland. Ed. by F. J. Pearson, Jr. et al. (Studies in Environmental Science: No. 43). 460p. 1991. 177.00 (*0-444-88983-3*) Elsevier.

Applied Journalism in Australia. John Avieson. 159p. (C). 1980. 35.00 (*0-86828-393-2*, Pub. by Deakin Univ AT) St Mut.

Applied Karst Geology: The Proceedings of the Fourth Multidisciplinary Conference on Sinkholes & the Engineering & Environmental Impacts of Karst. Ed. by Barry F. Beck. (Illus.). 294p. (C). 1993. text ed. 95.00 (*90-5410-305-1*, Pub. by A A Balkema NE) Ashgate Pub Co.

Applied Keyboarding. 3rd ed. Jerry W. Robinson et al. LC 93-7454. (YA). 1994. text ed. 19.95 (*0-538-62297-0*) S-W Pub.

Applied Keyboarding. 3rd ed. Jerry W. Robinson et al. LC 93-7454. (YA). 1994. text ed. 23.95 (*0-538-62298-9*) S-W Pub.

Applied Kinesiology. Tom Valentine & Carole Valentine. 1989. pap. 7.95 (*0-89281-328-8*) Inner Tradit.

Applied Kinesiology. 3rd ed. Clayne R. Jensen et al. (Illus.). 352p. (C). 1983. text ed. write for info. (*0-07-032469-7*) McGraw.

Applied Kinesiology: Synopsis. David S. Walther. (Illus.). 584p. 1988. text ed. 95.00 (*0-929721-00-4*) Systems DC.

Applied Kinesiology, Vol. 4: Orthopedic Conditions. David S. Walther. (Illus.). 600p. Date not set. text ed. 95.00 (*0-929721-02-0*) Systems DC.

***Applied Knowledge Acquisition.** Ting-Peng Liang & Jae K. Lee. Date not set. 44.95 (*1-55860-202-X*); disk 25.00 (*1-55860-204-6*) Morgan Kaufmann.

***Applied Knowledge Acquisition.** Paul R. Watkins. Date not set. text ed., disk 64.95 (*1-55860-205-4*) Morgan Kaufmann.

Applied Laboratory Medicine. Ed. by Norbert W. Tietz et al. LC 92-13381. 1992. pap. text ed. 29.50 (*0-7216-6474-1*) Saunders.

Applied Laser Spectroscopy. Ed. by W. Demtroder & M. Inguscio. LC 90-23596. (NATO ASI Series B, Physics: Vol. 241). (Illus.). 500p. 1991. 135.00 (*0-306-43717-1*, Plenum Pr) Plenum.

Applied Laser Spectroscopy: Techniques, Instrumentation, & Applications. Ed. by David L. Andrews & David A. Andrews. LC 92-38383. 472p. 1992. 125.00 (*1-56081-023-8*) VCH Pubs.

Applied Laser Tooling. Ed. by Oliverio D. Soares & M. Perez-Amor. (C). 1987. lib. bdg. 107.00 (*90-247-3486-X*) Kluwer Ac.

Applied Lettering: Rendering Roman, Sans Serif, & Brush Script Letterforms for Display Work. George Evans & Christine Cash. (Illus.). 80p. 1989. pap. 8.95 (*0-8230-0239-X*, Watsn-Guptill) Watsn-Guptill.

Applied Life Data Analysis. Wayne Nelson. LC 81-14779. (Probability & Mathematical Statistics: Applied Probability & Statistics Section Ser.). 634p. 1982. text ed. 112.00 (*0-471-09458-7*, Wiley-Interscience) Wiley.

Applied Linear Algebra. Usmani. (Pure & Applied Mathematics Ser.: Vol. 105). 272p. 1987. 65.00 (*0-8247-7622-4*) Dekker.

Applied Linear Algebra. 3rd ed. Ben Noble & James W. Daniel. (Illus.). 500p. (C). 1987. text ed. write for info. (*0-13-041260-0*) P-H.

Applied Linear Regression. 2nd ed. Sanford Weisberg. LC 85-5356. (Probability & Mathematical Statistics: Applied Probability & Statistics Section Ser.). 324p. 1985. text ed. 64.95 (*0-471-87957-6*) Wiley.

Applied Linear Regression Models. 2nd ed. John Neter et al. 688p. (C). 1988. text ed. 69.95 (*0-256-07068-7*) Irwin.

Applied Linear Statistical Models. 3rd ed. John Neter et al. 1184p. (C). 1990. text ed. 72.95 (*0-256-08338-X*) Irwin.

***Applied Linguistics.** T.. Van Els. 256p. 1984. pap. 24.95 (*0-7131-6422-0*, Pub. by E Arnld UK) St Martin.

Applied Liquid Crystal Polymers: A Special Issue of the Journal Molecular Crystals & Liquid Crystals. Ed. by M. Takeda et al. vi, 192p. 1989. pap. 181.00 (*0-685-47160-8*) Gordon & Breach.

Applied Liquid Crystal Research. Masatami Takeda & Shunsuke Kobayashi. (Molecular Crystals & Liquid Crystals Ser.). 239p. 1983. pap. text ed. 156.00 (*0-677-06295-8*) Gordon & Breach.

Applied Liquid Crystals Research II. Ed. by Shunsuke Kobayashi et al. 187p. 1986. pap. text ed. 116.00 (*2-88124-174-3*) Gordon & Breach.

***Applied Logic: How, What & Why: Logical Approaches to Natural Language.** Ed. by Laszlo Polos & Michael Masuch. LC 95-11570. (Synthese Library: Vol. 247). 400p. (C). 1995. lib. bdg. 115.00 (*0-7923-3432-9*) Kluwer Ac.

Applied Logistic Regression. David W. Hosmer & Stanley Lemeshow. LC 08-931893. 1989. text ed. 69.95 (*0-471-61553-6*) Wiley.

***Applied Logistic Regression Analysis.** Scott Menard. (Quantitative Applications in the Social Science Ser.: Vol. 108). 96p. (C). 1995. pap. 9.95 (*0-8039-5757-2*) Sage.

Applied Mac Scripting. Tom Trinko. LC 94-24955. 896p. 1995. pap. 34.95 (*1-55828-330-7*) H Holt & Co.

Applied Macroeconomics. 2nd ed. C. F. Pratten. (Illus.). 320p. 1990. 55.00 (*0-19-828331-8*) OUP.

Applied Magnetism. Ed. by Richard Gerber et al. LC 93-38822. 1993. lib. bdg. 199.00 (*0-7923-2622-9*) Kluwer Ac.

Applied Management in Hospital Pharmacy. Ed. by C. Richard Talley. 200p. 1991. text ed. 20.00 (*1-879907-03-8*) Am Soc Hlth-Syst.

***Applied Management Science & Spreadsheet Modeling.** Francis J. Clauss. LC 95-2889. 1996. text ed. 54.95 (*0-534-25842-5*) PWS Pubs.

Applied Many-Body Methods in Spectroscopy & Electronics. Ed. by D. Mukherjee. (Illus.). 292p. (C). 1992. 89.50 (*0-306-44193-4*, Plenum Pr) Plenum.

Applied Marine Hydraulics. Perry A. Stutman. LC 87-47737. (Illus.). 256p. 1988. text ed. 25.00 (*0-87033-366-6*) Cornell Maritime.

***Applied Marketing.** Bern Wisner. LC 95-3262. 1996. write for info. (*0-13-437914-4*) P-H.

Applied Marketing & Social Research. 2nd ed. Ute Bradley. LC 86-32447. 488p. 1987. text ed. 104.50 (*0-471-91356-1*) Chichester Pub.

Applied Marketing Problems. Peter F. Kaminski & David R. Rink. 128p. 1986. teacher ed write for info. (*0-201-10888-7*) Addison-Wesley.

Applied Marketing Research. Luiz Moutinho & Martin Evans. LC 92-17238. 1992. 34.00 (*0-201-56504-8*) Addison-Wesley.

Applied Materials Characterization, Vol. 48. Ed. by W. Katz & P. Williams. (MRS Symposium Proceedings Ser.: Vol. 48). 1985. text ed. 50.00 (*0-931837-13-8*) Materials Res.

Applied Math Concepts: Lines & Perimeters Area & Volume. rev. ed. CMSP Projects. (Illus.). 91p. (YA). reprint ed. pap. text ed. write for info. (*0-942851-01-3*) CMSP Projects.

Applied Math for Business, Economics, Life Sciences & Social Sciences. rev. ed. Raymond A. Barnett & Michael R. Ziegler. (Illus.). (C). 1991. 11.25 (*0-02-334384-2*) Dellen Pub.

Applied Math for Business, Economy, Life Science, & Social Science, Solutions Manual. 5th ed. 824p. (C). 1993. pap. write for info. (*0-02-334371-0*) Dellen Pub.

Applied Math for Wastewater Plant Operators. Joanne K. Price. LC 90-71881. 488p. 1991. student ed 38.50 (*0-87762-809-2*); write for info. (*0-87762-810-6*) Technomic.

Applied Math for Water Plant Operators. Joanne K. Price. LC 91-65983. 535p. 1991. 38.50 (*0-87762-874-2*); write for info. (*0-87762-875-0*) Technomic.

Applied Mathematics: Getting Started, Getting It Done. William T. Shaw & Jason Tigg. LC 93-13908. (Illus.). 320p. (C). 1994. text ed. 31.25 (*0-201-54217-X*) Addison-Wesley.

Applied Mathematical Demography: Texts in Statistics Ser. 2nd ed. Nathan Keyfitz. (Illus.). xxi, 441p. 1985. reprint ed. 49.80 (*0-387-96155-0*) Spr-Verlag.

Applied Mathematical Ecology. Ed. by S. A. Levin et al. (Biomathematics Ser.: Vol. 18). (Illus.). 505p. 1989. 64. 00 (*0-387-19465-7*, 2440) Spr-Verlag.

Applied Mathematical Programming. Stephen P. Bradley et al. LC 76-10426. (Illus.). (C). 1977. text ed. 65.75 (*0-201-00464-X*) Addison-Wesley.

Applied Mathematical Programming for Production & Engineering Management. Turgut M. Ozan. 656p. 1986. teacher ed write for info. (*0-8359-0028-2*, Reston); text ed. 63.00 (*0-8359-0026-6*, Reston) P-H.

Applied Mathematics. R. Jesse Phagan. (Illus.). 320p. 1992. text ed. 29.28 (*0-87006-822-9*) Goodheart.

Applied Mathematics. S. A. Sherif. 240p. (C). 1991. pap. 60.00 (*1-85352-692-4*, Pub. by HLT Pubns UK) St Mut.

Applied Mathematics: A Contemporary Approach. J. David Logan. LC 87-13318. 572p. 1987. text ed. 91.95 (*0-471-85083-7*) Wiley.

Applied Mathematics: A Workshop Presenter's Guide for Teacher Training. Center for Occupational Research & Development Staff. (Illus.). 1993. pap. text ed. write for info. (*1-55502-482-3*) CORD Commns.

An Asterisk (*) at the beginning of an entry indicates that the title is appearing in BIP for the first time.

387

***Applied Mathematics & Modeling for Chemical Engineers.** Richard G. Rice & Duong D. Do. 1994. text ed. 41.50 (*0-471-30377-1*) Wiley.

Applied Mathematics for Business & Home. Fred Justus. (Math Ser.). 24p. (gr. 6 up). 1979. student ed 5.00 (*0-8209-0117-2*, A-27) ESP.

Applied Mathematics for Business & the Social & Natural Sciences. Chester Piascik. Ed. by Pullins. 966p. (C). 1992. text ed. 67.50 (*0-314-83981-X*) West Pub.

Applied Mathematics for Business, Economics, & the Social Sciences. 4th ed. Frank S. Budnick. LC 92-30009. 1993. text ed. write for info. (*0-07-008902-7*) McGraw.

Applied Mathematics for Business, Economics, & the Social Sciences. 4th ed. Frank S. Budnick. 1993. Student Manual. student ed, pap. text ed. write for info. (*0-07-008904-3*) McGraw.

Applied Mathematics for Business, Economics, Life Sciences, & Social Sciences. 5th ed. Raymond A. Barnett & Michael R. Ziegler. LC 93-8897. (College Mathematics Ser.). 1099p. (C). 1993. write for info. (*0-02-306501-X*) Dellen Pub.

Applied Mathematics for Earth Scientists. Tsuneji Rikitake et al. 1987. lib. bdg. 162.50 (*90-277-1796-6*) Kluwer Ac.

Applied Mathematics for Economics. Jati K. Sengupta. (C). 1987. lib. bdg. 88.00 (*90-277-2588-8*) Kluwer Ac.

Applied Mathematics for Engineers. A. S. Cakmak & J. F. Botha. LC 94-70415. 320p. (C). 1995. 72.00 (*1-56252-199-3*) Computational Mech MA.

***Applied Mathematics for Engineers.** A. S. Cakmak & J. F. Botha. LC 94-70415. 320p. (C). 1995. pap. 32.00 (*1-56252-306-6*) Computational Mech MA.

Applied Mathematics for Engineers - Solutions Manual. A. S. Cakmak & J. F. Botha. 110p. (C). 1996. 15.00 (*1-56252-065-2*) Computational Mech MA.

Applied Mathematics for Management, Life & Social Sciences. Lawrence E. Spence & Charles L. Vanden Eynden. (C). 1989. text ed. 70.50 (*0-673-18837-X*) HarpCollege.

Applied Mathematics for Technical Programs: Algebra. Robert G. Moon. LC 73-75638. (C). 1973. pap. write for info. (*0-675-08943-3*, Merrill Pub Co) Macmillan.

Applied Mathematics for Technical Programs: Arithmetic & Geometry. Robert G. Moon. (C). 1973. pap. write for info. (*0-675-08983-2*, Merrill Pub Co) Macmillan.

Applied Mathematics for the Petroleum & Other Industries. 3rd rev. ed. Ed. by Mildred Gerding. (Illus.). 276p. (C). 1985. pap. text ed. 30.00 (*0-88698-085-2*, 1. 60030) PETEX.

Applied Mathematics in Aerospace Science & Engineering. Ed. by A. Miele & A. Salvetti. (Mathematical Concepts & Methods in Science & Engineering Ser.: Vol. 44). (Illus.). 500p. (C). 1994. 110.00 (*0-306-44754-1*, Plenum Pr) Plenum.

Applied Mathematics Student Resource Book. Center for Occupational Research & Development Staff. (Applied Mathematics Ser.). (Illus.). 1989. pap. text ed. write for info. (*1-55502-370-3*) CORD Commns.

Applied Mathematics Student Resource Book. 2nd ed. Center for Occupational Research & Development Staff. (Illus.). 1993. pap. text ed. write for info. (*1-55502-481-5*) CORD Commns.

Applied Mathematics, Unit A: "Getting to Know Your Calculator" Center for Occupational Research & Development Staff. (Illus.). 1989. teacher ed write for info. (*1-55502-338-X*); pap. text ed. write for info. (*1-55502-337-1*) CORD Commns.

Applied Mathematics, Unit B: "Naming Numbers in Different Ways" Center for Occupational Research & Development Staff. (Illus.). 1989. teacher ed write for info. (*1-55502-340-1*); pap. text ed. write for info. (*1-55502-339-8*) CORD Commns.

Applied Mathematics, Unit C: "Finding Answers with Your Calculator" Center for Occupational Research & Development Staff. (Illus.). 1989. teacher ed write for info. (*1-55502-342-8*); pap. text ed. write for info. (*1-55502-341-X*) CORD Commns.

Applied Mathematics, Unit 1: "Learning Problem-Solving Techniques" Center for Occupational Research & Development Staff. (Illus.). 1989. teacher ed write for info. (*1-55502-298-7*); pap. text ed. write for info. (*1-55502-297-9*) CORD Commns.

Applied Mathematics, Unit 10: "Working with Scale Drawings" Center for Occupational Research & Development Staff. (Illus.). 1989. teacher ed write for info. (*1-55502-312-6*); pap. text ed. write for info. (*1-55502-311-8*) CORD Commns.

Applied Mathematics, Unit 11: "Using Signed Numbers & Vectors" Center for Occupational Research & Development Staff. (Illus.). 1989. teacher ed write for info. (*1-55502-314-2*); pap. text ed. write for info. (*1-55502-313-4*) CORD Commns.

Applied Mathematics, Unit 12: "Using Scientific Notation" Center for Occupational Research & Development Staff. (Illus.). 1989. teacher ed write for info. (*1-55502-316-9*); pap. text ed. write for info. (*1-55502-315-0*) CORD Commns.

Applied Mathematics, Unit 13: "Precision, Accuracy, & Tolerance" Center for Occupational Research & Development Staff. (Illus.). 1989. teacher ed write for info. (*1-55502-318-5*); pap. text ed. write for info. (*1-55502-317-7*) CORD Commns.

Applied Mathematics, Unit 14: "Solving Problems with Powers & Roots" Center for Occupational Research & Development Staff. (Illus.). 1989. teacher ed write for info. (*1-55502-320-7*); pap. text ed. write for info. (*1-55502-319-3*) CORD Commns.

Applied Mathematics, Unit 15: "Using Formulas to Solve Problems" Center for Occupational Research & Development Staff. (Illus.). 1989. teacher ed write for info. (*1-55502-322-3*); pap. text ed. write for info. (*1-55502-321-5*) CORD Commns.

Applied Mathematics, Unit 16: "Solving Problems That Involve Linear Equations" Center for Occupational Research & Development Staff. (Illus.). 1989. teacher ed write for info. (*1-55502-324-X*); pap. text ed. write for info. (*1-55502-323-1*) CORD Commns.

Applied Mathematics, Unit 17: "Graphing Data" Center for Occupational Research & Development Staff. (Illus.). 1989. teacher ed write for info. (*1-55502-326-6*); pap. text ed. write for info. (*1-55502-325-8*) CORD Commns.

Applied Mathematics, Unit 18: "Solving Problems That Involve Nonlinear Equations" Center for Occupational Research & Development Staff. (Illus.). 1989. teacher ed write for info. (*1-55502-328-2*); pap. text ed. write for info. (*1-55502-327-4*) CORD Commns.

Applied Mathematics, Unit 19: "Working with Statistics" Center for Occupational Research & Development Staff. (Illus.). 1989. teacher ed write for info. (*1-55502-330-4*); pap. text ed. write for info. (*1-55502-329-0*) CORD Commns.

Applied Mathematics, Unit 2: "Estimating Answers" Center for Occupational Research & Development Staff. (Illus.). 1989. teacher ed write for info. (*1-55502-300-2*); pap. text ed. write for info. (*1-55502-299-5*) CORD Commns.

Applied Mathematics, Unit 20: "Working with Probabilities" Center for Occupational Research & Development Staff. (Illus.). 1989. teacher ed write for info. (*1-55502-332-0*); pap. text ed. write for info. (*1-55502-331-2*) CORD Commns.

Applied Mathematics, Unit 21: "Using Right-Triangle Relationships" Center for Occupational Research & Development Staff. (Illus.). 1989. teacher ed write for info. (*1-55502-334-7*); pap. text ed. write for info. (*1-55502-333-9*) CORD Commns.

Applied Mathematics, Unit 22: "Using Trigonometric Functions" Center for Occupational Research & Development Staff. (Illus.). 1989. teacher ed write for info. (*1-55502-336-3*); pap. text ed. write for info. (*1-55502-335-5*) CORD Commns.

Applied Mathematics, Unit 23: Factoring. Center for Occupational Research & Development Staff. (Illus.). 53p. 1991. teacher ed write for info. (*1-55502-431-9*); student ed, pap. text ed. write for info. (*1-55502-442-4*) CORD Commns.

Applied Mathematics, Unit 24: Patterns & Functions. Center for Occupational Research & Development Staff. (Illus.). 60p. 1991. teacher ed write for info. (*1-55502-432-7*); student ed, pap. text ed. write for info. (*1-55502-443-2*) CORD Commns.

Applied Mathematics, Unit 25: Quadratics. Center for Occupational Research & Development Staff. (Illus.). 59p. 1991. teacher ed write for info. (*0-318-68939-1*); student ed, pap. text ed. write for info. (*1-55502-444-0*) CORD Commns.

Applied Mathematics, Unit 26: "Systems of Equations" Center for Occupational Research & Development Staff. (Illus.). 1992. teacher ed write for info. (*1-55502-434-3*); pap. text ed. write for info. (*1-55502-445-9*) CORD Commns.

Applied Mathematics, Unit 27: "Inequalities" Center for Occupational Research & Development Staff. (Illus.). 1992. teacher ed write for info. (*1-55502-435-1*); pap. text ed. write for info. (*1-55502-446-7*) CORD Commns.

Applied Mathematics, Unit 28: "Geometry in the Workplace I" Center for Occupational Research & Development Staff. (Illus.). 1992. teacher ed write for info. (*1-55502-436-X*); pap. text ed. write for info. (*1-55502-447-5*) CORD Commns.

Applied Mathematics, Unit 29: "Geometry in the Workplace II" Center for Occupational Research & Development Staff. (Illus.). 1992. teacher ed write for info. (*1-55502-437-8*); pap. text ed. write for info. (*1-55502-448-3*) CORD Commns.

Applied Mathematics, Unit 3: Measuring in English & Metric Units. Center for Occupational Research & Development Staff. (Illus.). 1989. teacher ed write for info. (*1-55502-302-9*); pap. text ed. write for info. (*1-55502-301-0*) CORD Commns.

Applied Mathematics, Unit 30: Solving Problems with Computer Spreadsheets. Center for Occupational Research & Development Staff. (Illus.). 1992. teacher ed write for info. (*1-55502-438-6*); pap. text ed. write for info. (*1-55502-449-1*) CORD Commns.

Applied Mathematics, Unit 31: Solving Problems with Computer Graphics. Center for Occupational Research & Development Staff. (Illus.). 1992. teacher ed write for info. (*1-55502-439-4*); pap. text ed. write for info. (*1-55502-450-5*) CORD Commns.

Applied Mathematics, Unit 32: Quality Assurance & Process Control 1. Center for Occupational Research & Development Staff. (Illus.). 1992. teacher ed write for info. (*1-55502-440-8*); pap. text ed. write for info. (*1-55502-451-3*) CORD Commns.

Applied Mathematics, Unit 33: Quality Assurance & Process Control 2. Center for Occupational Research & Development Staff. (Illus.). 1992. teacher ed write for info. (*1-55502-441-6*); pap. text ed. write for info. (*1-55502-452-1*) CORD Commns.

Applied Mathematics, Unit 4: "Using Graphs, Charts, & Tables" Center for Occupational Research & Development Staff. (Illus.). 1989. teacher ed write for info. (*1-55502-304-5*); pap. text ed. write for info. (*1-55502-303-7*) CORD Commns.

Applied Mathematics, Unit 5: "Dealing with Data" Center for Occupational Research & Development Staff. (Illus.). 1989. teacher ed write for info. (*1-55502-294-4*); pap. text ed. write for info. (*1-55502-292-8*) CORD Commns.

Applied Mathematics, Unit 6: "Working with Lines & Angles" Center for Occupational Research & Development Staff. (Illus.). 1989. teacher ed write for info. (*1-55502-306-1*); pap. text ed. write for info. (*1-55502-305-3*) CORD Commns.

Applied Mathematics, Unit 7: "Working with Shapes in Two Dimensions" Center for Occupational Research & Development Staff. (Illus.). 1989. teacher ed write for info. (*1-55502-295-2*); pap. text ed. write for info. (*1-55502-293-6*) CORD Commns.

Applied Mathematics, Unit 8: "Working with Shapes in Three Dimensions" Center for Occupational Research & Development Staff. (Illus.). 1989. teacher ed write for info. (*1-55502-308-8*); pap. text ed. write for info. (*1-55502-307-X*) CORD Commns.

Applied Mathematics, Unit 9: "Using Ratios & Proportions" Center for Occupational Research & Development Staff. (Illus.). 1989. teacher ed write for info. (*1-55502-310-X*); pap. text ed. write for info. (*1-55502-309-6*) CORD Commns.

Applied Matrix Algebra in the Statistical Sciences. Alexander Basilevskyh. 390p. 1983. 57.00 (*0-444-00756-3*) Elsevier.

Applied Maximizing. Hans Bleiker & Annemarie Bleiker. 1988. write for info. (*0-925368-03-2*) IPMP.

Applied Measurement Engineering: How to Design Effective Mechanical Measurement Systems. Charles Wright. LC 94-1636. 432p. 1994. text ed. 60.00 (*0-13-253477-0*) P-H.

Applied Measurements in Mineral & Metallurgical Processing: Proceedings of IFAC Workshop, Transvaal, South Africa, 11-14 October 1988. Ed. by G. Sommer. (IFAC Publication Ser.: No. 87). 1989. 94.00 (*0-08-036385-7*, Pergamon Pr) Elsevier.

Applied Mechanical Vibrations. David V. Hutton. (Mechanical Engineering Ser.). (Illus.). 416p. 1981. text ed. write for info. (*0-07-031549-3*) McGraw.

Applied Mechanics. Charles E. Smith. Incl. Dynamics. 1976. text ed. 21.95 (*0-471-80178-X*); Statics. 1976. text ed. 21.95 (*0-471-80460-6*); 1976. Set text ed. write for info. (*0-318-56419-X*) Wiley.

Applied Mechanics. Patrick D. Collins & A. Jackson. LC 75-301190. (Illus.). 341p. reprint ed. pap. 97.20 (*0-8357-5680-7*, 2030352) Bks Demand.

Applied Mechanics: Proceedings of the International Conference on Applied Mechanics, Beijing, China, 21-25 August 1989, 3 vols. Ed. by Zheng Zhemin. (International Academic Publishers Ser.). 1992p. 1990. 475.00 (*0-08-037886-2*, Pergamon Pr) Elsevier.

Applied Mechanics Vol. 4: Soviet Review. Mikhailov. 1994. write for info. (*0-8493-9329-9*) CRC Pr.

Applied Mechanics & Soviet Reviews, Vol. 1. G. K. Mikhailov & Parton. 1989. 197.00 (*0-89116-718-8*) Taylor & Francis.

Applied Mechanics Aspects of Nuclear Effects in Materials: Presented at the Winter Annual Meeting of ASME, Washington, D. C., Dec. 2, 1971. Ed. by Conrad C. Wan. LC 77-182577. 210p. reprint ed. pap. 59.90 (*0-8357-5681-5*, 2016863) Bks Demand.

Applied Mechanics for Engineering Technology. 4th ed. Keith M. Walker. 560p. 1990. text ed. 48.00 (*0-13-040585-X*) P-H.

Applied Mechanics of Machine Elements. Broersma. (C). 1967. 225.00 (*0-85950-040-3*, Pub. by S Thornes Pubs UK) St Mut.

Applied Mechanics: Soviet Reviews, Vol. 2: Electromagnetoelasticity. Ed. by G. K. Mikhailov & V. Z. Parton. 360p. 1990. 145.00 (*0-685-40762-4*) Hemisp Pub.

Applied Mechanics, Soviet Reviews, Vol. 2: Stability & Analytical Mechanics. G. K. Mikhailov & Parton. 1990. 178.00 (*0-89116-720-X*) Hemisp Pub.

Applied Medical Microbiology. 2nd ed. J. G. Collee. (Illus.). 158p. 1981. pap. text ed. 24.95 (*0-632-00853-9*) Blackwell Sci.

Applied Metallography. George F. Vander Voort. 1986. text ed. 67.95 (*0-442-28836-0*) Chapman & Hall.

Applied Methods of Structural Reliability. Milik Tichy. LC 93-17751. (Topics in Safety, Reliability, & Quality Ser.: Vol. 2). 416p. (C). 1993. lib. bdg. 150.00 (*0-7923-2349-1*) Kluwer Ac.

Applied Methods of the Theory of Random Functions. A. G. Sveshnikov & J. Berry. LC 66-18233. (International Series Mono on Pure & Applied Mathematics: Vol. 89). 1966. 133.00 (*0-08-010869-5*, Pub. by Pergamon Repr UK) Franklin.

Applied Microbiology. Pam Caddow. (Illus.). 262p. 1989. pap. 23.50 (*1-871364-08-6*) Ishiyaku Euro.

Applied Microeconomics. 1992. 89.95 (*0-409-10015-3*, Pub. by Buttrwrth Can Acad CN) Buttrwrth-Heinemann.

Applied Microeconomics. Edwin Mansfield. LC 92-47402. (C). 1993. text ed. 59.95 (*0-393-96431-0*) Norton.

Applied Microeconomics & Games: The Learning System. Ed. by Lynn Gillette. (Illus.). 443p. (C). 1991. pap. 34. 95 (*0-9622521-2-3*) Econotex Pr.

Applied Micropaleontology. Ed. by David G. Jenkins. LC 93-18856. 284p. (C). 1993. lib. bdg. 99.00 (*0-7923-2264-9*) Kluwer Ac.

Applied Mineralogical Thermodynamics Selected Topics. N. D. Chatterjee. (Illus.). 328p. 1991. pap. text ed. 64.00 (*0-387-53215-3*) Spr-Verlag.

Applied Mineralogy. Meurig P. Jones. (Illus.). 250p. 1987. lib. bdg. 108.00 (*0-86010-510-5*); pap. text ed. 48.50 (*0-86010-511-3*) G & T Inc.

Applied Mineralogy: A Quantitative Approach. Meurig P. Jones. (C). 1987. lib. bdg. 79.00 (*0-317-58375-1*, Pub. by Graham & Trotman UK) Kluwer Ac.

Applied Mineralogy: Proceedings of the Second International Congress on Applied Mineralogy in the Minerals Industry, Los Angeles, California, February 22-25, 1984. International Congress on Applied Mineralogy in the Minerals Industry Staff. Ed. by Won C. Park et al. LC 84-29437. 1210p. reprint ed. pap. 180. 00 (*0-8357-2597-9*, 2052377) Bks Demand.

***Applied Mining Geology.** fac. ed. Society of Mining Engineers of AIME Staff. Ed. by A. J. Erickson, Jr. LC 84-81473. (Illus.). 232p. 1984. reprint ed. pap. 66.20 (*0-7837-7837-6*, 2047597) Bks Demand.

Applied Mining Geology, 3 vols. in 1. Ed. by A. J. Erickson, Jr. et al. (Illus.). 624p. 1992. reprint ed. pap. 70.00 (*0-87335-109-6*, 109-6) SMM&E Inc.

***Applied Mining Geology: General Studies: Problems of Sampling & Grade Control: Ore Reserve Estimation.** Ed. by A. J. Erickson, Jr. et al. (Illus.). reprint ed. pap. 175.60 (*0-7837-9176-3*, 2049875) Bks Demand.

Applied Mining Geology: Ore Reserve Estimation. Ed. by D. E. Ranta. LC 86-61399. 212p. (Orig.). reprint ed. pap. 60.50 (*0-8357-3483-8*, 2039742) Bks Demand.

Applied Mining Geology: Problems of Sampling & Grade Control. Ed. by R. A. Metz. LC 85-71945. 173p. reprint ed. pap. 49.40 (*0-8357-3414-5*, 2039671) Bks Demand.

Applied Modeling in Catchment Hydrology. Ed. by Vijay P. Singh. LC 81-71292. 1982. 38.00 (*0-918334-43-8*) WRP.

Applied Modeling of Hydrologic Time Series. J. D. Salas et al. LC 80-53334. 1981. reprint ed. 38.00 (*0-918334-37-3*) WRP.

Applied Modelling & Simulation: Proceedings of the International Symposium Held in Lugano, Switzerland, June 18-20, 1990. Ed. by M. H. Hamza. 167p. 1990. 50.00 (*0-88986-154-4*, 164) Acta Pr.

Applied Modelling & Simulation - AMS '84: Proceedings, IASTED Symposium, Nice, France, June 19-21, 1984. Ed. by M. H. Hamza. 170p. 1984. 60.00 (*0-88986-063-7*, 070) Acta Pr.

Applied Modelling & Simulation of Technological Systems: Proceedings of the 1st IMACS Symposium on Modelling & Simulation for Control of Lumped & Distributed Parameter Systems, Lille, France, 3-6 June, 1986. Ed. by Pierre Borne & Spyros G. Tzafestas. 726p. 1987. 133.50 (*0-444-70249-0*, North Holland) Elsevier.

Applied Molecular Genetics of Filamentous Fungi. Ed. by James R. Kinghorn & G. Turner. LC 92-3980. 232p. 1992. 159.95 (*0-7514-0058-0*, A6873, Pub. by Blackie Acad & Prof UK) Routledge Chapman & Hall.

Applied Molecular Genetics of Fungi. Ed. by J. F. Peberdy et al. (British Mycological Society Symposium Ser.: No. 18). (Illus.). 200p. (C). 1991. 64.95 (*0-521-41571-3*) Cambridge U Pr.

Applied Mossbauer Spectroscopy: Theory & Practice for Geochemists & Archeologists. S. Mitra. (Physics & Chemistry of the Earth Ser.: Vol. 18). 400p. 1993. 500. 00 (*0-08-042199-7*, Pergamon Pr) Elsevier.

Applied Multiple Regression - Correlation Analysis for the Behavioral Sciences: Correlation Analysis for the Behavioral Sciences. 2nd ed. Jacob Cohen & Patricia Cohen. 545p. 1983. text ed. 39.95 (*0-89859-268-2*) L Erlbaum Assocs.

Applied Multivariate Analysis. J. H. Bernstein et al. (Illus.). 510p. 1988. 65.00 (*0-387-96542-4*) Spr-Verlag.

Applied Multivariate Analysis. John E. Overall & C. James Klett. LC 81-20944. 522p. (C). 1983. reprint ed. lib. bdg. 48.50 (*0-89874-325-7*) Krieger.

Applied Multivariate Analysis in SAR & Environmental Studies. Ed. by J. Devillers & Walter Karcher. (C). 1991. lib. bdg. 157.50 (*0-7923-1290-2*) Kluwer Ac.

Applied Multivariate Data Analysis: Regression & Experimental Design. J. D. Jobson. Ed. by Stephen E. Fienberg & Ingram Olkin. (Texts in Statistics Ser.: Vol. I). (Illus.). xxv, 621p. 1994. disk 59.00 (*0-387-97660-4*) Spr-Verlag.

Applied Multivariate Data Analysis Vol. 2: Categorical & Multivariate Methods. J. D. Jobson. Ed. by Stephen E. Fienberg & Ingram Olkin. (Texts in Statistics Ser.). (Illus.). 752p. 1994. disk 59.00 (*0-387-97804-6*) Spr-Verlag.

Applied Multivariate Statistical Analysis. 3rd ed. Richard A. Johnson & Dean W. Wichern. 656p. 1992. text ed. 78.00 (*0-13-041773-4*) P-H.

Applied Multivariate Statistics for the Social Sciences. 2nd ed. James P. Stevens. 648p. (C). 1992. text ed. 99.95 (*0-8058-1154-0*); pap. 39.95 (*0-8058-1197-4*) L Erlbaum Assocs.

***Applied Multivariate Statistics for the Social Sciences.** 3rd ed. James P. Stevens. 650p. 1995. text ed. 130.00 (*0-8058-1670-4*) L Erlbaum Assocs.

***Applied Multivariate Statistics for the Social Sciences.** 3rd ed. James P. Stevens. 650p. 1995. pap. 65.00 (*0-8058-1671-2*) L Erlbaum Assocs.

***Applied Multivariate Techniques.** Subhash Sharma. LC 95-12400. 1996. text ed. write for info. (*0-471-31064-6*) Wiley.

Applied Mutation Breeding for Vegetatively Propagated Crops: Developments in Crop Science. Ed. by C. Broertjes & A. M. Van Harten. 350p. 1988. 179.50 (*0-444-42786-4*) Elsevier.

Applied Mycology of Fusarium. J. E. Smith. Ed. by M. O. Moss. LC 83-5337. (British Mycological Society Symposium Ser.: No. 7). 300p. 1984. 99.95 (*0-521-25398-5*) Cambridge U Pr.

Applied Myrmecology: A World Perspective. Ed. by Robert K. Vander Meer et al. 741p. (C). 1990. text ed. 124.50 (*0-8133-7785-4*) Westview.

Applied N Equals One Supergravity. Pran Nath et al. (ICIP Lecture Series in Theoretical Physics Lectures: Vol. 1). 116p. 1984. text ed. 36.00 (*9971-966-48-4*); pap. text ed. 15.00 (*9971-966-49-2*) World Scientific Pub.

Applied Natural Language Processing. Steven P. Shwartz. (Illus.). 240p. 1987. text ed. 29.95 (*0-89433-304-6*, NO. 8232); pap. text ed. 24.95 (*0-89433-260-0*) Petrocelli.

Applied Network Optimization. C. Mandel. LC 79-40808. 1980. text ed. 101.00 (*0-12-468350-9*) Acad Pr.

An Asterisk (*) at the beginning of an entry indicates that the title is appearing in BIP for the first time.

An Asterisk (*) at the beginning of an entry indicates that the title is appearing in BIP for the first time.

Applied Radiation & Isotopes, Vol 39, No. 8 see Radioactivity Measurements: Principles & Practice

Applied Radiation Chemistry: Radiation Processing. Robert J. Woods & Alexei K. Pikaev. LC 93-8042. 535p. 1993. text ed. 79.95 (0-471-54452-3) Wiley.

Applied Radiochemistry. Jean-Pierre Adloff & Robert Guillaumont. 1993. 95.00 (0-8493-4244-9, QD601) CRC Pr.

Applied Radiographic Calculations. Cynthia A. Dennis & Ronald L. Eisenberg. LC 92-28280. (Illus.). 192p. 1993. pap. text ed. 30.50 (0-7216-6596-9) Saunders.

Applied Radionuclide Metrology: Proceedings of the International Committee for Radionuclide Metrology Seminar, Geel, Belgium, 16-17 May 1983. Ed. by G. C. Mann et al. (International Journal of Applied Radiation & Isotopes Ser.: Vol. 34, No. 8). 286p. 1984. pap. 28.00 (0-08-030271-8, Pergamon Pr) Elsevier.

Applied Regression: An Introduction. Michael S. Lewis-Beck. (Quantitative Applications in the Social Sciences Ser.: Vol. 22). (Illus.). 79p. 1980. pap. 9.95 (0-8039-1494-6) Sage.

Applied Regression Analysis. 2nd ed. Norman R. Draper & Harry Smith. LC 80-17951. (Probability & Mathematical Statistics Ser.). 709p. 1981. text ed. 82.95 (0-471-02995-5) Wiley.

Applied Regression Analysis: A Research Tool. John O. Rawlings. LC 88-20638. 553p. (C). 1988. text ed. 62.95 (0-534-09246-2) Intl Thomson.

Applied Regression Analysis & Experimental Design. Brook. (Statistics: Textbooks & Monographs: Vol. 62). 256p. 1985. 59.75 (0-8247-7252-0) Dekker.

Applied Regression Analysis & Other Multivariable Methods. 2nd ed. David G. Kleinbaum et al. 736p. (C). 1988. text ed. 54.95 (0-87150-123-6) Intl Thomson.

Applied Regression Analysis for Business & Economics. Terry E. Dielman. 573p. (C). 1991. text ed. 56.95 (0-534-92238-4) Intl Thomson.

Applied Regression Analysis in Econometrics. Doran. (Statistics: Textbooks & Monographs: Vol. 102). 392p. 1989. 125.00 (0-8247-8049-3) Dekker.

Applied Rehabilitation Counseling. T. F. Riggar & Arnold W. Wolf. LC 86-21923. (Series on Rehabilitation). 424p. 1986. pap. 33.95 (0-8261-5370-4) Springer Pub.

Applied Reliability. 2nd ed. Paul A. Tobias & David C. Trindade. LC 85-20220. (Electrical Engineering Ser.). (Illus.). 400p. 1995. text ed. 64.95 (0-442-00469-9) Van Nos Reinhold.

Applied Reliability Assessment in Electric Power Systems. Ronald N. Allan. Ed. by R. Billinton et al. LC 90-40180. (Illus.). 560p. (C). 1991. 69.95 (0-87942-264-5, PC02519) Inst Electrical.

Applied Remote Sensing. Chor Pang Lo. 1986. text ed. 49.95 (0-470-20689-6) Wiley.

Applied Research Design: A Practical Guide. Terry E. Hedrick et al. (Applied Social Research Methods Ser.: Vol. 32). (Illus.). 160p. (C). 1993. text ed. 37.00 (0-8039-3233-2); pap. text ed. 16.95 (0-8039-3234-0) Sage.

Applied Research for Social Policy: The United States & the Federal Republic of Germany Compared. Ed. by Kenneth J. Arrow et al. 332p. 1984. reprint ed. lib. bdg. 77.50 (0-8191-4094-5) U Pr of Amer.

Applied Research in Coaching & Athletics Annual 1990. Ed. by Warren K. Simpson et al. 249p. (Orig.). 1990. pap. text ed. 23.95x (0-89641-191-5) American Pr.

Applied Research in Coaching & Athletics Annual 1991. Ed. by Warren K. Simpson et al. 323p. (Orig.). (C). 1991. pap. text ed. 23.75x (0-89641-215-6) American Pr.

***Applied Research in Coaching & Athletics Annual 1992.** Ed. by Warren Simpson. (Illus.). 240p. (Orig.). 1992. pap. text ed. 23.75x (0-89641-250-4) American Pr.

***Applied Research in Coaching & Athletics Annual 1993.** Ed. by Warren K. Simpson. 260p. (Orig.). 1993. pap. text ed. 23.75x (0-89641-260-1) American Pr.

***Applied Research in Coaching & Athletics Annual 1994.** Ed. by Warren K. Simpson. 264p. (Orig.). 1994. pap. text ed. 25.00x (0-89641-269-5) American Pr.

***Applied Research in Fuzzy Technology: Results of the Laboratory for International Fuzzy Engineering (LIFE)** Ed. by Anca L. Ralescu. LC 94-34459. (International Series in Intelligent Technologies). 480p. (C). 1994. lib. bdg. 120.00 (0-7923-9496-8) Kluwer Ac.

Applied Research in Gerontology. William J. McAuley. (Illus.). 288p. (C). 1987. text ed. 44.95 (0-442-26468-2) Van Nos Reinhold.

***Applied Research in Nursing.** Wilson. (Health & Life Science Ser.). 1995. pap. 24.95 (0-8273-6264-1) Delmar.

***Applied Research in Residential Treatment.** Ed. by Gordon Northrup. LC 94-24683. 99p. 1994. 29.95 (1-56024-687-1) Haworth Pr.

Applied Robotic Analysis. Robert Parkin. 448p. 1991. text ed. 91.00 (0-13-773391-7) P-H.

Applied Sampling. Seymour Sudman. (Quantitative Studies in Social Relations). 1976. text ed. 66.00 (0-12-675750-X) Acad Pr.

Applied Science - Built Environment (Fifth) 1992. 40.00 (1-56638-038-3) Math Sci Nucleus.

Applied Science - Built Environment (Second) 1992. 25.00 (1-56638-018-9) Math Sci Nucleus.

Applied Science - Built Environment (Sixth) 1992. 50.00 (1-56638-046-4) Math Sci Nucleus.

Applied Science - Built Environment (Third) 1992. 58.00 (1-56638-024-3) Math Sci Nucleus.

Applied Science - Literature Books (K-Sixth) 1992. 294.95 (1-56638-200-9) Math Sci Nucleus.

Applied Science - Our Technological World. J. R. Blueford et al. 1992. 23.95 (1-56638-000-6) Math Sci Nucleus.

Applied Science - Physics (Fifth A) 1992. 40.00 (1-56638-034-0) Math Sci Nucleus.

Applied Science - Physics (Fifth B) 1992. 30.00 (1-56638-035-9) Math Sci Nucleus.

Applied Science - Physics (First A) 1992. 30.00 (1-56638-007-3) Math Sci Nucleus.

Applied Science - Physics (First B) 1992. 25.00 (1-56638-008-1) Math Sci Nucleus.

Applied Science - Physics (Fourth A) 1992. 45.00 (1-56638-027-8) Math Sci Nucleus.

Applied Science - Physics (Fourth B) 1992. 45.00 (1-56638-028-6) Math Sci Nucleus.

Applied Science - Physics (KB) 1992. 60.00 (1-56638-005-7) Math Sci Nucleus.

Applied Science - Physics (Second A) 1992. 25.00 (1-56638-014-6) Math Sci Nucleus.

Applied Science - Physics (Second B) 1992. 40.00 (1-56638-015-4) Math Sci Nucleus.

Applied Science - Physics (Sixth A) 1992. 50.00 (1-56638-042-1) Math Sci Nucleus.

Applied Science - Physics (Sixth B) 1992. 50.00 (1-56638-043-X) Math Sci Nucleus.

Applied Science - Physics (Third A) 1992. 35.00 (1-56638-021-9) Math Sci Nucleus.

Applied Science - Physics (Third B) 1992. 40.00 (1-56638-022-7) Math Sci Nucleus.

Applied Science - Science & Math (Fifth A) 1992. 25.00 (1-56638-031-6) Math Sci Nucleus.

Applied Science - Science & Math (Fifth B) 1992. 25.00 (1-56638-032-4) Math Sci Nucleus.

Applied Science - Science & Math (Fifth C) 1992. 40.00 (1-56638-033-2) Math Sci Nucleus.

Applied Science - Science & Math (Fourth A) 1992. 35.00 (1-56638-025-1) Math Sci Nucleus.

Applied Science - Science & Math (Fourth C) 1992. 35.00 (1-56638-026-X) Math Sci Nucleus.

Applied Science - Science & Math (KA) 1992. 95.00 (1-56638-001-4) Math Sci Nucleus.

Applied Science - Science & Math (KB) 1992. 25.00 (1-56638-002-2) Math Sci Nucleus.

Applied Science - Science & Math (KC) 1992. 25.00 (1-56638-003-0) Math Sci Nucleus.

Applied Science - Science & Math (Second A) 1992. 25.00 (1-56638-011-1) Math Sci Nucleus.

Applied Science - Science & Math (Second B) 1992. 25.00 (1-56638-012-X) Math Sci Nucleus.

Applied Science - Science & Math (Second C) 1992. 25.00 (1-56638-013-8) Math Sci Nucleus.

Applied Science - Science & Math (Sixth A) 1992. 35.00 (1-56638-039-1) Math Sci Nucleus.

Applied Science - Science & Math (Sixth B) 1992. 25.00 (1-56638-040-5) Math Sci Nucleus.

Applied Science - Science & Math (Sixth C) 1992. 50.00 (1-56638-041-3) Math Sci Nucleus.

Applied Science - Science & Math (Third A) 1992. 25.00 (1-56638-019-7) Math Sci Nucleus.

Applied Science - Science & Math (Third B) 1992. 40.00 (1-56638-020-0) Math Sci Nucleus.

Applied Science - Science & Math (1A) 1992. 35.00 (1-56638-006-5) Math Sci Nucleus.

Applied Science - Technology (Fifth A) 1992. 35.00 (1-56638-036-7) Math Sci Nucleus.

Applied Science - Technology (Fifth B) 1992. 25.00 (1-56638-037-5) Math Sci Nucleus.

Applied Science - Technology (First A) 1992. 30.00 (1-56638-009-X) Math Sci Nucleus.

Applied Science - Technology (First B) 1992. 45.00 (1-56638-010-3) Math Sci Nucleus.

Applied Science - Technology (Fourth A) 1992. 40.00 (1-56638-029-4) Math Sci Nucleus.

Applied Science - Technology (Fourth B) 1992. 50.00 (1-56638-030-8) Math Sci Nucleus.

Applied Science - Technology (KA) 1992. 30.00 (1-56638-004-9) Math Sci Nucleus.

Applied Science - Technology (Second A) 1992. 25.00 (1-56638-016-2) Math Sci Nucleus.

Applied Science - Technology (Second B) 1992. 25.00 (1-56638-017-0) Math Sci Nucleus.

Applied Science - Technology (Sixth B) 1992. 50.00 (1-56638-045-6) Math Sci Nucleus.

Applied Science - Technology (Third A) 1992. 35.00 (1-56638-023-5) Math Sci Nucleus.

Applied Science & Technology Index: 1958-1994, 1958-1990. LC 14-5408. 240.00 (0-685-22228-4) Wilson.

Applied Science & Technology Index: 1958-1994, Vols. 1986-1994. LC 14-5408. write for info. (0-318-56449-1) Wilson.

Applied Science for the Aviation Technician. Ed. by IAP, Inc. LC 92-24395. (Illus.). 179p. 1985. pap. 10.95 (0-89100-085-2, EA-AS) IAP.

Applied Science in the Casting of Metals. K. Strauss. 1970. 225.00 (0-08-015711-4, Pub. by Pergamon Repr UK) Franklin.

Applied Science of the Soul. Eugen Rosenstock-Huessy. 40p. 1984. pap. text ed. 3.95 (0-910727-04-X) Golden Phoenix.

Applied Science Review Series, 13 vols. Springhouse Publishing Staff. Date not set. Per. vol. pap. text ed. 11.95 (0-685-65228-9) Springhouse Pub.

Applied Science, 1991. Ed. by Eleanor C. Goldstein. (SIRS Science Ser.). 1991. ring bd. 85.00 (0-89777-430-2) Sirs Inc.

Applied Science, 1992. Ed. by Eleanor Goldstein. (Social Issues Resources Ser.). 1992. 85.00 (0-89777-435-3) Sirs Inc.

Applied Science, 1993. Ed. by Eleanor Goldstein. (Resources Ser.). 1993. 85.00 (0-89777-440-X) Sirs Inc.

***Applied Science, 1994.** Ed. by Eleanor Goldstein. (Social Issues Resources Ser.). 1994. 85.00 (0-614-01899-4) Sirs Inc.

Applied Sciences Research & Utilization of Lunar Resources. Frank J. Malina. 1970. 89.00 (0-08-015565-0, Pub. by Pergamon Repr UK) Franklin.

Applied Scientific Inquiry in the Health Professions: An Epistemological Orientation. Anne C. Mosey. 280p. (C). 1992. pap. text ed. 38.00 (0-910317-74-7) Am Occup Therapy.

Applied Screen Film Mammography. Gini Wentz. (Illus.). 192p. 1991. text ed. 62.01 (0-08-040686-6, Pub. by PPI UK); pap. text ed. 40.01 (0-08-040687-4, Pub. by PPI UK) McGraw.

Applied Security Management. Clay E. Higgins. (Illus.). 282p. (C). 1990. text ed. 49.95x (0-398-05713-3) C C Thomas.

Applied Sedimentology. 3rd ed. Richard C. Selley. 446p. 1988. text ed. 106.00 (0-12-636365-X); pap. text ed. 49.00 (0-12-636366-8) Acad Pr.

Applied Seismic Wave Theory. A. J. Berkhout. (Advances in Seismic Wave Theory Ser.: Vol. 1). 1987. 82.00 (0-444-42898-4) Elsevier.

Applied Sensory Analysis of Foods, Vol. I. Ed. by Howard Moskowitz. 272p. 1988. 174.00 (0-8493-6705-0, TX546) CRC Pr.

Applied Sensory Analysis of Foods, Vol. II. Ed. by Howard Moskowitz. 192p. 1988. 174.00 (0-8493-6706-9, TX546) CRC Pr.

Applied Signal Processing: IASTED Symposium, Paris, France, June 19-21, 1985. Ed. by M. H. Hamza. 356p. 1985. 90.00 (0-88986-083-1, 086A) Acta Pr.

Applied Simulation & Modelling: Proceedings of IASTED Symposium, Galveston, Texas, U. S. A., May 18-20, 1988. Ed. by M. H. Hamza. 269p. 1988. 65.00 (0-88986-105-6, 147) Acta Pr.

Applied Simulation & Modelling - ASM '83: Proceedings, IASTED Symposium, San Francisco, May 16-18, 1983. Ed. by M. H. Hamza. 216p. 1983. 60.00 (0-88986-043-2, 051) Acta Pr.

Applied Simulation & Modelling - ASM '84: Proceedings, IASTED Symposium, San Francisco, U. S. A., June 4-6, 1984. Ed. by M. H. Hamza. 198p. 1984. 70.00 (0-88986-061-0, 069) Acta Pr.

Applied Simulation & Modelling - ASM '85: Proceedings, IASTED Symposium, Montreal, Canada, June 3-5, 1985. Ed. by D. O. Koval & M. H. Hamza. 345p. 1985. 75.00 (0-88986-081-5, 089) Acta Pr.

Applied Simulation & Modelling - ASM '86: Proceedings, IASTED Symposium, Vancouver, Canada, June 4-6, 1986. Ed. by D. O. Koval. 598p. 1986. 75.00 (0-88986-088-2, 098) Acta Pr.

Applied Simulation & Modelling - ASM '87: Proceedings IASTED Symposium, Santa Barbara, California, U. S. A., May 27-29, 1987. Ed. by D. O. Koval & M. H. Hamza. 350p. 1987. 100.00 (0-88986-104-8, 109) Acta Pr.

Applied Simulation & Modelling - ASM '89: Proceedings of IASTED Symposium, Santa Barbara, California, U. S. A., November 13-15, 1989. Ed. by M. H. Hamza. 197p. 1989. 60.00 (0-88986-133-1, 156) Acta Pr.

Applied Sketching & Technical Drawing. Ronald J. Lutz. (Illus.). 224p. 1991. text ed. 29.28 (0-87006-764-8) Goodheart.

Applied Social & Political Philosophy. Comp. by Elizabeth Smith & Gene Blocker. 552p. 1994. pap. text ed. write for info. (0-13-816448-7) P-H.

Applied Social Psychology. Stuart Oskamp. (Illus.). 464p. (C). 1984. text ed. write for info. (0-13-043273-3) P-H.

Applied Social Psychology. James M. Weyant. (Illus.). 256p. 1986. 24.95 (0-19-504072-4) OUP.

Applied Social Psychology & Organizational Settings. John Carroll. 240p. (C). 1990. text ed. 49.95 (0-8058-0541-9) L Erlbaum Assocs.

Applied Social Psychology Annual, 4 vols., 2. Applied Social Psychology Annual Staff. LC 80-645341. 294p. pap. 83.80 (0-8357-8474-6, 2034742) Bks Demand.

Applied Social Psychology Annual, 4 vols., 3. Applied Social Psychology Annual Staff. LC 80-645341. 294p. pap. 86.70 (0-8357-8475-4, 2034742) Bks Demand.

Applied Social Psychology Annual, 4 vols., 4. Applied Social Psychology Annual Staff. LC 80-645341. 294p. pap. 79.80 (0-8357-8476-2, 2034742) Bks Demand.

Applied Social Psychology Annual, 4 vols., 5. Applied Social Psychology Annual Staff. LC 80-645341. 294p. pap. 82.10 (0-8357-8477-0, 2034742) Bks Demand.

Applied Social Psychology in India. Ed. by Girishwar Misra. 320p. (C). 1990. 27.50 (0-8039-9645-4) Sage.

Applied Social Research. Herbert Rubin. 384p. (C). 1983. write for info. (0-675-09793-2, Merrill Pub Co); 15.75 (0-675-20048-2, Merrill Pub Co) Macmillan.

Applied Social Research: Tool for the Human Services. 2nd ed. Duane R. Monette et al. 512p. (C). 1990. text ed. 44.75 (0-03-026293-3) HB Coll Pubs.

Applied Sociological Perspectives. Ed. by R. J. Anderson & W. W. Sharrock. (Illus.). 192p. 1984. pap. text ed. 15.95 (0-04-301168-3) Routledge Chapman & Hall.

Applied Sociology. Ed. by Howard E. Freeman et al. LC 82-49035. (Jossey-Bass Social & Behavioral Science Ser.). 518p. reprint ed. pap. 147.70 (0-7837-0168-3, 2040465) Bks Demand.

Applied Sociology: A Treatise on the Conscious Improvement of Society by Society. Lester Ward. LC 73-14187. (Perspectives in Social Inquiry Ser.). 406p. 1974. reprint ed. 23.95 (0-405-05530-7) Ayer.

Applied Sociology: Research & Critical Thinking. Thomas J. Sullivan. 240p. (Orig.). (C). 1991. pap. write for info. (0-02-418355-5) Macmillan.

***Applied Sociology: Sociological Understanding & Its Application.** Jerry S. Maneker. 70p. (Orig.). (C). 1994. pap. text ed. 14.50 (0-8191-9777-7) U Pr of Amer.

Applied Sociology of Sport. Ed. by Andrew Yiannakis & Susan L. Greendorfer. LC 90-29002. (Illus.). 288p. (Orig.). (C). 1992. text ed. 32.00x (0-87322-320-9, BYIA0320) Human Kinetics.

Applied Software Measurement: Assuring Productivity & Quality. Capers Jones. 624p. 1991. text ed. 50.00 (0-07-032813-7) McGraw.

Applied Soil Biology & Ecology. G. K. Veeresh & D. Rajagopal. 1987. 10.00 (0-8364-2291-0, Pub. by Oxford IBH II) S Asia.

Applied Soil Physics. R. J. Hanks & G. L. Ashcroft. (Advanced Series in Agricultural Sciences: Vol. 8). (Illus.). 159p. 1986. pap. 40.00 (0-387-90927-3) Spr-Verlag.

Applied Soil Physics: Soil Water & Temperature Applications. 2nd ed. R. J. Hanks. LC 92-14798. (Illus.). 200p. 1992. 39.95 (0-387-97850-X) Spr-Verlag.

Applied Solar Energy: An Introduction. Aden B. Meinel & Marjorie P. Meinel. 400p. (C). 1976. text ed. write for info. (0-201-04719-5) Addison-Wesley.

Applied Solid Dynamics. D. G. Gorman & W. Kennedy. (Illus.). 208p. 1988. pap. text ed. 54.95 (0-408-02309-0) Buttrwrth-Heinemann.

Applied Solid Mechanics Vol. 1: Proceedings from the First Applied Solid Mechanics Conference, University of Strathclyde, Glasgow, U. K., 26-27 March 1985. Ed. by A. S. Tooth & J. Spence. 476p. 1986. 122.50 (0-85334-415-9) Elsevier.

Applied Solid Mechanics Vol. 2: Proceedings of the Second Applied Solid Mechanics Confernece, Glasgow UK, 7-8 April 1987. Ed. by A. S. Tooth & J. Spence. 612p. 1988. 176.50 (1-85166-158-1) Elsevier.

Applied Solid Mechanics, Vol. 3: Contains Papers Presented at Conf. held at the Univ. of Surrey, Guildford, UK, 6-7 April 1989. Ed. by I. M. Allison & C. Ruiz. 474p. 1990. 117.00 (1-85166-435-1) Elsevier.

Applied Solid State Science: Advances in Materials & Device Research, Vols. 4-6. Incl. Vol. 5. 1975. lib. bdg. 120.00 (0-12-002974-X); Vol. 6. 1977. lib. bdg. 90.00 (0-12-002976-6); (Serial Publication Ser.). write for info. (0-318-50230-5) Acad Pr.

Applied Specialties in Psychology. Elizabeth M. Altmaier & Merle E. Meyer. 500p. 1985. text ed. 39.95 (0-89859-714-5) L Erlbaum Assocs.

Applied Specialties in Psychology. Elizabeth M. Altmaier & Merle Meyer. 600p. (C). 1985. text ed. write for info. (0-07-554880-1) McGraw.

Applied Spectroscopy in Materials Science. Ed. by W. G. Golden. 1992. 42.00 (0-8194-0782-8, 1636) SPIE.

Applied Spectroscopy in Materials Science, Vol. 1437. D. D. Saperstein. 1991. 53.00 (0-8194-0527-2) SPIE.

Applied Spectroscopy Reviews, Vol. 6. Ed. by Edward G. Brame. LC 68-23774. (Illus.). 391p. reprint ed. pap. 111.50 (0-8357-5689-0, 2027987) Bks Demand.

Applied Spectroscopy Reviews, Vol. 7. Ed. by Edward G. Brame. LC 68-23774. (Illus.). 397p. reprint ed. pap. 113.20 (0-8357-5690-4, 2027985) Bks Demand.

***Applied Speech Technology.** A. Syrdal et al. LC 94-26882. 1994. write for info. (0-8493-9456-2) CRC Pr.

Applied Sport Psychology: Personal Growth to Peak Performance. 2nd ed. Ed. by Jean M. Williams. LC 92-35585. 383p. (Orig.). (C). 1993. pap. text ed. 35.95 (1-55934-132-7) Mayfield Pub.

Applied Statics & Strength of Materials. 2nd ed. Leonard Spiegel & George F. Limbrunner. LC 93-7468. (Illus.). 758p. (C). 1994. text ed. write for info. (0-02-414961-6, Merrill Pub Co) Macmillan.

Applied Statistical Mechanics. Keith E. Gubbins & Thomas M. Reed. (Chemical Engineering (Reprint) Ser.). 528p. 1991. reprint ed. pap. text ed. 39.95 (0-7506-9136-0) Buttrwrth-Heinemann.

Applied Statistical Principles. Gench & Hinson. 91p. (C). 1993. 16.16 (1-56870-080-6) RonJon Pub.

Applied Statistical Thermodynamics. K. Lucas. (Illus.). xvii, 514p. 1991. 198.00 (0-387-52007-4) Spr-Verlag.

Applied Statistics. 3rd ed. John Neter et al. 1006p. (C). 1988. student ed 19.00 (0-685-18748-9, H03312); Instr's. manual. teacher ed write for info. (0-205-10331-6, H03296); boxed 56.00 (0-205-10328-6, H03288); write for info. (0-318-62190-8, H03304) Allyn.

Applied Statistics. 4th ed. John Neter et al. 1040p. (C). 1992. text ed. 61.00 (0-205-13478-5) Allyn.

Applied Statistics: A First Course. Mark L. Berenson et al. (Illus.). 448p. (C). 1988. text ed. write for info. (0-13-041476-X) P-H.

Applied Statistics: A Handbook of BMDP Analysis. D. R. Cox & E. J. Snell. 120p. 1987. pap. text ed. 19.50 (0-412-28410-3, 9985) Chapman & Hall.

Applied Statistics: A Handbook of Techniques. 2nd ed. L. Sachs. Tr. by Z. Reynarowych. (Series in Statistics). (Illus.). xxviii, 670p. 1984. 69.00 (0-387-90976-1) Spr-Verlag.

Applied Statistics: Analysis of Variance & Regression. 2nd ed. Olive J. Dunn & Virginia A. Clark. LC 86-24649. (Probability & Mathematical Statistics: Applied Probability & Statistics Section Ser.). 445p. 1987. text ed. 89.95 (0-471-81269-2) Wiley.

Applied Statistics: Principles & Examples. D. R. Cox. 1981. pap. 27.50 (0-412-16570-8, NO.6548) Chapman & Hall.

Applied Statistics & Probability for Engineers. Douglas C. Montgomery & George C. Runger. LC 93-29954. 896p. 1994. text ed. write for info. (0-471-54041-2) Wiley.

Applied Statistics & the SAS Programming Language. 3rd ed. R. P. Cody & J. K. Smith. 424p. 1991. pap. 29.50 (0-444-01619-8) P-H.

Applied Statistics for Business & Economics. Allen L. Webster. 1024p. (C). 1991. text ed. 66.95 (0-256-07314-7) Irwin.

Applied Statistics for Business & Finance. 2nd ed. Allen L. Webster. LC 94-17704. (Series in Statistics). 1072p. (C). 1994. text ed. 66.95 (0-256-14022-7) Irwin.

An Asterisk (*) at the beginning of an entry indicates that the title is appearing in BIP for the first time.

An Asterisk (*) at the beginning of an entry indicates that the title is appearing in BIP for the first time.

***Applying Environmental Economics in Africa.** Frank J. Convery. LC 95-1897. (World Bank Technical Paper: No. 277). 176p. 1995. pap. 10.95 (*0-8213-3190-6*, 13190) World Bank.

Applying Ethics: A Text with Readings. 4th ed. Jeffrey Olen & Vincent Barry. 470p. (C). 1992. pap. 34.95 (*0-534-16470-6*) Intl Thomson.

***Applying Ethics: A Text with Readings.** 5th ed. Jeffrey Olen & Vincent Barry. LC 95-11852. 1996. pap. 35.95 (*0-534-26316-X*) Intl Thomson.

Applying Expert System Technology to Business. Patrick J. Lyons. 269p. (C). 1994. pap. 27.95 (*0-534-20538-0*); disk, 5.25 hd 36.95 (*0-534-20540-2*); disk 36.95 (*0-534-20541-0*) Boyd & Fraser.

Applying Expert Systems in Business. Dimitris N. Chorafas. 256p. 1987. text ed. 36.95 (*0-07-010880-3*) McGraw.

Applying Family Therapy: A Practical Guide for Social Workers. H. C. Masson & P. O'Byrne. (Social Work Ser.). (Illus.). 134p. 1984. 68.00 (*0-08-030186-X*, 26-56, Pub. by Pergamon Repr UK) Franklin.

***Applying for Federal Jobs: A Guide to Writing Successful Applications & Resumes for the Job You Want in Government.** rev. ed. Patricia B. Wood. Ed. by Michelle Macie. LC 95-7816. (Illus.). 224p. (Orig.). 1995. pap. 16.95 (*0-943641-11-X*) Bookhaven Pr.

***Applying for Research Funding: Getting Started & Being Funded.** Joanne B. Ries & Karl G. Leukefeld. 252p. 1994. 38.00 (*0-8039-5364-X*); pap. 18.95 (*0-8039-5365-8*) Sage.

Applying Fractals in Astronomy. Ed. by Andre Heck et al. (Lecture Notes in Physics Ser.: Vol. M3). x, 210p. 1991. 30.00 (*0-387-54353-8*) Spr-Verlag.

Applying GAAP & GAAS, 2 vols. Paul Munter & Thomas A. Ratcliffe. LC 84-72343. 1985. Looseleaf updates avail. ring bd. write for info. (*0-8205-1012-2*) Bender.

Applying General Equilibrium. John B. Shoven & John Whalley. (Surveys of Economic Literature Ser.). (Illus.). 304p. (C). 1992. 59.95 (*0-521-26655-6*); pap. 24.95 (*0-521-31986-2*) Cambridge U Pr.

Applying Government Accounting Principles. Mortimer A. Dittenhofer. 1990. Looseleaf updates avail. ring bd. write for info. (*0-8205-1680-5*, 680) Bender.

Applying Government Auditing Standards. Mortimer A. Dittenhofer. 1990. Looseleaf updates avail. ring bd. write for info. (*0-8205-1853-0*, 853) Bender.

Applying Health & Safety Training Methods: A Study Guide to Accompany Behavioral Engineering Through Safety Training. James P. Kohn & Douglas L. Timmons. 78p. (C). 1988. spiral bd. 12.95x (*0-398-05473-8*) C C Thomas.

Applying Information Science & Consensus-Formation Technology Utilization to Do Zeitgeist-Sector Modeling, Scenario Reality Planning Bibliography, No. 3, Nos. 1172-1173. R. H. Martin. 1976. 12.50 (*0-686-20416-6*) CPL Biblios.

Applying Information Technology in Small Libraries: Proceedings of the 19th Annual Conference, APLIC. Ed. by Jane Vanderlin & William Barrows. LC 87-1061. 150p. (Orig.). 1987. pap. text ed. 15.00 (*0-933438-12-5*) APLIC Intl.

Applying Instrumentation & Automation in Environmental Engineering: Water & Wastewater. Ed. by J. E. Alleman et al. 145p. 1992. pap. 30.00 (*1-55617-016-5*) Instru Soc.

Applying Lotus 1-2-3 Release 2.2. Nelda Shelton & Sharon Burton. (C). 1992. write for info. (*0-395-56970-2*) HM Soft Schl Col Div.

Applying Machine Vision. Nello Zuech. LC 88-10145. 265p. 1988. text ed. 69.95 (*0-471-60070-9*) Wiley.

Applying Macintosh: Solutions, Ideas & Tools. Neil J. Salkind. 544p. (C). 1991. pap. write for info. (*0-675-22133-1*, Merrill Pub Co) Macmillan.

Applying Methods & Techniques of Futures Research. Ed. by James L. Morrison et al. LC 82-84194. (New Directions for Institutional Research Ser.: No. IR 39). 1983. pap. 16.95x (*0-87589-957-9*) Jossey-Bass.

Applying Moral Theories. 2nd ed. C. E. Harris, Jr. 214p. (C). 1992. pap. 19.95 (*0-534-16962-7*) Intl Thomson.

Applying MS Works 2.0. Nelda Shelton & Sharon Burton. (C). 1991. write for info. (*0-395-56982-6*) HM Soft Schl Col Div.

Applying Multiple Criteria Aid for Decision to Environmental Management: Based on the Papers Presented at the 38th Meeting of the European Working Group 'Multicriteria Aid for Decision,' Held at the Joint Research Centre, Ispra, Italy, October 7-8, 1993. Ed. by M. Paruccini. LC 94-12573. (Eurocourses: Environmental Management Ser.: Vol. 3). 374p. (C). 1994. lib. bdg. 134.00 (*0-7923-2922-8*) Kluwer Ac.

Applying Nursing Process: A Step-By-Step Guide. 3rd ed. Rosalinda A. Alfaro-Lefevre. (Illus.). 304p. (C). 1994. pap. text ed. 23.95 (*0-397-55023-5*, Lippincott Nursing) Lippincott.

***Applying OMT: A Practical Step-by-Step Guide to Using the Object Modeling Technique.** Kurt W. Derr. (Advances in Object Technology Ser.: Vol. 8). (Illus.). 550p. (Orig.). 1995. pap. 39.00 (*1-884842-10-0*) SIGS Bks.

Applying Pesticides. (Illus.). 80p. 1988. 9.00 (*0-89606-244-9*, 204); teacher ed 3.00 (*0-89606-060-8*, 204TK) Am Assn Voc Materials.

***Applying Psychology.** Virginia N. Quinn. 1994. write for info. (*0-615-00106-8*) McGraw.

***Applying Psychology.** 3rd ed. Virginia N. Quinn. 1994. text ed. write for info. (*0-615-00105-X*) McGraw.

Applying Psychology: Critical & Creative Thinking. 3rd ed. Robert C. Beck. 480p. (C). 1991. pap. text ed. write for info. (*0-13-040635-X*) P-H.

Applying Psychology: Individual & Organizational Effectiveness. 4th ed. Andrew J. DuBrin. LC 93-9097. Orig. Title: Effective Business Psychology. 1993. text ed. 51.00 (*0-13-241530-5*) P-H.

Applying Psychology: Understanding People. 2nd ed. Robert C. Beck. (Illus.). 496p. (C). 1985. pap. text ed. write for info. (*0-13-043480-9*) P-H.

Applying Psychology in Business: The Manager's Handbook. John W. Jones et al. (Issues in Organization & Management Ser.). 896p. 1990. text ed. 150.00 (*0-669-15838-0*) Free Pr.

Applying Psychology in Today's World: Strategies for Personal Growth. Ronald Evans & Laura Hubbs-Tait. 448p. (C). 1991. boxed write for info. (*0-318-68287-7*) P-H.

***Applying RCS & SCCS: From Source Control to Project Control.** Don Bolinger & Tan Bronson. Ed. by Mike Loukides. (Illus.). 500p. (Orig.). 1995. 29.95 (*1-56592-117-8*) OReilly & Assocs.

Applying Research to Hydraulic Practice. Ed. by P. E. Smith. LC 82-72777. 743p. 1982. pap. 59.00 (*0-87262-316-5*) Am Soc Civil Eng.

Applying Research to Practice: How to Use Data Collection & Research to Improve Library Management Decision-Making. Ed. by Leigh S. Estabrook. 1993. 25.00 (*0-87845-090-4*) U of Ill Lib Info Sci.

Applying Retail Management: A Strategic Approach Readings, Exercises, Problems. 5th ed. Barry Berman & Joel R. Evans. (Illus.). 336p. (C). 1992. pap. write for info. (*0-02-308625-4*) Macmillan.

Applying Soft Systems Methodology to an SSADM Feasibility Study. 126p. 1993. pap. 60.00 (*0-11-330601-6*, HM06016, Pub. by HMSO UK) UNIPUB.

Applying SQL in Business. Levi Reiss. 1992. text ed. write for info. (*0-07-051842-4*) McGraw.

Applying Statistics in Institutional Research. Ed. by Bernard D. Yancey. LC 85-645339. (New Directions for Institutional Research Ser.: No. IR 58). 1988. 16.95 (*1-55542-921-1*) Jossey-Bass.

Applying Structured Learning Therapy. Arnold P. Goldstein et al. LC 76-16518. 1977. 46.00 (*0-08-021109-7*, Pergamon Pr) Elsevier.

***Applying Successful Training Techniques: A Practical Guide to Coaching & Facilitating Skills.** Joe B. Wilson. (High Impact Training Ser.). (Illus.). 120p. 1994. pap. 12.95 (*1-883553-37-7*) R Chang Assocs.

Applying Technology to Record Systems: A Media Guideline. (Illus.). 132p. (Orig.). (C). 1994. pap. text ed. 30.00 (*0-7881-0585-X*) Diane Pub.

Applying the Bible to Life. Paul Woods. (Active Bible Curriculum Ser.). (Illus.). 48p. 1991. pap. 9.99 (*1-55945-116-5*) Group Pub.

Applying the Children Act in Boarding & Residential Environments, 1989. Ed. by Ewan W. Anderson & Alan J. Davison. 208p. 1993. pap. 36.00 (*1-85346-257-8*, Pub. by D Fulton UK) Taylor & Francis.

Applying the Deming Method to Higher Education. Ed. by Richard I. Miller. 133p. 1991. 27.00 (*0-910402-98-1*) Coll & U Personnel.

Applying the Humanities. Ed. by Daniel Callahan et al. LC 85-9479. (Hastings Center Series in Ethics). 346p. 1985. 49.50 (*0-306-41968-8*, Plenum Pr) Plenum.

Applying the New National Electrical Code. Gregory P. Bierals. LC 86-46141. 300p. 1990. text ed. 58.00 (*0-88173-038-6*) Fairmont Pr.

Applying the Seven Principles for Good Practice in Undergraduate Education. Ed. by Arthur W. Chickering & Zelda F. Gamson. LC 85-644763. (New Directions for Teaching & Learning Ser.: No. 47). 1991. 16.95 (*1-55542-781-2*) Jossey-Bass.

Applying the 1993 National Electric Code. Gregory Bierals. 233p. 1994. text ed. 68.00 (*0-13-300609-3*) P-H.

Applying the 1993 National Electrical Code. Gregory P. Bierals. LC 93-42491. 228p. 1994. 68.00 (*0-88173-167-6*) Fairmont Pr.

***Applying Total Quality to Sales.** Cas Welch & Pete Geissler. LC 94-23665. 53p. 1994. 15.00 (*0-87389-283-6*) ASQC Qual Pr.

Applying Transputer Based Parallel Machines: Proceedings of the 10th Occam User Group Technical Meeting, Enschede, Netherlands, April 3-5, 1989. Ed. by A. Bakkers. (Transputer & Occam Engineering Ser.). 317p. 1989. 65.00 (*90-5199-011-1*, Pub. by IOS Pr NE) IOS Press.

Applying Universal Principles for Self-Empowerment: Co-Creation Course 1. Meredith L. Young. LC 87-63011. 50p. 1988. Incls. 6 audiotapes plus a wkbk. bdr. & wkbk. in soft case. 89.95 (*0-913299-57-X*) Stillpoint.

Applying WordPerfect 5.1. Michael T. Kilkenny. (Illus.). 272p. (C). 1992. text ed. 29.95 (*0-256-11298-3*, 14-3783-01) Irwin.

Applying WordPerfect 5.1: Desk Top Publishing Edition. Sharon Burton & Nelda Shelton. (C). 1993. pap. 27.56 (*0-395-60620-9*) HM.

Applying WordPerfect 5.1-5.0. Nelda Shelton & Sharon Burton. (C). 1991. write for info. (*0-395-56974-5*) HM Soft Schl Col Div.

Applying Zortech C. Scott R. Ladd. 1992. pap. write for info. (*0-201-56302-9*) Addison-Wesley.

Applying Zortech C Plus Plus with Disks. Scott R. Ladd. 1992. pap. write for info. (*0-201-56303-7*) Addison-Wesley.

APPN Networks. Jesper Nilausen. LC 93-50760. 1994. pap. text ed. 42.95 (*0-471-94447-5*) Wiley.

Appogiatures. Jean Cocteau. 1988. 8.95 (*0-318-41299-3*) Man-Root.

Appogiatures. deluxe ed. Jean Cocteau. 1988. write for info. (*0-318-64673-0*) Man-Root.

Appointed. Walter H. Stowers & William H. Anderson. LC 70-158255. reprint ed. 36.50 (*0-404-00001-0*) AMS Pr.

Appointed Executive Local Government: The California Experience. John C. Bollens. LC 52-12988. (Illus.). xi, 233p. 1970. reprint ed. text ed. 59.75 (*0-8371-8068-6*, BOAE, Greenwood Pr) Greenwood.

Appointed to Die. Kate Charles. 368p. 1994. 19.95 (*0-89296-548-7*) Mysterious Pr.

***Appointed to Die.** Kate Charles. 352p. 1995. mass mkt. 5.99 (*0-446-40361-X*, Mysterious Paperbk) Warner Bks.

Appointing a Proxy for Health Care Decisions: Analysis & Chart of State Laws. pap. 5.00 (*0-318-37787-X*) Soc Right to Die.

Appointment. W. Somerset Maugham. LC 92-391. (Illus.). (J). (ps-3). 1993. 16.00 (*0-671-75887-X*, Green Tiger S&S) S&S Childrens.

Appointment at Dusk. Carolyn Hilliard. (C). 1990. pap. 30.00 (*0-7223-2587-8*, Pub. by A H S Ltd UK) St Mut.

Appointment at Gettysburg: Sergeant George W. Heilig 151st Pennsylvania Volunteers & the Civil War. John H. Walker. Ed. by Joel Radcliffe. LC 94-65042. (Illus.). 75p. 1994. text ed. 50.00 (*0-9623780-5-4*) Ars Obscura.

Appointment Congo. rev. ed. Virginia L. Shell. 320p. 1985. pap. 5.95 (*0-9615700-0-8*) Shell House.

Appointment for Murder. Susan C. Bakos. 1989. pap. 3.95 (*1-55817-238-6*, Pinnacle NY) Windsor NY.

Appointment in Dallas: The Final Solution to the Assassination of JFK. Hugh C. McDonald. (Illus.). 210p. (Orig.). 1992. mass mkt. 3.99 (*0-8217-3893-3*) Zebra.

Appointment in Japan: Memories of Sixty Years. G. C. Allen. (Illus.). 196p. (C). 1983. text ed. 35.00 (*0-485-11237-X*, Pub. by Athlone Pr UK) Humanities.

Appointment in Jerusalem. Lydia Prince. LC 75-19469. 189p. reprint ed. pap. 8.99 (*0-8007-9090-1*) Chosen Bks.

***Appointment in Normandy: 50th Anniversary of D-Day. Walter W. Jaffee. LC 95-76272. (Illus.). 590p. 1995. 31.95 (*0-9637586-4-0*) Glencannon Pr.**

The story of the Liberty ship JEREMIAH O'BRIEN'S epic voyage to Normandy for D-Day 50th anniversary June 6, 1994. As the last survivor of D-Day landings, the O'BRIEN was an honored guest. Be aboard for the President's visit, Queen's review in the Solent, D-Day plus 50 ceremonies in England & France. Experience the stunning outpouring of gratitude for U.S. help during WWII in London, Portsmouth, Southampton, Normandy, Rouen, Cherbourg. Be aboard "the centerpiece" at L'ARMADA DE LA LIBERTE, a great gathering of tall ships celebrating 50th anniversary of France's liberation. This 18,000 mile, 5 1/2 month voyage--San Francisco, Panama & across the Atlantic--with a volunteer crew of WWII veterans, average age 71, was also a journey back to a time when people, not computers, ran ships. The old-time camaraderie of the sea, meals from a coal-fired galley stove, tending the triple-expansion steam engine, beer sessions on no. 4 hatch: the O'BRIEN'S voyage back -- & forward -- into history was the trip of a lifetime. Note: THE LAST LIBERTY, by the same author, is the O'BRIEN'S history 1943-1993. Atlantic convoys, D-Day preparations, the Normandy landings, an "ammo ship" in the Pacific, lay-up & restoration. 490 pp, 110 photos, wartime extracts & other info. (0-9637586-0-8). $29.95. The Glencannon Press, Box 341, Palo Alto, CA 94302. (415) 323-3731. ***Publisher Provided Annotation.***

Appointment in Paradise. Glenn Cunningham. 1993. 16.95 (*0-8062-4911-0*) Carlton.

Appointment in Samarra. John O'Hara. LC 82-40029. 256p. 1982. pap. 10.00 (*0-394-71192-0*) Random.

Appointment in Samarra. John O'Hara. 1994. 13.50 (*0-679-60110-4*, Modern Lib) Random.

Appointment in Samarra. John O'Hara. 1993. reprint ed. lib. bdg. 89.00 (*0-7812-5481-7*) Rprt Serv.

Appointment in Sarajevo see My Enemy, My Love

Appointment in Venice. large type ed. Hilary Grenville. 1990. pap. 12.95 (*0-7089-6910-0*, Linford) Ulverscroft.

Appointment of Judges: The Johnson Presidency. 2nd ed. Neil D. McFeeley. (Administrative History of the Johnson Presidency Ser.). 213p. 1986. text ed. 28.50 (*0-292-70377-5*) U of Tex Pr.

***Appointment on the Hill: American Autobiography.** Dorothy Detzer. 262p. 1995. lib. bdg. 79.00 (*0-7812-8499-6*) Rprt Serv.

Appointment with a Stranger. Jean Thesman. 176p. 1990. reprint ed. pap. 3.50 (*0-380-70864-7*, Flare) Avon.

Appointment with Danger. large type ed. Judy Chard. (Linford Romance Library). 1991. pap. 13.95 (*0-7089-7115-6*) Ulverscroft.

***Appointment with Death.** Ruby Christian. 280p. 1995. 10.00 (*0-916620-39-5*) Portals Pr.

Appointment with Death. Agatha Christie. Ed. by Jayne Pliner. 224p. 1988. pap. text ed. 4.99 (*0-425-10858-9*, Berkley-Pacer) Berkley Pub.

Appointment with Death. large type ed. Agatha Christie. 296p. 1992. text ed. 19.95 (*0-8161-4529-6*) G K Hall.

Appointment with Death. large type ed. Agatha Christie. LC 91-31110. 336p. 1993. pap. 15.95 (*0-8161-4530-X*) G K Hall.

***Appointment with Destiny: Real Life Case Histories.** De. 1995. 17.95 (*1-885142-14-5*) J & B Editions.

Appointment with Doctor Death. Michael Betzold. 360p. 1993. 21.95 (*1-879094-37-1*); pap. 14.95 (*1-879094-42-8*) Momentum Bks.

Appointment with God. Michael Scanlan. (Orig.). 1987. pap. text ed. 3.95 (*0-940535-07-6*, UP106) Franciscan U Pr.

Appointment with Somerset Maugham: And Other Encounters with Literary Life. Richard H. Costa. LC 94-12375. (Illus.). 224p. 1994. 35.00 (*0-89096-618-4*); pap. 15.95 (*0-89096-619-2*) Tex A&M Univ Pr.

***Appointment with the Squire: A Novel.** Don Davis. 333p. 1995. 24.95 (*1-55750-157-2*) Naval Inst Pr.

Appointment You Will Keep. John Reisinger. pap. 6.00 (*0-87377-125-7*) GAM Pubns.

Appointments. Jerry Belch. Ed. by Valerie Harris. (Simulating the Medical Office). 60p. 1993. Appointments, 60p. 7.98 (*0-89262-315-2*) Career Pub.

Appointments with Power. Greg Rushford. 1994. pap. 29.00 (*1-884828-00-0*) Legal Times.

***Appomattox.** Andre Trudeau. (Civil War Ser.). 56p. (Orig.). 1994. pap. 3.95 (*0-915992-66-3*) Eastern Acorn.

Appomattox: The Last Campaign. Burleigh C. Rodick. 220p. 1988. reprint ed. 25.00 (*0-942211-58-8*) Olde Soldier Bks.

Appomattox Paroles April 9-15, 1865. William G. Nine & Ronald G. Wilson. (Virginia Civil War Battles & Leaders Ser.). (Illus.). 236p. 1989. 19.95 (*0-930919-69-6*) H E Howard.

***Appomattox River Seay Stories: Reminiscences of James Washington Seay, the Last of the Appomattox River Batteaumen.** Ed. by William E. Trout, Jr. & R. Dulaney Ward, Jr. (Illus.). (Orig.). (C). 1992. pap. 12.00 (*1-882365-00-3*) Hist Petersbrg Fnd.

Apportioning Groundwater Beneath the U. S.-Mexico Border. Stephen P. Mumme. (Research Report Ser.: No. 45). 54p. 1988. ring bd. 5.00 (*0-935391-79-7*, RR-45) UCSD Ctr US-Mex.

Apportionment & Representative Government. Alfred De Grazia. LC 83-12719. viii, 180p. 1983. reprint ed. text ed. 39.75 (*0-313-23375-6*, DGRA, Greenwood Pr) Greenwood.

Apportionment Cases. Richard C. Cortner. LC 75-100408. 296p. reprint ed. pap. 84.40 (*0-8357-5692-0*, 2023168) Bks Demand.

Apportionment of Death Taxes. John E. MacKenty. 1988. write for info. (*0-318-61708-0*) Am Coll Trust & Est.

***Apportionment Problem: The Search for the Perfect Democracy.** Bennett et al. (Hi Map Ser.: No. 8). (Illus.). 60p. Date not set. pap. text ed. 11.99 (*0-614-05319-6*, HM 5608) COMAP Inc.

Apposition in Contemporary English. Charles F. Meyer. (Studies in English Language). (Illus.). 152p. (C). 1992. 44.95 (*0-521-39475-9*) Cambridge U Pr.

Appproach Quickstart. Walt Bruce. 1994. pap. 21.95 (*1-56529-680-X*) Que.

Appraisal: Routes to Improved Performance. Clive Fletcher. 160p. (C). 1993. 45.00 (*0-85292-514-X*, Pub. by IPM Hse UK) St Mut.

Appraisal & Professional Development in Primary Schools. Christopher W. Day et al. 256p. 1987. 80.00 (*0-335-15542-1*, Open Univ Pr); pap. 27.00 (*0-335-15541-3*, Open Univ Pr) Taylor & Francis.

Appraisal & Staff Development in Schools. Jeff Jones. 160p. 1993. pap. 29.00 (*1-85346-279-9*, Pub. by D Fulton UK) Taylor & Francis.

Appraisal & Target Setting: A Handbook for Teacher Development. David Trethowan. 224p. (C). 1987. pap. 36.00 (*0-06-318363-3*, Pub. by P Chapman Pub UK) St Mut.

Appraisal by Objectives: Coaching & Appraising. Didactic Systems Staff. (Simulation Game Ser.). 1970. pap. 26.25 (*0-89401-003-4*) Didactic Syst.

***Appraisal Checklist: Helping Your Team to Get Results.** Brian Watling. (Institute of Management Ser.). 250p. 1995. pap. 36.50 (*0-273-60909-2*, Pub. by Pitman Pub Ltd UK) Trans-Atl Phila.

Appraisal Diagnosis of Speech & Language Disorders. 3rd ed. Harold A. Peterson & Thomas P. Marquardt. LC 93-33657. 1994. text ed. write for info. (*0-13-200149-7*) P-H.

***Appraisal Discussion.** Ian Mackay. (C). 1992. pap. 18.00x (*0-85171-099-9*, Pub. by IPM Hse UK) St Mut.

Appraisal Guidelines for Right of Way - Condemnation Appraisal Assignments. 41p. 1989. 20.00 (*0-317-01821-3*) Natl Assn Real Estate.

Appraisal Interview: An Approach to Training for Teachers & School Management. Eric Hewton. 120p. 1989. 80.00 (*0-335-09523-2*, Open Univ Pr); pap. 27.00 (*0-335-09522-4*, Open Univ Pr) Taylor & Francis.

Appraisal Investigator. Jack Rudman. (Career Examination Ser.: C-452). 1994. pap. 29.95 (*0-8373-0452-0*) Nat Learn.

Appraisal Journal Bibliography, 1932-1969. 171p. 1970. pap. 5.00 (*0-911780-22-X*) Appraisal Inst.

***Appraisal M. D.** (Valusource Accounting Software Products Ser.). 995.00 (*0-471-10962-2*) Wiley.

Appraisal, Market Analysis, & Public Policy in Real Estate: Essays in Honor of James A. Graaskamp. Ed. by James De Lisle. LC 93-16953. 512p. (C). 1994. lib. bdg. 95.00 (*0-7923-9344-9*) Kluwer Ac.

An Asterisk (*) at the beginning of an entry indicates that the title is appearing in BIP for the first time.

An Asterisk (*) at the beginning of an entry indicates that the title is appearing in BIP for the first time.

Approach to the Analysis of Political Systems. David Easton. (Reprint Series in Social Sciences). (C). 1993. reprint ed. pap. text ed. 1.90 (*0-8290-3919-8*, P-68) Irvington.

Approach to the Book of Mormon. 3rd ed. Hugh Nibley. LC 88-3585. (Collected Works of Hugh Nibley: Vol. 6). xvii, 541p. 1988. 19.95 (*0-87579-138-7*) Deseret Bk.

Approach to the Metaphysics of Plato Through the Parmenides. William F. Lynch. LC 68-23310. 255p. 1968. reprint ed. text ed. 55.00 (*0-8371-4833-2*, LYMP, Greenwood Pr) Greenwood.

Approach to the New Testament. James Moffatt. LC 77-27150. (Hibbert Lectures: 1921). reprint ed. 35.00 (*0-404-60420-X*) AMS Pr.

Approach to the Sacred in the Thought of Schopenhauer. Robert A. Gonzales. LC 92-4106. 332p. 1992. lib. bdg. 99.95 (*0-7734-9818-4*) E Mellen.

Approach to the Selberg Trace Formula via the Selberg Zeta-Function. J. Fischer. (Lecture Notes in Mathematics Ser.: Vol. 1253). iii, 184p. 1987. pap. 31.30 (*0-387-15208-3*) Spr-Verlag.

Approach to the Study of the Quran. N. Jung. pap. 5.00 (*0-935782-37-0*) Kazi Pubns.

Approach to the Theory of Income Distribution. Sidney Weintraub. LC 72-2572. (Illus.). 214p. 1973. reprint ed. text ed. 35.00 (*0-8371-6420-6*, WEID, Greenwood Pr) Greenwood.

Approach to Understanding of Islam. Ali Shariati. Tr. by Venus Kiavantash. 26p. 1980. pap. 2.00 (*0-941722-14-7*) Book Dist Ctr.

Approach to Urban Planning. Gerald W. Breese & Dorothy E. Whiteman. LC 73-90474. 147p. 1969. reprint ed. text ed. 49.75 (*0-8371-2284-8*, BRUP, Greenwood Pr) Greenwood.

Approach to Vedanta. Christopher Isherwood. 1970. pap. 4.95 (*0-87481-003-5*) Vedanta Pr.

Approach to World Order Studies & the World System. Richard A. Falk & Samuel Kim. (Working Papers: No. 22). 33p. 1982. pap. 12.95 (*0-911646-27-2*) Transaction Pubs.

***Approach 3 for Windows for Dummies.** Doug Lowe. 1994. pap. 19.99 (*1-56884-233-3*) IDG Bks.

Approached by Fur. deluxe limited ed. Lissa McLaughlin. (Burning Deck Poetry Ser.). (Illus.). 1976. 20.00 (*0-930900-25-1*) Burning Deck.

Approaches & Methods in Language Teaching: A Description & Analysis. Jack C. Richards & Theodore S. Rodgers. (Cambridge Language Teaching Library). (Illus.). 176p. 1986. 39.95 (*0-521-32093-3*); pap. 16.95 (*0-521-31255-8*) Cambridge U Pr.

Approaches & Methods in Neurotoxicology. Louis W. Chang & William Slikker. 1994. text ed. 149.00 (*981-02-1798-6*) World Scientific Pub.

Approaches & Options for Integrating Students with Disabilities: A Decision Tool. Research Triangle Institute Staff. 466p. 1993. teacher ed 25.00 (*0-944584-65-9*) Sopris.

Approaches de la Critique de la Raison Pure. Robert Theis. (Studien und Materialien Zur Geschichte der Philosophie Ser.: No. XXXI). viii, 199p. 1991. write for info. (*3-487-09435-5*, Pub. by Georg Olms GW) Lubrecht & Cramer.

Approaches for Incorporating Drought & Salinity Resistance in Crop Plants. V. L. Chopra & R. S. Paroda. 1986. 15.00 (*81-204-0151-4*, Pub. by Oxford IBH II) S Asia.

***Approaches for the Remediation of Federal Facility Sites Contaminated with Explosive or Radioactive Wastes: A Handbook.** Edwin Barth. (Illus.). 110p. (Orig.). (C). 1994. pap. text ed. 50.00x (*0-7881-1460-3*) Diane Pub.

Approaches in Linguistic Methodology. Ed. by Irmengard Rauch & Charles T. Scott. 168p. 1967. 21.50 (*0-299-04240-5*) U of Wis Pr.

***Approaches in Urologic Surgery.** LC 94-30311. 1994. write for info. (*0-86577-543-5*) Thieme Med Pubs.

***Approaches in Urologic Surgery.** G. Bartsch. Tr. by Terry C. Telger. LC 94-30311. (Illus.). 1994. write for info. (*3-13-129301-2*) Thieme Med Pubs.

***Approaches of Assessment of Information Technology.** A. R. Bakker. LC 94-73350. 336p. 1994. 93.00 (*90-5199-200-9*) IOS Press.

Approaches to Absence. Pasquale Verdicchio. 80p. 1994. pap. 8.00 (*1-55071-006-0*) Guernica Editions.

Approaches to Academic Reading & Writing. Martin L. Arnaudet & Mary E. Barrett. (Illus.). 288p. (C). 1983. pap. text ed. 18.00 (*0-13-043679-8*) P-H.

Approaches to Administrative Training in Education. Ed. by Joseph Murphy & Philip Hallinger. LC 86-14579. (Educational Leadership Ser.). 291p. 1987. 64.50 (*0-88706-433-7*); pap. 24.95 (*0-88706-434-5*) State U NY Pr.

Approaches to Adult ESL Literacy Instruction. Pat Rigg et al. Ed. by Joann Crandall & Joy K. Peyton. LC 93-30665. (Language in Education Ser.: Vol. 82). 98p. (Orig.). 1993. pap. text ed. 13.50 (*0-937354-82-1*) Delta Systems.

Approaches to Ancient Judaism. Jacob Neusner. (New Ser.: Vol. 2). 215p. 1990. 59.95 (*1-55540-545-2*, 24 00 17) Scholars Pr GA.

Approaches to Ancient Judaism, Vol. IV. William S. Green. (Brown Judaic Studies). 208p. 1983. pap. 18.00 (*0-89130-673-0*, 14 00 27) Scholars Pr GA.

Approaches to Ancient Judaism, Vol. V. Ed. by William S. Green. (Brown Judaic Studies: No. 32). (C). 1985. pap. 18.25 (*0-89130-798-2*) Scholars Pr GA.

Approaches to Ancient Judaism: Theory & Practice. Ed. by William S. Green. LC 76-57656. (Brown Judaic Studies: No. 1). 273p. reprint ed. pap. 77.90 (*0-7837-5464-7*, 2045229) Bks Demand.

Approaches to Ancient Judaism II. William S. Green. LC 76-57656. (Brown Judaic Studies). (C). 1980. 16.00 (*0-89130-447-9*, 14-00-09); pap. 11.50 (*0-89130-448-7*) Scholars Pr GA.

Approaches to Ancient Judaism III. Ed. by William S. Green. LC 76-57656. (Brown Judaic Studies). 220p. 1981. pap. 16.00 (*0-89130-553-X*, 14 00 11) Scholars Pr GA.

Approaches to Ancient Judaism, New Series, Vol. 3. Jacob Neusner. (USF Studies in the History of Judaism). 249p. 1993. 64.95 (*1-55540-830-3*, 240056) Scholars Pr GA.

Approaches to Ancient Judaism, New Series, Vol. 4: Religious & Theological Studies. Jacob Neusner. (South Florida Studies in the History of Judaism). 198p. 1993. 17.00 (*1-55540-868-0*, 240081) Scholars Pr GA.

Approaches to Ancient Judaism, New Series, Vol. 5: Historical, Literary, & Religious Studies. Herbert W. Basser. (USF Studies in the History of Judaism). 178p. 1993. 59.95 (*1-55540-869-9*, 240082) Scholars Pr GA.

Approaches to Anti-Viral Agents. Michael R. Harnden. LC 85-13851. 326p. 1985. lib. bdg. 130.00 (*0-89573-522-9*) VCH Pubs.

***Approaches to Antisemitism: Context and Curriculum.** Ed. by Michael Brown. LC 94-33857. 1994. write for info. (*0-87495-106-2*) Am Jewish Comm.

Approaches to Archaeological Ceramics. C. M. Sinopoli. (Illus.). 246p. 1991. 42.50 (*0-306-43852-6*, Plenum Pr); pap. 22.50 (*0-306-43575-6*, Plenum Pr) Plenum.

Approaches to Art in Education. Laura H. Chapman. 444p. (C). 1978. text ed. 37.25 (*0-15-502896-0*) HB Coll Pubs.

Approaches to Art Therapy: Theory & Technique. Ed. by Judith A. Rubin. LC 86-26376. 362p. 1987. 33.95 (*0-87630-452-8*) Brunner-Mazel.

Approaches to Auschwitz: The Holocaust & Its Legacy. John K. Roth & Richard L. Rubenstein. LC 86-27749. 420p. 1987. 20.00 (*0-8042-0778-X*, John Knox); pap. 18.99 (*0-8042-0777-1*, John Knox) Westminster John Knox.

Approaches to Beowulfian Scansion: Four Essays by John Miles Foley, Winfred P. Lehmann, Robert Creed, & Dolores Warwick Frese. Ed. by Alain Renoir & Ann Hernandez. (Old English Colloquium Ser.: No. 1). 64p. 1985. reprint ed. pap. text ed. 15.00 (*0-8191-4518-1*) U Pr of Amer.

Approaches to Breast Cancer Prevention. Ed. by Basil A. Stoll. (Developments in Oncology Ser.). 256p. 1991. lib. bdg. 115.00 (*0-7923-0995-2*) Kluwer Ac.

Approaches to Canadian History. Ed. by Carl Berger. LC 23-16213. (Canadian Historical Readings Ser.: No. 1). 1967. pap. 10.95 (*0-8020-1459-3*) U of Toronto Pr.

Approaches to Case Management for People with Disabilities. Doria Pilling. (Disability & Rehabilitation Ser.: No. 1). 220p. 1992. 57.00 (*1-85302-099-0*, Pub. by J Kingsley Pubs UK) Taylor & Francis.

Approaches to Case Study: A Handbook for Those Entering the Therapeutic Field. Robin Higgins. 250p. 1993. pap. 27.50 (*1-85302-182-2*, Pub. by J Kingsley Pubs UK) Taylor & Francis.

Approaches to Child Treatment. Johnson. (C). 1986. 55.95 (*0-205-14380-6*, H4380) Allyn.

Approaches to Child Treatment. Johnson. (C). 1992. pap. text ed. 28.95 (*0-205-14379-2*, H4379) Allyn.

Approaches to Clinical Supervision: Alternatives for Improving Instruction. Edward Pajak. 352p. (C). 1993. text ed. 42.95 (*0-926842-27-7*) CG Pubs Inc.

Approaches to Cognition: Contrasts & Controversies. Ed. by Terry Knapp & Lynn C. Robertson. 344p. (C). 1985. text ed. 69.95 (*0-89859-623-8*) L Erlbaum Assocs.

Approaches to Collecting. (Illus.). 24p. 1982. 5.00 (*0-88321-049-5*) Am Craft.

Approaches to Computer Writing Classrooms: Learning from Practical Experience. Ed. by Linda Myers. LC 92-32896. (SUNY Series, Literacy, Culture, & Learning: Theory & Practice). (Illus.). 225p. (C). 1993. 59.50 (*0-7914-1567-8*); pap. 19.95 (*0-7914-1568-6*) State U NY Pr.

Approaches to Criminal Justice Training. 2nd ed. John Fay. 280p. (Orig.). 1988. pap. 16.50 (*0-89854-128-X*) U of GA Inst Govt.

Approaches to Curriculum Management. Ed. by Margaret Preedy. (Management in Education Ser.). 192p. 1989. 85.00 (*0-335-09249-7*, Open Univ Pr); pap. 27.00 (*0-335-09248-9*, Open Univ Pr) Taylor & Francis.

Approaches to Database Translation. 1986. lib. bdg. 79.95 (*0-8490-3746-8*) Gordon Pr.

Approaches to Discourse: Language As Social Interaction. Deborah Schiffrin. (Blackwell Textbooks in Linguistics Ser.). 480p. 1994. 59.95 (*0-631-16622-X*); pap. 24.95 (*0-631-16623-8*) Blackwell Pubs.

Approaches to Discourse, Poetics & Psychiatry: Papers from the 1985 Utrecht Summer School of Critical Theory. Ed. by Iris M. Zavala et al. LC 87-20936. (Critical Theory Ser.: Vol. 4). vi, 235p. (C). 1988. 74.00 (*1-55619-013-1*); pap. 22.95 (*1-55619-059-X*) Benjamins North Am.

Approaches to Early Childhood Education. 2nd ed. Ed. by J. L. Roopnarine & J. E. Johnson. LC 92-14849. 416p. (C). 1992. pap. write for info. (*0-02-403545-9*, Merrill Pub Co) Macmillan.

Approaches to Earth Survey Problems Through the Use of Space Techniques. P. Bock. LC 73-94252. 1977. 213.00 (*0-08-021996-9*, Pub. by Pergamon Repr UK) Franklin.

Approaches to Elucidate Mechanisms in Teratogenesis. Frank Welsch. (Chemical Industry Institute of Toxicology Ser.). (Illus.). 220p. 1987. 110.00 (*0-89116-584-3*) Hemisp Pub.

Approaches to Emotion. Ed. by Klaus R. Scherer & Paul Ekman. 448p. (C). 1984. pap. 39.95 (*0-89859-406-5*) L Erlbaum Assocs.

Approaches to Environmental Accounting. Ed. by A. Franz & C. Stahmer. (Contributions to Economics Ser.). (Illus.). viii, 542p. 1993. pap. write for info. (*3-7908-0719-2*) Spr-Verlag.

Approaches to Environmental Accounting: Proceedings of the IARIW Conference on Environmental Accounting, Baden, Austria, 27-29 May, 1991. Ed. by A. Franz & C. Stahmer. (Contributions to Economics Ser.). (Illus.). viii, 542p. 1993. pap. 119.00 (*0-387-91469-2*) Spr-Verlag.

Approaches to Environmental Geology: A Colloquium & Workshop. Ed. by E. G. Wermund. (Report of Investigations Ser.: RI 81). (Illus.). 268p. 1974. 3.50 (*0-318-03211-2*) Bur Econ Geology.

Approaches to Ethics: Representative Selection from Classic Times to the Present. 3rd ed. William Jones et al. (Illus.). 1977. text ed. write for info. (*0-07-033005-0*) McGraw.

Approaches to Exchange Rate Policy: Strategic Choices. IMF Institute. Ed. by Richard Barth. LC 94-3937. xi, 298p. 1994. 22.00 (*1-55775-364-4*) Intl Monetary.

Approaches to God. Jacques Maritain. Tr. by Peter O'Reilly. LC 78-16555. 128p. 1978. reprint ed. text ed. 55.00 (*0-313-20606-6*, MATG, Greenwood Pr) Greenwood.

Approaches to Grammaticalization, Set. Ed. by Elizabeth C. Traugott & Bernd Heine. LC 91-3650. (Typological Studies in Language: Vols. 19: 1, 19: 2). 1991. 265.00x (*1-55619-404-8*); pap. 69.00 (*1-55619-405-6*) Benjamins North Am.

Approaches to Grammaticalization, Vol. 1: Theoretical & Methodological Issues. Ed. by Elizabeth C. Traugott & Bernd Heine. LC 91-3650. (Typological Studies in Language: Vols. 19: 1, 19: 2). xii, 360p. 1991. 124.00x (*1-55619-400-5*); pap. 32.95 (*1-55619-401-3*) Benjamins North Am.

Approaches to Grammaticalization, Vol. 2: Types of Grammatical Markers. Ed. by Elizabeth C. Traugott & Bernd Heine. LC 91-3650. (Typological Studies in Language: Vols. 19: 1, 19: 2). xii, 538p. 1991. 162.00x (*1-55619-402-1*); pap. 36.95 (*1-55619-403-X*) Benjamins North Am.

Approaches to Gramsci. Anne S. Sassoon. 14.95 (*0-906495-55-5*); pap. 7.95 (*0-906495-56-3*) Writers & Readers.

Approaches to Greater Flexibility of Exchange Rates: The Burgenstock Papers. C. F. Bergsten et al. LC 78-11633. 1970. 70.00 (*0-691-04196-2*) Princeton U Pr.

***Approaches to Greater Flexibility of Exchange Rates: The Burgenstock Papers, Arranged by C. Fred Bergsten, George N. Halm, Fritz Machlup, Robert V. Roosa.** C. Fred Bergsten. Ed. by George N. Halm. LC 78-11633. reprint ed. pap. 128.30 (*0-7837-9377-4*, 2060121) Bks Demand.

Approaches to Greek Myth. Ed. by Lowell Edmunds. LC 89-45482. (Illus.). 512p. 1989. text ed. 55.00 (*0-8018-3863-0*); pap. text ed. 16.95x (*0-8018-3864-9*) Johns Hopkins.

Approaches to Guidance in Contemporary Education. 2nd ed. Joseph Zaccaria & Stephen Bopp. LC 80-12986. 320p. 1980. 23.50 (*0-910328-31-5*); pap. 16.50 (*0-910328-32-3*) Sulzburger & Graham Pub.

Approaches to History: A Symposium. Ed. by H. P. Finberg. LC 76-449880. (Canadian University Paperbooks Ser.: No. 93). 231p. reprint ed. pap. 65.90 (*0-8357-4155-9*, 2036929) Bks Demand.

Approaches to Iconology: Visible Religions: Annual for Religious Iconography, Vol. IV & V. x, 325p. 1986. pap. 103.00 (*90-04-07772-3*) E J Brill.

Approaches to Implementing Solid Waste Recycling Facilities. Marc J. Rogoff & John F. Williams. LC 94-3865. (Illus.). 216p. 1994. 48.00 (*0-8155-1352-6*) Noyes.

Approaches to Individualized Education. Ed. by Jan Jeter. LC 80-67363. 85p. (Orig.). 1980. pap. 4.75 (*0-87120-101-1*, 611-80204) Assn Supervision.

Approaches to Industrial Policy Within the EC & Its Impact on European Integration. Fritz Franzmeyer. 180p. 1982. text ed. 58.95 (*0-566-00358-9*) Ashgate Pub Co.

Approaches to Innovation in Social Work Education. 1974. 3.85 (*0-685-21313-7*, 74-650-04) Coun Soc Wk Ed.

***Approaches to Intentionality.** William Lyons. 304p. 1995. 49.95 (*0-19-823526-7*) OUP.

***Approaches to International Law: An Interdisciplinary Anthology.** Robert J. Beck et al. (Illus.). 352p. 1996. 39.95 (*0-19-508539-6*); pap. text ed. 21.95 (*0-19-508540-X*) OUP.

Approaches to Interpretation of Sedimentary Environments. Ed. by Douglas J. Cant & Frances J. Hein. (Reprint Ser.: No. 11). 265p. 1987. pap. 21.00 (*0-918985-65-X*) SEPM.

Approaches to Islam in Reglious Studies. Ed. by Richard C. Martin. LC 85-1099. 243p. 1985. 30.00 (*0-8165-0868-2*) U of Ariz Pr.

Approaches to Joyce's Portrait: Ten Essays. Ed. by Thomas F. Staley & Bernard Benstock. LC 76-6670. 253p. reprint ed. pap. 72.20 (*0-8357-5694-7*, 2024331) Bks Demand.

Approaches to Judaism in Medieval Times, Vol. I. David R. Blumenthal. LC 83-18886. (Brown Judaic Studies). 188p. (C). 1984. pap. 15.95 (*0-89130-659-5*, 14 00 54) Scholars Pr GA.

Approaches to Judaism in Medieval Times, Vol. II. David R. Blumenthal. (Brown Judaic Studies). 1985. 24.95 (*0-89130-848-2*, 14-00-57); pap. 19.95 (*0-89130-849-0*) Scholars Pr GA.

Approaches to Language. R. Harris. LC 82-12390. (Language & Communication Library: Vol. 4). (Illus.). 192p. 1983. 76.00 (*0-08-028910-X*, Pub. by Pergamon Repr UK) Franklin.

Approaches to Language: Anthropological Issues. William C. McCormack & Stephen A. Wurm. (World Anthropology Ser.). xiv, 674p. 1978. 93.50 (*90-279-7660-0*) Mouton.

Approaches to Language Testing. Ed. by Bernard Spolsky. LC 78-62080. (Advances in Language Testing Ser.: No. 2). 80p. reprint ed. pap. 25.00 (*0-8357-3356-4*, 2039593) Bks Demand.

***Approaches to Language Typology.** Ed. by Masayoshi Shibatani & Theodora Bynon. (Illus.). 320p. 1995. 70.00 (*0-19-824271-9*) OUP.

Approaches to Literature Through Authors. Elizabeth Wildberger. LC 92-42266. (Reading Motivation Ser.). 256p. 1993. pap. 29.95 (*0-89774-776-3*) Oryx Pr.

Approaches to Literature Through Genre. Lucille Van Vliet. LC 92-13073. (Reading Motivation Ser.). 288p. 1992. pap. 29.95 (*0-89774-773-9*) Oryx Pr.

Approaches to Literature Through Literary Form. Paul K. Montgomery. (Reading Motivation Ser.). 184p. 1995. pap. 29.95 (*0-89774-775-5*) Oryx Pr.

Approaches to Literature Through Subject. Paula K. Montgomery. LC 93-967. (Reading Motivation Ser.). 256p. 1993. pap. 29.95 (*0-89774-774-7*) Oryx Pr.

Approaches to Literature Through Theme. Paula K. Montgomery. LC 92-13072. (Reading Motivation Ser.). 132p. 1992. pap. 29.95 (*0-89774-772-0*) Oryx Pr.

Approaches to Local History. 2nd ed. Alan Rogers. LC 76-54265. 283p. reprint ed. pap. 80.70 (*0-8357-5695-5*, 2025253) Bks Demand.

Approaches to Marx. Cowling & Wilde. 1989. 90.00 (*0-335-15622-3*, Open Univ Pr); pap. 32.00 (*0-335-15621-5*, Open Univ Pr) Taylor & Francis.

Approaches to Modeling of Friction & Wear. Ed. by Frederick F. Ling & C. H. Pan. (Illus.). xiii, 173p. 1987. 73.00 (*0-387-96656-0*) Spr-Verlag.

Approaches to Modern Judaism, Vol. II. Ed. by Marc L. Raphael. (Brown Judaic Studies: No. 56). 128p. (C). 1985. 20.95 (*0-89130-793-1*, 14 00 56); pap. 17.95 (*0-89130-794-X*) Scholars Pr GA.

Approaches to Modern Judaism. Ed. by Marc L. Raphael. (Brown Judaic Studies). 1983. pap. 16.00 (*0-89130-647-1*, 14 00 49) Scholars Pr GA.

Approaches to Moral Development: New Research & Emerging Themes. Ed. by Andrew Garrod. LC 92-44918. 236p. (C). 1993. text ed. 44.00 (*0-8077-3247-8*); pap. text ed. 18.95 (*0-8077-3246-X*) Tchrs Coll.

Approaches to National Health Planning. H. E. Hilleboe et al. (Public Health Papers: No. 46). 1972. pap. 2.80 (*92-4-130046-9*) World Health.

Approaches to Natural Language: Proceedings of the Workshop on Grammar & Semantics, Stanford, 1970. Grammar & Semantics Workshop Staff. Ed. by K. J. Hintikka et al. LC 72-179892. (Synthese Library: No. 49). (Illus.). 526p. 1973. lib. bdg. 121.50 (*90-277-0220-9*) Kluwer Ac.

Approaches to Natural Language: Proceedings of the Workshop on Grammar & Semantics, Stanford, 1970. Grammar & Semantics Workshop Staff. Ed. by K. J. Hintikka et al. LC 72-179892. (Synthese Library: No. 49). (Illus.). 526p. 1978. pap. text ed. 62.00 (*90-277-0233-0*) Kluwer Ac.

Approaches to Nature in the Middle Ages. Ed. by Lawrence D. Roberts. LC 82-8264. (Medieval & Renaissance Texts & Studies: Vol. 16). (Illus.). 1982. 20.00 (*0-86698-051-2*) MRTS.

Approaches to New Leads for Insecticides: Proceedings in Life Sciences. Ed. by H. C. Von Keyserlingk et al. (Illus.). 184p. 1986. 50.00 (*0-387-15952-5*) Spr-Verlag.

Approaches to Numerical Relativity: Proceedings of the International Workshop on Numerical Relativity, Southhampton, December 1991. Ed. by Ray A. D'Inverno. (Illus.). 400p. (C). 1993. 79.95 (*0-521-43976-0*) Cambridge U Pr.

Approaches to Old Testament Interpretation. rev. ed. John Goldingay. LC 90-37126. 208p. 1990. pap. 13.99 (*0-8308-1303-9*, 1303) InterVarsity.

Approaches to Organic Form. Ed. by Frederick Burwick. (C). 1987. lib. bdg. 117.00 (*90-277-2541-1*) Kluwer Ac.

Approaches to Organizing. Robert T. Golembiewski. LC 81-70133. (PAR Classics Ser.: No. 3). (Illus.). 280p. reprint ed. pap. 79.80 (*0-8357-4220-2*, 2037005) Bks Demand.

Approaches to Participation in Rural Development. Peter Oakley & David Marsden. (WEP Study Ser.). x, 91p. (Orig.). 1990. pap. 14.00 (*92-2-103594-8*) Intl Labour Office.

Approaches to Patient Care Assessment in a Multihospital System: Report of the Sisters of Mercy Health Corporation. LC 86-81892. 96p. 1987. pap. text ed. 30.00 (*0-86688-108-5*) Joint Comm Hlthcare.

Approaches to Peace: An Intellectual Map. Ed. by W. Scott Thompson & Kenneth M. Jensen. LC 89-26871. (Orig.). 1991. pap. text ed. 29.95 (*1-878379-01-1*) US Inst Peace.

Approaches to Physical Measurements in Biotechnology. B. C. Blake-Coleman. (Illus.). 224p. 1993. text ed. 53.50 (*0-12-103610-3*) Acad Pr.

Approaches to Planned Change: Orienting Perspectives & Micro-Level Interventions. Robert T. Golembiewski. LC 92-18639. (Classics in Organization & Management Ser.). 380p. (C). 1992. reprint ed. pap. 24.95 (*1-56000-646-3*) Transaction Pubs.

Approaches to Planning: Introducing Current Planning Theories, Concepts & Issues. E. R. Alexander. 136p. 1986. 35.00 (*2-88124-140-9*) Gordon & Breach.

Approaches to Planning & Design of Health Care Facilities in Developing Areas, Vol. 5. Ed. by B. M. Kleczkowski et al. (WHO Offset Publication Ser.: No. 91). 106p. 1985. pap. 6.60 (*92-4-170091-2*) World Health.

An Asterisk (*) at the beginning of an entry indicates that the title is appearing in BIP for the first time.

An Asterisk (*) at the beginning of an entry indicates that the title is appearing in BIP for the first time.

Approaches to Traditional Chinese Medical Literature: Proceedings of an International Symposium on Translation Methodologies & Terminologies. Ed. by Paul U. Unschuld. (C). 1989. lib. bdg. 99.00 (1-55608-041-7) Kluwer Ac.

Approaches to Training & Development. 2nd ed. Dugan Laird. LC 84-24480. 320p. 1985. 24.95 (0-201-04498-6) Addison-Wesley.

Approaches to Urban Archaeology. Martin Biddle. (Illus.). 300p. 1988. 45.00 (0-85224-597-1, Pub. by Edinburgh U Pr UK) Col U Pr.

*Approaches to World Order. Robert W. Cox. (Studies in International Relations: No. 40). (Illus.). 370p. (C). Date not set. write for info. (0-521-46114-6) Cambridge U Pr.

Approaches to Writing. 2nd ed. Paul Horgan. LC 88-14051. 279p. 1988. pap. 15.95 (0-8195-6221-1, Wesleyan Univ Pr) U Pr of New Eng.

Approaches Toward Church Unity. Norman Smyth & Williston Walker. 1919. 59.50 (0-686-37862-8) Elliots Bks.

Approaching. Parker P. Huang. Ed. by Stanley H. Barken & Diana Chang. (Review Asian-American Writers Chapbook Ser.: No. 1). (Illus.). 48p. 1989. 15.00 (0-89304-625-6); 15.00 (0-89304-627-2); pap. 5.00 (0-89304-626-4); pap. 5.00 (0-89304-628-0); audio 10.00 (0-89304-629-9) Cross-Cultrl NY.

Approaching an Action Against a Real Estate Broker (Evaluating the Claim Before Filing) Winter 1993, Action Guide. Barry L. Goldner et al. Ed. by Carolyn J. Stein. 92p. 1993. pap. text ed. 47.00 (0-88124-610-7, RE-11511) Cont Ed Bar-CA.

Approaching Construction Disputes: Summer 1992 Action Guide. Richard A. Holderness. Ed. by Ellen C. Lester. 80p. 1992. pap. 47.00 (0-88124-509-7, RE-11271) Cont Ed Bar-CA.

Approaching Earth. Daniel Noel. (Chrysalis Bks.). 192p. (Orig.). 1986. pap. 12.95 (0-916349-12-8) Amity Hse Inc.

*Approaching Economics. Adrian Perry. 448p. (C). 1989. 59.00x (0-7478-0370-6, Pub. by S Thornes Pubs UK) St Mut.

Approaching Economics. P. Perry. (C). 1989. 120.00 (0-685-37700-8, Pub. by S Thornes Pubs UK) St Mut.

*Approaching Environmental Issues in the Classroom. Margaret T. Pennock & Lisa V. Bardwell. Ed. by Martha C. Monroe & David Cappaert. (EEToolbox Resource Manual Ser.). (Illus.). 60p. 1994. 8.00 (1-884782-05-1) Natl Consort EET.

Approaching Equality. Frank Bowe. 1991. pap. 12.95 (0-932666-39-6) T J Pubs.

Approaching God: Daily Readings in Systematic Theology. Paul Enns. 1991. 16.99 (0-8024-0654-8) Moody.

Approaching Hoofbeats: The Four Horsemen of the Apocalypse. Billy Graham. 288p. 1985. pap. 3.95 (0-380-69921-4) Avon.

Approaching Hoofbeats: The Four Horsemen of the Apocalypse. Billy Graham. 1985. write for info. (0-8499-4170-9) Word Inc.

Approaching Human Geography: An Introduction to Contemporary Theoretical Debates. Paul J. Cloke et al. LC 91-2656. (Mappings: Society - Theory - Space Ser.). 240p. (Orig.). 1991. pap. text ed. 19.95 (0-89862-490-8) Guilford Pr.

Approaching Hysteria: Disease & Its Interpretations. Mark S. Micale. LC 94-16596. 1994. 29.95 (0-691-03717-5) Princeton U Pr.

Approaching Infinity: Selected Mathematical Writings of Rabeynu Shlomo of Chelme (Author of Mirkeves Hamishna) Tr. by M. Littman. 1989. pap. 12.95 (0-685-29637-7) Feldheim.

*Approaching Jehovah's Witnesses in Love: How to Witness Effectively Without Arguing. Wilbur Lingle. 250p. (Orig.). 1994. pap. 8.95 (0-87508-702-7) Chr Lit.

Approaching Macintosh. Michael Tchao et al. 356p. (C). 1986. pap. text ed. write for info. (0-201-16496-5) Addison-Wesley.

Approaching Macintosh: A Guide to Learning Macintosh Software. 2nd ed. Michael Tchao et al. (Illus.). 500p. (C). 1991. pap. text ed. 40.95 (0-201-52584-4) Addison-Wesley.

Approaching Nada. Vassar Miller. Ed. by Joseph J. Lomax. LC 77-20734. 1977. 15.00 (0-930324-03-X) Wings Pr.

*Approaching Peace: American Interests in Israeli-Palestinian Final-Status Talks. Ed. by Robert Satloff. LC 94-33594. 1994. write for info. (0-944029-58-2) Wash Inst NEP.

Approaching Precalculus Mathematics Discretely: Explorations in a Computer Environment. Philip G. Lewis. (Explorations in Logo Ser.). 350p. (Orig.). 1989. 47.50x (0-262-12138-7); pap. 24.95x (0-262-62063-4) MIT Pr.

Approaching Promise. Salaheddin Ali Nader Shah Anglia. 71p. (Orig.). (C). 1989. pap. text ed. 13.50 (0-8191-7403-3) U Pr of Amer.

Approaching Re-Creation: A Form for Seeing the Delicate Threads. Eric C. Fimbres. LC 82-90184. (Illus.). 208p. (Orig.). 1982. pap. 5.95 (0-9608946-0-8) Life Sustaining.

Approaching Snow. Joyce Herbert. 41p. 1983. pap. 8.95 (0-907476-23-6) Dufour.

Approaching Sociology. rev. ed. Margaret Coulson & Carol Riddell. 144p. 1980. pap. 12.95 (0-7100-0575-X) Routledge.

Approaching Storm: One Woman's Story of Germany 1934-1938. Nora Waln. LC 92-44480. 380p. 1993. 30.00 (0-939149-80-X); pap. 14.00 (0-939149-81-8) Soho Press.

Approaching Storm: U-Boats off the Virginia Coast During World War II. Alpheus J. Chewning. Ed. by Robert H. Pruett. LC 93-42262. 192p. (Orig.). 1994. pap. 18.95 (0-9627635-9-4) Brandylane.

*Approaching Suharto's Indonesia from the Margins. Ed. by Takashi Shiraishi. (Translation Ser.: No. 4). (Orig.). (C). 1995. pap. text ed. 14.00 (0-87727-403-7) Cornell SE Asia.

Approaching the Bible. Michael Penny. LC 92-70157. 348p. 1992. pap. 15.00 (1-880573-03-2) Grace WI.

*Approaching the Culture of Toys in Swedish Child Care: A Literature Survey & a Toy Inventory. Birgitta Almqvist. (Uppsala Studies in Education: No. 54). 175p. (Orig.). 1994. pap. 42.50x (91-554-3260-3, Pub. by Almqv & Wiksell SW) Coronet Bks.

Approaching the Gospels Together: A Leaders' Guide to Group Gospels Study. Mary C. Morrison. LC 86-62204. (Orig.). 1987. pap. 10.95 (0-87574-910-0) Pendle Hill.

Approaching the Guitar. Gene Bertoncini. 88p. 1990. pap. text ed. 14.95 (0-8497-6326-6, GE56) Kjos.

Approaching the Magic Hour: Memories of Walter Anderson. Agnes G. Anderson. Ed. by Patti C. Black. LC 89-5407. 224p. 1989. 19.95 (0-87805-394-8) U Pr of Miss.

*Approaching the Magic Hour: Memories of Walter Anderson. Agnes G. Anderson. Ed. by Patti C. Black. (Illus.). 178p. 1995. pap. 15.95 (0-87805-803-6) U Pr of Miss.

Approaching the Past: Historical Anthropology Through Irish Case Studies. Ed. by Marilyn Silverman & Philip H. Gulliver. (Illus.). 464p. 1992. text ed. 49.50 (0-231-07920-6); pap. text ed. 19.50 (0-231-07921-4) Col U Pr.

Approaching the Third Millennium: The Church's Ethical Challenge. Howard W. Roberts. LC 92-25109. 192p. 1992. pap. 10.95 (1-880837-04-8) Smyth & Helwys.

Approaching Theatre. Ed. by Andre Helbo et al. LC 90-43691. (Advances in Semiotics Ser.). (Illus.). 240p. 1991. 39.95 (0-253-32723-7) Ind U Pr.

*Approaching 2000: The Corporation in Transition. Ed. by Dennis Campbell. LC 94-42391. 1994. write for info. (90-411-0007-5) Kluwer Law Tax Pubs.

Approaching Vagueness. Ed. by T. T. Ballmer. (Linguistic Ser.: Vol. 50). 430p. 1983. 87.25 (0-444-86745-7, I-252-83, North Holland) Elsevier.

Approaching Vietnam: From World War II Through Dienbienphu. Lloyd C. Gardner. 1989. pap. 9.95 (0-393-30578-3) Norton.

Approaching Zanzibar. Tina Howe. 112p. (Orig.). 1990. pap. 8.95 (1-55936-008-9) Theatre Comm.

*Approaching Zanzibar: And Other Plays. Tina Howe. 224p. (Orig.). 1995. pap. 13.95 (1-55936-104-2) Theatre Comm.

Approaching Zero. P. Mungo & B. Clough. 1993. 22.00 (0-679-40938-6) McKay.

Approaching Zion. Hugh Nibley. LC 89-38824. (Collected Works of Hugh Nibley: Vol. 9). 631p. 1989. 19.95 (0-87579-252-9) Deseret Bk.

Approches, Drogues et Ivresse. Ernst Junger. 570p. (FRE.). 1991. pap. 18.95 (0-7859-2252-0, 2070326381) Fr & Eur.

Approches Sans Entraves. Jacques Maritain. 595p. (FRE.). 1973. 39.95 (0-7859-5534-8) Fr & Eur.

Appropiate Products, Employment & Technology: Case-Studies on Consumer Choice & Basic Needs in Developing Countries. Ed. by Wouter Van Ginneken & Christopher Baron. LC 83-40122. 384p. 1984. text ed. 45.00 (0-312-04671-5) St Martin.

Appropiate Technology: Choice & Development. Ed. by Mathew J. Betz et al. LC 84-8187. xi, 164p. 1984. lib. bdg. 37.00 (0-8223-0573-9) Duke.

Appropriate Biotechnology in Small-Scale Agriculture: How to Reorient Research & Development. Ed. by Joske F. Bunders & Jacqueline E. Broerse. 160p. (Orig.). 1991. pap. 23.75 (0-85198-770-2) CAB Intl.

Appropriate Development for Basic Needs. Ed. by D. P. Maguire. 360p. 1991. text ed. 76.00 (0-7277-1618-2, Pub. by T Telford UK) Am Soc Civil Eng.

Appropriate Macroeconomic Management in Indonesia's Open Economy. Sadiq Ahmed. LC 92-47503. (Discussion Paper Ser.: No. 191). 33p. 1993. 6.95 (0-8213-2338-5, 12338) World Bank.

Appropriate Methodologies for Development & Management of Groundwater Resources in Developing Countries: Proceedings of the International Workshop, Hyderabad, India, 28 February - 4 March 1989, 3 vols., Set. Ed. by C. P. Gupta et al. (Illus.). 1360p. (C). 1989. text ed. 160.00 (90-6191-963-0, Pub. by A A Balkema NE) Ashgate Pub Co.

Appropriate Methodology & Social Context. Adrian Holliday. LC 93-34915. (Cambridge Language Teaching Library Ser.). 247p. (C). 1994. 42.95 (0-521-43156-5); pap. 16.95 (0-521-43745-8) Cambridge U Pr.

Appropriate Remuneration in Developing Countries: Three-Dimensional Models for Executives & Workers. Rama M. Kuppachi. (Illus.). 244p. 1991. 27.50 (0-8039-9661-6) Sage.

Appropriate Technologies for Rural Development in India. Floris P. Blankenberg. (C). 1991. 35.00 (81-7022-371-7, Pub. by Concept II) S Asia.

Appropriate Technology. (Illus.). 73p. 1985. pap. 14.00 (0-7279-0157-5, Pub. by Brit Med Assn UK) Amer Coll Phys.

Appropriate Technology: A Focus for the Nineties. Ed. by Robert W. Stevens. 180p. (Orig.). 1991. pap. text ed. 19.50 (0-942850-30-0) Intermediate Tech.

Appropriate Technology: Problems & Promises, Part I (The Major Policy Issues) Nicolas Jequier. 1977. pap. text ed. 2.50 (0-917704-04-5) Volunteers Asia Pr.

Appropriate Technology: Scope for Co-Operation among the Countries of the West African Economic Community. J. C. Woillet. ii, 104p. (Orig.). 1981. pap. 12.00 (92-2-102359-1) Intl Labour Office.

Appropriate Technology at Work: Outstanding Projects Funded by the U. S. Department of Energy Appropriate Technology Small Grants Program 1978-1981. 25p. 1983. 3.00 (0-317-53923-X, MIS4) NCAT.

Appropriate Technology for Developing Countries. 3rd ed. W. Riedjik. Ed. by W Riedjik. 368p. (Orig.). 1987. pap. text ed. 32.50 (90-6275-085-0, Pub. by Delft U Pr NE) Coronet Bks.

Appropriate Technology for the Treatment of Wastewaters for Small Rural Communities. (EURO Reports & Studies: No. 90). 62p. 1985. pap. 4.80 (92-890-1256-0) World Health.

Appropriate Technology for Water Supply & Sanitation: A Summary of Technical & Economic Options. John M. Kalbermatten et al. 38p. 1980. write for info. (0-318-70274-6, 10049) World Bank.

Appropriate Technology in Industrialized Countries. Ed. by Willem Riedijk. (Illus.). 372p. (Orig.). 1989. pap. 42.50 (90-6275-284-5, Pub. by Delft U Pr NE) Coronet Bks.

Appropriate Technology in Resource Conservation & Recovery. ASCE National Convention, Environmental Analysis Research Council, Atlanta, 1980. Ed. by Charles G. Gunnerson & John M. Kalbermatten. LC 80-65304. 218p. 1980. pap. 21.00 (0-87262-035-2) Am Soc Civil Eng.

Appropriate Technology in Third World Development. Ed. by Pradip K. Ghosh & Denton E. Morrison. LC 83-26682. xiv, 494p. 1984. text ed. 89.50 (0-313-24150-3, GAT/, Greenwood Pr) Greenwood.

Appropriate Technology in Vector Control. Ed. by C. F. Curtis. 256p. 1989. 179.00 (0-8493-4755-6, RA639) CRC Pr.

Appropriate Technology Management Information System. 750p. 1984. 15.00 (0-317-53922-1, MIS2) NCAT.

Appropriate Technology Sourcebook: A Guide to Practical Books for Village & Small Community Technology. rev. ed. Ken Darrow & Mike Saxenian. (Illus.). 800p. 1993. reprint ed. 29.95 (0-917704-18-5); reprint ed. pap. 23.95 (0-917704-17-7) Volunteers Asia Pr. The APPROPRIATE TECHNOLOGY SOURCEBOOK is your complete & up-to-date guide to sustainable living. Since 1975, the AT SOURCEBOOK has been the standard reference for people interested in simple, small scale, sustainable technologies. The AT SOURCEBOOK catalogues & reviews over 1000 of the most useful books to help you do-it-yourself. The AT SOURCEBOOK can help you design a solar greenhouse or water heater, start an organic farm, set up a woodcraft shop, & even equip your home with an independent, environmentally friendly energy system such as photovoltaics, wind energy or small hydro power. The AT SOURCEBOOK also serves as a fully indexed & annotated guide to the Appropriate Technology Microfiche Library, which includes 1000 books in their entirety in microfiche form. Contact the publisher for free information, VIA Press, Appropriate Technology Project, P.O. Box 4543, Stanford, CA 94309, (800) 648-8043 or FAX (415) 725-1805. ***Publisher Provided Annotation.***

Appropriate Use of Fluorides for Human Health. 136p. 1986. pap. 10.20 (92-4-154203-9) World Health.

*Appropriate Weed Control in Southeast Asia. Ed. by S. S. Sastroutomo & B. A. Auld. 120p. 1995. pap. 27.50 (0-85198-991-8) CAB Intl.

Appropriate Well Drilling Technologies. 96p. 1978. 8.75 (1-56034-000-2, K007) Natl Water Well.

Appropriated Voice: Narrative Authority in Conrad, Forster & Woolf. Bette London. LC 89-48925. 208p. 1990. text ed. 37.50 (0-472-10160-9) U of Mich Pr.

Appropriateness & Effectiveness of Vocational Rehabilitation in Florida: Costs, Referrals, Services, & Outcomes. John A. Gardner. 1988. 25.00 (0-935149-12-0, WC-88-2) Workers Comp Res Inst.

Appropriateness of Selected Medical & Surgical Procedures: Relationships to Geographic Variations. Mark R. Chassin et al. LC 89-85022. 159p. 1989. pap. 28.00 (0-910701-52-0, 0881) Health Admin Pr.

*Appropriateness of Spinal Manipulation for Low-Back Pain: Data Collection Instruments & A Manual for Their Use. Paul G. Shekelle et al. 131p. 1995. pap. text ed. 10.00 (0-8330-1656-3) Rand Corp.

Appropriating Australian Folk Dances into Sacred Dance. Doug Adams. 1987. pap. 3.00 (0-941500-45-4) Sharing Co.

Appropriating Hegel. Crawford Elder. Ed. by Andrew Brennan & William Lyons. (Scots Philosophical Monographs: Vol. 3). 116p. 1981. 17.00 (0-08-025729-1, Pergamon Pr) Elsevier.

Appropriating Literacy: Writing & Reading in English As a Second Language. Judith Rodby. LC 92-18835. 151p. 1992. pap. text ed. 18.50 (0-86709-308-0) Boynton Cook Pubs.

*Appropriating Old Cultures. Geraldine Forte. 176p. 1994. pap. 16.95 (1-57087-082-9) Prof Pr NC.

Appropriating Shakespeare: Contemporary Critical Quarrels. Brian Vickers. LC 92-38549. 528p. (C). 1993. 47.00 (0-300-05415-7) Yale U Pr.

Appropriating Shakespeare: Contemporary Critical Quarrels. Brian Vickers. (Illus.). 528p. 1994. pap. 18.00 (0-300-06105-6) Yale U Pr.

Appropriating the Lonergan Idea. Frederick E. Crowe. Ed. by Michael Vertin. LC 87-33855. 410p. 1989. 49.95 (0-8132-0668-5) Cath U Pr.

*Appropriating the Lonergan Idea. Frederick E. Crowe. Ed. by Michael Vertin. LC 87-33855. reprint ed. pap. 120.90 (0-7837-9186-0, 2049886) Bks Demand.

Appropriating the Weather: Vilhelm Bjerknes & the Construction of a Modern Meteorology. Robert M. Friedman. LC 88-47729. (Illus.). 280p. 1989. 39.95 (0-8014-2062-8) Cornell U Pr.

Appropriating the Weather: Vilhelm Bjerknes & the Construction of a Modern Meteorology. Robert M. Friedman. LC 88-47729. (Illus.). 280p. 1993. pap. 16.95 (0-8014-8160-0) Cornell U Pr.

Appropriation Act, 1988, Chapter 38. 1988. pap. 13.00 (0-10-543888-X, HM3990, Pub. by HMSO UK) UNIPUB.

Appropriation of Nature: Essays on Human Ecology & Social Relations. Tim Ingold. LC 86-51130. (Illus.). 297p. 1987. text ed. 36.00 (0-87745-167-2) U of Iowa Pr.

Appropriation of Shakespeare: Post-Renaissance Reconstructions of the Works & the Myth. Derek Cohen. Ed. by Jean I. Marsden & Clive Bloom. LC 91-29982. (Insights Ser.). 230p. 1992. text ed. 45.00 (0-312-07198-1) St Martin.

Approval Motive: Studies in Evaluative Dependence. Douglas P. Crowne & David Marlowe. LC 80-475. (Illus.). xii, 233p. 1980. reprint ed. text ed. 55.00 (0-313-22365-3, CRAM, Greenwood Pr) Greenwood.

Approval Process: Recreation & Resort Development Experience. Ed. by Frank Schnidman. LC 83-50488. 48p. (Orig.). reprint ed. pap. 25.00 (0-7837-5767-0, 2045432) Bks Demand.

Approval Voting. Stephen Brams & Peter Fishburn. LC 82-17849. 224p. 1983. pap. 19.50 (0-8176-3124-0) Birkhauser.

Approved ADA Language Commentaries. Ed. by Gerry Fisher. (ADA Letters Ser.: Vol. 9, No. 3). 354p. 1989. pap. text ed. 30.00 (0-89791-311-6, 825890) Assn Compu Machinery.

Approved Bioequivalency Codes, 1993. Facts & Comparisons Staff. 1992. ring bd. 69.95 (0-932686-75-3) Facts & Comparisons.

Approved Lists of Bacterial Names (Amended Edition) Ed. by V. B. Skerman et al. 272p. 1989. text ed. 55.00 (1-55581-014-4) Am Soc Microbio.

*Approved Methods of the American Association of Cereal Chemists. 9th ed. Comp. by Approved Methods Committee Staff. LC 82-46081. 1200p. 1995. 475.00x (0-913250-86-4) Am Assn Cereal Chem.

Approved Practices in Beef Cattle Production. 5th ed. Elwood M. Juergenson. LC 72-97974. (Illus.). 470p. (gr. 9-12). 1980. 26.60 (0-8134-2093-8, 2093) Interstate.

*Approved Practices in Beef Cattle Production. 5th ed. Elwood M. Juergenson. LC 72-97974. (Illus.). 470p. (YA). (gr. 9-12). 1980. text ed. 19.95x (0-685-02530-6) Interstate.

Approved Practices in Crop Production. 2nd ed. E. A. Brickbaurer & W. P. Mortenson. (Illus.). xx, 396p. 1978. 26.60 (0-8134-1975-1) Interstate.

*Approved Practices in Crop Production. 2nd ed. E. A. Brickbaurer & W. P. Mortenson. (Illus.). xx, 396p. 1978. text ed. 19.95 (0-685-50792-0) Interstate.

Approved Practices in Dairying. 4th ed. E. M. Juergenson & W. P. Mortenson. (Illus.). xii, 356p. 1977. 26.60 (0-8134-1954-9) Interstate.

*Approved Practices in Dairying. 4th ed. E. M. Juergenson & W. P. Mortenson. (Illus.). xii, 356p. 1977. text ed. 19.95 (0-685-50793-9) Interstate.

Approved Practices in Pasture Management. 4th ed. Don W. Graffis et al. 1985. text ed. 19.95 (0-8134-2449-6) Interstate.

*Approved Practices in Pasture Management. 4th ed. Don W. Graffis et al. 1985. 26.60 (0-685-10594-6) Interstate.

Approved Practices in Sheep Production. 4th ed. E. M. Juergenson. (Illus.). x, 455p. 1981. 26.60 (0-8134-2163-2) Interstate.

*Approved Practices in Sheep Production. 4th ed. E. M. Juergenson. (Illus.). x, 455p. 1981. text ed. 19.95 (0-685-50794-7) Interstate.

Approved Practices in Soil Conservation. 5th ed. Albert B. Foster & Duane Bosworth. (Illus.). 470p. 1982. 26.60 (0-8134-2170-5, 2170); teacher ed 4.95 (0-8134-2337-6) Interstate.

*Approved Practices in Soil Conservation. 5th ed. Albert B. Foster & Duane Bosworth. (Illus.). 470p. 1982. text ed. 19.95x (0-685-02531-4) Interstate.

Approved Practices in Swine Production. 6th ed. J. K. Baker & E. M. Juergenson. LC 79-142330. 438p. 1979. 26.60 (0-8134-2038-5, 2038) Interstate.

*Approved Practices in Swine Production. 6th ed. J. K. Baker & E. M. Juergenson. 438p. 1979. text ed. 19.95x (0-685-02532-2) Interstate.

Approved Products for Farmers & Growers see Pesticides 19-(Yr) 1992

Approved Products for Farmers & Growers see Pesticides 19-(Yr) 1993

Approved unto God. Oswald Chambers. 1991. pap. 5.95 (0-906330-38-6) Chr Lit.

Approving Software Products: Proceedings of the IFIP WG5.4 Working Conference, Garmisch-Partenkirchen, FRG, 17-19 Sept., 1990. Ed. by W. D. Ehrenberger. 350p. 1990. 87.25 (0-444-88843-8, North Holland) Elsevier.

An Asterisk (*) at the beginning of an entry indicates that the title is appearing in BIP for the first time.

An Asterisk (*) at the beginning of an entry indicates that the title is appearing in BIP for the first time.

April Calls: The Sailing Adventure of a Lifetime. Chris Marshall. 144p. (Orig.). 1993. pap. 9.95 (*0-9637347-3-3*) C W Pub.

*__April '65: Confederate Covert Action in th American Civil War.__ William A. Tidwell. LC 94-33226. (Illus.). 280p. 1995. 30.00 (*0-87338-515-2*) Kent St U Pr.

April Fifteenth: The Most Pernicious Attack upon English Liberty. rev. ed. Donald W. MacPherson. 210p. 1983. pap. 12.00 (*0-9617124-2-2*) Winning St Paul.

April Fish, & the Wooing of Lady Sunday: Two Short Plays. Ted Pezzulo. 1975. pap. 4.75 (*0-8222-0062-7*) Dramatists Play.

April Fool! Francine Pascal. (Sweet Valley Twins Ser.: No. 28). (J). 1989. pap. 3.50 (*0-553-15688-8*) Bantam.

April Fools. Richie T. Cusick. 1990. pap. 3.25 (*0-590-43115-3*, Point) Scholastic Inc.

April Fools: An Insider's Account of the Rise & Collapse of Drexel Burnham. Dan G. Stone. 1990. 19.95 (*1-55611-228-9*) D I Fine.

April Fool's Day. Emily Kelley. LC 82-23559. (Carolrhoda On My Own Bks.). (Illus.). 48p. (J). (gr. k-3). 1983. lib. bdg. 15.95 (*0-87614-218-8*, Carolrhoda) Lerner Group.

April Fool's Day. Emily Kelley. LC 82-23559. (Carolrhoda On My Own Bks.). (Illus.). 48p. (J). (gr. k-4). 1983. pap. 3.95 (*0-87614-481-4*, Carolrhoda) Lerner Group.

April Fool's Day Mystery. Marion M. Markham. 64p. (J). 1993. pap. 3.50 (*0-380-71716-6*, Camelot Young) Avon.

April Fool's Day Mystery. Marion M. Markham. LC 90-41318. (Illus.). 48p. (J). (gr. 2-6). 1991. 13.95 (*0-395-56235-X*) HM.

April Gold. Grace L. Hill. 19.95 (*0-89190-057-8*, Am Repr) Amereon Ltd.

April Gold. Grace L. Hill. 304p. 1992. pap. text ed. 4.99 (*0-8423-0011-2*) Tyndale.

April Harvest. Lillian Budd. 1991. reprint ed. lib. bdg. 18.95 (*1-56849-048-8*) Buccaneer Bks.

April Hopes. William Dean Howells. LC 75-184525. (Selected Edition of W. D. Howells Ser.). 400p. 1975. 29.95 (*0-253-30770-8*) Ind U Pr.

April Hopes. William Dean Howells. (Notable American Authors Ser.). 1992. reprint ed. lib. bdg. 75.00 (*0-7812-3240-6*) Rprt Serv.

April Idea Book: A Creative Idea Book for the Elementary Teacher, Ps-6. Karen Sevaly. (Illus.). 112p. (Orig.). 1988. pap. 9.95 (*0-943263-07-7*, TF 400) Teachers Friend Pubns.

*__April Is Forever.__ Doris E. Fell. LC 94-35254. (Seasons of Intrigue Ser.). 352p. (Orig.). 1995. pap. 9.99 (*0-89107-828-2*) Crossway Bks.

April Lady. Georgette Heyer. 1991. mass mkt. 3.99 (*0-06-100242-9*, Harp PBks) HarpC.

April Lady. large type ed. Georgette Heyer. 419p. 1992. reprint ed. lib. bdg. 18.95 (*1-56054-203-9*) Thorndike Pr.

*__April Mist.__ C. L. Tench. 110p. (Orig.). 1995. pap. write for info. (*1-885591-66-7*) Morris Pubng.

April Monthly Activities. Janet Hale. (Illus.). 80p. (J). (gr. 1-5). 1990. student ed 8.95 (*1-55734-158-3*) Tchr Create Mat.

April Morning. Howard M. Fast. (gr. 6 up). 1983. mass mkt. 4.99 (*0-553-27322-1*) Bantam.

*__April Morning.__ Barbara Reeves. Ed. by J. Friedland & R. Kessler. (Novel-Ties Ser.). (YA). 1992. student ed, pap. text ed. 15.95 (*0-88122-714-5*) Lrn Links.

April of Her Age: The Buried Treasure of Robert Louis Stevenson & Princess Victoria Kaiulani. John C. Mebane. (Illus.). 248p. (Orig.). 1994. pap. 14.95 (*0-9641844-1-9*) Windward HI.

April Poem. Bob Grumman. 16p. (Orig.). 1989. pap. 1.00 (*0-926935-16-X*) Runaway Spoon.

April Rabbits. David Cleveland. (Illus.). 32p. (J). (gr. k-3). 1986. pap. 2.95 (*0-590-42369-X*) Scholastic Inc.

*__April Rain.__ Elsa W. Cromer. (Illus.). 40p. (Orig.). 1994. pap. text ed. 6.95 (*1-56315-035-2*) Sterling Hse.

April Showers. George Shannon. LC 94-6266. (Illus.). 24p. (J). (ps up). 1995. lib. bdg. 14.93 (*0-688-13122-0*) Greenwillow.

April Showers. George Shannon. LC 94-6266. (Illus.). 24p. (J). (ps up). 1995. 15.00 (*0-688-13121-2*) Greenwillow.

April Snow. Lillian Budd. 1991. reprint ed. lib. bdg. 18.95 (*1-56849-047-X*) Buccaneer Bks.

April Squire. large type ed. Emily Wynn. 1990. pap. 12.95 (*0-7089-6890-2*, Linford) Ulverscroft.

April Twilights. Willa Cather. 1976. 16.95 (*0-88411-127-X*, Aeonian Pr) Amereon Ltd.

April Twilights. rev. ed. Willa Cather. LC 76-14216. (Landmark Edition Ser.). xlviii, 88p. 1990. reprint ed. 30.00 (*0-8032-1448-0*) U of Nebr Pr.

April Twilights. Willa Cather. 1990. reprint ed. lib. bdg. 15.95 (*0-89968-492-0*) Buccaneer Bks.

April Wars. Beth Joselow. LC 83-60018. 62p. 1983. pap. 6.00 (*0-911809-00-7*) Moon Lake Bks.

April Wind & Other Poems. Frederick Turner. 1992. 16.50 (*0-8139-1358-6*) U Pr of Va.

April Witch. Ray Bradbury. (Ray Bradbury Ser.). 1987. lib. bdg. 13.95 (*0-88682-105-3*) Creative Ed.

April 1914. (Southern Historical Society Papers: Vol. XXXIX). (Illus.). 220p. 1991. reprint ed. 40.00 (*1-56837-142-X*) Broadfoot.

*__April's Christmas.__ Janeen S. DeBoard & Hazel A. Williams. 1994. 17.95 (*0-8034-9083-6*, 094521) Bouregy.

April's Grave. Susan Howatch. 1985. mass mkt. 4.99 (*0-449-20994-6*) Fawcett.

April's Kittens. Clare T. Newberry. LC 40-32442. (Illus.). 32p. (J). (gr. k-3). 1940. 17.00 (*0-06-024400-3*); lib. bdg. 16.89 (*0-06-024401-1*) HarpC Child Bks.

Apritsails & Lugsails. John Leather. (Illus.). 392p. 1989. text ed. 45.00 (*0-87742-998-7*) Intl Marine.

Aprobado. Carthew & Webb. 1986. pap. text ed. 17.04 (*0-582-33178-1*, 72067); audio 22.61 (*0-582-33177-3*, 72066) Longman.

Apron: Its Traditions, History & Secret Significances (1914) Frank C. Higgins. 1993. reprint ed. pap. 9.95 (*1-56459-418-1*) Kessinger Pub.

Apron Full of Gold: The Letters of Mary Jane Megquier from San Francisco, 1849-1856. 2nd ed. Ed. by Polly W. Kaufman. LC 93-29907. (Illus.). 128p. 1994. pap. 15.95 (*0-8263-1500-3*) U of NM Pr.

Apron Strings. Ed. by Jan Carlton. (Illus.). 396p. 1983. pap. 10.95 (*0-9613752-0-5*) Womens Com Rich.

Apropos of Africa: Sentiments of Negro American Leaders on Africa from the 1800's to the 1950's. Ed. by A. Cromwell Hill & Martin Kilson. 390p. 1969. 35.00 (*0-7146-1757-1*, Pub. by F Cass Pubs UK) Intl Spec Bk.

Apropos of Lady Chatterley's Lover. D. H. Lawrence. LC 73-8959. (English Literature Ser.: No. 33). 1973. reprint ed. lib. bdg. 75.00 (*0-8383-1702-2*) M S G Haskell Hse.

Aproximaciones a la Literatura Hispanoamericana. Manuel Gomez-Reinoso. LC 92-73237. (Coleccion Polymita Ser.). 158p. (Orig.). (SPA.). 1993. pap. 19.00 (*0-89729-649-4*) Ediciones.

Aproximaciones al Estudio de la Literatura Hispanica. 3rd ed. Carmelo Virgilo et al. 1994. pap. text ed. write for info. (*0-07-067518-X*) McGraw.

APS, Vol. 16, 1986. 1990. 46.25 (*0-316-06179-4*) Little.

APS, Vol. 18, 1987. 1990. 46.25 (*0-316-06180-8*) Little.

APS, Vol. 19, 1987. 1990. 46.25 (*0-316-06181-6*) Little.

APS, Vol. 20, 1988. 1990. 46.25 (*0-316-06182-4*) Little.

APS, Vol. 21, 1988. 1990. 46.25 (*0-316-06183-2*) Little.

APS, Vol. 22, 1989. 1990. 46.25 (*0-316-06184-0*) Little.

APS, Vol. 23, 1989. 1990. 46.25 (*0-316-06277-4*) Little.

APS, Vol. 24, 1990. 1990. 46.25 (*0-316-06282-0*) Little.

APS, Vol. 25, 1990. 1991. 46.25 (*0-316-04804-6*) Little.

APS Stamp Identifier. American Philatelic Society Staff. 66p. 1982. pap. 2.00 (*0-933580-10-X*) Am Philatelic Society.

Apsaalooka: The Crow Nation Then & Now. rev. ed. Mickey Old Coyote & Helene Smith. Ed. by Catherine Snyder. LC 92-82527. (Illus.). 251p. (Orig.). 1993. pap. 24.95 (*0-945437-11-0*) MacDonald-Sward.

*__APSCOM '93: Proceedings on the International Conference on Advances in Power System Control, Operation & Management, 2 vols.__ 2nd ed. (Conference Publication Ser.: No. 388). 987p. 1994. pap. 264.00 (*0-85296-569-9*) Inst Elect Eng.

*__APT for Libraries 1995: Alternative Press Titles for the General Reader.__ annuals Ed. by Charles Willett. 100p. (Orig.). 1995. pap. 15.00 (*0-9640119-2-1*) Crises Press.

Apterygota to Thysanoptera see Insects of Hawaii

Aptitude - Achievement Distinction: Proceedings. Conference on Issues in Educational Measurement, 2nd, Carmel, Cal., 1974 Staff. Ed. by Donald R. Green. LC 73-20415. 1974. text ed. 9.50 (*0-07-024272-0*, 99815) McGraw.

Aptitude, Learning & Instruction Vol. 3: Cognitive & Affective Process Analysis. Ed. by Richard E. Snow & Marshall J. Farr. 384p. 1987. text ed. 59.95 (*0-89859-721-8*) L Erlbaum Assocs.

Aptitude Tests: Index of Modern Information. Bobby J. Greenhalgh. LC 88-47868. 150p. 1988. 39.50 (*0-88164-920-1*); pap. 34.50 (*0-88164-921-X*) ABBE Pubs Assn.

Aptitudes & Instructional Methods: A Handbook for Research on Interactions. Lee J. Cronbach & Richard E. Snow. LC 76-5510. (Illus.). 1981. pap. text ed. 24.95 (*0-8290-0103-4*) Irvington.

Apuleius: Concordantia in Apulei Apologiam et Florides, Vol. 1. Ed. by P. Fleury & M. Zuinghedau. (Alpha-Omega, Reihe A Ser.: Vol. LXVI). 350p. Date not set. 75.00 (*0-685-74649-6*, Pub. by Georg Olms GW) Lubrecht & Cramer.

Apuleius - Concordantia in Apulei Apologiam et Florides. Ed. by P. Fleury & M. Zuinghedau. Bd. LXVI. 350p. Date not set. write for info. (*0-318-70665-2*, Pub. by Georg Olms GW) Lubrecht & Cramer.

Apuleius & His Influence. Elizabeth H. Haight. LC 63-10290. (Our Debt to Greece & Rome Ser.). (Illus.). 190p. 1963. reprint ed. 57.00 (*0-8154-0108-6*) Cooper Sq.

Apuleius Madaurensis Metamorphoses, Bks. IV, 1-27: Text, Introduction & Commentary. B. L. Hijmans, Jr. et al. (Groningen Commentaries on Apuleius Ser.). (Illus.). xvi, 247p. 1977. 47.00 (*90-6088-059-5*, Pub. by Boumas Boekhuis NE) Benjamins North Am.

Apuleius Madaurensis Metamorphoses, Bks. VI, 25-32 & VII: Text, Introduction & Commentary. B. L. Hijmans, Jr. et al. (Groningen Commentaries on Apuleius Ser.). xv, 325p. 1981. 54.50 (*90-6088-079-X*, Pub. by Boumas Boekhuis NE) Benjamins North Am.

Apuleius Madaurensis, Metamorphoses Book VIII: Text, Introduction, Commentary. B. L. Hijmans, Jr. et al. xiv, 335p. (C). 1985. 69.00 (*90-6980-005-5*, Pub. by Egbert Forsten NE) Benjamins North Am.

Apuleius on the God of Socrates. Apuleius. Tr. by Thomas Taylor. (LAT.). 1984. reprint ed. pap. 6.95 (*0-916411-25-7*, Pub. by Alexandrian Pr) Holmes Pub.

Apuleius on Trial at Sabratha. 2nd ed. Philip Ward. (Libya Past & Present Ser.: Vol. 7). 1969. pap. 4.95 (*0-902675-09-5*) Oleander Pr.

Apuleius Philosophus Platonicus: Untersuchungen zur Apologie (De magia) und zu De Mundo. Frank Regen. (Untersuchungen zur Antiken Literatur und Geschichte Ser.: Vol. 10). 123p. (C). 1971. 54.65 (*3-11-003678-9*) De Gruyter.

Apuleius: The Metamorphoses: A Commentary on Book Three. R. T. Van der Paardt. xvi, 218p. 1971. pap. 47.00 (*90-256-0573-7*, Pub. by A M Hakkert NE) Benjamins North Am.

Apuntamientos para la Historia Natural de los Quadrupedos del Paraguay y Rio de la Plata, 2 vols. in one. Don Felix De Azara. Ed. by Keir B. Sterling. LC 77-81077. (Biologists & Their World Ser.). (SPA.). 1978. reprint ed. lib. bdg. 57.95 (*0-405-10645-9*) Ayer.

Apuntando A la Torre: Aiming at the Watch Tower. Juan A. Monroy. (SPA.). 7.25 (*84-7645-225-X*, 223314, Pub. by Edit Clie SP) TSELF.

Apuntes: Reflexiones Acerca de las Interrogantes Que Agobian Al Pueblo Latinoamericano. Alina Miyares. LC 92-62950. 80p. (Orig.). (SPA.). 1993. pap. 8.00 (*1-882573-01-3*) Serena Bay.

Apuntes Desde el Destierro. Teresa Fernandez-Soneira. LC 88-83552. (Coleccion Cuba y Sus Jueces Ser.). (Illus.). 291p. (Orig.). (SPA.). 1989. pap. 15.00 (*0-89729-520-X*) Ediciones.

Apuntes Para un Joven Responsable: Notes for Mature Youth. Jose M. Zorilla. (SPA.). 5.95 (*84-7645-509-7*, 223427, Pub. by Edit Clie SP) TSELF.

Apuros Escolares. Charles M. Schulz. (Peanuts Ser.). 64p. (SPA.). (J). 1971. 4.95 (*0-8288-4504-2*) Fr & Eur.

Apus & Incas: A Cultural Walking & Trekking Guide to Cuzco, Peru. 2nd ed. Charles Brod. Ed. by Karen Boush. LC 88-83843. (Illus.). 160p. (Orig.). 1989. pap. 10.95 (*0-9618296-1-3*) Inca Expedns.

Apu's Initiation. Rupendra Guha Majumdar. (Redbird Ser.). 45p. 1976. lib. bdg. 9.00 (*0-89253-090-1*); 4.80 (*0-89253-130-4*) Ind-US Inc.

Apvaizdos Skirtuoju Keliu. Ed. by Viktoras Rimselis. (Illus.). 47p. (LIT.). 1977. pap. write for info. (*0-933820-02-X*) Marian Fathers.

APWA Equipment Code. 7.00 (*0-917084-15-2*) Am Public Works.

APWA Paver Pavement Condition Index Field Manual, Pt. 1: For Asphalt Pavements. M. Y. Shahin & S. D. Kohn. (Illus.). 76p. 1984. pap. text ed. 15.00 (*0-917084-26-8*) Am Public Works.

APWA Paver Pavement Condition Index Field Manual, Pt. 2: For Concrete Pavements. M. Y. Shahin & S. D. Kohn. (Illus.). 72p. (Orig.). 1984. pap. text ed. 15.00 (*0-917084-30-6*) Am Public Works.

APX 286 Programmers Reference Manual see Eighty Thousand Two Hundred Eighty-Six - Eighty Thousand Two Hundred Eighty-Seven Programmers Reference Manual

AP12 Programming Techniques. Norman Thomson. 1994. 39.95 (*0-387-94213-0*) Spr-Verlag.

AP4 & Other Dinucleoside Polyphosphates. McClennan. 1992. 173.00 (*0-8493-5918-X*, QP625) CRC Pr.

Aqrarian Reform & Public Enterprise in Mexico: The Political Economy of Yucatan's Henequen Industry. Jeffrey T. Brannon & Eric N. Baklanoff. LC 85-24506. (Illus.). 264p. 1986. 37.50 (*0-8173-0282-4*) U of Ala Pr.

Aqua Aerobics: A Scientific Approach. Thomas Kinder & Julie See. 108p. 1992. pap. 14.95 (*0-945483-20-1*) E Bowers Pub.

Aqua Aerobics Today. Carole M. Casten. Ed. by Clyde Perlee. 200p. (C). 1993. pap. text ed. 20.00 (*0-314-93454-5*) West Pub.

*__Aqua Expeditions I: A Global Travel Guide for the Scuba Diver & Snorkeler.__ Wendy C. Church. 320p. 1994. pap. text ed. 24.95 (*0-9643711-0-3*) Heathcoat Pub.

Aqua Kid Saves the Day: The Good News Kids Learn about Peace. Dorothy Mock. (Good News Kids Ser.). (Illus.). 32p. (Orig.). (J). (ps-2). 1992. pap. 3.99 (*0-570-04718-8*) Concordia.

Aquablue, Bk. 1. Thierry Cailleteau & Olivier Vatine. Ed. by Mike Richardson. Tr. by Randy Lofficier & Jean-marc Lofficier. (Illus.). 48p. 1988. reprint ed. pap. 6.95 (*1-878574-00-0*) Dark Horse Comics.

Aquablue, Bk. 2: The Blue Planet. Thierry Cailleteau & Olivier Vatine. Ed. by Mike Richardson. Tr. by Randy Lofficier & Jean-Marc Lofficier. (Illus.). 48p. 1990. reprint ed. write for info. (*2-906187-30-5*); reprint ed. pap. 8.95 (*1-878574-04-3*) Dark Horse Comics.

Aquaboogie: A Novel in Stories. Susan Straight. LC 90-41192. (National Fiction Prize Ser.). 196p. (Orig.). 1990. pap. 12.95 (*0-915943-59-X*) Milkweed Ed.

Aquacises: Terri Lee's Water Workout Book. Terri Lee. 256p. 1984. spiral bd. 22.50 (*0-8359-0152-1*, Reston) P-H.

Aquacises: Terri Lee's Water Workout Book. Terri Lee. (Illus.). 240p. 1990. reprint ed. pap. text ed. 22.50 (*0-9627703-0-2*) Lee Pub AZ. 600 illustrated water exercises for muscular strength, flexibility, endurance & cardio-respiratory fitness. Full color, plastic-coated cover. Publishers Weekly --"Terri Lee's Aquacises & the benefits of exercising in the water are convincing...a complete shape-up plan which can be pursued modestly or energetically depending on one's initial fitness level...appropriate for beginning & advanced athletes, young - ages 12 & up - or old ...intelligent & worthwhile book." Booklist --"Recommended for most fitness collections." Karl G. Stoedefalke Ph.D., Fellow American College of Sports Medicine --"Aquacises is literally a pharmacopoeia of body movements to be performed in the water. Components of physical or motor fitness such as flexibility, muscle strength, or coordination are identified with each exercise. Exercises are applicable to children & adults with medically defined disabilities & can also be used by fitness-oriented swimmers in their routines...a text for everyone. Only a lifetime of teaching & experimentation could have produced this text. Terri Lee's enthusiasm for aquatics is visible throughout. Her penchant for detail is commendable, & I recommend this text as the bridge between the science & art of aquatic exercise." ***Publisher Provided Annotation.***

Aquacktic Safety. American Red Cross Staff. 1992. pap. 3.95 (*0-8016-7686-X*) Mosby Yr Bk.

*__Aquacultural Development: Social Dimensions of an Emerging Industry.__ Jentoft & Sinclair. Ed. by Bailey. (C). 1995. pap. text ed. 42.00 (*0-8133-8942-9*) Westview.

Aquacultural Engineering. Frederick W. Wheaton. LC 84-21820. 728p. (C). 1993. reprint ed. lib. bdg. 74.50 (*0-89464-786-5*) Krieger.

Aquaculture. Richard K. Miller & Terri C. Walker. LC 88-80910. (Survey on Technology & Markets Ser.: No. 27). 50p. 1989. pap. text ed. 200.00 (*1-55865-026-1*) Future Tech Surveys.

Aquaculture: A Guide to Federal Government Programs. 52p. (Orig.). (C). 1994. pap. text ed. 30.00 (*1-56806-704-6*) Diane Pub.

Aquaculture: A Review of Recent Experience. OECD Staff. (Aquaculture Ser.). 331p. (Orig.). 1989. pap. 52.50 (*92-64-13218-X*) OECD.

Aquaculture: A Source Guide. 1991. lib. bdg. 250.00 (*0-8490-4875-3*) Gordon Pr.

Aquaculture: An Introduction. J. S. Lee & M. E. Newman. (Illus.). 464p. 1992. 39.95 (*0-8134-2911-0*); teacher ed 6.95 (*0-8134-2912-9*); pap. 29.95 (*0-685-38488-8*) Interstate.

Aquaculture: Developing a New Industry. OECD Staff. 126p. (Orig.). 1989. pap. 34.00 (*92-64-13206-6*) OECD.

Aquaculture: Fundamental & Applied Research. Ed. by B. Lahlou & P. Vitiello. LC 93-38053. (Coastal & Estuarine Studies: Vol. 43). 1993. 42.00 (*0-87590-257-X*) Am Geophysical.

Aquaculture: Models & Economics. Ed. by Upton Hatch & Henry Kinnucan. LC 93-20191. 288p. (C). 1993. Acid-free paper. pap. text ed. 47.50 (*0-8133-8534-2*) Westview.

*__Aquaculture: Principles & Practices.__ 1991. pap. write for info. (*0-85238-202-2*) Blackwell Sci.

Aquaculture: The Farming & Husbandry of Freshwater & Marine Organisms. John E. Bardach et al. LC 72-2516. 868p. 1974. pap. text ed. 74.95 (*0-471-04826-7*) Wiley.

Aquaculture & the Environment. T. V. Pillay. 189p. 1992. text ed. 69.95 (*0-470-21849-5*) Halsted Pr.

Aquaculture & Water Quality. Ed. by David E. Brune & Joseph R. Tomasso. (Advances in World Aquaculture Ser.: Vol. 3). (Illus.). 606p. (C). 1991. text ed. 60.00 (*0-9624529-2-0*) World Aquaculture.

Aquaculture Audio-Visual Films Catalog. Lee Emery. 12p. 1982. pap. 3.50 (*0-913235-17-2*) Am Fisheries Soc.

Aquaculture Development: Progress & Prospects. T. V. R. Pillay. LC 94-16593. 1994. 59.95 (*0-470-23432-6*) Halsted Pr.

Aquaculture Economic Analysis: An Introduction. Yung C. Shang. (Advances in World Aquaculture Ser.: Vol. 2). (Illus.). 211p. (C). 1990. text ed. 50.00 (*0-9624529-1-2*) World Aquaculture.

Aquaculture Engineering: Technologies for the Future. Mike Walker. (European Federation of Chemical Engineering Ser.). 350p. 1989. 172.00 (*0-89116-945-8*) Hemisp Pub.

Aquaculture for Veterinarians: Fish Husbandry & Medicine. Ed. by Lydia Brown. LC 92-41237. 1993. text ed. 136.00 (*0-08-040835-4*, Pergamon Pr); pap. text ed. 70.00 (*0-08-040836-2*, Pergamon Pr) Elsevier.

Aquaculture in Alaska: A Resource Potential. write for info. (*0-914500-03-1*) U of AK Inst Marine.

Aquaculture in Asia. Ed. by I Cjiu Liao et al. 102p. 1993. pap. 15.00 (*92-833-2122-7*, APO1227, Pub. by Asian Prod Organ) UNIPUB.

Aquaculture in Southeast Asia: A Historical Overview. Shao-Wen Ling. Ed. by Laura Mumaw. LC 77-3828. (Washington Sea Grant Ser.). (Illus.). 108p. 1977. pap. 10.00 (*0-295-95563-5*) U of Wash Pr.

Aquaculture in Taiwan. Lo Chai Chen. (Illus.). 273p. 1990. 65.00 (*0-85238-165-4*) Blackwell Sci.

Aquaculture Management. Meade. 1989. text ed. 60.95 (*0-442-20570-8*) Chapman & Hall.

Aquaculture Manual. R. Creswell. 1992. text ed. 39.95 (*0-442-01081-8*) Chapman & Hall.

Aquaculture of Milkfish Chanos Chanos: State of the Art. Cheng-Sheng Lee et al. (Illus.). 284p. (Orig.). 1986. pap. write for info. (*0-9617016-0-9*) Oceanic Inst.

Aquaculture of Striped Bass. Ed. by Joseph P. McCraren. 6.50 (*0-943676-16-9*) MD Sea Grant Col.

Aquaculture Practices in Taiwan. T. P. Chen. 1978. 100.00 (*0-685-63392-6*) St Mut.

Aquaculture Productivity. V. R. Sinha. 1991. 50.00 (*81-204-0559-5*, Pub. by Oxford IBH II) S Asia.

Aquaculture Project Formulation. David Insull & Colin E. Nash. (Fisheries Technical Papers: No. 316). 140p. 1991. pap. 17.00 (*92-5-103019-7*, F0197) UNIPUB.

Aquaculture Research Needs for Two Thousand. (Illus.). 430p. (C). 1992. text ed. 85.00 (*90-5410-215-2*, Pub. by A A Balkema NE) Ashgate Pub Co.

*__Aquaculture Science.__ Rick Parker. LC 94-34435. 672p. 1995. 33.95 (*0-8273-6454-7*) Delmar.

An Asterisk (*) at the beginning of an entry indicates that the title is appearing in BIP for the first time.

***Aquaculture Science.** 2nd abr. rev. ed. Vaughn Parker. 384p. 1995. text ed. 62.50 (*0-8273-6976-X*) Delmar.

Aquaculture Sourcebook: A Guide to North American Species. Edwin S. Iversen & Kay K. Hale. LC 92-12536. 1992. text ed. 49.95 (*0-442-00992-5*) Chapman & Hall.

Aquaculture Systems Engineering. LC 91-61892. 138p. 1991. 31.00 (*0-929355-14-8*) Am Soc Ag Eng.

Aquaculture Systems Modeling. M. L. Cuenco. 1989. pap. 5.25 (*971-10-2277-X*, Pub. by ICLARM PH) Intl Spec Bk.

Aquaculture Training Manual. 2nd ed. Donald R. Swift. (Illus.). 176p. 1993. pap. 29.95 (*0-85238-194-8*) Blackwell Sci.

***Aquaculture Water Reuse Systems: Engineering Design & Management.** Ed. by Michael B. Timmons & Thomas M. Losordo. LC 94-31158. (Developments in Aquaculture & Fisheries Science Ser.: 27). 1994. write for info. (*0-444-89585-X*) Elsevier.

Aquaculturists' Guide to Harmful Australian Microalgae. Gustaaf M. Hallegraeff. 111p. Date not set. pap. 30.00 (*0-643-05184-8*, Pub. by CSIRO AT) Intl Spec Bk.

Aquaerobics Sr. Easy Pool Exercises for Seniors. Dorothy V. Kelly. Ed. by Alina Nguyen & Judith Powell. LC 93-17459. (Illus.). 160p. (Orig.). 1993. pap. 12.95 (*1-56087-039-7*) Top Mtn Pub.

Aquamancer. Don Callander. 304p. (Orig.). 1993. mass mkt. 4.99 (*0-441-02816-0*) Ace Bks.

Aquamarine. Carol Anshaw. 1993. pap. 10.00 (*0-671-79586-4*, WSP) PB.

Aquametry: A Treatise on Methods for the Determination of Water, Pt. 1. John Mitchell & Donald M. Smith. LC 77-518. (Chemical Analysis Ser.: Vol. 5). 646p. reprint ed. pap. 180.00 (*0-7837-2402-0*, 2040087) Bks Demand.

Aquarelle. Lois Breumer. 95p. (C). 1990. 90.00 (*0-86439-121-8*, Pub. by Boolarong Pubns AT) St Mut.

Aquarian Age Healing: From Bio-Mechanics to Bio-Engineering, 2 vols., Set. J. Hurley & H. Sanders. (Alternative Medicine Ser.). 1991. lib. bdg. 175.95 (*0-8490-4534-7*) Gordon Pr.

Aquarian-Age Healing, Bk. 2: Bio-Engineering. John Hurley & Helen Sanders. 340p. 1970. reprint ed. spiral bd. 19.25 (*0-7873-1116-2*) Mokelumne.

Aquarian Age Philosophy. E. Doane. 128p. 1969. 7.00 (*0-86690-078-0*, D1075-014) Am Fed Astrologers.

Aquarian Anastasis. Lew P. Price. LC 65-9503. 1975. pap. 15.00 (*0-917578-01-5*) L Paxton Price.

Aquarian Book of Change. Patricia E. West. LC 81-90541. (Illus.). 178p. (gr. 8-12). 1982. pap. 4.50 (*0-942384-00-8*) Red Dragon.

Aquarian Conspiracy: Personal & Social Transformation in Our Time. rev. ed. Marilyn Ferguson. 464p. 1987. pap. 14.95 (*0-87477-458-6*) J P Tarcher.

Aquarian Gospel of Jesus Christ. Levi. 1972. 18.95 (*0-87516-041-7*); pap. 14.95 (*0-87516-168-5*) DeVorss.

Aquarian Guide to African Mythology. Jan Knappert. 1991. pap. 14.00 (*0-85030-885-2*, Pub. by Aquarian Pr UK) Thorsons SF.

Aquarian Guide to Native American Mythology. Page Bryant. (Illus.). 224p. 1991. pap. 13.95 (*1-85538-028-5*, Pub. by Aquarian Pr UK) Thorsons SF.

***Aquarian Revelation Vol. 1: Into the 4th Dimension.** Jeremiah. 500p. (Orig.). 1995. pap. 15.95 (*0-9639053-4-1*) Univ Truth Pr.

***Aquarian Revelation Vol. 2: Becoming One with God.** Jeremiah. 425p. (Orig.). Date not set. pap. 15.95 (*0-9639053-5-X*) Univ Truth Pr.

Aquarian Rosary: Reviving the Art of Mantra Yoga. Carol W. Parrish-Harra. LC 87-63437. (Illus.). 136p. 1988. pap. 8.95 (*0-945027-01-X*) Sparrow Hawk Pr.

Aquarian Runes. Zera Starchild. 104p. (Orig.). 1993. 15.00 (*0-9632970-2-3*) Doorway.

Aquarian Tarot. David Palladini. 16p. 1970. 12.95 (*0-913866-69-5*) US Games Syst.

Aquarian Tarot Deck-Book Set. David Palladini & Craig Junjulas. (Illus.). 126p. 1985. 23.95 (*0-88079-592-1*) US Games Syst.

Aquarium. (Colorguide Ser.). 1982. pap. 6.95 (*0-940842-05-X*) South Group.

Aquarium: Bringing the Seas Inside. Linda C. Riley. LC 93-16341. (Illus.). (J). (gr. 3 up). 1995. text ed. 17.95 (*0-7167-6509-8*, Sci Am Yng Rdrs) W H Freeman.

Aquarium Atlas. Rudiger Riehl & Hans Baensch. (Illus.). 994p. 39.95 (*3-88244-050-3*, 16050) Tetra Pr.

Aquarium Atlas 2. Hans A. Baensch. (Illus.). 1216p. 1993. 49.95 (*1-56465-114-2*, 16821) Tetra Pr.

Aquarium Book. George Ancona. (Illus.). 48p. (J). (gr. 3-6). 1991. 15.95 (*0-89919-655-1*, Clarion Bks) HM.

***Aquarium Book.** George Ancona. (J). (gr. 3-6). 1994. pap. 6.95 (*0-395-69940-1*, Clarion Bks) HM.

Aquarium Creatures. Kaye Quinn. (Facts 'n Fun Ser.). 80p. (Orig.). (J). 1991. pap. 2.95 (*0-8431-2719-8*) Price Stern.

Aquarium Encyclopedia. Ed. by Gunther Sterba. (Illus.). 608p. 1983. 45.00x (*0-262-19207-1*) MIT Pr.

Aquarium Fish. U. Erich Friese. (Illus.). 96p. 1989. 9.95 (*0-86622-766-0*, KW-026) TFH Pubns.

Aquarium Fish. Burkard Kahl. (Mini Fact Finders Ser.). 64p. 1990. pap. 4.95 (*0-8120-4447-9*) Barron.

Aquarium Fish. Dick Mills. LC 93-3155. (Eyewitness Handbks.). (Illus.). 304p. 1993. 29.95 (*1-56458-294-9*); Flexibinding. 17.95 (*1-56458-293-0*) Dorling Kindersley.

Aquarium Fish of the World: Natural Sciences of the World. Ivan Petrovicky. (Illus.). 500p. 1989. 22.99 (*0-517-67903-5*) Random Hse Value.

Aquarium Fish of the World: The Comprehensive Guide to 800 Species. Atsushi Sakurai. (Illus.). 296p. 1992. 29.95 (*0-8118-0269-8*) Chronicle Bks.

Aquarium Fish Survival Manual. Brian Ward. (Illus.). 176p. 1985. 23.95 (*0-8120-5686-8*) Barron.

Aquarium Keeping...Easy As ABC. Werner Weiss. Ed. by Herbert R. Axelrod. Tr. by Christa Ahrens. (Illus.). 112p. reprint ed. 14.95 (*0-86622-100-X*, PS-831) TFH Pubns.

Aquarium of Women. Bjorg Vik. Tr. by Janet Garton. LC 88-60362. 108p. 1988. pap. 16.95 (*0-317-67956-2*, Pub. by Norvik Pr UK) Dufour.

Aquarium of Women. Bjorg Vik. 1987. pap. 17.95 (*1-870041-04-6*) Dufour.

Aquarium Plants. Gerhard Brunner. Tr. by Gwynne Vevers. 1973. 29.95 (*0-87666-455-9*, H-966) TFH Pubns.

Aquarium Plants. Burkard Kahl. (Mini Fact Finders Ser.). 64p. 1992. pap. 4.95 (*0-8120-4707-9*) Barron.

Aquarium Plants Manual. Ines Scheurmann. 96p. 1993. pap. 5.95 (*0-8120-1687-4*) Barron.

Aquarium Take-Along Book. Sheldon L. Gerstenfeld. LC 93-23059. (Illus.). 128p. (J). (gr. 2-5). 1994. 14.99 (*0-670-84386-5*) Viking Child Bks.

Aquarium Take-along Book. Sheldon L. Gerstenfeld. (Illus.). 128p. (J). (gr. 2-5). 1994. pap. 5.99 (*0-14-036019-0*) Puffin Bks.

Aquariums. Wolfgang Ostermoller. (Illus.). 80p. 1984. pap. 5.95 (*0-86622-144-1*, PB-101) TFH Pubns.

Aquariums: Look & Learn. Herbert R. Axelrod. (Illus.). 64p. 1993. 7.95 (*0-7938-0070-6*, KD017) TFH Pubns.

Aquariums & Terrariums. Ray Broekel. LC 82-4428. (New True Bks.). (J). (gr. k-4). 1982. lib. bdg. 13.50 (*0-516-01660-1*) Childrens.

Aquariums for Those Who Care. Herbert Axelrod. (Illus.). 32p. 1994. pap. 3.95 (*0-7938-1375-1*, B101) TFH Pubns.

Aquariums for Your New Pet. Mary Sweeney. (Illus.). 64p. (Orig.). 1990. pap. 5.95 (*0-86622-624-9*, TU-016) TFH Pubns.

Aquariums of North America: A Guidebook to Appreciating North America's Aquatic Treasures. James M. Hillard. LC 94-18440. 199p. 1995. 27.50 (*0-8108-2923-1*) Scarecrow.

***Aquarius.** 272p. (Orig.). Date not set. pap. text ed. 6.50 (*0-515-11689-0*) Jove Pubns.

***Aquarius.** 208p. (Orig.). 1995. pap. text ed. 4.50 (*0-425-14896-3*) Berkley Pub.

***Aquarius.** 256p. (Orig.). 1995. pap. text ed. 4.99 (*0-425-14912-9*) Berkley Pub.

Aquarius. Astrology World Staff. (Day by Day Horoscopes, 1995 Ser.). 208p. (Orig.). 1994. pap. text ed. 3.99 (*0-425-15820-9*) Berkley Pub.

Aquarius. Lucille Callard. (Astro-Pups: Your Sign, Your Dogs Ser.). (Illus.). 60p. 1991. pap. 9.95 (*1-881038-10-6*) Penzance Pr.

Aquarius. James A. Lely. (Sun Sign Ser.). 40p. (J). (gr. 4). 1989. lib. bdg. 13.95 (*0-88682-258-0*) Creative Ed.

Aquarius. Sylvia J. Michaelson. (Illus.). 1987. pap. 3.00 (*0-9617005-2-1*) Ministering Angel.

Aquarius. Derek Parker & Julia Parker. LC 92-52794. (Sun & Moon Signs Library). (Illus.). 64p. 1992. 8.95 (*1-56458-094-6*) Dorling Kindersley.

Aquarius: A Coming of Age. Dianthus. LC 88-90502. 128p. (Orig.). 1991. pap. 8.75 (*0-9622160-0-3*) Dianthus.

Aquarius: Astro-Numerology. 2nd ed. Michael J. Kurban. 50p. 1991. pap. 8.00 (*0-938863-19-3*) Libra Press Chi.

Aquarius: Little Birth Sign. Andrews & McMeel. 1994. 4.95 (*0-8362-3069-8*) Andrews & McMeel.

Aquarius: The Artful Astrologer. Lee Holloway. 1993. 4.99 (*0-517-08260-8*) Random Hse Value.

Aquarius: Through the Numbers. Paul Rice & Valeta Rice. 64p. 1983. pap. 3.95 (*0-87728-575-6*) Weiser.

Aquarius Revisited: Seven Who Created the Sixties Counterculture That Changed America. Peter O. Whitmer. 1991. pap. 10.95 (*0-8065-1222-9*, Citadel Pr) Carol Pub Group.

Aquarius Transfer. Robert F. Joseph. 288p. 1982. pap. 2.95 (*0-449-14467-4*, GM) Fawcett.

Aquarius, 1987. Sydney Omarr. 1987. pap. 2.95 (*0-317-47657-2*, Sig) NAL-Dutton.

Aquascape, Vol. II. (Illus.). 224p. 1994. 89.95 (*4-89331-719-9*, Pub. by Process Archit JA) Bks Nippan.

Aquatecture: Architecture & Water. Anthony Wylson. (Illus.). 216p. 1986. 69.95 (*0-85139-727-1*) Buttrwrth-Heinemann.

Aquatic Activities Handbook. Sova. (Fitness & Health Ser.). 224p. (C). 1992. pap. text ed. 21.25 (*0-86720-280-7*) Jones & Bartlett.

Aquatic Adephaga (Coleoptera) of Fennoscandia & Denmark, Pt. 1: Gyrinidae, Haliplidae, Hygrbiidae & Noteridae. Modens Holmen. (Fauna Entomologica Scandinavica Ser.: No. 20). (Illus.). 173p. 1987. text ed. 45.00 (*90-04-08185-2*) Lubrecht & Cramer.

Aquatic & Wetland Plants of Southeastern United States: Dicotyledons. Robert K. Godfrey & Jean W. Wooten. LC 80-16452. (Illus.). 944p. 1981. 45.00 (*0-8203-0532-4*) U of Ga Pr.

Aquatic & Wetland Plants of Southeastern United States: Monocotyledons. Robert K. Godfrey & Jean W. Wooten. LC 76-2894. (Illus.). 736p. 1979. 40.00 (*0-8203-0420-4*) U of Ga Pr.

Aquatic Animals in the Wild & in Captivity. Patricia Curtis. (Illus.). 64p. (J). (gr. 3-8). 1992. 16.00 (*0-525-67384-9*, Lodestar Bks) Dutton Child Bks.

Aquatic Applications of Ozone. 28.00 (*0-317-07460-1*) Pan Am Intl Ozone.

Aquatic Beetle Subfamily Larainae (Coleoptera: Elmidae) in Mexico, Central America, & the West Indies. Paul J. Spangler & Silvia Santiago-Fragoso. LC 92-5590. (Smithsonian Contributions to Zoology Ser.: No. 528). (Illus.). 80p. reprint ed. pap. 25.00 (*0-7837-3405-0*, 2043365) Bks Demand.

Aquatic Bioenvironmental Studies: The Hanford Experience, 1944-1984. Ed. by C. D. Becker. (Studies in Environmental Science: No. 39). 350p. 1990. 114.50 (*0-444-88653-2*) Elsevier.

Aquatic Biology & Hydroelectric Power Development in New Zealand. Ed. by Paul R. Henriques. 288p. 1987. 65.00 (*0-19-558145-8*) OUP.

Aquatic Biotechnology & Food Safety. OECD Staff. 100p. (Orig.). 1994. pap. 18.00 (*92-64-14063-8*) OECD.

Aquatic Birds in the Trophic Web of Lakes: Proceedings of a Symposium Held in Sackville, New Brunswick, Canada, in August 1991. Ed. by JosephJ. Kerekes. LC 94-1387. 1994. lib. bdg. 257.00 (*0-7923-2751-9*) Kluwer Ac.

Aquatic Chemical Kinetics: Reaction Rates of Processes in Natural Waters. Ed. by Werner Stumm. (Environmental Science & Technology Ser.). 1990. text ed. 110.00 (*0-471-51029-7*) Wiley.

Aquatic Chemistry: An Introduction Emphasizing Chemical Equilibria in Natural Waters. 2nd ed. Werner Stumm & James J. Morgan. 1981. pap. text ed. 67.95 (*0-471-09173-1*) Wiley.

***Aquatic Chemistry: Interfacial & Interspecies Processes.** Ed. by C. P. Huang et al. LC 94-41862. (Advances in Chemistry Ser.: No. 244). (Illus.). 500p. 1994. 124.95 (*0-8412-2921-X*) Am Chemical.

Aquatic Chemistry Concepts. James F. Pankow. 1000p. 1991. 69.95 (*0-87371-150-5*, GB855) Lewis Pubs.

Aquatic Chemistry Problems. James F. Pankow. (Illus.). 500p. (Orig.). 1992. pap. 34.95 (*0-9627452-3-5*) Titan Pr OR.

Aquatic Ecosystems: An Operational Research Approach. Jan E. Beyer. LC 79-57217. (Illus.). 328p. 1981. 25.00 (*0-295-95719-0*) U of Wash Pr.

Aquatic Ecotoxicology: Fundamental Concepts & Methodologies, 2 Vols., Vol. I. Ed. by Alain Boudou & Francis Ribeyre. 320p. 1989. 228.00 (*0-8493-4828-5*, QH541) CRC Pr.

Aquatic Ecotoxicology: Fundamental Concepts & Methodologies, 2 Vols., Vol. II. Ed. by Alain Boudou & Francis Ribeyre. 272p. 1989. 228.00 (*0-8493-4829-3*, QH541) CRC Pr.

Aquatic Entomology: The Fisherman's & Ecologists Illustrated Guide to Insects & Their Relatives. W. Patrick McCafferty. (Illus.). 448p. (C). 1982. pap. 50.00 (*0-86720-017-0*) Jones & Bartlett.

Aquatic Entomology: The Fisherman's & Ecologists Illustrated Guide to Insects & Their Relatives. deluxe ed. W. Patrick McCafferty. (Illus.). 448p. (C). 1982. 300.00 (*0-86720-010-3*) Jones & Bartlett.

Aquatic Exercise. Sova. (Fitness & Health Ser.). 128p. (C). 1992. pap. text ed. 9.95 (*0-86720-754-X*) Jones & Bartlett.

Aquatic Fitness Everyone. Elder. 1993. pap. text ed. 18.95 (*0-88725-190-0*) Hunter Textbks.

***Aquatic Habitats: Hands on Elementary School Science.** Linda Poore. 38p. 1994. teacher ed 35.00 (*1-883410-03-7*) L Poore.

Aquatic Humic Substances: Influence on Fate & Treatment of Pollution. Ed. by I. H. Suffet & Patrick MacCarthy. LC 88-38029. (Advances in Chemistry Ser.: No. 219). (Illus.). ix, 844p. 1989. 109.95 (*0-8412-1428-X*) Am Chemical.

Aquatic Injuries: Evaluation & Strategy. Ronald R. Gilbert. LC 89-18414. (ATLA Monograph Ser.). 54p. (Orig.). 1990. pap. 14.00 (*0-941916-56-1*) ATLA Pr.

Aquatic Insect Ecology, Pt. 1: Biology & Habitat. J. V. Ward. 456p. 1991. text ed. 89.95 (*0-471-55007-8*) Wiley.

Aquatic Insects. Dennis Lehmkuhl et al. (Pictured Key Nature Ser.). 180p. (C). 1979. spiral bd. write for info. (*0-697-04767-9*) Wm C Brown Pubs.

Aquatic Insects. D. Williams & B. Feltmate. 360p. 1992. 46.50 (*0-85198-782-6*) CAB Intl.

Aquatic Insects of California, with Keys to North American Genera & California Species. Ed. by Robert L. Usinger. (Illus.). 1956. 60.00 (*0-520-01293-3*) U CA Pr.

Aquatic Insects of North America. 2nd ed. Richard W. Merritt & Kenneth W. Cummins. 768p. (C). 1995. pap. text ed. 69.95 (*0-8403-7588-3*) Kendall-Hunt.

Aquatic Invertebrate Bioassays- STP 715. Ed. by Buikema, Jr. & Cairns, Jr. 218p. 1980. 24.00 (*0-8031-0802-8*, 04-715000-16) ASTM.

Aquatic Life. LC 92-25074. (Understanding Science & Nature Ser.). 176p. (J). 1993. 18.60 (*0-8094-9679-8*); lib. bdg. 24.60 (*0-8094-9680-1*) Time-Life.

Aquatic Life in the John G. Shedd Aquarium: A Guide to Exhibit Animals. Nora L. Deans. (Illus.). 272p. (Orig.). 1983. pap. 6.95 (*0-9611074-0-5*) Shedd Aquarium.

Aquatic Mecocosm Studies in Ecological Risk Assessment. Graney. 1993. 95.00 (*0-87371-592-6*, QH541) Lewis Pubs.

Aquatic Microbial Ecology: Biochemical & Molecular Approaches. Ed. by Jurgen Overbeck et al. (Contemporary Bioscience Ser.). 224p. 1990. 49.00 (*0-387-97222-6*) Spr-Verlag.

Aquatic Microbial Ecology: Proceedings of the ASM Conference. Ed. by Rita R. Colwell & J. Foster. pap. 4.95 (*0-943676-07-X*) MD Sea Grant Col.

Aquatic Microbiology. Ed. by Frederick A. Skinner & M. J. Shewan. (Society of Applied Bacteriology Symposia Ser.: No. 6). 1978. text ed. 163.00 (*0-12-648030-3*) Acad Pr.

Aquatic Microbiology. 4th ed. G. Rheinheimer. 363p. 1991. text ed. 99.95 (*0-471-92695-7*, Wiley-Liss) Wiley.

Aquatic Microbiology: An Ecological Approach. Timothy E. Ford. (Illus.). 544p. 1993. 49.95 (*0-86542-225-7*) Blackwell Sci.

Aquatic Oligochaeta. Ed. by G. Bonomi & C. Erseus. (Developments in Hydrobiology Ser.). 1984. lib. bdg. 152.50 (*90-6193-775-2*) Kluwer Ac.

Aquatic Oligochaeta. Ed. by R. O. Brinkhorst & R. J. Diaz. (Developments in Hydrobiology Ser.). (C). 1988. lib. bdg. 132.00 (*0-317-66657-6*) Kluwer Ac.

Aquatic Oligochaete Biology: Proceedings of the 4th International Symposium on Aquatic Oligochaete Biology. Ed. by J. L. Caster. (Developments in Hydrobiology Ser.). 264p. (C). 1989. reprint ed. lib. bdg. 175.50 (*0-7923-0283-4*) Kluwer Ac.

Aquatic Oligochaete Biology V: Proceedings of the 5th Symposium, Held in Tallinn, Estonia, 1991. Ed. by T. B. Reynoldson & K. A. Coates. LC 93-47117. (Developments in Hydrobiology Ser.). 328p. (C). 1994. lib. bdg. 185.50 (*0-7923-2686-5*) Kluwer Ac.

Aquatic Organisms As Indicators of Environmental Pollution. Ed. by Joan A. Browder. (American Water Resources Association Monograph Ser.: No. 12). (Illus.). 94p. reprint ed. pap. 26.80 (*0-8357-3161-8*, 2039424) Bks Demand.

Aquatic Organization & Management. John A. Torney, Jr. & Robert D. Clayton. 190p. 1981. pap. text ed. write for info. (*0-8087-3624-8*) Macmillan.

Aquatic Plant Book. C. D. Cook. (Illus.). 228p. 1990. pap. 65.00 (*90-5103-043-6*, Pub. by SPB Acad Pub NE) Koeltz Sci Bks.

Aquatic Plants. 2nd ed. G. W. Prescott et al. (Pictured Key Nature Ser.). 176p. (C). 1979. spiral bd. write for info. (*0-697-04775-X*) Wm C Brown Pubs.

Aquatic Plants for Water Treatment & Resource Recovery. Ed. by K. R. Reddy & W. H. Smith. LC 87-61397. (Illus.). 1088p. 1987. 140.00 (*0-941463-00-1*) Magnolia FL.

Aquatic Plants of Illinois. rev. ed. Glen S. Winterringer & Alvin C. Lopinot. (Popular Science Ser.: Vol. VI). (Illus.). 142p. 1977. pap. 6.00 (*0-89792-068-6*) Ill St Museum.

Aquatic Pollutants & Biologic Effects with Emphasis on Neoplasia, Vol. 298. Ed. by H. F. Kraybill et al. (Annals Ser.). 604p. 1977. 54.00 (*0-89072-044-4*) NY Acad Sci.

Aquatic Pollutants Transformation & Bio Effects: Proceedings 2nd International Symposium Aquatic Pollutants, Netherlands 9-77. O. Hutzinger & I. Lelyveld. LC 77-30670. (Pergamon Series on Environmental Science). 1978. 220.00 (*0-08-022059-2*, Pub. by Pergamon Repr UK) Franklin.

Aquatic Pollution. Edward A. Laws. (Illus.). 496p. (C). reprint ed. text ed. 60.00 (*1-878907-09-3*, RAN) TechBooks.

Aquatic Pollution: An Introductory Text. 2nd ed. Edward S. Laws. LC 92-26501. (Environmental Science & Technology: A Wiley-Interscience Series of Texts & Monographs). 611p. 1993. pap. text ed. 64.95 (*0-471-58883-0*, Wiley-Interscience) Wiley.

Aquatic Readiness: Developing Water Competence in Young Children. Stephen J. Langendorfer & Lawrence D. Bruya. LC 93-42159. (Illus.). 224p. 1995. pap. text ed. 28.00 (*0-87322-663-1*, BLAN0663) Human Kinetics.

Aquatic Sciences. Ed. by John C. Baiardi & George D. Ruggieri. (Annals Ser.: Vol. 245). 70p. 1974. 17.00 (*0-89072-759-7*) NY Acad Sci.

Aquatic Snails of the Family Hydrobiidae of Peninsular Florida. Fred G. Thompson. LC 68-9707. 284p. reprint ed. pap. 81.00 (*0-7837-5832-4*, 2045551) Bks Demand.

Aquatic Surface Chemistry: Chemical Processes at the Particle-Water Interface. Ed. by Werner Stumm. LC 86-28078. (Environmental Science & Technology: A Wiley-Interscience Series of Texts & Monographs). 544p. 1987. text ed. 105.00 (*0-471-82995-1*, Wiley-Interscience) Wiley.

Aquatic Therapy: Various Uses & Techniques. Roxane L. McNeal. (Illus.). 134p. 1988. pap. 39.95 (*0-685-27210-9*) Aquatic Therapy.

***Aquatic Therapy Using PNF Patterns.** Lynette Jamison & David Ogden. (Illus.). 160p. 1994. pap. text ed. 39.00 (*0-88450-035-7*, 4345) Commun Skill.

Aquatic Therapy; Various Uses & Techniques: Patient Manual. Roxane L. McNeal. (Illus.). 56p. 1988. pap. text ed. 11.95 (*0-685-27211-7*) Aquatic Therapy.

Aquatic Toxicology, Vol. 2. Ed. by Lavern J. Weber. 240p. 1984. text ed. 86.00 (*0-89004-927-0*) Raven.

Aquatic Toxicology: Molecular, Biochemical, & Cellular Perspectives. Ed. by Donald C. Malins & Gary K. Ostrander. LC 93-6117. 512p. 1993. 60.00 (*0-87371-545-4*, QH90) Lewis Pubs.

Aquatic Toxicology: 2nd Conference- STP 667. Ed. by L. L. Marking & R. A. Kimerke. 403p. 1979. 37.75 (*0-8031-0279-8*, 667, 04-667000-16) ASTM.

Aquatic Toxicology: 3rd Conference- STP 707. Ed. by J. G. Eaton et al. 417p. 1980. 39.50 (*0-8031-0280-1*, 707, 04-707000-16) ASTM.

***Aquatic Toxicology Vol. 1.** fac. ed. Ed. by Lavern J. Weber. LC 81-23474. (Illus.). 237p. Date not set. pap. 67.60 (*0-7837-7143-6*, 2047151) Bks Demand.

Aquatic Toxicology & Environmental Fate, Vol. 9. Ed. by Ted M. Poston & Rich Purdy. LC 86-14648. (Special Technical Publication Ser.: No. 921). (Illus.). x, 535p. 1986. text ed. 64.00 (*0-8031-0489-8*, 04-921000-16) ASTM.

Aquatic Toxicology & Environmental Fate, Vol. 11. Ed. by Glen W. Suter, II & Michael A. Lewis. (Special Technical Publication Ser.: No. STP 1007). (Illus.). 610p. 1989. text ed. 74.00 (*0-8031-1180-0*) ASTM.

Aquatic Toxicology & Hazard Assessment, Vol. 12. Ed. by U. M. Cowgill & L. R. Williams. (Special Technical Publication Ser.: No. STP 1027). (Illus.). 445p. 1989. text ed. 65.00 (*0-8031-1253-X*, 04-010270-48) ASTM.

Aquatic Toxicology & Hazard Assessment: Eighth Symposium STP 891. Ed. by Rita Bahner et al. LC 85-23014. (Illus.). 485p. 1985. text ed. 52.00 (*0-8031-0437-5*, 04-891000-16) ASTM.

Aquatic Toxicology & Hazard Assessment: Seventh Symposium- STP 854. Ed. by Rick D. Cardwell et al. LC 84-70338. (Illus.). 590p. 1985. text ed. 60.00 (*0-8031-0410-3*, 04-854000-16) ASTM.

A

An Asterisk (*) at the beginning of an entry indicates that the title is appearing in BIP for the first time. 399

A

Aquatic Toxicology & Hazard Assessment - STP 802: Sixth Symposium. Ed. by W. E. Bishop et al. LC 82-73772. 560p. 1983. text ed. 59.00 (*0-8031-0255-0*, 04-802000-16) ASTM.

Aquatic Toxicology & Hazard Assessment (Fifth Conference)- STP 766. Ed. by Pearson et al. 414p. 1982. 44.50 (*0-8031-0796-X*, 04-766000-16) ASTM.

Aquatic Toxicology & Hazard Assessment (Fourth Conference)- STP 737. Ed. by D. R. Branson & K. L. Dickson. 466p. 1981. 43.00 (*0-8031-0799-4*, 04-737000-16) ASTM.

Aquatic Toxicology & Hazard Assessment, Vol. 10: STP 971. Ed. by William J. Adams et al. (Special Technical Publication Ser.). (Illus.). 960p. 1988. text ed. 64.00 (*0-8031-0978-4*, 04-971000-16) ASTM.

Aquatic Toxicology & Hazard Evaluation: First Conference- STP 634. Ed. by F. L. Mayer & J. L. Hamelink. 315p. 1977. 30.75 (*0-8031-0278-X*, 04-634000-16) ASTM.

Aquatic Toxicology & Risk Assessment, Vol. 13. Ed. by W. G. Landis & W. H. Van der Schalie. (Special Technical Publication Ser.: No. 1096). (Illus.). 380p. 1990. text ed. 86.00 (*0-8031-1460-5*, 04-010960-16) ASTM.

Aquatic Toxicology & Risk Assessment: Fourteenth Volume. Ed. by M. A. Mayes & M. G. Barrow. (Special Technical Publication Ser.: No. 1124). (Illus.). 385p. 1992. text ed. 89.00 (*0-8031-1425-7*, 04-011240-16) ASTM.

Aquatic Toxicology & Water Quality Management. Ed. by Jerome O. Nriagu & J. S. Lakshminarayana. LC 88-7282. (Advances in Environmental Science & Technology Ser.). 292p. 1989. text ed. 135.00 (*0-471-61551-X*) Wiley.

Aquatic Weed Management: Their Menace & Control. 2nd rev. ed. O. P. Gupta. (Illus.). 272p. 1987. 59.00 (*1-55528-148-6*, Messers Today & Tomorrow) Scholarly Pubns.

Aquatic Weeds: The Ecology & Management of Nuisance Aquatic Vegetation. Arnold H. Pieterse & Kevin J. Murphy. (Illus.). 616p. 1994. reprint ed. pap. 49.95 (*0-19-854840-0*) OUP.

Aquatic Weeds of North-East Region of India. M. M. Islam. 1989. 100.00 (*81-7089-099-3*, Pub. by Intl Bk Distr II) St Mut.

Aquatic Weeds of North-East Region of India. M. M. Islam. 163p. (C). 1989. 150.00 (*0-685-61471-9*, Pub. by Intl Bk Distr II) St Mut.

Aquatics. Sova. (Fitness & Health Ser.). 1991. boxed, text ed. 45.00 (*0-86720-184-3*) Jones & Bartlett.

Aquatics: A Revived Approach to Pediatric Management. Ed. by Faye H. Dulcy. LC 83-85. (Physical & Occupational Therapy in Pediatrics Ser.: Vol. 3, No. 1). 92p. 1983. text ed. 24.95 (*0-86656-215-X*) Haworth Pr.

Aquatics for All: The Next Quarter Century, 1976-CNCA 19th National Aquatic Conference, Urbana-Champaign, IL. Council for National Cooperation in Aquatics Staff. Ed. by Bernard E. Empleton. (Illus.). 116p. reprint ed. pap. 33.10 (*0-8357-3834-5*, 2036559) Bks Demand.

Aquatics for Special Populations. YMCA of the U. S. A. Staff. LC 86-28288. 168p. (Orig.). 1987. pap. text ed. 19.00x (*0-87322-097-8*, LYMC4880, YMCA USA) Human Kinetics.

Aquatics in the Eighty's: The Conservation, Education, & Research: CNCA 21st National Aquatic Conference, November 20-23, 1980, Atlanta Biltmore Hotel, Georgia Institute of Technology. Council for National Cooperation in Aquatics Staff. Ed. by E. Louise Priest. (Illus.). 164p. reprint ed. pap. 46.80 (*0-8357-3836-1*, 2036561) Bks Demand.

***Aquavideo: Locating Underground Water.** Cameron Verne L. & Bill Cox. (Illus.). 116p. 1970. pap. 8.95 (*0-88234-009-3*) Life Understanding.

Aquavideo: Locating Underground Water, a Complete Dowsing Method by the World Renowned Master. Verne L. Cameron. Ed. by Bill Cox. LC 77-139236. (Illus.). 116p. 1970. pap. 7.95 (*0-88234-005-0*) Life Understanding.

Aqueduct. Tobey Hiller. (Illus.). 48p. (Orig.). 1993. pap. 7.50 (*0-9631207-1-9*) Clear Mtn Pr.

Aqueducts of Ancient Rome. Raffaelo Fabretti. (Printed Sources of Western Art Ser.). (Illus.). 216p. (LAT.). 1981. reprint ed. boxed, pap. 50.00 (*0-915346-51-6*) A Wofsy Fine Arts.

***Aqueous Biphasic Separations: Biomolecules to Metal Ions.** Ed. by Robin D. Rogers & Mark A. Eiteman. 200p. 1995. 79.50 (*0-306-45019-4*) Plenum.

Aqueous Cleaning As an Alternative to CFC & Chlorinated Solvent-Based Cleaning. Carl D. D'Ruiz. LC 91-12464. (Illus.). 119p. 1991. 45.00 (*0-8155-1285-6*) Noyes.

Aqueous Coatings for Printing. 108p. 1981. student ed, audio 373.00 (*0-685-45515-7*, 0103HS05) TAPPI.

Aqueous Cytoplasm. Ed. by Alec D. Keith. LC 79-980. (Contemporary Biophysics Ser.: No. 1). (Illus.). 244p. reprint ed. pap. 69.60 (*0-8357-6023-5*, 2034543) Bks Demand.

Aqueous Phase Behavior of Surfactants. Robert G. Laughlin. (Colloid Science Ser.). (Illus.). 558p. 1994. text ed. 105.00 (*0-12-437745-9*) Acad Pr.

Aqueous Polymeric Coatings for Pharmaceutical Dosage Forms. McGinity. (Drugs & the Pharmaceutical Sciences Ser.: Vol. 36). 424p. 1989. 170.00 (*0-8247-7907-X*) Dekker.

Aqueous Silver Chloride Systems. Woolley. 1993. 105.31 (*0-08-023923-4*, Pergamon Pr) Elsevier.

Aqueous Size-Exclusion Chromatography. Ed. by P. L. Dubin. (Journal of Chromatography Library: Vol. 40). 454p. 1988. 141.00 (*0-444-42957-3*) Elsevier.

Aqueous Solubility: Methods of Estimation for Organic Compounds. Ed. by Yalkowsky & Banerjee. 304p. 1991. 125.00 (*0-8247-8615-7*) Dekker.

Aqueous Solutions: Data for Inorganic & Organic Compounds, 2 vols., Vol. 1: 1976. Rolf K. Freier. (C). Vol. 1, 1976. 238.50 (*3-11-001627-3*) De Gruyter.

Aqueous Solutions: Data for Inorganic & Organic Compounds, 2 vols., Vol. 2: 1978. Rolf K. Freier. (C). Vol. 2, 1978. 238.50 (*3-11-006537-1*) De Gruyter.

***Aqueous Two-Phase Partitioning: Physical Chemistry & Bioanalytical Applications.** Boris Y. Zaslavsky. LC 94-22868. 1994. 195.00 (*0-8247-9461-3*) Dekker.

Aqueous Wastes: From Petroleum & Petrochemical Plants. Milton R. Beychok. LC 67-19834. 380p. reprint ed. 108.30 (*0-8357-9839-9*, 2051229) Bks Demand.

Aqueus & Other Tales. Carol Spelius. Ed. by Rita Turow. 228p. 1990. pap. 8.95 (*0-941363-10-4*) Lake Shore Pub.

Aqui, Alla y Aculla: Conversacion y Composician. 2nd ed. Vincent A. Serpa et al. LC 88-86. 223p. 1988. Net. pap. text ed. write for info. (*0-471-60183-7*) Wiley.

Aqui Cuentan las Mujeres: Muestra y Estudio de Cinco Narradoras Puertorriquenas. Ed. by Maria M. Sola. LC 90-81211. 177p. 1990. pap. 8.50 (*0-929157-03-6*) Ediciones Huracan.

Aqui Esta Fido. Lynn Salem & Josie Stewart. Tr. by Mariana Robles. (Illus.). 8p. (J). (gr. 1). 1994. pap. 3.50 (*1-880612-18-6*) Seedling Pubns.

Aqui Estamos...Y No Nos Vamos: Here We Are...& We're Not Leaving. Contrib by Joe Moran et al. LC 90-32219. (Illus.). 40p. (Orig.). 1990. pap. 10.00 (*0-945486-07-3*) CSU SBUAG.

***Aqui Viene el Que Se Poncha!** Leonard Kessler. Tr. by Tomas Gonzalez. LC 94-13856. (I Can Read Bk.). (Illus.). 64p. (SPA.). (J). (gr. 1-3). 1995. 13.95 (*0-06-025437-8*); pap. 3.50 (*0-06-444189-X*, Trophy) HarpC Child Bks.

Aqui y Ahora. Barbara Mujica. (SPA.). (C). 1979. text ed. 21.50 (*0-03-042396-1*) HB Coll Pubs.

Aquifer Restoration: State of the Art. R. C. Knox et al. LC 85-25846. (Pollution Technology Review Ser.: No. 131). (Illus.). 750p. 1986. 64.00 (*0-8155-1069-1*) Noyes.

Aquifer Testing: Design & Analysis of Pumping & Slug Tests. Karen J. Dawson & Athan D. Istok. 280p. 1991. 5.25 hd 95.00 (*0-87371-501-2*, GB1197) Lewis Pubs.

Aquifers of the Caribbean Islands: Regional Aquifer Systems of the United States. Ed. by Fernando Gomez-Gomez et al. (Monograph Ser.: No. 15). (Illus.). 110p. (Orig.). 1991. pap. 10.00 (*1-882132-17-3*) Am Water Resources.

***Aquifers of the Far West: Papers Presented at AWRA Symposium on Water Supply & Water Reuse: 1992 & Beyond, June 2-6, 1991, San Diego, CA.** American Water Resouces Association Staff. Ed. by Keith R. Prince & A. Ivan Johnson. (AWRA Monograph Ser.: Vol. 16). (Illus.). 131p. Date not set. reprint ed. pap. 37.40 (*0-7837-9227-1*, 2049978) Bks Demand.

Aquifers of the Far West: Regional Aquifer Systems of the United States. Ed. by Keith R. Prince & A. Ivan Johnson. (Monograph Ser.: No. 16). (Illus.). 127p. (Orig.). 1992. pap. 11.00 (*1-882132-21-1*) Am Water Resources.

Aquifers of the Midwestern Area: Regional Aquifer Systems of the United States. Ed. by L. A. Swain & A. Ivan Johnson. (Monograph Ser.: No. 13). (Illus.). 252p. (Orig.). 1989. pap. 18.00 (*1-882132-10-6*) Am Water Resources.

***Aquifers of the Southern & Eastern States: Papers Presented at AWRA 27th Annual Conference & Symposium, September 8-13, 1991, New Orleans, LA.** American Water Resources Association Staff. Ed. by William R. Hotchkiss & A. Ivan Johnson. (AWRA Monograph Ser.: Vol. 17). (Illus.). 119p. Date not set. reprint ed. pap. 34.00 (*0-7837-9228-X*, 2049979) Bks Demand.

Aquifers of the Southern & Eastern States: Regional Aquifer Systems of the United States. Ed. by William R. Hotchkiss & A. Ivan Johnson. (Monograph Ser.: No. 17). (Illus.). 115p. (Orig.). 1992. pap. 11.00 (*1-882132-22-X*) Am Water Resources.

Aquifers of the Western Mountain Area: Regional Aquifer Systems of the United States. Ed. by John S. McLean & A. Ivan Johnson. (Monograph Ser.: No. 14). (Illus.). 229p. (Orig.). 1989. pap. 18.00 (*1-882132-05-X*) Am Water Resources.

Aquila, Vol. 3. N. R. Cartier. (Aquila Chestnut Hill Studies in Modern Languages & Literatures Ser.). 1976. lib. bdg. 65.50 (*90-247-1797-3*) Kluwer Ac.

AQUILA: A Digital Image Acquisition Program for Use at the Telescope. John R. Engel & Eric R. Craine. (Astronomy & Astrophysics Ser.). (Illus.). 24p. 1988. pap. 20.00 (*0-934525-12-9*); disk 225.00 (*0-934525-13-7*) West Research.

Aquila & the Iron Horse. S. P. Somtau. (Aquiliad Ser.: Vol. II). 256p. 1988. pap. 3.50 (*0-345-33868-5*, Del Rey) Ballantine.

Aquinas. F. C. Copleston. 272p. 1956. pap. 8.95 (*0-14-020349-4*, Penguin Bks) Viking Penguin.

Aquinas. Anthony Kenny. (Past Masters Ser.). 1983. pap. 7.95 (*0-19-287500-0*) OUP.

Aquinas Against the Averroists: On There Being Only One Intellect. Ralph McInerny. LC 92-16179. (Series in the History of Philosophy). 240p. 1993. 32.00 (*1-55753-028-9*); pap. 14.95 (*1-55753-029-7*) Purdue U Pr.

***Aquinas & the Jews.** John Y. Hood. LC 95-5296. (Middle Ages Ser.). 168p. 1995. text ed. 29.95 (*0-8122-3305-0*); pap. text ed. 14.95 (*0-8122-1523-0*) U of Pa Pr.

Aquinas & the Jews. John Y. B. Hood. LC 94-952. (American University Studies: History: Ser. IX, Vol. 158). 1994. write for info. (*0-8204-2443-9*) P Lang Pubs.

Aquinas Lecture Series Vols. 1-59, Set. 354.00 (*0-87462-150-X*) Marquette.

Aquinas on Human Action: A Theory of Practice. Ralph McInerny. LC 90-27754. 244p. 1992. pap. text ed. 19.95 (*0-8132-0761-4*) Cath U Pr.

Aquinas on Mind. Anthony Kenny. LC 92-12224. (Topics in Medieval Philosophy Ser.). 192p. 1993. 35.00 (*0-415-04415-4*, A9863) Routledge.

***Aquinas on Mind.** Anthony Kenny. (Topics in Medieval Philosophy Ser.). 192p. 1994. pap. 13.95 (*0-415-11306-7*, B4513) Routledge.

Aquinas on Nature & Grace. Ed. by A. M. Fairweather. LC 54-10259. (Library of Christian Classics). 382p. 1978. pap. 14.99 (*0-664-24155-7*, Westminster) Westminster John Knox.

***Aquinas on the Nature & Treatment of Animals.** Judith A. Barad. (Catholic Scholars Press Ser.). 234p. 1995. 64.95 (*1-57309-007-7*); pap. 44.95 (*1-57309-006-9*) Intl Scholars.

Aquinas Reader. Intro. by Mary T. Clark. LC 72-76709. 597p. (C). 1988. reprint ed. pap. text ed. 15.00 (*0-8232-1206-8*) Fordham.

Aquinas' Summa: An Introduction & Interpretation. Edward J. Gratsch. LC 85-15842. 305p. (Orig.). 1985. pap. 12.95 (*0-8189-0485-2*) Alba.

Aquinas to Whitehead: Seven Centuries of Metaphysics of Religion. Charles Hartshorne. LC 76-5156. (Aquinas Lectures). 1976. 10.00 (*0-87462-141-0*) Marquette.

Aquino Alternative. Ed. by M. Rajaretnam. 158p. 1986. pap. text ed. 17.25 (*9971-988-46-1*, Pub. by Inst SE Asian Studies SI) Ashgate Pub Co.

Aquino Assassination: The True Story & Analysis. Gerald N. Hill et al. (Illus.). 232p. 1983. pap. 8.95 (*0-912133-04-X*) Hilltop Pub Co.

Aquis Submersus. Theodor Storm. Ed. by Patricia M. Boswell. (German Texts Ser.). 146p. 1974. pap. 17.95 (*0-631-01920-0*, Pub. by Duckworth UK) Focus Info Gr.

Aquitaine & Ireland in the Middle Ages. Ed. by Jean-Michel Picard. 240p. 1994. boxed, text ed. 39.50 (*1-85182-135-X*, Pub. by Four Cts Pr IE) Intl Spec Bk.

Aquitaine Progression. Robert Ludlum. 704p. 1985. mass mkt. 6.99 (*0-553-26256-4*) Bantam.

Aquitaine Progression. Robert Ludlum. LC 83-19078. 752p. 1984. 17.95 (*0-394-53674-6*) Random.

AR Creative Directory. 1992. write for info. (*0-942454-35-9*) Black Bk.

AR One Hundred Award Showbook, No. 8. 280p. Date not set. 60.00 (*0-942454-42-1*) Black Bk.

Ar-Rafed: Arabic-Arabic Dictionary. Al-Amir Nasiruddin. 1971. 19.95 (*0-86685-101-1*) Intl Bk Ctr.

Ar-Ti-Facts. Kirk Robertson. Ed. by Coco Gordon. 20p. (Orig.). 1985. pap. 12.00 (*0-931956-17-X*) Water Mark.

AR 100 - The Seventh Annual Report Show. 40.00 (*0-942454-36-7*) Black Bk.

AR-15 - M16 Super Systems. Duncan Long. (Illus.). 144p. 1989. pap. 19.95 (*0-87364-511-1*) Paladin Pr.

AR-15-M16: A Practical Guide. Duncan Long. LC 85-160984. (Illus.). 168p. 1985. pap. 16.95 (*0-87364-321-6*) Paladin Pr.

AR-7 Advanced Weapons System. (Illus.). 64p. 1990. pap. 16.00 (*0-87364-563-4*) Paladin Pr.

AR-7 Super Systems. Duncan Long. (Illus.). 144p. 1990. pap. 17.00 (*0-87364-573-1*) Paladin Pr.

***Ara Pacis Augustae & the Imagery of Abundance in Later Greek & Early Roman Imperial Art.** David Castriota. LC 94-23503. 1995. write for info. (*0-691-03715-9*) Princeton U Pr.

Arab Administration. S. A. Hussaini. 300p. (C). 1985. text ed. 16.50 (*1-56744-218-8*) Kazi Pubns.

***Arab Airforces.** Charles Stafarace. (Foreign Airforces Ser.). (Illus.). 64p. 1994. pap. 9.95 (*0-89747-326-4*) Squad Sig Pubns.

Arab-American Almanac. 4th ed. Ed. by Joseph R. Haiek. 448p. 1992. pap. 19.95 (*0-915652-08-0*) News Circle.

Arab-American Bibliographic Guide. Philip M. Kayal. LC 85-11253. (Bibliography Ser.: No. 4). 42p. (Orig.). (C). 1985. pap. 5.00 (*0-937694-66-5*) Assn Arab-Amer U Grads.

***Arab Americans.** Chelsea Staff. 1995. (*0-7910-3371-6*) Chelsea Hse.

Arab Americans. Alixa Naff. (Peoples of North America Ser.). (Illus.). 112p. (J). (gr. 5 up). 1988. lib. bdg. 17.95 (*0-87754-861-7*) Chelsea Hse.

Arab Americans: Continuity & Change. Ed. by Baha Abu-Laban & Michael W. Suleiman. (Monograph Ser.: No. 24). 314p. (Orig.). 1989. pap. 19.75 (*0-937694-82-7*) Assn Arab-Amer U Grads.

Arab & African Film Making. Lizbeth Malkmus & Roy Armes. 256p. (C). 1991. text ed. 69.95 (*0-86232-916-7*, Pub. by Zed Books UK); pap. 25.00 (*0-86232-917-5*, Pub. by Zed Books UK) Humanities.

Arab & Jew: Wounded Spirits in a Promised Land. David K. Shipler. (Illus.). 608p. 1987. pap. 10.95 (*0-14-010376-7*, Penguin Bks) Viking Penguin.

Arab & Jew in Jerusalem: Explorations in Community Mental Health. Gerald Caplan. LC 79-27832. 308p. 1980. 32.00 (*0-674-04315-4*) HUP.

Arab & Persian Painting in the Fogg Art Museum, Vol. II. Marianna S. Simpson. Ed. by Peter Walsh & Andrea Kaliski. LC 80-10525. (Fogg Art Museum Handbooks Ser.). (Illus.). 125p. (C). 1980. pap. 8.50 (*0-916724-10-7*) Harvard Art Mus.

Arab & Regional Politics in the Middle East. P. J. Vatikiotis. LC 84-40051. 300p. 1984. text ed. 39.95 (*0-312-04692-8*) St Martin.

Arab & the African. S. Tristram Pruen. 368p. 1986. 250.00 (*1-85077-136-7*, Darf Pubs Ltd) St Mut.

Arab Apocalypse. Etel Adnan. (Poetry Ser.). Orig. Title: L' Apocalypse Arabe. (Illus.). 80p. (Orig.). 1989. pap. 13.50 (*0-942996-09-7*) Post Apollo Pr.

Arab Armies of the Middle East Wars, Vol. 2. Sam Katz. (Men-at-Arms Ser.: No. 194). (Illus.). 48p. pap. 11.95 (*0-85045-800-5*, 9127, Pub. by Osprey UK) Stackpole.

Arab Attitudes to Israel. Yehoshafat Harkabi. 527p. 1974. boxed 39.95x (*0-87855-168-9*) Transaction Pubs.

Arab Awakening. George Antonius. 1976. lib. bdg. 250.00 (*0-8490-1444-1*) Gordon Pr.

Arab Awakening: The Story of the Arab National Movement. George Antonius. 1969. 24.95 (*0-86685-000-7*) Intl Bk Ctr.

Arab Boycott of Israel. L. Meo et al. (Other Works Ser.: No. 2). 35p. (Orig.). 1976. pap. text ed. 2.00 (*0-937694-12-6*) Assn Arab-Amer U Grads.

Arab Brain Drain. Ed. by A. B. Zahlan. 309p. 1981. 25.00 (*0-903729-62-8*, Pub. by Ithaca UK) Evergreen Dist.

Arab Bulletin, 1916-1919, 4 vols., Set. Archives Research Ltd. Staff. 1900p. (C). 1987. text ed. 2,000.00 (*1-85207-025-0*, Pub. by Archive Res Ltd UK) St Mut.

Arab Bureau: British Policy in the Middle East, 1916-1920. Bruce C. Westrate. (Illus.). 256p. 1992. text ed. 35.00 (*0-271-00794-X*) Pa St U Pr.

Arab Business Yearbook, 1986. Ed. by Graham & Trotman Ltd. Staff. (Illus.). 450p. 1986. lib. bdg. 96.00 (*0-86010-671-3*); pap. text ed. 76.50 (*0-86010-672-1*) G & T Inc.

Arab Child Picture Dictionary: Arabic - English - French. (J). 1990. 19.95 (*0-86685-462-2*) Intl Bk Ctr.

Arab Christian: A History in the Middle East. Kenneth Cragg. 320p. 1991. 30.00 (*0-664-21945-4*) Westminster John Knox.

***Arab Cities of North Africa.** Maria Cordoba. LC 94-39399. (World Heritage Ser.). (ARC & ENG.). (J). 1995. lib. bdg. 15.00 (*0-516-08394-5*) Childrens.

Arab Civilization. J. Hell. 16.95 (*0-935782-38-9*) Kazi Pubns.

Arab Civilization: Challenges & Responses: Studies in Honor of Dr. Constantine Zurayk. Ed. by George N. Atiyeh & Ibrahim M. Oweiss. LC 87-18452. 365p. 1988. 74.50 (*0-88706-698-4*); pap. 24.95 (*0-88706-699-2*) State U NY Pr.

Arab Civilization to A.D. 1500. Douglas Dunlop. (Arab Background Ser.). 1971. 42.00 (*0-86685-012-0*) Intl Bk Ctr.

Arab Comic Strips: Politics of an Emerging Mass Culture. Allen Douglas & Fedwa Malti-Douglas. LC 93-103. 1993. 39.95 (*0-253-31814-9*); pap. 19.95 (*0-253-20831-9*) Ind U Pr.

Arab Comparative & Commercial Law, Vol. 1: The International Approach. Ed. by International Bar Association Staff. (C). 1987. lib. bdg. 112.50 (*0-86010-977-1*, Pub. by Graham & Trotman UK) Kluwer Ac.

Arab Conquest of Egypt. Alfred J. Butler. (C). 1988. 135.00 (*1-85077-205-3*, Darf Pubs Ltd) St Mut.

Arab Conquest of Egypt & the Last Thirty Years of the Roman Dominion. Alfred J. Butler. LC 72-180327. reprint ed. 67.50 (*0-404-56219-1*) AMS Pr.

Arab Conquest of Spain: 710-797. Roger Collins. (History of Spain Ser.). 224p. 1989. text ed. 59.95 (*0-631-15923-1*) Blackwell Pubs.

Arab Conquest of Spain: 710-797. Roger Collins. 1994. pap. 19.95 (*0-631-19405-3*) Blackwell Pubs.

Arab Conquest of the Western Sahara. H. T. Norris. 309p. 1986. 42.00 (*0-86685-596-3*) Intl Bk Ctr.

Arab Conquests in Central Asia. Hamilton A. Gibb. LC 75-11477. (BCL Ser.: I). reprint ed. 16.00 (*0-404-02718-0*) AMS Pr.

Arab Construction Industry. A. B. Zahlan. LC 83-13793. 288p. 1984. text ed. 39.95 (*0-312-04694-4*) St Martin.

Arab Contemporaries: The Role of Personalities in Politics. Majid Khadduri. LC 72-12576. (Illus.). 265p. 1973. 34.00 (*0-8018-1453-7*) Johns Hopkins.

Arab Development Funds in the Middle East. Soliman Demir. LC 79-503. (Policy Studies). 1979. 74.00 (*0-08-022489-X*, Pergamon Pr) Elsevier.

Arab Economy in Israel. Raja Khalidi. 224p. (C). 1987. 49.00 (*0-7099-1583-7*, Pub. by Croom Helm UK) Routledge Chapman & Hall.

Arab Education in Israel. Sami K. Mar'I. 1978. 39.95x (*0-8156-0145-X*) Syracuse U Pr.

Arab Family. Roderic Dutton. LC 85-10272. (Families the World Over Ser.). (Illus.). 32p. (J). (gr. 2-5). 1985. lib. bdg. 14.95 (*0-8225-1660-8*, Lerner Publctns) Lerner Group.

Arab Folktales. Ed. & Tr. by Inea Bushnaq. LC 85-9569. 416p. 1987. pap. 16.00 (*0-394-75179-5*) Pantheon.

Arab Foreign Aid. Andre Simmons. LC 80-65281. 192p. 1981. 25.00 (*0-8386-3019-7*) Fairleigh Dickinson.

Arab Gold: Heritage of the UaE. Peter Vine & Paula Casey. 160p. (C). 1990. 150.00 (*0-907151-39-6*, Pub. by IMMEL Pubng UK) St Mut.

Arab Gulf & the West. Ed. by Brian R. Pridham. LC 85-18298. 251p. 1985. text ed. 39.95 (*0-312-04703-7*) St Martin.

Arab Gulf States: A Travel Survival Kit. Gordon R. Robinson. (Illus.). 352p. (Orig.). 1993. pap. 15.95 (*0-86442-120-6*) Lonely Planet.

Arab Gulf States: Steps Toward Political Participation. J. E. Peterson. LC 87-25836. (Washington Papers: No. 131). 176p. 1988. text ed. 45.00 (*0-275-92881-0*, C2881, Praeger Pubs); pap. text ed. 13.95 (*0-275-92882-9*, B2882, Praeger Pubs) Greenwood.

Arab Gulf States & Japan: Prospects for Co-Operation. Ed. by Walid Sharif. LC 85-12819. 240p. 1986. 39.95 (*0-7099-3393-2*, Pub. by Croom Helm UK) Routledge Chapman & Hall.

Arab Heritage. Ed. by Nabih A. Faris. LC 84-27929. (Illus.). xii, 279p. 1985. reprint ed. text ed. 85.00 (*0-313-23371-3*, FAAH, Greenwood Pr) Greenwood.

Arab Historians of the Crusades. Francesco Gabrieli. (Dorset Press Reprints Ser.). 362p. 1990. reprint ed. 19.95 (*0-88029-452-3*) Dorset Pr.

400

An Asterisk (*) at the beginning of an entry indicates that the title is appearing in BIP for the first time.

Arab Historians of the Crusades. Ed. & Tr. by Francesco Gabrieli. LC 68-23783. 1978. reprint ed. pap. 14.00 (*0-520-05224-2*) U CA Pr.

Arab History & the Nation State. Youssef M. Choueiri. 272p. 1989. 56.95 (*0-415-03113-3*) Routledge.

Arab Horse. Borden. 1949. 16.00 (*0-87505-112-X*) Borden.

Arab Horse Stud Book: Containing the Entries of Arab Stallions & Mares, 6 vols. Arab Horse Society Staff. 1976. lib. bdg. 634.95 (*0-8490-1445-X*) Gordon Pr.

Arab Horses. Kay Wilson. (J). (gr. 2-9). 1986. 7.95 (*0-86685-481-9*) Intl Bk Ctr.

Arab Image in the U. S. Press, Vol. 1. Issam S. Mousa. LC 83-49021. (American University Studies: Communications: Ser. XV). 201p. (Orig.). 1984. pap. text ed. 19.20 (*0-8204-0069-6*) P Lang Pubs.

Arab Immigrant & Experience. (YA). (gr. 10-12). 1981. 6.00 (*0-317-56413-7*) UM Ctr MENAS.

Arab in Israeli Literature. Gila Ramras-Rauch. LC 88-46017. (Jewish Literature & Culture Ser.). 256p. 1989. 35.00 (*0-253-34832-3*) Ind U Pr.

***Arab Industrialization in Israel: Ethnic Entrepreneurship in the Periphery.** Izhak Schnell et al. LC 95-13916. (C). 1995. text ed. write for info. (*0-275-94856-0*, Praeger Pubs) Greenwood.

Arab Influence Upon Medieval Europe. Ed. by Dionisius Agius & Richard Hitchcock. (Middle East Culture Ser.: Vol. 18). 1993. 55.00 (*0-86372-161-3*, Pub. by Ithaca UK) Paul & Co Pubs.

Arab Intellectuals & the West: The Formative Years 1875-1914. Hisham B. Sharabi. LC 78-108384. 151p. reprint ed. pap. 43.10 (*0-8357-5699-8*, 2003895) Bks Demand.

Arab Invasion of Egypt: And the Last 30 Years of the Roman Dominion. Alfred J. Butler & John H. Clarke. 563p. 1992. pap. text ed. write for info. (*1-881316-06-8*) A&B Bks.

Arab Investors Sourcebook. Middle East Executive Reports, Ltd. Staff. Ed. by William Hearn. 650p. 1989. pap. 345.00 (*0-915797-01-1*) Intl Exec Reports.

***Arab Islamic Banking & the Renewal of Islamic Law.** Nicholas D. Ray. LC 95-9842. (Arab & Islamic Law Ser.). 1995. write for info. (*1-85966-104-1*, Pub. by Graham & Trotman UK) Kluwer Ac.

Arab-Israel Conflict & Its Resolution: Selected Documents. Ruth Lapidoth & Moshe Hirsh. 388p. (C). 1992. lib. bdg. 140.50 (*0-7923-1300-3*) Kluwer Ac.

Arab-Israel War, the Chinese Civil War & the Korean War. LC 87-1159. (West Point Military History Ser.). 146p. 1987. 25.00 (*0-89529-322-6*) Avery Pub.

Arab-Israel War, the Chinese Civil War & the Korean War. LC 87-1159. (West Point Military History Ser.). 146p. 1987. pap. 19.95 (*0-89529-274-2*) Avery Pub.

Arab-Israeli Armistice Agreements: February-July 1949: U. N. Text & Annexes. 40p. 1967. pap. 2.95 (*0-88728-069-2*) Inst Palestine.

Arab-Israeli Conflict. Deakin University Press Staff. (C). 1988. 40.00 (*0-7300-0596-8*, Pub. by Deakin Univ AT) St Mut.

Arab-Israeli Conflict. Paul J. Deegan. LC 91-73073. (War in the Gulf Ser.). 202p. (J). (gr. 4 up). 1991. lib. bdg. 13.99 (*1-56239-028-7*) Abdo & Dghtrs.

***Arab-Israeli Conflict.** T. G. Fraser. LC 95-15358. 1995. write for info. (*0-312-12757-X*); pap. write for info. (*0-312-12759-6*) St Martin.

Arab-Israeli Conflict. Gerald Kurland. Ed. by D. Steve Rahmas. LC 72-89221. (Topics of Our Times Ser.: No. 2). 32p. (Orig.). (YA). (gr. 7-12). 1973. lib. bdg. 4.95 (*0-87157-802-6*) SamHar Pr.

Arab-Israeli Conflict. Alvin Z. Rubinstein. (C). 1990. pap. text ed. 29.50 (*0-673-46405-9*) HarpCollege.

Arab-Israeli Conflict: A History. 3rd ed. Ian J. Bickerton & M. N. Pearson. 1993. pap. text ed. 23.32 (*0-582-90892-2*, 79916) Longman.

Arab-Israeli Conflict: A Politico-Legal Analysis. Gainsborough. 1986. text ed. 59.95 (*0-566-00818-1*, Pub. by Dartmth Pub UK) Ashgate Pub Co.

Arab Israeli Conflict: An Annotated Bibliography. Hatem I. Hussaini. (Bibliography Ser.: No. 1). 81p. (Orig.). 1975. pap. text ed. 2.00 (*0-937694-14-2*) Assn Arab-Amer U Grads.

***Arab-Israeli Conflict: An Historical Encyclopedia.** Ed. by Bernard Reich. LC 95-6684. 1996. text ed. write for info. (*0-313-27374-X*, Greenwood Pr) Greenwood.

Arab-Israeli Conflict, Vol. IV: The Difficult Search for Peace, 1975-1988, 2 pts. Ed. by John N. Moore. (American Society of International Law Ser.). 1992. 99.50 (*0-691-05672-2*) Princeton U Pr.

Arab-Israeli Conflict, Vol. IV: The Difficult Search for Peace, 1975-1988, 2 pts., Pt. 2. Ed. by John N. Moore. (American Society of International Law Ser.). 1992. 99.50 (*0-691-05678-1*) Princeton U Pr.

Arab Israeli Conflict, 1947-1967. Richard Lawless. (Living Through History Ser.). (Illus.). 64p. 1990. 19.95 (*0-7134-5990-5*, Pub. by Batsford UK) Trafalgar.

Arab-Israeli Confrontation of June 1967: An Arab Perspective. Ed. by Ibrahim Abu-Lughod. LC 74-107607. 215p. reprint ed. pap. 61.30 (*0-8357-5700-5*, 2014772) Bks Demand.

Arab-Israeli Dilemma. 3rd ed. Fred J. Khouri. LC 68-20483. (Contemporary Issues in the Middle East Ser.). 640p. (Orig.). 1985. text ed. 39.95x (*0-8156-2339-9*); pap. 17.95 (*0-8156-2340-2*) Syracuse U Pr.

Arab-Israeli Issue. LC 86-20259. (Flashpoints Ser.). (Illus.). (YA). (gr. 7 up). 1988. 18.60 (*0-86592-029-X*) Rourke Corp.

Arab-Israeli Military Balance since October, 1973. Dale R. Tahtinen. LC 74-81729. (Foreign Affairs Study Ser.: No. 11). 50p. reprint ed. pap. 25.00 (*0-8357-5701-3*, 2017044) Bks Demand.

Arab-Israeli Relations: Historical Background & Origins of the Conflict. Ed. by Ian S. Lustick. LC 93-50089. 424p. 1994. reprint ed. 66.00 (*0-8153-1581-3*) Garland.

Arab-Israeli Relations in World Politics, Vol. 10. Ed. by Ian S. Lustick. LC 93-49876. 360p. 1994. reprint ed. 59.00 (*0-8153-1590-2*) Garland.

Arab-Israeli Search for Peace. Ed. by Steven L. Spiegel. LC 92-19864. 200p. 1992. pap. text ed. 11.50 (*1-55587-313-8*) Lynne Rienner.

Arab-Israeli Security Agreements: Negotiating Asymmetric Reciprocity. Geoffrey Kemp. 1993. pap. 9.95 (*0-87003-021-3*) Carnegie Endow.

Arab-Israeli War, Nineteen Forty-Eight. Edgar O'Ballance. LC 79-2877. (Illus.). 220p. 1983. reprint ed. 24.50 (*0-8305-0045-6*) Hyperion Conn.

Arab-Israeli Wars. Ken Hills. (Wars That Changed the World Ser.: Group 2). (Illus.). 32p. (J). (gr. 3-9). 1991. lib. bdg. 10.95 (*1-85435-261-X*) Marshall Cavendish.

Arab-Israeli Wars: War & Peace in the Middle East, from the War of Independence Through Lebabon. Chaim Herzog. LC 83-5846. (Illus.). 464p. 1983. pap. 15.00 (*0-394-71746-5*) Random.

Arab-Jewish Relations in Israel: A Quest in Human Understanding. John E. Hofman. LC 87-51005. (C). 1987. text ed. 39.95 (*1-55605-025-9*); pap. text ed. 29.95 (*1-55605-026-7*) Wyndhall Pr.

Arab-Jewish Unity: Testimony Before the Anglo-American Inquiry for the Ihud (Union) Judah L. Magnes & Martin Buber. LC 75-7678. (Rise of Jewish Nationalism & the Middle East Ser.). 96p. 1975. reprint ed. 15.00 (*0-88355-348-1*) Hyperion Conn.

Arab-Latin American Relations: Energy, Trade & Investment. Ed. by Fehmy Saddy. LC 83-440. 205p. 1983. 34.95x (*0-87855-475-0*) Transaction Pubs.

Arab League & Peacekeeper in the Lebanon. Istvan S. Pogany. LC 87-12873. 224p. 1988. text ed. 45.00 (*0-312-00782-5*) St Martin.

Arab Linguistics: An Introductory Classical Text with Translation & Notes. Ed. by M. G. Carter. (Studies in the History of Linguistics: No. 24). x, 485p. 1981. 97.00x (*90-272-4506-1*) Benjamins North Am.

Arab Manpower. J. S. Birks & C. A. Sinclair. LC 80-12416. 450p. 1980. text ed. 59.95 (*0-312-04708-8*) St Martin.

Arab Medicine & Surgery: A Study of the Healing Art in Algeria. Melville W. Hilton-Simpson. LC 75-23721. reprint ed. 29.50 (*0-404-13279-0*) AMS Pr.

***Arab Middle East & the United States.** Kaufman. 1994. pap. 22.95 (*0-8057-9211-2*, Twayne) Macmillan.

Arab Military Industry. Yezid Sayigh. 268p. 1992. text ed. 67.00 (*0-08-041777-9*, Pub. by Brasseys UK) Brasseys Inc.

Arab Military Option. Saad E. Shazly. (Illus.). 329p. 1986. 26.00 (*0-9604562-1-X*) Am Mideast.

Arab Minority in Israel, 1967-1991: Political Aspects. Jacob M. Landau. LC 92-26238. (Illus.). 256p. 1993. 38.00 (*0-19-827712-1*, Clarendon Pr) OUP.

Arab Minority in Israel's Economy: Patterns of Ethnic Inequality. Noah Lewin-Epstein & Moshe Semyonov. 169p. (C). 1993. text ed. 50.00 (*0-8133-1525-5*) Westview.

Arab Moslems in the United States. Abdo A. Elkholy. 1966. 16.95 (*0-8084-0052-5*); pap. 12.95 (*0-8084-0053-3*) NCUP.

Arab Nationalism: A Critical Enquiry. 2nd ed. Bassam Tibi. Tr. by Marion F. Sluglett & Peter Sluglett. LC 89-24392. 334p. 1990. text ed. 49.95 (*0-312-04234-5*) St Martin.

Arab Nationalism: A Critical Enquiry. 2nd enl. ed. Bassam Tibi. Ed. by Marion F. Sluglett & Peter Sluglett. Tr. by Peter Sluglett. LC 89-24392. 343p. (C). 1991. pap. 19.95 (*0-312-06155-2*) St Martin.

Arab Nationalism: An Anthology. Ed. by Sylvia G. Haim. LC 62-11492. 1974. reprint ed. pap. 12.00 (*0-520-03043-5*) U CA Pr.

***Arab Nationalism: Birth, Evolution, & the Present Delemma.** Aparjita Gogoi & Gazi I. Abdulghafour. (C). 1995. 32.00x (*81-7095-043-0*, Pub. by Lancers Bks II) S Asia.

Arab Nationalism & the Future of the Arab World. Ed. by Hani A. Faris. LC 86-10824. (Monograph Ser.: No. 22). 159p. 1986. pap. text ed. 13.00 (*0-937694-75-4*) Assn Arab-Amer U Grads.

Arab Nationalism, Oil, & the Political Economy of Dependency. Abbas Alnasrawi. LC 90-25225. (Contributions in Economics & Economic History Ser.: No. 120). 232p. 1991. text ed. 55.00 (*0-313-27610-2*, AAQ/, Greenwood Pr) Greenwood.

Arab Navigation. S. Nadvi. 15.95 (*0-935782-39-7*) Kazi Pubns.

Arab Nonviolent Political Struggle in the Middle East. Philip Grant & Saad E. Ibrahim. Ed. by Ralph Crow. LC 90-31413. 136p. 1990. lib. bdg. 32.00 (*1-55587-222-0*) Lynne Rienner.

Arab Oil: Impact on Arab Countries & Global Implications. Ed. by Naiem A. Sherbiny & Mark A. Tessler. LC 75-19820. (Special Studies). 344p. 1976. text ed. 65.00 (*0-275-90251-X*, C0251, Praeger Pubs) Greenwood.

Arab Oil & United States Energy Requirements. Abbas Alnasrawi. (Monograph Ser.: No. 16). 88p. (Orig.). 1982. pap. 5.95 (*0-937694-52-5*) Assn Arab-Amer U Grads.

Arab Oil Embargo: Ten Years Later. Ed. by Bettina Silber. (Americans for Energy Independence Energy Policy Ser.). 50p. (Orig.). 1984. pap. 6.00 (*0-934458-07-3*) Americans Energy Ind.

Arab Oil Policies in the 1970s: Opportunity & Responsibilty. Yusif A. Sayigh. LC 83-8016. 288p. (C). 1983. 42.00x (*0-8018-3035-4*) Johns Hopkins.

Arab Oil Weapon. Albert P. Blaustein & Jordon J. Paust. LC 77-2937. 370p. 1977. 30.00 (*0-379-00797-5*) Oceana.

Arab Peace-Efforts & the Solution of the Arab-Israeli Problem. George Haddad. (Information Papers: No. 18). 82p. (Orig.). (C). 1976. pap. 2.00 (*0-937694-34-7*) Assn Arab-Amer U Grads.

Arab Perceptions of American Foreign Policy During the October War. William A. Rugh. LC 76-45494. (Special Study Ser.: No. 2). 1976. pap. 2.50 (*0-916808-13-0*) Mid East Inst.

Arab Personalities in Politics. Majid Khadduri. LC 81-62184. 363p. reprint ed. pap. 103.50 (*0-8357-5702-1*, 2025921) Bks Demand.

Arab Petropolitics. Abdulaziz Al-Sowayegh. LC 83-40196. 224p. 1984. text ed. 35.00 (*0-312-04718-5*) St Martin.

Arab Philosophy of History: Selections from the Prolegomena of Ibn Khaldun of Tunis (1332-1406) Tr. & Intro. by Charles Issawi. LC 86-29199. xiv, 192p. 1987. lib. bdg. 12.95 (*0-87850-056-1*) Darwin Pr.

Arab Political Humor. Khalid Kishtainy. 204p. 1993. 17.95 (*0-7043-2485-7*, Pub. by Quartet UK) Interlink Pub.

Arab Politics: Class, Power & International Involvement. Timothy C. Niblock. 256p. 1990. write for info. (*0-312-01972-6*); pap. write for info. (*0-312-01973-4*) St Martin.

Arab Politics: The Search for Legitimacy. Michael C. Hudson. LC 77-75379. 1979. pap. 18.00 (*0-300-02411-8*) Yale U Pr.

Arab Politics in the Soviet Mirror. Aryeh Yodfat. 331p. 1973. boxed 39.95x (*0-87855-159-X*) Transaction Pubs.

***Arab Population in the Israeli Economy: 1949 to the Present.** Azid Haidar. 208p. 1994. 42.00 (*0-312-12523-2*) St Martin.

Arab Predicament: Arab Political Thought & Practice since 1967. Fouad Ajami. (Canto Book Ser.). 384p. (C). 1992. 49.95 (*0-521-43243-X*); pap. 12.95 (*0-521-43833-0*) Cambridge U Pr.

Arab Press: News Media & Political Process in the Arab World. 2nd rev. ed. William A. Rugh. (Contemporary Issues in the Middle East Ser.). (Illus.). 256p. (C). 1987. pap. text ed. 17.95x (*0-8156-2420-4*) Syracuse U Pr.

Arab Press in the Middle East: A History. Ami Ayalon. (Studies in Middle Eastern History). 288p. 1995. 59.00 (*0-19-508780-1*) OUP.

Arab Radicals. Adeed Dawisha. 192p. 1986. 17.50 (*0-87609-020-X*) Coun Foreign.

Arab Rebirth: Pain & Ecstasy. Jacques Berque. Tr. by Quintin Hoare. Orig. Title: Les Arabes. 138p. (Orig.). 1984. 21.00 (*0-86356-105-5*, Pub. by Saqi Books UK); pap. 10.95 (*0-86356-015-6*) Evergreen Dist.

Arab Rediscovery of Europe: A Study in Cultural Encounters. Ibrahim A. Abu-Lughod. LC 62-21102. (Princeton Studies on the Near East). 199p. reprint ed. pap. 56.80 (*0-8357-5703-X*, 2000599) Bks Demand.

Arab Regional Organizations. Frank A. Clements. 250p. (C). 1992. 49.95 (*1-56000-057-0*) Transaction Pubs.

Arab Relations in the Middle East: The Road to Realignment. Ed. by Colin Legum & Haim Shaked. LC 78-20888. (Middle East Affairs Ser.: No. 1). 104p. (C). 1979. pap. 12.50 (*0-8419-0447-2*) Holmes & Meier.

Arab Relations with Jewish Immigrants & Israel, 1891-1991: The Hundred Year's Conflict. Lilly Weissbrod. LC 91-45792. 236p. 1992. lib. bdg. 89.95 (*0-7734-9461-8*) E Mellen.

Arab Republic of Egypt: An Agricultural Strategy for the 1990s. (Country Study Ser.). 148p. 1993. 9.95 (*0-8213-2337-7*, 12337) World Bank.

Arab Republic of Egypt Military Decorations & Medals, 1953-1983. Republic of Egypt, Cabinet of the Grand Chamberlain Staff & David V. Olson. (Illus.). 50p. (Orig.). 1989. reprint ed. pap. 20.00 (*0-929757-26-2*) Regt QM.

Arab Resources: The Transformation of a Society. Ed. by Ibrahim Ibrahim. 304p. (Orig.). (C). 1983. pap. text ed. 10.95 (*0-932568-07-6*) GU Ctr CAS.

***Arab Seafaring: In the Indian Ocean in Ancient & Early Medieval Times.** George F. Hourani. 1995. pap. write for info. (*0-691-00032-8*) Princeton U Pr.

***Arab Seafaring in the Indian Ocean in Ancient & Early Medieval Times.** George F. Hourani & John Carswell. (Princeton Paperbacks Ser.). 1995. write for info. (*0-691-00170-7*) Princeton U Pr.

Arab Social Life in the Middle Ages: An Illustrated Study. Shirley Guthrie. (Illus.). 320p. 1994. 69.95 (*0-86356-043-1*, Pub. by Saqi Bks UK) Interlink Pub.

Arab Society in Transition. Ed. by Nicholas S. Hopkins & Saad E. Ibrahim. 1986. pap. 22.50 (*977-424-126-6*, Pub. by Am Univ Cairo Pr UA) Col U Pr.

Arab State. Ed. by Giacomo Luciani. 1989. 45.00 (*0-520-06432-1*); pap. 14.00 (*0-520-06434-8*) U CA Pr.

Arab States & the Palestine Conflict. Barry Rubin. LC 81-5829. (Contemporary Issues in the Middle East Ser.). (Illus.). 328p. 1981. pap. 14.95 (*0-8156-0170-0*) Syracuse U Pr.

Arab States & the Palestine Question: Between Ideology & Self-Interest. Aaron D. Miller. LC 86-931. (Washington Papers: No. 120). 114p. 1986. text ed. 45.00 (*0-275-92215-4*, C2215, Praeger Pubs); pap. text ed. 14.95 (*0-275-92216-2*, B2216, Praeger Pubs) Greenwood.

Arab Strategies & Israel's Response. Yehoshafat Harkabi. LC 77-70273. 1977. 22.95 (*0-02-913760-8*); pap. 9.95 (*0-02-913780-2*) Free Pr.

"Arab" Street? Public Opinion in the Arab World. David Pollock. LC 92-44065. 1992. write for info. (*0-944029-21-3*) Wash Inst NEP.

Arab Studies for Teachers: A Critical Guide to Curricular Materials. Mostafa A. Hefny. LC 86-50416. (Illus.). 120p. (Orig.). 1987. pap. 5.00 (*0-9617535-0-1*) Wayne Cnty Inter Schl.

Arab-Syrian Gentleman & Warrior in the Period of the Crusades. Ibn M. Usamah. Tr. by Philip K. Hitti. LC 78-63514. reprint ed. 37.50 (*0-404-17158-3*) AMS Pr.

Arab-Syrian Gentleman & Warrior in the Period of the Crusades: Memoirs of Usamah Ibn-Munqidh. Tr. by Phillip K. Hitti. (Illus.). 288p. 1987. pap. text ed. 15.95 (*0-691-02269-0*) Princeton U Pr.

Arab Tells His Story; a Study in Loyalties. Edward S. Atiyah. LC 79-3071. (Illus.). 229p. 1981. reprint ed. 21.50 (*0-8305-0023-5*) Hyperion Conn.

Arab, the Horse of the Future. T. P. Boucaut. (Illus.). xx, 249p. reprint ed. write for info. (*0-318-71575-9*, Pub. by Georg Olms GW) Lubrecht & Cramer.

Arab Travellers & Geographers. Pier G. Donini. 108p. (C). 1990. 150.00 (*0-907151-35-3*, Pub. by IMMEL Pubng UK) St Mut.

Arab Tribes in the Vicinity of Eden. F. M. Hunter & C. W. Scaley. 368p. 1986. 300.00 (*1-85077-097-2*, Darf Pubs Ltd) St Mut.

Arab-Turkish Relations & the Emergence of Arab Nationalism. Zeine N. Zeine. LC 80-25080. 156p. 1981. reprint ed. text ed. 52.50 (*0-313-22705-5*, ZEAT, Greenwood Pr) Greenwood.

***Arab-United Kingdom Corporate Handbook.** (Illus.). 300p. (Orig.). 1995. pap. 395.00 (*0-7605-1555-7*) Rector Pr.

Arab Versus European: Diplomacy & War in Nineteenth-Century East Central Africa. Norman R. Bennett. 350p. 1985. 49.50 (*0-8419-0861-3*, Africana) Holmes & Meier.

Arab Village: A Social Structural Study of a Transjordanian Peasant Community. Richard T. Antoun. LC 70-633555. (Indiana University Social Science Ser.: Vol. 29). 208p. reprint ed. pap. 59.30 (*0-8357-5704-8*, 2056022) Bks Demand.

Arab Voices: Human Rights & Culture. Kevin Dwyer. 350p. 1991. 45.00 (*0-520-07490-4*); pap. 14.00 (*0-520-07491-2*) U CA Pr.

Arab Women. Lewis B. Sckolnick. (Civil Rights Reporter Ser.). (Illus.). 60p. (Orig.). (C). 1994. pap. 45.00 (*1-57205-149-3*) Rector Pr.

Arab Women: Old Boundaries, New Frontiers. Ed. by Judith E. Tucker. LC 92-33583. (Indiana in Arab & Islamic Studies). 1993. 35.00 (*0-253-36096-X*); pap. 14.95 (*0-253-20776-2*) Ind U Pr.

Arab Women in the Field: Studying Your Own Society. Ed. by Soraya Altorki & Camillia F. El-Solh. 200p. 1988. 39.95x (*0-8156-2449-2*); pap. 15.95 (*0-8156-2450-6*) Syracuse U Pr.

Arab Women Novelists: The Formative Years & Beyond. Joseph T. Zeidan. LC 94-1007. (Middle Eastern Studies). 416p. 1994. 74.50 (*0-7914-2171-6*); pap. 24.95 (*0-7914-2172-4*) State U NY Pr.

Arab World. 308p. 1985. pap. 110.00 (*1-85077-074-3*, Darf Pubs Ltd) St Mut.

Arab World. Gerald Butt. 152p. (C). 1988. pap. 18.95 (*0-534-10500-9*) Intl Thomson.

Arab World: Libraries & Librarianship 1960-1976; a Bibliography. Veronica S. Pantelidis. 116p. 1979. pap. 70.00 (*0-7201-0821-7*, Mansell Pub) Cassell.

Arab World: Nation, State & Democracy. Fawzy Mansour. Tr. by Michael Wolfers. LC 90-47485. (Studies in African Political Economy). 176p. (C). 1992. text ed. 17.50 (*0-86232-884-5*, Pub. by Zed Books UK); pap. 17.50 (*0-86232-885-3*, Pub. by Zed Books UK) Humanities.

Arab World: Personal Encounters. Elizabeth W. Fernea & Robert A. Fernea. (Illus.). 384p. 1987. reprint ed. pap. 14.00 (*0-385-23973-4*, Anchor NY) Doubleday.

Arab World: Society, Culture, & State. Halim Barakat. LC 92-23342. 1993. 30.00 (*0-520-07907-8*) U CA Pr.

Arab World: Society, Culture, & State. Halim Barakat. (C). 1993. pap. 15.00 (*0-520-08427-6*) U CA Pr.

Arab World after Desert Storm. Muhammad Faour. LC 93-29014. 1993. 24.95 (*1-878379-30-5*); pap. 15.95 (*1-878379-31-3*) US Inst Peace.

Arab World & Asia Between Development & Change: Dedicated to the XXXIst International Congress of Human Sciences in Asia & Northern Africa. Ed. by Gunter Barthel & Lothar Rathman. 304p. 1983. 55.00 (*0-317-53804-7*, Pub. by Collets UK) Pro-Am Music.

Arab World & Israel. Ahmad El Kodsy & Eli Lobel. LC 70-129571. (Illus.). 144p. 1970. pap. 4.50 (*0-85345-168-0*) Monthly Rev.

Arab World Notebook: Secondary School Level. Ed. by Audrey Shabbas & Ayad Al-Qazzaz. 1989. 39.95 (*0-685-29959-7*) Najda WCME.

Arab World Today. William R. Polk. 538p. 1991. pap. text ed. 14.95 (*0-674-04320-0*, POLARY) HUP.

Arab World Today. Ed. by Dan Tschirgi. LC 93-29379. 274p. 1994. lib. bdg. 45.00 (*1-55587-459-2*); pap. text ed. 18.95 (*1-55587-479-7*) Lynne Rienner.

Arab World's Legacy. Charles Issawi. LC 81-3279. 378p. 1981. pap. 14.95 (*0-87850-040-5*) Darwin Pr.

Arabaische Quellenbeitraege: Zur Geschichte der Kreuzzuge. xxiii, 295p. 1975. reprint ed. write for info. (*3-487-05590-2*, Pub. by Georg Olms GW) Lubrecht & Cramer.

Arabba, Gah, Zee, Marissa & Me! Ruth Rosner. Ed. by Ann Fay. LC 86-15904. (Illus.). 32p. (J). (ps-3). 1987. lib. bdg. 13.95 (*0-8075-0442-4*) A Whitman.

Arabbers of Baltimore. Roland L. Freeman. LC 88-40561. (Illus.). 192p. 1989. 19.95 (*0-87033-397-6*, Tidewtr Pubs) Cornell Maritime.

***Arabbin' Man.** Monalisa DeGross. LC 94-49520. (Illus.). (J). 1996. write for info. (*0-7868-0160-3*); lib. bdg. write for info. (*0-7868-2132-9*) Hyprn Child.

***Arabe-Express Dictionnaire, Guide de Conversation et Grammaire de l'Arabe Moderne.** 4th ed. Antranik Patanian. 159p. (ARA & FRE.). 1989. pap. 32.95 (*0-7859-7947-6*, 2716310076) Fr & Eur.

Arabe-Francais Dictionnaire. Jabbour Abdel-Nour. 1983. 39.95 (*0-86685-334-0*) Intl Bk Ctr.

Arabe Francais Dictionnaire, 2 vols. A. Kazirmski. (ARA & FRE.). 1983. reprint ed. 95.00 (*0-86685-110-0*) Intl Bk Ctr.

Arabe Sans Peine (One) Arabic for French Speakers. Assimil Staff. (ARA & FRE.). 1990. 28.95 (*0-8288-4353-8*, M14741); audio 125.00 (*0-8288-9050-1*, M14740) Fr & Eur.

An Asterisk (*) at the beginning of an entry indicates that the title is appearing in BIP for the first time.

Arabe Sans Peine (Two) et Livret Phonetique: Arabic for French Speakers. Assimil Staff. (ARA & FRE.). 1990. 28.95 (*0-7859-0380-1*, M14742); audio 125.00 (*0-8288-9051-X*) Fr & Eur.

***Arabe Sin Esfuerzo.** Tr. by J. J. Schmidt & Fortunato Riloba. (Sin Esfuerzo Ser.). (Illus.). 1982. 19.95 (*2-7005-0101-2*, Pub. by ASSIMIL FR) Distribks Inc.

***Arabe Sin Esfuerzo.** Tr. by J. J. Schmidt & Fortunato Riloba. (Sin Esfuerzo Ser.). 1982. audio 49.95 (*2-7005-1154-9*, Pub. by ASSIMIL FR) Distribks Inc.

Arabe Sin Esfuerzo: Arabic for Spanish Speakers. Assimil Staff. (ARA & SPA.). 1990. 28.95 (*0-8288-4360-0*, S25814); audio 125.00 (*0-8288-9029-3*, F19960) Fr & Eur.

Arabella. Georgette Heyer. 1976. 21.95 (*0-8488-0811-8*) Amereon Ltd.

Arabella. Georgette Heyer. 1992. mass mkt. 4.50 (*0-06-100444-8*, Harp PBks) HarpC.

Arabella. Richard Strauss. Ed. by Nicholas John. LC 82-1822. (English National Opera Guide Series: Bilingual Libretto, Articles: No. 30). (Illus.). 112p. (Orig.). (C). 1985. pap. 9.95 (*0-7145-4062-5*) Riverrun NY.

Arabella. large type ed. Georgette Heyer. LC 91-26433. 445p. 1992. reprint ed. lib. bdg. 18.95 (*1-56054-204-7*) Thorndike Pr.

Arabella, Lyrische Komodie in Drei Aufzugen. Hugo Von Hofmannsthal. Ed. by Hugo Schmidt. (C). 1963. pap. text ed. 2.95 (*0-393-09605-X*) Norton.

Arabella the Itchy Witch. Martha Smith. Ed. by Helen Graves. LC 85-40893. 86p. (J). (gr. 3 up). 1986. 6.95 (*1-55523-007-5*) Winston-Derek.

Araber in Palastina: Geschite und Herkunft. Michael Assaf. 68p. (GER.). reprint ed. pap. 5.95 (*0-935005-91-9*) Lincoln-Rembrandt.

Araber und Sein Pferd. Carl Raswan & R. H. Seydel. (Documenta Hippologica Ser.). (Illus.). 166p. 1990. reprint ed. write for info. (*3-487-08234-9*, Pub. by Georg Olms GW) Lubrecht & Cramer.

Arabes see Arab Rebirth: Pain & Ecstasy

Arabesk Debate: Music & Musicians in Modern Turkey. Martin Stokes. (Oxford Studies in Social & Cultural Anthropology). (Illus.). 288p. 1993. 56.00 (*0-19-827367-3*) OUP.

Arabesque. Deborah Satinwood. 416p. 1994. mass mkt. 4.50 (*0-8217-4476-3*) Zebra.

Arabesque: An Artist's Perspective. Leyla Farr. 112p. (C). 1990. 150.00 (*0-907151-14-0*, Pub. by IMMEL Pubng UK) St Mut.

Arabesque & Honeycomb. Sacheverell Sitwell. LC 78-37124. (Essay Index Reprint Ser.). 1977. reprint ed. 27.95 (*0-8369-2522-X*) Ayer.

Arabesques. braille ed. Anton Shammas. 443p. 1991. vinyl bd. 35.44 (*1-56956-186-9*, BR7489) W A T Braille.

Arabesques: More Tales of the Arabian Nights. Ed. by Susan Shwartz. 272p. 1988. pap. 3.50 (*0-380-75319-7*) Avon.

Arabesques 2. Ed. by Susan Shwartz. 384p. (Orig.). 1989. pap. 3.95 (*0-380-75570-X*) Avon.

Arabia. Jonathan Raban. (Illus.). 352p. 1991. pap. 11.00 (*0-671-74880-7*, Touchstone Bks) S&S Trade.

Arabia. David G. Hogarth. LC 79-2862. 139p. 1985. reprint ed. 18.00 (*0-8305-0036-7*) Hyperion Conn.

Arabia: Sand, Sea & Sky. Michael McKinnon. 224p. (C). 1990. 100.00 (*0-907151-63-9*, Pub. by IMMEL Pubng UK) St Mut.

Arabia: Sand, Sea, Sky. Michael McKinnon. (Illus.). 224p. 1992. 29.95 (*0-563-36106-9*, BBC-Parkwest) Parkwest Pubns.

Arabia: The Cradle of Islam, Studies in the Geography, People & Politics of the Peninsula. Samuel M. Zwemer. 1980. lib. bdg. 75.00 (*0-8490-3135-4*) Gordon Pr.

Arabia & the Bible. rev. ed. James A. Montgomery. (Library of Biblical Studies). 1969. 25.00 (*0-87068-090-0*) Ktav.

Arabia & the Gulf in Original Photographs Eighteen Eighty to Nineteen Fifty. Andrew Wheatcroft. 200p. 1983. 49.95 (*0-685-06164-7*, 00166) Routledge Chapman & Hall.

Arabia Before Mohammed. Lacy E. O'Leary. 1973. 59.95 (*0-87968-651-0*) Gordon Pr.

Arabia Before Muhammad. De Lacy E. O'Leary. LC 74-180373. (Illus.). reprint ed. 39.50 (*0-404-56313-9*) AMS Pr.

Arabia-Cradle of Islam. S. M. Zwemer. 482p. 1986. 350.00 (*1-85077-111-1*, Darf Pubs Ltd) St Mut.

Arabia Deserta. Alois Musil. LC 77-87085. (American Geographical Society Oriental Explorations & Studies: No. 2). (Illus.). reprint ed. 74.50 (*0-404-60232-0*) AMS Pr.

Arabia Imperilled: The Security Imperatives of the Arab Gulf States. Mazher A. Hameed & James R. Schlesinger. (Illus.). 189p. 1986. pap. 14.95 (*0-937783-00-5*) Mid East Assess.

Arabia in Early Maps. G. R. Tibbetts. (Arabia Past & Present Ser.: Vol. 4). (Illus.). 75p. 1978. 71.00 (*0-902675-58-3*) Oleander Pr.

Arabia of the Wahhabis. Harry S. Philby. LC 73-6297. (Middle East Ser.). 1977. reprint ed. 36.95 (*0-405-05355-X*) Ayer.

Arabia of the Wahhabis. H. St. John Philby. (Illus.). 422p. 1977. reprint ed. 35.00 (*0-7146-3073-X*, Pub. by F Cass Pubs UK) Intl Spec Bk.

Arabia Petraea: Reisebericht, 3 vols. Alois Musil. (Illus.). xxxix, 1636p. 1989. reprint ed. Vol. I: Moab. write for info. (*0-318-71536-8*, Pub. by Georg Olms GW) Lubrecht & Cramer.

Arabia Petraea: Reisebericht, 3 vols., Set. Alois Musil. (Illus.). xxxix, 1636p. 1989. reprint ed. write for info. (*3-487-06480-4*, Pub. by Georg Olms GW) Lubrecht & Cramer.

Arabia Petraea: Reisebericht, 3 vols., Vol. II. Alois Musil. (Illus.). xxxix, 1636p. 1989. reprint ed. write for info. (*0-318-71537-6*, Pub. by Georg Olms GW) Lubrecht & Cramer.

Arabia Petraea: Reisebericht, 3 vols., Vol. III. Alois Musil. (Illus.). xxxix, 1636p. 1989. reprint ed. write for info. (*0-318-71538-4*, Pub. by Georg Olms GW) Lubrecht & Cramer.

Arabian: A Guide for Owners. Sharon Byford. LC 86-72633. (Illus.). 352p. 1987. 35.95 (*0-931866-27-8*) Alpine Pubns.

Arabian & Islamic Studies: Articles. Ed. by R. L. Bidwell & Rex Smith. LC 83-12027. (Illus.). 320p. (C). 1984. text ed. 45.95 (*0-582-78308-9*) Longman.

Arabian Boundaries: Primary Documents, 1854-1959, 29 vols., Set. R. N. Schofield & G. H. Blake. 16000p. (C). 1987. text ed. 20,000.00 (*1-85207-130-3*, Pub. by Archive Res Ltd UK) St Mut.

Arabian Boundaries, Vols. 27-29: Continuation Volumes for 1959, 3 vols., Set. Richard Schofield & Gerald Blakes. (C). 1987. text ed. 1,500.00 (*0-685-38765-8*, Pub. by Archive Res Ltd UK) St Mut.

Arabian Collection: Artifacts from the Eastern Province. Grace Burkholder. (Illus.). 224p. (Orig.). (C). 1984. pap. text ed. write for info. (*0-9613535-0-3*) GB Pubns.

***Arabian Cuisine.** Anne M. Weiss-Armosh. 403p. 1984. write for info. (*0-9642489-0-5*) Dar An-Nafaes.

Arabian Cuisine. Anne M. Weiss-Armush. (Illus.). 400p. 1984. 30.00x (*0-86685-456-8*) Intl Bk Ctr.

Arabian Days. Edna O'Brien. 15.95 (*0-7043-2150-5*, Pub. by Quartet UK) Charles River Bks.

Arabian Delights: Mediterranean Cuisines from Mecca to Marrakesh. Anne M. Weiss-Armush. LC 93-33659. 320p. 1994. 25.00 (*1-56565-126-X*) Lowell Hse.

***Arabian Delights Cookbook.** Anne M. Weiss-Armush. 320p. 1995. pap. 15.00 (*1-56565-219-3*) Lowell Hse.

Arabian Desert: A Chronicle of Contrast. John Carter. 112p. (C). 1990. 110.00 (*0-907151-06-X*, Pub. by IMMEL Pubng UK) St Mut.

***Arabian Epic: Heroic & Oral Storytelling.** M. C. Lyons. (University of Cambridge Oriental Publications Ser.: 52). (C). 1995. write for info. (*0-521-48354-9*) Cambridge U Pr.

***Arabian Epic: Heroic & Oral Storytelling Vol. 1: Introduction.** M. C. Lyons. (University of Cambridge Oriental Publications: 49). 192p. (C). 1995. write for info. (*0-521-47428-0*) Cambridge U Pr.

***Arabian Epic: Heroic & Oral Storytelling Vol. 2: Analysis.** M. C. Lyons. (University of Cambridge Oriental Publications Ser.: 49). 500p. (C). 1995. write for info. (*0-521-47449-3*) Cambridge U Pr.

***Arabian Epic: Heroic & Oral Storytelling Vol. 3: Texts.** M. C. Lyons. (University of Cambridge Oriental Publications Ser.: 49). 500p. (C). 1995. write for info. (*0-521-47450-7*) Cambridge U Pr.

Arabian Fairy Tales. Amina Shah. 212p. (Orig.). 1989. pap. 12.50 (*0-86304-048-9*) ISHK Bk Service.

Arabian Financial Review: Saudi Arabia & Bahrain. Immel Staff. 148p. (C). 1990. pap. 90.00 (*0-907151-47-7*, Pub. by IMMEL Pubng UK) St Mut.

Arabian Gulf in Antiquity, Vol. 1: From Prehistory to the Fall of the Achamenid Empire. D. T. Potts. (Illus.). 460p. 1991. 110.00 (*0-19-814390-7*) OUP.

Arabian Gulf in Antiquity, Vol. 2: Alexander the Great to the Coming of Islam. D. T. Potts. (Illus.). 408p. 1991. 98.00 (*0-19-814391-5*) OUP.

Arabian Gulf Intelligence. Ed. by Robert H. Thomas. (Arabia Past & Present Ser.: Vol. 17). (Illus.). 728p. 1985. 95.00 (*0-900891-54-8*) Oleander Pr.

Arabian Gulf Oil Concessions, 1911-1953, 12 vols., Set. Archive Editions Staff. 7000p. (C). 1987. text ed. 8,500.00 (*1-85207-210-5*, Pub. by Archive Res Ltd UK) St Mut.

Arabian Highlands. J. B. Philby. LC 76-10643. (Middle East in the 20th Century Ser.). 1976. reprint ed. lib. bdg. 75.00 (*0-306-70765-9*) Da Capo.

Arabian History with Precious Gold in Saudi Arabia. Heather C. Ross. (Illus.). 180p. 1994. 80.00 (*2-88373-003-2*, Pub. by Arabesque Comm SZ) Empire Pub Srvs.

***Arabian Horse.** (Learning about Horses Ser.). 48p. (J). (gr. 3-4). 1994. lib. bdg. 13.35 (*1-56065-244-6*) Capstone Pr.

Arabian Horse. Rosemary Archer. 160p. 1990. 52.00 (*0-85131-549-6*, Pub. by J A Allen & Co UK) St Mut.

***Arabian Horse.** Stewart. (J). 1995. pap. 5.95 (*0-516-40244-7*) Childrens.

Arabian Horse. Reginald S. Summerhays. 1979. pap. 7.00 (*0-87980-183-2*) Wilshire.

Arabian Horse: His Country & People. W. Tweedie. (Arab Background Ser.). 1972. 35.00 (*0-86685-170-4*) Intl Bk Ctr.

***Arabian Horse Bibliography: A Project of the Arabian Horse Trust.** 180p. 1985. 12.00 (*0-614-04190-2*) Arabian Horse Trust.

***Arabian Horses.** Janet L. Gammie. LC 95-3369. (Horses Ser.). (J). 1995. lib. bdg. 9.95 (*1-56239-440-1*) Abdo & Dghtrs.

Arabian Jazz. Diana Abu-Jaber. LC 92-41532. 1993. 21.95 (*0-15-107862-9*) HarBrace.

Arabian Jazz. Diana Abu-Jaber. 1994. pap. 10.95 (*0-15-600048-2*) HarBrace.

Arabian Knights. Rene Bull. (J). (gr. 2-6). 1986. 8.98 (*0-685-16864-6*, 619342) Random Hse Value.

Arabian Link. James Warner. (Illus.). 448p. 1993. 22.95 (*0-89896-304-4*) Larksdale.

Arabian Love Poems. Nizar Kabbani. 240p. 1993. 28.00 (*0-89410-744-5*); pap. 15.00 (*0-89410-745-3*) Three Continents.

Arabian Mammals: A Natural History. Jonathan Kingdon. 279p. 1991. text ed. 150.00 (*0-12-408350-1*) Acad Pr.

Arabian Medicine. Edward Brown. 19.95 (*0-935782-19-2*) Kazi Pubns.

Arabian Medicine. Edward G. Browne. LC 79-2852. (Illus.). 138p. 1985. reprint ed. 18.50 (*0-8305-0028-6*) Hyperion Conn.

Arabian Medicine & Its Influence on the Middle Ages, 2 vols., Set. Donald E. Campbell. LC 74-180330. reprint ed. 84.50 (*0-404-56235-3*) AMS Pr.

Arabian Moons: Passages in Time Through Yemen. Dominique Champault. (Illus.). 160p. 1988. text ed. 45.00 (*0-7103-0318-1*, Pub. by Kegan Paul Intl UK) Routledge Chapman & Hall.

Arabian Mosaic: Short Stories by Arab Women Writers. Dalya Cohen-Mor. (C). 1993. 24.95 (*1-880613-08-5*); pap. 15.95 (*1-880613-06-9*) Sheba Pr.

Arabian Nightmare. Robert Irwin. (Dedalus European Fiction Ser.). (Illus.). 282p. 1990. 11.95 (*0-946626-14-6*, Pub. by Dedalus Bks UK) Hippocrene Bks.

Arabian Nightmare. Created by Warren Murphy & Richard Sapir. (Destroyer Ser.: No. 86). 256p. 1991. pap. 4.50 (*0-451-17060-1*, Sig) NAL-Dutton.

Arabian Nights. 25.95 (*0-8488-0866-5*) Amereon Ltd.

Arabian Nights. Tr. by Husain Haddawy. 1990. 27.95 (*0-393-02707-4*) Norton.

Arabian Nights. Laurence Housman. 176p. 1981. 35.00 (*0-913870-91-9*) Abaris Bks.

Arabian Nights. Jack Marshall. LC 86-19273. 101p. (Orig.). 1986. pap. 8.95 (*0-918273-28-5*) Coffee Hse.

Arabian Nights. Illus. by Sheila Moxley. LC 94-9137. 160p. (YA). (gr. 5 up). 1994. 19.95 (*0-531-06868-4*) Orchard Bks Watts.

Arabian Nights. Lowell Swortzell. 1977. 3.00 (*0-87129-223-8*, A18) Dramatic Pub.

Arabian Nights. Ed. by Jack D. Zipes. 464p. 1991. pap. 5.95 (*0-451-52542-6*, Sig Classics) NAL-Dutton.

Arabian Nights. deluxe ed. Mark Twain. (Illus.). (J). (gr. 4-9). 1981. reprint ed. 13.95 (*0-448-06006-X*, G&D) Putnam Pub Group.

Arabian Nights. Ed. by Richard Burton. (Illus.). 390p. 1992. reprint ed. lib. bdg. 31.95 (*1-877767-64-6*) Univ Publng Hse.

***Arabian Nights.** Tr. by Husain Haddawy. 464p. 1995. reprint ed. pap. 14.95 (*0-393-31367-0*, Norton Paperbks) Norton.

Arabian Nights: A Companion. Robert Irwin. 352p. 1994. 24.95 (*0-7139-9105-4*) Allen Lane.

***Arabian Nights: Tales Told by Sheherezade During a Thousand Nights & One Night.** Brian Alderson. LC 94-40945. (Books of Wonder). (Illus.). (J). 1995. 20.00 (*0-688-14219-2*) Morrow Jr Bks.

Arabian Nights: The Thousand & One Nights. Tr. by Husain Haddawy. (C). 1990. pap. text ed. 12.95 (*0-393-95906-6*) Norton.

Arabian Nights: The Thousand & One Nights. Mushin Mahdi. 1992. 17.00 (*0-679-41338-3*, Everymans Lib) Knopf.

Arabian Nights: Their Best-Known Tales. limited ed. Ed. by Kate D. Wiggin & Nora A. Smith. LC 92-38552. (Scribner's Illustrated Classics Ser.). (Illus.). 368p. (J). 1993. 75.00 (*0-684-19588-7*, C Scribner Sons Young); text ed. 25.00 (*0-684-19589-5*, C Scribner Sons Young) S&S Childrens.

Arabian Nights & Days. Naguib Mahfouz. Tr. by Denys Johnson-Davies. LC 94-6457. 1995. 22.95 (*0-385-46888-1*) Doubleday.

Arabian Nights Entertainment. G. F. Townsend. 672p. 1985. 350.00 (*1-85077-059-X*, Darf Pubs Ltd) St Mut.

Arabian Nights Entertainments. Ed. by Andrew Lang. 25.95 (*0-89190-085-3*, Am Repr) Amereon Ltd.

Arabian Nights Entertainments. Andrew Lang. (Illus.). 19.25 (*0-8446-0752-5*) Peter Smith.

***Arabian Night's Entertainments.** Ed. by Robert Mack. (World's Classics Ser.). 1300p. 1995. pap. 14.95 (*0-19-282832-0*) OUP.

Arabian Nights Entertainments. Ed. by Andrew Lang. LC 69-17098. (Illus.). xv, 424p. (J). (gr. k-6). 1969. reprint ed. pap. 6.95 (*0-486-22289-6*) Dover.

***Arabian Nights II: Sinbad & Other Popular Stories.** Tr. by Husain Haddawy. LC 95-1664. 1995. 27.50 (*0-393-03815-7*) Norton.

Arabian Oasis City: The Transformation of 'Unayzah. Soraya Altorki & Donald P. Cole. (Modern Middle East Ser.: No. 15). 284p. 1989. 35.00 (*0-292-78517-8*); pap. 14.95 (*0-292-78518-6*) U of Tex Pr.

Arabian Oil Ventures. J. B. Philby. LC 65-110. 1964. 7.50 (*0-916808-05-X*) Mid East Inst.

Arabian Peninsula. Richard H. Sanger. LC 76-117891. (Select Bibliographies Reprint Ser.). 1977. 31.95 (*0-8369-5344-4*) Ayer.

Arabian Peninsula: A Selected Annotated List of Periodicals, Books & Articles in English. 1980. lib. bdg. 49.95 (*0-8490-3134-6*) Gordon Pr.

Arabian Personalities of the Early 20th Century. Intro. by Robin L. Bidwell. (Arabia Past & Present Ser.: Vol. 19). (Illus.). 380p. 1986. 60.00 (*0-906672-39-2*) Oleander Pr.

Arabian Plate Hydrocarbon Geology & Potential - A Plate Tectonic Approach. Z. R. Beydoun. (Studies in Geology: No. 33). (Illus.). 77p. (Orig.). 1991. pap. 27.00 (*0-89181-041-2*) AAPG.

Arabian Poetry. William A. Clouston. 560p. 1986. 350.00 (*1-85077-137-5*, Darf Pubs Ltd) St Mut.

Arabian Princess Between Two Worlds: Memoirs, Letters Home, Sequels to My Memoirs: Syrian Customs & Usages. Sayyida Salme & Emily Ruete. LC 92-10573. (Arab History & Civilization, Studies & Texts: Vol. 3). 1992. 143.00 (*90-04-09615-9*) E J Brill.

Arabian Sands. Wilfred Thesiger. (Nonfiction Ser.). 1985. pap. 9.95 (*0-14-009514-4*, Penguin Bks) Viking Penguin.

Arabian Sands. braille ed. Wilfred Thesiger. 696p. 1991. vinyl bd. 55.68 (*1-56956-187-7*, BR8451) W A T Braille.

Arabian Society in the Middle Ages: Studies from One Thousand & One Nights. Edward W. Lane. 300p. 1989. text ed. 27.50 (*81-207-0939-X*, Pub. by Sterling Pubs II) Apt Bks.

Arabian Society in the Middle Ages: Studies from the 1001 Nights. Lane. (C). 1987. pap. 19.95 (*0-7007-0195-8*, Pub. by Curzon Pr UK) Humanities.

Arabian Studies, Vol. 8. Ed. by R. B. Serjeant & R. L. Bidwell. (University of Cambridge Oriental Publications: No. 42). (Illus.). 200p. (C). 1990. 69.95 (*0-521-37344-1*) Cambridge U Pr.

Arabian Wisdom. John Wortabet. 64p. (C). 1988. pap. text ed. 3.50 (*1-56744-219-6*) Kazi Pubns.

Arabia's Frontiers: The Story of Britain's Blue & Violet Lines. John Wilkinson. 405p. 1991. text ed. 89.50 (*1-85043-356-9*, Pub. by I B Tauris UK) St Martin.

Arabic. (Hugo's Phrasebks.). 128p. (Orig.). 1989. pap. 4.95 (*0-85285-141-3*) Hunter NJ.

Arabic. rev. ed. Frank Hill. (LanguageCard Pac Ser.). 1993. Incl. 4 language cards. 4.00 (*0-88699-060-2*) Travel Sci.

Arabic: Eastern. Frank A. Rice & Majed F. Sa'id. 400p. 1979. audio 175.00 (*0-88432-201-7*, AFA450); 19.95 (*0-685-73880-9*) Audio-Forum.

Arabic: Egyptian-Arabic Manual for Self-Study. 18th ed. E. A. Elias & E. E. Elias. 240p. pap. 13.00 (*0-88431-358-1*) IBD Ltd.

Arabic: Elias' Practical Grammar & Vocabulary of Colloquial Arabic. 3rd ed. A. E. Elias & E. E. Elias. 103p. pap. 10.00 (*0-88431-009-4*) IBD Ltd.

Arabic: Modern Written, Vol. I. Foreign Service Institute Staff. 419p. 1980. 245.00x (*0-88432-039-1*, AFA269); 29.95 (*0-88432-797-3*, AFA993) Audio-Forum.

Arabic: Modern Written, Vol. II. Foreign Service Institute Staff. 385p. (C). 1980. audio 175.00x (*0-88432-088-X*, AFA320); 29.95 (*0-88432-798-1*, AFA995) Audio-Forum.

Arabic: Phonology & Script. Al-Ani & Shammas. 1980. 14.95 (*0-917062-04-3*) Intl Bk Ctr.

Arabic: Teach Yourself. A. T. Ayyad. 1982. 16.95x (*0-86685-343-X*) Intl Bk Ctr.

Arabic: VocabuLearn, Level 1. (ARA & ENG.). 1990. 15.95 (*0-939001-76-4*) Penton Overseas.

Arabic Adeni Reader. Habaka J. Feghali. Ed. by Alan S. Kaye. LC 89-85773. (Arabic Dialect Series, Yemen). 265p. 1990. 49.00 (*0-931745-58-6*) Dunwoody Pr.

Arabic Adeni Textbook. Habaka J. Feghali. Ed. by Alan S. Kaye. LC 88-51590. (Arabic Dialect Series, Yemen). 233p. 1991. 44.00 (*0-931745-46-2*); audio 15.00 (*0-931745-52-7*) Dunwoody Pr.

Arabic Alphabet. Nazih Girgis. (Illus.). 57p. (ARA & ENG.). (J). (gr. k-12). 1983. audio, pap. 15.00 (*0-86685-340-5*) Intl Bk Ctr.

Arabic Alphabet: How to Read & Write It. Nicholas Awde & Putros Samano. 96p. 1987. pap. 6.00 (*0-8184-0430-2*) Carol Pub Group.

Arabic Alphabet Coloring Book. M. A. Qazi. 20p. (J). (ps). 1984. pap. 3.50 (*1-56744-220-X*) Kazi Pubns.

Arabic & Persian Periodicals in the Middle East Collection. 108p. 1985. pap. 5.00 (*0-930214-15-3*) U TX Austin Gen Libs.

Arabic & Persian Poems. Tr. by Omar Pound. LC 72-122106. (Orig.). 1970. 7.50 (*0-8112-0358-1*) New Directions.

Arabic & Persian Poems in English. Omar Pound. 124p. (Orig.). 1986. 12.95 (*0-915032-09-0*) Natl Poet Foun.

Arabic & Persian Poems in English. Ed. by Omar Pound. LC 85-50527. 123p. (Orig.). 1986. boxed 22.00 (*0-89410-466-7*) Three Continents.

Arabic-Arabic: A Contextual Arabic Dictionary. Sieny-Yusuf. 1991. 24.95 (*0-86685-502-5*) Intl Bk Ctr.

Arabic-Arabic Dictionary. Al Fara'id & As-Samarra'i. 1984. 17.95 (*0-86685-501-7*) Intl Bk Ctr.

Arabic-Arabic Dictionary. Mukhtar us-Sihah & Ar'Rhazi. 1990. 24.95 (*0-86685-375-8*) Intl Bk Ctr.

Arabic-Arabic Dictionary Muhit Al Muhit. Butrus Al-Bustani. (ARA.). 1983. 65.00 (*0-86685-096-1*) Intl Bk Ctr.

Arabic-Arabic Dictionary of the Names of Towns & Villages in Lebanon. Annis Freyha. 1974. 24.95 (*0-86685-099-6*) Intl Bk Ctr.

Arabic As Spoken in Lebanon. 2nd ed. Khalil El-Sayed. LC 89-91527. 124p. (ARA, ENG, FRE & SPA.). 1990. reprint ed. pap. text ed. 8.95 (*0-9624579-1-4*) K El-Sayed.

Arabic as Spoken in Saudi Arabia & Kuwait. Khalil El-Sayed & Ridha Al-Khayyat. LC 91-91958. 150p. 1991. 9.95 (*0-9624579-2-2*) K El-Sayed.

Arabic at a Glance. 448p. 1986. pap. 5.95 (*0-8120-2979-8*) Barron.

Arabic Authors. F. F. Arbuthnot. 262p. 1984. 200.00 (*1-85077-091-3*, Darf Pubs Ltd) St Mut.

Arabic Book. Johannes Pederson. Ed. by Robert Hillenbrand. Tr. by Geoffrey French. LC 82-61379. (Modern Classics in Near Eastern Studies). Orig. Title: Den Arabiske Bog. (Illus.). 220p. 1984. 35.00 (*0-691-06564-0*) Princeton U Pr.

Arabic Books Published in Egypt in the Nineteenth Century. Aida I. Nosseir. 1990. text ed. 50.00 (*0-685-37649-4*, Pub. by Am Univ Cairo Pr UA) Col U Pr.

Arabic Cassette Pack. Berlitz Editors. (Cassette Packs Ser.). 1991. Incl. cass. 15.95 (*2-8315-1046-5*) Berlitz.

Arabic Childbirth Picture Book. Fran P. Hosken. (Illus.). 84p. (Orig.). 1984. pap. 7.00 (*0-942096-06-1*) WINNEWS.

Arabic Christianity in the Monasteries of 9th Century. Sidney H. Griffith. (Collected Studies: Vol. CS380). 352p. 1992. 89.95 (*0-86078-337-5*, Pub. by Variorum UK) Ashgate Pub Co.

402 An Asterisk (*) at the beginning of an entry indicates that the title is appearing in BIP for the first time.

Arabic Coins & How to Read Them. R. J. Plante. (Illus.). 1981. pap. 20.00 (*0-686-45249-6*, Pub. by Seaby UK) S J Durst.

Arabic Coins & How to Read Them. 2nd ed. Richard Plant. (Illus.). 151p. 1980. 22.95 (*0-900652-52-7*, Pub. by Seaby UK) Trafalgar.

Arabic Computer Dictionary. Mohamed F. Ghanayem. Ed. by Taher Aboulnaga & Maan R. Al-Ubaidi. (Illus.). 702p. (ARA & ENG.). 1986. write for info. (*0-937127-00-0*) Intl Hse Pubns.

Arabic Conversation. Mounir Ghandour. 1976. audio 30.00 (*0-86685-338-3*); pap. 5.00 (*0-86685-041-4*) Intl Bk Ctr.

Arabic Culture: Through Its Language & Literature. Muhammed H. Bakalla. 365p. (Orig.). 1982. pap. 17.95 (*0-7103-0027-1*, Pub. by Kegan Paul Intl UK) Routledge Chapman & Hall.

Arabic Designs in Color. D'Avennes Prisse. (Pictorial Archive Ser.). (Illus.). 1978. pap. 7.95 (*0-486-23658-7*) Dover.

***Arabic Dialect Identification Course.** Margaret K. Nydell. 223p. 1995. pap. text ed. 59.95 (*0-9628410-9-9*) DLS VA.

Arabic Dictionary. (Handy Dictionaries Ser.). 120p. (Orig.). (ARA.). 1991. pap. 8.95 (*0-87052-960-9*) Hippocrene Bks.

Arabic Dictionary: Al Munjid fi al-Lugha Wal 'Alam. Dar El Mashreq. (ARA.). 1979. 65.00 (*2-7214-2124-7*) Intl Bk Ctr.

Arabic Dictionary of Pseudonyms & the Writers Who Use Them. Yusuf Dagher. (ARA.). 1982. 16.00 (*0-86685-300-6*) Intl Bk Ctr.

Arabic, Egyptian: Spoken. Samia Mehrez. 250p. (Orig.). 1985. audio 175.00 (*0-88432-131-2*, AFA400); 15.95 (*0-88432-539-3*, AFA999) J Norton Pubs.

Arabic Encyclopaedic Dictionary of Cultural Terms. Okasha. 1990. 48.00 (*0-86685-500-9*) Intl Bk Ctr.

Arabic Encyclopedia for Children: (Arabic-Arabic) Ahmed Khatib. 1984. 30.00 (*0-86685-351-0*) Intl Bk Ctr.

***Arabic-English - English-Arabic Standard Dictionary.** Wortabet. 1995. pap. (*0-7818-0383-7*) Hippocrene Bks.

Arabic-English Advanced Learners Dictionary. Anthony Salmone. 1978. 35.00 (*0-86685-089-9*) Intl Bk Ctr.

Arabic-English & English-Arabic Dictionaries in the Library of Congress. Comp. by George D. Selim. 213p. (ARA & ENG.). 1992. 6.50 (*0-16-036092-7*, 030-000-00234-2) Lib Congress.

Arabic-English Collegiate Dictionary. Elias. (ARA & ENG.). 1990. 31.50 (*977-73210-5-8*) Colton Bk.

Arabic-English Dictionary. (ARA & ENG.). 39.50 (*0-87557-002-X*, 002-X) Saphrograph.

Arabic-English Dictionary. D. Cameron. 1979. 23.00x (*0-86685-084-8*) Intl Bk Ctr.

***Arabic-English Dictionary.** J. Hava. (Al Faraid Ser.). (ARA.). 1982. 39.95 (*0-86685-643-9*) Intl Bk Ctr.

Arabic-English Dictionary. F. Steingass. (ARA & ENG.). 1987. 59.95 (*0-8288-0436-2*, F90) Fr & Eur.

Arabic-English Dictionary. Hans Wehr. Ed. by J. M. Cowan. 1990. 25.00 (*0-685-66742-1*, 174) Tahrike Tarsile Quran.

Arabic-English Dictionary. 3rd rev. ed. Hans Wehr. Ed. by J Milton Cowan. LC 75-24236. 1110p. (ARA & ENG.). 1976. pap. 15.00 (*0-87950-001-8*) Spoken Lang Serv.

Arabic English Dictionary. John Wortabet & Harvey Porter. 450p. 1993. reprint ed. pap. 14.95 (*0-7818-0153-2*) Hippocrene Bks.

Arabic-English Dictionary: Colloquial Arabic of Egypt. Socrates Spiro. 1973. 35.00 (*0-86685-090-2*) Intl Bk Ctr.

Arabic-English Dictionary: Hava's Al: Faraid. 1974. 39.95 (*2-7214-2106-9*) Intl Bk Ctr.

Arabic-English Dictionary of Agricultural Terms & Allied Terminology. Ahmad Khatib. (ARA & ENG.). 1978. pap. 14.95 (*0-86685-274-3*) Intl Bk Ctr.

Arabic-English Dictionary of Arabic Topography & Placenames. Nigel Groom. 1983. 39.95 (*0-86685-331-6*) Intl Bk Ctr.

Arabic-English Dictionary of Legal Terms. Mary Armstrong. (ARA & ENG.). (C). 1988. 350.00x (*0-685-49138-2*) St Mut.

Arabic-English Dictionary of Modern Written Arabic. Hans Wehr. Ed. by J. Milton Cowan. Orig. Title: A Dictionary of Modern Written Arabic. xvii, 1301p. (ARA & ENG.). 1993. reprint ed. 45.00 (*0-87950-003-4*) Spoken Lang Serv.

Arabic-English, English-Arabic Computer Dictionary. Routledge. 350p. (ARA & ENG.). 1986. 125.00 (*0-8288-0227-0*, F62951) Fr & Eur.

Arabic-English, English-Arabic Dictionary of Civil Engineering. Routledge. (ARA & ENG.). 1986. 150.00 (*0-7859-0639-8*, F76990) Fr & Eur.

Arabic English, English-Arabic Pocket Dictionary. A. E. Elias. 947p. (ARA & ENG.). 18.00 (*0-88431-992-X*) IBD Ltd.

Arabic-English, English-Arabic School Dictionary. 10th ed. A. E. Elias. (Illus.). 800p. (ARA & ENG.). 24.00 (*0-88431-425-1*) IBD Ltd.

Arabic-English (Faruqi's) Law Dictionary. 3rd ed. H. Faruqi. 380p. 1986. 74.00 (*0-88431-072-8*, Pub. by U Politecnica) IBD Ltd.

Arabic-English Learners Dictionary. F. Steingass. (ARA & ENG.). 1972. 45.00x (*0-86685-087-2*) Intl Bk Ctr.

Arabic English Learner's Dictionary. F. Steingass. 466p. 1993. 24.95 (*0-7818-0155-9*) Hippocrene Bks.

Arabic English Lexicon, 8 vols. E. W. Lane. (ARA & ENG.). 1985. reprint ed. 195.00 (*0-8288-8455-2*) Fr & Eur.

Arabic-English Lexicon, 8 vols., Set. Madd A. Qamus & Edward Lane. (ARA & ENG.). 1980. 370.00 (*0-685-02567-5*) Intl Bk Ctr.

Arabic-English Lexicon, 2 vols., Set. Edward W. Lane. 1984. reprint ed. 320.00x (*0-946621-04-7*) Intl Bk Ctr.

***Arabic-English Lexicon, Vol. 1.** Lane. 1995. 275.00 (*0-946621-03-9*) Artium Bks.

Arabic-English Lexicon, Vol. I. E. W. Lane-Poole. 1500p. (C). 1993. text ed. 165.00 (*1-56744-491-1*) Kazi Pubns.

Arabic-English Lexicon, Vol. II. E. W. Lane-Poole. 1520p. (C). 1993. text ed. 165.00 (*1-56744-492-X*) Kazi Pubns.

Arabic-English Modern. 17th ed. 869p. 1991. 42.00 (*0-88431-503-7*) IBD Ltd.

Arabic-English Modern Dictionary. Elias Elias. (ARA & ENG.). 1981. 45.00x (*0-86685-287-5*) Intl Bk Ctr.

***Arabic-English Pocket Dictionary.** Wortabet & Porter. (ARA.). 1979. 7.95 (*0-86685-093-4*) Intl Bk Ctr.

Arabic-English Pocket Dictionary. John Wortabet & H. Porter. 1980. pap. 7.95x (*0-86685-093-7*) Intl Bk Ctr.

***Arabic Essays, 2 pts., Set.** Ed. by Rashid L. Bashshur et al. (Contemporary Arabic Readers Ser.: Vol. II). 1976. 7.50 (*0-916798-12-7*) Intl Bk Ctr.

Arabic Essays Pt. 1: Texts, 2 pts. Ed. by Rashid L. Bashshur et al. (Contemporary Arabic Readers Ser.: Vol. II). vi, 78p. 1976. write for info. (*0-318-51699-3*) UM Dept NES.

Arabic Essays Pt. 2: Notes & Glossaries, 2 pts. Ed. by Rashid L. Bashshur et al. (Contemporary Arabic Readers Ser.: Vol. II). iv, 208p. 1976. write for info. (*0-318-51700-0*) UM Dept NES.

Arabic First Handwriting Workbook. Lily Sayegh. 1982. audio 6.00x (*0-917062-03-5*); audio 10.00x (*0-86685-630-7*) Intl Bk Ctr.

***Arabic for Beginners.** Syed Ali. (C). 1994. 6.75x (*81-85273-01-4*, Pub. by UBS Pubs Dist II) S Asia.

Arabic for Beginners. A. H. Siddiqui. pap. 14.95 (*0-935782-16-8*) Kazi Pubns.

Arabic for Daily Use. M. A. Qazi. 20p. (Orig.). (ARA.). 1986. pap. 2.00 (*1-56744-221-8*) Kazi Pubns.

Arabic for English Speaking Students. M. A. Rauf. 1991. 22.95 (*0-935782-21-4*) Kazi Pubns.

Arabic for English Speaking Students. rev. ed. Muhammad A. Rauf. 434p. (C). 1993. reprint ed. pap. text ed. 20.00 (*1-881963-00-4*) Al-Saadawi Pubns.

Arabic-French-Arabic Dictionary: Dictionnaire Arabe-Francais-Arabe. Edward Elias. 1318p. (ARA & FRE.). 1982. 39.95 (*0-8288-0441-9*, F370) Fr & Eur.

Arabic-French Dictionary, 2 vols., Set. Auguste Cherbonneau. (ARA & FRE.). 1973. 29.95 (*0-86685-103-8*) Intl Bk Ctr.

Arabic-French Dictionary: Dictionnaire Arabe-Francais, Dialectes de Syrie: Alep, Damas, Liban, Jerusalem. Adrien Barthelemy. 1100p. (ARA & FRE.). 1983. 225. 00 (*0-8288-0438-9*, F369) Fr & Eur.

Arabic-French, French-Arabic Dictionary: Dictionnaire Arabe-Francais-Arabe. Daniel Reig. 1448p. (ARA & FRE.). 1983. 95.00 (*0-8288-0442-7*, F290) Fr & Eur.

Arabic Geometrical Pattern & Design. J. Bourgoin. (Illus.). 224p. 1973. reprint ed. pap. 8.95 (*0-486-22924-6*) Dover.

Arabic-German Dictionary: Woerterbuch Arabisch-Deutsch. Gunther Krahl & M. Gharieb. 864p. (ARA & GER.). 1984. 175.00 (*0-8288-0443-5*, F19921) Fr & Eur.

Arabic Grammar. G. W. Thatcher. LC 60-9106. 300p. 1981. 50.00 (*0-8044-0646-4*, F Ungar Bks) Continuum.

Arabic Grammar. G. M. Wickens. LC 77-82523. 180p. 1980. pap. 27.95 (*0-521-29301-4*) Cambridge U Pr.

Arabic Grammar. G. W. Thatcher. 470p. (ARA & ENG.). 1992. reprint ed. 29.95 (*0-8288-8500-1*) Fr & Eur.

Arabic Grammar: Arabic-English Pocket Dictionary. F. Du Pre Thornton. 1992. 14.95 (*0-86685-551-3*) Intl Bk Ctr.

Arabic Grammar & Qur'anic Exegesis in Early Islam. C. H. Versteegh. LC 93-7248. (Studies in Semitic Languages & Linguistics: Vol. 19). xi, 230p. 1993. 51.50 (*90-04-09845-3*) E J Brill.

Arabic Grammar of the Written Language. G. W. Thatcher. 560p. 1993. reprint ed. pap. 19.95 (*0-87052-101-2*) Hippocrene Bks.

Arabic Hijazi Reader. Habaka J. Feghali. Ed. by John D. Murphy. LC 91-70530. (Arabic Dialect Series, Saudi Arabia). 193p. 1991. 44.00 (*0-931745-72-1*); digital audio 20.00 (*0-931745-87-X*) Dunwoody Pr.

Arabic Historical Phraseology: Supplement to Written Arabic: an Approach to the Basic Structures. Alfred F. Beeston. LC 68-18342. 150p. reprint ed. pap. 42.80 (*0-8357-5705-6*, 2022439) Bks Demand.

Arabic Historical Thought in the Classical Period. Tarif Khalidi. (Cambridge Studies in Islamic Civilization). 256p. (C). 1995. 54.95 (*0-521-46554-0*) Cambridge U Pr.

Arabic in Three Months. (Hugo's Language Courses Ser.). 224p. (Orig.). 1990. audio 49.95 (*1-55650-254-0*); pap. 7.95 (*0-85285-159-6*) Hunter NJ.

Arabic Inscriptions in Jerusalem. A. Walls & Amal Abu'l-Hajj. (Illus.). 48p. 1986. pap. 9.95 (*0-905035-28-3*) Interlink Pub.

Arabic-Islamic Cities: Building & Planning Principles. Besim S. Hakim. (Illus.). 450p. 1986. lib. bdg. 85.00 (*0-7103-0094-8*, Pub. by Kegan Paul Intl UK) Routledge Chapman & Hall.

Arabic Key Reader: 1001 Nights. Michel Nicola. (ARA & ENG.). 1985. 6.95x (*0-86685-349-9*) Intl Bk Ctr.

Arabic Key Words: The Basic Two Thousand-Word Vocabulary Transliterated & Arranged by Frequency in a Hundred Units. David Quitregard. (Language & Literature Ser.: Vol. 16). 144p. (Orig.). 1993. pap. 14.95 (*0-906672-27-9*) Oleander Pr.

Arabic Language & Grammar, 4 vols. in 1. Jochanan Kapliwatzky. LC 72-180351. reprint ed. 38.00 (*0-404-56283-3*) AMS Pr.

Arabic Language in America. Ed. by Aleya Rouchdy. LC 91-30156. 345p. 1992. 44.95 (*0-8143-2283-2*); pap. 19.95 (*0-8143-2284-0*) Wayne St U Pr.

Arabic Legal & Administrative Documents in the Cambridge Genizah Collections. Ed. by Geoffrey Khan. LC 93-1047. (Genizah Ser.: No. 10). 608p. (C). 1993. 180.00 (*0-521-45169-8*) Cambridge U Pr.

Arabic, Levantine: Pronunciation. Foreign Service Institute Staff. 100p. (ARA.). 1980. audio 185.00x (*0-88432-038-3*, AFA244); 10.95 (*0-88432-805-8*, AFA992) Audio-Forum.

***Arabic Lexicography: Problems & Solutions.** Adnan Al-Khatib. 91p. (ARA.). 1994. 18.95 (*0-86685-653-6*) Intl Bk Ctr.

Arabic Linguistic Tradition. Georges Bohas et al. 208p. 1990. 55.00 (*0-415-01904-4*, A4246) Routledge.

Arabic Literature: Then & Now. Ed. by Fran Ringold et al. (Nimrod Ser.). (Illus.). 149p. (C). 1981. pap. text ed. 5.50 (*0-942374-07-X*) Art & Human Council Tulsa.

Arabic Literature of Africa. Ed. by J. O. Hunwick & R. S. O'Fahey. LC 93-33250. 1993. 120.00 (*90-04-09450-4*) E J Brill.

Arabic Literature to the End of the Umayyad Period. Ed. by Alfred F. Beeston et al. LC 82-23528. (Cambridge History of Arabic Literature Ser.). (Illus.). 570p. 1984. 120.00 (*0-521-24015-8*) Cambridge U Pr.

Arabic Logic: Ibn al-Tayyib on Porphyry's "Eisagoge" Ed. & Tr. by Kwame Gyekye. LC 76-4071. 245p. 1979. 59. 50 (*0-87395-308-8*) State U NY Pr.

Arabic Made Easy. Abul Hashim. (Orig.). (ARA & ENG.). Date not set. pap. 15.75 (*0-935782-15-X*) Kazi Pubns.

Arabic Made Easy. Mouncef Saheb-Ettaba & Caroline Squire. 1959. pap. text ed. 10.95 (*0-679-50905-4*) McKay.

Arabic Manuscripts in the Yale University Library. Leon Nemoy. (Connecticut Academy of Arts & Sciences Ser., Trans.: Vol. 40). 1956. pap. 100.00 (*0-685-22894-0*) Elliots Bks.

Arabic Military Dictionary. Ernest Kay. 320p. 1987. 195. 00 (*0-8288-1904-1*, F18700) Fr & Eur.

Arabic, Moroccan. Harrell et al. 395p. 1980. audio 245.00 (*0-88432-052-9*, AFA300); 19.95 (*0-685-73353-X*) Audio-Forum.

Arabic Moroccan Reader. Habaka J. Feghali & Alan Kaye. LC 88-51591. 143p. 1989. 39.00 (*0-931745-47-0*); audio 15.00 (*0-931745-51-9*) Dunwoody Pr.

Arabic Novel: An Historical & Critical Introduction. 2nd ed. Roger Allen. (Contemporary Issues in the Middle East Ser.). 184p. (C). 1994. pap. text ed. 17.95 (*0-8156-2641-X*) Syracuse U Pr.

Arabic Papyri: Selected Material from the Khalili Collection. Geoffrey Khan. (Studies in the Khalili Collection of Islamic Art: Vol. I). (Illus.). 264p. 1992. 65.00 (*0-19-727500-1*) OUP.

Arabic Parts in Astrology: Lost Key to Prediction. Robert Zoller. 256p. 1989. pap. 14.95 (*0-89281-250-8*) Inner Tradit.

Arabic Philosophy & the West: Continuity & Interaction. Ed. by Therese-Anne Druart. 156p. (Orig.). 1988. pap. text ed. 12.95 (*0-932568-15-7*) GU Ctr CAS.

Arabic Phonetics. K. I. Semaan. pap. 4.50 (*0-935782-40-0*) Kazi Pubns.

Arabic Phonetics: The Points of Articulation of the Speech-Sounds Translated from Medieval Arabic. Khalil Semaan. 1977. 4.95 (*0-86685-424-X*) Intl Bk Ctr.

Arabic Phonology: An Acoustical & Physiological Investigation. Salman H. Al-Ani. (Janua Linguarum, Ser. Practica: No. 61). 104p. 1970. pap. text ed. 41.55 (*90-279-0727-7*) Mouton.

Arabic Phrase Book. Berlitz Editors. (Phrase Book Ser.). (Illus.). 192p. 1990. 5.95 (*2-8315-0751-0*) Berlitz.

Arabic Poetry: A Primer for Students. Ed. by Arthur J. Arberry. LC 65-11206. 183p. reprint ed. pap. 52.20 (*0-8357-5706-4*, 2024405) Bks Demand.

Arabic Political Memoirs & Other Studies. Elie Kedourie. 320p. 1974. 37.50 (*0-7146-3041-1*, Pub. by F Cass Pubs UK) Intl Spec Bk.

Arabic Proverbs. J. L. Burckhardt. 296p. (C). 1988. 200.00 (*1-85077-183-9*, Darf Pubs Ltd) St Mut.

Arabic Proverbs: Manners & Customs of the Modern Egyptians. J. L. Burckhardt. (ARA & ENG.). 1993. 18. 00 (*0-86685-561-0*) Intl Bk Ctr.

Arabic Proverbs: Or the Manners & Customs of the Modern Egyptians, Illustrated from Their Proverbial Sayings Current at Cairo, Translated & Explained. J. L. Burckhardt. 296p. (C). 1984. pap. 19.95 (*0-7007-0185-0*, Pub. by Curzon Pr UK) Humanities.

Arabic Qaidah (Yasserna-Al-Qur'an) Rhythmic Methods of Learning Quranic Arabic with English Pronunciations & Important Doas for Daily Islamic Life. rev. ed. Muhammad S. Haque. LC 85-63835. (Illus.). vi, 74p. (Orig.). 1992. pap. text ed. 4.00 (*0-933057-03-2*) Namuk Intl Inc.

Arabic Reader for Beginners. Ed. by George J. Koury. 1977. pap. text ed. 11.00 (*0-918266-05-X*) Smyrna.

Arabic-Russian Dictionary. Z. Baranov. (ARA & RUS.). 1984. 49.95 (*0-8288-0787-6*, F47635) Fr & Eur.

Arabic-Russian Learner's Phrasebook. Ia. Korshunova & A. Shakhbaz. 696p. (C). 1983. 90.00 (*0-685-37117-4*, Pub. by Collets) St Mut.

Arabic Short Stories. Tr. by Denys Johnson-Davies. 208p. 1987. 14.95 (*0-7043-2367-2*, Pub. by Quartet UK) Interlink Pub.

Arabic Short Stories. Tr. by Denys Johnson-Davies. LC 94-14365. 1994. 32.00 (*0-520-08563-9*); pap. 12.00x (*0-520-08944-8*) U CA Pr.

Arabic Short Stories Nineteen Forty-Five to Nineteen Sixty-Five. Ed. by Mahmoud Manzaloui. 1986. pap. 20. 00 (*977-424-121-5*, Pub. by Am Univ Cairo Pr UA) Col U Pr.

Arabic Sociolinguistics: Issues & Perspectives. Ed. by Yasir Suleiman. 256p. (C). 1994. text ed. 70.00 (*0-7007-0307-1*, Pub. by Curzon Pr UK) Humanities.

Arabic Spain. B. Wishaw & E. M. Wishaw. 1974. 59.95 (*0-87968-652-9*) Gordon Pr.

Arabic Spain. B. Wishaw & E. M. Wishaw. 460p. 1986. 300.00 (*1-85077-101-4*, Darf Pubs Ltd) St Mut.

Arabic-Spanish Period see History of Jewish Literature

Arabic-Speaking People in Rhode Island: A Centenary Celebration. Eleanor A. Doumato. (Rhode Island Ethnic Heritage Pamphlet Ser.). (Illus.). 48p. (Orig.). 1987. pap. 4.75 (*0-917012-84-4*) RI Pubns Soc.

Arabic Standard Atlas Book. Mohammed Nasr. (ARA.). 1983. pap. 14.95 (*0-86685-164-X*) Intl Bk Ctr.

Arabic Student Dictionary. Munjid Al Tulab & Dar El Mashreq. (ARA.). 1979. 25.00 (*2-7214-2118-2*) Intl Bk Ctr.

Arabic Text of the Apocalypse of Baruch: Edited & Translated with a Parallel Translation of the Syriac Text. F. Leemhuis et al. viii, 154p. 1986. 43.50 (*90-04-07608-5*) E J Brill.

Arabic Thought & Islamic Society. Aziz Al-Azmeh. 320p. 1986. 59.95 (*0-7099-0584-X*, Pub. by Croom Helm UK) Routledge Chapman & Hall.

Arabic Thought & Its Place in History. rev. ed. De Lacy E. O'Leary. LC 80-1917. 1981. reprint ed. 35.00 (*0-404-18982-2*) AMS Pr.

Arabic Thought in the Liberal Age, 1798-1939. Albert Hourani. LC 83-1788. 416p. 1983. pap. 27.95 (*0-521-27423-0*) Cambridge U Pr.

Arabic Travel Pack. (Hugo's Travel Packs Ser.). 128p. (Orig.). 1990. Includes audio cassette. 14.95 (*0-85285-145-6*) Hunter NJ.

Arabic-Ugaritic Lexical Studies. Fred Renfroe. (Abhandlungen Zur Literatur Alt-Syrien-Palastinas Ser.: Vol. 5). xii, 198p. 1992. text ed. 49.00 (*3-927120-09-X*, Pub. by UGARIT GW) Eisenbrauns.

Arabic Verb Frequency: Analytic & Synthetic Observations. Don Y. Lee. (C). 1991. text ed. 49.00 (*0-939758-22-9*) Eastern Pr.

***Arabic with Ease.** J. J. Schmidt. Tr. by Stephen Geist. (With Ease Ser.). (Illus.). 343p. 1979. 19.95 (*2-7005-0087-3*, Pub. by ASSIMIL FR) Distribks Inc.

***Arabic with Ease, Incl. 3 60-min. cassettes.** J. J. Schmidt. Tr. by Stephen Geist. (With Ease Ser.). 343p. 1979. audio 59.95 (*2-7005-1311-8*, Pub. by ASSIMIL FR) Distribks Inc.

Arabic with Ease: Arabic for English Speakers. Assimil Staff. (ARA & ENG.). 1990. 28.95 (*0-8288-4359-7*, M14743); audio 125.00 (*0-685-53027-2*) Fr & Eur.

Arabic Words in English see Needed Words

Arabic Writing for Beginners: Part One. Z. H. Qureshi. pap. 3.75 (*0-935782-06-0*) Kazi Pubns.

Arabic Writing for Beginners: Part Three. Z. H. Qureshi. pap. 3.75 (*0-935782-18-4*) Kazi Pubns.

Arabic Writing for Beginners: Part Two. Z. H. Qureshi. pap. 3.75 (*0-935782-11-7*) Kazi Pubns.

Arabic Writing Today: Drama. Ed. by Mahmoud Manzaloui. (American Research Center in Egypt, Publications Ser.: Vol. 2). 643p. (Orig.). 1977. pap. 12.50 (*0-936770-00-7*, Pub. by Amer Res Ctr Egypt UA) Eisenbrauns.

Arabic Yemeni Reference Grammar. Hamdi Qafisheh. LC 91-77058. 308p. 1992. 59.00 (*0-931745-83-7*) Dunwoody Pr.

***Arabidopsis.** Ed. by Elliot M. Meyerowitz & Chris R. Somerville. (Monographs: No. 27). (Illus.). 1270p. (C). 1994. 175.00 (*0-87969-428-9*) Cold Spring Harbor.

Arabidopsis: An Atlas of Morphology & Development. John L. Bowman. LC 93-5262. 1994. 79.00 (*0-387-94089-8*) Spr-Verlag.

Arabidopsis Thaliana as a Model for Plant-Pathogen Interactions. Ed. by Keith R. Davis & Raymond Hammerschmidt. LC 93-71322. (Symposium Ser.). (Illus.). viii, 136p. (Orig.). 1993. pap. 28.00 (*0-89054-153-1*) Am Phytopathol Soc.

Arabisch Ohne Muhe Heute: Arabic for German Speakers. Assimil Staff. (ARA & GER.). 1990. 29.95 (*0-8288-4358-9*, F11959); audio 125.00 (*0-685-53026-4*) Fr & Eur.

Arabisch Zonder Moeite: Arabic for Dutch Speakers. Assimil Staff. (ARA & DUT.). 1990. 28.95 (*0-8288-4365-1*, M10749); audio 125.00 (*0-8288-9030-7*, M10749) Fr & Eur.

Arabische Bahram-Roman: Untersuchungen zur Quellen - und Stoffgeschichte. Mechthild Pantke. (Studien zur Sprache, Geschichte und Kultur des Islamischen Orients: Vol. 6). 230p. (C). 1973. 115.40 (*3-11-003990-7*) De Gruyter.

Arabische Dialekt der Sukriyya Im Ostsudan. Stefan Reichmuth. (Studien Zur Sprachwissenschaft Ser.: Vol. 2). 325p. 1983. write for info. (*3-487-07457-5*, Pub. by Georg Olms GW) Lubrecht & Cramer.

Arabische Literature der Juden. Moritz Steinschneider. (Bibliotheca Arabico-Judaica Ser.). liv, 348p. 1986. reprint ed. write for info. (*3-487-00743-6*, Pub. by Georg Olms GW) Lubrecht & Cramer.

Arabischen, Perischen, Turkischen Handschriften der k. u. k. Hofbibliothek Zu Wien, 3 vols., Set. Gustav Flugel. lxxxii, 1990p. 1977. reprint ed. write for info. (*3-487-06412-X*, Pub. by Georg Olms GW) Lubrecht & Cramer.

Arabischer Adel. Sehen - Werten - Erkennen. die Beurteilung des Vollblutaraberpferdes, 1990. Otto Saenger. (Documenta Hippologica Ser.). (Illus.). 76p. (GER.). 1990. lib. bdg. 25.50 (*3-487-08313-2*, Pub. by Georg Olms GW) Lubrecht & Cramer.

Arabism & Islam: A Study of Islamic & Arabic History & Conflicts in the Middle East. 1991. lib. bdg. 250.00 (*0-8490-4214-3*) Gordon Pr.

Arabism & Islam: Stateless Nations & Nationless States. 52p. (Orig.). (C). 1993. pap. text ed. 25.00 (*1-56806-881-6*) Diane Pub.

Arabistan: The Land of the Arabian Nights. W. M. Fogg. 352p. 1984. 220.00 (*1-85077-023-9*, Darf Pubs Ltd) St Mut.

Arabists: The Romance of an American Elite. Robert D. Kaplan. LC 93-4321. 1993. text ed. 24.95 (*0-02-916785-X*) Free Pr.

An Asterisk (*) at the beginning of an entry indicates that the title is appearing in BIP for the first time.

A

***Arabists: The Romance of an American Elite.** Robert D. Kaplan. 1995. pap. 14.00 (*0-02-874023-8*) Free Pr.

Arabs. Peter Mansfield. 1990. pap. 9.95 (*0-14-013574-X*, Penguin Bks) Viking Penguin.

Arabs. Maxime Rodinson. Tr. by Arthur Goldhammer. LC 80-25916. (Illus.). 208p. (C). 1981. pap. text ed. 10.95 (*0-226-72356-9*) U Ch Pr.

Arabs. rev. ed. Peter Mansfield. (Pelican Ser.). 528p. 1985. pap. 8.95 (*0-14-022561-7*, Penguin Bks) Viking Penguin.

Arabs. rev. ed. Peter Mansfield. 560p. 1992. reprint ed. pap. 12.00 (*0-14-014768-3*, Penguin Bks) Viking Penguin.

Arabs: A Compact History. Francesco Gabrieli. Tr. by Salvator Attanasio. LC 81-4226. (Illus.). viii, 215p. 1981. reprint ed. text ed. 55.00 (*0-313-23032-3*, GATA, Greenwood Pr) Greenwood.

Arabs: A Short History. Philip K. Hitti. LC 85-7603. 1956. pap. 9.95 (*0-89526-982-1*) Regnery Pub.

Arabs: In the Golden Age. Mokhtar Moktefi. Tr. by Mary K. LaRose. LC 92-4989. (People of the Past Ser.). (Illus.). 64p. (J). (gr. 4-6). 1992. lib. bdg. 15.90 (*1-56294-201-8*) Millbrook Pr.

Arabs: Journeys Beyond the Mirage. David Lamb. LC 86-10136. (Illus.). 320p. 1987. 19.95 (*0-394-54433-1*) Random.

Arabs: Journeys Beyond the Mirage. David Lamb. LC 87-45914. 320p. 1988. pap. 13.00 (*0-394-75758-0*, Pub. by Avebury Pub UK) Random.

Arabs: Their History, Culture & Place in the Modern World. Arnold Hottinger. LC 82-6177. (Illus.). 344p. 1982. reprint ed. text ed. 69.50 (*0-313-23501-5*, HOTA, Greenwood Pr) Greenwood.

Arabs & Africa. Ed. by Khair E. Haseeb. LC 84-23151. 717p. 1985. 59.95 (*0-7099-3413-0*, Pub. by Croom Helm UK) Routledge Chapman & Hall.

Arabs & Israel for Beginners. Ron David. 1993. pap. 9.95 (*0-86316-161-8*) Writers & Readers.

Arabs & Israelis: A Dialogue. Saul Friedlander & Mahmoud Hussein. Tr. by Paul Auster & Jean Lacoutre. LC 75-9147. 224p. 1975. 24.50 (*0-8419-0208-9*) Holmes & Meier.

Arabs & Jews in Israel, Vol. 2: Change & Continuity in Mutual Intolerance, Vol. 2. Sammy Smooha. 357p. (C). 1992. pap. text ed. 47.50 (*0-8133-0756-2*) Westview.

***Arabs & Nubians in New Halfa: A Study of Settlement & Irrigation.** Muneera Salem-Murdock. LC 88-23246. 221p. 1989. pap. 63.00 (*0-7837-8554-2*, 2049369) Bks Demand.

Arabs & the Stars: Texts & Traditions on the Fixed Stars & Their Influence in Medieval Europe. Paul Kunitzsch. (Collected Studies: No. CS307). (Illus.). 350p. (ENG & GER.). (C). 1989. reprint ed. text ed. 95.00 (*0-86078-255-7*, Pub. by Variorum UK) Ashgate Pub Co.

Arabs & Zionism Before World War One. Neville Mandel. LC 73-78545. 1977. pap. 11.00 (*0-520-03940-8*) U CA Pr.

Arabs, Christians & Jews: Whose Side Is God On? rev. ed. James Hefley & Marti Hefley. 224p. 1991. reprint ed. pap. 10.95 (*0-929292-20-0*) Hannibal Bks.

Arabs in Exile: Yemeni Migrants in Urban Britain. Fred Halliday. (Illus.). 256p. 1992. text ed. 59.50 (*1-85043-499-9*, Pub. by I B Tauris UK) St Martin.

Arabs in History. Bernard Lewis. 1960. pap. text ed. 12.00 (*0-06-131029-8*, TB 1029, Torch) HarpC.

Arabs in History. rev. ed. Bernard Lewis. 200p. 1991. reprint ed. lib. bdg. 20.00x (*0-8095-9079-4*) Borgo Pr.

Arabs in History. 6th ed. Bernard Lewis. LC 92-43000. 256p. (C). 1993. 12.95 (*0-19-285258-2*) OUP.

Arabs in Israel. Sabri Jiryis. Tr. by Inea Bushnaq. LC 75-15347. 334p. reprint ed. pap. 95.20 (*0-8357-6024-3*, 2034342) Bks Demand.

Arabs in Tent & Town: An Intimate Account. Adela M. Goodrich-Freer. LC 77-87616. reprint ed. 26.00 (*0-404-16438-2*) AMS Pr.

Arabs in the Jewish State: Controlling a National Minority. 1991. lib. bdg. 63.00 (*0-8490-4444-8*) Gordon Pr.

Arabs in the Jewish State: Israel's Control of a National Minority. Ian Lustick. LC 79-22311. (Modern Middle East Ser.: No. 6). (Illus.). 399p. reprint ed. pap. 113.80 (*0-7837-1105-0*, 2041634) Bks Demand.

Arabs in the New World: Studies on Arab - American Communities. Abraham. 1983. 7.95 (*0-86685-386-3*) Intl Bk Ctr.

Arabs in the United States: Reference Guide. George D. Selim. 1984. lib. bdg. 79.95 (*0-87700-494-3*) Revisionist Pr.

Arabs, Oil, & Armageddon. Edgar C. James. pap. 6.99 (*0-8024-0510-X*) Moody.

Arabs under Israeli Occupation, 1972. 78p. 1973. 5.00 (*0-88728-047-1*) Inst Palestine.

Arabs under Israeli Occupation, 1973. 114p. 1974. 5.95 (*0-88728-053-6*) Inst Palestine.

Arabs under Israeli Occupation, 1974. 127p. 1977. 5.95 (*0-88728-054-4*) Inst Palestine.

Arabs under Israeli Occupation, 1975. 120p. 1977. 10.00 (*0-88728-050-1*) Inst Palestine.

Arabs under Israeli Occupation, 1977. Ed. by Leila Baroody. 128p. 1979. 5.95 (*0-88728-059-5*) Inst Palestine.

Arabs under Israeli Occupation, 1978. 136p. 1979. 5.95 (*0-88728-061-7*) Inst Palestine.

Arabs under Israeli Occupation, 1979. 156p. 1980. 5.95 (*0-88728-063-3*) Inst Palestine.

Arabs under Israeli Occupation, 1980. 130p. 1981. 5.95 (*0-88728-065-X*) Inst Palestine.

Arabs under Israeli Occupation, 1981. 110p. 1984. 10.00 (*0-88728-062-5*) Inst Palestine.

Arabs 1984-85: Atlas & Almanac. rev. ed. John C. Kimball. (Arabs Ser.). (Illus.). 108p. (Orig.). (C). 1984. reprint ed. pap. 7.95 (*0-318-01308-8*) Am Educ Trust.

Arabula: The Divine Guest. Andrew J. Davis. 403p. 1971. reprint ed. spiral bd. 13.75 (*0-7873-0247-3*) Mokelumne.

Arachidonate Metabolism in Immunologic Systems. Ed. by L. Levine. (Progress in Allergy Ser.: Vol. 44). (Illus.). viii, 216p. 1988. 118.50 (*3-8055-4773-0*) S Karger.

Arachidonic Acid Metabolism & Tumor Initiation. Lawrence J. Marnett. (Prostaglandins, Leukotrienes, & Cancer Ser.). 1985. lib. bdg. 75.50 (*0-89838-729-9*) Kluwer Ac.

Arachidonic Acid Metabolism & Tumor Promotion. Ed. by Susan M. Fischer & Thomas J. Slaga. (Prostaglandins, Leukotrienes, & Cancer Ser.). 1985. lib. bdg. 85.50 (*0-89838-724-8*) Kluwer Ac.

Arachidonic Acid Metabolites. Ed. by Ruth J. Hegyeli. LC 85-14607. (Atherosclerosis Reviews Ser.: Vol. 13). 182p. 1985. text ed. 72.50 (*0-88167-131-2*) Raven.

Arachne. Lisa Mason. 272p. 1992. mass mkt. 4.50 (*0-380-70911-2*, AvoNova) Avon.

Arachne's Tapestry: The Transformation of Myth in Seventeenth-Century Spain. Marcia L. Welles. 185p. 25.00 (*0-939980-11-8*) Trinity U Pr.

Arachnida from Panama. Alexander Petrunkevitch. (Connecticut Academy of Arts & Sciences Ser., Trans.: Vol. 27). 1925. pap. 100.00 (*0-685-22818-5*) Elliots Bks.

Arachnida Ixodid Ticks (Ixodae) B. I. Pomerantzev. Tr. by A. Elbl & G. Anastos. 1959. 17.95 (*0-934454-08-6*) Lubrecht & Cramer.

Arachnoidea: Tyroglyphoidea (Acari) A. A. Zakhvatkin. Ed. by A. Ratcliffe & A. M. Hughes. Tr. by A. M. Hughes. 1959. 28.95 (*0-934454-09-4*) Lubrecht & Cramer.

Arachnomania: The General Care & Maintenance of Tarantulas & Scorpions. Philippe De Vosjoli. 79p. 1991. pap. text ed. 8.50 (*1-882770-10-2*) Adv Vivarium.

Aradia: Gospel of the Witches. Charles G. Leland. 135p. 1989. pap. 5.95 (*0-919345-10-7*) Phoenix WA.

Aradia or the Gospel of the Witches. Charles G. Leland. Ed. by Nelson White & Anne White. LC 85-52307. 100p. (Orig.). 1986. pap. 10.00 (*0-939856-54-9*) Tech Group.

Arado Ar 196. Hans-Peter Dabrowski & Volker Koos. Tr. by Don Cox. (Illus.). 48p. (Orig.). 1993. pap. 7.95 (*0-88740-481-2*) Schiffer.

Arado Two Thirty-Four Blitz. J. Richard Smith & Eddie J. Creek. Ed. by Sarah A. Hitchcock. (Monarch Ser.: No. 1). (Illus.). 264p. 1992. 49.95 (*0-914144-51-0*) Monogram Aviation.

Aradus. Carol Dixon. LC 93-49597. 176p. (Orig.). 1994. pap. 6.99 (*1-56722-019-3*) Word Aflame.

Arafat: A Biography. Andrew Gowers & Tony Walker. LC 91-25963. (Illus.). 464p. 1994. pap. 14.95 (*1-56656-158-2*, Olive Branch Pr) Interlink Pub.

Arafat: A Political Biography. Alan Hart. LC 88-45748. 560p. 1989. 39.95 (*0-253-32711-3*); pap. 18.95 (*0-253-20516-6*, MB-516) Ind U Pr.

Arafat: In the Eyes of the Beholder. Janet Wallach & John Wallach. (Illus.). 1990. 21.95 (*0-8184-0533-3*, L Stuart) Carol Pub Group.

Arafat: In the Eyes of the Beholder. Janet Wallach & John Wallach. (Illus.). 480p. 1991. pap. 15.95 (*1-55958-120-4*) Prima Pub.

Arafat & the Palestine Liberation Organization. Diana Reische. LC 90-46868. (Illus.). 160p. (YA). (gr. 9-12). 1991. lib. bdg. 15.33 (*0-531-11000-1*) Watts.

Aragones 3-D. Sergio Aragones & Ray Zone. (Illus.). 64p. (Orig.). (YA). (gr. 9-12). 1989. pap. 4.95 (*0-317-93126-1*) Three-D Zone.

Aragonese Arch at Naples, 1443-1475. George L. Hersey. LC 72-91297. (Yale Publications in the History of Art: No. 24). (Illus.). 190p. reprint ed. pap. 54.20 (*0-8357-5707-2*, 2022005) Bks Demand.

Aragonese Version of the Secreto Secretorum. Pseudo Aristotle. (Dialect Ser.: No. 3). 1985. 12.00 (*0-942260-30-9*) Hispanic Seminary.

Arakelov Geometry. C. Soule et al. (Cambridge Studies in Advanced Mathematics: No. 33). 200p. (C). 1992. 49.95 (*0-521-41669-8*) Cambridge U Pr.

Arakin, 1 vol. (ENG & HEB.). 15.00 (*0-910218-83-8*) Bennet Pub.

Aralkyl Compounds: Their Derivatives & Oxidation Products see Rodd's Chemistry of Carbon Compounds

Aram & Israel or, Aramaeans in Syria & Mesopotamia. Emil G. Kraeling. LC 18-9797. (Columbia University. Oriental Studies: No. 13). reprint ed. 17.00 (*0-404-50503-1*) AMS Pr.

Aram Khachaturyan. Ed. by Collet's Holdings, Ltd. Staff. Tr. by Nicholas Kournokoff & Vladimi Bobrov. LC 85-18265. (Illus.). 286p. 1985. 19.95 (*0-943071-00-3*) Sphinx Pr.

Aramaic Bibliography, Part I: Old, Official, & Biblical Aramaic. Joseph A. Fitzmyer & Stephen A. Kaufman. (Comprehensive Aramaic Lexicon Ser.). 368p. 1992. text ed. 48.50 (*0-8018-4312-X*) Johns Hopkins.

Aramaic-English Interlinear New Testament: Acts-Philemon, Vol. II. Ed. by Way International Research Team Staff. LC 88-50024. 687p. 1988. 16.95 (*0-910068-74-7*) Am Christian.

Aramaic-English Interlinear New Testament: Hebrews-Revelation, Vol. III. Ed. by Way International Research Team Staff. LC 88-50024. 281p. 1989. 8.95 (*0-910068-75-5*) Am Christian.

Aramaic-English Interlinear New Testament: Matthew-John, Vol. I. Ed. by Way International Research Team Staff. LC 88-50024. 779p. 1988. 16.95 (*0-910068-73-9*) Am Christian.

Aramaic New Testament. LC 83-71100. 524p. 1983. 24.95 (*0-910068-47-X*) Am Christian.

Aramaic of Daniel in the Light of Old Aramaic. Stefanovic Zdravko. (JSOT Supplement Ser.: No. 129). 130p. (C). 1992. 20.00 (*1-85075-351-2*, Pub. by Sheffield Acad UK) CUP Services.

Aramaic Ritual Texts from Persepolis. Raymond A. Bowman. LC 65-55148. (Oriental Institute Publications: No. 91). 1970. lib. bdg. 35.00 (*0-226-62194-4*) U Ch Pr.

Aramaic Version of Jonah. 2nd ed. Etan Levine. LC 76-27614. 1979. pap. 14.75 (*0-87203-068-7*) Hermon.

Aramaic Version of Lamentations. Etan Levine. LC 76-276212. 203p. 1981. pap. 16.25 (*0-87203-065-2*) Hermon.

Aramaic Version of Qohelet. Etan Levine. 1979. pap. 16.25 (*0-87203-087-3*) Hermon.

Aramaic Version of the Bible: Contents & Context. Etan Levine. xiv, 258p. (C). 1988. lib. bdg. 95.40 (*0-89925-459-4*) De Gruyter.

***Aramaic Version of the Bible: Contents & Context.** Etan Levine. xiv, 258p. (C). 1988. lib. bdg. 55.40 (*3-11-011474-7*) De Gruyter.

***Aramaische Chrestomathie: Ausgewalte Texte (Inschriften, Ostraka und Papyri) Bis Zum 3. Jahrhundert N. Chr.** J. J. Koopmans. 1962. pap. text ed. 29.00 (*0-614-04000-0*, Pub. by Netherlands Inst NE) Eisenbrauns.

Aramaischen Framdworter Im Arabischen. Siegmund Fraenkel. xxii, 327p. 1982. reprint ed. write for info. (*3-487-00319-8*, Pub. by Georg Olms GW) Lubrecht & Cramer.

Aramco Reports on Al Hasa & Oman, 1950-1955, 4 vols., Set. Archives Research Ltd. Staff. (C). 1987. text ed. 1,600.00 (*1-85207-225-3*, Pub. by Archive Res Ltd UK) St Mut.

Aramco, the United States, & Saudi Arabia: A Study of the Dynamics of Foreign Oil Policy, 1933-1950. Irvine H. Anderson. LC 80-8535. 276p. reprint ed. pap. 78.70 (*0-7837-0045-8*, 2040292) Bks Demand.

Aramid (Kevlar) Fibers: Properties & Applications, 1977-1986. 110p. 1983. 85.00 (*0-686-48271-9*, LS108) T-C Pubns CA.

Araminta & the Coyotes. Paul Metcalf. 1990. pap. 10.00 (*0-912330-73-2*) Jargon Soc.

Araminta's Paint Box. Karen Ackerman. LC 88-35033. (Illus.). 32p. (J). (gr. 1-3). 1990. text ed. 13.95 (*0-689-31462-0*, Atheneum Bks Young) S&S Childrens.

***Arams of Idaho: Pioneers of the Camas Prairie & Joseph Plains.** Kristi M. Youngdahl. 200p. (Orig.). 1995. pap. 17.95 (*0-89301-186-X*) U of Idaho Pr.

Aran Island Knitting. pap. 11.95 (*0-85532-688-3*, Pub. by Search Pr UK) A Schwartz & Co.

Aran Islands. John Millington Synge. 208p. 1992. 9.95 (*0-14-018432-5*, Penguin Classics) Viking Penguin.

Aran Islands. John Millington Synge. LC 89-60940. 190p. 1989. reprint ed. pap. 9.95 (*0-910395-54-3*) Marlboro Pr.

Aran Reader. Ed. by Breandon Heithir & Ruairi O. Heithir. 320p. 1991. 31.95 (*0-946640-54-8*, Pub. by Lilliput Pr Ltd IE) Irish Bks Media.

Arana Encantadora - Spider Magic. LC 90-62626. (Finger Magic Book Ser.). (Illus.). 12p. (J). 1991. bds. 5.95 (*1-877779-21-0*) Schneider Educational.

***Arana Pequenita Vol. 11: Pasitos Spanish Language Development Books.** Darlyne F. Schott. (Pasitos Hacia la Lectura Ser.). 11p. (J). (ps-1). 1994. pap. text ed. 11.00 (*1-56537-080-5*) D F Schott Educ.

Aranas. Norman S. Barrett. LC 90-70883. (Picture Library). (Illus.). 32p. (SPA.). (J). (gr. k-4). 1990. lib. bdg. 12.60 (*0-531-07901-5*) Watts.

Arangetral. S. Santhi. (Indian Poetry Ser.). 66p. 1974. lib. bdg. 6.95 (*0-88253-463-7*) Ind-US Inc.

Aranmen All. Tom O'Flaherty. 192p. 1991. reprint ed. pap. 9.95 (*0-86322-123-8*, Pub. by Brandon Bk Pubs IE) Irish Bks Media.

Aransas. Stephen Harrigan. LC 86-5963. (Contemporary Fiction Ser.). 260p. 1986. reprint ed. pap. 8.95 (*0-87719-057-7*, Lone Star Bks) Gulf Pub.

Arapaho. Loretta Fowler. (Indians of North America Ser.). (Illus.). 128p. (J). (gr. 5 up). 1989. 17.95 (*1-55546-690-7*) Chelsea Hse.

Arapaho. Loretta Fowler. 1994. pap. 7.95 (*0-7910-0371-X*) Chelsea Hse.

Arapaho. Alfred L. Kroeber. LC 83-5749. (Illus.). xx, 495p. 1983. pap. 13.95 (*0-8032-7754-7*) U of Nebr Pr.

Arapaho. Alfred L. Kroeber. 150p. 1975. 14.95 (*0-87770-158-X*) Ye Galleon.

***Arapaho Child Life & Its Cultural Backgrounds.** M. Inez Hilger. (Bureau of American Ethnology Bulletins Ser.). 253p. 1995. lib. bdg. 89.00 (*0-7812-4148-0*) Rprt Serv.

Arapaho Indians. (Junior Library of American Indians). (Illus.). 80p. (J). (gr. 3-7). 1993. lib. bdg. 14.95 (*0-7910-1657-9*) Chelsea Hse.

Arapaho Indians. Vick Haluska. (Junior Library of American Indians). (Illus.). 80p. (J). (gr. 3-7). 1994. pap. 6.95 (*0-7910-1960-8*) Chelsea Hse.

Arapaho Indians: A Research Guide & Bibliography. Comp. by Zdenek Salzmann. LC 87-32274. (Bibliographies & Indexes in Anthropology Ser.: No. 4). 123p. 1988. text ed. 47.95 (*0-313-25354-4*, SZA/, Greenwood Pr) Greenwood.

Arapaho Revenge. George G. Gilman. (Edge Ser.: No. 43). 192p. 1992. pap. 3.50 (*1-55817-627-6*, Pinnacle NY) Windsor NY.

Arapahoe City to Fairmount: From a Ghost Town to a Community. Joyce A. Manley. 128p. (Orig.). 1989. pap. write for info. (*0-318-65759-7*) J A Manley.

Arapahoe Politics, 1851-1978: Symbols in Crises of Authority. Loretta Fowler. LC 81-10368. (Illus.). xxii, 373p. (C). 1982. reprint ed. 35.00 (*0-8032-1956-3*) U of Nebr Pr.

Arapahoes, Our People. Virginia C. Trenholm. LC 86-7111. (Civilization of the American Indian Ser.: Vol. 105). (Illus.). 1986. reprint ed. pap. 18.95 (*0-8061-2022-3*) U of Okla Pr.

Arapesh. Reo F. Fortune. LC 75-32817. (American Ethnological Society Publications: No. 19). reprint ed. 37.50 (*0-404-14121-8*) AMS Pr.

Ararapikva: Traditional Karuk Indian Literature from Northwestern California. Julian Lang. (Illus.). 112p. 1993. 30.00 (*0-930588-69-X*); pap. 10.95 (*0-930588-65-7*) Heyday Bks.

Ararapikva: Traditional Karuk Indian Literature from Northwestern California. Ed. by Julian Lang. 122p. (C). 1993. reprint ed. lib. bdg. 29.00x (*0-8095-4981-6*) Borgo Pr.

Ararat. Louise Gluck. 72p. 1990. 17.95 (*0-88001-247-1*) Ecco Pr.

Ararat. Louise Gluck. 72p. 1992. pap. 9.95 (*0-88001-248-X*) Ecco Pr.

Ararat: A Collection of Hungarian-Jewish Short Stories. Ed. & Tr. by Andrew Handler. LC 75-5244. 153p. 1978. 18.00 (*0-8386-1733-6*) Fairleigh Dickinson.

Ararat Conspiracy: A Novel. Jim Doblins & Ellie Gordon. 168p. 1988. pap. 5.95 (*0-943247-03-9*) UCS Press.

Ararat Papers. James C. Baloian. LC 79-50729. 1979. 6.95 (*0-933706-06-5*); pap. 3.95 (*0-933706-07-3*) Ararat Pr.

Ara's Amazing Spinning Wheel. David R. Collins. (Illus.). (J). (ps-2). 1991. lib. bdg. 8.99 (*0-8136-5181-6*); pap. 4.79 (*0-8136-5681-8*) Modern Curr.

Aras, die Arten und Rassen - ihre Haltung und Zucht. Dieter Hoppe. (Illus.). 167p. (GER.). 1983. lib. bdg. 34.95 (*3-8001-7081-7*) Lubrecht & Cramer.

Arata Isozaki: Architecture, 1960-1990. Arata Isozaki. LC 90-50795. (Illus.). 304p. 1991. 60.00 (*0-8478-1318-5*); pap. 35.00 (*0-8478-1319-3*) Rizzoli Intl.

Aratea. Ciceron Cicero. xi, 542p. 1966. reprint ed. write for info. (*0-318-71329-2*, Pub. by Georg Olms GW) Lubrecht & Cramer.

Aratea Cum Scholiis. Germanicus Caesar. Ed. by A. Breysig. xxxvi, 260p. 1967. reprint ed. write for info. (*0-318-71128-1*, Pub. by Georg Olms GW) Lubrecht & Cramer.

Arati Songs. Harshananda. 1990. 2.95 (*0-87481-235-6*) Vedanta Pr.

Arator. John Taylor. LC 76-58030. 1977. 15.00 (*0-913966-25-8*); pap. 7.00 (*0-913966-26-6*) Liberty Fund.

Arator on the Acts of the Apostles: A Baptismal Commentary. Richard Hillier. LC 92-31716. (Oxford Early Christian Studies). (C). 1993. 49.95 (*0-19-814786-4*, Clarendon Pr) OUP.

Arator's De Actibus Apostolorum. Ed. by J. L. Roberts, III et al. Tr. by John F. Makowski et al. LC 87-9661. (American Academy of Religion, Classics in Religious Studies). 100p. 1988. 19.95 (*1-55540-133-3*, 01-05-06) Scholars Pr GA.

Aratrika Hymns & Ramanam. Swami Tapasyananda. 1979. pap. 1.95 (*0-87481-476-6*, Pub. by Ramakrishna Math II) Vedanta Pr.

Aratus: Index Verborum in Arati Phaenomena. Aratus. Ed. by Malcolm Campbell. (Alpha-Omega, Reihe A Ser.: Vol. XC). v, 96p. (GER.). 1988. 37.70 (*3-487-09016-3*, Pub. by Georg Olms GW) Lubrecht & Cramer.

Araucanians see Pre-Columbian America

Araygnement of Paris see Dramatic Works of George Peele

Arbat Trilogy, Vol. 2: Fear. Anatoli Rybakov. 1992. 24.95 (*0-316-76377-2*) Little.

Arbeidsreg - Die Vernaamste Wette en Regulasies: Labour Law - the Key Statutes & Regulations. C. R. Thompson. 315p. 1991. pap. write for info. (*0-7021-2310-2*, Pub. by Juta SA) W W Gaunt.

Arbeit und Sitte in Palastina, 8 vols. in 7, Set. Gustaf Dalman. lxxxix, 3033p. 1987. reprint ed. write for info. (*3-487-00480-1*, Pub. by Georg Olms GW) Lubrecht & Cramer.

Arbeiten Uber Humor und Witz, Komik und Komodie in der Antike. Musa Iocosa. xx, 253p. 1974. write for info. (*3-487-05118-4*, Pub. by Georg Olms GW) Lubrecht & Cramer.

Arbeiten zur Ethnographie Sibiriens und Volkskunde Zentral-Europas. Hans Findeisen. (Asian Folklore & Social Life Monographs: No. 51). 228p. (GER.). 1973. 14.00 (*0-89986-048-6*) Oriental Bk Store.

Arbeiter in der Schweiz im 19. Jahrhundert. Erich Gruner. (Helvetia Politica Series A: Vol. III). 1990. reprint ed. 120.00 (*3-262-01930-5*) Periodicals Srv.

Arbeiterfrage: The Labor Question: with Particular Consideration of the Social Psychological Side of Modern Large-Scale Industry & Its Psycho-Physical Effect on Workers. Adolf Levenstein. LC 74-25767. (European Sociology Ser.). 410p. 1975. reprint ed. 34.95 (*0-405-06521-3*) Ayer.

Arbeiterschaft in Krieg und Inflation: Soziale Schichtung und Lage der Arbeiter in Augsburg und Linz 1910-1925. Merith Niehuss. (Veroeffentlichungen der Historischen Kommission zu Berlin, Band 67, Beitraege zu Inflation und Wiederaufbau in Deutschland und Europa 1914-1924: Band 3). xiv, 308p. (GER.). 1985. 89.25 (*3-11-009660-9*) De Gruyter.

Arbeitsdiagnose - Neue Wege der Chirurgischen Diagnose und Therapie. M. Hobsley. Tr. by Caroline Seemann. Orig. Title: Pathways in Surgical Management. 480p. (GER.). 1981. pap. 31.25 (*3-8055-0747-X*) S Karger.

Arbeitstagung Bonn, 1984. Ed. by F. Hirzebruch et al. (Lecture Notes in Mathematics Ser.: Vol. 1111). v, 481p. 1985. pap. 53.80 (*0-387-15195-8*) Spr-Verlag.

Arbie Williams Transforms the Britches Quilt: Contemporary Britches Quilts in the African-American Tradition. Eli Leon. (Illus.). (Orig.). (C). 1993. pap. text ed. 8.00 (*0-939982-19-6*) Sesnon Art Gall.

Arbitrage: Elements of Financial Economics. Michael Allingham. 184p. 1991. text ed. 69.95 (*0-312-06202-8*) St Martin.

Arbitrage Rebate Manual. Orrick Herrington & Sutcliffe Staff. 300p. (Orig.). 1990. pap. text ed. 25.00 (*0-936093-41-2*) Packard Pr Fin.

An Asterisk (*) at the beginning of an entry indicates that the title is appearing in BIP for the first time.

An Asterisk (*) at the beginning of an entry indicates that the title is appearing in BIP for the first time.

A

***Arcana Coelestia, Vol. 10.** Emanuel Swedenborg. (Standard Edition of Writings of Emanuel Swedenborg Ser.). 746, viiip. 1995. 15.00 (*0-87785-256-1*) Swedenborg.

Arcana Coelestia (Heavenly Secrets), Vol. 1. Emanuel Swedenborg. 539p. 1981. pap. 3.95 (*0-87785-053-4*) Swedenborg.

Arcana Mundi: Magic & the Occult in the Greek & Roman Worlds. Georg Luck. LC 84-28852. 416p. (Orig.). 1985. pap. text ed. 15.95 (*0-8018-2548-2*) Johns Hopkins.

Arcana of Christianity, 3 pts. in 2 vols., Set. Thomas L. Harris. LC 72-2955. reprint ed. 92.00 (*0-404-10720-6*) AMS Pr.

Arcana of Freemasonry. Albert Churchward. 327p. (Orig.). 1992. pap. 27.50 (*1-56459-106-9*) Kessinger Pub.

Arcane Eye of Hogarth. Burne Hogarth. 144p. 1992. 34.95 (*1-56097-095-2*); pap. 19.95 (*1-56097-087-1*) Fantagraph Bks.

Arcane Formulas: Mental Alchemy. Arcane Book Company Staff. 109p. 1969. reprint ed. spiral bd. 5.50 (*0-7873-0038-1*) Mokelumne.

Arcane Schools: A Review of Their Origin & Antiquity with a General History of Freemasonry & Its Relation to the Theosophic, Scientific, & Philosophic Mysteries. John Yarker. 582p. 1993. pap. 39.95 (*1-56459-306-1*) Kessinger Pub.

Arcane Seventeen. Andre Breton. 12.95 (*0-685-37228-6*, F89460) Fr & Eur.

Arcanum 17. Andre Breton. Tr. by Zack Rogow. (Sun & Moon Classics Ser.: No. 51). 250p. (Orig.). 1994. pap. 12.95 (*1-55713-170-8*) Sun & Moon CA.

Arcata Conference on Representations of Finite Groups, Pt. I. Ed. by P. Fong. LC 87-19348. (Proceedings of Symposia in Pure Mathematics Ser., Humboldt State University, Arcata, CA, July 29-August 16, 1974: Vol. 47.1). 487p. 1987. 75.00 (*0-8218-1477-X*, PSPUM 47.1) Am Math.

Arcata Conference on Representations of Finite Groups, Pt. II. Ed. by P. Fong. LC 87-19348. 552p. 1987. 82.00 (*0-8218-1478-8*, PSPUM 47.2) Am Math.

Arcata Conference on Representations of Finite Groups, Set. Ed. by P. Fong. LC 87-19348. 1039p. 1987. 149.00 (*0-8218-1479-6*, PSPUM 47) Am Math.

Arceuthobium in the United States. Lake S. Gill. (Connecticut Academy of Arts & Sciences Ser., Trans.: Vol. 32). 1935. pap. 89.50 (*0-685-44368-X*) Elliots Bks.

***ARCH: Selected Readings.** Ed. by R. F. Engle. (Advanced Texts in Econometrics Ser.). 384p. 1995. 65.00 (*0-19-877431-1*); pap. 29.95 (*0-19-877432-X*) OUP.

Arch Books Aloud, Set. LC 59-2142. (Continued Applied Christianity Ser.). (J). (gr. k-4). 1983. pap. 6.99 (*0-570-08091-6*); pap. 6.99 (*0-570-08092-4*); pap. 6.99 (*0-570-08093-2*); pap. 6.99 (*0-570-08094-0*); pap. 6.99 (*0-570-08095-9*); pap. 6.99 (*0-570-08096-7*) Concordia.

Arch Books Aloud, Sets 42 - 47. (J). (gr. k-4). 1983. write for info. (*0-318-56993-0*); audio (*0-318-56994-9*) Concordia.

Arch Books Series 20, 6 bks., Set. Incl. Stranger at Jacob's Well. Vivian Dede. LC 59-1277. 1983. pap. 1.69 (*0-570-06164-4*); Little Shepherd & the First Christmas. LC 59-1277. 1983. pap. 1.69 (*0-570-06169-5*); Father Who Forgave. Robert Baden. LC 59-1277. 1983. pap. 1.69 (*0-570-06165-2*); King Solomon's Dream. J. K. Eger. LC 59-1277. 1983. pap. 1.69 (*0-570-06166-0*); Two Cities That Burned. Lucille B. Golphenen. LC 59-1277. 1983. pap. 1.69 (*0-570-06168-7*); Boy Who Came Back to Life. Roberta Parseghian. LC 59-1277. 1983. pap. 1.69 (*0-570-06167-9*); LC 59-1277. (J). (gr. k-4). 1983. Set pap. 5.20 (*0-570-06170-9*) Concordia.

Arch Cape Chronicles. David English & Alma English. LC 93-72487. (Illus.). 357p. (Orig.). 1993. pap. 24.95 (*0-939116-38-3*) Frontier OR.

Arch Celebration: Commemorating the Twenty-Fifth Anniversary of the Gateway Arch, 1965-1990. Tom Ebenhoh. LC 90-60650. (Illus.). 96p. 1990. 29.95 (*0-9625509-4-9*) Spiritgraphics.

Arch Dams: Proceedings of the International Workshop Coimbra, 5 - 9 April 1987. Ed. by J. Laginha Serafim & R. W. Clough. (Illus.). 574p. (C). 1990. text ed. 130.00 (*90-6191-842-1*, Pub. by A A Balkema NE) Ashgate Pub Co.

***Arch Drawing of the Old Exec.** E. Santoyo. 1989. pap. 19.95 (*1-55835-012-8*) AIA Press.

Arch in Public Space. Mark Lilla. 1986. pap. write for info. (*0-02-919170-X*) Macmillan.

Arch Lectures: Eighteen Discourses on a Great Variety of Subjects. Claude Bragdon. LC 77-92505. (Essay Index in Reprint Ser.). (Illus.). 1978. reprint ed. 19.75 (*0-8486-3000-9*) Roth Pub Inc.

Arch of Fire: A Child in Nazi Germany. Siegfried Streufert. 224p. 1995. 19.98 (*0-9644318-0-7*) Aina Kai Bks. Seventy-two tales tell of experiences with Nazis & of the impact of the Second World War. They tell of a child who lived with fear, yet, at other times, would think, feel & love like children do anywhere at any time. Readers aged 12 to 90 called these tales fascinating, gripping, yet informative about life during war & oppression. "In short autobiographic stories, this book describes the experiences of a child living in Germany fifty years ago. It speaks of a childhood during the Hitler regime, about all the horrific experiences of a family that refused to go along with the system. Added to the trauma of the Nazi inspired war with its hunger & bombs, a war that led Germany into catastrophe, was the arrest of the child's father & his death in a concentration camp. ARCH OF FIRE belongs in the hands of younger people, those for whom this era is already a distant past, & those who harbor doubts about the heinous thoughts & actions of the Nazis. May these very lively descriptions of the barbaric aspects of that time help them understand what personal courage & humaneness means even in the face of a dictatorship. May this book help them develop a measure of responsibility for their own actions." Helmut Schmidt, Chancellor of (West) Germany. Order from Aina Kai Books, 4615 Custer Dr., Harrisburg, PA 17110-3209; 717-232-0772; FAX 717-232-7015.** ***Publisher Provided Annotation.

Arch of Knowledge. David Oldroyd. (C). 1990. pap. 24.95 (*0-86840-049-1*, Pub. by New South Wales Univ Pr AT) Intl Spec Bk.

Arch Rivals: Ninety Years of Welcome Arches in Small-Town America. Bernard C. Winn. LC 90-79396. (Illus.). 128p. (Orig.). 1994. pap. 13.95 (*0-9615161-7-8*) Incline Pr.

Archabet: An Architectural Alphabet. Photos by Balthazar Korab. LC 84-26335. (Illus.). 64p. 1985. 15.95 (*0-89133-117-4*) Preservation Pr.

Archabet: An Architectural Postcard Book. Photos by Balthazar Korab. (Illus.). 26p. (Orig.). 1992. pap. 7.95 (*0-89133-192-1*) Preservation Pr.

***Archaea: A Laboratory Manual.** Ed. by Frank T. Robb et al. 1048p. (C). 1995. 375.00 (*0-87969-397-5*) Cold Spring Harbor.

***Archaea: A Laboratory Manual: Halophiles.** Ed. by Shiladitya DasSarma & Esther M. Fleischmann. (Illus.). 264p. (C). 1995. pap. 65.00 (*0-87969-438-6*) Cold Spring Harbor.

***Archaea: A Laboratory Manual: Methanogens.** Ed. by Kevin R. Sowers & Harold J. Schreier. (Illus.). 520p. (C). 1995. pap. 95.00 (*0-87969-439-4*) Cold Spring Harbor.

***Archaea: A Laboratory Manual: Thermophiles.** Ed. by Frank T. Robb & Allen R. Place. (Illus.). 264p. (C). 1995. pap. 65.00 (*0-87969-440-8*) Cold Spring Harbor.

Archaean Geochemistry. Ed. by A. Kroener et al. (Illus.). 290p. 1984. 78.00 (*0-387-13746-7*) Spr-Verlag.

Archaebacteria: Biochemistry & Biotechnology. Ed. by M. J. Danson et al. (Biochemical Society Symposium Ser.: Vol. 58). 212p. 1992. 90.00 (*1-85578-010-0*, Pub. by Portland Pr Ltd UK) Ashgate Pub Co.

Archaebacteria: Proceedings of the 1st International Workshop on Archebacteria, Munich 1981. O. Kandler. (Illus.). 366p. 1982. text ed. 72.00 (*3-437-10797-6*) Lubrecht & Cramer.

Archaebacteria 85. Kandler & Zillig. 432p. 1987. pap. text ed. 130.00 (*0-89574-228-4*) G F Verlag.

Archaebacteria 85: Proceedings of the EMBO Workshop on Molecular Genetics of Archaebacteria & the International Workshop on Biology & Biochemistry of A..., Munich, June 1985. Ed. by O. Kandler & W. Zillig. (Illus.). 434p. 1987. lib. bdg. 96.50 (*3-437-11057-8*) Lubrecht & Cramer.

***Archaelogical Findings on the Ark of the Covenant.** Lawrence. Date not set. write for info. (*0-614-07375-8*, Red River Pr) Archival Servs.

Archaelogical Investigations in West-Central New Mexico, Vol. 2: Historic Cultural Resources, Bureau of Land Management, New Mexico State Office. Klara Kelley. Ed. by Barbara L. Daniels & Marilu Waybourn. (Cultural Resources Ser.: No. 4). (Illus.). 130p. (Orig.). 1988. pap. write for info. (*1-878178-05-9*) Bureau of Land Mgmt NM.

Archaelogy of Africa. Ed. by Thurstan Shaw et al. LC 92-13921. (Foods, Metals & Towns Ser.). (Illus.). 800p. 1993. 99.95 (*0-415-08444-X*) Routledge.

Archaelogy of Quelepa, El Salvador. E. Wyllys Andrews, IV. (Publication Ser.: No. 42). (Illus.). xii, 199p. 1976. 25.00 (*0-939238-47-0*) Tulane MARI.

Archaen Codex. Stephan M. Sechi. (Talislanta Ser.). (Illus.). 180p. (Orig.). 1992. pap. 15.00 (*1-880992-06-X*) Wizards Coast.

Archaeoastronomy. Ronald Mc Coy. (Plateau Ser.). 32p. 1992. pap. 6.95 (*0-89734-109-0*) Mus Northern Ariz.

Archaeoastronomy in Pre-Columbian America. Ed. by Anthony F. Aveni. LC 74-17622. (Illus.). 452p. reprint ed. pap. 128.90 (*0-8357-6659-4*, 2035328) Bks Demand.

Archaeobotanik: Ympisium der Universitaet Hohenheim (Stuttgart), July 1988. Ed. by U. Koerber-Grohne & H. Kuester. (Dissertationes Botanicae Ser.: Vol. 133). (Illus.). 216p. (ENG & GER.). 1989. pap. 54.00 (*3-443-64045-1*, Pub. by Cramer GW) Lubrecht & Cramer.

Archaeologica Graeca: Or, the Antiquities of Greece, 2 vols., Set. John Potter. Ed. by Burton Feldman & Robert Richardson. LC 78-60893. (Myth & Romanticism Ser.: Vol. 19). (Illus.). 1979. lib. bdg. 15.00 (*0-8240-3568-2*) Garland.

Archaeological Adventure in Israel: A Practical Guide. Arnold J. Flegenheimer. LC 86-90465. 1987. pap. 9.95 (*0-87957-009-1*) Roth Pub.

Archaeological & Historical Studies at Simpson Pass, Churchill County, Nevada. Eugene Hattori & Alvin McLane. (Illus.). 40p. 1980. 5.00 (*0-945920-12-1*) Desert Rsch Inst.

Archaeological & Historical Survey of Myrtle Point, St. Mary's County, Maryland. Stuart A. Reeve et al. (Occasional Papers: No. 3). (Illus.). 209p. 1991. 18.00 (*1-878399-09-8*) Div Hist Cult Progs.

Archaeological & Linguistic Reconstruction of African History. Ed. by Christopher Ehret & Merrick Posnansky. LC 82-8431. (Illus.). 311p. reprint ed. pap. 88.70 (*0-7837-4818-3*, 2044465) Bks Demand.

Archaeological & Paleoenvironmental Investigations in the Ash Meadows National Wildlife Refuge, Nye County, Nevada. Stephanie D. Livingston & Fred L. Nials. (Illus.). 212p. 1990. 25.00 (*0-945920-70-9*) Desert Rsch Inst.

Archaeological & Paleoenvironmental Investigations in the Dutchess Quarry Caves, Orange County, New York. Robert E. Funk & David W. Steadman. LC 94-18959. (Monographs in Archaeology). (Illus.). 128p. (Orig.). (C). 1994. pap. 16.95x (*1-882903-02-1*) Persimmon NY.

***Archaeological Approaches to Cultural Identity.** Ed. by S. J. Shennan. (One World Archaeology Ser.). 352p. 1994. pap. 24.95 (*0-415-09557-3*, B4516) Routledge.

Archaeological Approaches to Medieval Europe. Ed. by Kathleen Biddick. LC 84-14759. (Studies in Medieval Culture: No. 28). 1984. 27.95 (*0-918720-53-2*); pap. 16.95 (*0-918720-52-4*) Medieval Inst.

Archaeological Assessment of "Las Huertas", Socorro, New Mexico. Amy Earls. (Maxwell Museum Papers: No. 3). (Illus.). 125p. 1987. pap. 10.00 (*0-912535-04-0*) Max Mus.

Archaeological Autobiography. L. V. Grinsell. (Illus.). 144p. 1993. text ed. 33.00 (*0-86299-658-9*) A Sutton Pub.

Archaeological Bibliography for Eastern North America. Ed. by Roger W. Moeller. 198p. 1977. pap. 7.00 (*0-936322-03-9*) Am Indian Arch.

Archaeological Ceramics of Becan, Campeche, Mexico. Joseph W. Ball. (Publication Ser.: No. 43). (Illus.). xiv, 190p. 1977. 20.00 (*0-939238-48-9*) Tulane MARI.

Archaeological Chemistry. Ed. by Curt W. Beck. LC 74-22372. (Advances in Chemistry Ser.: No. 138). 254p. 1974. 43.95 (*0-8412-0211-7*) Am Chemical.

Archaeological Chemistry, Vol. II. Ed. by Giles F. Carter. LC 78-26128. (Advances in Chemistry Ser.: No. 171). 389p. 1978. 60.95 (*0-8412-0397-0*) Am Chemical.

Archaeological Chemistry, Vol. III. Ed. by Joseph B. Lambert. LC 83-15736. (Advances in Chemistry Ser.: No. 205). 487p. 1983. lib. bdg. 89.95 (*0-8412-0767-4*) Am Chemical.

Archaeological Chemistry IV. Ed. by Ralph O. Allen. LC 88-7953. (Advances in Chemistry Ser.: No. 220). vii, 524p. 1988. 89.95 (*0-8412-1449-2*) Am Chemical.

Archaeological Collection of the Johns Hopkins University. Ellen R. Williams. LC 83-31180. (Illus.). 224p. (C). 1984. text ed. 45.00 (*0-8018-3050-8*) Johns Hopkins.

Archaeological Collections from the Western Eskimos. Therkel Mathiassen. LC 76-21673. (Thule Expedition, 5th, 1921-1924 Ser.: Vol. 10, No. 1). reprint ed. 37.50 (*0-404-58325-3*) AMS Pr.

Archaeological Curatorship. Susan M. Pearce. LC 90-9519. (Leicester Museum Studies Ser.). 224p. 1990. 35.00 (*0-87474-813-5*) Smithsonian.

Archaeological Data Recovery at Drill Pad U19an, Nye County, Nevada. Gregory H. Henton & Lonnie C. Pippin. (Social Sciences Center Technical Report Ser.: No. 49). (Illus.). 101p. (Orig.). (C). 1987. pap. 4.00 (*0-945920-49-0*) Desert Rsch Inst.

Archaeological Data Recovery at Drill Pad U19au, Nye County, Nevada. Gregory H. Henton & Lonnie C. Pippin. (Illus.). 197p. 1991. 20.00 (*0-945920-55-5*) Desert Rsch Inst.

Archaeological Data Recovery at Drill Pad U19ay, Nye County, Nevada. Comp. by Cari L. Lockett. (Illus.). 94p. 1991. 10.00 (*0-945920-62-8*) Desert Rsch Inst.

Archaeological Discoveries in South Arabia. Richard L. Bowen & Frank Albright. LC 57-12447. (American Foundation for the Study of Man Ser.: Vol. 2). 342p. reprint ed. pap. 97.50 (*0-8357-5710-2*, 2001863) Bks Demand.

Archaeological Encyclopedia of the Holy Land. 3rd ed. Ed. by Avraham Negev. (Illus.). 400p. 1990. 29.95 (*0-13-044090-6*) P-H Gen Ref & Trav.

Archaeological Essays in Honor of Irvin B. Rouse. Robert C. Dunnell & Edwin C. Hall. 1979. 67.70 (*90-279-7834-4*) Mouton.

Archaeological Ethnography in Western Iran. Patty J. Watson. LC 78-5853. (Viking Fund Publications in Anthropology: No. 57). 343p. reprint ed. pap. 97.80 (*0-7837-5058-7*, 2044737) Bks Demand.

Archaeological Excavations at Kukulik, St. Lawrence Island, Alaska. Otto W. Geist. reprint ed. 32.50 (*0-404-11641-8*) AMS Pr.

Archaeological Excavations at the Fitzgibbons Site, Gallatin County, Illinois. Cathy A. Robison. LC 86-72024. (Center for Archaeological Investigations Research Paper Ser.: No. 53). (Illus.). xxi, 294p. 1986. pap. 18.50 (*0-88104-061-4*) Center Archaeo.

Archaeological Excavations at the Jackson Landing - Mulatto Bayou Earthwork. Mark Williams. (Mississippi Department of Archives & History Archaeological Reports). (Illus.). 73p. (Orig.). 1987. pap. 5.00 (*0-938896-50-4*) Mississippi Archives.

Archaeological Excavations at the Kruse Bluffbase No. 3 Site, Monroe County, Illinois. Phillip D. Neusius. LC 85-71910. (Center for Archaeological Investigations Research Paper Ser.: No. 51). (Illus.). x, 95p. 1985. pap. 6.50 (*0-88104-057-6*) Center Archaeo.

Archaeological Excavations in New Caledonia. Edward W. Gifford & Dick Shutler. LC 56-4866. (University of California, Anthropological Records: Vol. 18, No. 1). 152p. reprint ed. pap. 43.40 (*0-8357-5711-0*, 2021315) Bks Demand.

Archaeological Excavations in Southern Greece. Dorothy Leekley & Robert Noyes. LC 76-17378. 150p. 1977. 15.00 (*0-8155-5048-0*, NP) Noyes.

Archaeological Excavations in Thailand: A Survey of Recent Finds. Sorensen. (C). 1988. text ed. 60.00 (*0-7007-0179-6*, Pub. by Curzon Pr UK) Humanities.

Archaeological Excavations in Yap. Edward W. Gifford. LC 60-63050. (University of California, Anthropological Records: Vol. 18, No. 2). 80p. reprint ed. pap. 25.00 (*0-8357-5712-9*, 2021316) Bks Demand.

Archaeological Excavations at the Antietam Iron Furnace Complex, Washington County Maryland. Susan W. Frye. (Manuscript Ser.: No. 37). 228p. 1984. spiral bd. 10.00 (*1-878399-39-X*) Div Hist Cult Progs.

Archaeological Explanantion: The Scientific Method in Archaeology. Patty J. Watson et al. LC 84-5014. 384p. 1984. text ed. 37.50 (*0-231-06028-9*) Col U Pr.

Archaeological Explorations in Caves of the Point of Pines Region, Arizona. James C. Gifford. LC 79-9180. (Anthropological Papers: No. 36). 218p. 1980. pap. 22.95 (*0-8165-0360-5*) U of Ariz Pr.

Archaeological Explorations in El Peten, Guatemala. Ian Graham. (Publication Ser.: No. 33). (Illus.). 107p. 1967. 20.00 (*0-939238-37-3*) Tulane MARI.

Archaeological Explorations in Southern Nevada. M. R. Harrington et al. (Illus.). 126p. 1970. reprint ed. pap. 5.00 (*0-318-18303-X*) Southwest Mus.

Archaeological Explorations on the Middle Chinlee. Noel Morss. LC 28-11557. (American Anthropological Association Memoirs Ser.). 1927. pap. 16.00 (*0-527-00533-9*) Periodicals Srv.

Archaeological Fieldwork Opportunities Bulletin, 1994. AIA (Mesiter) Staff. 128p. 1993. per. 10.50 (*0-8403-9192-7*) Kendall-Hunt.

Archaeological Finds from Han Tombs at Guangdong & Hong Kong. Institute of Chinese Studies Staff. (Illus.). 260p. (Orig.). (CHI & ENG.). 1983. pap. text ed. 47.50x (*0-317-65566-3*, Pub. by Chinese Univ HK) Coronet Bks.

Archaeological Finds from Pre-Qin Sites in Guangdong. Institute of Chinese Studies Staff. (Illus.). 298p. (Orig.). (CHI & ENG.). 1984. pap. text ed. 52.50x (*0-317-65567-1*, Pub. by Chinese Univ HK) Coronet Bks.

Archaeological Finds from the Jin to the Tang Periods in Guangdong. Institute of Chinese Studies Staff. (Illus.). 248p. (Orig.). (CHI & ENG.). 1985. pap. text ed. 47.50 (*0-317-65569-8*, Pub. by Chinese Univ HK) Coronet Bks.

Archaeological Fishbones Collected by E. W. Gifford in Fiji. H. W. Fowler. (BMB Ser.: No. 214). 1972. reprint ed. pap. 15.00 (*0-527-02322-1*) Periodicals Srv.

Archaeological Geology. Ed. by George Rapp, Jr. & John A. Gifford. LC 84-40201. 455p. 1985. reprint ed. pap. 129.70 (*0-7837-3326-7*, 2057732) Bks Demand.

Archaeological Geology of North America. Ed. by N. P. Lasca & J. Donahue. (DNAG Centennial Special Volumes Ser.: Vol. 4). (Illus.). 543p. 1990. 62.50 (*0-8137-5304-X*) Geol Soc.

***Archaeological Geology of the Archaic Period in North America.** Ed. by E. Arthur Bettis, III. LC 94-49522. (Special Papers: Vol. 297). 1995. pap. 45.00 (*0-8137-2297-7*) Geol Soc.

Archaeological Guide to Mexico's Yucatan Peninsula. Joyce Kelly. LC 92-50715. 364p. 1993. 50.00 (*0-8061-2499-7*); pap. 19.95 (*0-8061-2585-3*) U of Okla Pr.

Archaeological Guide to Taxila. J. A. Marshall. 1987. reprint ed. 95.00 (*81-85046-15-8*, Scientific) St Mut.

Archaeological Haggadah. Ed. by Benno Rothenberg. LC 86-1052. (Illus.). 1986. 24.95 (*0-915361-36-1*) Modan-Adama Bks.

Archaeological Hammers & Theories. Ed. by James A. Moore & Arthur S. Keene. LC 82-11669. 1983. text ed. 59.00 (*0-12-505980-9*) Acad Pr.

Archaeological Heritage Management in the Modern World. Ed. by Henry Cleere. LC 88-20865. (One World Archaeology Ser.: No. 9). 318p. 1989. 65.00 (*0-04-445028-1*) Routledge Chapman & Hall.

Archaeological History of Iran. E. E. Herzfeld. 1976. lib. bdg. 59.95 (*0-8490-1446-8*) Gordon Pr.

Archaeological History of Iran. E. E. Herzfeld. (British Academy, London, Schweich Lectures on Biblical Archaeology Series, 1930). 1972. reprint ed. pap. 20.00 (*0-8115-1276-2*) Periodicals Srv.

Archaeological History of New York, 2 vols. in 1. Arthur C. Parker. LC 76-43800. (New York State Museum Bulletin Ser.: Nos. 235, 236, 237, 238). reprint ed. 53.50 (*0-404-15656-8*) AMS Pr.

Archaeological History of Religions of Indian Asia. Jack Finegan. (Illus.). 735p. 1989. 75.00 (*0-913729-43-4*) Paragon Hse.

Archaeological History of the Hocking Valley. rev. ed. James L. Murphy. LC 73-92906. (Illus.). 390p. (C). 1989. pap. 21.95 (*0-8214-0920-4*) Ohio U Pr.

Archaeological Illustration. Lesley Adkins & Roy Adkins. (Cambridge Manuals in Archaeology Ser.). (Illus.). (C). 1989. 74.95 (*0-521-35478-1*) Cambridge U Pr.

Archaeological Implications on the Role of Salt As an Element of Cultural Diffusion, Vol. 26. Richard O. Keslin. Ed. by Robert T. Bray. (Missouri Archaeologist Ser.). (Illus.). 181p. (Orig.). 1964. pap. 3.00 (*0-943414-42-3*) MO Arch Soc.

Archaeological Insights into the Custer Battle: An Assessment of the 1984 Field Season. Douglas D. Scott & Richard A. Fox, Jr. LC 86-40606. (Illus.). 128p. (Orig.). 1987. pap. 16.95 (*0-8061-2065-7*) U of Okla Pr.

406

An Asterisk (*) at the beginning of an entry indicates that the title is appearing in BIP for the first time.

***Archaeological Institute of America, Papers, 6 vols., Set Vols. 1-5, Index to Vols. 3-4.** Adolf F. Bandelier. 278. 00 (0-404-58050-5) AMS Pr.

Archaeological Investigation of Buckeye Hills East, Maricopa County, Arizona. J. Rodgers. (Anthropological Research Papers: No. 10). (Illus.). vii, 116p. 1976. 10.00 (0-685-19295-4) AZ Univ ARP.

Archaeological Investigation of the Historic Black Settlement at Mobile, Arizona. Mark T. Swanson. (Statistical Research Technical Ser.: No. 34). (Illus.). 95p. 1992. per., pap. text ed. 15.00 (1-879442-32-9) Stats Res.

Archaeological Investigation of the Marquette Mission Site. Lyle M. Stone. Ed. by David A. Armour. LC 74-171070. (Reports in Mackinac History & Archaeology: No. 1). (Illus.). 33p. (Orig.). 1972. pap. 6.00 (0-911872-17-5) Mackinac Island.

Archaeological Investigation on the Loboi Plain, Baringo District, Kenya. William R. Farrand et al. (Technical Reports: No. 4). (Illus.). 1976. pap. 2.00 (0-932206-13-1) U Mich Mus Anthro.

Archaeological Investigations along the Granite Reef Aqueduct, Cave Creek Archaeological District, Arizona. J. Rodgers. (Anthropological Research Papers: No. 12). (Illus.). ix, 185p. 1977. 15.00 (0-685-19296-2) AZ Univ ARP.

Archaeological Investigations along the Waurika Pipeline. Towana Spivey et al. (Contributions of the Museum of the Great Plains Ser.: No. 5). (Illus.). 1977. pap. 10.50 (0-685-88670-0) Mus Great Plains.

Archaeological Investigations at AZ U: 6: 61 (ASU), a Prehistoric Limited Activity Site in South-Central Arizona, No. 21. Patricia E. Brown & A. E. Rogge. (Anthropological Research Papers: No. 21). (Illus.). viii, 83p. 1980. 10.00 (0-685-19304-7) AZ Univ ARP.

Archaeological Investigations at CA-FRE-1333, in the White Creek Drainage, Western Fresno County, CA. Gary S. Breschini & Trudy Haversat. (Archives of California Prehistory Ser.: No. 12). (Illus.). vi, 102p. (Orig.). 1987. pap. text ed. 7.45 (1-55567-045-8) Coyote Press.

Archaeological Investigations at El-Hibeh 1980: Preliminary Report. Robert J. Wenke. (American Research Center in Egypt, Reports: Vol. 9). xii, 142p. 1984. text ed. 35.50 (0-89003-155-X, Pub. by Amer Res Ctr Egypt UA); pap. text ed. 25.50 (0-89003-154-1, Pub. by Amer Res Ctr Egypt UA) Eisenbrauns.

Archaeological Investigations at French Farm Lake in Northern Michigan, 1981-1982: A British Colonial Farm Site. Donald P. Heldman. LC 83-199610. (Archaeological Completion Report Ser.: No. 6). (Illus.). 142p. (Orig.). 1983. pap. 10.00 (0-911872-46-9) Mackinac Island.

Archaeological Investigations at Lee Canyon: Kayenta Anasazi Farmsteads in the Upper Basin, Coconino County, Arizona. Ed. by Stephanie M. Whittlesey. (Statistical Research Technical Ser.: No. 38). (Illus.). 242p. 1993. per., pap. text ed. 15.00 (1-879442-36-1) Stats Res.

Archaeological Investigations at Los Esteros Reservoir, Northeastern New Mexico. Ed. by John D. Schelberg & Jerold G. Widdison. (Contributions to Anthropological Studies: No. 4). 1987. 35.00 (0-932752-08-X) Ctr Anthrop Studies.

***Archaeological Investigations at Los Morteros, AA:12:57 (ASM), Locus 1, in the Northern Tucson Basin.** Mary Bernard-Shaw. (Technical Reports: No. 87-8). (Illus.). 103p. (Orig.). 1987. pap. 8.00 (1-886398-00-3) Desert Archaeol.

Archaeological Investigations at Seneca Lake, San Carlos Indian Reservation, Arizona. R. C. Stafford. (Anthropological Research Papers: No. 14). (Illus.). vi, 96p. 1978. 10.00 (0-685-19299-7) AZ Univ ARP.

Archaeological Investigations at Susquehanna: A 19th Century Farm Complex Aboard Patuxent River Naval Air Station, St. Mary's County, Maryland. Julia A. King. LC 89-622654. (Occasional Papers: No. 2). (Illus.). 137p. 1989. pap. 15.00 (1-878399-02-0) Div Hist Cult Progs.

Archaeological Investigations at the Harrison Branch & Bat Creek Sites. Gerald F. Schroedl. (UT Department of Anthropology Publication Ser.: No. 10). (Illus.). 284p. 1976. pap. 25.00x (0-87049-225-X) U of Tenn Pr.

***Archaeological Investigations at the Lonetree Site, AA:12:120 (ASM), in the Northern Tucson Basin.** Mary Bernard-Shaw. (Technical Reports: No. 90-1). (Illus.). 294p. (Orig.). 1990. pap. 12.00 (1-886398-03-8) Desert Archaeol.

Archaeological Investigations at the Morton Village & Norris Farms 36 Cemetery. Sharron K. Santure et al. (Reports of Investigations Ser.: No. 45). (Illus.). 258p. 1990. pap. 15.00 (0-89792-128-3) Ill St Museum.

Archaeological Investigations at the Owl Canyon Site (CA-SBr-3801), Mojave Desert, California. Mark Q. Sutton. Ed. by Gary S. Breschini & Trudy Haversat. (Archives of California Prehistory Ser.: No. 9). (Illus.). iv, 72p. (Orig.). 1986. pap. text ed. 6.20 (1-55567-042-3) Coyote Press.

Archaeological Investigations at the Pike's Point Site (4-LAS-537) Eagle Lake, Lassen County, California. Lonnie Pippin et al. (Social Sciences Center Technical Report Ser.: No. 7). (Illus.). 182p. (C). 1979. spiral bd. 18.50 (0-945920-07-5) Desert Rsch Inst.

***Archaeological Investigations at the Redtail Site, AA:12:149 (ASM) in the Northern Tucson Basin.** Mary Bernard-Shaw. (Technical Reports: No. 89-8). (Illus.). 289p. (Orig.). 1989. pap. 12.00 (1-886398-02-X) Desert Archaeol.

Archaeological Investigations for the Hard Times Timber Sale, Union County, Illinois. James S. Penny, Jr. LC 87-71350. (Center for Archaeological Investigations Research Paper Ser.: No. 56). (Illus.). viii, 52p. 1987. pap. 8.50 (0-88104-067-3) Center Archaeo.

Archaeological Investigations for the West Sinter Project, Southern Cortez Mountains, Eureka County, Nevada. Christopher Pierce & Nicholas Chapin. (Social Sciences Center Technical Report Ser.: No. 54). (Illus.). 51p. (Orig.). (C). 1987. pap. 5.00 (0-945920-54-7) Desert Rsch Inst.

Archaeological Investigations in Central Utah. John Gillin. (HU PMP Ser.: Vol. 17, No. 2). 1972. reprint ed. pap. 15.00 (0-527-01243-2) Periodicals Srv.

Archaeological Investigations in El Salvador. J. M. Longyear, 3rd. (HU PMM Ser.: Vol. 9, No. 2). 1972. reprint ed. 20.00 (0-527-01173-8) Periodicals Srv.

Archaeological Investigations in Highway Construction Borrow Pits in Marion & Monroe Counties, Illinois. James S. Penny, Jr. LC 85-71883. (Center for Archaeological Investigations Research Paper Ser.: No. 50). (Illus.). ix, 57p. 1985. pap. 6.50 (0-88104-056-8) Center Archaeo.

Archaeological Investigations in Jefferson County, Missouri. Robert M. Adams. Ed. by Carl H. Chapman. (Missouri Archaeologist Ser.: Vol. 11, Nos. 3 & 4). (Illus.). 71p. (Orig.). 1949. pap. 2.50 (0-943414-28-8) MO Arch Soc.

Archaeological Investigations in Northeastern Xuzestan, 1976. Henry T. Wright. (Technical Reports: No. 10). (Illus.). (Orig.). 1979. pap. 3.00 (0-932206-80-8) U Mich Mus Anthro.

Archaeological Investigations in the Aleutian Islands. Vladimir I. Iokhel'Son. LC 74-5850. reprint ed. 82.50 (0-404-11657-4) AMS Pr.

Archaeological Investigations in the Cave Creek Area, Maricopa County, South-Central Arizona. T. Kathleen Henderson & James B. Rodgers. (Anthropological Research Papers: No. 17). (Illus.). xii, 198p. 1979. 17.50 (0-685-19301-2) AZ Univ ARP.

Archaeological Investigations in the Department of Jutiapa, Guatemala. Robert Wauchope & Margaret N. Bond. LC 89-13171. (Illus.). xiii, 214p. 1989. 30.00 (0-939238-85-3) Tulane MARI.

Archaeological Investigations in the Northern Maya Highlands, Guatemala: Interaction & Development of Maya Civilization. Robert J. Sharer & David W. Sedat. (University Museum Monographs: No. 59). (Illus.). 487p. 1987. text ed. 95.00 (0-934718-59-8) U PA Mus Pubns.

Archaeological Investigations in the Thebes Gap Vicinity, Alexander County, Illinois. Paul A. Webb et al. LC 89-60245. (Center for Archaeological Investigations Research Paper Ser.: No. 55). (Illus.). xvii, 167p. (Orig.). 1989. pap. 10.00 (0-88104-065-7) Center Archaeo.

Archaeological Investigations in the Upper Susquehanna Valley, New York State. Robert E. Funk. LC 93-25158. (Monographs in Archaeology). 1993. 66.95 (0-9615462-9-8) Persimmon NY.

Archaeological Investigations in West-Central New Mexico, Vol. 3: Report of the First Field Season Bureau of Land Management, New Mexico State Office. David Kayser & Charles Carroll. Ed. by Marilu Waybourn. (Cultural Resources Ser.: No. 5). (Illus.). 249p. (Orig.). 1988. pap. write for info. (1-878178-06-7) Bureau of Land Mgmt NM.

Archaeological Investigations near Treaty Hill, Humboldt County, Nevada. Jonathan O. Davis et al. (Social Sciences Center Technical Report Ser.: No. 2). (Illus.). 92p. (Orig.). (C). 1976. pap. 9.50 (0-945920-01-6) Desert Rsch Inst.

***Archaeological Investigations of Cantil, Fremont Valley, Western Mojave Desert, California.** Mark Q. Sutton. (CSU Bakersfield Museum of Anthropology Occasional Papers in Anthropology). (Illus.). 225p. (Orig.). (C). 1991. pap. text ed. 10.00 (0-9632633-0-7) CSU Bakerfld Mus.

Archaeological Investigations of Fort Knox II, Knox County, Indiana, 1803-1813. Marlesa A. Gray. (Glenn A. Black Laboratory of Archaeology Research Reports: No. 9). (Illus.). 312p. (Orig.). 1988. pap. 32.00 (0-87195-015-4) Ind Hist Soc.

Archaeological Investigations of the Kiowa & Comanche Indian Agency Commissaries 34-Cm 232. Daniel J. Crouch. (Contributions of the Museum of the Great Plains Ser.: No. 7). (Illus.). 1978. pap. 11.30 (0-685-91362-7) Mus Great Plains.

Archaeological Investigations of the Weber I (20SA581) & Weber II (20SA582) Sites, Frankenmuth Township, Saginaw County, Michigan. Margaret U. Anderson et al. Ed. by William Lovis. (Illus.). 388p. (C). 1989. pap. text ed. write for info. (0-318-65399-0) MI Dept Trans.

Archaeological Investigations on Mackinac Island 1983: The Watermain & Sewer Project. Earl J. Prahl & Mark Branster. LC 85-622249. (Archaeological Completion Report Ser.: No. 8). (Illus.). 125p. (Orig.). 1984. pap. 10. 00 (0-911872-50-7) Mackinac Island.

Archaeological Investigations on the Buckboard Mesa Road Project. Daniel S. Amick et al. (Illus.). 134p. 1991. 14. 00 (0-945920-69-5) Desert Rsch Inst.

Archaeological Investigations on the North Coast of Rota, Mariana Islands. Ed. by Brian M. Butler. LC 88-70301. (Center for Archaeological Investigations Research Paper Ser.: No. 23). (Illus.). xxxii, 504p. (Orig.). 1988. pap. 18.00 (0-88104-066-5) Center Archaeo.

Archaeological Method. Evzen Neustupny. LC 92-1711. (Illus.). 192p. (C). 1993. 44.95 (0-521-38076-6) Cambridge U Pr.

Archaeological Method & Theory, No. 2. Ed. by Michael B. Schiffer. 300p. 1990. 35.00 (0-8165-1147-0) U of Ariz Pr.

Archaeological Method & Theory, Vol. 1. Ed. by Michael B. Schiffer. 273p. 1989. 35.00 (0-8165-1101-2) U of Ariz Pr.

Archaeological Method & Theory, Vol. 3. Ed. by Michael B. Schiffer. (Illus.). 298p. 1991. 35.00 (0-8165-1239-6) U of Ariz Pr.

Archaeological Method & Theory, Vol. IV. Ed. by Michael B. Schiffer. (Illus.). 288p. 1992. 40.00 (0-8165-1305-8) U of Ariz Pr.

Archaeological Method & Theory, Vol. 5. Ed. by Michael B. Schiffer. (Illus.). 286p. 1993. 40.00 (0-8165-1363-5) U of Ariz Pr.

Archaeological Overview of the Northern Channel Islands, California: Including Santa Barbara Island. Michael A. Glassow. (Illus.). vi, 249p. (Orig.). (C). 1986. pap. 20.60 (1-55567-025-3) Coyote Press.

Archaeological Perspective of Panay Island, Philippines. Peter J. Coutts. (San Carlos Humanities Ser.: No. 13). (Illus.). 342p. (Orig.). 1983. pap. 17.50 (971-10-0043-1, Pub. by San Carlos Univ PH) Cellar.

Archaeological Perspectives on the Battle of Little Bighorn: The Final Report. Douglas D. Scott et al. LC 88-40547. (Illus.). 328p. 1989. 29.95 (0-8061-2179-3) U of Okla Pr.

Archaeological Reconnaissance in Campeche, Quintana Roo, & Peten. Karl Ruppert & John H. Denison, Jr. LC 77-11517. (Carnegie Institution of Washington. Publications: No. 543). reprint ed. 44.00 (0-404-16277-0) AMS Pr.

Archaeological Reconnaissance in Sonora. Monroe Amsden. LC 76-43642. (Southwest Museum Papers: No. 1). reprint ed. write for info. (0-404-15476-X) AMS Pr.

Archaeological Reconnaissance in Sonora. Monroe Amsden. (Illus.). 51p. 1970. reprint ed. pap. 5.00 (0-318-18302-1) Southwest Mus.

Archaeological Reconnaissance in the Palau Archipelago, Western Caroline Islands, Micronesia. George J. Gumerman et al. (Center for Archaeological Investigations Research Paper Ser.: No. 23). (Illus.). xx, 141p. 1981. pap. 7.50 (0-88104-029-0) Center Archaeo.

Archaeological Reconnaissance of Fort Sill, Oklahoma. C. R. Ferring et al. (Contributions of the Museum of the Great Plains Ser.: No. 6). (Illus.). 1978. pap. 20.30 (0-685-91361-9) Mus Great Plains.

Archaeological Reconnaissance of Portage Open Bay in Southeast Missouri. James F. Hopgood. Ed. by Carl H. Chapman. (Memoir Ser.: No. 7). (Illus.). 71p. (Orig.). 1969. pap. 2.50 (0-943414-22-9) MO Arch Soc.

Archaeological Reconnaissance of the Groom Range, Lincoln County, Nevada. Ronald L. Reno & Lonnie C. Pippin. (Social Sciences Center Technical Report Ser.: No. 46). (Illus.). 270p. (Orig.). (C). 1986. pap. 25.00 (0-945920-46-6) Desert Rsch Inst.

Archaeological Reconnaissance of the NNWSI Yucca Mountain Project Area Southern Nye County, Nevada. Lonnie Pippin et al. (Social Sciences Center Technical Report Ser.: No. 28). (Illus.). 120p. (C). 1982. spiral bd. 12.00 (0-945920-28-8) Desert Rsch Inst.

Archaeological Reconnaissance of the Proposed Mohawk Valley Subdivision, Plumas County, California. Donald L. Zerga. (Illus.). 42p. 1980. 5.00 (0-945920-18-0) Desert Rsch Inst.

Archaeological Reconnaissance of the Salt Plains Areas of Northwestern Oklahoma. C. Reid Ferring et al. (Contributions of the Museum of the Great Plains Ser.: No. 4). (Illus.). 1976. pap. 3.65 (0-685-85503-1) Mus Great Plains.

Archaeological Reconnaissance of Yucca Flat, Nye County, Nevada. Ronald L. Reno & Lonnie C. Pippin. (Social Sciences Center Technical Report Ser.: No. 35). (Illus.). 211p. (Orig.). (C). 1985. pap. 20.00 (0-945920-35-0) Desert Rsch Inst.

Archaeological Reconnaissance, Survey & Testing in Connection with Proposed Alton, Utah - Las Vegas, Nevada Pipeline Corridor. Thomas H. Turner et al. (Social Sciences Center Technical Report Ser.: No. 1). (Illus.). 50p. (Orig.). (C). 1975. pap. 7.00 (0-945920-00-8) Desert Rsch Inst.

Archaeological Regions of Colombia: A Ceramic Survey. Wendell C. Bennett. 1976. lib. bdg. 59.95 (0-8490-1447-6) Gordon Pr.

Archaeological Remains in the Area of Kansas City: The Woodland Period, Early, Middle, & Late. J. M. Shippee. Ed. by Carl H. Chapman. (Research Ser.: No. 5). (Illus.). 93p. (Orig.). 1967. pap. 3.00 (0-943414-08-3) MO Arch Soc.

Archaeological Remains in Western India. R. C. Agrawal. (C). 1989. 72.00 (0-8364-2417-4, Pub. by Agam II) S Asia.

Archaeological Reports for 1977-1978, Vol. 24. Prag. 1991. pap. write for info. (0-318-68517-5, Pub. by Aris & Phillips UK) David Brown.

Archaeological Reports for 1978-1979, Vol. 25. Prag. 1991. pap. write for info. (0-318-68518-3, Pub. by Aris & Phillips UK) David Brown.

Archaeological Reports for 1979-1980, Vol. 26. Prag. 1991. pap. write for info. (0-318-68516-7, Pub. by Aris & Phillips UK) David Brown.

Archaeological Reports for 1980-1981, Vol. 27. Prag. 1991. pap. write for info. (0-318-68519-1, Pub. by Aris & Phillips UK) David Brown.

Archaeological Reports from the Tabqa Dam Project - Euphrates Valley, Syria. Ed. by David N. Freedman. LC 78-12251. (Annual of the American Schools of Oriental Research Ser.: Vol. 44). 182p. 1979. text ed. 30. 00 (0-89757-044-8) Am Sch Orient Res.

Archaeological Reports of Frederic Ward Putnam. Frederic W. Putnam. LC 78-178422. (Harvard University. Peabody Museum of Archaeology & Ethnology. Antiquities of the New World Ser.: No. 8). (Illus.). reprint ed. 62.50 (0-404-57308-8) AMS Pr.

Archaeological Research at Aztec-Period Rural Sites in Morelos, Mexico, Vol. 1: Excavations & Architecture. Michael E. Smith. (Memoirs in Latin American Archaeology Ser.: No. 4). (Illus.). 450p. (ENG & SPA.). 1992. pap. 32.00 (1-877812-06-4) UPLAAP.

Archaeological Research at 40RE107, 40RE108, & 40RE124 in the Clinch River Breeder Reactor Plant Area, Tennessee. Gerald F. Schroedl. LC 90-42302. (Publications in Anthropology: Vol. 53). 1990. pap. text ed. write for info. (0-87077-006-3) TVA.

Archaeological Research in the El Cajon Region, Vol. 1: Prehistoric Cultural Ecology. Ed. by Kenneth Hirth et al. (University of Pittsburgh Memoirs in Latin American Archaeology Ser.: No. 1). (Illus.). xxii, 282p. (ENG & SPA.). 1989. pap. 15.00 (1-877812-00-5) UPLAAP.

Archaeological Researches in Yucatan. E. H. Thompson. (HU PMM Ser.: Vol. 3, No. 1). 1972. reprint ed. 20.00 (0-527-01159-2) Periodicals Srv.

Archaeological Researches on the Pacific Coast of Costa Rica. Carl V. Hartman. LC 76-44733. (Pittsburgh. Carnegie Museum. Memoirs Ser.: Vol. 3, No. 1). reprint ed. 34.50 (0-404-15932-X) AMS Pr.

Archaeological Resource Management Plan for the Southern Maryland Region. Dennis J. Pogue & Michael A. Smolek. (Manuscript Ser.). 165p. 1985. reprint ed. spiral bd. 10.00 (1-878399-07-1, NO. 30) Div Hist Cult Progs.

Archaeological Results from Accelerator Dating. Ed. by John Gowlett & Robert Hedges. (Illus.). 176p. 1987. pap. 25.00 (0-947816-11-9, Pub. by Univ Comm Archeology UK) David Brown.

Archaeological Sciences 89. Ed. by P. Budd et al. (Illus.). 408p. 1991. pap. 42.00 (0-946897-28-X, Pub. by Oxbow Bks UK) David Brown.

Archaeological Sediments in Context. Ed. by Julie K. Stein & William R. Farrand. 147p. 1985. pap. 22.00 (0-912933-01-1) Ctr Study First Am.

Archaeological Settlement Pattern Data from the Chalco, Xochimilco, Ixtapalapa, Texcoco, & Zumpango Regions, Mexico. Jeffrey R. Parsons et al. LC 84-21935. (Technical Reports: No. 14). (Illus.). 222p. 1983. pap. 8.00 (0-932206-98-0) U Mich Mus Anthro.

Archaeological Site at Easton Lane, Winchester. P. J. Fasham et al. (Illus.). 180p. 1993. pap. text ed. 55.00 (0-907473-06-7) A Sutton Pub.

Archaeological Sites in Their Setting. Claudio Vita-Finzi. (Illus.). 1978. 19.95 (0-500-02090-6) Thames Hudson.

Archaeological Studies among the Ancient Cities of Mexico. W. H. Holmes. (Chicago Field Museum of Natural History Fieldiana Anthropology Ser.: Vol. 1). 1972. reprint ed. 45.00 (0-527-01861-9) Periodicals Srv.

Archaeological Studies at Drill Pad U20az, Pahute Mesa, Nye County, Nevada. Alan H. Simmons. (Illus.). 142p. 1991. 15.00 (0-945920-67-9) Desert Rsch Inst.

***Archaeological Studies in Rosamond, Western Mojave Desert, California.** Ed. by Mark Q. Sutton. (CSU Bakersfield Museum of Anthropology Occasional Papers in Anthropology). (Illus.). 157p. (Orig.). (C). 1993. pap. text ed. 8.00 (0-9632633-2-3) CSU Bakerfld Mus.

***Archaeological Studies in the Goose Lake Area, Southern San Joaquin Valley, California.** Ed. by Mark Q. Sutton. (CSU Bakersfield Museum of Anthropology Occasional Papers in Anthropology). (Illus.). 117p. (Orig.). (C). 1992. pap. text ed. 6.00 (0-9632633-1-5) CSU Bakerfld Mus.

Archaeological Studies of the Liberty to Gila Bend 230 KV Transmission System. Richard A. Brook et al. Ed. by Pat Stein. (Research Ser.). 54p. 1977. pap. 4.50 (0-685-14690-1, RS-5) Mus Northern Ariz.

Archaeological Studies on the Southeast Wisconsin Uplands, Kenosha County. David F. Overstreet et al. (Case Studies in Great Lakes Archaeology). 143p. (C). 1992. pap. 15.00 (1-881354-00-8) Gt Lks Archaeol.

Archaeological Study of Churches. Ed. by Peter Addyman & Richard Morris. LC 77-365546. (Council for British Archaeology Research Report Ser.: No. 13). (Illus.). 96p. reprint ed. pap. 27.40 (0-8357-5713-7, 2014021) Bks Demand.

Archaeological Study of the Mississippi Choctaw Indians. John H. Blitz. LC 85-620004. (Archaeological Report Ser.: No. 16). (Illus.). vi, 116p. (Orig.). 1985. pap. text ed. 7.50 (0-938896-44-X) Mississippi Archives.

Archaeological Survey at Beowawe, Nevada, Pt. A; Archaeological Reconnaissance of the Beowawe Prospect Lander & Eureka Counties, Nevada, Pt. B: A BLM Class III Cultural Resources Inventory of 14 Proposed Geothermal Drill Sites & Access Roads at Beowawe Geysers, Eureka County, Nevada. Elizabeth Budy & Alvin McLane. (Illus.). 27p. 1980. 4.00 (0-945920-13-X) Desert Rsch Inst.

Archaeological Survey at the McDermitt Caldera, Malheur County, Oregon. Eugene Hattori. (Illus.). 47p. 1980. 5.00 (0-945920-11-3) Desert Rsch Inst.

Archaeological Survey Between Beatty, Nye County, & Indian Springs, Clark County, Nevada. Eugene Hattori & Alvin McLane. (Illus.). 43p. 1982. 5.00 (0-945920-32-6) Desert Rsch Inst.

Archaeological Survey Between Lathrop Wells, Nye County, Nevada & the Nevada-California State Line. Eugene Hattori & Alvin McLane. (Illus.). 26p. 1981. 4.00 (0-945920-22-9) Desert Rsch Inst.

Archaeological Survey of a Proposed Buried Telephone Route Between Austin Summit & Kingston Canyon, Lander County, Nevada. Eugene Hattori & Alvin McLane. (Illus.). 11p. 1981. 2.00 (0-945920-25-3) Desert Rsch Inst.

Archaeological Survey of Artpark & the Lower Landing, Lewiston, NY. Ed. by Patricia K. Scott et al. LC 93-12486. (Illus.). 264p. 1993. text ed. 89.95 (0-7734-9280-1) E Mellen.

An Asterisk (*) at the beginning of an entry indicates that the title is appearing in BIP for the first time. 407

A

Archaeological Survey of Five Geothermal Well Sites & Access Roads in the Steamboat Hills, Washoe County, Nevada. Eugene Hattori. (Illus.). 14p. 1981. 2.00 (*0-945920-21-0*) Desert Rsch Inst.

Archaeological Survey of Mineral Prospecting Lands in the Shawnee National Forest, Southern Illinois, 1983. James S. Penny, Jr. (Center for Archaeological Investigations Research Paper Ser.: No. 45). (Illus.). vii, 86p. 1984. pap. 7.50 (*0-88104-017-7*) Center Archaeo.

Archaeological Survey of Saint Leonard's Town. Robert J. Hurry. (Occasional Papers: No. 5). (Illus.). 82p. 1990. 10.00 (*1-878399-11-X*) Div Hist Cult Progs.

Archaeological Survey of Southwest Virginia. Charlton G. Holland. LC 76-601580. (Smithsonian Contributions to Anthropology Ser.: No. 12). 215p. reprint ed. pap. 61.30 (*0-8357-5714-5*, 2051625) Bks Demand.

Archaeological Survey of Texas. E. B. Sayles. 1993. reprint ed. lib. bdg. 75.00 (*0-7812-5974-6*) Rprt Serv.

Archaeological Survey of the American Bottoms & Adjacent Bluffs, Illinois, 2 pts. Patrick J. Munson & Alan D. Harn. (Reports of Investigations Ser.: No. 21). (Illus.). 123p. 1971. pap. 3.00 (*0-89792-046-5*) Ill St Museum.

Archaeological Survey of the Keban Reservoir Area of East-Central Turkey. Robert E. Whallon. (Memoirs Ser.: No. 11). (Orig.). 1979. pap. 5.00 (*0-932206-84-0*) U Mich Mus Anthro.

Archaeological Survey of the Kerak Plateau. Ed. by J. Maxwell Miller. 354p. 1991. 115.00 (*1-55540-642-4*, 80 00 01) Scholars Pr GA.

Archaeological Survey of the Macoupin Valley. Kenneth B. Farnsworth. (Reports of Investigations Ser.: No. 26). (Illus.). 54p. 1979. pap. 3.00 (*0-89792-050-3*) Ill St Museum.

Archaeological Survey of the Northern Northwest Coast. Philip Drucker. (Shorey Indian Ser.). (Illus.). 133p. reprint ed. pap. 9.95 (*0-8466-4061-9*, I61) Shorey.

Archaeological Survey of Three Geothermal Drill Pads Near Borax Lake, Pueblo Valley, Harney County, Oregon. Alvin McLane. (Illus.). 14p. 1981. 2.00 (*0-945920-23-7*) Desert Rsch Inst.

Archaeological Survey of Wheeler Basin on the Tennessee River in Northern Alabama. William S. Webb. 1988. reprint ed. lib. bdg. 75.00 (*0-7812-0254-X*) Rprt Serv.

Archaeological Test Excavations at 4-PLU-369 Near Chester, Plumas County, California. Lonnie Pippin. (Illus.). 39p. 1979. 7.00 (*0-945920-09-1*) Desert Rsch Inst.

Archaeological Testing at the Sharrow Site: A Deeply Stratified Early to Late Holocene Cultural Sequence in Central Maine. James B. Petersen. (Occasional Publications in Maine Archaeology). (Illus.). 165p. (C). 1991. pap. text ed. 15.00 (*0-935447-08-3*) ME Hist Preserv.

Archaeological Testing for the Smithland Pool, Illinois. Steven Ahler et al. (Center for Archaeological Investigations Research Paper Ser.: No. 13). (Illus.). xii, 290p. 1980. pap. 12.00 (*0-88104-027-4*) Center Archaeo.

Archaeological Theory: Progress or Posture? Ed. by Iain M. MacKenzie. (Worldwide Archaeology Ser.). 192p. 1994. 51.95 (*1-85628-710-6*, Pub. by Avebury Pub UK) Ashgate Pub Co.

Archaeological Theory: Who Sets the Agenda? Ed. by Norman Yoffee & Andrew Sherratt. LC 92-25825. (New Directions in Archaeology Ser.). (Illus.). 240p. (C). 1993. 54.95 (*0-521-44014-9*); pap. 17.95 (*0-521-44958-8*) Cambridge U Pr.

Archaeological Theory in Europe: The Last Three Decades. Ed. by Ian Hodder. 272p. 1991. 59.95 (*0-415-06521-6*, A5752) Routledge.

Archaeological Thought in America. Ed. by C. C. Lamberg-Karlovsky. (Illus.). 350p. (C). 1991. pap. 27.95 (*0-521-40643-9*) Cambridge U Pr.

Archaeological Typology & Practical Reality: A Dialectical Approach to Artifact Classification & Sorting. William Y. Adams & Ernest W. Adams. (Illus.). 496p. (C). 1991. 29.95 (*0-521-39334-5*) Cambridge U Pr.

Archaeological Use & Distribution of Mollusca in the Maya Lowlands. E. Wyllys Andrews, IV. (Publication Ser.: No. 34). (Illus.). 115p. 1969. 20.00 (*0-939238-38-1*) Tulane MARI.

Archaeological Views from the Countryside: Village Communities in Early Complex Societies. Ed. by Glenn M. Schwartz & Steven E. Falconer. LC 93-28140. (Archaeological Inquiry Ser.). (Illus.). 320p. (C). 1994. text ed. 65.00 (*1-56098-319-1*) Smithsonian.

Archaeological Wood. Ed. by Roger M. Rowell & R. James Barbour. LC 89-39451. (Advances in Chemistry Ser.: No. 225). 488p. 1989. 79.95 (*0-8412-1623-1*) Am Chemical.

***Archaeological...Bulletin (95)** Meister & AIA Staff. 128p. 1994. per., pap. text ed. 10.50 (*0-7872-0303-3*) Kendall-Hunt.

Archaeologie und Geschichte: Beitraege zur siedlungsarchaeologischen Forschung, Vol.1. Herbert Jankuhn. xii, 323p. (C). 1976. 115.40 (*3-11-002003-3*) De Gruyter.

Archaeologische Hermeneutik: Anleitung Zur Deutung Klassischer Bildwerke. Carl Robert. LC 75-10652. (Ancient Religion & Mythology Ser.). (Illus.). (GER.). 1976. reprint ed. 32.95 (*0-405-07276-7*) Ayer.

Archaeologist at Large. Graham Webster. (Illus.). 192p. 1991. 60.00 (*0-7134-6803-3*, Pub. by Batsford UK) Trafalgar.

***Archaeologists Dig Square Holes.** Kate Duke. LC 95-10684. (Let's Read-&-Find Out Science Ser.: Stage 2). (J). 1997. 14.95 (*0-06-027056-X*); lib. bdg. 14.89 (*0-06-027057-8*) HarpC.

Archaeologist's Guide to Chert & Flint. Barbara E. Luedtke. LC 92-46805. (Archaeological Research Tools Ser.: No. 7). (Illus.). 176p. (C). 1992. 18.75 (*0-917956-75-3*) UCLA Arch.

***Archaeologists' Pocket Companion: A Compendium of Mathematical, Statistical & Cartographic Tables, Formulae, Conversion Factors & Symbols Commonly Consulted During Field Survey.** Peter L. Eidenbach. 76p. 1991. pap. 5.00 (*1-887523-02-2*) Human Systs Res.

Archaeology. Barbara Cork. (Young Scientist Ser.). (Illus.). 32p. (J). (gr. 5-8). 1985. lib. bdg. 13.96 (*0-88110-220-2*, Usborne); pap. 6.95 (*0-86020-865-6*, Usborne) EDC.

Archaeology. Dennis B. Fradin. LC 83-7309. (New True Bks.). 48p. (J). (gr. k-4). 1983. lib. bdg. 12.90 (*0-516-01691-1*); pap. 4.95 (*0-516-41691-X*) Childrens.

Archaeology. Harvard University Library Staff. (Widener Library Shelflist: No. 56). 442p. 1979. text ed. 45.00 (*0-674-04318-9*) HUP.

Archaeology. Hayden. LC 92-20551. (C). 1995. text ed. write for info. (*0-7167-2449-9*) W H Freeman.

Archaeology. Raintree Publishers Staff. LC 87-28634. (Science & Its Secrets Ser.). (Illus.). 64p. (Orig.). (J). (gr. 5-9). 1988. lib. bdg. 11.95 (*0-8172-3077-7*) Raintree Steck-V.

Archaeology. William L. Rathje & Michael B. Schiffer. 434p. (C). 1982. text ed. 42.75 (*0-15-502950-9*) HB Coll Pubs.

Archaeology. rev. ed. Joey Tanner. Tr. & Illus. by Stephany Grassinger. (Learning Packets - Anthropology Ser.). 86p. 1983. pap. text ed. 19.95 (*0-913705-02-0*) Zephyr Pr AZ.

Archaeology. 2nd ed. David H. Thomas. 512p. (C). 1989. text ed. 44.75 (*0-03-022728-3*) HB Coll Pubs.

Archaeology: A Brief Introduction. 5th ed. Brian M. Fagan. LC 93-17382. (C). 1993. text ed. 22.00 (*0-673-52336-5*) HarpCollege.

Archaeology: A Cultural-Evolutionary Approach. Frank W. Eddy. (Illus.). 384p. (C). 1984. pap. text ed. write for info. (*0-13-044057-4*) P-H.

Archaeology: A Cultural-Evolutionary Approach. 2nd ed. Frank W. Eddy. 336p. (C). 1990. text ed. write for info. (*0-13-044082-5*) P-H.

Archaeology: A Reference Handbook. Alan E. Day. LC 77-21938. 319p. reprint ed. pap. 91.00 (*0-7837-5292-X*, 2045046) Bks Demand.

Archaeology: Biologia Centrali-America or, Contibutions to the Knowledge of the Fauna & Flora of Mexico & Central America. A. P. Maudslay. Ed. by F. Ducane Godman & Osbert Salvin. LC 74-30688. (Illus.). 907p. 1983. 285.00 (*0-8061-9919-9*, Milpatron Publishing Corp) U of Okla Pr.

Archaeology: Discovering Our Past. 2nd ed. Robert J. Sharer & Wendy Ashmore. LC 92-10838. 684p. (C). 1993. text ed. 47.95 (*1-55934-041-X*) Mayfield Pub.

Archaeology: Down to Earth. abr. ed. David H. Thomas. (Illus.). 240p. (C). 1992. pap. text ed. 29.50 (*0-03-047584-8*) HB Coll Pubs.

Archaeology: The Historical Development of Civilizations. 2nd ed. Thomas C. Patterson. LC 92-16556. 416p. 1992. pap. text ed. 40.00 (*0-13-044298-4*) OUP.

***Archaeology: The History, Principles, & Methods of Modern Archaeology.** rev. ed. Kevin Greene. LC 95-6800. (Illus.). 192p. 1995. pap. text ed. 19.95 (*0-8122-1570-2*) U of Pa Pr.

Archaeology: The Science of Once & Future Things. Brian Hayden. LC 92-20551. (C). 1995. pap. text ed. write for info. (*0-7167-2307-7*) W H Freeman.

Archaeology: Theories, Methods & Practice. Colin Renfrew & Paul Bahn. LC 90-70289. (Illus.). 544p. (C). 1991. pap. text ed. 34.95 (*0-500-27605-6*) Thames Hudson.

Archaeology - a Thematic Unit. Mary E. Sterling. (Thematic Units Ser.). (Illus.). 80p. (Orig.). 1994. student ed, pap. 8.95 (*1-55734-296-2*) Tchr Create Mat.

Archaeology after Structuralism. Ed. by Ian Bapty & Tim Yates. 352p. (C). 1991. text ed. 74.00 (*0-415-04500-2*, A5539) Routledge.

Archaeology & a Science of Man. Wilfred T. Neill. 1978. text ed. 50.00 (*0-231-03661-2*) Col U Pr.

Archaeology & Bible History. rev. ed. Joseph Free. 352p. 1992. pap. 17.99 (*0-310-47961-4*) Zondervan.

Archaeology & Ceramics at the Marksville Site. Alan Toth. (Anthropological Papers: No. 56). (Illus.). 1975. pap. 2.00 (*0-932206-54-9*) U Mich Mus Anthro.

Archaeology & Ethnohistory of the Central Quiche. Dwight T. Wallace & Robert M. Carmack. (Monographs: No. 1). (Illus.). 118p. (Orig.). 1977. pap. text ed. 10.00 (*0-942041-00-3*) SUNYA Inst Mesoam.

Archaeology & Ethnohistory of the Omaha Indians: The Big Village Site. John O'Shea & John Ludwickson. LC 89-35986. (Studies in the Anthropology of North American Indians). (Illus.). xviii, 374p. 1992. 40.00 (*0-8032-3556-9*) U of Nebr Pr.

Archaeology & Fertility Cult in the Ancient Mediterranean: Papers Presented at the First International Conference on Archaeology of the Ancient Mediterranean. Anthony Bonanno. (Illus.). xii, 356p. (Orig.). 1986. pap. 55.00 (*90-6032-288-6*, Pub. by B R Gruener NE) Benjamins North Am.

***Archaeology & Geographic Information Systems: A European Perspective.** Ed. by Gary Lock & Zoran Stancic. 400p. 1995. 99.50x (*0-7484-0208-X*, Pub. by Tay Francis Ltd UK) Taylor & Francis.

Archaeology & Geomorphology of Northern Asia: Selected Works. Ed. by Henry N. Michael. LC 65-1456. (Arctic Institute of North America-Anthropology of the North; Translation from Russian Sources Ser.: No. 5). 528p. reprint ed. pap. 150.50 (*0-8357-5715-3*, 2019174) Bks Demand.

Archaeology & History of Glastonbury Abbey. Ed. by Lesley Abrams & James P. Carley. (Illus.). 361p. (C). 1991. text ed. 99.00 (*0-85115-284-8*) Boydell & Brewer.

Archaeology & History of Upper Galum Creek, Perry County, Illinois. Daniel R. Haas & Michael J. McNerney. LC 86-71980. (Preservation Ser.: No. 2). (Illus.). 241p. (Orig.). 1986. pap. 13.75 (*0-913415-01-4*) Am Resources.

Archaeology & History of White Walnut Creek. Michael J. Higgins et al. (Preservation Ser.: No. 1). (Illus.). 206p. (Orig.). 1984. pap. 13.75 (*0-913415-00-6*) Am Resources.

Archaeology & Language: The Puzzle of Indo-European Origins. Colin Renfrew. (Illus.). 325p. (C). 1990. pap. 19.95 (*0-521-38675-6*) Cambridge U Pr.

***Archaeology & Religion: With Slides.** Dan P. Cole. Ed. by Hershel Shanks. 55p. (Orig.). 1991. pap. text ed. 99.50 (*1-880317-31-1*, 5094-AC) Biblical Arch Soc.

Archaeology & the Bible. Bill Humble. (Illus.). 145p. 1990. pap. 6.99 (*0-89225-370-3*) Gospel Advocate.

Archaeology & the Bible: The Best of BAR Series, 2 vols., Set. Ed. by Dan Cole. (Illus.). (C). 1992. reprint ed. pap. 35.95 (*0-9613089-3-1*) Biblical Arch Soc.

Archaeology & the Bible: The Best of BAR Series, 2 vols., Vol. I: Early Israel. Ed. by Dan Cole. (Illus.). 324p. (C). 1992. reprint ed. pap. 18.95 (*0-9613089-5-8*) Biblical Arch Soc.

Archaeology & the Bible: The Best of BAR Series, 2 vols., Vol. II: Archaeology in the World of Herod, Jesus. Ed. by Dan Cole. (Illus.). 293p. (C). 1992. reprint ed. pap. 18.95 (*0-9613089-6-6*) Biblical Arch Soc.

Archaeology & the Colonial Gardener. Audrey Noel Hume. LC 73-80008. (Archaeological Ser.: No. 7). (Illus.). 93p. (Orig.). 1974. pap. 5.95 (*0-87935-012-1*) Colonial Williamsburg.

Archaeology & the Information Age. Ed. by Paul Reilly & Sebastian Rahtz. (One World Archaeology Ser.: No. 20). (Illus.). 415p. 1992. 89.95 (*0-415-07858-X*, A8152) Routledge.

Archaeology & the M3: A Multi-Period Gravel Site. P. J. Fasham & R. J. Whinney. (Illus.). 196p. 1993. pap. text ed. 55.00 (*0-907473-07-5*) A Sutton Pub.

Archaeology & the New Testament. John McRay. LC 91-11663. 480p. (Orig.). 1990. text ed. 39.99 (*0-8010-6267-5*) Baker Bk.

Archaeology & the Old Testament. James B. Pritchard. LC 58-10053. 279p. reprint ed. pap. 79.60 (*0-8357-5716-1*, 2016011) Bks Demand.

Archaeology & Wetherburn's Tavern. Ivor Noel Hume. LC 76-84024. (Archaeological Ser.: No. 3). (Illus.). 47p. (Orig.). 1969. pap. 5.95 (*0-910412-08-1*) Colonial Williamsburg.

***Archaeology & You.** rev. ed. George E. Stuart & Francis P. McManamon. 48p. 1995. pap. write for info. (*0-932839-11-8*) Soc Am Arch.

Archaeology, Annales, & Ethnohistory. Ed. by A. Bernard Knapp. (New Directions in Archaeology Ser.). (Illus.). 168p. (C). 1992. 59.95 (*0-521-41174-2*) Cambridge U Pr.

Archaeology As Anthropology: A Case Study. William A. Longacre. LC 79-113089. (Anthropological Papers: No. 17). 57p. 1970. pap. 6.95 (*0-8165-0219-6*) U of Ariz Pr.

Archaeology As Human Ecology: Methods & Theory for a Contextual Approach. Karl W. Butzer. LC 81-21576. (Illus.). 380p. 1982. pap. 27.95 (*0-521-28877-0*) Cambridge U Pr.

Archaeology at Cerros, Belize, Central America: An Interim Report, Vol. 1. Ed. by David A. Freidel & Robin A. Robertson. LC 86-3843. (Archaeology at Cerros, Belize, Central America Ser.). (Illus.). 166p. 1986. pap. text ed. 22.50x (*0-87074-214-0*) SMU Press.

Archaeology at Cerros, Belize, Central America: The Artifacts, Vol. II. James F. Garber. LC 86-3843. (Illus.). 166p. 1989. pap. text ed. 22.50 (*0-87074-285-X*) SMU Press.

Archaeology at Cerros, Belize, Central America, Vol. III: The Settlement System in a Late Preclassic Maya Community. Vernon L. Scarborough. LC 86-3843. (Illus.). 224p. 1991. pap. text ed. 22.50 (*0-87074-307-4*) SMU Press.

Archaeology at French Colonial Cahokia. Bonnie L. Gums. Ed. by Thomas Emerson & Evelyn Moore. (Studies in Illinois Archaeology: No. 3). (Illus.). (Orig.). (C). 1988. pap. text ed. write for info. (*0-942579-02-X*) IHPA.

Archaeology at New Market. Barbara Liggett. 1978. pap. 5.00 (*0-916530-09-4*) Athenaeum Phila.

Archaeology at San Luis: Broad-Scale Testing, 1984-1985. Gary Shapiro et al. (Florida Archaeology Ser.: No. 3). (Illus.). 271p. 1987. pap. 10.00 (*0-923308-03-2*) FL Bur Archaeol.

Archaeology Economy & Society. David Hinton. (Illus.). 245p. 1990. 39.95 (*1-85264-049-9*, Pub. by Seaby UK) Trafalgar.

Archaeology Explained. Keith Branigan. 121p. 1988. pap. 13.95 (*0-7156-2011-8*) Focus Info Gr.

Archaeology for Money. Clement W. Meighan. LC 86-24607. (Illus.). 151p. (Orig.). (C). 1986. pap. text ed. 10. 95 (*0-937523-01-1*) Wormwood Pr.

Archaeology for Museologists. Alfonz Lengyel. (Museum Study Ser.: No. 2). (Illus.). 158p. (Orig.). 1993. pap. 15. 00 (*0-9626500-1-3*) Fudan Mus Fndtn.

***Archaeology for Young Explorers.** Patricia Samford & David L. Ribblett. LC 94-40017. (J). 1995. write for info. (*0-87935-089-X*) Colonial Williamsburg.

Archaeology, Geology, & Paleobiology of Stanton's Cave, Grand Canyon NP, AZ. Ed. by Robert C. Euler. LC 84-80572. 141p. 1984. pap. 15.00 (*0-938216-21-X*) GCNHA.

Archaeology Handbook: A Field Manual & Resource Guide. Bill McMillon. 272p. 1991. text ed. 24.95 (*0-471-55015-9*); pap. text ed. 16.95 (*0-471-53051-4*) Wiley.

Archaeology, History, & Custer's Last Battle: The Little Big Horn Reexamined. Richard A. Fox, Jr. LC 92-31269. 1993. 29.95 (*0-8061-2496-2*) U of Okla Pr.

Archaeology in Adventist Literature, 1937-1980. Lloyd A. Willis. (Andrews University Dissertation Ser.: Vol. 7). x, 680p. 1984. pap. 19.99 (*0-943872-39-1*) Andrews Univ Pr.

Archaeology in Bath 1976-1985: Excavations at Orange Grove, Swallow Street, The Crystal Palace, Abbey Street. Ed. by Peter Davenport. (Illus.). 170p. 1991. write for info. (*0-318-68532-9*, Pub. by Univ Comm Archeology UK) David Brown.

Archaeology in British Towns. Patrick Ottoway. LC 91-41071. (Illus.). 208p. 1992. 69.95 (*0-415-00068-8*, A7637) Routledge.

Archaeology in Jordan. Henry O. Thompson. (American University Studies: History: Ser. IX, Vol. 55). 260p. (C). 1989. text ed. 47.95 (*0-8204-1070-5*) P Lang Pubs.

Archaeology in the City: A Hohokam Village in Phoenix, Arizona. Michael H. Bartlett et al. LC 86-918. 80p. (Orig.). 1986. pap. 8.95 (*0-8165-0970-0*) U of Ariz Pr.

Archaeology in the Connecticut College Arboretum. Harold D. Juli. (Connecticut College Arboretum Bulletin Ser.: No. 33). (Illus.). 56p. (C). 1992. pap. 5.00 (*1-878899-03-1*) CT Coll Arboretum.

Archaeology in the "Cradle of Civilization" Charles K. Maisels. LC 92-2777. (Experience of Archaeology Ser.). 224p. 1992. 75.00 (*0-415-04742-0*, A6070) Routledge.

Archaeology in the Holy Land. 4th ed. Kathleen M. Kenyon. (Illus.). (C). 1979. text ed. 10.95 (*0-393-01285-9*) Norton.

Archaeology in the Lowland American Tropics: Current Analytical Methods & Recent Applications. Ed. by Peter W. Stahl. (Illus.). 336p. (C). 1995. 59.95 (*0-521-44486-1*) Cambridge U Pr.

Archaeology in the Upper Delaware Valley: A Study of the Cultural Chronology of the Tocks Island Reservoir. Ed. by W. Fred Kinsey. LC 72-169104. (Pennsylvania Historical & Museum Commission Anthropological Ser.: No. 2). (Illus.). 499p. 1972. 15.00 (*0-911124-68-3*) Pa Hist & Mus.

Archaeology in the 70's -- Mitigating the Impact, Vol. 35, No. 1-2. Carl H. Chapman et al. Ed. by Robert T. Bray. (Missouri Archaeologist Ser.). (Illus.). 71p. (Orig.). 1973. pap. 1.00 (*0-943414-51-2*) MO Arch Soc.

Archaeology of Aboriginal Culture Change in the Interior Southeast: Depopulation During the Early Historic Period. Marvin T. Smith. LC 92-9365. (Ripley P. Bullen Monographs in Anthropology & History: No. 6). (Illus.). 198p. 1992. reprint ed. lib. bdg. 29.95 (*0-8130-0846-8*); reprint ed. pap. 17.95 (*0-8130-1158-2*) U Press Fla.

***Archaeology of Africa: Food, Metals & Towns.** Ed. by Thurstan Shaw et al. (One World Archaeology Ser.). (Illus.). 896p. 1994. pap. 35.00 (*0-415-11585-X*, B4517) Routledge.

Archaeology of Alamo Lake, Arizona: A Cultural Resources Sample Survey. David A. Gregory. (Statistical Research Technical Ser.: No. 13). (Illus.). 195p. 1988. spiral bd. 14.00 (*1-879442-11-6*) Stats Res.

Archaeology of Alkali Ridge, Southeastern Utah. J. O. Brew. (HU PMP Ser.: Vol. 21). 1946. 79.00 (*0-685-02850-X*) Periodicals Srv.

Archaeology of Alta California. Ed. by Leo R. Barker & Julia Costello. LC 91-45783. (Spanish Borderlands Sourcebooks Ser.: Vol. 15). 488p. 1992. 80.00 (*0-8240-1964-4*) Garland.

***Archaeology of Ancestors: Tomb Cult & Hero Cult in Early Greece.** Calra M. Antonaccio. (Greek Studies: Interdisciplinary Approaches). 240p. (C). 1994. lib. bdg. 39.50 (*0-8476-7941-1*) Rowman.

***Archaeology of Ancestors: Tomb Cult & Hero Cult in Early Greece.** Calra M. Antonaccio. (Greek Studies: Interdisciplinary Approaches). 240p. (C). 1994. pap. text ed. 17.95 (*0-8476-7942-X*) Rowman.

Archaeology of Ancient China. Kwang-Chih Chang. LC 86-9186. 544p. 1987. text ed. 60.00 (*0-300-03782-1*); pap. 25.00x (*0-300-03784-8*) Yale U Pr.

***Archaeology of Ancient Indian Cities.** Dilip K. Chakrabarti. (Illus.). 300p. 1995. 25.00 (*0-19-563472-1*) OUP.

Archaeology of Ancient Israel. Ed. by Amnon Ben-Tor. Tr. by R. Greenberg. (Illus.). 416p. (C). 1992. pap. 27.50 (*0-300-05919-1*) Yale U Pr.

Archaeology of Ancient Sicily. R. Ross Holloway. (Illus.). 304p. 1991. 49.95 (*0-415-01909-5*, A5755) Routledge.

Archaeology of Anglo-Saxon England. David M. Wilson. (Illus.). 532p. 1981. pap. 32.50 (*0-521-28390-6*) Cambridge U Pr.

Archaeology of Animals. Simon J. Davis. LC 87-50831. 224p. 1987. 35.00 (*0-300-04065-2*) Yale U Pr.

Archaeology of Architecture: Charles Robert Cockerell in Southern Europe & the Levant, 1810-1817. Pieter B. Broucke. LC 93-60063. (Illus.). 23p. 1993. pap. 4.95 (*0-930606-69-8*) Yale Ctr Brit Art.

Archaeology of Arnold Research Cave, Callaway County, Missouri, Vol. 28. J. M. Shippee. Ed. by Robert T. Bray. (Missouri Archaeologist Ser.). (Illus.). 107p. (Orig.). 1966. pap. 3.50 (*0-943414-46-6*) MO Arch Soc.

***Archaeology of Athens & Attica under the Democracy.** Ed. by W. D. Coulson et al. (Oxbow Monographs in Archaeology: No. 37). (Illus.). 250p. 1994. 75.00 (*0-946897-67-0*, Pub. by Oxbow Bks UK) David Brown.

Archaeology of Australia's History. Graham Connah. (Illus.). 192p. (C). 1994. pap. 29.95 (*0-521-45475-1*) Cambridge U Pr.

Archaeology of Beekeeping. Eva Crane. LC 82-74021. (Illus.). 320p. 1983. 46.50 (*0-8014-1609-4*) Cornell U Pr.

Archaeology of Beringia. Frederick H. West. LC 81-6160. (Illus.). 294p. reprint ed. pap. 83.80 (*0-8357-4583-X*, 2037514) Bks Demand.

An Asterisk (*) at the beginning of an entry indicates that the title is appearing in BIP for the first time.

***Archaeology of CA-Mno-2122: A Study of Pre-Contact & Post-Contact Lifeways among the Mono Basin Paiute.** Brooke S. Arkush. LC 95-3282. (Publications in Anthropology: Vol. 31). 1995. pap. 40.00 (*0-520-09793-9*) U CA Pr.

Archaeology of California. Joseph L. Chartkoff & Kerry K. Chartkoff. LC 82-60182. (Illus.). 480p. 1984. 55.00 (*0-8047-1157-7*); pap. 19.95 (*0-8047-1483-5*) Stanford U Pr.

Archaeology of Cape Nome, Alaska. John Bockstoce. (University Museum Monographs: No. 38). (Illus.). xiii, 133p. (Orig.). (C). 1979. pap. 25.00 (*0-934718-27-X*) U PA Mus Pubns.

Archaeology of Coastal New York. Carlyle S. Smith. LC 76-43833. (AMNH. Anthropological Papers: Vol. 43, Pt. 2). reprint ed. 14.50 (*0-404-15687-8*) AMS Pr.

Archaeology of Colorado. E. Steve Cassells. LC 83-82868. (Illus.). 330p. 1983. pap. 16.95 (*0-933472-76-5*) Johnson Bks.

Archaeology of Cook Inlet, Alaska. Frederica De Laguna. LC 74-5832. reprint ed. 67.50 (*0-404-11637-X*) AMS Pr.

Archaeology of Crete. John D. Pendlebury. LC 63-18049. (Illus.). 1969. 28.00 (*0-8196-0121-7*) Biblo.

Archaeology of Cyprus: Recent Developments. Ed. by Noel Robertson. LC 75-34930. 232p. 1976. 24.00 (*0-8155-5039-1*, NP) Noyes.

***Archaeology of Disease.** 2nd ed. Charlotte Roberts & Keith Manchester. LC 95-15961. (Illus.). 256p. 1995. 39.95 (*0-8014-3220-0*) Cornell U Pr.

***Archaeology of Early Historic South Asia: The Emergence of Cities & States.** Raymond Allchin. (Illus.). 300p. (C). 1995. write for info. (*0-521-37547-9*); pap. write for info. (*0-521-37695-5*) Cambridge U Pr.

Archaeology of Early Medieval Ireland. Nancy Edwards. LC 90-40298. (Middle Ages Ser.). (Illus.). 240p. (C). 1990. 41.95 (*0-8122-3085-X*, Pub. by B T B UK) U of Pa Pr.

Archaeology of Early Rome & Latium. R. Ross Holloway. LC 93-11279. 1994. write for info. (*0-415-08065-7*) Routledge.

***Archaeology of Eastern India: Chhotanagpur Plateau & West Bengal.** Dilip K. Chakrabarti. (C). 1993. 42.00x (*81-215-0601-8*, Pub. by Munshiram Manoharial II) S Asia.

***Archaeology of Eastern North America: Papers in Honor of Stephen Williams.** Ed. by James B. Stoltman. LC 93-620339. (Mississippi Department of Archives & History Archaeological Reports: No. 25). (Illus.). xi, 382p. (Orig.). 1993. pap. text ed. write for info. (*0-938896-62-8*) Mississippi Archives.

Archaeology of Economic Ideas. S. Todd Lowry. LC 87-15507. (Illus.). xviii, 366p. (C). 1988. lib. bdg. 57.00 (*0-8223-0774-X*) Duke.

Archaeology of English. Martyn Wakelin. LC 88-7827. (Illus.). 176p. (C). 1989. lib. bdg. 53.00 (*0-389-20859-0*, N8417) B&N Imports.

Archaeology of Etna Cave, Lincoln County, Nevada & Prehistory of Southeastern Nevada, 2 vols. in 1. Sidney M. Wheeler. (Publications in the Social Sciences Ser.: Nos. 6 & 7). (Illus.). 201p. (Orig.). (C). 1973. pap. 5.00 (*0-945920-89-X*) Desert Rsch Inst.

Archaeology of Frontier Taverns on the St. Louis-Vincennes Trace. Mark J. Wagner & Mary R. McCorvie. (Popular Science Ser.: Vol. XI). (Illus.). 56p. 1993. pap. 3.50 (*0-89792-139-9*) Ill St Museum.

Archaeology of Frontiers & Boundaries. Ed. by Stanton W. Green & Stephen M. Perlman. LC 84-9325. (Studies in Archaeology). 1985. text ed. 77.00 (*0-12-298780-2*) Acad Pr.

Archaeology of Garden & Field. Ed. by Naomi F. Miller & Kathryn L. Gleason. (Illus.). 248p. (C). 1994. text ed. 28.95 (*0-8122-3244-5*) U of Pa Pr.

Archaeology of Gender: Separating the Spheres in Urban America. Diana D. Wall. LC 93-44321. (Interdisciplinary Contributions to Archaeology Ser.). 241p. 1994. 37.50 (*0-306-44551-4*, Plenum Pr) Plenum.

Archaeology of Greece: An Introduction. rev. ed. William R. Biers. LC 87-5447. (Illus.). 344p. (C). 1987. 52.50 (*0-8014-2082-2*); pap. 19.95 (*0-8014-9406-0*) Cornell U Pr.

Archaeology of Greece: The Present State & Future Scope of a Discipline. Anthony M. Snodgrass. LC 86-19702. (Sather Classical Lectures: No. 53). (Illus.). 420p. 1980. 38.00 (*0-520-05855-0*) U CA Pr.

Archaeology of Greece: The Present State & Future Scope of a Discipline. Anthony M. Snodgrass. (Sather Classical Lectures: No. 53). (C). 1987. pap. 13.00 (*0-520-07892-6*) U CA Pr.

***Archaeology of Greek Colonisation Essays Dedicated to Sir John Boardman.** Ed. by Gocha R. Tsetskhladze & Franco De Angelis. (Oxford University Committee for Archaeology Monograph Ser.: No. 40). (Illus.). 160p. 1994. 34.50 (*0-947816-40-2*, Pub. by Oxbow Bks UK) David Brown.

Archaeology of Hampshire. Ed. by S. J. Shennan & R. T. Schadla-Hall. (Illus.). 130p. 1993. pap. text ed. 19.00 (*0-907473-00-8*) A Sutton Pub.

Archaeology of Human Origins: Papers by Glynn Isaac. Glynn L. Isaac. Ed. by Barbara Isaac. (Illus.). 480p. (C). 1990. 79.95 (*0-521-36573-2*) Cambridge U Pr.

Archaeology of India: A Survey of Indian Prehistory. Agrawal. (C). 1985. pap. 39.95 (*0-7007-0140-0*, Pub. by Curzon Pr UK) Humanities.

Archaeology of Indian Trade Routes up to the Century 200 B. C. Resource Use, Resource Access & Lines of Communication. Nayanjot Lahiri. (Illus.). 475p. 1992. 32.00 (*0-19-562814-4*) OUP.

Archaeology of Inequality. Ed. by Randall H. McGuire & Robert Paynter. (Social Archaeology Ser.). 256p. 1991. pap. 21.95 (*0-631-17959-3*) Blackwell Pubs.

Archaeology of Ireland. rev. ed. Robert A. Macalister. LC 70-172160. (Illus.). 1972. reprint ed. 36.95 (*0-405-08758-6*, Pub. by Blom Pubns UK) Ayer.

Archaeology of Israelite Samaria. Ron E. Tappy. LC 92-32945. (Harvard Semitic Studies: No. 44). 295p. 1992. 44.95 (*1-55540-770-6*, 04 04 44) Scholars Pr GA.

Archaeology of James Creek Shelter. Ed. by Robert G. Elston & Elizabeth E. Budy. LC 89-40598. (Anthropological Papers: No. 115). (Illus.). 344p. (Orig.). 1990. pap. text ed. 27.50 (*0-87480-339-X*) U of Utah Pr.

Archaeology of Jordan & Other Studies: Presented to Siegfried H. Horn. Ed. by Lawrence T. Geraty & Larry G. Herr. LC 86-72165. 732p. 1986. text ed. 49.99 (*0-943872-27-8*) Andrews Univ Pr.

Archaeology of Knowledge: Includes the Discourse on Language. Michel Foucault. Tr. by A. M. Sheridan-Smith. LC 72-1135. 1972. 29.50 (*0-394-47118-0*) Irvington.

Archaeology of Korea. Sarah Nelson. (World Archaeology Ser.). (Illus.). 288p. (C). 1993. 69.95 (*0-521-40443-6*); pap. 27.95 (*0-521-40783-4*) Cambridge U Pr.

Archaeology of la Calsada: A Rockshelter in the Sierra Madre Oriental, Mexico. C. Roger Nance. LC 91-41040. (Texas Archaeology & Ethnography Ser.). (Illus.). 256p. 1992. text ed. 35.00x (*0-292-70427-5*) U of Tex Pr.

Archaeology of Lytton, British Columbia. Harlan I. Smith. LC 73-3512. (Jesup North Pacific Expedition. Publications: Vol. 1, Pt. 3). reprint ed. 22.50 (*0-404-58114-5*) AMS Pr.

Archaeology of Mainland Southeast Asia. Charles Higham. (World Archaeology Ser.). (Illus.). 280p. 1989. 74.95 (*0-521-25523-6*); pap. 29.95 (*0-521-27525-3*) Cambridge U Pr.

Archaeology of Mangareva & Neighboring Atolls. Kenneth P. Emory. (BMB Ser.: No. 163). 1972. reprint ed. 20.00 (*0-527-02271-3*) Periodicals Srv.

Archaeology of Medieval Ireland. T. B. Barry. 256p. 1989. pap. 15.95 (*0-415-01104-3*, A2717) Routledge.

Archaeology of Mississippi. Calvin S. Brown. LC 72-5011. (Antiquities of the New World Ser.: Vol. 16). (Illus.). reprint ed. 76.50 (*0-404-57316-9*) AMS Pr.

Archaeology of New York State. William A. Ritchie. LC 94-12299. 357p. 1994. pap. 25.00 (*0-935796-52-5*) Purple Mnt Pr.

Archaeology of Newark Cave, White Pine County, Nevada & Archaeological Survey in Eastern Nevada, 1966, 2 vols. in 1. Don D. Fowler. (Publications in the Social Sciences Ser.: Nos. 2 & 3). (Illus.). 99p. (Orig.). (C). 1968. pap. 2.00 (*0-945920-87-3*) Desert Rsch Inst.

Archaeology of Nihoa & Necker Islands. Kenneth P. Emory. (BMB Ser.: No. 53). 1972. reprint ed. 25.00 (*0-527-02159-8*) Periodicals Srv.

Archaeology of North America. Dean Snow. 1992. pap. 7.95 (*0-7910-0353-1*) Chelsea Hse.

Archaeology of North America. Dean R. Snow. (Indians of North America Ser.). (Illus.). 144p. (YA). (gr. 5 up). 1989. 17.95 (*1-55546-691-5*) Chelsea Hse.

Archaeology of North-Eastern India. J. P. Singh & G. Sengupta. 1991. text ed. 50.00 (*0-7069-5463-7*, Pub. by Vikas II) S Asia.

Archaeology of Northeast China: Beyond the Great Wall. Ed. by Sarah M. Nelson. LC 94-9966. 1995. 65.00x (*0-415-11755-0*, B4521, Routledge NY) Routledge.

Archaeology of Northwestern Venezuela. A. Kidder, 2nd. (HU PMP Ser.: Vol. 26, No. 1). 1972. reprint ed. 23.00 (*0-527-01264-5*) Periodicals Srv.

Archaeology of Pacific Nicaragua. Frederick W. Lange et al. LC 90-23536. (Illus.). 344p. 1992. 49.95x (*0-8263-1260-8*) U of NM Pr.

Archaeology of Palestine. rev. ed. William F. Albright. 19.00 (*0-8446-0003-2*) Peter Smith.

Archaeology of Pataliputa & Nalanda. Kumar Brajmohan. 236p. 1987. 54.00 (*0-8364-2032-2*, Pub. by Usha II) S Asia.

Archaeology of Petaga Point: The Preceramic Component. Peter Bleed. LC 75-626260. (Minnesota Prehistoric Archaeology Ser.: No. 2). (Illus.). 51p. 1969. pap. 3.00 (*0-87351-049-6*) Minn Hist.

Archaeology of Plants. Julie M. Hansen. 1994. write for info. (*0-8493-8878-3*) CRC Pr.

Archaeology of Political Structure: Settlement Analysis in a Classic Maya Polity. Olivier De Montmollin. (Illus.). 300p. (C). 1989. 69.95 (*0-521-36232-6*) Cambridge U Pr.

Archaeology of Pre-Columbian Florida. Jerald T. Milanich. LC 93-36888. (Illus.). 496p. (C). 1994. lib. bdg. 49.95 (*0-8130-1272-4*); pap. 24.95 (*0-8130-1273-2*) U Press Fla.

Archaeology of Prehistoric Coastlines. Ed. by G. N. Bailey & J. Parkington. (New Directions in Archaeology Ser.). (Illus.). 200p. 1988. 59.95 (*0-521-25036-6*) Cambridge U Pr.

Archaeology of Rank. Paul K. Wason. LC 93-42094. (New Studies in Archaeology). (Illus.). 240p. (C). 1994. 54.95 (*0-521-38072-3*) Cambridge U Pr.

Archaeology of Regions: The Case for Full-Coverage Survey. Ed. by Suzanne K. Fish & Stephen A. Lowalewski. LC 89-6249. (Archaeological Inquiry Ser.: No. 7). (Illus.). 220p. (C). 1989. 42.00 (*0-87474-404-0*) Smithsonian.

Archaeology of Religious Places: Churches & Cemeteries in Britain. rev. ed. Warwick Rodwell. LC 89-24964. (Illus.). 208p. (C). 1990. text ed. 37.95x (*0-8122-8244-2*) U of Pa Pr.

Archaeology of Ritual & Magic. Ralph Merrifield. (Illus.). 224p. (C). 1988. 25.00 (*0-941533-25-5*); pap. 15.95 (*0-941533-26-3*) New Amsterdam Bks.

Archaeology of Roman Pannonia. Ed. by A. Lengyel & G. T. Radan. LC 81-51021. (Illus.). 674p. 1981. 55.00 (*0-8131-1370-9*) U Pr of Ky.

Archaeology of Santa Leticia & the Rise of Maya Civilization. Arthur Demarest. LC 84-62189. (Publication Ser.: No. 52). 272p. 1986. 42.50 (*0-939238-81-0*) Tulane MARI.

Archaeology of Santa Marta, Colombia: The Tairona Culture. J. A. Mason. (Chicago Field Museum of Natural History Fieldiana Anthropology Ser.: Vol. 20). 1972. reprint ed. 73.00 (*0-527-01880-5*) Periodicals Srv.

Archaeology of Section 20, North Valmy Power Plant, Humboldt County, Nevada. Robert Elston et al. (Social Sciences Center Technical Report Ser.: No. 19). (Illus.). 235p. (C). 1981. spiral bd. 15.00 (*0-945920-19-9*) Desert Rsch Inst.

Archaeology of Seventeenth Century Virginia: A Synthesis. Ed. by Theodore R. Reinhart & Dennis J. Pogue. (SP Ser.: No. 30). 402p. 1993. pap. 25.00 (*1-884626-13-0*) Archeolog Soc.

***Archaeology of Shirley Plantation.** fac. ed. Ed. by Theodore R. Reinhart. LC 84-15245. (Illus.). 238p. 1984. reprint ed. pap. 67.90 (*0-7837-7983-6*, 2047739) Bks Demand.

Archaeology of Slavery & Plantation Life. Ed. by Theresa A. Singleton. (Studies in Historical Archaeology). 1985. text ed. 55.00 (*0-12-646480-4*) Acad Pr.

Archaeology of Smith Creek Canyon, Eastern Nevada. Ed. by Donald R. Tuohy & Doris L. Rendall. (Illus.). 394p. 1979. pap. 16.50 (*0-685-50178-7*) Ctr Study First Am.

***Archaeology of Smith Creek Canyon, Eastern Nevada.** Ed. by Donald R. Tuohy & Doris L. Rendell. 394p. 1979. pap. 16.50 (*1-55889-825-5*) OR St U CSFA.

Archaeology of Social Disintegration in Skunk Hollow: A Nineteenth-Century Rural Black Community. Joan H. Geismar. (Studies in Historical Archaeology). 230p. 1982. text ed. 53.00 (*0-12-279020-0*) Acad Pr.

Archaeology of Society in the Holy Land. Ed. by Thomas Levy. (Illus.). 460p. 1994. 80.00 (*0-8160-2855-9*) Facts on File.

Archaeology of South India: Tamilnadu. K. S. Ramachandran. 1980. 40.00 (*0-8364-0669-9*, Pub. by Sundeep II) S Asia.

***Archaeology of Spanish & Mexican Colonialism in the American Southwest No. 3: Guides to the Archaeological Literature of the Immigrant Experience in America.** Comp. by James E. Ayres. (Columbian Quincentenary Ser.). 150p. (Orig.). 1995. pap. write for info. (*1-886818-01-0*) Society Hist Arch.

Archaeology of Summer Island: Changing Settlement Systems in Northern Lake Michigan. David S. Brose. LC 71-633183. (Museum of Anthropology, University of Michigan, Anthropological Papers: No. 41). (Illus.). 281p. reprint ed. pap. 80.10 (*0-7837-4773-X*, 2044528) Bks Demand.

***Archaeology of the African Diaspora in the Americas.** Ed. by Theresa A. Singleton & Mark D. Bograd. (Columbian Quincentenary Ser.: No. 2). (Illus.). 87p. (Orig.). 1995. pap. 10.00 (*1-886818-00-2*) Society Hist Arch.

Archaeology of the Arabian Gulf. Michael Rice. LC 93-7006. 1994. write for info. (*0-415-03268-7*) Routledge.

Archaeology of the Arizona Public Service 345 KV Line. Alan P. Olson. (Bulletin Ser.). 71p. 1971. pap. 2.50 (*0-685-14710-X*, BS-46) Mus Northern Ariz.

Archaeology of the Arkansas River Valley. Warren K. Moorehead. LC 76-43780. reprint ed. write for info. (*0-404-15634-7*) AMS Pr.

Archaeology of the British Isles: With a Gazeteer of Sites in England, Wales, Scotland, & Ireland. Andrew Hayes. LC 93-4856. 1993. text ed. 49.95 (*0-312-10205-4*); pap. 18.95 (*0-312-10248-8*) St Martin.

Archaeology of the Cahokia Mounds, ICT-Two: Site Structure. James M. Collins. Ed. by Thomas E. Emerson & Evelyn Taylor. (Illinois Cultural Resources Study: No. 10). (Illus.). 260p. (Orig.). 1990. pap. 14.00 (*0-942579-10-0*) IHPA.

Archaeology of the Cahokia Palisade: East Palisade Investigations & South Palisade Investigations. William R. Iseminger et al. Ed. by Thomas E. Emerson & Evelyn Taylor. (Illinois Cultural Resources Study: No. 14). (Illus.). 119p. (Orig.). 1990. pap. 16.00 (*0-942579-09-7*) IHPA.

Archaeology of the Central Eskimos, 2 pts. in 1 vol. Therkel Mathiassen. LC 76-21669. (Thule Expedition, 5th, 1921-1924 Ser.: No. 4). reprint ed. 137.50 (*0-404-58315-6*) AMS Pr.

Archaeology of the Central Salt River Valley: An Overview of the Prehistoric Occupation, Vol. 46. M. J. O'Brien. (Missouri Archaeologist Ser.). 1985. 8.00 (*0-943414-66-0*) MO Arch Soc.

Archaeology of the Collective East: Greece, Asia Minor, Egypt, Lebanon, Mesopatamia, Syria, Palestine, an Annotated Bibliography. Jill M. Phillips. 1977. lib. bdg. 250.00 (*0-8490-1362-3*) Gordon Pr.

Archaeology of the Consumer Society: The Second Industrial Revolution in Britain. Kenneth Hudson. LC 83-5560. (Illus.). 144p. 1983. 45.00 (*0-8386-3200-9*) Fairleigh Dickinson.

Archaeology of the Cultural Landscape: Field Work & Research in a South Swedish Rural Region. Ed. by Lars Larsson et al. (Acta Archaeologica Ludensia Ser.: Vol. 4.0, No. 19). (Illus.). 498p. 1993. 120.00x (*91-22-01550-7*, Pub. by Almqv & Wiksell SW) Coronet Bks.

Archaeology of the Cuneiform Inscriptions. A. H. Sayce. 220p. 1977. 25.00 (*0-89005-228-X*) Ares.

Archaeology of the Delaware Valley. E. Volk. (Harvard University Peabody Museum of Archaeology & Ethnology Papers). 1972. reprint ed. 47.00 (*0-527-01204-1*) Periodicals Srv.

Archaeology of the Dreamtime: The Story of Prehistoric Australia & Its People. Josephine Flood. 304p. (C). 1991. 40.00x (*0-300-04924-2*) Yale U Pr.

Archaeology of the Early Anglo-Saxon Kingdoms. C. J. Arnold. 224p. (C). 1988. lib. bdg. 59.95 (*0-415-00349-0*, A2385) Routledge.

Archaeology of the Early Anglo-Saxon Kingdoms. C. J. Arnold. 224p. 1989. 17.95 (*0-415-03248-2*, A3235) Routledge.

Archaeology of the English Civil War. Peter Harrington. 1989. pap. 25.00 (*0-7478-0156-8*, Pub. by Shire UK) St Mut.

Archaeology of the Florida Gulf Coast. Gordon R. Willey. 1982. reprint ed. 45.00 (*0-317-27694-8*) Kallman.

Archaeology of the Grand Canyon: The Bright Angel Site. Douglas W. Schwartz et al. LC 79-63535. (Grand Canyon Archaeological Ser: Vol. 1). (Illus.). 122p. (Orig.). 1979. pap. 6.95 (*0-933452-00-4*) Schol Am Res.

Archaeology of the Grand Canyon: The Walhalla Plateau. Douglas W. Schwartz et al. LC 81-5730. (Grand Canyon Archaeological Ser.: Vol. 3). (Illus.). 265p. (Orig.). 1981. pap. 15.00 (*0-933452-06-3*) Schol Am Res.

Archaeology of the Grand Canyon: Unkar Delta. Douglas W. Schwartz et al. LC 80-21667. (Grand Canyon Archaeological Ser.: Vol. 2). (Illus.). 421p. (Orig.). 1981. pap. 15.00 (*0-933452-04-7*) Schol Am Res.

Archaeology of the Gulf of Georgia & Puget Sound. Harlan I. Smith. LC 73-3521. (Jesup North Pacific Expedition. Publications: Vol. 2, Pt. 6). reprint ed. 34.50 (*0-404-58122-6*) AMS Pr.

Archaeology of the Hopi Buttes District, Arizona. George J. Gumerman. LC 87-73015. (Center for Archaeological Investigations Research Paper Ser.: No. 49). (Illus.). xxiv, 234p. (Orig.). 1988. pap. 18.50 (*0-88104-059-2*) Center Archaeo.

Archaeology of the Imagination. Ed. by Charles Winquist. (JAAR Thematic Studies). 1981. pap. 18.95 (*0-89130-679-X*, 01-24-82) Scholars Pr GA.

Archaeology of the Jerusalem Area. W. Harold Mare. LC 85-73719. 1986. 19.99 (*0-8010-6126-1*) Baker Bk.

Archaeology of the Land of Israel. Yohanan Aharoni. Ed. by Miriam Aharoni. Tr. by Anson F. Rainey. LC 81-14742. (Illus.). 364p. (C). 1982. reprint ed. pap. 21.99 (*0-664-24430-0*, Westminster) Westminster John Knox.

Archaeology of the Land of the Bible: 10,000-586 B. C. E. Amihai Mazar. (Anchor Bible Reference Library). 1990. 37.50 (*0-385-23970-X*, Anchor Bible) Doubleday.

Archaeology of the Lapita Cultural Complex: A Critical Review. Ed. by Patrick V. Kirch & Terry L. Hunt. (Illus.). 186p. 1989. pap. 17.00 (*0-295-96821-4*) U of Wash Pr.

Archaeology of the Lower Ohio River Valley. Jon Muller. LC 85-15050. (New World Archaeological Record Ser.). 1986. pap. text ed. 58.00 (*0-12-510331-X*) Acad Pr.

Archaeology of the Marianas Islands. L. Thompson. (BMB Ser.: No. 100). 1972. reprint ed. 15.00 (*0-527-02206-3*) Periodicals Srv.

Archaeology of the Marquesas Islands. Ralph Linton. (BMB Ser.: No. 23). 1972. reprint ed. 30.00 (*0-527-02126-1*) Periodicals Srv.

Archaeology of the Medieval English Monarchy. John Steane. (Illus.). 226p. 1994. 75.00 (*0-7134-7246-4*, Pub. by Batsford UK) Trafalgar.

Archaeology of the Mind. George Frankl. (Social History of the Unconscious Ser.: Vol. 1). 232p. 1993. pap. 18.95 (*1-871871-16-6*, Pub. by Open Gate Pr UK) Paul & Co Pubs.

Archaeology of the Moody Dune Site, 26Ny4844, Tonopah Test Range, Nye County, Nevada. Ronald L. Reno & Lonnie C. Pippin. (Illus.). 30p. 1986. 2.50 (*0-945920-48-2*) Desert Rsch Inst.

***Archaeology of the Nile Delta, Egypt: Problems & Priorities.** Edwin C. Van den Brink. xv, 325p. 1988. pap. text ed. 58.00 (*90-70556-30-8*, Pub. by Netherlands Inst NE) Eisenbrauns.

Archaeology of the North Coast of Honduras. Doris Stone. (HU PMM Ser.: Vol. 9, No. 1). 1972. reprint ed. 20.00 (*0-527-01172-X*) Periodicals Srv.

Archaeology of the Old Landmark: Nineteenth-Century Taverns along the St. Louis-Vincennes Trace in Southern Illinois. Ed. by Mark J. Wagner & Mary R. McCorvie. LC 93-1071. (Illus.). 1993. 20.00 (*0-942118-34-0*) Ctr Amer Arche.

Archaeology of the Olympics: The Olympics & Other Festivals in Antiquity. Ed. by Wendy J. Raschke. LC 87-40150. (Wisconsin Studies in Classics). 312p. reprint ed. pap. 89.00 (*0-7837-1984-1*, 2042258) Bks Demand.

Archaeology of the Oneida Iroquois. Peter P. Pratt. (Occasional Publications in Northeastern Anthropology: No. 1). 1976. 5.50 (*0-686-30586-8*) Fund Anthrop.

Archaeology of the Oneida Iroquois, Vol. 1. Peter P. Pratt. (Occasional Publications in Northeastern Anthropology: No. 1). (Illus.). xii, 303p. 5.50 (*0-318-22319-8*) F Pierce College.

Archaeology of the Pacific Equatorial Islands. Kenneth P. Emory. (BMB Ser.: No. 123). 1972. reprint ed. pap. 15.00 (*0-527-02229-2*) Periodicals Srv.

Archaeology of the Point St. George Site, & Tolowa Prehistory. Richard A. Gould. LC 67-63726. (U. C. Publ. in Anthropology Ser.: Vol. 4). 149p. reprint ed. 42.50 (*0-8357-9626-4*, 2014837) Bks Demand.

***Archaeology of the Pueblo Grande Platform Mound & Surrounding Features Vol. 1: Introduction to the Archival Project & History of Archaeological Research.** David R. Abbott et al. LC 93-85695. (Pueblo Grande Museum Anthropological Papers: No. 1). (Illus.). 350p. (Orig.). 1993. pap. 25.00 (*1-882572-03-3*) Pueblo Grande Mus.

An Asterisk (*) at the beginning of an entry indicates that the title is appearing in BIP for the first time.

409

*Archaeology of the Pueblo Grande Platform Mound & Surrounding Features Vol. 1: Introduction to the Archival Project & History of Archaeological Research. David R. Abbott et al. LC 93-85695. (Pueblo Grande Museum Anthropological Papers: No. 1). (Illus.). 350p. (Orig.). 1993. 43.00 (1-882572-02-5) Pueblo Grande Mus.

*Archaeology of the Pueblo Grande Platform Mound & Surrounding Features Vol. 2: Features in the Central Precinct of the Pueblo Grande Community. David A. Gregory et al. (Pueblo Grande Museum Anthropological Papers: No. 1). xvi, 451p. (Orig.). 1994. 48.00 (1-882572-04-1); pap. 30.00 (1-882572-05-X) Pueblo Grande Mus.

Archaeology of the Roman Economy. Kevin Greene. (Illus.). 192p. 1991. pap. 17.00 (0-520-07401-7) U CA Pr.

Archaeology of the Sierra Blanca Region of Southeastern New Mexico. Jane H. Kelley. (Anthropological Papers: No. 74). (Illus.). 527p. 1984. pap. text ed. 15.00 (0-932206-96-4) U Mich Mus Anthro.

Archaeology of the Southeastern United States: Paleoindian to World War I. Judith A. Bense. (Illus.). 388p. 1994. text ed. 75.00 (0-12-089060-7); pap. text ed. 34.95 (0-12-089061-5) Acad Pr.

Archaeology of the Southern Gobi-Mongolia: An Exploration of Ancient Civilization in Mongolia. Walter A. Fairservis, Jr. LC 92-71957. (Centers of Civilization Ser.). (Illus.). 280p. 1993. 75.00 (0-89089-498-1) Carolina Acad Pr.

Archaeology of the Spanish Missions of Texas. Anne A. Fox. LC 90-22360. (Spanish Borderlands Sourcebooks Ser.: Vol. 21). 400p. 1991. reprint ed. 61.00 (0-8240-2097-9) Garland.

Archaeology of the Thompson River Region, British Columbia. Harlan I. Smith. LC 73-3515. (Jesup North Pacific Expedition. Publications: Vol. 1, Pt. 6). reprint ed. 24.50 (0-404-58117-X) AMS Pr.

Archaeology of the Transjordan in the Bronze & Iron Ages. Rudolph H. Dornemann. LC 83-61718. (Publications in Anthropology & History: No. 4). (Illus.). 288p. 1983. pap. text ed. 50.00 (0-89326-053-3) Milwaukee Pub Mus.

Archaeology of the United States. Samuel F. Haven. LC 72-4999. (Harvard University. Peabody Museum of Archaeology & Ethnology. Antiquities of the New World Ser.: No. 3). reprint ed. 62.50 (0-404-57303-7) AMS Pr.

Archaeology of the Wetlands. John Coles. 120p. 1984. pap. 10.00 (0-85224-503-3, Pub. by Edinburgh U Pr UK) Col U Pr.

Archaeology of Three Springs Valley: A Study in Functional Cultural History. Ed. by Brian D. Dillon & Matthew A. Boxt. LC 88-28259. (Monograph: No. 30). (Illus.). 196p. (Orig.). 1989. pap. text ed. 19.00 (0-917956-62-1) UCLA Arch.

Archaeology of Tonga. W. C. McKern. (BMB Ser.: No. 60). 1972. reprint ed. 25.00 (0-527-02166-0) Periodicals Srv.

Archaeology of Two Northern California Sites. Delmer E. Sanburg, Jr. et al. (Monograph: No. 22). (Illus.). 92p. 1983. pap. 7.00 (0-917956-41-9) UCLA Arch.

Archaeology of Urban America: The Search for Pattern & Process. Ed. by Roy S. Dickens, Jr. (Studies in Historical Archaeology). 1982. text ed. 70.00 (0-12-214980-7) Acad Pr.

Archaeology of V. Gordon Childe. Ed. by David R. Harris. 172p. 1994. 49.95 (0-522-84622-X) Intl Spec Bk.

Archaeology of V. Gordon Childe: Contemporary Perspectives. Ed. by David R. Harris. LC 93-45011. (C). 1994. 42.00 (0-226-31759-5) U Ch Pr.

*Archaeology of Weapons: Arms & Armour from Prehistory to the Age of Chivalry. Ewart Oakeshott. LC 94-40355. (Illus.). 1994. 53.00 (0-85115-559-6, Boydell Pr) Boydell & Brewer.

Archaeology of Western Iran: Settlement & Society from Prehistory to the Islamic Conquest. Ed. by Frank Hole. LC 86-42576. (Archaeological Inquiry Ser.). (Illus.). 332p. 1987. 55.00 (0-87474-526-8, HOAW) Smithsonian.

Archaeology of William Henry Holmes. Ed. by David J. Meltzer & Robert C. Dunnell. LC 91-27847. (Illus.). 736p. (Orig.). (C). 1992. pap. text ed. 34.95 (1-56098-152-0) Smithsonian.

*Archaeology on Film. AIA Staff. 112p. 1994. per., pap. text ed. 13.50 (0-8403-9016-5) Kendall-Hunt.

Archaeology Studies of World War II. Ed. by W. Raymond Wood. (Illus.). 67p. 1991. 10.00 (0-913134-29-5) Mus Anthro MO.

Archaeology, Volcanism, & Remote Sensing in the Arenal Region, Costa Rica. Ed. by Payson D. Sheets & Brian R. McKee. LC 93-15655. (Illus.). 384p. 1994. text ed. 45.00x (0-292-77667-5) U of Tex Pr.

Archaeology Workbook. Steve Daniels & Nicholas David. LC 81-43519. (Illus.). 120p. (Orig.). (C). 1982. pap. 19.95 (0-8122-1125-1) U of Pa Pr.

Archaeomagnetic Dating. Ed. by Jeffrey L. Eighmy & Robert S. Sternberg. LC 90-11110. 446p. 1990. 70.00 (0-8165-1132-2) U of Ariz Pr.

Archaeometry: An Introduction to Physical Methods in Archaeology & the History of Art. Ulrich Leute. LC 87-22689. (Illus.). 176p. 1987. lib. bdg. 40.00 (0-89573-612-8) VCH Pubs.

Archaeometry: Proceedings of the 25th International Symposium. Ed. by Y. Maniatis. 720p. 1989. 143.75 (0-444-87333-3) Elsevier.

Archaeometry, '90. Ed. by E. Pernicka & G. Wagner. 880p. 1990. 163.50 (0-8176-2522-4) Birkhauser.

Archaeometry of Pre-Columbian Sites & Artifacts. Ed. by David A. Scott & Pieter Meyers. LC 94-18548. (Illus.). 432p. 1994. pap. 55.00 (0-89236-249-9) J P Getty Trust.

Archaeopteryx. Oliver. (Dinosaur Library: Set II). (Illus.). 24p. (J). 1984. lib. bdg. 14.00 (0-86592-209-8) Rourke Enter.

Archaeopteryx: The First Bird. Elizabeth Sandell. Ed. by Marjorie Oelerich & Harlan S. Hansen. LC 88-39803. (Dinosaur Discovery Era Ser.). (Illus.). 32p. (J). (gr. k-5). 1989. lib. bdg. 12.95 (0-944280-13-7); pap. text ed. 5.95 (0-944280-19-6) Bancroft-Sage.

Archaepteryx. David Hawcock. (J). 1994. 5.95 (0-8050-3194-4) H Holt & Co.

Archaic & Classical Greece: A Selection of Ancient Sources in Translation. Ed. by Michael Crawford & David Whitehead. LC 82-4355. 700p. 1983. 99.95 (0-521-22775-5); pap. 34.95 (0-521-29638-2) Cambridge U Pr.

Archaic & Classical Greek Coins. C. Kraay. (Illus.). 1990. reprint ed. lib. bdg. 80.00 (0-685-36400-3) S J Durst.

Archaic & Woodland Cemeteries at the Elizabeth Site in the Lower Illinois Valley. Ed. by Douglas K. Charles et al. LC 88-14982. (Kampsville Archeological Center Research Ser.: Vol. 7). (Illus.). 340p. (Orig.). 1988. pap. 15.95 (0-942118-27-8) Ctr Amer Arche.

Archaic Bookkeeping: Early Writing & Techniques of the Economic Administration of the Ancient Near East. Hans J. Nissen et al. Tr. by Paul Larsen. LC 93-909. (Illus.). 224p. 1993. 34.95 (0-226-58659-6) U Ch Pr.

Archaic Corinthian Pottery & the Anaploga Well. D. A. Amyx & Patricia Lawrence. LC 75-4551. (Corinth Ser.: Vol. 7, Pt. 2). (Illus.). xvi, 177p. 1976. 40.00 (0-87661-072-6) Am Sch Athens.

Archaic Cyprus: A Study of the Textual & Archaeological Evidence. A. T. Reyes. LC 93-26237. (Oxford Monographs on Classical Archaeology). (Illus.). 320p. (C). 1994. 75.00 (0-19-813227-1, Clarendon Pr) OUP.

Archaic Dictionary. W. R. Cooper. 1971. 59.95 (0-87968-653-7) Gordon Pr.

Archaic Economy & Modern Society: The Sinhalese System of Castes, Kinship & Property. Eva B. Ernfors & Runar F. Ernfors. (Studia Sociologica Upsaliensia: No. 31). 340p. (Orig.). 1990. pap. 52.50x (91-554-2604-2, Pub. by Almqv & Wiksell SW) Coronet Bks.

Archaic Egypt. W. B. Emery. (Illus.). 320p. 1974. pap. 7.95 (0-14-020462-8, Penguin Bks) Viking Penguin.

Archaic Features of the Cannanite Personal Names in the Hebrew Bible. Scott C. Layton. (Harvard Semitic Monographs). 314p. 1990. 29.95 (1-55540-513-4, 04 00 47) Scholars Pr GA.

Archaic Figure. Amy Clampitt. 1987. 15.95 (0-394-55919-3); pap. 12.95 (0-394-75090-X) Knopf.

Archaic Gravestones of Attica. Gisela M. Richter. (Illus.). 184p. 1988. reprint ed. 55.00 (0-86516-211-5); reprint ed. pap. text ed. 30.00 (0-86516-189-5) Bolchazy-Carducci.

Archaic Greece: The Age of Experiment. Anthony M. Snodgrass. (Orig.). 1980. pap. 14.00 (0-520-04373-1) U CA Pr.

Archaic Greek Poetry: An Anthology. Tr. & Sel. by Barbara H. Fowler. LC 92-50251. (Studies in Classics). 360p. (Orig.). (C). 1992. lib. bdg. 50.00 (0-299-13510-1); pap. 16.95 (0-299-13514-4) U of Wis Pr.

Archaic History of the Human Race. Gertrude W. Van Pelt. (Study Ser.: No. 3). 1980. pap. 3.00 (0-913004-36-7) Point Loma Pub.

Archaic Hunters & Gatherers in the American Midwest. James A. Brown. Ed. by James L. Phillips. (New World Archaeological Record Ser.). 1983. text ed. 60.00 (0-12-553980-0) Acad Pr.

Archaic Inscriptions see Remains of Old Latin

Archaic of Northeastern Ohio. Olaf H. Prufer & Dana A. Long. LC 86-33. (Kent State Research Papers in Archaeology: No. 6). 95p. reprint ed. pap. 27.10 (0-7837-1344-4, 2041492) Bks Demand.

Archaic Period, Eleven Hundred to Four Hundred Seventy-Nine B C. Ed. by George A. Christopoulos & John C. Bastias. Tr. by Philip Sherrard. LC 75-27171. (History of the Hellenic World Ser.: Vol. 2). (Illus.). 620p. 1977. 65.00 (0-271-01214-5) Pa St U Pr.

Archaic Period in the Mid-South: Proceedings of the 1989 Mid-South Archaeological Conference. Ed. by Charles H. McNutt. LC 91-620836. (Mississippi Department of Archives & History Archaeological Reports: No. 24). (Illus.). 95p. 1991. 8.00 (0-938896-60-1) Mississippi Archives.

Archaic Revival: Collected Essays & Conversations. Terrence McKenna. 1991. pap. 14.95 (0-8065-1240-7, Citadel Pr) Carol Pub Group.

Archaic Revival: Speculations on Psychedelic Mushrooms, the Amazon, Virtual Reality, UFOs, Evolution, Shamanism, the Rebirth of the Goddess, & the End of History. Terence McKenna. LC 91-55290. (Illus.). 288p. 1992. pap. 14.00 (0-06-250613-7) Harper SF.

Archaic Smile of Herodotus. Stewart Flory. LC 86-32584. 204p. 1987. 29.95 (0-8143-1827-4) Wayne St U Pr.

Archaic Style in Greek Sculpture. 2nd rev. ed. B. Ridgway. (Illus.). xxviii, 497p. (C). 1993. pap. text ed. 55.00 (0-89005-516-5) Ares.

Archaic Times to the End of the Peloponnesian War. Ed. by Charles W. Fornara. LC 79-54018. (Translated Documents of Greece & Rome Ser.: No. 1). 232p. 1983. pap. 22.95 (0-521-29946-2) Cambridge U Pr.

Archaic, Woodland & Historic Period Occupations of the Liberty Bridge Locale. Nancy N. Cleland et al. Ed. by William A. Lovis. (Michigan Cultural Resource Investigation Ser.). 449p. 1993. pap. write for info. (0-9623670-2-8) MI Dept Trans.

Archaique Racine. Solange Guenoun. LC 90-37392. (American University Studies: Romance Languages & Literature: Ser. II, Vol. 128). 249p. (C). 1990. text ed. 49.95 (0-8204-1144-2) P Lang Pubs.

Archaism, Modernism, & the Art of Paul Manship. Susan Rather. LC 92-14217. (American Studies Ser.). (Illus.). 284p. (C). 1993. text ed. 42.50 (0-292-76035-3) U of Tex Pr.

Archaistic Style in Roman Statuary. Mark D. Fullerton. LC 90-2135. (Mnemosyne Ser.: Supplement 110). (Illus.). xiv, 215p. 1990. pap. 41.25 (90-04-09146-7) E J Brill.

Archangel. Michael Conner. 352p. 1995. 21.95 (0-312-85743-8) Tor Bks.

*Archangel. Michael Conner. 1996. pap. write for info. (0-614-05545-8) Tor Bks.

*Archangel. Paul Watkins. LC 95-2656. 1995. write for info. (0-679-44391-6) Random.

Archangel. large type ed. Gerald Seymour. 480p. 1983. 23.95 (0-7089-8135-6, Charnwood) Ulverscroft.

Archangel! A Defense Against the Ray Lopez. Ron Henley & Paul Hodges. (ChessBase University Power Play! Ser.). (Illus.). 64p. (Orig.). 1993. pap. 10.95 (1-883358-01-9) R&D Pub NJ.

Archangel Blues. Eluki Bes Shahar. (Hellflower Ser.: Bk. 3). 256p. (Orig.). 1993. mass mkt. 4.50 (0-88677-543-4) DAW Bks.

Archangel Michael: His Mission & Ours. Rudolf Steiner. Tr. by Marjorie Spock. 288p. 1994. pap. 17.95 (0-88010-378-7) Anthroposophic.

Archaologisches Worterbuch Zur Erklarung der in Den Schriften Uber Christliche Kunstalterthumer Vorkommenden Kunstausdrucke. Heinrich Otte. viii, 488p. 1978. reprint ed. write for info. (3-487-06455-3, Pub. by Georg Olms GW) Lubrecht & Cramer.

Archaos du le Jardin Etincelant. Christiane Rochefort. 448p. (FRE.). 1984. pap. 11.95 (0-7859-1465-X, 2253001074) Fr & Eur.

Archbishop: The Life & Times of Robert Runcie. Jonathan Mantle. (Illus.). 360p. 1992. 29.95 (1-85619-058-7, Sinclair-Stevenson) Trafalgar.

Archbishop Cranmer's Immortal Bequest: The Book of Common Prayer of the Church of England: An Evangelistic Liturgy. Samuel Leuenberger. 400p. (Orig.). (C). 1990. pap. 24.99 (0-8028-0474-8) Eerdmans.

Archbishop George Matulaitis. abr. ed. Anthony Kucas. Tr. by Stanley C. Gaucias. (Illus.). 346p. 1981. write for info. (0-318-69852-8) Marian Fathers.

Archbishop Green: His Life & Opinions. A. J. Edwards. 109p. (C). 1986. pap. 20.00x (0-86383-254-7, Pub. by Gomer Pr UK) St Mut.

Archbishop Lefebvre & Religious Liberty. Michael Davies. 17p. 1980. pap. 1.50 (0-89555-143-8) TAN Bks Pubs.

Archbishop Oscar Romero: A Shepherd's Diary. Tr. by Irene B. Hodgson. 552p. 1993. 24.95 (0-86716-170-1) St Anthony Mess Pr.

Archbishop Romero: Memories & Reflections. Jon Sobrino. LC 89-48221. 1990. pap. 14.95 (0-88344-667-7) Orbis Bks.

Archbishop Romero, Martyr of Salvador. Placido Erdozain. Tr. by John McFadden & Ruth Warner. LC 81-2007. 128p. reprint ed. pap. 36.50 (0-8357-8805-9, 2033464) Bks Demand.

*Archbishop Theodore: Commemorative Studies on His Life & Influence. Ed. by Michael Lapidge. (Cambridge Studies on Anglo-Saxon England: No. 11). 354p. (C). 1995. 59.95 (0-521-48077-9) Cambridge U Pr.

Archbishop Theophan of Poltava: Selected Letters Together with a Memorial Address. Archbishop Theophan of Poltava. Tr. by Antonina L. Janda. 80p. (Orig.). 1989. pap. 4.50 (0-912927-31-3, X031) St John Kronstadt.

Archbishop Tutu of South Africa. Judith Bentley. LC 88-410. (Illus.). 96p. (J). (gr. 6 up). 1988. lib. bdg. 16.95 (0-89490-180-X) Enslow Pubs.

Archbishop William Laud. Charles Carlton. 320p. 1987. lib. bdg. 65.00 (0-7102-0463-9, RKP) Routledge.

Archbishop's Ceiling. Arthur Miller. 1985. pap. 4.75 (0-8222-0064-3) Dramatists Play.

Archbishop's Daughter. Norma Hubbard. 729p. (Orig.). 1992. pap. 11.95 (0-9631969-0-1) Wimberley Bks.

Archbishops of York from Paulinus to Maclagan. A. Tindal Hart. (C). 1988. 100.00 (1-85072-002-9, Pub. by W Sessions UK) St Mut.

Archbold Criminal Pleading Evidence & Practice. 1,994th ed. Ed. by P. J. Richardson. 1993. 317.00 (0-421-47000-3, Pub. by Sweet & Maxwll) W W Gaunt.

*Archbold Pleading, Evidence & Practice in Criminal Cases, 2 vols., Set. 36th ed. T. R. Butler & Marston Garsia. 1995. 225.00 (1-56169-109-7) W W Gaunt.

Archduke Rudolf, Beethoven's Patron, Pupil & Friend: His Life & Music. Susan Kagan. 1992. pap. 36.00 (0-945193-45-9) Pendragon NY.

Arche de Noe. Jules Supervielle. 188p. (FRE.). 1938. pap. 10.95 (0-7859-1327-0, 2070261417) Fr & Eur.

*Archean & Early Proterozoic Tectonic Framework of North-Central United States & Adjacent Canada. P. K. Sims. (U.S. Geological Survey Bulletin & Contributions to Precambrian Geology of Lake Superior Ser.: Vol. 1904). 1995. write for info. (0-615-00321-4) US Geol Survey.

*Archean Crustal Evolution. Ed. by K. C. Condie. (Developments in Precambrian Geology Ser.: Vol. 11). 1994. write for info. (0-444-81621-6) Elsevier.

Archean Greenstone Belts. K. C. Condie. (Developments in Precambrian Geology Ser.: Vol. 3). 434p. 1981. 151.50 (0-444-41854-7) Elsevier.

*Archeologic Investigations in James & Potomac Valleys. Gerard Fowke. (Bureau of American Ethnology Bulletins Ser.). 80p. 1995. lib. bdg. 79.00 (0-7812-4023-9) Rprt Serv.

*Archeological Excavations at Jamestown Virginia. rev. ed. John L. Cotter. (Special Publication Ser.: No. 32). 349p. (C). 1994. pap. 35.00 (1-884626-23-8) Archeolog Soc.

Archeological Excavations at Willow Beach, Arizona, 1950. Albert H. Schroeder. (Utah Anthropological Papers: No. 50). reprint ed. 35.00 (0-404-60650-4) AMS Pr.

Archeological Explanation: The Scientific Methods in Archeology. Patty J. Watson et al. LC 84-5014. (Illus.). 325p. reprint ed. pap. 92.70 (0-8357-6865-1, 2035563) Bks Demand.

Archeological Exploration of Patawomeke: The Indian Town Site (44St2) Ancestral to the One (44St1) Visited in 1608 by Captain John Smith. Thomas D. Stewart. LC 92-28885. (Smithsonian Contributions to Anthropology Ser.: No. 36). (Illus.). 116p. reprint ed. pap. 33.10 (0-7837-4380-7, 2044120) Bks Demand.

*Archeological Explorations in Northeastern Arizona. Alfred Kidder & Samuel Guernsey. (Bureau of American Ethnology Bulletins Ser.). 228p. 1995. lib. bdg. 89.00 (0-7812-4065-4) Rprt Serv.

Archeological Explorations in Southern Nevada. M. R. Harrington et al. (Illus.). 126p. 1970. reprint ed. 5.00 (0-916561-06-2) Southwest Mus.

Archeological Explorations on San Nicolas Island. Bruce Bryan. (Illus.). 160p. 1970. 12.50 (0-916561-07-0) Southwest Mus.

Archeological History of New York, 2 vols., Set. A. C. Parker. 1993. reprint ed. lib. bdg. 150.00 (0-7812-5163-X) Rprt Serv.

Archeological Investigation of the Shannon Site, Montgomery County, Virginia. Joseph L. Benthall. (Publication Ser.: No. 32). xi, 152p. 1969. pap. 7.95 (0-88490-063-0) VA State Lib.

*Archeological Investigations at Buena Vista Lake, Kern County, California. Ed. by Waldo R. Wedel. (Bureau of American Ethnology Bulletins Ser.). 194p. 1995. lib. bdg. 79.00 (0-7812-4130-8) Rprt Serv.

Archeological Investigations at Crow Creek Site (39bf11) Fort Randall Reservoir Area, South Dakota. Marvin F. Kivett & Richard E. Jensen. (Publications in Anthropology: No. 7). 1976. pap. 6.00 (0-686-20017-9) Nebraska Hist.

*Archeological Investigations at the Mouth of the Amazon. Betty Meggers & Clifford Evans. (Bureau of American Ethnology Bulletins Ser.). 664p. 1995. lib. bdg. 149.00 (0-7812-4167-7) Rprt Serv.

Archeological Investigations at the Red Willow Reservoir. Roger T. Grange, Jr. (Publications in Anthropology: No. 9). (Illus.). 238p. (Orig.). 1980. pap. 10.00 (0-686-28124-1) Nebraska Hist.

*Archeological Investigations in British Guiana. Clifford Evans & Betty Meggers. (Bureau of American Ethnology Bulletins Ser.). 418p. 1995. lib. bdg. 109.00 (0-7812-4177-4) Rprt Serv.

*Archeological Investigations in the Parita & Santa Maria Zones of Panama. John Ladd. (Bureau of American Ethnology Bulletins Ser.). 291p. 1995. lib. bdg. 89.00 (0-7812-4193-6) Rprt Serv.

Archeological Investigations in West-Central New Mexico, Vols. 1-3. (Cultural Resources Ser.: Nos. 3-5). (Illus.). 648p. (Orig.). 1988. pap. write for info. (1-878178-03-2) Bureau of Land Mgmt NM.

Archeological Investigations in West-Central New Mexico, Vol. 1: Report of the First Field Season Bureau of Land Management, New Mexico State Office. Eileen Camilli et al. Ed. by Barbara L. Daniels & Marilu Waybourn. (Cultural Resources Ser.: No. 3). (Illus.). 269p. (Orig.). 1988. pap. write for info. (1-878178-04-0) Bureau of Land Mgmt NM.

Archeological Investigations Within the Central Little River Draining Basin, Cleveland & Pottawatomie Counties, Oklahoma. Michael C. Moore et al. (Archeological Resource Survey Report Ser.: No. 31). (Illus.). 186p. (C). 1988. pap. text ed. 6.00 (1-881346-20-X) Univ OK Archeol.

Archeological Notes on Stansbury Island. Sydney J. Jameson. (Utah Anthropological Papers: No. 34). reprint ed. 20.00 (0-404-60634-2) AMS Pr.

*Archeological Observations. Gerard Fowke. (Bureau of American Ethnology Bulletins Ser.). 204p. 1995. lib. bdg. 89.00 (0-7812-4076-X) Rprt Serv.

*Archeological Observations North of the Rio Colorado. Neil M. Judd. (Bureau of American Ethnology Bulletins Ser.). 171p. 1995. lib. bdg. 79.00 (0-7812-4082-4) Rprt Serv.

Archeological Reconnaissance in Sonora. Monroe Amsden. (Illus.). 51p. 1970. reprint ed. 5.00 (0-916561-08-9) Southwest Mus.

Archeological Reconnaissance of the Upper Little River Basin in Cleveland County, Oklahoma, 1984. Terry L. Steinacher. (Archeological Resource Survey Report Ser.: No. 25). (Illus.). 150p. (C). 1986. pap. text ed. 6.00 (1-881346-17-X) Univ OK Archeol.

Archeological Reconnaissance of the Wolf Creek Drainage Basin, Ellis County, Oklahoma. Richard R. Drass & Christopher L. Turner. (Archeological Resource Survey Report Ser.: No. 35). (Illus.). 205p. (C). 1989. pap. text ed. 9.00 (1-881346-23-4) Univ OK Archeol.

*Archeological Remains in the Whitewater District, Eastern Arizona. Frank Roberts, Jr. (Bureau of American Ethnology Bulletins Ser.). 276p. 1995. lib. bdg. 89.00 (0-7812-4121-9); lib. bdg. 79.00 (0-7812-4126-X) Rprt Serv.

Archeological Resource Management in the U. K. An Introduction. Ed. by John Hunter & Ian Ralston. LC 93-20574. 288p. 1993. 34.00 (0-7509-0275-2) A Sutton Pub.

Archeological Resource Protection. Sherry Hutt et al. LC 92-18656. (Illus.). 176p. (Orig.). 1992. pap. 19.95 (0-89133-199-9) Preservation Pr.

*Archeological Resources for the Classroom: A Guide for Virginia Teachers. rev. ed. Martha R. Williams. (Special Publications: Vol. 27). 40p. 1994. pap. 12.95 (1-884626-25-4) Archeolog Soc.

410

An Asterisk (*) at the beginning of an entry indicates that the title is appearing in BIP for the first time.

Archeological Resources in the Bird Creek Basin, Rogers, Tulsa, & Osage Counties, Oklahoma. Richard R. Drass. (Archeological Resource Survey Report Ser.: No. 21). (Illus.). 165p. (C). 1985. pap. text ed. 5.00 (*1-881346-14-5*) Univ OK Archeol.

Archeological Salvage & Survey in Nebraska. Gayle F. Carlson & Richard E. Jensen. (Publications in Anthropology: No. 5). 191p. 1973. pap. 6.00 (*0-686-20018-7*) Nebraska Hist.

Archeological Society of Virginia: A Forty-Year History, No. 21. Howard A. Maccord, Sr. 66p. 1991. pap. 15.00 (*1-884626-07-6*) Archeolog Soc.

Archeological Survey along the Red River: The Kemp Bottoms Area, Bryan County, Oklahoma. Lois E. Albert. (Archeological Resource Survey Report Ser.). (Illus.). 166p. (C). 1984. pap. text ed. 5.00 (*1-881346-12-9*) Univ OK Archeol.

Archeological Survey & Settlement Pattern Models in Central Illinois. Donna C. Roper. (Scientific Papers: Vol. XVI). (Illus.). 156p. 1979. pap. 4.50 (*0-89792-081-3*) Ill St Museum.

Archeological Survey in the James Fork Watershed, LeFlore County, Oklahoma. Lois E. Albert. (Archeological Resource Survey Report Ser.: No. 28). (Illus.). 204p. (C). 1987. pap. text ed. 7.00 (*1-881346-19-6*) Univ OK Archeol.

Archeological Survey of Clearcut Areas along Little River, McCurtain & Pushmataha Counties, Oklahoma. Larry Neal. Ed. by Preston George. (Archeological Resource Survey Report Ser.: No. 32). (Illus.). 201p. (C). 1988. pap. text ed. 6.00 (*1-881346-21-8*) Univ OK Archeol.

***Archeological Survey of Pickwick Basin in the Adjacent Portions of the States of Alabama, Mississippi & Tennessee.** Webb & DeJarnette. (Bureau of American Ethnology Bulletins Ser.). 536p. 1995. lib. bdg. 119.00 (*0-7812-4129-4*) Rprt Serv.

Archeological Survey of the Flaming Gorge Reservoir Area, Wyoming-Utah. Kent C. Day & David S. Dibble. (Upper Colorado Ser.: No. 9). reprint ed. 22.50 (*0-404-60665-2*) AMS Pr.

Archeological Survey of the Fremont Area. James H. Gunnerson. (Utah Anthropological Papers: No. 28). reprint ed. 35.00 (*0-404-60628-8*) AMS Pr.

Archeological Survey of the La Sal Mountain Area, Utah. Alice Hunt. (Utah Anthropological Papers: No. 14). reprint ed. 38.50 (*0-404-60614-8*) AMS Pr.

***Archeological Survey of the Norris Basin in Eastern Tennessee.** Ed. by William S. Webb. (Bureau of American Ethnology Bulletins Ser.). 398p. 1995. lib. bdg. 99.00 (*0-7812-4118-9*) Rprt Serv.

***Archeological Survey of the Spiro Vicinity, Le Flore County, Oklahoma.** Dennis A. Peterson et al. (Archaeological Resource Survey Report: No. 37). (Illus.). 87p. (C). 1993. pap. text ed. 3.50 (*1-881346-29-3*) Univ OK Archeol.

Archeological Survey of Western Utah. Jack R. Rudy. (Utah Anthropological Papers: No. 12). reprint ed. 34.50 (*0-404-60612-1*) AMS Pr.

***Archeological Survey of Wheeler Basin on the Tennessee River in Northern Alabama.** William S. Webb. (Bureau of American Ethnology Bulletins Ser.). 214p. 1995. lib. bdg. 89.00 (*0-7812-4122-7*) Rprt Serv.

Archeologie du Savoir. Michel Foucault. (Gallimard Ser.). 257p. (FRE.). 1987. pap. 39.95 (*2-07-026999-X*) Schoenhof.

Archeology. Hayden. (C). 1995. text ed. write for info. (*0-7167-2377-8*) W H Freeman.

Archeology. Jane McIntosh. LC 94-9378. (Eyewitness Books). (J). 1994. 16.00 (*0-679-86572-1*); pap. 17.99 (*0-679-96572-6*) Knopf.

Archeology & the Bible. John Bowden. 24p. 1982. reprint ed. 4.00 (*0-910309-00-0*, 5032) Am Atheist.

Archeology & the Living Word see Arqueologia y la Palabra Viva

Archeology & Volcanism in Central America: The Zapotitan Valley of El Salvador. Ed. by Payson D. Sheets. (Texas Pan American Ser.). (Illus.). 317p. 1983. text ed. 40.00 (*0-292-78708-1*) U of Tex Pr.

Archeology; Dictionary of Terms & Techniques: Archeologia; Dizionario di Termini e Techniche. Sara Champion. 224p. (ITA.). 1983. 39.95 (*0-8288-1200-4*, F31850) Fr & Eur.

Archeology in Kansas. Patricia J. O'Brien. (Public Education Ser.: No. 9). (Illus.). vii, 144p. (Orig.). 1984. pap. 12.95 (*0-89338-020-2*) U of KS Mus Nat Hist.

Archeology Notes. Bonnie Henderson. (Illus.). 1978. 8.00 (*0-910042-33-0*); pap. 3.00 (*0-910042-32-2*) Allegheny.

Archeology of Cape Denbigh. James L. Giddings. LC 63-10231. (Illus.). 505p. reprint ed. pap. 144.00 (*0-8357-5717-X*, 2030023) Bks Demand.

Archeology of Fuga Moro. Bryan E. Snow & Richard Shutler. (San Carlos Humanities Ser.: No. 15). 1986. 17.50 (*971-10-0047-4*) Cellar.

Archeology of Knowledge. Michel Foucault. 1982. pap. 9.56 (*0-394-71106-8*) Pantheon.

Archeology of Mississippi. Calvin S. Brown. LC 92-28657. (Illus.). 384p. 1992. reprint ed. 42.00 (*0-87805-602-5*); reprint ed. pap. 19.95 (*0-87805-603-3*) U Pr of Miss.

Archeology of Pleistocene Lake Mohave. Elizabeth W. Campbell & William H. Campbell. 118p. 1963. reprint ed. pap. 5.00 (*0-916561-09-7*) Southwest Mus.

***Archeology of the Atomic Bomb.** 1995. lib. bdg. 251.95 (*0-8490-6744-8*) Gordon Pr.

Archeology of the Cahokia Mounds, ICT-Two: Ceramics. George R. Holley. Ed. by Thomas E. Emerson & Evelyn Taylor. (Illinois Cultural Resources Study: No. 11). (Illus.). 468p. (Orig.). 1989. pap. 24.00 (*0-942579-14-3*) IHPA.

Archeology of the Death Valley Salt Pan, California. Alice Hunt. (Utah Anthropological Papers: No. 47). reprint ed. 23.00 (*0-404-60647-4*) AMS Pr.

Archeology of the Florida Gulf Coast. Gordon R. Willey. LC 72-5013. (Harvard University. Peabody Museum of Archaeology & Ethnology. Antiquities of the New World Ser.: No. 18). (Illus.). reprint ed. 72.50 (*0-404-57318-5*) AMS Pr.

Archeology of the Frivolous: Reading Condillac. Jacques Derrida. Tr. by John P. Leavey, Jr. LC 86-25106. vi, 143p. 1987. reprint ed. 25.00 (*0-8032-1678-5*); reprint ed. pap. 8.95 (*0-8032-6571-9*) U of Nebr Pr.

Archeology of the Frobisher Voyages. Ed. by William W. Fitzhugh & Jacqueline S. Olin. LC 92-6561. (Illus.). 288p. (C). 1993. text ed. 45.00 (*1-56098-171-7*) Smithsonian.

Archeology of the Land of the Bible: 10,000-586 B.C.E. Amihai Mazar. 1992. pap. 20.00 (*0-385-42590-2*) Doubleday.

Archeology of the Mixed Grass Prairie Phase I: Quartermaster Creek. Susan M. Berta et al. Ed. by Timothy G. Baugh. (Archeological Resource Survey Report Ser.: No. 20). (Illus.). 313p. (C). 1984. pap. text ed. 8.00 (*1-881346-13-7*) Univ OK Archeol.

Archeology of the Mixed Grass Prairie, Phases II & III: Hay & Cyclone Creeks Surveys & Predictive Modeling in the Quartermaster Watershed. Michael C. Moore. (Archeological Resource Survey Report Ser.: No. 33). (Illus.). 244p. (C). 1988. pap. text ed. 10.00 (*1-881346-22-6*) Univ OK Archeol.

Archeology of the New Testament: The Life of Jesus & the Beginning of the Church. Jack Finegan. (Illus.). 400p. 1992. text ed. 65.00 (*0-691-03608-X*); pap. text ed. 29.95 (*0-691-00220-7*) Princeton U Pr.

***Archeology of the Yakutat Bay Area, Alaska.** Frederica De Laguna. (Bureau of American Ethnology Bulletins Ser.). 245p. 1995. lib. bdg. 89.00 (*0-7812-4192-8*) Rprt Serv.

Archeology of Zion Park. Albert H. Schroeder. (Utah Anthropological Papers: No. 22). reprint ed. 22.50 (*0-404-60622-9*) AMS Pr.

Archeology Search Book. Thomas F. Snyder. Ed. by Martha O'Neill. (Search Ser.). (Illus.). 32p. (J). (gr. 4-12). 1982. pap. text ed. 8.08 (*0-07-059467-8*) McGraw.

Archeosophy: A New Science. Edmond B. Szekely. (Illus.). 32p. 1973. pap. 5.95 (*0-89564-057-0*) IBS Intl.

Archer & the Princess: A Comedy Based on a Russian Folk Tale. Patricia B. Rumble. (Stage Magic Play Ser.). (Illus.). 48p. (Orig.). (J). (gr. 4-10). 1990. pap. 3.00 (*0-88680-334-9*) I E Clark.

***Archer Daniels Midland Co. (ADM) A Report on the Company's Environmental Policies & Practices.** (Illus.). 17p. (C). 1994. reprint ed. pap. text ed. 200.00x (*0-7881-0933-2*, Coun on Econ) Diane Pub.

Archer in Jeopardy, 3 bks., Set. Ross Macdonald. Incl. Doomsters. LC 79-63807. 1979. (*0-318-54004-5*); Instant Enemy. LC 79-63807. 1979. (*0-318-54005-3*); Zebra-Striped Hearse. LC 79-63807. 1979. (*0-318-54006-1*); LC 79-63807. 1979. 24.95 (*0-394-50804-1*) Knopf.

Archer in the Marrow. Peter Viereck. 1987. pap. 6.95 (*0-393-30326-8*) Norton.

Archer Milton Huntington. Beatrice G. Proske. (Illus.). 1965. 5.00 (*0-87535-098-4*) Hispanic Soc.

Archers. Jock Gallager. (Illus.). 128p. 1990. 19.95 (*0-563-36001-1*, Pub. by BBC UK) Parkwest Pubns.

Archer's & Bowhunter's Bible. H. Lea Lawrence. LC 93-16901. 1993. 12.00 (*0-385-42221-0*) Doubleday.

Archer's Bible. rev. ed. Fred Bear. LC 79-7585. (Outdoor Bible Ser.). (Illus.). 1980. pap. 11.00 (*0-385-15155-1*) Doubleday.

Archer's Compound Interest & Annuity Tables, Vol. I: Rates from One-Half to 3 percent. Shaw & Sons Ltd. Staff. (C). 1988. 195.00 (*0-7219-0273-1*, Scientific) St Mut.

Archer's Compound Interest & Annuity Tables, Vol. III: Rates from 6 to 12 percent. Shaw & Sons Ltd. Staff. (C). 1988. write for info. (*0-7219-0271-5*, Scientific) St Mut.

Archer's Compound Interest & Annuity Tables, Vol. III: Rates from 6 to 12 percent, Set. Shaw & Sons Ltd. Staff. (C). 1988. 500.00 (*0-317-92371-4*, Scientific) St Mut.

Archer's Compound Interest & Annuity Tables, Vol. II: Rates from 3 to 6 percent. Shaw & Sons Ltd. Staff. (C). 1988. 195.00 (*0-317-92370-6*, Scientific) St Mut.

***Archer's Digest.** 6th ed. Roger Combs. LC 77-148722. (Illus.). 256p. (Orig.). 1995. pap. 18.95 (*0-87349-167-X*) DBI.

Archer's Directory of Genealogical Software, 1993. George W. Archer. 122p. (Orig.). 1993. pap. text ed. 22.00 (*1-55613-918-7*) Heritage Bk.

Archer's Directory of Genealogical Utility Software: 1993 Edition. George W. Archer. 138p. (Orig.). 1993. pap. text ed. 23.50 (*1-55613-919-5*) Heritage Bk.

Archer's Goon. Diana W. Jones. LC 83-17199. 256p. (J). (gr. 7 up). 1984. 10.25 (*0-688-02582-X*) Greenwillow.

Archers Quizbook. Comp. by Loz Rigbey. 128p. 1990. pap. 3.95 (*0-563-20709-4*, Pub. by BBC UK) Parkwest Pubns.

Archery. Boy Scouts of America. (Illus.). 56p. (J). (gr. 6-12). 1986. pap. 1.85 (*0-8395-3381-0*, 33259) BSA.

Archery. 2nd ed. Dewayne J. Johnson & Robert A. Oliver. (Illus.). 53p. 1990. pap. text ed. 5.95x (*0-89641-187-7*) American Pr.

Archery. 3rd ed. Jean A. Barrett. (Illus.). 132p. (C). 1991. reprint ed. pap. text ed. 8.95 (*0-88133-537-1*) Waveland Pr.

Archery: Steps to Success. Kathleen M. Haywood & Catherine F. Lewis. LC 88-647. (Steps to Success Activity Ser.). (Illus.). 208p. (Orig.). (C). 1989. pap. text ed. 14.95 (*0-88011-324-3*, PHAY0324) Human Kinetics.

Archery: The Badminton Library of Sports & Pastimes. C. J. Longman & H. Walrond. Ed. by Duck of Beauford. (Legends of the Longbow Ser.: Vol. 1). (Illus.). 540p. (YA). (gr. 10 up). 1992. reprint ed. 39.95 (*1-56416-087-4*) Derrydale Pr.

Archery at the Dark of the Moon: Poetic Problems in Homer's Odyssey. Norman Austin. LC 73-94442. 311p. reprint ed. pap. 88.70 (*0-7837-4762-4*, 2044509) Bks Demand.

Archery by Elmer. Robert P. Elmer. (Legends of the Longbow Ser.: Vol. 11). (Illus.). 458p. 1993. reprint ed. 39.95 (*1-56416-097-1*) Derrydale Pr.

Archery Equipment & Supplies - Retail, 1995. American Business Directories Staff. 1995. spiral bd., pap. 275.00 (*1-56105-574-3*) Am Busn Direct.

Archery Instruction Manual. 4th rev. ed. Bolnick et al. Ed. by Donald W. Campbell. (Illus.). 272p. (C). 1993. 16.00 (*0-8403-8402-5*) Kendall-Hunt.

Archery Techniques. Carolyn F. Addison. 116p. (C). 1989. pap. text ed. 6.95x (*0-89641-181-8*) American Pr.

Archery the Technical Side. Ed. by C. N. Hickman et al. (Legends of the Longbow Ser.: Vol. 5). (Illus.). 281p. (YA). (gr. 10 up). 1992. reprint ed. 39.95 (*1-56416-091-2*) Derrydale Pr.

Arches: The Story Behind the Scenery. David W. Johnson. LC 85-80445. (Illus.). 48p. (Orig.). 1985. pap. 6.95 (*0-88714-002-5*) KC Pubns.

Arches & Pergolas. Robert Ditchfield. (Letts Guides to Garden Design Ser.). (Illus.). 64p. 1993. 9.95 (*1-55859-550-3*, Canopy Bks) Abbeville Pr.

Arches, Continuous Frames, Columns, & Conduits: Selected Papers. Hardy Cross. LC 63-17046. (Illus.). 275p. reprint ed. pap. 78.40 (*0-8357-5718-8*, 2019044) Bks Demand.

Arches National Park. John Hoffman. LC 85-50727. 1985. pap. 9.95 (*0-934148-02-3*) Wstrn Rec Pubns.

***Arches National Park.** Ed. by Jeff Nicholas. (Wish You Were Here Postcard Bks.). (Illus.). 32p. (Orig.). 1995. pap. 4.95 (*0-939365-48-0*) Sierra Pr CA.

Arches National Park, UT. rev. ed. Ed. by Trails Illustrated Staff. (Illus.). 1994. Folded topographical map. 8.99 (*0-925873-12-8*) Trails Illustrated.

Arches of the Years. Marzieh Gail. (Illus.). 360p. 1991. 32.95 (*0-85398-325-9*); pap. 20.95 (*0-85398-326-7*) G Ronald Pub.

Arches Tables for Statistical Analyses. J. Szymczyk. LC 61-14042. 1961. write for info. (*0-08-009336-1*, Pub. by Pergamon Repr UK) Franklin.

Archetypal Actions of Ritual: An Essay on Ritual Illustrated by the Jain Rite of Worship. Caroline Humphrey & James A. Laidlaw. (Studies in Social & Cultural Anthropology). (Illus.). 248p. 1994. 45.00 (*0-19-927947-0*); pap. 19.95 (*0-685-72939-7*) OUP.

***Archetypal Constable: National Identity & the Geography of Nostalgia.** Peter Bishop. LC 95-210. 1995. write for info. (*0-8386-3645-4*) Fairleigh Dickinson.

Archetypal Consultation: A Service Delivery Model for Native Americans. Eduardo Duran. (American University Studies: Psychology: Ser. VIII, Vol. 2). 168p. (Orig.). 1984. pap. text ed. 16.85 (*0-8204-0082-3*) P Lang Pubs.

Archetypal Forms in Teaching: A Continuum. William A. Reinsmith. LC 91-44433. (Contributions to the Study of Education Ser.: No. 56). 232p. 1992. text ed. 47.95 (*0-313-28405-9*, RTG/, Greenwood Pr) Greenwood.

Archetypal Imagination: Glimpses of the Gods in Life & Art. Noel Cobb. 256p. (Orig.). 1992. pap. 16.95 (*0-940262-47-9*) Lindisfarne Pr.

Archetypal Kingdom. Ann R. Colton. LC 88-70974. (Illus.). 450p. 1988. 21.95 (*0-917189-07-8*) Colton Found.

Archetypal Medicine. Alfred J. Ziegler. Tr. by Gary V. Hartman. LC 83-4757. Orig. Title: Morbismus: von der Besten aller Gesundheiten. 169p. (Orig.). (C). 1983. pap. 13.50 (*0-88214-322-0*) Spring Pubns.

Archetypal Patterns in Women's Fiction. Annis Pratt et al. LC 81-47167. 221p. reprint ed. pap. 63.00 (*0-8357-5719-6*, 2056716) Bks Demand.

Archetypal Process: Self & Divine in Whitehead, Jung & Hillman. Ed. by David Griffin. 290p. 1989. pap. 16.95 (*0-8101-0816-X*) Northwestern U Pr.

Archetypal Psychology: A Brief Account. rev. ed. James Hillman. LC 82-19663. 103p. (Orig.). 1983. pap. 13.50 (*0-88214-321-2*) Spring Pubns.

Archetypal Signifance of Gilgamesh. Rivkah Scharf-Kluger. 1995. pap. 15.95 (*3-85630-523-8*, Pub. by Daimon Verlag SZ) Atrium Pubs.

Archetypal World of Henry Moore. Erich Neumann. Tr. by R. F. Hull. (Bollingen Ser.: Vol. LXVIII). (Illus.). 216p. 1984. text ed. 35.00 (*0-691-09702-X*) Princeton U Pr.

Archetype & Allegory in the Dream of the Red Chamber. Andrew H. Plaks. LC 75-3469. (Illus.). 280p. reprint ed. pap. 79.80 (*0-8357-7893-2*, 2036312) Bks Demand.

Archetype, Architecture, & the Writer. Bettina L. Knapp. LC 84-47790. (Illus.). 224p. 1986. 29.95 (*0-253-30857-7*) Ind U Pr.

Archetype of the Unconscious & the Transfiguration of Therapy: Reflections On Jungian Psychology. Charles Ponce. 120p. (Orig.). 1990. pap. 9.95 (*1-55643-070-1*) North Atlantic.

Archetype West. William Everson. 1977. 8.95 (*0-685-79488-1*); pap. 3.95 (*0-685-79489-X*) Oyez.

Archetypes: A Natural History of the Self. Anthony Stevens. LC 83-3040. (Illus.). 336p. 1983. reprint ed. pap. 12.00 (*0-688-01976-5*, Quill) Morrow.

Archetypes & Ancestors: Palaeontology in Victorian London 1850-1875. Adrian Desmond. LC 83-18104. (Illus.). 288p. 1986. pap. text ed. 11.95 (*0-226-14344-9*) U Ch Pr.

Archetypes, Imprecators, & Victims of Fate: Origins & Developments of Satire in Black Drama. Femi Euba. LC 89-7542. (Contributions in Afro-American & African Studies: No. 126). 216p. 1989. text ed. 49.95 (*0-313-25557-1*, ETE/, Greenwood Pr) Greenwood.

Archetypes in Japanese Film: The Sociopolitical & Religious Significance of the Principal Heroes & Heroines. Gregory Barrett. LC 87-43126. (Illus.). 256p. 1989. 50.00 (*0-941664-93-7*) Susquehanna U Pr.

Archetypes of Conversion: The Spiritual Autobiographies of St. Augustine, John Bunyan, & Thomas Merton. Anne O. Hawkins. LC 83-46156. 192p. 1985. 33.50 (*0-8387-5079-6*) Bucknell U Pr.

Archetypes of the Zodiac. Kathleen Burt. LC 87-45743. (Modern Astrology Library). (Illus.). 576p. (Orig.). 1988. pap. 14.95 (*0-87542-088-5*) Llewellyn Pubns.

Archetypes of Wisdom: An Introduction to Philosophy. Douglas J. Soccio. 605p. (C). 1992. text ed. 42.95 (*0-534-14226-5*) Intl Thomson.

***Archetypes of Wisdom: An Introduction to Philosophy.** 2nd ed. Douglas J. Soccio. LC 94-22217. 678p. 1995. text ed. 43.95 (*0-534-21690-0*) Intl Thomson.

Archetypes on the Tree of Life: The Tarot as Pathwork. Madonna Compton. LC 91-27605. (Spiritual Perspectives Ser.). (Illus.). 334p. (Orig.). 1991. pap. 12.95 (*0-87542-104-0*) Llewellyn Pubns.

Archibald & the Crunch Machine. Jenny Nelson. (Illus.). 40p. (J). (gr. 2-4). 1990. pap. 5.95 (*1-55037-114-2*, Pub. by Annick CN) Firefly Bks Ltd.

Archibald Cary Coolidge: Life & Letters. Harold J. Coolidge & Robert H. Lord. LC 70-179512. (Select Bibliographies Reprint Ser.). 1977. reprint ed. 26.95 (*0-8369-6641-4*) Ayer.

Archibald Constable & His Literary Correspondents, 3 vols., Set. Thomas Constable. LC 70-148766. reprint ed. 210.00 (*0-404-07640-8*) AMS Pr.

Archibald Frisby. Michael Chesworth. (J). 1994. 15.00 (*0-374-30392-4*) FS&G.

Archibald Garrod & the Individuality of Man. Alexander G. Bearn. LC 92-27504. (Illus.). 256p. 1993. 49.95 (*0-19-262145-9*, Clarendon Pr) OUP.

Archibald Grimke: Portrait of a Black Independent. Dickson D. Bruce, Jr. LC 92-42703. (Southern Biography Ser.). (Illus.). 312p. (C). 1993. text ed. 27.50x (*0-8071-1796-X*) La State U Pr.

Archibald Lampman. Len R. Early. (Twayne's World Authors Ser. Canada: 770). 192p. 1986. text ed. 22.95 (*0-8057-6621-9*, Twayne) Macmillan.

Archibald Lampman: An Annotated Bibliography. George Wicken. 146p. (C). 1980. pap. text ed. 9.00 (*0-920763-55-3*, Pub. by ECW Press CN) Genl Dist Srvs.

Archibald MacLeish. Signi L. Falk. (Twayne's United States Authors Ser.). 1965. pap. 13.95x (*0-8084-0054-1*, T93) NCUP.

Archibald MacLeish. Grover C. Smith. LC 70-635457. (University of Minnesota Pamphlets on American Writers Ser.: No. 99). 48p. (Orig.). reprint ed. pap. 25.00 (*0-7837-2864-6*, 2057591) Bks Demand.

Archibald MacLeish: A Checklist. Edward J. Mullaly. LC 72-619620. (Serif Series: Bibliographies & Checklists: No. 26). 109p. reprint ed. pap. 31.10 (*0-8357-5576-2*, 2035203) Bks Demand.

Archibald MacLeish: Reflections. Ed. by Bernard A. Drabeck & Helen E. Ellis. LC 85-28912. (Illus.). 312p. 1988. 32.50 (*0-87023-517-7*); pap. 16.95 (*0-87023-623-7*) U of Mass Pr.

Archibald MacLeish Symposium, May 7-8, 1982: Proceedings. Ed. by Bernard A. Drabeck et al. LC 88-1290. 160p. (C). 1988. lib. bdg. 35.00 (*0-8191-6913-7*) U Pr of Amer.

Archibald Robertson, Lieutenant-General Royal Engineers. Archibald Robertson. LC 70-140879. (Eyewitness Accounts of the American Revolution Ser., No. 1). 1971. reprint ed. 20.95 (*0-405-01224-1*) Ayer.

Archibald the Great. Eve Tharlet. Tr. by Andrew Clements. (Illus.). 28p. (J). (gr. k up). 1993. 14.95 (*0-88708-267-X*, Picture Book Studio) S&S Childrens.

Archibald the Horse: A Children's Illustrated Story Book. Ann O. Campbell. (Illus.). 1982. 4.95 (*0-938686-25-9*) H Spriggle.

Archibald Yell. William W. Hughes. LC 87-6043. (Illus.). 218p. (Orig.). 1988. 22.00 (*0-938626-93-0*) U of Ark Pr.

Archidamian War. Donald Kagan. LC 89-28639. (Illus.). 400p. 1974. 44.50 (*0-8014-0889-X*) Cornell U Pr.

Archidamian War. Donald Kagan. LC 89-28639. (Illus.). 400p. 1990. pap. 16.95 (*0-8014-9714-0*) Cornell U Pr.

Archidoxes of Magic: Of the Supreme Mysteries of Nature, of the Spirits of Planets, Secrets of Alchemy, Occult Philosophy, Signs of the Zodiac, Magical Cure of Diseases, & Celestial Medicines. Theophrastus Paracelsus. 160p. 1992. pap. 17.95 (*1-56459-171-9*) Kessinger Pub.

Archie: His First Fifty Years. Charles Phillips. 128p. 1993. 15.98 (*0-89660-035-1*, Artabras) Abbeville Pr.

Archie Americana Series: Best of the Fifties. Ed. by Paul Castiglia. (Illus.). 96p. (Orig.). Date not set. pap. 8.95 (*1-879794-01-2*) Archie Comic.

Archie Americana, Vol. 1: The 1940's. Intro. by Scott Fulop. (Illus.). 128p. (YA). 1991. pap. 8.95 (*1-879794-00-4*, Archie Comics) Archie Comic.

Archie & Edith, Mike & Gloria: The Tumultuous History of "All in the Family" Donna McCrohan. LC 87-42743. 280p. 1988. pap. 7.95 (*0-89480-527-4*, 1527) Workman Pub.

***Archie & the Listers.** Robert Edwards. (Illus.). 256p. 1995. 44.95 (*1-85260-469-7*, Pub. by J H Haynes & Co UK) Motorbooks Intl.

Archie, Follow Me. Lynne Cherry. LC 89-77160. (Illus.). 32p. (J). (ps-1). 1990. 12.95 (*0-525-44647-8*, DCB) Dutton Child Bks.

An Asterisk (*) at the beginning of an entry indicates that the title is appearing in BIP for the first time.

Archie Givens Sr. Collection Curriculum Guide. Kevin Leuning. x, 30p. (J). (ps-12). 1988. pap. text ed. write for info. (*0-9632976-0-0*) A Givens Sr Collect.

Archie Moore, The White Slave or, Memoirs of a Fugitive. Richard Hildreth. LC 69-16309. (Illus.). xxii, 408p. 1971. reprint ed. lib. bdg. 45.00 (*0-678-00756-X*) Kelley.

Archie Moore..."The Ole Mongoose" Marilyn G. Douroux. (Illus.). 240p. 1991. 19.95 (*0-8283-1942-1*) Branden Pub Co.

Archie Moore..."The Ole Mongoose" limited ed. Marilyn G. Douroux. (Illus.). 240p. 1991. 39.95 (*0-8283-1944-8*) Branden Pub Co.

Archigram. P. Cook et al. 144p. 1991. pap. 44.00 (*0-8176-2447-3*) Birkhauser.

Archigram: Life & Times of the Archigram Group. Dennis Crompton. (Illus.). 144p. 1993. 50.00 (*1-85490-299-7*, Academy Edits); pap. 35.00 (*1-85490-300-4*, Academy Edits) St Martin.

Archilochus of Paros. H. D. Rankin. LC 77-6157. (Noyes Classical Studies). 136p. 1978. 15.00 (*0-8155-5053-7*, NP) Noyes.

Archimedes. E. J. Dijksterhuis. 434p. 1987. pap. 18.95 (*0-691-02400-6*) Princeton U Pr.

Archimedes & Arthur. Z. Racic. 300p. 1989. boxed, text ed. 53.33 (*0-13-044074-4*) P-H.

Archimedes & Me. John E. Schwab. LC 88-70022. 193p. (Orig.). 1988. pap. 4.95 (*0-945533-00-4*) Pinnacle Pr.

***Archimedes & the Sands of Space & Time.** Henry Sonneborn, 3rd. 192p. 1994. 15.95 (*0-9644050-0-8*) Eagle Pr NY.

Archimedes in the Middle Ages, Vol. 1. Arabo-Latin Tradition. Marshall Clagett. LC 62-7218. (Medieval Science Pubns., No. 6). (Illus.). 752p. reprint ed. 180.00 (*0-8357-9771-6*, 2012629) Bks Demand.

Archimedes in the Middle Ages, Vol. 3, P1-2. Archimedes. Ed. by Marshall Clagett. LC 62-7218. 302p. (ENG & LAT.). reprint ed. pap. 86.10 (*0-7837-6706-4*, 2046339) Bks Demand.

Archimedes in the Middle Ages, Vol. 3, P3. Archimedes. Ed. by Marshall Clagett. LC 62-7218. 958p. (ENG & LAT.). reprint ed. pap. 180.00 (*0-7837-6707-2*, 2046339) Bks Demand.

Archimedes in the Middle Ages, Vol. 3, P4. Archimedes. Ed. by Marshall Clagett. LC 62-7218. 340p. (ENG & LAT.). reprint ed. pap. 96.90 (*0-7837-6708-0*, 2046339) Bks Demand.

Archimedes in the Middle Ages, Vol. 4, P1. Archimedes. Ed. by Marshall Clagett. LC 62-7218. 469p. (ENG & LAT.). reprint ed. pap. 133.70 (*0-7837-6709-9*, 2046339) Bks Demand.

Archimedes in the Middle Ages, Vol. 4, P2. Archimedes. Ed. by Marshall Clagett. LC 62-7218. 106p. (ENG & LAT.). reprint ed. pap. 30.30 (*0-7837-6710-2*, 2046339) Bks Demand.

Archimedes in the Middle Ages, Vol. 5, P1-4. Archimedes. Ed. by Marshall Clagett. LC 62-7218. 613p. (ENG & LAT.). reprint ed. pap. 174.80 (*0-7837-6711-0*, 2046339) Bks Demand.

Archimedes in the Middle Ages, Vol. 5, P5. Archimedes. Ed. by Marshall Clagett. LC 62-7218. 118p. (ENG & LAT.). reprint ed. pap. 33.70 (*0-7837-6712-9*, 2046339) Bks Demand.

Archimedes' Revenge. Paul E. Hoffman. 288p. 1989. mass mkt. 5.99 (*0-449-21750-7*, Crest) Fawcett.

Archimedes Russell, Upstate Architect. Evamaria Hardin. LC 80-23601. (York State Book Ser.). (Illus.). 108p. reprint ed. pap. 30.80 (*0-7837-1194-8*, 2041724) Bks Demand.

Archimedes' Troubles: Sculptures & Drawings by Italo Scanga. William Zimmer & Burnett Miller. LC 83-81162. 12p. 1983. 4.00 (*0-934418-18-7*) Mus Contemp Art.

***Arching Backward: The Mystical Initiation of a Contemporary Woman.** Janet Adler. (Illus.). 128p. 1995. pap. 14.95 (*0-89281-546-9*, Destiny Bks) Inner Tradit.

Arching into the Afterlife. Pablo Medina. LC 90-24943. 96p. 1991. pap. 9.00 (*0-927534-12-6*) Biling Rev-Pr.

***Archipelago.** Arthur Sze. 80p. (Orig.). 1995. pap. 12.00 (*1-55659-100-4*) Copper Canyon.

Archipelago. deluxe limited ed. R. A. Lafferty. (Lost Manuscript Ser.). 283p. 1979. 100.00 (*0-936414-02-2*) Manuscript Pr.

Archipenko: Themes & Variations, 1908-1963. Donald Karshan. (Illus.). 100p. 1989. 35.00 (*0-933053-03-7*) Museum Art Sciences.

Architect. Jack Rudman. (Career Examination Ser.: C-17). 1994. pap. 29.95 (*0-8373-0017-7*) Nat Learn.

Architect, 2 vols. William Ranlett. LC 69-16664. (Architecture & Decorative Art Ser.). (Illus.). 1976. reprint ed. lib. bdg. 110.00 (*0-306-70799-3*) Da Capo.

Architect? A Candid Guide to the Profession. Roger K. Lewis. (Orig.). 1985. pap. 15.00x (*0-262-62048-0*) MIT Pr.

Architect: Chapters in the History of the Profession. Ed. by Spiro Kostof. LC 75-46368. (Illus.). 1986. pap. 14.95 (*0-19-504044-9*) OUP.

Architect: The First Ten Years. John Donaghey. LC 80-66726. (Illus.). 96p. (Orig.). (C). (gr. 12 up). 1980. pap. text ed. 5.00 (*0-9604298-0-8*) J Donaghey.

Architect, Actor & Audience. Ian Mackintosh. (Illus.). 208p. 1992. 49.95 (*0-415-03182-6*, A7956); pap. 14.95 (*0-415-03183-4*, A7960) Routledge.

Architect & Engineer Liability: Claims Against Design Professionals. Ed. by Robert F. Cushman & Thomas G. Bottum. LC 87-2010. 426p. 1987. text ed. 118.00 (*0-471-81297-8*) Wiley.

Architect & Engineer Liability: Claims Against Design Professionals. suppl. ed. Ed. by Robert F. Cushman & Thomas G. Bottum. LC 87-2010. 173p. 1987. Cumulataive suppl., 1993, 173p. pap. text ed. 55.00 (*0-471-58375-8*) Wiley.

Architect & the American Country House, 1890-1940. Mark A. Hewitt. (Illus.). 304p. (C). 1990. 55.00 (*0-300-04740-1*) Yale U Pr.

Architect Engineer Liability: A Growth Period. American Bar Association, Public Contract Law Section Staff. 45p. 1985. pap. 20.00 (*0-89707-170-0*, 539-0043) Amer Bar Assn.

Architect-Engineer Quality Control Manual. 63p. 1957. 15.00 (*0-318-17059-0*); 8.00 (*0-318-17060-4*) Natl Soc Prof Engrs.

Architect-Engineer's Role under Superfund & Selecting a Professional Liability Insurance Policy. ABA, Public Contract Law Section Staff. 88p. 1985. pap. 25.00 (*0-89707-169-7*, 539-0044) Amer Bar Assn.

Architect in Employment. 1987. 69.95 (*0-85139-798-0*) Buttrwrth-Heinemann.

Architect in History. Martin S. Briggs. LC 69-15613. (Architecture & Decorative Art Ser.). (Illus.). 400p. 1974. reprint ed. lib. bdg. 45.00 (*0-306-70584-2*) Da Capo.

Architect in Italy. Caroline Mauduit. (Illus.). 112p. 1988. 4.99 (*0-517-05595-3*) Random Hse Value.

Architect in Practice. 5th ed. Arthur J. Willis & W. N. George. 325p. 1974. text ed. 34.95 (*0-8464-0144-4*) Beekman Pubs.

Architect in Practice. 7th ed. David Chappell & Christopher Willis. (Illus.). 331p. 1992. pap. 39.95 (*0-632-02267-1*) Blackwell Sci.

Architect Looks at Downtown Portland. Richard E. Ritz. 102p. 1991. pap. 19.95 (*0-9629661-1-8*) Greenhills.

Architect of Genocide: Himmler & the Final Solution. Richard Breitman. LC 90-52956. 352p. 1991. 22.50 (*0-394-56841-9*) Knopf.

Architect of Genocide: Himmler & the Final Solution. Richard Breitman. LC 92-53857. (Tauber Institute Ser.: Vol. 14). 348p. 1992. pap. 15.95 (*0-87451-596-3*) U Pr of New Eng.

Architect of Ruins. Herbert Rosendorfer. Tr. by Mike Mitchell. (Dedalus European Fiction Classics Ser.). 384p. 1992. pap. 14.95 (*0-7818-0001-3*, Pub. by Dedalus Bks UK) Hippocrene Bks.

Architect of the Roman Empire, 2 vols., Set. Thomas R. Holmes. LC 75-41139. reprint ed. 42.50 (*0-404-14960-X*) AMS Pr.

Architect of Unity. William J. Schmidt. 1978. pap. 9.95 (*0-377-00079-5*) Friendship Pr.

Architect or Bee? The Human-Technology Relationship. Mike Cooley. 150p. 1980. reprint ed. pap. 7.00 (*0-89608-131-1*) South End Pr.

Architect, or Practical House Carpenter (1844) Asher Benjamin. 192p. 1988. pap. 9.95 (*0-486-25802-5*) Dover.

Architect Overseas Practice Standards: A Guide to Selected Countries. NCARB Staff. 115p. (Orig.). 1987. pap. text ed. 5.00 (*0-941575-02-0*) NCARB.

Architecte et l'Empereur de l'Assyrie. Fernando Arrabal. 320p. (FRE.). 1986. pap. 16.95 (*0-7859-3639-4*, 2267007869) Fr & Eur.

Architectonic for Science. Wolfgang Balzer et al. (C). 1987. lib. bdg. 157.50 (*90-277-2403-2*) Kluwer Ac.

***Architectonic Illusion: Photographs by Beatrice Helg.** Alison D. Nordstrom. 68p. 1994. pap. text ed. 20.00 (*1-887040-09-9*) SE Mus Photo.

Architectonics of Meaning: Foundations of the New Pluralism. Walter Watson. LC 93-9213. xx, 206p. (C). 1993. pap. text ed. 13.95 (*0-226-87506-7*) U Ch Pr.

Architectonics of the Cerebral Cortex. Ed. by Mary A. Brazier & Hellmuth Petsche. LC 77-83694. (International Brain Research Organization Monograph Ser.: Vol. 3). 502p. 1978. 124.50 (*0-89004-140-7*) Raven.

Architector, 2 vols. Francois Bucher. LC 77-86233. 170.00 (*0-913870-47-1*) Abaris Bks.

Architectronics: Revolutionary Technologies for Masterful Building Through Design. M. Winn. 336p. 1987. text ed. 25.00 (*0-07-071072-4*) McGraw.

Architects & Builders' Handbook: Date for Architects, Structural Engineers, Contractors & Draughtsmen. 18th ed. Frank E. Kidder. LC 31-32398. 2341p. reprint ed. pap. 180.00 (*0-8357-5720-X*, 2056356) Bks Demand.

Architects & Builders in North Carolina: A History of the Practice of Building. Catherine W. Bishir et al. LC 89-22521. (Illus.). xvi, 540p. (C). 1990. 39.95 (*0-8078-1898-4*) U of NC Pr.

Architects & Craftsmen in History: Essays in the Honor of Abott Payson Usher. 186p. 1956. pap. text ed. 29.50 (*0-685-14121-7*, Pub. by J C B Mohr GW) Coronet Bks.

Architects & Designers Graph Paper. 80p. 1992. pap. 16.95 (*0-8230-0238-1*, Whitney Lib) Watsn-Guptill.

Architects & Engineers. 2nd ed. James Acret. LC 84-5314. (Constuction Law: Land Use-Environmental Publications). 508p. 1984. text ed. 95.00 (*0-07-000222-3*) Shepards-McGraw.

Architects & Engineers: Their Professional Responsibilities. James Acret. LC 77-6379. 1984. text ed. 95.00 (*0-07-000187-1*, Shepards-McGraw) McGraw.

Architects & Firms: A Sociological Perspective on Architectural Practices. Judith R. Blau. 208p. 1987. reprint ed. 25.00 (*0-262-02209-5*); reprint ed. pap. 13.50x (*0-262-52128-8*) MIT Pr.

***Architects & Their Practices: A Changing Profession.** Martin Symes et al. LC 95-1183. 1995. pap. write for info. (*0-7506-1299-1*, Butterwrth Archit) Buttrwrth-Heinemann.

***Architect's AutoCAD. Robert H. Hsu. LC 94-79540. 264p. (Orig.). 1995. pap. 26.95 (*1-886280-00-2*) Macrostone Intl.**

There are dozens of AutoCAD reference books in the bookstores now. Unfortunately, none of them are written for architects & other AutoCAD users to enjoy the beauty & essence of AutoCAD. Besides, who has all the time in the world to browse through those 500 pages, thick like a wall, heavy like a dinosaur, & hard-to-read references! Architect's AutoCAD is a concise reference written & designed specifically for architects & all AutoCAD users to enjoy the beauty & essence of AutoCAD with ease & satisfaction. Written by an architect with over 20,000 hours AutoCAD experience in design, drafting, & management, this 200-page dynamo covers over 200 most useful AutoCAD features that architects & all AutoCAD users will be' using all the time. While many books about computers are difficult to enjoy, this ARCHITECT'S AutoCAD is truly an exception. ARCHITECT'S AutoCAD is the first book of our five book series for architects & all AutoCAD users. The other four books in the series are: ARCHITECT'S AutoCAD QUICK REFERENCE, ARCHITECT'S AutoCAD DATABASE, ARCHITECT'S AutoCAD RENDERING, & ARCHITECT'S AutoLISP. Volume discounts are available. Macrostone International, P.O. Box 4071, 3424 96th Ave. NE, Bellevue, WA 98009; 206-688-1093; FAX 206-635-0474. ***Publisher Provided Annotation.***

***Architect's AutoCAD Database.** Robert H. Hsu. 210p. 1995. pap. 26.95 (*1-886280-02-9*) Macrostone Intl.

***Architect's AutoCAD Quick Reference.** Robert H. Hsu. 206p. 1995. pap. 12.95 (*1-886280-01-0*) Macrostone Intl.

***Architect's AutoCAD Rendering.** Robert H. Hsu. 182p. 1995. pap. 36.95 (*1-886280-06-1*) Macrostone Intl.

***Architect's AutoLISP.** Robert H. Hsu. 192p. 1995. pap. 24.95 (*1-886280-03-7*) Macrostone Intl.

***Architect's DataCAD.** Robert H. Hsu. 226p. 1996. pap. 26.95 (*1-886280-07-X*) Macrostone Intl.

***Architect's DataCAD Quick Reference.** Robert H. Hsu. 198p. 1996. pap. 9.95 (*1-886280-08-8*) Macrostone Intl.

Architect's Detail Library. Fred A. Stitt. (Illus.). 608p. 1990. text ed. 109.95 (*0-442-20529-5*) Van Nos Reinhold.

Architects' Drawings from the Collection of Barbara Pine. Deborah Nevins et al. (Illus.). 48p. (Orig.). 1987. pap. 15.00 (*0-941680-05-3*) M&L Block.

Architect's Dream: Houses for the Next Millenium. Daniel Friedman et al. (Illus.). 70p. (Orig.). 1993. pap. 18.95 (*0-917562-66-6*) Contemp Arts.

Architects, Engineers & the Law: Commentary & Materials. J. R. Cooke. xxxiv, 314p. 1989. pap. 45.50 (*0-455-20946-4*, Pub. by Law Bk Co) W W Gaunt.

Architect's Guide to Computer-Aided Design. Mark L. Crosley. LC 87-13308. 202p. 1988. pap. text ed. 39.95 (*0-471-85336-4*) Wiley.

Architect's Guide to Florence. Bruno Giovannetti & Roberto Martucci. (Guidebooks Ser.). (Illus.). 160p. 1994. pap. 19.95 (*0-7506-1272-X*, Butterwrth Archit) Buttrwrth-Heinemann.

Architect's Guide to Florence. Renzo Salvadori. (Illus.). 120p. 1989. pap. 16.95 (*0-408-50069-7*) Buttrwrth-Heinemann.

Architect's Guide to London. Renzo Salvadori. (Illus.). 119p. 1990. pap. 19.95 (*0-408-50056-5*, Butterwrth Archit) Buttrwrth-Heinemann.

Architect's Guide to Rome. Renzo Salvadori. (Illus.). 144p. 1990. pap. 19.95 (*0-408-50054-9*, Butterwrth Archit) Buttrwrth-Heinemann.

***Architect's Guide to Running a Job.** Green. 1995. pap. write for info. (*0-7506-2206-7*, Focal) Buttrwrth-Heinemann.

Architect's Guide to Running a Job. 4th ed. Green. 1987. 47.95 (*0-85139-061-7*, Butterwrth Archit) Buttrwrth-Heinemann.

Architect's Guide to Venice. Renzo Salvadori. (Illus.). 122p. 1990. pap. 19.95 (*0-408-50055-7*, Butterwrth Archit) Buttrwrth-Heinemann.

Architect's Handbook for Client Briefing. Frank Salisbury. (Illus.). 198p. 1990. pap. text ed. 79.95 (*0-408-50020-4*, Butterwrth Archit) Buttrwrth-Heinemann.

Architect's Handbook of Construction Detailing. David K. Ballast. 496p. 1990. text ed. 85.00 (*0-13-044694-7*) P-H.

Architect's Handbook of Formulas, Tables & Mathematical Calculations. David K. Ballast. 544p. 1988. text ed. 74.25 (*0-13-044686-6*, Busn) P-H.

Architect's Handbook of Professional Practice. 12th ed. David Haviland. 750p. 1994. 200.00 (*1-55835-117-5*) AIA Press.

Architects House Themselves. Michael Webb. LC 93-32477. (Illus.). 224p. 1994. 39.95 (*0-89133-241-3*) Preservation Pr.

Architect's Legal Handbook: The Law for Architects. 5th ed. Anthony Speaight & Gregory Stone. (Illus.). 336p. 1991. pap. text ed. 115.00 (*0-7506-1219-3*, Butterwrth Archit) Buttrwrth-Heinemann.

Architects Make Zigzags: Looking at Architecture from A to Z. Illus. by Roxie Munro. LC 84-9679. 64p. (Orig.). (J). (gr. 3 up). 1986. pap. 9.95 (*0-89133-121-2*) Preservation Pr.

***Architect's Microstation.** Robert H. Hsu. 236p. 1995. pap. 26.95 (*1-886280-04-5*) Macrostone Intl.

***Architect's Microstation Quick Reference.** Robert H. Hsu. 212p. 1995. pap. 12.95 (*1-886280-05-3*) Macrostone Intl.

***Architects of Affluence: The Tsutsumi Family & the Seibu Enterprises in Twentieth-Century Japan.** Thomas R. Havens. (Harvard East Asian Monographs: No. 166). (Illus.). 351p. 1994. pap. text ed. 45.00 (*0-674-04360-X*, HAVARC) HUP.

Architects of Aviation. Maurice Holland & Thomas M. Smith. LC 70-148218. (Biography Index Reprint Ser.). 1977. 25.95 (*0-8369-8065-4*) Ayer.

Architects of Charleston. Beatrice St. Julien Ravenel. LC 91-34126. (Illus.). 337p. 1992. reprint ed. pap. 21.95 (*0-87249-828-X*) U of SC Pr.

Architects of Fortune: Mies van der Rohe & the Third Reich. Elaine S. Hochman. LC 90-3451. (Illus.). 382p. 1990. reprint ed. pap. 11.95 (*0-88064-121-5*) Fromm Intl Pub.

Architects of Golf: A Survey of Golf Course Design from Its Beginnings to the Present, with an Encyclopedic Listing of Golf Architects & Their Courses. rev. ed. Geoffrey S. Cornish & Ronald E. Whitten. LC 91-58372. (Illus.). 656p. 1993. 50.00 (*0-06-270082-0*, Harper Ref) HarpC.

Architects of Hyperspace. Thomas R. McDonough. 272p. 1987. pap. 2.95 (*0-380-75144-5*) Avon.

Architects of Ideas: The Story of the Great Theories of Mankind. Ernest R. Trattner. LC 75-20117. (Illus.). 426p. 1975. reprint ed. text ed. 35.00 (*0-8371-8296-4*, TRAI, Greenwood Pr) Greenwood.

Architects of Reform: Congregation & Community Leadership, Emanu-El of San Francisco, 1849-1980. Fred Rosenbaum. LC 80-54032. 241p. 1980. 19.95 (*0-943376-14-9*); pap. 9.95 (*0-943376-13-0*) Magnes Mus.

Architects of Worship. Robert W. McClelland. 1990. pap. 18.40 (*1-55673-216-3*) CSS OH.

Architects of Yiddishism at the Beginning of the Twentieth Century: A Study in Jewish Cultural History. Emanuel S. Goldsmith. LC 73-2894. 309p. 1976. 38.50 (*0-8386-1384-5*) Fairleigh Dickinson.

Architects on Architecture. rev. ed. Paul Heyer. 1994. pap. 39.95 (*0-442-01751-0*) Van Nos Reinhold.

***Architect's Other Hat: A Mystery.** Bernice Speight. 128p. (Orig.). 1995. pap. 9.95 (*1-56474-135-4*) Fithian Pr.

Architect's Paris. Thomas Carlson-Reddig. LC 92-36977. (Architecture-Travel Ser.). (Illus.). 176p. 1993. 17.95 (*0-8212-1953-7*) Bulfinch Pr.

Architects' People. Ed. by Russell Ellis & Dana Cuff. (Illus.). 320p. 1989. 45.00 (*0-19-505495-4*) OUP.

***Architect's Portable Handbook.** John P. Guthrie. LC 94-33398. 1994. 45.50 (*0-07-025302-1*) McGraw.

Architect's Responsibilities in the Project Delivery Process. 3rd ed. H. L. Murvin. (Illus.). 375p. 1989. pap. 44.50 (*0-9608498-3-1*) H L Murvin.

Architect's Rome. John M. McGuire, Jr. LC 94-1268. (Architecture-Travel Ser.). (Illus.). 176p. 1994. pap. 18.95 (*0-8212-1954-5*) Bulfinch Pr.

Architect's Room Design Data Handbook. Fred A. Stitt. (Illus.). 360p. 1992. reprint ed. text ed. 79.95 (*0-442-00716-7*) Van Nos Reinhold.

Architect's Sketchbook of Underground Buildings & Earth Shelters. Malcolm Wells. (Illus.). 192p. (C). 1990. pap. 14.95 (*0-9621878-1-X*) Malcolm Wells.

***Architect's Studio Companion: Rules of Thumb for Preliminary Design.** 2nd ed. Edward Allen & Joseph Iano. LC 95-16412. 1995. text ed. 54.95 (*0-471-04069-X*) Wiley.

Architect's Studio Companion: Simplified Guidelines for Building Design. Edward Allen & Joseph Iano. 1989. text ed. 59.95 (*0-471-63220-1*) Wiley.

Architectura. Jan V. De Vries. 1973. reprint ed. write for info. (*3-487-05854-5*, Pub. by Georg Olms GW) Lubrecht & Cramer.

Architectural Acoustics. M. David Egan. (Illus.). 304p. 1988. text ed. write for info. (*0-07-019111-5*) McGraw.

Architectural Acoustics. Anita Lawrence. (Illus.). xiii, 235p. 1970. 63.00 (*0-444-20059-2*, Pub. by Elsevier Applied Sci UK) Elsevier.

Architectural Aerodynamics. R. M. Aynsley et al. (Illus.). 254p. 1977. 74.00 (*0-85334-698-4*, Pub. by Elsevier Applied Sci UK) Elsevier.

Architectural Album: Chicago's North Shore. Ed. by Susan S. Benjamin. (Illus.). 208p. 1988. 35.00 (*0-9621602-0-2*) JL Evanston.

Architectural Album: Chicago's North Shore. rev. ed. Ed. by Susan S. Benjamin. (Illus.). 208p. 1991. reprint ed. 35.00 (*0-9621602-1-0*) JL Evanston.

Architectural Alternatives for Exploring Parallelism. David Lilja. LC 91-33298. (Illus.). 464p. (C). 1992. text ed. 65.00 (*0-8186-2642-9*, 2642) IEEE Comp Soc.

Architectural & Interior Models. 2nd ed. Sanford Hohauser. (Illus.). 320p. 1984. pap. 49.95 (*0-442-23668-9*) Van Nos Reinhold.

Architectural & Ornament Drawings of the Sixteenth to the Early Nineteenth Centuries in the Collection of the University of Michigan Museum of Art. Richard P. Wunder. (Illus.). 112p. 1965. 3.00 (*0-912303-90-5*) Michigan Mus.

Architectural & Perspective Designs. Giuseppe Bibiena. (Illus.). 1740. pap. 8.95 (*0-486-21263-7*) Dover.

An Asterisk (*) at the beginning of an entry indicates that the title is appearing in BIP for the first time.

Architectural & Social History of Cooperative Living. Lynn F. Pearson. LC 87-26409. 284p. 1988. text ed. 45.00 (*0-312-01293-4*) St Martin.

Architectural Antiquities of Western India. H. Cousens. (Illus.). 1983. text ed. 34.00 (*0-685-14107-1*) Coronet Bks.

Architectural Brickwork. David Jenkins. 1990. 29.98 (*1-55521-630-7*) Bk Sales Inc.

Architectural, Building, & Mechanical System Acoustics: A Guide to Technical Literature, Volume I Applications. James R. Ramsey. LC 86-63348. viii, 95p. 1986. 28.00 (*0-940737-00-0*) RT Books.

Architectural, Building, & Mechanical System Acoustics: A Guide to Technical Literature, Volume II Technology. James R. Ramsey. LC 86-63349. viii, 83p. 1986. 25.00 (*0-940737-01-9*) RT Books.

Architectural CAD Lab Manual. Thomas Obermeyer. 216p. 1985. text ed. 15.95 (*0-07-047509-1*) McGraw.

Architectural Ceramics: Eight Concepts. Michael Rubin. Ed. by Terry Van Shaik. LC 85-50004. (Illus.). 28p. (Orig.). 1985. pap. 5.00 (*0-936316-10-1*) Wash U Gallery.

Architectural Competitions in Nineteenth-Century England. Joan Bassin. Ed. by Stephen Foster. LC 84-2599. (Architecture & Urban Design Ser.: No. 6). 260p. reprint ed. 73.90 (*0-8357-1565-5*, 2070464) Bks Demand.

Architectural Compositions. Rob Krier. LC 88-42691. (Illus.). 320p. 1989. 65.00 (*0-8478-0965-X*) Rizzoli Intl.

Architectural Concrete: Design & Construction Practices. (Illus.). 48p. 1982. pap. 13.00 (*0-924659-14-9*, 1010) Aberdeen Group.

Architectural Conservation in the Czech & Slovak Republics. 168p. (Orig.). 1992. pap. 6.00 (*0-9627931-2-4*) World Monuments.

Architectural Contract Administration. Edmond Pachner. 248p. 1992. pap. text ed. 64.95 (*0-471-55004-3*) Wiley.

Architectural Contract Document Production. Thomas V. Berg. 448p. 1992. text ed. 58.00 (*0-07-004857-6*) McGraw.

Architectural Control: Design Review. 2nd ed. Byron R. Hanke & Thomas S. Kenny. (GAP Report Ser.: No. 2). 16p. (C). 1994. reprint ed. pap. 14.50 (*0-944715-30-3*) CAI.

Architectural Delineation: Photographic Approach to Presentation. 3rd ed. Ernest E. Burden. 1992. pap. text ed. 29.95 (*0-07-008939-6*) McGraw.

Architectural Delineation: Professional Shortcuts. Ivo Drpic. (Illus.). 224p. 1988. text ed. 49.95 (*0-442-22105-3*) Van Nos Reinhold.

Architectural Delineation: Professional Shortcuts. Ivo Drpic. 1993. pap. 29.95 (*0-442-01352-3*) Van Nos Reinhold.

Architectural Design: Integration of Structural & Environmental Systems. Carl Bovill. (Illus.). 208p. 1991. text ed. 34.95 (*0-442-00440-0*) Van Nos Reinhold.

Architectural Design & Indoor Microbial Pollution. Ed. by Ruth B. Kundsin. (Illus.). 328p. 1988. 49.95 (*0-19-504436-3*) OUP.

Architectural Design Collaborators, No. 3. Ed. by Robert W. Perlman & Arthur Y. Furst. (Illus.). 256p. 1992. pap. write for info. (*0-9624219-4-4*) Perlman Stearns.

Architectural Design Collaborators: The First Comprehensive Sourcebook. (Illus.). 1990. pap. 50.00 (*0-9624219-0-1*, Watsn-Guptill); spiral bd. 55.00 (*0-685-29108-1*) Perlman Stearns.

Architectural Design Collaborators Two: The Comprehensive Sourcebook for the Architectural & Design Communities. Ed. by Perlman-Stearns Inc. Staff. (Illus.). 320p. 1991. write for info. (*0-318-68296-6*); Japanese version. write for info. (*0-318-68298-2*); spiral bd. write for info. (*0-318-68297-4*) Perlman Stearns.

***Architectural Design-Drawing: Types & Methods.** rev. ed. Rendow Yee. LC 92-60528. (Illus.). 560p. (C). 1995. pap. text ed. 50.00 (*0-9631984-5-9*) RDW Pubns.

Architectural Detail. Jim Kemp. LC 92-5487. (Illus.). 176p. 1992. 17.95 (*0-681-41600-9*) Longmeadow Pr.

Architectural Detailing: Function, Constructability, Aesthetics. Edward Allen. LC 92-19378. (Illus.). 350p. 1992. text ed. 59.95 (*0-471-54792-1*) Wiley.

Architectural Detailing for Commercial Construction. Gene Farmer. 1991. pap. text ed. 41.95 (*0-07-019983-3*) McGraw.

Architectural Detailing in Contract Interiors. Wendy W. Staebler. (Illus.). 256p. 1988. 49.95 (*0-8230-0242-X*, Whitney Lib) Watsn-Guptill.

Architectural Details for Insulated Buildings. Ronald R. Brand. 1990. text ed. 69.95 (*0-442-23674-3*) Van Nos Reinhold.

Architectural Details from Old New England Homes. Stanley Schuler. LC 87-62395. (Illus.). 144p. 1987. 25.00 (*0-88740-114-7*) Schiffer.

Architectural Details from the Early Twentieth Century. Philip G. Knobloch. (Illus.). 240p. 1991. 19.95 (*1-55835-034-9*) AIA Press.

Architectural Drafting. Edwin Auilles. LC 79-730976. 1980. student ed 6.00 (*0-8064-0289-X*, 725); audio 279.00 (*0-8064-0290-3*) Bergwall.

Architectural Drafting. James H. Earle. (gr. 11 up). 1975. 8.95 (*0-932702-50-3*); teacher ed 3.50 (*0-932702-45-7*) Creative Texas.

Architectural Drafting. Jack Rudman. (Occupational Competency Examination Ser.: OCE-4). 1994. 39.95 (*0-8373-5754-3*); pap. 23.95 (*0-8373-5704-7*) Nat Learn.

Architectural Drafting. 2nd ed. Herbert F. Bellis & Walter A. Schmidt. LC 77-133389. 1971. text ed. 37.95 (*0-07-004418-X*) McGraw.

Architectural Drafting: Functional Planning & Creative Design. 2nd ed. George K. Stegman & Harry J. Stegman. LC 73-75303. (Illus.). 638p. reprint ed. pap. 180.00 (*0-7837-6798-6*, 2046630) Bks Demand.

Architectural Drafting & Construction. rev. ed. Ernest R. Weidhaas. (Illus.). 656p. 1989. teacher ed write for info. (*0-318-63885-1*) P-H.

Architectural Drafting & Design. 2nd ed. Alan Jefferis & David A. Madsen. 896p. 1991. teacher ed 14.00 (*0-8273-3675-6*); 18.95 (*0-8273-4649-2*); 18.95 (*0-8273-4648-4*); 18.95 (*0-8273-4647-6*); text ed. 49.95 (*0-8273-3674-8*); disk 12.95 (*0-8273-4751-0*); write for info. (*0-8273-4750-2*) Delmar.

Architectural Drafting II. Edwin Auilles. LC 80-730728. 1981. student ed 6.00 (*0-8064-0291-1*, 726); audio 279.00 (*0-8064-0292-X*) Bergwall.

Architectural Draftsman. Jack Rudman. (Career Examination Ser.: C-1092). 1994. pap. 23.95 (*0-8373-1092-X*) Nat Learn.

Architectural Drawing. Tom Porter. 1990. text ed. 19.95 (*0-442-30304-1*) Van Nos Reinhold.

Architectural Drawing: Options for Design. Paul Laseau. (Illus.). 192p. 1990. 27.95 (*0-8306-7008-4*, 50008, Design Pr); pap. 18.95 (*0-8306-8008-X*, Design Pr) TAB Bks.

Architectural Drawing: Options for Design. Paul Laseau. 1991. text ed. 27.95 (*0-07-036497-4*); pap. text ed. 18.95 (*0-07-036496-6*) McGraw.

Architectural Drawing & Light Construction. 4th ed. Edward J. Muller & James G. Fausett. 592p. 1993. text ed. 60.00 (*0-13-045477-X*) P-H.

Architectural Drawing & Planning. 3rd ed. William T. Goodban et al. (Illus.). 1979. text ed. 39.95 (*0-07-023771-9*) McGraw.

Architectural Drawing in the R. I. B. A. J. C. Palmes. pap. 7.95 (*0-685-20562-2*) Transatl Arts.

Architectural Drawing Masterclass: Graphic Techniques of the World's Leading Architecture. Tom Porter. LC 93-13558. (Illus.). 160p. 1993. pap. 50.00 (*0-684-19521-6*, Scribners) S&S Trade.

Architectural Drawings by Helmut Jacoby, 1968-1976. Intro. by Derek Walker. (Illus.). 1977. 22.95 (*0-8038-0016-9*) Archit CT.

Architectural Drawings Collection of King's College, Cambridge. Allan Doig. (Illus.). 160p. 1980. 50.00 (*0-86127-501-2*) Eastview.

Architectural Drawings of Alva Aalto, 1917-1939, Vol. 6: Aalto's Own Home in Helsinki, Finnish Pavilion at the 1937 World's Fair in Paris, & Other Buildings & Projects, 1932-1937. LC 94-27504. 424p. 1994. 180.00 (*0-685-74789-1*) Garland.

Architectural Drawings of Alvar Aalto, 1917-1939, Vol. 1: Buildings & Projects, 1917-1926. Alvar Aalto Foundation Staff et al. LC 93-27504. (Illus.). 560p. 1993. 180.00 (*0-8153-0590-7*) Garland.

Architectural Drawings of Alvar Aalto, 1917-1939, Vol. 2: Muurame Church, Southwestern Finland Agric. Alvar Aalto Foundation Staff et al. LC 93-27504. (Illus.). 560p. 1993. 180.00 (*0-8153-0591-5*) Garland.

Architectural Drawings of Alvar Aalto, 1917-1939, Vol. 3: Viipuri City Library, Turun Sanomat Buildi. Alvar Aalto Foundation Staff et al. LC 93-27504. (Illus.). 464p. 1993. 180.00 (*0-8153-0592-3*) Garland.

Architectural Drawings of Alvar Aalto, 1917-1939, Vol. 4: Paimio Tuberculosis Sanatorium, City of Tu. Alvar Aalto Foundation Staff et al. LC 93-27504. (Illus.). 560p. 1993. 180.00 (*0-8153-0593-1*) Garland.

Architectural Drawings of Alvar Aalto, 1917-1939, Vol. 5: Helsinki Stadium, Zagreb Central Hospital. Alvar Aalto Foundation Staff et al. LC 93-27504. (Illus.). 424p. 1993. 180.00 (*0-8153-0594-X*) Garland.

Architectural Drawings of Alvar Aalto, 1917-1939 Vol. 6: Aalto's Own Home in Helsinki, Finnish Pavilion at the 1937 World's Fair in Paris, & Other Buildings & Projects, 1932-1937. Alvar Aalto Archive Staff et al. LC 93-27504. (Illus.). 512p. 1994. Vol. 6. 180.00 (*0-8153-0595-8*) Garland.

Architectural Drawings of Alvar Aalto, 1917-1939 Vol. 6: Aalto's Own Home in Helsinki, Finnish Pavilion at the 1937 World's Fair in Paris, & Other Buildings & Projects, 1932-1937, 2 vols., 8. Alvar Aalto Archive Staff et al. LC 93-27504. (Illus.). 512p. 1994. write for info. (*0-8153-0597-4*) Garland.

Architectural Drawings of Alvar Aalto 1917-1939, Vol. 10: Villa Mairea 1938, Villa Mairea, 1938-1939. Aalto, Alvar, Foundation Staff. LC 93-27504. (Illus.). 384p. 1994. 180.00 (*0-8153-0599-0*) Garland.

Architectural Drawings of Alvar Aalto 1917-1939, Vol. 11: Tallinn Art Museum, Kauttua Terrace House, Finnish Pavilion at the 1939 World's Fair in New York, & Other Buildings & Projects, 1937-1939. Aalto, Alvar, Foundation Staff. LC 93-27504. (Illus.). 368p. 1994. 180.00 (*0-8153-0600-8*) Garland.

Architectural Drawings of Alvar Aalto 1917-1939, Vol. 7: Buildings & Plans for the A. Ahlstrom Company in Varkaus, & Tupe Houses, 1937-1939. Aalto, Alvar, Foundation Staff. LC 93-27504. (Illus.). 450p. 1994. 180.00 (*0-8153-0596-6*) Garland.

Architectural Drawings of Alvar Aalto 1917-1939, Vol. 9: Buildings for the Tampella Company, Inkeroinen Elementary School, & Other Buildings & Projects, 1936-1939. Aalto, Alvar, Foundation Staff. LC 93-27504. (Illus.). 424p. 1994. 180.00 (*0-8153-0598-2*) Garland.

Architectural Drawings of Antonio da Sangallo the Younger & His Circle. Christoph L. Frommel. Ed. by Nicholas Adams. LC 93-25102. (Architectural History Foundation Ser.). (Illus.). 572p. 1993. 95.00 (*0-262-06155-4*) MIT Pr.

Architectural Drawings of Benjamin Henry Latrobe. Jeffrey A. Cohen & Charles E. Brownell. Vol. 2. (Illus.). Date not set. write for info. (*0-318-72581-9*) Yale U Pr.

Architectural Drawings of Henri Sauvage: The Works of an Architect-Decorator in the Collections of the Institut Francais d'Architecture & the Archives de Paris. Institut Francais d'Architecture & the Archives de Paris Staff. LC 94-10133. (Architectural Works, c. 1905-c. 1931: Vol. II). (Illus.). 528p. 1994. 225.00 (*0-8153-0755-1*) Garland.

Architectural Drawings of Henri Sauvage: The Works of an Architect-Decorator in the Collections of the Institut Francais d'Architecture & the Archives de Paris. Institute Francais d'Architecture & the Archives de Paris Staff. LC 94-10133. (Non Architectural Drawings & Architectural Works c. 1898-c. 1905: Vol. I). (Illus.). 424p. 1994. 225.00 (*0-8153-0754-3*) Garland.

Architectural Drawings of R. M. Schindler: The Architectural Drawing Collection, University Art Museum, University of California, Santa Barbara, Vol. 1: July 1993. Ed. by David Gebhard. LC 92-39997. (Illus.). 672p. 1993. 300.00 (*0-8153-0863-9*) Garland.

Architectural Drawings of R. M. Schindler: The Architectural Drawing Collection, University Art Museum, University of California, Santa Barbara, Vol. 2. Ed. by David Gebhard. LC 92-39997. (Illus.). 688p. 1993. 300.00 (*0-8153-0864-7*) Garland.

Architectural Drawings of R. M. Schindler: The Architectural Drawing Collection, University Art Museum, University of California, Santa Barbara, Vol. 3. Ed. by David Gebhard. LC 92-39997. (Illus.). 632p. 1993. 300.00 (*0-8153-0865-5*) Garland.

Architectural Drawings of R. M. Schindler: The Architectural Drawing Collection, University Art Museum, University of California, Santa Barbara, Vol. 4. Ed. by David Gebhard. LC 92-39997. (Illus.). 672p. 1993. 300.00 (*0-8153-0866-3*) Garland.

Architectural Drawings of the Regency Period, 1790-1837. Giles Worsley. (Illus.). 164p. 1992. 24.95 (*1-55835-044-6*) AIA Press.

***Architectural Drawings of the Russian Avant-Garde.** Catherine Cooke & I. A. Kazus. (Illus.). 144p. 1990. 37.50 (*0-8109-6000-1*) Abrams.

Architectural Drawings of the Russian Avant-Garde. Catherine Cooke & I. A. Kazus. (Illus.). 144p. 1990. pap. 24.95 (*0-8109-6137-7*) Abrams.

Architectural Drawings of the Russian Avant-Garde. Catherine Cooke & I. A. Kazus. (Illus.). 144p. 1990. 37.50 (*0-87070-545-8*) Mus of Modern Art.

***Architectural Drawings of the Russian Avant-Garde.** Catherine Cooke & I. A. Kazus. (Illus.). 144p. 1990. pap. 24.95 (*0-87070-556-3*) Mus of Modern Art.

Architectural Economics for Small-Scale Design & Construction. Donald P. Grant. (Illus.). x, 240p. (Orig.). 1988. pap. 32.50 (*0-911215-03-4*) Small Master.

Architectural Education & Boston: Centennial Publication of the Boston Architectural Center 1889-1989, with Highlights of 100 Years by Architects & Historians. Margaret H. Floyd. (Illus.). 200p. (Orig.). 1989. pap. 25.00 (*0-9624098-1-2*) Boston Arch Ctr.

***Architectural Education & Boston: Centennial Publication of the Boston Architectural Center 1889-1989, with Highlights of 100 Years by Architects & Historians.** Margaret H. Floyd. (Illus.). 200p. (Orig.). 1989. 50.00 (*0-9624098-0-4*) Boston Arch Ctr.

Architectural Education & the Built Future: Faculty Essay Competition, 1992. NIAE Staff. 80p. 1992. pap. text ed. 12.00 (*0-8403-8169-7*) Kendall-Hunt.

Architectural Electromagnetic Shielding Handbook: A Design & Specification Guide. Leland H. Hemming. LC 91-21458. (Illus.). 240p. (C). 1992. text ed. 59.95 (*0-87942-287-4*, PC0282-4) Inst Electrical.

Architectural Ensembles of Armenia. O. Khalpakhchian. 480p. 1980. 99.00 (*0-569-08690-6*, Pub. by Collets UK) St Mut.

Architectural Estimator. Jack Rudman. (Career Examination Ser.: C-3114). 1994. pap. 27.95 (*0-8373-3114-5*) Nat Learn.

***Architectural Follies in America.** Headley. 1995. 16.95 (*0-89133-260-X*) Preservation Pr.

Architectural Graphic Standards. deluxe ed. Charles G. Ramsey & Harold R. Sleeper. 233p. 1990. text ed. 125.00 (*0-471-51940-5*) Wiley.

Architectural Graphic Standards. 8th ed. Ed. by John R. Hoke, Jr. LC 94-5028. 1994. Student edition. student ed, pap. text ed. 79.95 (*0-471-01284-X*) Wiley.

Architectural Graphic Standards. 8th suppl. ed. Charles G. Ramsey & Harold R. Sleeper. LC 87-31746. 320p. 1993. pap. 81.50 (*0-471-59456-3*) Wiley.

Architectural Graphic Standards Facsimile. Charles G. Ramsey & Harold R. Sleeper. 233p. 1990. text ed. 195.00 (*0-471-51556-6*) Wiley.

Architectural Graphics. 2nd ed. Frank Ching. (Illus.). 192p. 1985. pap. 24.95 (*0-442-21864-8*) Van Nos Reinhold.

Architectural Graphics & Communication. 2nd ed. Robert I. Duncan. (Illus.). 256p. 1991. per. write for info. (*0-8403-6797-X*) Kendall-Hunt.

Architectural Graphics & Communication Problems. 2nd ed. Robert I. Duncan. 288p. (C). 1992. pap. text ed., spiral bd. 22.95 (*0-8403-7960-9*) Kendall-Hunt.

***Architectural Graphics Standards: 1995 Supplement.** 9th ed. Ramsey & Sleeper. 1995. pap. text ed. 75.00 (*0-471-11472-3*) Wiley.

Architectural Guidebook to New York City. Francis Morrone. LC 93-42964. (Illus.). 400p. 1994. pap. 21.95 (*0-87905-629-0*) Gibbs Smith Pub.

Architectural Heritage. Ed. by Deborah Howard. (Illus.). 96p. 1990. 29.00 (*0-7486-0206-2*, Pub. by Edinburgh U Pr UK) Col U Pr.

Architectural Heritage III: Mackintosh & His Contemporaries. Ed. by John Lowrey. (Architectural Heritage Ser.). (Illus.). 128p. 1992. text ed. 49.00 (*0-685-57098-3*, Pub. by Edinburgh U Pr UK); pap. 20.00 (*0-7486-0382-4*, Pub. by Edinburgh U Pr UK) Col U Pr.

Architectural Heritage of Bulgaria. Stefan Stamov & R. Angreova. Ed. by N. Caneva-Decevska. (Import Ser.). (Illus.). 227p. 1974. lib. bdg. 55.00 (*0-306-70675-X*) Da Capo.

Architectural Heritage of Genesee County, New York. Catherine Roth. (Illus.). 339p. 1989. 40.00 (*0-685-29181-2*); per. 29.50 (*0-685-29182-0*) Lndmrk Soc Genesee.

Architectural Heritage of St. Louis 1803-1891. Lawrence Lowic. LC 81-71595. (Illus.). 160p. 1982. pap. 10.00 (*0-936316-02-0*) Wash U Gallery.

Architectural Heritage of the Piscataqua: Houses & Gardens of the Portsmouth District. John M. Howells. (Illus.). 244p. 1988. reprint ed. lib. bdg. 34.50 (*0-929590-00-7*) Whalesback Bks.

***Architectural Heritage of the Roanoke Valley.** fac. ed. William L. Whitwell & Lee W. Winborne. LC 81-12987. (Illus.). 236p. 1982. reprint ed. pap. 67.30 (*0-7837-7986-0*, 2047742) Bks Demand.

Architectural Heritage on the Lands of Bulgaria. P. Berbenliev. 320p. (C). 1988. text ed. 300.00 (*0-569-09175-6*, Pub. by Collets) St Mut.

Architectural Heritage, 1991, Vol. II: Scottish Architects Abroad. Ed. by Deborah Howard. (Illus.). 128p. 1991. text ed. 49.00 (*0-7486-0295-X*, Pub. by Edinburgh U Pr UK); pap. text ed. 20.00 (*0-685-49607-4*, Pub. by Edinburgh U Pr UK) Col U Pr.

Architectural History of Carbondale, Illinois. Susan E. Maycock. LC 82-19189. (Illus.). 256p. 1983. pap. 15.95 (*0-8093-1120-8*) S Ill U Pr.

***Architectural History of Harford County, Maryland.** Christopher Weeks. LC 95-5325. 1996. write for info. (*0-8018-4913-6*) Johns Hopkins.

Architectural History of Haverhill. Howard W. Curtis & Gregory H. Laing. (Illus.). 40p. (Orig.). 1976. pap. text ed. 10.00 (*0-318-50095-7*) HPL Pr.

Architectural History of Norwich Cathedral. Eric Fernie. (Clarendon Studies in the History of Art). (Illus.). 224p. 1993. 95.00 (*0-19-817502-7*) OUP.

Architectural History of the South Carolina College, 1801-1855. John M. Bryan. LC 76-54242. xxxii, 158p. 1976. pap. 15.95 (*0-87249-353-9*) U of SC Pr.

Architectural History of the University of Cambridge & Colleges of Cambridge & Eton, 3 Vols., Set. Robert Willis & John W. Clark. (Illus.). 1989. 295.00 (*0-521-35323-8*) Cambridge U Pr.

Architectural History of the University of Cambridge & Colleges of Cambridge & Eton, 3 Vols., Set. Robert Willis & John W. Clark. (Illus.). 1990. pap. 95.00 (*0-521-35851-5*) Cambridge U Pr.

Architectural History of the University of Cambridge & Colleges of Cambridge & Eton, 3 vols., Vol. 1. Robert Willis & John W. Clark. (Illus.). 825p. 1988. 135.00 (*0-521-35320-3*) Cambridge U Pr.

Architectural History of the University of Cambridge & Colleges of Cambridge & Eton, 3 vols., Vol. 1. Robert Willis & John W. Clark. (Illus.). 825p. 1989. pap. 37.95 (*0-521-35848-5*) Cambridge U Pr.

Architectural History of the University of Cambridge & Colleges of Cambridge & Eton, 3 vols., Vol. 2. Robert Willis & John W. Clark. (Illus.). 744p. 1988. 135.00 (*0-521-35321-1*); pap. 37.95 (*0-521-35849-3*) Cambridge U Pr.

Architectural History of the University of Cambridge & Colleges of Cambridge & Eton, 3 vols., Vol. 3. Robert Willis & John W. Clark. (Illus.). 865p. 1988. 135.00 (*0-521-35322-X*) Cambridge U Pr.

Architectural History of the University of Cambridge & Colleges of Cambridge & Eton, 3 vols., Vol. 3. Robert Willis & John W. Clark. (Illus.). 865p. 1989. pap. 37.95 (*0-521-35850-7*) Cambridge U Pr.

Architectural Illustrations in Watercolor. Stephan Hoffpauir & Joyce Rosner. (Illus.). 160p. 1989. 39.95 (*0-8230-0247-0*, Whitney Lib) Watsn-Guptill.

Architectural Interior Systems Workbook. Jack A. Kremers. (Illus.). 176p. 1992. pap. 19.95 (*0-442-00162-2*) Van Nos Reinhold.

***Architectural Journeys.** Antoine Predock. (Illus.). 144p. 1995. 35.00 (*0-8478-1904-3*) Rizzoli Intl.

Architectural Judgement. Peter Collins. (Illus.). 1971. 34.95 (*0-7735-0114-2*, Pub. by McGill CN) U of Toronto Pr.

Architectural Lighting Design. Frederic H. Jones. LC 90-80857. (Illus.). 200p. 1990. pap. 21.95 (*0-931961-93-9*, CX93) Crisp Pubns.

Architectural Lighting Design. Gary R. Steffy. 1990. text ed. 44.95 (*0-442-20761-1*) Van Nos Reinhold.

Architectural Lighting for Commercial Interiors. P. C. Sorcar. LC 87-2210. 352p. 1987. text ed. 59.95 (*0-471-01168-1*) Wiley.

Architectural Management. Ed. by M. P. Nicholson. 418p. 1992. 109.95 (*0-442-31598-8*) Chapman & Hall.

***Architectural Metal Pack.** Zahner. Date not set. text ed. 99.95 (*0-471-12302-1*) Wiley.

***Architectural Metals: A Guide to Selection, Specification, & Performance.** L. William Zahner. LC 94-40182. 1995. text ed. 89.95 (*0-471-04506-3*) Wiley.

Architectural Models. T. Saito et al. (Illus.). 144p. 1993. pap. 42.95 (*4-7661-0727-6*, Pub. by Graphic Sha JA) Bks Nippan.

Architectural Models: Guide to Construction Techniques. Wolfgang Knoll & Martin Hechinger. Tr. by R. M. Diamant. LC 92-27801. (Illus.). 1993. text ed. 39.95 (*0-07-071543-2*) McGraw.

An Asterisk (*) at the beginning of an entry indicates that the title is appearing in BIP for the first time.

Architectural Monuments of Leningrad Suburbs. 616p. 1983. 320.00 (*0-317-57262-8*, Pub. by Collets UK) St Mut.

Architectural Monuments of Moscow, 18th-19th Centuries. M. Il'In. (Illus.). 1973. 55.00 (*0-685-86586-X*) St Mut.

Architectural, Ornament, Landscape & Figure Drawing. Richard P. Wunder. 1975. pap. 12.50 (*0-910408-16-5*) Coll Store.

***Architectural Perspective Grids: An Easy Method of Three Dimensional Design & Perspective Construction.** John Chen & Tim Cooper. 1995. disk 44.95 (*0-07-011133-2*) McGraw.

***Architectural Photography.** Michael G. Harris. LC 94-32564. (Illus.). 144p. 1995. pap. 39.95 (*0-240-51377-0*, Focal) Buttrwrth-Heinemann.

Architectural Planning of St. Petersburg. Iurii A. Egorov. Tr. by Eric Dluhosch. LC 67-24283. 275p. reprint ed. pap. 78.40 (*0-8357-5721-8*, 2006064) Bks Demand.

Architectural Plans for Adding on or Remodeling. Jerold L. Axelrod. 1992. 26.95 (*0-07-157845-5*); pap. 19.95 (*0-07-157844-7*) McGraw.

Architectural Plans for Adding on or Remodeling. Jerold L. Axelrod. 336p. 1992. 26.95 (*0-8306-3930-6*, 2803); pap. 19.95 (*0-8306-3929-2*, 2803) TAB Bks.

Architectural Plates from the "Encyclopedie" Denis Diderot. 1994. pap. 10.95 (*0-486-27954-5*) Dover.

Architectural Practice: A Critical View. Robert Gutman. LC 88-804. (Illus.). 160p. (Orig.). 1988. pap. 11.95 (*0-910413-45-2*) Princeton Arch.

Architectural Practice in Mexico City: A Manual for Journeyman Architects of the Eighteenth Century. Mardith K. Schuetz. LC 87-3456. 137p. 1987. 25.95 (*0-8165-1000-8*) U of Ariz Pr.

***Architectural Practice Management, Set.** F. Stasiowski. 1993. text ed. 225.00 (*0-471-02410-4*) Wiley.

Architectural Presentations. Eisuke Tanaka. 120p. (ENG & JPN.). 1990. pap. 46.95 (*4-7661-0555-9*, Pub. by Graphic Sha JA) Bks Nippan.

Architectural Principles in the Age of Historicism. Robert J. Van Pelt & Carroll W. Westfall. (Illus.). 384p. (C). 1991. text ed. 42.50 (*0-300-04999-4*) Yale U Pr.

Architectural Principles in the Age of Historicism. Robert J. Van Pelt & Carroll W. Westfall. (Illus.). 384p. (C). 1993. pap. 18.00 (*0-300-05788-1*) Yale U Pr.

Architectural Principles in the Age of Humanism. Rudolf Wittkower. (Academy Editions Ser.). (Illus.). 160p. 1988. 35.00 (*0-312-02082-1*) St Martin.

Architectural Principles in the Age of Humanism. Rudolf Wittkower. 1971. pap. 9.95 (*0-393-00599-2*) Norton.

Architectural Programming: A Performance Approach to the Design Process. Donna Duerk. LC 93-10180. 1993. pap. 44.95 (*0-442-01026-5*) Van Nos Reinhold.

***Architectural Programming: Creative Techniques for Design Professionals.** Kumlin. 1995. disk 68.00 (*0-07-035972-5*) McGraw.

Architectural Progress in the Renaissance & Baroque: Sojourns in & Out of Italy. Ed. by Henry A. Millon & Susan S. Munshower. (Papers in Art History: Vol. VIII). (Illus.). 929p. (Orig.). 1992. pap. 70.00 (*0-915773-07-4*) Penn St Univ Dept Art Hist.

Architectural Reflections. Colin S. Wilson. (Illus.). 256p. 1992. pap. 24.95 (*0-7506-1283-5*) Buttrwrth-Heinemann.

***Architectural Remains: Anuradhapura, Ceylon.** James G. Smither. (C). 1994. text ed. 98.00 (*81-206-0883-6*, Pub. by Asian Educ Servs II) S Asia.

Architectural Rendering. E. D. Levinson. LC 82-17151. 256p. 1983. text ed. 29.95 (*0-07-037413-9*) McGraw.

Architectural Rendering, No. 120. Takenaka Corp. Staff. (Illus.). 144p. 1994. 55.00 (*4-7661-0767-5*, Pub. by Graphic Sha JA) Bks Nippan.

Architectural Rendering: An International Perspective. Philip Crowe. LC 92-13108. 224p. 1992. text ed. 54.95 (*0-07-014712-4*) McGraw.

Architectural Rendering: The Techniques of Contemporary Presentation. 3rd ed. Albert O. Halse. 1988. text ed. 69.95 (*0-07-025629-2*) McGraw.

Architectural Rendering in Tempera. Richard Baehr. (Illus.). 160p. 1995. text ed. 49.95 (*0-442-01261-6*) Van Nos Reinhold.

Architectural Rendering Techniques: A Color Reference. Mike W. Lin. LC 84-25812. (Illus.). 256p. 1985. text ed. 54.95 (*0-442-25953-0*) Van Nos Reinhold.

Architectural Restoration at Uxmal, 1986-1987. A. Barrera & J. Huchim. (University of Pittsburgh Latin American Archaeology Reports: No. 1). (Illus.). 1990. Incl. Spanish translation. pap. 13.00 (*1-877812-02-1*) UPLAAP.

Architectural Sculpture in New York City. Stephen M. Jacoby. (Illus.). 11.25 (*0-8446-5203-2*) Peter Smith.

Architectural Shades & Shadows. Henry McGoodwin. (Illus.). 120p. (Orig.). (C). 1991. 29.95 (*1-55835-053-5*) AIA Press.

***Architectural Sketches of the Spanish Era Forts of Guam: From the Holdings of the Servicio Historico Militar, Madrid.** Ed. by Thomas B. McGrath. Tr. by Marjorie G. Driver & Omaira Brunal-Perry. (MARC Educational Ser.: No. 17). 62p. 1994. 20.00 (*1-878453-18-1*); pap. 10.00 (*0-614-07000-7*) Univ Guam MAR Ctr.

Architectural Sketching & Rendering: Techniques for Designers & Artists. Stephen Kliment. (Illus.). 192p. 1984. pap. 18.95 (*0-8230-7053-0*, Whitney Lib) Watsn-Guptill.

Architectural Sketching in Markers. Harold Linton. 1991. pap. 39.95 (*0-442-31883-9*) Van Nos Reinhold.

Architectural Specifications Writer. Jack Rudman. (Career Examination Ser.: C-3222). 1994. pap. 29.95 (*0-8373-3222-2*) Nat Learn.

Architectural Studies: Step-by-Step Guide to Rendering & Techniques. Richard F. Koplar. 1993. text ed. 44.95 (*0-07-035868-0*) McGraw.

Architectural Study Drawings: Their Characteristics & Their Properties As a Graphic Medium for Thinking in Design. Daniel M. Herbert. LC 92-26750. 1993. pap. 34.95 (*0-442-01204-7*) Van Nos Reinhold.

Architectural Supervision on Site. A. A. MacFarlane. (Illus.). iv, 189p. 1973. 47.00 (*0-85334-574-0*, Pub. by Elsevier Applied Sci UK) Elsevier.

Architectural Systems: A Needs, Resources, & Design Approach. Ezra D. Ehrenkrantz. (Illus.). 256p. 1989. text ed. 48.00 (*0-07-019100-X*) McGraw.

Architectural Technology. Thomas Obermeyer. 1976. text ed. 39.95 (*0-07-047496-6*) McGraw.

Architectural Technology up to the Scientific Revolution: The Art & Structure of Large-Scale Buildings. Ed. by Robert Mark. (New Liberal Arts Ser.). 272p. 1994. pap. 19.95x (*0-262-63157-1*) MIT Pr.

***Architectural Terracottas from the Regia.** Susan B. Downey. (Papers & Monographs of the American Academy in Rome Ser.). 200p. 1995. text ed. 45.00x (*0-472-10571-X*) U of Mich Pr.

Architectural Theory & Practice from Alberti to Ledoux. 2nd ed. Ed. & Intro. by Dora Wiebenson. LC 82-70938. (Illus.). 124p. 1983. pap. 25.00 (*0-9608208-0-9*, 89573-4) Arch Pubns.

Architectural Theory of Viollet-le-Duc: Readings & Commentaries. Eugene-Emmanuel Viollet-de-Duc & M. F. Hearn. (Illus.). 308p. 1990. pap. 18.00x (*0-262-72013-2*) MIT Pr.

Architectural Treasures of Early America, 8 Vols, Set. 1978. 110.95 (*0-405-10063-9*, 26) Ayer.

Architectural Uncanny: Essays in the Modern Unhomely. Anthony Vidler. (Illus.). 264p. 1992. 30.00 (*0-262-22044-X*) MIT Pr.

Architectural Uncanny: Essays in the Modern Unhomely. Anthony Vidler. (Illus.). 278p. 1994. pap. 13.50x (*0-262-72018-3*) MIT Pr.

Architectural Woodwork. S. Major. 1995. pap. 49.95 (*0-442-01402-3*) Van Nos Reinhold.

Architectural Working Drawings. 3rd ed. Ralph W. Liebing. 1990. text ed. 69.95 (*0-471-50181-6*) Wiley.

Architectural Working Drawings: Residential & Commercial Buildings. William P. Spence. 1992. text ed. 64.95 (*0-471-57488-0*) Wiley.

Architecturally Speaking. Eugene Raskin. (Illus.). 1970. reprint ed. pap. 7.95 (*0-8197-0003-7*) Bloch.

Architecture. Boy Scouts of America. (Illus.). 46p. (J). (gr. 6-12). 1966. pap. 1.85 (*0-8395-3321-7*, 33321) BSA.

Architecture. Robert Gardner. (Yesterday's Science, Today's Technology Ser.). (Illus.). 96p. (J). (gr. 5-8). 1994. lib. bdg. 16.98 (*0-8050-2855-2*) TFC Bks NY.

***Architecture.** Paula B. Pratt. LC 94-23499. (World History Ser.). (J). 1995. 16.95 (*1-56006-286-X*) Lucent Bks.

Architecture. Eleanor Van Zandt. LC 89-21973. (Arts Ser.). (Illus.). 48p. (J). (gr. 6-11). 1990. lib. bdg. 11.95 (*0-8114-2362-X*) Raintree Steck-V.

Architecture. Forrest Wilson. 1990. text ed. 24.95 (*0-442-23948-3*) Van Nos Reinhold.

***Architecture.** Richard Wood. (Legacies Ser.). (Illus.). 48p. (J). (gr. 2-6). 1995. 15.95 (*1-56847-273-0*) Thomson Lrning.

Architecture. Thomas G. Jackson. (Select Bibliographies Reprint Ser.). 1977. reprint ed. 48.95 (*0-8369-9938-X*) Ayer.

***Architecture, Vol. 5.** Steven M. Lehar et al. Ed. by Omid M. Omidvar & Charles L. Wilson. (Progress in Neural Networks Ser.). 256p. 1995. write for info. (*1-56750-045-5*) Ablex Pub.

Architecture: A Modern View. Richard Rogers. LC 90-71314. (Walter Neurath Memorial Lecture Ser.). (Illus.). 64p. 1991. 14.95 (*0-500-55022-0*) Thames Hudson.

Architecture: A Modern View. Richard Rogers. LC 90-71314. (Walter Neurath Memorial Lecture Ser.). (Illus.). 64p. 1992. pap. 9.95 (*0-500-27651-X*) Thames Hudson.

Architecture: A Place for Women. Ed. by Ellen P. Berkeley & Matilda McQuaid. LC 88-29299. (Illus.). 256p. (C). 1989. pap. 19.95 (*0-87474-231-5*) Smithsonian.

Architecture: A Window on the Past. Ed. by Richard Voelkel. (Orange Countiana Ser.). 159p. Date not set. 40.00 (*1-881860-02-7*); pap. 32.00 (*1-881860-03-5*) Orange Cnty Hist.

Architecture: Design Engineering Drafting. William P. Spence. 1991. 38.64 (*0-02-677123-3*) Macmillan.

Architecture: Drafting & Design. 3rd ed. Donald E. Hepler & Paul I. Wallach. (YA). (gr. 9-12). 1976. text ed. 36.32 (*0-07-028291-9*) McGraw.

Architecture: Drafting & Design. 4th ed. Donald E. Hepler et al. (Illus.). 608p. (YA). (gr. 10-12). 1982. text ed. 34.24 (*0-07-028301-X*) McGraw.

Architecture: Drafting & Design. 5th ed. Donald E. Helper & Paul I. Wallach. 608p. 1987. text ed. 32.53 (*0-07-028318-4*) McGraw.

Architecture: Drafting & Design. 5th ed. Donald E. Hepler & Paul I. Wallach. 1987. text ed. write for info. (*0-07-028340-0*) McGraw.

Architecture: Expression & Meaning. Harold Kemp. 176p. (C). 1994. pap. text ed. 19.95 (*0-8403-9104-8*) Kendall-Hunt.

Architecture: Form Space & Order. 2nd ed. Ching. 1994. pap. 29.95 (*0-442-01792-8*) Van Nos Reinhold.

Architecture: From Pre-History to Post-Modernism. Marvin Trachtenberg & Isabelle Hyman. (Illus.). 608p. (C). 1986. text ed. 60.95 (*0-13-044702-1*) P-H.

Architecture: From Prehistory to Post-Modernism. Marvin Trachtenberg & Isabelle Hyman. (Illus.). 608p. 1986. 60.00 (*0-8109-1077-2*) Abrams.

Architecture: Meaning & Expression Interim Edition. Harold W. Kemp. 144p. (C). 1993. per., pap. text ed. 14.95 (*0-8403-8730-X*) Kendall-Hunt.

***Architecture: Meaning & Expression Selected Readings.** Harold Kemp. 144p. (C). 1994. per., pap. text ed. 19.95 (*0-8403-9739-9*) Kendall-Hunt.

Architecture: Meaning & Place. Christian Norberg-Schulz. LC 87-45387. (Illus.). 256p. 1988. pap. 29.95 (*0-8478-0847-5*) Rizzoli Intl.

Architecture: Nineteenth & Twentieth Centuries. 4th ed. Henry-Russell Hitchcock. (Pelican History of Art Ser.). (Illus.). 696p. (C). 1989. reprint ed. pap. text ed. 28.50 (*0-300-05320-7*) Yale U Pr.

Architecture: Process & Composition. Geoffrey Broadbent. (Illus.). 144p. 1994. pap. 30.00 (*1-85490-360-8*, Academy Edits) St Martin.

***Architecture: Residential Drawing & Design.** rev. ed. LC 94-30266. (Illus.). 688p. 1995. text ed. 45.28 (*1-56637-122-8*) Goodheart.

Architecture: Reversible Sites-Reversible Density: Architectural Experiments after Auschwitz-Hiroshima. Arakawa & Madeline Gins. (Illus.). 120p. 1995. pap. 38.00 (*1-85490-279-2*, Academy Edits) St Martin.

Architecture: Space, Form & Order. Francis D. Ching. 350p. 1979. pap. 29.95 (*0-442-21535-5*) Van Nos Reinhold.

Architecture: The Natural & the Man-Made. Vincent Scully. (Illus.). 408p. 1993. pap. 24.95 (*0-312-09742-5*) St Martin.

Architecture: The Story of Practice. Dana Cuff. (Illus.). 300p. 1992. reprint ed. pap. 20.00 (*0-262-53112-7*) MIT Pr.

Architecture: Theory. Ed. by Carol Digrappa. 132p. (Orig.). 1985. 17.95 (*0-912810-48-3*) Lustrum Pr.

Architecture see Colonial Art

Architecture - Art or Profession? Three Hundred Years of Architectural Education in Britain. Mark Crinson & Jules Lubbock. LC 93-49014. 1994. text ed. 69.95 (*0-7190-4171-6*, Pub. by Manchester Univ Pr UK); text ed. 19.95 (*0-7190-4172-4*, Pub. by Manchester Univ Pr UK) St Martin.

Architecture Address Book. (Illus.). 112p. 1992. 19.95 (*0-8478-5608-9*) Rizzoli Intl.

Architecture after Richardson: Regionalism Before Modernism; Longfellow, Alden, & Harlow in Boston & Pittsburgh. Margaret H. Floyd. LC 92-43959. (Illus.). 455p. (C). 1994. 75.00 (*0-226-25410-0*) U Ch Pr.

Architecture, Ambition, & Americans: A Social History of American Architecture. rev. ed. Wayne Andrews. LC 78-50786. (Illus.). 1979. pap. text ed. 14.95 (*0-02-900750-X*) Free Pr.

Architecture American see American Victorian Architecture

Architecture & Allied Design: An Environmental Design Perspective. Anthony C. Antoniades. (Illus.). 512p. 1992. per. 34.95 (*0-8403-5820-2*) Kendall-Hunt.

Architecture & Architectural Sculpture in the Roman Empire. Ed. by Martin Henig. (Illus.). 176p. 1990. 65.00 (*0-947816-29-1*, Pub. by Univ Comm Archeology UK) David Brown.

***Architecture & Art of Southern India: Vijayanagara & the Successor States, 1350-1750.** George Michell. (New Cambridge History of India Ser.: No. I:6). (Illus.). 288p. (C). Date not set. write for info. (*0-521-44110-2*) Cambridge U Pr.

Architecture & Building Dictionary: English-French-German-Arabic. deluxe ed. Abd El Gaward. 465p. (ARA, ENG, FRE & GER.). 1976. 75.00 (*0-8288-5575-7*, M9753) Fr & Eur.

Architecture & Community: Building of the Islamic World Today. Ed. by Renata Holod & Darl Rastorfer. LC 83-71377. (Illus.). 255p. 1989. 64.95 (*0-89381-123-8*, Butterwrth Archit) Buttrwrth-Heinemann.

Architecture & Community Variability Within the Antelope Creek Phase of the Texas Panhandle. Christopher R. Lintz. (Studies in Oklahoma's Past). (Illus.). 380p. (C). 1986. pap. text ed. 13.00 (*1-881346-07-2*) Univ OK Archeol.

Architecture & Construction Management in the Highland & Remote Areas of Nepal. Ed. by Joel M. Boch-Isaacson. 166p. (C). 1987. 125.00 (*0-89771-095-9*, Pub. by Ratna Pustak Bhandar) St Mut.

Architecture & Critical Imagination. Wayne Attoe. 208p. reprint ed. pap. 59.30 (*0-8357-5722-6*, 2026685) Bks Demand.

Architecture & Democracy. Claude Bragdon. 1971. 59.95 (*0-87968-654-5*) Gordon Pr.

Architecture & Design, 1970-1990: New Ideas in America. Beverly Russell. (Illus.). 144p. 1989. 29.95 (*0-685-28261-9*) Abrams.

Architecture & Disjunction. Bernard Tschumi. (Illus.). 280p. 1994. 30.00x (*0-262-20094-5*) MIT Pr.

Architecture & Dynamics of Developing Mind: Experiential Structuralism As a Frame for Unifying Cognitive Developmental Theories. Andreas Demetriou et al. (Monographs of the Society for Research in Child Development). 158p. 1993. pap. text ed. 18.50 (*0-226-14247-7*) U Ch Pr.

Architecture & Film. (Architectural Design Ser.: No. 112). 120p. 1995. pap. 26.95 (*1-85490-246-6*, Academy Edits) St Martin.

Architecture & Ideology in Early Medieval Spain. Jerrilynn Dodds. LC 88-43437. (Illus.). 256p. (C). 1994. lib. bdg. 45.00 (*0-271-00671-4*); pap. text ed. 25.00 (*0-271-01325-7*) Pa St U Pr.

Architecture & Ideology in Eastern Europe During the Stalin Era: An Aspect of Cold War History. Anders Aman. (American History Foundation Ser.). (Illus.). 356p. 1992. 40.00x (*0-262-01130-1*) MIT Pr.

***Architecture & Inner Structure of the Coriandrum Sativum** L. J. Szujko-Lacza. 116p. 1994. 60.00 (*963-05-6771-7*, Pub. by Akad Kiado HU) St Mut.

Architecture & Its Image: Four Centuries of Architectural Representation Works from the Collection of the Canadian Centre for Architecture. Ed. by Eve Blau & Edward Kaufman. (Illus.). 400p. 1989. 75.00x (*0-262-02289-3*) MIT Pr.

***Architecture & Meaning on the Athenian Acropolis.** Robin F. Rhodes. (Illus.). 240p. (C). 1995. 60.00 (*0-521-47024-2*); pap. 16.95 (*0-521-46981-3*) Cambridge U Pr.

Architecture & Medicine: I. M. Pei Designs the Kirklin Clinic, University of Alabama at Birmingham Medical Center. Aaron Betsky. LC 92-28149. 144p. (C). 1993. lib. bdg. 29.95 (*0-8191-8878-6*) U Pr of Amer.

Architecture & Nature. Ed. by Werner Blaser. 160p. (ENG, FRE & GER.). (C). 1983. text ed. 59.95 (*3-7643-1524-5*) Birkhauser.

Architecture & Nihilism: On the Philosophy of Modern Architecture. Massimo Cacciari. Tr. by Stephen Sartarelli. LC 92-33713. (Theoretical Perspectives in Architectural History & Criticism Ser.). (Illus.). 288p. (C). 1993. text ed. 35.00 (*0-300-05215-4*) Yale U Pr.

Architecture & Operating Systems. Thom Luce. 384p. (C). 1989. text ed. write for info. (*0-394-39194-2*) Knopf.

Architecture & Order: Approaches to Social Space. Ed. by Michael P. Pearson & Colin Richards. LC 93-18491. (Material Cultures Ser.). 1993. write for info. (*0-415-06728-6*) Routledge.

Architecture & Ornament. Anthony White & Bruce Robertson. 1991. 21.95 (*0-07-158196-0*) McGraw.

Architecture & Ornament. Anthony White & Bruce Robinson. 1991. pap. text ed. 12.95 (*0-07-016955-1*) McGraw.

Architecture & Ornament. Antony White & Bruce Robertson. 110p. 1991. 21.95 (*0-685-48964-7*, Design Pr); pap. 12.95 (*0-8306-1827-9*, Design Pr) TAB Bks.

***Architecture & Panelling: The James A. de Rothschild Collection at Waddersan Manors.** Bruno Pons. (Illus.). 680p. 1996. 290.00 (*0-302-00669-9*) Scala Books.

Architecture & Planning in China, Mongolia & Korea, Nos. 1055-56. M. Hugo-Brunt. 1976. 8.00 (*0-686-20399-2*) CPL Biblios.

Architecture & Planning of Classical Moscow. Albert J. Schmidt. LC 88-71549. (Memoirs Ser.: Vol. 181). (Illus.). 200p. (C). 1988. 38.00 (*0-87169-181-7*, M181-SCA) Am Philos.

Architecture & Planning of Graham, Anderson, Probst & White, 1912-1936: Transforming Tradition. Sally A. Chappell. LC 91-9162. (Chicago Architecture & Urbanism Ser.). (Illus.). 356p. 1992. 65.00 (*0-226-10134-7*) U Ch Pr.

Architecture & Politics in Germany, 1918-1945. Barbara M. Lane. LC 85-8550. 292p. 1985. pap. 17.50 (*0-674-04370-7*) HUP.

Architecture & Power: The Town Hall & the English Urban Community c. 1500-1640. Robert Tittler. (Illus.). 232p. 1992. 65.00 (*0-19-820230-X*) OUP.

Architecture & Programming 80x86, Vol. 2: Architecture Reference. Rakesh Agarwal. 656p. 1990. pap. text ed. 61.00 (*0-13-245432-7*) P-H.

***Architecture & Protocols for High-Speed Networks.** Ed. by Otto Spaniol. LC 94-31167. 304p. (C). 1994. lib. bdg. 97.50 (*0-7923-9512-3*) Kluwer Ac.

Architecture & Rural Life in Central Delaware, 1700-1900. Bernard L. Herman. LC 86-14608. (Illus.). 288p. 1987. 42.50 (*0-87049-519-4*); pap. 24.95 (*0-87049-632-8*) U of Tenn Pr.

Architecture & Sculpture of Oaxaca. Robert J. Mullen. (Monographs). (Illus.). 456p. (Orig.). (C). 1995. per. 60.00 (*0-87918-079-X*) ASU Lat Am St.

Architecture & Society: Selected Essays of Henry Van Brunt. Henry Van Brunt. Ed. by William A. Coles. LC 69-18028. (Illus.). 580p. 1969. text ed. 53.00 (*0-674-04325-1*) Belknap Pr.

Architecture & the After-Life. Howard Colvin. (Illus.). 432p. (C). 1992. text ed. 70.00 (*0-300-05098-4*) Yale U Pr.

Architecture & the Corporation: The Creative Intersection. Thomas Walton. 208p. 1988. text ed. 37.95 (*0-02-933931-6*) Free Pr.

Architecture & the Crisis of Modern Science. Alberto Perez Gomez. (Illus.). 416p. 1983. reprint ed. pap. 20.00 (*0-262-66055-5*) MIT Pr.

Architecture & the Decorative Arts: The A. Lawrence Kocher Collection of Books at the Colonial Williamsburg Foundation. Cynthia Z. Stiverson. LC 88-36398. 235p. (C). 1989. lib. bdg. 30.00 (*0-933951-24-8*) Locust Hill Pr.

Architecture & the Environment: A Personal View. HRH the Prince of Wales. Ed. by Christopher Martin. (Architectural Design Ser.: No. 101). (Illus.). 150p. (Orig.). 1993. pap. 26.95 (*1-85490-143-5*, Academy Edits) St Martin.

Architecture & the Esthetics of Plenty. James M. Fitch. LC 84-27922. (Illus.). xii, 304p. 1985. reprint ed. text ed. 89.50 (*0-313-24798-6*, FIAR, Greenwood Pr) Greenwood.

Architecture & the Human Dimension. Peter F. Smith. LC 79-307569. 239p. reprint ed. pap. 68.20 (*0-8357-5723-4*, 2027713) Bks Demand.

***Architecture & the (New) Public Sphere.** (Modulus Ser.). (Illus.). 160p. 1995. pap. text ed. 24.95 (*1-56898-030-2*) Princeton Arch.

Architecture & the Phenomena of Transition: The Three Space Conceptions in Architecture. Siegfried Giedion. LC 71-95921. (Illus.). 318p. reprint ed. pap. 90.70 (*0-8357-5724-2*, 2021592) Bks Demand.

Architecture & the Text: The Scrypts of Joyce & Piranesi. Jennifer Bloomer. LC 92-31624. (Theoretical Perspectives in Architectural History & Criticism Ser.). 248p. (C). 1993. text ed. 35.00 (*0-300-04927-7*) Yale U Pr.

Architecture & Urban Space. Ed. by Servando Alvarez et al. 872p. (C). 1991. lib. bdg. 235.00 (*0-7923-1418-2*) Kluwer Ac.

An Asterisk (*) at the beginning of an entry indicates that the title is appearing in BIP for the first time.

An Asterisk (*) at the beginning of an entry indicates that the title is appearing in BIP for the first time.

415

Architecture of Henry John Klutho: The Prairie School in Jacksonville. Robert C. Broward. LC 83-6460. (Illus.). 379p. 1984. 49.95 (*0-8130-0731-3*) U Press Fla.

Architecture of Hesiodic Poetry. Richard Hamilton. LC 88-46117. (American Journal of Philology Monographs: No. 3). 144p. 1989. text ed. 28.00 (*0-8018-3819-3*) Johns Hopkins.

Architecture of High Performance Computers, Vol. I. R. N. Ibbett & Nigel P. Topham. 212p. 1989. pap. 40.00 (*0-387-91352-1*) Spr-Verlag.

Architecture of High Performance Computers, Vol. II. R. N. Ibbett & Nigel P. Topham. (Illus.). 216p. 1989. pap. 36.00 (*0-387-91353-X*) Spr-Verlag.

Architecture of Historic Richmond. Paul S. Dulaney. LC 68-14089. 222p. reprint ed. pap. 63.30 (*0-7837-2430-6*, 2042578) Bks Demand.

Architecture of Humanism: A Study in the History of Taste. Geoffrey Scott. 11.50 (*0-8446-1399-1*) Peter Smith.

Architecture of Humanism: A Study in the History of Taste. Geoffrey Scott. (Illus.). 224p. 1974. pap. 8.95 (*0-393-00734-0*) Norton.

Architecture of Ideology: Neo-Confucian Imprinting on Cheju Island, Korea. David J. Nemeth. (UC Publications in Geography: Vol. 26). (Orig.). 1988. pap. 50.00 (*0-520-09713-0*) U CA Pr.

Architecture of Imagery in Alberto Moravia's Fiction. Janice M. Kozma. LC 92-56385. (Studies in the Romance Languages & Literatures: No. 244). 1993. 20.00 (*0-8078-9248-3*) U of NC Pr.

Architecture of Incarceration. Ed. by Iona Spens. (Illus.). 144p. 1994. 50.00 (*1-85490-358-6*, Academy Edits) St Martin.

Architecture of Integrated Information Systems: Foundations of Enterprise Modelling. August-Wilhelm Scheer. LC 92-19895. (Illus.). 220p. 1992. 59.00 (*3-540-55131-X*); 59.00 (*0-387-55131-X*) Spr-Verlag.

Architecture of Islamic Iran: The Il Khanid Period. Donald N. Wilber. LC 72-88972. 208p. 1969. reprint ed. text ed. 36.75 (*0-8371-2504-9*, WIII, Greenwood Pr) Greenwood.

Architecture of Japan. Arthur Drexler. LC 55-5987. (Museum of Modern Art Publications in Reprint). (Illus.). 1967. reprint ed. 19.95 (*0-405-01516-X*) Ayer.

Architecture of Jeremiah, 1-20. William L. Holladay. 204p. 1976. 29.50 (*0-8387-1523-0*) Bucknell U Pr.

Architecture of John Wellborn Root. Donald Hoffman. (Illus.). xviii, 264p. 1988. pap. 16.95 (*0-226-34793-1*) U Ch Pr.

Architecture of Matter. Stephen E. Toulmin & June Goodfield. LC 81-71397. (Phoenix Ser.). 398p. 1982. pap. text ed. 15.95 (*0-226-80840-8*) U Ch Pr.

Architecture of Maximilian Godefrey. Robert L. Alexander. LC 74-6810. (Johns Hopkins Studies in Nineteenth-Century Architecture). (Illus.). 266p. reprint ed. pap. 75.90 (*0-8357-5725-0*, 2020331) Bks Demand.

Architecture of McKim Mead & White in Photographs Plans & Elevations. Mckim. 1990. pap. 21.95 (*0-486-26556-0*) Dover.

Architecture of Medieval Britain: A Social History. Colin Platt. (Illus.). 352p. (C). 1991. text ed. 60.00 (*0-300-04953-6*) Yale U Pr.

Architecture of Michelangelo. James S. Ackerman. LC 85-8671. (Illus.). 384p. 1986. pap. text ed. 19.95 (*0-226-00240-3*) U Ch Pr.

Architecture of Microprocessors. Francois Anceau. 320p. (C). 1986. text ed. 36.75 (*0-201-14401-8*) Addison-Wesley.

Architecture of Middle Tennessee. Ed. by Thomas B. Brumbaugh et al. LC 72-2879. (Historic American Building Survey Ser.). (Illus.). 184p. 1974. 19.95 (*0-8265-1184-8*) Vanderbilt U Pr.

Architecture of Minard Lafever. Jacob Landy. LC 69-19461. (Illus.). 313p. 1970. text ed. 63.00 (*0-231-03132-7*) Col U Pr.

Architecture of Minard Lafever. Jacob Landy. LC 69-19461. 227p. reprint ed. pap. 64.70 (*0-7837-0420-8*, 2040743) Bks Demand.

Architecture of Mott B. Schmidt. Mark A. Hewitt. LC 91-10615. (Illus.). 176p. 1991. 50.00 (*0-8478-1399-1*) Rizzoli Intl.

Architecture of Mughal India. Catherine B. Asher. (New Cambridge History of India Ser.: I: 4). (Illus.). 384p. (C). 1992. 89.95 (*0-521-26728-5*) Cambridge U Pr.

***Architecture of New Prague, 1895-1945.** Rostislav Svacha. Tr. by Alexandra Buchler. (Illus.). 544p. 1995. 50.00 (*0-262-19358-2*) MIT Pr.

Architecture of New York City: Histories & Views of Important Structures, Sites & Symbols. rev. ed. Donald M. Reynolds. LC 94-5705. 1994. pap. text ed. 29.95 (*0-471-01439-7*) Wiley.

Architecture of Novgorod. I. I. Kushnir. 144p. 1982. pap. 35.00 (*0-317-57206-7*, Pub. by Collets UK) St Mut.

Architecture of Petra. Judith McKenzie. (British Academy Monographs in Archaeology: No. 1). (Illus.). 494p. 1991. 145.00 (*0-19-727000-X*) OUP.

Architecture of Pipelined Computers. Peter M. Kogge. 334p. 1981. 62.00 (*0-89116-494-4*) Hemisp Pub.

***Architecture of Rebecca Binder & Associates.** Date not set. 19.99 (*1-56496-151-6*) Rockport Pubs.

Architecture of Religion: A Theoretical Essay. Paul Wiebe. (Monograph Series in Religion: Vol. VIII). 155p. write for info. (*0-939980-07-X*) Trinity U Pr.

Architecture of Richard Morris Hunt. Ed. by Susan R. Stein. LC 85-16523. (Illus.). 224p. 1986. 35.95 (*0-226-77168-7*); pap. 19.95 (*0-226-77169-5*) U Ch Pr.

Architecture of Richard Neutra: From International Style to California Modern. Arthur Drexler & Thomas Hines. LC 82-81426. (Illus.). 112p. 1982. pap. 14.95 (*0-87070-506-7*, 0-8109-6007-9) Mus of Modern Art.

***Architecture of Richard Rogers.** Deyan Sudjic. (Illus.). 160p. 1995. 39.95 (*0-8109-1954-0*) Abrams.

Architecture of Ripon Cathedral. Lynn Harrison. (C). 1988. 45.00 (*0-900657-52-9*, Pub. by W Sessions UK) St Mut.

Architecture of Robert & James Adam, 1758-1794, 2 vols., Set. A. T. Bolton. (Illus.). 880p. reprint ed. 195.00 (*0-907462-49-9*) Antique Collect.

Architecture of Sevastopol. E. V. Venikeev. 208p. 1983. 40.00 (*0-317-57209-1*, Pub. by Collets UK) St Mut.

Architecture of Sir Christopher Wren. Viktor Furst. LC 56-36662. 244p. 1956. reprint ed. 49.00 (*0-686-01441-3*) Somerset Pub.

Architecture of Sir Roger Pratt. Roger Pratt. Ed. by R. T. Gunther. LC 72-177516. (Illus.). 1979. reprint ed. 23.95 (*0-405-08862-0*, Pub. by Blom Pubns UK) Ayer.

Architecture of Small Computer Systems. 2nd ed. Arthur Lippiatt & Graham Wright. (Illus.). 240p. (C). 1986. pap. text ed. 19.95 (*0-13-044744-7*) P-H.

Architecture of Social Integration in Prehistoric Pueblos. Ed. by William D. Lipe & Michelle Hegmon. LC 89-81117. (Occasional Paper Ser.: No. 1). (Illus.). 175p. (Orig.). 1990. pap. text ed. 21.95x (*0-9624640-0-7*) Crow Canyon Archaeol.

Architecture of Solids. G. E Bacon. LC 81-9762. (Wykeham Science Ser.: No. 58). 138p. 1981. pap. 18.00 (*0-8448-1397-4*, Crane Russak) Taylor & Francis.

Architecture of Solitude: Cistercian Abbeys in Twelfth-Century England. Peter Fergusson. LC 83-43072. (Illus.). 370p. 1984. 89.00 (*0-691-04024-9*) Princeton U Pr.

Architecture of Sound: Planning & Designing Auditoria. Peter Lord & Duncan Templeton. (Illus.). 176p. 1986. text ed. 79.95 (*0-85139-726-3*) Buttrwrth-Heinemann.

Architecture of Supercomputers: Titan Case Study. Daniel P. Siewiorek & Philip J. Koopman, Jr. 202p. 1991. text ed. 49.95 (*0-12-643060-8*) Acad Pr.

Architecture of Symbolic Computing. Peter M. Kogge. 768p. 1991. text ed. write for info. (*0-07-035596-7*) McGraw.

Architecture of Systems Problem Solving. George J. Klir. LC 85-9283. 556p. 1985. 110.00 (*0-306-41867-3*, Plenum Pr) Plenum.

***Architecture of Tall Buildings.** Ed. by Council on Tall Buildings & Urban Habitats Staff et al. LC 94-47110. (Tall Buildings & Urban Environment Ser.). 1995. text ed. 75.00 (*0-07-012540-6*) McGraw.

Architecture of the Arkansas Ozarks. Donald Harington. (Illus.). 1987. pap. 7.95 (*0-15-607880-5*, Harvest Bks) HarBrace.

Architecture of the City. Aldo Rossi. Tr. by Diane Ghirardo. 252p. 1982. pap. 16.95x (*0-262-68043-2*) MIT Pr.

Architecture of the Eighteenth Century. John Summerson. LC 85-50749. (World of Art Ser.). (Illus.). 1986. pap. 14.95 (*0-500-20202-8*) Thames Hudson.

Architecture of the French Enlightenment. Allan Braham. 1980. pap. 30.00 (*0-520-06739-8*) U CA Pr.

Architecture of the Greenwich Village Waterfront. Ed. by Regina M. Kellerman. 128p. 1989. 55.00x (*0-8147-4603-9*) NYU Pr.

Architecture of the Imagination. Thomas W. Schaller. (Architecture Ser.). 1992. text ed. write for info. (*0-442-00993-3*) Van Nos Reinhold.

Architecture of the Islamic World: Its History & Social Meaning. Ed. by George Michell. LC 84-50341. (Illus.). 1984. 40.00 (*0-500-34076-5*) Thames Hudson.

***Architecture of the Islamic World: Its History & Social Meaning.** Ed. by George Michell. LC 84-50341. (Illus.). 288p. 1995. pap. 29.95 (*0-500-27847-4*) Thames Hudson.

Architecture of the Italian Renaissance. Jacob Burckhardt. Ed. by Peter Murray. Tr. by James Palmes. LC 83-18113. (Illus.). 320p. 1987. pap. 24.95 (*0-226-08049-8*) U Ch Pr.

Architecture of the Italian Renaissance. rev. ed. Peter Murray. LC 85-26243. (Illus.). 252p. 1986. 16.00 (*0-8052-0807-0*) Schocken.

Architecture of the Kariye Camii in Istanbul. Robert G. Ousterhout. LC 87-22279. (Dumbarton Oaks Studies: Vol. 25). (Illus.). 292p. 1988. 45.00 (*0-88402-165-3*) Dumbarton Oaks.

Architecture of the Old South. Mills Lane. LC 93-1550. 1993. 55.00 (*1-55859-044-7*) Abbeville Pr.

Architecture of the Old South: Georgia. Mills Lane. (Illus.). 264p. 1990. 34.95 (*1-55859-021-8*) Abbeville Pr.

***Architecture of the Old South: Kentucky & Tennessee.** Mills Lane. (Illus.). 245p. 1993. 55.00 (*0-88322-022-9*) Beehive GA.

Architecture of the Old South: Louisiana. Mills Lane. (Illus.). 264p. 1990. 34.95 (*1-55859-022-6*) Abbeville Pr.

Architecture of the Old South: Mississippi & Alabama. Mills Lane. (Illus.). 264p. 1989. 34.95 (*1-55859-008-0*) Abbeville Pr.

Architecture of the Old South: North Carolina. Mills Lane. (Illus.). 264p. 1990. 34.95 (*1-55859-009-9*) Abbeville Pr.

Architecture of the Old South: South Carolina. Mills Lane. (Illus.). 264p. 1989. 34.95 (*1-55859-004-8*) Abbeville Pr.

Architecture of the Old South: Virginia. Mills Lane. (Illus.). 240p. 1989. 34.95 (*0-89659-970-1*) Abbeville Pr.

Architecture of the Private Streets of St. Louis: The Architects & the Houses They Designed. Charles C. Savage. LC 86-16476. (Illus.). 256p. 1987. 29.95 (*0-8262-0485-6*) U of Mo Pr.

Architecture of the Roman Empire: An Introductory Study. rev. ed. William L. MacDonald. LC 81-16513. (Publications in the History of Art: No. 17). (Illus.). 372p. 1982. pap. 25.00 (*0-300-02819-9*, Y-429) Yale U Pr.

Architecture of the Roman Empire: An Urban Appraisal, Vol. II. William L. MacDonald. LC 81-16513. (History of Art Ser.: No. 35). 328p. 1986. 55.00 (*0-300-03456-3*) Yale U Pr.

Architecture of the Roman Empire: An Urban Appraisal, Vol. 2. rev. ed. William MacDonald. LC 81-16513. 320p. (C). 1988. reprint ed. pap. 25.00 (*0-300-03470-9*) Yale U Pr.

***Architecture of the Shakers.** LC 94-23258. 1995. pap. 28.00 (*0-88150-337-1*) Countryman.

***Architecture of the Shakers.** Julie Nicoletta. LC 94-23258. (Illus.). 176p. 1995. 40.00 (*0-88150-310-X*) Countryman.

Architecture of the Soul: The Use of Myth & Fairytale in Depth Psychology. Ed. by Dolores E. Brien. (PAJA Papers Nineteen Ninety). 1992. pap. 8.00 (*1-882275-01-2*) Rnd Table Pr.

Architecture of the Southwest: Indian, Spanish, American. Trent E. Sanford. LC 76-100242. (Illus.). 312p. 1970. reprint ed. text ed. 59.75 (*0-8371-4012-9*, SAAS, Greenwood Pr) Greenwood.

Architecture of the Stalin Era. Alexei Tarkhanov & Sergei Kavtaradze. (Illus.). 1992. 50.00 (*0-8478-1473-4*) Rizzoli Intl.

Architecture of the Twentieth Century. Udo Kultermann. LC 92-26734. 1993. text ed. 39.95 (*0-442-00942-9*) Van Nos Reinhold.

Architecture of the Well-Tempered Environment. rev. ed. Reyner Banham. LC 84-156. (Illus.). 320p. (C). 1984. pap. text ed. 22.95 (*0-226-03698-7*) U Ch Pr.

Architecture of the Well-Tempered Environment. 2nd rev. ed. Reyner Banham. LC 84-156. (Illus.). 320p. (C). 1984. lib. bdg. 30.00 (*0-226-03697-9*) U Ch Pr.

Architecture of the West Building of the National Gallery of Art. Christopher A. Thomas. LC 92-11234. 1992. write for info. (*0-89468-184-2*) Natl Gallery Art.

***Architecture of the 20th Century.** Hollingsworth. 1995. 17.99 (*0-517-12022-4*) Random Hse Value.

Architecture of Transformation: Transcending the Paralysis of Power. Carolyn J. Barthelenghi. 200p. 1991. 35.00 (*0-9629235-0-8*) Stonecrest Ent.

Architecture of Transportation. (Architectural Design Ser.: No. 109). (Illus.). 120p. (Orig.). 1994. pap. 26.95 (*1-85490-240-7*, Academy Edits) St Martin.

Architecture of Victorian London. John Summerson. LC 75-16130. (Illus.). 109p. 1976. 14.95 (*0-8139-0592-3*) U Pr of Va.

Architecture of Western Gardens: A Design History from the Renaissance to the Present Day. Monique Mosser & Georges Teyssot. (Illus.). 544p. 1991. 135.00x (*0-262-13264-8*) MIT Pr.

Architecture of William Morgan. Paul D. Spreiregen. (Illus.). 262p. 1987. 60.00 (*0-292-79023-6*) U of Tex Pr.

Architecture on Screen: Films & Videos on Architecture, Landscape Architecture, Historic Preservation, City & Regional Planning. Ed. by Nadine Covert & Vivian Wick. LC 93-36811. 300p. 1994. 65.00 (*0-8161-0593-6*); pap. 35.00 (*0-8161-0625-8*) G K Hall.

Architecture, Poetry, & Number in the Royal Palace at Caserta. George L. Hersey. (Illus.). 384p. 1983. 47.50 (*0-262-08121-0*) MIT Pr.

Architecture, Power, & National Identity. Lawrence J. Vale. (Illus.). 288p. (C). 1992. text ed. 47.50 (*0-300-04958-7*) Yale U Pr.

Architecture Records in the San Francisco Bay Area: A Guide to Research. Ed. by Waverly Lowell. LC 89-16904. (Reference Library of the Humanities). 370p. 1988. lib. bdg. 54.00 (*0-8240-6614-6*) Garland.

Architecture, Ritual Practice & Co-Determination in the Swedish Office. Dennis Doxtater. (Ethnoscapes Ser.). 400p. 1994. 81.95 (*1-85628-558-8*, Pub. by Avebury Pub UK) Ashgate Pub Co.

Architecture Shapes. Michael J. Crosbie & Steve Rosenthal. (Illus.). 26p. (J). (ps). 1993. 6.95 (*0-89133-211-1*) Preservation Pr.

Architecture, Society & Space - The High-Density Question Re-Examined. A. R. Cuthbert. (Illus.). 90p. 1985. pap. 22.00 (*0-08-033227-7*, Pub. by PPL UK) Elsevier.

Architecture Studio: Cranbrook Academy of Art. Dan Hoffman. LC 93-43292. 224p. 1994. 45.00 (*0-8478-1796-2*) Rizzoli Intl.

Architecture Subjects Itself. Prod. by Southern California Institute of Architecture Staff. (Offramp Ser.: Vol. 1, Issue 4). (Illus.). 100p. (Orig.). 1993. pap. 24.00 (*1-878271-87-3*) Princeton Arch.

Architecture Through the Looking Glass. J. Robinson. 1992. pap. write for info. (*0-442-01003-6*) Van Nos Reinhold.

Architecture, Time & Eternity: A Studies in the Stellar & Temporal Symbolism of Trraditional Buildings, 2 vols., Set. Adrian Snodgrass. 1990. 140.00 (*81-85179-30-1*, Pub. by Aditya Prakashan II) S Asia.

Architecture Today. rev. ed. Charles Jencks. LC 80-27124. (Illus.). 360p. 1988. 75.00 (*0-8109-1883-8*) Abrams.

Architecture Transformed: A History of the Photography of Buildings from 1839 to the Present. Cervin Robinson & Joel Herschmann. (Illus.). 224p. 1990. reprint ed. pap. 32.50x (*0-262-68064-5*) MIT Pr.

Architecture Vivante, 5 vols., Set. Ed. by Jean Badovici. LC 75-5874. (Architecture & Decorative Art Ser.). (Illus.). 885p. 1975. 750.00 (*0-306-70540-0*) Da Capo.

Architecture Without Architects: A Short Introduction to Non-Pedigreed Architecture. Bernard Rudofsky. LC 87-10778. (Illus.). 162p. 1987. reprint ed. pap. 16.95 (*0-8263-1004-4*) U of NM Pr.

***Architecture Without Kings: The Rise of Puritan Classicism under Cromwell.** Timothy Mowl & Brian Earnshaw. LC 94-43001. 1995. text ed. write for info. (*0-7190-4678-5*, Pub. by Manchester Univ Pr UK) St Martin.

Architecture Without Rules: The Houses of Marcel Breuer & Herbert Beckhard. David Masello. LC 92-32187. 1993. 35.00 (*0-393-03491-7*) Norton.

***Architecture Without Rules: The Houses of Marcel Breuer & Herbert Beckhard.** David Masello. (Illus.). 176p. 1995. pap. 19.95 (*0-393-31375-1*, Norton Paperbks) Norton.

Architecture 101: A Guide to the Design Studio. Andy Pressman. 179p. 1993. pap. text ed. 29.95 (*0-471-57318-3*) Wiley.

Architectureproduction. Ed. by Beatriz Colomina. (Revisions, Papers in Architectural Theory & Criticism Ser.: Vol. 2). 192p. 1988. pap. 14.95 (*0-910413-20-7*) Princeton Arch.

Architectures & Compilation Techniques for Fine & Medium Grain Parallelism: Proceedings of the IFIP WG 10.3 Working Conference, Orlando, Florida, U. S. A., 20-22 January 1993. Ed. by Michel Cosnard et al. LC 93-16960. (IFIP Transactions A: Computer Science & Technology Ser.: Vol. A-23). xii, 330p. 1993. pap. 111.50 (*0-444-88464-5*, North Holland) Elsevier.

Architectures for Intelligence. Ed. by Kurt VanLehn. (Carnegie Mellon Symposia on Cognition Ser.). 448p. (C). 1991. text ed. 89.95 (*0-8058-0405-6*); pap. 36.00 (*0-8058-0406-4*) L Erlbaum Assocs.

***Architectures in Love.** Ed. by Kim Shkapich. LC 94-36407. (Illus.). 72p. 1995. 35.00 (*0-8478-1859-4*) Rizzoli Intl.

Architectures of Herzog & De Meuron: Portraits by Thomas Ruff. Steven Holl et al. Tr. by Catherine Schelbert. (Illus.). 200p. 1994. pap. 65.00 (*0-935875-12-3*) P Blum Edit.

Architektur in Der DDR. A. Behr. 212p. 1980. 81.00 (*0-317-57201-6*, Pub. by Collets UK) St Mut.

Architektur zur Zwischenkriegszeit, 4 Bks. Ed. by O. M. Ungers & Liselotte Ungers. 1972. 400.00 (*0-8115-3507-X*) Periodicals Srv.

Architettura Civile. Ferdinando G. Da Bibiena. LC 68-57184. (Illus.). (ITA.). 1972. 55.95 (*0-405-08268-1*, Pub. by Blom Pubns UK) Ayer.

Architext: An Introduction. Gerard Genette. Tr. by Jane E. Lewin. 95p. 1992. 28.00 (*0-520-04498-3*); pap. 13.00 (*0-520-07661-3*) U CA Pr.

Architexture: A Shelter Word. rev. ed. Sally J. Patton & Dianne Maxon. 56p. (J). (gr. 2-6). 1989. reprint ed. pap. text ed. 14.95 (*0-913705-38-1*) Zephyr Pr AZ.

Archiv Fur Lateinische Lexikographie und Grammatik Mit Einschluss Des Alteren Mittellateins, 15 vols. Ed. by Eduard Von Wolfflin. cxcvi, 9212p. 1967. reprint ed. Index, Vols. 1-10. write for info. (*0-318-71070-6*, Pub. by Georg Olms GW) Lubrecht & Cramer.

Archiv Fur Lateinische Lexikographie und Grammatik Mit Einschluss Des Alteren Mittellateins, 15 vols., Set. Ed. by Eduard Von Wolfflin. cxcvi, 9212p. 1967. reprint ed. write for info. (*0-318-71069-2*, Pub. by Georg Olms GW) Lubrecht & Cramer.

***Archival Administration.** Ed. by Larence et al. 256p. 1995. 12.95 (*0-614-07377-4*, 82-003, Red River Pr) Archival Servs.

Archival Administration. Kevin Sandifer. Ed. by Rowland P. Gill. 96p. (C). 1994. pap. text ed. 15.25 (*0-910653-17-8*, Red River Pr) Archival Servs.

Archival Appraisal. Frank Boles & Julia M. Young. 275p. 1991. pap. text ed. 39.95 (*1-55570-064-0*) Neal-Schuman.

***Archival Appraisal: Theory & Practice.** Barbara L. Craig. 232p. 1996. 60.00 (*1-85739-009-1*) Bowker-Saur.

Archival Doc. July 40 - Dec 41: A Documentary History of the Relocation & Incarceration of Japanese Americans, 1942-1945, Vol. 1. Ed. by Roger Daniels. 1989. 50.00 (*0-8240-2791-4*) Garland.

Archival Documents, April, 1942. Roger Daniels. LC 88-37350. (American Concentration Camps Ser.: Vol. 4). 262p. 1989. 50.00 (*0-8240-2794-9*) Garland.

Archival Documents, February 20, 1942-March 31, 1942. Roger Daniels. LC 88-37350. (American Concentration Camps Ser.: Vol. 3). 382p. 1989. 60.00 (*0-8240-2793-0*) Garland.

Archival Documents, January 1, 1942-February 19, 1942. Roger Daniels. LC 88-37350. (American Concentration Camps Ser.: Vol. 2). 364p. 1989. 60.00 (*0-8240-2792-2*) Garland.

Archival Documents, June 1942-December 1942. Roger Daniels. LC 88-37350. (American Concentration Camps Ser.: Vol. 6). 254p. 1989. 60.00 (*0-8240-2796-5*) Garland.

Archival Documents, May, 1942. Roger Daniels. LC 88-37350. (American Concentration Camps Ser.: Vol. 5). 436p. 1989. 60.00 (*0-8240-2795-7*) Garland.

Archival Documents, 1943. Roger Daniels. LC 88-37350. (American Concentration Camps Ser.: Vol. 7). 382p. 1989. 70.00 (*0-8240-2797-3*) Garland.

Archival Enterprise: Modern Archival Principles, Practices, & Management Techniques. Bruce W. Dearstyne. LC 92-24279. 270p. (C). 1992. text ed. 55.00 (*0-8389-0602-8*) ALA.

***Archival Management of Electronic Records.** Ed. by David Bearman. (Technical Reports). 56p. 1991. pap. text ed. 20.00 (*1-885626-02-9*) Archives & Mus.

***Archival Methods.** David Bearman. (Technical Reports). 67p. 1989. pap. 20.00 (*1-885626-00-2*) Archives & Mus.

Archival Principles & Practice: A Cartoon Guide to Archives Management. Jeanette W. Ford. LC 89-49030. 160p. 1990. pap. 17.50x (*0-89950-480-9*) McFarland & Co.

***Archival Services.** Ed. by Larence et al. 256p. 1995. 12.00 (*0-910653-22-4*) Archival Servs.

Archival Strategies & Techniques. Michael R. Hill. (Qualitative Research Methods Ser.: Vol. 31). (Illus.). 96p. (C). 1993. text ed. 21.50 (*0-8039-4824-7*); pap. text ed. 9.50 (*0-8039-4825-5*) Sage.

An Asterisk (*) at the beginning of an entry indicates that the title is appearing in BIP for the first time.

An Asterisk (*) at the beginning of an entry indicates that the title is appearing in BIP for the first time.

417

Arctic Geology & Petroleum Potential: Proceedings of the Norwegian Petroleum Society Conference Held at 15-17 August 1990, Troms, Norway. Ed. by T. O. Vorren. LC 92-5691. (Norwegian Petroleum Society (NPF) Special Publication Ser.: Vol. 2). 1992. write for info. (0-444-88943-4) Elsevier.

Arctic Harpooner: A Voyage on the Schooner Abbie Bradford 1878-1879. Robert Ferguson. Ed. by Leslie D. Stair. (Seafaring Men: Their Ships & Times Ser.). (Illus.). 1980. reprint ed. text ed. 19.50 (0-930576-29-2) E M Coleman Ent.

Arctic Heart: A Poem Cycle. Gretel Ehrlich. LC 92-15095. (Illus.). 70p. (Orig.). 1992. pap. 12.95 (0-88496-357-8) Capra Pr.

Arctic Heart: A Poem Cycle. Gretel Ehrlich. (Illus.). 84p. (Orig.). (C). 1992. reprint ed. lib. bdg. 33.00x (0-8095-4098-3) Borgo Pr.

Arctic Herd. John Morgan. LC 83-9130. (Alabama Poetry Ser.). x, 64p. 1984. 15.95x (0-8173-0195-X) U of Ala Pr.

Arctic Homeland: Kinship, Community, & Development in Northwest Greenland. Mark Nuttal. (Anthropological Horizons Ser.: No. 2). (Illus.). 256p. 1992. 50.00 (0-8020-2886-1); pap. 19.95 (0-8020-7391-3) U of Toronto Pr.

Arctic Hunter. Diane Hoyt-Goldsmith. LC 92-2563. (Illus.). 32p. (J). (gr. 3-7). 1992. lib. bdg. 15.95 (0-8234-0972-4) Holiday.

Arctic Hunter. Diane Hoyt-Goldsmith. (J). 1994. pap. 6.95 (0-8234-1124-9) Holiday.

Arctic Hunters. J. C. King. 32p. (J). 1991. pap. 8.95 (0-88894-834-4, Pub. by Groundwood-Douglas & McIntyre CN) Firefly Bks Ltd.

Arctic Imperative: Is Canada Losing Its North? John Honderich. (Illus.). 270p. 1987. 30.00 (0-8020-5763-2) U of Toronto Pr.

Arctic in History. Richard Vaughn. (Illus.). 256p. 1994. text ed. 44.00 (0-7509-0177-2) A Sutton Pub.

Arctic Journeys: A History of Exploration for the Northwest Passage. Miller Graf. LC 91-30738. (American University Studies: History: Ser. IX, Vols. 121). 377p. (C). 1992. text ed. 56.95 (0-8204-1745-9) P Lang Pubs.

Arctic Land. Bobbie Kalman. (Arctic World Ser.). (Illus.). 56p. (J). (gr. 3-4). 1988. 15.95 (0-86505-144-5); pap. 7.95 (0-86505-154-2) Crabtree Pub Co.

Arctic Languages: An Awakening. 450p. 1990. pap. 45.00 (92-3-102661-5, U6615) UNIPUB.

Arctic Leverage: Canadian Sovereignty & Security. Nathanial F. Caldwell, Jr. LC 90-31362. 144p. 1990. text ed. 45.00 (0-275-93453-5, C3453, Praeger Pubs) Greenwood.

Arctic Life: Challenge to Survive. Ed. by Martina M. Jacobs & James B. Richardson, III. LC 82-73756. (Illus.). 208p. (Orig.). 1983. pap. 19.95 (0-911239-02-2) Carnegie Mus.

Arctic Memories. Normee Ekoomiak. LC 89-39194. (Illus.). 32p. (J). (gr. 3 up). 1990. 15.95 (0-8050-1254-0, Bks Young Read) H Holt & Co.

Arctic Memories. Normee Ekoomiak. LC 89-39194. (Illus.). 32p. (J). (gr. 3 up). 1992. pap. 5.95 (0-8050-2347-X, Bks Young Read) H Holt & Co.

Arctic Mirrors: Russia & the Small Peoples of the North. Yuri Slezkine. (Illus.). 480p. 1994. 32.95 (0-8014-2976-5) Cornell U Pr.

Arctic National Wildlife Debate. Ed. by Thomas Stern & Britt David. LC 87-71270. (Orig.). 1987. pap. 5.00 (0-934458-09-X) Americans Energy Ind.

Arctic National Wildlife Refuge. Alaska Geographic Society Staff. Ed. by Penny Rennick. (Alaska Geographic Ser.: Vol. 20, No. 3). (Illus.). 96p. (Orig.). 1993. pap. 18.95 (1-56661-012-5) Alaska Geog Soc.

Arctic National Wildlife Refuge. Alexandra Siy. LC 91-3882. (Circle of Life Ser.). (Illus.). 80p. (J). (gr. 5 up). 1991. text ed. 14.95 (0-87518-468-5, Dillon Silver Burdett) Silver Burdett Pr.

Arctic Ocean Issues in the 1980s. Ed. by Douglas M. Johnston. (Law of the Sea Workshop Ser.: No. W6). 1982. 5.00 (0-911189-03-3) Law Sea Inst.

Arctic Ocean Region. Ed. by A. Grantz et al. (DNAG, Geology of North America Ser.: Vol. L). (Illus.). 654p. 1990. 85.00 (0-8137-5211-6) Geol Soc.

***Arctic Odyssey: The Diary of Diamond Jenness, 1913-1916.** Diamond Jenness & Stuart E. Jenness. (Illus.). 860p. 1995. pap. 29.95 (0-660-12905-1) U of Wash Pr.

Arctic Ordeal: The Journal of John Richardson, Surgeon-General with Franklin, 1820-1822. Ed. by C. Stuart Houston. (Illus.). 384p. 1984. 49.95 (0-7735-0418-4, Pub. by McGill CN) U of Toronto Pr.

***Arctic Ordeal: The Journal of John Richardson, Surgeon-Naturalist with Franklin, 1820-1822.** Ed. by C. Stuart Houston. (Illus.). 384p. 1994. pap. 22.95 (0-7735-1223-3, Pub. by McGill CN) U of Toronto Pr.

***Arctic Peoples.** Alexandra Parsons. LC 95-10399. (Make It Work! Ser.: History Ser.). (J). 1995. 18.95 (1-56847-138-6) Thomson Lrning.

Arctic Politics: Conflict & Cooperation in the Circumpolar North. Oran R. Young. LC 92-53869. (Arctic Visions Ser.). (Illus.). 303p. (C). 1992. text ed. 35.00 (0-87451-605-6); pap. 17.95 (0-87451-606-4) U Pr of New Eng.

Arctic Prairies: A Canoe-Journey of 2,000 Miles in Search of the Caribou Being the Account of a Voyage to the Region North of Aylmer Lake. Ernest T. Seton. (Illus.). 308p. (YA). 1994. pap. 18.95 (1-885529-04-X) Stevens Pub.

Arctic Rendezvous. Graham McGill. 293p. 1993. pap. 13.95 (0-87604-305-8, 388) ARE Pr.

Arctic Roads & Summer Sun: (For Older Travelers) Philip R. Petersen. (Illus.). 100p. (Orig.). 1988. pap. 14.50 (0-9621726-0-X) Raven Pubs.

Arctic Roads & Summer Sun: Business Supplement. rev. ed. Philip R. Petersen. LC 89-831737. (Illus.). 108p. 1990. pap. 9.95 (0-9621726-1-8) Raven Pubs.

Arctic Schoolteacher: Kulukak, Alaska, 1931-1933. Abbie M. Madenwald. LC 92-54129. (Western Frontier Library: Vol. 59). (Illus.). 224p. 1992. 21.95 (0-8061-2469-5) U of Okla Pr.

Arctic Schoolteacher: Kulukak, Alaska, 1931-1933. Abbie M. Madenwald. LC 92-54129. (Western Frontier Library: Vol. 59). (Illus.). 224p. 1994. pap. 11.95 (0-8061-2611-6) U of Okla Pr.

Arctic Searching Expedition: A Journal of a Boat Voyage Through Rupert's Land & the Arctic Sea, in Search of the Discovery Ships under Command of Sir John Franklin, 2 Vols, Set. John Richardson. LC 68-55214. 1971. reprint ed. text ed. 75.00 (0-8371-3858-2, RIAS) Greenwood.

Arctic Seas. Y. Herman. 1989. text ed. 109.95 (0-442-23171-7) Chapman & Hall.

***Arctic Son.** Jean Aspen. 1995. 19.95 (0-89732-173-1) Menasha Ridge.

Arctic Spring. Sue Vyner. LC 92-32280. (Illus.). (J). (ps-3). 1993. 13.99 (0-670-84934-0) Viking Child Bks.

Arctic Summer. Downs Matthews. LC 92-25376. (Illus.). 40p. (J). (gr. 2-5). 1993. pap. 14.00 (0-671-79539-2, S&S Bks Young Read) S&S Childrens.

Arctic Summer & Other Fiction. E. M. Forster. LC 80-26199. (Abinger Edition of E. M. Forster Ser.: Vol. 9). 342p. 1981. 54.50 (0-8419-0670-X) Holmes & Meier.

Arctic Treachery. Richard Woodman. 232p. 1987. 15.95 (0-8027-0948-6) Walker & Co.

Arctic Trip. Drew Bjorke. (Illus.). 12p. (J). (ps). 1993. 4.95 (1-56828-035-1) Red Jacket Pr.

Arctic Tundra. L. Stone. (Ecozones Ser.). (Illus.). 48p. (J). (gr. 4-8). 1988. lib. bdg. 15.94 (0-86592-436-8); lib. bdg. 11.95 (0-685-58568-9) Rourke Corp.

Arctic Twilight: Old Finnish Tales. Samuli Paulaharju. Ed. by Robert W. Matson. Tr. by Allan M. Pitkanen. (Illus.). 1982. 15.00 (0-943478-00-6) Finnish Am Lit.

Arctic Underwater Operations. Ed. by Louis Rey. 360p. 1985. lib. bdg. 115.50 (0-86010-631-4) G & T Inc.

Arctic Village: A Nineteen Thirties Portrait of Wiseman, Alaska. Robert Marshall. LC 90-27265. (Illus.). xxviii, 399p. 1991. 28.00 (0-912006-47-1); pap. 20.00 (0-912006-51-X) U of Alaska Pr.

Arctic Wars, Animal Rights, Endangered Peoples. Finn Lynge. Tr. by Marianne Stenbaek. LC 92-1516. (Arctic Visions Ser.). (Illus.). 134p. 1993. 16.95 (0-87451-588-2) U Pr of New Eng.

Arctic Water Pollution Research: Applications of Science & Technology: Proceedings of an IAWPRC Conference Held in Yellowknife, Canada, 28 April-1 May 1985. Ed. by W. A. Bridgeo & H. R. Eisenhauer. LC 82-645900. (Illus.). 194p. 1986. pap. 52.00 (0-08-034149-7, Pub. by PPL UK) Elsevier.

Arctic Whalers. Basil Lubbock. (C). 1987. 138.00 (0-85174-107-X, Pub. by Brwn Son Ferg) St Mut.

Arctic Whales & Whaling. Bobbie Kalman. (Arctic World Ser.). (Illus.). 56p. (J). (gr. 3-4). 1988. 15.95 (0-86505-146-1); pap. 7.95 (0-86505-156-9) Crabtree Pub Co.

Arctic Whaling Diary: The Journal of Captain George Comer in Hudson Bay, 1903-1905. George Comer. Ed. by W. Gillies Ross. LC 84-217794. (Illus.). 303p. reprint ed. pap. 86.40 (0-8357-3649-0, 2036377) Bks Demand.

Arctic Whaling Sketchbook. William Gilkerson. (Illus.). 56p. 1983. ring bd. 185.00 (0-9617194-2-7) E J Lefkowicz.

***Arctic Wilderness: The 5th World Wilderness Congress.** Ed. by Vance Martin & Nicholas Tyler. (Illus.). 320p. (Orig.). (C). 1995. pap. text ed. 32.00 (1-55591-931-6, North Amer Pr) Fulcrum Pub.

Arctic Wolf: Living with the Pack. L. David Mech. (Illus.). 128p. 1992. pap. 19.95 (0-89658-211-6) Voyageur Pr.

Arctic Zoology, 2 vols. in one. Thomas Pennant. LC 73-17835. (Natural Sciences in America Ser.). (Illus.). 1012p. 1974. reprint ed. 76.95 (0-405-05758-X) Ayer.

Arctic, 1927. A. Y. Jackson. 140p. 1982. 26.00 (0-920806-37-6, Pub. by Penumbra Pr CN) U of Toronto Pr.

Arcturus, Set. reprint ed. lib. bdg. 225.00 (0-404-19503-2) AMS Pr.

***ArcView Developer's Guide.** Amir H. Razavi. (Illus.). 300p. 1995. pap. 49.95 (1-56690-059-X, 4202, OnWord Pr) High Mtn.

ArcView User's Guide: Motif Version. 1992. pap. text ed. write for info. (1-879102-09-9) ERS Inst.

ArcView User's Guide: Sun Version. 1992. pap. text ed. write for info. (1-879102-08-0) ERS Inst.

***ARDA Education Institute Resource Manual.** 2nd ed. (Industry Issues Ser.). 120p. 1994. 95.00 (0-614-04623-8, 54706) ARDA.

Ardath, the Story of a Dead Self. Marie Corelli. 602p. 1993. spiral bd. 11.00 (0-7873-0208-2) Mokelumne.

Ardele, Ou la Marguerite. Jean Anouilh. (Folio Ser.: No. 1057). (FRE.). 1970. pap. 8.95 (2-07-037057-7) Schoenhof.

Ardele ou la Marguerite see Pieces Grincantes

***Arden: Plays One.** Arden. 448p. 1995. pap. 15.95 (0-413-68800-3, A0703, Pub. by Methuen UK) Heinemann.

***Arden: Plays Two.** John Arden. 1995. pap. 15.95 (0-413-68810-0, A0704, Pub. by Methuen UK) Heinemann.

Arden-D'Arcy: Plays One. John Arden & Margaretta D'Arcy. (Methuen World Dramatists Ser.). 432p. (Orig.). 1991. pap. 15.95 (0-413-64940-7, AO564, Pub. by Methuen UK) Heinemann.

Arden Graff's Interior Design Kit. Arden Graff. (Illus.). (Orig.). (C). 1979. student ed. 9.95 (0-934892-00-8) Interiors.

Arden of Feversham. Ed. by Martin White. (New Mermaid Ser.). (C). 1984. pap. text ed. 6.95 (0-393-95236-3) Norton.

Arden of Feversham. LC 73-133633. (Tudor Facsimile Texts. Old English Plays Ser.: No. 61). reprint ed. 49.50 (0-404-53361-2) AMS Pr.

Arden on File. Comp. by Malcolm Page. (Methuen Writer-Files Ser.). 96p. 1988. pap. 10.95 (0-413-56280-8, A0011, Pub. by Methuen UK) Heinemann.

***Ardennes: Battle of the Bulge, 2 vols., Set.** 1995. lib. bdg. 600.95 (0-8490-6673-5) Gordon Pr.

Ardennes Tapes. Timothy B. Benford. 1989. pap. 3.95 (1-55817-230-0, Pinnacle NY) Windsor NY.

Ardennes 1944: Hitler's Last Gamble in the West. James Arnold. (Campaign Ser.: No. 5). (Illus.). 96p. pap. 14.95 (0-85045-959-1, 9504, Pub. by Osprey UK) Stackpole.

Ardennes 1944: Peiper & Skorzeny. Jean-Paul Pallud. (Elite Ser.: No. 11). (Illus.). 64p. pap. 12.95 (0-85045-740-8, 9410, Pub. by Osprey UK) Stackpole.

Arden's Touch. Beth Henderson. LC 90-20177. (Novel of Romance Ser.). 192p. 1990. 15.95 (0-87131-640-4) M Evans.

Ardent Apparitions. Ellen Fitzgerald. (Regency Romance Ser.). 224p. 1992. 19.95 (0-8027-1209-6) Walker & Co.

Ardent Eighties: Reminiscences of an Interesting Decade. Gregory Weinstein. LC 74-29529. (Modern Jewish Experience Ser.). (Illus.). 1975. reprint ed. 24.95 (0-405-06753-4) Ayer.

Ardent Eighties & After: Reminiscences of an Interesting Decade. Gregory Weinstein. (American Biography Ser.). 242p. 1991. reprint ed. lib. bdg. 69.00 (0-7812-8408-2) Rprt Serv.

Ardent Spirits: The Rise & Fall of Prohibition. John Kobler. (Illus.). 416p. 1993. reprint ed. pap. 14.95 (0-306-80512-X) Da Capo.

Ardhoka Thanaka: Half a Tale. Ed. by Lath Mukund. 1983. 28.50 (0-8364-1087-4) S Asia.

Ardi's Country Painting, Bk. 1. Ardi Hansen. (Illus.). 32p. 1985. pap. 6.50 (0-941284-26-3) J Shaw Studio.

Ardi's Country Painting, Bk. 2. Ardi Hansen. (Illus.). 24p. 1986. pap. 6.95 (0-941284-30-1) J Shaw Studio.

Ardi's Country Painting, Bk. 3. Ardi Hansen. (Illus.). 32p. 1986. pap. 6.95 (0-941284-36-0) J Shaw Studio.

Ardi's Country Painting, Bk. 4. Ardi Hansen. (Illus.). 32p. 1987. pap. 6.95 (0-941284-41-7) J Shaw Studio.

Ardors. Robert Gibbons. (Orig.). 1986. pap. 4.95 (0-911623-04-3) I Klang.

Ardor's Hut. Abby Rosenthal. 64p. (Orig.). 1990. 15.00 (0-934184-22-4); pap. 7.00 (0-934184-21-6) Alembic Pr.

Ardreys. Kay Vernon. (Illus.). 1979. pap. 1.95 (0-89083-483-0) Zebra.

Arduin Grimoire IV: The Lost Grimoire. David A. Hargrave. (Illus.). 150p. 1984. pap. 11.95 (0-940918-10-2, STK 82-006) Dragon Tree.

Arduin Grimoire V: Dark Dreams. David A. Hargrave. (Illus.). 100p. 1985. pap. 11.95 (0-940918-19-6, STK 82-007) Dragon Tree.

Arduin Grimoire VI: House of the Rising Sun. David A. Hargrave. (Illus.). 95p. 1986. pap. 11.95 (0-940918-20-X, STK 82-008) Dragon Tree.

Arduin Grimoire VII: Shadowlands. David A. Hargrave. (Illus.). 1987. 11.95 (0-940918-46-3, STK 82-016) Dragon Tree.

Arduin Grimoire VIII: The Winds of Chance. David A. Hargrave. (Illus.). 107p. 1988. pap. 11.95 (0-940918-45-5, STK 82-017) Dragon Tree.

Are All Christians Ministers? John N. Collins. 176p. (Orig.). 1992. pap. text ed. 11.95 (0-8146-2168-6) Liturgical Pr.

Are All Italians Lousy Lovers. Costanzo Costantini. Tr. by Eugene Walter. LC 74-28697. 212p. 1975. 6.95 (0-8184-0207-5) Carol Pub Group.

Are All the Giants Dead? Mary Norton. LC 78-6622. (Illus.). 123p. (J). (gr. 3-7). 1978. pap. 9.95 (0-15-607888-0, Voyager Bks) HarBrace.

Are Americans on a Consumption Binge? The Evidence Reconsidered. Robert A. Blecker. 71p. 1990. 12.00 (0-944826-22-9) Economic Policy Inst.

Are Australian Ecosystems Different? Ed. by J. Dodson & M. Westoby. 280p. (C). 1985. text ed. 110.00 (0-685-63248-2, Pub. by Surrey Beatty & Sons AT) St Mut.

Are Blacks Spiritually Inferior to Whites? The Dispelling of an American Myth. Anthony T. Evans. 160p. (Orig.). 1992. pap. 7.95 (0-9625605-3-7) Renais Prodns.

Are Bureaucrats Different: A Study of Political Attitudes & Political Behavior. James C. Garand. (Bureaucracies, Public Administration & Public Policy Ser.). 256p. 1995. 56.95 (1-56324-160-9); pap. text ed. 23.95 (1-56324-161-7) M E Sharpe.

Are Chemicals in Drinking Water Menacing Your Health? Raymond W. Bernard. 26p. 1955. reprint ed. spiral bd. 4.95 (0-7873-1115-4) Mokelumne.

Are Clowns Hatched? Life of Chucko the Clown. Mildred M. Runyon. LC 93-80477. (Illus.). 180p. (Orig.). 1994. pap. 19.95 (1-884431-09-7) Gold Ring Pubng.

***Are Evangelicals Born Again? The Character Traits of True Faith.** rev. ed. R. Kent Hughes. LC 94-36901. 160p. 1995. reprint ed. pap. 8.99 (0-89107-798-7) Crossway Bks.

Are Families Forever? Understanding Your Family. Fran Sciacca & Jill Sciacca. (Lifelines Ser.). 64p. (YA). 1992. pap. 3.99 (0-310-48071-X) Zondervan.

Are Foreign-Owned Subsidiaries Good for the United States? Raymond Vernon. (Orig.). Date not set. pap. text ed. write for info. (1-56708-037-5) Grp of Thirty.

Are Gay Rights Right? Making Sense of the Controversy. Roger Magnuson. 149p. 1990. pap. 8.99 (0-88070-336-9, Multnomah Bks) Questar Pubs.

Are Gays Really "Gay"? A Sociological, Scientific, & Theological Analysis. Firpo W. Carr. 110p. (Orig.). Date not set. write for info. (0-9631293-0-9) ScholarTech.

Are Genes Us? The Social Consequences of the New Genetics. Ed. by Carl F. Cranor. LC 94-14617. 260p. (C). 1994. text ed. 45.00 (0-8135-2123-8); pap. text ed. 18.95 (0-8135-2124-6) Rutgers U Pr.

Are Jewish Families Different? Andrew Cherlin & Carin Celebuski. 12p. 1982. pap. 1.00 (0-686-91970-X) Am Jewish Comm.

***Are Men Born Sinners? The Myth of Original Sin.** Alfred T. Overstreet. 275p. (Orig.). 1995. pap. 19.95 (0-9644832-0-3) Evangel Bks Pub.

Are Mormons Christians? Stephen E. Robinson. 1991. 8.95 (0-88494-784-X) Bookcraft Inc.

Are Mothers Really Necessary? Bob Mullan. 224p. 1988. 60.00 (1-85283-200-2, Pub. by Boxtree Ltd UK); pap. 30.00 (1-85283-210-X, Pub. by Boxtree Ltd UK) St Mut.

Are My Children Going to Make It? Real Help for Teaching the Gospel in the Home. R. Wayne Boss & Leslee S. Boss. LC 91-15674. 244p. 1991. 13.95 (0-87579-517-X) Deseret Bk.

Are Nicaragua's Trades Free: A Response to the AIFLD Report. 5.00 (0-685-14984-6) Natl Lawyers Guild.

Are Our Kids All Right? Susan B. Dynerman. 384p. 1994. 19.95 (1-56079-334-1) Petersons Guides.

Are Policy Variables Exogenous? The Econometric Implications of Learning While Maximizing. B. Horvath. Ed. by Martin J. Beckmann & W. Krelle. (Lecture Notes in Economics & Mathematical Systems Ser.: Vol. 364). (Illus.). xii, 162p. 1991. pap. 31.00 (0-387-54287-6) Spr-Verlag.

ARE Practice Exam, Non-Graphic Divisions: A, D-F, E, G, H, I. Larry A. Paul. 120p. (Orig.). 1994. pap. 24.95 (0-912045-69-8) Prof Pubns CA.

Are Prisons Any Better: Twenty Years of Correctional Reform. Ed. by John W. Murphy & Jack E. Dison. (Criminal Justice System Annuals Ser.: Vol. 26). (Illus.). 240p. (C). 1990. 49.95 (0-8039-3569-2); pap. 24.00 (0-8039-3570-6) Sage.

Are Professors Professional? The Organisation of University Examinations. David W. Piper. LC 93-38452. (Higher Education Policy Ser.: No. 25). 252p. 1994. 60.00 (1-85302-540-2, Pub. by J Kingsley Pubs UK) Taylor & Francis.

Are Quanta Real? A Galilean Dialogue. J. M. Jauch. LC 72-79907. 130p. 1990. 24.95 (0-253-30862-3); pap. 7.95 (0-253-20545-X, MB-545) Ind U Pr.

Are Seventh-Day Adventists False Prophets? A Former Insider Speaks Out. Wallace D. Slattery. 64p. 1990. pap. 4.99 (0-87552-445-1) Presby & Reformed.

Are Southern Baptists "Evangelicals"? James L. Garrett, Jr. & E. Glenn Hinson. LC 82-18870. 247p. 1983. 14.95 (0-86554-033-0, MUP-H44) Mercer Univ Pr.

Are Takeover Targets Undervalued? An Empirical Examination of the Financial Characteristics of Target Companies. John Pound. 39p. 1986. pap. 35.00 (0-931035-54-6) IRRC Inc DC.

Are the Children Safe? Dan Cates. LC 90-55261. (Illus.). 120p. (Orig.). 1991. pap. 9.00 (1-56002-070-9) Aegina Pr.

Are the Dead Alive Now? Victor P. Wierwille. LC 82-70237. 110p. 1982. 7.95 (0-910068-40-2) Am Christian.

Are the Jews a Race? Karl Kautsky. LC 72-97288. 255p. 1972. reprint ed. text ed. 59.75 (0-8371-2609-6, KAJR, Greenwood Pr) Greenwood.

Are the New Super Sprays Endangering Your Health? Raymond W. Bernard. 48p. 1956. reprint ed. spiral bd. 4.95 (0-7873-1142-1) Mokelumne.

Are the Stars Causes? Plotinus. 1985. pap. 3.95 (0-916411-93-1, Pub. by Alexandrian Pr) Holmes Pub.

Are the Stars Out Tonight? The Story of the Famous Ambassador & Cocoanut Grove ... Hollywood's Hotel. Margaret T. Burk. (Illus.). 190p. 1980. text ed. 15.00 (0-937806-00-5) M Burk.

Are There Any Questions? Denys Cazet. LC 91-42977. (Illus.). 32p. (J). (ps-2). 1992. 15.95 (0-531-05451-9); lib. bdg. 15.99 (0-531-08601-1) Orchard Bks Watts.

Are There Better Ways to Resolve Tax Disputes, Conference on Alternative Despute Resolution. 259p. 1992. pap. text ed. 35.00 (1-56986-174-9) Federal Bar.

***Are There Diamonds in My Backyard? First Questions & Answers about the Earth.** Time-Life for Children Staff. Ed. by Sara Mark. LC 95-12423. (Time-Life Library of First Questions & Answers). (Illus.). 48p. (J). (ps-k). 1995. write for info. (0-7835-0902-2) Time-Life.

Are There Hippos on the Farm? Ethel Kessler & Leonard Kessler. (Illus.). 32p. (J). (ps-00). 1986. ring bd. 4.95 (0-671-62066-5, Litl Simon S&S) S&S Childrens.

Are There Really Tannaitic Parallels to the Gospels? A Refutation of Morton Smith. Jacob Neusner. (USF Studies in the History of Judaism). 186p. 1993. 59.95 (1-55540-867-2, 240080) Scholars Pr GA.

Are There Seals in the Sandbox? Ethel Kessler & Leonard Kessler. (Super Chubby Board Bks.). (Illus.). 24p. (J). (ps). 1990. ring bd. 4.95 (0-671-70539-3, Litl Simon S&S) S&S Childrens.

Are There Stripes in Heaven. Lee Klein. LC 94-16351. 32p. (J). 1994. pap. 4.95 (0-8091-6618-6) Paulist Pr.

Are There Too Many Lawyers? And Other Vexatious Questions. Joseph S. Fulda. xiv, 121p. (Orig.). 1993. pap. 12.95 (0-910614-84-9) Foun Econ Ed.

***Are There Two Ways of Atonement? Confronting the Controversies.** Louis Goldberg. 32p. 1990. pap. 3.95 (1-880226-05-7) Lederer Pubns.

Are These the Last Days? Robert G. Gromacki. LC 75-42165. 149p. 1970. reprint ed. pap. 4.95 (0-87227-019-X) Reg Baptist.

An Asterisk (*) at the beginning of an entry indicates that the title is appearing in BIP for the first time.

An Asterisk (*) at the beginning of an entry indicates that the title is appearing in BIP for the first time.

***Area Adjacent to the Turkey Creek Caldera, Cochise County, Arizona: Analytic Data & Geologic Sample Catalog.** Edward A. Du Bray & John S. Pallister. LC 95-15400. (Bulletins Ser., Vol. 2021: Geologic Sampling of the Chiricahua Mountains, Arizona Ser.: Ch. E). 1996. write for info. (*0-615-00733-3*) US Geol Survey.

Area & Volume. Marion Smoothey. LC 92-10579. (Let's Investigate Ser.). (Illus.). (J). 1992. 16.95 (*1-85435-460-4*) Marshall Cavendish.

Area Array, CCD, Image Sensor Products Data Book. Texas Instruments Engineering Staff. 479p. 1991. 18.95 (*0-685-62524-9*, SOCS030) Tex Instr Inc.

***Area Board Manual: Legal Responsibilities & Liabilities of Area Mental Health, Developmental Disabilities, & Substance Abuse Boards.** Mark F. Botts. (Orig.). (C). Date not set. pap. text ed. write for info. (*1-56011-247-6*, 95.16) Institute Government.

Area Classification in Hazardous, Classified, Dust Locations. rev. ed. 1988. reprint ed. pap. 30.00 (*1-55617-095-5*, S12.10) Instru Soc.

***Area Code Guide.** 60p. (Orig.). 1994. pap. 19.95 (*0-7605-0550-0*) Rector Pr.

Area Code Handbook, 1994. rev. ed. AT&T-General Staff. (Illus.). 66p. 1994. 2.95 (*0-932764-18-5*, 999-600-111) AT&T Customer Info.

Area, Development Policy, & the Middle City in Malaysia. James Osborn. LC 73-92650. (Research Papers Ser.: No. 153). (Illus.). 291p. (C). 1974. pap. 12.00 (*0-89065-060-8*) U Chicago Comm Geo.

Area di San Domenico. Barbara W. Dodsworth. LC 93-43459. (Intercultural Studies: Vol. 2). 224p. (C). 1995. text ed. 47.95 (*0-8204-2452-8*) P Lang Pubs.

Area-Efficient VLSI Computation. Charles E. Leiserson. (Association for Computing Machinery Doctoral Dissertation Award Ser.). (Illus.). 152p. 1983. pap. 32.50x (*0-262-12102-6*) MIT Pr.

Area Eighty-Eight. Kaoru Shintani. Ed. by Seiji Horibuchi. Tr. by James D. Hudnall & Satoru Fujii. (Illus.). 200p. (Orig.). 1991. pap. 12.95 (*0-929279-44-1*) Viz Commns Inc.

Area Handbook for the Republic of Tunisia see Tunisia: A Country Study

Area Labor - Management Committees. Rita Bosek. Ed. by Juyne Linger. 8p. (Orig.). 1977. pap. 8.00 (*0-317-04918-6*) Natl Coun Econ Dev.

Area Lighting: Solar Electric Area Lighting. David Arrowood & William Cirrito. 144p. 1993. 49.95 (*0-9636559-0-6*) Photocomm.

Area Maintenance Technician (USPS) Jack Rudman. (Career Examination Ser.: C-3429). 1994. pap. 29.95 (*0-8373-3429-2*) Nat Learn.

Area of Darkness. V. S. Naipaul. 1993. 20.50 (*0-8446-6680-7*) Peter Smith.

Area of Darkness. V. S. Naipaul. 288p. 1992. pap. 10.00 (*0-14-002895-1*, Penguin Bks) Viking Penguin.

Area of Suspicion. John D. MacDonald. 208p. 1986. pap. 3.95 (*0-449-13099-1*, GM) Fawcett.

Area Services Coordinator. Jack Rudman. (Career Examination Ser.: C-18). 1994. pap. 34.95 (*0-8373-0018-5*) Nat Learn.

Area-Stratified Regional Econometric Model. Norman J. Glickman. (Discussion Paper Ser.: No. 58). 1972. pap. 10.00 (*1-55869-010-7*) Regional Sci Res Inst.

***Area under Vines Second Basic Community Survey - Main Results.** European Communities Staff. 406p. 1994. pap. 45.00 (*92-826-7431-2*, CA82-94-505-2AC, Pub. by Europ Com) UNIPUB.

Areal-Typological Study of American Indian Languages North of Mexico. J. Sherzer. (North-Holland Linguistic Ser.: Vol. 20). 1976. pap. 31.00 (*0-444-10911-0*, North Holland) Elsevier.

Areas for Growth: A Drama Approach to PSE. Jerome Hanratty. LC 94-9924. 1994. pap. 49.95 (*0-521-46910-4*) Cambridge U Pr.

Areas of Cooperation in Library Development in Asian & Pacific Regions. Ed. by Sally C. Tseng et al. LC 84-71838. 90p. 1985. pap. 10.00 (*0-930691-00-8*) Chinese Lib.

Areas under Vines Results of the Annual Surveys: 1979-1990. Eurostat Staff. 220p. 1992. pap. 45.00 (*92-826-4871-0*, CA-76-92-358-EN-C, Pub. by Europ Com) UNIPUB.

Areawide Planning for Independent Living for Older People. Southern Conference on Gerontology Staff. LC 73-8869. (Center for Gerontological Studies & Programs Ser.: No. 22). 152p. reprint ed. pap. 43.40 (*0-7837-4895-7*, 2044560) Bks Demand.

Arecaceae, Pt. I: Introduction & the Iriarteinae. Andrew Henderson. (Flora Neotropica Monograph Ser.: No. 53). (Illus.). 104p. 1990. pap. text ed. 22.00 (*0-89327-353-8*) NY Botanical.

***Arena.** John G. Abeln. 350p. 1995. pap. 9.95 (*1-56901-759-X*) NW Pub.

Arena. Ignatius Brianchianinov. Tr. by Archimandrite Lazarus Moore. 300p. (Orig.). 1982. 15.00 (*0-88465-009-X*); pap. 12.00 (*0-88465-011-1*) Holy Trinity.

Arena. Bruce Jones. 48p. 1989. 5.95 (*0-87135-557-4*) Marvel Entmnt.

Arena. Dennis Phillips. (New American Poetry Ser.: No. 10). 137p. (Orig.). 1991. pap. 10.95 (*1-55713-127-9*) Sun & Moon CA.

Arena. John Preston. (Orig.). 1993. pap. 4.95 (*1-56333-083-0*) Masquerade.

Arena. Shmarya Levin. Tr. by Maurice Samuel. LC 74-27999. (Modern Jewish Experience Ser.). (ENG.). 1975. reprint ed. 28.95 (*0-405-06726-7*) Ayer.

Arena: The History of the Federal Theatre. Hallie Flanagan. LC 65-23693. (Illus.). 1972. reprint ed. 35.95 (*0-405-08521-4*, Pub. by Blom Pubns UK) Ayer.

Arena Adventure: The First Forty Years. Ed. by Laurence Maslon. 108p. (Orig.). 1990. pap. 24.95 (*1-55783-092-4*) Applause Theatre Bk Pubs.

***Arena Ball: The Building of Virginia's Soccer Dynasty - Collector's Edition.** limited ed. Robert Daniels. (Illus.). 128p. 1994. 30.00 (*1-885758-01-4*) Quality Sports.

Arena Beach. Donna Staples. LC 92-36302. (YA). 1993. 14.95 (*0-395-65366-5*) HM.

Arena Birds: Sexual Selection & Behavior. Paul A. Johnsgard. LC 93-8131. (Illus.). 384p. 1994. 39.95 (*1-56098-315-9*) Smithsonian.

Arena of Greed: The Great Chicago Commodity Market Scam. William E. Fitzgerald. 535p. 1990. 24.95 (*0-9627407-0-5*) DeVin Pubs.

Arena of International Finance. Charles A. Coombs. LC 76-19093. (Illus.). 263p. reprint ed. pap. 75.00 (*0-8357-5728-5*, 2016463) Bks Demand.

Arena of Jerusalem. Ivan Schwebel. LC 86-3570. (Illus.). 1987. 39.95 (*0-915361-43-4*) Modan-Adama Bks.

Arena of Khazan. Ken St. Andre. (Illus.). 1979. 5.95 (*0-940244-12-8*) Flying Buffalo.

Arena of Masculinity: Sports, Homosexuality, & the Meaning of Sex. Brian Pronger. (Stonewall Inn Editions Ser.). (Illus.). 320p. 1992. pap. 14.95 (*0-312-06293-1*) St Martin.

Arena of Masculinity; Sports: Sports, Homosexuality, & the Meaning of Sex. Brian Pronger. 1990. 22.95 (*0-312-05053-4*) St Martin.

Arena Theatre: Dimensions for the Space Age. Edwin M. Grove. LC 87-50838. 143p. 1989. 16.00 (*0-87875-344-3*) Whitston Pub.

***Arena Warriors.** Jennifer DiMarco. (Illus.). 8p. (Orig.). 1995. pap. 9.00 (*1-886383-04-9*) Pride OH.

Arenas of Language Use. Herbert H. Clark. LC 92-38874. 440p. (C). 1993. lib. bdg. 47.50 (*0-226-10781-7*); pap. text ed. 19.95 (*0-226-10782-5*) U Ch Pr.

Arenas of the Mind: Critical Reading for Writing. Lillian Back & Merla Wolk. LC 92-18244. (C). 1992. 18.00 (*0-673-46312-5*) HarpCollege.

Arenas, Stages & Spaces: A Guide to Theatres in Chicago & Vicinity. Bruce Mays & Cynthis Maltbie. (Illus.). 117p. (Orig.). 1982. pap. 6.95 (*0-941906-00-0*) Diversity Pr.

Arenaviridae. Ed. by M. S. Salvato. (Viruses Ser.). (Illus.). 426p. (C). 1993. 85.00 (*0-306-44272-8*, Plenum Pr) Plenum.

Arenaviruses: Perspectives in Medical Virology, Vol. 2. C. R. Howard. 266p. 1986. 132.50 (*0-444-80715-2*) Elsevier.

***Arendt & Heidegger: The Fate of the Political.** Dana R. Villa. LC 95-13293. 1995. write for info. (*0-691-04401-5*); pap. write for info. (*0-691-04400-7*) Princeton U Pr.

Arendt, Camus, & Modern Rebellion. Jeffrey C. Isaac. LC 92-8593. 304p. (C). 1992. text ed. 35.00 (*0-300-05203-0*) Yale U Pr.

Arendt, Camus, & Modern Rebellion. Jeffrey C. Isaac. 304p. 1994. pap. 16.00 (*0-300-06054-8*) Yale U Pr.

Aren't You Coming Too? Eve Rice. LC 86-33506. (Illus.). 32p. (J). (ps-3). 1988. 11.95 (*0-688-06446-9*); lib. bdg. 11.88 (*0-688-06447-7*) Greenwillow.

Aren't You Forgetting Something, Fiona? (Parents Magazine Press Read-Aloud Library). (J). 1994. 14.60 (*0-8368-0981-5*) Gareth Stevens Inc.

Aren't You Forgetting Something, Fiona? Joanna Cole. LC 83-13457. (Illus.). 48p. (J). (ps-3). 1984. 5.95 (*0-8193-1121-9*) Parents.

Areography: Geographical Strategies of Species. Eduardo H. Rapoport. (Publications of Fundacion Bariloche: Vol. 1). (Illus.). 250p. 1982. 120.00 (*0-08-028914-2*, G135, H110, Pub. by Pergamon Repr UK) Franklin.

Areopagatica. John Milton. 80p. 1972. reprint ed. 15.00 (*0-87556-219-1*) Saifer.

Areopagitica. John Milton. Ed. by Richard C. Jebb. LC 72-170811. reprint ed. 22.50 (*0-404-03556-6*) AMS Pr.

Areopagitica: Freedom of the Press. rev. ed. John Milton. Ed. by A. S. Ash. LC 86-64056. (Humanist Classics Ser.). Orig. Title: Areopagitica. 48p. 1990. pap. 4.00 (*0-942208-04-8*) Bandanna Bks.

Areopagitica see Areopagitica: Freedom of the Press

Areopagitica & Of Education. John Milton. Ed. by George H. Sabine. (Crofts Classics Ser.). 128p. 1951. pap. text ed. write for info. (*0-88295-057-6*) Harlan Davidson.

Areopagos Council, to Three Hundred Seven B. C. Robert W. Wallace. LC 88-9397. 320p. 1989. text ed. 42.50 (*0-8018-3646-8*) Johns Hopkins.

Arete: Ancient Writers, Papyri, & Inscriptions on the History & Ideals of Greek Athletics & Games. S. Miller. 120p. 1979. pap. 12.50 (*0-89005-313-8*) Ares.

Arete: Greek Sports from Ancient Sources. Stephen G. Miller. LC 90-28646. (Illus.). 239p. 1991. 40.00 (*0-520-07508-0*); pap. 15.00 (*0-520-07509-9*) U CA Pr.

***Aretha Franklin: Lady Soul.** Leslie Gourse. LC 94-29074. (Impact Biographies Ser.). (Illus.). 160p. (YA). (gr. 7-12). 1995. lib. bdg. 15.47 (*0-531-13037-1*) Watts.

***Aretha Franklin: Lady Soul.** Leslie Gourse. (Impact Biographies Ser.). (Illus.). 160p. (YA). (gr. 7-12). 1995. pap. 8.00 (*0-614-07257-3*) Watts.

Aretha Franklin: The Queen of Soul. Mark Bego. 1989. 18.95 (*0-312-02863-6*) St Martin.

Aretino's Dialogues. Pietro Aretino. Tr. by Raymond Rosenthal. 420p. 1994. pap. 16.95 (*0-941419-96-7*) Marsilio Pubs.

ARexx: "Some Issues in Programming" Jere M. Marrs. LC 93-186535. 164p. 1993. pap. text ed. 30.00 (*0-9636575-0-X*) Tech Res NW.

ARexx Cookbook: A Tutorial Guide to the ARexx Language on the Commodore Amiga Personal Computer. Merrill Callaway. LC 92-81371. (Illus.). 251p. (Orig.). 1992. pap. 24.95 (*0-9632773-0-8*); disk, pap. 49.95 (*0-9632773-2-4*); disk 9.95 (*0-9632773-1-6*) Whitestone NM.

ARexx from the Beginning: A Self-Study Workbook. Jere M. Marrs. 200p. (Orig.). 1994. pap. text ed. 20.00 (*0-9636575-1-8*) Tech Res NW.

Argal: Or, the Silver Devil, 2 vols. in one. George Hadley. Ed. by R. Reginald & Douglas Menville. LC 76-1461. (Supernatural & Occult Fiction Ser.). 1976. reprint ed. lib. bdg. 35.95 (*0-405-08420-X*) Ayer.

***Argalis.** deluxe limited ed. R. Medem. (Illus.). 304p. 1994. boxed 150.00 (*1-57157-027-6*) Safari Pr.

Argalus & Parthenia. Francis Quarles. Ed. by David Freeman. LC 86-45041. (Renaissance English Text Society Ser.: Series 6, No. 11). (Illus.). 240p. 1987. 30.00 (*0-918016-90-8*) Folger Bks.

Argent. Charles Peguy. 252p. (FRE.). 1932. pap. 34.95 (*0-7859-1292-4*, 2070249743) Fr & Eur.

Argent. Emile Zola. (FRE.). 1975. pap. 11.95 (*0-7859-2970-3*) Fr & Eur.

Argent. Emile Zola. (Folio Ser.: No. 1222). (FRE.). 1975. 12.95 (*2-07-037222-7*) Schoenhof.

Argent. Emile Zola. (FRE.). 1980. pap. 13.95 (*0-7859-1634-2*, 2070372227) Fr & Eur.

Argent: Last of the Swamp Rats. Mallory H. Ferrell. Ed. by Pacific Fast Mail Staff. (Illus.). 144p. 1994. write for info. (*0-915713-27-6*) Pac Fast Mail.

Argent, la Sexualite et le Pou. Richard J. Foster. 240p. (FRE.). 1990. 9.95 (*0-8297-1432-4*) Life Pubs Intl.

Argentina. Alan Biggins. (World Bibliographical Ser.). 1991. lib. bdg. 112.50 (*1-85109-109-2*) ABC-CLIO.

Argentina. Dominique Bona. 374p. (FRE.). 1986. pap. 12.95 (*0-7859-2034-X*, 2070377342) Fr & Eur.

Argentina. Nicholas Caistor. LC 91-7215. (World in View Ser.). (Illus.). 96p. (YA). (gr. 6-11). 1991. lib. bdg. 24.26 (*0-8114-2443-X*) Raintree Steck-V.

Argentina. Marcelo Cavarozzi. 1996. text ed. 30.00 (*0-8133-0343-5*) Westview.

Argentina. Ethel C. Gofen. LC 90-23159. (Cultures of the World Ser.: Group 2: Latin America). (Illus.). 128p. (YA). (gr. 5-9). 1991. lib. bdg. 21.95 (*1-85435-381-0*) Marshall Cavendish.

Argentina. Martin Hintz. LC 85-2638. (Enchantment of the World Ser.). (Illus.). 127p. (J). (gr. 4-6). 1985. lib. bdg. 20.55 (*0-516-02752-2*) Childrens.

Argentina. Karen Jacobsen. LC 90-36526. (New True Bks.). (Illus.). 48p. (J). (gr. k-4). 1990. lib. bdg. 12.90 (*0-516-01101-4*); pap. 4.95 (*0-516-41101-2*) Childrens.

Argentina. Sol Liebowitz. (Let's Visit Places & Peoples of the World Ser.). (Illus.). 128p. (J). (gr. 5 up). 1990. 14.95 (*0-7910-1106-2*) Chelsea Hse.

Argentina. Marion Morrison. (People & Places Ser.). (Illus.). 48p. (J). (gr. 4-8). 1989. lib. bdg. 12.95 (*0-382-09793-9*) Silver Burdett Pr.

Argentina. G. Pendle. 1976. lib. bdg. 59.95 (*0-8490-1448-4*) Gordon Pr.

Argentina. Rosa Q. Mesa. LC 73-180800. (Latin American Serial Documents Ser.: Vol. 5). 726p. reprint ed. pap. 180.00 (*0-8357-5729-3*, 2013547) Bks Demand.

Argentina: A City & a Nation. James R. Scobie. (Latin American Histories Ser). (C). 1971. pap. text ed. 15.95 (*0-19-501480-4*) OUP.

Argentina: A Nation at the Crossroads of Myth & Reality. Ricardo Zinn. 15.95 (*0-8315-0179-0*); pap. 5.95 (*0-8315-0180-4*) Speller.

Argentina: A Study of the Educational System & a Guide to the Placement of Students in Educational Institutions in the United States. Liz A. Reisberg. (World Education Ser.). (Illus.). 150p. 1993. pap. text ed. 45.00 (*0-929851-17-X*) Am Assn Coll Registrars.

Argentina: A Wild West Heritage. Marge Peterson & Rob Peterson. LC 89-11707. (Discovering Our Heritage Ser.). (Illus.). 128p. (J). (gr. 5 up). 1990. text ed. 14.95 (*0-87518-413-8*, Dillon Silver Burdett) Silver Burdett Pr.

***Argentina: Business Financing Handbook.** (Illus.). 70p. (Orig.). 1994. pap. 295.00 (*0-7605-1179-9*) Rector Pr.

Argentina: Business Risk Overview. Ed. by Lewis B. Sckolnick. 125p. (Orig.). (C). 1994. pap. text ed. 495.00 (*1-57205-566-9*) Rector Pr.

***Argentina: Commercial Law.** 300p. (Orig.). 1994. pap. 295.00 (*0-7605-1223-X*) Rector Pr.

Argentina: Country Reporter. Lewis B. Sckolnick. (Illus.). 60p. 1994. pap. 895.00 (*1-57205-173-6*) Rector Pr.

Argentina: Foreign Financing Reporter. Ed. by Lewis B. Sckolnick. (Illus.). 60p. (Orig.). 1994. pap. 225.00 (*1-57205-234-1*) Rector Pr.

Argentina: From Insolvency to Growth. LC 93-4348. (Country Study Ser.). 382p. 1993. write for info. (*0-8213-2463-2*, 12463) World Bank.

Argentina: Illusions & Realities. 2nd rev. ed. Gary W. Wynia. LC 86-9839. 290p. 1992. 18.95 (*0-8419-1296-3*) Holmes & Meier.

Argentina: In the Hour of the Furnaces. (Illus.). 105p. 1974. pap. 3.00 (*0-916024-08-3*) NA Cong Lat Am.

Argentina: Political Culture & Instability. Susan Calvert & Peter Calvert. LC 89-40048. (Illus.). 342p. 1991. pap. 19.95 (*0-8229-6097-4*) U of Pittsburgh Pr.

Argentina: Provincial Government Finances. (Country Study Ser.). 244p. 1990. 13.95 (*0-8213-1634-6*, 11634) World Bank.

Argentina: Provincial Government Finances. (Country Study Ser.). (SPA.). 1991. 13.95 (*0-8213-1762-8*, 11762) World Bank.

Argentina: Reallocating Resources for the Improvement of Education. (Country Study Ser.). 102p. 1991. 7.95 (*0-8213-1752-0*, 11752) World Bank.

Argentina: Reasignacion De los Recursos Para el Mejorimiento De la Educacion. (Country Study Ser.). 102p. (SPA.). 1991. 7.95 (*0-8213-1753-9*, 11753) World Bank.

Argentina: Tax Policy for Stabilization & Economic Recovery. (Country Study Ser.). 164p. (ENG & SPA.). 1990. English. 10.95 (*0-8213-1541-2*, 11541); Spanish. 10.95 (*0-8213-1542-0*, 11542) World Bank.

Argentina: The Economic Crisis in the 1980s. Berhard Fischer. 112p. 1985. lib. bdg. 44.00 (*3-16-345017-2*, Pub. by J C B Mohr GW) Coronet Bks.

***Argentina: The Great Estancias.** Thomas de Elia et al. LC 95-8168. (Illus.). 228p. 1995. 60.00 (*0-8478-1905-1*) Rizzoli Intl.

Argentina: The Malvinas & the End of Military Rule. Alejandro Dabat & Luis Lorenzano. Tr. by Ralph Johnstone. 205p. 1984. text ed. 39.95 (*0-86091-085-7*, Pub. by Verso UK); pap. text ed. 14.95 (*0-86091-790-8*, Pub. by Verso UK) Routledge Chapman & Hall.

Argentina: The Military Junta & Human Rights. Amnesty International Staff. 99p. (Orig.). 1987. pap. 5.00 (*0-939994-34-8*, Pub. by Amnesty Intl Pubns UK) Amnesty Intl USA.

Argentina: Trade, Licensing & Investing Rules & Regulations. Ed. by Lewis B. Sckolnick. (Illus.). 80p. (Orig.). (C). 1994. pap. 225.00 (*1-57205-051-9*) Rector Pr.

Argentina & Her People of Today. N. Winter. 1976. lib. bdg. 69.95 (*0-8490-1449-2*) Gordon Pr.

Argentina & Its Human Rights. 1982. lib. bdg. 69.95 (*0-8490-3224-5*) Gordon Pr.

Argentina & Peron: 1970-75. Ed. by Lester A. Sobel. LC 75-20835. (Interim History Ser.). 175p. reprint ed. pap. 49.90 (*0-8357-5730-7*, 2022895) Bks Demand.

Argentina & the Failure of Democracy: Conflict among Political Elites, 1904-1955. Peter H. Smith. LC 74-5907. (Illus.). 239p. reprint ed. pap. 68.20 (*0-8357-6025-1*, 2034272) Bks Demand.

Argentina & the Jews: A History of Jewish Immigration. Haim Avni. (Judaic Studies Ser.). 288p. 1991. 32.95 (*0-8173-0554-8*) U of Ala Pr.

Argentina & the United States. Clarence H. Haring. LC 83-45779. 77p. (C). 1984. reprint ed. text ed. 49.75 (*0-313-24431-6*, HARG, Greenwood Pr) Greenwood.

Argentina & the United States: A Conflicted Relationship. Joseph S. Tulchin. (Twayne's International History Ser.: No. 5). 224p. (C). 1990. pap. 14.95 (*0-8057-9204-X*, Twayne) Macmillan.

Argentina & the United States: A Conflicted Relationship. Joseph S. Tulchin. Ed. by Akira Iriye. (Twayne's International History Ser.: No. 5). (Illus.). 1990. text ed. 26.95 (*0-8057-7900-0*, 576, Twayne) Macmillan.

Argentina & Uruguay. Gordon Ross. 1976. lib. bdg. 59.95 (*0-87968-655-3*) Gordon Pr.

Argentina Between the Great Powers, 1936-46. Ed. by Guido Di Tella & D. Cameron Watt. LC 89-49237. (Latin American Ser.). 226p. 1990. 49.95 (*0-8229-1159-0*) U of Pittsburgh Pr.

Argentina Business Forecaster. Ed. by Lewis B. Sckolnick. 70p. (Orig.). (C). 1994. pap. 675.00 (*1-57205-365-8*) Rector Pr.

***Argentina Business Intelligence Handbook.** (Illus.). 70p. (Orig.). 1994. pap. 295.00 (*0-7605-1068-7*) Rector Pr.

***Argentina Business Risk Outlook.** 70p. (Orig.). 1994. pap. 495.00 (*0-7605-1381-3*) Rector Pr.

***Argentina Commercial Law.** 150p. (C). 1994. pap. 295.00 (*0-7605-0069-X*) Rector Pr.

Argentina Company Handbook, 1993. Ed. by IMF Editora Staff. 76p. 1995. pap. 29.95 (*1-878753-38-X*) Ref Press.

Argentina Confronts Politics: Political Culture & Public Opinion in the Argentine Transition to Democracy. Edgardo Catterberg. LC 90-42450. 136p. 1991. lib. bdg. 30.00 (*1-55587-248-4*) Lynne Rienner.

Argentina from Anarchism to Peronism: Workers, Unions & Politics, 1855-1985. Ronaldo Munck et al. (Illus.). 276p. (C). 1987. text ed. 45.00 (*0-86232-570-6*, Pub. by Zed Books UK); pap. 17.50 (*0-86232-571-4*, Pub. by Zed Books UK) Humanities.

Argentina in Pictures. Ed. by Lerner Publications, Department of Geography Staff. (Visual Geography Ser.). (Illus.). 64p. (YA). (gr. 5 up). 1988. lib. bdg. 18.95 (*0-8225-1807-4*, Lerner Publctns) Lerner Group.

Argentina, Nineteen Forty-Six to Eighty-Three: The Economic Ministers Speak. Guido Di Tella & Carlos R. Braun. LC 89-48069. 270p. 1990. text ed. 65.00 (*0-312-03620-5*) St Martin.

Argentina since Independence. Ed. by Leslie Bethell. LC 92-26994. (Illus.). 300p. (C). 1993. 59.95 (*0-521-43376-2*) Cambridge U Pr.

Argentina since Independence. Ed. by Leslie Bethell. LC 92-26994. (Illus.). 300p. (C). 1993. pap. 18.95 (*0-521-43988-4*) Cambridge U Pr.

***Argentina Tax Law.** 150p. (C). 1994. pap. 295.00 (*0-7605-0068-1*) Rector Pr.

Argentina, Uruguay & Paraguay: A Travel Survival Kit. Wayne Bernhardson & Maria Massolo. (Illus.). 616p. (Orig.). 1992. pap. 16.95 (*0-86442-140-0*) Lonely Planet.

Argentina's Capitalist Revolution Revisited: Confronting the Social Costs of Statist Mistakes. William Ratliff & Roger Fontaine. LC 93-28402. (Essays in Public Policy Ser.: No. 41). 55p. 1993. pap. 5.00 (*0-8179-5462-7*) Hoover Inst Pr.

Argentina's "Dirty War" An Intellectual Biography. Donald C. Hodges. 407p. 1991. 42.50 (*0-292-70423-2*) U of Tex Pr.

***Argentina's Lost Patrol: Armed Struggle, 1969-1979.** Maria J. Moyano. LC 94-35509. 1995. 25.00 (*0-300-06122-6*) Yale U Pr.

Argentina's Privatization Program. World Bank Staff. LC 93-31978. (Development in Practice Ser.). 44p. 1993. 6.95 (*0-8213-2586-8*, 12586) World Bank.

Argentine. Hugo Miatello. 1976. lib. bdg. 35.00 (*0-87968-656-1*) Gordon Pr.

Argentine Anarchism & La Protesta. Fernando Quesada. 1975. lib. bdg. 250.00 (*0-87968-657-X*) Gordon Pr.

Argentine Crisis. Oscar Camilion. (Critical Issues 1990 Ser.: No. 4). 32p. 1990. pap. 4.95 (*0-87609-092-7*) Coun Foreign.

An Asterisk (*) at the beginning of an entry indicates that the title is appearing in BIP for the first time.

An Asterisk (*) at the beginning of an entry indicates that the title is appearing in BIP for the first time.

A

Argus de l'Autographe et du Manuscrit. Argus. 130p. (FRE.). 1992. 125.00 (*0-8288-7226-0*, 2765404984) Fr & Eur.

Argus du Livre de Collection: Repertoire Bibliographique, 1992. Argus. 852p. (FRE.). 1992. 350.00 (*0-8288-7225-2*, 2765404976) Fr & Eur.

Argus Guide to Antiques. Y. Gairaud. 512p. (FRE.). 1992. 150.00 (*0-8288-7306-2*, 2859170464) Fr & Eur.

Argus Guide to Doll Collecting. F. Theimer. 260p. (FRE.). 1992. 125.00 (*0-8288-7310-0*, 2859170316) Fr & Eur.

Argus Guide to Primitive Art. R. Wilhelem. 304p. (FRE.). 1992. 150.00 (*0-8288-7307-0*, 2859170413) Fr & Eur.

Argus Guide to Regional Furniture. Y. Gairaud. 304p. (FRE.). 1992. 150.00 (*0-8288-7308-9*, 2859170898) Fr & Eur.

Argus Guide to Toys. F. Theimer. 280p. (FRE.). 1991. 150.00 (*0-8288-7309-7*, 2859171045) Fr & Eur.

Argus Leader South Dakota 99. Argus Leader of Sioux Falls Staff. LC 89-7713. (Illus.). 280p. 1989. 29.99 (*0-944287-05-0*); 39.99 (*0-944287-06-9*) Ex Machina.

Argus Leader South Dakota 99. deluxe ed. Argus Leader of Sioux Falls Staff. LC 89-7713. (Illus.). 280p. 1989. pap. 19.99 (*0-944287-04-2*) Ex Machina.

Argy Rousseau. Janine Bloch-Dermant. LC 91-65285. (Illus.). 248p. 1991. 85.00 (*0-500-23626-7*) Thames Hudson.

Argyle. Brooks B. Wallace. LC 91-76021. (Illus.). 32p. (J). (ps-3). 1992. 13.95 (*1-56397-043-0*) Boyds Mills Pr.

Argyle Patent: And Accompanying Documents. Jennie M. Patten. 68p. 1991. reprint ed. pap. 9.00 (*0-685-60412-8*, 4520) Clearfield Co.

Argyll - Mid Argyll & Cowal, Vol. 7: Medieval & Later Monuments. 628p. 1992. 280.00 (*0-11-494094-0*, HM40940, Pub. by HMSO UK) UNIPUB.

Argyll: An Inventory of the Monuments: Mid Argyll & Cowal: Prehistoric & Early Historic Monuments, Vol. 6. (Royal Commission on the Ancient & Historical Monuments of Scotland Ser.). (Illus.). 228p. 1988. 130.00 (*0-11-493384-7*, HM4078, Pub. by HMSO UK) UNIPUB.

Arhats in China & Japan. Marinus W. De Visser. LC 78-70136. reprint ed. 27.50 (*0-404-17406-X*) AMS Pr.

Aria. Peter Elbing. (Illus.). 32p. (J). 1994. 13.99 (*0-670-85062-4*) Viking Child Bks.

Aria. Lydia Raurell. 12p. (Orig.). 1975. pap. 1.00 (*0-934776-01-6*) Bard Pr.

Aria: The Knights of Aquarius. M. Weyland. Tr. by Chris Tanz & Jean-Paul Bierny. (Illus.). 48p. 1987. reprint ed. pap. 12.95 (*0-89865-508-0*, Starblaze) Donning Co.

Aria Barocca: Medium High Voice. John G. Paton. 110p. (Orig.). 1986. pap. text ed. 8.95 (*0-9602296-5-5*) Leyerle Pubns.

Aria Barocca: Medium Low Voice. John G. Paton. 110p. 1987. pap. text ed. 8.95 (*0-9602296-7-1*) Leyerle Pubns.

Aria Takes off. 2nd ed. M. Weyland. Ed. by Kay Reynolds. Tr. by Chris Tanz & Jean-Paul Bierny. (Aria Ser.). (Illus.). 56p. 1986. reprint ed. 6.95 (*0-89865-468-8*, Starblaze) Donning Co.

Ariadne. Robert Kelly. 24p. 1991. pap. 4.00 (*0-685-56985-3*) St Lazaire.

Ariadne. Batya Podos. LC 80-70233. 52p. (Orig.). 1980. pap. 3.00 (*0-9603628-2-7*) Frog in Well.

Ariadne: A Tragedy in Five Acts. Thomas Corneille. Tr. by Oscar Mandel. LC 80-24597. (Illus.). 95p. reprint ed. pap. 27.10 (*0-7837-4948-1*, 2044614) Bks Demand.

Ariadne auf Naxos: Gotha, Seventeen Seventy-Five. Georg A. Benda. Ed. by Thomas Bauman. Bd. with Ino: Leipzig, Seventeen Seventy-Nine. (German Opera Ser., 1770-1800: Vol. 4). 315p. 1986. Set lib. bdg. 15.00 (*0-8240-8853-0*) Garland.

Ariadne auf Naxos see Alceste

Ariadne Auf Naxos of Hugo von Hofmannsthal & Richard Strauss. Donald G. Daviau & George J. Buelow. LC 74-14835. (University of North Carolina Studies in Comparative Literature: No. 80). 282p. reprint ed. pap. 80.40 (*0-7837-2074-2*, 2042348) Bks Demand.

Ariadne, Awake! Doris Orgel. LC 93-24123. (Illus.). 80p. (J). (ps-3). 1994. lib. bdg. 15.99 (*0-670-85158-2*) Viking Child Bks.

***Ariadne's Lives.** Nina D. Nichols. LC 94-31366. 1995. write for info. (*0-8386-3582-2*) Fairleigh Dickinson.

Ariadne's Thread. Susan Bassnett. LC 88-80462. 1988. pap. 16.95 (*0-948259-40-X*) Dufour.

Ariadne's Thread: A Workbook of Goddess Magic. Shekhinah Mountainwater. 250p. (Orig.). 1991. pap. 14.95 (*0-89594-475-8*) Crossing Pr.

Ariadne's Thread: Essays in History & Philosophy. Joseph A. Schufle. (Illus.). x, 306p. (C). 1989. 45.00 (*0-945407-03-3*) Meadow Pr NM.

Ariadne's Thread: In Search of a Greener Future. Mary E. Clark. 400p. 1989. pap. 24.95 (*0-312-01586-0*) St Martin.

Ariadne's Thread: Story Lines. J. Hillis Miller. 320p. (C). 1992. text ed. 37.50x (*0-300-05216-2*) Yale U Pr.

Arian Controversy. Henry M. Gwatkin. LC 77-84702. reprint ed. 34.00 (*0-404-16109-X*) AMS Pr.

***Arian Debate.** Augustine of Hippo. Ed. by John E. Rotelle. Tr. & Pref. by Roland J. Teske. (Works of Saint Augustine). 520p. 1995. 39.00 (*1-56548-038-4*) New City.

Ariana. Edward Stewart. 1992. mass mkt. 4.99 (*0-440-21207-3*) Dell.

Ariana Olisvos: Her Last Works & Days. David Dwyer. LC 76-8752. 80p. 1976. lib. bdg. 15.00 (*0-87023-218-5*) U of Mass Pr.

Ariane. Gabrielle DuPre. 1988. pap. 4.50 (*0-317-67195-2*) St Martin.

Ariane & Bluebeard (Adapted from the Opera) Russell. (Illus.). 1990. pap. 3.95 (*0-913035-71-8*) Eclipse Bks.

Ariane Mnouchkine & the Theatre du Soleil. Adrian Kiernander. LC 92-32954. (Directors in Perspective Ser.). (Illus.). 212p. (C). 1993. 59.95 (*0-521-36139-7*) Cambridge U Pr.

Arianism: Historical & Theological Reassessments. Ed. & Intro. by Robert C. Gregg. LC 85-81654. (Patristic Monograph: No. 11). viii, 380p. 1985. pap. 12.00 (*0-915646-10-2*) N Amer Patristic Soc.

***Arianism after Arius: Essays on the Development of the 4th Century Trinitarian Conflicts.** Ed. by Michel R. Barnes & Daniel H. Williams. 280p. 1993. text ed. 39.95 (*0-567-09641-6*, Pub. by T & T Clark UK) Bks Intl VA.

Arianrhod, a Welsh Myth Retold. Barbara Donley. LC 87-90724. (Illus.). 136p. (Orig.). 1987. pap. 10.00 (*0-9618699-1-7*) Stone Circle.

Arias in Silence. Gordon Parks. LC 93-47352. (Illus.). 128p. 1994. 40.00 (*0-8212-2120-5*) Bulfinch Pr.

Aric Database Initialization Book, Vol. 1. Mary Bahr-Jones. Ed. by M. James Bahr. (Aric Nursing Database Management System Ser.). (Illus.). 98p. 1991. write for info. (*1-879115-00-X*) J Bahr Assocs.

Aric Reports Generation Book, Vol. 1. Bahr, James, Associates Staff. (Illus.). 166p. 1991. write for info. (*0-318-68309-1*) J Bahr Assocs.

Arid & Semi-Arid Lands: A Preview. 63p. 1967. 0.75 (*0-318-14551-0*, 1) Intl Ctr Arid & Semi-Arid.

Arid & Semiarid Rangelands: Guidelines for Development. R. Dennis Child et al. Ed. by R. Katherine Jones. (Illus.). 291p. 1987. per. 11.50 (*0-933595-08-5*) Winrock Intl.

Arid Australia. Ed. by H. G. Cogger & E. E. Cameron. 338p. (C). 1989. text ed. 75.00 (*0-7305-0222-8*, Pub. by Surrey Beatty & Sons AT) St Mut.

Arid Domain. William S. Greever. Ed. by Stuart Bruchey. LC 78-56663. (Management of Public Lands in the U. S. Ser.). (Illus.). 1979. reprint ed. lib. bdg. 17.95 (*0-405-11334-X*) Ayer.

Arid-Land Ecosystems: Structure, Functioning & Management, Vol. 2. Ed. by D. W. Goodall & R. A. Perry. LC 77-84810. (International Biological Programme Ser.: No. 17). 550p. 1981. 180.00 (*0-521-22988-X*) Cambridge U Pr.

Arid Land Plant Resources. Ed. by J. R. Goodin & David K. Northington. 724p. 1979. 15.00 (*0-318-14552-9*, 79-1) Intl Ctr Arid & Semi-Arid.

Arid-Lands Research Institutions: A World Directory, 1977. Ed. by Patricia Paylore. LC 67-20092. 317p. 1977. pap. 17.95 (*0-8165-0631-0*) U of Ariz Pr.

***Arid Shrubland Plants of Western Australia.** Andrew Mitchell & David Wilcox. Date not set. 55.00 (*1-875560-47-5*, Pub. by Univ of West Aust Pr AT); pap. 45.00 (*1-875560-22-X*, Pub. by Univ of West Aust Pr AT) Intl Spec Bk.

Arid Shrublands: Proceedings US-Australia Workshop No. 3. Ed. by D. Hyder. 148p. 3.00 (*0-318-16597-X*) Soc Range Mgmt.

Arid Waters: Photographs from the Water in the West Project. Ed. by Peter Goin. LC 92-20023. (Illus.). 104p. (C). 1992. pap. 17.95 (*0-87417-199-7*) U of Nev Pr.

Arid Zone Geomorphology. Ed. by David S. Thomas. 1989. text ed. 75.95 (*0-470-21341-8*) Halsted Pr.

Arid Zone Geomorphology. David S. Thomas. 382p. (C). 1991. 850.00 (*81-7089-139-6*, Pub. by Intl Bk Distr II) St Mut.

Arid Zone Research & Development. H. S. Mann. 531p. 1980. 300.00 (*0-317-62029-0*, Scientific) St Mut.

Arid Zone Research & Development: (International Symposium 1978) Scientific Publishers Staff. (C). 1980. text ed. 200.00 (*81-85046-03-4*, Pub. by Scientific Pubs II) St Mut.

Arid Zone Settlement in Australia: A Focus on Alice Springs. 129p. 10.00 (*92-808-0506-1*) UN.

Arid Zone Settlement Planning: The Israeli Experience. Ed. by Gideon S. Golany. (Policy Studies). 1979. 140.00 (*0-08-023378-3*, Pergamon Pr) Elsevier.

Arie Antiche English Translations. Ed. by Dorothy Richardson & Tina Ruta. LC 90-62112. 150p. 1990. pap. text ed. 18.95 (*1-55725-017-0*) Paraclete MA.

Arie Selenger's Power Volleyball. Arie Selenger. (Illus.). 352p. 1987. pap. 17.95 (*0-312-04915-3*) St Martin.

Ariel. Ed. by Erika Boehm & W. Darrell Semelroth. (Poetry Anthology Ser.). 1983. 2.95 (*0-931672-05-8*) Triton Coll.

Ariel. Sylvia Plath. LC 66-15738. 1981. pap. 10.00 (*0-06-090890-4*, CN890, PL) HarpC.

Ariel. Jose E. Rodo. Tr. by Margaret S. Peden. 156p. 1988. 16.95 (*0-292-70395-3*); pap. 8.95 (*0-292-70396-1*) U of Tex Pr.

Ariel: Estudio Critico de Leopoldo Alas (Clarin) Jose E. Rodo. (Nueva Austral Ser.: Vol. 216). (SPA.). 1991. pap. text ed. 24.95x (*84-239-7216-X*) Elliots Bks.

Ariel: Poems. Sylvia Plath. 94p. 1991. reprint ed. lib. bdg. 25.00x (*0-8095-9056-5*) Borgo Pr.

Ariel & Sebastian: Serpent Teen. (Illus.). 48p. (J). (gr. 3-7). 1992. pap. 2.95 (*1-56115-266-8*, 21807, Golden Pr) Western Pub.

Ariel & the Police: Michel Foucault, William James, Wallace Stevens. Frank Lentricchia. LC 87-18885. 208p. (C). 1987. text ed. 27.50 (*0-299-11540-2*) U of Wis Pr.

Ariel & the Police: Michel Foucault, William James, Wallace Stevens. Frank Lentricchia. LC 87-18885. 208p. 1989. pap. text ed. 14.95 (*0-299-11544-5*) U of Wis Pr.

Ariel Controversy: Religion & "The Negro Problem" Ed. by John D. Smith. LC 92-32358. (Anti-Black Thought, 1863-1925 Ser.: Vol. 5). 392p. 1993. 61.00 (*0-8153-0977-5*) Garland.

Ariel Custer. Grace L. Hill. 336p. reprint ed. lib. bdg. 19.95 (*0-89190-033-0*, Rivercity Pr) Amereon Ltd.

Ariel Custer, No. 8. Grace L. Hill. 1989. pap. 4.99 (*0-8423-1686-8*) Tyndale.

Ariel Guitar Library: Bach Lute Suites for Guitar. Date not set. pap. 12.95 (*0-8256-9979-7*) Music Sales.

Ariel II. Ed. by W. Darrell Semelroth & Erika Boehm. (Poetry Anthology Ser.). 1983. 2.95 (*0-931672-06-6*) Triton Coll.

Ariel III. Ed. by Erika Boehm & W. Darrell Semelroth. (Poetry Anthology Ser.). 1984. 3.95 (*0-931672-07-4*) Triton Coll.

***Ariel on la Vie de Shelley.** Andre Maurois. (Coll. Diamant). 1970. pap. write for info. (*0-7859-5275-6*) Fr & Eur.

Ariel the Spy. M. J. Carr. LC 92-54512. (Little Mermaid Novels Ser.). (Illus.). 80p. (J). (gr. 1-4). 1993. pap. 3.50 (*1-56282-372-8*) Disney Pr.

Ariel, Zed & the Secret of Life. Anna Fienberg. (J). (gr. 4-7). 1994. pap. 5.95 (*1-86373-276-4*, Pub. by Allen & Unwin Aust Pty AT) IPG Chicago.

Arielle & the Hanukkah Surprise. Devra Speregen. (J). 1992. pap. 2.50 (*0-590-46125-7*, Cartwheel) Scholastic Inc.

***Ariel's World: An Exploration of Lake Ontario.** Susan J. Peterson. (Illus.). 164p. (Orig.). 1995. pap. 11.95 (*0-9646149-0-1*) Ariel Assocs.

***Aries.** 272p. (Orig.). Date not set. pap. text ed. 6.50 (*0-515-11661-0*) Jove Pubns.

***Aries.** 208p. (Orig.). 1995. pap. text ed. 4.50 (*0-425-14886-6*) Berkley Pub.

***Aries.** 256p. (Orig.). 1995. pap. text ed. 4.99 (*0-425-14902-1*) Berkley Pub.

Aries. Berkley Publishing Staff. (Day by Day Horoscopes, 1995 Ser.). 208p. (Orig.). 1994. pap. text ed. 3.99 (*0-425-14345-7*) Berkley Pub.

Aries. Lucille Callard. (Astro-Pups: Your Sign, Your Dogs Ser.). (Illus.). 60p. (Orig.). 1991. pap. 9.95 (*1-881038-00-9*) Penzance Pr.

Aries. Derek Parker & Julia Parker. LC 92-52784. (Sun & Moon Signs Library). (Illus.). 64p. (Orig.). 1992. 8.95 (*1-56458-084-9*) Dorling Kindersley.

Aries. Kathleen Paul. (Sun Sign Ser.). 40p. (J). (gr. 4). 1989. lib. bdg. 13.95 (*0-88682-255-6*) Creative Ed.

Aries: Astro-Numerogia. Michael J. Kurban. Tr. by Loretta H. Kurban. LC 86-91267. (Illus.). (Orig.). (SPA.). 1992. pap. 8.00 (*0-938863-45-2*) Libra Press Chi.

Aries: Astro-Numerology. 2nd ed. Michael J. Kurban. (Illus.). 50p. 1991. pap. 8.00 (*0-938863-09-6*) Libra Press Chi.

Aries: Little Birth Sign. Andrews & McMeel. 1994. 4.95 (*0-8362-3070-1*) Andrews & McMeel.

Aries: The Artful Astrologer. Lee Holloway. 1993. 4.99 (*0-517-08247-0*) Random Hse Value.

Aries: Through the Numbers. Paul Rice & Valeta Rice. 64p. 1983. pap. 3.95 (*0-87728-565-9*) Weiser.

Aries Womyn. Esther Heggie. (Orig.). 1987. pap. text ed. 2.00 (*0-938885-02-2*) Shu Pub.

***Ariesmar.** LC 95-94119. 100p. (Orig.). 1995. pap. text ed. 15.00 (*1-887303-01-4*) Blu Lantern Pub.

Arigo: Surgeon of the Rusty Knife. John G. Fuller. 274p. 1975. 16.95 (*0-8159-5020-9*) Devin.

Arikara Narrative of the Campaign Against the Hostile Dakotas: June 1876. Ed. by O. G. Libby. (Illus.). 1920. 20.00 (*0-914074-00-8*, J M C & Co) Amereon Ltd.

Arikha. Duncan Thomson. (Illus.). 240p. 1994. 49.95 (*0-7148-3010-0*, Pub. by Phaidon Press UK) Chronicle Bks.

Arikha: Texts by Samuel Beckett, Robert Hughes, Barbara Rose, Jane Livingston, Richard Channin, & Andre Fermigier. (Illus.). 223p. 1986. 50.00 (*0-500-09171-4*) Thames Hudson.

Arimaspian Eye. David L. Hall. LC 91-45682. (SUNY Series, The Margins of Literature). 436p. 1992. 39.50 (*0-7914-1307-1*); 19.95 (*0-7914-1308-X*) State U NY Pr.

Ariodanto & Ieneura see Sources of Much Ado About Nothing

***Arion & the Dolphin.** Vikram Seth. LC 94-33177. 1995. 15.99 (*0-525-45384-9*) Dutton Child Bks.

Ariosto. C P Brand. 206p. 1974. 18.00 (*0-85224-246-8*, Pub. by Edinburgh U Pr UK) Col U Pr.

Ariosto. Chelsea Q. Yarbro. 368p. 1988. pap. 3.95 (*0-8125-5852-9*) Tor Bks.

Ariosto & Boiardo: The Origins of "Orlando Furioso" Peter V. Marinelli. LC 87-4993. 256p. 1987. text ed. 31.00 (*0-8262-0636-0*) U of Mo Pr.

Ariosto's Bitter Harmony: Crisis & Evasion in the Italian Renaissance. Albert R. Ascoli. 384p. 1987. text ed. 59.50 (*0-691-05479-7*) Princeton U Pr.

Ariostos Seven Planets Governing Italie, or His Satyrs. Ludovico Ariosto. LC 76-57350. (English Experience Ser.: No. 770). 1977. reprint ed. lib. bdg. 20.00 (*90-221-0770-1*) Walter J Johnson.

Arisal of the Clear: A Simple Guide to Healthy Eating According to Traditional Chinese Medicine. Bob Flaws. Ed. by Honora Wolfe. LC 91-73954. 75p. (Orig.). 1991. pap. 8.95 (*0-936185-27-9*) Blue Poppy.

Arise: A Christian Psychology of Love. Chester P. Michael & Marie C. Norrisey. 162p. (Orig.). 1981. pap. 3.95 (*0-940136-00-7*) Open Door Inc.

Arise & Eat. Wayne Monbleau. 20p. (Orig.). 1991. pap. 2.00 (*0-944648-08-8*) Loving Grace Pubns.

Arise & Evangelize. Don J. Jennings. 1975. pap. 1.25 (*0-914012-17-7*) Sword of Lord.

***Arise & Walk.** Barry Gifford. 1995. 11.95 (*0-385-31472-8*, Delta) Dell.

Arise & Walk: A Novel. Barry Gifford. LC 93-33768. 176p. 1994. 19.95 (*0-7868-6013-8*) Hyperion.

***Arise, Misanthrope, Take Stand Against the Race.** Brendan Tripp. 32p. 1981. pap. 5.00 (*1-57353-005-0*) Eschaton Prods.

Arise Ye Mighty People! Gender, Class, & Race in Popular Struggles. Ed. by Terisa E. Turner & Bryan J. Ferguson. LC 93-36486. 250p. 1994. 45.95 (*0-86543-300-3*); pap. 14.95 (*0-86543-301-1*) Africa World.

***Arising from Flames.** Lama. (Timeless Wisdom Ser.). 1995. 15.95 (*1-882519-01-9*) WisdomKeepers.

ARIST 26: Annual Review of Information Science & Technology. Ed. by Martha E. Williams. 1991. 87.00 (*0-938734-55-5*) Learned Info.

ARIST 27: Annual Review of Information Science & Technology. Ed. by Martha E. Williams. 427p. 1992. 89.00 (*0-938734-66-0*) Learned Info.

ARIST 28: Annual Review of Information Science & Technology. Ed. by Martha E. Williams. 493p. 1993. 92.50 (*0-938734-75-X*) Learned Info.

***ARIST 29: Annual Review of Information Science & Technology.** Ed. by Martha E. Williams. 455p. 1994. 95.00 (*0-938734-91-1*) Learned Info.

Aristarchs Homerische Textkritik, 2 vols., Set. Arthur Ludwich. viii, 1409p. 1971. reprint ed. write for info. (*3-487-04082-4*, Pub. by Georg Olms GW) Lubrecht & Cramer.

Aristarchus of Samos, the Greek Copernicus. Thomas Heath. (Illus.). 434p. 1981. reprint ed. pap. 9.95 (*0-486-24188-2*) Dover.

Arista's New Boyfriend. M. J. Carr. LC 92-54511. (Little Mermaid Novels Ser.). (Illus.). 80p. (J). (gr. 1-4). 1993. pap. 3.50 (*1-56282-371-X*) Disney Pr.

Aristeas to Philocrates (Letter to Aristeas) Hadas. 1988. 25.00 (*0-87068-229-6*) Ktav.

Aristide: An Autobiography. Jean-Bertrand Aristide. Tr. by Linda Maloney. LC 92-34558. (Illus.). 216p. 1993. reprint ed. 14.95 (*0-88344-845-9*) Orbis Bks.

Aristide Maillol: The Artist & The Book. Alan Wofsy. (Illus.). 1975. 20.00 (*0-915346-01-X*) A Wofsy Fine Arts.

Aristide Maillol: 1861-1944. John Rewald. LC 75-42576. (Illus.). 140p. 1975. pap. 9.95 (*0-89207-000-5*) S R Guggenheim.

Aristides, Vol. 1. Aristides. Tr. by C. A. Behr. (Loeb Classical Library: No. 458). 594p. 1973. text ed. 18.95 (*0-674-99505-8*) HUP.

Aristides - Concordantia in Orationem Quae Aristidis Fertur Esse Eis Basilea. Ed. by Stephen A. Stertz. (Alpha-Omega, Reihe A Ser.: Bd. XVII). 195p. 1988. write for info. (*3-487-07874-0*, Pub. by Georg Olms GW) Lubrecht & Cramer.

Aristides, (Opera), 3 vols., Set. Ed. by Guilielmi Dindorfii. clxvii, 2541p. 1964. reprint ed. write for info. (*0-318-70854-X*, Pub. by Georg Olms GW) Lubrecht & Cramer.

Aristo & the Classical Smile. Kristen O. Murtaugh. (Studies in Romance Languages: No. 36). 206p. (C). 1981. 12.50 (*0-674-04487-8*) HUP.

Aristocats. (Classics Ser.). 96p. (J). 1988. 6.98 (*1-57082-032-5*) Mouse Works.

Aristocats. Walt Disney. (Disney Animated Ser.). (J). 1988. 5.99 (*0-517-66195-0*) Random Hse Value.

Aristocats. Walt Disney Staff. (Penguin-Disney Ser.). 1988. 6.98 (*0-8317-0394-6*) Viking Penguin.

Aristocracy & People: Britain, Eighteen Fifteen to Eighteen Sixty Five in Germany. Norman Gash. (New History of England Ser.). 383p. 1981. pap. 16.50 (*0-674-04491-6*) HUP.

Aristocracy & the Middle-Classes in Germany: Social Types in German Literature, 1830-1900. Ernest K. Bramsted. LC 64-15031. 388p. (Orig.). reprint ed. pap. 110.60 (*0-8357-5731-5*, 2020035) Bks Demand.

Aristocracy in America: From the Sketch-Book of a German Nobleman. Fracis J. Grund. 11.75 (*0-8446-0666-9*) Peter Smith.

Aristocracy in England, 1660-1914. John V. Beckett. 528p. 1988. pap. 29.95 (*0-631-16072-8*) Blackwell Pubs.

Aristocracy in Europe, 1815-1914. Dominic Lieven. 1994. pap. 15.00 (*0-231-08113-8*) Col U Pr.

Aristocracy in Europe, 1815-1914. Dominic C. Lieven. LC 92-23071. 308p. (C). 1993. 29.50 (*0-231-08112-X*); pap. 15.00 (*0-685-63514-7*) Col U Pr.

Aristocracy of Everyone: The Politics of Education & the Future of America. Benjamin R. Barber. LC 92-53157. 272p. 1992. 19.50 (*0-345-37040-6*, Ballantine Trade) Ballantine.

Aristocracy of Everyone: The Politics of Education & the Future of America. Benjamin R. Barber. LC 92-53157. 320p. 1994. reprint ed. pap. 11.95 (*0-19-509154-X*) OUP.

Aristocracy of Labor: The Position of Skilled Craftsmen in the American Class Structure. Gavin Mackenzie. LC 73-80484. (Cambridge Studies in Sociology: Vol. 7). 218p. reprint ed. pap. 62.20 (*0-8357-5732-3*, 2027244) Bks Demand.

Aristocracy of the Long Robe: The Origins of Judicial Review in America. Jack M. Sosin. LC 88-37581. (Contributions in Legal Studies: No. 52). 369p. 1989. text ed. 65.00 (*0-313-26733-2*, SJR/, Greenwood Pr) Greenwood.

Aristocracy of the Mind, a Precious Heritage: A Biography of Jorge Bocobo. Celia B. Olivar. (Illus.). 124p. 1981. pap. 6.50 (*0-686-32580-X*, Pub. by New Day Pub PH) Cellar.

***Aristocracy's Outlaw: The Doc Holliday Story.** Sylvia D. Lynch. (Illus.). 332p. 1995. 29.95x (*0-9645781-0-7*, Iris Press); pap. 24.00x (*0-9645781-1-5*, Iris Press) Tenn Iris Pr.

Aristocrat. Catherine Coulter. 1993. mass mkt. 4.50 (*0-373-48261-2*, 5-48261-7) Harlequin Bks.

***Aristocrat.** Ernst Weiss. Tr. by Martin Chalmers. 210p. (Orig.). 1995. pap. 13.99 (*1-85242-262-9*) Serpents Tail.

Aristocrat As Art. Domna C. Stanton. LC 79-16657. 320p. 1980. text ed. 50.00 (*0-231-03903-4*) Col U Pr.

An Asterisk (*) at the beginning of an entry indicates that the title is appearing in BIP for the first time.

An Asterisk (*) at the beginning of an entry indicates that the title is appearing in BIP for the first time.

423

A

Aristotle on Substance: The Paradox of Unity. Mary L. Gill. 295p. 1991. text ed. 45.00 (0-691-07334-1); pap. text ed. 16.95 (0-691-02070-1) Princeton U Pr.

Aristotle on the Constitution of Athens. 2nd ed. Tr. by E. Poste. xiv, 172p. 1992. reprint ed. 27.50 (0-8377-2520-8) Rothman.

Aristotle on the Goals & Exactness of Ethics. Georgios Anagnostopoulos. 474p. 1994. 50.00 (0-520-08125-0) U CA Pr.

Aristotle on the Human God. Richard Kraut. 388p. 1991. text ed. 49.50 (0-691-07349-X); pap. text ed. 17.95 (0-691-02071-X) Princeton U Pr.

Aristotle on the Many Senses of Priority. John J. Cleary. LC 87-32202. (Journal of the History of Philosophy Monograph Ser.). 148p. (Orig.). (C). 1988. pap. text ed. 15.95 (0-8093-1465-7) S Ill U Pr.

Aristotle on the Perfect Life. Anthony Kenny. 184p. 1992. 49.95 (0-19-824017-1) OUP.

*__Aristotle on the Perfect Life.__ Anthony Kenny. 184p. 1995. pap. 19.95 (0-19-823603-4) OUP.

Aristotle on Tragic & Comic Mimesis. Leon Golden. LC 92-12593. (American Classical Studies: No. 29). 125p. 1992. 24.95 (1-55540-718-8, 40 04 29); pap. 14.95 (1-55540-719-6) Scholars Pr GA.

Aristotle, Rhetoric I: A Commentary. William M. Grimaldi. LC 79-53372. viii, 362p. 1980. 65.00x (0-8232-1048-0) Fordham.

Aristotle, Rhetoric II: A Commentary. William M. Grimaldi. LC 79-53372. x, 377p. 1989. 65.00x (0-8232-1049-9) Fordham.

Aristotle Selected Works. 3rd ed. Hippocrates G. Apostle & Lloyd P. Gerson. LC 91-62514. 723p. 1991. text ed. 27.20 (0-911589-14-7); pap. text ed. 13.60 (0-911589-13-9) Peripatetic.

Aristotle. The Nicomachean Ethics: A Commentary. H. Henry Joachim. Ed. by D. A. Rees. LC 85-7665. 304p. 1985. reprint ed. text ed. 52.50 (0-313-24837-0, JOAT, Greenwood Pr) Greenwood.

Aristotle the Philosopher. Ed. by J. L. Ackrill. (Oxford Paperbacks University Ser.). (Orig.). 1981. pap. text ed. 15.95 (0-19-289118-9) OUP.

Aristotle to Zoos: A Philosophical Dictionary of Biology. P. B. Medawar & J. S. Medawar. (Illus.). 319p. 1983. 34. 50 (0-674-04535-1) HUP.

Aristotle to Zoos: A Philosophical Dictionary of Biology. P. B. Medawar & J. S. Medawar. LC 84-16529. 319p. 1985. pap. text ed. 12.50 (0-674-04537-8) HUP.

Aristotle Transformed: The Ancient Commentators & Their Influence. Ed. by Richard Sorabji. LC 89-37190. (Illus.). 556p. 1990. 69.95 (0-8014-2432-1) Cornell U Pr.

Aristotle, Verb Meaning & Functional Grammar: Towards a New Typology of States of Affairs. Albert Rijksbaron. vi, 54p. (Orig.). 1989. pap. 16.00 (90-5063-039-1, Pub. by Gieben NE) Benjamins North Am.

Aristotle (394-322 B.C.) Mark Blaug. (Pioneers in Economics Ser.: Vol. 2). 304p. 1991. text ed. 97.95 (1-85278-464-4, Pub. by E Elgar Pub UK) Ashgate Pub Co.

Aristotle's Art of Poetry: A Greek View of Poetry & Drama. Intro. by Aristoteles & W. Hamilton Fyfe. LC 83-45409. reprint ed. 20.00 (0-404-20007-9) AMS Pr.

Aristotle's Categories & Propositions (De Interpretatione) H. G. Apostle. LC 80-80777. (Apostle Translations of Aristotle's Works: Vol. 3). 157p. (Orig.). 1980. text ed. 14.00 (0-9602870-4-3); pap. text ed. 7.60 (0-9602870-5-1) Peripatetic.

Aristotle's Concept of Soul, Sleep, & Dreams. H. Wijsenbeek-Wijler. 260p. 1978. pap. text ed. 57.50 (0-317-54427-6, Pub. by A M Hakkert SP) Coronet Bks.

Aristotle's Concept of the Universal. George Brakas. (Studien und Materialien Zur Geschichte der Philosophie Ser.: Bd. 26). vi, 114p. (GER.). 1988. lib. bdg. 32.37 (3-487-07996-8, Pub. by Georg Olms GW) Lubrecht & Cramer.

Aristotle's Constitution of Athens. 2nd enl. rev. ed. Aristotle. LC 78-155630. (BCL Ser.: No. 1). reprint ed. 36.50 (0-404-00368-0) AMS Pr.

Aristotle's Constitution of Athens. 2nd rev. ed. Aristotle. LC 72-9302. (Philosophy of Plato & Aristotle Ser.). (ENG & GRE.). 1974. reprint ed. 25.95 (0-405-04857-2) Ayer.

Aristotles Contra Augustinum, Zur Frage Nach Dem Verhaltnis Von Zeit und Seele Bei Den Antiken Aristoteleskommentatoren, Im Arabischen Aristotelismus und Im 13 Jahrhundert. Ed. by Udo R. Jeck. LC 93-41209. (Bochumer Studien zur Philosophie Ser.: No. 21). xvi, 521p. (GER.). 1993. 89.00 (90-6032-339-4, Pub. by Gruner NE) Benjamins North Am.

Aristotle's Contribution to the Practice & Theory of Historiography: Howison Lecture, 1957. Kurt Von Fritz. LC 58-9957. (University of California Publications in Social Welfare: Vol. 28, No. 3). 28p. reprint ed. pap. 25.00 (0-8357-5733-1, 2021177) Bks Demand.

Aristotle's De Anima. Aristotle. Ed. by G. Bos. Tr. by Zerahyah Hen. (Aristoteles Semitico-Latinus Ser.: No. 6). 202p. (HEB.). 1993. 77.25 (90-04-09937-9, NLG135) E J Brill.

Aristotle's De Anima in Focus. Ed. by Michael Durrant. LC 92-23551. (Philosophers in Focus Ser.). 224p. 1993. 59. 95 (0-415-05339-0, B0693, Routledge NY); pap. 16.95 (0-415-05340-4, B0697, Routledge NY) Routledge.

Aristotle's "De Motu Animalium" Martha C. Nussbaum. LC 77-72132. 456p. 1985. pap. text ed. 29.95 (0-691-02035-3) Princeton U Pr.

*__Aristotle's Economic Thought.__ Scott Meikle. 200p. 1995. 36.00 (0-19-815002-4) OUP.

Aristotle's Ethics. J. O. Urmson. 128p. 1988. pap. text ed. 19.95 (0-631-15946-0) Blackwell Pubs.

Aristotle's Ethics Notes. Robert Milch. (Orig.). 1966. pap. 4.25 (0-8220-0889-0) Cliffs.

Aristotle's Eudaemonia, Terminal Illness, & the Question of Life Support. Juliet C. Rothman. LC 92-17507. (American University Studies: Philosophy: Ser. V, Vol. 141). 149p. (C). 1993. text ed. 44.95 (0-685-71440-3) P Lang Pubs.

Aristotle's First Principles. Terence Irwin. 720p. 1990. reprint ed. pap. 36.00 (0-19-824290-5) OUP.

Aristotle's Metaphysics. H. G. Apostle. LC 79-88598. (Apostle Translations of Aristotle's Works: Vol. 1). 498p. 1979. reprint ed. text ed. 24.00 (0-9602870-0-0); reprint ed. pap. text ed. 12.00 (0-9602870-1-9) Peripatetic.

*__Aristotle's Modal Logic: Essence & Entailment in the Organon.__ Richard Patterson. (Illus.). 304p. (C). 1995. 54.95 (0-521-45168-X) Cambridge U Pr.

Aristotle's Mother. Herbert E. Read. (Dramascripts Ser.: Vol. 1). 1961. pap. 4.95 (0-900891-03-3) Oleander Pr.

Aristotle's Nicomachean Ethics. 2nd ed. H. G. Apostle. LC 84-60009. (Apostle Translations of Aristotle's Works: Vol. 6). 372p. 1984. reprint ed. pap. 12.00 (0-911589-03-1); reprint ed. pap. text ed. 24.00 (0-911589-02-3) Peripatetic.

Aristotle's Nicomachean Ethics. Tr. by D. P. Chase. 357p. reprint ed. pap. 9.95 (0-935005-83-8) Lincoln-Rembrandt.

Aristotle's On the Soul (De Anima) H. G. Apostle. LC 81-86481. (Apostle Translations of Aristotle's Works: Vol. 5). 225p. (Orig.). (C). 1982. text ed. 18.00 (0-9602870-8-6); pap. text ed. 9.00 (0-9602870-9-4) Peripatetic.

*__Aristotle's Organon in Epitome, the Poetics, the Rhetoric, the Analytics: Aristotle's Tool-Kit.__ Victorino Tejera. LC 95-7507. 1995. write for info. (0-7734-8847-2) E Mellen.

*__Aristotle's Organon in Epitome, the Poetics, the Rhetoric, the Analytics: Aristotle's Tool-Kit.__ Victorino Tejera. LC 95-7507. (Studies in Classics: Vol. 2). 216p. 1995. text ed. 89.95 (0-7734-8884-7) E Mellen.

Aristotle's Philosophy of Friendship. Suzanne Stern-Gillet. LC 94-10399. (SUNY Series in Ancient Greek Philosophy). 192p. 1995. text ed. 49.50 (0-7914-2341-7); pap. 16.95 (0-7914-2342-5) State U NY Pr.

Aristotle's Physics. H. G. Apostle. LC 80-80037. (Apostle Translations of Aristotle's Works: Vol. 2). 386p. 1980. reprint ed. text ed. 24.00 (0-9602870-2-7); reprint ed. pap. text ed. 12.00 (0-9602870-3-5) Peripatetic.

Aristotle's Physics: A Collection of Essays. Ed. by Lindsay Judson. 304p. 1992. 65.00 (0-19-824844-X) OUP.

*__Aristotle's Physics: A Collection of Essays.__ Ed. by Lindsay Judson. 304p. 1995. pap. 22.50 (0-19-823602-6) OUP.

*__Aristotle's Physics: A Guided Study.__ Joe Sachs. (Masterworks of Discovery Ser.). 280p. 1995. text ed. 52.00 (0-8135-2191-2); pap. text ed. 18.00 (0-8135-2192-0) Rutgers U Pr.

Aristotle's Physics & Its Medieval Varieties. Helen S. Lang. LC 91-35652. (Ancient Greek Philosophy Ser.). 322p. (C). 1992. 59.50 (0-7914-1083-8); pap. 19.95 (0-7914-1084-6) State U NY Pr.

Aristotle's Physics & Its Reception in the Arabic World: With An Edition of the Unpublished Parts of Ibn Bajja's Commentary on the Physics. P. Lettinck. LC 93-46583. (Aristoteles Semitico-Latinus Ser.: Vol. 7). 1994. 171.50 (90-04-09960-3) E J Brill.

Aristotle's Poetics. Aristotle. Tr. by S. H. Butcher. (Mermaid Dramabook Ser.). 118p. (Orig.). 1961. pap. 5.95 (0-8090-0527-1) Hill & Wang.

Aristotle's Poetics. Aristotle & James Hutton. Ed. by G. M. Kirkwood. 120p. (Orig.). (C). 1982. pap. text ed. 7.95 (0-393-95216-9) Norton.

Aristotle's Poetics. Stephen Halliwell. LC 86-4299. xi, 369p. 1986. 39.95 (0-8078-1710-4) U of NC Pr.

Aristotle's Poetics: A Course of Eight Lectures. Humphrey House. LC 77-27445. 128p. 1978. reprint ed. text ed. 35. 00 (0-8371-9095-9, HOAP, Greenwood Pr) Greenwood.

Aristotle's Poetics: A Translation & Commentary for Students of Literature. Leon Golden & O. B. Hardison, Jr. LC 81-14829. 1981. reprint ed. pap. 22.95 (0-8130-0720-8) U Press Fla.

Aristotle's Poetics: The Poetry of Philosophy. Michael Davis. 256p. (C). 1992. text ed. 55.00 (0-8476-7741-9); pap. text ed. 19.95 (0-8476-7742-7) Rowman.

Aristotle's Poetics & English Literature: A Collection of Critical Essays. Elder Olson. LC 65-24430. (Gemini Bks: Patterns of Literary Criticism). 264p. reprint ed. pap. 75.30 (0-8357-5734-X, 2026737) Bks Demand.

Aristotle's Poetics, No. 8: Apostle Translations of Aristotle's Works. Hippocrates G. Apostle et al. LC 89-64029. 167p. 1990. pap. text ed. 6.80 (0-911589-09-0) Peripatetic.

Aristotle's Politics. H. G. Apostle & L. P. Gerson. LC 86-60430. (Apostle Translations of Aristotle's Works: Vol. 7). 399p. (Orig.). 1986. text ed. 24.00 (0-911589-04-X); pap. text ed. 12.00 (0-911589-05-8) Peripatetic.

Aristotle's Posterior Analytics. H. G. Apostle. LC 81-80233. (Apostle Translations of Aristotle's Works: Vol. 4). 328p. (Orig.). (C). 1981. text ed. 24.00 (0-9602870-6-X); pap. text ed. 12.00 (0-9602870-7-8) Peripatetic.

Aristotle's Psychology. Daniel N. Robinson. 160p. 1989. text ed. 31.50 (0-231-07002-0) Col U Pr.

Aristotle's Psychology. Aristotle. LC 75-13253. (History of Ideas in Ancient Greece Ser.). (ENG & GRE.). 1976. reprint ed. 30.95 (0-405-07290-2) Ayer.

Aristotle's Rhetoric: An Art of Character. Eugene Garver. 328p. 1995. lib. bdg. 53.95 (0-226-28424-7); pap. text ed. 18.95 (0-226-28425-5) U Ch Pr.

Aristotle's Secret. Charles R. La Dow. (Illus.). 92p. (Orig.). 1986. pap. 8.95 (0-9617232-0-3) C R LaDow.

Aristotle's Theory of Actuality. Zev Bechler. LC 94-1045. (SUNY Series in Ancient Greek Philosophy). 384p. (C). 1995. text ed. 69.50 (0-7914-2239-9); pap. 23.95 (0-7914-2240-2) State U NY Pr.

*__Aristotle's Theory of Material Substance.__ Gad Freudenthal. 256p. 1995. text ed. 45.00 (0-19-824093-7) OUP.

Aristotle's Theory of Poetry & Fine Art. 4th ed. Samuel H. Butcher. (C). 1955. pap. 9.95 (0-486-20042-6) Dover.

Aristotle's Theory of the State. Curtis N. Johnson. LC 89-37268. 288p. 1990. text ed. 55.00 (0-312-03678-7) St Martin.

Aristotle's Two Systems. Daniel W. Graham. (Illus.). 384p. 1988. 79.00 (0-19-824970-5) OUP.

Aristotle's Vision of Nature. Frederick J. Woodbridge. Ed. by John H. Randall, Jr. LC 83-12756. xxii, 169p. 1983. reprint ed. text ed. 49.75 (0-313-24131-7, WOAR, Greenwood Pr) Greenwood.

Aristotle's Voice: Rhetoric, Theory, & Writing in America. Jasper Neel. LC 94-9931. 264p. (C). 1994. 34.95 (0-8093-1933-0) S Ill U Pr.

Arithmancy. Ed. by Nelson White & Anne White. LC 81-84893. (Illus.). 50p. (Orig.). 1981. pap. 9.00 (0-939856-23-9) Tech Group.

Arithmestics. Caleb Gattegno. (Illus.). 28p. 1971. pap. 3.00 (0-87825-019-0) Ed Solutions.

*__Arithmetic.__ Donna Burk et al. (Box It or Bag It Mathematics Ser.). (Illus.). 97p. (C). 1988. teacher ed 11.75 (1-886131-07-4, BB6) Math Lrning.

Arithmetic. Carl Sandburg. LC 32-5291. (J). (gr. 4-7). 1993. 15.95 (0-15-203865-5) HarBrace.

Arithmetic. Alan Wise & Carol Wise. LC 85-799. (College Outline Ser.). 406p. (C). 1986. pap. text ed. 12.50 (0-15-601529-3) HB Coll Pubs.

Arithmetic. 4th ed. Mervin L. Keedy. LC 82-18492. (Illus.). 560p. 1983. teacher ed write for info. (0-201-14781-5); pap. text ed. write for info. (0-201-14780-7); student ed write for info. (0-201-14782-3); student ed write for info. (0-201-15075-1); disk write for info. (0-201-15264-9); Apple II write for info. (0-201-15263-0); write for info. (0-201-14784-X); write for info. (0-201-14960-5) Addison-Wesley.

Arithmetic. Charles Godfrey & E. A. Price. 485p. reprint ed. pap. 138.30 (0-8357-5735-8, 2051353) Bks Demand.

Arithmetic, Vol. 1. Ed. by Michael Artin & John Tate. (Progress in Mathematics Ser.). 350p. 1983. 49.50 (0-8176-3132-1) Birkhauser.

Arithmetic: A Guided Approach. Irving Drooyan & William Rosen. LC 85-3192. 364p. (C). 1986. text ed. 39.95 (0-471-80814-8) P-H.

Arithmetic: A Programmed Worktext. 4th ed. Arthur H. Heywood. LC 81-10231. (Mathematics Ser.). 460p. (C). 1982. pap. 42.95 (0-8185-0490-0) Brooks-Cole.

Arithmetic: A Review. J. Louis Nanney & Richard D. Shaffer. LC 75-93297. 316p. reprint ed. pap. 90.10 (0-8357-5736-6, 2023213) Bks Demand.

Arithmetic: A Straightforward Approach. Martin M. Zuckerman. (Illus.). 394p. 1985. pap. text ed. 28.95 (0-912675-07-1); disk write for info. (0-912675-33-0); write for info. (0-912675-09-8) Ardsley.

Arithmetic: An Innovative Approach. Heschel Shapiro. 1992. per. 28.00 (0-88252-138-1) Paladin Hse.

Arithmetic: In a Flash. Elizabeth Burchard. (Exambusters Ser.). 425p. (J). (gr. 7-12). 1994. pap. 9.95 (1-881374-16-5) Flash Blasters.

Arithmetic Algebraic Geometry. J. L. Colliot-Thelene et al. Ed. by E. Ballico. LC 93-28781. (Lecture Notes in Mathematics Ser.: Vol. 1553). 1994. 37.00 (0-387-57110-8) Spr-Verlag.

Arithmetic Algebraic Geometry. Gerard Van der Geer et al. 1990. 63.00 (0-8176-3513-0) Birkhauser.

Arithmetic Algebraic Geometry: Lectures Given at the 2nd Session of the Centro Internazionale Matematico Estivo Held in Trento, Italy, June 24-July 2, 1991. J. L. Colliot-Thelene et al. (Lecture Notes in Mathematics Ser.: Vol. 1553). vii, 223p. 1993. pap. write for info. (3-540-57110-8) Spr-Verlag.

Arithmetic & Algebra. 3rd ed. Rosanne Proga. 688p. 1992. pap. 49.95 (0-534-92997-4) PWS Pubs.

Arithmetic & Algebra Again. Brita Immergut & Jean B. Smith. LC 93-15956. 1994. pap. text ed. 14.95 (0-07-031720-8) McGraw.

Arithmetic & Algebra Again. Brita Immergut & Jean B. Smith. 1994. Solutions Manual. teacher ed, pap. text ed. 6.00 (0-07-031721-6) McGraw.

Arithmetic & Beginning Algebra. 2nd ed. Allyn J. Washington. 1984. pap. text ed. 27.95 (0-8053-9540-7) Addison-Wesley.

Arithmetic & Combinatorics: Kant & His Contemporaries. Gotfried Martin. Ed. & Tr. by Judy Wubnig. LC 84-5476. (Philosophical Explorations Ser.). 272p. 1985. text ed. 29.95 (0-8093-1184-4) S Ill U Pr.

Arithmetic & Spectral Analysis of Poincare Series. James Cogdell & Ilya Piatetski-Shapiro. (Perspectives in Mathematics Ser.). 182p. 1990. text ed. 44.00 (0-12-178590-4) Acad Pr.

Arithmetic Complexity of Computations. S. Winograd. LC 79-93154. (CBMS-NSF Regional Conference Ser.: No. 33). iii, 93p. 1980. pap. text ed. 20.00 (0-89871-163-0) Soc Indus-Appl Math.

Arithmetic Drill & Practice: Grades 1-6. Frank Taylor. 1988. 5.95 (0-89108-183-6, 8806) Love Pub Co.

Arithmetic Duality Theorems. James S. Milne. (Perspectives in Mathematics Ser.). 230p. 1986. text ed. 73.00 (0-12-498040-6) Acad Pr.

Arithmetic, Elementary Algebra, Geometry: A Guided Approach. Irving Drooyan & Bill Rosen. LC 85-22735. 620p. 1986. pap. text ed. 38.95 (0-471-82129-2) P-H.

Arithmetic Exercises: Grade Eight. Fred Justus. (Math Ser.). 24p. (gr. 8). 1978. student ed 5.00 (0-8209-0098-2, A-8) ESP.

Arithmetic Exercises: Grade Five. Fred Justus. (Math Ser.). 24p. (gr. 5). 1979. student ed 5.00 (0-8209-0095-8, A-5) ESP.

Arithmetic Exercises: Grade Four. Fred Justus. (Math Ser.). 24p. (gr. 4). 1979. student ed 5.00 (0-8209-0094-X, A-4) ESP.

Arithmetic Exercises: Grade Seven. Fred Justus. (Math Ser.). 24p. (gr. 7). 1979. student ed 5.00 (0-8209-0097-4, A-7) ESP.

Arithmetic Exercises: Grade Six. Fred Justus. (Math Ser.). 24p. (gr. 6). 1977. student ed 5.00 (0-8209-0096-6, A-6) ESP.

Arithmetic for College Students. 5th ed. D. Franklin Wright. LC 86-82101. 384p. (C). 1987. teacher ed 2.00 (0-669-12190-8); text ed. 28.00 (0-669-12189-4) Heath.

Arithmetic for College Students. 6th ed. D. Franklin Wright. 528p. (C). 1991. text ed. write for info. (0-669-24470-8); Student solutions guide. student ed write for info. (0-669-24476-7); Instr.'s guide. teacher ed write for info. (0-669-24472-4); Test item file. teacher ed write for info. (0-669-27153-5) Heath.

Arithmetic for Commerce. A. Greer. 256p. (C). 1986. 49.00 (0-85950-566-9, Pub. by S Thornes Pubs UK) St Mut.

Arithmetic for Rig Personnel. Eldon Holcomb. 64p. (Orig.). (C). 1979. pap. text ed. 10.00 (0-88698-106-9, 1.61010) PETEX.

Arithmetic for the Mature Student. F. H. George. LC 66-19075. 1966. 144.00 (0-08-011904-2, Pub. by Pergamon Repr UK) Franklin.

Arithmetic for the Modern Age. Aaron Bakst. LC 60-53374. 349p. reprint ed. pap. 99.50 (0-8357-5737-4, 2007243) Bks Demand.

Arithmetic Functions & Integer Products. P. D. Elliot. (Grundlehren der Mathematischen Wissenschaften Ser.: Vol. 272). xv, 461p. 1984. 120.00 (0-387-96094-5) Spr-Verlag.

Arithmetic Geometry. Ed. by Cornell & J. Silverman. 370p. 1986. 49.95 (0-387-96311-1) Spr-Verlag.

Arithmetic Is Fun: The Arithmetic Example Handbook of Grade-School Math. Michael A. Salant. LC 91-90203. (Illus.). 128p. (Orig.). (J). (gr. 1-6). 1995. 16.95 (0-9609288-5-5); spiral bd., pap. 10.95 (0-9609288-4-7) M A Salant.

Arithmetic Made Simple. rev. ed. Robert Belge. LC 87-24716. 1988. pap. 12.00 (0-385-23938-6) Doubleday.

Arithmetic Module Series: One Volume Non-Programmed Edition. Thomas J. McHale & Paul T. Witzke. 400p. (C). 1976. pap. text ed. write for info. (0-201-04757-8); write for info. (0-318-50126-0) Addison-Wesley.

Arithmetic Modules. Thomas J. McHale & Paul T. Witzke. 125p. (C). 1975. Module 1, whole nos. pap. text ed. 18. 25 (0-201-04751-9); Module 2, fractions. pap. text ed. 20.50 (0-201-04752-7); Module 3, decimals. pap. text ed. 20.50 (0-201-04753-5); Module 4, perfect ratio. pap. text ed. 20.50 (0-201-04754-3); Module 5. pap. text ed. 15.16 (0-201-04756-X) Addison-Wesley.

Arithmetic of Al-Uqlidisi. Abu Al-Hasan & Ahmed-Ibn Ibrahim. Tr. by A. S. Saidan. 1978. lib. bdg. 201.00 (90-277-0752-9) Kluwer Ac.

*__Arithmetic of Algebraic Curves.__ Serguei A. Stepanov. LC 94-42129. (Monographs in Contemporary Mathematics). 425p. 1995. 115.00 (0-306-11036-9, Consultants) Plenum.

Arithmetic of Blowup Algebras. Wolmer V. Vasconcelos. (London Mathematical Society Lecture Note Ser.: No. 195). 400p. (C). 1994. pap. 34.95 (0-521-45484-0) Cambridge U Pr.

Arithmetic of Complex Manifolds. Ed. by W. P. Barth & H. Lange. (Lecture Notes in Mathematics Ser.: Vol. 1399). v, 171p. 1989. pap. 29.20 (0-387-51729-4, 3568) Spr-Verlag.

*__Arithmetic of Diagonal Hypersurfaces over Finite Fields.__ Fernando Q. Gouvea & Noriko Yui. (London Mathematical Society Lecture Note Ser.: No. 209). (Illus.). 182p. (C). 1995. pap. 32.95 (0-521-49834-1) Cambridge U Pr.

Arithmetic of Dosages & Solutions: A Programmed Presentation. 7th ed. Laura K. Hart. (Illus.). 128p. 1989. 18.95 (0-8016-3498-9) Mosby Yr Bk.

Arithmetic of Elliptic Curves. J. H. Silverman. (Graduate Texts in Mathematics Ser.: Vol. 106). (Illus.). xii, 400p. 1994. reprint ed. 49.50 (0-387-96203-4) Spr-Verlag.

Arithmetic of Elliptic Curves II. Joseph H. Silverman. LC 94-21787. (Graduate Texts in Mathematics Ser.). 1994. 59.00 (0-387-94325-0) Spr-Verlag.

*__Arithmetic of Elliptic Curves II, 151.__ J. H. Silverman. Ed. by J. H. Ewing et al. LC 94-21787. (Graduate Texts in Mathematics Ser.). 535p. 1994. pap. text ed. 39.00 (0-387-94328-5) Spr-Verlag.

Arithmetic of Finite Fields. Charles Small. (Pure & Applied Mathematics Ser.: Vol. 148). 240p. 1991. 110.00 (0-8247-8526-6) Dekker.

Arithmetic of Function Fields: Proceedings of the Workshop at the Ohio State University, June 17-26, 1991. Ed. by David Goss et al. LC 92-29651. (Ohio State Mathematical Research Institute Publications: Vol. 2). viii, 482p. (C). 1992. lib. bdg. 65.95 (3-11-013171-4) De Gruyter.

Arithmetic of God, Vol. 1. 3rd ed. Ed. by Don Kistler. 187p. (Orig.). 1976. pap. 6.00 (0-940532-00-X) AOG.

Arithmetic of Heaven see Numbers in the Bible: God's Unique Design in Biblical Numbers

Arithmetic of p-Adic Modular Forms. Fernando Q. Gouvea. (Lecture Notes in Mathematics Ser.: Vol. 1304). viii, 121p. 1988. pap. 28.90 (0-387-18946-7) Spr-Verlag.

Arithmetic of Probability Distributions, & Characterization Problems on Abelian Groups. G. M. Feldman. Ed. by Simeon Ivanov. Tr. by Yu Lyiubarskii. LC 92-45025. (Translations of Mathematical Monographs: Vol. 116). 223p. 1993. 127.00 (0-8218-4593-4) Am Math.

An Asterisk (*) at the beginning of an entry indicates that the title is appearing in BIP for the first time.

An Asterisk (*) at the beginning of an entry indicates that the title is appearing in BIP for the first time.

·425·

A

Arizona Energy: A Framework for Decision. Ed. by Ellen Hale. LC 76-20232. 160p. 1976. pap. 3.50 (0-8165-0562-4) U of Ariz Pr.

Arizona Environmental Law Handbook. Brown & Bain. (State Environmental Law Ser.). 310p. 1993. pap. text ed. 74.00 (0-86587-333-X) Gov Insts.

Arizona Favorites: Southwest Traditional to Light Modern Cooking. Dorie F. Pass & Dorothy Tegeler. LC 92-52501. (Illus.). 176p. (Orig.). 1992. pap. 8.95 (0-935182-55-1) Gem Guides Bk.

Arizona Federal Census Index, 1860 (Every Name) Ronald V. Jackson. LC 78-56238. (Illus.). 1978. lib. bdg. 48.00 (0-89593-211-3) Accelerated Index.

Arizona Federal Census Index, 1870 (Every Name) Ronald V. Jackson. LC 78-56236. (Illus.). 1978. lib. bdg. 79.00 (0-89593-210-5) Accelerated Index.

Arizona Federal Census Index, 1880 (Every Name) Ronald V. Jackson. (Illus.). 1980. lib. bdg. 135.00 (0-89593-709-3) Accelerated Index.

Arizona Festival Fun for Kids! Carole Marsh. (Carole Marsh Arizona Bks.). (Illus.). (YA). (gr. 3-12). 1994. lib. bdg. 24.95 (0-7933-3932-4); pap. 14.95 (0-7933-3933-2); disk 29.95 (0-7933-3934-0) Gallopade Pub Group.

Arizona Film & Video Production Directory. 96p. 1990. 18.95 (0-318-50059-0) PHG AZ.

Arizona Flora. 2nd rev. ed. Thomas H. Kearney et al. (Illus.). 1960. 70.00 (0-520-00637-2) U CA Pr.

Arizona Game Birds. David E. Brown. LC 88-27797. (Illus.). 307p. 1989. 25.95 (0-8165-1019-9) U of Ariz Pr.

Arizona Gathering Two, 1950-1969: An Annotated Bibliography. Donald M. Powell. LC 72-82946. 214p. reprint ed. pap. 61.00 (0-8357-4764-6, 2037691) Bks Demand.

Arizona Glimpses. Barb Browning. LC 88-92218. (Illus.). 36p. (Orig.). 1988. 6.50 (0-9622076-0-8); pap. 3.50 (0-9622076-1-6) Bobarb Pr.

Arizona Gold Placers & Placering. Eldred Wilson. (Illus.). 148p. 1989. reprint ed. pap. 6.95 (0-89632-003-0) Gem Guides Bk.

Arizona Golf Guide: A Comprehensive Guide to Every Golf Course in Arizona. Stephan Harper. (Illus.). 302p. (Orig.). 1993. 21.95 (1-883415-00-4) Teebox.

Arizona Government. Jay J. Wagoner. LC 84-23543. (Illus.). 176p. (Orig.). 1985. pap. text ed. 7.95 (0-87905-183-3) Gibbs Smith Pub.

Arizona Governors, 1912-1990. Ed. by John L. Myers et al. LC 89-80719. 208p. (C). 1989. 29.95 (0-929690-05-2) Herit Pubs AZ.

Arizona Gun Owner's Guide. Alan Korwin. (Illus.). 128p. (Orig.). 1989. pap. 6.95 (0-9621958-0-4) Bloomfield Pr.

Arizona Gun Owner's Guide. rev. ed. Alan Korwin. (Illus.). 128p. (Orig.). 1994. pap. 9.95 (0-9621958-2-0) Bloomfield Pr.

***Arizona Gun Owner's Guide.** 11th rev. ed. Alan Korwin. 160p. (Orig.). 1994. pap. 10.95 (0-9621958-3-9) Bloomfield Pr.

Arizona Hardcase. Jory Sherman. (Gunn Ser.: No. 13). (Orig.). 1982. pap. 2.25 (0-8217-1039-7) Zebra.

Arizona Health Care Perspective, 1994. Ed. by Kathleen O. Morgan et al. 24p. 1994. 18.00 (1-56692-152-X) Morgan Quitno Corp.

***Arizona Health Care Perspective 1995.** Ed. by Kathleen O. Morgan et al. 24p. 1995. 18.00 (1-56692-402-2) Morgan Quitno Corp.

Arizona Health Insurance Licensing Course. James J. Smith. 1990. ring bd. 35.00 (1-877723-49-5, 26753) Rough Notes.

Arizona Heart Institute Foundation Cookbook: A Renaissance in Good Eating. Arizona Heart Institute Foundation Staff. 576p. 1993. pap. 19.95 (0-9635767-1-2) AZ Heart Inst.

***Arizona Heat.** Jennifer Greene. 1995. mass mkt. 3.25 (0-373-05966-3, 1-05966-6) Silhouette.

Arizona Heat. Judith Steel. 448p. 1992. mass mkt. 4.50 (0-8217-3955-7) Zebra.

Arizona Highways Album: The Road to Statehood. Dean Smith et al. LC 86-82099. 176p. 1987. 19.95 (0-916179-10-9) Ariz Hwy.

Arizona Highways Heritage Cookbook. Louise Dewald. Ed. by Wesley Holden & Bob Dyer. (Illus.). 176p. (Orig.). 1988. 13.95 (0-916179-16-8) Ariz Hwy.

Arizona Highways Presents Desert Wildflowers. Desert Botanical Garden Staff. Ed. by James E. Cook & Wesley Holden. (Illus.). 112p. (Orig.). 1988. pap. 9.95 (0-916179-15-X) Ariz Hwy.

Arizona Hot Air Balloon Mystery. Carole Marsh. (Carole Marsh Arizona Bks.). (Illus.). (J). (gr. 2-9). 1994. 24.95 (0-7933-2336-3); pap. 14.95 (0-7933-2337-1); disk 29.95 (0-7933-2338-X) Gallopade Pub Group.

Arizona Humoresque: A Century of Arizona Humor. Ed. by C. L. Sonnichsen. LC 91-29733. (Illus.). 306p. 1992. 16.95 (0-88289-869-8); pap. 9.95 (0-88289-900-7) Pelican.

Arizona in Literature. Mary Boyer. LC 78-129967. (American History & Americana Ser.: No. 47). 1970. reprint ed. lib. bdg. 62.95 (0-8383-1168-7) M S G Haskell Hse.

Arizona in Perspective, 1994. Ed. by Kathleen O. Morgan et al. 26p. 1994. 18.00 (1-56692-202-X) Morgan Quitno Corp.

***Arizona in Perspective 1995.** Ed. by Kathleen O. Morgan et al. 26p. 1995. pap. 18.00 (1-56692-452-9) Morgan Quitno Corp.

Arizona Index: A Subject Index to Periodical Articles About the State, 2 vols. Ed. by University of Arizona Library Staff. 1978. lib. bdg. 195.00 (0-8161-0090-X, Hall Library) G K Hall.

Arizona Industrial Directory, 1994. 432p. 1994. disk write for info. (0-318-72680-7) Database Pub Co.

Arizona Industrial Directory, 1994. 432p. 1995. pap. 85.00 (0-929695-71-2) Database Pub Co.

Arizona Is for Kids. Roberta Salts. (Illus.). 32p. (J). (gr. 1-4). 1988. pap. 2.95 (0-685-21928-3) Double B Pubns.

Arizona Is Hot. Kaitlin M. Smith. (Illus.). 14p. (J). (gr. k-3). 1992. pap. 10.95 (1-895583-18-7) MAYA Pubs.

Arizona Jeopardy! Answers & Questions about Our State! Carole Marsh. (Carole Marsh Arizona Bks.). (Illus.). (J). (gr. 3-12). 1994. lib. bdg. 24.95 (0-7933-4085-3); pap. 14.95 (0-7933-4086-1); disk 29.95 (0-7933-4087-X) Gallopade Pub Group.

Arizona Jim. Charles A. Seltzer. 279p. 1975. reprint ed. lib. bdg. 21.95 (0-88411-101-6, Aeonian Pr) Amereon Ltd.

Arizona "Jography" A Fun Run Thru Our State! Carole Marsh. (Carole Marsh Arizona Bks.). (Illus.). (YA). (gr. 3-12). 1994. lib. bdg. 24.95 (1-55609-498-1); pap. 14.95 (1-55609-497-3); disk 29.95 (0-7933-1359-7) Gallopade Pub Group.

Arizona Justice & the Lonely Gun. large type ed. Gordon D. Shirreffs. Bd. with Lonely Gun. (Western Ser.). 484p. 1983. 21.95 (0-7089-1034-3) Ulverscroft.

Arizona Justice of the Peace Courts: Technical Assistance Project. National Center for State Courts Staff. 138p. 1984. 9.00 (0-685-15016-X, WRO, T/A-501) Natl Ctr St Courts.

Arizona Kid. Ron Koertge. 224p. (YA). (gr. 7 up). 1989. reprint ed. mass mkt. 3.99 (0-380-70776-4, Flare) Avon.

Arizona Kid's Cookbook: Recipes, How-to, History, Lore & More! Carole Marsh. (Carole Marsh Arizona Bks.). (Illus.). (YA). (gr. 3-12). 1994. lib. bdg. 24.95 (0-7933-0130-0); pap. 14.95 (0-7933-0129-7); disk 29.95 (0-7933-0131-9) Gallopade Pub Group.

***Arizona Land Surveying Law: Questions & Answers.** John E. Keen. 53p. 1995. pap. text ed. 20.00 (1-56569-015-X) Land Survey.

Arizona Land Use Law. Douglas A. Jorden & Michael D. House. 1990. ring bd. 85.00 (0-88726-007-1) AZ St Bar.

Arizona Landlord's Deskbook. Carlton C. Casler. 254p. (C). 1992. pap. text ed. 19.95 (1-881436-00-4) Consumer Law Bks.

Arizona Landmarks. James Cook. Ed. by John W. Holden. LC 84-73392. (Illus.). 160p. (Orig.). 1985. 35.00 (0-916179-04-4) Ariz Hwy.

Arizona Law of Medical Malpractice. Robert Stephen, Jr. 320p. 1988. 88.00 (0-317-99664-9) Medilex Co.

Arizona Law Review: 1959-1991, 35 vols., Set. 1,562.50 (0-8377-9022-0) Rothman.

Arizona Legal Research Guide. Ed. by Kathy Shimpock-Vieweg & Marianne S. Alcorn. LC 91-40052. x, 330p. 1992. 38.50 (0-89941-784-1, 306770) W S Hein.

Arizona Legal Services Practice Manual, Set. Ed. by Ann M. Davis. 1991. ring bd. 130.00 (0-685-49409-8) AZ St Bar.

Arizona Legal Services Practice Manual, Vol. I. 2nd ed. Ed. by Ann M. Davis. 480p. 1989. 75.00 (0-88726-015-2) AZ St Bar.

Arizona Legends & Lore. Dorothy D. Anderson. LC 91-10594. (Illus.). 176p. (Orig.). 1991. pap. 6.95 (0-914846-55-8) Golden West Pub.

Arizona Library Book: A Surprising Guide to the Unusual Special Collections in Libraries Across Our State for Students, Teachers, Writers & Publishers - Includes Reproducible Mailing Labels Plus Activities for Young People! Carole Marsh. (Carole Marsh Arizona Bks.). (Illus.). 1994. lib. bdg. 24.95 (0-7933-3014-9); pap. 14.95 (0-7933-3015-7); disk 29.95 (0-7933-3016-5) Gallopade Pub Group.

Arizona Life Insurance Licensing Course. James J. Smith. 1990. ring bd. 35.00 (1-877723-13-4, 26535) Rough Notes.

Arizona Lovestorm. Wendy Garrett. 1991. mass mkt. 4.25 (0-8217-3482-2) Zebra.

Arizona, Magnificent Wilderness. Larry Ulrich. (Illus.). 112p. 1987. 27.95 (0-942394-40-2); pap. 17.95 (0-929969-66-9) Westcliffe Pubs Inc.

Arizona Marketplace for Writers & Photographers. Carol O. Brown. 160p. (Orig.). 1990. pap. 7.95 (0-914846-49-3) Golden West Pub.

Arizona Marriage Dissolution Manual. Arizona Law Institute Staff et al. LC 83-112484. 510p. 1982. 34.35 (0-910039-01-1) AZ Law Inst.

Arizona Media Book: A Surprising Guide to the Amazing Print, Broadcast & Online Media of Our State for Students, Teachers, Writers & Publishers - Includes Reproducible Mailing Labels Plus Activities for Young People! Carole Marsh. (Carole Marsh Arizona Bks.). (Illus.). 1994. lib. bdg. 24.95 (0-7933-3167-6); pap. 14.95 (0-7933-3168-4); disk 29.95 (0-7933-3169-2) Gallopade Pub Group.

Arizona Medical Association: The First Hundred Years. John W. Kenendy. Ed. by Kathy Bailey. (C). 1993. text ed. write for info. (0-318-70335-1) Herit Pubs AZ.

Arizona Medicine & Other Historical Essays. John W. Kennedy. Ed. by Robert K. Kravetz. 256p. (C). 1990. 29.95 (0-929690-09-5) Herit Pubs AZ.

Arizona Memories. Ed. by Anne H. Morgan & Rennard Strickland. LC 84-8853. 354p. 1984. 40.00 (0-8165-0869-0) U of Ariz Pr.

Arizona Mileposts. William Hafford. 204p. 1993. pap. 15.95 (0-916179-38-9) Ariz Hwy.

***Arizona Military Installations: 1752-1992.** Richard Nearing & David Hoff. (Illus.). 80p. (Orig.). 1995. pap. 20.00 (0-9635455-1-5) GEM Pub AZ.

Arizona Minerals & How to Find Them. Raymond Merriam. (Illus.). 73p. (Orig.). 1995. pap. 4.95 (0-918080-40-1) Treas Chest Bks.

Arizona Museums: Your Guide to Arizona's Treasures. 2nd ed. Al Fischer & Mildred Fischer. 240p. 1993. pap. 9.95 (0-914846-73-6) Golden West Pub.

Arizona Mystery Van Takes Off! Book 1: Handicapped Arizona Kids Sneak Off on a Big Adventure. Carole Marsh. (Carole Marsh Arizona Bks.). (Illus.). (J). (gr. 3-12). 1994. 24.95 (0-7933-4970-2); pap. 14.95 (0-7933-4971-0); disk 29.95 (0-7933-4972-9) Gallopade Pub Group.

Arizona-New Mexico Automotive Directory. Ed. by T. L. Spelman. 1985. 24.95 (1-55527-001-8) Auto Contact Inc.

Arizona Nights. Stewart E. White. 1976. lib. bdg. 15.75 (0-89968-124-7, Lghtyr Pr) Buccaneer Bks.

Arizona Notary Law Primer. National Notary Magazine Editors. LC 93-85882. 1993. pap. 10.95 (0-933134-29-0) Natl Notary.

Arizona Odyssey: Bibliographic Adventures in Nineteenth Century Magazines. David M. Goodman. LC 73-94875. 1969. 20.00 (0-910152-02-0) AZ Hist Foun.

Arizona 101: An Irreverent Short Course for New Arrivals. James Cook. (Illus.). 70p. 1981. pap. 3.95 (0-9606366-0-9) Gem Guides Bk.

Arizona Outdoor Guide. Ernest E. Snyder. LC 85-11454. (Illus.). 128p. (Orig.). 1985. pap. 6.95 (0-914846-20-5) Golden West Pub.

Arizona Panhandle. Richard Clarke. 192p. 1989. 18.95 (0-8027-4098-7) Walker & Co.

Arizona Pathways: Study Guide. 32p. (Orig.). (J). (gr. 6-8). 1990. student ed 9.95 (0-911981-65-9) Cloud Pub.

Arizona Photographers: The Snell & Wilmer Collection. Contrib by Terence Pitts. (Illus.). 80p. (Orig.). 1990. pap. 15.00 (0-938262-19-X) Ctr Creat Photog.

Arizona Place Names. Will C. Barnes. LC 87-35835. 503p. 1988. reprint ed. pap. 18.95 (0-8165-1074-1) U of Ariz Pr.

Arizona Probate: Arizona Practice Systems Library Manual, Vol. 1. Ed. by Thomas S. Wiley. LC 79-11140. 1980. 97.50 (0-317-00624-X) Lawyers Cooperative.

Arizona Probate: Arizona Practice Systems Library Manual, Vol. 1. suppl. ed. Ed. by Thomas S. Wiley. LC 79-91140. 1980. Suppl. 1985. 33.50 (0-317-03224-0) Lawyers Cooperative.

Arizona Probate Code Practice Manual & Forms Diskette. 3rd ed. Jeannette K. Geiser et al. 570p. 1989. ring bd. 90.00 (0-88726-012-8); disk 35.00 (0-88726-013-6) AZ St Bar.

Arizona Project: How a Team of Investigative Reporters Got Revenge on Deadline. rev. ed. Michael F. Wendland. 304p. 1988. pap. 10.95 (0-945165-02-1) Blue Sky Pr Inc.

Arizona Property & Casualty Insurance Licensing Course. James J. Smith. 50.00 (0-942326-70-9, 26841) Rough Notes.

Arizona Puzzles. John McLean. 64p. 1991. pap. 6.95 (0-9631657-0-4) AZ Puzzles.

Arizona Quarterly Illustrated, 1880-1881: A Reprint With Introduction & Index. Ed. by Lonnie E. Underhill. (Orig.). (C). 1985. reprint ed. 95.00 (0-933234-06-6); reprint ed. 135.00 (0-933234-07-4) Roan Horse.

Arizona Quiz Bowl Crash Course! Carole Marsh. (Carole Marsh Arizona Bks.). (Illus.). (YA). (gr. 3-12). 1994. lib. bdg. 24.95 (1-55609-505-8); pap. 14.95 (1-55609-504-X); disk 29.95 (0-7933-1368-6) Gallopade Pub Group.

Arizona Ranch Houses: Southern Territorial Style, 1867-1900. Janet A. Stewart. LC 87-14553. 121p. 1987. reprint ed. pap. 14.95 (0-8165-1045-8) U of Ariz Pr.

Arizona Range Grasses: Their Description, Forage Value & Management. Robert R. Humphrey. LC 79-13764. (Illus.). 159p. reprint ed. pap. 45.40 (0-8357-5740-4, 2056388) Bks Demand.

Arizona Rangers. Bill O'Neal. Ed. by Edwin M. Eakin. (Illus.). 288p. 1988. pap. 15.95 (0-89015-610-7) Sunbelt Media.

Arizona Rental Rights: A Guide Book for Tenants, Landlords, & Mobile Home Users. David A. Peterson & Andrew M. Hull. LC 93-78484. (Illus.). 96p. (Orig.). 1993. pap. 6.95 (0-935182-63-2) Gem Guides Bk.

Arizona Revised Statutes, 1991, 4 vols., Set. Michie Company Staff. pap. 120.00 (0-87473-675-7) Michie Butterworth.

Arizona Road Atlas. Arizona Department of Transportation Staff. (Illus.). 56p. 1989. 4.95 (0-916179-21-4) Ariz Hwy.

Arizona Rollercoasters! Carole Marsh. (Carole Marsh Arizona Bks.). (Illus.). (YA). (gr. 3-12). 1994. lib. bdg. 24.95 (0-7933-5230-4); pap. 14.95 (0-7933-5231-2); disk 29.95 (0-7933-5232-0) Gallopade Pub Group.

Arizona Rough Riders. Charles Herner. LC 73-121894. 287p. reprint ed. pap. 81.80 (0-8357-5741-2, 2024317) Bks Demand.

Arizona Rural Health Provider Atlas. 2nd rev. ed. Rena J. Gordon. (Illus.). iv, 152p. (C). 1987. pap. text ed. 24.95 (0-945463-01-4) U Arizona Rural Hlth Office.

Arizona Saddles. large type ed. Brett Austin. (Linford Western Library). 1991. pap. 13.95 (0-7089-7017-6) Ulverscroft.

Arizona Scenic Drives. Stewart Green. (Falcon Guide Ser.). (Illus.). 184p. (Orig.). 1992. pap. 12.95 (1-56044-111-9) Falcon Pr MT.

Arizona School Trivia: An Amazing & Fascinating Look at Our State's Teachers, Schools & Students! Carole Marsh. (Carole Marsh Arizona Bks.). (Illus.). (YA). (gr. 3-12). 1994. lib. bdg. 24.95 (0-7933-0127-0); pap. 14.95 (0-7933-0126-2); disk 29.95 (0-685-45932-2) Gallopade Pub Group.

***Arizona Select.** Randy Vogel. (Southwest Rock Climbing Ser.). (Illus.). 200p. 1995. pap. 20.00 (0-934641-78-1) Chockstone Pr.

Arizona Silly Basketball Sportsmysteries, Vol. I. Carole Marsh. (Carole Marsh Arizona Bks.). (Illus.). (YA). (gr. 3-12). 1994. lib. bdg. 24.95 (0-7933-0124-6); pap. 14.95 (0-7933-0123-8); disk 29.95 (0-7933-0125-4) Gallopade Pub Group.

Arizona Silly Basketball Sportsmysteries, Vol. II. Carole Marsh. (Carole Marsh Arizona Bks.). (Illus.). (YA). (gr. 3-12). 1994. lib. bdg. 24.95 (0-7933-1568-9); pap. 14.95 (0-7933-1569-7); disk 29.95 (0-7933-1570-0) Gallopade Pub Group.

Arizona Silly Football Sportsmysteries, Vol. I. Carole Marsh. (Carole Marsh Arizona Bks.). (Illus.). (YA). (gr. 3-12). 1994. lib. bdg. 24.95 (1-55609-501-5); pap. 14.95 (1-55609-500-7); disk 29.95 (0-7933-1361-9) Gallopade Pub Group.

Arizona Silly Football Sportsmysteries, Vol. II. Carole Marsh. (Carole Marsh Arizona Bks.). (Illus.). (YA). (gr. 3-12). 1994. lib. bdg. 24.95 (0-7933-1362-7); pap. 14.95 (0-7933-1363-5); disk 29.95 (0-7933-1364-3) Gallopade Pub Group.

Arizona Silly Trivia! Carole Marsh. (Carole Marsh Arizona Bks.). (Illus.). (YA). (gr. 3-12). 1994. lib. bdg. 24.95 (1-55609-496-5); pap. 14.95 (1-55609-495-7); disk 29.95 (0-7933-1358-9) Gallopade Pub Group.

Arizona Slaughter. Jon Sharpe. (Trailsman Ser.: No. 118). 176p. (Orig.). 1991. pap. 3.50 (0-451-17067-9, Sig) NAL-Dutton.

Arizona Small Game Cookbook. Lee Fischer & Bruce Fischer. Ed. by Evelyn Bates. (Illus.). 128p. (Orig.). 1992. pap. 5.95 (0-914846-74-4) Golden West Pub.

Arizona Soils. David M. Hendricks. Ed. by Richard A. Haney. LC 85-6724. (Illus.). 280p. (Orig.). 1985. pap. 45.00 (0-932913-02-4) Univ AZ Agriculture.

Arizona Star. large type ed. Faith Baldwin. LC 93-34587. 1994. 17.95 (1-56054-319-1) Thorndike Pr.

Arizona Star. Faith Baldwin. 1976. reprint ed. lib. bdg. 22.95 (0-88411-601-8, Aeonian Pr) Amereon Ltd.

***Arizona State Business Handbook.** 400p. (C). 1995. text ed. 395.00 (0-7605-1917-X) Rector Pr.

Arizona State Constitution: A Reference Guide. John D. Leshy. LC 92-35922. (Reference Guides to the State Constitutions of the United States Ser.: No. 15). 456p. 1993. text ed. 85.00 (0-313-27266-2, LAH/, Greenwood Pr) Greenwood.

Arizona State University K-6 Drama Theatre Curriculum Guide. Lin Wright. 1992. 8.00 (0-317-05168-7) U IL Sch Music.

***Arizona Statutes: 1993 Edition, 4 vols., Set.** rev. ed. Date not set. 125.00 (1-55834-040-8) Michie Butterworth.

Arizona Strip: Christmas on the Homestead & Other Stories. Jean Luttrell. (Illus.). 40p. (Orig.). 1988. pap. 4.25 (0-9617609-1-5) Shade Tree NV.

Arizona: Studies: Blackline Masters. Michael McCabe. (Illus.). 41p. 1990. teacher ed 27.95 (0-911981-64-0) Cloud Pub.

Arizona: Studies: Map Skills Program. Darryl Stacy & Michael McCabe. (Illus.). 59p. (J). (gr. 4-6). 1990. ring bd. 45.95 (0-911981-53-5) Cloud Pub.

Arizona Studies Program: Activity Manual. 2nd ed. Carol Shockley & Phelps Wilkins. Ed. by Eunice A. Combs. (Illus.). 176p. 1983. 95.00 (0-943068-83-5) Graphic Learning.

Arizona Studies Program: Teacher's Guide. 2nd ed. Carol Shockley & Phelps Wilkins. Ed. by Eunice A. Combs. (Illus.). 28p. 1983. teacher ed 10.00 (0-943068-84-3) Graphic Learning.

Arizona Superior Courts: Proposed Classification & Salary Plans. National Center for State Courts Staff. 456p. 1980. write for info. (0-318-61224-0, WRO-047) Natl Ctr St Courts.

Arizona Survival. Betty L. Hall. 160p. (Orig.). (gr. 10-12). 1982. pap. text ed. 5.84 (0-318-19358-2) Westwood Pr.

Arizona Teacher Proficiency Examination Workbook. rev. ed. 96p. 1995. pap. 11.95 (0-935810-52-8) Primer Pubs.

Arizona Temptation. Garda Parker. 1992. mass mkt. 4.25 (0-8217-3763-5) Zebra.

Arizona Territorial Census Index 1864. Ronald V. Jackson. LC 78-56235. (Illus.). 1978. lib. bdg. 45.00 (0-89593-209-1) Accelerated Index.

Arizona Territorial Census Index 1866. Ronald V. Jackson. (Illus.). 1982. lib. bdg. 45.00 (0-89593-706-9) Accelerated Index.

Arizona Territorial Census Index 1867. Ronald V. Jackson. (Illus.). 1983. lib. bdg. 45.00 (0-89593-707-7) Accelerated Index.

Arizona Territorial Census Index 1869. Ronald V. Jackson. (Illus.). 1982. lib. bdg. 51.00 (0-89593-708-5) Accelerated Index.

Arizona Territorial Cookbook: The Food & Lifestyles of a Frontier. Melissa R. Weiner & Budge Ruffner. Ed. by Robyn Browder. LC 82-2489. (Regional Cookbks.). (Illus.). 232p. 1983. pap. 8.95 (0-89865-312-6, AACR2) Donning Co.

Arizona Territorial Deed Records 1864-1869. Dora M. Whiteside. 50p. (Orig.). 1986. pap. 8.00 (0-938353-05-5) D M Whiteside.

Arizona Territorial Great Register 1876 of Yavapai County Arizona. Dora M. Whiteside. (Orig.). 1987. pap. 4.00 (0-938353-07-1) D M Whiteside.

Arizona Territorial Hospital Records 1890-1910. Dora M. Whiteside. 61p. (Orig.). 1985. pap. 8.00 (0-938353-04-7) D M Whiteside.

Arizona Territorial Marriage Records Index, 1895-1912: Yavapai County, Arizona. Dora M. Whiteside. 24p. (Orig.). 1986. pap. 4.00 (0-938353-06-3) D M Whiteside.

Arizona Territorial Poll Tax Records, 1873-1876. Dora M. Whiteside. 44p. (Orig.). 1984. pap. 4.50 (0-938353-03-9) D M Whiteside.

Arizona Territory. abr. ed. Eileen Barish. 346p. 1994. pap. 9.95 (1-56901-520-1) NW Pub.

Arizona Territory Cookbook. Daphne Overstreet. 1995. pap. 5.95 (0-914846-75-2) Golden West Pub.

Arizona Territory, 1863-1912: A Political History. Jay J. Wagoner. LC 69-16331. (Illus.). 599p. reprint ed. pap. 170.80 (0-7837-1916-7, 2042120) Bks Demand.

An Asterisk (*) at the beginning of an entry indicates that the title is appearing in BIP for the first time.

A

An Asterisk (*) at the beginning of an entry indicates that the title is appearing in BIP for the first time.

A

Arkansas CSA Soldiers, Vol. 3: Surnames M-Z. Bobbie J. McLane & Capitola Glazner. 200p. (Orig.). 1979. pap. 25.00 (*0-929604-30-X*) Arkansas Ancestors.

Arkansas' Damned Yankees: An Index to Union Soldiers in Arkansas Regiments. Comp. by Desmond W. Allen. 220p. 1987. 34.00 (*0-941765-12-1*); pap. 22.00 (*0-685-50068-3*) Arkansas Res.

Arkansas Delta: Land of Paradox. Ed. by Jeannie Whayne & Willard B. Gatewood. LC 92-43140. (Illus.). 336p. (C). 1993. 32.00 (*1-55728-287-0*) U of Ark Pr.

Arkansas Democratic Politics, 1896-1920. Richard L. Niswonger. LC 89-5195. 344p. 1990. 29.95 (*1-55728-116-5*) U of Ark Pr.

Arkansas Diamonds. Thomas P. Terry. (Illus.). 40p. (Orig.). 1977. pap. 3.95 (*0-939850-04-4*) Spec Pub.

Arkansas Digest: Covering Cases from State & Federal Courts. West Publishing Company Staff. write for info. (*0-318-60691-7*) West Pub.

Arkansas Dingbats! Bk. 1: A Fun Book of Games, Stories, Activities & More about Our State That's All in Code! for You to Decipher. Carole Marsh. (Carole Marsh Arkansas Bks.). (Illus.). (J). (gr. 3-12). 1994. lib. bdg. 24.95 (*0-7933-3782-8*); pap. 14.95 (*0-7933-3783-6*); disk 29.95 (*0-7933-3784-4*) Gallopade Pub Group.

Arkansas Eighteen Forty Census: Surnames in Census Order, Vol. 2. Comp. by Berniece D. Coyle & Thomas E. Coyle. 278p. 1994. pap. text ed. 35.00 (*1-56088-055-4*) Coyle Data Co.

Arkansas Eighteen Forty Census Alphabetically Listed by Surname, Vol. 1. Comp. by Berniece D. Coyle & Thomas E. Coyle. 252p. 1994. pap. text ed. 35.00 (*1-56088-054-6*) Coyle Data Co.

Arkansas Federal Census Index, 1820. Ronald V. Jackson. (Illus.). lib. bdg. 48.00 (*0-89593-710-7*) Accelerated Index.

Arkansas Federal Census Index, 1830. Ronald V. Jackson. (Illus.). 1981. lib. bdg. 54.00 (*0-89593-212-1*) Accelerated Index.

Arkansas Federal Census Index, 1840. Ronald V. Jackson. LC 77-85784. (Illus.). 1981. lib. bdg. 54.00 (*0-89593-004-8*) Accelerated Index.

Arkansas Federal Census Index, 1850. Ronald V. Jackson. LC 77-85793. (Illus.). 1981. lib. bdg. 65.00 (*0-89593-005-6*) Accelerated Index.

Arkansas Federal Census Index, 1860. Ronald V. Jackson. (Illus.). 1991. lib. bdg. 129.00 (*0-89593-711-5*) Accelerated Index.

Arkansas Federal Census Index, 1870. (Illus.). 1987. lib. bdg. 240.00 (*0-89593-223-7*) Accelerated Index.

Arkansas Festival for Kids! Carole Marsh. (Carole Marsh Arkansas Bks.). (Illus.). (YA). (gr. 3-12). 1994. lib. bdg. 24.95 (*0-7933-3935-9*); pap. 14.95 (*0-7933-3936-7*); disk 29.95 (*0-7933-3937-5*) Gallopade Pub Group.

Arkansas Folklore Sourcebook. Ed. by W. K. McNeil & William M. Clements. LC 92-5544. (Illus.). 288p. 1992. 30.00 (*1-55728-254-4*) U of Ark Pr.

Arkansas Fundamental Court Improvement Project. National Center for State Courts Staff. 1981. pap. write for info. (*0-318-61187-2*, SRO-006) Natl Ctr St Courts.

Arkansas Gazette Obituaries Index, 1819-1879. Stephen J. Chism. 120p. 1990. 27.50 (*0-89308-398-4*, AR 23) Southern Hist Pr.

Arkansas Geography: The Physical Landscape & the Historical-Cultural Setting. Gerald Hanson & Hubert Stroud. LC 80-52075. (Illus.). 100p. (Orig.). (gr. 7-12). 1981. pap. 17.95 (*0-914546-34-1*) Rose Pub.

Arkansas Geography: The Physical Landscape & the Historical-Cultural Setting. Gerald Hanson & Hubert Stroud. LC 80-52075. (Illus.). 100p. (Orig.). (YA). (gr. 7-12). 1981. pap. write for info. (*0-914546-63-5*) Rose Pub.

Arkansas Governments Performance Standards, 1990. Ed. by Greg Michels. (Governments Performance Standards Ser.). (Illus.). 150p. 1990. text ed. 125.00 (*1-55507-475-8*) Municipal Analysis.

Arkansas Handbook on Environmental Laws. Chisenhall, Nestrud & Julian Staff. (State Environmental Law Ser.). 145p. 1990. pap. text ed. 65.00 (*0-86587-214-7*) Gov Insts.

Arkansas Health Care Perspective, 1994. Ed. by Kathleen O. Morgan et al. 24p. 1994. 18.00 (*1-56692-153-8*) Morgan Quitno Corp.

***Arkansas Health Care Perspective 1995.** Ed. by Kathleen O. Morgan et al. 24p. 1995. 18.00 (*1-56692-403-0*) Morgan Quitno Corp.

Arkansas Health Course. James J. Smith. Date not set. 32.00 (*1-56461-065-9*, 26259) Rough Notes.

Arkansas Heritage: Fifth Grade History Textbook. Ruth Mitchell. LC 85-63310. (Illus.). 192p. 1986. 18.00 (*0-914546-62-7*) Rose Pub.

Arkansas Heritage: Recipes Past & Present. American Cancer Society, Arkansas Division, Inc. Staff. LC 92-32004. 1992. write for info. (*0-87197-356-1*) Favorite Recipes.

Arkansas Hiking Trails: A Guide to Seventy Plus Selected Trails in the Natural State. 2nd ed. Tim Ernst. (Illus.). 192p. 1994. pap. 16.95 (*1-882906-12-8*) Ernst Wilderness.

Arkansas Hiking Trails: A Guide to 70 Selected Trails in "The Natural State" Tim Ernst. 176p. 1992. pap. text ed. 14.99 (*1-882906-00-4*) Ernst Wilderness.

Arkansas Historical & Biographical Index, Vol. 1. Ronald V. Jackson. LC 78-53686. (Illus.). 1984. lib. bdg. 30.00 (*0-89593-171-0*) Accelerated Index.

***Arkansas Historical Dance Series.** David Peterson. 80p. 1995. bmax, pap. 25.50 (*0-944436-50-1*) Univ Central AR Pr.

Arkansas Historical Math Facts. Linda Payne. LC 90-63448. 72p. (J). (gr. 3-6). 1986. spiral bd. 25.00 (*0-914546-84-8*) Rose Pub.

***Arkansas History: An Annotated Bibliography.** Comp. by Michael B. Dougan et al. LC 95-7477. (Bibliographies of the States of the United States Ser.: No. 5). 400p. 1995. text ed. 75.00 (*0-313-28226-9*, Greenwood Pr) Greenwood.

Arkansas History for Young People. T. Harri Baker & Jane Browning. (YA). (gr. 8). 1991. student ed 28.00 (*1-55728-083-5*); teacher ed write for info. (*1-55728-201-3*) U of Ark Pr.

Arkansas Hot Air Balloon Mystery. Carole Marsh. (Carole Marsh Arkansas Bks.). (Illus.). (J). (gr. 2-9). 1994. 24.95 (*0-7933-2345-2*); pap. 14.95 (*0-7933-2346-0*); disk 29.95 (*0-7933-2347-9*) Gallopade Pub Group.

Arkansas in Perspective 1994. Ed. by Kathleen O. Morgan et al. 26p. 1994. 18.00 (*1-56692-203-8*) Morgan Quitno Corp.

***Arkansas in Perspective 1995.** Ed. by Kathleen O. Morgan et al. 26p. 1995. pap. 18.00 (*1-56692-453-7*) Morgan Quitno Corp.

Arkansas in the Guilded Age, Eighteen Seventy-four to Nineteen Hundred. Waddy W. Moore. (Illus.). 229p. 1976. pap. 14.95 (*0-914546-08-2*) J W Bell.

Arkansas... Its Land & People. Matt Bradley. LC 80-81993. (Illus.). 112p. 1984. 35.00 (*0-9604642-0-4*) Mus Sci & Hist.

Arkansas Jeopardy! Answers & Questions about Our State! Carole Marsh. (Carole Marsh Arkansas Bks.). (Illus.). (J). (gr. 3-12). 1994. lib. bdg. 24.95 (*0-7933-4088-8*); pap. 14.95 (*0-7933-4089-6*); disk 29.95 (*0-7933-4090-X*) Gallopade Pub Group.

Arkansas "Jography" A Fun Run Thru Our State! Carole Marsh. (Carole Marsh Arkansas Bks.). (Illus.). (YA). (gr. 3-12). 1994. lib. bdg. 24.95 (*1-55609-485-X*); pap. 14.95 (*1-55609-088-9*); disk 29.95 (*0-7933-1375-9*) Gallopade Pub Group.

Arkansas JPC Judicial Article Task Force: Judicial Personnel. National Center for State Courts Staff. 33p. write for info. (*0-318-61226-7*, SRO-019) Natl Ctr St Courts.

Arkansas JPC Judicial Article Task Force: The Financing of Arkansas Courts. James R. James. 51p. write for info. (*0-318-61216-X*, SRO-020) Natl Ctr St Courts.

Arkansas Kid's Cookbook: Recipes, How-to, History, Lore & More! Carole Marsh. (Carole Marsh Arkansas Bks.). (Illus.). (YA). (gr. 3-12). 1994. lib. bdg. 24.95 (*0-7933-0154-8*); pap. 14.95 (*0-7933-0153-X*); disk 29.95 (*0-7933-0155-6*) Gallopade Pub Group.

Arkansas Land Patents: Arkansas, Chicot, & Desha Counties (Granted Through 30 June 1908) Desmond W. Allen & Bobbie J. McLane. (County Ser.). (Illus.). 126p. (Orig.). 1991. pap. 16.00 (*1-56546-001-4*) Arkansas Res.

Arkansas Land Patents: Ashley County (Granted Through 30 June 1908) Desmond W. Allen & Bobbie J. McLane. (County Ser.). (Illus.). 89p. (Orig.). 1991. pap. 14.00 (*1-56546-003-0*) Arkansas Res.

Arkansas Land Patents: Baxter County (Granted Through 30 June 1908) Desmond W. Allen & Bobbie J. McLane. (County Ser.). (Illus.). 80p. (Orig.). 1991. pap. 14.00 (*1-56546-004-9*) Arkansas Res.

Arkansas Land Patents: Benton County (Granted Through 30 June 1908) Desmond W. Allen & Bobbie J. McLane. (County Ser.). (Illus.). 156p. (Orig.). 1991. pap. 18.00 (*1-56546-005-7*) Arkansas Res.

Arkansas Land Patents: Boone County (Granted Through 30 June 1908) Desmond W. Allen & Bobbie J. McLane. (County Ser.). (Illus.). 116p. (Orig.). 1991. pap. 16.00 (*1-56546-006-5*) Arkansas Res.

Arkansas Land Patents: Bradley County (Granted Through 30 June 1908) Desmond W. Allen & Bobbie J. McLane. (County Ser.). (Illus.). 97p. (Orig.). 1991. pap. 14.00 (*1-56546-007-3*) Arkansas Res.

Arkansas Land Patents: Calhoun County (Granted through 30 June 1908) Desmond W. Allen & Bobbie J. McLane. (County Ser.). (Illus.). 79p. (Orig.). 1991. pap. 14.00 (*1-56546-008-1*) Arkansas Res.

Arkansas Land Patents: Carroll County (Granted through 30 June 1908) Desmond W. Allen & Bobbie J. McLane. (County Ser.). (Illus.). 116p. (Orig.). 1991. pap. 16.00 (*1-56546-009-X*) Arkansas Res.

Arkansas Land Patents: Clark County (Granted through 30 June 1908) Desmond W. Allen & Bobbie J. McLane. (County Ser.). (Illus.). 83p. (Orig.). 1991. pap. 14.00 (*1-56546-010-3*) Arkansas Res.

Arkansas Land Patents: Cleburne County (Granted through 30 June 1908) Desmond W. Allen & Bobbie J. McLane. (County Ser.). (Illus.). 78p. (Orig.). 1991. pap. 14.00 (*1-56546-011-1*) Arkansas Res.

Arkansas Land Patents: Cleveland County (Granted through 30 June 1908) Desmond W. Allen & Bobbie J. McLane. (County Ser.). (Illus.). 72p. (Orig.). 1991. pap. 14.00 (*1-56546-012-X*) Arkansas Res.

Arkansas Land Patents: Columbia County (Granted through 30 June 1908) Desmond W. Allen & Bobbie J. McLane. (County Ser.). (Illus.). 115p. (Orig.). 1991. pap. 16.00 (*1-56546-013-8*) Arkansas Res.

Arkansas Land Patents: Conway, Faulkner, & Perry Counties (Granted through 30 June 1908) Desmond W. Allen & Bobbie J. McLane. (County Ser.). (Illus.). 142p. (Orig.). 1990. pap. 18.00 (*1-56546-014-6*) Arkansas Res.

Arkansas Land Patents: Crawford County (Granted Through 30 June 1908) Desmond W. Allen & Bobbie J. McLane. (County Ser.). (Illus.). 68p. (Orig.). 1991. pap. 14.00 (*1-56546-015-4*) Arkansas Res.

Arkansas Land Patents: Dallas County (Granted through 30 June 1908) Desmond W. Allen & Bobbie J. McLane. (County Ser.). (Illus.). 57p. (Orig.). 1991. pap. 14.00 (*1-56546-016-2*) Arkansas Res.

Arkansas Land Patents: Drew County (Granted through 30 June 1908. Desmond W. Allen & Bobbie J. McLane. (County Ser.). (Illus.). 90p. (Orig.). 1991. pap. 14.00 (*1-56546-017-0*) Arkansas Res.

Arkansas Land Patents: Eastern Arkansas Counties (Granted Through 30 June 1908) Desmond W. Allen & Bobbie J. McLane. (County Ser.). (Illus.). 234p. (Orig.). 1991. pap. 24.00 (*1-56546-002-2*) Arkansas Res.

Arkansas Land Patents: Franklin County (Granted through 30 June 1908) Desmond W. Allen & Bobbie J. McLane. (County Ser.). (Illus.). 73p. (Orig.). 1991. pap. 14.00 (*1-56546-018-9*) Arkansas Res.

Arkansas Land Patents: Fulton County (Granted through 30 June 1908) Desmond W. Allen & Bobbie J. McLane. (County Ser.). (Illus.). 99p. (Orig.). 1991. pap. 14.00 (*1-56546-019-7*) Arkansas Res.

Arkansas Land Patents: Garland County (Granted through 30 June 1908) Desmond W. Allen & Bobbie J. McLane. (County Ser.). (Illus.). 99p. (Orig.). 1991. pap. 14.00 (*1-56546-020-0*) Arkansas Res.

Arkansas Land Patents: Grant & Saline Counties (Granted through 30 June 1908) Desmond W. Allen & Bobbie J. McLane. (County Ser.). (Illus.). 128p. (Orig.). 1991. pap. 16.00 (*1-56546-021-9*) Arkansas Res.

Arkansas Land Patents: Hempstead County (Granted through 30 June 1908) Desmond W. Allen & Bobbie J. McLane. (County Ser.). (Illus.). 91p. (Orig.). 1991. pap. 14.00 (*1-56546-022-7*) Arkansas Res.

Arkansas Land Patents: Hot Spring County (Granted through 30 June 1908) Desmond W. Allen & Bobbie J. McLane. (County Ser.). (Illus.). 62p. (Orig.). 1991. pap. 14.00 (*1-56546-023-5*) Arkansas Res.

Arkansas Land Patents: Howard County (Granted through 30 June 1908) Desmond W. Allen & Bobbie J. McLane. (County Ser.). (Illus.). 102p. (Orig.). 1991. pap. 14.00 (*1-56546-024-3*) Arkansas Res.

Arkansas Land Patents: Independence County (Granted through 30 June 1908) Desmond W. Allen & Bobbie J. McLane. (County Ser.). (Illus.). 111p. (Orig.). 1991. pap. 14.00 (*1-56546-025-1*) Arkansas Res.

Arkansas Land Patents: Izard County (Granted through 30 June 1908) Desmond W. Allen & Bobbie J. McLane. (County Ser.). (Illus.). 108p. (Orig.). 1991. pap. 14.00 (*1-56546-026-X*) Arkansas Res.

Arkansas Land Patents: Jackson, Lawrence, & Woodruff Counties (Granted through 30 June 1908) Desmond W. Allen & Bobbie J. McLane. (County Ser.). (Illus.). 81p. (Orig.). 1991. pap. 14.00 (*1-56546-027-8*) Arkansas Res.

Arkansas Land Patents: Jefferson County (Granted through 30 June 1908) Desmond W. Allen & Bobbie J. McLane. (County Ser.). (Illus.). 80p. (Orig.). 1991. pap. 14.00 (*1-56546-028-6*) Arkansas Res.

Arkansas Land Patents: Johnson County (Granted through 30 June 1908) Desmond W. Allen & Bobbie J. McLane. (County Ser.). (Illus.). 72p. (Orig.). 1991. pap. 14.00 (*1-56546-029-4*) Arkansas Res.

Arkansas Land Patents: Lafayette County (Granted through 30 June 1908) Desmond W. Allen & Bobbie J. McLane. (County Ser.). (Illus.). 73p. (Orig.). 1991. pap. 14.00 (*1-56546-030-8*) Arkansas Res.

Arkansas Land Patents: Lincoln County (Granted through 30 June 1908) Desmond W. Allen & Bobbie J. McLane. (County Ser.). (Illus.). 64p. (Orig.). 1991. pap. 14.00 (*1-56546-031-6*) Arkansas Res.

Arkansas Land Patents: Little River County (Granted through 30 June 1908) Desmond W. Allen & Bobbie J. McLane. (County Ser.). (Illus.). 66p. (Orig.). 1991. pap. 14.00 (*1-56546-032-4*) Arkansas Res.

Arkansas Land Patents: Logan County (Granted through 30 June 1908) Desmond W. Allen & Bobbie J. McLane. (County Ser.). (Illus.). 91p. (Orig.). 1991. pap. 14.00 (*1-56546-033-2*) Arkansas Res.

Arkansas Land Patents: Lonoke & Prairie Counties (Granted through 30 June 1908) Desmond W. Allen & Bobbie J. McLane. (County Ser.). (Illus.). 75p. (Orig.). 1991. pap. 14.00 (*1-56546-034-0*) Arkansas Res.

Arkansas Land Patents: Madison County (Granted through 30 June 1908) Desmond W. Allen & Bobbie J. McLane. (County Ser.). (Illus.). 151p. (Orig.). 1991. pap. 18.00 (*1-56546-035-9*) Arkansas Res.

Arkansas Land Patents: Marion County (Granted through 30 June 1908) Desmond W. Allen & Bobbie J. McLane. (County Ser.). (Illus.). 107p. (Orig.). 1991. pap. 14.00 (*1-56546-036-7*) Arkansas Res.

Arkansas Land Patents: Miller County (Granted through 30 June 1908) Desmond W. Allen & Bobbie J. McLane. (County Ser.). (Illus.). 63p. (Orig.). 1991. pap. 14.00 (*1-56546-037-5*) Arkansas Res.

Arkansas Land Patents: Montgomery County (Granted through 30 June 1908) Desmond W. Allen & Bobbie J. McLane. (County Ser.). (Illus.). 73p. (Orig.). 1991. pap. 14.00 (*1-56546-038-3*) Arkansas Res.

Arkansas Land Patents: Nevada County (Granted through 30 June 1908) Desmond W. Allen & Bobbie J. McLane. (County Ser.). (Illus.). 81p. (Orig.). 1991. pap. 14.00 (*1-56546-039-1*) Arkansas Res.

Arkansas Land Patents: Newton County (Granted through 30 June 1908) Desmond W. Allen & Bobbie J. McLane. (County Ser.). (Illus.). 99p. (Orig.). 1991. pap. 14.00 (*1-56546-040-5*) Arkansas Res.

Arkansas Land Patents: Ouachita County (Granted through 30 June 1908) Desmond W. Allen & Bobbie J. McLane. (County Ser.). (Illus.). 101p. (Orig.). 1991. pap. 14.00 (*1-56546-041-3*) Arkansas Res.

Arkansas Land Patents: Pike County (Granted through 30 June 1908) Desmond W. Allen & Bobbie J. McLane. (County Ser.). (Illus.). 85p. (Orig.). 1991. pap. 14.00 (*1-56546-042-1*) Arkansas Res.

Arkansas Land Patents: Polk County (Granted through 30 June 1908) Desmond W. Allen & Bobbie J. McLane. (County Ser.). (Illus.). 95p. (Orig.). 1991. pap. 14.00 (*1-56546-043-X*) Arkansas Res.

Arkansas Land Patents: Pope County (Granted through 30 June 1908) Desmond W. Allen & Bobbie J. McLane. (County Ser.). (Illus.). 83p. (Orig.). 1991. pap. 14.00 (*1-56546-044-8*) Arkansas Res.

Arkansas Land Patents: Pulaski County (Granted through 30 June 1908) Desmond W. Allen & Bobbie J. McLane. (County Ser.). (Illus.). 82p. (Orig.). 1991. pap. 14.00 (*1-56546-045-6*) Arkansas Res.

Arkansas Land Patents: Randolph County (Granted through 30 June 1908) Desmond W. Allen & Bobbie J. McLane. (County Ser.). (Illus.). 84p. (Orig.). 1991. pap. 14.00 (*1-56546-046-4*) Arkansas Res.

Arkansas Land Patents: Scott County (Granted through 30 June 1908) Desmond W. Allen & Bobbie J. McLane. (County Ser.). (Illus.). 77p. (Orig.). 1991. pap. 14.00 (*1-56546-047-2*) Arkansas Res.

Arkansas Land Patents: Searcy County (Granted through 30 June 1908) Desmond W. Allen & Bobbie J. McLane. (County Ser.). (Illus.). 87p. (Orig.). 1991. pap. 14.00 (*1-56546-048-0*) Arkansas Res.

Arkansas Land Patents: Sebastian County (Granted through 30 June 1908) Desmond W. Allen & Bobbie J. McLane. (County Ser.). (Illus.). 80p. (Orig.). 1991. pap. 14.00 (*1-56546-049-9*) Arkansas Res.

Arkansas Land Patents: Sevier County (Granted through 30 June 1908) Desmond W. Allen & Bobbie J. McLane. (County Ser.). (Illus.). 88p. (Orig.). 1991. pap. 14.00 (*1-56546-050-2*) Arkansas Res.

Arkansas Land Patents: Sharp County (Granted through 30 June 1908) Desmond W. Allen & Bobbie J. McLane. (County Ser.). (Illus.). 97p. (Orig.). 1991. pap. 14.00 (*1-56546-051-0*) Arkansas Res.

Arkansas Land Patents: Stone County (Granted through 30 June 1908) Desmond W. Allen & Bobbie J. McLane. (County Ser.). (Illus.). 75p. (Orig.). 1991. pap. 14.00 (*1-56546-052-9*) Arkansas Res.

Arkansas Land Patents: Union County (Granted through 30 June 1908) Desmond W. Allen & Bobbie J. McLane. (County Ser.). (Illus.). 140p. (Orig.). 1991. pap. 18.00 (*1-56546-053-7*) Arkansas Res.

Arkansas Land Patents: Van Buren County (Granted through 30 June 1908) Desmond W. Allen & Bobbie J. McLane. (County Ser.). (Illus.). 83p. (Orig.). 1991. pap. 14.00 (*1-56546-054-5*) Arkansas Res.

Arkansas Land Patents: Washington County (Granted through 30 June 1908) Desmond W. Allen & Bobbie J. McLane. (County Ser.). (Illus.). 199p. (Orig.). 1991. pap. 22.00 (*1-56546-055-3*) Arkansas Res.

Arkansas Land Patents: White County (Granted through 30 June 1908) Desmond W. Allen & Bobbie J. McLane. (County Ser.). (Illus.). 77p. (Orig.). 1991. pap. 14.00 (*1-56546-056-1*) Arkansas Res.

Arkansas Land Patents: Yell County (Granted through 30 June 1908) Desmond W. Allen & Bobbie J. McLane. (County Ser.). (Illus.). 85p. (Orig.). 1991. pap. 14.00 (*1-56546-057-X*) Arkansas Res.

***Arkansas Land Surveying Law: Questions & Answers.** John E. Keen. 41p. 1995. pap. text ed. 20.00 (*1-56569-016-8*) Land Survey.

Arkansas Library Book: A Surprising Guide to the Unusual Special Collections in Libraries Across Our State for Students, Teachers, Writers & Publishers - Includes Reproducible Mailing Labels Plus Activities for Young People! Carole Marsh. (Carole Marsh Arkansas Bks.). (Illus.). 1994. lib. bdg. 24.95 (*0-7933-3017-3*); pap. 14.95 (*0-7933-3018-1*); disk 29.95 (*0-7933-3019-X*) Gallopade Pub Group.

Arkansas Life & Health Course. James J. Smith. Date not set. 35.00 (*1-56461-086-1*, 26994) Rough Notes.

Arkansas Life Course. James J. Smith. Date not set. 32.00 (*1-56461-070-5*, 26296) Rough Notes.

Arkansas Made: A Survey of the Decorative, Mechanical, & Fine Arts Produced in Arkansas, 1819-1870, Vol. II. Swannee Bennett & William B. Worthen. LC 89-20508. 229p. 1991. 50.00 (*1-55728-183-1*); pap. 35.00 (*1-55728-184-X*) U of Ark Pr.

Arkansas Made, Vol. I: A Survey of the Decorative, Mechanical, & Fine Arts Produced in Arkansas, 1819-1870. Swannee Bennett & William B. Worthen. LC 89-20508. 232p. 1990. 45.00 (*1-55728-138-6*); pap. 30.00 (*1-55728-139-4*) U of Ark Pr.

Arkansas Mammals. John A. Sealander. (Illus.). 313p. 1979. 26.50 (*0-318-19454-6*) River Road Pr.

Arkansas Mammals: Their Natural History, Classification & Distribution. John A. Sealander & Gary A. Heidt. LC 89-4795. (Illus.). 308p. 1990. 50.00 (*1-55728-102-5*); pap. 30.00 (*1-55728-103-3*) U of Ark Pr.

Arkansas Marriage Records, 1808-1835. James L. Morgan. 90p. reprint ed. pap. 15.00 (*0-941765-91-1*) Arkansas Res.

Arkansas Marriages, Early to 1850. Liahona Research, Inc. Staff. Ed. by Jordan Dodd. 1990. lib. bdg. 60.00 (*1-877677-25-6*) Precision Indexing.

Arkansas Media Book: A Surprising Guide to the Amazing Print, Broadcast & Online Media of Our State for Students, Teachers, Writers & Publishers - Includes Reproducible Mailing Labels Plus Activities for Young People! Carole Marsh. (Carole Marsh Arkansas Bks.). (Illus.). 1994. lib. bdg. 24.95 (*0-7933-3170-6*); pap. 14.95 (*0-7933-3171-4*); disk 29.95 (*0-7933-3172-2*) Gallopade Pub Group.

Arkansas Merchant Tokens. Tom H. Robinson. Ed. by David E. Schenkman. LC 85-51498. (Illus.). 259p. 1985. 32.50 (*0-918492-07-6*) TAMS.

Arkansas' Mexican War Soldiers. Desmond W. Allen. 135p. 1988. pap. 18.00 (*0-941765-38-5*) Arkansas Res.

An Asterisk (*) at the beginning of an entry indicates that the title is appearing in BIP for the first time.

Arkansas Military Bounty Grants War of 1812. Katheren Christensen. 265p. (Orig.). 1971. pap. 25.00 (*0-929604-23-7*) Arkansas Ancestors.

Arkansas Model Criminal Jury Instructions. Arkansas Supreme Court Committee on Criminal Jury Instructions. (State Practice Publications Ser.). 389p. 1979. Incl. hardcover binder & 1982 supplement. ring bd. 65.00 (*0-672-83758-7*) Michie Butterworth.

Arkansas Model Criminal Jury Instructions. suppl. ed. Arkansas Supreme Court Committee on Criminal Jury Instructions. (State Practice Publications Ser.). 389p. 1979. Nineteen Eighty-Two supplement only. 25.00 (*0-87215-628-1*) Michie Butterworth.

***Arkansas Model Jury Instructions - Criminal, 2 vols., Set.** 2nd ed. Arkansas Supreme Court Committee on Criminal Jury Instructions. 1994. ring bd. 140.00 (*1-55834-143-9*) Michie Butterworth.

Arkansas Mystery Van Takes Off! Book 1: Handicapped Arkansas Kids Sneak Off on a Big Adventure. Carole Marsh. (Carole Marsh Arkansas Bks.). (Illus.). (J). (gr. 3-12). 1994. 24.95 (*0-7933-4973-7*); pap. 14.95 (*0-7933-4974-5*); disk 29.95 (*0-7933-4975-3*) Gallopade Pub Group.

Arkansas Natural Area Plan. Arkansas Department of Planning Staff. (Illus.). xvii, 248p. (Orig.). 1974. pap. 11. 95 (*0-912456-07-8*) Ozark Soc Bks.

Arkansas Newspaper Abstracts, 1819-1845. James L. Morgan. 364p. 1992. reprint ed. text ed. 42.00 (*0-941765-74-1*); reprint ed. pap. 32.00 (*0-941765-73-3*) Arkansas Res.

Arkansas Newspaper Index, 1819-1845. James L. Morgan. 100p. 1992. reprint ed. pap. 16.00 (*0-941765-75-X*) Arkansas Res.

Arkansas Odyssey: The Saga of Arkansas from Prehistoric Times to Present. Michael Dougan. Ed. by Carol Griffee. LC 88-62036. (Illus.). 684p. (C). 1995. text ed. 79.95 (*0-914546-65-1*) Rose Pub.

ARKANSAS ODYSSEY interprets Arkansas history through modernization theory. It covers over three thousand topics, including geology, geographic regions, paleo & modern Indians, French & Spanish exploration, Colonial Arkansas, Territorial Arkansas, statehood, slavery, farm, plantation & hill life, Civil War, religion, women, Reconstruction, architecture, settlements & society, education, New South Era, Populist Era, Progressive Era, 1920s, the 1927 & 1937 Mississippi River Floods, Great Depression, World War II, Post-War, integration, Central High, modernization, culture, literature, music, Equal Rights Amendment, legislature, courts, & cults. This narrative history is rich in detail & examines the problems & promise of Arkansas, including the question of why one of the poorest states has produced some of the richest companies & people in the U. S., as well as the forty-second President of the United States. Rose Publishing Company, Inc., 2723 Foxcroft Road, #208, Little Rock, AR 72227, (501) 227-8104, FAX (501) 224-4442, hardcover, $79.95. Comprehensive history of Arkansas, 36p. index, census data, governors, economic profile, chronology. ***Publisher Provided Annotation.***

***Arkansas: Off the Beaten Path: A Guide to Unique Places.** 2nd ed. Patti DeLano. LC 95-17258. (Illus.). 160p. 1995. pap. 9.95 (*1-56440-645-8*) Globe Pequot.

Arkansas Pensioners, Eighteen Eighteen to Nineteen Hundred: Records of Some Arkansas Residents Who Applied to the Federal Government for Benefits Arising from Services in Federal Military Organizations. Dorothy Payne. 226p. 1985. 26.50 (*0-89308-537-5*) Southern Hist Pr.

Arkansas Pike County Biographies 1890. Courtney York & Gerlene York. 59p. 1974. reprint ed. pap. 12.00 (*0-916660-18-4*) Hse of York.

Arkansas Politics & Government: Do the People Rule? Diane D. Blair. LC 87-31423. (Politics & Governments of the American States Ser.). (Illus.). xxvi, 362p. 1988. 40.00x (*0-8032-1188-0*); pap. 16.95 (*0-8032-6073-3*) U of Nebr Pr.

Arkansas Portfolio: Twenty Years of Wilderness. Photos by Tim Ernst. LC 94-94452. (Illus.). 128p. 1994. 50.00 (*1-882906-14-4*) Ernst Wilderness.

Arkansas Property & Casualty Course. James J. Smith. Date not set. 50.00 (*1-56461-080-2*, 26975) Rough Notes.

Arkansas Quiz Bowl Crash Course! Carole Marsh. (Carole Marsh Arkansas Bks.). (Illus.). (YA). (gr. 3-12). 1994. lib. bdg. 24.95 (*1-55609-492-7*); pap. 14.95 (*1-55609-491-4*); disk 29.95 (*0-7933-1384-8*) Gallopade Pub Group.

Arkansas Raiders. Bryce Harte. (Creed Ser.: No. 10). 208p. (Orig.). 1993. pap. 3.99 (*0-425-13809-7*) Berkley Pub.

Arkansas River. Jory Sherman. (Rivers West Ser.: No. 06). 1991. pap. 4.99 (*0-553-29180-7*) Bantam.

Arkansas Roadkill Cookbook. Bruce Carlson. (Illus.). 112p. 1992. pap. 7.95 (*1-878488-73-2*) Quixote Pr IA.

Arkansas Roadsides: A Guidebook for the State. Bill Earngey. (Illus.). 176p. 1988. pap. 9.95 (*0-9619592-0-7*) East Mntn Pr.

Arkansas Rollercoasters! Carole Marsh. (Carole Marsh Arkansas Bks.). (Illus.). (YA). (gr. 3-12). 1994. lib. bdg. 24.95 (*0-7933-5233-9*); pap. 14.95 (*0-7933-5234-7*); disk 29.95 (*0-7933-5235-5*) Gallopade Pub Group.

Arkansas Rules of Evidence: With Commentary & Annotations. Mort Gitelman et al. 1988. 50.00 (*0-943099-02-1*) M&M Pr.

Arkansas School Trivia: An Amazing & Fascinating Look at Our State's Teachers, Schools & Students! Carole Marsh. (Carole Marsh Arkansas Bks.). (Illus.). (YA). (gr. 3-12). 1994. lib. bdg. 24.95 (*0-7933-0151-3*); pap. 14.95 (*0-7933-0150-5*); disk 29.95 (*0-7933-0152-1*) Gallopade Pub Group.

Arkansas Sheriff's Census Index, 1823 & 1829. Ronald V. Jackson. LC 77-94182. (Illus.). 1972. lib. bdg. 51.00 (*0-89593-167-2*) Accelerated Index.

Arkansas Silly Basketball Sportsmysteries, Vol. I. Carole Marsh. (Carole Marsh Arkansas Bks.). (Illus.). (YA). (gr. 3-12). 1994. lib. bdg. 24.95 (*0-7933-0149-1*); pap. 14.95 (*0-7933-0147-5*); disk 29.95 (*0-685-45933-0*) Gallopade Pub Group.

Arkansas Silly Basketball Sportsmysteries, Vol. II. Carole Marsh. (Carole Marsh Arkansas Bks.). (Illus.). (YA). (gr. 3-12). 1994. lib. bdg. 24.95 (*0-7933-1571-9*); pap. 14.95 (*0-685-45934-9*); disk 29.95 (*0-7933-1573-5*) Gallopade Pub Group.

Arkansas Silly Football Sportsmysteries, Vol. I. Carole Marsh. (Carole Marsh Arkansas Bks.). (Illus.). (YA). (gr. 3-12). 1994. lib. bdg. 24.95 (*1-55609-488-4*); pap. 14.95 (*1-55609-487-6*); disk 29.95 (*0-7933-1377-5*) Gallopade Pub Group.

Arkansas Silly Football Sportsmysteries, Vol. II. Carole Marsh. (Carole Marsh Arkansas Bks.). (Illus.). (YA). (gr. 3-12). 1994. lib. bdg. 24.95 (*0-7933-1378-3*); pap. 14.95 (*0-7933-1379-1*); disk 29.95 (*0-7933-1380-5*) Gallopade Pub Group.

Arkansas Silly Trivia! Carole Marsh. (Carole Marsh Arkansas Bks.). (Illus.). (YA). (gr. 3-12). 1994. lib. bdg. 24.95 (*1-55609-484-1*); pap. 14.95 (*1-55609-083-8*); disk 29.95 (*0-7933-1374-0*) Gallopade Pub Group.

Arkansas' Spanish-American War Soldiers. Desmond W. Allen. (Illus.). 273p. 1988. pap. 24.00 (*0-941765-32-6*) Arkansas Res.

***Arkansas State Business Handbook.** 400p. (C). 1995. text ed. 395.00 (*0-7605-1918-8*) Rector Pr.

Arkansas State Constitution: A Reference Guide. Kay C. Goss. LC 92-30034. (Reference Guides to the State Constitutions of the United States Ser.: No. 10). 274p. 1993. text ed. 65.00 (*0-313-27472-X*, GSQ/, Greenwood Pr) Greenwood.

Arkansas Tax List Index 1819 to 1829. Ronald V. Jackson. LC 77-95000. (Illus.). 1976. lib. bdg. 48.00 (*0-89593-168-0*) Accelerated Index.

Arkansas Tax List Index 1830 to 1839. Ronald V. Jackson. (Illus.). 1981. lib. bdg. 79.00 (*0-89593-169-9*) Accelerated Index.

Arkansas Timeline: A Chronology of Arkansas History, Mystery, Trivia, Legend, Lore & More. Carole Marsh. (Carole Marsh Arkansas Bks.). (Illus.). (J). (gr. 3-12). 1994. lib. bdg. 24.95 (*0-7933-5884-1*); pap. 14.95 (*0-7933-5885-X*); disk 29.95 (*0-7933-5886-8*) Gallopade Pub Group.

Arkansas Township Digest: Minor Civil Divisions, 1820-1990. Desmond W. Allen. (Illus.). 1994. 43.00 (*0-941765-93-8*); pap. 32.00 (*0-941765-92-X*) Arkansas Res.

Arkansas Union Soldiers Pension Application Index. Desmond W. Allen. 182p. 1987. 32.00 (*0-941765-94-6*); pap. 20.00 (*0-941765-14-8*) Arkansas Res.

Arkansas Voices. 2nd ed. Intro. by Sarah Fountain. 288p. (C). 1989. lib. bdg. 28.95 (*0-9615143-7-X*) Univ Central AR Pr.

Arkansas Volunteers of 1836-1837. James L. Morgan. 81p. 1992. reprint ed. pap. 14.00 (*0-941765-79-2*) Arkansas Res.

Arkansas Wildlife. Susan Morrison. LC 80-52076. 64p. 1980. 14.95 (*0-914546-32-5*) Rose Pub.

***Arkansas 1850 Census Every-Name Index.** Bobbie J. McLane & Desmond W. Allen. 480p. 1995. 49.50 (*1-56546-063-4*) Arkansas Res.

Arkansas's (Most Devastating!) Disasters & (Most Calamitous!) Catastrophies! Carole Marsh. (Carole Marsh Arkansas Bks.). (Illus.). (YA). (gr. 3-12). 1994. lib. bdg. 24.95 (*0-7933-0139-4*); pap. 14.95 (*0-7933-0138-6*); disk 29.95 (*0-7933-0140-8*) Gallopade Pub Group.

Arkansas's Unsolved Mysteries (& Their "Solutions") Includes Scientific Information & Other Activities for Students. Carole Marsh. (Carole Marsh Arkansas Bks.). (Illus.). (J). (gr. 3-12). 1994. lib. bdg. 24.95 (*0-7933-5731-4*); pap. 14.95 (*0-7933-5732-2*); disk 29.95 (*0-7933-5733-0*) Gallopade Pub Group.

Arkansaw Bear. Aurand Harris. (Orig.). (J). (gr. 5 up). 1980. 5.00 (*0-87602-226-3*) Anchorage.

Arkful of Animals. William E. Cole. (J). (gr. 4-7). 1992. pap. 3.95 (*0-395-61618-2*) HM.

Arkham House Companion: Fifty Years of Arkham House. Sheldon Jaffery. LC 89-31701. (Starmont Reference Guide Ser.: No. 9). xvi, 184p. 1989. lib. bdg. 41.00x (*1-55742-005-X*); pap. 31.00x (*1-55742-004-1*) Borgo Pr.

Arkham Unveiled: A New England Haven for Investigators. Keith Herber et al. Ed. by Lynn Willis. (Call of Cthulhu Roleplaying Game System Ser.). (Illus.). 160p. (Orig.). 1990. pap. 17.95 (*0-933635-62-1*, 2325) Chaosium.

Arkhangel Skoye: Country Estate of the 18th & 19th Centuries. Valery Rapaport. 148p. 1984. 104.00 (*0-317-61209-3*, Pub. by Collets UK) Pro-Am Music.

Arkhangelsk System in the Ruy Lopez. Jerzy Konikowski. Tr. by Paul Janicki. 89p. (Orig.). 1987. pap. 6.00 (*0-931462-67-3*) Chess Ent Inc.

Arkhivy Strashnogo Suda. Igor Yefimov. LC 82-15469. 302p. (RUS.). 1982. pap. 8.50 (*0-938920-25-1*) Hermitage.

Arkiyskupas Jurgis Matulaitis Matulevicius: Gyvosios Krikscionybes Apastalas. Antanas Kucas. (Illus.). 592p. (LIT.). 1979. write for info. (*0-933820-04-6*) Marian Fathers.

Arktos: The Polar Myth in Science, Symbolism & Nazi Survival. Joscelyn Godwin. LC 92-32626. (Illus.). 265p. (Orig.). 1993. pap. 16.95 (*0-933999-46-1*) Phanes Pr.

Arktouros: Hellenic Studies Presented to Bernard M. W. Knox on the Occasion of His 65th Birthday. Ed. by Glen W. Bowersock et al. 471p. 1979. 150.00 (*3-11-007798-1*) De Gruyter.

Arkwright of Cromford. John N. Merrill. 36p. 1987. 25.00 (*0-907496-35-0*, Pub. by JNM Pubns UK) St Mut.

Arkwrights: Spinners of Fortune. R. S. Fitton. 336p. 1989. text ed. 24.95 (*0-7190-2783-7*) St Martin.

ARL - RLG Interlibrary Loan Cost Study. M. Roche. 64p. 1993. 10.00 (*0-918006-70-8*) ARL.

ARLD: The American Record Label Directory & Dating Guide, 1940-1959. Comp. by Galen Gart. 270p. 1989. spiral bd. 42.00 (*0-936433-11-6*) Big Nickel.

Arlen Ness: Master Harley Customizer. Timothy Remus. (Illus.). 128p. 1990. pap. 19.95 (*0-87938-407-7*) Motorbooks Intl.

Arlen Roth's Complete Acoustic Guitar. Arlen Roth. (Illus.). 208p. 1985. pap. 18.95 (*0-02-872150-0*) Schirmer Bks.

Arlen Roth's Heavy Metal Guitar. Arlen Roth. 186p. (YA). 1990. pap. 16.95 (*0-02-870010-4*) Schirmer Bks.

Arlene Alda's ABC. Arlene Alda. LC 93-24999. (Illus.). 32p. (J). (ps up). 1993. reprint ed. 12.95 (*1-883672-01-5*) Tricycle Pr.

Arlene Dahl's Lovescopes. Arlene Dahl. 1983. 15.95 (*0-02-529370-2*) Macmillan.

Arlene Dahl's Lovescopes. Arlene Dahl. LC 83-6387. 224p. 1983. write for info. (*0-672-52770-7*) Macmillan.

Arlequin Poli par L'Amour. Pierre C. De Marivaux. 32p. (FRE.). 1951. 7.95 (*0-8288-9602-X*, F48130) Fr & Eur.

Arlesienne. Alphonse Daudet. 11.00 (*0-685-34888-1*) Fr & Eur.

Arlesienne. Alphonse Daudet. 170p. (FRE.). 1986. pap. 24. 95 (*0-7859-4665-9*) Fr & Eur.

Arlie the Alligator. Sandra Warren & Deborah B. Pfleger. LC 91-73758. (Illus.). 48p. (J). (ps-3). 1992. audio 19.90 (*1-880175-11-8*); boxed, lib. bdg. 13.95 (*1-880175-13-4*); audio 5.95 (*1-880175-12-6*) Arlie Enter.

Arlington: A Novel, 3 vols. in 2, 1. Thomas H. Lister. LC 79-8154. reprint ed. write for info. (*0-404-61980-0*) AMS Pr.

Arlington: A Novel, 3 vols. in 2, 2. Thomas H. Lister. LC 79-8154. reprint ed. write for info. (*0-404-61981-9*) AMS Pr.

Arlington: A Novel, 3 vols. in 2, Set. Thomas H. Lister. LC 79-8154. reprint ed. 84.50 (*0-404-61979-7*) AMS Pr.

Arlington Dictionary of Electronics. Ed. by Harold R. Rodgers et al. (Illus.). 1971. text ed. 25.00 (*0-8464-0146-0*) Beekman Pubs.

Arlington House: The Robert E. Lee Memorial. Nancy G. Brooks. LC 85-18925. (Handbook Ser.: No. 133). (Illus.). 48p. (Orig.). 1986. pap. 2.00 (*0-912627-23-9*) Natl Park Serv.

Arlington National Cemetary: A Moment of Silence. Owen Andrews. LC 93-27115. (Illus.). 1994. 14.95 (*0-89133-223-5*) Preservation Pr.

Arlington National Cemetery. Catherine Reef. LC 91-17183. (Places in American History Ser.). (Illus.). 72p. (J). (gr. 4-6). 1991. text ed. 14.95 (*0-87518-471-5*, Dillon Silver Burdett) Silver Burdett Pr.

***Arlington National Cemetery.** R. Conrad Stein. LC 95-6307. (Cornerstones of Freedom Ser.). (J). 1995. write for info. (*0-516-06625-0*) Childrens.

Arlington National Cemetery: Shrine to America's Heros. James E. Peters. LC 86-50284. 335p. 1988. pap. 13.95 (*0-933149-04-2*) Woodbine House.

Arly. Robert N. Peck. (History Series for Young People). 160p. (J). (gr. 5 up). 1989. 16.95 (*0-8027-6856-3*) Walker & Co.

Arlyn Hackett's Menu Magic: Health-Wise Cuisine. Arlyn Hackett. 1994. pap. 19.95 (*0-8038-9355-8*) Hastings.

Arly's Run. Robert N. Peck. 160p. (J). (gr. 5-9). 1991. 16.95 (*0-8027-8120-9*) Walker & Co.

Arm & Darkness. Taylor Caldwell. 1983. pap. 3.50 (*0-449-20321-2*) Fawcett.

Arm & the Darkness. Taylor Caldwell. 1974. reprint ed. lib. bdg. 32.95 (*0-88411-151-2*, Aeonian Pr) Amereon Ltd.

Arm Chair Chemistry. Alyea. (Illus.). 1990. teacher ed write for info. (*1-877991-16-3*, AP4272); student ed write for info. (*1-877991-15-5*, AP1801) Flinn Scientific.

Arm Injuries: Medical Analysis Index with Research Bibliography. Trudy W. Vaughn. LC 85-47573. 150p. 1987. 39.50 (*0-88164-320-3*); pap. 34.50 (*0-88164-321-1*) ABBE Pubs Assn.

Arm of God. Barbara Wood. 32p. 1989. pap. 2.95 (*0-88144-139-2*) Christian Pub.

Arm of the Starfish. Madeleine L'Engle. 240p. (YA). (gr. 7 up). 1980. mass mkt. 3.99 (*0-440-90183-9*, LFL) Dell.

Arm of the Starfish. Madeleine L'Engle. LC 65-10919. 256p. (J). (gr. 7 up). 1965. 18.00 (*0-374-30396-7*) FS&G.

ARM Pricing Considerations & Yield Simulations. 60p. 1985. 10.00 (*0-929097-01-7*, 17988) Sav & Comm Bank.

Arm Risc Chip: A Programmer's Guide. Alex Van Someren. (C). 1993. pap. text ed. 37.75 (*0-201-62410-9*) Addison-Wesley.

ARMA Model Identification. B. Choi. Ed. by J. O. Berger et al. (Series in Statistics - Subseries: Probability & Its Applications). 216p. 1992. 39.95 (*0-387-97795-3*) Spr-Verlag.

Arma Samaj: An Account of Its Origin, Doctrines & Activities. Rai Lajpat & Lala Lajpat. (C). 1989. 47.00 (*81-85199-30-2*, Pub. by Renaiss Publng Hse II) S Asia.

Armada. Garrett Mattingly. 464p. 1974. pap. 11.95 (*0-395-08366-4*, 17, SenEd) HM.

Armada. Peter Padfield. LC 87-63369. (Illus.). 192p. 1988. 28.95 (*0-87021-006-8*) Naval Inst Pr.

Armada Campaign 1588. John Tincey. (Elite Ser.: No. 15). (Illus.). 64p. pap. 12.95 (*0-85045-821-8*, 9415, Pub. by Osprey UK) Stackpole.

Armada in Ireland. Niall Fallon. LC 77-95546. (Illus.). 246p. reprint ed. pap. 72.40 (*0-8357-5742-0*, 2056666) Bks Demand.

Armada in the Public Records. N. A. Rodger. LC 88-179916. (Illus.). 75p. 1988. 5.95 (*0-11-440215-9*, HM1919, Pub. by HMSO UK) UNIPUB.

Armada of Flanders: Spanish Maritime Policy & European War, 1568-1668. R. A. Stradling. (Studies in Early Modern History). (Illus.). 328p. (C). 1992. 64.95 (*0-521-40534-3*) Cambridge U Pr.

Armada of Thirty Whales. Daniel G. Hoffman. LC 73-144757. (Yale Series of Younger Poets: No. 51). reprint ed. 18.00 (*0-404-53851-7*) AMS Pr.

Armadale. Wilkie Collins. Ed. by Catherine Peters. (World's Classics Ser.). (Illus.). 720p. 1990. pap. 10.95 (*0-19-281802-3*) OUP.

***Armadale.** Wilkie Collins. Ed. & Intro. by John Sutherland. 752p. 1995. 10.95 (*0-14-043411-9*, Penguin Classics) Viking Penguin.

Armadale, 2 vols., Set. Wilkie Collins. 1988. reprint ed. lib. bdg. 150.00 (*0-7812-0752-5*) Rprt Serv.

Armadale, 2 vols., Set. Wilkie Collins. LC 70-107168. (Illus.). 1972. reprint ed. 69.00 (*0-403-00433-0*) Scholarly.

Armadeus Prophecy & Teaching in the New Ages, Bk. 1. Ronald G. Kaufmann. LC 91-133189. (Illus.). 264p. (Orig.). 1986. pap. 14.95 (*0-940539-00-4*) Heridonius.

Armadeus Prophecy & Teaching in the New Ages, Bk. 2. Ronald G. Kaufmann. LC 91-133189. 192p. (Orig.). 1987. 12.95 (*0-940539-02-0*) Heridonius.

Armadeus Prophecy & Teaching in the New Ages, Bk. 3. Ronald G. Kaufmann. LC 91-133189. (Illus.). 180p. (Orig.). 1987. pap. 12.95 (*0-940539-04-7*) Heridonius.

Armadillo. Mary E. Monsell. LC 90-19135. (Illus.). 32p. (J). (ps-1). 1991. text ed. 13.95 (*0-689-31676-3*, Atheneum Bks Young) S&S Childrens.

Armadillo. Seliesa Pembleton. LC 91-43731. (Remarkable Animals Ser.). (Illus.). 60p. (J). (gr. 4 up). 1992. text ed. 13.95 (*0-87518-507-X*, Dillon Silver Burdett) Silver Burdett Pr.

Armadillo Book. Bill Bryant. LC 82-18938. (Illus.). 128p. 1983. pap. 6.95 (*0-88289-383-1*) Pelican.

Armadillo from Amarillo. Lynne Cherry. LC 93-11185. (J). 1994. 14.95 (*0-15-200359-2*, Gulliver Bks) HarBrace.

***Armadillo Ray Contemplates the Moon.** John Beifuss. LC 94-44527. (Illus.). (J). 1995. 13.95 (*0-8118-0334-1*) Chronicle Bks.

***Armadillo Rodeo.** Jan Brett. LC 94-42425. (Illus.). (J). 1995. write for info. (*0-399-22803-9*, Putnam) Putnam Pub Group.

***Armadillos.** Don Patton. (Nature Bks.). (Illus.). 32p. (J). (gr. 2-6). 1995. lib. bdg. 22.79 (*1-56766-182-3*) Childs World.

Armadillos & Old Lace. Friedman. 1994. 21.00 (*0-671-86923-X*) S&S Trade.

Armadillos & Other Unusual Animals. Q. L. Pearce. Ed. by Jane Steltenpohl. (Amazing Science Ser.). (Illus.). 64p. (J). (gr. 4-6). 1989. lib. bdg. 12.98 (*0-671-68528-7*, Julian Messner); pap. 5.95 (*0-671-68645-3*, Julian Messner) Silver Burdett Pr.

Armageddon. Marilyn Hickey. 1994. pap. 3.95 (*1-56441-050-1*) M Hickey Min.

Armageddon. Gordon Lindsay. (Revelation Ser.: Vol. 14). 1962. 1.95 (*0-89985-047-2*) Christ for the Nations.

Armageddon: Appointment with Destiny. Grant R. Jeffrey. 1990. 4.99 (*0-553-28537-8*) Bantam.

Armageddon: The Diary of Vladimir Brezynski. Gerry Nelson. 198p. 1983. 12.95 (*0-914701-00-2*) New Comet.

***Armageddon: The Second World War.** Clive Ponting. LC 95-2995. 1995. 25.00 (*0-679-43602-2*) Random.

Armageddon: The World War in Literature. E. W Lohrke. 1971. 69.95 (*0-87968-660-X*) Gordon Pr.

Armageddon Again? A Reply to Hal Lindsey. rev. ed. Stafford North. 124p. (Orig.). 1991. pap. 4.95 (*0-9631138-0-1*) Landmark Bks.

Armageddon Box. Robert Weinberg. 368p. (Orig.). 1991. pap. 4.50 (*0-8439-3222-8*) Dorchester Pub Co.

Armageddon by Morning. Nicky Cruz. LC 92-81424. 272p. (Orig.). 1992. pap. 8.95 (*0-89221-224-1*) New Leaf.

Armageddon-Dead Ahead. C. C. Cribb. LC 77-70212. pap. 2.95 (*0-932046-03-7*) Manhattan Ltd NC.

Armageddon in the Classroom: An Examination of Nuclear Education. Herbert I. London. 146p. (Orig.). 1987. pap. text ed. 18.50 (*0-8191-6548-4*) U Pr of Amer.

***Armageddon in Waco: Critical Perspectives on the Branch Davidian Conflict.** Ed. by Stuart A. Wright. LC 95-8872. 1995. write for info. (*0-226-90844-5*); pap. write for info. (*0-226-90845-3*) U Ch Pr.

Armageddon Inheritance. David Weber. 368p. 1993. mass mkt. 4.99 (*0-671-72197-6*) Baen Bks.

Armageddon Network. Michael Saba. LC 84-72241. 288p. (Orig.). 1984. pap. 9.95 (*0-915597-07-1*) Amana Bks.

Armageddon, Nineteen Hundred Eighteen. Cyril B. Falls. 18.95 (*0-405-13280-8*) Ayer.

An Asterisk (*) at the beginning of an entry indicates that the title is appearing in BIP for the first time.

A

Armageddon Now! The Premillenarian Response to Russia & Israel since 1917. Dwight Wilson. LC 91-39999. 274p. 1991. reprint ed. 25.00 (*0-930464-58-3*); reprint ed. pap. 9.95 (*0-930464-57-5*) Inst Christian.

Armageddon off Vesta. M. S. Murdock. LC 88-51716. (Buck Rogers: Martian Wars Trilogy Ser.: Bk. 3). (Illus.). 288p. (Orig.). (J). 1989. pap. 3.95 (*0-88038-761-0*) TSR Inc.

Armageddon Rag. George R. Martin. LC 83-13597. 335p. 1983. 25.00 (*0-89366-150-3*) Ultramarine Pub.

Armageddon Revisited: A World War I Journal. Amos N. Wilder. LC 93-33296. 208p. 1994. 23.50 (*0-300-05560-9*) Yale U Pr.

Armageddon Run. David Robbins. (Endworld Ser.: No. 7). 256p. (Orig.). 1987. pap. 2.95 (*0-8439-2527-2*) Dorchester Pub Co.

Armageddon Script: Prophecy in Action. Peter Lemesurier. (Illus.). 270p. 1993. write for info. (*0-906540-19-4*); pap. 15.95 (*0-906540-37-2*) Element MA.

Armageddon Soon? William MacDonald. 1992. pap. 3.50 (*0-937396-89-3*) Walterick Pubs.

Armageddon, the Future of Planet Earth. Jimmy Swaggart. 1987. 12.95 (*0-935113-06-1*) Swaggart Ministries.

***Armageddon Virus.** Daniel L. Idema. 160p. (Orig.). Date not set. pap. 7.95 (*0-7610-0369-X*) NW Pub.

Armagedon (Armageddon) El Climax de la Historia (The Climax of History) Luis Palau. (SPA.). 1992. 3.50 (*0-8423-6476-5*, 498020) Editorial Unilit.

***Armagh & the Royal Centres in Early Medieval Ireland: Monuments, Cosmology & the Past.** N. B. Aitchison. (C). 1994. text ed. 71.00 (*1-873448-02-3*, Pub. by Cruithne Pr UK) Boydell & Brewer.

Armalite & Ballot Box: An Irish-American Republican Primer. Robert E. Connolly. 130p. 1985. pap. 7.00 (*0-9614659-0-5*) Cuchullain Pubns.

Armament & Disarmament in the 1980s. Ed. & Intro. by Wolfgang Mallmann. LC 92-21182. (Library of Contemporary History, Stuttgart). 288p. 1995. 52.95 (*0-85496-383-9*) Berg Pubs.

Armaments & Arbitration. Alfred T. Mahan. Bd. with Great Illusion: A Reply to Rear Admiral A. T. Mahan. LC 77-147583. LC 77-147583. (Library of War & Peace; Int'l. Organization, Arbitration & Law). 1972. Set lib. bdg. 46.00 (*0-8240-0347-0*) Garland.

Armaments & Disarmament: Commonly Used Terms & Acronyms. 54p. (Orig.). (C). 1993. pap. text ed. 19.95 (*1-56806-562-0*) Diane Pub.

Armaments & Politics in France on the Eve of the First World War: The Introduction of Three-Year Conscription 1913-1914. Gerd Krumeich. Tr. by Stephen Conn. LC 84-73480. 307p. (C). 1987. 64.00 (*0-907582-15-X*); pap. 19.95 (*0-907582-34-6*) Berg Pubs.

Arman. Kyoichi Tsuzuki. (Art Random Ser.: No. 79). (Illus.). 48p. 1991. 32.95 (*4-7636-8581-3*, Pub. by Kyoto Shoin JA) Bks Nippan.

Arman. Jan Van der Marck. (Illus.). 128p. 1990. 69.95 (*0-89659-423-8*) Abbeville Pr.

Arman: Monochrome Accumulations 1986-1989. Donald Kuspit. (Illus.). 139p. 1991. 40.00 (*91-7970-951-6*) Abbeville Pr.

Arman Selected Works. Jan V. D. Marck. LC 74-18537. (Illus.). 48p. 1974. 8.00 (*0-686-99820-0*) Mus Contemp Art.

Arman 1955-1991: A Retrospective. Alison D. Greene & Pierre Restany. (Illus.). 144p. 1992. write for info. (*0-89090-052-3*); pap. write for info. (*0-89090-050-7*) Mus Fine TX.

Armance. Stendhal. 320p. 1975. write for info. (*0-318-63430-9*) Fr & Eur.

Armance. Stendhal. 320p. (FRE.). 1987. pap. 10.95 (*0-7859-1633-4*, 2070366863) Fr & Eur.

Armance. Stendhal. (Folio Ser.: No. 686). 320p. (FRE.). 1975. 8.95 (*2-07-036686-3*) Schoenhof.

Armance. Stendhal, pseud. Tr. by Scott Moncrief. 255p. 1986. reprint ed. pap. 14.95 (*0-948166-03-7*, Pub. by Soho Bk Co UK) Dufour.

Armand Gatti in the Theatre. Dorothy Knowles. LC 88-28744. (Illus.). 336p. 1989. 38.50 (*0-8386-3371-4*) Fairleigh Dickinson.

Armand Hammer Collection: Five Centuries of Masterpieces. Ed. by John Walker. (Illus.). 296p. 1981. 85.00 (*0-8109-1069-1*) Abrams.

Armand Hammer Collection: Four Centuries of Masterpieces. Pref. by Robert T. Buck, Jr. 1978. 10.00 (*0-685-46368-0*) Buffalo Acad.

Armando Asked "Why?" Jay Hulbert & Sid Kantor. (Ready-Set-Read Ser.). (Illus.). 24p. (J). (ps-2). 1990. lib. bdg. 17.84 (*0-8172-3576-0*); pap. 4.95 (*0-8114-6739-2*) Raintree Steck-V.

Armando Palacio Valdes: Alone, & Other Stories. Armando P. Valdes. Tr. by Robert M. Fedorchek. LC 92-54400. (Illus.). 144p. 1993. 29.50 (*0-8387-5251-9*) Bucknell U Pr.

Armar la Historia. Gervasio L. Garcia. LC 89-80368. 127p. 1989. pap. 8.50 (*0-940238-99-3*) Ediciones Huracan.

***Armarium.** Ed. by Dezsenyi et al. 382p. (C). 1976. 72.00 (*963-05-1016-2*) St Mut.

Armas Para la Lucha Espiritual. Larry Lea. 240p. (SPA.). 1990. 4.95 (*0-8297-0366-7*) Life Pubs Intl.

***Armas Secretas.** Cortazar. 1995. pap. 12.50 (*0-679-76099-7*) Random Hse Value.

Armature of Conquest: Spanish Accounts of the Discovery of America, 1492-1589. Beatriz P. Bodmer. Tr. by Lydia L. Hunt. LC 91-39494. 344p. (C). 1992. 49.50x (*0-8047-1977-2*) Stanford U Pr.

***Armature of Conquest: Spanish Accounts of the Discovery of America, 1492-1589.** Beatriz P. Bodmer. Tr. by Lydia L. Hunt. 340p. 1995. pap. 16.95 (*0-8047-2470-9*) Stanford U Pr.

Armature Winder. Jack Rudman. (Career Examination Ser.: C-2481). 1994. pap. 29.95 (*0-8373-2481-5*) Nat Learn.

Armature Winding & Motor Repair. Daniel H. Braymer. 1986. reprint ed. pap. 16.95 (*0-917914-43-0*) Lindsay Pubns.

***Armchair Angler.** Terry Brykczynski. 1994. 9.98 (*0-88365-876-3*) Galahad Bks.

Armchair Angler. Ed. by Terry Brykczynski et al. (Illus.). 404p. 1993. reprint ed. pap. 15.00 (*0-02-017801-8*, Collier S&S) S&S Trade.

Armchair Climbers Guide to Yosemite. Brad Asmus. (Illus.). 56p. 1993. pap. 8.95 (*0-9631113-2-9*) Four Mile Pr.

Armchair Conductor. Dan Carlinsky. 1991. mass mkt. 10.00 (*0-440-50415-5*, Dell Trade Pbks) Dell.

Armchair Detective, 5 vols. Incl. Vol. 18, No. 3. 1985. (*0-89296-327-1*); Vol. 18, No. 4. 1985. (*0-89296-328-X*); Vol. 19, No. 1. 1986. (*0-89296-329-8*); Vol. 19, No. 2. 1986. (*0-89296-330-1*); Vol. 19, No. 3. 1986. (*0-89296-331-X*); (Illus.). 6.00 (*0-318-59462-5*); Incl. Vol. 18, No. 3. (*0-89296-327-1*); Vol. 18, No. 4. (*0-89296-328-X*); Vol. 19, No. 1. (*0-89296-329-8*); Vol. 19, No. 2. (*0-89296-330-1*); Vol. 19, No. 3. (*0-89296-331-X*); 6.00 (*0-318-59463-3*); Incl. Vol. 18, No. 3. (*0-89296-327-1*); Vol. 18, No. 4. (*0-89296-328-X*); Vol. 19, No. 1. (*0-89296-329-8*); Vol. 19, No. 2. (*0-89296-330-1*); Vol. 19, No. 3. (*0-89296-331-X*); 6.00 (*0-318-59464-1*); Incl. Vol. 18, No. 3. (*0-89296-327-1*); Vol. 18, No. 4. (*0-89296-328-X*); Vol. 19, No. 1. (*0-89296-329-8*); Vol. 19, No. 2. (*0-89296-330-1*); Vol. 19, No. 3. (*0-89296-331-X*); 6.00 (*0-318-59465-X*) FS&G.

Armchair Detective, 5 vols. Incl. Vol. 18, No. 3. 1985. (*0-89296-327-1*); Vol. 18, No. 4. 1985. (*0-89296-328-X*); Vol. 19, No. 1. 1986. (*0-89296-329-8*); Vol. 19, No. 2. 1986. (*0-89296-330-1*); Vol. 19, No. 3. 1986. (*0-89296-331-X*); (Illus.). 6.00 (*0-318-59461-7*) Hill & Wang.

Armchair Detective, Vol. 1. Allen J. Hubin. LC 82-643921. viii, 158p. (C). 1981. reprint ed. lib. bdg. 27.00x (*0-941028-00-3*, Brownstone Bks) Borgo Pr.

Armchair Detective, Vol. 16. 1987. 6.00 (*0-89296-320-4*) Armchair Detective.

Armchair Detective, Vol. 18. 1987. 6.00 (*0-89296-325-5*); 6.00 (*0-89296-326-3*) Armchair Detective.

Armchair Detective, Vol. 19. 1986. 6.00 (*0-89296-332-8*) Armchair Detective.

Armchair Detective, Vol. 20. 1987. 6.00 (*0-89296-336-0*) Armchair Detective.

Armchair Detective, Vol. 20, No. 3. 1987. pap. 6.00 (*0-89296-335-2*) Armchair Detective.

Armchair Detective, Vol. 21. 1988. 6.00 (*0-89296-339-5*) Armchair Detective.

Armchair Detective, Vol. 21. 1988. 6.00 (*0-89296-340-9*) Armchair Detective.

Armchair Detective, Vol. 22. 1989. 6.00 (*0-89296-341-7*) Armchair Detective.

Armchair Detective, Vol. 22. 1989. 6.00 (*0-89296-342-5*) Armchair Detective.

Armchair Detective, Vol. 22. 1989. 6.00 (*0-89296-343-3*) Armchair Detective.

Armchair Detective, Vol. 22. 1989. 6.00 (*0-89296-344-1*) Armchair Detective.

Armchair Detective, Vol. 23. 1990. 7.50 (*0-89296-405-7*) Armchair Detective.

Armchair Detective, Vol. 23. 1990. 7.50 (*0-89296-406-5*) Armchair Detective.

Armchair Detective, Vol. 23. 1990. 7.50 (*0-89296-407-3*) Armchair Detective.

Armchair Detective, Vol. 24. 1991. 7.50 (*0-89296-409-X*) Armchair Detective.

Armchair Detective: The First Ten Years, IX. Ed. by Allen J. Hubin. lib. bdg. 40.00 (*0-8240-4898-9*) Garland.

Armchair Detective: The First Ten Years, Set. Ed. by Allen J. Hubin. lib. bdg. 280.00 (*0-8153-0195-2*) Garland.

Armchair Detective: The First Ten Years, VII. Ed. by Allen J. Hubin. lib. bdg. 40.00 (*0-8240-4896-2*) Garland.

Armchair Detective: The First Ten Years, VIII. Ed. by Allen J. Hubin. lib. bdg. 40.00 (*0-8240-4897-0*) Garland.

Armchair Detective: The First Ten Years, Vols. I & II. Ed. by Allen J. Hubin. lib. bdg. 40.00 (*0-8240-4893-8*) Garland.

Armchair Detective: The First Ten Years, Vols. III & IV. Ed. by Allen J. Hubin. lib. bdg. 40.00 (*0-8240-4894-6*) Garland.

Armchair Detective: The First Ten Years, x. Ed. by Allen J. Hubin. lib. bdg. 40.00 (*0-8240-4899-7*) Garland.

Armchair Detective: Your Guide Through the Maze of the JFK Assassination. James Butman & Brian Sprinkle. Ed. by Betty Wright. LC 92-16855. 128p. 1992. pap. 12. 95 (*0-935834-86-9*) Rainbow Books.

***Armchair Detective Book of Lists.** Kate Stine. 1995. pap. 12.95 (*1-883402-98-0*) S&S Trade.

Armchair Detective Index: Volumes 1-20, 1967-1987. Ed. by Steven A. Stilwell. 184p. 1992. 29.95 (*1-56287-043-2*); pap. 19.95 (*1-56287-044-0*) Armchair Detective.

***Armchair Economist: Economics & Everyday Life.** Stephen E. Landsburg. 1995. pap. 12.00 (*0-02-917776-6*) Free Pr.

Armchair Economist: The Economics of Everyday Experience. Steven E. Landsburg. 260p. 1993. text ed. 22.95 (*0-02-917775-8*) Free Pr.

Armchair Fitness. Manor Healthcare Corporation Staff & Betty Switkes. (Illus.). 64p. 1984. write for info. (*0-917025-00-8*) Manor Health.

Armchair Football: A Fan's Guide to the Rules, Plays & Strategy of America's Favorite Pastime. Donna P. Foehr. (Illus.). 160p. 1991. pap. 9.95 (*0-915765-91-8*) Krantz Co.

Armchair Golf. Jim Becker. 1993. mass mkt. 9.95 (*0-440-50510-0*) Dell.

Armchair Magician. Barbara L. Thaw & Stephen J. Ronson. LC 94-5766. 1994. 9.95 (*0-440-50671-9*) Dell.

Armchair Millionaire. Frederick H. Vice. 120p. 1981. pap. 10.00 (*0-87364-204-X*) Paladin Pr.

Armchair Millionaire: How to Get Maximun Return on Minimum Investment. F. H. Vice. 1986. lib. bdg. 79.95 (*0-8490-3718-2*) Gordon Pr.

Armchair Mountaineer: The Triumphs & Tragedies of Ascent, from Fact & Fiction. Ed. by David Reuther & John Thorn. (Illus.). 324p. 1989. reprint ed. pap. 12.95 (*0-89732-092-1*) Menasha Ridge.

Armchair Quarterback's Guide to the Football Cards of the Denver Broncos. Rusty Morse. (Illus.). 24p. (Orig.). 1986. pap. 3.00 (*0-943714-02-8*) Cmdrs-Rusty's.

Armchair Research. Nancy K. Kepley. (Illus.). 50p. 1988. pap. text ed. 7.50 (*0-9625964-0-X*) Root All.

***Armchair Retreat.** David M. Knight. 180p. 1994. reprint ed. pap. 5.95 (*0-942971-23-X*) His Way.

Armchair Sailor. Bob Fisher. 170p. 1994. 29.95 (*1-85310-426-4*) Voyageur Pr.

Armchair Traveler. Bette G. Wahfeldt. (Illus.). 178p. 1986. pap. 6.50 (*0-9616280-1-4*) BW Enterprises.

Armchair Universe: An Exploration of Computer Worlds. A. K. Dewdney. LC 87-25046. 320p. 1995. pap. text ed. write for info. (*0-7167-1939-8*) W H Freeman.

Arme Heinrich nebst einer Auswahl aus der Klage, dem Gregorius und Den liedern: Mit einem Woerterverzeichnis. 2nd rev. ed. Hartmann Von Aue. Ed. by Friedrich Mauer. (Sammlung Goeschen Ser.: No. 18). 1968. 6.00 (*3-11-002723-2*) De Gruyter.

Armed America. Elaine Landau. (Illus.). 128p. (YA). (gr. 6 up). 1990. lib. bdg. 12.98 (*0-671-72386-3*, Julian Messner); pap. 5.95 (*0-671-72387-1*, Julian Messner) Silver Burdett Pr.

Armed & Considered Dangerous: A Survey of Felons & Their Firearms. James D. Wright & Peter H. Rossi. (Social Institutions & Social Change Ser.). (Illus.). 263p. (C). 1986. pap. text ed. 19.95 (*0-202-30331-4*) Aldine de Gruyter.

***Armed & Considered Dangerous: A Survey of Felons & Their Firearms.** James D. Wright & Peter H. Rossi. (Social Institutions & Social Change Ser.). (Illus.). 263p. (C). 1986. pap. text ed. 19.95 (*0-202-30542-2*) Aldine de Gruyter.

Armed & Dangerous. Ken Abraham. 1993. pap. 3.97 (*1-55748-241-1*) Barbour & Co.

Armed & Dangerous: A Writer's Guide to Weapons. Michael Newton. (Howdunit Ser.). 186p. 1990. pap. 15. 99 (*0-89879-370-X*) Writers Digest.

Armed & Dangerous: Answers for Teens from the Bible! (YA). pap. 7.95 (*1-55748-242-X*) Barbour & Co.

Armed & Dangerous: My Undercover Struggle Against Apartheid. Ronnie Kasrils. (African Writers Ser.). 240p. 1993. pap. 15.95 (*0-435-90983-5*) Heinemann.

Armed & Dangerous: The Rise of the Survivalist Right. James Coates. 1988. pap. 8.95 (*0-374-52125-5*) FS&G.

***Armed & Dangerous: Why the Pentagon Declared War on Lesbians & Gays.** Rebeca Toledo. 26p. 1993. pap. 2.50 (*0-89567-117-4*) World View Forum.

Armed & Female: Twelve Million American Women Own Guns, Should You? Paxton Quigley. 1993. mass mkt. 4.99 (*0-312-95150-7*) St Martin.

***Armed-Citizen Solution to Crime in the Streets: Many Criminals, So Few Bullets.** Mack Tanner. 200p. 1994. pap. 12.00 (*0-87364-806-4*) Paladin Pr.

Armed Communist Movements in Southeast Asia. Ed. by Lim Joo-Jock & Vani. S. LC 83-40149. 300p. 1984. text ed. 35.00 (*0-312-04943-9*) St Martin.

Armed Conflict in Lebanon, 1982: Humanitarian Law in a Real World Setting. Sally V. Mallison & W. Thomas Mallison. (Illus.). 86p. 1985. pap. 8.95 (*0-318-01034-8*) Am Educ Trust.

Armed Defense: Gunfight Survival for the Householder & Businessman. Burt Rapp. LC 89-84029. 205p. 1989. pap. text ed. 14.95 (*1-55950-014-X*) Loompanics.

Armed for Action: Library Response to Citizen Information Needs. Joan Durrance. LC 83-15400. 190p. 1984. 39.95 (*0-918212-71-5*) Neal-Schuman.

Armed for Spiritual Warfare. Jamie Buckingham. 105p. (Orig.). 1989. student ed. pap. 6.95 (*1-55725-010-3*); Incls. video. student ed, vhs 34.95 (*1-55725-011-1*) Paraclete MA.

***Armed Force: (The Arms Trilogy)** (Executioner Ser.). 1995. mass mkt. 3.50 (*0-373-61197-8*, 1-61197-9) Harlequin Bks.

Armed Forces. Robert Italia. Ed. by Rosemary Wallner. LC 91-73075. (War in the Gulf Ser.). 202p. (J). (gr. 4 up). 1991. lib. bdg. 13.99 (*1-56239-026-0*) Abdo & Dghtrs.

Armed Forces & Democratic Accountability: Human Rights & Civil-Military Relations in Argentina, Brazil & Uruguay. (Human Rights Report Ser.: No. 2). 100p. 1990. pap. 10.00 (*0-929513-09-6*) WOLA.

Armed Forces & Modern Counter-Insurgency. Ed. by Ian F. Beckett & John Pimlott. LC 84-22850. 224p. 1987. pap. 14.95 (*0-312-00449-4*) St Martin.

Armed Forces & Political Power in Eastern Europe: The Soviet-Communist Control System. Bradley R. Gitz. LC 91-28743. (Contributions in Political Science Ser.: No. 292). 208p. 1992. text ed. 49.95 (*0-313-27723-0*, GLK/, Greenwood Pr) Greenwood.

Armed Forces & Society in Spain Past & Present: A Collaborative Study. Ed. by Thomas M. Barker & Rafael B. Martinez. 320p. 1988. text ed. 48.00 (*0-88033-959-4*) East Eur Quarterly.

Armed Forces & the Welfare Societies: Challenges in the 1980s. Gwyn Harries-Jenkins. LC 82-10500. 256p. 1983. text ed. 32.50 (*0-312-04926-9*) St Martin.

Armed Forces' Foreign Language Teaching. Paul F. Angiolillo. 440p. 1947. 15.95 (*0-913298-57-3*) S F Vanni.

Armed Forces Guide to Personal Financial Planning. 3rd ed. J. Kevin Berner & Thomas V. Daula. 416p. 1994. pap. 22.95 (*0-8117-2501-4*) Stackpole.

Armed Forces in Transition. Andreas Behnke. (SIPRI Research Reports: No. 7). 150p. 1995. 39.95 (*0-19-829180-9*); pap. 23.00 (*0-19-829183-3*) OUP.

Armed Forces of the U. S. S. R. 4th rev. ed. Harriet F. Scott & William F. Scott. (C). 1929. text ed. 60.00 (*0-8133-0886-0*); pap. text ed. 22.50 (*0-8133-0887-9*) Westview.

Armed Forces on a Northern Frontier: The Military in Alaska's History, 1867-1987. Jonathan M. Nielson. LC 87-31781. (Contributions in Military Studies: No. 74). 301p. 1988. text ed. 49.95 (*0-313-26030-3*, NAE/, Greenwood Pr) Greenwood.

Armed Forces on the West Coast. Ed. by John Langellier. (Illus.). 76p. (Orig.). 1981. pap. text ed. 15.00 (*0-89745-023-X*) Sunflower U Pr.

Armed Forces Radio Service Basic Musical Library, "P" Series, 1-1000. Larry F. Kiner & Harry Mackenzie. LC 90-40207. (Discographies Ser.: No. 39). 352p. 1990. text ed. 65.00 (*0-313-27527-0*, KAW, Greenwood Pr) Greenwood.

Armed Forces Tests (AFT-ASVAB) Jack Rudman. (Admission Test Ser.: ATS-34). 1994. pap. 29.95 (*0-8373-5034-4*) Nat Learn.

Armed Love. Eleanor Lerman. LC 73-6013. (Wesleyan Poetry Program Ser.: Vol. 68). 64p. 1973. pap. 10.95 (*0-8195-1068-8*, Wesleyan Univ Pr) U Pr of New Eng.

Armed Memory. Jim Young. 256p. 1995. 21.95 (*0-312-85766-7*) Tor Bks.

Armed Nation: The Brazilian Military Corporate Mystique. Robert A. Hayes. LC 87-32558. 300p. (C). 1988. 20.00 (*0-87918-069-2*) ASU Lat Am St.

Armed Option: Zen in the Art of Combat Pistolcraft. Warren W. Buttler. LC 93-70315. 160p. 1993. pap. 14. 95 (*0-939427-75-3*) Alpha Pubns OH.

Armed Robbery: Cops, Robbers & Victims. Thomas Gabor et al. (Illus.). 244p. 1987. 46.95x (*0-398-05328-6*) C C Thomas.

Armed Robbery Orgasm: A Lovemap Autobiography of Masochism. Ronald W. Keyes & John Money. (New Concepts in Human Sexuality Ser.). (Illus.). 164p. 1993. 23.95 (*0-87975-856-2*) Prometheus Bks.

Armed Struggle in Africa: With the Guerrillas in "Portuguese" Guinea. Gerard Chaliand. LC 72-81789. 160p. 1969. pap. 2.95 (*0-85345-179-6*) Monthly Rev.

Armed Transport Bounty. John McKay. LC 88-62459. (Anatomy of the Ship Ser.). (Illus.). 120p. 1989. 36.95 (*0-87021-280-X*) Naval Inst Pr.

Armed Virginia Sloop of Seventeen Sixty-Eight. Clayton A. Feldman. (Illus.). 140p. (Orig.). 1991. pap. 19.95 (*0-9615021-7-7*) Phoen Pubns.

Armed Vision: A Study in the Methods of Modern Literary Criticism. Stanley E. Hyman. LC 77-29139. 417p. 1978. reprint ed. text ed. 57.50 (*0-313-20273-7*, HYAV, Greenwood Pr) Greenwood.

Armed with Cameras: The American Military Photographers of World War II. Peter Maslowski. LC 93-7957. 1993. text ed. 29.95 (*0-02-920265-5*) Free Pr.

Armed with the Constitution: Jehovah's Witnesses in Alabama & the U. S. Supreme Court, 1939-1946. Merlin O. Newton. LC 94-3993. 1995. 29.95 (*0-8173-0736-2*) U of Ala Pr.

Armee des Ombres. Joseph Kessel. (FRE.). 1986. pap. 10. 95 (*0-7859-3234-8*, 2266036513) Fr & Eur.

Armee du Salut: Cite de Refuge, Vol. VI. Le Corbusier. Ed. by H. Allen Brooks. LC 83-9075. (Le Corbusier Archive Ser.). 440p. 1983. lib. bdg. 260.00 (*0-8240-5055-X*) Garland.

Armee Romaine d'Afrique et l'Occupation Militaire de lAfrique sous les Empereurs. Rene L. Cagnat. LC 75-7306. (Roman History Ser.). (Illus.). (FRE.). 1975. reprint ed. 66.95 (*0-405-07187-6*) Ayer.

Armenia. Ed. by Lerner Geography Department Staff. (Then & Now Ser.). (Illus.). 64p. (YA). (gr. 5 up). 1993. lib. bdg. 21.50 (*0-8225-2806-1*, Lerner Publctns) Lerner Group.

Armenia. Nersessian. (World Bibliographical Ser.). 1993. lib. bdg. 92.00 (*1-85109-144-0*) ABC-CLIO.

Armenia: Annual Volume Review of National Literatures. Ed. by Vahe Oshagan et al. 260p. 1984. 43.00 (*0-685-06985-0*); pap. 23.00 (*0-918680-22-0*) Bagehot Council.

Armenia: Travels & Studies, 2 vols., Set. H. F. Lynch. 1990. reprint ed. 70.00 (*0-86685-461-4*) Intl Bk Ctr.

***Armenia: U. S. Non Profit Aid.** 70p. (Orig.). 1995. pap. 125.00 (*0-7605-1534-4*) Rector Pr.

Armenia & Karabagh: The Struggle for Unity. Christopher Walker et al. 176p. 1991. 49.95 (*1-873194-20-X*, Pub. by Minority Rts Pubns UK); pap. 17.95 (*1-873194-00-5*, Pub. by Minority Rts Pubns UK) Paul & Co Pubs.

Armenia & the Bible: Papers Presented to the International Symposium Held at Heidelberg, 16-19 July 1990. Christoph Burchard. (University of Pennsylvania Armenian Texts & Studies). 262p. 1993. 49.95 (*1-55540-597-5*, 210212) Scholars Pr GA.

Armenia & the Crusades: Tenth to Twelfth Centuries - The Chronicle of Matthew of Edessa. Ara E. Dostourian. 392p. 1993. lib. bdg. 59.50 (*0-8191-8953-7*) U Pr of Amer.

Armenia & the Near East. Fridtjof Nansen. LC 76-25120. (Middle East in the 20th Century Ser.). 1976. reprint ed. lib. bdg. 37.50 (*0-306-70760-8*) Da Capo.

Armenia at the Crossroads: Democracy & Nationhood in the Post-Soviet Era. Ed. by Gerard J. Libaridian. LC 91-70342. 172p. 1991. 29.95 (*0-9628715-1-6*); pap. 14.95 (*0-9628715-0-8*) Blue Crane Bks.

An Asterisk (*) at the beginning of an entry indicates that the title is appearing in BIP for the first time.

An Asterisk (*) at the beginning of an entry indicates that the title is appearing in BIP for the first time.

Armies of the Hasmonaeans & Herod - from Hellenistic to Roman Frameworks. Israel Shatzman. (Texte und Studien zum Antiken Judentum Ser.: No. 25). 380p. 1990. 117.50 (*3-16-145617-3*, Pub. by J C B Mohr GW) Coronet Bks.

Armies of the Muslim Conquest. David Nicolle. (Men-at-Arms Ser.: No. 255). (Illus.). 48p. pap. 11.95 (*1-85532-279-X*, 9226, Pub. by Osprey UK) Stackpole.

Armies of the Night. Norman Mailer. 1968. pap. 6.99 (*0-451-14070-2*, AE2317, Sig) NAL-Dutton.

Armies of the Night: History As a Novel - The Novel As History. Norman Mailer. 304p. 1995. pap. 11.95 (*0-452-27279-3*, Plume) NAL-Dutton.

Armies of the Ottoman Turks 1300-1774. David Nicolle. (Men-at-Arms Ser.: No. 140). (Illus.). 48p. pap. 11.95 (*0-85045-511-1*, 9072, Pub. by Osprey UK) Stackpole.

Armies of the Poor: Determinants of Working-Class Participation in the Parisian Insurrection of June, 1848. Mark Traugott. LC 85-3511. (Illus.). 304p. 1985. 49.50x (*0-691-09414-4*); pap. 17.95x (*0-691-10173-6*) Princeton U Pr.

***Armies of the Poor: Determinants of Working-Class Participation in the Parisian Insurrection of June 1848.** Mark Traugott. LC 85-3511. reprint ed. 89.50 (*0-7837-9292-1*, 2060031) Bks Demand.

Armies of the Raj: From the Great Indian Mutiny to Independence, 1858-1947. Byron Farwell. (Illus.). 400p. 1991. pap. 13.95 (*0-393-30802-2*) Norton.

Armies of the Vietnam War, Vol. 2. Lee E. Russell. (Men-at-Arms Ser.: No. 143). (Illus.). 48p. pap. 11.95 (*0-85045-514-6*, 9075, Pub. by Osprey UK) Stackpole.

Armies of the Vietnam War 1962-75. Philip Katcher. (Men-at-Arms Ser.: No. 104). (Illus.). 48p. pap. 11.95 (*0-85045-360-7*, 9037, Pub. by Osprey UK) Stackpole.

Armies of the World: Britains Ltd. Lead Soldiers (1925-1941) Joseph T. Wallis. LC 92-91023. (Illus.). 419p. (Orig.). 1993. pap. 40.00 (*0-9605950-2-3*) J Wallis.

***Armies of U.S. Grant.** James R. Arnold. (Illus.). 320p. 1995. 29.95 (*1-85409-177-8*, Pub. by Arms & Armour UK) Sterling.

Armies of Wellington. Philip J. Haythornthwaite. (Illus.). 288p. 1994. 29.95 (*1-85409-175-1*) Sterling.

Armies on the Danube, Eighteen Hundred Nine. Scott Bowden & Charles Tarbox. LC 80-65117. (Armies of the Napoleonic Wars Research Ser.). (Illus.). 198p. 1980. 19.95 (*0-913037-00-1*) Empire Games Pr.

Armies on the Danube, Eighteen Hundred Nine. exp. rev. ed. Scott Bowden & Charles Tarbox. LC 80-65117. (Armies of the Napoleonic Wars Research Ser.). (Illus.). 256p. 1989. 26.95 (*0-913037-08-7*) Empire Games Pr.

Armies on the Danube 1809. 2nd rev. ed. Scott Bowden & Charles Tarbox. 1989. reprint ed. 26.95 (*0-9626655-0-9*) Emperors Pr.

Armin. Mark Dunster. 22p. (Orig.). 1982. pap. 4.00 (*0-89642-094-9*) Linden Pubs.

Armin Hofmann Graphic Design. Hans Wichmann. 192p. 1991. 54.00 (*0-8176-2339-6*) Birkhauser.

Armin Landeck: The Catalogue Raisonne of His Prints. 2nd enl. rev. ed. June K. Kraeft & Norman Kraeft. LC 91-46827. (Illus.). 240p. (C). 1994. 50.00 (*0-8093-1740-0*) S Ill U Pr.

Armin T. Wegner. Johanna Wernicke-Rothmayer. (European University Studies: German Language & Literature: Ser. 1, Vol. 503). 435p. (GER.). 1982. 67.70 (*3-8204-5789-5*) P Lang Pubs.

Arming & Fitting of English Ships of War, 1600-1815. Brian Lavery. LC 87-62011. (Illus.). 288p. 1988. 59.95 (*0-87021-009-2*) Naval Inst Pr.

Arming for Peace? Syria's Elusive Quest for Strategic Parity. Michael Eisenstadt. LC 92-19732. (Policy Papers: No. 31). 104p. (Orig.). 1992. pap. 11.95 (*0-944029-19-1*) Wash Inst NEP.

Arming for Spiritual Warfare: How Christians Can Prepare to Fight the Enemy. George Mallone. LC 90-46663. 200p. (Orig.). 1991. pap. 9.99 (*0-8308-1734-4*, 1734) InterVarsity.

Arming Military Justice, Vol. I: The Origins of the United States Court of Military Appeals, 1775-1950. Jonathan Lurie. (Illus.). 280p. 1992. text ed. 45.00 (*0-691-06944-1*) Princeton U Pr.

Arming Our Allies: Cooperation & Competition in Defense Technology. (Illus.). 121p. 1990. per., pap. 5.00 (*0-16-022063-7*, S/N 052-003-011) USGPO.

Arming the Dragon: U. S. Security Ties with the People's Republic of China. A. James Gregor. LC 87-24493. 140p. (Orig.). (C). 1988. pap. text ed. 12.75 (*0-89633-120-2*) Ethics & Public Policy.

Arming the Fleet: U. S. Navy Ordnance in the Muzzle-Loading Era. Spencer Tucker. (Illus.). 336p. 1989. 49.95 (*0-87021-007-6*) Naval Inst Pr.

Arming the Free World: The Origins of the United States Military Assistance Program, 1945-1950. Chester J. Pach, Jr. LC 90-41120. x, 322p. 1991. pap. text ed. 14.95x (*0-8078-1943-3*) U of NC Pr.

Arming the Luftwaffe: The Reich Air Ministry & the German Aircraft Industry, 1919-39. Edward L. Homze. LC 75-38055. (Illus.). 314p. reprint ed. pap. 89.50 (*0-7837-4646-6*, 2044370) Bks Demand.

Arming the Suckers. Ken Baumann. 1989. 29.95 (*0-89029-529-8*) Morningside Bkshop.

Arminius or the Rise of a National Symbol. Richard Kuehnemund. LC 79-181942. (North Carolina. University. Studies in the Germanic Languages & Literatures: No. 8). reprint ed. 27.00 (*0-404-50908-8*) AMS Pr.

Arminius Vambery: His Life & Adventures. Arminius Vambery. LC 73-6307. (Middle East Ser.). 1973. reprint ed. 31.95 (*0-405-05369-X*) Ayer.

Armistead Family, 1635-1910. Virginia Armistead Garber. LC 85-73795. 324p. 1986. reprint ed. 160.00 (*0-916497-77-1*); reprint ed. fiche 6.00 (*0-916497-76-3*) Burnett Micro.

Armistice & Other Memories: Forming a Pendant to the 'Spanish Farm Trilogy' Ralph H. Mottram. LC 79-160946. (Short Story Index Reprint Ser.). 1977. reprint ed. 19.95 (*0-8369-3925-5*) Ayer.

Armless Maiden. Ed. by Terri Windling. 384p. 1995. 22.95 (*0-312-85234-7*) Tor Bks.

Armlet of the Gods. Jack L. Chalker. 368p. (Orig.). 1986. pap. 3.95 (*0-345-32463-3*, Del Rey) Ballantine.

Armoires Vides. Annie Ernaux. (Folio Ser.: No. 1600). (FRE.). 1989. pap. 8.95 (*2-07-037600-1*) Schoenhof.

Armoires Vides. Annie Ernaux. 192p. (FRE.). 1984. pap. 10.95 (*0-7859-2496-5*, 2070376001) Fr & Eur.

Armonia De los Cuatro Evangelios. A. T. Robertson. Tr. by W. F. Patterson. Orig. Title: Harmony of the Four Gospels. 259p. (SPA.). 1986. reprint ed. pap. 7.25 (*0-311-04302-X*) Casa Bautista.

Armonia Familiar. Al Compton. 32p. 1988. reprint ed. pap. 1.75 (*0-311-46078-X*) Casa Bautista.

Armonia, 1856-1859. Ed. by H. Robert Cohen. (Repertoire International de la Presse Musicale Ser.). 367p. (ITA.). 1989. 120.00 (*0-8357-0889-6*) Univ Microfilms.

Armor. John Steakley. 432p. 1984. mass mkt. 5.99 (*0-88677-368-7*) DAW Bks.

Armor. Charlotte Yue & David Yue. LC 93-50601. (J). 1994. 14.95 (*0-395-68101-4*) HM.

Armor & Ashes. Miriam Marx. Ed. by Elizabeth Klein. (Chapbook Ser.: No. 13). 23p. 1983. pap. 3.00 (*0-932884-12-1*) Red Herring.

Armor Attacks Tank Platoon. John Antal. 1991. 14.95 (*0-89141-383-9*) Presidio Pr.

Armor in Vietnam: A Pictorial History. Jim Mesko. (Vietnam Studies Group). (Illus.). 80p. 1982. pap. 10.95 (*0-89747-126-1*, 6033) Squad Sig Pubns.

Armor Logistics. 1989. lib. bdg. 79.95 (*0-8490-3969-X*) Gordon Pr.

Armor of Light. Ed. by Merle Meeter. 208p. (Orig.). (C). 1979. pap. 6.95 (*0-932914-01-2*) Dordt Coll Pr.

Armor of Light: Stained Glass in Western France, 1250-1325, Vol. 23. Meredith P. Lillich. LC 92-30564. (California Studies in the History of Art). 1993. 150.00 (*0-520-05186-6*) U CA Pr.

Armor Quest: The Search for the Armor of God. Ed. by Sara Anderson. 150p. Date not set. 79.95 (*0-917851-96-X*) Bristol Hse.

***Armored Cav: A Guided Tour of an Armored Cavalry Regiment.** Tom Clancy. 352p. (Orig.). 1994. pap. 15.00 (*0-425-15836-5*, Berkley Trade) Berkley Pub.

Armored Combat in Vietnam. Donn A. Starry. LC 80-69325. 1981. 15.00 (*0-672-52673-5*, Bobbs) Macmillan.

Armored Fist. rev. ed. Time-Life Books Editors. (New Face of War Ser.). (Illus.). 200p. 1991. write for info. (*0-8094-8704-7*); lib. bdg. write for info. (*0-8094-8705-5*) Time-Life.

***Armored Fist: Official Strategy Guide.** Ed Dille. 1994. pap. 19.95 (*1-55958-761-X*) Prima Pub.

Armored Forces: History & Sourcebook. Robert M. Citino. LC 94-4784. (Histories & Sourcebooks on Combat Forces Ser.). 328p. 1994. text ed. 75.00 (*0-313-28500-4*, Greenwood Pr) Greenwood.

***Armored Hearts: New & Selected Poems.** David Bottoms. LC 95-6256. 150p. (Orig.). 1995. 25.00x (*1-55659-073-3*); pap. 14.00 (*1-55659-072-5*) Copper Canyon.

Armored Scale Insects of Ohio. Michael Kosztarab. (Bulletin New Ser.: Vol. 2, No. 2). 1963. 5.00 (*0-86727-049-7*) Ohio Bio Survey.

Armored Scale Insects, Vols. A & B: Their Biology, Natural Enemies & Control, 2 vols., Vol. A. D. Rosen. (World Crop Pests Ser.: Vol. 4). 386p. 1991. 159.00 (*0-444-42854-2*) Elsevier.

Armored Scale Insects, Vols. A & B: Their Biology, Natural Enemies & Control, 2 vols., Vol. B. D. Rosen. (World Crop Pests Ser.: Vol. 4). 616p. 1991. 200.00 (*0-444-42902-6*) Elsevier.

Armored Ships. Illus. & Text by Ian Marshall. 180p. 1993. pap. 28.95 (*0-943231-63-9*) Howell Pr VA.

Armored Ships. Ian H. Marshall. Ed. by Kathleen D. Valenzi. LC 90-81634. (Illus.). 180p. 1990. 39.95 (*0-943231-34-5*) Howell Pr VA.

Armored Warfare. John F. Fuller. LC 83-45766. reprint ed. 23.50 (*0-404-20102-4*, UG446) AMS Pr.

Armored Warfare: An Annotated Edition of Lectures on F. S. R. III, Operations Between Mechanized Forces. John F. Fuller. LC 83-8247. xix, 189p. 1983. reprint ed. text ed. 65.00 (*0-313-24067-1*, FUAR, Greenwood Pr) Greenwood.

Armorial Bruno Bernard Heim. Bernard B. Heim. (Illus.). 1981. 50.00 (*0-905715-16-0*, Pub. by Colin Smythe Ltd UK) Dufour.

***Armorial Du Canada Francais: (Armorial of French-Canada), 2 vols., Set.** Edouard Z. Massicotte & Regis Roy. (Illus.). 332p. 1994. pap. 28.50 (*0-614-00921-9*, 3790) Clearfield Co.

Armory of Swords. Ed. by Fred Saberhagen & Martin H. Greenberg. 320p. 1995. 21.95 (*0-312-85414-5*) Tor Bks.

Armory Show 1913, 3 vols, Set. LC 72-165525. (Arno Series of Contemporary Art). 1972. reprint ed. 69.95 (*0-405-00828-7*) Ayer.

Armour & His Times. Harper Leech & John C. Carroll. LC 79-179528. (Select Bibliographies Reprint Ser.). 1977. reprint ed. 29.95 (*0-8369-6657-0*) Ayer.

Armour & Weapons in the Middle Ages. Charles Ashdown. (C). 1988. 240.00 (*0-900470-63-1*, Pub. by New Holland Pubs UK) St Mut.

Armour & Weapons in the Middle Ages. Charles H. Ashdown. (Illus.). pap. 25.00 (*0-87556-603-0*) Saifer.

Armour Book in Honcho-Gunkiko. rev. ed. Arai Hakuseki. Ed. by H. Russell Robinson. 132p. (C). 1988. 200.00 (*0-87556-164-0*, Pub. by New Holland Pubs UK) St Mut.

Armour of the Pacific War. Steven J. Zaloga. (Vanguard Ser.: No. 35). (Illus.). 48p. pap. 10.95 (*0-85045-523-5*, 9324, Pub. by Osprey UK) Stackpole.

Armour Tactics in the Second World War: Panzer Army Campaigns in German War Diaries. Rudolf Steiger. (Studies in Military History). 288p. 1992. 59.95 (*0-85496-694-3*) Berg Pubs.

Armoured Train 14-69. Vsevolod V. Ivanov. Tr. by Gibson-Cowan & A. T. Grant. LC 83-10882. viii, 59p. 1983. reprint ed. text ed. 45.00 (*0-313-24132-5*, IVAR, Greenwood Pr) Greenwood.

Armoured Warfare. Ed. by J. P. Harris & F. H. Toase. LC 90-38797. 224p. 1990. text ed. 39.95 (*0-312-05231-6*) St Martin.

Armourer & His Craft. Charles J. Ffoulkes. LC 67-13328. (Illus.). 1972. reprint ed. 33.95 (*0-405-08501-X*) Ayer.

Armourer & His Craft: From XIth to the XVIth Century. Charles Ffoulkes. 240p. 1988. pap. 10.95 (*0-486-25851-3*) Dover.

Armourers. Matthias Pfaffenbichler. (Medieval Craftsmen Ser.). (Illus.). 72p. (Orig.). 1992. pap. 18.95 (*0-8020-7732-3*) U of Toronto Pr.

Armoury of Light Verse. Richard Armour. (Orig.). 1962. pap. 3.95 (*0-8283-1424-1*, 25, Intl Pocket Lib) Branden Pub Co.

Arms Across the Pacific: Security & Trade Issues Across the Pacific. Malcolm McIntosh. LC 87-32120. 189p. 1988. text ed. 45.00 (*0-312-01868-1*) St Martin.

Arms Across the Sea. Philip J. Farley et al. LC 77-91804. 144p. reprint ed. pap. 41.10 (*0-8357-5743-9*, 2027965) Bks Demand.

Arms Act, Nineteen Fifty-Nine with Rules, 1962. annot. ed. P. L. Malik. 160p. 1984. 60.00 (*0-317-54868-9*) St Mut.

Arms Act, 1959. Eastern Book Co. Staff. (C). 1988. 59.00 (*0-685-22633-6*) St Mut.

Arms Act, 1959: With Rules, 1962. 6th ed. P. L. Malik. (C). 1990. 45.00 (*0-685-39798-X*) St Mut.

Arms Act, 1959, with Rules, 1962 (Annotated) P. L. Malik. (C). 1992. 75.00 (*0-89771-775-9*, Pub. by Eastern Book II) St Mut.

Arms, Ammunitions & Explosives. A. N. Gaur. (C). 1990. 95.00 (*0-685-39354-2*) St Mut.

***Arms & Armor.** (Ultimate Sticker Bks.). (Illus.). 20p. (J). (ps-3). 1995. pap. 6.95 (*0-7894-0008-1*) Dorling Kindersley.

Arms & Armor. Michele Byam. LC 87-26449. (Eyewitness Bks.). (Illus.). 64p. (J). (gr. 5 up). 1988. 16.00 (*0-394-89622-X*) Knopf Bks Yng Read.

Arms & Armor. Michele Byam. LC 87-26449. (Eyewitness Bks.). (Illus.). 64p. (J). (gr. 5 up). 1988. lib. bdg. 16.99 (*0-394-99622-4*) Knopf Bks Yng Read.

Arms & Armor. Christopher Gravett. LC 94-7938. (Pointers Ser.). (Illus.). 32p. (J). (gr. 4-6). 1994. lib. bdg. 19.97 (*0-8114-6190-4*) Raintree Steck-V.

***Arms & Armor: A Pictorial Archive from Nineteenth-Century Sources.** Ed. by Carol B. Grafton. 128p. 1995. 7.95 (*0-486-28561-8*) Dover.

***Arms & Armor: In the Art Institute of Chicago.** Art Institute of Chicago Staff. (Illus.). 128p. 1995. 35.00 (*0-8212-2205-8*) Bulfinch Pr.

***Arms & Armor in the Art Institute of Chicago.** Walter J. Karcheski, Jr. (Illus.). 120p. 1995. 35.00 (*0-86559-142-3*); pap. 24.95 (*0-86559-143-1*) Art Inst Chi.

Arms & Armor of Medieval Knights. David Edge. 1993. 17.99 (*0-517-10319-2*) Random Hse Value.

Arms & Armor of the Medieval Knight. Stephen R. Turnbull. LC 87-33101. 1988. 14.99 (*0-517-64468-1*) Random Hse Value.

Arms & Armor of the Pilgrims. Harold L. Peterson. 1990. reprint ed. 2.00 (*0-940628-04-X*) Pilgrim Soc.

Arms & Armor of the Samurai. I. Bottomley. 1993. 17.99 (*0-517-10318-4*) Random Hse Value.

Arms & Armor of the Samurai. Stephen R. Turnbull. LC 87-32828. 1988. 14.99 (*0-517-64467-3*) Random Hse Value.

Arms & Armour of Arabia in the 18th, 19th & 20th Centuries. Robert Elgood. LC 93-12321. 152p. 1994. 99.50 (*0-85967-972-1*, Pub. by Scolar Pr UK) Ashgate Pub Co.

Arms & Artificial Intelligence: Weapon & Arms Control Applications of Advanced Computing. Ed. by Allan M. Din. (SIPRI Publication Ser.). (Illus.). 248p. 1988. 59.00 (*0-19-829122-1*) OUP.

Arms & Empire: Imperial Patterns Before World War II - The Link to Today's Global Chaos. Richard Krooth. 1980. pap. 5.95 (*0-939074-07-9*) Harvest Pubns.

Arms & Equipment Guide. TSR Staff. (Advanced Dungeons & Dragons Ser.). 1991. pap. 15.00 (*1-56076-109-1*) TSR Inc.

Arms & Equipment of the Civil War. Jack Coggins. (Illus.). 160p. 1994. reprint ed. pap. 12.95 (*0-916107-61-2*) Broadfoot.

Arms & Explosives. A. Aiyar. (C). 1988. 275.00 (*0-685-27926-X*) St Mut.

Arms & Hunger. William K. Brandt. Tr. by Victor Gollancz, Ltd. Staff. 208p. 1987. pap. 8.95x (*0-262-52127-X*) MIT Pr.

Arms & Independence: The Military Character of the American Revolution. Ed. by Ronald Hoffman & Peter J. Albert. LC 83-14599. (Perspectives on the American Revolution Ser.). 255p. reprint ed. pap. 72.70 (*0-8357-5744-7*, 2026734) Bks Demand.

Arms & Influence. Thomas C. Schelling. (Henry L. Stimson Lecture Ser.). (C). 1967. pap. 15.00 (*0-300-00221-1*, Y190) Yale U Pr.

Arms & Influence. Thomas C. Schelling. LC 76-41307. 293p. 1977. reprint ed. text ed. 59.75 (*0-8371-8980-2*, SCAI, Greenwood Pr) Greenwood.

Arms & Insecurity: A Mathematical Study of the Causes & Origins of War. Lewis F. Richardson. Ed. by Nicolas Rashevsky & Ernesto Trucco. LC 78-27901. 335p. reprint ed. pap. 95.50 (*0-8357-5745-5*, 2017006) Bks Demand.

Arms & Judgment: Law, Morality, & the Conduct of War in the 20th Century. Sheldon M. Cohen. 226p. (C). 1989. pap. text ed. 17.95 (*0-8133-0703-1*) Westview.

Arms & Men: A Study of American Military History. Walter Millis. LC 84-4711. 365p. (C). 1984. reprint ed. pap. 15.00 (*0-8135-0931-9*) Rutgers U Pr.

Arms & Oil: U. S. Military Strategy & the Persian Gulf. Thomas L. McNaugher. LC 84-45850. 226p. 1985. 31.95 (*0-8157-5624-0*); pap. 12.95 (*0-8157-5623-2*) Brookings.

Arms & Shoulders. (Fit Self-Improvement Ser.). 1983. pap. 7.95 (*0-89037-269-1*) Anderson World.

Arms & the African. William J. Foltz & Henry S. Bienen. LC 84-40670. 240p. 1987. pap. 15.00x (*0-300-03925-5*) Yale U Pr.

Arms & the Child. Saadet Deger & Somnath Sen. (SIPRI Strategic Issue Papers). 176p. 1995. 39.95 (*0-19-829151-5*) OUP.

Arms & the Enlisted Woman. Judith H. Stiehm. LC 87-33645. (Illus.). 352p. (C). 1989. 34.95 (*0-87722-565-6*) Temple U Pr.

Arms & the Enlisted Woman. Judith H. Stiehm. (Illus.). 352p. 1990. pap. 18.95 (*0-87722-705-5*) Temple U Pr.

Arms & the Man. George Bernard Shaw. 88p. 1990. pap. 1.00 (*0-486-26476-9*) Dover.

Arms & the Man. George Bernard Shaw. Ed. by Louis Crompton. LC 68-22306. 1969. pap. 5.50 (*0-672-61087-6*, Bobbs) Macmillan.

Arms & the Man. George Bernard Shaw. LC 91-52609. 60p. 1992. pap. 6.00 (*0-88734-230-2*) Players Pr.

Arms & the Man. George Bernard Shaw. (Penguin Plays Ser.). (YA). (gr. 9 up). 1950. pap. 4.95 (*0-14-048102-8*) Viking Child Bks.

Arms & the Man: Studies in Roman & Medieval Warfare & Society. John M. Carter. 146p. 1984. pap. 23.00 (*0-89126-123-0*) MA-AH Pub.

Arms & the Man; & John Bull's Other Island. George Bernard Shaw. 1993. mass mkt. 4.50 (*0-553-21421-7*) Bantam.

Arms & the Physicist. Herbert F. York. LC 94-13099. (Masters of Modern Physics Ser.). 1994. write for info. (*1-56396-099-0*) Am Inst Physics.

***Arms & the State: Patterns of Military Production & Trade.** Keith Krause. (Studies in International Relations: No. 22). (Illus.). 317p. (C). Date not set. pap. write for info. (*0-521-55866-2*) Cambridge U Pr.

Arms & the State: Patterns of Military Production & Trade. Keith Krause. (Studies in International Relations: No. 22). (Illus.). 320p. (C). 1992. 59.95 (*0-521-39446-5*) Cambridge U Pr.

Arms & the Woman: War, Gender, & Literary Representation. Helen M. Cooper et al. LC 89-5246. xxii, 348p. (C). 1989. 39.95 (*0-8078-1860-7*); pap. 14.95 (*0-8078-4256-7*) U of NC Pr.

Arms & Warfare: Escalation, De-Escalation & Negotiation. Michael Brzoska & Frederic S. Pearson. LC 93-46038. 230p. (C). 1994. text ed. 39.95 (*0-87249-982-0*) U of SC Pr.

Arms, Armies & Fortifications in the Hundred Years War. Ed. by Anne Curry & Michael Hughes. (Illus.). 288p. (C). 1994. text ed. 71.00 (*0-85115-365-8*, Boydell Pr) Boydell & Brewer.

Arms at Rest: Peacemaking & Peacekeeping in American History. Ed. by Joan R. Challinor & Robert L. Beisner. LC 86-14954. (Contributions in American History Ser.: No. 121). 238p. 1987. text ed. 55.00 (*0-313-24642-4*, BEW/, Greenwood Pr) Greenwood.

Arms, Autarky, & Aggression. William Carr. (Foundations of Modern History Ser.). 136p. 1973. reprint ed. pap. 1.95 (*0-393-09361-1*) Norton.

Arms Buildup in the Persian Gulf. Morris M. Mottale. 244p. (Orig.). (C). 1986. pap. text ed. 24.00 (*0-8191-5203-X*) U Pr of Amer.

Arms Control. American Assembly Staff. LC 75-117750. (Essay Index Reprint Ser.). 1977. 20.95 (*0-8369-1780-4*) Ayer.

Arms Control: A Guide to Negotiations & Agreements. Jozef Goldblat. 800p. (C). 1994. text ed. 140.00 (*0-8039-7751-4*) Sage.

Arms Control: Alliances, Arms Sales, & the Future. Ed. by Kenneth W. Thompson. (W. Alton Jones Foundation Series on Arms Control: Vol. XIX). 190p. (Orig.). (C). 1993. lib. bdg. 46.50 (*0-8191-8936-7*, Pub. by White Miller Center); pap. text ed. 18.50 (*0-8191-8937-5*, Pub. by White Miller Center) U Pr of Amer.

Arms Control: Has the West Lost Its Way? Robin Brown. (C). 1990. 45.00 (*0-907967-86-8*, Pub. by Inst Euro Def & Strat UK) St Mut.

Arms Control: Improved Coordination of Arms Control Research Needed. (Illus.). 68p. (Orig.). (C). 1993. pap. text ed. 40.00 (*1-56806-390-3*) Diane Pub.

Arms Control: Issues for the Public. American Assembly Staff. LC 61-14148. (Illus.). 223p. reprint ed. pap. 63.60 (*0-8357-3825-6*, 2036547) Bks Demand.

Arms Control: Moral, Political & Historical Lessons, Vol. XV. Ed. by Kenneth W. Thompson. LC 89-39847. (W. Alton Jones Foundation Series on Arms Control). 162p. (Orig.). (C). 1990. lib. bdg. 41.50 (*0-8191-7628-1*, Pub. by White Miller Center); pap. text ed. 22.00 (*0-8191-7629-X*, Pub. by White Miller Center) U Pr of Amer.

Arms Control: Myth Versus Reality. Ed. by Richard F. Staar. (Publication Ser.: No. 304). xxii, 211p. 1984. pap. 4.38 (*0-8179-8042-3*) Hoover Inst Pr.

An Asterisk (*) at the beginning of an entry indicates that the title is appearing in BIP for the first time.

An Asterisk (*) at the beginning of an entry indicates that the title is appearing in BIP for the first time.

433

Army & Civil Disorder: Federal Military Intervention in Labor Disputes, 1877-1900. Jerry M. Cooper. LC 79-7064. (Contributions in Military History Ser.: No. 19). 284p. 1980. text ed. 55.00 (*0-313-20958-8*, CAD/, Greenwood Pr) Greenwood.

***Army & Economic Mobilization.** 1995. lib. bdg. 263.95 (*0-8490-6585-2*) Gordon Pr.

Army & Industrial Manpower. Byron Fairchild & Jonathan Grossman. LC 86-25738. (Illus.). 306p. 1987. reprint ed. text ed. 67.50 (*0-313-25480-X*, FAAR, Greenwood Pr) Greenwood.

Army & Navy Store Co., Inc. Catalogue: 1918. 1989. reprint ed. 4.00 (*0-913150-97-5*) Pioneer Pr.

Army & Politics in Argentina, 1928-1945: Yrigoyen to Peron. Robert A. Potash. LC 69-13182. (Illus.). xiv, 314p. 1969. 42.50 (*0-8047-0683-2*) Stanford U Pr.

Army & Politics in Argentina, 1945-1962: Peron to Frondizi. Robert A. Potash. LC 79-64220. (Illus.). xiv, 418p. 1980. 49.50 (*0-8047-1056-2*) Stanford U Pr.

***Army & Politics in Argentina, 1962-1973 Vol. 3: From Frondizi's Fall to the Peronist Restoration.** Robert A. Potash. (Illus.). 592p. Date not set. 55.00x (*0-8047-2414-8*) Stanford U Pr.

Army & Politics in Indonesia. Harold Crouch. LC 88-47777. (Politics & International Relations of Southeast Asia Ser.). 376p. 1988. reprint ed. pap. 14.95 (*0-8014-9506-7*) Cornell U Pr.

Army & Romanian Society. 444p. 1980. 39.00 (*0-686-97592-8*, Pub. by Collets UK) St Mut.

Army & Social Progress. D. Volkogonov. 160p. (C). 1987. 55.00 (*0-685-31539-8*, Pub. by Collets UK) Pro-Am Music.

Army & the Law. Garrard Glenn. LC 72-168168. reprint ed. 20.00 (*0-404-02819-5*) AMS Pr.

Army & the Navajo: The Bosque Redondo Reservation Experiment, 1863-68. Gerald Thompson. LC 75-8457. (Illus.). 208p. reprint ed. pap. 59.30 (*0-7837-1914-0*, 2042118) Bks Demand.

Army & Vietnam. Andrew F. Krepinevich, Jr. LC 85-45865. 344p. 1988. reprint ed. pap. text ed. 14.95 (*0-8018-3657-3*) Johns Hopkins.

Army & You. Dorothy Hole. LC 92-2214. (Armed Forces Ser.). (Illus.). 48p. (J). (gr. 5-6). 1993. text ed. 12.95 (*0-89686-765-X*, Crstwood Hse) Silver Burdett Pr.

***Army Ants: The Biology of Social Predation.** William H. Gotwald. LC 94-32642. (Series in Anthropod Biology). 1995. pap. write for info. (*0-8014-9932-1*) Cornell U Pr.

***Army Ants: The Biology of Social Predation.** William H. Gotwald, Jr. LC 94-32642. (Illus.). 320p. 1995. 39.95x (*0-8014-2633-2*, Comstock Pub) Cornell U Pr.

Army, Aristocracy, Monarchs: War, Society & Government in Austria, 1618-1780. Thomas M. Barker. LC 81-85645. (Studies on Society in Change, No. 16 - War & Society in East Central Europe: Vol. VII). 1982. text ed. 42.00 (*0-930888-14-6*, 106) Col U Pr.

Army at War. Boston Publishing Co. Staff. Ed. by Robert Manning. (Vietnam Experience Ser.: Vol. 22). (Illus.). 192p. 1987. 16.95 (*0-939526-23-9*) Boston Pub Co.

Army Aviation: Cub to Comanche. Ed. by William R. Harris. 68p. (Orig.). 1991. pap. 5.00 (*0-9629073-0-8*) Army Aviatn.

***Army Aviation in Combat Operations.** 1995. lib. bdg. 259.95 (*0-8490-6563-1*) Gordon Pr.

Army Aviation's Leaders: Who Are They? Where Are They? Ed. by Lynn Coakley. 300p. (C). 1993. ring bd. 175.00 (*0-9629073-1-6*) Army Aviatn.

Army Badges & Insignia, Bk. 2: World War 1. Rosignoli. 10.95 (*0-02-605080-3*) Macmillan.

***Army Badges Insignia World War 2.** Rosignoli. 1974. pap. (*0-7137-0697-X*, Pub. by Blandford Pr UK) Sterling.

Army Basic Training. Bryan J. Stanley. 1992. 15.95 (*0-533-10281-2*) Vantage.

Army Battlefield Guide Belgium & Northern France. Richard Holmes. 200p. 1994. pap. 24.95 (*0-11-772762-8*, HM27628, Pub. by HMSO UK) UNIPUB.

Army Behind the Army. Edward A. Powell. LC 74-75242. (United States in World War I Ser.). (Illus.). xiii, 470p. 1974. reprint ed. lib. bdg. 48.95 (*0-89198-107-1*) Ozer.

Army Blue. Lucian K. Truscott. 1990. mass mkt. 5.95 (*0-446-35980-7*) Warner Bks.

Army Brat. William J. Smith. (Illus.). 225p. 1991. reprint ed. pap. 14.95 (*0-934257-50-7*) Story Line.

Army Budget Fiscal Year 1993: An Analysis. (Illus.). 67p. (Orig.). (C). 1993. pap. text ed. 30.00 (*1-56806-586-8*) Diane Pub.

Army Called It Home: Military Interiors of the 19th Century. William L. Brown, III. (Illus.). 232p. (C). 1992. text ed. 29.95 (*0-939631-42-3*) Thomas Publications.

Army-Chaplain Schmelzle's Journey to Flaetz & Life of Quintus Fixlein. Jean P. Richter. Tr. by Thomas Carlyle. (Studies in German Literature, Linguistics & Culture: Vol. 57). 240p. 1991. 59.00 (*0-938100-89-0*) Camden Hse.

Army Corps of Engineers & the Evolution of Federal Flood Plain Management Policy. Jamie W. Moore & Dorothy P. Moore. Ed. by Sylvia Dane. (Environment & Behavior Program, Special Publication Ser.: No. 20). 200p. (Orig.). (C). 1989. pap. 15.00 (*1-877943-00-2*) Natural Hazards.

Army Correspondence of Colonel John Laurens in the Years 1777-1778. John Laurens. Ed. by Peter Decker. LC 78-77106. (Eyewitness Accounts of the American Revolution Ser., No. 1). 1969. reprint ed. 18.95 (*0-405-01160-1*) Ayer.

Army Dictionary & Desk Reference. Tim Zurick. LC 91-28377. 288p. 1992. pap. 14.95 (*0-8117-2435-2*) Stackpole.

Army Doctor. Elizabeth Seifert. 1973. reprint ed. lib. bdg. 20.95 (*0-88411-006-0*, Aeonian Pr) Amereon Ltd.

***Army Doctor's Wife on the Frontier: Letters from Alaska & the Far West, 1874-1878.** Emily M. FitzGerald. Ed. by Abe Laufe & Russell J. Ferguson. LC 62-7757. (Illus.). 370p. 1962. reprint ed. pap. 105.50 (*0-7837-8941-6*, 2049651) Bks Demand.

Army Experiences with Deployment Planning in Operation Desert Shield. James P. Stucker & Iris M. Kameny. LC 93-3573. 1993. write for info. (*0-8330-1364-5*, MR-164-A/OSD) Rand Corp.

Army Exploration in the American West, 1803-1863. William H. Goetzman. 1991. pap. 19.95 (*0-87611-110-X*) Tex St Hist Assn.

Army Exploration in the American West, 1803-1863. limited ed. William H. Goetzman. 1991. 39.95 (*0-87611-111-8*) Tex St Hist Assn.

Army for Empire: The United States Army in the War with Spain. 2nd rev. ed. Graham A. Cosmas. LC 93-48947. (Illus.). (C). 1994. 29.95 (*0-942597-49-4*) White Mane Pub.

Army Force Structure: Future Reserve Roles Shaped by New Strategy, Base Force Mandates, & Gulf War. (Illus.). 66p. (Orig.). (C). 1993. pap. text ed. 37.95 (*1-56806-535-3*) Diane Pub.

Army Generals & Reconstruction: Louisiana, 1862-1877. Joseph G. Dawson, III. LC 81-11735. (Illus.). xvi, 312p. 1994. pap. 14.95 (*0-8071-1960-1*) La State U Pr.

Army Gets an Air Force: Tactics of Insurgent Bureaucratic Politics. Frederic A. Bergerson. LC 79-18191. (Illus.). 232p. reprint ed. pap. 66.20 (*0-7837-4260-6*, 2043952) Bks Demand.

***Army in India & Its Evolution: Including an Account of the Establishment of the Royal Air Force in India.** Picton Publ. Ltd. Staff. 1992. 79.95 (*0-948251-68-9*, Pub. by Picton UK) St Mut.

Army in Texas during Reconstruction, 1865-1870. William L. Richter. LC 86-30056. (Military History Ser.: No. 3). 280p. 1987. 32.50 (*0-89096-282-0*) Tex A&M Univ Pr.

Army in the Air. Anthony Farrar-Hockley. (Illus.). 256p. 1994. 38.00 (*0-7509-0617-0*) A Sutton Pub.

Army in the Service of the State. Tom Bowden. 168p. 1976. 32.95x (*0-87855-219-7*) Transaction Pubs.

Army in Victorian Society. Gwyn Harries-Jenkins. LC 77-362735. (Studies in Social History). 332p. reprint ed. pap. 94.70 (*0-8357-5748-X*, 2026523) Bks Demand.

Army, Industry & Labour in Germany, 1914-1918. Gerald D. Feldman. 580p. 1992. pap. 22.95 (*0-85496-764-8*) Berg Pubs.

Army Lawyer: A History of the Judge Advocate General's Corps, 1775-1975, with Finding Aids. LC 93-78311. 356p. 1993. reprint ed. 45.00 (*0-89941-845-7*, 307890) W S Hein.

Army Letters. Oliver W. Norton. 397p. 1990. 30.00 (*0-89029-094-6*) Morningside Bkshop.

Army Letters from an Officer's Wife, 1871-1888. Frances M. Roe. LC 81-7571. (Illus.). xxii, 387p. 1981. pap. 11.95 (*0-8032-8905-7*) U of Nebr Pr.

Army Letters from an Officer's Wife, 1871-1888. Frances M. Roe. Ed. by Richard H. Kohn. LC 78-22395. (American Military Experience Ser.). (Illus.). 1980. reprint ed. lib. bdg. 30.95 (*0-405-11871-6*) Ayer.

Army Library, 6 bks., Set. John Nicholaus. (Illus.). 288p. (J). (gr. 3-8). 1989. lib. bdg. 111.60 (*0-86592-417-1*) Rourke Corp.

***Army Life: A Private's Reminiscences of the Civil War in the 20th Maine Infantry Regiment.** Theodore Gerrish. 1995. write for info. (*0-614-07228-X*) Stan Clark Military.

Army Life: A Private's Reminiscences of the Civil War in the 20th Maine Infantry Regiment. Theodore Gerrish. 400p. 1995. reprint ed. 25.00 (*1-879664-27-5*) Stan Clark Military. One of the most famous regiments of the Civil War was the Twentieth Regiment of Maine Volunteers. Formed in 1862, the regiment saw action in some of the fiercest campaigns & battles of the war; Fredericksburg, Gettysburg, the Wilderness, Spotsylvania, Petersburg, Five Forks & Appomattox, where it had the distinct honor of being one of the regiments to receive the surrender of the Confederate Army. Originally commanded by Colonel Adelbert Ames, leadership of the regiment soon fell upon the shoulders of the most famous civilian soldier of the war - Colonel Joshua Lawrence Chamberlain. At Gettysburg, Chamberlain & the 20th Maine anchored the Union line on Little Round Top & saved the day, & the battle, for the Federal cause. The regiment fought with excellence in several later campaigns, but will always be known for its brilliant & heroic performance at Gettysburg. After the war only one veteran of the unit attempted to chronicle the exploits of the 20th Maine Infantry. ARMY LIFE appeared in its first edition in 1882. Although there are brief, scattered accounts written by other veterans of the unit's wartime activities, this remains the only full-length book, purposely published by a veteran of the 20th Maine Infantry Regiment. Stan Clark Military Books, 915 Fairview Avenue, Gettysburg, PA 17325. (717) 337-1728.** ***Publisher Provided Annotation.

Army Life in a Black Regiment. Thomas W. Higginson. 296p. 1971. reprint ed. 24.00 (*0-87928-022-0*) Corner Hse.

Army Life in a Black Regiment. Thomas W. Higginson. (American Biography Ser.). 296p. 1991. reprint ed. lib. bdg. 75.00 (*0-7812-8183-0*) Rprt Serv.

Army Life in a Black Regiment. Thomas W. Higginson. (Notable American Authors Ser.). 1992. reprint ed. lib. bdg. 75.00 (*0-7812-3102-7*) Rprt Serv.

Army Life in a Black Regiment. Thomas W. Higginson. 228p. 1984. reprint ed. pap. 9.95 (*0-393-30157-5*) Norton.

Army Life on the Pacific. Lawrence Kip. 200p. Date not set. write for info. (*0-87770-016-8*) Ye Galleon.

Army Life on the Western Frontier: Selections From the Official Reports Made Between 1826 & 1845. George Croghan. Ed. by Francis P. Prucha. LC 58-11600. (Illus.). 232p. reprint ed. pap. 66.20 (*0-8357-5749-8*, 2004767) Bks Demand.

Army List, 1993, Pt. 1. 534p. 1993. pap. 35.00 (*0-11-772657-5*, HM26575, Pub. by HMSO UK) UNIPUB.

***Army Maintenance Management System.** 1995. lib. bdg. 257.96 (*0-8490-6607-7*) Gordon Pr.

Army Manuals & Publications. 1992. lib. bdg. 289.95 (*0-8490-5589-X*) Gordon Pr.

Army Material Command: Factors Influencing Retirement Decisions During 1990 Reduction in Force. (Illus.). 73p. (Orig.). (C). 1993. pap. text ed. 35.00 (*1-56806-312-1*) Diane Pub.

***Army Medical Department, 1818-1865.** 1995. lib. bdg. 299.75 (*0-8490-7574-2*) Gordon Pr.

Army Medical Department, 1818-1865. Mary C. Gillett. LC 87-600095. (Army Historical Series, Center for Military History Publication: No. 330-5). (Illus.). 385p. (Orig.). 1987. pap. 17.00 (*0-16-001954-0*, 008-029-00152-7) USGPO.

***Army Morale, Welfare & Recreation Programs in the Future: Maximizing Soldier Benefits in Times of Austerity.** Susan Way-Smith. LC 94-35043. 1994. write for info. (*0-8330-1582-6*, MR491A) Rand Corp.

Army of Alexander the Great. Nick Sekunda. (Men-at-Arms Ser.: No. 148). (Illus.). 48p. pap. 11.95 (*0-85045-539-1*, 9080, Pub. by Osprey UK) Stackpole.

Army of Amateurs. Philippe De Vomecourt. (Classics of World War II: The Secret War Ser.). 1991. reprint ed. write for info. (*0-8094-8575-3*); reprint ed. lib. bdg. write for info. (*0-8094-8576-1*) Time-Life.

Army of Flanders & the Spanish Road: 1567-1659. Geoffrey Parker. LC 76-180021. (Cambridge Studies in Early Modern History). (Illus.). 288p. 1975. pap. 24.95 (*0-521-09907-2*) Cambridge U Pr.

Army of Gustavus Adolphus, Vol. 1: Infantry. R. Brzezinski. (Men-at-Arms Ser.: No. 235). (Illus.). 48p. pap. 11.95 (*0-85045-997-4*, 9193, Pub. by Osprey UK) Stackpole.

Army of Gustavus Adolphus (2) Cavalry. Richard Brzezinski. (Men-at-Arms Ser.). (Illus.). 48p. 1993. pap. 11.95 (*1-85532-350-8*, 9233, Pub. by Osprey UK) Stackpole.

Army of India Medal Roll, 1799-1826. Picton Publishing Staff. 123p. (C). 1987. 120.00 (*0-317-90450-7*, Pub. by Picton UK) St Mut.

Army of Manifest Destiny: The American Soldier in the Mexican War, 1846-1848. James M. McCaffrey. (American Social Experience Ser.). (Illus.). 275p. (C). 1992. 50.00 (*0-8147-5468-6*); pap. 17.95 (*0-8147-5505-4*) NYU Pr.

Army of Northern Virginia. Philip Katcher. (Men-at-Arms Ser.: No. 37). (Illus.). 48p. pap. 11.95 (*0-85045-210-4*, 9003, Pub. by Osprey UK) Stackpole.

Army of Northern Virginia Memorial Volume. John W. Jones. (Illus.). 1975. reprint ed. 30.00 (*0-89029-029-6*) Morningside Bkshop.

Army of Peter the Great (1) Infantry. Angus Konstam. (Men-at-Arms Ser.). (Illus.). 48p. 1993. pap. 11.95 (*1-85532-315-X*, 9231, Pub. by Osprey UK) Stackpole.

Army of Robert E. Lee. Philip Katcher. (Illus.). 320p. 1994. 29.95 (*1-85409-174-3*) Sterling.

Army of Shadows. large type ed. John Harris. 1978. 15.95 (*0-7089-0127-1*) Ulverscroft.

Army of Tennessee. Stanley F. Horn. LC 53-5478. (C). 1993. pap. 17.95 (*0-8061-2565-9*) U of Okla Pr.

Army of the Aged. Richard L. Neuberger & Kelley Loe. LC 72-2379. (FDR & the Era of the New Deal Ser.). 332p. 1973. reprint ed. lib. bdg. 39.50 (*0-306-70518-4*) Da Capo.

Army of the Caesars. Michael Grant. LC 92-6179. 386p. 1992. 19.95 (*0-87131-705-2*) M Evans.

Army of the French Revolution: From Citizen-Soldiers to Instrument of Power. Jean-Paul Bertaud. Tr. by R. R. Palmer. (Illus.). 384p. 1989. 59.50 (*0-691-05537-8*) Princeton U Pr.

Army of the Future. Charles De Gaulle. LC 74-5925. 179p. 1977. reprint ed. text ed. 35.00 (*0-8371-7525-9*, GAAF, Greenwood Pr) Greenwood.

Army of the Heartland: The Army of Tennessee, 1861-1862. Thomas L. Connelly. LC 67-21373. (Illus.). xvi, 306p. 1967. 29.95 (*0-8071-0404-3*) La State U Pr.

Army of the Indian Mughals. William Irvine. 1962. reprint ed. text ed. 20.00 (*0-685-14067-9*) Coronet Bks.

Army of the Potomac. Philip Katcher. (Men-at-Arms Ser.: No. 38). (Illus.). 48p. pap. 11.95 (*0-85045-208-2*, 9004, Pub. by Osprey UK) Stackpole.

Army of the Potomac: Part 1. LC 76-41427. (Civil War Monographs). 1977. reprint ed. lib. bdg. 52.00 (*0-527-17550-1*); reprint ed. pap. 42.00 (*0-527-17548-X*) Periodicals Srv.

Army of the Potomac: Part 2. LC 76-41428. (Civil War Monographs). 1977. reprint ed. pap. 34.00 (*0-527-17552-8*) Periodicals Srv.

Army of the Sutlej: Casualty Roll, 1845-46. Ed. by Picton Publishing Staff. 50p. (C). 1987. 105.00 (*0-317-90445-0*, Pub. by Picton UK) St Mut.

Army Officer's Guide. 46th ed. Lawrence P. Crocker. (Illus.). 624p. 1993. pap. 19.95 (*0-8117-2510-3*) Stackpole.

***Army Pictorial Techniques, Equipments & Systems Still Photography.** 1995. lib. bdg. 265.99 (*0-8490-6657-3*) Gordon Pr.

Army, Politics & Society in Germany, 1933-45: Studies in the Army's Relation to Nazism. Phil K. Muller. LC 87-16333. 130p. 1987. text ed. 35.00 (*0-312-00918-6*) St Martin.

Army Politics in Cuba, 1898-1958. Louis A. Perez. LC 75-35440. (Pitt Latin American Ser.). 256p. reprint ed. pap. 73.00 (*0-8357-5750-1*, 2025443) Bks Demand.

Army Register of the Volunteer Forces, 8 vols., Set. 1987. reprint ed. write for info. (*0-942211-06-5*) Olde Soldier Bks.

Army Register of the Volunteer Forces, Vol. 1. 1987. reprint ed. 150.00 (*0-942211-07-3*) Olde Soldier Bks.

Army Register of the Volunteer Forces, Vol. 2. 1987. reprint ed. 150.00 (*0-942211-08-1*) Olde Soldier Bks.

Army Register of the Volunteer Forces, Vol. 3. 1987. reprint ed. 150.00 (*0-942211-09-X*) Olde Soldier Bks.

Army Register of the Volunteer Forces, Vol. 4. 1987. reprint ed. 150.00 (*0-942211-10-3*) Olde Soldier Bks.

Army Register of the Volunteer Forces, Vol. 5. 1987. reprint ed. 150.00 (*0-942211-11-1*) Olde Soldier Bks.

Army Register of the Volunteer Forces, Vol. 6. 1987. reprint ed. 150.00 (*0-942211-12-X*) Olde Soldier Bks.

Army Register of the Volunteer Forces, Vol. 7. 1987. reprint ed. 150.00 (*0-942211-13-8*) Olde Soldier Bks.

Army Register of the Volunteer Forces, Vol. 8. 1987. reprint ed. 150.00 (*0-942211-14-6*) Olde Soldier Bks.

Army Reserve Component Accessions from Personnel Completing Their First Active-Duty Enlistment. Richard Buddin & Stephen J. Kirin. LC 93-25903. 1993. write for info. (*0-8330-1419-6*, MR-258-A) Rand Corp.

Army Science: The New Frontiers: Military & Civilian Application. Ed. by Daphne Kamely & Robert Sasmor. LC 93-9121. 1993. write for info. (*0-943255-36-8*) Portfolio Pub.

Army, State & Society in Italy, 1830-1915. John Gooch. LC 88-23368. 290p. 1989. text ed. 45.00 (*0-312-02523-8*) St Martin.

Army Surgeon's Manual. William Grace. (American Civil War Medical Ser.: No. 10). 200p. 1992. reprint ed. 45.00 (*0-930405-41-2*) Norman SF.

Army Surveillance in America, 1775-1980. Joan M. Jensen. 304p. (C). 1991. text ed. 35.00 (*0-300-04668-5*) Yale U Pr.

Army Tactical Weather. 1991. lib. bdg. 79.95 (*0-8490-4088-4*) Gordon Pr.

***Army Tactical Weather.** 1995. lib. bdg. 250.95 (*0-8490-6669-7*) Gordon Pr.

Army That Buell Built. Ed. by Richard J. Reid. LC 94-92107. 78p. (Orig.). 1994. pap. write for info. (*1-877713-05-8*) R J Reid.

Army Times Book of Great Land Battles: From the Civil War to the Gulf War. J. D. Morelock. Ed. by Walter J. Boyne. LC 94-8373. 352p. 1994. 29.95 (*0-425-14371-6*) Berkley Pub.

Army Training of Illiterates in World War Two. Samuel Goldberg. LC 74-176810. (Columbia University, Teachers College. Contributions to Education Ser.: No. 966). reprint ed. 37.50 (*0-404-55966-2*) AMS Pr.

Army Transportation Services in a Theater of Operations. 1991. lib. bdg. 79.95 (*0-8490-4080-9*) Gordon Pr.

***Army Transportation Services in a Theater of Operations.** 1995. lib. bdg. 250.95 (*0-8490-6634-4*) Gordon Pr.

***Army Uniforms of World War 2.** Mollo. 1980. (*0-7137-0611-2*, Pub. by Blandford Pr UK) Sterling.

Army Vehicle Identification Numbers. 4th ed. Ed. by Dennis R. Spence. (Military Vehicles Reference Ser.: No. 2). 1994. 39.95 (*0-938242-10-5*) Portrayal.

Army Vehicle Manuals. 4th ed. Ed. by Dennis R. Spence. (Military Vehicles Reference Ser.: No. 1). 136p. 1989. 34.95 (*0-938242-09-1*) Portrayal.

Army Vehicle Parts Guide. Comp. by Dennis R. Spence. (Military Vehicles Reference Ser.: No. 4). 60p. 1987. pap. 15.95 (*0-938242-19-9*) Portrayal.

Army Vehicle Publications. Ed. by Dennis R. Spence. LC 85-155001. (Military Vehicles Reference Ser.: No. 3). 1985. 21.95 (*0-938242-11-3*) Portrayal.

***Army Water Transport Operations.** 1995. lib. bdg. 250.55 (*0-8490-6621-2*) Gordon Pr.

Army Wife Handbook: A Complete Social Guide. 2nd ed. Ann Crossley & Carol A. Keller. LC 93-73172. (Illus.). 432p. (Orig.). 1994. pap. 20.00 (*0-9626228-2-6*) ABI Pr.

Army Wife's Cookbook. Alice K. Grierson. Ed. by Mary L. Williams. LC 72-91099. 72p. 1972. spiral bd. 4.95 (*0-911408-27-4*) SW Pks Mnmts.

Army's Nuclear Power Program: The Evolution of a Support Agency. Lawrence H. Suid. LC 89-25700. (Contributions in Military Studies: No. 98). 152p. 1990. text ed. 47.95 (*0-313-27226-3*, SND/, Greenwood Pr) Greenwood.

Army's Role in Domestic Disaster Support: An Assesment of Policy Choices. John Y. Schrader. LC 93-26504. 1993. write for info. (*0-8330-1423-4*, MR-303-A) Rand Corp.

434

An Asterisk (*) at the beginning of an entry indicates that the title is appearing in BIP for the first time.

An Asterisk (*) at the beginning of an entry indicates that the title is appearing in BIP for the first time.

Aromatic Amino Acids in the Brain. Ciba Foundation Staff. LC 73-91643. (Ciba Foundation Symposium: New Ser.: No. 22). 406p. reprint ed. pap. 115.80 (*0-8357-5752-8*, 2022152) Bks Demand.

Aromatic & Heteroaromatic Chemistry, Vols. 1-6. Incl. Vol. 1. 1971-72 Literature. LC 70-616637. 1973. 42.00 (*0-85186-753-7*); Vol. 2. 1972-73 Literature. LC 70-616637. 1974. 47.00 (*0-85186-763-4*); Vol. 3. 1973-74 Literature. LC 72-95095. 1975. 53.00 (*0-85186-773-1*); Vol. 4. 1974-75 Literature. LC 70-616637. 1976. 70.00 (*0-85186-783-9*); Vol. 5. 1975-76 Literature. LC 70-616637. 1977. 87.00 (*0-85186-793-6*); Vol. 6. 1976-77 Literature. LC 74-615720. 1978. 70.00 (*0-85186-803-7*); LC 72-95095. write for info. (*0-318-50462-6*, Pub. by Royal Soc Chem UK) Am Chemical.

Aromatic Chemistry. M. Sainsbury. (Oxford Chemistry Primers Ser.: No. 4). (Illus.). 96p. (C). 1992. pap. text ed. 9.95 (*0-19-855674-8*) OUP.

Aromatic Compounds with Fused Carbocyclic Ring Systems see Rodd's Chemistry of Carbon Compounds

Aromatic Heterocyclic Chemistry. David T. Davies. (Oxford Chemistry Primers Ser.: No. 2). (Illus.). 96p. (C). 1992. pap. text ed. 9.95 (*0-19-855660-8*) OUP.

Aromatic High Strength Fibers. H. H. Yang. (Society of Plastics Engineers Monographs). 873p. 1989. text ed. 235.00 (*0-471-62988-X*) Wiley.

Aromatic Hydrocarbons: Vol. I, Pt. 7, Vapor-Liquid Equilibrium Data Collection. J. Gmehling et al. Ed. by D. Behrens & R. Eckermann. (Dechema Chemistry Data Ser.). 564p. 1980. text ed. 201.00 (*3-921567-23-8*, Pub. by Dechema GW) Scholium Intl.

Aromatic Sextet. Erich J. Clar. LC 72-616. 138p. reprint ed. pap. 39.40 (*0-8357-5753-6*, 2023998) Bks Demand.

Aromatic Substitution by the SRN1 Mechanism. Ed. by Roberto A. Rossi & Rita H. Rossi. LC 82-22829. (ACS Monograph: No. 178). 300p. 1983. lib. bdg. 54.95 (*0-8412-0648-1*) Am Chemical.

Aromatic Thermotropichi Fluid Crystal Polyesters. Bessonov. 1992. write for info. (*0-8493-6703-4*, CRC Reprint) Franklin.

Aromatica Encyclopaedia. Data Notes Staff. 65p. 1992. ring bd. 32.95 (*0-911569-94-4*) Prosperity & Profits.

Aromaticity & Antiaromaticity: Electronic & Structural Aspects. Vladimir Minkin et al. 336p. 1994. text ed. 79.95 (*0-471-59382-6*, Wiley-Interscience) Wiley.

***Aromatics.** Angela Flanders. 1995. 25.00 (*0-517-70194-4*, C P Pubs) Crown Pub Group.

Aron Nimzowitsch: Master of Planning. Raymond Keene. (Illus.). 352p. 1991. pap. 19.95 (*0-7134-6898-X*, Pub. by Batsford UK) Trafalgar.

Aroostook: A Century of Logging in Northern Maine. Richard W. Judd. LC 88-27774. (Illus.). 375p. 1989. text ed. 32.50 (*0-89101-997-9*) U Maine Pr.

Around. Peter Downsbrough. LC 78-65770. (Illus.). 1978. pap. text ed. 4.50 (*0-9602192-0-X*) P Downsbrough.

Around Africa & Asia by Sea. (Trade & Travel Routes Ser.). (Illus.). 128p. (YA). 1990. 17.95 (*0-8160-1875-8*) Facts on File.

Around Atlanta with Children. rev. ed. Denise Black & Janet Schwartz. LC 93-81141. 312p. 1994. pap. 12.95 (*1-56352-133-4*) Longstreet Pr Inc.

Around Burnside. A. I. Kostrikin. (Ergebnisse der Mathematik und Ihrer Grenzgebiete Ser.: Vol. 20). 256p. 1990. 89.00 (*0-387-50602-0*, 3165) Spr-Verlag.

Around California in 1891. Terence Emmons. (Portable Stanford Book Ser.). (Illus.). 208p. (Orig.). 1991. pap. 12.95 (*0-916318-46-X*) Stanford Alumni Assn.

***Around California 1891.** T. Emmons. 1994. pap. 3.99 (*0-517-13384-9*) Random.

Around Cinemas. James Agate. LC 72-169323. (Literature of Cinema, Ser. 2). (Illus.). 286p. 1972. reprint ed. 20.95 (*0-405-03888-7*) Ayer.

Around Cinemas: Second Series. James Agate. LC 76-169324. (Literature of Cinema, Ser. 2). (Illus.). 300p. 1978. reprint ed. 24.95 (*0-405-03889-5*) Ayer.

Around Classification Theory of Models. S. Shelah. (Lecture Notes in Mathematics Ser.: Vol. 1182). vii, 279p. 1986. pap. 43.80 (*0-387-16448-0*) Spr-Verlag.

Around Douglas & Beyond: A Collection of Columns about the People of Douglas County. Jane A. Lehrman. Ed. by Sally Lehrman. (Illus.). 123p. (Orig.). 1990. lib. bdg. 27.50 (*0-685-46926-3*); pap. text ed. 24.50 (*0-922082-01-4*) Desk Top Pubs Inc.

Around Helston in the Old Days. A. S. Oates. (C). 1989. text ed. 30.00 (*0-907566-46-4*, Pub. by Dyllansow Truran UK) St Mut.

Around Home in Unicoi County. William W. Helton. (Illus.). 636p. 1994. reprint ed. pap. 17.95 (*1-57072-002-9*) Overmountain Pr.

Around Ireland. John Rea. LC 82-84237. 1982. pap. 7.00 (*0-918702-05-4*) Eilean Ban Pub.

Around Me. Erica Magnus. LC 90-26459. (Illus.). 32p. (J). (ps-3). 1992. 13.00 (*0-688-09756-1*); lib. bdg. 12.93 (*0-688-09753-7*) Lothrop.

Around Nineteen Eighty-One: Academic Feminist Literary Theory. Jane Gallop. 288p. 1991. 42.50 (*0-415-90189-8*, A3653, Routledge NY); pap. 13.95 (*0-415-90190-1*, A3657, Routledge NY) Routledge.

Around Old Bethany. R. L. Berry. 83p. pap. 1.00 (*0-686-29097-6*) Faith Pub Hse.

Around on Cape Cod, No. 27. Noel W. Beyle. (Illus.). 48p. (Orig.). 1986. pap. 0.95 (*0-912609-10-9*) First Encounter.

Around Proust. Richard E. Goodkin. 179p. 1991. text ed. 39.50 (*0-691-06894-1*); pap. text ed. 11.95 (*0-691-01508-2*) Princeton U Pr.

Around Scotland. John Rea. LC 78-54125. 1978. pap. 4.00 (*0-918702-03-8*) Eilean Ban Pub.

Around the Absurd: Essays on Modern & Postmodern Drama. Ed. by Enoch Brater & Ruby Cohn. (Theater: Theory - Text - Performance Ser.). 328p. (C). 1992. pap. text ed. 16.95 (*0-472-08193-4*) U of Mich Pr.

Around the Advent Wreath: Devotions for Families Using the Advent Wreath. Nancy L. Sasser. 40p. (Orig.). 1984. pap. 4.99 (*0-8066-2074-9*, 10-20749, Augsburg) Augsburg Fortress.

Around the Banks of Pimlico. Marvin Johnston. (Illus.). 144p. (Orig.). (C). 1985. pap. 11.95 (*0-946211-15-9*, Pub. by Attic IE) InBook.

***Around the Block with Judy Hopkins.** Judy Hopkins. Ed. by Laura Reinstatler. (Illus.). 116p. (Orig.). 1994. pap. 18.95 (*1-56477-079-6*) That Patchwork.

Around the Buoys: A Manual of Sailboat Racing Tactics & Strategy. Michael Huck. LC 93-36786. (Illus.). 1994. pap. text ed. 17.95 (*0-07-030817-9*) Intl Marine.

Around the Cape of Good Hope: Poems of the Sea by Nordahl Grieg. Nordahl Grieg. Tr. by Lars Egede-Nissen. (Illus.). 1979. pap. 3.25 (*0-933748-01-9*) Nordic Bks.

Around the Cat's Back. Jerry Gildemeister. (Illus.). 128p. (J). (gr. 4-12). 1989. 32.50 (*0-936376-06-6*) Bear Wallow Pub.

Around the Church, Around the Year: Unitarian Universalism for Children. Jan Evans-Tiller. Ed. by Kathryn Lewis et al. (Illus.). 144p. (Orig.). (J). (gr. k-3). 1990. pap. text ed. 30.00 (*1-55896-174-7*) Unitarian Univ.

Around the Circle in 1892: A Thousand Miles by Rail Through the Rocky Mountains. S. K. Hooper. Ed. by William R. Jones. (Illus.). 1978. pap. 4.95 (*0-89646-049-5*) Vistabooks.

Around the Clock. Elizabeth Bartlett. 100p. (Orig.). 1989. pap. 10.00 (*0-932662-76-5*) St Andrews NC.

Around the Community: Activity Book. K. Hollenbeck. (Graphic Learning Integrated Social Studies Ser.). 90p. (J). 1993. 5.25 (*0-87746-376-X*) Graphic Learning.

Around the Community: Copy Masters File. K. Hollenbeck. (Graphic Learning Integrated Social Studies Ser.). 90p. 1993. 85.00 (*0-87746-377-8*) Graphic Learning.

Around the Community: Literature Set, 6 stories. Ed. by L. Johnson. (Graphic Learning Integrated Social Studies Ser.). (Illus.). (ENG & SPA.). 1993. 225.00 (*0-87746-321-2*) Graphic Learning.

Around the Community: Teacher's Guide. K. Hollenbeck. (Graphic Learning Integrated Social Studies Ser.). (Illus.). 300p. 1993. 75.00 (*0-87746-375-1*) Graphic Learning.

Around the Corner: Tenth Anniversary Anthology. Manuscriptors Guild Members. Ed. by Dot Fowler & Pat Price. (Illus.). 150p. (Orig.). Date not set. pap. text ed. 12.50 (*0-9637150-1-1*) Talent By Lb.

Around the Cragged Hill: A Personal & Political Philosophy. George F. Kennan. LC 92-9936. 288p. 1993. 22.95 (*0-393-03411-9*) Norton.

Around the Cragged Hill: A Personal & Political Philosophy. Goerge F. Kennan. 1994. pap. 12.95 (*0-393-31145-7*) Norton.

Around the Drums Compleatly. Joel Rothman. 1976. 30.00 (*0-913952-05-2*) J R Pubns.

Around the Golden Ring of Russia. Yu Bychkov & V. Desatnikov. 255p. (C). 1988. 120.00 (*0-569-22234-6*, Pub. by Collets UK) Pro-Am Music.

Around the Horn to the Sandwich Islands & California 1845-1850. Chester S. Lyman. (American Biography Ser.). 328p. 1991. reprint ed. lib. bdg. 79.00 (*0-7812-8255-1*) Rprt Serv.

Around the Horn to the Sandwich Islands & California 1845-50. Chester S. Lyman. Ed. by Frederick J. Teggart. LC 70-152992. (Select Bibliographies Reprint Ser.). 1977. reprint ed. 25.95 (*0-8369-5744-X*) Ayer.

Around the House. (What Can You Find? Ser.). 10p. (J). (ps). 1995. 4.95 (*1-56458-268-X*) Dorling Kindersley.

Around the House. Chatham River. (Fun with Words Ser.). 48p. 1990. 4.99 (*0-517-68880-8*) Random Hse Value.

Around the Keys. Hazel Cobb. 32p. 1991. pap. text ed. 5.95 (*0-87487-663-X*) Summy-Birchard.

Around the Keys Again. Hazel Cobb. 32p. 1991. pap. text ed. 5.95 (*0-87487-664-8*) Summy-Birchard.

Around the Oak. Gerda Muller. LC 93-32310. (J). (gr. 3 up). 1994. 14.99 (*0-525-45239-7*, DCB) Dutton Child Bks.

Around the Palma Sola Loop. Fred Hall. (Illus.). (Orig.). 1986. pap. 6.95 (*0-8200-1033-2*) Great Outdoors.

Around the Rugged Rock. Elizabeth Cadell. 20.95 (*0-88411-390-6*, Aeonian Pr) Amereon Ltd.

***Around the Rugged Rock.** large type ed. Elizabeth Cadell. LC 94-26165. 1995. pap. 19.95 (*0-7862-0290-4*) Thorndike Pr.

Around the Shores of Lake Michigan: A Guide to Historic Sites. Margaret B. Bogue. LC 84-40490. (Illus.). 400p. 1985. pap. text ed. 19.95 (*0-299-10004-9*) U of Wis Pr.

Around the Square: An Architectural Hunt in the Environs of Harvard Square. Bettina A. Norton. (Neighborhood Trivia Hunt Ser.). (Illus.). 80p. (Orig.). 1992. pap. 11.95 (*0-938357-08-5*) BAN Pub Boston.

Around the Stove in Roscoe's General Store - 1866. Nancy L. Lonsinger. (Illus.). 48p. (Orig.). 1976. pap. 2.00 (*1-880443-00-7*) Roscoe Village.

Around the Table: Family Stories of Sholom Aleichem. Tr. & Sel. by Aliza Shevrin. LC 90-49273. (Illus.). 96p. (J). (gr. 5-8). 1991. text ed. 12.95 (*0-684-19237-3*, C Scribner Sons Young) S&S Childrens.

Around the Ward in Eighty Days. Joni Hilton. LC 92-76069. 1993. pap. 10.95 (*1-55503-531-0*, 0111191) Covenant Comms.

Around the Wicket Gate. C. H. Spurgeon. 1992. pap. 4.95 (*1-56186-301-7*) Pilgrim Pubns.

Around the World. Beverly Caruso. 378p. 1993. pap. 9.99 (*0-927545-46-2*) YWAM Pub.

Around the World. Fannon. (Women Today Ser.). (J). 1991. 12.95 (*0-86593-119-4*) Rourke Corp.

Around the World: An Atlas of Maps & Pictures. LC 94-9997. (J). 1994. 14.95 (*0-528-83691-9*) Rand McNally.

Around the World: Pictures for Practice. Marjorie Fuchs et al. Ed. by Joanne Dresner. (Yes (Pictures for Practice) Ser.: No. 2). (Illus.). 80p. (Orig.). 1986. pap. text ed. 14.89 (*0-582-90723-3*, 75236) Longman.

Around the World - One Bite at a Time: An International Collection of Party Foods. Rebecca B. Karavatakis. 240p. 1987. 15.98 (*0-9618812-0-8*) Peligator Pubns.

Around-the-World Cooky Book. Lois L. Sumption & Marguerite L. Ashbrook. (Illus.). 1979. reprint ed. pap. 3.95 (*0-486-23802-4*) Dover.

Around the World Crafts for Church & Home. Susan Addington. (Bible Craft Ser.). 96p. (J). (gr. k-6). 1994. 9.95 (*1-56417-001-2*, SS3823, Shining Star Pubns) Good Apple.

Around the World in a Hundred Years: Henry the Navigator - Magellan. Jean Fritz. LC 92-27042. (Illus.). 128p. (J). (gr. 2-6). 1994. 17.95 (*0-399-22527-7*, Putnam) Putnam Pub Group.

Around the World in Cross Stitch. Jan Eaton. (Illus.). 176p. 1994. 27.50 (*0-943955-85-8*, Trafalgar Sq Pub) Trafalgar.

Around the World in Eighteen Holes. Tom Callahan & Dave Kindred. LC 93-51075. 1994. 23.00 (*0-385-47315-X*) Doubleday.

Around the World in Eighty Days. Michael Hulett. (Illus.). 48p. (Orig.). (J). (gr. 4 up). 1985. pap. 4.00 (*0-88680-233-4*) I E Clark.

***Around the World in Eighty Days.** Michael Palin. LC 94-41914. (Illus.). 288p. 1995. pap. 17.95 (*0-912333-39-1*) KQED.

Around the World in Eighty Days. Jules Verne. (Airmont Classics Ser.). (J). (gr. 8 up). 1964. pap. 2.25 (*0-8049-0024-8*, CL-24) Airmont.

Around the World in Eighty Days. Jules Verne. 18.95 (*0-88411-917-3*, Aeonian Pr) Amereon Ltd.

Around the World in Eighty Days. Jules Verne. Tr. by George M. Towle. 176p. 1984. pap. 2.95 (*0-553-21356-3*, Bantam Classics) Bantam.

Around the World in Eighty Days. Jules Verne. (Illustrated Classics Collection 3). 64p. 1994. pap. 3.60 (*1-56103-519-X*) Lake Pub Co.

Around the World in Eighty Days. Jules Verne. LC 87-62829. (Books of Wonder). (Illus.). 256p. (J). (gr. 5 up). 1988. 19.95 (*0-688-07508-8*) Morrow Jr Bks.

Around the World in Eighty Days. Jules Verne. 256p. 1991. pap. 3.95 (*0-451-52545-0*, Sig Classics) NAL-Dutton.

***Around the World in Eighty Days.** Jules Verne. Ed. & Tr. by Williams Butcher. (World's Classics Ser.). 296p. 1995. pap. 8.95 (*0-19-283093-7*) OUP.

Around the World in Eighty Days. Jules Verne. (J). 1990. pap. 3.25 (*0-590-43053-X*) Scholastic Inc.

Around the World in Eighty Days. Jules Verne. 224p. (YA). (gr. 9-12). 1990. pap. 2.50 (*0-8125-0430-5*) Tor Bks.

Around the World in Eighty Days. Jules Verne. pap. 2.95 (*0-89375-608-3*) Troll Assocs.

***Around the World in Eighty Days.** Jules Verne. (Puffin Classics Ser.). 272p. (YA). (gr. 5 up). 1995. pap. 3.99 (*0-14-036711-X*) Puffin Bks.

Around the World in Eighty Days. abr. ed. Jules Verne. Ed. by D'Ann Calhoun. (Now Age Illustrated III Ser.). (Illus.). (J). (gr. 4-12). 1977. pap. text ed. 2.95 (*0-88301-261-8*) Pendulum Pr.

Around the World in Eighty Days. deluxe limited ed. Jules Verne. LC 87-62829. (Books of Wonder). (Illus.). 256p. (J). (gr. 5 up). 1988. 175.00 (*0-688-08257-2*) Morrow Jr Bks.

Around the World in Eighty Days. large type ed. Michael Palin. 1991. 23.95 (*0-7089-8573-4*, Charnwood) Ulverscroft.

Around the World in Eighty Days: Classic Story Books. Jules Verne. (J). 1994. 4.98 (*0-8317-1645-2*) Smithmark.

Around the World in Eighty Days: Student Activity Book. Marcia Sohl & Gerald Dackerman. (Now Age Illustrated Ser.). (Illus.). (gr. 4-12). 1976. student ed 1.25 (*0-88301-285-5*) Pendulum Pr.

Around the World in Eighty Days Readalong. Jules Verne. (Illustrated Classics Collection 3). 64p. 1994. audio, pap. 13.50 (*1-56103-521-1*) Lake Pub Co.

Around the World in Eighty Dishes. Polly Van der Linde & Tasha Van der Linde. LC 71-160447. (Illus.). 88p. (J). (gr. k-7). 10.95 (*0-87592-007-1*) Scroll Pr.

Around the World in Eighty Ways. Hans G. Guggenheim. (Orig.). 1988. 30.00 (*0-317-43635-X*, Pub. by Regency Press) St Mut.

Around the World in Old Ironsides: The Voyage of U. S. S. Constitution, 1844-1846. Henry G. Thomas. Ed. by Alan B. Flanders. LC 93-15295. 164p. 1993. 24.95 (*0-9627635-5-1*); pap. 19.95 (*0-9627635-6-X*) Brandylane.

Around the World in Seventy-Two Days: The Race Between Pulitzer's Nellie Bly & Cosmopolitan's Elizabeth Bisland. Jason Marks. LC 92-73586. (Illus.). 261p. (Orig.). 1993. pap. 12.95 (*0-9633696-1-X*) Gemittarius.

Around the World in Seventy-Two Days: The Race Between Pulitzer's Nellie Bly & Cosmopolitan's Elizabeth Bisland. Jason Marks. LC 92-73586. (Illus.). 261p. (Orig.). 1993. pap. 12.95 (*0-9633696-2-8*) Gemittarius.

A little more than one hundred years ago, two American women journalists raced around the world chasing a phantom. His name was Phileas Fogg, a fictional character in Jules Verne's AROUND THE WORLD IN EIGHTY DAYS. On November 14, 1889, Nellie Bly (pen name of Elizabeth Cochrane), a dynamic 22-year-old newspaper reporter, sailed from New York as a circulation-boosting stunt for the NEW YORK WORLD. That same day, Elizabeth Bisland, a dignified, alluring associate editor of COSMOPOLITAN magazine, was dispatched in the other direction, boarding a train that would take her across the continent to San Francisco. Nellie had promised her readers to girdle the globe in seventy-five days--whereupon Miss Bisland's publisher expressed confidence that his woman could do it in less. A media war ensued, with each publication sparing no effort or expense to ensure that its lady finished first. The adventures of these two dauntless women in strange far-off lands & over stormy seas rigorously tested their powers of resourcefulness & determination. Traveling without companion or chaperone, they risked the opprobrium of their male-dominated Victorian society. They were, unquestionably, extraordinary pioneers of the Women's Rights Movement, not only in America but around the world they traversed. To order: Publishers Distribution Service (PDS), (800) 507-BOOK, Baker & Taylor, Ingram, Pacific Pipeline. Special library hardcover discount. ***Publisher Provided Annotation.***

Around the World in Sixty Years. Olivia Casberg. 1993. pap. 12.00 (*0-933380-14-3*) Olive Pr Pubns.

Around the World in Twenty Legends. Priscilla L. McQueen. (Basic Readers Ser.). 1970. teacher ed 3.25 (*0-685-36208-6*); student ed 2.30 (*0-685-36209-4*) McQueen.

***Around the World in 18 Holes.** Kindred. 1995. pap. (*0-385-47848-8*) Doubleday.

***Around the World in 45 Years: Charlie Brown's Anniversary Celebration.** Charles Schulz. (Illus.). 180p. 1994. 19.95 (*0-8362-1772-1*) Andrews & McMeel.

***Around the World in 45 Years: Charlie Brown's Anniversary Celebration.** Charles M. Schulz. (Illus.). 180p. 1994. pap. 12.95 (*0-8362-1766-7*) Andrews & McMeel.

Around the World Magic Pen Book. (J). (gr. 3 up). 1991. pap. 1.97 (*1-56297-134-4*) Lee Pubns KY.

Around the World on a Stationary Bicycle. Albert M. Freiberg. 1992. 15.95 (*0-533-10169-7*) Vantage.

Around the World on the "Kamchatka," 1817-1819. V. N. Golovnin. Tr. by Ella L. Wiswell. LC 79-15230. (Illus.). 392p. 1979. text ed. 20.00 (*0-8248-0640-9*) UH Pr.

Around the World on the QE II. LC 81-5921. 1981. 12.95 (*0-9603174-7-3*) Bks of Value.

Around the World Program Series. Hilary L. Hopper. (J). (gr. 4 up). 1993. Smyth sewn casebound. 17.95 (*0-939923-28-9*); Family ed. 48.00 (*0-939923-26-2*); Perfect bdg. per. 7.95 (*0-939923-27-0*) M & W Pub Co.

Around the World Rally: Thirty-Six World Cruising Skippers Interviewed in the Most Comprehensive Equipment Survey Ever Undertaken. Jimmy Cornell. (Illus.). 208p. (Orig.). 1993. pap. 16.50 (*0-924486-47-3*) Sheridan.

Around the World Single-Handed: The Cruise of the Islander. Harry Pidgeon. 288p. 1989. pap. 5.95 (*0-486-25946-3*) Dover.

Around the World, Vol. 1: Mexico. Betsy Franco. (Illus.). 48p. (J). (gr. 1-3). 1993. pap. text ed. 7.95 (*1-55799-256-8*) Evan-Moor Corp.

Around the World, Vol. 2: Japan. Betsy Franco. (Illus.). 48p. (J). (gr. 1-3). 1993. pap. text ed. 7.95 (*1-55799-257-6*) Evan-Moor Corp.

Around the World, Vol. 3: Russia. Betsy Franco. (Illus.). 48p. (J). (gr. 1-3). 1993. pap. text ed. 7.95 (*1-55799-258-4*) Evan-Moor Corp.

Around the World with a King. William N. Armstrong. (Pacific Basin Bks.). 320p. 1988. pap. 14.95 (*0-7103-0291-6*, Pub. by Kegan Paul Intl UK) Routledge Chapman & Hall.

Around the World with a Stiff Knee. Sue Spencer. 1993. pap. 11.95 (*0-685-67185-2*) Knowledge Bk Pubs.

Around the World with Ant & Bee. Angela Banner. (Illus.). 96p. (J). (ps-1). 1989. 6.95 (*0-434-92958-1*, Pub. by W Heinemann Ltd) Trafalgar.

Around the World with Auntie Mame. Patrick Dennis. 1976. 21.95 (*0-8488-1287-5*) Amereon Ltd.

Around the World with Auntie Mame. Patrick Dennis. 1992. reprint ed. lib. bdg. 27.95 (*0-89966-939-5*) Buccaneer Bks.

Around the World with God's Friends: Mission Education Activity Book - Elementary Grades. Wendy Miller. (Illus.). 24p. (Orig.). (J). (gr. 1-5). 1990. pap. text ed. 1.50 (*1-877736-06-6*, Mission Focus) MB Missions.

Around the World with Jesus. Dorothy Cross. 0.60 (*0-88027-102-7*) Firm Foun Pub.

Around the World with My Recorder. Dexter. 1990. 6.95 (*0-685-32161-4*, T072) Hansen Ed Mus.

436

An Asterisk (*) at the beginning of an entry indicates that the title is appearing in BIP for the first time.

An Asterisk (*) at the beginning of an entry indicates that the title is appearing in BIP for the first time.

437

Arrow to the Heart. large type ed. Jill Murray. (Linford Romance Library). 1990. pap. 12.95 (0-7089-6824-4, Linford) Ulverscroft.
Arrow to the Sun: A Pueblo Indian Tale. Gerald McDermott. (Picture Puffins Ser.). (Illus.). (J). (gr. 1 up). 1977. pap. 4.99 (0-14-050211-4, Puffin) Puffin Bks.
Arrow to the Sun: A Pueblo Indian Tale. Gerald McDermott. LC 73-16172. (Illus.). 48p. (J). (gr. 1 up). 1974. pap. 15.99 (0-670-13369-8) Viking Child Bks.
Arrow Zip Code Directory. 1994. pap. 6.75 (0-913450-85-5) Arrow Map.
Arrowhead-Big Bear: The Alps of Southern California. LC 89-92581. 1990. 14.95 (0-933692-24-2) A R Collings.
Arrowhead Cattle Company. Richard Clarke. 1988. 16.95 (0-8027-4079-0) Walker & Co.
Arrowhead Mills Natural Foods Cookbook: Healthy Homestyle Cooking from America's Heartland. Vicki R. Chelf. LC 93-17146. 296p. 1993. pap. 14.95 (0-89529-546-6) Avery Pub.
Arrowheads & Projectile Points. Lar Hothem. (Illus.). 224p. 1991. pap. 7.95 (0-89145-228-1) Collector Bks.
Arrowheads & Spear Points in the Prehistoric Southeast: A Guide to Understanding Cultural Artifacts. Linda C. Culberson. LC 93-8455. (Illus.). 160p. 1993. text ed. 29.95 (0-87805-643-2); pap. 12.95 (0-87805-638-6) U Pr of Miss.
Arrowheads & Stone Artifacts. C. G. Yeager. LC 85-31179. (Illus.). 158p. (Orig.). 1986. pap. 11.95 (0-87108-709-X) Pruett.
Arrowheads of the Neolithic Levant: A Seriation Analysis. Avi Gopher. LC 93-20369. (American Schools of Oriental Research Dissertation Ser.: Vol. 10). xviii, 325p. 1994. text ed. 49.50 (0-931464-76-5) Eisenbrauns.
Arrows: Selected Poetry, 1957-1992. David Meltzer. LC 94-26540. 180p. (Orig.). (C). 1994. 25.00 (0-87685-939-2); pap. 13.00 (0-87685-938-4) Black Sparrow.
Arrows: Selected Poetry, 1957-1992, signed ed. deluxe ed. David Meltzer. LC 94-26540. 180p. (Orig.). (C). 1994. 30.00 (0-87685-940-6) Black Sparrow.
Arrow's Complete Guide to Mail Order Foods. Nancy J. Kocs. LC 87-71024. 157p. (Orig.). 1987. pap. 19.95 (0-944894-07-0) Arrow Clearinghouse.
Arrow's Complete Guide to Mail Order Sporting Goods. Catherine A. Kocs. LC 92-70783. 152p. (Orig.). 1992. pap. 19.95 (0-944894-11-9) Arrow Clearinghouse.
Arrow's Fall. Mercedes Lackey. (Heralds of Valdemar Ser.: Bk. 3). 320p. 1988. reprint ed. pap. 4.99 (0-88677-400-4) DAW Bks.
Arrow's Flight. Mercedes Lackey. (Heralds of Valdemar Ser.: Bk. 2). 320p. 1987. reprint ed. mass mkt. 4.99 (0-88677-377-6) DAW Bks.
Arrows of Desire: The Films of Michael Powell & Emeric Pressburger. Ian Christie. (Illus.). 144p. (Orig.). 1994. pap. 14.95 (0-571-16271-1) Faber & Faber.
***Arrows of the Almighty: The Story of William Bromley, Pioneer Missionary to Papua New Guinea.** A. A. Berg. (Illus.). 96p. Date not set. pap. write for info. (0-8341-1531-X) Nazarene.
Arrows of the Queen. Misty Lackey. (Heralds of Valdemar Ser.: Bk. 1). 320p. 1987. reprint ed. mass mkt. 4.99 (0-88677-378-4) DAW Bks.
Arrows of the Sun. Judith Tarr. 512p. 1993. 24.95 (0-312-85263-0) Tor Bks.
Arrows of the Sun. Judith Tarr. 512p. 1995. mass mkt. 5.99 (0-8125-5060-9) Tor Bks.
Arrows, Structures & Functors: The Categorical Imperative. Ed. by Michael A. Arbib & Ernest G. Manes. 1975. text ed. 63.00 (0-12-059060-3) Acad Pr.

Arrows Swift & Far: Guiding Your Child Through School. Nancy Devlin. 100p. (Orig.). 1993. pap. text ed. 9.95 (0-9635217-0-5) Archr Pub NJ. What "Doc Spock" does for children's health care, Dr. Devlin does for children's education. Her book serves to relieve parents' anxiety when things are normal, to alert parents to problems, & to give them practical advice & the words to use when working with the school system. It is a must for hurried parents who want to do the best for their children but feel powerless when dealing with the complex school bureaucracy. ARROWS SWIFT & FAR urges parents to be activists. Starting with parents' first contact with the school, Dr. Devlin points out how they can & should take the initiative to ensure that the school understands their child. Only with this understanding can the school fulfill its mandate. Dr. Devlin stresses that parents are the authority on their own child, they know him best & must be his advocate. Ten chapters take parents through the range of situations which can positively or negatively affect their child's education. Parents need this information because, while they can delegate some responsibility for their child's education to the school, they cannot abdicate it. Order From: Nancy Devlin & Assoc., P.O. Box 7776, North Brunswick, NJ 08902. *Publisher Provided Annotation.*

Arrow's Theorem, the Paradox of Social Choice: A Case Study in the Philosophy of Economics. Alfred F. MacKay. LC 79-26445. 152p. reprint ed. pap. 43.40 (0-8357-5754-4, 2056644) Bks Demand.
Arrows to the Heart. Gwendolyn A. Jansma-Gwenana. LC 92-74744. 1993. pap. 10.95 (0-87212-260-3) Libra.
Arrowsmith. Sinclair Lewis. 1976. 22.95 (0-8488-0825-8) Amereon Ltd.
Arrowsmith. Sinclair Lewis. LC 25-78. (Modern Classic Ser.). 132p. 1990. 15.95 (0-15-108216-2) HarBrace.
Arrowsmith. Sinclair Lewis. 1961. pap. 5.95 (0-451-52225-7, Sig Classics) NAL-Dutton.
***Arrowsmith.** Sinclair Lewis. 1994. reprint ed. lib. bdg. 26.95x (0-89966-402-4) Buccaneer Bks.
Arrowsmith Notes. Salibelle Royster. (Orig.). 1982. pap. 4.50 (0-8220-0201-9) Cliffs.
Arroz Con Leche. Lulu Delacre. (Illus.). (J). 1992. pap. 4.95 (0-590-41886-6, Blue Ribbon Bks); audio 4.95 (0-590-60035-4, Blue Ribbon Bks) Scholastic Inc.
Arroz Con Leche: Popular Songs & Rhymes from Latin America. Lulu Delacre. (Illus.). (J). (ps-3). 1989. pap. 14.95 (0-590-41887-4) Scholastic Inc.
Arroz y Tartana. Vicente Blasco Ibanez. 300p. (SPA.). 1978. 10.00 (0-8288-8560-5) Fr & Eur.
***ARRT Examination in Computed Tomography (CT)** (Admission Test Ser.). Date not set. pap. 39.95 (0-8373-5816-7) Nat Learn.
***ARRT Examination in Computed Tomography (CT)** (Admission Test Ser.). Date not set. 55.95 (0-8373-5866-3) Nat Learn.
Ars Amandi: The Erotic of Extremes in Thomas Mann & Marguerite Duras. Ursula W. Schneider. LC 93-20475. (Studies in European Thought: Vol. 6). 280p. (C). 1995. text ed. 51.95 (0-8204-2188-X) P Lang Pubs.
Ars Amatoria, Bk. 1. Ovid. (Illus.). 196p. 1989. reprint ed. pap. 24.95 (0-19-814736-8) OUP.
Ars Amatoria see Amores
Ars Cantus Mensurabilis Mensurata Per Modos Iuris. Ed. by C. Matthew Balensuela. (Greek & Latin Music Theory Ser.). xii, 331p. 1994. 30.00 (0-8032-1245-3) U of Nebr Pr.
"Ars Componendi Sermones" of Ranulph Higden, O.S.B. Ed. by Margaret Jennings. LC 87-23925. (Davis Medieval Texts & Studies: No. 6). xlix, 82p. 1991. 45.75 (90-04-06862-7) E J Brill.
***Ars Et Musica in Liturgia: Essays Presented to Casper Harders on His Seventieth Birthday.** Ed. by Frans Brouwer & Robin A. Leaver. (Studies in Liturgical Musicology Ser.: No. 1). 214p. 1994. 29.50 (0-8108-2948-7) Scarecrow.
Ars Impressoria-Entstehung & Entwicklung des Buchdrucks. Ed. by Hans Limburg Universitats & Stadtbibliothek Koln. 200p. 1985. lib. bdg. 62.00 (3-598-10587-8) K G Saur.
ARS Legendi for Chaucer's Canterbury Tales: A Re-Constructive Reading. Delores W. Frese. 320p. 1991. lib. bdg. 37.95 (0-8130-1041-1); pap. text ed. 17.95 (0-8130-1060-8) U Press Fla.
Ars Magna: Or The Rules of Algebra. Girolamo Cardano. (Illus.). xxiv, 267p. 1993. reprint ed. pap. text ed. 8.95 (0-486-67811-3) Dover.
Ars Moriendi, That Is to Saye the Craft for to Deye for the Helthe of Mannes Sowle. LC 74-80159. (English Experience Ser.: No. 639). 1974. reprint ed. 25.00 (90-221-0639-X) Walter J Johnson.
Ars Nova & the Renaissance, Thirteen Hundred to Fifteen Hundred Forty see New Oxford History of Music
Ars Orientalis: The Arts of Islam & the East, Vols. 3-11. (Illus.). write for info. (0-318-51916-X) Freer.
Ars Reck Vivendi: Being Essays Contributed to "the Easy Chair" George W. Curtis. LC 72-4608. (Essay Index Reprint Ser.). 1977. reprint ed. 18.95 (0-8369-2941-1) Ayer.
Ars Rhetorica. Aristotle. Ed. by W. David Ross. (Oxford Classical Texts Ser.). 1959. 23.00 (0-19-814557-8) OUP.
Ars Rhetorica Quae Vulgo Fertur Aristotelis Ad Alexandrum. Anaximenes. (Illus.). xii, 275p. 1981. reprint ed. write for info. (3-487-07052-9, Pub. by Georg Olms GW) Lubrecht & Cramer.
Ars Sacra, 800-1200. Peter Lasko. (Pelican History of Art Ser.). (Illus.). 320p. 1995. 65.00 (0-300-06048-3) Yale U Pr.
Ars Sacra, 800-1200. 2nd ed. Peter Lasko. LC 93-28559. 1994. 55.00 (0-300-05367-3) Yale U Pr.
Arsace (Sarri) see Italian Opera Librettos, Vol. III, 1640-1770
***Arsen, Elemente in der Awuatischen Umwelt II Vol. 75: Biotische Un Abiotische Systeme.** F. R. Atri. (Schriftenreihe des Vereins Fuer Wassrt-Boden Und Lufthygiene). 198p. 1987. pap. text ed. 30.00x (3-437-30576-X) Lubrecht & Cramer.
Arsenal. Jerry Ahern. (Survivalist Ser.: No. 16). 240p. 1988. pap. 2.95 (0-8217-2355-3) Zebra.
Arsenal Greats. Keith Fisher. 200p. (C). 1989. pap. text ed. 21.00 (0-85976-314-5, Pub. by J Donald) St Mut.
Arsenal, No. 4: Surrealist Subversion. Franklin Rosemont. (Illus.). 224p. (Orig.). 1989. lib. bdg. 27.50 (0-941194-28-0); pap. 17.00 (0-941194-27-2) Black Swan Pr.
Arsenal of Democracy: The Story of American War Production. Donald M. Nelson. LC 72-2378. (FDR & the Era of the New Deal Ser.). 439p. 1973. reprint ed. lib. bdg. 45.00 (0-685-01352-9) Da Capo.
Arsenal of Freedom: The Springfield Armory, 1890-1948. Comp. by William S. Brophy. (Illus.). 400p. 1992. pap. 29.95 (0-917218-51-5) A Mowbray.

***Arsenic in the Environment, 2 pts.** Incl. Cycling & Characterization. Jerome O. Nriagu. LC 93-23141. 560p. 1994. text ed. 95.00 (0-471-57929-7); Human Health & Ecosystem Effects. Ed. by Jerome O. Nriagu. LC 93-23141. 345p. 1994. text ed. 85.00 (0-471-30436-0); (Advances in Environmental Science & Technology Ser.: Vols. 26-27). 154.00 (0-471-11231-3) Wiley-Interscience.
Arsenic Metallurgy, Fundamentals & Applications: Proceedings of Symposium Sponsored by the TMS-AIME Physical Chemistry Committee & Mackay Mineral Research Institute, University of Nevada-Reno, at the 1988 TMS Annual Meeting & Exhibition, Phoenix, Arizona, January 25-28, 1988. Metallurgical Society of AIME Staff. Ed. by Ramana G. Reddy et al. LC 87-43300. 544p. reprint ed. pap. 155.10 (0-7837-1438-6, 2052412) Bks Demand.
Arsenical Pesticides: A Symposium Sponsored by the Division of Pesticide Chemistry at the 168th Meeting of the American Chemical Society, Atlantic City, NJ: Sept. 9, 1974. E. A. Woolson. LC 74-31378. (ACS Symposium Ser.: No. 7). 184p. reprint ed. pap. 52.50 (0-8357-5755-2, 2052228) Bks Demand.
Arsenij I Arsenity. I. E. Troitskij. 552p. (C). 1973. reprint ed. lib. bdg. 126.00 (0-902089-47-1, Pub. by Variorum UK) Ashgate Pub Co.
Arsenio: The Prince of Late Night. Aileen Joyce. 1993. mass mkt. 4.99 (0-06-104282-X, Harp PBks) HarpC.
Arsenio Hall. Norman King. 1993. 20.00 (0-688-10827-X) Morrow.
Arshile Gorky. Melvin P. Lader. LC 84-24268. (Modern Masters Ser.). (Illus.). 128p. 1985. 32.95 (0-89659-525-0); pap. 22.95 (1-55859-249-0) Abbeville Pr.
Arshile Gorky. William C. Seitz. LC 75-169313. (Museum of Modern Art Publications in Reprint). (Illus.). 60p. 1979. reprint ed. 17.95 (0-405-01571-2) Ayer.
***Arshile Gorky: The Breakthrough Years.** Michael Auping et al. LC 94-22795. (Illus.). 1995. write for info. (0-914782-92-4) Buffalo Acad.
***Arshile Gorky: The Breakthrough Years.** Michael Auping. LC 94-22795. (Illus.). 192p. 1995. 45.00 (0-8478-1875-6) Rizzoli Intl.
Arshile Gorky: The Implications of Symbols. Harry Rand. LC 90-47360. (Illus.). 270p. 1991. 60.00 (0-520-06371-6); pap. 25.00 (0-520-06345-7) U CA Pr.
Arshile Gorky: The Man, the Times, the Idea. Harold Rosenberg. LC 62-11237. (Illus.). 144p. 1981. reprint ed. pap. 7.95 (0-935296-20-4) Sheep Meadow.
Arshile Gorky: Three Decades of Drawings. Contrib by Melvin P. Lader. LC 90-62329. (Illus.). 72p. 1990. pap. 20.00 (0-935037-38-1) G Peters Gallery.

***Arshile Gorky & the Genesis of Abstraction: Drawings from the Early 1930s. Matthew Spender et al. LC 94-78407. (Illus.). 112p. (Orig.). 1994. pap. 30.00 (1-886055-00-9) S Mazoh. This exhibition catalogue of thirty-nine drawings, many neither shown nor published before, displays the richness of Arshile Gorky's production as a draftsman over several years crucial to his development. Documenting the emergence of Gorky's unmistakably unique & intensely personal pictorial language, the exhibition examines the complex relationship among these six themes developed in these drawings & their eventual connection to Gorky's 1934 proposed mural project for the Public Works of Art Project (PWAP). These drawings reveal the evolution of Gorky's highly inventive imagery, offering deep insight into a synthetic creative process that draws from both Renaissance & contemporary sources. The drawings not only mark the origins of Gorky's genius, they also reveal his working methods, demonstrating his systematic rearrangement of self-referential motifs which became major iconographic & thematic sources throughout his working life. Introducing the catalogue are essays by Matthew Spender & Barbara Rose, & individual entries for the drawings are by Melvin P. Lader, Joseph P. Ruzicka, Sarah E. Lawrence & Martin Kline. The venues for the exhibition include The Art Museum, Princeton University, Milwaukee Art Museum, & The Baltimore Museum of Art.** *Publisher Provided Annotation.*

***Arshile Gorky & the Genesis of Abstraction: Drawings from the Early 1930s.** Matthew Spender & Barbara Rose. (Illus.). 104p. 1995. pap. 30.00 (0-295-97424-9) U of Wash Pr.
Arshile Gorky, Nineteen Four to Nineteen Forty-Eight: A Retrospective. Diane Waldman. LC 80-52992. (Illus.). 286p. 1981. 19.95 (0-89207-025-0) S R Guggenheim.
Arson! Cap Iversen. (Dakota Ser.: No. 1). 233p. (Orig.). 1992. pap. 7.95 (1-55583-197-4) Alyson Pubns.

Arson: A Multi-Dimensional Problem. Nicholas Borg & Leonard David. 1976. 2.50 (0-686-17606-5, TR 76-4) Society Fire Protect.
Arson: A Review of the Psychiatric Literature. Ann Barker. (Maudsley Monographs: No. 35). (Illus.). 132p. 1994. 42.50 (0-19-262526-8) OUP.
Arson Investigation. Robert E. Carter. 286p. (C). 1978. text ed. write for info. (0-02-472400-9) Macmillan.
***Arson Investigation: The Step-by-Step Procedure.** Thomas J. Bouquard. 132p. 1983. pap. 15.95 (0-398-06025-8) C C Thomas.
Arson Investigation: The Step-by-Step Procedure. Thomas J. Bouquard. 132p. 1983. 28.95x (0-398-04839-8) C C Thomas.
Arson Investigation Guide. (Illus.). 152p. (Orig.). (C). 1993. pap. text ed. 30.00x (1-56806-840-9) Diane Pub.
Arson Investigation Guide: A Manual for Arson Investigators. 1992. lib. bdg. 88.95 (0-8490-8854-2) Gordon Pr.
Arson Legislation Reference Manual. 1985. ring bd. write for info. (0-318-66134-9, 549-0049-01) Amer Bar Assn.
Arson 1976. R. G. Provencher. 1976. 3.25 (0-686-17605-7, TR 76-3) Society Fire Protect.
Art. Boy Scouts of America. (Illus.). 48p. (J). (gr. 6-12). 1968. pap. 1.85 (0-8395-3320-9, 33320) BSA.
Art. L. Ron Hubbard. 228p. 1992. 62.50 (0-88404-483-1) Bridge Pubns Inc.
Art. Bob Reese. LC 92-12187. (School Days Ser.). (Illus.). 24p. (J). (ps-2). 1992. lib. bdg. 9.75 (0-516-05578-X) Childrens.
Art, Vol. I. 3rd ed. Frederick N. Hartt. 560p. (C). 1988. pap. text ed. 50.00 (0-13-048646-9) P-H.
Art, Vol. II. 3rd ed. Frederick N. Hartt. 608p. (C). 1988. pap. text ed. 32.95 (0-13-048703-1) P-H.
Art: A Comparative Study. Jed Jackson. 384p. (C). 1994. pap. text ed. 59.95 (0-8403-8989-2) Kendall-Hunt.
Art: A History of Painting, Sculpture, Architecture. 4th ed. Frederick N. Hartt. LC 92-12068. 1993. 60.00 (0-8109-1921-4) Abrams.
Art: A History of Painting, Sculpture, Architecture. 4th ed. Frederick N. Hartt & Nan Rosenthal. LC 92-13200. 1128p. 1993. text ed. 60.95 (0-13-052432-8) P-H.
Art: A History of Painting, Sculpture, Architecture, 2 vols., 1. 4th ed. Frederick N. Hartt. LC 92-5809. (Illus.). 1992. pap. text ed. 43.95 (0-13-052416-6) P-H.
Art: A History of Painting, Sculpture, Architecture, 2 vols., 2. 4th ed. Frederick N. Hartt. LC 92-5809. (Illus.). 1992. pap. text ed. 43.95 (0-13-052424-7) P-H.
Art: A History of Painting, Sculpture, Architecture, Vol. I. 2nd ed. Frederick N. Hart. (Abrams Book Ser.). (Illus.). 496p. (C). 1985. pap. text ed. 27.95 (0-13-047374-X) P-H.
Art: African American. 2nd rev. ed. Samella Lewis. (Illus.). 312p. (Orig.). (C). 1990. reprint ed. pap. text ed. 25.00 (0-941248-08-9) Hancraft.
Art: An Introduction. 5th ed. Dale G. Cleaver. (Illus.). 491p. (C). 1988. pap. text ed. 35.25 (0-15-503434-0); sl. write for info. (0-318-64529-7) HB Coll Pubs.
Art: Basic for Young Children. Lila Lasky & Rose Mukerji. LC 80-82565. (Illus.). 164p. (Orig.). 1980. pap. text ed. 5.00 (0-912674-73-3, NAEYC NO. 106) Natl Assn Child Ed.
Art: Context & Criticism. John D. Kissick. 512p. (C). 1993. pap. text ed. write for info. (0-697-11650-6) Brown & Benchmark.
Art: Ideas for Elementary Classroom Teachers; Bulletin Board Suggestions; Patterns; Ideas for Holidays. Laura S. Crosby. (Illus.). 1985. spiral bd. 25.00 (0-915114-04-6) Lewis-Sloan.
***Art: Images & Ideas.** (Discover Art Ser.). 1992. teacher ed, text ed. 49.10 (0-87192-271-1) Davis Mass.
Art: Images & Ideas. Laura Chapman. (Discover Art Ser.). (Illus.). (J). (gr. 8). 1992. text ed. 33.80 (0-87192-231-2) Davis Mass.
Art: Making a School Policy. Bill Michael. (C). 1989. 69.00 (1-85098-377-1, Pub. by Jordanhill College UK) St Mut.
***Art: Open-Ended Art.** (1-2-3 Ser.). (Illus.). 160p. (J). 1995. 14.95 (0-614-06799-5, WPH 0401) Totline Bks.
Art: Tempo of Today. rev. ed. Jean M. Morman. (Illus.). 1978. teacher ed 4.70 (0-685-62931-7); text ed. 17.20 (0-912242-14-0) Art Educ.
Art: The Way It Is. 3rd ed. John A. Richardson. (Illus.). 400p. (C). 1986. pap. text ed. 33.95 (0-13-046533-X) P-H.
Art: The Way It Is. 4th ed. John A. Richardson. (Illus.). 416p. 1992. 49.50 (0-8109-1911-7) Abrams.
Art: The Way It Is. 4th ed. John A. Richardson. 384p. 1991. pap. text ed. 45.95 (0-13-040437-3) P-H.
Art - The Veil. David Meltzer. (Illus.). 64p. 1982. pap. 5.00 (0-87924-040-7) Membrane Pr.
Art a la Carte: Decorative Imagery in Maps, 1600-1900. Museum Practice Program, Graduate Students Staff. (Illus.). 22p. 1979. pap. 2.00 (0-912303-17-4) Michigan Mus.
Art Aardvark. Roberta West-Naus. (Holiday & Art Ser.). (Illus.). 72p. (J). (gr. 1-6). 1981. 7.95 (0-88160-041-5, LW 226) Learning Wks.
Art Across America: Two Centuries of Regional Painting, 3 vols., Set. William H. Gerdts. (Illus.). 1224p. 1990. 495.00 (1-55859-033-1) Abbeville Pr.
Art after Modernism. Ed. by Brian Wallis. 485p. 1984. pap. 19.95 (0-87923-632-9) Godine.
Art after Philosophy & After: Collected Writings 1966-1990. Joseph Kosuth. (Illus.). 312p. 1991. 35.00 (0-262-11157-8) MIT Pr.
Art after Philosophy & After: Collected Writings 1966-1990. Joseph Kosuth. (Illus.). 312p. 1993. 17.95x (0-262-61091-4) MIT Pr.
Art Against War: Four Hundred Years of Protest Art. D. J. Bruckner et al. LC 83-6342. (Illus.). 128p. 1984. pap. 22.50 (0-89659-389-4) Abbeville Pr.

An Asterisk (*) at the beginning of an entry indicates that the title is appearing in BIP for the first time.

An Asterisk (*) at the beginning of an entry indicates that the title is appearing in BIP for the first time.

Art & History: Images Their Meaning. Ed. by Robert I. Rotberg & Theodore K. Rabb. (Studies in Interdisciplinary History). (Illus.). 310p. 1988. pap. 17.95 (*0-521-33569-8*) Cambridge U Pr.

Art & History: Images Their Meaning. Ed. by Robert I. Rotberg & Theodore K. Rabb. (Studies in Interdisciplinary History). (Illus.). 310p. 1988. 59.95 (*0-521-34018-7*) Cambridge U Pr.

Art & History of Book Printing: A Topical Bibliography. Comp. by Vito J. Brenni. LC 83-20696. v, 147p. 1984. text ed. 49.95 (*0-313-24306-9*, BHI/, Greenwood Pr) Greenwood.

Art & History of Books. Norma Levarie. LC 82-8984. (Illus.). 328p. 1995. 45.00 (*1-884718-02-7*) Oak Knoll.

Art & History of Books. Norma Levarie. LC 82-8984. (Quality Paperbacks Ser.). (Illus.). 315p. 1982. reprint ed. pap. 24.50 (*0-306-80181-7*) Da Capo.

Art & History of Frames. Henry Heydenryk. 128p. 1993. pap. 22.95 (*1-55821-265-5*) Lyons & Burford.

Art & Holy Powers in the Early Christian House. Eunice D. Maguire et al. (Illinois Byzantine Studies: No. II). (Illus.). 264p. 1989. pap. 24.95 (*0-252-06095-4*) U of Ill Pr.

Art & Human Consciousness. Gottfried Richter. Tr. by Margaret Frohlich. (Illus.). 300p. (Orig.). 1985. 30.00 (*0-88010-108-3*) Anthroposophic.

Art & Human Intelligence. Victorino Tejera. LC 65-15781. (Century Philosophy Ser.). (Illus.). 1965. 39.50 (*0-89197-030-4*); pap. text ed. 9.95 (*0-89197-031-2*) Irvington.

Art & Iconography of Late Post-Classic Central Mexico: Conference at Dumbarton Oaks, October 22 & 23, 1977. LC 82-2541. (Illus.). 264p. 1982. 24.00 (*0-88402-110-6*) Dumbarton Oaks.

Art & Iconography of Vishnu-Narayana. Nanditha Krishna. (Illus.). xiv, 122p. (C). 1981. text ed. 45.00 (*0-86590-025-6*, Pub. by Taraporevala II) Apt Bks.

Art & Idea in the Novels of Bernard Malamud: Toward "The Fixer" Robert Ducharme. (Studies in American Literature: No. 13). 1974. pap. text ed. 37.70 (*90-279-3212-3*) Mouton.

Art & Identity in Oceania. Ed. by F. Allan Hanson & Louise Hanson. LC 90-32710. (Illus.). 400p. 1990. text ed. 39.00 (*0-8248-1304-9*) UH Pr.

Art & Ideology in Revolutionary China. David Holm. (Studies on Contemporary China). (Illus.). 424p. 1991. 69.00 (*0-19-828716-X*) OUP.

***Art & Illusion: a Guide to Crossdressing Vol. 1: Face & Hair.** 3rd ed. JoAnn Roberts. (Illus.). 40p. 1994. pap. 15.00 (*1-880715-05-8*) Creat Des Srvs.

***Art & Illusion: a Guide to Crossdressing Vol. 2: Fashion & Style.** 3rd ed. JoAnn Roberts. (Illus.). 40p. 1994. pap. 15.00 (*1-880715-08-2*) Creat Des Srvs.

Art & Illusion in The Winter's Tale. B. J. Sokol. LC 94-12627. 283p. 1995. text ed. 69.95 (*0-7190-3857-X*, Pub. by Manchester Univ Pr UK) St Martin.

Art & Imagination: A Study in the Philosophy of Mind. Roger Scruton. 256p. 1982. reprint ed. pap. 16.95 (*0-7100-9014-5*, RKP) Routledge.

Art & Imagination of Langston Hughes. R. Baxter Miller. LC 89-5645. 160p. 1990. 18.00 (*0-8131-1662-7*) U Pr of Ky.

Art & Industry of Sandcastles. Jan Adkins. (Illus.). 64p. (Orig.). (gr. k up). 1982. reprint ed. pap. 9.95 (*0-8027-7205-6*) Walker & Co.

Art & Inquiry. Berel Lang. LC 74-18240. 227p. 1975. lib. bdg. 24.00 (*0-8143-1531-3*) Ridgeview.

Art & Inquiry. Berel Lang. LC 74-18240. 229p. reprint ed. pap. 65.30 (*0-8357-5756-0*, 2032712) Bks Demand.

Art & Interaction: An Academic Fieldwork Program for Colleges. Judith Peck. (Activities Program for Institutions Ser.). (Illus.). 179p. (C). 1990. pap. text ed. 19.95 (*0-685-35355-9*) Ramapo College.

Art & Interreligious Dialogue: Six Perspectives. Michael S. Bird. (Illus.). 160p. (C). reprint ed. lib. bdg. 46.50 (*0-8191-9554-5*); reprint ed. pap. text ed. 19.50 (*0-8191-9555-3*) U Pr of Amer.

Art & Islamic Literacy among the Hausa of Northern Nigeria. Salah M. Hassan. LC 92-24451. (African Studies: Vol. 27). (Illus.). 400p. 1992. text ed. 99.95 (*0-7734-9581-9*) E Mellen.

Art & Its Objects: Second Edition with Six Supplementary Essays. Richard Wolheim. (Canto Book Ser.). 286p. (C). 1992. pap. 11.95 (*0-521-43778-4*) Cambridge U Pr.

Art & Its Significance: An Anthology of Aesthetic Theory. Ed. by Stephen D. Ross. LC 83-9683. (SUNY Series in Philosophy). 574p. 1984. 59.50 (*0-87395-764-4*) State U NY Pr.

Art & Its Significance: An Anthology of Aesthetic Theory. 2nd rev. ed. Ed. by Stephen D. Ross. LC 83-9683. 638p. (C). 1987. pap. 19.95 (*0-88706-600-3*) State U NY Pr.

Art & Its Significance: An Anthology of Aesthetic Theory. 3rd ed. Stephen D. Ross. 692p. (C). 1994. pap. 19.95 (*0-7914-1852-9*) State U NY Pr.

Art & Knowledge. Joseph Chiari. LC 76-57236. 132p. 1977. 35.00 (*0-87752-208-1*) Gordian.

Art & Labor: Ruskin, Morris, & the Craftsman Ideal in America. Eileen Boris. (Illus.). 288p. (C). 1988. pap. 19.95 (*0-87722-563-X*) Temple U Pr.

***Art & Lies.** Winterson. Date not set. pap. write for info. (*0-679-76270-1*) Random Hse Value.

***Art & Lies.** Jeanette Winterson. 1995. 22.00 (*0-679-44181-6*) Knopf.

Art & Life in Africa: Selections from the Stanley Collection, Exhibitions of 1985 & 1992. Christopher D. Roy. (Illus.). 280p. 1993. pap. 40.00 (*0-295-97241-6*) U of Wash Pr.

Art & Life in India: The Last Four Decades. Ed. by Josef James. (C). 1989. 26.00 (*81-7018-567-X*, Pub. by BR Pub II) S Asia.

Art & Life in New Guinea. Raymond W. Firth. LC 75-32815. reprint ed. 30.00 (*0-404-14119-6*) AMS Pr.

***Art & Life of G. O'Keefe.** Jan G. Castro. 1995. 24.00 (*0-517-88387-2*) Random.

Art & Life of Georgia O'Keeffe. Jan G. Castro. LC 84-12099. (Illus.). 1985. 35.00 (*0-517-55058-X*, Crown) Crown Pub Group.

Art & Life of W. Herbert Dunton, 1878-1936. Julie Schimmel. LC 84-11932. (Illus.). 268p. 1984. 45.00 (*0-292-77031-6*) U of Tex Pr.

***Art & Life of Weaver Hawkins.** Eileen Chanin & Steven Miller. 1995. 75.00 (*976-8097-67-1*) IPG Chicago.

Art & Life on the Upper Mississippi, 1890-1915. Michael Conforti. (Illus.). 384p. 1994. 65.00 (*0-87413-560-5*) U Delaware Pr.

Art & Literature: Studies in Relationship. William S. Heckscher & Egon Verheyen. ii, 528p. 1985. 45.50 (*0-8223-0630-1*) Duke.

Art & Literature in Spain, 1600-1800: Studies in Honour of Nigel Glendinning. Ed. by Charles Davis & Paul J. Smith. (Series A: Monagrafias: Vol. 148). (Illus.). 264p. (C). 1993. text ed. 63.00 (*1-85566-013-X*, Pub. by Tamesis Bks Ltd UK) Boydell & Brewer.

Art & Literature under the Bolsheviks, Vol. 1: The Crisis of Renewal, 1917-1924. Brandon Taylor. (Illus.). 213p. (C). 1991. text ed. 52.50 (*0-7453-0293-9*, Pub. by Pluto Pr UK) Westview.

Art & Literature under the Bolsheviks, Vol. 2, Vol. 2. Brandon Taylor. (C). 1993. text ed. 55.50 (*0-7453-0556-3*, Pub. by Pluto Pr UK) Westview.

Art & Magic in the Court of the Stuarts. Vaughan Hart. LC 94-2272. (Illus.). 256p. 1994. 59.95x (*0-415-09031-8*, B3435) Routledge.

Art & Mainstreaming: Art Instruction for Exceptional Children in Regular School Classes. fac. ed. Claire B. Clements & Robert D. Clements. (Illus.). 186p. (C). 1984. pap. 28.95x (*0-398-04891-6*) C C Thomas.

Art & Man. Clementina Anstruther-Thomson. LC 74-93314. (Essay Index Reprint Ser.). 1977. 27.95 (*0-8369-1270-5*) Ayer.

Art & Man: Essays & Fragments. Clementina Anstruther-Thomson. LC 74-93314. (Essay Index Reprint Ser.). (Illus.). 371p. reprint ed. lib. bdg. 21.00 (*0-8290-0470-X*) Irvington.

Art & Mass Media. R. Heartfield. (C). 1989. 100.00 (*0-685-34321-9*, Pub. by Collets) St Mut.

***Art & Mass Media.** Robert Pelfrey. 400p. (C). 1995. pap. text ed. 45.95 (*0-7872-0488-9*) Kendall-Hunt.

Art & Math Throughout the Year. Jimmie Aydelott. (J). (gr. 1-6). 1989. pap. 8.99 (*0-8224-0104-5*) Fearon Teach Aids.

Art & Method of the Violin Maker: Principles & Practices. Henry A. Strobel. LC 92-93940. (Illus.). 78p. (Orig.). 1992. pap. 19.50 (*0-9620673-5-0*) H A Strobel.

Art & Miracles in Medieval Byzantium: The Crypt as Hosios Loukas & Its Frescoes. Carolyn L. Connor. (Illus.). 136p. 1991. text ed. 67.50 (*0-691-04084-2*) Princeton U Pr.

Art & Money: Visual & Economic Representation. Marc Shell. LC 93-29238. 229p. 1993. 35.00 (*0-226-75213-5*) U Ch Pr.

Art & Morality. Kitaro Nishida. Tr. by David A. Dilworth & Valdo H. Viglielmo. LC 72-92067. 228p. reprint ed. pap. 65.00 (*0-8357-6026-X*, 2034642) Bks Demand.

Art & Music. Time-Life Inc. Editors. Ed. by Jean Crawford. (Child's First Library of Learning). (Illus.). 88p. (J). (gr. k-3). 1994. write for info. (*0-8094-9474-4*); lib. bdg. write for info. (*0-8094-9475-2*) Time-Life.

Art & Music: Therapy & Research. Ed. by Andrea Gilroy & Colin Lee. LC 94-9637. (Illus.). 288p. 1994. 59.95x (*0-415-10044-5*, B4390); pap. 18.95 (*0-415-10045-3*, B4394) Routledge.

Art & Music of John Lennon. John Robertson. 1991. 17.95 (*1-55972-076-X*, Birch Ln Pr) Carol Pub Group.

Art & Music of John Lennon. John Robertson. 232p. 1993. pap. 12.95 (*0-8065-1438-8*, Citadel Pr) Carol Pub Group.

Art & Mystery of Historical Archaeology. Beaudry. 1992. 79.95 (*0-8493-8854-6*, E159) CRC Pr.

Art & Mystery of Tennessee Furniture & Its Makers Through 1850. Nathan Harsh & Derita C. Williams. (Artisans & the Arts Ser.). (Illus.). 345p. 1988. lib. bdg. 42.50 (*0-9615966-2-7*) TN His Soc.

Art & Myth in Ancient Greece. Thomas H. Carpenter. LC 88-51326. (World of Art Ser.). (Illus.). 1991. pap. 14.95 (*0-500-20236-2*) Thames Hudson.

Art & Nationalism in Colonial India: Occidental Orientations. Partha Mitter. (Illus.). 512p. (C). 1995. 89.95 (*0-521-44354-7*) Cambridge U Pr.

Art & Nature: An Illustrated Anthology of Nature Poetry. Comp. by Kate Farrell. (Illus.). 176p. 1992. 17.95 (*0-8212-1979-0*) Bulfinch Pr.

Art & Nonart: Reflections on an Orange Crate & a Moose Call. Marcia M. Eaton. LC 81-65462. (Illus.). 176p. 1983. 45.00 (*0-8386-3084-7*) Fairleigh Dickinson.

Art & Otherness: Crisis in Cultural Identity. Thomas McEvilley. LC 92-7120. 176p. 1992. 20.00 (*0-929701-21-6*) McPherson & Co.

***Art & Otherness: Crisis in Cultural Identity.** Thomas McEvilley. LC 92-7120. 174p. 1995. reprint ed. pap. 12.00 (*0-929701-48-8*) McPherson & Co.

Art & Patronage in the Caroline Courts: Essays in Honour of Sir Oliver Millar. Ed. by David Howarth. LC 92-576. (Illus.). 304p. (C). 1993. 69.95 (*0-521-43185-9*) Cambridge U Pr.

Art & Philosophy. Timothy Taubes. 121p. 1993. 22.95 (*0-87975-865-1*) Prometheus Bks.

Art & Philosophy: Brancusi: the Courage to Love. Florence M. Hetzler. LC 91-18624. (American University Studies: Fine Arts: Ser. XX, Vol. 17). 251p. 1992. 58.95 (*0-8204-1599-5*) P Lang Pubs.

Art & Photography. Aaron Scharf. (Illus.). 400p. 1991. pap. 16.95 (*0-14-013132-9*, Penguin Bks) Viking Penguin.

Art & Photography: Forerunners & Influences. Heinrich Schwarz. Ed. by William E. Parker. LC 87-10763. (Illus.). 158p. (C). 1987. pap. text ed. 12.95 (*0-226-74234-2*) U Ch Pr.

Art & Physics: Experiments in Space, Time, & Light. Leonard Shlain. (Illus.). 480p. Date not set. 25.00 (*0-688-09752-9*) Morrow.

Art & Physics: Parallel Visions in Space, Time, & Light. Leonard Shlain. LC 92-24714. 1993. 12.00 (*0-688-12305-8*, Quill) Morrow.

Art & Poetry of Charles-Ferdinand Ramuz. David Bevan. (Language & Literature Ser.). 1977. 25.00 (*0-902675-47-8*) Oleander Pr.

Art & Political Expression in Early China. Martin J. Powers. (Illus.). 352p. 1992. text ed. 50.00 (*0-300-04767-3*) Yale U Pr.

Art & Politics. Leslie W. Hedley. 72p. (Orig.). 1994. pap. 10.00 (*0-933515-16-2*) Exile Pr.

***Art & Politics.** Richard Wagner. Tr. by William A. Ellis. 436p. 1995. pap. 15.00 (*0-8032-9774-2*, Bison Books) U of Nebr Pr.

Art & Politics see Richard Wagner's Prose Works

Art & Politics in Late Medieval & Early Renaissance Italy, 1250-1500. Ed. by Charles M. Rosenberg. LC 89-40744. (Conferences in Medieval Studies: Vol. 2). (C). 1992. pap. text ed. 22.95 (*0-268-00628-8*) U of Notre Dame Pr.

Art & Politics in Renaissance Italy: British Academy Lectures. Ed. by George Holmes. (British Academy Ser.). (Illus.). 416p. 1994. 59.00 (*0-19-726126-4*) OUP.

***Art & Politics in Renaissance Italy: British Academy Lectures.** Intro. & Sel. by George Holmes. (British Academy Ser.). (Illus.). 416p. 1995. pap. 19.95 (*0-19-726159-0*) OUP.

Art & Politics in Wolfgang Koeppen's Postwar Trilogy. Richard L. Gunn. LC 83-48753. (American University Studies: Germanic Languages & Literature: Ser. I, Vol. 26). 232p. (Orig.). (C). 1983. pap. text ed. 25.25 (*0-8204-0048-3*) P Lang Pubs.

Art & Politics of College Teaching: A Practical Guide for the Beginning Professor. Ed. by R. McLaren Sawyer et al. LC 91-33003. 347p. (C). 1992. text ed. 29.95 (*0-8204-1684-3*) P Lang Pubs.

Art & Politics of the Second Empire: The Universal Expositions of 1855 & 1867. Patricia Mainardi. LC 87-6262. 248p. 1987. text ed. 50.00 (*0-300-03871-2*) Yale U Pr.

Art & Politics of the Second Empire: The Universal Expositions of 1855 & 1867. Patricia Mainardi. 248p. (C). 1990. reprint ed. 22.50 (*0-300-04747-9*) Yale U Pr.

Art & Politics of Wana Shamanship. Jane M. Atkinson. (Illus.). 365p. (C). 1989. pap. 16.00 (*0-520-07877-2*) U CA Pr.

Art & Popular Religion in Evangelical America, 1915-1940. Robert L. Gambone. LC 88-17444. (Illus.). 304p. 1989. 42.50 (*0-87049-588-7*) U of Tenn Pr.

Art & Power: Renaissance Festivals, 1450-1650. Roy Strong. (Illus.). 346p. (Orig.). (C). 1995. pap. text ed. 25.00 (*0-85115-247-3*) Boydell & Brewer.

Art & Practice of Astral Projection. Ophiel. 124p. (Orig.). 1974. pap. 8.95 (*0-87728-246-3*) Weiser.

Art & Practice of Children's Orthopaedics. Dennis R. Wenger & Mercer Rang. 768p. 1993. 152.50 (*0-88167-867-8*) Raven.

Art & Practice of Compassion & Empathy. Margot Lasher. 224p. (Orig.). 1992. pap. 11.95 (*0-87477-710-0*) J P Tarcher.

Art & Practice of Getting Material Things Through Creative Visualization. rev. ed. Ophiel. 120p. 1975. pap. 8.95 (*0-87728-279-X*) Weiser.

Art & Practice of Hawking. E. B. Michell. (Illus.). 303p. 1983. pap. 25.00 (*0-87556-656-1*) Saifer.

Art & Practice of Loving. Frank Andrews. 236p. 1992. pap. 10.95 (*0-87477-690-2*) J P Tarcher.

Art & Practice of Low Vision. Freeman. 165p. 1991. pap. text ed. 34.95 (*0-7506-9010-0*) Buttrwrth-Heinemann.

Art & Practice of Public Administration: Papers by Louis J. Kroeger. Louis J. Kroeger. Ed. by Harriet Nathan. LC 78-634565. 344p. (Orig.). reprint ed. pap. 98.10 (*0-7837-2131-5*, 2042413) Bks Demand.

Art & Practice of Silver Printing. Henry P. Robinson & W. D. Abney. LC 72-9227. (Literature of Photography Ser.). 1973. reprint ed. 18.95 (*0-405-04933-1*) Ayer.

Art & Prudence. Mortimer J. Adler. Ed. by Garth S. Jowett. LC 77-11371. (Aspects of Film Ser.). 1978. reprint ed. lib. bdg. 54.95 (*0-405-11126-6*) Ayer.

Art & Prudence: Studies in the Thought of Jacques Maritain. Ralph McInerny. LC 88-18826. (C). 1988. text ed. 21.95 (*0-268-00619-9*); pap. text ed. 9.95 (*0-268-00620-2*) U of Notre Dame Pr.

Art & Psyche: A Study in Psychoanalysis & Aesthetics. Ellen H. Spitz. 192p. (C). 1989. reprint ed. pap. 14.00 (*0-300-04620-0*) Yale U Pr.

Art & Psychoanalysis. Laurie S. Adams. LC 92-56205. (Illus.). 320p. 1993. 35.00 (*0-06-430297-0*, HarpT) HarpC.

Art & Psychoanalysis. Laurie S. Adams. 1994. pap. 20.00 (*0-06-430206-7*) HarpC.

Art & Psychoanalysis. Peter Fuller. (Art Ser.). (Illus.). 250p. 1981. 12.95 (*0-906495-24-5*); pap. 6.95 (*0-906495-32-6*) Writers & Readers.

Art & Reality: Ways of the Creative Process. Joyce Cary. LC 77-128218. (Essay Index Reprints - World Perspectives Ser.: Vol. 20). 1977. reprint ed. 21.95 (*0-8369-1906-8*) Ayer.

Art & Reflections of Rupert Conrad: The Naked Dawn. Ed. by Ruth Conrad. LC 89-24024. (Illus.). 216p. 1991. 40.00 (*0-8453-4824-8*, Cornwall Bks) Assoc Univ Prs.

Art & Revolution. rev. ed. Leon Trotsky. Ed. by Paul N. Siegel. LC 72-795611. Orig. Title: Leon Trotsky on Literature & Art. (Illus.). 252p. 1992. reprint ed. pap. 20.95 (*0-87348-738-9*) Pathfinder NY.

Art & Revolution in Modern China: The Lingnan (Cantonese) School of Painting, 1906-1951. Ralph C. Croizier. (Center for Chinese Studies, UC Berkeley: No. 29). 1988. 42.50 (*0-520-05909-3*) U CA Pr.

Art & Ritual of the Byzantine Church. Christopher Walter. (Birmingham Byzantine Ser.). (Illus.). 302p. (C). 1982. lib. bdg. 87.95 (*0-86078-104-6*, Pub. by Variorum UK) Ashgate Pub Co.

Art & Scholasticism: With Other Essays. Jacques Maritain. Tr. by J. F. Scanlan. LC 70-152196. (Essay Index Reprint Ser.). 1977. reprint ed. 16.95 (*0-8369-2241-7*) Ayer.

Art & Science. Ed. by Stephen R. Graubard. LC 87-25250. (Daedalus Library). (Illus.). 212p. (Orig.). (C). 1988. lib. bdg. 45.00 (*0-8191-6677-4*); pap. text ed. 22.50 (*0-8191-6678-2*) U Pr of Amer.

Art & Science Connection. Kimberly Tolley. 1994. text ed. 24.95 (*0-201-45545-5*) Addison-Wesley.

Art & Science Connection: Hands-On Activities for Primary Students. Kimberly Tolley. 1993. pap. 24.95 (*0-201-45544-7*) Addison-Wesley.

Art & Science in German Landscape Painting 1770-1840. Timothy F. Mitchell. (Clarendon Studies in the History of Art: No. 11). (Illus.). 256p. 1994. 105.00 (*0-19-817507-8*) OUP.

Art & Science of Aggressive Baserunning. Cliff Petrak. LC 85-30039. 197p. 1986. text ed. 21.95 (*0-13-047671-4*, Parker Publishing Co) P-H.

***Art & Science of Analog Circuit Design.** Jim Williams. 392p. 1995. 49.95 (*0-7506-9505-6*, Focal) Buttrwrth-Heinemann.

***Art & Science of Assessment in Psychotherapy.** Ed. by Chris J. Mace. LC 94-46785. 208p. 1995. 59.95x (*0-415-10538-2*, C0459); pap. 17.95 (*0-415-10539-0*, C0465) Routledge.

Art & Science of Basic Handgun Accuracy. W. W. Butler. LC 91-71671. (Illus.). 72p. 1991. pap. 10.00 (*0-939427-74-5*, 07076) Alpha Pubns OH.

Art & Science of Bedside Diagnosis. Joseph D. Sapira & Jane M. Orient. (Illus.). 650p. 1990. 75.00 (*0-683-07520-9*) Williams & Wilkins.

Art & Science of Book Publishing. Herbert S. Bailey, Jr. LC 90-7103. 232p. 1990. reprint ed. pap. text ed. 14.95 (*0-8214-0970-0*) Ohio U Pr.

***Art & Science of Burn Care.** fac. ed. Ed. by John A. Boswick, Jr. LC 86-25923. (Illus.). 413p. Date not set. pap. 117.80 (*0-7837-7441-9*, 2047235) Bks Demand.

Art & Science of C: An Introduction to Computer Science. Eric S. Roberts. LC 94-16744. (Illus.). 700p. (C). 1995. pap. text ed. 45.25 (*0-201-54322-2*) Addison-Wesley.

***Art & Science of Child Care: Research, Policy & Practice in European Union.** Ed. by Matthew Colton et al. 279p. 1995. 42.95 (*1-85742-285-6*, Pub. by Ashgate UK) Ashgate Pub Co.

***Art & Science of Coaching Lin.** J. Sandusky. 1994. pap. 13.95 (*0-915611-62-7*) Sagamore Pub.

Art & Science of Computer Animation. Stuart Mealing. 320p. (Orig.). 1992. pap. text ed. 37.95 (*1-871516-16-1*, Pub. by Intellect Bks UK) Cromland.

***Art & Science of Cooking.** Mary Michael. 1995. 16.95 (*0-8062-5265-0*) Carlton.

Art & Science of Counseling & Psychotherapy. Michael S. Nystul. 460p. (C). 1993. pap. write for info. (*0-675-21212-X*, Merrill Pub Co) Macmillan.

Art & Science of Culinary Preparation: A Culinarian's Manual. Jerald W. Chesser. Ed. by Stephen C. Fernald & William B. Jacoby. LC 91-76371. (Illus.). 586p. (C). 1992. text ed. 32.00 (*0-9631023-1-1*) ACF Educ Inst.

Art & Science of Cytopathology. Richard DeMay. 1995. write for info. (*0-89189-322-9*) Am Soc Clinical.

Art & Science of Decision Making. Melvin Tainiter. (Commuter Series in Management Science). 80p. (Orig.). 1971. pap. 3.25 (*0-87974-001-9*) Timetable Pr.

Art & Science of Decision Making. Melvin Tainiter. 115p. 1986. 9.95 (*0-934577-02-1*) Softext Pub.

Art & Science of Dumpster Diving. John Hoffman. LC 92-74645. (Illus.). 254p. (Orig.). 1993. pap. 12.95 (*1-55950-088-3*, 14099) Loompanics.

Art & Science of Fly Fishing. Lennox Dick et al. (Illus.). 130p. 1993. pap. 19.95 (*1-878175-41-6*) F Amato Pubns.

Art & Science of Fly Fishing. Lenox Dick. 1977. pap. 5.95 (*0-8065-0587-7*, Citadel Pr) Carol Pub Group.

Art & Science of Footwear Manufacturing. 36p. 1983. 18.00 (*0-318-20639-0*) Footwear Indus.

Art & Science of Geography: U. S. & Soviet Perspectives. Ed. by V. V. Annenkov & George J Demko. 159p. (C). 1992. text ed. 37.00 (*0-8133-8516-4*) Westview.

Art & Science of Innovation Management: An International Perspective, Proceedings of the 4th International Conference on Product, Innovation Management, Innsbruck, Austria, Aug., 26-28, 1985. Ed. by Heinz Hubner. 452p. 1986. 123.00 (*0-444-42647-7*) Elsevier.

Art & Science of Inventing. 2nd ed. Gilbert Kivenson. 256p. 1982. text ed. 42.95 (*0-442-24583-1*) Chapman & Hall.

Art & Science of Lecture Demonstration. Charles Taylor. (Illus.). 200p. 1988. pap. text ed. 21.90 (*0-85274-323-8*) IOP Pub.

Art & Science of Logic. Daniel Bonevac. 676p. (C). 1990. text ed. 47.95 (*0-87484-805-9*) Mayfield Pub.

***Art & Science of Logic.** Daniel Bonevac. 676p. (C). 1990. teacher ed, text ed. write for info. (*1-55934-966-2*); teacher ed, text ed. write for info. (*0-87484-966-7*) Mayfield Pub.

Art & Science of Love. Albert Ellis. 1960. 7.95 (*0-8184-0009-9*) Carol Pub Group.

An Asterisk (*) at the beginning of an entry indicates that the title is appearing in BIP for the first time.

An Asterisk (*) at the beginning of an entry indicates that the title is appearing in BIP for the first time.

***Art at the Edge: Contemporary Art from Poland.** Intro. by David Elliott. 1988. pap. 24.00 (0-905836-66-9, Pub. by Museum Modern Art UK) St Mut.

Art at the Edge: Daniel Reeves. Linda Dubler. (Illus.). 16p. 1990. 7.50 (0-939802-65-1) High Mus Art.

Art at the Edge: Elisa D'Arrigo. Carrie Przybilla. LC 90-84884. (Illus.). 16p. 1990. 4.00 (0-939802-66-X) High Mus Art.

Art at the Edge: Ida Applebroog. LC 89-85649. (Illus.). 24p. 1989. 7.50 (0-939802-68-6) High Mus Art.

Art at the Edge: Jorge Tacla. Carrie Przybilla. LC 91-75674. (Illus.). 24p. 1991. pap. 6.00 (0-939802-71-6) High Mus Art.

Art at the Service of War: Canada, Art, & the Great War. Maria Tippett. (Illus.). 192p. 1984. 15.95 (0-8020-2541-2) U of Toronto Pr.

Art at Work: The New Renaissance in Corporate Collecting. Marjory Jacobson. LC 93-18707. 1993. 60.00 (0-87584-363-8) Harvard Busn.

Art au Point de Vue Sociologique: Art from the Sociological Point of View. 11th ed. Marie J. Guyau. LC 74-25756. (European Sociology Ser.). 442p. 1975. reprint ed. 35.95 (0-405-06510-8) Ayer.

Art au Siecle de Pericles. Pierre Devambez. (Illus.). 112p. (FRE.). 1955. lib. bdg. write for info. (0-8288-3944-1) Fr & Eur.

***Art Auction Records International 1994.** (Illus.). 2200p. (C). 1994. 295.00 (0-7605-0630-2) Rector Pr.

Art Auction Trends: Major Nineteenth Century American Artists. Ed. by James M. Coleman. 342p. 1992. pap. 31.95 (0-9631671-0-3) Connemara-Coleman.

Art Awaiting the Saviour. Ali Shariati. Tr. by Homa Fardjadi. 23p. 1980. pap. 2.00 (0-941722-16-3) Book Dist Ctr.

Art, Beauty, & Pornography. Jon Huer. LC 87-2472. 239p. 1987. 34.95 (0-87975-397-8) Prometheus Bks.

Art Beyond the Gallery in Early Twentieth Century England. Richard Cork. LC 84-52240. (Illus.). 352p. 1985. 75.00 (0-300-03236-6) Yale U Pr.

***Art Book: An A-Z of Artists.** (Illus.). 1994. 35.00 (0-7148-3032-1) Chronicle Bks.

***Art Book: An A-Z of Artists.** rev. ed. Phaidon Staff. (C). 1994. 35.00 (0-7148-2984-6, Pub. by Phaidon Press UK) Chronicle Bks.

Art, Books & Children: Art Activities Based on Children's Literature. Joan Frost. (Illus.). 88p. (J). (gr. 1-6). 1984. spiral bd. 13.95 (0-938594-03-6) Spec Lit Pr.

Art Books from the U. S. S. R. Ilya Glazunov. 268p. 1981. 75.00 (0-569-08519-5, Pub. by Collets UK) Pro-Am Music.

Art Books, 1876-1949: Including an International Index of Current Serial Publications. Frwd. by J. M. Edelstein. 780p. 1981. 99.00 (0-8352-1370-6) Bowker.

Art Books, 1950-1979: Including an International Directory of Museum Permanent Collection Catalogs. Frwd. by J. M. Edelstein. 1500p. 1979. 99.00 (0-8352-1189-4) Bowker.

Art Books, 1980-1984: Including International Serials. Frwd. by J. M. Edelstein. 571p. 1985. 99.00 (0-8352-1819-8) Bowker.

Art Bronzes. Michael Forrest. LC 87-63481. (Illus.). 493p. 1988. 95.00 (0-88740-122-8) Schiffer.

Art Business Encyclopedia. Leonard DuBoff. LC 93-71921. (Illus.). 320p. (Orig.). 1994. 29.95 (1-880559-14-5); pap. 18.95 (1-880559-13-7) Allworth Pr.

Art by Accident. Alan Burns. (Illus.). 350p. 1996. 32.95 (0-7145-4195-8) Riverrun NY.

Art by Chance: Fortuitous Impressions. George L. McKenna. LC 89-30073. (Illus.). 96p. 1989. pap. 14.95 (0-942614-13-5) Nelson-Atkins.

Art by Design: Reflections of Finland: An Exhibition in Collaboration with the Finnish Society. Barbara Kulvih & Antti Siltavuori. (Illus.). 48p. 1988. 12.00 (0-915171-08-2) Katonah Gal.

Art by Metamorphosis: Selections of African Art from the Spelman College Collection. Dele Jegede. (Illus.). 100p. (Orig.). (C). 1988. pap. write for info. (0-9621349-0-2) Spelman Coll Art.

Art C. A. R. T. Art Correlated Activities As Resources for Teachers. M. Madeline Ullom. Ed. by Art In-Forms Staff. (Illus.). 160p. (gr. k-5). 1988. Grades K-5. teacher ed 25.00 (0-911835-07-5) Art In-Forms.

Art Calendar Guide to Making a Living As an Artist. Ed. by Carolyn Blakeslee & Drew Steis. (Illus.). 220p. (Orig.). 1992. pap. 17.95 (0-945388-01-2) Art Calendar.

Art Center of Corpus Christi Cookbook. Illus. by Sally Pomeroy & Mary A. Tanner. 102p. (Orig.). 1991. spiral bd. 9.00 (0-9629702-0-4) Art Ctr Corpus Christi.

Art Center Workbook. Henry Sanoff. (Illus.). 82p. (C). 1984. pap. text ed. 9.95 (0-317-93290-X) H Sanoff.

***Art-Centered Education & Therapy for Children with Disabilities.** Frances E. Anderson. LC 93-33203. (Illus.). 284p. 1994. pap. 29.95 (0-398-06006-1) C C Thomas.

Art-Centered Education & Therapy for Children with Disabilities. Frances E. Anderson. LC 93-33203. (Illus.). 284p. (C). 1994. text ed. 44.95x (0-398-05896-2) C C Thomas.

Art Chronicles, 1954-1966. Frank O'Hara. LC 74-77526. 1990. pap. 14.95 (0-8076-0756-8) Braziller.

Art Cinematographique, 8 vols., Set. LC 70-124019. (Illus.). 1970. reprint ed. 51.95 (0-405-01625-5) Ayer.

Art Circle: A Theory of Art. George Dickie. LC 83-83295. 1984. 45.00 (0-930586-37-9) Haven Pubns.

Art Class. Gina Ingoglia. LC 91-58786. (Disney's First Readers Ser.). (Illus.). 48p. (J). (gr. k-3). 1992. 9.95 (1-56282-047-8); lib. bdg. 9.89 (1-56282-227-6) Disney Pr.

Art Class: A Beginner's Complete Guide to Painting & Drawing. Ed. by Ken Howard. (Illus.). 240p. 1989. 32.50 (0-8230-0256-X, Watsn-Guptill) Watsn-Guptill.

Art Collection at Potsdam. John C. Riordan. (Illus.). 118p. (Orig.). 1982. pap. 10.00 (0-942746-04-X) SUNYP R Gibson.

Art Collection in the Heylshof at Worms. 56p. 1984. pap. 5.00 (0-318-17312-3) Stein Coll Intl.

Art Collections of Great Britain & Ireland: The National Art Collections Fund Book of Art Galleries & Museums. Jeannie Chapel & Charlotte Gere. (Illus.). 352p. 1986. 45.00 (0-8109-0941-3) Abrams.

Art Collectors of Russia: Private Treasures Revealed. Christina Burrus. (Illus.). 256p. 1994. 69.00 (1-85043-740-8, Pub. by I B Tauris UK) St Martin.

Art Colony Nurse. large type ed. Jane Converse. (Linford Romance Library). 256p. 1989. pap. 11.95 (0-7089-6703-5, Linford) Ulverscroft.

Art Concepts for Children. Carol B. Small. LC 89-14917. (Children's Resources Ser.). (Illus.). 112p. (Orig.). (J). (gr. 6 up). 1989. pap. 8.95 (0-938267-04-3) Bold Prodns.

Art Connections. Kimberly B. Thompson & Diana S. Loftus. (Illus.). 176p. (Orig.). (J). (gr. 4-8). 1994. pap. 12.95 (0-673-36080-6) GdYrBks.

Art Contemporain Sovietique Selection d'Oeuvres Provenant de la Collection KNIGA. C. Forge. (C). 1990. 195.00 (0-685-34379-0, Pub. by Collets) St Mut.

Art Course. Tom Robb. 1990. 15.99 (0-517-05380-2) Random Hse Value.

Art, Creativity & the Sacred: An Anthology in Religion & Art. Ed. by Diane Apostolos-Cappadona. (Illus.). 352p. 1983. pap. 19.95 (0-8245-0609-X) Crossroad NY.

***Art, Creativity & the Sacred: An Anthology in Religion & Art.** rev. ed. Ed. by Diane Apostolos-Cappadona. LC 95-15413. (Illus.). 352p. 1995. pap. text ed. 19.95 (0-8264-0829-X) Continuum.

Art Crime. John E. Conklin. LC 93-11869. 322p. 1994. text ed. 49.95 (0-275-94771-8, Praeger Pubs) Greenwood.

Art Critic & the Art Historian. Quentin Bell. LC 75-314718. (Leslie Stephen Lecture Ser.: 1973). 34p. reprint ed. pap. 25.00 (0-8357-5757-9, 2051369) Bks Demand.

Art Criticism. John Ruskin. Ed. by R. L. Herbert. 13.25 (0-8446-0694-4) Peter Smith.

Art Criticism & Its Institutions in Nineteenth-Century France. Ed. by Michael R. Orwicz. LC 93-46023. 1994. text ed. 69.95 (0-7190-3859-6, Pub. by Manchester Univ Pr UK) St Martin.

Art Criticism from a Laboratory. Alan Burroughs. LC 70-110267. 277p. 1971. reprint ed. text ed. 59.75 (0-8371-4493-0, BUAC, Greenwood Pr) Greenwood.

Art Criticism in the Sixties. Ed. by Brandeis University - Poses Institute of Fine Arts Staff. 1965. pap. 3.25 (0-8079-0008-7) October.

Art Criticism of John Ruskin. Ed. by Robert L. Herbert. (Quality Paperbacks Ser.). 465p. 1987. reprint ed. pap. 12.95 (0-306-80310-0) Da Capo.

Art Criticism of Paul Claudel. Marie-Therese Killiam. LC 89-2366. (American University Studies: Fine Arts: Ser. XX, Vol. 11). 413p. (C). 1990. text ed. 68.95 (0-8204-0902-2) P Lang Pubs.

Art Criticism of Theophile Gautier. Spencer. 23.50 (0-685-34914-4) Fr & Eur.

Art Crusade. Peter C. Marzio. LC 75-20404. (Smithsonian Studies in History & Technology: No. 34). (Illus.). 102p. reprint ed. pap. 29.10 (0-8357-5758-7, 2004691) Bks Demand.

Art, Culture & Enterprise. Justin Lewis. 196p. 1990. 52.00 (0-415-04449-X, A4234); pap. 14.95 (0-415-04450-2, A4238) Routledge.

Art, Culture, & Environment: A Catalyst for Teaching. June K. McFee & Rogena M. Degge. 416p. (C). 1992. per. 29.95 (0-8403-7418-6) Kendall-Hunt.

Art, Culture, & Ethnicity. Ed. by Bernard Young. 278p. (C). 1990. pap. text ed. 20.00 (0-937652-54-7) Natl Art Ed.

Art Curriculum Activities Kit: Intermediate Level, Grades 5-8. Barbara M. Reuther & Diane Fogler. (Illus.). 208p. 1988. pap. text ed. 24.95 (0-13-047184-4, Parker Publishing Co) P-H.

Art Curriculum Activities Kit: Primary Level, Grades 1-4. Barbara M. Reuther & Diane Fogler. (Illus.). 204p. 1988. pap. text ed. 24.95 (0-13-047143-7, Parker Publishing Co) P-H.

Art D'amours. Tr. by Lawrence Blonquist. LC 84-48065. 224p. 1987. lib. bdg. 20.00 (0-8240-8915-4) Garland.

Art D'aujourd'Jhui: Peintures, Dessins, Estampes Scuptures de Notre Temps, 6 vols, Set. LC 69-9225. (Illus.). (FRE.). 1969. reprint ed. 165.95 (0-405-00709-4) Ayer.

Art de Dictier. Eustache Deschamps. Ed. by Deborah Sinnreich-Levi. (Medieval Texts & Studies: No. 17). 160p. 1994. 28.00 (0-937191-33-7) Colleagues Pr Inc.

Art de la Conversation. 2nd ed. Lenard. 1985. pap. 30.95 (0-8384-3702-8) Heinle & Heinle.

Art de l'Aimer, Les Remedes a l'Amour, Les Produits de Beaute. Ovide. (FRE.). 1974. pap. 10.95 (0-7859-4024-3) Fr & Eur.

Art de Lire. Quentin M. Hope. 575p. (C). 1988. pap. text ed. write for info. (0-13-087966-5) P-H.

Art de Naviguer. Pedro De Medina. LC 92-15326. 1992. 100.00 (0-8201-1470-7) Schol Facsimiles.

Art de Roger Martin du Gard. Renee F. Wehrmann. LC 85-61601. 129p. (FRE.). 1986. 18.95 (0-917786-38-6) Summa Pubns.

Art de Vivre. Andre Maurois. 256p. (FRE.). 1973. 6.95 (0-7859-0110-8, M3759) Fr & Eur.

Art de Vivre: Decorative Arts & Design in France, 1789-1989. David R. McFadden et al. Ed. by Nancy Aakre. LC 88-63278. (Illus.). 256p. 1989. text ed. 60.00 (0-86565-976-1) Vendome.

Art Dealers: Powers Behind the Scene Tell How the Art World Really Works. Ed. by Laura de Coppet & Alan Jones. (Illus.). 320p. 1984. pap. 17.95 (0-517-55302-3, C P Pubs) Crown Pub Group.

Art Deco. Alastair Duncan. LC 88-50231. (World of Art Ser.). (Illus.). 210p. 1988. pap. 14.95 (0-500-20230-3) Thames Hudson.

Art Deco. Katharine M. McClinton. 1986. pap. 14.95 (0-517-54599-3, C P Pubs) Crown Pub Group.

Art Deco. Richard Striner. LC 94-18571. (Stylebooks Ser.). 1994. write for info. (1-55859-824-3) Abbeville Pr.

Art Deco. rev. ed. Victor Arwas. (Illus.). 316p. 1992. 75.00 (0-8109-1926-5) Abrams.

Art Deco: Les Maitres de Mobilier, le Decor des Paquebots. Pierre Kjellberg. (Illus.). 238p. (FRE.). 1992. lib. bdg. 195.00 (0-7859-3645-9, 2859170545) Fr & Eur.

Art Deco Advertising, No. 1. Ed. by Leslie Cabarga. LC 88-82915. 48p. 1988. 5.75 (0-88108-061-6) Art Dir.

Art Deco Advertising, No. 2. Ed. by Leslie Cabarga. LC 88-82915. 48p. 1988. 5.75 (0-88108-062-4) Art Dir.

Art Deco Advertising, No. 3. Ed. by Leslie Cabarga. LC 88-82915. 48p. 1988. 5.75 (0-88108-063-2) Art Dir.

Art Deco Advertising, No. 4. Ed. by Leslie Cabarga. LC 88-82915. 48p. 1990. 5.75 (0-88108-078-0) Art Dir.

Art Deco Advertising, No. 5. Ed. by Leslie Cabarga. LC 88-82915. 48p. 1990. 5.75 (0-88108-079-9) Art Dir.

***Art Deco & Modernist Ceramics.** Karen McCready. LC 94-61467. (Illus.). 192p. 1995. 45.00 (0-500-01669-0) Thames Hudson.

Art Deco & Other Figures. Bryan Catley. (Illus.). 344p. 1978. 89.50 (0-902028-57-X) Antique Collect.

Art Deco & Streamline Vermont: A Catalog of Urban Architecture, Historic Preservation Program. University of Vermont Staff. (Illus.). 55p. (Orig.). 1985. pap. write for info. (0-9614365-0-6) U of VT Dept Hist.

Art Deco Architecture: Design, Decoration, & Detail from the Twenties & Thirties. Patricia Bayer. (Illus.). 224p. 1992. 49.50 (0-8109-1923-0) Abrams.

Art Deco Chrome, Bk. 2: A Collector's Guide, Industrial Design in the Chase Era. Richard J. Kilbride. (Illus.). 138p. 1991. pap. 27.95 (0-937791-05-9) JO-D Bks.

Art Deco Chrome, the Chase Era. Richard J. Kilbride. LC 87-83509. (Illus.). 104p. 1988. pap. 24.95 (0-937791-04-0) JO-D Bks.

Art Deco Cut & Use Stencils. Theodore Menten. (J). 1977. pap. 4.95 (0-486-23551-3) Dover.

Art Deco Designs: A Design Sourcebook. (Illus.). 224p. 1991. 24.99 (0-517-01490-4) Random Hse Value.

Art Deco Designs & Motifs. Marcia Loeb. (Pictorial Archive Ser.). (Illus.). 96p. (Orig.). 1972. pap. 5.95 (0-486-22826-6) Dover.

Art Deco Designs in Color. Ed. by Charles R. Fry. LC 75-17173. (Illus.). 48p. 1975. pap. 7.95 (0-486-23216-6) Dover.

Art Deco Display Alphabets. Dan X. Solo. 1983. 12.75 (0-8446-6008-6) Peter Smith.

Art Deco Display Alphabets: 100 Complete Fonts. Dan X. Solo. (Pictorial Archive Ser.). (Illus.). 104p. (Orig.). 1982. pap. 6.95 (0-486-24372-9) Dover.

Art Deco Fashion: French Designers Nineteen Eight to Nineteen Twenty-Five. Martin Battersby. (Illus.). 112p. 1984. pap. 10.95 (0-312-05181-6) St Martin.

Art Deco Floral Patterns in Full Color. E. A. Seguy. LC 74-77178. (Illus.). 40p. 1974. reprint ed. pap. 7.95 (0-486-23041-4) Dover.

Art Deco Furniture: The French Designers. Alastair Duncan. LC 91-67310. (Illus.). 192p. 1992. reprint ed. pap. 24.95 (0-500-27660-9) Thames Hudson.

Art Deco Identification & Price Guide. 2nd enl. rev. ed. Tony Fusco. (Illus.). 440p. 1993. pap. 16.00 (0-380-77012-1, Confident Collect) Avon.

Art Deco Interiors in Color. Charles R. Fry. LC 77-75887. (Illus.). 1977. pap. 7.95 (0-486-23527-0) Dover.

Art Deco Jewelry. Melissa Gabardi. (Illus.). 360p. 1989. 79.50 (1-85149-065-5) Antique Collect.

Art Deco Jewelry Designs in Full Color. Idees Staff. LC 93-10730. (Pictorial Archive Ser.). 1993. pap. write for info. (0-486-27694-5) Dover.

***Art Deco Ornamental Ironwork.** Henri Martinie. LC 94-47177. (Illus.). 1995. write for info. (0-486-28535-9) Dover.

***Art Deco Paper Doll Wardrobe 1920-1939.** Norma Meehan. (Illus.). 1994. 4.95 (0-87588-422-9, 4734) Hobby Hse.

Art Deco Skyscraper in New York. rev. ed. Norbert Messler. (Illus.). 224p. (C). 1986. text ed. 14.80 (0-8204-0158-7) P Lang Pubs.

Art Deco Skyscraper in New York, Vol. 25. Norbert Messler. (European University Studies: Ser. 28). 234p. 1983. 44.60 (3-8204-7562-1) P Lang Pubs.

Art Deco Spot Illustrations & Motifs: 513 Original Designs. William Rowe. LC 85-6843. 62p. (Orig.). 1985. pap. 5.95 (0-486-24924-7) Dover.

Art Deco Stained Glass Pattern Book. Ed Sibbett, Jr. LC 77-77051. (Illus.). 1977. pap. 4.95 (0-486-23550-5) Dover.

Art Deco Style in Household Objects, Architecture, Sculpture, Graphics, Jewelry. Ed. by Theodore Menten. (Illus.). 192p. (Orig.). 1972. pap. 9.95 (0-486-22824-X) Dover.

Art Deco Style in Household Objects, Architecture, Sculpture, Graphics, Jewelry. Theodore Menten. (Illus.). (Orig.). 20.50 (0-8446-4586-9) Peter Smith.

Art d'ecrire. Etiemble. 26.15 (0-7859-0624-X, F140180) Fr & Eur.

Art, Design, & the Modern Corporation: The Collection of Container Corp. of America, a Gift to the National Museum of American Art. Neil Harris & Martina R. Norelli. LC 85-14431. (Illus.). 136p. (Orig.). 1985. pap. 22.50 (0-87474-509-8, HAADP) Smithsonian.

Art, Dialogue, & Outrage: Essays on Literature & Culture. Wole Soyinka. 336p. 1994. 25.00 (0-679-40065-6) Pantheon.

***Art Diary International 1995.** Giancarlo Politi. 500p. 1995. pap. 25.00 (88-7816-058-X) Dist Art Pubs.

Art Dictionary: Woerterbuch der Kunst. 11th ed. Johannes Jahn. 932p. (GER.). 1989. 59.95 (0-8288-1420-1, M6986) Fr & Eur.

Art Dictionary of Military History: Dictionnaire d'Art et d'Histoire Militaires. Andre Corvisier. 896p. (FRE.). 1988. 195.00 (0-8288-1905-X, F33200) Fr & Eur.

Art Directing Photography. Hugh Marshall. (Illus.). 144p. 1989. 27.95 (0-89134-259-1, 30162) North Light Bks.

Art Direction for Film & Video. Robert Olson. (Illus.). 160p. 1993. pap. 19.95 (0-240-80189-X, Focal) Buttrwrth-Heinemann.

Art Directors Annual, 66th. (Illus.). 848p. 1987. 44.95 (0-937414-07-7) ADC Pubns.

***Art Directors' Index to Illustrators, No. 15.** RotoVision Staff. 1995. (0-8230-6434-4) Watsn-Guptill.

Art Directors' Index to Photographers, Set. Rotovision, S. A. Staff. (Illus.). 1994. boxed 135.00 (0-8230-6334-8, Watsn-Guptill) Watsn-Guptill.

Art Directors' Index to Photographers, 2 vols., Vol. 1: Europe. Rotovision, S. A. Staff. (Illus.). 400p. 1994. 67.50 (0-8230-6323-2, Watsn-Guptill) Watsn-Guptill.

***Art Directors' Index to Photographers, Vol. 1, No. 20.** RotoVision Staff. 1995. (0-8230-6430-1) Watsn-Guptill.

***Art Directors' Index to Photographers, Vol. 2, No. 20.** RotoVision Staff. 1995. (0-8230-6429-8) Watsn-Guptill.

Art Directors' Index to Photographers, 2 vols., Vol. 2: The Americas, Asia & Australasia. Rotovision, S. A. Staff. (Illus.). 300p. 1994. 67.50 (0-8230-6324-0, Watsn-Guptill) Watsn-Guptill.

Art Directors' Workbook of Type Faces see Classic Type Faces & How to Use Them: Including 91 Complete Fonts

Art Discourse - Discourse in Art. Jessica Prinz. LC 90-19388. (Illus.). 225p. (C). 1991. text ed. 35.00 (0-8135-1673-0); pap. text ed. 15.00 (0-8135-1734-6) Rutgers U Pr.

Art Documentation Cumulative Index, Vols. 1-6, 1982-1987. Ed. by Lynette M. Korenic. 44p. (Orig.). 1989. pap. text ed. 10.00 (0-942740-07-6) Art Libs Soc.

***Art Does Not Exist.** Drexler. 1995. pap. text ed. 10.95 (0-932511-99-6) Fiction Coll.

Art du luthier. Auguste Tolbecque. (Illus.). 316p. (FRE.). 1969. reprint ed. lib. bdg. 55.00 (0-8450-2583-X) Broude.

***Art du XIXe Siecle: Larousse Dictionnaire de Peinture et de Sculpture.** Jean-Philippe Breuille. 777p. (FRE.). 1993. 225.00 (0-7859-8610-3, 203511313x) Fr & Eur.

***Art du XXe Siecle Dictionnaire de Peinture et De Sculpture.** Jean-Philippe Breuille. 896p. (FRE.). 1991. 225.00 (0-7859-7670-1, 2035113083) Fr & Eur.

Art Education. Jack Rudman. (National Teachers Examination Ser.: NT-13). 1994. pap. 23.95 (0-8373-8423-0) Nat Learn.

Art Education: A Critical Necessity. Albert W. Levi & Ralph A. Smith. (Disciplines in Art Education, Contexts of Understanding Ser.). (Illus.). 280p. 1991. 39.95 (0-252-01813-3); pap. 16.95 (0-252-06185-3) U of Ill Pr.

Art Education: A Guide to Information Sources. Ed. by Clarence Bunch. LC 73-17518. (Art & Architecture Information Guide Ser.: Vol. 6). 348p. 1978. 68.00 (0-8103-1272-7) Gale.

Art Education: Elementary Education. Andra Johnson. 222p. 1992. pap. 20.00 (0-937652-61-X) Natl Art Ed.

Art Education & Human Development. Howard Gardner. LC 90-2955. (Illus.). 80p. (Orig.). 1990. pap. 7.50 (0-89236-179-4) J P Getty Trust.

Art Engine Texts. Fred Truck. 88p. 1989. Incl. software disk. disk 200.00 (0-938236-10-5) Electric Bank.

Art Epochs & Their Leaders: A Survey of the Genesis of Modern Art. Oscar Hagen. LC 75-165637. (Select Bibliographies Reprint Ser.). 1977. reprint ed. 42.95 (0-8369-5946-9) Ayer.

Art et l'Amour, 2 vols. Florent Fels. (Illus.). (FRE.). 1952. Vol. 1, 226p. write for info. (0-318-68956-1); Vol. 2, 309p. write for info. (0-318-68957-X) Fr & Eur.

Art et l'Amour, 2 vols., Set. Florent Fels. (Illus.). (FRE.). 1952. lib. bdg. 125.00 (0-8288-3940-9) Fr & Eur.

Art et Scolastique. 4th ed. Jacques Maritain. 280p. (FRE.). 1965. 19.95 (0-8288-9854-5, F111960) Fr & Eur.

Art Exhibition by California Artists: Illustrated Catalogue. limited ed. (Illus.). 1983. reprint ed. pap. 25.00 (0-318-00405-4) K Starosciak.

Art Experience. Vicci Sperry. LC 68-26914. (Illus.). 1969. 24.95 (0-912158-60-3); pap. 7.95 (0-912158-61-1) Hennessey.

Art Experience, Grades 4-6. Willet Ryder. 1991. pap. 12.95 (0-673-46353-2) GdYrBks.

Art Experiences & Criticism. Squires. 1991. 22.00 (0-536-57955-5) Ginn Pr.

***Art Experiences for Young Children.** Naomi Pile. (Illus.). 112p. (C). 1990. reprint ed. pap. text ed. 16.50 (0-87411-444-6) Copley Pub.

Art Facts: A Book of Contexts. B. P. Nichol. LC 89-667. 168p. (Orig.). (C). 1990. pap. 15.00 (0-925904-00-7) Chax Pr.

Art Fever: Passages Through the Western Art Trade. James Parsons. Ed. by Steve Fox & Nancy Schlede. LC 81-83141. (Illus.). 111p. 1981. 300.00 (0-9610550-1-4); 29.95 (0-9610550-0-6) Gallery West.

***Art File, No. 3.** (Illus.). 240p. 1995. 64.95 (4-938586-59-2, Pub. by PIE Bks JA) Bks Nippan.

Art for a Fairer World. Oxfam Publications Staff. (C). 1992. pap. text ed. 21.00 (0-85598-208-X, Pub. by Oxfam Pubns UK) St Mut.

Art for a Purpose: The Artists' International Association 1933-1953. Robert Radford. 205p. 1991. 17.95 (0-9506783-7-6, Pub. by Winchester Schl Art Pr UK) Paul & Co Pubs.

An Asterisk (*) at the beginning of an entry indicates that the title is appearing in BIP for the first time.

An Asterisk (*) at the beginning of an entry indicates that the title is appearing in BIP for the first time.

Art in Progress: A Survey Prepared for the Fifteenth Anniversary of the Museum of Modern Art, New York Staff. Museum of Modern Art Library Staff. 1981. 35. 95 (*0-405-12882-7*) Ayer.

Art in Public Places. John Beardsley. Ed. by Andy L. Harney. LC 81-85019. (Illus.). 149p. (Orig.). 1981. pap. 12.00 (*0-941182-05-3*) Partners Livable.

Art in Review: Puerto Rico. Ed. by Muna Lee. (Puerto Rico Ser.). 1979. lib. bdg. 59.95 (*0-8490-2868-X*) Gordon Pr.

Art in Revolution. John Berger. LC 68-26045. (Illus.). 1969. pap. 14.00 (*0-394-41562-0*) Pantheon.

Art in Seattle's Public Places: An Illustrated Guide. James M. Rupp. LC 90-32846. (Illus.). 320p. (Orig.). 1992. pap. 19.95 (*0-295-97100-2*) U of Wash Pr.

Art in Seventeenth Century New England. Phillip Johnson. (Illus.). 73p. 1977. pap. 1.50 (*0-317-13609-7*) Wadsworth Atheneum.

Art in Small-Scale Societies. 2nd ed. Richard L. Anderson. 304p. 1988. pap. text ed. write for info. (*0-13-047762-1*) P-H.

Art in Small-Scale Societies: Contemporary Readings. 3rd ed. Richard L. Anderson & Karen L. Field. LC 92-14754. 480p. 1992. pap. text ed. 35.00 (*0-13-045451-6*) P-H.

Art in Structural Design: An Introduction & Sourcebook. Alan Holgate. (Illus.). 272p. 1986. 49.95 (*0-19-856167-9*); pap. 24.95 (*0-19-856177-6*) OUP.

Art in Switzerland Nineteen Ninety-One: Celebrating 700 Years Towards Democracy. Ed. by Jean-Pierre Golay & Russell Panczenko. (Illus.). 46p. 1991. 8.95 (*0-932900-27-5*) Elvejhem Mus.

Art in Teaching Art. Manfred L. Keiler. LC 61-5497. (Illus.). 262p. reprint ed. pap. 74.70 (*0-7837-6027-2*, 2045839) Bks Demand.

Art in the Age of Aquarius, 1955-1970. William C. Seitz. LC 90-26271. (Illus.). 272p. 1992. 49.95 (*0-87474-868-2*) Smithsonian.

Art in the Age of Mass Media. John A. Walker. LC 94-254. 1994. text ed. 40.50 (*0-8133-2216-2*) Westview.

Art in the Age of Mass Media. John A. Walker. LC 94-254. (C). 1994. pap. text ed. 19.95 (*0-8133-2217-0*) Westview.

Art in the Age of the Mass Media. John Walker. 124p. 1983. pap. text ed. 17.95 (*0-86104-718-4*, Pub. by Pluto Pr UK) Westview.

***Art in the American South 1733-1989: Selections from the Roger Houston Collection.** Paul Grootkerk. Ed. by Herman Mhire. (Illus.). 87p. 1993. 20.00 (*0-936819-07-3*) USL Art Museum.

Art in the Cold War. Christine Lindey. (Illus.). 224p. (C). 1991. 30.00 (*1-56131-010-7*) New Amsterdam Bks.

***Art in the Elementary School: Drawing, Painting & Creating for the Classroom.** Marlene G. Linderman. 272p. (C). 1995. pap. write for info. (*0-697-12500-9*) Brown & Benchmark.

Art in the Elementary School: Drawing, Painting, & Creating for the Classroom. 4th ed. Marlene G. Linderman. 320p. (C). 1990. pap. write for info. (*0-697-03341-4*) Brown & Benchmark.

Art in the Environment in the United States. Emma L. Fundaburk & Mary D. Foreman. (Illus.). 220p. 1975. reprint ed. 15.00 (*0-9617083-0-1*) Am Bicent Mus.

Art in the Hellenistic Age. J. J. Pollitt. (Illus.). 352p. 1986. pap. 34.95 (*0-521-27672-1*) Cambridge U Pr.

Art in the Humanities. 2nd ed. Patrick D. De Long. (C). 1970. pap. text ed. 20.50 (*0-13-046979-3*) P-H.

Art in the Light of Conscience: Eight Essays on Poetry by Marina Tsvetaeva. Marina Tsvetaeva. 214p. (C). 1992. 32.00 (*0-674-04802-4*) HUP.

Art in the Making: Italian Painting Before 1400. David Bomford et al. (Illus.). 1990. pap. text ed. 30.00 (*0-300-06144-7*) Yale U Pr.

Art in the Making: Rembrandt. David Bomford et al. (National Gallery Publications). (Illus.). 1990. pap. text ed. 30.00 (*0-300-06145-5*) Yale U Pr.

Art in the Massachusetts State House. Massachusetts Art Commission Staff. LC 86-63635. (Illus.). 78p. (Orig.). 1986. pap. write for info. (*0-9617851-0-1*) Mass Art Comm.

Art in the National Curriculum: Wales. HMSO Staff. 66p. (ENG & WEL.). 1992. pap. 14.00 (*0-11-701686-1*, HM16861, Pub. by HMSO UK) UNIPUB.

Art in the Nineteenth Century: Art & Artists. Jillian Powell. (Art & Artists Ser.). (Illus.). 48p. (J). (gr. 6-10). 1994. 16.95 (*1-56847-219-6*) Thomson Lrning.

Art in the Public Interest. Intro. by Arlene Raven. LC 89-16719. (Studies in the Fine Arts: Criticism: No. 32). 380p. 1990. pap. 108.10 (*0-8357-1970-7*, 2070756) Bks Demand.

Art in the Public Interest. Ed. by Arlene Raven. (Illus.). 380p. 1993. reprint ed. pap. 14.95 (*0-306-80539-1*) Da Capo.

***Art in the Roman Empire.** Michael Grant. LC 95-5440. 1995. write for info. (*0-415-12031-4*) Routledge.

Art in the San Francisco Bay Area, 1945-1980: An Illustrated History. Thomas Albright. LC 84-24112. 360p. 1985. 75.00 (*0-520-05193-9*); pap. 37.50 (*0-520-05518-7*) U CA Pr.

Art in the Science Dominated World: Science, Logic & Art. Ed. by E. L. Feinberg & P. N. Lebedev. (Studies in Cybernetics: Vol. 13). 177p. 1987. text ed. 51.00 (*2-88124-141-7*) Gordon & Breach.

Art in the Service of Religion. Text by Naomi R. Kline. write for info. (*0-9601342-3-9*) PSC Art Gall.

Art in the Seventh Power. Corinne Robins. (Illus.). 72p. (Orig.). 1984. pap. 5.00 (*0-930557-00-X*) Pratt Press.

Art in the Seventies. Edward Lucie-Smith. (Illus.). 128p. 1980. 45.00 (*0-8014-1328-1*); pap. 19.95 (*0-8014-9194-0*) Cornell U Pr.

Art in the Soviet Union: Major Works by Soviet Artists from 1917 to the 1970's Painting, Sculpture, Graphic Arts. O. Sopotsinsky. 502p. 1977. 90.00 (*0-317-14219-4*, Pub. by Collets UK) St Mut.

Art in the White House: A Nation's Pride. William Kloss. (Illus.). 376p. 1992. 49.50 (*0-8109-3965-7*) White House Hist.

Art in the White House: A Nation's Pride. William Kloss. LC 92-68463. 1992. write for info. (*0-912308-46-X*) White House Hist.

Art in the World. 3rd ed. Stella P. Russell. (Illus.). (C). 1989. pap. text ed. 42.75 (*0-03-028672-7*) HB Coll Pubs.

Art in the World. 4th ed. Stella Russell. LC 92-70938. (Illus.). 550p. (C). 1992. pap. text ed. write for info. (*0-03-276543-6*) HB Coll Pubs.

Art in Theory, 1900-1990. Ed. by Charles Harrison & Paul Wood. 1216p. 1993. pap. 24.95 (*0-631-16575-4*) Blackwell Pubs.

Art in Transition: Post-Impressionist Prints & Drawings from the Achenbach Foundation for Graphic Arts. Evelyn Lincoln. LC 88-80186. (Illus.). 15p. (C). 1988. pap. 4.00 (*0-88401-058-9*) Fine Arts Mus.

Art in Ulster, No. 1: 1557-1957. John Hewitt. (Illus.). 190p. reprint ed. pap. 29.00 (*0-85640-128-5*, Pub. by Blackstaff Pr IE) Dufour.

Art in Ulster, No. 2: 1957-1977. Mike Catto. (Illus.). 190p. 1992. reprint ed. pap. 29.00 (*0-85640-129-3*, Pub. by Blackstaff Pr IE) Dufour.

Art in Unexpected Places. Ed. by Rebecca L. Lawrence & Audrey V. Sylvester. LC 88-64115. (Illus.). 96p. (Orig.). 1989. pap. 10.00 (*0-9621915-0-7*) NH SCA.

Art in Vienna: Klimt, Kokoschka, Schiele & Their Contemporaries. Peter Vergo. (Illus.). 256p. (Orig.). (C). 1994. pap. 24.95 (*0-7148-2967-6*, Pub. by Phaidon Press UK) Chronicle Bks.

Art in Vienna 1898-1918: Klimt, Kokoschka, Schiele, & Their Contemporaries. Peter Vergo. LC 81-66147. (Illus.). 253p. 1981. pap. 22.95 (*0-8014-9226-2*) Cornell U Pr.

Art in Wales, AD1850-1980: An Illustrated History. Eric Rowan. 128p. 1985. 65.00 (*0-7083-0854-6*, Pub. by U of Wales UK) Bks Intl VA.

Art in Your Visual Environment. 2nd ed. Gerald F. Brommer & George F. Horn. LC 84-73494. (Illus.). 256p. (J). (gr. 7-8). 1985. text ed. 23.80 (*0-87192-169-3*) Davis Mass.

Art in Your World. 2nd ed. Gerald F. Brommer & George F. Horn. LC 84-73493. (Illus.). 256p. (J). (gr. 7-8). 1985. text ed. 23.80 (*0-87192-168-5*) Davis Mass.

Art Inc: American Paintings from Corporate Collections. Montgomery Museum of Fine Arts Staff. Ed. by Mitchell D. Kahan. LC 78-65838. (Illus.). (ps-12). 1979. 15.00 (*0-89616-008-4*); pap. 15.00 (*0-89616-009-2*) Montgomery Mus.

Art Index, 1938-1953. LC 31-7513. 225.00 (*0-685-22229-2*) Wilson.

Art Index, 1953-1990. LC 31-7513. 250.00 (*0-685-22230-6*) Wilson.

Art Index, 1990-1994. LC 31-7513. write for info. (*0-685-22231-4*) Wilson.

Art Information. 3rd ed. Lois S. Jones. 400p. (C). 1993. per. 34.95 (*0-8403-5713-3*) Kendall-Hunt.

Art Inscribed: Essays on Ekphrasis in Spanish Golden Age Poetry. Emilie L. Bergmann. LC 79-966. (Studies in Romance Languages: No. 35). (Illus.). 362p. 1979. 20.00 (*0-674-04805-9*) HUP.

Art Institute of Chicago: The Essential Guide. Sel. by James N. Wood & Teri J. Edelstein. LC 93-11195. (Illus.). 260p. (Orig.). 1993. pap. 17.95 (*0-86559-120-2*) Art Inst Chi.

Art Institute of Chicago Museum Studies, Vol. 15, No. 2. Ed. by Rachel Dressler. (Illus.). 86p. 1990. pap. 8.50 (*0-685-31189-9*) U Ch Pr.

***Art Institute of Chicago Museum Studies Vol. 19, No. I: One Hundred Years at the Art Institute: A Centennial Celebration.** (Illus.). 112p. 1993. 14.95 (*0-86559-107-5*) Art Inst Chi.

***Art Institute of Chicago Museum Studies Vol. 20, No. 2: The Joseph Winterbotham Collection.** (Illus.). 96p. 1994. 14.95 (*0-86559-124-5*) Art Inst Chi.

***Art Institute of Chicago Museum Studies Vol. 20, No. I: Ancient Art at the Art Instutite of Chicago.** (Illus.). 96p. 1994. 14.95 (*0-86559-122-9*) Art Inst Chi.

***Art Institute of Chicago Museum Studies Vol. 21, No. I: Notable Acquisitions since 1980.** (Illus.). 96p. 1995. 10. 50 (*0-86559-140-7*) Art Inst Chi.

Art Instruction in English Public Schools. Charles H. Sawyer. (Illus.). 73p. 1937. write for info. (*1-879886-02-2*) Addison Gallery.

***Art into Life: Collected Papers from the Kresge Art Museum Medieval Symposia.** Ed. by Carol Fisher & Kathleen L. Scott. LC 94-45563. 1995. 45.00 (*0-87013-365-9*) Mich St U Pr.

Art into Life, an Interpretation of Contemporary Trends in Painting. Frank A. Wilson. LC 59-25976. (Illus.). 244p. reprint ed. pap. 69.60 (*0-8357-5761-7*, 2015654) Bks Demand.

Art into Pop. Simon Frith & Howard Horne. (Illus.). 192p. 1988. pap. 11.95 (*0-416-41540-7*, A1956) Routledge Chapman & Hall.

***Art Is a Way of Knowing.** Pat B. Allen. 1995. pap. 12.00 (*1-57062-078-4*) Shambhala Pubns.

Art Is Action. Baker Brownell. LC 73-90616. (Essay Index Reprint Ser.). 1977. 18.95 (*0-8369-1250-0*) Ayer.

Art Is Boring for the Same Reason We Stayed in Vietnam. Stephen P. Miller. (Post- & Pre-Everything Ser.). 120p. (Orig.). 1992. pap. 9.00 (*0-934450-50-1*) Unmuzzled Ox.

Art Is Composition. (Illus.). 16p. 1992. pap. text ed. 52.50 (*0-935493-63-8*) Modern Learn Pr.

Art Is Elementary: Teaching Visual Thinking Through Art Concepts. Ivan E. Cornia et al. (Illus.). 464p. 1994. teacher ed 39.95 (*0-87905-138-8*, Peregrine Smith) Gibbs Smith Pub.

Art Is Line. (Illus.). 16p. 1992. pap. text ed. 52.50 (*0-935493-58-1*) Modern Learn Pr.

Art Isn't Easy: The Achievement of Stephen Sondheim. Joanne Gordon. LC 88-6543. (Illus.). 336p. (C). 1990. 39.95 (*0-8093-1407-X*) S Ill U Pr.

Art Isn't Easy: The Theatre of Stephen Sondheim. Joanne Gordon. (Illus.). 357p. 1992. reprint ed. pap. 16.95 (*0-306-80468-9*) Da Capo.

***Art-Istry for Children: Color.** Kate McSwain. 212p. (Orig.). (J). (gr. 1-6). 1992. pap. 29.95 (*1-878347-39-X*) NL Assocs.

Art Japanese Style. Charlene S. McCree. LC 92-62005. (Illus.). 64p. (Orig.). 1994. pap. 8.00 (*1-56002-239-6*, Univ Edtns) Aegina Pr.

Art-Journal Illustrated Catalogue see Crystal Palace Exhibition Illustrated Catalogue: London, 1851

Art Law, 2 vols., 1. Feldman. 1986. 165.00 (*0-316-09296-7*) Little.

Art Law, 2 vols., 2. Feldman. 1986. 165.00 (*0-316-09297-5*) Little.

Art Law: Representing Artists, Dealers & Collectors. Robert E. Duffy. LC 89-63038. 766p. 1989. text ed. 110. 00 (*0-87224-000-2*, G6-2005) PLI.

Art Law: Rights & Liabilities of Creators & Collectors. Franklin Feldman et al. 1401p. 1986. 160.00 (*0-316-09298-3*) Little.

Art Law: The Guide for Collectors, Investors, Dealers, & Artists - 1992. 2nd ed. Ralph E. Lerner & Judith Bresler. 478p. 1992. pap. 50.00 (*0-685-69381-3*) PLI.

Art Law, Domestic & International. Ed. by Leonard D. DuBoff. LC 75-7668. (Illus.). x, 627p. 1975. text ed. 27. 50 (*0-8377-0503-7*) Rothman.

Art Law in a Nutshell. 2nd ed. Leonard D. DuBoff. (Nutshell Ser.). 350p. 1992. pap. text ed. 17.00 (*0-314-01335-0*) West Pub.

Art Law Primer. Caryn Leland. 32p. 1981. pap. 5.00 (*0-933032-03-X*) Foun Commun Artists.

Art Law Primer. Linda F. Pinkerton & John T. Guardalabene. 224p. 1988. pap. 9.95 (*1-55821-002-4*) Lyons & Burford.

***Art Learning & Teaching: Glorifying God Through Art.** Janis Fogt. (Illus.). 88p. 1994. pap. 14.95 (*0-9644506-7-4*) Janis Fogt.

Art Lesson. Tomie De Paola. (Illus.). 32p. (J). (ps-3). 1989. 13.95 (*0-399-21688-X*, Putnam) Putnam Pub Group.

Art Lesson. Tomie DePaola. (Illus.). 32p. (J). (ps-3). 1994. pap. 5.95 (*0-399-22761-X*) Putnam Pub Group.

Art Lessons. Eleanor Schick. LC 86-243. (Illus.). 48p. (J). (gr. k-3). 1987. 11.75 (*0-688-05120-0*); lib. bdg. 11.88 (*0-688-05121-9*) Greenwillow.

***Art Lessons: The Rise & Fall of Public Arts Funding.** Alice G. Goldfarb. LC 94-40365. 1995. 25.00 (*0-465-00437-7*) Basic.

Art Lessons from Around the World. Alice Escobar. LC 82-7952. 224p. 1982. pap. 15.95 (*0-13-047399-5*, Busn) P-H.

Art Libraries & Information Services: Development, Organization, & Management. Lois S. Jones & Sarah S. Gibson. (Library & Information Science Ser.). 1986. text ed. 69.00 (*0-12-389170-1*) Acad Pr.

Art-Life of William Morris Hunt. Helen M. Knowlton. LC 75-173172. 1972. reprint ed. 18.95 (*0-405-08714-4*, Pub. by Blom Pubns UK) Ayer.

Art, Literature, Religion: Life on the Borders. Ed. by Robert Detweiler. LC 82-3319. (American Academy of Religion, Thematic Studies). 208p. (C). 1983. 34.95 (*0-89130-578-5*, 01 24 92) Scholars Pr GA.

***Art Lover: A Novel.** Carole Maso. LC 94-43655. 1995. write for info. (*0-88001-410-5*) Ecco Pr.

Art Lover's Book of Days. Comp. by Laurie Lebo & Lydia Staub. LC 86-62498. 176p. 1986. 12.95 (*0-87846-275-9*) Mus Fine Arts Boston.

Art Lovers Quotations. Ed. by Helen Exley. (Quotable Quotations Ser.). (Illus.). 60p. 1994. 6.99 (*1-85015-316-7*) Exley Giftbooks.

Art Made Tongue-Tied by Authority: Elizabethan & Jacobean Dramatic Censorship. John D. Clare. (Revels Plays Companion Library). 1990. text ed. 49.95 (*0-7190-2434-X*, Pub. by Manchester Univ Pr UK) St Martin.

Art-Makers: An Informal History of Painting, Sculpture & Architecture in 19th Century America. Russell Lynes. 1983. 18.25 (*0-8446-5930-4*) Peter Smith.

Art Makers: An Informal History of Painting, Sculpture, & Architecture in 19th Century America. Russell Lynes. (Illus.). xii, 514p. 1982. reprint ed. pap. 10.95 (*0-486-24239-0*) Dover.

Art Making & Education. Maurice Brown & Diana Korzenik. LC 92-35667. (Disciplines in Art Education Ser.). 240p. (C). 1993. 39.95 (*0-252-02007-3*); pap. 16.95 (*0-252-06312-0*) U of Ill Pr.

Art Marketing Handbook: Marketing Art in the Nineties. 6th rev. ed. Calvin J. Goodman. Ed. by Florence J. Goodman. (Illus.). 531p. 1991. 60.00 (*0-917232-26-7*) Gee Tee Bee.

Art Marketing Handbook for the Fine Artist. Constance Franklin-Smith. 192p. 1992. per. 24.95 (*0-940899-21-3*) ArtNetwork.

Art Marketing Sourcebook for the Fine Artist. Ed. by Constance Franklin-Smith. 336p. 1992. per. 21.95 (*0-940899-19-1*) ArtNetwork.

Art Materialized: Selections from the Fabric Workshop. Sarah McFadden & Carter Ratcliff. LC 81-84586. (Illus.). 60p. 1982. 10.00 (*0-916365-04-2*) Ind Curators.

Art Maxims in a Bronx Fedora. Barry McCallion. 1973. pap. 1.75 (*0-911856-06-4*) Abyss.

Art Meets Science & Spirituality. Ed. by Andreas Papadakis. (Academy Editions Ser.). (Illus.). 96p. (Orig.). 1991. pap. 21.95 (*0-312-06172-2*) St Martin.

Art Metal & Enameling. Leslie V. Hawkins. 234p. (J). (gr. 9-12). 1974. text ed. 17.60 (*0-02-662240-8*) Bennett IL.

Art Metalwork. John Nagle. LC 78-730845. 1977. student ed 9.00 (*0-8064-0233-4*, 508); audio 279.00 (*0-8064-0234-2*) Bergwall.

Art Metalwork see Metalwork for Craftsmen: A Step by Step Guide with 55 Projects

***Art Miami 95.** International Fine Art Expositions Staff. (Illus.). 348p. Date not set. write for info. (*1-886639-01-9*) Internat Fine Art.

Art, Mimesis & the Avant-Garde: Aspects of a Philosophy of Difference. Andrew Benjamin. (Illus.). 256p. 1991. 49.95 (*0-415-06047-8*, A5718); pap. 18.95 (*0-415-06627-1*, A6218) Routledge.

Art, Mind, & Brain: A Cognitive Approach to Creativity. Howard Gardner. LC 82-70846. 380p. 1984. pap. 20.00 (*0-465-00445-8*) Basic.

Art, Mind, & Education: Research from Project Zero. Ed. by Howard Gardner & D. N. Perkins. LC 88-29583. 183p. reprint ed. pap. 52.20 (*0-7837-5736-0*, 2045397) Bks Demand.

Art Moderne: Certains. Joris-Karl Huysmans. 448p. (FRE.). 1976. 17.95 (*0-7859-0033-0*, F88080) Fr & Eur.

Art, Modernity & Faith: Towards a Theology of Art. George Pattison. LC 90-48916. 208p. 1991. text ed. 45. 00 (*0-312-05707-5*) St Martin.

Art Monograms & Lettering. 20th ed. J. M. Bergling. LC 63-22577. 1964. 24.95 (*0-910222-02-9*) Gem City Coll.

Art Monumental roman en France: Coll. Art et Geoge. Aubart et al. 21.95 (*0-685-38374-1*) Fr & Eur.

***Art Museum: Sophie Calle, Louise Lawler, Richard Misrach, Diane Neumaiger, Richard Ross.** Trudy W. Stack. (Illus.). 64p. 1995. pap. 16.95 (*0-938262-26-2*) Ctr Creat Photog.

Art Museum of Georgia-TBLISI. Tamaz Sanikidze. 176p. 1985. 69.00 (*0-317-61215-8*, Pub. by Collets UK) Pro-Am Music.

Art Museums & Galleries in Missouri: An Annotated Illustrated Directory. 2nd enl. rev. ed. Ed. by Sharon K. Hanson. (Illus.). 144p. 1994. reprint ed. pap. 14.95 (*0-9610626-4-9*) Sheba Rev.

Art Museums of Louis I. Kahn. Patricia C. Loud. LC 89-51072. (Illus.). 304p. (Orig.). (C). 1989. text ed. 63.00 (*0-8223-0989-0*); pap. 32.00 (*0-8223-0998-X*) Duke.

Art Museums of the World, 2 vols., 1. Ed. by Virginia Jackson et al. LC 85-5578. 1696p. 1987. text ed. 125.00 (*0-313-25876-7*, COA/01) Greenwood.

Art Museums of the World, 2 vols., Set. Ed. by Virginia Jackson et al. LC 85-5578. 1696p. 1987. text ed. 195.00 (*0-313-21322-4*, COA/) Greenwood.

Art Museums of the World, 2 vols., Vol. 2. Ed. by Virginia Jackson et al. LC 85-5578. 1696p. 1987. text ed. 125.00 (*0-313-25877-5*, COA/02) Greenwood.

Art Music in the American Society: The Condition of Art Music in the Late Twentieth Century. Nicholas E. Tawa. LC 86-31486. 285p. 1987. 26.00 (*0-8108-1976-7*) Scarecrow.

Art Musical, 5 vols. Ed. by H. Robert Cohen. (Repertoire International de la Presse Musicale Ser.). (FRE.). 1988. 600.00 (*0-685-46005-3*) Univ Microfilms.

Art, Myth, & Culture. H. A. Shapiro. LC 81-82732. (Greek Vases from Southern Collections). (Illus.). 175p. 1981. pap. 15.95 (*0-89494-012-0*) New Orleans Mus Art.

Art, Myth, & Ritual: The Path to Political Authority in Ancient China. K. C. Chang. (Illus.). 160p. (C). 1983. 32.00 (*0-674-04807-5*) HUP.

Art, Myth & Ritual: The Path to Political Authority in Ancient China. K. C. Chang. 160p. 1988. reprint ed. pap. 11.50 (*0-674-04808-3*) HUP.

Art Nouveau. Alastair Duncan. LC 93-61372. (World of Art Ser.). (Illus.). 216p. 1994. pap. 14.95 (*0-500-20273-7*) Thames Hudson.

***Art Nouveau.** Constance M. Greiff. LC 95-15025. (Stylebks.). 1995. write for info. (*0-7892-0024-4*) Abbeville Pr.

Art Nouveau. Lara-Vinca Masini. (Illus.). 414p. 1991. 29.99 (*0-517-64175-5*) Random Hse Value.

Art Nouveau: An Annotated Bibliography. Richard Kempton. Incl. Vol. 1. Austria, Belgium & France. LC 77-3689. 1977. (*0-318-53291-3*); LC 77-3689. (Art & Architecture Bibliographies Ser.: No. 4). 1977. 39.95 (*0-912158-59-X*) Hennessey.

Art Nouveau: An Anthology. Edmund V. Gillon, Jr. (Illus.). (Orig.). 1969. pap. 4.95 (*0-486-22388-4*) Dover.

Art Nouveau: An Art of Transition from Individualism to Mass Society. Gabriele Sterner. Tr. by Frederick G. Peters & Diana S. Peters. (Pocket Art Ser.). (Illus.). 189p. 1982. pap. 6.95 (*0-8120-2105-3*) Barron.

Art Nouveau: Art & Design at the Turn of the Century. Ed. by Peter H. Selz & Mildred Constantine. LC 72-169315. (Museum of Modern Art Publications in Reprint). 1972. reprint ed. 36.95 (*0-405-01573-9*) Ayer.

Art Nouveau: Jugenstil Architecture in Europe. Ed. by Hans-Dieter Dyroff. 244p. 1989. lib. bdg. 37.50 (*3-598-10818-4*) K G Saur.

Art Nouveau Abstract Designs. Rebecca Mckillip. (International Design Library). (Illus.). 48p. (Orig.). 1983. pap. 5.95 (*0-88045-023-1*) Stemmer Hse.

Art Nouveau & Art Deco Bookbinding: French Masterpieces, 1880-1940. Alastair Duncan & Georges De Bartha. (Illus.). 200p. 1989. 67.50 (*0-685-25301-5*) Abrams.

Art Nouveau & Art Deco Jewelry. Lillian Baker. (Illus.). 176p. 1990. pap. 9.95 (*0-89145-158-7*) Collector Bks.

Art Nouveau & Early Art Deco Type & Design. Ed. by Theodore Menten. (Pictorial Archive Ser.). (Illus.). 96p. (Orig.). 1972. pap. 4.95 (*0-486-22825-8*) Dover.

An Asterisk (*) at the beginning of an entry indicates that the title is appearing in BIP for the first time.

Art Nouveau Animal Designs & Patterns: Sixty Plates in Full Color. M. P. Verneuil. LC 92-13000. (Pictorial Archive Ser.). 1992. pap. write for info. (*0-486-27218-4*) Dover.

Art Nouveau Architecture: Residential Masterpieces, 1892-1911. Junichi Shimomura. Ed. by Seiji Horibuchi. Tr. by Satoru Fujii. (Illus.). 188p. 1992. 34.95 (*0-929279-82-4*, Cadence Bks) Viz Commns Inc.

Art Nouveau Decorative Ironwork: One Hundred & Fifty Photographic Illustrations. Theodore Menten. (Illus.). 144p. 1981. pap. 7.95 (*0-486-23986-1*) Dover.

Art Nouveau Designs in Color. Alphonse M. Mucha et al. (Illus.). 90p. (Orig.). 1974. pap. 6.95 (*0-486-22885-1*) Dover.

Art Nouveau Display Alphabets: One Hundred Complete Fonts. Dan X. Solo. LC 76-18408. (Pictorial Archive Ser.). (Illus.). (Orig.). 1976. pap. 5.95 (*0-486-23386-3*) Dover.

Art Nouveau Domestic Metalwork in Pewter & Silver Plate from Wurtemberg Metal Fabriken 1906. (Illus.). 448p. 1989. reprint ed. 79.50 (*1-85149-066-3*) Antique Collect.

Art Nouveau Floral Ornament in Color. M. P. Verneuil et al. Ed. by Charles R. Fry. LC 76-29490. (Illus.). 48p. 1976. pap. 6.95 (*0-486-23409-6*) Dover.

Art Nouveau Floral Stencil Designs in Full Color. M. P. Verneuil. LC 92-32083. (Pictorial Archive Ser.). 1993. write for info. (*0-486-27440-3*) Dover.

Art Nouveau Floral Stickers & Seals. Ed Sibbett. 1985. pap. 3.50 (*0-486-24933-6*) Dover.

Art Nouveau Frames & Borders: 250 Copyright-Free Illustrations for Artists & Craftsmen. Ed. by Carol B. Grafton. (Pictorial Archive Ser.). (Illus.). 128p. 1983. pap. 6.95 (*0-486-24513-6*) Dover.

Art Nouveau Glass & Pottery. Thomas Piche. Ed. by Faith Meyer. (Illus.). 16p. (Orig.). 1982. pap. text ed. 4.00 (*0-932660-06-1*) U of NI Dept Art.

Art Nouveau in Fin-de-Siecle France: Politics, Psychology, & Style. Debora L. Silverman. (Studies on the History of Society & Culture: No. 7). 450p. 1989. 45.00 (*0-520-06322-8*) U CA Pr.

Art Nouveau in Fin-de-Siecle France: Politics, Psychology & Style. Debora L. Silverman. 1992. pap. 20.00 (*0-520-08088-2*) U CA Pr.

Art Nouveau in Hungary. J. Szabadi. (Illus.). 158p. (C). 1989. text ed. 300.00 (*0-685-40282-7*, Pub. by Collets) St Mut.

Art Nouveau in Munich. Ed. by Kathryn B. Hiesinger. LC 88-25265. (Illus.). 179p. (Orig.). 1988. pap. 12.95 (*0-87633-076-6*) Phila Mus Art.

Art Nouveau Jewelry & Fans. Gabriel Mourey et al. (Illus.). 150p. 1973. reprint ed. pap. 8.95 (*0-486-22961-0*) Dover.

Art Nouveau Lamps & Fixtures. 192p. 1989. 19.99 (*0-517-67883-7*) Random Hse Value.

Art Nouveau Motifs & Vignettes. Ed. by Carol B. Grafton. (Illus.). 48p. 1989. pap. 3.95 (*0-486-25936-6*) Dover.

Art Nouveau Posters & Graphics. Roger Sainton. (Illus.). 96p. 1984. pap. 9.95 (*0-312-05274-X*) St Martin.

Art Nouveau Stained Glass for Today. Bill Hillman. 38p. 1993. pap. 13.95 (*0-935133-41-0*) CKE Pubns.

Art Nouveau Stained Glass Pattern Book. Ed Sibbett, Jr. LC 77-87497. (Pictorial Archive Ser.). (Illus.). 1978. pap. 4.95 (*0-486-23577-7*) Dover.

Art Nouveau Style: In Jewelry, Metalwork, Glass, Ceramics, Textiles, Architecture & Furniture. Ed. by Roberta Waddell. LC 77-80034. (Illus.). (Orig.). 1977. pap. 12.95 (*0-486-23515-7*) Dover.

Art Nouveau Style Book of Alphonse Mucha. Alphonse M. Mucha. (Illus.). 80p. 1980. pap. 9.95 (*0-486-24044-4*) Dover.

Art Nouveau Tarot. Matt Myers. 24p. 1989. 14.00 (*0-88079-375-9*) US Games Syst.

Art Nouveau Typographic Ornaments. Dan X. Solo. (Pictorial Archive Ser.). (Illus.). 100p. (Orig.). 1982. pap. 4.95 (*0-486-24366-4*) Dover.

Art Nouveau Typographic Ornaments. Dan X. Solo. (Orig.). 1983. 12.75 (*0-8446-6010-8*) Peter Smith.

Art Observations. Charles B. Rogers. (Illus.). 64p. 1980. pap. 5.95 (*0-686-64396-8*) Rogers Hse Mus.

Art of a Changing Society: British Watercolors & Drawings, 1775-1900. Howard E. Wooden. LC 83-51132. (Illus.). 120p. 1983. pap. 10.00 (*0-939324-11-3*) Wichita Art Mus.

Art of a Vanished Race: The Mimbres Classic Black-on-White. Victor M. Giammattei & N. Greer Reichert. LC 75-28600. (Illus.). 96p. 1975. pap. 12.00 (*0-916280-00-4*) Dillon-Tyler Pubs.

Art of a Vanished Race: The Mimbres Classic Black-on-White. 3rd ed. Victor Giammattei & Nanci Reichert. LC 75-28600. (Illus.). 100p. 1993. pap. 11.95 (*0-944383-21-1*) High-Lonesome.

Art of Accompanying: Master Lessons from the Repertoire. Robert Spillman. 384p. (Orig.). 1985. spiral bd. 30.00 (*0-02-872380-5*) Schirmer Bks.

Art of Accompanying & Coaching. K. Adler. LC 79-147128. (Music Reprint Ser.). 260p. 1971. reprint ed. lib. bdg. 35.00 (*0-306-70360-2*); reprint ed. pap. 15.95 (*0-306-80027-6*) Da Capo.

Art of Achieving Quality. G. Frederick Bolling. 171p. 1995. 32.95 (*0-566-07462-1*, Pub. by Gower UK) Ashgate Pub Co.

Art of Achieving Success. John D. Hawkes. 128p. 1971. pap. 8.95 (*0-89036-008-1*) Hawkes Pub Inc.

Art of Acting. John Dolman. LC 79-109289. 313p. 1971. reprint ed. text ed. 59.75 (*0-8371-3832-9*, DOAA, Greenwood Pr) Greenwood.

Art of Acting: From Basic Exercises to Multi-Dimensional Performances. Carlton Colyer. Ed. by Arthur L. Zapel. LC 89-27928. 224p. (Orig.). (C). 1989. pap. text ed. 14.95 (*0-916260-62-3*, B171) Meriwether Pub.

Art of Adaptation: Fact & Fiction into Film. Linda Seger. 256p. 1992. pap. 14.95 (*0-8050-1626-0*, Owl) H Holt & Co.

Art of Administration. Kenneth E. Eble. LC 78-62572. (Jossey-Bass Series in Higher Education). 176p. reprint ed. pap. 50.20 (*0-7837-2525-6*, 2042684) Bks Demand.

Art of Administration: A Guide for Academic Administrators. Kenneth E. Eble. LC 78-62572. (Policy, Leadership & Administration Ser.). 176p. 1992. reprint ed. pap. 20.00 (*1-55542-436-8*) Jossey-Bass.

Art of Adoption. Linda C. Burgess. LC 77-55. 1977. 12.50 (*0-87491-066-8*) Acropolis.

Art of Adoption. Linda C. Burgess. 176p. 1981. pap. 6.95 (*0-393-00036-2*) Norton.

Art of Advice: How to Give It & How to Take It. Jeswald W. Salacuse. 1994. 18.00 (*0-8129-2102-X*, Times Bks) Random.

Art of Advocacy. Lloyd Stryker. LC 79-15312. reprint ed. 25.00 (*0-89201-043-6*) Zenger Pub.

Art of Advocacy: Demonstrative Evidence. Ashley S. Lipson. 1988. ring bd. write for info. (*0-8205-1082-3*) Bender.

Art of Advocacy: Jury Instruction. Baldwin et al. 1989. Looseleaf updates available. ring bd. write for info. (*0-8205-1029-7*) Bender.

Art of Advocacy: Jury Selection. E. W. Wagner, Jr. (Art of Advocacy Ser.). 1981. ring bd. write for info. (*0-8205-1040-8*) Bender.

Art of Aeschylus. Thomas G. Rosenmeyer. LC 81-1289. (Illus.). 393p. (C). 1982. pap. 14.00 (*0-520-04608-0*) U CA Pr.

Art of Aesthetic Plastic Surgery, 2 vols., Set. Lewis. 1989. 360.00 (*0-316-52344-5*) Little.

Art of Africa. Jacques Kerchache et al. LC 92-27689. (Illus.). 620p. 1993. 175.00 (*0-8109-0628-7*) Abrams.

Art of Aging. Evelyn Mandel. Ed. by Miriam Frost. Orig. Title: The Gray Matter. (Illus.). 176p. (Orig.). 1982. 14.95 (*0-86683-754-X*) Harper SF.

Art of Aging: A Celebration of Old Age in Western Art. Patrick McKee & Heta Kauppinen. (Illus.). 208p. 1986. 29.95 (*0-89885-304-4*) Human Sci Pr.

Art of AIDS: From Stigma to Conscience. Rob Baker. (Illus.). 252p. 1994. 12.95 (*0-8264-0653-X*) Continuum.

Art of Airbrushing. Maynard Clark. LC 90-63279. 54p. 1990. pap. 5.95 (*0-916809-46-3*) Scott Pubns MI.

***Art of Ajanta & Sopocani.** Om D. Upadhya. (Comparative Study, an Enquiry in Prana Aesthetics Ser.). (C). 1994. text ed. 72.00 (*81-208-0990-4*, Pub. by Motilal Banarsidass II) S Asia.

Art of Al Frueh. Thomas P. Bruhn. (Illus.). 16p. 1983. 2.00 (*0-918386-35-7*) W Benton Mus.

***Art of Alchemy, 4 vols., Set.** Adiramled, pseud. 1994. pap. 16.95 (*1-55818-310-8*, Pub. by Alchemical Pr) Holmes Pub.

Art of Alchemy, or The Generation of Gold, Pt. II, Lessons 4-6. Delmar Bryant. 1990. pap. 5.95 (*1-55818-170-9*) Holmes Pub.

Art of Alchemy, or The Generation of Gold, Pt. III, Lessons 7-9. Delmar Bryant. 1990. pap. 5.95 (*1-55818-171-7*) Holmes Pub.

Art of Alchemy, or The Generation of Gold, Pt. IV, Lessons 10-12. Delmar Bryant. 1990. pap. 5.95 (*1-55818-172-5*) Holmes Pub.

Art of Alchemy or the Generation of Gold: A Course of Practical Lessons in Metallic Transmutation for the Use of Occult Students Being a New Illumination Regarding the Secret Science of the Sages. Adiramled. 73p. 1993. pap. 12.95 (*1-56459-319-3*) Kessinger Pub.

Art of Alchemy, or The Generation of Gold, Pt. I, Lessons 1-3: A Course of Practical Lessons in Metallic Transmutation. Delmar Bryant. 1990. pap. 5.95 (*1-55818-169-5*) Holmes Pub.

Art of Alexander & John Cozens. Kim Sloan. LC 86-50738. 192p. 1987. text ed. 37.50 (*0-300-03826-7*) Yale U Pr.

Art of Alfred Hitchcock. Donald Spoto. (Illus.). 1992. pap. 18.00 (*0-385-41813-2*, Anchor NY) Doubleday.

Art of Algebra: Simplified Account Numbers, Equations Groups, Continued Fractions. R. North. LC 64-66139. 1965. 98.00 (*0-08-010694-3*, Pub. by Pergamon Repr UK) Franklin.

Art of All Nations, 1850-1873: The Emerging Role of Exhibitions & Critics, Vol. 2. Ed. by Elizabeth G. Holt. LC 81-47989. (Illus.). 684p. 1982. reprint ed. 75.00 (*0-691-03996-8*) Princeton U Pr.

Art of Allusion in Victorian Fiction. Michael Wheeler. LC 79-11861. 182p. 1979. text ed. 44.00 (*0-06-497587-8*, N6737) B&N Imports.

Art of Ama Ata Aidoo: Polylectics & Reading Against Neocolonialism. Vincent O. Odamtten. LC 93-35009. (Illus.). 216p. (C). 1994. lib. bdg. 32.95 (*0-8130-1276-7*); pap. 16.95 (*0-8130-1277-5*) U Press Fla.

***Art of American Automobile.** Nick Georgano. (Illus.). 268p. 1995. 24.98 (*0-8317-0677-5*) Smithmark.

Art of American Car Design: The Profession & Personalities. C. Edson Armi. LC 86-43251. (Illus.). 320p. 1988. 37.50 (*0-271-00479-7*) Pa St U Pr.

Art of American Indian Cooking. Yeffe Kimball & Jean Anderson. 224p. pap. 9.95 (*1-55821-004-0*) Lyons & Burford.

Art of Amusing. Frank Bellew. LC 74-15725. (Popular Culture in America Ser.). (Illus.). 328p. 1975. reprint ed. 28.95 (*0-405-06362-8*) Ayer.

Art of Ancestor Hunting in the Philippines. Luciano P. Santiago. 36p. (Orig.). 1991. pap. 8.50 (*971-10-0437-2*, Pub. by New Day Pub PH) Cellar.

Art of Ancient Greece: Sources & Documents. J. J. Pollitt. (Illus.). 296p. (C). 1990. pap. 24.95 (*0-521-27366-8*) Cambridge U Pr.

Art of Ancient Greece: Sources & Documents. J. J. Pollitt. (Illus.). 296p. (C). 1990. 74.95 (*0-521-25368-3*) Cambridge U Pr.

Art of Ancient India: Buddhist, Hindu, Jain. Susan L. Huntington & John C. Huntington. (Illus.). 852p. 1985. 80.00 (*0-8348-0183-3*) Weatherhill.

Art of Angling. Guiniad Charfy. LC 91-76499. 134p. 1992. 18.00 (*1-56541-201-X*) Chalidze.

Art of Animal Drawing: Construction, Action, Analysis, Caricature. Ken Hultgren. LC 92-33086. (Illus.). 144p. 1993. reprint ed. pap. 7.95 (*0-486-27426-8*) Dover.

***Art of Animated Image.** Charles Solomon. 1988. pap. 7.95 (*0-941710-24-6*) Packard.

Art of Annemieke Mein: Wildlife Artist in Textiles. Annemmieke Mein. (Illus.). 160p. 1995. 50.00 (*1-879504-03-0*, 403-0) A Schwartz & Co.

Art of Appreciation: A Cultural Awareness Perspective. Max R. Rennels. 160p. 1992. per. 24.95 (*0-8403-7078-4*) Kendall-Hunt.

Art of Arabian Costume: A Saudi Arabian Profile. Heather C. Ross. (Illus.). 188p. 1990. 65.00 (*0-907513-00-X*, Pub. by Arabesque Comm SZ) Empire Pub Srvs.

Art of Arabian Costume: A Saudi Arabian Profile. Heather C. Ross. LC 93-26337. 1993. 65.00 (*0-88734-640-5*) Players Pr.

Art of Arabian Costume: A Saudi Arabian Profile. Heather C. Ross. (Illus.). 188p. 1982. 50.00 (*0-7103-0031-X*, Pub. by Kegan Paul Intl UK) Routledge Chapman & Hall.

Art of Arbitration: Essays on International Arbitration Liber Amicorum. Pieter Sanders. Ed. by Jan C. Schultz et al. 344p. 1982. 75.00 (*90-6544-054-2*) Kluwer Law Tax Pubs.

Art of Archibald J. Motley, Jr. Wendy Greehouse & Jontyle Robinson. pap. 24.95 (*0-913820-15-6*) Chicago Hist.

Art of Architectural Illustration. 226p. 1994. 49.99 (*1-56496-074-9*) Rockport Pubs.

Art of Architecture, a Poem: In Imitation of Horace's Art of Poetry. Intro. by William A. Gibson. LC 92-22687. (Augustan Reprints Ser.: No. 144 (1970)). reprint ed. 12.00 (*0-404-70144-2*, PR3505.G94A89) AMS Pr.

Art of Argument. Carlos L. Hunsinger. LC 79-15660. 1981. 19.95 (*0-87949-154-X*) Ashley Bks.

Art of Argument. Giles St. Aubyn. LC 84-9739. (J). (gr. 9 up). 1960. 12.95 (*0-87523-133-0*) Emerson.

Art of Arnold Bennett. J. Hepburn. LC 72-6783. (Studies in Fiction: No. 34). 1972. reprint ed. lib. bdg. 75.00 (*0-8383-1667-0*) M S G Haskell Hse.

Art of Aromatherapy. 13th ed. R. B. Tisserand. 320p. pap. 20.95 (*0-8464-4213-2*) Beekman Pubs.

Art of Aromatherapy: The Beautifying & Healing Properties of the Essential Oils of Flowers & Herbs. Robert B. Tisserand. LC 77-20493. (Illus.). 336p. 1987. pap. 10.95 (*0-89281-001-7*, Destiny Bks) Inner Tradit.

Art of Arousal. Ruth Westheimer. LC 92-25989. 1993. 35.00 (*1-55859-330-6*) Abbeville Pr.

Art of Art for Children's Books. Diana Klemin. LC 82-80362. (Illus.). 128p. (C). 1982. reprint ed. pap. 16.95 (*0-9608042-0-X*) Murton Pr.

Art of Art Therapy. Judith A. Rubin. LC 84-9344. 224p. 1984. 33.95 (*0-87630-371-8*) Brunner-Mazel.

Art of Arthur Boyd. Ursula Hoff. (Illus.). 256p. 1986. 70.00 (*0-233-97824-0*, Pub. by A Deutsch UK) Trafalgar.

Art of Asking: How to Solicit Philanthropic Gifts. Paul H. Schneiter. LC 85-80786. (Illus.). 176p. 1985. 25.00 (*0-930807-00-6*, 600180) Fund Raising.

Art of Astronomical Navigation. S. M. Burton. (C). 1987. 45.00 (*0-85174-257-2*, Pub. by Brwn Son Ferg) St Mut.

Art of Asylum-Keeping: Thomas Story Kirkbride & the Origins of American Psychiatry. Nancy Tomes. LC 93-49742. (Studies in Health, Illness, & Caregiving). Orig. Title: A Generous Confidence. (Illus.). 424p. (Orig.). 1994. reprint ed. pap. text ed. 14.95 (*0-8122-1539-7*) U of Pa Pr.

Art of Attack. H. S. Cowper. (Illus.). 1977. reprint ed. 24.00 (*0-7158-1212-2*) Charles River Bks.

Art of Attack in Chess. V. Vukovic. 440p. 1965. 27.00 (*0-08-011197-1*, Pergamon Pr); pap. 19.90 (*0-08-011196-3*, Pergamon Pr) Elsevier.

Art of Attracting Women: Finding Exactly What You Want. Jonathan Yarnold. Ed. by Elletro Productions Staff. LC 93-83491. 120p. (Orig.). 1993. pap. 8.95 (*1-56875-041-2*, 041-2) R & E Pubs.

Art of Aubrey Beardsley. Catherine Slessor. 1989. 10.98 (*1-55521-449-5*) Bk Sales Inc.

Art of Authorial Presence: Hawthorne's Provincial Tales. G. R. Thompson. LC 92-33301. 334p. (C). 1993. lib. bdg. 49.95 (*0-8223-1306-5*); pap. text ed. 19.95 (*0-8223-1321-9*) Duke.

Art of Auto Fellatio. Gary Griffin. (Illus.). 96p. 1993. pap. 9.95 (*1-879967-11-1*) Added Dimensns.

***Art of Awakening Spirit.** Carol Kurtz-Walsh. 288p. (Orig.). 1994. pap. 14.95 (*0-9642967-0-5*) Spiritology Pubns.

Art of Bacchylides. Anne P. Burnett. (Martin Classical Lectures: No. 29). 224p. 1985. 25.00 (*0-674-04666-8*) HUP.

Art of Badi az-Zaman Al Hamadhani: As Picaresque Narrative. James T. Monroe. 175p. (Orig.). 1984. pap. text ed. 15.00 (*0-8156-6070-7*, Am U Beirut) Syracuse U Pr.

Art of Balcony Gardening. Yvonne Rees. (Illus.). 144p. 1991. 24.95 (*0-7063-6999-8*, Pub. by Ward Lock UK) Sterling.

Art of Ballroom Dancing. D. J. Fallon. (Ballroom Dance Ser.). 1986. lib. bdg. 79.95 (*0-8490-3322-5*) Gordon Pr.

Art of Ballroom Dancing. D. J. Fallon. (Ballroom Dance Ser.). 1985. lib. bdg. 69.00 (*0-87700-766-7*) Revisionist Pr.

Art of Barbie. Ed. by Craig Yoe & Ruth Sullivan. (Illus.). 128p. 1994. 30.00 (*1-56305-691-7*) Workman Pub.

***Art of Barbie.** Craig Yoe. 1994. pap. 19.95 (*1-56305-751-4*) Workman Pub.

Art of Bassoon Playing. rev. ed. William Spencer. Ed. by Frederick A. Mueller. (Illus.). 72p. 1969. pap. text ed. 11.95 (*0-87487-073-9*) Summy-Birchard.

Art of Batik. Margaret Hone. 1990. pap. 10.95 (*0-85532-619-0*, Pub. by Search Pr UK) A Schwartz & Co.

Art of Beauty - De Medicamine Faciei Femihae. limited ed. Ovid. (Illus.). 18p. 1990. 350.00 (*0-923980-28-8*) Arundel Pr.

Art of Bedouin Jewellery: A Saudi Arabian Profile. Heather C. Ross. (Illus.). 133p. 1990. 65.00 (*0-907513-01-8*, Pub. by Arabesque Comm SZ) Empire Pub Srvs.

Art of Bedouin Jewelry: A Saudi Arabian Profile. Heather C. Ross. LC 93-35828. 1994. 65.00 (*0-88734-641-3*) Players Pr.

Art of Being. Erich Fromm. LC 92-14010. 144p. 1992. 16.95 (*0-8264-0614-9*) Continuum.

Art of Being. rev. ed. Erich Fromm. 144p. (C). 1994. pap. text ed. 11.95 (*0-8264-0673-4*) Continuum.

***Art of Being a Catechist: Giving the Word to Children.** Michael Salamolard & Jean-Loys Ory. 207p. 1993. pap. 40.00 (*0-85439-467-2*, Pub. by St Paul Pubns UK) St Mut.

Art of Being an Executive. Louis B. Lundborg. 275p. 1981. 19.95 (*0-02-919300-1*) Free Pr.

Art of Being & Becoming. Hazrat I. Khan. 296p. 1990. pap. 15.00 (*0-930872-41-X*) Omega Pubns NY.

Art of Being Human. 4th ed. Richard P. Janaro. (C). 1993. student ed, pap. text ed. 15.00 (*0-06-501765-X*) HarpCollege.

Art of Being Human: The Humanities As a Technique for Living. 3rd ed. Richard P. Janaro & Thelma C. Altshuler. 575p. (C). 1990. pap. text ed. 30.00 (*0-06-043252-7*) HarpCollege.

Art of Being Human: The Humanities As a Technique for Living. 4th ed. Richard P. Janaro & Thelma C. Altshuler. LC 92-21354. (C). 1993. 48.00 (*0-06-500282-2*); teacher ed 10.00 (*0-06-500283-0*) HarpCollege.

Art of Being Ruled. Wyndham Lewis. LC 88-32776. (Illus.). 464p. (C). 1989. reprint ed. 25.00 (*0-87685-754-3*); reprint ed. pap. 15.00 (*0-87685-753-5*) Black Sparrow.

Art of Being Ruled. Wyndham Lewis. LC 72-39603. (English Literature Ser.: No. 33). 1972. reprint ed. lib. bdg. 75.00 (*0-8383-1376-0*) M S G Haskell Hse.

Art of Being Well Informed: What You Need to Know to Gain the Winning Edge in Business. Andrew P. Garvin. LC 93-20090. 192p. 1993. pap. 12.95 (*0-89529-576-8*) Avery Pub.

Art of Being Yourself. Frank E. Richelieu. LC 92-53722. 320p. (Orig.). 1992. pap. 12.95 (*0-917849-15-9*) Sci of Mind.

Art of Betting Horses & Winning Consistently. J. J. Clarkin. 32p. 1985. pap. 6.95 (*0-934650-08-X*) Sunnyside.

Art of Bev Doolittle. Illus. by Bev Doolittle. 1990. 60.00 (*0-553-07009-6*) Bantam.

Art of Biblical History. V. Philips Long. (Foundations of Contemporary Interpretation Ser.: Vol. 5). 160p. 1994. pap. 17.99 (*0-310-43180-8*) Zondervan.

Art of Biblical Narrative. Robert Alter. LC 80-68958. 208p. 1983. pap. text ed. 13.00 (*0-465-00427-X*) Basic.

Art of Biblical Poetry. Robert Alter. LC 85-47550. 228p. 1987. pap. 14.00 (*0-465-00431-8*) Basic.

Art of Bill Alexander & Buck Paulson, Series 15. Toby Willis-Camp. (Illus.). 92p. 1992. pap. text ed. write for info. (*1-883576-14-8*) Alexander Art.

Art of Bill Alexander & Buck Paulson, Series 16. Toby Willis-Camp. (Illus.). 92p. 1992. pap. text ed. write for info. (*1-883576-15-6*) Alexander Art.

Art of Bill Alexander & Robert Warren, Series 7. Patricia Perrault-Mattison. (Illus.). 84p. 1989. pap. text ed. write for info. (*1-883576-06-7*) Alexander Art.

Art of Bill Alexander & Robert Warren, Series 8. Patricia Perrault-Mattison. (Illus.). 84p. 1989. pap. text ed. write for info. (*1-883576-07-5*) Alexander Art.

Art of Bill Alexander & Robert Warren, Series 9. Patricia Perrault-Mattison. (Illus.). 78p. 1990. pap. text ed. write for info. (*1-883576-08-3*) Alexander Art.

Art of Bill Alexander & Robert Warren, Series 10. John Hartman. (Illus.). 80p. 1990. pap. text ed. write for info. (*1-883576-09-1*) Alexander Art.

Art of Bill Alexander & Robert Warren, Series 11. John Hartman. (Illus.). 92p. 1990. pap. text ed. write for info. (*1-883576-10-5*) Alexander Art.

Art of Bill Alexander & Robert Warren, Series 12. John Hartman. (Illus.). 90p. 1991. pap. text ed. write for info. (*1-883576-11-3*) Alexander Art.

Art of Bill Alexander & Robert Warren, Series 13. Toby Willis-Camp. (Illus.). 88p. 1991. pap. text ed. write for info. (*1-883576-12-1*) Alexander Art.

Art of Bill Alexander & Sharon Perkins, Series 14. Toby Willis-Camp. (Illus.). 84p. 1991. pap. text ed. write for info. (*1-883576-13-X*) Alexander Art.

Art of Billing & Collecting. 2nd ed. Sally Bozich & Suzanne Rian. (Illus.). 140p. 1988. spiral bd. 39.95 (*0-962419-1-1*) S & S Kenmore.

Art of Biography. Paul M. Kendall & Stephen B. Oates. LC 83-49162. 1985. reprint ed. pap. 4.95 (*0-393-00411-2*) Norton.

Art of Birds. Pablo Neruda. Tr. by Jack Schmitt. LC 84-7585. (Texas Pan American Ser.). (Illus.). 87p. 1985. reprint ed. 19.95 (*0-292-70371-6*) U of Tex Pr.

Art of Black American Women: Works of Twenty-Four Artists of the Twentieth Century. Robert Henkes. LC 92-50955. 271p. 1993. lib. bdg. 35.00 (*0-89950-818-9*) McFarland & Co.

Art of Black & White Photography. John Garrett. (Illus.). 160p. 1990. pap. 22.50 (*0-8174-3534-4*, Amphoto) Watsn-Guptill.

An Asterisk (*) at the beginning of an entry indicates that the title is appearing in BIP for the first time.

445

*Art of Blacksmithing. Bealer. 1995. (0-7858-0395-5) Bk Sales Inc.

Art of Bonsai. Peter D. Adams. (Illus.). 224p. 1992. pap. 17.95 (0-7063-7116-X, Pub. by Ward Lock UK) Sterling.

Art of Bookbinding, Its Rise & Progress. Edward Walker. Ed. by Paul Koda. LC 84-5242. (History of the Book Ser.). 111p. 1984. reprint ed. text ed. 30.00 (0-938768-07-7) Oak Knoll.

Art of Botanical Illustration. Wilfrid Blunt. (Illus.). 320p. 1994. 59.50 (1-85149-177-5) Antique Collect.

Art of Botanical Illustration: An Illustrated History. unabridged ed. Wilfred Blunt. (Illus.). 372p. 1993. reprint ed. pap. 14.95 (0-486-27265-6) Dover.

Art of Botanical Illustrations. Martyn Rix. 1990. 85.00 (0-685-33410-4); pap. 29.99 (0-517-69628-2) Random Hse Value.

Art of Bowing: Fifty Variations on a Gavotte by Corelli for Unaccompanied Violin. Giuseppe Tartini. Ed. by Edith Winn. (Carl Fischer Music Library: No. 398). (Illus.). 1905. pap. 7.50 (0-8258-0068-4) Fischer Inc NY.

Art of Brachygraphie: That Is, to Write As Fast As a Man Speaketh Treatably, Writing but One Letter for a Word. Peter Bales. LC 70-38146. (English Experience Ser.: No. 426). 120p. 1972. reprint ed. 20.00 (90-221-0426-5) Walter J Johnson.

Art of Brazilian Cookery. Dolores Botafogo. (International Cookbook Classics Ser.). 240p. 1993. pap. 9.95 (0-7818-0130-3) Hippocrene Bks.

Art of Breathing. Leo Kofler. 1991. lib. bdg. 79.95 (0-87700-932-5) Revisionist Pr.

*Art of Breathing: A Course of Six Simple Lessons to Improve Performance. 2nd ed. Nancy Zi. LC 94-60023. 159p. 1994. pap., vhs 39.95 (1-884872-64-6) ViVi CA.

*Art of Breathing: A Course of Six Simple Lessons to Improve Performance & Well Being. 2nd ed. Nancy Zi. LC 94-60023. 1994. pap. 9.95 (1-884872-62-X) ViVi CA.

Art of Brian Friel: Neither Dreams Nor Reality. Elmer Andrews. LC 93-39876. 1994. write for info. (0-312-12046-X) St Martin.

Art of Bridge Building. Wesley Nelson. 1989. pap. 3.95 (0-910452-69-5) Covenant.

Art of Buck Paulson, Series 1. Patricia Perrault-Mattison. (Illus.). 96p. 1989. pap. text ed. write for info. (1-883576-16-4) Alexander Art.

Art of Buck Paulson, Series 2. Patricia Perrault-Mattison. (Illus.). 88p. 1990. pap. text ed. write for info. (1-883576-17-2) Alexander Art.

Art of Building Cities: City Building According to Its Artistic Fundamentals. Camillo Sitte. Tr. by Charles T. Stwart. LC 78-14144. (Illus.). 1992. reprint ed. 29.50 (0-88355-817-3) Hyperion Conn.

Art of Business Credit Investigation, Vol. I: When Red Flags Appear & "It Just Doesn't Feel Right" I N V E S T I G A T E. Peggy E. Mound. 152p. (Orig.). 1990. pap. 26.95 (0-9627792-6-1) Advanced Verification.

Art of Business Negotiation. Harvard Business Review Staff. (Help for the General Manager Ser.). 93p. 1991. pap. 19.95 (0-87584-288-7) Harvard Busn.

Art of Business Negotiation. Harvard Business School Press Staff. 1991. pap. text ed. 19.95 (0-07-103348-3) McGraw.

Art of Business Programming. Shimon Schocken. 1992. text ed. write for info. (0-07-056919-3) McGraw.

Art of Byzantium. V. Likhacheva. 310p. (RUS.). 1981. 24.00 (0-317-57213-X, Pub. by Collets UK) St Mut.

Art of C: Elegant Programming Solutions. Herbert Schildt. 412p. 1991. 5.25 hd, pap. text ed. 39.95 (0-07-881691-2) Osborne-McGraw.

*Art of Calligraphy. David Harris. LC 94-26722. (Illus.). 128p. 1995. 24.95 (1-56458-849-1) Dorling Kindersley.

Art of Calligraphy: Joining Heaven & Earth. Chogyam Trungpa. Ed. by Judith L. Lief. LC 94-6361. 1994. 50.00 (0-87773-591-3) Shambhala Pubns.

Art of Cameroon. 2nd ed. Tamara Northern. LC 83-20306. (Illus.). 208p. 1984. pap. 19.95 (0-86528-026-6, NOACP) SITES.

Art of Captain Cook's Voyages, 2 vols., Vol. 2. Rudiger Joppien & Bernard Smith. LC 84-52812. (Illus.). 274p. 1985. 75.00 (0-300-03451-2) Yale U Pr.

Art of Captain Cook's Voyages: The Voyage of the Resolution & the Discovery 1776-1780, Vol. III. Rudiger Joppien & Bernard Smith. LC 87-21947. 300p. (C). 1988. text ed. 225.00 (0-300-04105-5) Yale U Pr.

Art of Card Reading at Bridge. Fred L. Karpin. (Bridge & Other Card Game Ser.). 232p. 1982. reprint ed. pap. 5.95 (0-486-21787-6) Dover.

Art of Caricature. Dick Gautier. LC 85-9462. (Illus.). (Orig.). 1985. pap. 11.00 (0-399-51132-6, Perigree Bks) Berkley Pub.

Art of Cartooning. Jack Markow. (Illus.). 80p. 1990. pap. 9.00 (0-399-51626-3, Perigree Bks) Berkley Pub.

Art of Case Analysis: A Guide to the Diagnosis of Business Situations. 3rd ed. Robert Ronstadt. 1994. pap. 9.95 (0-685-69348-1) Lord Pub.

*Art of Case Study Research: Perspectives on Practice. Robert E. Stake. 208p. 1995. text ed. 39.95 (0-8039-5766-1); pap. text ed. 17.95 (0-8039-5767-X) Sage.

Art of Catching & Cooking Crabs. Lynette Walther. (Illus.). 96p. 1985. pap. 7.95 (0-911145-07-9) Liberty Pub.

Art of Catching & Cooking Crabs. Lynette L. Walthers. Ed. by Robert H. Robinson. LC 83-61595. (Illus.). 100p. 1983. pap. 5.95 (0-911145-05-2) Sussex Prints.

Art of Catching & Cooking Shrimp. Lynette L. Walther. (Illus.). 124p. 1986. pap. 7.95 (0-911145-08-7) Liberty Pub.

Art of Catching & Cooking Shrimp. Lynette L. Walther. 120p. 1986. pap. 5.95 (0-685-17370-4) Sussex Prints.

Art of Celebration. Alfred Appel, Jr. LC 92-53167. 1992. 37.50 (0-679-40007-9) Knopf.

Art of Celebration. Ed. by Rachel Reeder. (Liturgy Ser.). 96p. (Orig.). 1990. pap. 10.95 (0-918208-50-5) Liturgical Conf.

Art of Cello Playing. Louis Potter, Jr. (Illus.). 236p. (Orig.). (C). 1980. pap. text ed. 24.95 (0-87487-071-2) Summy-Birchard.

Art of Cello Teaching. Gordon Epperson. 8.00 (0-318-18105-3) Am String Tchrs.

*Art of Celtia. Courtney Davis. (Illus.). 128p. 1995. pap. 14.95 (0-7137-2307-6, Pub. by Blandford Pr UK) Sterling.

Art of Central Africa: Masterpieces from the Berlin Ethnographic Museum. Hans-Joachim Koloss. (Illus.). 96p. 1990. pap. 19.95 (0-8109-2462-5) Abrams.

Art of Central Africa: Masterpieces from the Berlin Ethnographic Museum. Hans-Joachim Koloss. (Illus.). 88p. 1990. 5.95 (0-87099-590-1, Abrams) Metro Mus Art.

Art of Central Banking. 2nd ed. Ralph G. Hawtrey. 484p. 1970. reprint ed. 35.00 (0-7146-1227-8, Pub. by F Cass Pubs UK) Intl Spec Bk.

Art of Cezanne. Kurt Badt. LC 84-82410. (Illus.). 346p. 1985. reprint ed. lib. bdg. 50.00 (0-87817-302-1) Hacker.

Art of Change: Strategic Therapy & Hypnotherapy Without Trance. Georgio Nardone & Paul Watzlawick. Tr. by Sally Davis & Michael Wyatt. LC 92-32436. (Social & Behavioral Science Ser.). 164p. 1993. 30.95 (1-55542-499-6) Jossey-Bass.

Art of Chaperoning Student Group Travel. Nancy M. Childress & Martha M. Cofer. LC 92-27159. 160p. 1993. pap. 14.95 (0-935834-92-3) Rainbow Books.

Art of Charcuterie. Jane Grigson. 384p. (Orig.). (C). 1991. pap. 14.95 (0-88001-272-2) Ecco Pr.

Art of Charles Partridge Adams. Dorothy Dines et al. LC 93-22386. (Illus.). 154p. 1993. 37.95 (1-55591-163-3) Fulcrum Pub.

Art of Charles Prendergast from the Collections of the Williams College Museum of Art & Mrs. Charles Prendergast. Nancy M. Mathews. LC 93-22826. (Exhibit Catalog Ser.). (Illus.). 120p. (Orig.). 1993. pap. 25.00 (0-913697-16-8) Williams Art.

Art of Chart Interpretation: A Step-by-Step Method of Analyzing, Synthesizing & Understanding the Birth Chart. Tracy Marks. LC 86-9683. 180p. (Orig.). 1986. pap. 9.95 (0-916360-29-6) CRCS Pubns CA.

Art of Chart Synthesis. Tracy Marks. LC 78-68664. 1979. pap. 6.00 (0-933620-03-9) Sag Rising.

Art of Cheese Cookery. rev. ed. Nika S. Hazelton. (Cookery Ser.). 1978. reprint ed. pap. 9.95 (0-89496-003-2) Ross Bks.

Art of Chemical Process Design. G. L. Wells & L. M. Rose. (Computer Aided Chemical Engineering Ser.: No. 2). 1986. 118.00 (0-444-42699-X) Elsevier.

Art of Chess. 3rd ed. James Mason. Ed. by Fred Reinfeld & Sidney Bernstein. pap. 6.95 (0-486-20463-4) Dover.

Art of Chess Combination: A Guide for All Players of the Game. Eugene Znosko-Borovsky. Tr. by Philip W. Sergeant. (Illus.). 1936. pap. 5.95 (0-486-20583-5) Dover.

Art of Chi Kung: Making the Most of Your Vital Energy. Wong K. Kit. 1993. pap. 18.95 (1-85230-403-0) Element MA.

*Art of Children's Picture Books: A Selective Reference Guide. 2nd ed. Sylvia S. Marantz & Kenneth A. Marantz. LC 94-16308. (Garland Reference Library of the Humanities Ser.). 320p. 1994. 38.00 (0-8153-0937-6, H1636) Garland.

Art of Chinese Gardens. Chung Wah-nan. (Illus.). 268p. 1982. 57.50 (962-209-059-1, Pub. by Hong Kong Univ Pr HK) Coronet Bks.

Art of Chinese Miniature Landscape. H. Yunhua. (Illus.). 162p. (C). 1989. text ed. 495.00 (0-685-40286-X, Pub. by Collets) St Mut.

Art of Chinese Poetry. James J. Liu. LC 62-7475. xii, 164p. 1966. pap. text ed. 10.95 (0-226-48687-7) U Ch Pr.

Art of Christian Listening. Thomas N. Hart. LC 80-82810. 132p. (Orig.). 1981. pap. 6.95 (0-8091-2345-2) Paulist Pr.

Art of Christian Riese Lassen. 1993. pap. 21.95 (1-55912-376-1) CEDCO Pub.

*Art of Christmas Crafts. Milly MacLeod. 1994. 15.99 (0-517-12088-7) Random Hse Value.

Art of Cinema. Jean Cocteau. Tr. by Robin Buss. (Illus.). 240p. 1992. 35.00 (0-7145-2947-8) M Boyars Pubs.

Art of Cinema. Jean Cocteau. Tr. by Robin Buss. (Illus.). 240p. 1993. pap. 17.95 (0-7145-2974-5) M Boyars Pubs.

Art of Cinema: Selected Essays. George Amberg et al. LC 75-124020. (Arno Press Cinema Program Ser.). (Illus.). 106p. 1975. reprint ed. 15.95 (0-405-03924-7) Ayer.

Art of Clarinet Playing. Keith Stein. (Illus.). 80p. 1958. pap. text ed. 12.95 (0-87487-023-2) Summy-Birchard.

Art of Classical Guitar Playing. Charles Duncan. (Art of Ser.). (Illus.). 132p. (Orig.). 1980. pap. text ed. 19.95 (0-87487-079-8) Summy-Birchard.

Art of Classroom Inquiry: A Handbook for Teacher Researchers. Ruth S. Hubbard & Brenda M. Power. LC 92-27603. 184p. 1993. pap. text ed. 17.50 (0-435-08762-2, 08762) Heinemann.

Art of Claud Lovat Fraser. Clive E. Driver. LC 72-179649. (Illus.). 78p. 1971. pap. 6.30 (0-939084-01-5) R Mus & Lib.

Art of Clay: Timeless Pottery of the Southwest. Intro. by Lee Cohen & Roger Kenedy. LC 91-58828. (Illus.). 144p. 1993. 34.95 (0-940666-19-7) Clear Light.

*Art of Clifford Possum Tjapaltjarri. (Illus.). 180p. (C). 1994. text ed. 195.00 (0-7605-0482-2) Rector Pr.

Art of Closing Any Deal: How to Be a "Master Closer" in Everything You Do. James W. Pickens. LC 89-32619. 1989. 18.95 (0-944007-40-6) Sure Sellers.

Art of Closing Any Deal: How to Be a Master Closer in Everything You Do. James W. Pickens. 1991. pap. 12.99 (0-446-39098-4) Warner Bks.

Art of Co-Therapy: How Therapists Work Together. William Roller & Vivian Nelson. LC 90-44744. 256p. 1991. lib. bdg. 33.50 (0-89862-557-2) Guilford Pr.

Art of Coaching Track & Field. Ken Brauman. LC 85-29784. 206p. 1986. text ed. 21.95 (0-13-046640-9, Parker Publishing Co) P-H.

Art of Coalition Building: A Guide for Community Leaders. Cherie R. Brown. LC 84-70911. 56p. 1984. pap. 3.50 (0-87495-053-8) Am Jewish Comm.

Art of Coarse Acting. rev. ed. Michael Green. LC 87-17039. (Illus.). 128p. (Orig.). 1988. reprint ed. pap. 10.95 (0-87910-111-3) Limelight Edns.

Art of Coins & Their Photography. J. Hoberman. (Illus.). 1982. lib. bdg. 85.00 (0-686-43399-8) S J Durst.

Art of Collage. Gerald F. Brommer. LC 77-92192. (Illus.). 176p. 1978. 23.00 (0-87192-096-4) Davis Mass.

Art of Collecting African Art. Robert Nooter & Nancy Nooter. Ed. by Susan M. Vogel. LC 88-7253. (Illus.). 64p. (Orig.). (C). 1988. pap. text ed. 14.50 (0-9614587-9-8) Museum African.

Art of Color. Johannes Itten. (Illus.). 156p. 1973. text ed. 79.95 (0-442-24037-6) Van Nos Reinhold.

*Art of Combination. Maxim V. Blokh. (Illus.). 171p. (Orig.). 1994. pap. 15.95 (1-879479-18-4) ICE WA.

Art of Communicating: Achieving Interpersonal Impact on Business. Bert Decker. Ed. by Michael G. Crisp. LC 87-73186. (Fifty-Minute Ser.). 80p. (Orig.). 1988. pap. 9.95 (0-931961-45-9) Crisp Pubns.

Art of Communicating Ideas. William Grace & Joan Grace. 1952. 10.00 (0-8159-5014-4) Devin.

*Art of Communication. 68p. (CHI.). 1987. pap. 4.50 (1-56582-103-3) Christ Renew Min.

Art of Community. Spencer H. MacCallum. LC 78-112866. 118p. 1970. 10.00 (0-317-06383-9) Heather Foun.

Art of Compiler Design: Theory & Practice. Thomas Pittman & James Peters. 368p. 1991. text ed. 60.00 (0-13-048190-4) P-H.

Art of Composition, Vol. 1. S. N. Rizvi et al. 202p. 1990. pap. 30.00 (81-209-0772-8, Pub. by Pitambar Pub II) St Mut.

Art of Comprehension, Vol. 2. S. N. Rizvi et al. 122p. 1990. pap. 30.00 (81-209-0767-1, Pub. by Pitambar Pub II) St Mut.

Art of Computer Conversation. Brian R. Gaines & Mildred L. Shaw. (Illus.). 224p. 25.95 (0-13-047332-4) P-H.

Art of Computer Designing. Osamu Sato. (Illus.). 128p. 1993. pap. 36.95 (4-7661-0736-5, Pub. by Graphic Sha JA) Bks Nippan.

Art of Computer Graphics. Peter R. Sorensen. (Illus.). 192p. 1993. 49.95 (0-8306-4062-2, 4197, Windcrest) TAB Bks.

Art of Computer Programming: Semi-Numerical Algorithms, Vol. 2. 2nd ed. Donald E. Knuth. (C). 1981. text ed. 50.50 (0-201-03822-6) Addison-Wesley.

Art of Computer Programming, Vol. 1: Fundamental Algorithms. 2nd ed. Donald E. Knuth. LC 73-1830. 640p. (C). 1973. text ed. 50.50 (0-201-03809-9) Addison-Wesley.

Art of Computer Programming, Vol. 3: Sorting & Searching. Donald E. Knuth. (C). 1973. text ed. 50.50 (0-201-03803-X) Addison-Wesley.

Art of Computer Systems Performance Analysis: Techniques for Experimental Design, Measurement, Simulation & Modeling. Raj Jain. 1991. text ed. 64.95 (0-471-50336-3) Wiley.

Art of Condolence: What to Write, What to Say, What to Do at a Time of Loss. Leonard M. Zunin & Hilary S. Zunin. LC 90-55945. 288p. 1992. reprint ed. pap. 12.00 (0-06-092166-8, PL) HarpC.

Art of Conducting. 2nd ed. Donald Hunsberger & Roy Ernst. 384p. (C). 1991. pap. text ed. write for info. (0-07-031326-1) McGraw.

Art of Conducting. Michael Bowles. LC 74-23419. (Music Ser.). 210p. 1975. reprint ed. lib. bdg. 29.50 (0-306-70718-7) Da Capo.

Art of Confident Public Speaking. Grant G. Gard. LC 85-16980. 228p. 1986. text ed. 21.95 (0-13-046897-5, Busn) P-H.

Art of Conflict Prevention: Theory & Practice. Ed. by Werner Bauwens & Luc Reychler. (Brassey's Atlantic Commentaries Ser.). 232p. (Orig.). 1994. 21.00 (1-85753-105-1) Macmillan.

Art of Construction: Projects & Principles for Beginning Engineers & Architects. 3rd ed. Mario Salvadori. LC 89-49406. (Illus.). 144p. (J). (gr. 5 up). 1990. pap. 9.95 (1-55652-080-8) Chicago Review.

Art of Contemplation. Ramon Lull, pseud. Tr. by Allison Peers. 1976. lib. bdg. 250.00 (0-8490-1451-4) Gordon Pr.

Art of Contemporary English Culture. George H. Gilpin, Jr. LC 90-8369. 250p. 1991. text ed. 45.00 (0-312-04496-8) St Martin.

Art of Contemporary Travis Picking: How to Play the Alternating-Bass Fingerpicking Style. Mark D. Hanson. LC 85-82658. (Illus.). 64p. (Orig.). 1986. audio, pap. 18.95 (0-936799-00-5); audio (0-318-60428-0) Accent Music.

Art of Continental Knitting. Fray Metcalfe & Maria Long. (Illus.). 69p. (Orig.). 1986. pap. text ed. 9.95 (0-318-22298-1) Merriway Co.

Art of Contrary Thinking. 4th ed. Humphrey B. Neill. LC 54-7837. 1963. pap. 7.95 (0-87004-110-X) Caxton.

Art of Conversation. Peter Burke. LC 93-10831. 178p. 1993. 39.95 (0-8014-2956-0); pap. 13.95 (0-8014-8167-8) Cornell U Pr.

Art of Conversation. Morris. 1986. pap. 7.95 (0-671-63275-2) S&S Trade.

Art of Conversation: The Magic Key to Personal & Social Popularity. James A. Morris, Jr. 1976. 19.95 (0-13-046698-0) P-H.

Art of Conveyancing & Pleading. Murli Manohar. 290p. 1974. 45.00 (0-317-54573-6) St Mut.

Art of Conveyancing & Pleading. Murli Manohar. (C). 1990. 35.00 (0-685-39760-2) St Mut.

Art of Conveyancing & Pleadings. Ed. by Murli Manohar. (C). 1989. reprint ed. 65.00 (0-685-37458-0) St Mut.

*Art of Cookery in the Middle Ages. Terrence Scully. 256p. 1995. text ed. 45.00 (0-85115-611-8) Boydell & Brewer.

Art of Cookery Made Plain & Easy. Hannah Glasse. 472p. 1994. reprint ed. 25.00 (0-9633659-2-4) US Hist Res Srv.

Art of Cooking, Vol. I. Jacques Pepin. 1993. 35.00 (0-8446-6718-8) Peter Smith.

Art of Cooking, Vol. II. Jacques Pepin. 1993. 35.00 (0-8446-6719-6) Peter Smith.

Art of Cooking for the Diabetic. Mary A. Hess & Katharine Middleton. 512p. 1979. pap. 5.99 (0-451-16118-1, Sig) NAL-Dutton.

Art of Cooking for the Diabetic. Mary A. Hess & Katharine Middleton. 528p. 1993. pap. 5.99 (0-451-17574-3, Sig) NAL-Dutton.

Art of Cooking for the Diabetic. Katharine Middleton & Mary A. Hess. LC 77-23701. 384p. 1979. 15.95 (0-685-01188-7); pap. 11.95 (0-8092-7222-9) Contemp Bks.

Art of Cooking for the Diabetic. rev. ed. Mary A. Hess & Katherine Middlleton. 448p. 1988. pap. 14.95 (0-8092-4653-8) Contemp Bks.

Art of Cooking with Certified Angus Beef. Anne Byrn. Ed. by Franz Mitterer. LC 89-61562. (Illus.). 80p. 1989. write for info. (0-9623729-0-0) Culinaire.

Art of Cooking with Quinoa: A Complete Vegetable Protein. Maria B. Kijac. 52p. 1991. pap. 7.95 (0-9633303-0-6) PM Pub IL.

Art of Cook's Voyages, 2 vols., II. Bernard Smith & Rudiger Joppien. (Illus.). 1984. 98.00 (0-19-554456-0) OUP.

*Art of Coping. Frederica R. Halligan. 192p. (Orig.). 1995. pap. 15.95 (0-8245-1487-4) Crossroad NY.

Art of Coppersmithing: A Practical Treatise on Working Sheet Copper into All Forms. John Fuller, Sr. (Illus.). 352p. 1993. reprint ed. pap. 25.00 (1-879335-37-9) Astragal Pr.

Art of Counseling. rev. ed. Rollo May. LC 88-30155. 1990. text ed. 23.95 (0-89876-156-5) Gardner Pr.

Art of Counterpoint. Charles H. Kitson. LC 75-4973. (Music Reprint Ser.). 344p. 1975. reprint ed. lib. bdg. 42.50 (0-306-70668-7) Da Capo.

Art of Counterpoint. Gioseffo Zarlino. Tr. by Guy A. Marco & Claude V. Palisca. LC 82-14900. (Music Reprint Ser.). (Illus.). xxvi, 294p. (C). 1983. reprint ed. lib. bdg. 35.00 (0-306-76206-4) Da Capo.

Art of Counterpoint: Le Istitutioni Harmoniche, 1558, Pt. 3. Gioseffo Zarlino. Tr. by Guy A. Marco & Claude V. Palisca. LC 68-13923. (Music Theory Translation Ser.). (Illus.). 322p. reprint ed. pap. 91.80 (0-8357-8029-5, 2033933) Bks Demand.

Art of Courtly Dancing in the Early Renaissance. Ingrid Brainard. LC 91-58192. (Studies in the Renaissance: No. 33). 1993. write for info. (0-404-62333-6) AMS Pr.

Art of Courtly Love. Andreas Capellanus. 192p. 1990. pap. text ed. 13.00 (0-231-07305-4) Col U Pr.

Art of Courtship. 1991. lib. bdg. 75.00 (0-8490-4186-4) Gordon Pr.

Art of Crafting Potpourri: A Book about Making Potpourri. Elizabeth Johnson & Bob Johnson. 32p. 1991. pap. 8.95 (0-9631353-0-9) Cameron Pk Bot.

Art of Craftsmanship. Philip Trupp. (Illus.). 72p. 1976. pap. 3.50 (0-87491-043-9) Acropolis.

*Art of Creating Collectors. Zella Jackson. 128p. 1994. pap. 49.95 (0-913069-49-3) Consultant Pr.

Art of Creating Monotypes. John S. Fredericks. Ed. by Beverly Fredericks. (Illus.). 135p. (C). 1991. vhs 89.00 (1-878988-10-7) HR Prodns.

Art of Creating Monotypes. John S. Fredericks. Ed. by Beverly Fredericks. (Illus.). 135p. (C). 1991. 30.00 (1-878988-08-5) HR Prodns. Elliot Rating..."One of the ten best teachers on tape."--ARTIST'S MAG. The work is a comprehensive procedural text discussing methods & techniques for creating monotypes, as well as a valuable reference tool. Includes a chronological sketch that involves artists & their methods throughout the monotype's brief 400-year history. A 120-minute video with four contemporary American artists - Beverly Fredericks, Martin Green, Florence Putterman, & Karen Vernon - demonstrating their techniques is available as a text/video set by the same title. "Technical questions, terminology, techniques, recipes, subsidiary information dealing with health hazards, archival integrity, documentation, & details concerning each of the four artists' methods are found in the...textbook. Because the book is available for...reference, the viewer can simply sit back & enjoy the video, absorbing the experience of watching artists at work without having to memorize what is being said...a lastingly useful teaching tool for artists, teachers, workshops, & therapists in

An Asterisk (*) at the beginning of an entry indicates that the title is appearing in BIP for the first time.

search of a painterly, creative method for making monotypes. It is unusual to find in any single class, workshop, or studio, as many inventive techniques as there are in this videotape & book."-- Mary Carroll Nelson, Contributing Editor, AMERICAN ARTIST. To order contact: HR Productions, (310) 670-7566. ***Publisher Provided Annotation.***

Art of Creative Critical Thinking. John C. Kim. 396p. (C). 1993. lib. bdg. 49.50 (*0-8191-8847-6*); pap. text ed. 27. 50 (*0-8191-8848-4*) U Pr of Amer.

***Art of Creative Critical Thinking.** rev. ed. John C. Kim. LC 94-12765. 430p. (C). 1994. lib. bdg. 49.50 (*0-8191-9597-9*) U Pr of Amer.

Art of Creative Critical Thinking. rev. ed. John C. Kim. LC 94-12765. 430p. 1994. pap. text ed. 29.50 (*0-8191-9598-7*) U Pr of Amer.

Art of Creative Thinking. Wilferd A. Peterson. Ed. by Dan Olmos. LC 90-71111. 208p. (Orig.). 1991. pap. 10.00 (*1-56170-004-5*, 131) Hay House.

Art of Creative Writing. Lajos Egri. 224p. 1995. pap. 8.95 (*0-8065-0200-2*, C263, Citadel Pr) Carol Pub Group.

***Art of Creole Cookery.** William Kaufman. 230p. 1995. pap. 8.95 (*0-7610-0314-2*) NW Pub.

***Art of Crisis Management.** Robert Foster. 240p. (Orig.). Date not set. pap. 8.95 (*0-7610-0270-7*) NW Pub.

Art of Criticism. Dominique Bouhours. LC 81-8900. 1981. reprint ed. 50.00 (*0-8201-1364-6*) Schol Facsimiles.

Art of Criticism: Henry James on the Theory & the Practice of Fiction. Henry James. Ed. by William Veeder & Susan Griffin. LC 85-24544. vi, 518p. 1986. pap. text ed. 16.95 (*0-226-39197-3*) U Ch Pr.

Art of Cross-Examination. LC 76-20426. 32p. 1976. pap. 8.50 (*0-685-42960-1*, 531-0001) Amer Bar Assn.

Art of Cross Examination. Henry B. Rothblatt. 1971. 5.00 (*1-55917-014-X*, 881); audio 50.00 (*1-55917-012-3*); vhs 350.00 (*1-55917-013-1*) Natl Prac Inst.

Art of Cross-Examination. Francis L. Wellman. 1976. lib. bdg. 300.00 (*0-8490-1386-0*) Gordon Pr.

Art of Cross-Examination. 4th enl. rev. ed. Francis L. Wellman. 480p. 1962. pap. 9.00 (*0-02-074960-0*, Collier S&S) S&S Trade.

Art of Cross Examination, Civil & Criminal. Ed. by A. Aiyar. (C). 1990. 225.00 (*0-89771-248-X*) St Mut.

Art of Crossing Cultures. Craig Storti. LC 89-84387. 130p. 1990. pap. 15.95 (*0-933662-85-8*) Intercult Pr.

Art of Cuba in Exile. Jose G. Sicre. Tr. by Ralph E. Dimmick. (Illus.). 215p. 1987. 59.00 (*0-89729-467-X*) Ediciones.

***Art of Cuisine.** Henri De Toulouse-Lautrec & Maurice Joyant. Tr. by Margery Weiner. LC 95-13390. 1995. write for info. (*0-8050-4110-9*) H Holt & Co.

Art of Curing, Pickling & Smoking Meat & Fish. James Robinson. 1973. 250.00 (*0-87968-053-9*) Gordon Pr.

Art of Cutting & History of English Costume (1887) Edward B. Giles. LC 87-42830. (Illus.). 240p. 1987. reprint ed. pap. 19.95 (*0-914046-05-5*) R L Shep.

Art of Cutwork & Applique: Historic, Modern & Kuna Indian. Herta Puls. (Illus.). 240p. 1978. 19.50 (*0-8231-4256-6*) Branford.

Art of Cycle Analysis: Solar & Lunar Cycles. Ed. by Diane Epperson. 85p. 1989. pap. 70.00 (*1-879192-05-5*) Fndtn Study Cycles.

Art of Daghestan: Decorative Applied Art, Paintings, Scultpture & Graphics. D. M. Magomedov. 200p. 1981. 125.00 (*0-317-14220-8*, Pub. by Collets UK) St Mut.

Art of Daily Activism. Judith L. Boice. LC 92-478. 240p. (Orig.). 1992. pap. 13.95 (*0-914728-74-1*) Wingbow Pr.

Art of Dance. Harvey Edwards. (Illus.). 1989. 35.00 (*0-8212-1734-8*) Little.

***Art of Dance: A Journal.** Nancy Van Norman Baer. (Illus.). 128p. 1994. 17.95 (*0-87654-084-1*) Pomegranate Calif.

Art of Dancing. Edward Ferrero. (Series in Dance). 1990. 35.00 (*0-306-76293-5*) Da Capo.

Art of Dapping. J. Johnston Mann. 1989. 25.00 (*0-7223-2094-9*, Pub. by A H S Ltd UK) St Mut.

***Art of Darkness: A Poetics of Gothic.** Anne Williams. LC 94-30949. 1995. lib. bdg. 39.00 (*0-226-89906-3*); pap. text ed. 14.95 (*0-226-89907-1*) U Ch Pr.

Art of Darkness: The After Dark Companion. Erfert Fenton. (Illus.). 128p. 1992. disk, pap. 19.95 (*1-56609-012-1*) Peachpit Pr.

***Art of Data Recording.** John Watkinson. 512p. 1994. 59. 95 (*0-240-51309-6*, Focal) Buttrwrth-Heinemann.

Art of Dealing Poker, Vol. II. Michael A. Mangarella. Ed. by Gina I. Mangarella. (Illus.). 208p. (Orig.). (C). 1991. pap. 9.95 (*1-877725-12-9*) Video One Prodns.

Art of Death: Visual Culture in the English Death Ritual, c. 1500-1800. Nigel Llewellyn. (Illus.). 160p. 1991. pap. 22.95 (*0-948462-16-7*) U of Wash Pr.

Art of Deception. Nora Roberts. (NR Flowers Ser.: No. 27). 1993. mass mkt. 3.59 (*0-373-51027-6*, 1-51027-0) Silhouette.

Art of Deception. 3rd rev. ed. Nicholas Capaldi. LC 87-62207. 222p. 1987. pap. 16.95 (*0-87975-424-9*) Prometheus Bks.

Art of Decision-Making. M. Davis. (Illus.). viii, 92p. 1985. 39.00 (*0-387-96228-X*) Spr-Verlag.

Art of Decision Making: Issues & Cases in Higher Education. Patricia R. Plante. (ACE-Oryx Series on Higher Education). 224p. 1987. 27.95 (*0-02-924550-8*, ACE-Oryx) Oryx Pr.

Art of Defence in Bridge. Terence Reese & Roger Trezel. 80p. 1988. pap. 9.95 (*0-575-02598-0*, Pub. by V Gollancz UK) Trafalgar.

Art of Defence in Chess: Defence & Counterattack Techniques in Chess. Lyev Polugayevsky & I. Damsky. (Russian Chess Ser.). (Illus.). 270p. 1988. 29.95 (*0-08-032059-7*, Pergamon Pr); pap. 19.90 (*0-08-032058-9*, Pergamon Pr) Elsevier.

Art of Defense in Chess. Andrew Soltis. LC 74-25728. 1983. 13.00 (*0-679-14108-1*) McKay.

Art of Deliberalizing: A Handbook for True Professionals. Wayne C. Booth. 13p. 1990. 5.00 (*0-911696-48-2*) Assn Am Coll.

***Art of Democracy: A Concise History of Popular Culture in the United States.** Jim Cullen. (Illus.). 352p. 1995. 36.00 (*0-85345-919-3*, CL9193); pap. 18.00 (*0-85345-920-7*, PB9207) Monthly Rev.

Art of Demosthenes. Lionel Pearson. LC 81-16752. (American Philological Association Special Publications Ser.). (C). 1982. pap. 24.00 (*0-89130-551-3*, 40-05-04) Scholars Pr GA.

Art of Derek Walcott. Stewart Brown. LC 90-3799. 220p. 1991. 35.00 (*0-8023-1290-X*) Dufour.

Art of Derek Walcott. Ed. by Stewart Brown. (Illus.). 231p. 1991. pap. 19.95 (*1-85411-027-6*, Pub. by Poetry Wales Pr UK) Dufour.

Art of Describing: Dutch Art in the Seventeenth Century. Svetlana Alpers. LC 82-6969. (Illus.). (C). 1983. lib. bdg. 42.50 (*0-226-01512-2*) U Ch Pr.

Art of Describing: Dutch Art in the Seventeenth Century. Svetlana Alpers. LC 82-6969. (Illus.). (C). 1984. pap. text ed. 24.95 (*0-226-01513-0*) U Ch Pr.

Art of Devotion, 1330-1500. Henk Van Os. LC 94-15506. 1994. 49.50 (*0-691-03793-0*) Princeton U Pr.

***Art of Diamond Cutting.** Basil Watermeyer & Sofus S. Michelsen. LC 94-1804. 137p. 1994. pap. 27.95 (*0-412-98411-3*, Blackie & Son-Chapman NY) Routledge Chapman & Hall.

***Art of Diana Armfield.** Julian Halsby. (Illus.). 128p. 1995. 40.00 (*0-7153-0233-7*, Pub. by D & C Pub UK) Sterling.

Art of Dictation. Eva Roman. (Illus.). 135p. 1971. pap. 11. 95 (*0-8464-1077-X*) Beekman Pubs.

Art of Digital Audio. John Watkinson. (Illus.). 484p. 1988. 56.95 (*0-240-51270-7*, Focal) Buttrwrth-Heinemann.

Art of Digital Audio. 2nd ed. John Watkinson. (Illus.). 490p. 1994. 59.95 (*0-240-51320-7*, Focal) Buttrwrth-Heinemann.

Art of Digital Design: An Introduction to Top-Down Design. 2nd ed. Franklin P. Prosser & David E. Winkel. (Illus.). 560p. 1986. text ed. 78.00 (*0-13-046780-4*) P-H.

Art of Digital Drumming. Steve DeFuria & Joe Scacciaferro. (Ferro Technologies Ser.). (Illus.). 120p. (Orig.). 1989. pap. 19.95 (*0-88188-869-9*, HL 00237455) H Leonard.

Art of Digital Video. John Watkinson. (Illus.). 580p. 1990. 54.95 (*0-240-51287-1*, Focal) Buttrwrth-Heinemann.

Art of Digital Video. 2nd ed. John Watkins. 608p. 1994. 59. 95 (*0-240-51369-X*, Focal) Buttrwrth-Heinemann.

Art of Dining: A History of Cooking & Eating. Sara Paston-Williams. 1994. 49.50 (*0-8109-1940-0*) Abrams.

Art of Diplomacy: The American Experience. Thomas A. Bailey. LC 68-11680. (C). 1968. 29.50 (*0-89197-032-0*); pap. text ed. 16.95 (*0-89197-033-9*) Irvington.

Art of Directing. John W. Kirk & Ralph A. Bellas. (Illus.). 240p. (C). 1990. reprint ed. pap. text ed. 18.00 (*0-9627402-0-9*) Ad Hoc Prodns.

Art of Discipline, Thought & Control. Terry Prueher. Ed. by Jennifer Nemetz. 112p. (C). 1993. pap. 9.95 (*0-936417-35-8*) Axelrod Pub.

Art of Distributed Applications: Programming Techniques for Remote Procedure Calls. John R. Corbin. (Sun Technical Reference Library). ix, 321p. 1990. 39.95 (*0-685-48006-2*) Spr-Verlag.

Art of Divination. Scott Cunningham. 160p. 1993. pap. 12. 95 (*0-89594-623-8*) Crossing Pr.

***Art of Domination.** Anna Riva. 32p. (Orig.). 1995. pap. text ed. 3.95 (*0-943832-23-3*) Intl Imports.

Art of Dora Carrington. Jane Hill. LC 93-61838. (Illus.). 144p. 1994. 24.95 (*0-500-09244-3*) Thames Hudson.

***Art of Dora Carrington.** Jane Hill. LC 93-61838. (Illus.). 144p. 1995. pap. 15.95 (*0-500-27857-1*) Thames Hudson.

Art of Dostoevesky: Deliriums & Nocturnes. Robert L. Jackson. LC 81-47136. 392p. 1981. 55.00x (*0-691-06484-9*) Princeton U Pr.

Art of Double Bass Playing. Warren A. Benfield & James S. Dean, Jr. (Illus.). 40p. 1973. pap. text ed. 8.95 (*0-87487-081-X*) Summy-Birchard.

Art of Doubles: Winning Tennis Strategies. Pat Blaskower. 144p. (Orig.). 1994. pap. 14.99 (*1-55870-330-6*) Betterway Bks.

Art of Dragon Magazine. Ed. by Jean Blashfield. LC 87-51356. (Illus.). 1988. pap. 16.95 (*0-88038-537-5*) TSR Inc.

Art of Drama. Ronald Peacock. LC 73-3026. 263p. 1974. reprint ed. text ed. 35.00 (*0-8371-6825-2*, PEAD, Greenwood Pr) Greenwood.

Art of Dramatic Writing. Lajos Egri. 1972. pap. 10.95 (*0-671-21332-6*, Touchstone Bks) S&S Trade.

Art of Drawing. Walter Koschatzky. Date not set. 59.50 (*0-89835-265-7*) Abaris Bks.

Art of Drawing. 3rd ed. Bernard Chaet. LC 82-15404. (C). 1983. pap. text ed. 38.00 (*0-03-062028-7*) HB Coll Pubs.

Art of Drawing. Willy Pogany. (Quality Paperback Ser.: No. 257). (Illus.). 128p. 1976. reprint ed. pap. 9.95 (*0-8226-0257-1*) Littlefield.

Art of Drawing: Old Masters from the Crocker Art Museum. Jeffrey Ruda. LC 92-71560. (Illus.). 200p. (Orig.). 1992. pap. 50.00 (*0-939896-00-1*) Flint Inst Arts.

Art of Drawing in France. Ed. by Per Bjurstrom. (Illus.). 224p. 1987. 47.50 (*0-85667-328-5*, Pub. by P Wilson Pubs) Sothebys Pubns.

Art of Drawing with the Pen, & Limning with Water Colours. Henry Peacham. LC 71-25631. (English Experience Ser.: No. 230). 70p. 1970. reprint ed. 35.00 (*90-221-0230-0*) Walter J Johnson.

Art of Drawn Work. Butterick Publishing Company Staff. Ed. by Kaethe Kliot. 128p. (C). 1989. reprint ed. pap. 11.00 (*0-916896-29-3*) Lacis Pubns.

Art of Dreadlocks. Wanda Johnson. (Illus.). 35p. (Orig.). 1991. pap. 4.50 (*1-56411-031-1*) Untd Bros & Sis.

Art of Dreaming. Carlos Castaneda. LC 92-56194. 256p. 1993. 22.00 (*0-06-017051-4*, HarpT) HarpC.

Art of Dreaming. Carlos Castaneda. 1994. pap. 12.00 (*0-06-092554-X*, PL) HarpC.

***Art of Dress: Fashion in England & France 1750 to 1820.** Aileen Ribeiro. LC 94-35347. 1995. write for info. (*0-300-06287-7*) Yale U Pr.

Art of Dress Modelling. Lily Silberberg & Martin Shoben. (Illus.). 280p. 1992. pap. 44.95 (*0-7506-0257-0*) Buttrwrth-Heinemann.

***Art of Dried & Scented Flowers.** Anneliese Ott. (Illus.). 160p. 1995. 14.95 (*0-304-34661-6*, Pub. by Cassell UK) Sterling.

Art of Dried Flowers. Rob Wood & Lucy Wood. LC 90-52875. (Illus.). 128p. 1992. reprint ed. 12.98 (*1-56138-168-3*) Courage Bks.

***Art of Drowning.** Billy Collins. LC 95-3297. (Pitt Poetry Ser.). 1995. write for info. (*0-8229-3893-6*); pap. write for info. (*0-8229-5567-9*) U of Pittsburgh Pr.

Art of Dying. Oscar Hahn. Ed. by Yvette E. Miller. Tr. by James Hoggard. LC 87-82268. 96p. (ENG & SPA.). 1987. pap. 10.00 (*0-935480-32-3*) Lat Am Lit Rev Pr.

Art of Earthmoving: Equipment & Methods. 3rd ed. Jagman Singh. 604p. (C). 1986. text ed. 95.00 (*90-6191-476-0*, Pub. by A A Balkema NE) Ashgate Pub Co.

Art of Easy Entertaining. rev. ed. Susan Walter et al. LC 93-39093. (California Culinary Academy Ser.). 256p. 1994. reprint ed. pap. 18.95 (*1-56426-056-9*, Calif Culinary Acad) Cole Group.

Art of Eating. M. F. Fisher. 1994. 25.75 (*0-8446-6728-5*) Peter Smith.

Art of Eating. M. F. Fisher. 780p. 1990. pap. 16.00 (*0-02-032220-8*, Collier S&S) S&S Trade.

Art of Eating In: Fast, Easy & Fabulous. California Culinary Academy Staff. 1993. 12.95 (*1-56426-000-3*, Calif Culinary Acad) Cole Group.

Art of Eating in France: Manners & Menus in the 19th Century. Jean-Paul Aron. 1975. 29.95 (*0-7206-0493-1*, Pub. by Peter Owen Ltd UK) Dufour.

Art of Editing. 5th ed. Floyd K. Baskette et al. (Illus.). 528p. (C). 1991. text ed. write for info. (*0-02-306295-9*) Macmillan.

Art of Editing. 5th ed. Floyd K. Baskette et al. (Illus.). 528p. (C). 1991. student ed, pap. write for info. (*0-02-315141-2*) Macmillan.

***Art of Education: Reclaiming Your Family, Community, & Self.** Linda Dobson. LC 95-4148. 1995. 14.75 (*0-945097-26-3*) Home Educ Pr.

Art of Educational Evaluation: A Personal View. Elliot W. Eisner. (Illus.). 275p. 1985. 55.00 (*0-905273-62-1*, Falmer Pr); pap. 28.00 (*0-905273-61-3*, Falmer Pr) Taylor & Francis.

Art of Edward Thomas. Ed. by Jonathan Barker. LC 87-60969. 150p. 1987. 25.00 (*0-907476-66-X*, Pub. by Poetry Wales Pr UK) Dufour.

Art of Effective Doctor-Patient Communication. 2nd rev. ed. David Singer. Ed. by Karen Hadley. 90p. Date not set. pap. 19.95 (*0-9636712-0-0*) D Singer Ent.

Art of Effective Fracture Fixation with Rush Pins. F. Robert Brueckmann. (Illus.). 144p. 1989. text ed. 59.00 (*0-86577-323-8*) Thieme Med Pubs.

Art of Efficient Reading. 4th ed. George D. Spache & Paul C. Berg. 400p. (C). 1984. pap. write for info. (*0-02-414050-3*) Macmillan.

Art of EKG Interpretation: A Self-Instructional Text. 83th ed. Karen S. Ehrat. 432p. 1992. spiral bd. 32.95 (*0-8403-7469-0*) Kendall-Hunt.

Art of Electronics. 2nd ed. Paul Horowitz & Winfield Hill. (Illus.). 800p. (C). 1989. 59.95 (*0-521-37095-7*) Cambridge U Pr.

Art of Electronics: Student Manual. Paul Horowitz. 1989. pap. 29.95 (*0-521-37709-9*) Cambridge U Pr.

Art of Electrostatic Precipitation. 3rd ed. Jacob Katz. LC 79-90504. (Illus.). 399p. (C). 1989. pap. text ed. 45.00 (*0-9603986-2-7*) J Katz.

Art of Embroidery in the Nineties. Coleman Schneider. (Illus.). 468p. (C). 1991. 36.00 (*0-9601662-4-6*) C Schneider.

Art of Emily Bronte. Ed. by Anne Smith. LC 76-19859. (Barnes & Noble Critical Studies). 1976. text ed. 44.00 (*0-85478-483-7*); pap. text ed. 16.00 (*0-389-20054-9*) B&N Imports.

Art of Emily Dickinson's Early Poetry. David T. Porter. LC 66-13182. 222p. reprint ed. pap. 63.30 (*0-7837-4125-1*, 2057948) Bks Demand.

Art of Empire: Painting & Architecture of the Byzantine Periphery: A Comparative Study of Four Provinces. Annabel J. Wharton. LC 86-43039. (Illus.). 250p. 1988. lib. bdg. 45.00 (*0-271-00495-9*) Pa St U Pr.

Art of Encouraging Invention: A New Approach to Government Innovation Policy. Stefan Folster. (Industrial Institute for Economic & Social Research Report Ser.). 133p. (Orig.). 1991. pap. 46.50x (*91-7204-365-2*, Pub. by Almqv & Wiksell SW) Coronet Bks.

Art of Engagement: How to Build a Strong Foundation of Communication for Marriage. David Epstein & Shelia Epstein. (Illus.). 306p. 1983. 19.95 (*0-914615-00-9*) I Nathan Pub Co.

Art of English Shooting. limited ed. George Edie. 48p. 1993. 125.00 (*0-685-69869-6*) Arion Pr.

Art of Enhancing the Universe Within: A Course in Mind Management from a Spiritual Point of View. James H. Fedor. (Orig.). 1989. pap. 9.95 (*0-929896-04-1*) MindArt Pub.

Art of Enlightenment. Yeshe De Project Staff & Tarthang Tulku. (Illus.). 32p. 1987. pap. 4.95 (*0-89800-198-6*) Dharma Pub.

Art of Enlightenment see Sacred Art Tibetan Thanka Portfolios

Art of Entering Sweepstakes & Winning Consistently. Edward F. Ryder. (Orig.). 1979. pap. 6.95 (*0-934650-00-4*) Sunnyside.

Art of Ercole de' Roberti. Joseph Manca. (C). 1992. 150.00 (*0-521-39462-7*) Cambridge U Pr.

Art of Eric Carle. Eric Carle. LC 91-646. (Illus.). 124p. (J). (gr. k up). 1993. pap. 29.95 (*0-88708-176-2*, Picture Book Studio) S&S Childrens.

Art of Erotic Massage. Andrew Yorke. (Illus.). 160p. (Orig.). 1989. pap. 14.95 (*0-7137-1988-5*, Pub. by Blandford Pr UK) Sterling.

Art of Etching. E. S. Lumsden. (Illus.). 1924. pap. 7.50 (*0-486-20049-3*) Dover.

Art of Etching. E. S. Lumsden. (Illus.). 19.25 (*0-8446-2497-7*) Peter Smith.

***Art of Ethics.** Elizabeth Z. McGrath. LC 93-36798. (Values & Ethics Ser.: Vol. VII). 163p. 1993. 13.95 (*0-8294-0804-5*, Campion Bks) Loyola.

Art of Exaggeration: Piranesi's Perspectives on Rome. Eunice D. Howe et al. (Illus.). 78p. (Orig.). (C). 1995. pap. 15.00 (*0-945192-16-9*) USC Fisher Gallery.

Art of Excess: Mastery in Contemporary American Fiction. Tom LeClair. LC 88-31582. 256p. 1989. pap. 15.95 (*0-252-06102-0*) U of Ill Pr.

Art of Exclusion: Representing Blacks in the Nineteenth Century. Albert Boime. LC 89-4213. (Illus.). 251p. 1990. pap. 24.95 (*0-87474-257-9*) Smithsonian.

Art of Experimental Physics. Dietz Preston. 432p. 1991. Net. pap. text ed. write for info. (*0-471-84748-8*) Wiley.

Art of F. G. Cooper. Ed. by Leslie Cabarga. LC 95-75684. (Illus.). 128p. 1992. pap. text ed. 27.50 (*0-88108-097-7*) Art Dir.

***Art of Facilitation.** Hunter. 1995. pap. text ed. 17.95 (*1-55561-101-X*) Fisher Bks.

Art of Fact: Contemporary Artists of Nonfiction. Barbara Lounsberry. LC 89-17222. (Contributions to the Study of World Literature Ser.: No. 53). 232p. 1990. text ed. 55.00 (*0-313-26893-2*, LCB/, Greenwood Pr) Greenwood.

Art of Falconry. Frederick II of Hohenstaufen. Ed. by Casey A. Wood & F. Marjorie Fyfe. (Illus.). cxi, 637p. 1943. 79.50 (*0-8047-0374-4*) Stanford U Pr.

Art of Falconry. G. Lascelles. 176p. 17.50 (*0-87556-647-2*) Saifer.

Art of Falling. Patrick T. Madden. 30p. (Orig.). 1989. pap. text ed. write for info. (*0-318-65571-3*) Quest Pr.

***Art of Falling Apart.** rev. ed. Frederic F. Flach. 150p. 1995. pap. 9.95 (*1-886330-03-4*) Hatherleigh.

Art of Fashion Accessories. Joanne D. Ball & Dorothy H. Torem. LC 92-63102. (Illus.). 240p. 1993. 59.95 (*0-88740-461-8*) Schiffer.

Art of Fashion Draping. Connie A. Crawford. (Illus.). 320p. (C). 1988. text ed. 32.00 (*0-87005-634-4*) Fairchild.

Art of Fear Management: Living, Loving, Laughing, Life Long Lessons, Free From Fear (How to Control Your Fears & Start Caring for Yourself) Rhonda R. Burgs. 250p. 1993. 15.95 (*1-882682-00-9*) Jim Co Counsel.

Art of Fiction. David Lodge. 288p. 1994. 10.95 (*0-14-017492-3*, Penguin Bks) Viking Penguin.

Art of Fiction. 4th ed. Ed. by R. F. Dietrich & Roger H. Sundell. 453p. (C). 1983. pap. text ed. 20.75 (*0-03-060546-6*) HB Coll Pubs.

Art of Fiction: Notes on Craft for Young Writers. John C. Gardner. LC 83-47850. 256p. 1984. 17.95 (*0-394-50469-0*) Knopf.

Art of Fiction: Notes on Craft for Young Writers. John C. Gardner. LC 90-55698. 240p. 1991. pap. 9.00 (*0-679-73403-1*, Vin) Random.

Art of Fiction in the Heart of Dixie: An Anthology of Alabama Writers. Philip D. Beidler. LC 86-6919. 352p. (C). 1986. 27.50 (*0-8173-0313-8*); pap. 19.95 (*0-8173-0314-6*) U of Ala Pr.

Art of Film Music. George Burt. 288p. 1994. text ed. 35.00 (*1-55553-193-8*) NE U Pr.

Art of Filo Cookbook: International Entrees, Appetizers, & Desserts Wrapped in Flaky Pastry. Marti Sousanis. (Illus.). 143p. (Orig.). 1983. pap. 12.50 (*0-201-10871-2*) Addison-Wesley.

Art of Filo Cookbook: International Entrees, Appetizers, & Desserts Wrapped in Flaky Pastry. Marti Sousanis. LC 83-3917. (Illus.). 143p. (Orig.). 1983. pap. 9.95 (*0-943186-05-6*) Aris Bks.

Art of Fine Furniture Building: A Guide to Designing, Constructing, & Finishing High Quality Furniture. Kathy Prochnow & Dave Prochnow. (Illus.). 176p. (Orig.). 1993. pap. 16.95 (*1-55870-282-2*) Betterway Bks.

Art of Fingerstyle Guitar. Comp. by Stefan Grossman. (Guitar Workshop Ser.). 1993. 9.95 (*1-56222-333-X*, 94638); audio 9.98 (*1-56222-373-9*, 94638) Mel Bay.

Art of Finnish Cooking. Taimi Previdi. 290p. 1994. 19.95 (*0-7818-0284-9*) Hippocrene Bks.

Art of Firing. Nils Lou. 120p. 1995. pap. text ed. 30.00 (*0-9638064-0-8*) Clay Pacific.

Art of Flamenco. D. E. Pohren. 1985. lib. bdg. 250.00 (*0-8490-3248-2*) Gordon Pr.

Art of Flamenco. rev. ed. Don Pohren. (Illus.). 225p. 1990. text ed. 24.95 (*0-685-46241-2*, Pub. by Soc Sp Studies SP) Bold Strummer Ltd.

Art of Flight Instruction. Don Gladney. (Illus.). 200p. (Orig.). 1989. pap. write for info. (*0-318-65361-3*) ATDI.

An Asterisk (*) at the beginning of an entry indicates that the title is appearing in BIP for the first time.

447

Art of Floral Design. Norah T. Hunter. 59p. 1994. teacher ed 12.00 (*0-8273-5090-2*) Delmar.

Art of Floral Design. Norah T. Hunter & Herb Mitchell. LC 93-31901. 566p. 1994. text ed. 51.95 (*0-8273-5089-9*) Delmar.

Art of Floral Painting with Lowell Speers, Series 1. John Hartman. (Illus.). 76p. 1990. pap. text ed. write for info. (*1-883576-19-9*) Alexander Art.

Art of Floral Painting with Lowell Speers, Series 2. Toby Willis-Camp. (Illus.). 72p. 1991. pap. text ed. write for info. (*1-883576-20-2*) Alexander Art.

Art of Florence, 2 vols., Set. Glenn Andres et al. LC 83-6394. (Illus.). 1348p. 1989. 385.00 (*0-89659-402-5*) Abbeville Pr.

Art of Flower Arranging. Jan Hall & Sarah Waterkeyn. 1992. 14.98 (*0-8317-0423-3*) Smithmark.

Art of Flute Playing. Edwin Putnik. LC 75-146521. (Illus.). 96p. 1970. pap. 14.95 (*0-87487-077-1*) Summy-Birchard.

*__Art of Fly Tying.__ Cy. 1994. pap. text ed. write for info. (*0-86573-046-6*) Cy De Cosse.

Art of Fly Tying. John Van Vliet. LC 94-12559. (Hunting & Fishing Library). 128p. 1994. 19.95 (*0-86573-043-1*) Cy De Cosse.

Art of Flying. Robert N. Buck. LC 91-46647. 193p. 1992. 24.95 (*1-56566-005-6*) Thomasson-Grant.

Art of Forecasting. Sophia Mason. 60p. 1977. 7.00 (*0-86690-330-5*, M1322-034) Am Fed Astrologers.

Art of Framing. Charlene Brown. Ed. by Sydney Sprague. (Artist's Library). (Illus.). 64p. (Orig.). 1991. pap. 6.95 (*1-56010-070-2*, AL19) W Foster Pub.

Art of Frank C. McCarthy. Text by Elmer Kelton. (Illus.). 160p. 1992. 60.00 (*0-688-11883-6*) Morrow.

Art of Frank Norris, Storyteller. Barbara Hochman. LC 87-19201. 160p. 1988. text ed. 22.00 (*0-8262-0663-8*) U of Mo Pr.

Art of Fredda Burwell Holt. 2nd rev. ed. John D. Holt. 1975. pap. 2.95 (*0-914916-02-5*) Ku Paa.

Art of Freehand Pinstriping. Dick Bird. 66p. 1994. pap. 14.95 (*0-9641470-0-9*) Eastwood PA.

Art of French Calotype: With a Critical Dictionary of Photographers, 1845-1870. Andre Jammes & Eugenia P. Janis. LC 82-47600. (Illus.). 376p. 1983. 120.00x (*0-691-04002-8*) Princeton U Pr.

Art of French Horn Playing. Philip Farkas. (Illus.). 96p. 1956. pap. 14.95 (*0-87487-021-6*) Summy-Birchard.

Art of Freshwater Fishing. Dick Sternberg. LC 82-141019. (Hunting & Fishing Library). (Illus.). 160p. 1982. 19.95 (*0-86573-010-5*) Cy De Cosse.

Art of Friendship: The Idealization of Friendship in Medieval & Early Renaissance Literature. Reginald Hyatte. LC 94-3014. (Studies in Intellectual History: Vol. 50). 1994. 74.50 (*90-04-10018-0*) E J Brill.

Art of Fund Raising. 3rd ed. Irving R. Warner. 193p. 1993. text ed. 19.95 (*0-930807-27-8*, 600322) Fund Raising.

*__Art of Fund-Raising: What Every Health Care Trustee Needs to Know.__ Edward H. Bovich et al. LC 94-24891. 199p. 1994. 35.00 (*1-55648-123-5*, 196128) AHPI.

Art of G. K. Chesterton. Alzina S. Dale. LC 85-18165. (Illus.). 136p. (C). 1985. 24.95 (*0-8294-0516-X*) Loyola Univ Pr.

Art of Gardening. Thomas Hill. LC 79-84117. (English Experience Ser.: No. 936). 276p. 1979. reprint ed. lib. bdg. 30.00 (*0-686-71070-3*) Walter J Johnson.

Art of Gardening in Pots. Elisabeth De Lestrieux. (Illus.). 207p. 1990. 59.50 (*1-85149-131-7*) Antique Collect.

Art of Gardening Through the Ages. T. Wengel. 272p. (C). 1987. 395.00 (*0-685-34467-3*, Pub. by Collets) St Mut.

Art of Gardening with Roses. Graham S. Thomas. 160p. 1991. 27.50 (*0-8050-1533-7*) H Holt & Co.

Art of Garnishing. Inja Nam & Arno Schmidt. LC 93-7905. (Illus.). 1994. text ed. 34.95 (*0-442-01084-2*) Van Nos Reinhold.

Art of Gelato: Frozen Italian Desserts & Pastries. Frank C. Daniele. 1994. 14.95 (*0-8062-4824-6*) Carlton.

Art of Gem Cutting. 7th ed. Henry C. Dake. (Illus.). 96p. pap. 3.50 (*0-910652-07-4*) Gembooks.

Art of General Practice. David Morrell. (Illus.). 168p. 1991. 45.00 (*0-19-261988-8*); pap. 19.95 (*0-19-261990-X*) OUP.

Art of Geoffrey Chaucer. John L. Lowes. LC 70-114910. (Select Bibliographies Reprint Ser.). 1930. 6.00 (*0-8369-5315-0*) Ayer.

*__Art of George du Maurier.__ (Illus.). 250p. (C). 1995. text ed. 85.95 (*0-85967-977-2*, Pub. by Scolar Pr UK) Ashgate Pub Co.

Art of George Eliot. William J. Harvey. LC 78-786. 254p. 1978. reprint ed. text ed. 35.00 (*0-313-20267-2*, HAAGE, Greenwood Pr) Greenwood.

Art of Gerald Brockhurst. Thomas Brumbaugh et al. LC 92-39990. 1993. 20.00 (*0-915977-11-7*) Georgia Museum of Art.

*__Art of Getting Even.__ Brodsky. 1995. 4.98 (*1-55521-663-3*) Bk Sales Inc.

Art of Getting Things Done: A Practical Guide to the Use of Power. Richard W. Brislin. LC 90-47542. 266p. 1991. text ed. 22.95 (*0-275-93761-5*, C3761, Praeger Pubs) Greenwood.

Art of Getting Well. Anthony di Fabio. LC 87-62790. (Illus.). 141p. 1987. pap. 25.00 (*0-9615437-1-X*) Rheumatoid.

Art of Getting Your Own Sweet Way. 2nd ed. Philip B. Crosby. (Illus.). 240p. 1982. pap. text ed. 7.95 (*0-07-014527-X*) McGraw.

*__Art of Giancarlo Impiglia.__ Ronny Cohen & Giancarlo Impiglia. LC 95-15118. (Illus.). 128p. 1995. 50.00 (*0-8478-1903-5*) Rizzoli Intl.

Art of Giftwrapping: A Guide to Gifts That Look Great. Alexandra Eames & Carol Spier. (Illus.). 72p. 1993. 9.98 (*0-8317-3860-X*) Smithmark.

*__Art of Giovanni Antonio da Pordenone: Between Dialect & Language.__ Charles E. Cohen. (Cambridge Studies in the History of Art). (Illus.). 512p. (C). 1992. write for info. (*0-521-30630-2*) Cambridge U Pr.

Art of Giving Quality Service. Mary Gober & Robert Tannehill. 104p. (Orig.). 1984. pap. 7.00 (*0-685-29372-6*) Tannehill-Gober.

Art of Giving Quality Service in the Motor Carrier Industry. Charles W. Clowdis, Jr. & American Trucking Association Sales & Marketing Council. 108p. 1984. pap. text ed. 10.00 (*0-88711-080-0*) Am Trucking Assns.

Art of Glass: Selections from Columbus Collections. Columbus Museum of Art Staff. (Illus.). 96p. (Orig.). 1981. pap. 6.50 (*0-918881-09-9*) Columbus Mus Art.

*__Art of Goaltending.__ Vladislav Tretiak. (Illus.). 160p. (Orig.). 1995. pap. 14.95 (*0-920985-03-3*, Pub. by Polestar Bk Pubs CN) Orca Bk Pubs.

*__Art of Goldfish Keeping.__ Peter Cole. (Illus.). 128p. 1995. pap. 12.95 (*0-7137-2451-X*, Pub. by Blandford Pr UK) Sterling.

Art of Golf. rev. ed. Walter Simpson. (Illus.). 1992. reprint ed. 28.00 (*0-940889-35-8*) Classics Golf.

Art of Golf 1754-1940: Timeless, Enchanting Illustrations & Narrative of Golf's Formative Years. Gary H. Schwartz. LC 89-28182. (Illus.). 160p. (Orig.). 1990. pap. 19.95 (*0-9623000-2-0*) Wood River CA.

Art of Good Bidding. Terence Reese & David Bird. 192p. (Orig.). 1993. pap. 10.95 (*0-571-16716-0*) Faber & Faber.

*__Art of Good Cooking.__ Ruby Vencill. 240p. 1995. write for info. (*1-886029-06-7*) Spider Hill Pr.

Art of Gothic: Ann Radcliffe's Major Novels. Nelson C. Smith. Ed. by Devendra P. Varma. LC 79-8481. (Gothic Studies & Dissertations). 1980. lib. bdg. 28.95 (*0-405-12680-8*) Ayer.

Art of Government. James Reichley. (Reprint Series in Sociology). (Illus.). 1972. reprint ed. lib. bdg. 26.50 (*0-697-00222-5*); reprint ed. pap. 9.95 (*0-89197-664-7*) Irvington.

Art of Graphics for the IBM PC. J. McGregor & A. Watt. 448p. (C). 1986. pap. text ed. 31.25 (*0-201-18089-8*) Addison-Wesley.

Art of Graphology. 2nd ed. Marie Bernard. LC 85-51385. (Illus.). 416p. 1994. pap. 25.00 (*0-685-72776-9*) Whitston Pub.

Art of Greece & Rome. Harry J. Carroll. (Illus.). 12p. 1972. 1.00 (*0-915478-30-7*) Galleries Coll.

Art of Gregory Gillespie. Ed. by K. R. Eagles-Smith. (Illus.). 30p. (Orig.). 1992. pap. text ed. 15.00 (*0-941576-19-1*) Harcourts Contemporary.

Art of Grill & Smoker Cooking. J. E. Matthews. Ed. by James B. Van Treese. 280p. 1993. pap. 9.95 (*1-56901-052-8*) NW Pub.

Art of Grilling: A Menu Cookbook. Kelly McCune. LC 89-45792. (Illus.). 108p. 1990. pap. 17.00 (*0-06-096462-6*, PL) HarpC.

Art of Growing Older: Writers on Living & Aging. Sel. by Wayne C. Booth. LC 92-22720. (Illus.). 320p. 1992. 22.00 (*0-671-78192-8*) S&S Trade.

Art of Gupta India: Empire & Province. Joanna G. Williams. LC 81-13783. (Illus.). 400p. 1982. 79.50 (*0-691-03988-7*) Princeton U Pr.

*__Art of Gupta India: Empire & Province.__ Joanna G. Williams. LC 81-13783. (Illus.). 381p. 1982. reprint ed. pap. 108.60 (*0-7837-8599-2*, 2049414) Bks Demand.

Art of Gustave Moreau: Theory, Style, & Content. Julius D. Kaplan. LC 82-6980. (Studies in the Fine Arts: The Avant-Garde: No. 33). (Illus.). 221p. reprint ed. pap. 63.00 (*0-8357-1350-4*, 2070234) Bks Demand.

Art of Hair Work: Hair Braiding & Jewelry of Sentiment. Mark Campbell. Ed. by Kaethe Kliot. 208p. (C). 1993. reprint ed. pap. 20.00 (*0-916896-31-5*) Lacis Pubns.

*__Art of Hairdressing Success.__ Linda McGinnis. 208p. 1995. pap. text ed. 18.95 (*1-886203-64-4*) Paradime Pubng.

Art of Hand Applique. Laura L. Fritz. 1990. pap. 14.95 (*0-89145-964-2*) Collector Bks.

Art of Hand-Lettering: Its Mastery & Practice. Helm Wotzkow. (Illus.). 320p. (YA). (gr. 9-12). pap. 6.95 (*0-486-21797-3*) Dover.

Art of Hand-Tying Coil Springs: A Set of How-to Diagrams. National Association of Professional Upholsterers Staff. (Illus.). 22p. 1985. pap. text ed. 30.00 (*0-9615307-0-7*) Nat Assn Pro Upholsterers.

Art of Handel's Operas. Hugo Meynell. LC 86-5406. (Studies in the History & Interpretation of Music: Vol. 1). 264p. 1986. lib. bdg. 89.95 (*0-88946-425-1*) E Mellen.

Art of Hanna-Barbera: Fifty Years of Creativity. Ted Sennett. LC 88-40627. (Illus.). 288p. 1989. 50.00 (*0-670-82978-1*, Viking Studio) Studio Bks.

Art of Hanna-Barbera: Fifty Years of Creativity. deluxe limited ed. Ted Sennett. LC 88-40627. (Illus.). 288p. 1989. boxed 300.00 (*0-670-83071-2*, Viking Studio) Studio Bks.

Art of Happiness or the Teachings of Epicurus. Henry D. Sedgwick. LC 70-117841. (Essay Index Reprint Ser.). 1977. 24.95 (*0-8369-1814-2*) Ayer.

Art of Harmony. Sang H. Kim. LC 93-43077. 160p. (Orig.). 1994. pap. 6.95 (*1-880336-03-0*) Turtle CT.

Art of Hating. Gerald Schoenewolf. LC 90-45054. 224p. 1990. 27.50 (*0-87668-693-5*) Aronson.

Art of Hawaiian Featherwork. John D. Holt. (Illus.). 180p. (Orig.). 1985. text ed. 29.95 (*0-914916-68-8*) Ku Paa.

Art of Hawaiian Steel Guitar. Stacy Phillips. 1993. 15.00 (*1-56222-103-5*, 94383); 9.98 (*1-56222-877-3*, 94383) Mel Bay.

Art of Healing. Lewis Mehl & Gayle Peterson. 350p. text ed. write for info. (*0-8290-1804-2*); audio (*0-318-61266-6*) Irvington.

Art of Healing with Transcendental Energy. Raymond G. Jaegers. (Illus.). 66p. 1976. pap. text ed. 5.00 (*0-318-33043-1*) Aries Prod.

Art of Hebrew Lettering. pap. 9.95 (*0-686-76480-3*) Feldheim.

Art of Helping, Vol. VII. Robert R. Carkhuff. 140p. 1993. teacher ed 12.95 (*0-87425-232-6*); student ed 12.95 (*0-87425-233-4*); pap. text ed. 24.95 (*0-87425-231-8*) Human Res Dev Pr.

Art of Henry Ossawa Tanner (1859-1937) (Illus.). 1970. 2.50 (*0-686-27125-4*) Mus African Art.

Art of Heraldry: An Encyclopaedia of Armory. Arthur C. Fox-Davies. LC 68-56481. (Illus.). 1972. reprint ed. 66.95 (*0-405-08530-3*, Pub. by Blom Pubns UK) Ayer.

Art of Hiring in America's Colleges & Universities. Ed. by Ronald H. Stein & Stephen J. Trachenberg. (Frontiers in Education Ser.). 188p. (C). 1993. 33.95x (*0-87975-786-8*) Prometheus Bks.

Art of History: A Study of Four Great Historians of the Eighteenth Century. John B. Black. 1976. lib. bdg. 59.95 (*0-8490-1452-2*) Gordon Pr.

Art of Hitting Three Hundred. rev. ed. Charles Lau & Alfred Glossbrenner. 1992. pap. 18.95 (*0-14-015335-7*, Penguin Bks) Viking Penguin.

Art of Holly Hobbie. Holly Hobbie. LC 86-2065. (Illus.). 128p. 1986. 12.95 (*0-394-54862-0*) Random.

*__Art of Home Conversion: Transforming Uncommon Properties into Stylish Homes.__ Lorrie Mack. (Illus.). 160p. 1995. pap. 17.95 (*0-304-34591-1*, Pub. by Cassell UK) Sterling.

Art of Hospitality. Yvonne G. Baker. LC 86-70117. 196p. 1986. pap. 8.99 (*0-89636-208-6*, LifeJourney) Chariot Family.

Art of Hot-Air Ballooning. Roger Bansemer. (Illus.). 165p. 1992. write for info. (*0-944201-00-8*) Gollum Pr.

Art of Howard Terpning. Elmer Kelton. 1992. 60.00 (*0-553-08113-6*) Bantam.

Art of Human Computer Interface. Brenda Laurel. 1990. pap. 32.95 (*0-201-51797-3*) Addison-Wesley.

Art of Hungarian Cooking. Paul P. Bennett & Velma Clark. 221p. 1993. reprint ed. pap. 8.95 (*0-7818-0202-4*) Hippocrene Bks.

Art of Hunger. Paul Auster. 270p. 1991. 21.95 (*1-55713-056-6*); 40.00 (*1-55713-059-0*) Sun & Moon CA.

Art of Hunger: Essays, Prefaces, Interviews & the Red Notebook. Paul Auster. LC 93-2048. 352p. 1993. pap. 12.00 (*0-14-017168-1*, Penguin Bks) Viking Penguin.

Art of Hunting. Norman Strung. LC 83-72752. (Hunting & Fishing Library). (Illus.). 160p. 1984. 19.95 (*0-86573-008-3*) Cy De Cosse.

*__Art of Hypnotherapy.__ C. Roy Hunter. 328p. 1994. per., pap. text ed. 24.95 (*0-7872-0515-X*) Kendall-Hunt.

Art of I. Denton. Ivan Denton. LC 88-1162. (Illus.). 104p. (Orig.). 1988. 29.95 (*1-55728-009-6*); pap. 15.95 (*1-55728-010-X*) U of Ark Pr.

*__Art of Independence.__ Scott Ashin. Date not set. pap. write for info. (*0-345-38410-5*) Ballantine.

Art of Indexing. Larry S. Bonura. LC 93-30966. (Technical Communication Library). 1994. text ed. 26.95 (*0-471-01449-4*) Wiley.

Art of India. Sivaramurti. 1993. 175.00 (*0-8109-0630-9*) Abrams.

Art of India from the Williams College Museum of Art. Christopher Noey & Janet Temos. LC 93-41492. (Illus.). 136p. (Orig.). 1994. pap. 35.00 (*0-913697-18-4*) Williams Art.

Art of Indonesia. Bambang Sumadio. LC 93-4481. 1993. 60.00 (*0-86565-142-6*) Vendome.

Art of Indoor Bonsai: Cultivation Tropical, Sub-Tropical & Tender Bonsai. John Ainsworth. 128p. 1992. reprint ed. pap. 19.95 (*0-943955-58-0*, Trafalgar Sq Pub) Trafalgar.

Art of Information Gathering. 2nd ed. Barry Zalma. 338p. 1994. ring bd. 35.95 (*1-884770-08-8*) Claimschool.

Art of Infrared Photography: A Comprehensive Guide to the Use of Black & White Infrared Film. Joseph Paduano. (Illus.). 1995. pap. 17.95 (*0-936262-32-X*) Amherst Media.

Art of Inlay: Contemporary Design & Technique. Larry Robinson. LC 94-12076. (Illus.). 112p. 1994. text ed. 24.95 (*0-87930-332-8*) Miller Freeman.

Art of Inner Listening. Jessie K. Crum. LC 74-21643. (Orig.). 1975. pap. 4.95 (*0-8356-0303-2*, Quest) Theos Pub Hse.

Art of Instructing the Infant Deaf & Dumb see Essay on the Principles of Education, Physiologically Considered

Art of Instrument Flying. Jerry R. Williams. (Practical Flying Ser.). (Illus.). 272p. 1988. 24.95 (*0-8306-2018-4*, 2418); pap. 16.95 (*0-8306-2418-X*) TAB Bks.

Art of Instrument Flying. 2nd ed. J. R. Williams. 1991. text ed. 31.95 (*0-07-070583-6*); pap. text ed. 19.95 (*0-07-070582-8*) McGraw.

Art of Instrument Flying. 2nd ed. J. R. Williams. (Practical Flying Ser.). (Illus.). 352p. 1991. 26.95 (*0-8306-7654-6*, 3654, TAB-Aero); pap. 19.95 (*0-8306-3654-4*, TAB-Aero) TAB Bks.

Art of Interactive Teaching: With Cases, Simulations, Games & Other Interactive Methods. Hans E. Klein. (Illus.). 650p. 1995. 56.00 (*1-877868-06-X*) WACRA. Interdisciplinary, International, Intercultural CONTRIBUTIONS from around the world EXPLORE & DISCUSS THE LATEST DEVELOPMENTS IN DESIGN, PRODUCTION, IMPLEMENTATION, RESEARCH, EVALUATION, & PEDAGOGICAL INNOVATIONS USING CASES, SIMULATIONS, GAMES, VIDEOS & OTHER INTERACTIVE TEACHING METHODS. Topics included: A Dialogue of the Deaf - Deepening Cultural Competence Through International, Live, Case-based Teaching - Compressing the Cultural Adaptation Learning Curve - Strategic Management: Evaluating the Case Method - Teaching Interrelationships Among Disciplines - Development of Reflective Thought Processes - Problem Solving & the Core Curriculum - Criteria for Case Selection - Learning Effects on Students - Interaction-based Self-Assessment - Teamwork Among Social Work Students - Service Learning in Higher Ed - Managing Across Cultural Boundaries - International Management of Change - Contingency & Case-design - Managing & Coaching Critical Thinking - Effective Case-writing - Case Research in a Global Environment - Case Development & Case-teaching in the Context of Scarce Resources. Other volumes: CASE METHOD RESEARCH & APPLICATION: INNOVATION THROUGH COOPERATION (ISBN 1-877868-05-1), FORGING NEW PARTNERSHIPS (ISBN 1-877868-04-3), MANAGING CHANGE (ISBN 1-877868-03-5), PROBLEM SOLVING (ISBN 1-877868-02-7), NEW VISTAS (ISBN 1-877868-01-9). Contact: World Association for Case Method Research & Application, 23 Mackintosh Ave., Needham, MA 02191; 617-444-8982; FAX 617-444-1548; HKLEIN@BENTLEY.EDU.** ***Publisher Provided Annotation.

Art of Intercession. Zacharias T. Fomum. 1989. 14.95 (*0-533-07884-9*) Vantage.

Art of Interference: Stresses Readings in Verbal & Visual Texts. Mary A. Caws. (Illus.). 341p. 1990. text ed. 50.00 (*0-691-06839-9*); pap. text ed. 15.95 (*0-691-01478-7*) Princeton U Pr.

Art of Interior Architecture: 1979-1989. Stanley Abercrombie et al. Ed. by Catharine Weese. LC 89-61547. (Illus.). 150p. 1989. 39.95 (*0-929862-01-5*) CCAIA.

Art of Intervention in Dynamic Psychotherapy. Bert Kaplan. LC 88-6238. 263p. 1988. 35.00 (*0-87668-983-7*) Aronson.

Art of Interviewing for Television, Radio & Film. Irv Broughton. LC 79-9399. (Illus.). 1981. 18.95 (*0-8306-9743-8*) TAB Bks.

Art of Inventing: How to Invent & How to Solve Technical Problems. Henry Altov. Tr. by Lev Shulyak. LC 93-60989. (Illus.). 170p. (Orig.). 1994. 40.00 (*0-9640740-1-X*) Tech Innovat.

Art of Investing School District Funds, No. 9005: The Rules of the Game, No. 9005. Jeffrey Flynn. (Series). 110p. 1990. pap. 15.00 (*0-910170-54-1*) Assn Sch Busn.

Art of Investing While Collecting: An Authoritative Guide to Quality, Value & All Aspects of Collecting Fine Art & Tangibles. Robert Johanningmeier. LC 82-70884. (Illus.). 234p. 1983. pap. 14.95 (*0-943188-07-5*) Art & Comm.

Art of Islam. Nurhan Atasoy et al. (Illus.). 176p. 1992. 50.00 (*2-08-013510-4*, Pub. by Flammarion) Abbeville Pr.

Art of Island Southeast Asia: The Fred & Rita Richman Collection in the Metropolitan Museum of Art. Florina H. Capistrano-Baker. LC 93-51050. (Illus.). 156p. 1994. 60.00 (*0-87099-697-5*); pap. 29.95 (*0-87099-698-3*) Metro Mus Art.

Art of Israeli Cooking. Aldo Nahoum. (International Cooking Classics Ser.). 274p. 1992. pap. 8.95 (*0-7818-0096-X*) Hippocrene Bks.

Art of Italian Cooking. Giorgetto Giugiaro. 1988. 19.95 (*0-671-09307-X*) S&S Trade.

*__Art of Italian Regional Cooking.__ Francesco Antonucci et al. LC 94-45007. (Illus.). 224p. 1995. pap. 17.95 (*0-8069-0849-1*) Sterling.

*__Art of Ivan Gantschev.__ Illus. by Ivan Gantschev. 108p. (YA). 1994. 39.95 (*1-55858-231-2*) North-South Bks NYC.

Art of Jack B. Yeats. T. G. Rosenthal. (Illus.). 305p. 1994. 65.00 (*0-233-98849-1*, Pub. by A Deutsch UK) Trafalgar.

Art of Jack Davis. Hank Harrison. (Illus.). 144p. (Orig.). 1987. 18.95 (*0-941613-01-1*); pap. 9.95 (*0-941613-00-3*) Stabur Pr.

Art of James Bama. Text by Elmer Kelton. LC 92-46673. 1993. 60.00 (*0-553-09305-3*) Bantam.

Art of James Branch Cabell. H. Walpole. 1971. 59.95 (*0-87968-661-8*) Gordon Pr.

Art of Japan. Yoshiko Kakudo. (Illus.). 256p. 1991. 45.00 (*0-8118-0055-5*); pap. 29.95 (*0-8118-0040-7*) Chronicle Bks.

An Asterisk (*) at the beginning of an entry indicates that the title is appearing in BIP for the first time.

A

An Asterisk (*) at the beginning of an entry indicates that the title is appearing in BIP for the first time.

449

A

Art of Memory: A Treatise Useful for Such as Are to Speak in Public. Marius D'Assigny. LC 83-46046. (Scientific Awakening in the Restoration Ser.: No. 1). 128p. 1985. reprint ed. 45.00 (*0-404-63301-3*) AMS Pr.

Art of Memory...As It Dependeth upon Places & Ideas. John Willis. LC 73-6172. (English Experience Ser.: No. 634). 104p. 1973. reprint ed. 25.00 (*90-221-0634-9*) Walter J Johnson.

Art of Mental Prayer. Bede Frost. LC 87-28281. 288p. 1988. reprint ed. pap. 9.95 (*0-8192-1422-1*) Morehouse Pub.

Art of Mesoamerica. Mary E. Miller. LC 85-51916. (World of Art Ser.). (Illus.). 1986. pap. 14.95 (*0-500-20203-6*) Thames Hudson.

Art of Metal in Africa. Ed. by Marie-Therese Brincard. LC 82-72765. (Illus.). 148p. 1982. pap. 18.00 (*0-89192-347-0*) Interbk Inc.

Art of Mexican Cooking: Traditional Mexican Cooking for Aficionados. Diana Kennedy. 1989. 24.95 (*0-553-05706-5*) Bantam.

Art of Michael Whelan: Scenes, Visions. Michael Whelan. LC 93-12706. (Illus.). 1993. 60.00 (*0-553-07447-4*) Bantam.

Art of Mickey Mouse: Artists Interpret the World's Favorite Mouse. Ed. by Craig Yoe & Janet Morra-Yoe. LC 91-23545. (Illus.). 128p. 1992. 35.00 (*1-56282-994-7*) Hyperion.

Art of Mickey Mouse: Artists Interpret the World's Favorite Mouse. Craig Yoe & Janet Morra-Yoe. (Illus.). 128p. 1993. pap. 19.95 (*1-56282-744-8*) Hyperion.

***Art of Mickey Mouse: Artists Interpret the World's Favorite Mouse.** Craig Yoe & Janet Morra-Yoe. (Illus.). 144p. 1995. 9.95 (*0-7868-6188-6*) Hyperion.

Art of Microelectronic Systems. Apostolas Dollas. 350p. 1995. text ed. 49.95 (*1-56881-031-8*) AK Peters.

Art of Midwifery: Early Modern Midwives in Europe. Ed. by Hilary Marland. LC 92-49026. (Wellcome Institute Series in the History of Medicine). (Illus.). 256p. 1993. 74.50 (*0-415-06425-2*, B2344, Routledge NY) Routledge.

Art of Mingling: Easy, Proven Techniques for Mastering Any Room. Jeanne Martinet. 160p. (Orig.). 1992. pap. 8.95 (*0-312-08316-5*) St Martin.

Art of Mixing Work & Play. Steve Wilson. 137p. 1992. pap. 17.95 (*0-89894-052-4*) Advocate Pub Group.

Art of Modeling Dynamic Systems: Forecasting for Chaos, Randomness, & Determinism. Foster Morrison. (Scientific & Technical Computation Ser.). 387p. 1991. text ed. 69.95 (*0-471-52004-7*) Wiley.

Art of Moebius. Moebius. (Illus.). 96p. 1989. 14.95 (*0-87135-610-4*) Marvel Entmnt.

Art of Mohiniyattam. Bharati Shivaji. 1986. 38.00 (*0-8364-1925-1*, Pub. by Lancer II) S Asia.

Art of Monetary Policy. Ed. by David C. Colander & Dewey Daane. 232p. 1994. text ed. 50.00 (*1-56324-346-6*); pap. text ed. 21.95 (*1-56324-347-4*) M E Sharpe.

Art of Money Making. James D. Mills. LC 73-2524. (Big Business; Economic Power in a Free Society Ser.). 1973. reprint ed. 28.95 (*0-405-05103-4*) Ayer.

Art of Motherhood. Susan B. Tobey. (Illus.). 180p. 1991. 29.95 (*1-55859-105-2*) Abbeville Pr.

Art of Mughal India: Painting & Precious Objects. Stuart C. Welch. LC 74-27421. (Asia Society Ser.). (Illus.). 1980. reprint ed. 35.95 (*0-405-06569-8*) Ayer.

Art of Multi-Image. LC 82-87973. 144p. 1978. 16.00 (*0-685-00547-X*); pap. 18.50 (*0-89240-025-0*) Assn Ed Comm Tech.

Art of Murder. Ed. by Jonathan Goodman. 240p. 1992. pap. 10.95 (*0-8184-0562-7*, L Stuart) Carol Pub Group.

Art of Music. Francisco C. Fagundes. LC 87-50759. 91p. (Orig.). 1988. pap. 6.00 (*0-916383-42-3*, Univ Edtns) Aegina Pr.

Art of Music. Simms. (C). 1993. student ed 10.00 (*0-673-46839-9*) HarpCollege.

Art of Music, 14 vols., Set. Ed. by Daniel G. Mason. LC 74-26067. reprint ed. 525.00 (*0-404-13020-8*) AMS Pr.

Art of Music: An Introduction. Bryan R. Simms. LC 92-16878. (C). 1992. 44.50 (*0-673-38916-2*) HarpCollege.

Art of Music & Other Essays: (A Travers Chants) Hector Berlioz. Ed. & Tr. by Elizabeth Csicsery-Ronay. LC 93-3752. 1994. 29.95 (*0-253-31164-0*) Ind U Pr.

Art of Music Cassettes. Simms. (C). 1993. Pkg. of 6. text ed. 31.00 (*0-673-46863-1*) HarpCollege.

Art of Music Copying & Basic Notation. Sammy Casale. 1993. 5.95 (*1-56222-606-1*, 93852) Mel Bay.

Art of Music Licensing. Al Kohn & Bob Kohn. LC 92-589. 1992. 95.00 (*0-13-068792-8*) Aspen Law.

***Art of Musical Drumming.** Barry James. Ed. by Dale Sinclair. (Illus.). 220p. 1994. pap. 14.95 (*3-902210-41-9*) Promise Corp.

Art of Naming. Anne Ferry. 232p. 1988. 29.95 (*0-226-24464-4*) U Ch Pr.

Art of Native American Basketry: A Living Legacy. Ed. by Frank W. Porter, III. LC 89-26008. (Contributions to the Study of Anthropology Ser.: No. 5). 368p. 1990. text ed. 69.50 (*0-313-26716-2*, PAH/, Greenwood Pr) Greenwood.

Art of Natural Family Planning. 3rd ed. John F. Kippley & Sheila K. Kippley. LC 75-328470. (Illus.). 254p. 1989. pap. 8.95 (*0-9601036-6-X*) Couple to Couple.

***Art of Natural Farming & Gardening.** 3rd ed. Ed. by Ralph Engelken & Rita Engelken. LC 83-73572. (Illus.). 208p. (Orig.). 1981. pap. 9.95 (*0-942066-00-6*) Barrington IA.

Art of Natural History. S. Peter Dance. 1990. 85.00 (*0-685-33411-2*); pap. 29.99 (*0-517-69629-0*) Random Hse Value.

***Art of Natural Living.** John P. Wagner. (Illus.). 64p. 1993. pap. text ed. 29.95 (*0-9636805-1-X*) Events Unltd.

***Art of Nature: Reflections of the Grand Design.** Tim McNulty. (Illus.). 1994. pap. 24.95 (*0-930861-07-8*) Prior Pub Co.

Art of Nature: Reflections on the Grand Design. Bruce Heinemann. (Illus.). 1993. 49.95 (*0-930861-05-1*) Prior Pub Co.

Art of Nautical Illustration. Michael Leek. 1991. 29.98 (*1-55521-737-0*) Bk Sales Inc.

Art of Negotiating. Nierenbe. 1981. pap. 7.95 (*0-671-62999-9*) S&S Trade.

Art of Negotiating. Gerard I. Nierenberg. 1989. mass mkt. 5.99 (*0-671-70499-0*) PB.

Art of Negotiating. Gerard I. Nierenberg. 1990. student ed, audio 69.95 (*0-924967-00-5*) Intl Ctr Creat Think.

Art of Nepal: A Catalogue of the Los Angeles County Museum of Art Collection. Pratapaditya Pal. 1985. pap. 38.00 (*0-520-05407-5*) U CA Pr.

Art of Netsuke Carving. Masatoshi. (Illus.). 236p. 1992. reprint ed. 80.00 (*0-8348-0265-1*) Weatherhill.

Art of Netting. Ed. by Kaethe Kliot. 112p. (Orig.). 1989. pap. 10.00 (*0-916896-30-7*) Lacis Pubns.

***Art of New American Cooking.** Seilhac & Feltman. 1995. 9.98 (*1-884822-17-7*) Blck Dog & Leventhal.

Art of New Guinea: Cultural Traditions of the Sepik River: Selections from the Marion & Samuel Spring Collection. Eric K. Silverman. (Illus.). 48p. 1989. pap. 8.95 (*0-8130-0924-3*) U Press Fla.

Art of Newspaper Making. Charles A. Dana. LC 71-125689. (American Journalists Ser.). 1974. reprint ed. 16.95 (*0-405-01666-2*) Ayer.

Art of Nijinsky. Geoffrey Whitworth. LC 72-83753. (Illus.). 1972. reprint ed. 23.95 (*0-405-09073-0*) Ayer.

Art of Noises. Luigi Russolo. Tr. by Barclay Brown. LC 85-28413. (Monographs in Musicology: No. 6). 87p. 1987. lib. bdg. 31.00 (*0-918728-57-6*) Pendragon NY.

Art of Norman Rockwell. 1993. 4.95 (*0-8362-3033-7*) Andrews & McMeel.

Art of Northwest New Guinea. Ed. by Suzanne Greub. LC 90-35048. (Illus.). 224p. 1993. 50.00 (*0-8478-1295-2*) Rizzoli Intl.

Art of Nursing. 2nd ed. Wynona Bice-Stephens. 64p. 1992. 9.95 (*0-8059-3254-2*) Dorrance.

Art of Nurturing. E. E. White. 87p. 1977. pap. 6.95 (*0-917962-42-7*) Whitenwife Pubns.

Art of Nutritional Cooking. Michael Baskette. (Illus.). 350p. 1992. pap. 24.95 (*0-442-00190-8*) Van Nos Reinhold.

Art of Oboe Playing. Robert Sprenkle & David A. Ledet. (Illus.). 96p. 1961. pap. text ed. 14.95 (*0-87487-040-2*) Summy-Birchard.

Art of Ogata Kenzan: Persona & Production in Japanese Ceramics. Richard Wilson. (Illus.). 272p. 1991. 49.95 (*0-8348-0240-6*) Weatherhill.

Art of Old Peru. Walter Lehmann. LC 72-87767. (Illus.). 1975. reprint ed. 60.00 (*0-87817-119-3*) Hacker.

Art of Oliver Goldsmith. Ed. by Andrew Swarbrick. LC 84-374. (Critical Studies). 200p. 1984. 42.00 (*0-389-20462-5*, N8023) B&N Imports.

Art of Olivia: Let Them East Cheesecake. Olivia De Berardinis. Ed. by Joel Beren. (Illus.). 108p. 1995. 29.95 (*0-929643-06-2*) Ozone Prodns.

Art of Orchestration: Principles of Tone Color in Modern Scoring. Bernard Rogers. LC 73-97353. 198p. 1970. reprint ed. text ed. 49.75 (*0-8371-2969-9*, ROAO, Greenwood Pr) Greenwood.

Art of Organ Accompaniment in the Church Services. Walter L. Twinning. 1976. lib. bdg. 39.00 (*0-403-03786-7*) Scholarly.

Art of Organ Accompaniment in the Church Services. Walter L. Twinning. 1988. reprint ed. lib. bdg. 49.00 (*0-7812-0177-2*) Rprt Serv.

Art of Organ Building, 2 vols. George A. Audsley. Incl. Vol. 1. Proem. (Illus.). x, 600p. 14.95 (*0-486-21314-5*); Vol. 2. Specifications of Organs. (Illus.). iv, 750p. 14.95 (*0-486-21315-3*); write for info. (*0-318-51748-5*) Dover.

Art of Organ Voicing. L. G. Monette. LC 92-23871. 1992. 35.00 (*0-932826-25-3*) New Issues MI.

***Art of OS-2 Version 3-C Programming.** 2nd ed. Kathleen Panov & Larry Salomon. Date not set. text ed. 44.95 (*0-471-08633-9*) Wiley.

Art of OS-2 2.1 C Programming. Kathleen Panov et al. 320p. 1993. disk, pap. 39.95 (*0-471-58802-4*) Wiley.

Art of OS-2 2.1 C Programming. Kathleen Panov et al. 1993. pap. 39.95 (*0-89435-446-9*) Wiley.

Art of Oscar Wilde. Epifanio San Juan. LC 77-18910. 238p. 1978. reprint ed. text ed. 35.00 (*0-313-20211-7*, SJAO, Greenwood Pr) Greenwood.

Art of Otomo. Katsuhiro Otomo. 1991. 35.00 (*0-685-59751-2*) Marvel Entmnt.

Art of Our Necessities: Form & Consciousness in Shakespeare. Harvey Birenbaum. (American University Studies: English Language & Literature: Ser. IV, Vol. 84). 320p. (C). 1989. text ed. 43.80 (*0-8204-0799-2*) P Lang Pubs.

Art of Our Own: The Spiritual in 20th Century Art. B. Lipsey. (C). 1990. 320.00 (*0-685-34378-2*, Pub. by Collets) St Mut.

***Art of Our Time.** B. John Zavrel. Ed. by Marco Bodenstein. (Illus.). 58p. (Orig.). 1987. pap. 5.00 (*0-914301-10-1*) West-Art.

***Art of Our Time.** deluxe ed. B. John Zavrel. Ed. by Marco Bodenstein. (Illus.). 58p. (Orig.). 1987. pap. 80.00 (*0-914301-11-X*) West-Art.

Art of Outdoor Photography: Techniques for the Advanced Amateur & Professional. Boyd Norton. LC 92-35905. (Illus.). 152p. 1993. 35.00 (*0-89658-159-4*) Voyageur Pr.

Art of Painting. Charles A. Du Fresnoy. LC 76-88819. (Art Histories Collection Ser.). 1969. reprint ed. 25.95 (*0-405-02221-2*) Ayer.

Art of Painting Animals on Rocks. Lin Wellford. LC 94-7944. (Illus.). 128p. (Orig.). 1994. pap. 21.99 (*0-89134-572-8*) North Light Bks.

Art of Painting on Silk. Ed. & Tr. by Gisela Banbury. (Illus.). 128p. 1987. pap. 16.95 (*0-85532-597-6*, Pub. by Search Pr UK) A Schwartz & Co.

Art of Painting on Silk, Vol. 2. pap. 16.95 (*0-85532-623-9*, Pub. by Search Pr UK) A Schwartz & Co.

Art of Painting On Silk, Vol. 3: Fashions. Pam Dawson. 1989. pap. 19.95 (*0-85532-628-X*, Pub. by Search Pr UK) A Schwartz & Co.

Art of Painting On Silk, Vol. 4: Potpourri. Pam Dawson. 1989. pap. 19.95 (*0-85532-646-8*, Pub. by Search Pr UK) A Schwartz & Co.

Art of Pantomime. Charles Aubert. LC 68-56484. (Illus.). 1972. reprint ed. 23.95 (*0-405-08226-6*, Pub. by Blom Pubns UK) Ayer.

Art of Paper Casting: With Rycraft Ceramic Stamps. Robin Rycraft & Carol Rycraft. (Illus.). 32p. 1994. pap. 7.00 (*0-9641345-0-0*) Rycraft.

Art of Paper Crafts. Cheryl Owen. 1994. 14.98 (*0-8317-0435-7*) Smithmark.

Art of Papermaking. Bernard Toale. LC 82-74003. (Illus.). 136p. 1983. 23.50 (*0-87192-140-5*) Davis Mass.

Art of Papermaking, 1890. Alexander Watt. (Illus.). 240p. 1983. pap. 25.00 (*0-87556-581-6*) Saifer.

Art of Parallel Programming. Bruce P. Lester. 464p. 1993. text ed. 62.00 (*0-13-045923-2*) P-H.

***Art of Partnering.** Ed Rigsbee. 192p. 1994. 24.95 (*0-8403-9343-1*) Kendall-Hunt.

Art of Passing Over: An Invitation to Living Creatively. Francis Dorff. 224p. 1988. pap. 10.95 (*0-8091-2958-2*) Paulist Pr.

Art of Pastel Painting. Alan Flattman. (Illus.). 176p. 1986. 29.95 (*0-671-61318-9*) P-H.

***Art of Pastoring: Contemplative Reflections.** William C. Martin. 92p. (Orig.). 1994. pap. 7.95 (*1-885121-00-8*) CTS Press.

Art of Pastoring: Ministry Without All the Answers. David Hansen. LC 94-409. 192p. (Orig.). 1994. pap. 10.99 (*0-8308-1669-0*, 1669) InterVarsity.

Art of Patinas for Bronze. Michael S. Edge. 120p. (C). 1990. pap. 24.95 (*1-879257-00-9*) Artesia Pr.

Art of Paul Sandby. E. Bruce Robertson. LC 85-40260. (Illus.). 112p. (Orig.). 1985. pap. 12.95 (*0-930606-47-7*) Yale Ctr Brit Art.

Art of Paul Sawyier. Arthur F. Jones. LC 75-41988. 208p. 1976. 35.00 (*0-8131-1340-7*) U Pr of Ky.

Art of Peace. George Ohsawa. Ed. by Sandy Rothman. Tr. by William Gleason. LC 90-82077. 152p. (Orig.). 1990. pap. 7.95 (*0-918860-50-4*) G Ohsawa.

***Art of Peace: A Personal Manual on Peacemaking & Creativity.** Stephen L. Fiske. (Illus.). (Orig.). 1995. pap. 20.00 (*0-932727-83-2*, N Paradigm Bks) Hope Pub Hse.

Art of Peace: Teachings of the Founder of Aikido. Morihei Ueshiba. Ed. & Tr. by John Stevens. LC 92-50118. (Pocket Classics Ser.). 140p. (Orig.). 1992. pap. 6.00 (*0-87773-851-3*) Shambhala Pubns.

Art of Pencil Drawing. Gene Franks. (Collector's Ser.). (Illus.). 144p. 1994. pap. 19.95 (*1-56010-186-5*, CS01-S) W Foster Pub.

Art of Pencil Drawing. Ernest W. Watson. (Illus.). 160p. 1985. pap. 12.95 (*0-8230-0276-4*, Watsn-Guptill) Watsn-Guptill.

Art of Perfect Parenting & Other Absurd Ideas. Andrew G. Yellen. 122p. (Orig.). 1993. pap. text ed. 10.95 (*0-9639499-0-X*) Yellen & Assocs.

***Art of Performing Bamboo Instruments of Bali, Bk. 1.** Julia Hansen. (JPN.). 1992. pap. 12.00 (*0-614-04568-1*) Linaria Pr.

***Art of Performing Bamboo Instruments of Bali, Bk. 2.** Julia Hansen. 1994. pap. 12.00 (*0-614-04569-X*) Linaria Pr.

Art of Perfume: Discovering & Collecting Perfume Bottles. Christie M. Lefkowith. LC 94-60270. (Illus.). 208p. 1994. 60.00 (*0-500-23686-0*) Thames Hudson.

Art of Persian Cooking. Forough Hekmat. (International Cookbook Classics Ser.). 190p. 1994. pap. 9.95 (*0-7818-0241-5*) Hippocrene Bks.

Art of Persian Music. J. During et al. LC 90-43217. 280p. 1990. disk 100.00 (*0-934211-22-1*); disk 100.00 (*0-685-58481-X*) Mage Pubs Inc.

Art of Personal Filmmaking. Bastian Cleve. (Illus.). 230p. 1989. spiral bd., vhs 49.95 (*0-9623848-1-X*); spiral bd., vhs 49.95 (*0-9623848-2-8*); spiral bd. 24.95 (*0-9623848-0-1*) Images Intl.

Art of Personal Prayer. Lance Webb. (Abingdon Classics Ser.). 160p. 1992. pap. 4.95 (*0-687-01920-6*) Abingdon.

Art of Persuasion: A National Review Rhetoric for Writers. Linda Bridges & William F. Rickenbacker. LC 91-67486. 144p. 1993. pap. text ed. 8.95 (*0-8264-0584-3*) Continuum.

Art of Persuasion: A National Review Rhetoric for Writers. Linda Bridges & William F. Rickenbacker. (Illus.). 144p. 1991. write for info. (*0-9627841-0-9*) Natl Review.

Art of Persuasion: Political Propaganda from Aeneas to Brutus. Jane D. Evans. LC 91-42665. (Illus.). 220p. (C). 1992. text ed. 39.50 (*0-472-10282-6*) U of Mich Pr.

Art of Persuasion in Greece. George A. Kennedy. LC 63-7070. 362p. reprint ed. pap. 103.20 (*0-8357-6027-8*, 2034658) Bks Demand.

Art of Peter Scott: Images from a Lifetime. Sel. by Peter Scott. (Illus.). 168p. 1993. 55.00 (*1-85619-100-1*, Sinclair-Stevenson) Trafalgar.

***Art of Peter Voulkos.** Rose Slivka & Karen Tsujimoto. Ed. by Barry Lancet. (Illus.). 192p. 1995. 70.00 (*4-7700-1807-X*) Kodansha.

Art of Philosophizing & Other Essays. Bertrand Russell. (Quality Paperback Ser.: No. 273). 119p. 1977. reprint ed. pap. 9.95 (*0-8226-0273-3*) Littlefield.

Art of Photographic Lighting. Michael Busselle. (Illus.). 192p. 1993. 27.95 (*0-7153-9805-9*, Pub. by D & C Pub UK) Sterling.

***Art of Photographic Lighting.** Michael Busselle. (Illus.). 192p. 1995. pap. 19.95 (*0-7153-0282-5*, Pub. by D & C Pub UK) Sterling.

Art of Photographing Nature. Photos by Art Wolfe. 1993. 27.50 (*0-517-88034-2*, Crown) Crown Pub Group.

Art of Photographing North America. W. Jeklin. 1992. 14.98 (*0-88365-706-6*) Galahad Bks.

***Art of Photography.** Bruce Barnbaum. 176p. 1994. per., pap. text ed. 32.95 (*0-8403-9647-3*) Kendall-Hunt.

Art of Photoplay Making. Victor O. Freeburg. LC 72-124006. (Literature of Cinema Ser.). 1970. reprint ed. 21.95 (*0-405-01612-3*) Ayer.

Art of Piano Playing. Heinrich Neuhaus. Tr. by K. A. Leibovitch. LC 89-2585. 240p. 1989. 32.00 (*0-89341-556-1*, Longwood Academic) Hollowbrook.

***Art of Piano Playing.** Heinrich Neuhaus. Tr. by K. A. Leibovitch. LC 89-2585. 240p. 1995. pap. 22.50 (*0-89341-756-4*, Longwood Academic) Hollowbrook.

Art of Piano Playing: A Scientific Approach. George Kochevitsky. (Illus.). 80p. (J). (gr. 9 up). 1967. pap. text ed. 11.95 (*0-87487-068-2*) Summy-Birchard.

Art of Pilotage. John Mellor. (Illus.). 192p. 1990. 27.50 (*0-924486-04-X*) Sheridan.

Art of Pitching. Tom Seaver & Lee Lowenfish. LC 83-83031. (Illus.). 224p. 1984. 17.00 (*0-688-02663-X*) Hearst Bks.

Art of Pitching. Tom Seaver. 1994. pap. 10.00 (*0-688-13226-X*) Hearst Bks.

Art of Pizza Making: Trade Secrets & Recipes. Dominick A. DeAngelis. LC 92-90099. (Illus.). 100p. (Orig.). 1992. pap. 6.95 (*0-9632034-0-1*) Creat Pizza.

***Art of Planned Giving: Understanding Donors & the Culture of Giving.** White. (Nonprofit Law, Finance & Management Ser.). Date not set. text ed. 49.95 (*0-471-08149-3*) Wiley.

Art of Planning: Selected Essays of Harvey S. Perloff. Ed. by Leland S. Burns & John Friedmann. LC 85-12470. (Environment, Development, & Public Policy: Public Policy & Social Services Ser.). 378p. 1985. 60.00 (*0-306-42030-9*, Plenum Pr) Plenum.

Art of Planting, Vol. 1. Rosemary Verey. 1990. 40.00 (*0-316-89976-3*) Little.

***Art of Plato: Ten Essays in Platonic Interpretation.** R. B. Rutherford. LC 94-41991. 352p. (C). 1995. text ed. 45.00 (*0-674-04811-3*) HUP.

Art of Play: An Adult's Guide to Reclaiming Imagination & Spontaneity. Adam Blatner & Allee Blatner. LC 86-27419. 203p. 1987. 32.95 (*0-89885-355-9*); pap. 20.95 (*0-89885-359-1*) Human Sci Pr.

Art of Playing Bingo & Winning Consistently. B. A. Hartwell. (Orig.). 1980. pap. 6.95 (*0-934650-01-2*) Sunnyside.

Art of Playing on the Violin, 1751. Francesco Geminiani. Ed. by David D. Boyden. 1952. 24.95 (*0-19-322200-0*) OUP.

Art of Playing Real Life Monopoly: The Wage Earner's Guide to Building an Estate. Duncan Lindsey. (Illus.). 224p. (Orig.). 1986. pap. 9.95 (*0-936667-00-1*) Oregon Pr.

***Art of Playing Rock Guitar.** Richard Daniels. (Illus.). 180p. Date not set. pap. 18.95 (*0-89524-895-6*, 02509127) Cherry Lane.

Art of Playing Second Fiddle. Theodore W. Schroeder. 96p. 1985. pap. 5.99 (*0-570-03950-9*, 12-2884) Concordia.

Art of Playing the Fantasia. Thomas De Sancta Maria. Tr. by Warren E. Hultberg & Almonte C. Howell, Jr. LC 90-29326. (Illus.). 850p. 1991. 99.95 (*0-935480-52-8*) Lat Am Lit Rev Pr.

Art of Playing the Flute: Breath Control. Roger Mather. LC 80-52140. (Series of Workbooks: Vol. 1). (Illus.). 88p. (Orig.). (C). 1980. pap. 8.95 (*0-9604640-0-X*) Romney Pr.

Art of Playing the Flute: Embouchure, Vol. 2. Roger Mather. LC 80-52140. (Illus.). 112p. (Orig.). (C). 1981. pap. 9.95 (*0-9604640-1-8*) Romney Pr.

Art of Playing the Piano: Conversations with Mortimer Markoff. Mortimer Markoff & Frederic W. Platt. Ed. by Merlyn Holmes. LC 93-38483. (Illus.). 144p. (Orig.). 1993. pap. 14.95 (*0-9639221-7-3*) London Rd Bks.

Art of Playing the Recorder. Daniel Waitzman. LC 77-78321. 1990. 22.50 (*0-404-16010-7*); pap. 9.50 (*0-404-16011-5*) AMS Pr.

Art of Playwriting: Lectures Delivered at the University of Pennsylvania on the Mask & Wig Foundation. LC 67-22051. (Essay Index Reprint Ser.). 1977. reprint ed. 18.95 (*0-8369-0159-2*) Ayer.

***Art of Pocahontas.** Steven Rebello. (Illus.). 200p. 1995. 50.00 (*0-7868-6158-4*) Hyperion.

Art of Poetry. Denise Folliot. 1989. pap. 12.95 (*0-691-01880-4*) Princeton U Pr.

Art of Poetry. Peter Levi. 336p. (C). 1991. 37.00 (*0-300-04847-5*) Yale U Pr.

Art of Poetry. Ed. & Tr. by Burton Raffel. LC 78-171176. 83p. (ENG & LAT.). 1974. 19.50 (*0-87395-240-5*) State U NY Pr.

Art of Poetry. Horace. LC 79-158320. (Augustan Translators Ser.). reprint ed. 49.50 (*0-404-54123-2*) AMS Pr.

Art of Poetry: Seven Lectures, 1920-1922. William P. Ker. LC 67-26752. (Essay Index Reprint Ser.). 1977. 18.95 (*0-8369-0590-3*) Ayer.

Art of Poetry Writing: A Guide for Poets, Students, & Readers. William Packard. 240p. 1992. 18.95 (*0-312-07641-X*) St Martin.

Art of Poland. Irena G. Piotrowska. LC 75-179736. (Biography Index Reprint Ser.). 1977. reprint ed. 38.95 (*0-8369-8104-9*) Ayer.

Art of Polish Cooking. Alina Zeranska. (Illus.). 384p. 1989. reprint ed. 17.95 (*0-88289-709-8*) Pelican.

An Asterisk (*) at the beginning of an entry indicates that the title is appearing in BIP for the first time.

An Asterisk (*) at the beginning of an entry indicates that the title is appearing in BIP for the first time.

451

***Art of Sexual Magic.** Margo Anand. LC 95-11379. 1995. write for info. (0-87477-814-X, J P T-Putnam) Putnam Pub Group.

Art of Shakespeare. Ed. by Georgina Callan. (Illus.). 136p. 1989. write for info. (0-318-64075-9) Corky Inc.

Art of Shan-Shan Sheng. Joan Cohen & Jeff Hantover. (Illus.). 96p. (Orig.). Date not set. 28.00 (0-9634729-3-3); pap. 16.00 (0-9634729-6-8) East West Art.

Art of Sharing Your Faith. Joel D. Heck. LC 90-48506. 1991. pap. 8.99 (0-8007-5387-9) Revell.

***Art of Shelling: A Complete Guide to Finding Shells & Other Beach Collectibles at Shelling Locations from Florida to Maine.** Chuck Robinson & Debbie Robinson. LC 95-69822. (Illus.). 152p. (Orig.). 1995. pap. 14.95 (0-9647267-6-9) Old Squan Vill Pub.

Art of Shetland Lace. Sarah Don. (Illus.). 119p. 1991. reprint ed. pap. 26.00 (0-916896-34-X) Lacis Pubns.

Art of Shiatsu. Cowmeadow. 1992. pap. 16.95 (1-85230-328-X) Element MA.

Art of Shibata Zeshin: The Mr. & Mrs. James E. O'Brien Collection. Text by Howard A. Link. LC 79-24341. (Illus.). 195p. 1995. 25.00 (0-903697-05-X, 237) Honolu Arts.

Art of Shibata Zeshin: The Mr. & Mrs. James E. O'Brien Collection at the Honolulu Academy of Arts. Howard A. Link. (Illus.). 196p. (C). 1979. 25.00 (0-937426-23-7) Honolu Arts.

Art of Ship & Boat Handling. Robert D. Moss. Ed. by Neal Kimel. LC 93-206641. (Illus.). 150p. 1991. 49.95 (1-883121-00-0) Onboard Marine.

Art of Shooting Baskets: From the Free Throw to the Slam Dunk. Ted St. Martin & Frank Frangie. LC 92-20264. (Illus.). 160p. 1992. pap. 9.95 (0-8092-4009-2) Contemp Bks.

Art of Showing Art. rev. ed. James K. Reeve. LC 86-61319. (Illus.). 144p. (Orig.). 1992. pap. 14.95 (0-933031-67-X) Coun Oak Bks.

Art of Shrinking. Jerome J. Klinman. LC 83-733313. (Illus.). 176p. 1984. 17.95 (0-915417-00-6) Argent Pr.

Art of Side Saddle: History, Etiquette, Showing. Rosamund Owen. 176p. 1989. 90.00 (0-9509663-0-4) St Mut.

Art of Silence: Meditating the Western Way. Elizabeth Baron & Sandra Frazier-Delsignore. (Illus.). 187p. (Orig.). 1992. pap. 12.95 (1-884039-00-6) DOrlamonde Prods.

Art of Silk Ribbon Embroidery. Judith B. Montano. Ed. by Louise O. Townsend. LC 92-53801. (Illus.). 80p. 1993. pap. 21.95 (0-914881-55-8) C & T Pub.

Art of Simon Dinnerstein. LC 89-20625. (Illus.). 268p. 1990. 50.00 (1-55728-142-4); pap. 35.00 (1-55728-143-2) U of Ark Pr.

Art of Simpling. W. Coles. 114p. 1986. spiral bd. 9.90 (0-7873-0189-2) Mokelumne.

Art of Sinclair Lewis. David J. Dooley. LC 65-17173. 302p. reprint ed. pap. 86.10 (0-7837-6024-8, 2045836) Bks Demand.

Art of Singing. W. J. Henderson. LC 78-4953. (Music Reprint Ser.: 1978). 1978. reprint ed. lib. bdg. 49.50 (0-306-77593-X) Da Capo.

Art of Singing: How to Sing, 2 vols. in 1. Enrico Caruso & Louisa Tetrazzini. LC 74-23417. (Music Reprint Ser.). 1975. reprint ed. lib. bdg. 29.50 (0-306-70674-1) Da Capo.

Art of Singing & Voice Technique. Viktor Fuchs. (Illus.). 160p. (Orig.). 1986. pap. 12.95 (0-7145-0032-1) Riverrun NY.

Art of Single Living: A Guide to Goin' It Alone in the 90's. Ruthe Stein. 1993. reprint ed. pap. 9.99 (1-56171-234-5, S P I Bks) Sure Sellers.

Art of Single Living: A Guide to Going It Alone in the '90s. Ruthe Stein. 276p. 1990. 16.95 (1-56171-001-6) Sure Sellers.

Art of Single String Soloing. Sal Salvador. (Sal Salvador Jazz Guitar Ser.). 1993. 7.95 (0-685-64253-4, 94186); audio 9.98 (0-685-64254-2, 94186) Mel Bay.

Art of Skiing 1856-1936: Timeless, Enchanting Illustrations & Narrative of Skiing's Formative Years. Gary H. Schwartz. LC 89-50585. (Illus.). 172p. (Orig.). 1989. pap. 19.95 (0-9623000-1-2) Wood River CA.

Art of Slave Narrative: Original Essays in Criticism & Theory. Ed. by John Sekora & Darwin T. Turner. (Essays in Literature Book Ser.: Bk. 5). 144p. 1982. pap. text ed. 8.00 (0-934312-04-4) WIU Essays Lit.

Art of Smooth Pasting. Avinash Dixit. LC 92-45249. (Fundamentals of Pure & Applied Economics Ser.: Vol. 55). 1993. pap. text ed. 18.00 (3-7186-5384-2) Gordon & Breach.

Art of Soapmaking. Merilyn Mohr. 128p. 1989. pap. 9.95 (0-920656-03-X, Pub. by Camden Hse CN) Firefly Bks Ltd.

***Art of Soccer: A Better Way to Play.** rev. ed. Player Picker Staff & Mark G. Catlin. 206p. (Orig.). 1993. 24.95 (0-9626834-2-6) Soccer Bks.

Art of Social Dancing. L. Hostetler. (Ballroom Dance Ser.). 1986. lib. bdg. 79.95 (0-8490-3302-0) Gordon Pr.

Art of Social Dancing. L. Hostetler. (Ballroom Dance Ser.). 1985. lib. bdg. 74.00 (0-87700-666-0) Revisionist Pr.

Art of Software Design. Isensee. 1995. text ed. 42.95 (0-442-01848-7) Van Nos Reinhold.

Art of Software Testing. Glenford J. Myers. LC 78-12923. (Business Data Processing Ser.). 177p. 1979. text ed. 53.95 (0-471-04328-1, Wiley-Interscience) Wiley.

Art of Solo Fingerpicking. rev. ed. Mark Hanson. 80p. 1992. audio, pap. text ed. 18.95 (0-936799-02-1) Accent Music.

Art of Solving Word Problems. Clarence J. Wallen. 60p. 1992. per. 8.95 (0-8403-7395-3) Kendall-Hunt.

Art of Soul-Winning. 2nd exp. rev. ed. Murray W. Downey. LC 57-9523. 1989. 9.99 (0-8010-2985-6) Baker Bk.

Art of Sound Building. William Halfpenny & John Halfpenny. LC 69-13236. (Illus.). 1972. reprint ed. 15.95 (0-405-08587-7, Pub. by Blom Pubns UK) Ayer.

Art of Sound Effects Editor. Ed. by Marvin Kerner. (Illus.). 118p. 1989. pap. 21.95 (0-240-80008-7, Focal) Buttrwrth-Heinemann.

Art of South American Cooking. Felipe Rojas-Lombardi. LC 90-56395. 416p. 1991. 30.00 (0-06-016425-5, HarpT) HarpC.

Art of South India. Andhra Pradesh & Rajendra Prasad. (C). 1980. 35.00 (0-8364-2466-2, Pub. by Sundeep II) S Asia.

Art of South India: Tamilnadu & Kerala. K. V. Rajan. (C). 1988. 32.50 (0-8364-2465-4, Pub. by Sundeep II) S Asia.

Art of South Indian Cooking. Aroona Reejhsinghani. 141p. 1982. 6.95 (0-318-36302-X) Asia Bk Corp.

Art of Southeast Asia: Cambodia, Vietnam, Thailand, Laos, Burma, Java & Bali. Philip Rawson. LC 89-52204. (World of Art Ser.). (Illus.). 252p. 1990. pap. 14.95 (0-500-20060-2) Thames Hudson.

Art of Southern Sung China. James Cahill. LC 74-27411. (Asia Society Ser.). (Illus.). 1976. reprint ed. lib. bdg. 26.95 (0-405-06560-4) Ayer.

Art of Spanking. Milo Manara. Tr. by Elisabeth Bell. 96p. 1993. pap. 17.95 (1-56163-090-X, Eurotica) NBM.

Art of Speculation. rev. ed. Philip L. Carret. LC 75-2625. (Wall Street & the Security Market Ser.). 1975. reprint ed. 34.95 (0-405-06951-0) Ayer.

Art of Speculation. Philip L. Carret. LC 84-73108. 1979. reprint ed. 20.00 (0-87034-050-6) Fraser Pub Co.

Art of Speech. 11th ed. Dora Krummel. 172p. (C). 1990. pap. 35.00 (0-908175-30-2, Pub. by Boolarong Pubns AT) St Mut.

Art of Speech: A Handbook of Elocution. 4th rev. ed. Kathleen Rich. 108p. 1984. 25.00 (0-905418-38-7, Pub. by Gresham Bks UK) St Mut.

Art of Spiderwebbing on a Cloak of Black. Syrinx. Ed. by Thorguard Templar. 74p. (Orig.). 1993. 20.00 (1-883147-99-9) Intern Guild ASRS.

Art of Spiritual Guidance: A Contemporary Approach to Growing in the Spirit. Carolyn Gratton. 264p. 1993. reprint ed. pap. 14.95 (0-8245-1223-5) Crossroad NY.

Art of Spiritual Healing. Keith Sherwood. LC 85-10224. (New Age Ser.). (Illus.). 224p. (Orig.). 1985. pap. 7.95 (0-87542-720-0) Llewellyn Pubns.

Art of Spiritual Healing. Joel S. Goldsmith. 192p. 1992. reprint ed. pap. 10.00 (0-06-250364-2) Harper SF.

***Art of Sports Officiating.** Kathryn L. Davis. LC 95-2559. 1996. write for info. (0-615-00483-0) Allyn.

Art of Stage Dancing: A Manual of Stagecraft. N. Wayburn. 1976. lib. bdg. 59.95 (0-8490-1454-9) Gordon Pr.

Art of Stage Lighting. 3rd ed. Frederick Bentham. (Illus.). 1976. 24.95 (0-87830-009-0, Theatre Arts Bks) Routledge Chapman & Hall.

Art of Stained Glass Made Easy. Barry Bier. (Illus.). 96p. 1994. pap. 14.95 (1-85368-226-8, Pub. by New Holland Pubs UK) Sterling.

Art of Star Wars. Carol W. Titelman. (Illus.). 1985. 17.95 (0-345-33217-2, Ballantine Trade) Ballantine.

Art of Star Wars: A New Hope. Ed. by Carol Titelman. (Illus.). 176p. 1994. pap. 18.00 (0-345-39202-7, Del Rey) Ballantine.

Art of Star Wars: Return of the Jedi. (Illus.). 160p. 1994. pap. 18.00 (0-345-39204-3) Ballantine.

Art of Star Wars: The Empire Strikes Back. Ed. by Deborah Call. (Illus.). 176p. 1994. pap. 18.00 (0-345-39203-5) Ballantine.

Art of Star Wars Galaxy. G. Gerani. 1993. pap. 19.95 (1-883313-01-5) Topps Comics.

***Art of Star Wars Galaxy Vol. II.** Gary Gerani. (Illus.). 128p. (Orig.). 1994. pap. 19.95 (1-883313-03-1) Topps Comics.

Art of Statistical Science: A Tribute to G. S. Watson. Ed. by K. V. Mardia. (Probability & Mathematical Statistics: Applied Probability & Statistics Section Ser.: No. 1345). 317p. 1992. text ed. 190.00 (0-471-93110-1) Wiley.

Art of Staying Sane. Joseph Barth. LC 70-117757. (Essay Index Reprint Ser.). 1977. 20.95 (0-8369-1783-9) Ayer.

Art of Staying Together. Michael S. Broder. 256p. 1994. reprint ed. mass mkt. 5.50 (0-380-72263-1) Avon.

Art of Stencilling. Lynn Le Grice. (Illus.). 1990. pap. 17.95 (0-517-58016-0, C P Pubs) Crown Pub Group.

Art of Stephen Hickman. Stephen Hickman. (Illus.). 120p. 1989. pap. 12.95 (0-89865-760-1) Donning Co.

Art of Stepmothering. Pearl Prilik. 256p. 1994. 19.95 (1-56796-042-1) WRS Group.

Art of Steve Hanks: Poised Between Heartbeats. Keith G. Olson. (Illus.). 128p. 1994. 69.95 (0-9618978-2-1) Hadley Hse.

Art of Steve Hanks: Poised Between Heartbeats. deluxe limited ed. Keith G. Olson. (Illus.). 128p. 1994. 200.00 (0-9618978-3-X) Hadley Hse.

Art of Storytelling. Elaine M. Ward. 1990. pap. 9.95 (1-877871-07-9) Ed Ministries.

Art of Storytelling: Creative Ideas for Preparation & Performance. Marsh Cassady. LC 94-12938. 1994. 12.95 (1-56608-002-9) Meriwether Pub.

Art of Strategic Planning for Information Technology: Crafting Strategy for the 90's. Bernard H. Boar. LC 93-9880. 320p. 1993. text ed. 39.95 (0-471-59918-2) Wiley.

Art of Strategy: A New Translation of Sun Tzu's Classic The Art of War. R. L. Wing. LC 87-37465. (Illus.). 168p. 1988. pap. 15.95 (0-385-23784-7, Dolp) Doubleday.

Art of Stretching & Kicking. James Lew. LC 80-106144. (Illus.). 104p. 1977. pap. 7.95 (0-86568-007-8, 206) Unique Pubns.

Art of Strict Musical Composition. Jonann P. Kirnberger. Ed. by David Beach. Tr. by Jurgen Thyme. LC 81-853. (Yale Music Theory Translation Ser.: No. 4). 448p. (C). 1982. 50.00 (0-300-02483-5) Yale U Pr.

Art of String Quartet Playing. M. Herter Norton. 1966. pap. 4.95 (0-393-00360-4) Norton.

Art of Study: The Sorbonne Method. Edmond B. Szekely. (Illus.). 40p. 1973. pap. 3.50 (0-89564-065-1) IBS Intl.

Art of Styling Paragraphs. Robert M. Esch & Roberta R. Walker. (Illus.). 224p. (C). 1990. Incl. instr's. manual. pap. write for info. (0-02-334310-9) Macmillan.

Art of Styling Sentences: Twenty Patterns for Success. 3rd ed. Marie L. Waddell et al. LC 92-34542. 150p. 1993. pap. 8.95 (0-8120-1448-0) Barron.

Art of Sub-Saharan Africa: The Fred & Rita Richman Collection. Christine M. Kreamer. Ed. by Amanda Woods & Kelly Morris. LC 86-82472. (Illus.). 96p. (Orig.). 1986. 16.95 (0-939802-25-2) High Mus Art.

Art of Success - in the Ruins. Nick Dear. (Methuen New Theatrescripts Ser.). 100p. (Orig.). (C). 1989. pap. 13.95 (0-685-44877-0, A0705, Pub. by Methuen UK) Heinemann.

***Art of Success & in the Ruins.** Nick Dear. 100p. (C). 1994. pap. 13.95 (0-413-68230-7, A0705, Pub. by Methuen UK) Heinemann.

Art of Successful Deer Hunting. Francis E. Sell. 188p. 1980. pap. 5.95 (0-932558-13-5) Willow Creek Pr.

Art of Successful Praying. Gordon Lindsay. 1967. 1.95 (0-89985-079-0) Christ for the Nations.

***Art of Successful Rhythm Piano-Keyboard Playing.** Andrew D. Gordon. 1994. 19.95 (1-882146-36-0) A D G Prods.

***Art of Successful Self-Management, Writing & Self-Publishing.** Clayton A. Stahlka. (Illus.). 204p. 1995. spiral bd. 24.95 (0-9645791-0-3) Stahlka Assocs.

Art of Successful Teaching: A Blend of Content & Context. Tim Lautzenheiser. LC 91-77572. 240p. 1992. 19.95 (0-941050-29-7, G-3722) GIA Pubns.

Art of Supportive Leadership: A Practical Handbook for People in Positions of Responsibility. J. Donald Walters. LC 88-129718. (Illus.). 110p. (Orig.). 1987. pap. 7.95 (0-916124-20-7, CCP3) Crystal Clarity.

Art of Surgical Technique. Milton T. Edgerton. (Illus.). 218p. 1988. pap. 40.00 (0-683-02749-2) Williams & Wilkins.

Art of Survival. A. E. Maxwell. 1993. mass mkt. 4.99 (0-06-104115-7, Harp PBks) HarpC.

Art of Survival. James D. Quinn. LC 93-93947. 112p. 1994. pap. 7.00 (1-56002-357-0, Univ Edtns) Aegina Pr.

Art of Survival in East Africa: The Kerebe & Long-Distance Trade, 1800-1895. Gerald Hartwig. LC 74-84653. 250p. 1976. 49.50 (0-8419-0182-1, Africana) Holmes & Meier.

Art of Swedish Massage. Bertild Ravald. (Illus.). 120p. 1984. pap. 14.95 (0-930267-18-4) Bergh Pub.

Art of Swimming, Sixteen Ninety-Six. 3rd ed. Melchisedec Thevenot. LC 72-87722. (Illus.). 1972. reprint ed. lib. bdg. 11.95 (0-405-09027-7, Pub. by Blom Pubns UK) Ayer.

Art of Synthesis. Alan Leo. (Astrologer's Library). 318p. 1989. pap. 12.95 (0-89281-178-1) Inner Tradit.

Art of Syrian Cookery. Helen Corey. (International Cooking Classics Ser.). (Illus.). 186p. 1992. pap. 8.95 (0-7818-0095-1) Hippocrene Bks.

Art of Syrian Cookery. Helen E. Corey. 190p. 1993. pap. 12.95 (0-9626376-2-9) Charlyn Pub Hse.

Art of T. S. Eliot. Helen Gardner. 196p. 1980. pap. 9.95 (0-571-08527-X) Faber & Faber.

Art of Tai Chi: A Practical Guide. Paul Crompton. (Home Library of Alternative Medicine). (Illus.). 160p. 1993. pap. 16.95 (1-85230-430-8) Element MA.

Art of Taking Minutes. Delores Dochterman. LC 82-42639. 208p. 1982. 21.00 (0-9609526-0-8) Snyder Pub Co.

Art of Talking So That People Will Listen: Getting Through to Family, Friends, & Associates. Paul Swets. (Illus.). 188p. 1986. pap. 8.95 (0-13-047837-7) P-H.

Art of Talking to Yourself & Others. Harry Hazel. LC 87-62196. 150p. 1987. pap. 7.95 (1-55612-081-8) Sheed & Ward MO.

***Art of Talking with Your Teenager.** rev. ed. Paul W. Swets. 224p. 1995. pap. 9.95 (1-55850-478-8) Adams Pubng.

Art of Tantra. Philip Rawson. (World of Art Ser.). (Illus.). 216p. 1985. pap. 14.95 (0-500-20166-8) Thames Hudson.

***Art of Tarot.** Christina Olsen. LC 95-15102. 1995. write for info. (0-7892-0016-3) Abbeville Pr.

***Art of Tassel Making.** Susan Dickens. (Illus.). 1995. text ed. 29.95 (1-86373-618-2) IPG Chicago.

***Art of Taste: A Gourmet Guide to Vegeterian Cooking.** Beatrix Rohlsen. (Illus.). 141p. 1994. pap. 19.95 (0-9643302-0-2) Gourmet Creat.

Art of Tatting. Katharin L. Hoare. Ed. by Jules Kliot. (Illus.). 128p. 1982. reprint ed. 30.00 (0-916896-19-6) Lacis Pubns.

Art of Teaching. Gilbert Highet. 1989. pap. 10.00 (0-679-72314-5, Vin) Random.

Art of Teaching: Sixteenth-Century Allegorical Prints & Drawings. Patricia A. Emison. Ed. by Elise K. Kenney. LC 86-50993. (Illus.). 103p. (Orig.). 1986. pap. 10.00 (0-318-42457-6) Yale Art Gallery.

Art of Teaching Art: A Complete Art Curriculum Planning Guide. Sandra Woodworth. 80p. (C). 1993. pap. 22.50 (1-884651-01-1) Show & Tell.

Art of Teaching Ballroom Dancing. J. Lanza. (Ballroom Dance Ser.). 1986. lib. bdg. 99.95 (0-8490-3326-8) Gordon Pr.

Art of Teaching Craft: A Complete Handbook. Joyce Spencer & Deborah Kneen. (Illus.). 80p. 1994. pap. 9.95 (1-86351-106-7, Pub. by S Milner AT) Sterling.

Art of Teaching Dance Technique. Joan Schlaich & Betty DuPont. (Illus.). 112p. (Orig.). (C). 1993. pap. text ed. 17.95 (0-88314-544-8) AAHPERD.

Art of Teaching ESL: Staff Development Program. 1992. pap. text ed. 53.27 (0-201-50172-4); teacher ed, vhs 158.67 (0-201-19525-9) Longman.

Art of Teaching Writing. Lucy M. Calkins. LC 85-21922. (Illus.). 347p. (C). 1985. pap. text ed. 21.50 (0-435-08246-9) Heinemann.

Art of Teaching Writing. 2nd ed. Calkins. 544p. 1994. text ed. 35.95 (0-435-08817-3) Heinemann.

Art of Teaching Writing. 2nd ed. Calkins. LC 93-21095. 544p. (C). 1994. pap. text ed. 25.00 (0-435-08809-2) Heinemann.

Art of Technical Documentation. Katherine Haramundanis. (Software Development Ser.). (Illus.). 267p. (Orig.). 1991. pap. 28.95 (1-55558-080-7, EY-H892E-DP, Digital DEC) Buttrwrth-Heinemann.

Art of Telling: Essays on Fiction. Frank Kermode. 240p. 1985. pap. text ed. 12.95 (0-674-04829-6) HUP.

Art of Tennis, 1874-1940: Timeless, Enchanting, Illustrations & Narrative of Tennis' Formative Years. Gary H. Schwartz. (Illus.). 172p. (Orig.). 1990. pap. 19.95 (0-9623000-4-7) Wood River CA.

Art of Terry Redlin: Opening Windows to the Wild. 4th deluxe limited ed. Keith G. Olson. (Illus.). 132p. 1991. ring bd. 400.00 (0-9618978-1-3) Hadley Hse.

Art of Terry Redlin: Opening Windows to the Wild. 4th ed. Keith G. Olson. (Illus.). 132p. 1991. 65.00 (0-9618978-0-5) Hadley Hse.

Art of the Actor-Manager: Wilson Barrett & the Victorian Theatre. James M. Thomas. LC 83-17864. (Theater & Dramatic Studies: No. 15). (Illus.). 215p. reprint ed. pap. 61.30 (0-8357-1492-6, 2070580) Bks Demand.

Art of the Advanced Dungeons & Dragons Fantasy Game, Bk. II. Ed. by Mary Kirchoff. LC 85-51039. (Illus.). 128p. (Orig.). 1989. pap. 16.95 (0-88038-605-3) TSR Inc.

Art of the Aeneid. William S. Anderson. Ed. by John H. Betts. 121p. (C). 1989. reprint ed. pap. 11.00 (0-86516-237-9) Bolchazy-Carducci.

Art of the Affair. Charles Creed. 80p. (Orig.). 1980. pap. 3.95 (0-933180-10-1) Ellis Pr.

Art of the Amateur. Robert T. Hogan & Richard Burnham. 368p. 1984. 52.50 (0-85105-372-6, Pub. by Colin Smythe Ltd UK) Dufour.

Art of the American Indian. Levin et al. Ed. by Vandervelde. 1973. 1.25 (0-89992-077-2) Coun India Ed.

***Art of the American Indian Frontier: A Portfolio.** David W. Penney. LC 94-42820. 24p. 1995. 18.95 (1-56584-251-0) New Press NY.

Art of the American Indian Frontier: The Chandler-Pohrt Collection. David W. Penny. LC 91-37736. (Illus.). 368p. 1993. pap. 35.00 (0-295-97318-8) U of Wash Pr.

***Art of the Amplifier.** Michael Doyle. (Illus.). 80p. (Orig.). 1995. pap. text ed. 22.95 (0-7935-3989-7, HL00330002) H Leonard.

Art of the Ancient Near East. Pierre Amiet. (Illus.). 620p. 1980. 150.00 (0-8109-0638-4, 0638-4) Abrams.

Art of the Ancient World. H. A. Groenewegen-Frankfort & Bernard Ashmole. (Janson Art History Ser.). (Illus.). 512p. (C). 1971. text ed. 59.95 (0-13-047001-5) P-H.

Art of the Ancient World: A Guide for the Collector & Investor, Vol. IV. Jerome M. Eisenberg. LC 82-168565. (Illus.). 208p. 1985. 20.00 (0-934749-00-0); pap. 15.00 (0-934749-01-9) Eisenberg Inc.

Art of the Anglo-Saxon Age. Esther Jackson. 1964. 20.00 (0-87233-827-4) Bauhan.

Art of the Architectural Model. Akiko Busch. (Illus.). 128p. 1991. 39.95 (0-8306-9969-4, 50009, Design Pr) TAB Bks.

Art of the Autochrome: The Birth of Color Photography. John Wood. LC 92-38758. (Illus.). 202p. 1993. 65.00 (0-87745-413-2) U of Iowa Pr.

Art of the Autonomous Republics of the Russian Federation. E. Golubova. 1973. 65.00 (0-317-14221-6, Pub. by Collets UK) St Mut.

Art of the Avant-Garde in Russia: Selections from the George Costakis Collection. Margit Rowell & Angelica Rudenstine. LC 81-52858. (Illus.). 320p. 1981. pap. 17.00 (0-686-81458-4) S R Guggenheim.

Art of the Avant-Garde in Russia - Selections from the G. Costakis-Solomon Guggenheim Museum Exhibition. B. Lipsey. (C). 1990. pap. 170.00 (0-685-34377-4, Pub. by Collets) St Mut.

Art of the Ballets Russes: The Russian Seasons in Paris, 1908-1929. Militsa Pozharskaya & Tatiana Volodina. (Illus.). 288p. 1991. 49.95 (1-55859-151-6) Abbeville Pr.

Art of the Barovier. Ed. by Marina Barovier. (Illus.). 216p. 1993. 75.00 (88-7743-126-1, Pub. by Arsenale Editrice IT) Antique Collect.

***Art of the Beautiful: Decorative Art of the Huichol Indians.** Pablo De la Cruz & Carl Lumholtz. Ed. & Intro. by Bruce Finson. (Illus.). 100p. 1994. pap. 20.00 (0-943907-14-4) Bruce Finson.

Art of the Bedchamber: The Chinese Sexual Yoga Classics Including Women's Solo Meditation Texts. Douglas Wile. LC 90-28707. 299p. 1992. 59.50 (0-7914-0885-X); pap. 19.95 (0-7914-0886-8) State U NY Pr.

Art of the Brontes. Christine Alexander & Jane Sellars. (Illus.). 300p. (C). 1995. 79.95 (0-521-43248-0) Cambridge U Pr.

Art of the Brontes. Christine Alexander & Jane Sellars. (Illus.). 300p. (C). 1995. pap. 34.95 (0-521-43841-1) Cambridge U Pr.

Art of the Bronze Age: Southeastern Iran, Western Central Asia, & the Indus Valley. Holly Pittman. (Orig.). 1994. pap. 7.95 (0-8109-6446-5) Abrams.

An Asterisk (*) at the beginning of an entry indicates that the title is appearing in BIP for the first time.

An Asterisk (*) at the beginning of an entry indicates that the title is appearing in BIP for the first time.

453

Art of the Turkish Tale. Barbara K. Walker. LC 90-39477. 1993. pap. 17.50 (*0-89672-316-X*) Tex Tech Univ Pr.

Art of the Turkish Tale, Vol. 2. Barbara K. Walker. (Illus.). 286p. 1993. 27.50 (*0-89672-265-1*); pap. 18.50 (*0-89672-317-8*) Tex Tech Univ Pr.

***Art of the Turnaround: How to Rescue Your Troubled Business from Creditors, Predators, & Competitors.** Jerry S. White & Matthew L. Schuchman. LC 94-27095. 224p. 1994. 24.95 (*0-8144-0260-7*) AMACOM.

Art of the Twenties. LC 78-71872. (Illus.). 69p. (Orig.). 1978. pap. 5.00 (*0-939896-14-1*) Flint Inst Arts.

Art of the Victorian Stage. Alfred Darbyshire. LC 76-91898. 1972. 20.95 (*0-405-08429-3*, Pub. by Blom Pubns UK) Ayer.

***Art of the Vineyard.** Gary Conway. LC 95-7532. 1995. write for info. (*1-885203-10-1*) Jrny Editions.

Art of the Violin. Pierre Baillot. Tr. by Louise Goldberg. 540p. 1991. pap. 29.95 (*0-8101-0754-6*) Northwestern U Pr.

Art of the Weathervane. Steve Miller. LC 83-51742. (Illus.). 160p. 1984. 35.00 (*0-88740-005-1*) Schiffer.

Art of the Western World. 39.95 (*0-8373-6561-9*, DANTES-61) Nat Learn.

Art of the Western World. Ed. by Denise Hooker. 464p. (C). 1990. 150.00 (*1-85283-248-7*, Pub. by Boxtree Ltd UK) St Mut.

Art of the Western World: From Ancient Greece to Post-Modernism. Bruce Cole & Adelheid Gealt. (Illus.). 368p. 1991. pap. 16.00 (*0-671-74728-2*, Touchstone Bks) S&S Trade.

Art of the Woman: The Life & Work of Elisabet Ney. Emily F. Cutrer. LC 87-19077. (Women in the West Ser.). (Illus.). xvi, 271p. 1988. 30.00 (*0-8032-1438-3*) U of Nebr Pr.

Art of the World's Greatest Watercolorists. Fiona Hackney. 1990. 12.98 (*1-55521-568-8*) Bk Sales Inc.

Art of the Writer: Essays, Excerpts, & Translations. enl. rev. ed. Ed. by Lane Cooper. LC 73-37837. (Essay Index Reprint Ser.). 1977. reprint ed. 25.95 (*0-8369-2586-6*) Ayer.

Art of Theatre. Dennis J. Sporre. LC 92-24835. 432p. (C). 1992. pap. text ed. write for info. (*0-13-052291-0*) P-H.

Art of Theatrical Makeup for Stage & Screen. Michael G. Westmore. (Illus.). (C). 1972. pap. text ed. 37.95 (*0-07-069485-0*) McGraw.

Art of Theological Reflection. Patricia O. Killen & John De Beer. 160p. (Orig.). 1994. pap. 14.95 (*0-8245-1401-7*) Crossroad NY.

Art of Theorem Painting: A History & Complete Instruction Manual. Linda C. Lefko & Barbara Knickerbocker. (Illus.). 112p. 1992. 30.00 (*0-525-93532-0*, Dutton Studio); pap. 20.00 (*0-525-48596-1*, Dutton Studio) Studio Bks.

Art of Thinking. Allen F. Harrison & Robert M. Bramson. 240p. 1987. pap. 4.95 (*0-425-10568-7*) Berkley Pub.

Art of Thinking. Dagobert D. Runes. (Orig.). pap. 0.95 (*0-685-19398-5*, 92, Citadel Pr) Carol Pub Group.

Art of Thinking. 3rd ed. Ruggerio. (C). 1990. pap. text ed. 25.00 (*0-06-045668-X*) HarpCollege.

***Art of Thinking: A Guide to Critical & Creative Thought.** 4th rev. ed. Vincent R. Ruggiero. LC 94-27207. (C). 1994. 17.50 (*0-673-99325-6*) HarpC.

Art of This Century. Ed. by Peggy Guggenheim. LC 68-9242. (Contemporary Art Ser.). (Illus.). 1968. reprint ed. 15.95 (*0-405-00721-3*) Ayer.

Art of This Century: The Guggenheim Collections. Thomas Krens et al. (Illus.). 240p. 1992. 60.00 (*0-89207-072-2*) S R Guggenheim.

***Art of This Century: The Guggenheim Museum & Its Collection.** Thomas Krens. 1994. 65.00 (*0-8109-6865-7*) Abrams.

Art of Thomas Cole: Ambition & Imagination. Elwood C. Parry, III. LC 85-40511. (Illus.). 424p. 1989. 95.00 (*0-87413-214-2*) U Delaware Pr.

Art of Thomas Hardy. Lionel Johnson. LC 72-11548. (Studies in Thomas Hardy: No. 14). 1969. reprint ed. lib. bdg. 75.00 (*0-8383-0575-X*) M S G Haskell Hse.

Art of Thomas Hardy. Lionel P. Johnson. (BCL1-PR English Literature Ser.). 276p. 1992. reprint ed. lib. bdg. 79.00 (*0-7812-7554-7*) Rprt Serv.

Art of Thomas Merton. Ross Labrie. LC 79-1341. 188p. 1979. pap. 9.95 (*0-912646-55-1*) Tex Christian.

Art of Thornton Wilder. Malcolm Goldstein. LC 65-10239. 191p. reprint ed. pap. 54.50 (*0-8357-6835-X*, 2035522) Bks Demand.

Art of Three Dimensional Design: How to Create Space Figures. Louis Wolchonok. LC 34-9269. 1969. reprint ed. pap. 8.95 (*0-486-22201-2*) Dover.

Art of Throwing Weapons. James W. Madden. LC 91-60071. (Illus.). 104p. (Orig.). 1991. pap. 8.95 (*0-9628825-3-4*) Patrick Las Vegas.

Art of Tibet: A Catalogue of the Los Angeles County Museum of Art Collection. Pratapaditya Pal. (Illus.). 328p. 1990. 60.00 (*0-8109-1899-4*) Abrams.

Art of Tipping: Customs & Controversies. John E. Schein et al. LC 84-23953. (Illus.). 260p. 1984. 14.95 (*0-9612552-1-8*); pap. 7.95 (*0-9612552-2-6*) Tippers Intl.

Art of Tom Lea. Tom Lea. LC 88-23425. (Illus.). 272p. 1989. 50.00 (*0-89096-366-5*) Tex A&M Univ Pr.

Art of Tom Lovell: An Invitation to History. Don Hedgpeth. LC 92-47465. (Illus.). 1993. 60.00 (*0-688-12645-6*) Morrow.

***Art of Touch: A Massage Manual for Young People.** Chia Martin. (Illus.). (J). (gr. 4-12). 1995. pap. write for info. (*0-934252-57-2*) Hohm Pr.

***Art of Touch: A Massage Manual for Young People.** Chia Martin. 50p. 1995. pap. 11.95 (*0-614-06937-8*) Hohm Pr.

Art of Transcribing for Guitar. Dave Celentano. 76p. 1991. audio, pap. text ed. 15.95 (*0-931759-56-0*) Centerstream Pub.

Art of Transcribing for the Organ. Herbert F. Ellingford. 158p. 1992. pap. 27.95 (*1-881162-00-1*) W Leupold Edits.

Art of Translating Poetry. Burton Raffel. LC 87-43124. 220p. 1988. lib. bdg. 27.50 (*0-271-00626-9*) Pa St U Pr.

Art of Translating Prose. Burton Raffel. LC 93-20439. 184p. (C). 1994. 29.95 (*0-271-01080-0*) Pa St U Pr.

Art of Translation: Kornei Chukovsky's A High Art. Kornei Chukovsky. Ed. & Tr. by Lauren G. Leighton. LC 83-6457. 327p. reprint ed. pap. 93.20 (*0-8357-6542-3*, 2035905) Bks Demand.

Art of Translation: Voices from the Field. Ed. by Rosanna Warren. 288p. 1989. text ed. 37.50 (*1-55553-048-6*) NE U Pr.

Art of Travel. Henry James. Ed. by Morton D. Zabel. LC 76-111839. (Essay Index Reprint Ser.). 1977. 35.95 (*0-8369-1663-8*) Ayer.

Art of Travel: Essays on Travel Writing. Ed. by Philip Dodd. 172p. 1982. text ed. 25.00 (*0-7146-3205-8*, Pub. by F Cass Pubs UK) Intl Spec Bk.

Art of Trenton Falls. Paul D. Schweizer et al. (Illus.). 72p. 1990. 18.95 (*0-915895-08-0*) Munson Williams.

Art of Trombone Playing. Edward Kleinhammer. (Illus.). 112p. 1963. pap. 16.95 (*0-87487-058-5*) Summy-Birchard.

Art of True Healing. Israel Regardie. Ed. by Marc Allen. LC 91-21732. (Classic Wisdom Collection). 96p. 1991. 9.95 (*0-931432-76-6*) New Wrld Lib.

Art of Trust: Healing Your Heart & Opening Your Mind. Lee Jampolsky. LC 93-38547. 1994. 9.95 (*0-89087-710-6*) Celestial Arts.

Art of Tuba & Euphonium. William Winkle & Harvey Phillips. (Illus.). 90p. 1992. pap. text ed. 14.95 (*0-87487-682-6*) Summy-Birchard.

Art of Turkish Cooking. Neset Eren. 303p. 1993. reprint ed. pap. 9.95 (*0-7818-0201-6*) Hippocrene Bks.

Art of Tying the Dry Fly. Skip Morris. (Illus.). 112p. (Orig.). 1993. 39.95 (*1-878175-37-8*); pap. 29.95 (*1-878175-36-X*) F Amato Pubns.

Art of Tying the Nymph. Skip Morris. 112p. 1994. pap. 29.95 (*1-878175-51-3*) F Amato Pubns.

Art of Tympanist & Drummer. Andrew A. Shivas. 96p. 1988. pap. 15.00 (*0-85224-574-2*, Pub. by Edinburgh U Pr UK) Col U Pr.

***Art of Typography.** Martin Solomon. Date not set. 29.95 (*0-88108-119-1*) Art Dir.

Art of Understanding Your Mate. Cecil G. Osborne. 192p. 1988. pap. 8.99 (*0-310-30601-9*, 10481P, Pyranee) Zondervan.

Art of Unknowing: Dimensions of Openness in Analytic Therapy. Stephen Kurtz. LC 88-39471. 280p. 1989. 35.00 (*0-87668-860-1*) Aronson.

Art of Using Your Whole Brain. 2nd ed. I. Katherine Benziger & Anne Sohn. (Illus.). 304p. (Orig.). 1991. pap. text ed. 16.95 (*1-880931-00-1*) KBA Pub.

Art of Using Your Whole Brain: Extroversion, Introversion & Adaption, Vol. 2. I. Katherine Benziger. (Illus.). 300p. (Orig.). 1992. pap. 16.95 (*1-880931-03-6*) KBA Pub.

***Art of Utopia: A New Direction in Contemporary Aboriginal Art.** (Illus.). 180p. (C). 1994. text ed. 195.00 (*0-7605-0484-9*) Rector Pr.

Art of Van Gogh. (Illus.). 80p. 1992. 4.95 (*0-8362-3018-3*) Andrews & McMeel.

Art of Vase-Painting in Classical Athens. Martin Robertson. (Illus.). 364p. (C). 1992. 94.95 (*0-521-33010-6*) Cambridge U Pr.

Art of Vase-Painting in Classical Athens. Martin Robertson. (Illus.). 364p. (C). 1994. pap. 34.95 (*0-521-33881-6*) Cambridge U Pr.

Art of Vergil: Image & Symbol in the "Aeneid" Viktor Poschl. Tr. by Gerda Seligson. LC 85-27077. 222p. 1986. reprint ed. text ed. 45.50 (*0-313-25053-7*, POAV, Greenwood Pr) Greenwood.

Art of Versification. Matthaeus Vindocinensis. Tr. & Intro. by Aubrey E. Galyon. LC 79-28313. 135p. reprint ed. pap. 38.50 (*0-8357-5765-X*, 2029998) Bks Demand.

***Art of Veterinary Practice: A Guide to Client Communication.** Myrna M. Milani. LC 94-40919. 312p. 1995. text ed. 29.95 (*0-8122-3260-7*) U of Pa Pr.

Art of Viktoras Petravicius Vol. 1: Early Works: 1935-1949. Ed. by Algimantas Kezys. (ENG & LIT.). 1990. 25.00 (*0-9617756-3-7*) Galerija.

Art of Violin Playing, Bk. 1. rev. ed. Carl Flesch. Tr. by Frederick H. Martens. (Illus.). 188p. (J). 1924. pap. 24.95 (*0-8258-0135-4*, 01317) Fischer Inc NY.

Art of Violin Playing: Artistic Realization & Instruction, Book 2. Carl Flesch. Tr. by Frederick H. Martens. 237p. (J). 1930. pap. 24.95 (*0-8258-0136-2*, 0 2046) Fischer Inc NY.

Art of Violincello Playing. E. Van der Straeten. reprint ed. lib. bdg. 49.00 (*0-403-03864-2*) Scholarly.

Art of Violincello Playing. Edmund S. Van der Straeten. 1988. reprint ed. lib. bdg. 59.00 (*0-7812-0798-3*) Rprt Serv.

Art of Vogue Covers. W. Packer. 256p. 1984. 9.98 (*0-517-44647-2*) Random Hse Value.

Art of Vogue Covers: 1909 to 1940. William Packer. (Illus.). 256p. 1980. 10.98 (*0-517-53838-5*) Random Hse Value.

Art of Voltaire's Theater: An Exploration of Possibility. Marie Wellington. (American University Studies: Romance Languages & Literature: Ser. II, Vol. 61). 260p. (C). 1987. text ed. 40.95 (*0-8204-0483-7*) P Lang Pubs.

Art of Walking. Ed. by Edwin V. Mitchell. LC 77-92512. (Essay Index in Reprint Ser.). (Illus.). 1978. reprint ed. 16.75 (*0-8486-3009-2*) Roth Pub Inc.

Art of Walt Disney: From Mickey Mouse to the Magic Kingdoms. Christopher Finch. LC 73-4639. (Illus.). 458p. 1983. pap. 39.98 (*0-8109-8052-5*, Abradale Pr) Abrams.

Art of Walt Disney: From Mickey Mouse to the Magic Kingdoms. Christopher Finch. 1988. 4.99 (*0-517-66474-7*) Random Hse Value.

***Art of Walt Disney: From Mickey Mouse to the Magic Kingdoms.** rev. ed. Christopher Finch. LC 95-1746. 1995. write for info. (*0-8109-1962-1*) Abrams.

***Art of War.** (Illus.). 77p. Date not set. pap. 4.50 (*0-614-06500-3*) Heian Intl.

Art of War. Sun Tzu. Ed. by James Clavell. 1983. 14.95 (*0-385-29216-3*) Delacorte.

Art of War. Sun Tzu. Ed. by James Clavell. 1989. pap. 9.95 (*0-385-29985-0*, Delta) Dell.

Art of War. Sun Tzu. Tr. & Intro. by Samuel B. Griffith. 1971. pap. 7.95 (*0-19-501476-6*) OUP.

Art of War. Sun Tzu. (Illus.). 222p. (Orig.). 1988. 17.95 (*0-19-501540-1*) OUP.

Art of War. Sun Tzu. Tr. & Intro. by Thomas Cleary. LC 88-15813. (Dragon Editions Ser.). 250p. (Orig.). 1988. pap. 11.00 (*0-87773-452-6*) Shambhala Pubns.

Art of War. Sun Tzue. 16.95 (*0-8488-0113-X*, Amereon Hse) Amereon Ltd.

Art of War. rev. ed. Niccolo Machiavelli. Tr. by Ellis Farneworth. LC 64-66078. (Orig.). (C). 1965. pap. write for info. (*0-672-60434-5*, LLA196, Bobbs) Macmillan.

Art of War. 2nd abr. ed. Sun Tzu. Ed. & Tr. by Thomas Cleary. LC 90-52805. (Pocket Classics Ser.). 120p. 1991. pap. text ed. 6.00 (*0-87773-537-9*) Shambhala Pubns.

Art of War. Henri Jomini. LC 68-54793. 410p. 1971. reprint ed. text ed. 65.00 (*0-8371-5014-0*, JOAW, Greenwood Pr) Greenwood.

Art of War. Niccolo Machiavelli. Tr. by Ellis Farneworth. (Quality Paperbacks Ser.). 336p. 1990. reprint ed. pap. 12.95 (*0-306-80412-3*) Da Capo.

Art of War. Niccolo Machiavelli. Tr. by Peter Whitehorne. Bd. with Prince. LC 73-172705. LC 73-172705. (Tudor Translations, First Ser.: No. 39). reprint ed. 115.00 (*0-404-51951-2*) AMS Pr.

Art of War. Sun Tzu. 197p. (Orig.). 1990. reprint ed. lib. bdg. 25.95 (*0-89966-660-4*) Buccaneer Bks.

Art of War: Waterloo to Mons. William L. McElwee. LC 74-17459. 352p. 1975. pap. 10.95 (*0-253-20214-0*, MB-214) Ind U Pr.

Art of War & Englands Traynings. Edward Davies. LC 68-54633. (English Experience Ser.: No. 37). 1968. reprint ed. 45.00 (*90-221-0037-5*) Walter J Johnson.

Art of War & Renaissance England. John R. Hale. LC 79-65983. (Folger Guides to the Age of Shakespeare Ser.). 1979. pap. 4.95 (*0-918016-10-X*) Folger Bks.

***Art of War for Executives.** Donald G. Krause. LC 94-29606. (Orig.). 1995. pap. 12.00 (*0-399-51902-5*, Perigree Bks) Berkley Pub.

Art of War for the Christian Soldier. 2nd ed. Frank W. Sandford. LC 66-29707. 165p. 1966. 6.00 (*0-910840-12-1*) Kingdom.

Art of War in Italy, 1494-1529. F. L. Taylor. LC 92-41767. 256p. 1993. 35.00 (*1-85367-142-8*, 5461) Stackpole.

Art of War in Italy, 1494-1529. Frederick L. Taylor. LC 76-84284. (Illus.). 228p. 1971. reprint ed. text ed. 35.00 (*0-8371-5025-6*, TAWI, Greenwood Pr) Greenwood.

Art of War in Medieval India. J. N. Sarkar. (Illus.). 1984. text ed. 30.00 (*0-685-13608-6*) Coronet Bks.

***Art of War in Spain: The Conquest of Granada, 1481-1492.** William H. Prescott. Ed. & Intro. by Albert D. McJoynt. (Illus.). 288p. 1995. 40.00 (*1-85367-193-2*, Pub. by Greenhill Bks UK) Stackpole.

Art of War in the Age of Peace: U. S. Military Posture for the Post-Cold War World. Michael E. O'Hanlon. LC 91-47086. 176p. 1992. text ed. 45.00 (*0-275-94259-7*, C4259, Praeger Pubs) Greenwood.

Art of War in the Middle Ages: A.D. 378-1515. rev. ed. Charles W. Oman. Ed. by John H. Beeler. (Illus.). 194p. 1960. pap. 9.95 (*0-8014-9062-6*) Cornell U Pr.

Art of War in the Western World. Archer Jones. (Illus.). 768p. 1989. pap. 21.50 (*0-19-506241-8*) OUP.

Art of War in the Western World. Archer Jones. LC 86-25017. (Illus.). 768p. 1987. 39.95 (*0-252-01380-8*) U of Ill Pr.

Art of War in World History: From Antiquity to the Nuclear Age. Comp. by Gerard Chaliand. LC 92-20153. 1993. write for info. (*0-520-07963-9*); pap. write for info. (*0-520-07964-7*) U CA Pr.

***Art of Warfare in the Age of Marlborough.** David Chandler. (Illus.). 320p. 1995. 29.95 (*1-885119-14-3*) Sarpedon.

Art of Warfare in the Age of Napoleon. Gunther E. Rothenberg. LC 77-86495. (Illus.). 280p. 1978. 29.95 (*0-253-31076-8*); pap. 10.95 (*0-253-20260-4*, MB-260) Ind U Pr.

Art of Wargaming. Peter P. Perla, III. LC 89-28818. (Illus.). 416p. 1990. 29.95 (*0-87021-050-5*) Naval Inst Pr.

Art of Watching Films. Joseph M. Boggs. (C). 1991. teacher ed, pap. text ed. write for info. (*1-55934-087-8*) Mayfield Pub.

Art of Watching Films. 3rd rev. ed. Joseph M. Boggs. 459p. (C). 1991. pap. text ed. 33.95 (*0-87484-982-9*) Mayfield Pub.

Art of Watching Films: Computerized Test Bank. rev. ed. Joseph M. Boggs. (C). 1991. disk write for info. (*0-318-68359-8*) Mayfield Pub.

Art of Watercolor. rev. ed. Charles Le Clair. LC 93-38097. (Illus.). 144p. 1994. 29.95 (*0-8230-0291-8*, Watsn-Guptill) Watsn-Guptill.

***Art of Watercolor: A Guide to the Skills & Techniques.** Ray C. Smith. LC 94-35426. (Illus.). 128p. 1995. 24.00 (*0-89577-654-5*) RD Assn.

Art of Weaving. Else Regensteiner. LC 86-61293. (Illus.). 192p. 1986. reprint ed. pap. 19.95 (*0-88740-079-5*) Schiffer.

Art of Welding. W. A. Vause. (Workshop Practice Ser.: No. 7). (Illus.). 96p. (Orig.). 1985. pap. 18.50 (*0-85242-846-4*, Pub. by Argus Books UK) Trans-Atl Phila.

Art of Wen Cheng-ming (Fourteen Seventy to Fifteen Fifty-Nine) Richard Edwards. 262p. reprint ed. pap. 74.70 (*0-8357-5766-8*, 2023748) Bks Demand.

Art of Western Riding. Susan N. Jones. 1980. pap. 7.00 (*0-87980-273-1*) Wilshire.

Art of Western Riding. Bob Mayhew & John Birdsall. Ed. by Sean Frawley. 160p. 1990. 24.00 (*0-87605-886-1*) Howell Bk.

Art of Whistling. Jack W. Chartier. (Illus.). 40p. (J). (gr. 1 up). 1993. lib. bdg. 4.95 (*0-9636343-1-3*) Chartier.

Art of Willa Cather. Ed. by Bernice Slote & Virginia Faulkner. LC 74-78479. (Illus.). xii, 267p. 1974. 25.00 (*0-8032-0841-3*) U of Nebr Pr.

Art of William Alexander & Buck Paulson, Series 17. Shirley Tucker. Ed. by John Hartman. (Illus.). 40p. 1993. pap. text ed. write for info. (*1-883576-33-4*, BK-117); pap. text ed. write for info. (*1-883576-34-2*, BK-118); pap. text ed. write for info. (*1-883576-35-0*, BK-119) Alexander Art.

Art of William Alexander & Lowell Speers, Ser. 1. Laurie Layton-Anderson. (Illus.). 76p. 1987. pap. text ed. write for info. (*1-883576-00-8*) Alexander Art.

Art of William Alexander & Lowell Speers, Series 2. Laurie Layton-Anderson. (Illus.). 80p. 1987. pap. text ed. write for info. (*1-883576-01-6*) Alexander Art.

Art of William Alexander & Lowell Speers, Series 3. Julia Somers-Arthur. (Illus.). 83p. 1988. pap. text ed. write for info. (*1-883576-02-4*) Alexander Art.

Art of William Alexander & Lowell Speers, Series 4. Julia Somers-Arthur. (Illus.). 76p. 1988. pap. text ed. write for info. (*1-883576-03-2*) Alexander Art.

Art of William Alexander & Lowell Speers, Series 5. John Hartman. (Illus.). 76p. 1988. pap. text ed. write for info. (*1-883576-04-0*) Alexander Art.

Art of William Alexander & Lowell Speers, Series 6. John Hartman. (Illus.). 79p. 1989. pap. text ed. write for info. (*1-883576-05-9*) Alexander Art.

Art of William Morris. Aymer Vallance. (Fine Art Ser.). (Illus.). 264p. 1988. reprint ed. pap. 18.95 (*0-486-25647-2*) Dover.

***Art of William S. Phillips: The Glory of Flight.** Text by Edwards Park. (Illus.). 160p. 1994. 60.00 (*0-86713-022-9*) Greenw Pr Ltd.

Art of Wind Playing. Arthur Weisberg. (Illus.). 138p. (C). 1993. 19.95 (*0-9639728-0-4*) Satco.

Art of Winning, Vol. 1. Dennis Conner. 1990. mass mkt. 4.95 (*0-312-92098-9*) St Martin.

Art of Wise Investing. John Moody. 93p. reprint ed. 16.95 (*0-931133-07-6*, Busn Class) Pac Pub Grp.

Art of Wondering: A Revisionist Return to the History of Rhetoric. William A. Covino. LC 87-37561. 141p. (Orig.). 1988. pap. text ed. 17.50 (*0-86709-193-2*) Boynton Cook Pubs.

Art of Wood Turning. (Illus.). 48p. 1983. 8.00 (*0-88321-050-9*) Am Craft.

***Art of Woodworking: Advanced Routing.** LC 95-12164. 1995. write for info. (*0-8094-9541-4*) Time-Life.

Art of Woodworking & Furniture Appreciation. 2nd ed. Laszlo Katz. (Illus.). 1980. 50.00 (*0-686-00808-1*) PFC.

***Art of Wordperfect 6.0 for DOS.** Kathleen Stewart. 1995. write for info. (*0-87709-626-0*) Boyd & Fraser.

Art of Work. Roger Coleman. 182p. (C). 1988. text ed. 21.00 (*0-7453-0168-1*, Pub. by Pluto Pr UK) Westview.

Art of World Religions: Buddhism. Michael Ridley. (Illus.). 184p. 1978. 49.95 (*0-7137-0886-7*) Asia Bk Corp.

Art of Worldly Wisdom. Balthasar Gracian. Tr. by Joseph Jacobs. LC 92-50738. 272p. 1993. pap. 6.00 (*0-87773-921-8*, Sham Pocket Class) Shambhala Pubns.

Art of Worldly Wisdom: A Pocket Oracle. Baltazar Gracian. Tr. by Christopher Maurer. 1992. 17.50 (*0-385-42131-1*) Doubleday.

Art of Worship. Robert G. Davidson. 20p. 1987. pap. 5.50 (*0-940754-45-2*) Ed Ministries.

***Art of Wrist-Spin Bowling.** Peter Philpott. (Illus.). 128p. 1995. 24.95 (*1-85223-870-4*, Pub. by Crowood Pr UK) Trafalgar.

Art of Writing. Gerard Manley Hopkins. Tr. by Andre Maurois. LC 72-3375. (Essay Index Reprint Ser.). 1977. reprint ed. 20.95 (*0-8369-2914-4*) Ayer.

***Art of Writing: An Illustrated Journal.** 1995. pap. text ed. 5.95 (*1-56138-558-1*) Running Pr.

Art of Writing: Lu Chi's Wen Fu. Lu Chi. Tr. by Sam Hamill. LC 90-25970. 64p. (Orig.). 1991. pap. 6.95 (*0-915943-62-X*) Milkweed Ed.

Art of Writing Advertising. Ed. by Denis Higgins. 126p. 1965. pap. 9.95 (*0-8442-3100-2*, NTC Busn Bks) NTC Pub Grp.

Art of Writing Effective Letters. Rosemary T. Fruehling & Sharon Bouchard. 1972. text ed. 14.95 (*0-07-022345-9*) McGraw.

Art of Writing for Publication. Kenneth T. Henson. 1994. 24.95 (*0-205-15769-6*, Longwood Div) Allyn.

Art of Writing Letters. Helen Gregory. Date not set. write for info. (*0-941973-11-5*) Pinstripe Pub.

Art of Writing Music. John Cacavas. LC 93-2594. 1993. write for info. (*0-88284-619-1*, 4163); pap. write for info. (*0-88284-618-3*, 4161) Alfred Pub.

Art of Writing Non-Fiction. 2nd rev. ed. Andre Fontaine & William A. Glavin, Jr. 232p. 1987. text ed. 39.95 (*0-8156-2403-4*) Syracuse U Pr.

Art of Writing Nonfiction. 2nd ed. Andre Fontaine & William A. Glavin, Jr. 232p. (C). 1990. pap. text ed. 14.95 (*0-8156-2509-X*) Syracuse U Pr.

Art of Written Forms see Calligraphy: The Art of Written Forms

Art of Wyland. Wyland. (Illus.). 32p. (J). 1992. pap. text ed. 7.95 (*0-9631793-2-2*) Wyland Galleries.

454

An Asterisk (*) at the beginning of an entry indicates that the title is appearing in BIP for the first time.

An Asterisk (*) at the beginning of an entry indicates that the title is appearing in BIP for the first time.

455

Art Therapy & Dramatherapy: Their Relation & Practice. Sue Jennings & Ase Minde. 176p. 1992. 49.95 (*1-85302-027-3*, Pub. by J Kingsley Pubs UK) Taylor & Francis.

Art Therapy & Group Work: An Annotated Bibliography. Comp. by Kathleen M. Hanes. LC 81-13442. xx, 191p. 1982. text ed. 49.95 (*0-313-23172-9*, HAW/, Greenwood Pr) Greenwood.

Art Therapy for Groups: A Handbook of Themes, Games & Exercises. Marian Liebmann. (Illus.). 226p. (Orig.). 1986. pap. text ed. 19.95 (*0-914797-24-7*) Brookline Bks.

Art Therapy in Practice. Ed. by Marian Liebmann. 176p. 1990. 56.00 (*1-85302-057-5*, Pub. by J Kingsley Pubs UK); pap. 27.00 (*1-85302-058-3*, Pub. by J Kingsley Pubs UK) Taylor & Francis.

Art Therapy in the United States. Elinor Ulman et al. (Illus.). 40p. 1977. pap. 3.95 (*0-8391-1164-9*) Art Therapy.

Art Therapy, Vol. 10, No. 1: Journal of the American Art Therapy Association. Ed. by Cathy Malchiodi. (Illus.). 64p. (Orig.). (C). 1993. 16.00 (*1-882147-17-0*) Am Art Therapy.

Art Therapy, Vol. 9, No. 4: Journal of the American Art Therapy Association. Ed. by Cathy A. Malchiodi. (Illus.). 56p. (Orig.). (C). 1992. pap. 18.00 (*1-882147-15-4*) Am Art Therapy.

Art Therapy with Families in Crisis: Overcoming Resistance Through Nonverbal Expression. Ed. by Debra Linesch. LC 92-27839. (Illus.). 192p. 1993. 25.00 (*0-87630-638-5*) Brunner-Mazel.

Art Therapy with Offenders. Ed. by Marian Liebmann. 220p. 1994. pap. 36.00 (*1-85302-171-7*, Pub. by J Kingsley Pubs UK) Taylor & Francis.

Art Through Children's Literature: Creative Art Lessons for Caldecott Books. Debi Englebaugh. (Illus.). 190p. 1994. pap. text ed. 22.50 (*1-56308-154-7*) Teacher Ideas Pr.

Art Through History: (Levels I, II, III, & IV) rev. ed. Wendy Slatkin et al. (Illus.). 350p. 1988. ring bd., sl. 1,050.00 (*0-923960-10-4*) ATHP.

Art Through History, Level I: An Introduction to Painting, Sculpture & Architecture. rev. ed. Wendy Slatkin et al. (Illus.). 100p. 1986. ring bd., sl. 325.00 (*0-923960-14-7*) ATHP.

Art Through History, Level II: America, from the Colonial Era to the Present. rev. ed. Wendy Slatkin et al. (Illus.). 100p. 1986. ring bd., sl. 325.00 (*0-923960-15-5*) ATHP.

Art Through History, Level III: World History: Ancient Civilizations. rev. ed. Wendy Slatkin et al. (Illus.). 50p. 1988. ring bd., sl. 175.00 (*0-923960-16-3*) ATHP.

Art Through History, Level IV: World History: From Medieval to Modern Times. rev. ed. Wendy Slatkin et al. (Illus.). 100p. 1988. ring bd., sl. 350.00 (*0-923960-17-1*) ATHP.

Art Through Nature: An Integrated Approach to Teaching Art & Nature Study to Young Children. Jane A. Kane. LC 83-83315. 128p. (Orig.). 1984. pap. text ed. 19.95 (*0-918452-44-9*) Learning Pubns.

Art to Choke Hearts - Pissing in the Gene Pool. Rollins. 254p. (Orig.). 1992. reprint ed. pap. 15.00 (*1-880985-10-1*) Two Thirteen Sixty-one.

Art to Wear. Julie S. Dale. LC 86-14041. (Illus.). 320p. 1986. 95.00 (*0-89659-664-8*) Abbeville Pr.

Art-to-Wear. Ruth Seeley-Scheel. (Illus.). 1986. pap. 6.95 (*0-9619815-0-4*) Laugh Goose.

Art to Wear: The Complete Jewelry. Erte. (Illus.). 192p. 1991. 75.00 (*0-525-93361-1*, Dutton Studio) Studio Bks.

***Art Today.** Edward Lucie-Smith. (Illus.). 500p. (C). 1995. 59.95 (*0-7148-3201-4*, Pub. by Phaidon Press UK) Chronicle Bks.

Art Today: An Introduction to the Visual Arts. 6th ed. Ray Faulkner et al. 496p. (C). 1987. pap. text ed. 40.00 (*0-03-064039-3*) HB Coll Pubs.

***Art Treasures from the Imperial Collections.** (Illus.). 35p. 1975. pap. 12.00 (*0-614-02675-X*) Japan Soc.

Art Treasures from the Museums of the Moscow Kremlin. I. Sizov Nenarkomova. 111p. 1980. 75.00 (*0-569-08692-2*, Pub. by Collets UK) St Mut.

Art Treasures in China. Mary Tregear & Shelagh Vainker. LC 94-5162. 1994. write for info. (*0-8109-1949-4*) Abrams.

Art Treasures of Dubrovnik. C. Fishovic et al. (C). 1992. text ed. 140.00 (*0-7855-0121-5*, Pub. by Collets) St Mut.

Art Treasures of Herceg Novi. L. Sefarovic. (Illus.). 158p. (C). 1984. text ed. 275.00 (*0-685-47838-6*, Pub. by Collets) St Mut.

Art Treasures of Seoul: With Walking Tours. Edward B. Adams. (Illus.). 272p. 1980. 25.00 (*0-89860-018-9*) Eastview.

Art Treasures of Slovenia. Lev Menase. 208p. 1981. 131.00 (*0-317-57218-0*, Pub. by Collets UK) St Mut.

Art Treasures of the Moscow Kremlin. Aida Nasibova & William Mendeleyev. 200p. 1984. 275.00 (*0-317-61218-2*, Pub. by Collets) St Mut.

Art Treasures of the Moscow Kremlin. Aida Nasibova. (Illus.). 238p. (C). 1988. text ed. 300.00 (*0-685-40303-3*, Pub. by Collets) St Mut.

***Art under Duress: El Salvador, 1980-Present.** Arizona State University Art Museum Staff. LC 94-47049. 1995. write for info. (*0-9644646-0-8*) Ariz St U Art Mus.

Art under Stalin. Matthew C. Bown. LC 91-11281. (Illus.). 256p. 1991. 40.00 (*0-8419-1299-8*) Holmes & Meier.

Art Ventures: A Guide for Families to Impressionism & Post-Impressionism. Bay Hallowell. Ed. by Vicky A. Clark. LC 89-37006. (Illus.). 24p. 1989. pap. 5.95 (*0-88039-020-4*) Mus Art Carnegie.

Art Ventures: A Guide for Families to Ten Works of Art in the Carnegie Museum of Art. Bay Judson et al. LC 87-858. (Illus.). 24p. (Orig.). (J). (gr. 4-6). 1987. pap. text ed. 5.95 (*0-88039-014-X*) Mus Art Carnegie.

Art Walk. (TapeGuide Ser.). 1993. 6.95 (*1-56015-030-0*) Penton Overseas.

Art with Found Materials. John Lancaster. LC 91-2875. (Fresh Start Ser.). (Illus.). 48p. (J). (gr. 5-8). 1991. lib. bdg. 12.95 (*0-531-14204-3*) Watts.

Art Without Epoch: Works of Distant Times Which Still Appeal to Modern Taste. Ludwig Goldscheider. LC 76-42710. reprint ed. 34.00 (*0-404-15361-5*) AMS Pr.

***Art Without Rejection.** Sheila Reid. (Illus.). 242p. (Orig.). 1993. 39.00 (*0-9646268-1-0*); pap. 18.00 (*0-9646268-0-2*) Rush Eds.

***Art Wolfe's Guide to Better Outdoor, Action, Travel, & Adventure Photography.** Art Wolfe & Mark Gardner. (Illus.). 96p. Date not set. pap. 6.95 (*0-89886-430-5*) Mountaineers.

Art Work: Artists in the New England Labor Market. Gregory Wassall et al. LC 83-17459. 191p. 1983. pap. 8.95 (*0-915400-46-4*, ACA Bks) Am Council Arts.

Art Work: How Produced, How Reproduced. John Petrina. LC 70-107733. (Essay Index Reprint Ser.). 1977. 20.95 (*0-8369-1531-3*) Ayer.

***Art Work of Augusta.** 2nd ed. Charles E. Jones. (Illus.). 196p. Date not set. reprint ed. 60.00 (*0-9643639-0-9*) Magnolia Bookshop.

Art Work of Louis C. Tiffany. (Illus.). 91p. reprint ed. 70.00 (*0-938290-06-1*) Apollo.

Art-Work of the Future & Other Works. Richard Wagner. Tr. by W. Ashton Ellis. LC 93-25288. xxx, 422p. 1993. pap. 15.00 (*0-8032-9752-1*, Bison Books) U of Nebr Pr.

Art Workmanship of the Maori Race in New Zealand. Augustus Hamilton. LC 75-35255. (Illus.). reprint ed. 84.00 (*0-404-14427-6*) AMS Pr.

Art World at Your Fingertips: For Artists, Students, Art Dealers & Their Patrons & Essential for Those Interested in the Visual Arts. Charles L. Rosenthal. (Illus.). 100p. 1991. text ed. 17.50 (*0-9629041-1-2*); pap. 8.95 (*0-9629041-0-4*); spiral bd., pap. 8.95 (*0-9629041-2-0*) J-C Ranch Pr.

Art Worlds. Howard S. Becker. LC 81-2694. (Illus.). 408p. 1982. pap. 14.00 (*0-520-05218-8*) U CA Pr.

***Art Year 1995: Fall - Winter.** 360p. Date not set. pap. 13.95 (*88-7757-059-8*) Dist Art Pubs.

***Art Year 1995: The International Exhibition Guide.** 300p. 1995. pap. 13.95 (*88-7757-055-5*) Dist Art Pubs.

Art Young: His Life & Times. Arthur H. Young. Ed. by John N. Beffel. LC 75-352. (Radical Tradition in America Ser.). (Illus.). 479p. 1975. reprint ed. 32.45 (*0-88355-255-8*) Hyperion Conn.

Art Young: His Life & Times. Arthur H. Young. (American Biography Ser.). 467p. 1991. reprint ed. lib. bdg. 89.00 (*0-7812-8432-5*) Rprt Serv.

Art Young's Inferno: A Journey Thru Hell Six Hundred Years After Dante. Art Young. (Illus.). 1971. reprint ed. 15.00 (*0-87556-421-6*) Saifer.

ARTA Travel Agent Manual. Douglas Thompson & Alexander Anolik. 1993. disk 85.00 (*0-936831-14-6*) Dendrobium Bks.

Artabgrenzung durch DNA-Analyse bei eingen Vertretern der Strophariaceae (Basidiomycetes) K. D. Jahnke. (Illus.). 186p. (GER.). 1984. pap. text ed. 36.00 (*3-7682-1419-2*) Lubrecht & Cramer.

Artaserse. Johann C. Bach. LC 83-48734. (Johann Christian Bach: The Collected Works). 550p. 1986. lib. bdg. 140.00 (*0-8240-6050-4*) Garland.

Artaserse (Graun) see Italian Opera Librettos, Vol. III, 1640-1770

Artaud: Collected Works, 6 vols., Vol. 1. Antonin Artaud. Tr. by Alastair Hamilton & Victor Corti. (Orig.). (FRE.). 1997. pap. 13.95 (*0-7145-0170-0*) Riverrun NY.

Artaud: Collected Works, 6 vols., Vol. 2. Antonin Artaud. Tr. by Alastair Hamilton & Victor Corti. (Orig.). (FRE.). 1997. pap. 13.95 (*0-7145-0172-7*) Riverrun NY.

Artaud: Collected Works, 6 vols., Vol. 3. Antonin Artaud. Tr. by Alastair Hamilton & Victor Corti. (Orig.). (FRE.). 1997. pap. 13.95 (*0-7145-0779-2*) Riverrun NY.

Artaud: Collected Works, 6 vols., Vol. 4. Antonin Artaud. Tr. by Alastair Hamilton & Victor Corti. (Orig.). (FRE.). 1997. pap. 13.95 (*0-7145-0623-0*) Riverrun NY.

Artaud: Collected Works, 6 vols., Vol. 5. Antonin Artaud. Tr. by Alastair Hamilton & Victor Corti. (Orig.). (FRE.). 1997. pap. 13.95 (*0-7145-3660-1*) Riverrun NY.

Artaud: Collected Works, 6 vols., Vol. 6. Antonin Artaud. Tr. by Alastair Hamilton & Victor Corti. (Orig.). (FRE.). 1997. pap. 13.95 (*0-7145-3656-3*) Riverrun NY.

Artaud: Four Texts. Antonin Artaud. Tr. by Clayton Eshleman. (Illus.). 100p. 1982. 16.95 (*0-915572-57-5*); pap. 6.95 (*0-915572-56-7*) Panjandrum.

Artaud & the Gnostic Drama. Jane Goodall. (Illus.). 240p. (C). 1994. 42.00 (*0-19-815186-1*, 6327) OUP.

Artaud on Theatre. Ed. by Claude Schumacher. 210p. (Orig.). 1991. pap. 25.95 (*0-413-65270-X*, A0589, Pub. by Methuen UK) Heinemann.

Artaud What. Nico Vassilakis. 11p. (Orig.). 1994. pap. 3.00 (*0-926935-93-3*) Runaway Spoon.

Arte Barbaro y Preromanico: Desde el Siglo IV Hasta el Ano 1000. Jose Pijoan. (Summa Artis Ser.: Vol. 8). 600p. 1989. 295.00x (*84-239-5208-8*) Elliots Bks.

Arte Barroco en Francia, Italia y Aemania, Siglos XVII y XVIII. Jose Pijoan. (Summa Artis Ser.: Vol. 16). 600p. 1989. 295.00x (*84-239-5216-9*) Elliots Bks.

Arte Chicano: A Comprehensive Annotated Bibliography of Chicano Art, 1965-1981. Ed. by Shifra M. Goldman & Tomas Ybarra-Frausto. (Chicano Studies Library Publications: No. 11). (Illus.). 778p. (C). 1985. 90.00 (*0-685-08355-1*); pap. text ed. 35.00 (*0-918520-09-6*) Chicano Stud Lib.

Arte Contemporaneo: Movimientos y Artistas. Antonio Landauro. (Illus.). 160p. (Orig.). (SPA.). (C). 1994. pap. text ed. write for info. (*1-56259-031-6*) Editorial Amer.

Arte Cristiano Primitivo. Arte Bizantino: Hasta el Saqueo de Constantinopla por los Cruzados el Ano 1204. Jose Pijoan. (Summa Artis Ser.: Vol. 7). 600p. 1989. 295.00x (*84-239-5207-X*) Elliots Bks.

Arte de Agradar: Art of Pleasing Others. Salvador Iserte. (SPA.). 3.25 (*84-7228-396-8*, 220046, Pub. by Edit Clie SP) TSELF.

Arte de Ensenar. C. H. Benson. Tr. by Fernando P. Villalobos. (Curso para Maestros Cristianos Ser.: No. 5). 128p. (SPA.). 1971. pap. 4.50 (*0-89922-016-9*) Edit Caribe.

Arte de Escribir. Fay F. Rogg & Emilia Borsi. 1994. pap. text ed. write for info. (*0-07-053543-4*) McGraw.

Arte de la China. Jean R. Riviere. (Summa Artis Ser.: Vol. 20). 600p. 1989. 295.00x (*84-239-5220-7*) Elliots Bks.

Arte de la Conversacion - el Arte de la Composicion. 5th ed. Ponce De Leon. 1991. pap. 33.95 (*0-8384-3749-4*) Heinle & Heinle.

Arte de la India. Jean R. Riviere. (Summa Artis Ser.: Vol. 19). 600p. 1989. 295.00x (*84-239-5219-3*) Elliots Bks.

Arte de los Pueblos Aborigenes. Jose Pijoan. (Summa Artis Ser.: Vol. 1). 600p. 1989. 295.00x (*84-239-5201-0*) Elliots Bks.

Arte de Morir: Poemas. Oscar Hahn. 180p. 1977. 5.00 (*0-935318-03-8*) Edins Hispamerica.

***Arte de Papua y Nueva Guinea.** Eudald Serra & Alberto Folch. (Illus.). 224p. (SPA.). 1993. 100.00 (*84-343-0175-X*) Elliots Bks.

Arte De Pensar Positivamente. 160p. 1989. pap. 4.99 (*0-934664-47-1*) Yoga Res Foun.

Arte de Ser - La Mujer Encantadora: (Fascinating Womanhood) Helen A. Andelin. 234p. (Orig.). (SPA.). 1981. pap. 7.95 (*0-685-56459-2*) Pacific Santa Barbara.

***Arte del Africa Negra.** Elsy Leuzinger. (Illus.). 388p. (ENG, FRE, GER & SPA.). 1993. 100.00x (*84-343-0176-8*) Elliots Bks.

Arte del Asia Occidental, Sumeria, Babilonia, Asiria, Hititia, Fenicia, Persia, Partia, Sasania, Escitia. Jose Pijoan. (Summa Artis Ser.: Vol. 2). 600p. 1989. 295.00x (*84-239-5202-9*) Elliots Bks.

Arte Del Contrapunto. Giovanni M. Artusi. 80p. 1969. reprint ed. write for info. (*0-318-71579-1*, Pub. by Georg Olms GW) Lubrecht & Cramer.

Arte del Japon. Fernando G. Gutierrez. (Summa Artis Ser.: Vol. 21). 600p. 1989. 295.00x (*84-239-5221-5*) Elliots Bks.

***Arte del Objeto Japones.** Maria L. Borras. (Illus.). 244p. (ENG, FRE, GER & SPA.). 1993. 100.00x (*84-343-0049-4*) Elliots Bks.

Arte del Periodo Humanistico: Trecento y Cuatrocento. Jose Pijoan. (Summa Artis Ser.: Vol. 13). 600p. 1989. 295.00x (*84-239-5213-4*) Elliots Bks.

Arte del Renacimiento en el Centro y Norte de Europe. Jose Pijoan. (Summa Artis Ser.: Vol. 15). 600p. 1989. 295.00x (*84-239-5215-0*) Elliots Bks.

Arte di Comunicare. Rosetta D'Angelo & Paola Blelloch. 352p. (C). 1993. per. 39.95 (*0-8403-8782-2*) Kendall-Hunt.

Arte e la Scienza della Totalita. Herbert L. Bierele. 1986. pap. 14.95 (*0-940480-32-8*) UNI Press.

Arte Egipcio: Hasta la Conquista Romana. Jose Pijoan. (Summa Artis Ser.: Vol. 3). 600p. 1989. 295.00x (*84-239-5203-7*) Elliots Bks.

***Arte en la Escuela: Expresion Plastica.** Esther Boix & Ricard Creus. (Illus.). 116p. (SPA.). 1993. 100.00 (*84-343-0465-1*) Elliots Bks.

Arte Espanol del Siglo XVIII. Jose Camon Aznar. (Summa Artis Ser.: Vol. 27). 600p. 1989. 295.00x (*84-239-5227-4*) Elliots Bks.

Arte Europeo de los Siglos XIX y XX. Jose Pijoan et al. (Summa Artis Ser.: Vol. 23). 600p. 1989. 295.00x (*84-239-5223-1*) Elliots Bks.

Arte Gotico de la Europa Occidental: Siglos XIII, XIV y XV. Jose Pijoan. (Summa Artis Ser.: Vol. 11). 600p. 1989. 295.00x (*84-239-5211-8*) Elliots Bks.

Arte Griego: Hasta la Toma de Corinto por los Romanos (146 a. de J. C.) Jose Pijoan. (Summa Artis Ser.: Vol. 4). 600p. 1989. 295.00x (*84-239-5204-5*) Elliots Bks.

Arte Iberoamericano desde la Colonizacion a la Independencia, Pt. I. Santiago Sebastian Lopez et al. (Summa Artis Ser.: Vol. 28). 600p. 1989. 295.00x (*84-239-5228-2*) Elliots Bks.

Arte Iberoamericano desde la Colonizacion a la Independencia, Pt. II. Santiago Sebastian Lopez et al. (Summa Artis Ser.: Vol. 29). 600p. 1989. 295.00x (*84-239-5229-0*) Elliots Bks.

***Arte Indio y Esquimal del Canada.** Ian C. Clark. (Illus.). 212p. (ENG, FRE, GER & SPA.). 1993. 100.00x (*84-343-0053-2*) Elliots Bks.

Arte Islamico. Jose Pijoan. (Summa Artis Ser.: Vol. 12). 600p. 1989. 295.00x (*84-239-5212-6*) Elliots Bks.

Arte Nuevo de Hacer Comedias. Lope De Vega. 153p. (SPA.). 1981. 9.95 (*0-8288-7163-9*, S9043) Fr & Eur.

Arte of English Poesie. George Puttenham. Ed. by Gladys D. Willcock & Alice Walker. 471p. reprint ed. pap. 134.30 (*0-8357-5768-4*, 2024510) Bks Demand.

Arte of English Poesie. George Puttenham. LC 79-26413. (English Experience Ser.: No. 342). 258p. 1971. reprint ed. 30.00 (*90-221-0342-0*) Walter J Johnson.

Arte of English Poesie: Contriued into Three Bookes: The First of Poets & Poesie, the Second of Proportion, the Third of Ornament. Richard Puttenham. LC 71-85107. (Kent English Reprints, the Renaissance Ser.). 340p. reprint ed. pap. 96.90 (*0-7837-6150-3*, 2045872) Bks Demand.

Arte of Limning. Nicholas Hilliard. Ed. by R. K. Thornton & T. G. Cain. (Illus.). 139p. lib. bdg. 35.00 (*0-85635-294-2*) Hacker.

Arte of Navigation. Martin Cortes. LC 92-16475. (Scholars' Facsimiles & Reprints Ser.: Vol. 471). 1992. reprint ed. 75.00 (*0-8201-1471-5*) Schol Facsimiles.

Arte of Rhetorique. Thomas Wilson. LC 62-7014. 1977. reprint ed. 50.00 (*0-8201-1259-3*) Schol Facsimiles.

Arte of Warre, (Certain Waies of the Orderyng of Souldiours) Niccolo Macchiavelli. Tr. by P. Whitehorne. LC 79-26097. (English Experience Ser.: No. 135). 1969. reprint ed. 85.00 (*90-221-0135-5*) Walter J Johnson.

Arte or Crafte of Rhethoryke. Leonard Cox. Ed. by Frederic I. Carpenter. LC 73-136371. (Chicago. University. English Studies: No. 5). reprint ed. 29.50 (*0-404-50265-2*) AMS Pr.

Arte Poetica, Ou Regras Da Verdadiera Poesia Em Geral, 2 vols. in 1. Francisco J. Friere. 554p. 1977. reprint ed. write for info. (*3-487-06470-7*, Pub. by Georg Olms GW) Lubrecht & Cramer.

Arte Portugues. Jose A. Franca et al. (Summa Artis Ser.: Vol. 30). 600p. (SPA.). 1989. 295.00x (*84-239-5230-4*) Elliots Bks.

Arte Precolombino, Mexicano y Maya. Jose Pijoan. (Summa Artis Ser.: Vol. 10). 600p. 1989. 295.00x (*84-239-5210-X*) Elliots Bks.

Arte Prehistorico Europeo. Jose Pijoan. (Summa Artis Ser.: Vol. 6). 600p. 1989. 295.00x (*84-239-5206-1*) Elliots Bks.

Arte Romanico: Siglos XI y XII. Jose Pijoan. (Summa Artis Ser.: Vol. 9). 5p. 1989. 295.00x (*84-239-5209-6*) Elliots Bks.

Arte Romano: Hasta la Muerte de Diocleciano: Arte Etrusco y Arte Helenistico Despues de la Toma de Corinto. Jose Pijoan. (Summa Artis Ser.: Vol. 5). 600p. 1989. 295.00x (*84-239-5205-3*) Elliots Bks.

Arte y Ciencia de la Manicura. Alice R. Cimaglia. (Illus.). 144p. (SPA.). pap. 21.50 (*0-87350-431-3*) Milady Pub.

Arte y Sensualidad: Cincuenta Imagenes Del Hombre y De la Tierra. Esteban Tollinchi. LC 79-19403. (Illus.). 710p. 1981. 20.00 (*0-8477-2111-6*); pap. 16.00 (*0-8477-2112-4*) U of PR Pr.

Artefactos: Colombian Crafts from the Andes to the Amazon. Benjamin Villegas & Liliana Villegas. LC 91-37255. (Illus.). 240p. 1992. 45.00 (*0-8478-1503-X*) Rizzoli Intl.

Artefacts As Categories: A Study of Ceramic Variability in Central India. Daniel Miller. (New Studies in Archaeology). (Illus.). 250p. 1985. 64.95 (*0-521-30522-5*) Cambridge U Pr.

Arteffects. Jean D. Green. (Illus.). 208p. (Orig.). 1993. pap. 29.95 (*0-8230-2529-2*, Watsn-Guptill) Watsn-Guptill.

Artemia Biology. Robert Browne et al. (Illus.). 352p. 1990. 240.00 (*0-8493-6729-8*, QL444) CRC Pr.

***Artemis: The Goddess of the Hunt.** Manuela Dunn-Mascetti. LC 95-11684. 1996. write for info. (*0-8118-0939-0*) Chronicle Bks.

***Artemis Chronicles.** Lillian R. Yeshe. LC 95-90234. 512p. (Orig.). 1995. pap. 17.95 (*0-9646369-0-5*) L R Yeshe.

Artemis in the Park. Eloise K. Healy. LC 91-11670. 88p. (Orig.). 1991. lib. bdg. 18.95 (*0-932379-91-5*); pap. 8.95 (*0-932379-90-7*) Firebrand Bks.

Artemis Speaks: VBAC Stories & Natural Childbirth Information. Nan Koehler. LC 85-70586. 1985. 14.95 (*0-9614679-0-8*) Jerald Brown.

Artemis Speaks: V.B.A.C. Stories & Natural Childbirth Information. 2nd ed. Nan Koehler. (Illus.). 551p. 1989. pap. 12.95 (*0-9623851-0-7*) N U Koehler.

Artemisia. Anna Banti. Tr. by Shirley D. Caracciolo. LC 88-6498. (European Women Writers Ser.). viii, 219p. 1988. 30.00x (*0-8032-1203-8*) U of Nebr Pr.

***Artemisia.** Anna Banti. vi, 219p. 1995. pap. 10.00 (*0-8032-6119-5*) U of Nebr Pr.

Artemisia Gentileschi. Mary D. Garrard. LC 92-34329. (Rizzoli Art Ser.). (Illus.). 24p. (Orig.). 1993. 7.95 (*0-8478-1652-4*) Rizzoli Intl.

Artemisia Gentileschi: The Image of the Female Hero in Italian Baroque Art. Mary D. Garrard. (Illus.). 632p. 1991. text ed. 99.50 (*0-691-04050-8*); pap. text ed. 35.00 (*0-691-00285-1*) Princeton U Pr.

Artemisia, Scaevola, Santalum, & Vaccinium of Hawaii. C. Skottsberg. (BMB Ser.: No. 43). 1972. reprint ed. 15.00 (*0-527-02146-6*) Periodicals Srv.

Artemistempel im Delion auf Paros: Mit Einem Beitrag von A. Ohnesorg. Manfred Schuller. (Denkmaeler Antiker Architektur Ser.: Band 18, No. 1). (Illus.). x, 140p. (GER.). (C). 1991. lib. bdg. 190.80 (*3-11-012442-4*) De Gruyter.

Artemus & the Alphabet. Scott Bassett & Tammy Bassett. (Illus.). 32p. (J). (ps-00). 1980. 6.95 (*0-9605548-0-7*); lib. bdg. 6.95 (*0-9605548-1-5*) Bassett & Brush.

Artemus Ward. James C. Austin. (Twayne's United States Authors Ser.). 1964. pap. 13.95x (*0-8084-0055-X*, T51) NCUP.

Artemus Ward: His Book. Charles F. Browne. (Works of Charles Farrar Browne). 1989. reprint ed. lib. bdg. 79.00 (*0-7812-2091-2*) Rprt Serv.

Artemus Ward: His Travels. Artemus Ward. (Illus.). 120p. 1992. pap. 6.95 (*0-932458-48-3*) Star Rover.

Artemus Ward: His Travels. Charles F. Browne. (Works of Charles Farrar Browne). 1989. reprint ed. lib. bdg. 79.00 (*0-7812-2092-0*) Rprt Serv.

Artemus Ward among the Fenians. Charles F. Browne. 1973. 59.95 (*0-87968-662-6*) Gordon Pr.

Artemus Ward (Charles Farrar Browne) A Biography & Bibliography. Don C. Seitz. (American Newspapermen 1790-1933 Ser.). (Illus.). 338p. 1974. reprint ed. 28.00 (*0-8464-0009-X*) Beekman Pubs.

Artemus Ward in London. Charles F. Browne. (Works of Charles Farrar Browne). 1989. reprint ed. lib. bdg. 79.00 (*0-7812-2093-9*) Rprt Serv.

Artemus Ward in London & Other Papers. Artemus Ward, pseud. LC 73-134318. (Illus.). reprint ed. 35.00 (*0-404-06829-4*) AMS Pr.

An Asterisk (*) at the beginning of an entry indicates that the title is appearing in BIP for the first time.

An Asterisk (*) at the beginning of an entry indicates that the title is appearing in BIP for the first time.

Arthropod-Borne & Rodent-Borne Viral Diseases. (Technical Report Ser.: No. 719). 116p. 1985. pap. 6.00 (*92-4-120719-1*) World Health.

Arthropod-Borne Viruses: Proceedings of the WHO Scientific Group, Geneva, 1960. WHO Staff. (Technical Report Ser.: No. 219). 68p. (ENG, FRE, RUS & SPA.). 1961. pap. 2.00 (*92-4-120219-X*) World Health.

Arthropod-Borne Viruses of Vertebrates: An Account of the Rockefeller Foundation Virus Program, 1951-1970. Max Theiler & W. G. Downs. LC 72-91308. 606p. reprint ed. pap. 172.80 (*0-8357-5771-4*, 2022044) Bks Demand.

Arthropod Brain: Its Evolution, Development, Structure, & Functions. Ed. by Ayodhya P. Gupta. LC 87-8253. 588p. 1987. text ed. 109.95 (*0-471-82811-4*) Wiley.

Arthropod Cell Culture Systems. Ed. by Arthur H. McIntosh & Karl Maramorosch. LC 93-38285. 1994. 169.95 (*0-8493-7642-4*) CRC Pr.

***Arthropod Management Tests.** A. Burditt. 403p. 1994. 45. 00 (*0-614-01938-9*) Entomol Soc.

Arthropod Phylogeny. H. Bruce Boudreaux. LC 84-3960. 328p. (C). 1987. reprint ed. lib. bdg. 37.00 (*0-89874-746-5*) Krieger.

***Arthropod Species in Culture in the U. S. & Other Countries.** D. Edward et al. 49p. 1987. 7.00 (*0-614-01937-0*) Entomol Soc.

Arthropods & Human Skin. J. O'Donel Alexander. (Illus.). 430p. 1984. 210.00 (*0-387-13235-X*) Spr-Verlag.

Arthropods of Medical & Veterinary Importance: A Checklist of Preferred Names & Allied Terms. Comp. by A. R. Pittaway. 160p. 1991. pap. 31.00 (*0-85198-741-9*) CAB Intl.

Arthropods of Medical & Veterinary Importance: A Checklist of Preferred Names & Allied Terms. A. R. Pittaway. 192p. 1991. pap. 59.95 (*0-8288-7365-8*, 851987419) Fr & Eur.

Arthroscopic Atlas of the Temporomandibular Joint. David I. Blaustein & Leslie B. Heffez. LC 89-13158. (Illus.). 117p. 1990. 89.00 (*0-8121-1242-3*); text ed. 89.00 (*0-685-48046-1*) Williams & Wilkins.

Arthroscopic Findings in the Knee Joint. A. Gachter. (Slide Ser.). (Illus.). 75p. 1988. pap. 253.00 (*0-387-92593-7*) Spr-Verlag.

Arthroscopic Laser Surgery: Clinical Implications. Allen T. Brillhart. LC 93-38570. (Illus.). 288p. 1994. 125.00 (*0-387-94186-X*) Spr-Verlag.

Arthroscopic Management of the Knee. 2nd ed. David J. Dandy. (Illus.). 236p. 1987. text ed. 82.00 (*0-443-02958-X*) Churchill.

Arthroscopic Shoulder Surgery: And Related Procedures. Harvard Ellman & Gary Gartsman. (Illus.). 350p. 1993. text ed. 175.00 (*0-8121-1492-2*) Williams & Wilkins.

Arthroscopic Surgery. J. Serge Parisien. (Illus.). 400p. 1988. text ed. 165.00 (*0-07-048474-0*) Hlth Prof Div.

Arthroscopic Surgery: The Shoulder & Elbow. Esch & Baker. 1993. text ed. 125.00 (*0-397-51182-5*) Lippincott.

Arthroscopic Surgery: The Wrist. Whipple. (Illus.). 208p. 1992. text ed. 95.00 (*0-397-51023-3*) Lippincott.

Arthroscopy: Diagnostic & Surgical Practice. S. Ward Casscells. LC 83-11289. 206p. reprint ed. pap. 58.80 (*0-7837-2694-5*, 2043072) Bks Demand.

Arthroscopy of the Knee. R. Aigner & J. Gillquist. (Flexibook Ser.). (Illus.). 228p. 1991. text ed. 27.00 (*0-86577-342-4*) Thieme Med Pubs.

Arthroscopy of the Knee. Vincent Chassaing et al. Tr. by Reginald A. Elson. (Illus.). 156p. 1988. text ed. 88.00 (*0-88167-427-3*) Raven.

Arthroscopy of the Knee: Diagnosis & Treatment. W. Norman Scott. (Illus.). 528p. 1990. text ed. 125.00 (*0-7216-8032-1*) Saunders.

Arthroscopy of the Knee Joint. H. R. Henche. Tr. by P. A. Casey. (Illus.). 1979. 81.00 (*0-387-09314-1*) Spr-Verlag.

Arthroscopy of the Shoulder: Diagnosis & Therapy. H. Resch & E. Beck. Tr. by M. L. Antoft & B. Marschall. (Illus.). 190p. 1992. 128.00 (*0-387-82339-5*) Spr-Verlag.

Arthroscopy of the Wrist & Elbow. Ed. by Gary G. Poehling et al. LC 93-42821. 200p. 1995. 98.00 (*0-7817-0194-5*) Raven.

Arthrosonography. H. Sattler & U. Harland. (Illus.). 175p. 1990. 104.00 (*0-387-19482-7*) Spr-Verlag.

***Arthur.** Amanda Graham. 32p. (J). 1995. 4.95 (*0-947212-16-7*, Pub. by ERA Pubns AT) Pubs Dist MI.

Arthur. Stephen R. Lawhead. LC 89-50337. (Pendragon Cycle Ser.). 445p. 1989. pap. 11.99 (*0-89107-475-9*) Crossway Bks.

Arthur. Stephen R. Lawhead. (Pendragon Cycle Ser.: Bk. 3). 448p. 1995. reprint ed. mass mkt. 5.99 (*0-380-70890-6*, AvoNova) Avon.

Arthur: Tales of the Young King. C. Brim. (Illus.). 32p. (J). (gr. 2-6). 1989. 10.95 (*0-88625-236-9*) Durkin Hayes Pub.

Arthur: The King of Light. Allen Artos. (Illus.). 100p. (Orig.). 1986. pap. 6.00 (*0-934852-29-4*) Lorien Hse.

A.R.T.H.U.R. The Life & Opinions of a Digital Computer. Laurence Lerner. LC 74-21241. 66p. 1975. reprint ed. pap. 8.95 (*0-87023-181-2*) U of Mass Pr.

Arthur A. Pilgrim. Arthur Blessitt. LC 85-71322. (Orig.). 1985. pap. 5.00 (*0-934461-00-7*, BP601) Blessitt Pub.

Arthur Adamov. John H. Reilly. LC 74-2162. (Twayne's World Authors Ser.). 177p. (C). 1974. lib. bdg. 17.95 (*0-8057-2005-7*) Irvington.

Arthur Alfonso Schomburg: Black Bibliophile & Collector, a Biography. Elinor Des Verney Sinnette. LC 88-29001. (African American Life Ser.). 262p. (C). 1989. 34.95 (*0-8143-2156-9*); pap. 16.95 (*0-8143-2157-7*) Wayne St U Pr.

Arthur & Clementine. Adela Turin & Nella Bosnia. (Feminist Fables for Children Ser.). Orig. Title: Arturo E Clementina. (Illus.). 32p. (J). (gr. 3-6). 1980. 6.95 (*0-904613-19-4*) Writers & Readers.

Arthur & Gorlagon. George L. Kittredge. LC 73-100768. (Arthurian Legend & Literature Ser.: No. 1). 1970. reprint ed. pap. 75.00 (*0-8383-0049-9*) M S G Haskell Hse.

Arthur & the Anglo-Saxon Wars. David Nicolle. (Men-at-Arms Ser.: No. 154). (Illus.). 48p. pap. 11.95 (*0-85045-548-0*, 9086, Pub. by Osprey UK) Stackpole.

Arthur & the Dragon. Pauline Cartwright. LC 90-10091. (Highgate Collection). (Illus.). 32p. (J). (gr. 1-4). 1990. lib. bdg. 17.28 (*0-8114-2689-0*) Raintree Steck-V.

***Arthur & the Sword.** Thomas Malory. LC 95-9968. (J). 1995. write for info. (*0-689-31987-8*, Atheneum S&S) S&S Trade.

Arthur & Tristan: On the Intersection of Legends in German Medieval Literature. William C. McDonald. LC 91-40230. 308p. 1992. lib. bdg. 99.95 (*0-7734-9448-0*) E Mellen.

Arthur Andersen European Community Sourcebook: The Most Authoritative, Comprehensive Reference Guide Ever Assembled on the European Market. Arthur Andersen et al. 500p. 1991. lib. bdg. 150.00 (*0-9624436-4-6*) Triumph Bks.

Arthur Andersen North American Business Sourcebook: The Most Comprehensive, Authoritative Reference Guide Ever Assembled on NAFTA & the North American Market. Arthur Andersen. 600p. 1993. lib. bdg. 195.00 (*1-880141-51-5*) Triumph Bks.

Arthur! Arthur! More Comic Sketches from the Master's Pen. Arthur Black. 233p. 1991. 24.95 (*0-7737-2513-X*, Pub. by Stoddart Pubng CN) Genl Dist Srvs.

Arthur Ashe. Ed Weissberg. (Black Americans of Achievement Ser.). (Illus.). 112p. (YA). (gr. 5 up). 1991. lib. bdg. 17.95 (*0-7910-1115-1*) Chelsea Hse.

Arthur Ashe. Ted Weissberg. 1993. pap. 3.95 (*0-87067-781-0*, Melrose Sq) Holloway.

Arthur Ashe: Against the Wind. David R. Collins. (People in Focus Ser.). (J). 1994. text ed. 13.95 (*0-87518-647-5*, Dillon Silver Burdett) Silver Burdett Pr.

Arthur Ashe: Black Americans of Achievement. Ted Weissberg. (J). (gr. 4-7). 1992. pap. 7.95 (*0-7910-1141-0*) Chelsea Hse.

Arthur Ashe: Champion of Dreams & Motion. Stuart A. Kallen. LC 93-8623. (I Have a Dream Ser.). 48p. 1993. lib. bdg. 14.96 (*1-56239-255-7*) Abdo & Dghtrs.

Arthur Ashe: Portrait in Motion. Arthur Ashe & Frank Deford. (Illus.). 304p. 1993. pap. 11.95 (*0-7867-0050-5*) Carroll & Graf.

Arthur Ashe & His Match with History. Robert Quackenbush. (J). (gr. 4-7). 1994. pap. 4.95 (*0-671-88182-5*, S&S Bks Young Read) S&S Childrens.

Arthur Ashe & His Match with History. Robert Quackenbush. LC 93-14945. (J). (gr. 5 up). 1994. pap. 14.00 (*0-671-86597-8*, S&S Bks Young Read) S&S Childrens.

***Arthur Ashe on Tennis: Strokes, Strategy, Traditions, Players, Psychology, & Wisdom.** Arthur Ashe & Alexander McNab. LC 94-29542. 1995. 20.00 (*0-679-43797-5*) Knopf.

***Arthur Ashe, Tennis Legend.** Jim Spence. LC 95-5361. (Great Comeback Champions Ser.). (J). 1995. write for info. (*1-57103-004-2*) Rourke Pr.

Arthur Aylsworth & His Descendants in America, with Notes, Historical & Genealogical, Relating to the Family, from Early English Records. James N. Arnold. (Illus.). 632p. 1988. reprint ed. lib. bdg. 105.00 (*0-8328-0146-1*); reprint ed. pap. 95.00 (*0-8328-0147-X*) Higginson Bk Co.

Arthur B. Carles: "Painting with Color" Barbara A. Wolanin. (Illus.). 208p. (Orig.). 1983. 19.95 (*0-943836-01-8*) Penn Acad Art.

Arthur B. Metzner: A Special Issue in His Honor. R. K. Gupta & K. F. Wissburn. 228p. 1987. pap. text ed. 427. 00 (*2-88124-258-8*) Gordon & Breach.

***Arthur Babysits.** Marc Brown. (Illus.). (J). (ps-3). 1994. pap. text ed. 4.95 (*0-316-11442-1*) Little.

Arthur Babysits. Marc T. Brown. (Illus.). 32p. (J). (ps-3). 1992. 14.95 (*0-316-11293-3*, Joy St Bks) Little.

Arthur Baker's Historic Calligraphic Alphabets. Arthur Baker. (Pictorial Archive Ser.). (Illus.). 96p. (Orig.). 1980. pap. 4.95 (*0-486-24054-1*) Dover.

Arthur Beaumont: Naval Artist, 1890-1978. Alison Beaumont. (Illus.). 64p. 1989. pap. 20.00 (*0-685-25995-1*) Beaumont Pub.

Arthur Berriedale Keith 1879-1944: The Chief Ornament of Scottish Learning. Ridgeway F. Shinn, Jr. (Illus.). 1990. text ed. 50.00 (*0-08-037737-8*, Pub. by Aberdeen U Pr) Macmillan.

Arthur Bliss: A Bio-Bibliography. Stewart R. Craggs. LC 88-10975. (Bio-Bibliographies in Music Ser.: No. 13). 190p. 1988. text ed. 49.95 (*0-313-25739-6*, CSB/, Greenwood Pr) Greenwood.

Arthur Bloomfield's Restaurant Book: A Celebration of Dining in the Bay Area & Beyond. Arthur Bloomfield. (Illus.). 225p. 1987. pap. 10.95 (*0-317-60779-0*) Aris Bks.

***Arthur Boyd: Retrospective.** Barry Pearce. (Illus.). 200p. (C). 1994. 80.00 (*0-947349-08-1*, Pub. by Lund Humphries UK) Antique Collect.

Arthur Boyd at Bundanon. Janet McKenzie. (Illus.). 144p. 1994. 50.00 (*1-85490-337-3*, Academy Edits) St Martin.

Arthur Boyd at Bundanon. Janet McKenzie. (Illus.). 144p. 1994. pap. 38.00 (*1-85490-338-1*, Academy Edits) St Martin.

Arthur Burns & the Successor Generation: Selected Writings of & about Arthur Burns. Hans N. Tuch. LC 88-20595. 76p. (Orig.). (C). 1989. lib. bdg. 29.00 (*0-8191-7143-3*); pap. text ed. 11.50 (*0-8191-7144-1*) U Pr of Amer.

Arthur C. Clarke. 2nd ed. Eric S. Rabkin. Ed. by Roger C. Schlobin. LC 79-84709. (Starmont Reader's Guide Ser.: Vol. 1). 80p. 1980. lib. bdg. 20.00 (*0-916732-22-3*); pap. 10.00 (*0-916732-21-5*) Borgo Pr.

Arthur C. Clarke: The Authorized Biography. Neil McAleer. 448p. 1993. pap. 12.95 (*0-8092-3720-2*) Contemp Bks.

Arthur C. Clarke's Venus Prime, Vol. 6: The Shining Ones. Paul Preuss. 272p. (Orig.). 1991. pap. 3.95 (*0-380-75350-2*) Avon.

Arthur Campbell: Pioneer & Patriot of the "Old Southwest" Hartwell L. Quinn. LC 89-43628. (Illus.). 207p. 1990. lib. bdg. 27.50x (*0-89950-509-0*) McFarland & Co.

Arthur Conan Doyle. Don R. Cox. LC 84-28050. (Literature & Life Ser.). 250p. (C). 1985. 19.95 (*0-8044-2146-3*, F Ungar Bks) Continuum.

Arthur Conan Doyle. Jacqueline A. Jaffe. (English Authors Ser.). 160p. 1987. text ed. 21.95 (*0-8057-6954-4*, Twayne) Macmillan.

Arthur Conan Doyle: Great British & Irish Short Stories I. Illus. by James McConnell. LC 94-75351. (Classic Short Stories Ser.). 80p. 1994. pap. 4.50 (*1-56103-026-0*) Lake Pub Co.

Arthur Conan Doyle Mystery Theatre. 1983. 19.95 (*0-943748-03-8*) Ekay Music.

Arthur D. Little Forecast on Information Technology & Productivity. Norman Weizer. 1991. text ed. 39.95 (*0-471-52511-1*) Wiley.

Arthur Davies: A Catalogue Raisonne of the Prints. Joseph S. Czestochowski. LC 83-40542. (American Art Ser.). (Illus.). 256p. 1987. 85.00 (*0-87413-242-8*) U Delaware Pr.

Arthur Dobbs, Esquire, 1689-1765: Surveyor-General of Ireland, Prospector & Governor of North Carolina. Desmond Clarke. LC 58-14501. 232p. reprint ed. pap. 66.20 (*0-7837-2078-5*, 2042352) Bks Demand.

Arthur Dove: Nature as Symbol. Sherrye Cohn. LC 85-5848. (Studies in the Fine Arts: The Avant-Garde: No. 49). 254p. reprint ed. pap. 72.40 (*0-8357-2018-7*, 2070658) Bks Demand.

Arthur Dove & Helen Torr: The Huntington Years. Anne C. DePietro & Mary T. Rehm. Ed. by Penny Jones. LC 89-80260. (Illus.). 100p. (Orig.). 1989. pap. text ed. 16. 95 (*1-879195-03-8*) Heckscher Mus.

***Arthur Evans & the Palace at Minos.** Ann Brown. (Illus.). 110p. 1995. 19.95 (*0-907849-50-4*, 9504, Pub. by Ashmolean Mus UK); pap. 15.95 (*0-900090-92-8*, 0928, Pub. by Ashmolean Mus UK) A Schwartz & Co.

Arthur Evans & the Palace of Minos. A. C. Brown. (Illus.). 110p. 1989. pap. 15.95 (*0-900909-22-6*, Pub. by Ashmolean Mus UK) A Schwartz & Co.

Arthur Ewert: A Life for the Comintern. David P. Hornstein. 328p. (C). 1993. lib. bdg. 48.50 (*0-8191-9258-9*) U Pr of Amer.

Arthur Fiedler: Papa, the Pops & Me. Johanna Fiedler. LC 94-7676. 1994. 24.95 (*0-385-42391-8*) Doubleday.

Arthur Fitzwilliam Tai: Artist in the Adirondacks. Warder H. Cadbury & Henry F. Marsh. LC 82-40437. (American Art Ser.). (Illus.). 344p. 1986. 95.00 (*0-87413-224-X*) U Delaware Pr.

***Arthur Flemming Crusader at Large.** Frwd. by Elliot L. Richardson. 371p. 1992. 25.00 (*0-9628363-2-X*) Caring Pub.

***Arthur Foote, 1853-1937.** Arthur Foote. (American Autobiography Ser.). 135p. 1995. reprint ed. lib. bdg. 69. 00 (*0-7812-8519-4*) Rprt Serv.

Arthur Foote, 1853-1937: An Autobiography. Arthur Foote. LC 78-2021. (Music Reprint Ser.: 1978). (Illus.). 1978. reprint ed. lib. bdg. 32.50 (*0-306-77531-X*) Da Capo.

Arthur, for the Very First Time. Patricia MacLachlan. LC 79-2007. (Illus.). 128p. (J). (gr. 4-7). 1980. lib. bdg. 14. 89 (*0-06-024047-4*) HarpC Child Bks.

Arthur, for the Very First Time. Patricia MacLachlan. LC 79-2007. (Trophy Bk.). (Illus.). 128p. (J). (gr. 3-6). 1989. pap. 3.95 (*0-06-440288-6*, Trophy) HarpC Child Bks.

***Arthur Frommer's Branson: The Complete Guide to What's Good & What's Bad in the Nation's Newest Music Capital.** 320p. 1995. pap. text ed. 13.95 (*0-02-860256-0*) Macmillan.

Arthur G. Dove: Pastels, Charcoals, Watercolors. Debra B. Balken. (Illus.). 50p. (Orig.). 1993. pap. text ed. 15.00 (*0-9635932-0-X*) T Dintenfass Gal.

Arthur Ganson: Diverse Machinery. Nick Capasso. (Illus.). 8p. (Orig.). 1992. pap. 1.00 (*0-945506-11-2*) DeCordova Mus.

***Arthur Giron's Edith Stein: A Dramaturgical Sourcebook.** Ed. by Donald Marinelli. (Dramaturgical Sourcebook Ser.). (Illus.). 210p. 1994. pap. 15.95 (*0-88748-178-7*) Carnegie-Mellon.

Arthur Goes to Camp. Marc T. Brown. LC 81-15588. (Illus.). 32p. (J). (ps-3). 1984. mass mkt. 4.95 (*0-316-11058-2*, Joy St Bks) Little.

***Arthur Goes to School.** Brown. (J). 10.00 (*0-679-86734-1*) Random.

Arthur Henderson. Chris Wrigley. Ed. by K. O. Morgan. (Political Portraits Ser.). xii, 210p. 1990. 32.00 (*0-7083-1083-4*, Pub. by U of Wales UK) Bks Intl VA.

Arthur, High King of Britain. Michael Morpurgo. LC 93-33620. (Illus.). 144p. (J). (gr. 4-9). 1995. 19.95 (*0-15-200080-1*) HarBrace.

Arthur Hill: Western Actor, Miner, & Law Officer. John Moring. (Illus.). 115p. 1994. pap. text ed. 16.95 (*0-89745-175-9*) Sunflower U Pr.

Arthur Hugh Clough. Wendell V. Harris. (Twayne's English Authors Ser.). (C). 1968. lib. bdg. 17.95 (*0-8057-1096-5*) Irvington.

Arthur Hugh Clough. Samuel Waddington. LC 70-148321. reprint ed. 42.50 (*0-404-08921-6*) AMS Pr.

Arthur Hugh Clough: Growth of a Poet's Mind. Evelyn B. Greenberger. LC 78-116735. 282p. 1970. 32.00 (*0-674-04849-0*) HUP.

Arthur Irwin: A Biography. David MacKenzie. LC 93-93699. 323p. 1993. 45.00 (*0-8020-2632-X*) U of Toronto Pr.

Arthur J. Balfour & Ireland, 1874-1922. Catherine B. Shannon. LC 87-6543. 362p. 1988. 38.95 (*0-8132-0636-7*) Cath U Pr.

***Arthur J. Balfour & Ireland, 1874-1922.** Catherine B. Shannon. LC 87-6543. (Illus.). reprint ed. pap. 108.30 (*0-7837-9187-9*, 2049887) Bks Demand.

Arthur Jacobson: Interviewed by Irene Kahn Atkins. Arthur Jacobson. LC 91-27516. (Directors Guild of America Oral History Ser.). (Illus.). 270p. 1991. 29.50 (*0-8108-2468-X*) Scarecrow.

Arthur Jensen: Consensus & Controversy. Ed. by Sohan Modgil & Celia Modgil. (International Master Minds Challenged Ser.). 410p. 1987. 125.00 (*1-85000-093-X*, Falmer Pr) Taylor & Francis.

***Arthur J.Goldberg: New Deal Liberal.** David Stebenne. (Illus.). 576p. 1996. 45.00 (*0-19-507105-0*) OUP.

***Arthur, King.** D. L. Anderson. 1995. pap. 4.99 (*0-06-105433-X*, Prism Bks) P-H.

Arthur Kitson: Money Reformer. L. Wise. 1982. lib. bdg. 69.95 (*0-87700-375-0*) Revisionist Pr.

Arthur Lord Collection. Pilgrim Society Collection Staff. 1971. 2.00 (*0-940628-08-2*) Pilgrim Soc.

Arthur M. Sackler Museum, Harvard University. John Coolidge & John M. Rosenfield. (Illus.). 50p. (Orig.). 1985. pap. 9.95 (*0-916724-59-X*) Harvard Art Mus.

Arthur M. Schlesinger, Jr., & the Ideological History of American Liberalism. Stephen P. Depoe. LC 93-5806. (Studies in Rhetoric & Communication). 216p. 1994. 29. 95 (*0-8173-0718-4*) U of Ala Pr.

Arthur Machen: A Bibliography. Henry Danielsson. LC 74-130267. (Reference Ser.: No. 44). 1970. reprint ed. lib. bdg. 52.95 (*0-8383-1174-1*) M S G Haskell Hse.

Arthur Machen & Montgomery Evans: Letters of a Literary Friendship, 1923-1947. Ed. by Sue S. Hassler & Donald M. Hassler. LC 93-30315. (Illus.). 208p. 1994. lib. bdg. 26.00 (*0-87338-489-X*) Kent St U Pr.

Arthur Meets the President. Marc T. Brown. (J). (ps-3). 1991. 14.95 (*0-316-11265-8*) Little.

Arthur Meets the President: An Arthur Adventure. Marc T. Brown. (J). (ps-3). 1992. mass mkt. 4.95 (*0-316-11291-7*, Joy St Bks) Little.

Arthur Meighen: The Door of Opportunity. Roger Graham. 341p. 1968. 8.50 (*0-7720-0130-8*, Pub. by Stoddart Pubng CN) Genl Dist Srvs.

Arthur Mervyn. Charles B. Brown. Ed. by Frank Cabo. (Masterworks of Literature Ser.). 1991. pap. 17.95 (*0-8084-0446-6*) NCUP.

Arthur Mervyn, 2 vols., Set. Charles B. Brown. 1993. reprint ed. lib. bdg. 150.00 (*0-7812-5436-1*) Rprt Serv.

Arthur Mervyn: Or the Memoirs of the Year 1793. Charles B. Brown. (Works of Charles Brockden Brown). 1989. reprint ed. lib. bdg. 79.00 (*0-7812-2069-6*) Rprt Serv.

Arthur Miller. Intro. by Harold Bloom. (Modern Critical Views Ser.). 164p. 1987. 29.95 (*0-87754-711-4*) Chelsea Hse.

Arthur Miller. Neil Carson. LC 88-15750. (Modern Dramatists Ser.). 180p. (Orig.). 1988. pap. 12.95 (*0-312-02381-2*) St Martin.

Arthur Miller. Bruce S. Glassman. (Genius Ser.). (Illus.). 128p. (J). (gr. 7-9). 1990. 12.95 (*0-382-09904-4*); pap. 7.95 (*0-382-24032-4*) Silver Burdett Pr.

Arthur Miller. rev. ed. Leonard Moss. (United States Authors Ser.: No. 115). 200p. 1980. text ed. 20.95 (*0-8057-7311-8*, Twayne) Macmillan.

Arthur Miller & Company. Ed. by Christopher Bigsby. 240p. (Orig.). (C). 1990. pap. 17.95 (*0-413-65050-2*, A0544, Pub. by Methuen UK) Heinemann.

Arthur Miller in Conversation. Steve Centola. LC 92-37358. 1993. 13.95 (*0-935061-51-7*) Contemp Res.

Arthur Miller's All My Sons. Intro. by Harold Bloom. (Modern Critical Interpretations Ser.). 160p. 1988. lib. bdg. 24.95 (*1-55546-060-7*) Chelsea Hse.

Arthur Miller's Death of a Salesman. Ed. by Harold Bloom. (Modern Critical Interpretations Ser.). 152p. 1988. lib. bdg. 29.95 (*1-55546-061-5*) Chelsea Hse.

***Arthur Miller's Death of a Salesman.** Ed. & Intro. by Harold Bloom. LC 95-13561. (Bloom's Notes Ser.). 1995. write for info. (*0-7910-3656-1*); pap. write for info. (*0-7910-3681-2*) Chelsea Hse.

Arthur Morgan: A Biography & Memoir. Walter Kahoe. LC 77-84817. (Illus.). 180p. 1977. 7.95 (*0-916178-01-3*) Whimsie Pr.

Arthur Morgan Remembered. Ernest Morgan. 1991. 6.00 (*0-910420-31-9*) Comm Serv OH.

Arthur Murray's Dance Secrets. Arthur Murray. (Ballroom Dance Ser.). 1986. lib. bdg. 79.95 (*0-8490-3371-3*) Gordon Pr.

Arthur Murray's Dance Secrets. Arthur Murray. (Ballroom Dance Ser.). 1985. lib. bdg. 100.00 (*0-87700-698-9*) Revisionist Pr.

Arthur O. Lovejoy & the Quest for Intelligibility. Daniel J. Wilson. LC 79-25902. 266p. reprint ed. pap. 75.90 (*0-7837-2457-8*, 2042610) Bks Demand.

Arthur of the English Poets. Howard Maynadier. 454p. (C). 1966. text ed. 75.00 (*0-8383-0670-5*) M S G Haskell Hse.

Arthur of the Welsh: A Collaborative Study of the Arthurian Legend in Medieval Welsh Literature. Ed. by Rachel Bromwich et al. 322p. 1993. reprint ed. 55.00 (*0-7083-1107-5*, Pub. by U of Wales UK) Bks Intl VA.

Arthur-Peacemaker. Arthur Blessitt. LC 85-71322. (Orig.). 1986. pap. 5.00 (*0-934461-02-3*, BP603) Blessitt Pub.

Arthur Pigou, 1877-1959. Ed. by Mark Blaug. (Pioneers in Economics Ser.: Vol. 36). 208p. 1992. 72.95 (*1-85278-499-7*, Pub. by E Elgar Pub UK) Ashgate Pub Co.

458
An Asterisk (*) at the beginning of an entry indicates that the title is appearing in BIP for the first time.

Arthur Rackham: A Bibliography. 3rd ed. Sarah B. Latimore & Grace C. Haskell. 111p. 1987. reprint ed. 21.00 (*0-935259-01-5*) San Marco Bk.

Arthur Rackham: A Biography. James Hamilton. (Illus.). 199p. 1990. 45.00 (*1-55970-096-3*) Arcade Pub Inc.

Arthur Rackham: A Biography. James Hamilton. (Illus.). 199p. 1994. pap. 29.95 (*1-85145-708-9*, Pub. by Pavilion UK) Trafalgar.

***Arthur Rackham: A Life with Illustration.** James Hamilton. (Illus.). 199p. 1995. pap. 24.95 (*1-85793-634-5*, Pub. by Pavilion UK) Trafalgar.

Arthur Rackham Fairy Book. Illus. by Arthur Rackham. 271p. (J). (gr. 2-10). 1991. 3.99 (*0-517-24213-3*) Random Hse Value.

Arthur Ransome. Peter Hunt. (Twayne's English Authors Ser.: No. 484). 200p. 1991. text ed. 21.95 (*0-8057-7003-8*, Twayne) Macmillan.

Arthur Redman Wilfley: Miner, Inventor, & Entrepreneur. Jay E. Niebur & James E. Fell, Jr. (Illus.). xii, 245p. 1981. pap. 8.95 (*0-942576-25-X*) CO Hist Soc.

Arthur Rimbaud. F. C. St. Aubyn. (World Authors Ser.: No. 369). 184p. 1988. text ed. 23.95 (*0-8057-8227-3*, TWAS 369 (FRANCE), Twayne) Macmillan.

Arthur Rimbaud. rev. ed. Enid Starkie. LC 61-18478. (Illus.). 1968. reprint ed. pap. 14.95 (*0-8112-0197-X*, NDP254) New Directions.

Arthur Rothstein's America in Photographs, 1930-1980. Arthur Rothstein. LC 84-6147. 96p. 1984. pap. 7.95 (*0-486-24735-X*) Dover.

Arthur S. Dewing Collection of Greek Coins, 2 Vols. Ed. by Leo Mildenberg & Silvia Hurter. (ACNAC (American Coins in North American Collections)). (Illus.). 336p. 1985. boxed 120.00 (*0-89722-206-7*) Am Numismatic.

***Arthur Schnitzler.** Sol Liptzin. LC 94-48728. (Studies in Austrian Literature, Culture, & Thought). 1995. pap. 19.95 (*1-57241-013-2*) Ariadne CA.

Arthur Schnitzler. Reinhard Urbach. Tr. by Donald Daviau. LC 73-178165. (Literature & Life Ser.). (Illus.). 192p. (C). 1973. 19.95 (*0-8044-2936-7*, F Ungar Bks) Continuum.

Arthur Schnitzler & Politics. Adrian C. Roberts. (Studies in Austrian Literature, Culture, & Thought. Translation Ser.). 214p. 1989. 29.00 (*0-929497-06-6*); pap. 23.00 (*0-929497-14-7*) Ariadne CA.

Arthur Schnitzler Berta Garlan. Tr. & Intro. by G. J. Weinberger. (American University Studies: Germanic Languages & Literature: Ser. I, Vol. 62). 208p. (C). 1987. text ed. 33.00 (*0-8204-0549-3*) P Lang Pubs.

Arthur Schopenhauer's English Schooling. Patrick Bridgwater. 416p. (C). 1988. lib. bdg. 77.00 (*0-415-00743-7*, A2467) Routledge.

Arthur Sets Sail. Libor Schaffer. LC 87-1594. (Illus.). 32p. (J). (gr. k-3). 1987. 14.95 (*1-55858-059-X*) North-South Bks NYC.

Arthur Shawcross: The Genesee River Killer. Joel Norris. 1992. mass mkt. 4.99 (*1-55817-578-4*, Pinnacle NY); audio 5.99 (*1-55817-592-X*, Pinnacle NY) Windsor NY.

Arthur Shepherd: American Composer. Richard Loucks. LC 79-22143. (Illus.). 1980. lib. bdg. 19.95 (*0-8425-1706-5*) BYU Scholarly.

Arthur Sherburne Hardy: Man of American Letters. E. Kate Stewart. 31.50 (*0-916379-38-8*) Scripta.

Arthur Site: Settlement & Subsistence Structure at a Washita River Phase Village. Robert L. Brooks. (Studies in Oklahoma's Past). (Illus.). 170p. (C). 1987. pap. text ed. 6.50 (*1-881346-08-0*) Univ OK Archeol.

Arthur Stories. Winifred Warren. 1988. 8.95 (*0-941363-01-5*) Lake Shore Pub.

Arthur Sullivan: A Victorian Musician. Arthur Jacobs. 496p. 1987. pap. 13.95 (*0-19-282033-8*) OUP.

Arthur Sullivan: A Victorian Musician. Arthur Jacobs. (Illus.). 502p. 1992. 49.95 (*0-931340-51-9*, Amadeus Pr) Timber.

Arthur Symons. John M. Munro. Ed. by Sylvia E. Bowman. LC 68-17234. (Twayne's English Authors Ser.). 174p. (C). 1969. lib. bdg. 17.95 (*0-8290-1721-6*) Irvington.

Arthur Symons. T. Earle Welby. LC 74-6467. (English Literature Ser.: No. 33). 1974. lib. bdg. 48.95 (*0-8383-1972-6*) M S G Haskell Hse.

Arthur Symons: A Bibliography. Karl Beckson et al. LC 89-84406. (British Authors, 1880-1920 Ser.). 330p. (C). 1990. 30.00 (*0-944318-04-5*) ELT Pr.

Arthur Symons: A Life. Karl Beckson. (Illus.). 416p. 1987. 79.00 (*0-19-812882-7*) OUP.

Arthur Symons: Critic of the Seven Arts. Lawrence W. Markert. Ed. by Donald Kuspit. LC 87-22802. (Studies in the Fine Arts: Criticism: No. 25). 190p. reprint ed. 54.20 (*0-8357-1845-X*, 2070739) Bks Demand.

Arthur Symons: Selected Letters, 1880-1935. Ed. by Karl Beckson & John M. Munro. LC 87-51647. (Illus.). 321p. 1989. text ed. 44.95 (*0-87745-213-X*) U of Iowa Pr.

Arthur Symons, a Critical Study. Thomas E. Welby. (BCL1-PR English Literature Ser.). 147p. 1992. reprint ed. lib. bdg. 69.00 (*0-7812-7684-5*) Rprt Serv.

Arthur Symons, Poetry & Prose. Arthur Symons. 98p. 9.95 (*0-85635-058-3*) Dufour.

Arthur the King. Graeme Fife. LC 90-24599. (Illus.). 200p. 1994. pap. 14.95 (*0-8069-8345-0*) Sterling.

***Arthur Throws a Tantrum.** Ginette Anfousee. (First Novels Ser.). (Illus.). 64p. (J). (gr. 1-4). 1995. pap. 4.95 (*0-88780-221-4*); bds. 14.95 (*0-88780-222-2*) Formac Dist Ltd.

***Arthur Tress: A Monograph.** Peter Weiermair. 140p. Date not set. 49.95 (*3-905514-71-0*) Dist Art Pubs.

***Arthur Tress: Requiem for a Paperweight.** David A. Mellor. Ed. & Intro. by Constance W. Glenn. (Illus.). 16p. (Orig.). 1994. pap. 10.00 (*0-936270-33-0*) CA St U LB Art.

Arthur W. Kincade: Banker, Philanthropist & Civic Leader. James H. Thomas. (Illus.). 209p. 10.00 (*0-685-10135-5*) Wichita Ctr Entrep SBM.

Arthur W. Pink - Born to Write. Richard P. Belcher. 165p. 1993. reprint ed. pap. write for info. (*1-883265-01-0*) Richbarry Pr.

Arthur W. Pink - Letters from Spartanburg, 1917-1920. Ed. by Richard P. Belcher. 287p. 1993. write for info. (*1-883265-00-2*) Richbarry Pr.

***Arthur W. Pink - Letters of an Itinerant Preacher 1920-21.** Ed. by Richard P. Belcher. 1994. pap. write for info. (*1-883265-09-6*) Richbarry Pr.

Arthur War Lord. Dafydd ab Hugh. 400p. (Orig.). 1994. mass mkt. 4.99 (*0-380-77028-8*, AvoNova) Avon.

Arthur War Lord Bk. 2: Far Beyond the Wave. Dafydd A. Hugh. 352p. (Orig.). 1994. mass mkt. 4.99 (*0-380-77717-7*, AvoNova) Avon.

Arthur Wing Pinero & Henry Arthur Jones. Penny Griffin. Ed. by Bruce King & Adele King. LC 90-43259. (Modern Dramatists Ser.). 254p. 1991. text ed. 29.95 (*0-312-05572-2*) St Martin.

Arthur Young Guide to Rating Venture Capital. Steven G. Burrill & Craig T. Norback. 192p. 1988. 24.95 (*0-8306-3014-7*) TAB Bks.

Arthur Young on Industry & Economics. Arthur Young. LC 72-38271. (Evolution of Capitalism Ser.). 188p. 1972. reprint ed. 15.95 (*0-405-04142-X*) Ayer.

Arthurian & Other Studies Presented to Shunichi Noguchi. Ed. by Takashi Suzuki & Tsuyoshi Mukai. LC 92-40726. (Illus.). 295p. (C). 1993. text ed. 89.00 (*0-85991-380-5*, DS Brewer) Boydell & Brewer.

Arthurian Bibliography II: Subject Index, No. II. Ed. by C. E. Pickford et al. (Arthurian Studies: Vol. VI). 144p. 1983. 71.00 (*0-85991-099-7*) Boydell & Brewer.

Arthurian Bibliography Three, 1978-1992. Ed. by Caroline Palmer. (Arthurian Studies: Vol. 31). 694p. (C). 1995. text ed. 108.00 (*0-85991-399-6*) Boydell & Brewer.

Arthurian Book of Days. Eddison Sadd et al. Ed. by Elisa Petrini. (Illus.). 192p. 1990. text ed. 22.95 (*0-02-606675-0*) Macmillan Info.

Arthurian Dictionary. Charles Moorman & Ruth Minary. 1990. pap. 8.95 (*0-89733-348-9*) Academy Chi Pubs.

Arthurian Drama: An Anthology. Ed. by Alan Lupack. LC 90-20122. 358p. 1991. 48.00 (*0-8240-3424-4*, 90-20122) Garland.

Arthurian Encyclopedia. Ed. by Norris J. Lacy et al. LC 87-47756. (Illus.). 650p. 1987. 16.95 (*0-87226-164-6*) P Bedrick Bks.

Arthurian Epic. S. Humphreys Gurteen. LC 65-26457. (Arthurian Legend & Literature Ser.: No. 1). 1969. reprint ed. lib. bdg. 75.00 (*0-8383-0562-8*) M S G Haskell Hse.

Arthurian Fictions: Rereading the Vulgate Cycle. E. Jane Burns. LC 85-7325. 185p. 1985. 40.00 (*0-8142-0387-6*) Ohio St U Pr.

Arthurian Legend & Literature: An Annotated Bibliography: Renaissance to Present, Vol. II. Ed. by Edmund Reiss et al. LC 83-47612. (Publications in Medieval Studies). 400p. lib. bdg. 54.00 (*0-8240-9122-1*) Garland.

Arthurian Legend in the Literatures of the Spanish Peninsula. William S. Entwistle. LC 75-6563. 278p. 1975. reprint ed. 50.00 (*0-87753-059-9*) Phaeton.

Arthurian Legend in the Seventeenth Century. Roberta F. Brinkley. (BCL1-PR English Literature Ser.). 228p. 1992. reprint ed. lib. bdg. 79.00 (*0-7812-7038-3*) Rprt Serv.

Arthurian Legends. Richard Barber. (Illus.). 224p. (C). 1993. text ed. 34.00 (*0-85115-110-8*) Boydell & Brewer.

Arthurian Legends: An Illustrated Anthology. Intro. by Richard Barber. (Reprints Ser.). (Illus.). 224p. 1988. 28.50 (*0-88029-050-1*) Dorset Pr.

***Arthurian Legends: An Illustrated Anthology.** Richard Barber. (Illus.). 1994. pap. 18.00 (*0-85115-252-X*, Boydell Pr) Boydell & Brewer.

Arthurian Legends: An Illustrated Anthology, No. 600. Ed. by Richard Barber. (Illus.). 224p. 1979. 53.50 (*0-8226-0600-3*) Littlefield.

Arthurian Literature, No. XII. Ed. by James P. Carley & Felicity Riddy. (Illus.). 224p. (C). 1993. text ed. 63.00 (*0-85991-397-X*, Boydell Pr) Boydell & Brewer.

Arthurian Literature, Vol. II. Neil Wright et al. Ed. by Richard Barber. (Illus.). 176p. 1982. 65.00 (*0-85991-095-4*) Boydell & Brewer.

Arthurian Literature, Vol. III. Claude Lutrell et al. Ed. by Richard Barber. 224p. 1983. 63.00 (*0-85991-149-7*) Boydell & Brewer.

Arthurian Literature, Vol. IV. David Dumville et al. 256p. 1985. 65.00 (*0-85991-163-2*) Boydell & Brewer.

Arthurian Literature, Vol. V. Martin Puhvel et al. Ed. by Richard Barber. 192p. 1985. 63.00 (*0-85991-191-8*) Boydell & Brewer.

Arthurian Literature, Vol. VII. Ed. by Richard Barber. (Illus.). 1987. 63.00 (*0-85991-242-6*) Boydell & Brewer.

Arthurian Literature, Vol. VIII. Ed. by Richard Barber. 224p. 1989. 63.00 (*0-85991-283-3*) Boydell & Brewer.

Arthurian Literature, Vol. IX. Ed. by Richard Barber. (Arthurian Literature Ser.). 160p. (C). 1989. 63.00 (*0-85991-291-4*) Boydell & Brewer.

Arthurian Literature, Vol. X. Ed. by Richard Barber. 168p. 1991. 63.00 (*0-85991-308-2*) Boydell & Brewer.

Arthurian Literature XI. Ed. by Richard Barber. 160p. (C). 1992. text ed. 63.00 (*0-85991-350-3*) Boydell & Brewer.

***Arthurian Literature XIII.** Ed. by James P. Carley & Felicity Riddy. (Arthurian Literature Ser.). 224p. (C). 1995. text ed. 63.00 (*0-85991-449-6*, DS Brewer) Boydell & Brewer.

Arthurian Material in the Chronicles of Great Britain & France. Robert Fletcher. LC 68-2114. (Arthurian Legend & Literature Ser.: No. 1). 1969. reprint ed. lib. bdg. 75.00 (*0-8383-0551-2*) M S G Haskell Hse.

Arthurian Myth of Quest & Magic: A Festchrift in Honor of Lavon B. Fulwiler. William E. Tanner et al. (Illus.). 200p. (Orig.). 1993. pap. text ed. 14.75 (*0-9635769-0-9*) Caxtons Mod Art.

Arthurian Poets: Algernon Charles Swinburne. Intro. by James Carley. 256p. (Orig.). 1990. pap. 19.00 (*0-85115-546-4*) Boydell & Brewer.

Arthurian Poets: Charles Williams. Intro. by David L. Dodds. (Arthurian Poets Ser.: No. XXIII). 352p. (Orig.). (C). 1991. text ed. 79.00 (*0-85991-327-9*); pap. text ed. 29.00 (*0-85115-291-0*) Boydell & Brewer.

Arthurian Poets: Edwin Arlington Robinson. Intro. by James P. Carley. 384p. (Orig.). 1990. pap. text ed. 21.00 (*0-85115-545-6*) Boydell & Brewer.

Arthurian Poets: John Masefield. David L. Dodds. (Arthurian Studies: Vol. 32). 256p. (C). 1994. text ed. 63.00 (*0-85991-408-9*); pap. text ed. 23.00 (*0-85115-363-1*) Boydell & Brewer.

Arthurian Poets: Matthew Arnold & William Morris. Intro. by James P. Carley. 96p. 1994. pap. 13.00 (*0-85115-544-8*) Boydell & Brewer.

Arthurian Revival: Essays on Form, Tradition, & Transformation. Ed. by Debra N. Mancoff. LC 92-8108. (Illus.). 360p. 1992. 49.00 (*0-8153-0060-3*, H1419) Garland.

Arthurian Romance & Modern Poetry & Music. William A. Nitze. LC 76-122995. (Arthurian Legend & Literature Ser.: No. 1). (C). 1970. reprint ed. lib. bdg. 37.95 (*0-8383-1128-8*) M S G Haskell Hse.

Arthurian Romances. Chretien De Troyes. Ed. & Tr. by D. D. Owen. 550p. 1993. pap. 7.95 (*0-460-87389-X*) C E Tuttle.

Arthurian Romances. Chretien De Troyes. Tr. by William W. Kibler & Carleton W. Carroll. 528p. 1991. pap. 9.95 (*0-14-044521-8*) Viking Penguin.

Arthurian Romances of Chretien de Troyes: Once & Future Fictions. Donald Maddox. (Cambridge Studies in Medieval Literature: No. 12). 220p. (C). 1991. 54.95 (*0-521-39450-3*) Cambridge U Pr.

Arthurian Romances Unrepresented in Malory's "Morte D'Arthur", 8 Vols, Set. Tr. by Jessie L. Weston. reprint ed. 180.00 (*0-404-00470-9*) AMS Pr.

Arthurian Saga, 4 vols. Mary Stewart. 1985. Boxed set. boxed 23.80 (*0-449-20941-5*) Fawcett.

Arthurian Tarot Course: A Quest for All Seasons. Caitlin Matthews. 1993. pap. 17.00 (*1-85538-258-X*, Pub. by Aquarian Pr UK) Thorsons SF.

Arthurian Torso: Containing the Posthumous Fragment of the Figure of Arthur. Charles Williams. LC 83-45486. 1948. 27.00 (*0-404-20290-X*, PN685) AMS Pr.

Arthurian Tradition. J. Matthews. 1994. 19.95 (*1-85230-567-3*) Element MA.

***Arthurian Tradition.** John Matthews. 1995. pap. 14.95 (*1-85230-713-7*) Element MA.

Arthurian Tradition: Essays in Convergence. Mary F. Braswell & John M. Bugge. LC 86-24945. (Illus.). 232p. 1988. 27.50 (*0-8173-0347-2*) U of Ala Pr.

Arthurian Yearbook, Vol. II. Ed. by Keith Busby. (Illus.). 350p. 1992. 37.00 (*0-8153-0337-8*, 1458) Garland.

Arthurian Yearbook, Vol. 3. Ed. by Keith Busby. 286p. 1993. 43.00 (*0-8153-1539-2*, H18113) Garland.

Arthurian Yearbook One. Ed. by Keith Busby. LC 10-533877. (Illus.). 260p. 1991. 35.00 (*0-8240-7209-X*, 1247) Garland.

***Arthur's April Fool.** (J). (ps-3). 1995. audio 8.95 (*0-316-11181-3*) Little.

Arthur's April Fool. Marc T. Brown. LC 82-20368. (Illus.). 32p. (J). (ps-3). 1983. 15.95 (*0-316-11196-1*, Joy St Bks) Little.

Arthur's April Fool. Marc T. Brown. LC 82-20368. (Illus.). 32p. (J). (ps-3). 1985. mass mkt. 4.95 (*0-316-11234-8*, Joy St Bks) Little.

Arthur's Baby. (Illus.). (J). (ps-3). 1993. audio, mass mkt. 7.95 (*0-316-11336-0*) Little.

Arthur's Baby. Marc Brow. (J). (ps-3). 1990. 4.95 (*0-316-11007-8*, Joy St Bks) Little.

***Arthur's Baby.** Garrett Christopher. Ed. by J. Friedland & R. Kessler. (Novel-Ties Ser.). (J). (gr. k-1). 1995. student ed, pap. text ed. 14.95 (*1-56982-235-2*) Lrn Links.

Arthur's Baby, Vol. 1. Marc T. Brown. 32p. (J). 1987. 14.95 (*0-316-11123-6*, Joy St Bks) Little.

***Arthur's Big Buy.** Marc Brown. LC 94-48816. (J). 1995. 14.95 (*0-316-10919-3*) Little.

Arthur's Birthday. (Illus.). (J). (ps-3). 1993. audio, pap. 7.95 (*0-316-11337-9*) Little.

Arthur's Birthday. Marc T. Brown. (Illus.). 32p. (J). (ps-3). 1989. 15.95 (*0-316-11073-6*, Joy St Bks) Little.

Arthur's Birthday. Marc T. Brown. (J). (ps-3). 1991. mass mkt. 4.95 (*0-316-11074-4*) Little.

Arthur's Britain. Leslie Alcock. 1970. pap. 8.95 (*0-14-021396-1*, Penguin Bks) Viking Penguin.

Arthur's Britian The Land & the Legend. Derek Brewer & Ernest Frank. (C). 1987. text ed. 75.00 (*0-907115-26-8*, Pub. by Pevensey UK) St Mut.

Arthur's Camp-Out. Lillian Hoban. LC 91-27528. (I Can Read Bk.). (Illus.). 64p. (J). (gr. k-3). 1993. 14.00 (*0-06-020525-3*); lib. bdg. 13.89 (*0-06-020526-1*) HarpC Child Bks.

Arthur's Camp-Out. Lillian Hoban. LC 91-27528. (I Can Read Bk.). (Illus.). 64p. (J). (gr. k-3). 1994. pap. 3.75 (*0-06-444175-X*, Trophy) HarpC Child Bks.

Arthur's Chicken Pox. Marc Brown. LC 93-22996. (J). 1994. 15.95 (*0-316-11384-0*) Little.

Arthur's Christmas. Marc T. Brown. LC 84-4373. (Illus.). (J). (ps-3). 1984. 15.95 (*0-316-11180-5*, Joy St Bks) Little.

Arthur's Christmas. Marc T. Brown. LC 84-4373. (Illus.). (J). (ps-3). 1985. mass mkt. 4.95 (*0-316-10993-2*, Joy St Bks) Little.

Arthur's Christmas Cookies. Lillian Hoban. LC 72-76496. (Harper I Can Read Bk.). (Illus.). 64p. (J). (gr. k-3). 1972. lib. bdg. 14.89 (*0-06-022368-5*) HarpC Child Bks.

Arthur's Christmas Cookies. Lillian Hoban. LC 72-76596. (Trophy I Can Read Book). (Illus.). 64p. (J). (gr. k-3). 1984. pap. 3.50 (*0-06-444055-9*, Trophy) HarpC Child Bks.

Arthur's Christmas Cookies. unabridged ed. Lillian Hoban. (I Can Read Book Ser.). (Illus.). (J). (ps-3). 1990. audio, pap. 6.95 (*1-55994-217-7*, Caedmon) HarperAudio.

***Arthur's Companions: Sonnets from the Welsh.** deluxe limited ed. W. Nicholas Knight. (Illus.). 150p. 1994. 19.95 (*1-882935-11-X*) Rolla Fine Arts.

***Arthur's Dad.** Ginette Anfousee. (First Novels Ser.). (Illus.). 64p. (J). (gr. 1-4). 1995. pap. 4.95 (*0-88780-094-7*); bds. 14.95 (*0-88780-095-5*) Formac Dist Ltd.

Arthur's Eyes. (Illus.). (J). (ps-3). 1993. audio, mass mkt. 7.95 (*0-316-11338-7*) Little.

Arthur's Eyes. Marc T. Brown. LC 79-11734. (Illus.). (J). (ps-3). 1979. lib. bdg. 14.95 (*0-316-11063-9*, Joy St Bks) Little.

Arthur's Eyes. Marc T. Brown. (Reading Rainbow Featured Ser.). (Illus.). 32p. (J). (ps-3). 1986. mass mkt. 4.95 (*0-316-11069-8*, Joy St Bks) Little.

Arthur's Family Vacation. Marc T. Brown. LC 92-26650. (J). 1993. 15.95 (*0-316-11312-3*) Little.

***Arthur's Family Vacation: An Arthur Adventure.** Marc Brown. (Illus.). (J). (ps-3). 1995. pap. 4.95 (*0-316-10958-4*) Little.

Arthur's First Sleepover. Marc Brown. LC 93-46113. (J). 1994. 15.95 (*0-316-11445-6*) Little.

Arthur's Funny Money. Lillian Hoban. LC 80-7903. (Harper I Can Read Bk.). (Illus.). 64p. (J). (gr. k-3). 1981. lib. bdg. 14.89 (*0-06-022344-8*) HarpC Child Bks.

Arthur's Funny Money. Lillian Hoban. LC 80-7903. (Trophy I Can Read Book & Cassette Set). (Illus.). 64p. (J). (gr. k-3). 1984. pap. 3.50 (*0-06-444048-6*, Trophy) HarpC Child Bks.

Arthur's Funny Money. unabridged ed. Lillian Hoban. (I Can Read Book Ser.). (Illus.). (J). (ps-3). 1990. audio, pap. 6.95 (*1-55994-218-5*, Caedmon) HarperAudio.

Arthur's Great Big Valentine. Lillian Hoban. LC 88-21202. (Harper I Can Read Bk.). (Illus.). 64p. (J). (gr. k-3). 1989. lib. bdg. 14.89 (*0-06-022407-X*) HarpC Child Bks.

Arthur's Great Big Valentine. Lillian Hoban. LC 88-21202. (Trophy I Can Read Bk.). (Illus.). 64p. (J). (gr. k-3). 1991. pap. 3.50 (*0-06-444149-0*, Trophy) HarpC Child Bks.

Arthur's Halloween. Marc T. Brown. LC 82-14286. (Illus.). 32p. (J). (ps-3). 1982. 15.95 (*0-316-11116-3*, Joy St Bks) Little.

Arthur's Halloween. Marc T. Brown. LC 82-14286. (Illus.). 32p. (J). (ps-3). 1983. mass mkt. 4.95 (*0-316-11059-0*, Joy St Bks) Little.

Arthur's Halloween Costume. Lillian Hoban. LC 83-49465. (Harper I Can Read Bk.). (Illus.). 64p. (J). (gr. k-3). 1984. lib. bdg. 14.89 (*0-06-022391-X*) HarpC Child Bks.

Arthur's Halloween Costume. Lillian Hoban. LC 83-49465. (Trophy I Can Read Bk.). (Illus.). 64p. (J). (gr. k-3). 1986. pap. 3.50 (*0-06-444101-6*, Trophy) HarpC Child Bks.

Arthur's Honey Bear. Lillian Hoban. LC 73-14325. (Harper I Can Read Bk.). (Illus.). 64p. (J). (gr. k-3). 1974. 14.95 (*0-06-022369-3*); lib. bdg. 14.89 (*0-06-022370-7*) HarpC Child Bks.

Arthur's Honey Bear. Lillian Hoban. LC 73-14324. (Trophy I Can Read Book & Cassette Set). (Illus.). 64p. (J). (gr. k-3). 1982. pap. 3.50 (*0-06-444033-8*, Trophy) HarpC Child Bks.

Arthur's Honey Bear. unabridged ed. Lillian Hoban. (I Can Read Book Ser.). (Illus.). (J). (ps-3). 1990. audio, pap. 6.95 (*1-55994-219-3*, Caedmon) HarperAudio.

Arthur's Loose Tooth. Lillian Hoban. LC 85-42611. (I Can Read Bk.). (Illus.). 64p. (J). (ps-3). 1985. lib. bdg. 14.89 (*0-06-022354-5*) HarpC Child Bks.

Arthur's Loose Tooth. Lillian Hoban. LC 85-42611. (Trophy I Can Read Bk.). (Illus.). 64p. (J). (gr. k-3). 1987. pap. 3.50 (*0-06-444093-1*, Trophy) HarpC Child Bks.

Arthur's New Power. Russell Hoban. LC 77-11550. (Illus.). (J). (gr. 1-5). 1978. lib. bdg. 12.89 (*0-690-01371-X*, Crowell Jr Bks) HarpC Child Bks.

Arthur's Nose. Marc T. Brown. (Illus.). 32p. (J). (ps-3). 1976. lib. bdg. 14.95 (*0-316-11193-7*, Joy St Bks) Little.

Arthur's Nose. Marc T. Brown. (Illus.). 32p. (J). (ps-3). 1986. mass mkt. 4.95 (*0-316-11070-1*, Joy St Bks) Little.

Arthur's Pen Pal. Lillian Hoban. (I Can Read Bk. & Cassette). 32p. (J). (ps-2). 1990. pap. 6.95 (*0-00-004236-6*, Caedmon) HarperAudio.

Arthur's Pen Pal. Lillian Hoban. LC 75-6289. (Harper I Can Read Bk.). (Illus.). 64p. (J). (gr. k-3). 1976. lib. bdg. 14.89 (*0-06-022372-3*) HarpC Child Bks.

Arthur's Pen Pal. Lillian Hoban. LC 75-6289. (Trophy I Can Read Bk.). (Illus.). 64p. (J). (gr. k-3). 1982. pap. 3.50 (*0-06-444032-X*, Trophy) HarpC Child Bks.

Arthur's Pen Pal. unabridged ed. Lillian Hoban. (I Can Read Book Ser.). (Illus.). (J). (ps-3). 1990. audio, pap. 6.95 (*1-55994-238-X*, Caedmon) HarperAudio.

***Arthur's Pet Business.** (J). (ps-3). 1995. 8.95 (*0-316-11182-1*) Little.

Arthur's Pet Business. Marc T. Brown. (J). (ps-3). 1990. 14.95 (*0-316-11262-3*, Joy St Bks) Little.

Arthur's Pet Business. Marc T. Brown. (J). (ps-3). 1993. mass mkt. 4.95 (*0-316-11316-6*) Little.

Arthur's Prize Reader. Lillian Hoban. LC 77-25637. (Harper I Can Read Bk.). (Illus.). 64p. (J). (ps-3). 1978. lib. bdg. 14.89 (*0-06-022380-4*) HarpC Child Bks.

An Asterisk (*) at the beginning of an entry indicates that the title is appearing in BIP for the first time.

Arthur's Prize Reader. Lillian Hoban. LC 77-25637. (Trophy I Can Read Book & Cassette Set). (Illus.). 64p. (J). (ps-3). 1984. pap. 3.50 (*0-06-444049-4*, Trophy) HarpC Child Bks.

Arthur's Prize Reader. unabridged ed. Lillian Hoban. (I Can Read Book Ser.). (Illus.). (J). (ps-3). 1990. audio, pap. 6.95 (*1-55994-220-7*, Caedmon) HarperAudio.

***Arthur's Problem Puppy.** Ginette Anfousee. (First Novels Ser.). (Illus.). 64p. (J). (gr. 1-4). 1995. pap. 4.95 (*0-88780-276-1*); bds. 14.95 (*0-88780-277-X*) Formac Dist Ltd.

Arthur's Puppy. Marc T. Brown. LC 92-46342. (J). (gr. 1-8). 1993. 15.95 (*0-316-11355-7*, Joy St Bks) Little.

***Arthur's Teacher Trouble.** Marc Brown. 1994. pap. 29.50 (*1-57135-017-9*) Living Bks.

Arthur's Teacher Trouble. Marc T. Brown. (Illus.). 32p. (J). (ps-3). 1987. 15.95 (*0-316-11244-5*, Joy St Bks) Little.

Arthur's Teacher Trouble. Marc T. Brown. (Illus.). 32p. (J). (ps-3). 1989. mass mkt. 4.95 (*0-316-11186-4*, Joy St Bks) Little.

Arthur's Thanksgiving. Marc T. Brown. LC 83-798. (Illus.). 32p. (J). (gr. 1-3). 1983. 15.95 (*0-316-11060-4*, Joy St Bks) Little.

Arthur's Thanksgiving. Marc T. Brown. LC 83-798. (Illus.). 32p. (J). (gr. 1-3). 1984. mass mkt. 4.95 (*0-316-11232-1*, Joy St Bks) Little.

Arthur's Tooth. (Illus.). (J). (ps-3). 1993. audio, mass mkt. 7.95 (*0-316-11339-5*) Little.

Arthur's Tooth. Marc T. Brown. (Illus.). 32p. (J). (ps-3). 1985. 15.95 (*0-316-11245-3*, Joy St Bks) Little.

Arthur's Tooth, Vol. 1. Marc T. Brown. (J). (ps-3). 1986. mass mkt. 4.95 (*0-316-11246-1*) Little.

Arthur's Valentine. Marc T. Brown. (Illus.). (Orig.). (J). (ps-3). 1980. 15.95 (*0-316-11062-0*, Joy St Bks) Little.

Arthur's Valentine. Marc T. Brown. (Illus.). 32p. (Orig.). (J). (ps-3). 1988. mass mkt. 4.95 (*0-316-11187-2*, Joy St Bks) Little.

Artic Blends to Go: A Language-Based Articulation Program, 5 bks., Set. Janet R. Lanza et al. 1992. 29.95 (*1-55999-236-0*) LinguiSystems.

***Artic Plus.** Jean G. DeGaetano. 100p. 1987. pap. text ed. 29.95 (*1-886143-00-5*) Grt Ideas Tching.

Artic to Go: A Two-in-One Therapy Program: Language Based Articulation Exercises, 5 booklets. Janet R. Lanza et al. 1988. 29.95 (*1-55999-016-3*) LinguiSystems.

Artichoke. Joanna M. Glass. 1979. pap. 4.75 (*0-8222-0067-8*) Dramatists Play.

Artichoke & Other Poems. Phyllis Thompson. LC 75-76763. 76p. 1969. 6.00 (*0-87022-791-2*) UH Pr.

***Artichoke Blank Book.** 80p. 1995. 7.00 (*1-882835-28-X*) STA-Kris.

Artichoke Cookbook. Patricia Rain. LC 85-5771. (Illus.). 180p. (Orig.). 1985. pap. 11.95 (*0-89087-415-8*) Celestial Arts.

Article & Noun in English: An Essay in Psychomechanical Analysis. John Hewson. LC 70-173385. (Janua Linguarum, Ser. Practica: No. 104). 137p. (Orig.). 1972. pap. text ed. 30.80 (*90-279-2149-6*) Mouton.

Article & the Concept of Definiteness in Language. Jiri Kramsky. (Janua Linguarum, Ser. Minor: No. 125). 1972. 36.95 (*90-279-2119-9*) Mouton.

Article Five Convention Process: A Symposium. P. G. Kauper et al. LC 70-150510. (Symposia on Law & Society Ser.). 1971. reprint ed. lib. bdg. 25.00 (*0-306-70185-5*) Da Capo.

Article Writing: A Creative Challenge. Ann Saling. 208p. 1982. pap. 5.95 (*0-910455-00-7*) ANSAL Pr.

Article Writing: How to Plan an Article, Learn from Models, & Polisy Your Final Words. David C. Cook Foundation Staff. (Interlit Imprint Ser.: Unit 3). 40p. 1993. pap. text ed. 5.95 (*1-884752-02-0*) D C Cook Fnd.

Article Writing Guidelines. John Nemec. 14p. 1987. 1.75 (*0-9618998-2-4*) Nemec Pub.

Article 177 EEC: Experiences & Problems: Proceedings of the TMC Colloquium, The Hague, September 5-6, 1985. Ed. by Henry G. Schermers et al. 490p. 1987. 102.75 (*0-444-70086-2*, North Holland) Elsevier.

***Article 2(7) Revisited: Principles & Realities.** Abiodun Williams et al. (Reports & Papers 1994 Ser.: Vol. 5). 81p. (C). 1994. pap. text ed. write for info. (*1-880660-09-1*) Acad Coun UN Syst.

Articles Agreed on in the National Synode of the Reformed Churches of France. LC 76-57381. (English Experience Ser.: No. 799). 1977. reprint ed. lib. bdg. 17.50 (*90-221-0799-X*) Walter J Johnson.

Articles de Paris. Sisley Huddleston. LC 75-90646. (Essay Index Reprint Ser.). 1977. 20.95 (*0-8369-1265-9*) Ayer.

Articles, Etc. Through Pictures. Harris Winitz. (Language Through Pictures Ser.). (Illus.). 70p. (gr. 2-12). 1982. pap. 4.75 (*0-939990-34-2*) Intl Linguistics.

Articles Exhibited in Parliament Against William, Archbishop of Canterbury. William Laud. LC 72-212. (English Experience Ser.: No. 333). 16p. 1971. reprint ed. 20.00 (*90-221-0333-1*) Walter J Johnson.

Articles from the New England Journal of Medicine on Drug Therapy, Vol. 8. Ed. by Edwin W. Salzman. (NEJM Reprint Collection). (Illus.). 300p. 1991. reprint ed. text ed. 49.00 (*0-910133-33-6*); reprint ed. pap. text ed. 34.00 (*0-910133-23-9*) MA Med Soc.

Articles in English: A Structural Analysis of Usage. Sayo Yotsukura. LC 72-108144. (Janua Linguarum, Ser. Practica: No. 49). (Orig.). 1970. pap. text ed. 42.35 (*90-279-0724-2*) Mouton.

Articles of Agreement of the International Bank for Reconstruction & Development. 38p. (ENG, FRE & SPA.). write for info. (*0-8213-1469-6*, 11469); write for info. (*0-8213-1470-X*, 11470); write for info. (*0-318-70275-4*, 11471) World Bank.

Articles of Agreement of the International Development Association. 42p. English. write for info. (*0-8213-1472-6*, 11472); French. write for info. (*0-8213-1473-4*, 11473); Spanish. write for info. (*0-8213-1474-2*, 11474) World Bank.

Articles of Agreement of the International Finance Corporation. 26p. English. write for info. (*0-8213-1475-0*, 11475); French. write for info. (*0-8213-1476-9*, 11476); Spanish. write for info. (*0-8213-1477-7*, 11477) World Bank.

Articles of Belief & Acts of Religion. Benjamin Franklin. (Notable American Authors Ser.). 1992. reprint ed. lib. bdg. 75.00 (*0-7812-2885-9*) Rprt Serv.

***Articles of Business.** Vivian C. Kistler. 166p. 1994. pap. text ed. 20.00 (*0-938655-28-0*) Columba Pub.

Articles of Confederation: An Interpretation of the Social Constitutional History of the American Revolution, 1774-1781. Merrill Jensen. 310p. (C). 1959. pap. 15.50 (*0-299-00204-7*) U of Wis Pr.

Articles of Faith. James E. Talmage. LC 80-22041. (Classics in Mormon Literature Ser.). 482p. 1981. 14.95 (*0-87747-838-4*) Deseret Bk.

Articles of Faith. James E. Talmage. LC 80-22041. x, 482p. 1984. pap. 5.95 (*0-87579-325-8*) Deseret Bk.

***Articles of Faith Activity & Idea Book.** Karen Finch. (Illus.). 64p. (Orig.). (J). (ps-7). 1994. 7.95 (*1-885476-07-8*) Finch Fmly Games.

***Articles of Faith Activity & Idea Book, Vol. 2.** Karen Finch. (Illus.). 64p. (Orig.). (J). (ps-7). 1994. 7.95 (*1-885476-08-6*) Finch Fmly Games.

Articles of Faith, Articles of Peace: The Religious Liberty Clauses & the American Public Philosophy. Ed. by James D. Hunter & Os Guinness. 168p. 1990. 22.95 (*0-8157-3828-5*) Brookings.

Articles of Faith Learning Book. Ann Laemmlen & Jackie Owen. 171p. (J). (gr. 3-6). 1990. student ed, pap. 7.95 (*0-87579-400-9*) Deseret Bk.

Articles of Islamic Acts: Tawzih-ul-masail. rev. ed. Ayattullah A. Al-Khoei. Ed. by Amir A. Aini. Tr. by Muhammad F. Haq. 664p. (C). 1991. reprint ed. 18.00 (*0-941724-21-2*) Islamic Seminary.

Articles of Military Discipline. LC 71-76430. (English Experience Ser.: No. 77). 16p. 1969. reprint ed. 30.00 (*90-221-0077-4*) Walter J Johnson.

Articles of Peace: In a Treatie. LC 71-171753. (English Experience Ser.: No. 378). 1971. reprint ed. 20.00 (*90-221-0378-1*) Walter J Johnson.

Articles of War: A Collection of Poetry about World War Two. Ed. by Leon Stokesbury. 259p. 1990. 24.95 (*1-55728-148-3*); pap. 12.95 (*1-55728-149-1*) U of Ark Pr.

Articles of War: The Statutes Which Governed Our Fighting Navies 1661-1749 & 1866. N. A. Rodger. 62p. 1987. 40.00 (*0-85937-275-8*, Pub. by K Mason Pubns Ltd UK) St Mut.

Articles on Britain. Karl Marx & Friedrich Engels. 466p. 1971. 25.00 (*0-8464-0153-3*) Beekman Pubs.

Articles on Mathematical Statistics & the Theory of Probability. Ed. by Jurii V. Linnik. LC 66-26640. (Proceedings of the Steklov Institute of Mathematics Ser.: No. 79). 259p. 1966. 75.00 (*0-8218-1879-1*, STEKLO-79) Am Math.

Articles on the Middle East, 1947-1971: A Cumulation of Bibliographies from the Middle East Journal, 4 vols., Set. Ed. by Peter M. Rossi & Wayne E. White. LC 79-91337. (Cumulated Bibliography Ser.: No. 7). 1980. 180.00 (*0-87650-030-0*) Pierian.

Articles on Twentieth Century Literature: An Annotated Bibliography, 1954-1970, 7 vols., Set. Comp. by David E. Pownall. LC 73-6588. lib. bdg. 630.00 (*0-527-72150-6*) Kraus Intl.

Articles on Women Writers, 1976-1984: A Bibliography, Vol. 2. Narda L. Schwartz. LC 85-7484. 304p. 1986. lib. bdg. 26.00 (*0-87436-438-8*) ABC-CLIO.

Articles to Be Inquired of, in the First Metropolitical Visitation of the Most Reverend Father Richarde... Archbishop of Canterbury. Church of England Staff. LC 74-28851. (English Experience Ser.: No. 732). 1975. reprint ed. 3.50 (*90-221-0732-9*) Walter J Johnson.

Articling Handbook. Rosen et al. 192p. 1988. pap. 42.00 (*0-409-80480-0*) Butterworth Legal Pubs.

Articu-ACTION. Denise Grigas. (Illus.). 144p. 1993. teacher ed 14.95 (*0-937857-37-8*, 1524) Speech Bin.

Articular Cartilage & Knee Joint Function: Basic Science & Arthroscopy. J. Whit Ewing. (Bristol-Myers - Squibb-Zimmer Orthopaedic Research Symposia Ser.). 392p. 1990. 114.00 (*0-88167-542-3*) Raven.

Articular Cartilage & Osteoarthritis. Klaus E. Kuettner et al. 800p. 1992. 100.00 (*0-88167-862-7*) Raven.

Articular Cartilage Biochemistry. Ed. by Klaus E. Kuettner et al. (Illus.). 478p. 1986. text ed. 88.00 (*0-88167-204-1*) Raven.

Articular Synovium. Ed. by P. Franchimont. (Illus.). viii, 184p. 1982. pap. 91.25 (*3-8055-3461-2*) S Karger.

Articulate Body. Anne Dennis. 224p. 1994. pap. 19.95 (*0-89676-133-9*) Drama Bk.

Articulate Body. Pavel Machotka & John P. Spiegel. (Illus.). 250p. 1982. 29.50 (*0-8290-0229-4*) Irvington.

Articulate Body. Pavel Machotka & John P. Spiegel. (Illus.). 250p. (C). 1985. reprint ed. pap. text ed. 12.95 (*0-8290-1662-7*) Irvington.

Articulate Energy: An Inquiry into the Syntax of English Poetry. Donald Davie. 1988. reprint ed. lib. bdg. 59.00 (*0-7812-0488-7*) Rprt Serv.

Articulate Energy: An Inquiry into the Syntax of English Poetry. Donald Davie. LC 77-158901. 1971. reprint ed. 45.00 (*0-403-01316-X*) Scholarly.

Articulate Executive. Harvard Business School Press Staff. 1991. pap. text ed. 19.95 (*0-07-103328-9*) McGraw.

Articulate Executive: Orchestrating Effective Communication. Pref. by Fernando Bartolome. LC 93-23956. (Harvard Business Review Book Ser.). 1993. 29.95 (*0-87584-433-2*) Harvard Busn.

Articulate Executive: Orchestrating Effective Communication. Fernando Bartolome. 1993. text ed. 29.95 (*0-07-103425-0*) McGraw.

Articulate Flesh: Male Homo-Eroticism & Modern Poetry. Gregory Woods. LC 87-10646. 320p. 1988. 35.00 (*0-300-03872-0*) Yale U Pr.

Articulate Flesh: Male Homo-Eroticism & Modern Poetry. Gregory Woods. 278p. (C). 1990. reprint ed. pap. 17.00 (*0-300-04752-5*) Yale U Pr.

Articulate Images: The Sister Arts from Hogarth to Tennyson. Ed. by Richard Wendorf. LC 83-5798. (Illus.). 296p. reprint ed. pap. 84.40 (*0-8357-5772-2*, 2033246) Bks Demand.

Articulate Mammal. 3rd ed. Jean Aitchison. 292p. 1989. pap. text ed. 16.95 (*0-04-445355-8*) Routledge Chapman & Hall.

Articulate Person: A Guide to Everyday Public Speaking. Bruce E. Gronbeck. LC 82-20477. 304p. reprint ed. pap. 86.70 (*0-7837-3009-8*, 2042931) Bks Demand.

Articulate Professional. V. J. Singal et al. LC 93-86505. 200p. (Orig.). 1993. spiral bd., pap. 24.50 (*0-9639001-0-2*) Sequoia Career.

Articulate Silences. Shiv K. Kumar. (Writers Workshop Redbird Ser). 34p. 1975. 6.75 (*0-88253-500-5*); pap. text ed. 4.00 (*0-88253-499-8*) Ind-US Inc.

Articulate Silences: Hisaye Yamamoto, Maxine Hong Kingston, Joy Kogawa. King-Kok Cheung. LC 92-46452. (Reading Women Writing Ser.). (Illus.). 216p. 1993. 35.00 (*0-8014-2415-1*); pap. 14.95 (*0-8014-8147-3*) Cornell U Pr.

***Articulate Voice: An Introduction to Voice & Diction.** 2nd ed. Lynn K. Wells. 225p. 1993. pap. text ed. 33.00 (*0-89787-347-5*) Gorsuch Scarisbrick.

Articulated Agricultural Development: Traditional & Capitalist Agricultures in Papua, New Guinea. Mike Donaldson & Kenneth Good. 170p. 1988. text ed. 54.95 (*0-566-05469-8*, Pub. by Avebury Pub UK) Ashgate Pub Co.

Articulated Steam Locomotives of North America: A Catalogue of "Giant Steam" Robert A. LeMassena. (Illus.). 416p. 1979. 55.00 (*0-913582-26-3*) Sundance.

***Articulating Change in the "Last Unknown"** Frederick K. Errington. (C). 1995. pap. text ed. 19.95 (*0-8133-2454-8*) Westview.

***Articulating Change in the "Last Unknown"** Frederick K. Errington & Deborah B. Gewertz. LC 94-45532. 1995. text ed. 59.95 (*0-8133-2453-X*) Westview.

***Articulating Hidden Histories: Exploring the Influence of Eric R. Wolf.** Ed. by Jane Schneider & Rayna Rapp. LC 94-22055. 1995. 45.00 (*0-520-08581-7*); pap. 18.00 (*0-520-08582-5*) U CA Pr.

Articulating the Elephant Man: Joseph Merrick & His Interpreters. Peter W. Graham & Fritz H. Oehlschlaeger. (Parallax). 208p. 1992. 32.00 (*0-8018-4357-X*) Johns Hopkins.

Articulation: A Physiological Approach. Samuel G. Fletcher. (Illus.). (Orig.). (C). 1992. pap. text ed. 45.00 (*1-879105-89-6*) Singular Publishing.

Articulation: Poems. Timothy Kelly. LC 93-26569. 1993. 18.50 (*0-89924-085-2*); pap. 9.50 (*0-89924-084-4*) Lynx Hse.

Articulation & Phonological Disorders. 3rd ed. John E. Bernthal & Nicholas W. Bankson. LC 92-22821. 432p. (C). 1992. text ed. write for info. (*0-13-052408-5*) P-H.

Articulation & Voice: Effective Communication, No. 20. Joseph A. DeVito et al. LC 74-14615. 127p. (C). 1975. pap. write for info. (*0-672-61350-6*, SC20, Bobbs) Macmillan.

Articulation Between For-Profit Private Occupational Schools & Secondary Vocational Programs: Colleges & Universities. Max Lerner. 39p. 1987. 5.25 (*0-318-23410-6*, IN315) Ctr Educ Trng Employ.

***Articulation Curriculum I.** Jean G. DeGaetano. 120p. 1987. pap. text ed. 29.95 (*1-886143-01-3*) Grt Ideas Tching.

***Articulation Curriculum II.** Jean G. DeGaetano. 100p. 1987. pap. text ed. 29.95 (*1-886143-02-1*) Grt Ideas Tching.

***Articulation Curriculum Super Pack.** Jean G. DeGaetano. 139p. 1993. pap. text ed. 29.95 (*1-886143-03-X*) Grt Ideas Tching.

Articulation in English Between the High School & College. William E. Vaughan. LC 73-177673. (Columbia University. Teachers College. Contributions to Education Ser.: No. 370). reprint ed. 37.50 (*0-404-55370-2*) AMS Pr.

Articulation of Sound Forms in Time. Susan Howe. (Illus.). 56p. (Orig.). 1987. pap. 8.00 (*0-942433-11-4*) Awede Pr.

***Articulation Screening Assessment.** rev. ed. Jean G. DeGaetano. 15p. 1989. pap. text ed. 16.95 (*1-886143-04-8*) Grt Ideas Tching.

Articulations: The Body & Illness in Poetry. Ed. by Jon Mukand. LC 94-16528. 452p. (Orig.). 1994. pap. 19.95 (*0-87745-478-7*) U of Iowa Pr.

Articulator Features & Portuguese Vowel Height. Wayne J. Redenbarger. (Studies in Romance Languages: No. 37). (Illus.). 197p. (C). 1981. pap. 9.00 (*0-674-04815-6*) HUP.

Articulatory Organization: From Phonology to Speech Signals. Ed. by O. Fujimura. (Journal: Phonetica: Vol. 45, No. 2-4, 1988). (Illus.). iv, 122p. 1989. reprint ed. 46.50 (*3-8055-5150-9*) S Karger.

Articulatory Organization from Phonology to Speech Signals: Journal: Phonetica, Vol. 45, No. 2-4, 1988. Ed. by O. Fujimura. 128p. 1989. pap. 46.50 (*3-8055-5015-4*) S Karger.

Articulatory Phonology. R. L. Diehl. (Journal Phonetica: Vol. 49, No. 3-4, 1992). (Illus.). 108p. 1992. pap. 43.25 (*3-8055-5724-8*) S Karger.

Articulos de Costumbres. Mariano J. De Larra. Ed. by Luis F. Diaz Larios. (Nueva Austral Ser.: Vol. 99). (SPA.). 1991. pap. text ed. 24.95 (*84-239-1899-8*) Elliots Bks.

Articulos Olvidados Sobre Espana Y la Primera Guerra Mundial. Miguel De Unamuno. Ed. by Christopher Cobb. (Serie B: Textos, XXII). (Illus.). 217p. (Orig.). (SPA.). (C). 1976. pap. 45.00 (*0-7293-0022-6*, Pub. by Tamesis Bks Ltd UK) Boydell & Brewer.

Articulos Politicos en la Revista de Espana, 1871-1872. Benito P. Galdos. Ed. by Brian J. Dendle & Joseph Schraibman. xii, 159p. (Orig.). 1982. 9.75 (*0-9608168-0-1*) Dendle & Schraibman.

ArticuMAZEment: A Pathfinding Game for Articulation & Language Practice, 4 bklts., Set. Lori Hickman. (J). (gr. 5-10). 1990. bds. 34.95 (*1-55999-101-1*) LinguiSystems.

ArticuMAZING Stories & Activities. Susan R. Simms. 1992. student ed, spiral bd. 29.95 (*1-55999-217-4*) LinguiSystems.

Artie. Wil Denson. (Illus.). 32p. (Orig.). (YA). (gr. 7-12). 1988. pap. 4.00 (*0-88680-292-X*) I E Clark.

Artie, & Pink Marsh: Eighteen Ninety-Six to Eighteen Ninety-Seven. George Ade. LC 63-22584. (Chicago in Fiction Ser). (Illus.). 236p. reprint ed. pap. 67.30 (*0-8357-9641-8*, 2015748) Bks Demand.

Artie's Big Surprise. Anna Mattingly. 1994. 8.95 (*0-8062-5034-8*) Carlton.

Artie's Brief: The Whole Truth & Nothing But. Christi Killien. 112p. (J). 1990. pap. 2.95 (*0-380-71108-7*, Camelot) Avon.

Artifact. W. Michael Gear. 1990. mass mkt. 5.99 (*0-88677-406-3*) DAW Bks.

Artifact: Notebooks from Hell 1974-1980. Richard Hell. (Illus.). 172p. (Orig.). 1990. pap. 5.95 (*0-937815-39-X*) Hanuman Bks.

***Artifact & Assemblage: The Finds from a Regional Survey of the Southern Argolid, Greece Vol. 1: The Prehistoric & Early Iron Age Pottery & the Lithic Artifacts.** Ed. by Curtis Runnels et al. LC 94-25691. 1995. 65.00 (*0-8047-2065-7*) Stanford U Pr.

Artifact Collective - Texts, No. 1. Mike MisKowski & Jack Foley. Ed. by Jake Berry. 20p. (Orig.). (YA). (gr. 7 up). 1988. pap. 3.00 (*0-944215-02-5*) Abscond Pubs.

Artifact, Unit One: Field Notebook. Nan McNutt. (Project Archeology Series: Saving Traditions). (J). (gr. 5-8). 1987. student ed 1.25 (*0-944584-01-2*) Sopris.

Artifacts: Poems by B. J. Buckley. B. J. Buckley. (Illus.). 80p. (Orig.). 1987. pap. 8.95 (*0-939635-02-X*) Willow Bee Pub.

Artifacts see **Excavations at Seibal: Department of Peten, Guatemala**

Artifacts & the American Past. Thomas J. Schlereth. LC 80-19705. (Illus.). 1981. pap. 18.95 (*0-942063-00-7*) AASLH.

Artifacts, Art Works & Agency. Randall R. Dipert. (Arts & Their Philosophies Ser.). 288p. (C). 1993. 44.95 (*0-87722-990-2*) Temple U Pr.

Artifacts in Biological Electron Microscopy. Ed. by R. F. Crang & K. L. Klomparens. LC 88-15217. (Illus.). 254p. 1988. 69.50 (*0-306-42863-6*, Plenum Pr) Plenum.

Artifacts of Dzibilchaltun, Yucatan, Mexico: Shell, Polished Stone, Bone, Wood, & Ceramics. Jennifer T. Taschek. 1994. write for info. (*0-939238-80-2*) Tulane MARI.

Artifacts of R. Buckminster Fuller - A Comprehensive Collection of His Designs & Drawings: Dymaxion Deployment, 1929-1946, Vol. 2. R. Buckminster Fuller. Ed. by William Marlin. 450p. 1985. lib. bdg. 120.00 (*0-8240-5083-5*) Garland.

Artifacts of R. Buckminster Fuller - A Comprehensive Collection of His Designs & Drawings: The Dymaxion Experiment, 1926-1943, Vol. 1. R. Buckminster Fuller. Ed. by William Marlin. 450p. 1985. lib. bdg. 120.00 (*0-8240-5082-7*) Garland.

Artifacts of R. Buckminster Fuller-A Comprehensive Collection of His Designs & Drawings: Designs, 1947-1960, Vol. 3. R. Buckminster Fuller. Ed. by William Marlin. 450p. 1985. lib. bdg. 120.00 (*0-8240-5084-3*) Garland.

Artifacts of R. Buckminster Fuller-A Comprehensive Collection of His Designs & Drawings: Designs, 1960-1983, Vol. 4. R. Buckminster Fuller. Ed. by William Marlin. 450p. 1985. lib. bdg. 120.00 (*0-8240-5085-1*) Garland.

Artifacts of the Northwest Coast Indians. Hilary Stewart. (Illus.). 172p. pap. 12.95 (*0-88839-098-X*) Hancock House.

Artifacts of the Spanish Colonies of Florida & the Caribbean, 1500-1800: Ceramics, Glassware, & Beads, Vol. 1. Kathleen Deagan. LC 86-24772. (Illus.). 208p. 1987. 39.95 (*0-87474-392-3*); pap. 19.95 (*0-87474-393-1*) Smithsonian.

Artifacts of Uaxactun, Guatemala. Alfred V. Kidder. LC 77-11502. (Carnegie Institution of Washington. Publications: No. 576). reprint ed. 17.50 (*0-404-16265-7*) AMS Pr.

Artifacts, Representations, & Social Practice: Essays for Marx Wartofsky. Ed. by Carol C. Gould & Robert S. Cohen. LC 93-38216. (Boston Studies in the Philosophy of Science). 568p. (C). 1994. lib. bdg. 186.00 (*0-7923-2481-1*) Kluwer Ac.

Artifacture. James Taylor. (Illus.). 64p. (Orig.). (C). 1989. pap. 7.00 (*0-940475-88-X*) Dolphin-Moon.

Artifex: Sketches & Ideas. Richard Aldington. (Essay Index Reprint Ser.). 1977. 23.95 (*0-8369-1438-4*) Ayer.

An Asterisk (*) at the beginning of an entry indicates that the title is appearing in BIP for the first time.

An Asterisk (*) at the beginning of an entry indicates that the title is appearing in BIP for the first time.

461

***Artificial Intelligence Applications to Traffic Engineering.** Ed. by M. Bielli et al. 332p. 1994. 125.00 (*90-6764-171-5*, Pub. by VSP NE) Coronet Bks.

Artificial Intelligence Applications, 8th Conference (CAIA '92) LC 86-649003. 450p. 1992. 70.00 (*0-8186-2690-9*, 2690) IEEE Comp Soc.

Artificial Intelligence Approach to Integrated Circuit Floorplanning. M. A. Jabri. (Lecture Notes in Engineering Ser.: Vol. 66). (Illus.). 162p. 1991. pap. 34.00 (*0-387-53958-1*) Spr-Verlag.

Artificial Intelligence Approach to Test Generation. Narinder Singh. 1987. lib. bdg. 57.00 (*0-89838-185-1*) Kluwer Ac.

Artificial Intelligence Approach to Visit Design. Thaddeus Kowalski. (C). 1985. reprint ed. lib. bdg. 65.00 (*0-89838-169-X*) Kluwer Ac.

Artificial Intelligence Approach to VLSI Routing. Rostam Joobbani. 1985. lib. bdg. 67.50 (*0-89838-205-X*) Kluwer Ac.

Artificial Intelligence at MIT: Expanding Frontiers, 1. Ed. by Patrick H. Winston & Sarah A. Shellard. 1200p. 1990. 45.00x (*0-262-23150-6*) MIT Pr.

Artificial Intelligence at MIT: Expanding Frontiers, 2. Patrick H. Winston & Sarah A. Shellard. 1200p. 1990. 45.00x (*0-262-23151-4*) MIT Pr.

Artificial Intelligence at MIT: Expanding Frontiers, Set. Ed. by Patrick H. Winston & Sarah A. Shellard. 1200p. 1990. 80.00x (*0-262-23154-9*) MIT Pr.

Artificial Intelligence, Culture & Language: On Education & Work. Ed. by Bo Goranzon & M. Florin. (Artificial Intelligence & Society Ser.). (Illus.). 288p. 1990. pap. 59.00 (*0-387-19573-4*) Spr-Verlag.

Artificial Intelligence Debate: False Starts, Real Foundations. Ed. by Stephen R. Graubard. 328p. (Orig.). 1988. pap. 14.00 (*0-262-57074-2*) MIT Pr.

Artificial Intelligence Developments & Applications. Ed. by J. S. Gero & R. Stanton. 364p. 1988. 84.75 (*0-444-70465-5*, North Holland) Elsevier.

Artificial Intelligence Dictionary: A Dictionary Specifically for Artificial Intelligence Users & Specialists. Ellen Thro. Ed. by Lance A. Leventhal. LC 89-43542. (Lance A. Leventhal Microtrend Ser.). 352p. (Orig.). 1991. pap. 24.95 (*0-915391-36-8*, Microtrend) Slawson Comm.

Artificial Intelligence Experience: An Introduction. Susan J. Scown. 183p. 1988. pap. text ed. 18.00 (*0-13-048091-6*) P-H.

Artificial Intelligence, Expert Systems & Languages in Modelling & Simulation: Proceeding of the First IMACS Symposium, Barcelona, Spain, 2-4 June, 1987. Ed. by C. A. Kulikowski et al. 374p. 1988. 95.00 (*0-444-70482-5*, North Holland) Elsevier.

Artificial Intelligence, Expert Systems, & Symbolic Computing. Ed. by Elias N. Houstis & John R. Rice. LC 92-31962. 1992. write for info. (*0-444-89703-8*) Elsevier.

Artificial Intelligence, Expert Systems, Computer Vision, & Natural Language Processing. William B. Gevarter. LC 84-6014. (Illus.). 226p. 1984. 36.00 (*0-8155-0994-4*) Noyes.

***Artificial Intelligence Finance & Industry: Theory & Application in Portfolio Management.** Robert R. Trippi & Jae K. Lee. 250p. 1995. 65.00 (*1-55738-868-7*) Probus Pub Co.

***Artificial Intelligence for Applications, 11th Conference on (CAIA '95)** 384p. 1995. pap. text ed. 80.00 (*0-8186-7070-3*, PR07070) IEEE Comp Soc.

Artificial Intelligence for Applications, 9th Conference on (CAIA '93) LC 89-649003. 488p. 1993. pap. text ed. 70.00 (*0-8186-3840-0*, 3840) IEEE Comp Soc.

Artificial Intelligence for Engineering. Ed. by Graham Winstanley. 434p. 1991. pap. text ed. 49.95 (*0-471-92603-5*) Wiley.

Artificial Intelligence for Engineering, Design, & Manufacturing. Ed. by S. H. Rubin. 218p. 1992. pap. 30.00 (*1-55617-017-3*) Instru Soc.

Artificial Intelligence for Microcomputers. Mickey Williamson. 1985. 24.95 (*0-89303-071-6*) S&S Trade.

Artificial Intelligence for Military Applications. Barry B. Silverman & William P. Hutzler. (Topics in Operations Research Ser.). 200p. 1986. pap. 10.00 (*0-685-64802-8*) Op Res Soc.

Artificial Intelligence for Society. Ed. by Karamjit S. Gill. LC 85-29596. 280p. 1986. text ed. 76.95 (*0-471-90930-0*) Wiley.

Artificial Intelligence for Society. Ed. by Karamjit S. Gill. LC 85-29596. 304p. reprint ed. pap. 86.70 (*0-7837-4018-2*, 2043848) Bks Demand.

Artificial Intelligence for Space Station Automation: Crew Safety, Productivity, Autonomy, Augumented Capability. Oscar Firschein et al. LC 86-5149. (Illus.). 386p. 1986. 48.00 (*0-8155-1078-0*) Noyes.

Artificial Intelligence Frontiers in Statistics: AI & Statistics III. Ed. by D. J. Hand. LC 92-34777. 1992. write for info. (*0-412-40710-8*) Chapman & Hall.

Artificial Intelligence Handbook, 2 vols., Set. A. E. Nisenfeld. Ed. by J. R. Davis. 1989. text ed. 98.00 (*1-55617-135-8*, A135-8) Instru Soc.

Artificial Intelligence Handbook, 2 vols., Vol. 1: Principles. A. E. Nisenfeld. Ed. by J. R. Davis. 250p. 1989. Vol. 1, Principles, 250p. text ed. 45.00 (*1-55617-133-1*, A133-1) Instru Soc.

Artificial Intelligence Handbook, 2 vols., Vol. 2: Applications. A. E. Nisenfeld. Ed. by J. R. Davis. 350p. 1989. Vol. 2, Applications, 350p. text ed. 65.00 (*1-55617-134-X*, A134X) Instru Soc.

Artificial Intelligence II - Methodology, Systems, Applications: Proceedings of the 2nd International Conference, Varna, Bulgaria, 16-19 September, 1986. Ed. by P. Jorrand & V. Sgurev. 406p. 1987. 87.25 (*0-444-70205-9*, North Holland) Elsevier.

Artificial Intelligence III - Mehtodology, Systems, Applications: Proc. of the 3rd Internat. Conf. (AIMSA '88), Varna, Bulgaria, 20-23 Sept., 1988. Ed. by Tim O'Shea & V. Sgurev. 444p. 1988. 92.50 (*0-444-70508-2*, North Holland) Elsevier.

Artificial Intelligence in Accounting & Auditing: Using Expert Systems. Intro. by Miklos A. Vasarhelhiyi. (Rutgers Series in Accounting Research). 340p. (C). 1994. text ed. 59.95 (*1-55876-055-5*) Wiener Pubs Inc.

Artificial Intelligence in Accounting & Auditing - Using Expert Systems, 1994. Intro. by Miklos A. Vasarhelyi. (Rutgers Series in Accounting Research: Vol. 3). (Illus.). 322p. (C). 1994. text ed. 59.95x (*1-55876-078-4*) Wiener Pubs Inc.

Artificial Intelligence in Accounting & Auditing-Using Expert Systems. Miklos A. Vasarhelyi. LC 87-40223. 560p. 1988. text ed. 59.95 (*0-910129-72-X*) Wiener Pubs Inc.

Artificial Intelligence in Action: Commodore 64. Charles Platt. 1985. pap. 12.99 (*0-89824-119-7*) Trillium Pr.

Artificial Intelligence in Chemical Engineering. Thomas E. Quantrille & Y. A. Liu. (Illus.). 609p. 1992. text ed. 59.95 (*0-12-569550-0*) Acad Pr.

Artificial Intelligence in Chemistry: Structure Elucidation & Simulation of Organic Reactions. Z. Hippe. (Studies in Physical & Theoretical Chemistry: No. 73). 272p. 1991. 137.00 (*0-444-98746-0*) Elsevier.

Artificial Intelligence in Databases & Information Systems (DS-3) Proc. of the TC2WG2.6 - TC8WG8.1 Working Conf., Guangzhou, China 4-8 July, 1988. Ed. by R. A. Meersman et al. 584p. 1990. 110.25 (*0-444-88645-1*, North Holland) Elsevier.

Artificial Intelligence in Design. Ed. by D. T. Pham. (Artificial Intelligence in Industry Ser.). (Illus.). 520p. 1991. 129.00 (*0-387-50634-9*) Spr-Verlag.

Artificial Intelligence in Design. Ed. by G. Rzevski. LC 89-61419. (AIENG Ser.: Vol. 4). 564p. 1989. 107.00 (*0-945824-20-3*) Computational Mech MA.

Artificial Intelligence in Design 'Ninety-One. Gero. 1991. 165.00 (*0-7506-1188-X*) Buttrwrth-Heinemann.

Artificial Intelligence in Design 'Ninety-Two. Ed. by J. S. Gero. LC 92-15405. 940p. (C). 1992. lib. bdg. 247.00 (*0-7923-1799-8*) Kluwer Ac.

***Artificial Intelligence in Design '94: Proceedings of the Third International Conference, Held August 1994 in Lausanne, Switzerland.** Ed. by John S. Gero & Fay Sudweeks. LC 94-22248. (Diverse Ser.). 784p. (C). 1994. lib. bdg. 237.00 (*0-7923-2994-5*) Kluwer Ac.

Artificial Intelligence in Economics & Management. Ed. by Louis F. Pau. 292p. 1986. 69.25 (*0-444-87961-7*, North Holland) Elsevier.

Artificial Intelligence in Education, 1993. Ed. by Paul Brna et al. (Illus.). 616p. (Orig.). 1993. pap. 45.00 (*1-880094-08-8*) Assn Advan Comput Educ.

***Artificial Intelligence in Engineering, 3 vols.** Ed. by D. Sriram & R. A. Adey. (AIENG Ser.: Vol. 2). 1987. 245.00 (*1-85312-195-9*) Computational Mech MA.

Artificial Intelligence in Engineering: Design. Ed. by John S. Gero. LC 88-71239. (AIENG Ser.: Vol. 3). 465p. 1988. 129.00 (*0-931215-97-8*) Computational Mech MA.

Artificial Intelligence in Engineering: Diagnosis & Learning. Ed. by John S. Gero. LC 88-71238. (AIENG Ser.: Vol. 3). 422p. 1988. 119.00 (*0-931215-99-4*) Computational Mech MA.

Artificial Intelligence in Engineering: Proceedings of the 3rd International Conf., Palo Alto CA, 8-11 Aug., 1988, Pt. I: Design. Ed. by J. S. Gero. 465p. 1988. Part I: Design; 465p. 141.00 (*0-444-70469-8*) Elsevier.

Artificial Intelligence in Engineering: Proceedings of the 3rd International Conf., Palo Alto CA, 8-11 Aug., 1988, Pt. II: Robotics & Processes. Ed. by J. S. Gero. 404p. 1988. Part II: Robotics & Processes; 404p. 128.25 (*0-444-70470-1*) Elsevier.

Artificial Intelligence in Engineering: Proceedings of the 3rd International Conf., Palo Alto CA, 8-11 Aug., 1988, Pt. III: Diagnosis & Learning. Ed. by J. S. Gero. 422p. 1988. Part III: Diagnosis & Learning; 422p. 131.00 (*0-444-70471-X*) Elsevier.

Artificial Intelligence in Engineering: Proceedings of the 3rd International Conf., Palo Alto CA, 8-11 Aug., 1988, Set. Ed. by J. S. Gero. 1988. 381.50 (*0-685-22683-2*) Elsevier.

Artificial Intelligence in Engineering: Robotics & Processes. Ed. by John S. Gero. LC 88-71240. (AIENG Ser.: Vol. 3). 403p. 1988. 117.00 (*0-931215-98-6*) Computational Mech MA.

Artificial Intelligence in Engineering: Tools & Techniques. Ed. by D. Sriram & Robert A. Adey. LC 87-71288. (AIENG Ser.: Vol. 2). 416p. 1987. 84.00 (*0-931215-80-3*) Computational Mech MA.

Artificial Intelligence in Engineering Design. Ed. by R. A. Adey. LC 91-77556. (Progress in Engineering Ser.: Vol. 12). 186p. 1993. pap. 72.00 (*0-945824-62-9*) Computational Mech MA.

Artificial Intelligence in Engineering Design, Vol. 1: Design Representation & Models of Routine Design. Ed. by Christopher Tong & Duvvuru Sriram. (Illus.). 473p. 1992. text ed. 44.95 (*0-12-660561-0*) Acad Pr.

Artificial Intelligence in Engineering Design, Vol. 2: Models of Innovative Design, Reasoning about Physical Systems, & Reasoning about Geometry. Ed. by Christopher Tong & Duvvuru Sriram. (Illus.). 524p. 1992. text ed. 49.95 (*0-12-660562-9*) Acad Pr.

Artificial Intelligence in Engineering Design, Vol. 3: Knowledge Acquisition, Commercial Systems, & Integrated Environments. Ed. by Christopher Tong & Duvvuru Sriram. (Illus.). 388p. 1992. text ed. 49.95 (*0-12-660563-7*) Acad Pr.

Artificial Intelligence in Engineering VIII, Set. Ed. by G. Rzevski et al. LC 93-71020. (AIENG Ser.: Vol. 8). 1472p. 1993. 480.00 (*1-56252-159-4*) Computational Mech MA.

Artificial Intelligence in Engineering VIII, Vol. 1: Design, Methods & Techniques. Ed. by G. Rzevski et al. LC 93-71020. (AIENG Ser.). 608p. 1993. 198.00 (*1-56252-180-2*) Computational Mech MA.

Artificial Intelligence in Engineering VIII, Vol. 2: Applications & Techniques. Ed. by G. Rzevski et al. LC 93-71020. (AIENG Ser.). 864p. 1993. 282.00 (*1-56252-181-0*) Computational Mech MA.

Artificial Intelligence in Higher Education: CEPES-UNESCO International Symposium, Prague, CSFR, October 23-25, 1989 Proceedings. Ed. by V. Marik et al. (Lecture Notes in Computer Science, Lecture Notes in Artificial Intelligence Ser.: Vol. 451). ix, 247p. 1990. pap. 33.00 (*0-387-52952-7*) Spr-Verlag.

***Artificial Intelligence in Industrial Decision Making, Control, & Automation.** Ed. by Spyros G. Tzafestas & Henk B. Verbruggen. LC 94-46547. (International Series on Microprocessor-Based & Intelligent Systems Engineering: Vol. 14). 1995. lib. bdg. 317.00 (*0-7923-3320-9*) Kluwer Ac.

Artificial Intelligence in Maintenance. Ed. by J. Jeffrey Richardson. LC 85-15394. (Illus.). 485p. 1986. 48.00 (*0-8155-1042-X*) Noyes.

Artificial Intelligence in Manufacturing. Ed. by G. Rzevski. LC 89-61419. (AIENG Ser.: Vol. 4). 476p. 1989. 107.00 (*0-945824-22-X*) Computational Mech MA.

Artificial Intelligence in Manufacturing: Key to Integration? Proceedings of the Technology Assessment & Management Conference of the Gottlieb Duttweiler Institute, Ruschlikon, Zurich, Switzerland, November 7-8, 1985. Ed. by T. Bernold. (Technology Assessment & Management Ser.: No. 3). 326p. 1987. 99.00 (*0-444-70154-0*, North Holland) Elsevier.

Artificial Intelligence in Mathematics. Ed. by J. H. Johnson et al. (Institute of Mathematics & Its Applications Conference Series, New Ser.: Vol. 51). (Illus.). 352p. 1994. 67.50 (*0-19-853686-0*) OUP.

Artificial Intelligence in Medicine. Ed. by I. De Lotto & M. Stefanelli. 226p. 1986. 64.00 (*0-444-87843-2*, North Holland) Elsevier.

Artificial Intelligence in Medicine: Proceedings of the 4th Conference on Artificial Intelligence in Medicine Europe, Munich, Germany, October 3-6, 1993, Vol. 10. Ed. by Steen Andreassen et al. LC 93-61133. (Studies in Health Technology & Informatics). 508p. 1993. 116.00 (*90-5199-141-X*, Pub. by IOS Pr NE) IOS Press.

***Artificial Intelligence in Medicine: Interpreting Clinical Data: Papers from the 1994 Spring Symposium.** Ed. by Isaac Kohane & Serdar Uckun. (Technical Reports). (Illus.). 168p. (Orig.). 1994. pap. 25.00x (*0-929280-57-1*) Amer Artificial.

Artificial Intelligence in Operational Research. Ed. by Ray J. Paul. (Illus.). 375p. 1992. text ed. 120.00 (*0-333-55117-6*, Pub. by Macmill Press UK) Scholium Intl.

Artificial Intelligence in Optimal Design & Manufacturing. Ed. by Dong Zuomin. LC 93-552. 1993. text ed. 68.00 (*0-13-037540-3*) P-H.

***Artificial Intelligence in Organization Design, Planning & Control.** Ed. by Robert W. Blanning & David R. King. LC 94-48549. 1995. pap. text ed. 55.00 (*0-8186-7069-X*, BP07069) IEEE Comp Soc.

Artificial Intelligence in Perspective. Ed. by Daniel G. Bobrow. LC 93-21601. (Special Issues of Artificial Intelligence Ser.). 472p. 1994. pap. 37.50 (*0-262-52186-5*, Bradford Bks) MIT Pr.

Artificial Intelligence in Process Engineering. Ed. by Michael L. Mavrovouniotis. 367p. 1990. text ed. 73.00 (*0-12-480575-2*) Acad Pr.

Artificial Intelligence in Psychology: Interdisciplinary Essays. Margaret A. Boden. (Explorations in Cognitive Science Ser.). 172p. 1989. 25.00 (*0-262-02285-0*, Bradford Bks); pap. 12.95 (*0-262-52140-7*, Bradford Bks) MIT Pr.

***Artificial Intelligence in Real Time Control 1994: A Postprint Volume from the IFAC Symposium, Valencia, Spain, 3-5 October 1994.** Ed. by A. Crespo & IFAC Symposium on Artificial Intelligence in Real Time Control Staff. LC 95-7031. 1995. pap. 82.00 (*0-08-042236-5*, Pergamon Pr) Elsevier.

Artificial Intelligence in the Ada Environment. Louis Baker. (Illus.). 320p. 1989. text ed. 44.00 (*0-07-003350-1*) McGraw.

***Artificial Intelligence in the Capital Markets: State-of-the-Art Applications.** Roy A. Freedman. 1994. 85.00 (*1-55738-811-3*) Probus Pub Co.

Artificial Intelligence in the Pacific Rim: Proceedings of Pacific Rim International Conference on Artificial Intelligence, Nagoya 1990. Ed. by Hozumi Tanaka. 940p. 1991. 140.00 (*90-5199-053-7*, Pub. by IOS Pr NE) IOS Press.

Artificial Intelligence Information-Control Systems of Robots '94. I. Plander. 432p. 1994. text ed. 109.00 (*981-02-1877-X*) World Scientific Pub.

Artificial Intelligence: Methodology, Systems, Applications: Proceedings of the International Conference on Artificial Intelligence Varna, Bulgaria, 17-20 Sept., 1984. Ed. by W. Bible & B. Petkoff. 248p. 1985. 78.50 (*0-444-87743-6*, North Holland) Elsevier.

Artificial Intelligence Methods & Applications. N. G. Bourbakis. (Advanced Series on Artificial Intelligence). 732p. 1992. text ed. 116.00 (*981-02-1057-4*) World Scientific Pub.

***Artificial Intelligence Planning Systems.** James Hendler & Drew McDermott. 600p. 1996. 59.95 (*1-55860-280-1*) Morgan Kaufmann.

Artificial Intelligence Planning Systems: Proceedings of the First International Conference, June 15-17, 1992, College Park, Maryland. Ed. by James Hendler. LC 92-13636. 1992. 49.95 (*1-55860-250-X*) Morgan Kaufmann.

Artificial Intelligence Programming. 2nd ed. Ed. by Eugene Charniak et al. 552p. (C). 1988. text ed. 49.95 (*0-89859-609-2*) L Erlbaum Assocs.

Artificial Intelligence Project for Commodore. O'Malley. 1991. 19.95 (*0-8306-6420-3*) TAB Bks.

Artificial Intelligence, Simulation & Modeling. Lawrence E. Widman et al. 1989. text ed. 70.00 (*0-471-60599-9*) Wiley.

Artificial Intelligence Technique for Information & Fact Retrieval: An Application in Medical Knowledge Processing. Nicholas V. Findler. (Information Systems Ser.). (Illus.). 176p. 1992. pap. 25.00 (*0-262-56060-7*) MIT Pr.

Artificial Intelligence Through Search. Chris Thornton & Benedict Du Boulay. LC 92-20255. (Diverse Ser.). 384p. (C). 1992. lib. bdg. 115.50 (*0-7923-1868-4*) Kluwer Ac.

Artificial Intelligence Through Search. Christopher Thornton & Benedict Du Boulay. 364p. 1992. pap. text ed. 22.95 (*1-871516-24-2*, Pub. by Intellect Bks UK) Cromland.

Artificial Intelligence Tools & Techniques for Civil & Structural Engineers. Civil Comp Editors. 303p. 1989. pap. 150.00 (*0-948749-13-X*, Pub. by Civil-Comp UK) St Mut.

Artificial Intelligence Tools in Education: Proceedings of the IFIP TC3 Working Conference, Frascati, Italy, 26-28 May 1987. Ed. by P. Ercoli & R. Lewis. 236p. 1988. 61.75 (*0-444-70354-3*, North Holland) Elsevier.

Artificial Intelligence (TRR 1399) Ed. by Naomi Kassabian. (Transportation Research Record Ser.). (Illus.). 56p. 1993. pap. text ed. 20.00 (*0-309-05471-0*) Transport Res Bd.

Artificial Intelligence Vocabulary: A French-English Terminology. 184p. (Orig.). (ENG & FRE.). (C). 1994. pap. text ed. 85.00 (*0-7881-0762-3*) Diane Pub.

Artificial Intelligence, Vol. 4: Proceedings of the International Conference on Methodology, Systems Applications, 4th, Albena, Bulgaria, 19-22 Sept. 1990. Ed. by P. Jorrand & V. Sgurev. 434p. 1990. 95.00 (*0-444-88771-7*, North Holland) Elsevier.

Artificial Intelligence with Common LISP: Fundamentals of Symbolic & Numeric Processing. James L. Noyes. 542p. (C). 1992. text ed. write for info. (*0-669-19473-5*); Instr.'s guide. teacher ed write for info. (*0-669-19474-3*); Instr.'s diskette 5-1/2". write for info. (*0-669-32648-8*); Instr.'s diskette 3-1/2". write for info. (*0-669-28244-8*) Heath.

Artificial Intelligence with Statistical Pattern Recognition. Edward Patrick & James Fattu. 363p. 1986. text ed. 59.95 (*0-13-049131-4*, Busn) P-H.

Artificial Larynx. Y. Lebrun. (Neurolinguistics Ser.: Vol. 1). 90p. 1973. 18.50 (*90-265-0173-0*, Pub. by Swets Pub Serv NE) Taylor & Francis.

Artificial Life: A Report from the Frontier Where Computers Meet Biology. Steven Levy. LC 92-50600. 1993. pap. 13.00 (*0-679-74389-8*, Vin) Random.

***Artificial Life: An Overview.** Ed. by Christopher G. Langton. (Complex Adaptive Systems Ser.). (Illus.). 336p. 1995. 42.00 (*0-262-12189-1*, Bradford Bks) MIT Pr.

Artificial Life: How Computers Are Transforming Our Understanding of Evolution & the Future of Life. Steven Levy. LC 91-50749. (Illus.). 320p. 1992. 24.50 (*0-679-40774-X*) Pantheon.

Artificial Life: Proceedings of an Interdisciplinary Workshop on the Synthesis & Simulation of Living Systems. Ed. by Christopher G. Langton. (Santa Fe Institute Ser.). 688p. (C). 1989. pap. 34.95 (*0-201-09356-1*, Adv Bk Prog) Addison-Wesley.

***Artificial Life & Virtual Reality.** Roy F. Baumeister. 1994. pap. 16.95 (*0-89862-152-6*) Guilford Pubns.

Artificial Life & Virtual Reality. Ed. by Nadia M. Thalman & Daniel Thalmann. LC 94-12672. 1994. text ed. 49.95 (*0-471-95146-3*) Wiley.

Artificial Life Explorer's Kit. Ellen Thro. 1993. disk, pap. 24.95 (*0-672-30301-9*) Sams.

Artificial Life II. Christopher G. Langton et al. (Santa Fe Institute Ser.). (Illus.). 500p. (C). 1992. 54.95 (*0-201-52570-4*, Adv Bk Prog); pap. 34.95 (*0-201-52571-2*, Adv Bk Prog) Addison-Wesley.

Artificial Life III. Christopher G. Langton. (Illus.). (C). 1993. 55.95 (*0-201-62492-3*) Addison-Wesley.

Artificial Life III. Christopher G. Langton. (Proceedings, Santa Fe Institute Studies in the Sciences of Complexity: Vol. 17). (Illus.). 599p. (C). 1993. pap. 34.95 (*0-201-62494-X*) Addison-Wesley.

Artificial Life IV. Ed. by Rodney A. Brooks & Pattie Maes. (Bradford Series in Complex Adaptive Systems). (Illus.). 740p. 1994. pap. 60.00x (*0-262-52190-3*, Bradford Bks) MIT Pr.

Artificial Life Lab. Rudy Rucker. (Illus.). 250p. (Orig.). 1993. disk, pap. 34.95 (*1-878739-48-4*) Waite Group Pr.

Artificial Life Playhouse: Evolution at Your Fingertips. Stephen Prata. (Illus.). 190p. (Orig.). 1993. disk, pap. 23.95 (*1-878739-32-8*) Waite Group Pr.

Artificial Life Route to Artificial Intelligence: Building Embodied, Situated Agents. Ed. by Luc Steels & Rodney Brooks. 352p. 1994. text ed. 69.95 (*0-8058-1518-X*); pap. 29.95 (*0-8058-1519-8*) L Erlbaum Assocs.

Artificial Lift. 190p. 1975. 10.80 (*0-317-32910-3*, 30512) Soc Petrol Engineers.

Artificial Lift. Richard W. Donnelly. Ed. by Charles Kirkley & Jodie Leecraft. (Oil & Gas Production Ser.). (Illus.). 71p. (Orig.). 1985. pap. text ed. 20.00 (*0-88698-086-0*, 3.31210) PETEX.

462

An Asterisk (*) at the beginning of an entry indicates that the title is appearing in BIP for the first time.

Artificial Lift Methods. (Well Servicing & Workover Ser.: Lesson 5). (Illus.). 45p. (Orig.). 1971. pap. text ed. 12.00 (*0-88698-061-5*, 3.70510) PETEX.

Artificial Limbs for Confederate Soldiers. Patrick J. McCawley. Ed. by Judith M. Brimelow. 40p. 1992. pap. write for info. (*1-880067-15-3*) SC Dept of Arch & Hist.

Artificial Liver Support: Proceedings. F. W. Schmidt. Ed. by G. Brunner. (Illus.). 332p. 1981. 70.00 (*0-387-10591-3*) Spr-Verlag.

***Artificial Minds: An Exploration of the Mechanisms of Mind.** Stan Franklin. 456p. 1995. 35.00 (*0-262-06178-3*, Bradford Bks) MIT Pr.

Artificial Morality: Virtuous Robots for Virtual Games. Peter Danielson. LC 91-30432. 256p. 1992. 69.95 (*0-415-03484-1*, A5029); pap. 15.95 (*0-415-07691-9*, A7338) Routledge.

***Artificial Neural Nets & Genetic Algorithms: Proceedings of the International Conference in Ales, France, 1995.** Ed. by D. W. Pearson et al. LC 95-10560. 1995. write for info. (*3-211-82692-0*) Spr-Verlag.

Artificial Neural Networks. (IEE Conference Publications: No. 349). 383p. 1991. pap. 109.00 (*0-85296-531-1*, Pub. by Peregrinus UK) Inst Elect Eng.

Artificial Neural Networks. (IEE Conference Publications: No. 372). 294p. 1993. pap. 100.00 (*0-85296-573-7*) Inst Elect Eng.

Artificial Neural Networks. HMSO Staff. 52p. 1992. pap. 25.00 (*0-11-430067-4*, HM00674, Pub. by HMSO UK) UNIPUB.

Artificial Neural Networks. T. Kohonen et al. 1991. 197.25 (*0-444-89178-1*) Elsevier.

***Artificial Neural Networks.** Dan Patterson. 1995. pap. text ed. 48.00 (*0-13-295353-6*) P-H.

Artificial Neural Networks: Approximation & Learning Theory. Halbert White. 320p. 1992. 49.95 (*1-55786-329-6*) Blackwell Pubs.

Artificial Neural Networks: Concepts & Control Apps. V. Rao Vemuri. LC 92-3326. 520p. 1992. text ed. 60.00 (*0-8186-9069-0*, 2069) IEEE Comp Soc.

Artificial Neural Networks: Concepts & Theory. Pankaj Mehra & Ben Wah. LC 91-46288. 680p. 1992. text ed. 70.00 (*0-8186-8997-8*, 1997) IEEE Comp Soc.

Artificial Neural Networks: International Workshop IWANN '91 Granada, Spain, September 17-19, 1991 Proceedings. Ed. by A. Prieto et al. (Lecture Notes in Computer Science Ser.: Vol. 540). xiii, 476p. 1991. pap. 44.00 (*0-387-54537-9*) Spr-Verlag.

Artificial Neural Networks: Learning Algorithms, Performance Evaluation, & Applications. N. B. Karayiannis & Anastasios N. Venetsanopoulos. LC 92-34614. (Kluwer International Series in Engineering & Computer Science: SECS 0209). 464p. (C). 1992. lib. bdg. 83.00 (*0-7923-9297-3*) Kluwer Ac.

Artificial Neural Networks: Oscillations, Chaos, & Sequence Processing. Lipo Wang & Daniel L. Alkon. LC 93-23137. (Neural Networks Technology Ser.). 127p. 1993. pap. text ed. 35.00 (*0-8186-4470-2*) IEEE Comp Soc.

Artificial Neural Networks: Paradigms, Applications, & Hardware Implementations. Ed. by Edgar Sanchez-Sinencio & Clifford Lau. LC 91-28273. (Illus.). 560p. 1992. text ed. 69.95 (*0-87942-289-0*, PC0284-0) Inst Electrical.

Artificial Neural Networks: Theoretical Concepts. V. Vemuri. LC 88-71053. (Neural Networks Technology Ser.). 145p. 1988. pap. 20.00 (*0-8186-0855-2*, 855) IEEE Comp Soc.

Artificial Neural Networks - Concept Learning. Joachim Diederich. (Neural Networks Technology Ser.). 120p. 1990. pap. 30.00 (*0-8186-2015-3*, 2015) IEEE Comp Soc.

Artificial Neural Networks - Electronic Implementation. Nelson Morgan. (Neural Networks Technology Ser.). 120p. 1990. pap. 32.00 (*0-8186-2029-3*, 2029) IEEE Comp Soc.

Artificial Neural Networks - Forecasting Time Series. V. Rao Vemuri & Robert D. Rogers. LC 94-37174. (Neural Networks Technology Ser.). 220p. 1993. pap. text ed. 35.00 (*0-8186-5120-2*, 5120) IEEE Comp Soc.

Artificial Neural Networks & Expert Systems (ANNES '93) LC 93-78211. 346p. 1993. pap. text ed. 70.00 (*0-8186-4260-2*, 4260) IEEE Comp Soc.

Artificial Neural Networks for Computer Vision. Y. T. Zhou & R. Chellappa. Ed. by Bart Kosko & Michael A. Arbib. (Research Notes in Neural Computing Ser.). (Illus.). 184p. 1991. pap. 39.95 (*0-387-97683-3*) Spr-Verlag.

Artificial Neural Networks for Image Understanding. Arun D. Kulkarni. 1994. text ed. 49.95 (*0-442-00921-6*) Van Nos Reinhold.

Artificial Neural Networks for Intelligent Manufacturing. Ed. by Cihan H. Dagli. LC 93-35422. 1993. write for info. (*0-412-48050-6*, Chap & Hall NY) Chapman & Hall.

Artificial Neural Networks for Speech & Vision. Ed. by Richard J. Mammone. LC 93-32966. 1993. write for info. (*0-412-54850-X*, Chap & Hall NY) Chapman & Hall.

Artificial Neural Networks, No. 2: Proceedings of the 1992 International Conference on Artificial Neural Networks, Brighton, United Kingdom, 4-7 September, 1992. Ed. by Igor Aleksander & John Taylor. LC 92-24523. 1992. write for info. (*0-444-89488-8*, North Holland) Elsevier.

Artificial Neural Systems: A Survey on Technology & Markets, No. 11. Richard K. Miller & Terri C. Walker. LC 88-80489. 44p. 1989. pap. text ed. 200.00 (*1-55865-010-5*) Future Tech Surveys.

Artificial Neural Systems: Theory & Practice. James A. Freeman & David M. Skapura. (Computation & Neural Systems Ser.). (Illus.). 608p. (C). 1991. text ed. 50.50 (*0-201-51376-5*) Addison-Wesley.

***Artificial Nutrition Support in Clinical Practice.** Ed. by David Silk et al. 608p. 1994. 216.75 (*1-56593-399-0*, 0812) Singular Publishing.

Artificial Organs. W. J. Kolff. 180p. 1975. text ed. 54.50 (*0-7065-1525-0*, Pub. by Keter Pub IS) Coronet Bks.

***Artificial Paradise: Science Fiction & American Reality.** Sharona Ben-Tov. LC 95-1033. (Studies in Literature & Science). 1995. 29.95 (*0-472-10580-9*) U of Mich Pr.

Artificial Paradises: Baudelaire's Masterpiece on Hashish. Charles Baudelaire. LC 94-17664. (FRE.). 1995. 9.95 (*0-8065-1483-3*, Citadel Pr) Carol Pub Group.

Artificial Perception & Music Recognition. Andranik S. Tangiuane. LC 93-21437. (Lecture Notes in Computer Science, Lecture Notes in Artificial Intelligence Ser.: Vol. 746). 1993. 39.00 (*0-387-57394-1*) Spr-Verlag.

Artificial Princess see Five Novels

Artificial Reality. Jeffrey Essmann. 1992. pap. 4.75 (*0-8222-0066-X*) Dramatists Play.

Artificial Reality. 2nd ed. Myron W. Krueger. (Illus.). 320p. (C). 1991. text ed. 29.25 (*0-201-52260-8*) Addison-Wesley.

Artificial Recharge. O'Hare. 1986. 59.95 (*0-87371-050-9*, TD404, CRC Reprint) Franklin.

Artificial Recharge of Ground Water. Ed. by A. I. Johnson & Donald J. Finlayson. 656p. 1989. pap. text ed. 54.00 (*0-87262-713-6*, 713) Am Soc Civil Eng.

***Artificial Red Cells: Materials, Performances, & Clinical Study As Blood Substitutes.** E. Tsuchida. LC 94-44053. 1995. 120.00 (*0-471-95614-7*) Wiley.

Artificial Reproduction & Reproductive Rights. Athena Nga Chee Liu. 200p. 1991. text ed. 59.95 (*1-85521-022-3*, Pub. by Dartmth Pub UK) Ashgate Pub Co.

Artificial Respiration. Ricardo Piglia. Tr. by Daniel Balderston. LC 93-29571. (Latin America in Translation - En Traduccion - Em Traducao Ser.). 192p. 1994. lib. bdg. 29.95 (*0-8223-1426-6*); pap. 12.95 (*0-8223-1414-2*) Duke.

Artificial Sand Fills in Water. (Illus.). 280p. (C). 1992. text ed. 175.00 (*90-5410-138-5*, Pub. by A A Balkema NE) Ashgate Pub Co.

Artificial Satellites: Helpers in Space. Jeanne Bendick. (Early Bird Astronomy Ser.). (Illus.). 32p. (J). (gr. k-2). 1991. lib. bdg. 13.90 (*1-56294-002-3*); pap. 4.95 (*1-878841-56-4*) Millbrook Pr.

Artificial Satellites of the Earth. V. Petrov. (Illus.). 288p. 1960. text ed. 176.00 (*0-677-20540-6*) Gordon & Breach.

Artificial Seawaters: Formulas & Methods. Joseph P. Bidwell & Stephen Spotte. LC 85-12556. 327p. 1985. boxed 100.00 (*0-86720-057-X*) Jones & Bartlett.

***Artificial Social Systems: 4th European Workshop on Modelling Autonomous Agents in a Multi-Agent World MAAMAW '92, S. Martino al Cimino, Italy, July 29-31 1992.** Ed. by Cristiano Castelfranchi & Eric Werner. LC 94-3556. (Lecture Notes in Computer Science: Vol. 830). 1994. 52.00 (*0-387-58266-5*) Spr-Verlag.

***Artificial Societies: The Computer Simulation of Social Life.** Ed. by Nigel Gilbert & Rosaria Conte. LC 94-47440. 1995. 75.00x (*1-85728-305-8*, Pub. by UCL Pr UK) Taylor & Francis.

Artificial Space Debris. Nicholas L. Johnson & Darren S. McKnight. LC 86-31247. 128p. 1987. lib. bdg. 47.50 (*0-89464-012-7*) Krieger.

Artificial Space Debris. enl. ed. Nicholas L. Johnson & Darren S. McKnight. (Orbit Ser.). 142p. (C). 1991. reprint ed. 52.50 (*0-89464-043-7*) Krieger.

Artificial Structures & Shorelines. Ed. by H. J. Walker. (C). 1988. lib. bdg. 212.00 (*90-277-2746-5*) Kluwer Ac.

Artificial Sweeteners: A Special Issue of the Journal Comments on Toxicology. Ed. by A. W. Hayes & W. O. Berndt. 100p. 1989. pap. text ed. 34.00 (*2-88124-395-9*) Gordon & Breach.

***Artificial Sweetners & Other Food Substitutes Market.** 159p. (Orig.). 1995. pap. 3,195.00 (*0-7605-2259-6*) Rector Pr.

***Artificial Systems for Insulin Delivery.** Ed. by P. Brunetti et al. LC 82-47688. (Serono Symposia Publications for Raven Press: No. 6). (Illus.). Date not set. reprint ed. pap. 180.00 (*0-7837-9545-9*, 2060294) Bks Demand.

Artificial Vision for Mobile Robots: Stereo Vision & Multisensory Perception. Nicholas Ayache. (Artificial Intelligence - Bobrow, Brady & Davis Ser.). (Illus.). 360p. 1991. 52.50x (*0-262-01124-7*) MIT Pr.

Artikel 12 Gg-Freiheit des Berufes und Grundrecht der Arbeit: Der Verwaltungsvorbehalt. Ed. by Hans-Peter Schneider et al. (Veroeffentlichungen der Historischen Kommission zu Berlin, Band 67, Beitraege zu Inflation und Wiederaufbau in Deutschland und Europa 1914-1924: Heft 43). 288p. (GER.). 1985. 66.15 (*3-11-010460-1*) De Gruyter.

Artillerist's Manual. John Gibbon. 1991. 75.00 (*0-89029-541-7*) Morningside Bkshop.

Artillerist's Manual. Comp. by John Gibbon. LC 74-84270. 500p. 1971. reprint ed. text ed. 48.50 (*0-8371-5007-8*, GIAM, Greenwood Pr) Greenwood.

Artillery. James R. Arnold. Ed. by Ian Ballantine. LC 86-47565. (Illustrated History of the Vietnam War Ser.). (Illus.). 160p. 1987. pap. 6.95 (*0-317-61484-3*) Bantam.

Artillery. Terry Gander. (Modern Military Techniques Ser.). (Illus.). 48p. (J). (gr. 5 up). 1987. lib. bdg. 14.95 (*0-8225-1380-3*, Lerner Publctns) Lerner Group.

Artillery. J. Nicholaus. (Army Library). (Illus.). 48p. (J). (gr. 3-8). 1989. lib. bdg. 18.60 (*0-86592-419-8*) Rourke Corp.

Artillery: Guns & Rocket Systems. T. J. O'Malley. LC 94-13570. (Military Manuals Ser.). 160p. 1994. 19.95 (*1-85367-188-6*, 5404) Stackpole.

Artillery at the Golden Gate: The Harbor Defenses of San Francisco in World War II. Brian B. Chin. LC 94-65848. (Illus.). 176p. 1994. pap. 12.95 (*0-929521-85-4*) Pictorial Hist.

Artillery Equipment of the Napoleonic Wars. Terence Wise. (Men-at-Arms Ser.: No. 96). (Illus.). 48p. pap. 11.95 (*0-85045-336-4*, 9032, Pub. by Osprey UK) Stackpole.

***Artillery Hell: The Employment of Artillery at Antietam.** Curt Johnson & Richard C. Anderson, Jr. LC 94-13226. (Military History Ser.: No. 38). (Illus.). 152p. 1995. 29.50x (*0-89096-622-2*); pap. 14.95x (*0-89096-623-0*) Tex A&M Univ Pr.

Artillery of Lies. large type ed. Derek Robinson. 1993. 39.95 (*0-7066-1018-0*, Pub. by Remploy Pr CN) St Mut.

Artillery of Nathan Bedford Forrest. John W. Morton. 374p. 1993. pap. 10.95 (*0-89176-042-3*, Bellum Edits) R Bemis Pub.

***Artillery of Nathan Bedford Forrest's Cavalry.** John W. Morton. 376p. 1994. 31.95 (*1-55793-019-8*) Guild Bindery Pr.

***Artillery of Nathan Bedford Forrest's Cavalry.** John W. Morton. 374p. 1909. 35.00 (*1-56013-008-3*) Olde Soldier Bks.

Artillery of the Press. James Reston. LC 67-11330. 128p. reprint ed. 36.50 (*0-8357-9150-5*, 2002159) Bks Demand.

Artillery Officer in the Mexican War, 1846-1847: Letters of Robert Anderson. Robert Anderson. LC 74-148870. (Select Bibliographies Reprint Ser.). 1977. reprint ed. 26.95 (*0-8369-5642-7*) Ayer.

***Artillery Through the Ages: A Short Illustrated History of Cannon, Emphasizing Types Used in America.** Albert Manucy. (Illus.). 92p. (Orig.). (C). 1994. pap. text ed. 45.00x (*0-7881-0745-3*) Diane Pub.

Artillery Through the Ages: A Short Illustrated History of Cannon, Emphasizing Types Used in America. Albert Manucy. (Illus.). 96p. (Orig.). 1985. reprint ed. pap. 2.75 (*0-16-003405-1*, S/N 024-005-00159-0) USGPO.

Artillerymen of Historic Fort Monroe, Virginia. Phyllis I. McClellan. (Illus.). 264p. (Orig.). 1992. pap. text ed. 20.00 (*1-55613-529-7*) Heritage Bk.

***ArtIntAct: A CD ROM Magazine.** Jean-Louis Boisser et al. 112p. 1995. text ed. 49.95 (*3-89322-675-3*) Dist Art Pubs.

***Artintact 2: An Interactive CD ROM Magazine.** 112p. Date not set. spiral bd. 49.95 (*3-89322-715-6*) Dist Art Pubs.

Artis Rhetoricae Epitome. Cornutus. Ed. by Johannes Graeven. 55p. 1973. write for info. (*3-296-12010-6*, Pub. by Georg Olms GW) Lubrecht & Cramer.

Artisan or Artist: History of Teaching of Art & Crafts in English Schools. G. Sutton. LC 67-19822. 1967. 138.00 (*0-08-012270-1*, Pub. by Pergamon Repr UK) Franklin.

Artisan Republic: Revolution, Reaction, & Resistance in Lyon, 1848-1851. Mary L. Stewart-McDougall. 232p. 1984. 44.95 (*0-7735-0426-5*, Pub. by McGill CN) U of Toronto Pr.

Artisans & Architects: The Ruskinian Tradition in Architectural Thought. Mark Swenarton. LC 88-14853. 224p. 1989. text ed. 45.00 (*0-312-02375-8*) St Martin.

Artisans & Industrialization: Indian Weaving in the Twentieth Century. Tirthankar Roy. (Illus.). 256p. 1994. 23.00 (*0-19-563100-5*) OUP.

Artisans & Machinery: Moral & Physical Condition of the Manufacturing Population. Peter Gaskell. 399p. 1968. 42.50 (*0-7146-1395-9*, Pub. by F Cass Pubs UK) Intl Spec Bk.

Artisans & Machinery: The Moral & Physical Condition of the Manufacturing Population Considered with Reference to Mechanical Substitutions for Human Labour. Peter Gaskell. LC 68-28259. xv, 399p. 1968. reprint ed. 45.00 (*0-678-05047-3*) Kelley.

Artisans & Merchants of Alexandria, Virginia 1780-1820, Vol. 1. T. Michael Miller. 428p. 1991. pap. 20.00 (*1-55613-389-8*) Heritage Bk.

Artisans & Merchants of Alexandria, Virginia 1780-1820, Vol. 2. T. Michael Miller. (Illus.). 545p. 1992. pap. 35.50 (*1-55613-598-X*) Heritage Bk.

Artisans Anthology of Drama. Intro. by Marion Perry. 134p. (Orig.). (C). 1994. pap. text ed. 12.00 (*0-9632200-3-9*) Marienhelz Artisans.

Artisans Appalachia U. S. A. David Gaynes. 1977. pap. 6.95 (*0-913239-13-5*) Appalach Consortium.

Artisans for Independence: Philadelphia Mechanics & the American Revolution. Charles S. Olton. (Illus.). 182p. 1975. 29.95x (*0-8156-0111-5*) Syracuse U Pr.

***Artisans in the North Carolina Backcountry.** Johanna M. Lewis. (Illus.). 240p. 1995. text ed. 34.95 (*0-8131-1908-1*) U Pr of Ky.

Artisans into Workers: Labor in Nineteenth-Century America. Bruce Laurie. 1989. pap. 9.95 (*0-374-52153-0*) FS&G.

Artisans of Banaras: Popular Culture & Identity, 1880-1986. Nita Kumar. (Illus.). 300p. 1988. 39.50 (*0-691-05531-9*) Princeton U Pr.

Artisans of Glory: Writers & Historical Thought in Seventeenth-Century France. Orest Ranum. LC 79-19248. (Illus.). xiii, 355p. 1980. 37.50 (*0-8078-1413-X*) U of NC Pr.

Artist. lib. bdg. 14.95 (*0-921285-29-9*, Pub. by Bungalo Bks CN); pap. 4.95 (*0-921285-28-0*, Pub. by Bungalo Bks CN) Firefly Bks Ltd.

Artist. Jan De Hartog. 1976. 17.95 (*0-8488-0980-7*) Amereon Ltd.

Artist: A Social History. 2nd ed. Edmund B. Feldman. LC 94-17482. 256p. 1994. pap. text ed. 24.67 (*0-13-303553-0*) P-H.

Artist - Lee Godie: A Twenty-Year Retrospective. Michael Bonesteel. Ed. by Pat Matsumoto. (Illus.). 34p. (Orig.). 1993. pap. 10.00 (*0-938903-16-0*) Chi Ofc Fine Arts.

Artist .., & the Legend: A Visit to China Is Remembered & the Legends Unfold... Ed. by Judith G. Werley. LC 74-81927. (Illus.). (J). (gr. 7 up). 1974. 25.00 (*0-933652-09-7*) Domjan Studio.

Artist & Audience. Terence Grieder. 416p. (C). 1990. pap. text ed. 42.75 (*0-03-014199-0*) HB Coll Pubs.

***Artist & Audience.** 3rd ed. Terence Grieder. 474p. (C). 1994. pap. text ed. write for info. (*0-697-27454-3*) Brown & Benchmark.

Artist & Audience: African Literature As a Shared Experience. Ed. by Richard Priebe & Thomas Hale. LC 79-89930. (Annual Selected Papers of the African Literature Association). 203p. (Orig.). 1979. pap. 14.00 (*0-89410-123-4*) Three Continents.

Artist & His Model: One Hundred Eighty Drawings. Pablo Picasso. LC 93-37470. 178p. 1993. pap. 12.95 (*0-486-27877-8*) Dover.

Artist & Patron in Postwar Japan. T. R. Havens. 1982. 49.50 (*0-691-05363-4*) Princeton U Pr.

Artist & Political Vision. Ed. by Benjamin Barber & Michael J. McGrath. LC 80-80317. 408p. (C). 1981. 39.95 (*0-87855-380-0*) Transaction Pubs.

Artist & Social Reform: France - Belgium, 1885-1898. Eugenia W. Herbert. LC 75-164605. (Select Bibliographies Reprint Ser.). 1980. reprint ed. 18.95 (*0-8369-5889-6*) Ayer.

Artist & the Book in Western Europe & the United States, Eighteen Sixty to Nineteen Sixty. Museum of Fine Arts, Boston & Harvard College Library. LC 81-81721. (Illus.). 332p. 1982. reprint ed. lib. bdg. 65.00 (*0-87817-277-7*) Hacker.

Artist & the Bully. Gillian Leggat. (Junior African Writers Ser.). (Illus.). (J). (gr. 5-6). 1992. pap. 3.95 (*0-7910-2913-1*) Chelsea Hse.

Artist & the Child: Exhibition of Children's Books & Original Illustrations. 1985. pap. 12.50 (*0-89073-065-2*) Boston Public Lib.

Artist & the City. Eugenio Trias. Tr. by Kenneth Krabbenhoft. LC 81-21730. (European Perspectives Ser.). 128p. 1982. text ed. 35.50 (*0-231-05286-3*) Col U Pr.

Artist & the Crow. Dan Stryk. LC 84-11551. (Illus.). 96p. (Orig.). 1984. pap. 5.25 (*0-911198-71-7*) Purdue U Pr.

Artist & the Decorator. D. M. Campana. (Illus.). 12.95 (*0-939608-16-2*) Campana Art.

Artist & the Tyrant: Vassily Aksenov's Works in the Brezhnev Era. Konstantin Kustanovich. 219p. (Orig.). 1992. pap. 17.95 (*0-89357-235-7*) Slavica.

Artist & the Unicorn: The Lives of Arthur B. Davies. Brooks Wright. LC 78-50903. 1978. 5.85 (*0-911183-00-0*) Rockland County Hist.

Artist Archetype in Gola Culture. Warren L. D'Azevedo. 1970. 5.00 (*0-686-11766-2*) Arden Assocs.

Artist, Architect & Patron. Ed. by Alexandra Artley. (Illus.). 96p. 1980. 22.50 (*0-85139-075-7*) Eastview.

Artist As a Channel. J. Donald Walters. LC 88-154656. 117p. (Orig.). 1988. pap. 9.95 (*0-916124-42-8*, CCP17) Crystal Clarity.

Artist As Anthropologist in Victorian England: The Representation of Type & Character in Victorian Art. Mary Cowling. (Illus.). (C). 1989. 89.95 (*0-521-35490-0*) Cambridge U Pr.

Artist As Autist. Jack Moskovitz. (Illus.). 59p. (Orig.). 1989. pap. 3.00 (*0-926935-14-3*) Runaway Spoon.

Artist As Critic: Critical Writings of Oscar Wilde. Oscar Wilde. Ed. by Richard Ellmann. LC 82-13361. (Phoenix Fiction Ser.). 474p. (C). 1982. reprint ed. pap. text ed. 18.95 (*0-226-89764-8*) U Ch Pr.

Artist As Native: Reinventing Regionalism. Alan Gussow. LC 93-24779. (Illus.). 120p. 1993. 30.00 (*1-56640-596-3*); pap. 24.00 (*1-56640-675-7*) Pomegranate Calif.

Artist As Politician: The Relationship Bewteen the Art & the Politics of the French Romantics. Ellie N. Schamber. LC 83-19741. 256p. (Orig.). 1984. pap. text ed. 24.00 (*0-8191-3619-0*) U Pr of Amer.

***Artist As Teacher: William Merritt Chase & Irving R. Wiles.** Katherine Cameron. (Illus.). 48p. (Orig.). 1994. pap. 10.00 (*0-933793-30-8*) Guild Hall.

Artist As Therapist. Arthur Robbins. LC 86-10466. 226p. 1987. 42.95 (*0-89885-322-2*); pap. 22.95 (*0-89885-439-3*) Human Sci Pr.

Artist As Thinker: From Shakespeare to Joyce. George Anastaplo. LC 82-6502. xvi, 499p. 1983. lib. bdg. 40.00 (*0-8040-0416-1*, Swallow); pap. 19.95 (*0-8040-0417-X*, Swallow) Ohio U Pr.

Artist at the Piano. George Woodhouse. 1988. reprint ed. lib. bdg. 49.00 (*0-7812-0074-1*) Rprt Serv.

Artist at the Piano. George Woodhouse. reprint ed. lib. bdg. 25.00 (*0-403-03855-3*) Scholarly.

Artist at War: The Journal of John Gaitha Browning. John G. Browning. Ed. by Oleta S. Toliver. LC 94-20152. (War & the Southwest Ser.: No. 3). (Illus.). 331p. 1994. 29.95 (*0-929398-76-9*) UNTX Pr.

Artist at Work. Louise Neaderland. 1982. 5.00 (*0-942561-08-2*) Bone Hollow.

Artist at Work: Narrative Technique in Chretien de Troyes. Evelyn Mullally. LC 88-71547. (Transactions Ser.: Vol. 78, Pt. 4). 240p. (Orig.). (C). 1988. pap. 30.00 (*0-87169-784-X*, T784-MUE) Am Philos.

Artist Beware. 2nd ed. Michael McCann. (Illus.). 480p. 1992. pap. 29.95 (*1-55821-175-6*) Lyons & Burford.

Artist Descending a Staircase see Albert's Bridge & Other Plays

Artist Game Bag. 2nd ed. Lynn B. Hunt. (Fifty Greatest Bks.). (Illus.). 106p. (YA). (gr. 10 up). 1990. reprint ed. 39.95 (*0-381-20045-0*) Derrydale Pr.

Artist Grows Old. Kenneth M. Clark. LC 72-898082. (Rede Lecture, 1970 Ser.). (Illus.). 36p. reprint ed. pap. 25.00 (*0-8357-5776-5*, 2051371) Bks Demand.

Artist, His Model, Her Image, His Gaze: Picasso's Pursuit of the Model. Karen L. Kleinfelder. (Illus.). 224p. (C). 1993. 50.00 (*0-226-43983-6*) U Ch Pr.

Artist in America. rev. ed. Thomas H. Benton. LC 82-20279. (Illus.). 418p. 1983. pap. 19.95 (*0-8262-0399-X*) U of Mo Pr.

Artist in American Society: The Formative Years, 1790-1860. Neil Harris. LC 81-19752. (C). 1982. pap. text ed. 19.95 (*0-226-31754-4*) U Ch Pr.

Artist in Business: Basic Business Practices. Craig Dreeszen. Ed. by Barbara S. Bacon & John Fiscella. 118p. (Orig.). 1988. pap. 10.00 (*0-945464-01-0*) Univ MA Arts.

Artist in Conrad's Fiction: A Psychocritical Study. Joseph Dobrinsky. Ed. by A. Walton Litz. LC 88-39247. (Studies in Modern Literature: No. 92). 152p. reprint ed. 43.10 (*0-8357-1873-5*, 2070709) Bks Demand.

Artist in Conservation. David Shepherd. (Illus.). 112p. 1993. 49.95 (*0-7153-9459-2*, Pub. by D & C Pub UK) Sterling.

Artist in Each of Us. Florence Cane. LC 83-14347. (Illus.). 380p. (C). 1983. reprint ed. pap. 18.95 (*0-9611462-0-6*) Art Therapy.

Artist in His Studio: The Heroes of Modern Art. enl. rev. ed. Alexander Liberman. LC 88-42661. (Illus.). 1988. 60.00 (*0-394-56567-3*) Random.

Artist in Iowa, a Life of Grant Wood. Darrell Garwood. LC 70-110827. (Illus.). 259p. 1971. reprint ed. text ed. 38.50 (*0-8371-3227-4*, GAAI, Greenwood Pr) Greenwood.

Artist in Love. large type ed. Hilda Durman. (Linford Romance Library). 272p. 1989. pap. 11.95 (*0-7089-6645-4*, Linford) Ulverscroft.

Artist in Modern German Drama, 1885-1939. R. S. Collins. 1974. 59.95 (*0-87968-663-4*) Gordon Pr.

Artist in the Garden: A Guide to Creating Small & Natural Gardens. Enid Munroe. LC 93-30053. 1994. 25.00 (*0-8050-2718-1*) H Holt & Co.

Artist in the Kitchen. Saint Louis Art Museum Staff. Ed. by Phoebe Burke & Mary Morgan. 224p. 1993. 25.95 (*0-89178-039-4*) St Louis Art Mus.

Artist in the Market Place: Making your Living in the Fine Arts. James Adams & Patricia Frischer. LC 80-11273. 168p. 1980. pap. 5.95 (*0-87131-323-5*) M Evans.

Artist in the University Medical Center: A Textile Technique from Laos. May H. Lesser. LC 89-51422. (Illus.). 192p. 1990. text ed. 35.00 (*0-295-97028-6*) U of Wash Pr.

Artist Observed: Twenty-Eight Interviews with Contemporary Artists. John Gruen. LC 95-12959. (Illus.). 344p. 1991. (*1-55652-103-0*) A cappella Bks.

Artist of the Actual: Essays on Paul Goodman. Ed. by Peter Parisi. LC 85-19583. 204p. 1986. 22.50 (*0-8108-1843-4*) Scarecrow.

***Artist of the American Renaissance: The Letters of Kenyon Cox, 1883-1919.** Ed. by H. Wayne Morgan. LC 95-1587. (Illus.). 312p. 1995. text ed. 35.00x (*0-87338-517-9*) Kent St U Pr.

Artist of the Floating World. Kazuo Ishiguro. 1989. pap. 10.00 (*0-679-72266-1*, Vin) Random.

Artist of the Nineteenth Century. Hutton Clement. reprint ed. lib. bdg. 75.00 (*0-7812-0122-5*) Rprt Serv.

Artist on the Goldfields: The Diary of Eugene Von Guerard. Ed. by Marjorie Tipping. 1992. text ed. 39.95 (*0-522-84503-7*) Intl Spec Bk.

Artist on the Witness Stand. Fritz Eichenberg. LC 84-61828. (Orig.). 1984. pap. 3.00 (*0-87574-257-2*) Pendle Hill.

Artist Outsider: Creativity & the Boundaries of Culture. Ed. by Michael D. Hall & Eugene W. Metcalf. LC 93-84474. (Illus.). 296p. (C). 1994. 55.00 (*1-56098-334-5*); pap. 24.95 (*1-56098-335-3*) Smithsonian.

Artist Project: Portraits of the Real Art World, New York Artists 1981-1990. Peter Bellamy. (Illus.). 256p. 1993. 45.00 (*1-55859-563-5*, Cross Riv Pr) Abbeville Pr.

Artist, the Book & the Child: An Exhibition of Original Art for Children's Books. (Illus.). 60p. (J). 1989. pap. 17.00 (*0-89792-120-8*) Ill St Museum.

Artist Was a Young Man: The Life Story of Peter Rindisbacher. Alvin M. Josephy, Jr. LC 75-101097. (Illus.). 102p. 1970. 12.50 (*0-88360-018-8*) Amon Carter.

Artist You Don't Have to Be! A Jewish Arts & Crafts Book. Joann Magnus & Howard I. Bogot. 1990. pap. 10.95 (*0-8074-0422-5*, 168504) UAHC.

***Artista (the Artist)** (Illus.). 32p. (SPA.). 1992. pap. 5.95 (*0-921285-22-1*, Pub. by Bungalo Bks CN) Firefly Bks Ltd.

***Artistas Cobra.** Jean-Clarence Lambert. Vol. 1. (Illus.). (SPA.). 1993. write for info. (*0-614-00039-4*) Elliots Bks.

***Artistas Cobra.** Jean-Clarence Lambert. Vol. 1. (Illus.). (SPA.). 1993. write for info. (*0-614-00145-5*) Elliots Bks.

***Artistas Cobra.** Jean-Clarence Lambert. Vol. 1. (Illus.). (SPA.). 1993. write for info. (*0-614-00250-8*) Elliots Bks.

Artiste de la Faim et Autres Rectis. Franz Kafka. (Parus Vivants Kafka Ser.: No. II). 249p. (FRE.). 1990. pap. 13.95 (*0-7859-2596-1*, 2070382818) Fr & Eur.

Artisthelp: The Artist's Guide to Work-Related Human & Social Services. Ed. by Joan Jeffri. 335p. (Orig.). 1990. pap. 45.00 (*1-55570-035-7*) Neal-Schuman.

Artistic Anatomy. Ed. by Walter F. Moses. 1939. pap. 8.95 (*0-685-00796-0*) Borden.

Artistic Anatomy. Paul Richer. Ed. by Robert B. Hale. (Illus.). 256p. 1986. pap. 22.50 (*0-8230-0297-7*, Watsn-Guptill) Watsn-Guptill.

Artistic Anatomy of Trees. 2nd ed. Rex V. Cole. (Illus.). 1951. pap. 8.95 (*0-486-21475-3*) Dover.

Artistic Cat. Ed. by Running Press Staff. LC 91-5063. (Miniature Editions Ser.). (Illus.). 108p. 1992. 4.95 (*1-56138-091-1*) Running Pr.

Artistic Change at St-Denis: Abbot Suger's Program & the Early Twelfth-Century Controversy over Art. Conrad Rudolph. 139p. 1990. text ed. 29.50 (*0-691-04068-0*) Princeton U Pr.

Artistic Collaboration in the Twentieth Century. Cynthia J. McCabe. LC 84-3090. (Illus.). 224p. 1984. pap. text ed. 29.95 (*0-87474-687-6*, MCACP) Smithsonian.

Artistic Country Seats, I. Ed. by George W. Sheldon. LC 78-17476. (Architecture & Decorative Art Ser.: 1978). (Illus.). 1979. reprint ed. lib. bdg. 85.00 (*0-306-77598-0*) Da Capo.

Artistic Country Seats, II. Ed. by George W. Sheldon. LC 78-17476. (Architecture & Decorative Art Ser.: 1978). (Illus.). 1979. reprint ed. lib. bdg. 85.00 (*0-306-77599-9*) Da Capo.

Artistic Country Seats, Set. Ed. by George W. Sheldon. LC 78-17476. (Architecture & Decorative Art Ser.: 1978). (Illus.). 1979. reprint ed. lib. bdg. 160.00 (*0-306-70829-9*) Da Capo.

Artistic Culture of the U. S. S. R. T. Cherniavskaia. 356p. (C). 1984. 125.00 (*0-685-37190-5*, Pub. by Collets) St Mut.

Artistic Culture of the U. S. S. R. Background Dictionary. T. N. Cherniavskaia. 356p. (C). 1984. 80.00 (*0-317-92418-4*, Pub. by Collets UK) Pro-Am Music.

Artistic Differences. Charlie Hauck. LC 92-43759. 1993. 21.00 (*0-688-12152-7*) Morrow.

Artistic Expression. Ed. by John Hospers. LC 71-142225. (Century Philosophy Ser.). (Illus.). (Orig.). (C). 1971. 39.50 (*0-89197-035-5*); pap. text ed. 12.50 (*0-89197-036-3*) Irvington.

Artistic Form & Yoga in the Sacred Images of India. Heinrich Zimmer. Tr. by Gerald Chapple et al. LC 84-42589. (Illus.). 319p. (Orig.). 1990. 45.00 (*0-691-07289-2*); pap. 16.95 (*0-691-02060-4*) Princeton U Pr.

Artistic Gymnastics: A Comprehensive Guide to Performing & Teaching Skills for Beginners & Advanced Beginners. Fred Turoff. 432p. (C). 1991. pap. write for info. (*0-697-10745-0*) Brown & Benchmark.

Artistic Heritage in a Changing Pacific. Ed. by Philip J. Dark & Roger G. Rose. LC 93-7844. (Illus.). 312p. (C). 1993. text ed. 39.00 (*0-8248-1573-4*) UH Pr.

Artistic History of Carlos Gardel: A Chronological Study with Filmography & Discography. Miguel A. Morena. (Latin American Music Ser.). 1980. lib. bdg. 75.00 (*0-8490-3059-5*) Gordon Pr.

Artistic Home. Todd London. LC 87-33600. 112p. (Orig.). (C). 1988. pap. 3.95 (*0-930452-76-3*) Theatre Comm.

Artistic Houses: Being a Series of Interior Views of a Number of the Most Beautiful & Celebrated Homes in the United States with a Description of the Art Treasures Contained Therein. LC 69-18531. (Illus.). 1977. 48.95 (*0-405-08215-0*, Pub. by Blom Pubns UK) Ayer.

Artistic Ingredients of the Longrifle. Joe Kindig, III. LC 88-92711. (Illus.). 102p. 1989. boxed 20.00 (*0-87387-104-9*) Shumway.

***Artistic Integration in Gothic Buildings.** Ed. by Virginia C. Raguin et al. (Illus.). 384p. 1995. 65.00 (*0-8020-0457-1*) U of Toronto Pr.

***Artistic Integration in Gothic Buildings.** Ed. by Virginia C. Raguin et al. (Illus.). 384p. 1995. pap. 24.95 (*0-8020-7477-4*) U of Toronto Pr.

Artistic Intelligences: Implications for Education. Ed. by William J. Moody. 240p. (C). 1990. text ed. 20.95 (*0-8077-3050-5*) Tchrs Coll.

Artistic Landscape Photography. Alfred H. Wall. LC 72-9243. (Literature of Photography Ser.). 1973. reprint ed. 17.95 (*0-405-04947-1*) Ayer.

Artistic Problems of the Italian Renaissance. M. Alpatov. 286p. 1976. 83.00 (*0-317-14222-4*, Pub. by Collets UK) St Mut.

Artistic Reflections of Women. Dell A. Mc Coy. 19.50 (*0-913582-41-7*) Sundance.

Artistic Relations: Literature & the Visual Arts in Nineteenth-Century France. Ed. by Peter Collier & Robert Lethbridge. LC 94-4503. (Illus.). 368p. 1994. 40.00 (*0-300-06009-2*) Yale U Pr.

Artistic Representation of Latin American Diversity: Sources & Collections. Ed. by Barbara J. Robinson. (Illus.). xviii, 518p. (Orig.). 1993. pap. 52.50 (*0-917617-32-0*) SALALM.

Artistic Side of Photography in Theory & Practice. A. J. Anderson. LC 72-9179. (Literature of Photography Ser.). 1978. reprint ed. 28.95 (*0-405-04890-4*) Ayer.

Artistic Strategy & the Rhetoric of Power: Political Uses of Art from Antiquity to the Present. Ed. by David Castriota. LC 85-27764. (Illus.). 280p. (C). 1986. text ed. 27.50 (*0-8093-1289-1*) S Ill U Pr.

Artistic Theory in Italy, 1450-1600. Anthony Blunt. 1962. reprint ed. 17.95 (*0-19-881050-4*) OUP.

***Artistic Touch.** 2nd ed. Christine M. Unwin. (Illus.). 144p. 1994. 29.95 (*0-9642712-0-6*) Creative Art Pr.

Artistic Trickery: The Tradition of Trompe l'Oeil Art. Michael Capek. LC 94-13902. (Art Beyond Borders Ser.). (Illus.). 64p. (YA). (gr. 5 up). 1995. lib. bdg. 21.50 (*0-8225-2064-8*, Lerner Publctns) Lerner Group.

Artistic Unity of the Russian Orthodox Church: Religion, Liturgy, Icons & Architecture. Jane M. De Vyuer. (Illus.). 80p. (Orig.). 1992. pap. 9.95 (*1-881211-01-0*) Firebird Pubs.

Artistic Voyagers: Europe & the American Imagination in the Works of Irving, Allston, Cole, Cooper, & Hawthorne. Joy S. Kasson. LC 81-23743. (Contributions in American Studies: No. 60). (Illus.). xii, 206p. 1982. text ed. 49.95 (*0-313-23089-7*, KAV/) Greenwood.

Artistic Woodturning. Dale L. Nish. LC 80-21302. (Illus.). 288p. 1980. 19.95 (*0-8425-1842-8*); pap. 15.95 (*0-8425-1826-6*) BYU Scholarly.

Artistically Cultivated Herbs. large type ed. Elise Felton. LC 90-12316. (Illus.). 196p. (Orig.). 1990. pap. 14.95 (*0-88007-180-X*) Woodbridge Pr.

Artistocrates. Michel De Saint Pierre. (FRE.). 1978. pap. 11.95 (*0-7859-4059-6*) Fr & Eur.

Artistry & Faith in the Book of Judith. Toni Craven. LC 82-25000. (Society of Biblical Literature Dissertation Ser.). 150p. (C). 1983. pap. 16.95 (*0-89130-612-9*, 06 01 70) Scholars Pr GA.

Artistry in Arms: The Art of Gunsmithing & Gun Engraving. Norton, R. W., Art Gallery Staff. LC 75-164699. (Illus.). 1971. pap. 2.50 (*0-9600182-4-7*) Norton Art.

Artistry in Avian Abodes: The Little Birdhouse Book - A Pot Pourri of Facts, Fun & Fancy. Dorothy F. Weber. (Back Porch Bks.). (Illus.). 64p. (Orig.). 1988. pap. 7.95 (*0-9620905-0-6*) D F Weber.

Artistry in Silver: An Exhibition of Sculpture by Charles M. Russell. Norton, R. W., Art Gallery Staff. LC 78-17945. (Illus.). 1970. pap. 1.00 (*0-9600182-1-2*) Norton Art.

Artistry in Singing: Lieder for the American Singer. G. Griffith. (Illus.). 1966. pap. 16.00 (*0-88431-124-4*) IBD Ltd.

Artistry in Single Action: The Dallas Six Gun. deluxe ed. Halton Henderson. Ed. by Bill Sloan. (Illus.). 125p. 1989. boxed 299.00 (*0-9626336-0-7*) Chama Pr.

Artistry in Teaching. Louis J. Rubin. 182p. (C). 1985. pap. text ed. write for info. (*0-07-554606-X*) McGraw.

Artistry of Aeschylus & Zeami: A Comparative Study of Greek Tragedy & No. Mae J. Smethurst. 507p. 1989. text ed. 57.50 (*0-691-06752-X*) Princeton U Pr.

Artistry of Marian McPartland. Marian McPartland. 1985. pap. 10.95 (*0-89898-415-7*) CPP Belwin.

Artistry of Political Literature: Essays on War, Commitment & Criticism. Holger Klein. LC 93-48022. 292p. 1994. 89.95 (*0-7734-9114-7*) E Mellen.

Artistry of Reconstructive Surgery: Selected Classic Case Studies. Brent. (Illus.). 1052p. 1987. 125.00 (*0-8016-0749-3*) Mosby Yr Bk.

Artistry of Reconstructive Surgery: Selected Classic Case Studies. limited ed. Brent. (Illus.). 1052p. 1987. 650.00 (*0-8016-0987-9*) Mosby Yr Bk.

***Artistry of the Mentally Ill: A Contribution to the Psychology & Psychopathology of Configuration.** Hans Prinzhorn. Tr. by Eric Von Brockdorff. LC 95-18. (ENG & GER.). 1995. 35.00 (*3-211-82639-4*) Spr-Verlag.

Artistry Series of Chess Encyclopedias, 5 vols., Set. E. A. Furst. 1991. 99.75 (*1-879394-05-7*) Caissas Pr.

Artistry: the Work of Artists. V. A. Howard. LC 81-6265. 222p. (C). 1982. 29.95 (*0-915145-06-5*); pap. 12.50 (*0-915145-07-3*) Hackett Pub.

Artists: A Kansas Collection. Patric Rowley. (Illus.). 108p. (YA). (gr. 7-12). 1989. 34.95 (*0-9623079-0-4*) Artists Registry.

***Artists, Advertising & the Borders of Art.** Michele H. Bogart. LC 94-43010. 1994. 48.00 (*0-226-06307-0*) U Ch Pr.

Artists Against War & Fascism: Papers of the First American Artists' Congress. Ed. by Matthew Baigell & Julia Williams. (Illus.). 200p. (C). 1986. 40.00 (*0-8135-1125-9*) Rutgers U Pr.

Artist's Album. Richard N. Matzen, Jr. (Illus.). 48p. (Orig.). 1985. pap. 5.95 (*0-9619926-2-X*) A Mann Enterps.

Artists All: Creativity, the University, & the World. Burton Raffel. 160p. 1991. 23.50 (*0-271-00760-5*) Pa St U Pr.

Artist's Alphabet: A Child's Activity Book for Language, Movement & Painting. Gael Roziere. 28p. (J). (ps-4). 1988. student ed. pap. 5.95 (*0-9619004-2-3*) M Press NM.

Artists & Aesthetics in Spain. Ann Livermore. (Tamesis Bks.). (Illus.). 168p. 1990. 45.00 (*0-7293-0294-6*) Boydell & Brewer.

Artists & Anatomists. A. Hyatt Mayor. 1994. 19.95 (*0-8109-6447-3*) Abrams.

Artists & Architects Collaborate: Designing the Wiesner Building. Robert Campbell & Jeffrey Cruikshank. (Illus.). 94p. (Orig.). 1985. pap. 10.00 (*0-938437-12-7*) MIT List Visual Arts.

Artists & Artisans. Irene M. Franck & David M. Brownstone. (Work Throughout History Ser.). (Illus.). 224p. 1986. 17.95 (*0-8160-1441-8*) Facts on File.

Artists & Artisans in Colorado. Ed. by Peggy Guanella. (Premier Edition Ser.: Vol. 1). (Illus.). 48p. (Orig.). 1988. pap. 6.00 (*0-317-91379-4*) Columbine Expressions.

Artists & Artisans in Delft: A Socio-Economic Study of the Seventeenth Century. John M. Montias. LC 81-11953. (Illus.). 445p. reprint ed. pap. 126.90 (*0-8357-2920-6*, 2039160) Bks Demand.

Artists & Aspects of the Contemporary Art Society of Queensland. Helen Fridemanis. 152p. (C). 1990. pap. 90.00 (*0-86439-127-7*, Pub. by Boolarong Pubns AT) St Mut.

Artist's & Craftsman's Guide to Reducing, Enlarging & Transferring Designs. Rita Weiss. (General Crafts Ser.). 64p. (Orig.). 1983. pap. 3.95 (*0-486-24142-4*) Dover.

Artists & Craftsmen in Central American Antiquities, Calendar Systems, & History. George C. Vaillant. (Illus.). 102p. 1973. reprint ed. 17.50 (*0-87917-037-9*) La Tienda.

Artists & Craftspeople. Arlene Hirschfelder. (American Indian Lives Ser.). (Illus.). 128p. (YA). (gr. 4-11). 1994. 16.95 (*0-8160-2960-1*) Facts on File.

Artists & Galleries in Hawaii. Paul Vogelsberger. (Illus.). 152p. 1994. 34.95 (*1-878101-02-1*) Printech HI.

Artist's & Graphic Designer's Market 1995. Ed. by Mary Cox. 720p. 1994. 23.99 (*0-89879-675-X*) Writers Digest.

Artists & Illustrators of the Old West 1850-1900. Robert Taft. LC 81-47991. (Illus.). 492p. (Orig.). (C). 1982. reprint ed. 65.00x (*0-691-03995-X*); reprint ed. pap. 22.95 (*0-691-00343-2*) Princeton U Pr.

Artists & Patrons: Some Social & Economic Aspects of Chinese Painting. Ed. by Chu-Tsing Li et al. LC 89-2688. (Illus.). 262p. 1991. text ed. 35.00 (*0-685-54317-X*); pap. 24.95 (*0-295-97148-7*) U of Wash Pr.

Artists & Photographic Installations. David R. White. Ed. by Susan Heroy. (Illus.). 16p. (Orig.). 1984. pap. text ed. 4.00 (*0-9613965-0-4*) One-Thousand-Seven-Hundred-&-Eight E.

Artists & Revolution: Dada & the Bauhaus, 1917-1925. Allan C. Greenberg. Ed. by Stephen Foster. LC 79-24156. (Studies in the Fine Arts: The Avant-Garde: No. 4). 300p. reprint ed. 85.00 (*0-8357-1080-7*, 2070312) Bks Demand.

Artists & Their Cats: In Their Own Voices. Ed. by Moore & Navaretta. LC 90-61443. (Illus.). 64p. (Orig.). 1990. pap. text ed. 10.00 (*1-877675-02-4*) Midmarch Arts-WAN.

Artists & Their Films of Modern Hindi Cinema: Cultural & Socio-Political Impact on Society 1931-91, 3 vols., 1. Ram A. Agnihotri. (C). 1992. write for info. (*81-7169-181-1*, Commonwealth) S Asia.

Artists & Their Films of Modern Hindi Cinema: Cultural & Socio-Political Impact on Society 1931-91, 3 vols., 2. Ram A. Agnihotri. (C). 1992. write for info. (*81-7169-182-X*, Commonwealth) S Asia.

Artists & Their Films of Modern Hindi Cinema: Cultural & Socio-Political Impact on Society 1931-91, 3 vols., 3. Ram A. Agnihotri. (C). 1992. write for info. (*81-7169-183-8*, Commonwealth) S Asia.

Artists & Their Films of Modern Hindi Cinema: Cultural & Socio-Political Impact on Society 1931-91, 3 vols., Set. Ram A. Agnihotri. (C). 1992. 110.00 (*81-7169-180-3*, Commonwealth) S Asia.

Artists & Their Friends in England 1700-1799, 2 vols. William T. Whitley. LC 68-56471. (Illus.). 1972. reprint ed. 60.95 (*0-405-09068-4*) Ayer.

Artists & Their Friends in England 1700-1799, 2 vols., 1. William T. Whitley. LC 68-56471. (Illus.). 1972. reprint ed. 30.95 (*0-405-09069-2*) Ayer.

Artists & Their Friends in England 1700-1799, 2 vols., 2. William T. Whitley. LC 68-56471. (Illus.). 1972. reprint ed. 30.95 (*0-405-09070-6*) Ayer.

Artists & Thinkers. Louis W. Flaccus. LC 67-23218. (Essay Index Reprint Ser.). 1977. 19.95 (*0-8369-0444-3*) Ayer.

Artists & Warfare in the Renaissance. John Hale. (Illus.). 288p. (C). 1991. text ed. 65.00 (*0-300-04840-8*) Yale U Pr.

Artists & Writers. Sanford Schwartz. LC 89-29036. (Illus.). 368p. 1990. 24.95 (*1-878274-02-3*); pap. 14.95 (*1-878274-01-5*) Yarrow Pr.

***Artists & Writers Colonies: Retreats, Residencies, & Respites for the Creative Mind.** Gail H. Bowler. (Illus.). 196p. (Orig.). 1995. pap. 15.95 (*0-936085-34-7*) Blue Heron.

Artists & Writers Market List. rev. ed. Ed. by Melanie S. Howard. (Illus.). 30p. 1986. 5.00 (*0-938369-01-6*) Greeting Card Assn.

Artists & Writers Market List, 1991: Greeting Card Creative Network's Artists & Writers' Market List. Ed. by Nancy Riviere & Patricia Farley. 50p. 1991. pap. 25.00 (*0-938369-12-1*) Greeting Card Assn.

Artists Annual Review. Fine Arts Index Staff. 1994. pap. 29.95 (*0-9629816-6-4*) Intl Art Ref.

Artists Anodizing Aluminum. David LaPlantz. LC 87-61000. (Illus.). 200p. (Orig.). 1988. pap. 19.95 (*0-942002-03-2*) Press LaPlantz.

Artists As Illustrators: An International Directory with Signatures & Monograms, 1800-Present. John Castagno. LC 88-34832. (Illus.). 645p. 1989. 127.50 (*0-8108-2168-0*) Scarecrow.

Artists at Gemini G.E.L. Celebrating the 25th Year. Mark Rosenthal. LC 92-43357. 1993. 60.00 (*0-8109-1933-8*) Abrams.

Artists at Work: Twenty-Five Northwest Glassmakers, Ceramists, & Jewelers. Susan Biskeborn & Kim Zumwalt. LC 90-1089. (Illus.). 172p. 1991. pap. 24.95 (*0-88240-405-9*) Alaska Northwest.

Artists Behind the Work: Life Histories of Nick Charles, Sr., Frances Demientieff, Lena Sours, & Jennie Thlunaut. Suzi Jones. (Illus.). 149p. (Orig.). 1986. pap. 17.50 (*0-931163-02-1*) U Alaska Museum.

Artists' Biographies for the Art Reference Guide. Shorewood Staff. 80p. (Orig.). 1986. 15.50 (*0-88185-027-6*) Shorewood Fine Art.

***Artists' Books.** Stephen Bury. (Illus.). 224p. 1995. 85.95 (*1-85928-163-X*, Pub. by Scolar Pr UK) Ashgate Pub Co.

Artists' Books: A Critical Anthology & Sourcebook. 3rd ed. Intro. by Joan Lyons. LC 85-3180. (Research, Fine Arts Ser.). (Illus.). 274p. (C). 1993. reprint ed. pap. text ed. 119.95 (*0-89822-041-6*, N74333A75) Visual Studies.

Artists by Themselves, 4 vols. Rachel Barnes. 1990. Monet. 16.95 (*0-394-58906-8*); Renoir. 16.95 (*0-394-58908-4*); Degas. 16.95 (*0-394-58907-6*) Knopf.

Artists by Themselves: Artists' Portraits from the National Academy of Design. National Academy of Design Staff. LC 83-62156. (Illus.). 176p. 1983. pap. 20.00 (*0-295-96143-0*) U of Wash Pr.

***Artists Colonies Retreats & Study Centers.** Cynthia Navaretta & Donna Marxer. 32p. 1995. 6.00 (*1-877675-17-2*) Midmarch Arts-WAN.

Artist's Complete Guide to Facial Expression. Gary Faigin. (Illus.). 304p. 1990. pap. 35.00 (*0-8230-1628-5*, Watsn-Guptill) Watsn-Guptill.

An Asterisk (*) at the beginning of an entry indicates that the title is appearing in BIP for the first time.

An Asterisk (*) at the beginning of an entry indicates that the title is appearing in BIP for the first time.

465

Arts & Crafts Lessons Anyone Can Teach. M. Elissa Brockley. 237p. 1982. 16.50 (*0-13-047043-0*, Parker Publishing Co) P-H.

Arts & Crafts Metalwork of Janet Payne Bowles. Barry Shifman. (Illus.). 136p. (Orig.). 1994. 34.95 (*0-253-35208-8*) Ind U Pr.

Arts & Crafts Metalwork of Janet Payne Bowles. Barry Shifman. LC 93-77202. (Illus.). 136p. (Orig.). (C). 1993. pap. write for info. (*0-936260-58-0*) Ind Mus Art.

Arts & Crafts Movement. Elizabeth Cumming & Wendy Kaplan. LC 90-70199. (World of Art Ser.). (Illus.). 252p. 1991. pap. 12.95 (*0-500-20248-6*) Thames Hudson.

Arts & Crafts Movement in America, 1876-1916. Robert J. Clark. (C). 1992. pap. 24.95 (*0-691-00294-0*) Princeton U Pr.

Arts & Crafts Movement in California: Living the Good Life. Ed. by Kenneth R. Trapp. LC 92-28352. 1993. 55.00 (*1-55859-393-4*) Abbeville Pr.

Arts & Crafts Movement in the Cotswold. Mary Greensted. (Illus.). 1993. text ed. 34.00 (*0-86299-942-1*) A Sutton Pub.

Arts & Crafts of Ancient China. Ed. by American Womans Club of Shanghai Staff. 1976. lib. bdg. 59.95 (*0-87968-666-9*) Gordon Pr.

Arts & Crafts of Chester County, Pa. Margaret B. Schiffer. LC 80-52028. (Illus.). 285p. 1981. 29.95 (*0-916838-35-8*) Schiffer.

Arts & Crafts of Hawaii: Canoes. Peter Buck & Te Rangi Hiroa. (Special Publication Ser.: No. 45 (6)). (Illus.). 41p. 1957. pap. 7.95 (*0-910240-39-6*) Bishop Mus.

Arts & Crafts of Hawaii: Clothing. Peter Buck & Te Rangi Hiroa. (Special Publication Ser.: No. 45 (5)). (Illus.). 97p. 1957. pap. 7.95 (*0-910240-38-8*) Bishop Mus.

Arts & Crafts of Hawaii: Death & Burial. Peter Buck & Te Rangi Hiroa. (Special Publication Ser.: No. 45 (13)). (Illus.). 26p. 1957. pap. 7.95 (*0-910240-46-9*) Bishop Mus.

Arts & Crafts of Hawaii: Fishing. Peter Buck & Te Rangi Hiroa. (Special Publication Ser.: No. 45 (7)). (Illus.). 78p. 1957. pap. 7.95 (*0-910240-40-X*) Bishop Mus.

Arts & Crafts of Hawaii: Food. Peter Buck & Te Rangi Hiroa. (Special Publication Ser.: No. 45 (1)). (Illus.). 83p. 1957. pap. 7.95 (*0-910240-34-5*) Bishop Mus.

Arts & Crafts of Hawaii: Games & Recreation. Peter Buck & Te Rangi Hiroa. (Special Publication Ser.: No. 45 (8)). (Illus.). 32p. 1957. pap. 7.95 (*0-910240-41-8*) Bishop Mus.

Arts & Crafts of Hawaii: Houses. Peter Buck & Te Rangi Hiroa. (Special Publication Ser.: No. 45 (2)). (Illus.). 52p. 1957. pap. 7.95 (*0-910240-35-3*) Bishop Mus.

Arts & Crafts of Hawaii: Index. Peter Buck & Te Rangi Hiroa. (Special Publication Ser.: No. 45 (14)). 19p. 1957. pap. 7.95 (*0-910240-47-7*) Bishop Mus.

Arts & Crafts of Hawaii: Musical Instruments. Peter Buck & Te Rangi Hiroa. (Special Publication Ser.: No. 45 (9)). 39p. 1957. pap. 7.95 (*0-910240-42-6*) Bishop Mus.

Arts & Crafts of Hawaii: Ornaments & Personal Adornment. Peter Buck & Te Rangi Hiroa. (Special Publication Ser.: No. 45 (12)). (Illus.). 40p. 1957. pap. 7.95 (*0-910240-45-0*) Bishop Mus.

Arts & Crafts of Hawaii: Plaiting. Peter Buck & Te Rangi Hiroa. (Special Publication Ser.: No. 45 (3)). (Illus.). 39p. 1957. pap. 7.95 (*0-910240-36-1*) Bishop Mus.

Arts & Crafts of Hawaii: Religion. Peter Buck & Te Rangi Hiroa. (Special Publication Ser.: No. 45 (11)). (Illus.). 77p. 1957. pap. 7.95 (*0-910240-44-2*) Bishop Mus.

Arts & Crafts of Hawaii: Twined Baskets. Peter Buck & Te Rangi Hiroa. (Special Publication Ser.: No. 45 (4)). (Illus.). 33p. 1957. pap. 7.95 (*0-910240-37-X*) Bishop Mus.

Arts & Crafts of Hawaii: War & Weapons. Peter Buck & Te Rangi Hiroa. (Special Publication Ser.: No. 45 (10)). (Illus.). 57p. 1957. pap. 7.95 (*0-910240-43-4*) Bishop Mus.

Arts & Crafts of India. Nicholas Barnard. (Illus.). 192p. 1994. 34.95 (*1-85029-504-2*, Pub. by Conrad Octopus) Trafalgar.

*__Arts & Crafts of India.__ Nicholas Barnard. (Illus.). 192p. 1995. pap. 24.95 (*1-85029-705-3*, Pub. by Conran Octopus UK) Trafalgar.

Arts & Crafts of India & Ceylon. A. K. Coomaraswamy. (Illus.). xxiv, 265p. 1987. reprint ed. 19.00 (*0-88065-044-3*, Messers Today & Tomorrow) Scholarly Pubns.

Arts & Crafts of Indonesia. Anne Richter. LC 93-10290. (Illus.). 160p. 1994. 35.00 (*0-8118-0454-2*); pap. 22.95 (*0-8118-0481-X*) Chronicle Bks.

Arts & Crafts of Mexico. Chloe Sayer. LC 90-35592. (Illus.). 160p. 1990. 35.00 (*0-87701-781-6*); pap. 19.95 (*0-87701-791-3*) Chronicle Bks.

*__Arts & Crafts of Morocco.__ James F. Jereb. LC 95-13389. 1995. write for info. (*0-8118-1157-3*) Chronicle Bks.

Arts & Crafts of Older Spain. Leonard Williams. 1977. 108.95 (*0-8369-6995-2*, 7872) Ayer.

Arts & Crafts of Rajasthan. Ed. by Aman Nath & Francis Wacziarg. (Illus.). 228p. 1987. 45.00 (*0-295-96465-0*) Mapin International Inc.

*__Arts & Crafts of South America.__ Lucy Davies & Mo Fini. 1995. text ed. 35.00 (*0-8118-0812-2*); pap. 22.95 (*0-8118-0837-8*) Chronicle Bks.

Arts & Crafts of Syria. Johannes Kalter et al. LC 92-80751. (Illus.). 240p. 1993. 45.00 (*0-500-97401-2*) Thames Hudson.

Arts & Crafts of Tamilnadu. Nanditha Krishna. LC 88-82472. (Living Traditions of India Ser.). (Illus.). 176p. 1992. 45.00 (*0-944142-21-4*) U of Wash Pr.

*__Arts & Crafts of Thailand.__ William Warren et al. LC 94-31817. 1996. write for info. (*0-8118-1026-7*); pap. write for info. (*0-8118-1001-1*) Chronicle Bks.

Arts & Crafts of the Cherokee. Rodney L. Leftwich. 160p. 1986. reprint ed. pap. 8.95 (*0-935741-11-9*) Cherokee Pubns.

Arts & Crafts of the Cook Islands. Peter H. Buck. (BMB Ser.: No. 179). 1972. reprint ed. 80.00 (*0-527-02287-X*) Periodicals Srv.

Arts & Crafts of the Swat Valley: Living Traditions in the Hindukush. Johannes Kalter. LC 90-70395. (Illus.). 180p. 1991. 39.95 (*0-500-97384-9*) Thames Hudson.

Arts & Crafts of Torres Strait. David R. Moore. 1989. pap. 25.00 (*0-7478-0007-3*, Pub. by Shire UK) St Mut.

Arts & Crafts of Turkestan. Johannes Kalter. LC 84-51235. (Illus.). 1985. 19.95 (*0-500-97316-4*) Thames Hudson.

Arts & Crafts Studio of Dirk Van Erp. Dorothy Lamoureux. LC 89-61391. (Illus.). 60p. (Orig.). 1989. pap. 15.00 (*1-877742-01-5*) SF Craft & Folk.

*__Arts & Crafts Style.__ Isabelle Anscombe. (Illus.). 240p. 1995. pap. 29.95 (*0-7148-3469-6*, Pub. by Phaidon Press UK) Chronicle Bks.

Arts & Crafts the Year Round, 2 Vols, Set. Ruth Sharon. (Illus.). 1965. 29.00 (*0-8381-0213-1*) United Syn Bk.

Arts & Culture in Taiwan. B. Kaulbach & B. Proksch. (Illus.). 128p. 1984. pap. 25.00 (*0-89986-368-X*) Oriental Bk Store.

Arts & Education Handbook. Ed. by Jonathan Katz. 1987. pap. 12.95 (*0-318-41108-3*) Natl Assem State.

Arts & Entertainment. LC 93-2390. (Picturepedia Ser.). 1993. write for info. (*1-56458-388-0*) Dorling Kindersley.

Arts & Entertainment Fads. Ed. by Frank W. Hoffmann & William G. Bailey. LC 89-24570. (Illus.). 379p. 1990. text ed. 39.95 (*0-86656-881-6*) Haworth Pr.

Arts & Entertainment FADS. Ed. by Frank W. Hoffmann & William G. Bailey. LC 89-24571. (Illus.). 379p. 1990. pap. 14.95 (*0-918393-72-8*) Harrington Pk.

*__Arts & 504: A Handbook for Accessible Arts Programming.__ (Illus.). 112p. (Orig.). (C). 1994. pap. text ed. 29.95x (*0-7881-0817-4*) Diane Pub.

Arts & Higher Education: SRHE Leverhulme V. Ed. by Ken Robinson. 220p. 1982. pap. 21.00 (*0-900868-89-9*, Open Univ Pr) Taylor & Francis.

Arts & Human Development. Howard Gardner. 1994. pap. 16.00 (*0-465-00440-7*) Basic.

*__Arts & Humanities in the Social Studies.__ Douglas Selwyn. LC 94-80080. (NCSS Bulletin Ser.: No. 90). 65p. (Orig.). 1995. pap. 14.95 (*0-87986-064-2*) Nat Coun Soc Studies.

Arts & Humanities under Fire: New Arguments for Government Support. 16p. 1990. pap. text ed. 3.00 (*0-915400-84-7*, ACA Bks) Am Council Arts.

Arts & Humanity: An Introduction to Applied Aesthetics. Ira P. Schwarz. 512p. 1986. pap. text ed. 18.95 (*0-8134-2610-3*) Interstate.

Arts & Ideas. 7th ed. William Fleming. 512p. (C). 1986. pap. text ed. 40.00 (*0-03-071592-X*) HB Coll Pubs.

Arts & Ideas. 8th ed. William Fleming. (C). 1991. pap. text ed. 45.25 (*0-03-040484-3*) HB Coll Pubs.

Arts & Ideas. 9th ed. William Fleming. (Illus.). 656p. (C). 1994. pap. text ed. write for info. (*0-15-501104-9*) HB Coll Pubs.

Arts & Ideas: Student Manual. Laurinda Dixon. 128p. (C). 1993. pap. text ed., spiral bd. 14.95 (*0-8403-8622-2*) Kendall-Hunt.

Arts & Inspiration: Mormon Perspectives. Ed. by Steven P. Sondrup. LC 80-21927. (Illus.). 240p. 1980. pap. 0.50 (*0-8425-1845-2*) BYU Scholarly.

Arts & Media in America: Freedom or Censorship? Ed. by Oliver Trager. (Editorials on File Bk.). 224p. (YA). 1991. 29.95 (*0-8160-2578-9*) Facts on File.

Arts & Personal Growth. Ed. by Malcolm Ross. LC 80-40260. (Curriculum Issues in Arts Education Ser.: Vol. 1). (Illus.). 136p. 1980. 58.00 (*0-08-024714-8*, Pub. by Pergamon Repr UK) Franklin.

*__Arts & Psychotherapy.__ Shaun McNiff. (Illus.). 258p. 1981. pap. 18.95 (*0-398-06277-3*) C C Thomas.

Arts & Psychotherapy. Shaun McNiff. (Illus.). 258p. 1981. 32.95 (*0-398-04112-1*) C C Thomas.

Arts & Public Policy in the U. S. Ed. by W. McNeil Lowry. LC 84-17686. 1984. reprint ed. 7.95 (*0-13-047689-7*) Am Assembly.

Arts & Sciences. Albert Goldbarth. LC 86-12493. (Poetry Ser.). 107p. 1986. 17.95 (*0-86538-056-2*); pap. 8.95 (*0-86538-057-0*) Ontario Rev NJ.

Arts & Sciences: A Sourcebook on Colonial America. Ed. by Carter Smith. (American Albums from the Collections of the Library of Congress). (Illus.). 96p. (J). (gr. 5-8). 1991. lib. bdg. 18.90 (*1-56294-037-6*); pap. 8.95 (*1-878841-67-X*) Millbrook Pr.

Arts & the American Home, 1890-1930. Ed. by Jessica H. Foy & Karal A. Marling. LC 93-32083. (Illus.). 224p. (C). 1994. text ed. 35.00 (*0-87049-825-8*) U of Tenn Pr.

Arts & the Art of Criticism. Theodore M. Greene. LC 73-16391. 690p. 1973. reprint ed. 75.00 (*0-87752-162-X*) Gordian.

Arts & the Basis of Education. Bruce E. Miller. 134p. (Orig.). (C). 1993. lib. bdg. 39.50 (*0-8191-9127-2*); pap. text ed. 17.50 (*0-8191-9128-0*) U Pr of Amer.

Arts & the Handicapped: An Issue of Access. LC 75-27022. (Illus.). 80p. 1975. pap. 4.00 (*0-89192-041-2*) Interbk Inc.

Arts & the World of Business. 2nd ed. Charlotte Georgi. LC 78-12103. 188p. 1979. lib. bdg. 22.50 (*0-8108-1174-X*) Scarecrow.

Arts & Their Interrelations. Ed. by Harry R. Garvin. LC 78-62038. (Bucknell Review Ser.: Vol. 24, No. 2). (Illus.). 186p. 1979. 22.00 (*0-8387-2355-1*) Bucknell U Pr.

Arts & Their Mission. Rudolf Steiner. Tr. by Monges. 125p. 1986. reprint ed. 16.00 (*0-910142-01-7*); reprint ed. pap. 9.95 (*0-685-13521-7*) Anthroposophic.

Arts & 504: A 504 Handbook for Accessible Arts Programming. Betsy Laslett. (Illus.). 101p. 1985. pap. 5.00 (*0-16-004283-6*, S/N 036-000-00047-3) USGPO.

*__Art's Anglo-American Paper Lion: John McLure Hamilton's Untold Story.__ Richard J. Alperin. (Illus.). 461p. 1993. 125.00x (*0-614-04381-6*) Junius Inc.

Art's Anglo-American Paper Lion: John McLure Hamilton's Untold Story. Richard J. Alperin. LC 93-91581. (Illus.). 461p. (C). 1993. lib. bdg. 125.00 (*0-9603932-6-9*) Junius Inc.

Arts As Education. Ed. by Merryl R. Goldberg & Ann Phillips. LC 92-72985. (Reprint Ser.: No. 24). (Illus.). 168p. (Orig.). (C). 1992. pap. 10.95 (*0-916690-26-1*) Harvard Educ Rev.

Arts As Industry: Their Economic Importance to the New York-New Jersey Metropolitan Region. Port Authority of New York & New Jersey Staff et al. (Illus.). 136p. (Orig.). 1983. pap. text ed. 12.00 (*0-912443-00-6*) Alliance Arts.

Arts at a New Frontier: The National Endowment for the Arts. Fannie Taylor & Anthony L. Barresi. (Nonprofit Management & Finance Ser.). 288p. 1984. 49.50 (*0-306-41569-0*, Plenum Pr) Plenum.

Arts at Black Mountain College. Mary E. Harris. (Illus.). 650p. 1989. Paperback published September 1989. pap. 32.50x (*0-262-58100-0*) MIT Pr.

*__Arts Boards: Creating a New Community Equation.__ rev. ed. Nello McDaniel & George Thorn. Ed. by Barbara Carlisle & Shelley Conger. 104p. (C). 1994. pap. text ed. 12.00 (*1-884345-03-4*) ARTS Action.

Arts Compared: An Aspect of Eighteenth-Century British Aesthetics. James S. Malek. LC 74-11088. 176p. reprint ed. pap. 50.20 (*0-7837-3602-9*, 2043467) Bks Demand.

Arts Decoratifs Bordelais: Mobiliers et Objets Domestiques (1714-1895) Jacqueline du Pasquier. 208p. (FRE.). 1993. lib. bdg. 195.00 (*0-7859-3647-5*, 2859171142) Fr & Eur.

*__Arts Education: Beliefs, Practices & Possibilities.__ Ed. by Edward P. Errington. 210p. 1993. pap. 78.00 (*0-949823-35-X*, Pub. by Deakin Univ AT) St Mut.

Arts, Education, & Aesthetic Knowing. Ed. by Bennett Reimer & Ralph A. Smith. (National Society for the Study of Education Publication Ser.). 288p. 1992. 27.50 (*0-226-60158-7*) U Ch Pr.

Arts Education Beyond the Classroom. Ed. by Judith H. Balfe & Joni C. Heine. LC 88-22346. (ACA Arts Research Seminar Series Paper). 104p. (Orig.). 1988. pap. 9.95 (*0-915400-63-4*, 0042, ACA Bks) Am Council Arts.

Arts et les Dieux. deluxe ed. Alain. 1488p. (FRE.). 1979. 110.00 (*0-8288-3412-1*, F80950) Fr & Eur.

Arts Express Teacher's Guide. Ed. by Luralyn Lahr & Harry Hinkle. (Arts Express TV Ser.). 56p. 1983. pap. 3.50 (*0-910475-93-8*) KET.

Arts Festival Planning Guide. Ed. by Robert L. Chapman & Ardath A. Goldstein. iv, 112p. 1975. pap. 3.00 (*0-86526-131-8*) NC Archives.

Arts Festival Work Kit. rev. ed. Pam Korza & Dian Magie. Ed. by Barbara S. Bacon & John Fiscella. (Illus.). 134p. 1988. pap. text ed. 14.95 (*0-945464-02-9*) Univ MA Arts.

Arts for Older Adults: An Enhancement of Life. Donald H. Hoffman. 208p. 1991. text ed. 52.00 (*0-13-048182-3*) P-H.

Arts from the Arctic: An Exhibition of Circumpolar Art by Indigenous from Alaska, Canada, Greenland, Sapmi, Lapland, & Russia. Ed. by Jan Steinbright & Caroline Atuk-Derrick. (Illus.). 80p. 1993. pap. write for info. (*1-883036-00-3*) Inst Alaska.

Arts from the Scholar's Studio Selected Oriental Masterpieces in Painting Lacquer, Glass, Ceramic, Wood, Metal & Stone. Ed. by Susan Ribeiro. (Illus.). 287p. 1988. lib. bdg. 150.00 (*0-7103-0321-1*, Pub. by Kegan Paul Intl UK) Routledge Chapman & Hall.

Arts Graduates, Their Skills & Their Employment: Perspectives for Change. Ed. by Heather Eggins. LC 92-16907. 224p. 1992. 80.00 (*0-7507-0062-9*, Falmer Pr); pap. 33.00 (*0-7507-0063-7*, Falmer Pr) Taylor & Francis.

Arts History. Richard Kostelanetz. 1981. 3.00 (*0-932360-53-X*) Archae Edns.

Arts, Ideas, & Civilization. Jack A. Hobbs & Robert L. Duncan. 272p. (C). 1988. pap. text ed. write for info. (*0-13-048711-2*) P-H.

Arts, Ideas, & Civilization. 2nd ed. Jack A. Hobbs & Robert L. Duncan. 560p. 1991. pap. text ed. 48.00 (*0-13-053562-1*) P-H.

Arts, Ideas & Civilization with Cassette. Jack A. Hobbs & Robert L. Duncan. 272p. 1992. pap. write for info. (*0-13-047888-1*) P-H.

Arts in Boston. Bernard Taper. LC 76-113186. (Joint Center for Urban Studies Publications). 182p. 1970. 22.00 (*0-674-04825-3*); pap. 10.95 (*0-674-04832-6*) HUP.

Arts in Canada: The Last Fifty Years. Ed. by W. J. Keith & B. Z. Shek. (Illus.). 165p. reprint ed. pap. 47.10 (*0-8357-5778-1*, 2020492) Bks Demand.

Arts in Crisis: The National Endowment for the Arts vs. America. Joseph W. Zeigler. LC 93-41465. (Illus.). 184p. 1994. 24.95 (*1-55652-204-5*); pap. 14.95 (*1-55652-203-7*) A cappella Bks.

Arts in Earnest: North Carolina Folklife. Ed. by Daniel Patterson & Charles G. Zugg, III. LC 89-22112. (Illus.). 324p. (Orig.). 1989. lib. bdg. 45.50 (*0-8223-0943-2*); pap. text ed. 20.95 (*0-8223-1021-X*) Duke.

Arts in Education: Some Research Studies. Ed. by Les Tickle. 240p. 1988. lib. bdg. 57.50 (*0-7099-4339-3*, Pub. by Croom Helm UK) Routledge Chapman & Hall.

Arts in Found Places. (Illus.). 140p. 1976. pap. 7.00 (*0-89192-042-0*) Interbk Inc.

Arts in Higher Adult Education: A Second Review of Programs. F. Goldman. 1967. 2.50 (*0-87060-021-4*, REP 117) Syracuse U Cont Ed.

Arts in Higher Education. Ed. by Lawrence E. Dennis & Renata M. Jacobs. LC 68-57442. (Jossey-Bass Higher Education Ser.). 176p. reprint ed. pap. 50.20 (*0-8357-5779-X*, 2013941) Bks Demand.

Arts in Lutheran Higher Education: Conference Proceedings. Ed. by Myron R. Falck. (Illus.). 11p. (Orig.). (C). 1989. pap. 10.00 (*0-943535-02-6*) Primarius Ltd.

Arts in Prehistoric Greece. Sinclair Hood. (Pelican History of Art Ser.). (Illus.). 311p. (C). 1988. reprint ed. pap. text ed. 25.00 (*0-300-05287-1*) Yale U Pr.

Arts in Renewal. Lewis Mumford et al. LC 70-84296. (Essay Index Reprint Ser.). 1977. 18.95 (*0-8369-1121-0*) Ayer.

Arts in Schools: State by State. rev. ed. Music Educators Staff. 104p. 1988. reprint ed. 17.50 (*0-940796-57-0*, 1005) Music Ed Natl.

Arts in Society. Ed. by Robert N. Wilson et al. LC 79-7031. (Perennial Works in Sociology Ser.). 1980. reprint ed. lib. bdg. 31.95 (*0-405-12129-6*) Ayer.

Arts in the Primary School. Glennis Andrews et al. (Library on Aesthetic Education). 224p. 1993. 80.00 (*1-85000-771-3*, Falmer Pr); pap. 30.00 (*1-85000-772-1*, Falmer Pr) Taylor & Francis.

*__Arts in the Religions of the Pacific: Symbols of Life.__ Albert C. Moore. LC 95-6217. (Illus.). 256p. 1995. 45.00 (*0-86187-186-3*, Pub. by Pinter Pubs UK) St Martin.

Arts in the World Economy: Public Policy & Private Philanthropy for a Global Cultural Community. Ed. by Olin Robison et al. LC 94-21200. 192p. 1994. 22.00 (*0-87451-698-6*) U Pr of New Eng.

Arts in the 1970s: Cultural Closure? Ed. by Bart Moore-Gilbert. LC 93-3712. 1993. write for info. (*0-415-09905-6*); pap. write for info. (*0-415-09906-4*) Routledge.

Arts in Theological Education: New Possibilities for Integration. Wilson Yates. LC 87-16701. (Studies in Religion). 207p. 1988. 20.95 (*1-55540-160-0*, 00-08-03); pap. 15.95 (*1-55540-163-5*) Scholars Pr GA.

Arts, Literature, & Society. Ed. by Arthur Marwick. (Social History Society Ser.). (Illus.). 320p. 1990. 87.50 (*0-415-01445-X*, A4567) Routledge.

Arts Management: A Guide to Finding Funds & Winning Audiences. Alvin H. Reiss. 267p. 1992. 45.00 (*0-930807-32-4*, 600321) Fund Raising.

Arts Management Bibliography. rev. ed. Arts Extension Service Staff. 17p. 1988. 3.00 (*0-945464-03-7*) Univ MA Arts.

Arts Management in the Nineties: The Essential Annotated Bibliography. Nik-ki Whittingham. 113p. (Orig.). 1990. pap. 29.95 (*0-915867-04-4*) ENAAQ Pubns.

Arts Management Reader. Alvin H. Reiss. 704p. 1979. 65.00 (*0-8247-6850-7*) Dekker.

Arts Mentor Program: A Manual for Sponsors. Melody Lewis-Kane et al. 58p. 1986. 4.50 (*0-910883-16-5*, 127) Natl Coun Aging.

Arts of Africa, Oceania, & the Americas: Selected Readings. Janet C. Berlo & Lee Anne Wilson. 384p. (C). 1992. pap. text ed. write for info. (*0-13-756230-6*) P-H.

Arts of Alasdair Gray. Ed. by Robert Crawford & Thom Nairn. (Illus.). 200p. 1991. pap. text ed. 29.00 (*0-7486-0294-1*, Pub. by Edinburgh U Pr UK) Col U Pr.

Arts of Beauty: Or, Secrets of a Lady's Toilet, with Hints to Gentlemen on the Art of Fascinating. Lola Montez. LC 77-19081. 1978. reprint ed. 4.95 (*0-912946-52-0*) Ecco Pr.

Arts of Beauty: Or, Secrets of a Lady's Toilet with Hints to Gentlemen on the Art of Fascination. Lola Montez. 125p. 1986. reprint ed. pap. 14.95 (*0-933883-01-3*) Aquarius Rising Pr.

Arts of Black Africa. Jean Laude. Tr. by Jean Decock. LC 71-125165. (African Studies Center, UCLA: No. 1). (Illus.). 1971. pap. 15.00 (*0-520-02358-7*) U CA Pr.

Arts of Black Folks. (Illus.). 1992. 14.95 (*0-87104-426-9*) NY Pub Lib.

Arts of Central Africa: An Annotated Bibliography. Daniel P. Biebuck. (Reference Bks.). 304p. 1987. lib. bdg. 49.00 (*0-8161-8601-4*) G K Hall.

Arts of Cheating, Swindling & Murder. Intro. by Jesse L. Bennett. (Criminology Ser.). 1992. lib. bdg. 82.95 (*0-8490-5307-2*) Gordon Pr.

Arts of Cheating, Swindling & Murder. Douglas Jerrold et al. Ed. by Jesse Lee Bennett. LC 74-10425. (Classics of Crime & Criminology Ser.). (Illus.). 153p. 1975. reprint ed. 16.00 (*0-88355-192-6*) Hyperion Conn.

Arts of China. 3rd ed. Michael Sullivan. LC 82-16027. (Illus.). 320p. (C). 1984. pap. 30.00 (*0-520-04918-7*) U CA Pr.

Arts of Impoverishment: Beckett, Rothko, Resnais. Leo Bersani & Ulysse Dutoit. LC 93-16603. 245p. 1994. 39.95 (*0-674-04875-X*); pap. 19.95 (*0-674-04876-8*) HUP.

Arts of Independence: The DAR Museum Collection. Elisabeth D. Garrett. (Museum Treasures Ser.). (Illus.). 200p. 1985. lib. bdg. 30.00 (*0-9602528-5-1*) Natl Soc DAR.

Arts of India. 5p. 1994. 30.00 (*1-56290-102-8*, 6043) Crystal.

Arts of India: Architecture, Sculpture, Painting, Music, Dance & Handicraft. Krishna Chaitanya. (Illus.). 107p. (C). 1987. 80.00 (*81-7017-209-8*, Pub. by Abhinav II) S Asia.

Arts of India: 1550-1990. Ed. by John Guy & Deborah Swallow. (Illus.). 240p. 1992. pap. 39.95 (*1-85177-022-4*, Pub. by Victoria & Albert Mus UK) Trafalgar.

Arts of Japan, 2 vols., Vol. I: Ancient & Medieval. Seiroku Noma. Tr. by John Rosenfield. LC 65-19186. (Illus.). 305p. 1978. 35.00 (*0-87011-335-6*) Kodansha.

An Asterisk (*) at the beginning of an entry indicates that the title is appearing in BIP for the first time.

An Asterisk (*) at the beginning of an entry indicates that the title is appearing in BIP for the first time.

467

A

Arzt und Heilkunde in den fruhmittelalterlichen Leges: Eine Wort- und Sachkundliche Untersuchung, Vol. 12. Annette Niederhellamnn. 3053p. 1983. 142.35 (3-11-009607-2) De Gruyter.

As: A Surfeit of Similes. Norton Juster. LC 88-8449. (Illus.). 80p. (J). 1989. 15.00 (0-688-08139-8); lib. bdg. 14.93 (0-688-08140-1) Morrow Jr Bks.

AS - 400 Architecture & Application: The Database Machine. Jill T. Lawrence. 1993. pap. text ed. 39.95 (0-471-58141-0) Wiley.

As a Cat Thinketh. Jim Proimos. (Illus.). 168p. (Orig.). 1994. pap. 5.95 (1-56245-089-1) Great Quotations.

As a Child: Safeguarding Children's Rights. Elizabeth D. Shetina. LC 92-9748. (Human Rights Ser.). 1992. 22.60 (0-86593-176-3); 16.95 (0-685-59324-X) Rourke Corp.

As a Child Grows: Reading Level 2-3. 1993. 2.50 (0-88336-511-1) New Readers.

As a Driven Leaf. Milton Steinberg. LC 75-32237. 1939. pap. 12.95x (0-87441-074-6) Behrman.

As a Driven Leaf. Milton Steinberg. LC 87-26981. 480p. 1994. reprint ed. 25.00 (0-87668-994-2) Aronson.

As a Father Loves His Children: The Image of God As Loving Father in Judaism, Christianity, & Islam. Gordon E. Pruett. LC 94-12974. (Catholic Scholars Press). 1994. 34.95 (1-883255-68-6); 54.95 (1-883255-69-4) Intl Scholars.

As a Favor. Susan Dunlap. 1991. mass mkt. 4.99 (0-440-20999-4) Dell.

As a Heron Unsettles a Quiet Pool: Nine Poems for Mary. Tim McNulty. 16p. 1988. 5.00 (1-882623-05-3) Exiled-Am Pr.

As-a-Land. Edie Boyer. 68p. 1982. pap. 6.95 (0-932298-19-2) Tri-State Pr Corp.

As a Last Resort, Read the Directions. Dick Squires. (Family Edition Ser.). (Illus.). 142p. (Orig.). 1990. per., pap. 6.00 (0-9624138-1-X) D Squires.

As a Man Grows Older. Italo Svevo. Tr. by Beryl De Zoete. (Sun & Moon Classics Ser.: No. 25). 245p. (Orig.). 1993. pap. 12.95 (1-55713-128-7) Sun & Moon CA.

As a Man Grows Older. Ettore Schmitz. LC 77-10842. 245p. 1977. reprint ed. text ed. 55.00 (0-8371-9819-4, SCAA, Greenwood Pr) Greenwood.

As a Man Sows, & Other Stories. Grace D. Litchfield. LC 77-160940. (Short Story Index Reprint Ser.). 1977. reprint ed. 23.95 (0-8369-3919-0) Ayer.

As a Man Speaketh, So Is He. Grant Von Harrison. (Personal Enrichment Ser.). 31p. 1989. pap. text ed. 2.95 (0-929985-09-5) Jackman Pubng.

As a Man Thinketh. J. Allen. 1987. 7.95 (0-933062-22-2) R H Sommer.

As a Man Thinketh. James Allen. 1993. pap. 1.49 (1-55748-424-4) Barbour & Co.

As a Man Thinketh. James Allen. 1985. 4.99 (0-915720-20-5) Brownlow Pub Co.

As a Man Thinketh. James Allen. pap. 2.50 (0-87516-000-X) DeVorss.

As a Man Thinketh. James Allen. (Illus.). 64p. 1993. 5.95 (0-681-41865-6) Longmeadow Pr.

As a Man Thinketh. James Allen. LC 77-77691. 1976. text ed. 10.00 (0-912472-21-9) Miller Bks.

As a Man Thinketh. James Allen. 64p. 1989. 1.95 (0-929896-05-X) MindArt Pub.

As a Man Thinketh. James Allen. 1948. 7.99 (0-88088-037-6) Peter Pauper.

As a Man Thinketh. James Allen. 1959. pap. 5.95 (0-399-12829-8, G&D) Putnam Pub Group.

As a Man Thinketh. James Allen. LC 88-43565. (Miniature Editions Ser.). 88p. 1989. 4.95 (0-89471-714-6) Running Pr.

As a Man Thinketh. James Allen. 88p. 1983. pap. 4.50 (0-89540-136-3, SB-136) Sun Pub.

As a Man Thinketh. James Allen. 4.99 (0-529-05908-8, F12); pap. 2.99 (0-529-05906-1, D6) World Bible.

As a Man Thinketh, Vol. 2. James Allen. Ed. by James H. Fedor. 148p. 1988. pap. 7.95 (0-929896-00-9) MindArt Pub.

As a Man Thinketh see Treasury of Christian Classics

As a Man Thinketh Journal. James Allen. Ed. by Running Press Staff. (Illus.). 96p. (Orig.). 1992. pap. 5.95 (1-56138-093-8) Running Pr.

As a Roaring Lion. Michael K. Sartin. Ed. by Lord of Host Books Staff. 200p. (Orig.). 1991. pap. text ed. 11.95 (0-9629558-0-9) First Pentecstl LA.

***As a Seal upon Your Heart: The Life of St. Paul of the Cross Founder of the Passionists.** Paul F. Spencer. 200p. 1992. pap. 24.95 (0-85439-485-0, Pub. by St Paul Pubns UK) St Mut.

As a Strong Bird on Pinions Free & Other Poems. Walt Whitman. 1971. 59.95 (0-87968-667-7) Gordon Pr.

As a Woman Thinketh. James Allen & Dorothy Hulst. 62p. (Orig.). 1982. pap. 2.50 (0-87516-483-8) DeVorss.

As above, So Below: Paths to Spiritual Renewal in Daily Life. New Age Journal Editors & Ronald S. Miller. 346p. (Orig.). 1992. pap. 14.95 (0-87477-659-7) J P Tarcher.

As Ancient Is This Hostelry: The Story of the Wayside Inn. Alison Ridley & Curtis F. Garfield. (Illus.). 338p. (Orig.). (YA). (gr. 7 up). 1989. reprint ed. pap. 15.00 (0-9621976-0-2) Porcupine Enter.

A's & B's of Academic Scholarships, 1995-96. 17th ed. Debra Wexler. 1994. pap. 7.00 (0-945981-85-6, TN7673) Octameron Assocs.

***A's & B's of Academic Scholarships, 1996-97.** 18th ed. 1995. pap. 7.50 (0-945981-97-X, TN772818) Octameron Assocs.

As Angels of Light. Rose Johnson & Don Ratzlaff. LC 80-82926. (Illus.). 143p. (Orig.). 1980. pap. 2.95 (0-937364-00-2) Kindred Prods.

As Battles Raged. Elizabeth Aspril. (Illus.). (Orig.). 1981. 12.95 (0-9604750-1-X); pap. 7.95 (0-9604750-0-1) E Keys.

As Befits a Legend: Building a Tomb for Napoleon, 1840-1861. Michael P. Driskel. LC 93-12099. (Illus.). 280p. 1994. lib. bdg. 32.00 (0-87338-484-9) Kent St U Pr.

As Big As a Whale. Melvin Berger. (Ranger Rick Science Spectacular Ser.). 16p. (J). (gr. 2-4). 1993. pap. 14.95 (1-56784-201-1) Newbridge Comms.

As Bill Sees It: Selected Writings of the A. A.'s Co-Founder. LC 87-402899. 332p. 1967. 3.35 (0-916856-03-8) AAWS.

As Bill Sees It - Como lo ve Bill. rev. ed. Alcoholics Anonymous World Services, Inc. Staff. (SPA.). 1993. 2.50 (0-916856-54-2) AAWS.

As Birds Flying: Jerusalem - Nineteen Seventeen. Andrew Adams. Ed. by E. Raymond. LC 91-76731. (Illus.). 160p. (Orig.). 1993. pap. 7.00 (0-934666-45-8) Artisan Sales.

As Boys Become Men: Learning New Male Roles. Doug Cooper Thompson. 81p. 1985. pap. 9.95 (0-8290-1591-4) Irvington.

As Bread That Is Broken. Peter G. Van Breemen. 1974. pap. 11.95 (0-87193-052-8) Dimension Bks.

As Built with Second Thoughts, Reforming What Was Old. David McCord. pap. 2.00 (0-686-70266-2) Boston Public Lib.

As Burns Said.... Arnold O'Hara. (C). 1988. 30.00 (0-907526-30-6, Alloway Pub) St Mut.

As by a New Pentecost. Patti G. Mansfield. 179p. 1992. pap. 9.95 (0-940535-44-0, UP 144) Franciscan U Pr.

As by Fire. Bertha B. Moore. 325p. 1977. reprint ed. lib. bdg. 14.95 (0-89966-277-3) Buccaneer Bks.

As Canadian As ... Possible ... under the Circumstances! Linda Hutcheon. 53p. (C). 1990. pap. text ed. 7.00 (1-55022-118-3, Pub. by ECW Press CN) Genl Dist Srvs.

As China Sees the World: Perceptions of Chinese Scholars. Ed. by Harish Kapur. LC 87-12845. 247p. 1987. text ed. 45.00 (0-312-00915-1) St Martin.

As Clean As a Whistle. Mary R. Palmer. LC 90-70148. 48p. (J). (ps-4). 1990. pap. 5.95 (0-932433-66-9) Windswept Hse.

***As Climate Changes: International Impacts & Implications.** Ed. by Kenneth M. Strzepek & Joel B. Smith. (Illus.). 340p. (C). 1995. write for info. (0-521-46224-X); pap. write for info. (0-521-46796-9) Cambridge U Pr.

As Cool As a Cucumber. Jaine Rodack. Ed. by Ellen Rolfes. (Something to Talk about Ser.). 96p. (J). (gr. k-6). 1993. spiral bd. 5.95 (1-879958-19-8) Tradery Hse.

As Daisies Do. Phillip Huntley-Franck. Ed. by James B. Van Treese. 300p. 1994. pap. 8.95 (1-56901-076-5) NW Pub.

As Ding Saw Hoover. Jay N. Darling. Ed. by John M. Henry. LC 54-11723. 139p. reprint ed. pap. 39.70 (0-8357-5780-3, 2000454) Bks Demand.

A's Dream. Aaron Shurin. LC 88-63269. 96p. 1989. 8.00 (0-929022-04-1) O Bks.

As Dreams Are Made On: Previews of the Human Mind. David P. Pace & E. C. Barksdale. LC 87-91102. 1988. 18.95 (0-87212-209-3) Libra.

As Eagles Fly. Barbara Cartland. 16.95 (0-685-10840-6, Am Repr) Amereon Ltd.

As Easy As One, Two, Three: A Mostly Macrobiotic Cookbook. Pamela Henkel & Lee Koch. Ed. by Laurel Ruggles. LC 90-82651. 127p. (Orig.). 1990. pap. 6.95 (0-918860-51-2) G Ohsawa.

As Easy As Pie. Susan G. Purdy. (Illus.). 448p. 1990. reprint ed. pap. 14.95 (0-02-036080-0, Collier S&S) S&S Trade.

As Ever. Jane Weinberger. LC 90-70519. (Illus.). 310p. (Orig.). 1991. pap. 9.95 (0-932433-74-X) Windswept Hse.

As Ever: The Collected Correspondence of Allen Ginsberg & Neal Cassady. Ed. by Barry Gifford. LC 77-82182. 275p. 1977. 15.00 (0-916870-09-X); pap. 5.95 (0-916870-08-1) Creat Arts Bk.

As Ever, Gene: The Letters of Eugene O'Neill to George Jean Nathan. Ed. by Nancy L. Roberts & Arthur W. Roberts. LC 86-45800. (Illus.). 248p. 1987. 42.50 (0-8386-3303-X) Fairleigh Dickinson.

As Evil Does. John Tigges. 384p. (Orig.). 1987. pap. 3.95 (0-8439-2521-3) Dorchester Pub Co.

As Far As Blood Goes. Rochelle N. Schwab. (Orig.). 1988. pap. 3.50 (0-87067-837-X) Holloway.

As Far As I Can See.... Frances Weaver. (Illus.). (Orig.). 1989. pap. 7.95 (0-9617930-3-1) Midlife Musings.

As Far as I Can See. Frances Weaver. (Illus.). 140p. (Orig.). 1989. pap. text ed. 7.95 (0-8431-2901-8) Midlife Musings.

As Far as I Can See: Contemporary Writing of the Middle Plains. Illus. by Robert L. Hanna. 242p. (Orig.). 1989. pap. 9.95 (0-931534-11-9) Windflower Pr.

As Far As Republican Principles Will Admit: Essays by Martin Diamond. Ed. by William A. Schambra. 412p. (C). 1991. 19.95 (0-8447-3784-4, AEI Pr) Am Enterprise.

As Far As the Eye Can See. David Brill. LC 90-45387. (Illus.). 190p. (C). 1990. 14.95 (1-55853-073-8) Rutledge Hill Pr.

As Far As You Can Go Without a Passport: Views from the End of the Road. Tom Bodett. 160p. 1986. pap. 10.58 (0-201-10673-6) Addison-Wesley.

As Far Away As China. Jay Boyer. LC 88-93039. 78p. (C). 1989. 8.95 (0-923707-02-6) Pratt CO.

As Fine As Melanctha (Nineteen Fourteen to Nineteen Thirty), Vol. Four Of Unpublished Works Of Gertrude Stein I. Gertrude Stein. LC 72-103661. (Select Bibliographies Reprint Ser.). 1980. 30.95 (0-8369-5161-1) Ayer.

As for Love: Poems & Translations. Macha L. Rosenthal. 64p. 1987. pap. 11.95 (0-19-505268-4) OUP.

***As for Me & My House.** Dolores Hayford. 1995. 12.99 (0-88419-389-6, Creation Hse) Strang Comms Co.

As for Me & My House. Lou Priolo. 228p. 1992. pap. 2.99 (0-88368-245-1) Whitaker Hse.

As for Me & My House. Emma L. Thayne. 8.95 (0-88494-716-5) Bookcraft Inc.

As for Me & My House: Some Redemptive Words for the Black Family. Alvin C. Bernstine. LC 94-10332. 1994. 8.95 (0-910683-24-7) Townsnd-Pr.

As for the Sky, Falling: A Critical Look at Psychiatry & Suffering. Supeene. (NFS Canada). Date not set. pap. 14.95 (0-929005-09-0, Pub. by Second Story Pr CN) InBook.

As for Us. David Gollub. 32p. (Orig.). 1989. pap. 3.00 (0-929730-16-X) Zeitgeist Pr.

***AS/400: Systems, Utilities, Database & Programming.** Geoge Lin & Gayla Stewart. LC 95-15988. 1995. text ed. 49.00 (0-13-382060-2) P-H.

AS-400 Budget Benchmarks. Elms Information Services Group Staff. (Illus.). 208p. (Orig.). Date not set. pap. 95.00 (0-685-70190-5) Elms Info Servs.

AS-400 CL by Example. Virgil Green. (By Example Ser.). (Illus.). 900p. (Orig.). 1995. pap. 119.00 (1-884322-19-0) Comp Applicatns.

***AS-400 Companion.** John Enck & Michael Ryan. (Illus.). 147p. (C). 1994. pap. text ed. 19.00 (1-878956-45-0) CBM Bks.

***AS-400 Data Management Fundamentals.** Robert W. Janson. LC 95-2330. 1995. write for info. (0-7895-0045-0) Boyd & Fraser.

AS-400 Programming. Bernard Coydon. LC 94-20005. 1994. write for info. (0-07-707745-8) McGraw.

***AS-400 Security in a Client-Server Environment.** Joseph S. Park. (Wiley Technical Communication Library). Date not set. pap. text ed. 39.95 (0-471-11683-1) Wiley.

AS-400 System Administration Guide. Jesse Gamble & Bill Merrow. 1994. text ed. 45.00 (0-07-022798-5) McGraw.

AS-Four Hundred Utilities Handbook. Louise Van Osdol. 1994. pap. text ed. write for info. (0-07-047986-0) McGraw.

As Free as an Eagle: The Inmate's Family Survival Guide. Daniel J. Bayse. 235p. (Orig.). 1991. pap. 16.75 (0-929310-63-2) Am Correctional.

As from Kemmel Hill: An Adjutant in France & Flanders, 1917 & 1918. Arthur Behrend. LC 75-3861. (Illus.). 176p. 1975. reprint ed. text ed. 39.75 (0-8371-8087-2, BEKH, Greenwood Pr) Greenwood.

As God Is My Witness. Gloria D. Benish. 118p. (Orig.). 1993. pap. 9.95 (0-9636100-0-7) Miracle MT.

As God Is My Witness. Carl Rosenberg. Ed. by Sol Lewis. LC 90-55237. (Illus.). 146p. 1991. 20.95 (0-89604-142-5); pap. 10.95 (0-89604-143-3) Holocaust Pubns.

As God Made Them: Portraits of Some Nineteenth-Century Americans. Gamaliel Bradford. (BCL1 - U. S. History Ser.). 294p. 1991. reprint ed. lib. bdg. 79.00 (0-7812-6028-0) Rprt Serv.

As Good As a Yarn with You: Letters Between Miles Franklin, Katharine Susannah Prichard, Jean Devanny, Marjorie Barnard, Flora Eldershaw & Eleanor Dark. Ed. by Carole Ferrier. (Illus.). 448p. (C). 1992. 74.95 (0-521-39314-0) Cambridge U Pr.

As Good As Any: Foreign Correspondence on American Radio, 1930-1940. David H. Hosley. LC 83-12730. (Contributions to the Study of Mass Media & Communications Ser.: No. 2). (Illus.). 165p. 1984. text ed. 45.00 (0-313-23782-4, HOG/) Greenwood.

As Good As Gold: Grand Prize Recipes from America's Cooking Contests. Linda Davis-O'Brien. LC 92-96945. 224p. 1993. Comb bdg. spiral bd. 16.95 (0-9634470-0-9) L Davis-OBrien.

As Grain Once Scattered: The History of Christ Episcopal Church Savannah, GA. Roger Warlick & Edward H. Morgan. (Illus.). 224p. 1987. 35.00 (0-9619270-0-3) Christ Episcopal.

As Grandfather Told Me. Ugadali. 1980. 4.95 (0-89992-076-4) Coun India Ed.

As Green As Emeraude: Collected Poems of Margo Skinner. Margo Skinner. 106p. (Orig.). 1990. pap. 15.00 (0-939790-04-1) Dawn Heron.

As Her Whimsey Took Her: Critical Essays on the Work of Dorothy L. Sayers. Ed. by Margaret P. Hannay. LC 79-10933. 319p. reprint ed. pap. 91.00 (0-7837-0576-X, 2040920) Bks Demand.

As I Am. 250p. (Orig.). 1988. pap. write for info. (1-55672-031-9) US HHS.

As I Crossed a Bridge of Dreams: Recollections of a Woman in Eleventh-Century Japan. Tr. & Intro. by Ivan Morris. 176p. 1989. pap. 7.95 (0-14-044282-0, Penguin Classics) Viking Penguin.

***As I Grow.** Helene Rothschild. LC 94-68702. 30p. 1994. pap. 3.95 (1-56875-092-7, 092-7) R & E Pubs.

***As I Have Loved You.** Kitty Deruyter. LC 94-33538. 1994. 13.95 (1-55503-707-0) Covenant Comms.

As I Have Loved You: Challenge of Christian Ethics. James P. Hanigan. 240p. (Orig.). 1986. pap. 12.95 (0-8091-2734-2) Paulist Pr.

As I Have Loved You: The Life of Catherine de Hueck Doherty. Omer Tanghe. Tr. by Robert Wild. 121p. (Orig.). 1988. pap. 9.95 (1-85390-055-9, Pub. by Veritas Pubns IE) Irish Bks Media.

As I Knew Them: Memoirs of James E. Watson. James E. Watson. (American Biography Ser.). 330p. 1991. reprint ed. lib. bdg. 79.00 (0-7812-8404-X) Rprt Serv.

As I Knew Them; Presidents & Politics from Grant to Coolidge, 2 vols., Set. Henry L. Stoddard. (American Biography Ser.). 1991. reprint ed. lib. bdg. 148.00 (0-7812-8367-1) Rprt Serv.

As I Lay Dying. Faulkner. (Book Notes Ser.). 1985. pap. 2.50 (0-8120-3502-X) Barron.

As I Lay Dying. William Faulkner. Ed. by Josef Blotner et al. (William Faulkner Manuscripts). 1987. lib. bdg. 65.00 (0-8240-6809-2) Garland.

As I Lay Dying. William Faulkner. 1964. 22.00 (0-394-41581-7) Random.

As I Lay Dying. William Faulkner. LC 90-50261. (Vintage International Ser.). 288p. 1991. pap. 9.00 (0-679-73225-X, Vin) Random.

As I Lay Dying. Anno. by Dianne C. Luce. (William Faulkner Annotations to Novels Ser.). 150p. 1990. 15.00 (0-8240-4233-6) Garland.

As I Lay Dying: Stories Out of Stories. Warwick Wadlington. LC 92-18053. (Masterwork Studies: No. 102). 200p. 1992. text ed. 21.95 (0-8057-8070-X, Twayne); pap. 12.95 (0-8057-8115-3, Twayne) Macmillan.

As I Lay Dying see Novels, 1930-1935

As I Lay Dying Notes. James Roberts. 1969. pap. 3.95 (0-8220-0210-8) Cliffs.

***As I Please: Selected Writings 1975-94.** Salleh B. Joned. (Skoob Pacifica Ser.). 1995. pap. 11.95 (1-871438-29-2) Atrium Pubs.

As I Recall: Sources in Western Civilization (Renaissance to the Present) 2nd ed. Kenneth Ostrand. 284p. (C). 1992. pap. text ed. 32.00 (0-9627173-5-5) Intl Horizons.

As I Recall: Sources in Western Civilization (to the Renaissance) 2nd ed. Kenneth Ostrand. 300p. (C). 1992. pap. text ed. 32.00 (0-9627173-4-7) Intl Horizons.

As I Recall...Sources in Western Civilization: Ancient Times to the Renaissance, Vol. 1. Kenneth D. Ostrand. 212p. (C). 1989. pap. text ed. 18.00 (0-318-41279-9) Le Storti Graphics.

As I Recall...Sources in Western Civilization, Vol. 2: Renaissance to Napoleon. Kenneth D. Ostrand. 164p. 1989. pap. text ed. 18.00 (0-317-01806-X) Le Storti Graphics.

As I Remember. Nina Swida. 60p. (Orig.). 1987. pap. text ed. 5.00 (0-930401-10-7) Artex Pub.

As I Remember. Arnold Benthe. Ed. by Robert A. Sobieszek & Peter C. Bunnell. LC 76-24684. (Sources of Modern Photography Ser.). (Illus.). 1979. reprint ed. lib. bdg. 35.95 (0-405-09660-7) Ayer.

As I Remember. Arnold Genthe. 1992. reprint ed. lib. bdg. 75.00 (0-7812-5037-4) Rprt Serv.

As I Remember: A Barge from Corregidor, a March from Bataan, a Fence of Cabanatuan. Edward E. Thomas. (Illus.). 280p. 1990. pap. 24.95 (0-9626789-0-2) E E Thomas.

As I Remember Baby Album: Remembering My 1st Years. Ed. by Kenn Hayes. 48p. 1993. 14.99 (0-529-07525-3) World Bible.

As I Remember Fordham: Selections from the Sesquicentennial Oral History Project. Office of the Sesquicentennial Fordham University Staff. LC 91-61628. 208p. 1991. 20.00 (0-8232-1338-2) Fordham.

***As I Remember Him.** Hans Zinsser. (American Autobiography Ser.). 443p. 1995. reprint ed. lib. bdg. 99.00 (0-7812-8671-9) Rprt Serv.

As I Remember Him: The Biography of R. S. Hans Zinsser. 11.75 (0-8446-0975-7) Peter Smith.

As I Remember It. Stanley Eskew. 1982. pap. 6.00 (0-941092-05-4) Mtn St Pr.

As I Remember It: A Detailed Description of the North Family of the Watervliet, N. Y. Shaker Community. Trudy R. Sherburne. (Illus.). (Orig.). (J). (gr. 5-10). 1987. pap. 4.95 (0-944178-00-6) World Shaker.

As I Remember Them. Galina Von Meck. (Illus.). 19.95 (0-89182-041-8) Charles River Bks.

As I Saw It. John J. McIntire. 1977. 18.95 (0-8369-9189-3, 9058) Ayer.

As I Saw It. Dean Rusk & Richard Rusk. Ed. by Daniel S. Papp. 672p. 1990. 29.95 (0-393-02650-7) Norton.

As I Saw It: The Tragedy of Hungary. Geza Lakatos. Tr. by Mario D. Fenyo. Orig. Title: Ahony en Lattam. (Illus.). 250p. 1993. write for info. (0-318-72265-8) Universe Pub Co.

As I See It. Donald F. Barnes. LC 91-62779. 262p. (Orig.). 1991. 39.95 (0-87218-496-X) Natl Underwriter.

As I See It. John H. Lounsbury. 102p. (Orig.). 1991. pap. text ed. 14.00 (1-56090-058-X) Natl Middle Schl.

As I See It: Contemporary Issues. Ed. by Henry R. Rust. 96p. (Orig.). 1991. pap. 10.95 (1-877871-21-4, 3542) Ed Ministries.

As I See It: Radial Keratotomy Before, During & After Surgery. Raymond J. Munna. (Illus.). 110p. 1986. pap. 9.95 (0-935669-07-8) A Granite Pubs.

As I See Religion. Harry E. Fosdick. LC 75-11835. 201p. 1975. reprint ed. text ed. 52.50 (0-8371-8142-9, FOAI, Greenwood Pr) Greenwood.

***As I See the World Today.** Simon Leong. 1994. pap. 6.95 (0-533-10937-X) Vantage.

As I Skillbooklet. Barbara J. Crane. (Crane Reading System-English Ser.). (Illus.). (gr. k-2). 1982. pap. text ed. 2.49 (0-89075-027-0) Bilingual Ed Serv.

As I Think. James Allen. Ed. by Art W. Christensen. 62p. 1991. 7.95 (0-87516-636-9) DeVorss.

***As I Walked Out One Evening.** W. H. Auden. 1995. pap. 12.00 (0-679-76170-5) Random.

As I Was Crossing Boston Common. Norma Farber. LC 75-6520. (Illus.). 32p. (J). (ps-2). 1991. reprint ed. 14.95 (0-525-25960-0, DCB) Dutton Child Bks.

As I Was Going Down Sackville Street. Oliver S. Gogarty. LC 75-41113. reprint ed. 34.50 (0-404-14715-1) AMS Pr.

As I Was Saying. Horace J. Bridges. LC 70-121451. (Essay Index Reprint Ser.). 1977. 21.95 (0-8369-1698-0) Ayer.

As I Was Saying. Gilbert K. Chesterton. LC 67-22085. (Essay Index Reprint Ser.). 1977. 19.95 (0-8369-0295-5) Ayer.

An Asterisk (*) at the beginning of an entry indicates that the title is appearing in BIP for the first time.

An Asterisk (*) at the beginning of an entry indicates that the title is appearing in BIP for the first time.

469

As Unions Mature: An Analysis of the Evolution of American Unionism. Richard A. Lester. 1958. pap. 11. 95x (0-691-02800-1) Princeton U Pr.

***As Unions Mature: An Analysis of the Evolution of American Unionism.** Richard A. Lester. LC 58-10048. reprint ed. pap. 52.20 (0-7837-9373-1, 2060117) Bks Demand.

As Various As Their Land. Stephanie G. Wolf. (Illus.). 320p. 1994. pap. 13.00 (0-06-092537-X, PL) HarpC.

As We Are. Don Clark. LC 87-72880. 180p. (Orig.). 1988. pap. 7.95 (1-55583-127-3) Alyson Pubns.

As We Are Now. May Sarton. 136p. 1973. 10.95 (0-393-08372-1) Norton.

As We Are Now. May Sarton. 128p. 1992. pap. 7.95 (0-393-30957-6) Norton.

As We Drifted & Other Poems. Robert Brandts. LC 72-87039. 1972. pap. 3.00 (0-87922-013-9) Christophers Bks.

As We Forgive Our Debtors: Bankruptcy & Consumer Credit in America. Teresa A. Sullivan et al. (Illus.). 384p. 1989. 29.95 (0-19-505578-0) OUP.

As We Forgive Our Debtors: Bankruptcy & Consumer Credit in America. Teresa A. Sullivan et al. (Illus.). 384p. 1991. reprint ed. pap. 11.95 (0-19-507004-6) OUP.

As We Go Marching. John T. Flynn. LC 79-172212. (Right Wing Individualist Tradition in America Ser.). 1972. reprint ed. 20.95 (0-405-00421-4) Ayer.

As We Know. John Ashbery. (Poet Ser.). 1986. pap. 15.00 (0-14-058591-5, Penguin Bks) Viking Penguin.

As We Live & Breathe: The Challenge of Our Environment. Ed. by Donald J. Crump. LC 74-151945. (Special Publications Series 6: No. 2). (Illus.). 1971. 12.95 (0-87044-097-7) Natl Geog.

As We Lived - Stories Told by Black Story Tellers. Jakie L. Pruett & Everett B. Cole. 1982. 9.95 (0-89015-309-4) Sunbelt Media.

As We Remember Zion. E. Alterman. Date not set. 25.00 (0-06-017041-7, HarpT) HarpC.

***As We Saw the Thirties: Essays on Social & Political Movements of a Decade.** Ed. by Rita J. Simon. LC 66-15475. 261p. 1967. reprint ed. pap. 74.40 (0-7837-8088-5, 2047841) Bks Demand.

As We Saw Them: The First Japanese Embassy to the United States (1860) Masao Miyoshi. Ed. by John Urda. (Illus.). 232p. 1994. pap. 13.00 (1-56836-028-2) Kodansha.

As We Saw Them: The First Japanese Embassy to the United States (1860) Masao Miyoshi. LC 78-62851. (Illus.). 244p. reprint ed. pap. 69.60 (0-7837-4841-8, 2044488) Bks Demand.

As We See It from Here, Vol. IV. Jesse H. Holmes. LC 79-90910. (Life's Energy Fields Ser.). (Illus.). 146p. 1980. 9.75 (0-935436-03-0) Metascience.

As We See Ourselves: A Look at Latin America by Latin Americans. Ed. by George Kilpatrick. 74p. 1985. pap. 4.00 (0-317-43432-2) Tulane Lat Am Lib.

As We Seek God: International Reflections on Contemporary Benedictine Monasticism. Ed. by Stephanie Campbell. (Cistercian Studies: No. 70). 1983. pap. 7.95 (0-685-01092-9) Cistercian Pubns.

As We Understood. Al-Anon Family Group Headquarters, Inc. Staff. LC 85-71379. 269p. 1985. 7.50 (0-910034-56-7) Al-Anon.

As We Went Marching On: A Story of the War. George W. Hosmer. LC 78-164567. (American Fiction Reprint Ser.). 1977. reprint ed. 25.95 (0-8369-7044-6) Ayer.

As We Were: Life in America 1814. Gaillard Hunt. 300p. 1993. pap. 14.95 (0-936399-54-6) Berkshire Hse.

As We Were: The Story of Old Elizabethtown, Vol. 13. Theodore Thayer. (Illus.). 280p. 1964. 20.00 (0-686-81820-2) NJ Hist Soc.

As We Were Told: (A Written & Oral History) 2nd rev. ed. Ed. by Jane Stenzel. LC 91-74028. (Illus.). 409p. (C). 1991. 40.00 (0-9626377-7-7) Coarsegold Hist Soc.

As Wind to Fire. large type ed. Jane A. Julian. 480p. 1992. 21.95 (0-7089-2628-2) Ulverscroft.

A's with Ease. Carlita Faxton. 52p. Date not set. pap. write for info. (0-9636553-3-7) C Faxton.

As Years Go By: The Sixties Revolution at British Decca. David Wedgbury & John Tracy. (Illus.). 112p. 1994. pap. 19.95 (1-85793-007-X, Pub. by Pavilion UK) Trafalgar.

***As Years Go By (Showcase)** Margaret Chittenden. 1995. mass mkt. 3.75 (0-373-70666-9) Harlequin Bks.

As You & the Abused Person Journey Together. Sharon E. Cheston. LC 94-30804. (Illumination Bks.). 80p. 1994. pap. 3.95 (0-8091-3513-2) Paulist Pr.

As You Believe. Barbara Dewey. LC 85-70370. (Illus.). 208p. 1989. pap. 14.95 (0-933123-03-5) Bartholomew Bks.

***As You Believe.** Herman Granberry. 390p. 1995. pap. 9.95 (1-56901-702-6) NW Pub.

As You Can See in the Text...Which Passages Do Literary Scholars Quote & Interpret in "Gulliver's Travels?" "Quotation Analysis" As an Aid to Understanding Comprehension Processes of Longer & Difficult Texts. Klaus Zollner. Ed. by Jurgen Klein. (Aspekte der Englischen Geistes- und Kulturgeschichte Ser.: Vol. 19). 349p. 1989. pap. 49.80 (3-631-40696-7) P Lang Pubs.

As You Desire. Madeline Moore. LC 93-84275. 180p. (Orig.). 1993. pap. 9.95 (0-933216-95-5) Spinsters Ink.

***As You Eat, So Your Baby Grows.** rev. ed. Nikki Goldbeck. (Illus.). 16p. 1994. 2.50 (0-9606138-8-9) Ceres Pr.

As You Eat So Your Baby Grows: A Guide to Nutrition in Pregnancy. Nikki Goldbeck. (Illus.). 24p. (C). 1978. pap. 2.00 (0-9606138-9-7) Ceres Pr.

As You Go. Waylon Bailey. LC 81-47888. 118p. (Orig.). 1981. pap. 4.00 (0-914520-15-6) Insight Pr.

As You Leave Home. Jerry B. Jenkins. LC 92-33485. 1993. write for info. (1-56179-132-6) Focus Family.

As You Like It. (New Swan Shakespeare Ser.). 1989. pap. 2.95 (0-582-52725-2) Longman.

As You Like It. Ed. by Alan Brissenden. LC 92-8422. (Oxford Shakespeare Ser.). (C). 1993. 55.00 (0-19-812948-3, Clarendon Pr) OUP.

As You Like It. Adapt. by I. E. Clark. (Illus.). 41p. 1967. pap. 10.00 (0-88680-007-2); pap. 2.00 (0-88680-006-4) I E Clark.

As You Like It. Richard Knowles. (New Variorum Edition of Shakespeare Ser.: Vol. 28). xxviii, 737p. 1977. 40.00 (0-87352-278-8, Z36) Modern Lang.

As You Like It. M. H. Publications Staff. 170p. 1990. 95.00 (1-872680-11-9, Pub. by M H Pubns UK) St Mut.

As You Like It. Ed. by A. L. Rowse. LC 84-15393. (Contemporary Shakespeare Ser.: Vol. II). 108p. (Orig.). 1985. pap. text ed. 3.45 (0-8191-3914-9) U Pr of Amer.

As You Like It. Shakespeare. (BBC Television Plays Ser.). 1978. pap. 4.95 (0-563-17614-8, Pub. by BBC UK) Parkwest Pubns.

As You Like It. William Shakespeare. (Airmont Shakespeare Ser.). (J). (gr. 10 up). 1965. pap. 1.25 (0-8049-1006-5, S-6) Airmont.

As You Like It. William Shakespeare. (Classics Ser.). 1988. pap. 3.50 (0-553-21290-7, Bantam Classics) Bantam.

As You Like It. William Shakespeare. (Book Notes Ser.). 1985. pap. 2.50 (0-8120-3503-8) Barron.

As You Like It. William Shakespeare. (Illustrated Classics Shakespeare Collection). 64p. 1994. pap. 3.60 (1-56103-655-2) Lake Pub Co.

As You Like It. William Shakespeare. Ed. by Albert Gilman. 1986. pap. 2.50 (0-451-52131-5, Sig Classics) NAL-Dutton.

As You Like It. William Shakespeare. Ed. by I. J. Bisson. (New Clarendon Shakespeare Ser.). 1976. 6.95 (0-19-831925-8) OUP.

As You Like It. William Shakespeare. Ed. by Roma Gill. (Oxford School Shakespeare Ser.). (Illus.). 144p. (YA). (gr. 6 up). 1994. pap. 7.50 (0-19-831979-7) OUP.

As You Like It. William Shakespeare. LC 92-38745. (Illustrated Shakespeare Ser.). 1993. 8.99 (0-517-06489-8) Random Hse Value.

As You Like It. William Shakespeare. Ed. by Ralph Sargeant. (Pelican Shakespeare Ser.). 1959. pap. 4.95 (0-14-071417-0, Pelican Bks) Viking Penguin.

As You Like It. William Shakespeare. Ed. by H. J. Oliver. (New Penguin Shakespeare Ser.). 1981. mass mkt. 5.50 (0-14-070714-X, Penguin Classics) Viking Penguin.

As You Like It. John P. Ward. LC 92-31505. (Twayne's New Critical Introduction to Shakespeare Ser.: Vol. 15). 224p. 1992. text ed. 22.95 (0-8057-8727-5, Twayne); pap. 13.95 (0-8057-8728-3, Twayne) Macmillan.

***As You Like It.** large type ed. William Shakespeare. 1994. pap. 24.95 (0-7089-4510-4, Charnwood) Ulverscroft.

As You Like It. 2nd ed. William Shakespeare. Ed. by Agnes Latham. LC 75-2896. (Arden Shakespeare Ser.). 224p. (C). 1975. 49.95 (0-416-17830-8, NO.2444); pap. 8.95 (0-416-17840-5, NO.2445) Routledge Chapman & Hall.

As You Like It. William Shakespeare. Ed. by Alan Brissenden. LC 93-25742. (World's Classics; The Oxford Shakespeare Ser.). (Illus.). 256p. (C). 1994. reprint ed. pap. 6.95 (0-19-281955-0) OUP.

As You Like It. William Shakespeare. Ed. by Diane Davidson. LC 83-60731. (Shakespeare on Stage Ser.: Vol. 7). (Illus.). 122p. (YA). (gr. 8-12). 1985. reprint ed. pap. 5.95 (0-934048-14-2) Swan Books.

As You Like It: Shakespeare for Everyone. Jennifer Mulherin. LC 90-478. (Illus.). 32p. (J). (gr. 3-7). 1990. lib. bdg. 12.95 (0-87226-339-8) P Bedrick Bks.

As You Like It Notes. Tom Smith. 1981. pap. 3.75 (0-8220-0007-5) Cliffs.

As You Like It Readalong. William Shakespeare. (Illustrated Classics Shakespeare Collection). 64p. 1994. audio, pap. 13.50 (1-56103-657-9) Lake Pub Co.

***As You Pass By: Architectural Musings on Salt Lake City.** Jack Goodman. (Illus.). 256p. (Orig.). 1995. 30.00x (0-87480-488-4); pap. 16.95x (0-87480-489-2) U of Utah Pr.

As You Think. 1991. 3.95 (0-929586-00-X) Meridian Learn Systs.

As You Think. James Allen. Ed. by Marc Allen. LC 91-21731. (Classic Wisdom Collection). 96p. 1991. 9.95 (0-931432-77-4) New Wrld Lib.

As You Think. rev. ed. James Allen. Ed. by Marc Allen. LC 91-40418. 96p. 1987. pap. 6.95 (0-931432-46-4) New Wrld Lib.

***As You Think, So Shall You Become.** James Allen. Ed. & Pref. by Mark Nolan. 90p. (Orig.). 1994. pap. 12.95 (1-881754-68-5) Dolphin Pubng.

As You Thinketh. rev. ed. James Allen & Tag Powell. Ed. by Judith L. Powell et al. LC 88-12347. (Illus.). 104p. 1988. pap. 6.95 (0-914295-69-1) Top Mtn Pub.

As You Were, Vol. 1. Howard D. Ashcraft. Ed. by Michelle Mullenax. LC 90-93204. (Illus.). 1990. 14.95 (0-9626936-0-X) Ashcraft Enter.

***As Your Parents Age: Your 94-Minute Guide to Information, Help, Peace of Mind, Set, book & audio tape.** Rita J. Putnam. 124p. (Orig.). 1994. digital audio, pap. 21.95 (1-886909-00-8) Dynam Comm.

AS-400: A Practical Guide to Programming & Operations. Donald G. Zeilenga & Donna M. Lenczycki. 1992. pap. 34.95 (0-89435-433-7) Wiley.

AS-400: A Practical Guide to Programming & Operations. Donald G. Zeilenga & Donna M. Lenczycki. 1993. pap. text ed. 39.95 (0-471-60309-0, GE4337) Wiley.

AS-400 Alternative: A S-370 to AS-400 Migration Sourcebook. David Andrews et al. (Illus.). (Orig.). 1990. pap. 265.00 (0-9622558-4-X) ADM Consulting.

AS-400 Alternative: A System-370 to AS-400 Migration Sourcebook. 2nd ed. David Andrews et al. (Illus.). 186p. 1992. pap. 265.00 (0-9622558-8-2) ADM Consulting.

AS-400 Architecture & Application: The Database Machine. Jill T. Lawrence. 1992. pap. 34.95 (0-89435-434-5) Wiley.

***AS-400 Client-Server Series Bk. 1: Introduction.** Alfred E. Nickles. 130p. 1994. 99.00 (1-887519-01-7) C-S Technol.

***AS-400 Client-Server Series Bk. 2: Getting Started.** Alfred E. Nickles. 182p. 1995. 99.00 (1-887519-02-5) C-S Technol.

AS-400 Concepts & Facilities. 2nd ed. Tony Baritz & David Dunne. (IBM Ser.). 408p. 1993. text ed. 45.00i (0-07-018303-1) McGraw.

AS/400 Control Language Guide. Brian Fu. 1994. pap. 39. 95 (0-89435-483-3) Wiley.

AS/400 Control Language Guide. Brian Fu. LC 94-1969. 252p. 1994. pap. text ed. 29.95 (0-471-61152-2) Wiley.

AS/400 Control Language Guide. Brian Fu. 1994. text ed. 45.00 (0-07-022629-6) McGraw.

AS-400 Control Language Programming. Bryan Meyers & Dan Riehl. 550p. (C). 1993. pap. text ed. 65.00 (1-882419-04-9, Duke Pr) Duke Commns Intl.

AS-400 Disk Saving Tips & Techniques. James R. Plunkett. (Quick Read Ser.). 74p. 1993. pap. text ed. 59.95 (1-884322-01-8) Comp Applicatns.

AS-400 Information Engineering. John Porter. (IBM Ser.). 352p. 1993. text ed. 45.00i (0-07-050623-X) McGraw.

AS-400 Revolution: Guide to the AS-400 & IBM Strategy. rev. ed. David Andrews. (Illus.). 186p. 1989. reprint ed. pap. 95.00 (0-9622558-2-3) ADM Consulting.

AS-400 Revolution: Guide to the AS-400 & IBM Strategy. 5th ed. David Andrews. Ed. by Doreen Simeone. (Illus.). 180p. 1990. pap. 95.00 (0-9622558-5-8) ADM Consulting.

AS-400 Revolution: Guide to the AS-400 & IBM Strategy. 6th ed. David Andrews. Ed. by Doreen Simeone. (Illus.). 180p. 1991. pap. 95.00 (0-9622558-7-4) ADM Consulting.

AS-400 Revolution: Guide to the AS-400 & IBM Strategy. 6th ed. David Andrews. Ed. by Doreen Simeone. Tr. by Voight Software & Unternehmensberatung GmbH Staff. 180p. (GER.). 1992. pap. 155.00 (0-9622558-9-0) ADM Consulting.

AS-400 Security Strategy: A Management Issue. Nora Craig. (Quick Read Ser.). 168p. 1993. pap. text ed. 59.95 (1-884322-03-4) Comp Applicatns.

***AS-400 Subfiles in RPG.** CAS Staff. (FastStart Ser.). (Illus.). 200p. (Orig.). 1994. pap. 59.95 (1-884322-24-7) Comp Applicatns.

ASA Annual Meeting Papers, 1986-1991. 1991. 6.00 (0-685-73869-8, Crossroads) African Studies Assn.

ASA Annual Meeting Papers, 1986-1991, Set. 1991. 375.00 (0-685-55856-8, Crossroads) African Studies Assn.

Asa, As I Knew Him. Susanna Kaysen. LC 86-46186. (Vintage Contemporaries Ser.). 128p. 1987. pap. 8.00 (0-394-74985-5, Vin) Random.

Asa, As I Knew Him. Susanna Kaysen. 1992. write for info. (0-394-75362-3) Random.

Asa, As I Knew Him. Susanna Kaysen. 1994. pap. 10.00 (0-679-75377-X, Vin) Random.

Asa Fitch & the Emergence of American Entomology, with an Entomological Bibliography & a Catalog of Taxonomic Names & Type Specimens. Jeffrey K. Barnes. (Bulletin Ser.: No. 461). (Illus.). 120p. (Orig.). 1988. pap. 12.50 (1-55557-006-2) NYS Museum.

Asa Gray: American Botanist, Friend of Darwin. A. Hunter Dupree. LC 88-45434. 526p. 1988. reprint ed. pap. text ed. 15.95 (0-8018-3741-3) Johns Hopkins.

Asa Griggs Candler: Founder of Coca-Cola. 2nd ed. Charles H. Candler. Ed. by Casey Watson. (Illus.). 512p. 1994. pap. 19.95 (1-57090-005-1) Alexander Bks.

Asad of Syria: The Struggle for the Middle East. Patrick Seale. 552p. 1989. 38.00 (0-520-06667-7); pap. 16.00 (0-520-06976-5) U CA Pr.

ASAE Standards 1994. 41th ed. 800p. 1994. 125.00 (0-929355-50-4, S0294) Am Soc Ag Eng.

Asafo! African Flags of the Fante. Peter Adler & Nicholas Barnard. LC 92-70869. (Illus.). 96p. 1992. pap. 19.95 (0-500-27684-6) Thames Hudson.

Asahel Curtis: Photographs of the Great Northwest. Richard Frederick & Jeanne Engerman. (Illus.). 72p. (Orig.). 1983. pap. 7.95 (0-917048-56-3) Wash St Hist Soc.

***Asahel Nettleton: Sermons from the Second Great Awakening.** Asahel Nettleton. 500p. 1995. 35.95 (0-9641803-3-2) Internat Outreach.

***Asahiflex & the Pre-1959 Asahi Pentax Cameras: A Guide to Identification & Collection.** Frederick C. Sherfy. (Illus.). 80p. (Orig.). 1994. pap. 14.95 (0-9641107-5-X) F C Sherfy.

Asalto. Reinaldo Arenas. LC 90-86232. 141p. 1991. 16.00 (0-89729-596-X) Ediciones.

Asang: Adaptations to Culture Contact in Miskito Community. Mary W. Helms. LC 70-630257. (Illus.). 276p. reprint ed. pap. 78.70 (0-8357-6717-5, 2035351) Bks Demand.

Asanga's Chapter on Ethics with the Commentary by Tsong-Kha-Pa: The Basic Path to Awakening, the Complete Bodhisattva. Mark Tatz. LC 86-8660. (Studies in Asian Thought & Religion: No. 4). 370p. 1986. lib. bdg. 99.95 (0-88946-054-X) E Mellen.

***Asante: The Gold Coast.** Philip Koslow. (Kingdoms of Africa Ser.). (Illus.). 64p. (J). (gr. 3 up). 1995. 14.95 (0-7910-3139-X); pap. 7.95 (0-7910-3140-3) Chelsea Hse.

Asante Africa. Carolyn Brock. 250p. 1990. 23.00 (0-8309-0580-4) Herald Hse.

Asante & Its Neighbours, Seventeen Hundred to Eighteen Seven. John K. Fynn. LC 77-175917. 127p. reprint ed. pap. 36.20 (0-8357-5781-1, 2016707) Bks Demand.

Asante & the Dutch, Seventeen Forty-Four to Eighteen Seventy-Three. Larry W. Yarak. (Oxford Studies in African Affairs). (Illus.). 336p. 1990. 72.00 (0-19-822156-8) OUP.

Asante in the Nineteenth Century. Ivor Wilks. LC 74-77834. (African Studies: No. 13). (Illus.). 872p. 1975. 110.00 (0-521-20463-1) Cambridge U Pr.

Asante in the Nineteenth Century. Ivor Wilks. LC 74-77834. (African Studies: No. 13). (Illus.). 872p. 1989. pap. 34.95 (0-521-37994-6) Cambridge U Pr.

Asante Resource Guide: Culture & Tradition. Beryle Banfield. (Illus.). 78p. 1988. 10.95 (0-914110-02-0) Blyden Pr.

ASAP: The Fastest Way to Create a Memorable Speech. William Mooney. 1992. 14.95 (0-8120-6280-9) Barron.

***Asay Doodles Goes to Town.** Chuck Asay. (Illus.). 160p. 1995. pap. text ed. 8.95 (1-56554-142-1) Pelican.

ASBDA Curriculum Guide. Ed. by American School Band Directors Association Staff. 1974. pap. 20.00 (0-913650-19-6) CPP Belwin.

ASBDA Curriculum Guide: Reference Book for School Band Directors. Ed. by American School Band Directors Association Staff. LC 73-75694. 1973. 25.00 (0-913650-00-5) CPP Belwin.

Asbestiform Fibers: Nonoccupational Health Risks. National Research Council U. S. Staff. LC 84-60249. 352p. reprint ed. pap. 100.40 (0-7837-2041-6, 2042308) Bks Demand.

***Asbestos.** 1995. lib. bdg. 256.75 (0-8490-6681-6) Gordon Pr.

Asbestos. Wayne Kline. 56p. (Orig.). 1989. pap. 6.00 (0-9619097-0-6) Edge Bks.

Asbestos. IARC Working Group on the Evaluation of the Carcinogenic Risk of Chemicals to Man (1976: Lyon, France) Staff. (IARC Monographs on the Evaluation of Carcinogenic Risk of Chemicals to Man: No. 14). 108p. reprint ed. pap. 30.80 (0-8357-6462-1, 2035833) Bks Demand.

Asbestos: A Source Guide. 1991. lib. bdg. 250.00 (0-8490-4897-4) Gordon Pr.

Asbestos: An Annotated Bibliography. Robert F. Nardini. (CompuBibs Ser.: No. 14). 1986. pap. 15.00 (0-914791-13-3) Vantage Info.

Asbestos: Directory of Research & Documentation Centres. Ed. by S. Amaducci. 1982. lib. bdg. 112.50 (90-277-1415-0) Kluwer Ac.

Asbestos: Directory of Unpublished Studies. S. Amaducci. 1982. lib. bdg. 99.00 (90-277-1414-2) Kluwer Ac.

Asbestos: Directory of Unpublished Studies. 2nd ed. Ed. by S. Amaducci. 222p. 1987. 54.00 (1-85166-073-9, Pub. by Elsevier Applied Sci UK) Elsevier.

Asbestos: Medical & Legal Aspects. 3rd ed. Barry I. Castleman. 798p. 1995. boxed 95.00 (0-13-048414-8) Aspen Law.

Asbestos: Properties, Applications, & Hazards, Vol. 1. Ed. by Leslie Michaels & S. S. Chissick. LC 78-16535. (Illus.). 572p. reprint ed. pap. 163.10 (0-8357-5782-X, 2052252) Bks Demand.

Asbestos: The Hazardous Fiber. Ed. by Benardes. 1989. 81. 00 (0-8493-6354-3, TA55) CRC Pr.

Asbestos: The Unseen Peril in Our Environment. Edwin Flatto. 1983. pap. 8.95 (0-935540-10-5) Plymouth Pr.

Asbestos - the Unseen Peril. 43p. 1990. pap. 8.95 (0-935540-09-1) Plymouth Pr.

Asbestos Abatement: Facility Survey & Building Systems. Univ. of Florida, TREEO Staff. 336p. 1989. 59.50 (0-8403-5683-8) Kendall-Hunt.

Asbestos Abatement: Risks & Responsibilities. 1987. 55.00 (0-87179-918-9) BNA.

Asbestos Abatement Vol. 1: Reference Manual. University of Florida (TREEO) Staff. 576p. 1990. 59.95 (0-8403-5647-1) Kendall-Hunt.

Asbestos Abatement Equipment. Richard K. Miller & Marcia E. Rupnow. LC 90-83848. (Survey on Technology & Markets Ser.: No. 143). 50p. 1991. pap. text ed. 200.00 (1-55865-168-3) Future Tech Surveys.

Asbestos Abatement Resource Guide. 2nd rev. ed. LC 89-9950. 1989. 250.00 (1-55871-101-5, BSP130) BNA.

Asbestos Abatement Rules: The Complete Resource Guide. 1988. ring bd. 110.00 (0-87179-948-0, BSP-80) BNA.

Asbestos Abatement, Vol. II: Reference Manual. University of Florida (TREEO) Staff. 464p. 1990. 54.95 (0-8403-5648-X) Kendall-Hunt.

Asbestos & Asbestosis: A Medical Subject Analysis & Research Index with Bibliography. Walter O. Braun. LC 83-70090. 140p. 1983. 39.50 (0-941864-84-7); pap. 34.50 (0-941864-85-5) ABBE Pubs Assn.

Asbestos & Disease. Irving J. Selikoff & Douglas H. Lee. LC 77-25735. (Environmental Science Ser.). 1978. text ed. 158.00 (0-12-636050-2) Acad Pr.

Asbestos & Jade in the Kobuk River Region of Alaska. Eskil Anderson. (Shorey Prospecting Ser.). 26p. reprint ed. pap. 3.95 (0-8466-0037-4, S37) Shorey.

Asbestos & Other Fibrous Materials: Mineralogy, Crystal Chemistry, & Health Effects. H. Catherine Skinner et al. (Illus.). 224p. 1988. 45.00 (0-19-503967-X) OUP.

Asbestos & Other Natural Mineral Fibres. (Environmental Health Criteria Ser.: No. 53). 194p. 1987. pap. 9.60 (92-4-154193-8) World Health.

Asbestos Cancer: One Man's Experience. Myrna J. Grove. LC 93-74752. 1995. 12.95 (0-8158-0498-9) Chris Mass.

Asbestos Claims: The Decision to Use Workers' Compensation & Tort. Robert I. Field & Richard B. Victor. 1988. 25.00 (0-935149-13-9, WC-88-5) Workers Comp Res Inst.

Asbestos Compliance Encyclopedia. Ed. by P. David Shafer & Barbara Kelly. 1987. ring bd. 149.95 (1-55645-322-1) Busn Legal Reports.

An Asterisk (*) at the beginning of an entry indicates that the title is appearing in BIP for the first time.

An Asterisk (*) at the beginning of an entry indicates that the title is appearing in BIP for the first time.

471

Ascomycetes of Ohio, Vol. I. Bruce Fink. (Bulletin Ser.: No. 5). 1915. 3.00 (*0-86727-004-7*) Ohio Bio Survey.

Ascomycetes of Ohio, Vols. IV & V. Bruce Fink & Leafy J. Corrington. (Bulletin Ser.: No. 10). 1921. 3.00 (*0-86727-009-8*) Ohio Bio Survey.

Asconius: Commentary on Five Speeches of Cicero. Simon Squires. (LAT.). 1989. pap. 16.00 (*0-86516-220-4*) Bolchazy-Carducci.

Ascorbic Acid: Chemistry, Metabolism, & Uses. Bert M. Tolbert. Ed. by Paul A. Seib. LC 82-13795. (ACS Advances in Chemistry Ser.: No. 200). 1982. 69.95 (*0-8412-0632-5*) Am Chemical.

Ascorbino Metric Titrations. L. Erdey & G. Svehla. 184p. 1973. 65.00 (*0-569-08055-X*, Pub. by Collets UK) Pro-Am Music.

ASCOT Simplified Archivage of Orthopedic Surgery & Traumatology: A-S-C-O-T Archivage Simplifie en Chirurgie Orthopedique et Traumatologie. L. E. Goutard. 144p. (FRE.). 1983. 49.95 (*0-8288-1808-8*, M15435) Fr & Eur.

Ascott, Quebec, Canada: 1825. Jay M. Holbrook. LC 80-117991. 1976. pap. 5.00 (*0-931248-06-X*) Holbrook Res.

ASCP Image Base: Cytopathology. 1992. vdisk 650.00 (*0-89189-319-9*, D69-3-001-00) Am Soc Clinical.

ASDA Handbook. annuals 100p. 4.00 (*0-318-17488-X*) Am Student Dent.

Asdell's Patterns of Mammalian Reproduction: A Compendium of Species-Specific Data. Virginia Hayssen et al. LC 92-56775. (Comstock Book Ser.). 952p. 1993. 75.00 (*0-8014-1753-8*) Cornell U Pr.

Ase Omo Osayin...Ewe Aye. Miguel Ramos. 113p. (Orig.). (SPA.). (C). 1982. pap. 11.99 (*0-685-26085-2*) M W Ramos.

ASE-OTC Dividend Reinvestment Handbook. P. Y. Feng. 100p. (Orig.). Date not set. pap. 7.95 (*0-934036-06-3*) PMF Research.

ASE Science Teacher's Handbook. Ed. by J. Nellist & B. Nicholl. (C). 1989. 140.00 (*0-09-156340-2*, Pub. by S Thornes Pubs UK) St Mut.

ASEAN: Its Role in the Development of Southeast Asia, 1985. Donald E. Weatherbee et al. Ed. by Mahendra Srivastava. 1990. 5.00 (*0-685-34495-9*) Southern Ctr Intl Stud.

ASEAN: The Association of South-East Asian Nations 20 Years. R. Nagi. (C). 1988. 28.50 (*81-7095-008-2*, Pub. by Lancers Books II) S Asia.

ASEAN - China Economic Relations: Developments in ASEAN & China. Ed. by Chia Siow Yue & Cheng Bifan. 339p. 1989. pap. text ed. 37.00 (*981-3035-31-5*, Pub. by Inst SE Asian Studies SI) Ashgate Pub Co.

ASEAN & China: An Evolving Relationship. Ed. by Joyce K. Kallgren et al. LC 88-80736. (Research Papers & Policy Studies: No. 24). 384p. (Orig.). 1988. pap. 20.00 (*1-55729-004-0*) IEAS.

ASEAN & the Diplomacy of Accommodation. Michael Antolik. LC 89-49026. 216p. 1990. 51.95 (*0-87332-630-X*) M E Sharpe.

ASEAN & the EC: The Impact of Nineteen Ninety-Two. Ed. by Norbert Wagner. 345p. 1990. pap. 28.00 (*981-3035-70-6*, Pub. by Inst SE Asian Studies SI) Ashgate Pub Co.

ASEAN & the EC: Trade in Tropical Agricultural Products. Ed. by Rolf J. Langhammer & Hans C. Rieger. 185p. 1988. pap. text ed. 13.75 (*9971-988-81-X*, Pub. by Inst SE Asian Studies SI) Ashgate Pub Co.

ASEAN & the Security of South-East Asia. Michael Leifer. 224p. (C). 1989. lib. bdg. 57.50 (*0-415-01008-X*, A2503) Routledge.

ASEAN & the United Nations System. 12.00 (*92-1-157067-0*) UN.

***ASEAN Business Directory.** 118p. (Orig.). 1995. pap. 165.00 (*0-7605-2361-4*) Rector Pr.

***ASEAN Business Guide.** 118p. (Orig.). 1995. pap. 165.00 (*0-7605-2384-3*) Rector Pr.

***ASEAN-China Economic Relations Vol. 4: Industrial Restructuring in ASEAN & China.** Ed. by Joseph L. Tan & Luo Zhaohong. (ASEAN-China Economic Relations Ser.). 273p. 1994. pap. 45.95 (*981-3016-89-2*) Ashgate Pub Co.

***ASEAN Coal Energy Technology Transfer Market Report.** 60p. (Orig.). 1995. pap. 165.00 (*0-7605-2386-X*) Rector Pr.

***ASEAN Demographics Report.** 60p. (Orig.). 1995. pap. 165.00 (*0-7605-2379-7*) Rector Pr.

ASEAN Economic Co-operation. Ed. by Chia S. Yue. (ASEAN Economic Research Unit Workshop Proceedings Ser.). 164p. (Orig.). 1980. pap. text ed. 25.00 (*9971-902-06-0*, Pub. by Inst SE Asian Studies SI) Ashgate Pub Co.

ASEAN Economic Co-operation: A Handbook. Comp. by Hans C. Reiger. 240p. 1991. pap. 23.95 (*981-3035-66-8*, Pub. by Inst SE Asian Studies SI) Ashgate Pub Co.

ASEAN Economic Cooperation: A New Perspective. Ed. by Hendra Esmara. 256p. 1989. text ed. 50.00 (*9971-68-141-2*, Pub. by Chopmen Singapore SI) Advent Bks Div.

***ASEAN Economic Report.** 60p. (Orig.). 1995. pap. 165.00 (*0-7605-2378-9*) Rector Pr.

ASEAN-EEC Trade in Services. Ed. by Jean Waelbroeck et al. 180p. 1986. pap. text ed. 28.60 (*9971-902-92-3*, Pub. by Inst SE Asian Studies SI) Ashgate Pub Co.

***ASEAN Electric Power Generation Markets.** 75p. (Orig.). 1995. pap. 165.00 (*0-7605-2387-8*) Rector Pr.

***ASEAN Energy Sector Market Report.** (Orig.). 1995. pap. 165.00 (*0-7605-2388-6*) Rector Pr.

***ASEAN Environment Plan Report.** 60p. (Orig.). 1995. pap. 165.00 (*0-7605-2391-6*) Rector Pr.

***ASEAN Environmental Sector Market Report.** 60p. (Orig.). 1995. pap. 165.00 (*0-7605-2389-4*) Rector Pr.

ASEAN Financial Co-operation: Developments in Banking, Finance & Insurance. Michael T. Skully. LC 84-8197. 256p. 1985. text ed. 35.00 (*0-312-05604-4*) St Martin.

***ASEAN Financing Development Report.** 62p. (Orig.). 1995. pap. 195.00 (*0-7605-2383-5*) Rector Pr.

***ASEAN Health Care Market Report.** 60p. (Orig.). 1995. pap. 165.00 (*0-7605-2377-0*) Rector Pr.

ASEAN in the Nineteen Nineties, New Challenges, New Directions. Perry L. Wood & Jimmy W. Wheeler. 76p. (Orig.). (C). 1990. pap. text ed. 8.50 (*1-55813-036-5*) Hudson Instit IN.

ASEAN into the 1990s. Ed. by Alison Broinowski. LC 90-30324. 321p. 1990. text ed. 59.95 (*0-312-04641-3*) St Martin.

ASEAN Negotiations: Two Insights. Pushpa Thambipillai & J. Saravanamuttu. 64p. 1985. pap. text ed. 10.00 (*9971-902-87-7*, Pub. by Inst SE Asian Studies SI) Ashgate Pub Co.

ASEAN Reader. Ed. by Sharon Siddique et al. 582p. 1992. 67.75 (*981-3016-42-6*, Pub. by Inst SE Asian Studies SI) Ashgate Pub Co.

ASEAN Report, 2 vols. Thomas W. Allen. Ed. by Barry Wain. Incl. Vol. 1. Comparative Assessment of the ASEAN Countries. 1980. (*0-318-56159-X*); Vol. 2. Evolution & Programs of ASEAN: The Asian Wall Street Journal. 1980. (*0-318-56160-3*); (Illus.). 414p. 1980. Set. Set pap. 125.00 (*0-295-95740-9*, 80-110683) U of Wash Pr.

ASEAN-South Asia Economic Relations. Mukul G. Asher. Ed. by Charan D. Wadhva. 396p. 1985. pap. text ed. 25.00 (*9971-902-98-2*, Pub. by Inst SE Asian Studies SI) Ashgate Pub Co.

ASEAN States: Coping with Dependence. Donald K Crone. LC 83-2433. 240p. 1983. text ed. 31.95 (*0-275-90962-X*, C0962, Praeger Pubs) Greenwood.

ASEAN Today-Your Partner of Tomorrow. 295p. 1981. pap. 18.00 (*0-89192-348-9*) Interbk Inc.

ASEAN-U. S. Economic Relations: Private Enterprise As a Means for Economic Development & Co-Operation. Ed. by Joseph L. Tan & Narongchai Akrasanee. 159p. 1991. pap. text ed. 27.25 (*981-3035-71-4*, Pub. by Inst SE Asian Studies SI) Ashgate Pub Co.

ASEAN-U. S. Initiative: Assessment & Recommendations for Improved Eco Relations. Seiji Naya et al. 206p. 1989. pap. 26.50 (*981-3035-22-6*, Pub. by Inst SE Asian Studies SI) Ashgate Pub Co.

***ASEAN Wastewater Treatment Market Report.** 75p. (Orig.). 1995. pap. 195.00 (*0-7605-2390-8*) Rector Pr.

ASEAN Who's Who, 3 vols., Set. (Illus.). 3000p. (C). 1994. 750.00 (*0-685-71763-1*) Rector Pr.

ASEAN Who's Who, Vol. 1. Ed. by Lewis B. Sckolnick. (Illus.). 1000p. (C). 1994. write for info. (*1-57205-020-9*) Rector Pr.

ASEAN Who's Who, Vol. 2. Ed. by Lewis B. Sckolnick. (Illus.). 1000p. (C). 1994. write for info. (*1-57205-021-7*) Rector Pr.

ASEAN Who's Who, Vol. 3. Ed. by Lewis B. Sckolnick. (Illus.). 1000p. (C). 1994. write for info. (*1-57205-022-5*) Rector Pr.

ASEE Membership Handbook, 1994. American Society for Engineering Education Staff. 250p. (Orig.). 1993. pap. write for info. (*0-87823-132-3*) Am Soc Eng Ed.

Aseff the Spy. Boris I. Nikolajewsky. (Russian Ser.: Vol. 11). 1969. 25.00 (*0-87569-011-4*) Academic Intl.

ASEN: Iron Altars of the Fon People of Benin. Edna G. Bay. (Illus.). 48p. 1985. pap. 8.00 (*0-317-58461-8*, Crossroads) African Studies Assn.

***Asentamientos Indigenas en el Valle de la Laguna.** Ana M. Boada. (Illus.). 197p. (SPA.). 1987. pap. 8.50 (*1-877812-17-X*) UPLAAP.

Asentamientos Indigenas en el Valle de la Laguna. Ana M. Rivas. 197p. 1987. 8.50 (*0-685-75379-4*) UPLAAP.

***Asentamientos Prehispanicos en la Costa Pacifica Caucana.** Diogenes Patino. (Illus.). 160p. (SPA.). 1988. pap. 8.50 (*1-877812-19-6*) UPLAAP.

Aseptic Food Processing & Packaging. Business Communications Co., Inc. Staff. (Illus.). 164p. 1986. pap. 1,750.00 (*0-89336-471-1*, GA-050R) BCC.

Aseptic Packaging of Food. H. Reuter. LC 89-50658. 284p. 1989. pap. 75.00 (*0-87762-694-4*) Technomic.

Aseptic Pharmaceutical Manufacturing: Technology for the 1990s. Ed. by W. Olson & M. Groves. 430p. 1987. 116.00 (*0-935184-06-6*) Interpharm.

***Aseptic Pharmaceutical Manufacturing II: Applications for the 1990s.** Ed. by Michael J. Groves & Ram Murty. 450p. 1995. 165.00 (*0-935184-77-5*) Interpharm.

Aseptic Processing of Foods. Ed. by Helmut Reuter. (Illus.). 313p. 1993. pap. 89.00 (*1-56676-058-5*, 760585) Technomic.

Aserah: Extrabiblical Evidence. Walter A. Maier, III. LC 86-15596. (Harvard Semitic Monographs). 274p. 1987. 24.95 (*1-55540-046-9*, 04-00-37) Scholars Pr GA.

Aseres Hadibros: The Ten Commandments. Avrohom C. Feuer. (ArtScroll Mesorah Ser.). 64p. 1981. 9.95 (*0-89906-179-6*); pap. 5.95 (*0-89906-180-X*) Mesorah Pubns.

Asessment of Children. 3rd rev. ed. Jerome M. Sattler. 1200p. (C). 1992. 58.00 (*0-9618209-2-6*) J M Sattler.

Asey Mayo Trio. Phoebe A. Taylor. 256p. 1990. reprint ed. pap. 5.95 (*0-88150-171-9*, Foul Play) Countryman.

***ASFE Contract Reference Guide.** Date not set. 60.00 (*0-614-05183-5*, BPCCRG01873.5M) ASFE.

ASFE Contract Reference Guide. 79p. 1986. 60.00 (*0-318-13491-8*) ASFE.

***ASFE Guide to the In-House Review of Reports.** 20p. Date not set. 25.00 (*0-614-05181-9*, PQC089125M) ASFE.

***ASFE Pocket Guide to OSHA Excavation Regulations.** 19p. Date not set. 10.00 (*0-614-05235-1*, PG006915M) ASFE.

ASFE Professional Liability Loss Prevention Education Program. 200p. 150.00 (*0-318-17771-4*) ASFE.

Asgard Run. Steve Vance. 320p. (Orig.). 1990. pap. 3.95 (*0-8439-2937-5*) Dorchester Pub Co.

***Ash: A Novel.** Lisa R. Fraustino. LC 94-33008. (Illus.). 176p. (C). (gr. 12 up). 1995. lib. bdg. 16.99 (*0-531-08739-5*) Orchard Bks Watts.

***Ash: A Novel.** Lisa R. Fraustino. LC 94-33008. (Illus.). 176p. (YA). (gr. 7 up). 1995. 16.95 (*0-531-06889-7*) Orchard Bks Watts.

Ash Circle. Martin Anderson. Ed. by Alana Sherman & Lorraine De Gennard. 48p. (Orig.). 1989. pap. text ed. 4.95 (*0-939689-06-5*) Alms Hse Pr.

Ash Deposits & Corrosion Due to Impurities in Combustion Gases: Proceedings of the Symposium, June 26-July 1, 1977, New England College, Henniker, New Hampshire. Ed. by Richard W. Bryers. LC 78-7001. (Illus.). 691p. 1978. text ed. 148.00 (*0-89116-074-4*) Hemisp Pub.

Ash Dieback, No. 88. 1966. 1.00 (*0-686-20700-9*) SUNY Environ.

Ash Flow Tuffs. Ed. by C. E. Chapin & W. E. Elston. LC 79-53022. (Special Paper Ser.: No. 180). (Illus.). 218p. 1979. pap. 22.00 (*0-8137-2180-6*) Geol Soc.

Ash Glazes. Phil Rogers. 144p. 1991. text ed. 29.95 (*0-8019-8243-X*) Chilton.

Ash Glazes. Robert Tichane. LC 86-63699. (Oriental Glaze Ser.). (Illus.). 216p. 1987. text ed. 22.00 (*0-914267-05-1*) NYS Inst Glaze.

Ash Is the Candle's Wick. John Judson. (W.N.J. Ser.: No. 1). 1975. pap. 6.00 (*1-55780-050-2*) Juniper Pr WI.

***Ash Ock.** Christopher Hinz. (Paratwa Saga Ser.: Bk. 2). 1995. mass mkt. 5.99 (*0-8125-3078-0*) Tor Bks.

Ash-Shafiis Risalah, Basic Ideas. K. I. Semaan. pap. 3.00 (*0-935782-41-9*) Kazi Pubns.

Ash Wednesday Supper. Giordano Bruno. Tr. by Stanley L. Jaki. (Illus.). 174p. 1975. text ed. 37.70 (*90-279-7581-7*) Mouton.

***Ash Wednesday Supper.** Giordano Bruno. Ed. by Edward A. Gosselin & Lawrence S. Lerner. Tr. by Lawrence S. Lerner. (Renaissance Society of America Reprints for Teaching Ser.). 238p. 1995. pap. 19.95 (*0-8020-7469-3*) U of Toronto Pr.

ASHA Membership Directory, 1988-1989. 700p. 1989. write for info. (*0-318-64434-7*) Am Speech Lang Hearing.

ASHA Membership Directory, 1989-90. Ed. by Frederick T. Spahr. 725p. 1989. text ed. 50.00 (*0-910329-45-1*); pap. 40.00 (*0-910329-44-3*) Am Speech Lang Hearing.

Ashamed of the Gospel: When the Church Becomes Like the World. John F. MacArthur, Jr. LC 93-23849. 1993. 17.99 (*0-89107-729-4*) Crossway Bks.

Ashana. E. P. Roesch. 1991. mass mkt. 5.99 (*0-345-37298-0*) Ballantine.

Ashana. E. P. Roesch. 1990. 19.95 (*0-394-56963-6*) Random.

Ashanti. Robert S. Rattray. LC 73-92759. (Illus.). 348p. 1971. reprint ed. text ed. 35.00 (*0-8371-2201-5*, RAA&, Negro U Pr) Greenwood.

Ashanti Brainwashing Test Manual: ABT Manual. Kwabena F. Ashanti. 80p. (Orig.). (C). 1991. pap. text ed. 12.95 (*0-911325-06-9*) Tone Bks Inc.

Ashanti, Eighteen Ninety-Five. Ian McInnes & Mark Fraser. (Illus.). 156p. (C). 1987. 126.00 (*0-948251-12-3*, Pub. by Picton UK) St Mut.

***Ashanti to Zulu: African Traditions.** Margaret Musgrove. (Illus.). (J). 1992. pap. 4.99 (*0-14-054604-9*) Puffin Bks.

Ashanti to Zulu: African Traditions. Margaret W. Musgrove. Ed. by Leo D. Dillon. LC 76-6610. (Pied Piper Bks.). (Illus.). (J). (gr. k-4). 1976. 17.00 (*0-8037-0357-0*); lib. bdg. 15.89 (*0-8037-0358-9*) Dial Bks Young.

Ashanti to Zulu: African Traditions. Margaret W. Musgrove. LC 76-6610. (Pied Piper Bks.). (Illus.). 32p. (J). (gr. k up). 1980. pap. 4.95 (*0-8037-0308-2*, Puff Pied Piper) Puffin Bks.

Ashanti War, 2 vols., Set. H. Brackenbury. 1968. 95.00 (*0-7146-1795-4*, Pub. by F Cass Pubs UK) Intl Spec Bk.

Asharah Mubasharah. Muhammad Iqbal Siddiqi. 200p. (Orig.). 1990. pap. 9.95 (*1-56744-223-4*) Kazi Pubns.

Ashbel Smith of Texas: Pioneer, Patriot, Statesman, 1805-1886. Elizabeth Silverthorne. LC 81-48380. (Centennial Series of the Association of Former Students: No. 11). (Illus.). 280p. 1982. 24.50 (*0-89096-127-1*) Tex A&M Univ Pr.

Ashbury People. large type ed. Doreen Wallace. 1976. 12.00 (*0-85456-500-0*) Ulverscroft.

Ashby. Maurice Valency. LC 88-31298. 277p. (C). 1988. reprint ed. pap. 11.95 (*0-941533-51-4*) New Amsterdam Bks.

Ashby Funeral Home Records, Vol. 1: 1916-1928. Shirlene M. Chilton. 81p. 1986. spiral bd. 13.75 (*0-945183-02-X*) Saline Cnty Hist Heritage Soc.

Ashby Guidebook for Study of the Paranormal. rev. ed. Robert H. Ashby. Ed. by Frank Tribbe. Orig. Title: Guidebook for Study of Psychical Research. 233p. 1987. pap. 10.95 (*0-87728-660-4*) Weiser.

Ashby Report (1954) M. D. Stephens. (C). 1990. 35.00 (*1-85041-032-1*, Pub. by Univ Nottingham UK) St Mut.

ASHE. Hermine Pinson. Ed. by J. Whitebird. (New Texas Poetry Sampler Ser.). 28p. (Orig.). 1992. pap. text ed. 10.00 (*0-930324-23-4*) Wings Pr.

ASHE: Finance in Higher Education. Dave Breneman. 34.00 (*0-536-05553-X*) Ginn Pr.

ASHE: Women in Higher Education a Feminist Perspective. Judith Glazer. 41.00 (*0-536-58351-X*) Ginn Pr.

Ashe County, North Carolina, Abstract of the 1880 Federal Census. Evelyn G. Waters. 311p. 1992. lib. bdg. 36.00 (*0-8328-2359-7*) Higginson Bk Co.

***Ashe County, North Carolina Marriage Bonds & Certificates, 1819-1871.** Francis T. Ingmire. 70p. 1994. lib. bdg. 27.00 (*0-8095-8009-8*); pap. 9.50 (*0-8095-8508-1*) Borgo Pr.

ASHE Reader on College Students. Ed. by George Kuh. 1989. 26.50 (*0-536-57317-4*) Ginn Pr.

ASHE Reader on Community Colleges. Ed. by James Ratcliff. 1992. 26.50 (*0-536-58226-2*) Ginn Pr.

ASHE Reader on Curriculum in Transition. Ed. by Clifton Conrad. 1990. 31.00 (*0-536-57792-7*) Ginn Pr.

ASHE Reader on Faculty & Faculty Issues in Colleges & Universities. 2nd ed. Martin J. Finkelstein. 1990. 31.50 (*0-536-05856-3*) Ginn Pr.

ASHE Reader on Finance in Higher Education. Richard E. Anderson & Larry L. Leslie. 1990. 33.00 (*0-536-05556-4*) Ginn Pr.

ASHE Reader on Organization & Governance in Higher Education. 4th ed. Ed. by Marvin Peterson. 1991. 32.50 (*0-536-57981-4*) Ginn Pr.

ASHE Reader on the History of Higher Education. Ed. by Lester Goodchild. 1989. 34.00 (*0-536-57566-5*) Ginn Pr.

Ashe, Traditional Religion & Healing in Sub-Saharan Africa & the Diaspora: A Classified International Bibliography. Comp. by John Gray. LC 89-2168. (Bibliographies & Indexes in Afro-American & African Studies: No. 24). 539p. 1989. text ed. 79.50 (*0-313-26500-3*, GAD) Greenwood.

Ashenden. W. Somerset Maugham. 256p. 1976. pap. 8.00 (*0-14-017431-1*, Penguin Classics) Viking Penguin.

Ashenden, or, the British Agent. W. Somerset Maugham. 22.95 (*0-89190-213-9*, Am Repr) Amereon Ltd.

Ashenden, or The British Agent. large type ed. W. Somerset Maugham. 512p. 1992. 22.95 (*1-85290-034-2*, Pub. by ISIS UK) Transaction Pubs.

Ashenden, or, The British Agent. W. Somerset Maugham. LC 76-178451. (Short Story Index Reprint Ser.). reprint ed. 14.50 (*0-8369-4052-0*) Ayer.

Ashenden, or, The British Agent. W. Somerset Maugham. LC 75-25348. (Works of W. Somerset Maugham Ser.). 1977. reprint ed. 27.95 (*0-405-07805-6*) Ayer.

Asher. William Wallis. LC 91-65500. 75p. (Orig.). (C). 1991. pap. 7.50 (*0-9627031-2-5*) Stone & Scott Pubs.

Asher & the Capmakers: A Hanukkah Story. Eric A. Kimmel. LC 92-37978. (Illus.). 32p. (J). (ps-3). 1993. lib. bdg. 15.95 (*0-8234-1031-5*) Holiday.

Asher B. Durand: An Engraver's & a Farmer's Art. James T. Flexner. LC 82-84455. (Illus.). 96p. (Orig.). 1983. pap. 5.00 (*0-943651-10-7*) Hudson Riv.

Asherah: Goddess of Israel. Richard J. Pettey. LC 90-35025. (American University Studies: Theology & Religion: Ser. VII, Vol. 74). 233p. (C). 1990. text ed. 41.95 (*0-8204-1306-2*) P Lang Pubs.

Asherah & the Cult of Yahweh in Israel. Saul Olyan. LC 88-19168. (Society of Biblical Literature Monographs). 144p. 1988. 20.95 (*1-55540-253-4*, 06 00 34); pap. 13.95 (*1-55540-254-2*, 06 00 34) Scholars Pr GA.

***Ashes: Terrifying True Horror of a Macabre Criminal Career.** James Joseph. 352p. (Orig.). 1994. pap. 5.99 (*0-425-13663-9*) Berkley Pub.

Ashes & Diamonds. Jerzy Andrzejewski. Tr. by D. J. Welsh. 239p. 1991. pap. 10.95 (*0-8101-0856-9*) Northwestern U Pr.

Ashes & Dust. George G. Gilman. (Edge Ser.: No. 19). (Orig.). 1990. pap. 3.50 (*1-55817-360-9*, Pinnacle NY) Windsor NY.

Ashes & Ecstasy. Catherine Hart. 480p. (Orig.). 1994. mass mkt., pap. text ed. 4.99 (*0-8439-3458-1*) Dorchester Pub Co.

Ashes & Fire. Jacob Pat. Tr. by Leo Steinberg. LC 48-1353. 254p. reprint ed. pap. 72.40 (*0-8357-5784-6*, 2010713) Bks Demand.

Ashes & Mead. Diane Robinson. Ed. by Roy Zarucchi & Carolyn Page. (Chapbook Ser.). (Illus.). 28p. (Orig.). 1991. pap. 5.00 (*1-879205-12-2*) Nightshade Pr.

Ashes & Sparks, Set. R. Dell Davis. LC 89-81718. (Illus.). 172p. (J). (gr. 1-8). 1989. audio, boxed 24.95 (*0-9616736-1-3*) J Franklin.

Ashes & Tears. James Bloom. Ed. by Michael Sherer. (Orig.). 1987. pap. 5.20 (*1-55673-018-7*, 8802) CSS OH.

Ashes, Ashes. Etienne Delessert. (Limited Editions Ser.). (Illus.). 32p. (YA). (gr. 1-12). 1990. lib. bdg. 17.95 (*0-88682-628-4*, 97855-098) Creative Ed.

Ashes, Ashes, All Fall Down. Joseph Robinette. 1982. 4.95 (*0-87129-251-3*, A29) Dramatic Pub.

Ashes at My Guru's Feet. Gurumayi Chidvilasananda. Ed. by Swami Kripananda. LC 90-30300. 96p. 1990. 19.95 (*0-911307-16-8*) SYDA Found.

Ashes for Gold: A Tale from Mexico. Katherine Maitland. LC 94-14349. (Mondo Folktales ser.). (Illus.). 24p. (Orig.). (J). (gr. k-4). 1994. 23.95 (*1-879531-14-3*); lib. bdg. 9.95 (*1-879531-43-7*); pap. 4.95 (*1-879531-22-4*) Mondo Pubng.

***Ashes from the Fire.** Joan Chittister. (Orig.). 1995. pap. write for info. (*1-55612-802-9*) Sheed & Ward MO.

Ashes in the Rain. Al Martinez. LC 89-4400. 256p. 1989. pap. 12.00 (*0-89229-019-6*) TQS Pubns.

Ashes in the Wind. Kathleen E. Woodiwiss. 672p. 1981. mass mkt. 5.99 (*0-380-76984-0*) Avon.

Ashes in the Wind: The Destruction of Dutch Jewry. Jacob Presser. Tr. by Arnold Pomerans. LC 88-225. (Illus.). 571p. 1988. reprint ed. 49.95 (*0-8143-2036-8*); reprint ed. pap. 19.95 (*0-8143-2037-6*) Wayne St U Pr.

Ashes, No. 9: Valor in the Ashes. William W. Johnstone. 432p. 1988. pap. 3.95 (*0-8217-2484-3*) Zebra.

***Ashes of Guilt.** Lorene Blaine. 274p. 1995. pap. 8.95 (*1-56901-540-6*) NW Pub.

Ashes of Izalco. Claribel Alegria & Darwin J. Flakoll. LC 89-62125. 192p. (Orig.). 1989. 17.95 (*0-915306-83-2*); pap. 9.95 (*0-915306-84-0*) Curbstone.

An Asterisk (*) at the beginning of an entry indicates that the title is appearing in BIP for the first time.

An Asterisk (*) at the beginning of an entry indicates that the title is appearing in BIP for the first time.

473

Asia in the Making of Europe Vol. III: A Century of Advance, 4 bks., Bk. 1. Donald F. Lach & Edwin J. Van Kley. (Illus.). 674p. 1993. 85.00 (*0-226-46753-8*) U Ch Pr.

Asia in the Making of Europe Vol. III: A Century of Advance, 4 bks., Bk. 2. Donald F. Lach & Edwin J. Van Kley. (Illus.). 544p. 1993. 75.00 (*0-226-46754-6*) U Ch Pr.

Asia in the Making of Europe Vol. III: A Century of Advance, 4 bks., Bk. 3. Donald F. Lach & Edwin J. Van Kley. (Illus.). 488p. 1993. 65.00 (*0-226-46755-4*) U Ch Pr.

Asia in the Making of Europe Vol. III: A Century of Advance, 4 bks., Bk. 4. Donald F. Lach & Edwin J. Van Kley. (Illus.). 560p. 1993. 85.00 (*0-226-46756-2*) U Ch Pr.

Asia in the Making of Europe Vol. III: A Century of Advance, 4 bks., Set. Donald F. Lach & Edwin J. Van Kley. (Illus.). 1993. 300.00 (*0-226-46757-0*) U Ch Pr.

Asia in the Making of Europe, Vol. I: The Century of Discovery, Book 1. Donald Lach. 568p. 1994. pap. text ed. 29.95 (*0-226-46731-7*) U Ch Pr.

Asia in the Making of Europe, Vol. I: The Century of Discovery, Book 2. Donald F. Lach. 504p. 1994. pap. text ed. 27.50 (*0-226-46732-5*) U Ch Pr.

Asia in the Making of Europe, Vol. II: A Century of Wonder, Book 1: The Visual Arts. Donald F. Lach. 1994. pap. text ed. 24.95 (*0-226-46730-9*) U Ch Pr.

Asia in the Making of Europe, Vol. II: A Century of Wonder, Book 2: The Literary Arts. Donald F. Lach. xxiv, 408p. 1994. pap. text ed. 24.95 (*0-226-46733-3*) U Ch Pr.

Asia in the Making of Europe, Vol II: A Century of Wonder, Book 3: The Scholarly Disciplines. Donald F. Lach. 440p. 1994. pap. text ed. 24.95 (*0-226-46734-1*) U Ch Pr.

Asia in the Nineteen Nineties: American & Soviet Perspectives. Ed. by Robert A. Scalapino & Gennady I. Chufrin. LC 90-86307. (Research Papers & Policy Studies: No. 36). xv, 272p. (Orig.). 1991. pap. 20.00 (*1-55729-025-3*) IEAS.

Asia in the 21st Century: Evolving Strategic Priorities. Ed. by Michael D. Bellows. 1994. write for info. (*0-318-72954-7*) USGPO.

Asia in Western & World History: A Guide for Teaching. Ed. by Ainslie T. Embree & Carol Gluck. (Columbia Project on Asia in the Core Curriculum Ser.). 768p. 1995. 75.00 (*1-56324-264-8*, East Gate Bk); pap. 27.50 (*1-56324-265-6*, East Gate Bk) M E Sharpe.

Asia in Western Fiction. Ed. by Robin W. Winks & James R. Rush. LC 89-20149. 224p. (Orig.). 1990. pap. text ed. 14.95 (*0-8248-1293-X*) UH Pr.

***Asia Intellectual Property Reports 1993.** Chew K. Ying & Ang K. Tiang. 724p. 1994. write for info. (*0-409-99708-0*) Butterworth Legal Pubs.

***Asia Key Indicators for Developing Countries.** (Illus.). 425p. 1995. pap. 295.00 (*0-7605-1694-4*) Rector Pr.

***Asia Media, Advertising, Marketing.** (Illus.). 500p. (C). 1994. 495.00 (*1-57205-828-5*) Rector Pr.

Asia Pacific: It's Role in the New World Disorder. Michael Dobbs-Higginson. 404p. 1994. 34.95 (*0-434-00081-7*, Pub. by W Heinemann Ltd) Trafalgar.

***Asia Pacific Business Directory.** (Illus.). 300p. (Orig.). 1994. pap. 295.00 (*0-7605-0716-3*) Rector Pr.

Asia Pacific Conference on Insurance Taxation. Ed. by Bernard B. Goodman. 205p. 1991. ring bd. 125.00 (*1-56423-004-X*) Ntl Ctr Tax Ed.

Asia Pacific Conference on Insurance Taxation, 1992. Ed. by Bernard B. Goodman. 200p. 1992. ring bd. 125.00 (*1-56423-014-7*) Ntl Ctr Tax Ed.

Asia Pacific Conference on Insurance Taxation, 1993. Ed. by Bernard B. Goodman. 200p. 1993. ring bd. 125.00 (*1-56423-025-2*) Ntl Ctr Tax Ed.

***Asia Pacific Confidence & Security Building Measures.** Ed. by Ralph A. Cossa. LC 95-12882. (Significant Issues Ser.: Vol. 17, No. 6). 159p. (C). 1995. pap. text ed. 19.95 (*0-89206-307-6*) CSI Studies.

Asia Pacific Connections - Telecommunications Assessment. Ed. by Marcel Werner. LC 93-78864. 124p. 1993. pap. 65.00 (*90-5199-139-8*, Pub. by IOS Pr NE) IOS Press.

***Asia-Pacific Construction Costs Handbook.** Langdon, Davis, Seah International Staff. 1994. 139.95 (*0-87629-346-1*) R S Means.

***Asia-Pacific Construction Law Reports, 1991.** Ed. by Vincent Powell-Smith. 575p. 1994. write for info. (*0-409-99705-6*) Butterworth Legal Pubs.

***Asia-Pacific Construction Law Reports 1992.** Ed. & Intro. by Vincent Powell-Smith. 548p. 1994. write for info. (*0-409-99653-X*) Butterworth Legal Pubs.

Asia Pacific Economic Cooperation: The Challenge Ahead. Richard L. Grant et al. (Significant Issues Ser.: Vol. 12, No. 4). 62p. 1990. pap. text ed. 7.95 (*0-89206-158-8*) CSI Studies.

Asia-Pacific Economies: Promises & Challenges, 2 Vol. set. Jan Dutta. (Research in International Business & Finance Ser.: Vol. 6). 1987. 113.00 (*0-89232-647-6*); Pt. A. write for info. (*0-89232-851-7*); Pt. B. write for info. (*0-89232-852-5*) Jai Pr.

Asia Pacific in the New World Politics. Ed. by James C. Hsiung. LC 93-12747. 274p. 1993. lib. bdg. 44.00 (*1-55587-323-5*); pap. text ed. 18.95 (*1-55587-355-3*) Lynne Rienner.

Asia-Pacific Literatures in English: Bibliographies. Robert E. McDowell et al. LC 78-62030. (Illus.). (Orig.). 1978. 26.00 (*0-89410-072-6*); pap. 15.00 (*0-89410-073-4*) Three Continents.

Asia-Pacific Microwave Conference, 1992. IEEE Microwave Theory & Techniques Society Staff. Ed. by IEEE Staff. LC 91-78086. 600p. 1992. pap. text ed. write for info. (*0-7803-0549-3*, 92TH0426-7); fiche write for info. (*0-7803-0550-7*) Inst Electrical.

Asia-Pacific Physics Conference: Proceedings of the Fifth Conference, 2 vols. S. P. Chia et al. 1404p. 1994. text ed. 213.00 (*981-02-1741-2*) World Scientific Pub.

Asia-Pacific Physics Conference: Proceedings of the First, 2 vols., 1. Ed. by A Arima et al. 1984. write for info. (*9971-978-00-8*) World Scientific Pub.

Asia-Pacific Physics Conference: Proceedings of the First, 2 vols., Set. Ed. by A Arima et al. 1984. 140.00 (*0-317-01258-4*) World Scientific Pub.

Asia Pacific Physics Conference: Proceedings of the Fourth, 2 vols. S. H. Ahn et al. 1568p. 1991. pap. 83.00 (*981-02-0542-2*) World Scientific Pub.

Asia Pacific Physics Conference: Proceedings of the Fourth, 2 vols., Set. S. H. Ahn et al. 1568p. 1991. text ed. 263.00 (*981-02-0538-4*) World Scientific Pub.

Asia-Pacific Report Nineteen Eighty-Seven thru Nineteen Eighty-Eight: Trends, Issues, Challenges. Ed. by Charles E. Morrison. LC 87-20074. vi, 84p. 1987. pap. 10.00 (*0-86638-098-1*) EW Ctr HI.

Asia-Pacific Report, 1986: Trends, Issues, Challenges. Ed. by Charles E. Morrison. LC 85-27538. viii, 104p. 1986. pap. 10.00 (*0-86638-071-X*) EW Ctr HI.

Asia-Pacific Report, 1989: Focus: China in the Reform Era. Ed. by Charles E. Morrison & Robert F. Dernberger. LC 89-1103. vi, 126p. 1989. pap. 15.00 (*0-86638-111-2*) EW Ctr HI.

Asia-Pacific Satellite Business Directory, 1994-95. (Illus.). 352p. 1994. pap. 74.95 (*0-929548-13-2*) MLE Inc.

Asia Pacific Securities Handbook 1993. Ed. by Karl Wilson. 240p. 1993. pap. 99.95 (*1-878753-47-9*, Pub. by P Jay Pub HK) Ref Press.

***Asia-Pacific Securities Handbook, 1994-95.** 2nd ed. 279p. 1994. pap. 99.95 (*1-878753-74-6*) Ref Press.

***Asia-Pacific Securities Handbook, 1995-1996.** 3rd ed. 279p. 1995. pap. 99.95 (*1-57311-002-7*) Ref Press.

***Asia-Pacific Software Engineering Conference, 1st (APSEC '94) Proceedings, Tokyo, Japan, December 1994.** LC 94-72781. 472p. 1994. pap. text ed. 90.00 (*0-8186-6960-8*, PR06960) IEEE Comp Soc.

Asia-Pacific Workshop on Advances in Motion Control. IEEE (Industrial Electronics Society & Singapore Section) Staff. Ed. by IEEE (Institute of Electrical & Electronics Engineers, Inc.) Staff. LC 93-77329. 240p. 1993. pap. write for info. (*0-7803-1223-6*, 93TH0541-3); fiche write for info. (*0-7803-1224-4*) Inst Electrical.

***Asia Rural Poverty Vol. I: Bangladesh, India & Sri Lanka.** (Illus.). 560p. (Orig.). 1995. pap. 295.00 (*0-7605-1687-1*) Rector Pr.

***Asia Rural Poverty Vol. II: Indonesia, Korea, Philippines & Thailand.** (Illus.). 560p. (Orig.). 1995. pap. 295.00 (*0-7605-1693-6*) Rector Pr.

Asia Society Guides: An Original Anthology. LC 74-27407. (Asia Society Ser.). (Illus.). 1976. reprint ed. lib. bdg. 48.95 (*0-405-06558-2*) Ayer.

Asia Society Reprint Collection. 428.50 (*0-405-06551-5*, 394) Ayer.

***Asia Stock Handbook 1994.** 200p. (Orig.). 1995. pap. 200.00 (*0-7605-1987-0*) Rector Pr.

Asia the Beautiful Cookbook. Jackie Passmore. LC 16-4. (Beautiful Cookbook Ser.). 256p. 1992. 45.00 (*0-00-255115-2*) Collins SF.

Asia: the People of China & Japan: Learning Center. Irene Handberg. (Multicultural Education Ser.). 64p. 1992. teacher ed write for info. (*1-56831-411-6*) Lrning Connect.

Asia: the People of China & Japan: Learning Center, Set. Irene Handberg. (Multicultural Education Ser.). 64p. 1992. write for info. (*1-56831-140-0*) Lrning Connect.

Asia Through the Back Door. 3rd ed. Rick Steves & John Gottberg. (Illus.). 336p. (Orig.). 1990. pap. 15.95 (*0-945465-48-3*) John Muir.

Asia Through the Back Door. 4th ed. Rick Steves & Bob Effertz. (Illus.). 352p. (Orig.). 1993. pap. 16.95 (*1-56261-109-7*) John Muir.

Asia Tobacco Markets. Ed. by Lewis B. Sckolnick. 360p. (Orig.). (C). 1994. pap. 1,795.00 (*1-57205-307-0*) Rector Pr.

***Asia Today: An Atlas of Reproducible Pages.** rev. ed. (Today Ser.). (Illus.). 210p. 1995. ring bd. 33.45 (*0-930141-57-1*) World Eagle.

Asia Today: Two Outlooks. Han Suyin. (Beatty Memorial Lectures Ser.). 1969. pap. 9.95 (*0-7735-0062-6*, Pub. by McGill CN) U of Toronto Pr.

Asia Today: Two Outlooks. Suyin Han. LC 77-91795. (Beatty Memorial Lectures). 115p. reprint ed. pap. 32.80 (*0-7837-1016-X*, 2041327) Bks Demand.

***Asia Trade Handbook 1994-1995.** (Illus.). 400p. (Orig.). 1994. pap. 595.00 (*0-7605-0998-0*) Rector Pr.

Asia Yearbook 1994. Ed. by Lewis B. Sckolnick. (Illus.). 247p. (Orig.). (C). 1994. 190.00 (*1-57205-016-0*); pap. 149.00 (*1-57205-017-9*) Rector Pr.

***Asia Yearbook 1995.** (Illus.). 250p. (Orig.). 1995. pap. 165.00 (*0-7605-1643-X*) Rector Pr.

***Asia Yearbook 1995.** 35th ed. Far Eastern Economic Review Staff. 240p. 1995. 59.95 (*962-7010-59-6*); pap. 45.00 (*962-7010-58-8*) Intl Pubns Serv.

***Asia 1994 Yearbook.** (Illus.). 320p. (Orig.). 1994. pap. 165.00 (*1-57205-738-6*) Rector Pr.

ASIAN: Business Opportunities Series. Metra Consulting Staff. 300p. 1984. 334.00 (*0-86033-248-9*) G & T Inc.

***Asian Advertising, Marketing & Media Data.** 306p. 1994. 470.00 (*0-86338-506-0*, Pub. by Euromonitor Pubns UK) Gale.

***Asian Affair.** Hubert Byrd. 150p. (YA). Date not set. pap. 7.95 (*0-7610-0222-7*) NW Pub.

Asian American: Chinese & Japanese in the United States since 1850. Roger Daniels. LC 88-5643. (Illus.). 402p. 1990. 18.95 (*0-295-97018-9*) U of Wash Pr.

***Asian American: Emerging Minorities.** 2nd ed. Harry H. Kitano & Roger Daniels. LC 94-22745. 208p. 1994. pap. text ed. write for info. (*0-13-315185-9*) P-H.

Asian American: How the Years Got Their Names. Ret. by Lynell Johnson. (Graphic Learning Multicultural Literature Program Ser.). (Illus.). (ENG & SPA.). (J). (gr. k-5). 1994. 39.00 (*0-87746-419-7*) Graphic Learning.

Asian American: Jade Snow Wong. K. Hollenbeck. (Graphic Learning Multicultural Literature Program Ser.). (Illus.). (ENG & SPA.). (J). (gr. k-5). 1994. 39.00 (*0-87746-413-8*) Graphic Learning.

Asian American: Minoru Yasui. Beth Lyons. (Graphic Learning Multicultural Literature Program Ser.). (Illus.). (ENG & SPA.). (J). (gr. k-5). 1994. 39.00 (*0-87746-416-2*) Graphic Learning.

Asian American: The Mole & the Great Man. Ret. by K. Hollenbeck. (Graphic Learning Multicultural Literature Program Ser.). (Illus.). (ENG & SPA.). (J). (gr. k-5). 1994. 39.00 (*0-87746-422-7*) Graphic Learning.

Asian American: The Way of the Tiger. Ret. by G. Davis. (Graphic Learning Multicultural Literature Program Ser.). (Illus.). (ENG & SPA.). (J). (gr. k-5). 1994. 39.00 (*0-87746-425-1*) Graphic Learning.

***Asian American Almanac, Vol. 1.** (Asian American Reference Library). 208p. (YA). 1995. 29.00 (*0-8103-9686-6*, UXL) Gale.

***Asian American Almanac: A Reference Work on Asians in the U. S.** Ed. by Susan Gall & Irene Natividad. 900p. 1995. 95.00 (*0-8103-9193-7*) Gale.

Asian-American Authors. Ed. by William Adams et al. (Multi-Ethnic Literature Ser.). 1976. teacher ed 6.08 (*0-685-02280-3*) HM.

***Asian American Biography, 2 vols.** (Asian American Reference Library). 416p. 1995. 55.00 (*0-8103-9687-4*, UXL) Gale.

***Asian American Chronology.** (Asian American Reference Library). (Illus.). 160p. 1995. text ed. 29.00 (*0-8103-9692-0*, UXL) Gale.

Asian American Educational Experience: A Sourcebook for Teachers & Students. Ed. by Don T. Nakanishi & Tina Y. Nishida. LC 94-16361. 352p. 1994. 55.00 (*0-415-90871-X*, B2999) Routledge.

Asian American Educational Experience: A Sourcebook for Teachers & Students. Ed. by Donald T. Nakanishi & Tina Y. Nishida. LC 94-16361. 416p. 1994. pap. 18.95 (*0-415-90872-8*, B3003) Routledge.

***Asian American Encyclopedia, 6 Vols.** Ed. by Franklin Ng. LC 94-33003. (Illus.). 1900p. (YA). 1994. lib. bdg. 449.95 (*1-85435-677-1*) Marshall Cavendish.

Asian American Experience, 15 vols., Set. Ronald Takaki. (Illus.). 1994. write for info. (*0-7910-2175-0*, Am Art Analog) Chelsea Hse.

Asian American Experiences in the United States: Oral Histories of First to Fourth Generation Americans from China, the Philippines, Japan, India, the Pacific Islands, Vietnam & Cambodia. Joann F. Lee. LC 90-53504. (Illus.). 240p. 1991. lib. bdg. 27.50x (*0-89950-585-6*) McFarland & Co.

***Asian American Indians.** Alexandra Bandon. LC 94-41698. (Footsteps to America Ser.). (J). 1995. 14.95 (*0-02-768144-0*, New Dscvry Bks) Silver Burdett Pr.

***Asian American Literature.** Wong. (Literary Mosiac Ser.). (C). 1995. text ed. write for info. (*0-673-46977-8*) HarpCollege.

Asian American Literature: A Thematic Resource for K-12. Maywan S. Krach. (Illus.). 28p. 1994. 4.95 (*1-885008-00-7*) Shens Bks.

Asian American Literature: An Annotated Bibliography. Ed. by King-Kok Cheung & Stan Yogi. LC 88-5355. x, 276p. 1988. 37.50 (*0-87352-960-X*, B202C); pap. 19.75 (*0-87352-961-8*, B202P) Modern Lang.

Asian-American Literature: An Introduction to the Writings & Their Social Context. Elaine Kim. 248p. 1984. pap. 19.95 (*0-87722-352-1*) Temple U Pr.

***Asian-American Market Handbook 1995.** 200p. (Orig.). 1995. pap. 2,195.00 (*0-7605-2006-2*) Rector Pr.

Asian American Movement: A Social History. William Wei. LC 92-29438. (Asian American History & Culture Ser.). (Illus.). 376p. 1994. 39.95 (*1-56639-049-4*) Temple U Pr.

Asian American Movement: A Social History. William Wei. LC 92-29438. (Asian American History & Literature Ser.). (Illus.). 376p. (C). 1994. pap. text ed. 18.95 (*1-56639-183-0*) Temple U Pr.

Asian American Panethnicity: Bridging Institutions & Identities. Yen L. Espiritu. (Asian American History & Culture Ser.). 240p. (C). 1992. pap. 18.95 (*1-56639-096-6*) Temple U Pr.

***Asian American Reference Library, 5 Vols.** 1995. text ed. 119.00 (*0-8103-9685-8*, UXL) Gale.

Asian American Studies: An Annotated Bibliography & Research Guide. Ed. by Hyung-Chan Kim. LC 89-1925. (Bibliographies & Indexes in American History Ser.: No. 11). 514p. 1989. text ed. 85.00 (*0-313-26026-5*, KAT, Greenwood Pr) Greenwood.

***Asian American Voices.** (Asian American Reference Library). 160p. (YA). 1995. 29.00 (*0-8103-9496-0*, UXL) Gale.

Asian-Americans: A Study Guide & Source Book. Lynn P. Dunn. LC 74-31620. 1975. pap. 9.95 (*0-88247-304-2*) R & E Pubs.

Asian Americans: Achievement Beyond IQ. James R. Flynn. 184p. 1991. text ed. 39.95 (*0-8058-1110-9*) L Erlbaum Assocs.

Asian Americans: An Interpretive History. Sucheng Chan. (Twayne's Immigrant Heritage of American Ser.). 240p. (C). 1991. text ed. 24.95 (*0-8057-8426-8*, Twayne); pap. 11.95 (*0-8057-8437-3*, Twayne) Macmillan.

Asian Americans: Comparative & Global Perspectives. Ed. by Shirley Hune et al. LC 91-56. (Association for Asian American Studies Ser.). 290p. (C). 1991. pap. 30.00 (*0-87422-071-8*) Wash St U Pr.

***Asian Americans: Contemporary Perspectives.** Ed. by Pyong Gap Min. (Focus Editions Ser.: Vol. 174). 304p. 1994. 49.95 (*0-8039-4335-0*) Sage.

***Asian Americans: Contemporary Perspectives.** Ed. by Pyong Gap Min. (Sage Focus Editions Ser.: Vol. 174). 304p. 1994. pap. 24.95 (*0-8039-4336-9*) Sage.

Asian Americans: Oral Histories of First to Fourth Generation Americans from China, Korea, the Philippines, Japan, India, the Pacific Islands, Vietnam, & Cambodia. Joann F. Lee. LC 92-53730. (Illus.). 256p. 1992. pap. 11.95 (*1-56584-023-2*) New Press NY.

Asian Americans: Personality Patterns, Identity, & Mental Health. Laura Uba. LC 93-41723. 302p. 1993. lib. bdg. 33.95 (*0-89862-372-3*) Guilford Pr.

Asian Americans & the Supreme Court: A Documentary History. Ed. by Hyung-Chan Kim. LC 92-3067. (Documentary Reference Collections). 1184p. 1992. text ed. 135.00 (*0-313-27234-4*, KAK/, Greenwood Pr) Greenwood.

Asian Americans in Higher Education & at Work. Jayjia Hsia. 256p. (C). 1987. text ed. 49.95 (*0-8058-0089-1*) L Erlbaum Assocs.

Asian Americans in the United States, Vol. I. Alexander Yamato et al. 320p. 1993. per., pap. 24.50 (*0-8403-8240-5*) Kendall-Hunt.

Asian Americans in the United States, Vol. 2. Yamato et al. 288p. (C). 1993. pap. text ed. 23.50 (*0-8403-8362-2*) Kendall-Hunt.

Asian Americans Information Directory. 2nd ed. Backus. 1993. 75.00 (*0-8103-8501-5*) Gale.

Asian & African Studies, Vol. 20. Ed. by Jozef Genzor. (C). 1984. text ed. 60.00 (*0-7007-0183-4*, Pub. by Curzon Pr UK) Humanities.

Asian & African Studies, Vol. 21. Ed. by Jozef Genzor. (C). 1985. text ed. 60.00 (*0-7007-0186-9*, Pub. by Curzon Pr UK) Humanities.

Asian & African Studies, Vol. 26, 1991. Ed. by Jozef Genzor & Viktor Krupa. 280p. (C). 1990. text ed. 60.00 (*0-7007-0226-1*, Pub. by Curzon Pr UK) Humanities.

Asian & African Studies, 1987. Ed. by Jozef Genzor & Viktor Krupa. (Asian & African Studies: Vol. 23). 328p. (C). 1987. text ed. 60.00 (*0-7007-0211-3*, Pub. by Curzon Pr UK) Humanities.

Asian & African Studies, 1990, Vol. 25. Ed. by Jozef Genzor & Viktor Krupa. 380p. (C). 1989. text ed. 60.00 (*0-7007-0223-7*, Pub. by Curzon Pr UK) Humanities.

Asian & African Systems of Slavery. Ed. by James L. Watson. LC 79-19728. 356p. reprint ed. pap. 101.50 (*0-7837-4803-5*, 2044450) Bks Demand.

Asian & Asian American Studies. 113p. 1993. 20.00 (*0-8389-7691-3*) Assn Coll & Res Libs.

***Asian & Australasian Companies: A Guide to Sources of Information.** Ed. by Richard Rickson. 334p. 1994. 94.95 (*0-900246-61-8*) CBD Res.

***Asian & Pacific Islander Americans & Drug & Alcohol Abuse: A Resource Guide.** 1995. lib. bdg. 251.95 (*0-8490-6786-3*) Gordon Pr.

Asian & Pacific Islander Migration to the United States: A Model for New Global Patterns. Elliott R. Barkan. LC 92-10619. (Contributions in Ethnic Studies: No. 30). 280p. 1992. text ed. 49.95 (*0-313-27538-6*, BAZ/, Greenwood Pr) Greenwood.

***Asian & Pacific Islander Population in the United States.** 1995. lib. bdg. 250.00 (*0-8490-6513-5*) Gordon Pr.

Asian & Pacific Islander Task Force Report on the Year 2000: Health Promotion Objectives & Recommendations for California. 68p. (Orig.). (C). 1993. pap. text ed. 40.00 (*0-7881-0089-0*) Diane Pub.

Asian Anthropologist in the South: Field Experiences with Blacks, Indians, & Whites. Choong S. Kim. LC 76-49448. 168p. 1977. pap. text ed. 12.00x (*0-87049-432-5*) U of Tenn Pr.

Asian Apiculture: Proceedings of the First International Conference on the Asian Honey Bees & Bee Mites. Ed. by Lawrence J. Connor et al. LC 93-29190. 1993. 79.95 (*1-878075-03-9*) Wicwas Pr.

Asian Appetizers: Easy, Exotic First Courses to Dress up Any Meal. Joyce Jue. LC 91-12906. (Illus.). 132p. (Orig.). 1991. pap. 16.95 (*0-9627345-1-9*, Astolat Bks) Harlow & Ratner.

Asian Arcady: The Land & Peoples of Northern Siam. Reginald S. Le May. LC 77-87041. reprint ed. 27.00 (*0-404-16833-7*) AMS Pr.

Asian Art. 3rd ed. John D. LaPlante. 304p. (C). 1992. pap. write for info. (*0-697-11591-7*) Brown & Benchmark.

Asian Art, Vol. 1, No. 3. 80p. 1989. pap. 10.00 (*0-19-505508-X*) OUP.

Asian Art: Selections from the Collection of Mr. & Mrs. John D. Rockefeller, 3rd. Sherman E. Lee. (Illus.). 1970. pap. text ed. 35.00 (*0-89192-278-4*); 25.00 (*0-685-02525-X*) Interbk Inc.

Asian Art in the Art Institute of Chicago. Elinor Pearlstein et al. (Illus.). 152p. 1993. pap. 24.95 (*0-86559-095-8*) Art Inst Chi.

Asian Art in the Art Institute of Chicago. Elinor Pearlstein et al. (Illus.). 152p. 1993. 35.00 (*0-8109-1916-8*) Abrams.

Asian Art in the Walters Art Gallery: A Selection. Hiram W. Woodward, Jr. (Illus.). 120p. (Orig.). 1991. pap. 25.00 (*0-911886-38-9*) Walters Art.

***Asian Art Motifs from Korea: Trees.** (Illus.). 200p. 1995. 40.00 (*89-7059-025-0*, Pub. by Ahn Graphics KN) Weatherhill.

Asian Art Museum: Selected Articles from "Orientations" Asian Art Museum Curators. (Illus.). 175p. 1993. reprint ed. pap. text ed. 15.00 (*0-939117-06-1*) Asian Art Mus.

***Asian Art Museum of San Francisco: Selected Works.** Asian Art Museum of San Francisco Curatorial Staff et al. LC 94-32735. (Illus.). 208p. 1994. pap. 15.00 (*0-295-97414-1*) Asian Art Mus.

***Asian Art Museum of San Francisco: Selected Works.** Asian Art Museum of San Francisco Curatorial Staff et al. (Illus.). 208p. 1994. 25.00 (*0-614-04697-1*) U of Wash Pr.

An Asterisk (*) at the beginning of an entry indicates that the title is appearing in BIP for the first time.

Asian Arts in America: Seeds of the Inner Life. Ed. by Paul R. La Chance. (West & the Wider World Ser.: Vol. 5). (Illus.). 380p. (C). 1988. 29.95 (*0-940121-11-5*) Cross Cultural Pubns.

*__Asian Blepharoplasty: Surgical Atlas.__ William P. Chen. LC 94-27419. 1994. write for info. (*0-7506-9496-3*) Buttrwrth-Heinemann.

Asian Bureaucratic Systems Emergent from the British Imperial Tradition. Ralph J. Braibanti et al. LC 66-27487. (Duke University, Commonwealth-Studies Center, Publication Ser.: No. 28). 761p. reprint ed. pap. 180.00 (*0-8357-5788-9*, 2023370) Bks Demand.

Asian Business & Environment in Transition: Selected Readings & Essays. Ed. by A. Kapoor. LC 73-20719. 667p. (C). 1976. 9.95 (*0-87850-020-0*) Darwin Pr.

Asian Californians. Sucheng Chan. Ed. by Norris Hundley, Jr. & John A. Schutz. (Golden State Ser.). 246p. 1991. 10.00 (*0-929651-00-6*) MTL.

Asian Capital Markets: Regional & Global Perspectives. Ed. by Lilia C. Clemente & Roberto S. Mariano. LC 92-71666. (Illus.). 249p. (Orig.). 1992. pap. 29.95 (*0-9633012-0-9*) Asian Securit.

Asian Capitalists in the European Mirror. M. Rutten. 65p. 1994. pap. 16.00 (*90-5383-270-X*, Pub. by VU Univ Pr NE) Paul & Co Pubs.

Asian Century: The Economic Ascent of the Pacific Rim - & What It Means for the West. Julian Weiss. LC 88-24605. 239p. reprint ed. pap. 68.20 (*0-7837-1577-3*, 2041869) Bks Demand.

Asian Christian Spirituality: Reclaiming Traditions. Ed. by Virginia Fabella et al. LC 91-38771. 160p. 1992. pap. 16.95 (*0-88344-800-9*) Orbis Bks.

*__Asian City: Processes of Development, Characteristics & Planning.__ Ed. by Ashok K. Dutt. LC 94-31375. (Geojournal Library Ser.). 408p. (C). 1994. lib. bdg. 176.00 (*0-7923-3135-4*) Kluwer Ac.

Asian Civilizations. Jean-Michel Coblence. Tr. by Jane C. Lamb. (Human Story Ser.). Orig. Title: Les Civilisations de L'Asie. (Illus.). 77p. (YA). (gr. 7 up). 1988. 12.95 (*0-382-09483-2*) Silver Burdett Pr.

Asian Communism: Continuity & Transition. Ed. by Robert A. Scalapino & Dalchoong Kim. LC 88-62372. (Korea Research Monographs: No. 15). 416p. (Orig.). (C). 1989. pap. 20.00 (*1-55729-007-5*) IEAS.

Asian Company Handbook. 279p. (C). 1993. text ed. 165.00 (*0-934393-35-4*) Rector Pr.

Asian Contributions to Psychology. Ed. by Anand C. Paranjpe et al. LC 88-2334. 307p. 1988. text ed. 69.50 (*0-275-92524-2*, C2524, Praeger Pubs) Greenwood.

Asian Cooking. Anne Willan. LC 93-37150. (Illus.). 128p. 1994. 19.95 (*1-56458-593-X*) Dorling Kindersley.

*__Asian Countries Gender Indicators.__ (Illus.). 250p. (Orig.). 1994. pap. 225.00 (*1-57205-815-3*) Rector Pr.

Asian Crafts. Judith H. Corwin. Ed. by Iris Rosoff. LC 91-13500. (Illus.). 48p. (J). (gr. 1-4). 1992. lib. bdg. 13.27 (*0-531-11013-3*) Watts.

Asian Crafts. St. Tamara. LC 71-86983. (Activity Bks.: Vol. 6). (Illus.). (J). (gr. 2-6). 1972. lib. bdg. 13.95 (*0-87460-148-7*) Lion Bks.

Asian Crucible: The Steel Industry in China & India. Gilbert Etienne et al. (Illus.). 368p. (C). 1992. text ed. 42.00 (*0-8039-9414-1*) Sage.

Asian Development: Economic Success & Policy Lessons. William James et al. LC 88-40191. (C). 1989. pap. text ed. 16.95 (*0-299-11784-7*) U of Wis Pr.

Asian Development: The Role of Development Assistance. John P. Lewis. (Asian Agenda Report Ser.: No. 7). (Illus.). 66p. (Orig.). 1987. pap. text ed. 8.50 (*0-8191-6590-5*, The Asia Society) U Pr of Amer.

*__Asian Development Bank.__ Nihal Kappagoda. LC 94-45003. 200p. 1995. lib. bdg. 35.00 (*1-55587-468-1*) Lynne Rienner.

*__Asian Development Bank.__ Nihal Kappagoda. LC 94-45003. (Multilateral Development Banks Ser.: Vol. 2). 200p. 1995. pap. text ed. 19.95 (*1-55587-494-0*) Lynne Rienner.

Asian Development Bank & Rural Development: Policy & Practice. Robert Wihtol. LC 87-32369. 256p. 1988. text ed. 59.95 (*0-312-01673-5*) St Martin.

Asian Development Model & the Caribbean Basin Initiative: Conference Papers. Ed. by John Tessitore & Susan Woolfson. 244p. (Orig.). 1985. pap. 50.00 (*0-87641-222-3*) Carnegie Ethics & Intl Affairs.

Asian Development Outlook, 1992. Asian Development Bank Staff. (Illus.). 334p. 1992. pap. 19.95 (*0-19-585742-9*) OUP.

Asian Development Outlook 1993. Asian Development Bank Staff. (Illus.). 296p. (C). 1993. pap. 19.95 (*0-19-585941-3*, 11799) OUP.

Asian Development Outlook 1994. Asian Development Bank Staff. (Illus.). 264p. 1994. pap. 19.95 (*0-19-586599-5*) OUP.

*__Asian Development Outlook 1995.__ Asian Development Bank Staff. (Illus.). 280p. 1995. pap. 19.95 (*0-19-587419-6*) OUP.

*__Asian Development Overlook 1994.__ (Illus.). 250p. (Orig.). 1994. pap. 225.00 (*1-57205-811-0*) Rector Pr.

Asian Development Styles. Ralph Pieris. LC 77-74486. 1977. 7.50 (*0-88386-831-8*) S Asia.

Asian Diaries with Photographs by Hedda Morrison. H. W. Arndt. (Asia-Pacific Monographs: No. 2). (Illus.). 284p. 1987. text ed. 45.00 (*9971-68-125-0*, Pub. by Chopmen Singapore SI) Advent Bks Div.

Asian Dilemma in U. S. Foreign Policy: National Interest versus Strategic Planning. K. Holly Maze Carter. LC 88-3416. 250p. (C). 1989. 62.95 (*0-87332-512-5*); pap. text ed. 25.95 (*0-87332-544-3*) M E Sharpe.

Asian Dimension of Soviet Policy. D. D. Narula & R. R. Sharma. 1986. 25.00 (*0-317-56324-6*, Patriot) S Asia.

*__Asian Dynamism Through Human Resource Development.__ Asian Productivity Organization Staff. (Illus.). 553p. 1993. pap. text ed. 15.00 (*92-833-2128-6*, 321286, Pub. by Asian Productvty Org JA) Qual Resc.

*__Asian Electric Utilities Handbook.__ (Illus.). 250p. (Orig.). 1994. pap. 225.00 (*1-57205-813-7*) Rector Pr.

Asian Elephant: An Action Plan for Its Conservation. Charles Santiapillai & Peter Jackson. (Illus.). 88p. (Orig.). 1990. pap. 18.00 (*2-88032-997-3*, Pub. by IUCN SZ) Island Pr.

Asian Elephant: Ecology & Management. R. Sukumar. (Studies in Applied Ecology & Resource Management). (Illus.). 252p. (C). 1993. pap. 34.95 (*0-521-43758-X*) Cambridge U Pr.

*__Asian Energy Indicators.__ (Illus.). 250p. (Orig.). 1994. pap. 225.00 (*1-57205-816-1*) Rector Pr.

Asian Energy Problems. Asian Development Bank Staff. LC 81-84610. 304p. 1982. text ed. 65.00 (*0-275-90757-0*, C0757, Praeger Pubs) Greenwood.

Asian Experience in North America Series: Chinese & Japanese, 47 bks, Set. Roger Daniels. (Illus.). 1979. reprint ed. lib. bdg. 1,345.50 (*0-405-18992-3*) Ayer.

Asian Experience in Trade & Industrial Reform. Mohammad Sadli. LC 93-33942. 1994. pap. 6.95 (*1-55815-307-1*) ICS Pr.

Asian Eyes. Ken Crowder. 296p. 1990. 18.95 (*0-8027-5746-4*) Walker & Co.

Asian Faces of Jesus. R. S. Sugirtharajah. LC 93-536. (Faith & Cultures Ser.). 280p. (Orig.). 1993. pap. 19.95 (*0-88344-833-5*) Orbis Bks.

Asian Film Industry. John A. Lent. (Film Studies). (Illus.). 320p. 1990. text ed. 32.50 (*0-292-70421-6*); pap. 17.95 (*0-292-70422-4*) U of Tex Pr.

Asian Flashpoint: Security & the Korean Peninsula. Ed. by Andrew Mack. 175p. 1994. pap. 24.95 (*1-86873-401-3*, Pub. by Allen Unwin AT) Paul & Co Pubs.

Asian Food Feasts. Sigrid M. Shepard. LC 78-15773. 455p. 1984. pap. 14.95 (*0-932722-07-5*) Solstice Pr.

Asian Gambit. James Goonewardene. 240p. 1986. pap. 9.00 (*81-7013-033-6*, Pub. by Navrang) S Asia.

Asian Grill. David Barich & Thomas Ingalls. (Illus.). 72p. 1994. 12.95 (*0-8118-0674-X*) Chronicle Bks.

Asian Heritage. Stanley Barkan & Diana Chang. 1991. boxed 75.00 (*0-89304-941-7*) Cross-Cultrl NY.

Asian History. 3rd ed. Intro. by Grant Goodman. (Selected Syllabi from American Colleges & Universities in History Ser.). 320p. 1993. pap. text ed. 16.95 (*1-55876-064-4*) Wiener Pubs Inc.

Asian History on File. Diagram Visual Information Staff. (On File Ser.). 288p. (J). (gr. 5-10). 1995. 155.00 (*0-8160-2975-X*) Facts on File.

Asian Homosexuality. Ed. by Wayne R. Dynes & Stephen Donaldson. LC 92-15208. (Studies in Homosexuality: Vol. 3). (Illus.). 392p. 1992. 60.00 (*0-8153-0548-6*) Garland.

*__Asian House: Contemporary Houses of Southeast Asia.__ Robert Powell. (Illus.). 176p. 1995. 55.00 (*981-00-3496-2*, Pub. by Select Bks SI) Weatherhill.

Asian Ideas of East & West: Tagore & His Critics in Japan. Stephen N. Hay. LC 73-89972. (Harvard East Asian Ser.: No. 40). 502p. reprint ed. pap. 143.10 (*0-7837-1517-X*, 2041794) Bks Demand.

Asian Indian Experience. Parmatma Saran. 129p. 1985. 18.95 (*0-87073-646-9*); pap. 11.95 (*0-87073-647-7*) Schenkman Bks Inc.

Asian Indians. Susan Gordon. LC 90-12275. (Recent American Immigrants Ser.). (Illus.). 64p. (J). (gr. 5-8). 1990. lib. bdg. 14.21 (*0-531-10976-3*) Watts.

*__Asian Indians, Filipinos, Other Asian Communities & the Law.__ Ed. by Charles McClain. LC 94-22629. (Asian Americans & the Law Ser.: No. 4). (Illus.). 424p. 1994. 63.00 (*0-8153-1851-0*) Garland.

Asian Indians in the United States: A 1980 Census Profile. Peter Xenos et al. (Papers of the East-West Population Institute: No. 111). viii, 54p. 1989. 3.00 (*0-86638-114-7*) EW Ctr HI.

Asian Indigenous Law. Masaji Chiba. 250p. 1987. text ed. 97.50 (*0-7103-0113-8*, 01138, Pub. by Kegan Paul Intl UK) Routledge Chapman & Hall.

*__Asian Industrialization & Africa: Studies in Policy Alternatives to Structural Adjustment.__ Ed. by Howard Stein. LC 94-31707. 1995. write for info. (*0-312-12433-3*) St Martin.

Asian Issues (Nineteen Eighty-Five) Eduardo Lachica et al. (Asian Agenda Report Ser.: No. 3). (Illus.). 86p. (Orig.). (C). 1986. lib. bdg. 28.00 (*0-8191-5342-7*); pap. 10.50 (*0-8191-5343-5*) U Pr of Amer.

Asian Journal of Thomas Merton. Thomas Merton. Ed. by Naomi B. Stone et al. LC 71-103370. (Illus.). 448p. 1973. pap. 12.95 (*0-8112-0570-3*, NDP394) New Directions.

*__Asian Key Development Indicators.__ (Illus.). 250p. (Orig.). 1994. pap. 225.00 (*1-57205-812-9*) Rector Pr.

Asian Mainland. J. W. Jamieson. (Atlas of Mankind Ser.: Vol. 4). (Illus.). 128p. 1995. 30.00 (*0-941694-35-6*) Cliveden Pr.

Asian Marine Biology, 8 Vols., Vol. 1: 1984. Brian Morton. 192p. (C). 1992. Vol. 1, 1984, 192p. pap. 80.00 (*962-209-113-X*, Pub. by Hong Kong U Pr HK) St Mut.

Asian Marine Biology, 8 Vols., Vol. 2: 1985. Brian Morton. 152p. (C). 1992. Vol. 2, 1985, 152p. pap. 80.00 (*962-209-126-1*, Pub. by Hong Kong U Pr HK) St Mut.

Asian Marine Biology, 8 Vols., Vol. 3: 1986. Brian Morton. 192p. (C). 1992. Vol. 3, 1986, 192p. pap. 80.00 (*962-209-187-3*, Pub. by Hong Kong U Pr HK) St Mut.

Asian Marine Biology, 8 Vols., Vol. 4: 1987. Brian Morton. 170p. (C). 1992. Vol. 4, 1987, 170p. pap. 80.00 (*962-209-198-9*, Pub. by Hong Kong U Pr HK) St Mut.

Asian Marine Biology, 8 Vols., Vol. 5: 1988. Brian Morton. 146p. (C). 1992. Vol. 5, 1988, 146p. pap. 80.00 (*962-209-218-7*, Pub. by Hong Kong U Pr HK) St Mut.

Asian Marine Biology, 8 Vols., Vol. 6: 1989. Brian Morton. 256p. (C). 1992. Vol. 6, 1989, 256p. pap. 80.00 (*962-209-240-3*, Pub. by Hong Kong U Pr HK) St Mut.

Asian Marine Biology, 8 Vols., Vol. 7: 1990. Brian Morton. 214p. (C). 1992. Vol. 7, 1990, 214p. pap. 80.00 (*962-209-273-X*, Pub. by Hong Kong U Pr HK) St Mut.

Asian Marine Biology, 8 Vols., Vol. 8: 1991. Brian Morton. 232p. (C). 1992. Vol. 8, 1991, 232p. pap. 80.00 (*962-209-297-7*, Pub. by Hong Kong U Pr HK) St Mut.

*__Asian Market Economies: Challenges of a Changing International Environment.__ Ross Garnaut. 65p. (Orig.). 1994. pap. 15.95 (*981-3016-78-7*, Pub. by Inst SE Asian Studies SI) Ashgate Pub Co.

*__Asian Market Economies: Challenges of a Changing International Environment.__ Ross Garnaut. 54p. (Orig.). (C). 1994. pap. 35.00x (*0-7881-1299-6*) Diane Pub.

Asian Markets: A Guide to Company & Industry Information Sources. 3rd ed. Washington Researchers Staff. LC 88-51452. (International Ser.). 380p. (Orig.). 1993. pap. 335.00 (*1-56365-024-X*) Wash Res.

Asian Mathematical Conference: Proceedings of the Conference, University of Hong Kong, 14-18 August 1990. Ed. by Li Zhong et al. LC 92-9105. 650p. (C). 1992. text ed. 114.00 (*981-02-0749-2*) World Scientific Pub.

Asian Migration to Australia: The Background to Exclusion, 1896-1923. A. T. Yarwood. LC 84-15839. 210p. 1984. reprint ed. text ed. 52.50 (*0-313-24063-9*, YAAM, Greenwood Pr) Greenwood.

Asian Mind Game: Unlocking the Hidden Agenda of the Asian Business Culture. Chin-ning Chu. LC 90-46045. 288p. 1991. text ed. 26.00 (*0-89256-352-4*, Rawson Assocs) Macmillan.

Asian Minorities in American Schools, Colleges & Universities: A Classified Bibliography. Rama K. Rao. (Social Science Resource Guides Ser.: No. 5). 19p. (C). 1991. 6.95 (*0-9628998-4-4*) Ramdil.

Asian Money Markets. David C. Cole et al. (Illus.). 464p. 1995. 75.00 (*0-19-507429-7*) OUP.

Asian Music in North America. Ed. by Nazir A. Jairazbhoy & Sue C. De Vale. LC 76-640181. (Selected Reports in Ethnomusicology: Vol. 6). (Illus.). 199p. (Orig.). 1985. pap. 16.95 (*0-88287-020-3*) UCLA Dept Ethnom.

Asian Mythologies. Tr. by Wendy Doniger et al. LC 92-39077. (Illus.). xxiv, 376p. (C). 1993. pap. 27.00 (*0-226-06456-5*) U Ch Pr.

Asian Natural Gas - A New Era: Proceedings of a Conference Held in 1989. Ed. by Donald L. Klass & Tadahiko Ohashi. vi, 463p. 1989. 75.00 (*0-910091-70-6*) Inst Gas Tech.

Asian Natural Gas - Development of the Domestic Industry. Ed. by D. L. Klass et al. viii, 626p. 1993. 80.00 (*0-910091-87-0*) Inst Gas Tech.

Asian Natural Gas - New Markets & Distribution Methods. Ed. by D. L. Klass et al. viii, 618p. 1992. 75.00 (*0-910091-83-8*) Inst Gas Tech.

Asian Natural Gas--For a Brighter '90s. Ed. by Donald L. Klass & Tadahiko Ohashi. viii, 593p. 1991. 75.00 (*0-910091-78-1*) Inst Gas Tech.

Asian Nephrology. Ed. by K. S. Chugh et al. (Illus.). 1000p. 1995. 160.00 (*0-19-563401-2*) OUP.

*__Asian NIESs & the Global Economy: Industrial Restructuring & Corporate Strategy in the 1990s.__ Gordon L. Clark & Won Bae Kim. 360p. 1995. text ed. 48.50x (*0-8018-5105-X*) Johns Hopkins.

Asian Observer. Leighton Willgerodt. 176p. (Orig.). 1991. pap. 8.75 (*0-930693-07-8*) Cross Cult Pr.

*__Asian Pacific: Political & Economic Development in a Global Context.__ Vera Simone & Anne T. Ferara. 418p. (Orig.). (C). 1995. pap. text ed. 28.50 (*0-8013-0895-X*) Longman.

Asian Pacific Financial Markets. Y. K. Ho et al. Date not set. write for info. (*0-409-99591-6*) Butterworth Legal Pubs.

Asian-Pacific Operations Research (APORS '88): New Challenges for OR-MS in the Asian-Pacific Region: Proceedings of the 1st Conference of the Association of Asian-Pacific Operational Research Societies (APORS), Within IFORS, Seoul, Korea, August 24-26 1988. Ed. by B. H. Ahn. 736p. 1990. 154.00 (*0-444-88652-4*, North Holland) Elsevier.

Asian-Pacific Regional Security. Ed. by June T. Dreyer. LC 90-12832. (Illus.). 264p. 1990. pap. text ed. 14.95 (*0-88702-053-4*) Washington Inst Pr.

*__Asian Pacific Rim & Globalization.__ Ed. by Sam O. Park & Richard LeHeron. 202p. 1995. boxed, pap. 55.95 (*1-85628-894-3*, Pub. by Avebury Pub UK) Ashgate Pub Co.

Asian-Pacific Security after the Cold War. Ed. by T. B. Millar & James Walter. 144p. (Orig.). 1993. pap. 24.95 (*1-86373-398-1*, Pub. by Allen Unwin AT) Paul & Co Pubs.

Asian Panorama. K. M. De Silva & Sirima Kiribamune. 1990. text ed. 50.00 (*0-7069-4959-5*, Pub. by Vikas II) S Asia.

Asian Pasta. Linda Burum. LC 85-15663. 175p. (Orig.). 1985. 22.95 (*0-943186-21-8*); pap. 12.95 (*0-943186-23-4*) Aris Bks.

Asian Pasta: A Cook's Guide to the Noodles, Wrappers & Pasta Creations of the East. Linda Burum. (Illus.). 224p. 1985. pap. 12.45 (*0-201-10833-X*) Addison-Wesley.

Asian Pear Varieties in California. William H. Griggs & Ben T. Iwakiri. 60p. 1977. pap. 3.25 (*0-931876-00-1*, 4068) ANR Pubns CA.

Asian Perceptions of Nature: A Critical Approach. Ed. by Ole Bruun & Arne Kalland. (Nordic Institute of Asian Studies, Studies in Asian Topics, No.18). 260p. (C). 1995. pap. 25.00 (*0-7007-0290-3*, Pub. by Curzon Pr UK) Humanities.

Asian Perceptions of Nature: A Critical Approach. Ed. by Ole Bruun & Arne Kalland. (Nordic Institute of Asian Studies, Studies in Asian Topics, No.18). 260p. (C). 1995. text ed. 70.00 (*0-7007-0301-2*, Pub. by Curzon Pr UK) Humanities.

Asian Perspectives on International Security. Ed. by Donald H. McMillen. LC 83-24576. 226p. 1984. text ed. 35.00 (*0-312-05643-5*) St Martin.

A

Asian Philosophy. Ed. by Guttorm Floistad. LC 92-10697. (Contemporary Philosophy, a New Survey Ser.: Vol. 7). (C). 1993. lib. bdg. 170.00 (*0-7923-1762-9*) Kluwer Ac.

Asian Philosophy Today. Ed. by Dale Riepe. 322p. 1981. text ed. 91.00 (*0-677-15490-9*) Gordon & Breach.

Asian Plays: Fanshen, Saigon, & A Map of the World. David Hare. 256p. 1986. pap. 14.95 (*0-571-13990-6*) Faber & Faber.

*__Asian Pocket Guide for International Environmental Executives.__ William A. Delphos. Ed. by Alan J. Beard et al. 64p. 1994. write for info. (*1-883917-04-2*) Venture Pub NA.

Asian Policy: The New Soviet Challenge in the Pacific - A Twentieth Century Fund Paper. Robert A. Manning. 150p. 1988. 18.95 (*0-87078-245-2*); pap. 8.95 (*0-87078-244-4*) TCFP-PPP.

Asian Political Dictionary. Lawrence Ziring & C. I. Kim. LC 85-5994. (Clio Dictionaries in Political Science Ser.: No. 10). 438p. 1985. pap. text ed. 20.50 (*0-87436-369-1*) ABC-CLIO.

Asian Political Institutionalization. Ed. by Robert A. Scalapino et al. LC 85-80562. (Research Papers & Policy Studies: No. 15). 312p. 1986. pap. 20.00 (*0-912966-79-3*) IEAS.

*__Asian Popular Culture.__ John A. Lent. LC 94-45530. (International Communication & Popular Culture Ser.). (C). 1995. pap. text ed. 19.95 (*0-8133-2049-6*) Westview.

*__Asian Popular Culture.__ Ed. by John A. Lent. LC 94-45530. (International Communication & Popular Culture Ser.). 1995. text ed. 69.95 (*0-8133-2048-8*) Westview.

Asian Power & Politics: The Cultural Dimensions of Authority. Lucian W. Pye & Mary W. Pye. LC 85-2581. 432p. 1988. reprint ed. pap. 17.50 (*0-674-04979-9*) HUP.

Asian Question Collection. Linda Schwartz. 120p. (J). (gr. 4-8). 1994. 7.95 (*0-88160-215-9*, LW200) Learning Wks.

Asian Resources in the Southeastern United States: Archival & Manuscript Resources on China & Japan in North Carolina. Ed. by Kenneth W. Berger. (Occasional Papers of the Southeast Conference, Association for Asian Studies: No. 1). 73p. (Orig.). pap. 10.00 (*0-941481-01-8*) SE Conf Assn Asian Studies.

Asian Resources in the Southeastern United States: Archival & Manuscript Resources on East Asia in Georgia. Ed. by Kenneth W. Berger. (Occasional Papers of the Southeast Conference, Association for Asian Studies: No. 2). 58p. (Orig.). 1985. pap. 10.00 (*0-941481-02-6*) SE Conf Assn Asian Studies.

Asian Revolutionary, the Life of Sen Katayama. Hyman Kublin. LC 63-7156. 386p. reprint ed. pap. 110.10 (*0-8357-5789-7*, 2000882) Bks Demand.

Asian Roots, Western Soil: Japanese Influences in American Culture. Robert Manamura. Ed. by Robert Schildgen. (Illus.). 32p. (Orig.). 1993. pap. 5.99 (*0-942744-02-0*) Berkeley Art.

*__Asian Rural Poverty.__ (Illus.). 300p. (Orig.). 1994. pap. 225.00 (*0-7605-0915-8*) Rector Pr.

Asian Rural Societies see Contemporary Change in Traditional Societies

Asian Security: The Great Debate. Attar Chand. 318p. 1987. 34.95 (*0-318-37224-X*) Asia Bk Corp.

Asian Security Issues: National Systems & International Relations. Ed. by Lawrence Ziring & David G. Dickason. LC 88-82224. (Asian Forum Ser.). 200p. (Orig.). (C). 1988. pap. text ed. 12.50 (*0-929901-00-2*) WMU IGP.

Asian Security, 1985. Ed. by Research Institute for Peace & Security Staff. 226p. 1985. 38.50 (*0-08-031208-X*, Pergamon Pr); pap. 19.95 (*0-08-031209-8*, Pergamon Pr) Elsevier.

Asian Security, 1986. Ed. by Research Institute for Peace & Security. (Asia Ser.: No. 2). 212p. 1986. 38.50 (*0-08-033610-8*, Pergamon Pr); pap. 19.95 (*0-08-033611-6*, Pergamon Pr) Elsevier.

Asian Security 1987-1988: Asia 3. Research Institute for Peace & Security Staff. (Asia Ser.: No. 3). 212p. 1987. 28.75 (*0-317-66310-0*, Pergamon Pr) Elsevier.

Asian Security, 1988-89. RIPS Staff. (Asian Security Ser.: No. 4). (Illus.). 200p. 1988. 31.95 (*0-08-036263-X*, Pergamon Pr); pap. 19.95 (*0-08-036703-8*, Pergamon Pr) Elsevier.

Asian Security, 1990-91. RIPS Staff. (Asian Security Ser.: No. 6). 250p. 1990. 39.00 (*0-08-040709-9*, Pub. by Brasseys UK) Brasseys Inc.

Asian Security 1991-1992. Research Institute for Peace & Security Staff. (Asia Seven Asian Security Ser.). 285p. 1991. 39.00 (*0-08-041312-9*, Pub. by Brasseys UK); pap. 20.00 (*0-08-041316-1*, Pub. by Brasseys UK) Brasseys Inc.

Asian Security 1992-93. Research Institute for Peace Studies Staff. 250p. 1992. 45.00 (*1-85753-042-X*, Pub. by Brasseys UK) Brasseys Inc.

Asian Security, 1993-94. Research Institute for Peace Studies Staff. Ed. by Kasaka Masataka & Sidney Bearman. 254p. 1993. 40.00 (*1-85753-028-4*, Pub. by Brasseys UK) Brasseys Inc.

Asian Security, 1994-95. Research Institute for Peace Studies Staff. 256p. 1994. 40.00 (*1-85753-074-8*) Macmillan.

Asian Seminar on Rural Development: The Indian Experience. M. L. Dantwala. 1986. 25.00 (*81-204-0150-6*, Pub. by Oxford IBH II) S Asia.

An Asterisk (*) at the beginning of an entry indicates that the title is appearing in BIP for the first time. 475

Asian Shade. Larry Ketron. 1983. pap. 4.75 (*0-8222-0071-6*) Dramatists Play.

Asian Socioeconomic Development: A National Accounts Approach. Ed. by Kazushi Ohkawa & Bernard Key. 326p. 1981. text ed. 27.50 (*0-8248-0743-X*) UH Pr.

Asian States' Relations with the Middle East & North Africa: A Bibliography, 1950-1993. Sanford R. Silverburg & Bernard Reich. LC 94-4544. (Author Bibliographies Ser.: No. 6). 173p. 1994. 22.50 (*0-8108-2872-3*) Scarecrow.

Asian Studies: A Catalogue of Asian Resources in Connecticut. Comp. by Colleen A. Kelly. (Area Studies Resource Guides). 94p. 1980. 6.50 (*0-685-09432-4*) I N Thut World Educ Ctr.

Asian Studies in the Southeast: A Twenty-Five Year Retrospective. Ed. by Kenneth W. Berger. LC 86-31351. (Occasional Papers of the Southeast Conference, Association for Asian Studies: No. 2). x, 78p. (Orig.). 1987. pap. 10.00 (*0-941481-04-2*) SE Conf Assn Asian Studies.

***Asian Teachers in British Schools: A Study of Two Generations.** Paul A. Ghuman. LC 94-29845. 1995. 69.95 (*1-85359-261-7*); pap. text ed. 24.00 (*1-85359-260-9*) Taylor & Francis.

Asian Test Conference, 1st (ATS '92) LC 92-71801. 272p. 1992. 66.00 (*0-8186-2985-1*, 2985) IEEE Comp Soc.

Asian Test Symposium, 2nd (ATS '93) LC 93-77783. 341p. 1993. 70.00 (*0-8186-3930-X*, 3930) IEEE Comp Soc.

Asian Trade & Civilisation. Ed. by Genevieve Bouchon & Pierre-Yves Manguin. 260p. (C). 1993. write for info. (*0-521-36448-5*) Cambridge U Pr.

Asian Trade & European Expansion in the Age of Mercantilism. Dietmar Rothermund. 1981. 17.50 (*0-8364-0812-8*, Pub. by Manohar II) S Asia.

Asian Trade Routes. Ed. by Haellquist. (Continental & Maritime Studies on Asian Topics: No. 13). (C). 1991. pap. 37.50 (*0-7007-0212-1*, Pub. by Curzon Pr UK) Humanities.

Asian Tragedy: America & Vietnam. David Detzer. LC 91-37228. (Illus.). 160p. (YA). (gr. 7 up). 1992. lib. bdg. 16.90 (*1-56294-066-X*) Millbrook Pr.

Asian Urbanization: A Hong Kong Casebook. D. J. Swyer. 218p. (C). 1971. text ed. 36.00 (*0-85656-004-9*, Pub. by Hong Kong U Pr HK) St Mut.

Asian Urbanization Problems & Processes. F. J. Costa et al. (Urbanization of the Earth Ser.: Vol. 5). (Illus.). 165p. 1988. lib. bdg. 52.00 (*3-443-37007-1*) Lubrecht & Cramer.

***Asian Values & the U. S. How Much Conflict?** David I. Hitchcock. (CSIS Report Ser.). 41p. (C). 1994. pap. text ed. 9.95 (*0-89206-311-4*) CSI Studies.

Asian Variations in Ramayana. Ed. by K. Srinivasa Iyengar. 1986. 14.00 (*0-8364-1571-X*, Pub. by National Sahitya Akademi) S Asia.

Asian Vegetables: Chinese Style Cooking. Carrie Brown. LC 93-33445. (Illus.). 48p. (Orig.). 1994. 8.00 (*0-87573-031-0*) Jain Pub Co.

Asian Vegetarian Feast: Tempting Vegetable & Pasta Recipes from the East. Ken Hom. LC 87-20738. (Illus.). 224p. 1988. 19.95 (*0-688-07753-6*) Morrow.

Asian Village Economy at the Crossroads: An Economic Approach to Institutional Change. Yujiro Hayami & Masao Kikuchi. LC 81-83546. 295p. reprint ed. pap. 84.10 (*0-7837-2183-8*, 2042521) Bks Demand.

Asian Visions of Authority: Religion & the Modern States of East & Southeast Asia. Charles F. Keyes et al. LC 93-37979. 380p. (C). 1994. text ed. 35.00 (*0-8248-1471-1*) UH Pr.

Asian Voices in Christian Theology. Gerald H. Anderson. LC 75-13795. 333p. reprint ed. pap. 95.00 (*0-8357-5790-0*, 2025115) Bks Demand.

Asian Voices in English. Ed. by Mimi Chan & Roy Harris. 224p. 1991. 47.50x (*962-209-282-9*, Pub. by Hong Kong Univ Pr HK) Coronet Bks.

***Asian Water Utilities Handbook.** (Illus.). 250p. (Orig.). 1994. pap. 225.00 (*1-57205-814-5*) Rector Pr.

Asian Way to Peace: A Story of Regional Cooperation. Michael Haas. LC 89-32262. 336p. 1989. text ed. 69.50 (*0-275-93216-8*, C3216, Praeger Pubs) Greenwood.

Asian Women. Lewis B. Sckolnick. (Civil Rights Reporter Ser.). (Illus.). 60p. (Orig.). (C). 1994. pap. 45.00 (*1-57205-152-3*) Rector Pr.

Asian Yearbook of International Law, 1991, Vol. I. Ed. by Ko Swan. 436p. (C). 1993. lib. bdg. 156.50 (*0-7923-1734-3*) Kluwer Ac.

Asian Yearbook of International Law, 1992, Vol. II. Ed. by Ko Swan Sik. 460p. (C). 1994. lib. bdg. 174.00 (*0-7923-2239-8*) Kluwer Ac.

Asianic Elements in Greek Civilisation, Gifford Lecture in the University of Edinburgh, 1915-1916. William M. Ramsay. LC 77-97894. reprint ed. 35.00 (*0-404-05209-6*) AMS Pr.

Asianic Elements in Greek Civilization. William Ramsay. 303p. 1976. 30.00 (*0-89005-173-9*) Ares.

Asianomics. Donald J. Senese. (JSPES Monograph: No. 5). 1982. pap. 15.00 (*0-930690-14-1*) Coun Soc Econ.

Asians: Their Evolving Heritage. 6th ed. Thomas Welty. 398p. (C). 1989. pap. text ed. 21.25 (*0-06-047001-1*) HarpCollege.

***Asians & Pacific Islanders in the United States.** 1995. lib. bdg. 250.00 (*0-8490-6520-8*) Gordon Pr.

Asians & Pacific Islanders in the United States. Herbert Barringer et al. LC 92-4867. (Population of the United States in the 1980s: A Census Monograph Ser.). (Illus.). 384p. 1992. 42.50 (*0-87154-095-9*) Russell Sage.

***Asians & Pacific Islanders in the United States.** Herbert Barringer et al. 384p. 1995. pap. 18.50 (*0-87154-096-7*) Russell Sage.

Asians in America: A Reader. Malcolm Collier. 208p. (C). 1993. per., pap. text ed. 19.95 (*0-8403-8507-2*) Kendall-Hunt.

Asians in Australia: The Dynamics of Migration & Settlement. Ed. by Christine Inglis et al. 240p. 1992. 33.25 (*981-3016-34-5*, Pub. by Inst SE Asian Studies SI) Ashgate Pub Co.

Asians in Britain. Patrick Sookhdeo. 64p. 1977. pap. 5.00 (*0-85364-207-9*) Attic Pr.

Asians in East Africa: Jayhind & Uhuru. Agehananda Bharati. LC 72-85882. 368p. 1972. 39.95 (*0-911012-49-4*) Nelson-Hall.

Asians in the United States: Abstracts of the Psychological & Behaviorial Literature, 1967-1991. Ed. by Frederick T. Leong & James R. Whitfield. LC 92-17379. (Bibliographies in Psychology Ser.: No. 11). 226p. 1992. pap. 27.50 (*1-55798-178-7*) Am Psychol.

Asia's Cultural Mosaic: An Anthropological Introduction. Grant Evans. 384p. (C). 1993. pap. text ed. 18.00 (*0-13-052812-9*) P-H.

Asia's Environmental Crisis. Ed. by Michael C. Howard. 293p. (C). 1993. pap. text ed. 47.50 (*0-8133-8808-2*) Westview.

Asia's International Role in the Post-Cold War Era, Pts. I & II. (Adelphi Paper Ser.). 1993. write for info. (*1-85753-068-3*, 275); write for info. (*1-85753-073-X*, 276) Macmillan.

Asia's Leading Two Hundred Companies. Ed. by Lewis B. Sckolnick. (Illus.). 274p. 1994. pap. 245.00 (*1-57205-018-7*) Rector Pr.

Asia's "Miracle" Economies. 2nd ed. Jon Woronoff. LC 91-4178. 304p. (C). 1992. 46.95 (*0-87332-883-3*); pap. text ed. 21.95 (*0-87332-884-1*) M E Sharpe.

Asia's New Giant: How the Japanese Economy Works. Ed. by Hugh Patrick & Henry Rosovsky. LC 75-42304. 957p. reprint ed. pap. 180.00 (*0-8357-5791-9*, 2030002) Bks Demand.

Asia's New Industrial World: Will the East Win? Michael Smith et al. 192p. (Orig.). (C). 1985. pap. 11.95 (*0-416-38920-1*, 9375) Routledge Chapman & Hall.

Asia's Next Giant: South Korea & Late Industrialization. Alice H. Amsden. 400p. 1992. reprint ed. pap. 14.95 (*0-19-507603-6*) OUP.

***Asia's Rising Economic Tide: Unique Opportunities for the U. S.** Erland Heginbotham. 148p. (Orig.). 1993. pap. text ed. 15.00 (*0-89068-122-8*, CIR 25) Natl Planning.

***Asia's Rural Cooperatives.** Ed. by K. K. Taimni. 336p. (C). 1994. text ed. 56.50 (*0-8133-2229-4*) Westview.

Asia's Struggle for Full Humanity: Towards a Relevant Theology: Papers from the Asian Theological Conference, January 7-20, 1979, Wennappuwa, Sri Lanka. Asian Theological Conference Staff. Ed. by Virginia Fabella. LC 80-14923. 208p. reprint ed. pap. 59.30 (*0-8357-4049-8*, 2036739) Bks Demand.

Asiatic Elephant. Carl R. Green & William R. Sanford. LC 87-20200. (Wildlife Habits & Habitats Ser.). (Illus.). 48p. (J). (gr. 5). 1987. text ed. 12.95 (*0-89686-333-6*, Crstwood Hse) Silver Burdett Pr.

Asiatic Mode of Production in China. Ed. by Timothy Brook. LC 89-4247. (Chinese Studies on China Ser.). 230p. 1989. 62.95 (*0-87332-542-7*) M E Sharpe.

***Asiatic Mythology: A Description & Explanation of the Mythologies of All the Great Nations of Asia.** H. Maspero et al. (C). 1995. reprint ed. 98.00x (*81-206-0920-4*, Pub. by Asian Educ Servs II) S Asia.

Asiatic Palms: Lepidocaryeae, Pts. 1-2: The Species Daemonorops, 2 vols., Set. O. Beccari. (C). 1988. 1,140.00 (*0-685-22295-0*, Scientific) St Mut.

Asiatic Palms: Lepidocaryeae, Pts. 2-3: The Species of General Ceratolobus to Eugelssona, 2 vols., Set. O. Beccari. (C). 1988. 1,400.00 (*0-685-22294-2*, Scientific) St Mut.

Asiatic Palms: Lepidocarea, Part II & III: The Species of Genera Ceratobus to Eugelssona, 2 vols. O. Beccari. (Annals of Royal Botanic Garden, Calcutta Ser.: Vol. XII, Pt. 2). 231p. 1986. 825.00 (*1-55528-008-0*, Pub. by Today & Tomorrows P & P II) Scholarly Pubns.

Asiatic Palms: Lepidocaryeae, Part I: The Species of Calamus, 2 vols. O. Beccari. (Annals of Royal Botanic Garden, Calcutta Ser.: Vol. XI Supp.). 160p. 1986. 500.00 (*1-55528-003-X*, Pub. by Today & Tomorrows P & P II) Scholarly Pubns.

Asiatic Palms: Lepidocaryeary, Part I & II: The Species of Daemonorops, 2 vols. O. Beccari. (Annals of Royal Botanic Garden, Calcutta Ser.: Vol. XII). 239p. 1985. 650.00 (*0-317-64510-2*, Pub. by Today & Tomorrows P & P II) Scholarly Pubns.

Asiatic Researches: Essays, Tracts & Dissertations on Humanities & Sciences of India & Asia, 24 vols., Set. William Jones. (C). 1988. 1,900.00 (*0-7855-0052-9*, Pub. by Print Hse II) St Mut.

Asiatic Society of Bengal & the Discovery of India's Past, 1784-1838. O. P. Kejariwal. (Illus.). 312p. 1988. 26.00 (*0-19-562102-6*) OUP.

Asiatics: A Novel. Frederic Prokosch. LC 70-138620. (Illus.). 371p. 1972. reprint ed. text ed. 62.50 (*0-8371-5732-3*, PRAS, Greenwood Pr) Greenwood.

Asiatische Einfluesse auf Gunter Eich, Vol. 691. Keiko Yamane. (European University Studies: German Language & Literature: Ser. 1). 231p. (GER.). 1983. 44.60 (*3-8204-7793-4*) P Lang Pubs.

ASIC Guidebook. H. Scalf. 1991. text ed. write for info. (*0-442-00466-4*) Van Nos Reinhold.

ASIC Outlook 1994: An Application Specific IC Report & Directory. William J. McClean. (Illus.). 260p. 1993. per., pap. 485.00 (*1-877750-23-9*) ICE Corp.

ASID Professional Practice Manual. Ed. by Jo A. Thompson. 224p. 1992. 65.00 (*0-8230-0371-X*, Whitney Lib) Watsn-Guptill.

Aside from Teaching, What in the World Can You Do? Career Strategies for Liberal Arts Graduates. Dorothy K. Bestor. LC 82-2009. 352p. (Orig.). 1982. 30.00 (*0-295-95960-6*); pap. 15.00 (*0-295-95903-7*) U of Wash Pr.

Asie du Sud a l'Epoque des Grandes Decouvertes. Genevieve Bouchon. (Collected Studies: No. CS260). 342p. (FRE.). (C). 1987. reprint ed. lib. bdg. 106.95 (*0-86078-208-5*, Pub. by Variorum UK) Ashgate Pub Co.

ASIF - Technique for Internal Fixation of Fractures. Ed. by M. Allgower et al. 1975. ring bd. 291.00 (*0-387-92105-2*) Spr-Verlag.

Asil Araber Im Lichte Neuer Genetischer Erkenntnisse: The Asil Arabian in the Light of New Genetic Knowledge. Frederik Basils. (Documenta Hippologica Ser.). (Illus.). 51p. 1981. write for info. (*3-487-08224-1*, Pub. by Georg Olms GW) Lubrecht & Cramer.

Asil Araber, No. Three: Arabiens Edle Pferde. (Documenta Hippologica Ser.). (Illus.). 1008p. 1985. write for info. (*3-487-08266-7*, Pub. by Georg Olms GW) Lubrecht & Cramer.

Asil Arabians: The Noble Arabian Horses III - A Documentation. Ed. by Club Asil. (Documenta Hippologica Ser.). (Illus.). 1008p. (ARA, ENG & GER.). 1985. lib. bdg. 125.00 (*3-487-08267-5*) Lubrecht & Cramer.

***Asil Arabians IV: The Noble Arabian Horses.** Club Asil. (Documenta Hippologica Ser.). (Illus.). 923p. 1993. lib. bdg. 74.00 (*3-487-08340-X*) Lubrecht & Cramer.

Asilomar Conference on Signals, Systems, & Computers, 2 vols., Set. 27th ed. LC 89-640232. 1728p. 1994. pap. text ed. 140.00 (*0-8186-4120-7*, 4120) IEEE Comp Soc.

Asilomar Conference on Signals, Systems, & Computers, 25th. LC 89-640232. 1328p. 1992. 150.00 (*0-8186-2470-1*, 2470) IEEE Comp Soc.

Asilomar Conference on Signals, Systems, & Computers, 26th, 2 vols., Set. LC 89-640232. 1208p. 1993. 140.00 (*0-8186-3160-0*, 3160) IEEE Comp Soc.

Asimov Chronicles: Fifty Years of Isaac Asimov. Ed. by Martin H. Greenberg. 1989. 21.95 (*0-913165-44-1*) Dark Harvest.

Asimov Laughs Again: More Than 700 Favorite Jokes, Limericks, & Anecdotes. Isaac Asimov. LC 91-58353. 368p. 1993. reprint ed. pap. 12.00 (*0-06-092448-9*, PL) HarpC.

Asimov on Physics. Isaac Asimov. 1979. mass mkt. 4.95 (*0-380-41848-7*, Discus) Avon.

Asimov on Science: A Thirty Year Retrospective. Isaac Asimov. 1991. mass mkt. 4.99 (*1-55817-560-1*, Pinnacle NY) Windsor NY.

Asimov's Chronology of Science & Discovery. Isaac Asimov. LC 94-2504. (Illus.). 832p. 1994. 35.00 (*0-06-270113-4*, Harper Ref) HarpC.

Asimov's Chronology of the World. Isaac Asimov. LC 91-55007. 704p. 1991. 35.00 (*0-06-270036-7*, Harper Ref) HarpC.

Asimov's Dictionary of Scientific Terms. Ed. by Isaac Asimov. Date not set. 16.95 (*0-06-270009-X*, Harper Ref) HarpC.

Asimov's Guide to Earth & Space. Isaac Asimov. LC 91-11097. (Illus.). 304p. 1991. 19.50 (*0-679-40437-6*) Random.

Asimov's Guide to Shakespeare, 2 vols. in 1. Isaac Asimov. 1988. 17.99 (*0-517-26825-6*) Random Hse Value.

Asimov's Guide to Shakespeare. Isaac Asimov. 1991. reprint ed. lib. bdg. 39.95 (*1-56849-034-8*) Buccaneer Bks.

Asimov's Guide to the Bible, 2 vols. in 1. Isaac Asimov. 1988. 15.99 (*0-517-34582-X*) Random Hse Value.

Asimov's Guide to the Bible: The New Testament. Isaac Asimov. 640p. 1971. pap. 9.95 (*0-380-01031-3*) Avon.

Asimov's Guide to the Bible: The Old Testament. Isaac Asimov. 720p. 1971. pap. 10.95 (*0-380-01032-1*) Avon.

Asimov's New Guide to Science. rev. ed. Isaac Asimov. LC 83-46093. (Illus.). 992p. 1984. 40.00 (*0-465-00473-3*) Basic.

Asinano. Armando B. Rico. 155p. (ENG & SPA.). 1990. lib. bdg. 9.50 (*1-879219-00-X*) Veracruz Pubs.

***Asinano: A Bilingual Word Guide of the English & Spanish Language.** 2nd rev. ed. Armando B. Rico. 270p. (ENG & SPA.). 1995. pap. text ed. 18.00 (*1-879219-07-7*) Veracruz Pubs.

ASIS Annual Meeting: Celebrating Change; Information Management on the Move - Proceedings of the 55th Annual Meeting of the American Society for Information Science, October 26-28, 1992. Ed. by Debora Shaw. 375p. 1992. pap. 45.00 (*0-938734-69-5*) Learned Info.

ASIS Annual Meeting: Information & Technology - Planning for the Next 50 Years: Proceedings of the Annual Meeting of the American Society of Information Science, 51st, October 23-27, 1988. 264p. 1988. 50.00 (*0-938734-29-6*) Learned Info.

***ASIS Thesaurus of Information Science & Librarianship.** Jessica Milstead. 150p. 1994. pap. 34.95 (*0-938734-80-6*) Learned Info.

ASIS '90: "Information in the Year Two Thousand: From Research to Applications" - Proceedings of the 53rd Annual Meeting of the American Society for Information Science, Nov. 4-8, 1990. Ed. by Diane Henderson. 393p. 1990. 45.00 (*0-938734-48-2*) Learned Info.

ASIS '91: "Systems Understanding People" - Proceedings of the 54th Annual Meeting of the American Society for Information Science. Ed. by Jose-Marie Griffiths. 1991. 45.00 (*0-938734-56-3*) Learned Info.

ASIS '93: "Integrating Technologies, Converging Professions," Proceedings of the 56th Annual Meeting of the American Society for Information Science. Ed. by Susan Bonzi. 334p. 1993. 47.50 (*0-938734-78-4*) Learned Info.

***ASIS '94: The Economics of Information-Proceedings of the 57th Annual Meeting of the American Society for Information Science.** Ed. by Bruce Maxian. 115p. (Orig.). 1994. pap. 47.50 (*0-938734-93-8*) Learned Info.

Asiwinarong: Ethos, Image & Social Power among the Usen Barok of New Ireland. Roy Wagner. LC 85-43321. (Illus.). 288p. 1986. text ed. 45.00 (*0-691-09421-7*) Princeton U Pr.

Asiyih Khanum: The Most Exalted Leaf Entitled Navvab. Baharieh R. Ma'ani. 96p. 1993. 11.95 (*0-85398-353-4*, Pub. by G Ronald England UK) Bahai.

***ASJA Directory of Writers 1995.** 1995. pap. 75.00 (*1-880832-03-8*) Am Soc Jrnl & Auth.

***ASJA Directory of Writers 1996.** 1995. pap. 75.00 (*1-880832-04-6*) Am Soc Jrnl & Auth.

ASJA Handbook: A Writers' Guide to Ethical & Economic Issues. American Society of Journalists & Authors Staff. 1985. pap. 5.95 (*0-9612200-2-3*) Am Soc Jrnl & Auth.

ASJA Handbook: A Writer's Guide to Ethical & Economic Issues. 2nd rev. ed. Ed. by Murray T. Bloom et al. 90p. 1992. pap. 12.95 (*1-880832-00-3*) Am Soc Jrnl & Auth.

***Ask a Cactus Rose.** Adele Seronde. (Illus.). 40p. (J). (gr. 4-7). 1973. 12.00 (*0-911612-08-4*); pap. 8.00 (*0-911612-06-8*) Wenkart.

***Ask a Daffodil.** Adele Seronde. (Illus.). 40p. (J). (gr. 1-3). 1967. text ed. 12.00 (*0-911612-09-2*); pap. 8.00 (*0-911612-07-6*) Wenkart.

Ask a Riddle Big Book, Unit 4. (Networks Ser.). (J). (gr. 1). 1991. 29.50 (*0-88106-727-X*) Charlesbridge Pub.

***Ask about Animals.** Christine Lawrie. LC 94-28180. (Read All about It Ser.). (Illus.). (J). 1995. lib. bdg. write for info. (*0-8114-5729-X*) Raintree Steck-V.

Ask about Farm Animals. (Ask About Ser.). (Illus.). 64p. (J). (gr. 4-5). 1987. lib. bdg. 11.95 (*0-8172-2881-0*) Raintree Steck-V.

Ask about Prehistoric Life. (Ask About Ser.). (Illus.). 64p. (J). (gr. 4-5). 1987. lib. bdg. 11.95 (*0-8172-2879-9*) Raintree Steck-V.

Ask About Series, 10 titles, Set. (Illus.). 640p. (J). (gr. 4-5). 1987. lib. bdg. write for info. (*0-8172-2875-6*) Raintree Steck-V.

Ask about the Earth & the Sky. Ed. by Barbara J. Behm. (Ask About Ser.). (Illus.). 64p. (J). (gr. 4-5). 1987. lib. bdg. 11.95 (*0-8172-2876-4*) Raintree Steck-V.

Ask about the Home. (Ask About Ser.). (Illus.). 64p. (J). (gr. 4-5). 1987. lib. bdg. 11.95 (*0-8172-2882-9*) Raintree Steck-V.

Ask about the Human Body. (Ask About Ser.). (Illus.). 64p. (J). (gr. 4-5). 1987. lib. bdg. 11.95 (*0-8172-2884-5*) Raintree Steck-V.

Ask about the Mountains & the Sea. (Ask About Ser.). (Illus.). 64p. (J). (gr. 4-5). 1987. lib. bdg. 11.95 (*0-8172-2877-2*) Raintree Steck-V.

Ask about the World of Food. (Ask About Ser.). (Illus.). 64p. (J). (gr. 4-5). 1987. lib. bdg. 11.95 (*0-8172-2885-3*) Raintree Steck-V.

Ask about Volcanoes. (Ask About Ser.). (Illus.). 64p. (J). (gr. 4-5). 1987. lib. bdg. 11.95 (*0-8172-2878-0*) Raintree Steck-V.

Ask about Who I Am. (Ask About Ser.). (Illus.). 64p. (J). (gr. 4-5). 1987. lib. bdg. 11.95 (*0-8172-2883-7*) Raintree Steck-V.

Ask about Wild Animals. (Ask About Ser.). (Illus.). 64p. (J). (gr. 4-5). 1987. lib. bdg. 11.95 (*0-8172-2880-2*) Raintree Steck-V.

Ask: An Acronym for Prayer. Franklyn A. Simmonds. 159p. 1992. pap. 7.95 (*1-880753-92-8*) Lambs Bk Pub.

Ask & You Will Receive: Prayer & the Letter to the Hebrews. Norman P. Madsen. 136p. 1989. pap. 9.99 (*0-8272-0018-8*) Chalice Pr.

Ask Angela: Answers to Life's Mysteries from Man's Best Friend. Angela & Barbara Ackerman. LC 93-42461. 120p. (Orig.). 1994. pap. 9.95 (*0-8245-1355-X*) Crossroad NY.

Ask Anne & Nan. Anne Adams & Nancy Walker. Ed. by Castle Freeman & Barbara George. LC 88-51916. (Illus.). 192p. (Orig.). 1989. pap. 9.95 (*0-9621439-0-1*) Whetstone Pub.

Ask Another Question: The Story & Meaning of Passover. Miriam Chaikin. LC 84-12744. (Illus.). 96p. (J). (gr. 3-6). 1986. pap. 6.95 (*0-89919-423-0*, Clarion Bks) HM.

Ask Any Girl - STR. Winifred Wolfe. 1963. 4.95 (*0-87129-358-7*, A20) Dramatic Pub.

Ask Any Mother. Jean B. Boyce. 72p. 1991. 8.98 (*0-88290-423-X*) Horizon Utah.

Ask Anybody. Constance C. Greene. (Illus.). 160p. (YA). (gr. 5-9). 1991. pap. 3.95 (*0-14-034787-9*, Puffin) Puffin Bks.

Ask Audrey: The Author's Personal & Professional Experience in the Day-to-Day Living with Inflammatory Bowel Disease. Audrey Kron. 164p. 1992. pap. 12.00 (*0-9633877-0-7*) A Kron.

Ask Dale Murphy. Dale Murphy & Curtis Patton. (Illus.). 112p. 1987. pap. 8.95 (*0-912697-59-8*) Algonquin Bks.

Ask Dave: Dave Winfield Answers Kids' Questions about Baseball & Life. Dave Winfield. LC 94-225. (J). 1994. pap. 7.95 (*0-8362-8057-1*) Andrews & McMeel.

Ask Dougless: More Questions & Answers on Period Authenticity & Miniaturia. Dougless S. Bitler. (Ask Dougless Ser.: Vol. II). (Illus.). 113p. 1987. 9.95 (*0-938685-01-5*) Dees Delights.

Ask Dougless: More Questions & Answers on Period Authenticity & Miniaturia. Dougless S. Bitler. Ed. by Deanna Hacker. (Ask Dougless Ser.: Vol. III). (Illus.). 100p. 1990. pap. text ed. 9.95 (*0-938685-06-6*) Dees Delights.

Ask Dougless: One Hundred One Questions & Answers on Period Authenticity & Miniaturia. rev. ed. Dougless S. Bitler. LC 86-71018. (Ask Dougless Ser.: Vol. II). (Illus.). 64p. 1986. pap. 9.95 (*0-938685-00-7*) Dees Delights.

Ask Ernest! Ernest P. Worrell. LC 93-30370. 128p. (Orig.). 1993. pap. 7.95 (*1-55853-247-1*) Rutledge Hill Pr.

Ask for Nothing More. James Elward & Helen Van Slyke. 1985. pap. 3.95 (*0-8217-1643-3*) Zebra.

An Asterisk (*) at the beginning of an entry indicates that the title is appearing in BIP for the first time.

A

An Asterisk (*) at the beginning of an entry indicates that the title is appearing in BIP for the first time.

A

ASNT Nondestructive Testing Handbook, Vol. 4: Electromagnetic Testing. 2nd ed. Ed. by Paul McIntire & Michael Mester. (Illus.). 701p. 1986. 121.25 (*0-931403-01-4*, 129) Am Soc Nondestructive.

ASNT Nondestructive Testing Handbook, Vol. 5: Acoustic Emission Testing. Ed. by Ronnie K. Miller & Paul McIntire. (Illus.). 604p. 1987. 121.25 (*0-931403-02-2*, 130) Am Soc Nondestructive.

ASNT Nondestructive Testing Handbook, Vol. 6: Magnetic Particle Testing. Ed. by Thomas Schmidt et al. (Illus.). 454p. 1989. 121.25 (*0-931403-03-0*, 131) Am Soc Nondestructive.

ASNT Nondestructive Testing Handbook, Vol. 7: Ultrasonic Testing. 2nd ed. Ed. by Albert S. Birks et al. (Illus.). 915p. (C). 1991. text ed. 140.00 (*0-931403-04-9*, 132) Am Soc Nondestructive.

ASNT Nondestructive Testing Handbook, Vol. 8: Visual & Optical Testing. Ed. by Michael W. Allgaier et al. LC 93-521. 380p. 1993. 121.25 (*0-931403-05-7*, 133) Am Soc Nondestructive.

ASNT Training Program: Liquid Penetrant Method (Instructor Package) American Society for Nondestructive Testing (ASNT) Staff. (Illus.). 219p. (C). 1979. 189.25 (*0-931403-63-4*, 544) Am Soc Nondestructive.

ASNT Training Program: Liquid Penetrant Method (Student Package) American Society for Nondestructive Testing (ASNT) Staff. (Illus.). 219p. (C). 1979. 55.50 (*0-931403-62-6*, 543) Am Soc Nondestructive.

ASNT Training Program: Magnetic Particle Method (Instructor Package) ASNT Staff. (Illus.). 91p. (Orig.). 1979. pap. 239.50 (*0-931403-61-8*, 439) Am Soc Nondestructive.

ASNT Training Program: Magnetic Particle Method (Student Package) American Society for Nondestructive Testing (ASNT) Staff. (Illus.). 91p. (Orig.). 1979. pap. 64.50 (*0-931403-60-X*, 438) Am Soc Nondestructive.

ASNT Training Program: Radiography Method (Instructor Package) American Society for Nondestructive Testing (ASNT) Staff. (Illus.). 451p. (C). 264.75 (*0-931403-57-X*, 231) Am Soc Nondestructive.

ASNT Training Program: Radiography Method (Student Package) American Society for Nondestructive Testing (ASNT) Staff. (Illus.). 451p. (C). 1980. 72.50 (*0-931403-56-1*, 230) Am Soc Nondestructive.

ASO: Automated Systems Operations for MVS. Trevor Eddolls. LC 92-28693. 1992. text ed. 45.00 (*0-07-018994-3*) McGraw.

Asoka: The Buddhist Emperor of India. Vincent A. Smith. (C). 1990. reprint ed. 9.50 (*81-85418-11-X*, Pub. by Low Price II) S Asia.

Asoka & Indian Civilization. Helen Kanitkar & Hemant Kanitkar. Ed. by Malcolm Yapp et al. (World History Ser.). (Illus.). 32p. (YA). (gr. 6-11). 1980. reprint ed. pap. text ed. 4.35 (*0-89908-010-3*) Greenhaven.

Asoka Maurya. B. G. Gokhale. LC 66-16125. (Twayne's Rulers & Statesmen of the World Ser.). 194p. 1966. lib. bdg. 17.95 (*0-8290-1735-6*) Irvington.

Asoka, the Buddhist Emperor of India. 3rd enl. rev. ed. Vincent A. Smith. LC 78-70122. reprint ed. 31.00 (*0-404-17378-0*) AMS Pr.

Asolani. Pietro Bembo. Tr. by Rudolf B. Gottfried. LC 76-168501. (Select Bibliographies Reprint Ser.). 1977. reprint ed. 20.95 (*0-8369-5941-8*) Ayer.

***Asombroso Armadillo.** Dee Stuart. (Illus.). 48p. (SPA.). (J). (gr. 3-6). 1994. 19.95 (*0-87614-975-1*, Carolrhoda) Lerner Group.

***Asose Aworo Onile, a Yoruba Fortune Teller (English)** Taiyewo Ogunade. 4p. 1992. 3.50 (*1-881549-00-3*) Oluweri Pubns.

***Asose Aworo Onile, Oraculo Yoruba.** Taiyewo Ogunade. 4p. (SPA.). 1992. 3.50 (*1-881549-02-X*) Oluweri Pubns.

Asot Mishpat. Abraham Shumsky & Adaia Shumsky. (Mah Tov Hebrew Teaching Ser.: Bk. 1). (Illus.). (J). (gr. 4-6). 1969. teacher ed. 3.50 (*0-8074-0179-X*, 205302); student ed. 6.00 (*0-8074-0180-3*, 405300); text ed. 6.00 (*0-8074-0178-1*, 405301) UAHC.

Asp & the Angel Have Given Me Their Tongues. Neil Buckley. 1993. 8.95 (*0-533-10421-1*) Vantage.

***ASP-DAC'95-CHDL'95-VLSI'95 Proceedings.** IEEE (Circuits & Systems Society & Computer Society) Staff. Ed. by IEEE (Institute of Electrical & Electronics Engineers, Inc.) Staff. 1000p. 1995. pap. write for info. (*0-614-06706-5*, 95TH8102); mic. film write for info. (*0-7803-2763-2*, 95TH8102) Inst Electrical.

ASP Integrity Toolkit. F. Cohen. 120p. (Orig.). 1990. pap. 48.00 (*1-878109-12-X*) ASP PA.

ASP Tutorial & Student Guide. George H. Blackford. 96p. (C). 1992. 3.5 hd 29.95 (*1-881564-27-4*); 5.25 hd 24.95 (*1-881564-26-6*); 14.95 (*1-881564-25-8*) DMC Sftware.

ASP User's Manual (Version 2.00) George H. Blackford. 224p. (C). 1992. 29.95 (*1-881564-00-2*) DMC Sftware.

ASP 3.0 Technical Users' Manual. F. Cohen. (Orig.). (C). 1989. pap. 35.00 (*1-878109-09-X*) ASP PA.

ASPA Handbook of Personnel & Industrial Relations: Official Handbook of the American Society for Personnel Administration. Dale Yoder & Herbert G. Heneman, Jr. LC 79-9506. (Illus.). 1686p. reprint ed. pap. 180.00 (*0-7837-4612-1*, 2044331) Bks Demand.

Asparagus. E. Feher. 160p. (C). 1992. pap. 25.00 (*963-05-6083-6*, Pub. by A K HU) Intl Spec Bk.

***Asparagus: Can Do It for You!** Theodore A. Baroody. 56p. (Orig.). 1995. pap. 4.95 (*0-9619595-4-1*) Eclectic Pr NC.

Asparagus Cookbook. Stockton Asparagus Festival Cookbook Staff. LC 86-26918. 228p. (Orig.). 1990. pap. 9.95 (*0-89087-487-5*); spiral bd. 12.95 (*0-89087-537-5*) Celestial Arts.

Aspartame (NutraSweet) Is It Safe? H. J. Roberts. LC 89-81086. 328p. 1992. pap. 11.95 (*0-914783-58-0*) Charles.

Aspartame (NutraSweet) Is It Safe? H. J. Roberts. LC 89-81086. 328p. 1990. text ed. 19.95 (*0-914783-37-8*) Charles.

***Aspartic Proteinases: Structure, Function, Biology, & Biomedical Implications.** Ed. by Kenji Takahashi. LC 94-43762. (Advances in Experimental Medicine & Biology Ser.: Vol. 362). 620p. 1995. 139.50 (*0-306-44830-0*) Plenum.

Aspartic Proteinases & Their Inhibitors: Proceedings of the FEBS Advanced Course No. 84-07, Prague, Czechoslovakia, August 20-24, 1984. Ed. by Vladimir Kostka. (Illus.). xxiii, 613p. 1985. 234.65 (*0-89925-078-5*) De Gruyter.

***Aspartic Proteinases & Their Inhibitors: Proceedings of the FEBS Advanced Course No. 84-07, Prague, Czechoslovakia, August 20-24, 1984.** Ed. by Vladimir Kostka. (Illus.). xxiii, 613p. 1985. 234.65 (*3-11-010179-3*) De Gruyter.

***Aspartic Proteinases Physiology & Pathology.** Martin Fusek & Vaclav Vetvicka. 300p. 1995. write for info. (*0-8493-7660-2*, 7660) CRC Pr.

Aspatria. Anne U. Thomas. (Towns & Villages of England Ser.). (Illus.). 1994. pap. 12.50 (*0-7509-0498-4*) A Sutton Pub.

ASPCA Complete Cat Care Manual. Andrew Edney. LC 92-52783. (Illus.). 192p. (J). 1992. 24.95 (*1-56458-064-4*) Dorling Kindersley.

ASPCA Complete Dog Care Manual. Bruce Fogle. LC 92-53474. (Illus.). 192p. 1993. 24.95 (*1-56458-168-3*) Dorling Kindersley.

ASPCA Complete Dog Training Manual. Bruce Fogle. LC 93-28352. 1994. 22.95 (*1-56458-487-9*) Dorling Kindersley.

ASPE Convention Proceedings. Incl. ASPE Convention Proceedings 1982. (Illus.). 141p. 1982. (*0-318-60109-5*); ASPE Convention Proceedings 1984. (Illus.). 112p. 1984. (*0-318-60110-9*); 25.00 (*0-317-05982-3*); Incl. (*0-318-60109-5*); (*0-318-60110-9*); 15.00 (*0-318-18066-9*) Am Soc Plumb Eng.

ASPE Convention Proceedings 1982 see ASPE Convention Proceedings

ASPE Convention Proceedings 1984. (Illus.). 112p. 1984. 25.00 (*0-318-18064-2*); 15.00 (*0-318-18065-0*) Am Soc Plumb Eng.

ASPE Convention Proceedings 1984. see ASPE Convention Proceedings

ASPE Data Book, Vol. 1, 1979-80: Fundamentals of Plumbing Design. (Illus.). 312p. 75.00 (*0-318-13198-6*); 50.00 (*0-318-13199-4*) Am Soc Plumb Eng.

ASPE Data Book, Vol. 2, 1981-82: Special Plumbing Systems Design. rev. ed. (Illus.). 279p. 50.00 (*0-318-16984-3*); 25.00 (*0-318-16985-1*) Am Soc Plumb Eng.

Aspect & Georgian Medial Verbs. Dee A. Holisky. LC 81-17036. 224p. 1981. 35.00 (*0-88206-046-5*) Caravan Bks.

Aspect & Meaning in Slavic & Indic. Ranjit Chatterjee. LC 88-7602. (Current Issues in Linguistic Theory Ser.: Vol. 51). xxiii, 131p. (C). 1988. 47.00 (*90-272-3545-7*) Benjamins North Am.

Aspect Bound: A Voyage into the Realm of Germanic, Slavonic & Finno-Ugrian Aspectology. Ed. by C. De Groot & H. Tommola. viii, 283p. 1984. pap. 60.75 (*90-6765-031-5*) Mouton.

ASPECT Ninety Four: Advances in Subsea Pipeline Engineering & Technology. Ed. by Society for Underwater Technology Staff. LC 94-10377. (Advances in Underwater Technology, Ocean Science, & Offshore Engineering Ser.: Vol. 33). 256p. (C). 1994. lib. bdg. 99.00 (*0-7923-2822-1*) Kluwer Ac.

Aspect of Eternity. Bruce Bawer. LC 92-38919. 336p. 1993. 25.00 (*1-55597-187-3*) Graywolf.

Aspect of Plant Sciences, Vol. IV-V. 1982. 15.00 (*0-685-59943-4*, Messers Today & Tomorrow) Scholarly Pubns.

Aspect of Plant Sciences, Vol. VII. 1984. 19.00 (*1-55528-220-2*, Messers Today & Tomorrow) Scholarly Pubns.

Aspect of Plant Sciences, Vol. IX. 1987. 45.00 (*0-685-59944-2*, Pub. by Today & Tomorrows P & P II) Scholarly Pubns.

Aspect of Plant Sciences, Vol. XIII. 1991. 65.00 (*0-685-59945-0*, Messers Today & Tomorrow) Scholarly Pubns.

Aspect of the Fair: Aesthetics & Festival in Midwestern County Fairs. Leslie Prosterman. LC 93-49385. 1994. write for info. (*1-56098-408-2*) Smithsonian.

Aspectival Usage in Russian. A. Murphy & C. James. LC 64-66364. (Pergamon Oxford Russian Ser.). 1965. 72.00 (*0-08-010360-X*, Pub. by Pergamon Repr UK) Franklin.

Aspectos de Ingenieria de la Inyeccion de Agua. F. F. Craig, Jr. 132p. 1982. 30.00 (*0-89520-313-8*, 30453); 15.00 (*0-317-36517-7*) Soc Petrol Engineers.

Aspectos de Seguridad de la Cimentacion de Centrales Nucleares: Guia de Seguridad. (Coleccion Seguridad Ser.: No. 50-SG-S8). 80p. (SPA.). 1988. 35.00 (*92-0-324288-0*, ISP727S) UNIPUB.

Aspectos del Presupuesto Publico. Ed. by A. Premchand & A. L. Antonaya. x, 285p. 1988. pap. 12.50 (*1-55775-014-9*) Intl Monetary.

Aspectos Del Taller Poetico De Jaime Gil de Biedma. Gonzalo C. Marzol. Date not set. 44.70 (*0-685-69529-8*) Scripta.

***Aspectos Economic Os Sobre Transporte e Infraestructura Ante el Reto del Tratado de Libre Comercio de America del Norte.** Alejandro I. Yunez. (Special Publications Ser.: No. 2). 169p. (ENG & SPA.). 1994. 10.00 (*0-614-01224-4*) LBJ Sch Pub Aff.

Aspectroscopia Infrarroja. 2nd rev. ed. Jesus M. Rubio. (Serie de Quimica Monografia: No. 12). 80p. (C). 1981. pap. text ed. 3.50 (*0-8270-1419-8*) OAS.

Aspects: Beginner's Notebook. Jo Mullen. LC 85-71464. 90p. 1986. 7.50 (*0-86690-297-X*, M2357-014) Am Fed Astrologers.

Aspects Actuels de la Contraception Hormonale. Ed. by P. J. Keller. (Illus.). x, 88p. (GER.). 1991. pap. 36.00 (*3-8055-5263-7*) S Karger.

Aspects & Applications of the Random Walk. George H. Weiss. LC 94-4223. (Materials & Processes Ser.). 1994. write for info. (*0-444-81606-2*, North Holland) Elsevier.

Aspects & Houses in Analysis. Noel Tyl. LC 73-19912. (Principles & Practice of Astrology Ser.: Vol. 4). 176p. 1974. pap. 3.95 (*0-87542-803-7*) Llewellyn Pubns.

Aspects & Impressions. Edmund W. Gosse. LC 77-105016. (Essay Index Reprint Ser.). 1977. 21.95 (*0-8369-1469-4*) Ayer.

Aspects & Impressions. Edmund W. Gosse. LC 73-145048. 1971. reprint ed. 15.00 (*0-403-00992-8*) Scholarly.

***Aspects & Issues in the History of Children's Literature.** Ed. by Maria Nikolajeva. LC 94-43041. (Contributions to the Study of World Literature: Vol. 60). 224p. 1995. text ed. 55.00 (*0-313-29614-6*, Greenwood Pr) Greenwood.

Aspects & Personality. Karen Hamaker-Zondag. 320p. (Orig.). 1990. pap. 14.95 (*0-87728-650-7*) Weiser.

Aspects & Prospects of Theoretical Computer Science: Proceedings 6th International Meeting of Young Computer Scientists, Smolenice, Czechoslovakia, November 19-23, 1990. Ed. by J. Dassow et al. (Lecture Notes in Computer Science Ser.: Vol. 464). vi, 298p. 1990. pap. 38.00 (*0-387-53414-8*) Spr-Verlag.

Aspects & Treatments of Vulvar Cancer: Proceedings of the International Symposium, 1st, Madrid, 1971. International Symposium on Vulvar Cancer Staff. Ed. by L. Lopez De La Osa. (Illus.). 250p. 1972. 60.00 (*3-8055-1399-2*) S Karger.

***Aspects de la Biographie.** Andre Maurois. 1930. 13.95 (*0-7859-5271-3*) Fr & Eur.

Aspects De la Vie Monastique En France Au Moyen Age. Jacque Dubois. (Collected Studies: No. CS 395). 320p. 1993. 94.95 (*0-86078-360-X*, Pub. by Variorum UK) Ashgate Pub Co.

Aspects de l'Evolution Gouvernementale de l'Indochine Francaise. Roger Pinto. LC 77-179234. reprint ed. 22.50 (*0-404-54861-X*) AMS Pr.

Aspects for Treatment with Fosfomycin. Ed. by J. P. Guggenbichler. 150p. 1987. pap. 29.00 (*0-387-81986-X*) Spr-Verlag.

Aspects in Astrology. Sue Topmkins. 1990. pap. 25.00 (*1-85230-081-7*) Element MA.

Aspects in Vedic Astrology. Pandit G. Ojha et al. 180p. 1993. pap. 13.95 (*1-878423-15-0*) Morson Pub.

Aspects of a Cognitive-Pragmatic Theory of Language: On Cognition, Functionalism & Grammar. Jan Nuyts. LC 91-40002. (Pragmatics & Beyond New Ser.: No. 20). xii, 399p. 1992. 74.00x (*1-55619-288-6*) Benjamins North Am.

***Aspects of a Man.** Bill Mouser & Barbara Mouser. (Illus.). 160p. 1995. 10.00 (*0-614-07437-1*) Wine Pr Pub.

Aspects of a Southern Story. Robert Sargent. LC 82-51069. 72p. 1987. pap. text ed. 8.00 (*0-915380-15-3*) Word Works.

***Aspects of a Woman.** Bill Mouser & Barbara Mouser. (Illus.). 450p. 1995. 10.00 (*1-883893-16-X*) Wine Pr Pub.

Aspects of African Creativity: A Selected Annotated Bibliography of the Arts. Florence J Staats. 113p. (Orig.). 1991. pap. 13.95 (*0-9627366-2-7*) Arts & Comns NY.

Aspects of African Librarianship: A Collection of Writings. Ed. by M. Wise. 336p. 1985. text ed. 90.00 (*0-7201-1780-1*, Mansell Pub) Cassell.

Aspects of Aging. Ed. by Peter Kaim-Caudle et al. (Illus.). 184p. 1994. pap. 22.00 (*1-871177-58-8*, Pub. by Whiting & Birch UK) Paul & Co Pubs.

Aspects of Agrarian & Urban History of the Marathas. T. T. Mahajan. (C). 1991. 21.00 (*81-7169-162-5*, Pub. by Commonwealth II) S Asia.

Aspects of Altaic Civilization: Proceedings. Permanent International Altaistic Conference Staff. Ed. by David Francis & Denis Sinor. LC 80-28299. (Uralic & Altaic Ser.: Vol. 23). ix, 263p. 1981. reprint ed. text ed. 59.75 (*0-313-22945-7*, PIAA) Greenwood.

Aspects of Altaic Civilization II: Proceedings. Permanent International Altaistic Conference, 18th Meeting, Bloomington, June 29-July 5, 1975. Ed. by Paul A. Draghi & Larry V. Clark. (Uralic & Altaic Ser.: Vol. 134). 212p. 1978. 34.00 (*0-933070-02-0*) Res Inst Inner Asian Studies.

Aspects of Altaic Civilization Three: Proceedings of the Thirtieth Meeting of the Permanent International Altaistic Conference, Bloomington, Indiana, June 19-25, 1987. Ed. by Denis Sinor. LC 90-60745. (Uralic & Altaic Ser.: Vol. 145). ix, 265p. 1990. 32.00 (*0-933070-25-X*) Res Inst Inner Asian Studies.

Aspects of American Art, 7 vols. in one. (Illus.). 55p. (Orig.). 1981. pap. 20.00 (*1-879886-23-5*) Addison Gallery.

Aspects of American Film History Prior to 1920. Anthony Slide. LC 78-2912. 173p. 1978. 22.50 (*0-8108-1130-8*) Scarecrow.

Aspects of Apuleius' Golden Ass. Ed. by B. L. Hijmans, Jr. & R. T. Van Der Paardt. ix, 275p. 1978. 53.50 (*90-6088-061-7*, Pub. by Boumas Boekhuis NE) Benjamins North Am.

Aspects of Aristocracy: Grandeur & Decline in Modern Britain. David Cannadine. (Illus.). 352p. 1994. 32.00 (*0-300-05981-7*) Yale U Pr.

Aspects of Aristotle's Logic of Modalities. Jeroen Van Rijen. (C). 1988. lib. bdg. 107.50 (*0-7923-0048-3*) Kluwer Ac.

Aspects of Artificial Intelligence. Ed. by James H. Fetzer. (C). 1987. lib. bdg. 107.00 (*1-55608-037-9*); pap. text ed. 39.00 (*1-55608-038-7*) Kluwer Ac.

Aspects of Astronomy in America in the Nineteenth Century: An Original Anthology. Ed. by I. Bernard Cohen. LC 79-7948. (Three Centuries of Science in America Ser.). (Illus.). 1980. lib. bdg. 48.95 (*0-405-12529-1*) Ayer.

Aspects of Australian Fiction. Ed. by Alan Brissenden. 1991. pap. 17.95 (*0-85564-312-9*, Pub. by Univ of West Aust Pr AT) Intl Spec Bk.

Aspects of Authorship; or, Book Marks & Book Makers. Francis Jacox. LC 72-5751. (Essay Index Reprint Ser.). 1977. reprint ed. 30.95 (*0-8369-2994-2*) Ayer.

Aspects of Autism: Biological Research. Ed. by Lorna Wing. 120p. 1988. pap. 15.00 (*0-88048-630-9*, CG1A4125, Pub. by Royal Coll Psych UK) Am Psychiatric.

Aspects of Automated Natural Language Generation: Sixth International Workshop, Trento, Italy, April 5-7, 1992: Proceedings. Ed. by R. Dale et al. LC 92-9037. (Lecture Notes in Artificial Intelligence Ser.: Vol. 587). viii, 312p. 1992. pap. 48.00 (*0-387-55399-1*) Spr-Verlag.

***Aspects of Autonomy: The Autonomy Frustration Syndrome As Cause of Psychological Disorder & Autonomy Exercised As Precondition to Personal Well-Being & to the Good Society.** Henry Stern. 270p. (Orig.). 1995. pap. 15.00 (*0-9646379-4-4*) H Stern.

Aspects of Avian Endocrinology: Practical & Theoretical Implications. Ed. by C. G. Scanes. (Graduate Studies: No. 26). 411p. 1982. 59.95 (*0-89672-103-5*); pap. 29.95 (*0-89672-102-7*) Tex Tech Univ Pr.

Aspects of Balzac. W. Helm. 1971. 59.95 (*0-87968-669-3*) Gordon Pr.

Aspects of Balzac. W. Helm. LC 72-3677. (Studies in French Literature: No. 45). 1972. reprint ed. lib. bdg. 49.95 (*0-8383-1575-5*) M S G Haskell Hse.

Aspects of Bengali History & Society. Ed. by Rachel Baumer. LC 73-90491. (Asian Studies at Hawaii: No. 12). 1975. pap. text ed. 10.50 (*0-8248-0318-3*) UH Pr.

***Aspects of Bilingual Aphasia.** Ed. by Michael Paradis. LC 95-13571. 1995. text ed. 96.00 (*0-08-042570-4*, Pergamon Pr) Elsevier.

Aspects of Bilingualism in Wales. Colin Baker. 209p. 1985. 79.00 (*0-905028-51-1*, Pub. by Multilingual Matters UK); pap. 29.95 (*0-905028-50-3*, Pub. by Multilingual Matters UK) Taylor & Francis.

Aspects of British Calender Customs. Buckland & Wood. 190p. (C). 1991. 19.50 (*1-85075-243-5*, Pub. by Sheffield Acad UK) CUP Services.

Aspects of British Economic History. Arthur C. Pigou. 251p. 1971. reprint ed. 32.50 (*0-7146-2630-9*, Pub. by F Cass Pubs UK) Intl Spec Bk.

Aspects of British Foreign Policy. Arthur Willert. 1928. 59.50 (*0-686-83482-8*) Elliots Bks.

Aspects of British Political History, 1815-1914. Stephen J. Lee. LC 94-432. (Aspects of History Ser.). (Illus.). 368p. 1994. 59.95x (*0-415-09006-7*, B3977); pap. 16.95 (*0-415-09007-5*, B3981) Routledge.

Aspects of British Politics, 1904-1919. D. H. Collins. 1966. 161.00 (*0-08-010987-X*, Pub. by Pergamon Repr UK) Franklin.

Aspects of Bulgarian Syntax: Complementizers & WH Constructions. Catherine Rudin. iv, 232p. (Orig.). 1986. pap. 19.95 (*0-89357-156-3*) Slavica.

Aspects of Calculus. G. Klambauer. (Undergraduate Texts in Mathematics Ser.). (Illus.). 505p. 1986. text ed. 39.00 (*0-387-96274-3*) Spr-Verlag.

Aspects of Caste in South India, Ceylon & North West Pakistan. Edmund R. Leach. (Cambridge Papers in Social Anthropology: No. 2). (Illus.). 1971. pap. 16.95 (*0-521-09664-2*) Cambridge U Pr.

Aspects of Cell Motility. Society for Experimental Biology (Great Britain). Ed. by P. L. Miller. LC 76-415861. (Symposia of the Society for Experimental Biology Ser.: No. 22). 456p. reprint ed. pap. 130.00 (*0-8357-5793-5*, 2014671) Bks Demand.

Aspects of Central Bank Policy Making. Ed. by Z. Eckstein. (Illus.). xvi, 412p. 1991. 119.00 (*0-387-54281-7*) Spr-Verlag.

Aspects of Child Life & Education. G. Stanley Hall. Ed. by Theodate L. Smith. LC 74-21414. (Classics in Child Development Ser.). 342p. 1975. reprint ed. 29.95 (*0-405-06464-0*) Ayer.

Aspects of Childhood Nutrition. Ed. by G. H. Bourne. (World Review of Nutrition & Dietetics Ser.: Vol. 58). (Illus.). x, 166p. 1989. 118.50 (*3-8055-4918-0*) S Karger.

Aspects of Chinese Education. Ed. by C. T. Hu. LC 73-95245. (Columbia University, Center for Education in Asia, Publications). 109p. reprint ed. pap. 31.10 (*0-8357-5794-3*, 2026022) Bks Demand.

Aspects of Chinese Sociolinguistics: Essays by Yuen Ren Chao. Ed. by Anwar S. Dil. (Language Science & National Development Ser.). xvi, 416p. 1976. 52.50 (*0-8047-0909-2*) Stanford U Pr.

Aspects of Civil Engineering Contract Procedure. 3rd ed. R. J. Marks & R. Jackson. LC 84-25569. (International Library of Science, Technology, Engineering, & Social Studies Ser.). 1985. text ed. 121.00 (*0-08-031637-9*, Pub. by Pergamon Repr UK) Franklin.

Aspects of Climate Variability in the Pacific & the Western Americas. Ed. by D. H. Peterson. (Geophysical Monograph Ser.: Vol. 55). 445p. 1989. 50.00 (*0-87590-072-0*) Am Geophysical.

Aspects of Combinatorics: A Wide-Ranging Introduction. Victor W. Bryant. (Illus.). 256p. (C). 1993. 69.95 (*0-521-41974-3*); pap. 29.95 (*0-521-42997-8*) Cambridge U Pr.

An Asterisk (*) at the beginning of an entry indicates that the title is appearing in BIP for the first time.

An Asterisk (*) at the beginning of an entry indicates that the title is appearing in BIP for the first time.

Aspects of Mesozoic Geology & Paleontology on the Colorado Plateau. Ed. by Michael Morales. (Bulletin Ser.). 192p. 1993. pap. 19.95 (*0-89734-114-7*, BS-59) Mus Northern Ariz.

Aspects of Metaphor. Ed. by Jaakko Hintikka. LC 94-9742. (Synthese Library: Vol. 238). 1994. lib. bdg. 115.00 (*0-7923-2786-1*) Kluwer Ac.

Aspects of Microbial Metabolism & Ecology. Ed. by Geoffrey A. Codd. (Social Publication Society General Microbiology Ser.: No. 11). 1984. text ed. 138.00 (*0-12-178050-3*) Acad Pr.

Aspects of Mid-Cretaceous Regional Geology. Ed. by Richard A. Reyment & P. Bengston. LC 80-42379. 1981. text ed. 157.00 (*0-12-587040-X*) Acad Pr.

Aspects of Mind. Gilbert Ryle. Ed. by Rene Meyer. LC 92-21759. 256p. 1993. 44.95 (*0-631-18489-9*) Blackwell Pubs.

Aspects of Modern Architecture. Stephen Perrella. 1991. pap. 21.95 (*0-312-06705-4*) St Martin.

Aspects of Modern Art. Academy Editions Staff. 1990. pap. 21.95 (*0-312-04472-0*, Academy Edits) St Martin.

Aspects of Modern Drama. Edith Sitwell. LC 78-131833, 264p. 1972. reprint ed. 15.00 (*0-403-00720-8*) Scholarly.

Aspects of Modern Logic. E. W. Beth. Tr. by D. M. De Jongh & Susan De Jongh-Kearl. LC 79-135102. (Synthese Library: No. 32). 176p. 1970. lib. bdg. 62.00 (*90-277-0173-3*) Kluwer Ac.

Aspects of Modern Opera: Estimates & Inquiries. Lawrence Gilman. LC 68-25288. (Studies in Music: No. 42). 1969. reprint ed. lib. bdg. 56.95 (*0-8383-0302-1*) M S G Haskell Hse.

Aspects of Modern Otolaryngological Practice: First Congress of the Asian Otorhinolaryngological Federation, Pattaya, 1981. Ed. by S. Prasansuk et al. (Advances in Oto-Rhino-Laryngology Ser.: Vol. 29). (Illus.). xii, 236p. 1983. 131.25 (*3-8055-3592-9*) S Karger.

Aspects of Modern Poetry. Edith Sitwell. LC 74-117845. (Essay Index Reprint Ser.). 1977. 19.95 (*0-8369-1684-0*) Ayer.

Aspects of Modern Radar. Ed. by Eli Brookner. 576p. 1988. text ed. 79.00 (*0-89006-263-3*) Artech Hse.

Aspects of Modern Russian & Czech Literature: Selected Papers from the Third World Congress for Soviet & East European Studies. Ed. by Arnold McMillin. 239p. (Orig.). 1989. pap. 19.95 (*0-89357-194-6*) Slavica.

Aspects of Modern Swedish Literature. Ed. by Irene Scobbie. LC 88-61441. 376p. 1988. pap. 24.00 (*1-870041-02-X*, Pub. by Norvik Pr UK) Dufour.

Aspects of Modernism, from Wilde to Pirandello. Janko Lavrin. LC 68-22107. (Essay Index Reprint Ser.). 1977. reprint ed. 18.95 (*0-8369-0611-X*) Ayer.

Aspects of Motion Perception. Paul A. Kolers. LC 73-188746. 232p. 1972. 93.00 (*0-08-016843-4*, Pub. by Pergamon Repr UK) Franklin.

***Aspects of Mozart's Music in G Minor: Toward the Identification of Common Structural & Compositional Characteristics.** rev. ed. Steven B. Jan. LC 94-48095. (Outstanding Dissertations in Music from British Universities Ser.). 428p. 1995. 96.00 (*0-8153-1892-8*) Garland.

Aspects of Multilingualism: Proceedings from the Fourth Nordic Symposium on Bilingualism. Ed. by Erling Wande et al. (Studia Multiethnica Upsaliensia: No. 2). 437p. (Orig.). 1987. pap. text ed. 53.00x (*91-554-2066-4*, Pub. by Uppsala Univ Acta Univ Uppsaliensis SW) Coronet Bks.

Aspects of Multivariate Statistical Theory. Robb J. Muirhead. LC 82-1912. (Probability & Mathematical Statistics Ser.). 673p. 1982. text ed. 144.00 (*0-471-09442-0*, Wiley-Interscience) Wiley.

Aspects of Music in Canada. Ed. by Arnold Walter. LC 74-418249. 348p. reprint ed. pap. 99.20 (*0-8357-6371-4*, 2035725) Bks Demand.

***Aspects of Narration in Peter Carey's Novels: Deconstructing Colonialism.** Hermine Krassnitzer. LC 95-1687. (Salzburger Studies). 152p. 1995. text ed. 69.95 (*0-7734-1286-7*) E Mellen.

Aspects of National Health Service Acts. C. Seaton & W. A. Farndale. LC 66-25321. (Westminster Ser.: Vol. 3). 1966. 44.00 (*0-08-011971-9*, Pub. by Pergamon Repr UK) Franklin.

Aspects of Nature in Different Lands & Different Climates. Alexander Von Humboldt. Tr. by Sabine. LC 70-99251. 1970. reprint ed. 67.50 (*0-404-03385-7*) AMS Pr.

Aspects of Near East Society. Moishe Zeltzer. 1962. pap. 11.95 (*0-8084-0391-5*) NCUP.

Aspects of Nepalese Traditions. Ed. by Bernhard Kolvar. 250p. (Orig.). 1992. pap. 52.50 (*3-515-06129-0*) Coronet Bks.

Aspects of Neurogenesis see Studies on the Development of Behavior & the Nervous System

Aspects of Nominal Determination in Old Church Slavonic. Michael S. Flier. LC 72-88186. (Slavistic Printings & Reprintings Ser.: No. 172). 248p. 1974. text ed. 102.35 (*90-279-3242-5*) Mouton.

Aspects of Non-Equilibrium Thermodynamics. W. Muschik. (Series in Theoretical & Applied Mechanics: Vol. 9). 112p. 1989. text ed. 28.00 (*981-02-0087-0*) World Scientific Pub.

Aspects of Nonlinear Scattering Theory. G. Roach. LC 93-19958. (Pitman Monographs & Surveys in Pure & Applied Mathematics). 1993. write for info. (*0-582-09230-2*, Pub. by Longman UK) Longman.

Aspects of Nonverbal Communication. Ed. by W. Von Raffler-Engel. viii, 380p. 1983. pap. 30.00 (*90-265-0460-8*, Pub. by Swets Pub Serv NE) Taylor & Francis.

Aspects of Nuclear Reactor Safety: Proceedings of the International Colloquium on Irradiation Tests for Reactor Safety Programmes, Petten, Holland, June 1979. Peter Von der Hardt & H. Rottger. (European Applied Research Reports Special Topics Ser.). 646p. 1980. text ed. 186.00 (*3-7186-0016-1*) Gordon & Breach.

Aspects of Nutritional Physiology. Ed. by G. H. Bourne. (World Review of Nutrition & Dietetics Ser.: Vol. 56). (Illus.). x, 262p. 1988. 179.25 (*3-8055-4785-4*) S Karger.

Aspects of Obstetrics Today. Ed. by T. K. Eskes et al. 448p. 1975. 159.00 (*0-444-15151-6*, Excerpta Medica) Elsevier.

***Aspects of Oral Communication.** Ed. by Uta M. Quasthoff. LC 94-45206. (Research in Text Theory Ser.: No. 21). vi, 493p. (C). 1995. lib. bdg. 192.35 (*3-11-014465-4*) De Gruyter.

Aspects of Oral Molecular Biology. Ed. by D. B. Ferguson. (Frontiers of Oral Physiology Ser.: Vol. 8). (Illus.). xii, 144p. 1991. 124.00 (*3-8055-5261-0*) S Karger.

Aspects of Pacific Ethnohistory. Alan R. Tippett. LC 73-8820. (Illus.). 216p. (Orig.). 1973. pap. 6.95 (*0-87808-132-1*) William Carey Lib.

Aspects of Pacific Seismicity. Ed. by Emile A. Okal. 200p. 1991. reprint ed. pap. 27.50 (*0-8176-2589-5*) Spr-Verlag.

Aspects of Palynology. Ed. by Robert H. Tschudy & Richard A. Scott. LC 73-84968. 520p. reprint ed. pap. 148.20 (*0-7837-2375-X*, 2040061) Bks Demand.

Aspects of Pentecostal-Charismatic Origins. Ed. by Vinson Synan. LC 75-2802. 252p. 1975. 6.95 (*0-88270-111-8*) Bridge Pub.

Aspects of Personality Structure see Developments in the Rorschach Technique

Aspects of Philosophical Logic. Ed. by Uwe Monnich. 296p. 1981. lib. bdg. 99.00 (*90-277-1201-8*) Kluwer Ac.

Aspects of Plant Sciences, Vol. I. Ed. by P. K. Nair. 210p. 1976. 15.00 (*0-88065-170-9*, Messers Today & Tomorrow) Scholarly Pubns.

Aspects of Plant Sciences, Vol. II. Ed. by P. K. Nair. 164p. 1979. 15.00 (*0-88065-171-7*, Messers Today & Tomorrow) Scholarly Pubns.

Aspects of Plant Sciences, Vol. VI. Ed. by S. S. Bir. (Illus.). 261p. (C). 1983. 19.00 (*0-88065-235-7*, Pub. by Today & Tomorrows P & P II) Scholarly Pubns.

Aspects of Plant Sciences, Vol. III: Pteridophytes: Some Aspects - Their Structure & Morphology, Vol. III. S. S. Bir. 170p. 1980. 15.00 (*0-88065-172-5*, Messers Today & Tomorrow) Scholarly Pubns.

Aspects of Poetry: Being Lectures Delivered at Oxford. John C. Shairp. LC 72-4606. (Essay Index Reprint Ser.). 1977. reprint ed. 25.95 (*0-8369-2976-4*) Ayer.

Aspects of Police Work. Egon Bittner. 320p. 1990. text ed. 42.50 (*1-55553-069-9*) NE U Pr.

***Aspects of Political Censorship, 1914-1918.** Tania Rose. 104p. 1995. pap. 17.95 (*0-85958-632-4*, Pub. by Hull Univ Pr UK) Paul & Co Pubs.

Aspects of Political Ideas & Institutions in Ancient India. 3rd ed. Ram S. Sharma. (C). 1991. reprint ed. 24.00 (*81-208-0827-4*, Pub. by Motilal Banarsidass II) S Asia.

Aspects of Political Theory. K Valsangkar et al. (Illus.). 292p. 1981. pap. text ed. 8.95 (*0-86131-108-6*, Pub. by Orient Longman Ltd II) Apt Bks.

Aspects of Political Theory: Classical Concepts in an Age of Relativism. W. J. Stankiewicz. 175p. 1976. 29.95 (*0-02-977630-9*) Transaction Pubs.

Aspects of Positivity in Functional Analysis. Ed. by R. Nagel et al. (North Holland Mathematics Studies: Vol. 122). 274p. 1986. 59.00 (*0-444-87959-5*, North Holland) Elsevier.

Aspects of Practical Trust Administration. Michael Sladen & John Wilcox. 1985. 55.00 (*0-85297-074-9*, Pub. by Inst Bankers UK) St Mut.

Aspects of Preventive Psychiatry. Ed. by G. N. Christodoulou. (Bibliotheca Psychiatrica Ser.: No. 160). (Illus.). viii, 116p. 1981. 52.00 (*3-8055-1218-X*) S Karger.

Aspects of Primary Education in the Netherlands: A Paper by HMI. 44p. 1987. pap. 6.00 (*0-11-220631-X*, HM1716, Pub. by HMSO UK) UNIPUB.

Aspects of Printing from 1600. Ed. by Robin Myers & Michael Harris. (Illus.). 174p. 1987. pap. text ed. 28.00 (*0-902692-36-4*) Oak Knoll.

Aspects of Psychoanalytic Intervention see Alterations in Defenses During Psychoanalysis

Aspects of Public Administration in Nepal. Madhab Poudyal. 1986. 24.00 (*0-8364-1800-X*, Pub. by Somaiya) S Asia.

Aspects of Public Sector Employment Law. G. J. McCarry. xxi, 254p. 1988. pap. 49.50 (*0-455-20794-1*, Pub. by Law Bk Co) W W Gaunt.

Aspects of Quantum Field Theory in Curved Spacetime. Stephen A. Fulling. 300p. (C). 1989. pap. 29.95 (*0-521-37768-4*) Cambridge U Pr.

Aspects of Rabbinic Theology. Solomon Schechter. LC 92-43435. 432p. 1993. reprint ed. pap. 18.95 (*1-879045-24-9*) Jewish Lights.

Aspects of Radar Signal Processing. Bernard L. Lewis et al. 554p. 1986. text ed. 29.00 (*0-89006-197-1*) Artech Hse.

Aspects of Radiation Biophysics. Ed. by A. Mookherjee & S. B. Bhattacharjee. 120p. (C). 1984. 80.00 (*81-85017-16-6*, Pub. by Interprint II) St Mut.

Aspects of Reading Acquisition. Ed. by John T. Guthrie. LC 75-36956. (Hyman Blumberg Symposium Ser.: Fifth Ser.). (Illus.). 240p. 1976. 35.00 (*0-8018-1800-1*); pap. 13.95 (*0-8018-1801-X*) Johns Hopkins.

Aspects of Reading Education. Ed. by Susanna Pflaum-Connor. LC 77-95250. (National Society for the Study of Education Publication Ser.). 1978. 29.25 (*0-8211-1517-0*); text ed. write for info. (*0-685-03192-6*) McCutchan.

Aspects of Recent Price Movements. Frederick C. Mills. (NBER Bulletin Ser.: No. 48). 1933. reprint ed. 20.00 (*0-685-61158-2*) Natl Bur Econ Res.

Aspects of Relativism: Moral, Cognitive & Literary. James E. Bayley. 178p. (Orig.). (C). 1992. lib. bdg. 39.50 (*0-8191-8597-3*) U Pr of Amer.

Aspects of Religion Vol. 18: Essays in Honour of Ninian Smart. Ed. by Peter Masefield & Donald Wiebe. LC 94-15794. (Toronto Studies in Religion: Vol. 18). 417p. (C). 1994. text ed. 59.95 (*0-8204-2237-1*) P Lang Pubs.

Aspects of Religion in the United States of America. Isabella L. Bishop. LC 75-38438. (Religion in America, Ser. 2). 200p. 1979. reprint ed. 23.95 (*0-405-04059-8*) Ayer.

Aspects of Religious Belief & Practice in Babylonia & Assyria. Morris Jastrow. LC 68-56503. 1972. reprint ed. 27.95 (*0-405-08667-9*, Pub. by Blom Pubns UK) Ayer.

Aspects of Religious Propaganda in Judaism & Early Christianity. Ed. by Elizabeth S. Fiorenza. LC 74-27890. (University of Notre Dame, Center for the Study of Judaism & Christianity in Antiquity Ser.: No. 2). 205p. reprint ed. pap. 58.50 (*0-8357-5798-6*, 2029308) Bks Demand.

Aspects of Risk Theory. J. Grandell. Ed. by J. Gani & C. C. Heyde. (Applied Probability Ser.: Vol. 6). (Illus.). 192p. 1994. 49.00 (*0-387-97368-0*) Spr-Verlag.

Aspects of Rural Settlements & Rural Society in Early Medieval India. Brajadulal Chattopadhyay. (C). 1990. 19.00 (*81-7074-055-X*, Pub. by KP Bagchi IA) S Asia.

Aspects of Schenkerian Theory. David Beach. LC 82-13498. 240p. 1983. text ed. 14.00 (*0-300-02800-8*) Yale U Pr.

***Aspects of School Television in Europe: A Documentation.** (Communication Research & Broadcasting Ser.: Vol. 10). 596p. 1992. pap. 37.50 (*3-598-20209-1*) K G Saur.

Aspects of Scientific Explanation. Carl G. Hempel. LC 65-15441. 1970. pap. 19.95 (*0-02-914340-3*) Free Pr.

Aspects of Seismic Reflection Data Processing. Ed. by R. Marschall. (C). 1990. lib. bdg. 129.50 (*0-7923-0846-8*) Kluwer Ac.

Aspects of Semantic Opposition in English. Arthur Mettinger. (Studies in Lexicography & Lexicology). 216p. 1994. 39.95 (*0-19-824269-7*) OUP.

Aspects of Sino-American Relations since 1784. Ed. by Thomas H. Etzold. 173p. 1978. write for info. (*0-318-56378-9*); pap. 5.95 (*0-531-05609-0*) Wiener Pubs Inc.

Aspects of Slow & Persistent Virus Infections. Ed. by David A. Tyrrell. (New Perspectives in Clinical Microbiology Ser.: Vol. 2). 286p. 1979. lib. bdg. 84.00 (*90-247-2281-0*) Kluwer Ac.

Aspects of Small-Scale Fisheries Development. Ed. by Michael T. Morrissey & Richard B. Pollnac. 154p. (C). 1989. pap. 7.00 (*1-882027-00-0*) URI ICMRD.

Aspects of Social Anthropology in India. B. N. Sahay & P. K. Dutta. 272p. 1980. 23.95 (*0-318-36793-9*) Asia Bk Corp.

Aspects of Social Anthropology in India. Ed. by L. P. Vidyarthi et al. 275p. 1980. 23.95 (*0-940500-06-X*) Asia Bk Corp.

Aspects of Social Behavior in Ancient Rome. Tenney Frank. LC 69-20283. (Martin Classical Lectures Ser.: Vol. 2). 153p. 1969. reprint ed. 30.00 (*0-8154-0304-6*) Cooper Sq.

Aspects of Society & Economy of Medieval Mithila. Upendra Thakur. 1989. 20.00 (*81-7169-012-2*, Pub. by Commonwealth II) S Asia.

Aspects of Sociolinguistics in South Asia. Ed. by Bray B. Kachru & S. N. Shridar. (International Journal of the Sociology of Language Ser.: No. 16). 1978. pap. 60.00 (*90-279-7815-8*) Mouton.

Aspects of Solid-State & Semiconductor Physics Research in France & Germany. Norman J. Horing. (Illus.). 53p. (Orig.). (C). 1994. pap. text ed. 35.00 (*0-7881-0259-1*) Diane Pub.

Aspects of Some Vitamins, Minerals & Enzymes in Health & Disease. Ed. by G. H. Bourne. (World Review of Nutrition & Dietetics Ser.: Vol. 62). (Illus.). 216p. 1990. 173.00 (*3-8055-4994-6*) S Karger.

Aspects of South African Literature. Ed. by Christopher Heywood. LC 76-25033. 207p. 1976. 35.00 (*0-8419-0292-5*, Africana) Holmes & Meier.

Aspects of Soviet Culture: Voices of Glasnost 1960-1990. Jelena Mikojkovic-Djuric. 180p. 1991. text ed. 25.00 (*0-88033-204-2*) Col U Pr.

Aspects of Space Law. E. Van Bogaert. 140p. 1985. lib. bdg. 179.00 (*90-6544-048-8*) Kluwer Ac.

Aspects of Stroke Prevention. Ed. by J. D. Easton. (Journal: Cerebrovascular Diseases: Vol. 2, Suppl. 1, 1992). (Illus.). iv, 48p. 1992. pap. 21.00 (*3-8055-5584-9*) S Karger.

Aspects of Symmetry: Selected Erice Lectures. S. Coleman. (Illus.). 416p. 1985. 115.00 (*0-521-26706-4*) Cambridge U Pr.

Aspects of Symmetry: Selected Erice Lectures. Sidney Coleman. 402p. 1988. pap. 39.95 (*0-521-31827-0*) Cambridge U Pr.

Aspects of Synaptic Transmission: Acetylcholine, Sigma Receptors, CCK & Elcosanoids, Neurotoxins. Ed. by Trevor W. Stone. 250p. 1993. 99.00 (*0-7484-0063-X*) Taylor & Francis.

Aspects of Synaptic Transmission, Vol. 1: LTP, Galanin, Autonomic, Opioids & 5-HT. Ed. by Trevor W. Stone. 380p. 1991. 120.00 (*0-85066-828-X*, Pub. by Tay Francis Ltd UK) Taylor & Francis.

Aspects of Text Structure. M. Phillips. (Linguistic Ser.: Vol. 52). 1985. 84.75 (*0-444-87701-0*, North Holland) Elsevier.

Aspects of the Actual Novel. Marian Barbu. 300p. 1994. pap. text ed. 9.95 (*1-879585-67-7*) Xiquan Pubng.

Aspects of the Administration of International Justice. E. Lauterpacht. 200p. (C). 1991. 140.00 (*0-949009-90-3*, Pub. by Grotius Pubns UK) St Mut.

Aspects of the American West: Three Essays. Joe B. Frantz. LC 76-17973. (Essays on the American West, Sponsored by Elma Dill Russell Spencer Foundation Ser.: No. 1). 88p. 1976. 9.95 (*0-89096-023-2*) Tex A&M Univ Pr.

Aspects of the Analysis of Family Structure. Ansley J. Coale et al. LC 65-14308. 262p. reprint ed. pap. 74.70 (*0-7837-0231-0*, 2040539) Bks Demand.

Aspects of the Analysis of Plate Structures: A Volume in Honor of W. H. Whittrick. Ed. by D. J. Dawe et al. (Illus.). 138p. 1985. 75.00 (*0-19-856168-7*) OUP.

Aspects of the Ancient World: Essays & Reviews. Victor L. Ehrenberg. LC 72-7889. (Greek History Ser.). 1977. reprint ed. 28.95 (*0-405-04785-1*) Ayer.

Aspects of the Balkans: Continuity & Change. Henrik Birnbaum & V. Speros. (Slavistic Printings & Reprintings Ser.: No. 27). 1972. text ed. 126.95 (*90-279-2172-5*) Mouton.

Aspects of the Biology of Ageing. Society for Experimental Biology (Great Britain). LC 67-24943. (Symposia of the Society for Experimental Biology Ser.: No. 21). 660p. reprint ed. pap. 180.00 (*0-8357-5799-4*, 2014670) Bks Demand.

Aspects of the Computer-Based Patient Record. Ed. by M. H. Ball et al. (Computers in Health Care Ser.). (Illus.). xx, 316p. 1995. 49.50 (*0-387-97723-6*) Spr-Verlag.

Aspects of the Depression. Ed. by Felix Morley. LC 68-22932. (Essay Index Reprint Ser.). 1977. 17.95 (*0-8369-0719-1*) Ayer.

Aspects of the Development of Competence Vol. 14: The Minnesota Symposium on Child Psychology. Ed. by W. Andrew Collins. LC 80-20568. (Minnesota Symposium on Child Psychology Ser.). 288p. 1981. 49.95 (*0-89859-070-1*) L Erlbaum Assocs.

Aspects of the Eighteenth Century. Ed. by Earl R. Wasserman. (Illus.). 352p. 1965. 48.50x (*0-8018-0656-9*) Johns Hopkins.

Aspects of the Epic. Ed. by Tom Winnifrith et al. LC 82-10271. 200p. 1983. text ed. 29.95 (*0-312-05724-5*) St Martin.

Aspects of the Female Novel. Jacqueline M. Rogers. LC 91-6859. 200p. (C). 1991. text ed. 30.00 (*0-89341-663-0*); pap. text ed. 17.50 (*0-89341-664-9*) Hollowbrook.

Aspects of the Hague Rules. Clarke. 1976. pap. text ed. 89.00 (*90-247-1806-6*) Kluwer Ac.

***Aspects of the History of Psychology in America: 1892-1992.** Ed. by Helmut E. Adler & Robert W. Rieber. LC 94-42028. (Annals Ser.: Vol. 188). 1995. write for info. (*0-89766-866-9*); write for info. (*0-89766-867-7*) NY Acad Sci.

Aspects of the International Banking Safety Net. G. G. Johnson & Richard K. Abrams. (Occasional Paper Ser.: No. 17). 36p. 1983. pap. 5.00 (*1-55775-058-0*) Intl Monetary.

Aspects of the Iron Age in Central Southern Britain. Barry Cunliffe & David Miles. (Illus.). 315p. 1984. pap. 19.95 (*0-947816-02-X*, Pub. by Univ Comm Archeology UK) David Brown.

Aspects of the Kinetics & Dynamics of Surface Reactions. Ed. by Uzi Landman. LC 80-68004. (AIP Conference Proceedings Ser.: No. 61). 343p. 1980. lib. bdg. 22.25 (*0-88318-160-6*) Am Inst Physics.

Aspects of the Life & Thought of Sir John Frederick Herschel. John F. Herschel & Silvan S. Scheber. LC 80-2110. (Development of Science Ser.). (Illus.). 1981. lib. bdg. 104.95 (*0-405-13829-6*) Ayer.

Aspects of the Mapping Problem in Processor Networks. Peter A. Hilbers. (International Series on Parallel Computation: No. 2). (Illus.). 150p. (C). 1991. 39.95 (*0-521-40250-6*) Cambridge U Pr.

Aspects of the Mexican American Experience: An Original Anthology. Hill et al. Ed. & Intro. by Carlos E. Cortes. LC 76-1473. (Chicano Heritage Ser.). (Illus.). 1977. 49.95 (*0-405-09534-1*) Ayer.

Aspects of the Military Documents of the Ancient Egyptians. Anthony J. Spalinger. LC 81-14680. (Near Eastern Researches Ser.: No. 9). 261p. 1983. text ed. 40.00 (*0-300-02381-2*) Yale U Pr.

Aspects of the Modern European Mind. John Cruickshank. LC 75-422041. (Problems & Perspectives in History Ser.). 212p. reprint ed. pap. 60.50 (*0-8357-5800-1*, 2006381) Bks Demand.

Aspects of the Novel. E. M. Forster. LC 27-23181. 113p. 1956. pap. 7.95 (*0-15-609180-1*, Harvest Bks) HarBrace.

Aspects of the Novelist: E. M. Forster's Pattern & Rhythm. Audrey A. Lavin. LC 93-12338. (AUS IV: Vol. 151). 168p. (C). 1995. text ed. 35.95 (*0-8204-1966-4*) P Lang Pubs.

Aspects of the Rise of Economic Individualism: A Criticism of Max Weber & His School. Hector M. Robertson. LC 73-17059. (Reprints of Economic Classics Ser.). 1973. reprint ed. 35.00 (*0-678-00867-1*) Kelley.

Aspects of the Slavic Language Question: Church Slavonic-South Slavic-West Slavic,, Vol. 1. Ed. by Riccardo Picchio & Harvey Goldblatt. (Yale Russian & East European Publications: No. 4a). 416p. 1984. 35.00 (*0-936586-03-6*) Yale Russian.

Aspects of the Slavic Language Question: East Slavic, Vol. II. Ed. by Riccardo Picchio & Harvey Goldblatt. (Yale Russian & East European Publications: No. 4b). 367p. 1984. 35.00 (*0-936586-04-4*) Yale Russian.

Aspects of the Slavic Middle Ages & Slavic Renaissance Culture. Henrik Birnbaum. (American University Studies: Slavic Languages & Literature: Ser. XII, Vol. 4). 838p. (C). 1989. text ed. 110.95 (*0-8204-1057-8*) P Lang Pubs.

480

An Asterisk (*) at the beginning of an entry indicates that the title is appearing in BIP for the first time.

Aspects of the Social History of America. Theodore R. Sizer et al. LC 74-84297. (Essay Index Reprint Ser.). 1977. 14.95 (*0-8369-1074-5*) Ayer.

Aspects of the Theory of Heat Resistance of Metals & Alloys. K. A. Osipov. 256p. 1961. text ed. 67.00 (*0-7065-0165-9*, Pub. by Keter Pub IS) Coronet Bks.

Aspects of the Theory of International Capital Movements. 2nd ed. Carl Iversen. LC 67-27678. 1967. reprint ed. 49.50 (*0-678-00327-0*) Kelley.

Aspects of the Theory of Syntax. Noam Chomsky. 1965. reprint ed. pap. 13.50 (*0-262-53007-4*) MIT Pr.

Aspects of the Theory of Tariffs. Harry G. Johnson. LC 73-173414. 463p. 1971. 39.95 (*0-674-04991-8*) HUP.

Aspects of the Third Reich. Ed. by H. William Koch, Jr. LC 84-27592. 611p. 1986. pap. 19.95 (*0-312-00381-1*) St Martin.

Aspects of the Tongue (1828) Robert Froriep. Ed. by Charles Garton & Joseph D. Gerencser. (Arethusa Monographs: No. 9). (Illus.). xiii, 217p. 1982. pap. 15.00 (*0-930881-06-0*) Dept Classics.

Aspects of Time. George N. Schlesinger. LC 79-66954. 180p. (C). 1980. lib. bdg. 27.50 (*0-915144-69-7*); pap. text ed. 7.95 (*0-915144-70-0*) Hackett Pub.

Aspects of Trinity Division Geology. Ed. by Bob F. Perkins. LC 74-632779. (Geoscience & Man Ser.: Vol. 8). 228p. 1974. pap. 11.50 (*0-938909-07-X*) Geosci Pubns LSU.

Aspects of Tropical Mycology. Ed. by Susan Isaac et al. (British Mycological Society Symposium Ser.: No. 19). (Illus.). 350p. (C). 1994. 94.95 (*0-521-45050-0*) Cambridge U Pr.

Aspects of Uncertainty: A Tribute to D. V. Lindley. P. R. Freeman. Ed. by A. F. Smith. LC 93-33678. (Probability & Mathematical Statistics Ser.). 1994. text ed. 79.95 (*0-471-94347-9*) Wiley.

Aspects of Upper Great Lakes Anthropology: Papers in Honor of Lloyd A. Wilford. Ed. by Elden Johnson. LC 74-17003. (Minnesota Prehistoric Archaeology Ser.: No. 11). (Illus.). 190p. 1974. pap. 9.50 (*0-87351-087-9*) Minn Hist.

Aspects of Vagueness. Ed. by Heinz J. Skala et al. LC 83-26994. 1984. lib. bdg. 89.00 (*90-277-1692-7*) Kluwer Ac.

Aspects of Verdi. George W. Martin. LC 93-13748. (Illus.). 304p. 1993. reprint ed. pap. 15.95 (*0-87910-172-5*) Limelight Edns.

Aspects of Versification in Sanskrit Lyric Poetry. Sheldon Pollock. (American Oriental Ser.: Vol. 61). 1977. 12.00 (*0-940490-61-7*) Am Orient Soc.

Aspects of Vertebrate History: Essays in Honor of Edwin Harris Colbert. Ed. by Louis Jacobs. 412p. 1980. pap. 9.95 (*0-89734-053-1*, SP053-1) Mus Northern Ariz.

Aspects of Vietnamese History. Ed. by Walter F. Vella. LC 72-619626. (Asian Studies at Hawaii: No. 8). 288p. reprint ed. pap. 82.10 (*0-8357-5801-X*, 2029586) Bks Demand.

***Aspects of Visual Form Processing: Proceedings of the Second International Workshop on Visual Form.** Ed. by Carlo Arcelli et al. LC 94-31172. 632p. 1994. text ed. 162.00 (*981-02-2011-1*) World Scientific Pub.

Aspects of Vocal Multiphonics. B. Barnett. Date not set. 7.25 (*0-939044-19-6*) Lingua Pr.

Aspects of Wagner. 2nd ed. Bryan Magee. 112p. 1988. pap. 10.95 (*0-19-284012-6*) OUP.

Aspects of Welsh History: Selected Papers of Glyn Roberts. 345p. 1969. 17.50 (*0-904730-22-0*, Pub. by U of Wales UK) Bks Intl VA.

Aspects of Western Civilization: Problems & Sources in History, Vol. 1. 2nd ed. Perry M. Rogers. 480p. (C). 1991. pap. text ed. write for info. (*0-13-050758-X*) P-H.

Aspects of Western Civilization: Problems & Sources in History, Vol. 2. 2nd ed. Perry M. Rogers. 528p. (C). 1992. pap. text ed. write for info. (*0-13-051897-2*) P-H.

Aspects of Western Subanon Formal Speech. William C. Hall. Ed. by Virgil Poulter & Desmond C. Derbyshire. LC 87-62946. (Publications in Linguistics: No. 81). (Illus.). 191p. (Orig.). 1987. pap. 20.00 (*0-88312-093-3*); fiche 16.00 (*0-88312-427-0*) Summer Instit Ling.

Aspects of Wilde. Vincent O'Sullivan. 1976. lib. bdg. 59.95 (*0-8490-1460-3*) Gordon Pr.

Aspects of Wisdom in Judaism & Early Christianity. Ed. by Robert L. Wilken. LC 74-27888. (University of Notre Dame, Center for the Study of Judaism & Christianity in Antiquity Ser.: No. 1). 240p. reprint ed. pap. 68.40 (*0-8357-5802-8*, 2024365) Bks Demand.

***Aspects of Yoga.** H. Kumar Kaul. (C). 1994. 16.00 (*81-7018-810-5*, Pub. by BR Pub II) S Asia.

Aspects on the Johannine Literature. Ed. by Lars Hartman & Birger Olsson. (Coniectanea Biblica. New Testament Ser.: No. 18). 113p. (Orig.). 1987. pap. 33.50 (*91-22-00929-9*, Pub. by Almqv & Wiksell SW) Coronet Bks.

Aspects Sociologiques du Catholicisme Americain: Vie Urbaine et Institutions Religieuses. Francois Houtart. 1978. 33.95 (*0-405-10835-4*, 11841) Ayer.

Aspectual Function of the Rgvedic Present & Aorist. J. Gonda. (Disputationes Rheno-Trajectinae Ser.: No. 7). pap. 61.55 (*90-279-0033-7*) Mouton.

Aspectual Roles & the Syntax-Semantics Interface. Carol L. Tenny. LC 94-15056. (Studies in Linguistics & Philosophy: Vol. 52). 256p. (C). 1994. lib. bdg. 87.00 (*0-7923-2863-9*) Kluwer Ac.

Aspectual Roles & the Syntax-Semantics Interface. Carol L. Tenny. LC 94-15056. (Studies in Linguistics & Philosophy: Vol. 52). 256p. (C). 1994. pap. text ed. 34.50 (*0-7923-2907-4*) Kluwer Ac.

Aspectual Usage in Modern Russian. L. Pirogova. 320p. (C). 1988. 50.00 (*0-685-33700-6*, Pub. by Collets) St Mut.

Aspectual Usage in Modern Russian. O. Rassudova. 200p. (C). 1984. 55.00 (*0-685-33701-4*, Pub. by Collets); 33.00 (*0-685-39370-4*, Pub. by Collets) St Mut.

Aspectual Usage of the Dynamic Infinitive in Herodotus. Peter Stork. xviii, 535p. 1982. 61.00 (*90-6088-081-1*, Pub. by Boumas Boekhuis NE) Benjamins North Am.

Aspectus et Affectus: Essays & Editions in Grosseteste & Medieval Intellectual Life in Honor of Richard C. Dales. Ed. by Gunar Freibergs. LC 91-57962. (Studies in the Middle Ages: No. 23). 140p. 1993. 36.00 (*0-404-64163-6*) AMS Pr.

Aspekte: First-Year German Reader. 3rd ed. Robert E. Helbling et al. (GER.). 1983. text ed. 44.75 (*0-03-062506-8*) HB Coll Pubs.

Aspekte: Kultur, Politik, Alltag, Literatur. Robert E. Helbling et al. 130p. (GER.). (C). 1984. pap. text ed. 19.50 (*0-03-062591-2*) HB Coll Pubs.

Aspekte Amerikanischer Kultur. Jurgen Beneke et al. (Hildesheimer Beitrage Zu Den Erziehungs und Sozialwissenschaften Ser.: Vol. 31). viii, 190p. write for info. (*3-487-09223-9*, Pub. by Georg Olms GW) Lubrecht & Cramer.

Aspekte der Kontrastiven Syntax am Beispiel des Niederlaendischen und Deutschen. Jelle Stegemann. (Studia Linguistica Germanica). 201p. (C). 1979. text ed. 61.55 (*3-11-008017-6*) De Gruyter.

Aspekte der Sprachgestaltung bei Paul Celan. Edda D. Hodnett. LC 90-21534. (American University Studies: Germanic Languages & Literature: Ser. I, Vol. 89). 156p. (GER.). (C). 1991. text ed. 31.95 (*0-8204-1206-6*) P Lang Pubs.

Aspekte und Probleme der Minoischen Religion. Walter Potscher. (Religionswissenschaftliche Texte und Studien Ser.: Bd. 4). viii, 288p. 1990. write for info. (*3-487-09359-6*, Pub. by Georg Olms GW) Lubrecht & Cramer.

Aspekte Wissenschaftlicher Erklaerung. Carl G. Hempel. (Grundlagen der Kommunikation De Gruyter Studienbuch Ser.). (C). 1977. 26.15 (*3-11-004630-X*) De Gruyter.

***Aspen.** Lynn Erickson. (Mira Bks.). 1995. mass mkt. 4.99 (*1-55166-054-7*, 1-66054-7, Mira Bks) Harlequin Bks.

***Aspen.** Tracy Salcedo. (Twelve Short Hikes Ser.). (Illus.). 32p. 1995. pap. 4.95 (*0-934641-53-6*) Chockstone Pr.

Aspen: The History of a Silver-Mining Town, 1879-1893. Malcolm J. Rohrbough. (Illus.). 288p. 1988. pap. 10.95 (*0-19-505428-8*) OUP.

***Aspen: The Quiet Years.** Kathleen K. Daily & Gaylord Guenin. Ed. by Diane Borneman. (Illus.). 700p. 1994. 50.00 (*0-9641399-0-1*) Red Ink.

Aspen - Independence Pass, CO. rev. ed. (Illus.). 1993. 8.99 (*0-925873-81-0*) Trails Illustrated.

Aspen & Central Colorado Trails. Warren H. Ohlrich. LC 93-93820. (Illus.). 100p. (Orig.). 1993. pap. 9.95 (*0-9620046-9-3*) W H O Pr.

Aspen Book: A Complete Guide. Diane Tegmeyer. (Illus.). 1992. pap. 14.95 (*0-936399-31-7*) Berkshire Hse.

Aspen-Carbondale: Cross Country Map, CO. rev. ed. Ed. by Trails Illustrated Staff. 1988. 6.99 (*0-925873-61-6*) Trails Illustrated.

Aspen Dayhiker. Ruth Frey & Peter Frey. (Illus.). 160p. (Orig.). 1993. pap. 9.95 (*0-9636187-0-9*) Brush Creek.

Aspen Gold. Janet Dailey. 416p. 1992. mass mkt. 5.99 (*0-316-17153-0*) Little.

Aspen Gold. braille ed. Janet Daily. 675p. 1992. vinyl bd. 54.00 (*1-56956-039-0*, BR8646) W A T Braille.

Aspen Guide to Effective Health Care Correspondence. Aspen Reference Group Staff. Ed. by Kenneth E. Lawrence. LC 93-12612. 432p. 1993. text ed. 65.00 (*0-8342-0305-7*, 20305) Aspen Pub.

Aspen Handbook on the Media, 1977-1979 Edition. Ed. by William Rivers et al. 6.95 (*0-686-25999-8*) Aspen Inst Human.

Aspen High Country: The Geology, a Pictorial Guide to Roads & Trails. David Laing & Nicholas Lampiris. (Illus.). 144p. (Orig.). (J). (gr. 9-12). 1980. pap. write for info. (*0-9604274-0-6*) Thunder River.

Aspen in Color. Warren H. Ohlrich. LC 90-90323. (Illus.). 112p. 1990. 34.95 (*0-9620046-5-0*) W H O Pr.

Aspen Mountain Camping Equipment Company. 5th ed. Audrie M. Beck. 120p. (C). 1991. Manual practice set. pap. text ed. 20.95 (*0-256-09253-2*, 35-1345-05) Irwin.

***Aspen on Foot.** Ruth Frey. LC 95-94118. (Illus.). 208p. (Orig.). 1995. pap. 14.95 (*0-9636187-1-7*) Brush Creek.

Aspen, Portrait of a Rocky Mountain Town. Ed. by Warren H. Ohlrich. LC 92-90947. (Illus.). 112p. 1993. 29.95 (*1-882426-00-2*) W H O Pr.

Aspen, Portrait of a Rocky Mountain Town. Photographers Aspen Staff. Ed. by Warren H. Ohlrich. LC 92-90947. 112p. (Orig.). 1992. pap. 24.95 (*0-9620046-8-5*) W H O Pr.

***Aspen Potpourri: The People, Places & Food of Aspen.** Mary E. Hayes. 260p. 1990. 18.95 (*0-9641960-0-X*) Aspen Potpourri.

Aspen-Snowmass Cross Country Ski Trails. Warren H. Ohlrich. LC 89-51494. 56p. (Orig.). 1989. pap. 5.95 (*0-9620046-2-6*) W H O Pr.

Aspen-Snowmass Downhill Ski Trails. Warren H. Ohlrich. LC 89-90419. 104p. (Orig.). 1990. pap. 7.95 (*0-9620046-3-4*) W H O Pr.

Aspen-Snowmass Trails: A Hiking Trail Guide. Warren H. Ohlrich. LC 87-92228. 52p. (Orig.). 1988. pap. 7.95 (*0-9620046-0-X*) W H O Pr.

Aspen Visible: A Guidebook to the Natural & Man-Made Environment in & Around Aspen, Colorado. Joel Wurman. 1972. pap. 1.50x (*0-262-73050-2*) MIT Pr.

Aspen-Volare Nineteen Seventy-Six to Nineteen Eighty. LC 81-70240. (Illus.). 224p. 1982. pap. 15.95 (*0-8019-7193-4*) Chilton.

Aspergillus. Ed. by J. E. Smith. (Biotechnology Handbooks Ser.: Vol. 7). 1994. 69.50 (*0-306-44545-X*, Plenum Pr) Plenum.

Aspergillus: Biology & Industrial Applications. Ed. by Joan W. Bennett & Maren A. Klich. (Biotechnology Ser.). 432p. 1992. 46.00 (*0-7506-9124-7*) Buttrwrth-Heinemann.

***Aspergillus: 50 Years On.** Ed. by S. D. Martinelli & J. R. Kinghorn. (Progress in Industrial Microbiology Ser.: Vol. 29). 880p. 1994. text ed. 328.50 (*0-444-81762-X*) Elsevier.

Aspergillus & Aspergillosis. Ed. by H. Vanden Bossche et al. LC 88-4132. (Illus.). 342p. 1988. 85.00 (*0-306-42828-8*, Plenum Pr) Plenum.

Aspergillus Species on Stored Products. Z. Kozakiewicz. (CAB Intern'l Mycological Inst. Mycological Papers: No. 161). (Illus.). 188p. 1989. pap. 61.50 (*0-685-45057-0*, Pub. by CAB Commonwlth Agr UK) Lubrecht & Cramer.

Aspern Papers. Henry James. Bd. with Turn of the Screw. LC 76-158791.; Liar. LC 76-158791.; Two Faces. LC 76-158791. LC 76-158791. (Novels & Tales of Henry James Ser.: Vol. 12). xxiii, 412p. 1971. reprint ed. 45.00 (*0-678-02812-5*) Kelley.

Aspern Papers & Other Stories. Henry James. Ed. by Adrian Poole. (World's Classics Ser.). 1983. pap. 3.95 (*0-19-281622-5*) OUP.

Aspern Papers & Other Stories. Henry James. 1976. 20.95 (*0-8488-0541-0*) Amereon Ltd.

Aspern Papers & the Turn of the Screw. Henry James. Ed. by Anthony Curtis. (English Library). 240p. 1984. pap. 4.95 (*0-14-043224-8*, Penguin Classics) Viking Penguin.

***ASPG Graphics Supplement & Installation Guide.** George H. Blackford. (Illus.). 24p. 1994. 3.00 (*1-881564-01-0*) DMC Sftware.

Asphalt: A Strategic Plan. (SHRP Publication Ser.: No. 90ASPH). 56p. 1990. 5.00 (*0-685-41013-7*) Transport Res Bd.

Asphalt: Science & Technology. Edwin J. Barth. (Illus.). 720p. 1962. text ed. 336.00 (*0-677-00040-5*) Gordon & Breach.

Asphalt-Aggregate Mixture Analysis System (AAMAS) (National Cooperative Highway Research Program Report Ser.: No. 338). 185p. 1991. 20.00 (*0-309-04861-3*) Transport Res Bd.

Asphalt & Asphalt Additives. LC 92-23796. (Transportation Research Record Ser.: No. 1342). 100p. 1992. 22.00 (*0-309-05205-X*) Transport Res Bd.

Asphalt Cold-Mix Manual. (Illus.). 200p. 1991. pap. 16.00 (*0-318-13378-4*, MS-14) Asphalt Inst.

Asphalt Cold-Mix Recycling. 76p. 1983. 8.00 (*0-318-17742-0*, MS-21) Asphalt Inst.

***Asphalt Concrete Mix Materials (TRR 1436)** Ed. by Norman Solomon. (Transportation Research Record Ser.). (Illus.). 144p. 1994. pap. text ed. 29.00 (*0-309-05513-X*) Transport Res Bd.

Asphalt Concrete Mixtures (TRR 1417) Ed. by Norman Solomon. (Transportation Research Record Ser.). (Illus.). 196p. 1994. pap. text ed. 43.00 (*0-309-05565-2*) Natl Res Coun.

Asphalt Emulsions, No. 1079. Ed. by Harold W. Muncy. LC 89-49641. (Special Technical Publication Ser.). (Illus.). 122p. 1990. text ed. 32.00 (*0-8031-1457-5*, 04-010790-08) ASTM.

Asphalt Georgics. Hayden Carruth. LC 84-25499. 96p. 1985. 15.00 (*0-8112-0937-7*); pap. 6.95 (*0-8112-0938-5*, NDP591) New Directions.

Asphalt Handbook, 1989 Edition. 640p. 1989. 33.00 (*0-318-40049-9*, MS-4) Asphalt Inst.

Asphalt Hot-Mix Recycling. 2nd ed. (MS Ser.: No. 20). (Illus.). 52p. (C). 1986. pap. text ed. 8.00 (*0-317-03834-6*) Asphalt Inst.

Asphalt in Hydraulics. (Illus.). 80p. pap. 8.00 (*0-318-13379-2*, MS-12) Asphalt Inst.

Asphalt in Pavement Maintenance. (Illus.). 192p. 1983. pap. 12.00 (*0-318-13380-6*, MS-16) Asphalt Inst.

Asphalt Materials & Mixtures. (Research Record Ser.: No. 1115). 229p. 1987. 32.00 (*0-317-93780-4*) Transport Res Bd.

Asphalt Mix Materials & Mixtures 1990. (Transportation Research Record Ser.: No. 1269). 184p. 1990. 31.00 (*0-309-05050-2*) Transport Res Bd.

Asphalt Mixture Design. LC 92-30101. (Transportation Research Record Ser.: No. 1353). 107p. 1992. 22.00 (*0-309-05217-3*) Transport Res Bd.

Asphalt Mixtures & Asphalt Chemistry. (Transportation Research Record Ser.: No. 1228). 210p. 1989. 32.00 (*0-309-04823-0*) Transport Res Bd.

Asphalt Overlay Design Procedures. (National Cooperative Highway Research Program Report Ser.: No. 116). 46p. 1984. 8.40 (*0-309-03872-3*) Transport Res Bd.

Asphalt Overlays & Pavement Rehabilitation. (Illus.). 164p. 1983. 12.00 (*0-318-13381-4*, MS-17) Asphalt Inst.

Asphalt Pavement Repair Manuals of Practice. Kelly L. Smith et al. 73p. (Orig.). (C). 1993. pap. text ed. 15.00 (*0-309-05607-1*, SHRP-H-348) SHRP.

Asphalt Payment Construction: New Materials & Techniques - STP 724. Ed. by J. Scherocman. 136p. 1981. pap. 28.00 (*0-8031-0775-7*, 04-724000-08) ASTM.

Asphalt Pocketbook of Useful Information. 144p. 1982. 9.00 (*0-318-13384-9*, MS-6) Asphalt Inst.

Asphalt Properties & Relationship to Pavement Performance: Literature Review. (SHRP Interim Report Ser.: No. 015A). 1990. 5.00 (*0-685-41012-9*) Transport Res Bd.

Asphalt Recycling. Richard K. Miller & Marcia E. Rupnow. LC 90-84379. (Survey on Technology & Markets Ser.: No. 173). 50p. 1991. pap. text ed. 200.00 (*1-55865-225-6*) Future Tech Surveys.

Asphalt Rheology Relatonship to Mixture. Ed. by Oliver E. Briscoe. LC 87-1835. (Special Technical Publication Ser.: No. 941). (Illus.). viii, 200p. 1987. 34.00 (*0-8031-0938-5*, 0-941000-08) ASTM.

Asphalt Rivers. Bucky Sinister. 20p. (Orig.). 1994. pap. 3.00 (*0-916397-19-X*) Manic D Pr.

Asphalt Surface Treatments: Construction Techniques. (Illus.). 24p. 7.00 (*0-318-23657-5*, ES-12) Asphalt Inst.

Asphalt Surface Treatments - Specifications. (Illus.). 16p. 6.00 (*0-318-23656-7*, ES-11) Asphalt Inst.

Asphalt Worker. Jack Rudman. (Career Examination Ser.: C-19). 1994. pap. 23.95 (*0-8373-0019-3*) Nat Learn.

Asphaltene Particles in Fossil Fuel Exploration, Recovery, Refining & Production Processes. Ed. by M. K. Sharma & T. F. Yen. (Illus.). 244p. (C). 1994. 75.00 (*0-306-44709-6*, Plenum Pr) Plenum.

Asphaltenes & Asphalts, Vol. 1. Ed. by T. F. Yen & G. V. Chilingarian. LC 94-3116. (Developments in Petroleum Science Ser.: Vol. 40). 1994. write for info. (*0-444-88291-X*) Elsevier.

A

Asphodel. Ed. by Robert Spoo. LC 91-45620. 237p. 1992. lib. bdg. 42.50 (*0-8223-1240-9*); pap. 12.95 (*0-8223-1242-5*) Duke.

Asphodel Plantation Cookbook & Cook Box. Marcelle R. Couhig. LC 78-24263. 144p. 1980. spiral bd. 10.95 (*0-88289-194-4*); 30.00 (*0-911116-66-4*) Pelican.

Asphodel, That Greeny Flower & Other Love Poems. William Carlos Williams. LC 94-27083. (Bibelot Ser.). 64p. 1994. pap. 5.00 (*0-8112-1283-1*, NDP794) New Directions.

Asphyxiating Culture & Other Writings. Jean Dubuffet. Tr. by Carol Volk. LC 87-33680. (Illus.). 118p. 1988. 17.95 (*0-941423-09-3*) FWEW.

Asphyxiations - One to Forty. Ed. by Robert Hotchkiss. (Contemporary Poets Ser.). 49p. (Orig.). 1981. 9.95 (*0-686-30206-0*); pap. 4.00 (*0-686-30207-9*) Metron Pr.

Aspin Papers: Sanctions, Diplomacy & War in the Persian Gulf. Les Aspin. (Orig.). 8.95 (*0-89296-161-9*) Mysterious Pr.

Aspin Papers: Sanctions, Diplomacy, & War in the Persian Gulf. Les Aspin. LC 91-7361. (Significant Issues Ser.: Vol. 13, No. 2). 106p. reprint ed. pap. 30.30 (*0-7837-6057-4*, 2045870) Bks Demand.

Aspinall's Reports of Maritime Cases 1870-1940, 20 vols., Set. Aspinall. boxed 2,500.00 (*0-86205-264-5*) Butterworth Legal Pubs.

Aspinwall Empire. Duncan S. Somerville. (Illus.). xi, 129p. 1983. pap. 11.95 (*0-913372-29-3*) Mystic Seaport.

Aspinwall Genealogy. Algernon A. Aspinwall. 262p. 1988. reprint ed. lib. bdg. 44.50 (*0-8328-0140-2*); reprint ed. pap. 34.50 (*0-8328-0141-0*) Higginson Bk Co.

Aspiration Based Decision Support Systems. Ed. by A. Lewandowski & A. P. Wierzbicki. (Lecture Notes in Economics & Mathematical Systems Ser.: Vol. 331). x, 399p. 1989. pap. 50.60 (*0-387-51213-6*) Spr-Verlag.

Aspiration Biopsy. 2nd ed. Leopold G. Koss et al. LC 92-1467. (Illus.). 752p. 1992. 185.00 (*0-89640-212-6*) Igaku-Shoin.

Aspiration, Biopsy, Cytology, Part II: Cytology of Infradiaphragmatic Organs. J. Zajicek. (Monographs in Clinical Cytology: Vol. 7). (Illus.). 1979. 92.00 (*3-8055-2933-3*) S Karger.

Aspiration Levels in Bargaining & Economic Decision Making: Proceedings, Winzenhohl, FRG, 1982. Ed. by R. Tietz. (Lecture Notes in Economics & Mathematical Systems Ser.: Vol. 213). (Illus.). 406p. 1983. pap. 49.00 (*0-387-12277-X*) Spr-Verlag.

Aspiration Method for the Determination of Atmospheric-Ion Spectra. H. F. Tammet. 208p. 1971. text ed. 53.75 (*0-7065-0685-5*, Pub. by Keter Pub IS) Coronet Bks.

Aspiration Toward a Lost Natural Harmony in the Work of Three Italian Writers: Leopardi, Verga, & Moravia. Foscarina Alexander. LC 90-46357. (Studies in Italian Literature: Vol. 1). 136p. 1990. lib. bdg. 69.95 (*0-7734-9706-4*) E Mellen.

Aspiration vs. Opportunity: 'Careers' in the Inner City. Paul Bullock. LC 73-620101. (Policy Papers in Human Resources & Industrial Relations Ser.: No. 20). 180p. 1973. 10.00 (*0-87736-122-3*); pap. 5.00 (*0-87736-123-1*) U of Mich Inst Labor.

Aspiration Workbook. 1979. 4.95 (*1-55646-731-1*, XX-W, Career Aids OH) Opportunities Learn.

Aspirations & Anxieties: New England Workers & the Mechanized Factory System, 1815-1850. David A. Zonderman. (Illus.). 368p. 1992. 49.95 (*0-19-505747-3*) OUP.

Aspirations & Mentoring in an Academic Environment: Women Faculty in Library & Information Science. Mary N. Maack & Joanne Passet. LC 93-16200. (Contributions in Librarianship & Information Science Ser.: No. 75). 232p. 1994. Alk. paper. text ed. 49.95 (*0-313-27836-9*, MRL, Greenwood Pr) Greenwood.

Aspirations & Realities: A Documentary History of Economic Development Policy in Ireland since 1922. James L. Wiles & Richard B. Finnegan. LC 92-1123. (Contributions in Economics & Economic History Ser.: No. 137). 240p. 1992. text ed. 55.00 (*0-313-27440-1*, WAI/, Greenwood Pr) Greenwood.

Aspirations to Manifestations: From the Womb to the Void. Artis. LC 93-8430. 106p. 1993. pap. 13.50 (*0-938493-20-5*) Hulogosi Inc.

Aspire to the Heavens. Mary Higgins Clark. 216p. 1986. reprint ed. lib. bdg. 27.95 (*0-89966-533-0*) Buccaneer Bks.

Aspirin - Reports of Harmful & Unfavorable Effects Including Illness & Wayward Behavior: Index of New Information with Authors & Subjects. Roy R. Zimmerman. 180p. 1993. 49.50 (*1-55914-838-1*); pap. 44.50 (*1-55914-839-X*) ABBE Pubs Assn.

Aspirin a Day: What You Can Do to Prevent Heart Attack, Stroke, & Cancer. Michael Castleman. LC 92-36368. 192p. 1993. pap. 7.95 (*1-56282-880-0*) Hyperion.

Aspirin & Other Salicylates. Ed. by John R. Vane & Regina M. Botting. (Illus.). 672p. 1993. 149.95 (*0-412-32370-2*) Chapman & Hall.

An Asterisk (*) at the beginning of an entry indicates that the title is appearing in BIP for the first time. 481

A

Aspirin Handbook: A User's Guide to the Breakthrough Drug of the 90s. Joe Graedon. 1993. mass mkt. 4.99 (0-553-56119-7) Bantam.

Aspirin, Platelets & Stroke. William S. Fields & William K. Hass. LC 74-153915. (Illus.). 178p. 1971. 12.75 (0-87527-033-6) Green.

Aspirin Wars: Money, Medicine, & One Hundred Years of Rampant Competition. Charles C. Mann & Mark L. Plummer. LC 90-28735. (Illus.). 416p. 1991. 24.50 (0-394-57894-5) Knopf.

Aspirin Wars: Money, Medicine, & 100 Years of Rampant Competition. Charles C. Mann & Mark L. Plummer. 432p. 1993. pap. 16.95 (0-87584-401-4) Harvard Busn.

Aspirin Wars: Money, Medicine & 100 Yeas of Rampant Competition. Charles C. Mann & Mark L. Plummer. 1993. pap. text ed. 16.95 (0-07-103398-X) McGraw.

Aspiring Jazz Pianist: A Jazz Piano Method for Both the Solo & Combo Pianist with Play along Tape, Beginning through Intermediate. Debbie Denke. LC 91-90969. 156p. (Orig.). (C). 1991. pap. text ed. 31.95 (0-9629465-4-0) Wingspan Pubns.

Aspiring Mind of the Elizabethan Younger Generation. Anthony Esler. LC 66-26025. (Duke Historical Publications). 290p. reprint ed. pap. 82.70 (0-8357-5803-6, 2023379) Bks Demand.

Aspiring to Freedom: Commentaries on John Paul II's Encyclical "The Social Concerns of the Church" Peter L. Berger et al. Ed. by Kenneth A. Myers. LC 88-16563. 183p. reprint ed. pap. 52.20 (0-7837-0522-0, 2040846) Bks Demand.

Aspley Guise. Peter Clothier. 1970. 2.00 (0-88031-002-2) Invisible-Red Hill.

ASPM - Armed Services Pricing Manual, Vol. 2: Price Analysis. 200p. 1987. pap. 8.00 (0-318-35080-7, 5301) Commerce.

ASPM - Armed Services Pricing Manual, 1986. 368p. 1986. pap. 12.00 (0-318-35079-3, 5377) Commerce.

Aspring Women: Short Stories by Canadian Women, 1880-1900. Ed. by Sandra Campbell & Lorraine McMullen. 430p. (Orig.). 1993. pap. 17.00 (0-7766-0367-1, Pub. by Univ Ottawa Pr CN) Paul & Co Pubs.

***ASQ Questionnaires - English Version.** Bricker et al. 80p. 1995. boxed 115.00 (1-55766-181-2) P H Brookes.

***ASQ Questionnaires - Spanish Version.** Bricker et al. 80p. 1995. boxed 115.00 (1-55766-182-0) P H Brookes.

***ASQ User's Guide: A Parent-Completed, Child-Monitoring System.** Squires et al. 168p. (SPA.). 1995. spiral bd. 40.00 (1-55766-179-0) P H Brookes.

Asquith. Stephen E. Koss. LC 84-29285. (Illus.). 310p. 1985. pap. text ed. 16.00 (0-231-06155-2) Col U Pr.

***Asquith As War Leader.** George H. Cassar. LC 94-28401. 1994. write for info. (1-85285-117-1) Hambledon Press.

ASR: Astronomy. Snow. 1994. 11.95 (0-87434-606-1) Springhouse Pub.

ASR: Oceanography. Corso. 1994. 11.95 (0-87434-608-8) Springhouse Pub.

ASR: Organic Chemistry. Rutherford. 1994. 11.95 (0-87434-569-3) Springhouse Pub.

ASR: Physics. Mitchell. 1994. 11.95 (0-87434-573-1) Springhouse Pub.

***Asrael.** Lee Passarella. 25p. 1995. pap. 4.50 (0-9647127-1-7) Coreopsis Bks.

Asrama System: The History & Hermeneutics of a Religious Institution. Patrick Olivelle. LC 92-38998. 288p. (C). 1993. 49.95 (0-19-508327-X) OUP.

Ass & Bottom Parade: A Study of Sexuality, 2 vols., Set. (Sexual History Ser.). 1992. lib. bdg. 345.95 (0-8490-5339-0) Gordon Pr.

Assailing the Seven C's. Barbara B. Thatcher. Ed. by Sheryl York. LC 87-40261. 91p. (Orig.). (J). 1987. pap. 8.95 (1-55523-101-2) Winston-Derek.

Assam Challenge. K. M. Chhabra. 1993. text ed. 22.50 (81-220-0273-0, Pub. by Konark Pubs II) Advent Bks Div.

Assam Movement: Class, Ideology & Identity. Monirul Hassain. (Illus.). xv, 328p. (C). 1993. 42.00x (81-85445-29-X, Pub. by Manak Pubns Pvt Ltd) Nataraj Bks.

Assam Vaishnavism. Anima Dutta. (C). 1989. 24.00 (81-7099-173-0, Pub. by Mittal II) S Asia.

Assamese Self Taught. 160p. 1993. pap. 6.95 (0-7818-0223-7) Hippocrene Bks.

***Assamese Women in the Freedom Struggle.** Dipti Sharma. (C). 1993. 42.00 (81-85094-61-6, Pub. by Punthi Pus II) S Asia.

Assamoir: A Working Woman's Life. Lilian R. Furst. (Twayne's Masterworks Ser.). 144p. (C). 1990. text ed. 21.95 (0-8057-9444-1, Twayne); pap. 12.95 (0-8057-8132-3, Twayne) Macmillan.

Assassin. Liam O'Flaherty. 286p. 1988. reprint ed. pap. 8.95 (0-86327-006-9, Pub. by Wolfhound Pr IE) Dufour.

Assassin Est Mon Maitre. Henry De Montherlant. 312p. (FRE.). 1971. pap. 27.95 (0-8288-9886-3, F115560) Fr & Eur.

Assassin in the Greenwood: A Medieval Mystery Featuring Hugh Corbett. P. C. Doherty. LC 94-3325. 224p. 1994. 19.95 (0-312-11554-7) St Martin.

Assassin Legends: Myths of the Isma'ilis. Farhad Daftary. 200p. 1994. text ed. 59.95 (1-85043-705-X, Pub. by I B Tauris UK) St Martin.

Assassin of Paris. Louis C. Calman-Levy. 1994. 29.95 (0-226-10360-9) U Ch Pr.

Assassin on Stage: Brutus, Hamlet, & the Death of Lincoln. Albert Furtwangler. (Illus.). 192p. 1991. 24.95 (0-252-01746-3) U of Ill Pr.

Assassinating Hitler: Ethics & Resistance in Nazi Germany. Robert W. Whalen. LC 92-56704. 184p. 1993. 34.50 (0-945636-45-8) Susquehanna U Pr.

Assassination. Paul Metcalf. 16p. 1979. pap. 2.00 (0-930794-13-3) Station Hill Pr.

Assassination. deluxe limited ed. Paul Metcalf. 16p. 1979. 10.00 (0-930794-78-8) Station Hill Pr.

Assassination: Case Studies. Blythe F. Finke. Ed. by Sigurd C. Rahmas. (Topics of Our Times Ser.: No. 17). 32p. (Orig.). (YA). (gr. 7-12). 1982. lib. bdg. 4.95 (0-87157-818-2) SamHar Pr.

Assassination: The Death of the President. (Civil War Ser.). (Illus.). 176p. 1987. 19.93 (0-8094-4820-3); lib. bdg. 25.93 (0-8094-4821-1) Time-Life.

Assassination: The Murder of John F. Kennedy. Donald L. Kimball. LC 88-71929. 224p. (Orig.). 1988. pap. 10.00 (0-942698-08-8) Trends & Events.

***Assassination at the State House: The Unsolved Mystery of Governor William Goebel.** Ron Elliott. LC 94-78687. (Illus.). 256p. (C). 1994. 18.95 (0-913383-33-3) McClanahan Pub.

Assassination Bureau, LTD. Jack London et al. LC 94-9213. 208p. 1994. 8.95 (0-14-018677-8, Penguin Classics) Viking Penguin.

Assassination Bureau, Ltd. Jack London. reprint ed. lib. bdg. 18.95 (0-89190-655-X, Rivercity Pr) Amereon Ltd.

Assassination Chronicles. Edward J. Epstein. 704p. 1992. pap. 14.95 (0-88184-909-X) Carroll & Graf.

Assassination in Khartoum. David A. Korn. LC 92-46071. 1993. 24.95 (0-253-33202-8) Ind U Pr.

Assassination in Switzerland: The Murder of Vatslav Vorovsky. Alfred E. Senn. LC 80-53959. (Illus.). 232p. 1981. 32.50 (0-299-08550-3) U of Wis Pr.

Assassination of a British Prime Minister. Darwyn A. Byntt. 208p. 1994. 17.95 (0-8059-3436-7) Dorrance.

Assassination of a President: John F. Kennedy. Sue Hamilton. Ed. by John Hamilton. LC 89-84903. (Days of Tragedy Ser.). (Illus.). 32p. (J). (gr. 4). 1990. lib. bdg. 11.96 (0-939179-55-5) Abdo & Dghtrs.

***Assassination of a Prime Minister As It Happened.** S. Anandaram. (C). 1995. 22.00x (81-7094-096-6, Pub. by Vision) S Asia.

Assassination of Abraham Lincoln. Sue Hamilton. Ed. by John Hamilton. LC 89-84902. (Days of Tragedy Ser.). (Illus.). 32p. (J). (gr. 4). 1990. lib. bdg. 11.96 (0-939179-54-7) Abdo & Dghtrs.

Assassination of Abraham Lincoln. Robert E. Jakoubek. LC 92-10900. (Spotlight on American History Ser.). (Illus.). 64p. (J). (gr. 4-6). 1993. lib. bdg. 15.40 (1-56294-239-5); pap. 5.95 (1-56294-749-4) Millbrook Pr.

Assassination of Abraham Lincoln: Flight, Pursuit, Capture, & Punishment of the Conspirators. Osborn H. Oldroyd. (Illus.). 332p. 1990. reprint ed. pap. 22.50 (1-55613-360-X) Heritage Bk.

Assassination of Abraham Lincoln: Opposing Viewpoints. Michael O'Neal. LC 91-13682. (Great Mysteries Ser.). (Illus.). 112p. (J). (gr. 5-8). 1991. lib. bdg. 16.95 (0-89908-092-8) Greenhaven.

Assassination of Abraham Lincoln & Its Expiation. David M. Dewitt. (Select Bibliographies Reprint Ser.). 1977. 19.95 (0-8369-5574-9) Ayer.

Assassination of Gaitan: Public Life & Urban Violence in Columbia. Herbert Braun. LC 85-40362. (Illus.). 296p. 1986. text ed. 35.00x (0-299-10360-9) U of Wis Pr.

Assassination of General George Armstrong Custer: The True Story Behind the Battle of the Little Big Horn. Virgil Armstrong. Ed. by Patricia Whitman. 300p. (YA). (gr. 9-12). 1990. pap. write for info. (0-925390-22-4) Armstrong Assocs.

Assassination of Jesse James by the Coward Robert Ford. Ron Hansen. 1990. pap. 8.95 (0-393-30679-8) Norton.

Assassination of John F. Kennedy. R. Conrad Stein. LC 91-44546. (Cornerstones of Freedom Ser.). (Illus.). 32p. (J). (gr. 3-6). 1992. lib. bdg. 12.30 (0-516-06652-8) Childrens.

Assassination of John F. Kennedy. R. Conrad Stein. LC 91-44546. (Cornerstones of Freedom Ser.). (Illus.). 32p. (J). (gr. 3-6). 1993. pap. 3.95 (0-516-46652-6) Childrens.

Assassination of John F. Kennedy: A Complete Book of Facts. James P. Duffy & Vincent L. Ricci. 560p. 1992. pap. 14.95 (1-56025-042-9) Thunders Mouth.

Assassination of John F. Kennedy: A Comprehensive Historical & Legal Bibliography, 1963-1979. Comp. by DeLloyd J. Guth & David R. Wrone. LC 79-6184. (Illus.). lvi, 442p. 1980. text ed. 79.50 (0-313-21274-0, GJK/, Greenwood Pr) Greenwood.

Assassination of John F. Kennedy: An Annotated Film, TV, & Videography, 1963-1992. Comp. by Anthony Frewin. LC 93-24763. (Bibliographies & Indexes in Mass Media & Communications Ser.: No. 8). 192p. 1993. text ed. 49.95 (0-313-28982-4, GR8982, Greenwood Pr) Greenwood.

Assassination of Julius Caesar. Geroge Ochoa. (Turning Points in World History Ser.). (Illus.). 64p. (YA). (gr. 7 up). 1991. lib. bdg. 14.95 (0-382-24130-4); pap. 7.95 (0-382-24136-3) Silver Burdett Pr.

Assassination of Light: Modern Saudi Fiction. Ed. by Abu Bakr Ahmed Bagader. Tr. by Ava M. Heinrichsdorf & Abu Bakr Ahmed Bagader. LC 89-20596. 87p. (Orig.). (ARA.). 1990. 24.00 (0-89410-598-1); pap. 11.00 (0-89410-599-X) Three Continents.

Assassination of Lincoln: A History of the Great Conspiracy: Trial of the Conspirators by a Military Commission. T. M. Harris. (Sadie Rose Adventure Ser.). (Illus.). 420p. 1989. reprint ed. pap. 25.00 (1-55613-230-1) Heritage Bk.

Assassination of Lincoln: History & Myth. Lloyd Lewis. xviii, 367p. 1994. pap. 12.95 (0-8032-7949-3, Bison Books) U of Nebr Pr.

Assassination of Mahatma Gandhi. K. L. Gauba. 1969. pap. 3.50 (0-88253-140-9) Ind-US Inc.

Assassination of Malcolm X. 3rd ed. George Breitman et al. LC 76-47347. (Illus.). 196p. (C). 1992. reprint ed. pap. 14.95 (0-87348-632-3) Pathfinder NY.

Assassination of New York. Bob Fitch. 300p. 1993. 29.95 (0-86091-390-2, A9703, Pub. by Verso UK) Routledge Chapman & Hall.

Assassination of President John F. Kennedy. Patricia D. Netzley. LC 93-20818. (American Events Ser.). (Illus.). 96p. (J). (gr. 6 up). 1994. text ed. 14.95 (0-02-768127-0, New Dscvry Bks) Silver Burdett Pr.

Assassination of President Kennedy: Opposing Viewpoints. Jeffrey Waggoner. LC 89-37442. (Great Mysteries Ser.). (Illus.). 112p. (J). (gr. 5-8). 1989. lib. bdg. 16.95 (0-89908-068-5) Greenhaven.

Assassination of Rajiv Gandhi. Shashi Ahulwalia. (C). 1991. text ed. 22.00 (81-7099-315-6, Pub. by Mittal II) S Asia.

Assassination of Robert F. Kennedy: The Conspiracy & Coverup. William Turner & John G. Christian. 432p. 1993. pap. 13.95 (1-56025-058-5) Thunders Mouth.

Assassination of Robert Kennedy. Gerald Kurland. Ed. by D. Steve Rahmas. LC 72-89219. (Events of Our Times Ser.: No. 2). 32p. (Orig.). (gr. 7-12). 1973. lib. bdg. 4.95 (0-87157-702-X) SamHar Pr.

Assassination of the Black Male Image. Earl O. Hutchinson. LC 93-80991. 184p. (Orig.). 1994. pap. 9.95 (1-881032-11-6) Middle Passage.

Assassination Rhapsody. Derek Pell. (Illus.). 124p. 1989. pap. 6.00 (0-936756-54-3) Autonomedia.

Assassination Trilogy, 3 vols., Set. Philip Melanson & Carl Oglesby. 300p. 1993. pap. 15.00 (1-878825-09-7) Odonian Pr.

Assassinations & Executions: An Encyclopedia of Political Violence, 1865-1986. Harris M. Lentz, III. LC 87-46383. 296p. 1988. lib. bdg. 38.50x (0-89950-312-8) McFarland & Co.

Assassinations of John & Robert Kennedy. Leroy Hayman. (J). (gr. 4-7). 1993. pap. 2.95 (0-590-46539-2) Scholastic Inc.

Assassinations That Shook America. Edmund Lindop. LC 92-15082. (Illus.). 144p. (YA). (gr. 9-12). 1992. lib. bdg. 14.98 (0-531-11049-4) Watts.

Assassini. Thomas Gifford. 688p. 1991. mass mkt. 6.50 (0-553-28740-0) Bantam.

Assassins. 1994. pap. 18.95 (1-57007-004-0, XW1632) Astor Bks.

Assassins. Stephen Sondheim & John Weidman. LC 91-14809. 120p. 1991. 22.50 (1-55936-039-9); pap. 9.95 (1-55936-038-0) Theatre Comm.

Assassins. Time-Life Books Editors. Ed. by Janet Cave. (True Crime Ser.). 1994. 14.99 (0-7835-0033-5); lib. bdg. 17.45 (0-7835-0034-3) Time-Life.

Assassins. large type ed. F. M. Parker. (General Ser.). 350p. 1990. 18.95 (0-8161-4999-2, Large Print Bks) Hall.

Assassins: A Radical Sect in Islam. Bernard Lewis. 1987. pap. 9.95 (0-19-520550-2) OUP.

Assassins: A Study of the Cult of the Assassins in Persia & Islam. F. A. Ridley. (Islam Ser.). 1980. lib. bdg. 59.95 (0-8490-3077-3) Gordon Pr.

***Assassin's Apprentice.** Robin Hobb. LC 94-28942. (Farseer). 1995. pap. 12.95 (0-553-37445-1) Bantam.

Assassins at Large: Being a Fully Documented & Hitherto Unpublished Account of the Executions Outside Russia Ordered by the GPU. Hugo Dewar. LC 79-2898. 203p. 1980. reprint ed. 20.00 (0-8305-0069-3) Hyperion Conn.

Assassin's Express. Axel Kilgore. (They Call Me the Mercenary Ser.: No. 8). (Orig.). 1982. pap. 2.50 (0-89083-955-7) Zebra.

Assassins of Dol Amroth. Charlie Crutchfield. Ed. by Peter C. Fenlon, Jr. (Middle-Earth Ready-to-Run Adventure Supplement Ser.). (Orig.). (YA). (gr. 10-12). 1987. pap. 6.00 (0-915795-98-1, 8106) Iron Crown Ent Inc.

Assassins of Memory: Essays on the Denial of the Holocaust. Pierre Vidal-Naquet. Tr. by Jeffrey Mehlman. (European Perspectives Ser.). (Illus.). 224p. (FRE.). (C). 1993. text ed. 27.50 (0-231-07458-1) Col U Pr.

Assassins of Memory: Essays on the Denial of the Holocaust. Pierre Vidal-Naquet. 1994. pap. 15.95 (0-231-07459-X) Col U Pr.

Assassin's Play-Off. Warren Murphy. (Destroyer Ser.: No. 20). 1989. pap. 3.50 (1-55817-211-4, Pinnacle NY) Windsor NY.

Assata: An Autobiography. Assata Shakur. LC 87-23772. 290p. 1988. 18.95 (0-88208-221-3); pap. 9.95 (1-55652-074-3) L Hill Bks.

Assateague. 2nd ed. William H. Wroten, Jr. LC 72-79769. (Illus.). 64p. 1972. pap. 3.95 (0-87033-168-X, Tidewtr Pubs) Cornell Maritime.

Assateague: Island of the Wild Ponies. Andrea Jauck & Larry Points. LC 92-5908. (Illus.). 32p. (J). (gr. 1-5). 1993. text ed. 14.95 (0-02-774695-X, Mac Bks Young Read) S&S Childrens.

Assateague Island, National Seashore: Maryland & Virginia. William H. Amos. LC 79-607136. (National Park Service Handbook Ser.: No. 106). (Illus.). 175p. pap. 6.00 (0-16-003440-X, S/N 024-005-00776-8) USGPO.

Assateague Ponies. Ronald R. Keiper. LC 84-26682. (Illus.). 102p. 1985. 6.00 (0-87033-330-5, Tidewtr Pubs) Cornell Maritime.

Assault. Reinaldo Arenas. Tr. by Andrew Hurley. LC 93-32554. 144p. 1994. 20.95 (0-670-84066-1, Viking) Viking Penguin.

***Assault.** Reinaldo Arenas. Tr. by Andrew Hurley. 160p. 1995. pap. 10.95 (0-14-015718-2, Penguin Bks) Viking Penguin.

Assault. Harry Mulisch. Tr. by Claire White. LC 84-22623. 162p. 1986. pap. 13.00 (0-394-74420-9) Pantheon.

***Assault: Liberalism's Attack on Religion, Freedom, & Democracy.** Dale A. Berryhill. LC 94-79223. 208p. 1995. pap. 10.99 (1-56384-077-4) Huntington Hse.

***Assault & Logistics: Union Army Coastal & River Operations, 1861-1866.** Charles D. Gibson & E. Kay Gibson. LC 95-60239. (Army's Navy Ser.: Vol. 2). (Illus.). 680p. (C). 1995. 45.00 (0-9608996-3-4) Ensign Pr.

***Assault & Logistics: Union Army Coastal & River Operations, 1861-1866.** (Army's Navy Ser.). 1995. write for info. (0-614-06779-0) Ensign Pr.

Assault & Rape on Virginia's Campuses. 60p. (Orig.). (C). 1992. pap. text ed. 19.95 (1-56806-065-3) Diane Pub.

Assault from the Sea: Essays on the History of Amphibious Warfare. Merrill L. Bartlett. LC 83-2178. (Illus.). 453p. 1983. 34.95 (0-87021-088-2); pap. 17.95 (0-87021-076-9) Naval Inst Pr.

***Assault from the Sea: The Amphibious Landing at Inchon.** Curtis A. Utz. LC 94-34662. (U. S. Navy in the Modern World Ser.: Vol. 2). 1994. pap. write for info. (0-945274-27-0) Naval Hist Ctr.

Assault from the Sky. John Weeks. (Battle Standards Ser.). (Illus.). 236p. (C). 1989. reprint ed. lib. bdg. 25.00x (0-8095-7545-0) Borgo Pr.

Assault of Indian Tribalism: The General Allotment Law (Dawes Act) of 1887. Wilcomb E. Washburn. LC 85-12622. 88p. (C). 1985. reprint ed. pap. text ed. 8.50 (0-89874-877-1) Krieger.

Assault on a Queen. Jack Finney. 1994. reprint ed. lib. bdg. 29.95 (1-56849-375-4) Buccaneer Bks.

Assault on America's Children: Safeguarding Your Child from Becoming a Victim of Child Abuse. Donn Ferguson. LC 93-80373. 64p. (Orig.). 1994. pap. 5.95 (1-879560-30-5) Harbor Hse West.

Assault on Assimilation: John Collier & the Origins of Indian Policy Reform. Lawrence C. Kelly. LC 83-1288. 475p. reprint ed. pap. 135.40 (0-8357-8699-4, AU00373) Bks Demand.

Assault on Authority: Dialogue or Dilemma? William W. Meissner. LC 70-152878. 320p. reprint ed. pap. 91.20 (0-8357-8807-5, 2033465) Bks Demand.

Assault on Baghdad. Leo Kessler. 256p. 1992. 20.00 (0-7278-4278-1) Severn Hse.

Assault on Bordeaux. B. J. Hurwood. 176p. 1982. pap. 1.95 (0-8439-1075-5) Dorchester Pub Co.

Assault on Culture: Utopian Currents from Letrisme to Class War. Stuart Home. (Illus.). 128p. 1993. reprint ed. pap. 12.95 (1-873176-30-9, AK Pr San Fran) AK Pr Dist.

Assault on Culture: Utopian Currents from Lettrisme to Class War. Stewart Home. 115p. (Orig.). (C). 1991. pap. 13.00 (0-948518-88-X) Left Bank.

***Assault on Eden.** Virginia S. Owens. LC 95-3452. 176p. 1995. reprint ed. pap. 15.99 (0-8010-5241-6) Baker Bk.

Assault on Fellawi. A. Caillou. 1976. pap. 1.50 (0-380-00718-5) Avon.

Assault on French Literature & Other Essays. Percy M. Jones. LC 75-26214. 197p. 1976. reprint ed. text ed. 49.75 (0-8371-8401-0, JOAFL, Greenwood Pr) Greenwood.

Assault on Lake Casitas. Brad A. Lewis. Ed. by Ed Moran. LC 90-84461. (Illus.). 200p. (Orig.). 1990. pap. 11.95 (1-879174-00-6) Broad St Bks.

***Assault on Medical Freedom.** P. Joseph Lisa. 336p. (Orig.). 1994. pap. 14.95 (1-57174-003-1) Hampton Roads Pub Co.

Assault on Nicaragua: The Untold Story of the U. S. 'Secret War' Daniel Ortega & Daniel Sheehan. Ed. by Rod Holt. 115p. (Orig.). 1987. pap. write for info. (0-929405-00-5) Walnut Pub.

Assault on Normandy: First-Person Accounts from the Sea Services. Ed. by Paul Stillwell. LC 93-49791. (Illus.). 320p. 1994. 39.95 (1-55750-781-3) Naval Inst Pr.

Assault on Paradise: Social Change in a Brazilian Village. 2nd ed. Conrad Kottak. 1992. pap. text ed. write for info. (0-07-035766-8) McGraw.

Assault on Peleliu. Frank Hough. (Elite Unit Ser.: No. 25). (Illus.). 208p. 1990. reprint ed. 32.50 (0-89839-145-8) Battery Pr.

Assault on Raven's Ruin. TSR Staff. (Dungeons & Dragons Ser.). (Illus.). 1992. pap. 6.95 (1-56076-379-5) TSR Inc.

Assault on Religion. Russell Kirk. LC 86-656. 126p. (C). 1986. lib. bdg. 34.00 (0-8191-5294-3, Ctr for Judical Studies); pap. text ed. 15.00 (0-8191-5295-1, Ctr for Judical Studies) U Pr of Amer.

Assault on Society: Satirical Literature to Film. Donald W. McCaffrey. LC 92-4040. (Illus.). 293p. 1992. 35.00 (0-8108-2507-4) Scarecrow.

Assault on Society: Satirical Literature to Film. Donald W. McCaffrey. LC 92-4040. (Illus.). 293p. 1992. reprint ed. pap. 19.50 (0-8108-2594-5) Scarecrow.

Assault on the Crown. Danard Emanuelson. LC 89-81787. (Illus.). 358p. (Orig.). 1989. pap. 6.95 (0-9624917-0-5) Epsilon Bks.

Assault on the Liberty: The True Story of the Israeli Attack on an American Intelligence Ship. James M. Ennes, Jr. LC 79-4793. 1979. 14.95 (0-394-50512-3) Random.

Assault on the Media: The Nixon Years. William E. Porter. LC 75-14898. 330p. reprint ed. pap. 94.10 (0-7837-4720-9, 2059072) Bks Demand.

Assault on World Poverty: Problems of Rural Development, Education, & Health. International Bank for Reconstruction & Development Staff. LC 75-7912. 439p. reprint ed. pap. 125.20 (0-7837-4258-4, 2043948) Bks Demand.

Assault Pistols, Rifles & Submachine Guns. Duncan Long. 1987. pap. 12.95 (0-8065-1042-0, Citadel Pr) Carol Pub Group.

Assault Pistols, Rifles & Submachine Guns. Duncan Long. (Illus.). 152p. 1986. pap. 21.95 (0-87364-353-4) Paladin Pr.

Assault Upon Charles Sumner see Plays for a New Theatre: Playbook 2

An Asterisk (*) at the beginning of an entry indicates that the title is appearing in BIP for the first time.

An Asterisk (*) at the beginning of an entry indicates that the title is appearing in BIP for the first time.

483

Assertive Discipline Middle School Workbook. Lee Canter. (Illus.). 128p. 1992. student ed 8.95 (*0-939007-49-5*) Lee Canter & Assocs.

Assertive Discipline Parent Resource Guide. Lee Canter & Marlene Canter. (Illus.). 110p. 1985. student ed, pap. 8.95 (*0-9608978-7-9*, 1010) Lee Canter & Assocs.

Assertive Discipline Seasonal Motivators. Lee Canter. (Illus.). 96p. (Orig.). 1992. pap. 7.95 (*0-939007-47-9*) Lee Canter & Assocs.

Assertive Discipline Secondary Workbook. Lee Canter. (Illus.). 128p. 1992. student ed 8.95 (*0-939007-50-9*) Lee Canter & Assocs.

Assertive Formula. A. D. Russo. (Human Resources Book Ser.). 95p. 1982. pap. 4.00 (*0-9610708-0-3*) Twenty Fst CT.

Assertive Option: Your Rights & Responsibilities. Patricia Jakubowski & Arthur J. Lange. LC 78-62904. (Illus.). 348p. (Orig.). (C). 1978. pap. text ed. 19.95 (*0-87822-192-1*, 1921) Res Press.

Assertive Supervision: Building Involved Teamwork. Susanne S. Drury. LC 84-61001. 324p. (Orig.). (C). 1984. pap. text ed. 19.95 (*0-87822-233-2*, 2332) Res Press.

Assertive Teacher. Gwynne Wilson-Brown. 128p. 1994. 51.95 (*1-85742-217-1*, Pub. by Arena UK); pap. 20.95 (*1-85742-218-X*, Pub. by Arena UK) Ashgate Pub Co.

***Assertive Trainer: A Practical Handbook on Assertiveness for Trainers & Running Assertiveness Courses.** Liz Willis & Jenny Daisley. LC 94-36467. (McGraw-Hill Training Ser.). 1995. text ed. 24.95 (*0-07-709077-2*) McGraw.

Assertive Woman: A New Look. 2nd rev. ed. Stanlee Phelps & Nancy Austin. LC 87-16794. 256p. 1987. pap. 9.95 (*0-915166-61-5*) Impact Pubs CA.

Assertiveness. Henry Virkler. 308p. (Orig.). 1989. pap. 11.95 (*0-310-39471-6*, 11421P) Zondervan.

Assertiveness: A Positive Process. Barrie Hopson & Mike Scally. Ed. by JoAnn Padgett. LC 92-50989. 90p. 1993. pap. 7.95 (*0-89384-214-1*) Pfeiffer & Co.

Assertiveness for Managers. Terry Gillen. 257p. 1992. 53.95 (*0-566-02861-1*, Pub. by Gower UK) Ashgate Pub Co.

Assertiveness for Managers: Learning Effective Skills for Managing People. 3rd rev. ed. Diana Cawood. (Business Ser.). 168p. 1992. pap. 12.95 (*0-88908-996-5*, 9568) Self-Counsel Pr.

Assertiveness Is. A. D. Russo. (Illus.). 108p. (Orig.). 1985. pap. 4.00 (*0-9610708-1-1*) Twenty Fst CT.

Assertiveness Skills. Nelda Shelton & Sharon Burton. LC 93-18310. (Business Skills Express Ser.). 96p. 1993. pap. 10.00 (*1-55623-857-6*) Irwin Prof Pubng.

Assertiveness Training: And How to Instantly Read People. Dick Sutphen. 96p. pap. 3.95 (*0-87554-247-6*) Valley Sun.

Assesment of Crop Loss from Air Pollutants. Ed. by W. W. Heck et al. 558p. 1989. 144.00 (*1-85166-244-8*) Elsevier.

Assess Your Own Nutrient Status. Jeffrey Bland. (Self-Care Health Library). 32p. 1987. pap. 2.25 (*0-87983-395-5*) Keats.

***Assess Your Own Teaching Quality.** Sally Brown & Phil Race. (Teaching & Learning in Higher Education Ser.). 160p. 1995. pap. 29.95x (*0-7494-1370-0*, Pub. by Kogan Page Educ UK) Taylor & Francis.

Assess Your Strengths & Weaknesses: A Workbook for Evaluating Your Association. American Society of Association Executives Staff. 78p. (Orig.). 1988. pap. 50.00 (*0-88034-011-8*) Am Soc Assn Execs.

Assess Your True Potential. Created by DK Direct, Ltd. Staff. LC 92-37435. (Mindpower Ser.). (Illus.). 144p. 1993. 14.99 (*0-7835-1250-3*) Time-Life.

Assessing Academic Climates & Cultures. Ed. by William G. Tierney. LC 85-645339. (New Directions for Institutional Research Ser.: No. IR 68). 1990. 16.95 (*1-55542-810-X*) Jossey-Bass.

Assessing Achievement in the Arts. Malcolm Ross et al. LC 92-31892. (C). 1993. 90.00 (*0-335-19062-6*, Open Univ Pr); pap. 32.50 (*0-335-19061-8*, Open Univ Pr) Taylor & Francis.

Assessing Adolescent & Adult Intelligence. Alan S. Kaufman. 600p. 1990. teacher ed write for info. (*0-205-12391-0*, H23914); text ed. 65.27 (*0-205-12390-2*, H23906) Allyn.

Assessing Adolescents. Oster. (C). 1988. pap. 19.95 (*0-205-14444-6*, H4444) Allyn.

***Assessing Adult Learning: A Guide for Practitioners.** Joseph J. Moran. 1996. write for info. (*0-89464-938-8*) Krieger.

Assessing AIDS Prevention: Selected Papers Presented at the International Conference Held in Montreux (Switzerland), October 29-November 1, 1990. Ed. by F. Paccaud et al. x, 305p. 1992. 147.50 (*0-8176-2722-7*) Birkhauser.

Assessing & Controlling Bacterial Regrowth in Distribution Systems. 264p. 1990. pap. 25.00 (*0-89867-490-5*, 90567) Am Water Wks Assn.

Assessing & Correcting Classroom Reading Problems. J. Estill Alexander & Betty S. Heathington. (C). 1988. text ed. 52.00 (*0-673-39704-1*) HarpCollege.

Assessing & Guiding Young Children's Development & Learning. Oralie McAfee & Deborah Leong. LC 93-19943. 1993. pap. text ed. write for info. (*0-205-14018-1*) Allyn.

Assessing & Improving Student Achievement: Guidebook. National School Services Staff. (C). 1994. 25.00 (*0-932957-97-8*) Natl School.

Assessing & Improving Student Achievement: Training Manual. National School Services Staff. (C). 1994. 95.00 (*0-932957-85-4*) Natl School.

Assessing & Managing Behavior Disabilities. Ed. by Norris G. Haring. LC 87-16008. 344p. 1987. 50.00 (*0-295-96563-0*); pap. 25.00 (*0-295-96545-2*) U of Wash Pr.

Assessing & Programming Gross Motor Development for Children. 2nd ed. E. Michael Loovis & Walter F. Ersing. 1979. pap. text ed. 10.95 (*0-89917-495-7*) Tichenor Pub.

Assessing & Screening Preschoolers: Psychological & Educational Dimensions. Ena V. Nuttall et al. 512p. (C). 1992. text ed. 51.95 (*0-205-13280-4*, Longwood Div) Allyn.

Assessing & Treating Culturally Diverse Clients: A Practical Guide. Freddy A. Paniagua. LC 94-17662. (Multicultural Aspects of Counseling Ser.: Vol. 4). 136p. 1994. 36.00 (*0-8039-5495-6*); pap. 16.95 (*0-8039-5496-4*) Sage.

***Assessing Asian Language Performance: Guidelines for Evaluating Limited-English Proficient Students.** Li-Rong L. Cheng. 222p. 1991. pap. text ed. 29.95 (*0-614-04586-X*) Acad Comm.

***Assessing Ballistic Missile Proliferation & Its Control.** Ed. by John Harvey. 144p. (Orig.). 1991. pap. 14.00 (*0-935371-25-7*) CFISAC.

Assessing Bank Reform: FDICIA One Year Later. Ed. by George G. Kaufman & Robert E. Litan. LC 93-11151. 168p. (C). 1993. 29.95 (*0-8157-4874-4*); pap. 11.95 (*0-8157-4873-6*) Brookings.

Assessing Basic Academic Skills in Higher Education: The Texas Approach. Ed. by Richard Alpert et al. 288p. (C). 1988. text ed. 69.95 (*0-8058-0336-X*) L Erlbaum Assocs.

***Assessing Calculus Reform Efforts: A Report to the Community.** James Leitzel & Alan Tucker. LC 94-72962. 100p. (C). 1994. pap. text ed. 15.00 (*0-88385-093-1*, NTE37CAT) Math Assn.

Assessing Changing Food Consumption Patterns. National Research Council Assembly of Life Sciences-Food & Nutrition Board. 296p. (C). 1981. pap. text ed. 24.95 (*0-309-03135-4*) Natl Acad Pr.

Assessing Chemical Mutagens: The Risk to Humans. Ed. by Victor K. McElheny & Seymour Abrahamson. LC 79-998. (Banbury Report Ser.: No. 1). (Illus.). 367p. 1979. 44.00 (*0-87969-200-6*) Cold Spring Harbor.

Assessing Child & Adolescent Disorders: A Practice Manual. 2nd ed. Masud Hoghughi. (Illus.). 320p. (C). 1992. text ed. 65.00 (*0-8039-8296-8*); pap. text ed. 25.00 (*0-8039-8297-6*) Sage.

Assessing Child Maltreatment Reports: The Problem of False Allegations. Ed. by Michael Robin. LC 91-20799. (Child & Youth Services Ser.). (Illus.). 297p. 1991. lib. bdg. 39.95 (*0-86656-931-6*); pap. text ed. 19.95 (*1-56024-161-6*) Haworth Pr.

Assessing Children's Language in Naturalistic Contexts. 3rd ed. Nancy J. Lund & Judith F. Duchan. 384p. 1992. text ed. write for info. (*0-13-051905-7*) P-H.

Assessing Children's Learning. Mary J. Drummond. (Primary Curriculum Ser.). 160p. 1993. pap. 26.00 (*1-85346-198-9*, Pub. by D Fulton UK) Taylor & Francis.

Assessing Chronic Pain. Ed. by P. M. Camic & F. D. Brown. (Contributions to Psychology & Medicine Ser.). (Illus.). 250p. 1989. 65.00 (*0-387-96942-X*) Spr-Verlag.

Assessing Clinical Competence. Ed. by Victor R. Neufeld & Geoffrey R. Norman. LC 84-10555. (Medical Education Ser.: Vol. 7). 384p. 1984. 39.95 (*0-8261-3330-4*) Springer Pub.

Assessing Communication Education: A Handbook for Media, Speech, & Theatre Educators. Ed. by William G. Christ. (Communication Ser.). 400p. 1994. text ed. 69.95 (*0-8058-1622-4*); pap. 27.50 (*0-8058-1623-2*) L Erlbaum Assocs.

Assessing Community Health Needs & Coverage Module 2: Facilitator's Guide. Martine Hilton. (Primary Health Care Management Advancement Programme (PHC MAP) Modules Ser.). 59p. 1993. pap. text ed. write for info. (*1-882839-09-9*) Aga Khan Fnd.

Assessing Community Health Needs & Coverage Module 2: User's Guide. Jack Reynolds. (Primary Health Care Management Advancement Programme (PHC MAP) Modules Ser.). 227p. 1993. pap. text ed. write for info. (*1-882839-01-3*) Aga Khan Fnd.

***Assessing Competence in Higher Education.** Ed. by Anne Edwards & Peter Knight. (Staff & Education Development Ser.). 192p. 1995. pap. 34.00x (*0-7494-1458-8*, Pub. by Kogan Page Educ UK) Taylor & Francis.

Assessing Completeness & Accuracy of Criminal History Record Systems: Audit Guide. (Illus.). 50p. (Orig.). (C). 1993. pap. text ed. 30.00 (*1-56806-776-3*) Diane Pub.

Assessing Controlled Access Protection. (Illus.). 81p. (Orig.). (C). 1994. pap. text ed. 45.00 (*0-7881-0827-1*) Diane Pub.

Assessing Corporate Talent: A Key to Managerial Manpower Planning. Robert B. Finkle & William S. Jones. LC 71-120702. 260p. reprint ed. pap. 74.10 (*0-8357-9841-0*, 2012353) Bks Demand.

Assessing Cultural Anthropology. Ed. by Robert Borofsky. LC 93-5323. 1993. pap. text ed. write for info. (*0-07-006578-0*) McGraw.

Assessing Dangerousness: Violence by Sexual Offenders, Batterers & Child Abusers. Ed. by Jacquelyn C. Campbell. (Interpersonal Violence, the Practice Ser.: Vol. 8). 160p. 1994. 42.95 (*0-8039-3746-6*) Sage.

***Assessing Development - Global Education Programs: A Planning Model.** Roland Case & Walter Werner. 40p. (C). 1990. 5.00 (*0-614-03000-5*) Amer Forum.

Assessing Development Effectiveness: Evaluation in the World Bank & the International Finance Corporation. LC 94-15316. 1994. write for info. (*0-8213-2833-6*) World Bank.

Assessing Development Finance Institutions: A Public Interest Analysis. Jacob Yaron. LC 92-27380. (Discussion Paper Ser.: Vol. 174). 45p. 1992. 6.95 (*0-8213-2203-6*, 12203) World Bank.

Assessing Early Childhood Education. 99p. 1989. 9.75 (*0-685-30500-7*) Northwest Regional.

Assessing Ecological Risks of Biotechnology. Lev R. Ginzburg. (Illus.). 379p. 1990. text ed. 36.00 (*0-409-90199-7*) Buttrwrth-Heinemann.

Assessing Educational Achievement. Ed. by Desmond L. Nuttall. LC 85-20679. (Contemporary Analysis in Education Ser.: Vol. 10). 190p. 1986. pap. 30.00 (*1-85000-056-5*, Falmer Pr) Taylor & Francis.

Assessing Educational Outcomes. Ed. by Peter T. Ewell. LC 85-60832. (New Directions for Institutional Research Ser.: No. IR 47). (Orig.). 1985. pap. 16.95x (*0-87589-753-3*) Jossey-Bass.

Assessing Educational Outcomes: Third National Conference on Measurement & Evaluation in Nursing. Ed. by Margery Garbin. 144p. (Orig.). (C). 1991. pap. text ed. 29.95 (*0-88737-541-3*) Natl League Nurse.

***Assessing Educational Practices: The Contribution of Economics.** Ed. by William E. Becker & William J. Baumol. (Illus.). 285p. (C). 1995. 35.00x (*0-262-02398-9*) MIT Pr.

Assessing Elderly People for Residential Care: A Practical Guide. June Neill. (C). 1989. 59.00 (*0-685-28581-2*, Pub. by Natl Inst Soc Work); 30.00 (*0-685-40335-1*, Pub. by Natl Inst Soc Work); 35.00 (*0-902789-59-7*, Pub. by Natl Inst Soc Work); 40.00 (*0-7855-0087-1*, Pub. by Natl Inst Soc Work) St Mut.

Assessing Engineering Education in Sub-Saharan Africa. Ed. by Manuel Zymelman. LC 92-45128. (Technical Paper Ser.: No. 197). 183p. 1993. 10.95 (*0-8213-2371-7*, 12371) World Bank.

Assessing English. Brian Johnston. (English, Language & Education Ser.). 176p. 1987. pap. 27.00 (*0-335-15999-0*, Open Univ Pr) Taylor & Francis.

Assessing Evaluation Studies: The Case of Bilingual Education Strategies. National Research Council Staff. 138p. (C). 1992. pap. text ed. 22.00 (*0-309-04728-5*) Natl Acad Pr.

Assessing Excellence: A Guide for Studying the Middle Level School. Ed. by C. Bruce. (Orig.). 1988. pap. 7.00 (*0-88210-218-4*) Natl Assn Principals.

Assessing Experience in Psychotherapy: Personal Construct Alternatives. A. J. Faidley & L. M. Leitner. LC 92-48993. 232p. 1993. text ed. 55.00 (*0-275-94260-0*, C4260, Praeger Pubs) Greenwood.

Assessing Faculty Work: Enhancing Individual & Institutional Performance. Larry A. Braskamp & John C. Ory. LC 93-42904. (Higher & Adult Education Ser.). 355p. 1994. 32.95 (*1-55542-635-2*) Jossey-Bass.

Assessing Fault Model & Test Quality. Kenneth M. Butler & M. Ray Mercer. 160p. (C). 1991. lib. bdg. 65.50 (*0-7923-9222-1*) Kluwer Ac.

Assessing Fitness: Your Guide to a Healthy Lifestyle. Richard V. Schroeder. 176p. 1990. per., pap. text ed. 18.95 (*0-8403-5771-0*) Kendall-Hunt.

Assessing for Nursing Diagnoses: A Human Needs Approach. Evelyn M. Lyke. (Illus.). 222p. 1991. pap. 15.50 (*0-397-54819-2*) Lippincott.

Assessing for Special Educational Needs. Ed. by Sheila Wolfendale. (Special Needs in Ordinary Schools Ser.). (Illus.). 192p. 1993. pap. text ed. 30.00 (*0-304-32652-6*) Cassell.

Assessing for Special Educational Needs. Ed. by Sheila Wolfendale. (Special Needs in Ordinary Schools Ser.). (Illus.). 192p. 1993. 75.00 (*0-304-32654-2*) Weidner & Sons.

***Assessing Forest Ecosystem Health in the Inland West.** Ed. by R. Neil Sampson & David L. Adams. LC 94-32728. (Journal of Sustainable Forestry Ser.). (Illus.). 459p. 1994. lib. bdg. 69.95 (*1-56022-052-X*) Haworth Jrnl Co-Edits.

Assessing Genetic Risks: Implications for Health & Social Policy. Institute of Medicine, Committee on Assessing Genetic Risks Staff. 352p. (C). 1994. pap. text ed. 44.95 (*0-309-04798-6*) Natl Acad Pr.

Assessing Governmental Performance: An Analytical Framework. Eugene J. Meehan. LC 92-25740. (Contributions in Political Science Ser.: No. 310). 216p. 1992. text ed. 49.95 (*0-313-28720-1*, GM8720, Greenwood Pr) Greenwood.

Assessing Health & Human Services Needs: Concepts, Methods & Applications. Ed. by Roger Bell et al. LC 81-20249. (Community Psychology Ser.: Vol. VIII). (Illus.). 352p. 1983. 45.95 (*0-89885-057-6*) Human Sci Pr.

Assessing Health Care: A Study in Organizational Evaluation. Gilbert Smith & Caroline Cantly. LC 84-27215. 195p. 1985. 99.00 (*0-335-15072-1*, Open Univ Pr) Taylor & Francis.

Assessing Health Care Reform. Institute of Medicine, Committee on Assessing Health Care Reform Proposals Staff. 88p. (C). 1993. pap. text ed. 21.00 (*0-309-04926-1*) Natl Acad Pr.

Assessing Health Need Using the Life Cycle Framework. Chrissie Pickin & Selwyn St. Leger. LC 92-18760. 192p. 1992. 85.00 (*0-335-15743-2*, Open Univ Pr); pap. 27.50 (*0-335-15742-4*, Open Univ Pr) Taylor & Francis.

Assessing Higher Order Thinking in Mathematics. Ed. by Gerald Kulm. LC 90-572. 220p. (C). 1990. 24.95 (*0-87168-356-3*, 89-27S) AAAS.

***Assessing Higher Order Thinking in Mathematics.** Ed. by Gerald Kulm. 208p. 1994. per., pap. 19.95 (*0-8058-1876-6*) L Erlbaum Assocs.

Assessing Higher Order Thinking Skills. 92p. 1987. 9.75 (*0-317-66076-4*) Northwest Regional.

Assessing Housing Needs & Policy Alternatives in Developing Countries. Raymond J. Struyk. LC 88-17414. (Urban Institute Report Ser.: No. 88-4). 108p. (Orig.). (C). 1988. pap. text ed. 15.50 (*0-87766-423-4*) Urban Inst.

***Assessing Individual Differences in Human Behavior: New Concepts, Methods, & Findings.** Ed. by David Lubinski & Rene Dawis. LC 95-11398. 400p. (C). 1995. text ed. 49.95 (*0-89106-072-3*) Davies-Black.

Assessing Individual Needs: A Practical Approach. Harry Ayers et al. 64p. 1993. pap. 19.00 (*1-85346-285-3*, Pub. by D Fulton UK) Taylor & Francis.

Assessing Infants & Preschoolers with Handicaps. Donald B. Bailey, Jr. & Mark Wolery-Allegheny. 512p. (C). 1989. text ed. write for info. (*0-675-21008-9*, Merrill Pub Co) Macmillan.

Assessing Information Needs Module 1: Facilitator's Guide. Mary Millar. (Primary Health Care Management Advancement Programme (PHC MAP) Modules Ser.). 55p. 1993. pap. text ed. write for info. (*1-882839-08-0*) Aga Khan Fnd.

Assessing Information Needs Module 1: User's Guide. Jack Reynolds. (Primary Health Care Management Advancement Programme (PHC MAP) Modules Ser.). 54p. 1993. pap. text ed. write for info. (*1-882839-00-5*) Aga Khan Fnd.

Assessing Institutional Effectiveness: Issues, Methods, & Management. Frwd. by Cameron Fincher. 106p. (Orig.). (C). 1989. pap. 6.00 (*1-880647-01-X*) U GA Inst High Educ.

Assessing Institutional Effectiveness: Redirecting the Self-Study Process. Peter T. Ewell & Robert P. Lisensky. 110p. (Orig.). 1988. 16.95 (*1-879994-00-3*) Consortium Advan.

Assessing, Insuring & Disposing of Jazz Record Collections. Intro. by David Goldenberg. (IAJRC Monograph: No. 1). (Illus.). ix, 85p. (Orig.). (C). 1990. pap. 10.95 (*0-9625487-0-7*) Intl Assn Jazz Record.

Assessing Interventions: Traditional & Innovative Methods. Ed. by Fred Tudiver et al. (Research Methods for Primary Care Ser.: Vol. 4). (Illus.). 260p. (C). 1992. 49.95 (*0-8039-4770-4*); pap. 24.00 (*0-8039-4771-2*) Sage.

***Assessing Investment Opportunities in Economies in Transition.** OECD Staff. 186p. (Orig.). 1994. pap. 52.00x (*92-64-24252-X*) OECD.

Assessing Language Ability in the Classroom. 2nd ed. Andrew D. Cohen. LC 93-41932. 1994. pap. 23.95 (*0-8384-4262-5*) Heinle & Heinle.

Assessing Language Production in Children: Experimental Procedures. Jon F. Miller. (Illus.). 186p. (C). 1991. pap. text ed. 47.00 (*0-205-13546-3*) Allyn.

Assessing Leadership & Managerial Behavior. 85p. 1988. 9.75 (*0-318-41957-2*) Northwest Regional.

Assessing Learning Motivation. 85p. 1988. 9.75 (*0-318-41958-0*) Northwest Regional.

Assessing Learning Time at the Co-op Training Station. Jeanne Desy et al. 58p. 1985. 6.25 (*0-318-17849-4*, SN 50) Ctr Educ Trng Employ.

Assessing Learning with LOGO. Pat Nolan & Ken Ryba. 84p. 1986. teacher ed 12.50 (*0-924667-31-1*) Intl Society Tech Educ.

Assessing Local Government. Jeffrey Stanyer. 256p. 1985. write for info. (*0-85520-769-8*); pap. write for info. (*0-85520-770-1*) Blackwell Pubs.

Assessing Management People: A Practical Guide. J. A. Dukes. 176p. 1988. 34.50 (*0-89397-310-6*) Nichols Pub.

Assessing Medical Technologies. Institute of Medicine. 573p. 1985. text ed. 49.95 (*0-309-03583-X*) Natl Acad Pr.

Assessing Minority Students with Learning & Behavior Problems. Catherine Collier. LC 88-81254. 104p. 1988. pap. text ed. 11.00 (*0-940059-05-3*) Hamilton Pubns.

Assessing Molecular & Atomic Scale Technologies. Susan Hadden. (Special Project Report Ser.). 117p. 1989. 10.00 (*0-89940-866-4*) LBJ Sch Pub Aff.

Assessing Needs & Planning Care in Social Work. Brian J. Taylor & Toni Devine. LC 93-1817. 141p. 1993. 49.95 (*1-85742-139-6*, Pub. by Ashgate UK); pap. 21.95 (*1-85742-144-2*, Pub. by Ashgate UK) Ashgate Pub Co.

***Assessing Needs in Continuing Education: An Essential Tool for Quality Improvement.** Donna S. Queeney. LC 94-37102. (Higher & Adult Education Ser.). 304p. 1995. 30.95 (*0-7879-0059-1*) Jossey-Bass.

Assessing Needs in Educational & Social Programs. Belle R. Witkin. LC 84-48002. (Jossey-Bass Social & Behavioral Science Ser.). 437p. reprint ed. pap. 124.60 (*0-7837-0189-6*, 2040485) Bks Demand.

Assessing Neurotoxicity of Drugs of Abuse. 1994. lib. bdg. 250.00 (*0-8490-8604-3*) Gordon Pr.

Assessing New Pricing Concepts in Public Utilities: Proceedings of the Institute of Public Utilities Ninth Annual Conference. Michigan State University, Institute of Public Utilities Staff. Ed. by Harry M. Trebing. LC 78-620031. (MSU Public Utilities Papers). (Illus.). 528p. reprint ed. pap. 150.50 (*0-8357-5805-2*, 2056383) Bks Demand.

Assessing Object Relations Phenomena. Ed. by Morton Kissen. LC 86-10513. (Illus.). 400p. (C). 1986. text ed. 50.00 (*0-8236-0445-4*) Intl Univs Pr.

Assessing Organizational Effectiveness: Systems Change, Adaptation & Strategy. Raymond F. Zammuto. LC 81-9130. (Administrative Systems Ser.). 181p. (C). 1982. 64.50 (*0-87395-552-8*); pap. 21.95 (*0-87395-553-6*) State U NY Pr.

***Assessing Patients.** Springhouse Corporation Staff. LC 95-6497. (New Nursing Photobooks Ser.). 1995. pap. write for info. (*0-87434-808-0*) Springhouse Pub.

Assessing Pavement Maintenance Needs. (Research Record Ser.: No. 1109). 78p. 1987. 11.00 (*0-309-04459-6*) Transport Res Bd.

An Asterisk (*) at the beginning of an entry indicates that the title is appearing in BIP for the first time.

Assessing Pediatric Practice: A Critical Study. Raymond S. Duff. Ed. by Charles D. Cook. LC 90-5003. 237p. 1990. text ed. 33.00 (*0-910701-59-8*, 0819) Health Admin Pr.

***Assessing Physical Fitness & Physical Activity in Population-Based Surveys, 2 vols.** 1994. lib. bdg. 600. 75 (*0-8490-6432-5*) Gordon Pr.

***Assessing Physical Fitness & Physical Activity in Population-Based Surveys, 2 vols., Set.** 1995. lib. bdg. 602.99 (*0-8490-6729-4*) Gordon Pr.

Assessing Physically Disabled People at Home. Kathleen Maczka. Ed. by Jo Campling. (Therapy in Practice Ser.: No. 12). 128p. 1990. pap. 23.00 (*0-412-32480-6*, A4417) Chapman & Hall.

Assessing Pschopathology & Behavior Problems in Persons with Mental Retardation: A Review of Available Instruments. (Illus.). 239p. (Orig.). (C). 1994. pap. text ed. 45.00 (*0-7881-0529-9*) Diane Pub.

Assessing Public Concern for Landscape Quality: A Potential Model to Identify Visual Thresholds. Arthur W. Magill. (Illus.). 50p. (Orig.). (C). 1993. pap. text ed. 30.00 (*0-7881-0017-3*) Diane Pub.

Assessing Quality Circle Effectiveness. 36.95 (*0-685-08872-3*) IAQC Pr.

Assessing Quality Circles Effectiveness. IAAQC Press. 19. 95 (*0-317-69756-0*) IAQC Pr.

Assessing Quality Health Care: Perspectives for Clinicians. Richard P. Wenzel. (Illus.). 560p. 1992. 79.00 (*0-683-08924-2*) Williams & Wilkins.

Assessing Quality in Further & Higher Education. Allan Ashworth & Roger Harvey. (Higher Education Policy Ser.: No. 24). 176p. 1994. 49.50 (*1-85302-539-9*, Pub. by J Kingsley Pubs UK) Taylor & Francis.

Assessing Quality in Outpatient Psychotherapy: Implications for Designing & Selecting Cost-Efficient Mental Health Care Benefits. Robert J. Lueger. LC 93-77662. 75p. (Orig.). 1993. pap. 37.00 (*0-89154-463-1*) Intl Found Employ.

Assessing Radical Education. Nigel Wright. 256p. 1989. 90. 00 (*0-335-09228-4*, Open Univ Pr); pap. 32.00 (*0-335-09227-6*, Open Univ Pr) Taylor & Francis.

Assessing Reform in South Korea. Asia Watch Staff. 52p. 1988. pap. 5.00 (*0-929692-04-7*, Asia Watch) Hum Rts Watch.

Assessing Risk & Measuring Change in Families: The Family Risk Scales. Stephen Magura et al. 40p. 1987. pap. 16.95 (*0-87868-275-9*) Child Welfare.

Assessing Risk on Wall Street. Thomas A. Rorro. LC 83-51720. 224p. 1984. 19.95 (*0-89709-134-5*) Liberty Pub.

Assessing Risks to Health: Methodologic Approaches. Ed. by John C. Bailar, III et al. LC 88-6203. 344p. 1993. text ed. 49.95 (*0-86569-167-3*, T167, Auburn Hse) Greenwood.

Assessing Rural Needs: A Manual for Practitioners. Jeffrey Ashe. 129p. 1978. 7.75 (*0-86619-075-9*, 11058-BK) Vols Tech Asst.

Assessing Schizophrenic Thinking: A Clinical & Research Instrument for Measuring Thought Disorder. Mary H. Johnston & Philip S. Holzman. LC 79-88771. (Jossey-Bass Social & Behavioral Science Ser.). 328p. reprint ed. pap. 93.50 (*0-8357-4928-2*, 2037858) Bks Demand.

Assessing School & Classroom Climate. 91p. 1987. 9.75 (*0-317-66077-2*) Northwest Regional.

Assessing Sex Bias in Testing: A Review of the Issues & Evaluations of 74 Psychological & Educational Tests. Paula Selkow. LC 84-564. (Contributions in Psychology Ser.: No. 3). (Illus.). x, 264p. 1984. text ed. 59.95 (*0-313-24447-2*, SAX) Greenwood.

Assessing Special Students: Strategies & Procedures. 4th ed. James A. McLoughlin & Rena B. Lewis. 712p. (C). 1994. text ed. write for info. (*0-02-379492-5*, Merrill Pub Co) Macmillan.

Assessing Spiritual Needs: A Guide for Caregivers. George Fitchett. LC 93-18153. (Guides to Pastoral Care Ser.). 128p. 1993. pap. 9.99 (*0-8066-2629-1*, 9-2629) Augsburg Fortress.

Assessing Sport & Physical Education: Diagnosis & Projection. Earle F. Zeigler. 411p. (Orig.). 1986. pap. text ed. 18.80x (*0-87563-293-9*) Stipes.

Assessing Sport Skills. Bradford N. Strand & Rolayne Wilson. LC 92-22433. 176p. 1993. pap. 23.00x (*0-87322-377-2*, BSTR0377) Human Kinetics.

Assessing Stress in Children. Louis A. Chandler. LC 85-12188. 240p. 1985. text ed. 55.00 (*0-275-90072-X*, C0072, Praeger Pubs) Greenwood.

Assessing Structural Reform: Lessons for the Future. 260p. (Orig.). 1994. pap. 42.00 (*92-64-14090-5*) OECD.

Assessing Student Characteristics in Admissions to Higher Education: A Review of Procedures. Hunter M. Breland. (Research Monograph: No. 9). 144p. (Orig.). 1981. pap. 10.95 (*0-87447-138-9*) College Bd.

Assessing Student Learning & Development: A Guide to the Principles, Goals, & Methods of Determining College Outcomes. T. Dary Erwin. LC 90-22107. (Higher & Adult Education Ser.). 232p. 1991. 30.95 (*1-55542-325-6*) Jossey-Bass.

Assessing Student Outcomes: Performance Assessment Using the Dimensions of Learning Model. Robert J. Marzano et al. LC 93-41882. 138p. 1993. pap. 13.95 (*0-87120-225-5*, 611-93179) Assn Supervision.

Assessing Student Outcomes: Performance Assessment Using the Dimensions of Learning Model. Robert J. Marzano et al. LC 93-41882. 1993. write for info. (*0-08-720225-5*, Pergamon Pr) Elsevier.

Assessing Student Performance: Exploring the Purpose & Limits of Testing. Grant P. Wiggins. LC 93-29490. (Education-Higher Education Ser.). 336p. 1993. 29.95 (*1-55542-592-5*) Jossey-Bass.

Assessing Students' Learning. Ed. by James H. McMillan. LC 85-644763. (New Directions for Teaching & Learning Ser.: No. TL 34). 1988. 16.95 (*1-55542-929-7*) Jossey-Bass.

Assessing Students with Multiple Disabilities: Practical Guidelines for Practitioners. Donna Reavis. (Illus.). 110p. (C). 1990. text ed. 29.95x (*0-398-05683-8*) C C Thomas.

***Assessing Students with Multiple Disabilities: Practical Guidlines for Practitioners.** Donna Reavis. (Illus.). 110p. 1990. pap. 15.95 (*0-398-06339-7*) C C Thomas.

Assessing Success in Family Literacy Projects: Alternative Approaches to Assessment & Evaluation. Ed. by Daniel D. Holt. LC 94-2136. (Language in Education Ser.: No. 85). (Illus.). 142p. (Orig.). 1994. pap. text ed. 15.50 (*0-937354-85-6*) Delta Systems.

Assessing Surprises & Nonlinearities in Greenhouse Warming. Ed. by Joel Darmstadter & Michael A. Toman. 1993. pap. 25.00 (*0-915707-71-3*) Resources Future.

Assessing Tax Reform. Henry J. Aaron & Harvey Galper. LC 84-45979. (Studies of Government Finance). 145p. 1985. 26.95 (*0-8157-0038-5*); pap. 9.95 (*0-8157-0037-7*) Brookings.

Assessing Teacher Performance: Task Analysis & Evaluation. Robert C. Hawley. LC 80-67945. 112p. (Orig.). 1982. pap. 19.95 (*0-913636-12-6*) Educ Res MA.

Assessing the Abilities & Instructional Needs of Students: A Practical Guide for Educators, Psychologists, Speech Pathologists, & Diagnosticians. Ed. by Donald D. Hammill. LC 86-15133. (PRO-ED Assessment Ser.). (Illus.). 630p. 1987. text ed. 41.00 (*0-89079-137-6*, 1399) PRO-ED.

Assessing the Adversary: Estimates by the Eisenhower Administration of Soviet Intentions & Capabilities. Raymond L. Garthoff. 52p. (C). 1991. pap. text ed. 5.95 (*0-8157-3057-8*) Brookings.

Assessing the Base Force: How Much Is Too Much? William W. Kaufmann. 97p. (C). 1993. pap. 9.95 (*0-8157-4887-6*) Brookings.

Assessing the Canada - U. S. Free Trade Agreement. Ed. by Murray G. Smith & Frank Stone. 1989. pap. text ed. 15.00 (*0-88645-061-6*, Pub. by Inst Res Pub CN) Ashgate Pub Co.

***Assessing the Constitutional Route to Federal Budget Balance: The Balanced Budget Amendment: Toxic, Not Tonic.** Charles J. Whalen. 50p. (Orig.). 1995. pap. 3.00 (*0-941276-08-2*, J Levy Econ Inst) Bard Coll Pubns.

Assessing the Costs of Student Recruitment at Smaller Independent Colleges & Universities. Ed. by John Weber. 77p. 1989. 25.00 (*0-915164-47-7*) NACUBO.

Assessing the Demographic Impact of Developmental Projects: Conceptual, Methodological & Policy Issues. Amarjit S. Oberai. (International Labour Organisation Ser.). 128p. 1991. 74.50 (*0-415-06841-X*, A6190) Routledge.

Assessing the Driving Ability of the Elderly: A Preliminary Investigation. Ellen D. Taira et al. LC 88-35759. (Physical & Occupational Therapy in Geriatrics Ser.: Vol. 7, Nos. 1 & 2). (Illus.). 215p. 1989. text ed. 39.95 (*0-86656-895-6*) Haworth Pr.

***Assessing the Effects of Being Raised in a Dysfunctional Environment: Introducing the Classification System of Child Abuse & Neglect (CSCAN)** Anthony S. Dallmann-Jones. 100p. (Orig.). 1995. pap. 9.95 (*1-881952-48-7*) Three Blue Herons.

Assessing the Effects of Powerplant-Induced Mortality on Fish Populations: Proceedings. Ed. by Webster Van Winkle. LC 77-81956. 1977. 160.00 (*0-08-021950-0*, Pub. by Pergamon Repr UK) Franklin.

Assessing the Effects of the Uruguay Round. OECD Staff. 38p. (Orig.). 1993. pap. 11.00 (*92-64-14017-4*) OECD.

Assessing the Elderly: A Practical Guide to Measurement. Rosalie A. Kane & Robert L. Kane. LC 81-47065. (Rand Corporation Research Study). 320p. 1984. pap. text ed. 19.95 (*0-669-09780-2*) Free Pr.

***Assessing the Environmental Impact of Farm Policies.** Walter N. Thurman. (Studies in Agricultural Policy). 65p. (Orig.). 1995. pap. 9.95 (*0-8447-3915-4*) Am Enterprise.

Assessing the Future: A Sensitivity Analysis of Highway & Road Improvements on Growth in the San Francisco Bay Area. 46p. 1991. 35.00 (*0-317-05638-7*, PG1006PRO) Assn Bay Area.

Assessing the Future & Policy Planning. Ed. by W. A. Hahn & K. F. Gordon. LC 72-78920. 350p. 1973. text ed. 108.00 (*0-677-12650-6*) Gordon & Breach.

Assessing the Handicaps & Needs of Mentally Retarded Children. Ed. by Brian Cooper. LC 81-66374. 1981. text ed. 104.00 (*0-12-188020-6*) Acad Pr.

Assessing the Impact of Computer-Based Instruction: A Review of Recent Research. M. D. Roblyer et al. LC 88-24377. (Computers in the Schools Ser.: Vol. 5, Nos. 3-4). (Illus.). 149p. 1988. text ed. 39.95 (*0-86656-893-X*) Haworth Pr.

Assessing the Impact of Policy on Peruvian Small Ruminant Production Systems. Corinne Valdiva. Ed. by Karen Seckler. (Development Studies Paper). 23p. (Orig.). 1992. pap. 6.00 (*0-933595-67-0*) Winrock Intl.

Assessing the Impact of SFAS Number 116 & SFAS Number 117: A Guide for Colleges & Universities. KPMG Peat Marwick Staff. LC 94-1337. 1994. 64.95 (*0-915164-92-2*) NACUBO.

Assessing the Impact of Statutory Minimum Wages in Developing Countries: Four Country Studies. (Labour Management Relations Ser.: No. 67). vii, 160p. 1988. pap. 16.00 (*92-2-106204-X*) Intl Labour Office.

***Assessing the Impacts of Climate Change on Natural Resource Systems.** Ed. by Kenneth D. Frederick & Norman J. Rosenberg. LC 94-39503. 224p. (C). 1994. lib. bdg. 115.00 (*0-7923-3211-3*) Kluwer Ac.

Assessing the National Curriculum. Ed. by Philip O'Hear & John White. 128p. 1993. pap. 27.00 (*1-85396-232-5*, Pub. by Paul Chapman UK) Taylor & Francis.

Assessing the Nation's Earthquakes: The Health & Future of Regional Seismograph Networks. Commission on Geosciences, Environment & Resources Staff. 80p. 1990. pap. text ed. 15.00 (*0-309-04291-7*) Natl Acad Pr.

Assessing the Need for Judicial Resources: Guidelines for a New Process; Preliminary Draft. National Center for State Courts Task Force on Principles for Assessing Judicial Resources Staff. Ed. by Alexander B. Aikman & Victor E. Flango. 67p. 1983. pap. write for info. (*0-89656-069-4*, R-081) Natl Ctr St Courts.

***Assessing the Needs of Bilingual Pupils: Living in Two Languages (Resource Materials for Teachers)** Deryn Hall. 64p. 1995. pap. 17.95 (*1-85346-332-9*, Pub. by D Fulton UK) Taylor & Francis.

Assessing the New Testament Evidence for the Historicity of the Resurrection of Jesus. William L. Craig. LC 88-25838. (Studies in Bible & Early Christianity: Vol. 16). 462p. 1989. lib. bdg. 109.95 (*0-88946-616-5*) E Mellen.

Assessing the Nuclear Age. Ed. by Len Ackland & Steven McGuire. LC 85-82511. (Illus.). 400p. 1986. 24.95 (*0-941682-07-2*); pap. 12.95 (*0-941682-08-0*) Educ Found for Nucl Sci.

Assessing the President: The Media, Elite Opinion, & Public Support. Richard A. Brody. 208p. 1991. 29.50 (*0-8047-1907-1*) Stanford U Pr.

Assessing the President: The Media, Elite Opinion, & Public Support. Richard A. Brody. 208p. (C). 1992. pap. 10.95 (*0-8047-2096-7*) Stanford U Pr.

Assessing the Quality of Management Module 7: Facilitator's Guide. Mary Millar. (Primary Health Care Management Advancement Programme (PHC MAP) Modules Ser.). 47p. 1993. pap. text ed. write for info. (*1-882839-13-7*) Aga Khan Fnd.

Assessing the Quality of Management Module 7: User's Guide. Lori D. Brown. (Primary Health Care Management Advancement Programme (PHC MAP) Modules Ser.). 90p. 1993. pap. text ed. write for info. (*1-882839-05-6*) Aga Khan Fnd.

Assessing the Quality of Radioimmunoassay Systems: Approved Guideline, Vol. 5. National Committee for Clinical Laboratory Standards. 1985. 40.00 (*1-56238-073-7*, LA1-A) Natl Comm Clin Lab Stds.

Assessing the Quality of Services Module 6: Facilitator's Guide. Martine Hilton. (Primary Health Care Management Advancement Programme (PHC MAP) Modules Ser.). 45p. 1993. pap. text ed. write for info. (*1-882839-12-9*) Aga Khan Fnd.

Assessing the Quality of Services Module 6: User's Guide. Lori D. Brown. (Primary Health Care Management Advancement Programme (PHC MAP) Modules Ser.). 190p. 1993. pap. text ed. write for info. (*1-882839-04-8*) Aga Khan Fnd.

Assessing the Risk of Dangerousness: Potential for Further Violence of Sexual Offenders, Batterers & Child Abusers. Ed. by Jacquelyn C. Campbell. (Interpersonal Violence, the Practice Ser.: Vol. 7). 160p. 1994. pap. 18. 95 (*0-8039-3747-4*) Sage.

***Assessing the Risks of Re-Using Contaminated Land.** Tom Cairney. LC 94-46421. 1995. text ed. 79.95 (*0-471-94893-4*) Wiley.

Assessing the Significance of the Holocaust. Ed. by Abie I. Ingber & Benny Kraut. (Orig.). 1987. pap. 4.95 (*0-934393-05-2*) Hillel Jewish.

Assessing the Skeletal Maturity of the Hand-Wrist: FELS Method. Alex F. Roche et al. (Illus.). 348p. (C). 1988. text ed. 78.95x (*0-398-05452-5*) C C Thomas.

Assessing the State Legislative Response to Global Warming. Larry Morandi. (State Legislative Reports: Vol. 17, No. 6). 4p. 1992. pap. 5.00 (*1-55516-278-9*, 7302-1706) Natl Conf State Legis.

Assessing the 1984 "Ulysses" Ed. by George Sandulescu & Clive Hart. 224p. 1986. 53.00 (*0-389-20635-0*) B&N Imports.

Assessing Therapeutic Recreation Manpower: Guidelines for Using the Survey Questionnaire. Judith E. Goldstein & Peter J. Verhoeven. 26p. reprint ed. pap. 25.00 (*0-7837-1539-0*, 2041822) Bks Demand.

Assessing Timberland Investment Opportunities. 146p. 1986. 20.00 (*0-935018-31-X*) Forest Prod.

Assessing Trainer Effectiveness. Leslie Rae. 342p. 1991. 74. 95 (*0-566-07264-5*, Pub. by Gower UK) Ashgate Pub Co.

Assessing Training Needs, 5 vols. (Illus.). 672p. pap. write for info. (*0-318-59905-8*, NTDSP) Am Soc Train & Devel.

Assessing Transportation-Related Air Quality Impacts. (Special Report Ser.: No. 167). 167p. 1976. 8.40 (*0-309-02478-1*) Transport Res Bd.

Assessing Tropical Forest Lands: Suitability for Sustainable Uses. Richard A. Carpenter. 352p. 1982. text ed. 105. 00 (*0-907567-02-9*, Tycooly Pub); pap. text ed. 65.00 (*0-907567-07-X*, Tycooly Pub) Weidner & Sons.

Assessing Visually Handicapped People: An Introduction to Test Procedures. Michael Tobin. 112p. 1994. pap. 27.50 (*1-85346-295-0*, Pub. by D Fulton UK) Taylor & Francis.

Assessing Vocational Teachers. Elizabeth V. Dubravcic et al. 87p. 8.00 (*0-318-22040-7*, RD262) Ctr Educ Trng Employ.

Assessing What Professors Do: An Introduction to Academic Performance Appraisal in Higher Education. David A. Dilts et al. LC 93-30978. (Contributions to the Study of Education Ser.: Vol. 61). 220p. 1994. text ed. 49.95 (*0-313-26761-8*, Greenwood Pr) Greenwood.

Assessing Writers' Knowledge & Processes of Composing. Lester Faigley et al. Ed. by Marcia Farr. LC 84-28428. (Writing Research Ser.: Vol. 2). 288p. 1985. text ed. 45. 00 (*0-89391-226-3*); pap. 27.50 (*0-89391-320-0*) Ablex Pub.

Assessing Writing Skill. Hunter M. Breland et al. (Research Monograph: No. 11). 128p. (Orig.). 1987. pap. 14.95 (*0-87447-280-6*) College Bd.

Assessing Young Children with Special Needs: An Ecological Perspective. Susan M. Benner. 400p. (C). 1992. teacher ed write for info. (*0-8013-0489-X*, 78322); pap. text ed. 36.95 (*0-8013-0488-1*, 78321) Longman.

Assessing Your Leisurestyle & Formulating Strategies see Leisure Wellness Series

***Assessing Your Team: Seven Measures of Team Success Team Leader's Package.** Dick Richards & Susan Smyth. LC 94-65546. 32p. 1994. student ed, pap. 9.95 (*0-88390-420-9*) Pfeiffer & Co.

Assessing Your Team: Seven Measures of Team Success Team Leader's Package. Dick Richards & Susan Smyth. LC 94-65546. 72p. 1994. pap. 24.95 (*0-88390-437-3*) Pfeiffer & Co.

Assessment. Ed. by Diana O. Potter & Minnie B. Rose. LC 82-11760. (Nurse's Reference Library). (Illus.). 839p. 1982. text ed. 29.95 (*0-916730-39-5*) Springhouse Pub.

Assessment: A Sourcebook for Social Work Practice. Ed. by Julia B. Rauch. LC 93-27098. 416p. 1993. pap. 27.95 (*0-87304-267-0*) Families Intl.

Assessment: How Do We Know What They Know? WSASCD Staff. 112p. 1993. per., pap. text ed. 16.95 (*0-8403-8620-6*) Kendall-Hunt.

***Assessment: Policy to Practice.** Ed. by Ministry of Education of New Zealand Staff. (Illus.). 52p. (Orig.). (C). 1994. pap. text ed. 12.95x (*1-878450-95-6*, Pub. by Lrning Media NZ) R Owen Pubs.

Assessment: The Cornerstone of Activity Programs. Ruth Perschbacher. LC 93-85327. 145p. (C). 1993. pap. 24.95 (*0-910251-62-2*) Venture Pub PA.

Assessment: The Special Educator's Role. Cheri Hoy & Noel Gregg. LC 93-22949. 1994. text ed. 47.95 (*0-534-21132-1*) Brooks-Cole.

Assessment Across Disorders: Perspectives, Practices, & Procedures. Katharine G. Butler. LC 93-34702. (Topics in Language Disorders Ser.). 240p. 1994. 30.00 (*0-8342-0593-9*) Aspen Pub.

Assessment Administration Practices in the U.S. & Canada. 217p. 1992. pap. 50.00 (*0-88329-082-0*) IAAO.

Assessment Aide. Jack Rudman. (Career Examination Ser.: C-2180). 1994. pap. 23.95 (*0-8373-2180-8*) Nat Learn.

Assessment Alternatives in Mathematics: An Overview of Assessment Techniques That Promote Learning. Jean K. Stenmark. (Equals Ser.). (Illus.). 48p. (Orig.). 1989. pap. 5.00 (*0-912511-54-0*) Lawrence Science.

Assessment & Access: Hispanics in Higher Education. Ed. by Gary D. Keller et al. LC 90-48185. (United States Hispanic Studies). 333p. 1992. 64.50 (*0-7914-0779-9*); pap. 21.95 (*0-7914-0780-2*) State U NY Pr.

Assessment & Accountability. Jill Blackmore. 170p. (C). 1988. 54.00 (*0-7300-0591-7*, Pub. by Deakin Univ AT) St Mut.

Assessment & Accountability in Reference Work. Ed. by Susan G. Blandy et al. LC 92-26676. (Reference Librarian Ser.: No. 38). (Illus.). 320p. 1993. reprint ed. 49.95 (*1-56024-358-9*) Haworth Pr.

Assessment & Alert of Major Hazards. Ed. by Aspen Institute Staff. 48p. 1979. pap. text ed. 8.50 (*0-8191-5837-2*, Aspen Inst for Humanistic Studies) U Pr of Amer.

***Assessment & Care Co-Ordination.** NISW Staff. 1993. 105.00 (*1-873153-13-9*, Pub. by Natl Inst Soc Work) St Mut.

Assessment & Care Management for Adults in Residential & Supported Accomodation: A Handbook for Care Manager & Social Care Staff. Philip Seed & Gillian Kaye. LC 93-41412. 200p. 1994. pap. 27.50 (*1-85302-227-6*, Pub. by J Kingsley Pubs UK) Taylor & Francis.

Assessment & Care of the Fetus: Physiological, Clinical & Medicolegal Principles. Robert D. Eden & Frank H. Boehm. (Illus.). 1043p. 1990. boxed 98.00 (*0-8385-0436-1*, A0436-4) Appleton & Lange.

Assessment & Collection of Tax from Non-Residents. (Cahiers de Droit Fiscal International Ser.: Vol. LXXa). 650p. 1985. pap. 91.00 (*90-6544-218-9*) Kluwer Law Tax Pubs.

Assessment & Control of Biochemical Methods. Terry Hector. Ed. by Arthur M. James. (Analytical Chemistry by Open Learning Ser.). 150p. 1987. pap. text ed. 54.95 (*0-471-91279-4*) Wiley.

Assessment & Control of Non-Point Source Pollution of Aquatic Systems: A Practical Approach. Ed. by W. Rast et al. (Man & the Biosphere Ser.: Vol. 14). 300p. 1995. 75.00 (*1-85070-384-1*) Prthnon Pub.

Assessment & Control of Software Risks. Capers Jones. LC 93-36816. (Yourden Press Computing Ser.). 1993. text ed. 38.00 (*0-13-741406-4*, Yourdon) P-H.

Assessment & Control of VOC Emissions from Waste Treatment & Disposal Facilities. Thomas T. Shen et al. LC 92-26278. 1993. pap. 52.95 (*0-442-01229-2*) Van Nos Reinhold.

Assessment & Correction in the Elementary Language Arts. C. Glennon Rowell. LC 92-29658. 1993. text ed. write for info. (*0-205-13998-1*) Allyn.

Assessment & Curriculum Reform. Ed. by James L. Ratcliff & Elizabeth A. Jones. LC 85-644752. (New Directions for Higher Education Ser.: No. HE 80). 100p. 1992. 16. 95 (*1-55542-735-9*) Jossey-Bass.

***Assessment & Development Centres.** Iain Ballantyne & Nigel Povah. 200p. 1995. 54.95 (*0-566-07484-2*, Pub. by Gower UK) Ashgate Pub Co.

***Assessment & Development in Europe: Adding Value to Individuals & Organizations.** Mac Bolton. LC 95-2230. (Training Ser.). 1995. write for info. (*0-07-707928-0*) McGraw.

An Asterisk (*) at the beginning of an entry indicates that the title is appearing in BIP for the first time. 485

A

Assessment & Diagnosis in Child Psychopathology. Ed. by Michael Rutter et al. LC 87-12180. 477p. 1987. lib. bdg. 50.00 (0-89862-699-4) Guilford Pr.

Assessment & Evaluation for Student Centered Learning. 2nd ed. Ed. by Bill Harp. 296p. (J). (gr. k-6). 1994. pap. text ed. 28.95 (0-926842-39-0) CG Pubs Inc.

Assessment & Evaluation for Student Centered Learning: Expanded Professional Version. 2nd ed. Ed. by Bill Harp. 356p. (J). (gr. k-6). 1995. text ed. 38.95 (0-926842-40-4) CG Pubs Inc.

Assessment & Evaluation in Schooling. Bill Hannan. 141p. (C). 1985. 48.00 (0-7300-0300-0, Pub. by Deakin Univ AT) St Mut.

Assessment & Examination in the Secondary School. Richard Riding & Susan Butterfield. 256p. 1990. 55.00 (0-415-03108-7, A4318) Routledge.

Assessment & Instruction of Reading Disabilities. Lipson & Wixson. (C). 1991. text ed. 58.50 (0-673-18335-1) HarpCollege.

*Assessment & Instruction of Social Skills. Linda K. Elksnin & Nick Elksnin. (Illus.). 256p. (Orig.). (C). 1995. pap. text ed. 34.95 (1-56593-266-8, 0588) Singular Publishing.

Assessment & Intervention in Emergency Nursing. 3rd ed. Nedell E. Lanros. (Illus.). 669p. 1988. boxed, pap. 44.95 (0-8385-0435-3, A0435-6) Appleton & Lange.

Assessment & Learning of Mathematics. Ed. by Gilah Leder. (C). 1990. 75.00 (0-86431-122-2, Pub. by Aust Council Educ Res AT) St Mut.

Assessment & Management of Chemical Risks. Ed. by Joseph V. Rodricks & Robert C. Tardiff. LC 83-25851. (ACS Symposium Ser.: No. 239). 184p. 1984. lib. bdg. 44.95 (0-8412-0821-2) Am Chemical.

Assessment & Management of Emotional & Psychological Reactions to Brain Damage & Aphasia. Peter Wahrborg. (Illus.). 120p. (Orig.). (C). 1991. pap. text ed. 31.50x (1-879105-18-7, 0211) Singular Publishing.

Assessment & Management of Mainstreamed Hearing-Impaired Children: Principles & Practices. Mark Ross et al. LC 90-27495. 415p. (C). 1991. text ed. 38.00 (0-89079-458-8, 1969) PRO-ED.

Assessment & Management of the Suicidal Adolescent. Lawrence Clayton. 1989. pap. 5.95 (0-929240-18-9) Essential Med Info Syst Inc.

Assessment & Placement of Minority Students. 2nd ed. R. J. Samuda & S. L. Kong. Ed. by J. Cummins. Tr. by J. Pascual-Leone & J. Lewis. (Illus.). 244p. 1991. reprint ed. text ed. 39.90 (0-88937-024-9) Hogrefe & Huber Pubs.

Assessment & Prediction of Suicide. Ed. by Ronald W. Maris et al. LC 91-35408. 697p. 1992. lib. bdg. 55.00 (0-89862-791-5) Guilford Pr.

Assessment & Prevention of Failure Phenomena in Rock Engineering: Proceedings, Istanbul, April 1993. Ed. by A. G. Pasamehmetoglu et al. (Illus.). 800p. (C). 1993. text ed. 150.00 (90-5410-309-4, Pub. by A A Balkema NE) Ashgate Pub Co.

Assessment & Remediation of Articulatory & Phonological Disorders. 2nd ed. Nancy Creaghead et al. 432p. (C). 1989. write for info. (0-675-20653-7, Merrill Pub Co) Macmillan.

Assessment & Renovation of Concrete Structures. Ted Kay. (Longman Concrete Design & Construction Ser.). 224p. 1992. text ed. 183.00 (0-470-21864-9) Wiley.

*Assessment & Selection in Organizations: Methods & Practice for Recruitment & Appraisal. Neil Anderson & Peter Herriot. 1994. pap. text ed. 64.95 (0-471-93994-3) Wiley.

Assessment & Selection in Organizations: Methods & Practice for Recruitment & Appraisal. Peter Herriot. 700p. 1990. text ed. 160.95 (0-471-91640-4) Wiley.

Assessment & Tax Accounting Supervisor. (Career Examination Ser.: C-3270). 1994. pap. 39.95 (0-8373-3270-2) Nat Learn.

Assessment & Testing. Robert Wood. (Illus.). 288p. (C). 1993. pap. 37.00 (0-521-44997-9) Cambridge U Pr.

*Assessment & Testing: Myths & Realities. Ed. by Trudy H. Bers & Mary L. Mittler. LC 85-644753. (New Directions for Community Colleges Ser.: No. 88). 110p. (Orig.). 1994. pap. 16.95 (0-7879-9983-0) Jossey-Bass.

Assessment & the School Library Media Center. Carol C. Kuhlthau et al. 125p. 1994. pap. text ed. 18.00 (1-56308-211-X) Libs Unl.

*Assessment & Therapy for Young Dysfluent Children: Family Interaction. Lena Rustin et al. 200p. 1995. pap. 62.25 (1-56593-278-1, 0599) Singular Publishing.

*Assessment & Therapy of Disturbances in Infancy. Selma Fraiberg. LC 94-72520. 294p. 1994. pap. text ed. 35.00 (1-56821-338-7) Aronson.

Assessment & Therapy of Parkinsonism. Ed. by C. D. Marsden. (New Trends in Clinical Neurology Ser.). (Illus.). 105p. 1990. 65.00 (1-85070-318-3) Prthnon Pub.

Assessment & Treatment of Addictive Disorders. Ed. by Timothy B. Baker & Dale S. Cannon. LC 87-30537. 318p. 1988. text ed. 69.50 (0-275-92388-6, C2388, Praeger Pubs) Greenwood.

Assessment & Treatment of Adolescent Sex Offenders. Garry P. Perry & Janet Orchard. LC 92-14135. 160p. (Orig.). 1992. pap. 20.20 (0-943158-75-3, ATABP, Prof Resc Pr) Pro Resource.

Assessment & Treatment of Childhood Problems: A Clinician's Guide. Carolyn S. Schroeder & Betty N. Gordon. LC 91-20201. 512p. 1991. lib. bdg. 42.00 (0-89862-565-3) Guilford Pr.

Assessment & Treatment of Depression in Children & Adolescents. 2nd ed. Harvey F. Clarizio. LC 89-90917. 250p. 1994. pap. 31.95 (0-88422-103-2) Clinical Psych.

Assessment & Treatment of Emotional or Behavioral Disorders. H. A. Ninness et al. LC 93-20502. 192p. 1993. text ed. 55.00 (0-275-94098-5, C4098, Praeger Pubs) Greenwood.

Assessment & Treatment of Multiple Personality & Dissociative Disorders. James P. Bloch. Ed. by Harold H. Smith, Jr. LC 91-52545. (Practitioner's Resource Ser.). 112p. 1991. pap. 14.70 (0-943158-67-2, ATMBP, Prof Resc Pr) Pro Resource.

Assessment & Treatment of Panic Disorder & Agoraphobia. E. De Beurs. 206p. 1993. pap. 33.00 (90-5170-202-7, Pub. by Thesis Pubs NE) IBD Ltd.

*Assessment & Treatment of Patients with Coexisting Mental Illness & Alcohol & Other Drug Abuse. 1995. lib. bdg. 251.95 (0-8490-6831-2) Gordon Pr.

Assessment & Treatment of the Elderly Neuropsychiatric Patient. Ed. by Gabe J. Maletta & Francis J. Pirozzolo. LC 86-9507. (Advances in Neurogerontology Ser.: Vol. 4). 291p. 1986. text ed. 65.00 (0-275-92112-3, C2112, Praeger Pubs) Greenwood.

Assessment Assistant. Jack Rudman. (Career Examination Ser.: C-2181). 1994. pap. 23.95 (0-8373-2181-6) Nat Learn.

Assessment-Based Vocational Curriculum Manual: The Bridge Between School & Community. Marcia M. Warne & Wenden W. Waite. LC 86-28168. 190p. (Orig.). (C). 1987. pap. text ed. 37.00 (0-8191-5822-4) U Pr of Amer.

*Assessment Center Handbook. Brian T. Page. 1995. pap. 17.95 (0-87526-429-8) Gould.

Assessment Center Methods in Educational Administration: Past, Present & Future. Frederick C. Wendel & Ward Sybouts. Ed. by Miles T. Bryant. LC 89-114353. (UCEA Monograph Ser.). 48p. (Orig.). (C). 1988. pap. text ed. 3.50 (0-922971-09-9, MS3-AC) Univ Council Educ Admin.

Assessment Centers. George Thornton, III. (Human Resources Management Ser.). 256p. (C). 1992. pap. text ed. 26.95 (0-201-55403-8) Addison-Wesley.

Assessment Centers & Managerial Performance. George Thornton, III & William C. Byham. (Organizational & Occupational Psychology Ser.). 1982. text ed. 79.00 (0-12-690620-3) Acad Pr.

Assessment Centres. Charles Woodruffe. 240p. 1993. pap. 125.00 (0-85292-545-X, Pub. by IPM Hse UK) St Mut.

Assessment Centres. Charles Woodruffe. 250p. (C). 1990. 99.00 (0-85292-440-2, Pub. by IPM Hse UK) St Mut.

Assessment Centres: Identifying & Developing Competence. Charles Woodruffe. 192p. (C). 1993. pap. text ed. 79.00 (0-85292-499-2, Pub. by IPM Hse UK) St Mut.

Assessment Clerk. Jack Rudman. (Career Examination Ser.: C-2920). 1994. pap. 19.95 (0-8373-2920-5) Nat Learn.

Assessment Collection - Legal Remedies: Assessment Collection - Legal Remedies. rev. ed. Thomas J. Hindman. (GAP Report Ser.: Vol. 5). (C). 1992. pap. 14.50 (0-944715-21-4) CAI.

Assessment Companion: Communication Checklists for SLP's, Teachers, & Parents. Linda Zachman et al. (ps up). 1993. student ed, spiral bd. 27.95 (1-55999-257-3) LinguiSystems.

Assessment, Evaluation, & Programming System for Infants & Children, Vol. 1: Measurement for Birth to Three Years. Ed. by Diane Bricker. 352p. (C). 1992. spiral bd. 41.00 (1-55766-095-6) P H Brookes.

Assessment, Evaluation, & Programming System for Infants & Children, Vol. 1: Measurement for Birth to Three Years, AEPS Child Progress Record, 02/1994, pkg. of 30. Ed. by Diane Bricker. 352p. (C). 1992. lp 16.00 (1-55766-165-0) P H Brookes.

Assessment, Evaluation, & Programming System for Infants & Children, Vol. 1: Measurement for Birth to Three Years, Data Recording Forms, pkg. of 10. Ed. by Diane Bricker. 352p. (C). 1992. disk 21.00 (1-55766-097-2) P H Brookes.

Assessment, Evaluation, & Programming System for Infants & Children, Vol. 1: Measurement for Birth to Three Years, Family Report, pkg. of 10. Ed. by Diane Bricker. 352p. (C). 1992. 15.00 (1-55766-099-9) P H Brookes.

Assessment, Evaluation & Record Keeping. Aileen Duncan & Norman Smith. (C). 1989. 50.00 (1-85098-224-4, Pub. by Jordanhill College UK) St Mut.

Assessment for Decision, Vol. I. Ed. by Donald R. Peterson & Daniel B. Fishman. (Rutgers Symposia on Applied Psychology Ser.). 463p. (C). 1988. pap. text ed. 20.00 (0-8135-1247-6) Rutgers U Pr.

Assessment for Early Intervention: Best Practices for Professionals. Stephen J. Bagnato & John Neisworth. LC 91-6540. (Guilford School Practitioner Ser.). 260p. 1991. lib. bdg. 45.00 (0-89862-359-6); pap. text ed. 19.95 (0-89862-238-7) Guilford Pr.

Assessment for Excellence: The Philosophy & Practice of Assessment & Evaluation in Higher Education. Alexander W. Astin. LC 92-44619. 352p. 1991. boxed 27.95 (0-89774-805-0) Oryx Pr.

Assessment for Instruction in Early Literacy. Leslie Morrow & Jeffrey Smith. 256p. (C). 1989. Casebound. text ed. 54.00 (0-13-050428-9) P-H.

*Assessment for Learning in Higher Education. Ed. by Peter Knight & Sally Brown. (Staff & Educational Development Ser.). 192p. 1995. pap. 34.95 (0-7494-1532-0) Taylor & Francis.

Assessment for Teacher Development. John Wilson et al. 250p. 1989. 70.00 (1-85000-536-2, Falmer Pr); pap. 33.00 (1-85000-537-0, Falmer Pr) Taylor & Francis.

Assessment, Improvement, & Cooperation: The Challenge of Reform in Higher Education. Cameron Fincher. 76p. (Orig.). (C). 1991. pap. 6.00 (1-880647-03-6) U GA Inst High Educ.

Assessment in Adapted Physical Education & Therapeutic Recreation. Leonard Kalakian & Michael A. Horvat. 208p. (C). 1995. pap. text ed. write for info. (0-697-14953-6) Brown & Benchmark.

Assessment in Christian Higher Education: Rhetoric & Reality. Ed. by D. John Lee & Gloria G. Stronks. (Calvin College Ser.: Vol. II). 270p. (Orig.). Date not set. lib. bdg. 53.00 (0-8191-9408-5); pap. text ed. 24.50 (0-8191-9409-3) U Pr of Amer.

Assessment in Counseling: A Guide to the Use of Psychological Assessment Procedures. Albert B. Hood & Richard W. Johnson. 1991. 25.95 (1-55620-074-9) Am Coun Assn.

Assessment in Developmental Career Counseling. Linda Seligman. LC 80-13151. 480p. 1980. 27.00 (0-910328-30-7); pap. 21.50 (0-910328-34-X) Sulzburger & Graham Pub.

Assessment in Developmental Career Counseling. 2nd ed. Linda Seligman. 480p. 1994. 59.95 (0-8039-5803-X); pap. 28.95 (0-8039-5804-8) Sage.

Assessment in Early Childhood Education. Ed. by Geva M. Blenkin & A. V. Kelly. 200p. 1992. pap. 27.00 (1-85396-153-1, Pub. by Paul Chapman UK) Taylor & Francis.

Assessment in Higher Education. 2nd ed. Heywood. 464p. 1989. text ed. 115.95 (0-471-92032-0) Wiley.

*Assessment in Higher Education. 2nd ed. John Heywood. LC 88-14423. (Illus.). Date not set. reprint ed. pap. 122.60 (0-7837-9502-5, 2060252) Bks Demand.

Assessment in Higher Education. John Heywood. LC 76-12786. 303p. reprint ed. pap. 86.40 (0-8357-5806-0, 2030756) Bks Demand.

Assessment in Higher Education: Politics, Pedagogy, & Portfolios. Patrick L. Courts & Kathleen H. McInerney. LC 92-41612. 208p. 1993. text ed. 57.95 (0-275-94426-3, C4426, Praeger Pubs); pap. text ed. 16.95 (0-275-94427-1, B4427, Praeger Pubs) Greenwood.

Assessment in Mental Handicap: A Guide to Assessment Practices, Tests & Checklists. Ed. by James Hogg & Norma V. Raynes. (Illus.). 289p. 1987. 29.95 (0-914797-31-X) Brookline Bks.

*Assessment in Neuropsychology. Ed. by John R. Beech & Leonora Harding. LC 95-15757. (Assessment Library). 1995. write for info. (0-415-09390-2); pap. write for info. (0-415-12953-2) Routledge.

Assessment in Physical Education: A Teacher's Guide to the Issues. Bob Carroll. LC 93-27227. 152p. 1994. 75.00 (0-7507-0298-2, Falmer Pr); pap. 29.00 (0-7507-0299-0, Falmer Pr) Taylor & Francis.

*Assessment in Practice: Putting Principles to Work on College Campuses. Trudy W. Banta et al. LC 95-18627. (Higher & Adult Education Ser.). 1995. 34.95 (0-7879-0134-2) Jossey-Bass.

Assessment in Residential Treatment Settings: Principles & Methods to Support Cost-Effective Quality Operations. Ed. by Gordon L. Paul. LC 86-61550. (Assessment in Residential Treatment Settings Ser.: No. 1). 332p. (Orig.). 1986. pap. text ed. 24.95 (0-87822-275-8, 2758) Res Press.

Assessment in Schools. 2nd ed. David Satterly. (Theory & Practice in Education Ser.). (Illus.). 384p. 1989. pap. text ed. 26.95 (0-631-16982-2) Blackwell Pubs.

Assessment in Social Work Practice. Carol H. Meyer. 192p. (C). 1993. text ed. 27.50 (0-231-07556-1) Col U Pr.

Assessment in Special & Remedial Education. 5th ed. John Salvia & James E. Ysseldyke. (C). 1991. write for info. (0-395-54451-3) HM Soft Schl Col Div.

Assessment in Special Education. William H. Berdine & Stacie A. Meyer. (C). 1987. text ed. 47.50 (0-673-39146-9) HarpCollege.

Assessment in Special Education: The Education Evaluation. Linda J. Hargrove & James A. Poteet. (Illus.). 432p. (C). 1984. text ed. write for info. (0-13-049726-6) P-H.

Assessment in Specific Circumstances. Anthony Owens. (C). 1991. pap. 45.00x (0-7300-1336-7, ECT338, Pub. by Deakin Univ AT) St Mut.

Assessment in Speech & Language Therapy. Ed. by John R. Beech et al. LC 92-39593. (NFER Assessment Library). 224p. 1993. 59.95 (0-415-07881-4, B2459, Routledge NY); pap. 18.95 (0-415-07882-2, B2463, Routledge NY) Routledge.

Assessment in the Mathematics Classroom: 1993 Yearbook. Ed. by Norman L. Webb. (Illus.). 248p. 1993. text ed. 20.00 (0-87353-352-6) NCTM.

Assessment in the Primary School. Helen McMullen. Ed. by Cedric Cullingford. (Children, Teachers & Learning Ser.). 192p. 1993. text ed. 70.00 (0-304-32595-3); pap. text ed. 22.50 (0-304-32586-4) Cassell.

Assessment Issues in Child Neuropsychology. Ed. by M. G. Tramontana & S. R. Hooper. LC 88-22399. (Critical Issues in Neuropsychology Ser.). (Illus.). 408p. 1988. 54.50 (0-306-42898-9, Plenum Pr) Plenum.

*Assessment Log & Developmental Progress Chart for the Carolina Curriculum: 12 Months to 3 Years. Johnson-Martin et al. 28p. 1995. 23.00 (1-55766-221-5) P H Brookes.

Assessment Log & Developmental Progress Chart for the Carolina Curriculum for Preschoolers with Special Needs. Johnson-Martin et al. 28p. 1990. reprint ed. Pkg. of 10. 20.00 (1-55766-039-5) P H Brookes.

Assessment, Management, & Treatment of Suicide: Guidelines for Practice. Ed. by Bruce Bongar. (Illus.). 352p. 1992. 39.95 (0-19-506846-7) OUP.

Assessment Manual for Health & Physical Fitness: Fitness for Living. Mitchell Collins. 96p. (C). 1994. pap. text ed., spiral bd. 12.95 (0-8403-8772-5) Kendall-Hunt.

Assessment Manual for Medical Groups. 3rd ed. Stephen J. Williams & Julianne P. Sanchez. Ed. by Victoria Melton. 180p. (Orig.). (C). 1994. pap. text ed. 40.00 (0-933948-21-2, 4637) Ctr Res Ambulatory.

Assessment Measures in Medical School, Residency, & Practice: The Connections. Ed. by Joseph S. Gonnella et al. LC 93-35462. (Medical Education Ser.: Vol. 17). 168p. 1993. 37.95 (0-8261-8350-6) Springer Pub.

*Assessment Methodologies & Management Theme 5: Proceedings of the World Fisheries Congress. Ed. by Gary T. Sakagawa. 1995. text ed. write for info. (1-886106-10-X) Science Pubs.

Assessment Methods for Infants & Toddlers: Transdisciplinary Team Approaches. Doris Bergen. LC 94-12519. (Early Childhood Education Ser.). 336p. 1994. 52.00x (0-8077-3380-6) Tchrs Coll.

Assessment Methods for Infants & Toddlers: Transdisciplinary Team Approaches. Doris Bergen. LC 94-12519. (Early Childhood Education Ser.). 336p. (C). 1994. pap. text ed. 25.95x (0-8077-3379-2) Tchrs Coll.

Assessment of a Manual Case Monitoring System for the Third Judicial District Court, Salt Lake City, Utah. National Center for State Courts Staff. 41p. 1977. 2.46 (0-685-15451-3, MAB-017) Natl Ctr St Courts.

Assessment of Achievement Programme: Home Economics, Performance of Pupils at Secondary Two. 32p. 1989. pap. 10.00 (0-11-493469-X, HM469X, Pub. by HMSO UK) UNIPUB.

Assessment of Achievement Programme: Technical Education Performance of Pupils at Secondary Two. 44p. 1989. pap. 10.00 (0-11-493468-1, HM5102, Pub. by HMSO UK) UNIPUB.

Assessment of Addictive Behaviors. Ed. by Dennis M. Donovan & G. Alan Marlatt. LC 87-19674. (Guilford Behavioral Assessment Ser.). 497p. 1988. lib. bdg. 48.95 (0-89862-144-5) Guilford Pr.

*Assessment of Adolescent Alcohol & Drug Abuse. Ken C. Winters. 91p. 1994. 29.50 (0-87424-291-6, W-291) Western Psych.

Assessment of Adolescents with Special Needs: A Guide for Transition Planning. Margaret West. 1987. 50.00 (0-295-96626-2) U of Wash Pr.

Assessment of Agricultural Education in Mexico, Central America, & the Caribbean. Antonio Macias-Lopez. (Studies in Technology & Social Change; No. 18). (Illus.). 133p. (Orig.). (C). 1990. pap. 12.00 (0-945271-26-3) ISU-TSCP.

Assessment of & Surgery for Impacted Third Molars: A Self-Instructional Guide, Bk. 6. 3rd rev. ed. James R. Hooley & Robert J. Whitacre. (Illus.). 104p. 1983. pap. 19.95 (0-89939-061-7) Stoma Pr.

*Assessment of Animal Agriculture in Sub-Saharan Africa. 125p. (Orig.). (C). 1992. pap. text ed. 15.00x (0-933595-76-X) Winrock Intl.

Assessment of Aphasia & Related Disorders. 2nd ed. Harold Goodglass & Edith Kaplan. LC 83-9326. 102p. 1983. text ed. 49.50 (0-8121-0901-5); 20.00 (0-685-73569-5, 0000-1); 7.50 (0-685-73570-2, 0000-4); 12.50 (0-685-73571-0, 0000-2); 10.00 (0-685-73572-9, 0000-3) Williams & Wilkins.

*Assessment of Atlantic Bluefin Tuna. National Research Council, Committee to Review the Outer Continental Shelf Environmental Studies Program Staff. 168p. (Orig.). (C). 1994. pap. text ed. 29.00 (0-309-05181-9) Natl Acad Pr.

Assessment of Audio Recording System for the North Dakota Supreme Court. National Center for State Courts Staff. 24p. 1975. 1.44 (0-685-16272-9, MAB-018) Natl Ctr St Courts.

*Assessment of Authentic Performance in School Mathematics. Ed. by Richard Lesh & Susan J. Lamon. 456p. 1994. pap. 24.95 (0-8058-1877-4) L Erlbaum Assocs.

Assessment of Authentic Performance in School Mathematics. Ed. by Richard A. Lesh & Susan J. Lamon. LC 92-14967. 456p. 1992. pap. 39.95 (0-87168-500-0, 92-16S) AAAS.

Assessment of Behavioral, Emotional, & Social Problems: Direct & Objective Methods for Use with Children & Adolescents. Kenneth W. Merrell. LC 93-19109. 288p. (C). 1994. boxed, text ed. 56.95 (0-8013-1107-1, 79565) Longman.

Assessment of Bilingual Aphasia. Michel Paradis. 1987. 17.50 (0-8058-0849-3); 19.95 (0-8058-0848-5) L Erlbaum Assocs.

*Assessment of Bilingual Aphasia. Michel Paradis. 1987. 34.50 (0-8058-0850-7) L Erlbaum Assocs.

Assessment of Bilingual Aphasia. Michel Paradis & G. Libben. 264p. 1987. text ed. 45.00 (0-89859-650-5) L Erlbaum Assocs.

Assessment of Biological Age in Man. F. Bourliere. (Public Health Papers: No. 37). 67p. 1970. pap. 2.80 (92-4-130037-X, 60) World Health.

Assessment of Biological Mechanisms Across the Lifespan. Stephanie M. Clancy Dollinger. Ed. by Lisabeth F. DiLalla. 216p. 1995. 39.95 (0-8058-1486-8) L Erlbaum Assocs.

Assessment of Carbon-Carbon Composite Research in the Far East. Robert A. Meyer. 58p. (Orig.). (C). 1992. pap. text ed. 49.95 (1-56806-021-1) Diane Pub.

Assessment of Cell Proliferation in Clinical Practice. Ed. by P. A. Hall & Nicholas A. Wright. (Illus.). xviii, 210p. 1991. 105.00 (0-387-19700-1) Spr-Verlag.

Assessment of Child & Adolescent Functioning: A Practitioner's Instrument for Assessing Clients. Ray MacNair & Elizabeth McKinney. LC 83-26602. 75p. 1983. pap. 4.50 (0-911847-02-2) U GA Inst Community.

Assessment of Child & Adolescent Personality. Ed. by Howard M. Knoff. LC 85-30585. 686p. 1986. lib. bdg. 49.95 (0-89862-668-4) Guilford Pr.

Assessment of Children. 3rd ed. Jerome M. Sattler. LC 87-90484. (Illus.). 1023p. (C). 1988. text ed. 60.00 (0-9618209-0-X) J M Sattler.

An Asterisk (*) at the beginning of an entry indicates that the title is appearing in BIP for the first time.

Assessment of Children: Fundamental Methods & Practices. Joseph C. Witt et al. 544p. 1994. boxed write for info. (*0-697-17226-0*) Brown & Benchmark.

Assessment of Chronic Pain Patients with the MMPI-2. Laura S. Keller & James N. Butcher. (Illus.). 288p. (C). 1991. text ed. 29.95 (*0-8166-1861-5*) U of Minn Pr.

Assessment of Clinical Sensitivity & Specificity of Laboratory Tests. (Proposed Guideline Ser.: Vol. 7). 1987. 40.00 (*1-56238-029-X*, GP10-P) Natl Comm Clin Lab Stds.

Assessment of Cognitive Function in Epilepsy. W. Edwin Dodson et al. Ed. by Marcel Kinsbourne & Beat Hiltbrunner. 168p. 1992. 59.95 (*0-939957-45-0*) Demos Vermande.

Assessment of Cognitive Processes: The PASS Theory of Intelligence. Jagannath P. Das et al. LC 93-13843. 236p. 1993. 43.95 (*0-205-14164-1*, Longwood Div) Allyn.

Assessment of College Performance. Richard I. Miller. LC 79-83575. (Jossey-Bass Series in Higher Education). (Illus.). 392p. reprint ed. pap. 111.80 (*0-8357-4912-6*, 2037842) Bks Demand.

Assessment of Conceptual Organization: Improving Writing, Thinking & Reading. Christian Gerhard. 50p. 1991. teacher ed 29.95 (*1-56602-039-5*) Research Better.

Assessment of Criminal Behaviour in Secure Settings. Ed. by Mary McMurran & John Hodge. 200p. 1993. pap. 37. 50 (*1-85302-124-5*, Pub. by J Kingsley Pubs UK) Taylor & Francis.

Assessment of Cultural Resources of Lehman Caves National Monument, White Pine County, Nevada. Don D. Fowler. (Social Sciences Center Technical Report Ser.: No. 3a). (Illus.). 52p. (Orig.). (C). 1977. pap. 5.00 (*0-945920-02-4*) Desert Rsch Inst.

Assessment of Current & Alternative Methods of Court Reporting in the Ninth Judicial Circuit Court, Orlando, Florida. 144p. 1987. 9.00 (*0-685-19932-0*, SERO-037) Natl Ctr St Courts.

Assessment of Damages for Personal Injury & Death. 3rd ed. H. Luntz. 1990. Australia. 94.00 (*0-409-49544-1*) Butterworth Legal Pubs.

Assessment of Deficiencies & Preservation of Bridge Substructures Below the Waterline. (National Cooperative Highway Research Program Report Ser.: No. 251). 80p. 1982. 8.40 (*0-309-03421-3*) Transport Res Bd.

Assessment of Delaware County's Court of Common Pleas Courtroom Needs to Year 2000. National Center for State Courts Staff. 48p. 1979. 2.88 (*0-685-15156-5*, NERO-023) Natl Ctr St Courts.

Assessment of Diagnostic Technology in Health Care: Rationale, Methods, Problems, & Directions. Institute of Medicine Staff. 152p. 1989. pap. text ed. 17.50 (*0-309-04099-X*) Natl Acad Pr.

Assessment of DOD Fuel Standardization Policies. James P. Stucker et al. LC 94-19024. 1994. write for info. (*0-8330-1546-X*, MR376OSD) Rand Corp.

Assessment of Drunk Driving Policies in Texas & Other States. Contrib by Leigh Boske & Robert MacDonald. (Policy Research Project Report Ser.: No. 69). 322p. 1985. 10.00 (*0-89940-671-8*) LBJ Sch Pub Aff.

Assessment of Early Child Development. Dorothy Flapan & Peter B. Neubauer. LC 84-450013. 180p. 1994. pap. 25.00 (*1-56821-284-4*) Aronson.

Assessment of Early Mathematics. Aileen Duncan. (C). 1989. 55.00 (*1-85098-210-4*, Pub. by Jordanhill College UK) St Mut.

Assessment of Eating Disorders. Williamson. (Practitioner Guidebook Ser.). (C). 1990. 39.95 (*0-205-14508-6*, H4508, Longwood Div); pap. 25.95 (*0-205-14507-8*, H4507, Longwood Div) Allyn.

Assessment of Economic Policy Issues Raised by the European Community's Single Market Program. 50p. (Orig.). (C). 1993. pap. text ed. 35.00 (*0-7881-0025-4*) Diane Pub.

Assessment of Effectiveness Measures for Local Government Recreation Agencies in Oregon. Roger Delles. 99p. 1974. pap. 4.00 (*0-943272-09-2*) Inst Recreation Res.

Assessment of Energy Use in Multibuilding Facilities. (Illus.). 120p. (Orig.). (C). 1994. pap. text ed. 45.00 (*0-7881-0500-0*) Diane Pub.

Assessment of Energy Use in Multibuilding Facilities. (Orig.). 1994. lib. bdg. 250.00 (*0-8490-5777-9*) Gordon Pr.

Assessment of Erosion. Workshop on Assessment of Erosion in U. S. A. & Europe (1978: State University, Ghent) Staff. LC 80-41170. (Illus.). 581p. reprint ed. pap. 165.60 (*0-8357-3735-7*, 2036461) Bks Demand.

Assessment of Exceptional Students: Educational & Psychological Procedures. 3rd ed. Ronald L. Taylor. LC 92-15195. 1992. text ed. write for info. (*0-205-14142-0*) Allyn.

Assessment of Exceptional Students Educational & Psychological Procedures. 2nd ed. Ronald L. Taylor. 448p. (C). 1989. text ed. write for info. (*0-13-050170-0*) P-H.

Assessment of Existing & Developing Water Main Rehabilitation Practices. 186p. 1990. pap. 31.50 (*0-89867-552-9*, 90572) Am Water Wks Assn.

Assessment of Factors Affecting Requirements of Farm Livestock. D. Cuthbertson & H. Sinclair. LC 69-14229. (International Encyclopedia of Food & Nutrition Ser.: Vol. 17, Pt. 2). 1969. 341.00 (*0-08-012710-X*, Pub. by Pergamon Repr UK) Franklin.

Assessment of Family Violence: A Clinical & Legal Sourcebook. Robert T. Ammerman & Michel Hersen. (Series on Personality Processes). 400p. 1992. text ed. 64.95 (*0-471-52415-8*) Wiley.

Assessment of Foreign Investment in California Real Estate. (Illus.). 56p. (Orig.). (C). 1994. pap. text ed. 40. 00 (*0-7881-0761-5*) Diane Pub.

Assessment of Fossil Energy Materials Research Needs. (Illus.). 60p. (Orig.). (C). 1994. pap. text ed. 50.00 (*0-7881-0760-7*) Diane Pub.

***Assessment of Fracture Risk & Its Application to Screening for Postmenopausal Osteoporosis.** Ed. by World Health Organization Staff. (Technical Report Ser.). 129p. 1994. pap. 19.80 (*92-4-120843-0*) World Health.

Assessment of Grant Information & Tracking Systems: A Look at Selected Agencies of South Dakota State Government. C. Kenneth Meyer et al. 1978. 5.00 (*1-55614-021-5*) U of SD Gov Res Bur.

***Assessment of Hearing Disability.** King. 124p. 1992. pap. 47.75 (*1-56593-571-3*, 0317) Singular Publishing.

Assessment of Hormones & Drugs in Saliva in Biobehavioral. Ed. by C. Kirschbaum et al. (Illus.). 356p. 1993. 69.00 (*0-88937-050-8*) Hogrefe & Huber Pubs.

Assessment of Incineration of Industrial Wastes, EUR 14136. K. Maniatis. 114p. 1992. pap. 17.00 (*92-826-3855-3*, CD-NA-14136-EN-C, Pub. by Europ Com) UNIPUB.

Assessment of Individuals with Severe Disabilities: An Applied Behavior Approach to Life Skills Assessment. 2nd ed. Browder. 432p. 1994. pap. 34.00 (*1-55766-067-0*, 0670) P H Brookes.

Assessment of Infants & Young Children. Libby G. Cohen & Loraine J. Spenciner. LC 92-35208. 528p. (C). 1994. teacher ed write for info. (*0-8013-1248-5*, 79879); boxed, text ed. 47.95 (*0-8013-0965-4*, 79247) Longman.

Assessment of Intellectual Functioning. Lewis R. Aiken. 464p. 1986. teacher ed write for info. (*0-318-61510-X*, H88586) Allyn.

Assessment of Intellectual Functioning. Lewis R. Aiken. 464p. 1986. text ed. 67.00 (*0-205-08857-0*, H8857-8) Allyn.

***Assessment of Intelligence & Development of Infants & Young Children: With Specialized Measures.** Harold D. Love. 138p. 1991. pap. 19.95 (*0-398-06246-3*) C C Thomas.

Assessment of Intelligence & Development of Infants & Young Children: With Specialized Measures. Harold D. Love. 138p. (C). 1991. text ed. 34.95x (*0-398-05676-5*) C C Thomas.

Assessment of Internal Contamination Resulting from Recurrent or Prolonged Uptakes. International Commission on Radiological Protection. (International Commission of Radiological Protection Ser.: No. 10a). 1971. pap. 13.50 (*0-08-016772-1*, Pergamon Pr) Elsevier.

Assessment of Jury Management in Prince George's County, Maryland. 15p. 1986. 1.00 (*0-685-18268-1*, SERO-021) Natl Ctr St Courts.

Assessment of Land-Use Impacts of Highways in Small Urban Areas. Alan J. Horowitz et al. (Publications in Architecture & Urban Planning: No. R85-5). (Illus.). iv, 177p. 1985. 12.50 (*0-938744-43-7*) U of Wis Ctr Arch-Urban.

Assessment of Land Value: Proceedings. Ed. by Daniel M. Holland. (Committee on Taxation, Resources & Economic Development Ser.: No. 5). 306p. 1970. 30.00 (*0-299-05621-X*) U of Wis Pr.

Assessment of Laterality: Issues, Techniques, & Implications. Ed. by R. S. Dean & Cecil R. Reynolds. (Critical Issues in Neuropsychology Ser.). (Illus.). 230p. (C). 1994. write for info. (*0-306-44420-8*, Plenum Pr) Plenum.

Assessment of Learners with Special Needs: Concepts & Applications. Richard L. Luftig. 576p. 1988. text ed. 45. 00 (*0-205-11733-3*, H1733-8) Allyn.

Assessment of Learners with Special Needs: Concepts & Applications. Richard L. Luftig. 576p. 1989. teacher ed write for info. (*0-318-63879-7*, H17346) Allyn.

Assessment of Learning: Cognitive & Affective. David A. Payne. (C). 1974. text ed. 18.50 (*0-669-85209-0*) Heath.

Assessment of Learning Disabilities: Preschool Through Adulthood. Ed. by Larry B. Silver. LC 90-20024. 180p. (Orig.). (C). 1989. pap. text ed. 26.00 (*0-89079-393-X*, 1799) PRO-ED.

Assessment of Learning in the Classroom. John Izard. (C). 1991. pap. 50.00 (*0-7300-1337-5*, ECT338, Pub. by Deakin Univ AT) St Mut.

Assessment of Lives: Personality Evaluation in a Bureaucratic Society. LC 70-168860. (Jossey-Bass Behavioral Science Ser.). 262p. reprint ed. pap. 74.70 (*0-8357-5807-9*, 2013786) Bks Demand.

Assessment of Logging Costs from Forest Inventories in the Tropics, Pts. 1-11. Ed. by F. A. O. Staff. (C). 1991. text ed. 250.00 (*0-89771-613-2*, Pub. by Intl Bk Distr II) St Mut.

Assessment of Logging Costs from Forest Inventories in the Tropics, Pts. 1-11. FAO Staff. 1992. 175.00 (*81-7089-172-8*, Pub. by Intl Bk Distr II) St Mut.

Assessment of Long-Range Transboundary Air Pollution. (Air Pollution Studies: No. 7). 94p. 1991. 25.00 (*92-1-116505-9*, 91.II.E.18) UN.

Assessment of Lubricant Technology: Presented at the 1972 Spring Lubrication Symposium, June 6-8, 1972, Boston, MA. Spring Lubrication Symposium (1972, Boston). Ed. by B. D. McConnell. LC 72-93945. 148p. reprint ed. pap. 42.20 (*0-8357-5808-7*, 2026787) Bks Demand.

Assessment of Management Alternatives for LWR Wastes Cost & Radiological Impact Associated with Near-Surface Disposal of Reactor Waste, Vol. 8. EC Staff. (EUR Ser.: No. 14043). 1993. pap. 11.00 (*92-826-4892-3*, CD-NH-14043-EN-C, Pub. by Europ Com) UNIPUB.

Assessment of Manganese Nodule Resources. Ed. by Graham & Trotman Ltd. Staff. 79p. 1982. lib. bdg. 48.00 (*0-86010-347-1*) G & T Inc.

Assessment of Marital Discord: An Integration for Research & Practice. K. D. O'Leary. 392p. 1987. text ed. 79.95 (*0-89859-901-6*) L Erlbaum Assocs.

Assessment of Microfilm & Records Retention Programs in the Delaware County Court of Common Pleas, Media, Pennsylvania. National Center for State Courts Staff. 24p. 1978. 1.44 (*0-685-16557-4*, DPO, T/A-501) Natl Ctr St Courts.

***Assessment of Motor & Process Skills.** Anne G. Fisher. Date not set. pap. text ed. 25.00 (*0-9645127-0-X*) Three Star Pr.

Assessment of New Diamond Technology in Japan. 93p. (Orig.). (C). 1992. pap. text ed. 95.00 (*1-56806-072-6*) Diane Pub.

Assessment of Nutritional Status & Food Consumption Surveys: Proceedings of the European Nutritionists Group Symposium, 11th, Warsaw, April 1972. European Nutritionists Group Symposium Staff. Ed. by J. C. Somogyi. (Bibliotheca Nutritio et Dieta Ser.: No. 20). (Illus.). 224p. 1974. pap. 75.25 (*3-8055-1685-1*) S Karger.

***Assessment of NVQs & SVQs Series, 9 booklets, Set.** IPM Staff. (C). 1994. ring bd. 533.25x (*0-08-042154-7*, Pub. by IPM Hse UK) St Mut.

***Assessment of Parenting: Psychiatric & Psychological Contributions.** Ed. by Peter Reder & Clare Lucey. LC 95-7618. 1995. write for info. (*0-415-11453-5*); pap. write for info. (*0-415-11454-3*) Routledge.

Assessment of Performance & Competence: A Handbook for Teachers & Trainers. 2nd ed. Les Walklin. 224p. (C). 1991. pap. 51.00x (*0-7487-1115-5*, Pub. by S Thornes Pubs UK) St Mut.

Assessment of Personal Injury Damages. 2nd ed. Bruce. 320p. 1992. text ed. 79.95 (*0-409-89768-X*) Butterworth Legal Pubs.

Assessment of Personality & Behavior Problems: Infancy Through Adolescence. Roy P. Martin. LC 88-19030. 399p. 1988. lib. bdg. 45.00 (*0-89862-727-3*) Guilford Pr.

Assessment of Personality & Behavior Problems: Infancy Through Adolescence. Roy P. Martin. 399p. 1992. reprint ed. pap. text ed. 21.95 (*0-89862-026-0*) Guilford Pr.

Assessment of Persons. Norman D. Sundberg. (Illus.). 1977. text ed. write for info. (*0-13-049585-9*) P-H.

Assessment of Potable Water Membrane Applications & Research Needs. 184p. 1989. pap. 22.00 (*0-89867-491-3*, 90564) Am Water Wks Assn.

Assessment of Potential Markets for Small Satellites. Lawrence H. Stern et al. (Space Research & Development Ser.). 111p. (Orig.). (C). 1989. pap. 25.00 (*0-9625101-0-6*) VA Ctr Innovative Tech.

Assessment of Present Level of Historic Standing Structures Survey Coverage in Maryland Using U. S. Census of Housing Data. Maryland Historical Trust Staff. (White Papers Series on Preservation Planning: No. 5). 10p. 1987. 2.00 (*1-878399-23-3*) Div Hist Cult Progs.

Assessment of Pupil Achievement: Motivation & School Success. Ed. by P. R. Weston. 190p. 1991. 38.00 (*90-265-1147-7*, Pub. by Swets Pub Serv NE) Taylor & Francis.

Assessment of Quality of Life & Cancer Treatment: Proceedings of the International Workshop, Milan, December 11-13, 1985. Ed. by V. Ventafridda et al. 252p. 1987. 106.25 (*0-444-80838-8*) Elsevier.

Assessment of Quality-of-Work-Life Programs for the Transit Industry - Model Programs. (National Cooperative Transit Research Program Synthesis Ser.: No. 6). 37p. 1983. 6.80 (*0-309-03716-6*) Transport Res Bd.

Assessment of Quality-of-Work-Life Programs for the Transit Industry - Research Report. (National Cooperative Transit Research Program Synthesis Ser.: No. 5). 99p. 1983. 8.80 (*0-309-03715-8*) Transport Res Bd.

Assessment of Quality Software Development Tools, 2nd Symposium. LC 91-76563. 336p. 1992. 70.00 (*0-8186-2620-8*, 2620) IEEE Comp Soc.

Assessment of Quality Software Development Tools, 3rd Symposium. 350p. 1994. pap. text ed. 70.00 (*0-8186-5660-3*, 5660) IEEE Comp Soc.

***Assessment of Remedies: The Impact of Compensatory & Punitive Damages on Title Vi.** Edward E. Potter & Ann E. Reesman. 110p. 1990. pap. 10.00 (*0-614-06160-1*, 2019-PP-4040) EPF.

Assessment of Research-Doctorate Programs in the U. S. Engineering. National Research Council. 193p. (C). 1982. pap. text ed. 19.95 (*0-309-03336-5*) Natl Acad Pr.

Assessment of Research-Doctorate Programs in the United States: Humanities. National Research Council. 244p. (C). 1982. pap. text ed. 14.95 (*0-309-03333-0*) Natl Acad Pr.

Assessment of Research Needs for Wind Turbine Rotor Materials Technology. 120p. (C). 1991. pap. text ed. 19.00 (*0-309-04479-0*) Natl Acad Pr.

Assessment of Research on Natural Hazards. Gilbert F. White & J. Eugene Haas. LC 75-2058. (Environmental Studies). (Illus.). 487p. 1975. 45.00 (*0-262-08083-4*) MIT Pr.

Assessment of Resources & Needs in Highway Technology Education. Comp. by American Society of Civil Engineers Staff. 227p. 1975. pap. 12.00 (*0-87262-117-0*) Am Soc Civil Eng.

Assessment of School Needs for Low-Achieving Students: Staff Survey. Francine S. Beyer & Ronald L. Houston. 44p. 1989. reprint ed. pap. 16.95 (*1-56602-025-5*) Research Better.

Assessment of Selected Heat Pump Systems. Institute of Gas Technology Staff & J. Wurm. 192p. 1977. pap. 6.50 (*0-318-12587-0*, M58977) Am Gas Assn.

***Assessment of Sexual Function: A Guide to Interviewing.** Group for the Advancement of Psychiatry Staff. 100p. 1994. pap. 15.00 (*0-87668-128-3*) Aronson.

Assessment of Sexual Function: A Guide to Interviewing. Group for the Advancement of Psychiatry Staff. LC 74-158483. (Group for the Advancement of Psychiatry, Symposium Ser.: Vol. 8, No. 88). 96p. reprint ed. pap. 27.40 (*0-7837-2111-0*, 2042390) Bks Demand.

Assessment of Situation & Potential for Co-Firing Coal & Biomass in Energy Facilities. (Illus.). 96p. (Orig.). (C). 1994. pap. text ed. 45.00 (*0-7881-0615-5*) Diane Pub.

Assessment of Skeletal Maturity & Prediction of Adult Height. 2nd ed. Ed. by James M. Tanner et al. 1984. text ed. 121.00 (*0-12-683360-5*) Acad Pr.

Assessment of Space Shuttle Flight Software Development Processes. Commission on Engineering & Technical Systems Staff & National Research Council Staff. 208p. (Orig.). (C). 1993. pap. text ed. 35.00 (*0-309-04880-X*) Natl Acad Pr.

Assessment of Space Station Freedom Program: Audit Report. 53p. (Orig.). (C). 1994. pap. text ed. 60.00 (*0-7881-0381-4*) Diane Pub.

Assessment of Special Children: Tests & the Problem-Solving Process. Joseph C. Witt et al. (C). 1988. text ed. 34.50 (*0-673-39755-6*) HarpCollege.

Assessment of Special Education Needs: Responses to Emotional & Behavioural Difficulties. David Galloway et al. LC 93-39141. (Effective Teacher Ser.). 1994. write for info. (*0-582-08514-4*, Pub. by Longman UK) Longman.

Assessment of Special Educational Needs: An International Perspective. Ed. by Tony Cline. LC 92-6584. 224p. 1992. 72.50 (*0-415-07880-6*, A7523) Routledge.

***Assessment of Stroke Outcome: Round Table.** Ed. by J. M. Orgogozo & G. L. Lenzi. (Journal: Cerebrovascular Diseases Ser.: Vol. 4, Suppl. 2, 1994). (Illus.). iv, 30p. 1994. pap. 13.75 (*3-8055-6064-8*) S Karger.

Assessment of Structural Safety: A Comparative Statistical Study of the Evolution & Use of Levels 1, 2, & 3. Ezio Leporati. Tr. by Nicoletta Grimoldi. LC 79-50708. (Series in Cement & Concrete Research: No. 1). (Illus.). 143p. reprint ed. pap. 40.80 (*0-8357-8808-3*, 2033344) Bks Demand.

Assessment of the Adaptability of New PROMIS to a State Judicial Information System. National Center for State Courts Staff. 329p. 1979. 19.74 (*0-89656-034-1*, F-003) Natl Ctr St Courts.

Assessment of the Arctic Marine Environment: Selected Topics of the International Conference on Port & Ocean Engineering under Arctic Conditions, Third, Fairbanks, Alaska, August 11-15, 1975. International Conference on Port & Ocean Engineering under Artic Conditions Staff. Ed. by D. W. Hood & D. C. Burrell. LC 75-43209. (Occasional Studies: No. 4). (Illus.). 468p. 1976. 3.00 (*0-914500-07-4*) U of AK Inst Marine.

Assessment of the Carcinogenicity & Mutagenicity of Chemicals: Proceedings of the WHO Scientific Group, Geneva, 1972. WHO Staff. (Technical Report Ser.: No. 546). 1974. pap. 1.60 (*92-4-120546-6*) World Health.

Assessment of the Economic Impacts of California's Drought on Urban Areas: A Research Agenda. Nancy Y. Moore et al. LC 93-42318. 1993. write for info. (*0-8330-1489-7*, MR-251-CUWA) Rand Corp.

Assessment of the Effect in EC Member States of Implementation of Policy CO2 Red. 177p. 1994. pap. 45.00 (*92-826-6505-4*, CR-80-93-072-EN, Pub. by Europ Com) UNIPUB.

***Assessment of the Effectiveness of Derelict Land Grant in Reclaiming Land for Development.** HMSO Staff. 96p. 1994. pap. 40.00 (*0-11-752923-0*, HM29230, Pub. by HMSO UK) UNIPUB.

Assessment of the elections in Cameroon October 11, 1992. National Democratic Institute for International Affairs Staff. 260p. (ENG & FRE.). 1993. pap. 9.95 (*1-880134-19-5*) Natl Demo Inst.

Assessment of the Human Stress Response. George S. Everly, Jr. & Steven A. Sobelman. LC 86-47604. (Stress in Modern Society Ser.: No. 4). 1987. 32.50 (*0-404-63254-8*) AMS Pr.

Assessment of the Impact of Measures & Activities Accomplished During the International Youth Year: Participation, Development, Peace, 1985. 43p. 1987. pap. 6.00 (*92-1-130125-4*, E.87.IV.5) UN.

Assessment of the Judicial Customs of Nepal. Kaisher Bahadur KC. 303p. 1957. 10.00 (*0-318-12867-5*, 22) Am-Nepal Ed.

Assessment of the Juvenile Justice System in Philadelphia, 4 vols., Vol. I. National Center for State Courts Staff. 276p. 1984. 17.00 (*0-685-15037-2*, NERO-142) Natl Ctr St Courts.

Assessment of the Juvenile Justice System in Philadelphia, 4 vols., Vol. II. National Center for State Courts Staff. 41p. 1984. 3.00 (*0-685-15038-0*, NERO-143) Natl Ctr St Courts.

Assessment of the Juvenile Justice System in Philadelphia, 4 vols., Vol. III. National Center for State Courts Staff. 566p. 1984. 34.00 (*0-685-15039-9*, NERO-144) Natl Ctr St Courts.

***Assessment of the Lower Limb.** Ed. by Linda M. Merriman & David R. Tollafield. LC 94-44955. 1995. write for info. (*0-443-05030-9*) Churchill.

Assessment of the Massachusetts Motor Vehicle Tort Litigation Case Evaluation Program. Robert Lowe & Linda Walker. 61p. 1992. 4.00 (*0-685-55349-3*, NERO255) Natl Ctr St Courts.

Assessment of the Natural Gas Resource Base of the United States. R. J. Finley et al. (Illus.). 69p. 1988. 4.00 (*0-317-03114-7*, RI 179) Bur Econ Geology.

An Asterisk (*) at the beginning of an entry indicates that the title is appearing in BIP for the first time.

A

Assessment of the Newborn. Mohsen Ziai et al. 425p. 1983. text ed. 61.00 (0-318-37136-7) Little.

Assessment of the NIH Women's Health Initiative. Institute of Medicine, Food & Nutrition Board & Board on Health Sciences Policy staff. Ed. by Susan Thaul & Dana Hoftra. 160p. (Orig.). 1993. pap. text ed. 25.00 (0-309-04989-X) Natl Acad Pr.

Assessment of the Nutritional Status of the Community. D. B. Jelliffe. (Monograph Ser.: No. 53). (Illus.). 271p. (ENG, FRE, RUS & SPA.). 1966. 18.80 (92-4-140053-6) World Health.

Assessment of the Oil & Gas Potential of the Washington Outer Continental Shelf. Stephen P. Palmer & William S. Lingley, Jr. (Washington State & Offshore Oil & Gas Ser.). (Illus.). 88p. (Orig.). 1989. pap. 45.00 (0-934539-09-X, WSG89-2) Wash Sea Grant.

Assessment of the Performance of Automatic Sprinkler Systems. J. Kenneth Richardson. 1984. 4.35 (0-318-03819-6, TR84-2) Society Fire Protect.

Assessment of the Possible Health Effects of the Ground Wave Emergency Network. National Research Council, Commission on Life Sciences Staff. 180p. (Orig.). (C). 1993. pap. text ed. 33.00 (0-309-04777-3) Natl Acad Pr.

Assessment of the Primary Health Care Needs of North & South Omaha. Genevieve Burch. 159p. (Orig.). 1981. pap. 10.50 (1-55719-046-1) U NE CPAR.

Assessment of the Private Sector: A Case Study & Its Methodological Implications. Samuel Paul. (Discussion Paper Ser.: No. 93). 114p. 1990. 7.95 (0-8213-1597-8, 11597) World Bank.

Assessment of the Senegalese Electoral Code. National Democratic Institute for International Affairs Staff. 140p. (ENG & FRE.). 1991. pap. 6.00 (1-880134-07-1) Natl Demo Inst.

Assessment of the State-of-the-Art for Process Monitoring Sensors for Polymer Composites. Donald Hunston et al. (Illus.). 141p. (Orig.). (C). 1992. pap. text ed. 45.00 (0-941375-98-6) Diane Pub.

Assessment of the U. S. Outer Continental Shelf Environmental Studies Program, No. 3: Social & Economic Studies. National Research Council, Committee to Review the Outer Continental Shelf Environmental Studies Program Staff. LC 89-63847. 164p. (Orig.). (C). 1993. pap. text ed. 30.00 (0-309-04835-4) Natl Acad Pr.

Assessment of the U. S. Outer Continental Shelf Environmental Studies Program, Vol. 1: Physical Oceanography. National Research Council Staff. LC 89-63847. 153p. reprint ed. pap. 43.70 (0-7837-5037-4, 2044713) Bks Demand.

Assessment of the U. S. Outer Continental Shelf Environmental Studies Program, Vol. 2: Ecology. National Research Council Staff. 162p. 1992. pap. 21.00 (0-309-04598-3) Natl Acad Pr.

***Assessment of the Use of Single Cytochrome P450 Enzymes in Drug Research.** Ed. by M. R. Waterman & M. Hildebrand. LC 94-43228. (Ernst Schering Research Foundation Workshop Ser.: Vol. 13). (Illus.). 239p. 1994. text ed. 56.00 (0-387-58343-2) Spr-Verlag.

Assessment of Threatened Plants of India. S. K. Jain. (C). 1988. text ed. 40.00 (0-685-44245-4, Scientific) St Mut.

Assessment of Toxic Agents at the Workplace. Ed. by A. Berlin. 660p. 1983. lib. bdg. 249.00 (0-89838-613-6) Kluwer Ac.

Assessment of Tumor Response. B. W. Hancock. 1982. lib. bdg. 107.50 (90-247-2712-X) Kluwer Ac.

Assessment of United States Competitiveness in High Technology Industries. 1991. lib. bdg. 75.00 (0-8490-4389-1) Gordon Pr.

Assessment of Urinary Sediment by Electron Microscopy: Applications in Renal Disease. Anil K. Mandal. LC 87-14153. 284p. 1987. 69.50 (0-306-42521-1, Plenum Pr) Plenum.

Assessment of Variation in Scampania Nemorosa & Selected Related Species (Hepatophyta) Douglas R. Zehr. (Bryophytorum Bibliotheca Ser.: No. 15). (Illus.). 140p. 1980. pap. 24.00 (3-7682-1282-3) Lubrecht & Cramer.

Assessment of Ventricular Function. Ed. by D. H. Spodick. (Advances in Cardiology Ser.: Vol. 32). (Illus.). vi, 154p. 1985. 101.00 (3-8055-3993-2) S Karger.

Assessment of Vulnerable Groups in Mongolia: Strategies for Social Policy Planning. Caroline Harper. LC 93-44826. (Discussion Paper Ser.: No. 229). 88p. 1994. write for info. (0-8213-2748-8) World Bank.

Assessment of Young Developmentally Disabled Children. Ed. by Theodore D. Wachs & R. Sheehan. LC 88-2966. (Perspectives in Developmental Psychology Ser.). (Illus.). 438p. 1988. 59.50 (0-306-42733-8, Plenum Pr) Plenum.

Assessment, Placement, & Programming of Bilingual Exceptional Pupils: A Practical Approach. Maximino Plata. 54p. 1982. pap. 9.10 (0-86586-136-6, R259) Coun Exc Child.

Assessment Problems in Reading. Ed. by Walter H. MacGinitie. LC 73-84793. 107p. reprint ed. pap. 30.50 (0-8357-5809-5, 2026814) Bks Demand.

***Assessment Standards for School Mathematics.** National Council of Teachers of Mathematics Staff. LC 95-17267. (Illus.). 102p. (Orig.). 1995. pap. write for info. (0-87353-419-0) NCTM.

Assessment Strategies for Cognitive-Behavioral Intervention. Ed. by P. C. Kendall & Steven D. Hollon. 1980. text ed. 54.00 (0-12-404460-3) Acad Pr.

Assessment Techniques in Special Education. John Venn. LC 93-17272. (Illus.). 576p. (C). 1994. text ed. write for info. (0-675-21159-X, Merrill Pub Co) Macmillan.

***Assessment, Testing & Evaluation in Teacher Education.** Susan M. Brookhart et al. Ed. by Suzanne W. Soled. (Social & Policy Issues in Education Ser.). 1995. write for info. (1-56750-153-2); pap. write for info. (1-56750-154-0) Ablex Pub.

Assessment Testing in the Primary School. C. Connor. 1990. 70.00 (1-85000-551-6, Falmer Pr); pap. 33.00 (1-85000-552-4, Falmer Pr) Taylor & Francis.

Assessment Tools: For Practitioners, Managers, & Trainers. Armand Lauffer. LC 82-10552. (Sage Human Services Guides Ser.: No. 30). 192p. reprint ed. pap. 54.80 (0-7837-6576-2, 2046141) Bks Demand.

Assessment Tools for Recreational Therapy: Red Book, No. 1. Joan Burlingame & Tom Blaschko. 306p. (C). 1993. reprint ed. 40.00 (1-882883-02-0) Idyll Arbor.

Assessment Tools for Recreational Therapy, No. 1: Red Book. Joan Burlingame & Thomas M. Blaschko. (Illus.). 306p. 1990. text ed. 40.00 (0-939116-28-6) Frontier OR.

Assessment with Projective Techniques: A Concise Introduction. Albert Rabin. LC 80-26229. 352p. 1981. 35.95 (0-8261-3550-1) Springer Pub.

Assessments & Decisions: A Study of Information Gathering by Hermit Crabs. R. Elwood & S. Neil. (Studies in Behavioural Adaptation Ser.). 200p. (C). 1992. text ed. 69.95 (0-412-39110-4, A6081) Chapman & Hall.

***Assessments of Sex Offenders by Measures of Erectile Response: Psychometric Properties & Decision Making.** rev. ed. William D. Murphy & Howard E. Barbaree. 90p. (C). Date not set. pap. text ed. 10.00 (1-884444-14-8) Safer Soc.

Assessor. Jack Rudman. (Career Examination Ser.: C-20). 1994. pap. 23.95 (0-8373-0020-7) Nat Learn.

Assessor Training Manual for Public Sector Assessment Centers. 2nd ed. Patrick T. Maher. LC 93-84900. 225p. (C). 1993. text ed. 99.95 (0-943865-00-X); pap. text ed. 59.95 (0-943865-01-8) Persnl & Org Dev.

Asset Accumulation & Economic Activity: Reflections on Contemporary Macroeconomic Theory. James Tobin. LC 80-12844. (Illus.). xvi, 100p. 1982. pap. text ed. 5.95 (0-226-80502-6) U Ch Pr.

Asset Allocation: Balancing Financial Risk. Roger C. Gibson. 220p. 1989. text ed. 45.00 (1-55623-164-4) Irwin Prof Pubng.

***Asset Allocation & Financial Market Timing: Techniques for Investment Professionals.** Carroll D. Aby & Donald E. Vaughn. LC 94-45275. 376p. 1995. text ed. 69.50 (0-89930-761-2, Quorum Bks) Greenwood.

Asset Allocation for Institutional Portfolios. Mark P. Kritzman. 352p. 1990. text ed. 50.00 (1-55623-163-6) Irwin Prof Pubng.

Asset & Liability Management by Banks. OECD Staff. (Trends in Banking Structure & Regulation in OECD Countries Ser.). 176p. (Orig.). 1987. pap. 20.00 (92-64-13009-8) OECD.

Asset & Liability Management for Savings Institutions. Institute of Financial Education Staff. 1989. 47.95 (0-912857-50-1) Inst Finan Educ.

Asset Appreciation: Business Income & Price-Level Accounting, 1918-1935 - an Original Anthology. Stephen A. Zeff. LC 75-18487. (History of Accounting Ser.). (Illus.). 1980. reprint ed. 34.95 (0-405-07569-3) Ayer.

Asset-Based Financing: A Transactional Guide, 4 vols. Howard Ruda. LC 84-72027. 1985. ring bd. write for info. (0-8205-1059-9) Bender.

Asset-Based Lending. Intro. by Charlotte Weisman. (Special Collection from the Journal of Commercial Bank Lending). (Illus.). 120p. (Orig.). 1988. pap. text ed. 37.00 (0-936742-53-4, 36035) Robt Morris Assocs.

Asset-Based Lending: A Practical Guide to Secured Financing. 2nd ed. Peter H. Weil. 750p. 1992. 125.00 (0-685-69382-1) PLI.

Asset-Based Lending: An Introductory Guide to Secured Financing. Peter H. Weil. 783p. 1989. text ed. 25.00 (0-685-45802-4, A1-1410) PLI.

Asset-Based Lending: Commercial Finance & Acquisition Financing. (Commercial Law & Practice Ser.). 548p. 1992. pap. text ed. 70.00 (0-685-56860-1, A4-4360) PLI.

***Asset Based Lending: The Complete Guide to Originating, Evaluating & Managing Asset-Based Loans.** Peter S. Clarke. 350p. 1995. 60.00 (1-55738-754-0) Probus Pub Co.

Asset-Based Lending 1993 Including Commercial Finance & Acquisition Financing. (Commercial Law & Practice Course Handbook Ser.: Vol. 646). 549p. 1993. 70.00 (0-685-69702-9, A4-4412) PLI.

Asset Demands & Interest Rate Setting Equations in Imperfect Markets. C. J. Green. (Bank of England. Discussion Papers. Technical Ser.: No. 10). 23p. reprint ed. pap. 25.00 (0-8357-5810-9, 2031767) Bks Demand.

Asset Financial Set. Donald Rice. 1990. 145.00 (0-316-74311-9) Little.

Asset Financing. Michael D. Rice. 770p. 1989. 145.00 (0-316-74313-5) Little.

Asset Forfeiture Practice & Procedure: A Digest of Case Law. Judith E. Secher. 1994. 195.00 (0-379-21204-8) Oceana.

Asset Management. (Journal Reprint Ser.). 9.95 (0-944298-23-0, 861) Inst Real Estate.

Asset Management. reprint ed. 9.95 (0-685-71666-X, 861) Inst Real Estate.

***Asset Management: CEBS Study Manual - Course VII.** 2nd ed. Ed. by Glenn L. Wood. 321p. 1994. pap. 65.00 (0-89154-484-4) Intl Found Employ.

Asset Markets & Exchange Rates: Modeling an Open Economy. abr. ed. Polly R. Allen & Peter B. Kenen. LC 79-16874. 352p. 1983. pap. 29.95 (0-521-27406-0) Cambridge U Pr.

Asset Markets, Exchange Rates, & Economic Integration. Polly R. Allen & Peter B. Kenen. LC 79-16874. (Illus.). 1980. 105.00 (0-521-22982-0) Cambridge U Pr.

Asset Plays: Profiting from Undervalued Stock. New York Institute of Finance Staff. 1988. 29.95 (0-317-03938-5) NY Inst Finance.

Asset Plays: Profiting from Undervalued Stocks. New York Institute of Finance Staff. 1988. 24.95 (0-13-049819-X) P-H.

***Asset Protection: Domestic & International Law & Tactics.** Ed. by Duncan E. Osborne. LC 95-8267. 1995. write for info. (0-615-00663-9) Clark Boardman Callaghan.

Asset Protection: Legal & Estate Planning. Peter Spero. 1993. ring bd. 125.00 (0-685-69654-5, APLP) Warren Gorham & Lamont.

Asset Protection Secrets. Arnold S. Goldstein. Ed. by Mark T. Lauer. 332p. (Orig.). 1993. 39.95 (1-880539-50-0); pap. 29.95 (1-880539-00-4) Garrett FL.

Asset Protection Strategies: Tax & Legal Aspects. Lewis D. Solomon & Lewis J. Saret. LC 93-24353. (Business Practice Library). 1993. text ed. 128.00 (0-471-59266-8) Wiley.

Asset Securitization: International Finance & Legal Perspectives. Ed. by Joseph Norton & Paul Spellman. 350p. 1991. 74.95 (0-631-17808-2) Blackwell Pubs.

Asset Securitization: Principles & Practice. Ed. by David M. Morris. 1990. pap. 75.00 (1-55840-441-4) Exec Ent Pubns.

***Asset Securitization: Principles & Practice.** Ed. by David M. Morris. 1994. pap. text ed. 75.00 (0-471-11236-4) Wiley.

ASSET Test (Assessing Semantic Skills Through Everyday Themes) Mark Barrett et al. 1988. 64.95 (1-55999-017-1); 36.00 (1-55999-018-X) LinguiSystems.

Asset Valuation, 2 vols. McGraw-Hill Staff Shepard's. 1991. 150.00 (0-07-172326-9) McGraw.

Asset Valuation & Income Determination: A Consideration of the Alternatives. Ed. by Robert R. Sterling. LC 73-160580. 1971. text ed. 20.00 (0-914348-11-6) Scholars Bk.

Assets Analyst. Jack Rudman. (Career Examination Ser.: C-1851). 1994. pap. 27.95 (0-8373-1851-3) Nat Learn.

Assets & the Poor: A New American Welfare Policy. Michael Sherraden. LC 90-42236. 336p. 1991. pap. text ed. 20.95 (1-56324-066-1) M E Sharpe.

***Assets Unknown: How to Find Money You Didn't Know You Had.** David W. Folsom. 446p. (Orig.). 1994. write for info. (0-9641164-0-5) Fmly Values.

A--hole No More! Xavier Crement. 192p. 1990. pap. 11.95 (0-89804-804-4, Enthea Pr) Ariel GA.

A--holes Forever. Xavier Crement. 192p. 1992. pap. 11.95 (0-89804-807-9, Enthea Pr) Ariel GA.

A--holes: The People Who Make Life Hell. Roy Engstrom & Gary Engstrom. LC 92-90745. (Illus.). 144p. (Orig.). 1992. pap. 9.95 (0-9632620-5-X) Two Arts Pub.

ASSIA Thesaurus. 120p. 1991. 90.00 (1-85739-080-6) Bowker-Saur.

Assignation. Joyce Carol Oates. 221p. (C). 1988. 16.95 (0-88001-200-5) Ecco Pr.

Assignation. Joyce Carol Oates. LC 89-45126. 208p. 1989. reprint ed. pap. 7.95 (0-06-097246-7, PL 7246, PL) HarpC.

***Assigning Economic Value to Natural Resources.** National Research Council Commission on Natural Resources. 196p. (Orig.). (C). 1994. pap. text ed. 29.00 (0-309-05143-6) Natl Acad Pr.

Assigning Liability for Superfund Cleanups: An Analysis of Policy Options. Katherine N. Probst & Paul R. Portney. 62p. 1992. pap. text ed. 15.00 (0-915707-64-0) Resources Future.

***Assigning, Responding, Evaluation.** 3rd ed. John O. White. 192p. (C). 1995. pap. text ed. 15.96 (0-312-10217-8) St Martin.

Assigning Work. Didactic Systems Staff. (Simulation Game Ser.). 1973. pap. 26.25 (0-89401-006-9); pap. 21.50 (0-685-78097-X); pap. 35.00 (0-89401-096-4) Didactic Syst.

Assignment: Or on the Observing of the Observer of the Observers. Friedrich Durrenmatt. Tr. by Joel Agee. (International Ser.). 1989. pap. 7.95 (0-679-72233-5, Vin) Random.

***Assignment: Oswald.** James P. Hosty. 288p. 1995. 24.95 (1-55970-311-3) Arcade Pub Inc.

Assignment--Black Gold. Edward S. Aarons. (Assignment Ser.). 192p. (Orig.). 1980. pap. 1.95 (0-449-13354-0, GM) Fawcett.

Assignment--Ceylon. Edward S. Aarons. (Assignment Ser.). 208p. 1981. pap. 1.95 (0-449-13583-7, GM) Fawcett.

Assignment--the Girl in the Gondola. Edward S. Aarons. (Assignment Ser.). 1979. pap. 1.75 (0-449-14165-9, GM) Fawcett.

Assignment--Thirteenth Princess. Will B. Aarons. 1979. pap. 1.75 (0-449-13919-0, GM) Fawcett.

Assignment Andalusia. large type ed. Philip McCutchan. (Dales Mystery Ser.). 297p. 1993. pap. 16.95 (1-85389-388-9, Dales) Ulverscroft.

Assignment Burma. Lee O. Miller. 240p. 1986. reprint ed. pap. 2.95 (0-8439-2408-X) Dorchester Pub Co.

***Assignment Fenland.** large type ed. Philip McCutchan. (Dales Large Print Ser.). 1994. pap. 16.95 (1-85389-509-1, Pub. by Magna Print Bks) Ulverscroft.

Assignment Gaolbreak. Philip McCutchan. 240p. 1994. pap. 16.95 (1-85389-474-5, Dales) Ulverscroft.

Assignment in Brittany. Helen MacInnes. LC 42-17993. 1971. 24.95 (0-15-109620-1) HarBrace.

Assignment in Eternity. Robert A. Heinlein. 288p. 1987. mass mkt. 4.99 (0-671-65350-4) Baen Bks.

Assignment in Kashmir. Aamir Ali. (Orient Paperbacks Ser.). 200p. 1973. pap. 2.95 (0-88253-246-4) Ind-US Inc.

Assignment in Utopia. Eugene Lyons. 290p. (C). 1990. pap. 24.95 (0-88738-856-6) Transaction Pubs.

Assignment in Utopia. Eugene Lyons. LC 76-110271. 658p. 1971. reprint ed. text ed. 85.00 (0-8371-4497-3, LYAU, Greenwood Pr) Greenwood.

Assignment Jonesville: A News Reporting Workbook. 2nd ed. Nicholas N. Plasterer. xii, 210p. (C). 1971. pap. text ed. 12.95 (0-8071-0037-4) La State U Pr.

Assignment London. large type ed. Philip McCutchan. (Dales Ser.). 325p. 1994. pap. 16.95 (1-85389-432-X, Dales) Ulverscroft.

Assignment Maltese Maiden. large type ed. Edward S. Aarons. (Adventure Travel Guide Ser.). 368p. 1992. 21.95 (0-7089-2618-5) Ulverscroft.

Assignment Manchurian Doll. Edward S. Aarons. (Assignment Ser.). 1979. pap. 1.75 (0-449-13449-0, GM) Fawcett.

Assignment Methods in Combinational Data Analysis. Hubert. (Statistics: Vol. 73). 344p. 1987. 125.00 (0-8247-7617-8) Dekker.

***Assignment of the Glass Transition, STP 1249.** Ed. by Rickey J. Seyler. LC 94-27245. (Special Technical Publication Ser.: Vol. 1249). (Illus.). 314p. 1994. text ed. 75.00 (0-8031-1995-X, 04-012490-50) ASTM.

Assignment Palermo. large type ed. Edward S. Aarons. 1989. pap. 11.95 (0-7089-6741-8, Linford) Ulverscroft.

Assignment: Pentagon: The Insider's Guide to the Potomac Puzzle Palace. rev. ed. Perry M. Smith. (Association of the U. S. Army Book Ser.). 286p. 1993. pap. 16.00 (0-02-881017-1) Brasseys Inc.

Assignment: Pentagon: The Insider's Guide to the Potomac Puzzle Palace. 2nd rev. ed. Perry M. Smith. (Association of the U. S. Army Book Ser.). 286p. 1993. 30.00 (0-02-881018-X) Brasseys Inc.

***Assignment: Pentagon: The Insider's Guide to the Potomac Puzzle Palace.** 3rd rev. ed. P. Smith, III. (Association of the U. S. Army Book Ser.). 298p. 1997. 28.00 (1-57488-008-X) Brasseys Inc.

***Assignment: Pentagon: The Insider's Guide to the Potomac Puzzle Palace.** 3rd rev. ed. P Smith, III. (Association of the U. S. Army Book Ser.). 298p. 1997. pap. 16.00 (1-57488-009-8) Brasseys Inc.

Assignment Photography. American Society of Magazine Photography Staff. Ed. by David Halsey. 40p. 1991. pap. 14.00 (0-9605474-0-1) Am Soc Media.

Assignment Problems in Parallel & Distributed Computing. Shahid H. Bokhari. (C). 1987. lib. bdg. 56.00 (0-89838-240-8) Kluwer Ac.

Assignment Rescue: An Autobiography. Varian Fry. (YA). (gr. 7 up). 1993. pap. 3.50 (0-590-46970-3) Scholastic Inc.

Assignment to Disaster. large type ed. Edward S. Aarons. (Linford Mystery Library). 368p. 1993. pap. 14.95 (0-7089-7429-5, Linford) Ulverscroft.

Assignment: Tokyo. Gladys H. Hunter. 234p. (Orig.). 1980. 9.95 (0-931290-33-3) Nettleton Hse.

Assignment Washington II, Military Atlas, Maps & Charts of Washington Area Military Installations. William R. Crawford & Lela A. Crawford. (Illus.). 1992. 5.95 (0-914862-29-4) Military Marketing.

Assignments & Authorities: A Supplement for Legal Writing. 2nd ed. Deborah J. Klein. 136p. 1991. spiral bd. 12.95 (0-8403-6989-1) Kendall-Hunt.

Assignments, Arrangements & Compositions by Debtors with Precedents. 2nd ed. T. Irlicht. 1986. Australia. 65.00 (0-409-49065-2) Butterworth Legal Pubs.

Assignments in Applied Statistics. Ed. by Simon Conrad. 1989. text ed. 115.00 (0-471-92281-1) Wiley.

Assignments in Exposition. 11th enl. rev. ed. Clement Dunbar et al. LC 93-26540. (C). 1993. text ed. 25.00 (0-06-501273-9) HarpCollege.

Assignments in Trial Practice. 5th ed. Joseph Howe & Walker J. Blakey. 350p. 1986. 29.00 (0-316-37576-4) Little.

***Assignments to Fundamentals of Legal Research, Sixth Edition & Legal Research Illustrated, Sixth Edition.** J. Myron Jacobstein & Ray M. Mersky. Ed. by Donald J. Dunn. (University Textbook Ser.). 426p. 1994. teacher ed, pap. text ed. write for info. (1-56662-198-4) Foundation Pr.

***Assignments to Fundamentals of Legal Research, Sixth Edition & Legal Research Illustrated, Sixth Edition.** J. Myron Jacobstein & Roy M. Mersky. Ed. by Donald J. Dunn. (University Textbook Ser.). 221p. 1994. pap. text ed. 12.50 (1-56662-197-6) Foundation Pr.

Assimilate Partitioning & Carbohydrate Metal in Potato. Davies. 1995. write for info. (0-8493-6915-0) CRC Pr.

Assimilate Transport in Plants. A. L. Kursanov. 1984. 302.00 (0-444-80508-7, I-195-84) Elsevier.

Assimilating New Members. Lyle E. Schaller. LC 77-18037. (Creative Leadership Ser.). 1978. pap. 10.95 (0-687-01938-9) Abingdon.

Assimilation: The Ideal & the Reality. Brent A. Nelson. 27p. 1987. pap. 3.00 (0-936247-07-X) Amer Immigration.

Assimilation Acculturation, & Social Mobility. George Pozzetta. (Immigration & Ethnicity Ser.: Vol. 13). 368p. 1991. reprint ed. 61.00 (0-8240-7413-0) Garland.

Assimilation & Assertion: The Response to the Holocaust in Mordecai Richler's Writing. Rachel F. Brenner. (American University Studies: General Literature: Ser. XIX, Vol. 19). 219p. (C). 1989. text ed. 35.20 (0-8204-0811-5) P Lang Pubs.

Assimilation & Community: The Jews in Nineteenth-Century Europe. Ed. by Jonathan Frankel & Steven J. Zipperstein. (Illus.). 352p. (C). 1991. 54.95 (0-521-40284-0) Cambridge U Pr.

***Assimilation & Its Discontents.** Barry M. Rubin. LC 94-30991. 1995. 25.00 (0-8129-2293-X, Times Bks) Random.

An Asterisk (*) at the beginning of an entry indicates that the title is appearing in BIP for the first time.

Assimilation Blues: Black Families in a White Community. Beverly D. Tatum. LC 87-241. (Contributions in Afro-American & African Studies: No. 108). 128p. 1987. text ed. 45.00 (*0-313-25872-4*, TMB/, Greenwood Pr) Greenwood.

Assimilation Blues: Black Families in a White Community. Beverly D. Tatum. LC 87-241. 152p. (C). 1992. reprint ed. pap. text ed. 12.95 (*0-9632146-2-4*) Hazel-Maxwell.

Assimilation in American Life: The Role of Race, Religion & National Origins. Milton M. Gordon. 1964. pap. 15.95 (*0-19-500896-0*) OUP.

Assimilation of American Family Patterns by European Immigrants & Their Children. Alan E. Bayer. Ed. by Francesco Cordasco. LC 80-839. (American Ethnic Groups Ser.). 1981. lib. bdg. 19.95 (*0-405-13403-7*) Ayer.

Assimilation of Buddhism in Korea: Religious Maturity & Innovation in the Silla Dynasty. L. Lancaster & C. S. Yu. LC 87-71274. 264p. (C). 1991. text ed. 45.00 (*0-89581-878-7*, Asian Human Pr) Jain Pub Co.

Assimilation of Buddhism in Korea: Religious Maturity & Innovation in the Silla Dynasty. L. Lancaster & C. S. Yu. LC 87-71274. (Studies in Korean Religions & Culture: Vol. 4). 264p. (C). 1991. pap. text ed. 20.00 (*0-89581-889-2*, Asian Human Pr) Jain Pub Co.

Assimilation of Experience of Five American White Ethnic Novelists of the Twentieth Century. Betty A. Burch. LC 90-39828. (European Immigrants & American Society Ser.). 272p. 1990. reprint ed. 20.00 (*0-8240-7423-8*) Garland.

Assimilation of Leah Wennover. Stephanie T. Hoppe. 64p. (Orig.). 1993. pap. 6.95 (*0-9634514-2-1*) Evoe Pr.

Assimilation of the Italian Immigrant: An Original Anthology. John F. Carr & Sarah G. Pomeray. LC 74-17919. (Italian American Experience Ser.). (Illus.). 332p. 1975. reprint ed. 12.95 (*0-405-06392-X*) Ayer.

Assimilation of Yugoslavs in Franklin County, Ohio. Walter V. Babics. LC 73-155330. 1972. reprint ed. pap. 8.00 (*0-686-61035-0*) Ragusan Pr.

Assimilation vs. Separation: Joseph the Administrator & the Politics of Religion in Biblical Israel. Aaron Wildavsky. LC 92-20151. 475p. (C). 1992. 34.95 (*1-56000-081-3*) Transaction Pubs.

Assimlation in America: Theory & Reality. Milton M. Gordon. (Reprint Series in Social Sciences). (C). 1993. reprint ed. pap. text ed. 1.90 (*0-8290-2673-8*, S-407) Irvington.

Assiniboine. Robert H. Lowie. LC 74-7978. reprint ed. 22.45 (*0-404-11868-2*) AMS Pr.

Assisi Embroidery. Eva M. Leszner. (Illus.). 1988. 13.50 (*0-7134-5595-0*) Branford.

Assisi Embroidery. Pamela M. Ness. (Illus.). 1978. pap. 3.50 (*0-486-23743-5*) Dover.

Assisi Murders. Timothy Holme. 1988. 16.95 (*0-8027-5721-9*) Walker & Co.

Assisi Murders. large type ed. Timothy Holme. 368p. 1988. 15.95 (*0-7089-1848-4*) Ulverscroft.

Assisi Problem & the Art of Giotto. Alastair Smart. LC 81-81724. (Illus.). 310p. 1983. reprint ed. lib. bdg. 85.00 (*0-87817-283-1*) Hacker.

Assistance & Benefits Information Directory: A Guide to Programs & Printed Materials Describing Assistance Programs, Benefits, & Services Offered to Individuals by Federal & State Agencies, National Associations, & Other Organizations, 2 vols., Set. Kay Gill & Mary Emanoil. 1000p. 1992. lib. bdg. 190.00 (*1-55888-797-0*) Omnigraphics Inc.

Assistance & Benefits Information Directory, Publications: A Guide to Programs & Printed Materials Describing Assistance Programs, Benefits, & Services Offered to Individuals by Federal & State Agencies, National Associations, & Other Organizations, Vol. 2. Mary Emanoil. 200p. 1992. lib. bdg. 95.00 (*1-55888-756-3*) Omnigraphics Inc.

Assistance & Benefits Programs Directory: A Guide to Federal, State, & Organizational Programs, Public & Private, Providing Financial Assistance & Special Services to Individuals Covering the Fields of Cultural Affairs; Education; Employment, Labor, & Training; Housing & Home Energy; Law, Justice, & Legal Services; & Health & Social Services, Vol. 1: Programs. Kay Gill. 750p. 1992. lib. bdg. 125.00 (*1-55888-423-8*) Omnigraphics Inc.

Assistance Dogs: In Special Service. Elizabeth Ring. LC 93-735. (Good Dogs! Ser.). (Illus.). 32p. (J). (gr. 2-4). 1993. lib. bdg. 13.90 (*1-56294-290-5*) Millbrook Pr.

Assistance of Vice. Roslyn Dane. 168p. (Orig.). 1989. pap. 8.95 (*0-934411-19-0*, Banned Bks) Edward-William Austin.

***Assistance Strategies to Reduce Poverty.** 1991. 7.95 (*0-8213-1920-5*, 11920) World Bank.

Assistant. Bernard Malamud. 304p. 1980. mass mkt. 4.95 (*0-380-51474-5*, Bard) Avon.

Assistant. Bernard Malamud. 304p. 1993. pap. 10.00 (*0-380-72085-X*) Avon.

Assistant. Bernard Malamud. 1980. mass mkt. 4.95 (*0-380-68338-5*) Avon.

Assistant: New Tasks, New Opportunities. Elizabeth R. Murphy. LC 81-69370. 191p. reprint ed. pap. 54.50 (*0-8357-5811-7*, 2023532) Bks Demand.

Assistant Accountant. Jack Rudman. (Career Examination Ser.: C-21). 1994. pap. 23.95 (*0-8373-0021-5*) Nat Learn.

Assistant Accountant-Auditor. Jack Rudman. (Career Examination Ser.: C-2077). 1994. pap. 27.95 (*0-8373-2077-1*) Nat Learn.

Assistant Actuary. Jack Rudman. (Career Examination Ser.: C-22). 1994. pap. 34.95 (*0-8373-0022-3*) Nat Learn.

Assistant Administrative Director. Jack Rudman. (Teachers License Examination Ser.: S-12). 1994. pap. 39.95 (*0-8373-8112-6*) Nat Learn.

Assistant Administrator. Jack Rudman. (Career Examination Ser.: C-1093). 1994. pap. 27.95 (*0-8373-1093-8*) Nat Learn.

Assistant Air Pollution Control Engineer. Jack Rudman. (Career Examination Ser.: C-1094). 1994. pap. 27.95 (*0-8373-1094-6*) Nat Learn.

Assistant Architect. Jack Rudman. (Career Examination Ser.: C-77). 1994. pap. 29.95 (*0-8373-0077-0*) Nat Learn.

Assistant Architectural Draftsman. Jack Rudman. (Career Examination Ser.: C-1095). 1994. pap. 23.95 (*0-8373-1095-4*) Nat Learn.

Assistant Area Manager. Jack Rudman. (Career Examination Ser.: C-1096). 1994. pap. 29.95 (*0-8373-1096-2*) Nat Learn.

Assistant Area Manager of School Maintenance. Jack Rudman. (Career Exam Ser.: No. C-3523). 1994. 29.95 (*0-8373-3523-X*) Nat Learn.

Assistant Area Services Coordinator. Jack Rudman. (Career Examination Ser.: C-78). 1994. pap. 29.95 (*0-8373-0078-9*) Nat Learn.

Assistant Assessor. Jack Rudman. (Career Examination Ser.: C-23). 1994. pap. 23.95 (*0-8373-0023-1*) Nat Learn.

Assistant Attorney. Jack Rudman. (Career Examination Ser.: C-24). 1994. pap. 34.95 (*0-8373-0024-X*) Nat Learn.

Assistant Automotive Shop Supervisor. Jack Rudman. (Career Examination Ser.: C-529). 1994. pap. 27.95 (*0-8373-0529-2*) Nat Learn.

Assistant Bacteriologist. Jack Rudman. (Career Examination Ser.: C-25). 1994. pap. 27.95 (*0-8373-0025-8*) Nat Learn.

Assistant Bridge & Tunnel Maintainer. Jack Rudman. (Career Examination Ser.: C-27). 1994. pap. 23.95 (*0-8373-0027-4*) Nat Learn.

Assistant Bridge Operator. Jack Rudman. (Career Examination Ser.: C-26). 1994. pap. 23.95 (*0-8373-0026-6*) Nat Learn.

Assistant Bridge Operator Trainee. Jack Rudman. (Career Examination Ser.: C-79). 1994. pap. 19.95 (*0-8373-0079-7*) Nat Learn.

Assistant Budget Analyst. Jack Rudman. (Career Examination Ser.: C-1736). 1994. pap. 29.95 (*0-8373-1736-3*) Nat Learn.

Assistant Budget Director. Jack Rudman. (Career Examination Ser.: C-2991). 1994. pap. 39.95 (*0-8373-2991-4*) Nat Learn.

Assistant Budget Examiner. Jack Rudman. (Career Examination Ser.: C-28). 1994. pap. 29.95 (*0-8373-0028-2*) Nat Learn.

Assistant Building Construction Engineer. Jack Rudman. (Career Examination Ser.: C-3169). 1994. pap. 29.95 (*0-8373-3169-2*) Nat Learn.

Assistant Building Custodian. Jack Rudman. (Career Examination Ser.: C-66). 1994. pap. 23.95 (*0-8373-0066-5*) Nat Learn.

Assistant Building Electrical Engineer. Jack Rudman. (Career Examination Ser.: C-1909). 1994. pap. 29.95 (*0-8373-1909-9*) Nat Learn.

Assistant Building Inspector. (Career Examination Ser.: C-3382). 1994. pap. 29.95 (*0-8373-3382-2*) Nat Learn.

Assistant Building Mechanical Engineer. Jack Rudman. (Career Examination Ser.: C-2570). 1994. pap. 29.95 (*0-8373-2570-6*) Nat Learn.

Assistant Building Structural Engineer. Jack Rudman. (Career Examination Ser.: C-2567). 1994. pap. 34.95 (*0-8373-2567-6*) Nat Learn.

Assistant Buildings Superintendent. Jack Rudman. (Career Examination Ser.: C-1097). 1994. pap. 29.95 (*0-8373-1097-0*) Nat Learn.

Assistant Business Manager. Jack Rudman. (Career Examination Ser.: C-528). 1994. pap. 29.95 (*0-8373-0528-4*) Nat Learn.

Assistant Business Officer. Jack Rudman. (Career Examination Ser.: C-2075). 1994. pap. 29.95 (*0-8373-2075-5*) Nat Learn.

Assistant Buyer. Jack Rudman. (Career Examination Ser.: C-29). 1994. pap. 23.95 (*0-8373-0029-0*) Nat Learn.

Assistant Captain. Jack Rudman. (Career Exam Ser.: No. C-3524). 1994. 29.95 (*0-8373-3524-8*) Nat Learn.

Assistant Cashier. Jack Rudman. (Career Examination Ser.: C-30). 1994. pap. 19.95 (*0-8373-0030-4*) Nat Learn.

Assistant Chemical Engineer. Jack Rudman. (Career Examination Ser.: C-31). 1994. pap. 27.95 (*0-8373-0031-2*) Nat Learn.

Assistant Chemist. Jack Rudman. (Career Examination Ser.: C-32). 1994. pap. 27.95 (*0-8373-0032-0*) Nat Learn.

Assistant Civil Engineer. Jack Rudman. (Career Examination Ser.: C-33). 1994. pap. 23.95 (*0-8373-0033-9*) Nat Learn.

Assistant Civil Engineer (Structures) Jack Rudman. (Career Examination Ser.: C-1910). 1994. pap. 27.95 (*0-8373-1910-2*) Nat Learn.

Assistant Claims Examiner. Jack Rudman. (Career Examination Ser.: C-1098). 1994. pap. 23.95 (*0-8373-1098-9*) Nat Learn.

Assistant Clerk. Jack Rudman. (Career Examination Ser.: C-1099). 1994. pap. 19.95 (*0-8373-1099-7*) Nat Learn.

Assistant Community Development Project Supervisor. Jack Rudman. (Career Examination Ser.: C-907). 1994. pap. 29.95 (*0-8373-0907-7*) Nat Learn.

Assistant Community Organization Specialist (Urban Renewal) Jack Rudman. (Career Examination Ser.: C-1100). 1994. pap. 29.95 (*0-8373-1100-4*) Nat Learn.

Assistant Cook. Jack Rudman. (Career Examination Ser.: C-1101). 1994. pap. 23.95 (*0-8373-1101-2*) Nat Learn.

Assistant Coordinator of Volunteer Services. Jack Rudman. (Career Examination Ser.: C-3140). 1994. pap. 27.95 (*0-8373-3140-4*) Nat Learn.

Assistant Court Clerk. Jack Rudman. (Career Examination Ser.: C-34). 1994. pap. 27.95 (*0-8373-0034-7*) Nat Learn.

Assistant Custodial Work Supervisor. Jack Rudman. (Career Examination Ser.: C-2916). 1994. pap. 27.95 (*0-8373-2916-7*) Nat Learn.

Assistant Custodian. Jack Rudman. (Career Examination Ser.: C-35). 1994. pap. 23.95 (*0-8373-0035-5*) Nat Learn.

Assistant Custodian-Engineer. Jack Rudman. (Career Examination Ser.: C-36). 1994. pap. 23.95 (*0-8373-0036-3*) Nat Learn.

Assistant Departmental Attorney. Jack Rudman. (Career Examination Ser.: C-2233). 1994. pap. 39.95 (*0-8373-2233-2*) Nat Learn.

Assistant Deputy Superintendent of Women's Prisons. Jack Rudman. (Career Examination Ser.: C-1697). 1994. pap. 44.95 (*0-8373-1697-9*) Nat Learn.

Assistant Deputy Warden. Jack Rudman. (Career Examination Ser.: C-1698). 1994. pap. 44.95 (*0-8373-1698-7*) Nat Learn.

Assistant Director. Jack Rudman. (Career Examination Ser.: C-1102). 1994. pap. 34.95 (*0-8373-1102-0*) Nat Learn.

Assistant Director (Child Welfare) Jack Rudman. (Career Examination Ser.: C-1809). 1994. pap. 34.95 (*0-8373-1809-2*) Nat Learn.

Assistant Director of Building & Housing. Jack Rudman. (Career Examination Ser.: C-3086). 1994. pap. 39.95 (*0-8373-3086-6*) Nat Learn.

Assistant Director of Custodial & Security Services. Jack Rudman. (Career Examination Ser.: C-2922). 1994. pap. 34.95 (*0-8373-2922-1*) Nat Learn.

Assistant Director of Maintenance (Sewer District) Jack Rudman. (Career Examination Ser.: C-2908). 1994. pap. 34.95 (*0-8373-2908-6*) Nat Learn.

Assistant Director of Nursing Care. Jack Rudman. (Career Examination Ser.: C-2858). 1994. pap. 34.95 (*0-8373-2858-6*) Nat Learn.

Assistant Director of Social Services. Jack Rudman. (Career Examination Ser.: C-2798). 1994. pap. 34.95 (*0-8373-2798-9*) Nat Learn.

Assistant Director of Traffic Control. Jack Rudman. (Career Examination Ser.: C-1876). 1994. pap. 34.95 (*0-8373-1876-9*) Nat Learn.

Assistant Director of Traffic Safety. Jack Rudman. (Career Examination Ser.: C-458). 1994. pap. 34.95 (*0-8373-0458-X*) Nat Learn.

Assistant Director (Welfare) Jack Rudman. (Career Examination Ser.: C-1802). 1994. pap. 34.95 (*0-8373-1802-5*) Nat Learn.

Assistant District Attorney. Jack Rudman. (Career Examination Ser.: C-1103). 1994. pap. 34.95 (*0-8373-1103-9*) Nat Learn.

Assistant Electrical Engineer. Jack Rudman. (Career Examination Ser.: C-37). 1994. pap. 23.95 (*0-8373-0037-1*) Nat Learn.

Assistant Electronic Technician. Jack Rudman. (Career Examination Ser.: C-1982). 1994. pap. 27.95 (*0-8373-1982-X*) Nat Learn.

Assistant Employment & Training Program Administrator. Jack Rudman. (Career Examination Ser.: C-3075). 1994. pap. 34.95 (*0-8373-3075-0*) Nat Learn.

Assistant Engineering Technician. Jack Rudman. (Career Examination Ser.: C-931). 1994. pap. 27.95 (*0-8373-0931-X*) Nat Learn.

Assistant Federal & State Aid Coordinator. Jack Rudman. (Career Examination Ser.: C-1104). 1994. pap. 34.95 (*0-8373-1104-7*) Nat Learn.

Assistant Fire Marshal. Jack Rudman. (Career Examination Ser.: C-1105). 1994. pap. 29.95 (*0-8373-1105-5*) Nat Learn.

Assistant Floor Supervisor. Jack Rudman. (Career Examination Ser.: C-1106). 1994. pap. 29.95 (*0-8373-1106-3*) Nat Learn.

Assistant Foreman. Jack Rudman. (Career Examination Ser.: C-38). 1994. pap. 27.95 (*0-8373-0038-X*) Nat Learn.

Assistant Foreman (Department of Sanitation) Jack Rudman. (Career Examination Ser.: C-39). 1994. pap. 27.95 (*0-8373-0039-8*) Nat Learn.

Assistant Gardener. Jack Rudman. (Career Examination Ser.: C-40). 1994. pap. 23.95 (*0-8373-0040-1*) Nat Learn.

Assistant General Superintendent. Jack Rudman. (Career Examination Ser.: C-2109). 1994. pap. 39.95 (*0-8373-2109-3*) Nat Learn.

Assistant Head Custodian. Jack Rudman. (Career Examination Ser.: C-1822). 1994. pap. 29.95 (*0-8373-1822-X*) Nat Learn.

Assistant Health Insurance Administrator. Jack Rudman. (Career Examination Ser.: C-358). 1941. pap. 29.95 (*0-8373-0358-3*) Nat Learn.

Assistant Heating & Ventilating Engineer. Jack Rudman. (Career Examination Ser.: C-1912). 1994. pap. 29.95 (*0-8373-1912-9*) Nat Learn.

Assistant Hospital Administrator. Jack Rudman. (Career Examination Ser.: C-1107). 1994. pap. 34.95 (*0-8373-1107-1*) Nat Learn.

Assistant Housing Manager. Jack Rudman. (Career Examination Ser.: C-41). 1994. pap. 29.95 (*0-8373-0041-X*) Nat Learn.

Assistant Labor Relations Specialist. Jack Rudman. (Career Examination Ser.: C-2057). 1994. pap. 34.95 (*0-8373-2057-7*) Nat Learn.

Assistant Land Surveyor. Jack Rudman. (Career Examination Ser.: C-3031). 1994. pap. 29.95 (*0-8373-3031-9*) Nat Learn.

Assistant Landscape Architect. Jack Rudman. (Career Examination Ser.: C-42). 1994. pap. 29.95 (*0-8373-0042-8*) Nat Learn.

Assistant Landscape Engineer. Jack Rudman. (Career Examination Ser.: C-43). 1991. pap. 22.00 (*0-8373-0043-6*) Nat Learn.

Assistant Library Director. Jack Rudman. (Career Examination Ser.: C-1108). 1994. pap. 29.95 (*0-8373-1108-X*) Nat Learn.

Assistant Library Director I. Jack Rudman. (Career Examination Ser.: C-2783). 1994. pap. 29.95 (*0-8373-2783-0*) Nat Learn.

Assistant Library Director II. Jack Rudman. (Career Examination Ser.: C-2784). 1994. pap. 34.95 (*0-8373-2784-9*) Nat Learn.

Assistant Library Director III. Jack Rudman. (Career Examination Ser.: C-2785). 1994. pap. 34.95 (*0-8373-2785-7*) Nat Learn.

Assistant Library Director IV. Jack Rudman. (Career Examination Ser.: C-2786). 1994. pap. 34.95 (*0-8373-2786-5*) Nat Learn.

Assistant Library Director V. Jack Rudman. (Career Examination Ser.: C-2787). 1994. pap. 34.95 (*0-8373-2787-3*) Nat Learn.

Assistant Management Analyst. Jack Rudman. (Career Examination Ser.: C-2094). 1994. pap. 34.95 (*0-8373-2094-1*) Nat Learn.

Assistant Mechanical Construction Engineer. Jack Rudman. (Career Examination Ser.: C-2706). 1994. pap. 27.95 (*0-8373-2706-7*) Nat Learn.

Assistant Mechanical Engineer. Jack Rudman. (Career Examination Ser.: C-44). 1994. pap. 23.95 (*0-8373-0044-4*) Nat Learn.

Assistant Microbiologist. Jack Rudman. (Career Examination Ser.: C-1811). 1994. pap. 27.95 (*0-8373-1811-4*) Nat Learn.

Assistant Notes. Mordecai Marcus. 1972. pap. 4.50 (*0-8220-0214-0*) Cliffs.

Assistant Office Services Supervisor. Jack Rudman. (Career Examination Ser.: C-3048). 1994. pap. 27.95 (*0-8373-3048-3*) Nat Learn.

Assistant Park Supervisor. Jack Rudman. (Career Examination Ser.: C-1564). 1994. pap. 27.95 (*0-8373-1564-6*) Nat Learn.

Assistant Pathologist. Jack Rudman. (Career Examination Ser.: C-1109). 1994. pap. 39.95 (*0-8373-1109-8*) Nat Learn.

Assistant Payroll Supervisor. Jack Rudman. (Career Examination Ser.: C-1110). 1994. pap. 27.95 (*0-8373-1110-1*) Nat Learn.

Assistant Personnel Examiner. Jack Rudman. (Career Examination Ser.: C-1661). 1994. pap. 34.95 (*0-8373-1661-8*) Nat Learn.

Assistant Physicist. Jack Rudman. (Career Examination Ser.: C-2087). 1994. pap. 34.95 (*0-8373-2087-9*) Nat Learn.

Assistant Plan Examiner. Jack Rudman. (Career Examination Ser.: C-932). 1994. pap. 29.95 (*0-8373-0932-8*) Nat Learn.

Assistant Planner. Jack Rudman. (Career Examination Ser.: C-933). 1994. pap. 27.95 (*0-8373-0933-6*) Nat Learn.

Assistant Plant Facilities Administrator. Jack Rudman. (Career Examination Ser.: C-2757). 1994. pap. 34.95 (*0-8373-2757-1*) Nat Learn.

Assistant Plumbing Engineer. Jack Rudman. (Career Examination Ser.: C-2705). 1994. pap. 29.95 (*0-8373-2705-9*) Nat Learn.

Assistant Power Plant Operator. Jack Rudman. (Career Examination Ser.: C-1905). 1994. pap. 27.95 (*0-8373-1905-6*) Nat Learn.

Assistant Press Secretary. Jack Rudman. (Career Examination Ser.: C-1111). 1994. pap. 27.95 (*0-8373-1111-X*) Nat Learn.

Assistant Principal: Leadership Choices & Challenges. Catherine Marshall. 144p. 1991. pap. 18.00 (*0-8039-6110-3*, D1478) Corwin Pr.

Assistant Principal, Elementary School. Jack Rudman. (Teachers License Examination Ser.: S-1). 1994. pap. 39.95 (*0-8373-8101-0*) Nat Learn.

Assistant Principal, Jr. H. S. Jack Rudman. (Teachers License Examination Ser.: S-2). 1994. pap. 39.95 (*0-8373-8102-9*) Nat Learn.

Assistant Procurement Coordinator. Jack Rudman. (Career Examination Ser.: C-916). 1994. pap. 29.95 (*0-8373-0916-6*) Nat Learn.

Assistant Program Manager. Jack Rudman. (Career Examination Ser.: C-934). 1994. pap. 34.95 (*0-8373-0934-4*) Nat Learn.

Assistant Program Specialist (Correction) Jack Rudman. (Career Examination Ser.: C-1996). 1994. pap. 34.95 (*0-8373-1996-X*) Nat Learn.

Assistant Project Coordinator. Jack Rudman. (Career Examination Ser.: C-2590). 1994. pap. 27.95 (*0-8373-2590-0*) Nat Learn.

Assistant Public Buildings Manager. Jack Rudman. (Career Examination Ser.: C-2718). 1994. pap. 27.95 (*0-8373-2718-0*) Nat Learn.

Assistant Public Health Engineer. Jack Rudman. (Career Examination Ser.: C-2232). 1994. pap. 27.95 (*0-8373-2232-4*) Nat Learn.

Assistant Purchasing Agent. Jack Rudman. (Career Examination Ser.: C-935). 1994. pap. 23.95 (*0-8373-0935-2*) Nat Learn.

Assistant Radiologist. Jack Rudman. (Career Examination Ser.: C-1112). 1994. pap. 34.95 (*0-8373-1112-8*) Nat Learn.

Assistant Real Estate Agent. Jack Rudman. (Career Examination Ser.: C-2178). 1994. pap. 23.95 (*0-8373-2178-6*) Nat Learn.

Assistant Real Estate Appraiser. (Career Examination Ser.: C-3365). 1994. pap. 23.95 (*0-8373-3365-2*) Nat Learn.

Assistant Recreation Supervisor. Jack Rudman. (Career Examination Ser.: C-45). 1994. pap. 29.95 (*0-8373-0045-2*) Nat Learn.

A

An Asterisk (*) at the beginning of an entry indicates that the title is appearing in BIP for the first time.

Assistant Rent Examiner. Jack Rudman. (Career Examination Ser.: C-936). 1994. pap. 23.95 (0-8373-0936-0) Nat Learn.

Assistant Resident Buildings Superintendent. Jack Rudman. (Career Examination Ser.: C-1058). 1994. pap. 29.95 (0-8373-1058-X) Nat Learn.

Assistant Retirement Benefits Examiner. Jack Rudman. (Career Examination Ser.: C-1557). 1994. pap. 27.95 (0-8373-1557-3) Nat Learn.

Assistant Sanitary Engineer. Jack Rudman. (Career Examination Ser.: C-1969). 1994. pap. 27.95 (0-8373-1969-2) Nat Learn.

Assistant School Custodian-Engineer. Jack Rudman. (Career Examination Ser.: C-46). 1994. pap. 27.95 (0-8373-0046-0) Nat Learn.

Assistant School Transportation Supervisor. Jack Rudman. (Career Examination Ser.: C-112). 1994. pap. 27.95 (0-8373-0112-2) Nat Learn.

Assistant Signal Circuit Engineer. Jack Rudman. (Career Examination Ser.: C-47). 1994. pap. 29.95 (0-8373-0047-9) Nat Learn.

Assistant Social Worker. Jack Rudman. (Career Examination Ser.: C-1113). 1994. 23.95 (0-8373-1113-6) Nat Learn.

Assistant State Accounts Auditor - Examiner of Municipal Affairs. Jack Rudman. (Career Examination Ser.: C-1991). 1994. pap. 34.95 (0-8373-1991-9) Nat Learn.

Assistant Station Supervisor. Jack Rudman. (Career Examination Ser.: C-48). 1994. pap. 23.95 (0-8373-0048-7) Nat Learn.

Assistant Stationary Engineer. Jack Rudman. (Career Examination Ser.: C-2279). 1994. pap. 27.95 (0-8373-2279-0) Nat Learn.

Assistant Statistician. Jack Rudman. (Career Examination Ser.: C-49). 1994. pap. 27.95 (0-8373-0049-5) Nat Learn.

Assistant Stockman. Jack Rudman. (Career Examination Ser.: C-50). 1994. pap. 23.95 (0-8373-0050-9) Nat Learn.

Assistant Superintendent (Buses & Shops) Jack Rudman. (Career Examination Ser.: C-1725). 1994. pap. 34.95 (0-8373-1725-8) Nat Learn.

Assistant Superintendent (Cars & Shops) Jack Rudman. (Career Examination Ser.: C-2015). 1994. pap. 34.95 (0-8373-2015-1) Nat Learn.

Assistant Superintendent of Alarms. Jack Rudman. (Career Examination Ser.: C-2964). 1994. pap. 34.95 (0-8373-2964-7) Nat Learn.

Assistant Superintendent of Buildings & Grounds. Jack Rudman. (Career Examination Ser.: C-937). 1994. pap. 29.95 (0-8373-0937-9) Nat Learn.

Assistant Superintendent of Construction. Jack Rudman. (Career Examination Ser.: C-1114). 1994. pap. 34.95 (0-8373-1114-4) Nat Learn.

Assistant Superintendent of Public Works. Jack Rudman. (Career Examination Ser.: C-2306). 1994. pap. 34.95 (0-8373-2306-1) Nat Learn.

Assistant Superintendent of Sanitation. Jack Rudman. (Career Examination Ser.: C-2456). 1994. pap. 34.95 (0-8373-2456-4) Nat Learn.

Assistant Superintendent of Water Works. Jack Rudman. (Career Examination Ser.: C-2003). 1994. pap. 34.95 (0-8373-2003-8) Nat Learn.

Assistant Superintendent (Power) Jack Rudman. (Career Examination Ser.: C-2016). 1994. pap. 34.95 (0-8373-2016-X) Nat Learn.

Assistant Superintendent (Signals) Jack Rudman. (Career Examination Ser.: C-2017). 1994. pap. 34.95 (0-8373-2017-8) Nat Learn.

Assistant Superintendent (Structures) Jack Rudman. (Career Examination Ser.: C-2018). 1994. pap. 34.95 (0-8373-2018-6) Nat Learn.

Assistant Superintendent (Surface Transportation) Jack Rudman. (Career Examination Ser.: C-1770). 1994. pap. 34.95 (0-8373-1770-3) Nat Learn.

Assistant Superintendent (Track) Jack Rudman. (Career Examination Ser.: C-2019). 1994. pap. 34.95 (0-8373-2019-4) Nat Learn.

Assistant Supervisor (Air Conditioning, Rolling Stock) Jack Rudman. (Career Examination Ser.: C-2063). 1994. pap. 29.95 (0-8373-2063-1) Nat Learn.

Assistant Supervisor (Buses & Shops) Jack Rudman. (Career Examination Ser.: C-1115). 1994. pap. 29.95 (0-8373-1115-2) Nat Learn.

Assistant Supervisor (Cars & Shops) Jack Rudman. (Career Examination Ser.: C-1975). 1994. pap. 29.95 (0-8373-1975-7) Nat Learn.

Assistant Supervisor (Child Welfare) Jack Rudman. (Career Examination Ser.: C-51). 1994. pap. 29.95 (0-8373-0051-7) Nat Learn.

Assistant Supervisor (Electrical Power) Jack Rudman. (Career Examination Ser.: C-1976). 1994. pap. 29.95 (0-8373-1976-5) Nat Learn.

Assistant Supervisor (Electronic Equipment) Jack Rudman. (Career Examination Ser.: C-2192). 1994. pap. 29.95 (0-8373-2192-1) Nat Learn.

Assistant Supervisor (Elevators & Escalators) Jack Rudman. (Career Examination Ser.: C-1727). 1994. pap. 29.95 (0-8373-1727-4) Nat Learn.

Assistant Supervisor (Lighting) Jack Rudman. (Career Examination Ser.: C-2006). 1994. pap. 29.95 (0-8373-2006-2) Nat Learn.

Assistant Supervisor of Electrical Installations. Jack Rudman. (Career Examination Ser.: C-1116). 1994. pap. 29.95 (0-8373-1116-0) Nat Learn.

Assistant Supervisor of Mechanical Installations. Jack Rudman. (Career Examination Ser.: C-1117). 1994. pap. 29.95 (0-8373-1117-9) Nat Learn.

Assistant Supervisor of Youth Services. Jack Rudman. (Career Examination Ser.: C-1659). 1994. pap. 29.95 (0-8373-1659-6) Nat Learn.

Assistant Supervisor (Power Distribution) Jack Rudman. (Career Examination Ser.: C-1777). 1994. pap. 29.95 (0-8373-1777-0) Nat Learn.

Assistant Supervisor (Stores, Materials & Supplies) Jack Rudman. (Career Examination Ser.: C-1814). 1994. pap. 29.95 (0-8373-1814-9) Nat Learn.

Assistant Supervisor (Structures) Jack Rudman. (Career Examination Ser.: C-1977). 1994. pap. 29.95 (0-8373-1977-3) Nat Learn.

Assistant Supervisor (Structures) - Group C. Jack Rudman. (Career Examination Ser.: C-1972). 1994. pap. 29.95 (0-8373-1972-2) Nat Learn.

Assistant Supervisor (Track) Jack Rudman. (Career Examination Ser.: C-1728). 1994. pap. 29.95 (0-8373-1728-2) Nat Learn.

Assistant Supervisor (Turnstiles) Jack Rudman. (Career Examination Ser.: C-2007). 1994. pap. 29.95 (0-8373-2007-0) Nat Learn.

Assistant Supervisor (Ventilation & Drainage) Jack Rudman. (Career Examination Ser.: C-2091). 1994. pap. 29.95 (0-8373-2091-7) Nat Learn.

Assistant Supervisor (Welfare) Jack Rudman. (Career Examination Ser.: C-52). 1994. pap. 29.95 (0-8373-0052-5) Nat Learn.

Assistant Surveyor. Jack Rudman. (Career Examination Ser.: C-1972). 1994. pap. 29.95 (0-8373-1792-4) Nat Learn.

Assistant Tax Valuation Engineer. Jack Rudman. (Career Examination Ser.: C-3196). 1994. pap. 27.95 (0-8373-3196-X) Nat Learn.

Assistant Teacher. Jack Rudman. (Career Examination Ser.: C-1118). 1994. pap. 23.95 (0-8373-1118-7) Nat Learn.

Assistant Tenant Supervisor. Jack Rudman. (Career Examination Ser.: C-542). 1994. pap. 27.95 (0-8373-0542-X) Nat Learn.

Assistant to Assessor. Jack Rudman. (Career Examination Ser.: C-2182). 1994. pap. 27.95 (0-8373-2182-4) Nat Learn.

Assistant to City Clerk. Jack Rudman. (Career Examination Ser.: C-930). 1994. pap. 23.95 (0-8373-0930-1) Nat Learn.

Assistant to Commissioner. Jack Rudman. (Career Examination Ser.: C-1119). 1994. pap. 34.95 (0-8373-1119-5) Nat Learn.

Assistant to Director. Jack Rudman. (Career Examination Ser.: C-3092). 1994. pap. 34.95 (0-8373-3092-0) Nat Learn.

Assistant to Director, Bureau of Vehicle Maintenance. Jack Rudman. (Career Examination Ser.: C-3111). 1994. pap. 34.95 (0-8373-3111-0) Nat Learn.

Assistant to Planning Director. Jack Rudman. (Career Examination Ser.: C-3155). 1994. pap. 34.95 (0-8373-3155-2) Nat Learn.

Assistant to Superintendent. Jack Rudman. (Career Examination Ser.: C-2210). 1994. pap. 34.95 (0-8373-2210-3) Nat Learn.

Assistant to the Town Comptroller. Jack Rudman. (Career Examination Ser.: C-3128). 1994. pap. 34.95 (0-8373-3128-5) Nat Learn.

Assistant Town Engineer. Jack Rudman. (Career Examination Ser.: C-211). 1994. pap. 29.95 (0-8373-0211-0) Nat Learn.

Assistant Train Dispatcher. Jack Rudman. (Career Examination Ser.: C-53). 1994. pap. 23.95 (0-8373-0053-3) Nat Learn.

Assistant Transit Management Analyst. Jack Rudman. (Career Examination Ser.: C-3280). 1994. pap. 29.95 (0-8373-3280-X) Nat Learn.

Assistant Urban Designer. Jack Rudman. (Career Examination Ser.: C-1120). 1994. pap. 27.95 (0-8373-1120-9) Nat Learn.

Assistant Warden. Jack Rudman. (Career Examination Ser.: C-1121). 1994. pap. 39.95 (0-8373-1121-7) Nat Learn.

Assistant Water Maintenance Foreman. Jack Rudman. (Career Examination Ser.: C-2919). 1994. pap. 27.95 (0-8373-2919-1) Nat Learn.

Assistant Water Service Foreman. Jack Rudman. (Career Examination Ser.: C-2924). 1994. pap. 27.95 (0-8373-2924-8) Nat Learn.

***Assistant Workers' Compensation Supervisor.** (Career Examination Ser.: Series 1). Date not set. pap. 34.95 (0-8373-3679-1) Nat Learn.

Assistant Workmen's Compensation Examiner. Jack Rudman. (Career Examination Ser.: C-1643). 1994. pap. 27.95 (0-8373-1643-X) Nat Learn.

Assistant Youth Corps Project Director. Jack Rudman. (Career Examination Ser.: C-2207). 1994. pap. 34.95 (0-8373-2207-3) Nat Learn.

Assistant Youth Guidance Technician. Jack Rudman. (Career Examination Ser.: C-938). 1994. pap. 29.95 (0-8373-0938-7) Nat Learn.

Assistantships & Graduate Fellowships in the Mathematical Science. (MISC Ser.: Vol. ASST). 137p. 1993. Annual updates. 18.00 (0-8218-0180-5) Am Math.

Assisted Circulation, No. 3. Ed. by F. Unger. (Illus.). 660p. 1989. 207.00 (0-387-50722-1, 2642) Spr-Verlag.

***Assisted Circulation 4.** Ed. by F. Unger. 416p. 1995. 178.00 (3-540-58547-8) Spr-Verlag.

Assisted Human Reproductive Technology. Ed. by E. S. Hafez. (Reproductive Health Technology Ser.). 248p. 1991. 116.00 (1-56032-148-2) Hemisp Pub.

Assisted Living For the Aged & Frail: Innovations in Design, Management, & Financing. Victor Regnier et al. LC 93-38639. 271p. 1994. 35.00 (0-231-08276-2) Col U Pr.

Assisted Living Housing for the Elderly: Innovations in Design & Planning. Victor Regnier. LC 92-43118. 1993. text ed. 39.95 (0-442-00702-7) Van Nos Reinhold.

Assisted Reproduction, Vol. 5. Ed. by Y. Boutaleb & A. Gzouli. (Recent Developments in Fertility & Sterility Ser.). (Illus.). 250p. (C). 1991. 85.00 (1-85070-288-8) Prthnon Pub.

***Assisted Reproduction Progress in Research & Practice.** Robert W. Shaw. (Advances in Reproductive Endocrinology Ser.: Vol. 7). (Illus.). 150p. 1995. 65.00 (1-85070-679-4) Prthnon Pub.

Assisted Reproductive Technologies. Ed. by Richard P. Marrs. LC 93-1410. 1993. 80.00 (0-86542-203-6) Blackwell Sci.

Assisted Vaginal Delivery: Obstetric Forceps & Vacuum Extraction Techniques. Leonard E. Laufe & Michael Berkus. (Illus.). 160p. 1992. pap. text ed. 42.00 (0-07-105412-X) Hlth Prof Div.

Assisted Ventilation. John Moxham. (Illus.). 93p. 1991. pap. 22.00 (0-7279-0306-3, Pub. by Brit Med Assn UK) Amer Coll Phys.

Assisted Ventilation at Home: A Practical Guide. W. J. Kinnear. LC 93-33019. (Oxford Medical Publications). 112p. (C). 1994. 33.00 (0-19-262400-8) OUP.

Assisted Ventilation of the Neonate. 2nd ed. Jay P. Goldsmith & Edward H. Karotkin. (Illus.). 460p. 1988. text ed. 80.50 (0-7216-1527-9) Saunders.

Assisting & Assessing Educational Personnel: The Impact of Clinical Supervision. Saundra J. Tracy & Robert H. MacNaughton. LC 92-15196. 1992. text ed. write for info. (0-205-13767-9) Allyn.

Assisting & Encouraging Crime: A Consultation Paper. (Law Commission Consultation Paper Ser.: No. 131). 216p. 1993. pap. 25.00 (0-11-730214-7, HM02147, Pub. by HMSO UK) UNIPUB.

Assisting Displaced Workers: Do the States Have a Better Idea? Duane E. Leigh. LC 89-5844. 172p. 1989. text ed. 22.00 (0-88099-073-2); pap. text ed. 12.00 (0-88099-074-0) W E Upjohn.

Assisting in Long-Term Care. 2nd ed. Barbara Hegner & Esther Caldwell. LC 92-22067. 1993. 28.95 (0-8273-5285-9) Delmar.

Assisting in Long-Term Care. 2nd ed. Barbara Hegner & Esther Caldwell. 776p. 1994. teacher ed 49.95 (0-8273-5280-8); pap. text ed. 28.95 (0-8273-5258-1); disk 39.95 (0-8273-5476-2) Delmar.

Assisting in Long-Term Care: Student Workbook. 2nd ed. Barbara Hegner. 454p. 1994. 16.95 (0-8273-5443-6) Delmar.

Assisting Insiders with Federal Securities Law Compliance: A Guide for the Corporate Secretary. American Society of Corporate Secretaries Staff. write for info. (0-318-61652-1) Am Soc Corp Sec.

Assisting Small Business Clients in Obtaining Funds. 55p. 1983. pap. 14.00 (0-686-84210-3) Am Inst CPA.

***Assisting Sustainable Food Production: Action or Apathy?** Ed. by Robert Paarlberg & Steven Breth. 92p. (Orig.). (C). 1994. pap. text ed. 9.95x (0-933595-95-6) Winrock Intl.

Assisting the Beginning Teacher. Leslie Huling-Austin et al. 1989. pap. 12.50 (0-685-41075-7) Assn Tchr Ed.

Assisting the Victims of Armed Conflict & Other Disasters. Ed. by Frits Kalshoven. (C). 1989. lib. bdg. 105.50 (0-7923-0163-3) Kluwer Ac.

***Assisting Workers Displaced by Structural Change.** Duane E. Leigh. 220p. 1995. text ed. 25.00 (0-88099-154-2); pap. text ed. 15.00 (0-88099-153-4) W E Upjohn.

Assistive Devices: Doorways to Independence. Cynthia L. Compton. 67p. 1991. pap. text ed. 25.00 (0-9638716-0-9) VanComp Assocs.

***Assistive Devices for Persons with Hearing Impairment.** Donald J. Schum. Ed. by Richard S. Tyler. LC 94-26290. 1994. 42.95 (0-205-15126-4, Longwood Div) Allyn.

Assistive Listening Devices & Systems. Ed. by Trudy Snope. (Professional Practices Ser.). 114p. 1985. pap. text ed. 20.00 (0-910329-31-1) Am Speech Lang Hearing.

Assistive Technologies: Principles & Practice. Cook & Hussey. LC 94-30291. 496p. 1993. 45.95 (0-8016-1038-9) Mosby Yr Bk.

***Assistive Technology: A Resource for School, Work, & Community.** Flippo et al. 272p. 1995. pap. 34.00 (1-55766-189-8) P H Brookes.

Assistive Technology for Persons with Disabilities: The Role of Occupational Therapy. William C. Mann & Joseph P. Lane. 300p. (C). 1991. pap. text ed. 38.00 (0-910317-71-2) Am Occup Therapy.

Assistive Technology in Traumatic Brain Injury Vocational Rehabilitation. C. Gerald Warren. Ed. by Robert Fraser & David Clemmons. LC 91-73659. (Traumatic Brain Injury Rehabilitation Training Ser.). 42p. (Orig.). 1991. spiral bd., pap. 14.95 (1-878205-07-2) GR Press.

***Assists for Illnesses & Injuries.** Concept by L. Ron Hubbard. 48p. 1994. pap. 4.00 (0-88404-913-2) Bridge Pubns Inc.

***Assists Processing Handbook.** L. Ron Hubbard. 408p. 1994. spiral bd. 55.00 (0-88404-826-8) Bridge Pubns Inc.

Associate Accountant. Jack Rudman. (Career Examination Ser.: C-1798). 1994. pap. 29.95 (0-8373-1798-3) Nat Learn.

Associate Administrative Analyst. (Career Examination Ser.: C-3425). 1994. pap. 34.95 (0-8373-3425-X) Nat Learn.

Associate Administrator. Jack Rudman. (Career Examination Ser.: C-1122). 1994. pap. 29.95 (0-8373-1122-5) Nat Learn.

Associate Advisor, PEDC (U. S. P. S.) Jack Rudman. (Career Examination Ser.: C-2118). 1994. pap. 34.95 (0-8373-2118-2) Nat Learn.

Associate Analytical Chemist. Jack Rudman. (Career Examination Ser.: C-3194). 1994. pap. 34.95 (0-8373-3194-3) Nat Learn.

Associate Attorney. Jack Rudman. (Career Examination Ser.: C-2269). 1994. pap. 34.95 (0-8373-2269-3) Nat Learn.

Associate Biostatistician. Jack Rudman. (Career Examination Ser.: C-2292). 1994. pap. 34.95 (0-8373-2292-8) Nat Learn.

Associate Budget Analyst. Jack Rudman. (Career Examination Ser.: C-3172). 1994. pap. 34.95 (0-8373-3172-2) Nat Learn.

Associate Business Promotion Coordinator. Jack Rudman. (Career Examination Ser.: C-2526). 1994. pap. 39.95 (0-8373-2526-9) Nat Learn.

Associate Capital Program Analyst. Jack Rudman. (Career Examination Ser.: C-2039). 1994. pap. 34.95 (0-8373-2039-9) Nat Learn.

Associate Cashier. Jack Rudman. (Career Examination Ser.: C-2005). 1994. pap. 23.95 (0-8373-2005-4) Nat Learn.

Associate Chemist. Jack Rudman. (Career Examination Ser.: C-3362). 1994. pap. 29.95 (0-8373-3362-8) Nat Learn.

Associate Civil Engineer (Structures) Jack Rudman. (Career Examination Ser.: C-1911). 1994. pap. 34.95 (0-8373-1911-0) Nat Learn.

Associate Claim Examiner. Jack Rudman. (Career Exam Ser.: No. C-3504). 1994. 27.95 (0-8373-3504-3) Nat Learn.

Associate Computer Programmer. Jack Rudman. (Career Examination Ser.: C-2206). 1994. pap. 29.95 (0-8373-2206-5) Nat Learn.

Associate Computer Programmer-Analyst. Jack Rudman. (Career Examination Ser.: C-3218). 1994. pap. 29.95 (0-8373-3218-4) Nat Learn.

Associate Computer Systems Analyst. Jack Rudman. (Career Examination Ser.: C-939). 1994. pap. 29.95 (0-8373-0939-5) Nat Learn.

Associate Court Clerk. Jack Rudman. (Career Examination Ser.: C-2587). 1994. pap. 27.95 (0-8373-2587-0) Nat Learn.

Associate Degree Nursing: Facilitating Competency Development. Ed. by Marian M. Pettengill. 1987. write for info. (0-318-68852-2) Midwest Alliance Nursing.

Associate Degree Nursing & the Nursing Home. 216p. 1988. pap. 22.95 (0-88737-423-9, 15-2241) Natl League Nurse.

Associate Degree Nursing Education: An Historical Annotated Bibliography, 1942-1988. Patricia T. Haase. LC 89-23713. 316p. (C). 1990. text ed. 52.50 (0-8223-0983-1) Duke.

Associate Degree Preferred. Ed. by Dale Parnell. 88p. (Orig.). reprint ed. pap. 25.10 (0-7837-2484-5, 2042641) Bks Demand.

Associate Economist. Jack Rudman. (Career Examination Ser.: C-2497). 1994. pap. 34.95 (0-8373-2497-1) Nat Learn.

Associate Education Analyst. Jack Rudman. (Career Examination Ser.: C-3046). 1994. pap. 39.95 (0-8373-3046-7) Nat Learn.

Associate Education Officer. Jack Rudman. (Career Examination Ser.: C-3051). 1994. pap. 39.95 (0-8373-3051-3) Nat Learn.

Associate Engineering Technician. Jack Rudman. (Career Examination Ser.: C-2467). 1994. pap. 29.95 (0-8373-2467-X) Nat Learn.

Associate Environmental Analyst. Jack Rudman. (Career Examination Ser.: C-3033). 1994. pap. 29.95 (0-8373-3033-5) Nat Learn.

Associate Graphic Artist. Jack Rudman. (Career Examination Ser.: C-1525). 1994. pap. 29.95 (0-8373-1525-5) Nat Learn.

Associate Industrial Hygienist. Jack Rudman. (Career Examination Ser.: C-3037). 1994. pap. 44.95 (0-8373-3037-8) Nat Learn.

Associate Information & Referral Coordinator. Jack Rudman. (Career Examination Ser.: C-2926). 1994. pap. 34.95 (0-8373-2926-4) Nat Learn.

Associate Inspector (Construction) Jack Rudman. (Career Exam Ser.: No. C-3502). 1994. 34.95 (0-8373-3502-7) Nat Learn.

Associate Inspector (Electrical) (Career Examination Ser.: C-3360). 1994. pap. 34.95 (0-8373-3360-1) Nat Learn.

Associate Inspector (Highways & Sewers) Jack Rudman. (Career Exam Ser.: No. C-3519). 1994. 34.95 (0-8373-3519-1) Nat Learn.

Associate Inspector (Housing) Jack Rudman. (Career Examination Ser.: C-3011). 1994. pap. 34.95 (0-8373-3011-4) Nat Learn.

***Associate Inspector (Plumbing)** (Career Examination Ser.: Series 1). Date not set. pap. 34.95 (0-8373-3666-X) Nat Learn.

Associate Investigator. Jack Rudman. (Career Exam Ser.: No. C-3503). 1994. 34.95 (0-8373-3503-5) Nat Learn.

Associate Labor Relations Specialist. Jack Rudman. (Career Examination Ser.: C-1946). 1994. pap. 39.95 (0-8373-1946-3) Nat Learn.

Associate Management Analyst. Jack Rudman. (Career Examination Ser.: C-1234). 1994. pap. 39.95 (0-8373-1234-5) Nat Learn.

Associate Management Auditor. (Career Examination Ser.: C-3426). 1994. pap. 39.95 (0-8373-3426-8) Nat Learn.

Associate Manpower Program Coordinator. Jack Rudman. (Career Examination Ser.: C-2317). 1994. pap. 39.95 (0-8373-2317-7) Nat Learn.

Associate Marketing Representative. Jack Rudman. (Career Examination Ser.: C-2040). 1994. pap. 34.95 (0-8373-2040-2) Nat Learn.

Associate Medical Examiner. Jack Rudman. (Career Examination Ser.: C-2722). 1994. pap. 39.95 (0-8373-2722-9) Nat Learn.

Associate Methods Analyst. Jack Rudman. (Career Examination Ser.: C-1735). 1994. pap. 39.95 (0-8373-1735-5) Nat Learn.

An Asterisk (*) at the beginning of an entry indicates that the title is appearing in BIP for the first time.

Associate Occupational Analyst. Jack Rudman. (Career Examination Ser.: C-2550). 1994. pap. 39.95 (*0-8373-2550-1*) Nat Learn.

Associate Park Service Worker. Jack Rudman. (Career Examination Ser.: C-2469). 1994. pap. 27.95 (*0-8373-2469-6*) Nat Learn.

Associate Personnel Administrator. (Career Examination Ser.: C-3322). 1994. pap. 39.95 (*0-8373-3322-9*) Nat Learn.

***Associate Public Health Sanitarian.** (Career Examination Ser.: Series 1). Date not set. pap. 34.95 (*0-8373-3690-2*) Nat Learn.

Associate Public Information Specialist. Jack Rudman. (Career Exam Ser.: No. C-3520). 1994. 34.95 (*0-8373-3520-5*) Nat Learn.

Associate Public Records Officer. Jack Rudman. (Career Examination Ser.: No. C-3521). 1994. 34.95 (*0-8373-3521-3*) Nat Learn.

Associate Quality Assurance Specialist. Jack Rudman. (Career Rxamination Ser.: No. C-3522). 1994. 39.95 (*0-8373-3522-1*) Nat Learn.

***Associate Radiological Health Specialist.** (Career Examination Ser.: Series 1). Date not set. pap. 39.95 (*0-8373-3692-9*) Nat Learn.

Associate Real Property Manager. Jack Rudman. (Career Examination Ser.: C-2890). 1991. pap. 22.00 (*0-8373-2890-X*) Nat Learn.

Associate Reformed Presbyterian Death & Marriage Notices from the Christian Magazine of the South, the Erskine Miscellany, & the Due West Telescope 1843-1863. Lowry Ware. 209p. 1993. 25.00 (*0-913363-13-8*) SCMAR.

Associate Safety Professional Home Study Workbook: Safety Fundamentals (Core), 2 vols. rev. ed. James P. Watts. (Illus.). 1989. Vol. I, 326p. write for info. (*0-9630668-3-8*); Vol. II, 278p. write for info. (*0-9630668-4-6*) LV Safe Wkshps.

Associate Safety Professional Home Study Workbook: Safety Fundamentals (Core), 2 vols., Set. rev. ed. James P. Watts. (Illus.). 1989. 150.00 (*0-9630668-5-4*) LV Safe Wkshps.

Associate Sanitation Enforcement Agent. Jack Rudman. (Career Examination Ser.: C-3216). 1994. pap. 29.95 (*0-8373-3216-8*) Nat Learn.

Associate Series: Understanding Financial Statements, Understanding Workouts, Basic Issues in Drafting Corporate Agreements, Basic Securities Law - Due Diligence. (Corporate Law & Practice Ser.). 706p. 1991. pap. text ed. 17.50 (*0-685-56882-2*, B4-6982) PLI.

Associate Social Services Management Specialist. Jack Rudman. (Career Examination Ser.: C-454). 1994. pap. 34.95 (*0-8373-0454-7*) Nat Learn.

Associate Space Analyst. Jack Rudman. (Career Examination Ser.: No. C-3518). 1994. 39.95 (*0-8373-3518-3*) Nat Learn.

Associate Staff Analyst. Jack Rudman. (Career Examination Ser.: C-1552). 1994. pap. 39.95 (*0-8373-1552-2*) Nat Learn.

Associate Statistician. Jack Rudman. (Career Examination Ser.: C-940). 1994. pap. 34.95 (*0-8373-0940-9*) Nat Learn.

Associate Superintendent of Construction. Jack Rudman. (Career Examination Ser.: C-1518). 1994. pap. 34.95 (*0-8373-1518-2*) Nat Learn.

Associate Tax Auditor. Jack Rudman. (Career Examination Ser.: C-2314). 1994. pap. 34.95 (*0-8373-2314-2*) Nat Learn.

Associate Traffic Enforcement Agent. Jack Rudman. (Career Examination Ser.: C-215). 1994. pap. 29.95 (*0-8373-0215-3*) Nat Learn.

Associate Transit Management Analyst. Jack Rudman. (Career Examination Ser.: C-3423). 1994. pap. 34.95 (*0-8373-3423-3*) Nat Learn.

Associate Urban Park Ranger. Jack Rudman. (Career Examination Ser.: C-3179). 1994. pap. 29.95 (*0-8373-3179-X*) Nat Learn.

Associate Water Use Inspector. (Career Examination Ser.). 1994. pap. 29.95 (*0-8373-3583-3*, C3583-3) Nat Learn.

Associate Word Processor. Jack Rudman. (Career Examination Ser.: C-3183). 1994. pap. 29.95 (*0-8373-3183-8*) Nat Learn.

Associate Worker's Compensation Review Analyst. Jack Rudman. (Career Examination Ser.: C-309). 1994. pap. 29.95 (*0-8373-0309-5*) Nat Learn.

Associate Workmen's Compensation Examiner. Jack Rudman. (Career Examination Ser.: C-1547). 1994. pap. 29.95 (*0-8373-1547-6*) Nat Learn.

Associated Graded Algebra of a Gorenstein Artin Algebra. Anthony A. Iarrobino. LC 93-39027. (Memoirs of the American Mathematical Society Ser.: No. 514). 132p. 1994. pap. 30.00 (*0-8218-2576-3*) Am Math.

Associated Press Book of World's Richest People. Chet Currier. 1991. 19.99 (*0-517-02013-0*) Random Hse Value.

Associated Press Coverage of a Major Disaster: The Crash of Delta Flight 1141. Thomas Fensch. (Communication Textbook Series, Journalism Subseries). 456p. 1989. text ed. 89.95 (*0-8058-0519-2*); pap. text ed. 49.95 (*0-8058-0518-4*) L Erlbaum Assocs.

Associated Press Crossword Puzzle Book, No. 5. Associated Press Editors. 1989. pap. 5.95 (*0-8092-4429-2*) Contemp Bks.

Associated Press Guide to News Writing. Rene J. Cappon. 1991. pap. 11.00 (*0-13-053679-2*) P-H.

Associated Press History of Television. Norm Goldstein. 1991. 19.99 (*0-517-02011-4*) Random Hse Value.

Associated Press Photojournalism Stylebook. Associated Press Staff. 1990. pap. 16.35 (*0-201-13235-4*) Addison-Wesley.

Associated Press Pictorial History of Baseball. Hal Brock. 208p. 1994. write for info. (*0-9640034-1-4*) World Pubns.

Associated Press Stylebook & Libel Manual. Associated Press Staff. 288p. 1982. pap. 8.95 (*0-201-10091-6*) Addison-Wesley.

Associated Press Stylebook & Libel Manual. 3rd ed. Associated Press Staff. 1992. pap. 11.49 (*0-201-56760-1*) Addison-Wesley.

Associated Press Stylebook & Libel Manual. 4th ed. Ed. by Norm Goldstein. (Illus.). 352p. 1994. pap. 13.46 (*0-201-62704-3*) Addison-Wesley.

Associated Press Stylebook & Libel Manual: The Journalist's Bible. rev. ed. Associated Press Staff. LC 87-3572. (Illus.). 336p. 1987. pap. 10.53 (*0-201-10433-4*) Addison-Wesley.

Associated Press Sunday Crossword Puzzle, Bk. 3. Associated Press Editors. 96p. (Orig.). 1986. pap. 5.95 (*0-8092-4985-5*) Contemp Bks.

Associated Press Sunday Crossword Puzzle Book, Bk. 6. Editors of the Associated Press Staff. (Illus.). 96p. (Orig.). 1991. pap. 7.95 (*0-8092-4108-0*) Contemp Bks.

Associated Systems Theory: A Systematic Approach to Cognitive Representations of Persons. Ed. by Robert S. Wyer. (Advances in Social Cognition Ser.). 256p. 1994. text ed. 49.95 (*0-8058-1473-6*); pap. 22.50 (*0-8058-1474-4*) L Erlbaum Assocs.

Association: British Extraparliamentary Political Organization, 1769-1793. Eugene C. Black. LC 63-17195. (Historical Monographs: No. 54). (Illus.). 358p. 1963. 30.00 (*0-674-05000-2*) HUP.

Association: Or, a Concise Exposition of the Practical Part of Fourier's Social Science. Albert Brisbane. LC 72-2947. (Communal Societies in America Ser). reprint ed. 29.50 (*0-404-10713-3*) AMS Pr.

Association see **On Sensations from Pressure & Impact**

Association, Club & Organization, Group Tours As a Travel Business: A Possibility Reference. rev. ed. Carrol, Frieda, Research Division Staff. 1992. ring bd. 21.95 (*0-317-04789-2*, Pub. by Frieda Carrol) Prosperity & Profits.

Association Education Evaluation Workbook. American Society & Association Executives Education Section Council. 75p. 1987. GBC Binding. 30.00 (*0-88034-014-2*) Am Soc Assn Execs.

Association Education Handbook. American Society of Association Executives Staff. 173p. 1984. pap. 55.00 (*0-88034-015-0*) Am Soc Assn Execs.

Association Executive Compensation Study. 7th ed. American Society of Association Executives Staff. pap. 150.00 (*0-88034-017-7*) Am Soc Assn Execs.

Association Football on Different Continents. Ed. by Stephen Wagg. 240p. 1994. 55.00 (*0-7185-1677-X*, Pub. by Leicester Univ Pr) St Martin.

Association for Advancement of Behavior Therapy Membership Directory. 196p. 1994. pap. 50.00 (*0-318-13401-2*) Assn Advance Behav Therapy.

Association for Asian Studies Membership Directory: 1992. rev. ed. Ed. by Carol M. Hansen. 140p. 1992. pap. 15.00 (*0-924304-08-1*) Assn Asian Studies.

Association for Asian Studies Membership Directory, 1993. Ed. by Carol M. Hansen. 140p. 1993. 20.00 (*0-685-62327-0*); pap. 9.00 (*0-924304-12-X*) Assn Asian Studies.

Association for Geographic Information Yearbook 1991. Ed. by James Cadoux-Hudson & Ian Heywood. 420p. 1991. pap. 60.00 (*0-7484-0028-1*, Pub. by Tay Francis Ltd UK) Taylor & Francis.

***Association for Population-Family Planning Libraries & Information Centers-International (APLIC-I) Union List of Serials.** APLIC-I Staff. Ed. & Comp. by Michael F. Zimmerman. LC 95-3107. (Special Publication Ser.: No. 7). 1995. write for info. (*0-933438-22-2*) APLIC Intl.

Association for Practitioners in Infection Control Curriculum, Vol. I & II. APIC Staff. 1136p. 1989. spiral bd. 80.00 (*0-8403-5313-8*) Kendall-Hunt.

Association for Practitioners in Infection Control Self-Development Education Program. APIC Staff. 256p. (C). 1990. 40.00 (*0-8403-6202-1*) Kendall-Hunt.

Association International Activity. Ed. by John M. Crawford & Anne Ballen. 120p. (Orig.). 1988. pap. 40.00 (*0-88034-029-0*) Am Soc Assn Execs.

***Association Law.** 350p. (C). 1994. 395.00 (*0-7605-0682-5*) Rector Pr.

Association Management: Association Management, No. 1. rev. ed. (GAP Report Ser.: Vol. 1). (C). 1992. pap. 14.50 (*0-944715-18-4*) CAI.

Association Meeting Trends 1992. American Society of Association Executives Staff. 146p. (Orig.). Date not set. pap. 110.00 (*0-88034-055-X*) Am Soc Assn Execs.

Association Oath Rolls of the British Plantations: New York, Virginia, Etc., A.D. 1696, Being a Contribution to Political History. William Gandy. LC 93-3795. (Stokvis Studies in Historical Chronology & Thought: No. 10). (Illus.). 86p. 1993. lib. bdg. 23.00x (*0-8095-0100-7*, Sidewinder Press); pap. 13.00x (*0-8095-1100-2*, Sidewinder Press) Borgo Pr.

Association Oath Rolls of the British Plantations (New York, Virginia, Etc.) A. D. 1696. Wallace Gandy. 96p. 1993. reprint ed. pap. 10.00 (*0-685-69922-6*, 9126) Clearfield Co.

Association of American Feed Control Officials Incorporated, Official Publication 1992. rev. ed. Association of American Feed Control Officials, Inc. Staff. Ed. by Earl M. Haas. 324p. 1992. 20.00 (*1-878341-02-2*) AAFCO.

Association of American Geographers: The First Seventy-Five Years. Preston E. James & Geoffrey J. Martin. LC 78-74887. (Illus.). 1979. 15.00 (*0-89291-134-4*) Assn Am Geographers.

***Association of American Universities Research Libraries Project: Reports of the AAU Task Forces.** 1994. pap. 12.00 (*0-918006-24-4*) ARL.

***Association of American University Press Directory 1994-1995.** 1994. pap. text ed. 14.95 (*0-945103-08-5*) U Ch Pr.

Association of American University Presses Directory, 1990-1991. Association of American University Staff. LC 54-43046. 1990. pap. 14.95 (*0-945103-03-4*) Assn Am Univ.

Association of British Health Care Industries Directory 1992-93: Guide to Health Care Equipment, Services & Supplies. Association for British Health Care Industries Staff. 112p. 1992. pap. 85.00 (*1-85302-173-3*, Pub. by J Kingsley Pubs UK) Taylor & Francis.

Association of Evangelical Friends. Arthur O. Roberts. 1975. pap. 3.50 (*0-913342-04-1*) Barclay Pr.

Association of Human Mortality with Air Pollution 1984. Frederick W. Lipfert. Ed. by Eustace A. Dixon. (Illus.). 240p. (C). 1984. pap. 15.95 (*0-942848-03-9*) Eureka Pubns.

***Association of Law Societies Practice Manual, 10 pts., Set.** A. Botha. Date not set. ring bd. 176.00 (*0-409-00644-0*, SA) Butterworth Legal Pubs.

Association of MBAs Guide to Business Schools. 10th ed. Ed. by Godfrey Golzen & Laura McGeary. 192p. (C). 1993. pap. 37.50x (*0-273-60340-X*, Pub. by Pitman Pub Ltd UK) Trans-Atl Phila.

***Association of MBAs Guide to Business Schools, 1995-96 Edition.** Ed. by Golzen McGeary & Laura McGeary. 350p. 1995. pap. 49.50 (*0-273-61306-5*, Pub. by Pitman Pub Ltd UK) Trans-Atl Phila.

***Association of Pacific Coast Geographers Yearbook 56.** Ed. by Daniel E. Turbeville, 3rd. 232p. (Orig.). 1995. pap. text ed. 15.00 (*0-87071-290-X*) Oreg St U Pr.

Association of South-East Asian Nations (ASEAN) annuals Ed. by Kenneth R. Simmonds & Brian H. Hill. (Law & Practice under the GATT & Other Trading Arrangements Ser.). 1991. Annual release. ring bd. 150.00 (*0-379-00822-X*) Oceana.

Association Operating Ratio Report. 8th ed. American Society of Association Executives Staff. 90p. 1989. pap. 100.00 (*0-88034-019-3*) Am Soc Assn Execs.

Association Technology Trends 1990. American Society of Association Executives Staff. 85p. (Orig.). 1990. pap. 60.00 (*0-88034-046-0*) Am Soc Assn Execs.

Association Theory: The Phases of Matter & Their Transformations. R. Ginell. (Studies in Physical & Theoretical Chemistry: Vol. 1). 224p. 1979. 59.00 (*0-444-41753-2*) Elsevier.

***Associational WMU Guide.** Carol Noffsinger. Ed. by Judith Edwards. 44p. (Orig.). 1995. pap. text ed. 3.95 (*1-56309-123-2*) Womans Mission Union.

Associationalism among Baptists in America: 1707-1814. Walter B. Shurden. Ed. by Edwin S. Gaustad. LC 79-52577. (Baptist Tradition Ser.). 1980. lib. bdg. 28.95 (*0-405-12445-7*) Ayer.

Associations: The Memory Book. Barry Roth. LC 92-70949. (Illus.). 90p. (Orig.). 1993. pap. 6.95 (*1-881140-01-6*) Benidee Prods.

Associations & Law: The Classical & Early Christian Stages. Otto F. Gierke. Ed. & Tr. by George Heiman. LC 76-48741. 174p. reprint ed. pap. 49.60 (*0-8357-8030-9*, 2033994) Bks Demand.

***Associations & the Global Marketplace.** Kimberly A. Svevo-Cianci & American Society of Association Executives Staff. 353p. 1995. pap. 82.95 (*0-88034-092-4*) Am Soc Assn Execs.

***Associations & the Global Marketplace: Profiles of Success.** Kimberly Svevo-Cianci. LC 95-6201. 1995. write for info. (*0-88034-100-9*) Am Soc Assn Execs.

Associations Between Insects & Plants. T. R. New. 113p. 1990. pap. 19.95 (*0-86840-099-8*, Pub. by New South Wales Univ Pr AT) Intl Spec Bk.

Associations et Societes Secretes sous la Deuxieme Republique, 1848-1851. J. Tchernoff. LC 77-176137. reprint ed. 55.00 (*0-404-07185-6*) AMS Pr.

Associations in Action: The Washington, D. C. Higher Education Community. Harland G. Bloland. Ed. & Frwd. by Jonathan D. Fife. LC 85-72833. (ASHE-ERIC Higher Education Report Ser.: No. 2, 1985). 135p. (Orig.). 1985. pap. 10.00 (*0-913317-21-7*) GWU Schl E&HD.

Associations Legislation in Australia & New Zealand. A. S. Sievers. 145p. 1989. pap. 24.00 (*1-86287-004-7*, Pub. by Federation Pr AU) W W Gaunt.

Associative Algebras. Richard S. Pierce. (Graduate Texts in Mathematics Ser.: Vol. 88). 416p. 1982. 59.00 (*0-387-90693-2*) Spr-Verlag.

Associative Array Processor. C. Fernstrom et al. (Lecture Notes in Computer Science Ser.: Vol. 216). xii, 323p. 1986. pap. 39.00 (*0-387-16445-6*) Spr-Verlag.

***Associative Card Code: A Tested ESP Methodology Manual.** Katharine C. Sabin. (Illus.). 65p. (Orig.). 1995. pap. 40.00 (*1-884715-03-6*) Mindreach Pubng.

Associative Computing: A Programming Paradigm for Massively Parallel Computers. J. L. Potter. (Frontiers of Computer Science Ser.). (Illus.). 336p. 1991. 59.50 (*0-306-43987-5*, Plenum Pr) Plenum.

Associative Democracy: New Forms of Economic & Social Governance. Paul Hirst. LC 93-36878. 232p. 1994. 45.00x (*0-87023-896-5*); pap. 16.95 (*0-87023-897-3*) U of Mass Pr.

Associative Engines: Connectionism, Concepts, & Representational Change. Andy Clark. LC 93-18722. (Illus.). 272p. 1993. 32.50 (*0-262-03210-4*) MIT Pr.

Associative Memory Using Artificial Neural Networks. A. N. Michel et al. 300p. 1995. text ed. 74.00 (*981-02-1581-9*) World Scientific Pub.

Associative N-Two Fixation, Vol. 1. Ed. by Peter B. Vose & Alaides P. Ruschel. 232p. 1981. 132.00 (*0-8493-6130-3*, S651, CRC Reprint) Franklin.

Associative N-Two Fixation, Vol. 2. Ed. by Peter B. Vose & Alaides P. Ruschel. 288p. 1981. 143.00 (*0-8493-6131-1*, CRC Reprint) Franklin.

Associative Networks: The Representation & Use of Knowledge by Computers. Ed. by Nicholas V. Findler. LC 78-31318. 1979. text ed. 106.00 (*0-12-256380-8*) Acad Pr.

Associative Neural Memories: Theory & Implementation. Ed. by Mohamad H. Hassoun. LC 92-30660. 376p. 1993. 85.00 (*0-19-507682-6*) OUP.

Assommoir. Emile Zola. 1955. write for info. (*0-318-63431-7*) Fr & Eur.

Assommoir. Emile Zola. Ed. by Jacques Dubois. 568p. (FRE.). 1990. pap. 11.95 (*0-7859-1486-2*, 2266033646) Fr & Eur.

***Assommoir.** Emile Zola. Ed. by Robert Lethbridge. Tr. by Margaret Mauldon. (World's Classics Ser.). (Illus.). 520p. 1995. pap. 6.95 (*0-19-282983-1*) OUP.

Assommoir. Emile Zola. (Folio Ser.: No. 1051). 1955. pap. 12.95 (*2-07-037051-8*) Schoenhof.

Assommoir. Emile Zola. (Classics Ser.). 1970. mass mkt. 6.95 (*0-14-044231-6*, Penguin Classics) Viking Penguin.

Assommoir, Zola: Critical Monographs in English. Roger Clark. 88p. 1993. pap. 32.00 (*0-85261-268-0*, Pub. by Univ of Glasgow UK) St Mut.

Assorted Articles. D. H. Lawrence. LC 68-29223. (Essay Index Reprint Ser.). 1977. reprint ed. 21.95 (*0-8369-0612-8*) Ayer.

Assorted Goods. Helen Sventitsky. Ed. by Edward Mycue. (Took Modern Poetry in English Ser.: No. 6). (Illus.). 28p. (Orig.). 1991. pap. 4.00 (*0-9625855-6-4*) Norton Coker Pr.

***Assorted Lives: A Collection of Poetry.** Roswita B. Davis. (Orig.). Date not set. pap. write for info. (*0-9632687-5-9*) PenRose Pub.

Assorted Prose. John Updike. 1965. 24.95 (*0-394-41473-X*) Knopf.

Assorted Stories. Lee Harwood. (Morning Coffee Chapbook Ser.). (Illus.). 12p. (Orig.). 1987. pap. 10.00 (*0-918273-37-4*) Coffee Hse.

Assorted Tales & Other Lies. Susan R. Spears. LC 92-82994. 120p. 1992. pap. 12.95 (*0-9635302-0-8*) Cracker Pub.

Assortment of Quotable Mindbenders. Hugh Sedditt & Noah Kidding. 1978. pap. 52.00 (*0-685-66988-2*) Arthur Owned.

***Assu of Cape Mudge: Recollections of a Coastal Indian Chief.** Joy Inglis. 184p. 1989. 19.95 (*0-7748-0333-9*) U of Wash Pr.

Assumed Identity. David Morrell. 512p. 1994. mass mkt. 6.50 (*0-446-60070-9*, Warner Vision) Warner Bks.

Assumed Identity. large type ed. David Morrell. 1994. 23.95 (*0-7927-1959-X*, Paragon Lrg Print) Chivers N Amer.

***Assumed Name.** Ricardo Piglia. Ed. by Yvette E. Miller. Tr. by Sergio Waisman. (Discoveries Ser.). 160p. Date not set. pap. 15.95 (*0-935480-71-4*) Lat Am Lit Rev Pr.

Assuming the Guise: African Masks Considered & Reconsidered. Suzanne Bach. LC 91-50617. (Illus.). 80p. (Orig.). 1991. pap. text ed. 14.95 (*0-913697-13-3*, U of Pa Pr) Williams Art.

Assumption-Based Planning: A Planning Tool for Very Uncertain Times. James A. Dewar et al. LC 93-7133. 1993. write for info. (*0-8330-1341-6*, MR-114-A) Rand Corp.

Assumption Cathedral of the Moscow Kremlin. T. V. Tolstaya. 132p. 1981. 105.00 (*0-686-73050-X*, Pub. by Collets UK) St Mut.

Assumption of Guilt. Harold Mehling. 352p. 1994. reprint ed. pap. text ed. 5.99 (*0-515-11450-2*) Jove Pubns.

Assumption of Moses: A Critical Edition with Commentary. Johannes Tromp. LC 92-39790. (Studia in Veteris Testamenti Pseudepigrapha Ser.: Vol. 10). 1992. 80.00 (*90-04-09779-1*) E J Brill.

Assumption of Our Lady. St. Dimitry of Rostov. 1976. pap. 1.50 (*0-317-30435-6*) Holy Trinity.

Assumption of Risk. Michael A. Stackpole. (BattleTech Ser.). 288p. 1993. pap. 4.99 (*0-451-45283-6*, ROC) NAL-Dutton.

Assumption of Rogues & Rascals. Elizabeth Smart. 1992. write for info. (*0-679-73803-7*) McKay.

Assumptions about Human Nature: A Social-Psychological Approach. 2nd ed. Lawrence S. Wrightsman. 368p. (C). 1991. text ed. 48.00 (*0-8039-2774-6*); pap. text ed. 22.95 (*0-8039-2775-4*) Sage.

Assumptions & Perceptions in Disarmament. Daniel Frei. 321p. pap. 14.00 (*92-9045-006-1*, G.11.84.0.4) UN.

Assumptions of Social Psychology: A Reexamination. Robert E. Lana. 160p. (C). 1991. text ed. 34.50 (*0-8058-1022-6*); pap. 16.50 (*0-8058-1023-4*) L Erlbaum Assocs.

Assur 14446: La famiglia "A" C. Saporetti. (Cybernetica Mesopotamica, Data Sets: Cuneiform Texts Ser.: Vol. 1). 140p. 1979. pap. 15.00 (*0-89003-036-7*) Undena Pubns.

Assurance. C. H. Spurgeon. 1976. pap. 2.00 (*1-56186-404-8*) Pilgrim Pubns.

***Assurance - Maladie d'Aujourd'hui.** Ed. by Joel V. Basarich. (FLMI Insurance Education Program Ser.). (FRE.). (C). 1994. pap. text ed. 25.00 (*0-939921-64-2*) LOMA.

Assurance of Adequate Disinfection, or C-T of Not C-T. 128p. 1987. pap. 17.50 (*0-89867-406-9*, 20013) Am Water Wks Assn.

Assurance of Faith: Calvin, English Puritanism, & the Dutch Second Reformation. Joel R. Beeke. LC 90-22089. (American University Studies: Theology & Religion: Ser. VII, Vol. 89). 518p. (C). 1994. pap. text ed. 39.95 (*0-8204-1428-X*) P Lang Pubs.

An Asterisk (*) at the beginning of an entry indicates that the title is appearing in BIP for the first time.

Assurance of Faith: Conscience in the Theology of Martin Luther & John Calvin. Randall C. Zachman. LC 92-12726. 272p. (C). 1992. text ed. 28.00 (*0-8006-2574-9*, 1-2574, Fortress Pr) Augsburg Fortress.

Assurance of Salvation. John R. Mumaw. 1989. pap. 4.95 (*0-87813-955-9*) Christian Light.

Assurance of Things Hoped For: A Theology of Christian Faith. Avery Dulles. LC 93-29720. 336p. 1994. 00 (*0-19-508302-4*) OUP.

Assurance Sciences: An Introduction to Quality Control & Reliability. S. Halpern. 1978. text ed. 77.00 (*0-13-049601-4*) P-H.

Assurance Technologies: Principles & Practices. Dev G. Raheja. (Engineering & Technology Management Ser.). 1991. text ed. 55.00 (*0-07-051212-4*) McGraw.

Assurance That Christ Is in You. Bill Freeman. (Illus.). 18p. (Orig.). 1984. pap. 0.50 (*0-914271-05-9*) Mnstry Wrd.

Assurances of the Heart: Faith-Building Devotions on Questions Christians Ask. Cornelius Plantinga, Jr. 304p. 1993. reprint ed. pap. 12.99 (*0-310-38641-1*) Zondervan.

Assurances Sur la Mort. James M. Cain. (FRE.). Date not set. pap. 11.95 (*0-7859-1966-X*, 2070374327) Fr & Eur.

Assuring Child Support: An Extension of Social Security. Irwin Garfinkel. LC 92-15042. (Illus.). 160p. 1992. 32.50x (*0-87154-300-1*) Russell Sage.

Assuring Child Support: An Extension of Social Security. Irwin Garfinkel. (Illus.). 172p. 1994. reprint ed. pap. 14.95 (*0-87154-301-X*) Russell Sage.

Assuring Control of Nuclear Weapons: The Evolution of Permissive Action Links. Peter Stein & Peter D. Feaver. (Occasional Papers: No. 2). (Illus.). 124p. (Orig.). 1987. lib. bdg. 38.00 (*0-8191-6336-8*); pap. text ed. 16.50 (*0-8191-6337-6*) U Pr of Amer.

Assuring Freedom to the Free: A Century of Emancipation in the U. S. A. Arnold M. Rose. LC 63-14634. 311p. reprint ed. pap. 88.70 (*0-7837-3789-0*, 2043609) Bks Demand.

Assuring Learning with Self-Instructional Packages, or Up the Up Staircase. Rita B. Johnson & Stuart R. Johnson. (C). 1973. reprint ed. pap. text ed. write for info. (*0-201-03327-5*) Addison-Wesley.

Assuring Quality for the Social Studies in Our Schools. Paul R. Hanna. (Publication Series: Education & Society). 126p. (C). 1987. pap. text ed. 6.78 (*0-8179-8502-6*) Hoover Inst Pr.

Assuring Quality Out-Patient Care for Children: Guidelines & a Management System. Charles D. Cook & Jane Heidt. 224p. 1987. 39.50 (*0-19-504993-4*) OUP.

Assuring Structural Integrity of Steel Reactor Pressure Boundary Components: Proceedings of the Fifth International Seminar, Held in Davos, Switzerland, 24-25 Aug., 1987. Ed. by K. E. Stahlkopf & L. E. Steele. 374p. 1989. 126.00 (*1-85166-242-1*) Elsevier.

Assuring Structural Integrity of Steel Reactor Pressure Vessels. L. E. Steele & K. E. Stahlkopf. (Illus.). 220p. 1980. 66.75 (*0-85334-906-1*, Pub. by Elsevier Applied Sci UK) Elsevier.

Assyria & Hanigalbat: A Historical Reconstruction of Bilateral Relations from the Middle of the Fourteenth to the End of the Twelfth Centuries B. C. Amir Harrak. (Texte und Studien Zur Orientalistik Ser.: Vol. 4). xviii, 315p. 1987. 31.20 (*3-487-07948-8*, Pub. by Georg Olms GW) Lubrecht & Cramer.

Assyrian & Babylonian Empires, 8th-6th Centuries B. C. (Cambridge Ancient History Ser.: Vol. 2, Pt. 2). 1991. 150.00 (*0-521-08691-4*) Cambridge U Pr.

Assyrian & Hebrew Hymns of Praise. Charles G. Cumming. LC 34-3318. (Columbia University. Oriental Studies: No. 12). reprint ed. 16.50 (*0-404-50502-3*) AMS Pr.

Assyrian Colonies in Cappadocia. Louis L. Orlin. (Orig.). 1970. pap. text ed. 67.70 (*3-10-800110-8*) Mouton.

Assyrian Connection. Phillip Goodman. LC 93-84463. 306p. 1993. pap. 12.99 (*0-933451-15-6*) Prescott Pr.

Assyrian Deeds & Documents, 4 vols., Set. Ed. by Claude H. Johns. LC 78-72742. (Ancient Mesopotamian Texts & Studies). reprint ed. 195.00 (*0-404-18180-5*) AMS Pr.

Assyrian Dictionary of the Oriental Institute of the University of Chicago, 2 pts., Pt. 1 & 2. Ed. by Erica Reiner et al. LC 56-58292. 1980. lib. bdg. 110.00 (*0-918986-17-6*) Orientl Inst Pr IT.

Assyrian Dictionary of the Oriental Institute of the University of Chicago, Vol. 1, A, Pt. 1. Ed. by A. Leo Oppenheim & Erica Reiner. LC 56-58292. (AKK.). 1964. lib. bdg. 40.00 (*0-918986-06-0*) Orientl Inst Pr IT.

Assyrian Dictionary of the Oriental Institute of the University of Chicago, Vol. 1, A, Pt. 2. Ed. by A. Leo Oppenheim & Erica Reiner. LC 56-58292. (AKK.). 1989. reprint ed. lib. bdg. 60.00 (*0-918986-07-9*) Orientl Inst Pr IT.

Assyrian Dictionary of the Oriental Institute of the University of Chicago, Vol. 2, B. Ed. by A. Leo Oppenheim et al. LC 56-58292. (AKK.). 1966. lib. bdg. 35.00 (*0-918986-08-7*) Orientl Inst Pr IT.

Assyrian Dictionary of the Oriental Institute of the University of Chicago, Vol. 3, D. Ed. by A. Leo Oppenheim & Erica Reiner. (AKK.). 1989. reprint ed. lib. bdg. 25.00 (*0-918986-09-5*) Orientl Inst Pr IT.

Assyrian Dictionary of the Oriental Institute of the University of Chicago, Vol. 4, E. Ed. by A. Leo Oppenheim & Erica Reiner. (AKK.). 1974. reprint ed. lib. bdg. 45.00 (*0-918986-10-9*) Orientl Inst Pr IT.

Assyrian Dictionary of the Oriental Institute of the University of Chicago, Vol. 5, G. Ed. by A. Leo Oppenheim. LC 56-58292. (AKK & ENG.). 1956. lib. bdg. 20.00 (*0-918986-11-7*) Orientl Inst Pr IT.

Assyrian Dictionary of the Oriental Institute of the University of Chicago, Vol. 6, H. Ed. by A. Leo Oppenheim. LC 56-58292. (AKK & ENG.). 1956. lib. bdg. 25.00 (*0-918986-12-5*) Orientl Inst Pr IT.

Assyrian Dictionary of the Oriental Institute of the University of Chicago, Vol. 7, I/J. Ed. by A. Leo Oppenheim & Erica Reiner. (AKK.). 1989. reprint ed. lib. bdg. 40.00 (*0-918986-13-3*) Orientl Inst Pr IT.

Assyrian Dictionary of the Oriental Institute of the University of Chicago, Vol. 8, K. Ed. by A. Leo Oppenheim et al. LC 56-58292. 1971. lib. bdg. 65.00 (*0-918986-14-1*) Orientl Inst Pr IT.

Assyrian Dictionary of the Oriental Institute of the University of Chicago, Vol. 9, L. Ed. by A. Leo Oppenheim & Erica Reiner. (AKK.). 1978. reprint ed. lib. bdg. 35.00 (*0-918986-15-X*) Orientl Inst Pr IT.

Assyrian Dictionary of the Oriental Institute of the University of Chicago, Vol. 10, M, Pts. 1 & 2. Ed. by A. Leo Oppenheim & Erica Reiner. LC 56-58292. (AKK.). 1991. reprint ed. lib. bdg. 110.00 (*0-918986-16-8*) Orientl Inst Pr IT.

Assyrian Dictionary of the Oriental Institute of the University of Chicago, Vol. 13, Q. Ed. by Erica Reiner et al. LC 56-58292. xxiv, 332p. 1982. text ed. 60.00 (*0-918986-24-9*) Orientl Inst Pr IT.

Assyrian Dictionary of the Oriental Institute of the University of Chicago, Vol. 15, S. Ed. by Erica Reiner et al. LC 56-58292. xxiv, 428p. 1984. text ed. 65.00 (*0-918986-40-0*) Orientl Inst Pr IT.

Assyrian Dictionary of the Oriental Institute of the University of Chicago, Vol. 16, S. Ed. by A. Leo Oppenheim & Erica Reiner. LC 56-58292. (AKK.). 1989. reprint ed. lib. bdg. 30.00 (*0-918986-18-4*) Orientl Inst Pr IT.

Assyrian Dictionary of the Oriental Institute of the University of Chicago, Vol. 17, S, Pt. 1. Ed. by Erica Reiner et al. LC 56-58292. xxviii, 492p. 1989. 85.00 (*0-918986-55-9*) Orientl Inst Pr IT.

Assyrian Dictionary of the Oriental Institute of the University of Chicago, Vol. 17, S, Pt. 2. Ed. by Erica Reiner et al. LC 56-58292. xxiii, 453p. 1992. lib. bdg. 115.00 (*0-918986-78-8*) Orientl Inst Pr IT.

Assyrian Dictionary of the Oriental Institute of the University of Chicago, Vol. 21, Z. Ed. by A. Leo Oppenheim & Erica Reiner. LC 56-58292. 1961. lib. bdg. 20.00 (*0-918986-19-2*) Orientl Inst Pr IT.

Assyrian Doomsday Book, or, Liber Censualis of the District Round Harran in the Seventh Century B.C. Ed. by Claude H. Johns. LC 78-72741. (Ancient Mesopotamian Texts & Studies). reprint ed. 27.50 (*0-404-18179-1*) AMS Pr.

Assyrian Empire: Prehistory of the Balkans, & the Middle East & the Aegean World, 10th-8th Centuries B. C. 2nd ed. Ed. by John Boardman et al. LC 75-85719. (Cambridge Ancient History Ser.: Vol. 3, Pt. 1). (Illus.). 1059p. 1982. 150.00 (*0-521-22496-9*) Cambridge U Pr.

Assyrian Empire: The Assyrian & Babylonian Empires & Other States of the New East, 8th-6th Centuries B. C. Ed. by John Boardman. LC 75-85719. (Cambridge Ancient History Ser.: Vol. 3, Pt. 2). (Illus.). 912p. 1992. 140.00 (*0-521-22717-8*) Cambridge U Pr.

Assyrian Empire: The Expansion of the Greek World, 8th-6th Centuries B. C. 2nd ed. Ed. by John Boardman & N. G. Hammond. (Cambridge Ancient History Ser.: Vol. 3, Pt. 3). (Illus.). 530p. 1982. 94.95 (*0-521-23447-6*) Cambridge U Pr.

Assyrian Grammar. Samuel A. Mercer. LC 22-17308. (Columbia University. Oriental Studies: No. 29). reprint ed. 15.00 (*0-404-50519-8*) AMS Pr.

Assyrian Invasions & Deportations of Israel. 2nd ed. J. Llewllyn Thomas. 48p. 1989. pap. 3.00 (*0-934666-33-4*) Artisan Sales.

Assyrian Language. Leonard W. King. LC 73-18448. reprint ed. 32.50 (*0-404-11351-6*) AMS Pr.

Assyrian Medical Texts from the Originals in the British Museum. Ed. by Reginald C. Thompson. LC 78-72766. (Ancient Mesopotamian Texts & Studies). (Illus.). 120p. reprint ed. 37.50 (*0-404-18220-8*) AMS Pr.

Assyrian National Question at the United Nation: (A Historical Injustice Redressed) Sargon O. Dadesho. (Illus.). 308p. 1987. text ed. 25.00 (*0-9618344-0-4*) Bet Nahrain.

***Assyrian Origins: Discoveries of Ashor on the Tigris: Antiquities from the Vorderasiatisches Museum, Berlin.** Prudence O. Harper et al. (Illus.). 1995. pap. 25.00 (*0-87099-743-2*) Metro Mus Art.

Assyrian Primer: An Inductive Method of Learning the Cuneiform Characters. J. Dyneley Prince. LC 17-31948. (Columbia University. Contributions to Oriental History & Philology Ser.: No. 3). reprint ed. 20.00 (*0-404-50533-3*) AMS Pr.

Assyrian Primer & Assyrian Texts. J. D. Prince & E. A. Budge. 104p. 1978. pap. 15.00 (*0-89005-226-3*) Ares.

Assyrian Rulers of the Early First Millennium BC: I (1114-859 BC) A. Kirk Grayson. (Royal Inscriptions of Mesopotamia, Assyrian Periods Ser.: No. 2). (Illus.). 448p. 1991. 150.00 (*0-8020-5965-1*) U of Toronto Pr.

Assyrian Rulers of the Third & Second Milenia BC. A. Kirk Grayson. (Royal Inscriptions of Mesopotamia Ser.). 356p. 1987. 90.00 (*0-8020-2605-2*) U of Toronto Pr.

Assyrian Sculpture. Julian Reade. (British Museum Paperbacks Ser.). (Illus.). 72p. 1983. pap. 12.50 (*0-674-05016-9*) HUP.

Assyrians. Richard Morris. 112p. (Orig.). pap. 10.95 (*0-912292-92-X*) The Smith.

Astadhyayi of Panini. Panini. Tr. by Sumitra M. Katre. (Texas Linguistics Ser.). 1376p. 1987. text ed. 100.00 (*0-292-70394-5*) U of Tex Pr.

Astadhyayi of Panini, 2 vols., Set. Tr. by Srisa C. Vasu. 1980. reprint ed. 78.50 (*81-208-0409-0*, Pub. by Motilal Banarsidass II) S Asia.

Astadhyayi of Panini, Vol. 1. Rama N. Sharma. (C). 1988. 37.00 (*81-215-0052-4*, Pub. by Munshiram Manoharial II) S Asia.

Astadhyayi of Panini, Vol. 2. Rama N. Sharma. 1990. 75.00 (*0-685-37839-X*, Pub. by Munshiram Manoharial II) S Asia.

***Astadhyayi of Panini Vol. 1.** Tr. by S. D. Joshi. (C). 1992. 17.50x (*81-7201-166-0*, Pub. by Sahitya Akademi II) S Asia.

Astaire Dancing. John Mueller. (Illus.). 448p. 1991. reprint ed. 24.99 (*0-517-06075-2*) Random Hse Value.

Astaire Dancing: The Musical Films. John Mueller. LC 84-47874. (Illus.). 448p. 1985. 45.00 (*0-394-51654-0*) Knopf.

Astanga Yoga, an Aerobic Yoga System: Sequential Movement Synchronized with Breathing. Paltabhi Jois & Ray Rosenthal. (Illus.). 160p. 1989. Incl. video cass. cass. & instructional bk. write for info. (*0-923064-00-1*); pap. text ed. write for info. (*0-923064-01-X*) Hart Prodns.

Astanga Yoga, an Aerobic Yoga System, Taught by K. Paltabhi Jois. Ray Rosenthal. 1988. vhs 39.95 (*0-685-23252-2*) Hart Prodns.

Asta's Book. Barbara Vine. LC 93-11384. 1994. 24.95 (*0-7927-1759-7*, Paragon Lrg Print); pap. 23.95 (*0-7927-1758-9*, Paragon Lrg Print) Chivers N Amer.

Astavakra Samhita. Astavakra. Tr. by Swami Nityaswarupananda. (ENG & SAN.). 1940. pap. 2.95 (*0-87481-165-1*, Pub. by Advaita Ashrama II) Vedanta Pr.

ASTC ICIMUSET Directory, 1994. 158p. pap. 38.00 (*0-944040-38-1*) AST Ctrs.

ASTC Salary Survey, 1993. Comp. by Andrea Peek. 68p. 1993. 125.00 (*0-944040-33-0*) AST Ctrs.

ASTC Science Center Survey Report Series (1988-89), 3 vols., Set. write for info. (*0-685-29590-7*) AST Ctrs.

ASTC Science Center Survey Report Series (1988-89), 3 vols., Vol. 1: Exhibits Report & Directory. Vol. 1, Exhibits Report & Directory. 20.00 (*0-944040-14-4*) AST Ctrs.

ASTC Science Center Survey Report Series (1988-89), 3 vols., Vol. 2: Education Report & Directory. Vol. 2, Education Report & Directory. 20.00 (*0-944040-15-2*) AST Ctrs.

ASTC Science Center Survey Report Series (1988-89), 3 vols., Vol. 3: Administration & Finance Report. Vol. 3, Administration & Finance Report. 15.00 (*0-944040-16-0*) AST Ctrs.

***ASTD Assess (Version 1.1) Software for Training Needs Assessment Surveys.** Ed. by John Wilcox. LC 94-78628. (Illus.). 97p. 1994. disk 395.00 (*1-56286-010-0*) Am Soc Train & Devel.

ASTD Handbok of Instructional Technology. Ed. by George M. Piskurich. LC 92-23142. 1992. 59.95 (*0-07-001531-7*) Am Soc Train & Devel.

ASTD Reference Guide to Professional Human Resource Development Roles & Competencies. 2nd ed. William J. Rothwell & Henry J. Sredl. 1000p. 1992. 79.95 (*0-87425-177-X*) Human Res Dev Pr.

ASTD Research Ser., 5 vols. Ed. by Richard D. Peterson. (ASTD Research Ser.). 384p. 11.95 (*0-318-13264-8*); pap. 14.95 (*0-318-13263-X*, PEDPP) Am Soc Train & Devel.

***ASTD Technical & Skills Training Handbook: American Society for Training & Development.** Ed. by Leslie Kelly. LC 94-28037. 1994. 59.50 (*0-07-033899-X*) McGraw.

Astella & Pipturus of Hawaii. C. Skottsberg. (BMB Ser.: No. 117). 1972. reprint ed. 20.00 (*0-527-02223-3*) Periodicals Srv.

Aster Aardvark's Alphabet Adventures. Steven Kellogg. LC 87-5715. (Illus.). 40p. (J). (gr. k up). 1987. 15.00 (*0-688-07256-9*); lib. bdg. 14.93 (*0-688-07257-7*) Morrow Jr Bks.

Aster Aardvark's Alphabet Adventures. Steven Kellogg. LC 87-5715. (Illus.). 40p. (J). (gr. 1 up). 1992. pap. 3.95 (*0-688-11571-3*, Mulberry) Morrow.

***Asteraceae.** E. Lamont. (Memoirs of the New York Botanical Garden Ser.: Vol. 72). (Illus.). 1995. pap. write for info. (*0-89327-391-0*) NY Botanical.

Asteraceae: Cladistics & Classification. Kare Bremer. LC 93-28134. (Illus.). 752p. 1994. 79.95 (*0-88192-275-7*) Timber.

Asteraceae of the High Mountains of New Guinea. P. Van Royen. (Illus.). 318p. 1983. lib. bdg. 65.00 (*3-7682-1355-2*) Lubrecht & Cramer.

Asteraceae, Vol. 1: Vascular Flora of the Southeastern United States. Arthur Cronquist. LC 79-769. xv, 261p. 1980. 45.00 (*0-8078-1362-1*) U of NC Pr.

Asterion, the Minotaur: A Book of Suspicion, Resentment, Confusion, Regret, Poor Memory, Tales, Poetry, & Conversation. Paul Majkut. LC 93-16136. 1993. write for info. (*0-9632702-3-0*) Lightning.

Asteriscos. Jose Ferrer Canales. LC 90-30571. 314p. (Orig.). 1990. pap. 5.95 (*0-8477-3616-4*) U of PR Pr.

Asterisk! Jerome Weidman. 1969. pap. 4.75 (*0-8222-0072-4*) Dramatists Play.

Asterisk Destiny. Campbell Armstrong. 1991. mass mkt. 4.95 (*0-06-100160-0*, Harp PBks) HarpC.

***Asterisked Materials in the Greek Job.** Peter J. Gentry. LC 94-49392. (Septuagint & Cognate Studies Series - Society of Biblical Literature: No. 38). 1995. write for info. (*0-7885-0093-7*); pap. write for info. (*0-7885-0094-5*) Scholars Pr GA.

Asterix: Comment Obelix est Tombe dans la Marmite du Druide Quand Il Etait Petit. Rene De Goscinny & M. Uderzo. (FRE.). (J). 1990. 19.95 (*0-8288-8597-4*) Fr & Eur.

Asterix: How Obelix Fell into the Magic Cauldron When He Was a Little Boy. Rene De Goscinny & M. Uderzo. (J). 1990. 19.95 (*0-8288-8594-X*) Fr & Eur.

Asterix - Obelix & Company. Rene De Goscinny. (Illus.). pap. 9.95 (*0-340-25307-X*) Intl Lang.

Asterix - The Twelve Tasks Of. Goscinny. (Illus.). pap. 9.95 (*0-340-27647-9*) Intl Lang.

Asterix Aetepekioe en Oayammie. Rene De Goscinny & A. Uderzo. (GRE.). 1992. 19.95 (*0-7859-1040-9*, 9602202661) Fr & Eur.

Asterix als Gladiator. Rene De Goscinny & M. Uderzo. (Illus.). (GER.). (J). (gr. 7-10). 1992. 19.95 (*0-8288-4923-4*) Fr & Eur.

Asterix als Legionar. Rene De Goscinny & M. Uderzo. (Illus.). (GER.). (J). (gr. 7-10). 1992. 19.95 (*0-8288-4924-2*) Fr & Eur.

Asterix & Caesar's Gift. Rene De Goscinny & M. Uderzo. (Illus.). (J). (gr. 7-10). 1990. 19.95 (*0-8288-4915-3*) Fr & Eur.

Asterix & Caesar's Gift. Rene De Goscinny. (Asterix Ser.). (J). 1977. pap. 9.95 (*0-317-00093-4*) Intl Lang.

Asterix & Caesar's Gilt. Goscinny. (Illus.). pap. 9.95 (*0-340-23301-X*) Intl Lang.

Asterix & Cleopatra. Rene De Goscinny & M. Uderzo. (Illus.). (J). (gr. 7-10). 1990. 19.95 (*0-8288-4916-1*) Fr & Eur.

Asterix & Cleopatra. Rene De Goscinny. (Asterix Ser.). (Illus.). (J). 1976. pap. 9.95 (*0-340-17220-7*) Intl Lang.

Asterix & Maestria. Rene De Goscinny & A. Uderzo. (GER.). 1992. 19.95 (*0-7859-1025-5*, 3770400291) Fr & Eur.

Asterix & Operation Getafix. Rene De Goscinny & M. Uderzo. (J). 1990. 19.95 (*0-8288-8570-2*) Fr & Eur.

Asterix & Son. Rene De Goscinny & M. Uderzo. (J). 1990. 19.95 (*0-8288-8568-0*) Fr & Eur.

Asterix & Son. Rene De Goscinny & A. Uderzo. 1992. 19.95 (*0-7859-1047-6*, 0-340-330082) Fr & Eur.

Asterix & the Banquet. Rene De Goscinny & M. Uderzo. (J). 1990. 19.95 (*0-8288-8590-7*) Fr & Eur.

Asterix & the Banquet. Rene De Goscinny & A. Uderzo. 1992. 19.95 (*0-7859-1042-5*, 0-340-231742) Fr & Eur.

Asterix & the Banquet. Goscinny. (Illus.). pap. 9.95 (*0-340-26429-2*) Intl Lang.

Asterix & the Big Fight. Rene De Goscinny & M. Uderzo. (Illus.). (J). (gr. 7-10). 1990. 19.95 (*0-8288-4917-X*) Fr & Eur.

Asterix & the Big Fight. Rene De Goscinny. (Asterix Ser.). (Illus.). (J). 1976. pap. 9.95 (*0-340-19167-8*) Intl Lang.

Asterix & the Black Gold. Rene De Goscinny & M. Uderzo. (J). 1990. 19.95 (*0-8288-8592-3*) Fr & Eur.

Asterix & the Black Gold. Rene De Goscinny & A. Uderzo. 1992. 19.95 (*0-7859-1046-8*, 0-340-27476X) Fr & Eur.

Asterix & the Cauldron. Rene De Goscinny. (Asterix Ser.). (Illus.). (J). 1976. pap. 9.95 (*0-340-22711-7*) Intl Lang.

Asterix & the Chieftain's Shield. Rene De Goscinny & M. Uderzo. (Illus.). (J). (gr. 7-10). 1990. 19.95 (*0-8288-4918-8*) Fr & Eur.

Asterix & the Chieftain's Shield. Rene De Goscinny. (Asterix Ser.). (Illus.). (J). 1977. pap. 9.95 (*0-340-22710-9*) Intl Lang.

Asterix & the Golden Sickle. Rene De Goscinny. (Asterix Ser.). (Illus.). (J). 1976. pap. 9.95 (*0-340-21209-8*) Intl Lang.

Asterix & the Goths. Rene De Goscinny & M. Uderzo. (Illus.). (J). (gr. 7-10). 1990. 19.95 (*0-8288-4919-6*) Fr & Eur.

Asterix & the Great Crossing. Rene De Goscinny. (Asterix Ser.). (Illus.). (J). 1976. pap. 9.95 (*0-340-21589-5*) Intl Lang.

Asterix & the Great Divide. Rene De Goscinny & M. Uderzo. (J). 1990. 19.95 (*0-8288-8567-2*) Fr & Eur.

Asterix & the Great Divide. Rene De Goscinny & A. Uderzo. 1992. 19.95 (*0-7859-1045-X*, 0-340-259884) Fr & Eur.

Asterix & the Laurel Wreath. Rene De Goscinny & M. Uderzo. (Illus.). (J). (gr. 7-10). 1990. 19.95 (*0-8288-4920-X*) Fr & Eur.

Asterix & the Laurel Wreath. Rene De Goscinny. (Asterix Ser.). (Illus.). (J). 1976. pap. 9.95 (*0-340-20699-3*) Intl Lang.

Asterix & the Magic Carpet. Rene De Goscinny & M. Uderzo. (J). 1990. 19.95 (*0-8288-8569-9*) Fr & Eur.

Asterix & the Magic Carpet. Rene De Goscinny & A. Uderzo. 1992. 19.95 (*0-7859-1048-4*, 0-340-409576) Fr & Eur.

Asterix & the Normans. (Illus.). pap. 9.95 (*0-02-497290-8*) Intl Lang.

Asterix & the Normans. Rene De Goscinny & M. Uderzo. (Illus.). (J). (gr. 7-10). 1990. 19.95 (*0-8288-4921-8*) Fr & Eur.

Asterix & the Roman Agent. Rene De Goscinny & M. Uderzo. (Illus.). (J). (gr. 7-10). 1990. 19.95 (*0-8288-4922-6*) Fr & Eur.

Asterix & the Roman Agent. Rene De Goscinny. (Asterix Ser.). (Illus.). (J). 1976. pap. 9.95 (*0-340-19168-6*) Intl Lang.

Asterix & the Soothsayer. Rene De Goscinny. (Asterix Ser.). (Illus.). (J). 1976. pap. 9.95 (*0-340-20697-7*) Intl Lang.

Asterix Apud Brittannos. Rene De Goscinny & A. Uderzo. (LAT.). 1992. 19.95 (*0-7859-1029-8*, 3770400593) Fr & Eur.

Asterix apud Gothos. Rene De Goscinny & M. Uderzo. (Illus.). (LAT.). (J). (gr. 7-10). 1990. lib. bdg. 19.95 (*0-8288-4925-0*) Fr & Eur.

Asterix at the Olympic Games. Rene De Goscinny & M. Uderzo. (Illus.). (J). (gr. 7-10). 1990. 19.95 (*0-8288-4926-9*) Fr & Eur.

Asterix at the Olympic Games. Rene De Goscinny. (Asterix Ser.). (Illus.). (J). 1976. pap. 9.95 (*0-340-19169-4*) Intl Lang.

Asterix Atque Olla Cypria. Rene De Goscinny & A. Uderzo. (LAT.). 1992. 19.95 (*0-7859-1033-6*, 3770400666) Fr & Eur.

An Asterisk (*) at the beginning of an entry indicates that the title is appearing in BIP for the first time.

Asterix auf Korsika. Rene De Goscinny & M. Uderzo. (Illus.). (GER.). (J). (gr. 7-10). 1990. lib. bdg. 19.95 (*0-8288-4927-7*) Fr & Eur.

Asterix aux Jeux Olympiques. Rene De Goscinny. (FRE.). (J). (gr. 7-9). 1990. 19.95 (*0-8288-5109-3*, FC884) Fr & Eur.

Asterix aux Jeux Olympiques. Rene De Goscinny & A. Uderzo. (FRE.). 1992. 19.95 (*0-7859-0986-9*, 2205003208) Fr & Eur.

Asterix bei den Briten. Rene De Goscinny & M. Uderzo. (Illus.). (GER.). (J). (gr. 7-10). 1990. lib. bdg. 19.95 (*0-8288-4928-5*) Fr & Eur.

Asterix bei den Olympischen Spielen. Rene De Goscinny & M. Uderzo. (Illus.). (GER.). (J). (gr. 7-10). 1990. lib. bdg. 19.95 (*0-8288-4929-3*) Fr & Eur.

Asterix bei den Schweizern. Rene De Goscinny & M. Uderzo. (Illus.). (GER.). (J). (gr. 7-10). 1990. lib. bdg. 19.95 (*0-8288-4930-7*) Fr & Eur.

Asterix Certamen Principum. Rene De Goscinny & A. Uderzo. (LAT.). 1992. 19.95 (*0-7859-1027-1*, 3770400577) Fr & Eur.

Asterix chez les Belges. Rene De Goscinny & M. Uderzo. (Illus.). (FRE.). (J). (gr. 7-10). 1990. 19.95 (*0-8288-4931-5*) Fr & Eur.

Asterix Chez les Bretons. Rene De Goscinny. (FRE.). (J). (gr. 7-9). 1990. 19.95 (*0-8288-5108-5*, FC880) Fr & Eur.

Asterix Chez les Bretons. Rene De Goscinny & A. Uderzo. (FRE.). 1992. 19.95 (*0-7859-1075-1*, 220500185X) Fr & Eur.

Asterix Chez les Helvetes. Rene De Goscinny. (Illus.). (FRE.). (J). (gr. 7-9). 1990. 19.95 (*0-8288-5110-7*, FC889) Fr & Eur.

Asterix Chez les Helvetes. Rene De Goscinny & A. Uderzo. (FRE.). 1992. 19.95 (*0-7859-0989-3*, 2205005162) Fr & Eur.

Asterix Chez Rahazade. Rene De Goscinny & M. Uderzo. (FRE.). (J). 1990. 19.95 (*0-8288-8572-9*) Fr & Eur.

Asterix Chez Rahazade. Rene De Goscinny & A. Uderzo. (FRE.). 1992. 19.95 (*0-7859-1016-6*, 2864970201) Fr & Eur.

Asterix Clipeus Arvernus. Rene De Goscinny & A. Uderzo. (LAT.). 1992. 19.95 (*0-7859-1077-8*, 377040064X) Fr & Eur.

Asterix der Gallier. Rene De Goscinny & M. Uderzo. (Illus.). (GER.). (J). (gr. 7-10). 1990. lib. bdg. 19.95 (*0-8288-4932-3*) Fr & Eur.

Asterix el Galo. Rene De Goscinny & M. Uderzo. (Illus.). (SPA.). (J). (gr. 7-10). 19.95 (*0-8288-4933-1*) Fr & Eur.

Asterix en Bretana. Rene De Goscinny & M. Uderzo. (Illus.). (SPA.). (J). (gr. 7-10). 1990. lib. bdg. 19.95 (*0-8288-4934-X*) Fr & Eur.

Asterix en Corcega. Rene De Goscinny & M. Uderzo. (Illus.). (SPA.). (J). (gr. 7-10). 1990. lib. bdg. 19.95 (*0-8288-4935-8*) Fr & Eur.

Asterix en Corse. Rene De Goscinny & M. Uderzo. (Illus.). (FRE.). (J). (gr. 7-10). 1990. 19.95 (*0-8288-4936-6*) Fr & Eur.

Asterix en Corse. Rene De Goscinny & A. Uderzo. (FRE.). 1992. 19.95 (*0-7859-0991-5*, 2205006940) Fr & Eur.

Asterix en Helvecia. Rene De Goscinny & M. Uderzo. (Illus.). (SPA.). (J). (gr. 7-10). 1990. lib. bdg. 19.95 (*0-8288-4937-4*) Fr & Eur.

Asterix en Hispania. Rene De Goscinny & A. Uderzo. (SPA.). 1992. 19.95 (*0-7859-1039-5*, 8475100287) Fr & Eur.

Asterix en Hispanie. Rene De Goscinny. (Illus.). (FRE.). (J). (gr. 7-9). 1990. 19.95 (*0-8288-5111-5*, FC887) Fr & Eur.

Asterix en los Juegos Olimpicos. Rene De Goscinny & M. Uderzo. (Illus.). (SPA.). (J). (gr. 7-10). 1990. lib. bdg. 19.95 (*0-8288-4938-2*) Fr & Eur.

Asterix et Cleopatra. Rene De Goscinny & A. Uderzo. (LAT.). 1992. 19.95 (*0-7859-1026-3*, 3770400569) Fr & Eur.

Asterix et Cleopatre. Rene De Goscinny. (FRE.). (J). (gr. 7-9). 1990. 19.95 (*0-8288-5112-3*, FC878) Fr & Eur.

Asterix et Cleopatre. Rene De Goscinny & A. Uderzo. (FRE.). 1992. 19.95 (*0-7859-0981-8*, 2205001574) Fr & Eur.

Asterix et Hispanie. Rene De Goscinny & A. Uderzo. (FRE.). 1992. 19.95 (*0-7859-0988-5*, 2205003941) Fr & Eur.

Asterix et la Rose et le Glaive. Rene De Goscinny & M. Uderzo. (FRE.). (J). 1990. 19.95 (*0-8288-8573-7*) Fr & Eur.

Asterix et la Serpe d'or. Rene De Goscinny. (Illus.). (FRE.). (J). (gr. 3-8). 1990. 19.95 (*0-8288-4939-0*) Fr & Eur.

Asterix et la Surprise de Cesar. Rene De Goscinny & A. Uderzo. (FRE.). 1992. 19.95 (*0-7859-0993-1*, 2205030044) Fr & Eur.

Asterix et la Surprise de Cesar. Rene Goscinny & Uderzo Goscinny. 64p. (FRE.). 1993. lib. bdg. 19.95 (*0-7859-3651-3*, 2865030044) Fr & Eur.

Asterix et le Chaudron. Rene De Goscinny. (Illus.). (FRE.). (J). (gr. 7-9). 1990. 19.95 (*0-8288-5113-1*, FC885) Fr & Eur.

Asterix et le Chaudron. Rene De Goscinny & A. Uderzo. (FRE.). 1992. 19.95 (*0-7859-0987-7*, 2205003364) Fr & Eur.

Asterix et les Goths. Rene De Goscinny. (FRE.). (J). (gr. 7-9). 1990. 19.95 (*0-8288-5114-X*, FC875) Fr & Eur.

Asterix et les Normands. Rene De Goscinny. (FRE.). (J). (gr. 7-9). 1990. 19.95 (*0-8288-5115-8*, FC881) Fr & Eur.

Asterix et les Normands. Rene De Goscinny & A. Uderzo. (FRE.). 1992. 19.95 (*0-7859-0983-4*, 2205001906) Fr & Eur.

Asterix et Normanni. Rene De Goscinny & A. Uderzo. (LAT.). 1992. 19.95 (*0-7859-1031-X*, 3770400615) Fr & Eur.

Asterix Gallus. Rene De Goscinny & M. Uderzo. (Illus.). (LAT.). (J). (gr. 7-10). 1990. lib. bdg. 19.95 (*0-8288-4941-2*) Fr & Eur.

Asterix Gladiador. Rene De Goscinny & M. Uderzo. (Illus.). (SPA.). (J). (gr. 7-10). 1990. lib. bdg. 19.95 (*0-8288-4942-0*) Fr & Eur.

Asterix Gladiateur. Rene De Goscinny. (FRE.). (J). (gr. 7-9). 1990. 19.95 (*0-8288-5116-6*, FC876) Fr & Eur.

Asterix Gladiateur. Rene De Goscinny & A. Uderzo. (FRE.). 1992. 19.95 (*0-7859-0980-X*, 2205001345) Fr & Eur.

Asterix Gladiator. Rene De Goscinny & M. Uderzo. (Illus.). (LAT.). (J). 1990. 19.95 (*0-8288-4943-9*) Fr & Eur.

Asterix in Belgium. Rene De Goscinny & M. Uderzo. (J). 1990. 19.95 (*0-8288-8591-5*) Fr & Eur.

Asterix in Belgium. Rene De Goscinny & A. Uderzo. 1992. 19.95 (*0-7859-1044-1*, 0-340-257350) Fr & Eur.

Asterix in Belgium. Goscinny. (Illus.). pap. 9.95 (*0-340-27753-X*) Intl Lang.

Asterix in Britain. Rene De Goscinny & M. Uderzo. (Illus.). (J). 1990. 19.95 (*0-8288-4944-7*) Fr & Eur.

Asterix in Britain. Rene De Goscinny. (Asterix Ser.). (Illus.). (J). 1976. pap. 9.95 (*0-340-17221-5*) Intl Lang.

Asterix in Corsica. Rene De Goscinny & M. Uderzo. (J). 1990. 19.95 (*0-8288-8566-4*) Fr & Eur.

Asterix in Corsica. Rene De Goscinny & A. Uderzo. 1992. 19.95 (*0-7859-1043-3*, 240741) Fr & Eur.

Asterix in Corsica. Goscinny. (Illus.). pap. 9.95 (*0-340-27754-8*) Intl Lang.

Asterix in Hispania. Rene De Goscinny & A. Uderzo. (LAT.). 1992. 19.95 (*0-7859-1034-4*, 3770400674) Fr & Eur.

Asterix in Spain. Rene De Goscinny & M. Uderzo. (Illus.). (J). 1990. 19.95 (*0-8288-4945-5*) Fr & Eur.

Asterix in Spain. Rene De Goscinny. (Asterix Ser.). (Illus.). (J). 1976. pap. 9.95 (*0-340-18326-8*) Intl Lang.

Asterix in Spanien. Rene De Goscinny & M. Uderzo. (Illus.). (GER.). (J). 1990. lib. bdg. 19.95 (*0-8288-4946-3*) Fr & Eur.

Asterix in Switzerland. Rene De Goscinny & M. Uderzo. (Illus.). (J). 1990. lib. bdg. 19.95 (*0-8288-4947-1*) Fr & Eur.

Asterix in Switzerland. Rene De Goscinny. (Asterix Ser.). (Illus.). (J). 1976. pap. 9.95 (*0-340-19270-4*) Intl Lang.

Asterix iter Gallicum. Rene De Goscinny & M. Uderzo. (Illus.). (LAT.). (J). 1990. lib. bdg. 19.95 (*0-8288-4948-X*) Fr & Eur.

Asterix la Rosa y la Espada. Rene De Goscinny & A. Uderzo. (SPA.). 1992. 19.95 (*0-7859-1038-7*, 8474199123) Fr & Eur.

Asterix la Rose et le Glaive. Rene De Goscinny & A. Uderzo. (FRE.). 1992. 19.95 (*0-7859-1017-4*, 2864970538) Fr & Eur.

Asterix la Zizanie. Rene De Goscinny. (Illus.). (FRE.). (J). (gr. 7-9). 1990. 19.95 (*0-8288-5117-4*, FC888) Fr & Eur.

Asterix le Gaulois. Rene De Goscinny. (FRE.). (J). (gr. 7-9). 1990. 19.95 (*0-8288-5118-2*, FC873) Fr & Eur.

Asterix le Gaulois. Rene De Goscinny & A. Uderzo. (FRE.). 1992. 19.95 (*0-7859-0979-6*, 2205000969) Fr & Eur.

Asterix Legionario. Rene De Goscinny & M. Uderzo. (Illus.). (SPA.). (J). 1990. lib. bdg. 19.95 (*0-8288-4949-8*) Fr & Eur.

Asterix Legionnaire. Rene De Goscinny. (FRE.). (J). (gr. 7-9). 1990. 19.95 (*0-8288-5119-0*, FC882) Fr & Eur.

Asterix Legionnaire. Rene De Goscinny & A. Uderzo. (FRE.). 1992. 19.95 (*0-7859-0984-2*, 2205002309) Fr & Eur.

Asterix, Obelix & Company. Rene De Goscinny & M. Uderzo. (J). 1990. 19.95 (*0-8288-8565-6*) Fr & Eur.

Asterix Olympius. Rene De Goscinny & A. Uderzo. (LAT.). 1992. 19.95 (*0-7859-0959-1*, 0-377-040658) Fr & Eur.

Asterix Orientalis. Rene De Goscinny & A. Uderzo. (LAT.). 1992. 19.95 (*0-7859-1035-2*, 3770400682) Fr & Eur.

Asterix the Gaul. Rene De Goscinny & M. Uderzo. (Illus.). (J). 1990. 19.95 (*0-8288-4950-1*) Fr & Eur.

Asterix the Gaul. Goscinny. (Illus.). pap. 9.95 (*0-340-17210-X*) Intl Lang.

Asterix the Gladiator. Rene De Goscinny & M. Uderzo. (Illus.). (J). 1990. 19.95 (*0-8288-4951-X*) Fr & Eur.

Asterix the Gladiator. Rene De Goscinny. (Asterix Ser.). (Illus.). (J). 1976. pap. 9.95 (*0-340-18320-9*) Intl Lang.

Asterix the Legionary. Rene De Goscinny & M. Uderzo. (Illus.). (J). 1990. 19.95 (*0-8288-4952-8*) Fr & Eur.

Asterix the Legionary. Rene De Goscinny. (Asterix Ser.). (Illus.). (J). 1976. pap. 9.95 (*0-340-18321-7*) Intl Lang.

Asterix und die Goten. Rene De Goscinny & M. Uderzo. (Illus.). (GER.). (J). 1990. lib. bdg. 19.95 (*0-8288-4953-6*) Fr & Eur.

Asterix und Kleopatra. Rene De Goscinny & M. Uderzo. (Illus.). (GER.). (J). 1990. lib. bdg. 19.95 (*0-8288-4954-4*) Fr & Eur.

Asterix vs Caesar. Rene De Goscinny & M. Uderzo. (J). 1990. 19.95 (*0-8288-8593-1*) Fr & Eur.

Asterix y Cleopatra. Rene De Goscinny & M. Uderzo. (Illus.). (SPA.). (J). 1990. lib. bdg. 19.95 (*0-8288-4955-2*) Fr & Eur.

Asterix y el Caldero. Rene De Goscinny & M. Uderzo. (Illus.). (SPA.). (J). 1990. lib. bdg. 19.95 (*0-8288-4956-0*) Fr & Eur.

Asterix y los Godos. Rene De Goscinny & M. Uderzo. (Illus.). (SPA.). (J). 1990. lib. bdg. 19.95 (*0-8288-4957-9*) Fr & Eur.

Asterix y los Normandos. Rene De Goscinny & M. Uderzo. (Illus.). (SPA.). (J). 1990. lib. bdg. 19.95 (*0-8288-4958-7*) Fr & Eur.

Asteroid & Spacecraft Dynamics: Proceedings of the Topical Meetings of the COSPAR Interdisciplinary Scientific Commission B & P (Meetings B4 & P1) of the COSPAR 28th Plenary Meeting held in The Hague, The Netherlands, 25 June - 6 July 1990. Ed. by W-H. Ip et al. (Advances in Space Research Ser.: Vol. 11, No. 6). (Illus.). 225p. 1991. pap. 160.00 (*0-08-041160-6*, Pergamon Pr) Elsevier.

Asteroid Ephemeris, Eighteen Eighty-Three to Nineteen Ninety-Nine. Zipporah P. Dobyns. 180p. (Orig.). 1977. pap. text ed. 18.00 (*0-685-28051-9*) TIA Pubns.

Asteroid Goddesses. rev. ed. Demetra George & Douglas Bloch. (Illus.). 408p. 1990. pap. 16.95 (*0-935127-15-1*) ACS Pubns.

Asteroid Mechanics, 2 vols., Vol. 2, Ed. by Martha Lang-Wescott. 80p. (Orig.). 1991. pap. 15.95 (*0-9619852-4-0*) Treehouse Mtn.

Asteroid Mechanics One. Ed. by Martha Wescott. 80p. (Orig.). 1990. pap. 15.95 (*0-9619852-6-7*) Treehouse Mtn.

***Asteroid Name Encyclopedia.** Jacob Schwartz. LC 95-103. (Illus.). 448p. 1995. pap. 19.95 (*1-56718-609-2*) Llewellyn Pubns.

Asteroids. Ed. by Tom Gehrels et al. LC 79-19686. (Illus.). 1193p. reprint ed. pap. 180.00 (*0-8357-4765-4*, 2037692) Bks Demand.

Asteroids: Invaders from Space. Robert Kraske. LC 94-8072. (Illus.). (J). 1995. text ed. 14.95 (*0-689-31860-X*, Atheneum S&S) S&S Trade.

Asteroids, Comets & Meteors, Vol. 3: Proceedings of a Meeting Held at the Astronomical Observatory of Uppsala University, June 12-16, 1989. Ed. by C. I. Lagerkvist et al. (Illus.). 620p. (Orig.). 1990. pap. 375. 00x (*91-506-0777-4*, Pub. by Almqv & Wiksell SW) Coronet Bks.

Asteroids, Comets, & Meteors 1993: Proceedings of the 160th Symposium of the International Astronomical Union, Held in Belgirate, Italy, June 14-18, 1993. Ed. by A. Milani et al. LC 94-16936. (International Astronomical Union Symposia Ser.). 503p. (C). 1994. lib. bdg. 147.50 (*0-7923-2880-9*); pap. text ed. 75.00 (*0-7923-2881-7*) Kluwer Ac.

Asteroids II. Ed. by Richard P. Binzel et al. LC 89-20223. (Space Science Ser.). 1258p. 1990. 65.00 (*0-8165-1123-3*) U of Ariz Pr.

Asteroids in Midpoints. Emma B. Donath. LC 83-71149. 160p. 1982. 13.00 (*0-86690-242-2*, 2291-01) Am Fed Astrologers.

Asteroids in Synastry. Emma B. Donath. 96p. 1977. 10.00 (*0-86690-082-9*, D1080-024) Am Fed Astrologers.

Asteroids in the Birthchart. Emma B. Donath. 104p. 1979. 9.00 (*0-86690-081-0*, D1079-024) Am Fed Astrologers.

Asteroids in the U. S. A. Emma B. Donath. 144p. 1979. 11. 00 (*0-86690-083-7*, D1081-024) Am Fed Astrologers.

Asteroids to Quasars: A Symposium for the 60th Birthday of William Liller. Ed. by Phyllis Lugger. 280p. (C). 1991. 69.95 (*0-521-35231-2*) Cambridge U Pr.

Asthetic Surgery of the Breast. Georgiade et al. (Illus.). 768p. 1990. text ed. 235.00 (*0-7216-3207-6*) Saunders.

Asthetik. Franz Von Kutschera. vi, 583p. (C). 1989. lib. bdg. 98.50x (*3-11-011416-X*); pap. text ed. 36.95x (*3-11-012194-8*) De Gruyter.

Asthma. Ed. by P. J. Barnes. (British Medical Bulletin Ser.: Vol. 48, 1). (Illus.). 320p. 1992. text ed. 130.00 (*0-443-04718-9*) Churchill.

Asthma. M. Eric Gershwin & E. L. Klingelhofer. 1986. pap. 10.53 (*0-201-11581-6*) Addison-Wesley.

Asthma. Ed. by G. Jariwalla. (Practical Clinical Medicine Ser.). (C). 1988. lib. bdg. 63.00 (*0-85200-672-1*) Kluwer Ac.

***Asthma.** A. J. Wardlaw. (Medieval Mediterranean Ser.). (Illus.). 206p. (Orig.). 1993. pap. 52.50x (*1-872748-26-0*, Pub. by Bios Scientific UK) Coronet Bks.

Asthma. 3rd ed. Ed. by T. J. Clark et al. (Illus.). 550p. 1992. 95.95 (*0-442-31582-1*) Chapman & Hall.

Asthma: A Complete Guide to Self-Management of Asthma & Allergies for Patients & Their Families. Allan M. Weinstein. 384p. 1988. mass mkt. 5.99 (*0-449-21562-8*, Crest) Fawcett.

Asthma: A Practical Guide for Physicians. 72p. 37.60 (*0-685-11547-X*, 0060) Am Lung Assn.

***Asthma: An Epidemiological Overview.** HMSO Staff. 64p. 1995. pap. 25.00 (*0-11-321897-4*, HM18974, Pub. by HMSO UK) UNIPUB.

Asthma: Basic Mechanisms & Clinical Management. 2nd ed. Ed. by P. J. Barnes et al. (Illus.). 804p. 1992. text ed. 165.00 (*0-12-079026-2*) Acad Pr.

Asthma: Current Studies in Therapy. Ed. by Vincent J. Fontana et al. 1978. 29.00 (*0-8422-7289-5*) Irvington.

Asthma: Immunopathology & Immunotherapy - Immunopathologie und Immunotherapie. Ed. by F. Kummer. (Illus.). 192p. 1993. pap. 737.00 (*0-387-82454-5*) Spr-Verlag.

Asthma: Its Pathogenesis & Treatment. Kaliner et al. (Lung Biology in Health & Disease Ser.). 808p. 1990. 210.00 (*0-8247-8217-8*) Dekker.

Asthma: Physiology, Immunopharmacology & Treatment. Ed. by A. Barry Kay et al. 1984. text ed. 161.00 (*0-12-402750-4*) Acad Pr.

Asthma: Psysiology, Immunopharmacology & Treatment, Fourth International Symposium. Ed. by S. T. Holgate et al. (Illus.). 464p. 1993. text ed. 99.00 (*0-12-352330-3*) Acad Pr.

***Asthma: Questions & Answers.** Paul Thomas. (Illus.). 100p. 1995. pap. 29.95 (*1-873413-90-4*) Merit Pub Intl.

***Asthma: Questions You Have...Answers You Need.** Paula Brisco. LC 94-23176. (Orig.). 1994. pap. 10.95 (*1-882606-16-7*) Peoples Med Soc.

Asthma: Stop Suffering, Start Living. 2nd ed. M. Eric Gershwin & E. L. Klingelhofer. (Illus.). 240p. 1992. pap. 12.50 (*0-201-60847-2*) Addison-Wesley.

***Asthma & Allergies: The Natural Way of Healing.** Natural. 1995. mass mkt. 4.99 (*0-440-21662-1*) Dell.

Asthma & Allergy in Pregnancy & Early Infancy. Ed. by Michael Schatz & Robert S. Zeiger. LC 92-48684. (Allergic Disease & Therapy Ser.: Vol. 7). 656p. 1993. 180.00 (*0-8247-8795-1*) Dekker.

Asthma & Bronchial Hyperreactivity. Ed. by H. Herzog & A. P. Perruchoud. (Progress in Respiration Research Ser.: Vol. 19). (Illus.). xii, 520p. 1985. 75.25 (*3-8055-4036-1*) S Karger.

Asthma & Bronchitis. Jan DeVries. (By Appointment Only Ser.). 144p. 1992. pap. 11.95 (*1-85158-394-7*, Pub. by Mnstream UK) Trafalgar.

Asthma & Emotion. Abraham Stern. 216p. 1980. 35.00 (*0-89876-002-X*) Gardner Pr.

Asthma & Exercise. Nancy Hogshead & Gerald S. Couzens. 256p. 1991. pap. 9.95 (*0-8050-1688-0*, Owl) H Holt & Co.

Asthma & Hay Fever: Proven Drug-Free Methods to Combat the Causes. Leon Chaitow. 1990. pap. 2.95 (*0-7225-1899-4*) Thorsons SF.

Asthma & Rhinitis. Holgate Busse. 1440p. 1994. 195.00 (*0-86542-246-X*) Blackwell Sci.

Asthma As an Inflammatory Disease. Ed. by O'Byrne. (Allergic Disease & Therapy Ser.: Vol. 2). 336p. 1990. 140.00 (*0-8247-8220-8*) Dekker.

Asthma Attack by Bo B. Bear. Charlotte L. Casterline. (Illus.). (Orig.). (J). (ps-6). 1988. pap. 5.95 (*0-9617218-2-0*) Info All Bk.

Asthma, Catarrh, Hayfever & Sinusitus. Ed. by Health Research Staff. 63p. 1994. reprint ed. spiral bd. 4.95 (*0-7873-1260-6*) Mokelumne.

Asthma in Children & Adolescents: Pediatrician Journal, Vol. 18, No. 4. Ed. by D. W. Kaplan & E. F. Ellis. (Illus.). iv, 80p. 1992. pap. 47.25 (*3-8055-5523-7*) S Karger.

***Asthma in Control.** 1995. write for info. (*0-941549-11-9*) Creative Hlth.

Asthma in the Workplace. Bernstein et al. 664p. 1993. 199. 00 (*0-8247-8799-4*) Dekker.

Asthma Reviews, Vol. 1. John Morley. 181p. 1988. text ed. 60.00 (*0-12-040921-6*) Acad Pr.

Asthma Reviews, Vol. 2. Ed. by John Morley. 209p. 1989. text ed. 92.00 (*0-12-040922-4*) Acad Pr.

Asthma Self-Care Book. Geri Harrington. LC 90-55538. 288p. 1992. reprint ed. pap. 11.00 (*0-06-092270-2*, PL) HarpC.

Asthma Self-Help Book. 2nd rev. ed. Paul J. Hannaway. LC 93-36384. 1994. pap. 12.95 (*1-55958-434-3*) Prima Pub.

Asthma Self-Help Book: A Comprehensive Guide to Management of Asthma in Children & Adults. Paul J. Hannaway. Ed. by Nancy Savles. LC 89-80071. (Illus.). 265p. (C). 1991. reprint ed. text ed. 18.95 (*0-9621799-0-6*) Lighthse MA.

Asthma Self-Help Book: How to Live a Normal Life in Spite of Your Condition. 2nd ed. Paul J. Hannaway. 250p. (Orig.). 1992. 19.95 (*1-55958-166-2*) Prima Pub.

Asthma Storm: One Family's Journey from Asthma Diagnosis to Control. Barbara L. Westmoreland. 206p. 1994. pap. 14.95 (*0-9639398-0-7*) Lane Press.

Asthma, the Natural Way. Roy Ridgeway. (Natural Way Ser.). 1994. pap. 5.95 (*1-85230-492-8*) Element MA.

Asthma Treatment: A Multidisciplinary Approach. Ed. by D. Olivieri et al. (NATO ASI Series A, Life Sciences: Vol. 299). (Illus.). 296p. (C). 1992. 85.00 (*0-306-44215-9*, Plenum Pr) Plenum.

Asthmatic's Action Plan: Practical Advice for Gaining Relief from Distressing Symptoms. John Chapman. 1991. pap. 8.95 (*0-7225-2163-4*) Thorsons SF.

Astley's Amphitheatre. Jacqueline S. Bratton & Jane Traies. (Theatre in Focus Ser.). 65p. (Orig.). 1980. pap. text ed., sl. 105.00 (*0-85964-059-0*) Chadwyck-Healey.

ASTM & Other Specifications & Classifications for Petroleum Products & Lubricants: Fuels & Oils, Bituminous Materials, Solvents. 6th ed. ASTM Committee D-2 on Petroleum Products & Lubricants. LC 93-36967. 516p. 1993. pap. 100.00 (*0-8031-1783-3*, 03-402093-12) ASTM.

ASTM & Other Specifications & Classifications for Petroleum Products & Lubricants: Fuels & Oils, Bituminous Materials, Solvents. American Society for Testing & Materials Staff. LC 89-6452. 505p. reprint ed. pap. 144.00 (*0-7837-5979-7*, 2045783) Bks Demand.

ASTM Annual Book of Standards, 1986, 48 pts.

ASTM Building & Economic Standards. 2nd ed. 1992. 39. 00 (*0-317-05721-9*) AACE Intl.

ASTM Chemical & Spectrometric Test Methods for Steel. Contrib by ASTM Committee A-1 on Steel, Stainless Steel, & Related Alloys Staff & ASTM Committee E-1 on Analytical Chemistry for Metals, Ores, & Related Materials Staff. LC 92-15058. 1992. 71.00 (*0-8031-1758-2*, 03-501192-50) ASTM.

ASTM Fire Test Standards. 3rd ed. American Society for Testing & Materials Staff. LC 90-34084. (Illus.). 904p. reprint ed. pap. 180.00 (*0-7837-6055-8*, 2045868) Bks Demand.

ASTM Fire Test Standards. 4th ed. ASTM Staff. LC 93-36985. 1993. 110.00 (*0-8031-1781-7*, 03-505093-31) ASTM.

ASTM Painting Inspection Standards for Field or Shop Applications. American Society for Testing Materials Staff. LC 94-21809. 1994. 54.00 (*0-8031-1797-3*, 03-433094-14) ASTM.

ASTM Performance Standards for Textile Fabrics. ASTM Subcommittee D13.56 Staff. LC 88-6294. 249p. 1988. pap. text ed. 32.00 (*0-8031-1200-9*, 03-413088-18) ASTM.

An Asterisk (*) at the beginning of an entry indicates that the title is appearing in BIP for the first time.

493

ASTM Power Plant Water Analysis Manual. 232p. 1984. pap. text ed. 43.00 (*0-8031-0200-3*, 03-419084-16); Lab Manual. teacher ed 48.00 (*0-8031-0201-1*, 03-419184-16) ASTM.

ASTM Protective Coating Standards for Use in Nuclear Power Plants. 60p. 1991. pap. 35.00 (*0-8031-1242-4*, 03-433091-14) ASTM.

ASTM Specifications for Carbon & Alloy Steel Plates for Pressure Vessels: (Excluding Corrosion Resisting Steel Plates) American Society for Testing & Materials Staff. 186p. reprint ed. pap. 53.10 (*0-8357-6029-4*, 2034434) Bks Demand.

ASTM Specifications for Structural Steel. American Society for Testing & Materials Staff. 234p. reprint ed. pap. 66.70 (*0-8357-5812-5*, 2023991) Bks Demand.

ASTM Standard on Building Economics. 3rd ed. LC 94-20473. 1994. 45.00 (*0-8031-1795-7*, 03-506094-10) ASTM.

ASTM Standards & Other Specifications & Test Methods on the Quality Assurance of Landfill Liner Systems. LC 94-11664. 1994. pap. 77.00 (*0-8031-1784-1*) ASTM.

ASTM Standards for Clean Rooms. ASTM Staff. LC 92-35359. 1993. 65.00 (*0-8031-1768-X*, 03-601093-46) ASTM.

ASTM Standards for Corrosion Testing of Metals. 370p. 1990. pap. 51.00 (*0-8031-1235-1*, 03-701090-27) ASTM.

ASTM Standards for Environmentally Degradable Plastics. LC 93-30768. 1993. 47.00 (*0-8031-1779-5*, 03-42009319) ASTM.

ASTM Standards for Fence Materials & Products. 5th ed. 172p. 1990. pap. 28.00 (*0-8031-1241-6*, 03-614090-02) ASTM.

ASTM Standards in ACI 301, 318, & 349. 307p. 1989. 99.75 (*0-686-95238-3*, SP-71(89)) ACI.

ASTM Standards in Building Codes: Specifications, Test Methods, Practices, Classifications, Definitions, 1. 19th ed. reprint ed. pap. 160.00 (*0-8357-5813-3*, 2021524) Bks Demand.

ASTM Standards in Building Codes: Specifications, Test Methods, Practices, Classifications, Definitions, 2. 19th ed. 2040p. reprint ed. pap. 180.00 (*0-8357-5814-1*) Bks Demand.

ASTM Standards in Building Codes: Specifications, Test Methods, Practices, Classifications, Terminology, 4 vols., Vol. 1. 28th ed. American Society for Testing & Materials Staff. LC 83-641658. 1850p. reprint ed. pap. 180.00 (*0-7837-4880-9*, 2044834) Bks Demand.

ASTM Standards in Building Codes: Specifications, Test Methods, Practices, Classifications, Terminology, 4 vols., Vol. 2. 28th ed. American Society for Testing & Materials Staff. LC 83-641658. 1955p. reprint ed. pap. 180.00 (*0-7837-4881-7*, 2044834) Bks Demand.

ASTM Standards in Building Codes: Specifications, Test Methods, Practices, Classifications, Terminology, 4 vols., Vol. 3. 28th ed. American Society for Testing & Materials Staff. LC 83-641658. 1950p. reprint ed. pap. 180.00 (*0-7837-4882-5*, 2044834) Bks Demand.

ASTM Standards in Building Codes: Specifications, Test Methods, Practices, Classifications, Terminology, 4 vols., Vol. 4. 28th ed. American Society for Testing & Materials Staff. LC 83-641658. 1792p. reprint ed. pap. 180.00 (*0-7837-4883-3*, 2044834) Bks Demand.

ASTM Standards in Building Codes, 1992, 4 vols., Set. 28th ed. 7080p. 1992. pap. 395.00 (*0-8031-1751-5*, 03-002592-10) ASTM.

ASTM Standards on Amusement Rides & Devices. 4th ed. LC 92-24021. 1992. 19.00 (*0-8031-1765-5*, 03-624092-47) ASTM.

ASTM Standards on Aquatic Toxicology & Hazard Evaluation. ASTM Committee E-47 on Biological Effects & Environmental Fate. LC 93-5098. 535p. 1993. pap. text ed. 86.00 (*0-8031-1778-7*, 03-547093-16) ASTM.

ASTM Standards on Building Economics. 2nd ed. ASTM Subcommittee E06.81 on Building Economics Staff. LC 92-3763. 155p. 1992. pap. 39.00 (*0-8031-1752-3*, TH153) ASTM.

ASTM Standards on Building Economics. American Society for Testing & Materials Staff. LC 90-295. (Illus.). 68p. reprint ed. pap. 25.00 (*0-7837-4704-7*, 2044851) Bks Demand.

ASTM Standards on Catalysts. 3rd rev. ed. ASTM Staff. LC 88-23729. (ASTM Standards Ser.). 110p. 1988. pap. 26.00 (*0-8031-1210-6*, 03-432088-12) ASTM.

ASTM Standards on Chromatography. 2nd ed. ASTM Staff. LC 89-6803. 824p. 1989. pap. 76.00 (*0-8031-1219-X*, 03-519089-50) ASTM.

ASTM Standards on Chromatography: Gas Chromatography, Liquid Chromatography, Thin-Layer Chromatography, Steric Exclusion Chromatography. American Society for Testing & Materials Staff. LC 40-10712. 772p. reprint ed. pap. 180.00 (*0-8357-5815-X*, 2029163) Bks Demand.

ASTM Standards on Color & Appearance Measurement. ASTM Committee. LC 94-9964. 1994. pap. 69.00 (*0-8031-1794-9*) ASTM.

ASTM Standards on Color & Appearance Measurement. 2nd ed. American Society for Testing & Materials Staff. LC 83-641658. 359p. reprint ed. pap. 102.40 (*0-7837-4705-5*, 2044845) Bks Demand.

ASTM Standards on Color & Appearance Measurement. 3rd ed. (ASTM Standards Ser.). 384p. 1987. pap. 55.00 (*0-8031-1245-9*, 03-512091-14) ASTM.

ASTM Standards on Computerized Systems. 2nd ed. 202p. 1986. pap. 32.00 (*0-8031-0974-1*, 03-531086-32) ASTM.

ASTM Standards on Durability Testing of Nonmetallic Materials. LC 93-36359. 364p. 1993. 77.00 (*0-8031-1780-9*) ASTM.

ASTM Standards on Electrical Protective Equipment for Workers. 8th ed. 137p. 1991. pap. 29.00 (*0-8031-1247-5*, 03-618091-21) ASTM.

ASTM Standards on Electrical Protective Equipment for Workers. 8th ed. American Society for Testing & Materials Staff. LC 91-22201. 140p. reprint ed. pap. 39.90 (*0-7837-5980-0*, 2045784) Bks Demand.

ASTM Standards on Electrical Protective Equipment for Workers. 9th ed. ASTM Committee F-18 on Electrical Protective Equipment for Workers. LC 93-5097. 1993. 32.00 (*0-8031-1776-0*, 03-618093-21) ASTM.

*__ASTM Standards on Emergency Medical Systems.__ ASTM Committee F-30 on Emergency Medical Systems & American Society for Testing & Materials Staff. 300p. 1994. 59.00 (*0-8031-1799-X*) ASTM.

*__ASTM Standards on Environmental Sampling.__ ASTM Staff. LC 95-895. 1995. write for info. (*0-8031-1806-6*) ASTM.

ASTM Standards on Fasteners. American Society for Testing & Materials, Committee F-16 on Fasteners. LC 78-108362. 336p. reprint ed. pap. 95.80 (*0-8357-5816-8*, 2015509) Bks Demand.

ASTM Standards on Gaskets. 3rd ed. American Society for Testing & Materials Staff. LC 83-641658. 107p. reprint ed. pap. 30.50 (*0-8357-5817-6*, 2031946) Bks Demand.

ASTM Standards on Gaskets. 5th ed. LC 84-641658. (Compilations of ASTM Standards Ser.). 100p. 1990. pap. 28.00 (*0-8031-1226-2*, 03-603090-20) ASTM.

ASTM Standards on Gaskets. 6th ed. LC 93-36966. 1993. 45.00 (*0-8031-1782-5*, 03-603093-20) ASTM.

ASTM Standards on Geosynthetics. 2nd ed. 122p. 1991. pap. 43.00 (*0-8031-1239-4*, 03-435091-38) ASTM.

ASTM Standards on Geosynthetics. 3rd ed. ASTM, Committee D-35 on Geosynthetics Staff. LC 92-46796. 1993. 49.00 (*0-8031-1769-8*, 03-435093-38) ASTM.

ASTM Standards on Geosynthetics. American Society for Testing & Materials Staff. LC 91-148. (Illus.). 111p. reprint ed. pap. 31.70 (*0-7837-6095-7*, 2059141) Bks Demand.

ASTM Standards on Geotextiles. ASTM Staff. LC 88-39583. 1988. pap. 29.00 (*0-8031-1214-9*) ASTM.

ASTM Standards on Ground Water & Vadose Zone Investigation. 1992. write for info. (*0-318-69345-3*) ASTM.

ASTM Standards on Ground Water & Vadose Zone Investigations. 2nd ed. ASTM Committee D-18 on Soil & Rock. LC 93-39811. 1994. write for info. (*0-8031-1786-8*) ASTM.

ASTM Standards on Ground Water & Vadose Zone Investigations. American Society for Testing & Materials Staff. LC 92-16915. (Illus.). 174p. reprint ed. pap. 49.60 (*0-7837-6293-3*, 2046008) Bks Demand.

ASTM Standards on Hazardous Substances & Oil Spill Response. 119p. 1990. pap. 40.00 (*0-8031-1237-8*, 03-620090-48) ASTM.

*__ASTM Standards on Hazardous Substances & Oil Spill Response.__ 2nd ed. Ed. by ASTM, Committee F-20, Hazardous Substances & Oil Spill Response Staff. LC 94-36691. (Haz Ser.: Vol. 94). 1994. 54.00 (*0-8031-1798-1*, 03-620094-48) ASTM.

*__ASTM Standards on Lead-Based Paint Assessment in Buildings.__ Comp. by ASTM Committee E-6 on Performance of Buildings. LC 94-33687. 168p. 1994. 69.00 (*0-8031-1802-3*) ASTM.

ASTM Standards on Liquid Particles & Sprays: Sponsored by ASTM Subcommittee E29.04 on Liquid Particle Measurement. LC 92-18055. 1992. 25.00 (*0-8031-1762-0*, 03-529092-34) ASTM.

ASTM Standards on Manufactured Carbon & Graphite Products, 1981. American Society for Testing & Materials Staff. (Illus.). 94p. reprint ed. pap. 26.80 (*0-8357-6877-5*, 2052317) Bks Demand.

ASTM Standards on Masonry. ASTM Staff. LC 89-18301. 197p. 1990. pap. 42.00 (*0-8031-1224-6*, 03-315090-60) ASTM.

ASTM Standards on Masonry. 2nd ed. ASTM Committees C-12 on Mortars for Unit Masonry & C-15 on Manufactured Masonry Units Staff. LC 92-24837. 1992. 45.00 (*0-8031-1763-9*, 03-315092-60) ASTM.

ASTM Standards on Masonry. American Society for Testing & Materials Staff. LC 89-18301. 200p. reprint ed. pap. 57.00 (*0-7837-4797-7*, 2044838) Bks Demand.

ASTM Standards on Materials & Environmental Microbiology. 2nd ed. LC 92-47143. 1993. 68.00 (*0-8031-1771-X*, 03-535093-48) ASTM.

ASTM Standards on Materials & Environmental Microbiology. American Society for Testing & Materials Staff. LC 87-27054. (Illus.). 313p. reprint ed. pap. 89.30 (*0-7837-4786-1*, 2044823) Bks Demand.

ASTM Standards on Precision & Bias for Various Applications. 4th ed. LC 92-11911. 1992. 49.00 (*0-8031-1757-4*, 03-511092-34) ASTM.

ASTM Standards on Protective Clothing. 297p. 1990. pap. 59.00 (*0-8031-1236-X*, 03-623090-55) ASTM.

ASTM Standards on Sensory Evaluation of Materials & Products. LC 88-10535. 76p. 1988. pap. 26.00 (*0-8031-1203-3*, 03-518088-36) ASTM.

ASTM Standards on Skiing. LC 85-641658. (Compilations of ASTM Standards Ser.). 64p. pap. text ed. 14.00 (*0-8031-0434-0*, PCN03-602700-47) ASTM.

ASTM Standards on Soil Compaction. 2nd ed. LC 93-1146. 180p. 1993. pap. 45.00 (*0-8031-1774-4*, 03-418093-38) ASTM.

ASTM Standards on Soil Compaction. American Society for Testing & Materials Staff. LC 91-36474. 179p. reprint ed. pap. 51.10 (*0-7837-5978-9*, 2045782) Bks Demand.

ASTM Standards on Soil Stabilization with Admixtures. 2nd ed. LC 92-23293. 1992. 39.00 (*0-8031-1764-7*, 03-418292-38) ASTM.

ASTM Standards on Technical Aspects of Products Liability Litigation. 2nd ed. 16p. 1988. pap. 15.00 (*0-8031-1211-4*, 03-540088-41) ASTM.

ASTM Standards on Technical Aspects of Products Liability Litigation. American Society for Testing & Materials Staff. LC 83-641658. 18p. reprint ed. pap. 25.00 (*0-8357-5818-4*, 2031945) Bks Demand.

ASTM Standards on the Building of Materials Databases. American Society for Testing Materials. LC 93-24406. 105p. 1993. pap. 43.00 (*0-8031-1777-9*, 03-549093-63) ASTM.

ASTM Standards on Thermocouples. 2nd ed. LC 83-641658. (Compilations of ASTM Standards Ser.). 257p. pap. text ed. 37.00 (*0-8031-0838-9*, 03-520086-40) ASTM.

ASTM Standards on Tires. LC 83-641658. (Compilations of ASTM Standards Ser.). 116p. pap. text ed. 18.00 (*0-8031-0420-0*, PCN03-609084-20) ASTM.

ASTM Standards on Viscosity Tables for Kinematic Viscosity Conversions. 42p. 1987. pap. 20.00 (*0-8031-0990-3*, 03-043040-12) ASTM.

ASTM Viscosity Index Calculated from Kinematic Viscosity. American Society for Testing & Materials Staff. LC 65-24834. (American Society for Testing & Materials: No. DS 39a). 959p. reprint ed. pap. 180.00 (*0-8357-5819-2*, 2019952) Bks Demand.

*__Aston Martin.__ Alan Archer. (C). 1989. pap. 25.00x (*0-85263-980-5*, Pub. by Shire UK) St Mut.

Aston Martin & Lagonda. Chris Harvey. (Illus.). 245p. 34.95 (*0-902280-68-6*, P068, Pub. by Oxford Ill Pr) Haynes Pubns.

*__Aston-Martin & Lagonda.__ 2nd ed. Chris Harvey. (Illus.). 288p. Date not set. 44.95 (*1-85509-239-5*, Pub. by J H Haynes & Co UK) Motorbooks Intl.

Aston Martin & Lagonda, Vol. 2. Paul Chudecki. (Collector's Guide Ser.). (Illus.). 128p. 1990. 27.95 (*0-947981-41-1*, Pub. by Motor Racing UK) Motorbooks Intl.

Aston Martin & Lagonda: Six-Cylinder DB Models, Vol. 1. A. Whyte. (Collector's Guide Ser.). (Illus.). 144p. 1984. text ed. 27.95 (*0-900549-83-1*, Pub. by Motor Racing UK) Motorbooks Intl.

*__Aston Martin & Lagonda: The V-Engined Cars.__ David G. Styles. (Illus.). 200p. 1995. 34.95 (*1-85223-808-9*, Pub. by Crowood UK) Motorbooks Intl.

Aston Martin V8 Race Cars. Paul Chuderki. (Illus.). 192p. 1990. 34.95 (*0-85045-973-7*, Pub. by Osprey Pubng Ltd UK) Motorbooks Intl.

Aston Martin, 1913-1947: An English Thoroughbred. Edward I. Hunter & Archer. (Illus.). 320p. 1992. 69.95 (*1-85532-203-X*, Pub. by Osprey Pubng Ltd UK) Motorbooks Intl.

Astonish Me, Yahweh! Lura J. Geiger et al. (Illus.). 128p. (Orig.). 1983. student ed 11.95 (*0-931055-01-6*) LuraMedia.

Astonish Me, Yahweh! Leader's Guide. Lura J. Geiger. (Illus.). 128p. (Orig.). 1984. 15.95 (*0-931055-02-4*) LuraMedia.

Astonish Us in the Morning: Tyrone Guthrie Remembered. Alfred Rossi. LC 80-11855. (Illus.). 322p. reprint ed. pap. 91.80 (*0-8357-5820-6*, 2033175) Bks Demand.

Astonished Hours. Peter Cooley. (Poetry Ser.). 70p. (Orig.). 1992. lib. bdg. 16.95 (*0-88748-130-2*); pap. 9.95 (*0-88748-131-0*) Carnegie-Mellon.

Astonished Muse. Reuel Denny. 300p. 1989. pap. 21.95 (*0-88738-762-4*) Transaction Pubs.

Astonished Traveler: William Darby, Frontier Geographer & Man of Letters. J. Gerald Kennedy. LC 81-3711. xiv, 242p. 1981. text ed. 35.00 (*0-8071-0886-3*) La State U Pr.

Astonishing Armadillo. Dee Stuart. LC 92-25970. (J). (gr. 2-5). 1993. 19.95 (*0-87614-769-4*, Carolrhoda) Lerner Group.

Astonishing Armadillo. Dee Stuart. (J). (gr. 2-5). 1994. pap. 6.95 (*0-87614-630-2*, Carolrhoda) Lerner Group.

Astonishing Curriculum: Integrating Science & Humanities Through Language. Ed. by Stephen Tchudi. 168p. (Orig.). 1993. pap. 14.95 (*0-8141-0210-7*) NCTE.

Astonishing Hypothesis: The Scientific Search for the Soul. Francis Crick. Ed. by B. Grossman. (Illus.). 352p. 1994. text ed. 25.00 (*0-684-19431-7*, Scribners) S&S Trade.

*__Astonishing Hypothesis: The Scientific Search for the Soul.__ Francis Crick. 1995. pap. 14.00 (*0-684-80158-2*, Touchstone Bks) S&S Trade.

Astonishing Mr. Scripps: The Turbulent Life of America's Penny Press Lord. Vance H. Trimble. LC 90-22401. (Illus.). 560p. 1992. 39.95 (*0-8138-0679-6*) Iowa St U Pr.

Astonishing Undersea Creatures. Ken Hoy. (Dare to Find Out About Ser.). (Illus.). 10p. (J). (ps-3). 1994. 12.95 (*1-57102-002-0*, Ideals Child) Hambleton-Hill.

*__Astonishing Weight of the Dead.__ Tom Wayman. 160p. (Orig.). 1995. pap. 12.95 (*0-919591-08-6*, Pub. by Polestar Bk Pubs CN) Orca Bk Pubs.

Astonishing World: Essays. Barbara G. Harrison. 384p. 1992. 22.95 (*0-395-59105-8*) Ticknor & Fields.

Astonishing World: The Selected Poems of Angel Gonzalez, 1956 to 1986. Ed. & Tr. by Steven F. Brown. Tr. by Gutierrez Revuelta. LC 93-9273. 264p. (ENG & SPA.). 1993. pap. 14.95 (*0-915943-58-1*) Milkweed Ed.

Astonishment & Power: Kongo Minkisi - The Art of Renee Stout. Wyatt MacGaffey & Michael D. Harris. (Illus.). 224p. (Orig.). 1993. pap. 34.95 (*1-56098-274-8*) Smithsonian.

Astoria. Washington Irving. LC 67-25439. (Illus.). 498p. 1967. 19.95 (*0-8323-0101-9*) Binford Mort.

Astoria, 2 vols. Washington Irving. 1971. 200.00 (*0-87968-671-5*) Gordon Pr.

*__Astoria.__ Robert Viscusi. (Prose Ser.: No. 26). 313p. 1995. 18.00 (*0-920717-93-4*) Guernica Editions.

Astoria & Empire. James P. Ronda. LC 89-38464. (Illus.). xiv, 400p. 1990. 27.50 (*0-8032-3896-7*); pap. 12.95 (*0-8032-8942-1*) U of Nebr Pr.

Astorian. Roger T Tetlow. LC 75-25323. (Illus.). 192p. 1975. pap. 4.95 (*0-8323-0263-5*) Binford Mort.

Astorian Adventure: The Journal of Alfred Seton, 1811-1815. Ed. by Robert F. Jones. (Illus.). 224p. 1993. 25.00 (*0-8232-1503-2*) Fordham.

Astors: Landscape with Millionaires. Derek Wilson. (Illus.). 448p. 1993. 24.95 (*0-312-09744-1*) St Martin.

Astound & Risible. 1988. 7.00 (*0-317-90533-3*) Inkblot Pubns.

Astounding Diary of Dr. John G. Lake. Gordon Lindsay. 1987. per. 2.95 (*0-89985-273-4*) Christ for the Nations.

*__Astounding New Discoveries.__ Noah W. Hutchings. 29p. (Orig.). 1994. pap. 2.50 (*1-879366-62-2*) Hearthstone OK.

Astounding Optical Illusions. Katherine Joyce. LC 93-43911. (J). 1994. 13.95 (*0-8069-0431-3*) Sterling.

*__Astounding Optical Illusions.__ Katherine Joyce. (Illus.). 116p. 1995. pap. 4.95 (*0-8069-0432-1*) Sterling.

Astounding Truth. Allen Tolbert. 1989. pap. 6.00 (*0-318-41031-1*) AOG.

Astra. Grace L. Hill. reprint ed. lib. bdg. 21.95 (*0-89190-034-9*, Rivercity Pr) Amereon Ltd.

Astraea: The Imperial Theme in the Sixteenth Century. Frances A. Yates. (Illus.). 1985. pap. 9.95 (*0-7448-0025-0*, 0250W) Routledge Chapman & Hall.

Astraea: The Imperial Theme in the Sixteenth Century. Frances A. Yates. (Illus.). 233p. 1994. pap. 19.95 (*0-7126-9894-9*, Pub. by Pimlico) Trafalgar.

Astrakhan Cloak. Nuala Ni Dhomhnaill. Tr. by Paul Muldoon. LC 92-51047. 112p. 1993. 15.95 (*0-916390-55-1*); pap. 10.95 (*0-916390-54-3*) Wake Forest.

Astral Body. Arthur E. Powell. LC 73-4775. (Classics Ser.). 280p. 1973. reprint ed. pap. 12.00 (*0-8356-0438-1*, Quest) Theos Pub Hse.

Astral Light: Nature's Amazing Picture Gallery. Henry T. Edge. Ed. by W. Emmett Small & Helen Todd. (Theosophical Manual Ser.: No. 10). 62p. 1975. reprint ed. pap. 2.50 (*0-913004-20-0*) Point Loma Pub.

*__Astral Magic in Babylonia.__ Erica Reiner. LC 95-76539. (Transactions Ser.: Vol. 85, Pt. 4). (Illus.). 80p. (C). 1995. pap. 20.00 (*0-87169-854-4*, T854-ree) Am Philos.

Astral Medicine: A Practical Treatise & Therapeutics Combining Astrology, Diet & Homeopathic Medicine. M. Duz. 1991. lib. bdg. 67.95 (*0-8490-4305-0*) Gordon Pr.

Astral Mirror. Ben Bova. 288p. (Orig.). 1985. pap. 2.95 (*0-8125-3217-1*) Tor Bks.

Astral Plane. Charles W. Leadbeater. 1973. 7.95 (*81-7059-067-1*) Theos Pub Hse.

Astral Plane. C. W. Leadbeater. 100p. 1972. reprint ed. spiral bd. 4.95 (*0-7873-1122-7*) Mokelumne.

Astral Projection. Oliver Fox. 160p. 1974. reprint ed. pap. 4.95 (*0-8065-0463-3*, Citadel Pr) Carol Pub Group.

Astral Projection (Modus Operandi) John Mittl. 8p. 1993. reprint ed. spiral bd. 3.30 (*0-7873-0620-7*) Mokelumne.

Astral Projection (Out of Body Experience) Arden C. Rizer, Jr. Ed. by A. S. A. Staff. 25p. 1991. pap. 6.92 (*0-939795-41-8*) Amer Spirit.

Astral Projection, Ritual Magic & Alchemy. Ed. by Francis King. 288p. (Orig.). 1987. pap. 10.95 (*0-89281-164-1*, Destiny Bks) Inner Tradit.

Astral Projection Workbook. James H. Brennan. LC 89-29668. 160p. (Orig.). 1990. pap. 12.95 (*0-8069-7306-4*) Sterling.

Astral Projections. Brad Steiger. LC 82-81928. 1982. pap. 12.95 (*0-914918-36-2*, Whitford Pr) Schiffer.

Astral Travel: Your Guide to the Secrets of Out-of-the-Body Experience. Gavin Frost & Yvonne Frost. LC 85-52006. 240p. 1986. reprint ed. pap. 8.95 (*0-87728-336-2*) Weiser.

Astral World. Swami Panchadasi. pap. 3.00 (*0-911662-36-7*) Yoga.

Astral Worship. J. H. Hill. 128p. 1971. reprint ed. spiral bd. 4.95 (*0-7873-0408-5*) Mokelumne.

*__Astral Zoo.__ Bill Morris. 190p. (Orig.). 1995. pap. 11.95 (*0-9639775-1-2*) New Sun Pubns.

Astralogos. D. R. Fosso. 72p. 1987. pap. 6.00 (*0-913773-20-4*) S Wright.

*__Astrea Pt. I: Honore d'Urfe.__ Tr. & Intro. by Steven Rendall. LC 94-32421. (Medieval & Renaissance Texts & Studies Ser.: 134). 416p. 1995. 30.00 (*0-86698-142-X*) MRTS.

Astree. Honore D. Urfe. (Folio Ser.: No. 1523). 442p. (FRE.). 1984. pap. 15.95 (*2-07-037523-4*) Schoenhof.

Astrid Janette Presenta: Cocina Internacional. Astrid Perez. LC 92-60604. (Illus.). 448p. (SPA.). 1992. 19.95 (*0-9633213-1-5*) Veva Pub.

Astrid Klein. Klaus Ottmann. (Illus.). 12p. 1991. pap. 6.00 (*0-929687-08-6*) E & C Zilkha Gal.

Astrid Lindgren. Johanna Hurwitz. (Illus.). 64p. (J). (gr. 2-6). 1991. 3.95 (*0-14-032692-8*) Puffin Bks.

Astrid Lindgren. Eva-Marie Metcalf. LC 94-20503. (Twayne's World Author Ser.: No. 851). 184p. 1994. text ed. 22.95x (*0-8057-4525-4*, Twayne) Macmillan.

Astride the Nightmare. Elinor C. Flewellen. (Illus.). 74p. (Orig.). 1987. pap. 7.95 (*0-943457-00-9*) Hagar Tave Pr.

***Astride the Winged Horse. James H. Albertson. 152p. 1995. pap. 12.50 (*0-9645358-0-7*) Candlewood Pub. ASTRIDE THE WINGED HORSE is a piece of critical thinking designed to emphasize that man plays a major role in the creation of his own reality. His world is not some foreign imposition. In fact, the light which lights the world emanates not FROM the world, but from that life which has exposed it. We see, for example, that a mouse's world is revealed to the mouse by the mouse. Its**

An Asterisk (*) at the beginning of an entry indicates that the title is appearing in BIP for the first time.

494

vision is its cage. Man, of course, suffers a similar fate: His world is simply a reflection of his power TO BE THERE. It is the signifier of what he is. But more telling yet is the fact that the world must fist flare before the intellect can come into play. There must be revelation before analysis. Life's basic task, therefore, requires far more of us than this endless investigation which Aristotle so carefully delineated. Unquestionably, its great task is to push onward, ever repeating the methods of its history so that it may again travel that route which carried us all upward from the fungi. Assuredly, it is in this journey wherein we find the real action of the world, for it is here that life builds within life & creates that growth from which new worlds are born. To order contact: Candlewood Publishers, 2700 Gold Creek Rd., Sand Point ID, 83864-6718. ***Publisher Provided Annotation.***

Astro-Alchemy: Making the Most of Your Transits. Joan Negus. 156p. 1985. pap. 9.95 (*0-917086-82-1*) ACS Pubns.

Astro Blue: A Member of Our Family. Aaron E. Freeman. LC 83-73197. (Illus.). 144p. (J). (gr. 6 up). 1984. lib. bdg. 9.95 (*0-915509-00-8*); pap. 6.95 (*0-915509-01-6*) Argos Pub Co.

Astro-Change. Aten Hati. 53p. 1981. pap. 5.00 (*0-935146-64-4*) Morningland.

Astro-Compatibility. Gail A. Guttman. 216p. 1986. pap. 10.95 (*0-87500-020-7*) RKM Pub Co.

Astro-Cycles & Speculative Markets. L. J. Jensen. (Illus.). 1978. 35.00 (*0-939093-11-1*) Lambert Gann Pub.

Astro Data, No. IV. Lois Rodden. pap. 35.00 (*0-86690-355-0*, 3045-014) Am Fed Astrologers.

Astro Data Two. rev. ed. Lois Rodden. 1993. pap. 29.00 (*0-917086-23-6*) Am Fed Astrologers.

Astro-Data V: Profiles in Crime. Lois M. Rodden. 238p. 1992. pap. text ed. 36.00 (*0-9633716-0-6*) Data News Pr.

Astro-Degree Tables: Zodiacal Data. Iain McLaren-Owens. LC 94-96299. (Astro-Degrees Ser.). 200p. 1994. pap. text ed. 24.00 (*1-885500-00-9*, AD2) Astro-Cards.

Astro-Diagnosis: A Guide to Healing. 9th ed. Max Heindel et al. Ed. by Rosicrucian Fellowship Staff. (Illus.). 446p. (C). 1976. reprint ed. pap. text ed. 9.95 (*0-911274-06-5*) Rosicrucian.

Astro-Dome Book: 3-D Map of the Night Sky. Klaus Hunig. Ed. by Lori Solensten. Orig. Title: Sternenhimmel. (Illus.). 56p. (Orig.). (J). (gr. 4 up). 1983. pap. 9.95 (*0-913319-00-7*) Sunstone Pubns.

Astro-Dots: Find the Constellations. Illus. by Jesse Zerner. 64p. (Orig.). (J). (ps-7). 1985. pap. 3.95 (*0-913319-01-5*) Sunstone Pubns.

Astro-Economics: A Study of Astrology & the Business Cycle. David Williams. 64p. 1959. reprint ed. pap. 3.00 (*0-87542-882-7*) Llewellyn Pubns.

Astro Essentials: Planets in Signs, Houses & Aspects. Maritha Pottenger. 416p. (Orig.). 1991. pap. 19.95 (*0-935127-14-3*) ACS Pubns.

Astro-Guide to Nutrition. Lynne Palmer. 1993. 12.00 (*0-86690-438-7*) Am Fed Astrologers.

Astro-Logical Love. Naura Hayden. 287p. 1982. 14.95 (*0-942104-00-5*, 01258-370) Bibli O'Phile Pub Co.

Astro-Logical Love. Naura Hayden. 12.95 (*0-317-01095-6*, Dutton) NAL-Dutton.

Astro-Logos, Language of Life: The True Story of a Man & the People & Planets Around Him. James T. Braha. (Illus.). 352p. 1989. pap. text ed. 12.95 (*0-935895-01-9*) Hermetician Pr.

Astro Metrics: Of Undiscovered Planets & Intelligent Life Forms. Yari Danjo. (Illus.). 355p. (C). Date not set. 29.95 (*0-9638989-0-6*) Privately Pub.

Astro Noesis. Ed. by Wisdom's Goldenrod Staff. (Illus.). Date not set. 16.95 (*0-943914-00-0*) Larson Pubns.

Astro-Numerology. Rose Murray. 48p. 1991. 6.00 (*0-86690-400-X*, M3172-014) Am Fed Astrologers.

Astro Organizer: Easy Learning Reference Guide for Astrological Charts & Graphs. D. L. Thomas. (Illus.). (Orig.). 1992. pap. 19.95 (*0-9635359-0-0*) Astrographix.

Astro-Tarot. S. Mikielle Chatman. 140p. 1992. pap. 8.00 (*1-881146-19-7*) Fat Chance.

Astro-Theology: or a Demonstration of Being & Attributes of God, from a Survey of the Heavens. William Derham. (Anglistica & Americana Ser.: No. 78). xxvi, 246p. 1976. reprint ed. 50.70 (*3-487-06132-5*, Pub. by Georg Olms GW) Lubrecht & Cramer.

Astro-Weather, 1993: Central Time Edition. Guy Spiro. 127p. 1992. pap. 9.95 (*1-880127-05-9*) TMA Pub.

Astro-Weather, 1993: Eastern Time Edition. Guy Spiro. 127p. 1992. pap. 9.95 (*1-880127-04-0*) TMA Pub.

Astro-Weather, 1993: Pacific Time Edition. Guy Spiro. 127p. 1992. pap. 9.95 (*1-880127-06-7*) TMA Pub.

Astro-Weather 1994. Guy Spiro. (Orig.). 1994. pap. 9.95 (*1-880127-08-3*) TMA Pub.

***Astro Weather 1995: Central Time Edition.** Guy Spiro. 144p. (Orig.). 1994. pap. 9.95 (*1-880127-12-1*) TMA Pub.

***Astro Weather 1995: Eastern Time Edition.** Guy Spiro. 144p. (Orig.). 1994. pap. 9.95 (*1-880127-11-3*) TMA Pub.

***Astro Weather 1995: Mountain Time Edition.** Guy Spiro. 144p. (Orig.). 1994. pap. 9.95 (*1-880127-13-X*) TMA Pub.

***Astro Weather 1995: Pacific Time Edition.** Guy Spiro. 144p. (Orig.). 1994. pap. 9.95 (*1-880127-14-8*) TMA Pub.

Astroanalysis. American AstroAnalysts Institute. Incl. Sagittarius. (Orig.). 1977. (*0-448-12564-1*); 360p. 1977. Set pap. 8.95 (*0-685-01830-X*, G&D) Putnam Pub Group.

Astroanalysis: Aquarius. 256p. 1988. pap. 10.95 (*0-425-11216-0*) Berkley Pub.

Astroanalysis: Aries. 256p. 1988. pap. 10.95 (*0-425-11206-3*) Berkley Pub.

Astroanalysis: Cancer. 1988. pap. 10.95 (*0-425-11209-8*) Berkley Pub.

Astroanalysis: Capricorn. 256p. 1988. pap. 10.95 (*0-425-11215-2*) Berkley Pub.

Astroanalysis: Gemini. 256p. 1988. pap. 10.95 (*0-425-11208-X*) Berkley Pub.

Astroanalysis: Leo. 256p. 1988. pap. 10.95 (*0-425-11210-1*) Berkley Pub.

Astroanalysis: Libra. 256p. 1988. pap. 10.95 (*0-425-11212-8*) Berkley Pub.

Astroanalysis: Pisces. 256p. 1988. pap. 10.95 (*0-425-11217-9*) Berkley Pub.

Astroanalysis: Sagittarius. 256p. 1988. pap. 10.95 (*0-425-11214-4*) Berkley Pub.

Astroanalysis: Scorpio. 256p. 1988. pap. 10.95 (*0-425-11213-6*) Berkley Pub.

Astroanalysis: Taurus. 256p. 1988. pap. 10.95 (*0-425-11207-1*) Berkley Pub.

Astroanalysis: Virgo. 256p. 1988. pap. 10.95 (*0-425-11211-X*) Berkley Pub.

Astrobusiness: A Guide to the Commerce & Law of Outer Space. Edward R. Finch, Jr. & Amanda L. Moore. LC 84-18203. 176p. 1984. text ed. 55.00 (*0-275-91155-1*, C1155, Praeger Pubs) Greenwood.

Astrocartography Book of Maps: The Astrology of Relocation: How 136 Famous People Found Their Place. Jim Lewis & Ariel Guttman. LC 89-8070. (Modern Astrology Library). 336p. (Orig.). 1989. pap. 15.95 (*0-87542-434-1*) Llewellyn Pubns.

Astrochemistry. Ed. by M. S. Vardya & S. P. Tarafdar. 1986. lib. bdg. 172.50 (*90-277-2359-1*); pap. text ed. 69.50 (*90-277-2360-5*) Kluwer Ac.

Astrochemistry of Cosmic Phenomena: Proceedings of the 150th Symposium of the International Astronomical Union, Held at Campos do Jordao, Sao Paulo, Brazil, August 5-9, 1991. Ed. by P. D. Singh. LC 92-17224. 536p. (C). 1992. lib. bdg. 150.00 (*0-7923-1824-2*); pap. text ed. 75.00 (*0-7923-1825-0*) Kluwer Ac.

Astrocytes, Vol. 2. Sergey Federoff & Antonia Vernadakis. (Cellular Neurobiology Ser.). 1987. text ed. 128.00 (*0-12-250452-6*) Acad Pr.

Astrocytes, Vol. 3. Sergey Federoff & Antonia Vernadakis. (Cellular Neurobiology Ser.). 1987. text ed. 143.00 (*0-12-250453-4*) Acad Pr.

Astrocytes: Normal, Reactive, & Neoplastic. Philip E. Duffy. (Illus.). 236p. 1983. text ed. 81.00 (*0-89004-996-3*) Raven.

Astrocytes: Pharmacology & Function. Sean Murphy. (Illus.). 457p. 1993. text ed. 99.00 (*0-12-511370-6*) Acad Pr.

Astrocytes, Vol. 1: Development, Morphology & Regional Specialization of Astrocytes. Sergey Federoff & Antonia Vernadakis. (Cellular Neurobiology Ser.). 1987. text ed. 128.00 (*0-12-250451-8*) Acad Pr.

Astrocytomas: Diagnosis, Treatment, & Biology. Ed. by Peter M. Black et al. LC 92-10543. (Contemporary Issues in Neurological Surgery Ser.). (Illus.). 1993. 80.00 (*0-86542-217-6*) Blackwell Sci.

***Astrodynamics--Concepts, Quantities & Symbols: Recommended Practice.** American Institute of Aeronautics & Astronautics Staff & American National Standards Institute Staff. 1994. write for info. (*0-615-00107-6*) AIAA.

Astrodynamics & Astrionics: Proceedings of the Nineteenth International Astronautical Congress, New York, 1968. M. Lunc & P. Contensou. LC 58-23647. (International Astronautical Congress Ser.: Vol. 2). 1970. 248.00 (*0-08-006930-4*, Pub. by Pergamon Repr UK) Franklin.

Astrodynamics, 1975. Ed. by William F. Powers et al. (Advances in the Astronautical Sciences Ser.: Vol. 33). (Illus.). 1976. lib. bdg. 35.00 (*0-87703-079-0*, Pub. by Am Astro Soc); fiche 40.00 (*0-87703-142-8*, Pub. by Am Astro Soc) Univelt Inc.

Astrodynamics, 1979, Pt. 1. Ed. by P. A. Penzo et al. (Advances in the Astronautical Sciences Ser.). (Illus.). 494p. 1980. Part 1, 494pp. lib. bdg. 45.00 (*0-87703-107-X*, Pub. by Am Astro Soc); pap. 35.00 (*0-87703-108-8*, Pub. by Am Astro Soc) Univelt Inc.

Astrodynamics, 1979, Pt. 2. Ed. by P. A. Penzo et al. (Advances in the Astronautical Sciences Ser.). (Illus.). 502p. 1980. Part 2,502pp. 45.00 (*0-87703-109-6*, Pub. by Am Astro Soc); pap. 35.00 (*0-87703-110-X*, Pub. by Am Astro Soc) Univelt Inc.

Astrodynamics, 1979, Vol. 40. Ed. by P. A. Penzo et al. (Advances in the Astronautical Sciences Ser.). (Illus.). 1980. fiche 20.00 (*0-87703-139-8*, Pub. by Am Astro Soc) Univelt Inc.

Astrodynamics 1981. Ed. by Alan L. Friedlander et al. (Advances in the Astronautical Sciences Ser.: Vol. 46). (Illus.). 1124p. (Orig.). 1982. fiche 40.00 (*0-87703-163-0*, Pub. by Am Astro Soc) Univelt Inc.

Astrodynamics 1981, Pt. 1. Ed. by Alan L. Friedlander et al. (Advances in the Astronautical Sciences Ser.: Vol. 46). (Illus.). 1124p. (Orig.). 1982. lib. bdg. 55.00 (*0-87703-159-2*, Pub. by Am Astro Soc) Univelt Inc.

Astrodynamics 1981, Pt. 1. Ed. by Alan L. Friedlander et al. (Advances in the Astronautical Sciences Ser.: Vol. 46). (Illus.). 1124p. (Orig.). 1982. pap. text ed. 45.00 (*0-87703-160-6*, Pub. by Am Astro Soc) Univelt Inc.

Astrodynamics 1981, Pt. 2. Ed. by Alan L. Friedlander et al. (Advances in the Astronautical Sciences Ser.: Vol. 46). (Illus.). 1124p. (Orig.). 1982. lib. bdg. 55.00 (*0-87703-161-4*, Pub. by Am Astro Soc); pap. text ed. 45.00 (*0-87703-162-2*, Pub. by Am Astro Soc) Univelt Inc.

Astrodynamics, 1983. Ed. by G. T. Tseng et al. (Advances in the Astronautical Sciences Ser.: Vol. 54, Pts. I & II). (Illus.). 1984. lib. bdg. 120.00 (*0-87703-190-8*, Pub. by Am Astro Soc); pap. text ed. 90.00 (*0-87703-191-6*, Pub. by Am Astro Soc); fiche 40.00 (*0-87703-192-4*, Pub. by Am Astro Soc) Univelt Inc.

Astrodynamics 1985, 2 Pts. Ed. by Bernard Kaufman et al. (Advances in the Astronautical Sciences Ser.: Vol. 58). (Illus.). 1556p. 1986. lib. bdg. 140.00 (*0-87703-245-9*, Pub. by Am Astro Soc); pap. 110.00 (*0-87703-246-7*, Pub. by Am Astro Soc); fiche 60.00 (*0-87703-247-5*, Pub. by Am Astro Soc) Univelt Inc.

***Astrodynamics 1993.** Arun Misra et al. LC 57-43769. (Advances in the Astronautical Sciences Ser.: 85, I, II & III). (Illus.). 2750p. 1994. lib. bdg. 390.00x (*0-87703-380-3*, Pub. by Am Astro Soc) Univelt Inc.

Astroelectronics. McLean. 1992. text ed. 45.00 (*0-86187-662-8*, Pub. by Pinter Pubs UK) St Martin.

Astrofinance Reference Guide, Vol. I. Hermes. Ed. by James E. Schildgen. LC 91-72965. (Illus.). 150p. 1991. pap. 50.00 (*0-939397-01-3*) Capital Futures Assocs.

Astrofisica. (Monografia: No. 10). 108p. (SPA.). 1982. pap. 3.50 (*0-8270-1902-5*) OAS.

Astrogenesis: Secrets of the Playing Cards with Keys to Astrology. Barbara B. Allen. 160p. 1991. reprint ed. bds. 34.95 (*0-9627429-0-2*) M David Pub.

Astrogram Astrology I. Jayne & Kellye. LC 80-51518. 96p. 1980. 5.50 (*0-86690-117-5*, J1224-014) Am Fed Astrologers.

Astrolabium Vranicum Generale: Nova Orbis Terrarum Descripto (A Map to Accompany the Astrolabium) John Blagrave. LC 78-38156. (English Experience Ser.: No. 435). (Illus.). 69p. 1972. reprint ed. 20.00 (*90-221-0435-4*) Walter J Johnson.

Astrolagaster: or The Figvre-Caster. John Melton. LC 92-550. (Augustan Reprints Ser.: No. 174X (1975)). reprint ed. 12.00 (*0-404-70173-6*, BF1681) AMS Pr.

Astrologer Looks at Murder. Barbara Watters. LC 70-83978. 192p. 1969. 2.50 (*0-86690-167-1*, W1510-024) Am Fed Astrologers.

Astrologer's Day & Other Stories. R. K. Narayan. 229p. 1981. reprint ed. 4.95 (*0-88253-105-0*) Ind-US Inc.

Astrologer's Guide. Tr. by Guido Bonatus & Henry Coley. 105p. 1965. spiral bd. 7.15 (*0-7873-0115-9*) Mokelumne.

Astrologer's Guide. William Lilly. 112p. 1970. 7.00 (*0-86690-123-X*, L1294-014) Am Fed Astrologers.

Astrologer's Guide: Being the One Hundred & Forty-Six Considerations of the Famous Astrologer, Guido Bonatus. Guido Bonatus. Ed. by William Lilly. Tr. by Henry Coley. reprint ed. 35.00 (*1-55818-211-X*) Holmes Pub.

***Astrologer's Handbook.** Julie Parker. (Illus.). 256p. (Orig.). 1995. pap. 10.95 (*0-916360-59-8*) CRCS Pubns CA.

Astrologer's Handbook. Frances Sakoian & Louis S Acker. 21.95 (*0-685-41889-8*) Wehman.

Astrologer's Node Book. Donna Van Toen. 95p. 1981. pap. 5.95 (*0-87728-521-7*) Weiser.

Astrologer's Notebook on Aspects of the Transiting Planets. Mary Elsnau. 225p. 1969. reprint ed. spiral bd. 7.70 (*0-7873-0313-5*) Mokelumne.

Astrologer's Question Box. Doris C. Doane. 200p. 1984. 13.00 (*0-86690-284-8*, D2554-014) Am Fed Astrologers.

Astrologi Halucinati Stars & the End of the World in Luther's Time: Papers Presented at the International Seminar Held at the Wissenschaftskolleg zu Berlin, 28-29 May, 1984. Ed. by Paola Zambelli. x, 294p. 1986. lib. bdg. 115.40 (*3-11-010317-6*) De Gruyter.

Astrologia: Que Dice la Biblia? I. D. Thomas et al. Tr. by Jose Luis Martinez Diaz. (Coleccion Doctrinas Modernas Ser.). Orig. Title: Astrology & the Bible. 32p. 1986. reprint ed. pap. 1.25 (*0-311-05031-X*, Edit Mundo) Casa Bautista.

***Astrologia Espiritual.** Jan Spiller & Karen McCoy. (ENG & SPA.). 1995. pap. 12.00 (*0-684-81329-7*) S&S Trade.

***Astrologia Gallica Book Twenty-Two Directions.** Jean-Baptiste Morin. Tr. by James H. Holden. 294p. 1994. 16.00 (*0-86690-425-5*, M3463-014) Am Fed Astrologers.

Astrologia y Biblia: Astrology & the Bible. William Petersen. (SPA.). 2.95 (*84-7228-232-5*, 220050, Pub. by Edit Clie SP) TSELF.

***Astrological Almanac for 1995.** Lynne Palmer. 134p. 1994. 12.00 (*0-86690-443-3*) Am Fed Astrologers.

Astrological Americana. 150p. 1949. 7.50 (*0-86690-050-0*, A1001-014) Am Fed Astrologers.

***Astrological & Predictive Almanac, 1995.** Foulsham Editors. 1994. pap. 5.99 (*0-572-02029-5*, Pub. by W Foulsham UK) Trans-Atl Phila.

Astrological Aphorisms of Cardan. Ed. by William Lilly. 1990. reprint ed. pap. 3.95 (*1-55818-101-6*, Sure Fire) Holmes Pub.

Astrological Aspects. Leyla Rael & Dane Rudhyar. 244p. 1980. pap. 14.00 (*0-943358-00-0*) Aurora Press.

Astrological Aspects. Charles E. Carter. 190p. 1966. reprint ed. spiral bd. 6.60 (*0-7873-0160-4*) Mokelumne.

Astrological Aspects: Your Inner Dialogues. Jeanne Avery. LC 84-21086. 384p. 1995. pap. 16.95 (*0-385-18857-9*, A 2642-014, Dolp) Am Fed Astrologers.

Astrological Body Types: Face, Form & Expression. Judith A. Hill. (Illus.). 168p. (Orig.). 1993. pap. 17.95 (*1-883376-21-1*) Stellium Pr.

Astrological Compatibility. Lynne Palmer. LC 76-25674. 352p. 1976. 14.00 (*0-86690-139-6*, P1366-014) Am Fed Astrologers.

***Astrological Cookbook: Your Culinary Guide to Celestial Harmony.** Rana Birkmeier. Ed. by Ruth Dejauregui & Bill Yenne. (Illus.). 128p. 1994. text ed. 12.95 (*0-912517-11-5*) Bluewood Bks.

Astrological Counsel. Noel Tyl. LC 73-19927. (Principles & Practice of Astrology Ser.: Vol. 10). 192p. (Orig.). 1975. pap. 3.95 (*0-87542-809-6*) Llewellyn Pubns.

Astrological Counseling: The Path to Self-Actualization. Ed. by Joan McEvers. LC 90-46437. (New World Astrology Ser.). 304p. (Orig.). 1990. pap. 14.95 (*0-87542-385-X*) Llewellyn Pubns.

Astrological Degrees of Life. Harold Hason. 214p. 1985. 8.95 (*0-931345-04-9*, H2574-014) Am Fed Astrologers.

Astrological Diary of the Seventeenth Century: Samuel Jeake of Rye 1652-1699. Samuel Jeake. Ed. by Michael Hunter & Annabel Gregorg. (Illus.). 304p. 1988. 85.00 (*0-19-822962-3*) OUP.

Astrological Essays. Manly P. Hall. pap. 4.00 (*0-89314-302-2*) Philos Res.

***Astrological Foundation of the Christ Myth.** Malik H. Jabbar. (Illus.). 128p. (Orig.). 1995. pap. 8.95 (*1-57154-002-4*) Rare Bks Dist.

Astrological Games People Play. Bernie Ashman. 368p. (Orig.). 1987. pap. 12.95 (*0-917086-74-0*) ACS Pubns.

Astrological Gardening: The Ancient Wisdom of Successful Planting & Harvesting by the Stars. Louise Riotte. LC 89-11987. (Illus.). 224p. 1989. pap. 11.95 (*0-88266-561-8*, Garden Way Pub) Storey Comm Inc.

***Astrological Gardening: The Ancient Wisdom of Successful Planting & Harvesting by the Stars.** Louise Riotte. LC 94-24541. (Illus.). 1994. 6.99 (*0-517-12272-3*) Random Hse Value.

***Astrological Geomancy in Africa.** J. A. Cole. Ed. by Kali Sichen. (Illus.). 61p. 1990. pap. 9.95 (*0-916299-12-0*) North Scale Co.

Astrological Guidance to Occupations. S. P. Malia. 83p. 1983. pap. text ed. 5.95 (*0-86590-232-1*, Pub. by Taraporevala II) Apt Bks.

Astrological Guide to Health: For Each of the Twelve Sun Signs. Ariel Gordon. 50p. 1988. reprint ed. pap. 4.00 (*0-89540-172-X*, SB-172, Sun Bks) Sun Pub.

Astrological Guide to Self-Awareness. 2nd rev. ed. Donna Cunningham. 204p. 1994. pap. 9.95 (*0-916360-57-1*) CRCS Pubns CA.

Astrological Guide to Successful Everyday Living. Sybil Leek. 288p. 1988. 6.99 (*0-517-67664-8*) Random Hse Value.

Astrological Healing: The History & Practice of Astromedicine. Reinhold Ebertin. (Illus.). 416p. 1990. pap. 19.95 (*0-87728-711-2*) Weiser.

Astrological Healing Gems. Shivaji Bhattacharjee. 128p. (Orig.). (C). 1990. pap. 7.95 (*1-878423-07-X*) Morson Pub.

***Astrological Herbal for Women.** Elisabeth Brooke. (Illus.). 248p. 1995. pap. 10.95 (*0-89594-740-4*) Crossing Pr.

Astrological History of Mashaallah. Edward S. Kennedy & David Pingree. LC 72-113185. (Harvard Monographs in the History of Science). (Illus.). 220p. reprint ed. pap. 63.30 (*0-7837-1706-7*, 2057235) Bks Demand.

Astrological Houses: The Spectrum of Individual Experience. Dane Rudhyar. LC 74-180105. 216p. 1986. reprint ed. pap. 12.95 (*0-916360-24-5*) CRCS Pubns CA.

Astrological Insights into Personality. Betty Lundsted. 368p. (Orig.). 1980. pap. 14.95 (*0-917086-22-8*) ACS Pubns.

Astrological Insights into the Spiritual Life. Dane Rudhyar. 154p. 1979. pap. 10.95 (*0-943358-09-4*) Aurora Press.

Astrological Investigations: How to Estimate the Important Areas of Life. W. Frankland. 99p. 1994. pap. 8.00 (*0-89540-235-1*, SB-235, Sun Bks) Sun Pub.

Astrological Key to Mahabharata. Paule Lemer. (C). 1989. 21.00 (*81-208-0453-8*, Pub. by Motilal Banarsidass II) S Asia.

Astrological Keywords. Manly P. Hall. (Quality Paperback Ser.: No. 299). (Illus.). 229p. (Orig.). 1975. pap. 11.95 (*0-8226-0299-7*) Littlefield.

Astrological Keywords. Manly P. Hall. (Orig.). 8.95 (*0-89314-503-3*) Philos Res.

Astrological Let Me Be Book. Florence Nelson. (Illus.). 1977. pap. 2.50 (*0-918328-01-2*) Carma.

Astrological Life Scripts: Mythological Archtypes in the Natal Horoscope. John Muzzio. 190p. 1986. pap. 7.95 (*0-930706-17-X*) Seek-It Pubns.

Astrological Lore in the Buddhist Sardulakarnavadana. Sharmishta Sharma. (C). 1992. 17.50 (*0-8364-2810-2*, Pub. by Eastern Bk Linkers II) S Asia.

Astrological Lore of All Ages. Elbert Benjamine. LC 93-10699. 1993. 9.95 (*0-87887-366-X*) Church of Light.

Astrological Mandala: The Cycle of Transformations & Its 360 Symbolic Phases. Dane Rudhyar. 1974. pap. 10.00 (*0-394-71992-1*, Vin) Random.

Astrological Megatrends 1996. Edward J. Kluska. 200p. 1986. pap. 9.95 (*0-9615748-0-1*) New World OH.

Astrological Patterns. Frances Sakoian. 1988. pap. 7.95 (*0-06-080921-3*, PL) HarpC.

Astrological Pioneers of America. Holden & Hughes. 238p. 1988. 17.95 (*0-86690-351-8*, H2830-014) Am Fed Astrologers.

Astrological Prediction. P. J. Harwood. 215p. 1993. pap. 18.00 (*0-89540-242-4*, SB-242, Sun Bks) Sun Pub.

Astrological Psychosynthesis: The Integration of Personality, Love, & Intelligence in the Horoscope. Bruno Huber. (Illus.). 1992. pap. 23.00 (*1-85538-041-2*, Pub. by Aquarian Pr UK) Thorsons SF.

A

An Asterisk (*) at the beginning of an entry indicates that the title is appearing in BIP for the first time.

495

Astrological Reports to Assyrian Kings. Ed. by Hermann Hunger. (State Archives of Assyria Ser.: Vol. 8). (Illus.). xxix, 384p. 1992. text ed. 80.00 (*951-570-131-7*, Pub. by Helsinki Univ Pr FI); pap. text ed. 59.50 (*951-570-130-9*, Pub. by Helsinki Univ Pr FI) Eisenbrauns.

***Astrological Research Methods: An ISAR Anthology, Vol. 1.** Ed. by Mark Pottengen. (Illus.). 428p. (C). 1995. pap. text ed. write for info. (*0-9646366-0-3*) ISAR MI.

Astrological Secrets of the Hebrew Sages: To Rule Both Day & Night. Joel C. Dobin. LC 77-8288. 256p. 1983. reprint ed. pap. 12.95 (*0-89281-052-1*) Inner Tradit.

***Astrological Signatures: Evolution of the Soul & the Nature of Astrological Energies.** C. C. Zain. LC 94-32270. (Brotherhood of Light Ser.: Course 2). (Illus.). 248p. 1995. pap. 14.95 (*0-87887-372-4*) Church of Light.

Astrological Study of the Bach Flower Remedies. Peter Damian. 88p. (Orig.). Date not set. pap. 8.95 (*0-8464-4212-4*) Beekman Pubs.

Astrological Symbolism in Spenser's "The Shepheardes Calender" The Cultural Background of a Literary Text. J. M. Richardson. LC 88-8436. (Studies in Renaissance Literature: Vol. 1). (Illus.). 1989. 119.95 (*0-88946-144-9*) E Mellen.

***Astrological Symbols & & African Gods.** Anthony K. Andoh & Kali Sichen. (Illus.). 1995. pap. 14.95 (*0-916299-05-8*) North Scale Co.

Astrological Techniques, Vol. 1: Fundamental Considerations & Natal Astrology. John Quinn. LC 87-90722. (Illus.). 159p. (Orig.). 1988. pap. 19.95 (*0-944189-01-6*) Quinn TX.

Astrological Thesaurus, Vol. 1. Michael Munkasey. LC 92-34334. (Llewellyn's Modern Astrology Library). 490p. 1992. 19.95 (*0-87542-579-8*) Llewellyn Pubns.

Astrological Triptych. Dane Rudhyar. 296p. 1978. pap. 14.00 (*0-943358-10-8*) Aurora Press.

Astrological Types. Howard Duff. 52p. 1948. 4.00 (*0-86690-084-5*, D1083-024) Am Fed Astrologers.

Astrological Voids: Exploring the Missing Components in the Birth Chart. Janis Huntley. (Illus.). 192p. 1991. pap. 14.95 (*1-85230-227-5*) Element MA.

Astrological Works. Abraham Ibn Ezra. 1972. lib. bdg. 250.00 (*0-87968-525-5*) Krishna Pr.

***Astrologkical Magick.** Estelle Daniels. (Illus.). 352p. (Orig.). 1995. pap. 14.95 (*0-87728-826-7*) Weiser.

***Astrology.** Ariel Books Staff. (Illus.). 40p. 1995. 6.95 (*0-8362-4742-6*) Andrews & McMeel.

Astrology, Pt. 1, Vol. 18. Readings Research Dept. Staff. (Library). 611p. 1985. lib. bdg. 24.95 (*0-87604-159-4*, 1118) ARE Pr.

Astrology, Pt. 2, Vol. 19. Readings Research Dept. Staff. (Library). 330p. 1985. lib. bdg. 22.95 (*0-87604-176-4*, 1119) ARE Pr.

Astrology, 9 vols., Set. 3rd ed. Elman Bacher. 907p. (C). 1990. reprint ed. pap. text ed. 40.00 (*0-911274-99-5*) Rosicrucian.

Astrology: A Guide to the Signs. (Illus.). 80p. 1992. 4.95 (*0-8362-3014-0*) Andrews & McMeel.

***Astrology: A Key to Personality.** Jeff Mayo. 384p. 1995. 13.95 (*0-14-019489-4*, Arkana) Viking Penguin.

Astrology: A New Age Guide. Ed Perrone. LC 83-70690. 219p. (Orig.). 1983. pap. 8.95 (*0-8356-0579-5*, Quest) Theos Pub Hse.

Astrology: An Echo of the Future, Vol. I. Philip S. Berg. 224p. (C). 1992. write for info. (*0-943688-14-0*); pap. write for info. (*0-943688-15-9*) Res Ctr Kabbalah.

Astrology: History, Symbols, & Signs. Solange De Mailly Nesle. (Illus.). 197p. (Orig.). 1985. pap. 14.95 (*0-89281-105-6*) Inner Tradit.

Astrology: How to Cast Your Horoscope. D. C. Davidson. 235p. 1979. 9.95 (*0-583-13082-8*) Asia Bk Corp.

Astrology: How to Chart Your Horoscope. Max Heindel. 1978. pap. 7.00 (*0-87980-005-4*) Wilshire.

Astrology: How to Make & Read Your Own Horoscope. Sepharial. 145p. 1981. pap. 12.00 (*0-89540-097-9*, SB-097, Sun Bks) Sun Pub.

***Astrology: Is Your Future in the Stars.** Stacey J. Farley. 68p. (YA). (gr. 7-12). 1993. pap. write for info. (*1-57515-024-7*) PPI Pubng.

Astrology: Its Techniques & Ethics. C. A. Libra. (Arcana Ser.). (Illus.). 272p. 1981. reprint ed. pap. 5.95 (*0-87877-035-6*, P-35) Newcastle Pub.

Astrology: Its Techniques & Ethics. C. Aq. Libra. LC 80-23764. xii, 259p. 1980. reprint ed. lib. bdg. 27.00x (*0-89370-635-3*) Borgo Pr.

Astrology: Key to Holistic Health. Marcia Starck. Ed. by Arlene Robertson. 220p. (Orig.). 1982. per., pap. 12.95 (*0-930706-11-0*) Seek-It Pubns.

Astrology: Mundane & Spiritual, 2 vols., Set. S. R. Parchment. 1968. reprint ed. spiral bd. 30.25 (*0-7873-0657-6*) Mokelumne.

Astrology: Mundane, Astral, Occult. Noel Tyl. LC 73-19926. (Principles & Practice of Astrology Ser.: Vol. 11). 192p. (Orig.). 1975. pap. 3.95 (*0-87542-810-X*) Llewellyn Pubns.

Astrology: Off the Top. Sydney Omarr. 128p. 1975. 6.50 (*0-86690-135-3*, O1362-014) Am Fed Astrologers.

Astrology: Opposing Viewpoints. Mary P. Royer. LC 91-21657. (Great Mysteries Ser.). (Illus.). 112p. (J). (gr. 5-8). 1991. lib. bdg. 16.95 (*0-89908-090-1*) Greenhaven.

Astrology: Tables of Houses, Latitude Zero to Sixty-Six Degrees. Max Heindel. Ed. by Rosicrucian Fellowship Staff. 293p. 1992. reprint ed. pap. text ed. 9.95 (*0-911274-37-5*) Rosicrucian.

Astrology: The Celestial Mirror. Warren Kenton. (Art & Imagination Ser.). (Illus.). 1989. pap. 11.95 (*0-500-81004-4*) Thames Hudson.

Astrology: The Classic Guide to Understanding Your Horoscope. Ronald C. Davison. LC 64-10326. (Illus.). 204p. (Orig.). 1988. reprint ed. pap. 9.95 (*0-916360-37-7*) CRCS Pubns CA.

Astrology: The Music of Life. Lew P. Price. 1984. pap. 25.00 (*0-917578-05-8*) L Paxton Price.

Astrology: The Mystery of the Ductless Glands. 2nd rev. ed. Rosicrucian Fellowship Staff. (Illus.). 87p. (C). 1983. reprint ed. pap. text ed. 4.50 (*0-911274-68-5*) Rosicrucian.

Astrology: The Star Science from A to Z & Astro-Rhythms. Milo Kovar. (Illus.). (Orig.). 1985. pap. 7.95 (*0-941208-07-9*) Milo Kovar.

Astrology: Thirty Years Research. Doris C. Doane. 328p. 1956. 14.00 (*0-86690-070-5*, D1065-014) Am Fed Astrologers.

Astrology: True or False? rev. ed. Roger B. Culver & Philip A. Ianna. 228p. 1988. pap. 18.95 (*0-87975-483-4*) Prometheus Bks.

Astrology: Worlds Visible & Invisible. Everett Blackman. 100p. 1974. 7.50 (*0-86690-059-4*, B1104-034) Am Fed Astrologers.

Astrology, a Cosmic Science. 2nd rev. ed. Isabel M. Hickey. 370p. 1992. pap. 12.95 (*0-916360-52-0*) CRCS Pubns CA.

Astrology, Alchemy, & the Tarot. John Sandbach. Ed. by Arlene Robertson. 80p. (Orig.). 1981. per., pap. 4.95 (*0-930706-08-0*) Seek-It Pubns.

Astrology Alive! Experiential Astrology, Astrodrama & the Healing Arts. Barbara Schermer. (Illus.). 224p. 1988. pap. 9.95 (*0-85030-703-1*, Pub. by Aquarian Pr UK) Thorsons SF.

***Astrology & Alchemy.** Frances Palgrave. 1994. pap. 6.95 (*1-55818-295-0*) Holmes Pub.

Astrology & Alchemy; Two Fossil Sciences. Mark A. Graubard. LC 79-8611. reprint ed. 40.00 (*0-404-18475-8*) AMS Pr.

***Astrology & Consciousness.** Rio Olesky. (Illus.). 384p. (Orig.). 1995. pap. 14.95 (*1-56184-123-4*) New Falcon Pubns.

Astrology & Health. Sheila Geddes. 1995. pap. 7.95 (*0-572-01822-3*, Pub. by Foulsham UK) Atrium Pubs.

***Astrology & Heredity: The Thread of Life.** Rosemary J. Peel. (Illus.). 128p. 1995. pap. 9.95 (*0-7137-2477-3*, Pub. by Blandford Pr UK) Sterling.

Astrology & Its Practical Application. Elsa Parker. (Arcana Ser.). 1977. pap. 5.95 (*0-87877-039-9*) Newcastle Pub.

Astrology & Its Practical Application. Tr. by E. Parker & Coba Goedhart. 202p. 1970. reprint ed. spiral bd. 9.35 (*0-7873-0658-4*) Mokelumne.

Astrology & Past Lives. Mary Devlin. LC 86-62344. 304p. 1989. 18.95 (*0-914918-71-0*, Whitford Pr) Schiffer.

Astrology & Prediction. Eric Russell. 182p. 1975. reprint ed. pap. 2.95 (*0-8065-0446-3*, Citadel Pr) Carol Pub Group.

***Astrology & Psychics.** Andre Kole & Terry Holley. (Zondervan Guide to Cults & Religious Movements Ser.). 96p. 1995. 4.99 (*0-310-48921-0*) Zondervan.

Astrology & Reincarnation. Manly P. Hall. pap. 3.00 (*0-89314-303-0*) Philos Res.

***Astrology & Reincarnation.** Manly P. Hall. Date not set. pap. 4.00 (*0-89314-805-9*) Philos Res.

Astrology & Reincarnation. Donald Yott. 256p. (Orig.). 1989. pap. 9.95 (*0-87728-701-5*) Weiser.

Astrology & Relationships. Mary Devin & Julie Lockhart. LC 88-50300. (Illus.). 300p. (Orig.). 1988. pap. 16.95 (*0-914918-77-X*, Whitford Pr) Schiffer.

Astrology & Religion among the Greeks & Romans. Franz Cumont. 1912. pap. 4.50 (*0-486-20581-9*) Dover.

***Astrology & Religion among the Greeks & Romans.** Franz Cumont. 208p. 1994. pap. 16.95 (*1-56459-459-9*) Kessinger Pub.

Astrology & Religion in Indian Art. Swami Sivapriyananda. 1990. 49.50 (*81-7017-231-4*, Pub. by Abhinav II) S Asia.

Astrology & Sexual Analysis. Morris C. Goodman. 1984. pap. 7.00 (*0-87980-405-X*) Wilshire.

Astrology & Spiritual Awakening. Gregory C. Bogart. LC 93-73696. (Illus.). 244p. (Orig.). 1994. pap. 19.95 (*0-9639068-3-6*) Dawn Mtn Pr.

Astrology & Spiritual Development. Donna Cunningham. (Illus.). 144p. (Orig.). 1989. pap. 9.95 (*0-945946-03-1*) Cassandra Pr.

Astrology & Stock Market Forecasting. Louis McWhirter. Ed. by H. Weingarten. 1977. reprint ed. 35.00 (*0-88231-034-8*) ASI Pubs Inc.

Astrology & the Bible see Astrologia: Que Dice la Biblia?

***Astrology & the Cards.** 2nd ed. E. H. Bailey. (Astro-Cards Reprints Ser.). 60p. 1994. pap. text ed. 9.00 (*1-885500-08-4*, AR6) Astro-Cards.

Astrology & the Games People Play: A Tool for Self-Understanding in Work & Relationships. Spencer Grendahl. LC 93-48354. 1994. 12.95 (*1-56718-338-7*) Llewellyn Pubns.

***Astrology & the Seventeenth-Century Mind: William Lilly & the Language of the Stars.** Ann Geneva. LC 94-27757. 1995. text ed. write for info. (*0-7190-4154-6*, Pub. by Manchester Univ Pr UK) St Martin.

Astrology & the Spiritual Path: The Spiritual Significance of Age Progression. Bruno Huber & Louise Huber. 215p. (Orig.). 1990. pap. 12.95 (*0-87728-706-6*) Weiser.

Astrology & Vibrational Healing. Donna Cunningham. (Illus.). 168p. (Orig.). 1988. pap. 9.95 (*0-9615875-8-X*) Cassandra Pr.

Astrology & Vocational Aptitude. H. Von Klockler. 100p. 1974. 10.00 (*0-86690-166-3*, V1509-014) Am Fed Astrologers.

Astrology & You. Carroll Righter. 1989. pap. 5.00 (*0-87980-422-X*) Wilshire.

Astrology & Your Cat. Marian Futterman. Ed. by Jacob Futterman. (Illus.). 1977. pap. write for info. (*0-930140-01-X*) Jay Pub.

Astrology & Your Past Lives. Jeanne Avery. 1987. pap. 11.00 (*0-671-63294-9*, Fireside) S&S Trade.

Astrology As a Business. Doris C. Doane. LC 85-73309. 96p. 1986. 8.00 (*0-86690-303-8*, D2344-014) Am Fed Astrologers.

Astrology As Science: A Statistical Approach. Urban-Lurain. LC 83-71419. 88p. 1984. 13.00 (*0-86690-042-X*, U2313-014) Am Fed Astrologers.

Astrology Beginner's Notebook. Jo Mullen. LC 83-73608. 80p. 1984. 7.50 (*0-86690-269-4*, M2531-014) Am Fed Astrologers.

Astrology Beyond Ego. Tim Lyons. LC 86-40123. 204p. (Orig.). 1986. pap. 6.95 (*0-8356-0612-0*, Quest) Theos Pub Hse.

Astrology Can Make Sense. Ellen Lagerwerff. 84p. 1985. 6.00 (*0-86690-260-0*, L2457-014) Am Fed Astrologers.

Astrology Carousel for Junior Astrologers. Dona Shaw. (Illus.). 101p. (J). 1993. pap. text ed. 10.00 (*1-884776-02-7*) Lazuli Prods.

Astrology Disproved. Lawrence E. Jerome. LC 77-90138. (Science & the Paranormal Ser.). 233p. 1977. 23.95 (*0-87975-067-7*) Prometheus Bks.

Astrology Drawn to Life. J. Willingham-French. 1993. 14.00 (*0-86690-437-9*) Am Fed Astrologers.

Astrology Encyclopedia. James R. Lewis. 550p. 1994. 45.00 (*0-8103-8900-2*, 101561) Gale.

Astrology Encyclopedia. James R. Lewis. 550p. 1994. pap. 19.95 (*0-8103-9460-X*) Visible Ink Pr.

Astrology for All. Alan Leo. (Astrologer's Library). 348p. 1989. pap. 12.95 (*0-89281-175-7*) Inner Tradit.

Astrology for All. Alan Leo. 336p. 1973. reprint ed. spiral bd. 8.80 (*0-7873-0553-7*) Mokelumne.

Astrology for Beginners: An Easy Guide to Understanding & Interpreting Your Chart. William W. Hewitt. LC 91-36399. (Modern Astrology Ser.). 304p. (Orig.). 1991. pap. 9.95 (*0-87542-307-8*) Llewellyn Pubns.

Astrology for Cats. Walter Reiner. 1993. pap. 7.95 (*0-425-13863-1*) Berkley Pub.

Astrology for Dogs. Linda Lacy. LC 89-29516. (Other Dog Bks.). (Illus.). 1990. 12.95 (*0-87714-142-8*) Denlingers.

Astrology for Lovers. Liz Greene. 368p. (Orig.). 1989. pap. 12.95 (*0-87728-702-3*) Weiser.

Astrology for the Light Side of the Brain: A User-Friendly Guide. Kim Rogers-Gallagher. 300p. (Orig.). 1995. pap. 12.95 (*0-935127-35-6*) ACS Pubns.

Astrology for the Millions. 6th ed. Grant Lewi. LC 90-31242. (Classics of Astrology Library). 464p. 1990. pap. 12.95 (*0-87542-438-4*) Llewellyn Pubns.

Astrology for the New Age: An Intuitive Approach. Marcus Allen. LC 79-10433. 128p. (Orig.). 1984. reprint ed. pap. 7.95 (*0-916360-22-9*) CRCS Pubns CA.

Astrology for Yourself: How to Understand & Interpret Your Own Horoscope. Demetra George & Douglas Bloch. LC 86-18966. (Illus.). 288p. (Orig.). 1987. pap. 20.95 (*0-914728-61-X*) Wingbow Pr.

Astrology from A to Z: An Illustrated Source Book. Eleanor Bach. LC 91-17601. 224p. 1992. pap. 14.95 (*0-87131-674-9*) M Evans.

Astrology Handbook: A Guide to Interpretation. Jeanie Innis. 158p. 1994. student ed 8.95 (*1-882811-06-2*) Skyline Pubns.

Astrology, How & Why It Works: An Introduction to Basic Astrology. Marc E. Jones. (Illus.). 437p. 1993. reprint ed. pap. 16.95 (*0-943358-38-8*) Aurora Press.

Astrology in a Nutshell. A. E. Partridge. 72p. 1969. 1.75 (*0-86690-018-7*, P2262-034) Am Fed Astrologers.

Astrology in a Nutshell. C. H. Webber. 132p. 1969. reprint ed. spiral bd. 8.80 (*0-7873-0939-7*) Mokelumne.

Astrology in Action: How Astrology Works in Practice, Demonstrated by Transits, Progressions & Major Chart Themes in Famous People's Lives. Paul Wright. 1989. pap. 12.95 (*0-916360-44-X*) CRCS Pubns CA.

Astrology in Medicine. C. A. Mercier. 1972. 35.00 (*0-87968-672-3*) Gordon Pr.

Astrology in Mesopotamian Culture. A. E. Thierens. 1977. lib. bdg. 59.95 (*0-8490-1461-1*) Gordon Pr.

Astrology in Modern Language: An In-Depth Interpretation of the Birth Chart, Focusing on the Houses & Their Ruling Planets. 2nd ed. Richard B. Vaughan. LC 70-171475. (Illus.). 336p. 1992. reprint ed. pap. 12.95 (*0-916360-50-4*) CRCS Pubns CA.

Astrology in One Day. Magnus Jensen. 35p. 1970. reprint ed. spiral bd. 3.85 (*0-7873-1123-5*) Mokelumne.

Astrology in Relation to Mind & Character. 61p. 1967. reprint ed. spiral bd. 4.40 (*0-7873-0012-8*) Mokelumne.

Astrology in Relation to Mind & Character: A Mental Specialist. 61p. 1994. pap. 5.00 (*0-89540-238-6*, SB-238, Sun Bks) Sun Pub.

Astrology in Roman Law & Politics. Frederick H. Cramer. LC 54-6119. (American Philosophical Society, Philadelphia. Memoirs Ser.: Vol. 37). 303p. reprint ed. pap. 86.40 (*0-8357-5821-4*, 2000352) Bks Demand.

Astrology Inside Out. Bruce E. Nevin. (Illus.). 320p. (Orig.). 1982. pap. 18.95 (*0-914918-19-2*, Whitford Pr) Schiffer.

Astrology, Karma & Transformation: The Inner Dimensions of the Birth Chart. 2nd rev. ed. Stephen Arroyo. (Illus.). 272p. 1992. pap. 12.95 (*0-916360-54-7*) CRCS Pubns CA.

Astrology Kit. Created by Grant Lewi & Liz Greene. 1987. 26.95 (*0-312-01350-7*, Pub. by Thomas Dunne Bks) St Martin.

***Astrology Looks at History.** Ed. by Noel Tyl. (Llewellyn's New World Astrology Ser.). (Illus.). 464p. 1995. pap. 16.95 (*1-56718-868-0*) Llewellyn Pubns.

Astrology Lost Magic. Intro. by Luanna C. Blagrove. (Illus.). 250p. 1988. 24.95 (*0-939776-38-3*) Blagrove Pubns.

Astrology Made Easy. Astarte. 1977. pap. 7.00 (*0-87980-009-7*) Wilshire.

Astrology Made Easy: The Influence of the Stars & Planets upon Human Life. 55p. 1972. reprint ed. spiral bd. 4.40 (*0-7873-0364-X*) Mokelumne.

Astrology, Numerology, & Biorhythms. rev. ed. Marie L. Betz. 1994. 15.95 (*0-533-10745-8*) Vantage.

Astrology, Nutrition & Health. Robert C. Jansky. Ed. by Margaret Anderson. 1977. pap. 12.95 (*0-914918-08-7*, Whitford Pr) Schiffer.

Astrology of Accidents. Carter. 1978. pap. 10.00 (*0-7229-5059-4*) Theos Pub Hse.

Astrology of Childbirth. Doris C. Doane. 1988. pap. 16.95 (*0-86690-380-1*, 3035-014) Am Fed Astrologers.

Astrology of Choice. Roy Alexander. LC 83-6486. (Illus.). 192p. 1983. pap. 7.95 (*0-87728-563-2*) Weiser.

Astrology of Death. Richard Houck. LC 94-77043. (Illus.). 400p. (Orig.). 1994. pap. 21.95 (*0-9641612-5-7*) Grndswell Pr.

Astrology of Deep Space. Philip Sedgwick. 226p. 1985. per. 12.95 (*0-930706-15-3*) Seek-It Pubns.

Astrology of Dreams. Beth Koch. 1990. pap. 16.95 (*0-86690-374-7*, 3042-014) Am Fed Astrologers.

Astrology of Fate. Liz Greene. LC 84-51742. (Illus.). 378p. (Orig.). 1985. pap. 12.95 (*0-87728-636-1*) Weiser.

Astrology of Genius: A Study of the Nobel Prize Winners. 3rd ed. Roy Tate. LC 88-141308. 142p. reprint ed. pap. 40.50 (*0-8357-6030-8*, 2033584) Bks Demand.

Astrology of Genius: A Study of the Nobel Prize Winners. 3rd ed. Roy Tate. 138p. (C). 1988. reprint ed. pap. 9.95 (*0-9620703-0-0*) Evlntry Pubns.

Astrology of Genius: A Study of the Nobel Prizewinners. 5th rev. ed. Roy Tate. 141p. 1990. reprint ed. pap. text ed. 9.95 (*0-9620703-2-7*) Evlntry Pubns.

Astrology of I Ching. W. K. Chu. 1993. pap. 14.00 (*0-14-019439-8*, Arkana) Viking Penguin.

Astrology of Identity. Reed Hayes. LC 85-71466. 278p. 1986. 17.95 (*0-86690-298-8*, H2348-014) Am Fed Astrologers.

Astrology of Personality. Dane Rudhyar. 445p. 1991. 18.95 (*0-943358-25-6*) Aurora Press.

Astrology of Self-Discovery: An In-Depth Exploration of the Potentials Revealed in the Birth Chart. Tracy Marks. LC 85-7844. 288p. (Orig.). 1986. pap. 13.95 (*0-916360-20-2*) CRCS Pubns CA.

Astrology of Sexuality. Martin Schulman. LC 82-159118. 162p. 1982. pap. 8.95 (*0-87728-481-4*) Weiser.

Astrology of the Four Horsemen: How You Can Heal Yourself & Planet Earth. Elizabeth C. Prophet. (Pocketbook Ser.). 640p. 1990. pap. 5.95 (*0-922729-06-9*) Summit Univ.

Astrology of the Macrocosm: New Directions in Mundane Astrology. Ed. by Joan McEvers. LC 90-35088. (New World Astrology Ser.). 420p. (Orig.). 1990. pap. 14.95 (*0-87542-384-1*) Llewellyn Pubns.

Astrology of the Old Testament. Karl Anderson. 502p. 1970. spiral bd. 22.00 (*0-7873-0033-0*) Mokelumne.

Astrology of the Seers. David Frawley. 342p. (Orig.). (C). 1990. pap. 18.95 (*1-878423-05-3*) Passage Pr.

Astrology of Theosophy. Edward Wilson. LC 82-70432. 80p. 1982. 8.00 (*0-86690-033-0*, W2601-014) NAL-Dutton.

Astrology of Transformation. Dane Rudhyar. LC 80-51553. 1980. pap. 10.00 (*0-8356-0542-6*, Quest) Theos Pub Hse.

Astrology Plus Insight. Gavin McClung. LC 83-72571. 136p. 1984. 12.00 (*0-86690-259-7*, M2427-014) Am Fed Astrologers.

Astrology, Psychology & the Four Elements: An Energy Approach to Astrology & Its Use in the Counseling Arts. Stephen Arroyo. LC 75-27828. 208p. (Orig.). 1975. pap. 10.95 (*0-916360-01-6*) CRCS Pubns CA.

***Astrology Really Works!** Magi Society Staff. Ed. by Jill Kramer. (Illus.). 300p. (Orig.). 1995. pap. 12.95 (*1-56170-134-3*, 170) Hay House.

Astrology Reborn. John M. Addey. 40p. 1971. 7.00 (*0-86690-192-2*, A1007-014) Am Fed Astrologers.

Astrology, Reincarnation & Psychics. Gordon Lindsay. (Sorcery in America Ser.: Vol. 2). 1968. 1.95 (*0-89985-951-8*) Christ for the Nations.

Astrology, Romance, You & the Stars. Anthony Norvell. 1979. pap. 10.00 (*0-87980-011-9*) Wilshire.

Astrology Simplified & Life Delineator. Lyman E. Stowe. 100p. 1972. reprint ed. spiral bd. 4.40 (*0-7873-1126-X*) Mokelumne.

Astrology, Simplified Scientific... 19th ed. Max Heindel. Ed. by Rosicrucian Fellowship Staff. (Illus.). 198p. (C). 1984. reprint ed. pap. text ed. 8.95 (*0-911274-01-4*) Rosicrucian.

Astrology Study Guide, Vol. 2. Katalin Williams. 112p. 1981. 10.00 (*0-685-18406-4*, W1528-014) Am Fed Astrologers.

Astrology Test. Dan Pape. (Illus.). 32p. (Orig.). (C). 1993. pap. text ed. write for info. (*1-882330-17-X*) Magni Co.

Astrology: The Message of the Stars: An Esoteric Exposition of Natal & Medical Astrology. 19th ed. Max Heindel & Augusta F. Heindel. Ed. by Rosicrucian Fellowship Staff. (Illus.). 728p. (C). 1989. reprint ed. pap. text ed. 15.95 (*0-911274-18-9*) Rosicrucian.

Astrology the Sacred Science. Joan Hodgson. 243p. 1991. pap. 12.95 (*0-916360-06-7*) CRCS Pubns CA.

Astrology, the Supernatural & the Beyond. Sri Chinmoy. LC 74-75131. 123p. (Orig.). 1974. pap. 5.95 (*0-88497-037-X*) Aum Pubns.

Astrology Then & Now. Robert Hughes. LC 85-73304. 156p. 1986. 16.95 (*0-86690-308-9*, H2352-014) Am Fed Astrologers.

Astrology Theologized: The Spiritual Hermeneutics of Astrology & Holy Writ Being a Treatise upon the Influence of the Stars on Man & on the Art of Ruling Them by the Law of Grace (1885) Anna K. Bonus. 121p. 1993. reprint ed. pap. 16.95 (*1-56459-409-2*) Kessinger Pub.

Astrology, Vol. I: Your Child's Horoscope. 2nd ed. Max Heindel. Ed. by Rosicrucian Fellowship Staff. 97p. (C). 1990. reprint ed. pap. text ed. 2.50 (*0-911274-21-9*) Rosicrucian.

An Asterisk (*) at the beginning of an entry indicates that the title is appearing in BIP for the first time.

Astrology, Vol. II: Your Child's Horoscope. Max Heindel. Ed. by Rosicrucian Fellowship Staff. 96p. (C). 1973. pap. text ed. 2.50 (*0-911274-22-7*) Rosicrucian.

Astrology's Special Measurements: How to Expand the Meaning of the Horoscope. Ed. by Noel Tyl. LC 93-48976. (New World Astrology Ser.). 352p. 1994. pap. 12.00 (*1-56718-864-8*) Llewellyn Pubns.

Astrometric Binaries: Reprinted from Astrophysics & Space Science, Vol. 110, No. 1. Zdenek Kopal & Jurgen Rahe. 1985. lib. bdg. 97.50 (*90-277-1970-5*) Kluwer Ac.

Astrometric Techniques. Ed. by Heinrich K. Eichhorn & Robert J. Leacock. 1986. lib. bdg. 237.50 (*90-277-2256-0*) Kluwer Ac.

Astrometric Techniques. Ed. by Heinrich K. Eichhorn & Robert J. Leacock. 1986. pap. text ed. 100.50 (*90-277-2257-9*) Kluwer Ac.

Astromony in Color. Brown. 6.95 (*0-02-567700-4*) Macmillan.

Astronaut Primer. William R. Pogue. (Illus.). (Orig.). 1986. pap. 5.50 (*0-935291-00-8*) Nat Space Soc.

Astronaut to Zodiac: A Young Stargazer's Alphabet. Roger Ressmeyer. LC 92-9615. (Illus.). 32p. (J). (gr. k-6). 1992. 15.00 (*0-517-58805-6*); lib. bdg. 15.99 (*0-517-58806-4*) Crown Bks Yng Read.

Astronaut Training Book for Kids. Kim Long. (Illus.). 160p. (J). (gr. 5-p). 1990. 15.95 (*0-525-67296-6*, Lodestar Bks) Dutton Child Bks.

Astronautical Multilingual Dictionary. International Academy of Astronautics Staff. 936p. (CZE, ENG, FRE, GER, ITA, RUS & SPA.). 1970. 215.50 (*0-444-40830-4*) Elsevier.

Astronautical Multilingual Dictionary. International Academy of Astronautics Staff. 936p. (CZE, ENG, FRE, GER, ITA, RUS & SPA.). 1969. 395.00 (*0-8288-9249-0*, M7701) Fr & Eur.

Astronautical Research: International Astronautical Congress. Ed. by Luigi G. Napolitano et al. Incl. Proceedings, 1975 - Space & Energy. 1976. (*0-318-55139-X*); write for info. (*0-318-55138-1*, Pub. by Pergamon Repr UK) Franklin.

Astronautical Research 1971: Proceedings. Congress of the International Astronautical Federation, 22nd, Brussels, Sept. 1971. Ed. by L. G. Napolitano. LC 72-92536. (Illus.). 586p. 1973. lib. bdg. 154.50 (*90-277-0306-X*) Kluwer Ac.

Astronautical Research 1972: Proceedings of the International Astronautical 23rd Congress, 1972. International Astronautical Congress Staff. Ed. by L. G. Napolitano et al. LC 72-97959. 300p. 1973. lib. bdg. 136.50 (*90-277-0333-7*) Kluwer Ac.

Astronautics Convention, 1979: Proceedings, 2 pts. Ed. by Geoff Davies. 314p. (Orig.). 1981. pap. text ed. 40.00 (*0-9596726-5-6*, Pub. by Astronautical Soc W Australia AT) Univelt Inc.

Astronautics for Peace & Human Progress: Proceedings of the International Astronautical 29th Congress, Dubrovnik, October 1-8, 1978. International Astronautical Congress Staff. Ed. by L. G. Napolitano. LC 79-40049. (Illus.). 1979. 182.00 (*0-08-024732-6*, Pub. by Pergamon Repr UK) Franklin.

Astronautics Year 1965: International Astronautical & Military Space - Missile Review. D. Howard. LC 64-240090. 1966. 144.00 (*0-08-012071-7*, Pub. by Pergamon Repr UK) Franklin.

Astronauts. Jonathan Burch. Ed. by Rebecca Stefoff. LC 91-45925. (Living Dangerously Ser.). (Illus.). 32p. (J). (gr. 5-9). 1992. lib. bdg. 17.26 (*1-56074-041-8*) Garrett Ed Corp.

Astronauts. Mike Goodman. LC 89-31222. (At Risk Ser.). (Illus.). 48p. (J). (gr. 5-6). 1989. lib. bdg. 11.95 (*0-89686-430-8*, Crstwood Hse) Silver Burdett Pr.

Astronauts. Carol Greene. LC 83-23142. (New True Bks.). (Illus.). 48p. (J). (gr. k-4). 1984. lib. bdg. 12.90 (*0-516-01722-5*); pap. 4.95 (*0-516-41722-3*) Childrens.

Astronauts. Dinah Moche. LC 78-54955. (Pictureback Ser.). (Illus.). (J). (ps-3). 1979. pap. 2.25 (*0-394-83901-3*) Random Bks Yng Read.

Astronauts. Bill Yenne. 1991. pap. 14.95 (*0-671-08194-2*) S&S Trade.

Astronauts: Canada's Voyageurs in Space. Lydia Dotto. (Illus.). 176p. 1993. 22.95 (*0-7737-2707-8*, Pub. by Stoddart Pubng CN) Genl Dist Srvs.

Astronauts & Spacecraft. Gabriele. (J). 1985. pap. 1.95 (*0-911211-62-4*) Penny Lane Pubns.

***Astronauts Are Sleeping.** Natalie Standiford. 1996. write for info. (*0-679-86999-9*, Apple Soup Bks) Knopf Bks Yng Read.

Astronaut's Diary. Jeffrey A. Hoffman. 54p. (Orig.). 1986. pap. 9.95 (*0-936897-00-7*) Caliban.

Astronaut's Diary. limited ed. Jeffrey A. Hoffman. 54p. (Orig.). 1986. 150.00 (*0-936897-01-5*) Caliban.

***Astronauts Flying T-38 Jets: An Audit Report of Johnson Space Center-NASA.** (Illus.). 87p. (Orig.). (C). 1994. pap. text ed. 45.00x (*0-7881-1144-2*) Diane Pub.

Astronauts of Ancient Japan. Illus. by Vaughn M. Greene. LC 78-78289. 164p. 1978. 7.95 (*0-318-03043-8*) Merlin Engine Wks.

***Astronauts of Inner Space: Experiences of the Pure Self Within.** Ed. by Dawn King. 250p. (Orig.). 1995. pap. 19.95 (*0-941848-01-9*) Builders Pub.

Astronauts: Space Jokes & Riddles. Charles Keller. (J). (gr. 4-7). 1991. pap. 2.95 (*0-671-73984-0*, Litl Simon S&S) S&S Childrens.

Astronauts to Diving Ducks. Christopher Carrie. (Crayola Encyclopedia of Coloring Fun Bks.). (Illus.). 40p. (Orig.). (J). (gr. k up). 1989. pap. 1.49 (*0-86696-219-0*) Binney & Smith.

Astronomer. Jack Rudman. (Career Examination Ser.: C-54). 1994. pap. 29.95 (*0-8373-0054-1*) Nat Learn.

***Astronomer & Other Stories.** Doris Betts. (Voices of the South Ser.). 242p. 1995. pap. 11.95 (*0-8071-2010-3*) La State U Pr.

Astronomer As Natural Philosopher: An Inaugural Lecture. Alan H. Cook. LC 73-89007. (Illus.). 39p. reprint ed. pap. 25.00 (*0-8357-5822-2*, 2051372) Bks Demand.

Astronomers. Donald Goldsmith. (Illus.). 376p. 1993. pap. 14.95 (*0-312-09245-8*) St Martin.

Astronomer's Garden & Beached. Kevin Hood. (Methuen New Theatrescripts Ser.). 122p. (Orig.). 1991. pap. 11.95 (*0-413-65080-4*, AO536, Pub. by Methuen UK) Heinemann.

Astronomer's Night Sky. Brian Jones. 1990. 9.99 (*0-517-01991-4*) Random Hse Value.

Astronomer's Universe: Stars, Galaxies, & Cosmos. Herbert Friedman. 1990. 24.95 (*0-393-02818-6*) Norton.

Astronomic & Grid Azimuth. R. B. Buckner. (Illus.). 255p. 1989. pap. text ed. 34.00 (*0-910845-22-0*, 955) Landmark Ent.

Astronomica. Manilius. (Loeb Classical Library: No. 469). 510p. (C). 1978. text ed. 18.95 (*0-674-99516-3*) HUP.

Astronomica, 5 vols. in 2, Set. Marcus Manilius. cxcvii, 627p. 1972. reprint ed. write for info. (*3-487-04271-1*, Pub. by Georg Olms GW) Lubrecht & Cramer.

Astronomical Activities: Observing, Recording, & Interpreting Celestial Phenomena. 2nd ed. Lon C. Hill. 256p. (C). 1994. per., pap. text ed. 34.95 (*0-8403-9334-2*) Kendall-Hunt.

Astronomical Algorithms. Meeus. 1991. 24.95 (*0-943396-35-2*) Willmann-Bell.

Astronomical Almanac for the Year Nineteen Ninety-Four. 552p. 1993. 34.95 (*0-11-886944-2*, HM69442, Pub. by HMSO UK) UNIPUB.

Astronomical Almanac for the Year 1990. (Illus.). 540p. 1989. boxed 23.00 (*0-16-002107-3*, S/N 008-054-001) USGPO.

Astronomical Almanac for the Year, 1993. 552p. 1993. 28.95 (*0-11-886943-4*, HM69434, Pub. by HMSO UK) UNIPUB.

Astronomical Almanac for the Year, 1995. 552p. 1994. 40.00 (*0-11-886949-3*, HM69493, Pub. by HMSO UK) UNIPUB.

***Astronomical & Astrophysical Objectives of Sub-Milliarcsecond Optical Astrometry: Proceedings of the 166th Symposium of the International Astronomical Union Held in the Hague, the Netherlands, August 15-19, 1994.** Ed. by Erik Hog. (International Astronomical Union Symposia Ser.). 452p. (C). 1995. pap. 78.00 (*0-7923-3443-4*) Kluwer Ac.

***Astronomical & Astrophysical Objectives of Sub-Milliarcsecond Optical Astrometry: Proceedings of the 166th Symposium of the International Astronomical Union Held in the Hague, the Netherlands, August 15-19, 1994.** International Astronomical Union Staff. Ed. by Erik Hog & P. Kenneth Seidelmann. LC 95-11844. (International Astronomical Union Symposia Ser.). 452p. (C). 1995. lib. bdg. 192.00 (*0-7923-3442-6*) Kluwer Ac.

***Astronomical Calendar 1995.** Guy Ottewell. 1994. pap. 16.00 (*0-934546-30-4*) Astron Wkshp.

Astronomical CCD Observing & Reduction Techniques. Ed. by S. Howell. (ASP Conference Series Publications: Vol. 23). 329p. 1992. 40.00 (*0-937707-42-2*) Astron Soc Pacific.

Astronomical Centers of the World. Kevin Krisciunas. (Illus.). 350p. 1988. 34.95 (*0-521-30278-1*) Cambridge U Pr.

***Astronomical Code of the RgVeda.** Subhash Kak. (C). 1994. 16.50 (*81-85689-98-9*, Pub. by Aditya Prakashan II) S Asia.

Astronomical Companion. Guy Ottewell. (Illus.). (C). 1979. pap. 12.00 (*0-934546-01-0*) Astron Wkshp.

Astronomical Cuneiform Texts, 3 vols. (Sources in the History of Mathematics & Physical Sciences Ser.: Vol. 5). (Illus.). 799p. 1983. 175.00 (*0-387-90812-9*) Spr-Verlag.

Astronomical Data Analysis Software & Systems. Ed. by D. Worall et al. (ASP Conference Series Publications: Vol. 25). 551p. 1992. 40.00 (*0-937707-44-9*) Astron Soc Pacific.

***Astronomical Data Analysis Software & Systems III No. 61.** Ed. by Dennis R. Crabtree et al. 576p. 1994. 40.00 (*0-937707-80-5*) Astron Soc Pacific.

Astronomical Description of the Late Comet. John Bainbridge. LC 74-28828. (English Experience Ser.: No. 710). 1975. reprint ed. 20.00 (*90-221-0710-8*) Walter J Johnson.

Astronomical Formulae for Calculators. 4th ed. Meeus. 1988. pap. 14.95 (*0-943396-22-0*) Willmann-Bell.

Astronomical Image Comparator: An Astronomical Video Image Comparator System. Eric R. Craine & Neil T. Wemple. (Astronomy & Astrophysics Ser.). (Illus.). 26p. 1988. pap. 20.00 (*0-934525-07-2*); disk 225.00 (*0-934525-08-0*) West Research.

Astronomical Infrared Spectroscopy: Future Observational Directions. Ed. by S. Kwok. (ASP Conference Series Publications: Vol. 41). 418p. 1993. 40.00 (*0-937707-60-0*) Astron Soc Pacific.

Astronomical Knowledge of the Maori, Genuine & Empirical. Elsdon Best. Bd. with Maori Division of Time. LC 75-35226. LC 75-35226. reprint ed. 39.50 (*0-404-14405-5*) AMS Pr.

Astronomical Lore in Chaucer. Florence M. Grimm. LC 73-168207. (University of Nebraska Studies in Language, Literature & Criticism). 1970. reprint ed. 27.50 (*0-404-02919-1*) AMS Pr.

Astronomical Masers. Moshe Elitzur. (C). 1992. lib. bdg. 94.00 (*0-7923-1216-3*); pap. text ed. 47.00 (*0-7923-1217-1*) Kluwer Ac.

Astronomical Notes on the Maya Codices. R. W. Willson. (Harvard University Peabody Museum of Archaeology & Ethnology Papers: Vol. 6, No. 3). 1972. reprint ed. 12.00 (*0-527-01208-4*) Periodicals Srv.

Astronomical Observations: An Optical Perspective. Gordon Walker. (Illus.). 400p. 1987. pap. 37.95 (*0-521-33907-3*) Cambridge U Pr.

Astronomical Optics. Daniel J. Schroeder. 352p. 1987. text ed. 73.00 (*0-12-629805-X*) Acad Pr.

Astronomical Phenomena for the Year 1991. (Illus.). 77p. 1989. pap. 3.25 (*0-16-002119-7*, S/N 008-054-00142-4) USGPO.

Astronomical Phenomena for the Year 1992. (Illus.). 78p. 1990. pap. 3.50 (*0-16-002116-2*, S/N 008-054-00139-4) USGPO.

Astronomical Phenomena for the Year, 1992. 74p. 1991. pap. 11.00 (*0-11-886936-1*, HM9361) UNIPUB.

Astronomical Phenomena for the Year, 1994. 74p. 1993. pap. 10.00 (*0-11-886946-9*, HM69469, Pub. by HMSO UK) UNIPUB.

Astronomical Photoelectric Photometry. American Association for the Advancement of Science Staff. Ed. by Frank B. Wood. LC 53-12745. 149p. reprint ed. pap. 42.50 (*0-8357-5823-0*, 2000204) Bks Demand.

Astronomical Photometry, a Guide. Christiaan Sterken. (Astrophysics & Space Science Library). 288p. (C). 1992. lib. bdg. 100.00 (*0-7923-1653-3*); pap. text ed. 50.00 (*0-7923-1776-9*) Kluwer Ac.

Astronomical Photometry, Text & Handbook for the Advanced & Professional Astronomer. Hendon & Kaitchuck. 1990. 24.95 (*0-943396-25-5*) Willmann-Bell.

Astronomical Principles of Religion, Natural & Reveal'd. William Whiston. (Anglistica & Americana Ser.: No. 109). 304p. 1983. reprint ed. 76.70 (*3-487-07327-7*, Pub. by Georg Olms GW) Lubrecht & Cramer.

Astronomical Problems: Introductory Course in Astronomy. B. Vel'Yaminov & P. Rabbitt. LC 67-22828. 1969. 134.00 (*0-08-010893-8*, Pub. by Pergamon Repr UK) Franklin.

***Astronomical Religion: Ancient Astrology As Key to Symbolic Worship.** W. B. Crow. 1994. reprint ed. pap. text ed. 6.95 (*1-55818-311-6*, Sure Fire) Holmes Pub.

Astronomical Revolution: Copernicus - Kepler - Borelli. Alexandre Koyre. (Illus.). 531p. 1992. reprint ed. pap. 12.95 (*0-486-27095-5*) Dover.

Astronomical Scrapbook. Joseph Ashbrook. (Illus.). 480p. 1984. text ed. 18.95 (*0-933346-24-7*) Sky Pub.

Astronomical Scrapbook: Skywatchers, Pioneers & Seekers in Astronomy. Joseph Ashbrook. (Illus.). 384p. 1985. 34.95 (*0-521-30045-2*) Cambridge U Pr.

Astronomical Tables of the Sun, Moon, & Planets. Jean Meeus. LC 83-5762. 400p. (Orig.). 1983. pap. text ed. 19.95 (*0-943396-02-6*) Willmann-Bell.

***Astronomical Tables of the Sun, Moon & Planets.** 2nd ed. Jean Meeus. LC 95-3657. 1995. write for info. (*0-943396-45-X*) Willmann-Bell.

Astronomical Works of Gregory Chioniades, Vol. 1, Pt. 1: The Zij Al-Ala Text, Translation, Commentary. David Pingree. (Corpus des Astronomes Byzantins Ser.: Vol. II). 412p. (Orig.). (C). 1985. pap. 69.00 (*90-70265-65-6*, Pub. by Gieben NE) Benjamins North Am.

Astronomical Works of Gregory Chioniades, Vol. 1, Pt. 2: The Zii Al-Ala Tables. David Pingree. (Corpus des Astronomes Byzantins Ser.: Vol. II). 235p. (Orig.). (C). 1986. pap. 85.00 (*90-70265-50-8*, Pub. by Gieben NE) Benjamins North Am.

Astronomie. Evry L. Schatzman. 1860p. write for info. (*0-318-51927-5*) Fr & Eur.

Astronomies & Cultures. Ed. by Clive Ruggles & Nicholas Saunders. (Illus.). 320p. 1993. text ed. 39.95 (*0-87081-319-6*) Univ Pr Colo.

***Astronomy.** Stuart Atkinson. (Understanding Science Ser.). (Illus.). 48p. (YA). (gr. 6-12). 1995. pap. 7.95 (*0-7460-1361-2*, Usborne) EDC.

***Astronomy.** Stuart Atkinson. (Understanding Science Ser.). (Illus.). 48p. (YA). (gr. 6-12). 1995. lib. bdg. 14.96 (*0-88110-741-7*, Usborne) EDC.

Astronomy. Boy Scouts of America. (Illus.). 80p. (J). (gr. 6-12). 1983. pap. 1.85 (*0-8395-3303-9*, 33303) BSA.

Astronomy. Peter L. Brown. LC 84-1654. (World of Science Ser.). (Illus.). 64p. (YA). (gr. 7 up). 1985. 15.95 (*0-87196-985-8*) Facts on File.

Astronomy. Dennis B. Fradin. LC 82-19722. (New True Bks.). (Illus.). 48p. (J). (gr. k-4). 1983. lib. bdg. 12.90 (*0-516-01673-3*); pap. 4.95 (*0-516-41673-1*) Childrens.

Astronomy. Ian Graham. LC 94-13835. (Science Spotlight Ser.). (J). 1995. lib. bdg. write for info. (*0-8114-3841-4*) Raintree Steck-V.

Astronomy. Kristen Lippincott. LC 93-33102. (Eyewitness Science Ser.). (J). 1994. 15.95 (*1-56458-680-4*) Dorling Kindersley.

Astronomy. OECD Staff. 150p. (Orig.). 1993. pap. 40.00 (*92-64-13928-1*) OECD.

Astronomy. Graham Peacock & Dennis Ashton. (Science Activities Ser.). (Illus.). 32p. (J). (gr. 2-4). 1994. 14.95 (*1-56847-191-2*) Thomson Lrning.

Astronomy. Raintree Publishers Staff. LC 87-28780. (Science & Its Secrets Ser.). (Illus.). 64p. (Orig.). (J). (gr. 5-9). 1988. lib. bdg. 11.95 (*0-8172-3080-7*) Raintree Steck-V.

Astronomy. Ian Ridpath. (American Nature Guide Ser.). 1992. 9.98 (*0-8317-6969-6*) Smithmark.

Astronomy. Jack Rudman. (DANTES Ser.: No. 1). 1994. pap. 23.95 (*0-8373-6601-1*) Nat Learn.

***Astronomy.** Jack Rudman. (DANTES Ser.: No. 1). 1994. 39.95 (*0-8373-6501-5*) Nat Learn.

Astronomy. Philip Steele. LC 90-20633. (Pocket Facts Ser.). (Illus.). 32p. (J). (gr. 5-6). 1991. text ed. 11.95 (*0-89686-586-X*, Crstwood Hse) Silver Burdett Pr.

Astronomy. Whittingham. 1984. pap. 8.00 (*0-8331-1800-5*) Hubbard Sci.

Astronomy. Lisa Wroble. (Science Fair Projects Ser.). (Illus.). 48p. (J). (gr. 3-6). Date not set. lib. bdg. 12.95 (*1-56065-110-5*) Capstone Pr.

Astronomy. 6th ed. E. G. Ebbighausen & Robert L. Zimmerman. (Illus.). 208p. (C). 1992. pap. write for info. (*0-02-331330-7*) Macmillan.

***Astronomy: A Beginner's Guide to the Universe.** Eric Chaisson & Stephen McMillan. LC 94-3511. 1994. pap. text ed. 46.00 (*0-13-644063-0*) P-H.

Astronomy: A Physical Perspective. Marc Kutner. 576p. 1987. Net. text ed. write for info. (*0-471-60499-2*) Wiley.

Astronomy: A Self Teaching Guide. 4th ed. Dinah L. Moche. 368p. 1993. pap. text ed. 17.95 (*0-471-53001-8*) Wiley.

Astronomy: A Student Study Guide. William R. Luebke. 196p. (C). 1993. pap. text ed., spiral bd. 19.95 (*0-8403-9126-9*) Kendall-Hunt.

Astronomy: An Introduction. Herman Von Baravalle. 1991. pap. 6.95 (*0-945803-15-X*) R Steiner Col Pubns.

Astronomy: Exploring Beyond Earth. rev. ed. Carolyn Zolg. (Learning Packets - Anthropology Ser.). (Illus.). 72p. 1993. pap. text ed. 19.95 (*0-913705-03-9*) Zephyr Pr AZ.

Astronomy: From Stonehenge to Quasars. Michael W. Friedlander. (Illus.). 640p. (C). 1985. text ed. write for info. (*0-13-049867-X*) P-H.

Astronomy: From the Earth to the Universe. 4th ed. Jay M. Pasachoff. (C). 1991. pap. text ed. 43.00 (*0-03-031329-5*) SCP.

Astronomy: In Quest of the Universe. Karl F. Kuhn. Ed. by Westby. 518p. (C). 1991. pap. text ed. 44.50 (*0-314-78700-3*) West Pub.

Astronomy: Lab Manual for Non-Scientists, 1995. William Cocke et al. 144p. (C). 1994. pap. text ed., spiral bd. 16.95 (*0-8403-9352-0*) Kendall-Hunt.

Astronomy: Laboratory Manual. 3rd ed. University of Minnesota Staff. 96p. 1991. per. 9.95 (*0-8403-7080-6*) Kendall-Hunt.

Astronomy: Principles & Practice. A. E. Roy & D. Clarke. (Illus.). 376p. 1988. pap. 36.00 (*0-85274-393-9*) IOP Pub.

Astronomy: Principles & Practice. 3rd ed. A. E. Roy & D. Clarke. (Illus.). 376p. 1988. 129.00 (*0-85274-394-7*) IOP Pub.

Astronomy: Structure of the Universe. 3rd ed. A. E. Roy & D. Clarke. (Illus.). 316p. 1989. 129.00 (*0-85274-082-4*); pap. 35.00 (*0-85274-083-2*) IOP Pub.

Astronomy: The Cosmic Journey. 5th ed. William K. Hartmann & Chris Impey. 728p. 1994. text ed. 49.95 (*0-534-21192-5*) Intl Thomson.

Astronomy: The Cosmic Journey, 1991 ed. William K. Hartmann. 693p. (C). 1991. text ed. 47.95 (*0-534-14946-4*) Intl Thomson.

Astronomy: The Cosmic Perspective. 2nd ed. Michael Zeilik & John E. Gaustad. 864p. 1990. write for info. (*0-471-51864-6*) Wiley.

Astronomy: The Evolving Universe. 6th ed. Incl. 168p. teacher ed 16.50 (*0-471-53487-0*); trans. 275.55 (*0-471-54629-1*); disk 25.00 (*0-471-55766-8*); disk 1.00 (*0-471-54576-7*); 1.00 (*0-471-54575-9*); sl. 123.55 (*0-471-54628-3*); 99.50 (*0-471-53488-9*); 1991. Net. Set text ed. write for info. (*0-471-52267-8*); Incl. teacher ed 16.50 (*0-471-53487-0*); trans. 275.55 (*0-471-54629-1*); disk 25.00 (*0-471-55766-8*); disk 1.00 (*0-471-54576-7*); 1.00 (*0-471-54575-9*); sl. 123.55 (*0-471-54628-3*); 99.50 (*0-471-53488-9*); Net. Set pap. text ed. write for info. (*0-471-53856-6*) Wiley.

Astronomy: The Evolving Universe. 7th ed. Michael Zeilik. LC 93-39216. 1993. pap. text ed. write for info. (*0-471-59739-2*) Wiley.

***Astronomy: Through Space & Time.** Sune Engelbrektson. 88p. 1994. student ed, spiral bd. write for info. (*0-697-27236-2*) Wm C Brown Pubs.

Astronomy: Through Time & Space. Sune Engelbrektson. (Illus.). 464p. (C). 1993. pap. text ed. write for info. (*0-697-10923-2*) Wm C Brown Pubs.

Astronomy No. 17: Extending Science. Bernard Abrams & Patrick Moore. 152p. (C). 1994. pap. 21.00x (*0-85950-938-9*, Pub. by S Thornes Pubs UK) St Mut.

Astronomy a Laboratory Textbook. John W. Wilson. (Illus.). 218p. (Orig.). (C). 1992. pap. text ed. 21.95x (*0-89892-099-X*) Contemp Pub Co of Raleigh.

Astronomy Activity Book. Dennis Schatz. (J). (gr. 4-7). 1991. pap. 6.95 (*0-671-70449-4*, Litl Simon S&S) S&S Childrens.

Astronomy Adventures. National Wildlife Federation Staff. (J). (gr. k-8). 1991. pap. 7.95 (*0-945051-31-X*, 75022) Natl Wildlife.

Astronomy & Astrophysics. National Research Council. (Space Science in the Twenty-First Century Series: Imperatives for the Decades 1995 to 2015). 84p. 1988. pap. text ed. 14.95 (*0-309-03875-8*) Natl Acad Pr.

Astronomy & Astrophysics. Ed. by Morton S. Roberts. LC 85-13380. (AAAS Publication Ser.: No. 84-5). (Illus.). 407p. reprint ed. pap. 116.00 (*0-7837-6742-0*, 2046370) Bks Demand.

Astronomy & Astrophysics: A Source Guide. 1991. lib. bdg. 250.00 (*0-8490-4862-1*) Gordon Pr.

Astronomy & Astrophysics: Interstellar Matter, Galaxy, Universe. Ed. by K. Schaifers & H. H. Voigt. (Landolt-Boernstein, New Ser.: Group VI, Vol. 2, Subvol. C). (Illus.). 490p. 1982. 867.00 (*0-387-10977-3*) Spr-Verlag.

Astronomy & Astrophysics: Methods-Constants-Solar System. Ed. by K. H. Hellwege. (Landolt-Boernstein Ser.: Vol. 2). (Illus.). 320p. 1981. 558.00 (*0-387-10054-7*) Spr-Verlag.

Astronomy & Astrophysics: Stars & Star Clusters. Ed. by H. H. Voigt & K. Schaifers. (Landolt-Boernstein Ser.: Group VI, Vol. 2, Subvolume b). (Illus.). 480p. 1981. 830.00 (*0-387-10976-5*) Spr-Verlag.

An Asterisk (*) at the beginning of an entry indicates that the title is appearing in BIP for the first time.

Astronomy & Astrophysics Abstacts, Vol. 1: Literature 1969, Part 1. Ed. by S. Boehme et al. vii, 435p. 1969. 57.00 (*0-387-04421-3*) Spr-Verlag.

***Astronomy & Astrophysics Abstracts.** Ed. by G Burkhardt & U. Esser. 2208p. 1994. 327.00 (*3-540-58554-0*) Spr-Verlag.

Astronomy & Astrophysics Abstracts, Vol. 37. Ed. by S. Boehme et al. Tr. by Lutz D. Schmadel. (Literature 1984 Ser.: Pt. 1). 920p. 1985. 127.00 (*0-387-13937-0*) Spr-Verlag.

Astronomy & Astrophysics Abstracts: Literature, Vol. 32; 1982, Pt. 2. Ed. by S. Boehme. 848p. 1983. 99.00 (*0-387-12516-7*) Spr-Verlag.

Astronomy & Astrophysics Abstracts: Literature 1979, Pt. 2, Vol. 26. Ed. by S. Boehme et al. 794p. 1980. 80.00 (*0-387-10134-9*) Spr-Verlag.

Astronomy & Astrophysics Abstracts: Vol. 23-24. Ed. by S. Boehme et al. 1127p. 1980. 79.00 (*0-387-09830-5*) Spr-Verlag.

Astronomy & Astrophysics Abstracts: Vols. 35-36, Author & Subject Indexes to Vols. 25-34, Literature 1979-1983. Ed. by I. Heinrich & Lutz D. Schmadel. (Astronomy & Astrophysics Abstracts Ser.). 915p. 1984. 127.00 (*0-387-13651-7*) Spr-Verlag.

Astronomy & Astrophysics Abstracts, Vol. 10: Literature 1973, Pt. 2. Ed. by S. Boehme et al. viii, 661p. 1974. 58.00 (*0-387-06795-7*) Spr-Verlag.

Astronomy & Astrophysics Abstracts, Vol. 2: Literature 1969, Pt. 2. Ed. by S. Boehme et al. x, 516p. 1970. 57.00 (*0-387-04773-5*) Spr-Verlag.

Astronomy & Astrophysics Abstracts, Vol. 21: Literature 1978, Pt. 1. Ed. by S. Boehme et al. viii, 834p. 1978. 65.00 (*0-685-07582-6*) Spr-Verlag.

Astronomy & Astrophysics Abstracts, Vol. 22: Literature 1978, Pt. 2. Ed. by S. Boehme et al. viii, 849p. 1979. 64.00 (*0-387-09464-4*) Spr-Verlag.

Astronomy & Astrophysics Abstracts, Vol. 25: Literature 1979, Pt. 1. Ed. by S. Boehme et al. x, 871p. 1979. 82.00 (*0-387-09831-3*) Spr-Verlag.

Astronomy & Astrophysics Abstracts, Vol. 27: Literature 1980, Pt. 1. Ed. by S. Boehme et al. 939p. 1980. 80.00 (*0-387-10479-8*) Spr-Verlag.

Astronomy & Astrophysics Abstracts, Vol. 28: Literature 1980, Pt. 2. Ed. by S. Boehme et al. 841p. 1981. 79.00 (*0-387-10799-1*) Spr-Verlag.

Astronomy & Astrophysics Abstracts, Vol. 29: Literature 1981,, Pt. 1. Ed. by S. Boehme. 853p. 1981. 79.00 (*0-387-11264-2*) Spr-Verlag.

Astronomy & Astrophysics Abstracts, Vol. 3: Literature 1970, Pt. 1. Ed. by S. Boehme. x, 490p. 1970. 57.00 (*0-387-05314-X*) Spr-Verlag.

Astronomy & Astrophysics Abstracts, Vol. 30: Literature, 1981. Ed. by S. Boehme et al. 792p. 1982. 99.00 (*0-387-11721-0*) Spr-Verlag.

Astronomy & Astrophysics Abstracts, Vol. 31: Literature 1982, Pt. 1. S. Boehme et al. x, 776p. 1982. 99.00 (*0-387-12072-6*) Spr-Verlag.

Astronomy & Astrophysics Abstracts, Vol. 4: Literature 1970, Pt. 2. Ed. by S. Boehme. x, 562p. 1971. 57.00 (*0-387-05514-2*) Spr-Verlag.

Astronomy & Astrophysics Abstracts, Vol. 42: Literature, 1986, Pt. 2. Ed. by E. Bohme et al. 1130p. 1987. 153.00 (*0-387-17898-8*) Spr-Verlag.

Astronomy & Astrophysics Abstracts, Vol. 5: Literature 1971, Pt. 1. Ed. by S. Boehme. x, 505p. 1971. 57.00 (*0-387-05701-3*) Spr-Verlag.

Astronomy & Astrophysics Abstracts, Vol. 50 A & B: Literature 1989, Pt. 2, Set. Ed. by G. Burkhardt et al. xxvii, 1429p. 1990. 270.00 (*0-387-52889-X*) Spr-Verlag.

Astronomy & Astrophysics Abstracts, Vol. 52: Literature 1990, Pt. 2, Vols. A & B, 2 vols., Set. Ed. by G. Burkhardt et al. 1556p. 1991. 298.00 (*0-387-54336-8*) Spr-Verlag.

Astronomy & Astrophysics Abstracts, Vol. 53: Literature 1991, Pt. 1. Ed. by G. Burkhardt et al. xviii, 1625p. 1992. 349.00 (*0-387-55314-2*) Spr-Verlag.

Astronomy & Astrophysics Abstracts, Vol. 54: Literature 1991, 2 vols., Set. Ed. by G. Burkhardt et al. 1648p. 1992. 349.00 (*0-387-55795-4*) Spr-Verlag.

Astronomy & Astrophysics Abstracts, Vol. 55A & 55B: Literature, 1992, Pt. 1, 2 vols., Set. Ed. by G. Burkhardt et al. x, 1447p. 1993. 369.00 (*0-387-56436-5*) Spr-Verlag.

Astronomy & Astrophysics Abstracts, Vol. 6: Literature 1971, Pt. 2. Ed. by S. Boehme. x, 560p. 1972. 57.00 (*0-387-05888-5*) Spr-Verlag.

Astronomy & Astrophysics Abstracts, Vol. 7: Literature 1972, Pt. 1. Ed. by S. Boehme et al. x, 526p. 1972. 57.00 (*0-387-06072-3*) Spr-Verlag.

Astronomy & Astrophysics Abstracts, Vol. 8: Literature 1972, Pt. 2. Ed. by S. Boehme et al. x, 594p. 1973. 57.00 (*0-387-06352-8*) Spr-Verlag.

Astronomy & Astrophysics Abstracts, Vol. 9: Literature 1973, Pt. 1. Ed. by S. Boehme et al. vii, 610p. 1973. 57.00 (*0-387-06560-1*) Spr-Verlag.

Astronomy & Astrophysics for the Nineteen Eighties: Reports of the Astronomy Survey Committee, 2 vols., Vol. 1: 1982. 189p. 1983. Vol. 1, 1982, 189p. pap. 19.95 (*0-309-03249-0*) Natl Acad Pr.

Astronomy & Astrophysics for the Nineteen Eighties: Reports of the Astronomy Survey Committee, 2 vols., Vol. II: 1983. 442p. 1983. Vol. II, 1983 442pgs. pap. text ed. 32.00 (*0-309-03334-9*) Natl Acad Pr.

Astronomy & Ceremony in the Prehistoric Southwest. John Carlson et al. (Maxwell Museum Papers: No. 2). (Illus.). 232p. 1987. pap. 21.00 (*0-912535-03-2*) Max Mus.

Astronomy & Cosmology. John North. 1994. 35.00 (*0-393-03656-1*); pap. 18.95 (*0-393-31193-7*) Norton.

***Astronomy & Empire in the Ancient Andes: The Cultural Origins of Inca Sky Watching.** Brian S. Bauer & David S. Dearborn. LC 95-3565. 1995. 37.50 (*0-292-70829-7*); pap. 14.95 (*0-292-70837-8*) U of Tex Pr.

Astronomy & History: Selected Essays. O. Neugebauer. (Illus.). 538p. 1983. pap. 48.00 (*0-387-90844-7*) Spr-Verlag.

Astronomy & Optics from Pliny to Descartes: Texts, Diagrams & Conceptual Structures. Bruce S. Eastwood. (Collected Studies: No. CS291). 312p. (C). 1989. lib. bdg. 89.95 (*0-86078-239-5*, Pub. by Variorum UK) Ashgate Pub Co.

Astronomy & Philately. 76p. 1977. 5.00 (*0-318-13295-8*) Am Topical Assn.

Astronomy & Physics see Comprehensive Dissertation Index 1861-1972

Astronomy & Space Science from the Moon: Proceedings of Symposium E4 of the COSPAR 29th Plenary Meeting Held in Washington, DC, 28 August-5 September, 1992, No. 14/6. B. H. Foing. (Advances in Space Research Ser.: No. 14/6). 290p. 1994. pap. 165.00 (*0-08-042483-X*, Pergamon Pr) Elsevier.

Astronomy & the Bible: Questions & Answers. Donald B. DeYoung. LC 89-39. 1989. pap. 7.99 (*0-8010-2991-0*) Baker Bk.

Astronomy & the Imagination: A New Approach to Man's Experience of the Stars. Norman Davidson. 238p. 1990. pap. 12.95 (*0-7102-1179-1*, 1251, RKP) Routledge.

Astronomy & the Maya Calendar Correlation. Paul D. Campbell. (Illus.). 127p. (Orig.). (C). 1992. lib. bdg. 40.30 (*0-89412-195-2*); pap. 30.80 (*0-89412-194-4*) Aegean Park Pr.

Astronomy As a Hobby. Andrew Fraknoi et al. (Illus.). 28p. 1986. pap. 4.00 (*0-937707-09-0*, IP 101) Astron Soc Pacific.

Astronomy at Yale 1701-1968. Dorrit Hoffleit. LC 91-70522. (Memoirs of the Connecticut Academy of Arts & Sciences Ser.: Vol. 23). (Illus.). 230p. 1992. 40.00 (*1-878508-02-4*) CT Acad Arts & Sciences.

Astronomy Basics. Karen Liptak. (Illus.). 48p. (J). (gr. 3-7). 1986. 10.95 (*0-13-049966-8*) P-H.

Astronomy Before the Telescope, Part III: Stars, Constellations, & Cosmology. N. Bobrovnikoff. pap. write for info. (*0-318-60790-5*) Pachart Pub Hse.

Astronomy, Cosmology & Fundamental Physics. Ed. by Michele Caffo et al. (C). 1989. lib. bdg. 155.00 (*0-7923-0258-3*) Kluwer Ac.

Astronomy for All Ages: Discovering the Universe Through Activities for Children & Adults. Phillip Harrington & Edward Pascuzzi. LC 93-46751. 160p. 1994. pap. 17.95 (*1-56440-388-2*) Globe Pequot.

Astronomy for Kids: Milky Way & Mars Bars. Carole Marsh. (Quantum Leap Ser.). (Illus.). (J). 1994. 24.95 (*0-7933-0012-6*); pap. 14.95 (*0-7933-0013-4*); disk 29.95 (*0-7933-0014-2*) Gallopade Pub Group.

Astronomy for the Beginner. Patrick Moore. (Illus.). 48p. (C). 1992. 12.95 (*0-521-41833-X*) Cambridge U Pr.

Astronomy for the Inquiring Mind: The Growth & Use of Theory in Science. Eric M. Rogers. LC 81-47286. (Illus.). 173p. reprint ed. pap. 49.40 (*0-8357-2921-4*, 2039161) Bks Demand.

***Astronomy for the Masses.** David Lamp. 80p. (C). 1994. pap. text ed., spiral bd. 9.95 (*0-7872-0304-1*) Kendall-Hunt.

Astronomy from a Space Platform. Ed. by George W. Morgenthaler & Howard D. Greyber. (Science & Technology Ser.: Vol. 28). 1972. lib. bdg. 35.00 (*0-87703-061-8*, Am Astronaut) Univelt Inc.

Astronomy from A to Z: A Dictionary of Celestial Objects & Ideas. Charles A. Schweighauser. LC 91-7124. (Illus.). 192p. (Orig.). 1991. pap. 14.95 (*0-9620873-5-1*) Illinois Issues.

Astronomy from Kepler to Newton: Historical Studies. Curtis Wilson. (Collected Studies: No. CS290). 302p. (C). 1989. lib. bdg. 8,939.55 (*0-86078-238-7*, Pub. by Variorum UK) Ashgate Pub Co.

Astronomy from Space: Proceedings of the Topical Meeting of the COSPAR Interdisciplinary Scientific Commission E (Meetings E3, E4, & E5) of the COSPAR 25th Plenary Meeting held in Graz, Austria, 25 June - 7 July 1984. Ed. by G. G. Fazio et al. (Illus.). 220p. 1985. pap. 54.00 (*0-08-033192-0*, Pub. by PPL UK) Elsevier.

Astronomy from Space: Sputnik to Space Telescope. Ed. by James Cornell & Paul Gorenstein. 264p. 1983. reprint ed. 27.50 (*0-262-03097-7*) MIT Pr.

***Astronomy, from the Earth to the Universe.** 95th ed. Jay M. Pasachoff. LC 94-33449. (Golden Sunburst Ser.). (C). 1994. pap. text ed. 48.75 (*0-03-001667-3*) Saunders.

Astronomy from Wide-Field Imaging: Proceedings of the 161st Symposium of the International Astronomical Union, Held in Potsdam, Germany, August 23-27, 1993. Ed. by H. T. MacGillivray. LC 94-12286. (International Astronomical Union Symposia Ser.). 792p. (C). 1994. lib. bdg. 215.50 (*0-7923-2878-7*); pap. text ed. 105.00 (*0-7923-2879-5*) Kluwer Ac.

Astronomy in Our World. Kaler. (C). 1994. text ed. 57.00 (*0-06-500004-8*) HarpCollege.

Astronomy in the Old Testament. Giovanni Sciaparelli. 1972. 59.95 (*0-87968-673-1*) Gordon Pr.

Astronomy in the Service of Islam. David A. King. (Collected Studies: No. CS 416). 352p. 1993. 94.95 (*0-86078-357-X*, Pub. by Variorum UK) Ashgate Pub Co.

Astronomy Labs for the Personal Computer. Michael J. Ruiz & Randy A. Booker. 96p. (C). 1994. pap. text ed., spiral bd. 17.95 (*0-8403-9068-8*) Kendall-Hunt.

Astronomy Made Simple. 3rd ed. Michael Hamburg. 1976. pap. 12.00 (*0-385-26582-4*) Doubleday.

Astronomy of Levi Ben Gerson, 1288-1344. B. R. Goldstein. LC 85-2751. (Studies in the History of Mathematics & Physical Sciences: Vol. 11). (Illus.). 300p. 1985. 119.00 (*0-387-96132-1*) Spr-Verlag.

Astronomy of Milton's Paradise Lost. Thomas N. Orchard. LC 68-4178. (Studies in Milton: No. 22). (Illus.). 1969. reprint ed. lib. bdg. 75.00 (*0-8383-0672-1*) M S G Haskell Hse.

Astronomy on the Personal Computer. O. Montenbruck & T. Pfleger. Tr. by S. Dunlop. (Illus.). 272p. 1991. disk 51.00 (*0-387-52754-0*) Spr-Verlag.

Astronomy on the Personal Computer. 2nd ed. O. Montenbruck. 1994. disk 59.00 (*0-387-57700-9*) Spr-Verlag.

Astronomy One Hundred: A Handbook. Michael Chriss & Judith K. Brooks. LC 79-92143. (Illus.). 250p. (Orig.). 1980. pap. text ed. 11.20 (*0-936064-00-5*) Perspicilli Pr.

Astronomy Simply Explained for Beginners. F. W. Murray. (C). 1987. 45.00 (*0-85174-485-0*, Pub. by Brwn Son Ferg) St Mut.

Astronomy Simulations from Dance of the Planets Book. Arc Science Simulations Staff. 1992. 3.5 hd 21.33 (*0-13-052697-5*) P-H.

Astronomy Study Guide & Exercises for Distance Education. 4th ed. John L. Safko. 400p. (C). 1994. per., pap. text ed. 29.95 (*0-8403-9174-9*) Kendall-Hunt.

***Astronomy: The Evolving Universe: With Sky Wheel, Set.** 7th ed. Michael Zeilik. 1995. pap. text ed. write for info. (*0-471-12150-9*) Wiley.

Astronomy Today. Eric J. Chaisson & Steve McMillan. LC 92-37428. 1993. write for info. (*0-13-050832-2*) P-H.

Astronomy Today. Eric J. Chaisson & Steve McMillan. 704p. (C). 1993. text ed. write for info. (*0-13-050824-1*) P-H.

Astronomy Today: Planets, Stars, Space Exploration. Dinah Moche. LC 82-5211. (Library of Knowledge). (Illus.). 96p. (J). (gr. 5 up). 1982. pap. 13.00 (*0-394-84423-8*) Random Bks Yng Read.

Astronomy Versus Astrology. rev. ed. Ivan Kelly et al. (Illus.). 16p. 1989. 4.00 (*0-937707-00-7*, IP 500) Astron Soc Pacific.

***Astronomy with Millimeter & Submillimeter Wave Interferometry No. 59.** Ed. by M. Ishiguro & William J. Welch. 464p. 1994. 40.00 (*0-937707-78-3*) Astron Soc Pacific.

Astronomy with Schmidt-Type Telescopes. Ed. by Massimo Capaccioli. 1984. lib. bdg. 182.00 (*90-277-1756-7*) Kluwer Ac.

Astronomy with Your Personal Computer. 2nd ed. Peter J. Duffett-Smith. (Illus.). 300p. (C). 1990. 59.95 (*0-521-38093-6*); pap. 27.95 (*0-521-38995-X*) Cambridge U Pr.

Astronomy 201. Wayne State University Staff. (C). 1993. 10.00 (*1-881592-05-7*) Hayden-McNeil.

Astroparticle Physics. Ed. by D. V. Nanopoulos. 500p. (C). 1991. text ed. 128.00 (*981-02-0582-1*); pap. 46.00 (*981-02-0583-X*) World Scientific Pub.

Astrophotography. 2nd ed. Barry Gordon. LC 83-138189. (Illus.). 224p. 1985. pap. text ed. 18.95 (*0-943396-07-7*) Willmann-Bell.

***Astrophotography: An Introduction.** H. J. Arnold. LC 94-42325. (Sky & Telescope Observer's Guides). 192p. 1995. pap. 18.95 (*0-933346-73-5*) Sky Pub.

Astrophotography for the Amateur. rev. ed. Michael A. Covington. (Illus.). 176p. (C). 1991. 49.95 (*0-521-41305-2*); pap. 18.95 (*0-521-40984-5*) Cambridge U Pr.

Astrophotography II. Martinez. (Illus.). 172p. 1987. text ed. 18.95 (*0-943396-13-1*) Willmann-Bell.

Astrophotography with the Schmidt Telescope. Siegfried Marx & Werner Pfau. Tr. by Phillip Lamble. (Illus.). 168p. (C). 1992. 59.95 (*0-521-39549-6*) Cambridge U Pr.

Astrophysical & Laboratory Spectroscopy. Ed. by R. Brown & J. Lang. (Scottish Universities Summer School in Physics, a NATO Advanced Study Institute Ser.: No. 33). (Illus.). 416p. 1987. 96.00 (*0-905945-16-6*) IOP Pub.

Astrophysical Aspects of the Most Energetic Cosmic Rays. Ed. by M. Nagano & F. Takahara. 516p. (C). 1991. text ed. 118.00 (*981-02-0686-0*) World Scientific Pub.

Astrophysical Concepts. Martin D. Harwit. Ed. by Rudolph Kippenhahn & J. P. Zahn. (Astronomy & Astrophysics Library). (Illus.). xv, 626p. 1992. reprint ed. 59.00 (*0-387-96683-8*) Spr-Verlag.

Astrophysical Data: Planets & Stars. Kenneth R. Lang. (Illus.). 956p. 1993. 59.00 (*0-387-97109-2*) Spr-Verlag.

Astrophysical Directions. Michael Erlewine. 140p. 1977. 13.00 (*0-86690-097-7*, E1104-034) Am Fed Astrologers.

Astrophysical Disks. Ed. by S. F. Dermott et al. LC 92-44412. 1992. write for info. (*0-89766-739-5*); pap. write for info. (*0-89766-740-9*) NY Acad Sci.

Astrophysical Fluid Dynamics. Eduardo Battaner. (Illus.). 288p. (C). 1994. write for info. (*0-521-43166-2*); pap. write for info. (*0-521-43747-4*) Cambridge U Pr.

Astrophysical Fluid Dynamics. Ed. by J. P. Zahn & J. Zinn-Justin. (Lse Houches Summer School Proceedings Ser.: Vol. 47). 550p. 1994. 248.50 (*0-444-81797-2*, North Holland) Elsevier.

Astrophysical Jets. Ed. by D. Burgarella et al. (Space Telescope Science Institute Symposium Ser.: No. 6). (Illus.). 328p. (C). 1994. 59.95 (*0-521-44221-4*) Cambridge U Pr.

Astrophysical Jets. Ed. by Attilio Ferrari & A. G. Pacholczyk. 1983. lib. bdg. 103.00 (*90-277-1627-7*) Kluwer Ac.

Astrophysical Jets & Their Engines. Ed. by Wolfgang Kundt. (C). 1987. lib. bdg. 92.00 (*90-277-2548-9*) Kluwer Ac.

Astrophysical Masers: Proceedings, Arlington, Virginia, March 9-11, 1992. Ed. by Andrew W. Clegg & Gerald E. Nedoluha. LC 92-46270. (Lecture Notes in Physics Ser.: Vol. 412). 1993. 81.00 (*0-387-56343-1*) Spr-Verlag.

Astrophysical Parameters for Globular Clusters: IAU Colloquium, No. 68. Ed. by A. G. Davis Philip & D. S. Hayes. 614p. (Orig.). 1982. 31.00 (*0-9607902-2-5*); pap. 27.00 (*0-9607902-1-7*) L Davis Pr.

Astrophysical Quantities. 3rd ed. C. W. Allen. 310p. (C). 1976. text ed. 80.00 (*0-485-11150-0*, Pub. by Athlone Pr UK) Humanities.

Astrophysical Radiation Hydrodynamics. Ed. by Karl-Heinz A. Winkler & Michael L. Norman. 1986. lib. bdg. 172.50 (*90-277-2335-4*) Kluwer Ac.

Astrophysical Techniques. 2nd ed. C. R. Kitchin. (Illus.). 496p. 1991. 160.00 (*0-7503-0137-6*); pap. 39.00 (*0-7503-0138-4*) IOP Pub.

Astrophysics. G. Boerner et al. LC 25-9130. (Tracts in Modern Physics Ser.: Vol. 69). (Illus.). iv, 120p. 1973. 53.00 (*0-387-06376-5*) Spr-Verlag.

Astrophysics, Vol. 1: Stars. Richard Bowers & Terry Deeming. (Illus.). 343p. (C). 1984. Vol. 1, Stars 343pps. pap. 45.00 (*0-86720-018-9*) Jones & Bartlett.

Astrophysics, Vol. 2: Interstellar Matter & Galaxies. Richard Bowers & Terry Deeming. (Illus.). 300p. (C). 1984. Vol. 2, Interstellar Matter & Galaxies, 300pps. pap. 45.00 (*0-86720-047-2*) Jones & Bartlett.

Astrophysics & Space Physics Reviews, Vol. 1. Ed. by R. A. Syunyaev. (Soviet Scientific Reviews Ser.: Section E). 326p. 1981. text ed. 342.00 (*3-7186-0021-8*) Gordon & Breach.

Astrophysics & Space Physics Reviews, Vol. 2. Ed. by R. A. Syunyaev. (Soviet Scientific Reviews Ser.: Section E). 480p. 1983. text ed. 342.00 (*3-7186-0070-6*) Gordon & Breach.

Astrophysics & Space Physics Reviews, Vol. 3. R. A. Syunyaev. (Soviet Scientific Reviews Ser.: Section E). 359p. 1984. text ed. 312.00 (*3-7186-0092-7*) Gordon & Breach.

Astrophysics & Space Physics Reviews, Vol. 4. R. A. Syunyaev. (Soviet Scientific Reviews Ser.: Section E). 328p. 1985. text ed. 312.00 (*3-7186-0125-7*) Gordon & Breach.

Astrophysics & Space Physics Reviews, Vol. 5. Ed. by R. A. Syunyaev. (Soviet Scientific Reviews Ser.: Section E). 260p. 1986. text ed. 323.00 (*3-7186-0214-8*) Gordon & Breach.

Astrophysics & Space Physics Reviews, Vol. 6. R. A. Syunyaev. (Soviet Scientific Reviews Ser.: Section E). 106p. 1988. Pt. 1: The Phobus Project, 106p. pap. text ed. 74.00 (*3-7186-4837-7*); Pt. 2: Cosmology, 94p. pap. text ed. 68.00 (*3-7186-4838-5*); Pt. 3: Supernovae, 122p. pap. text ed. 87.00 (*3-7186-4839-3*); Pt. 4: Nuclear Process, 120p. pap. text ed. 87.00 (*3-7186-4840-7*); Pt. 5: Plasma Theory, 150p. pap. text ed. 106.00 (*3-7186-4841-5*) Gordon & Breach.

Astrophysics & Space Physics Reviews: Supernova 1987A, Vol. 8. V. S. Imshennik & D. K. Nadezhin. Ed. by R. A. Syunyaev. (Soviet Scientific Reviews Ser.: Vol. 8, Pt. 1). ii, 154p. 1989. pap. text ed. 101.00 (*3-7186-4952-7*) Gordon & Breach.

Astrophysics & Space Physics Reviews: The Distribution of Mass & Angular Momentum in the Solar System, Vol. 8. L. S. Marochnik et al. Ed. by R. A. Syunyaev. (Soviet Scientific Reviews Ser.: Vol. 8, Pt. 3). ii, 62p. 1989. pap. text ed. 40.00 (*3-7186-4986-1*) Gordon & Breach.

Astrophysics & Space Physics Reviews: Thermonuclear Burning & the Explosion of Degenerate Matter in Supernovae, Vol. 8. A. M. Khokhlov. Ed. by R. A. Syunyaev. (Soviet Scientific Reviews Ser.: Vol. 8, Pt. 2). ii, 82p. 1989. pap. text ed. 55.00 (*3-7186-4981-0*) Gordon & Breach.

Astrophysics & Twentieth-Century Astronomy to 1950, Vol. 4, Pt. A. Ed. by Owen Gingerich. LC 83-10164. (General History of Astronomy Ser.). 206p. 1984. 44.95 (*0-521-24256-8*) Cambridge U Pr.

Astrophysics from Spacelab. Remo Ruffini. Ed. by Pier L. Bernacca. (Astrophysics & Space Science Library: No. 81). 720p. 1980. lib. bdg. 103.00 (*90-277-1064-3*) Kluwer Ac.

Astrophysics from the Moon. Ed. by Michael J. Mumma & Harlan J. Smith. LC 90-55582. (Conference Proceeding Ser.: No. 207). (Illus.). 696p. 1990. 85.00 (*0-88318-770-1*) Am Inst Physics.

Astrophysics in Antarctica. Ed. by D. Mullan et al. LC 89-46421. (AIP Conference Proceedings Ser.: No. 198). 288p. 1989. lib. bdg. 80.00 (*0-88318-398-6*) Am Inst Physics.

Astrophysics of Brown Dwarfs. J. C. Kafatos et al. 276p. 1986. 75.00 (*0-521-32337-1*) Cambridge U Pr.

Astrophysics of Cosmic Rays. V. S. Berezinskii et al. 500p. 1991. 165.75 (*0-444-88641-9*, North Holland) Elsevier.

Astrophysics of Cosmic Rays. V. L. Ginzburg. 72p. 1970. text ed. 28.50 (*0-7065-0705-3*, Pub. by Keter Pub IS) Coronet Bks.

Astrophysics of Cosmic Rays. 2nd rev. suppl. ed. Vitalii L. Ginzburg. Ed. by Ron Hardin. LC 73-606893. (U. S. National Aeronautics & Space Administration. NASA Technical Translation Ser.: TT F-561). 68p. reprint ed. pap. 25.00 (*0-8357-5825-7*, 2003731) Bks Demand.

Astrophysics of Gaseous Nebulae & Active Galactic Nuclei. Donald E. Osterbrock. (Illus.). 325p. (C). 1989. text ed. 36.00 (*0-935702-22-9*) Univ Sci Bks.

Astrophysics of Neutron Stars. M. Lipunov. Ed. by Gerhard Borner et al. Tr. by R. S. Wadhwa. (Astronomy & Astrophysics Library). 344p. (C). 1992. text ed. 98.00 (*0-387-53568-3*) Spr-Verlag.

Astrophysics of Quasi-Stellar Objects & Active Galactic Nuclei. J. S. Miller. 519p. (C). 1985. text ed. 30.00 (*0-935702-21-0*) Univ Sci Bks.

An Asterisk (*) at the beginning of an entry indicates that the title is appearing in BIP for the first time.

An Asterisk (*) at the beginning of an entry indicates that the title is appearing in BIP for the first time.

Asymptotic Systems. Rabi N. Bhattacharya & Manfred Denker. (DMV Seminar Ser.: Vol. 14). 122p. 1990. 29.50 (0-8176-2282-9); pap. 19.50 (0-685-45915-2) Birkhauser.

***Asymptotic Theories for Plates & Shells.** Ed. by R. P. Gilbert & K. Hackl. LC 94-46989. (Pitman Research Notes in Mathematics Ser.: Vol. 319). 1995. write for info. (0-615-00453-9) Wiley.

Asymptotic Theory for Econometricians. Halbert White. (Economic Theory, Econometrics & Mathematical Economics Ser.). 1984. text ed. 72.00 (0-12-746650-9) Acad Pr.

Asymptotic Theory for Empirical Reliability & Concentration Processes. Miklos Csorgo et al. (Lecture Notes in Statistics Ser.: Vol. 33). v, 171p. 1986. pap. 32.00 (0-387-96359-6) Spr-Verlag.

Asymptotic Theory of Extreme Order Statistics. 2nd ed. Janos Galambos. LC 86-7207. 430p. (C). 1987. text ed. 49.50 (0-89874-957-3) Krieger.

Asymptotic Theory of Statistical Inference. B. L. Rao. LC 86-15735. (Probability & Mathematical Statistics Ser.). 464p. 1987. text ed. 127.00 (0-471-84335-0) Wiley.

Asymptotic Wave Theory. M. Roseau. LC 74-26167. (Applied Mathematics & Mechanics Ser.: Vol. 20). 349p. 1976. 97.50 (0-444-10798-3, North Holland) Elsevier.

Asymptotic Waveform Evaluation & Moment Matching for Interconnect Analysis. Eli Chiprout. LC 93-37220. (International Series in Engineering & Computer Science, VLSI, Computer Architecture, & Digital Screen Processing). 216p. (C). 1993. lib. bdg. 78.00 (0-7923-9413-5) Kluwer Ac.

Asymptotics Beyond All Orders. Ed. by H. Segur et al. (NATO ASI Series B, Physics: Vol. 284). (Illus.). 388p. 1992. 105.00 (0-306-44112-8, Plenum Pr) Plenum.

Asymptotics in Statistics: Some Basic Concepts. Lucien M. Le Cam & G. Lo Yang. Ed. by J. O. Berger et al. (Series in Statistics). (Illus.). viii, 180p. 1990. 32.00 (0-387-97372-9) Spr-Verlag.

Asymptotics of Analytic Difference Equations. G. K. Immink. (Lecture Notes in Mathematics Ser.: Vol. 1085). v, 134p. 1984. pap. 28.10 (0-387-13867-6) Spr-Verlag.

Asymptotics of Operator & Pseudo-Differential Equations. V. P. Maslov & V. E. Nazaikinskii. LC 88-3984. (Monograph in Contemporary Mathematics). (Illus.). 320p. 1988. 95.00 (0-306-11014-8, Consultants) Plenum.

Asymtotics for Orthogonal Polynomials. W. Van Assche. (Lecture Notes in Mathematics Ser.: Vol. 1265). vi, 201p. 1987. pap. 30.00 (0-387-18023-0) Spr-Verlag.

Asynchonous Transfer Mode: Solution for Broadband ISDN. 2nd ed. Martin De Prycker. LC 93-25395. 1993. 48.00 (0-13-178542-7) P-H.

Asynchronous Circuit Design for VLSI Signal Processing. Ed. by Teresa H. Meng & Sharad Malik. LC 93-33160. 184p. (C). 1994. lib. bdg. 115.00 (0-7923-9397-X) Kluwer Ac.

***Asynchronous Circuits.** Janusz A. Brzozowski & Carl-Johan Seger. LC 94-42873. (Monographs in Computer Science). 1995. write for info. (0-387-94420-6) Spr-Verlag.

Asynchronous Design Methodologies: Proceedings of the IFIP WG10.5 Working Conference on Asynchronous Design Methodologies, Manchester, UK, 31 March-2 April, 1993. Ed. by Stephen B. Furber & Martyn D. Edwards. LC 93-25344. (IFIP Transactions A: Computer Science & Technology Ser.: Vol. A-28). 1993. write for info. (0-444-81599-6, North Holland) Elsevier.

***Asynchronous Digital Circuit Design.** Ed. by G. Birtwistle & A. Davis. LC 95-1009. (Workshops in Computing Ser.). 1995. write for info. (3-540-19901-2) Spr-Verlag.

Asynchronous Sequential Switching Circuit. Stephen H. Unger. LC 82-18014. 304p. 1983. reprint ed. 30.50 (0-89874-565-9) Krieger.

Asynchronous Transfer Mode. Martin DePrycker. (Ellis Horwood Series in Computer Communications & Networking). 250p. 1991. 53.00 (0-13-053513-3, 270602) P-H.

Asynchronous Transfer Mode. IGIC, Inc. Staff. 1991. 2,995.00 (0-918435-62-5) Info Gatekeepers.

Asynchronous Transfer Mode Networks: Performance Issues. Raif O. Onvural. LC 93-30130. 260p. 1993. 65.00 (0-89006-662-0) Artech Hse.

Asynchronous Transfer Mode Networks: Proceedings of the TRICOMM '93 Conference Held April 20-22, in Raleigh, North Carolina. Ed. by Yannis Viniotis & Raif O. Onvural. LC 93-12807. 236p. 1993. 75.00 (0-306-44486-0, Plenum Pr) Plenum.

Asyst 88 International Conference Proceedings: Connecting Users & Applications. Intro. by Kirsten Bartles. (Illus.). 300p. (Orig.). 1989. pap. 25.00 (0-924729-00-7) Keithley Asyst.

AS2 Skillbooklet. Barbara J. Crane. (Crane Reading System-English Ser.). (Illus.). (gr. k-2). 1982. pap. text ed. 2.49 (0-89075-029-7) Bilingual Ed Serv.

AS400 Security, Audit & Control. K. Lester. 140p. 1993. 261.00 (1-85617-182-5) Elsevier.

***At a Century's Ending: Reflections 1982-1995.** George F. Kennan. 350p. 1995. 25.00 (0-393-03882-3) Norton.

At a Dollar a Year: Ripples on the Edge of the Maelstrom. Robert L. Raymond. LC 76-157794. (Short Story Index Reprint Ser.). 1977. reprint ed. 19.95 (0-8369-3906-9) Ayer.

At a Foreign University: An International Study of Adaptation & Coping. Otto Klineberg & W. Frank Hull, IV. LC 79-18170. 223p. 1979. text ed. 55.00 (0-275-90377-X, C0377, Praeger Pubs) Greenwood.

At-a-Glance Doll Inventory Cards. 100p. 1984. pap. 3.95 (0-87588-212-9, 1018) Hobby Hse.

At-a-Glance Nutrition Counter. Patricia Hausman. 256p. 1984. mass mkt. 4.95 (0-345-90191-6) Ballantine.

At a Journal Workshop: The Basic Text & Guide for Using the Intensive Journal Process. Ira Progoff. LC 75-13932. 320p. 1975. pap. 15.95 (0-87941-006-X) Dialogue Hse.

At a Journal Workshop: Writing to Access the Power of the Unconscious & Evoke Creative Ability. rev. ed. Ira Progoff. 432p. (Orig.). 1992. pap. 15.95 (0-87477-638-4) J P Tarcher.

At a Loss. Mike Martone. 1977. 2.00 (0-685-67942-X) Windless Orchard.

At a New Mining Camp: Creede of Colorado, 1892. Richard H. Davis. Ed. by William R. Jones. (Illus.). 32p. 1977. reprint ed. pap. 3.95 (0-89646-018-5) Vistabooks.

At a Theater Near You: Screen Entertainment from a Christian Perspective. Thomas Patterson. LC 94-13363. (Wheaton Literary Ser.). 216p. 1994. pap. 9.99 (0-87788-041-7) Shaw Pubs.

***At a Theater or Drive-in Near You: The History, Culture, & Politics of the American Exploitation Film.** rev. ed. Randall Clark. LC 94-39322. (Studies in American Popular History & Culture). 248p. 1995. 50.00 (0-8153-1951-7) Garland.

At a Winter's Fire. Bernard E. Capes. LC 78-101793. (Short Story Index Reprint Ser.). 1977. 20.95 (0-8369-3181-5) Ayer.

***At a Zoo.** Henny Wenkart. (Teaching Jonny's Sister to Read Ser.: Vol. 1). (Illus.). 23p. (J). (gr. k-3). 1960. pap. 2.95 (0-911612-01-7) Wenkart.

***At Adair's House: More Columns from America's Favorite Former Single Mom.** Adair Lara. LC 94-33727. 1995. pap. 11.95 (0-8118-0498-4) Chronicle Bks.

At All Began with a Doormat. Rachel Atkins. (Illus.). 32p. (J). 1994. 11.95 (1-56062-236-9) CIS Comm.

***At All Costs: Stories of Impossible Victories.** Bryan Perrett. (Illus.). 240p. 1995. pap. 14.95 (1-85409-276-6) Sterling.

At All Costs! Stories of Impossible Victories. Bryon Perrett. (Illus.). 240p. 1993. 24.95 (1-85409-157-3) Sterling.

At All Times & in All Places. Richard Holden. 272p. (C). 1989. text ed. 60.00 (1-872795-43-9, Pub. by Pentland Pr UK) St Mut.

At All Times, in Every Age. Eusebe Menard. 122p. 1977. 2.95 (0-8199-0663-8, Frncscn Herld) Franciscan Pr.

At America's Service. Karl Albrecht. 1992. pap. 12.99 (0-446-39316-9) Warner Bks.

***At an Elevation: On the Poetry of Robert Pack.** Ed. by David H. Bain & Sydney L. Plum. LC 94-78295. 205p. (Orig.). Date not set. pap. 13.95x (0-910408-10-6) Coll Store.

AT & T Reliability Manual. D. J. Klinger et al. (Illus.). 200p. 1990. text ed. 64.95 (0-442-31848-0) Van Nos Reinhold.

At Any Cost - Love, Life & Death at Sea. Peter Tangvald. Ed. by Nancy Scott et al. (Illus.). 264p. 1991. 19.95 (0-944428-07-X); pap. write for info. (0-944428-09-6) Cruising Guide.

At Any Price. David Drake. (Hammer's Slammers Ser.). 288p. 1985. reprint ed. mass mkt. 4.95 (0-671-55978-8) Baen Bks.

At Babci's Knee. Ed. by Alicja Padzik. Tr. by Aska Zurawiecka. LC 85-51371. (Little La Ser.). (Illus.). 165p. (Orig.). (ENG & POL.). (J). (ps). 1985. pap. 25.00 (0-935003-01-0); audio (0-935003-00-2) Talent-Ed.

At Baoshan. Simon Schuchat. (Morning Coffee Chapbook Ser.). (Illus.). 16p. (Orig.). 1987. pap. 7.50 (0-918273-39-0) Coffee Hse.

At Bertram's Hotel. Agatha Christie. (Agatha Christie Ser.). 329p. 1991. text ed. 19.95 (0-8161-4531-8) G K Hall.

At Bertram's Hotel. large type ed. Agatha Christie. (Agatha Christie Ser.). 329p. 1992. pap. 14.95 (0-8161-4532-6) G K Hall.

At Bertram's Hotel: A Miss Marple Mystery. Agatha Christie. 1992. mass mkt. 4.99 (0-06-100363-8, Harp PBks) HarpC.

At Book. Stephanie Moretti. (Window on Words Ser.). (Illus.). 18p. (J). (ps-1). 1991. 18.95 (1-879567-08-3, Valeria Bks) Wonder Well.

At Camp Kee Tov: Ethics for Jewish Juniors. Helen Fine. (Illus.). (J). (gr. 4-6). 6.95 (0-8074-0128-5, 121711) UAHC.

At Christmas Be Merry. Illus. & Sel. by P. K. Roche. 32p. (J). (ps-1). 1989. pap. 3.95 (0-14-050680-2, Puffin) Puffin Bks.

At Christmas the Heart Goes Home: A Holiday Treasury. Marjorie Holmes. 1991. 15.00 (0-385-41292-4) Doubleday.

At Christmas Time. (Illus.). 157p. (J). 1992. 5.98 (0-8317-0367-9) Smithmark.

At Christmas Time. J. Alex Munro. 80p. 1982. write for info. (0-9601670-4-8) J Alex Munro.

At Christmas Time the World Grows Young. Amy B. Almy. LC 70-116926. (Short Story Index Reprint Ser.). 1977. 16.95 (0-8369-3428-8) Ayer.

At Christmastime. Valerie Worth. LC 92-52693. (Michael di Capua Bks.). (Illus.). 32p. (J). (gr. k up). 1992. lib. bdg. 14.89 (0-06-205020-6) HarpC Child Bks.

At Close Range. Francis H. Smith. LC 75-37560. (Short Story Index Reprint Ser.). 1977. reprint ed. 21.95 (0-8369-4119-5) Ayer.

At Creation's Open Door. Eleanor Fitzgibbons. LC 93-60358. 65p. 1994. pap. 5.95 (1-55523-622-7) Winston-Derek.

At Daddy's on Saturdays. Linda W. Girard. Ed. by Abby Levine. LC 87-2126. (Albert Whitman Concept Bks.). (Illus.). 32p. (J). (gr. k-3). 1987. lib. bdg. 13.95 (0-8075-0475-0); pap. 5.95 (0-8075-0473-4) A Whitman.

At Daggers Drawn. Lois J. Menzel. 1989. pap. 2.95 (0-449-21601-2) Fawcett.

***At Dark of the Moon.** large type ed. Alice C. Ley. 352p. 1995. 23.95 (0-7089-3263-0) Ulverscroft.

At Dawn We Slept: The Untold Story of Pearl Harbor. Gordon W. Prange. 892p. 1982. pap. 15.95 (0-14-006455-9, Penguin Bks) Viking Penguin.

At Dawn We Slept: The Untold Story of Pearl Harbor. enl. rev. ed. Gordon W. Prange et al. LC 91-50176. (Illus.). 944p. 1991. pap. 18.95 (0-14-015734-4, Penguin Bks) Viking Penguin.

***At Day's End.** Ed. by Caroline Sullivan. 856p. 1994. 69.95 (1-56167-253-X) Nat Lib Poetry.

At Day's End: Book-Related Activities for Small Groups. Harriet R. Kinghorn & Fay H. Smith. LC 88-2249. 236p. 1988. lib. bdg. 21.50 (0-87287-654-3) Libs Unl.

***At Dead of Night.** Amey. 1995. mass mkt. (0-553-56474-9) Bantam.

At Death's Door. Joyce R. Badger. 14p. (Orig.). 1988. pap. 1.50 (0-929688-10-4) Bear Hse Pub.

At Dunkard Creek. D. W. Faulkner. (Hollow Spring Poetry Ser.). 60p. (Orig.). 1983. pap. 6.95 (0-686-39715-0) Hollow Spring Pr.

At Dusk on Naskeag Point. Tina Barr. LC 84-28621. 1984. pap. 4.00 (0-913984-0-X) Flume Pr.

At Duty's Call: A Study in Obsolete Patriotism. W. J. Reader. LC 87-32142. (Studies in Imperialism). 160p. 1988. text ed. 59.95 (0-7190-2395-5, Pub. by Manchester Univ Pr UK) St Martin.

At Duty's Call: A Study in Obsolete Patriotism. W. J. Reader. LC 87-32142. (Studies in Imperialism). 160p. 1991. text ed. 19.95 (0-7190-2409-9, Pub. by Manchester Univ Pr UK) St Martin.

At Ease: A Fluency Builder. Stacy Hagen. 128p. 1994. pap. text ed. 14.50 (0-13-293077-3) P-H.

At Ease: Stories I Tell to Friends. Dwight D. Eisenhower. (Military Classics Ser.). (Illus.). 400p. 1988. 23.95 (0-8306-4003-7, 40003) TAB Bks.

At Ease: Stories I Tell to Friends. Dwight D. Eisenhower. 400p. 1981. reprint ed. pap. 7.95 (0-915992-04-3) Eastern Acorn.

At Ease in the White House: The Uninhibited Memoirs of a Presidential Social Aide. Stephen M. Bauer. 1991. 19.95 (1-55972-061-1, Birch Ln Pr) Carol Pub Group.

At Ease in Zion: A Social History of Southern Baptists, 1865-1900. Rufus B. Spain. LC 66-10367. 1967. 17.50 (0-8265-1096-5) Vanderbilt U Pr.

At Ease Professionally: An Etiquette Guide for the Business World (at Home & Abroad) Hilka Klinkenberg. (Illus.). 268p. 1992. 18.95 (0-929387-55-4) Bonus Books.

At Ease under Pressure: James I, II Peter. (New Horizons Bible Study Ser.). 48p. 1982. teacher ed, pap. 2.35 (0-89367-072-3); student ed 2.95 (0-89367-073-1) Light & Life.

At Ease with Microsoft (R) FoxPro (TM) 2.5 for Windows. Ray E. Werner & Susan Klopfer. LC 93-8045. 1993. 24.60 (0-8306-4510-1, Windcrest) TAB Bks.

At Ease with Stress. Wanda Nash. LC 91-65006. 224p. (Orig.). 1991. pap. 9.95 (0-89622-482-1, C55) Twenty-Third.

At Ease with the Dead. Walter Satterthwait. 1993. mass mkt. 3.99 (0-373-83266-4, 1-83266-6) Harlequin Bks.

At Egypt. Clark Coolidge. 1988. per. 7.50 (0-935724-35-4) Figures.

***At Eighty-Two: A Journal.** May Sarton. LC 95-7744. 1995. 23.00 (0-393-03889-0) Norton.

At Every Gate a Pearl. Shirley Boll. 1986. pap. 3.25 (0-87813-525-1) Christian Light.

At Every Wedding Someone Stays Home: Poems. Dannye R. Powell. LC 93-38795. 96p. 1994. 18.00 (1-55728-315-X); pap. 10.00 (1-55728-316-8) U of Ark Pr.

At Face Value: Autobiographical Writing in Spanish America. Sylvia Molloy. (Studies in Latin American & Iberian Literature: No. 4). 320p. (C). 1991. 49.95 (0-521-33195-1) Cambridge U Pr.

At Face Value: The Life & Times of Eliza McCormack-John White. Don Akenson. 264p. (C). 1990. 39.95 (0-7735-0765-5, Pub. by McGill CN); pap. 17.95 (0-7735-0948-8, Pub. by McGill CN) U of Toronto Pr.

At Fault see Collected Works of Kate Chopin

***At Fenway.** Shaughnessy. write for info. (0-517-70104-9) Random Hse Value.

At Foot of Rainbow. Porter. 20.95 (0-685-71942-1) Amereon Ltd.

At Forty: Poems from the Heart of Judith Liff Goldstein. Judith L. Goldstein. (Illus.). 64p. (Orig.). 1987. pap. 4.95 (0-9618389-0-6) Sharone Pr.

At Freedom's Edge: Black Mobility & the Southern White Quest for Racial Control, 1861-1915. William Cohen. LC 90-44493. 340p. 1991. text ed. 45.00 (0-8071-1621-1); pap. text ed. 16.95 (0-8071-1652-1) La State U Pr.

At General Howe's Side, 1776-1778. Friedrich Von Muenchhausen. LC 73-94002. (Revolutionary War Bicentennial Ser.). (Illus.). 84p. 1974. lib. bdg. 15.95 (0-912480-09-2) Freneau.

At Gettysburg; or What a Girl Saw & Heard of the Battle. Tillie P. Alleman. (Illus.). 128p. 1994. reprint ed. 15.00 (1-879664-20-8) Stan Clark Military.

At God's Altar: Rite One. Enid M. Chadwick. Ed. by Eugenia Schuler. (Illus.). 1978. pap. 1.50 (0-934502-01-3) Thursday Pubs.

At Grammy's House. Eve Rice. LC 89-34617. (Illus.). 32p. (J). (ps up). 1990. 12.95 (0-688-08874-0); lib. bdg. 12.88 (0-688-08875-9) Greenwillow.

At Grandma's House: Story Book for Young Children in Sign Language. Sue Johnson. (Talking Fingers Bks.). (Illus.). 28p. (J). 1985. pap. 4.50 (0-916708-14-4) Modern Signs.

At Grandma's Knee. Ginny Dustin. (Illus.). 48p. (Orig.). 1992. pap. text ed. write for info. (1-880551-03-9) Silver Hill.

At Great Price: The Story of Tamsen Donner. Mabel H. Chapman. 156p. (Orig.). 1992. pap. 5.95 (0-9634580-0-0) M Chapman Pub.

At Ground Level. Ruth Burgess. 1987. 20.00 (0-947988-21-1, Pub. by Wild Goose Pubns UK) St Mut.

At Half-Past Eight: Essays on the Theatre 1921-1922. James Agate. LC 70-91308. 1972. reprint ed. 24.95 (0-405-08182-0, Pub. by Blom Pubns UK) Ayer.

At Hard Labor: Inmate Labor at the Colorado State Penitentiary, 1871-1940. Elinor M. McGinn. LC 92-34581. (American University Studies: History: Ser. IX, Vol. 137). 171p. (C). 1994. text ed. 39.95 (0-8204-2097-2) P Lang Pubs.

At Heaven's Gate. Robert Penn Warren. LC 84-18980. (Revived Modern Classics Ser.). 400p. 1985. reprint ed. pap. 11.95 (0-8112-0933-4, NDP588) New Directions.

At Her Captain's Command. Patricia Chandler. (American Romance Ser.). 1993. mass mkt. 3.50 (0-373-16497-1, 1-16497-9) Harlequin Bks.

At His Feet: Lessons Learned from the Master. Madge Beckon. 198p. (Orig.). 1994. pap. 8.95 (1-882701-06-2) Gospel Folio.

At Holy Mother's Feet see In the Company of the Holy Mother

At Home. (Learn-a-Word Board Bks.). (Orig.). (J). (gr. 2-6). 1986. 3.99 (0-517-05403-5, 614952) Random Hse Value.

At Home. (Babar & His Friends Ser.). (Illus.). 48p. (Orig.). (J). 1991. 6.99 (0-517-05210-5) Random Hse Value.

At Home. Kyle Carter. LC 94-18133. (J). 1994. write for info. (1-57103-080-8) Rourke Pr.

At Home. Etienne Delessert. LC 93-27456. (Yok-Yok Ser.). (Illus.). 32p. (J). (gr. 1-8). 1994. lib. bdg. 10.95 (0-88682-646-2, 97934-098) Creative Ed.

At Home. Mark Haddon. (Baby Dinosaurs Ser.). (Illus.). 14p. (J). (ps). 1994. 3.95 (0-307-17575-8, Artsts Writrs) Western Pub.

At Home. Gerald Hawksley. (Count a Round Ser.). (Illus.). 10p. (J). (ps). 1990. bds. 4.95 (1-878624-18-0) McClanahan Bk.

At Home. Illus. by Tony Tallarico. (Tiny Bks.). 28p. (J). (ps-1). 1984. bds. 2.95 (0-448-48818-3, Tuffy) Putnam Pub Group.

At Home. Sian Tucker. (Nursery Board Bks.). 14p. (J). (ps). 1991. pap. 2.95 (0-671-73399-0, Litl Simon S&S) S&S Childrens.

At Home: Essays 1982-1988. Gore Vidal. 1990. pap. 9.95 (0-679-72528-8, Vin) Random.

At Home: Essays, 1983-1987. Gore Vidal. LC 88-42670. (Illus.). 288p. 1988. 18.95 (0-394-57020-0) Random.

At Home: Memoirs. William C. Plomer. LC 79-179737. (Biography Index Reprint Ser.). 1977. reprint ed. 18.95 (0-8369-8106-5) Ayer.

At Home: The American Family, 1750-1870. Elisabeth D. Garrett. (Illus.). 304p. 1990. 49.50 (0-8109-1894-3) Abrams.

At-Home Activities for Math & Science: Hundreds of Activities to Increase Children's Love of Learning. Robyn F. Spizman & Marianne D. Garber. (Illus.). 160p. (J). (gr. k-3). 1994. 13.95 (0-86653-816-X, GA1508) Good Apple.

At-Home Activities for Reading, Language Arts, & Social Studies: Hundreds of Activities to Increase Children's Love of Learning. Robyn F. Spizman & Marianne D. Garber. (Illus.). 160p. (J). (gr. k-3). 1994. 13.95 (0-86653-817-8, GA1509) Good Apple.

At Home among Strangers: Exploring the Deaf Community in the United States. Jerome D. Schein. LC 89-35384. 254p. 1989. 24.95 (0-930323-51-3) Gallaudet Univ Pr.

At Home & Abroad. braille ed. V. S. Pritchett. 719p. 1991. vinyl bd. 57.52 (1-56956-188-5, BR8318) W A T Braille.

At Home & Abroad: Images from a Time of Change. Domenic J. Iacono & David L. Pince. (Illus.). 20p. 1989. pap. 6.00 (0-318-41896-7) SUNYP R Gibson.

At Home & at School: Activity Book. K. Hollenbeck. (Graphic Learning Integrated Social Studies Ser.). 40p. 1993. 3.25 (0-87746-368-9) Graphic Learning.

At Home & at School: Copy Masters File. K. Hollenbeck. (Graphic Learning Integrated Social Studies Ser.). 40p. 1993. 60.00 (0-87746-369-7) Graphic Learning.

At Home & at School: Literature Set, 6 stories. Ed. by L. Johnson. (Graphic Learning Integrated Social Studies Ser.). (Illus.). (ENG & SPA.). 1993. 225.00 (0-87746-319-0) Graphic Learning.

At Home & at School: Resource Book. K. Hollenbeck. (Graphic Learning Integrated Social Studies Ser.). 48p. 1993. 5.75 (0-87746-370-0) Graphic Learning.

At Home & at School: Teacher's Guide. K. Hollenbeck. (Graphic Learning Integrated Social Studies Ser.). 236p. 1993. 75.00 (0-87746-367-0) Graphic Learning.

At Home & at Work: Architects' & Designers' Empowered Spaces. Carol S. King. LC 93-18655. Orig. Title: Empowered Spaces. 1993. 45.00 (0-86636-249-5) PBC Intl Inc.

At Home & at Work: The Family's Allocation of Labor. Michael Geerken & Walter R. Gove. LC 82-21467. (New Perspectives on Family Ser.). 167p. reprint ed. pap. 47.60 (0-8357-4794-8, 2037731) Bks Demand.

At Home & Beyond: New Essays on Spanish Poets of the Twenties. Ed. by Salvador Jimenez-Fajardo & John C. Wilcox. LC 82-60341. 125p. (ENG & SPA.). reprint ed. pap. 35.70 (0-7837-5169-9, 2044898) Bks Demand.

At Home & School. Margaret Hargreaves & Pat Davis. (Illus.). (J). (gr. 1). 1988. 259.00 (0-318-41078-8) Southwinds Pr.

***At Home at School: A Child's Transition.** Kathleen Shannon. 105p. (Orig.). 1995. 14.95 (0-7802-2485-X) Wright Group.

At Home in a Boarding House: Report of an Independent Working Group. 1981. 40.00 (0-317-05774-X, Pub. by Natl Inst Soc Work) St Mut.

An Asterisk (*) at the beginning of an entry indicates that the title is appearing in BIP for the first time.

An Asterisk (*) at the beginning of an entry indicates that the title is appearing in BIP for the first time.

At-Risk Students: Reaching & Teaching Them. Richard Sagor. LC 92-62101. 330p. (Orig.). 1993. pap. 39.95 (*0-9628917-1-1*) Watersun MA.

At-Risk Students & School Restructuring. Ed. by Keith M. Kershner & John A. Connolly. 144p. 1991. pap. text ed. 21.95 (*1-56602-000-X*) Research Better.

At-Risk Students & Their Families. Carolyn Lavely et al. 1993. 15.95 (*1-55691-103-3*, 033) Learning Pubns.

At-Risk Students & Thinking: Perspectives from Research. Ed. by Barbara Z. Presseisen. 160p. 1988. 14.95 (*0-8106-1483-9*) NEA.

***At-Risk Students in Elementary Education: Effective Schools for Disadvantaged Learners.** Merlyn S. Swanson. 102p. 1991. pap. 15.95 (*0-398-06450-4*) C C Thomas.

At-Risk Students in Elementary Education: Effective Schools for Disadvantaged Learners. Merlyn S. Swanson. 102p. (C). 1991. text ed. 28.95x (*0-398-05737-0*) C C Thomas.

At-Risk Youth: A Comprehensive Response. Jeffries McWhirter et al. LC 92-26966. 1993. pap. 25.95 (*0-534-19842-2*) Brooks-Cole.

At-Risk Youth: Identification, Programs, & Recommendations. Shirley Wells. (Illus.). 158p. 1990. lib. bdg. 24.50 (*0-87287-812-0*) Libs Unl.

At Risk Youth in Crises: A Team Approach in the Schools. Sharon R. Morgan. LC 93-41948. (C). 1994. pap. 28.00 (*0-89079-574-6*, 6719) PRO-ED.

At-Risk Youth in Crisis: A Handbook for Collaboration Between Schools & Social Services, 2 vols., Vol. 1: Introduction & Resources. viii, 59p. 1991. 7.50 (*0-86552-108-5*) U of Oreg ERIC.

At-Risk Youth in Crisis: A Handbook for Collaboration Between Schools & Social Services, 2 vols., Vol. 2: Suicide. x, 74p. 1991. 7.50 (*0-86552-109-3*) U of Oreg ERIC.

At-Risk Youth in Crisis: A Handbook for Collaboration Between Schools & Social Services, 3 vols., Vol. 3: Child Abuse. x, 54p. 1991. 7.50 (*0-86552-111-5*) U of Oreg ERIC.

At-Risk Youth in Crisis: A Handbook for Collaboration Between Schools & Social Services, 3 vols., Vol. 4: Substance Abuse. x, 53p. 1991. 7.50 (*0-86552-112-3*) U of Oreg ERIC.

At-Risk Youth in Crisis: A Handbook for Collaboration Between Schools & Social Services, 3 vols., Vol. 5: Attendance Services. x, 60p. 1991. 7.50 (*0-86552-119-0*) U of Oreg ERIC.

At Road's End: Transportation & Land Use Choices for Communities. Daniel Carlson et al. 288p. (C). 1995. pap. text ed. 37.50 (*1-55963-338-7*) Island Pr.

At School. (Learn-a-Word Board Bks.). (J). (gr. 2-6). 1986. 3.99 (*0-517-05404-3*, 614960) Random Hse Value.

At Sea. Toby Olson. LC 92-42395. 256p. 1993. 19.00 (*0-671-73641-8*) S&S Trade.

At Sea & in Port Approaches. ICS Staff et al. (C). 1983. 75.00 (*0-900886-81-1*, Pub. by Witherby & Co UK) St Mut.

At Sea with Joseph Conrad. J. G. Sutherland. LC 71-174692. (Studies in Conrad: No. 8). 1971. reprint ed. lib. bdg. 49.95 (*0-8383-1347-7*) M S G Haskell Hse.

At Sea with the Scientifics: The Challenger Letters of Joseph Matkin. Ed. by Philip F. Rehbock. (Illus.). 424p. (C). 1993. text ed. 38.00 (*0-8248-1424-X*) UH Pr.

At Seventy. May Sarton. 336p. 1993. pap. 9.95 (*0-393-31030-2*) Norton.

At Seventy: More About the 'New Yorker' & Me. Ely J. Kahn, Jr. 1988. 19.95 (*0-317-67524-9*) Viking Penguin.

At Speed. Bond Parkhurst. (Illus.). 158p. write for info. (*0-87880-013-1*) At Speed Pr.

At Stalin's Side: His Interpreter's Memoirs from the October Revolution to the Fall of the Dictator's Empire. Valentin M. Berezhkov. Tr. by Sergei M. Mikheyev. LC 94-19044. 1994. 22.50 (*1-55972-212-6*, Birch Ln Pr) Carol Pub Group.

At Sunset. Julia W. Howe. (Notable American Authors Ser.). 1992. reprint ed. lib. bdg. 75.00 (*0-7812-3225-2*) Rprt Serv.

At Swim-Two-Birds. Flann O'Brien. 1976. pap. 12.00 (*0-452-25913-4*, Plume) NAL-Dutton.

At Sword's Point. Scott MacMillan. (Knights of the Blood Ser.: No. 2). 352p. (Orig.). 1994. pap. 4.99 (*0-451-45407-3*, ROC) NAL-Dutton.

At Taliesin: Newspaper Columns by Frank Lloyd Wright & the Taliesin Fellowship, 1934-1937. Comment & Comp. by Randolph C. Henning. LC 91-3501. (Illus.). 304p. 1992. 39.95 (*0-8093-1709-5*) S Ill U Pr.

At That Time: Cycles & Seasons in the Life of a Christian. Ed. by James A. Wilde. (Font & Table Ser.). (Illus.). 118p. 1989. pap. 6.95 (*0-930467-87-6*) Liturgy Tr Pubns.

At the Alamo: Captain Navarro's Memoirs. Tr. by C. D. Huneycutt. (Illus.). 75p. (Orig.). 1988. pap. 6.95 (*0-915153-32-7*) Gold Star Pr.

***At the Altar of Their God: African American Catholics in Cleveland, 1922-1961.** Dorothy A. Blatnica. LC 94-32943. (Studies in African American History & Culture). (Illus.). 272p. 1994. 54.00 (*0-8153-1933-9*) Garland.

***At the Alter: Matrimonial Tales.** Montgomery. 1995. mass mkt. 4.99 (*0-553-56748-9*) Bantam.

At the Amusement Park. (Babar & His Friends Ser.). (Illus.). 48p. (J). 1991. 6.99 (*0-517-05209-1*) Random Hse Value.

At the Back of the North Wind. (Young Reader's Christian Library). (Illus.). (J). (gr. 3 up). per., pap. 2.50 (*1-55748-188-1*) Barbour & Co.

At the Back of the North Wind. MacDonald. 1986. lib. bdg. 9.49 (*0-8167-2876-3*); pap. 2.95 (*0-8167-0470-8*) Troll Assocs.

At the Back of the North Wind. George Macdonald. LC 64-21758. (Airmont Classics Ser.). (Illus.). (YA). (gr. 5 up). 1966. pap. 1.50 (*0-8049-0100-7*, CL-100) Airmont.

At the Back of the North Wind. George MacDonald. 7.99 (*1-55748-024-9*, Christian Lib) Barbour & Co.

At the Back of the North Wind. George MacDonald. LC 87-45455. (Illus.). 320p. (J). 1988. 18.95 (*0-87923-703-1*) Godine.

At the Back of the North Wind. George MacDonald. LC 88-63292. (Books of Wonder). (Illus.). 352p. (J). (gr. 5 up). 1989. 17.95 (*0-688-07808-7*) Morrow Jr Bks.

At the Back of the North Wind. George MacDonald. 352p. 1990. 12.99 (*0-517-69120-5*) Random Hse Value.

***At the Back of the North Wind.** George MacDonald. (Victorian Children's Classics Ser.). 370p. (YA). Date not set. pap. 4.95 (*0-88270-556-3*) Bridge Pub.

At the Back of the North Wind. rev. ed. George MacDonald. Ed. by Michael Phillips. 176p. (J). (ps-2). 1991. 10.99 (*1-55661-196-X*) Bethany Hse.

At the Back of the North Wind. George MacDonald. (George MacDonald Original Works: Series II). (Illus.). 378p. (YA). 1992. reprint ed. 16.00 (*1-881084-07-8*) Johannesen.

At the Ball Game. S. A. Kramer. LC 93-31845. (Pictureback Ser.). (Illus.). 32p. (Orig.). (J). (ps-3). 1994. pap. 2.50 (*0-679-85291-3*) Random Bks Yng Read.

***At the Bar.** David Margolick. 1995. pap. 13.00 (*0-671-88787-4*, Touchstone Bks) S&S Trade.

At the Bargaining Table: The Status of Public Sector Supervisory, Managerial & Confidential Employees. Joel M. Douglas. (Public Employee Relations Library: No. 70). 96p. 1989. 14.00 (*0-685-33388-4*) Intl Personnel Mgmt.

At the Battle of San Jacinto: With Rip Cavitt. Kathryn T. Carter. (Illus.). 64p. (J). (gr. 4-7). 1987. 9.95 (*0-89015-374-4*) Sunbelt Media.

***At the Beach.** Kathie Atkinson. (J). (ps-3). 1994. pap. 3.95 (*1-86373-590-9*) IPG Chicago.

At the Beach. John Holladay. (What's Wrong Ser.). 1992. 4.98 (*0-8317-9365-1*) Smithmark.

At the Beach. Babette Katz. (Artists' Bks.). (Illus.). 40p. 1990. pap. 10.00 (*0-89822-055-6*) Visual Studies.

At the Beach. Huy-Voun Lee. LC 93-25462. (Illus.). 32p. (J). 1994. 14.95 (*0-8050-2768-8*) H Holt & Co.

At the Beach. Sam Malvaney. LC 85-62693. (Illus.). 104p. 1985. 12.95 (*0-935180-17-6*) Mutual Pub HI.

At the Beach. Anne Rockwell. LC 86-2943. (Illus.). 24p. (J). (ps-1). 1987. text ed. 13.95 (*0-02-777940-8*, Mac Bks Young Read) S&S Childrens.

At the Beach. Wren & Maile. (Keiki's First Bks.). (Illus.). 10p. (ENG & HAW.). (J). (ps). 1992. bds. 4.95 (*1-880188-04-X*) Bess Pr.

At the Beach. Anne Rockwell. LC 90-45620. (Illus.). 24p. (J). (ps-1). 1991. reprint ed. pap. 3.95 (*0-689-71494-7*, Aladdin Paperbacks) S&S Childrens.

At the Bedside: Innovations in Hospital Nursing. David A. Gould & Mathy D. Mezey. (Paper Ser.: No. 19). 32p. 1991. 10.00 (*0-934459-68-1*) United Hosp Fund.

***At the Beginning.** Wiener. 1995. 30.00 (*0-02-872066-0*) Macmillan.

At the Beginning of a Pig. Nicola Moon. LC 93-41504. (Illus.). 24p. (J). (ps-00). 1994. 8.95 (*1-85697-977-6*, Kingfisher LKC) LKC.

At the Bend in the River Mankato: An Illustrated History. Vernard E. Lundlin. 128p. 1990. 25.95 (*0-89781-339-1*) Preferred Mktg.

At the Best of Times: Libyan Poems. Philip Ward. (Modern Poets Ser.: Vol. 9). 1968. pap. 4.95 (*0-902675-07-9*) Oleander Pr.

At the Blue Bell Inn. Joseph S. Fletcher. LC 79-122697. (Short Story Index Reprint Ser.). 1977. 17.95 (*0-8369-3530-6*) Ayer.

At the Border: Winter Lights. Carol Reposa. (Signature Ser.: Vol. 1). (Orig.). 1989. pap. 5.00 (*0-317-93651-4*) Pecan Grove.

At the Bottom: A Woman's Life in Central America. Luisa Gonzalez. Ed. by Robert French. Tr. & Intro. by Regina Pustan. 121p. 1994. pap. 9.95 (*0-915117-12-6*) New Earth Pubns.

At the Bottom of the River. Jamaica Kincaid. LC 83-16445. 96p. 1983. 15.00 (*0-374-10660-6*) FS&G.

At the Bottom of the River. Jamaica Kincaid. 96p. 1992. reprint ed. pap. 7.95 (*0-452-26754-4*, Plume) NAL-Dutton.

At the Boundaries: Proceedings of the Northeastern Center for Literary Studies, Vol. 1. Ed. by Herbert L. Sussman. LC 83-21007. 56p. 1983. pap. 6.95 (*0-930350-54-5*) NE U Pr.

At the Boundaries of Law: Feminism & Legal Theory. Ed. by Martha A. Fineman & Nancy S. Thomadsen. 368p. 1990. 49.50 (*0-415-90305-X*, A4372, Routledge NY); pap. 15.95 (*0-415-90306-8*, A4376, Routledge NY) Routledge.

At the Bridge Table: Popular Point Count Bidding. Jo Woods. 50p. 1958. write for info. (*0-318-53737-0*) J Woods Pubns.

At the Brink of War & Peace: The Tito-Stalin Split in a Historic Perspective. Ed. by Wayne S. Vucinich. 341p. 1983. text ed. 54.00 (*0-914710-98-2*) East Eur Quarterly.

At the Center of the Human Drama: The Philosophical Anthropology of Karol Wojtyla - Pope John Paul II. Kenneth L. Schmitz. LC 93-18202. (Michael J. McGivney Lectures of the John Paul II Institutes for Studies on Marriage & Family: No. 1991). 176p. (Orig.). 1994. 24.95 (*0-8132-0779-7*); pap. 11.95 (*0-8132-0780-0*) Cath U Pr.

At the Center of the World: Polar Symbolism Discovered in Celtic, Norse & Other Ritualized Landscapes. John Michell. LC 93-61809. (Illus.). 184p. 1994. 24.95 (*0-500-01607-0*) Thames Hudson.

At the Centre of Political Storms: Memoirs of a Soviet Diplomat. Ed. by L. Kutakov. 358p. (C). 1986. 60.00 (*0-685-31594-0*, Pub. by Collets UK) Pro-Am Music.

At the Chelsea. Florence Turner. 1987. 13.95 (*0-15-109780-1*, Harvest Bks) HarBrace.

At the Circus. Jane Launchberry. 1988. 2.98 (*0-671-09596-X*) S&S Trade.

At the Circus. Meredith Corporation-Better Homes & Gardens Staff. (Max the Dragon Project Book Ser.). (Illus.). 32p. (J). (ps-12). 1991. lib. bdg. 10.95 (*1-878363-57-5*) Forest Hse.

At the City Limits. James Magorian. LC 86-72766. (Illus.). 34p. (J). (gr. 3-5). 1987. pap. 3.00 (*0-930674-22-7*) Black Oak.

At the Controls: Women in Aviation. Carole S. Briggs. (Space & Aviation Ser.). (Illus.). 72p. (YA). (gr. 5 up). 1991. lib. bdg. 21.50 (*0-8225-1593-8*, Lerner Publctns) Lerner Group.

At the Court of Yearning. Lucian Blaga. Tr. & Intro. by Andrei Codrescu. 216p. 1989. 35.00 (*0-8142-0489-9*); pap. 18.50 (*0-8142-0496-1*) Ohio St U Pr.

At the Crack of the Bat. Illus. by Steve Cieslawski. LC 91-28946. 64p. (J). (gr. 2-5). 1992. 14.95 (*1-56282-176-8*); lib. bdg. 14.89 (*1-56282-177-6*) Hyprn Child.

At the Crack of the Bat. Lillian Morrison. LC 91-28946. (Illus.). 64p. (J). (gr. 3-7). 1994. pap. 5.95 (*1-56282-670-0*) Hyprn Ppbks.

At the Creation of a New Germany. George McGhee. LC 88-18029. 256p. (C). 1989. 32.00 (*0-300-04250-7*) Yale U Pr.

***At the Crest of the Tidal Wave: A Forecast for the Great Bear Market.** Robert R. Prechter, Jr. LC 95-68295. (Illus.). 1995. 49.00 (*0-932750-39-7*) New Classics Lib.

At the Cross. Charles Ludwig. 1990. pap. 5.95 (*0-87162-596-2*, D1379) Warner Pr.

At the Crossroads. Rachel Isadora. LC 90-30751. (Illus.). 32p. (J). (ps up). 1991. 16.00 (*0-688-05270-3*); lib. bdg. 15.93 (*0-688-05271-1*) Greenwillow.

At the Crossroads. Rachel Isadora. (Illus.). 32p. (J). (ps up). 1994. reprint ed. pap. 4.95 (*0-688-13103-4*, Mulberry) Morrow.

At the Crossroads: A Celebration of Diversity. Douglas Watson. (Monograph Ser.: No. 15). 379p. 15.00 (*0-914494-18-X*) Am Deaf & Rehab.

At the Crossroads: A History of Central Point 1850-1900. Linda M. Genaw. (Illus.). 124p. (Orig.). 1988. pap. text ed. 8.00 (*0-9620652-2-6*) L M Genaw.

At the Crossroads: Education in the Middle East. Adnan Badran. 335p. 1989. 34.95 (*0-943852-46-3*) Prof World Peace.

At the Crossroads: Essays on Ahad Ha'am. Ed. by Jacques Kornberg. LC 83-368. (Modern Jewish History Ser.). 242p. (C). 1984. 64.50 (*0-87395-738-5*); pap. 21.95 (*0-87395-739-3*) State U NY Pr.

At the Crossroads: Fertility of Mexican-American Women. Elizabeth H. Stephen. LC 89-37797. (Studies in Historical Demography). 210p. 1989. 15.00 (*0-8240-3397-3*) Garland.

***At the Crossroads: Librarians on the Information Superhighway.** Herbert S. White. 380p. 1995. lib. bdg. 55.00 (*1-56308-165-2*) Libs Unl.

At the Crossroads: Memories from a Rural Ethnic Community: The Saukville, Wisconsin Area. John Boatman. Ed. by Angela M. Schefft. 628p. (Orig.). (C). 1993. pap. text ed. 18.45 (*0-685-72296-1*) U Pr of Amer.

At the Crossroads: Michilimackinac During the American Revolution. David A. Armour & Keith R. Widder. (Illus.). 249p. 1978. 18.00 (*0-911872-24-8*) Mackinac Island.

At the Crossroads: The Mineral Problems of the United States. Eugene N. Cameron. 320p. 1986. pap. text ed. 39.95 (*0-471-83982-5*) Wiley.

At the Crossroads: The Mineral Problems of the United States. Eugene N. Cameron. LC 85-29587. (Wiley-Interscience Publication Ser.). 344p. reprint ed. pap. 98.10 (*0-7837-2389-X*, 2040074) Bks Demand.

At the Crossroads of Faith & Reason: An Essay on Pierre Bayle. Karl C. Sandberg. LC 66-18531. 135p. reprint ed. pap. 38.50 (*0-8357-5827-3*, 2027388) Bks Demand.

At the Crossroads of Infinities. E. I. Parnov. Tr. by Vladimir Talmy. 397p. 1971. 19.95 (*0-8464-0159-2*) Beekman Pubs.

***At the Crossroads of the Earth & the Sky: An Andean Cosmology.** fac. ed. Gary Urton. LC 81-4331. (Latin American Monographs). (Illus.). 268p. 1994. pap. 76.40 (*0-7837-7700-0*, 2047457) Bks Demand.

At the Crossroads of the Earth & the Sky: An Andean Cosmology. Gary Urton. (Latin American Monographs: No. 55). (Illus.). 268p. 1988. reprint ed. pap. 14.95 (*0-292-70404-6*) U of Tex Pr.

At the Crossroads, 1967. Janet Kardon et al. 104p. (Orig.). 1988. pap. 17.00 (*0-88454-042-1*) U of Pa Contemp Art.

At the Dawn of a New Age. Rudolf Hauschka. 104p. 1990. pap. 12.95 (*0-919924-25-5*, 1016, Pub. by Steiner Book Centre CN) Anthroposophic.

At the Dawn of Glasnost: Soviet Portraits. Photos by Proctor Jones, Jr. LC 88-92601. (Illus.). 136p. (Orig.). 1988. pap. 19.95 (*0-9608860-5-2*) Proctor Jones.

At the Dawn of Tyranny: The Origins of Individualism, Political Oppression & the State. Eli Sagan. 421p. 1993. pap. text ed. 12.00 (*1-882231-02-3*) FishDrum Mag.

At the Death of a Child: Words of Comfort & Hope. Donald L. Deffner. LC 93-3739. 1993. 2.75 (*0-570-04608-4*) Concordia.

At the Departure Gate with a Citizen of the Cosmos. Beredene Jocelyn. 1981. pap. 2.50 (*0-916786-61-7*, Saint George Pubns) R Steiner Col Pubns.

At the Dog in Dulwich. Ed. by Clive Murphy. 200p. 1987. 30.95 (*0-436-29671-3*, Pub. by Seck & Warburg UK) Trafalgar.

At the Door: Selected Literature for ESL Students. Sandra L. McKay & Dorothy Petitt. (Illus.). 208p. (C). 1983. pap. text ed. 16.95 (*0-13-049676-6*) P-H.

At the Drop of a Veil. Marianne Alireza. 1993. reprint ed. lib. bdg. 23.95 (*1-56849-013-5*) Buccaneer Bks.

At the Earth's Core. Edgar Rice Burroughs. 224p. 1990. pap. 3.95 (*0-345-36668-9*, Del Rey) Ballantine.

At the Earth's Core see Pellucidar Novels

At the Edge. Michael Behrens. 208p. (YA). (gr. 7 up). 1988. pap. 2.95 (*0-380-75610-2*, Flare) Avon.

***At the Edge.** Douglas Carlson. 98p. (Orig.). 1989. pap. 9.00 (*0-614-07022-8*) White Pine Pr Inc.

***At the Edge.** Jennifer DiMarco. 110p. (Orig.). 1994. pap. 9.95 (*1-886383-11-1*) Pride OH.

At the Edge: Molecular & Cellular Endocrinology. J. Funder. 150p. 1991. 45.75 (*0-444-89170-6*) Elsevier.

At the Edge of History - Passages about Earth: Passages about Earth. William I. Thompson. 446p. 1990. reprint ed. pap. 15.95 (*0-940262-32-0*) Lindisfarne Pr.

At the Edge of History & Passages about Earth. William I. Thompson. 490p. 1989. reprint ed. pap. text ed. 15.95 (*0-929660-07-2*) Morningtown.

At the Edge of Megalopolis: A History of Salem, N. H. 1900-1974. LC 74-21031. (Illus.). 1974. 12.00 (*0-914016-11-3*) Phoenix Pub.

At the Edge of Prehistory: Huber Phase Archaeology in the Chicago Area. Ed. by James A. Brown & Patricia J. O'Brien. LC 90-20801. (Illus.). (Orig.). 1990. pap. 15.95 (*0-942118-30-8*) Ctr Amer Arche.

At the Edge of Southeast Asian History: Essays. James F. Warren. (Illus.). 228p. (Orig.). (C). 1988. pap. 12.50 (*971-10-0263-9*, Pub. by New Day Pub PH) Cellar.

At the Edge of Space: The X-15 Flight Program. Milton O. Thompson. LC 91-23701. (Illus.). 384p. 1992. 29.95 (*1-56098-107-5*) Smithsonian.

At the Edge of the Chopping There Are No Secrets. John Thompson. 51p. (Orig.). 1973. pap. 3.95 (*0-88784-027-2*, Pub. by Hse of Anansi Pr CN) Genl Dist Srvs.

At the Edge of the Orchard Country. Robert Morgan. LC 85-29506. (Wesleyan Poetry Ser.). 75p. 1987. 22.50 (*0-8195-5158-9*, Wesleyan Univ Pr); pap. 10.95 (*0-8195-6164-9*, Wesleyan Univ Pr) U Pr of New Eng.

At the Edge of the Pond. Jennifer Dewey. (Illus.). 48p. (J). (gr. 1-5). 1987. 14.95 (*0-316-18208-7*) Little.

At the Edge of Town. John Davies. 76p. (C). 1981. 20.00x (*0-85088-923-5*, Pub. by Gomer Pr UK) St Mut.

At the Edges of Life: A Holistic Vision of the Human Adventure. Bruce G. Epperly. 1992. pap. 13.99 (*0-8272-0020-X*) Chalice Pr.

At the End of the Car Line. Ben H. Lampman. 1965. reprint ed. 20.00 (*0-8323-0145-0*) Binford Mort.

At the End of the Open Road: Poems. Louis Simpson. LC 63-17792. (Wesleyan Poetry Program Ser.: Vol. 20). 70p. 1963. pap. 10.95 (*0-8195-1020-3*, Wesleyan Univ Pr) U Pr of New Eng.

***At the End of the Rainbow? Gold, Land, & People in the Brazilian Amazon.** Gordon MacMillan. LC 95-139. (Methods & Cases in Conservation Science Ser.). 1995. write for info. (*0-231-10354-9*); pap. write for info. (*0-231-10355-7*) Col U Pr.

***At the End of the Road: The Rise & Fall of Austin-Healy, MG & Triumph Sports Cars.** Timothy R. Whisler. LC 95-3148. (Industrial Development & the Social Fabric Ser.: Vol. 13). 1995. write for info. (*1-55938-906-0*) Jai Pr.

At the Essence of Learning: Multicultural Education. Geneva Gay. LC 94-13977. 176p. (Orig.). 1994. pap. 15.00 (*0-912099-14-3*) Kappa Delta Pi.

At the Expense of Victory: A Desert Storm Diary of News Media Coverage. Ed DeMello. LC 94-77217. (Illus.). 336p. (Orig.). 1994. pap. 18.95 (*0-9640530-0-4*) Kenobi Prods.

At the Extremity of Civilization: A Meticulously Descriptive Diary of an Illinois Physician's Journey in 1849 along the Oregon Trail to the Goldmines & Cholera of California, Thence in Two Years to Return by Boat Via Panama. Israel S. Lord. Ed. by Necia D. Liles. (Illus.). 441p. 1995. lib. bdg. 45.00 (*0-7864-0000-5*) McFarland & Co.

At the Fair. John Holladay. (What's Wrong Ser.). 1992. 4.98 (*0-8317-9364-3*) Smithmark.

At the Fair: The Boston Immigrant Experience. Alan Seaburg. LC 90-60862. (Illus.). 128p. 1990. text ed. 24.95 (*0-9625794-0-8*) A Miniver Pr.

At the Fall of Somoza. Lawrence Pezzullo & Ralph Pezzullo. LC 93-1006. (Latin American Ser.). (Illus.). 328p. (C). 1993. text ed. 34.95 (*0-8229-3756-5*) U of Pittsburgh Pr.

At the Falls: Richmond, Virginia & Its People. Marie Tyler-McGraw. LC 94-5727. (Illus.). 450p. 1994. 39.95 (*0-8078-2163-2*); pap. 19.95 (*0-8078-4476-4*) U of NC Pr.

At the Farm. (Babar & His Friends Ser.). (Illus.). 48p. (J). 1991. 6.99 (*0-517-05211-3*) Random Hse Value.

At the Farm. Outlet Staff. (Learn-a-Word Board Bks.). (J). 1991. bds. 3.99 (*0-517-05401-9*) Random Hse Value.

At the Feet of Mahatma Gandhi. Rajendra Prasad. LC 79-156204. 1971. reprint ed. text ed. 69.50 (*0-8371-6154-1*, PRMG, Greenwood Pr) Greenwood.

At the Feet of the Master. Alcyone. 1986. 2.75 (*81-7059-125-2*) Theos Pub Hse.

At the Feet of the Master. Alcyone. pap. text ed. 4.00 (*0-911662-17-0*) Yoga.

At the Feet of the Master. Osho. Ed. by Ma D. Sarito. (Initiation Talks Ser.). (Illus.). 404p. 1993. 28.95 (*3-89338-112-0*, Pub. by Rebel Hse GW) Osho Chidvilas.

At the Feet of the Master. Alcyone. 1970. reprint ed. pap. 5.95 (*0-8356-0196-X*, Quest) Theos Pub Hse.

At the Field's End: Interviews with Twenty Pacific Northwest Writers. Nicholas O'Connell. LC 87-7053. 336p. 1987. pap. 12.95 (*0-88089-026-6*) Madrona Pubs.

An Asterisk (*) at the beginning of an entry indicates that the title is appearing in BIP for the first time.

An Asterisk (*) at the beginning of an entry indicates that the title is appearing in BIP for the first time.

At Their Word: Essays on the Arts of Language, Vol. 2. Cid Corman. LC 76-48282. 220p. (Orig.). 1978. 14.00 (*0-87685-308-4*); pap. 5.00 (*0-87685-307-6*) Black Sparrow.

At Their Word: Essays on the Arts of Language, Vol. 2, signed ed. deluxe ed. Cid Corman. LC 76-48282. 220p. (Orig.). 1978. 17.50 (*0-87685-309-2*) Black Sparrow.

At This Evening's Performance. Nagle Jackson. 1984. pap. 4.75 (*0-8222-0074-0*) Dramatists Play.

At This Very Moment - En Este Preciso Momento. Margot Pepper. Ed. by Ben Clarke. Tr. by Adriana F. Lopez & Javier Torres. (Poetry & Prose from San Francisco's Tenderloin District Ser.). (Illus.). 77p. (Orig.). (ENG & SPA.). 1992. pap. text ed. 6.00 (*0-9625153-3-7*) Freedom Voices Pubns.

At Timberline: A Nature Guide to the Mountains of the Northeast. Frederic L. Steele. (Illus.). 288p. 1982. pap. 13.95 (*0-910146-39-X*) AMC Books.

At Twelve: Portraits of Young Women. Sally Mann. (Illus.). 56p. 1988. pap. 19.95 (*0-89381-330-3*) Aperture.

At Twelve: Portraits of Young Women. Sally Mann. (Illus.). 56p. 1988. 35.00 (*0-89381-296-X*) Aperture.

At War for Peace. Thomas K. Siemer. 308p. 1986. pap. 12.95 (*0-940157-00-4*) Abbeyhills O C.

At War in the Gulf: A Chronology. Arthur H. Blair. 144p. (Orig.). 1992. pap. 9.95 (*0-89096-507-2*) Tex A&M Univ Pr.

At War in the Shadow of Vietnam: United States Military Aid to the Royal Lao Government, 1955-1975. Timothy Castle. LC 92-44151. 250p. (C). 1993. text ed. 47.50 (*0-231-07976-1*) Col U Pr.

At War with Friends. Eric Torgersen. LC 73-156274. 57p. 1972. pap. 2.95 (*0-87886-023-1*, Greenfld Rev Pr) Greenfld Rev Lit.

At Water's Edge: The Birds of Florida. Roger Bansemer & Bill Renc. LC 92-37447. (Illus.). 128p. 1993. 24.95 (*0-87833-821-7*) Taylor Pub.

At Weddings & Wakes. Alice McDermott. 1993. mass mkt. 5.99 (*0-440-21523-4*) Dell.

At Weddings & Wakes. Alice McDermott. 1992. 19.00 (*0-374-10674-6*) FS&G.

At Weddings & Wakes. large type ed. Alice McDermott. LC 92-31035. (General Ser.). 320p. 1993. 20.95 (*0-8161-5570-4*); pap. 16.95 (*0-8161-5571-2*) G K Hall.

At What Cost. S. Knappe & C. Brusaw. 1992. pap. write for info. (*0-517-58895-1*) Random Hse Value.

At What Price? Privacy, Libel, & Freedom of the Press. Barbara Dill. 1993. pap. 9.95 (*0-87078-179-0*) TCFP-PPP.

At What Price? Privacy, Libel, & Freedom of the Press. Barbara Dill & Martin London. LC 93-2350. (Perspectives on the News Ser.). 1993. 9.95 (*0-87078-356-4*) TCFP-PPP.

At-Will Employment & the Handsome American: The Second Annual Benjamin Aaron Lecture. Theodore J. St. Antoine. (Benjamin Aaron Annual Lecture Ser.). 20p. 1993. reprint ed. 7.00 (*0-89215-154-4*) U Cal LA Indus Rel.

At Wit's End. Erma Bombeck. 1986. mass mkt. 5.99 (*0-449-21184-3*, Crest) Fawcett.

At Wolfe's Door: The Nero Wolfe Novels of Rex Stout. J. Kenneth Van Dover. LC 88-34363. (Milford Ser.: Popular Writers of Today: Vol. 52). 120p. 1991. reprint ed. lib. bdg. 25.00x (*0-89370-189-0*, 18907358); reprint ed. pap. 15.00x (*0-89370-289-7*, 18907358) Borgo Pr.

At Women's Expense: State Power & the Politics of Fetal Rights. Cynthia R. Daniels. LC 93-4102. 191p. 1993. text ed. 19.95 (*0-674-05043-6*) HUP.

At Work in Homes: Household Workers in World Perspective. Ed. by Roger Sanjek & Shellee Colen. (American Ethnological Society Monograph Ser.: No. 3). 1990. 21.00 (*0-913167-39-8*) Am Anthro Assn.

At Work in the Electronic Office. Sanders. 192p. (C). 1991. pap. text ed. write for info. (*0-13-019522-7*) P-H.

***At Work with Grotowski on Physical Actions.** Thomas Richards. LC 94-23889. (ENG & ITA.). 1995. write for info. (*0-415-12491-3*); pap. write for info. (*0-415-12492-1*) Routledge.

***At World's End: A Daughter's Story.** Louise Kehoe. LC 95-7535. 1995. 22.00 (*0-8052-4122-1*) Schocken.

At Your Command: A Basic English Workbook. 2nd ed. Patricia Licklider. (C). 1987. pap. text ed. 24.00 (*0-673-39276-7*) HarpCollege.

At Your Door: A Modern-Day Campaign. L. N. Isynwill et al. Ed. by Lynn Willis & Keith Herber. (Call of Cthulhu Roleplaying Game System Ser.). (Illus.). 162p. (Orig.). (YA). (gr. 12 up). 1990. pap. 17.95 (*0-933635-64-8*, 2326) Chaosium.

At Your Fingertips: A Resource Guide for Office Personnel. Barbara B. Halpern. 54p. (C). 1988. pap. text ed. 10.00 (*0-15-504195-9*) HB Coll Pubs.

At Your Fingertips: A Resource Guide for Office Personnel. 2nd ed. Barbara B. Halpern. LC 94-70094. 86p. (C). 1994. pap. text ed. 10.50 (*0-03-098009-7*) Dryden Pr.

At Your Fingertips: The Care & Maintenance of a Vagina. Ed. by Deborah Werksman. (Illus.). (Orig.). 1994. pap. 4.95 (*0-9629162-6-9*) Quayle Quart.

At Your Own Risk. Marty Crisp. 1993. 13.95 (*0-8034-8981-1*) Bouregy.

At Your Own Risk: A Saint's Testament. Derek Jarman. LC 92-24387. (Illus.). 144p. 1994. 19.95 (*0-87951-473-6*); pap. 10.95 (*0-87951-538-4*) Overlook Pr.

ATA Accounting Service for Class I or Class II Motor Carriers. American Trucking Association National Accounting & Finance Council. 550p. 1989. ring bd. 95.00 (*0-88711-022-3*) Am Trucking Assns.

ATA Annual Meeting: Horizons - Proceedings of the 32nd Annual Conference of the American Translators Association. Ed. by A. Leslie Willson. 1991. 50.00 (*0-685-59471-8*) Learned Info.

***ATA Truck Driving Championships Rules & Procedures: State & National 1995.** (Illus.). 143p. 1995. pap. 3.50 (*0-88711-264-1*) Am Trucking Assns.

ATA Trucking Salaried Employees Compensation Study 1993, 2 vols., Set. American Trucking Association Staff. 529p. 1993. 400.00 (*0-88711-174-2*) Am Trucking Assns.

ATA Vehicle Maintenance Reporting Standards Handbook. 1985. text ed. 110.00 (*0-88711-178-5*) Am Trucking Assns.

ATA '88: "Languages at Crossroads" - Proceedings of the Annual American Translators Association Conference, 29th, October 12-16, 1988. 540p. 1988. 50.00 (*0-938734-28-8*) Learned Info.

ATA '89: "Coming of Age" - Proceedings of the 30th Annual Conference of the American Translators Association, October 11-15, 1989, Washington, DC. 582p. 1989. pap. 50.00 (*0-938734-39-3*) Learned Info.

ATA '90: "Looking Ahead" - Proceedings of the 31st Annual Conference of the American Translators Association, Oct. 17-21, 1990. Ed. by A. Leslie Willson. 475p. 1990. 50.00 (*0-938734-47-4*) Learned Info.

ATA '92: "Frontiers" - Proceedings of the 33rd Annual Conference of the American Translators Association, November 4-8, 1992. Ed. by Edith F. Losa. 399p. 1992. pap. 50.00 (*0-938734-68-7*) Learned Info.

***ATA '94: Vistas-Proceedings of the 35th Annual Conference of the American Translators Association.** Ed. by Peter W. Krawutschke. 441p. 1994. pap. 55.00 (*0-938734-92-X*) Learned Info.

Atacama: Desert of Chile & Peru. James W. Cornett. (Illus.). 19p. (Orig.). 1985. pap. 4.95 (*0-937794-07-4*) Nature Trails.

Atacames Special Area Management Plan: Atacames-Sua Muisne. Stephen Olsen et al. 68p. 1994. write for info. (*1-885454-01-5*) Coastal Res.

***Atahita Journal: A Collection of Prose & Poetry from the Southern Mountains.** Ed. by Barbara S. McRae. 78p. (Orig.). Date not set. pap. 8.00 (*0-9638930-1-7*) Teresita Pr.

Atahualpa. Frederick Howay. (Illus.). 28p. 1978. 3.95 (*0-87770-197-0*) Ye Galleon.

Atala. Francois-Rene De Chateaubriand. Ed. by Fernand Letessier. Bd. with Rene.; Aventures du Dernier Abencerage. (Class. Garnier Ser.). Set pap. 10.95 (*0-8288-9344-6*, F58479) Fr & Eur.

Atala: Avec: Rene, Le Dernier Abencerage. Rene De Chateaubriand & Fernand Letessier. 512p. (FRE.). 1958. 10.95 (*0-8288-9096-X*, F58476) Fr & Eur.

Atala: Edition Critique. Rene De Chateaubriand. 208p. 1952. 7.95 (*0-8288-9091-9*, F58720) Fr & Eur.

Atala see Oeuvres Romanesques et Voyages

Atala & Rene. Francois-Rene De Chateaubriand. Tr. by Irving Putter. 1952. pap. 12.00 (*0-520-00223-7*) U CA Pr.

Atala; Rene; Les Aventures du Dernier Abencerage. Francois R. Chateaubriand. (Folio Ser.: No. 1017). (Orig.). (FRE.). pap. 8.95 (*2-07-037017-8*) Schoenhof.

Atalanta: An Anthology of Creative Work Celebrating Women's Athletic Achievements. Ed. by Sandra K. Martz. 54p. (Orig.). 1984. pap. 4.00 (*0-918949-00-9*) Papier-Mache Press.

Atalanta Fugiens: An Edition of the Emblems, Fugues & Epigrams. Michael Maier. Tr. by Joscelyn Godwin. LC 89-34804. (Magnum Opus Hermetic Sourceworks Ser.: No. 22). (Illus.). 215p. (Orig.). 1989. And cassette. 50.00 (*0-933999-81-X*); And cassette. pap. 26.00 (*0-933999-82-8*) Phanes Pr.

Atalanta in Calydon, a Tragedy. Algernon C. Swinburne. (BCL1-PR English Literature Ser.). 79p. 1992. reprint ed. lib. bdg. 59.00 (*0-7812-7676-4*) Rprt Serv.

Atalanta (Seventeen Seventy-Seven) & Savannah (Seventeen Eighty) Robert Colvill. LC 87-4553. 1987. 50.00 (*0-8201-1421-9*) Schol Facsimiles.

Atalanta's Race: A Greek Myth. Illus. by Alexander Koshkin. LC 93-26734. (J). 1995. 15.95 (*0-395-67322-4*, Clarion Bks) HM.

Atalante. Marina Warner. (Illus.). 80p. 1994. pap. 9.95 (*0-85170-357-7*, Pub. by British Film Inst UK) Ind U Pr.

Atalantis Major. Daniel Defoe. LC 92-2368. (Augustan Reprints Ser.: No. 198 (1979)). reprint ed. 12.00 (*0-404-70198-1*, DA496 1711.D39) AMS Pr.

Atalaya de las Coronicas. Alfonso Martinez de Toledo. Ed. by James B. Larkin. (Spanish Ser.: No. 10). (Illus.). xvi, 157p. 1983. fiche 24.00 (*0-942260-29-5*) Hispanic Seminary.

AT&T: The Story of Industrial Conquest. Noobar R. Danielian. LC 74-7672. (Telecommunications Ser.). 486p. 1974. reprint ed. 33.95 (*0-405-06038-6*) Ayer.

AT&T Computer Software Catalog: UNIX R System V Software. AT&T Information Systems, Inc. Staff. 1987. 24.95 (*0-13-050154-9*) P-H.

AT&T Computer Software Guide PC 6300. AT&T Information Systems, Inc. Staff. write for info. (*0-318-59648-2*) S&S Trade.

AT&T Computer Software Guide 3B2-3B5-3B20 UNIT PC. AT&T Information Systems, Inc. Staff. write for info. (*0-318-59649-0*) S&S Trade.

AT&T Documentation Guide. 155p. (Orig.). (C). 1993. pap. text ed. 45.00 (*1-56806-792-5*) Diane Pub.

***AT&T Global Messaging.** Ira Hertzoff. 1995. text ed. 45.00 (*0-07-028459-8*) McGraw.

AT&T PC 6300 Made Easy. Martin D. Seyer & Leo J. Scanlon. (Illus.). 144p. 1985. pap. 28.95 (*0-13-050329-0*) P-H.

AT&T Quality Improvement Cycle. Ed. by Susan Annitto. (AT&T Quality Library). 68p. (Orig.). 1988. pap. 29.95 (*0-932764-20-7*, 500-031) AT&T Customer Info.

AT&T Toll-Free Eight Hundred Directory, 1992. Ed. by Dave Williams. 1993. Business ed. 14.95 (*0-938963-10-4*); Consumer ed. 9.95 (*0-938963-11-2*) AT&T Eight.

AT&T Toll-Free Eight Hundred Directory, 1993. Ed. by Kathryn Sullivan. 1993. Business edition. 14.95 (*0-938963-17-1*); Consumer edition. 9.95 (*0-938963-18-X*) AT&T Eight.

Ataque del Mundo de los Espiritus: Attack from the Spirit World. (SPA.). 5.50 (*84-7228-288-0*, 220048, Pub. by Edit Clie SP) TSELF.

Ataques Contra la Prensa: Un Informe Internacional. Committee to Protect Journalists Staff. Ed. by Jan Ellis. Tr. by Maria Negroni & Joel Solomon. 177p. (SPA.). 1991. pap. 10.00 (*0-944823-03-3*) Comm to Protect Jrnlists.

Atari, Vol. 1. Nancy Taitt. (Thinking-Learning-Creating: TLC for Growing Minds Ser.). 55p. (J). (gr. 4-12). 1983. pap. text ed. 11.95 (*0-88193-071-7*) Create Learn.

Atari, Vol. 2. Nancy Taitt. (Thinking-Learning-Creating: TLC for Growing Minds Ser.). 64p. (J). (gr. 4-12). 1984. pap. text ed. 11.95 (*0-88193-072-5*) Create Learn.

Atari, Vol. 3. Henry A. Taitt & Jennifer Taitt. (Thinking-Learning-Creating: TLC for Growing Minds Ser.). 47p. (J). (gr. 5-12). 1983. pap. text ed. 11.95 (*0-88193-073-3*) Create Learn.

Atari, Vol. 4. Henry A. Taitt & Jennifer Taitt. (Thinking-Learning-Creating: TLC for Growing Minds Ser.). 51p. (J). (gr. 5-12). 1983. pap. text ed. 11.95 (*0-88193-074-1*) Create Learn.

Atari Assembly Language Programmer's Guide. Allan Moose & Marian Lorenz. 288p. 1986. pap. 26.95 (*0-938862-54-5*) Weber Systems.

Atari BASIC: Faster & Better. Carl M. Evans. 300p. 19.95 (*0-936200-29-4*) Blue Cat.

Atari BASIC: Learning by Using. Thomas E. Rowley. 73p. 7.95 (*0-936200-35-9*) Blue Cat.

Atari Compendium. Scott Sanders. 880p. 1993. pap. 49.95 (*0-9638331-0-3*) Sftware Dev.

***Atari Jaguar: Official Gamer's Guide.** J. Douglas Arnold & Zach Meston. (Gaming Mastery Ser.). (Illus.). 240p. (Orig.). 1995. pap. 16.95 (*1-884364-13-6*) Sandwich Islands.

Atari LOGO in the Classroom. Donna Bearden. 1984. pap. text ed. 14.95 (*0-8359-0121-1*, Reston) P-H.

Atari ST: The Advanced Programmer's Guide. Harrison. 287p. 1986. 21.90 (*1-85058-053-7*, Pub. by Sigma Pr UK) Bk Clearing Hse.

Atari ST Programmer's Guide. Gilbert Held. 350p. (Orig.). 1987. pap. 26.95 (*0-938862-79-0*) Weber Systems.

Atari XE User's Handbook. Weber Systems, Inc. Staff. 300p. (Orig.). 1985. pap. 26.95 (*0-938862-41-3*) Weber Systems.

Atari XL User's Handbook. Weber Systems, Inc. Staff. LC 84-50834. (User's Handbooks to Personal Computers Ser.). 300p. 1985. pap. 26.95 (*0-938862-08-1*) Weber Systems.

Atariba & Niguayona. Harriet Rohmer & Jesus Guerrero Rea. LC 76-17495. (Illus.). 24p. (ENG & SPA.). (J). (gr. 2-6). 1988. 13.95 (*0-89239-026-3*) Childrens Book Pr.

Atarron. Christopher McGlothlin. 360p. 1994. pap. 5.95 (*0-9639383-0-4*) Delacroix Pubng.

Atat Urk. A. L. Macfie. LC 93-33763. (Profiles in Power Ser.). (C). 1994. text ed. 47.50 (*0-582-07862-8*) Longman.

Atat Urk. A. L. Macfie. LC 93-33763. (Profiles in Power Ser.). (C). 1995. pap. text ed. 17.95 (*0-582-07863-6*) Longman.

Ataturk: A Biography of Mustafa Kemal, Father of Modern Turkey. Lord Kinross. (Illus.). 640p. 1992. pap. 15.00 (*0-688-11283-8*, Quill) Morrow.

Ataud Para el Vivo y el Talamo Para el Muerto. Andres De Claramonte. (Textos Ser.: B37). 160p. (C). 1993. pap. text ed. 35.00 (*1-85566-019-9*, Pub. by Tamesis Bks Ltd UK) Boydell & Brewer.

Ataxia-Telangiectasia. Richard A. Gatti & Robert B. Painter. (NATO ASI Series H: Cell Biology: Vol. 77). (Illus.). 283p. 1993. write for info. (*3-540-56792-5*) Spr-Verlag.

Ataxia Telangiectasia: A Cellular & Molecular Link Between Cancer, Neuropathology & Immune Deficiency. Ed. by B. A. Bridges & D. G. Harnden. LC 81-13146. (Wiley-Medical Publication Ser.). (Illus.). 422p. reprint ed. pap. 120.30 (*0-8357-6031-6*, 2034215) Bks Demand.

Ataxia-Telangiectsia. Ed. by Richard A. Gatti & Robert B. Painter. LC 93-20625. (NATO ASI Series H: Cell Biology: Vol. 77). 1993. 129.00 (*0-387-56792-5*) Spr-Verlag.

A.T.C. Communications for V.F.R. Pilots Cassette Cross Country Flight with Written Transcript. 1994. 15.00 (*0-941456-17-X*) Aviation Lang Sch.

***ATCC Cell Lines & Hybridomas.** 8th ed. Ed. by Robert Hay et al. 632p. 1994. pap. text ed. write for info. (*0-930009-54-1*) ATCC.

***ATCC Guide to Packaging & Shipping of Biological Materials.** rev. ed. Ed. by E. M. Brown & R. P. Simione. (Illus.). 32p. 1994. pap. text ed. write for info. (*0-930009-55-X*) ATCC.

ATCC Yeasts. 19th ed. Ed. by S. C. Jong & M. J. Edwards. 230p. 1995. pap. text ed. write for info. (*0-930009-33-9*) ATCC.

Atchafalaya. C. C. Lockwood. 1984. 35.00 (*0-87511-695-7*) Claitors.

Atchison, Topeka & Santa Fe. Pamela Berkman. (Railroad Histories Ser.). (Illus.). 128p. 1988. 12.98 (*0-517-63350-7*, Crescent) Random Hse Value.

Atchison, Topeka & Santa Fe Railway. Ed. by Richard E. Cox. (Illus.). 40p. (Orig.). 1984. pap. 5.97 (*0-912935-00-6*) Vanishing Vistas.

ATCP - TAPPI Wastewater Treatment Seminar, 1992: Torremar Hotel, Veracruz, Mexico, November 12-13. Technical Association of the Pulp & Paper Industry Staff. (TAPPI Notes Ser.). reprint ed. pap. 40.00 (*0-7837-4484-6*, 2044260) Bks Demand.

Atelier Contemporain. Francis Ponge. 361p. (FRE.). 1977. pap. 59.95 (*0-7859-1595-8*, 207029630X) Fr & Eur.

Atelier d'Alberto Giacometti. Jean Genet. (FRE.). pap. 19.95 (*0-8288-9772-7*, F101960) Fr & Eur.

***Atelier Gerhard Richter: Photographs by Benjamin Katz.** Henning Widmann & Benjamin Katz. (Illus.). 108p. 1995. pap. 25.00 (*3-89322-607-9*) Dist Art Pubs.

Atencingo: The Politics of Agrarian Struggle in a Mexican Ejido. David Ronfeldt. LC 74-190528. xii, 284p. 1973. 37.50 (*0-8047-0820-7*) Stanford U Pr.

Ateneo Cientifico, Literario y Artistico de Madrid (1835-1885) Antonio R. Salvador. (Serie A: Monagrafias, XXV). 186p. (Orig.). (SPA.). (C). 1971. pap. 36.00 (*0-900411-29-5*, Pub. by Tamesis Bks Ltd UK) Boydell & Brewer.

Aterrizaje en la Luna. Herge. (Illus.). 62p. (SPA.). (J). 19.95 (*0-8288-5010-0*) Fr & Eur.

ATF Firearms Inspections: Use of Results to Improve Inspection Targeting Has Been Limited. 70p. (Orig.). (C). 1993. pap. text ed. 40.00 (*1-56806-904-9*) Diane Pub.

Atget Paris. Laure Beaumont-Maillet. Tr. by David Britt. (Illus.). 788p. (Orig.). (C). 1993. pap. 55.00 (*3-927258-07-5*) Gingko Press.

Atget's Seven Albums. Molly Nesbit. (Illus.). 440p. (C). 1994. text ed. 60.00 (*0-300-03580-2*) Yale U Pr.

Atget's Seven Albums. Molly Nesbit. (Illus.). 440p. (C). 1994. pap. 30.00 (*0-300-05916-7*) Yale U Pr.

ATH: Its Use & Meaning: A Study in the Greek Poetic Tradition from Homer to Euripides. Richard E. Doyle. LC 83-80059. 200p. reprint ed. pap. 57.00 (*0-7837-5596-1*, 2045502) Bks Demand.

Athabasca. Alistair MacLean. 288p. 1982. mass mkt. 4.95 (*0-449-20001-9*, Crest) Fawcett.

Athabaskan, Eyak & Tlingit Sonorants. Michael E. Krauss. (Alaska Native Language Center Research Papers Ser.: No. 5). 210p. 1981. pap. text ed. 12.00 (*0-933769-35-0*) Alaska Native.

Athabaskans: People of the Boreal Forest. Yvonne Yarber & Carol E. Choy. Ed. by Terry P. Dickey & Mary B. Smetzer. 39p. (Orig.). (J). (gr. 7-12). 1983. teacher ed 4.00 (*0-931163-10-2*); pap. 9.95 (*0-931163-09-9*) U Alaska Museum.

Athalie. Jean B. Racine. (Illus.). 128p. (FRE.). 1985. pap. 10.95 (*0-7859-1587-7*, 204016071X) Fr & Eur.

Athanasian Christology. Kannengiess. Date not set. 19.95 (*0-06-064238-6*, HarpT) HarpC.

***Athanasiana: Zu Leben und Lehre des Athanasius.** Martin Tetz. (Beihefte Zur Zeitschrift Fuer die Neutestamentliche Wissenschaft Ser.: No. 78). viii, 314p. (GER.). 1995. lib. bdg. 113.85 (*3-11-014611-8*) De Gruyter.

Athanasius: The Life of Antony & the Letter to Marcellinus. Ed. by Robert C. Gregg. LC 79-56622. (Classics of Western Spirituality Ser.). 192p. 1980. 15.95 (*0-8091-0309-5*); pap. 14.95 (*0-8091-2295-2*) Paulist Pr.

Athanasius & Constantius: Theology & Politics in the Constantinian Empire. Timothy D. Barnes. LC 92-33050. 363p. (C). 1993. text ed. 49.95 (*0-674-05067-3*) HUP.

***Athanasius & the Politics of Asceticism.** David Brakke. (Oxford Early Christian Studies). 384p. 1995. 55.00 (*0-19-826816-5*) OUP.

Athanasius: De Incarnatione Verbi: Einleitung, Ubersetzung, Kommentar. E. P. Meijering. 431p. (Orig.). (GER.). (C). 1989. pap. 83.00 (*90-5063-023-5*, Pub. by Gieben NE) Benjamins North Am.

Athapaskan Linguistics: Current Perspectives on a Language Family. Ed. by Eung D. Cook & Keren Rice. (Trends in Linguistics, State-of-the-Art Reports). viii, 645p. (C). 1989. lib. bdg. 176.95 (*0-89925-282-6*) Mouton.

Athar-Veda (Summary) 5.00 (*0-938924-32-X*) Sri Shirdi Sai.

Atharva Veda. Bibek Debroy. (Great Epics of India Ser.: Veda 4). (C). 1992. pap. 3.00 (*0-8364-2774-2*, Pub. by BR Pub II) S Asia.

Atharvaveda, Vol. 1. Tr. by Acharya V. Shastri. xii, 827p. 1984. 15.00 (*0-685-72926-5*, Pub. by Sarvadeshik Arya II) Nataraj Bks.

Atharvaveda, Vol. 2. Tr. by Acharya V. Shastri. xii, 736p. 1984. 15.00 (*0-685-72927-3*, Pub. by Sarvadeshik Arya II) Nataraj Bks.

Atharvaveda: Sanskrit Text with English Translation. Tr. by Devi Chand. (C). 1982. 44.00 (*0-8364-2418-2*, Pub. by Munshiram Manoharial II) S Asia.

Atheism: A Philosophical Justification. Michael Martin. 1992. pap. 24.95 (*0-87722-943-0*) Temple U Pr.

Atheism: Collected Essays, 1943-1949. Bertrand Russell. LC 71-169217. (Atheist Viewpoint Ser.). 232p. 1976. reprint ed. 22.95 (*0-405-03808-9*) Ayer.

Atheism: The Case Against God. George H. Smith. LC 79-2726. (Skeptic's Bookshelf Ser.). 355p. (C). 1979. pap. 18.95 (*0-87975-124-X*) Prometheus Bks.

Atheism & Liberation. Antonio Perez Esclarin. Tr. by John Drury. LC 78-731. 208p. reprint ed. pap. 59.30 (*0-8357-4074-9*, 2036764) Bks Demand.

Atheism & Other Addresses. Joseph Lewis. LC 72-161333. (Atheist Viewpoint Ser.). (Illus.). 510p. 1972. reprint ed. 35.95 (*0-405-03800-3*) Ayer.

Atheism & Theism. Errol E. Harris. LC 92-32787. 176p. (C). 1993. reprint ed. pap. 15.00 (*0-391-03799-4*) Humanities.

Atheism, Ayn Rand, & Other Heresies. George H. Smith. 324p. (C). 1991. 24.95 (*0-87975-577-6*) Prometheus Bks.

An Asterisk (*) at the beginning of an entry indicates that the title is appearing in BIP for the first time.

An Asterisk (*) at the beginning of an entry indicates that the title is appearing in BIP for the first time.

Atherosclerosis Reviews, Vol. 9. Ed. by Antonio M. Gotto, Jr. & Rodolfo Paoletti. 174p. 1982. text ed. 58.00 (0-89004-751-0) Raven.

Atherosclerosis Reviews, Vol. 11. Ed. by Antonio M. Gotto, Jr. & Rodolfo Paoletti. 264p. 1983. text ed. 104.50 (0-89004-910-6) Raven.

*__Atherosclerosis Reviews Vol. 3.__ Atherosclerosis Reviews Staff. Ed. by Rodolfo Paoletti & Antonio M. Gotto, Jr. LC 76-640124. (Illus.). 279p. Date not set. pap. 79.60 (0-7837-7174-6, 2047125) Bks Demand.

*__Atherosclerosis Reviews Vol. 4.__ fac. ed. Atherosclerosis Reviews Staff. Ed. by Rudolfo Paoletti & Antonio M. Gotto, Jr. LC 76-640124. (Illus.). 277p. Date not set. pap. 79.00 (0-7837-7173-8, 2047125) Bks Demand.

Atherosclerosis Reviews, Vol. 14: 1987. Atherosclerosis Reviews Staff. LC 76-640124. 233p. reprint ed. pap. 66.50 (0-7837-7118-5, 2046947) Bks Demand.

*__Atherosclerosis X: Proceedings of the 10th International Symposium on Atherosclerosis, Montreal, October 9-14, 1994.__ Ed. by J. Davignon et al. LC 95-12158. (International Congress Ser.: No. 1066). 1995. write for info. (0-444-82007-8, Excerpta Medica) Elsevier.

*__Atherosclerosis III: Recent Advances in Atherosclerosis Research.__ Saratoga International Conference on Atherosclerosis Staff. Ed. by Fujio Numano & Robert W. Wissler. LC 94-46619. (Annals Ser.: Vol. 748). 1995. write for info. (0-89766-811-1); pap. write for info. (0-89766-812-X) NY Acad Sci.

Atherosclerosis V: Proceedings of the Fifth International Symposium. Ed. by Antonio M. Gotto, Jr. et al. (Illus.). 848p. 1980. 136.00 (0-387-90473-5) Spr-Verlag.

Atherosclerosis VI: Proceedings. Ed. by F. G. Schettler et al. (Illus.). 982p. 1982. 81.50 (0-387-11450-5) Spr-Verlag.

Atherosclerosis VII. Ed. by N. H. Fidge & P. J. Nestel. 720p. 1987. 176.00 (0-444-80815-9, Excerpta Medica) Elsevier.

Atherosclerosis VIII: Proceedings of the 8th International Symposium on Atherosclerosis, Rome, Italy, 9-13, Oct., 1988. Ed. by G. Crepaldi et al. (International Congress Ser.: No. 817). 868p. 1989. 188.75 (0-444-81078-1, Excerpta Medica) Elsevier.

Atherosclerotic Cardiovascular Disease, Hemostasis, & Endothelial Function. Ed. by Robert B. Francis, Jr. LC 92-23024. (Fundamental & Clinical Cardiology Ser.: Vol. 8). 376p. 1992. 150.00 (0-8247-8726-9) Dekker.

Atherosclerotic Plaques: Advances in Imaging for Sequential Quantitative Evaluation. Ed. by R. W. Wissler et al. (NATO ASI Series A, Life Sciences: Vol. 219). (Illus.). 304p. 1992. 89.50 (0-306-44083-0, Plenum Pr) Plenum.

Athgreany Stone Circle - The Stones of Time. Helen O'Cleary. (Illus.). 203p. (Orig.). 1991. pap. 38.00 (0-9626761-0-1) Al H Morrison.

Athiest Trap. Joseph R. Mixie. 56p. (C). 1994. pap. text ed. 12.75 (0-8191-9548-0) U Pr of Amer.

Athlete. James Humphrey. 80p. (Orig.). 1988. pap. 10.00 (0-936641-16-9) Poets Alive Pr.

Athlete: A Computerized Accounting Practice Set for Use with BPI Systems General Accounting Program. Thomas F. George. Ed. by Mary E. George. (Illus.). 111p. (Orig.). (C). 1988. teacher ed 12.95 (0-929683-06-4); pap. text ed. 22.95 (0-929683-00-5) Servs by George.

Athlete II: A Computerized Accounting Practice Set for Use with BPI Systems General Accounting Program. Thomas F. George. Ed. by Mary E. George. (Illus.). 186p. (Orig.). (C). 1989. pap. text ed. 25.95 (0-929683-03-X) Servs by George.

Athlete III: A Computerized Accounting Practice Set for Use with BPI (Other) General Accounting System Programs. Thomas F. George. Ed. by Mary E. George. (Illus.). 150p. (Orig.). (C). 1989. pap. text ed. 25.95 (0-929683-10-2) Servs by George.

Athlete Within: A Personal Guide to Total Fitness. Harvey Simon. 1987. 19.95 (0-316-52250-3) Little.

Athletes. Nathan Aaseng. LC 94-12469. (American Indian Lives Ser.). (J). 1995. write for info. (0-8160-3019-7) Facts on File.

Athletes. Kyle Carter. LC 94-12386. (Performers Discovery Library). (J). 1994. write for info. (1-57103-061-1) Rourke Pr.

Athletes: Photographs, 1860-1986. Ed. by Ruth Silverman. LC 87-45203. 176p. 1987. 35.00 (0-394-55104-4) Knopf.

*__Athletes: Professional Athlete's Image Study.__ 150p. (Orig.). 1995. pap. 495.00 (0-7605-1997-8) Rector Pr.

Athletes Afire. Rick Arndt. LC 85-71182. 161p. 1985. pap. 3.95 (0-88270-590-3) Bridge Pub.

Athletes & Artists. Agnes Rossi. (Creative Writers Ser.). 92p. 1987. 27.50x (0-8147-7400-8) NYU Pr.

Athletes & Artists: Stories. Agnes Rossi. 72p. 1987. pap. 6.95 (0-89255-115-1) Persea Bks.

Athletes & Athletics: Sports Almanac-U. S. A. G. Keith Dolan. 383p. 1984. text ed. 14.95 (0-9613548-0-1) Footprint Pub.

Athletes & Drugs: A No-Win Combination. Community Intervention, Inc. Staff. 36p. (Orig.). 1986. pap. 3.95 (0-9613416-2-9) Comm Intervention.

Athletes & Oracles: The Transformation of Olympia & Delphi in the Eighth Century B. C. Catherine Morgan. (Illus.). 270p. (C). 1990. 54.95 (0-521-37451-0) Cambridge U Pr.

Athletes & the American Hero Dilemma. Janet C. Harris. LC 93-29253. (HK Sport Science Monograph Ser.: Vol. 4). (Illus.). 168p. 1994. 26.00x (0-87322-537-6, BHAR0537) Human Kinetics.

Athletes Away. Harrington E. Crissey, Jr. (Illus.). 75p. (Orig.). 1984. pap. 8.95 (0-9608878-3-0) H E Crissey.

Athlete's Body. Ken Sprague. 1980. 6.95 (0-685-02281-1) HM.

*__Athlete's Cookbook.__ U. S. A. Gymnastics Staff. Ed. by Michelle Dusserre. (Illus.). 224p. (Orig.). 1995. pap. 14.95 (1-57028-052-5) Masters Pr IN.

Athlete's Guide to Agents. Robert H. Ruxin. 208p. 1993. pap. text ed. 14.95 (0-86720-779-5) Jones & Bartlett.

Athletes' Guide to Mental Training. Robert M. Nideffer. LC 85-4305. 164p. (C). 1985. pap. text ed. 14.95 (0-931250-96-X, BNID0096) Human Kinetics.

Athlete's Guide to Sports Psychology: Mental Skills for Physical People. Dorothy V. Harris & Bette L. Harris. LC 83-80735. 200p. (Orig.). 1984. pap. 18.00 (0-88011-206-9, PHAR0206) Human Kinetics.

Athlete's Health Care Book: From the Hip Down. Myles J. Schneider & Mark D. Sussman. (Illus.). 160p. 1986. pap. 7.95 (0-87491-809-X) Acropolis.

Athlete's Shoulder. Ed. by Andrews & Kevin E. Wilk. (Illus.). 600p. 1993. text ed. 125.00 (0-443-08847-0) Churchill.

Athletes Tell Their Unforgettable Moments in Sport. Robert M. Sterling & Mark Looy. LC 84-47521. (Illus.). 200p. (Orig.). 1986. pap. 11.95 (0-88011-234-4, PSTE0234) Human Kinetics.

*__Athlete's Topical Bible.__ Gordon Thiessen. 168p. (Orig.). (YA). (gr. 6 up). 1993. pap. 8.95 (1-887002-06-5) Cross Trng.

*__Athletic & Recreational Facilities, Vol. 4.__ (Illus.). 224p. 1995. 75.00 (4-87246-317-X, Pub. by Meisei Co Ltd JA) Bks Nippan.

Athletic Connection: Guidebook. Damon J. Sprock. LC 83-83000. (Illus.). 160p. (Orig.). 1984. pap. 5.95 (0-915981-00-9) Jupiter Prods.

Athletic Development of the Dressage Horse: Manege Patterns. Charles De Kunffy. (Illus.). 224p. 1992. 28.00 (0-87605-896-9) Howell Bk.

*__Athletic Drug Reference '95.__ Ed. by Robert J. Fuentes et al. 1995. 9.95 (1-881011-04-6) Clean Data.

Athletic Female. American Orthopaedic Society for Sports Medicine Staff. Ed. by Arthur J. Pearl. LC 92-27038. (Illus.). 328p. 1993. text ed. 42.00x (0-87322-410-8, BPEA0410) Human Kinetics.

*__Athletic Footwear Market, 4 Vols., Set.__ 1000p. (Orig.). 1995. pap. 795.00 (0-7605-2059-3) Rector Pr.

Athletic Horse: Principles & Practice of Equine Sports Medicine. David R. Hodgson & Reuben J. Rose. LC 94-7652. (Illus.). 512p. 1994. text ed. 89.50 (0-7216-3759-0) Saunders.

Athletic Hunter: Sports Medicine for Outdoorsman. Jeffry A. Metheny. (Illus.). 128p. (Orig.). 1992. pap. text ed. 12.95 (0-9634193-0-7) Double Guage.

Athletic Injuries: Guidebook for Medicine & Research. Harold J. Martini. LC 87-47678. 150p. 1987. 39.50 (0-88164-660-1); pap. 34.50 (0-88164-661-X) ABBE Pubs Assn.

Athletic Injuries of the Foot & Ankle. Anunziato Amendola. 432p. 1995. text ed. 70.00 (0-07-001219-9) Hlth Prof Div.

Athletic Injuries of the Shoulder. Frank A. Pettrone. 402p. 1994. text ed. 85.00 (0-07-049742-7) Hlth Prof Div.

Athletic Injuries to the Head, Neck & Face. Torg. 704p. 1991. 75.00 (0-8151-8846-3, Yr Bk Med Pubs) Mosby Yr Bk.

Athletic Injury Assessment. 2nd ed. Booher & Thibodeau. (Illus.). 688p. (C). 1989. text ed. 44.95 (0-8016-2561-0) Mosby Yr Bk.

Athletic Injury Assessment. 3rd ed. Booher & Thibodeau. 704p. 1993. 44.95 (0-8016-7674-6) Mosby Yr Bk.

Athletic Injury Care: And Sports Conditioning. Gary Shankman. 1992. pap. 13.95 (0-9630564-0-9) Sports Hlth.

Athletic Massage. Rich Phaigh & Paul J. Perry. 176p. 1986. pap. 12.00 (0-671-60303-5, Fireside) S&S Trade.

*__Athletic Scholarships: A Complete Guide.__ Intro. by John Green & Kathleen M. Parker. 561p. (Orig.). 1994. pap. 20.95 (1-884669-05-0) Conway Greene.

Athletic Scholarships: Making Your Sports Pay. David Lahey. 200p. (YA). 1992. pap. 12.95 (1-895629-06-3, Pub. by Warwick Pub CN) Firefly Bks Ltd.

Athletic Scholarships: Thousands of Grants & Over 200 Million Dollars for College-Bound Athletes. 3rd ed. Andy Clark. LC 93-16812. Orig. Title: The Directory of Athletic Scholarships. 288p. 1993. reprint ed. 24.95 (0-8160-2892-3) Facts on File.

Athletic Scholarships: Thousands of Grants & Over 200 Million Dollars for College-Bound Athletes. Andy Clark. LC 93-16812. Orig. Title: The Directory of Athletic Scholarships. 288p. 1993. reprint ed. pap. write for info. (0-8160-2893-1) Facts on File.

Athletic Shoe. Jeff MacNelly. 1991. pap. 6.95 (0-312-04873-4) St Martin.

Athletic Shorts. Chris Crutcher. LC 91-4418. (YA). (gr. 12 up). 1991. 14.00 (0-688-10816-4) Greenwillow.

Athletic Shorts: Six Short Stories. Chris Crutcher. 160p. (J). (gr. 7 up). 1992. pap. 3.99 (0-440-21390-8, LFL) Dell.

Athletic Shorts: Six Short Stories. large type ed. Chris Crutcher. LC 93-12. 202p. 1993. reprint ed. lib. bdg. 15.95 (1-56054-687-5) Thorndike Pr.

Athletic Skier. Warren Witherell & David Evrard. LC 93-30516. (Illus.). 288p. (Orig.). 1993. pap. 24.95 (1-55566-117-3) Johnson Bks.

*__Athletic Taping: Canadian Version.__ Sports Medicine Council of British Columbia Staff. (Illus.). 128p. (C). 1995. pap. text ed. 20.00 (0-8036-0116-6) Davis Co.

*__Athletic Taping & Bracing.__ Donald R. Hellison. LC 95-1522. (Illus.). 112p. 1995. pap. text ed. write for info. (0-87322-654-2, BHEL0654) Human Kinetics.

*__Athletic Taping & Bracing.__ David H. Perrin. LC 95-1519. (Illus.). 136p. 1995. text ed. write for info. (0-87322-502-3, BPER0502) Human Kinetics.

Athletic Training: A Study & Laboratory. Arnheim. Date not set. write for info. (0-8016-0331-5) Mosby Yr Bk.

Athletic Training: Principles & Practice. Thomas Fahey. 1986. teacher ed, text ed. write for info. (0-87484-804-0) Mayfield Pub.

Athletic Training: Principles & Practice. Thomas Fahey. 564p. (C). 1986. text ed. 48.95 (0-87484-582-3); trans. write for info. (0-318-60140-0) Mayfield Pub.

Athletic Training & Conditioning. rev. ed. O. William Dayton. 397p. reprint ed. pap. 113.20 (0-8357-5831-1, 2055670) Bks Demand.

Athletic Training & Sports Medicine. 2nd ed. Ed. by Letha Y. Hunter-Griffin. LC 91-70295. 1027p. 1991. 49.00 (0-89203-044-5) Amer Acad Ortho Surg.

Athletic Training & Sports Medicine Instructor Manual. Ed. by Letha Y. Hunter-Griffin. 515p. 1992. 19.95 (0-89203-067-4) Amer Acad Ortho Surg.

Athletics. (Illus.). 22p. (J). (gr. 6-12). 1964. pap. 1.85 (0-8395-3324-1, 33324) BSA.

Athletics. P. Woods. 1989. pap. 6.95 (0-7460-0247-5, Usborne) EDC.

Athletics & Academe: An Anatomy of Abuses & a Prescription for Reform. Wilford S. Bailey & Taylor D. Littleton. (ACE-Oryx Series on Higher Education). 160p. 1991. 27.95 (0-02-897028-4, ACE-Oryx) Oryx Pr.

Athletics & Mathematics in Archaic Corinth: An Early Design of the Greek Stadion. David G. Romano. LC 92-75705. (Memoirs Ser.: Vol. 206). (Illus.). 117p. (C). 1993. 25.00 (0-87169-206-6, M206-ROD) Am Philos.

Athletics Congress's Track & Field Coaching Manual. 2nd ed. Ed. by Vern Gambetta. LC 88-32160. (Illus.). 240p. 1989. pap. 21.00x (0-88011-332-4, PTAC0332) Human Kinetics.

Athletics, Growth, & Development in Children: The University of Western Australia Study. Brian A. Blanksby et al. LC 93-47059. 1994. text ed. 45.00 (3-7186-0578-3) Gordon & Breach.

Athletics in Ancient Athens. 2nd rev. ed. Donald G. Kyle. LC 92-42730. (Mnemosyne, Bibliotheca Classica Batava Ser.: No. 95). (Illus.). xiv, 240p. 1993. 74.50 (90-04-09759-7) E J Brill.

Athletics in Children & Adolescents. Ed. by Elizabeth Coryllos et al. (Illus.). 450p. Date not set. 65.00 (0-8121-1305-5) Williams & Wilkins.

Athletics in the Classroom: Fun Teaching, Fun Learning. Walt Trask. 96p. 1992. pap. 9.95 (0-9633975-3-2) Derivative.

Athletics of the Ancient World. E. Norman Gardiner. (Illus.). 232p. 1980. pap. 20.00 (0-89005-257-3) Ares.

*__Athletics of Voice: A Handbook for Teachers & Students of Singing.__ Brad Newsom. Ed. by Shirley Windward. (Illus.). 108p. (C). 1995. pap. text ed. 15.00 (0-9644358-0-2) NewWind.

Athlit Ram. Ed. by Lionel Casson et al. LC 90-10804. (Nautical Archaeology Ser.: No. 3). (Illus.). 112p. 1991. 72.50 (0-89096-451-3) Tex A&M Univ Pr.

Athol Fugard. Dennis Walder. Ed. by Bruce King & Adele King. (Modern Dramatists Ser.). 152p. 1990. pap. 11.95 (0-333-30904-9) St Martin.

Athos: The Holy Mountain. Philip Sherrard. LC 84-16571. (Illus.). 176p. 1985. 35.00 (0-87951-988-6) Overlook Pr.

*__Athos Sixty.__ Gareth Morgan. 144p. 1994. pap. 10.95 (1-57087-069-1) Prof Pr NC.

Athyra. Steven Brust. 256p. (Orig.). 1993. mass mkt. 4.99 (0-441-03342-3) Ace Bks.

Atid Bibliography. pap. 5.00 (0-686-96097-1) United Syn Bk.

Atitlan: An Archaeological Study of Ancient Remains on the Borders of Lake Atitlan, Guatemala. Samuel K. Lothrop. LC 77-11509. (Carnegie Institution of Washington. Publications: No. 444). reprint ed. 22.00 (0-404-16268-1) AMS Pr.

Atiyah-Patodi-Singer Index Theorem. Richard Melrose. LC 93-1405. (Research Notes in Mathematics Ser.). 392p. (C). 1993. text ed. 59.95 (1-56881-002-4) AK Peters.

Atiyah's Accidents, Compensation & the Law. Peter Cane. (Law in Context Ser.). xxiii, 639p. 1987. 75.00 (0-297-79052-8) Rothman.

*__Atiyah's Accidents, Compensation, & the Law.__ 5th ed. Hugh Collins. (Law in Context Ser.). 428p. (C). 1994. pap. text ed. 43.95 (0-406-03146-0, Trans) Northwestern U Pr.

ATK Dataprocessing Dictionary, Finnish, English, French, Russian, Swedish, German: ATK Sanakirja Suomi-Englanti-Franska-Ruotsi-Saksa-Venaja. ATK Staff. 233p. (ENG, FIN, FRE, GER, RUS & SWE.). 1986. 125.00 (0-8288-0262-9, F23900) Fr & Eur.

Atka, an Ethnohistory of the Western Aleutians. Lydia T. Black. (Alaska History Ser.: No. 24). (Illus.). 219p. 1984. 28.50 (0-919642-99-3) Limestone Pr.

Atkins - Knopfler: Neck & Neck. Ed. by David C. Olsen. 132p. 1991. pap. text ed. 16.95 (0-89898-635-4) CPP Belwin.

Atkin's Encyclopaedia of Court Forms in Civil Proceedings, 43 vols. 2nd ed. Ed. by Jack I. Jacob et al. 3,200.00 (0-406-01020-X, U.K.) Butterworth Legal Pubs.

Atkins, Joseph Atkins: The Story of a Family. F. H. Atkins. 158p. 1992. reprint ed. lib. bdg. 35.00 (0-8328-2621-9); reprint ed. pap. 25.00 (0-8328-2622-7) Higginson Bk Co.

Atkins Solution Manual for Physical Chemistry. 4th ed. Peter W. Atkins. 510p. 1990. 17.95 (0-685-47291-4) W H Freeman.

Atkinson Heritage. large type ed. Mollie Hardwick. 455p. 1981. 12.00 (0-7089-0670-2) Ulverscroft.

*__Atkinson Reproduced in Color.__ (Illus.). 112p. 1995. pap. 34.95 (0-944094-04-X) ST Pubns.

Atkinson Sign Painting. (Illus.). 256p. 1983. reprint ed. 25.00 (0-911380-62-0) ST Pubns.

Atkinson's Correlative Atlas of Colposcopy, Cytology, & Histopathology. Robert L. Giuntoli et al. LC 65-7511. (Illus.). 288p. 1987. text ed. 147.00 (0-397-50589-2, Lippincott Medical) Lippincott.

Atkisson Ancestry of West Tennessee: Featuring Grandmother Annie, Her Family & Her Poetry. Suzanne L. Stanfill. 128p. 1994. per., pap. text ed. 12.00 (1-880799-01-4) Heirloom CA.

ATKOL Comprehensive Guide to Adult Male Video. ATKOL Staff. Ed. by Jeff Satkin. LC 90-83641. 184p. 1990. pap. text ed. write for info. (1-878176-00-5) ATKOL.

ATL-Sanasto Suomi-Englanti-Suomi. ATL Staff. 171p. (ENG & FIN.). 1985. 75.00 (0-8288-0261-0, F24011) Fr & Eur.

ATLA Index: 1951-1992. 2nd ed. Ed. by ATLA Press Staff. 300p. 1993. pap. 52.00 (0-941916-67-7) ATLA Pr.

ATLA Trial Notebook. 2nd ed. Tom Vesper. ring bd. 69.00 (0-941916-66-9) ATLA Pr.

Atlaidai: Lithuanian Pilgrimages. Ed. by Algimantas Kezys. (Illus.). 190p. (ENG & LIT.). 1990. 19.95 (0-8294-0639-5) Loyola Univ Pr.

Atlanta. (Insight Guide Ser.). (Illus.). 360p. 1994. pap. 21.95 (0-395-71052-9) HM.

Atlanta. Jacob D. Cox. 1987. 20.00 (0-89029-089-X) Morningside Bkshop.

Atlanta. David K. Gleason. LC 94-14529. (Illus.). 168p. 1994. 39.95 (0-8071-1937-7) La State U Pr.

Atlanta. N. Loewen. (Great Cities of the U. S. A. Ser.). (Illus.). 48p. (J). (gr. 5 up). 1989. lib. bdg. 15.94 (0-86592-543-7); lib. bdg. 11.95 (0-685-58591-3) Rourke Corp.

*__Atlanta.__ Sara Orwig. 384p. (Orig.). 1995. mass mkt., pap. 4.99 (0-451-40343-6, Onyx) NAL-Dutton.

Atlanta. Pegeen Snow. LC 88-20243. (Downtown America Bks.). (Illus.). 60p. (J). (gr. 3 up). 1989. text ed. 13.95 (0-87518-389-1, Dillon Silver Burdett) Silver Burdett Pr.

Atlanta. Jacob D. Cox. (Illus.). 274p. 1989. reprint ed. 25.00 (0-916107-59-0) Broadfoot.

Atlanta: A Brave & Beautiful City. Peter Beney. (Illus.). 144p. 1994. 35.00 (1-56145-098-7); pap. 19.95 (1-56145-095-2) Peachtree Pubs.

Atlanta: A City of Neighborhoods. Photos by Joseph F. Thompson. LC 93-8089. (Illus.). 126p. 1993. 49.95 (0-87249-979-0) U of SC Pr.

Atlanta: A City of the Modern South. Federal Writers' Project Staff & Writers Program-WPA Staff. (American Guide Ser.). 1989. reprint ed. lib. bdg. 69.00 (0-7812-1050-X, 1050) Rprt Serv.

Atlanta: A City of the Modern South. Federal Writers' Project Staff. LC 72-84460. (American Guidebook Ser.). 1980. reprint ed. lib. bdg. 69.00 (0-403-02200-2) Somerset Pub.

*__Atlanta: A Vision for the New Millennium.__ Phyllis S. Fraley. (Illus.). 256p. 1995. 39.95 (1-56352-265-9) Longstreet Pr Inc.

Atlanta: City of Dreams, Vol. II. (Illus.). 102p. 1990. pap. 17.95 (1-56145-015-4) Peachtree Pubs.

Atlanta: Or the True Blessed Island of Poetry. Thomas Holley Chivers. (Works of Thomas Holley Chivers Ser.). 1990. reprint ed. lib. bdg. 79.00 (0-7812-2289-3) Rprt Serv.

Atlanta: Welcome! Rosanne Knorr. LC 93-81138. (Illus.). 128p. 1994. pap. 14.95 (1-56352-132-6) Longstreet Pr Inc.

Atlanta see Sherman's Battle for Atlanta

Atlanta & Environs: A Chronicle of Its People & Events, Vol. 2. Franklin M. Garrett. LC 54-14260. 1080p. 1969. 44.95 (0-8203-0264-3) U of Ga Pr.

Atlanta & Environs: A Chronicle of Its People & Events, Vol. 2: 1880s-1930s. Franklin M. Garrett. LC 54-14260. 1080p. 1969. 44.95 (0-8203-0263-5) U of Ga Pr.

Atlanta & Environs: A Chronicle of Its People & Events, Vol. 3: Years of Change & Challenge, 1940s-1970s. Harold H. Martin. LC 86-16158. (Illus.). 632p. 1987. 39.95 (0-8203-0913-3) U of Ga Pr.

Atlanta & Its Lawyers: A Century of Vision: 1888-1988. Lea Agnew & Jo A. Haden-Miller. (Illus.). 200p. 1988. 29.95 (0-9621443-0-4) Atlanta Bar.

*__Atlanta & the War.__ Webb Garrison. 400p. 1995. 19.95 (1-55853-339-7) Rutledge Hill Pr.

Atlanta Architecture Vol. I: Art Deco to Modern Classic, 1929-1959. Robert M. Craig. LC 94-2732. 160p. 1995. 29.95 (0-88289-961-9) Pelican.

Atlanta Area Jobhunter's Companion. Fred Bonner. 80p. (Orig.). 1984. pap. 2.95 (0-9613020-0-3) Jobhunter's Comp.

Atlanta Area School Directory: Your Complete Guide to Greater Atlanta Area Public & Private Education. 3rd ed. Oskar Rogg. 240p. 1994. pap. text ed. 9.95 (0-9631939-5-3) Care Solutions.

Atlanta at Home. Frances Schultz. (Illus.). 160p. 1994. 39.95 (0-941711-23-4) Wyrick & Co.

Atlanta Braves. Michael Goodman. (Baseball: The Great American Game Ser.). 48p. (J). (gr. 4-10). 1992. lib. bdg. 14.95 (0-88682-460-5) Creative Ed.

Atlanta Braves Album & Autograph Book. Stan Hosler. 72p. (Orig.). 1992. pap. 7.95 (0-9628530-5-4) Bookmark GA.

Atlanta Campaign: A Civil War Driving Tour of Atlanta-Area Battlefields with a Reader's Guide to the Atlanta Campaign. J. Britt McCarley et al. Ed. by Bradley R. Rice & Jane P. Weldon. LC 88-18941. (Illus.). 112p. (Orig.). 1989. reprint ed. pap. 9.95 (0-87797-160-9) Cherokee.

Atlanta Campaign: May-November 1864. John Cannan. (Great Campaigns Ser.). (Illus.). 176p. 1991. 24.95 (0-938289-05-5) Combined Bks.

Atlanta Century. Norman Shavin. (Illus.). 272p. 1986. 36.95 (0-910719-03-9) Capricorn Corp.

Atlanta Chefs Book. William Struns. Ed. by R. McMinn. 120p. (Orig.). 1989. pap. text ed. 6.95 (0-935201-90-4) Affordable Adven.

An Asterisk (*) at the beginning of an entry indicates that the title is appearing in BIP for the first time.

Atlanta Color Tour Book. Bonechi. (Illus.). 72p. (Orig.). (C). 1989. pap. text ed. 7.95 (*0-936672-78-1*) Aerial Photo.

Atlanta Diary 1994. 200p. Date not set. 15.00 (*0-914975-43-9*) Per Annum.

Atlanta Diary 1994. deluxe ed. 200p. Date not set. 30.00 (*0-914975-42-0*) Per Annum.

Atlanta Diary 1995. 180p. Date not set. 15.00 (*0-914975-60-9*) Per Annum.

Atlanta Diary 1995. deluxe ed. 180p. Date not set. 30.00 (*0-914975-59-5*) Per Annum.

***Atlanta Distributers, Inc. Version C & D: General Accounting Application.** Elliott L. Slocum & Pamela J. Duke. LC 94-3699. 1994. write for info. (*0-88406-277-5*) GA St U Busn Pr.

Atlanta Distributors, Inc. Time-Sharing Financial Accounting Modules. Elliott L. Slocum, Jr. et al. LC 79-10926. (Research Monograph: No. 81). 235p. (C). 1979. spiral bd. 25.00 (*0-88406-120-5*) GA St U Busn Pr.

Atlanta Distributors, Inc. General Accounting Application. Elliot L. Slocum & Pamela J. Duke. 225p. 1992. pap. 35.00 (*0-88406-251-1*, RM105) GA St U Busn Pr.

Atlanta Eldercare Sourcebook: A Resource Guide for Older Adults, Caregivers & Eldercare Professionals. 2nd ed. Carla S. Rogg & Oskar H. Rogg. 1993. pap. 19.95 (*0-9631939-2-9*) Care Solutions.

Atlanta Epicure. Anne Byrn. Ed. by Gretchen Weidenbach. (American Epicure Ser.). 160p. 1986. pap. 7.95 (*0-89716-156-4*) P B Pubng.

Atlanta Exposition Cookbook. Comp. by Henry L. Wilson. LC 83-24252. (Brown Thrasher Bks.). 166p. 1984. reprint ed. 14.95 (*0-8203-0708-4*) U of Ga Pr.

Atlanta Falcons. Richard Rambeck. (NFL Today Ser.). (Illus.). 48p. (J). (gr. 4 up). 1991. lib. bdg. 14.95 (*0-88682-359-5*) Creative Ed.

***Atlanta Georgia.** 6th ed. Frommer Staff. 1995. pap. 5.95 (*0-671-89158-8*) Macmillan.

Atlanta Hawks. rev. ed. Richard Rambeck. (NBA Today Ser.). (Illus.). 32p. (J). (gr. 4 up). 1993. lib. bdg. 14.95 (*0-88682-560-1*) Creative Ed.

Atlanta in Eighteen Ninety: The Gate City. Atlanta Historical Society. LC 86-12463. (Illus.). xxx, 98p. 1986. 19.95 (*0-86554-241-4*, H-211) Mercer Univ Pr.

Atlanta in 88 Pictures: Self-Guided Tours in 88 Pictures. Lisa D. Hoff. (Cities in Color Pictorial Guidebooks Ser.). (Illus.). 80p. (Orig.). 1993. pap. 9.95 (*0-9617959-9-9*) Cities in Color.

***Atlanta JobBank, 1995.** 384p. 1994. 15.95 (*1-55850-447-8*) Adams Pubng.

Atlanta Jobs. Stephen E. Hines. 1991. pap. 13.95 (*0-929255-05-4*) CareerSource.

Atlanta Jobs: A Practical Guide for College Graduates. Stephen E. Hines & Phil Cunningham. 88p. (C). 1988. 4.95 (*0-685-19971-1*) CareerSource.

Atlanta Jobs: The Career Search Systems. Stephen E. Hines. (Illus.). 175p. (Orig.). 1988. pap. 10.95 (*0-929255-01-1*) CareerSource.

Atlanta Jobs, 1983. Stephen E. Hines. 1993. pap. 15.95 (*0-929255-10-0*) CareerSource.

Atlanta Jobs, 1990. Stephen E. Hines. (Career Search System Ser.). 215p. (Orig.). 1990. pap. 10.95 (*0-929255-02-X*) CareerSource.

Atlanta Jobs, 1992. Steve Hines. 304p. 1992. pap. 15.95 (*0-929255-08-9*) CareerSource.

Atlanta Jobs, 1994. Steve Hines. 254p. 1993. pap. 15.95 (*0-929255-13-5*) CareerSource.

***Atlanta Jobs, 1995.** Steve Hines. 400p. 1995. pap. 15.95 (*0-929255-15-1*) CareerSource.

Atlanta Life Insurance Company: Guardian of Black Economic Dignity. Alexa B. Henderson. LC 88-34000. (Illus.). 256p. 1990. 31.95 (*0-8173-0441-X*) U of Ala Pr.

Atlanta Municipal Court Operations Assessment. 31p. 1986. 2.00 (*0-685-18269-X*, SERO-024) Natl Ctr St Courts.

Atlanta Offering: Poems. Frances E. Harper. LC 70-79027. (Black Heritage Library Collection). 1977. 16.95 (*0-8369-8588-5*) Ayer.

Atlanta Picture Book. 40p. (J). (ps-12). 1986. pap. 3.50 (*0-936672-05-6*) Aerial Photo.

***Atlanta Restaurant Guide.** Christiane Lauterbach. 1995. pap. 9.95 (*1-56554-031-X*) Pelican.

Atlanta Restaurant Guide. 2nd ed. William Cutler & Christiane Lauterbach. LC 87-32802. 272p. 1988. pap. 7.95 (*0-88289-662-8*) Pelican.

Atlanta Run. David Robbins. (Endworld Ser.: No. 17). 192p. 1989. pap. 2.95 (*0-8439-2816-6*) Dorchester Pub Co.

Atlanta Run - Memphis Run, 2 vols. in 1. David Robbins. (Endworld Double Edition Ser.). 384p. 1992. pap. 4.50 (*0-8439-3299-6*) Dorchester Pub Co.

***Atlanta Small Business Capital Handbook.** Waleed Farah. 35p. 1995. pap. 9.95 (*1-881439-14-3*) Info S Pubns.

***Atlanta Small Business Handbook.** Waleed Farah. 176p. 1995. pap. 13.50 (*1-881439-12-7*) Info S Pubns.

Atlanta University Publications: Nos. 1, 2, 4, 8, 9, 11, & 13-18, Set. Atlanta University Staff. LC 68-28965. (American Negro: His History & Literature, Ser. No. 1). 1969. reprint ed. 32.95 (*0-405-01804-5*) Ayer.

Atlanta University Publications: Nos. 3, 5-7, 10, 12, 19 & 20, Set. Atlanta University Staff. LC 68-28985. (American Negro: His History & Literature, Ser. No. 3). 1970. reprint ed. 27.95 (*0-405-01914-9*) Ayer.

Atlanta Walks: A Guide to Walking, Running, & Bicycling Historic & Scenic Atlanta. Ren Davis & Helen Davis. (Illus.). 240p. 1993. pap. 9.95 (*1-56145-078-2*) Peachtree Pubs.

Atlanta, 1847-1890: City Building in the Old South & the New. James M. Russell. LC 87-29946. (Illus.). xiii, 314p. 1988. text ed. 40.00 (*0-8071-1413-8*) La State U Pr.

***Atlanta 1995.** Frommer Staff. 1995. pap. 12.95 (*0-02-860044-4*) Macmillan.

Atlanta's Best Bargains: The Quality Guide for Smart Shoppers. Trey Pope & Carter Griffin. LC 92-18853. 80p. (Orig.). 1992. pap. 8.95 (*0-87797-243-5*) Cherokee.

Atlanta's Business & Employment Guide. Silver Reede. (Illus.). 240p. (C). 1991. per. 29.95 (*0-944449-08-5*) Silver Reede Servs.

Atlanta's Children: Tragic Variations. (Orig.). 1981. pap. 2.00 (*0-9616146-1-7*) Small-Small Pr.

Atlanta's Top Decision Makers, Vol. 1. Jeanne R. Graves. (Illus.). 1991. pap. 79.95 (*0-9617375-4-9*) Res Comns Group.

Atlanta's Top Networking Channels, Vol. 2. Jeanne R. Graves. (Illus.). 1991. pap. 49.95 (*0-9617375-5-7*) Res Comns Group.

Atlanta's Urban Trails, Vol. 1: City Tours. Ren Davis. (Orig.). 1989. pap. 6.95 (*0-932419-19-4*) Susan Hunter.

Atlanta's Urban Trails, Vol. 2: Country Tours. Ren Davis & Helen Davis. Ed. by Phyllis Mueller. LC 88-8811. (Illus.). 136p. (Orig.). 1988. pap. 9.95 (*0-932419-20-8*) Cherokee.

Atlante Garzanti Biology Dictionary: Atlante Biologico Garzanti. 4th ed. G. Vogel & H. Angermann. 576p. (ITA.). 1982. pap. 24.95 (*0-8288-1223-3*, M14442) Fr & Eur.

Atlante Garzanti Dictionary of History, Universal Historical Chronology: Atlante Storico Garzanti, Cronologia della Storia Universale. 10th ed. Garzanti. 632p. (ITA.). 1982. 24.95 (*0-8288-1494-5*, M14437) Fr & Eur.

Atlante Garzanti Geography Encyclopedia: Atlante Enciclopedia Geografica Garzanti. Ed. by Garzanti. 1280p. (ITA.). 1982. pap. write for info. (*0-8288-1461-9*, M14445) Fr & Eur.

Atlantean Chronicles. Eichner. 1972. 9.50 (*0-686-02510-5*) Fantasy Pub Co.

Atlantean Document. Stephen L. Smoke. 1982. 19.95 (*0-88280-077-9*) ETC Pubns.

Atlantean Press Review, 1992. Ed. by Patricia LeChevalier. (Illus.). 230p. 1992. pap. 12.00 (*0-9626854-4-5*)

***Atlantic: District of Columbia, Virginia, West Virginia.** Thomas G. Aylesworth & Virginia L. Aylesworth. LC 94-40423. (State Studies). 1995. write for info. (*0-7910-3400-3*); pap. write for info. (*0-7910-3418-6*) Chelsea Hse.

Atlantic: Virginia, W. Virginia, District of Columbia. Thomas G. Aylesworth & Virginia L. Aylesworth. (State Reports). (Illus.). 64p. (J). (gr. 3 up). 1991. lib. bdg. 16.95 (*0-7910-1041-4*) Chelsea Hse.

Atlantic Alcidae: The Evolution, Distribution & Biology of the Auks Inhabiting the Atlantic Ocean & Adjacent Water Areas. Ed. by David N. Nettleship & Tim R. Birkhead. 1986. text ed. 108.00 (*0-12-515670-7*); pap. text ed. 39.95 (*0-12-515671-5*) Acad Pr.

Atlantic Alliance & Its Critics. Ed. by Robert W. Tucker & Linda Wrigley. LC 82-15072. 204p. 1983. text ed. 49.95 (*0-275-91094-6*, C1094, Praeger Pubs) Greenwood.

Atlantic Alliance & the Middle East. Ed. by Joseph I. Coffey & Gianni Bonvicini. LC 88-20605. (Policy & Institutional Studies). 328p. 1989. 49.95 (*0-8229-1154-X*) U of Pittsburgh Pr.

Atlantic Alliance & U. S. Global Strategy. Jacquelyn K. Davis & Robert L. Pfaltzgraff, Jr. LC 83-18642. (Special Report Ser.). 44p. 1983. pap. 11.95 (*0-89549-051-X*) Inst Foreign Policy Anal.

Atlantic Alliance, Nuclear Weapons, & European Attitudes: Reexamining the Conventional Wisdom. Wallace J. Thies. LC 83-82915. (Policy Papers in International Affairs Ser.: No. 19). (Illus.). vii, 59p. (C). 1983. pap. 4.50 (*0-87725-519-9*) U of Cal IAS.

Atlantic Alliance Transformed. David M. Abshire et al. (CSIS Significant Issues Ser.). (C). 1992. pap. text ed. 18.50 (*0-89206-204-5*) Westview.

Atlantic American Societies: From Columbus Through Abolition, 1492 to 1988. Ed. by Alan L. Karras & John McNeill. LC 92-11919. 208p. 1992. 49.95 (*0-415-08072-X*, A7829); pap. 15.95 (*0-415-08073-8*, A7833) Routledge.

Atlantic & Gulf Coasts. William H. Amos & Stephen H. Amos. LC 84-48676. (Audubon Society Nature Guides Ser.). (Illus.). 670p. 1985. pap. 19.00 (*0-394-73109-3*) Knopf.

Atlantic Anthology, Vol. 3: Critical Essays. Ed. by Terry Whalen. 308p. (C). 1985. pap. text ed. 5.00 (*0-920304-41-9*, Pub. by ECW Press CN) Genl Dist Srvs.

Atlantic Archipelago: A Political History of the British Isles. Richard S. Tompson. LC 74-19840. (Studies in British History: Vol. 1). 433p. 1986. lib. bdg. 109.95 (*0-88946-455-3*) E Mellen.

Atlantic Barrier Reef Ecosystem at Carrie Bow Cay, Belize, III-New Marine Isopods. Brian Kensley. LC 84-600999. (Smithsonian Contributions to the Marine Sciences Ser.: No. 24). 85p. reprint ed. pap. 25.00 (*0-8357-5832-X*, 2024355) Bks Demand.

Atlantic Barrier Reef Ecosystem at Carrie Bow Cay, Belize Vol. I: Structure & Communities. Ed. by Klaus Ruetzler & Ian G. Macintyre. LC 81-607039. (Smithsonian Contributions to the Marine Sciences Ser.). (Illus.). 554p. (C). 1982. 27.00 (*0-87474-850-X*) Smithsonian.

***Atlantic Bed & Breakfasts.** 192p. 1995. pap. 19.95 (*0-88780-330-X*) Formac Dist Ltd.

Atlantic Blue Riband: Evolution of the Express Liner. C. Mackenzie-Kennedy. 1993. 68.00 (*1-85072-133-5*, Pub. by W Sessions UK) St Mut.

Atlantic Canada & Confederation: Essays in Canadian Political Economy. David G. Alexander. 176p. 1983. 27.50 (*0-8020-2487-4*); pap. 10.95 (*0-8020-6512-0*) U of Toronto Pr.

***Atlantic Canada Handbook: New Brunswick, Nova Scotia, Newfoundland, Prince Edward Island & Labrador.** Mark Morris & Nan Drosdick. (Moon Travel Handbooks Ser.). (Illus.). 450p. (Orig.). 1995. pap. 17.95 (*1-56691-007-2*) Moon Pubns CA.

Atlantic Canadian Imprints, 1801-1820: A Bibliography. Patricia L. Fleming. 189p. 1991. 95.00 (*0-8020-5872-8*) U of Toronto Pr.

Atlantic Charter. David R. Facey-Crowther. Ed. by Douglas Brinkley. LC 93-36838. (Franklin & Eleanor Roosevelt Institute Series on Diplomatic & Economic History: Vol. 8). 1994. text ed. 39.95 (*0-312-08930-9*) St Martin.

Atlantic Charter. Cecil King. LC 72-4504. (Essay Index Reprint Ser.). 1977. reprint ed. 33.95 (*0-8369-2955-1*) Ayer.

Atlantic City: One Hundred Twenty-Five Years of Ocean Madness. Vicki G. Levi & Lee Eisenberg. LC 93-46513. 1994. 18.95 (*0-89815-613-0*) Ten Speed Pr.

Atlantic City Behind the Tables. John Alcamo. 256p. 1991. pap. 5.95 (*0-914839-22-5*) Gollehon Pr.

Atlantic City Diary, 1880-1985: A Century of Memories. Ed Davis. (Illus.). 172p. reprint ed. pap. 9.95 (*0-9622645-1-2*) Atlantic City News Pub.

Atlantic City Gamble: Twentieth-Century Fund Report. George Sternlieb & James W. Hughes. 227p. 1985. pap. 13.50x (*0-674-05126-2*) HUP.

Atlantic City Proof. large type ed. Christopher C. Gilmore. 402p. 1981. 12.00 (*0-7089-0683-4*) Ulverscroft.

Atlantic City, Vol. 1: The Transition: A Picture Story. John K. Schwarz. (Orig.). 1989. pap. 3.50 (*0-9623462-0-9*) J K Schwarz.

Atlantic Coast. Daniel Ammen. (Illus.). 273p. 1990. reprint ed. 25.00 (*0-916107-83-3*) Broadfoot.

Atlantic Coast Conference Football: A History Through 1991. Tom Perrin. LC 92-50315. 480p. 1992. lib. bdg. 43.50x (*0-89950-749-2*) McFarland & Co.

Atlantic Coast Conference 1953-1978: Silver Anniversary. Bruce A. Corrie. LC 78-67832. (Illus.). 246p. 1978. 12.95 (*0-89089-025-0*) Carolina Acad Pr.

Atlantic Coast Fishing Vessel Safety Manual. Kateleen Castro & Joseph DeAlteris. (Illus.). 320p. (Orig.). (C). 1991. pap. text ed. 25.00 (*1-882027-03-5*) URI ICMRD.

Atlantic Coast Line Motive Power. 256p. 1989. 45.00 (*0-9618503-4-5*) Withers Pub.

Atlantic Connection: Prospects, Problems & Policies. Philip H. Trezise. LC 75-19321. 110p. reprint ed. pap. 31.40 (*0-8357-5833-8*, 2025413) Bks Demand.

Atlantic Continental Margin: U. S. Ed. by R. E. Sheridan & J. A. Grow. (DNAG, Geology of North America Ser.: Vol. I2). (Illus.). 620p. 1988. 49.50 (*0-8137-5204-3*) Geol Soc.

Atlantic County (NJ) Clerk's Office Criminal Case Operations: Final Report. National Center for State Courts Staff. 67p. 1980. 4.02 (*0-685-15455-6*, NERO-071) Natl Ctr St Courts.

Atlantic Cross Guide. 3rd ed. Anne Hammick. 1993. text ed. 34.95 (*0-07-025911-9*) McGraw.

Atlantic Crossing Guide. 2nd ed. RCC Pilotage Foundation Staff. Ed. by Philip Allen. (Illus.). 280p. 1988. 29.95 (*0-87742-979-0*) Intl Marine.

Atlantic Crossing Guide. 2nd rev. ed. Phillip Allen. 1990. text ed. 32.95 (*0-87742-255-9*) Intl Marine.

Atlantic Crossing Guide. 3rd ed. Anne Hammick. 1993. 29.95 (*0-87742-371-7*) Intl Marine.

Atlantic Cruise in Wanderer III. large type ed. Eric Hiscock. (General Practice Library). (Illus.). 320p. 1993. 21.95 (*0-7089-2895-1*) Ulverscroft.

Atlantic Double-Cross: American Literature & British Influence in the Age of Emerson. Robert Weisbuch. LC 86-6922. 360p. (C). 1987. 29.95 (*0-226-89149-6*) U Ch Pr.

Atlantic Double-Cross: American Literature & British Influence in the Age of Emerson. Robert Weisbuch. LC 86-6922. 360p. (C). 1989. pap. text ed. 14.95 (*0-226-89151-8*) U Ch Pr.

Atlantic Economy & Colonial Maryland's Eastern Shore: From Tobacco to Grain. Paul G. Clemens. LC 79-26181. (Illus.). 256p. 1980. 34.00 (*0-8014-1251-X*) Cornell U Pr.

Atlantic Empires: The Network of Trade & Revolution, 1713-1826. Peggy K. Liss. LC 82-13099. (Johns Hopkins Studies in Atlantic History & Culture Ser.). 364p. reprint ed. pap. 103.80 (*0-8357-6908-9*, 2037966) Bks Demand.

Atlantic Empires of France & Spain: Louisburg & Havana, 1700-1763. John R. McNeill. LC 85-1105. xvii, 329p. 1985. 45.00 (*0-8078-1669-8*) U of NC Pr.

Atlantic Encounter. Eric Collenette. 192p. 1987. 15.95 (*0-8027-0962-1*) Walker & Co.

Atlantic Essays. Thomas W. Higginson. (Notable American Authors Ser.). 1992. reprint ed. lib. bdg. 75.00 (*0-7812-3110-8*) Rprt Serv.

Atlantic Fish: An Educational Coloring Book. Spizzirri Publishing Inc Staff. Ed. by Linda Spizzirri. (Illus.). 32p. (J). (gr. 1-8). 1989. pap. 1.75 (*0-86545-135-4*) Spizzirri.

Atlantic Fishermans Handbook. Ed. by Richard B. Allen. (Illus.). 482p. (Orig.). 1982. pap. 9.00 (*0-9608932-0-2*) Fisheries Comm.

Atlantic Fishes of Canada. W. B. Scott & M. G. Scott. (Illus.). 761p. 1988. 50.00 (*0-8020-5712-8*) U of Toronto Pr.

Atlantic Four-Master: The Story of the Schooner Herbert L. Rawding, 1919-1947. Francis E. Bowker. x, 96p. 1986. 19.95 (*0-913372-41-2*); pap. 13.95 (*0-913372-42-0*) Mystic Seaport.

Atlantic Free Balloon Race. Thom Roberts. (J). (gr. 3-7). 1986. pap. 2.50 (*0-380-89868-3*, Camelot) Avon.

Atlantic Frontier: Colonial American Civilization (1607-1763) Louis B. Wright. (Illus.). 387p. 1963. pap. 15.95 (*0-8014-9043-X*) Cornell U Pr.

Atlantic Frontier: Colonial American Civilization, 1607-1763. Louis B. Wright. LC 79-27846. (Illus.). x, 354p. 1980. reprint ed. text ed. 49.75 (*0-313-22320-3*, WRAF, Greenwood Pr) Greenwood.

Atlantic Fury. Hammond Innes. 308p. 1985. pap. 3.50 (*0-88184-143-9*) Carroll & Graf.

Atlantic Fury. Hammond Innes. 320p. reprint ed. lib. bdg. 22.95 (*0-88411-178-4*, Aeonian Pr) Amereon Ltd.

Atlantic Gray Whale. Jan Mell. LC 89-7868. (Gone Forever Ser.). (Illus.). 48p. (J). (gr. 5-6). 1989. text ed. 12.95 (*0-89686-458-8*, Crstwood Hse) Silver Burdett Pr.

***Atlantic Hearth: Early Homes & Families of Nova Scotia.** Mary Byers & Margaret McBurney. (Illus.). 364p. 1994. 60.00 (*0-8020-2935-3*); pap. 24.95 (*0-8020-7762-5*) U of Toronto Pr.

Atlantic Heights: A World War I Shipbuilders Community. Richard M. Candee. LC 85-3644. (Portsmouth Marine Society Ser.: No. 7). (Illus.). 136p. 1985. 19.95 (*0-915819-06-6*) Portsmouth Marine Soc.

Atlantic High. William F. Buckley, Jr. (Illus.). 280p. 1983. pap. 17.95 (*0-316-11440-5*) Little.

Atlantic Hydrophysical Polygon-70: Meteorological & Hydrophysical Investigations. Ed. by V. G. Kort & V. S. Samoilenko. 404p. (ENG.). (C). 1984. text ed. 125.00 (*90-6191-423-X*, Pub. by A A Balkema NE) Ashgate Pub Co.

Atlantic Islanders of the Azores & Madeiras. Francis M. Rogers. LC 78-72837. (Illus.). 1979. 17.50 (*0-8158-0373-7*) Chris Mass.

***Atlantic Islands: A Study of the Faeroe Life & Scene.** Kenneth Williamson. (Illus.). 385p. 1970. 79.50x (*0-7100-6911-1*) Elliots Bks.

Atlantic Islands: Azores, Madeira, Canaries & Cape Verde Islands. 2nd ed. RCC Pilotage Foundation Staff. (Illus.). 232p. 1994. 74.95 (*0-85288-267-X*, Pub. by Imray Laurie Norie & Wilson UK) Bluewater Bks.

Atlantic Jeopardy: PQ17 Convoy to Hell, Trawlers Go to War, & Night of the U-Boats, 3 vols. in 1. Paul Lund & Harry Ludlam. 720p. 1995. 29.95 (*0-572-01577-1*, Pub. by Foulsham UK) Atrium Pubs.

Atlantic Journal & Friend of Knowledge. C. S. Rafinesque. (Illus.). 1946. pap. 20.00 (*0-685-42244-5*) Lubrecht & Cramer.

Atlantic Meets Pacific: A Global View of Pidginization & Creolization. Selected Papers from the Society for Pidgin & Creole Linguistics. Ed. by Francis Byrne & John Holm. LC 92-37121. (Creole Language Library: No. 11). ix, 465p. 1992. 97.00x (*1-55619-165-0*) Benjamins North Am.

Atlantic Merchant-Apothecary: Letters of Joseph Cruttenden 1710-1717. Joseph Cruttenden. Ed. by I. K. Steele. LC 77-2832. 161p. reprint ed. pap. 45.90 (*0-8357-5834-6*, 2026443) Bks Demand.

Atlantic Mine: Photographs from the Harold H. Heikkinen Collection. (Copper Country Local History Ser.: Vol. 45). (Illus.). 128p. 1993. 3.00 (*0-942363-44-2*) C J Monette.

Atlantic Ocean. C. H. Cotter. (C). 1987. 30.00 (*0-85174-212-2*, Pub. by Brwn Son Ferg) St Mut.

Atlantic Ocean. Susan Heinrichs. LC 86-9578. (New True Bks.). (Illus.). 48p. (J). (gr. k-4). 1986. lib. bdg. 12.90 (*0-516-01289-4*) Childrens.

Atlantic Ocean. H. G. King. (World Bibliographical Ser.: No. 61). 252p. 1985. lib. bdg. 65.00 (*1-85109-004-5*) ABC-CLIO.

Atlantic Ocean: History & Oceanography of the Bridge Between Two Worlds. Kay F. George. 1977. lib. bdg. 69.95 (*0-8490-1462-X*) Gordon Pr.

Atlantic Pacific's Dictionary of Trucking Industry Terms. Lew Grill. (Illus.). 124p. (Orig.). Date not set. pap. 11.95 (*1-881912-06-X*) Atlantic Pac Res.

Atlantic Pact Forty Years Later: A Historical Reappraisal. Ed. by Ennio Di Nolfo. viii, 268p. (C). 1991. lib. bdg. 106.15 (*3-11-012738-5*, 168-91) De Gruyter.

Atlantic Peeks: An Ethnographic Guide to the Portuguese-Speaking Islands. Jean E. Ludtke. LC 87-70196. 1989. 24.95 (*0-8158-0441-5*) Chris Mass.

***Atlantic Pilot Atlas.** James Clarke. (Illus.). 80p. Date not set. spiral bd. 85.00 (*0-7136-3640-8*) Sheridan.

Atlantic Port Cities: Economy, Culture, & Society in the Atlantic World, 1650-1850. Ed. by Franklin W. Knight & Peggy K. Liss. LC 90-37698. 320p. 1991. text ed. 44.00x (*0-87049-657-3*) U of Tenn Pr.

Atlantic Provinces: Newfoundland, Nova Scotia, New Brunswick, Prince Edward Island. William F. Morley. LC 68-90634. (Canadian Local Histories to 1950: A Bibliography Ser.: No. 1). 183p. reprint ed. pap. 52.20 (*0-8357-8031-7*, 2034020) Bks Demand.

Atlantic Provinces in Confederation. Ed. by E. R. Forbes & D. A. Muise. LC 92-95005. 628p. 1993. 60.00 (*0-8020-5886-8*); pap. 29.95 (*0-8020-6817-0*) U of Toronto Pr.

Atlantic Records: A Discography, 4 vols., 1. Comp. by Michel Ruppli. LC 78-75237. 1979. text ed. 95.00 (*0-313-21171-X*, RAL/1) Greenwood.

Atlantic Records: A Discography, 4 vols., Set. Comp. by Michel Ruppli. LC 78-75237. 1979. text ed. 275.00 (*0-313-21170-1*, RAL/) Greenwood.

Atlantic Records: A Discography, 4 vols., Vol. 2. Comp. by Michel Ruppli. LC 78-75237. 1979. text ed. 95.00 (*0-313-21172-8*, RAL/2) Greenwood.

Atlantic Records: A Discography, 4 vols., Vol. 3. Comp. by Michel Ruppli. LC 78-75237. 1979. text ed. 95.00 (*0-313-21173-6*, RAL/3) Greenwood.

An Asterisk (*) at the beginning of an entry indicates that the title is appearing in BIP for the first time.

507

Atlantic Records: A Discography, 4 vols., Vol. 4. Comp. by Michel Ruppli. LC 78-75237. 1979. text ed. 95.00 (*0-313-21174-4*, RAL/4) Greenwood.
Atlantic Reef Corals: A Handbook of the Common Reef & Shallow-Water Corals of Bermuda, the Bahamas, Florida, the West Indies & Brazil. rev. ed. F. G. Smith. LC 75-125663. (Illus.). 1971. 10.95 (*0-87024-179-6*) U of Miami Pr.
Atlantic Region to Confederation: A History. Ed. by Phillip A. Buckner & John C. Reid. (Illus.). 600p. (C). 1994. 60.00 (*0-8020-0553-5*); pap. 29.95 (*0-8020-6977-0*) U of Toronto Pr.
Atlantic Relations: Beyond the Reagan Era. Ed. by Stephen Gill. 288p. 1989. text ed. 49.95 (*0-312-03268-4*) St Martin.
Atlantic Revisited. Pierre Zoelly. 80p. 1992. 14.50 (*0-8176-2695-6*) Birkhauser.
***Atlantic Richfield (ARCO) A Report on the Company's Environmental Policies & Practices.** (Illus.). 33p. (C). 1994. reprint ed. pap. text ed. 200.00x (*0-7881-0975-8*, Coun on Econ) Diane Pub.
Atlantic Run. Bart Davis. Ed. by Paul McCarthy. 304p. (Orig.). 1993. mass mkt. 5.50 (*0-671-76904-9*, Pocket Star Bks) PB.
Atlantic Salmon. Gerald Hausman & Alice Winston. (Illus.). Date not set. write for info. (*0-89166-009-7*) Cobblesmith.
Atlantic Salmon. Bianca Lavies. LC 91-27990. (Illus.). 32p. (J). (gr. 2-5). 1992. 14.50 (*0-525-44860-8*, DCB) Dutton Child Bks.
Atlantic Salmon. W. Shearer. 1992. 65.00 (*0-85238-188-3*) Blackwell Sci.
Atlantic Salmon. Lee Wulff. LC 82-20253. (Illus.). 288p. 1988. 35.00 (*0-8329-0267-5*) Lyons & Burford.
Atlantic Salmon: A Fly Fishing Primer. Paul C. Marriner. LC 92-31271. 192p. 1992. 24.95 (*0-8329-0473-2*) New Win Pub.
Atlantic Salmon: Natural History, Exploration, & Future Management. W. M. Shearer. LC 92-18941. 244p. 1992. text ed. 69.95 (*0-470-21947-5*) Halsted Pr.
Atlantic Salmon Fishing. Charles Phair. (Fifty Greatest Bks.). (Illus.). 193p. 1993. reprint ed. 50.00 (*1-56416-049-1*) Derrydale Pr.
***Atlantic Salmon Flies & Fishing.** Joseph D. Bates. (Illus.). 400p. 1995. 34.95 (*0-8117-0181-6*) Stackpole.
Atlantic Salmon Fly: The Tyers & Their Art. Judith Dunham. (Illus.). 144p. 1991. 39.95 (*0-87701-800-6*) Chronicle Bks.
Atlantic Seafaring: Ten Centuries of Exploration & Trade in the North Atlantic. Roger Morris. (Illus.). 1992. 29.95 (*0-87742-337-7*, 60334) Intl Marine.
Atlantic Seafaring: Ten Centuries of Exploration & Trade in the North Atlantic. Roger Morris. 1992. 34.95 (*0-07-043298-8*) McGraw.
Atlantic Shore. John Hay & Peter Farb. (Illus.). 246p. 1982. reprint ed. pap. 7.95 (*0-940160-14-5*) Parnassus Imprints.
***Atlantic Slave Trade.** David Northrup. (Problems in World History Ser.). 221p. (C). 1994. pap. text ed. write for info. (*0-669-33145-7*) Heath.
Atlantic Slave Trade: A Census. Philip D. Curtin. 358p. 1972. 35.00 (*0-299-05400-4*); pap. 16.95 (*0-299-05404-7*) U of Wis Pr.
Atlantic Slave Trade: Effects on Economies, Societies, & Peoples in Africa, the Americas, & Europe. Ed. by Joseph E. Inikori & Stanley L. Engerman. 418p. 1992. lib. bdg. 48.00 (*0-8223-1230-1*); pap. text ed. 18.95 (*0-8223-1243-3*) Duke.
Atlantic Spain & Portugal. Oz Robinson & Mike Sadler. (Illus.). 196p. (C). 1990. 64.95 (*0-85288-150-9*, Pub. by Imray Laurie Norie & Wilson UK) Bluewater Bks.
Atlantic System; the Story of Anglo-American Control of the Seas. Forrest Davis. (History - United States Ser.). 363p. 1993. reprint ed. lib. bdg. 89.00 (*0-7812-4862-0*) Rprt Serv.
Atlantic Tide & Current Almanac: Northeast Edition, 1993. Ed. by Joseph Kawaky. (Illus.). 512p. (Orig.). 1993. pap. 14.95 (*1-878258-31-1*) Marine Trade.
Atlantic Turkey Shoot: U-Boats off the Outer Banks in World War II. James T. Cheatham. (Illus.). 1990. pap. 9.95 (*0-92705-09-X*) Gan Prodns.
Atlantic (Virginia, West Virginia, District of Columbia) Thomas G. Aylesworth & Virginia L. Aylesworth. (Let's Discover the States Ser.). (Illus.). 64p. (Orig.). (J). 1990. lib. bdg. 16.95 (*1-55546-555-2*); pap. 6.95 (*0-7910-0533-X*) Chelsea Hse.
Atlantic Vision: Olaus Rudbeck & Baroque Science. Gunnar Eriksson. (Uppsala Studies in History of Science: Vol. 19). (Illus.). 208p. (C). 1994. 27.95 (*0-88135-158-X*, Sci Hist) Watson Pub Intl.
Atlantic Wall: Hitler's Defenses in the West, 1941-1944. Alan F. Wilt. LC 75-27748. (Replica Edition Ser.). 254p. reprint ed. pap. 72.40 (*0-8357-5835-4*, 2027799) Bks Demand.
Atlantic Wall & Other Poems. Rosalie L. Colie. LC 74-2963. 100p. 1974. 21.95 (*0-691-06273-0*); pap. 9.95 (*0-691-01314-4*) Princeton U Pr.
Atlantic War Remembered: An Oral History Collection. John T. Mason, Jr. LC 90-43436. (Illus.). 380p. 1990. 36.95 (*0-87021-523-X*) Naval Inst Pr.
Atlantic Wrecks, Bk. 1. John N. Rasuso. Ed. by Linda Barrett. (Fisherman Library). (Illus.). 176p. (Orig.). 1992. pap. text ed. 17.95 (*0-923155-15-5*) Fisherman Lib.
Atlantil! Alice Lane. (Illus.). 296p. (Orig.). 1993. pap. 14.95 (*0-9636665-0-9*) Altre Pub.
Atlantis. Geoffrey Ashe. LC 91-67306. (Art & Imagination Ser.). (Illus.). 96p. 1992. pap. 14.95 (*0-500-81039-7*) Thames Hudson.
Atlantis. Reading Research Dept. Staff. (Library: Vol. 22). 480p. 1987. 24.95 (*0-87604-204-3*, 1122) ARE Pr.
Atlantis. Kevin Siembieda. Ed. by Alex Marciniszyn & Thomas Bartold. (Rifts World Book Ser.: No. 2). (Illus.). 160p. (Orig.). (YA). (gr. 8 up). 1992. pap. 15.95 (*0-916211-54-1*, 804) Palladium Bks.
Atlantis. Grant Sutherland. 155p. (C). 1990. 30.00 (*0-7316-1967-6*, Pub. by Pascoe Pub AT) St Mut.
Atlantis: An Interpretation. Manly P. Hall. pap. 4.50 (*0-89314-375-8*) Philos Res.
Atlantis: Myth or Reality? Murray Hope. (Illus.). 368p. 1991. pap. 12.95 (*0-14-019232-8*, Arkana) Viking Penguin.
Atlantis: Opposing Viewpoints. Wendy Stein. LC 88-24470. (Great Mysteries Ser.). (Illus.). 112p. (J). (gr. 5-8). 1989. lib. bdg. 16.95 (*0-89908-056-1*) Greenhaven.
Atlantis: Role Playing Simulations for the Study of American Politics. W. Robert Gump & James R. Woodworth. LC 85-5309. 219p. (C). 1986. teacher ed write for info. (*0-8304-1176-3*); spiral bd. 18.95 (*0-8304-1137-2*) Nelson-Hall.
Atlantis: Selected Poems, Nineteen Fifty-Three to Nineteen Eighty-Two. Slavko Mihalic. Tr. by Charles Simic & Peter Kastmiler. LC 83-81610. 48p. 1984. pap. 5.00 (*0-912678-61-5*, Greenfld Rev Pr) Greenfld Rev Lit.
Atlantis: The Antediluvian World. Ignatius Donnelly. (Illus.). 512p. 1987. pap. 17.00 (*0-89345-226-2*, Steinerbks) Garber Comm.
Atlantis: The Antediluvian World. Ignatius Donnelly. 1973. lib. bdg. 300.00 (*0-87968-055-5*) Krishna Pr.
Atlantis: The Antediluvian World. Ignatius Donnelly. 1990. 7.99 (*0-517-49002-1*) Random Hse Value.
Atlantis: The Antediluvian World. Ignatius Donnelly. Ed. by E. F. Bleiler. LC 76-24138. 518p. 1976. reprint ed. pap. 8.95 (*0-486-23371-5*) Dover.
Atlantis: The Antediluvian World. Ignatius Donnelly. (Notable American Authors Ser.). 1992. reprint ed. lib. bdg. 75.00 (*0-7812-2667-8*) Rprt Serv.
Atlantis: The Antediluvian World. Ignatius Donnelly. (Collector's Library of the Unknown). (Illus.). 490p. 1991. reprint ed. write for info. (*0-8094-8083-2*); reprint ed. lib. bdg. write for info. (*0-8094-8084-0*) Time-Life.
Atlantis: The Eighth Continent. Charles Berlitz. 256p. 1985. mass mkt. 4.95 (*0-449-20742-0*, Crest) Fawcett.
Atlantis: The Making of Myth. Phyllis Y. Forsyth. (Illus.). 256p. 1980. 34.95 (*0-7735-0355-2*, Pub. by McGill CN) U of Toronto Pr.
Atlantis: The Making of Myth. Phyllis Y. Forsyth. LC 80-508878. (Illus.). 227p. reprint ed. pap. 64.70 (*0-7837-6921-0*, 2046750) Bks Demand.
Atlantis: The Missing Continent. David McMullen. LC 77-22138. (Great Unsolved Mysteries Ser.). (Illus.). 48p. (J). (gr. 4 up). 1983. reprint ed. lib. bdg. 21.36 (*0-8172-1047-4*) Raintree Steck-V.
***Atlantis: Three Tales.** Samuel R. Delany. 288p. 1995. 24.95 (*0-8195-5283-6*, Wesleyan Univ Pr) U Pr of New Eng.
Atlantis & Egypt with Other Selected Essays. J. Gwyn Griffiths. 340p. 1991. 88.00 (*0-7083-1071-0*, Pub. by U of Wales UK) Bks Intl VA.
Atlantis & Lemuria. Rudolf Steiner. 131p. 1963. spiral bd. 6.60 (*0-7873-0828-5*) Mokelumne.
Atlantis & Lemuria. Rudolf Steiner. 1989. pap. 9.95 (*0-932298-75-3*) Tri-State Pr Corp.
Atlantis-Europe: The Secret of the West. Dimitri Merezhkovsky & Paul M. Allen. LC 71-157506. 456p. 1989. reprint ed. pap. 16.50 (*0-89345-243-2*, Steinerbks) Garber Comm.
Atlantis, Fact or Fiction? Ed. by Edwin S. Ramage. LC 77-23624. 224p. reprint ed. pap. 63.90 (*0-8357-5836-2*, 2056248) Bks Demand.
Atlantis in America. Lewis Spence. 248p. 1981. pap. 20.00 (*0-89540-119-3*, SB-119) Sun Pub.
Atlantis in Ireland: Round Towers of Ireland. Henry O'Brien. LC 73-94419. (Illus.). 536p. 1989. reprint ed. pap. 18.00 (*0-89345-245-9*, Steinerbks) Garber Comm.
***Atlantis in Spain.** Elena Whitshaw. (Illus.). 284p. 1994. pap. text ed. 15.95 (*0-932813-22-4*) Adventures Unltd.
Atlantis in the Light of Modern Research. Z. Kukal. LC 84-3981. 224p. 1984. reprint ed. 89.75 (*0-444-99616-8*) Elsevier.
***Atlantis in Wisconsin: New Revelations about the Lost City.** Frank Joseph. (Illus.). 224p. (Orig.). 1995. pap. 12.95 (*1-880090-12-0*) Galde Pr.
Atlantis Mystery. Edgar P. Jacobs. Tr. by Dwight Decker. (Adventures of Blake & Mortimer Ser.). (Illus.). 64p. 1990. pap. 8.95 (*0-87416-094-4*, Comcat Comics) Catalan Communs.
Atlantis of the Sands: The Search for the Lost City of Ubar. Ranulph Fiennes. (Illus.). 192p. 1993. 24.95 (*0-7475-1327-9*, Pub. by Bloomsbury Pub Ltd UK) Trafalgar.
Atlantis Station. V. E. Mitchell. (Star Trek: The Next Generation, Starfleet Academy Ser.). (YA). 1994. mass mkt. 3.99 (*0-671-88449-2*, Minstrel Bks) PB.
Atlantis the Submarine: Coloring & Activity Book. Mark A. Wagenman. (Illus.). 24p. (J). (ps-00). 1990. pap. 2.95 (*0-89610-168-1*) Island Heritage.
Atlantis Two, Three, Four, Five & One -- Includes Atlantis Times Two, Back Flash & Sky Mite in One Volume. R. C. Rapier. (Illus.). 1978. 30.00 (*0-9600589-2-3*) R C Rapier.
Atlas. (Picturepedia Ser.). (Illus.). 48p. (J). (gr. k-3). 1994. write for info. (*1-56458-799-1*) Dorling Kindersley.
***Atlas.** (DK Pockets Ser.). 160p. (J). 1995. 7.95 (*0-7894-0215-7*, 5-70628) Dorling Kindersley.
Atlas. Time-Life Books Editors. (Voyage Through the Universe Ser.). 144p. 1991. write for info. (*0-8094-6945-6*); lib. bdg. write for info. (*0-8094-6946-4*) Time-Life.
Atlas: The Biomechanics of the Normal & Diseased Hip. F. Pauwels. Tr. by R. J. Furlong & P. Maguet. LC 75-31723. (Illus.). 280p. 1976. 261.00 (*0-387-07428-7*) Spr-Verlag.
Atlas: The Heart. J. Willis Hurst. (Illus.). 400p. 1988. text ed. 49.00 (*0-07-031501-9*) McGraw.
Atlas see New Cambridge Modern History
Atlas & Catalogue of Infrared Sources in the Magellanic Clouds. P. Schwering & F. P. Israel. (C). 1990. lib. bdg. 123.00 (*0-7923-0654-6*) Kluwer Ac.
Atlas & Catalogue of the Diatom Types of Friedrich Hustedt, 3 vols. Reimer Simonsen. (Illus.). 526p. 1987. lib. bdg. 620.00 (*3-443-50007-2*) Lubrecht & Cramer.
Atlas & Dissection Guide for Comparative Anatomy. 5th ed. Saul Wischnitzer. LC 92-30800. (C). 1995. pap. text ed. write for info. (*0-7167-2374-3*) W H Freeman.
Atlas & Manual of Plant Pathology. Ervin H. Barnes. LC 79-10575. 344p. 1979. spiral bd. 49.50 (*0-306-40168-1*, Plenum Pr) Plenum.
Atlas & Outline of the Acts of the Apostles. Duane S. Crowther. LC 83-80528. 114p. 1983. pap. 9.98 (*0-88290-219-9*) Horizon Utah.
Atlas & Outline of the Life of Christ. Duane S. Crowther. LC 83-82414. 120p. (Orig.). 1983. pap. 9.98 (*0-88290-207-5*) Horizon Utah.
Atlas & Sourcebook of the Lesser Bushbaby, Galago Senegalensis. Haines Edgerton & James L. Stevens. 320p. 1982. 143.00 (*0-8493-6320-9*, QL737, CRC Reprint) Franklin.
Atlas & Text of Aspiration Biopsy. Kenneth C. Suen. (Illus.). 288p. 1990. 85.00 (*0-683-08024-5*) Williams & Wilkins.
Atlas Biblico Portavoz. Tim Dowley. (SPA.). 1991. pap. 8.99 (*0-8254-1168-8*) Kregel.
Atlas Celeste. rev. ed. John Bevis. (Mapping of the Stars Ser.). (Illus.). 126p. (C). 1989. reprint ed. 765.00 (*1-85297-023-5*, Pub. by Archival Facs UK) St Mut.
Atlas Copco AB & Desoutter Brothers (Holdings) PLC: Report on Proposed Merger. 76p. 1990. pap. 16.00 (*0-10-109592-9*, HM5929) UNIPUB.
Atlas de Anatomia. 6th ed. Victor Pauchet & S. Dupret. 520p. 1989. pap. 24.95 (*0-7859-5797-9*) Fr & Eur.
Atlas de Anatomia: Cuerpo Humano. 25th ed. E. Ferran de los Reyes. (Illus.). 84p. (SPA.). 1991. pap. 24.95 (*0-7859-4944-5*) Fr & Eur.
Atlas de Estructura Vegetal. Bracegirdle & Miles. 126p. (SPA.). 1975. pap. 29.95 (*0-8288-5788-1*, S37583) Fr & Eur.
Atlas de Farn & Bluetenpflanzen der Bundesrepublik Deutschlands. 2nd ed. H. Haeupler & P. Schoenfeld. (Illus.). 768p. (GER.). 1989. lib. bdg. 50.00 (*3-8001-3453-5*, Pub. by Ulmer Verlog GW) Lubrecht & Cramer.
Atlas de Histologia. 2nd ed. Daniel B. Freeman & Bracegirdle. (Illus.). 144p. (SPA.). 1981. pap. 24.95 (*0-7859-5100-8*) Fr & Eur.
Atlas de Histopatologia. R. C. Curran. 96p. (SPA.). 1979. 95.00 (*0-8288-4720-7*, S37588) Fr & Eur.
Atlas de l'Art Egyptien: Atlas of Egyptian Art. rev. ed. Emile Prisse d'Avennes. 405p. (FRE.). 1993. reprint ed. lib. bdg. 495.00 (*0-7859-3710-2*, 9775170001) Fr & Eur.
Atlas de las Enfermedades Cromosomicas. J. Grouchy & C. Turleau. 356p. (SPA.). 1978. 150.00 (*0-8288-4861-0*, S31931) Fr & Eur.
Atlas de los Estilos Artisticos. R. Fradera Veiga. 84p. (SPA.). 1979. pap. 24.95 (*0-8288-4721-5*, S36298) Fr & Eur.
Atlas de Monnaies Gauloises. H. De La Tour. 1968. 20.00 (*0-685-51536-2*) S J Durst.
Atlas de Patologia Macroscopica. R. C. Curran & E. L. Jones. 148p. (SPA.). 1978. 85.00 (*0-8288-4862-9*, S37589) Fr & Eur.
Atlas der Chirurgischen Schnitt-und Nahttechnik. 2nd ed. J. Zoltan. (Illus.). 176p. 1980. 77.00 (*3-8055-0439-X*) S Karger.
Atlas Der Diatomaceekunde, 3 vols. Begruendet Von Adolf Schmidt et al. xvi, 586p. 1984. reprint ed. 1,770.00 (*3-87429-220-7*) Koeltz Sci Bks.
Atlas der Diatomaceenkunde, I-X. Adolf Schmidt et al. (Illus.). 1984. ring bd. 2,640.00 (*3-87429-034-4*) Lubrecht & Cramer.
Atlas der Elektrokardiographie. 5th ed. O. Ritter & V. Fattorusso. 1976. 39.25 (*3-8055-2416-1*) S Karger.
Atlas der Hautersatzverfahren. J. Zoltan. (Illus.). 304p. 1984. 128.00 (*3-8055-3447-7*) S Karger.
Atlas der Kaltformgebungseigenschaften - Atlas of Cold Working Properties, 3 Vols., Set. (Illus.). (ENG & GER.). 1987. 390.00 (*0-685-67646-3*, Pub. by DGM Metallurgy Info GW) IR Pubns.
Atlas der Kaltformgebungseigenschaften - Atlas of Cold Working Properties, 3 Vols., Vol. 1: Aluminum Materials. (Illus.). 157p. (ENG & GER.). 1987. spiral bd. 140.00 (*3-88355-114-7*, Pub. by DGM Metallurgy Info GW) IR Pubns.
Atlas der Kaltformgebungseigenschaften - Atlas of Cold Working Properties, 3 Vols., Vol. 2: Copper Materials. (Illus.). 287p. (ENG & GER.). 1987. spiral bd. 160.00 (*3-88355-115-5*, Pub. by DGM Metallurgy Info GW) IR Pubns.
Atlas der Kaltformgebungseigenschaften - Atlas of Cold Working Properties, 3 Vols., Vol. 3: Precious Metals. (Illus.). 280p. (ENG & GER.). 1987. spiral bd. 155.00 (*3-88355-116-3*, Pub. by DGM Metallurgy Info GW) IR Pubns.
Atlas der Plastischen Chirurgie. F. Burian. Tr. by H. Sostmann & A. Schertel. Incl. Vol. 1. Allgemeiner Teil und Einfuehrung in den Speziellen Teil. 1977. (*0-318-55580-8*); Vol. 2. Kopf. 1977. (*0-318-55581-6*); Vol. 3. Rumpf und Extremitaeten. 1977. (*0-318-55582-4*); Illus.). (GER.). 1977. 434.50 (*3-8055-1434-4*) S Karger.
Atlas der Topographischen und Angewamdten Anatomie Des Menschen see Atlas of Topographical & Applied Human Anatomy
Atlas Emergency Procedures. Susan M. Dunmire & Paul M. Paris. LC 93-25118. (Illus.). 240p. 1994. text ed. 68.50 (*0-7216-3682-9*) Saunders.
Atlas Florae Europaeae, Vol. III: Distribution of Vascular Plants in Europe: Caryophyllaceae. Ed. by J. Jalas & J. Suominen. (C). 1989. 120.00 (*0-521-34272-4*) Cambridge U Pr.
Atlas Florae Europaeae, 2 vols., Vol. I: Distribution of Vasculer Plants in Europe. Ed. by J. Jalas & J. Sudminen. 164p. 1989. Vol. I: Distribution of Vascular Plants in Europe--Pteridophyta, Gymnospermae, 164p. 79.95 (*0-521-34270-8*) Cambridge U Pr.
Atlas Florae Europaeae, 2 vols., Vol. II: Distribution of Vascular Plants in Europe. Ed. by J. Jalas & J. Sudminen. 314p. 1989. 94.95 (*0-521-34271-6*) Cambridge U Pr.
Atlas for Applied Veterinary Anatomy. 2nd ed. Robert Getty. LC 65-7104. 382p. reprint ed. pap. 108.90 (*0-8357-5837-0*, 2055944) Bks Demand.
Atlas for Marine Policy in East Asian Seas. Ed. by Joseph R. Morgan & Mark J. Valencia. LC 91-29923. (C). 1992. 175.00 (*0-520-07798-9*) U CA Pr.
Atlas for Marine Policy in Southeast Asian Seas. Ed. by Joseph R. Morgan & Mark J. Valencia. LC 83-47891. (Illus.). 1983. 160.00 (*0-520-05005-3*) U CA Pr.
Atlas for Staging Mammalian & Chick Embryos. H. Butler & B. H. Juurlink. 224p. 1987. 186.00 (*0-8493-6629-1*, QL959) CRC Pr.
***Atlas for the Differential Diagnosis of AIDS.** M. Lipman et al. LC 94-21470. (Encyclopedia of Visual Medicine Ser.). 1994. 78.00 (*1-85070-474-0*) Prthnon Pub.
***Atlas for Today's World.** Rand McNally Staff. Date not set. pap. 7.95 (*0-528-83777-X*) Rand McNally.
***Atlas Great Britain & Ireland.** 6th ed. Michelin Staff. (Orig.). 1994. pap. 20.00 (*2-06-112106-3*) Michelin.
Atlas Historico Westminster de la Biblia. Wright Filson. 134p. 1990. reprint ed. pap. 24.95 (*0-311-15030-6*) Casa Bautista.
Atlas Ichthylogique des Indes Orientales Neerlandaises, Vol. VIII: Percoides II, Serranidae, Lutjanidae, Haemulidae, Sparidae. Pieter Bleeker. LC 82-80033. (Illus.). 156p. 1988. 50.00 (*0-87474-224-2*) Smithsonian.
Atlas Ichthyologique des Indes Orientales Neerlandaise: Atlas of Fishes of the Dutch East Indies, Vol. IX. Pieter Bleeker. LC 82-80033. (Illus.). 80p. 1989. reprint ed. 50.00 (*0-87474-297-8*) Smithsonian.
Atlas Ichtyologique des Indes Orientales Neerlandaises, Vol. I. Pieter Bleeker. 168p. 1977. reprint ed. 50.00 (*0-87474-234-X*, BLA1) Smithsonian.
Atlas Ichtyologique des Indes Orientales Neerlandaises, Vol. II. Pieter Bleeker. 112p. 1979. reprint ed. 50.00 (*0-87474-236-6*, BLA2) Smithsonian.
Atlas Ichtyologique des Indes Orientales Neerlandaises, Vol. III. Pieter Bleeker. 150p. 1981. reprint ed. 50.00 (*0-87474-237-4*, BLA3) Smithsonian.
Atlas Ichtyologique des Indes Orientales Neerlandaises: Atlas of fishes of The Dutch East Indies, Vol. VII. Pieter Bleecker. LC 82-80033. (Illus.). 126p. (C). 1988. 50.00 (*0-87474-266-8*) Smithsonian.
Atlas Ichtyologique des Indes Orientales Neerlandaises, Vol. IV: Murenes, Symbranches, et Leptocephales. 2nd ed. Pieter Bleeker. LC 82-80033. (Illus.). 132p. (FRE.). 1985. reprint ed. 50.00 (*0-87474-226-9*, BLA4) Smithsonian.
Atlas Ichtyologique des Indes Orientales Neerlandaises, Vol. V: Baudroies, Ostracions, Gymnodontes, Balistes (Atlas of Fishes of the Dutch East Indies) Pieter Bleeker. LC 82-80033. (Illus.). 152p. 1986. reprint ed. 50.00 (*0-87474-242-0*, BLA5) Smithsonian.
Atlas Ichtyologique des Indes Orientales Neerlandaises, Vol. VI: Atlas of Fishes of the Dutch East Indies. Pieter Bleeker. LC 82-80033. (Illus.). 175p. (C). 1987. reprint ed. 50.00 (*0-87474-296-X*) Smithsonian.
Atlas Ichtyologique Indes Orientales Neerlandaises, Vols. XI-XIV. Pieter Bleeker. (Atlas of Fishes of the Dutch East Indies Ser.). (Illus.). 200p. 1983. text ed. 250.00 (*0-87474-240-4*, BLAV) Smithsonian.
Atlas Linguistique et Ethnographique du Jura et des Alpes du Nord, Tome I. Martin & Tuaillon. (FRE.). 175.00 (*0-8288-9901-0*, F136320) Fr & Eur.
Atlas Manual de Anatomia. 6th ed. V. Pauchet & S. Dupret. Ed. by Ignacio Rodrigo Garcia. 518p. (SPA.). 1978. pap. 29.95 (*0-8288-4863-7*, S12343) Fr & Eur.
Atlas Most Important Ore Paragenese under Microscope. O. Oelsner & B. J. Hazzard. LC 65-15381. 1966. 131.00 (*0-08-011201-3*, Pub. by Pergamon Repr UK) Franklin.
Atlas Mundial. Ed. by American Map Corp. Staff. (Illus.). (J). (gr. 7-12). 1992. pap. 2.95 (*0-8416-9555-5*, 695555) Am Map.
Atlas of Abdominal Surgery. Braasch et al. (Illus.). 480p. 1990. text ed. 121.00 (*0-7216-5601-3*) Saunders.
Atlas of Abdominal Ultrasonography in Children. Gary F. Gates. LC 78-18743. (Illus.). 303p. reprint ed. pap. 86.40 (*0-8357-6565-2*, 2035937) Bks Demand.
***Atlas of Acupuncture.** Mann. Date not set. (*0-7506-1678-4*) Butterwrth-Heinemann.
Atlas of Acupuncture: Points & Meridians in Relation to Surface Anatomy. Felix Mann. 656p. 1966. text ed. 55.00 (*0-433-20301-3*) Buttrwrth-Heinemann.
Atlas of Adirondack Caterpillars. Timothy L. McCabe. (Bulletin Ser.: No. 470). (Illus.). 114p. (Orig.). (C). 1991. pap. text ed. 19.95 (*1-55557-185-9*) NYS Museum.
Atlas of Adult Cardiac Surgery. William A. Gay, Jr. (Surgical Practice Illustrated Ser.). (Illus.). 189p. 1990. text ed. 135.00 (*0-443-08598-6*) Churchill.
***Atlas of Adult Electroencephalography.** Warren T. Blume & Masako Kaibara. LC 94-31100. 292p. 1995. 99.00 (*0-7817-0162-7*) Raven.

An Asterisk (*) at the beginning of an entry indicates that the title is appearing in BIP for the first time.

An Asterisk (*) at the beginning of an entry indicates that the title is appearing in BIP for the first time.

509

Atlas of Deformational & Metamorphic Rock Fabrics. Ed. by G. J. Borradaile et al. (Illus.). 530p. 1982. 174.00 (*0-387-11278-2*) Spr-Verlag.

Atlas of Dental & Maxillofacial Radiology. Gregory. 256p. 1993. 75.00 (*0-8151-1284-X*, Yr Bk Med Pubs) Mosby Yr Bk.

Atlas of Dental Radiographic Anatomy. 4th ed. Myron J. Kasle. LC 93-2762. (Illus.). 336p. 1993. pap. text ed. 39.50 (*0-7216-4858-4*) Saunders.

Atlas of Dentition in Childhood: Spanish Edition. Duterloo. (SPA.). 1992. 58.90 (*0-7234-1763-6*) Mosby Yr Bk.

Atlas of Dermatology. 3rd ed. Gernot Rassner. (Illus.). 512p. 1993. text ed. 85.00 (*0-8121-1601-1*) Williams & Wilkins.

***Atlas of Dermatopathology.** George F. Murphy & Arlene Hurtzberg. LC 95-1014. (Illus.). 312p. 1995. text ed. write for info. (*0-7216-4886-X*) Saunders.

Atlas of Dermatopathology. Ed. by Ronald P. Rapini & Robert E. Jordon. (Illus.). 456p. 1987. 115.00 (*0-8151-7087-4*, ATD-1, Yr Bk Med Pubs) Mosby Yr Bk.

Atlas of Descriptive Embryology. 4th ed. Willis W. Mathews. 302p. (C). 1986. pap. write for info. (*0-02-377140-2*) Macmillan.

Atlas of Developmental Embryology. Emil S. Szebenyi. LC 75-388. (Illus.). 338p. (C). 1976. 65.00 (*0-8386-1710-7*) Fairleigh Dickinson.

Atlas of Diagnostic Cytopathology. Barbara F. Atkinson. (Illus.). 706p. 1992. text ed. 210.00 (*0-7216-3528-8*) Saunders.

Atlas of Diagnostic Ocular Microbiology. Wilhelmus & Osato. 200p. 1993. 54.95 (*0-8016-6494-2*) Mosby Yr Bk.

Atlas of Diagnostic Radiology of Exotic Pets. Rubel et al. 1991. text ed. 155.00 (*0-7216-3493-1*) Saunders.

Atlas of Digital Spectra of Cool Stars. D. E. Turnshek et al. (Astronomy & Astrophysics Ser.). (Illus.). 92p. 1985. pap. 30.00 (*0-934525-00-5*) West Research.

Atlas of Discus of the World. Herbert R. Axelrod et al. (TS Ser.). (Illus.). 368p. 1991. text ed. 100.00 (*0-86622-543-9*, TS-164) TFH Pubns.

Atlas of Disease & Pests in Beets. Ed. by J. Benada et al. (Illus.). 272p. (ENG, FRE & GER.). 1987. 133.50 (*0-444-99501-3*) Elsevier.

Atlas of Disease Distribution. Andrew Cliff & Peter Haggett. 400p. 1992. pap. 36.95 (*0-631-18529-1*) Blackwell Pubs.

Atlas of Diseases of the Ear in Dog & Cat. Orsher. 1994. write for info. (*0-397-51199-X*) Lippincott.

Atlas of Diseases of the Eye. 3rd ed. E. S. Perkins et al. (Illus.). 208p. (Orig.). 1986. pap. text ed. 50.00 (*0-443-02961-X*) Churchill.

Atlas of Dog Breeds. Bonnie Wilcox & Chris Walkowicz. (Illus.). 912p. 1992. lib. bdg. 129.95 (*0-86622-855-1*, H1091) TFH Pubns.

***Atlas of Dream Places.** Marshall Editions Staff. 1995. 39.95 (*0-528-83774-5*) Rand McNally.

Atlas of Drosophila Genes: Sequences & Molecular Features. Gustavo Maroni. LC 92-35001. 432p. 1993. 80.00 (*0-19-507116-6*) OUP.

Atlas of Drug Reactions. Collins R. Douglas. LC 85-11033. (Illus.). 431p. reprint ed. pap. 122.90 (*0-7837-6232-1*, 2045946) Bks Demand.

Atlas of Duplex Scanning. John J. Cranley & Karkow. 352p. 1989. text ed. 160.00 (*0-7216-2303-4*) Saunders.

Atlas of Duplex Scanning: Extremities. John J. Cranley. (Illus.). 426p. 1992. text ed. 155.00 (*0-7216-3466-4*) Saunders.

Atlas of Duplex Ultrasonography: Essential Images of the Vascular System. Sergio Salles-Cunha & George Andros. LC 87-30729. (Illus.). 200p. 1988. text ed. 79.00 (*0-941022-08-0*) Appleton Davies.

Atlas of Ear, Nose & Throat Pathology. L. Michaels. (C). 1990. lib. bdg. 190.00 (*0-7923-8934-4*) Kluwer Ac.

Atlas of Early American History: The Revolutionary Era, 1760-1790. Ed. by Lester Cappon. 1976. 250.00 (*0-911028-00-5*) Newberry.

Atlas of Early American History: The Revolutionary Era, 1760-1790. Lester J. Cappon. LC 75-2982. 1975. 275.00x (*0-691-04634-4*) Princeton U Pr.

Atlas of Early Man. Jaquetta Hawkes. (Illus.). 256p. 1993. pap. 18.95 (*0-312-09746-8*) St Martin.

Atlas of Early Maps of the Midwest. W. Raymond Wood. (Scientific Papers: Vol. XVIII). (Illus.). (Orig.). 1983. pap. 10.00 (*0-89792-096-1*) Ill St Museum.

Atlas of Eastern Europe. (Illus.). 54p. (Orig.). (C). 1994. pap. text ed. 50.00 (*1-56806-272-9*) Diane Pub.

***Atlas of Eastern Europe in the Twentieth Century.** Richard J. Crampton & Ben Crampton. LC 95-4172. 1995. write for info. (*0-415-06689-1*) Routledge.

Atlas of Echocardiography. 2nd ed. Ernesto Salcedo. (Illus.). 445p. 1985. text ed. 83.95 (*0-7216-7899-8*) Saunders.

Atlas of Economic Indicators: A Visual Guide to Market Forces & the Federal Reserve. W. Stansbury Carnes & Stephen D. Slifer. LC 91-58515. (Illus.). 240p. 1992. reprint ed. pap. 15.00 (*0-88730-537-7*) Harper Busn.

Atlas of Economic Issues. Charles Elliott. (World Contemporary Issues Ser.). (Illus.). 64p. 1992. 16.95 (*0-8160-2481-2*) Facts on File.

Atlas of Economic Structure & Policies, Vol. 2. P. S. Florence. LC 68-30840. 1970. 80.00 (*0-08-013218-9*, Pub. by Pergamon Repr UK) Franklin.

***Atlas of EEG in the First Months of Life.** A. W. De Weerd. LC 95-14334. (Illus.). 1995. write for info. (*0-444-89946-4*) Elsevier.

Atlas of Egyptian Art. E. Prisse d'Avennes. (Illus.). 426p. 1991. 270.00 (*977-5170-00-1*) U of Wash Pr.

Atlas of Electro-Encephalography in the Dog & Cat. Richard W. Redding & Charles E. Knecht. LC 83-13693. (Illus.). 400p. 1984. text ed. 75.00 (*0-275-91448-8*, C1448, Praeger Pubs) Greenwood.

Atlas of Electrochemical Equilibria in Aqueous Solutions. LC 65-11670. (Illus.). 644p. 1974. 75.00 (*0-915567-98-9*, 51082) NACE Intl.

Atlas of Electroencephalography. Alan Guberman. 1989. 168.00 (*0-316-33074-4*) Little.

Atlas of Electroencephalography, 3 vols., Set. 1993. write for info. (*0-444-81180-X*) Elsevier.

Atlas of Electron Microscopy of Clay Minerals & Their Admixtures. H. Beutelspacher & H. Van Der Marel. 333p. 1968. 192.50 (*0-444-40041-9*) Elsevier.

Atlas of Electron Spin Resonance Spectra: Theoretically Calculated Multicomponent Symmetrical Spectra Staff, Vol. 1. Akademiia Nauk SSSR Staff et al. LC 63-21216. 233p. reprint ed. pap. 66.50 (*0-8357-5841-9*, 2003355) Bks Demand.

Atlas of Electronic Spectra of Five-Nitrofuran Compounds. J. Eidus et al. 169p. 1970. text ed. 45.50 (*0-7065-0759-2*, Pub. by Keter Pub IS) Coronet Bks.

Atlas of Emergency Trauma Surgical Procedures. Norman McSwain & Drue N. Ware. LC 90-4546. (Illus.). 184p. 1994. 98.50 (*0-89640-179-0*) Igaku-Shoin.

Atlas of Endangered Animals. Stephen Pollock. LC 92-20387. (Environmental Atlas Ser.). (Illus.). 64p. (J). (gr. 6-9). 1993. 16.95 (*0-8160-2856-7*) Facts on File.

***Atlas of Endangered Peoples.** Steve Pollock. LC 94-35296. 1995. 16.95 (*0-8160-3283-1*) Facts on File.

Atlas of Endangered Places. Steve Pollock. LC 92-20388. (Environmental Atlas Ser.). (Illus.). 64p. (YA). 1993. 16.95 (*0-8160-2857-5*) Facts on File.

***Atlas of Endangered Resources.** Steve Pollock. LC 94-32549. (J). 1995. 16.95 (*0-8160-3284-X*) Facts on File.

Atlas of Endangered Species. John Burton. 256p. 1991. text ed. 95.00 (*0-02-897081-0*) Macmillan.

Atlas of Endocrine Organs: Vertebrates & Invertebrates. Ed. by Akira Matsumoto & Susumu Ishii. Tr. by A. Urano. LC 92-28888. (Illus.). 320p. 1992. 200.00 (*0-387-53158-0*) Spr-Verlag.

Atlas of Endometriosis. R. W. Shaw. (Encyclopedia of Visual Medicine Ser.). (Illus.). 100p. 1993. 70.00 (*1-85070-390-6*) Prthnon Pub.

Atlas of Endoscopic Sinonasal Surgery. Dinesh Mehta. (Illus.). 118p. 1992. text ed. 95.00 (*0-8121-1471-X*) Williams & Wilkins.

***Atlas of Endoscopic Spine Surgery.** John Regan et al. 1995. 145.00 (*0-942219-73-2*) Quality Med Pub.

Atlas of Endourology. Kurt Amplatz. (Illus.). 256p. 1986. 155.00 (*0-8151-0160-0*, QMG-1, Yr Bk Med Pubs) Mosby Yr Bk.

Atlas of Endourology. Kurt Amplatz. 1991. write for info. (*0-8151-0137-6*, Yr Bk Med Pubs) Mosby Yr Bk.

***Atlas of Endovascular Surgery.** Richard M. Green. (Illus.). 368p. 1989. text ed. 150.00 (*0-07-024292-5*) Hlth Prof Div.

Atlas of English Literature. Clement G. Goode & E. F. Shannon. 1971. 75.00 (*0-87968-287-6*) Gordon Pr.

***Atlas of Environment.** Geoffrey Lean. Date not set. write for info. (*0-09-177433-0*) Random.

Atlas of Environmental Issues. Nick Middleton. (World Contemporary Issues Ser.). (Illus.). 64p. (YA). (gr. 6 up). 1989. 16.95 (*0-8160-2023-X*) Facts on File.

Atlas of Esophageal Surgery. David B. Skinner. (Surgical Practice Illustrated Ser.). (Illus.). 186p. 1991. text ed. 133.95 (*0-443-08610-9*) Churchill.

Atlas of Experimental Immunobiology & Immunopathology. Byron H. Waksman. LC 73-81434. (Illus.). 1970. 75.00 (*0-300-01154-7*) Yale U Pr.

Atlas of Experimental Toxicological Pathology. C. Gopinath et al. (Current Histopathology Ser.). 176p. 1987. lib. bdg. 204.50 (*0-85200-332-3*) Kluwer Ac.

Atlas of Extraocular Muscle Surgery. 2nd ed. John A. Dyer & David A. Lee. LC 84-18090. 256p. 1984. text ed. 59.95 (*0-275-91427-5*, C1427, Praeger Pubs) Greenwood.

Atlas of Eyelid Surgery. Gary E. Borodic & Daniel J. Townsend. (Illus.). 160p. 1993. text ed. 99.95 (*0-7216-3640-3*) Saunders.

Atlas of Facial Expression. Stephen R. Peck. (Illus.). 176p. 1990. pap. 10.95 (*0-19-506322-8*) OUP.

Atlas of Fatigue Curves. Ed. by Howard E. Boyer. 518p. 1985. 188.00 (*0-87170-214-2*) ASM.

Atlas of Feline Anatomy for Veterinarians. Lola C. Hudson & William P. Hamilton. LC 93-12640. (Illus.). 224p. 1993. text ed. 89.50 (*0-7216-4004-4*) Saunders.

Atlas of Feline Ophthalmology. Kerry L. Ketring & Mary B. Glaze. 1994. pap. text ed. 75.00 (*1-884254-13-6*) Vet Lrn Syst.

Atlas of Feline Surgery. Alexander. 32p. Date not set. pap. 4.99 (*1-55664-391-8*) Mosby Yr Bk.

Atlas of Female Cancer Surgery. Wheeless. 1991. write for info. (*0-8151-9291-6*, Yr Bk Med Pubs) Mosby Yr Bk.

Atlas of Female Infertility Surgery. Robert B. Hunt. 560p. 1992. 125.00 (*0-8151-4739-2*, Yr Bk Med Pubs) Mosby Yr Bk.

Atlas of Fetal Diagnosis. Ed. by Zoltan Papp. LC 92-14609. 1992. 249.75 (*0-444-98675-8*) Elsevier.

Atlas of Fetal Sectional Anatomy. G. Isaacson. (Illus.). 195p. 1986. 149.00 (*0-387-96248-4*) Spr-Verlag.

Atlas of Fetal Skeletal Radiology & Morphology. Ed. by Asher Ornoy et al. (Illus.). 160p. 1988. 89.00 (*0-8151-6544-7*, ATF-1, Yr Bk Med Pubs) Mosby Yr Bk.

Atlas of Fetal Ultrasonographic Anatomy. Richard A. Bowerman. (Illus.). 172p. 1986. 69.95 (*0-8151-1104-5*, QMO-1, Yr Bk Med Pubs) Mosby Yr Bk.

Atlas of Figure Drawings, Vol. 3. Caroline B. Thomas et al. (Illus.). 922p. 1966. 45.00 (*0-8018-0624-0*) Johns Hopkins.

Atlas of Film-Screen Mammography. 2nd enl. rev. ed. Ellen S. De Paredes. LC 88-20633. (Illus.). 628p. 1992. 150.00 (*0-683-06758-3*) Williams & Wilkins.

Atlas of Fine Structure of Human Sperm Penetration, Eggs & Embryos Cultured In Vitro. Henry A. Sathananthan et al. LC 85-6400. 302p. 1985. text ed. 75.00 (*0-275-91308-2*, C1308, Praeger Pubs) Greenwood.

Atlas of Finite Groups: Maximal Subgroups & Ordinary Characters for Simple Groups. Ed. by John H. Conway et al. LC 85-11559. 250p. (C). 1986. text ed. 59.00 (*0-19-853199-0*) OUP.

***Atlas of Fish Histology: Normal & Pathological Features.** 2nd ed. Fumio Takashima & Takashi Hibiya. 1994. write for info. (*1-56081-412-8*) VCH Pubs.

Atlas of Fish Histology Normal & Pathological Features. Takashi Hibiya. (Illus.). 147p. 1982. lib. bdg. 98.00 (*3-437-30388-0*, Pub. by G Fischer Verlag GW) Lubrecht & Cramer.

Atlas of Five-Day Normal Sea-Level Pressure Charts for the Northern Hemisphere. James F. Lahey et al. 80p. 1958. spiral bd. 50.00 (*0-299-01663-3*) U of Wis Pr.

Atlas of Five Hundred Millibar Wind Characteristics for the Northern Hemisphere. James F. Lahey et al. 96p. 1958. spiral bd. 50.00 (*0-299-01703-6*) U of Wis Pr.

Atlas of Florence. (Illus.). 384p. 1994. 185.00 (*1-56886-006-4*) Marsilio Pubs.

Atlas of Florida. Ed. by Edward A. Fernald. (Illus.). 276p. 1981. 27.50 (*0-9606708-0-7*) Florida State U Inst.

Atlas of Florida. rev. ed. Ed. by Edward A. Fernald & Elizabeth Purdum. (Illus.). 288p. 1992. 39.95 (*0-8130-1131-0*) U Press Fla.

***Atlas of Florida Fossil Shells.** Edward J. Petich. (Illus.). 408p. 1994. text ed. 60.00 (*1-886094-04-7*) Chicago Spectrum.

Atlas of Fluorescein Angiography. Alexandre E. Jalkh & Jose M. Celorio. (Illus.). 272p. 1993. text ed. 155.00 (*0-7216-3641-1*) Saunders.

Atlas of Food Crops. Jacques Bertin et al. (Ecoles Practiques des Hautes Etudes Ser.: Section 6). (Illus.). 41p. 1971. text ed. 78.50 (*90-279-1798-1*) Mouton.

Atlas of Foot & Ankle Surgery. Michael J. Shereff. LC 92-19403. (Illus.). 320p. 1993. text ed. 93.95 (*0-7216-3537-7*) Saunders.

Atlas of Foot Radiology. Montagne. 1981. 81.50 (*0-89352-097-7*) Mosby Yr Bk.

Atlas of Foot Surgery. Trott. 1991. 89.50 (*0-941158-81-0*) Mosby Yr Bk.

Atlas of Foot Surgery, Vol. II: Rear Foot Surgery. O. A. Mercado. 75.00 (*0-940542-04-8*) Carolando.

Atlas of Forearm & Hand Cross-Sectional Anatomy with Computed Tomography & Magnetic Resonance Imaging Correlation. Roy A. Meals & Leanne L. Seeger. (Illus.). 199p. 1991. text ed. 59.95 (*0-443-08805-5*) Churchill.

Atlas of Foreshortening: The Artist's Model in Deep Perspective. John Cody. LC 84-3644. (Illus.). 352p. 1984. pap. 29.95 (*0-442-21595-9*) Van Nos Reinhold.

Atlas of Freshwater & Marine Catfishes: A Preliminary Survey of the Siluriformes. Warren E. Burgess. (Illus.). 784p. 1989. lib. bdg. 100.00 (*0-86622-891-8*, H 1097); pap. 49.95 (*0-86622-131-X*) TFH Pubns.

***Atlas of Fullerenes.** P. W. Fowler & D. E. Manolopoulos. (International Series of Monographs on Chemistry: No. 30). (Illus.). 400p. 1995. 98.00 (*0-19-855787-6*) OUP.

Atlas of Functions. Jerome Spanier & Keith B. Oldham. 700p. 1987. 199.50 (*0-89116-573-8*) Hemisp Pub.

Atlas of Fungal Pathology. Karlhanns Salfelder. (Current Histopathology Ser.). (C). 1990. lib. bdg. 190.00 (*0-7923-8935-2*) Kluwer Ac.

***Atlas of Galaxies Useful for Measuring the Cosmological Distance Scale.** 1994. lib. bdg. 260.95 (*0-8490-6419-8*) Gordon Pr.

Atlas of Galaxies Useful for Measuring the Cosmological Distance Scale. Allan Sandage & John Bedke. LC 88-600056. (Illus.). 103p. 1988. boxed 80.00 (*0-16-004227-5*, S/N 033-000-01020-6) USGPO.

Atlas of Garden Ponds. Herbert R. Axelrod et al. (Illus.). 285p. 1992. text ed. 49.95 (*0-86622-343-6*, TS178) TFH Pubns.

Atlas of Gastric Surgery. Michael J. Zinner. (Surgical Practice Illustrated Ser.). (Illus.). 242p. 1991. text ed. 133.95 (*0-443-08770-9*) Churchill.

Atlas of Gastroenterology. Tadataka Yamada. (Illus.). 624p. 1992. text ed. 195.00 (*0-397-50977-4*) Lippincott.

***Atlas of Gastrointestinal Cancer Staging by Endosonography.** T. L. Tio. LC 94-21375. (Illus.). 216p. 1994. 149.50 (*0-89640-267-3*) Igaku-Shoin.

Atlas of Gastrointestinal Endoscopy. Ottenjann & Classen. (Illus.). 550p. (C). 1990. 165.00 (*1-55664-203-2*) Mosby Yr Bk.

Atlas of Gastrointestinal Endoscopy. Fred E. Silverstien & Guido N. Tytgat. (Illus.). 272p. 1987. text ed. 185.00 (*0-03-012792-0*) Saunders.

Atlas of Gastrointestinal Motility in Health & Disease. Ed. by Marvin M. Schuster. LC 93-12116. (Illus.). 384p. 1994. 95.00 (*0-683-07623-X*) Williams & Wilkins.

Atlas of Gastrointestinal Pathology. David A. Owen & James K. Kelly. LC 94-989. 1994. text ed. 185.00 (*0-7216-6730-9*) Saunders.

Atlas of General Laparoscopic Surgery. Joseph Sanfilippo et al. (Illus.). 450p. (C). 1994. text ed. 150.00 (*0-397-51268-6*, Lippincott Medical) Lippincott.

Atlas of General Small Animal Surgery. Caywood & Lipowitz. (Illus.). 376p. 1988. 64.00 (*0-8016-1166-0*) Mosby Yr Bk.

Atlas of General Surgery. David C. Sabiston, Jr. LC 92-48756. (Illus.). 928p. 1993. text ed. 155.00 (*0-7216-7883-1*) Saunders.

Atlas of General Surgery. 2nd ed. Ed. by Hugh Dudley & David Carter. (Illus.). 1000p. 1986. text ed. 95.00 (*0-407-00377-0*) Buttrwrth-Heinemann.

Atlas of General Thoracic Surgery. Kaiser. 250p. 1994. 79.95 (*0-8016-6380-6*) Mosby Yr Bk.

Atlas of General Thoracic Surgery. Mark M. Ravitch & Felician M. Steichen. (Illus.). 400p. 1988. text ed. 195.00 (*0-7216-7474-7*) Saunders.

Atlas of Georgia. Thomas W. Hodler & Howard A. Schretter. Ed. by Rebecca McCarthy. (Illus.). 288p. 1986. 47.50 (*0-911847-03-0*) U GA Inst Community.

Atlas of Germ Cell Tumours. A. Talerman. (Illus.). 220p. 1989. 115.00 (*87-16-06490-9*, Yr Bk Med Pubs) Mosby Yr Bk.

Atlas of German Wine. Hugh Johnson & Ian Jamieson. (Illus.). 232p. 1986. 29.95 (*0-685-16684-8*) S&S Trade.

Atlas of Glaucoma Surgery. Obstbaum. (Illus.). 210p. (C). 1991. boxed 125.00 (*0-8385-3270-5*, A3270-4) Appleton & Lange.

Atlas of Glomerular Histopathology. P. H. Schillings & H. J. Schuurmans Stekhoven. (Illus.). 1980. 78.50 (*3-8055-0201-X*) S Karger.

***Atlas of Great Britain & Ireland.** Michelin Staff. (Orig.). 1994. spiral bd., pap. 20.00 (*2-06-112206-X*) Michelin.

Atlas of Great Lakes Indian History. Ed. by Helen H. Tanner. LC 86-4353. (Civilization of the American Indian Ser.: Vol. 174). (Illus.). 240p. 1987. 85.00 (*0-8061-1515-7*); pap. 45.00 (*0-8061-2056-8*) U of Okla Pr.

Atlas of Groin Dissection. Douglas E. Johnson & Frederick C. Ames. (Illus.). 170p. 1985. 54.95 (*0-8151-4886-0*, QMY-1, Yr Bk Med Pubs) Mosby Yr Bk.

Atlas of Gross Neuropathology. Robert E. Slemmer. (Illus.). 320p. (C). 1983. 48.50 (*0-87527-239-8*) Green.

Atlas of Gross Pathology. Fletcher. 1987. 35.00 (*0-906923-47-6*) Mosby Yr Bk.

Atlas of Growth in the Aging Craniofacial Skeleton. Behrents. (Craniofacial Growth Ser.: Vol. 18). (Illus.). 125p. 1986. 20.00 (*0-929921-14-3*) UM CHGD.

Atlas of Gynecologic & Obstetric Surgery. Hoskins. Date not set. 189.00 (*1-55664-340-3*) Mosby Yr Bk.

Atlas of Gynecologic Pathology. 2nd ed. J. Donald Woodruff et al. LC 65-40256. 328p. 1993. 147.00 (*0-7817-0056-6*) Raven.

Atlas of Gynecologic Surgery. Raymond A. Lee. (Illus.). 367p. 1992. text ed. 88.50 (*0-7216-3358-7*) Saunders.

Atlas of Haematology. 5th ed. George A. McDonald et al. (Illus.). 296p. 1989. text ed. 110.00 (*0-443-02560-6*) Churchill.

Atlas of Hand Cancels, 1875-1975. William F. Rapp. (Illus.). 95p. (Orig.). 1991. pap. 5.50 (*0-916170-39-X*) J-B Pub.

Atlas of Hand Splinting. Colleen C. Tenney & Janet M. Lisak. (Illus.). 208p. 1986. 36.95 (*0-316-85070-5*) Little.

Atlas of Hand Surgery, Vol. 2. Robert A. Chase. (Illus.). 496p. 1984. text ed. 175.00 (*0-7216-2497-9*) Saunders.

Atlas of Hawaii. 2nd deluxe ed. Department of Geography, University of Hawaii. LC 82-675462. (Illus.). 238p. 1983. pap. 29.95 (*0-8248-0837-1*) UH Pr.

Atlas of Head & Neck Pathology. Bruce Wenig. (Illus.). 448p. 1993. text ed. 169.00 (*0-7216-4032-X*) Saunders.

Atlas of Head & Neck Surgery. Ed. by Carl E. Silver. (Illus.). 325p. 1986. text ed. 126.00 (*0-443-08307-X*) Churchill.

Atlas of Head & Neck Surgery. 3rd ed. John M. Lore. (Illus.). 1219p. 1988. text ed. 172.00 (*0-7216-5816-4*) Saunders.

Atlas of Head & Neck Surgery, Vol. 2. Johns. 1990. 125.00 (*1-55664-254-7*) Mosby Yr Bk.

Atlas of Head & Neck Surgery: Mandible, Oral Cavity. Johns et al. Date not set. 125.00 (*1-55664-256-3*) Mosby Yr Bk.

Atlas of Head & Neck Surgery: Skin & Local Flaps. Johns et al. Date not set. 125.00 (*1-55664-255-5*) Mosby Yr Bk.

***Atlas of Heart Diseases: Heart Failure: Cardiac Function & Dysfunction.** Wilson Colucci. LC 94-41113. (Atlas of Heart Diseases Ser.: No. 4). (Illus.). 272p. 1995. text ed. 95.00 (*1-878132-27-X*) Current Med.

***Atlas of Heart Diseases Vol. 5: Chronic Ischemic Heart Disease.** George A. Beller. LC 95-1751. (Atlas of Heart Diseases Ser.: Vol. 5). (Illus.). 264p. 1995. text ed. 99.95 (*1-878132-29-6*) Current Med.

Atlas of Heart-Lung Transplantation. Amar S. Kapoor & Hillel Laks. (Illus.). 212p. 1994. text ed. 165.00 (*0-07-033708-X*) Hlth Prof Div.

Atlas of Hernia Surgery. George E. Wantz. (Illus.). 240p. 1991. 127.50 (*0-88167-724-8*) Raven.

Atlas of Histology. Johannes G. Rhodin. (Illus.). 1975. text ed. 45.00 (*0-19-501944-X*) OUP.

Atlas of Histopathology of the Cervix Uteri. Ed. by Gisela Dallenbach-Hellweg & Hemming Poulsen. (Illus.). 200p. 1991. 149.00 (*0-387-52295-6*) Spr-Verlag.

An Asterisk (*) at the beginning of an entry indicates that the title is appearing in BIP for the first time.

An Asterisk (*) at the beginning of an entry indicates that the title is appearing in BIP for the first time.

511

A

Atlas of Microvascular Surgery: Anatomy of Operative Approaches. Berish Strauch et al. LC 92-401. 560p. 1993. 199.00 (*0-86577-436-6*) Thieme Med Pubs.

Atlas of Microvascular Surgery in Head & Neck Reconstruction. Hayden. (Illus.). 350p. 1990. 85.00 (*0-8016-1682-4*) Mosby Yr Bk.

Atlas of Middle-Earth. rev. ed. Karen W. Fonstad. (Illus.). 224p. 1992. pap. 18.95 (*0-395-53516-6*) HM.

Atlas of Military Strategy. David G. Chandler. 1985. 29.95 (*0-02-905750-7*) Macmillan.

Atlas of Military Strategy. David G. Chandler. (Illus.). 1980. reprint ed. 29.95 (*0-685-01677-3*) Free Pr.

Atlas of Mineral Resources of the Escap Region - Laos People's Democratic Republic. 20p. 1990. 12.00 (*92-1-119572-1*, 90.II.F.14) UN.

Atlas of Mineral Resources of the ESCAP Region, Vol. 5: Sri Lanka. 45p. 1990. 12.00 (*92-1-119541-1*, 89.II.F.14) UN.

Atlas of Mineralized Bone Histology. H. H. Malluche & Marie-Claude Faugere. (Illus.). xiii, 136p. 1986. 191.25 (*3-8055-4201-1*) S Karger.

Atlas of Mobile Lang-Term EEG Recordings: Atlas Mobiler Langzeit EEG-Ableitungen. H. Stefan & W. Burr. (Illus.). 275p. (ENG & GER.). 1986. lib. bdg. 125.00 (*3-437-11005-5*, Pub. by G Fischer Verlag GW) Lubrecht & Cramer.

Atlas of Models of Crystal Surfaces. J. F. Nicholas. 238p. 1965. text ed. 255.00 (*0-677-00580-6*) Gordon & Breach.

Atlas of Modern History. Ed. by Hayden Middleton & Derek Heater. (Illus.). 64p. (YA). (gr. 7 up). 1991. bds. 15.95 (*0-19-831677-1*) OUP.

Atlas of Modern Jewish History. Evyatar Friesel. (Studies in Jewish History). (Illus.). 160p. 1990. 55.00 (*0-19-505393-1*) OUP.

Atlas of Mortality in Scotland: Including the Geography of Selected Socio-Economic Characteristics. Owen Lloy et al. (Illus.). 192p. 1987. 140.00 (*0-7099-4122-6*, Pub. by Croom Helm UK) Routledge Chapman & Hall.

Atlas of Mouse Development. M. H. Kaufman. (Illus.). 512p. 1992. text ed. 172.00 (*0-12-402035-6*) Acad Pr.

Atlas of MRI Artifacts & Variants. Mirowtiz. 1994. 115.00 (*0-8016-7670-3*) Mosby Yr Bk.

***Atlas of Myocardial Infarction: And Related Cardiovascular Complications.** Duncan S. Dymond. LC 94-21976. (Encyclopedia of Visual Medicine Ser.). 1994. 78.00 (*1-85070-505-4*) Prthnon Pub.

Atlas of Natural Conservation in China. Ed. by Changchun Institute of Geography Staff. (Illus.). 256p. 1990. 150.00 (*7-03-000367-5*, Pub. by Science Pr CH) Intl Spec Bk.

Atlas of Natural Wonders. Rupert O. Matthews. (Illus.). 240p. 1988. 35.00 (*0-8160-1993-2*) Facts on File.

***Atlas of Natural World.** Wood. 1994. 5.99 (*0-517-13555-8*) Random Hse Value.

Atlas of Naval Warfare 480 BC - 1975 AD see History of War at Sea: An Atlas & Chronology of Conflict at Sea from 480 B. C. to the Present

***Atlas of Nazi Germany: A Political, Economic & Social Anatomy of the Third Reich.** 2nd ed. Michael Freeman. LC 94-47233. (C). 1996. pap. text ed. 16.95 (*0-582-23924-9*) Longman.

Atlas of Near Infrared Spectra. LC 80-52913. 1981. 275.00 (*0-8456-0063-X*) Sadtler Res.

Atlas of Neonatal Anatomy. Jean-Pierre Lassau. (Illus.). 180p. 1982. 73.00 (*0-89352-139-6*, MA139, Yr Bk Med Pubs) Mosby Yr Bk.

Atlas of Neonatal Electroencephalography. 2nd ed. Janet E. Stockard-Pope et al. 416p. 1992. 103.00 (*0-88167-851-1*) Raven.

Atlas of Neotropical Lepidoptera Series, Set. 1993. write for info. (*0-945417-25-X*) Sci Pubs.

Atlas of Neptune. Garry E. Hunt & Patrick Moore. (Illus.). 128p. (C). 1994. 27.95 (*0-521-37478-2*) Cambridge U Pr.

Atlas of Neuroanatomy for Radiologists: Surface & Sectional, with CT Scanning Correlation. William B. Dublin & Arthur B. Dublin. LC 79-50199. (Illus.). 260p. (C). 1982. 62.50 (*0-87527-204-5*) Green.

Atlas of Neuropathology. 2nd rev. ed. Nathan Malamud & Asao Hirano. (Illus.). 1974. 120.00 (*0-520-02221-1*) U CA Pr.

***Atlas of Neuroradiology.** Steven J. Willing. (Illus.). 560p. 1995. text ed. 135.00 (*0-7216-4219-5*) Saunders.

Atlas of Neurosurgical Anatomy. J. L. Fox. (Illus.). 208p. 1989. 303.00 (*0-387-96838-5*) Spr-Verlag.

Atlas of Neurosurgical Techniques. John M. Tew, Jr. & Harry R. Van Loveren. LC 92-49097. 1993. text ed. 205.00 (*0-7216-3560-1*) Saunders.

Atlas of Neurotologic Skull Base Surgery. Smith. 1990. 95.00 (*0-8016-4716-9*) Mosby Yr Bk.

***Atlas of Nevada Confiers: A Phytogeographic Reference.** David A. Charlet. (Illus.). 240p. (Orig.). 1995. pap. text ed. 35.00 (*0-87417-265-9*) U of Nev Pr.

***Atlas of New Hampshire Trout Ponds.** 2nd ed. Northern Cartographic Staff. (Illus.). 164p. Date not set. pap. 14.95 (*0-944187-33-1*) N Cartographic.

Atlas of New York State Ferns: Contribution to a Flora of New York State, Checklist II. Richard S. Mitchell. (Bulletin Ser.: No. 456). 1984. pap. 2.50 (*1-55557-002-X*) NYS Museum.

Atlas of Normal & Variant Angiographic Anatomy. Saadoon Kadir. (Illus.). 544p. 1990. text ed. 119.00 (*0-7216-2894-X*) Saunders.

Atlas of Normal Developmental Roentgen Anatomy. 2nd ed. Theodore E. Keats. 800p. 1987. 159.00 (*0-8151-5045-8*, Yr Bk Med Pubs) Mosby Yr Bk.

Atlas of Normal Fetal Ultrasonographic Anatomy. 2nd ed. Bowerman. 338p. 1991. 75.00 (*0-8151-1046-4*, Yr Bk Med Pubs) Mosby Yr Bk.

Atlas of Normal Human Skin. W. Montagna et al. (Illus.). 384p. 1994. 125.00 (*0-387-97769-4*) Spr-Verlag.

Atlas of Normal Magnetic Resonance Anatomy. Bryan. 1991. 65.00 (*0-8151-1300-5*, Yr Bk Med Pubs) Mosby Yr Bk.

Atlas of Normal Radiographic Anatomy. Richard S. Snell & Alvin C. Wyman. LC 75-36765. 1976. 40.00 (*0-316-80207-7*) Little.

Atlas of Normal Roentgen Variants That May Simulate Disease. Keats. (Illus.). (SPA.). 1992. 147.30 (*0-8016-6731-3*) Mosby Yr Bk.

Atlas of Normal Roentgen Variants That May Simulate Disease. 5th ed. T. E. Keats. 983p. 1991. 175.00 (*0-8151-5048-2*, Yr Bk Med Pubs) Mosby Yr Bk.

***Atlas of North America: A Practical Atlas to the United States, Canada, & Mexico.** (Miniature Editions Ser.). (Illus.). 128p. 1995. 4.95 (*1-56138-548-4*) Running Pr.

Atlas of North America: Space Age Portrait of a Continent. (Illus.). 264p. 1988. 39.95 (*0-87044-605-3*); 51.95 (*0-87044-607-X*) Natl Geog.

Atlas of North American Astragalus, 2 vols, 1. Rupert C. Barneby. (Memoirs Ser.: Vol. 13). (Illus.). 1188p. 1964. write for info. (*0-89327-226-4*) NY Botanical.

Atlas of North American Astragalus, 2 vols, 2. Rupert C. Barneby. (Memoirs Ser.: Vol. 13). (Illus.). 1188p. 1964. write for info. (*0-89327-227-2*) NY Botanical.

Atlas of North American Astragalus, 2 vols, Set. Rupert C. Barneby. (Memoirs Ser.: Vol. 13). (Illus.). 1188p. 1964. 40.00 (*0-89327-225-6*); pap. 35.00 (*0-89327-224-8*) NY Botanical.

Atlas of North American Freshwater Fishes. D. S. Lee et al. LC 80-620039. (Illus.). 867p. 1980. 25.00 (*0-917134-03-6*) NC Natl Sci.

Atlas of North American Freshwater Fishes: 1983 Supplement. D. S. Lee et al. (Occasional Papers of the North Carolina Biological Survey: 1983-6). (Illus.). 67p. 1991. reprint ed. 10.00 (*0-917134-06-0*) NC Natl Sci.

***Atlas of North American Indians.** Gilbert Legay. LC 95-13019. (Illus.). 1995. write for info. (*0-8120-6515-8*) Barron.

Atlas of North European Vascular Plants: North of the Tropic of Cancer, 3 vols., Set. Eric Hulten & Magnus Fries. (Illus.). xvi, 1172p. 1986. reprint ed. 481.00 (*3-87429-263-0*) Koeltz Sci Bks.

Atlas of Northampton County, Pennsylvania. D. G. Beers. 56p. 1990. reprint ed. pap. 15.00 (*1-877701-16-5*) NCH&GS.

Atlas of Nuclear Medicine. Douglas Van Nostrand & Sheldon Baum. LC 65-9541. (Illus.). 1988. text ed. 95.00 (*0-397-50789-5*, Lippincott Medical) Lippincott.

Atlas of Nuclear Medicine Artifacts & Variants. 2nd ed. Ryo. 320p. 1989. 95.00 (*0-8151-7490-X*, Yr Bk Med Pubs) Mosby Yr Bk.

Atlas of Nuclear Medicine Imaging. 2nd ed. Sheldon Baum. (Illus.). 470p. (C). 1993. text ed. 185.00 (*0-8385-0449-3*, A0449-7) Appleton & Lange.

Atlas of Nursing: Atlas de la Enfermera. Ana M. Cimorra. (Illus.). 86p. (SPA.). 1987. pap. 19.95 (*0-7859-4943-7*) Fr & Eur.

Atlas of Nutritional Support Techniques. John L. Rombeau. 1989. 51.00 (*0-316-75575-3*) Little.

Atlas of Obstetrical Ultrasound. Carol Benson et al. LC 65-9855. (Illus.). 512p. 1988. text ed. 61.95 (*0-397-50820-4*, Lippincott Medical) Lippincott.

Atlas of Ocular Motility. Nelson & Robert A. Catalano. 256p. 1989. text ed. 121.00 (*0-7216-2628-9*) Saunders.

Atlas of Odor Character Profiles: DS-61. LC 85-15068. (ASTM Data Series Publication). (Illus.). 354p. 1985. text ed. 55.00 (*0-8031-0456-1*, 05-061000-36) ASTM.

Atlas of Office Surgery, Vol. 1. Ed. by Robert B. Benjamin. LC 88-32646. 156p. reprint ed. pap. 44.50 (*0-7837-2691-0*, 2043069) Bks Demand.

***Atlas of Oklahoma Climate.** Howard L. Johnson & Claude E. Duchon. LC 94-38763. (Illus.). 152p. 1995. 29.95x (*0-8061-2689-2*) U of Okla Pr.

Atlas of Oncology. R. W. Raven. (Encyclopedia of Visual Medicine Ser.). (Illus.). 200p. 1993. 85.00 (*1-85070-363-9*) Prthnon Pub.

Atlas of Operative Andrology: Selected Operations on Male Genitalia & Their Accessory Glands. Alpay Kelami. 202p. 1980. 142.35 (*3-11-008180-6*) De Gruyter.

Atlas of Operative Microsurgery, Vol. 1: Cerebrovascular Procedures. John M. Tew, Jr. & Harry R. Van Loveren. (Illus.). 304p. 1993. text ed. write for info. (*0-318-70149-9*) Saunders.

Atlas of Operative Neurosurgical Technique, Vol. 1. Long. (Illus.). 390p. 1989. 240.00 (*0-683-05148-2*) Williams & Wilkins.

Atlas of Operative Surgery: Esophagus, Stomach & Duodedum. Ed. by K. Kremer et al. (Illus.). 380p. 1989. text ed. 179.00 (*0-86577-291-6*) Thieme Med Pubs.

Atlas of Operative Surgery, Vol. II: Gallbladder, Bile Ducts, Pancreas. Ed. by K. Kremer et al. Tr. by Gerhard S. Sharon. LC 92-405. (Illus.). 149.00 (*0-86577-434-X*) Thieme Med Pubs.

Atlas of Operative Trauma Surgery. Trunkey. 200p. Date not set. 200.00 (*1-55664-278-4*) Mosby Yr Bk.

Atlas of Ophthalmic Surgery: Cornea Gloucorna Lens, Vol. II. George I. Spaeth & Douglas D. Koch. Ed. by Klaus Heilmann & David Patton. (Illus.). 272p. 1986. text ed. 159.00 (*0-86577-180-4*) Thieme Med Pubs.

Atlas of Ophthalmic Surgery: Vol. 1: Lids, Orbits, Extraocular Muscles. Charles Beyer-Machule & Gunter K. Von Noorden. Ed. by Klaus Heilmann & David Patton. (Illus.). 250p. 1984. text ed. 159.00 (*0-86577-179-0*) Thieme Med Pubs.

Atlas of Ophthalmic Surgery Vol. III: Strabismus. Buckley & Shields. 160p. 1994. 95.00 (*0-8016-7444-1*) Mosby Yr Bk.

Atlas of Ophthalmic Surgery Vol. IV: Vitreo-Ret. Meredith. 192p. 1994. 95.00 (*0-8016-6798-4*) Mosby Yr Bk.

Atlas of Ophthalmic Surgery, Vol. 1: Surgery of the Anterior Segment. Anderson et al. (Illus.). 240p. 1990. 99.00 (*0-8016-0172-X*) Mosby Yr Bk.

Atlas of Ophthalmic Surgery, Vol. 2: Oculoplastic, Lacrimal, & Orbital Surgery. Dutton. (Illus.). 342p. 1992. 125.00 (*0-8016-1464-3*) Mosby Yr Bk.

Atlas of Optic Nerve Disorders. Thomas C. Spoor. 192p. 1992. 142.00 (*0-88167-875-9*) Raven.

Atlas of Oral Diagnostic Imaging. Tomomitsu Higashi et al. Ed. by Brian W. Cochran. (Illus.). 270p. 1990. 42.50 (*0-912791-81-0*) Ishiyaku Euro.

Atlas of Oral Histology & Embryology. Gerrit Bevelander. LC 67-29213. 391p. reprint ed. pap. 111.50 (*0-8357-5843-5*, 2056325) Bks Demand.

Atlas of Oral Implantology. Ed. by A. N. Cranin et al. LC 93-781. (Illus.). 342p. 1993. text ed. 179.00 (*0-86577-449-8*) Thieme Med Pubs.

Atlas of Oral Pathology. R. D. Lucas & John W. Eveson. (Current Histopathology Ser.). 1985. lib. bdg. 234.50 (*0-85200-328-5*) Kluwer Ac.

Atlas of Oral Pathology. William G. Young & Heddie O. Sedano. LC 80-29439. (Illus.). 237p. (C). 1981. 44.95 (*0-8166-1040-1*) U of Minn Pr.

***Atlas of Orchids Pollination: European Orchids.** N. A. Van der Cingel. 200p. 1995. 85.00 (*90-5410-190-3*) Balkema RSA.

Atlas of Ore Minerals. P. Picot & Z. Johan. (Illus.). 460p. 1991. 187.50 (*0-444-99684-2*) Elsevier.

Atlas of Oregon Lakes. Ed. by Daniel M. Johnson et al. LC 84-675319. (Illus.). 328p. (C). 1985. pap. 25.95 (*0-87071-343-4*) Oreg St U Pr.

Atlas of Organ Transplantation. Ed. by M. Wayne Flye. LC 93-44256. 1994. text ed. 140.00 (*0-7216-4611-5*) Saunders.

Atlas of Orthodontics: Principles & Clinical Applications. Anthony D. Viazis. 256p. 1993. text ed. 169.00 (*0-7216-6643-4*) Saunders.

Atlas of Orthopaedic Surgical Approaches. C. L. Colton & A. J. Hall. (Illus.). 216p. 1993. pap. 49.95 (*0-7506-1702-0*) Buttrwrth-Heinemann.

Atlas of Orthopedic Pathology. Wold et al. (Illus.). 320p. 1990. text ed. 169.00 (*0-7216-2911-3*) Saunders.

Atlas of Orthopedic Surgery, Set. Laurin. (Illus.). 1992. 249.00 (*0-8151-5347-3*, Yr Bk Med Pubs) Mosby Yr Bk.

Atlas of Orthopedic Surgery, Vol. II: Upper Extremity. C. A. Laurin et al. (Illus.). 456p. 1990. 99.50 (*0-8151-5343-0*, Yr Bk Med Pubs) Mosby Yr Bk.

Atlas of Orthopedic Surgery, Vol. 1: General. Laurin. 1989. 99.50 (*0-8151-5344-9*, Yr Bk Med Pubs) Mosby Yr Bk.

Atlas of Orthopedic Surgery, Vol. 3: Lower Extremity. Riley Laurin & Camille Roy. (Illus.). 751p. 1992. 95.00 (*0-8151-5345-7*) Mosby Yr Bk.

Atlas of Orthopedic Surgical Approaches. Ed. by C. L. Colton & A. J. Hall. 250p. 1991. text ed. 145.00 (*0-7506-1338-6*) Buttrwrth-Heinemann.

Atlas of Osteoarthritis. Allen D. Meisel et al. LC 83-253444. 208p. reprint ed. pap. 59.30 (*0-7837-2727-5*, 2043107) Bks Demand.

Atlas of Osteoporosis. J. Stevenson. (Encyclopedia of Visual Medicine Ser.). (Illus.). 100p. 1992. 70.00 (*1-85070-329-9*) Prthnon Pub.

Atlas of Otologic Surgery. Goycoolea. 432p. 1989. text ed. 138.00 (*0-7216-2337-9*) Saunders.

Atlas of Outpatient & Office Surgery. 2nd ed. Robert B. Benjamin. (Illus.). 290p. 1993. 89.50 (*0-8121-1540-6*) Williams & Wilkins.

Atlas of Ovarian Tumors. Liane Deligdisch et al. LC 93-27160. 182p. 1994. 95.00 (*0-89640-240-1*) Igaku-Shoin.

Atlas of Ozone Spectral Parameters from Microwave to Medium Infrared. Jean-Marie Flaud et al. 599p. 1990. text ed. 121.00 (*0-12-259890-3*) Acad Pr.

Atlas of Paediatric Endoscopy: Upper Respiratory Tract & Oesophagus. Bruce Benjamin. (Illus.). 1982. text ed. 60.00 (*0-19-261179-8*) OUP.

Atlas of Palaeobiogeography, 1972. A. Hallam. 531p. 1973. 154.00 (*0-444-40975-0*) Elsevier.

Atlas of Palaeogeography & Lithofacies. Ed. by J. C. Cope et al. Tr. by J. K. Ingham & P. F. Rawson. (Geological Society Memoirs Ser.: No. 13). (Illus.). 176p. 1991. 493.00 (*0-903317-65-6*, Pub. by Geol Soc Pub Hse UK) AAPG.

Atlas of Pancreatic Exocrine Tumors: Morphology, Biology, & Diagnosis, with an International Guide for Tumor Classification. Ed. by P. M. Pour et al. LC 94-9950. 1994. write for info. (*0-387-70129-X*) Spr-Verlag.

Atlas of Pancreatic Surgery. Ed. by Howard A. Reber. (Illus.). 265p. 1988. 79.95 (*0-8151-7160-9*, ATR-1, Yr Bk Med Pubs) Mosby Yr Bk.

Atlas of Paramedic Skills. Brian Bedsloe. 1986. pap. 21.95 (*0-685-14608-1*, Reston) P-H.

Atlas of Paramedic Skills. Bryan E. Bledsoe. (Illus.). 448p. 1987. pap. 30.50 (*0-89303-444-4*) P-H.

Atlas of Paranasal Sinus Surgery. Frank N. Ritter & Michael H. Fritsch. LC 91-7018. (Illus.). 296p. 1992. 110.00 (*0-89640-194-4*) Igaku-Shoin.

Atlas of Parasitic Pathology. Karlhanns Salfelder et al. LC 92-49790. (Current Histopathology Ser.: Vol. 20). 192p. (C). 1992. lib. bdg. 195.00 (*0-7923-8998-0*) Kluwer Ac.

Atlas of Parrots. David Alderton. (H Ser.). (Illus.). 544p. 1991. 139.95 (*0-86622-120-4*, H-1109) TFH Pubns.

Atlas of Pathological Computer Tomography: Computer Tomography of Neck, Chest, Spine & Limbs, Vol. 3. L. Jeanmart et al. (Illus.). 210p. 1983. 270.00 (*0-387-11439-4*) Spr-Verlag.

Atlas of Pathological Computer Tomography Vol. 1: Cranio-Cerebral Computed Tomography, Set. A. Wackenheim et al. (Illus.). 150p. 1980. 261.00 (*0-387-09879-8*) Spr-Verlag.

Atlas of Pediatric Dermatology. Carlo Meneghini & E. Bonifazi. (Illus.). 172p. 1986. 44.95 (*0-8151-5759-2*, GZM-1, Yr Bk Med Pubs) Mosby Yr Bk.

Atlas of Pediatric Electroencephalography. Warren T. Blume. 344p. 1982. text ed. 179.50 (*0-89004-564-X*) Raven.

Atlas of Pediatric Neurosurgical Techniques: Atlas de Technicas Quirurgicas en Neurocirugia Infantil. F. J. Villarejo. Tr. by D. Applewhite. (Illus.). xii, 224p. 1984. 119.25 (*3-8055-3455-8*) S Karger.

Atlas of Pediatric Oncology. Sinniah. 1991. write for info. (*0-8151-7819-0*, Yr Bk Med Pubs) Mosby Yr Bk.

Atlas of Pediatric Ophthalmic Surgery. Joseph H. Calhoun et al. (Illus.). 320p. 1987. text ed. 98.95 (*0-7216-1104-4*) Saunders.

Atlas of Pediatric Ophthalmology & Strabismus Surgery. Monte A. Del Monte. (Illus.). 232p. 1992. text ed. 63.95 (*0-443-08708-3*) Churchill.

Atlas of Pediatric Orthopaedic Surgery. Morrissy. (Illus.). 800p. 1992. text ed. 150.00 (*0-397-50969-3*) Lippincott.

Atlas of Pediatric Orthopaedic Surgery, 2 vols. Mihran O. Tachdjian. (Illus.). 1664p. 1994. text ed. 289.00 (*0-7216-3733-7*) Saunders.

Atlas of Pediatric Otolaryngology. Charles D. Bluestone & Sylvan E. Stool. LC 93-40737. 1994. text ed. 159.00 (*0-7216-3711-6*) Saunders.

Atlas of Pediatric Surgery. Keith W. Ashcraft & Thomas M. Holder. LC 93-1848. 336p. 1994. text ed. 132.50 (*0-7216-3720-5*) Saunders.

Atlas of Pediatric Surgical Urology. George Kaplan. 1991. 55.00 (*0-8151-4984-0*, Yr Bk Med Pubs) Mosby Yr Bk.

Atlas of Pediatric Ultrasound. Ed. by R. D. Schulz & U. V. Willi. (Illus.). 214p. 1991. text ed. 99.00 (*0-86577-417-X*) Thieme Med Pubs.

Atlas of Pediatric Urologic Surgery. Frank Hinman, Jr. LC 94-4205. 1994. text ed. 175.00 (*0-7216-4231-4*) Saunders.

Atlas of Pelvic Surgery. 2nd ed. Clifford R. Wheeless, Jr. LC 87-3933. (Illus.). 475p. 1988. text ed. 135.00 (*0-8121-1080-3*) Williams & Wilkins.

Atlas of Pennsylvania. Ed. by David J. Cuff et al. 304p. (C). 1989. 120.00 (*0-87722-618-0*) Temple U Pr.

Atlas of Perception. Edwin Schlossberg. LC 92-13412. 1992. 40.00 (*0-394-58940-8*) Random.

Atlas of Perinatology. Silvio Aladjem & D. Vidyasagar. (Illus.). 508p. 1982. text ed. 155.00 (*0-7216-1080-3*) Saunders.

Atlas of Periodontics: Spanish Edition. Waite. (SPA.). 1992. 50.10 (*0-7234-1871-3*) Mosby Yr Bk.

Atlas of Phlebography of the Lower Limbs. Jacques Chermet. 256p. 1982. lib. bdg. 149.50 (*90-247-2525-9*) Kluwer Ac.

Atlas of Planar & Spect Bone Scans. Fogelman & Collier. 1989. 99.00 (*0-8016-3296-X*) Mosby Yr Bk.

Atlas of Plant Structure, 2 vols., 1. Brian Bracegirdle & Patricia H. Miles. 1971. text ed. 27.95 (*0-435-60312-4*) Heinemann.

Atlas of Plant Structure, 2 vols., 2. Brian Bracegirdle & Patricia H. Miles. 1971. text ed. 22.50 (*0-435-60314-0*) Heinemann.

Atlas of Plant Viruses, Vol. I. R. I. Francki et al. 240p. 1985. 191.00 (*0-8493-6501-5*, QR351) CRC Pr.

Atlas of Plant Viruses, Vol. II. R. I. Francki et al. 304p. 1985. 191.00 (*0-8493-6502-3*, QR351) CRC Pr.

Atlas of Podiatric Anatomy see Mercado Atlas of Foot Anatomy

Atlas of Podiatric Surgery: Forefoot Surgery, Vol. 1. O. A. Mercado. (Illus.). 290p. 1980. 75.00 (*0-940542-03-X*) Carolando.

***Atlas of Point Contact Spectra of Electron-Phanon Interactions in Metals.** A. V. Khotkevich. 168p. (C). 1994. lib. bdg. 125.00 (*0-7923-9526-3*) Kluwer Ac.

Atlas of Polymer & Plastics Analysis, 3 vols. large type ed. Dieter O. Hummel & Friedrich Scholl. Incl. Polymers, Structures, & Spectra. (Illus.). 671p. 1979. 480.00 (*0-89573-001-4*); Plastics, Fibres, Rubbers, Resins; Starting & Auxiliary MAterials, Degradation Products. (Illus.). 1035p. 1984. Parts A-1: Introduction, Classification, Spectra; A-2 Spectra, Indexes; 1035p 1984. 480.00 (*0-89573-013-8*); Additives & Processing Aids. 687p. 1981. 480.00 (*0-89573-014-6*); (Illus.). write for info. (*0-318-56335-5*) VCH Pubs.

Atlas of Polymer & Plastics Analysis, Set. 3rd ed. Dieter O. Hummel. 1000p. 1991. write for info. (*1-56081-189-7*) VCH Pubs.

Atlas of Polymer & Plastics Analysis, Vol. 1, Pts. A-B. 3rd ed. Dieter O. Hummel. 1000p. 1991. lib. bdg. 525.00 (*0-89573-973-9*); 435.00 (*0-685-56323-5*) VCH Pubs.

Atlas of Polymer & Plastics Analysis, Vol. 1: Parts A & B. 3rd ed. D. O. Hummel. 1200p. 1990. 525.00 (*0-685-49344-X*) VCH Pubs.

Atlas of Polymer Morphology. Arthur E. Woodward. 531p. (C). 1988. text ed. 184.50 (*1-56990-111-2*) Hanser-Gardner.

Atlas of Polymer Morphology. Arthur E. Woodward. 531p. (C). 1989. 495.00 (*0-685-36109-8*, Pub. by Textile Institue UK) St Mut.

Atlas of Porcelain Restorations. H. Denissen. (Illus.). 94p. 1990. 50.00 (*88-299-0831-2*, Pub. by Piccin Nueva Libraria) Ishiyaku Euro.

Atlas of Porcelain Restorations. H. Denissen et al. 94p. 1990. text ed. 50.00 (*1-57235-012-1*) Piccin NY.

Atlas of Practical Proctology. 2nd enl. rev. ed. Alexander Neiger. LC 89-71714. 170p. 1990. text ed. 98.00 (*0-920887-76-7*) Hogrefe & Huber Pubs.

Atlas of Practical Radiology. D. S. Grant. (Encyclopedia of Visual Medicine Ser.). (Illus.). 150p. 1993. 70.00 (*1-85070-397-3*) Prthnon Pub.

Atlas of Prehistoric Britain. John Manley. (Illus.). 160p. 1989. 39.95 (*0-19-520807-2*) OUP.

Atlas of Prenatal Development in Conceptions with Chromosomal Anomalies. Dorothy Warburton et al. (Oxford Monographs on Medical Genetics: No. 27). (Illus.). 144p. 1991. 85.00 (*0-19-505145-9*) OUP.

An Asterisk (*) at the beginning of an entry indicates that the title is appearing in BIP for the first time.

An Asterisk (*) at the beginning of an entry indicates that the title is appearing in BIP for the first time.

513

***Atlas of the Dissolved Oxygen Content of the Atlantic Ocean Vol. 9: Scientific Results of the German Atlantic Expedition of the Research Vessel "Meteor", 1925-1927, Atlas.** Hermann Wattenberg. 76p. 1993. 115.00 (*90-5410-240-3*) Balkema RSA.

Atlas of the English Civil War. P. R. Newman. (Illus.). 144p. 1985. text ed. 35.00 (*0-02-906540-2*) Macmillan.

Atlas of the Entomopathogenic Fungi. R. A. Samson et al. 220p. 1988. 129.00 (*0-387-18831-2*) Spr-Verlag.

Atlas of the Environment. Geoffrey Lean & Don Hinrichsen. 192p. 1994. lib. bdg. 39.50 (*0-87436-768-9*) ABC-CLIO.

Atlas of the Environment. Raintree Steck-Vaughn Staff. Ed. by Roger Coote. LC 92-8196. (Illus.). 96p. (J). (gr. 6-7). 1992. lib. bdg. 26.99 (*0-8114-7250-7*) Raintree Steck-V.

Atlas of the Great Caves of the World. Paul Courbon et al. LC 89-15722. (Illus.). 369p. 1989. 30.00 (*0-939748-29-0*); pap. 20.00 (*0-939748-21-5*) Cave Bks MO.

Atlas of the Greek & Roman World in Antiquity. Ed. by Nicholas G. Hammond. LC 81-675203. (Illus.). 64p. 1982. 48.00 (*0-8155-5060-X*, NP) Noyes.

Atlas of the Greek World. Peter Levi. (Cultural Atlas Ser.). (Illus.). 240p. 1981. 45.00 (*0-87196-448-1*) Facts on File.

Atlas of the Growth, Mortality & Recruitment of Philippine Fishes. Jose Inglese & Daniel Pauly. (ICLARM Technical Reports: No. 13). 127p. (Orig.). 1984. pap. 10. 90 (*971-10-2212-5*, Pub. by ICLARM PH) Intl Spec Bk.

***Atlas of the Holocaust.** 1995. 39.95 (*0-02-897451-4*) Macmillan.

Atlas of the Holocaust. Martin Gilbert. LC 92-33895. 1993. 20.00 (*0-688-12364-3*) Morrow.

Atlas of the Human Body. LC 94-4162. 1994. pap. 20.00 (*0-06-273297-8*, Harper Ref) HarpC.

Atlas of the Human Brain. 3rd ed. D. H. Ford et al. 1978. 43.00 (*0-444-80008-5*) Elsevier.

***Atlas of the Human Brainstem.** Ed. by George Paxinos & Xu F. Huang. (Illus.). 160p. 1995. spiral bd. write for info. (*0-12-547615-9*) Acad Pr.

Atlas of the Islamic World since 1500. Francis Robinson. (Cultural Atlas Ser.). (Illus.). 240p. 1982. 45.00 (*0-87196-629-8*) Facts on File.

Atlas of the Jewish World. Nicholas de Lange. (Cultural Atlas Ser.). (Illus.). 240p. 1984. 45.00 (*0-87196-043-5*) Facts on File.

Atlas of the Living Olive Shells of the World. Edward J. Petush & Dennis M. Sargent. (Illus.). 1986. 68.50 (*0-938415-00-X*) CERF Inc.

Atlas of the Menopause. M. I. Whitehead et al. (Encyclopedia of Visual Medicine Ser.). (Illus.). 900p. (C). 1993. 70.00 (*1-85070-388-4*) Prthnon Pub.

Atlas of the Mid-Atlantic Ridge Rift Valley. R. D. Ballard & J. G. Moore. (Illus.). 1977. 73.00 (*0-387-90247-3*) Spr-Verlag.

Atlas of the Middle East. (Illus.). 76p. (C). 1994. pap. text ed. 95.00 (*0-7881-0196-X*) Diane Pub.

Atlas of the Middle East. 1988. 65.00 (*0-318-32913-1*, Scribners) S&S Trade.

Atlas of the Middle East. Hammond Staff. 1991. pap. 5.95 (*0-8437-2516-8*) Hammond Inc.

Atlas of the Middle East. Israel Map & Publishing Co., Ltd. Staff. Ed. by Moshe Brawer. (Illus.). 140p. 1988. text ed. 75.00 (*0-02-905271-8*) Macmillan.

Atlas of the Moon. Antonin Rukl. Ed. by T. W. Rackham. (Illus.). 224p. 1992. 29.95 (*0-913135-17-8*) Kalmbach.

Atlas of the Mouth. 2nd ed. Maury Massler & Isaac Schour. (Illus.). (C). 22.40 (*0-685-05572-8*) Am Dental.

Atlas of the Myocardium. Roberto Ferrari & Lionel H. Opie. 188p. 1992. 68.50 (*0-88167-870-8*) Raven.

Atlas of the Mysterious in North America. Rosemary E. Guiley. LC 93-41985. (Illus.). 208p. 1994. (*0-8160-2876-1*) Facts on File.

Atlas of the Mysterious in North America. Rosemary E. Guiley. LC 93-41985. (Illus.). 208p. 1995. pap. 17.95 (*0-8160-2882-6*) Facts on File.

Atlas of the Natural World. Nick Middleton. (World Contemporary Issues Ser.). (Illus.). 64p. (YA). 1990. 16. 95 (*0-8160-2131-7*) Facts on File.

Atlas of the Netherlands Flora: Extinct & Very Rare Species, No. 1. Ed. by J. Mennema et al. (Illus.). 266p. 1980. lib. bdg. 117.00 (*90-6193-605-5*) Kluwer Ac.

Atlas of the Neuropathology of HIV Infection. Ed. by Francoise Gray. LC 92-48766. (Illus.). 320p. (C). 1993. 125.00 (*0-19-854776-5*) OUP.

Atlas of the Newborn. N. O'Doherty. 1985. lib. bdg. 82.00 (*0-85200-924-0*) Kluwer Ac.

Atlas of the Night Sky. S. Dunlop. (Illus.). 1991. Incl. maps of moon & planets. 9.99 (*0-517-44479-8*) Random Hse Value.

Atlas of the North American Indian. Carl Waldman. (Illus.). 288p. 1985. 35.00 (*0-87196-850-9*) Facts on File.

Atlas of the North American Indian. Carl Waldman. 1989. pap. 17.95 (*0-8160-2136-8*) Facts on File.

Atlas of the Northwest Coasts of America. Mikhail D. Teben'kov. Ed. & Tr. by Richard A. Pierce. (Alaska History Ser.: No. 21). (Illus.). (RUS.). 1981. 22.00x (*0-919642-55-1*) Limestone Pr.

Atlas of the Oceans. Martyn B. Bramwell. 1990. 5.00 (*0-517-03046-2*) Random Hse Value.

***Atlas of the Oceans.** rev. ed. Ed. by John Pernetta. LC 94-22176. 1994. 29.95 (*0-528-83703-6*) Rand McNally.

***Atlas of the Oceans' Wind & Wave Climate.** Comp. by I. R. Young & G. J. Holland. LC 94-43942. 1995. 240.01 (*0-08-042519-4*, Pergamon Pr) Elsevier.

Atlas of the Pacific Northwest. rev. ed. Ed. by Philip Jackson & A. Jon Kimerling. (Illus.). 160p. 1993. pap. 21.95 (*0-87071-415-5*) Oreg St U Pr.

Atlas of the Pacific Northwest. 8th rev. ed. Ed. by Philip Jackson & A. Jon Kimerling. (Illus.). 160p. 1993. text ed. 35.95 (*0-87071-416-3*) Oreg St U Pr.

Atlas of the Peripheral Ocular Fundus. 2nd ed. William L. Jones & Robert W. Reidy. LC 84-14984. (Illus.). 160p. 1992. text ed. 79.95 (*0-7506-9050-X*) Buttrwrth-Heinemann.

Atlas of the Peripheral Retina. Frank C. Bell & William J. Stenstrom. (Illus.). 244p. 1983. text ed. 145.00 (*0-7216-1669-0*) Saunders.

Atlas of the Planets. Vincent De Callatay & Audouin Dollfus. LC 76-350431. 160p. reprint ed. pap. 45.60 (*0-8357-5844-3*, 2026381) Bks Demand.

Atlas of the Polar Regions. CIA Staff. 66p. 1985. reprint ed. boxed 100.00 (*0-86720-061-8*) Jones & Bartlett.

Atlas of the Prenatal Mouse Brain. Uta B. Schambra et al. (Illus.). 327p. 1991. text ed. 89.00 (*0-12-622585-0*) Acad Pr.

Atlas of the Quabbin Valley: Past & Present. 2nd rev. ed. J. R. Greene. (Illus.). 28p. 1983. pap. 4.95 (*0-9609404-2-1*) J R Greene.

Atlas of the Quabbin Valley & Ware River Diversion. rev. ed. J. R. Greene. (Illus.). 32p. 1989. pap. 4.95 (*0-9609404-7-2*) J R Greene.

Atlas of the Rabbit Brain & Spinal Cord. Judy W. Shek et al. (Illus.). xvi, 140p. 1985. 285.00 (*3-8055-3814-6*) S Karger.

Atlas of the Republic of Georgia CIS: In Colour. (Illus.). 60p. (RUS.). (C). 1989. pap. text ed. 475.00 (*0-934393-56-7*) Rector Pr.

Atlas of the Roman World. Tim Cornell & John Matthews. (Cultural Atlas Ser.). (Illus.). 240p. 1982. 45.00 (*0-87196-652-2*) Facts on File.

Atlas of the Sand Hills. Ed. by Ann Bleed & Charles Flowerday. 1990. write for info. (*1-56161-000-3*) U NE Inst Agr & Nat Resc.

Atlas of the Skeletal Muscles. Robert J. Stone & Judith A. Stone. 224p. (C). 1990. spiral bd. write for info. (*0-697-10618-7*) Wm C Brown Pubs.

Atlas of the Solar System. Bill Yenne. 1987. 12.98 (*0-671-08926-9*) S&S Trade.

***Atlas of the States.** Mattson. Date not set. 70.00 (*0-13-324708-2*) P-H.

***Atlas of the Strange.** Querida L. Pearce. LC 94-41537. (Illus.). (J). 1995. write for info. (*1-56565-223-1*) Lowell Hse Juvenile.

***Atlas of the Stratification & Circulation of the Atlantic Ocean Vol. 6: Scientific Results of the German Atlantic Expedition of the Research Vessel "Meteor", 1925-1927, Atlas.** Georg Wust & Albert Defant. 98p. 1994. 115.00 (*90-5410-239-X*) Balkema RSA.

Atlas of the Surface Heat Balance of the Continents: Components & Parameters Estimated from Climatological Data. Dieter Henning. (Illus.). 402p. 1989. lib. bdg. 125.00 (*3-443-01025-3*, Pub. by Gebruder Borntraeger GW) Lubrecht & Cramer.

***Atlas of the Surface Microscopy of Pigmented Skin Tumors.** S. W. Menzies et al. (Illus.). 208p. 1995. text ed. 98.00 (*0-07-470206-8*) Hlth Prof Div.

Atlas of the Surgical Techniques of Oliver H. Beahrs. Oliver H. Beahrs et al. LC 84-1231. (Illus.). 332p. 1985. text ed. 91.95 (*0-7216-1602-X*) Saunders.

Atlas of the Textural Patterns of Basic & Ultrabasic Rocks & Their Genetic Significance. S. S. Augustithis. (C). 1979. 207.70x (*3-11-006571-1*) De Gruyter.

Atlas of the Textural Patterns of Granites, Gneisses & Associated Rock Types. S. S. Augustithis. 378p. 1973. 154.00 (*0-444-40977-7*) Elsevier.

***Atlas of the Textural Patterns of Ore Minerals & Metallogenic Processes.** Stylianos-Sarvas P. Augustithis. LC 94-41197. x, 664p. (C). 1995. lib. bdg. 346.45 (*3-11-013639-2*) De Gruyter.

Atlas of the Third World. 2nd ed. George T. Kurian. (Illus.). 400p. 1989. 125.00 (*0-8160-1930-4*) Facts on File.

Atlas of the Three-Dimensional Structure of Drugs. J. P. Tollenaere et al. (Janssen Research Foundation Ser.: Vol. 1). 322p. 1979. 67.25 (*0-444-80145-6*) Elsevier.

Atlas of the U. S. A Thematic & Comparative Approach. Nomad Publishers, Ltd. Staff. (Illus.). 128p. 1986. 50.00 (*0-02-922830-1*) Macmillan.

Atlas of the Ultrastructure of Viruses of Lepidopteran Pests of Plants. M. G. Chukhri. Tr. by V. Kothekar. (Russian Translation Ser.: No. 65). 251p. 1988. text ed. 70.00 (*90-6191-496-5*, Pub. by A A Balkema NE) Ashgate Pub Co.

Atlas of the Ultrastructure of Viruses of Lepidopteran Pests of Plants. M. G. Chukhrii. (C). 1988. 27.00 (*81-7087-002-X*, Pub. by Oxford IBH II) S Asia.

Atlas of the Ultraviolet Sky. Richard C. Henry et al. LC 88-45403. (Illus.). 464p. 1988. text ed. 70.00 (*0-8018-3738-3*) Johns Hopkins.

Atlas of the Universe. Kevin Krisciunas & Bill Yenne. (Illus.). 112p. 1991. 12.99 (*0-517-06527-4*, Crescent) Random Hse Value.

***Atlas of the Universe.** Patrick Moore. LC 94-22177. 1994. 29.95 (*0-528-83704-4*) Rand McNally.

Atlas of the Vascular Flora of Louisiana, Vol. I: Ferns & Ferns Allies, Conifers, & Monocotyledons. R. Dale Thomas & Charles M. Allen. 218p. (Orig.). 1993. pap. 10.00 (*0-9638600-0-3*) LA Dept Wldlife.

Atlas of the World. 2nd ed. LC 93-676838. (Illus.). 400p. (C). 1993. 65.00 (*0-19-521025-5*, 9236) OUP.

***Atlas of the World: Masterpiece Edition.** Rand McNally Staff. LC 94-22280. 1994. write for info. (*0-528-83715-X*) Rand McNally.

Atlas of the World Economy. Michael Freeman. Ed. by Derek H. Aldcroft. (Illus.). 184p. 1991. 50.00 (*0-13-050741-5*); 35.00 (*0-685-48175-1*) P-H.

Atlas of the World with Geophysical Boundaries Showing Oceans, Continents, & Tectonic Plates in Their Entirety. Athelstan Spilhaus. LC 91-55024. (Memoirs Ser.: Vol. 196). (Illus.). 100p. (C). 1991. 45.00 (*0-87169-196-5*, M196-SPA) Am Philos.

Atlas of the World's Languages. Ed. by Chris Moseley & R. E. Asher. (Illus.). 182p. 1993. 599.95 (*0-415-01925-7*, A7190) Routledge.

Atlas of the Young Kingdoms: The Northern Continent. Chaosium, Inc. Staff. Ed. by Lynn Willis. (Elric Roleplaying Game Ser.). (Illus.). 128p. 1995. pap. 16.95 (*1-56882-021-6*, 2905) Chaosium.

Atlas of the 1990 Census. Mark Uattson. 176p. 1992. text ed. 95.00 (*0-02-897302-X*) Macmillan.

***Atlas of the 1994 California General Election: Statewide Offices & Measures by County.** Ed. by Alan W. Miller. LC 95-77910. (Illus.). 133p. (Orig.). 1995. pap. text ed. 29.95 (*0-9645318-1-X*) Klipsan Pr.

Atlas of Therapeutic Proctology. Emilio De Los Rios. 185p. 1984. text ed. 142.00 (*0-7216-3036-7*) Saunders.

Atlas of Thoracic Surgery. Harold C. Urschel, Jr. & Joel D. Cooper. (Surgical Practice Illustrated Ser.). (Illus.). 240p. 1994. text ed. 159.95 (*0-443-08539-0*) Churchill.

Atlas of Thoracoscopic Surgery. Mark J. Krasna & Michael J. Mack. LC 93-34146. 1994. 175.00 (*0-942219-45-7*) Quality Med Pub.

Atlas of Thoroscopic Surgery. Ed. by William T. Brown. LC 93-36925. 1994. text ed. 145.00 (*0-7216-3793-0*) Saunders.

Atlas of Three Hundred Millibar Wind Characteristics for the Northern Hemisphere. James F. Lahey et al. 128p. 1960. spiral bd. 50.00 (*0-299-01963-2*) U of Wis Pr.

Atlas of Time-Temperature Diagrams for Irons & Steels. G. VanderVoort. 804p. 1991. 164.00 (*0-87170-415-3*, 6150) ASM.

Atlas of Time-Temperature Diagrams for Nonferrous Alloys. 300p. 1991. 164.00 (*0-87170-428-5*) ASM.

Atlas of Topographical Anatomy of the Brain & Surrounding Structures. Wolfgang Seeger. (Illus.). vii, 544p. 1985. pap. 71.00 (*0-387-81851-0*) Spr-Verlag.

Atlas of Topographical & Applied Human Anatomy, 2 vols., Set. 2nd ed. Eduard Pernkopf. Ed. by Helmut Ferner. Tr. by Harry Monsen. LC 79-25264. Orig. Title: Atlas der Topographischen und Angewamdten Anatomie Des Menschen. (Illus.). 1981. reprint ed. text ed. 355.00 (*0-7216-7196-9*) Saunders.

Atlas of Topographical & Applied Human Anatomy, 2 vols., Set. 3rd enl. rev. ed. Eduard Pernkopf. Ed. by Werner Platzer. Tr. by Harry Monsen. Orig. Title: Atlas der Topographischen und Angewamdten Anatomie Des Menschen. (Illus.). 804p. 1990. 295.00 (*0-683-06854-7*) Williams & Wilkins.

Atlas of Topographical & Applied Human Anatomy, 2 vols., Vol. 1: Head & Neck. 2nd ed. Eduard Pernkopf. Ed. by Helmut Ferner. Tr. by Harry Monsen. LC 79-25264. Orig. Title: Atlas der Topographischen und Angewamdten Anatomie Des Menschen. (Illus.). 1980. reprint ed. text ed. 179.00 (*0-7216-7198-5*) Saunders.

Atlas of Topographical & Applied Human Anatomy, 2 vols., Vol. 2: Thorax, Abdomen & Extremities. 2nd ed. Eduard Pernkopf. Ed. by Helmut Ferner. Tr. by Harry Monsen. LC 79-25264. Orig. Title: Atlas der Topographischen und Angewamdten Anatomie Des Menschen. (Illus.). 1980. reprint ed. text ed. 179.00 (*0-7216-7199-3*) Saunders.

Atlas of Topographical & Applied Human Anatomy, Vol. II: Thorax, Abdomen & Extremities. 3rd enl. rev. ed. Eduard Pernkopf. Ed. by Werner Platzer. Tr. by Harry Monson. (Illus.). 424p. 1990. text ed. 175.00 (*0-683-06853-9*) Williams & Wilkins.

Atlas of Topographical & Applied Human Anatomy, Vol. 1: Head & Neck. 3rd enl. rev. ed. Eduard Pernkopf. Ed. by Werner Platzer. Tr. by Harry Monsen. (Illus.). 380p. 1989. 175.00 (*0-683-06852-0*) Williams & Wilkins.

***Atlas of Tranesophageal Color Doppler Echocardiography & Intraoperative Imaging.** r. DeSimone et al. 200p. 1994. 125.00 (*0-387-57938-9*) Spr-Verlag.

Atlas of Transsphenoidal Microsurgery in Pituitary Tumors. Jules Hardy. LC 90-4654. (Illus.). 96p. 1990. 86.00 (*0-89640-183-9*) Igaku-Shoin.

Atlas of Transvaginal Color Doppler: The Current State of the Art. Ed. by Asim Kurjak. LC 93-35739. (Encyclopedia of Visual Medicine Ser.). (Illus.). 144p. 1993. text ed. 145.00 (*1-85070-459-7*) Prthnon Pub.

Atlas of Transvaginal Sonography. Jonathon Carter. LC 93-48347. 1994. 125.00 (*0-397-51460-3*) Lippincott.

Atlas of Trauma. Carrico. 1991. 65.00 (*0-8151-1447-8*, Yr Bk Med Pubs) Mosby Yr Bk.

Atlas of Trauma Management: The First Hour. B. A. Landon & J. D. Goodall. (Encyclopedia of Visual Medicine Ser.). (Illus.). 100p. 1993. 70.00 (*1-85070-411-2*) Prthnon Pub.

Atlas of Trauma Surgery. Donovan. 350p. 1994. 89.95 (*0-8016-6677-5*) Mosby Yr Bk.

Atlas of Tribal India: With Computed Tables of District-Level Data & Its Geographic Interpretation. Monis Raza. 1990. 100.00 (*0-685-34762-1*, Pub. by Concept II) S Asia.

Atlas of Trichoptera of the SW Pacific: Australian Region. Arthur Neboiss. (Entomologica Ser.). 1986. lib. bdg. 154. 50 (*90-6193-575-X*) Kluwer Ac.

Atlas of Tumor Pathology: Extragonadal Teratomas. F. Gonzalez-Crussi. (Second Ser.: Fascicle 18). (Illus.). 214p. 1990. per., pap. 15.00 (*0-16-001851-X*, S/N 008-023-000) USGPO.

Atlas of Tumor Pathology: Intraosseous & Parosteal, Tumors of the Jaws. Seymour Hoffman et al. (Illus.). 252p. 1990. per., pap. 11.00 (*0-16-001863-3*, S/N 008-023-001) USGPO.

Atlas of Tumor Pathology: Tumors & Pseudotumors of the Serous Membranes. W. T. McCaughey. (Second Ser.: Fascicle 20). (Illus.). 136p. 1990. per., pap. 10.00 (*0-16-001857-9*, S/N 008-023-000) USGPO.

Atlas of Tumor Pathology: Tumors of the Adrenal. rev. ed. David L. Page et al. (Second Ser.: Fascicle 23). (Illus.). 279p. 1990. per., pap. 20.00 (*0-16-001862-5*, S/N 008-023-001) USGPO.

Atlas of Tumor Pathology: Tumors of the Breast, Fascicle 2. Robert W. McDivitt. (Second Ser.). (Illus.). 158p. 1990. reprint ed. per., pap. 8.50 (*0-16-001829-3*, S/N 008-023-000) USGPO.

Atlas of Tumor Pathology: Tumors of the Cardiovascular System. Hugh A. McAllister, Jr. & John J. Fenoglio, Jr. (Second Ser.: Fascicle 15). (Illus.). 157p. 1990. per., pap. 8.00 (*0-16-001839-0*, S/N 008-023-000) USGPO.

Atlas of Tumor Pathology: Tumors of the Central Nervous System. Lucien J. Rubinstein. (Second Ser.: Fascicle 6). (Illus.). 418p. 1990. reprint ed. per., pap. 20.00 (*0-16-001832-3*, S/N 008-023-000) USGPO.

Atlas of Tumor Pathology: Tumors of the Esophagus & Stomach. Si-Chun Ming. (Second Ser.: Fascicle 7, Supplement). (Illus.). 70p. 1990. pap. 4.75 (*0-16-001859-5*, S/N 008-023-00097-2) USGPO.

Atlas of Tumor Pathology: Tumors of the Exocrine Pancreas. Antonio L. Cubilla & Patrick J. Fitzgerald. (Second Ser.: Fascicle 19). (Illus.). 301p. 1990. per., pap. 16.00 (*0-16-001856-0*, S/N 008-023-000) USGPO.

Atlas of Tumor Pathology: Tumors of the Extra-Adrenal Paraganglion System (Including Chemoreceptors) George G. Glenner & Philip M. Grimley. (Second Ser.: Fascicle 9). (Illus.). 90p. 1990. reprint ed. per., pap. 5.50 (*0-16-001834-X*, S/N 008-023-000) USGPO.

Atlas of Tumor Pathology: Tumors of the Gallbladder & Extrahepatic Bile Ducts. Jorge Albores-Saavedra & Donald E. Henson. (Second Ser.: Fascicle 22). (Illus.). 220p. 1990. per., pap. 16.00 (*0-16-001861-7*, S/N 008-023-000) USGPO.

Atlas of Tumor Pathology: Tumors of the Kidney, Renal Pelvis, & Ureter. James L. Bennington & J. Bruce Beckwith. (Second Ser.: Fascicle 12). (Illus.). 369p. 1990. reprint ed. per., pap. 8.50 (*0-16-001837-4*, S/N 008-023-000) USGPO.

Atlas of Tumor Pathology: Tumors of the Liver & Intrahepatic Bile Ducts. John R. Craig. (Second Ser.: Fascicle 26). (Illus.). 292p. 1990. per. 22.00 (*0-16-021180-8*, S/N 008-023-00103-1) USGPO.

Atlas of Tumor Pathology: Tumors of the Lower Respiratory Tract. Darryl Carter & Joseph C. Eggleston. (Second Ser.: Fascicle 17). (Illus.). 371p. 1990. reprint ed. per., pap. 15.00 (*0-16-001848-X*, S/N 008-023-000) USGPO.

Atlas of Tumor Pathology: Tumors of the Major Salivary Glands. A. C. Thackray & R. B. Lucas. (Second Ser.: Fascicle 10). (Illus.). 156p. 1990. reprint ed. per., pap. 8.00 (*0-16-001835-8*, S/N 008-023-000) USGPO.

Atlas of Tumor Pathology: Tumors of the Male Genital System. F. K. Mostofi. (Second Ser.: Fascicle 8). (Illus.). 324p. 1990. reprint ed. per., pap. 15.00 (*0-16-001833-1*, S/N 008-023-000) USGPO.

Atlas of Tumor Pathology: Tumors of the Ovary & Maldeveloped Gonads. Robert E. Scully. (Second Ser.: Fascicle 16). (Illus.). 427p. 1990. reprint ed. per., pap. 18.00 (*0-16-001845-5*, S/N 008-023-000) USGPO.

Atlas of Tumor Pathology: Tumors of the Parathyroid Glands. Benjamin Castleman & Sanford I. Roth. (Second Ser.: Fascicle 14). (Illus.). 102p. 1990. per., pap. 6.50 (*0-16-001838-2*, S/N 008-023-000) USGPO.

Atlas of Tumor Pathology: Tumors of the Peripheral Nervous System. James C. Harkin & Richard J. Reed. (Second Ser.: Fascicle 3). (Illus.). 176p. 1990. reprint ed. per., pap. 11.00 (*0-16-001846-3*, S/N 008-023-000) USGPO.

Atlas of Tumor Pathology: Tumors of the Peripheral Nervous System, Supplement. James C. Harkin & Richard J. Reed. (Second Ser.: Fascicle 3). (Illus.). 60p. 1990. per., pap. 4.25 (*0-16-001853-6*, S/N 008-023-000) USGPO.

Atlas of Tumor Pathology: Tumors of the Pituitary Gland. Kalman Kovacs & Eva Horvath. (Second Ser.: Fascicle 21). (Illus.). 281p. 1990. per., pap. 20.00 (*0-16-001860-9*, S/N 008-023-000) USGPO.

Atlas of Tumor Pathology: Tumors of the Soft Tissues. rev. ed. Raffaele Lattes. (Second Ser.: Fascicle 1). (Illus.). 282p. 1990. per., pap. 14.00 (*0-16-001828-5*, S/N 008-023-000) USGPO.

Atlas of Tumor Pathology: Tumors of the Thymus. Juan Rosai & Gerald D. Levine. (Second Ser.: Fascicle 13). (Illus.). 240p. 1990. reprint ed. per., pap. 8.50 (*0-16-001843-9*, S/N 008-023-000) USGPO.

Atlas of Tumor Pathology: Tumors of the Thyroid Gland. William A. Meissner. (Second Ser.: Fascicle 4, Supplement). (Illus.). 52p. 1990. per., pap. 4.50 (*0-16-001855-2*, S/N 008-023-000) USGPO.

Atlas of Tumor Pathology: Tumors of the Upper Respiratory Tract & Ear. Vincent J. Hyams. (Second Ser.: Fascicle 25). (Illus.). 355p. 1990. per., pap. 20.00 (*0-16-001864-1*, S/N 008-023-001) USGPO.

Atlas of Tumor Pathology: Tumors of the Urinary Bladder. Leopold G. Koss. (Second Ser.: Fascicle 11, Supplement). (Illus.). 58p. 1990. per., pap. 3.25 (*0-16-001858-7*, S/N 008-023-000) USGPO.

Atlas of Tumor Pathology: Tumors of the Urinary Bladder. Leopold G. Koss. (Second Ser.: Fascicle 11). (Illus.). 132p. 1990. reprint ed. per., pap. 7.00 (*0-16-001836-6*, S/N 008-023-000) USGPO.

Atlas of Tumor Pathology of the Fischer Rat. Ed. by Sherman F. Stinson et al. 496p. 1990. 282.00 (*0-8493-5462-5*, SF910) CRC Pr.

Atlas of Tumors of the Facial Skeleton. Ed. by J. Prein et al. (Illus.). 180p. 1986. 246.00 (*0-387-16167-8*) Spr-Verlag.

Atlas of Twentieth-Century World-History. Anna Bramwell. 1991. 29.95 (*0-06-016009-8*, HarpT) HarpC.

An Asterisk (*) at the beginning of an entry indicates that the title is appearing in BIP for the first time.

An Asterisk (*) at the beginning of an entry indicates that the title is appearing in BIP for the first time.

515

A

Atmospheric Effects of Chemical Rocket Propulsion: Public Policy Workshop Report. 52p. 1992. 14.95 (0-685-75200-3, PP-20) AIAA.

Atmospheric Effects on Radar Target Identification & Imaging: Proceedings of the NATO Advanced Study Institute, Goslar, 1975. NATO Advanced Study Institute Staff. Ed. by H. Jeske. (Mathematical & Physical Sciences Ser.: No. 27). 1976. lib. bdg. 112.50 (90-277-0769-3) Kluwer Ac.

Atmospheric Electricity. 2nd ed. J. Chalmers & D. Terr Haar. LC 66-29669. (International Series of Monographs in Natural Philosophy: Vol. 11). 1967. 224.00 (0-08-012005-9, Pub. by Pergamon Repr UK) Franklin.

Atmospheric Electrostatics. abr. ed. Lars Wahlin. Ed. by J. F. Hughes. (C). reprint ed. 12.00 (0-86380-042-4, QC961.W34); reprint ed. lib. bdg. 12.00 (0-685-33377-9) Colutron Research.

Atmospheric Environment. William R. Frisken. LC 73-8139. 78p. reprint ed. pap. 25.00 (0-8357-5846-X, 2020961) Bks Demand.

Atmospheric Environment: A Study of Comfort & Performance. Andris Auliciems. LC 72-80647. (University of Toronto, Department of Geography Research Publications: No. 8). 182p. reprint ed. pap. 51.90 (0-8357-5847-8, 2026482) Bks Demand.

Atmospheric Factors Affecting the Corrosion of Engineering Metals, STP 646. Ed. by S. Coburn. 238p. 1978. 24.50 (0-8031-0286-0, 04-646000-27) ASTM.

***Atmospheric Fluidized Bed Coal Combustion: Research, Development, & Application.** Ed. by M. Valk. LC 94-39741. (Coal Science & Technology Ser.: Vol. 22). 1994. write for info. (0-444-81932-0) Elsevier.

Atmospheric Halos. Walter Tape. LC 93-29785. (Antarctic Research Ser.: Vol. 60). 143p. 1994. 40.00 (0-87590-834-9) Am Geophysical.

Atmospheric Humidity in Electrical Cost-of-Service: An Outline Bibliography. Michael A. Weinberg. 1982. 1.77 (0-9601014-7-0) Weinberg.

Atmospheric Interactions. Martin & Steila. 192p. (C). 1992. pap. text ed. 26.95 (0-8403-8052-6) Kendall-Hunt.

Atmospheric Interactions. Walter E. Martin & Donald Steila. 192p. (C). 1993. per., pap. text ed. 26.95 (0-8403-8717-2) Kendall-Hunt.

Atmospheric Ionization. H. W. Braun. 1986. pap. 3.95 (0-685-24739-2) Research Analysts.

Atmospheric Landscapes in Watercolor. Aubrey Phillips. 1990. pap. 4.95 (0-85532-655-7, Pub. by Search Pr UK) A Schwartz & Co.

Atmospheric Methane: Sources, Sinks, & Role in Global Change. Ed. by M. A. Khalil. LC 93-31890. (NATO ASI Series I: Global Environmental Change: Vol. 13). 1993. 226.00 (0-387-54584-0) Spr-Verlag.

Atmospheric Microbial Aerosols: Theoretical & Applied Aspects. Ed. by Bruce Lighthart & J. A. Mohr. LC 93-2375. 397p. 1994. 95.00 (0-412-03181-7) Chapman & Hall.

Atmospheric Motion & Air Pollution: An Introduction for Students of Engineering & Science. Richard A. Dobbins. LC 79-952. (Environmental Science & Technology Ser.). (Illus.). 341p. reprint ed. pap. 97.80 (0-8357-5848-6, 2056601) Bks Demand.

Atmospheric Optics, Vol. VI. Ed. by Nikolai B. Divari. Tr. by Stephen B. Dresner. LC 69-18138. 184p. reprint ed. pap. 52.50 (0-8357-5849-4, 2020682) Bks Demand.

Atmospheric Oxidation & Antioxidants, 3 vols., Set. 2nd ed. Ed. by Gerald Scott. LC 92-39907. 1993. 557.00 (0-444-89618-X) Elsevier.

Atmospheric Oxidation & Antioxidants, 3 vols., Vol. I. 2nd ed. Ed. by Gerald Scott. LC 92-39907. xii, 234p. 1993. 182.75 (0-444-89615-5) Elsevier.

Atmospheric Oxidation & Antioxidants, 3 vols., Vol. II. 2nd ed. Ed. by Gerald Scott. LC 92-39907. xiv, 542p. 1993. 254.25 (0-444-89616-3) Elsevier.

Atmospheric Oxidation & Antioxidants, 3 vols., Vol. III. 2nd ed. Ed. by Gerald Scott. LC 92-39907. xiv, 376p. 1993. 220.00 (0-444-89617-1) Elsevier.

Atmospheric Oxidation Rate Program. Howard. 1992. 520.00 (0-87371-779-1, T) Lewis Pubs.

Atmospheric Ozone. A. K. Khrgian et al. 96p. 1967. pap. text ed. 28.50 (0-7065-0516-6, Pub. by Keter Pub IS) Coronet Bks.

Atmospheric Ozone Research & Its Policy Implications: Proceedings of the 3rd U. S.-Dutch International Symposium Nijmegen, the Netherlands, May 9-13, 1988. Ed. by T. Schneider et al. (Studies in Environmental Science: No. 35). 1048p. 1989. 202.75 (0-444-87266-3) Elsevier.

Atmospheric Particles & Nuclei. E. Meszaros et al. (Illus.). 273p. (C). 1991. text ed. 38.00 (963-05-5682-0, Pub. by A K HU) Intl Spec Bk.

Atmospheric Phenomena. C. Suits & H. Way. LC 60-7068. (Collected Works of Irving Langmuir: Vol. 10). 1961. 195.00 (0-08-009362-0, Pub. by Pergamon Repr UK) Franklin.

Atmospheric Physics. J. V. Iribarne & H. R. Cho. xii, 208p. 1980. lib. bdg. 36.50 (90-277-1033-3) Kluwer Ac.

Atmospheric Physics from Spacelab. Ed. by Jan J. Burger et al. (Astrophysics & Space Science Library: No. 61). 1976. lib. bdg. 121.50 (90-277-0768-5) Kluwer Ac.

Atmospheric Planetary Boundary Layer Physics: Proceedings of the International Course Held in Erice, Sicily, February, 1978. A. Longhetto. (Developments in Atmospheric Science Ser.: Vol. 11). 424p. 1980. 110.25 (0-444-41885-7) Elsevier.

Atmospheric Pollutants in Forest Areas. Ed. by H. W. Georgii. 1986. lib. bdg. 103.00 (90-277-2317-6) Kluwer Ac.

Atmospheric Pollution. E. E. Pickett. (Arab School of Science & Technology Ser.). 257p. 1987. 99.50 (0-89116-680-7) Hemisp Pub.

Atmospheric Pollution: Its History, Origins & Prevention. 4th ed. A. R. Meetham et al. (Illus.). 288p. 1981. 105.00 (0-08-024003-8, Pub. by Pergamon Repr UK) Franklin.

Atmospheric Pollution Research in the U. S. S. R. Frada Grinberg. Ed. by Ben Armfield. 142p. (Orig.). 1986. pap. text ed. 75.00 (1-55831-016-9) Delphic Associates.

Atmospheric Pollution, 1980: Proceedings of the 14th International Colloqium, Paris, May 1980. Ed. by M. M. Benarie. (Studies in Environmental Science: Vol. 8). 440p. 1980. 125.75 (0-444-41889-X) Elsevier.

Atmospheric Pollution, 1982. M. M. Benarie. (Studies in Environmental Science: Vol. 20). 404p. 1982. 131.00 (0-444-42083-5) Elsevier.

Atmospheric Processes in the High Latitudes of the Southern Hemisphere. P. D. Astapenko. 224p. 1964. text ed. 73.50 (0-7065-0261-2, Pub. by Keter Pub IS) Coronet Bks.

Atmospheric Processes over Complex Terrain. Ed. by William Blumen. (Meteorological Monographs: No. 45). (Illus.). 394p. 1990. 60.00 (1-878220-01-2) Am Meteorological.

Atmospheric Radiation: Theoretical Basis. 2nd ed. Richard M. Goodwin & Y. L. Yung. (Illus.). 528p. 1989. 95.00 (0-19-505134-3) OUP.

***Atmospheric Radiation: Theoretical Basis.** 2nd ed. R. M. Goody & Y. L. Yung. (Illus.). 544p. 1995. reprint ed. pap. 55.00 (0-19-510291-6) OUP.

Atmospheric Radiation--Progress & Prospects: Proceedings of the Beijing International Radiation Symposium, Beijing, China, August 26-30, 1986. Ed. by Liou Kuo-nan & Xiuji Zhou. (Illus.). 699p. 1987. 50.00 (7-03-000208-3, Pub. by Science Pr CH) Intl Spec Bk.

Atmospheric Radiation Studies. Ed. by K. Y. Kondrat'ev. 224p. 1974. text ed. 59.50 (0-7065-1447-5, Pub. by Keter Pub IS) Coronet Bks.

Atmospheric Radiation Tables. (Meteorological Monograph Ser.: No. 23). 1960. 12.00 (0-933876-11-4) Am Meteorological.

Atmospheric Radiative Transfer. Jacqueline Lenoble. LC 93-12711. (Illus.). 500p. 1993. 94.00 (0-937194-21-2) A Deepak Pub.

Atmospheric Remote Sensing by Microwave Radiometry. Michael A. Janssen. (Remote Sensing & Image Processing Ser.). 592p. 1993. text ed. 120.00 (0-471-62891-3) Wiley.

Atmospheric Science & Power Production. Ed. by Darryl Anderson. 855p. 1984. pap. 29.50 (0-87079-126-5, DOE/TIC-27601); fiche 9.00 (0-87079-231-8, DOE/TIC-27601) DOE.

Atmospheric Science & Public Policy. Ed. by David Atlas. 105p. 1976. pap. 11.00 (0-933876-43-2) Am Meteorological.

Atmospheric Sciences: An Introductory Survey. John M. Wallace & Peter V. Hobbs. 467p. 1977. text ed. 59.00 (0-12-732950-1) Acad Pr.

Atmospheric Sciences in Antartica. Ed. by J. W. Meriwether. 366p. 1989. 22.00 (0-685-38493-4) Am Geophysical.

Atmospheric Spectroscopy: Proceedings of the International Workshop SERC Rutherford Appleton Laboratory, Chilton, Didcot, Oxon, U. K., July 19-21, 1983. Ed. by Garry E. Hunt & J. Ballard. (Illus.). 120p. 1985. pap. 83.00 (0-08-030278-5, Pergamon Pr) Elsevier.

Atmospheric Sulfur & Nitrogen Oxides: Eastern North American Source Receptor Relationships. George M. Hidy. (Illus.). 447p. 1994. text ed. 125.00 (0-12-347255-5) Acad Pr.

Atmospheric Thermodynamics. 2nd ed. J. V. Iribarne & W. L. Godson. 255p. 1900. pap. text ed. 39.00 (90-277-1297-2) Kluwer Ac.

Atmospheric Tidal & Planetary Waves. Hans Volland. (C). 1988. lib. bdg. 150.00 (90-277-2630-2) Kluwer Ac.

Atmospheric Tides: Thermal & Gravitational. S. Chapman & Richard S. Lindzen. 210p. 1970. text ed. 156.00 (0-677-61810-7) Gordon & Breach.

Atmospheric Tracer Technology & Applications. Ed. by Jody H. Heiken. LC 86-5266. (Illus.). 368p. 1986. 42.00 (0-8155-1082-9) Noyes.

Atmospheric Transmission, Emission, & Scattering. Thomas G. Kyle. (Illus.). 300p. 1991. text ed. 79.00 (0-08-040287-9, Pergamon Pr) Elsevier.

Atmospheric Transmission, Emission, & Scattering. Thomas G. Kyle. (Illus.). 300p. 1993. pap. text ed. 41.00 (0-08-040288-7, Pergamon Pr) Elsevier.

Atmospheric Transport Processes Pt. 1: Energy Transfers & Transformations. Elmar R. Reiter. LC 76-603262. (DOE Critical Review Ser.). 253p. 1969. pap. 14.25 (0-87079-396-9, TID-24868); fiche 9.00 (0-87079-397-7) DOE.

Atmospheric Transport Processes, Pt. 2: Chemical Tracers. Elmar R. Reiter. LC 76-603262. (DOE Critical Review Ser.). 382p. 1971. pap. 17.50 (0-87079-140-0, TID-25314); fiche 9.00 (0-87079-141-9, TID-25314) DOE.

Atmospheric Transport Processes, Pt. 3: Hydrodynamic Tracers. Elmar R. Reiter. LC 76-603262. (DOE Critical Review Ser.). 216p. 1972. pap. 36.50 (0-87079-142-7, TID-25731); fiche 9.00 (0-87079-143-5, TID-25731) DOE.

Atmospheric Transport Processes, Pt. 4: Radioactive Tracers. Elmar R. Reiter. LC 76-603262. (DOE Critical Review Ser.). 615p. 1978. 23.50 (0-87079-114-1, TID-27114); fiche 9.00 (0-87079-145-1, TID-27114) DOE.

Atmospheric Turbulence & Air Pollution Modelling. rev. ed. Ed. by F. T. Nieuwstadt & Han Van Dop. 1984. lib. bdg. 49.00 (0-318-01663-X) Kluwer Ac.

Atmospheric Water Vapor Resources for Rainfall As They Are Related to Water-Synthesis in Plant-Life, Annotated Bibliography. Ed. by Michael Weinberg. 45p. 1978. 3.00 (0-9601014-5-4) Weinberg.

ATMs Post Debit Cards, Home Banking. Business Communications Co., Inc. Staff. 215p. 1988. 2,450.00 (0-89336-660-9, G-113A) BCC.

***ATM/Sonet Explained.** Sadie Lewis & Robert Hermes. 159p. (Orig.). 1995. pap. 12.95 (1-880548-53-4) Numidia Pr.

Atnatanas: Natives of Copper River, Alaska. Henry T. Allen. (Shorey Indian Ser.). 14p. 1970. reprint ed. pap. 2.95 (0-8466-4015-5) Shorey.

Atocha Treasure. S. Gennings. (Great Adventure Ser.). (Illus.). 32p. (J). (gr. 4 up). 1988. lib. bdg. 17.27 (0-86592-874-6); lib. bdg. 12.95 (0-685-58293-0) Rourke Corp.

Atoka Group (Lower-Middle Pennsylvanian), Northern Fort Worth Basin, Texas: Terrigenous Depositional Systems, Diagenesis, & Reservoir Distribution & Quality. D. M. Thompson. (Report of Investigations Ser.: RI 125). (Illus.). 62p. 1982. 2.50 (0-318-03270-8) Bur Econ Geology.

Atoll Culture: Ethnology of Ifaluk in the Central Carolines. Edwin G. Burrows. LC 79-11044. 355p. 1970. reprint ed. text ed. 59.75 (0-8371-4426-4, BUAT, Greenwood Pr) Greenwood.

Atom. Pierre Averous. (Focus on Science Ser.). (J). (gr. 6 up). 1988. 4.95 (0-8120-3837-1) Barron.

Atom. Darwin Gross. 130p. (Orig.). 1984. pap. 4.95 (0-931689-01-5) D Gross.

Atom: Heart & Science & Technology. Francis Leone. LC 86-81737. (Illus.). 177p. 1986. 24.95 (0-914587-03-X) Helix Pr.

Atom: Journey Across the Subatomic Cosmos. Isaac Asimov. (Illus.). 352p. 1991. 21.95 (0-525-24990-7) NAL-Dutton.

Atom: Journey Across the Subatomic Cosmos. Isaac Asimov. (Illus.). 336p. 1992. pap. 12.95 (0-452-26834-6, Plume-Truman Talley Bks) NAL-Dutton.

Atom & American Life. Allan M. Winkler. LC 92-20013. 1993. 30.00 (0-19-507821-7) OUP.

***Atom & Eve.** Elsie B. McMillan. 1995. 16.95 (0-533-11131-5) Vantage.

Atom & Individual in the Age of Newton: On the Genesis of the Mechanistic World View. Gideon Freudenthal. LC 85-14572. 1986. lib. bdg. 99.50 (90-277-1905-5) Kluwer Ac.

Atom & Organism: A New Approach to Theoretical Biology. Walter M. Elsasser. LC 66-21832. 153p. reprint ed. pap. 43.70 (0-8357-5850-8, 2014639) Bks Demand.

Atom & the Fault: Experts, Earthquakes, & Nuclear Power. Richard L. Meehan. 184p. 1986. reprint ed. 19.95x (0-262-13199-4) MIT Pr.

Atom & Void: Essays on Science & Community. J. Robert Oppenheimer. (Science Library). 164p. (C). 1989. text ed. 29.95 (0-691-08547-1); pap. text ed. 9.95 (0-691-02434-0) Princeton U Pr.

Atom-Atom Potential Method for Organic Molecular Solids. A. J. Pertsin & A. I. Kitaigorodsky. (Chemical Physics Ser.: Vol. 43). (Illus.). 400p. 1987. 91.00 (0-387-16246-1) Spr-Verlag.

Atom Besieged: Extraparliamentary Dissent in France & Germany. Dorothy Nelkin & Michael Pollak. (Illus.). 256p. 1981. pap. 9.95x (0-262-64021-X) MIT Pr.

***Atom Bomb.** Tom Seddon. (Illus.). 48p. (J). (gr. 2 up). 1995. text ed. 14.95 (0-7167-6582-9, Sci Am Yng Rdrs) W H Freeman.

Atom Bomb. David Killingray. Ed. by Malcolm Yapp et al. (World History Ser.). (Illus.). 32p. (YA). (gr. 6-11). 1980. reprint ed. pap. text ed. 4.35 (0-89908-210-6) Greenhaven.

Atom Clock. Lengyel. pap. 1.00 (0-686-00466-3) Fantasy Pub Co.

***Atom-Field Interactions & Dressed Atoms.** G. Compagno et al. (Cambridge Studies in Modern Optics Ser.: 17). (Illus.). 385p. (C). 1995. write for info. (0-521-41948-4) Cambridge U Pr.

Atom from A to Z. K. Gladkov. Tr. by Michael Zimmerman. 263p. 1971. 20.00 (0-8464-0160-6) Beekman Pubs.

Atom from the Sun of Knowledge. Lex Hixon. 389p. 1993. pap. 19.00 (1-879708-05-1) Pir Pubns.

Atom-Molecule Collision Theory: Guide for the Experimentalist. Ed. by R. B. Bernstein. LC 78-27380. (Physics of Atoms & Molecules Ser.). (Illus.). 1979. 155.00 (0-306-40121-5, Plenum Pr) Plenum.

Atom Photon Interactions: Basic Processes & Applications. Claude Cohen-Tannoudji et al. 416p. 1992. text ed. 84.95 (0-471-62556-6) Wiley.

Atom-Probe & Field Ion Microscopy: Field-Ion Emission & Surfaces & Interfaces at Atomic Resolution. Tien T. Tsong. 250p. (C). 1990. 105.00 (0-521-36379-9) Cambridge U Pr.

***Atom Probe Field Ion Microscopy.** M. K. Miller et al. (Monographs on the Physics & Chemistry of Materials). 544p. 1996. 120.00 (0-19-851387-9) OUP.

Atom Probe Microanalysis: Principles & Applications to Materials Problems. M. K. Miller & G. D. Smith. (Monograph). 278p. 1989. text ed. 47.00 (0-931837-99-5) Materials Res.

Atom-Smashing Power of Mind. Charles Fillmore. 204p. 1949. 7.95 (0-87159-001-8) Unity Bks.

***Atom-Smashing Power of Mind.** Charles Fillmore. 216p. 1995. reprint ed. 10.95 (0-87159-109-X) Unity Bks.

Atom Station. Halldor Laxness. 1976. 18.95 (0-8488-0177-6) Amereon Ltd.

Atom Station. Halldor Laxness. LC 81-85725. 206p. (C). 1982. reprint ed. pap. 16.95 (0-933256-31-0) Second Chance.

Atomic Absorption. Claude Veillon. LC 72-87851. (Handbook of Commercial Scientific Instruments Ser.: No. 1). (Illus.). 192p. reprint ed. pap. 54.80 (0-8357-5851-6, 2029017) Bks Demand.

Atomic Absorption & Emission Spectroscopy. Ed Metcalfe & F. Elizabeth Prichard. (Analytical Chemistry by Open Learning Ser.). 289p. 1987. pap. text ed. 49.95 (0-471-91385-5) Wiley.

Atomic Absorption Spectrometry: Techniques & Instrumentation in Analytical Chemistry. J. E. Cantle. 448p. 1982. 143.75 (0-444-42015-0) Elsevier.

Atomic Absorption Spectrometry in Occupational & Environmental Health Practice: Analytical Aspects & Health Significance, Vol. I. Ed. by D. L. Tsalev & Z. K. Zaprianov. 264p. 1984. 110.00 (0-8493-5603-2, QP534, CRC Reprint) Franklin.

Atomic Absorption Spectrometry in Occupational & Environmental Health Practice: Determination of Individual Elements, Vol. II. Ed. by D. L. Tsalev. 312p. 1984. 110.00 (0-8493-5604-0, QP534, CRC Reprint) Franklin.

***Atomic Absorption Spectrometry in Occupational & Environmental Health Practice Vol. III: Progress in Analytical Methodology.** Ed. by Dimiter L. Tsalev. 368p. 1995. 149.95 (0-8493-4999-0, 4999) CRC Pr.

Atomic Absorption Spectrophotometry. 2nd ed. W. T. Elwell & J. A. Gidley. 1966. 61.00 (0-08-012063-6, Pub. by Pergamon Repr UK) Franklin.

Atomic Absorption Spectroscopy. 2nd rev. ed. James W. Robinson. LC 75-328457. (Illus.). 197p. reprint ed. pap. 56.20 (0-7837-0896-3, 2041201) Bks Demand.

Atomic Absorption Spectroscopy: Applications in Agriculture, Biology & Medicine. Gary D. Christian & Fredric J. Feldman. LC 78-23204. 512p. 1979. reprint ed. lib. bdg. 39.50 (0-88275-797-0) Krieger.

Atomic Absorption Spectroscopy - Past, Present & Future: To Commemorate the 25th Anniversary of Alan Walsh's Landmark Paper in Spectrochimica Acta. P. W. Boumans. 248p. 1981. pap. 39.00 (0-08-026267-8, Pergamon Pr) Elsevier.

Atomic Absorption Spectroscopy: Past - Present & Future, Pt. 2: To Commemorate the 25th Anniversary of Alan Walsh's Landmark Paper in Spectrochimica Acta. Ed. by P. W. Boumans. (Spectrochimica Acta B Ser.: Vol. 36, No. 5). iv, 92p. 1981. pap. 19.25 (0-08-026287-2, Pergamon Pr) Elsevier.

Atomic Age, No. 1. Lovece & Okamoto. 48p. 1990. 4.50 (0-87135-709-7) Marvel Entmnt.

Atomic Age, No. 2. Lovece & Okamoto. 48p. 1990. 4.50 (0-87135-710-0) Marvel Entmnt.

Atomic Age, No. 3. Lovece & Okamoto. 48p. 1991. 4.50 (0-87135-711-9) Marvel Entmnt.

Atomic Age, No. 4. Lovece & Okamoto. 48p. 1991. 4.50 (0-87135-712-7) Marvel Entmnt.

Atomic & Electronic Structure of Surfaces: Theoretical Foundations. M. Lannoo & P. Friedel. Ed. by G. Ertl & R. Gomer. (Surface Sciences Ser.: Vol. 16). (Illus.). 272p. 1991. 64.00 (0-387-52682-X) Spr-Verlag.

Atomic & Ionic Spectra & Elementary Processes in Plasma. Ed. by I. I. Sobelman. (Proceedings of the Lebedev Physics Institute Ser.: Vol. 192). 242p. (C). 1992. lib. bdg. 115.00 (1-56072-071-9) Nova Sci Pubs.

Atomic & Laser Spectroscopy. Alan Corney. (Illus.). 1987. pap. 39.95 (0-19-851148-5) OUP.

Atomic & Molecular Beam Methods, Vol. 2. Ed. by Giacinto Scoles et al. (Illus.). 552p. 1992. 125.00 (0-19-504281-6) OUP.

Atomic & Molecular Beam Methods Vol. I: Basic Techniques & Molecular Scattering. Ed. by Giacinto Scoles. (Illus.). 752p. 1988. 125.00 (0-19-504280-8) OUP.

Atomic & Molecular Clusters. Ed. by E. R. Bernstein. (Studies in Physical & Theoretical Chemistry: No. 68). 806p. 1990. 254.00 (0-444-88193-X) Elsevier.

Atomic & Molecular Data for Space Astronomy Needs, Analysis, & Availability: A Selection of Papers Presented on the Joint Commission Meeting III of the 21st I.A.U. General Assembly, Held in Buenos Aires, Argentina, 23 July-1 August 1991. LC 92-31543. (Lecture Notes in Physics Ser.: Vol. 407). vii, 158p. 1992. 58.00 (0-387-97909-3) Spr-Verlag.

Atomic & Molecular Orbitals. George I. Sackheim. 1965. pap. 3.80 (0-87563-002-2) Stipes.

Atomic & Molecular Physics: Third U. S.-Mexico Symposium, Morelos, Mexico, 13-16 March 1991. Ed. by C. Cisneros & T. J. Morgan. 450p. 1991. text ed. 118.00 (981-02-0843-X) World Scientific Pub.

Atomic & Molecular Physics & Quantum Optics: Proceedings of the 5th Summer School. H. A. Bachor et al. 560p. 1993. text ed. 116.00 (981-02-1124-4) World Scientific Pub.

Atomic & Molecular Physics & the Interstellar Matter, 2 vols., Set. Ed. by R. M. Balian et al. LC 75-23253. (Les Houches Summer School Ser.: Vol. 26). 632p. 1975. 174.50 (0-444-10856-4, North Holland) Elsevier.

Atomic & Molecular Processes with Short Intense Laser Pulses. Ed. by A. D. Bandruk. LC 88-2509. (NATO ASI Series B, Physics: Vol. 171). (Illus.). 492p. 1988. 135.00 (0-306-42826-1, Plenum Pr) Plenum.

Atomic & Molecular Processing of Electronic & Ceramic Materials: Preparation, Characterization & Properties. Ed. by I. A. Aksay et al. (Materials Research Society Conference Proceedings Ser.). 1988. text ed. 40.00 (0-931837-85-5) Materials Res.

Atomic & Molecular Radiation Physics. L. G. Christophorou. LC 72-129159. (Wiley Monographs in Chemical Physics). 682p. reprint ed. pap. 180.00 (0-8357-5852-4, 2023999) Bks Demand.

Atomic & Molecular Spectroscopy: Basic Aspects & Practical Applications. Sune Svanberg. Ed. by G. Ecker et al. (Atoms & Plasmas Ser.: Vol. 6). (Illus.). 416p. 1991. 49.00 (0-387-52594-7) Spr-Verlag.

An Asterisk (*) at the beginning of an entry indicates that the title is appearing in BIP for the first time.

An Asterisk (*) at the beginning of an entry indicates that the title is appearing in BIP for the first time.

*Atomization of Liquids. (Illus.). 500p. (C). 1994. 295.00 (1-57205-858-7) Rector Pr.

Atomization of Melts. Andrew J. Yule & John J. Dunkley. LC 93-46239. (Oxford Series on Advanced Manufacturing: No. 11). (Illus.). 472p. (C). 1994. 90.00 (0-19-856258-6) OUP.

Atomospheric Ozone. Ed. by C. S. Zerefos & A. Ghazi. 1985. lib. bdg. 99.00 (0-318-04128-6) Kluwer Ac.

Atoms. Jean Perrin. Tr. by D. L. Hammick. LC 90-42918. xvi, 232p. 1990. reprint ed. 42.00 (0-918024-78-1); reprint ed. pap. 17.50 (0-918024-79-X) Ox Bow.

Atoms: Building Blocks of Matter. Timothy L. Biel. LC 90-13214. (Encyclopedia of Discovery & Invention Ser.). (Illus.). 96p. (J). (gr. 5-8). 1990. lib. bdg. 17.95 (1-56006-207-X) Lucent Bks.

*Atoms & Eskimo Kisses: A Memoir of Father & Son. Claudio G. Segre. LC 95-7629. (Illus.). 304p. 1995. 23.95 (0-670-86307-6, Viking) Viking Penguin.

Atoms & Men. Louis Leprince-Ringuet. Tr. by Elaine P. Halperin. LC 61-11292. 128p. reprint ed. pap. 36.50 (0-8357-5859-1, 2020200) Bks Demand.

Atoms & Molecules. Lisa Nestor. (C). 1993. 7.75 (1-56870-076-8) RonJon Pub.

Atoms & Molecules. P. Roxbee-Cox. (Understanding Science Ser.). (Illus.). 32p. (J). (gr. 6-9). 1993. lib. bdg. 13.96 (0-88110-589-9); pap. 6.95 (0-7460-0988-7) EDC.

Atoms & Molecules: An Introduction for Students of Physical Chemistry. M. Karplus & R. N. Porter. 620p. (C). 1970. pap. text ed. 35.50 (0-8053-5218-X) Benjamin-Cummings.

Atoms & Molecules in Electric Fields. Nils Ryde. (Illus.). 455p. 1976. 96.50x (0-685-13587-X) Coronet Bks.

Atoms & Plasmas. V. S. Lisitsa. LC 93-46645. (Atoms & Plasmas Ser.: Vol. 14). 1994. 98.00 (0-387-57580-4) Spr-Verlag.

Atoms & Power: An Essay on Newtonian Matter-Theory & the Development of Chemistry. Arnold Thackray. LC 72-99521. (Harvard Monographs in the History of Science). (Illus.). 352p. reprint ed. pap. 100.40 (0-8357-9153-X, 2017756) Bks Demand.

Atoms & Quanta. Daphne F. Jackson. (Surrey University Press Ser.). 215p. 1990. pap. text ed. 42.00 (0-12-379075-1) Acad Pr.

Atoms & the Law. Edwin B. Stason et al. LC 59-63825. (Michigan Legal Publications). xxvii, 1512p. 1982. reprint ed. lib. bdg. 85.00 (0-89941-176-2, 302390) W S Hein.

*Atoms, Chemical Bonds & Bond Dissociation Energies. Sandor Fliszar. LC 94-27454. (Lecture Notes in Chemistry: Vol. 63). 1994. 42.00 (0-387-58237-1) Spr-Verlag.

Atoms, Electrons & Change. P. W. Atkins. (Scientific American Library). 1995. text ed. write for info. (0-7167-5028-7) W H Freeman.

*Atoms' Family. J. M. Patten. LC 94-47598. (Let's Wonder About Science Ser.). (J). 1995. write for info. (1-55916-125-6) Rourke Bk Co.

Atoms for Peace: Dwight D. Eisenhower's Address to the United Nations, 1954. Intro. by Jack M. Holl & Roger M. Anders. LC 88-600494. (Milestone Documents Ser.). (Illus.). 32p. 1990. pap. text ed. 3.50 (0-911333-76-2, 200016) National Archives & Recs.

Atoms for Peace & War, 1953-1961: Eisenhower & the Atomic Energy Commission. Richard G. Hewlett & Jack M. Holl. 1989. 65.00 (0-520-06018-0) U CA Pr.

Atoms for Power. Ed. by Philip C. Jessup. LC 58-6048. 1958. 1.95 (0-936904-01-1) Am Assembly.

Atoms for the World: United States Participation in the Conference on the Peaceful Uses of Atomic Energy. Laura Fermi. LC 57-6977. (Illus.). 263p. reprint ed. pap. 75.00 (0-8357-5860-5, 2011227) Bks Demand.

Atoms in Astrophysics. Ed. by P. G. Burke et al. LC 82-22517. (Physics of Atoms & Molecules Ser.). 374p. 1983. 95.00 (0-306-41097-4, Plenum Pr) Plenum.

Atoms in Contact. B. R. Jennings & V. J. Morris. (Oxford Paperbacks Ser.). (Illus.). 112p. (C). 1974. text ed. 16.95 (0-19-851809-9) OUP.

Atoms in Electromagnetic Fields. C. Cohen-Tannoudji. 684p. 1994. text ed. 124.00 (981-02-1242-9); pap. text ed. 61.00 (981-02-1243-7) World Scientific Pub.

Atoms in External Fields. S. Fraga & J. Muszynska. (Physical Sciences Data Ser.: Vol. 8). 558p. 1981. 161.75 (0-444-41936-5) Elsevier.

Atoms in Intense Laser Fields. Ed. by Mihai Gavrila. (Illus.). 516p. 1992. text ed. 95.00 (0-12-003901-X) Acad Pr.

Atoms in Molecules: A Quantum Theory. Richard F. Bader. (International Series of Monographs on Chemistry: No. 22). (Illus.). 456p. 1991. 120.00 (0-19-855168-1) OUP.

Atoms in Molecules: A Quantum Theory. Richard F. Bader. LC 93-46241. (International Series of Monographs on Chemistry: No. 22). (Illus.). 456p. (C). 1994. pap. 37.50 (0-19-855865-1, Clarendon Pr) OUP.

Atoms in Strong Fields. Ed. by C. A. Nicolaides et al. LC 89-48928. (NATO ASI Series B, Physics: Vol. 212). (Illus.). 550p. 1990. 135.00 (0-306-43414-8, Plenum Pr) Plenum.

Atoms in Strong Light Fields. N. B. Delone & Vladimir P. Krainov. (Chemical Physics Ser.: Vol. 28). (Illus.). 350p. 1985. 99.00 (0-387-12412-8) Spr-Verlag.

*Atoms in Strong Magnetic Fields: Quantum Mechanical Treatment & Applications in Astrophysics & Quantum Chaos. Hanns Ruder. LC 94-23259. 1994. write for info. (0-387-57699-1); write for info. (3-540-57699-1) Spr-Verlag.

Atoms in the Family: My Life with Enrico Fermi. Laura Fermi. (History of Modern Physics & Astronomy Ser.). (Illus.). 280p. 1987. 32.00 (0-88318-524-5) Am Inst Physics.

Atoms in the Family: My Life with Enrico Fermi. Laura Fermi. (Illus.). xiv, 268p. 1994. pap. 13.95 (0-226-24367-2) U Ch Pr.

*Atoms in the Field. Don Cooper. (Illus.). 218p. (C). 1989. text ed. 29.95x (1-55059-000-6) Temeron Bks.

Atoms in Unusual Situations. Ed. by Jean P. Briand. LC 86-22495. (NATO ASI Series B, Physics). 450p. 1986. 95.00 (0-306-42399-5, Plenum Pr) Plenum.

Atoms, Ions, & Molecules: New Results in Spectral Line Astrophysics. Ed. by A. Haschick & P. Ho. (ASP Conference Series Publications: Vol. 16). 474p. 1991. 25.00 (0-937707-35-X) Astron Soc Pacific.

Atoms, Men & Stars: A Survey of the Latest Developments of Physical Science & Their Relation to Life. Rogers D. Rusk. LC 70-156712. (Essay Index Reprint Ser.). 1977. reprint ed. 26.95 (0-8369-2332-4) Ayer.

Atoms, Metaphors & Paradoxes: Niels Bohr & the Construction of a New Physics. Sandro Petruccioli. Tr. by Ian McGilvray. LC 93-177. 240p. (C). 1994. 54.95 (0-521-40259-X) Cambridge U Pr.

Atoms, Molecules, & Reactions: An Introduction to Chemistry. Ronald J. Gillespie et al. LC 93-42571. 1993. text ed. 42.00 (0-13-088790-0) P-H.

Atoms of Empire. Charles J. Hyne. LC 77-103519. (Short Story Index Reprint Ser.). 1977. 20.95 (0-8369-3261-7) Ayer.

Atoms of Hope. Mohan S. Rajan. 155p. 1980. 15.95 (0-940500-39-6, Pub. by Allied Pubs II) Asia Bk Corp.

Atoms, Pleasure, Virtue: The Philosophy of Epicurus. Avraam Koen. LC 94-1151. (American University Studies: Ser. V, Vol. 152). 176p. (C). 1995. pap. text ed. 39.95 (0-8204-2234-7) P Lang Pubs.

Atoms, Pneuma, & Tranquillity: Epicurean & Stoic Themes in European Thought. Ed. by Margaret J. Osler. 288p. (C). 1991. 59.95 (0-521-40048-1) Cambridge U Pr.

Atoms, Radiation & Radiation Protection. James E. Turner. 346p. 1986. pap. text ed. 45.00 (0-07-105320-4) Hlth Prof Div.

*Atoms, Radiation, & Radiation Protection. 2nd ed. James E. Turner. LC 94-33123. 555p. 1995. text ed. 69.95 (0-471-59581-0) Wiley.

Atoms, Stars & Minds: Synthesizing an Elementary Particle That Comprehends Itself. Peter K. Bros. (Copernican Ser.: Vol. 1). 334p. (Orig.). 1992. pap. 14.95 (0-9627769-1-2) Fin Bk Partners.

Atoms, Stars & Nebulae. rev. ed. Lawrence H. Aller. LC 76-134951. (Harvard Books on Astronomy). (Illus.). reprint ed. pap. 90.80 (0-8357-5861-3, 2019508) Bks Demand.

Atoms, Stars, & Nebulae. 3rd ed. Lawrence H. Aller. (Illus.). 250p. (C). 1991. pap. 34.95 (0-521-31040-7) Cambridge U Pr.

Atoms, Stars, & Nebulae. 3rd ed. Lawrence H. Aller. (Illus.). 250p. (C). 1991. 89.95 (0-521-32512-9) Cambridge U Pr.

*Atoms, Whales & Rivers: Global Environmental Security & International Organization. Stoett. 207p. 1995. lib. bdg. 67.00 (1-56072-235-5) Nova Sci Pubs.

Atoms Within Us. rev. ed. Ernest Borek. LC 80-19010. 272p. 1980. text ed. 46.00 (0-231-04386-4); pap. text ed. 17.50 (0-231-04387-2) Col U Pr.

Atonement. Leon Morris. LC 83-20649. 219p. 1984. pap. 14.99 (0-87784-826-2, 826) InterVarsity.

*Atonement. Michael Winter. LC 94-32617. (Problems in Theology Ser.). 1994. 17.95 (0-8146-5852-0) Liturgical Pr.

*Atonement. 2nd rev. ed. Gordon H. Clark. Ed. & Intro. by John W. Robbins. (Illus.). 163p. 1995. pap. 8.95 (0-940931-87-7) Trinity Found.

Atonement & Incarnation: An Essay in Universalism & Particularity. Vernon White. 144p. (C). 1991. 54.95 (0-521-40031-7); pap. 15.95 (0-521-40732-X) Cambridge U Pr.

Atonement & Justification: English Evangelical Theology, 1640-1790: An Evaluation. Alan C. Clifford. (Illus.). 288p. 1990. 68.00 (0-19-826195-0) OUP.

Atonement of George Fox. Emilia Fogelklou-Norlind. Ed. by Eleanore P. Mather. LC 75-84675. (Orig.). 1969. pap. 3.00 (0-87574-166-5) Pendle Hill.

Atonement of Mindy Wise. Marilyn Kaye. Ed. by Liz Van Doren. 160p. (YA). (gr. 7 up). 1991. 15.95 (0-15-200402-5, Gulliver Bks) HarBrace.

Atoning Gospel. James E. Tull. LC 81-18732. 221p. 1982. 15.50 (0-86554-029-2, MUP-H28) Mercer Univ Pr.

Atop the Urban Hierarchy. Robert A. Beauregard. LC 88-18467. (Illus.). 324p. (C). 1989. 56.00 (0-8476-7554-8, R7554) Rowman.

Atopic Palmoplantar Eczema. H. J. Schwanitz. (Illus.). 150p. 1988. pap. 66.00 (0-387-17863-5) Spr-Verlag.

Atopula, Guerrero & Olmec Horizons in Mesoamerica. John S. Henderson. LC 79-65060. (Publications in Anthropology: No. 77). 1979. pap. 13.50 (0-913516-10-4) Yale U Anthro.

ATP - Airline Transport Pilot: A Comprehensive Text & Workbook for the ATP Written Exam. 4th ed. K. T. Boyd. LC 94-18373. 174p. 1994. pap. 24.95 (0-8138-0085-4) Iowa St U Pr.

ATP-FAR 135, Airline Transport Pilot. 3rd ed. K. T. Boyd. LC 94-20778. 202p. 1994. pap. 24.95 (0-8138-0508-2) Iowa St U Pr.

ATP Practical Test Standards FAA S-8081-5: Airplane & Helicopter. FAA Staff. (Practical Test Standards Ser.). (Illus.). 1988. reprint ed. pap. text ed. 4.95 (1-56027-042-X, ASA-8081-5) Av Suppl & Acad.

ATP Test Prep ATP-17A. rev. ed. ASA Staff. (Illus.). 409p. 1993. pap. 29.95 (1-56027-177-9, ASA-TP17A) Av Suppl & Acad.

ATP Tour. Ed. by Richard Evans. (Illus.). 240p. 1993. 55.00 (0-7475-1128-4, Pub. by Bloomsbury Pub Ltd UK) Trafalgar.

*ATP Tour Official Player Guide: Official Guide to IBM-ATP Tour. ATP Tour Staff. (Illus.). 432p. (YA). 1995. pap. 12.95 (1-57243-055-9) Triumph Bks.

*ATP Tour Official Player Guide: Official Guide to IBM-ATP Tour. ATP Tour Staff. (Illus.). 432p. (YA). 1995. lib. bdg. 24.95 (1-57243-072-9) Triumph Bks.

Atractyl Oxide: Chemistry, Biochemistry & Toxicology. R. Santi & S. Luciani. 136p. 1978. text ed. 16.00 (1-57235-061-X) Piccin NY.

*Atre e Storie a Sciacca, Celtabellotta, e Burgio del XV el XVII Secolo: Italian Stories & Art. Ed. by Ignazio Navarra. xvi, 144p. 1986. pap. 15.00 (0-89304-554-3) Cross-Cultrl NY.

*Atrevase a Sonar De Nuevo: Manual Del Adulto. Chapel of the Air Ministries Staff. Tr. by Anna Berglund et al. (1994 50-Day Spiritual Adventure Ser.). (Illus.). 64p. (Orig.). 1994. student ed. pap. text ed. 4.99 (1-879050-44-7) Chapel of Air.

*Atrevete a Cambiar. Nahum Rosario. 45p. (Orig.). (SPA.). 1995. pap. 5.00 (0-9634761-6-5) Pub Maranatha.

Atrevete a Dar Amor (Dare to Give Love) A. Mottesi. (SPA.). Date not set. 1.79 (1-56063-099-X, 498144) Editorial Unilit.

Atrevete a Sonar (Dare to Dream) F. Littauer. (SPA.). Date not set. 7.99 (1-56063-143-0, 498516) Editorial Unilit.

Atrevete Con la Vida: Dare to Live Now. Bruce Larson. (SPA.). 3.95 (84-7228-141-8, 220054, Pub. by Edit Clie SP) TSELF.

Atria. 1988. pap. 36.00 (0-86022-220-9, Pub. by Build Servs Info Assn UK) St Mut.

Atria. C. Hancock & J. G. Littler. (C). 1987. 100.00 (0-685-33092-3, Pub. by Interntl Solar Energy Soc UK) St Mut.

Atria (C49) C. J. Hancock & J. G. Littler. (C). 1987. 125.00 (0-685-30232-6, Pub. by Interntl Solar Energy Soc UK) St Mut.

Atrial Arrhythmias: Current Concepts & Management. Touboul & Waldo. (Illus.). 521p. 1990. 79.00 (0-8016-5092-5) Mosby Yr Bk.

*Atrial Arrhythmias: State of the Art. Ed. by John P. DiMarco & Eric N. Prystowsky. (Illus.). 448p. 1994. 70.00 (0-87993-604-5) Futura Pub.

Atrial Fibrillation. J. Loscalzo & M. E. Mendelson. 1994. 45.00 (0-86542-100-5) Blackwell Sci.

Atrial Fibrillation. J. Rawles. (Illus.). xii, 243p. 1991. 105.00 (0-387-19699-4) Spr-Verlag.

Atrial Fibrillation: A Treatable Disease? Ed. by J. H. Kingma et al. LC 92-49554. (Developments in Cardiovascular Medicine Ser.: Vol. 139). 1992. lib. bdg. 99.00 (0-7923-2008-5) Kluwer Ac.

*Atrial Fibrillation: Facts from Yesterday - Ideas for Tomorrow. Ed. by Henri E. Kulbertus et al. (Bakken Research Center Ser.). (Illus.). 184p. 1994. 55.00 (0-87993-097-7) Futura Pub.

Atrial Fibrillation: Mechanisms & Management. Ed. by Rodney H. Falk & Philip J. Podrid. 448p. 1992. 100.00 (0-88167-831-7, 2312) Raven.

Atrial Fibrillation: Mechanisms & Therapeutic Strategies. S. Bertil Olsson et al. LC 94-4682. (Illus.). 432p. 1994. 79.00 (0-87993-587-1) Futura Pub.

*Atrial Fibrillation for the Clinician. Ed. by Francis D. Murgatroyd & A. John Camm. LC 95-176. (Clinical Approaches to Tachyarrhythmias Ser.: Vol. 4). (Illus.). 152p. 1995. 19.00 (0-87993-614-2) Futura Pub.

Atrial Hormones & Other Natriuretic Factors. Ed. by Patrick J. Mulrow & Robert W. Schrier. (American Physiological Society Book). (Illus.). 186p. 1988. 44.50 (0-19-520687-8) OUP.

Atrial Natriuretic Hormones. David L. Vesely & James A. Haley. 256p. 1991. text ed. 76.00 (0-13-050584-6) P-H.

Atrial Natriuretic Peptides. Ed. by Barry M. Brenner & Jay H. Stein. (Contemporary Issues in Nephrology Ser.: Vol. 21). (Illus.). 276p. 1990. text ed. 83.00 (0-443-08669-9) Churchill.

Atrial Natriuretic Peptides. Ed. by Willis K. Samson & Remi Quirion. 336p. 1989. 216.00 (0-8493-6249-0, QP572) CRC Pr.

*Atrial Natriuretic Peptides. fac. ed. Ed. by Barry M. Brenner & Jay H. Stein. LC 89-22191. (Contemporary Issues in Nephrology Ser.: No. 21). (Illus.). 286p. 1989. reprint ed. pap. 81.60 (0-7837-7897-X, 2047653) Bks Demand.

Atributos de Dios. Arthur W. Pink. 131p. 1990. reprint ed. 4.95 (0-85151-540-1) Banner of Truth.

Atrioventricular Conduction in Congenital: Heart Disease - Surgical Anatomy. H. Kurosawa & A. E. Becker. 290p. 1987. 310.00 (0-387-70015-3) Spr-Verlag.

Atrium. Werner Blaser. (Illus.). 205p. 1985. 49.00 (3-85977-080-2, Pub. by Wepf & Co SZ) Interbk Inc.

Atrium Buildings. 2nd ed. 1986. 67.95 (0-85139-051-X) Buttrwrth-Heinemann.

Atrium Comes of Age. Richard Saxon. 95p. 1994. text ed. 52.95 (0-470-22127-5) Halsted Pr.

Atrium in Health & Disease. Ed. by Patrick Attuel et al. (Illus.). 286p. 1989. 60.00 (0-87993-346-1) Futura Pub.

Atrocities & Other Conditions in Concentration Camps in Germany. (Witness to the Holocaust Ser.: No. 3). 21p. 1980. 1.00 (0-685-13968-9) Witness Holocaust.

Atrocity see Moni: A Novel

Atrocity & Amnesia: The Political Novel since 1945. Robert Boyers. LC 85-13745. 275p. 1987. pap. 19.95 (0-19-505082-7) OUP.

Atrocity Book. Joan Colby. LC 84-17078. 69p. 1986. pap. 8.00 (0-89924-045-3) Lynx Hse.

Atrocity Exhibition. J. G. Ballard. (Illus.). 140p. 1990. 50.00 (0-940642-19-0) Re Search Pubns.

Atrocity Exhibition. rev. ed. J. G. Bullard. Ed. by V. Vale & Andrea Juno. (Illus.). 141p. 1990. pap. text ed. 13.99 (0-940642-18-2) Re Search Pubns.

Atrocity Propaganda, 1914-1919. James M. Read. LC 72-4676. (International Propaganda & Communications Ser.). 333p. 1977. reprint ed. 20.95 (0-405-04760-6) Ayer.

Atropos. William L. DeAndrea. 1990. 18.95 (0-89296-208-9) Mysterious Pr.

ATSDR Public Health Assessment Guidance Manual. 1992. 55.00 (0-87371-857-7, RA566) Lewis Pubs.

*ATSDR's Toxicological Profiles on CD-ROM: Agency for Toxic Substances & Disease Registry. 20p. 1995. 125.00 (1-56670-154-6, L1154) Lewis Pubs.

*ATSF Color Guide to Freight & Passenger Equipment. Lloyd E. Stagner. (Illus.). 1995. 49.95 (1-878887-45-9) Morning NJ.

Attaboy, Sam! Lois Lowry. (J). (gr. 4-7). 1993. pap. 3.50 (0-440-40816-4) Dell.

Attaboy, Sam! Lois Lowry. (Illus.). 128p. (J). (gr. 2-6). 1992. 14.95 (0-395-61588-7) HM.

Attache Adventures Abroad: The Postwar Decade in Turkey, Greece, Palestine & Equatorial Africa. Gilbert E. Bursley. (Illus.). 252p. (Orig.). 1994. pap. 15.50 (0-9638532-0-1) Cleary Coll.

Attached Deck with Screened in Porch. Ed. by Workbench Magazine Staff. (Workbench Plans Ser.). (Illus.). 15p. Date not set. 16.95 (0-86675-075-4) KC Pub.

Attached to Doctor Marchmont. large type ed. Juliet Shore. 336p. 1986. pap. 11.95 (0-7089-6297-1, Linford) Ulverscroft.

Attachment. 2nd ed. John Bowlby. LC 83-71445. 425p. 1983. pap. text ed. 20.00 (0-465-00543-8) Basic.

Attachment: A Life Span Concept, Proceedings of the American Psychological Association Symposium, New Orleans, 1974. American Psychological Association Symposium Staff. Ed. by T. Antonucci. (Human Development Journal: Vol. 19, No. 3). 1976. 20.00 (3-8055-2619-9) S Karger.

Attachment Across the Life Cycle. Ed. by Colin M. Parkes et al. (Illus.). 336p. 1991. 99.95 (0-415-05650-0, A5199, Tavistock) Routledge.

Attachment Across the Life Cycle. Ed. by Colin M. Parkes et al. 336p. 1993. pap. 25.00 (0-415-05651-9, B0621) Routledge.

Attachment & Early Hospitalization: An Experiment in the Prevention of Posthospital Disturbance in Infants. J. Fahrenfort. 144p. 1993. pap. 23.50 (90-5170-215-9, Pub. by Thesis Pubs NE) IBD Ltd.

Attachment & Perfection of Article 9 Security Interests. Harry J. Haynsworth, IV. 1988. ring bd. 15.00 (0-943856-23-X, 510) SC Bar CLE.

Attachment & the Therapeutic Process: Essays in Honor of Otto Allen Will, Jr. M.D. Ed. by James L. Sacksteder et al. 500p. (C). 1987. text ed. 50.00 (0-8236-0447-0) Intl Univs Pr.

Attachment Behaviour & the Schoolchild: An Introduction to Educational Therapy. Muriel Barrett & Jane Trevitt. (Illus.). 272p. 1991. 69.95 (0-415-04797-8, A5404); pap. 19.95 (0-415-04798-6, A5408) Routledge.

Attachment in Adults: Clinical & Developmental Perspectives. Ed. by Michael B. Sperling & William H. Berman. LC 94-2524. 360p. 1994. lib. bdg. 38.95 (0-89862-547-5, C2547) Guilford Pubns.

Attachment in Social Networks: Contributions to the Bowlby-Ainsworth-Attachment Theory. Ed. by L. W. C. Tavecchio & M. H. Van Ijzendoorn. (Advances in Psychology Ser.: No. 44). 484p. 1987. 105.25 (0-444-70156-7, North Holland) Elsevier.

Attachment in the Preschool Years: Theory, Research, & Intervention. Ed. by Mark T. Greenberg et al. LC 89-49657. (John D. & Catherine T. MacArthur Foundation Series on Mental Health & Development). xx, 508p. (C). 1993. pap. text ed. 22.95 (0-226-30630-5) U Ch Pr.

Attachment of Organisms to the Gut Mucosa, Vol. I. Ed. by Edgar C. Boedeker. 240p. 1984. 143.00 (0-8493-5286-X, QR171, CRC Reprint) Franklin.

Attachment of Organisms to the Gut Mucosa, Vol. II. Ed. by Edgar C. Boedeker. 272p. 1984. 143.00 (0-8493-5287-8, CRC Reprint) Franklin.

*Attachment Theory: Social, Developmental, & Clinical Perspectives. Ed. by Susan Goldberg et al. 1995. write for info. (0-88163-184-1) Analytic Pr.

*Attachments for Prosthetic Dentistry: Introduction & Application. Michael Sherring-Lucas & Paul Martin. 84p. 1995. pap. 38.00 (1-85097-036-X) Quintessence.

Attack. Clay Coleman. (Escape from Lost Island Ser.: No. 2). (YA). (gr. 9-12). 1990. pap. 2.95 (0-06-106022-4, PL) HarpC.

Attack: And Other Papers. Richard H. Tawney. LC 70-152216. (Essay Index Reprint Ser.). 1977. reprint ed. 20.95 (0-8369-2376-6) Ayer.

Attack Aircraft. Roy Braybrook. (Illus.). 176p. 1990. 29.95 (0-85429-711-1, Pub. by J H Haynes & Co UK) Motorbooks Intl.

Attack & Defense. Seven-Dan Ishida Akira & James Davies. (Elementary Go Ser.: Vol. 5). 1980. 13.95 (4-87187-014-6, G14) Ishi Pr Intl.

Attack & Defense of Little Round Top, Gettysburg, July 2, 1863. Oliver W. Norton. (Illus.). 350p. 1992. reprint ed. 25.00 (1-879664-07-0); reprint ed. pap. 12.95 (1-879664-08-9) Stan Clark Military.

Attack & Defense of Little Roundtop, Gettysburg, July 2, 1863. Norton & Pullen. 350p. 1983. 25.00 (0-89029-041-5) Morningside Bkshop.

Attack & Die: Civil War Military Tactics & the Southern Heritage. Grady McWhiney & Perry D. Jamieson. LC 81-902. (Illus.). xvii, 232p. 1982. pap. 14.50 (0-8173-0229-8) U of Ala Pr.

*Attack Asthma: How to Conquer Environmental Illnesses & Allergies Without Drugs. William Vayda. 170p. (Orig.). 1995. pap. 14.95 (0-85091-626-7, Pub. by Lothian Pub AT) Seven Hills Bk.

An Asterisk (*) at the beginning of an entry indicates that the title is appearing in BIP for the first time.

An Asterisk (*) at the beginning of an entry indicates that the title is appearing in BIP for the first time.

Attention Deficit Hyperactivity Disorder: What Every Parent Wants to Know. Ed. by David L. Wodrich. LC 93-31107. 320p. 1993. pap. 19.95 (*1-55766-141-3*) P H Brookes.

***Attention-Deficit Hyperactivity Disorder in Adults.** Paul H. Wender. (Illus.). 224p. 1995. 25.00 (*0-19-509227-9*) OUP.

***Attention-Deficit/Hyperactivity Disorder: Abstracts of the Psychological & Behavioral Literature, 1971-1994.** Ed. by Robert J. Resnick & Kathleen McEvoy. (Bibliographies in Psychology Ser.: No. 14). 204p. 1994. 27.50 (*1-55798-274-0*) Am Psychol.

***Attention-Deficit/Hyperactivity Disorder in the Classroom: A Practical Guide for Teachers.** Carol A. Dowdy et al. 250p. (Orig.). (C). 1995. pap. text ed. 27.00 (*0-89079-665-3*, 6961) PRO-ED.

Attention Deficits & Hyperactivity in Children. Stephen P. Hinshaw. (Developmental Clinical Psychology & Psychiatry Ser.: Vol. 29). (C). Date not set. text ed. 37.00 (*0-8039-5195-7*); pap. text ed. 16.95 (*0-8039-5196-5*) Sage.

Attention Deficits, Learning Disabilities, & Ritalin: A Practical Guide. 2nd ed. Robert B. Johnston. (Illus.). 189p. (Orig.). (C). 1991. pap. text ed. 24.50 (*1-879105-12-8*, A037) Singular Publishing.

***Attention Disorders in Children: School-Based Assessment, Diagnosis, & Treatment.** Richard Morriss. 1995. 49.50 (*0-614-06076-1*, W-314A) Western Psych.

Attention Getting Headings. (Easy-to-Make Photocopier Bks.). (Orig.). 1983. pap. 19.95 (*0-87280-034-2*, 781, Asher-Gallant) Caddylak Systs.

Attention-Getting Headings II. (Easy-to-Make Photocopier Bks.). (Orig.). 1984. pap. 19.95 (*0-87280-024-5*, 753, Asher-Gallant) Caddylak Systs.

***Attention, Good Listeners!** Jean G. DeGaetano. 52p. 1986. pap. text ed. 24.95 (*1-886143-07-2*) Grt Ideas Tching.

Attention in Learning: Theory & Research. Tom Trabasso & Gordon H. Bower. LC 74-26681. 266p. 1975. reprint ed. 22.50 (*0-88275-231-6*) Krieger.

Attention in Neurophysiology: An International Conference. Ed. by C. R. Evans & T. B. Mulholland. LC 73-154650. 471p. reprint ed. pap. 134.30 (*0-8357-5863-X*, 2025737) Bks Demand.

***Attention, Memory, & Executive Function.** G. Reid Lyon & Norman A. Krasnegor. LC 95-2540. 432p. 1995. boxed 43.00 (*1-55766-198-7*) P H Brookes.

***Attention Training & Healing: What Other Books Didn't Tell You.** Ruth Rosbach-Chandler. 64p. Date not set. pap. text ed. 9.95 (*0-9645303-0-9*) Olympic Press.

Attention, Voluntary Contraction & Event-Related Cerebral Potentials. Ed. by J. E. Desmedt. (Progress in Clinical Neurophysiology Ser.: Vol. 1). 1977. 78.50 (*3-8055-2438-2*) S Karger.

Attentional Correlates of Schizophrenia & Related Disorders. R. J. Van Den Bosch. xvi, 312p. 1982. 31.00 (*90-265-0433-0*, Pub. by Swets Pub Serv NE) Taylor & Francis.

***Attentional Deficit Disorder in Children & Adolescents.** Jack L. Fadely & Virginia N. Hosler. 292p. 1992. pap. 30.95 (*0-614-02075-1*) C C Thomas.

Attentional Deficit Disorder in Children & Adolescents. Jack L. Fadely & Virginia N. Hosler. 292p. (C). 1992. text ed. 51.95x (*0-398-05792-3*) C C Thomas.

***Attentional Processing: The Brain's Art of Mindfulness.** David LaBerge. LC 94-38071. (Illus.). 256p. 1995. text ed. 35.00 (*0-674-05268-4*, LABATT) HUP.

***Attentive & Committed.** Ellen Larson. Ed. by Debbie Bible. (Value Builders Ser.). (J). 1995. 7.95 (*0-7814-5100-0*, 10454) Cook.

Attentive Heart: Conversations with Trees. Stephanie Kaza. LC 92-97478. (Illus.). 208p. 1993. 17.50 (*0-449-90779-1*, Columbine) Fawcett.

Attenzione Prego! C. Flynn. (C). 1988. 45.00 (*0-85950-651-7*, Pub. by S Thornes Pubs UK); audio 220.00 (*0-85950-652-5*, Pub. by S Thornes Pubs UK) St Mut.

Attestation of Many Learned, Godly, & Famous Divines... Justifying...That the Church Government Ought to Be Always with the Peoples Free Consent. Henry Jacob. LC 74-28868. (English Experience Ser.: No. 747). 1975. reprint ed. 30.00 (*90-221-0747-7*) Walter J Johnson.

Atthasalini, Buddhaghosa's Commentary on the Dhammasangani. Buddhaghosa. Ed. by Edward Muller. LC 78-72383. reprint ed. 39.50 (*0-404-17245-8*) AMS Pr.

Atthis: The Local Chronicles of Ancient Athens. Felix Jacoby. LC 72-7897. (Greek History Ser.). 1977. reprint ed. 44.95 (*0-405-04796-7*) Ayer.

Atti Del XIV Congresso Internationale Di Linguistica E Filologia Romanza, 5 vols. Ed. by Alberto Varvaro. 1981. pap. 475.00 (*90-272-0941-3*) Benjamins North Am.

Attic. Katherine Dunn. 1990. pap. 9.99 (*0-446-39152-2*) Warner Bks.

Attic. T. S. Rue. (Nightmare Inn Ser.: No. 4). (YA). 1993. mass mkt. 3.50 (*0-06-106157-3*, Harp PBks) HarpC.

Attic. Jack Scaparro. 1991. mass mkt. 4.50 (*0-8217-3471-7*) Zebra.

Attic: A Memoir. Curtis Harnack. LC 93-12920. (Iowa Heritage Collection). (Illus.). 192p. (C). 1993. pap. 14.95 (*0-8138-2146-0*) Iowa St U Pr.

Attic, Basement & Garage Conversion. Paul Bianchina. 1989. text ed. 24.95 (*0-07-157442-5*) McGraw.

Attic, Basement & Garage Conversion: A Do-It-Yourselfer's Guide. Paul Bianchina. (Illus.). 208p. 1989. 24.95 (*0-8306-9271-1*); pap. 16.95 (*0-8306-3271-9*) TAB Bks.

Attic Black Figure Vase-Painters. J. D. Beazley. LC 75-44909. 1978. reprint ed. lib. bdg. 45.00 (*0-87817-191-6*) Hacker.

Attic Black-Figured Neck-Amphorae. Mary B. Moore & Dietrich Von Bothmer. LC 75-25613. (Illus.). 86p. 1976. 9.95 (*0-87099-134-5*) Metro Mus Art.

Attic Black-Figured Pottery. Mary B. Moore & Mary Z. Philippides. LC 86-20615. (Athenian Agora Ser.: Vol. 23). (Illus.). xvi, 382p. 1986. 60.00 (*0-87661-223-0*) Am Sch Athens.

Attic Book fo Contracts & Diary. (Illus.). 192p. (C). 1994. pap. 9.99 (*1-85594-046-9*, Pub. by Attic IE) InBook.

Attic Book of Special Days for Women. Attic Pr Staff. (Illus.). 224p. (C). 1993. 29.99 (*1-85594-011-6*, Pub. by Attic IE) InBook.

***Attic Document Reliefs: Art & Politics in Ancient Athens.** Carol L. Lawton. (Oxford Monographs on Classical Archaeology). (Illus.). 256p. 1995. 96.00 (*0-19-814955-7*) OUP.

***Attic Dolls.** Linda Carroll. (Milner Craft Ser.). (Illus.). 64p. 1995. 19.95 (*1-86351-128-8*, Pub. by S Milner AT) Sterling.

Attic Dreamer. Michael Monahan. LC 68-20321. (Essay Index Reprint Ser.). 1977. 20.95 (*0-8369-0711-6*) Ayer.

Attic Festivals of Demeter & Their Relation to the Agricultural Year. Allaire C. Brumfield. Ed. by W. R. Connor. LC 80-2643. (Monographs in Classical). 1981. lib. bdg. 29.00 (*0-405-14031-2*) Ayer.

Attic Grave Reliefs That Represent Women in the Dress of Isis, No. 22. Elizabeth J. Walters. LC 88-6237. (Hesperia Supplement Ser.: No. 22). (Illus.). xvi, 135p. 1988. pap. 40.00 (*0-87661-522-1*) Am Sch Athens.

Attic Letter-Cutters of 229-86 B.C. Stephen V. Tracy. LC 89-20286. (Hellenistic Culture & Society Ser.: No. 6). (Illus.). 3315p. 1990. 45.00 (*0-520-06806-8*) U CA Pr.

Attic Letters: Ume Tsuda's Correspondence to Her American Mother. Yoshiko Furuki. 492p. 1991. 32.50 (*0-8348-0244-9*) Weatherhill.

Attic Nights, 3 vols., Vol. 1, Bks. 1-4. Aulus Gellius. (Loeb Classical Library: No. 195, 200, 212). 528p. 1927. 18.95 (*0-674-99215-6*) HUP.

Attic Nights, 3 vols., Vol. 2, Bks. 6-13. Aulus Gellius. (Loeb Classical Library: No. 195, 200, 212). 570p. 1927. 18.95 (*0-674-99220-2*) HUP.

Attic Nights, 3 vols., Vol. 3, Bks. 14-20. Aulus Gellius. (Loeb Classical Library: No. 195, 200, 212). 530p. 1927. 18.95 (*0-674-99234-2*) HUP.

Attic Nights of Aulus Gellius: An Intermediate Reader - Grammar Review. 2nd ed. P. L. Chambers. (Latin Alive & Well Ser.). (Illus.). 82p. (LAT.). (C). 1994. pap. text ed. 15.95 (*0-9628450-3-5*) P L Chambers.

***Attic Nights of Aulus Gellius, Teacher Key.** 2nd ed. 1994. 5.95 (*0-9628450-4-3*) P L Chambers.

Attic Odyssey: Letters Tell a Tale or Two. Winifred W. Fiero. Ed. by Dorothy Bruno. (Illus.). 144p. 1986. write for info. (*0-9621626-0-4*); text ed. 10.00 (*0-685-24023-1*) W W Fiero.

Attic of an Ignoramus. Robert Q. Widener. LC 76-7846. 1976. 6.95 (*0-685-68660-4*) Courier Pr.

***Attic Orators.** M. Edwards. (Classical World Ser.). 94p. 1994. pap. text ed. 13.95 (*1-85399-413-8*) Focus Info Gr.

Attic Pyxis. Sally Roberts. 366p. 1978. 50.00 (*0-89005-210-7*) Ares.

Attic Quiz Book. G. Healy & P. O'Connor. (C). 1989. 39.00 (*0-946211-89-2*, Pub. by Attic Pr IE) St Mut.

Attic Red-Figure Vase-Painters, 3 Vols., Set. J. D. Beazley. 2036p. 1983. reprint ed. 125.00 (*0-87817-289-0*) Hacker.

Attic Theatre: A Description of the Stage & Theatre of the Athenians. Arthur E. Haigh. LC 68-24965. (Studies in Drama: No. 39). (Illus.). 1969. reprint ed. lib. bdg. 75.00 (*0-8383-0951-8*) M S G Haskell Hse.

Attic Treasure. Steve McKinstry. (Illus.). 32p. 1982. 6.95 (*0-317-62219-6*) Lucy & Co.

Attic Windows - A Contemporary View. Diana Leone. 64p. 1988. pap. 16.95 (*0-942786-09-2*) Leone Pubns.

Atticismus in Seinen Hauptvertretern Von Dionysius Von Halikarnass Bis Auf Den Zweiten Philostratus Dargestellt, 4 vols., Set. Wilhelm Schmid. xix, 2064p. 1964. reprint ed. write for info. (*0-318-71022-6*, Pub. by Georg Olms GW) Lubrecht & Cramer.

Atticshe Mittlere Komodie: Ihre Stellung in der Antiken Literatur & Literaturgeschichte. Heinz-Gunther Nesselrath. (Untersuchungen zur Antiken Literatur und Geschichte Ser.: No. 36). x, 395p. (GER.). (C). 1990. lib. bdg. 166.15 (*3-11-012196-4*) De Gruyter.

Attila. Pierre Corneille. 1965. pap. 5.95 (*0-7859-0590-1*, F36030) Fr & Eur.

Attila. Steven B. Vardy. (World Leaders - Past & Present Ser.). (Illus.). 112p. (YA). (gr. 5 up). 1991. 17.95 (*1-55546-803-9*) Chelsea Hse.

Attila: A Barbarian's Bedtime Story. Peter Hargitai. LC 93-84984. 283p. (Orig.). 1994. pap. 6.95 (*0-915951-20-7*) Puski-Corvin.

Attila & the Nomad Hordes. David Nicolle. (Elite Ser.: No. 30). (Illus.). 64p. pap. 12.95 (*0-85045-996-6*, 9430, Pub. by Osprey UK) Stackpole.

***Attila, King of the Huns: The Man & the Myth.** Patrick Howarth. (Illus.). 256p. 1994. 47.50x (*0-09-471930-6*, Pub. by Constable Pubs UK) Trans-Atl Phila.

***Attila the Pun: A Magic Moscow Story.** Daniel Pinkwater. (Illus.). (J). (gr. 3-6). 1995. pap. 3.95 (*0-689-71764-4*, Aladdin Paperbacks) S&S Childrens.

Attische Beredsamkeit, 3 vols. in 4, Set. Friedrich Blass. 2321p. 1979. reprint ed. write for info. (*3-487-00305-8*, Pub. by Georg Olms GW) Lubrecht & Cramer.

Attische Genealogie. Iohannes Toepffer. LC 72-7906. (Greek History Ser.). (GER.). 1973. reprint ed. 35.95 (*0-405-04802-5*) Ayer.

Attische Process. Moritz H. Meier & Georg F. Schomann. Ed. by Gregory Vlastos. LC 78-19370. (Morals & Law in Ancient Greece Ser.). (GER & GRE.). 1979. reprint ed. lib. bdg. 61.95 (*0-405-11561-X*) Ayer.

Attische Recht und Rechtsverfahren, 3 vols. in 1. Justus H. Lipsius. iv, 1041p. 1984. reprint ed. write for info. (*3-487-01434-3*, Pub. by Georg Olms GW) Lubrecht & Cramer.

Attiscshe Feste. Ludwig Deubner. 269p. 1969. reprint ed. write for info. (*0-318-70909-0*, Pub. by Georg Olms GW) Lubrecht & Cramer.

Attitude: Uncollected Poems of the Seventies. Michael Lally. 1982. pap. 7.50 (*0-914610-31-7*) Hanging Loose.

***Attitude: Your Most Priceless Possession.** 3rd ed. Elwood N. Chapman. (Orig.). 1995. pap. 9.95 (*1-56052-317-4*) Crisp Pubns.

***Attitude Adjustment: Manners Based on the 12 Principles of Character.** Kathryn B. Johnson. 64p. (YA). (gr. 7-12). 1994. pap. 9.95 (*0-9643045-0-3*) Attitude Adjustment.

Attitude & Attitude Change. Harry C. Triandis. LC 76-140555. (Wiley Foundations in Social Psychology Ser.). 248p. reprint ed. pap. 70.70 (*0-8357-5864-8*, 2055949) Bks Demand.

Attitude & Attitude Change: The Social Judgment-Involvement Approach. Carolyn W. Sherif. LC 81-13265. (Illus.). xxi, 264p. 1982. reprint ed. text ed. 59.75 (*0-313-23260-1*, SHAC, Greenwood Pr) Greenwood.

Attitude & Attitudes: Psychological & Medical Subject Analysis with Research Index & Bibliography. Vicky W. Holibrook. LC 83-71649. 159p. 1984. 39.50 (*0-88164-026-3*); pap. 34.50 (*0-88164-027-1*) ABBE Pubs Assn.

Attitude & Opinion Research. 3rd ed. Walter K. Lindenmann. 83p. 1983. 24.00 (*0-89964-221-7*) Coun Adv & Supp Ed.

***Attitude Awareness: Creating Your Own Healthy Outlook.** Paul Pratt. LC 94-69092. 160p. (Orig.). 1995. pap. 12.95 (*0-9643578-0-1*) C O R E Ent.

Attitude Change: The Competing Views. Ed. by Peter Suedfeld. (Controversy Ser.). 259p. 1971. pap. text ed. 6.95 (*0-202-25082-2*) Lieber-Atherton.

Attitude Change; a Review & Bibliography of Selected Research see Cinema & Social Sciences: A Survey of Ethnographic & Sociological Films

Attitude Connection: Focus on Quality. Joseph T. Black. Ed. by Stacey Witt. LC 90-92235. (Illus.). 144p. 1991. 14.95 (*0-9628474-2-9*) Life Vision Bks.

Attitude Consensus & Conflict in an Interest Group: An Assessment of Cohesion. Norman R. Luttbeg & Harmon Zeigler. (Reprint Series in Social Sciences). (C). 1993. reprint ed. pap. text ed. 1.00 (*0-8290-3351-3*, PS-395) Irvington.

Attitude Development for Retail Management. Larry K. Christiansen & James W. Strate. (Gregg-McGraw-Hill Marketing Ser.). (Illus.). 256p. 1981. student ed 12.50 (*0-07-010820-X*) McGraw.

Attitude du Lyrisme Contemporain. Tancrede De Visan. LC 78-64058. (Des Imagistes: Literature of the Imagist Movement Ser.). reprint ed. 35.00 (*0-404-17112-5*) AMS Pr.

Attitude Formation & Change. James D. Halloran. LC 75-41501. (Television Research Committee Working Paper Ser.: No. 2). 167p. 1976. reprint ed. text ed. 49.75 (*0-8371-8700-1*, HAFC, Greenwood Pr) Greenwood.

Attitude in Relation to Learning see Iowa University Studies in Psychology

***Attitude Is Everything.** Keith Harrell. 176p. 1994. boxed 24.95 (*0-7872-0447-1*) Kendall-Hunt.

Attitude of a Servant: Servant Heart - A Sign of Strength & Inner Peace Like Jesus. Michael Landsman. 1991. 3.50 (*0-88270-700-0*) Bridge Pub.

Attitude of American Courts in Labor Cases. George G. Groat. LC 78-77993. (Columbia University. Studies in the Social Sciences: No. 108). reprint ed. 32.50 (*0-404-51108-2*) AMS Pr.

Attitude of American Jewry Towards East European Jewish Immigration, 1881-1914. Myron Berman. Ed. by Francesco Cordasco. LC 80-842. (American Ethnic Groups Ser.). 1981. lib. bdg. 60.95 (*0-405-13406-1*) Ayer.

Attitude of American Jews to World War I, the Russian Revolution of 1917, and Communism, 1917 to 1945 see Jews, War & Communism

Attitude of Giving: Notes & Other Things. 2nd ed. Christopher. (Illus.). 1975. pap. 1.00 (*0-916940-02-0*) World Light.

Attitude of Gratitude: The Adaptation to Aging of the Elderly Japanese in America. Randall J. Kendis. LC 88-46191. (Immigrant Communities & Ethnic Minorities in the U. S. & Canada Ser.: No. 33). 1989. 45.00 (*0-404-19443-5*) AMS Pr.

Attitude of Gratitude: The Life of Wilfred Watson. Virginia G. Tait. LC 92-25808. 1992. write for info. (*1-877607-56-8*) Redeemer Bks.

Attitude of Parsi Women to Marriage. H. M. Billimoria. (C). 1991. 24.00 (*81-7040-430-4*, Pub. by Manohar II) S Asia.

Attitude of the Catholic Church Toward Witchcraft & the Allied Practices of Sorcery & Magic. Antoinette M. Pratt. LC 79-8116. 144p. reprint ed. 32.50 (*0-404-18429-4*) AMS Pr.

Attitude of the Congress of Vienna Toward Nationalism in Germany, Italy & Poland. Hannah A. Straus. (Columbia University. Studies in the Social Sciences: No. 558). reprint ed. 20.00 (*0-404-51558-4*) AMS Pr.

Attitude of Voltaire to Magic & the Sciences. M. S. Libby. 1971. 59.95 (*0-87968-676-6*) Gordon Pr.

Attitude of Voltaire to Magic & the Sciences. Margaret S. Libby. LC 35-10134. (Columbia University. Studies in the Social Sciences: No. 408). reprint ed. 10.00 (*0-404-51408-1*) AMS Pr.

Attitude Organization & Change: An Analysis of Consistency among Attitude Components. Milton J. Rosenberg et al. LC 80-14704. (Yale Studies in Attitude & Communication: Vol. 3). (Illus.). x, 239p. 1980. reprint ed. text ed. 59.75 (*0-313-22435-8*, ROAT) Greenwood.

Attitude Research Enters the '80s: Proceedings of the Attitude Research Conference, 11th, Carlsbad, CA, 1980. Attitude Research Conference Staff. Ed. by Richard W. Olshavsky. LC 80-20621. (American Marketing Association, Proceedings Ser.). 206p. reprint ed. pap. 58.80 (*0-8357-5865-6*, 2023355) Bks Demand.

Attitude Research Plays for High Stakes: Proceedings of the Attitude Research Conference, 8th, Las Vegas, NV, 1977. Attitude Research Conference Staff. Ed. by John C. Maloney & Bernard Silverman. LC 78-14033. (American Marketing Association, Proceedings Ser.). 287p. reprint ed. pap. 81.80 (*0-8357-5866-4*, 2023349) Bks Demand.

Attitude Research under the Sun: Proceedings of the Attitude Research Conference, 9th, Tarpon Springs, FL, 1978. Attitude Research Conference Staff. Ed. by John Eighmey. LC 78-13992. (American Marketing Association, Proceedings Ser.). 225p. reprint ed. pap. 64.20 (*0-8357-5867-2*, 2023348) Bks Demand.

***Attitude Strength: Antecedents & Consequences.** Ed. by Richard E. Petty & Jon A. Krosnick. 504p. 1995. text ed. 90.00 (*0-8058-1086-2*) L Erlbaum Assocs.

***Attitude Strength: Antecedents & Consequences.** Ed. by Richard E. Petty & Jon A. Krosnick. 504p. 1995. pap. 45.00 (*0-8058-1087-0*) L Erlbaum Assocs.

Attitude Structure & Function. Ed. by Anthony R. Pratkanis et al. 472p. 1989. text ed. 89.95 (*0-89859-991-1*); pap. text ed. 39.95 (*0-8058-0323-8*) L Erlbaum Assocs.

Attitude Treasury: One Hundred One Inspiring Quotations. Ed. by Marty Maskall. LC 90-84617. (Illus.). 128p. 1991. pap. 9.95 (*0-9627670-2-6*) Attitude Works.

Attitude: Your Most Priceless Possession. Elwood N. Chapman. 1988. 6.95 (*0-318-33264-7*, 117) Am Bartenders.

Attitudes. 2nd rev. ed. D. W. Rajecki. LC 89-38465. (Illus.). 522p. (C). 1990. pap. text ed. 27.95 (*0-87893-787-0*) Sinauer Assocs.

Attitudes. Paul Tanaquil. LC 70-144721. (Yale Series of Younger Poets: No. 14). reprint ed. 18.00 (*0-404-53814-2*) AMS Pr.

Attitudes & Avowals with Some Retrospective Reviews. Richard Le Gallienne. LC 71-99640. (Essay Index Reprint Ser.). 1977. 28.95 (*0-8369-1418-X*) Ayer.

Attitudes & Behavior: An Annotated Bibliography. David R. Siebold & Daniel J. Canary. LC 84-3389. 234p. 1984. text ed. 55.00 (*0-275-91137-3*, C1137, Praeger Pubs) Greenwood.

Attitudes & Behavioral Decisions. Ed. by A. Upmeyer. (Psychology Ser.). (Illus.). 310p. 1988. 73.00 (*0-387-96727-3*) Spr-Verlag.

Attitudes & Decisions. J. Richard Eiser & Joop Van Der Pligt. 192p. 1989. pap. 14.95 (*0-415-01112-4*, A3516) Routledge.

Attitudes & Emotions, Part III. Association for Research & Enlightment, Readings Research Department Staff. (Library: Vol. 15). 442p. 1982. 22.95 (*0-87604-141-1*, 1115) ARE Pr.

Attitudes & Emotions Pt. I. Comp. by Association for Research & Enlightenment, Readings Research Dept. (Library: Vol. 13). 445p. 1981. 22.95 (*0-87604-138-1*, 1113) ARE Pr.

Attitudes & Emotions, Pt. II. Comp. by Association for Research & Enlightenment, Readings Research Dept. (Library: Vol. 14). 393p. 1982. 22.95 (*0-87604-140-3*, 1114) ARE Pr.

Attitudes & Languages. Colin Baker. (Multilingual Matters Ser.: No. 83). 198p. 1992. 69.00 (*1-85359-143-2*, Pub. by Multilingual Matters UK); pap. 24.95 (*1-85359-142-4*, Pub. by Multilingual Matters UK) Taylor & Francis.

Attitudes & Opinions. 2nd ed. Stuart Oskamp. 496p. (C). 1990. text ed. write for info. (*0-13-050592-7*) P-H.

Attitudes & Persuasion. Richard E. Petty & John T. Cacioppo. 332p. 1981. pap. write for info. (*0-697-06551-0*) Brown & Benchmark.

Attitudes & Social Relations of Foreign Students in the United States. Claire Selltiz et al. LC 63-13885. 448p. reprint ed. pap. 127.70 (*0-8357-5868-0*, 2055913) Bks Demand.

Attitudes Are Contagious ... Are Yours Worth Catching? Dennis E. Mannering. Ed. by Virgina Mason & Christopher Samson. 68p. reprint ed. pap. text ed. 3.50 (*0-945890-00-1*) Options Unltd.

Attitudes, Chaos & the Connectionist Mind. J. Richard Eiser. (Illus.). 288p. 1994. 49.95 (*0-631-19129-1*); pap. 22.95 (*0-631-19131-3*) Blackwell Pubs.

***Attitudes, Concerns, & Priorities of Oregon Coast Residents Regarding Tourism & Economic Development: Results from Surveys of Residents in Eight Communities.** Kreg Lindberg et al. 48p. 1994. pap. 6.00 (*1-881826-04-X*) OR Sea Grant.

Attitudes, Goals & Priorities. Ed. by Michal R. Belknap. LC 91-3629. (Civil Rights, White House & Justice Dept. Ser.: Vol. 1). 488p. 1991. 119.00 (*0-8240-3366-3*) Garland.

Attitudes I. Virgil Leach. 1979. pap. 5.50 (*0-89137-803-0*) Quality Pubns.

Attitudes II. Virgil Leach. 1981. pap. 5.50 (*0-89137-804-9*) Quality Pubns.

***Attitudes in Teaching & Education.** William Hare. 136p. (Orig.). (C). 1993. pap. text ed. 17.95x (*1-55059-067-7*) Temeron Bks.

Attitudes, Interaction & Personality. L. Kardos. 150p. 1980. 45.00 (*0-569-08628-0*, Pub. by Collets UK) Pro-Am Music.

520

An Asterisk (*) at the beginning of an entry indicates that the title is appearing in BIP for the first time.

Attitudes of Americans on Coping with Interdependence: Findings of Opinion Research Organizations. Michael W. Moynihan. 20p. 1976. pap. text ed. 10.50 (0-8191-5859-3, Aspen Inst for Humanistic Studies) U Pr of Amer.

Attitudes of Colonial Powers Toward the American Indian. Ed. by Howard H. Peckham & Charles Gibson. LC 77-99793. (University of Utah Publications in the American West: No. 2). 147p. reprint ed. pap. 41.90 (0-8357-4380-2, 2037211) Bks Demand.

Attitudes of Educated Women Towards Social Issues. V. Mehta. 126p. 1979. 15.95 (0-318-37044-1) Asia Bk Corp.

Attitudes of Educators Toward Exceptional Children. Norris G. Haring et al. LC 77-25983. 238p. 1978. reprint ed. text ed. 65.00 (0-313-20070-X, HAAO, Greenwood Pr) Greenwood.

Attitudes of Entitlement: Theoretical & Clinical Issues. Ed. by Vamik D. Volkan & Terry C. Rodgers. LC 87-29579. (Virginia Psychoanalytic Society Book Ser.: No. 1). 106p. 1988. 19.95 (0-8139-1161-3) U Pr of Va.

Attitudes of Industrial Managers to Product Design. Design Council Staff. (C). 1988. pap. text ed. 95.00 (0-85072-232-2) St Mut.

Attitudes of Martin Bucer Toward the Bigamy of Philip of Hesse. Hastings Eells. LC 83-45611. reprint ed. 32.50 (0-404-19829-5) AMS Pr.

Attitudes of Religions & Ideologies Toward the Outsider: The Other. Ed. by Leonard Swidler & Paul Mojzes. LC 90-23415. (Religions in Dialogue Ser.: Vol. 1). 220p. 1990. lib. bdg. 89.95 (0-88946-270-4) E Mellen.

Attitudes of the Beatitudes. R. L. Brandt. LC 93-79319. 105p. (Orig.). 1993. pap. 6.95 (0-88270-647-0) Bridge Pub.

Attitudes of Voters & Planning Commissioners Toward Regional Planning, No. 1088. Walter J. Raymond. 1976. 5.50 (0-686-20403-4) CPL Biblios.

Attitudes, Personality, & Behavior. Icek Ajzen. 175p. (C). 1989. text ed. 28.95 (0-534-10948-9); pap. 20.95 (0-534-10949-7) Brooks-Cole.

Attitudes Through Idioms. 2nd ed. Thomas W. Adams & Susan R. Kuder. LC 93-9042. 1993. pap. 18.95 (0-8384-3975-6) Heinle & Heinle.

Attitudes to Criticism. Andor H. Gomme. LC 66-10057. (Crosscurrents-Modern Critiques Ser.). 192p. 1966. 7.95 (0-8093-0194-6) S Ill U Pr.

Attitudes to Death & Dying: Medical Analysis Index with Reference Bibliography. Katie L. Holt. LC 85-47582. 150p. 1987. 39.50 (0-88164-338-6); pap. 34.50 (0-88164-339-4) ABBE Pubs Assn.

Attitudes to Nature. Ed. by Jean Holm & John Bowker. LC 94-15087. (Themes in Religious Studies Ser.). 1994. 45.00 (1-85567-092-5, Pub. by Pinter Pubs UK); pap. 16.95 (1-85567-093-3, Pub. by Pinter Pubs UK) St Martin.

***Attitudes to Rape.** Colleen Ward. (Gender & Psychology Ser.). (Illus.). 224p. (C). 1995. 65.00 (0-8039-8593-2); pap. 19.95 (0-8039-8594-0) Sage.

Attitudes to Social Structure & Mobility in Upper Canada 1815-1840. Peter Russell. LC 89-34205. (Canadian Studies: Vol. 6). 211p. 1989. lib. bdg. 89.95 (0-88946-193-7) E Mellen.

Attitudes Toward American Foreign Policy: West Germany, 1962. Survey Research Center Staff. 1973. write for info. (0-89138-063-9) ICPSR.

Attitudes Toward Blind Persons. Irving F. Lukoff et al. LC 72-82239. 80p. reprint ed. pap. 25.00 (0-7837-5187-7, 2044921) Bks Demand.

Attitudes Toward Foreign Colonization: The Evolution of Nineteenth-Century Guatemalan Immigration Policy see Applied Enlightenment: Nineteenth Century Liberalism, 1800-1839

Attitudes Toward Handicapped Students: Professional, Peer & Parent Reactions. Marcia D. Horne. (School Psychology Ser.). 288p. (C). 1985. text ed. 59.95 (0-89859-584-3) L Erlbaum Assocs.

Attitudes Toward History. 3rd ed. Kenneth Burke. 1984. pap. 12.00 (0-520-04148-8) U CA Pr.

Attitudes Toward Mental Patients. Alexander Askenasy & Marisa Zavalloni. (New Babylon Studies in the Social Sciences). 1974. text ed. 44.65 (90-279-7891-3) Mouton.

Attitudes Toward Persons with Disabilities. Ed. by Harold E. Yuker. LC 87-23471. 352p. (C). 1988. 40.95 (0-8261-6190-1) Springer Pub.

Attitudes Toward Self-Inflicted Suffering in the Middle Ages. Giles Constable & John Brademas. (Stephen J. Brademas Lectures). 28p. (Orig.). pap. text ed. 2.50 (0-916586-87-1) Hellenic Coll Pr.

***Attitudes toward the Environment: Twenty-Five Years After Earth Day.** Everett Carll Ladd & Karlyn H. Bowman. (AEI Studies in Public Policy Ser.). 55p. (Orig.). 1995. pap. 9.95 (0-8447-7032-9) Am Enterprise.

Attitudes Toward the Outdoors: An Annotated Bibliography of U. S. Survey & Poll Research Concerning the Environment, Wildlife & Recreation. Dena J. Jolma. 277p. 1994. lib. bdg. 45.00 (0-89950-958-4) McFarland & Co.

Attitudes Toward Wildlife in Botswana. A. Richard Mordi. LC 91-20257. (Environment: Problems & Solutions Ser.). 240p. 1991. 58.00 (0-8240-0471-X) Garland.

Attitudinal Healing: A Guide for Groups & Individuals. Genevieve Weirich. 200p. (C). 1991. reprint ed. pap. text ed. 13.95 (0-9626466-1-X); reprint ed. write for info. (0-9626466-0-1) Cambrdg.

Attitudinal Judgement. Ed. by J. R. Eider. (Social Psychology Ser.). (Illus.). 275p. 1984. 64.00 (0-387-90911-7) Spr-Verlag.

***Attlee.** Kenneth Harris. 640p. 1995. pap. 29.95 (0-297-81574-1, Pub. by Weidenfeld) Trafalgar.

Attlee & Churchill Administrations & Industrial Unrest, 1945-55. Justin D. Smith. 208p. 1993. pap. 15.95 (1-85567-179-4, Pub. by Pinter Pubs UK) St Martin.

Attlee & Churchill Administrations & Industrial Unrest, 1945-55: A Study in Post-War Consensus. Justin D. Smith. 224p. 1990. text ed. 45.00 (0-86187-101-4, Pub. by Pinter Pubs UK) St Martin.

Attlee Government, 1945-1951. Ed. by Lewis Johnman & Nick Tiratsoo. 256p. 1992. text ed. 55.00 (0-86187-822-1, Pub. by Pinter Pubs UK) St Martin.

Attlee Years. Ed. by Nick Tiratsoo. 224p. 1994. text ed. 17.95 (1-85567-180-8, Pub. by Pinter Pubs UK) St Martin.

Attlee's Labour Governments, 1945-51. Robert D. Pearce. LC 93-15764. (Lancaster Pamphlets Ser.). 1994. write for info. (0-415-08893-3) Routledge.

ATTN: A&R: A Step-by-Step Guide into the Recording Industry. Teri Muench & Susan Pomerantz. Ed. by Sandy Feldstein & Patrick Wilson. (Illus.). 120p. (Orig.). 1988. pap. 16.95 (0-88284-361-3, 2260) Alfred Pub.

Attorney. Jack Rudman. (Career Examination Ser.: C-56). 1994. pap. 39.95 (0-8373-0056-8) Nat Learn.

Attorney - Departmental. Jack Rudman. (Career Examination Ser.: C-2234). 1994. pap. 44.95 (0-8373-2234-0) Nat Learn.

Attorney-Client Privilege & the Work-Product Doctrine: A Project of the Trial Evidence Committee, Section of Litigation. 176p. 1989. pap. 45.00 (0-89707-406-8, 531-0062) Amer Bar Assn.

Attorney-Client Privilege & the Work Product Doctrine: Corporate Applications. Herbert E. Milstein. (Corporate Practice Ser.: No. 22). 1980. 92.00 (1-55871-254-2) BNA.

Attorney-Client Privilege Under Siege: Preserving & Protecting It in Civil Cases. 761p. 1989. pap. 84.95 (0-89707-458-0, 519-0092-01) Amer Bar Assn.

Attorney-Client Privileges in the U. S. Paul R. Rice. 1993. ring bd. 105.00 (0-317-05382-5) Lawyers Cooperative.

Attorney-Client Relationship after Kaye, Scholer. (Corporate Law & Practice Course Handbook, 1985-86 Ser.). 527p. 1992. pap. 70.00 (0-685-69383-X) PLI.

Attorney Conspiracy. Jerry Cline. 1984. pap. 3.50 (0-449-20431-6) Fawcett.

Attorney Corporate Client Privilege. John W. Gergacz. 475p. 1990. text ed. 95.00 (0-07-172301-3) Shepards-McGraw.

Attorney Fee Awards. suppl. ed. Herbert B. Newberg. 1986. Supplemented semiannually. text ed. 95.00 (0-07-046344-1) Shepards-McGraw.

Attorney Fee Awards. 2nd rev. ed. Alba Conte. LC 93-44595. (Trial Practice Ser.). 1993. text ed. 190.00 (0-07-172504-0) Shepards-McGraw.

Attorney Fees in Washington with Collected Statutes & Case Summaries. Philip A. Talmadge. 280p. 1992. ring bd. 95.00 (0-409-20088-3) Michie Butterworth.

Attorney Fees in Washington with Collected Statutes & Case Summaries. suppl. ed. Philip A. Talmadge. 280p. 1992. Latest supp. 7/92. 35.00 (0-88063-999-7) Butterworth Legal Pubs.

***Attorney for the Damned: A Lawyer's Life with the Criminally Insane.** Woychuk. 1996. 22.95 (0-02-935607-5) Free Pr.

Attorney for the Damned: Clarence Darrow in the Courtroom. Clarence Darrow. Ed. by Arthur Weinberg. LC 88-39520. xxiv, 552p. 1989. pap. 16.95 (0-226-13649-3) U Ch Pr.

Attorney General, Politics & the Public Interest. John J. Edwards. LC 92-72472. xxxi, 533p. 1992. reprint ed. 95.00 (1-56169-023-6) W W Gaunt.

Attorney General Through Janet Reno. John Hamilton. LC 93-1967. (All the President's Men & Women Ser.). 32p. 1993. lib. bdg. 13.99 (1-56239-251-4) Abdo & Dghtrs.

Attorney General's Lawyer: Inside the Meese Justice Department. Douglas W. Kmiec. LC 91-44006. 248p. 1992. text ed. 49.95 (0-275-93983-9, C3983, Praeger Pubs) Greenwood.

Attorney General's Manual of the Administrative Procedure Act. Tom C. Clark. LC 72-9770. 139p. 1973. reprint ed. pap. 20.00 (0-912004-11-8) W W Gaunt.

Attorney General's National Committee to Study Antitrust Laws: Final Report, Vol. 1. U. S. Attorney General National Committee. LC 81-85310. xii, 393p. 1981. reprint ed. lib. bdg. 45.00 (0-89941-231-9, 201360) W S Hein.

Attorney General's Survey of Release Procedures, Vol. 2: Probation. United States Department of Justice Staff. LC 74-3859. (Criminal Justice in America Ser.). 1974. reprint ed. 40.95 (0-405-06176-5) Ayer.

Attorney General's Survey of Release Procedures, Vol. 4: Parole. United States Department of Justice Staff. LC 74-3860. (Criminal Justice in America Ser.). 1974. reprint ed. 51.95 (0-405-06175-7) Ayer.

Attorney in Eighteenth-Century England. Robert Robson. LC 85-48164. (Cambridge Studies in English Legal History). 194p. 1986. reprint ed. 47.00 (0-912004-34-7) W W Gaunt.

***Attorney Looks at the Secular Foundation for Clergy Sexual Misconduct Policies.** Anne Underwood. Date not set. pap. 7.50 (1-56699-139-0, OD109) Alban Inst.

Attorney Malpractice Law & Procedure. David J. Meiselman. LC 79-89562. 1980. 135.00 (0-685-59903-5) Clark Boardman Callaghan.

Attorney Trainee. Jack Rudman. (Career Examination Ser.: C-57). 1994. pap. 29.95 (0-8373-0057-6) Nat Learn.

***Attorneys: Audit Technique Guides.** (IRS Tax Audit Information Ser.). 88p. 1994. pap. 14.50 (1-57402-102-8) Athena Info Mgt.

Attorneys Academy, or the Manner of Proceeding upon Any Suite. Thomas Powell. LC 74-80209. (English Experience Ser.: No. 684). 1974. reprint ed. 30.00 (90-221-0684-5) Walter J Johnson.

Attorney's & Lender's Guide to Common Interest Ownership Acts: Condominiums, Cooperatives, & Planned Communities. LC 89-85243. 207p. 1989. pap. 39.95 (0-89707-491-2, 543-0301) Amer Bar Assn.

Attorneys As Activists: Evaluating the American Bar Association's BASICS Program. Ross F. Conner & C. Ronald Huff. LC 79-19830. (Contemporary Evaluation Research Ser.: Vol. 1). 264p. reprint ed. pap. 75.30 (0-8357-5869-9, 2021878) Bks Demand.

Attorney's Complete Guide to Practice Development: How to Build Your Practice & Career. Roger F. Smith & James H. Mitchell. 464p. 1991. text ed. 51.00 (0-13-558982-7) P-H.

Attorney's Desk Library. Richard A. Boswell. 1994. write for info. (0-318-72688-2) Clark Boardman Callaghan.

Attorneys' Dictionary & Handbook of Economics & Statistics. Les Seplaki. 384p. 1991. pap. text ed. write for info. (0-318-68147-1) Prof Homzons Pr.

Attorneys' Dictionary of Medicine, 5 vols. 16th ed. J. E. Schmidt. 1962. Updates available. ring bd. write for info. (0-8205-1609-0) Bender.

Attorney's Dictionary of Patent Claims: Legal Materials & Practice Commentaries, 2 vols., Set. Irwin M. Aisenberg. 1985. ring bd. write for info. (0-8205-1546-9) Bender.

Attorneys' Fees, 2 vols. Stuart M. Speiser. 1973. 160.00 (0-318-12019-4) Lawyers Cooperative.

Attorneys' Fees, 2 vols. suppl. ed. Stuart M. Speiser. 1973. Suppl. 1992. 59.50 (0-317-03273-9) Lawyers Cooperative.

Attorney's Fees & Law Office Management: A Selected Bibliography. Comp. by Judith L. Gutglass. LC 82-236288. (Washington University Law Library Bibliography Ser.: No. 3). vi, 24p. (Orig.). 1982. pap. text ed. 8.00 (0-318-01099-2) Wash U Law Lib.

Attorney's Fees in Florida, 1989-1994, 4 vols. suppl. ed. James Hauser. 1200p. 1991. Suppl. 01/1991. 42.50 (0-685-25481-X) Butterworth Legal Pubs.

Attorney's Fees in Florida, 1989-1994, 4 vols. suppl. ed. James Hauser. 1200p. 1993. 46.00 (0-685-74076-5) Butterworth Legal Pubs.

***Attorney's Fees in Florida, 1989-1994.** suppl. ed. James Hauser. 1994. ring bd. 47.00 (0-614-03176-1) Butterworth Legal Pubs.

Attorney's Fees in Florida, 1989-1994, 4 vols., Set. James C. Hauser. 1200p. 1995. ring bd. 280.00 (0-409-26875-5, D & S Pub) Michie Butterworth.

Attorneys General & New Methods of Dispute Resolution. 204p. 1990. 30.00 (0-317-05766-9, PB04) Natl Attys General.

Attorney's Guide to California Construction Contracts & Disputes. James Acret. LC 90-82521. 490p. 1990. 115.00 (0-88124-303-5, RE-31440) Cont Ed Bar-CA.

Attorney's Guide to California Professional Corporations. suppl. ed. 310p. 1989. 29.00 (0-685-20138-4, TX-30932) Cont Ed Bar-CA.

Attorney's Guide to California Professional Corporations. 4th ed. 310p. 1987. ring bd. 105.00 (0-685-20137-6, TX-30930) Cont Ed Bar-CA.

Attorney's Guide to California Professional Corporations: April 1991 Revisions. 4th ed. Kenneth H. Wennergren & Kathryn T. Mondon. Ed. by Christopher D. Dworin. LC 87-71434. 134p. 1991. ring bd. 35.00 (0-88124-386-8, TX-30933) Cont Ed Bar-CA.

Attorney's Guide to California Professional Corporations: June 1992 Update. 4th ed. Lawrence S. Branton. Ed. by Christopher D. Dworin. LC 87-71434. 220p. 1992. ring bd. 42.00 (0-88124-512-7, TX-30934) Cont Ed Bar-CA.

Attorney's Guide to Competitive Business Practices see Competitive Business Practices

Attorney's Guide to Forensic Engineering in the Maritime Environment. Ephraim E. Kaufman. (Illus.). 79p. 1992. pap. text ed. 12.95 (0-88450-089-6) Lawyers & Judges.

***Attorney's Guide to Oncology Cases, Vol. 2.** Melvin Shiffman et al. (Personal Injury Library: Vol. 2). 1994. text ed. 225.00 (0-471-11209-7) Wiley.

Attorney's Guide to Pension & Profit-Sharing Plans. 3rd ed. Richard A. Gilbert et al. 1985. 150.00 (0-88124-130-X, TX-30730) Cont Ed Bar-CA.

Attorney's Guide to Social Security Disability Claims. Kenneth F. Laritz. LC 86-10210. (Regulatory Manual Ser.). 451p. 1986. text ed. 110.00 (0-07-008461-0) Shepards-McGraw.

***Attorney's Guide to State Bar Admission Requirements.** 2nd ed. Ed. by Richard L. Hermann & Linda P. Sutherland. 144p. 1995. 17.95 (0-614-04284-4) Federal Reports Inc.

Attorney's Guide to Trade Secrets. California Continuing Education of the Bar Staff. LC 79-181871. 202p. 1971. 70.00 (0-88124-014-1, BU-30030) Cont Ed Bar-CA.

Attorney's Guidebook of Trial Forms & Techniques for Successful Handling of Personal Injury Cases. Paul N. Luvera, Jr. 1979. 89.50 (0-13-050294-4) Exec Reports.

Attorney's Handbook of Accounting. 3rd ed. Henry Sellin. 1979. Looseleaf updates available. ring bd. write for info. (0-8205-1032-7) Bender.

Attorney's Handbook on Consumer Bankruptcy & Chapter 13. 16th ed. John H. Williamson. 352p. 1992. pap. 21.95 (1-880730-02-2); pap. text ed. 17.00 (0-685-51790-X) Argyle Pub.

Attorney's Handbook on Consumer Bankruptcy & Chapter 13. 17th ed. John H. Williamson. 352p. 1993. pap. 21.95 (1-880730-04-9); pap. text ed. 17.00 (0-685-63424-8) Argyle Pub.

Attorney's Handbook on Consumer Bankruptcy & Chapter 13, 1994. 18th ed. John H. Williamson. 352p. 1994. pap. 21.95 (1-880730-06-5); pap. text ed. 18.00 (0-685-71512-4) Argyle Pub.

Attorney's Handbook on Drinking Driving Defense. John H. Williamson. (Illus.). 416p. 1991. pap. 29.95 (1-880730-00-6); pap. text ed. 20.00 (0-685-51789-6) Argyle Pub.

Attorney's Handbook on Small Business Reorganization under Chapter 11. 3rd ed. John H. Williamson. 336p. 1992. pap. 27.95 (1-880730-03-0); pap. text ed. 20.00 (0-685-51791-8) Argyle Pub.

Attorney's Handbook to Government Studies & Reports. Ed. by Bender's Editorial Staff. 1984. write for info. (0-8205-1064-5) Bender.

Attorney's Master Guide to Courtroom Psychology: How to Apply Behavioral Science Techniques for New Trial Success. David L. Herbert & Roger K. Barrett. 1980. 69.50 (0-13-050443-2) Exec Reports.

Attorney's Master Guide to Expediting Top Dollar Case Settlements. Charles E. Robbins. 1975. 69.50 (0-13-050526-9) Exec Reports.

Attorney's Master Guide to Successful Solo Law Practice. R. Sam Rea. LC 83-18652. 288p. 1983. text ed. 49.50 (0-87624-024-4, Inst Busn Plan) P-H.

***Attorney's Medical Advisor-Atlas, 10 vols., Set.** Lee Russ et al. LC 94-60666. 1994. ring bd. 1,650.00 (0-614-07290-5) Clark Boardman Callaghan.

Attorney's Medical Deskbook, 3 vols. 3rd ed. Dan J. Tennenhouse. LC 93-74118. 1993. ring bd. 345.00 (0-685-74752-2) Clark Boardman Callaghan.

Attorney's Medical Handbook. Samuel J. Faber & Stuart J. Faber. 256p. (Orig.). 1981. pap. text ed. 32.50 (0-89074-085-2) Lega Bks.

Attorneys' Medical Reference. 4th ed. Barry Creighton et al. 270p. 1984. ring bd. 85.00 (0-9614995-0-8) Michie Butterworth.

Attorney's Practice Guide to Negotiations. Philip Sperber. LC 85-11019. 1985. 65.00 (0-685-10775-2) Clark Boardman Callaghan.

Attorneys' Textbook of Medicine, 17 vols. 3rd ed. Roscoe N. Gray & Louise J. Gordy. 1934. Updates available. ring bd. write for info. (0-8205-1300-8) Bender.

Attorney's Textbook of Medicine: Manual of Traumatic Injuries, 3 vols., Set. 1989. write for info. (0-8205-1009-2) Bender.

***Attorney's Umbrella Book, 3 vols., Set.** rev. ed. Ed. by Warren, McVeigh & Griffin, Inc. Staff. (Illus.). 1500p. 1979. ring bd. 500.00 (0-941360-03-2) Griffin Comns.

Attracting & Feeding Wild Birds in the Prescott Area. David L. Harner. (Illus.). 96p. (Orig.). (YA). (gr. 12). 1989. pap. 3.95 (0-685-26081-X) Harner Pubns.

***Attracting Backyard Birds: Inviting Projects to Entice Your Feathered Friends.** Sandy Cortright & Will Pokriots. LC 94-47291. (Illus.). 128p. 1995. 19.95 (0-8069-0892-0) Sterling.

Attracting Birds to Southern Gardens. Neil Odenwald et al. LC 93-7572. 176p. 1993. 24.95 (0-87833-830-6) Taylor Pub.

Attracting, Organizing & Keeping Members. American Society of Association Executives Staff. Ed. by Wilford A. Butler. 170p. (Orig.). 1989. pap. 50.00 (0-88034-032-0) Am Soc Assn Execs.

Attracting Purple Martins. J. L. Wade. (Illus.). 240p. 1987. 19.95 (0-9616774-0-6) Nature Soc.

Attracting Romance: The Secrets to Successful Relationships. Lowell J. Arthur. LC 92-6891. (Illus.). 208p. 1992. pap. 14.95 (0-942963-20-2) Distinctive Pub.

Attracting the Affluent: The First Guide to America's Ultimate Market. Research Alert Editors. LC 91-10939. 320p. 1991. boxed 49.95 (0-942061-23-3, Financial Sourcebks) Sourcebks.

***Attracting Wildlife to Your Garden.** Rodger Elliot. (Orig.). Date not set. pap. 12.95 (0-85091-621-6) Intl Spec Bk.

***Attracting Wildlife to Your Garden.** Rodger Elliot. Ed. by John Patrick. (Lothian Australian Garden Ser.). (Illus.). 64p. (Orig.). 1995. pap. 9.95 (0-85091-628-3, Pub. by Lothian Pub AT) Seven Hills Bk.

Attraction & Attachment: Understanding Styles of Relationships. Ed. by Barbara J. Brothers. LC 93-42448. (Journal of Couples Therapy). (Illus.). 160p. 1994. lib. bdg. 29.95 (1-56024-620-0) Haworth Pr.

Attraction of Gravitation: New Studies in the History of General Relativity. Ed. by J. Earman et al. (Einstein Studies: Vol. 5). (Illus.). 400p. 1993. 125.00 (0-8176-3624-2) Spr-Verlag.

Attraction of Moths to Light & Infrared Radiation. H. S. Hsiao. (Illus.). 1972. 10.00 (0-911302-21-2) San Francisco Pr.

Attraction of Opposites: Thought & Society in a Dualistic Mode. Ed. by David Maybury-Lewis & Uri Almagor. 50p. 1989. 52.50 (0-472-10094-7); pap. 21.95 (0-472-08086-5) U of Mich Pr.

Attraction of the Cross Gardiner Spring. 1983. 18.95 (0-85151-387-5) Banner of Truth.

Attraction Paradigm. Donn E. Byrne. (Personality & Psychopathology Ser.: Vol. 11). 1971. text ed. 65.00 (0-12-148650-8) Acad Pr.

Attractions. Joy Bennett. 30p. (Orig.). 1992. pap. write for info. (0-9632649-1-5) J Bennett.

Attractions of Fascism: Social Psychology & Aesthetics of the "Triumph of the Right" Ed. by John Milfull. LC 89-28950. 326p. 1990. 68.00 (0-85496-613-7) Berg Pubs.

Attractive & Easy-to-Build Wood Projects. Robert B. Russell. (Illus.). 64p. (Orig.). 1980. pap. 3.95 (0-486-23965-9) Dover.

Attractive Cross Stitch Designs. Ondori Publishing Company Staff. LC 81-80834. (Illus.). 104p. (Orig.). 1981. pap. 13.95 (0-87040-501-2) Japan Pubns USA.

Attractive Molecules in Organic Chemistry. Fritz Vogtle. 402p. 1992. text ed. 220.00 (0-471-93147-0) Wiley.

Attractive Woman: A Physical Fitness Approach to Emotional & Spiritual Well-Being. Marvel Harrison-Davis & Catharine Stewart-Roache. 191p. 1988. 9.95 (0-913478-07-5) Hermosa.

Attractors for Semi-Groups & Evolution Equations. Olga A. Ladyzhenskaya. (Lezioni Lincee Lectures). 100p. (C). 1991. 44.95 (0-521-39030-3); pap. 17.95 (0-521-39922-X) Cambridge U Pr.

An Asterisk (*) at the beginning of an entry indicates that the title is appearing in BIP for the first time.

Attractors of Quasiperiodically Forced Systems. Tomasz Kapitaniak & Jerzy Wojewoda. 100p. 1994. text ed. 40.00 (*981-02-1525-8*) World Scientific Pub.

Attractors Representing Turbulent Flows. P. S. Constantin et al. LC 84-24623. (Memoirs of the AMS Ser. No. 314: No. 53/314). 67p. 1988. reprint ed. text ed. 18.00 (*0-8218-2315-9*, MEMO 53/314) Am Math.

Attribute Acrobatics. Betty Sternberg. (Illus.). (Orig.). (J). (gr. 1-9). 1974. pap. 9.95 (*0-918932-01-7*) Activity Resources.

Attribute Grammar Inversion & Source-to-Source Translation. Daniel M. Yellin. (Lecture Notes in Computer Science Ser.: Vol. 302). viii, 176p. 1988. pap. 30.00 (*0-387-19072-4*) Spr-Verlag.

Attribute Grammars. P. Deransart et al. (Lecture Notes in Computer Science Ser.: Vol. 323). ix, 232p. 1988. pap. 33.00 (*0-387-50056-1*) Spr-Verlag.

Attribute Grammars & Their Applications: International Workshop WAGA Paris, France, September 19-21, 1990 Proceedings. Ed. by P. Deransart et al. (Lecture Notes in Computer Science Ser.: Vol. 461). viii, 358p. 1990. pap. 40.00 (*0-387-53101-7*) Spr-Verlag.

Attribute Grammars, Applications & Systems: International Summer School SAGA Prague, Czechoslovakia, June 4-13, 1991 Proceedings. Ed. by H. Albias et al. (Lecture Notes in Computer Science Ser.: Vol. 545). ix, 513p. 1991. pap. 48.00 (*0-387-54572-7*) Spr-Verlag.

Attribute Pattern Boards. Linda Partee. (Illus.). 80p. 1982. 10.95 (*0-9607366-4-6*, KP114) Kino Pubns.

Attribute Sampling Plans, Tables of Tests & Confidence Limits for Proportions. Odeh & Owen. (Statistics: Textbooks & Monographs: Vol. 49). 384p. 1983. 125.00 (*0-8247-7136-2*) Dekker.

Attribute-Value Logic & the Theory of Grammar. Mark Johnson. LC 88-25120. (CSLI Lecture Notes Ser.: No. 16). 180p. 1988. 37.50 (*0-937073-37-7*); pap. 15.95 (*0-937073-36-9*) Ctr Study Language.

Attributes of God. G. Edmund Gibbs. (C). 1989. 29.00 (*0-7223-2238-0*, Pub. by A H S Ltd UK) St Mut.

Attributes of God. Arthur W. Pink. 1988. pap. 4.99 (*0-8010-6989-0*) Baker Bk.

Attributes of God. Lewis R. Farnell. LC 77-27205. (Gifford Lectures: 1924-25). 296p. reprint ed. 34.50 (*0-404-60475-7*) AMS Pr.

Attributes of Magnesium for Automobile Design: SAE International Congress & Exposition 1994, 14 papers. (Special Publications). 1994. pap. 44.00 (*1-56091-474-2*, SP-1022) Soc Auto Engineers.

Attribution. Gifford Weary et al. (Illus.). 260p. 1989. 61.00 (*0-387-96917-9*) Spr-Verlag.

Attribution: Basic Issues & Applications. Ed. by John H. Harvey & Gifford Weary. 1985. text ed. 79.00 (*0-12-329960-8*) Acad Pr.

Attribution: Perceiving the Causes of Behavior. Edward E. Jones et al. (Illus.). 200p. reprint ed. pap. 57.00 (*0-7837-5186-9*, 2044919) Bks Demand.

Attribution & Dating of Armenian Bilingual Trams. Y. T. Nercessian. (Illus.). 48p. (Orig.). 1983. 6.75 (*0-9606842-1-2*) ANS.

Attribution of Blame. Kelly G. Shaver. (Social Psychology Ser.). (Illus.). 210p. 1985. 63.00 (*0-387-96120-8*) Spr-Verlag.

Attribution Theory: An Organizational Perspective. Mark Martinko. (Illus.). 260p. 1995. 39.95 (*1-884015-19-0*) St Lucie Pr.

Attribution Theory: Applications to Achievement, Mental Health, & Interpersonal Conflict. Ed. by Sandra Graham & Valerie S. Folkes. (Applied Social Psychology Ser.). 232p. 1990. 49.95 (*0-8058-0531-1*) L Erlbaum Assocs.

Attribution Theory & Research. Ajit K. Dalal. (C). 1988. pap. 25.00 (*81-224-0093-0*, Pub. by Wiley Eastern II) S Asia.

Attribution Theory & Research: Conceptual, Developmental & Social Dimensions. J. Jaspars et al. 1983. text ed. 105.00 (*0-12-380980-0*) Acad Pr.

Attribution Theory in Clinical Psychology. Forsterling. LC 88-5696. (Clinical Psychology Ser.). 187p. 1988. text ed. 104.00 (*0-471-91604-8*) Wiley.

Attributional Theory of Motivation & Emotion. B. Weiner. (Social Psychology Ser.). (Illus.). 340p. 1986. 65.00 (*0-387-96312-X*) Spr-Verlag.

Attributions, Accounts & Close Relationships. Ed. by John H. Harvey et al. (Illus.). 304p. 1991. 44.00 (*0-387-97461-X*) Spr-Verlag.

Attributions & Psychological Change: Application of Attributional Theories to Clinical & Educational Practice. Ed. by Charles Antaki & Chris Brewin. LC 81-71575. (Illus.). 1982. text ed. 80.00 (*0-12-058780-7*) Acad Pr.

Attrition: Forecasting Battle Casualties & Equipment Losses in Modern War. Trevor N. Dupuy. 1990. pap. 19.95 (*0-915979-26-8*) NOVA Pubns.

Attrition of French As a Foreign Language. Bert Weltens. (Studies on Language Acquisition). vi, 148p. 1989. pap. 30.80 (*90-6765-402-7*) Mouton.

Attualita di Pirandello: Atti Del Simposio Diretto Da Philip Cordaro. Ed. by Philip Cordaro. LC 91-38800. 88p. (ITA.). 1991. lib. bdg. 49.95 (*0-7734-9709-9*) E Mellen.

Attune Your Body with Dao-In. Hua-Ching Ni. LC 90-62781. (Master's Series of Taoist Internal Arts). 1992. pap. 14.95 (*0-937064-40-8*) SevenStar Comm.

Attune Your Body with Dao-In: Taoist Exercise for a Long & Happy Life. Hua-Ching Ni. LC 94-12296. (Masters Series of Taoist Internal Practices: Bk. 1). 1994. 14.95 (*0-937064-72-6*) SevenStar Comm.

Attunement Through the Body. Shigenori Nagatomo. LC 91-39372. (SUNY Series, The Body in Culture, History, & Religion). 305p. 1992. 59.50 (*0-7914-1231-8*); pap. 19.95 (*0-7914-1232-6*) State U NY Pr.

Attunement with Life. Bill Wilkinson. xii, 84p. (Orig.). 1986. pap. text ed. 5.95 (*0-932869-02-5*) Emissaries.

Attunement with Life. 2nd ed. Bill Wilkinson. x, 83p. (Orig.). 1992. pap. 5.95 (*0-932869-05-X*, Eden Valley) Emissaries.

Attwater History & Genealogy. Charles H. Attwater. LC 85-71715. 316p. reprint ed. 150.00 (*0-916497-57-7*); reprint ed. fiche 6.00 (*0-916497-56-9*) Burnett Micro.

*__Atunes y Peces Espada: Los Peces Sin Patria.__ 3rd ed. James Joseph et al. (Illus.). vii, 46p. 1986. pap. 9.95 (*0-614-04383-2*) Inter-Am Tropical.

ATV Safety Training Manual. (Illus.). 1985. pap. 2.00 (*0-916682-45-5*) Outdoor Empire.

ATV's. Paul Estrem. LC 87-19900. (Super-Charged Ser.). (Illus.). 48p. (J). (gr. 5-6). 1987. text ed. 11.95 (*0-89686-348-4*, Crstwood Hse) Silver Burdett Pr.

Atwood-Coffee Catalogue of United States & Canadian Transportation Tokens, 2 Vols., Set. 4th ed. Ed. by J. M. Coffee. 1348p. 1982. 55.00 (*0-318-13314-8*) Am Vecturist.

Atwood-Coffee Catalogue of United States & Canadian Transportation Tokens, Vol. III. Ed. by J. M. Coffee. 946p. 1986. 50.00 (*0-318-21989-1*) Am Vecturist.

Atya-like Shrimps of the Indo-Pacific Region (Decapoda: Atyidae) Fenner A. Chace. LC 83-600083. (Smithsonian Contributions to Zoology Ser.: No. 384). 58p. reprint ed. pap. 25.00 (*0-8357-5870-2*, 2021866) Bks Demand.

Atypical Adolescence. Max Sugar. 1990. 29.95 (*0-393-70109-3*) Norton.

Atypical Cognitive Deficits in Developmental Disorders: Implications for Brain Function. Ed. by Sarah H. Broman & Jordan Grafman. LC 93-12499. 352p. 1993. text ed. 75.00 (*0-8058-1180-X*) L Erlbaum Assocs.

Atypical Employment in the EC. Daniele Meulders et al. (Illus.). 280p. (C). 1994. text ed. 57.95 (*1-85521-426-1*, Pub. by Dartmth Pub UK) Ashgate Pub Co.

Atypical Infant Development. Ed. by Marci J. Hanson. LC 83-14741. (Illus.). 421p. (C). 1984. text ed. 39.00 (*0-89079-195-3*, 1245) PRO-ED.

Atypical Orthopedic Radiographic Procedures. Gary L. Watkins & Thomas F. Moore. LC 92-49255. 176p. 1992. 41.95 (*0-8016-6270-2*) Mosby Yr Bk.

Atypical Stutterer: Principles & Practices of Rehabilitation. Ed. by Kenneth O. St. Louis. (Speech, Language, & Hearing Ser.). 1985. pap. text ed. 49.00 (*0-12-661621-3*) Acad Pr.

Atys. Jean-Baptiste Lully. Ed. by Theodore D. De Lajarte. (Chefs-d'oeuvre classiques de l'opera francaise Ser.: Vol. 18). (Illus.). 362p. (FRE.). 1970. reprint ed. pap. 37.50 (*0-8450-1118-9*) Broude.

Atys, Tragedie Lyrique. Niccolo Piccinni. Ed. by Julian Rushton. LC 91-757502. (French Opera in the 17th & 18th Centuries Ser.: No. 7, Vol. LXV). (Illus.). 1991. lib. bdg. 86.00 (*0-945193-21-1*) Pendragon NY.

Atzompa: A Pottery Producing Village of Southern Mexico in the Mid-1950's. Jean C. Hendry. Ed. by Ronald Spores et al. (Publications in Anthropology: No. 40). 150p. (Orig.). 1992. pap. 20.00 (*0-935462-31-7*) Vanderbilt Pubns.

Au & Ag Heap & Dump Leaching Practice: With Panel Discussion, Water Chemistry of Heap Leaching Operations. Ed. by J. Brent Hiskey. LC 84-71234. 168p. reprint ed. pap. 47.90 (*0-8357-3413-7*, 2039670) Bks Demand.

Au Bon Beurre. Jean Dutourd. (Folio Ser.: No. 260). 375p. (FRE.). 1952. pap. 9.95 (*2-07-036260-4*) Schoenhof.

Au Bon Buerre Ou Dix Ans De la Vie d'un Cremier. Jean Dutourd. (FRE.). 1982. pap. 11.95 (*0-7859-1717-9*, 2070362604) Fr & Eur.

Au Bonheur Des Chiens. Remo Forlani. (FRE.). 1984. pap. 10.95 (*0-7859-2646-1*, 207037534X) Fr & Eur.

Au Bonheur des Dames. Emile Zola. 480p. (FRE.). 1985. pap. 11.95 (*0-685-74007-2*, 2266015311) Fr & Eur.

Au Bonheur des Dames. Emile Zola. (Folio Ser.: No. 1272). 1971. 12.95 (*2-07-037242-1*) Schoenhof.

Au Bord de l'Eau, Vol. 1. Luo Guan-Zhong. (FRE.). 1978. lib. bdg. 95.00 (*0-8288-3522-5*, F120800) Fr & Eur.

Au Bord de l'Eau, Vol. 2. Luo Guan-Zhong. (FRE.). 1978. lib. bdg. 89.98 (*0-8288-3523-3*, M5576) Fr & Eur.

Au Bord de l'Eau: Chapitre 47 a 92, Epilogue, Vol. 2. Shi Nai-An & Luo Guan-Zhong. 1376p. 55.95 (*0-686-56570-3*) Fr & Eur.

Au Bord de l'Eau: Prologue Chapitre 1 a 46, Vol. 1. Shi Nai-An & Luo Guan-Zhong. 1408p. 55.95 (*0-686-56569-X*) Fr & Eur.

Au Chateau d'Argol. Julien Gracq. 180p. (FRE.). 1990. reprint ed. pap. write for info. (*0-7859-4593-8*) Fr & Eur.

Au Coeur du Monde, Feuilles de Route: Sud-Americaines, Poemes Divers. Blaise Cendrars. (FRE.). 1979. pap. 10.95 (*0-8288-3818-6*, F92191) Fr & Eur.

Au Courant. Robert J. Johnson. 1991. pap. 16.95 (*0-8442-1419-1*, Passport Bks) NTC Pub Grp.

Au Courant: Teaching French Vocabulary & Culture Using the Mass Media. Jean-Pierre Berwald. (Language in Education Ser.). 156p. 1987. pap. text ed. 12.50 (*0-13-050600-1*) P-H.

Au-Dela de Cette Limite Votre Ticket N'est Plus Valable. Romain Gary. (Folio Ser.: No. 1048). 264p. 1975. 8.95 (*2-07-037048-8*) Schoenhof.

Au-dela de Cette Limite Votre Ticket n'est plus Valable. Romain Gary. 247p. (FRE.). 1978. pap. 10.95 (*0-7859-2406-X*, 2070370887) Fr & Eur.

Au-Dela des Chiffres. Paul Y. Cho & R. Whitney Manzano. Ed. by Annie Cosson. Tr. by Elvire Cousin. Orig. Title: More Than Numbers. 208p. (FRE.). 1986. 4.95 (*0-8297-0529-5*) Life Pubs Intl.

*__Au-dela des Mots: Authentic Texts for Advanced Students of French.__ Brian McCarthy. 96p. (C). 1989. pap. 9.95 (*0-521-31964-1*) Cambridge U Pr.

Au-Dela Du Deshonneur. James M. Cain. 183p. (FRE.). 1985. pap. 11.95 (*0-7859-2024-2*, 2070377016) Fr & Eur.

Au-Dela Du Renversement Copernicien. M. Richir. (Phaenomenologica Ser.: No. 73). 1977. lib. bdg. 94.00 (*90-247-1903-8*) Kluwer Ac.

Au-Dessous de Volcan. Malcolm Lowry. (FRE.). 1973. pap. 17.95 (*0-7859-4004-9*) Fr & Eur.

Au Harem d'Archi Ahmed. Mehdi Charef. (Folio Ser.: No. 1958). 184p. (FRE.). 1988. pap. 8.95 (*2-07-038041-6*) Schoenhof.

Au Harem d'Archi Ahmed. Mehdi Charef. 184p. (FRE.). 1988. pap. 10.95 (*0-7859-2093-5*, 2070380416) Fr & Eur.

Au Moment Voulu see When the Time Comes

Au Nom du Fils. Herve Bazin. (FRE.). 1979. pap. 12.95 (*0-7859-3055-8*) Fr & Eur.

Au Pair American Style. Cindy F. Miller & Wendy J. Slossburg. 150p. (Orig.). 1986. pap. 5.95 (*0-915765-35-7*) Natl Pr Bks.

Au Pair Girl. Monica Ware. (Romance Ser.). 240p. 1994. pap. 14.95 (*0-7089-7537-2*, Linford) Ulverscroft.

Au Pays de Mes Racines. Marie Cardinal. (FRE.). 1982. pap. 10.95 (*0-7859-3107-4*) Fr & Eur.

Au Rendez-Vous Allemand. Paul Eluard. 80p. (FRE.). 1976. 10.95 (*0-8288-9971-1*, F60213) Fr & Eur.

Au Revoir les Enfants. Louis Malle. Tr. by Anselm Hollo. (Illus.). 224p. 1988. pap. 8.95 (*0-8021-3114-X*) Grove-Atltic.

Au Revoir les Enfants. Louis Malle. (Gallimard Ser.). 132p. (FRE.). 1987. pap. 27.95 (*2-07-071187-0*) Schoenhof.

Au Seuil d'un Nouveau Paradigme: Le Baroque a la Lueur des Theories Lupasquiennes. Yvette G. Thomas. (American University Studies: Romance Languages & Literature: Ser. II, Vol. 27). 214p. (C). 1985. text ed. 28.35 (*0-8204-0237-0*) P Lang Pubs.

Au Texas: With the Great West & European Colonization in Texas. Victor P. Considerant. LC 74-32216. (American Utopian Adventure Ser.). 432p. (FRE.). 1975. reprint ed. lib. bdg. 50.00 (*0-87991-021-6*) Porcupine Pr.

AUAA (American Urological Association Allied) Urologic Nursing: Principles & Practice. American Urological Association Allied Staff. Ed. by Karen A. Karlowicz. LC 92-49388. (Illus.). 736p. 1994. text ed. 79.00 (*0-7216-2731-5*) Saunders.

Aubade: A Teacher's Notebook. Wallace Fowlie. LC 83-14095. vi, 216p. 1983. 37.00 (*0-8223-0566-6*); pap. 15.95 (*0-8223-0588-7*) Duke.

Auberge of the Flowering Hearth. Roy A. De Groot. 464p. 1992. pap. 14.95 (*0-88001-278-1*) Ecco Pr.

Aubrey Beardsley. Ian Fletcher. (English Authors Ser.). 194p. 1987. text ed. 26.95 (*0-8057-6958-7*, Twayne) Macmillan.

Aubrey Beardsley. Hans Hofstatter. LC 79-13369. (Pocket Art Ser.). (Illus.). 1979. pap. 6.95 (*0-8120-2104-5*) Barron.

Aubrey Beardsley: Catalog of Drawings & Bibliographies. A. E. Gallatin. (Illus.). 148p. 1980. reprint ed. 15.00 (*0-911858-39-3*) Appel.

*__Aubrey Beardsley: Dandy of the Grotesque.__ Chris Snodgrass. (Illus.). 400p. 1995. text ed. 45.00 (*0-19-509062-4*) OUP.

Aubrey Beardsley: Imp of the Perverse. Stanley Weintraub. LC 75-27231. (Illus.). 480p. 1976. pap. 16.95 (*0-271-01216-1*) Pa St U Pr.

Aubrey Beardsley: Symbol, Mask & Self-Irony. Milly Heyd. (American University Studies: English Language & Literature: Ser. IV, Vol. 35). 250p. 1987. text ed. 34.00 (*0-8204-0277-X*) P Lang Pubs.

Aubrey Beardsley Bookplates. Aubrey Beardsley. Ed. by Menten Theodore. pap. 3.50 (*0-486-23350-2*) Dover.

Aubrey Beardsley Designs from the Age of Chivalry. Barbara Holdridge. (International Design Library). (Illus.). 48p. (Orig.). 1983. pap. 5.95 (*0-88045-022-3*) Stemmer Hse.

Aubrey Beardsley Greeting Card Book. Aubrey Beardsley. Ed. by Theodore Menten. (Illus.). 64p. 1975. pap. 4.95 (*0-486-23173-9*) Dover.

*__Aubrey-Maturin Series, 16 vols., Set.__ Patrick O'Brian. (C). 1994. 360.00 (*0-393-03749-5*) Norton.

Aubrey the Snowflake. Marina C. Stockdale. (Stage Magic for Children's Theatre Ser.). (Illus.). 24p. (Orig.). (gr. k-6). 1987. pap. 2.00 (*0-88680-287-3*); 10.00 (*0-88680-288-1*) I E Clark.

Auburn. Photos by Tommy Thompson. (First Edition Ser.). (Illus.). 112p. 1988. 39.00 (*0-916509-39-7*) Harmony Hse Pub LO.

Auburn: A Look down Main Street. Josephine E. Vine. (Illus.). 1990. 12.00 (*0-9625523-0-5*) City Auburn.

Auburn & Placer County: Crossroads of a Golden Era. A. Thomas Homer. (Illus.). 136p. (YA). (gr. 7 up). 1988. 27.95 (*0-89781-237-9*) Preferred Mktg.

Auburn, Cord, Duesenberg. Don Butler. (Illus.). 352p. 1992. 39.95 (*0-87938-701-7*) Motorbooks Intl.

Auburn-Dover-Wakarusa. 56p. 1958. 5.50 (*0-686-46440-0*) Shawnee County Hist.

Auburn Entertains. Ed. by Helen Baggett et al. LC 86-6557. (Illus.). 322p. 1986. spiral bd. 14.95 (*0-934395-20-9*) Rutledge Hill Pr.

Auburn Fan's Guidebook to Understanding Alabama Mentality. Ed. by Eula M. Smitten. (Illus.). 104p. (Orig.). 1991. pap. 4.95 (*0-9630297-1-1*) Sassafras Creek.

Auburn-Georgia Football: A Hundred Years of Rivalry. George Scherer. LC 92-50318. 280p. 1992. pap. 39.95 (*0-89950-751-4*) McFarland & Co.

Auburn, Reo, Franklin & Pierce-Arrow vs. Cadillac, Chrysler, Lincoln & Packard. Brooks T. Brierley. (Illus.). 160p. 1994. 39.95 (*0-9615791-1-0*) Garrett & String.

Auburn University Walking Tour Guide. R. G. Millman. 128p. 1991. pap. 9.95 (*0-8173-0523-8*) U of Ala Pr.

Aucassin & Nicolette: Kritischer Text Mit Paradigmen & Glossar. Ed. by Hermann Suchier & Walther Suchier. LC 80-2239. reprint ed. 31.00 (*0-404-19035-9*) AMS Pr.

Aucassin & Nicolette with Other Romances. Eugene Mason. LC 70-172850. (Illus.). reprint ed. 37.50 (*0-404-07774-9*) AMS Pr.

Aucassin et Nicolette. Albert Pauphilet. 171p. 1971. 9.95 (*0-8288-7472-7*) Fr & Eur.

Auchenorrhyncha (Homoptera) of Fennoscandia & Denmark, Pt. 1: Introduction, Infraorder Fulgoromorpha. F. Ossiannilsson. (Fauna Entomologica Scandinavica Ser.: No. 7-1). (Illus.). 222p. 1978. text ed. 42.00 (*87-87491-24-9*) Lubrecht & Cramer.

Auchenorrhyncha (Hompotera) of Fennoscandia & Denmark, Pt. 2z: The Families Cicadidae, Cercopidae, Membracidae, & Cicadellidae (Excluding Deltocephalinae) F. Ossiannilsson. (Fauna Entomologica Scandinavica Ser.: No. 7-2). (Illus.). 408p. 1981. text ed. 53.00 (*87-87491-36-2*) Lubrecht & Cramer.

Auctarium. Die griechischen Personenamen in Rom. Ein Namenbuch., Vol. I-III. Heikki Solin. (C). 1980. 438.50 (*3-11-004635-0*) De Gruyter.

Auction. Jan Andrews. LC 90-41378. (Illus.). 32p. (J). (ps-3). 1991. text ed. 13.95 (*0-02-705535-3*, Mac Bks Young Read) S&S Childrens.

Auction. Bill Hubbard. (Illus.). 225p. (Orig.). 1989. pap. 14.95 (*0-912395-16-8*) Millers River Pub Co.

Auction. large type ed. Justin Scott. 478p. 1986. 23.95 (*0-7089-8376-6*) Ulverscroft.

Auction - Law & Practice. Brian W. Harvey & F. Meisel. 1985. U.K. pap. 86.00 (*0-406-52660-5*) Butterworth Legal Pubs.

Auction Action! A Survival Companion for Any Auction Goer. Ralph Roberts. (Illus.). 192p. 1986. pap. 12.95 (*0-8306-2752-9*, NO. 2752) TAB Bks.

Auction Action: A Survival Companion for Any Auction Goer. Ralph Roberts. 1986. pap. 12.95 (*0-07-156628-7*) McGraw.

Auction Book: A Comprehensive Fundraising Resource for Nonprofit Organizations. 3rd rev. ed. Betsy Beatty & Libby Kirkpatrick. LC 85-70258. (Illus.). 164p. 1987. pap. 25.00 (*0-9613483-2-1*) Auction Pr.

Auction Book: Automobile Auction Directory. Tim Johnson & Joy Johnson. LC 92-80998. (Illus.). 224p. (Orig.). 1993. pap. 12.95 (*1-880782-21-9*) Spirit Dance.

Auction Prices of American Artists, 1995. rev. ed. Richard Hislop. 393p. 1995. lib. bdg. 45.00 (*0-903872-50-1*, Pub. by Art Sales Index Ltd UK) Dealers Choice.

Auction Prices of Nineteenth Century: Artists, Impressionist & Old Masters, Set. Richard Hislop. 2800p. 1990. lib. bdg. 350.00 (*0-318-43154-8*, Pub. by Art Sales Index Ltd UK) Dealers Choice.

Auction Prices Realized: U. S. Coins, 1984. Ed. by Bob Wilhite. LC 83-642434. 1984. pap. 50.00 (*0-87341-042-4*) Krause Pubns.

Auction Prices Realized: U. S. Paper Money, 1983. Ed. by Bob Wilhite. 1983. pap. 40.00 (*0-87341-029-7*) Krause Pubns.

Auction Prices Realized Nineteen Eighty-Six, U. S. Coins. Ed. by Bob Wilhite. LC 83-642434. 1987. pap. 50.00 (*0-87341-085-8*) Krause Pubns.

Auction Prices Realized, U. S. Coins. Ed. by Robert E. Wilhite. LC 83-642434. 800p. 1982. pap. 50.00 (*0-87341-073-4*) Krause Pubns.

Auction Prices Realized: U. S. Coins, 1983. Ed. by Bob Wilhite. LC 83-642434. 1983. pap. 50.00 (*0-87341-030-0*) Krause Pubns.

Auction Prices Realized, U. S. Coins, 1991. Robert Wilhite. Ed. by Tom Michael. LC 83-642434. 800p. 1991. pap. 60.00 (*0-87341-154-4*) Krause Pubns.

Auction Prices Realized, 1985: U. S. Coins. Bob Wilhite. LC 83-642434. 1985. pap. 50.00 (*0-87341-048-3*) Krause Pubns.

Auction Prices Realized 1988. Ed. by Bob Wilhite. LC 83-642434. 1988. pap. 50.00 (*0-87341-104-8*) Krause Pubns.

Auction Prices Realized 1989. Ed. by Robert Wilhite. LC 83-642434. 864p. 1989. pap. 60.00 (*0-87341-121-8*) Krause Pubns.

Auction Prices Realized, 1990. Robert Wilhite. LC 83-642434. 1990. pap. 60.00 (*0-87341-132-3*) Krause Pubns.

Auction Prices Realized, 1992: U. S. Coins. 11th ed. Bob Wilhite. LC 83-642434. (Illus.). 800p. 1992. pap. 60.00 (*0-87341-186-2*) Krause Pubns.

Auction Prices Realized, 1993: U. S. Coins. Ed. by Robert Wilhite & Tom Michael. LC 83-642434. 416p. 1993. pap. 60.00 (*0-87341-251-6*) Krause Pubns.

Auction Prices Realized 87. Ed. by Bob Wilhite. LC 83-642434. 800p. 1987. pap. 50.00 (*0-87341-092-0*) Krause Pubns.

Auction Quotas & U.S. Trade Policy. C. Fred Bergsten et al. LC 87-12948. (Policy Analysis in International Economics Ser.: No. 19). 241p. 1987. pap. 10.00 (*0-88132-050-1*) Inst Intl Eco.

Auction Revolution: The Complete Guide to Buying & Selling Real Estate by Auction. Robert D. Friedman & Tim McIntire. 144p. 1993. per., pap. text ed. 14.95 (*0-9634922-0-9*); boxed 22.95 (*0-9634922-1-7*) GRP Pr.

Auctioning Radio Spectrum Licenses. 47p. (Orig.). (C). 1993. pap. text ed. 40.00 (*1-56806-770-4*) Diane Pub.

Auctions: The Social Construction of Value. Charles W. Smith. 288p. 1988. 23.99 (*0-318-37131-6*) Free Pr.

Auctions: The Social Construction of Value. Charles W. Smith. 237p. 1990. pap. 12.00 (*0-520-07201-4*) U CA Pr.

Auctions for Amateurs. Sandra Quinn-Musgrove & Edward J. Doherty. LC 93-71299. 166p. (Orig.). 1993. pap. 9.95 (*0-9628295-2-8*) Blue Hse TX.

Auctions of 1990. (Annual Supplement to the Blood-Horse Magazine Ser.). 500p. 1991. pap. 30.00 (*0-939049-38-4*) Blood-Horse.

An Asterisk (*) at the beginning of an entry indicates that the title is appearing in BIP for the first time.

Auctions of 1991. (Annual Supplement Ser.). (Illus.). 525p. (Orig.). 1992. pap. 35.00 (*0-939049-44-9*) Blood-Horse.
Auctions of 1992. 350p. 1993. pap. 35.00 (*0-939049-51-1*) Blood-Horse.
Auctions of 1993. Ed. by Raymond S. Paulick & Dan Mearns. (Illus.). 350p. (Orig.). 1994. pap. 35.00 (*0-939049-56-2*) Blood-Horse.
***Auctions of 1994: Annual Supplement to the Blood-Horse.** Ed. by Raymond S. Paulick & Dan Mearns. (Blood-Horse Supplement Ser.). (Illus.). 400p. (Orig.). 1995. pap. 40.00 (*0-939049-64-3*) Blood-Horse.
Auctor & Actor: A Narratological Reading of Apuleius' "The Golden Ass" John J. Winkler. 353p. 1991. reprint ed. pap. 15.00 (*0-520-07639-7*) U CA Pr.
Auctor Ludens: Essays on Play in Literature. Gerald Guinness & Andrew Hurley. LC 86-4247. (Cultura Ludens Ser: No. 2). ix, 204p. 1986. 52.00x (*0-915027-19-4*); pap. 27.95x (*0-915027-20-8*) Benjamins North Am.
Audacious Kids: Coming of Age in America's Classic Children's Books. Jerry Griswold. 304p. 1992. 25.00 (*0-19-505888-7*) OUP.
Audacious Poetry. Greta B. Lipson. (Illus.). 128p. (J). (gr. 6-12). 1992. student ed 11.95 (*0-86653-683-3*, 1417) Good Apple.
***Audacious Women: Early British Mormon Immigrants.** Rebecca C. Bartholomew. LC 94-23624. 303p. (Orig.). 1995. pap. 18.95 (*1-56085-066-3*) Signature Bks.
Audacity. Alan Evans. 1987. 16.95 (*0-8027-0995-8*) Walker & Co.
Audacity. large type ed. Alan Evans. 448p. 1987. 16.95 (*0-7089-1699-6*) Ulverscroft.
Audel Electric Motors. 5th rev. ed. Edwin P. Anderson. 672p. 1991. text ed. 35.00 (*0-02-501920-1*, Audel) Macmillan.
Auden. B. Everett. (Writers & Critics Ser.). 117p. 1980. 24.50 (*0-912378-04-2*) Chips.
Auden: A Carnival of Intellect. Edward Callan. 1983. 30.00 (*0-19-503168-7*) OUP.
Auden & After: The Liberation of Poetry, 1930-41. Francis Scarfe. 1988. reprint ed. lib. bdg. 49.00 (*0-7812-0412-7*) Rprt Serv.
Auden & After: The Liberation of Poetry, 1930-41. Francis Scarfe. reprint ed. 39.00 (*0-403-03312-8*) Somerset Pub.
Auden Generation: Literature & Politics in England in the 1930's. Samual Hynes. (Pimlico Ser.). 428p. 1993. reprint ed. pap. 22.95 (*0-7126-5250-7*, Pub. by Pimlico) Trafalgar.
Auden Generation: Literature & Politics in England in the 1930's. Samuel Hynes. LC 82-47627. 432p. 1982. reprint ed. 62.50 (*0-691-06516-0*); reprint ed. pap. 16.95 (*0-691-01395-0*) Princeton U Pr.
Auden's Apologies for Poetry. Lucy McDiarmid. 200p. 1990. text ed. 27.50 (*0-691-06784-8*) Princeton U Pr.
Audi Fox Service Manual, 1973-1979. Bentley, Robert, Inc. Staff. LC 79-53187. (Illus.). 1979. pap. 39.95 (*0-8376-0097-9*) Bentley.
Audi 100, 200 Official Factory Repair Manual: 1989-1991 Including Quattro & 20-Valve, 3 vols. Audi of America, Inc. Staff. 169.95 (*0-8376-0372-2*) Bentley.
Audi 4000 Coupe Official Factory Repair Manual 1980 to 1983. Audi of America, Inc. Staff. LC 83-70221. (Illus.). 880p. (Orig.). 1983. pap. 59.95 (*0-8376-0349-8*) Bentley.
Audi 4000s, 4000cs & Coupe GT Official Factory Repair Manual: 1984-1987, Including Quattro & Quattro Turbo. Audi of America. 1989. 94.95 (*0-8376-0373-0*) Bentley.
Audi 5000, 5000S Official Factory Repair Manual, Gasoline & Turbo Gasoline, Diesel & Turbo Diesel, 1977-1983. Audi of America, Inc. Staff. LC 83-71486. (Illus.). 992p. (Orig.). 1983. pap. 59.95 (*0-8376-0352-8*) Bentley.
Audi 5000S, 5000CS Official Factory Repair Manual: 1984-1988 Gasoline, Turbo, & Turbo Diesel, Including Wagon & Quattro, 2 vols. Audi of America. 139.95 (*0-8376-0370-6*) Bentley.
Audi 80, 90, Coupe Quattro Electrical Troubleshooting Manual: 1988-1992. (Illus.). 618p. 1992. pap. 79.95 (*0-8376-0375-7*) Bentley.
Audi 80, 90, Coupe Quattro Electrical Troubleshooting Manual: 1988-1990. (Illus.). 576p. (Orig.). 1990. pap. 59.95 (*0-8376-0383-8*) Bentley.
Audi 80, 90 Coupe Quattro Official Factory Repair Manual: 1988-1991, Including 80 Quattro, 90 Quattro & 20-Valve Models. Audi of America. (Illus.). 1222p. 89.95 (*0-8376-0367-6*) Bentley.
Audible Approach to Silence. David White. LC 91-91174. 110p. 1991. pap. 9.95 (*0-9630616-0-7*) Whitestone.
Audibles: My Life in Football. Joe Montana & Bob Raissman. 1990. pap. 3.95 (*0-380-71326-8*, Flare) Avon.
Audie. Dorothy P. Hoover. 112p. 1993. pap. 10.95 (*1-880365-82-0*) Prof Pr NC.
Audience. Herbert Blau. LC 89-30491. (Parallax: Re-Visions of Culture & Society Ser.). 432p. 1990. text ed. 60.00x (*0-8018-3844-4*); pap. text ed. 16.95x (*0-8018-3845-2*) Johns Hopkins.
Audience & Rhetoric: An Archaeological Composition of the Discourse Community. James E. Porter. 204p. 1991. pap. text ed. 26.60 (*0-13-050675-3*, 640601) P-H.
Audience Criticism & the Historical Jesus. J. Arthur Baird. 1969. 6.50 (*0-664-20846-0*) Biblical Res Assocs.
Audience Expectations & Teacher Demands. Robert Brooke & John Hendricks. LC 88-31210. (Studies in Writing & Rhetoric). 148p. (Orig.). (C). 1989. pap. 12.95 (*0-8093-1514-9*) S Ill U Pr.
Audience for American Art Museums. J. Mark Schuster. LC 90-20253. 72p. 1991. pap. 10.95 (*0-929765-00-1*, 1775) Seven Locks Pr.
Audience for Moral Philosophy? John T. Edelman. LC 90-36808. 136p. 1991. text ed. 45.00 (*0-312-04931-5*) St Martin.
Audience, Intention, & Rhetoric in Pascal & Simone Weil. Thomas Stokes. LC 93-14191. (Currents in Comparative Romance Languages & Literatures Ser.: vol. 22). 1993. write for info. (*0-8204-2260-6*) P Lang Pubs.
Audience of One. Gerald Barrax. LC 79-3050. (Contemporary Poetry Ser.). 94p. 1980. pap. 7.95 (*0-8203-0502-2*) U of Ga Pr.
Audience Participation: Theatre for Young People. Brian Way. (Illus.). 232p. (Orig.). 1980. pap. 11.95x (*0-87440-000-7*) W H Baker.
Audience Promotion Assistant. Jack Rudman. (Career Examination Ser.: C-1123). 1994. pap. 29.95 (*0-8373-1123-3*) Nat Learn.
Audience Ratings: Radio, Television, & Cable. rev. ed. Hugh M. Beville, Jr. (Communication Ser.). 424p. 1988. text ed. 79.95 (*0-8058-0175-8*); student ed, pap. 39.95 (*0-8058-0174-X*) L Erlbaum Assocs.
***Audience Reflected in the Medium of Law: A Critique of the Political Economy of Speech Rights in the United States.** Myles A. Ruggles. 208p. 1994. 39.95 (*0-89391-881-4*); pap. 22.50 (*0-89391-993-4*) Ablex Pub.
Audience Research Sourcebook. Ed. by Gerald Hartshorn. (Illus.). 192p. 1991. 50.00 (*0-89324-113-X*) Natl Assn Broadcasters.
Audience Responses to Media Diversification: Coping with Plenty. Ed. by L. B. Becker & K. Schoenbach. (Communication Ser.). 400p. 79.95 (*0-8058-0229-0*) L Erlbaum Assocs.
Audience, the Message, the Speaker. 5th ed. John Hasling. LC 92-15896. 1992. pap. text ed. write for info. (*0-07-026999-8*) McGraw.
Audiencemaking: How the Media Create the Audience. Ed. by James Ettema & D. Charles Whitney. (Annual Reviews of Communication Research Ser.: Vol. 22). 286p. 1994. 52.00 (*0-8039-4625-2*); pap. 24.00 (*0-8039-4626-0*) Sage.
Audiences & Intentions: A Book of Arguments. 2nd ed. Nancy M. Bradbury & Arthur Quinn. 659p. (C). 1994. pap. write for info. (*0-02-313202-7*) Macmillan.
Audiencia in the Spanish Colonies As Illustrated by the Audiencia in Manila, 1583-1800. Charles H. Cunningham. LC 72-131250. 479p. 1971. reprint ed. 75.00 (*0-87752-130-1*) Gordian.
Audiencia of New Galicia in the Sixteenth Century: A Study in Spanish Colonial Government. J. H. Parry, pseud. LC 85-10039. (Illus.). xii, 207p. 1985. reprint ed. text ed. 59.75 (*0-313-24957-1*, PANG, Greenwood Pr) Greenwood.
Audio: The International Market. Euromonitor Staff. 120p. 1989. 2,925.00 (*0-685-31232-1*, Pub. by Euromonitor Pubns UK) Gale.
Audio Algebra: Glob Principle & Algebra of Words. John M. Brown. (Illus.). 52p. 1987. audio, pap. text ed. 12.00 (*0-317-91301-8*) Educ Dy AZ.
***Audio Amateur Loudspeaker Projects.** Ed. by Audio Amateur Magazine Staff. LC 85-81547. (Illus.). 135p. 1985. pap. text ed. 20.00 (*0-8338-0193-7*) Audio Amateur.
***Audio & Media.** S. Alten. 1990. 45.95 (*0-534-12132-2*) Brooks-Cole.
Audio & Video Digital Radio Broadcasting Systems & Techniques: Proceedings of the Sixth Tirrenia International Workshop on Digital Communications, Tirrenia, Italy, 5-9 September, 1993. Ed. by Riccardo De Denzi & Marco Luise. LC 93-49576. 1994. write for info. (*0-444-81580-5*) Elsevier.
***Audio Anthology Vol. 1: When Audio Was Young.** Ed. by C. G. McProud. LC 87-62118. (Illus.). 124p. 1987. pap. text ed. 16.95 (*0-8338-0195-3*) Audio Amateur.
***Audio Anthology Vol. 2: When Audio Was Young.** Ed. by C. G. McProud. (Illus.). 124p. 1989. pap. text ed. 16.95 (*0-8338-0197-X*) Audio Amateur.
***Audio Anthology Vol. 3: When Audio Was Young.** Ed. by C. G. McProud. LC 90-80999. (Illus.). 124p. 1990. pap. text ed. 16.95 (*0-9624191-1-7*) Audio Amateur.
***Audio Anthology Vol. 4: When Audio Was Young.** Ed. by C. G. McProud. LC 91-72106. (Illus.). 144p. 1991. pap. text ed. 16.95 (*0-9624191-9-2*) Audio Amateur.
Audio Anthology, Vol. 5: When Audio Was Young. Radio Magazine Editors. (Illus.). 144p. (Orig.). 1993. reprint ed. pap. 16.95 (*1-882580-01-X*) Audio Amateur.
Audio Arts: Definitions of Practice. William Furlong. (Illus.). 144p. 1994. pap. 30.00 (*1-85490-363-2*, Academy Edits) St Martin.
Audio Book Breakthrough: Selection & Use in Public Libraries & Education. Preston Hoffman & Carol H. Osteyee. LC 93-1701. 208p. 1993. text ed. 39.95 (*0-313-28690-6*, Greenwood Pr) Greenwood.
Audio Control Handbook. 6th ed. Robert S. Oringel. (Illus.). 304p. 1989. pap. 34.95 (*0-240-80015-X*, Focal) Buttrwrth-Heinemann.
Audio Control Handbook: For Radio & Television Broadcasting. 5th enl. rev. ed. Robert S. Oringel. LC 83-6131. (Communication Arts Bks.). (Illus.). 380p. 1983. pap. text ed. 16.00 (*0-8038-0550-0*) Hastings.
Audio Design: Sound Recording Techniques for Film & Video. Anthony J. Zaza. 400p. 1991. text ed. 50.00 (*0-13-050733-4*) P-H.
Audio Designer's Tube Register. Tom Mitchell. (Common Low-Power Triodes Ser.: Vol. 1). (Illus.). 144p. 1993. 18.00 (*0-9628170-1-5*) Media Cncpt.
Audio Dictionary. Glenn D. White. 1987. 30.00 (*0-295-96527-4*) U of Wash Pr.
Audio Dictionary. 2nd rev. ed. Glenn D. White. LC 90-23471. 426p. 1991. reprint ed. pap. 19.95 (*0-295-97088-X*) U of Wash Pr.
***Audio Electronics.** John L. Hood. LC 94-41505. (Illus.). 240p. 1995. pap. 29.95 (*0-7506-2181-8*, Focal) Buttrwrth-Heinemann.
Audio Electronics Reference Book. Ed. by I. R. Sinclair. (Illus.). 624p. (C). 1988. text ed. 170.00 (*0-632-01929-8*) Buttrwrth-Heinemann.
Audio Engineering Handbook. Ed. by Blair K. Benson. (Illus.). 1040p. 1988. text ed. 94.50 (*0-07-004777-4*) McGraw.
Audio Engineer's Reference Book. Ed. by Michael Talbot-Smith. LC 94-6957. 480p. 1994. 99.95 (*0-7506-0386-0*, Focal) Buttrwrth-Heinemann.
***Audio Glossary.** J. Gordon Holt. LC 90-62135. (Illus.). 152p. 1990. pap. text ed. 9.95 (*0-9624191-4-1*) Audio Amateur.
Audio IC Circuits Manual. Marston. 1989. pap. 30.95 (*0-434-91210-7*, TK) CRC Pr.
***Audio IC Projects.** Maplin Staff. (Maplin Ser.). 208p. 1995. pap. 19.95 (*0-7506-2121-4*, Focal) Buttrwrth-Heinemann.
Audio in Media. 3rd ed. Stanley R. Alten. 644p. (C). 1990. text ed. 45.95 (*0-534-12134-9*) Intl Thomson.
Audio in Media. 4th ed. Stanley R. Alten. 670p. 1994. text ed. 47.95 (*0-534-19602-0*) Intl Thomson.
Audio Industry Consumer Study. 220p. 475.00 (*0-318-14036-5*) Elec Ind Assn.
Audio Production Techniques for Video. David M. Huber. (Illus.). 368p. 1987. pap. 34.95 (*0-240-80148-2*, Focal) Buttrwrth-Heinemann.
Audio Recording & Reproduction: Practical Measures for Audio Enthusiasts. Michael Talbot-Smith. LC 94-10165. (Illus.). 208p. 1994. pap. 22.95 (*0-7506-1917-1*) Buttrwrth-Heinemann.
Audio-Recording in the Superior Court of District of Columbia. National Center for State Courts Staff. (Paul Reardon Ser.). 17p. 1982. 1.02 (*0-685-16276-1*, PRS-026) Natl Ctr St Courts.
Audio Servicing: Theory & Practice. Andy J. Wells. (Illus.). 240p. (Orig.). 1979. text ed. 25.95 (*0-07-069246-7*) McGraw.
Audio Systems Design & Installation. Philip Giddings. 350p. 1990. 59.95 (*0-672-22672-3*, Bobbs) Macmillan.
Audio Tape Program: A Workbook. Anne Lindell. (C). 1983. pap. text ed. 13.95 (*0-472-08573-5*) U of Mich Pr.
Audio Tapes: E. S. Bird Library. Comp. by A. Charters. 1976. 3.75 (*0-686-63886-7*, MSS 22) Syracuse U Cont Ed.
Audio-Tutorial Introduction to Chemistry: Workbook. Paul Santiago. (Illus.). 192p. (C). 1985. reprint ed. pap. text ed. 18.95 (*0-88133-159-7*) Waveland Pr.
Audio-Tutorial System. James D. Russell. Ed. by Danny G. Langdon. LC 77-25454. (Instructional Design Library). (Illus.). 80p. 1978. 23.95 (*0-87778-107-9*) Educ Tech Pubns.
Audio-Typing: A Progressive Course. Edith Whicher. 136p. (Orig.). (C). 1975. Students' ed. student ed, pap. 22.00 (*0-8464-0161-4*) Beekman Pubs.
Audio, Video, & Data Telecommunications. David Petersen. LC 92-9766. 1992. write for info. (*0-07-707427-0*) McGraw.
Audio-Video Buying Guide. Consumer Reports Editors & Monte Florman. 208p. 1994. pap. 8.99 (*0-89043-766-1*) Consumer Reports.
Audio-Video Buying Guide. 2nd ed. Monte Florman & Consumer Reports Books Editors. 208p. (Orig.). 1993. pap. 8.99 (*0-89043-680-0*) Consumer Reports.
Audio-Video Discount & Wholesale Buyer's Guide. Warren Weagant. 64p. 1980. pap. write for info. (*0-933132-05-0*) Command Prods.
Audio-Video Production. Henry B. Aldridge & Lucy A. Liggett. 400p. 1989. text ed. 63.00 (*0-13-050774-1*) P-H.
Audio-Video Review Digest, 1989: Cumulation. Ed. by Susan L. Stetler. 325p. 1990. 156.00 (*0-8103-2991-3*) Gale.
Audio-Video Technology & the Courts: Guide for Court Managers. National Center for State Courts Staff et al. LC 78-105951. (Courts' Equipment Analysis Project Ser.). (Illus.). 76p. 1977. pap. 0.70 (*0-89656-022-8*, R-034) Natl Ctr St Courts.
Audio-Vision: Sound on Screen. Michel Chion. Ed. & Tr. by Claudia Gorbman. LC 93-23982. 1993. write for info. (*0-231-07898-6*); pap. write for info. (*0-231-07899-4*) Col U Pr.
Audio-Visual Aid Technician. Jack Rudman. (Career Examination Ser.: C-58). 1994. pap. 23.95 (*0-8373-0058-4*) Nat Learn.
Audio-Visual Aide. Jack Rudman. (Career Examination Ser.: C-2903). 1994. pap. 23.95 (*0-8373-2903-5*) Nat Learn.
Audio-Visual Aids in Health Biology: Index of Modern Information. Andy J. Cyrpinski. LC 88-47968. 150p. 1990. 39.50 (*1-55914-210-3*); pap. 34.50 (*1-55914-211-1*) ABBE Pubs Assn.
Audio Visual-Draughting, Office-Reproduction & Other Ancillary Equipment & Supplies: Equipment Planning Guide for Vocational & Technical Training & Education Programmes. 2nd rev. ed. (Illus.). v, 240p. 1985. pap. 32.00 (*92-2-103815-7*) Intl Labour Office.
Audio-Visual Equipment: A Technician's & User's Handbook. Ed. by Ian Robertson. (Illus.). 180p. 1991. text ed. 59.95 (*0-7506-0021-7*) Buttrwrth-Heinemann.
Audio-Visual Guide to American Holidays. Ed. by Carol A. Emmens & Harry Maglione. LC 78-6230. 284p. 1978. lib. bdg. 27.50 (*0-8108-1140-5*) Scarecrow.
Audio-Visual Guide to Sources of the African Past. Robinson et al. 1980. 280.00 (*0-8419-0537-1*, Africana) Holmes & Meier.
Audio-Visual Marketing Handbook for Independent Schools. Committee on Boarding Schools. 1987. pap. 16.00 (*0-934338-64-7*) NAIS.
Audio-Visual Primer. Carmel L. Morse. LC 82-84727. (Illus.). 75p. (Orig.). 1983. pap. 5.95 (*0-911997-00-8*) Backwoods Pubns.
Audio-Visual Program, No. 1-5. Anthony B. Colletti. (Keystone Publications' Audio-Visual Program Ser.). 1979. 250.00 (*0-912126-39-6*); teacher ed 7.07 (*0-912126-37-X*); student ed 1.79 (*0-912126-38-8*) Keystone Pubns.
Audio-Visual Programs Specialist. Jack Rudman. (Career Examination Ser.: C-3209). 1994. pap. 29.95 (*0-8373-3209-5*) Nat Learn.
Audio-Visual Specialist. Jack Rudman. (Career Examination Ser.: C-1826). 1994. pap. 23.95 (*0-8373-1826-2*) Nat Learn.
Audio-Visual Technician. Jack Rudman. (Career Examination Ser.: C-1894). 1994. pap. 23.95 (*0-8373-1894-7*) Nat Learn.
Audio-Visual Technology & Learning see Educational Technology Reviews Ser.
Audio Workbook. Danny G. Langdon. LC 77-25109. (Instructional Design Library). (Illus.). 80p. 1978. 23.95 (*0-87778-109-5*) Educ Tech Pubns.
Audio Worksheets, 4 vol. set. Los Angeles County Schools Ser. (Auditory Skills Instructional Planning System Ser.: 3rd Component). (Illus.). 356p. 1980. ring bd. 380.00 (*0-943292-13-1*) Foreworks.
Audio Worksheets, Vol. 1. Los Angeles County Schools Staff. (Illus.). 1980. 95.00 (*0-943292-09-3*) Foreworks.
Audio Worksheets, Vol. 2. Los Angeles County Schools Staff. (Illus.). 1980. 95.00 (*0-943292-10-7*) Foreworks.
Audio Worksheets, Vol. 3. Los Angeles County Schools Staff. (Illus.). 1980. 95.00 (*0-943292-11-5*) Foreworks.
Audio Worksheets, Vol. 4. Los Angeles County Schools Staff. (Illus.). 1980. 95.00 (*0-943292-12-3*) Foreworks.
Audio Writing. Richard Kostelanetz. 91p. (Orig.). 1984. pap. 10.00 (*0-932360-39-4*) Archae Edns.
***AudioBook Reference Guide, 1995-96.** Robin F. Whitten. 44p. 1995. pap. text ed. 9.95 (*0-9645649-0-4*) AudioFile.
***AudioBooks on the Go: A Listener's Guide to Books on Cassette.** AudioFile Editors. (Illus.). 200p. (Orig.). 1995. pap. 9.95 (*1-56626-088-4*) Country Rds.
Audiocassette & Compact Disc Finder. 3rd ed. 1500p. 1993. 125.00 (*0-937548-22-7*) Plexus Pub.
Audiocassette Finder: A Subject Guide to Educational & Literary Materials on Audiocassettes. 2nd ed. National Information Center for Educational Media Staff. Ed. by Stephanie Korney. 925p. 1989. 95.00 (*0-937548-14-6*) Natl Info Ctr NM.
AudioCraft: An Introduction to the Tools & Techniques of Audio Production. 2nd rev. ed. Randy Thom. LC 89-61191. (Illus.). 200p. (C). 1989. pap. text ed. 22.00 (*0-941209-02-4*) Natl Fed Com Broad.
Audioencyclopedia. Howard M. Tremaine. 984p. (SPA.). 1977. 150.00 (*0-7859-5831-2*, 8426702104) Fr & Eur.
Audioencyclopedia, 2 vols., Set. H. M. Tremaine. 1920p. (SPA.). 1977. 295.00 (*0-8288-5289-8*, S30775) Fr & Eur.
Audioencyclopedia, Vol. 2. Howard M. Tremaine. 936p. (SPA.). 1977. 150.00 (*0-7859-5832-0*, 8426702112) Fr & Eur.
***Audiological Rehabilitation of the Elderly.** Kriscos. 1995. 45.00 (*0-7506-9531-5*, Focal) Buttrwrth-Heinemann.
Audiologist. Jack Rudman. (Career Examination Ser.: C-1124). 1994. pap. 27.95 (*0-8373-1124-1*) Nat Learn.
Audiologist - Speech Pathologist. Jack Rudman. (Career Examination Ser.: C-59). 1994. pap. 27.95 (*0-8373-0059-2*) Nat Learn.
***Audiologists' Desk Reference.** Ed. by James W. Hall, 3rd & H. Gustav Mueller. 400p. 1995. 49.95 (*1-56593-269-2*, 0591) Singular Publishing.
Audiology. Jack Rudman. (National Teachers Examination Ser.: NT-34). 1994. pap. 23.95 (*0-8373-8444-3*) Nat Learn.
Audiology. 6th ed. Hayes A. Newby & Gerald R. Popelka. 512p. (C). 1992. text ed. write for info. (*0-13-051921-9*) P-H.
Audiology: The Fundamentals. Fred H. Bess & Larry E. Humes. (Illus.). 256p. 1990. pap. 39.00 (*0-683-00619-3*) Williams & Wilkins.
Audiology: The Fundamentals. 2nd ed. Fred H. Bess & Larry E. Humes. (Illus.). 336p. 1994. 48.00 (*0-683-00620-7*) Williams & Wilkins.
Audiology & Audiological Medicine. Ed. by H. A. Beagley. (Illus.). (C). 1982. text ed. 125.00 (*0-19-261154-2*) OUP.
Audiometric Interpretation: A Manual of Basic Audiometry. 2nd ed. Harriet Kaplan et al. LC 92-46331. 403p. 1993. pap. 44.50 (*0-205-14753-4*, Longwood Div) Allyn.
***Audiophile Loudspeaker.** Gene Healy. Ed. by Abigail Pattee et al. (Illus.). 164p. 1995. pap. 22.95 (*0-9647777-0-3*) Boston Post Pub Co.
Audiophile's Technical Guide to 78 rpm, Transcription, & Microgroove Recordings. James R. Powell, Jr. viii, 86p. 1992. pap. 50.00 (*0-9634921-2-8*) Gramophone.
Audiophilia: Tu-Be or Not Tu Be. 2nd ed. Henry L. Eisenson. (Illus.). 320p. (Orig.). 1996. pap. 29.95 (*1-56866-064-2*) Index Pub Grp.
Audiotex Directory & Buyer's Guide. Larry Podell & David Kaye. 1989. 40.00 (*0-317-93152-0*) ADBG Pub.
Audiovestibular Toxicity of Drugs, 2 vols., Vol. I. Jose A. De Oliviera. 256p. 1989. Volume I, 256p. 180.00 (*0-8493-6959-2*, RF285) CRC Pr.
Audiovestibular Toxicity of Drugs, 2 vols., Vol. II. Jose A. De Oliviera. 240p. 1989. Volume II, 240p. 168.00 (*0-8493-6960-6*, RF285) CRC Pr.
Audiovisual Combi, 8 vols., Set. Sven Lidman. 1991. 695.00 (*0-7859-6359-6*, 8485797302) Fr & Eur.
Audiovisual Combi, Vol. 1. Sven Lidman. 312p. 1991. 95.00 (*0-685-70609-5*, 8485797310) Fr & Eur.
Audiovisual Combi, Vol. 2. Sven Lidman. 312p. 1991. 95.00 (*0-7859-6361-8*, 8485797329) Fr & Eur.
Audiovisual Combi, Vol. 3. Sven Lidman. 296p. 1991. 95.00 (*0-7859-6362-6*, 8485797337) Fr & Eur.
Audiovisual Combi, Vol. 4. Sven Lidman. 304p. 1991. 95.00 (*0-7859-6363-4*, 8485797345) Fr & Eur.

A

An Asterisk (*) at the beginning of an entry indicates that the title is appearing in BIP for the first time.

Audiovisual Combi, Vol. 5. Sven Lidman. 312p. 1991. 95.00 (*0-7859-6364-2*, 8485797353) Fr & Eur.

Audiovisual Combi, Vol. 6. Sven Lidman. 296p. 1991. 95.00 (*0-7859-6365-0*, 8485797361) Fr & Eur.

Audiovisual Combi, Vol. 7. Sven Lidman. 312p. 1991. 95.00 (*0-7859-6499-1*) Fr & Eur.

Audiovisual Combi, Vol. 8. Sven Lidman. 304p. 1991. 95.00 (*0-7859-6366-9*, 8485797388) Fr & Eur.

Audiovisual Communication Handbook. 4.00 (*0-686-44171-0*) World Neigh.

Audiovisual Equipment & Materials: A Basic Repair & Maintenance Manual. Don Schroeder & Gary Lare. LC 79-384. 172p. 1979. pap. text ed. 18.50 (*0-8108-1206-1*) Scarecrow.

Audiovisual Equipment & Materials, Vol. II: A Basic Repair & Maintenance Manual. Don Schroeder & Gary Lare. LC 79-384. (Illus.). 141p. 1989. pap. 20.00 (*0-8108-2265-2*) Scarecrow.

Audiovisual Handbook: How to Save Money on AV Rentals. James A. Allen. Ed. by Gary Simon & Elizabeth Allen. (Illus.). 216p. (Orig.). 1993. pap. 39.95 (*0-9634718-0-5*) Allen Media.

Audiovisual Material Glossary. Nancy B. Olson. (Library, Information, & Computer Science Ser.: No. 7). (Illus.). 56p. (Orig.). 1988. pap. text ed. 8.50 (*1-55653-026-9*) OCLC Online Comp.

Audiovisual Policies in College Libraries. Kristine Brancolini. (CLIP Note Ser.: No. 14). 152p. (C). 1991. 18.95 (*0-685-58953-6*); pap. text ed. 21.95 (*0-8389-7495-3*) Assn Coll & Res Libs.

***Audiovisual Resources for Family Programming.** Barbara Jordan & Noreen Stockpole. LC 94-37388. 1994. write for info. (*1-55570-191-4*) Neal-Schuman.

Audiovisual Resources in a Hospital Medical Library: Their Organization & Management. J. Birnhack. 164p. 1988. text ed. 70.00 (*0-7201-1881-6*, Mansell Pub) Cassell.

Audiovisual Review Digest 1990 Sub, Pt. 3. Susan L. Stetler. 1990. write for info. (*0-8103-6997-4*) Gale.

Audiovisual Script Writing. Norton S. Parker. 1974. reprint ed. pap. 15.00 (*0-8135-0797-9*) Rutgers U Pr.

Audiovisual Technology Primer. Albert J. Casciero & Raymond G. Roney. (Library Science Text Ser.). 262p. 1988. lib. bdg. 25.50 (*0-87287-620-9*) Libs Unl.

Audiovisual Training Modules. Harold D. Stolovitch. Ed. by Danny G. Langdon. LC 77-25142. (Instructional Design Library). (Illus.). 104p. 1978. 23.95 (*0-87778-108-7*) Educ Tech Pubns.

Audit & Accounting Guide: Audits of Employee Benefit Plans. 2nd ed. 1989. 26.00 (*0-87051-064-9*) Am Inst CPA.

Audit & Accounting Guide: Audits of Finance Companies. 2nd rev. ed. American Institute of Certified Public Accountants Staff. 117p. 1988. pap. 26.00 (*0-87051-003-7*) Am Inst CPA.

Audit & Control of Advanced On-Line Systems, Manual. Ed. by Javier F. Kuong. 1983. 195.00 (*0-940706-00-8*, MAP-7) Management Advisory Pubns.

Audit & Control of Computerized Systems. Javier F. Kuong. 1983. 75.00 (*0-940706-01-6*, MAP-6) Management Advisory Pubns.

Audit & Control of Data Communication Networks, Map-24. Chester M. Winters. (Computer Security, Auditing & Controls Ser.). 250p. 1988. 59.00 (*0-940706-20-2*) Management Advisory Pubns.

Audit & Control of Distributed Data Processing Systems. Larry J. Duff. 1983. 33.00 (*0-89413-104-4*); 33.00 (*0-685-07007-7*) Inst Inter Aud.

Audit & Control of End-User Computing. Larry E. Rittenberg et al. 188p. 1990. 45.00 (*0-89413-205-9*) Inst Inter Aud.

Audit & Control of Systems Programming Activities. Bernard K. Plagman et al. (Illus.). 121p. 1985. pap. text ed. 33.00 (*0-89413-143-5*) Inst Inter Aud.

Audit & Reduction Manual for Industrial Emmissions & Wastes. (Technical Report Ser.: No. 7). 127p. 1991. 20.00 (*92-807-1303-5*, E.91.III.D.6) UN.

Audit & Security Issues with Expert Systems. Daniel O'Leary. LC 92-28385. (Information Technology Division Research Report Ser.). 1992. write for info. (*0-87051-124-6*) Am Inst CPA.

Audit Approaches for a Computerized Inventory System. American Institute of Certified Public Accountants Staff. (Computer Services Guidelines Ser.). (Illus.). 70p. reprint ed. pap. 25.00 (*0-8357-4260-1*, 2037056) Bks Demand.

Audit Clerk. Jack Rudman. (Career Examination Ser.: C-1907). 1994. pap. 19.95 (*0-8373-1907-2*) Nat Learn.

Audit Commission Annual Report: Year Ended 31 March 1993. 51p. 1993. pap. 17.00 (*0-11-886110-7*, HM61107, Pub. by HMSO UK) UNIPUB.

Audit Commission, Annual Report: Year Ender 31 March 1992. 51p. 1992. pap. 20.00 (*0-11-886086-0*, HM60860, Pub. by HMSO UK) UNIPUB.

Audit Committee: A Broader Mandate. Jeremy Bacon. (Report Ser.: No. 914). (Illus.). viii, 53p. (Orig.). 1988. pap. text ed. 60.00 (*0-8237-0358-4*) Conference Bd.

Audit Committee Handbook. 2nd ed. Louis Braiotta, Jr. LC 93-46345. 1994. text ed. 70.00 (*0-471-01028-6*) Wiley.

Audit Committees. Daniel J. McCauley. (Corporate Practice Ser.: No. 49). 1986. 92.00 (*1-55871-255-0*) BNA.

Audit, Control, & Security of Paperless Systems: Trends, Guidelines, Practices, & Techniques. Ed. by Lee A. Campbell. 140p. 1990. pap. 25.00 (*0-89413-234-2*) Inst Inter Aud.

Audit Decision Cases. Ed. by Richard S. Woods. LC 72-94944. 214p. reprint ed. pap. 61.00 (*0-8357-5871-0*, 2012399) Bks Demand.

Audit Director's Guide. Louis Braiotta, Jr. LC 84-3902. 320p. (C). 1984. reprint ed. lib. bdg. 35.00 (*0-89874-745-7*) Krieger.

Audit Documentation Guide - a Model Study Approach: Companion Volume to Audit Manual for Criminal History Record Systems. Paul L. Woodard et al. 1983. write for info. (*0-318-60292-X*) SEARCH Grp.

Audit Guide. 2nd ed. Stoy Hayward & Co. Staff. 1991. U.K. pap. 55.00 (*0-406-67823-5*) Butterworth Legal Pubs.

Audit Handbook: Improving Health Care Through Clinical Audit. I. K. Crombie et al. 225p. 1993. text ed. 72.95 (*0-471-93766-5*, Wiley-Liss) Wiley.

Audit Handbook of Human Resource Management. George E. Biles & Randall S. Schuler. 254p. 1986. ring bd. 60.00 (*0-685-53356-5*, PB36) Soc Human Resc Mgmt.

Audit in Action. Richard Smith et al. (Illus.). 245p. 1993. pap. text ed. 27.00 (*0-7279-0317-9*, Pub. by British Med Jrnl UK) Amer Coll Phys.

Audit in Obstetrics & Gynaecology. M. Maresh. (Illus.). 224p. 1994. write for info. (*0-632-03352-5*) Blackwell Sci.

***Audit Kit.** Kent A. Keeney. LC 94-33978. 1994. 35.00 (*0-87389-328-X*) ASQC Qual Pr.

Audit Manual for Criminal History Records Systems. Paul Woodard et al. 1982. write for info. (*0-318-60295-4*) SEARCH Grp.

Audit of Airport Security: Safety of Aircraft, Passengers, & Property in Airport Operating Areas. (Illus.). 52p. (Orig.). (C). 1994. pap. text ed. 40.00 (*0-7881-0356-3*) Diane Pub.

Audit of Flood Insurance Mapping Activities. 51p. (Orig.). (C). 1993. pap. text ed. 45.00 (*0-7881-0145-5*) Diane Pub.

Audit of the Case Study Method. Michael Masoner. LC 87-29293. 250p. 1988. text ed. 55.00 (*0-275-92761-X*, C2761, Praeger Pubs) Greenwood.

Audit Planning. American Institute of Certified Public Accountants Staff. (Technical Information for Practitioners Ser.: No. 2). 80p. 1989. 25.00 (*0-87051-063-0*) Am Inst CPA.

Audit Planning. 3rd ed. American Institute of Certified Public Accountants Staff. LC 89-6695. (Technical Information for Practitioners Ser.: No. 2). 80p. reprint ed. pap. 25.00 (*0-7837-6629-7*, 2046217) Bks Demand.

Audit Planning, Nineteen Eighty-Nine Revised Edition. rev. ed. Michael A. Tursi. LC 89-6695. (Technical Information for Practitioners Ser.: No. 2). (Illus.). 79p. reprint ed. pap. 25.00 (*0-8357-4597-X*, 2037529) Bks Demand.

***Audit Procedures Handbook 1994.** 900p. (Orig.). 1994. pap. 295.00 (*0-7605-1111-X*) Rector Pr.

Audit Process: Principles, Practice & Cases. I. H. Gray & S. Manson. 560p. 1990. pap. 36.95 (*0-412-02651-1*, A4431, Chap & Hall NY) Chapman & Hall.

Audit-Proof Tax Shelters. Donald J. Korn. 1993. pap. 17.95 (*0-13-050931-0*) P-H.

Audit Report. Leon Hopkins. 1984. pap. 39.00 (*0-406-01650-X*) Butterworth Legal Pubs.

***Audit Report.** 2nd ed. Leon Hopkins. 216p. 1994. pap. text ed. 55.00 (*0-406-02047-7*, UK) Butterworth Legal Pubs.

Audit Report on Bell Atlantic. 31p. 1986. 6.00 (*0-318-21752-X*) NARUC.

Audit Report on BellSouth. 131p. 1986. 17.00 (*0-317-01644-X*) NARUC.

Audit Report on Expenditures of the American Gas Association, 1993. 77p. 1994. 35.00 (*0-318-50045-0*) NARUC.

Audit Report on NYNEX Corporation & Affiliates. 130p. 1987. ring bd. 17.00 (*0-317-01643-1*) NARUC.

Audit Report on Pacific Telesis. 251p. 1986. 29.00 (*0-317-01645-8*) NARUC.

Audit Report on U. S. West. 60p. 1986. 10.00 (*0-317-01646-6*) NARUC.

Audit Report on United States Telephone Association. 74p. 1992. 35.00 (*0-318-50046-9*) NARUC.

Audit Report Writing Manual. Angela J. Maniak. 196p. 1990. pap. 49.00 (*1-55520-132-6*) Probus Pub Co.

Audit Risk & Audit Evidence: The Bayesian Approach to Statistical Auditing. Anthony Steele. (Illus.). 224p. 1992. pap. text ed. 42.50 (*0-12-664140-4*) Acad Pr.

Audit Sampling. (AICPA Audit Guides Ser.). 1983. 26.00 (*0-87051-031-2*) Am Inst CPA.

Audit Sampling: An Introduction. 3rd ed. Dan M. Guy et al. LC 93-30967. 1994. text ed. write for info. (*0-471-57462-7*) Wiley.

Audit Standards: A Comparative Analysis. 2nd ed. Walter Willborn. LC 92-46604. 80p. 1993. 19.95 (*0-87389-235-6*) ASQC Qual Pr.

Audit Standards in the Public Sector: An Analysis of Comparative Experience. 132p. 1987. 15.00 (*92-1-123108-6*, E.87.II.H.2) UN.

***Audit Technique Guides, 9 vols., Set.** (IRS Tax Audit Information Ser.). (Illus.). 1994. pap. 87.95 (*1-57402-009-9*) Athena Info Mgt.

Audit Trail Administration (UNIX SVR 4.2) UNIX Systems Staff. 192p. (C). 1993. pap. text ed. 24.00 (*0-13-066887-7*) P-H.

***Audit Trail Administration (UNIX SVR4.2 MP)** UNIX Staff. (Illus.). 160p. (C). 1994. pap. text ed. 34.00 (*0-13-158056-6*) P-H.

Auditing. 222p. pap. write for info. (*0-926709-26-7*) MicroMash.

***Auditing.** (CPA Review Ser.: Vol. II). 592p. 1995. pap. 32.95 (*0-538-84716-6*) S-W Pub.

Auditing. Nathan M. Bisk. (CPA Comprehensive Exam Review Ser.). 1994. pap. 31.95 (*0-88128-640-0*) Totaltape.

***Auditing.** Kurt Pany & O. Ray Whittington. 232p. (C). 1993. student ed, text ed. 25.50 (*0-256-11642-3*) Irwin.

Auditing. Kurt J. Pany & O. Ray Whittington. LC 93-4070. 752p. (C). 1993. Alk. paper. text ed. 68.95 (*0-256-11637-7*) Irwin.

Auditing. David N. Ricchiute. (C). 1991. text ed. write for info. (*0-538-81402-0*, AJ99CA) S-W Pub.

Auditing. Larry E. Rittenberg & Bradley J. Schwieger. LC 93-72825. 1153p. (C). 1994. text ed. 68.00 (*0-03-029919-5*) Dryden Pr.

Auditing. 2nd ed. James A. Cashin & Garland C. Owens. LC 63-9246. 857p. reprint ed. pap. 180.00 (*0-8357-5872-9*, 2012393) Bks Demand.

Auditing. 2nd ed. Dan M. Guy et al. 1033p. (C). 1990. text ed. 61.75 (*0-15-504295-5*) Dryden Pr.

Auditing. 2nd ed. Dan M. Guy et al. 364p. (C). 1990. pap. write for info. (*0-318-67018-6*) HarBrace.

Auditing. 3rd ed. Dan M. Guy et al. LC 92-82981. 1004p. (C). 1993. text ed. 60.00 (*0-03-096533-0*) Dryden Pr.

Auditing. 3rd ed. Dan M. Guy et al. LC 92-82981. 1004p. (C). 1993. disk 14.50 (*0-03-097887-4*); disk 14.50 (*0-03-097886-6*); disk 14.50 (*0-03-097888-2*) Dryden Pr.

Auditing. 3rd ed. Wanda A. Wallace. LC 94-17200. 1995. text ed. 63.95 (*0-538-82539-1*) S-W Pub.

Auditing. 4th ed. Thomas D. Hubbard et al. LC 90-84298. 919p. 1991. 52.95 (*0-87393-118-1*); student ed 18.95 (*0-87393-124-6*) Dame Pubns.

***Auditing.** 4th ed. David N. Ricchiute. LC 94-28905. 256p. 1995. text ed. 63.95 (*0-538-83883-3*) S-W Pub.

***Auditing.** 7th ed. Anthony Krzystofik. 344p. (C). 1992. student ed, text ed. 24.95 (*0-256-12092-7*) Irwin.

Auditing. 7th ed. Jack C. Robertson. LC 92-16451. 1152p. (C). 1992. text ed. 68.95 (*0-256-10318-6*) Irwin.

Auditing. 9th ed. Leslie Howard. 416p. (Orig.). 1992. pap. 36.50 (*0-7121-1037-2*, Pub. by Pitman Pub Ltd UK) Trans-Atl Phila.

Auditing: A Practical Manual for Auditors. Lawrence R. Dicksee. 1979. 26.95 (*0-405-07548-0*, 14231) Ayer.

Auditing: A Systems Approach. Richard Scott et al. (Illus.). 720p. (C). 1982. teacher ed write for info. (*0-8359-0239-0*, Reston); teacher ed write for info. (*0-8359-0274-9*, Reston); write for info. (*0-318-55514-X*, Reston) P-H.

Auditing: Advances in Behavioral Research. Ed. by L. A. Ponemon & D. R. Gadhart. (Recent Research in Psychology Ser.). (Illus.). x, 166p. 1991. pap. 49.00 (*0-387-97619-1*) Spr-Verlag.

Auditing: An Integrated Approach. 5th ed. Alvin A. Arens. 848p. 1991. text ed. 75.00 (*0-13-053380-7*) P-H.

Auditing: An Integrated Approach. 6th ed. Alvin Arens & James Loebbeck. 1994. pap. text ed. 72.00 (*0-13-289100-X*) P-H.

***Auditing: Campbell Williams CPA Review.** H. James Williams & Carole C. Williams. (C). 1994. 35.00 (*0-9635927-3-4*) C Williams Pub.

Auditing: Integrated Concepts & Procedures. 6th ed. Donald H. Taylor & G. William Glezen. LC 93-36581. 1993. text ed. write for info. (*0-471-59039-8*) Wiley.

***Auditing: Integrated Concepts & Procedures.** 6th ed. Donald H. Taylor & Patrick R. Delaney. 1994. text ed. write for info. (*0-471-02490-2*) Wiley.

Auditing: Practical Manual for Auditors, Authorized American Edition. Lawrence R. Dicksee. Ed. by Robert H. Montgomery. LC 75-18466. (History of Accounting Ser.). 1979. reprint ed. 29.95 (*0-405-07549-9*) Ayer.

Auditing: Selected Questions & Unofficial Answers Indexed to Content Specification Outline. American Institute of Certified Public Accountants Staff. Ed. by James D. Blum. 110p. reprint ed. pap. 31.40 (*0-8357-5873-7*, 2025096) Bks Demand.

Auditing a Quality System for the Defense Industry. Charles B. Robinson. (Auditing Ser.). (Illus.). 156p. (Orig.). 1990. pap. 29.95 (*0-87389-078-7*) ASQC Qual Pr.

Auditing Advertising Agencies. W. H. Ladd. Ed. by Lee A. Campbell. (Briefing Ser.). 44p. 1993. pap. text ed. 20.00 (*0-89413-279-2*) Inst Inter Aud.

Auditing & Accountability. Michael Sherer & David Kent. 200p. (C). 1983. pap. 36.00 (*1-85396-012-8*, Pub. by P Chapman Pub UK) St Mut.

***Auditing & Accounting Disclosure Handbook 1995.** (Illus.). 400p. (Orig.). 1994. pap. 295.00x (*0-7605-0620-5*) Rector Pr.

***Auditing & Accounting Disclosure Handbook 1995.** 400p. (C). 1994. 295.00 (*0-7605-0914-X*) Rector Pr.

Auditing & EDP Study Guide. 2nd ed. Gordon B. Davis et al. 246p. reprint ed. pap. 70.20 (*0-8357-2651-7*, 2040179) Bks Demand.

***Auditing & Systems Objective Questions & Explanations.** 6th ed. Irvin N. Gleim & William A. Hillison. LC 94-73044. (Illus.). 806p. 1995. pap. text ed. 16.95 (*0-917537-74-2*) Gleim Pubns.

Auditing ARM Portfolios: A Practical Guide. Carol Milner. 50p. (Orig.). 1993. pap. 20.00 (*0-945359-19-5*) Mortgage Bankers.

Auditing Assistant. Jack Rudman. (Career Examination Ser.: C-2092). 1994. pap. 27.95 (*0-8373-2092-5*) Nat Learn.

Auditing Concepts & Applications: A Risk-Analysis Approach. 2nd ed. Larry F. Konrath. Ed. by Burvikovs. LC 92-17895. 700p. (C). 1993. text ed. 65.75 (*0-314-01099-8*) West Pub.

***Auditing Concepts & Issues: Outlines & Notes Book.** 2nd ed. H. James Williams & Carole C. Williams. (C). 1993. text ed. 26.00 (*0-9635927-0-X*) C Williams Pub.

Auditing Concepts & Methods. 5th ed. Douglas R. Carmichael & John J. Willingham. 672p. 1989. text ed. write for info. (*0-07-009999-5*) McGraw.

Auditing Construction Costs. Alan Jacobson. (IIA Monograph). 31p. 1988. pap. text ed. 15.00 (*0-89413-184-2*) Inst Inter Aud.

Auditing Contracts: Assessing & Measuring Risk & Control. Andrew Chambers & Graham Rand. (Financial Times Management Ser.). 224p. 1994. 135.00x (*0-273-03767-6*, Pub. by Pitman Pubng UK) St Mut.

Auditing EDP Systems. 2nd ed. Donald A. Watne & Peter B. Turney. 640p. 1990. text ed. 75.00 (*0-13-051004-1*) P-H.

***Auditing for Environmental Quality Leadership: Beyond Compliance to Environmental Excellence.** Ed. by John T. Willig. 331p. 1995. text ed. 54.95 (*0-471-11492-8*) Wiley.

***Auditing Health Care Benefits: How to Effectively Manage Costs & Minimize Risk.** Michael A. Paolella. LC 95-12461. 1995. text ed. 105.00 (*0-471-11918-0*) Wiley.

Auditing Human Resources Management. Marilyn Dolenko. Ed. by Lee A. Campbell. 40p. 1990. pap. 15.00 (*0-89413-218-0*) Inst Inter Aud.

Auditing IBM's Customer Information Control System. Albert Marcella. 178p. 1991. pap. 20.00 (*0-89413-240-7*) Inst Inter Aud.

Auditing in a Microcomputer Environment: Student's Workbook. John R. Nelson. Ed. by Richard Holman. (Media-Assisted Training Ser.). 44p. 1986. pap. text ed. 15.00 (*0-89413-152-4*) Inst Inter Aud.

Auditing in a Microcomputer Environment: Videotape & Instructor's Guide. John R. Nelson. Ed. by Richard Holman. (Media-Assisted Training Ser.). 44p. 1986. pap. text ed. 400.00 (*0-89413-153-2*) Inst Inter Aud.

***Auditing in Common Computer Environments.** American Institute of Certified Public Accountants Staff. LC 94-41127. (Auditing Procedure Studies). 1995. write for info. (*0-87051-161-0*) Am Inst CPA.

Auditing in the Electronic Environment: Theory, Practice & Literature. Delroy L. Cornick. LC 80-81813. 316p. 1981. 29.75 (*0-912338-23-7*); fiche 14.75 (*0-912338-24-5*) Lomond.

Auditing Investment Businesses. Chris Morgan & Matthew Patient. 1989. U.K. pap. 101.00 (*0-406-53109-9*) Butterworth Legal Pubs.

Auditing Local Union Financial Records: A Guide for Local Union Trustees. John Lund. LC 92-27352. (ILR Bulletin Ser.: No. 67). 96p. 1992. pap. 9.95 (*0-87546-194-8*) ILR Pr.

Auditing Microcomputers. Maria Langer. Ed. by Lee A. Campbell. 71p. 1991. Tool kit. 200.00 (*0-89413-238-5*) Inst Inter Aud.

Auditing Non-U. S. Operations. William L. Thornhill. Ed. by Richard Holman. (IIA Monograph). 65p. 1984. pap. text ed. 15.00 (*0-89413-115-X*) Inst Inter Aud.

Auditing Principles & Practices. 16th ed. F. A. Attwood. (Illus.). 1977. 25.00 (*0-8464-0162-2*) Beekman Pubs.

Auditing Program Libraries for Change Controls. D. A. Dallas & S. R. Vallabhaneni. Ed. by Richard Holman. (IIA Monograph). 21p. 1986. pap. text ed. 15.00 (*0-89413-144-3*) Inst Inter Aud.

Auditing Purchased Software: Acquisition, Adaptation & Installation. S. Rao Vallabhaneni. Ed. by Richard Holman. (IIA Monograph). (Illus.). 55p. 1985. pap. text ed. 15.00 (*0-89413-129-X*) Inst Inter Aud.

Auditing Real Estate Practices: A Manual. Leopold J. Kovar. 63p. 1974. 1.00 (*0-318-15818-3*, N-3) Natl Neighbors.

Auditing Standards & Procedures Manual 1993. Douglas R. Carmichael. (Professional Accounting & Business Ser.). 688p. 1992. pap. text ed. 115.00 (*0-471-59071-1*) Wiley.

***Auditing Standards & Procedures Manual 1995.** D. R. Carmichael & Martin Benis. 1995. pap. text ed. 115.00 (*0-471-11519-3*) Wiley.

Auditing the Data Processing Function. Richard W. Lott. LC 79-54841. 222p. reprint ed. pap. 63.30 (*0-8357-5874-5*, 2023588) Bks Demand.

Auditing the Development of Computing Systems. B. J. Travis. 1987. pap. 87.00 (*0-406-50093-2*) Butterworth Legal Pubs.

Auditing the IT Environment: Assessing & Measuring Risk & Control. Andrew Chambers & Graham Rand. (Financial Times Management Ser.). 336p. 1993. 120.00x (*0-273-03769-2*, Pub. by Pitman Pub Ltd UK) Trans-Atl Phila.

Auditing the Maintenance of Software. S. Rao Vallabhaneni. (Illus.). 224p. 1987. text ed. 51.00 (*0-13-050964-7*) P-H.

Auditing the Marketing Function. Dale L. Flesher. Ed. by Lee A. Campbell. (Tool Kit Ser.). 133p. 1993. 200.00 (*0-89413-297-0*) Inst Inter Aud.

***Auditing Theory & Practice.** 3rd ed. Roger Hermanson et al. (C). 1983. 59.95 (*0-256-02917-2*) Irwin.

Auditing Theory & Practice. 6th ed. Roger H. Hermanson et al. LC 92-26342. 864p. (C). 1992. text ed. 65.95 (*0-256-12802-2*) Irwin.

Auditing Theory & Practice. Robert H. Montgomery. LC 75-18477. (History of Accounting Ser.). (Illus.). 1979. reprint ed. 53.95 (*0-405-07559-6*) Ayer.

Auditing Today. 5th ed. Emile Woold & Janice Riches. LC 93-44623. 1994. write for info. (*0-13-178559-1*) P-H.

Auditing with Computers. LC 94-17777. 1994. write for info. (*0-87051-152-1*) Am Inst CPA.

Auditing Your Customer Service: The Foundation for Success. John Leppard & Liz Molyneux. LC 93-41814. (Marketing for Managers Ser.). 144p. 1994. pap. 13.95 (*0-415-09732-0*, B3937) Routledge.

***Auditing Your Educational Strategic Plan: Making a Good Thing Better.** Roger Kaufman & Philip Grise. LC 95-796. (Illus.). 96p. 1995. 25.95 (*0-8039-6299-1*); pap. 12.95 (*0-8039-6237-1*) Corwin Pr.

Auditing 1 (V301) Competency Test. 3rd ed. CUNA Staff & Ewing. (VAP Ser.). 6p. 1994. 9.00 (*0-8403-9332-6*) Kendall-Hunt.

Auditing 2 (V302) Competency Test. 3rd ed. CUNA Staff & Ewing. (VAP Ser.). 6p. 1994. 9.00 (*0-8403-9333-4*) Kendall-Hunt.

Audition. Pierre Buser & Michel Imbert. Tr. by Roy H. Kay. (Illus.). 280p. 1992. 47.50 (*0-262-02331-8*) MIT Pr.

524

An Asterisk (*) at the beginning of an entry indicates that the title is appearing in BIP for the first time.

An Asterisk (*) at the beginning of an entry indicates that the title is appearing in BIP for the first time.

Audits of Providers of Health Care Services: As of December 31, 1990. American Institute of Certified Public Accountants Staff. (AICPA Audit & Accounting Guide Ser.). 276p. reprint ed. pap. 78.70 (0-7837-3558-8, 2043395) Bks Demand.

Audits of Providers of Health Care Services: Proposal Audit & Accounting Guide. American Institute of Certified Public Accountants Staff. (Exposure Draft Ser.). 185p. reprint ed. pap. 52.80 (0-8357-8033-3, 2034092) Bks Demand.

Audits of Providers of Health Care Services: With Conforming Changes As of May 1, 1992. American Institute of Certified Public Accountants Staff. (Audit & Accounting Guide Ser.). 249p. reprint ed. pap. 71.00 (0-7837-6651-3, 2046258) Bks Demand.

Audits of Savings & Loan Associations. (American Institute of CPAs Audit Guides Ser.). 1987. pap. 26.00 (0-87051-025-8) Am Inst CPA.

Audits of Savings Institutions: With Conforming Changes As of May 1, 1992. American Institute of Certified Public Accountants Staff. (Audit & Accounting Guide Ser.). 303p. reprint ed. pap. 86.40 (0-7837-6650-5, 2046257) Bks Demand.

***Audits of Savings Institutions: With Conforming Changes As of May 1, 1993.** American Institute of Certified Public Accountants Staff. (Audit & Accounting Guide Ser.). 307p. 1993. pap. 87.50 (0-7837-8473-2, 2049278) Bks Demand.

Audits of Savings Institutions: As of August 31, 1991, Includes: Audit Risk Alerts: Savings Institutions Industry Developments, 1991. American Institute of Certified Public Accountants Staff. (AICPA Audit & Accounting Guide Ser.). 343p. reprint ed. pap. 97.80 (0-7837-3559-6, 2043396) Bks Demand.

Audits of Small Businesses. American Institute of Certified Public Accountants. LC 85-171942. (Auditing Procedure Study Ser.). (Illus.). 108p. reprint ed. pap. 30.80 (0-8357-5881-8, 2033147) Bks Demand.

Audits of State & Local Governmental Units. 5th ed. (American Institute of CPAs Audit Guides Ser.). 1989. pap. 26.00 (0-87051-072-X) Am Inst CPA.

Audits of State & Local Governmental Units: Proposed Audit & Accounting Guide, May 17, 1993. American Institute of Certified Public Accountants Staff. (Exposure Draft Ser.). 202p. reprint ed. pap. 57.60 (0-7837-6700-5, 2046325) Bks Demand.

Audits of State & Local Governmental Units: With Conforming Changes As of May 1, 1992. American Institute of Certified Public Accountants Staff. (Audit & Accounting Guide Ser.). 291p. reprint ed. pap. 83.00 (0-7837-6656-4, 2046267) Bks Demand.

Audits of Stock Life Insurance Companies: Including Statements of Position Issued by Auditing Standards Division, & Statement of Financial Accounting Standards Issued by the Financial Accounting Standards Board. American Institute of Certified Public Accountants Staff. 266p. reprint ed. pap. 75.90 (0-7837-0076-8, 2040325) Bks Demand.

Audits of Stock Life Insurance Companies: With Conforming Changes As of May 1, 1992. American Institute of Certified Public Accountants Staff. (Industry Audit Guide Ser.). 216p. reprint ed. pap. 61.60 (0-7837-6654-8, 2046261) Bks Demand.

Audits of Voluntary Health & Welfare Organizations. 2nd ed. (American Institute of CPAs Audit Guides Ser.). 1988. pap. 26.00 (0-87051-027-4) Am Inst CPA.

Audits of Voluntary Health & Welfare Organizations: As of December 31, 1990. American Institute of Certified Public Accountants Staff. (AICPA Industry Audit Guide Ser.). 94p. reprint ed. pap. 26.80 (0-7837-3554-5, 2043391) Bks Demand.

Audits of Voluntary Health & Welfare Organizations: With Conforming Changes As of May 1, 1992. American Institute of Certified Public Accountants Staff. (Industry Audit Guide Ser.). 63p. reprint ed. pap. 25.00 (0-7837-6646-7, 2046253) Bks Demand.

***Audits of Voluntary Health & Welfare Organizations: With Conforming Changes As of May 1, 1993.** American Institute of Certified Public Accountants Staff. (Industry Audit Guide Ser.). 223p. 1993. pap. 63.60 (0-7837-8474-0, 2049279) Bks Demand.

Audrey. Charles Higham. 1984. 14.95 (0-02-551510-1) Macmillan.

Audrey. Mary Johnston. 1976. lib. bdg. 11.95 (0-89968-150-6, Lghtyr Pr) Buccaneer Bks.

Audrey. Mary Johnston. 418p. 1977. reprint ed. lib. bdg. 16.95 (0-89966-251-X) Buccaneer Bks.

***Audrey: Her Real Story.** Alexander Walker. 1994. 22.95 (0-312-11746-9) St Martin.

Audrey Flack: Sketchbook, 1985-1989. Thalia Gouma-Peterson. LC 92-80435. (Illus.). 80p. 1992. pap. 14.95 (0-940979-20-9) Natl Museum Women.

Audrey Flack on Painting. Audrey Flack. (Illus.). 116p. 1981. pap. 14.95 (0-8109-2235-5) Abrams.

Audrey Hepburn: A Bio-Bibliography. Davida Hofstede. LC 94-5823. (Bio-Bibliographies in the Performing Arts Ser.: No. 55). 256p. 1994. text ed. 45.00 (0-313-28909-3, Greenwood Pr) Greenwood.

Audrey Hepburn: A Biography. Warren Harris. (A Biography). 1994. 23.00 (0-671-75800-4) S&S Trade.

***Audrey Hepburn: A Biography.** large type ed. Warren G. Harris. LC 94-31165. (Large Print Book Ser.). 1994. 24.95 (1-56895-156-6) Wheeler Pub.

Audrey Hepburn: A Celebration. Sheridan Morley. (Illus.). 160p. 1994. 24.95 (1-85793-136-X, Pub. by Pavilion UK) Trafalgar.

***Audrey Hepburn: A Celebration.** Sheridan Morley. (Illus.). 192p. 1995. pap. 15.95 (1-85793-267-6, Pub. by Pavilion UK) Trafalgar.

Audrey Hepburn: An Intimate Portrait. Diana Maychick. (Illus.). 304p. 1993. 21.95 (1-55972-195-2, Birch Ln Pr) Carol Pub Group.

Audrey Hepburn: An Intimate Portrait. large type ed. Diana Maychick. LC 93-42995. 1994. 22.95 (0-7862-0103-7); pap. 13.95 (0-7862-0104-5) Thorndike Pr.

Audrey Hepburn's Symphonic Salad & the Coming of Autumn. Tom Weigel. Ed. by Maureen Owen. (Illus.). 56p. (Orig.). 1980. pap. 4.00 (0-916382-23-0) Telephone Bks.

Audrey Poppin. Robert Johnston. LC 89-92709. 223p. (Orig.). 1990. pap. 6.95 (0-9625321-3-4) Sand Castle Bks.

Audrey Thomas & Her Works. Barbara Godard. 89p. (C). 1989. pap. text ed. 9.95 (1-55022-036-5, Pub. by ECW Press CN) Genl Dist Srvs.

Audrey's Add No Salt Cookery. Audrey Greene. (Illus.). 1982. write for info. (0-9608892-0-5) Greene Pubns.

Audrey's Cookie Cookbook: Two Hundred Cookie & Bar Recipes. Audrey Buck. (Illus.). 219p. 1992. Comb. bdg. pap. 12.95 (0-9632507-0-1) Bayberry MO.

Audubon: Life Art in the American Wilderness. Shirley Streshinsky. LC 93-3665. (Illus.). 1993. 25.00 (0-679-40859-2, Villard Bks) Random.

Audubon: Natural Priorities. Roger DiSilvestro. LC 94-18452. 1994. 24.95 (1-878685-51-1) Turner Pub GA.

Audubon: The Kentucky Years. L. Clark Keating. LC 75-38216. (Kentucky Bicentennial Bookshelf Ser.). 104p. 1976. 10.00 (0-8131-0215-4) U Pr of Ky.

***Audubon & Early American Artists.** Kay Hyman. 64p. 1994. write for info. (0-9640034-9-X) World Pubns.

Audubon & His Journals, 2 vols. Elliott Coues. 1971. 250.00 (0-87968-677-4) Gordon Pr.

Audubon & His Journals, 2 vols., 1. John J. Audubon. Ed. by Maria Audubon. 1200p. 1986. reprint ed. pap. 8.95 (0-486-25143-8) Dover.

Audubon & His Journals, 2 vols, Set. John J. Audubon. Ed. by Maria R. Audubon. LC 75-38340. (Select Bibliographies Reprint Ser.). 1977. 62.95 (0-8369-6660-0) Ayer.

***Audubon & His Journals, Vol. I.** unabridged ed. Maria R. Audubon. (Illus.). 1994. pap. text ed. 12.95 (0-486-28391-7) Dover.

***Audubon & His Journals, Vol. II.** unabridged ed. Maria R. Audubon. (Illus.). 1994. pap. text ed. 12.95 (0-486-28392-5) Dover.

Audubon Ark: A History of the National Audubon Society. Frank Graham. 1990. 29.95 (0-394-58164-4) Knopf.

Audubon Ark: A History of the National Audubon Society. Frank Graham, Jr. LC 91-4384. 350p. 1992. pap. 14.95 (0-292-70440-2) U of Tex Pr.

Audubon Bird Prints: A Portfolio of 6 Self-Matted Full Color Prints. John J. Audubon. Date not set. pap. 3.95 (0-486-25773-8) Dover.

Audubon Birds in Cross Stitch. Ginnie Thompson. LC 93-6135. (Needlework Ser.). (Illus.). 1993. reprint ed. 3.95 (0-486-27603-1) Dover.

Audubon Birds of America Postcards. John J. Audubon. Date not set. pap. 3.95 (0-486-25457-7) Dover.

***Audubon Birds Stained Glass Pattern Book.** Carol Krez. LC 95-1406. (Illus.). 1995. pap. write for info. (0-486-28625-8) Dover.

Audubon Conservation Report No. 6: Report of the Advisory Panel on the California Condor. Ed. by Robert E. Ricklefs. (Audubon Conservation Report Ser.). (Illus.). 1978. pap. 3.00 (0-930698-04-5) Natl Audubon.

Audubon Field Guide to North American Mammals. Audubon Society Staff & John O. Whitaker, Jr. LC 79-3525. (Illus.). 752p. 1980. 19.00 (0-394-50762-2) Knopf.

Audubon Field Guide to North American Trees: Eastern Edition. Audubon Society Staff & Elbert L. Little, Jr. 1980. 19.00 (0-394-50760-6) Knopf.

Audubon Field Guide to North American Trees: Western Area. Audubon Society Staff & Elbert L. Little, Jr. 1980. 19.00 (0-394-50761-4) Knopf.

Audubon House: Building the Environmentally Responsible, Energy-Efficient Office. National Audubon Society Staff & Croxton Collaborative, Architects Staff. LC 93-46161. (Sustainable Design Ser.). 1994. text ed. 24.95 (0-471-02496-1) Wiley.

Audubon in Florida: With Selections from the Writings of John James Audubon. Kathryn H. Proby. LC 72-85114. (Illus.). 384p. 1974. pap. 15.95 (0-87024-301-2) U of Miami Pr.

Audubon Journal. Ed. by Running Press Staff. (Illus.). 160p. 1993. 19.95 (1-56138-182-9) Running Pr.

Audubon Perspectives: The Rebirth of Nature. Roger L. DiSilvestro. 288p. 1992. text ed. 34.95 (0-471-53208-8) Wiley.

Audubon Policy Report, No. 1: CO2 Diet for a Greenhouse Planet: A Citizen's Guide for Slowing Global Warming. John DeCicco et al. LC 90-61726. 75p. 1990. pap. 5.95 (0-930698-33-9) Natl Audubon.

Audubon Reader: The Best Writings of John James Audubon. Ed. by Scott R. Sanders. LC 85-45773. 256p. 1986. 29.95 (0-253-31081-4) Ind U Pr.

***Audubon Society Bird Garden.** National Audubon Society Staff & Stephen W. Kress. LC 95-6748. 176p. 1995. 24.95 (0-7894-0139-8, 6-70475) Dorling Kindersley.

***Audubon Society Birdfeeder Handbook.** Date not set. write for info. (0-7894-0337-4, 6-70523) Dorling Kindersley.

Audubon Society Encyclopedia of North American Birds. John K. Terres. (Illus.). 1136p. 1991. reprint ed. 39.99 (0-517-03288-0, Pub. by Wings Bks) Random Hse Value.

Audubon Society Field Guide to North American Butterflies. Audubon Society Staff & Robert M. Pyle. LC 80-84240. (Illus.). 864p. 1981. 19.00 (0-394-51914-0) Knopf.

Audubon Society Field Guide to North American Fishes, Whales, & Dolphins. Audubon Society Staff et al. LC 83-47962. (Illus.). 848p. 1983. 19.00 (0-394-53405-0) Knopf.

Audubon Society Field Guide to North American Fossils. Audubon Society Staff & Ida Thompson. LC 81-84772. (Illus.). 1982. 19.00 (0-394-52412-8) Knopf.

Audubon Society Field Guide to North American Insects & Spiders. Audubon Society Staff et al. LC 80-7620. (Illus.). 1008p. 1980. 19.00 (0-394-50763-0) Knopf.

Audubon Society Field Guide to North American Mushrooms. Audubon Society Staff & Gary H. Lincoff. LC 81-80827. (Illus.). 864p. 1981. 18.00 (0-394-51992-2) Knopf.

Audubon Society Field Guide to North American Reptiles & Amphibians. Audubon Society Staff et al. LC 79-2217. (Illus.). 1979. 19.00 (0-394-50824-6) Knopf.

Audubon Society Field Guide to North American Rocks & Minerals. Audubon Society Staff & Charles W. Chesterman. LC 78-54893. (Illus.). 1979. 19.00 (0-394-50269-8) Knopf.

Audubon Society Field Guide to North American Seashells. Audubon Society Staff & Harold A. Rehder. LC 80-84239. 1981. 19.00 (0-394-51913-2) Knopf.

Audubon Society Field Guide to North American Seashore Creatures. Audubon Society Staff & Norman A. Meinkoth. LC 81-80828. (Illus.). 1981. 18.00 (0-394-51993-0) Knopf.

Audubon Society Field Guide to North American Weather. David Ludlum. LC 91-52707. (Audubon Field Guide Ser.). (Illus.). 640p. 1991. 19.00 (0-679-40851-7) Knopf.

Audubon Society Field Guide to North American Wildflowers. Incl. Eastern Region William Niering & Nancy Olmstead. 1979. 19.00 (0-394-50432-1); Western Region Richard Spellenberg. 1979. 19.00 (0-394-50431-3); (Illus.). 1979. write for info. (0-318-54007-X) Knopf.

Audubon Society Field Guide to the Night Sky. Mark R. Chartrand, III. LC 91-52708. (Audubon Field Guide Ser.). (Illus.). 688p. 1991. 19.00 (0-679-40852-5) Knopf.

Audubon Society Field Guides, 19 vols. 1988. Set. write for info. (0-318-63751-0) Chanticleer.

Audubon Society Guide to North American Birds: Western Region. Audubon Society Staff & M. D. Udvardy. 1977. 18.00 (0-394-41410-1) Knopf.

Audubon Society Guides to North American Birds: Eastern Region. Audubon Society Staff et al. 1977. 18.00 (0-394-41405-5) Knopf.

Audubon Society Master Guide to Birding, 3 vols., Set. Ed. by John Farrand, Jr. Incl. Vol. 1. Gulls-Dippers. LC 83-47945. 447p. 1983. 16.95 (0-394-53382-8); Vol. 2. Loons-Sandpipers. LC 83-47945. 398p. 1983. 16.95 (0-394-53384-4); Vol. 3. Old-World Warblers-Sparrows. LC 83-47945. 399p. 1983. 16.95 (0-394-53383-6); LC 83-47945. (Illus.). 1984. 50.85 (0-394-54121-9) Knopf.

Audubon Society Pocket Guide Series of Familiar Birds, Trees, & Wildflowers. Audubon Society Staff. 1987. pap. 15.95 (0-394-75797-1) Knopf.

Audubon Society Pocket Guide to Dinosaurs. Joseph E. Wallace. LC 92-12162. (Audubon Society Pocket Guides Ser.). 1993. pap. 8.00 (0-679-74150-X) Knopf.

Audubon Society Pocket Guide to Familiar Butterflies of North America. Richard K. Walton. LC 90-52502. (Audubon Society Pocket Guide Ser.). (Illus.). (Orig.). 1990. pap. 5.95 (0-679-72981-X) Knopf.

Audubon Society Pocket Guide to Familiar Marine Mammals of North America. Stephen H. Amos. LC 90-52501. (Audubon Society Pocket Guides Ser.). (Illus.). (Orig.). 1990. pap. 5.95 (0-679-72982-8) Knopf.

Audubon Society Pocket Guide to Familiar Mushrooms of North America. Peter Katsaros. LC 90-52503. (Audubon Society Pocket Guides Ser.). (Illus.). (Orig.). 1990. pap. 9.00 (0-679-72984-4) Knopf.

Audubon Society Pocket Guide to Familiar Seashore Creatures. Stephen H. Amos. (Audubon Society Pocket Guides Ser.). (Orig.). 1990. pap. 5.95 (0-685-46222-6) Knopf.

Audubon Society Pocket Guide to North American Birds of Lakes & Rivers. Richard K. Walton. LC 93-21252. (Audubon Society Pocket Guides Ser.). (Illus.). 1994. 9.00 (0-679-74922-5) Random.

Audubon Society Pocket Guide to North American Birds of Prey. Richard K. Walton. LC 93-21253. (Audubon Society Pocket Guides Ser.). (Illus.). 1994. 9.00 (0-679-74923-3) Knopf.

Audubon Society Pocket Guide to North American Birds of Sea & Shore. Simon Perkins. LC 93-21251. (Audubon Society Pocket Guides Ser.). (Illus.). 1994. 9.00 (0-679-74921-7) Random.

Audubon Society Pocket Guide to North American SongBirds & Familiar Backyard Birds: Eastern Region. Wayne R. Petersen. LC 93-21254. (Audubon Society Pocket Guides Ser.). (Illus.). 1994. 9.00 (0-679-74926-8) Knopf.

Audubon Society Pocket Guide to North American Songbirds & Familiar Backyard Birds (Western Region) Western Region. Richard K. Walton. LC 93-21250. (Audubon Society Pocket Guides Ser.). 1994. 9.00 (0-679-74925-X) Knopf.

Audubon Society Pocket Guide to North American Waterfowl. Richard K. Walton. LC 93-21255. (Audubon Society Pocket Guides Ser.). (Illus.). 1994. 9.00 (0-679-74924-1) Knopf.

Audubon Society Pocket Guides, 31 vols. 1988. Set. write for info. (0-318-63750-2) Chanticleer.

Audubon to Xantus: The Lives of Those Commemorated in North American Bird Names. Barbara Mearns & Richard Mearns. (Illus.). 588p. 1992. text ed. 39.95 (0-12-487423-1) Acad Pr.

Audubon Wildlife Report, 1987. Ed. by Roger L. DiSilvestro et al. 690p. 1987. text ed. 92.00 (0-12-041000-1) Acad Pr.

Audubon Wildlife Report 1988-1989. Ed. by William J. Chandler et al. 817p. 1988. text ed. 92.00 (0-12-041001-X); pap. text ed. 47.00 (0-12-041002-8) Acad Pr.

Audubon Wildlife Report 1989-1990. Ed. by William J. Chandler & Lillian Labate. 585p. 1989. text ed. 92.00 (0-12-041003-6) Acad Pr.

Audubon's Birds. (Illus.). 80p. 1992. 4.95 (0-8362-3016-7) Andrews & McMeel.

Audubon's Birds. Ed. by Running Press Staff. LC 91-50906. (Miniature Editions Ser.). (Illus.). 128p. 1992. 4.95 (1-56138-090-3) Running Pr.

Audubon's Birds in Color for Decoupage. Ed. by Eleanor H. Rawlings. LC 77-70050. (Pictorial Archive Ser.). (Illus.). 1977. pap. 4.95 (0-486-23492-4) Dover.

Audubon's Birds of America. National Audubon Society Staff. (Illus.). 435p. 1989. write for info. (0-89659-425-4) Abbeville Pr.

Audubon's Birds of America. Roger T. Peterson. 1993. 100.00 (0-89660-040-8, Artabras) Abbeville Pr.

Audubon's Birds of America. deluxe ed. National Audubon Society Staff. (Illus.). 435p. 1989. ring bd. write for info. (0-89659-427-0) Abbeville Pr.

Audubon's Birds of America: The Audubon Society Baby Elephant Folio. rev. ed. Roger T. Peterson & Virginia M. Peterson. (Illus.). 694p. 1990. 250.00 (1-55859-128-1) Abbeville Pr.

***Audubon's Birds of America: The Royal Octavo Edition.** John J. Audubon. LC 94-30553. 1994. 49.95 (1-57145-012-2) Thunder Bay CA.

Audubon's Great National Work: The Royal Octavo Edition of Birds of America. Ron Tyler. LC 92-30793. (Illus.). 235p. (C). 1993. 45.00 (0-292-78129-6) U of Tex Pr.

Audubon's Western Journal: 1849-1850. John W. Audubon. 1992. reprint ed. lib. bdg. 75.00 (0-7812-5003-X) Rprt Serv.

Audubon's Western Journal, 1849-1850. John W. Audubon. LC 83-17860. (Illus.). 249p. 1984. reprint ed. 29.95 (0-8165-0840-2); reprint ed. pap. 10.95 (0-8165-0841-0) U of Ariz Pr.

Audubon. Constance Rourke. 1993. reprint ed. lib. bdg. 89.00 (0-7812-5826-X) Rprt Serv.

Auerbach Will. Stephen Birmingham. 432p. 1987. pap. 4.95 (0-425-10020-0) Berkley Pub.

Auf Deutsch, Bitte. Incl. Text 11985. 17.25 (0-8325-9686-8); Text 21971. text ed. 17.25 (0-8325-9689-2); Text 31972. text ed. 17.25 (0-8325-9692-2); 1971. 10.60 (0-8325-9687-6); Incl. 17.25 (0-8325-9686-8); text ed. 17.25 (0-8325-9689-2); text ed. 17.25 (0-8325-9692-2); 10.60 (0-685-02499-7); Incl. 17.25 (0-8325-9686-8); text ed. 17.25 (0-8325-9689-2); text ed. 17.25 (0-8325-9692-2); Set audio 10.60 (0-8325-9690-6); Incl. 17.25 (0-8325-9686-8); text ed. 17.25 (0-8325-9689-2); text ed. 17.25 (0-8325-9692-2); 10.60 (0-8325-9688-4); Incl. 17.25 (0-8325-9686-8); text ed. 17.25 (0-8325-9689-2); text ed. 17.25 (0-8325-9692-2); 10.60 (0-8325-9691-4) NTC Pub Grp.

Auf Deutsch, Bitte, No. 1. Incl. Text 11985. 17.25 (0-8325-9686-8); Text 21971. text ed. 17.25 (0-8325-9689-2); Text 31972. text ed. 17.25 (0-8325-9692-2); 1971. Set audio 233.35 (0-8325-9685-X) NTC Pub Grp.

Auf Deutsch, Bitte, No. 2. Incl. Text 11985. 17.25 (0-8325-9686-8); Text 21971. text ed. 17.25 (0-8325-9689-2); Text 31972. text ed. 17.25 (0-8325-9692-2); 1971. Set audio 233.35 (0-8325-9693-0) NTC Pub Grp.

Auf Geht's (Allemand) German for French Speakers. Assimil Staff. (FRE & GER.). 1991. 24.95 (0-8288-4477-1, F51170); audio 125.00 (0-8288-9031-5, M12686) Fr & Eur.

Aufbau der Werke des Tacitus. Guenther Wille. (Heurmeta Ser.: No. 9). 673p. (Orig.). 1983. pap. 46.00 (90-6032-229-0, Pub. by Gruner NE) Benjamins North Am.

Aufbau des Livianischen Geschichtswerks. Gunther Wille. (Heuremata Studien Zu Literatur, Sprachenn & Kultur der Antike). viii, 124p. 1973. pap. 24.00 (90-6032-026-3, Pub. by Gruner NE) Benjamins North Am.

Aufbau, Organisation und Funktion Eines Neuen Informationszentrums Am Beispiel der Vorarlberger Landesbibliothek. Ed. by Eberhard Tiefenthaler. (Bibliotheksstudien Ser.). 193p. (GER.). 1990. lib. bdg. 52.00 (3-598-11002-2) K G Saur.

Aufbruch & Verheissung: Gesammelte Aufsaetze zum Hebraerbrief. Erich Graesser. (Beihefte zur Zeitschrift fuer die Neuetestamentliche Wissenschaft Ser.: No. 65). viii, 367p. (GER.). (C). 1992. lib. bdg. 121.55 (3-11-013669-4) De Gruyter.

Aufgaben und Stellung der Intelligenz in der Gesellschaft: The Task & Position of Intellectuals in Society. Theodor Geiger. LC 74-25749. (European Sociology Ser.). 174p. 1975. reprint ed. 20.95 (0-405-06504-3) Ayer.

Aufgaben und Ziele der Vergleichenden Mythenforschung: Tasks & Goals of Comparative Mythology. Heinrich Lessmann. Ed. by Kees W. Bolle. LC 77-79138. (Mythology Ser.). (GER.). 1978. reprint ed. lib. bdg. 19.95 (0-405-10548-7) Ayer.

An Asterisk (*) at the beginning of an entry indicates that the title is appearing in BIP for the first time.

Aufgabensammlung zur Infinitesimalrechnung. Alexander Ostrowski. Incl. Vol. 1. Funktionen Einer Variablen. 341p. 1980. 68.00 (*0-8176-0290-9*); Vol. 2A. Differentialrechnung auf dem Gebiete Mehrerer Variblen. Aufgaben und Hinweise. 300p. 1980. 67.00 (*0-8176-0534-7*); Vol. 2B. Differentialrechnung auf dem Gebiete Mehrerer Variablen, Losungen. 233p. 1980. 50.00 (*0-8176-0572-X*); Vol. 3. Integralrechnung auf dem Gebiete Mehrerer Variablen: Differentialrechnung auf dem Gebiete Mehrerer Variablen, Losungen. 398p. 1977. 53.95 (*0-685-00763-4*); (Mathematische Reihe Ser.: Vols. 28, 38, 47 & 56). (GER.). write for info. (*0-318-51085-5*) Birkhauser.

Aufgehobene Zeit: Zeitstruktur und Zeitelemente in der Lyrik Johannes Bobrowkis. Werner Schulz. LC 83-48451. (American University Studies: Germanic Languages & Literature: Ser. I, Vol. 716). 222p. (Orig.). (GER.). (C). 1983. pap. text ed. 20.95 (*0-8204-0023-8*) P Lang Pubs.

Aufklaerung, Rokoko, Sturm und Drang see Geschichte der Deutschen Poetik

Aufklarung Catholicism 1780-1850: Liturgical & Other Reforms in the Catholic Aufklarung. Leonard J. Swidler. LC 78-2736. (American Academy of Religion. Studies in Religion: No. 17). 107p. reprint ed. pap. 30.50 (*0-7837-5479-5*, 2045244) Bks Demand.

Aufmacher: Des Mann, der bei Bild Hans Esser War. Gunter Wallraff. (New German Texts Ser.). 222p. 1991. text ed. 39.95 (*0-7190-3450-7*, Pub. by Manchester Univ Pr UK); text ed. 13.95 (*0-7190-2871-X*, Pub. by Manchester Univ Pr UK) St Martin.

***Aufsaetze Zum Alten Testament: Aus Vier Jahrzehnten.** Herbert Donner. (Beiheftze Zur Zeitschrift Fuer die Alttestamentliche Wissenschaft Ser.: Vol. 224). x, 284p. (GER.). (C). 1994. lib. bdg. 129.25 (*3-11-014097-7*) De Gruyter.

Aufsatze und Vortrage Nineteen Eleven to Nineteen Twenty. Edmund Husserl. Ed. by Nenon Sepp. (C). 1986. lib. bdg. 209.50 (*90-247-3216-6*) Kluwer Ac.

Aufsatze und Vortrage, 1922-1937. Edmund Husserl. Ed. by T. Nenon & H. R. Sepp. (C). 1989. lib. bdg. 172.00 (*90-247-3620-X*) Kluwer Ac.

Aufsatze Zur Fruhlateinischen Dichtung. ix, 89p. 1969. write for info. (*0-318-71171-0*, Pub. by Georg Olms GW) Lubrecht & Cramer.

Aufsteig & Neidergang der Roemischen Welt, ANRW - Rise & Decline of the Roman World, Teil II, Bd 37-1: Geschichte & Kultur Roms im Spiegel der Neueren Forschung. Ed. by Hildegard Temporini & Wolfgang Haase. xxii, 937p. (GER & LAT.). (C). 1993. lib. bdg. 515.40 (*3-11-013746-1*) De Gruyter.

Aufsteig & Niedergang der Roemischen Welt - Rise & Decline of the Roman World, Teil II, Principat, Band 34-2: Geschichte & Kultur Roms im Spiegel der Neueren Forschung. Ed. by Hildegard Temporini & Wolfgang Hasse. xvi, 1076p. (C). 1993. lib. bdg. 576.95 (*3-11-010390-7*) De Gruyter.

Aufsteig und Niedergang der Roemischen Welt (ANRW) Teil 2 Band 36-4. Ed. by Temporini & Haase. xviii, 990p. (C). 1990. lib. bdg. 515.40 (*3-11-012441-6*) De Gruyter.

Aufsteig und Niedergand der Roemischen Weit: Rise & Decline of the Roman World Teil II: Principat. Band 26-1. Ed. by Hildegard Temporini & Wolfgang Haase. xxvi, 812p. (GER.). 1992. lib. bdg. 444.65 (*3-11-010223-4*) De Gruyter.

Aufstieg und Niedergang der Roemischen Welt: Geschichte und Kultur Roms im Spiegel der neueren Forschung, Teil II, Ed. by Hildegard Temporini & Wolfgang Haase. x, 667p. 1986. lib. bdg. 280.00 (*0-89925-255-9*) De Gruyter.

Aufstieg und Niedergang der Roemischen Welt: Geschichte und Kultur Roms im Spiegel der neueren Forschung, Teil II, Principat. Band 32.4. Ed. by Hildegard Temporini & Wolfgang Haase. x, 611p. 1986. lib. bdg. 313.85 (*0-89925-249-4*) De Gruyter.

***Aufstieg und Niedergang der Roemischen Welt: Selection 2, Principat.**

Aufstieg und Niedergang der Roemischen Welt - Rise & Decline of the Roman World: Geschichte und Kultur Roms im Spiegel der Neuren Forschung. Tel II, Principat. Band 20-2 Religion. Ed. by Hildegard Temporini & Wolfgang Haase. (Hellenistisches Judentum in Roemischer Zeit, Ausgenommen Philon und Josephus Ser.: Pt. 2). 634p. 1987. lib. bdg. 326.95 (*3-11-011231-0*) De Gruyter.

Aufstieg und Niedergang der Roemischen Welt - Rise & Decline of the Roman World: Geschichte und Kultur Roms in Spiegel der Neuren Forschung. Teil II, Principat. Band: 20-1 Religion. Ed. by Hildegard Temporini & Wolfgang Haase. (Hellenistisches Judentum in Roemischer Zeit, Ausgenommen Philon und Josephus Ser.: Pt. 1). 668p. 1987. lib. bdg. 342.35 (*0-89925-235-4*) De Gruyter.

***Aufstieg und Niedergang der Roemischen Welt - Rise & Decline of the Roman World: Geschichte und Kultur Roms in Spiegel der Neuren Forschung. Teil II, Principat. Band: 20-1 Religion.** Ed. by Hildegard Temporini & Wolfgang Haase. (Hellenistisches Judentum in Roemischer Zeit, Ausgenommen Philon und Josephus Ser.: Pt. 1). 668p. 1987. lib. bdg. 342.35 (*3-11-010367-2*) De Gruyter.

Aufstieg und Niedergang der Roemischen Welt (ANRW) Rise & Decline of the Roman World. Ed. by Hildegard Temporini & Wolfgang Haase. (Philosophie (Stoiziamus) Ser.: Band 36: 3). xvi, 900p. (C). 1989. lib. bdg. 476.95 (*0-89925-254-0*) De Gruyter.

***Aufstieg und Niedergang der Roemischen Welt (ANRW) - Rise & Decline of the Roman World Teil II: Principat.** Ed. by Wolfgang Haase & Hildegard Temporini. xx, 1021p. (ENG, FRE & GER.). (C). 1994. lib. bdg. 561.55 (*3-11-013946-4*) De Gruyter.

Aufstieg und Niedergang der Roemischen Welt (ANRW) - Rise & Delcine of the Roman World: Geschichte und Kultur Roms Im Spiegel der Neueren Forschung. Ed. by H. Temporini & W. Hasse. (Teil II Ser.: Vol. 27.1). xvi, 762p. (GER.). (C). 1992. lib. bdg. 412.35 (*3-11-010372-9*) De Gruyter.

***Aufstieg und Niedergang der Roemischen Welt (ANRW)-- Rise & Decline of the Roman World.** Ed. by Wolfgang Haase. (Geschichte und Kultur Roms im Spiegel der Neueren Forschung: Band 36.1). xvi, 712p. (C). 1987. lib. bdg. 369.25x (*3-11-010378-8*) De Gruyter.

***Aufstieg und Niedergang der Roemischen Welt-Rise & Decline of the Roman World Teil II, Bd. 37.2: Geschichte und Kultur Roms im Spiegel der Neueren Forschung.** Ed. by Hildegard Temporini & Wolfgang Haase. xx, 1141p. (ENG & GER.). (C). 1994. lib. bdg. 643.10 (*3-11-014184-1*, 176-94) De Gruyter.

Aufstieg und Niedergang der Roemischen Welt (Rise & Decline of the Roman World), Tiel II, Bd 34.1: Geschichte und Kultur Roms im Spiegel der Neueren Forschung. Ed. by Hildegard Temporini & Wolfgang Haase. xii, 870p. (C). 1993. lib. bdg. 469.25 (*3-11-010376-1*) De Gruyter.

Aufstieg und Niedergang der Romanischen Welt Rise & Decline of the Roman World: Geschichte und Kultur Roms Im Spiegel der Neueren Forschung, Pt. 1. Ed. by Wolfgang Haase & Hildegard Temporini. (Teil II Ser.: Vol. 33, Pts. 1-5). xvi, 847p. (ENG, FRE, GER & ITA.). (C). 1991. lib. bdg. 436.15 (*3-11-010375-3*) De Gruyter.

Aufstieg und Niedergang der Romanischen Welt Rise & Decline of the Roman World: Geschichte und Kultur Roms Im Spiegel der Neueren Forschung, Pt. 2. Ed. by Wolfgang Haase & Hildegard Temporini. (Teil II Ser.: Vol. 33, Pts. 1-5). xii, 798p. (ENG, FRE, GER & ITA.). (C). 1991. lib. bdg. 407.70 (*3-11-010389-3*) De Gruyter.

Aufstieg und Niedergang der Romanischen Welt Rise & Decline of the Roman World: Geschichte und Kultur Roms Im Spiegel der Neueren Forschung, Pt. 4. Ed. by Wolfgang Haase & Hildegard Temporini. (Teil II Ser.: Vol. 33, Pts. 1-5). xvi, 876p. (ENG, FRE, GER & ITA.). (C). 1991. lib. bdg. 453.85 (*3-11-012716-4*) De Gruyter.

Aufstieg und Niedergang der Romanischen Welt Rise & Decline of the Roman World: Geschichte und Kultur Roms Im Spiegel der Neueren Forschung, Pt. 5. Ed. by Wolfgang Haase & Hildegard Temporini. (Teil II Ser.: Vol. 33, Pts. 1-5). xv, 698p. (ENG, FRE, GER & ITA.). (C). 1991. lib. bdg. 361.55 (*3-11-012793-8*) De Gruyter.

Aufstieg und Niedergang der romischen Welt: Section 1, von den Anfangen Roms bis zum Ausgang der Republik, 4 vols. Ed. by Hildegard Temporini. Incl. Vol. 1. Politische Geschichte. (Illus.). 1972. 296.70 (*3-11-001885-3*); Vol. 2. Sprache und Literatur bis zum Ende des. (Illus.). 1972. 366.70 (*3-11-004250-9*); Vol. 3. Sprache und Literatur 1. 1974. 265.35 (*3-11-004251-7*); Vol. 4, Pts. 1 & 2. Philosophie und Wissenschaften, Kuenste. (Illus.). 1975. 376.70 (*3-11-004570-2*); (C). write for info. (*0-318-51610-1*) De Gruyter.

Aufstieg und Niedergang der Romischen Welt - Rise & Decline of the Roman World: Geschichte und Kulture Roms im Spiegel der Neueren Forschung. Ed. by Hildegard Temporini & Wolfgang Hasse. (ANRW Teil II Ser.: Band 33.6). xv, 954p. (LAT.). (C). 1991. lib. bdg. 492.35 (*3-11-013489-6*, 268-91) De Gruyter.

Aufstieg und Niedergang der Romischen Welt (ANRW) Rise & Decline of the Roman World, Teil II: Principat, Vol. 36.5: Philosophie (Einzelne Autoren: Doxograp. Ed. by Hildegard Temporini & Wolfgand Hasse. xviii, 547p. (GER.). (C). 1992. lib. bdg. 301.55 (*3-11-012794-6*) De Gruyter.

Aufstieg und Niedergang der Romischen Welt (ANRW) Rise & Decline of the Roman World, Teil II: Principat, Vol. 36.6: Philosophie (Doxographica - Forts) Ed. by Hildegard Temporini & Wolfgand Hasse. xx, 618p. (GER.). (C). 1992. lib. bdg. 324.65 (*3-11-013699-6*) De Gruyter.

Aufstieg und Niedergang der Romischen Welt (ANRW) (Rise & Decline of the Roman World) Geschichte und Kultur Roms im Spiegel der Neueren Forschung. Ed. by Hildegard Temporini & Wolfgang Haase. (Three Tiele in Mehreren Einzelbanden und Gesamtregister Ser.). 1400p. (C). 1990. lib. bdg. 338.50 (*3-11-012630-3*) De Gruyter.

Aufstieg und Niedergang der Romischen Welt (ANRW)- Rise & Decline of the Roman World: Geschichte und Kultur Roms im Spiegel der Neueren Forschung Teil II, Vol. 33.3. Ed. by Wolfgang Haase. xii, 733p. (GER.). (C). 1991. lib. bdg. 383.10 (*3-11-012541-2*) De Gruyter.

***Aufwuchs-Diatomeen in Seen und Ihre Eignung als Indikatoren der Trophie.** G. Hofmann. (Bibliotheca Diatomologica Ser.: Vol. 30). (Illus.). 241p. (GER.). 1994. pap. 75.00x (*3-443-57021-6*, Pub. by Cramer-Borntraeger GW) Lubrecht & Cramer.

Augar's Daughter: A Story of Etruscan Life. Sybille Haynes. (Illus.). 238p. 1987. 29.95 (*0-948695-04-8*, Pub. by Rubicon Pr UK); pap. 19.95 (*0-948695-05-6*, Pub. by Rubicon Pr UK) Intl Spec Bk.

***Auge & Ohr: Studien zur Erforscgung der Sprache Am Menschen, 1700-1850.** Joachim Gessinger. xxv, 789p. (GER.). (C). 1994. lib. bdg. 267.70 (*3-11-013633-3*) De Gruyter.

Augenkommunikation. Methodenreflexion und Beispielanalyse. Konrad Ehlich & Jochen Rehbein. (Linguistik Aktuell Ser.: No. 2). viii, 150p. 1982. 43.00x (*90-272-2722-5*) Benjamins North Am.

Auger Effect & Other Radiationless Transitions. Ed. by E. H. Burhop. LC 79-23744. (Cambridge Monographs on Physics). 202p. 1980. reprint ed. lib. bdg. 22.00 (*0-88275-966-3*) Krieger.

Auger Microprobe Analysis. I. F. Ferguson. (Illus.). 400p. 1989. 170.00 (*0-85274-147-2*) IOP Pub.

Augers. Paula Rankin. LC 80-70565. (Poetry Ser.). 1981. pap. 9.95 (*0-915604-46-9*) Carnegie-Mellon.

***Auggie Wren's Christmas Story.** Paul Auster. (Illus.). 24p. 1992. pap. 40.00 (*1-884381-05-7*) W Drenttel NY.

***Auggie Wren's Christmas Story Signed.** Paul Auster. (Illus.). 24p. 1992. 110.00 (*1-884381-04-9*) W Drenttel NY.

Auglaize County, Ohio Marriage Records, Bks. 1-7: 1848-1899. Elmer C. Spear. 380p. 1993. pap. text ed. 24.95 (*1-55856-138-2*) Closson Pr.

Augmentation - Meta-Process or: Minimum Ingredients of Thorough, Rigorous Problem-Solving. Hans Bleiker & Annemarie Bleiker. 1988. ring bd. write for info. (*0-925368-05-9*) IPMP.

Augmentation of Convective Heat & Mass Transfer. Ed. by A. E. Bergles & R. L. Webb. LC 75-143215. 168p. reprint ed. pap. 47.90 (*0-8357-5882-6*, 2015856) Bks Demand.

Augmentative & Alternative Communication. Howard C. Shane & Maggie Sauer. Ed. by Harvey Halpern. LC 86-16919. (PRO-ED Studies in Communicative Disorders). 88p. (Orig.). 1986. pap. text ed. 9.00 (*0-89079-091-4*, 1381) PRO-ED.

Augmentative & Alternative Communication: Management of Severe Communication Disorders in Children & Adults. David R. Beukelman & Pat Mirenda. 448p. (C). 1992. reprint ed. text ed. 48.00 (*1-55766-094-8*) P H Brookes.

Augmentative & Alternative Communication Systems for Persons with Moderate & Severe Disabilities. Diane Baumgart et al. LC 90-33268. 272p. (Orig.). (C). 1990. pap. text ed. 24.00 (*1-55766-049-2*, 0492) P H Brookes.

Augmentative Communication: An Introduction. Ed. by Sarah Blackstone & Deborah M. Bruskin. LC 86-72931. 512p. 1986. pap. 35.00 (*0-910329-36-2*) Am Speech Lang Hearing.

Augmentative Communication: Implementation Strategies. Ed. by Sarah W. Blackstone et al. (Illus.). 900p. (C). 1989. 70.00 (*0-910329-47-8*) Am Speech Lang Hearing.

***Augmentative Communication in the Medical Setting.** Ed. by Kathryn M. Yorkston. 320p. 1992. pap. text ed. 49.00 (*0-88450-491-3*, 7735) Commun Skill.

Augmented Lagrangian & Operator-Splitting Methods in Nonlinear Methods. Roland Glowinski & Patrick Le Tallec. LC 89-11319. (Studies in Applied Mathematics: No. 9). x, 295p. 1989. 49.75 (*0-89871-230-0*) Soc Indus-Appl Math.

Augmented Lagrangian Methods: Applications to the Numerical Solution of Boundary-Value Problems. M. Fortin & R. Glowinski. (Studies in Mathematics & Its Applications: Vol. 15). 340p. 1983. pap. 92.50 (*0-444-86680-9*, I-168-83, North Holland) Elsevier.

Augmentin: Clavulanate Potentiated Amoxycillin. G. N. Rolinson & A. Watson. (International Congress Ser.: Vol. 544). 310p. 1981. 84.75 (*0-444-90188-4*, Excerpta Medica) Elsevier.

Augmenting Agents in Cancer Therapy. Ed. by Evan M. Hersh et al. (Progress in Cancer Research & Therapy Ser.: Vol. 16). 592p. 1981. text ed. 164.00 (*0-89004-525-9*) Raven.

Augsburg & Constantinople: The Correspondence Between Patriarch Jeremiah II & the Tubingen Theologians. George Mastrantonis. 424p. 1981. 22.95 (*0-916586-81-2*); pap. 14.95 (*0-916586-82-0*) Hellenic Coll Pr.

Augsburg Commentary on the New Testament: Acts. Gerhard A. Krodel. LC 86-10796. 528p. (Orig.). (C). 1986. kivar, pap. 20.00 (*0-8066-8884-X*, 10-9046, Augsburg) Augsburg Fortress.

Augsburg Commentary on the New Testament: Ephesians, Colossians. Ed. by Walter F. Taylor, Jr. & John H. Reumann. LC 85-7479. 176p. (Orig.). (C). 1985. kivar 17.00 (*0-8066-2165-6*, 10-9030, Augsburg) Augsburg Fortress.

Augsburg Commentary on the New Testament: First & Second James, Peter, Jude. John H. Elliott & R. A. Martin. LC 82-70962. 192p. (Orig.). 1982. kivar 17.00 (*0-8066-1937-6*, 10-9042, Augsburg) Augsburg Fortress.

Augsburg Commentary on the New Testament: First & Second Timothy, Titus, Second Thessalonians. Arland J. Hultgren & Roger Aus. LC 83-72126. (Augsburg Commentary on the New Testament Ser.). 224p. 1984. kivar 17.00 (*0-8066-8874-2*, 10-9032, Augsburg) Augsburg Fortress.

Augsburg Commentary on the New Testament: First Corinthians. Roy A. Harrisville. LC 87-17561. (Augsburg Commentary on the New Testament Ser.). 304p. (Orig.). 1987. kivar 17.00 (*0-8066-8866-1*, 10-9024, Augsburg) Augsburg Fortress.

Augsburg Commentary on the New Testament: First, Second, & Third John. Robert Kysar. LC 86-17416. 160p. (Orig.). (C). 1986. kivar, pap. 17.00 (*0-8066-8862-9*, 10-9044, Augsburg) Augsburg Fortress.

Augsburg Commentary on the New Testament: Galatians, Philippians, Philemon, First Thessalonians. Ed. by Edgar Krentz et al. LC 85-11116. 256p. (Orig.). (C). 1985. kivar 17.00 (*0-8066-2166-4*, 10-9028, Augsburg) Augsburg Fortress.

Augsburg Commentary on the New Testament: Hebrews. Robert H. Smith. LC 83-72125. (Augsburg Commentary on the New Testament Ser.). 208p. (Orig.). 1984. kivar, pap. 17.00 (*0-8066-8876-9*, 10-9034, Augsburg) Augsburg Fortress.

Augsburg Commentary on the New Testament: John. Robert Kysar. LC 85-26736. (Augsburg Commentary on the New Testament Ser.). 336p. (Orig.). 1986. kivar 17.00 (*0-8066-8860-2*, 10-9018, Augsburg) Augsburg Fortress.

Augsburg Commentary on the New Testament: Luke. David L. Tiede. LC 88-22292. 512p. (C). 1988. kivar, pap. 20.00 (*0-8066-8858-0*, 10-9016, Augsburg) Augsburg Fortress.

Augsburg Commentary on the New Testament: Mark. Donald H. Juel. LC 90-32876. 240p. (Orig.). 1990. kivar 17.00 (*0-8066-8856-4*, 10-9014) Augsburg Fortress.

Augsburg Commentary on the New Testament: Matthew. Robert H. Smith. LC 88-7767. (Commentary on the New Testament Ser.). 352p. (Orig.). (C). 1989. pap. 17.00 (*0-8066-8854-8*, 10-9012, Augsburg) Augsburg Fortress.

Augsburg Commentary on the New Testament: Revelation. Gerhard A. Krodel. LC 89-30828. (Augsburg Commentary on the New Testament Ser.). 392p. (Orig.). 1989. pap. 17.00 (*0-8066-8880-7*, 10-9038) Augsburg Fortress.

Augsburg Commentary on the New Testament: Romans. Roy A. Harrisville. LC 80-65550. 246p. (Orig.). 1980. kivar, pap. 17.00 (*0-8066-8864-5*, 10-9022, Augsburg) Augsburg Fortress.

Augsburg Commentary on the New Testament: Second Corinthians. Frederick W. Danker. LC 89-51. 256p. (Orig.). 1989. pap. 17.00 (*0-8066-8868-8*, 10-9026, Augsburg) Augsburg Fortress.

Augsburg Confession. Johann M. Reu. LC 83-45650. reprint ed. 76.50 (*0-404-19859-7*) AMS Pr.

Augsburg Confession: A Commentary. Ed. by Leif Grane. Tr. by John H. Rasmussen. LC 86-28832. 256p. (Orig.). 1987. pap. 18.99 (*0-8066-2252-0*, 10-0519, Augsburg) Augsburg Fortress.

Augsburg Historical Atlas of Christianity in the Middle Ages & Reformation. Charles S. Anderson. LC 67-11723. 70p. 1967. pap. 14.99 (*0-8066-1317-3*, 10-0521, Augsburg) Augsburg Fortress.

Augsburg Sermons for Children: Gospels, Series A. LC 92-27959. 112p. 1992. pap. 9.99 (*0-8066-2621-6*, 9-2621) Augsburg Fortress.

Augsburg Sermons for Children: Gospels Series C. Augsburg Fortress Staff. 1994. pap. 9.99 (*0-8066-2623-2*, 9-2623, Augsburg) Augsburg Fortress.

Augsburg Sermons Three: Gospels, Series A. LC 92-12758. 240p. 1992. 16.99 (*0-8066-2618-6*, 9-2618) Augsburg Fortress.

Augsburg Sermons 3: New Sermons on Gospel Texts: Gospels, Series C. LC 93-43919. 1994. 16.99 (*0-8066-2620-8*) Augsburg Fortress.

Augsburg Story Bible. Illus. by Annegert Fuchshuber. LC 92-2527. 272p. (J). (gr. 3-7). 1992. lib. bdg. 19.99 (*0-8066-2607-0*, 9-2607, Augsburg) Augsburg Fortress.

***Auguries & Omens.** Yvonne Aburrow. Date not set. pap. 22.95 (*1-898307-11-3*, Pub. by Capall Bann Pubng UK) Holmes Pub.

Auguries of Evocation: British Poetry During & after the Movement. Charu S. Singh. 239p. 1987. text ed. 35.00 (*81-7045-002-0*, Pub. by Associated Pub Hse II) Advent Bks Div.

Augury. Philip Garrison. LC 90-11255. 160p. 1991. 19.95 (*0-8203-1312-2*) U of Ga Pr.

August. Judith Rossner. 576p. 1989. mass mkt. 6.99 (*0-446-35224-1*) Warner Bks.

August. Knut Hamsun. Tr. by Eugene Gay-Tifft. 440p. 1990. reprint ed. lib. bdg. 45.00 (*0-86527-374-X*) Fertig.

***August & Marie Krogh: Lives in Science.** Bodil Schmidt-Nielsen. (An American Physiological Society Book Ser.). (Illus.). 304p. 1995. text ed. 49.95 (*0-19-509099-5*) OUP.

August Bebel, Shadow Emperor of the German Workers. William H. Maehl. LC 79-51544. (Memoirs of the American Philosophical Society Ser.: Vol. 138). 576p. reprint ed. pap. 164.20 (*0-7837-0542-5*, 2040870) Bks Demand.

August Belmont: A Political Biography. Irving Katz. LC 68-19751. (Illus.). 296p. 1968. text ed. 42.00 (*0-231-03112-2*) Col U Pr.

August Benziger: International Portrait Painter. Marieli Benziger & Janet Reberdy. LC 93-19230. (Illus.). 360p. 1993. 29.95 (*1-55612-614-X*) Sheed & Ward MO.

August Blanqui & the Art of Insurrection. Samuel Bernstein. 364p. 1971. 29.95 (*0-8464-1456-2*) Beekman Pubs.

August Break. Edith Heal. LC 84-40118. 144p. 1984. 12.95 (*0-940650-45-2*) Sun & Moon CA.

August Bride: A Narrative Travelogue of a Short Stay in the People's Republic of China. David W. Dippel. (Illus.). 485p. 1990. ring bd. 75.00 (*0-9627693-0-4*) D. W.D. Pubn.

August Celebration: A Molecule of Hope for a Changing World. Linda Grover. LC 93-80687. 168p. (Orig.). 1994. pap. text ed. 10.95 (*0-9639538-0-X*) Gilbert Hoover & Clarke.

August Coup: The Truth & the Lessons. braille ed. Mikhail Gorbachev. 178p. 1992. vinyl bd. 14.24 (*1-56956-041-2*, BR8741) W A T Braille.

August Derleth: A Bibliography. Alison M. Wilson. LC 82-24020. (Author Bibliographies Ser.: No. 59). 257p. 1983. 26.00 (*0-8108-1606-7*) Scarecrow.

August Derleth Reader. Intro. by Jim Stephens. LC 92-24433. 1992. pap. 16.95 (*1-879483-11-4*) Prairie Oak Pr.

August Edouart - A Quaker Album: American & English Duplicate Silhouettes 1827-1845. Helen Laughon & Nel Laughon. (Illus.). 144p. 1987. text ed. 29.95 (*0-9616686-0-1*) Cheswick Pr.

August Folly. Angela Thirkell. (Barsetshire Novels Ser.). 297p. 1988. pap. 4.95 (*0-88184-421-7*) Carroll & Graf.

***August Folly.** Angela Thirkell. 272p. 1995. pap. 11.95 (*0-7867-0272-9*) Carroll & Graf.

August Hermann Francke: Schriften und Predigten. Ed. by Erhard Peschke. (Texte zur Geschichte des Pietismus Ser.: Vol. 10, Sec. 2). xxvi, 639p. (C). 1989. lib. bdg. 273.10 (*3-11-007143-6*) De Gruyter.

An Asterisk (*) at the beginning of an entry indicates that the title is appearing in BIP for the first time.

527

August in Abiquiu. Diane Jackson. LC 80-11214. (Illus.). 64p. (Orig.). 1980. pap. 6.95 (0-913270-87-3) Sundial Pubns.

August in the Caribbean. Michael Gabriele. Ed. by James B. Van Treese. Tr. by Ingram. 266p. 1994. pap. 8.95 (1-56901-138-9) NW Pub.

August Macke: Tunisia: Postcard Book. (Illus.). 18p. 1993. pap. 8.95 (3-7913-1316-9, Pub. by Prestel) TeNeues.

*__August Magic.__ Katherine Applegate. (YA). (gr. 7 up). 1995. mass mkt. 3.99 (0-671-51032-0, Archway) PB.

August Monthly Activities. Janet Hale. (Illus.). 80p. (J). (gr. 1-5). 1990. student ed 8.95 (1-55734-166-4) Tchr Create Mat.

August Nights. Hugh Hood. 215p. 1985. pap. 14.95 (0-7737-5046-0, Pub. by Stoddart Pubng CN) Genl Dist Srvs.

August Nineteen Fourteen: The Red Wheel, Vol. 1. Aleksandr I. Solzhenitsyn. Tr. by H. T. Willetts. 896p. 1992. reprint ed. pap. 16.95 (0-14-007122-9, Penguin Bks) Viking Penguin.

August Nineteen Fourteen: The Red Wheel-I. Aleksandr Solzhenitsyn. Tr. by Harry T. Willetts. 1120p. 1989. pap. 19.95 (0-374-51999-4) FS&G.

August Norieri. Mary Davis. 1970. pap. 2.75 (0-911116-39-7) Pelican.

August-November, 1912, Vol. 25. Woodrow Wilson. LC 66-10880. (Papers of Woodrow Wilson). (Illus.). 1978. 69.50 (0-691-04650-6) Princeton U Pr.

August People. Ralph Graves. 448p. 1986. pap. 3.95 (0-8217-1863-0) Zebra.

August Sander: Photographs of an Epoch 1904-1959. deluxe limited ed. Comment by Robert Kramer. (Illus.). 128p. 600.00 (0-89381-062-2) Aperture.

August Seventeen Seventy-Four to August Seventeen Seventy-Five see Letters of Delegates to Congress, 1774-1789

August Sixteenth to December Thirty-First, Seventeen Seventy-Six see Letters of Delegates to Congress, 1774-1789

August Sleepwalker. Bei Dao. Tr. by Bonnie S. McDougall. LC 89-13694. 144p. 1990. 16.95 (0-8112-1131-2); pap. 8.95 (0-8112-1132-0, NDP692) New Directions.

August Snow. Reynolds Price. 1991. pap. 4.75 (0-8222-0075-9) Dramatists Play.

August Strindberg. Olof Lagercrantz. Tr. by Anselm Hollo. LC 84-42803. 400p. 1984. 25.50 (0-374-10685-1) FS&G.

August Strindberg. Martin Lamm. Ed. by Harry G. Carlson. LC 69-16323. 1972. 27.95 (0-405-08724-1) Ayer.

August Strindberg: A Psychoanalytic Study with Special Reference to the Oedipus Complex. Axel J. Uppvall. LC 79-117593. (Studies in European Literature: No. 56). (C). 1970. reprint ed. lib. bdg. 75.00 (0-8383-1026-5) M S G Haskell Hse.

August Thirty-Two, Two Thousand: And Other Essays for a New Millennium. John Newmeyer. LC 94-71771. (Illus.). 172p. 1994. 12.95 (0-9641233-0-4) Bright Moon.

August Tiesselinck: A Lifetime in Metal, 1890-1972. Isak Lindenauer. (Illus.). 82p. 1990. pap. 20.00 (0-9624994-0-4) Lindenauer.

August Travel, Devious Paths, Prose & Poetry by Herman Taube. Herman Taube. 250p. 1992. 15.95 (0-931848-83-0); pap. 9.95 (0-931848-84-9) Dryad Pr.

August von Kotzebue: The Comedy, the Man. Oscar Mandel. LC 88-43438. (Illus.). 44p. 1990. lib. bdg. 25.00 (0-271-00668-4) Pa St U Pr.

August Wilhelm Schlegel As a Translator of Shakespeare. Margaret E. Atkinson. LC 76-51367. (Studies in Shakespeare: No. 24). 1977. lib. bdg. 46.95 (0-8383-2135-6) M S G Haskell Hse.

*__August Wilson: A Casebook.__ Ed. by Marilyn Elkins. LC 94-27256. (Casebooks on Modern Dramatists Ser.: No. 15). 256p. 1994. 38.00 (0-8153-0922-8, H1626) Garland.

August Wilson: Three Plays. Pref. by August Wilson. LC 90-44105. 336p. (C). 1994. reprint ed. 29.95 (0-8229-3666-6) U of Pittsburgh Pr.

August Wilson & the African-American Odyssey. Kim Pereira. LC 94-25855. Date not set. write for info. (0-252-02137-1); pap. write for info. (0-252-06429-1) U of Ill Pr.

August Zero. Jane R. Miller. LC 93-4137. 96p. (Orig.). 1993. 22.00 (1-55659-060-1); pap. 11.00 (1-55659-061-X) Copper Canyon.

August 1794-December 1794 see Papers of Alexander Hamilton

August 1944. Robert A. Miller. (Illus.). 300p. 1988. 17.95 (0-89141-316-2) Presidio Pr.

Augusta. Federal Writers' Project, Georgia. LC 73-3606. (American Guide Ser.). reprint ed. 12.50 (0-404-57910-8) AMS Pr.

Augusta & the American Revolution: Events in the Georgia Back Country, 1773-1783. Edward J. Cashin & Heard Robertson. LC 74-28968. (Illus.). 1975. pap. 7.00 (0-685-04356-8) Richmond Cty Hist Soc.

Augusta & Trab. Christopher De Vinck. LC 93-7897. 144p. (J). (gr. 3-7). 1993. text ed. 13.95 (0-02-729945-7, Four Winds Pr) S&S Childrens.

Augusta Cotton. Margaret Erhart. LC 92-53830. 304p. 1992. 19.95 (0-944072-21-6) Zoland Bks.

Augusta County: Virginia Publick Claims. Janice L. Abercrombie & Richard Slatten. (Virginia Publick Claims Ser.). ix, 38p. (C). 1991. reprint ed. lib. bdg. 20.00x (0-8095-8304-6) Borgo Pr.

*__Augusta County: Virginia Publick Claims.__ Janice L. Abercrombie & Richard Slatten. (Virginia Publick Claims Ser.). ix, 38p. (C). 1991. reprint ed. pap. 5.00x (0-8095-8509-X) Borgo Pr.

Augusta County Marriages, Seventeen Forty-Eight to Eighteen Fifty: 1853. John Vogt & T. William Kethley, Jr. LC 88-34674. (Virginia Historic Marriage Register Ser.). (Illus.). xi, 414p. 1986. pap. 17.00x (0-935931-23-6) Borgo Pr.

*__Augusta County Marriages, Seventeen Forty-Eight to Eighteen Fifty: 1853.__ John Vogt & T. William Kethley, Jr. (Virginia Historic Marriage Register Ser.). xi, 414p. 1986. lib. bdg. 41.00x (0-8095-8209-0) Borgo Pr.

Augusta E. Stetson: Apostle to the World. Gail M. Weatherbe. LC 90-93332. (Illus.). xii, 322p. 1990. 16.00 (1-879135-06-X) Emma Pub Soc.

Augusta E. Stetson, C.S.D. 2nd ed. Gail M. Weatherbe. LC 93-201814. iii, 20p. 1991. pap. 3.00 (1-879135-00-0) Emma Pub Soc.

Augusta E. Stetson, C.S.D. Refutes the Statement of Mr. Clifford P. Smith, That She Is Not a Christian Scientist. Augusta E. Stetson. LC 94-71169. (Illus.). 48p. 1994. reprint ed. per., pap. 6.00 (1-879135-11-6) Emma Pub Soc.

*__Augusta, Sicily Earthquake of 13 December, 1990: A Field Report by EEFIT.__ R. E. Hughes et al. 36p. 1994. pap. 38.00 (0-615-00346-X) Am Soc Civil Eng.

Augusta Tabor: A Pioneering Woman. Betty Moynihan. LC 88-14962. (Illus.). 160p. (Orig.). 1988. pap. 9.95 (0-917895-23-1) Cordillera CO.

Augusta Tabor: Her Side of the Scandal. Caroline Bancroft. (Illus.). 16p. 1955. pap. 1.95 (0-933472-14-5) Johnson Bks.

Augustan America. Webb. Date not set. 17.95 (0-06-016797-1, HarpT) HarpC.

Augustan Court: Queen Anne & the Decline of Court Culture. R. O. Bucholz. LC 92-440. (Illus.). 356p. (C). 1993. 47.50 (0-8047-2080-0) Stanford U Pr.

Augustan Empire, Forty-Four B. C.-A. D. Seventy. (Cambridge Ancient History Ser.: Vol. 10). 1934. 150.00 (0-521-04492-8) Cambridge U Pr.

Augustan Historical Writing: Histories of England in the English Enlightenment. Laird Okie. 248p. (C). 1991. lib. bdg. 46.00 (0-8191-8050-5) U Pr of Amer.

Augustan Laws on Family Relations. P. Csillag. 276p. 1976. 58.00 (0-569-08371-0, Pub. by Collets UK) Pro-Am Music.

*__Augustan Laws on Family Relations.__ P. Csillag. 275p. (C). 1976. 48.00x (963-05-0376-X, Pub. by Akad Kiado HU) St Mut.

*__Augustan Rome.__ A. Wallace-Hadrill. (Classical World Ser.). 117p. 1993. pap. text ed. 13.95 (1-85399-138-4) Focus Info Gr.

Augustan Studies. Geoffrey Tillotson. LC 73-14037. 266p. 1974. reprint ed. text ed. 35.00 (0-8371-7140-7, TIAS, Greenwood Pr) Greenwood.

Augustan Studies: Essays in Honor of Irvin Ehrenpreis. Ed. by Douglas L. Patey & Timothy Keegan. LC 85-40084. (Illus.). 272p. 1986. 38.50 (0-87413-272-X) U Delaware Pr.

Augustan Translators: Restoration & Eighteenth Century English Translations of the Classics, 23 vols. in 26. Augustan Translators. 1666. reprint ed. 1,582.00 (0-404-54100-3) AMS Pr.

Augustana - A Profession of Faith: A History of Augustana College, 1860-1935. Conrad Bergendoff. LC 76-92170. (Augustana College Library Publication Ser.: No. 33). (Illus.). 220p. 1969. 5.95 (0-910182-33-7) Augustana Coll.

Augustana Book Concern & Christine Nilsson's Visit to Brockton, Mass. in November, 1870. Ernest W. Olson & Evald B. Lawson. (Augustana Historical Society Publication Ser.: Vol. 3). 96p. 1933. pap. 3.00 (0-910184-03-8) Augustana.

Augustana Ministerium: A Study of the Careers of the 2504 Pastors of the Augustana Evangelical Lutheran Synod-Church 1850-1962. Conrad Bergendoff. LC 80-66400. (Augustana Historical Society Publication Ser.: No. 28). 246p. 1980. 15.00 (0-910184-28-3) Augustana.

Augustans & Romantics, Sixteen Eighty-Nine to Eighteen Thirty. 2nd rev. ed. Henry V. Dyson & John E. Butt. reprint ed. 39.00 (0-403-03061-7) Somerset Pub.

Augustans & Romantics, Sixteen Eighty-Nine to Eighteen Thirty. Henry V. Dyson & B. Dyson. 1988. reprint ed. lib. bdg. 65.00 (0-7812-0133-0) Rprt Serv.

Auguste Comte: An Intellectual Biography, Vol. 1. Mary Pickering. LC 92-44510. 800p. (C). 1993. 49.95 (0-521-43405-X) Cambridge U Pr.

Auguste de Colbert: Aristocratic Survival in an Era of Upheaval, 1793-1809. Jeanne A. Ojala. LC 79-4872. 213p. reprint ed. pap. 60.80 (0-8357-5883-4, 2027169) Bks Demand.

Auguste Laurent & the Prehistory of Valence. Marya Novitski. LC 92-23090. (History of Science & Technology Ser.: Vol. 1). 1992. text ed. 58.00 (3-7186-5235-8) Gordon & Breach.

Auguste Rodin: Postcard Book. (Illus.). 18p. 1993. pap. 8.95 (3-7913-1311-8, Pub. by Prestel) TeNeues.

*__Auguste Rodin & Camille Claudel.__ Ed. by J. A. Schmoll. (Pegasus Library). (Illus.). 128p. 1994. 25.00 (3-7913-1382-7) TeNeues.

Auguste Rodin: Das Hoellentor: Skulpturen und Zeichnungen. Ed. by Manfred Fath. (Illus.). 170p. (GER.). 1991. 64.00 (3-7913-1162-X, Pub. by Prestel) TeNeues.

Auguste Rodin, Eighteen Forty to Nineteen Seventeen: B. G. Cantor Sculpture Center. Joan V. Miller. Ed. by Gary Marotta. (Illus.). 64p. (Orig.). 1981. pap. write for info. (0-939912-00-7) Cantor Art Found.

*__Auguste Rodin Erotic Watercolors.__ Anne-Marie Bonnet. (Illus.). 160p. 1995. 85.00 (1-55670-428-3) Stewart Tabori & Chang.

Augustin Bea: The Cardinal of Unity. Stjepan Schmidt. Tr. by Leslie Wearne. 816p. 1993. 49.00 (1-56548-016-3) New City.

Augustin, die Christliche Antike und das Mittelalter. Ernst Troeltsch. Ed. by J. P. Mayer. LC 78-67393. (European Political Thought Ser.). (GER.). 1980. reprint ed. lib. bdg. 17.95 (0-405-11746-9) Ayer.

Augustin-Louie Cauchy: A Biography. B. Belhoste. Ed. by G. J. Toomer. (Studies in the History of Mathematics & Physical Sciences: Vol. 16). (Illus.). 392p. 1991. 79.00 (0-387-97220-X) Spr-Verlag.

Augustine. Henry Chadwick. (Past Masters Ser.). 128p. 1986. pap. 7.95 (0-19-287534-5) OUP.

Augustine. Mary T. Clark. LC 93-36685. (C). 1994. 35.00 (0-87840-552-6) Georgetown U Pr.

Augustine. Christopher Kirwan. 224p. 1989. 75.00 (0-415-00812-3, A2593) Routledge.

Augustine. Christopher Kirwan. 256p. 1991. pap. 16.95 (0-415-06364-7, A5527) Routledge.

Augustine. James J. O'Donnell. LC 84-28133. (World Authors Ser.: No. 759). 168p. 1985. text ed. 23.95 (0-8057-6609-X, Twayne) Macmillan.

Augustine. Robert Van de Weyer. (Spiritual Classics Ser.). 64p. 1991. 4.99 (0-8007-7130-3) Revell.

Augustine: Ancient Thought Baptized. John M. Rist. LC 93-32394. 360p. (C). 1994. 59.95 (0-521-46084-0) Cambridge U Pr.

Augustine: Earlier Writings. Ed. by John S. Burleigh. LC 53-13043. (Library of Christian Classics). 410p. 1979. pap. 14.99 (0-664-24162-X, Westminster) Westminster John Knox.

Augustine: From Rhetor to Theologian. Joanne McWilliam et al. 200p. (C). 1992. text ed. 35.00 (0-88920-203-6, Pub. by Wilfrid Laurier CN) Humanities.

*__Augustine: His Thought in Context.__ T. Kermit Scott. LC 95-5573. 272p. (Orig.). 1995. pap. 14.95 (0-8091-3566-3) Paulist Pr.

Augustine: Later Works. Ed. by John Burnaby. LC 55-5022. (Library of Christian Classics). 356p. 1980. reprint ed. pap. 14.99 (0-664-24165-4, Westminster) Westminster John Knox.

Augustine: Mystic & Mystagogue. Ed. by Frederick Van Fleteren et al. LC 93-31502. (Collectanea Augustiniana Ser.). 648p. (C). 1994. text ed. 69.95 (0-8204-2290-8) P Lang Pubs.

Augustine: Presbyter Factus Sum. Joseph T. Lienhard et al. LC 93-16709. 590p. (C). 1994. text ed. 69.95 (0-8204-2199-5) P Lang Pubs.

Augustine: The Confessions & the City of God. Benedict J. Groeschel. (Spiritual Legacy Ser.). 160p. (Orig.). 1995. pap. 11.95 (0-8245-2505-1) Crossroad NY.

Augustine & the Arians: The Bishop of Hippo's Encounters with Ulfilan Arianism. William A. Sumruld. LC 92-50684. Date not set. write for info. (0-945636-46-6) Susquehanna U Pr.

*__Augustine & the Catechumenate.__ J. William Harmless. 300p. (Orig.). 1995. pap. text ed. 18.95 (0-8146-6132-7, Pueblo Bks) Liturgical Pr.

*__Augustine & the Limits of Politics.__ Jean B. Elshtain. LC 95-16515. (Frank M. Covey Jr. Loyola Lectures in Political Analysis). (C). 1996. text ed. 21.95 (0-268-00645-8) U of Notre Dame Pr.

Augustine & the Limits of Virtue. James Wetzel. 280p. (C). 1992. 59.95 (0-521-40541-6) Cambridge U Pr.

*__Augustine & the Making of a Christian Literature: Classical Tradition & Augustine Aesthetics.__ Robert J. Forman. LC 95-8717. (Texts & Studies in Religion: No. 65). 240p. 1996. text ed. 89.95 (0-7734-8904-5) E Mellen.

Augustine Baker. Anthony Low. LC 74-99527. (Twayne's English Authors Ser.). 170p. (C). 1970. lib. bdg. 17.95 (0-8290-1759-3) Irvington.

Augustine Baker's Inner Light: A Study in English Recusant Spirituality. James Gaffney. LC 89-50663. 1990. pap. 21.50 (0-940866-08-0) U Scranton Pr.

Augustine Day by Day. John E. Rotelle. (Orig.). 1986. pap. 4.50 (0-89942-170-9, 170-09) Catholic Bk Pub.

Augustine: De Fide et Symbolo: Introduction, Translation, Commentary. E. P. Meijering. 197p. (Orig.). (C). 1987. pap. 35.00 (90-70265-78-8, Pub. by Gieben NE) Benjamins North Am.

Augustine Heard & Company: American Merchants in China. Stephen C. Lockwood. LC 78-120318. (East Asian Monographs: No. 37). 171p. 1971. pap. 11.00 (0-674-05270-6) HUP.

Augustine Laure, S. J., Missionary to the Yakimas. Victor Garrand. 36p. 1977. pap. 7.50 (0-87770-187-3) Ye Galleon.

Augustine of Hippo. Peter Brown. 463p. 1987. 22.50 (0-88029-098-6) Dorset Pr.

Augustine of Hippo: A Biography. Peter Brown. 1967. reprint ed. pap. 15.00 (0-520-01411-1) U CA Pr.

Augustine of Hippo: Selected Writings. St. Augustine. Tr. by Mary T. Clark. (Classics of Western Spirituality Ser.). 544p. 1984. pap. 17.95 (0-8091-2573-0) Paulist Pr.

Augustine on Evil. G. R. Evans. 198p. (C). 1990. pap. 19.95 (0-521-39743-X) Cambridge U Pr.

Augustine on Music: An Interdisciplinary Collection of Essays. Ed. by Richard R. La Croix. LC 87-22012. (Studies in the History & Interpretation of Music: Vol. 6). 120p. 1988. lib. bdg. 59.95 (0-88946-431-6) E Mellen.

Augustine on Prayer. rev. ed. Thomas A. Hand. (Orig.). 1986. pap. 3.95 (0-89942-171-7, 171-04) Catholic Bk Pub.

Augustine on Romans: Propositions from the Epistle to the Romans & Unfinished Commentary on the Epistle to the Romans. Paula F. Landes. LC 82-10259. (Society of Biblical Literature Texts & Translations Ser.). 124p. (C). 1982. pap. 18.95 (0-89130-583-1, 06-02-23) Scholars Pr GA.

Augustine, the Harvest, & Theology (1300-1650) Essays Dedicated to Heiko Augustinus Oberman in Honor of His Sixtieth Birthday. Ed. by Kenneth Hagen. LC 90-49022. vii, 375p. (ENG & GER.). 1990. 91.50 (90-04-09319-2) E J Brill.

Augustine to Galileo. A. C. Crombie. (Illus.). 728p. 1980. 40.00 (0-674-05273-0) HUP.

Augustine Today. Ed. by Richard J. Neuhaus. (Encounter Ser.). 168p. (Orig.). (C). 1993. pap. text ed. 12.99 (0-8028-0216-8) Eerdmans.

Augustine's Conversion: A Guide to the Argument of Confessions I-IX. Colin Starnes. 320p. (C). 1990. text ed. 45.00 (0-88920-991-X, Pub. by Wilfrid Laurier CN) Humanities.

Augustine's Critique of Skepticism: A Study of Contra Academicos. Augustine J. Curley. LC 93-42013. 1994. write for info. (0-8204-2379-3) P Lang Pubs.

Augustine's De Civitate Dei: An Annotated Bibliography of Modern Criticism, 1960-1990. Dorothy F. Donnelly. LC 91-26511. (Augustinian Historical Institute Series of Villanova University). 109p. (C). 1992. text ed. 29.95 (0-8204-1607-X) P Lang Pubs.

Augustine's Heritage: Readings from the Augustinian Tradition, 3 vols., 1. Ed. by John E. Rotelle. 1986. 1.50 (0-89942-701-4, 701-04) Catholic Bk Pub.

Augustine's Heritage: Readings from the Augustinian Tradition, 3 vols., 2. Ed. by John E. Rotelle. 1986. write for info. (0-89942-702-2, 702-04) Catholic Bk Pub.

Augustine's Heritage: Readings from the Augustinian Tradition, 3 vols., 3. Ed. by John E. Rotelle. 1986. write for info. (0-89942-703-0, 703-04) Catholic Bk Pub.

Augustine's Ideal of the Religious Life. Adolar Zumkeller. LC 85-70093. 480p. reprint ed. pap. 136.80 (0-7837-5622-4, 2045531) Bks Demand.

Augustine's Laws. Norman R. Augustine. LC 83-22409. (Illus.). 241p. 1984. 29.95 (0-915928-81-7) AIAA.

Augustine's Love of Wisdom: An Introspective Philosophy. Vernon J. Bourke. LC 91-46448. (Series in the History of Philosophy). 240p. (C). 1992. 27.00 (1-55753-025-4); pap. 13.75 (1-55753-026-2) Purdue U Pr.

Augustine's Prayerful Ascent: An Essay on the Literary Form of the Confessions. Robert McMahon. LC 88-27893. 200p. 1989. 27.50 (0-8203-1126-X) U of Ga Pr.

Augustine's Quest of Wisdom. rev. ed. Vernon J. Bourke. LC 93-5192. 332p. 1993. pap. 14.00 (0-87343-054-9) Magi Bks.

Augustine's Rule. Adolar Zumkeller et al. LC 86-72341. 128p. (Orig.). 1987. pap. 4.95 (0-941491-06-4) Augustinian Pr.

Augustine's Trick. William Lazo. (Augustine Detective Ser.). 64p. (Orig.). (C). 1991. pap. 4.00 (1-880046-05-9) Baculite Pub.

Augustine's Works. Daley. (Monarch Ser.). 1989. pap. 4.25 (0-671-00537-5) S&S Trade.

Augustinian Bibliography, 1970-1980: With Essays on the Fundamentals of Augustinian Scholarship. Terry L. Miethe. LC 82-6173. xxiii, 218p. 1982. text ed. 59.95 (0-313-22629-6, MIA/, Greenwood Pr) Greenwood.

Augustinian Imperative: A Reflection on the Politics. William E. Connolly. (Modernity & Political Thought Ser.: Vol. 1). 176p. (C). 1993. text ed. 39.95 (0-8039-3636-2); pap. text ed. 17.95 (0-8039-3637-0) Sage.

Augustinian Law & Charism: The Life & Work of Clement of Osimo. Carlos Alonso. Ed. by John E. Rotelle. Tr. by Audrey Fellowes. LC 88-70366. (Augustinian Ser.). (Illus.). 72p. 1988. pap. 4.95 (0-941491-17-X) Augustinian Pr.

*__Augustinian Origins, Charism, & Spirituality.__ Balbino Rano. LC 94-32757. (Augustinian Ser.: Vol. 3). 1994. write for info. (0-941491-75-7); pap. text ed. write for info. (0-941491-76-5) Augustinian Pr.

Augustinian Piety & Catholic Reform: Augustine, Colet, & Erasmus. Peter I. Kaufman. LC 82-12491. 161p. 1982. text ed. 9.45 (0-86554-047-0, MUP-H46) Mercer Univ Pr.

Augustinian Studies: Papers Read at Recent Augustinian Educational Conferences. Augustinian Educational Conferences Staff. LC 67-22052. (Essay Index Reprint Ser.). 1977. 20.95 (0-8369-0163-0) Ayer.

Augustinus - Concordantia in Libros XIII Confessionum S. Aurelii Augustini, 2 vols., Set. Rodney H. Cooper et al. (Alpha-Omega, Reihe A Ser.: Bd. CXXIV). xx, 1191p. (GER.). 1991. write for info. (3-487-09489-4, Pub. by Georg Olms GW) Lubrecht & Cramer.

Augusto D'Halmar: Novelista (Estudio De Pasion y Muerte Del Cura Deusto) Ramon L. Acevedo. LC 76-8011. (Coleccion Mente y Palabra). 204p. (Orig.). (SPA.). 1976. 5.00 (0-8477-0530-7); pap. 4.00 (0-8477-0531-5) U of PR Pr.

Augusto Roa Bastos's "I The Supreme" A Dialogic Perspective. Helene C. Weldt-Basson. 264p. (C). 1993. text ed. 39.95 (0-8262-0888-6) U of Mo Pr.

*__Augustus.__ John Williams. LC 94-37249. 1995. write for info. (1-55728-343-5) U of Ark Pr.

Augustus & the Ancient Romans. Michael Poulton. LC 92-5824. (Life in the Time of Ser.). (Illus.). 63p. (J). (gr. 6-7). 1992. lib. bdg. 24.26 (0-8114-3350-1) Raintree Steck-V.

Augustus & the Greek World. Glen W. Bowersock. LC 81-13432. xii, 176p. 1982. reprint ed. text ed. 49.75 (0-313-23298-9, BOAG, Greenwood Pr) Greenwood.

Augustus Caesar. David Shotter. (Lancaster Pamphlets Ser.). 128p. 1991. pap. 9.95 (0-415-06048-6, A6678) Routledge.

Augustus Caesar. Nancy Z. Walworth & Arthur M. Schlesinger, Jr. (World Leaders - Past & Present Ser.). (Illus.). 112p. (YA). (gr. 5 up). 1989. 17.95 (1-55546-804-7) Chelsea Hse.

Augustus Caesar & the Organization of the Empire of Rome. John B. Firth. LC 73-14440. (Heroes of the Nations Ser.). reprint ed. 30.00 (0-404-58259-1) AMS Pr.

Augustus Caesar & the Organization of the Empire of Rome. John B. Firth. LC 70-38352. (Select Bibliographies Reprint Ser.). 1977. reprint ed. 34.95 (0-8369-6769-0) Ayer.

An Asterisk (*) at the beginning of an entry indicates that the title is appearing in BIP for the first time.

An Asterisk (*) at the beginning of an entry indicates that the title is appearing in BIP for the first time.

529

Aunt Wilhelmina's Will. Grant McBurnie & Michael Polack. LC 93-6570. (J). 1994. write for info. (0-383-03676-3) SRA Schl Grp.

Aunt Zeze's Tears see Brazilian Tales

Aunt Zinnia & the Ogre. (Beechwood Bunny Tales Ser.). (Illus.). 32p. (J). (gr. k-3). 1992. lib. bdg. 17.27 (0-8368-0910-6) Gareth Stevens Inc.

Aunt Zona's Web: Life of Arizona Hughes, a Pioneer Teacher. rev. ed. Tom Chapman. (Illus.). 1979. 5.00 (0-686-27735-X) Puddingstone.

Auntie Barbara's Tips for an Ordinary Life: A Celebration of a Kinder, Gentler Lifestyle. Barbara Hovanetz. 128p. 1992. pap. 8.00 (0-380-76126-2) Avon.

Auntie Mame. Patrick Dennis. 1976. 21.95 (0-8488-0475-9) Amereon Ltd.

Auntie Mame. Patrick Dennis. 1994. mass mkt. 5.99 (0-345-37650-1) Ballantine.

Auntie Mame. adapted ed. Patrick Dennis. Ed. by Robert E. Lee. 1960. pap. 4.75 (0-8222-0077-5) Dramatists Play.

Auntie Mame. Patrick Dennis. 275p. 1990. reprint ed. lib. bdg. 26.95 (0-89966-726-0) Buccaneer Bks.

Auntie Mame: An Irreverent Escapade. Patrick Dennis. LC 94-15275. 446p. 1994. 20.95 (0-8161-5987-4) Hall.

Aunties: A Collection of Recipes & Memories. Cheril Vendetti. (Illus.). 114p. 1987. write for info. (0-318-64839-3) Feathers Forever.

Auntiques & the Valentine Card. John Tissot & Matthew Carlin. 16p. (Orig.). (J). (gr. 2 up). 1991. pap. 3.00 (0-88680-357-8) I E Clark.

Aunts. Robert Liddell. LC 87-60977. (Illus.). 192p. 1987. 21.00 (0-7206-0665-9, Pub. by P Owen Ltd UK) Dufour.

Aunts. rev. ed. Isabella Halsted. Ed. by Bella Halsted. (Illus.). 188p. 1993. pap. 16.95 (0-9636116-0-7) Sharksmouth.

Aunt's Story. Patrick White. 288p. 1993. 10.95 (0-14-018653-0, Penguin Classics) Viking Penguin.

Aunty Poepe Letters. Maili Yardley. (Illus.). (Orig.). 1985. pap. text ed. 8.95 (0-914916-67-X) Ku Paa.

*__Aunty Pua's Dilemma.__ Ann K. Corum. 32p. 1994. 12.95 (1-56647-086-2) Mutual Pub HI.

Aunty Pua's Keiki Cookbook. Ann K. Corum. LC 91-70849. (Illus.). 80p. 1991. pap. 6.95 (0-935848-88-6) Bess Pr.

Aupha Manual of Health Services Management. Robert J. Taylor & Susan B. Taylor. 680p. 1993. boxed 69.00 (0-8342-0363-4, 20363) Aspen Pub.

Aur Sea. Jack Hirschman. 40p. (Orig.). 1974. pap. 5.00 (0-686-05773-2) Tree Bks.

Aura. Carlos Fuentes. Tr. by Lysander Kemp. LC 75-2417. 160p. (ENG & SPA.). 1986. pap. 10.00 (0-374-51171-3) FS&G.

Aura. Carlos Fuentes. (SPA.). 1989. 5.95 (0-8288-2564-5, S1404) Fr & Eur.

Aura & What It Means to You. Ed. by Health Research Staff. 108p. 1955. reprint ed. spiral bd. 9.35 (0-7873-0403-4) Mokelumne.

Aura Coloring Book. Levanah S. Bdolak. Ed. by Anita Wolff. (Illus.). 120p. (Orig.). 1991. pap. 11.95 (0-944278-01-9) Voyant.

Aura Literary - Arts Review: Fifteen-Year Author & Title Index, Nos. 1-25, 1974-1988. Anthony J. Schimizzi & Dieu Van Tong. (Friends of the Sterne Library Ser.: No. 2). ix, 170p. 1989. lib. bdg. 10.00 (0-9620942-1-8) M H Sterne Lib.

Aura Paradigm: Aura Phenomena & Human Prehistory. Michael Baran. Ed. by Dan Kassell. (Illus.). 66p. (Orig.). 1988. pap. 8.50 (0-9623889-0-4) Authentic Mktg.

Auraicept Na N-Eces. Ed. by George Calder. LC 78-72717. (Celtic Language & Literature Ser.: Goidelic & Brythonic). reprint ed. 47.50 (0-404-17558-4) AMS Pr.

Aural. Vassilis Zambaras. 24p. (Orig.). 1984. pap. 2.00 (0-935162-05-4) Singing Horse.

Aural Awareness. Pratt et al. 1990. 90.00 (0-335-09418-X, Open Univ Pr); pap. 29.00 (0-335-09417-1, Open Univ Pr) Taylor & Francis.

Aural Habilitation: The Foundations of Verbal Learning in Hearing-Impaired Children. Daniel Ling & Agnes H. Ling. LC 78-56077. 1978. pap. text ed. 24.95 (0-88200-121-3, C2441) Alexander Graham.

Aural Harmony. A. Eugene Ellsworth. LC 72-138243. 1970. spiral bd. 19.95 (0-910842-00-0, GE9) Kjos.

Aural Images of Lost Traditions: Sharps & Flats in the Sixteenth Century. Robert Toft. (Illus.). 256p. 1991. 60.00 (0-8020-5929-5) U of Toronto Pr.

Aural Literature Criticism. Ed. by Richard Kostelanetz. (Precisely Ser.). 192p. (Orig.). 1981. 15.00 (0-932360-42-4); pap. 6.00 (0-932360-43-2) Archae Edns.

*__Aural Rehabilitation.__ 2nd ed. Hull. 1991. 45.00 (1-879105-35-7, 0230) Singular Publishing.

Aural Rehabilitation. 2nd ed. Raymond H. Hull. (Illus.). 384p. (Orig.). (C). 1991. pap. text ed. 39.50 (1-879105-46-2, 0230) Singular Publishing.

Aural Rehabilitation: A Management Model. 2nd ed. Derek A. Sanders. (Illus.). 464p. (C). 1981. text ed. write for info. (0-13-053215-0) P-H.

Aural Rehabilitation Infants see Management of Hearing Handicap: Infants to Elderly

Aural Sex & Verbal Intercourse see Sex Information, May I Help You?

Aural Skills for Conductors. Wayne Bailey. 120p. (C). 1992. spiral bd. 23.95 (1-55934-068-1) Mayfield Pub.

Aurally Coded English Spelling Dictionary: ACE. David Museley & Catherine Nichol. 1989. pap. 70.00 (0-317-58012-4) St Mut.

Aurangzib & the Decay of the Mughal Empire. Stanley L. Poole. 1990. reprint ed. 9.50 (81-85418-10-1, Pub. by Low Price II) S Asia.

Auranofin in Rheumatoid Arthritis. Ed. by Norman L. Gottlieb. LC 87-73225. 128p. 1987. 30.00 (0-941741-00-1) Adis Pr Intl.

Auras: An Essay on the Meaning of Colors. Edgar Cayce. 20p. 1973. pap. 3.00 (0-87604-012-1, 206) ARE Pr.

Auras Tendrils. Ann F. Chandonnet. 72p. 1985. 7.95 (0-920806-45-7, Pub. by Penumbra Pr CN) U of Toronto Pr.

*__Aurat Durbar.__ Ed. by Fauzia Rafiq. Date not set. pap. 14.95 (0-929005-70-8) InBook.

Aurelia. Gerard De Nerval. Bd. with Pandora.; Chimeres. (Livre de Poche Classique Ser.). (FRE.). Set pap. 10.95 (0-8288-9653-4, F69730) Fr & Eur.

*__Aurelia.__ Kirsch et al. 112p. 1994. student ed 13.00 (3-468-49521-8); teacher ed 26.25 (3-468-49522-6); text ed. 16.50 (3-468-49520-X); trans. 112.95 (3-468-49525-0) Langenscheidt.

Aurelia. Gerard De Nerval. Tr. by Richard Aldington. LC 77-10265. (Illus.). 200p. reprint ed. 23.50 (0-404-16317-3) AMS Pr.

*__Aurelia, No. 1.1.__ Kirsch et al. 1994. audio 20.00 (3-468-49523-4) Langenscheidt.

*__Aurelia, No. 1.2.__ Kirsch et al. 1994. audio 20.00 (3-468-49524-2) Langenscheidt.

Aurelia see Oeuvres

Aurelia & Other Writings. Gerard De Nerval. Tr. by Geoffrey Wagner. 164p. (Orig.). 1995. pap. 13.95 (1-878972-09-X) Exact Change.

Aurelia Followed by Sylvie. 2nd rev. ed. Gerard De Nerval. Tr. by Kendall Lappin. 160p. 1993. pap. 9.95 (1-878580-07-8) Asylum Arts.

Aurelia, Les Chimeres, La Pandora. Gerard De Nerval. (Illus.). (FRE.). 1984. pap. 8.95 (0-7859-3079-5) Fr & Eur.

Aurelien (Le Monde Reel) Louis Aragon. 697p. (FRE.). 1986. pap. 20.95 (0-7859-2039-0, 2070377504) Fr & Eur.

Aurelio Galfetti Castelgrande, Bellinzona, no. 4. Frank Werner. (Opus Ser.). 1993. 39.00 (0-685-67320-0, Pub. by W Ernst Sohn) VCH Pubs.

Aurelius Victor: De Caesaribus. Tr. & Intro. by H. W. Bird. (Translated Texts for Historians Ser.). 256p. (Orig.). 1994. pap. text ed. 17.95 (0-85323-218-0, Pub. by Liverpool Univ Pr UK) U of Pa Pr.

Aureng-Zebe. John Dryden. Ed. by Frederick M. Link. LC 78-123119. (Regents Restoration Drama Ser.). 155p. reprint ed. pap. 44.20 (0-8357-7876-2, 2036294) Bks Demand.

Aurian. Maggie Furey. 1994. mass mkt. 5.99 (0-553-56525-7) Bantam.

Auricula Meretricula. rev. ed. Ann Cumming & Mary W. Blundell. (Focus Classical Library). (Illus.). 57p. (Orig.). 1993. pap. text ed. 5.95 (0-941051-35-8) Focus Info Gr.

Auricular Therapy: Theory & Practice. Beatrice Bartnett. (Illus.). 146p. (Orig.). 1992. pap. 29.95 (0-9622182-1-9) Lifestyle Inst.

Auriculas. Brenda Hyatt. (Classic Garden Plants Ser.). (Illus.). 144p. 1989. 19.95 (0-87106-522-3) Globe Pequot.

Auriculotherapy Manual: Chinese & Western Systems of Ear Acupuncture. Terry Oleson. (Illus.). 178p. 1990. pap. 35.00 (0-9629415-0-6) Hlth Care Altern.

Aurier's Symbolist Art Criticism & Theory. Patricia T. Mathews. LC 85-20944. (Studies in the Fine Arts: Criticism: No. 18). (Illus.). 230p. reprint ed. pap. 65.60 (0-8357-1686-4, 2070610) Bks Demand.

Auriol: Or, the Elixir of Life. William H. Ainsworth. Ed. by R. Reginald & Douglas Menville. LC 75-46248. (Supernatural & Occult Fiction Ser.). (Illus.). 1976. reprint ed. lib. bdg. 23.95 (0-405-08108-1) Ayer.

Aurobindo, Gandhi & Roy: A Yogi, a Mahatma & a Rationalist. Niranjan Dhar. 1986. 13.50 (0-8364-1578-7, Pub. by Minerva II) S Asia.

*__Aurobindo Ghose: Revolutionary & Reformer.__ S. R. Bakshi. (C). 1994. text ed. 26.00 (81-7041-702-3, Pub. by Anmol II) S Asia.

Aurobindo's Philosophy of Brahman. Stephen H. Phillips. xii, 200p. 1986. 41.25 (90-04-07765-0) E J Brill.

Aurobindran Yoga: A Revisioning. Som P. Ranchan. 1993. 12.95 (81-220-0308-7, Pub. by Konark Pubs Pvt Ltd II) Advent Bks Div.

Aurora. Jacob Boehme. 723p. (Orig.). 1992. pap. 39.95 (1-56459-115-8) Kessinger Pub.

Aurora. A. V. Jones. LC 74-26994. (Geophysics & Astrophysics Monographs: No.9). 301p. 1974. lib. bdg. 94.00 (90-277-0272-1) Kluwer Ac.

Aurora. Michael Leiris. Tr. by Anna Warby. 1991. pap. 12.50 (0-947757-25-2) Serpents Tail.

Aurora. Michel Leiris. (Imaginaire Ser.). 193p. (FRE.). 1977. pap. 11.95 (2-07-029647-4) Schoenhof.

*__Aurora.__ Ellene Pomerantz. 450p. Date not set. pap. 12.95 (0-7610-0382-7) NW Pub.

Aurora. Joan Smith. 1987. pap. 2.95 (0-449-21533-4, Crest) Fawcett.

Aurora, No. 7. Thomas Mallon. 246p. 1992. pap. 8.95 (0-393-30848-0) Norton.

Aurora: Sun-Earth Interactions. Neil Bone. 200p. 1991. text ed. write for info. (0-13-051392-X) P-H.

Aurora: The Dayspring, or Dawning of the Day in the East. Jacob Boehme. Ed. by C. J. Barker. Tr. by John Sparrow. 1992. reprint ed. pap. text ed. 34.95 (1-55818-181-4, Sure Fire) Holmes Pub.

*__Aurora: The Mysterious Northern Lights.__ Candace Savage. LC 94-1458. (Illus.). 144p. 1995. pap. 20.00 (0-87156-374-6) Sierra.

Aurora: The Mysterious Northern Lights. Candace C. Savage. LC 94-1458. 144p. 1994. 25.00 (0-87156-419-X) Sierra.

Aurora: The Pentagon's Secret Hypersonic Spyplane. Bill Sweetman. 1993. pap. 9.95 (0-87938-780-7) Motorbooks Intl.

Aurora Australis. Ernest Shackleton. (Antarctic Classics Ser.). (Illus.). 216p. (C). 1989. reprint ed. pap. 51.00 (0-948285-06-0, Pub. by Archival Facs UK) St Mut.

Aurora Bligh & Early Poems. Mary Fabilli. 1968. 5.00 (0-685-04661-3); pap. 2.50 (0-685-04662-1) Oyez.

Aurora Borealis. S. I. Akasofu. Ed. by Robert A. Henning et al. LC 72-92087. (Alaska Geographic Ser.: Vol. 6, No. 2). (Illus.). 95p. 1979. reprint ed. pap. 19.95 (0-88240-124-6) Alaska Geog Soc.

Aurora Consurgens, a Document Attributed to Thomas Aquinas on the Problem of Opposites in Alchemy. St. Thomas Aquinas. Ed. by Marie-Louise Von Franz. Tr. by R. F. Hull. LC 65-10405. 571p. reprint ed. pap. 162.80 (0-8357-5884-2, 2051598) Bks Demand.

*__Aurora Dawn.__ Herman Wouk. 1994. lib. bdg. 24.95x (1-56849-404-1) Buccaneer Bks.

Aurora Dawn. Herman Wouk. 288p. 1992. pap. 9.95 (0-316-95509-4) Little.

Aurora de la Redencion del Mundo. Erich Sauer. Orig. Title: The Dawn of World Redemption. 304p. (SPA.). 1967. pap. 9.50 (0-8254-1652-3) Kregel.

Aurora-Elgin Area Streetcars & Interurbans, 4 vols., Set. Hopkins S. Peffers. (Illus.). 776p. 1993. 198.00 (1-883461-05-7) Am Slide-Chart.

Aurora-Elgin Area Streetcars & Interurbans, Vol. 2: Aurora Elgin & Fox River Electric. Hopkins S. Peffers. (Illus.). 184p. 1993. 49.50 (1-883461-02-2) Am Slide-Chart.

Aurora-Elgin Area Streetcars & Interurbans, Vol. 1: Fox River Division. Hopkins S. Peffers. (Illus.). 168p. 1993. 49.50 (1-883461-01-4) Am Slide-Chart.

Aurora-Elgin Area Streetcars & Interurbans, Vol. 4: The Connecting Lines. Hopkins S. Peffers. (Illus.). 200p. 1993. 49.50 (1-883461-04-9) Am Slide-Chart.

Aurora-Elgin Area Streetcars & Interurbans, Vol. 3: The Third Rail Line. Hopkins S. Peffers. (Illus.). 224p. 1993. 49.50 (1-883461-03-0) Am Slide-Chart.

Aurora en Copacabana. Pedro Calderon de la Barca. (Textos Ser.: Series B, No. 36). (Illus.). 224p. (SPA.). (C). 1995. text ed. 53.00 (1-85566-015-6, Pub. by Tamesis Bks Ltd UK) Boydell & Brewer.

Aurora Leigh. Elizabeth Barrett Browning. 351p. 1992. pap. 12.00 (0-915864-85-1) Academy Chi Pubs.

Aurora Leigh. Elizabeth Barrett Browning. Ed. by Margaret Reynolds. LC 90-47489. (Illus.). 700p. 1991. text ed. 69.95 (0-8214-0956-5) Ohio U Pr.

Aurora Leigh. Elizabeth Barrett Browning. LC 92-28006. (World's Classics Ser.). 408p. 1993. pap. 11.95 (0-19-282875-4) OUP.

Aurora Leigh. Elizabeth Barrett Browning. Ed. by Margaret Reynolds. (Critical Editions Ser.). (C). 1994. pap. text ed. 12.95 (0-393-96298-9) Norton.

Aurora Means Dawn. Scott R. Sanders. LC 88-24127. (Illus.). 32p. (J). (gr. 1-5). 1989. text ed. 13.95 (0-02-778270-0, Bradbury S&S) S&S Childrens.

Aurora N. A. C. E. Cookbook 1994-1995. Anchorage Chapter National Assoc. of Catering Executives Staff. (Illus.). 200p. 1994. 15.00 (1-884234-01-1) Penmanship Plus.

Aurora of North Manitou Island. Donna Winters. Ed. by Anne Severance. (Great Lakes Romances Ser.). 288p. (Orig.). 1993. pap. 9.95 (0-923048-81-2) Bigwater Pub.

Aurora of the Philosophers. Paracelsus. Tr. by A. E. Waite. 1985. reprint ed. pap. 3.95 (0-916411-50-8) Holmes Pub.

Aurora Quest. James Axler. (Earthblood Ser.). 1994. mass mkt. 4.99 (0-373-63809-4, 1-63809-7) Harlequin Bks.

Aurora Se Acerca: The Dawn is Coming. Oswald Smith. (SPA.). 3.25 (84-7645-253-5, 223300, Pub. by Edit Clie SP) TSELF.

*__Aurora Sedeera Coralis.__ B. A. Willis. 500p. 1995. pap. 12.95 (0-7610-0144-1) NW Pub.

Aurora Stained Glass Patterns, Bk. 1: Knights & Dragons, etc. Amy Flores. (Illus.). 32p. (Orig.). 1985. pap. 6.95 (0-913417-01-7, F701) Aurora Pubns.

Aurora Stained Glass Patterns, Bk. 2: Frames & Mirrors. Amy Flores. (Illus.). 32p. (Orig.). 1985. pap. 6.95 (0-913417-02-5, F702) Aurora Pubns.

Aurora, Their Last Utopia: Oregon's Christian Commune, 1856-1883. Eugene E. Snyder. LC 93-74148. 148p. 1993. 19.95 (0-8323-0506-5); pap. 12.95 (0-8323-0507-3) Binford Mort.

Aurora Watcher's Handbook. T. Neil Davis. LC 91-43080. (Illus.). x, 231p. 1992. 35.00 (0-912006-59-5); pap. 20.00 (0-912006-60-9) U of Alaska Pr.

Auroral Phenomena: Experiments & Theory, Proceedings of the Lockheed Research Symposium on Space Science, 1st, Palo Alto, Calif., 1964. Lockheed Research Symposium on Space Science Staff. Ed. by Martin Walt. LC 78-17993. 180p. reprint ed. pap. 51.30 (0-8357-5885-0, 2015528) Bks Demand.

Auroral Physics. Ed. by C. I. Meng et al. (Illus.). 600p. (C). 1991. 140.00 (0-521-38049-9) Cambridge U Pr.

Auroral Plasma Dynamics. Ed. by Robert L. Lysak. LC 93-43462. (Geophysical Monograph Ser.: No. 80). 1993. 57.00 (0-87590-039-9) Am Geophysical.

Aurora's Motive: A Novel. Erich Hackl. Tr. by Edna McCown. LC 88-45318. 112p. 1989. 15.95 (0-394-57328-5) Knopf.

Aurora's Whole Realm Catalog. Anne B. Brown. (Advanced Dungeons & Dragons, Second Edition; Al-Qadim Ser.). (Illus.). 1992. pap. 7.95 (1-56076-327-2) TSR Inc.

Aurore Sourcebook. William N. Keith, Jr. (Traveller: 2300 Ser.: No. 2300). 96p. (Orig.). 1987. pap. 10.00 (0-943580-37-4) Game Designers.

Aurum Potabile, or the Receipt of Doctor Father Antonie. 1984. reprint ed. pap. 2.95 (0-916411-95-8) Holmes Pub.

Aus Alten Zeiten (Nimrods Tagebuch) Charles J. Apperley. (Documenta Hippologica Ser.). xvi, 245p. (GER.). 1992. reprint ed. write for info. (3-487-08161-X, Pub. by Georg Olms GW) Lubrecht & Cramer.

Aus Altromischen Priesterbuchern. Eduard Norden. LC 75-10644. (Ancient Religion & Mythology Ser.). (GER.). 1976. reprint ed. 25.95 (0-405-07019-5) Ayer.

Aus dem Leben der Deuschen Juden im Mittelalter. Abraham Berliner. Ed. by Steven Katz. LC 79-7127. (Jewish Philosophy, Mysticism & History of Ideas Ser.). 1980. reprint ed. lib. bdg. 17.95 (0-405-12241-1) Ayer.

Aus Dem Leben des Buchhandlers. Philipp E. Reich. reprint ed. write for info. (0-318-71732-8, Pub. by Georg Olms GW) Lubrecht & Cramer.

Aus Dem Schwarzspanierhause: Erinnerungen an Ludwig van Beethoven Aus Meiner Jugendzeit. Gerhard V. Breuning. viii, 221p. 1970. reprint ed. write for info. (0-318-71888-X, Pub. by Georg Olms GW) Lubrecht & Cramer.

Aus dem Tagebuch eines Emigranten und Anderes Osterreichisches Aus Amerika. Alfred Farau. LC 91-31472. (Austrian Culture Ser.: Vol. 4). 245p. (C). 1992. text ed. 49.95 (0-8204-1631-2) P Lang Pubs.

Aus Den Briefen der Herzogin Elisabeth Charlotte von Orleans An Die Kurfurstin Sophie von Hannover, 2 vols., Set. Elisabeth C. Von Orleans. 851p. reprint ed. write for info. (0-318-71458-2, Pub. by Georg Olms GW) Lubrecht & Cramer.

Aus Den Briefen der Herzogin Elisabeth Charlotte von Orleans An Etienne Polier De Bottens. Elisabeth C. Von Orleans. No. 231. 131p. reprint ed. write for info. (0-318-71457-4, Pub. by Georg Olms GW) Lubrecht & Cramer.

Aus Den Lebenserinnerungen. Hans Herzfeld. Ed. by Willy Real. (Veroeffentlichungen der Historischen Kommission zu Berlin, Band 67, Beitraege zu Inflation und Wiederaufbau in Deutschland und Europa 1914-1924: Vol. 81). x, 219p. (GER.). (C). 1992. lib. bdg. 36.95 (3-11-013520-5, 102-92) De Gruyter.

Aus Goldenem Kelch see Paymaneh-ye Zarin

Aus Lydien. Karl Buresch. (Subsidia Epigraphica Ser.: Vol. VII). xv, 226p. (GER.). 1977. reprint ed. write for info. (3-487-06264-X, Pub. by Georg Olms GW) Lubrecht & Cramer.

Aus Meinem Leben. E. Fischer. (Illus.). 260p. 1987. 56.00 (0-387-18002-8) Spr-Verlag.

Aus Schleiermachers Leben, in Briefen, 4 vols. F. Schleiermacher. xxxvi, 2006p. (GER.). (C). 1974. reprint ed. 480.75 (3-11-002261-3) De Gruyter.

Aus Theorie und Praxis der Geschichtswissenschaft: Festschrift fur Hans Herzfeld zum 80, Geburtstag. Ed. by Dietrich Kurze. (Veroeffentlichungen der Historischen Kommission zu Berlin, Band 67, Beitraege zu Inflation und Wiederaufbau in Deutschland und Europa 1914-1924: Vol. 37). xii, 445p. (GER.). (C). 1972. 192.30 (3-11-003813-7) De Gruyter.

Aus Unserer Zeit. 4th ed. Ed. by Ian C. Loram & Leland R. Phelps. (GER.). (C). 1988. pap. text ed. 19.95 (0-393-95614-8) Norton.

Ausable River, NY. Paul Marriner. (River Journal Ser.: Vol. 1, No. 4). (Illus.). 48p. 1994. pap. 14.95 (1-878175-43-2) F Amato Pubns.

Ausar Auset Nutrition Handbook. Ra Un Nefer Amen. 54p. (Orig.). 1988. pap. 6.00 (0-317-93991-2) Khamit.

Ausburg Confession: Anniversary Edition. Ed. & Tr. by Theodore G. Tappert. 64p. 1980. pap. 4.50 (0-8006-1385-6, 1-1385, Fortress Pr) Augsburg Fortress.

Auschwitz: A Doctor's Eyewitness Account. Miklow Nyiszli. Tr. by Tibere Kramer & Richard Seaver. 240p. (C). 1993. reprint ed. pap. 10.95 (1-55970-202-8) Arcade Pub Inc.

Auschwitz: A History in Photographs. Comp. by Teresa Swiebocka. LC 93-1083. (Illus.). 1993. 59.95 (0-253-35581-8) Ind U Pr.

Auschwitz: A Judge Looks at the Evidence. 2nd ed. Wilhelm Staeglich. Tr. by Thomas Francis. (Illus.). 376p. 1990. 19.95 (0-939484-32-3); pap. 11.95 (0-939484-33-1) Inst Hist Rev.

Auschwitz: True Tales from a Grotesque Land. Sara Nomberg-Przytyk. Ed. by Eli Pfefferkorn & David Hirsch. Tr. by Roslyn Hirsch. LC 84-17386. xii, 185p. 1985. pap. 9.95 (0-8078-4160-9) U of NC Pr.

Auschwitz - Beginning of a New Era? Reflections on the Holocaust. Ed. by E. Fleischner. 35.00 (0-87068-499-X); pap. 19.95 (0-685-02907-7) Ktav.

*__Auschwitz & After.__ Charlotte Delbo. Tr. by Rosette C. Lamont. 1995. write for info. (0-300-06208-7) Yale U Pr.

*__Auschwitz & After: Race, Culture & "The Jewish Question" in France.__ Ed. by Lawrence D. Kritzman. LC 94-27397. 1994. 55.00 (0-415-90440-4, A5762) Routledge.

*__Auschwitz & After: Race, Culture & "the Jewish Question" in France.__ Ed. by Lawrence D. Kritzman. LC 94-27397. 384p. 1994. pap. 17.95 (0-415-90441-2, A5766) Routledge.

Auschwitz & the Allies. Martin Gilbert. LC 80-28911. 368p. 1990. pap. 15.95 (0-8050-1462-4, Owl) H Holt & Co.

Auschwitz As Revelation. Michael B. Buser. LC 74-83300. 61p. reprint ed. pap. 25.00 (0-7837-6308-5, 2046023) Bks Demand.

Auschwitz Chimneys Smoke. rev. ed. M. Burk Necker. (Illus.). 140p. 1993. pap. 12.50 (1-877582-19-0) Ardor Pub.

Auschwitz Chronicle, Nineteen Thirty-Nine to Nineteen Forty-Five. Danuta Czech. LC 89-35351. (Illus.). 880p. 1990. 125.00 (0-8050-0938-8) H Holt & Co.

*__Auschwitz: The End of a Legend: A Critique of Jean-Claude Pressac.__ Carlo Mattogno. Tr. by Russ Granata. (Illus.). xiii, 138p. (Orig.). (C). 1994. pap. 12.95 (0-939484-50-1) Inst Hist Rev.

Auschwitz: The End of a Legend: How Was Such Mass Murder Technically Possible? Carlo Mattogno. (Critique on Pressac's Auschwitz Bks.). 150p. 1994. pap. 20.00 (0-9640716-0-6) Granata Pubng.

An Asterisk (*) at the beginning of an entry indicates that the title is appearing in BIP for the first time.

***Auschwitz 1940-1945.** rev. ed. Kazimierz Smolen. LC 95-67556. 125p. Date not set. reprint ed. pap. 8.95 (*0-9644293-1-4*) Route Sixty-Six.

Auscultation of the Heart. 3rd ed. Abe Ravin et al. LC 76-53227. 297p. reprint ed. pap. 84.70 (*0-8357-5886-9*, 2026506) Bks Demand.

Ausdrucke fur den Begriff des Wissens in der Vorplatonischen. Bruno Snell. LC 75-13295. (History of Ideas in Ancient Greece Ser.). (GER.). 1976. reprint ed. 12.95 (*0-405-07339-9*) Ayer.

Ausdrucksfunktion Extrem Verkurzter Figren. Kurt Rathe. (Warburg Institute Studies: Vol. 8). 1972. reprint ed. 30.00 (*0-8115-1386-6*) Periodicals Srv.

Auseinandersetzungen an der Pariser Universitaet im XIII Jahrhundert. (Miscellanea Mediaevalia Ser.: Vol. 10). (C). 1976. 173.10 (*3-11-005986-X*) De Gruyter.

Ausfuhrliches Handbuch der Photographie: 1891-93, 4 Vols., Set. Joseph M. Eder. (Illus.). 476p. 1933. reprint ed. pap. 300.00 (*0-87556-594-8*) Saifer.

Ausfuhrliches Lexikon der Griechischen und Romischen Mythologie, 10 vols. Wilhelm H. Roscher. (GER.). 1992. reprint ed. write for info. (*3-487-00915-3*, Pub. by Georg Olms GW) Lubrecht & Cramer.

Ausgefuhrte Bauten Und Entwurfe Von Frank Lloyd Wright see Drawings & Plans of Frank Lloyd Wright: The Early Period (1893-1909)

Ausgewaehlte Desserts. Olli Leeb. (Illus.). 197p. (GER.). 1985. 20.50 (*3-921799-84-8*, Pub. by Olli Leeb GW) Lubrecht & Cramer.

Ausgewaehlte Kapitel aus der Funktionentheorie. Wolfgang Fischer & Ingo Lieb. (Vieweg Studium: Aufbaukurs Mathematik Ser.: Vol. 48). (Illus.). ix, 328p. (GER.). (C). 1989. pap. 46.00 (*3-528-07248-2*, Pub. by Vieweg & Sohn GW) Ballen Bkslr.

Ausgewaehlte Sammlung Motetten Zu 4, 5, 6 und 8 Stimmen. Gregor Langius. Ed. by Reinhold Starke. Vol. XXV. (GER & LAT.). 1967. reprint ed. write for info. (*0-318-51196-7*) Broude.

Ausgewaehlte Werke. Johann C. Gottsched. Ed. by P. M. Mitchell. Incl. Vol. 1. Gedichte und Gedichtuebertragungen. vi, 533p. 1968. 352.00 (*3-11-000351-1*); Vol. 2. Saemtliche Dramen. iv, 481p. 1970. 315.00 (*3-11-000363-5*); Vol. 3. Saemtliche Dramenuebertragungen. vi, 393p. 1970. 259.00 (*3-11-000364-3*); Vol. 4. 481p. 1968. 315.00 (*3-11-000353-8*); (Ausgaben Deutscher Literatur des Fuenfzehnten bis Achtzehnten Jahrhunderts Ser.). (GER.). write for info. (*0-318-51612-8*) De Gruyter.

Ausgewaehlte Werke, Vol. 11. Johann C. Gottsched. 164p. (GER.). 1983. 113.85 (*3-11-007934-8*) De Gruyter.

Ausgewahlt Reden, 2 vols. in 1. Lysias. viii, 310p. 1963. write for info. (*3-296-14510-9*, Pub. by Georg Olms GW) Lubrecht & Cramer.

Ausgewahlte Kleine Schriften. Karl Deichgraber. x, 414p. 1984. write for info. (*3-615-00002-1*, Pub. by Georg Olms GW) Lubrecht & Cramer.

Ausgewahlte Kleine Schriften. Hans Drexler. (Collectanea Ser.: Vol. IX). viii, 436p. 1982. write for info. (*3-487-07143-6*, Pub. by Georg Olms GW) Lubrecht & Cramer.

Ausgewahlte Komodien, 3 vols. Plautus. Ed. by August O. Lorenz. 1981. Bd. 2: Mostellaria, 239p. write for info. (*3-296-15001-3*, Pub. by Georg Olms GW); Bd. 3: Miles Gloriosus, viii, 294p. write for info. (*0-318-71196-6*, Pub. by Georg Olms GW); Bd. 4: Pseudolus, viii, 289p. write for info. (*3-296-15003-X*, Pub. by Georg Olms GW) Lubrecht & Cramer.

Ausgewahlte Komodien, 3 vols., Set. Plautus. Ed. by August O. Lorenz. 1981. write for info. (*0-318-71195-8*, Pub. by Georg Olms GW) Lubrecht & Cramer.

***Ausgewahlte Probleme der Literarischen Ubersetzung Dargestellt Anhand der Ubersetzung Mittelwalisischer Texte Ins Deutsche.** Sabine Heinz. LC 94-21530. 208p. (GER.). 1995. text ed. 89.95 (*0-7734-9032-9*) E Mellen.

Ausgewahlte Reden. Demosthenes. xxii, 690p. 1973. reprint ed. write for info. (*3-487-04823-X*, Pub. by Georg Olms GW) Lubrecht & Cramer.

Ausgewahlte Schriften: Selected Papers. Goldstein. (Phaenomenologica Ser.: No. 43). 1972. lib. bdg. 103.00 (*90-247-5047-4*) Kluwer Ac.

Ausgewahlte Texte der Isis- und Sarapis-Religion. Maria Totti. (Subsidia Epigraphica Ser.: Bd. XII). viii, 231p. (GER.). 1985. write for info. (*3-487-07678-0*, Pub. by Georg Olms GW) Lubrecht & Cramer.

***Ausgezeichnete Autor: Staeditsche Literaturpreise und Kulturpolitik in Deutschland 1926-1971.** Hanna Leitgeb. (European Cultures Ser.: No. 4). 436p. (GER.). (C). 1994. lib. bdg. 124.65 (*3-11-014402-6*) De Gruyter.

Ausgrabungen von Khor Dehmit bis Bet el-Wali. Herbert Ricke et al. LC 68-15933. (Oriental Institute Nubian Expedition Publications: Vol. 2). (Illus.). 1968. lib. bdg. 30.00 (*0-226-62366-1*, OINE2) U Ch Pr.

Ausias March: Selected Poems. Ausias March. Ed. by Arthur Terry. LC 76-29514. (Edinburgh Bilingual Library). 1977. 20.00 (*0-292-70323-6*) Lib Soc Sci.

Ausman & Snyder's Medical Library, 11 vols. suppl. ed. 1993. Suppl. 1993. write for info. (*0-318-67052-6*) Lawyers Cooperative.

Ausman & Snyder's Medical Library, 11 vols., Set. write for info. (*0-318-67051-8*) Lawyers Cooperative.

AUSMAP Atlas of Australia. Ken Johnson. (Illus.). 96p. (C). 1993. pap. 33.50 (*0-521-42122-5*) Cambridge U Pr.

Ausonius: Concordantia in Ausonium, with Indices to Proper Nouns & Greek Forms. Ed. by L. J. Bolchazy & J. M. Sweeny. (Alpha-Omega, Reihe A Ser.: Bd. XLV). 908p. 1982. 154.70 (*3-487-07156-8*, Pub. by Georg Olms GW) Lubrecht & Cramer.

Ausonius of Bordeaux: Genesis of a Gallic Aristocracy. Hagith Sivan. LC 92-16629. (Illus.). 272p. 1993. 59.95 (*0-415-08614-0*, A9922, Routledge NY) Routledge.

***Auspicious Music in a Changing Society: Damai Musicians of Nepal.** Carol Tingey. (C). 1994. 48.00 (*81-7026-193-7*, Pub. by Heritage IA) S Asia.

***Auspicious Music in a Changing Society: The Damai Musicians of Nepal.** Carol Tingey. (C). 1994. 80.00 (*0-7286-0220-2*, Pub. by Sch Orient & African Stud UK) S Asia.

Auspicious Wisdom: The Texts & Traditions of Srividya Sakta Tantrism in South India. Douglas R. Brooks. LC 91-31730. (SUNY Series in Tantric Studies). 301p. 1992. 49.50 (*0-7914-1145-1*); pap. 16.95 (*0-7914-1146-X*) State U NY Pr.

Ausra, Jubiliejine Stovykla. Ed. by Juozas Toliusis. (Illus.). 72p. (LIT.). (J). (gr. 1 up). 1983. pap. write for info. (*0-9611488-1-0*) Lith Scouts.

Aussere Wirtschaftspolitik Osterreich-Ungarns: Mitteleuropaische Plane. Gustav Gratz & Richard Schuller. (Wirtschafts-Und Sozialgeschichte des Weltkrieges (Osterreichische Und Ungarische Serie)). (GER.). 1925. 150.00 (*0-317-27415-5*) Elliots Bks.

Aussie Boys: And Other True Homosexual Experiences from down Under. Rusty Winter. 192p. (Orig.). 1995. pap. 14.95 (*0-943595-01-0*) Leyland Pubns.

Aussie Hot: And Other True Homosexual Experiences. Rusty Winter. 160p. (Orig.). 1995. pap. 14.95 (*0-943595-13-4*) Leyland Pubns.

Aussie Soft Toys. Evelyn O'Neill. (Lothian Australian Craft Ser.). (Illus.). 64p. (Orig.). 1995. pap. 14.95 (*0-85091-483-3*, Pub. by Lothian Pub AT) Seven Hills Bk.

Aussprache des Fruehneuhochdeutschen nach Lesemeistern des 16. Jahrhunderts. Sigrid D. Painter. (Berkeley Insights in Linguistics & Semiotics Ser.: Vol. 1). 200p. 1989. text ed. 39.95 (*0-8204-0498-5*) P Lang Pubs.

Ausspracheworterbuch. (Duden Ser.: Vol. 6). 794p. 1993. 29.95 (*3-411-20916-X*, Pub. by Bibliogr Inst Brockhaus GW) Langenscheidt.

Austempered Ductile Iron: Your Means to Improved Performance, Productivity & Cost. International Conference on Austempered Ductile Iron (1st: 1984: Rosemont & Chicago, IL) Staff. LC 84-73332. (Illus.). 347p. reprint ed. pap. 98.90 (*0-8357-5887-7*, 2056399) Bks Demand.

Austempered Ductile Iron: Your Means to Improved Performance, Productivity & Cost: 2nd International Conference, 17-19 March 1986, Rackham School, University of Michigan, Ann Arbor, MI. International Conference on Austemperd Ductile Iron Staff. LC 86-71752. (Illus.). 454p. reprint ed. pap. 129.40 (*0-7837-5196-6*, 2057066) Bks Demand.

Austen Chamberlain: Gentleman in Politics. David Dutton. 373p. 1986. 39.95 (*0-685-12367-7*) Transaction Pubs.

***Austen Chamberlain Diary Letters: The Correspondence of Sir Austen Chamberlain with His Sisters Hilda & Ida, 1916-1937.** Ed. by Robert C. Self. (Camden Fifth Ser.: No. 5). 350p. (C). 1995. write for info. (*0-521-55157-9*) Cambridge U Pr.

Austenitic Stainless Steels: Microstructure & Mechanical Properties. Ed. by P. Marshall. 444p. 1984. 106.25 (*0-85334-277-6*, I-262-84, Pub. by Elsevier Applied Sci UK) Elsevier.

Austere Landscape: The Paintings of Hung-Jen. Jason C. Kuo. (Illus.). 288p. (Orig.). 1991. 39.95 (*957-9482-11-X*) U of Wash Pr.

Austerities. Charles Simic. LC 82-4289. (Braziller Poetry Ser.). 64p. 1982. 7.95 (*0-8076-1043-7*); pap. 4.95 (*0-8076-1044-5*) Braziller.

***Austerity.** Dan Siegel. 250p. 1995. pap. 8.95 (*0-7610-0035-6*) NW Pub.

Austerity Management in Academic Libraries. Ed. by John F. Harvey & Peter Spyers-Duran. LC 83-14428. 304p. 1984. text ed. 35.00 (*0-8108-1648-2*) Scarecrow.

Austerlitz, 1805. David Chandler. (Campaign Ser.: No. 2). (Illus.). 96p. 1990. pap. 14.95 (*0-85045-957-5*, 9501, Pub. by Osprey Pubng Ltd UK) Stackpole.

Austernpilz (Polyporaceae) Kochbuch: Ueber 100 Gerichte und Zubereitungstips mit Austernpilzen. Nora Richter. (Illus.). 72p. (GER.). 1984. pap. 7.50 (*0-318-19268-3*) Lubrecht & Cramer.

Austin. Dave Oliphant. 160p. (Orig.). 1985. lib. bdg. 13.95 (*0-933384-16-5*); pap. 9.95 (*0-933384-15-7*) Prickly Pear.

***Austin.** Photos & Text by Laurence Parent. LC 94-43909. (Texas Monthly Sights & Scenes Ser.). 64p. 1995. pap. 7.95 (*0-87719-260-X*, 9260) Gulf Pub.

Austin. 3rd ed. Richard Zelade. (Texas Monthly Guidebooks Ser.). 360p. 1992. pap. 16.95 (*0-87719-207-3*) Gulf Pub.

Austin: Its Architects & Architecture. 1986. pap. 14.95 (*0-9617412-0-1*) AIA Austin.

Austin: Lone Star Rising. John T. Davis & J. B. Colson. (Urban Tapestry Ser.). (Illus.). 350p. 1994. 39.50 (*1-881096-08-4*) Towery Pub.

Austin: The Son Becomes Father. Mary D. Wade. (Illus.). 64p. (J). (gr. 3-5). 1993. 10.95 (*1-882539-08-7*); teacher ed 5.00 (*1-882539-10-9*); pap. 4.95 (*1-882539-09-5*) Colophon Hse.

***Austin Affair.** D. J. Pollack. 276p. 1994. 19.95 (*1-55793-041-4*) Guild Bindery Pr.

Austin Album. Audray Bateman. (Illus.). 1979. 25.00 (*0-88426-056-9*) Encino Pr.

Austin & the Reese River Mining District: Nevada's Forgotten Frontier. Donald R. Abbe. LC 84-20966. (Wilbur S. Shepperson Series in History & Humanities: No. 19). (Illus.). 128p. (Orig.). 1985. pap. 10.95 (*0-87417-091-5*) U of Nev Pr.

Austin & Travis County: A Pictorial History, 1839-1939. Katherine Hart. (Waterloo Book Ser.). (Illus.). 168p. 1975. 25.00 (*0-88426-045-3*) Encino Pr.

Austin City Limits. Clifford Endres. LC 86-27215. (Illus.). 136p. 1987. 24.95 (*0-292-70378-3*); pap. 15.95 (*0-292-70398-8*) U of Tex Pr.

Austin Clarke: A Reference Guide. Lorraine Ricigliano. LC 92-42514. (Reference Publications in Literature). 180p. 1993. text ed. 45.00 (*0-8161-7384-2*, Hall Reference) Macmillan.

Austin Clarke 1886-1974: A Critical Introduction. Maurice Harmon. 224p. 1989. 56.00 (*0-389-20864-7*) B&N Imports.

***Austin Colony Pioneers: Including History of Bastrop, Fayette, Grimes, Montgomery & Washington Counties, Texas.** Worth S. Ray. (Illus.). 378p. 1995. reprint ed. 30.00 (*0-8063-1473-7*) Genealog Pub.

Austin Datebook. rev. ed. Kurt W. Kretsinger. 136p. 1991. 4.77 (*0-685-74013-7*) Datebook Pub.

Austin Elliot. Henry Kingsley. (BCL1-PR English Literature Ser.). 331p. 1992. reprint ed. lib. bdg. 89.00 (*0-7812-7578-4*) Rprt Serv.

Austin Environmental Handbook. Ecology Action Staff. 72p. 1994. pap. text ed. 3.00 (*0-9641303-0-0*) Ecology AOT.

Austin Farrer: The Essential Sermons. Ed. by Leslie Houlden. LC 91-8872. 211p. 1991. pap. 12.95 (*1-56101-042-1*) Cowley Pubns.

Austin-Healey Complete Official 100-Six & 3000, 1956-1968. British Leyland Motors Staff. LC 77-72588. (Illus.). 416p. (Orig.). 1977. pap. 45.00 (*0-8376-0133-9*) Bentley.

Austin-Healey Sprite MK 1 Driver's Handbook (1958-1961) British Leyland Motors, Staff. 16.00 (*0-8376-0545-8*) Bentley.

Austin-Healey 100. John Wheatley. (Super Profile Ser.). 56p. 1986. 11.95 (*0-85429-487-2*, F487, Pub. by G T Foulis Ltd) Haynes Pubns.

***Austin-Healey 100 & 3000 Series.** John Heilig. LC 95-13978. (Sports Car Color History Ser.). 1995. pap. write for info. (*0-7603-0060-7*) Motorbooks Intl.

***Austin-Healey 100 & 3000 Series.** Graham Robson. (Illus.). 200p. 1994. 35.95 (*1-85223-787-2*, Pub. by Crowood UK) Motorbooks Intl.

***Austin-Healey 100-4 Drivers.** Robert Bentley. 1994. 25.00 (*0-8376-0572-5*) Bentley.

Austin-Healey 100-4, 100-6, 3000 & Sprite Mk. I-IV, 1953-1972. Walter Zeichner. LC 89-63366. (Illus.). 96p. 1989. 19.95 (*0-88740-212-7*) Schiffer.

Austin-Healey 100-6 & 3000 All Big 6 Cylinder Models: Super Profile. John Wheatley. (Super Profile Ser.). (Illus.). 56p. 1987. 11.95 (*0-85429-574-7*, F574, Pub. by G T Foulis Ltd) Haynes Pubns.

***Austin-Healey 100-6 Drivers.** Robert Bentley. 1994. 25.00 (*0-8376-0573-3*) Bentley.

***Austin-Healey 300 Bk. 1: Handbook.** Robert Bentley. 1994. 25.00 (*0-8376-0574-1*) Bentley.

***Austin-Healey 300 Bk. 3: Handbook.** 1994. 25.00 (*0-8376-0575-X*) Bentley.

Austin Heritage Cook Book. Illus. by J. U. Salvant. 410p. Date not set. 12.95 (*0-9609134-0-8*) Herit Soc Austin.

***Austin Job Guide.** Madeline Bailey. (Illus.). 76p. (Orig.). 1992. pap. text ed. 12.95 (*0-9639688-0-7*) Q C C.

Austin Natural Science Association & Austin Natural Science Association Guild Yearbook, 1989-90. Ed. & Illus. by Silent Partners, Inc. Staff. 102p. (Orig.). 1989. pap. write for info. (*1-878353-07-1*) Silent Partners.

Austin Originals: Chats with Colorful Characters. Robyn Turner. (Illus.). 176p. 1982. 10.00 (*0-942376-05-6*) Paramount TX.

Austin Robinson: The Life of an Economic Advisor. Alec Cairncross. LC 92-36201. 256p. 1993. text ed. 69.95 (*0-312-09471-X*) St Martin.

Austin Seven Source Book. Bryan Purves. (Source Book Ser.). (Illus.). 592p. 1990. 150.00 (*0-85429-557-7*, Pub. by J H Haynes & Co UK) Motorbooks Intl.

Austin Seven Specials. 2nd ed. L. M. Williams. (Illus.). 176p. 1994. 29.95 (*0-85429-955-6*, Pub. by J H Haynes & Co UK) Motorbooks Intl.

Austin Sketchbook. Tony Crosby. (Illus.). 1978. 20.00 (*0-88426-053-4*) Encino Pr.

Austin, Vol. 1: The Pictorial. Lee E. Line et al. Ed. by Patrick D. Hudspeth & Barbara V. Cooke. 68p. (Orig.). 1989. 16.00 (*0-317-93913-0*); pap. 8.00 (*0-317-93914-9*) Strictly TX Inc.

Austin Weddings. 6th rev. ed. Gerri Samuels. (Coopwood & Fields Consumer Planning Guide Ser.). 208p. 1994. pap. 14.95 (*1-878991-13-2*) I Do Pub.

Austinian Theory of Law: Being an Edition of Lectures I, V, & VI of Austin's "Jurisprudence," & of Austin's "Essay on the Uses of the Study of Jurisprudence" with Critical Notes & Excursus. W. Jethro Brown. LC 83-22935. xv, 383p. 1983. reprint ed. lib. bdg. 37.50 (*0-8377-0342-5*) Rothman.

Austin's Hyde Park...the First 50 Years: 1891-1941. Sarah Sitton & Thad Sitton. 1993. pap. 9.25 (*0-9629206-0-6*) Hyde Pk Pubng.

***Austraica & Judaica: Essays & Translations.** Harry Zohn. LC 94-26810. (Austrian Culture Ser.: 15). 1995. write for info. (*0-8204-2567-2*) P Lang Pubs.

Australasia. Alfred R. Wallace. Ed. by A. H. Keane. LC 77-86976. 1977. reprint ed. 52.00 (*0-404-16785-3*) AMS Pr.

Australasian Caliciales. Leif Tibell. (Illus.). 280p. (Orig.). 1987. pap. 62.00x (*91-554-1987-9*, Pub. by Uppsala Univ Acta Univ Uppsaliensis SW) Coronet Bks.

Australasian Chalcidoidea (Hymenoptera) Z. Boucek. 832p. 1988. text ed. 190.00 (*0-85198-607-2*) CAB Intl.

Australasian Computerized Legal Information Handbook. G. Greenleaf et al. 1988. pap. 55.00 (*0-409-49445-3*) Butterworth Legal Pubs.

Australasian England. E. E. Morris. 1970. 59.95 (*0-87968-678-2*) Gordon Pr.

Australasian Marsupials & Monotremes: An Action Plan for Their Conservation. Ed. by M. Kennedy. 120p. 1992. 20.00 (*2-8317-0052-3*, Pub. by IUCN SZ) Island Pr.

Australasian Port & Harbour Conference, 4th, 1992: Shaping the Port of the Future. Intro. by N. V. Lawson. (Illus.). 315p. (Orig.). 1992. pap. 72.00 (*0-85825-555-3*) Accents Pubns.

Australasian Port & Harbour Engineering Conference, Third, 1990. Intro. by Bob Jones. (Illus.). 200p. (Orig.). 1990. pap. 62.50 (*0-85825-503-0*) Accents Pubns.

Australasian Serials: Current Developments in Bibliography. Ed. by Carol Mills & John Mills. LC 91-24326. (Australian & New Zealand Journal of Serials Librarianship). (Illus.). 93p. 1991. lib. bdg. 24.95 (*1-56024-195-0*) Haworth Pr.

Australasian Tax Reports, 19 vols. Butterworths Staff. Australia. ring bd. 1,419.00 (*0-409-42421-8*) Butterworth Legal Pubs.

Australasian Tokens & Coins. A. Andrews. (Illus.). 1982. reprint ed. lib. bdg. 35.00 (*0-942666-10-0*) S J Durst.

***Australia.** (American Geographical Society Around the World Program Ser.). 1994. lib. bdg. 17.95 (*0-614-04840-0*) Am Geographical.

***Australia.** (American Geographical Society Around the World Program Ser.). 1994. pap. 9.95 (*0-614-04841-9*) Am Geographical.

Australia. Caroline Aldrich-Langen. LC 83-19723. (World Education Ser.). (Illus.). 276p. (Orig.). 1983. pap. text ed. 12.00 (*0-910054-78-9*) Am Assn Coll Registrars.

***Australia.** Helen Arnold. LC 95-15225. (Postcards From Ser.). (J). 1995. write for info. (*0-8172-4010-1*) Raintree Steck-V.

Australia. Donna Bailey. LC 89-26124. (Where We Live Ser.). (Illus.). 32p. (J). (gr. 1-4). 1990. lib. bdg. 19.97 (*0-8114-2547-9*); pap. 3.95 (*0-8114-7175-6*) Raintree Steck-V.

Australia. Peter Cranshaw. LC 88-18426. (People & Places Ser.). (Illus.). 48p. (J). (gr. 4-8). 1988. lib. bdg. 12.95 (*0-382-09511-1*) Silver Burdett Pr.

Australia. Laura Dolce. (Let's Visit Places & Peoples of the World Ser.). (Illus.). 128p. (J). (gr. 5 up). 1990. 14.95 (*0-7910-1105-4*) Chelsea Hse.

***Australia.** Driving Tour. (Driving Tours Ser.). 1995. pap. 18.00 (*0-02-860073-8*) Macmillan.

Australia. Dan Garrett. LC 89-21726. (World in View Ser.). (Illus.). 96p. (YA). (gr. 6-12). 1990. lib. bdg. 24.26 (*0-8114-2429-4*) Raintree Steck-V.

Australia. D. V. Georges. LC 86-9587. (New True Bks.). (Illus.). 48p. (J). (gr. k-4). 1986. lib. bdg. 12.90 (*0-516-01290-8*); pap. 4.95 (*0-516-41290-6*) Childrens.

Australia. Helen Jonsen. (Language & Travel Guides Ser.). 250p. (Orig.). 1994. pap. 14.95 (*0-7818-0166-4*) Hippocrene Bks.

Australia. Emilie U. Lepthien. LC 82-4541. (Enchantment of the World Ser.). (Illus.). (J). (gr. 5-9). 1982. lib. bdg. 20.55 (*0-516-02751-4*) Childrens.

Australia. Jo E. Moore. (Illus.). 16p. (J). (gr. 3-6). 1993. pap. 5.95 (*1-55799-243-6*) Evan-Moor Corp.

Australia. Martin Nabhan. (World Partners Ser.). (Illus.). 64p. (YA). (gr. 7 up). 1990. lib. bdg. 17.27 (*0-86593-088-0*); lib. bdg. 12.95 (*0-685-36362-7*) Rourke Corp.

Australia. Lewis K. Parker. LC 94-4249. (Dropping in On Ser.). (J). 1994. write for info. (*1-55916-007-1*) Rourke Bk Co.

Australia. Vijeya Rajendra. LC 91-15864. (Cultures of the World Ser.: Group 3). (Illus.). 128p. (J). (gr. 5-9). 1991. lib. bdg. 21.95 (*1-85435-400-0*) Marshall Cavendish.

Australia. Ed. by Fran Ringold. 160p. 1993. pap. 6.95 (*0-685-65045-6*) Art & Human Council Tulsa.

Australia. Laurence Santrey. LC 84-2636. (Illus.). 32p. (J). (gr. 3-6). 1985. lib. bdg. 9.49 (*0-8167-0124-5*); pap. text ed. 2.95 (*0-8167-0125-3*) Troll Assocs.

Australia. rev. ed. Comp. by Nelles Verlag. (Nelles Guides Ser.). (Illus.). 256p. 1992. pap. 14.95 (*3-88618-372-6*, Pub. by Nelles Verlag GW) Seven Hills Bk.

Australia. 2nd ed. R. L. Heathcote. LC 93-36287. 1994. pap. text ed. 46.95 (*0-470-23344-3*) Halsted Pr.

Australia: A Cultural History. Rickard. (Present & the Past Ser.). (Illus.). 309p. (Orig.). (C). 1988. pap. text ed. 29.50 (*0-582-49330-7*, 73580) Longman.

Australia: A Picture Book to Remember. rev. ed. 1991. 6.99 (*0-517-25021-7*) Random Hse Value.

Australia: A Reader's Guide. Ed. by Peter Browne. (Illus.). 200p. 1995. 40.00 (*1-875589-24-4*) D W Thorpe.
This bibliographic survey of Australia's greatest writers & their works covers some 1,500 titles on every imaginable subject. From flights of fantasy to fact-based tomes...science & technology to philosophy & world religion...this comprehensive work is an essential starting point for anyone who wants to locate & select the greatest books from "down under". Each title is described in a 50-80 word annotation & accompanied by a photograph of its jacket cover.
Publisher Provided Annotation.

Australia: A Reissue of the Cambridge History of the British Empire, Vol. VII, Pt. I. Ed. by Ernest Scott. 800p. 1989. 94.95 (*0-521-35621-0*) Cambridge U Pr.

***Australia: A Travel Survival Kit.** 7th ed. Hugh Finlay et al. (Illus.). 944p. 1994. pap. 23.95 (*0-86442-233-4*) Lonely Planet.

Australia: A Traveler's Preview. Kit Lane & Art Lane. LC 89-62874. (Illus.). 80p. (Orig.). 1989. pap. 5.95 (*1-877703-15-X*) Pavilion Pr.

***Australia: Aboriginal Middens.** 70p. (Orig.). 1994. pap. 125.00 (*0-7605-0798-8*) Rector Pr.

An Asterisk (*) at the beginning of an entry indicates that the title is appearing in BIP for the first time.

531

Australia: Annual Volume Review of National Literatures. Ed. by L. A. Dobrez et al. 256p. 1980. pap. 23.00 (*0-918680-16-6*) Bagehot Council.

***Australia: Business Financing Handbook.** (Illus.). 70p. (Orig.). 1994. pap. 295.00 (*0-7605-1180-2*) Rector Pr.

Australia: Business Risk Overview. Ed. by Lewis B. Sckolnick. 125p. (Orig.). (C). 1994. pap. text ed. 495.00 (*1-57205-548-0*) Rector Pr.

Australia: Cadogan Guides. Nicholas Lush. LC 87-32998. (Illus.). 484p. (Orig.). 1988. pap. 14.95 (*0-87106-796-X*) Globe Pequot.

***Australia: Commercial Law.** 300p. (Orig.). 1994. pap. 295.00 (*0-7605-1224-8*) Rector Pr.

***Australia: Committee of the Inquiry into Defence & Defence Related Awards.** 100p. (Orig.). 1994. pap. 125.00 (*0-7605-0777-5*) Rector Pr.

***Australia: Conserving the National Estate.** 120p. (Orig.). 1994. pap. 125.00 (*0-7605-0789-9*) Rector Pr.

Australia: Country Reporter. Lewis B. Sckolnick. (Illus.). 60p. 1994. pap. 895.00 (*1-57205-182-5*) Rector Pr.

***Australia: Cultural Heritage of the Australian Alps.** 100p. (Orig.). 1994. pap. 125.00 (*0-7605-0793-7*) Rector Pr.

***Australia: Directory of New Business Opportunities.** 100p. (Orig.). 1994. pap. 125.00 (*0-7605-0778-3*) Rector Pr.

***Australia: Economic Implications of Emigration from Australia.** 100p. (Orig.). 1994. pap. 125.00 (*0-7605-0783-X*) Rector Pr.

Australia: Foreign Financing Reporter. Ed. by Lewis B. Sckolnick. (Illus.). 60p. (Orig.). 1994. pap. 225.00 (*1-57205-235-X*) Rector Pr.

Australia: Hippocrene Companion Guide. Graeme Newman & Tamsin Newman. 252p. 1992. pap. 16.95 (*0-7818-0041-2*) Hippocrene Bks.

***Australia: Immigration a Survey of the Issues.** 200p. (Orig.). 1994. pap. 145.00 (*0-7605-0782-1*) Rector Pr.

***Australia: Internal Migration 1981-1986.** 170p. (Orig.). 1994. pap. 145.00 (*0-7605-0786-4*) Rector Pr.

Australia: Land of Natural Wonders. Alberto De Larramendi Ruis. LC 94-17017. (World Heritage Ser.). (Illus.). 36p. (J). (gr. 3 up). 1994. lib. bdg. 15.00 (*0-516-08390-2*); pap. 6.95 (*0-516-48390-0*) Childrens.

***Australia: National Wilderness Inventory Handbook.** 70p. (Orig.). 1994. pap. 45.00 (*0-7605-0791-0*) Rector Pr.

Australia: OECD Economic Survey. Ed. by Lewis B. Sckolnick. (Illus.). 200p. (Orig.). (C). 1994. pap. text ed. 165.00 (*1-57205-630-4*) Rector Pr.

Australia: On the Other Side of the World. Penny Stanley-Baker. LC 87-34523. (Illus.). 38p. (J). (gr. k-5). 1988. 5.95 (*0-944589-15-4*, 154) Young Discovery Lib.

***Australia: One-Hundred-Fifty Percent R&D Tax Incentive Guide to Benefits.** 200p. (Orig.). 1994. pap. 149.95 (*0-7605-0781-3*) Rector Pr.

***Australia: Politics of Immigration.** 170p. (Orig.). 1994. pap. 125.00 (*0-7605-0785-6*) Rector Pr.

***Australia: Sites & Bytes: Recording Aboriginal Places.** 100p. (Orig.). 1994. pap. 125.00 (*0-7605-0792-9*) Rector Pr.

***Australia: Stone Artefac Quarries & Reduction Sites.** 112p. (Orig.). 1994. pap. 125.00 (*0-7605-0776-7*) Rector Pr.

Australia: Take a Bow. Brian Morris. 1990. pap. 5.00 (*0-517-03702-5*) Random Hse Value.

Australia: The Beautiful Cookbook. 240p. 1994. 45.00 (*0-00-255372-4*) Collins SF.

***Australia: The Forests of South-West Western Australia.** (Illus.). 140p. (Orig.). 1994. pap. 125.00 (*0-7605-0772-4*) Rector Pr.

***Australia: The Forests of the Central Highlands & East Gippsland Victoria.** (Illus.). 140p. (Orig.). 1994. pap. 125.00 (*0-7605-0773-2*) Rector Pr.

Australia: The Island Continent. 2nd ed. Carl Robinson. 1993. pap. 16.95 (*0-8442-9887-5*, Passport Bks) NTC Pub Grp.

Australia: The Photographer's View from the 1850's to the Bicentenary. Photos by Robert Coupe. (Illus.). 1988. 19.95 (*0-582-66357-1*) Longman.

Australia: Trade, Licensing & Investing Rules & Regulations. Ed. by Lewis B. Sckolnick. (Illus.). 80p. (Orig.). (C). 1994. pap. 225.00 (*1-57205-052-7*) Rector Pr.

***Australia: Unemployment & Immigration.** 100p. (Orig.). 1994. pap. 125.00 (*0-7605-0784-8*) Rector Pr.

***Australia: What Is Social Value?** 70p. (Orig.). 1994. pap. 45.00 (*0-7605-0797-X*) Rector Pr.

Australia: Where in the World to Now? Stan Karpowicz. 185p. (C). 1990. pap. 60.00 (*0-646-11256-2*, Pub. by Boolarong Pubns AT) St Mut.

Australia: Where the Fun Is. Lauren Goodyear & Thalassa Skinner. LC 88-60465. (Illus.). 432p. (Orig.). 1991. pap. 12.95 (*0-914457-20-9*) Mustang Pub.

Australia: Year by Year. Joycelyn Bayne. (Illus.). 87p. (C). 1989. 110.00 (*0-7316-3343-1*, J Bayne) St Mut.

Australia - New Zealand Restaurants & Night Life. Jim Kennedy & Lori Shorman. LC 88-84106. (Orig.). 1990. pap. 7.95 (*0-9622126-2-8*) Highlife Pubns.

Australia: A Lucky Land. Al Stark. LC 87-13424. (Discovering Our Heritage Ser.). (Illus.). 152p. (J). (gr. 5 up). 1988. text ed. 14.95 (*0-87518-365-4*, Dillon Silver Burdett) Silver Burdett Pr.

Australia & Britain: Studies in a Changing Relationship. Ed. by A. F. Madden & W. H. Morris-Jones. (Studies in Commonwealth Politics & History: No. 8). (Illus.). 214p. 1983. 32.50 (*0-7146-3149-3*, Pub. by F Cass Pubs UK) Intl Spec Bk.

Australia & China: The Ambiguous Relationship. E. M. Andrews. 328p. 1985. 29.95 (*0-522-84296-8*) Intl Spec Bk.

Australia & Indonesian Revolution. Margaret L. George. 236p. 1980. 29.95 (*0-522-84209-7*) Intl Spec Bk.

Australia & Its Urban Centres. B. Hofmeister. (Urbanization of the Earth Ser.: Vol. 6). (Illus.). 256p. 1988. lib. bdg. 85.00 (*0-933090-27-7*) Lubrecht & Cramer.

Australia & New Zealand, 1995: The Complete Guide with Outback Tours & Barrier Reef Resorts. Fodor's Travel Staff. (Illus.). 1994. pap. 18.00 (*0-679-02693-2*) Fodors Travel.

Australia & the Asia Game. Michael Byrnes. 288p. 1994. pap. 19.95 (*1-86373-662-X*, Pub. by Allen Unwin AT) Paul & Co Pubs.

***Australia & the European Imagination.** 60p. (Orig.). 1995. pap. 65.00 (*0-7605-1907-2*) Rector Pr.

Australia & the Indonesian Revolution. Margaret George. LC 80-670253. 235p. reprint ed. pap. 67.00 (*0-7837-1456-4*, 2052432) Bks Demand.

Australia & the League of Nations. W. J. Hudson. LC 81-670133. (Illus.). 238p. reprint ed. pap. 67.90 (*0-8357-5888-5*, 2019362) Bks Demand.

Australia & the Non-White Migrant. Ed. by Kenneth Rivett. 327p. 1975. 34.95 (*0-522-84078-7*) Intl Spec Bk.

Australia & the Pacific. Australian Institute Of International Affairs Staff. LC 70-106405. (Essay Index Reprint Ser.). 1977. 21.95 (*0-8369-1443-0*) Ayer.

Australia Antigen: Proceedings of the Hepatitis Associated Antigen & Corresponding Antibodies Symposium, Munich, 1970. Virus Hepatitis Antigens & Antibodies Symposium Staff. Ed. by J. P. Soulier. (Vox Sanguinis Ser.: Vol. 19, Nos. 3-4). 1970. pap. 48.00 (*3-8055-1088-8*) S Karger.

Australia Antigen & Viral Hepatitis: Proceedings of the International Symposium on Basic Progress in Blood Transfusion, 6th, Brussels, Feb., 1972. International Symposium on Basic Progress in Blood Transfusion Staff. Ed. by J. Desmyter & W. T. London. (Vox Sanguinis Ser.: Vol. 24). (Illus.). 1973. pap. 14.50 (*3-8055-1611-8*) S Karger.

Australia at the Polls: The National Elections of 1980 & 1983. Ed. by Howard R. Penniman. LC 82-73669. 361p. reprint ed. pap. 102.90 (*0-8357-4435-3*, 2037269) Bks Demand.

***Australia, Britain & Migration: A Study of Desperate Hopes, 1915-1940.** Michael Roe. (Studies in Australian History). (Illus.). 328p. (C). 1995. 59.95 (*0-521-46507-9*) Cambridge U Pr.

***Australia Business.** Edward Hinkelman. 340p. 1995. pap. 24.95 (*0-614-07190-9*) Wrld Trade Pr.

***Australia Business Executive Outlook.** 70p. (Orig.). 1994. pap. 295.00 (*0-7605-1375-9*) Rector Pr.

Australia Business Forecaster. Ed. by Lewis B. Sckolnick. 70p. (Orig.). (C). 1994. pap. 675.00 (*1-57205-333-X*) Rector Pr.

***Australia Business Intelligence Handbook.** (Illus.). 70p. (Orig.). 1994. pap. 295.00 (*0-7605-1007-5*) Rector Pr.

***Australia Business Telephone Directory.** 300p. (Orig.). 1994. pap. 295.00 (*0-7605-0587-X*) Rector Pr.

***Australia by Rail.** 2nd ed. Colin Taylor. (Bradt Guides Ser.). (Illus.). 144p. 1994. 15.95 (*1-56440-537-0*) Globe Pequot.

***Australia Commercial Law.** 150p. (C). 1994. pap. 295.00 (*0-7605-0072-X*) Rector Pr.

Australia Compared: People, Politics, & Policies. Ed. by Francis G. Castles. 224p. (Orig.). 1992. pap. text ed. 19.95 (*0-04-442339-X*, Pub. by Allen Unwin AT) Paul & Co Pubs.

Australia Cruising Guide. Alan Lucas. (Illus.). 1994. 39.95 (*0-85288-246-7*, Pub. by Imray Laurie Norie & Wilson UK) Bluewater Bks.

***Australia Directory of Family Services.** 140p. (Orig.). 1994. pap. 125.00 (*0-7605-0780-5*) Rector Pr.

Australia Discover Guide. Berlitz Editors. (Discover Guides Ser.). (Illus.). 336p. 1992. pap. 17.95 (*2-8315-0599-2*) Berlitz.

***Australia Editing Handbook.** 200p. (Orig.). 1994. pap. 125.00 (*0-7605-0800-3*) Rector Pr.

***Australia: Editing Texts: Papers from a Conference at the Humanities Research Centre.** 60p. (Orig.). 1995. pap. 65.00 (*0-7605-1908-0*) Rector Pr.

Australia Faces Southeast Asia: The Emergence of Foreign Policy. Amry Vandenbosch & Mary B. Vandenbosch. LC 67-29340. 183p. reprint ed. pap. 52.20 (*0-8357-5889-3*, 2003348) Bks Demand.

Australia Felix: or, Harlequin Laughing Jackass & the Magic Bat. Garnet Walch. (Paperbacks Ser.). 150p. (Orig.). 1989. pap. text ed. 9.95 (*0-7022-2151-1*, Pub. by Univ Queensland Pr AT) Intl Spec Bk.

Australia for Women. Ed. by Hawthorne & Klein. 1994. pap. 19.95 (*1-875559-27-2*, Pub. by SpiniFex Pr AT) InBook.

Australia for Women: Travel & Culture. Ed. by Susan Hawthorne & Renate Klein. LC 94-5906. 1994. pap. 17.95 (*1-55861-095-2*) Feminist Pr.

Australia Goes to Press. Willis S. Holden. LC 77-8449. (Illus.). 297p. 1977. text ed. 59.75 (*0-8371-9689-2*, HOAU, Greenwood Pr) Greenwood.

***Australia Government Publications Guide.** 70p. (Orig.). 1994. pap. 65.00 (*0-7605-0804-6*) Rector Pr.

***Australia Historic Coast.** 120p. (Orig.). 1994. pap. 125.00 (*0-7605-0794-5*) Rector Pr.

***Australia: History of Sexualities in Australia Project.** 60p. (Orig.). 1995. pap. 65.00 (*0-7605-1912-9*) Rector Pr.

Australia in Pictures. Ed. by Lerner Publications, Department of Geography Staff. (Visual Geography Ser.). (Illus.). 64p. (YA). (gr. 5 up). 1990. lib. bdg. 18.95 (*0-8225-1855-4*, Lerner Publctns) Lerner Group.

Australia in the International Economy in the Twentieth Century. David Meredith & Barrie Dyster. (Illus.). 352p. (C). 1990. 74.95 (*0-521-33496-9*); pap. 29.95 (*0-521-33689-9*) Cambridge U Pr.

Australia in the New World Order: Foreign Policy in the 1970s. Ed. by J. A. Mackie. LC 76-378596. 164p. reprint ed. pap. 46.80 (*0-7837-1455-6*, 2052431) Bks Demand.

Australia in the World Crisis, 1929-1933. Douglas B. Copland. LC 74-111474. (BCL Ser. I). reprint ed. 19.00 (*0-404-01718-5*) AMS Pr.

Australia in World Affairs, Vol. 3: 1961-65. Gordon Greenwood. Ed. by Norman Harper. LC 58-206. 511p. reprint ed. pap. 145.70 (*0-8357-5890-7*, 2056690) Bks Demand.

Australia in World Affairs, Vol. 4: 1966-70. Ed. by Gordon Greenwood & Norman Harper. LC 58-206. 501p. reprint ed. pap. 142.80 (*0-8357-5891-5*, 2056690) Bks Demand.

Australia in World Affairs, 1971-75. Ed. by W. J. Hudson. LC 80-66318. (Illus.). 440p. reprint ed. pap. 125.40 (*0-8357-5892-3*, 2019360) Bks Demand.

***Australia Institutions & Organizations.** 120p. (Orig.). 1994. pap. 125.00 (*0-7605-0799-6*) Rector Pr.

***Australia, New Guinea & Melanesia: Late Pleistocene Sites.** 70p. (Orig.). 1994. pap. 45.00 (*0-7605-0790-2*) Rector Pr.

Australia, New Zealand, & the Pacific Islands since the First World War. Ed. by William S. Livingston & W. Roger Louis. 261p. 1979. text ed. 20.00 (*0-292-70344-9*) U of Tex Pr.

Australia, New Zealand, & the United States: Internal Change & Alliance Relations in the Anzus States. Ed. by Richard W. Baker. LC 90-45198. 304p. 1991. text ed. 59.95 (*0-275-93797-6*, C3797, Praeger Pubs) Greenwood.

Australia, New Zealand, South Sea Islands Job Manual - Now Hiring. 5th rev. ed. Richard M. Zink. (Illus.). 64p. (YA). (gr. 9 up). 1994. pap. 14.95x (*0-939469-38-3*) Zinks Career Guide.

***Australia Phrasebook.** Ed. by Sally Steward. (Illus.). 148p. 1994. pap. 5.95 (*0-86442-256-3*) Lonely Planet.

Australia Pocket Guide. Berlitz Editors. (Pocket Guides). (Illus.). 256p. 1994. pap. 10.95 (*2-8315-2583-7*) Berlitz.

Australia R & R: Representations & Reinterpretations of Australia's War in Vietnam. Ed. by Jeff Doyle & Jeffrey Grey. (Vietnam Generation Ser.). 176p. (Orig.). (C). 1991. pap. text ed. 15.00 (*0-9628524-3-0*) Burning Cities Pr.

***Australia Rainforest Legacy Vol. 2: Flora & Fauna.** 170p. (Orig.). 1994. pap. 145.00 (*0-7605-0795-3*) Rector Pr.

Australia, Seventeen Eighty-Eight to Nineteen Eighty-Eight: The Creation of a Nation. Charles Wilson. (Illus.). 288p. 1987. 56.00 (*0-389-20768-3*, N8327) B&N Imports.

Australia South West & Our Future. Jan Taylor. (Orig.). 1992. pap. text ed. 12.95 (*0-86417-350-4*, Pub. by Kangaroo Pr AT) Seven Hills Bk.

***Australia Tax Law.** 150p. (C). 1994. pap. 295.00 (*0-7605-0071-1*) Rector Pr.

Australia Today. Caroline Arnold. LC 87-10660. (First Book Ser.). (Illus.). 96p. (J). (gr. 4-9). 1987. lib. bdg. 11.62 (*0-531-10377-3*) Watts.

Australia Travel Guide. Sunset Magazine & Book Editors. LC 86-82155. (Illus.). 128p. 1987. 12.99 (*0-376-06066-2*) Sunset Menlo Pk.

Australia Travellers Guide. 6th ed. Berlitz Editors. (Travellers Guides Ser.). (Illus.). 416p. 1993. 14.95 (*2-8315-1706-0*) Berlitz.

***Australia Welfare 1993: Services & Assistance.** 200p. (Orig.). 1994. pap. 145.00 (*0-7605-0779-1*) Rector Pr.

Australia, Willkommen: A History of the Germans in Australia. Jurgen Tampke & Colin Doxford. (Illus.). 281p. 1990. 34.95 (*0-86840-307-5*, Pub. by New South Wales Univ Pr AT) Intl Spec Bk.

Australia, 1939: The Gathering Storm. Susan Johnson & Lindsay Nation. (Illus.). 192p. 1989. pap. 22.50 (*0-86840-347-4*, Pub. by New South Wales Univ Pr AT) Intl Spec Bk.

Australia '92-'93. Elizabeth Hansen. (Frommer's Comprehensive Travel Guide Ser.). (Illus.). 528p. 1992. pap. 18.00 (*0-13-334798-2*, P-H Travel) P-H Gen Ref & Trav.

Australian. Diana Palmer. 1993. mass mkt. 4.50 (*0-373-48269-8*, 5-48269-0) Silhouette.

Australian Aboriginal. Herbert Basedow. LC 76-44687. (Illus.). reprint ed. 41.50 (*0-404-15904-4*) AMS Pr.

Australian Aboriginal Grammar. Barry J. Blake. 240p. 1986. 62.00 (*0-7099-3989-2*, Pub. by Croom Helm UK) Routledge Chapman & Hall.

Australian Aboriginal Languages. B. Blake. (C). 1991. pap. 29.95 (*0-7022-2353-0*, Pub. by Univ Queensland Pr AT) Intl Spec Bk.

Australian Aboriginal Words in English: Their Origin & Meaning. R. M. Dixon et al. (Illus.). 278p. 1991. 47.00 (*0-19-553099-3*) OUP.

Australian Aborigines. Richard Nile. LC 92-17044. (Threatened Cultures Ser.). (Illus.). 48p. (J). (gr. 5-6). 1992. lib. bdg. 22.80 (*0-8114-2303-4*) Raintree Steck-V.

Australian Acacias in Developing Countries. J. W. Turnbull. 196p. (Orig.). (C). 1986. text ed. 130.00 (*0-685-63249-0*, Pub. by ACIAR) St Mut.

Australian Accounting Standards Review Board: The Establishment of Its Participative Review Process. Asheq R. Rahman & Richard Brief. LC 91-41423. (New Works in Accounting History, 1992). 568p. 1992. 90.00 (*0-8153-0802-7*) Garland.

Australian Administrative Law. Roman Tomasic & Don Fleming. xxiii, 530p. 1991. pap. 69.00 (*0-455-20950-2*, Pub. by Law Bk Co) W W Gaunt.

Australian Administrative Law Decisions, 15 vols., Set. Ed. by D. C. Pearce. 1990. 2,239.00 (*0-409-42141-3*) Butterworth Legal Pubs.

Australian Adventure: Letters from an Ambassador's Wife. Anne Clark. LC 73-97905. 262p. reprint ed. pap. 74.70 (*0-7837-1011-9*, 2041322) Bks Demand.

Australian Aeronautical Conference, 1993, 2 vols. 5th ed. Intro. by Colin A. Martin. (National Conference Publication Ser.: No. 93-6). (Illus.). 610p. 1993. pap. text ed. 108.00 (*0-85825-576-6*, Pub. by Inst Engrs Aust-EA Bks AT) Accents Pubns.

Australian Agriculture. P. Scott. 150p. 1981. 70.00 (*0-569-08687-6*, Pub. by Collets UK) Pro-Am Music.

Australian American Security Relationship in Regional & International Perspective. Henry S. Albinski. 1982. text ed. 39.95 (*0-312-06119-6*) St Martin.

Australian & Canadian Federalism 1867-1985: A Study of Judicial Technique. Christopher Gibert. 280p. 1986. 49.95 (*0-522-84292-5*) Intl Spec Bk.

Australian & Indian Literature: Studies in Mutual Response. David Kerr & R. K. Dhwan. 200p. 1991. text ed. 35.00 (*81-85218-24-2*, Pub. by Prestige II) Advent Bks Div.

Australian & New Zealand Citator to U. K. Reports 1973-87. Butterworths Staff. 231.00 (*0-409-30900-1*) Butterworth Legal Pubs.

Australian & South Pacific Law: Structure & Legal Materials. Igor I. Kavass. LC 83-80470. xiv, 482p. 1983. pap. text ed. 48.50 (*0-89941-244-0*, 302880) W S Hein.

Australian Animals. Joanne Mattern. LC 92-41033. (Illus.). 24p. (J). (gr. k-2). 1993. 1.95 (*0-8167-3096-2*) Troll Assocs.

Australian Animals Discovery Library, 6 bks., Set. Lynn Stone. (Illus.). 144p. (J). (gr. k-5). 1990. lib. bdg. 71.64 (*0-86593-054-6*); lib. bdg. 53.70 (*0-685-36368-6*) Rourke Corp.

Australian Army at War 1899-1975. John Laffin. (Men-at-Arms Ser.: No. 123). (Illus.). 48p. pap. 11.95 (*0-85045-418-2*, 9056, Pub. by Osprey UK) Stackpole.

Australian Astronautics Convention Proceedings 1975. Ed. by Alan T. Philip. (Illus.). 1977. pap. text ed. 18.00 (*0-9596726-1-3*) Univelt Inc.

Australian Astronomer John Tebbutt: The Life & World of the Man on the 100 Dollar Note. Ragbir Bhathal. (Illus.). 112p. (Orig.). 1993. pap. 16.95 (*0-86417-522-1*, Pub. by Kangaroo Pr AT) Seven Hills Bk.

Australian Bar Review. Ed. by J. D. Heydon. Australia. ring bd. 186.00 (*0-409-48902-6*) Butterworth Legal Pubs.

Australian Bed & Breakfast Book, 1994. Ed. by J. Thomas. (International Guide Ser.). (Illus.). 272p. 1994. pap. 14.95 (*1-56554-009-3*) Pelican.

***Australian Bed & Breakfast Book, 1995.** Ed. by J. Thomas. (Illus.). 272p. 1995. pap. 14.95 (*1-56554-118-9*) Pelican.

Australian Beetles. John F. Lawrence & E. B. Britton. (Illus.). 184p. Date not set. 39.95 (*0-522-84519-3*) Intl Spec Bk.

Australian Birds in Stained Glass. Diane Coady. (Illus.). 48p. (Orig.). 1993. reprint ed. pap. 9.95 (*0-86417-393-8*, Pub. by Kangaroo Pr AT) Seven Hills Bk.

***Australian Blackletter Law Series: Contract Law.** P. Clarke & R. Krever. 270p. 1993. pap. 35.00 (*0-409-30818-8*, Austral) Butterworth Legal Pubs.

Australian Blattidae of the Subfamilies Chorisoneurinae & Ectobiinae (Orthoptera) Morgan Hebard. (Monograph: No. 4). (Illus.). 129p. (Orig.). 1943. pap. 10.00 (*0-910006-13-X*) Acad Nat Sci Phila.

Australian Books in Print 1994. 32th ed. 1400p. 1994. 115.00 (*1-875589-36-8*) D W Thorpe.

***Australian Books in Print 1995. 33th ed. 1400p. 1995. lib. bdg. 120.00 (*1-875589-58-9*) D W Thorpe. This unique reference provides detailed bibliographic information on over 60,000 in-print books published in --or about--Australia or written by Australian authors. There are also details on over 3,000 publishers & distributors whose titles are represented, as well as information on all trade associations, literary awards, & more.**
Publisher Provided Annotation.

Australian Brass: The Career of Lieutenant General Sir Horace Robertson. Jeffrey Grey. (Illus.). 320p. (C). 1992. 64.95 (*0-521-40157-7*) Cambridge U Pr.

Australian Breadmaking Handbook. Bread Research Institute of Australia Staff. (Illus.). 250p. 1990. pap. 24.95 (*0-908237-36-7*, Pub. by New South Wales Univ Pr AT) Intl Spec Bk.

Australian Business & Investment Guide 1987. 1987. 45.00 (*0-912289-78-3*) St James Pr.

Australian Business Dictionary. H. A. Ford et al. 1985. Australia. pap. 22.00 (*0-409-49254-X*) Butterworth Legal Pubs.

***Australian Business Taxation.** H. M. Rigney. 430p. 1990. pap. 69.00 (*0-409-30159-0*, Austral) Butterworth Legal Pubs.

Australian Buying Reference. 8th ed. Ed. by Deby Williams. 804p. 1987. 130.00 (*0-947060-06-5*) R W Cameron.

***Australian Capital Gains Tax.** 2nd ed. G. S. Cooper & M. W. Inglis. 1992. pap. 66.00 (*0-409-30492-1*, Australia) Butterworth Legal Pubs.

Australian Casebook of Study Centres in Distance Education. Deakin University Press Staff. 134p. (C). 1985. 48.00 (*0-7300-0213-6*, Pub. by Deakin Univ AT) St Mut.

Australian Cattle Dog Champions, 1980-1986. Camino E. E. & B. Co. Staff. (Illus.). 103p. 1987. pap. 36.95 (*0-940808-42-0*) Camino E E & Bk.

An Asterisk (*) at the beginning of an entry indicates that the title is appearing in BIP for the first time.

An Asterisk (*) at the beginning of an entry indicates that the title is appearing in BIP for the first time.

***Australian Media Law.** Jonathan Gill. 240p. 1995. pap. 29. 95 (*0-522-84548-7*) Paul & Co Pubs.

***Australian Melodramas: Thomas Keneally's Fiction.** Peter Pierce. (Studies in Australian Literature Ser.). 222p. 1995. pap. 14.95 (*0-7022-2813-3*, Pub. by Univ Queensland Pr AT) Intl Spec Bk.

***Australian Men & Women of Science, Engineering, & Technology.** 600p. 1995. 110.00 (*1-875589-64-3*) D W Thorpe.

***Australian Men & Women of Science, Engineering & Technology.** 592p. 1994. 110.00 (*1-875589-40-6*) K G Saur.

Australian Mine Directory. 200p. (Orig.). 1995. pap. 595. 00x (*1-57205-702-5*) Rector Pr.

Australian Movies & the American Dream. Glen Lewis. LC 87-14590. (Illus.). 229p. 1987. text ed. 49.95 (*0-275-92675-3*, C2675, Praeger Pubs) Greenwood.

Australian Multiculturalism: A Documentary History & Critique. Lois Foster & David Stockley. 240p. 1988. 79. 00 (*1-85359-008-8*, Pub. by Multilingual Matters UK); pap. 29.95 (*1-85359-007-X*, Pub. by Multilingual Matters UK) Taylor & Francis.

Australian Mushrooms & Toadstools: How to Identify Them. rev. ed. A. Wood. 53p. 1990. pap. 4.95 (*0-86840-044-0*, Pub. by New South Wales Univ Pr AT) Intl Spec Bk.

Australian National Dictionary: A Dictionary of Australianisms on Historical Principles. Ed. by W. S. Ramson. 830p. 1989. 85.00 (*0-19-554736-5*) OUP.

Australian National Playwrights Conference: A Retrospective. Harriet Persons. (C). 1990. 45.00 (*0-86819-241-4*, Pub. by Currency Pr AT) St Mut.

Australian National Political Attitudes, 1967. Donald Aitkin et al. 1975. write for info. (*0-89138-117-1*) ICPSR.

Australian Needlepoint Designs. Jenni Kirkham. (Illus.). 128p. 1994. 24.95 (*0-86417-553-1*, Pub. by Kangaroo Pr AT) Seven Hills Bk.

Australian, New Zealand, & United States Security Relations, 1951-1986. Thomas-Durell Young. 284p. (C). 1992. pap. text ed. 42.50 (*0-8133-8056-1*) Westview.

Australian Official Publications. Howard Coxon. LC 80-40046. (Guides to Official Publications: Vol. 5). (Illus.). 227p. 1980. 92.00 (*0-08-023131-4*, Pub. by Pergamon Repr UK) Franklin.

Australian Open Learning Information Network (Olin) Trials & Tribulations with Technology, but Powerful Potential for Participation. Ed. by Barry Smith. 99p. (C). 1987. 56.00 (*0-7300-0259-4*, Pub. by Deakin Univ AT) St Mut.

Australian Opinion Polls 1941-90: An Index, 2 vols., Set. Murray Goot. 300p. 1993. 115.00 (*1-875589-13-9*) D W Thorpe.

Australian Orchid Designs. Evelyn Hales. (Illus.). 120p. (Orig.). 1993. pap. 12.95 (*0-86417-381-4*, Pub. by Kangaroo Pr AT) Seven Hills Bk.

Australian Organic Gardener's Handbook. Keith V. Smith. (Illus.). 254p. (Orig.). 1995. pap. 19.95 (*0-85091-591-0*, Pub. by Lothian Pub AT) Seven Hills Bk.

***Australian Outback & Its People.** Kate Darian-Smith & David Lowe. (People & Places Ser.). (Illus.). 48p. (J). (gr. 5-8). 1995. 15.95 (*1-56847-337-0*) Thomson Lrning.

Australian Paniceae (Poaceae) Robert D. Webster. (Illus.). 322p. (C). 1987. pap. 84.00 (*3-443-50006-4*) Lubrecht & Cramer.

Australian People & Animals in Today's Dreaming: The Role of Comparative Psychology in the Management of Natural Resources. Ed. by David B. Croft. LC 90-21042. 144p. 1991. text ed. 45.00 (*0-275-93908-1*, C3908, Praeger Pubs) Greenwood.

Australian People, Seventeen Eighty-Eight to Nineteen Forty-Five. Brian Fitzpatrick. LC 81-13255. (Illus.). viii, 279p. 1982. reprint ed. text ed. 59.75 (*0-313-23016-1*, FIAU, Greenwood Pr) Greenwood.

***Australian Perceptions of Asia.** Ed. by David Walker & Julia Horne. 135p. 1994. 39.95 (*0-7855-0334-X*, Pub. by Deakin Univ AT) St Mut.

Australian Periodicals in Print 1994. 12th ed. 850p. 1994. pap. 55.00 (*1-875589-31-7*) D W Thorpe.

Australian Plants for Arts & Crafts. Gwen Elliot. 1992. pap. 24.95 (*0-947062-94-7*, Pub. by Hyland Hse AT) Intl Spec Bk.

Australian Plants for Your Garden. Glen Heyne & Peta Heyne. 184p. 1985. pap. 14.95 (*0-85091-221-0*, Pub. by Lothian Pub AT) Intl Spec Bk.

Australian Plants Identified. Gwen Elliot. (Illus.). 240p. 1990. pap. 24.95 (*0-947062-63-7*, Pub. by Hyland Hse AT) Intl Spec Bk.

Australian Plants of the Eighties: Series A. W. H. Payne. 384p. (C). 1991. text ed. 95.00 (*0-7855-0035-9*, Pub. by Surrey Beatty & Sons AT) St Mut.

Australian Poems in Perspective: A Collection of Poems & Critical Commentaries. Ed. by P. K. Elkin. 231p. 1978. pap. text ed. 18.95 (*0-7022-1025-0*, Pub. by Univ Queensland Pr AT) Intl Spec Bk.

Australian Pokerwork: A Guide. Helena Walsh. (Illus.). 56p. 1993. 21.95 (*0-86417-465-9*, Pub. by Kangaroo Pr AT) Seven Hills Bk.

Australian Policies & Attitudes Toward China. Henry S. Albinski. LC 66-10548. 527p. reprint ed. pap. 150.20 (*0-8357-8809-1*, 2052281) Bks Demand.

Australian Policing: Contemporary Issues. Duncan Chappell & Paul Wilson. 224p. (C). 1989. Australia. pap. 58.00 (*0-409-49489-5*) Butterworth Legal Pubs.

***Australian Politics.** Hugh V. Emy & Owen E. Hughes. 580p. 1995. pap. 36.95 (*0-7329-2788-9*, Pub. by Macmill Educ AT) Paul & Co Pubs.

***Australian Politics.** 3rd ed. Hugh V. Emy & Owen E. Hughes. 580p. 1995. 74.95 (*0-7329-2796-X*, Pub. by Macmill Educ AT) Paul & Co Pubs.

Australian Popular Culture. Ed. by Ian Craven. 240p. (C). 1994. 18.95 (*0-521-46667-9*) Cambridge U Pr.

Australian Private International Law. 3rd ed. E. I. Sykes & M. C. Pryles. 850p. 1991. 139.00 (*0-455-21039-X*, Pub. by Law Bk Co); pap. 99.50 (*0-455-21040-3*, Pub. by Law Bk Co) W W Gaunt.

***Australian Race Relations.** Andrew Markus. 266p. 1995. pap. 19.95 (*1-86373-554-2*, Pub. by Allen Unwin AT) Paul & Co Pubs.

***Australian Radiology: A History.** James F. Ryan et al. (Illus.). 150p. 1995. text ed. write for info. (*0-07-470207-6*) Hlth Prof Div.

***Australian Rainforest Legacy Vol. 3: History.** 170p. (Orig.). 1994. pap. 125.00 (*0-7605-0796-1*) Rector Pr.

Australian Rainforests. Paul Adam. (Monographs on Biogeography: No. 6). (Illus.). 328p. 1992. 85.00 (*0-19-854223-2*) OUP.

Australian Rainforests. Paul Adam. (Monographs on Biogeography: No. 6). (Illus.). 328p. 1994. reprint ed. pap. 35.00 (*0-19-854872-9*) OUP.

Australian Rainforests in New South Wales, Vol. 1. Alexander G. Floyd. 130p. (C). 1990. text ed. 110.00 (*0-949324-31-0*, Pub. by Surrey Beatty & Sons AT) St Mut.

Australian Rainforests in New South Wales, Vol. 2. Alexander G. Floyd. 128p. 1990. text ed. 175.00 (*0-949324-32-9*, Pub. by Surrey Beatty & Sons AT) St Mut.

Australian Real Property Law. Adrian Bradbrook et al. lxx, 800p. 1991. 125.00 (*0-455-20992-8*, Pub. by Law Bk Co); pap. 89.00 (*0-455-20993-6*, Pub. by Law Bk Co) W W Gaunt.

Australian Realism: The Systematic Philosophy of John Anderson. A. J. Baker. 120p. 1986. 49.95 (*0-521-32051-8*) Cambridge U Pr.

Australian Rock Art: A New Synthesis. Robert Layton. (Illus.). 256p. (C). 1992. 69.95 (*0-521-34666-5*) Cambridge U Pr.

Australian Scapegoat: Towards an Intopodean Aesthetic. Peter Fuller. 64p. (Orig.). 1986. pap. 15.00 (*0-85564-245-9*, Pub. by Univ of West Aust Pr AT) Intl Spec Bk.

Australian School Through Children's Eyes. J. J. Smolicz & M. J. Secombe. Ed. by R. J. Selleck. 135p. pap. 14.95 (*0-522-84233-X*) Intl Spec Bk.

Australian Science in the Making: A Bicentennial History, Published in Association with the Australian Academy of Science. Ed. by R. W. Home. (Illus.). 300p. 1990. 79. 95 (*0-521-35556-7*) Cambridge U Pr.

Australian Science in the Making: A Bicentennial History, Published in Association with the Australian Academy of Science. Ed. by R. W. Home. (Illus.). 440p. (C). 1990. pap. 32.95 (*0-521-39640-9*) Cambridge U Pr.

Australian Scuba Divers Illustrated Dictionary. Robert Berthold. (C). 1993. 79.00 (*0-646-07526-8*, Pub. by R Berthold Photo AT) St Mut.

Australian Security Intelligence Organization: An Unofficial History. Frank Cain. LC 92-38419. (Cass Series, Studies in Intelligence). (Illus.). 292p. (C). 1994. 40.00 (*0-7146-3477-8*, Pub. by F Cass Pubs UK); pap. 20.00 (*0-7146-4124-3*, Pub. by F Cass Pubs UK) Intl Spec Bk.

Australian Sheep & Wool Handbook. Cottle. 1991. 89.95 (*0-909605-60-2*) Buttrwrth-Heinemann.

***Australian Shepherd Dog: Champion of Versatility.** Liz Palika. LC 95-3753. 1995. 29.95 (*0-87605-039-9*) Howell Bk.

Australian Shepherds. Joseph Hartnagle. (KW Ser.). (Illus.). 192p. 1990. lib. bdg. 11.95 (*0-86622-609-5*, KW-191) TFH Pubns.

Australian Short Story: An Anthology from the 1890's to the 1980's. Ed. by Laurie Hergenhan. LC 85-1016. (UQP Australian Authors Ser.). 352p. 1986. pap. 18.95 (*0-7022-1787-5*) Intl Spec Bk.

Australian Snakes: A Natural History. Richard Shine. LC 91-26031. (Illus.). 224p. 1992. 36.00 (*0-8014-2737-1*) Cornell U Pr.

***Australian Snakes: A Natural History.** Richard Shine. (Comstock Book Ser.). (Illus.). 224p. 1995. pap. 27.50x (*0-8014-8261-5*) Cornell U Pr.

Australian Social Development. Clarence H. Northcott. LC 68-56676. (Columbia University. Studies in the Social Sciences: No. 189). reprint ed. 23.50 (*0-404-51189-9*) AMS Pr.

Australian Social Worker & the Law. 3rd ed. F. Bates et al. vii, 349p. 1991. pap. 49.00 (*0-455-21032-2*, Pub. by Law Bk Co) W W Gaunt.

Australian Softbill Management. Rosemary Hutton. 144p. (C). 1990. text ed. 90.00 (*0-9587727-3-8*, Pub. by Surrey Beatty & Sons AT) St Mut.

Australian Soil & Land Survey Field Handbook, Vol. 1. R. C. McDonald et al. 172p. 1984. pap. 30.00 (*0-909605-32-7*, Pub. by Inkata Pr AT) Intl Spec Bk.

Australian Soil & Land Survey Handbooks, Vol. 2: Guidelines for Conducting Surveys. Ed. by R. H. Gunn et al. 1988. 65.95 (*0-909605-44-0*, Pub. by Inkata Pr AT) Intl Spec Bk.

Australian Soils: The Human Impact. Ed. by J. S. Russell & R. F. Isbell. LC 85-16514. (Illus.). 522p. 1987. text ed. 50.00 (*0-7022-1968-1*, Pub. by Univ Queensland Pr AT) Intl Spec Bk.

Australian Sourcebooks: Social Sciences. Barbara Brady. 200p. 1992. 75.00 (*1-875589-03-1*) D W Thorpe.

Australian Squatters. Hubert De Castella. Ed. by C. B. Thornton-Smith. (Illus.). 212p. 1987. 34.95 (*0-522-84333-6*) Intl Spec Bk.

Australian Studies: Acquisition & Collection Development for Libraries. Ed. by G. E. Gorman. LC 92-10382. 360p. 1992. text ed. 80.00 (*0-7201-2134-5*, Z688, Mansell Pub) Cassell.

Australian Supplement to Borrie & Lowe's Law of Contempt. A. Shott. 132p. (C). 1989. Australia. pap. 49. 00 (*0-409-49459-3*, Austral) Butterworth Legal Pubs.

***Australian Tax Legislation 1994.** 1994. pap. 66.00 (*0-409-30839-0*, Austral) Butterworth Legal Pubs.

Australian Tea Tree Oil. Cynthia B. Olsen. (Illus.). 40p. (Orig.). 1989. pap. text ed. 3.95 (*0-9628882-0-6*) Kali Pr.

Australian Tea Tree Oil Guide. 2nd ed. Cynthia B. Olsen. LC 91-220651. 80p. 1991. pap. 6.95 (*0-9628882-1-4*) Kali Pr.

***Australian Teachers & the Law.** K. Trone. 208p. 1989. pap. 39.00 (*0-409-49437-2*, Austral) Butterworth Legal Pubs.

Australian Teachers Careers. Rupert Maclean & Phillip McKenzie. (C). 1990. 75.00 (*0-86431-077-3*, Pub. by Aust Council Educ Res AT) St Mut.

Australian Telescope: A Window on the Universe. Ed. by Australia Telescope National Facility, Commonwealth Scientific & Industrial Research Organization, Australia, Division of Radiophysics Staff. 1989. pap. text ed. 15.00 (*0-643-05021-3*, Pub. by CSIRO AT) Intl Spec Bk.

Australian Tertiary Deposits Containing Terrestrial Mammals. Ruben A. Stirton et al. LC 68-66225. (University of California Publications in Social Welfare: Vol. 77). (Illus.). 41p. reprint ed. pap. 25.00 (*0-8357-5893-1*, 2014696) Bks Demand.

Australian Themes. Barbara Nuttall. 1994. 17.95 (*0-533-10968-X*) Vantage.

Australian Themes in Cross Stitch. Vivienne Garforth. (Illus.). 80p. 1993. 19.95 (*0-86417-430-6*, Pub. by Kangaroo Pr AT) Seven Hills Bk.

Australian Themes in Machine Embroidery. Marilyn Townsend. (Lothian Australian Craft Ser.). (Illus.). 64p. (Orig.). 1995. pap. 14.95 (*0-85091-563-5*, Pub. by Lothian Pub AT) Seven Hills Bk.

Australian Tour Suggestions. Frank Stone. 1981. 23.00 (*0-7223-1434-5*, Pub. by A H S Ltd UK) St Mut.

Australian Tour to England 1948. Peter Griffiths & Peter Wynne-Thomas. 105p. 1992. pap. 60.00 (*1-874524-01-7*, Pub. by Limlow Bks UK) St Mut.

Australian Tour to England 1953. Peter Griffiths & Peter Wynne. 106p. 1993. pap. 55.00 (*1-874524-05-X*, Pub. by Limlow Bks UK) St Mut.

Australian Tour to England 1993. Peter Wynne-Thomas & Peter Griffiths. 90p. 1993. pap. 65.00 (*1-874524-06-8*, Pub. by Limlow Bks UK) St Mut.

***Australian Trade Practices Act 1974: Proscriptions & Prescriptions for a More Competitive Economy.** Ed. by David K. Round. (Studies in Industrial Organization: Vol. 19). 1995. lib. bdg. 75.00 (*0-7923-3228-8*) Kluwer Ac.

***Australian Travel & Tourism Law.** 2nd ed. A. J. Cordato. 300p. 1993. pap. 39.00 (*0-409-49082-2*, Austral) Butterworth Legal Pubs.

Australian Tropical Rainforests: Science - Values - Meaning. Ed. by L. J. Webb & J. Kikkawa. 1990. 60.00 (*0-643-05055-8*, Pub. by CSIRO AT) Intl Spec Bk.

Australian Tunnelling Conference, No. VII: The Underground Domain. Intro. by Paul Howlett. (Illus.). 334p. (Orig.). 1990. pap. 62.50 (*0-85825-504-9*) Accents Pubns.

Australian Vegetation. Ed. by R. H. Groves. (Illus.). 500p. (C). 1994. 79.95 (*0-521-41420-2*) Cambridge U Pr.

Australian Victories in France in 1918. John Monash. (Great War Ser.: No. 24). (Illus.). 424p. reprint ed. 39.95 (*0-89839-181-4*) Battery Pr.

***Australian Vintage Paperback Guide.** Graene Flanagan. 212p. 1994. 30.00 (*0-936071-41-9*); pap. 20.00 (*0-936071-38-9*) Gryphon Pubns.

Australian Visions: Nineteen Eighty-Four Exxon International Exhibition. Diane Waldman. (Illus.). 100p. 1984. pap. 12.50 (*0-89207-048-X*) S R Guggenheim.

Australian Voices: Writers & Their Work. Ray Willbanks. LC 91-8248. (Illus.). 243p. 1991. text ed. 45.00 (*0-292-70429-1*) U of Tex Pr.

Australian War Strategy, Nineteen Thirty-Nine to Nineteen Forty-Five: A Documentary History. John Robertson & John McCarthy. 612p. 1985. text ed. 49.95 (*0-7022-1924-X*, Pub. by Univ Queensland Pr AT) Intl Spec Bk.

Australian Waterbirds: A Field Guide. Richard Kingsford. (Illus.). 128p. (Orig.). 1994. pap. 15.95 (*0-86417-330-X*, Pub. by Kangaroo Pr AT) Intl Spec Bk.

Australian Way of Life. Ed. by George Caiger. LC 69-18921. (Essay Index Reprint Ser.). 1977. 19.95 (*0-8369-1026-5*) Ayer.

Australian Weevils, 8 vols., Set. E. C. Zimmerman. (Illus.). 1992. 750.00 (*0-643-05144-9*, Pub. by CSIRO AT) Intl Spec Bk.

Australian Weevils, Vol. 1. E. C. Zimmerman. (Illus.). 520p. 1992. 150.00 (*0-643-05145-7*, Pub. by CSIRO AT) Intl Spec Bk.

Australian Weevils, Vol. 2. E. C. Zimmerman. (Illus.). 520p. 1992. 150.00 (*0-643-05146-5*, Pub. by CSIRO AT) Intl Spec Bk.

Australian Weevils, Vol. 3. E. C. Zimmerman. (Illus.). 650p. 1992. 100.00 (*0-643-05147-3*, Pub. by CSIRO AT) Intl Spec Bk.

Australian Weevils, Vol. 4. E. C. Zimmerman. (Illus.). 650p. 1992. 100.00 (*0-643-05148-1*, Pub. by CSIRO AT) Intl Spec Bk.

Australian Weevils, Vol. 5. E. C. Zimmerman. (Illus.). 650p. 1991. 200.00 (*0-643-05149-X*, Pub. by CSIRO AT) Intl Spec Bk.

Australian Weevils, Vol. 6. E. C. Zimmerman. (Illus.). 650p. 1992. 200.00 (*0-643-05150-3*, Pub. by CSIRO AT) Intl Spec Bk.

Australian Welfare State. Michael A. Jones. LC 79-55030. 252p. reprint ed. pap. 71.90 (*0-8357-5894-X*, 2023184) Bks Demand.

Australian Wilderness. 1991. 19.99 (*0-517-03386-0*) Random Hse Value.

Australian Wildflowers in Stained Glass. Diane Coady. (Illus.). 48p. (Orig.). 1993. reprint ed. pap. 9.95 (*0-86417-435-7*, Pub. by Kangaroo Pr AT) Seven Hills Bk.

Australian Wildlife Year: A Month-by-Month Guide to Nature. Reader's Digest Editors. (Illus.). 336p. 1989. 34.95 (*0-86438-071-2*, Random) RD Assn.

Australian Women: Contemporary Feminist Thought. Ed. by Norma Grieve & Ailsa Burns. 400p. 1994. pap. 35.00 (*0-19-553503-0*) OUP.

Australian Women in Papua New Guinea: Colonial Passages 1920-1960. Chilla Bulbeck. (Illus.). 320p. (C). 1992. 69. 95 (*0-521-41285-4*) Cambridge U Pr.

Australian Words & Their Origins. Ed. by Joan Hughes. 680p. 1990. 29.95 (*0-19-553087-X*) OUP.

Australians & Egypt, Nineteen Fourteen to Nineteen Nineteen. Suzanne Brugger. 188p. 1980. 29.95 (*0-522-84175-9*) Intl Spec Bk.

Australians & the Gold Rush: California & Down Under, 1849-1854. Jay Monaghan. LC 66-23182. 345p. reprint ed. pap. 98.40 (*0-8357-5895-8*, 2031440) Bks Demand.

Australia's Age of Iron: History & Archaeology. Ian Jack & Aedeen Cremin. (Sydney University Press Publication Ser.). (Illus.). 192p. 1994. 47.00 (*0-424-00158-6*) OUP.

Australia's Animals Discovered. Peter Stanbury & Graeme Phipps. (Illus.). 120p. 1980. 33.00 (*0-08-024796-2*, Pergamon Pr) Elsevier.

Australia's Commonwealth Parliament, 1901-1988. G. S. Reid & M. A. Forrest. 1988. 24.95 (*0-522-84383-2*) Intl Spec Bk.

Australia's Defence Resources: A Compendium of Data. 3rd ed. Ernest McNamara et al. 192p. 1986. pap. 22.00 (*0-08-029881-8*, T110, T120, T130, K122, PPA) Elsevier.

Australia's External Relations in the 1980s: The Interaction of Economic, Political & Strategic Factors. Ed. by Paul Dibb. LC 83-40165. 224p. 1984. text ed. 29.95 (*0-312-06120-X*) St Martin.

Australia's Fan Heritage. Audrey North. 70p. (C). 1990. 75.00 (*0-86439-001-7*, Pub. by Boolarong Pubns AT) St Mut.

Australia's First Fabians: Middle-Class Radicals, Labour Activists, & the Early Labour Movement. Race Mathews. LC 92-45211. (Illus.). 288p. (C). 1993. 59.95 (*0-521-44133-1*); pap. write for info. (*0-521-44678-3*) Cambridge U Pr.

***Australia's Foreign Relations: In the World of the 1990's.** 2nd rev. ed. Gareth Evans & Bruce Grant. 448p. 1995. pap. 34.95 (*0-522-84657-2*) Intl Spec Bk.

Australia's Frontline: Remembering the 1939-45 War. Libby Connors et al. (Orig.). 1992. pap. 16.95 (*0-7022-2446-4*, Pub. by Univ Queensland Pr AT) Intl Spec Bk.

Australia's Greatest Asset. David Pope & Lee Alston. 336p. 1989. pap. 33.00 (*1-86287-013-6*, Pub. by Federation Pr AU) W W Gaunt.

Australia's Greenhouse Policy Seminar. Intro. by John Lessels. (Illus.). 137p. (Orig.). 1992. pap. text ed. 36.00 (*0-85825-569-3*, Pub. by Inst Engrs Aust-EA Bks AT) Accents Pubns.

Australia's Gulf War. Murray Goot & Rodney Tiffen. 1992. pap. 24.95 (*0-522-84463-4*) Intl Spec Bk.

Australia's Home: Its Origins, Builders & Occupiers. Robin Boyd. 224p. 1987. pap. 24.95 (*0-522-84358-1*) Intl Spec Bk.

Australia's Interests & Policies in the Far East. Jack Shepherd. LC 75-30114. (Institute of Pacific Relations Ser.). reprint ed. 34.50 (*0-404-59559-6*) AMS Pr.

Australia's Italians: Culture & Community in a Changing Society. Ed. by Castles et al. 272p. 1992. pap. text ed. 19.95 (*1-86373-170-9*, Pub. by Allen Unwin AT) Paul & Co Pubs.

Australia's Northern Neighbours: Independent or Dependent? Ed. by Edward P. Wolfers. LC 77-362478. 286p. reprint ed. pap. 81.60 (*0-8357-6825-2*, 2035511) Bks Demand.

Australia's Outback: Journeys & Discoveries. Jocelyn Burt. LC 92-32070. (Illus.). 144p. 1993. 35.00 (*0-395-66014-9*) HM.

Australia's Outlook on Asia. Werner Levi. LC 78-26904. 1979. text ed. 49.50 (*0-313-20897-2*, LEAO, Greenwood Pr) Greenwood.

Australia's Resources & Their Development. R. K. Wilson. 406p. (C). 1980. text ed. 120.00 (*0-685-50526-X*, Pub. by Australogia AT) St Mut.

***Australia's Rock Art.** 70p. (Orig.). 1994. pap. 45.00 (*0-7605-0788-0*) Rector Pr.

Australia's Spies & Their Secrets. David McKnight. 400p. 1994. pap. 24.95 (*1-86373-661-1*, Pub. by Allen Unwin AT) Paul & Co Pubs.

Australia's Timeless Land: Alice Springs, Ayers Rock, The Olgas. Max Colwell & David Colwell. 64p. (C). 1989. 50.00 (*0-9594393-5-8*, Pub. by M Colwell Pubns AT) St Mut.

***Australia's Trade Policies.** Ed. by Richard Pomfret. (Illus.). 256p. 1995. pap. 32.00 (*0-19-553536-7*) OUP.

Australia's Voltage Dilemma - 230 Volts Or 240 Volts. Intro. by David K. Sweeting. (National Conference Publication Ser.: No. 93-14). (Illus.). 42p. (Orig.). 1993. pap. text ed. 45.50 (*0-85825-594-4*, Pub. by Inst Engrs Aust-EA Bks AT) Accents Pubns.

Australia's Women: A Documentary History. Kay Daniels & Mary Murnane. (Illus.). 335p. 1989. pap. text ed. 29. 95 (*0-7022-2235-6*, Pub. by Univ Queensland Pr AT) Intl Spec Bk.

Australie-Boudhisme see Grande Encyclopedie

Austranimals. Jill B. Bruce. (Illus.). 32p. (Orig.). (J). (gr. k-4). 1994. 12.95 (*0-86417-569-8*, Pub. by Kangaroo Pr AT) Seven Hills Bk.

An Asterisk (*) at the beginning of an entry indicates that the title is appearing in BIP for the first time.

An Asterisk (*) at the beginning of an entry indicates that the title is appearing in BIP for the first time.

535

Authentic Development in Africa. Brian Walker. LC 85-82567. (Headline Ser.: No. 274). (Illus.). 72p. (Orig.). 1985. pap. 5.95 (*0-87124-102-1*) Foreign Policy.

Authentic Doctrine of the Eucharist. Teresa Whalen. LC 92-21577. 180p. (Orig.). 1992. pap. 12.95 (*1-55612-558-5*, LL1558) Sheed & Ward MO.

Authentic English-Hindi Dictionary. Joeseph DeCosta & A. R. Shukla. (ENG & HIN.). 59.95 (*0-8288-7692-4*, M3647) Fr & Eur.

Authentic Everyday Dress of the Renaissance: All 154 Plates from the "Trachtenbuch" Christoph Weiditz. LC 93-44628. (Illus.). 144p. 1994. reprint ed. pap. 10.95 (*0-486-27975-8*) Dover.

Authentic Existence. Ilija Poplasen. (Illus.). 454p. 1994. 20.00 (*0-935352-26-0*) MIR PA.

Authentic French Fashions of the Twenties. Ed. by JoAnne Olian. 144p. 1990. pap. 7.95 (*0-486-26187-5*) Dover.

Authentic French Provincial Furniture from Provence, Normandy, & Brittany. Text by Henri Algoud et al. LC 93-7055. (Illus.). 1993. pap. 12.95 (*0-486-27535-3*) Dover.

Authentic German Home Style Recipes. 4th ed. Gini Youngkrantz. 290p. 1994. 15.95 (*0-939593-03-3*) Divers Pubns. Duplicate German recipes as they are prepared in their kitchens & translated by the native German author. All recipes use ingredients commonly found in local U.S. grocery stores. This book answers the question asked by so many Americans of German ancestry & individuals who have been stationed or lived in Germany: "HOW CAN I PREPARE THOSE SPECIAL, DELICIOUS GERMAN RECIPES I HAVE TASTED IN THE PAST?" Two of just many testimonials: "Not only are your recipes easy to follow & turn out very successful, but the comments in your book are very entertaining too..."--J.E.R., Mililani, Hawaii & "We've been here almost three years & will be leaving this year. We will really miss our favorite German dishes but thanks to your book we will still be able to enjoy them once we leave Germany!"--by J.B., Ansbach, Germany. Call or write for ordering information: Diversified Publications, P.O. Box 548, Colorado City, CO 81019, (AC 719) 676-3090. ***Publisher Provided Annotation.***

Authentic Gilbert & Sullivan Songbook: 92 Unabridged Selections from All 14 Operas. Gilbert & Sullivan. Ed. by M. Binney & P. Lavender. 23.75 (*0-8446-5576-7*) Peter Smith.

Authentic Gilbert & Sullivan Songbook: 92 Unabridged Selections from All 14 Operas, Reproduced from Early Vocal Scores. William S. Gilbert & Arthur S. Sullivan. Ed. by James Spero. LC 76-55953. (Illus.). 1978. pap. 14.95 (*0-486-23482-7*) Dover.

***Authentic Gospel.** Jeffrey E. Wilson. 31p. 1990. pap. 1.75 (*0-85151-574-6*) Banner of Truth.

Authentic Guide to Drinks of the Civil War Era. Sharon Johnson & Byron Johnson. (Illus.). 216p. (C). 1992. pap. text ed. 14.95 (*0-939631-45-8*) Thomas Publications.

Authentic Guitar Style of Harry Chapin. Ed. by Milton Okun. (Illus.). 55p. (Orig.). 1990. pap. text ed. 10.95 (*0-89524-384-9*) Cherry Lane.

Authentic Guitar Style of Suzanne Vega. Ed. by Mark Phillips. (Illus.). 56p. (Orig.). 1990. pap. text ed. 12.95 (*0-89524-375-X*) Cherry Lane.

Authentic History of Lancaster County, Pennsylvania. J. I. Mombert. Ed. by William L. Iscrupe & Shirley G. Iscrupe. 760p. 1988. reprint ed. 45.00 (*0-944128-01-7*) SW PA Geneal Servs.

Authentic History of the Cato-Street Conspiracy. George T. Wilkinson. LC 75-39305. (Criminology: Historical Perspectives Ser.). (Illus.). 1972. reprint ed. 34.95 (*0-405-04157-8*) Ayer.

Authentic History of the Douglass Monument. John W. Thompson. LC 71-170705. (Black Heritage Library Collection). 1977. reprint ed. 25.95 (*0-8369-8895-7*) Ayer.

***Authentic Hot Rods: The Real "Good Old Days"** Don Montgomery. (Illus.). 208p. 1994. 32.95 (*0-9626454-4-3*) D Montgomery.

Authentic I-Ching: A New Translation. Tr. by Henry Wei. 425p. (Orig.). 1986. 12.95 (*0-87877-091-7*) Newcastle Pub.

Authentic Indian Designs. Ed. by Maria Naylor. LC 74-17711. (Illus.). 256p. 1975. reprint ed. pap. 9.95 (*0-486-23170-4*) Dover.

***Authentic Interpretations on the 1983 Code.** Lawrence G. Wrenn. 68p. (Orig.). 1993. pap. 6.50 (*0-943616-61-1*) Canon Law Soc.

Authentic Leadership: Courage in Action. Robert W. Terry. LC 93-17060. (Joint Publication in the Jossey-Bass Public Administration Series, the Jossey-Bass Nonprofit Sector Series, & the Jossey-Bass Management Ser.). 343p. 1993. 31.95 (*1-55542-547-X*) Jossey-Bass.

***Authentic Leadership: Lifetime Tools That Make a Difference.** J. W. Bizzack. Date not set. pap. 14.00 (*0-9630878-6-X*) Autumn Hse KY.

Authentic Letters of T. Kosciuszko. 15.00 (*0-318-03452-2*) Polish Museum Am.

Authentic Librettos of the French & German Operas. 1980. 19.95 (*0-405-13471-1*) Ayer.

Authentic Librettos of the Italian Operas. 1980. 19.95 (*0-405-13472-X*) Ayer.

Authentic Librettos of the Wagner Operas. Richard Wagner. 1980. 19.95 (*0-405-13470-3*) Ayer.

Authentic Life of Billy the Kid. Pat F. Garrett. LC 54-10053. (Western Frontier Library: No. 3). 1974. reprint ed. pap. 9.95 (*0-8061-1195-X*) U of Okla Pr.

Authentic Memoirs of William Augustus Bowles, Esquire, Ambassador from the United Nations of Creeks & Cherokees, to the Court of London. William A. Bowles. LC 73-146376. (First American Frontier Ser.). 1976. reprint ed. 22.95 (*0-405-02827-X*) Ayer.

Authentic Metaphysics in an Age of Unreality. Leo Sweeney et al. 465p. 1988. text ed. 39.80 (*0-8204-0464-0*) P Lang Pubs.

Authentic Metaphysics in an Age of Unreality. 2nd ed. Leo Sweeney. LC 93-981. 1993. write for info. (*0-8204-2278-9*) P Lang Pubs.

Authentic Mexican: Regional Cooking from the Heart of Mexico. Rick Bayless & Deann G. Bayless. Ed. by Maria D. Guarnaschelli. LC 86-12706. (Cookbook Library). (Illus.). 448p. 1987. 24.95 (*0-688-04394-1*) Morrow.

Authentic Mexican Cooking. Paula Holt & Helen Juarez. 256p. 1984. pap. 8.95 (*0-671-50496-7*, Fireside) S&S Trade.

Authentic Narrative of the Causes Which Led to the Death of Major Andre. Joshua H. Smith. Ed. by Peter Decker. LC 78-76239. (Eyewitness Accounts of the American Revolution Ser., No. 1). (Illus.). 1969. reprint ed. 25.95 (*0-405-01181-4*) Ayer.

Authentic Narrative of the Shipwreck & Sufferings of Mrs. Eliza Bradley. Eliza Bradley. 1986. 12.00 (*0-87770-371-X*) Ye Galleon.

Authentic North American Arctic Circle Indian Clothing for Special Times. (Little Bears Go Visiting Ser.: Bk. 11). (J). (ps-3). write for info. (*0-931363-10-1*) Celia Totus Enter.

Authentic North American California Indian Clothing for Special Times. (Little Bears Go Visiting Ser.: Bk. 10). (J). (ps-3). write for info. (*0-931363-09-8*) Celia Totus Enter.

Authentic North American Columbia River Plateau & California Indian Cradleboards. (Baby Bears Go Visiting Ser.: Bk. 16). (J). (ps-5). write for info. (*0-931363-15-2*) Celia Totus Enter.

Authentic North American Columbia River Plateau Indian Clothing for Special Times. (Little Bears Go Visiting Ser.: Bk. 2). (J). (ps-3). write for info. (*0-931363-01-2*) Celia Totus Enter.

Authentic North American Columbia River Plateau Yakima Indian Clothing for Special Times. (Little Bears Go Visiting Ser.: Bk. 1). (J). (ps-3). write for info. (*0-931363-00-4*) Celia Totus Enter.

Authentic North American Great Basin Indian Clothing for Special Times. (Little Bears Go Visiting Ser.: Bk. 7). (J). (ps-3). write for info. (*0-931363-06-3*) Celia Totus Enter.

Authentic North American Great Basin, Southwest, & Southeast Cradleboards. (Baby Bears Go Visiting Ser.: Bk. 14). (J). (ps-5). write for info. (*0-931363-13-6*) Celia Totus Enter.

Authentic North American Indian Baby Cradles. (Baby Bears Go Visiting Ser.: Bk. 17). (J). (ps-5). write for info. (*0-931363-16-0*) Celia Totus Enter.

Authentic North American Oregon Indian Clothing for Special Times. (Little Bears Go Visiting Ser.: Bk. 12). (J). (ps-3). write for info. (*0-931363-11-X*) Celia Totus Enter.

Authentic North American Pacific Northwest Coast Indian Clothing for Special Times. (Little Bears Go Visiting Ser.: Bk. 3). (J). (ps-3). write for info. (*0-931363-02-0*) Celia Totus Enter.

Authentic North American Pacific Northwest Coast, Woodlands & Arctic Circle Indian Cradles & Cradleboards. (Baby Bears Go Visiting Ser.: Bk. 15). (J). (ps-5). write for info. (*0-931363-14-4*) Celia Totus Enter.

Authentic North American Plains Indian Clothing for Special Times. (Little Bears Go Visiting Ser.: Bk. 4). (J). (ps-3). write for info. (*0-931363-03-9*) Celia Totus Enter.

Authentic North American Plains Indian Clothing for Special Times. (Little Bears Go Visiting Ser.: Bk. 6). (J). (ps-3). write for info. (*0-931363-05-5*) Celia Totus Enter.

Authentic North American Plains Indian Cradle Boards. (Baby Bears Go Visiting Ser.: Bk. 13). (J). (ps-3). write for info. (*0-931363-12-8*) Celia Totus Enter.

Authentic North American Southeast Indian Clothing for Special Times. (Little Bears Go Visiting Ser.: Bk. 8). (J). (ps-3). write for info. (*0-931363-07-1*) Celia Totus Enter.

Authentic North American Southwest Indian Clothing for Special Times. (Little Bears Go Visiting Ser.: Bk. 5). (J). (ps-3). write for info. (*0-931363-04-7*) Celia Totus Enter.

Authentic North American Woodland Indian Clothing for Special Times. (Little Bears Go Visiting Ser.: Bk. 9). (J). (ps-3). write for info. (*0-931363-08-X*) Celia Totus Enter.

Authentic Pasta Book. Fred Plotkin. 1989. pap. 14.00 (*0-671-68212-1*, Fireside) S&S Trade.

Authentic Public Speaking: A Personalized Approach. Loren D. Crane. 272p. 1986. per. 23.95 (*0-8403-4000-1*) Kendall-Hunt.

Authentic Reading Assessment: Practices & Possibilities. Ed. by Sheila W. Valencia et al. LC 93-11920. 328p. 1993. pap. 18.00 (*0-87207-765-9*) Intl Reading.

Authentic Records of Revival, Now in Progress in the United Kingdom. Ed. by William Reid. (Revival Library). viii, 478p. 1980. reprint ed. lib. bdg. 17.50 (*0-940033-17-8*) R O Roberts.

Authentic Records of Revivals Now in Progress in the United Kingdom. William Reid. 486p. 1980. 17.50 (*0-939464-33-0*) Labyrinth Pr.

Authentic Rubaiyyat of Sufi Poet Omar Khayaam. Omar Khayaam. Tr. by Omar Ali Shah. 100p. 1993. text ed. write for info. (*0-9636083-0-4*) Inst Diffusion.

***Authentic Rule of the World.** Ilija Poplasen. (Illus.). 480p. (YA). (gr. 12-12). 1995. 20.00 (*0-935352-35-X*) MIR PA.

***Authentic School Science: Knowing & Learning in Open-Inquiry Science Laboratories.** Michael-Wolff Roth. LC 94-30832. (Science & Technology Education Library Ser.: 1). 1995. lib. bdg. 106.00 (*0-7923-3088-9*) Kluwer Ac.

Authentic Self. Robert R. Ehman. 146p. 1994. 22.95 (*0-87975-846-5*) Prometheus Bks.

Authentic Self: Toward a Philosophy of Personality. Walter LaCentra. (American University Studies: Philosophy: Ser. V, Vol. 36). 211p. (C). 1987. text ed. 35.95 (*0-8204-0460-8*) P Lang Pubs.

Authentic Small Houses of the Twenties: Illustrations & Floor Plans of 254 Characteristic Homes. Robert T. Jones. x, 278p. 1987. reprint ed. pap. 12.95 (*0-486-25406-2*) Dover.

Authentic Story of Taiwan: An Illustrated History. Ed. by Marc Hutsebaut. (Illus.). 160p. 1991. 110.00 (*957-638-056-1*, HSB001, Pub. by SMC Pub CC) Oriental Bk Store.

Authentic Transformation: A New Vision of Christ & Culture. John H. Yoder et al. 224p. (Orig.). 1995. pap. 15.95 (*0-687-02273-8*) Abingdon.

Authentic Turkish Designs. Azade Akar. LC 92-4843. (Design Library). 1992. pap. write for info. (*0-486-27211-7*) Dover.

Authentic Vegetarian Cookery. John Bryant & Charray Bryant. (Illus.). 406p. (C). 1989. ring bd. 39.95 (*0-9622778-1-9*) Wild Thyme.

Authentic Victorian Decoration & Ornamentation in Full Color: 46 Plates from "Studies in Design" Christopher Dresser. (Pictorial Archive Ser.). 48p. (Orig.). 1986. pap. 7.95 (*0-486-25083-0*) Dover.

Authentic Victorian Stencil Designs. Ed. by Carol B. Grafton. (Illus.). 64p. (Orig.). 1982. pap. 4.95 (*0-486-24337-0*) Dover.

Authentic Victorian Stoves, Heaters, Ranges, Etc. An Unabridged Reprint of the Illustrated Floyd, Wells & Co. Catalog, ca. 1898. Floyd, Wells & Co., Staff. (Illus.). 192p. 1988. reprint ed. pap. 7.95 (*0-486-25610-3*) Dover.

Authentic Voices: Arkansas Culture, 1541-1860. Ed. & Intro. by Sarah Fountain. (Illus.). 325p. 1986. lib. bdg. 28.95 (*0-9615143-1-0*) Univ Central AR Pr.

Authentic Witnesses: Approaches to Medieval Texts & Manuscripts. Mary A. Rouse & Richard H. Rouse. LC 89-40389. (Mediaeval Studies: Vol. 27). (C). 1993. pap. text ed. 29.95 (*0-268-00623-7*) U of Notre Dame Pr.

Authentic Witnesses: Approaches to Medieval Texts & Manuscripts. Ed. by Richard H. Rouse & Mary A. Rouse. LC 89-40389. (Mediaeval Studies: No. 27). (C). 1990. text ed. 59.95 (*0-268-00622-9*) U of Notre Dame Pr.

Authentic Writer: Freshman Rhetoric & Composition. James C. Mellard & James C. Wilcox. 1977. pap. text ed. 14.00 (*0-669-85639-8*) Heath.

Authentic Writings of Ignatius: A Study of Linguistic Criteria. Milton P. Brown, Jr. LC 63-19458. 175p. reprint ed. pap. 49.90 (*0-8357-9096-7*, 2017888) Bks Demand.

***Authenticating Culture in Interwar Japan: Kuki Shuzo & the Rise of National Aesthetics.** Leslie Pincus. LC 95-12978. (Twentieth-Century Japan Ser.: Vol. 5). 1995. write for info. (*0-520-20134-5*) U CA Pr.

***Authenticities: Philosophical Reflections on Musical Performance.** Peter Kivy. LC 94-36842. (Illus.). 296p. 1995. 35.00x (*0-8014-3046-1*) Cornell U Pr.

Authenticity: The Being of the Self, the World, & the Other. Robert Kuhry. Ed. by Diane Parker. LC 92-50860. 200p. 1993. pap. 11.95 (*0-88247-978-4*, 978) R & E Pubs.

Authenticity & Early Music. Ed. by Nicholas Kenyon. (Illus.). 240p. 1989. pap. 19.95 (*0-19-816153-0*) OUP.

Authenticity & Islamic Liberalism. Jamal Khwaja. 150p. 1987. 14.00 (*0-8364-2150-7*, Pub. by Allied II) S Asia.

Authenticity & Learning: Nietzhe's Educational Philosophy. David E. Cooper. (Modern Revivals in Philosophy Ser.). 172p. 1992. 49.95 (*0-7512-0012-3*, Pub. by Gregg Revivals UK) Ashgate Pub Co.

Authenticity in Music. Raymond Leppard. 88p. (Orig.). 1988. pap. 8.50 (*0-931340-20-9*, Amadeus Pr) Timber.

Authenticity of Prometheus Bound. Mark Griffith. LC 76-14031. (Cambridge Classical Studies). 1977. 69.95 (*0-521-21099-2*) Cambridge U Pr.

Authenticity of the Pauline Epistles in the Light of Stylostatistical Analysis. Ken Neumann. (Society of Biblical Literature Dissertation Ser.). 403p. 1990. 25.95 (*1-55540-428-6*, 06 21 20); pap. 16.95 (*1-55540-429-4*) Scholars Pr GA.

Authigenic Albite in ta Jurassic Alkaline, Saline Lake Deposit, Colorado Plateau--Evidence for Early Diagenetic Origin. Neil S. Fishman et al. Date not set. write for info. (*0-318-72715-3*) US Geol Survey.

Author a Month (for Dimes) Sharron L. McElmeel. (Illus.). 175p. (Orig.). 1993. pap. text ed. 23.50 (*0-87287-952-6*) Teacher Ideas Pr.

Author a Month (for Nickels) Sharron L. McElmeel. (Illus.). 172p. 1990. pap. text ed. 24.00 (*0-87287-827-9*) Libs Unl.

Author a Month (for Pennies) Sharron L. McElmeel. (Illus.). 224p. 1988. pap. text ed. 24.50 (*0-87287-661-6*) Libs Unl.

Author & Added Entry Catalog of the American Missionary Association Archives, 3 vols., Set. LC 72-104397. 1970. text ed. 825.00 (*0-8371-3602-4*, AMA/, Greenwood Pr) Greenwood.

Author & Agent: Eudora Welty & Diarmuid Russell. Michael Kreyling. 1991. 22.95 (*0-374-10727-0*) FS&G.

Author & Agent: Eudora Welty & Diarmuid Russell. Michael Kreyling. (Illus.). 224p. 1992. pap. 9.00 (*0-374-52330-4*, Noonday) FS&G.

Author & Audience: A Readings & Workshops Guide. Ed. by Amy Holman. 108p. 1991. pap. 6.95 (*0-913734-24-1*) Poets & Writers.

Author & Audience in Latin Literature. Ed. by Tony Woodman & Jonathan Powell. 288p. (C). 1992. 64.95 (*0-521-38307-2*) Cambridge U Pr.

Author & Classified Catalogues of the Royal Botanic Gardens Library, 9 vols. Royal Botanic Gardens Library Staff, Kew, England. 1973. Author, 5 vols. lib. bdg. 545.00 (*0-8161-1086-7*, Hall Library); Classified, 4 vols. lib. bdg. 455.00 (*0-8161-1087-5*, Hall Library) G K Hall.

Author & Editor at Work: Making a Better Book. Elsie M. Stainton. 96p. 1981. pap. 7.95 (*0-8020-6449-3*) U of Toronto Pr.

Author & His Publisher. Siegfried Unseld. Tr. by Hunter Hannum & Hildegarde Hannum. LC 79-26021. 1980. 15.00 (*0-226-84189-8*) U Ch Pr.

Author & Key Word Index to Twenty-Four Conferences & Symposia on Environmental Design Research, Design Methods & Computer-Aided Design, Nos. 1034-1036. Donald P. Grant. 1976. 12.50 (*0-686-20395-X*) CPL Biblios.

Author & Printer in Victorian England. Allan C. Dooley. LC 92-10420. (Victorian Literature & Culture Ser.). 224p. (C). 1992. text ed. 30.00 (*0-8139-1401-9*) U Pr of Va.

Author & Subject Catalogues of the Library of the Peabody Museum of Archaeology & Ethnology, 54 vols, Set. Harvard University, Peabody Museum of Archaeology & Ethnology Staff. 1970. lib. bdg. 6,410.00 (*0-8161-0647-9*, Hall Library) G K Hall.

Author & Subject Catalogues of the Library of the Peabody Museum of Archaeology & Ethnology: Fourth Supplement, 7 vols. Peabody Museum of Archaeology & Ethnology Editors. 1979. lib. bdg. 1,080.00 (*0-8161-0253-8*, Hall Library) G K Hall.

Author & Subject Catalogues of the Library of the Peabody Museum of Archaeology & Ethnology, First Supplement, 12 vols, Set. Harvard University, Peabody Museum of Archaeology & Ethnology Staff. 1975. lib. bdg. 1,775.00 (*0-8161-0861-7*, Hall Library) G K Hall.

Author & Subject Catalogues of the Library of the Peabody Museum of Archaeology & Ethnology, Second Supplement, 6 vols, Set. Harvard University, Peabody Museum of Archaeology & Ethnology Staff. 1972. lib. bdg. 920.00 (*0-8161-0960-5*, Hall Library) G K Hall.

Author & Subject Catalogues of the Library of the Peabody Museum of Archaeology & Ethnology, Third Supplement, 7 vols., Set. Harvard University, Peabody Museum of Archaeology & Ethnology Staff. 1975. lib. bdg. 1,060.00 (*0-8161-1168-5*, Hall Library) G K Hall.

Author & Subject Catalogues of the Naval Library, Ministry of Defence, 5 vols., Set. London, Ministry of Defense, Naval Library Staff. 1970. lib. bdg. 545.00 (*0-8161-0755-6*, Hall Library) G K Hall.

Author & Subject Indexes, Combination Offer: Author & Subject Indexes of Mathematical Reviews, 1973-1979; Author & Subject Indexes of Mathematical Reviews, 1980-1984, 2 vols., Set. pap. 3,536.00 (*0-8218-0151-1*, MRCIN/73/84C) Am Math.

Author & Subject Indexes, Combination Offer: Author Index of Mathematical Reviews, 1940-1959; Cumulative Subject Index, 1940-1958, 2 vols., Set. pap. 667.00 (*0-8218-0150-3*, MRCIN/40/59C) Am Math.

Author & Subject Indexes of Mathematical Reviews: 1973-1979, 12 Vol. LC 42-4221. 8417p. 1981. pap. 1,858.00 (*0-8218-0035-3*, MREVIN 73/79) Am Math.

Author & Subject Indexes of Mathematical Reviews, 1980-1984, 12 vols., Set. LC 42-4221. 9878p. 1986. pap. 2,250.00 (*0-8218-0105-8*, MREVIN/80/84) Am Math.

Author & Subject Indices to Kansas State University Doctoral Dissertations, Masters Theses & Masters Reports. Evan W. Williams & Herbert H. Beckwith. LC 76-622728. (Libraries Bibliography: No. 5). 1969. 10.00 (*0-686-20804-8*) KSU.

Author & Subject Indices to Kansas State University Doctoral Dissertations, Masters Theses & Masters Reports: First Supplement 1969-1973. Evan W. Williams. LC 76-374570. (Libraries Bibliography: No. 5). 1975. 17.50 (*0-686-20805-6*) KSU.

Author, Art & the Market: Rereading the History of Aesthetics. Martha Woodmanesee. 1993. 29.50 (*0-231-08060-3*) Col U Pr.

Author As Character in the Works of Sholom Aleichem. Victoria Aarons. LC 84-22703. (Studies in Art & Religious Interpretation: Vol. 3). 192p. 1989. lib. bdg. 79.95 (*0-88946-553-3*) E Mellen.

Author! Author! Susan Terris. 1990. 14.95 (*0-374-34995-9*) FS&G.

Author Bibliography of English Language Fiction in the Library of Congress Through 1950, 8 vols., Set. 1976. lib. bdg. 870.00 (*0-8161-0966-4*, Hall Library) G K Hall.

Author Biographies Master Index. 4th ed. 1993. 260.00 (*0-8103-7582-6*) Gale.

Author Biographies Master Index, Vol. 1, A-K. 4th ed. 1993. write for info. (*0-8103-7891-4*) Gale.

Author Biographies Master Index, Vol. 2, L-Z. 4th ed. 1993. write for info. (*0-8103-7892-2*) Gale.

An Asterisk (*) at the beginning of an entry indicates that the title is appearing in BIP for the first time.

An Asterisk (*) at the beginning of an entry indicates that the title is appearing in BIP for the first time.

A

Authority of Jesus Christ. Frank E. Stranges. 12p. 1985. pap. text ed. 2.00 (0-933470-08-8) Intl Evang.

Authority of Language: Heidegger, Wittgenstein, & the Threat of Philosophical Nihilism. James C. Edwards. 272p. 1990. lib. bdg. 32.95 (0-8130-0942-1) U Press Fla.

Authority of Law: Essays on Law & Morality. Joseph Raz. 1983. pap. 26.00 (0-19-825493-8) OUP.

Authority of Publius: A Reading of the Federalist Papers. Albert Furtwangler. LC 83-18806. 152p. (C). 1984. 29.95 (0-8014-1643-4); pap. 10.95 (0-8014-9339-0) Cornell U Pr.

Authority of Scripture: A Study of the Reformation & Post-Reformation Understanding of the Bible. John K. Reid. LC 79-8716. 286p. 1981. reprint ed. text ed. 59.75 (0-313-22191-X, REAS, Greenwood Pr) Greenwood.

Authority of the Believer. A. L. Gill. 102p. 1990. spiral bd. 12.95 (0-941975-03-7) Power Hse Pub.

Authority of the Believer. A. L. Gill & Joyce Gill. 147p. (KOR.). 1993. spiral bd. 12.95 (0-941975-20-7) Power Hse Pub.

Authority of the Believer. J. A. MacMillan. LC 80-68065. 96p. 1981. pap. 2.99 (0-87509-152-0) Chr Pubns.

***Authority of the Bible.** Woodrow Kroll. 1994. pap. 2.50 (0-8474-0894-9) Back to Bible.

Authority of the Consumer. Ed. by Russell Keat et al. LC 93-24576. 1993. 50.00 (0-415-08918-2, Routledge NY); 17.95 (0-415-08919-0, Routledge NY) Routledge.

Authority of the New Testament Scriptures see Redemptive History & the New Testament Scriptures

Authority of the Old Testament. John Bright. LC 67-14989. (Twin Brooks Ser.). 272p. 1975. pap. 14.99 (0-8010-0637-6) Baker Bk.

Authority, Power & Leadership in the Jewish Community: Cases & Issues. Ed. by Daniel J. Elazar. 334p. 1991. 51.00 (0-8191-8128-5); pap. 30.00 (0-8191-8129-3) U Pr of Amer.

Authority, Power & Policy in the U. S. S. R. Essays Dedicated to Leonard Schapiro. Ed. by T. H. Rigby et al. 207p. 1985. pap. 10.95 (0-312-06135-8) St Martin.

Authority to Heal. Ken Blue. 168p. (Orig.). (C). 1987. pap. 8.99 (0-8308-1700-X, 1700) InterVarsity.

Authority Without Power: Law & the Japanese Paradox. John O. Haley. (Studies on Law & Social Control). 256p. 1994. reprint ed. pap. 15.95 (0-19-509257-0) OUP.

Authorization Agreements for Legal Services Clients. Legal Assistance Foundation of Chicago. 52p. 1987. pap. 5.00 (0-685-23156-9, 42,246) NCLS Inc.

Authorized Ben Treasury. John Troy. (Illus.). 240p. 1994. 14.95 (1-57223-010-X); pap. 9.95 (1-57223-011-8) Outlook Pubng.

Authorized Daily Prayer Book. Joseph H. Hertz. (ENG & HEB.). 1948. 30.00 (0-8197-0094-0) Bloch.

Authorized Insider's Guide to ACT. Douglas J. Wolf. 184p. 1992. 26.95 (0-8306-2455-4, 3856, Windcrest); pap. 16.95 (0-8306-2454-6, 3856, Windcrest) TAB Bks.

Authorized Insider's Guide to Act. Douglas J. Wolf. 1992. text ed. 26.95 (0-07-071331-6) McGraw.

Authorized Insider's Guide to Act! Douglas J. Wolf. 1992. pap. 16.95 (0-07-157804-8) McGraw.

Authorized King James Version of 1611 in Exegeses. Herb Jahn. LC 92-90034. 832p. 1992. pap. 20.00 (0-9631951-0-7) H Jahn.

***Authorized Persons Only.** Andrei Frolov. 1995. 13.95 (0-533-11178-1) Vantage.

***Authorized Texas Ranger Cookbook.** John B. Harris & Cheryl Harris. (Illus.). 222p. 1994. write for info. (0-9641614-0-0) Harris Farms.

Authorizing Fictions: Jose Donoso's "Casa de Campo" Marie Murphy. (Monografias Ser.: No. A 152). 160p. (C). 1992. text ed. 63.00 (1-85566-020-2, Pub. by Tamesis Bks Ltd UK) Boydell & Brewer.

Authorizing Petrarch. William J. Kennedy. 320p. 1995. 36.50x (0-8014-2974-9) Cornell U Pr.

Authorizing the Past: The Rhetoric of History in Seventeenth-Century New England. Stephen C. Arch. LC 94-8729. 256p. 1994. lib. bdg. 30.00 (0-87580-188-9) N Ill U Pr.

Authorizing Words: Speech, Writing, & Print in the English Renaissance. Martin Elsky. LC 89-42875. (Illus.). 272p. 1990. 34.95 (0-8014-2173-X) Cornell U Pr.

Authors. Karl Miller. 234p. 1991. reprint ed. pap. 14.95 (0-19-212277-0) OUP.

Authors: Critical & Biographical References. 2nd ed. Richard E. Combs & Nancy R. Owen. LC 93-774. 477p. 1993. 49.50 (0-8108-2679-8) Scarecrow.

Authors & Artists, Vol. 6. Agnes Garrett & Helga P. McCue. 1991. 69.00 (0-8103-5055-6) Gale.

Authors & Artists, Vol. 7. Collier. 1991. 69.00 (0-8103-5056-4) Gale.

Authors & Artists, Vol. 8. Agnes Garrett & Helga P. McCue. 1992. 69.00 (0-8103-7583-4) Gale.

Authors & Artists, Vol. 10. Agnes Garrett & Helga P. McCue. 1993. 69.00 (0-8103-8024-2) Gale.

Authors & Artists, Vol. 11. Agnes Garrett & Helga P. McCue. 1993. 69.00 (0-8103-8025-0) Gale.

Authors & Artists, Vol. 12. Collier. 1994. 69.00 (0-8103-8565-1, 003492) Gale.

Authors & Artists, Vol. 13. Collier. 1994. 69.00 (0-8103-8566-X, 003493) Gale.

***Authors & Artists, Vol. 14.** Ed. by E. A. DesChenes. 1994. 59.00 (0-8103-5730-5) Gale.

Authors & Artists for Young Adults, Vol. 1. Ed. by Anne Commire et al. (Illus.). 1988. 69.00 (0-8103-2763-5) Gale.

Authors & Artists for Young Adults, Vol. 2. Ed. by Anne Commire et al. 1989. 69.00 (0-8103-5051-3) Gale.

Authors & Artists for Young Adults, Vol. 3. Ed. by Agnes Garrett & Helga P. McCue. 1989. 69.00 (0-8103-5052-1, 003413-99584) Gale.

Authors & Artists for Young Adults, Vol. 9. Ed. by Laurie Collier. (Illus.). 240p. 1992. 69.00 (0-8103-7584-2, 003421) Gale.

Authors & Artists for Young Adults, Vol. 4: A Biographical Guide to Novelists, Poets, Playwrights, Screenwriters, Lyricists, Illustrators, Cartoonists, Animators, & Other Creative Artists, Vol. 4. Ed. by Agnes Garret & Helga P. McCue. 250p. 1990. 69.00 (0-8103-5053-X) Gale.

Authors & Artists for Young Adults, Vol. 5: A Biographical Guide to Novelists, Poets, Playwrights Screenwriters, Lyricists, Illustrators, Cartoonists, Animators, & Other Creative Artists, Vol. 5. Ed. by Agnes Garrett & Helga P. McCue. 1990. 69.00 (0-8103-5054-8) Gale.

Authors & Authenticity. Patrick Parrinder. 400p. 1991. text ed. 79.00 (0-231-07646-0); pap. text ed. 25.00 (0-231-07647-9) Col U Pr.

Authors & Friends. Anne Fields. LC 05-2567. 1991. 16.00 (0-403-00092-0) Scholarly.

Authors & Friends. Annie Fields. (Illus.). 1970. reprint ed. 18.00 (0-404-00596-9) AMS Pr.

Authors & Friends. Annie Fields. (Notable American Authors Ser.). 1992. reprint ed. lib. bdg. 75.00 (0-7812-2826-3) Rprt Serv.

Authors & Friends. Annie A. Fields. (BCL1-PS American Literature Ser.). 355p. 1992. reprint ed. lib. bdg. 89.00 (0-7812-6610-6) Rprt Serv.

Authors & I. Charles L. Hind. LC 68-54351. (Essay Index Reprint Ser.). 1977. 23.95 (0-8369-0543-1) Ayer.

Authors & Illustrators Through the Year: Ready-to-Use Literature Activities for Grades K-3. David J. Fiday. 320p. 1989. spiral bd. 26.95 (0-87628-001-7) Ctr Appl Res.

Authors & Others. Alice P. Cooper. LC 70-107689. (Essay Index Reprint Ser.). 1977. 21.95 (0-8369-1493-7) Ayer.

Authors & Owners: The Invention of Copyright. Mark Rose. LC 92-43010. 190p. (Orig.). 1993. text ed. 29.00 (0-674-05308-7) HUP.

***Authors & Owners: The Invention of Copyright.** Mark Rose. 192p. (Orig.). (C). 1995. pap. text ed. 14.95 (0-674-05309-5) HUP.

Authors & Publishers: Agreements & Legal Aspects of Publishing. 2nd ed. Sarna. 232p. 1987. 52.50 (0-409-80628-5) Butterworth Legal Pubs.

Authors & Texts in Byzantium. Alexander Kazdhan. (Collected Studies: No. CS 400). 336p. 1993. 92.00 (0-86078-362-6, Pub. by Variorum UK) Ashgate Pub Co.

Authors & the Book Trade. Frank A. Swinnerton. LC 79-117849. (Essay Index Reprint Ser.). 1977. 19.95 (0-8369-1723-5) Ayer.

Authors & Their Works. E. Cobham Brewer. 1971. 59.95 (0-87968-679-0) Gordon Pr.

Authors-at-Arms. Charles P. Hawkes. LC 70-107709. (Essay Index Reprint Ser.). 1977. 21.95 (0-8369-1511-9) Ayer.

Author's Chair & Beyond: Language & Literacy in a Primary Classroom. Ellen B. Karelitz. LC 92-37259. (Illus.). 217p. 1993. pap. text ed. 19.00 (0-435-08781-9, 08781) Heinemann.

Author's Choice. Elizabeth August. (Men Made in America Ser.). 1993. mass mkt. 3.59 (0-373-45158-X, 1-45158-2) Silhouette.

Author's Craft. Arnold Bennett. LC 74-5396. (Collected Works of Arnold Bennett: Vol. 5). 1977. reprint ed. 21.95 (0-518-19086-2) Ayer.

Author's Craft & Other Critical Writings of Arnold Bennett. Arnold Bennett. Ed. by Samuel Hynes. LC 68-12706. (Regents Critics Ser.). 301p. reprint ed. pap. 85.80 (0-7837-0230-2, 2040538) Bks Demand.

Author's Day. Daniel Pinkwater. LC 92-18154. (Illus.). 32p. (J). (gr. k-3). 1993. text ed. 13.95 (0-02-774642-9, Mac Bks Young Read) S&S Childrens.

Authors Dead & Living. Frank L. Lucas. LC 68-29226. (Essay Index Reprint Ser.). 1977. reprint ed. 20.95 (0-8369-0633-0) Ayer.

Author's Dimension: Selected Essays. Christa Wolf. Ed. by Alexander Stephan. Tr. by Jan Van Heurck. 1990. 27.50 (0-374-12302-0) FS&G.

***Author's Dimension: Selected Essays.** Christa Wolf. Ed. by Alexander Stephan. Tr. by Jan Van Heurck. xii, 336p. 1995. pap. 14.95 (0-226-90494-6) U Ch Pr.

Author's Farce. Henry Fielding. Ed. by Charles B. Woods. LC 65-27454. (Regents Restoration Drama Ser.). 171p. (Orig.). reprint ed. pap. 48.80 (0-7837-0152-7, 2040439) Bks Demand.

Authors for Children: A Calendar. Sharron L. McElmeel. 1992. 10.00 (0-931510-43-0) Hi Willow.

***Author's Guide to Biomedical Journals: Complete Manuscript Submission Instruction for 185 Leading Biomedical Periodicals.** Ed. by Mary A. Liebert. 628p. 1994. 164.00 (0-913113-61-1) M Liebert.

Author's Guide to Children's Book Promotion. rev. ed. Susan S. Raab. 58p. 1990. pap. 9.95 (0-9621211-1-8) Raab Assocs.

***Author's Guide to Children's Book Promotion.** rev. ed. Susan S. Raab & Johanna Bierwirth. 85p. 1994. pap. 12.95 (0-9621211-3-4) Raab Assocs.

Author's Guide to College Textbook Publishing. rev. ed. 1983. 1.00 (0-686-48071-6) AAP.

Author's Guide to Journals in the Behavioral Sciences. Alvin Wang. 496p. 1989. pap. 24.95 (0-8058-0313-0); 3.5 hd 49.95 (1-56321-053-3); 5.25 hd 49.95 (1-56321-054-1) L Erlbaum Assocs.

Author's Guide to Manuscript Preparation. McGraw-Hill, College Division Staff. 1992. pap. text ed. write for info. (0-07-046733-1) McGraw.

Author's Guide to Nursing Journals. Ed. by Susan C. Slaninka. (Orig.). (C). 1994. pap. text ed. 19.95 (0-9628084-3-1) Hlth Mngmnt Pubns.

Author's Guide to Publishing Better Articles in Better Journals in the Behavioral Sciences. Joel Kupfersmid & Donald M. Wonderly. 129p. (Orig.). (C). 1994. pap. text ed. 19.95 (0-88422-123-7) Clinical Psych.

Author's Guide to Social Work Journals. 3rd ed. Henry N. Mendelsohn. LC 90-20573. 284p. 1992. 26.95 (0-87101-219-7) Natl Assn Soc Wkrs.

Authors' Guide to the Journals of the American Meteorological Society. 2nd ed. (Illus.). 32p. 1992. pap. write for info. (1-878220-07-1) Am Meteorological.

Author's Handbook. Franklynn Peterson & Judi Kesselman-Turkel. 248p. 1982. pap. 8.95 (0-13-053900-7) P-H.

Author's Handbook. 4th ed. B. J. Lowe. 48p. (Orig.). 1992. pap. 10.00 (0-88415-050-X) Gulf Pub.

Authors' Insights: Turning Teenagers into Readers & Writers. Ed. by Donald R. Gallo. 131p. (YA). (gr. 9-12). 1992. pap. 14.95 (0-86709-294-7, 0294) Boynton Cook Pubs.

Authors of Books for Young People. 3rd ed. Martha E. Ward et al. LC 90-32569. 784p. 1990. 59.50 (0-8108-2293-8) Scarecrow.

Authors of Confusion. Robert R. Gustafson. pap. 1.45 (0-686-12743-9) Grace Pub Co.

Authors of Pictures, Draftsmen of Words. Ruth Hubbard. LC 88-34641. 176p. (C). 1989. pap. text ed. 18.50 (0-435-08491-7) Heinemann.

Authors of Plant Names: A List of Authors of Scientific Names of Plants with Recommended Standard Forms of Their Names, Including Abbreviations. R. K. Brummitt & C. E. Powell. 732p. 1992. lib. bdg. 75.00 (0-947643-44-3, Pub. by Royal Botanic Garden UK) Lubrecht & Cramer.

Authors of the Day: Studies in Contemporary Literature. Grant M. Overton. LC 75-156700. (Essay Index Reprint Ser.). 1977. reprint ed. 28.95 (0-8369-2289-1) Ayer.

***Authors of the Middle Ages Vol. II, Nos. 5-6: Historical & Religious Writers of the Latin West.** Mews Constant & Valerie I. Flint. Ed. by Patrick J. Geary. 192p. 1995. 55.50 (0-86078-488-6, Pub. by Variorum UK) Ashgate Pub Co.

Authors of Their Own Lives: Intellectual Autobiographies by Twenty American Sociologists. Ed. by Bennett M. Berger. 503p. 1990. 40.00 (0-520-06555-7) U CA Pr.

Authors of Their Own Lives: Intellectual Autobiographies by Twenty American Sociologists. Ed. by Bennett M. Berger. 1992. pap. 16.00 (0-520-06556-5) U CA Pr.

Authors on Film. Ed. by Harry M. Geduld. LC 72-75390. (Midland Bks.: No. 179). 319p. reprint ed. pap. 91.00 (0-8357-9197-1, 2013005) Bks Demand.

Author's Suggestions for the Use of Cases & Materials on Federal Courts. 9th ed. Charles T. McCormick et al. (University Casebook Ser.). 44p. (C). 1992. pap. text ed. write for info. (1-56662-054-6) Foundation Pr.

Authors Take Sides on the Spanish Civil War. W. H. Auden et al. 1971. 59.95 (0-87968-680-4) Gordon Pr.

Authors to Themselves: Milton & the Revelation of History. Marshall Grossman. 220p. 1988. 59.95 (0-521-34037-3) Cambridge U Pr.

Author's Voice. Richard Greenberg. 1987. pap. 2.75 (0-8222-0079-1) Dramatists Play.

Authorship. Ed. by Peter Davison et al. LC 77-90619. (Literary Taste, Culture & Mass Communication Ser.: Vol. 10). 385p. 1978. lib. bdg. 110.00 (0-85964-045-0) Chadwyck-Healey.

Authorship: The Dynamic Principles of Creative Writing. Doran W. Cannon. 224p. (C). 1993. teacher ed 19.95 (1-883636-12-4); lib. bdg. 24.95 (1-883636-07-8); pap. 15.95 (1-883636-10-8) Hannah Hse.

Authorship & Audience: Literary Performance in the American Renaissance. Stephen Railton. 247p. 1992. text ed. 37.50 (0-691-06925-5); pap. text ed. 13.95 (0-691-01516-3) Princeton U Pr.

Authorship & Copyright. David Saunders. LC 91-43745. 256p. 1992. 49.95 (0-415-04158-9, A7892) Routledge.

Authorship & Literary Subversions in the Romantic Period: Pushkin, Scott, Hoffman. David G. Kropf. LC 93-26838. 1994. 39.50 (0-8047-2300-1) Stanford U Pr.

Authorship of Shakespeare. James G. McManaway. LC 62-4031. (Folger Guides to the Age of Shakespeare Ser.). 1962. pap. 4.95 (0-918016-25-8) Folger Bks.

Authorship of Shakespeare, 2 vols., Set. Nathaniel Holmes. LC 77-135734. reprint ed. 105.00 (0-404-03316-4) AMS Pr.

Authorship of Shakespeare's Plays: A Socio-Linguistic Study. Jonathan Hope. LC 93-29834. (Illus.). 208p. (C). 1994. 49.95 (0-521-41737-6) Cambridge U Pr.

Authorship of the Equatorie of the Planetis. Kari A. Schmidt. (Chaucer Studies: Vol. 19). (Illus.). 320p. (C). 1993. text ed. 71.00 (0-85991-370-8) Boydell & Brewer.

Authorship of the Platonic Epistles. Reginald Hackforth. (Publications of the University of Manchester, Classical Ser.: No. 2). 203p. 1985. reprint ed. 25.87 (3-487-05451-5, Pub. by Georg Olms GW) Lubrecht & Cramer.

Authorship of the Vengement Alixandre & of the Venjance Alixandre. Edward C. Armstrong. (Elliott Monographs: Vol. 19). 1926. pap. 15.00 (0-527-02622-0) Periodicals Srv.

Authorship of Timon of Athens. Ernest H. Wright. (Authorship of "Timon of Athens" Ser.). reprint ed. 24.50 (0-404-07044-2) AMS Pr.

Authorship of Wuthering Heights. Irene Willis. LC 75-30845. (Studies in the Brontes: No. 64). 1975. lib. bdg. 75.00 (0-8383-2072-4) M S G Haskell Hse.

Authorware Academic: User's Guide & Models for Instructional Design. Mike Allen. 1994. pap. text ed. 45.00 (0-13-303470-4) P-H.

Authorware Academic for Macintosh. Inc. Macromedia. 1994. pap. text ed. 112.50 (0-13-289802-0) P-H.

Authorware Academic for Windows. Inc. Macromedia. 1994. pap. text ed. 113.00 (0-13-289794-6) P-H.

Authorware Academic User's Guide. Mike Allen. 1994. pap. text ed. 22.50 (0-13-303454-2) P-H.

Authorware Models for Instructional Design. Mike Allen. 1994. pap. text ed. 98.00 (0-13-303462-3) P-H.

***Authorware Professional 2.0.** Matthew Holtz. (Multimedia Workshop Ser.). 162p. 1995. pap. 18.95 (0-534-31060-5) Intl Thomson.

Autism. Laura Schreibman. (Developmental Clinical Psychology & Psychiatry Ser.: Vol. 15). 160p. (C). 1989. text ed. 37.00 (0-8039-2809-2); pap. text ed. 16.95 (0-8039-2810-6) Sage.

Autism: A Practical Guide for Those Who Help Others. John Gerdtz & Joel Bregman. 144p. 1990. 17.95 (0-8245-1288-X) Crossroad NY.

Autism: A Reappraisal of Concepts & Treatment. Ed. by Michael Rutter & Eric Schopler. LC 77-26910. (Illus.). 552p. 1978. 49.50 (0-306-31096-1, Plenum Pr) Plenum.

***Autism: An Introduction to Psychological Theory.** Francesca Happe. (Illus.). 160p. 1995. text ed. 24.95 (0-674-05312-5, HAPAUT) HUP.

Autism: Explaining the Enigma. Uta Frith. (Cognitive Development Ser.). 1992. pap. text ed. 18.95 (0-631-16824-9) Blackwell Pubs.

Autism: From Tragedy to Triumph. Carol Johnson & Julia Crowder. (Illus.). 188p. 1994. pap. 12.95 (0-8283-1965-0) Branden Pub Co.

***Autism: Handle with Care.** Gail Gillingham. 107p. 1995. pap. text ed. 24.95 (1-885477-14-7) Fut Educ.

Autism: Identification, Education, & Treatment. Ed. by Dianne E. Berkell. 328p. 1992. text ed. 69.95 (0-8058-0896-5); pap. 29.95 (0-8058-0897-3) L Erlbaum Assocs.

Autism: Information & Resources for Parents, Families, & Professionals. Richard L. Simpson & Paul Zionts. LC 92-1. 188p. 1992. pap. text ed. 24.00 (0-89079-538-X, 5192) PRO-ED.

Autism: Nature, Diagnosis, & Treatment. Ed. by Geraldine Dawson. LC 88-16356. 417p. 1989. lib. bdg. 46.00 (0-89862-724-9) Guilford Pr.

Autism: Nightmare Without End. Dorothy J. Beavers. Ed. by Debbie Hammond. LC 79-27669. 1982. 24.95 (0-87949-167-1) Ashley Bks.

Autism: Strategies for Change. Gerald Groden & M. Grace Baron. LC 87-8682. 256p. (C). 1991. pap. text ed. 23.95 (0-89876-184-0) Gardner Pr.

Autism: The Facts. Simon Baron-Cohen & Patrick Bolton. LC 92-49828. (The Facts Ser.). 128p. 1993. 19.95 (0-19-262328-1) OUP.

Autism: The Facts. Simon Baron-Cohen & Patrick Bolton. LC 92-49828. (The Facts Ser.). (Illus.). 122p. 1994. pap. 14.95 (0-19-262327-3) OUP.

Autism & Asperger Syndrome. Ed. by Uta Frith. (C). 1992. 54.95 (0-521-38448-6); pap. 18.95 (0-521-38608-X) Cambridge U Pr.

***Autism & the Crisis of Meaning.** Alexander During. 288p. (C). 1996. text ed. 59.50x (0-7914-2813-3); pap. 19.95x (0-7914-2814-1) State U NY Pr.

***Autism Handbook: Understanding & Treating Autism & Pervasive Developmental Disorders.** Bryna Siegal. (Illus.). 320p. 1995. 25.00 (0-19-507667-2) OUP.

Autism in Adolescents & Adults. Ed. by Eric Schopler & Gary B. Mesobov. LC 82-22314. (Current Issues in Autism Ser.). 456p. 1983. 52.50 (0-306-41057-5, Plenum Pr) Plenum.

***Autism in Children & Adults: Etiology, Assessment & Intervention.** Ed. by Johnny L. Matson. (Special Education Ser.). 420p. (C). 1993. text ed. 42.95 (0-534-23826-2) Sycamore Pub.

***Autism Society of America 1994 Conference: A New Dawn of Awakening.** Future Education Inc. Staff. Ed. by Polly A. McGlew. 389p. 1994. pap. 34.95 (1-885477-13-9) Fut Educ.

Autism Treatment Guide. Elizabeth K. Gerlach. LC 93-91648. 130p. (Orig.). 1993. pap. 9.95 (0-9637578-0-6) Four Leaf Pr.

Autisme Infantile-Infantile Autism. F. Gremy et al. (Colloque de L'INSERM Ser.: No. 146). 360p. (ENG & FRE.). 1987. lib. bdg. 33.00 (2-85598-316-9) S M P F Inc.

Autistic Adults at Bittersweet Farms. Norman S. Giddan & Jane J. Giddan. LC 90-41945. (Haworth Series on Social & Community Horticulture). 219p. 1991. text ed. 39.95 (1-56024-042-3); pap. text ed. 17.95 (1-56024-057-1) Haworth Pr.

Autistic Alienated American Misfits. Christina B. North. (Contemporary Ser.). (Illus.). 193p. 1982. 9.95 (0-686-35767-1) C B North.

Autistic Behaviors: Experimental Analysis & Treatment Applications. O. Ivar Lovaas et al. 450p. 1990. text ed. 39.50 (0-8290-2467-0) Irvington.

Autistic Child: Language Development Through Behavior Modification. O. Ivar Lovaas. LC 76-5890. (Illus.). 256p. 1984. pap. text ed. 16.95 (0-8290-1003-3) Irvington.

Autistic Child: Language Development Through Behavior Modification. O. Ivor Lovaar. LC 76-5890. (Illus.). 256p. (C). 1986. reprint ed. text ed. 29.95 (0-8290-0253-7) Irvington.

Autistic Children. Lorna Wing. 160p. 1974. reprint ed. pap. 7.95 (0-8065-0408-0, Citadel Pr) Carol Pub Group.

Autistic Children: A Guide for Parents & Professionals. 2nd ed. Lorna Wing. LC 84-29276. 176p. 1985. 27.95 (0-87630-391-2) Brunner-Mazel.

Autistic Children: A Working Diary. Florence Milnes Kozak. LC 86-7034. (Contemporary Community Health Ser.). 192p. 1986. 49.95 (0-8229-3539-2); pap. 14.95 (0-8229-5383-8) U of Pittsburgh Pr.

Autistic Gestures, an Experimental Study in Symbolic Movement see Serial Reactions Considered As Conditioned Reactions

Autistic States in Children. rev. ed. Francis Tustin. 1992. 69.95 (0-415-08128-9, A7785, Pub. by Tavistock UK); pap. 17.95 (0-415-08129-7, A7789, Pub. by Tavistock UK) Routledge Chapman & Hall.

538

An Asterisk (*) at the beginning of an entry indicates that the title is appearing in BIP for the first time.

Auto. (Meyers Kleine Kinderbibliothek Ser.). 1991. 13.25 (*3-411-08451-0*, Pub. by Bibliogr Inst Brockhaus GW) Langenscheidt.

Auto - Oil Air Quality Improvement Research Program. 468p. 1992. pap. 49.00 (*1-56091-237-5*, SP-920) Soc Auto Engineers.

Auto - Oil Air Quality Improvement Research Program, Vol. II. (International Fuels & Lubricants Meeting & Exposition, 1993 Ser.). pap. 34.00 (*1-56091-439-4*, SP-1000) Soc Auto Engineers.

***Auto Accident Checklist.** Jon R. Abele. LC 94-43879. 128p. (Orig.). 1995. pap. text ed. 21.00 (*0-913875-12-0*, 5120) Lawyers & Judges.

Auto Accident Law & Practice, 4 vols. Miller & Kulman. 1988. Updates available. ring bd. write for info. (*0-8205-1158-7*, 158) Bender.

Auto Air Conditioning. James H. Doolin. 48p. 1982. pap. 15.00 (*0-914626-03-5*) Doolco Inc.

Auto Air Conditioning Technology. John Althouse et al. (Illus.). 255p. 1991. text ed. 30.60 (*0-87006-815-6*) Goodheart.

Auto Analysis. Eugene Field. (Notable American Authors Ser.). 1992. reprint ed. lib. bdg. 75.00 (*0-7812-2654-6*) Rprt Serv.

Auto & Petrochemical Catalysts. Business Communications Co., Inc. Staff. 152p. 1987. pap. 1,750.00 (*0-89336-500-9*, C-023R) BCC.

Auto & Robot in Welding & Allied Procedures: Proceedings of the IIW Conference, Strasbourg, France, 2-3 September 1985. Ed. by International Institute of Welding, London, UK Staff. (Illus.). 432p. 1985. 179.00 (*0-08-032533-5*, Pub. by PPL UK) Franklin.

Auto & Truck Rental & Leasing Industry: Past Performance, Current Trends & Strategies for the Future. 235p. 1994. 995.00 (*0-317-55208-2*) Busn Trend.

Auto as Icon. Richard N. Masteller. (Illus.). (Orig.). (C). 1979. pap. 8.95 (*1-880269-02-3*) D H Sheehan.

***Auto Audio: Choosing, Installing, & Maintaining Car Stereo Systems.** Andrew Yoder. 1994. pap. text ed. 24.95 (*0-07-076536-7*) McGraw.

Auto-Biographical Discourses: Theory, Criticism, Practice. Laura Marcus. LC 93-47153. 1994. text ed. 79.95 (*0-7190-3642-9*, Pub. by Manchester Univ Pr UK) St Martin.

***Auto-Biographical I: The Theory & Practice of the Feminist Auto-Biography.** Liz Stanley. 304p. 1995. text ed. 19.95 (*0-7190-4649-1*, Pub. by Manchester Univ Pr UK) St Martin.

Auto-Biographical One: Theory & Practice of Feminist Auto-Biography. Liz Stanley. 1992. text ed. 69.95 (*0-7190-2980-5*, Pub. by Manchester Univ Pr UK) St Martin.

Auto Biography. S. Sundaresan. 141p. 1987. text ed. 22.50 (*81-207-0583-1*, Pub. by Sterling Pubs II) Apt Bks.

Auto Body Repair. Lester G. Duenk et al. (gr. 9-12). 1984. text ed. 26.00 (*0-02-662340-4*) Bennett IL.

Auto Body Repair. Charles Lauer. LC 85-702615. 1985. student ed 7.00 (*0-8064-0209-1*, 484); audio 239.00 (*0-8064-0210-5*) Bergwall.

Auto Body Repair. Jack Rudman. (Occupational Competency Examination Ser.: OCE-5). 1994. 23.95 (*0-8373-5705-5*) Nat Learn.

Auto Body Repair II. Robert Jenkins. LC 81-730636. 1981. student ed 5.00 (*0-8064-0151-6*, 443); audio 89.00 (*0-8064-0152-4*) Bergwall.

Auto Body Repairing & Refinishing. rev. ed. Bill Toboldt & Terry L. Richardson. LC 93-21748. Orig. Title: Auto Body Repairing & Repainting. (Illus.). 377p. 1993. text ed. 34.64 (*0-87006-018-X*) Goodheart.

Auto Body Repairing & Repainting see Auto Body Repairing & Refinishing

Auto Body Repairman. Jack Rudman. (Career Examination Ser.: C-1125). 1994. pap. 23.95 (*0-8373-1125-X*) Nat Learn.

Auto Body Tools Explained. Robert Jenkins. LC 82-730274. 1980. student ed 5.00 (*0-8064-0129-X*, 432); audio 109.00 (*0-8064-0130-3*) Bergwall.

Auto Book. 2nd ed. William H. Crouse & Donald L. Anglin. (Illus.). 1978. text ed. 35.95 (*0-07-014560-1*) McGraw.

Auto Book. 3rd ed. William H. Crouse & Donald L. Anglin. LC 83-16206. 640p. 1984. text ed. 35.95 (*0-07-014571-7*); student ed 16.95 (*0-07-014573-3*) McGraw.

***Auto-Carto Eleven.** Eleventh International Symposium on Computer-Assisted Cartography Staff. 443p. 1993. 35.00 (*0-614-06103-2*, T726) Am Congrs Survey.

***Auto Chassis: Suspension, Steering & Brakes.** Kalton C. Lahue. Ed. by Conty. 500p. (C). 1995. student ed, spiral bd. write for info. (*0-314-04694-1*) West Pub.

***Auto Component Locator Guide 81-85.** (Illus.). 600p. (C). 1994. 225.00 (*0-7605-0347-8*) Rector Pr.

Auto-Destruct & the Rhesus Umbrella. Jeff Wanshel. 1977. pap. 4.75 (*0-8222-0080-5*) Dramatists Play.

Auto Detailing for Show & Profit. 2nd ed. David H. Jacobs, Jr. (Illus.). 96p. 1994. pap. text ed. 11.95 (*0-87938-886-2*) Motorbooks Intl.

Auto Dictionary. John Edwards. (Illus.). 256p. 1993. 24.95 (*1-55788-067-0*) Price Stern.

Auto Drive Trains Technology. James E. Duffy & Chris Johanson. LC 94-1440. (Illus.). 675p. (C). 1995. pap. text ed. 35.96 (*1-56637-028-0*) Goodheart.

***Auto Electricity & Electronics Technology.** James E. Duffy. 1995. student ed 37.28 (*1-56637-053-1*) Goodheart.

***Auto Electronics Projects.** Maplin Staff. (Maplin Ser.). 208p. 1995. pap. 19.95 (*0-7506-2296-2*, Focal) Buttrwrth-Heinemann.

Auto Emissions Explained. Paul Tucker. Ed. by Kelly Gorham. (Automotive Ser.). 28p. (YA). (gr. 10 up). 1994. student ed 7.00 (*0-8064-0017-X*, A38); audio 299.00 (*0-8064-0016-1*) Bergwall.

Auto Engineman. Jack Rudman. (Career Examination Ser.: C-61). 1994. pap. 23.95 (*0-8373-0061-4*) Nat Learn.

Auto Engines of Tomorrow: Power Alternatives for Cars to Come. Harris E. Dark. LC 74-6518. 192p. reprint ed. pap. 54.80 (*0-8357-5903-2*, 2056223) Bks Demand.

Auto Engines Technology. James E. Duffy. (Illus.). 575p. 1993. text ed. 39.80 (*0-87006-068-6*) Goodheart.

Auto Equipment Inspector. Jack Rudman. (Career Examination Ser.: C-1126). 1994. pap. 27.95 (*0-8373-1126-8*) Nat Learn.

Auto Fleet Management. Hermann S. Botzow. LC 67-30632. 211p. reprint ed. pap. 60.20 (*0-8357-9842-9*, 2012354) Bks Demand.

Auto French, Advanced. (Advanced Auto Language Packages Ser.). 64p. 1993. audio, pap. 24.95 (*0-8120-7982-5*) Barron.

Auto Fuel & Emission Control Systems Technology. James E. Duffy & Howard Smith. LC 86-19592. (Illus.). 528p. 1992. 37.28 (*0-87006-932-2*) Goodheart.

Auto Fuel Economy Standards: Good for the Environment or a Cause of Highway Deaths. 1991. pap. 5.00 (*0-943802-90-3*, BG111) Natl Ctr Pol.

***Auto German Advanced.** Irene Guyomard & Chris Pohl. LC 94-22694. (ENG & GER.). 1995. write for info. (*0-8120-7981-7*); write for info. (*0-8120-1430-8*) Barron.

Auto Glass Installation: An Introductory Guide. (Illus.). 64p. 1989. teacher ed 39.95 (*1-56393-001-3*); pap. 29.95 (*1-56393-000-5*) National Glass Assn.

Auto Glass Supervision. National Glass Association Staff. Date not set. pap. text ed. 49.95 (*1-56393-007-2*) National Glass Assn.

Auto Glass Technician Manual: Instructor's Edition. National Glass Association Staff. 114p. 1993. pap. text ed. 69.95 (*1-56393-006-4*) National Glass Assn.

Auto Guide 1987. Duquet & Lachapell. 1988. pap. 17.95 (*0-8050-0881-0*) H Holt & Co.

Auto Handbook. 3rd ed. Robert Bosch. Date not set. pap. 31.95 (*0-8376-0330-7*) Bentley.

Auto ID in Manufacturing, Pt. 1: Case Histories of Inventory Control, Work-in-Process, Picking & Sorting, Shipping & Billing. ID Systems Magazine Editors. 128p. (Orig.). 1991. pap. 19.95 (*0-911261-04-4*) Helmers Pub.

Auto Industries of Europe, United States & Japan. Richard Phillips et al. LC 82-13856. (Economist Intelligence Ser.). 352p. 1982. 32.00 (*0-685-42673-4*) Harper Busn.

Auto Industry Ahead: Who's Driving? Ed. by Peter J. Arnesen. LC 89-506. (Michigan Papers in Japanese Studies: No. 18). x, 131p. 1989. pap. 9.00 (*0-939512-36-X*) U MI Japan.

***Auto Injuries: Claiming Behavior & Its Impact on Insurance Costs.** Insurance Research Council Staff. 126p. 1994. pap. text ed. 25.00 (*1-56594-001-6*) Ins Res Coun.

Auto-Instructional Text in Correct Writing, Form B. 2nd ed. Eugenia W. Butler et al. 476p. 1980. pap. text ed. 18.00 (*0-669-02484-8*); Answer key. teacher ed 2.00 (*0-669-02486-4*); Key for suppl. tests. teacher ed 2.00 (*0-669-04404-0*) Heath.

Auto-Instructional Text in Correct Writing, Form B. 2nd suppl. ed. Eugenia W. Butler et al. 476p. 1980. Suppl. tests. 2.00 (*0-669-04324-9*) Heath.

Auto Insurance Alert! Why the System Stinks, How to Fix It & What to Do in the Meantime. Andrew Tobias. 96p. (Orig.). 1993. pap. 4.75 (*0-671-79222-9*, Fireside) S&S Trade.

Auto Insurance & No-Fault Law. Robert H. Joost. LC 92-75017. 1992. ring bd. 135.00 (*0-685-59867-5*) Clark Boardman Callaghan.

Auto Insurance Database. 200p. (Orig.). (C). 1993. 50.00 (*0-89382-224-8*) Nat Assn Insu Comm.

Auto Insurance Database Report. 268p. 1994. spiral bd. 50.00 (*0-89382-260-4*) Nat Assn Insu Comm.

Auto Insurance Tricks & Repair Rip-Offs: A New & Different Kind of Owner's Manual. Ron Alford. 130p. (Orig.). 1994. pap. 9.95 (*0-924893-06-0*) Plan Pub.

Auto Italian, Advanced. (Advanced Auto Language Packages Ser.). 64p. 1993. audio, pap. 24.95 (*0-8120-8109-9*) Barron.

Auto Loan Payment Tables. Financial Publishing Co. Staff. 280p. 1986. pap. 9.00 (*0-87600-485-0*) Finan Pub.

Auto Machinist. Jack Rudman. (Career Examination Ser.: C-62). 1994. pap. 23.95 (*0-8373-0062-2*) Nat Learn.

Auto Maintenance Coordinator. Jack Rudman. (Career Examination Ser.: C-1127). 1994. pap. 29.95 (*0-8373-1127-6*) Nat Learn.

Auto Maintenance for Everyone. Kenneth Schock. Ed. by Al Hull. (Illus.). 263p. (C). 1988. 26.95 (*0-685-23255-7*) Sales Focus.

Auto Maintenance Record. Cedric C. Gutter, Sr. 52p. 1992. write for info. (*0-9635213-0-6*) C&L Manuals.

Auto Math Handbook. John Lawlor. 1991. pap. 14.95 (*1-55788-020-4*, HP Books) Berkley Pub.

Auto Mechanic. Douglas Florian. LC 90-48809. (Illus.). 24p. (J). (ps up). 1991. 13.95 (*0-688-10635-8*); lib. bdg. 13.88 (*0-688-10636-6*) Greenwillow.

Auto Mechanic. Jack Rudman. (Career Examination Ser.: C-63). 1994. pap. 23.95 (*0-8373-0063-0*) Nat Learn.

Auto Mechanic. Douglas Florian. LC 93-28802. (Illus.). 24p. (J). (ps up). 1994. reprint ed. pap. 4.95 (*0-688-13104-2*, Mulberry) Morrow.

Auto Mechanic (Diesel) Jack Rudman. (Career Examination Ser.: C-64). 1994. pap. 23.95 (*0-8373-0064-9*) Nat Learn.

Auto Mechanics. Jack Rudman. (DANTES Ser.: No. 2). 1994. pap. 23.95 (*0-8373-6602-X*) Nat Learn.

***Auto Mechanics.** Jack Rudman. (DANTES Ser.: No. 2). 1994. 39.95 (*0-8373-6502-3*) Nat Learn.

Auto Mechanics. Jack Rudman. (Occupational Competency Examination Ser.: No. 7). 1994. 23.95 (*0-8373-5707-1*) Nat Learn.

Auto Mechanics. 2nd ed. Jay Webster. 570p. 1986. 27.48 (*0-02-829900-0*) Glencoe.

Auto Mechanics Basic Engineering Guide. Bill Carroll. LC 70-102903. (Performance Engineering Handbooks Ser.). (Illus.). 228p. 1974. pap. 10.00 (*0-910390-19-3*) Auto Bk.

Auto Mechanics for the Complete Dummy. 2nd ed. Philip R. Martin. LC 82-62322. (Illus.). 192p. 1983. pap. 4.95 (*0-930968-02-6*) Motormatics.

Auto Mechanics Fundamentals. Martin W. Stockel. LC 81-20007. (Illus.). 606p. 1990. text ed. 35.96 (*0-87006-770-2*) Goodheart.

Auto Mechanics Refresher Course. Chek-Chart Staff. (C). student ed 42.00 (*0-88098-078-8*, H M Gousha) P-H Gen Ref & Trav.

***Auto-Money: A Guide to Automotive Awareness.** Paul Hanson & Susan Hanson. 136p. 1995. pap. 11.95 (*0-9646075-0-6*) Auto-Money.

Auto Museum Directory U. S. A. William R. Taylor. LC 83-82411. (Illus.). 112p. (Orig.). 1983. kivar 10.95 (*0-916447-01-4*) Edit Review.

Auto Museums Directory: U. S. A. Supplement with Canadian Museums. William R. Taylor. (Illus.). 56p. (Orig.). 1989. pap. 8.50 (*0-916447-03-0*) Edit Review.

Auto Opium: A Social History of American Automobile Design. David Gartman. LC 93-49738. 272p. 1994. 59.95x (*0-415-10571-4*, B3985); pap. 17.95 (*0-415-10572-2*, B3989) Routledge.

Auto Owner's Supply Book, 1929. Western Auto Supply Co. Staff. (Illus.). 128p. 1989. reprint ed. pap. 2.00 (*0-910667-03-9*) Northstar Bks.

Auto Parking in Marinas. (Illus.). 13p. 1989. 125.00 (*0-929803-09-4*) Intl Marina Inst.

***Auto Parts Market.** 700p. (Orig.). 1994. pap. 1,495.00 (*1-57205-926-5*) Rector Pr.

Auto Parts Storekeeper. Jack Rudman. (Career Examination Ser.: C-1128). 1994. pap. 23.95 (*0-8373-1128-4*) Nat Learn.

Auto RacePages, 1992: Vol. 1. Mark C. Youngson. (Professional Racing Ser.). 300p. 1991. pap. 21.95 (*0-9631788-0-6*) Youngson Pub.

***Auto Radio: Choosing, Installing, Maintaining & Repairing Car Stereo Systems.** Andrew Yoder. 1995. text ed. 34.95 (*0-07-076535-9*) TAB Bks.

***Auto Rental & Leasing Market.** 300p. (Orig.). 1994. pap. 1,295.00 (*1-57205-925-7*) Rector Pr.

Auto Repair. John Doyle. (Illus.). 381p. 1987. write for info. (*0-89434-088-3*) Ferguson.

Auto Repair for Dummies. rev. ed. Deanna Sclar. 480p. 1989. spiral bd. 17.95 (*0-89815-341-7*) Ten Speed Pr.

Auto Repair for Dummies. 2nd rev. ed. Deanna Sclar. 480p. 1989. 26.95 (*0-89815-347-6*) Ten Speed Pr.

Auto Repair for Dummies Glove Compartment Guide. Deanna Sclar. (Illus.). 144p. (Orig.). 1991. pap. 4.95 (*0-89815-435-9*) Ten Speed Pr.

Auto Repair Manual, 1990-94. Ed. by Chilton Staff. 1632p. 1993. text ed. 26.95 (*0-8019-7912-9*) Chilton.

Auto Repair Manual 1991-95. Ed. by Chilton Staff. 1648p. 1994. text ed. 26.95 (*0-8019-7915-3*) Chilton.

***Auto Repair Manual, 1992-96.** Ed. by Chilton Staff. 1680p. 1995. text ed. 26.95 (*0-8019-7916-1*) Chilton.

Auto Restoration From Junker to Jewel. Burt Mills. LC 79-24680. (Illus.). 291p. 1981. reprint ed. pap. 22.95 (*0-87938-098-5*) Motorbooks Intl.

Auto Restoration Tips & Techniques. Peterson's Staff. Ed. by Spence Murray. (Illus.). 256p. (Orig.). 1977. pap. 17.95 (*1-870642-42-2*) Motorbooks Intl.

***Auto Roadside Survival Guide to Dummies.** David Solomon. 1995. pap. 9.99 (*1-56884-377-1*) IDG Bks.

Auto Russian, Advanced. (Advanced Auto Language Packages Ser.). 64p. 1993. audio, pap. 24.95 (*0-8120-8110-2*) Barron.

Auto Sacramental & the Parable in Spanish Golden Age Literature. T. Dietz. (North Carolina Studies in the Romance Languages & Literatures). 205p. 1973. 20.00 (*0-88438-932-4*) Spanish Lit Pubns.

Auto Safety: Assessing America's Performance. John D. Graham. LC 88-26700. 258p. 1989. text ed. 55.00 (*0-86569-188-6*, Auburn Hse) Greenwood.

Auto Safety Regulation: The Cure or the Problem? Ed. by Henry G. Manne & Roger L. Miller. LC 76-1676. 1976. 15.95 (*0-913878-09-X*) T Horton & Dghts.

Auto Service & Repair. rev. ed. Martin W. Stockel & Martin T. Stockel. (Illus.). 960p. 1991. text ed. 43.92 (*0-87006-760-5*) Goodheart.

Auto Service Manual. Ed. by Chilton Staff. 2496p. 1994. text ed. 100.00 (*0-8019-8569-2*) Chilton.

Auto Service Manual 1987-91. Chilton Book Co. Staff. 1344p. (SPA.). 1992. 45.00 (*0-8019-8326-6*) Chilton.

Auto Service Manual 1989-93. Chilton Automotives Editorial Staff. 2304p. 1992. text ed. 95.00 (*0-8019-8290-1*) Chilton.

Auto Service Manual, 1990-94. Ed. by Chilton Staff. 2304p. 1993. text ed. 100.00 (*0-8019-8470-X*) Chilton.

Auto Shop Activity Guide. Glenn Harold. 1985. 11.95 (*0-02-829920-5*) Macmillan.

Auto Shop Foreman. Jack Rudman. (Career Examination Ser.: C-1129). 1994. pap. 27.95 (*0-8373-1129-2*) Nat Learn.

Auto Shop Supervisor. Jack Rudman. (Career Examination Ser.: C-1130). 1994. pap. 27.95 (*0-8373-1130-6*) Nat Learn.

Auto Shop Workbook. William H. Crouse et al. 256p. (C). 1984. pap. text ed. 16.95 (*0-07-014572-5*) McGraw.

Auto Slavery: The Labor Process in the American Automobile Industry, 1897-1950. David Gartman. (Class & Culture Ser.). 360p. (C). 1986. text ed. 45.00 (*0-8135-1181-X*) Rutgers U Pr.

Auto Spanish I, Advanced. (Advanced Auto Language Packages Ser.). 64p. 1993. audio, pap. 24.95 (*0-8120-8108-0*) Barron.

Auto Spanish II, Advanced. (Advanced Auto Language Packages Ser.). 64p. 1993. audio, pap. 24.95 (*0-8120-7983-3*) Barron.

Auto Standard Transmission. Peter Novellino. LC 76-732018. 1977. student ed 7.00 (*0-8064-0091-9*, 413); audio 299.00 (*0-8064-0092-7*) Bergwall.

Auto-Suggestion. Herbert A. Parkyn. 190p. 1993. pap. 15.00 (*0-89540-199-1*, SB-199) Sun Pub.

Auto Suppliers Sourcebook to Japanese Transplants. Annie M. Brewer & Donald E. Brewer. 187p. 1992. text ed. 148.50 (*0-9632341-2-9*) Whitefoord.

Auto Taming Tape. Gordon Yaswen. 1986. Audiocassette, 60 mins. audio 9.95 (*0-317-91168-6*) Yastek Servs.

Auto Tour Guide to the Lake Mead National Recreation Area. Douglas B. Evans. LC 76-160215. (Illus.). 40p. (Orig.). 1971. pap. 0.50 (*0-911408-22-3*) SW Pks Mnmts.

***Auto-Truck Interchange.** 32th ed. 1966. per. 68.00 (*0-614-07084-8*) ADP-Hollander.

***Auto-Truck Interchange: Foreign & Domestic: I. D. - Body, Set.** 61th ed. 1995. per. write for info. (*0-614-07078-3*) ADP-Hollander.

***Auto-Truck Interchange: Foreign & Domestic: Mechanical, Set.** 61th ed. 1995. per. write for info. (*0-614-07079-1*) ADP-Hollander.

***Auto-Truck Interchange: Foreign & Domestic: Wheel Cover Manual.** 216p. 1995. per. 42.00 (*1-882437-34-9*) ADP-Hollander.

***Auto-Truck Interchange: Foreign & Domestic: Wheel Manual.** 61th ed. 327p. 1995. per. 42.00 (*1-882437-35-7*) ADP-Hollander.

Auto-Urine-Therapy. Beatrice Bartnett. 50p. (Orig.). 1989. pap. write for info. (*0-9622182-0-0*) Lifestyle Inst.

Auto Work & Its Discontents. Ed. by B. J. Widick. LC 76-16095. (Policy Studies in Employment & Welfare: No. 25). 123p. reprint ed. pap. 35.10 (*0-8357-5904-0*, 2027377) Bks Demand.

Auto 2010: The Car Magazine from the Future. Paul Van Valkenburgh. (Illus.). 112p. (Orig.). 1990. pap. 14.95 (*0-9617425-1-8*) Van Valkenburgh.

Autoaesthetics: Strategies of the Self after Nietzshe. Stephen Barker. LC 91-35840. (Philosophy & Literary Theory Ser.). 392p. (C). 1992. text ed. 55.00 (*0-391-03748-X*) Humanities.

Autoantibodies to Immunoglobulins. Ed. by F. Shakib. (Monographs in Allergy: Vol. 26). (Illus.). x, 274p. 1989. 192.00 (*3-8055-4913-X*) S Karger.

Autoantibodies to Nuclear Antigens: Advances in Laboratory Tests & Significance in Systemic Rheumatic Diseases. 2nd ed. Robert M. Nakamura et al. LC 85-5992. 1985. 25.00 (*0-89189-188-9*) Am Soc Clinical.

Autoapprenticeship. William D. Barillas. LC 86-91046. (Orig.). 1987. pap. 7.00 (*0-940311-00-3*) Merganser Pr.

Autobio of My Mother. Rosellen Brown. 1994. mass mkt. 5.99 (*0-440-21694-X*) Dell.

Autobiographia. Walt Whitman. 1972. 69.95 (*0-87968-681-2*) Gordon Pr.

Autobiographic Memoirs, 2 vols., Set. Frederic Harrison. LC 75-30025. reprint ed. 125.00 (*0-404-13990-6*) AMS Pr.

Autobiographical Account by a Leading Sardinian Republican Politician of Resistance to Fascism in Sardinia from 1918-1930: Marcia su Roma e Dintorni (The March on Rome & Thereabouts) Emilio Lussu. Tr. by Roy W. Davis. LC 92-15142. 224p. 1992. lib. bdg. 89.95 (*0-7734-9558-4*) E Mellen.

Autobiographical Acts: The Changing Situation of a Literary Genre. Elizabeth W. Bruss. LC 76-13460. 192p. reprint ed. pap. 54.80 (*0-8357-5905-9*, 2029703) Bks Demand.

Autobiographical Eye. Ed. by David Halpern. LC 92-44646. (Illus.). 1993. pap. 12.95 (*0-88001-329-X*) Ecco Pr.

Autobiographical Memoir. Frank B. Long. 35p. (Orig.). pap. 4.95 (*0-318-04708-X*) Necronomicon.

Autobiographical Memoir of Petrus Borchardus Borcherds. Petrus B. Borcherds. LC 72-5526. (Black Heritage Library Collection). 1977. reprint ed. 40.95 (*0-8369-9135-4*) Ayer.

Autobiographical Memory. Ed. by David C. Rubin. (Illus.). 320p. 1988. pap. 24.95 (*0-521-36850-2*) Cambridge U Pr.

Autobiographical Memory: An Introduction. Martin A. Conway. 192p. 1990. 90.00 (*0-335-09849-5*, Open Univ Pr); pap. 32.00 (*0-335-09848-7*, Open Univ Pr) Taylor & Francis.

***Autobiographical Memory: Remembering What & Remembering When.** Charles P. Thompson et al. 225p. 1996. text ed. 35.00 (*0-8058-1514-7*) L Erlbaum Assocs.

Autobiographical Memory & the Validity of Retrospective Reports. Ed. by Norbert Schwarz & Seymour Sudman. LC 93-31775. 1993. 69.00 (*0-387-94167-3*) Spr-Verlag.

Autobiographical Notes. George Gissing. 1972. 59.95 (*0-87968-682-0*) Gordon Pr.

Autobiographical Notes: A Centennial Edition. Albert Einstein. Ed. & Tr. by Paul A. Schilpp. LC 78-13925. 95p. (C). 1991. pap. 9.95 (*0-8126-9179-2*) Open Court.

Autobiographical Notes & Notes on His Artistic & Poetic Circle of Friends, 1830-1882, 2 Vols, Set. William B. Scott. Ed. by W. Minto. LC 70-128417. (Illus.). 1970. reprint ed. 105.00 (*0-404-05643-1*) AMS Pr.

Autobiographical Notes of Charles Evans Hughes. Charles E. Hughes. Ed. by David J. Danelski & Joseph S. Tulchin. LC 72-88130. (Studies in Legal History). 383p. 1973. 38.00 (*0-674-05325-7*) HUP.

An Asterisk (*) at the beginning of an entry indicates that the title is appearing in BIP for the first time.

539

A

Autobiographical Notes, Verses & Other Writings. Andrew J. Graham. (American Biography Ser.). 265p. 1991. reprint ed. lib. bdg. 69.00 (*0-7812-8152-0*) Rprt Serv.

Autobiographical Novel. rev. ed. Kenneth Rexroth. Ed. by Linda Hamalian. LC 91-4785. (Revived Modern Classics Ser.). 528p. 1991. pap. 14.95 (*0-8112-1179-7*, NDP725) New Directions.

Autobiographical Novel of Co-Consciousness: Goncharov, Woolf, & Joyce. Galya Diment. LC 94-8385. (Florida James Joyce Ser.). 216p. 1994. lib. bdg. 29.95 (*0-8130-1304-6*) U Press Fla.

Autobiographical Passion: Studies in the Self on Show. Peter Steele. 1989. pap. 24.95 (*0-522-84363-8*) Intl Spec Bk.

Autobiographical Quests: Augustine, Montaigne, Rousseau, & Wordsworth. Elizabeth De Mijolla. LC 93-28201. (C). 1994. 29.50 (*0-8139-1468-X*) U Pr of Va.

Autobiographical Reflections. Eric Voegelin. LC 89-32051. xiv, 128p. 1989. 16.95 (*0-8071-1515-0*) La State U Pr.

Autobiographical Reflections. Colin Wilson. 49p. (C). 1990. reprint ed. lib. bdg. 23.00x (*0-8095-6753-9*) Borgo Pr.

***Autobiographical Reflections.** Colin Wilson. 49p. (C). 1990. reprint ed. pap. 13.00x (*0-946650-20-9*) Borgo Pr.

Autobiographical Reminiscences: With Family Letters & Notes on Music. Charles Gounod. LC 68-16235. (Music Ser.). 1970. reprint ed. lib. bdg. 35.00 (*0-306-71081-1*) Da Capo.

Autobiographical Reminiscences of Rev. Alvan Bond, D. D., 1793-1882. H. R. Bond. 214p. 1988. reprint ed. lib. bdg. 42.00 (*0-8328-0278-6*); reprint ed. pap. 32.00 (*0-8328-0279-4*) Higginson Bk Co.

Autobiographical Sketch. John Marshall. (History - United States Ser.). 48p. 1993. reprint ed. lib. bdg. 59.00 (*0-7812-4880-9*) Rprt Serv.

Autobiographical Sketch by John Marshall. John Marshall. Ed. by John S. Adams. LC 71-160849. (American Constitutional & Legal History Ser). (Illus.). 74p. 1973. reprint ed. lib. bdg. 19.50 (*0-306-70216-9*) Da Capo.

Autobiographical Sketch by John Marshall. John Marshall. (American Biography Ser.). 48p. 1991. reprint ed. lib. bdg. 59.00 (*0-7812-8271-3*) Rprt Serv.

Autobiographical Sketch of Mrs. John Drew. Louisa L. Drew. (American Biography Ser.). 200p. 1991. reprint ed. lib. bdg. 59.00 (*0-7812-8114-8*) Rprt Serv.

Autobiographical Sketches. Annie Besant. 1972. 59.95 (*0-87968-683-9*) Gordon Pr.

Autobiographical Sketches. Mathew Carey. LC 70-125683. (American Journalists Ser.). 1977. reprint ed. 23.95 (*0-405-01660-3*) Ayer.

Autobiographical Sketches. Mathew Carey. (American Biography Ser.). 156p. 1991. reprint ed. lib. bdg. 59.00 (*0-7812-8060-5*) Rprt Serv.

Autobiographical Sketches & Recollections. Theodore Clapp. (American Biography Ser.). 419p. 1991. reprint ed. lib. bdg. 89.00 (*0-7812-8070-2*) Rprt Serv.

Autobiographical Sketches & Recollections: During a 35 Years Residence in New Orleans. Theodore Clapp. LC 77-38346. (Select Bibliographies Reprint Ser.). 1977. reprint ed. 25.95 (*0-8369-6763-1*) Ayer.

Autobiographical Statements in Twentieth-Century Russian Literature. Ed. by Janet G. Harris. 312p. 1990. text ed. 39.50 (*0-691-06818-6*) Princeton U Pr.

***Autobiographical Story.** K. R. Terry. LC 95-60835. 398p. 1996. pap. 15.95 (*1-55523-747-9*) Winston-Derek.

Autobiographical Study. Sigmund Freud. Ed. & Tr. by James Strachey. 1989. reprint ed. pap. 4.95 (*0-393-00146-6*) Norton.

Autobiographical Subject: Gender & Ideology in Eighteenth-Century England. Felicity A. Nussbaum. LC 89-32587. 288p. 1989. text ed. 38.50x (*0-8018-3825-8*) Johns Hopkins.

***Autobiographical Subject: Gender & Ideology in Eighteenth-Century England.** Felicity A. Nussbaum. 288p. 1995. reprint ed. pap. text ed. 16.95x (*0-8018-5237-4*) Johns Hopkins.

Autobiographical Tightropes: Simone de Beauvoir, Nathalie Sarraute, Marguerite Duras, Monique Wittig & Maryse Conde. Leah D. Hewitt. LC 89-29319. x, 259p. 1990. reprint ed. pap. 12.95 (*0-8032-7258-8*) U of Nebr Pr.

Autobiographical Tightropes: Simone de Beauvoir, Nathalie Sarraute, Marguerite Duras, Monique Wittig & Maryse Conde. Leah D. Hewitt. LC 89-29319. x, 259p. 1992. reprint ed. 30.00 (*0-8032-2354-4*) U of Nebr Pr.

Autobiographical Voices: Race, Gender, Self-Portraiture. Francoise Lionnet. LC 88-43236. (Reading Women Writing Ser.). 280p. 1989. 34.95 (*0-8014-2091-1*) Cornell U Pr.

Autobiographical Voices: Race, Gender, Self-Portraiture. Francoise Lionnet. LC 88-43236. (Reading Women Writing Ser.). 280p. 1991. reprint ed. pap. 13.95 (*0-8014-9927-5*) Cornell U Pr.

Autobiographical Works of Washington Allston. Washington Allston. 1991. reprint ed. 50.00 (*0-8201-1450-2*) Schol Facsimiles.

Autobiographical Writings of Lewis Mumford: A Study in Literary Audacity. Frank G. Novak, Jr. LC 88-50558. (Biography Monographs). 72p. 1988. pap. text ed. 8.95 (*0-8248-1189-5*) UH Pr.

Autobiographics: A Feminist Theory of Women's Self Representation. Leigh Gilmore. LC 93-5982. (Reading Women Writing Ser.). 280p. 1994. 37.50 (*0-8014-2778-9*); pap. 14.95 (*0-8014-8061-2*) Cornell U Pr.

Autobiographics in Freud & Derrida. Ed. by Jane M. Todd. LC 90-34444. (Studies in Comparative Literature). 232p. 1990. reprint ed. 20.00 (*0-8240-0001-3*) Garland.

Autobiographie des Dolmetschers Osman Aga Aus Temeschwar. Kreutel. (Gibb Memorial New Ser.: Vol. 28). 1980. 55.00 (*0-906094-07-0*, Pub. by Aris & Phillips UK) David Brown.

Autobiographies. Alfred Corn. 128p. 1992. 19.00 (*0-670-84602-3*, Viking) Viking Penguin.

Autobiographies. Alfred Corn. 128p. 1993. pap. 12.50 (*0-14-058690-3*, Penguin Bks) Viking Penguin.

Autobiographies. Richard Kostelanetz. LC 79-87601. 1981. 20.00 (*0-918406-16-1*); pap. 8.00 (*0-918406-15-3*); 100.00 (*0-918406-17-X*) Future Pr.

***Autobiographies, Vol. 1.** Raine. 1995. pap. 24.95 (*1-871438-41-1*) Atrium Pubs.

Autobiographies: Narrative of a Life, My Bondage & My Freedom, Life & Times. Frederick Douglass. Ed. by Henry L. Gates, Jr. LC 93-24168. 1126p. 1994. 35.00 (*0-940450-79-8*) Library of America.

Autobiographies in Experimental Psychology. Ed. by Ronald Gandelman. LC 85-20585. 128p. (C). 1985. text ed. 29.95 (*0-89859-544-4*) L Erlbaum Assocs.

Autobiographies of Conversion. Joseph H. Fichter. LC 87-1634. (Studies in Religion & Society: Vol. 17). 256p. 1987. lib. bdg. 89.95 (*0-88946-857-5*) E Mellen.

Autobiographies of Noah Webster: From the Letters & Essays, Memoir & Diary. Intro. by Richard M. Rollins. 394p. 1989. lib. bdg. 39.95 (*0-87249-574-4*) U of SC Pr.

Autobiographies of Ten Religious Leaders: Alternatives in Christian Experience. Radoslav A. Tsanoff. LC 68-57880. 320p. reprint ed. pap. 91.20 (*0-8357-6353-6*, 2035628) Bks Demand.

Autobiographies of the Haymarket Martyrs. Ed. by Philip S. Foner. LC 77-85125. 198p. 1993. reprint ed. pap. 15.95 (*0-913460-58-3*) Pathfinder NY.

Autobiographische Tierbilder Bei Horaz. G. Warmuth. Bd. 22. Date not set. write for info. (*0-318-70700-4*, Pub. by Georg Olms GW) Lubrecht & Cramer.

Autobiographische Tierbilder Bei Horaz. Georg Warmuth. (Altertumswissenschaftliche Texte und Studien Ser.: Bd. 22). ix, 232p. (GER.). 1992. write for info. (*3-487-09568-8*, Pub. by Georg Olms GW) Lubrecht & Cramer.

Autobiography. Richard Avedon. LC 93-440. 1993. 100.00 (*0-679-40921-1*) Random.

Autobiography. Peter Brook. Date not set. pap. write for info. (*0-679-43327-9*) Random.

Autobiography. Benvenuto Cellini. (Classics Ser.). 1956. mass mkt. 8.95 (*0-14-044049-6*, Penguin Classics) Viking Penguin.

Autobiography. Agatha Christie. 1976. 34.95 (*0-8488-0458-9*) Amereon Ltd.

Autobiography. Robin G. Collingwood. 1983. 24.95 (*0-19-824694-3*) OUP.

Autobiography. Robert Creeley. (Illus.). 115p. (Orig.). 1990. pap. 5.95 (*0-937815-42-X*) Hanuman Bks.

Autobiography. Benedetto Croce. Tr. by Robin G. Collingwood. LC 79-114871. (Select Bibliographies Reprint Ser.). 1977. 16.95 (*0-8369-5276-6*) Ayer.

Autobiography. Olivia De Havilland. 1989. write for info. (*0-318-65586-1*, HarpT) HarpC.

Autobiography. Benjamin Franklin. 1990. pap. 8.50 (*0-679-72613-6*, Vin) Random.

Autobiography. Yukichi Fukuzawa. Tr. by Eiichi Kiyooka. LC 66-15468. (Illus.). 407p. 1980. pap. text ed. 19.00 (*0-231-08373-4*) Col U Pr.

Autobiography. James Goodwin. LC 93-11948. (Twayne's Studies in Genre). 175p. 1994. text ed. 22.95 (*0-8057-0954-1*, Twayne) Macmillan.

Autobiography. Joseph Jefferson. Ed. by Alan S. Downer. LC 64-16063. (John Harvard Library). (Illus.). 388p. 1964. 32.00 (*0-674-05350-8*) HUP.

Autobiography. John Stuart Mill. Ed. by John H. Robson. 240p. 1990. pap. 9.95 (*0-14-043316-3*, Penguin Classics) Viking Penguin.

Autobiography. Richard Morris. 1994. 15.00 (*0-939520-01-X*) Ghost Dance.

Autobiography. Colin Powell. 1995. 27.50 (*0-679-43296-5*) Random.

Autobiography. John C. Powys. 652p. 1994. pap. 22.95 (*0-912568-17-8*) Colgate U Pr.

Autobiography. Charles Rich. LC 90-52664. 143p. (Orig.). 1991. pap. 5.95 (*0-932506-80-1*) St Bedes Pubns.

Autobiography. William R. Shurtleff. 91p. (Orig.). 1990. Spiral bound. spiral bd. 49.95 (*0-942515-04-8*) Pine Hill CA.

***Autobiography.** J. Szavai. (Studies in Modern Philology: No. 1). 236p. (C). 1984. pap. 26.00x (*963-05-3659-5*, Pub. by Akad Kiado HU) St Mut.

Autobiography. Anthony Trollope. Ed. by P. D. Edwards. (World's Classics Ser.). (Illus.). 1980. pap. 6.95 (*0-19-281509-1*) OUP.

Autobiography. limited ed. Richard Avedon. 1993. Ltd. ed. 500.00 (*0-679-42964-6*) Random.

Autobiography. Charles F. Adams, Jr. (Works of Charles Francis Adams Jr. (1835-1915)). 1989. reprint ed. lib. bdg. 79.00 (*0-7812-1419-X*) Rprt Serv.

Autobiography. Neville Cardus. LC 75-37825. (Illus.). 288p. 1976. reprint ed. text ed. 59.75 (*0-8371-8577-7*, CAAU, Greenwood Pr) Greenwood.

Autobiography. John Cournos. LC 78-64010. (Des Imagistes: Literature of the Imagist Movement Ser.). (Illus.). 368p. reprint ed. 35.00 (*0-404-17084-6*) AMS Pr.

Autobiography. George Dewey. LC 74-108813. (BCL Ser. I). (Illus.). reprint ed. 17.50 (*0-404-02121-2*) AMS Pr.

Autobiography. Amos Kendall. (History - United States Ser.). 700p. 1993. reprint ed. lib. bdg. 109.00 (*0-7812-4827-2*) Rprt Serv.

Autobiography. Edwin Muir. (Memoir Ser.). 320p. (C). 1990. reprint ed. pap. 10.95 (*1-55597-128-8*) Graywolf.

Autobiography. Friedrich Paulsen. Tr. by Theodore Lorenz. LC 38-38641. reprint ed. 19.00 (*0-404-04945-1*) AMS Pr.

Autobiography. Margaret E. Sangster. Ed. by Annette K. Baxter. LC 79-8812. (Signal Lives Ser.). (Illus.). 1980. reprint ed. lib. bdg. 39.95 (*0-405-12857-6*) Ayer.

Autobiography, 2 vols. Louis Spohr. LC 69-12693. (Music Ser.). 1969. reprint ed. lib. bdg. 65.00 (*0-306-71222-9*) Da Capo.

Autobiography. Frank Lloyd Wright. (American Biography Ser.). 620p. 1991. reprint ed. lib. bdg. 109.00 (*0-7812-8431-7*) Rprt Serv.

Autobiography, 2 vols., Set. Lyman Beecher. (American Biography Ser.). 1991. reprint ed. lib. bdg. write for info. (*0-7812-8016-8*) Rprt Serv.

Autobiography, 2 vols, Set. Lew Wallace. 1972. reprint ed. 48.95 (*0-8422-8121-5*) Irvington.

Autobiography, 2 vols., Vol. 1. Samuel Bamford. Ed. by W. H. Chaloner. 364p. 1967. 35.00 (*0-7146-1055-0*, Pub. by F Cass Pubs UK) Intl Spec Bk.

Autobiography, 2 vols., Vol. 2. Samuel Bamford. Ed. by W. H. Chaloner. 580p. 1967. 35.00 (*0-7146-1056-9*, Pub. by F Cass Pubs UK) Intl Spec Bk.

Autobiography: A Reader for Writers. 2nd ed. Ed. by Robert Lyons. (C). 1984. pap. 18.95 (*0-19-503401-5*) OUP.

Autobiography: Centenary Edition. Jawaharlal Nehru. 640p. 1989. 19.95 (*0-19-562395-9*); pap. 9.95 (*0-19-562361-4*) OUP.

Autobiography: Intellectual, Moral, & Spiritual. Asa Mahan. (American Biography Ser.). 458p. 1991. reprint ed. lib. bdg. 89.00 (*0-7812-8262-4*) Rprt Serv.

Autobiography: Memoirs, & Experiences of Moncure Daniel Conway, 2 Vols. Moncure D. Conway. LC 76-87495. (American Public Figures Ser.). (Illus.). 1970. reprint ed. lib. bdg. 115.00 (*0-306-71402-7*) Da Capo.

Autobiography: Or, the Story of My Experiments with Truth. 2nd ed. M. K. Gandhi. Tr. by Mahadev Desai. 432p. (C). 1983. 12.00 (*0-934676-40-2*) Greenlf Bks.

Autobiography: Or the Story of My Experiments with Truth. 2nd ed. M. K. Gandhi. Tr. by Mahadev Desai. 432p. (C). 1984. pap. 5.00 (*0-934676-68-2*) Greenlf Bks.

Autobiography: The Rainbow Comes & Goes, the Lights of Common Day, Trumpets from the Steep. Diana Cooper. 752p. 1985. pap. 13.95 (*0-88184-131-5*) Carroll & Graf.

Autobiography: The Story of My Experiments with Truth. Mohandas K. Gandhi. LC 93-19758. 560p. 1993. pap. 10.95 (*0-8070-5909-9*) Beacon Pr.

Autobiography: The Story of My Experiments with Truth. Mohandas K. Gandhi. (Social Sciences Ser.). 480p. 1983. reprint ed. pap. 6.95 (*0-486-24593-4*) Dover.

Autobiography: The Story of My Experiments with Truth. Mohandas K. Gandhi. 535p. 1990. reprint ed. lib. bdg. 35.95 (*0-89966-746-5*) Buccaneer Bks.

Autobiography: The Story of the Lord's Dealings with Mrs. Amanda Smith, The Colored Evangelist, Containing an Account of Her Life Work of Faith, & Her Travels in America, England, Ireland, Scotland, India & Africa, as an Independent Missionary. Amanda B. Smith. (Schomburg Library of Nineteenth-Century Black Women Writers). 608p. 1988. 26.00 (*0-19-505261-7*) OUP.

Autobiography: To the Is-Land; An Angel at My Table; Envoy from Mirror City. Janet Frame. (Illus.). 400p. 1991. pap. 17.50 (*0-8076-1259-6*) Braziller.

Autobiography - Intellectual, Moral & Spiritual. Asa Mahan. LC 75-3269. reprint ed. 45.00 (*0-404-59257-0*) AMS Pr.

Autobiography & Correspondence of Mary Granville, Mrs. Delany, 6 Vols, Set. Mary Delany. Ed. by Lady Llanover. LC 75-163683. reprint ed. 300.00 (*0-404-02080-1*) AMS Pr.

Autobiography & Letters. James G. Ramsey. Ed. by William B. Hesseltine. LC 54-63080. 385p. reprint ed. pap. 109.80 (*0-8357-5906-7*, 2022216) Bks Demand.

Autobiography & Other Essays. George M. Trevelyan. LC 75-142707. (Essay Index Reprint Ser.). 1977. 20.95 (*0-8369-2205-0*) Ayer.

Autobiography & Other Writings. Benjamin Franklin. Ed. by Russel B. Nye. LC 85-12061. (YA). (gr. 9 up). 1958. pap. 9.96 (*0-395-05130-4*, RivEd) HM.

Autobiography & Other Writings. Benjamin Franklin. Ed. by Ormond Seavey. LC 92-14671. (World's Classics Ser.). (Illus.). 400p. (C). 1993. pap. 4.95 (*0-19-282733-2*, 13438) OUP.

Autobiography & Other Writings. Benjamin Franklin. Ed. by Peter Shaw. 304p. (gr. 9-12). 1982. pap. 3.95 (*0-553-21075-0*, Bantam Classics) Bantam.

Autobiography & Postmodernism. Ed. by Kathleen Ashley et al. LC 93-32437. 328p. (C). 1994. lib. bdg. 50.00 (*0-87023-899-X*); pap. 17.95 (*0-87023-900-7*) U of Mass Pr.

Autobiography & Questions of Gender. Ed. by Shirley Neuman. 1992. text ed. 29.50 (*0-7146-3422-0*, Pub. by F Cass Pubs UK) Intl Spec Bk.

Autobiography & Reminiscences. Sarah J. Cummins. 1987. reprint ed. 14.95 (*0-87770-042-7*) Ye Galleon.

Autobiography & Selected Letters. Charles Darwin. Ed. by Francis Darwin. 1892. pap. 6.95 (*0-486-20479-0*) Dover.

Autobiography & Selected Writings. Benjamin Franklin. Ed. by Dixon Wecter & Larzer Ziff. LC 59-14521. (Rinehart Editions Ser.). 317p. (C). 1949. pap. text ed. 14.75 (*0-03-009890-4*) HB Coll Pubs.

Autobiography & Selected Writings. Benjamin Franklin. 352p. 1961. pap. 3.50 (*0-451-52202-8*, Sig Classics) NAL-Dutton.

Autobiography & Selected Writings. Benjamin Franklin. (C). 1981. pap. 4.00 (*0-685-03395-3*, T18, Modern Lib) Random.

***Autobiography & the Existential Self: Studies in Modern French Writing.** Ed. by Terry Keefe & Edmund Smyth. LC 94-46864. 1995. write for info. (*0-312-12593-3*) St Martin.

Autobiography As Burla in the Guzman de Alfarache. Nina C. Davis. LC 91-55272. 160p. 1991. 29.50 (*0-8387-5221-7*) Bucknell U Pr.

Autobiography at the Trigger by Etelvina Astrada. Ed. by Timothy J. Rogers. LC 82-60922. 128p. 1984. 13.00 (*0-938972-04-9*) Spanish Lit Pubns.

Autobiography (Atmakatha) Mahesh Eklunchwar. (C). 1989. text ed. 8.50 (*81-7046-069-7*, Pub. by Seagull Bks II) S Asia.

Autobiography by Tan Kah Kee. Tan Kah Kee. 600p. 1993. pap. text ed. 15.00 (*1-879771-06-3*) Global Pub NJ.

Autobiography in Early Modern Spain. Ed. by Nicholas Spadaccini & Jenaro Talens. (Hispanic Issues Ser.: No. 2). 300p. (Orig.). (C). 1988. pap. 9.95 (*0-910235-24-4*) Prisma Bks.

Autobiography in Early Modern Spain. Ed. by Nicholas Spadaccini & Jenaro Talens. (Hispanic Issues Ser.: Vol. 2). (Orig.). 1988. pap. text ed. 14.95 (*0-8166-2009-1*) U of Minn Pr.

Autobiography in Poetry. Maurice H. Thatcher. 1974. 7.50 (*0-8315-0145-6*) Speller.

***Autobiography in Walker Percy: Repetition, Recovery, & Redemption.** Edward J. Dupuy. (Southern Literary Studies). (Illus.). 184p. (C). 1995. text ed. 25.00 (*0-8071-2012-X*) La State U Pr.

Autobiography, Letters, & Literary Remains of Mrs. Piozzi (Thrale), 2 vols., Set. Hester Piozzi. LC 70-178349. reprint ed. 115.00 (*0-404-56776-2*) AMS Pr.

Autobiography Memories & Experiences. Moncure D. Conway. (Works of Moncure Daniel Conway Ser.). 1990. reprint ed. lib. bdg. 79.00 (*0-7812-2346-6*) Rprt Serv.

Autobiography of a Black Activist, Feminist, Lawyer, Priest, & Poet. Pauli Murray. LC 88-20728. Orig. Title: Song in a Weary Throat; an American Pilgrimage. 464p. 1989. reprint ed. pap. 18.95 (*0-87049-596-8*) U of Tenn Pr.

Autobiography of a Brown Buffalo. Oscar Z. Acosta. 1989. pap. 10.00 (*0-679-72213-0*, Vin) Random.

Autobiography of a Business Woman. Alice F. MacDougall. Ed. by Annette K. Baxter. LC 79-8800. (Signal Lives Ser.). (Illus.). 1980. reprint ed. lib. bdg. 26.95 (*0-405-12847-9*) Ayer.

Autobiography of a Cheque. R. S. Metha. 136p. 1984. text ed. 15.00 (*0-86590-274-7*, Pub. by Sterling Pubs II) Apt Bks.

Autobiography of a Chinese Woman, Buwei Yang Chao. Chao Pu-Wei. Tr. by Chao Yuen-Ren. LC 72-100225. 327p. 1970. reprint ed. text ed. 35.00 (*0-8371-3712-8*, CHCW, Greenwood Pr) Greenwood.

Autobiography of a City in Arms: Augusta, Georgia, 1861-1865. Comp. by Berry Fleming. LC 76-12661. (Illus.). 1976. 14.50 (*0-937044-03-2*); pap. 6.50 (*0-685-04357-6*) Richmond Cty Hist Soc.

Autobiography of a Common Man: With Some Uncommon Experiences. Daniel G. Forbes. 1992. 16.95 (*0-533-10164-6*) Vantage.

Autobiography of a Criminal. 2nd ed. Henry Tufts. Ed. by Edmund Pearsons. LC 92-75830. (Illus.). 312p. 1993. reprint ed. pap. 12.95 (*1-55950-095-6*, 94202) Loompanics.

Autobiography of a Curmudgeon. Harold L. Ickes & Bernard Sternsher. LC 85-14850. xxv, 350p. 1985. reprint ed. text ed. 69.50 (*0-313-24988-1*, ICAU, Greenwood Pr) Greenwood.

Autobiography of a Face. Lucy Grealy. 256p. 1994. 19.95 (*0-395-65780-6*) HM.

***Autobiography of a Face.** Ludy Grealy. 1995. pap. 12.00 (*0-06-097673-X*, HarpT) HarpC.

***Autobiography of a Family Photograph.** Jacqueline Woodson. LC 94-3639. 1995. 17.95 (*0-525-93721-8*, Dutton-Truman Talley) NAL-Dutton.

Autobiography of a Farm Boy. Isaac P. Roberts. (American Biography Ser.). 207p. 1991. reprint ed. lib. bdg. 69.00 (*0-7812-8324-8*) Rprt Serv.

Autobiography of a Female Slave. Mattie Griffiths. LC 79-89412. (Black Heritage Library Collection). 1977. 17.95 (*0-8369-8584-2*) Ayer.

Autobiography of a Female Slave. Mattie Griffiths. 15.00x (*1-56675-011-3*) Mnemosyne.

Autobiography of a Female Slave. Mattie Griffiths. LC 71-92430. 1857. 49.00 (*0-403-00163-3*) Scholarly.

Autobiography of a Female Slave. Martha G. Browne. LC 71-92745. 401p. 1970. reprint ed. text ed. 45.00 (*0-8371-2194-9*, GRS&, Negro U Pr) Greenwood.

Autobiography of a Female Slave. Martha G. Browne. (American Biography Ser.). 401p. 1991. reprint ed. lib. bdg. 89.00 (*0-7812-8046-X*) Rprt Serv.

Autobiography of a Flea. 196p. 1983. reprint ed. pap. 3.95 (*0-88184-002-5*) Carroll & Graf.

Autobiography of a Flea, No. III. Paul Little. (Orig.). 1991. mass mkt. 4.95 (*1-878320-94-7*) Masquerade.

***Autobiography of a Flea & Other Tart Tales.** 320p. 1995. mass mkt. 5.95 (*0-7867-0292-3*) Carroll & Graf.

Autobiography of a French Detective from 1818 to 1858: Most Curious Revelations of the French Detective Police System. Louis Canler. LC 75-32738. (Literature of Mystery & Detection Ser.). 1976. reprint ed. 26.95 (*0-405-07866-8*) Ayer.

Autobiography of a Fugitive Negro. Samuel R. Ward. LC 68-29022. (American Negro: His History & Literature, Ser. No. 1). 1974. reprint ed. 37.95 (*0-405-01842-8*) Ayer.

Autobiography of a Fugitive Negro: His Anti-Slavery Labours in the United States, Canada, & England. Samuel R. Ward. (B. E. Ser.: No. 4). 1855. 42.00 (*0-8115-2955-X*) Periodicals Srv.

Autobiography of a Fugitive Negro: His Anti-Slavery Labours in the United States, Canada, England. Samuel R. Ward. (American Biography Ser.). 412p. 1991. reprint ed. lib. bdg. 89.00 (*0-7812-8401-5*) Rprt Serv.

An Asterisk (*) at the beginning of an entry indicates that the title is appearing in BIP for the first time.

Autobiography of a Happy Woman. Ed. by Leon Stein & Annette K. Baxter. LC 74-3926. (Women in America Ser.). 388p. 1974. reprint ed. 34.95 (*0-405-06073-4*) Ayer.

Autobiography of a Hunted Priest. John Gerard. Tr. by Philip Caraman. (Books to Live Ser.). 1988. reprint ed. 15.95 (*0-88347-223-6*) Thomas More.

Autobiography of a Magdalen. L. C. W. reprint ed. 9.75 (*0-87651-208-2*) Southern U Pr.

***Autobiography of a Mountain Man.** Stephen Meedk. (American Autobiography Ser.). 17p. 1995. reprint ed. lib. bdg. 69.00 (*0-7812-8590-9*) Rprt Serv.

Autobiography of a Philosopher. George H. Palmer. (American Biography Ser.). 137p. 1991. reprint ed. lib. bdg. 59.00 (*0-7812-8305-1*) Rprt Serv.

Autobiography of a Pioneer: or, The Nativity, Experience, Travels & Ministerial Labors of Rev. Jacob Young. Jacob Young. (American Biography Ser.). 528p. 1991. reprint ed. lib. bdg. 99.00 (*0-7812-8434-1*) Rprt Serv.

***Autobiography of a Plain Preacher.** Raymond Huse. (American Autobiography Ser.). 121p. 1995. reprint ed. lib. bdg. 69.00 (*0-7812-8562-3*) Rprt Serv.

Autobiography of a Quack & the Case of George Dedlow. Silas W. Mitchell. LC 68-57542. (Muckrakers Ser.). (Illus.). reprint ed. lib. bdg. 14.00 (*0-8398-1264-7*) Irvington.

Autobiography of a Revolutionary: Essays on Animal & Human Rights. Roberta Kalechofsky. LC 91-19709. 200p. 1991. pap. 11.95 (*0-916288-34-X*) Micah Pubns.

Autobiography of a Revolutionary Soldier. James P. Collins. Ed. by Richard H. Kohn. LC 78-22378. (American Military Experience Ser.). 1980. reprint ed. lib. bdg. 15.95 (*0-405-11855-4*) Ayer.

Autobiography of a Schizophrenic Girl: An Astonishing Memoir of Reality Lost & Regained. Frwd. by Frank Conroy. 192p. 1994. pap. 9.95 (*0-452-01133-7*, Mer) NAL-Dutton.

Autobiography of a Seventeenth-Century Venetian Rabbi: Leon Modena's Life of Judah. Tr. & Intro. by Mark R. Cohen. (Illus.). 272p. 1988. 49.50 (*0-691-05529-7*); pap. 16.95 (*0-691-00824-8*) Princeton U Pr.

Autobiography of a Shaker, & Revelation of the Apocalypse. enl. ed. Frederick W. Evans. LC 72-2986. reprint ed. 19.50 (*0-404-10748-6*) AMS Pr.

Autobiography of a Skeptic. Frank Farmer. 292p. (C). 1987. reprint ed. pap. 7.95 (*0-944386-06-7*) SOM Pub.

***Autobiography of a Slave: A Bilingual Edition.** Juan F. Manzano. Ed. by Ivan A. Schulman. Tr. by Evelyn P. Garfield. (Latin American Literature & Culture Ser.). 160p. (C). 1996. 34.95 (*0-8143-2537-8*); pap. 16.95 (*0-8143-2538-6*) Wayne St U Pr.

Autobiography of a Winnebago Indian. Paul Radin. 1920. pap. 3.50 (*0-486-20096-5*) Dover.

Autobiography of a Working Woman. Adelheid D. Popp. Tr. by E. C. Harvey. LC 79-2950. (Illus.). 135p. 1986. reprint ed. 21.00 (*0-8305-0113-4*) Hyperion Conn.

Autobiography of a Yaqui Poet. Refugio Savala. Ed. by Kathleen Sands. LC 79-19817. 228p. 1980. pap. 11.95 (*0-8165-0628-0*) U of Ariz Pr.

***Autobiography of a Yogi.** Paramahansa Yogananda. LC 78-151319. (HIN.). 1971. pap. 4.00x (*0-87612-077-X*) Self Realization.

Autobiography of a Yogi. Paramahansa Yogananda. LC 78-151319. (Illus.). 1971. French ed. pap. 28.50x (*0-87612-066-4*); Greek ed. pap. 21.00 (*0-87612-069-9*); Italian ed. pap. 11.00 (*0-87612-067-2*); Spanish ed. pap. 14.00 (*0-87612-068-0*); Hindi ed. pap. 22.50x (*85-323-0046-4*) Self Realization.

Autobiography of a Yogi. Paramahansa Yogananda. LC 78-151319. (Illus.). 1973. 4.00 (*0-87612-078-8*) Self Realization.

Autobiography of a Yogi. Paramahansa Yogananda. LC 78-151319. (Illus.). 608p. 1993. Bengali ed. 4.00 (*0-87612-071-0*); Dutch ed. 25.00 (*90-202-4016-1*); German ed. 19.00 (*3-502-62657-X*); Gujarati ed. 4.00 (*0-87612-072-9*); Japanese ed. 25.00 (*0-87612-073-7*); pap. 4.50 (*0-87612-079-6*) Self Realization.

Autobiography of a Yogi. Paramhasa Yogananda. LC 78-151319. 1993. pap. 12.95 (*1-56589-108-2*) Crystal Clarity.

Autobiography of a Yogi. 12th rev. ed. Paramahansa Yogananda. LC 80-52927. (Illus.). 520p. 1981. 18.50 (*0-87612-082-6*); pap. 11.50 (*0-87612-083-4*) Self Realization.

***Autobiography of a Young One.** Kita Antonia. 86p. (Orig.). 1994. pap. 12.00 (*1-887116-00-1*) Saxon West Pubns.

Autobiography of Adin Ballou 1803-1890. Adin Ballou. Ed. by William S. Heywood. LC 74-26603. (American Utopian Adventure Ser.). (Illus.). xviii, 586p. 1972. reprint ed. lib. bdg. 49.50 (*0-87991-033-X*) Porcupine Pr.

Autobiography of Admiral George Dewey. George Dewey. LC 86-23711. (Classics of Naval Literature Ser.). 297p. 1987. 32.95 (*0-87021-028-9*) Naval Inst Pr.

Autobiography of Albert Einstein. Gerhard Roth. Tr. by Malcolm Green. 120p. (Orig.). 1993. pap. 13.99 (*0-947757-47-3*) Serpents Tail.

Autobiography of Alfred Austin, Poet Laureate, 1835-1910, 2vols. in 1. Alfred Austin. LC 79-148744. (Illus.). reprint ed. 46.50 (*0-404-08717-5*) AMS Pr.

Autobiography of Alice B. Toklas. Gertrude Stein. 19.75 (*0-8446-3003-9*) Peter Smith.

Autobiography of Alice B. Toklas. Gertrude Stein. 1955. pap. 5.95 (*0-394-70133-X*) Random.

Autobiography of Alice B. Toklas. Gertrude Stein. 1990. pap. 10.00 (*0-679-72463-X*, Vin) Random.

Autobiography of Alice B. Toklas. Gertrude Stein. LC 93-15339. 1993. 14.50 (*0-679-60081-7*, Modern Library Prakashan) Random.

Autobiography of Amos Kendall. Amos Kendall. (American Biography Ser.). 700p. 1991. reprint ed. lib. bdg. 109.00 (*0-7812-8233-0*) Rprt Serv.

Autobiography of an Actress. Anna C. Mowatt. Ed. by Annette K. Baxter. LC 79-8807. (Signal Lives Ser.). (Illus.). 1980. reprint ed. lib. bdg. 50.95 (*0-405-12853-3*) Ayer.

Autobiography of an American Novelist. Thomas Wolfe. Ed. by Leslie Field. (Illus.). 168p. 1830. pap. text ed. 7.95x (*0-674-05317-6*) HUP.

Autobiography of an Androgyne. Earl Lind et al. LC 75-12333. (Homosexuality). 1975. reprint ed. 23.95 (*0-405-07400-X*) Ayer.

Autobiography of an Attitude. George J. Nathan. LC 76-145204. 1971. reprint ed. 39.00 (*0-403-00758-5*) Scholarly.

Autobiography of an Awakening. Andrew Cohen. 152p. (Orig.). 1992. pap. 10.95 (*0-9622678-4-8*) Moksha Found.

Autobiography of an Elderly Woman. 280p. 1994. 21.00 (*0-916366-79-0*) Pushcart Pr.

Autobiography of an Elderly Woman. Mary H. Vorse. LC 74-3977. (Women in America Ser.). 276p. 1974. reprint ed. 23.95 (*0-405-06125-0*) Ayer.

Autobiography of an Ex-Colored Man. James Weldon Johnson. LC 89-40439. 156p. 1989. pap. 9.00 (*0-679-72753-1*, Vin) Random.

***Autobiography of an Ex-Colored Man.** unabridged ed. James W. Johnson. (Thrift Editions Ser.). 96p. 1995. pap. text ed. 1.00 (*0-486-28512-X*) Dover.

Autobiography of an Ex-Coloured Man. James Weldon Johnson. (American Century Ser.). 224p. 1960. pap. 7.00 (*0-8090-0032-6*) Hill & Wang.

Autobiography of an Homosexual Englishman "Y" 176p. 1980. 40.00 (*0-89771-001-0*) St Mut.

Autobiography of an Idea. Louis H. Sullivan. (Illus.). 1924. pap. 7.95 (*0-486-20281-X*) Dover.

Autobiography of an Idea. Louis H. Sullivan. (American Biography Ser.). 329p. 1991. reprint ed. lib. bdg. 79.00 (*0-7812-8373-6*) Rprt Serv.

Autobiography of an Indian Monk. Shri P. Swami. (C). 1992. 18.00 (*81-215-0546-1*, Pub. by Munshiram Manoharial II) S Asia.

Autobiography of an Unknown Indian. Nirad C. Chaudhuri. 1989. pap. 16.30 (*0-201-15576-1*) Addison-Wesley.

Autobiography of Andrew Carnegie. Andrew Carnegie. 396p. 1986. reprint ed. pap. text ed. 15.95 (*1-55553-001-X*) NE U Pr.

Autobiography of Andrew Carnegie. Andrew Carnegie. 1993. reprint ed. lib. bdg. 89.00 (*0-7812-5441-8*) Rprt Serv.

Autobiography of Andrew T. Still with a History of the Discovery & Development of the Science of Osteopathy. Andrew T. Still. LC 78-180591. (Medicine & Society in America Ser.). 508p. 1972. reprint ed. 30.95 (*0-405-03973-5*) Ayer.

Autobiography of Anton Rubinstein, 1829-1889. Ed. by Anton Rubinstein. 1988. reprint ed. lib. bdg. 59.00 (*0-7812-0097-0*) Rprt Serv.

Autobiography of Arthur Young: With Selections from His Correspondence. Arthur Young. Ed. by M. Betham-Edwards. LC 67-29463. (Reprints of Economic Classics Ser.). (Illus.). 1967. reprint ed. 49.50 (*0-678-00339-4*) Kelley.

Autobiography of B. H. Roberts. Brigham H. Roberts. Ed. by Gary J. Bergera. LC 90-39781. 266p. 1991. pap. 12.95 (*1-56085-005-1*) Signature Bks.

Autobiography of Ben Franklin Notes. Merrill M. Skaggs. 1969. pap. 4.50 (*0-8220-0216-7*) Cliffs.

Autobiography of Benjamin Franklin. Benjamin Franklin. LC 80-26312. (Airmont Classics Ser.). (J). (gr. 8 up). 1965. pap. 2.75 (*0-8049-0071-X*, CL-71) Airmont.

Autobiography of Benjamin Franklin. Benjamin Franklin. 160p. 1962. pap. 4.95 (*0-02-002910-1*, Collier S&S) S&S Trade.

Autobiography of Benjamin Franklin. Benjamin Franklin. Ed. by Leonard W. Labaree et al. (Illus.). 1964. pap. 9.95 (*0-300-00147-9*, Y117) Yale U Pr.

Autobiography of Benjamin Franklin. Benjamin Franklin. Ed. by R. Jackson Wilson. LC 80-26312. (Modern Library College Editions). 223p. (C). 1981. pap. text ed. write for info. (*0-07-554271-4*) McGraw.

Autobiography of Benjamin Franklin. Benjamin Franklin. Ed. by Kenneth Silverman. LC 80-26312. (Classics Ser.). 320p. 1986. mass mkt. 5.95 (*0-14-039052-9*, Penguin Classics) Viking Penguin.

Autobiography of Benjamin Franklin. Intro. by Louis P. Masur. LC 92-72223. (Bedford Books in American History Ser.). 192p. (C). 1993. pap. text ed. 5.00 (*0-312-08446-3*, Bedford Bks) St Martin.

Autobiography of Benjamin Franklin. Intro. by Louis P. Masur. LC 92-72223. (Bedford Books in American History Ser.). 192p. (C). 1993. text ed. 35.00 (*0-312-09665-8*, Bedford Bks) St Martin.

Autobiography of Benjamin Franklin. Benjamin Franklin. 1981. reprint ed. lib. bdg. 21.95 (*0-89966-416-4*) Buccaneer Bks.

Autobiography of Benjamin Franklin. Benjamin Franklin. 1993. reprint ed. lib. bdg. 89.00 (*0-7812-5457-4*) Rprt Serv.

Autobiography of Benjamin Franklin. Benjamin Franklin. (American Biography Ser.). 228p. 1991. reprint ed. lib. bdg. 69.00 (*0-7812-8137-7*) Rprt Serv.

Autobiography of Benjamin Franklin: A Genetic Text. Benjamin Franklin. Ed. by J. A. Lemay & P. M. Zall. LC 78-25907. (Illus.). 352p. reprint ed. pap. 100.40 (*0-8357-8606-4*, 2035003) Bks Demand.

Autobiography of Benjamin Franklin: A Restoration of a "Fair Copy" by Max Farrand. Benjamin Franklin. (History - United States Ser.). 210p. 1993. reprint ed. lib. bdg. 79.80 (*0-7812-4832-9*) Rprt Serv.

Autobiography of Benjamin Franklin see Writings

Autobiography of Benjamin Rush: His Travels Through Life. Benjamin Rush. Ed. by George W. Corner. LC 72-100241. 399p. 1970. reprint ed. text ed. 65.00 (*0-8371-3037-9*, RUAR, Greenwood Pr) Greenwood.

Autobiography of Benvenuto Cellini. Benvenuto Cellini. Tr. by John A. Symonds. LC 85-4998. 485p. 1985. 12.95 (*0-394-60528-4*, Modern Lib) Random.

Autobiography of Bertrand Russell. Bertrand Russell. (Unwin Paperbacks Ser.). 1978. pap. 16.95 (*0-04-921022-X*) Routledge Chapman & Hall.

Autobiography of Bertrand Russell: Vol. 2, 1914-1944. Bertrand Russell. 1968. 34.95 (*0-04-921009-2*) Routledge Chapman & Hall.

Autobiography of Bertrand Russell: Vol. 3, 1944-1967. Bertrand Russell. 232p. 1981. reprint ed. 34.95 (*0-04-921010-6*) Routledge Chapman & Hall.

Autobiography of Black Chicago. Dempsey J. Travis. (Illus.). 560p. (Orig.). 1981. pap. 22.50 (*0-941484-01-7*) Urban Res Pr.

Autobiography of Black Jazz. Dempsey J. Travis. LC 82-83604. (Illus.). 560p. (Orig.). 1983. 35.10 (*0-941484-03-3*) Urban Res Pr.

Autobiography of Black Jazz. Dempsey J. Travis. (Illus.). 560p. (Orig.). 1983. pap. 22.50 (*0-941484-10-6*) Urban Res Pr.

Autobiography of Black Politics. Dempsey J. Travis. LC 85-15646. (Illus.). 704p. 1987. 27.50 (*0-941484-05-X*) Urban Res Pr.

Autobiography of Calvin Coolidge. Calvin Coolidge. LC 84-72055. (Illus.). 246p. (Orig.). (C). 1989. reprint ed. pap. 14.95 (*0-944951-03-1*) C Coolidge Memorial.

Autobiography of Calvin Coolidge. Calvin Coolidge. (History - United States Ser.). 246p. 1992. reprint ed. lib. bdg. 79.00 (*0-7812-6229-1*) Rprt Serv.

Autobiography of Carl Schurz. Carl Schurz. (American Biography Ser.). 331p. 1991. reprint ed. lib. bdg. 79.00 (*0-7812-8344-2*) Rprt Serv.

Autobiography of Cassandra, Princess & Prophetess of Troy. 2nd ed. Ursule Molinaro. LC 92-17468. 112p. 1992. pap. 9.00 (*0-929701-24-0*) McPherson & Co.

Autobiography of Charles Caldwell, M.D. Charles Caldwell. (American Biography Ser.). 454p. 1991. reprint ed. lib. bdg. 89.00 (*0-7812-8057-5*) Rprt Serv.

Autobiography of Charles Darwin, 1809-1882: With Original Omissions Restored. Charles Darwin. Ed. by Nora Barlow. LC 93-17940. 1993. reprint ed. pap. 8.95 (*0-393-31069-8*) Norton.

Autobiography of Charles G. Finney. Charles G. Finney. Ed. by Helen S. Wessel. LC 77-2813. 240p. 1977. pap. 8.99 (*0-87123-010-0*) Bethany Hse.

Autobiography of Charles G. Finney. Charles G. Finney. (American Biography Ser.). 230p. 1991. reprint ed. lib. bdg. 69.00 (*0-7812-8131-8*) Rprt Serv.

Autobiography of Charles Halle: With Correspondence & Diaries. Ed. by Michael Kennedy. (Illus.). 216p. 1981. reprint ed. lib. bdg. 29.50 (*0-306-76094-0*) Da Capo.

Autobiography of Clara Fisher Maeder. Clara F. Maeder. (American Biography Ser.). 138p. 1991. reprint ed. lib. bdg. 59.00 (*0-7812-8260-8*) Rprt Serv.

Autobiography of Colonel John Trumbull. John Trumbull. Ed. by T. Sizer. LC 79-116912. (Library of American Art Ser.). (Illus.). 1970. reprint ed. lib. bdg. 59.50 (*0-306-71242-3*) Da Capo.

Autobiography of Colonel John Trumbull, Patriot-Artist 1756-1843. John Trumbull. (American Biography Ser.). 404p. 1991. reprint ed. lib. bdg. 89.00 (*0-7812-8397-3*) Rprt Serv.

Autobiography of Daniel Evans Taylor: A Christian Ministry for Our Time. Daniel E. Taylor. LC 87-34838. 160p. 1987. pap. 49.95 (*0-88946-043-4*) E Mellen.

Autobiography of David Crockett. David Crockett. LC 80-2887. (BCL Ser.: No. I & II). reprint ed. 42.50 (*0-404-18059-0*) AMS Pr.

Autobiography of David Crockett. David Crockett. (BCL1 - United States Local History Ser.). 328p. 1991. reprint ed. lib. bdg. 89.00 (*0-7812-6314-X*) Rprt Serv.

***Autobiography of David Kinley.** David Kinley. (American Autobiography Ser.). 167p. 1995. reprint ed. lib. bdg. 69.00 (*0-7812-8571-2*) Rprt Serv.

Autobiography of Dayanand Saraswati. K. C. Yadav. (C). 1987. 17.00 (*0-685-19668-2*, Pub. by Manohar II) S Asia.

Autobiography of Denis Zachaire. T. L. Davis. 1993. pap. 6.95 (*1-55818-142-3*) Holmes Pub.

Autobiography of Dr. Karl Ernst von Baer. Ed. by Jane M. Oppenheimer. LC 86-1924. 1986. 25.00 (*0-88135-079-6*) Watson Pub Intl.

Autobiography of Du Pont De Nemours. Tr. by Elizabeth Fox-Genovese. LC 84-10645. Orig. Title: Fr. 298p. 1984. 40.00 (*0-8420-2132-9*) Scholarly Res Inc.

***Autobiography of Elder Helvecio Martins.** Helvecio Martins & Mark Grover. LC 94-37044. 131p. 1994. 12.95 (*1-56236-218-6*) Aspen Bks.

Autobiography of Elder Wilson Thompson: Embracing a Sketch of His Life, Travels, & Ministerial Labors, in Which Is Included a Concise History of the Old Order of Regular Baptist Churches. Wilson Thompson. (American Biography Ser.). 502p. 1991. reprint ed. lib. bdg. 99.00 (*0-7812-8385-X*) Rprt Serv.

Autobiography of Eleanor Roosevelt. Eleanor Roosevelt. (Illus.). 498p. 1992. reprint ed. pap. 15.95 (*0-306-80476-X*) Da Capo.

Autobiography of Emperor Haile Sellasie I: My Life & Ethiopia's Progress 1892-1937. Haile Sellasie I. Ed. & Tr. by Edward Ullendorff. (Illus.). 1976. 45.00 (*0-19-713589-7*) OUP.

Autobiography of Fukuzawa Yukichi. Fukuzawa Yukichi. Tr. by Kiyooka Eiichi. LC 92-8907. (Library of Japan). 448p. 1992. reprint ed. 29.95 (*0-8191-8295-8*) Madison Bks UPA.

Autobiography of George Dewey. George Dewey. (History - United States Ser.). 337p. 1992. reprint ed. lib. bdg. 89.00 (*0-7812-6212-7*) Rprt Serv.

Autobiography of George Dewey: Admiral of the Navy. George Dewey. (American Biography Ser.). 337p. 1991. reprint ed. lib. bdg. 79.00 (*0-7812-8107-5*) Rprt Serv.

Autobiography of George Muller. George Muller. 300p. 1984. pap. 5.99 (*0-88368-159-5*) Whitaker Hse.

Autobiography of Geraldine Farrar: Such Sweet Compulsion. Geraldine Farrar. (Music Book Index Ser.). 303p. 1992. reprint ed. lib. bdg. 89.00 (*0-7812-9492-4*) Rprt Serv.

Autobiography of Giambattista Vico. Giambattista Vico. Tr. by Max H. Fisch & Thomas G. Bergin. 240p. 1963. pap. 14.95 (*0-8014-9088-X*) Cornell U Pr.

Autobiography of God. L. J. Ogilvie. Tr. by Man-chong Fung. (CHI.). 1983. pap. write for info. (*0-941598-06-3*) Living Spring Pubns.

Autobiography of God. Lloyd J. Ogilvie. LC 78-53355. 324p. (C). 1981. pap. 8.99 (*0-8307-0791-3*, 5415106) Regal.

***Autobiography of God.** rev. ed. Herbert L. Beierle. 1995. pap. 12.95 (*0-940480-38-7*) UNI Press.

Autobiography of Harry S. Truman. Harry S. Truman. Ed. by Robert H. Ferrell. LC 80-66304. 1980. pap. 9.95 (*0-87081-091-X*) Univ Pr Colo.

Autobiography of Henry Fowle of Boston (1766-1837) Ed. by David H. Kilmer. (Illus.). xx, 248p. (Orig.). 1992. pap. 20.00 (*1-55613-482-7*) Heritage Bk.

Autobiography of Henry Merrell: Industrial Missionary to the South. Henry Merrell. Ed. by James L. Skinner, III. LC 90-10919. (Illus.). 592p. 1991. 50.00 (*0-8203-1253-3*) U of Ga Pr.

Autobiography of Henry VIII. Margaret George. 1987. pap. 15.00 (*0-345-34275-5*, Ballantine Trade) Ballantine.

Autobiography of Hercules. Paul F. Kirby. LC 86-71501. 134p. (Orig.). 1986. pap. 15.00 (*0-86516-174-7*) Bolchazy-Carducci.

Autobiography of Jack Woodford. Jack Woodford, pseud. LC 62-17697. (Illus.). 384p. 1989. pap. 13.95 (*0-9601574-5-X*) Woodford Mem.

Autobiography of James Gallier, Architect. James Gallier. LC 69-13715. (Architecture & Decorative Art Ser.). 1973. reprint ed. lib. bdg. 35.00 (*0-306-71247-4*) Da Capo.

Autobiography of James Gallier, Architect. James Gallier. (American Biography Ser.). 150p. 1991. reprint ed. lib. bdg. 59.00 (*0-7812-8141-5*) Rprt Serv.

Autobiography of James L. Smith: Including, Reminiscences of Slave Life, Recollections of the War, Education of Freedmen, Causes of Exodus, Etc. James L. Smith. LC 76-89430. (Black Heritage Library Collection). 1977. 15.95 (*0-8369-8652-0*) Ayer.

Autobiography of John C. Van Dyke: A Personal Narrative of American Life, 1861-1931. John C. Van Dyke. Ed. by Peter Wild. (Illus.). 320p. 1993. 34.95 (*0-87480-392-6*) U of Utah Pr.

Autobiography of John Gould Fletcher. Ed. by Lucas Carpenter. LC 87-34660. Orig. Title: Life Is My Song. 432p. 1988. reprint ed. 26.00 (*1-55728-031-2*) U of Ark Pr.

Autobiography of John Hays Hammond. John H. Hammond. (American Biography Ser.). 813p. 1991. reprint ed. lib. bdg. 129.00 (*0-7812-8164-4*) Rprt Serv.

Autobiography of John Hays Hammond, 2 vols. in 1, Vol. 17. John H. Hammond. LC 74-351. (Gold Ser.). (Illus.). 813p. 1974. reprint ed. 64.95 (*0-405-05913-2*) Ayer.

Autobiography of John Stuart Mill. John Stuart Mill. LC 24-27691. 240p. (C). 1960. pap. text ed. 15.50 (*0-231-08506-0*) Col U Pr.

Autobiography of John Stuart Mill. John Stuart Mill. Ed. by Jack Stillinger. (C). 1957. pap. 9.96 (*0-395-05120-7*, RivEd) HM.

Autobiography of Joseph Jefferson. Joseph Jefferson. (American Biography Ser.). 363p. 1991. reprint ed. lib. bdg. 79.00 (*0-7812-8216-0*) Rprt Serv.

Autobiography of Joseph Jefferson. Joseph Jefferson. 1993. reprint ed. lib. bdg. 89.00 (*0-7812-5473-6*) Rprt Serv.

Autobiography of Joseph Priestley. Joseph Priestley. 159p. 1990. 25.00 (*0-685-37308-8*) Fairleigh Dickinson.

Autobiography of Jurji Zaidan, with Four Letters to His Son. Jurji Zaidan. Ed. & Tr. by Thomas Philipp. LC 90-37911. 118p. 1991. reprint ed. 26.00 (*0-89410-652-X*); reprint ed. pap. 14.00 (*0-89410-653-8*) Three Continents.

Autobiography of Kim Dae Jung. Kim D. Jung. Ed. by R. Scholl. 256p. 1999. 22.95 (*0-471-57752-9*) Wiley.

***Autobiography of Larry Sanders.** Larry Sanders et al. 1995. 21.00 (*0-684-81204-5*) S&S Trade.

Autobiography of Lawrence C. Bryant. Lawrence C. Bryant. 230p. 1971. 15.00 (*0-686-01113-9*); pap. 10.00 (*0-686-01114-7*) L C Bryant.

Autobiography of Leigh Hunt, 2 Vols, 1. Leigh Hunt. LC 25-25547. reprint ed. write for info. (*0-404-03416-0*) AMS Pr.

Autobiography of Leigh Hunt, 2 Vols, 2. Leigh Hunt. LC 25-25547. reprint ed. write for info. (*0-404-03417-9*) AMS Pr.

Autobiography of Leigh Hunt, 2 Vols, Set. Leigh Hunt. LC 25-25547. reprint ed. 115.00 (*0-404-03415-2*) AMS Pr.

Autobiography of Leonard Woolf: Beginning Again: An Autobiography of the Years 1911-1918. Leonard Woolf. LC 75-9848. 263p. 1989. pap. 8.95 (*0-15-611680-4*, Harvest Bks) HarBrace.

Autobiography of Leonard Woolf: Downhill All the Way: An Autobiography of the Years 1919-1939. Leonard Woolf. LC 75-9821. (Illus.). 259p. 1989. pap. 8.95 (*0-15-626145-6*, Harvest Bks) HarBrace.

Autobiography of Leonard Woolf: Growing: An Autobiography of the Years 1904-1911. Leonard Woolf. LC 75-9832. (Illus.). 256p. 1989. pap. 8.95 (*0-15-637215-0*, Harvest Bks) HarBrace.

A

Autobiography of LeRoi Jones. Amiri Baraka. 335p. 1994. pap. 14.95 (1-55652-231-2) L Hill Bks.

Autobiography of Leroi Jones- Amiri Baraka. Amiri Baraka. 329p. 1984. 16.95 (0-88191-000-7) Freundlich.

Autobiography of Lincoln Steffens, 2 vols. Joseph L. Steffens. (American Biography Ser.). 1991. reprint ed. lib. bdg. 148.00 (0-7812-8360-4) Rprt Serv.

Autobiography of Lincoln Steffens, 2 Vols, 2. Lincoln Steffens. LC 67-7897. (Illus.). 353p. 1968. reprint ed. pap. 10.95 (0-15-609396-0, Harvest Bks) HarBrace.

Autobiography of Lord Alfred Douglas. Alfred Douglas. (Select Bibliographies Reprint Ser.). 1977. 21.95 (0-8369-5421-1) Ayer.

Autobiography of Lord Alfred Douglas. Alfred Douglas. reprint ed. lib. bdg. 79.00 (0-7812-0316-3) Rprt Serv.

Autobiography of Lord Alfred Douglas. Alfred Douglas. LC 71-144979. (Illus.). 340p. 1972. reprint ed. 69.00 (0-403-00796-8) Scholarly.

Autobiography of Lorenzo de' Medici the Magnificent: A Commentary on My Sonnets. Tr. by James W. Cook. LC 94-11190. (Medieval & Renaissance Texts & Studies: Vol. 129). 1994. 28.00 (0-86698-136-5) MRTS.

Autobiography of Malcolm X. Told to Alex Haley. 608p. 1992. pap. 12.00 (0-345-37671-4, Ballantine Trade) Ballantine.

Autobiography of Malcolm X. Malcolm X. 1987. mass mkt. 5.99 (0-345-90233-5) Ballantine.

Autobiography of Malcolm X. Malcolm X. (Black History Titles Ser.). 1981. mass mkt. 5.99 (0-345-35068-5, Del Rey) Ballantine.

Autobiography of Malcolm X. Malcom X & Alex Haley. 1976. 25.95 (0-89190-216-3, Am Repr) Amereon Ltd.

Autobiography of Malcolm X: With the Assistance of Alex Haley. Malcolm X. LC 92-52659. 464p. 1992. 20.00 (0-345-37975-6, One World) Ballantine.

Autobiography of Malcolm X Notes. Ray Shepard. 69p. (Orig.). (C). 1973. pap. text ed. 3.95 (0-8220-0802-5) Cliffs.

Autobiography of Margaret Oliphant: The Complete Text. Margaret O. Oliphant. Ed. by Elisabeth Jay. 208p. 1990. 39.95 (0-19-818615-0) OUP.

Autobiography of Mark Rutherford & Mark Rutherford's Deliverance. William H. White. (C). 1989. 39.95 (1-870352-00-9, Pub. by Libris UK) Paul & Co Pubs.

Autobiography of Mark Rutherford, Dissenting Minister, 1881. William H. White. Ed. by Robert L. Wolff. Bd. with Mark Rutherford's Deliverance, 1885. LC 75-1514. LC 75-1514. (Victorian Fiction Ser.). 1976. Set lib. bdg. 73.00 (0-8240-1587-8) Garland.

Autobiography of Mark Twain. Ed. by Charles Neider. LC 90-55053. (Illus.). 384p. 1990. reprint ed. pap. 13.00 (0-06-092025-4, PL) HarpC.

Autobiography of Martin Van Buren, 2 vols. in 1. Martin Van Buren. Ed. by John C. Fitzpatrick. LC 68-58656. 808p. 1969. reprint ed. 57.50 (0-678-00531-1) Kelley.

Autobiography of Martin Van Buren, 2 vols, Set. Martin Van Buren. Ed. by John Fitzpatrick. LC 72-75314. 820p. 1973. reprint ed. lib. bdg. 79.50 (0-306-71275-X) Da Capo.

Autobiography of Mary Magdalene. Beth Ingber-Irvin. LC 89-80564. (Illus.). 96p. (Orig.). 1989. pap. 8.95 (0-931892-65-1) B Dolphin Pub.

***Autobiography of Maud Gonne: A Servant of the Queen.** rev. ed. Maud G. MacBride. Ed. by A. Norman Jeffares & Anna M. White. LC 94-39713. 1995. lib. bdg. 32.00 (0-226-30251-2); pap. 14.95 (0-226-30252-0) U Ch Pr.

Autobiography of Maxim Gorky. Maxim Gorky. Tr. by Isidor Schneider. 1969. reprint ed. pap. 5.95 (0-8065-0199-5, Citadel Pr) Carol Pub Group.

Autobiography of Miss Jane Pittman. Ernest J. Gaines. 256p. 1982. mass mkt. 4.99 (0-553-26357-9) Bantam.

Autobiography of Mother Jones. Mary Jones. LC 71-89741. (American Labor, from Conspiracy to Collective Bargaining Ser., No. 1). 242p. 1974. reprint ed. 23.95 (0-405-02130-5) Ayer.

Autobiography of Mother Jones: Pittston Strike Commemorative Edition. Intro. by Clarence Darrow & Meridel LeSueur. (Labor Classics Ser.). (Illus.). 320p. (Orig.). 1990. reprint ed. 25.95 (0-88286-167-0); reprint ed. pap. 12.95 (0-88286-166-2) C H Kerr.

Autobiography of My Body. David Guy. 400p. 1992. 5.99 (0-451-17252-3, Sig) NAL-Dutton.

***Autobiography of My Body.** David Guy. 336p. 1995. 11.95 (0-452-27453-2, Plume) NAL-Dutton.

Autobiography of My Mother. Rosellen Brown. 272p. 1981. pap. 2.95 (0-345-28738-X) Ballantine.

Autobiography of My Mother. Jamaica Kincaid. 184p. 1995. 18.00 (0-374-10731-9) FS&G.

Autobiography of My Pictures: Hints to Young Painter. R. B. Kitaj. 1992. 24.95 (0-500-09202-8) Thames Hudson.

Autobiography of Oliver Otis Howard, 2 vols., Set. Oliver O. Howard. LC 73-170699. (Black Heritage Library Collection). 1977. reprint ed. 66.95 (0-8369-8889-2) Ayer.

Autobiography of Oliver Otis Howard, Major General, United States Army, 2 vols., Set. Oliver O. Howard. (American Biography Ser.). 1991. reprint ed. lib. bdg. 148.00 (0-7812-8196-2) Rprt Serv.

Autobiography of Osugi Sakae. Osugi Sakae. Tr. & Intro. by Byron K. Marshall. (Voices from Asia Ser.: No. 6). (C). 1992. 30.00 (0-520-07759-8); pap. 13.00 (0-520-07760-1) U CA Pr.

Autobiography of Parley P. Pratt. Parley P. Pratt. LC 85-10264. (Illus.). 447p. 1994. pap. 13.95 (0-87579-841-1) Deseret Bk.

Autobiography of Pat Robertson: Shout It from the Housetops! rev. ed. Pat Robertson & Jamie Buckingham. LC 72-76591. 275p. (Orig.). 1995. pap. 5.95 (0-88270-097-9) Bridge Pub.

Autobiography of Peggy Eaton. Margaret O. Eaton. Ed. by Annette K. Baxter. LC 79-8789. (Signal Lives Ser.). 1980. reprint ed. lib. bdg. 25.95 (0-405-12837-1) Ayer.

Autobiography of Peter Cartwright. Peter Cartwright. 349p. 1986. pap. 9.95 (0-687-02319-X) Abingdon.

Autobiography of Peter Cartwright: The Backwoods Preacher. Peter Cartwright. Ed. by W. P. Strickland. LC 70-38344. (Select Bibliographies Reprint Ser.). 1977. 38.95 (0-8369-6761-5) Ayer.

Autobiography of Rev. E. Mathews, the Father Dickson of Mrs. Stowe's 'Dred' Edward Mathews. LC 79-89392. (Black Heritage Library Collection). 1977. 27.95 (0-8369-8629-6) Ayer.

Autobiography of Rev. James Finley. W. P. Strickland. 1993. reprint ed. lib. bdg. 89.00 (0-7812-5405-1) Rprt Serv.

Autobiography of Robert A. Millikan. Robert A. Millikan. Ed. by I. Bernard Cohen. LC 79-7975. (Three Centuries of Science in America Ser.). (Illus.). 1980. reprint ed. lib. bdg. 29.95 (0-405-12558-5) Ayer.

Autobiography of Roy Cohn. Roy Cohn & Sidney Zion. (Illus.). 304p. 1988. 18.95 (0-8184-0471-X) Carol Pub Group.

Autobiography of Roy Cohn. Roy Cohn & Sidney Zion. 1988. mass mkt. 4.95 (0-312-91402-4) St Martin.

Autobiography of Saint Therese of Lisieux: The Story of a Soul. St. Teresa of Lisieux. 1987. mass mkt. 8.95 (0-385-02903-9, D56, Image Bks) Doubleday.

Autobiography of Sam Houston. Samuel Houston. Ed. by Donald Day & Harry H. Ullom. LC 80-18864. (Illus.). xviii, 298p. 1980. reprint ed. text ed. 38.50 (0-313-22704-7, HOAUS, Greenwood Pr) Greenwood.

Autobiography of Samuel Bamford, 2 vols., Set. Samuel Bamford. Ed. & Intro. by W. H. Chaloner. Incl. Vol. 1. Early Days. LC 67-23461. 1967. reprint ed. 45.00 (0-678-05233-6); Vol. 2. Passages in the Life of a Radical. 3rd ed. LC 67-23461. 1967. reprint ed. 45.00 (0-678-05234-4); LC 67-23461. 1967. 87.50 (0-678-05025-2) Kelley.

Autobiography of Samuel D. Gross, M. D. with Sketches of His Contemporaries, 2 vols., 1. Samuel D. Gross. LC 71-180576. (Medicine & Society in America Ser.). 898p. 1972. reprint ed. 28.95 (0-405-03980-8) Ayer.

Autobiography of Samuel D. Gross, M. D. with Sketches of His Contemporaries, 2 vols., 2. Samuel D. Gross. LC 71-180576. (Medicine & Society in America Ser.). 898p. 1972. reprint ed. 28.95 (0-405-03981-6) Ayer.

Autobiography of Samuel D. Gross, M. D. with Sketches of His Contemporaries, 2 vols., Set. Samuel D. Gross. LC 71-180576. (Medicine & Society in America Ser.). 898p. 1972. reprint ed. 56.95 (0-405-03953-0) Ayer.

***Autobiography of Santa Claus: It's Better to Give.** Jeff Guinn. Ed. by Mike Towle. LC 94-33027. (Illus.). 283p. 1994. 22.95 (1-56530-140-4) Summit TX.

Autobiography of Sir John Bramston. John Bramston. LC 10-2212. (Camden Society, London. Publications, First Ser.: No. 32). reprint ed. 95.00 (0-404-50132-X) AMS Pr.

Autobiography of Sir Walter Besant. Walter Besant. LC 76-144877. 1971. reprint ed. 39.00 (0-403-00864-6) Scholarly.

***Autobiography of Sol Bloom.** Sol Bloom. (American Autobiography Ser.). 345p. 1995. reprint ed. lib. bdg. 89.00 (0-7812-8460-0) Rprt Serv.

Autobiography of Special Agent Dale Cooper. Ed. by Sally Peters. 192p. 1991. pap. 8.95 (0-671-74400-3) PB.

Autobiography of St. Anthony Mary Claret. Anthony M. Claret. LC 85-51661. 227p. 1985. pap. 12.00 (0-89555-284-1) TAN Bks Pubs.

Autobiography of St. Ignatius. Ignacio Loyola. 1972. lib. bdg. 59.95 (0-87968-685-5) Gordon Pr.

Autobiography of St. Ignatius of Loyola, with Related Documents. Tr. by Joseph F. O'Callaghan. LC 92-32959. x, 113p. 1993. reprint ed. pap. 15.00 (0-8232-1480-X) Fordham.

Autobiography of St. Margaret Mary. Margaret M. Alacoque. Tr. by Sisters of the Visitation. LC 86-50148. 141p. 1986. reprint ed. pap. 4.00 (0-89555-295-7) TAN Bks Pubs.

Autobiography of Takahashi Chikuzan: Adventures of a Tsugaru-Jamiesen Musician. Tr. & Anno. by Gerald Groemer. LC 91-9875. (Detroit Monographs in Musicology: No. 10). 1991. 35.00 (0-89990-052-6) Info Coord.

***Autobiography of the African American Self.** Justin W. Fenwick. 155p. (J). (gr. 6-12). 1995. pap. text ed. 15.95 (0-9646262-0-9) TPFS Pr.

***Autobiography of the Angel of Death.** Charles Daniel. LC 94-71620. 242p. (Orig.). 1995. pap. 14.95 (1-56883-053-X) Colonial Pr AL.

Autobiography of the Moon. Dick Higgins. (Chapbook Ser.). (Orig.). 1991. pap. text ed. 5.00 (0-945112-13-0) Generator Pr.

Autobiography of the Supreme Court: Off-the-Bench Commentary by the Justices. Ed. by Alan F. Westin. LC 78-5165. 475p. 1978. reprint ed. text ed. 36.75 (0-313-20385-7, WESU, Greenwood Pr) Greenwood.

Autobiography of Theodore Edgar Potter. Theodore E. Potter. (Michigan Heritage Library: Vol. 1). 1978. reprint ed. 9.95 (0-915056-08-9) Hardscrabble Bks.

Autobiography of Theodore Roosevelt. Theodore Roosevelt. (Quality Paperbacks Ser.). 628p. 1985. reprint ed. pap. 15.95 (0-306-80232-5) Da Capo.

Autobiography of Thomas Collier Platt. Thomas C. Platt. LC 73-19172. (Politics & People Ser.). (Illus.). 580p. 1974. reprint ed. 44.95 (0-405-05894-2) Ayer.

Autobiography of Thomas Collier Platt. Thomas C. Platt. (American Biography Ser.). 556p. 1991. reprint ed. lib. bdg. 99.00 (0-7812-8317-5) Rprt Serv.

Autobiography of Thomas Jefferson see Writings

Autobiography of Thomas L. Chadbourne, Esq. Thomas L. Chadbourne. Ed. by C. C. Goetsch et al. LC 83-13469. (Ingram Documents in Legal History Ser.). 301p. (Orig.). 1985. lib. bdg. 40.00 (0-379-20846-6) Oceana.

Autobiography of Thoughts. Dom Martin. 150p. (Orig.). 1994. pap. 15.00 (0-9616078-3-1) Trans Gala Pubns.

Autobiography of Thurlow Weed, 2 vols., Set. Thurlow Weed. 1993. reprint ed. lib. bdg. 150.00 (0-7812-5204-0) Rprt Serv.

Autobiography of Thurlow Weed see Life of Thurlow Weed

Autobiography of Values. Charles A. Lindbergh. LC 77-7873. 448p. 1978. 19.95 (0-15-110202-3) HarBrace.

Autobiography of Values. Charles A. Lindbergh. 1992. pap. 14.95 (0-15-609402-9, Harvest Bks) HarBrace.

Autobiography of W. E. B. Du Bois: A Soliloquy on Viewing My Life from the Last Decade of Its First Century. W. E. B. Du Bois. LC 68-14103. 1976. reprint ed. 20.00 (0-527-25262-X) Kraus Intl.

Autobiography of W. E. Burghardt Du Bois: A Soliloquy on Viewing My Life from the Last Decade of Its First Century. W. E. B. Du Bois. Ed. by Herbert Aptheker. LC 68-14103. 448p. (C). 1968. 21.00 (0-7178-0235-3); pap. 10.95 (0-7178-0234-5) Intl Pubs Co.

Autobiography of Will Rogers. Donald Day. 1976. 26.95 (0-89190-330-5, Am Repr) Amereon Ltd.

Autobiography of Will Rogers. Will Rogers. Ed. by Donald Day. LC 76-6592. reprint ed. 39.50 (0-404-15293-7) AMS Pr.

Autobiography of William Allen White. abr. rev. ed. Ed. by Sally F. Griffith. LC 89-49050. (Illus.). xxiv, 368p. 1990. pap. 12.95 (0-7006-0471-5) U Pr of KS.

Autobiography of William Allen White. 2nd abr. rev. ed. Ed. by Sally F. Griffith. LC 89-49050. (Illus.). xxiv, 368p. 1990. 35.00x (0-7006-0470-7) U Pr of KS.

Autobiography of William Butler Yeats: Consisting of Reveries over Chilhood & Youth. William Butler Yeats. 416p. 1987. text ed. 50.00 (0-02-632710-4, Scribners) S&S Trade.

Autobiography of William Carlos Williams. William Carlos Williams. 1967. pap. 12.95 (0-8112-0226-7, NDP223) New Directions.

***Autobiography of William Carlos Williams.** William Williams. (American Autobiography Ser.). 402p. 1995. reprint ed. lib. bdg. 99.00 (0-7812-8663-8) Rprt Serv.

***Autobiography of William Colfax Markham.** William Markham. (American Autobiography Ser.). 241p. 1995. reprint ed. lib. bdg. 79.00 (0-7812-8586-0) Rprt Serv.

Autobiography of William Henry Johnson. William H. Johnson. LC 72-129569. (Studies in Black History & Culture: No. 54). 1970. reprint ed. lib. bdg. 63.95 (0-8383-1155-5) M S G Haskell Hse.

Autobiography of William Jay. William Jay. 1974. 17.95 (0-85151-177-5) Banner of Truth.

Autobiography of William Jerdan, 4 Vols, 1. William Jerdan. LC 70-170813. reprint ed. write for info. (0-404-07661-0) AMS Pr.

Autobiography of William Jerdan, 4 Vols, 2. William Jerdan. LC 70-170813. reprint ed. write for info. (0-404-07662-9) AMS Pr.

Autobiography of William Jerdan, 4 Vols, 3. William Jerdan. LC 70-170813. reprint ed. write for info. (0-404-07663-7) AMS Pr.

Autobiography of William Jerdan, 4 Vols, 4. William Jerdan. LC 70-170813. reprint ed. write for info. (0-404-07664-5) AMS Pr.

Autobiography of William Jerdan, 4 Vols, Set. William Jerdan. LC 70-170813. reprint ed. 306.00 (0-404-07660-2) AMS Pr.

Autobiography of William Zeckendorf. William Zeckendorf & Edward McCreary. LC 87-62947. (Illus.). 320p. 1988. reprint ed. 24.95 (0-9618972-0-1) Plaza Pr.

Autobiography of Worthington Whittredge. Worthington Whittredge. Ed. by John I. Baur. LC 74-85661. (Brooklyn Museum Publications in Reprint). 1969. reprint ed. 15.95 (0-405-00874-0) Ayer.

Autobiography, Politics, & Sexuality: Essays in Curriculum Theory, 1972-1992, Vol. 2. William F. Pinar. LC 94-132. (Counterpoints: Studies in the Postmodern Theory of Education: Vol. 2). 278p. (Orig.). (C). 1994. pap. text ed. 24.95 (0-8204-1849-8) P Lang Pubs.

Autobiography Studies in Modern Philology 1. Janos Szavi. 236p. 1984. 50.00 (0-569-08825-9, Pub. by Collets UK) Pro-Am Music.

Autobiography Vol. II, 1937-1960: Exile's Odyssey. Mircea Eliade. Tr. by Mac L. Ricketts. (Illus.). 248p. 1988. 19.95 (0-226-20411-1) U Ch Pr.

Autobiography, Vol. 1: Journey East, Journey West, 1907-1937. Mircea Eliade. Tr. by Mac L. Ricketts. LC 87-30230. (Illus.). xi, 336p. 1990. pap. 15.95 (0-226-20407-3) U Ch Pr.

Autobiography, with Letters. William L. Phelps. LC 76-29445. reprint ed. 57.50 (0-404-15320-8) AMS Pr.

Autobiography, 1791-1828. Benjamin Franklin. (Notable American Authors Ser.). 1992. reprint ed. lib. bdg. 75.00 (0-7812-2894-8) Rprt Serv.

Autobiography, 1829-1889. A. Rubinstein. LC 68-25303. (Studies in Music: No. 42). 1969. reprint ed. lib. bdg. 75.00 (0-8383-0315-3) M S G Haskell Hse.

Autobiography 1883. Anthony Trollope. (Penguin Trollope Ser.). 352p. 1994. 9.95 (0-14-043811-4, Penguin Classics) Viking Penguin.

Autobiography (1931-1967) Karan Singh. (Illus.). 354p. 1990. pap. 9.95 (0-19-562436-X) OUP.

Autobiolgraphy of a Kiowa Apache Indian. Ed. by Charles S. Brant. Orig. Title: Jim Whitewolf: The Life of a Kiowa Apache Indian. (Illus.). 160p. reprint ed. pap. 4.95 (0-486-26862-4) Dover.

Autobody Refinishing Handbook. Andre G. Deroche. (Illus.). 288p. 1987. text ed. 50.00 (0-13-054198-2) P-H.

Autobody Repair. Lester G. Duenk et al. 1984. student ed 5.00 (0-02-662320-X) Bennett IL.

Autobody Repair & Refinishing. Robert P. Schmidt. 350p. (C). 1981. teacher ed write for info. (0-8359-0248-X, Reston) P-H.

Autobody Stamping Applications & Analysis. 228p. 1992. pap. 60.00 (1-56091-214-6, SP-897) Soc Auto Engineers.

Autobody Stamping Technology Progress (SP-865) 1991. 29.00 (1-56091-129-8) Soc Auto Engineers.

***Autobus Magico Dentro de un Pastel.** (J). (ps-3). 1995. pap. 2.50 (0-590-22850-1) Scholastic Inc.

Autobus Magico en el Interior de la Tierra: The Magic School Bus Inside the Earth. Joanna Cole. Tr. by Maria Cordoba & Jose L. Cortes. (Illus.). (SPA.). (J). (gr. 1-4). 1993. pap. 5.95 (0-590-46342-X) Scholastic Inc.

***Autobus Magico en el Museo Encantado.** (J). (ps-3). 1995. pap. 2.50 (0-590-20549-8) Scholastic Inc.

***Autobus Magico Planta una Semilla.** (J). (ps-3). 1995. pap. 2.50 (0-590-22851-X) Scholastic Inc.

***Autobus Magico Salta Hasta Llegar a Casa.** (J). (ps-3). 1995. pap. 2.50 (0-590-20548-X) Scholastic Inc.

Autobus Magico Viaja por el Agua. Joanna Cole. Tr. by Isabel Cano & Jose L. Cortes. (Illus.). (SPA.). (J). (gr. 4-7). 1993. pap. 5.95 (0-590-46427-2) Scholastic Inc.

AutoCAD: A Concise Guide to Commands & Features for Release 12. 4th ed. Steven Elliot & Ronald W. Leigh. (Illus.). 696p. 1995. disk 27.95 (1-56604-139-2) Ventana Pr.

AutoCAD: A Problem-Solving Approach. Sham L. Tickoo. 1994. pap. 39.95 (0-8273-6015-0) Delmar.

***AutoCAD: A Visual Series, 2D Fundamentals.** Steven R. Foster. LC 94-43745. 1995. write for info. (0-8273-6899-2) Delmar.

***AutoCAD: A Visual Series, 3D Fundamentals.** Steven R. Foster. LC 94-45543. 1995. spiral bd. write for info. (0-8273-6901-8) Delmar.

AutoCAD: Methods & Macros. Jeff Guenther et al. (Illus.). 320p. 1988. 29.95 (0-8306-0189-9) TAB Bks.

Autocad: The Drawing Tool. Charles F. Rubenstein. 1992. teacher ed 20.00 (0-8273-4887-8) Delmar.

AutoCAD: The Drawing Tool. Charlie Rubenstein. 384p. 1992. pap. 28.95 (0-8273-4885-1) Delmar.

***AutoCAD: A Tutorial with Drafting Concepts.** A. Rudy Avizius. 700p. 1995. pap. text ed. 40.00 (0-314-04441-8) West Pub.

AutoCAD AME: Solid Modeling for Mechanical Design. Ted Saufley. LC 93-21491. 464p. 1994. text ed. 31.40 (0-87006-083-X) Goodheart.

***AutoCAD & Its Applications: Advanced, Release 13 for DOS.** Shumaker & Madsen. (Illus.). 950p. (Orig.). (C). 1995. pap. text ed. write for info. (1-56637-178-3) Goodheart.

***AutoCAD & Its Applications: Advanced, Release 13 for Windows.** Shumaker & Madsen. (Illus.). 950p. (Orig.). (C). 1995. pap. text ed. write for info. (1-56637-183-X) Goodheart.

***AutoCAD & Its Applications: Basics, Release 13 for Windows.** Shumaker & Madsen. (Illus.). 950p. (Orig.). (C). 1995. pap. text ed. write for info. (1-56637-182-1) Goodheart.

AutoCAD & its Applications: Release 12 for Windows. Terence M. Shumaker et al. (AutoCAD & its Applications ser.). (Illus.). 1276p. (Orig.). (YA). (gr. 8 up). 1994. pap. text ed. 37.00 (1-56637-020-5) Goodheart.

AutoCAD & Its Applications REL 10. Terence M. Shumaker & David A. Madsen. (Illus.). 1989. 31.00 (0-87006-683-8) Goodheart.

AutoCAD & Its Applications, Release 11. 2nd ed. Terence M. Shumaker & David A. Madsen. (Illus.). 944p. 1991. pap. text ed. 33.00 (0-87006-861-X) Goodheart.

AutoCAD & Its Applications Release 12 DOS Edition. Terence M. Shumaker & David A. Madsen. LC 92-38054. 1136p. 1993. 35.00 (0-87006-014-7) Goodheart.

AutoCAD Architectural Lab Manual. Thomas Obermeyer. 216p. 1987. spiral bd. 17.95 (0-07-047524-5) McGraw.

***AutoCAD Basics: Lesson Sets.** (Illus.). 700p. (C). Date not set. student ed 97.00 (0-8064-0446-9, TAV3) Bergwall.

AutoCAD Book: Drawing, Modeling, & Applications Including Release 12. 3rd ed. James M. Kirkpatrick. LC 92-39816. 688p. (C). 1993. pap. write for info. (0-02-364440-0, Merrill Pub Co) Macmillan.

***AutoCAD Book: Drawing, Modeling & Applications, Including Release 13.** 4th ed. James M. Kirkpatrick. LC 95-10211. 1996. write for info. (0-02-364474-5) P-H.

AutoCAD Command Practice Workbook. Charles F. Rubenstein. 60p. 1993. 15.95 (0-8273-6034-7) Delmar.

***AutoCAD Companion.** James A. Leach. LC 94-48563. (Graphics Ser.). 1995. write for info. (0-256-16137-2) Irwin.

AutoCAD Cookbook for the IBM (for MS & PC DOS) Christopher J. Delucchi. 446p. 1989. pap. text ed. 29.95 (0-471-60837-8) Wiley.

AutoCAD Course Manual. H. M. Allen & Fred Brasfield. 170p. (C). 1991. student ed 19.96 (1-56870-003-2) RonJon Pub.

***Autocad Designer: Tutorial 1.** Jacob K. Halim. Ed. by Dewey Thaise. (MCAD Ser.). (Illus.). 320p. 1995. pap. 39.95 (1-877928-04-6) Orange Fortune.

***AutoCAD Drafting.** Grout. 1995. 37.50 (0-02-677135-7) Glencoe.

AutoCAD Essentials. Terence M. Shumaker & David A. Madsen. 592p. 1993. 30.64 (0-87006-977-2) Goodheart.

***AutoCad Essentials: An Unintimidating Introduction to AutoCad & AutoCad Lt.** Bill Fane. 1994. pap. 19.95 (0-201-40909-7) Addison-Wesley.

AutoCAD Express. T. McCarthy. (Illus.). xiii, 312p. (C). 1991. pap. 29.00 (0-387-19590-4, 3781) Spr-Verlag.

AutoCAD Express. 2nd rev. ed. T. McCarthy. (Illus.). xvi, 335p. 1993. pap. 39.00 (0-387-19748-6) Spr-Verlag.

Autocad for Architecture. Alan Jefferis & Michael Jones. 133p. 1994. teacher ed 25.00 (0-8273-5432-0) Delmar.

542

An Asterisk (*) at the beginning of an entry indicates that the title is appearing in BIP for the first time.

AutoCAD for Architecture: Release 12. Alan Jefferis & Michael Jones. LC 93-21482. 664p. 1994. pap. text ed. 34.95 (*0-8273-5431-2*) Delmar.

AutoCAD for Beginners Release 13 for Windows. Michael Beall & Dennis Balagtas. (Illus.). 600p. (Orig.). 1995. pap. text ed. 30.00 (*1-56205-243-8*) New Riders Pub.

***Autocad for Dummies.** Bud Smith. 1995. pap. 19.99 (*1-56884-191-4*) IDG Bks.

AutoCAD for Engineering Graphics. Gary R. Bertoline. 350p. (C). 1989. pap. write for info. (*0-02-309030-8*) Macmillan.

AutoCAD for Engineering Graphics. 2nd ed. Gary R. Bertoline. 578p. (C). 1994. pap. write for info. (*0-02-309042-1*) Macmillan.

AutoCAD for Interior Design & Space Planning: Release 12 Version. 2nd ed. Beverly L. Kirkpatrick & James M. Kirkpatrick. LC 93-45438. 650p. (C). 1994. pap. write for info. (*0-02-364471-0*) Macmillan.

AutoCAD for Mechanical Engineers. Donald Barrus & Karl Grote. 1994. pap. text ed. 24.00 (*0-13-301383-9*) P-H.

AutoCAD for Mechanical Engineers & Designers. Peter Karaiskos. 1994. pap. text ed. 29.95 (*0-471-01779-5*) Wiley.

***AutoCAD for Success.** Stephen J. Ethier & Christine A. Ethier. LC 95-1408. 1995. pap. text ed. 39.00 (*0-02-334421-0*) P-H.

AutoCAD for the Apparel Industry. Phyllis B. Miller. LC 92-47249. 540p. 1994. pap. text ed. 34.95 (*0-8273-5224-7*) Delmar.

Autocad for the Apparel Industry: Instructor's Guide. Phyllis B. Miller. 64p. 1994. 15.00 (*0-8273-5928-4*) Delmar.

Autocad for the Mac Visual Guide. Genevieve Katz. LC 93-87707. 464p. 1994. pap. 26.99 (*0-7821-1516-0*) Sybex.

AutoCAD for Windows. A. Yarwood. LC 94-9030. 1995. pap. text ed. 29.95 (*0-470-23406-7*) Halsted Pr.

AutoCAD for Windows. A. Yarwood. LC 94-9030. 1995. write for info. (*0-582-23935-4*, Pub. by Longman UK) Longman.

AutoCAD for Windows Book. Ralph Grabowski. 296p. 1994. pap. text ed. 34.95 (*0-8273-5581-5*) Delmar.

***AutoCad for Windows Express.** Tim McCarthy. 1994. pap. 39.00 (*3-540-19865-2*) Spr-Verlag.

AutoCAD in Three Dimensions. Stephen Ethier. 522p. (C). 1994. pap. write for info. (*0-02-334232-3*) Macmillan.

AutoCAD in 3D. Forcade et al. 800p. 1995. 45.00 (*1-56205-248-9*) New Riders Pub.

AutoCAD in 3D. Frank J. Johnson. (Computing That Works Ser.). 464p. 1991. pap. text ed. 29.95 (*0-07-032645-2*) McGraw.

***AutoCad Instructor.** Leach. 1995. pap. 55.00 (*0-7863-0462-6*) Irwin Prof Pubng.

***AutoCAD Instructor.** James A. Leach. LC 94-29190. 968p. (C). 1994. 43.95 (*0-256-17144-0*) Irwin.

***AutoCAD Lexikon.** Dietmar Rudolph. 589p. (GER.). 1991. 135.00 (*0-7859-8697-9*, 387686240x) Fr & Eur.

***AutoCad Lt. The Complete Guide.** David S. Cohn. 1995. pap. 29.95 (*0-201-40908-9*) Addison-Wesley.

AutoCad Mechanical Lab Manual. Donald D. Voisinet. 176p. 1987. pap. text ed. 16.95 (*0-07-047526-1*) McGraw.

AutoCAD Methods & Macros. 2nd ed. Jeff Guenther & Ed Ocoboc. (Computer Graphics Technology & Management Ser.). 1991. pap. 24.95 (*0-07-155506-4*) McGraw.

AutoCAD Methods & Macros. 2nd ed. Jeff Guenther & Ed Ocoboc. (Computer Graphics Technology & Management Ser.). (Illus.). 380p. 1990. pap. 24.95 (*0-8306-3544-0*, TAB/TPR) TAB Bks.

***AutoCAD of Windows Express.** T. McCarthy. 328p. 1994. pap. text ed. 29.95 (*0-387-19865-2*) Spr-Verlag.

AutoCAD Power Tools. Bud E. Smith. 1993. disk, pap. 55.00 (*0-679-79145-0*) Random.

AutoCAD Productivity Book: For Releases 10, 11, & 12. 5th ed. James L. Brittain et al. LC 92-36880. 27.95 (*1-56604-026-4*) Ventana Pr.

AutoCAD Productivity Book: The Non-Programmer's Guide to Customizing AutoCAD. 6th ed. George O. Head. 1995. disk, pap. 34.95 (*1-56604-185-6*) Ventana Pr.

AutoCAD Professional's API Toolkit. 1993. disk, pap. 50.00 (*1-56205-162-8*) New Riders Pub.

AutoCAD Programming. Dennis N. Jump. 1991. pap. text ed. 24.60 (*0-07-155371-1*) McGraw.

AutoCAD Programming. Dennis N. Jump. (Computer Graphics Technology & Management Ser.). (Illus.). 352p. 1989. 39.95 (*0-8306-9093-X*, 3093); pap. 24.95 (*0-685-21468-0*) TAB Bks.

AutoCAD Programming. Dennis N. Jump. 1991. 24.95 (*0-8306-9393-9*) TAB Bks.

AutoCAD Programming. Dennis N. Jump. (Computer Graphics Technology & Management Ser.). (Illus.). 304p. 1991. pap. 29.95 (*0-8306-3779-6*) TAB Bks.

AutoCAD Programming. 2nd ed. Dennis N. Jump. 1991. text ed. 39.95 (*0-07-157741-6*); pap. text ed. 29.95 (*0-07-157740-8*) McGraw.

AutoCAD Programming. 2nd ed. Dennis N. Jump. (Computer Graphics Technology & Management Ser.). (Illus.). 304p. 1991. 34.95 (*0-8306-7779-8*, 3779) TAB Bks.

AutoCAD Reference Library, 7 vols., Set. 1991. pap. text ed. 307.75 (*0-940087-65-0*) Ventana Pr.

AutoCAD Release. Shawna D. Lockhart. LC 93-41523. (C). 1994. pap. text ed. 39.75 (*0-201-62344-7*) Addison-Wesley.

***Autocad Release II.** William Knapp. Ed. by Marcie Cohen. 26p. (YA). 1992. student ed 7.00 (*0-8064-0380-2*, D17) Bergwall.

***Autocad Release II, Vol. D.** William Knapp. Ed. by Marcie Cohen. (YA). 1992. vhs 299.00 (*0-8064-0379-9*, D17) Bergwall.

AutoCAD, Release 12: The Professional Reference. 2nd ed. NRP Staff. Ed. by Kurt Hampe et al. LC 93-20218. 1100p. 1993. 42.95 (*1-56205-059-1*) New Riders Pub.

Autocad Release 12 Certification Exam Preparation Manual. Alan J. Kalameja. 237p. 1994. pap. text ed. 34.95 (*0-8273-5920-9*) Delmar.

AutoCAD Release 12 Encyclopedia. David S. Cohn. 1993. pap. 36.95 (*0-201-62262-9*) Addison-Wesley.

AutoCAD Release 12 for Beginners. Jim Boyce & Vic Wright. (Illus.). (Orig.). 1992. pap. 19.95 (*1-56205-056-7*) New Riders Pub.

AutoCAD Release 12 for Students. Alfred Yarwood. LC 93-9049. 239p. 1993. pap. text ed. 32.95 (*0-470-20001-4*) Halsted Pr.

AutoCAD Release 12 for Windows Instant Reference. George Omura & B. Robert Callori. LC 93-83694. 321p. 1993. pap. 12.95 (*0-7821-1222-6*) Sybex.

AutoCAD Release 12 Instant Reference. George Omura & B. Robert Callori. LC 92-61598. 305p. 1992. 12.95 (*0-7821-1167-X*) Sybex.

AutoCAD Release 12 On-Screen Advisor. Hampe. 32p. 1993. 18.95 (*1-56205-208-X*) New Riders Pub.

AutoCAD Release 12 Quick Reference. Que Development Group Staff. (Quick Reference Ser.). (Illus.). (Orig.). 1992. pap. 9.95 (*1-56529-024-0*) Que.

AutoCAD Release 12 QuickStart. Nancy Fulton. (QuickStart Ser.). (Illus.). (Orig.). 1992. pap. 21.95 (*1-56529-006-2*) Que.

***AutoCad Rel.X (WIN & DOS)** George Omura et al. LC 94-68874. 350p. 1995. pap. 12.99 (*0-7821-1474-1*) Sybex.

AutoCAD Solid Modeling Workbook. Gary Bertoline et al. (Graphics Ser.). 250p. 1995. text ed. 19.95 (*0-256-12451-5*) Irwin.

AutoCAD Student Workbook & Instructor's Guide. Frank Conner. 200p. 1992. 175.00 (*1-56205-024-9*) New Riders Pub.

AutoCad Student Workbook with Disk. Frank Conner. 1991. pap. 39.95 (*1-56205-018-4*) New Riders Pub.

AutoCAD Technical Reference. Ralph Grabowski. 320p. 1992. pap. 32.95 (*0-8273-4820-7*) Delmar.

AutoCAD Tutor. Frank Conner. (Illus.). 450p. (Orig.). 1992. 29.95 (*1-56205-081-8*) New Riders Pub.

AutoCAD Tutor for Engineering Graphics. Alan J. Kalameja. 320p. 1992. pap. 28.95 (*0-8273-5081-3*) Delmar.

***AutoCAD Tutor for Engineering Graphics Release 13.** Kalameja. 96p. 1995. teacher ed, pap. text ed. 14.00 (*0-8273-5913-6*) Delmar.

AutoCAD Tutor for Engineering Graphics, Release 13. 2nd ed. Alan Kalameja. (Illus.). 800p. 1994. pap. 26.95 (*0-8273-5914-4*) Delmar.

AutoCAD Tutor Instructor's Guide. Connor. 1992. disk 175.00 (*1-56205-093-1*) New Riders Pub.

Autocad Workbook. Terry Wohlers. 1986. pap. 29.32 (*0-02-668070-X*); pap. 14.64 (*0-02-668080-7*) Macmillan.

***AutoCAD Workbook for Technical & Engineering Drawing.** Kathleen L. Kitto & James L. Wilson. 400p. 1995. pap. text ed. write for info. (*0-314-04676-3*) West Pub.

***AutoCad 13 Instant Reference.** Omura et al. 1995. 12.99 (*0-614-05127-4*) Sybex.

AutoCAD 3D Companion. George O. Head. (Illus.). 579p. 1993. pap. 27.95 (*1-56604-042-6*) Ventana Pr.

AutoCAD 3D Companion: The Illustrated Guide to AutoCAD's Third Dimension. 2nd ed. George O. Head. (Illus.). 648p. 1995. disk 34.95 (*1-56604-142-2*) Ventana Pr.

AutoCAD 3D Design & Presentation. New Riders Publishing Staff. (Illus.). 448p. (Orig.). 1991. 29.95 (*0-934035-81-4*) New Riders Pub.

AutoCarto Eleven: Eleventh International Symposium on Computer-Assisted Cartography. 456p. 1993. 35.00 (*1-57083-001-0*) ASP & RS.

AutoCarto Nine: Ninth International Symposium on Computer-Assisted Cartography. 879p. 1989. pap. 7.00 (*0-944426-55-7*) ASP & RS.

Autocarto Ten: Tenth International Symposium on Computer-Assisted Cartography. 444p. 1991. 15.00 (*0-944426-44-1*) ASP & RS.

Autocephaly of the Metropolia in America. Panagiotes N. Trempelas. Ed. by Robert G. Stephanopoulos & N. M. Vaporis. Tr. by George S. Bebis. 80p. 1974. pap. 2.50 (*0-916586-00-6*) Holy Cross Orthodox.

Autoclaved Aerated Concrete: Moisture & Properties. Ed. by F. H. Wittman. (Developments in Civil Engineering Ser.: No. 6). 380p. 1983. 161.75 (*0-444-42117-3*, I-481-82) Elsevier.

Autoclaved Aerated Concrete: Properties, Testing, & Design: RILEM Recommended Practices. RILEM Technical Committee 78-MCA Staff & RILEM Technical Committee 51-ALC Staff. LC 93-6890. 1993. Alk. paper. write for info. (*0-419-17960-7*, E & FN Spon) Routledge Chapman & Hall.

Autocourse History of the Grand Prix Car, 1945-1965. Doug Nye. (Illus.). 256p. 1993. 49.95 (*1-874557-50-0*, Pub. by Hazelton UK) Motorbooks Intl.

Autocourse History of the Grand Prix 66-91. Doug Nye. (Illus.). 304p. 1992. 59.95 (*0-905138-94-5*, Pub. by Hazelton UK) Motorbooks Intl.

***Autocourse 1995-1996.** annuals (Illus.). 288p. 1995. 49.95 (*1-874557-36-5*, Pub. by Hazelton UK) Motorbooks Intl.

Autocracy & Insurgency in Organized Labor. Ed. by Burton H. Hall. LC 70-164980. (New Politics Ser.). 355p. 1972. pap. 21.95x (*0-87855-504-8*); pap. text ed. 32.95x (*0-87855-004-6*) Transaction Pubs.

Autocracy, Capitalism, & Revolution in Russia. Tim McDaniel. LC 86-30790. 510p. 1987. pap. 17.00 (*0-520-06071-7*) U CA Pr.

Autocracy, Democracy & Communism. Marie B. Hall. 1988. pap. 12.00 (*0-938760-12-2*) Veritat Found.

Autocracy, Modernization & Revolution in Russia & Iran. Tim McDaniel. 256p. 1991. text ed. 49.50 (*0-691-03147-9*) Princeton U Pr.

Autocracy, Modernization, & Revolution in Russia & Iran. Tim McDaniel. 256p. 1993. pap. text ed. 15.95 (*0-691-02482-0*) Princeton U Pr.

Autocrat of the Breakfast-Table. Oliver W. Holmes. (Airmont Classics Ser.). (YA). (gr. 11 up). 1968. pap. 1.95 (*0-8049-0159-7*, CL-159) Airmont.

Autocrat of the Breakfast Table. Oliver W. Holmes. (Notable American Authors Ser.). 1992. reprint ed. lib. bdg. 75.00 (*0-7812-3156-6*) Rprt Serv.

Autocratic Tradition & Chinese Politics. Zhengyuan Fu. 432p. (C). 1994. 64.95 (*0-521-44228-1*) Cambridge U Pr.

Autocrine & Paracrine Mechanisms in Reproductive Endocrinology. Ed. by L. C. Krey et al. LC 90-6703. (Reproductive Biology Ser.). (Illus.). 214p. 1989. 69.50 (*0-306-43490-3*, Plenum Pr) Plenum.

Autocritique of Enlightenment: Rousseau & the Philosophes. Mark Hulliung. LC 94-1857. 309p. 1994. text ed. 45.00 (*0-674-05425-3*, HULAUT) HUP.

Autocross Racing. Sallie Stephenson. LC 91-13635. (Fast Track Ser.). (Illus.). 48p. (J). (gr. 5). 1991. text ed. 12.95 (*0-89686-692-0*, Crstwood Hse) Silver Burdett Pr.

***Autodesk Collection: Professional Design Software for Collegiate Users.** Shawna D. Lockhart & Kevin P. Reagh. 528p. (C). 1994. pap. text ed. write for info. (*0-201-65623-X*) Addison-Wesley.

Autoerotic Fatalities. Robert R. Hazelwood et al. LC 81-47692. 224p. 1983. text ed. 42.95 (*0-669-04716-3*) Free Pr.

Autofact Conference Proceedings, 1992: Sixty-Four Technical Papers. 820p. 1992. pap. text ed. 110.00 (*0-87263-430-2*) SME.

Autofact Five: Proceedings of the AUTOFACT FIVE Conference on Computer Integrated Manfaturing & the Automated Factory, Detroit, Mich., Nov. 1983. AUTOFACT FIVE Conference Staff. xvi, 1048p. 1983. 60.00 (*0-444-86820-8*) Elsevier.

Autofact Four: Proceedings of AUTOFACT FOUR Conference on Computer Integrated Manufacturing & the Automated Factory, Philadelphia, PA, Nov-Dec 1982. AUTOFACT FOUR Conference Staff. 688p. 1983. 60.00 (*0-444-86618-3*) Elsevier.

Autofact 1988: Conference Proceedings, Oct. 30 - Nov. 2, 1988. LC 88-62225. (Illus.). 700p. 1988. pap. text ed. 95.00 (*0-87263-328-4*) SME.

Autofact 1990: Conference Proceedings. Intro. by Edward J. Adlard. (Illus.). 933p. 1990. pap. text ed. 99.00 (*0-87263-389-6*) SME.

Autofact '85: Conference Proceedings, November 4-7, 1985, Detroit, MI. Autofact '85 (1985: Detroit, MI) Staff. LC 85-62651. (Illus.). 919p. reprint ed. pap. 180.00 (*0-8357-6502-4*, 2035873) Bks Demand.

Autofacts Yearbook, 1991, Vol. 1. William R. Pochiluk. Ed. by David Nash. 625p. 1991. text ed. 495.00 (*1-879800-00-4*) Autofacts.

Autofacts Yearbook, 1992. William R. Pochiluk & David Nash. 1000p. 1992. text ed. 495.00 (*1-879800-01-2*) Autofacts.

Autofacts Yearbook, 1992, Vol. 1. William Pochiluk & David Nash. 480p. 1992. text ed. 495.00 (*1-879800-02-0*) Autofacts.

Autofacts Yearbook, 1992, Vol. 2. William Pchiluk & David Nash. 500p. 1992. text ed. 495.00 (*1-879800-03-9*) Autofacts.

Autofacts Yearbook, 1993, 2 vols., Set. William Pochiluk. 1993. text ed. 595.00 (*0-9637549-0-4*) AUTOFACTS Intl.

Autofacts Yearbook, 1993, 2 vols., Vols. 1-2. William Pochiluk. 1993. Vol. 1, 523p. text ed. write for info. (*0-9637549-1-2*); Vol. 2, 480p. text ed. write for info. (*0-9637549-2-0*) AUTOFACTS Intl.

Autofacts Yearbook, 1994, Set. William Pochiluk. Ed. by Christopher Benko. 1125p. 1994. text ed. 1,190.00 (*0-9637549-5-5*) AUTOFACTS Intl.

Autofacts Yearbook, 1994, Vol. 1. William Pochiluk. Ed. by Christopher Benko. 525p. 1994. text ed. 595.00 (*0-9637549-3-9*) AUTOFACTS Intl.

Autofacts Yearbook, 1994, Vol. 2. William Pochiluk. Ed. by Christopher Benko. 600p. 1994. text ed. 595.00 (*0-9637549-4-7*) AUTOFACTS Intl.

***Autofacts 1995: Yearbook, Vol. 1.** William Pochiluk. Ed. by Mary Ruhl. 525p. 1995. text ed. 595.00 (*0-9637549-7-1*) AUTOFACTS Intl.

***Autofacts 1995: Yearbook, Vol. 2.** William Pochiluk. Ed. by Mary Ruhl. 490p. 1995. text ed. 595.00 (*0-9637549-8-X*) AUTOFACTS Intl.

***Autofacts 1995: Yearbook, 2 vols., Vols. 1-2.** William Pochiluk. Ed. by Mary Ruhl. 1115p. 1995. text ed. write for info. (*0-9637549-6-3*) AUTOFACTS Intl.

Autogenic Therapy, Vols. I, II, III. Incl. Vol. I. Autogenic Methods. Ed. by Wolfgang Luthe & Johannes H. Schultz. 272p. 1969. text ed. 72.00 (*0-8089-0270-9*, 792601); Vol. II. Medical Applications. Ed. by Wolfgang Luthe & Johannes H. Schultz. 232p. 1969. 48.50 (*0-8089-0271-7*, 792602); Vol. III. Applications in Psychotherapy. Ed. by Wolfgang Luthe & Johannes H. Schultz. 240p. 1969. text ed. 72.00 (*0-8089-0272-5*, 792603); Vol. IV. Research & Theory. LC 70-76888. 1970. 44.50 (*0-8089-0273-3*); Vol. V. Dynamics of Autogenic Neutralization. LC 70-76888. 368p. 1970. text ed. 83.00 (*0-8089-0664-X*, 792605); Vol. VI. Treatment with Autogenic Neutralization. LC 70-76888. 448p. 1973. text ed. 92.00 (*0-8089-0692-5*, 792606); write for info. (*0-318-52854-1*, Grune) Saunders.

Autogenic Therapy, Vols. IV, V & VI. Incl. Vol. I. Autogenic Methods. Ed. by Wolfgang Luthe & Johannes H. Schultz. 272p. 1969. text ed. 72.00 (*0-8089-0270-9*, 792601); Vol. II. Medical Applications. Ed. by Wolfgang Luthe & Johannes H. Schultz. 232p. 1969. 48.50 (*0-8089-0271-7*, 792602); Vol. III. Applications in Psychotherapy. Ed. by Wolfgang Luthe & Johannes H. Schultz. 240p. 1969. text ed. 72.00 (*0-8089-0272-5*, 792603); Vol. IV. Research & Theory. LC 70-76888. 1970. 44.50 (*0-8089-0273-3*); Vol. V. Dynamics of Autogenic Neutralization. LC 70-76888. 368p. 1970. text ed. 83.00 (*0-8089-0664-X*, 792605); Vol. VI. Treatment with Autogenic Neutralization. LC 70-76888. 448p. 1973. text ed. 92.00 (*0-8089-0692-5*, 792606); LC 70-76888. (Illus.). write for info. (*0-318-52855-X*, Grune) Saunders.

Autogenic Training: A Clinical Guide. Wolfgang Linden. LC 90-13970. 180p. 1990. lib. bdg. 40.00 (*0-89862-551-3*); pap. text ed. 17.95 (*0-89862-454-1*) Guilford Pr.

***Autograph Collecting Made Easy.** Allan Kaufman. 1995. 10.95 (*0-8062-5037-2*) Carlton.

Autograph Collector's Kit. Paul Hartunian. (Illus.). 176p. 1993. audio, ring bd. 49.95 (*0-685-65218-1*) Ultimate Secrets.

Autograph Letters & Manuscripts see Major Acquisitions of the Pierpont Morgan Library 1924-1974

Autograph of William Shakespeare. George Wise. LC 72-178312. reprint ed. 21.50 (*0-404-07002-7*) AMS Pr.

Autographs: A Key to Collecting. Mary A. Benjamin. 384p. 1986. reprint ed. pap. 10.95 (*0-486-25035-0*) Dover.

Autographs: Identification & Price Guide. George S. Lowry. (Illus.). 496p. (Orig.). 1994. pap. 15.00 (*0-380-77234-5*, Confident Collect) Avon.

Autographs: Verses from New England Autograph Albums, 1825-1925. Alice S. Fowler. LC 90-63183. (Illus.). 90p. 1990. 17.50 (*0-9621607-0-9*) Pioneer Bks.

Autographs for Freedom, 2 Vols. Ed. by Julia Griffiths. LC 71-83965. (Black Heritage Library Collection). 1977. 41.95 (*0-8369-8583-4*) Ayer.

Autographs of the Confederacy. Michael Reese, II. LC 81-68377. 225p. 1981. 54.95 (*0-940746-00-X*); 89.95 (*0-686-42866-8*) Cohasco.

Autographs Once in the Possession of Teresa Guicciolo, Don Juan, Cantos I-V, Vol. II. George Gordon Byron. Ed. by Jerome J. McGann & Alice Levine. LC 83-49281. (Manuscripts of the Younger Romantics & the Bodleian Shelley Manuscripts). 350p. 1985. lib. bdg. 102.00 (*0-8240-6251-5*) Garland.

Autographs Once in the Possession of Teresa Guicciolo, Poems 1807-1818, Vol. I. Byron. Ed. by Jerome J. McGann & Alice Levine. LC 83-49278. (Manuscripts of the Younger Romantics & the Bodleian Shelley Manuscripts). 320p. 1986. lib. bdg. 91.00 (*0-8240-6250-7*) Garland.

Autographs Once in the Possession of Teresa Guicciolo, Poems 1819-1822, Vol. III. Byron. Ed. by Jerome J. McGann & Alice Levine. LC 83-49282. (Manuscripts of the Younger Romantics & the Bodleian Shelley Manuscripts). 475p. 1984. lib. bdg. 183.00 (*0-8240-6252-3*) Garland.

Autoharp Book. Becky Blackley. LC 83-81145. (Illus.). 256p. (Orig.). 1983. pap. 19.95 (*0-912827-01-7*) I A D Pubns.

Autohydrogenation of Oil Gases. H A. Dirksen et al. (Research Bulletin Ser.: No. 25). iv, 75p. 1955. 5.00 (*0-685-18496-X*) Inst Gas Tech.

Autoimmune Disease. Ed. by Noel R. Rose & Ian R. Mackay. 1985. text ed. 154.00 (*0-12-596920-1*) Acad Pr.

Autoimmune Disease: Focus on Sjogren's Syndrome. Ed. by D. A. Isenberg & A. C. Horsfall. (University College, London, Molecular Pathology Ser.). 250p. 1994. 162.50x (*1-872748-23-6*, Pub. by Bios Scientific UK) Coronet Bks.

Autoimmune Disease Models: A Guidebook. Ed. by Irun R. Cohen & Ariel Miller. (Illus.). 329p. 1994. text ed. 64.95 (*0-12-178330-8*) Acad Pr.

Autoimmune Disease Therapeutic Markets: New Therapies Target Causes, Not Symptoms. Market Intelligence Staff. 320p. 1992. 1,895.00 (*1-56753-077-X*) Frost & Sullivan.

Autoimmune Diseases of the Endocrine System. Ed. by Volpe. 1990. 167.00 (*0-8493-6849-9*, RC649) CRC Pr.

Autoimmune Diseases Two. Ed. by Noel R. Rose & Ian R. Mackay. (Illus.). 444p. 1992. text ed. 99.95 (*0-12-596922-8*) Acad Pr.

Autoimmune Endocrine Disease. Anthony P. Weetman. (Reviews in Clinical Immunology Ser.: No. 1). (Illus.). 260p. (C). 1992. 64.95 (*0-521-40161-5*) Cambridge U Pr.

Autoimmune Hepatitis. Ed. by M. Nishioka et al. 360p. 1994. 177.25 (*0-444-88196-4*) Elsevier.

Autoimmune Liver Diseases. Edward L. Krawitt & Russell H. Wiesner. 288p. 1991. 98.50 (*0-88167-771-X*, 2252) Raven.

***Autoimmune Neurological Disease.** Michael P. Pender & Pamela A. McCombe. (Cambridge Reviews in Clinical Immunology Ser.). 286p. (C). 1994. write for info. (*0-521-46113-8*) Cambridge U Pr.

Autoimmune Thyroiditis: Approaches Towards Its Etiological Differentiation. Ed. by W. Scherbaum et al. (Illus.). 320p. 1991. pap. 79.00 (*0-387-53476-8*) Spr-Verlag.

Autoimmunity: Basic Concepts & Systemic & Selected Organ-Specific Diseases. Ed. by J. M. Cruse & R. E. Lewis. (Concepts in Immunopathology Ser.: Vol. 1). (Illus.). viii, 362p. 1985. 158.50 (*3-8055-3908-8*) S Karger.

Autoimmunity: Experimental & Clinical Aspects, Vol. 475. Ed. by Robert S. Schwartz & Noel R. Rose. 107.00 (*0-89766-345-4*); pap. 107.00 (*0-89766-346-2*) NY Acad Sci.

Autoimmunity: Experimental Aspects. Ed. by Moncef Zouali. LC 93-47074. (NATO ASI Series H: Cell Biology: Vol. 80). (Illus.). xvi, 304p. 1994. 136.00 (*0-387-57642-8*) Spr-Verlag.

Autoimmunity: Physiology & Disease. Ed. by Antonio Coutinho & Michel D. Kazatchkine. LC 93-12816. 468p. 1993. text ed. 92.95 (*0-471-59227-7*, Wiley-Liss) Wiley.

Autoimmunity & Autoimmune Disease: Symposium, No. 129. CIBA Foundation Symposium Staff. LC 87-10493. (CIBA Foundation Symposia Ser.). 1987. text ed. 75.00 (*0-471-91095-3*) Wiley.

Autoimmunity & Endocrine Disease. Ed. by Robert Volpe. LC 85-4607. (Basic & Clinical Endocrinology Ser.: No. 5). (Illus.). 487p. reprint ed. pap. 138.80 (*0-7837-0606-5*, 2040954) Bks Demand.

Autoimmunity & Endocrine Diseases. Ed. by A. Pinchera & L. Vanhaelst. (Journal: Hormone Research: Vol. 16, No. 5). (Illus.). 84p. 1982. pap. 33.00 (*3-8055-3658-5*) S Karger.

Autoimmunity & the Pathogenesis of Diabetes. Ed. by F. Ginsberg-Fellner & R. C. McEvoy. (Endocrinology & Metabolism: Progress in Research & Clinical Practice Ser.: Vol. 4). (Illus.). 288p. 1989. 119.00 (*0-387-96645-5*, 2060) Spr-Verlag.

Autoimmunity & Toxicology: Immune Disregulation Induced by Drugs & Chemicals. Ed. by M. E. Kammuller et al. 474p. 1989. 205.25 (*0-444-81023-4*) Elsevier.

Autoimmunity in Nephritis. Ed. by Francis W. Ballardie. LC 91-35410. 140p. 1992. text ed. 60.00 (*3-7186-5195-5*) Gordon & Breach.

Autoimmunity in Psoriasis. Ed. by Ernst H. Beutner. 328p. 1982. 132.00 (*0-8493-5473-0*, RL321, CRC Reprint) Franklin.

Autoimmunity, Rheumatoid Arthritis & Cyclosporin A (Sandimmun) Mizushima & Amor. 104p. (C). 1991. 35.00 (*1-85070-305-1*) Prthnon Pub.

Autoimmunoregulation & Autoimmune Disease. Ed. by J. M. Cruse & R. E. Lewis. (Concepts in Immunopathology Ser.: Vol. 4). (Illus.). viii, 304p. 1987. 222.50 (*3-8055-4406-5*) S Karger.

Autoionization: Recent Developments & Applications. Ed. by Aaron Temkin. LC 87-6947. (Physics of Atoms & Molecules Ser.). 274p. 1985. 85.00 (*0-306-41854-1*, Plenum Pr) Plenum.

Autokinesis. Ken Norris. 1980. pap. 3.50 (*0-916696-12-X*) Cross Country.

Autolexical Syntax: A Theory of Parallel Grammatical Relations. Jerrold M. Sadock. LC 90-11058. (Studies in Contemporary Linguistics). 200p. 1990. pap. text ed. 22.50 (*0-226-73345-9*) U Ch Pr.

Autolexical Syntax: A Theory of Parallel Grammatical Relations. Jerrold M. Sadock. LC 90-11058. (Studies in Contemporary Linguistics). 200p. 1990. lib. bdg. 45.00 (*0-226-73344-0*) U Ch Pr.

AutoLISP: Programming by Example. Gene Straka. 1992. text ed. 39.95 (*0-07-061975-1*) McGraw.

AutoLISP: Programming by Example. Gene Straka. (Computer Graphics Technology & Management Ser.). 352p. 1992. 39.95 (*0-8306-3992-6*, 4167, Windcrest); pap. 29.95 (*0-8306-3993-4*, 4167, Windcrest) TAB Bks.

AutoLISP in Plain English: A Practical Guide for Non-Programmers, for Release 13. 5th ed. George O. Head. (Illus.). 300p. 1994. pap. 23.95 (*1-56604-140-6*) Ventana Pr.

AutoLISP in Plain English: A Practical Guide for Non-Programmers for Releases 11 & 12. 4th ed. George O. Head. (Illus.). 262p. pap. 23.95 (*1-56604-009-4*) Ventana Pr.

***AutoLISP Programming: Principles & Techniques.** Rod Rawls. LC 95-8369. 500p. 1995. text ed. 33.00 (*1-56637-196-1*) Goodheart.

Autologic: Proof Theory & Automated Deduction. Neil Tennant. 256p. 1993. 55.00 (*0-7486-0358-1*, Pub. by Edinburgh U Pr UK) Col U Pr.

Autologous Blood Transfusion: Current Issues. Robert L. Thurer & Lieta Maffei. LC 88-39303. (C). 1989. pap. 7.00 (*0-915355-62-0*) Am Assn Blood.

***Autologous Bone Marrow Transplantation & Solid Tumors.** Ed. by J. Gordon McVie et al. LC 84-13380. (Monograph Series of the European Organization for Research on Treatment of Cancer: No. 14). (Illus.). Date not set. reprint ed. pap. 59.30 (*0-7837-9561-0*, 2060310) Bks Demand.

Autologous Tissue Heart Valves. J. W. Love. (Medical Intelligence Unit Ser.). 128p. 1993. 89.95 (*1-879702-52-5*) R G Landes.

Autologous Transfusion: Using Your Own Blood. B. G. Adhoute. (Illus.). x, 138p. 1992. 75.00 (*0-387-59554-6*) Spr-Verlag.

Autologous Transfusion Devices. 13p. 1991. 49.00 (*0-910275-62-9*, AT6-113) Assn Adv Med Instrn.

Autologous Transfusions. Taswell. 1991. 70.00 (*0-86542-062-9*) Blackwell Sci.

Autolycus' Pack & Other Light Wares. Arundell J. Esdaile. LC 70-86747. (Essay Index Reprint Ser.). 1977. 18.95 (*0-8369-1128-8*) Ayer.

Automach Australia '84: Conference Proceedings, 23-25 May 1984, Sydney, Australia. Society of Manufacturing Engineers Staff. LC 84-50595. 609p. reprint ed. pap. 173.60 (*0-8357-5907-5*, 2030899) Bks Demand.

Automach Australia '85: Conference Proceedings, July 2-5, 1985, Melbourne, Australia. Society of Manufacturing Engineers Staff. LC 85-50863. (Illus.). 599p. reprint ed. pap. 170.80 (*0-8357-6470-2*, 2035841) Bks Demand.

***Automagic Horse: An Adventure Story with a Touch of Magic.** L. Ron Hubbard. (Illus.). 104p. (J). (gr. 4-8). 1995. 17.95 (*0-88404-906-X*) Bridge Pubns Inc.

***Automagic Horse: An Adventure Story with a Touch of Magic.** L. Ron Hubbard. (Illus.). (J). 1995. audio 9.95 (*0-88404-932-9*) Bridge Pubns Inc.

Automania: The Complete Book of Automobile Trivia. Alan McPhee. (Illus.). 240p. 1990. pap. 12.95 (*0-929091-11-6*) Firefly Bks Ltd.

Automata: Theoretic Aspects of Formal Power Series. Arto Salomaa & M. Soittola. (Texts & Monographs in Computer Science). 1978. 59.50 (*0-387-90282-1*) Spr-Verlag.

Automata & Algebras in Categories. Jiri Adamek & Vera Trnkova. (C). 1990. lib. bdg. 218.50 (*0-7923-0010-6*) Kluwer Ac.

***Automata & Formal Languages: An Introduction.** Dean Kelley. LC 94-22953. 1995. text ed. 52.00 (*0-13-497777-7*) P-H.

Automata & Languages. John M. Howie. (Illus.). 320p. 1991. 65.00 (*0-19-853424-8*); pap. 29.95 (*0-19-853442-6*) OUP.

***Automata, Languages, & Programming.** Ed. by S. Abiteboul & E. Shamir. (Lecture Notes in Computer Science: Vol. 820). 644p. 1994. pap. 88.00 (*0-387-58201-0*) Spr-Verlag.

Automata, Languages & Programming. Ed. by G. Ausiello et al. (Lecture Notes in Computer Science Ser.: Vol. 372). xi, 788p. 1989. pap. 87.00 (*0-387-51371-X*, 3248) Spr-Verlag.

Automata, Languages, & Programming. Ed. by S. Even & O. Kariv. (Lecture Notes in Computer Science Ser.: Vol. 115). 552p. 1981. pap. 41.00 (*0-387-10843-2*) Spr-Verlag.

Automata, Languages & Programming. Ed. by L. Kott. (Lecture Notes in Computer Science Ser.: Vol. 226). ix, 474p. 1986. pap. 49.00 (*0-387-16761-7*) Spr-Verlag.

Automata, Languages & Programming. Ed. by T. Ottmann. (Lecture Notes in Computer Science Ser.: Vol. 267). (Illus.). x, 565p. 1987. pap. text ed. 57.00 (*0-387-18088-5*) Spr-Verlag.

Automata, Languages & Programming: Proceedings of ICALP International Colloquium, 18th, Madrid, Spain, July 8-12, 1991. Ed. by J. Leach Albert et al. (Lecture Notes in Computer Science Ser.: Vol. 510). xii, 763p. 1991. pap. 70.00 (*0-387-54233-7*) Spr-Verlag.

Automata, Languages & Programming: Proceedings of the 20th International Colloquium, ICALP 93, Lund, Sweden, July 5-9, 1993. Ed. by A. Lingas et al. (Lecture Notes in Computer Science Ser.: Vol. 700). vii, 697p. 1993. pap. 101.00 (*0-387-56939-1*) Spr-Verlag.

Automata, Languages & Programming: Proceedings 17th International Colloquium Warwick University, England, July 16-20, 1990. Ed. by M. S. Paterson et al. (Lecture Notes in Computer Science Ser.: Vol. 443). ix, 781p. 1990. pap. 77.00 (*0-387-52826-1*) Spr-Verlag.

Automata, Languages & Programming: Sixth Colloquium. Ed. by H. A. Maurer. (Lecture Notes in Computer Science Ser.: Vol. 71). 1979. pap. 48.00 (*0-387-09510-1*) Spr-Verlag.

Automata, Languages, & Programming: 19th International Colloquium, ICALP '91 Wien, Austria, July 13-17, 1992 Proceedings. Ed. by W. Kuich et al. LC 92-21890. (Lecture Notes in Computer Science Ser.: Vol. 623). xii, 721p. 1992. 102.00 (*0-387-55719-9*); pap. 98.00 (*3-540-55719-9*) Spr-Verlag.

Automata, Languages & Programming '78. Ed. by G. Ausiello & C. Boehm. (Lecture Notes in Computer Science Ser.: Vol. 62). 1978. pap. 29.00 (*0-387-08860-1*) Spr-Verlag.

Automata Networks in Computer Science. Ed. by Fogelman F. Soulie et al. (Non-Linear Science: Theory & Applications Ser.). (Illus.). 288p. 1987. text ed. 59.50 (*0-691-08479-3*) Princeton U Pr.

***Automata, Neural Networks & Parallel Machines: Some Emerging Principles.** K. Takir Shah. 500p. 1995. text ed. 86.00 (*981-02-1365-4*) World Scientific Pub.

Automata on Infinite Objects & Church's Problem. M. Rabin. LC 72-6749. (CBMS Regional Conference Series in Mathematics: No. 13). 22p. 1982. reprint ed. 18.00 (*0-8218-1663-2*, CBMS-13) Am Math.

Automata on Infinite Words. Ed. by Maurice Nivat & D. Perrin. (Lecture Notes in Computer Science Ser.: Vol. 192). iii, 216p. (ENG & FRE.). 1985. pap. 30.00 (*0-387-15641-0*) Spr-Verlag.

Automate: How to Understand Your Car. Ed. by H. Hillier. (C). 1989. 75.00 (*0-09-156821-8*, Pub. by S Thornes Pubs UK) St Mut.

Automated Accounting Systems & Procedures Handbook. Douglas A. Potter. 562p. 1991. text ed. 135.00 (*0-471-54466-3*) Wiley.

Automated Accounting Systems & Procedures Handbook. Douglas A. Potter. 576p. 1992. pap. text ed. 65.00 (*0-471-55939-3*) Wiley.

Automated Agriculture for the Twenty-First Century: Proceedings Symposium & Exhibition, December 1991. LC 91-76823. 540p. pap. 48.50 (*0-929355-21-0*, P1191) Am Soc Ag Eng.

Automated Analysis of Legal Texts: Edited Versions of Selected Papers from the International Conference, 2nd, Florence, Italy, September, 1985. Ed. by Antonio A. Martino & F. Socci Natali. 938p. 1986. 166.75 (*0-444-70111-7*, North Holland) Elsevier.

Automated & Algorithmic Debugging: Proceedings, First International Workshop, AADEBUG '93, Link Oping, Sweden, May 3-5, 1993. Ed. by Peter A. Fritzson. LC 93-38413. (Lecture Notes in Computer Science Ser.: Vol. 749). 1993. 54.00 (*0-387-57417-4*) Spr-Verlag.

Automated Assembly. Kenneth R. Treer. LC 78-75097. 469p. reprint ed. pap. 133.70 (*0-8357-5908-3*, 2055739) Bks Demand.

Automated Battlefield. Frank Barnaby. (Illus.). 185p. 1986. text ed. 27.95 (*0-02-901730-0*) Free Pr.

Automated Blood Counts & Differentials: A Practical Guide. J. David Bessman. LC 85-24108. (Contemporary Medicine & Public Health Ser.). (Illus.). 176p. 1986. text ed. 45.00 (*0-8018-3171-7*); pap. text ed. 28.50x (*0-8018-3173-3*) Johns Hopkins.

Automated Builder Dictionary - Encyclopedia of Industrialized Housing. rev. ed. Don O. Carlson. (Illus.). 224p. 1991. pap. text ed. 35.00 (*0-685-50697-5*) Automated Builder.

Automated Builder Dictionary - Encyclopedia of Industrialized Housing. 2nd rev. ed. Don O. Carlson. (Illus.). 224p. 1991. text ed. 35.00 (*0-9607408-1-3*) Automated Builder.

Automated Chemical Analysis. Peter Stockwell. 300p. 1994. text ed. 48.00 (*0-13-051400-4*) P-H.

Automated Court Report Production: Increasing the Volume, Improving the Quality. National Center for State Courts Staff. (Paul Reardon Ser.). 44p. 1983. 2.64 (*0-685-16285-0*, PRS-040) Natl Ctr St Courts.

Automated Data Retrieval in Astronomy. Ed. by Carlos Jaschek & Wulff D. Heintz. 1982. lib. bdg. 103.00 (*90-277-1435-5*) Kluwer Ac.

Automated Deduction, CADE-11: Eleventh International Conference on Automated Deduction, Saratoga Springs, NY, June 15-18, 1992 Proceedings. Ed. by Deepak Kapur & Joerg H. Siekmann. LC 92-16409. (Lecture Notes in Computer Science, Lecture Notes in Artificial Intelligence Ser.: Vol. 607). xv, 793p. 1992. pap. 102.00 (*0-387-55602-8*) Spr-Verlag.

Automated Deduction, CADE 12: Proceedings of the 12th International Conference on Automated Dedication, Nancy, France, June-July 1994. International Conference on Automated Deduction Staff. Ed. by Alan Bundy. LC 94-17912. (Lecture Notes in Computer Science, Vol. 814; Lecture Notes in Artificial Intelligence). 1994. 102.00 (*0-387-58156-1*) Spr-Verlag.

Automated Deduction in Multiple-Valued Logics. Reiner Hahnle. (International Series of Monographs on Computer Science: No. 10). (Illus.). 184p. 1994. 45.00 (*0-19-853989-4*) OUP.

Automated Deduction in Nonclassical Logics: Efficient Matrix Proof Methods for Modal & Intuitionistic Logics. Lincoln A. Wallen. (Artificial Intelligence Ser.). 300p. 1989. 37.50 (*0-262-23144-1*) MIT Pr.

***Automated Deduction in Nonstandard Logics.** Ed. by Peter Jackson & Rich Scherl. (Technical Reports). (Illus.). 169p. (Orig.). 1994. pap. 25.00x (*0-929280-50-4*) Amer Artificial.

Automated Defibrillation. 2nd ed. Al Weigel et al. 1993. text ed. 16.00 (*0-89303-068-6*) P-H.

Automated Design & Engineering for Electronics: Proceedings of the Technical Sessions, February 26-28, 1985, Anaheim, CA. Automated Design & Engineering for Electronics Staff. 389p. reprint ed. pap. 110.90 (*0-8357-5910-5*, 2025191) Bks Demand.

Automated Design & Engineering for Electronics: Proceedings of the Technical Sessions, Moscone Convention Center, San Francisco, CA, March 11-13, 1986. Automated Design & Engineering for Electronics. 320p. reprint ed. pap. 91.20 (*0-8357-5911-3*, 2027688) Bks Demand.

Automated Design & Engineering for Electronics: Proceedings of the Technical Sessions, October, 15-17, 1985 Boston, MA. Automated Design & Engineering for Electronics (1985 : Boston, MA). 415p. reprint ed. pap. 118.30 (*0-8357-5912-1*, 2027689) Bks Demand.

Automated Design & Engineering for Electronics--East: Proceedings of the Technical Sessions, World Trade Center, Boston, MA., Sept. 30 - Oct. 2, 1986. Automated Design & Engineering for Electronics Staff (1986, Boston, Ma). 449p. reprint ed. pap. 128.00 (*0-8357-5909-1*, 2029364) Bks Demand.

Automated Design & Engineering for Electronics-West: Proceedings of the Technical Sessions, March 31-April 2, 1987. Automated Design & Engineering for Electronics (1987: Anaheim, CA) Staff. (Illus.). 387p. pap. 110.30 (*0-8357-5913-X*, 2030236) Bks Demand.

Automated Design of Control Systems. C. W. Merriam. LC 73-86001. 356p. 1975. text ed. 195.00 (*0-677-04440-2*) Gordon & Breach.

Automated Development of Fundamental Mathematical Theories. Art Quaife. LC 92-34849. (Automated Reasoning Ser.: Vol. 2). 1992. lib. bdg. 123.00 (*0-7923-2021-2*) Kluwer Ac.

Automated DNA Sequencing & Analysis. Ed. by Mark D. Adams et al. (Illus.). 392p. 1994. text ed. 79.00 (*0-12-717010-3*) Acad Pr.

Automated Enzyme Assays, Vol. 2, Pt. 1. D. B. Roodyn. (Laboratory Techniques in Biochemistry & Molecular Biology Ser.). 1970. pap. 22.00 (*0-444-10056-3*, North Holland) Elsevier.

Automated Fabrication: Improving Productivity in Manufacturing. Burns Marshall. (Illus.). 400p. (C). 1993. text ed. 69.00 (*0-13-119462-3*) P-H.

Automated Fabrication of Mobility Aids (AFMA) Below-Knee CASD-CAM Testing & Evaluation Program Results. (Illus.). 52p. (Orig.). (C). 1993. pap. text ed. 19.95x (*1-56806-212-5*) Diane Pub.

Automated Factory Handbook: Technology & Management. David Cleland & Bopaya Bidanda. 1990. text ed. 69.95 (*0-07-155176-X*) McGraw.

Automated Factory Handbook: Technology & Management. David I. Cleland. 1990. 69.95 (*0-8306-9296-7*) TAB Bks.

Automated Farm Surface Irrigation Systems Worldwide. 92p. 1986. 10.00 (*81-85068-13-5*) US Comm Irrigation.

Automated Field Survey Data Collection System. (National Cooperative Highway Research Program Report Ser.: No. 295). 107p. 1987. 13.20 (*0-309-04564-9*) Transport Res Bd.

Automated Flight Control Systems. Vaughn Bradshaw & Burgess. 432p. boxed 54.80 (*0-13-050501-3*) P-H.

Automated Generation of Model-Based Knowledge-Acquisition Tools. Mark Musen. (Research Notes in Artificial Intelligence Ser.). 1989. 29.95 (*1-55860-090-6*) Morgan Kaufmann.

Automated Generation of Model Based Knowledge Acquisition Tools. Mark A. Musen. 300p. (C). 1989. pap. text ed. 200.00 (*0-273-08812-2*, Pub. by Pitman Pubng UK) St Mut.

Automated Guided Vehicle Systems. L. F. Gelders & R. H. Hollier. 300p. 1989. 133.00 (*0-387-50404-4*) Spr-Verlag.

Automated Guided Vehicle Systems: Proceedings of the 2nd International Conference on AGVS & 16th IPA Conference, Stuttgart, F. R. G. June 7-9, 1983. Ed. by H. J. Warnecke. iv, 346p. 1984. 102.75 (*0-444-86686-8*, I-507-83) Elsevier.

Automated Guided Vehicle Systems 3: Proceedings of the Third International Conference Stockholm, Sweden, 15-17 October 1985. Ed. by S. E. Andersson. 350p. 1986. 102.75 (*0-444-87815-7*, North Holland) Elsevier.

Automated Guided Vehicles: A Survey on Technology & Markets. Richard K. Miller & Terri C. Walker. LC 88-80495. 50p. 1989, pap. text ed. 200.00 (*1-55865-002-4*) Future Tech Surveys.

Automated Guided Vehicles & Automated Manufacturing. R. Miller. 192p. 1987. 34.00 (*0-87263-281-4*) SME.

Automated Highway - Intelligent Vehicle Systems: Technology & Socioeconomic Aspects. 1990. 59.00 (*1-56091-062-3*, SP-833) Soc Auto Engineers.

Automated Hospital Information Systems: Getting the Most from the System You Select. Dennis Strum. LC 84-60126. 352p. 1984. pap. text ed. 51.50 (*0-914957-00-7*) Precept Pr.

Automated Hospital Information Systems: How to Decide What You Want. Dennis Strum. LC 84-60127. 320p. 1984. pap. text ed. 47.25 (*0-914957-01-5*) Precept Pr.

Automated IC Manufacturing Seven. Ed. by V. Akins & H. Harada. LC 92-70529. (Proceedings Ser.: Vol. 92-8). 250p. 1992. 36.00 (*1-56677-004-1*) Electrochem Soc.

Automated Immunoanalysis, 2 pts., Pt. 1. Ed. by Robert F. Ritchie. LC 77-28836. (Clinical & Biochemical Analysis Ser.: No. 7). (Illus.). 349p. reprint ed. pap. 94.30 (*0-7837-0817-3*, 2041132) Bks Demand.

Automated Immunoanalysis, 2 pts., Pt. 2. Ed. by Robert F. Ritchie. LC 77-28836. (Clinical & Biochemical Analysis Ser.: No. 7). (Illus.). 303p. reprint ed. pap. 86.40 (*0-7837-0818-1*) Bks Demand.

Automated Information Retrieval in Libraries: A Management Handbook. Vicki Anders. LC 91-44401. (Library Management Collection). 264p. 1992. text ed. 59.95 (*0-313-27361-8*, AAO/, Greenwood Pr) Greenwood.

Automated Information Systems: Implementation Guidelines. National Center for State Courts, State Judicial Information Systems Project Staff. 46p. 1983. pap. write for info. (*0-89656-067-8*, R-077) Natl Ctr St Courts.

Automated Inspection & High-Speed Vision Architectures, Vol. 849. Ed. by R. Ahlers & M. J. Chen. 280p. 1988. 51.00 (*0-89252-884-2*) SPIE.

Automated Inspection & High Speed Vision Architectures, Vol. 1004. Ed. by M. J. Chen. 1988. 51.00 (*0-8194-0039-4*) SPIE.

Automated Inspection & High-Speed Vision Architectures III. Ed. by Michael J. Chen. 320p. 1990. 62.00 (*0-8194-0236-2*, VOL. 1197) SPIE.

Automated Inspection & Product Control: Proceedings of the International Conference, 7th, Birmingham, U. K., March 26-28, 1985. Ed. by P. A. McKeown. 400p. 1985. 107.75 (*0-444-87734-7*, North Holland) Elsevier.

Automated Inspection & Quality Assurance. Robinson & Miller. (Quality & Reliability Ser.: Vol. 16). 272p. 1989. 59.75 (*0-8247-8002-7*) Dekker.

Automated Instrumentation for Radioimmunoassay. Lemuel J. Bowie. 224p. 1980. 119.00 (*0-8493-5747-0*, QP519, CRC Reprint) Franklin.

Automated Inventory Management for the Distributor. Graham. 24.95 (*0-317-63814-9*) Van Nos Reinhold.

***Automated Knowledge Acquisition.** Sabrina Sestito. 250p. 1994. text ed. 53.00 (*0-13-301136-4*) P-H.

Automated Law Firm: A Complete Guide to Software & Systems. Richard L. Robbins. 254p. 1989. ring bd. 75.00 (*0-13-051038-6*) P-H.

Automated Law Firm: A Complete Guide to Software & Systems. 2nd ed. Richard L. Robbins. 590p. 1992. ring bd. 110.00 (*0-13-291352-6*) Aspen Law.

Automated Manufacturing-STP 862. Ed. by Leonard B. Gardner. LC 85-1243. (Illus.). 255p. 1985. text ed. 38.00 (*0-8031-0422-7*, 04-862000-32) ASTM.

Automated Manufacturing, 1983: Proceedings of the European Automated Manufacturing Conference, 2nd, Birmingham, UK, May 1983. European Automated Manufacturing Conference Staff. Ed. by B. Rooks. iv, 452p. 1983. 97.50 (*0-444-86687-6*, I-277-83, North Holland) Elsevier.

Automated Manufacturing 1985: Proceedings of the Third European Conference, Birmingham, U. K. 14-17 May 1985. Ed. by B. B. Hundy. 400p. 1985. 115.50 (*0-444-87772-X*, North Holland) Elsevier.

Automated Materials Handling. Ed. by R. H. Hollier. 310p. 1990. 128.00 (*0-387-51848-7*, 3655) Spr-Verlag.

Automated Materials Handling: Proceedings of the International Conference, 1st, London, U. K., April 1983. Ed. by R. H. Hollier. iv, 284p. 1983. 87.25 (*0-444-86666-3*, I-279-83, North Holland) Elsevier.

Automated Materials Handling 1985: Proceedings of the Second International Conference, Birmingham, U. K., 14-17 May 1985. Ed. by R. H. Hollier. 350p. 1985. 115.50 (*0-444-87770-3*, North Holland) Elsevier.

544 An Asterisk (*) at the beginning of an entry indicates that the title is appearing in BIP for the first time.

An Asterisk (*) at the beginning of an entry indicates that the title is appearing in BIP for the first time.

545

Automatic Flight Control. 4th ed. E. H. Pallett. LC 93-25282. 1993. pap. text ed. 45.00x (*0-632-03495-5*) Blackwell Pubs.

Automatic, General-Purpose EO Sterilizers & EO Sterilant Sources Intended for Use in Health Care Facilities. 1993. 49.00 (*1-57020-001-7*, ST24-113) Assn Adv Med Instrn.

Automatic Generation of Morphological Set Recognition Algorithms. R. C. Vogt. (Perception Engineering Ser.). (Illus.). 288p. 1989. 98.00 (*0-387-97049-5*, 3015) Spr-Verlag.

Automatic Government: The Politics of Indexation. R. Kent Weaver. LC 88-10562. 276p. 1988. 34.95 (*0-8157-9258-1*); pap. 14.95 (*0-8157-9257-3*) Brookings.

Automatic Heating. Jack Rudman. (Occupational Competency Examination Ser.: OCE-6). 1994. 39.95 (*0-8373-5756-X*); pap. 23.95 (*0-8373-5706-3*) Nat Learn.

Automatic I. D. Questions & Answers. rev. ed. Richard B. Meyers. 1992. pap. 29.95 (*0-929870-08-5*) Advanstar Commns.

Automatic Identification: Making It Pay. Kevin R. Sharp & Hake. 1990. text ed. 54.95 (*0-442-23775-8*) Van Nos Reinhold.

Automatic Identification & Data Collection Systems. Jonathan Cohen. LC 93-38078. 1994. text ed. 49.00 (*0-07-707914-0*) McGraw.

Automatic Litigation Support: A Practical Introduction. Fred Greguras. (Corporate Practice Ser.: No. 36). 1984. 92.00 (*1-55871-146-5*) BNA.

Automatic Logic Synthesis Techniques for Digital Systems. M. D. Edwards. 1992. text ed. 35.00 (*0-07-019417-3*) McGraw.

Automatic Mac. Fred Terry. (Illus.). (Orig.). 1992. pap. 39.95 (*0-13-052820-X*) Brady Compu Bks.

Automatic, Manual Transmissions, Transaxles, & Drive Trains. rev. ed. Bob Leigh et al. Ed. by Roger L. Fennema & Kalton C. Lahue. (Automobile Mechanics Refresher Course Ser.: Bk. 5). (Illus.). 84p. 1981. student ed, pap. 9.95 (*0-88098-066-4*, H M Gousha); audio 13.90 (*0-88098-072-9*, H M Gousha) P-H Gen Ref & Trav.

Automatic Mesh Generation: Applications to Finite Element Methods. P. L. George. 333p. 1992. text ed. 115.00 (*0-471-93097-0*) Wiley.

Automatic Meter Reading: An Opportunity Now? 48p. 1988. pap. 12.50 (*0-89867-422-0*, 20023) Am Water Wks Assn.

Automatic Methods of Analysis. M. Valcarcel & M. D. Luque de Castro. (Techniques & Instrumentation in Analytical Chemistry Ser.: No. 9). 560p. 1988. 128.25 (*0-444-43005-9*) Elsevier.

Automatic Natural Language Parsing. Karen Sprack-Jones & Yorick Wilks. LC 83-8601. 208p. 1985. 44.95 (*0-470-27460-3*) P-H.

Automatic Object Recognition. Ed. by Hatem N. Nasr. (Institute Ser.: Vol. IS07). 254p. 1991. 62.00 (*0-8194-0467-5*) SPIE.

Automatic Object Recognition, Vol. 1471. F. A. Sadjadi. 1991. 70.00 (*0-8194-0580-9*) SPIE.

Automatic Oracle. Peter Porter. (Oxford Poets Ser.). 80p. 1987. pap. 8.95 (*0-19-282088-5*) OUP.

Automatic Parallelization: New Approaches to Code Generation, Data Distribution, & Performance Prediction. Ed. by Christoph W. KeBler. xii, 221p. 1994. pap. 49.00 (*3-528-05401-8*, Pub. by Vieweg & Sohn GW) Ballen Bkslr.

Automatic Password Generator Standard. (Illus.). 60p. (Orig.). (C). 1994. pap. text ed. 60.00 (*0-7881-0759-3*) Diane Pub.

Automatic Perimetry in Glaucoma: A Practical Guide. Ed. by Stephen M. Drance & Douglas Anderson. LC 85-8069. 208p. 1985. text ed. 97.95 (*0-8089-1705-6*, 791062, Grune) Saunders.

Automatic Potentiometric Titrations. Gyula I. Svehla. 1978. 199.00 (*0-08-021590-4*, Pub. by Pergamon Repr UK) Franklin.

Automatic Product-People Identification. Business Communications Co., Inc. Staff. 181p. 1988. 2,250.00 (*0-89336-630-7*, G-112) BCC.

Automatic Program Construction. Alan W. Biermann et al. 1982. write for info. (*0-318-57142-0*) Elsevier.

Automatic Program Debugging for Intelligent Tutoring Systems. William Murray. (Research Notes in Artificial Intelligence Ser.). 347p. 1989. Research Monograph. 29.95 (*0-934613-98-2*) Morgan Kaufmann.

Automatic Program Debugging for Intelligent Tutoring Systems. Ed. by William Murray. 248p. (C). 1988. pap. text ed. 200.00 (*0-273-08795-9*, Pub. by Pitman Pubng UK) St Mut.

Automatic Programming Applied to VLSI CAD Software: A Case Study. Dorothy E. Setliff & Rob A. Rutenbar. (C). 1990. lib. bdg. 69.00 (*0-7923-9112-8*) Kluwer Ac.

Automatic Programming, Numerical Methods & Functional Analysis. Steklov Institute of Mathematics, Academy of Sciences, U. S. S. R. Staff. Ed. by V. N. Faddeeva. (Proceedings of the Steklov Institute of Mathematics Ser.: No. 96). 323p. 1970. 66.00 (*0-8218-1896-1*, STEKLO-96) Am Math.

Automatic Refinement of Expert System Knowledge Bases. Allen Ginsberg. (Research Notes in Artificial Intelligence Ser.). 176p. 1988. Research Monograph. 29.95 (*0-934613-96-6*) Morgan Kaufmann.

Automatic Refinement of Expert System Knowledge Bases. Ed. by Allen Ginsberg. 288p. (C). 1988. pap. text ed. 180.00 (*0-273-08794-0*, Pub. by Pitman Pubng UK) St Mut.

Automatic Revision of Storage Structures. Frances G. Gustavson. Ed. by Harold Stone. LC 82-6974. (Computer Science: Systems Programming Ser.: No. 11). 154p. reprint ed. 43.70 (*0-8357-1345-8*, 2070167) Bks Demand.

Automatic Semantic Interpretation. J. Van Bakel. x, 176p. 1984. pap. 42.35 (*90-6765-039-0*) Mouton.

Automatic Speech Recognition: The Development of the SPHINX Recognition System. Kai-Fu Lee. (International Series in Engineering & Computer Science, VLSI, Computer Architecture, & Digital Screen Processing). 224p. (C). 1988. lib. bdg. 85.50 (*0-89838-296-3*) Kluwer Ac.

Automatic Speech Recognition Research in the U. S. S. R. George Vysotsky. Ed. by Andrew A. Michta. (Illus.). 143p. (Orig.). 1986. pap. text ed. 75.00 (*1-55831-055-X*) Delphic Associates.

Automatic Sprinkler & Standpipe Systems. 2nd ed. John L. Bryan. Ed. by Gene A. Moulton & Deborah A. Shaw. 1990. 55.75 (*0-87765-368-2*, AUTO-90) Natl Fire Prot.

Automatic Sprinkler Systems Handbook. Ed. by Robert E. Solomon. 700p. 1994. 77.50 (*0-317-63582-4*, 13HB-94) Natl Fire Prot.

Automatic Steering of an Articulated Haul Truck for Underground Mining. J. D. Lane & R. H. King. 1994. write for info. (*0-318-72529-0*) US Interior.

Automatic Supervision in Manufacturing. Ed. by Maciej Szafarczyk. LC 93-46279. (Advanced Manufacturing Ser.). 1994. text ed. 145.00 (*0-387-19858-X*) Spr-Verlag.

Automatic Tax Planner. LC 85-6528. 150.00 (*0-916592-54-5*) Panel Pubs.

Automatic Teller Machines. John J. Williams. Ed. by Laurie Williams. (Illus.). 52p. (Orig.). 1990. pap. 39.00 (*0-934274-20-7*) Consumertronics.

Automatic Test Equipment. Keith Brindley. (Illus.). 240p. 1991. 32.95 (*0-7506-0130-2*) Buttrwrth-Heinemann.

Automatic Text Processing. Gerard Salton. (Computer Science Ser.). (Illus.). 450p. (C). 1989. pap. text ed. 45.25 (*0-201-12227-8*) Addison-Wesley.

Automatic Tools for Designing Office Information Systems: The TODOS Approach. Ed. by B. Pernici et al. (Research Reports ESPRIT, Project 813, TODOS: Vol. 1). ix, 321p. 1990. pap. 39.00 (*0-387-53284-6*) Spr-Verlag.

***Automatic Transaxles & Transmissions.** 2nd ed. J. Gary Campbell. LC 94-36828. 1995. text ed. 53.33 (*0-13-291147-7*) P-H Gen Ref & Trav.

Automatic Translation of Languages: Papers Presented NATO Summer School, Venice, July 1962. A. Ghizzetti. LC 65-28547. 1966. 99.00 (*0-08-011799-6*, Pub. by Pergamon Repr UK) Franklin.

Automatic Transmission. Peter Novellino. LC 77-731115. 1978. student ed 6.00 (*0-8064-0115-X*, 425); audio 279.00 (*0-8064-0116-8*) Bergwall.

***Automatic Transmission.** Tucker. Date not set. 27.95 (*0-8273-2606-8*) Delmar.

Automatic Transmission, 2 vols. 2nd ed. Chek-Chart Staff. (C). 1990. Vol. I--Classroom manual, 300 pgs.; Vol. II--Shop manual, 250 pgs. pap. text ed. 53.00 (*0-06-454012-X*, H M Gousha) P-H Gen Ref & Trav.

***Automatic Transmissions.** Jack Erjavec. (Today's Technician Ser.). (Illus.). 688p. 1995. 48.95 (*0-8273-6190-4*) Delmar.

Automatic Transmissions. 2nd ed. M. Brycha. 1982. pap. text ed. 41.00 (*0-13-054577-5*) P-H.

Automatic Transmissions & Transaxles. 3rd ed. Mathias F. Brejcha. 484p. 1992. pap. text ed. 51.00 (*0-13-051202-8*) P-H.

Automatic Transmissions Instructors Guide. John H. White. 1991. 12.00 (*0-8273-2607-6*) Delmar.

Automatic Tuning of PID Controllers. K. J. Astrom & T. Hagglund. LC 88-3010. 141p. 1988. 45.00 (*1-55617-081-5*, A081-5) Instru Soc.

Automatic Tuning of PID Controllers. 2nd ed. Karl J. Astrom & Tore H. Hagglund. LC 94-10795. 1994. write for info. (*1-55617-516-7*) Instru Soc.

Automatic Turning Machines. 1982. 50.00 (*0-85083-217-9*) St Mut.

Automatic Verification Methods for Finite State Systems. Ed. by J. Sifakis. (Lecture Notes in Computer Science Ser.: Vol. 407). vii, 382p. 1990. pap. 38.60 (*0-387-52148-8*, 3916) Spr-Verlag.

Automatic Washers. Ed. by A. Ross Sabin. (Illus.). 200p. (gr. 11). 1980. 20.00 (*0-938336-04-5*) Whirlpool.

Automatic Wristwatches from Switzerland: Watches That Wind Themselves. Heinz Hampel. LC 94-65607. (Illus.). 318p. 1994. 79.95 (*0-88740-609-2*) Schiffer.

Automatics: Fast Firepower, Tactical Superiority. Duncan Long. (Illus.). 144p. 1986. pap. 18.00 (*0-87364-397-6*) Paladin Pr.

Automating Business Process Re-Engineering: Computerized Quality & Productivity Improvement. Gregory A. Hansen. LC 93-31030. 256p. 1994. text ed., disk 53.00 (*0-13-079179-2*) P-H.

***Automating Instructional Design: Computer-Based Development & Delivery Tools.** Ed. by Robert D. Tennyson & Ann E. Barron. LC 95-82. (NATO ASI Series F, Computer & Systems Sciences: Vol. 140). 1995. 149.00 (*3-540-58765-9*) Spr-Verlag.

Automating Instructional Design: Concepts & Issues. Ed. by J. Michael Spector et al. LC 92-46057. (Illus.). 380p. 1993. 39.95 (*0-87778-259-8*) Educ Tech Pubns.

Automating Instructional Design, Development, & Delivery. Ed. by R. D. Tennyson. (NATO ASI Series F: Computer & Systems Sciences, Special Programme AET: Vol. 119). 290p. 1993. write for info. (*3-540-57022-5*) Spr-Verlag.

Automating Instructional Design, Development, & Delivery. R. D. Tennyson. (NATO ASI Series F: Computer & Systems Sciences, Special Programme AET: Vol. 119). 288p. 1994. 69.00 (*0-387-57022-5*) Spr-Verlag.

Automating Language Implementation: A Pragmatic Approach. Kai Koskimies. 228p. 1991. 43.00 (*0-13-053356-4*, 270108) P-H.

Automating Library Acquisitions: Issues & Outlook. Richard W. Boss. LC 82-8941. (Professional Librarian Ser.). 135p. 1982. pap. 30.50 (*0-86729-006-4*, Hall Reference) Macmillan.

Automating Library Procedures: A Survivor's Handbook. Ian Lovecy. LC 84-221628. (Illus.). 255p. reprint ed. pap. 72.70 (*0-7837-7014-6*, 2046828) Bks Demand.

Automating Literacy: A Challenge for Libraries. Linda Main & Char Whitaker. LC 90-47285. (New Directions in Information Management Ser.: No. 24). 144p. 1991. text ed. 45.00 (*0-313-27528-9*, MLX/, Greenwood Pr) Greenwood.

Automating Mainframe Management: Using Expert Systems with Examples from VM & MVS. Michael Seadle. 400p. 1991. text ed. 44.95 (*0-07-055911-2*) McGraw.

Automating Management Information Systems. Harry E. Burke. 1990. text ed. 99.95 (*0-442-20712-3*) Van Nos Reinhold.

Automating Managers. John Moss-Jones. 1991. text ed. 47.50 (*0-86187-837-X*, Pub. by Pinter Pubs UK) St Martin.

Automating Personnel Operations: The Human Resource Manager's Guide to Computerization. Gary J. Meyer. 1984. ring bd. 76.50 (*1-55645-416-3*) Busn Legal Reports.

Automating School Library Catalogs: A Reader. Catherine Murphy. 211p. 1992. lib. bdg. 27.00 (*0-87287-771-X*) Libs Unl.

Automating Software Design. Ed. by Michael Lowry & Robert McCartney. 394p. 1991. pap. 35.00x (*0-262-62080-4*) MIT Pr.

***Automating Solaris Installations.** Paul Kasper. 1995. disk, pap. text ed. 38.00 (*0-13-312505-X*) P-H.

Automating Systems Development. Ed. by D. Benyon & S. Skidmore. LC 88-17827. (Illus.). 516p. 1988. 110.00 (*0-306-42931-4*, Plenum Pr) Plenum.

Automating the Archives: A Beginner's Guide. Richard Kesner & Lisa Weber. 8p. 1991. pap. 3.50 (*0-685-51011-5*) Soc Am Archivists.

Automating the Design of Computer Systems. W. P. Birmingham et al. LC 91-44782. (Illus.). 296p. 1992. text ed. 54.95 (*0-86720-241-6*) AK Peters.

Automating the Lexicon: Research & Practice in a Multilingual Environment. Ed. by Donald E. Walker et al. LC 94-11746. (Illus.). 400p. 1995. 69.00 (*0-19-823950-5*) OUP.

Automating the Newspaper Clipping Files: A Practical Guide. Special Libraries Association, Newspaper Division Staff. (Illus.). 51p. (Orig.). 1987. pap. 37.50 (*0-87111-328-7*) SLA.

Automating the Personnel Function: A Human Resource Manager's Guide to Computerization. Robert C. Enderle. LC 86-83152. 80p. 1987. ring bd. 24.95 (*0-9618186-0-3*) Enderle Pub Co.

Automating the Physician's Office. Barry Wend. 60p. 1992. student ed, pap. 21.00 (*0-932223-14-1*) Churchill PC.

Automating the Sewing Room. 1982. 30.00 (*0-318-01187-5*, 13110) Indus Fabrics.

Automating the Small Law Office & Solo Practice. (Commercial Law & Practice Course Handbook Ser.). 1992. pap. 70.00 (*0-685-69384-8*) PLI.

Automating the Small Library. William Saffady. (Small Libraries Publications: No. 18). 16p. 1991. pap. 5.00 (*0-8389-5745-5*) ALA.

Automating Windows. Michael Utvich. 1993. pap. 24.95 (*0-679-79153-1*) Random.

Automating Your Office: Pathways to Management Succcess. Ed. by Lou Pilla. (Illus.). 158p. (Orig.). 1984. pap. 13.95 (*0-916323-02-1*) Admin Mgmt.

Automation. Mary Cress. (Science Ser.). 24p. (gr. 6 up). 1977. student ed 5.00 (*0-8209-0153-9*, S-15) ESP.

Automation: Its Impact on Business & People. Walter S. Buckingham. LC 81-20228. ix, 196p. 1982. reprint ed. text ed. 35.00 (*0-313-23339-X*, BUAU, Greenwood Pr) Greenwood.

Automation & Autoanalysis in Medicine: Research & Reference Guidebook. Kurt L. Reichert. LC 83-45002. 150p. 1985. 39.50 (*0-88164-180-4*); 34.50 (*0-88164-181-2*) ABBE Pubs Assn.

Automation & Control in Transport. 2nd rev. ed. F. T. Barwell. LC 82-18981. 400p. 1983. 168.00 (*0-08-026712-2*, Pub. by Pergamon Repr UK) Franklin.

Automation & Environmental Control in Plant Tissue Culture. Ed. by Jenny Aitken-Christie et al. LC 94-14890. 592p. (C). 1994. lib. bdg. 248.00 (*0-7923-2841-8*) Kluwer Ac.

Automation & Global Production: Automobile Engine Production in Mexico, the United States, & Canada. Harley Shaiken & Stephen Herzenberg. (Monograph Ser.: No. 26). (Illus.). 120p. 1987. pap. 12.50 (*0-935391-75-4*, MN-26) UCSD Ctr US-Mex.

Automation & Industrial Workers: A Fifteen Nation Study, 2 vols., Set. J. Forslin & Adam Sarapata. LC 79-40811. 1979. 237.00 (*0-08-028095-1*, Pub. by Pergamon Repr UK) Franklin.

Automation & Industrial Workers: A Fifteen Nation Study, 2 pts., Vol. 1, Pt. 1. Ed. by Jan Forslin et al. (Publications of the Vienna Centre). (Illus.). 721p. 1981. 108.00 (*0-08-023339-2*, Pub. by Pergamon Repr UK) Franklin.

Automation & Industrial Workers: A Fifteen Nation Study, 2 pts., Vol. 1, Pt. 2. Ed. by Jan Forslin et al. (Publications of the Vienna Centre). (Illus.). 721p. 1981. 129.00 (*0-08-024310-X*, Pub. by Pergamon Repr UK) Franklin.

Automation & Industrial Workers (Vol. 1 & Vol. 2) A Fifteen Nation Study & Cross-National Comparison, 4 pt. set. Ed. by Frank Adler et al. (Vienna Centre Ser.). 1484p. 1986. text ed. 295.00 (*0-08-033375-3*, Pub. by PPL UK) Elsevier.

Automation & Instrumentation, No. M2. 152p. 1983. pap. 29.00 (*0-89867-301-1*, 30002) Am Water Wks Assn.

Automation & Instrumentation: Proceedings of the 8th International Convention Milan, Milan 11-64. L. Dadda & U. Pellegrini. LC 66-27882. 1967. 301.00 (*0-08-011693-0*, Pub. by Pergamon Repr UK) Franklin.

Automation & Instrumentation for Power Plants: Proceedings of the IFAC Symposium, December 15-17, 1986, Bangalore, India. Ed. by M. Ramamoorty. (IFPS Proceedings Ser.: No. 8700). 360p. 1989. 140.00 (*0-08-034197-7*, Pergamon Pr) Elsevier.

Automation & Logistics in Precast Concrete. Ed. by A. J. Hogeslag et al. 252p. (Orig.). 1992. pap. 52.50 (*90-6275-811-8*, Pub. by Delft U Pr NE) Coronet Bks.

Automation & Organizational Change in Libraries. Peggy Johnson. (Professional Librarian Ser.). 245p. (C). 1991. text ed. 39.95 (*0-8161-1919-8*, Hall Reference); pap. 24.95 (*0-8161-1920-1*, Hall Reference) Macmillan.

Automation & Robotics in Construction X: Proceedings of the 10th International Symposium on Automation & Robotics in Construction (ISARC), Houston, Texas, U.S.A., 24-26 May, 1993. Ed. by George H. Watson et al. LC 93-1947. 1993. write for info. (*0-444-81523-6*) Elsevier.

Automation & Robotics in Construction XI: Proceedings of the Eleventh International Symposium on Automation & Robotics in Construction--ISARC, Brighton, UK, 24-26 May, 1994. Ed. by Denis Chamberlain. LC 94-14975. 716p. 1994. 317.25 (*0-444-82044-2*, North Holland) Elsevier.

Automation & Robotics in the Textile & Apparel Industries. Ed. by Gordon A. Berkstresser, III & David R. Buchanan. LC 86-5204. (Illus.). 328p. 1986. 45.00 (*0-8155-1077-2*) Noyes.

Automation & Systems Issues in Air Traffic Control. Ed. by J. A. Wise et al. (NATO ASI Series F: Computer & Systems Sciences, Special Programme AET: Vol. 73). (Illus.). xix, 592p. 1991. 139.00 (*0-387-53903-4*) Spr-Verlag.

Automation & Technological Change. Ed. by John T. Dunlop. LC 62-17597. 1962. 3.95 (*0-317-02946-0*, 05449-C) Am Assembly.

Automation & the Worker: A Study of Social Change in Power Plants. Floyd C. Mann & L. Richard Hoffman. LC 83-12978. (Illus.). xiv, 272p. 1983. reprint ed. text ed. 59.75 (*0-313-24222-4*, MAUW, Greenwood Pr) Greenwood.

Automation & the Workplace: Labor, Education & Training Issues. 1986. lib. bdg. 250.00 (*0-8490-3742-5*) Gordon Pr.

Automation Assessment & Management Review, Glynn County State Court. Don Hardenbergh & James R. James. 86p. 1985. 5.00 (*0-685-33607-7*, SERO-053) Natl Ctr St Courts.

Automation Based Creative Design: Research & Perspectives. Ed. by Alexander Tzonis & Ian White. LC 94-3098. 1994. write for info. (*0-444-89870-0*) Elsevier.

Automation Encyclopedia. Ed. by G. Graham. LC 87-63598. 597p. 1988. 99.00 (*0-87263-304-7*) SME.

Automation for Injection Molding. Application Automation Div. Staff. 1985. 5.00 (*0-910447-03-9*) Application Eng Corp.

Automation for Press Feed Operations. Walker. (Manufacturing Engineering & Materials Processing Ser.: Vol. 18). 176p. 1986. 99.75 (*0-8247-7350-0*) Dekker.

Automation for Safety in Shipping & Offshore Petroleum Operations. Ed. by Chengi Kuo et al. 514p. 1986. 110.25 (*0-444-70101-X*, North Holland) Elsevier.

Automation for School Libraries: How to Do It from Those Who Have Done It. Ed. by Gregory Zuct et al. 150p. 1994. pap. text ed. 18.00 (*0-8389-0637-0*) ALA.

Automation in Anesthesia: A Relief? A. P. Meijler. (Illus.). 210p. 1987. pap. 60.00 (*0-387-18204-7*) Spr-Verlag.

Automation in Animal Development. Ed. by Rosine Chandebois & J. Faber. (Monographs in Developmental Biology: Vol. 16). (Illus.). xii, 204p. 1983. 132.00 (*3-8055-3666-6*) S Karger.

Automation in Blood Transfusion: Proceedings of the Thirteenth Annual Symposium on Blood Transfusion, Groningen 1988. Ed. by Smith C. Sibinga et al. (Developments in Hematology & Immunology Ser.). (C). 1989. lib. bdg. 51.00 (*0-7923-0488-8*) Kluwer Ac.

Automation in Clinical Microbiology. Ed. by James H. Jorgensen. 240p. 1987. 191.00 (*0-8493-5108-1*, QR67, CRC Reprint) Franklin.

Automation in Developing Countries. x, 246p. 1974. 20.00 (*92-2-100158-X*) Intl Labour Office.

***Automation in Fatigue & Fracture: Testing & Analysis, STP 1231.** Ed. by Claude Amzallag. LC 94-36845. (Special Technical Publication Ser.: Vol. 1231). (Illus.). 670p. 1994. text ed. 119.00 (*0-8031-1985-2*, 04-012310-30) ASTM.

Automation in Housing & Systems Building News: Dictionary of Industrialized Manufactured Housing. Ed. by Don Carlson. (Illus.). 1981. 15.00 (*0-9607408-0-5*) Automated Builder.

Automation in Insurance. 2nd ed. Robert J. Anderson et al. LC 93-77522. 441p. (Orig.). (C). 1993. pap. 26.00 (*0-89462-077-0*) IIA.

Automation in Libraries. 2nd ed. Richard T. Kimber & A. Boyd. 1974. 104.00 (*0-08-017969-X*, Pub. by Pergamon Repr UK) Franklin.

Automation in Libraries, 1978-1982: A LITA Bibliography. Comp. by Anne G. Adler et al. LC 83-62104. (Library Hi Tech Monograph Ser.: No. 1). 1983. 40.00 (*0-87650-157-9*) Pierian.

Automation in Library Reference Services: A Handbook. Robert J. Carande. LC 92-19417. (Library Management Collection). 208p. 1992. text ed. 55.00 (*0-313-27837-7*, CHU, Greenwood Pr) Greenwood.

An Asterisk (*) at the beginning of an entry indicates that the title is appearing in BIP for the first time.

Automation in Mining Mineral & Metal Processing: Proceedings 2nd IFAC Symposium, Johannesburg 9-76. South Africa Council Automation Staff & F. Lancaster. LC 78-40123. 1978. 331.00 (*0-08-022441-5*, Pub. by Pergamon Repr UK) Franklin.

Automation in Mining, Mineral & Metal Processing 1980: Proceedings of the 3rd IFAC Symposium, Montreal, PQ, Canada, August, 1988. IFAC Symposium, 3rd, Montreal, PQ, Canada, Aug. 1980. Ed. by J. O'Shea & M. Polis. LC 80-40809. (Illus.). 712p. 1980. 277.00 (*0-08-026164-7*, Pub. by Pergamon Repr UK) Franklin.

Automation in Mining, Mineral & Metal Processing, 1992: Selected Papers from the 7th IFAC Symposium, Beijing, PRC, 26-28 August, 1992, No. 11. Ed. by Yan Gu & Zhen-Yu Chen. LC 93-8258. (IFAC Symposia Ser.: Vol. 1993). 1993. 130.00 (*0-08-041892-9*, Pergamon Pr) Elsevier.

Automation in Practice. Samuel E. Rusinoff. LC 57-13299. 269p. reprint ed. pap. 76.70 (*0-8357-5916-4*, 2052046) Bks Demand.

Automation in Quality Assurance. 2nd ed. Ed. by Bruce Brocka. (Illus.). 206p. 1988. write for info. (*0-318-65301-X*) Exec Sci Inst.

Automation in Space, Vol. I: Expert Systems in Space. Sloggett. 300p. 1993. text ed. write for info. (*0-13-053547-8*) P-H.

Automation in Space, Vol. II: Robots in Space. Sloggett. 300p. 1993. text ed. write for info. (*0-13-053554-0*) P-H.

Automation in the Design & Manufacture of Large Marine Systems. Ed. by Chryssostomos Chryssostomidis. 318p. 1990. 110.00 (*0-89116-960-1*) Hemisp Pub.

Automation in the Food Industry. C. A. Moore. 1991. text ed. 105.00 (*0-442-31432-9*) Chapman & Hall.

***Automation in the Laboratory.** Ed. by W. Jeffrey Hurst. LC 94-43002. 1995. write for info. (*1-56081-025-4*) VCH Pubs.

Automation in the Law School: Including Law Libraries. Betty W. Taylor & Dan F. Henke. (Law Library Information Reports: Vol. 7). 124p. 1986. pap. 100.00 (*0-87802-082-9*) Glanville.

Automation in Warehousing: Proceedings of the Sixth International Conference, Stockholm, Sweden, 15-17 October 1985. Ed. by R. H. Hollier. 330p. 1986. 102.75 (*0-444-87816-5*, North Holland) Elsevier.

Automation of America's Offices, Eighteen Eighty-Five to Two Thousand: An Assessment of the Consequences of the Rapid Introduction of Information & Telecommunications Technologies in the Office. 1986. lib. bdg. 250.00 (*0-8490-3734-4*) Gordon Pr.

Automation of Canal Irrigation Systems, 1993. 28.00 (*81-85068-44-5*) US Comm Irrigation.

Automation of Cervical Cancer Screening. Ed. by Heinz K. Grohs & O. A. Husain. LC 94-2501. (Illus.). 400p. 1994. 115.00 (*0-89640-255-X*) Igaku-Shoin.

Automation of Cytogenetics. Ed. by C. Lundsteen & J. Piper. (Illus.). 335p. 1989. 90.00 (*0-387-51105-9*, 2914) Spr-Verlag.

Automation of Mechanical Testing. Ed. by David T. Heberling. LC 93-16119. (STP Ser.: 1208). (Illus.). 105p. 1993. 31.00 (*0-8031-1868-6*, 04-012080-23) ASTM.

Automation of Pharmaceutical Operations. Ed. by David J. Fraade. LC 82-25962. 360p. 1983. 58.00 (*0-943330-02-5*) Advanstar Commns.

Automation of Pharmaceutical Operations: Supplement. Ed. by David J. Fraade. LC 85-6239. (Illus.). 106p. (Orig.). 1985. pap. 27.00 (*0-943330-06-8*) Advanstar Commns.

Automation of Reasoning I: Classical Papers on Computational Logic 1957-1966. Ed. by Joerg H. Siekmann & G. Wrightson. (Symbolic Computation Ser.). 525p. 1983. 104.00 (*0-387-12043-2*) Spr-Verlag.

Automation of Reasoning II: Classical Papers on Computational Logic 1967-1970. Ed. by Joerg H. Siekmann & G. Wrightson. (Symbolic Computation Ser.). 640p. 1983. 104.00 (*0-387-12044-0*) Spr-Verlag.

Automation of Securities Processing. Louis J. Karcher. 1990. 34.95 (*0-13-151598-5*) P-H.

Automation of Soviet Railroads: Selected Papers with Analysis. Ed. by Suzanne Possehl. (Illus.). 218p. (Orig.). 1990. pap. 100.00 (*1-55831-116-5*) Delphic Associates.

***Automation of the Tax Practice of the '90s.** American Institute of Certified Public Accountants Staff. 116p. 1991. pap. 33.10 (*0-7837-8477-5*, 2049282) Bks Demand.

Automation on Shipboard. G. Bonwick. 1969. text ed. 39.95 (*0-312-06195-1*) St Martin.

***Automation Pays! How to Automate Your Retail Business - Success Stories. Chuck Atkinson. Ed. by Sandra H. Record. 215p. (Orig.). 1995. pap. text ed. 19.95 (*0-917081-33-1*) Aces Four Pr. AUTOMATION PAYS! leads you through the sometimes scary process of switching from cash registers & manual methods to capturing information & managing with computers. AUTOMATION PAYS! includes success stories of businesses, from small to large, that have automated with profitable results. The book also lists may of the "pitfalls" to avoid. Selecting peripherals, such as bar code scanners & printers, receipt printers, cash drawers, networks, & credit card processing is made simple. The book includes lists of systems dealer organizations, publications & trade shows that will help locate the best solution for a business. All the benefits of automation, including inventory control, reduced manual processing, faster accounting, theft reduction, reduced employee hours & training & the optimum use of money are explained. Analyzing your needs, designing a system & selecting low cost equipment to manage your business are made clear with examples from the real world. Computers are affordable by any size business & have become necessary in most cases to gather & manage the information necessary to remain competitive & profitable. The author has developed software & systems for inventory & money management since 1978 & has been associated with the installation of over 10,000 systems. To order: 800-826-5009; FAX 817-560-8249.**

Publisher Provided Annotation.

Automation Plan for the Kansas Appellate Courts. National Center for State Courts Staff. 57p. 1982. write for info. (*0-318-61280-1*, NCRO-072) Natl Ctr St Courts.

Automation, Production Systems, & Computer-Integrated Manufacturing. Mikell P. Grover. (Illus.). 640p. 1987. text ed. 81.00 (*0-13-054652-6*) P-H.

Automation Requirements Analysis, Wichita Municipal Court. Don Hardenbergh & Doug Walker. 75p. 1985. 5.00 (*0-685-16646-5*, SERO-011) Natl Ctr St Courts.

Automation Requirements for the Superior Court of Guam, Vol. I: Functional Requirements. Susan Koenig et al. 194p. 1991. 12.00 (*0-685-50618-5*, WRO-128) Natl Ctr St Courts.

Automation Requirements for the Superior Court of Guam, Vol. II: Functional Checklists. Susan Koenig et al. 125p. 1991. 7.50 (*0-685-50619-3*, WRO-129) Natl Ctr St Courts.

Automation Requirements for the Superior Court of Guam, Vol. III: Data Element Dictionary. Susan Koenig et al. 64p. 1991. 4.00 (*0-685-50620-7*, WRO130) Natl Ctr St Courts.

Automation Services for Libraries: A Resource Handbook. rev. ed. Ernest A. Muro. (Library Management Ser.). (C). 1991. pap. 47.50 (*1-879491-00-1*) Vendor Rltns.

Automation Services for Libraries: A Resource Handbook - 92. 2nd ed. Intro. by Ernest A. Muro. (Library Management Ser.). 1992. pap. 57.50 (*1-879491-04-4*) Vendor Rltns.

Automation Services for Libraries: A Resource Handbook of Marketing & Sales. Ernest A. Muro. (C). 1991. pap. 47.50 (*1-879491-01-X*) Vendor Rltns.

Automation Services for Libraries: A Resource Handbook of Marketing & Sales - 92. 2nd ed. Ed. by Ernest A. Muro. (Illus.). 1995. pap. 57.50 (*1-879491-05-2*) Vendor Rltns.

Automation Services for Libraries: LATINET '91. Ernest A. Muro. Ed. by Jesus Lau & Martha Allan. Tr. by Martha Allan & Barbara Covitz. (Library Management Ser.). (Illus.). 347p. (ENG & SPA.). 1992. pap. 67.50 (*1-879491-03-6*) Vendor Rltns.

Automation Systems for Control & Data Acquisition. Lawrence T. Amy. (Resources for Measurement & Control Ser.). Orig. Title: Computer Automation: A Practical Approach for Instrument Control & Data Acquisition. 1992. 65.00 (*1-55617-390-3*) Instru Soc.

Automation Technical Assistance for Fairfield, Ohio Municipal Court: Final Report. 26p. 1986. 2.00 (*0-685-18270-3*, NERO,T/A-534) Natl Ctr St Courts.

Automation Technology & Industrial Renewal: Adjustment Dynamics in the U. S. Metalworking Sector. Donald A. Hicks. 160p. 1986. 39.75 (*0-8447-3598-1*) Am Enterprise.

Automation Technology in Management: In Selected Asian Countries. 112p. 1987. pap. 15.00 (*0-317-59545-8*, Pub. by APO JA) Qual Resc.

Automation, Tooling & Thermosets: Proceedings of the Society of Plastics Engineers, Ontario Section & Thermostat Division, Ramada Inn, Airport West, Mississauga, Ontario, Canada, March 3 & 4, 1983. Society of Plastics Engineers Staff. 209p. reprint ed. pap. 59.60 (*0-8357-5917-2*, 2021698) Bks Demand.

Automation User Survey. Automated Systems, NEMA Staff. 15.00 (*0-318-18039-1*) Natl Elec Mfrs.

Automation, Work Organisation & Occupational Stress. viii, 188p. 1986. 18.00 (*92-2-103866-1*) Intl Labour Office.

Automatisierung & Wandel der Betrieblichen Arbeitswelt. Guenter Spur et al. (Akademie der Wissenschaften zu Berlin, Forschungsbericht Ser.: No. 4). (Illus.). x, 314p. (Orig.). (GER.). (C). 1993. pap. text ed. 98.50 (*3-11-013939-1*) De Gruyter.

Automatism, Insanity, & the Psychology of Criminal Responsibility: A Philosophical Inquiry. Robert F. Schopp. (Studies in Philosophy & Law). 288p. (C). 1991. 47.95 (*0-521-40150-X*) Cambridge U Pr.

Automative Workers in Korea. Kyuhan Bae. (Institute of Social Sciences Korean Studies: No. 9). 230p. 1987. pap. text ed. 15.00 (*0-8248-1131-3*) UH Pr.

Automatizacija. 500p. (ENG, FRE, GER, RUS & SER.). 1985. 125.00 (*0-8288-0263-7*, F78580) Fr & Eur.

Automne a Pekin. Boris Vian. 320p. 1964. pap. 5.95 (*0-686-55683-6*) Fr & Eur.

Automne a Pekin. Boris Vian. 288p. (FRE.). 1980. pap. 14.95 (*0-7859-1513-3*, 2707303135) Fr & Eur.

Automobile: Inventions That Changed Our Lives. Barbara Ford. (J). (gr. 3-7). 1987. 10.95 (*0-8027-6724-9*); lib. bdg. 11.85 (*0-8027-6725-7*) Walker & Co.

Automobile Accident Compensation: Payments by Auto Insurers, Vol. II. 121p. 1985. 10.00 (*0-8330-0556-1*, R-3051-ICJ) Rand Corp.

Automobile Accident Compensation: Payments from All Sources, Vol. III. 63p. 1985. 7.50 (*0-8330-0586-3*, R-3052-ICJ) Rand Corp.

Automobile Accident Compensation: State Rules, Vol. IV. 61p. 1985. 7.50 (*0-8330-0557-X*, R-3053-ICJ) Rand Corp.

Automobile Accident Compensation: Who Pays How Much How Soon, Vol. I. 33p. 1985. pap. 4.00 (*0-8330-0622-3*, R-3050-ICJ) Rand Corp.

Automobile Accident Costs & Payments: Studies in the Economics of Injury Reparation. Alfred F. Conard et al. LC 64-17437. (Michigan Legal Publications). xxviii, 506p. 1983. reprint ed. lib. bdg. 47.50 (*0-89941-315-3*, 303080) W S Hein.

Automobile Accidents - Prevention & Control: Index of New Information with Authors & Subjects. Science & Life Consultants Association Staff. LC 92-54200. 180p. 1992. 44.50 (*1-55914-552-8*); pap. 39.50 (*1-55914-553-6*) ABBE Pubs Assn.

Automobile Aerobics: Exercise Your Right to Trim Thousands Off the Price of Your Next Automobile & Make the Dealership Sweat! Daniel J. Levy. 160p. 1994. pap. 9.95 (*0-9637628-8-5*) Tennyson Pub.

Automobile Age. James J. Flink. (Illus.). 472p. 1990. reprint ed. pap. 18.00x (*0-262-56055-0*) MIT Pr.

***Automobile Air Conditioner & Heater Guide: 1981-1983 U.S., 1975-1982 Import.** 6th ed. (Illus.). 600p. (C). 1994. 195.00 (*0-7605-0367-2*) Rector Pr.

***Automobile Air Conditioner & Heater Guide: 1984-1985 U. S., 1983-1984 Import.** 7th ed. (Illus.). 600p. (C). 1994. 195.00 (*0-7605-0368-0*) Rector Pr.

***Automobile Air Conditioner & Heater Guide: 1986 U. S., 1985 Import.** 8th ed. (Illus.). 600p. 1994. 195.00 (*0-7605-0369-9*) Rector Pr.

***Automobile Air Conditioner & Heater Guide: 1987 U. S., 1986 Import.** 9th ed. (Illus.). 600p. (C). 1994. 195.00 (*0-7605-0370-2*) Rector Pr.

***Automobile Air Conditioner & Heater Guide: 1988 U.S., 1987 Import.** 10th ed. (Illus.). 600p. (C). 1994. 195.00 (*0-7605-0371-0*) Rector Pr.

***Automobile Air Conditioner & Heater Guide: 1989 U. S., 1988 Import.** 11th ed. (Illus.). 600p. (C). 1994. 195.00 (*0-7605-0372-9*) Rector Pr.

***Automobile Air Conditioner & Heater Guide: 1990 U. S., 1991 Import.** 12th ed. (Illus.). 600p. (C). 1994. 195.00 (*0-7605-0373-7*) Rector Pr.

***Automobile Air Conditioner & Heater Guide: 1992-1993 U.S., 1991-1992 Import.** 13th ed. (Illus.). 600p. (C). 1994. 225.00 (*0-7605-0374-5*) Rector Pr.

***Automobile Air Conditioner & Heater Guide, 74-80.** 5th ed. (Illus.). 600p. (C). 1994. 195.00 (*0-7605-0366-4*) Rector Pr.

Automobile Almanac-Annual. 1981. 6.95 (*0-686-51337-1*); pap. 2.95 (*0-686-51338-X*) Monarch Ltd.

Automobile & Air Pollution. 1991. lib. bdg. 69.95 (*0-8490-4501-0*) Gordon Pr.

Automobile & American Culture. Ed. by David L. Lewis & Laurence Goldstein. 1983. pap. text ed. 19.95 (*0-472-08044-X*) U of Mich Pr.

Automobile & Culture. Gerald Silk et al. LC 83-22164. (Illus.). 320p. 1985. pap. 34.95 (*0-8109-2283-5*) Abrams.

***Automobile & Pollution.** Paul Degobert. (Illus.). 520p. (C). 1995. text ed. write for info. (*2-7108-0676-2*) Technip.

Automobile & The Environment. Maxine Rock. (Earth at Risk Ser.). (Illus.). (YA). (gr. 5 up). 1992. lib. bdg. 19.95 (*0-7910-1592-0*) Chelsea Hse.

Automobile & the Environment: An International Perspective. Organization for Economic Cooperation & Development Staff. (Transportation Studies). 1978. 55.00 (*0-262-07070-7*) MIT Pr.

Automobile Association Exploring Britain's Long Distance Paths. Automobile Association of England Staff. 1993. 45.00 (*0-393-03460-7*) Norton.

Automobile Association Illustrated Guide to France. Automobile Association of England Staff. 1992. 45.00 (*0-393-03456-9*) Norton.

***Automobile Automatic Transmission Guide, 64-82.** 9th ed. (Illus.). 600p. (C). 1994. 225.00 (*0-7605-0357-5*) Rector Pr.

Automobile Body Shop Equipment & Supplies, 1995. American Business Directories Staff. 1995. spiral bd., pap. 410.00 (*1-56105-575-1*) Am Busn Direct.

Automobile Body Shops (East North Central Region), 1995. American Business Directories Staff. 1995. spiral bd., pap. 810.00 (*1-56105-577-8*) Am Busn Direct.

Automobile Body Shops (Mountain Region), 1995. American Business Directories Staff. 1995. spiral bd., pap. 310.00 (*1-56105-578-6*) Am Busn Direct.

Automobile Body Shops (North East Region), 1995. American Business Directories Staff. 1995. spiral bd., pap. 1,035.00 (*1-56105-579-4*) Am Busn Direct.

Automobile Body Shops (Pacific Region), 1995. American Business Directories Staff. 1995. spiral bd., pap. 610.00 (*1-56105-580-8*) Am Busn Direct.

Automobile Body Shops (South Atlantic Region), 1995. American Business Directories Staff. 1995. spiral bd., pap. 785.00 (*1-56105-581-6*) Am Busn Direct.

Automobile Body Shops (South Central Region), 1995. American Business Directories Staff. 1995. spiral bd., pap. 800.00 (*1-56105-582-4*) Am Busn Direct.

Automobile Body Shops (West North Central Region), 1995. American Business Directories Staff. 1995. spiral bd., pap. 465.00 (*1-56105-583-2*) Am Busn Direct.

Automobile Body Shops (7 Regions), 1995. American Business Directories Staff. 1995. spiral bd., pap. 3,625.00 (*1-56105-576-X*) Am Busn Direct.

Automobile Book 1994. Consumer Guide Editors. 256p. (Orig.). 1993. pap. 9.99 (*0-451-82266-8*, Sig) NAL-Dutton.

Automobile Book 1995. Consumer Guide Editors. 256p. 1994. pap. 9.99 (*0-451-82277-3*, Sig) NAL-Dutton.

***Automobile Chemical Market.** 400p. (Orig.). 1994. pap. 1,895.00 (*1-57205-981-8*) Rector Pr.

Automobile Choice & Its Energy Implications. Ed. by Charles Lave. (Illus.). 137p. 1981. pap. write for info. (*0-08-027397-1*, Pergamon Pr) Elsevier.

Automobile Collection: Heritage Plantation of Sandwich. David Brownell. Ed. by G. Melber. LC 86-81676. (Illus.). 72p. (Orig.). 1986. pap. 9.95 (*0-939059-00-2*) Herit Plant Sandwich.

***Automobile Collision Repair Data Imported 92-94.** (Illus.). 600p. (C). 1994. 395.00 (*0-7605-0412-1*) Rector Pr.

***Automobile Collision Repair Data Imported 94.** (Illus.). 600p. (C). 1994. 295.00 (*0-7605-0415-6*) Rector Pr.

***Automobile Collision Repair Data Imported, 94, Non Laminated.** (Illus.). 600p. (C). 1994. 295.00 (*0-7605-0417-2*) Rector Pr.

***Automobile Collision Repair Data U. S. 92-94.** (Illus.). 600p. (C). 1994. 395.00 (*0-7605-0411-3*) Rector Pr.

***Automobile Collision Repair Data U. S. 94.** (Illus.). 600p. (C). 1994. 295.00 (*0-7605-0414-8*) Rector Pr.

***Automobile Collision Repair Data U. S., 94 Non Laminated.** (Illus.). 600p. (C). 1994. 295.00 (*0-7605-0416-4*) Rector Pr.

Automobile Compensation Plan. Patterson H. French. LC 68-58574. (Columbia University. Studies in the Social Sciences: No. 393). reprint ed. 21.00 (*0-404-51393-X*) AMS Pr.

***Automobile Component Locator Guide 86-87.** (Illus.). 600p. (C). 1994. 195.00 (*0-7605-0348-6*) Rector Pr.

***Automobile Component Locator Guide 88.** (Illus.). 600p. (C). 1994. 195.00 (*0-7605-0349-4*) Rector Pr.

***Automobile Component Locator Guide 89-90.** (Illus.). 600p. (C). 1994. 195.00 (*0-7605-0350-8*) Rector Pr.

***Automobile Component Locator Guide 91-92.** (Illus.). 600p. (C). 1994. 195.00 (*0-7605-0351-6*) Rector Pr.

***Automobile Component Locator Guide 93-94.** (Illus.). 600p. (C). 1994. 195.00 (*0-7605-0352-4*) Rector Pr.

***Automobile Crash Estimating Guide U. S.** (Illus.). 600p. 1994. 395.00 (*0-7605-0406-7*) Rector Pr.

Automobile Dealers - New (Eastern Region), 1995. American Business Directories Staff. 1995. spiral bd., pap. 1,135.00 (*1-56105-585-9*) Am Busn Direct.

Automobile Dealers - New (Two Regions), 1995. American Business Directories Staff. 1995. spiral bd., pap. 1,630.00 (*1-56105-584-0*) Am Busn Direct.

Automobile Dealers - New (Western Region), 1995. American Business Directories Staff. 1995. spiral bd., pap. 670.00 (*1-56105-586-7*) Am Busn Direct.

Automobile Design: Twelve Great Designers & Their Work. 2nd ed. Ronald Barker & Anthony Harding. 411p. 1992. 39.00 (*1-56091-210-3*, R-115) Soc Auto Engineers.

Automobile Design Liability, 3 vols., Set. 3rd ed. Center for Auto Safety Staff & Richard M. Goodman. LC 91-76912. 1991. ring bd. 370.00 (*0-685-59882-9*) Clark Boardman Callaghan.

***Automobile Early Model Crash Estimating Guide.** (Illus.). 600p. (Orig.). 1994. pap. 295.00 (*0-7605-0408-3*) Rector Pr.

Automobile Electronic Equipment 1970-71. Geoffrey W. Dummer & J. M. Robertson. LC 72-111933. 1970. 135.00 (*0-08-016037-9*, Pub. by Pergamon Repr UK) Franklin.

***Automobile Electronic Market.** 400p. (Orig.). 1994. pap. 2,295.00 (*1-57205-982-6*) Rector Pr.

Automobile Electronics. Shoichi Washino. (Japanese Technology Reviews Ser.: Vol. 1). 144p. 1989. pap. text ed. 48.00 (*2-88124-285-5*) Gordon & Breach.

***Automobile Emission Control Guide, 66-82.** 3rd ed. (Illus.). 600p. (C). 1994. 225.00 (*0-7605-0381-8*) Rector Pr.

***Automobile Emission Control Guide, 82-83.** 4th ed. (Illus.). 600p. (C). 1994. 195.00 (*0-7605-0382-6*) Rector Pr.

***Automobile Emission Control Guide, 83-84.** 5th ed. (Illus.). 600p. (C). 1994. 195.00 (*0-7605-0383-4*) Rector Pr.

***Automobile Emission Control Guide, 84-85.** 6th ed. (Illus.). 600p. (C). 1994. 195.00 (*0-7605-0384-2*) Rector Pr.

***Automobile Emission Control Guide, 86-87.** 7th ed. (Illus.). 600p. (C). 1994. 195.00 (*0-7605-0385-0*) Rector Pr.

***Automobile Emission Control Guide, 87-88.** 8th ed. (Illus.). 600p. (C). 1994. 195.00 (*0-7605-0386-9*) Rector Pr.

***Automobile Emission Control Guide, 88-89.** 9th ed. (Illus.). 600p. (C). 1994. 195.00 (*0-7605-0387-7*) Rector Pr.

***Automobile Emission Control Guide, 89-90.** 10th ed. (Illus.). 600p. (C). 1994. 195.00 (*0-7605-0388-5*) Rector Pr.

***Automobile Emission Control Guide, 92.** 12th ed. (Illus.). 600p. (C). 1994. 195.00 (*0-7605-0389-3*) Rector Pr.

***Automobile Emission Control System Application Guide 66-94.** (Illus.). 600p. (C). 1994. 195.00 (*0-7605-0390-7*) Rector Pr.

***Automobile Engine Tune up & Electronics 1991-94, 2 vols., Set.** 10th ed. (Illus.). 1200p. (C). 1994. 295.00 (*0-7605-0293-5*) Rector Pr.

Automobile Exhaust in Health & Disease: Medical Analysis Index with Reference Bibliography. Lyton L. Springer. LC 85-47572. 150p. 1987. 39.50 (*0-88164-318-1*); pap. 34.50 (*0-88164-319-X*) ABBE Pubs Assn.

Automobile Facts & Figures. Ed. by Hindustan Motors Ltd., Staff. 1967. 4.50 (*0-910824-16-9*) Kallman.

***Automobile Front End & Brake Guide 85-90.** (Illus.). 600p. (C). 1994. 195.00 (*0-7605-0375-3*) Rector Pr.

***Automobile Front End & Brake Guide 88-92.** (Illus.). 600p. (C). 1994. 195.00 (*0-7605-0376-1*) Rector Pr.

Automobile Frontal Impacts. 1989. 46.00 (*0-89883-439-2*, SP782) Soc Auto Engineers.

Automobile Fuels of the 1980's: A Survey. Jack Frazier. (Illus.). 1978. pap. 4.95 (*0-685-87593-8*) Solar Age Pr.

***Automobile Imported Car Parts & Time Guide 1986-93.** 12th ed. (Illus.). 600p. (C). 1994. 225.00 (*0-7605-0309-5*) Rector Pr.

***Automobile Imported Car Parts & Time Guide 1988-94.** 13th ed. (Illus.). 600p. (C). 1994. 245.00 (*0-7605-0310-9*) Rector Pr.

***Automobile Imported Car Repair Guide 1975-83.** 5th ed. (Illus.). 600p. (C). 1994. 195.00 (*0-7605-0301-X*) Rector Pr.

***Automobile Imported Car Repair Guide 1990-93, 2 vols., Set.** 15th ed. (Illus.). 1200p. (C). 1994. 325.00 (*0-7605-0303-6*) Rector Pr.

***Automobile Imported Car Repair Guide 1991-94, 2 vols., Set.** 16th ed. (Illus.). 1200p. (C). 1994. 325.00 (*0-7605-0304-4*) Rector Pr.

***Automobile Imported Car Repair Manual 1986-89.** 11th ed. (Illus.). 600p. (C). 1994. 195.00 (*0-7605-0302-8*) Rector Pr.

***Automobile Imported Component Locator Guide.** (Illus.). 600p. (C). 1994. 195.00 (*0-7605-0356-7*) Rector Pr.

***Automobile Imported Component Locator Guide.** (Illus.). 600p. (C). 1994. 195.00 (*0-7605-0355-9*) Rector Pr.

***Automobile Imported Component Locator Guide 81-86.** (Illus.). 600p. (C). 1994. 195.00 (*0-7605-0353-2*) Rector Pr.

***Automobile Imported Component Locator Guide 87-88.** (Illus.). 600p. (C). 1994. 195.00 (*0-7605-0354-0*) Rector Pr.

***Automobile Imported Crash Estimating Guide.** (Illus.). 600p. (Orig.). 1994. pap. 395.00 (*0-7605-0407-5*) Rector Pr.

***Automobile Imported Engine Tune up & Electronics Guide 1985-89.** 6th ed. (Illus.). 600p. (C). 1994. 195.00 (*0-7605-0305-2*) Rector Pr.

***Automobile Imported Engine Tune up & Electronics Guide 1989-91, 2 vols., Set.** 8th ed. (Illus.). 1200p. (C). 1994. 295.00 (*0-7605-0306-0*) Rector Pr.

***Automobile Imported Engine Tune up & Electronics Guide 1990-93, 2 vols., Set.** 10th ed. (Illus.). 1200p. (C). 1994. 295.00 (*0-7605-0307-9*) Rector Pr.

***Automobile Imported Engine Tune up & Electronics Guide 1991-94, 2 vols., Set.** 11th ed. (Illus.). 1200p. (C). 1994. 295.00 (*0-7605-0308-7*) Rector Pr.

***Automobile Imported Front End & Brake Guide 87-91.** (Illus.). 600p. (C). 1994. 195.00 (*0-7605-0377-X*) Rector Pr.

***Automobile Imported Front End & Brake Guide 89-92.** (Illus.). 600p. (C). 1994. 195.00 (*0-7605-0378-8*) Rector Pr.

***Automobile Imported Transmission Guide, 77-84.** 2nd ed. (Illus.). 600p. (C). 1994. 225.00 (*0-7605-0360-5*) Rector Pr.

***Automobile Imported Transmission Guide, 86-91.** 5th ed. (Illus.). 600p. (C). 1994. 225.00 (*0-7605-0362-1*) Rector Pr.

***Automobile Imported Transmission Guide, 89-93.** 6th ed. (Illus.). 600p. (C). 1994. 225.00 (*0-7605-0363-X*) Rector Pr.

***Automobile Imported Transmission, 85-89.** 4th ed. (Illus.). 600p. (C). 1994. 225.00 (*0-7605-0361-3*) Rector Pr.

***Automobile Imported Wiring Guide 1983-84.** 2nd ed. (Illus.). 600p. (C). 1994. 295.00 (*0-7605-0331-1*) Rector Pr.

***Automobile Imported Wiring Guide 1985-86.** 3rd ed. (Illus.). 600p. (C). 1994. 295.00 (*0-7605-0332-X*) Rector Pr.

***Automobile Imported Wiring Guide 1987.** 4th ed. (Illus.). 600p. (C). 1994. 295.00 (*0-7605-0333-8*) Rector Pr.

***Automobile Imported Wiring Guide 1988.** 5th ed. (Illus.). 600p. (C). 1994. 295.00 (*0-7605-0334-6*) Rector Pr.

***Automobile Imported Wiring Guide 1989.** 6th ed. (Illus.). 600p. (C). 1994. 295.00 (*0-7605-0335-4*) Rector Pr.

***Automobile Imported Wiring Guide 1990.** 7th ed. (Illus.). 600p. (C). 1994. 295.00 (*0-7605-0336-2*) Rector Pr.

***Automobile Imported Wiring Guide 1991.** 8th ed. (Illus.). 600p. (C). 1994. 295.00 (*0-7605-0337-0*) Rector Pr.

***Automobile Imported Wiring Guide 1992.** 9th ed. (Illus.). 600p. (C). 1994. 295.00 (*0-7605-0338-9*) Rector Pr.

***Automobile Imported Wiring Guide 1993.** 10th ed. (Illus.). 600p. (C). 1994. 295.00 (*0-7605-0339-7*) Rector Pr.

Automobile Industry: Its Economic & Commercial Development. Ralph C. Epstein. LC 72-5045. (Technology & Society Ser.). (Illus.). 429p. 1972. reprint ed. 29.95 (*0-405-04697-9*) Ayer.

Automobile Industry: The Coming of Age of Capitalism's Favorite Child. Edward D. Kennedy. LC 68-56238. (Library of Early American Business & Industry: No. 43). 333p. 1972. reprint ed. 39.50 (*0-678-00906-6*) Kelley.

Automobile Industry in Japan: A Study of Ancillary Firm Development. Konosuke Odaka et al. (Hitotsubashi University Economic Research Ser.: No. 26). 356p. 1988. 79.00 (*4-314-00487-8*) OUP.

Automobile Industry since 1945. Lawrence J. White. LC 76-148939. (Illus.). 362p. reprint ed. pap. 103.20 (*0-8357-5918-0*, 2051939) Bks Demand.

Automobile Industry, 1896-1920. Ed. by George S. May. 1989. 85.00 (*0-8160-2084-1*) Facts on File.

Automobile Industry, 1920-1980. Ed. by George S. May. (Encyclopedia of American Business History & Biography Ser.). (Illus.). 544p. 1989. 85.00 (*0-8160-2083-3*) Facts on File.

Automobile Insurance: A Long-Range Outlook. Sajjad A. Hashmi. LC 72-619522. (Sesquicentennial Insurance Ser.). (Illus.). 260p. 1972. 8.95 (*0-87925-000-3*) Ind U Busn Res.

Automobile Insurance: Actuarial Models. Jean Lemaire. (S. S. Huebner International Ser.). 1985. lib. bdg. 63.00 (*0-89838-166-5*) Huebner Foun Insur.

Automobile Insurance: Actuarial Models. Jean Lemaire. (C). 1985. 335.00 (*0-685-33794-4*, Pub. by Witherby & Co UK) St Mut.

Automobile Insurance & Road Accident Prevention. OECD Staff. 128p. (Orig.). 1990. pap. 32.00 (*92-64-13409-3*) OECD.

Automobile Insurance Database. 186p. (C). 1991. 50.00 (*0-89382-185-3*) Nat Assn Insu Comm.

Automobile Insurance in Ontario. O'Donnell. 472p. 1991. 90.00 (*0-409-89361-7*) Butterworth Legal Pubs.

Automobile Insurance Publications. Christian L. Wiktor. xiii, 220p. (Orig.). 1973. pap. text ed. 14.00 (*0-8377-1300-5*) Rothman.

Automobile Leasing vs. Financing: A Black & White Comparison. Curtis W. Sipe & Michael S. Waltemeyer. (Orig.). (C). 1988. pap. write for info. (*0-945694-00-8*) Curtis Assocs.

***Automobile Liability Claims: Insurance Company Philosophies & Practices.** Jerry Rosenbloom. (C). 1968. 9.50 (*0-256-00677-6*) Irwin.

Automobile Liability Insurance, 3 vols. 2nd ed. Irwin E. Schermer. LC 81-15532. 1981. ring bd. 395.00 (*0-87632-365-4*) Clark Boardman Callaghan.

Automobile Life Cycle Tools & Recycling Technologies: Twenty Papers. 1993. 56.00 (*1-56091-351-7*, SP-966) Soc Auto Engineers.

Automobile Mechanic Certification Tests. David Sharp. 12.95 (*0-685-11238-1*) S&S Trade.

***Automobile Parts & Time Guide 1987-94.** 66th ed. (Illus.). 600p. (C). 1994. 225.00 (*0-7605-0294-3*) Rector Pr.

Automobile Photography Handbook. Curt Scott. (Photographing Your Car for Publication Ser.). (Illus.). 8p. 1989. pap. 3.50 (*0-9614882-4-7*) Crown Pub CA.

Automobile Race Car Equipment, 1995. American Business Directories Staff. 1995. spiral bd., pap. 465.00 (*1-56105-587-5*) Am Busn Direct.

Automobile Radiator Repair Shops, 1995. American Business Directories Staff. 1995. spiral bd., pap. 700.00 (*1-56105-588-3*) Am Busn Direct.

Automobile Radio & Stereo Systems, 1995. American Business Directories Staff. 1995. spiral bd., pap. 505.00 (*1-56105-589-1*) Am Busn Direct.

Automobile Record Breakers: From Rocket to road Car. David Tremayne. 1989. 12.98 (*1-55521-454-1*) Bk Sales Inc.

***Automobile Repair Guide: Early Model 69-75.** 6th ed. (Illus.). 600p. (C). 1994. 195.00 (*0-7605-0393-1*) Rector Pr.

***Automobile Repair Guide: Early Model 74-79.** 8th ed. (Illus.). 600p. (C). 1994. 195.00 (*0-7605-0394-X*) Rector Pr.

***Automobile Repair Guide Vintage I 35-53.** (Illus.). 600p. (C). 1994. 195.00 (*0-7605-0391-5*) Rector Pr.

***Automobile Repair Guide Vintage II 53-61.** (Illus.). 600p. (C). 1994. 195.00 (*0-7605-0392-3*) Rector Pr.

***Automobile Repair Guide, 80-86.** 49th ed. (Illus.). 600p. (C). 1994. 195.00 (*0-7605-0395-8*) Rector Pr.

***Automobile Repair Guide, 83-89.** 52nd ed. (Illus.). 600p. (C). 1994. 195.00 (*0-7605-0396-6*) Rector Pr.

***Automobile Repair Manual 1991-94, 2 vols., Set.** 57th ed. (Illus.). 1200p. (C). 1994. 295.00 (*0-7605-0292-7*) Rector Pr.

***Automobile Replacement Assemblies Crash Estimating Guide Imported.** 12th ed. (Illus.). 600p. (C). 1994. 195.00 (*0-7605-0410-5*) Rector Pr.

***Automobile Replacement Assemblies Crash Estimating Guide U. S.** 12th ed. (Illus.). 600p. (C). 1994. 195.00 (*0-7605-0409-1*) Rector Pr.

Automobile Revolution: The Impact of an Industry. Jean P. Bardou et al. Tr. by James M. Laux. LC 81-11571. (Illus.). 352p. reprint ed. pap. 100.40 (*0-8357-3903-1*, 2036637) Bks Demand.

Automobile Safety: Present & Future Technology, Nine Papers. 1992. 35.00 (*1-56091-280-4*, SP-925) Soc Auto Engineers.

Automobile Sales Manager's Complete Success Formula: A Current Guide to Managing a Profitable Car Dealership. Jon McCormick. 330p. (Orig.). 1994. 39.95 (*1-57002-003-5*); pap. 29.95 (*1-57002-004-3*) Univ Publng Hse.

***Automobile Specification Guide 1987-93.** (Illus.). 600p. (C). 1994. 165.00 (*0-7605-0290-0*) Rector Pr.

***Automobile Specification Guide 1988-94.** (Illus.). 600p. (C). 1994. 165.00 (*0-7605-0291-9*) Rector Pr.

***Automobile Technical Service Guides 80-83 Imports.** (Illus.). 600p. (C). 1994. pap. 195.00 (*0-7605-0400-8*) Rector Pr.

***Automobile Technical Service Guides 84-85 U. S. Cars & Light Trucks.** (Illus.). 600p. (C). 1994. text ed. 195.00 (*0-7605-0398-2*) Rector Pr.

***Automobile Technical Service Guides 84-86 Imports.** (Illus.). 600p. (C). 1994. pap. 195.00 (*0-7605-0401-6*) Rector Pr.

***Automobile Technical Service Guides 86-93 U. S. Cars & Light Trucks.** (Illus.). 600p. (C). 1994. pap. 195.00 (*0-7605-0399-0*) Rector Pr.

***Automobile Technical Service Guides 87-89 Imports.** (Illus.). 600p. (C). 1994. pap. 195.00 (*0-7605-0402-4*) Rector Pr.

***Automobile Technical Service Guides 89-93 Imports.** (Illus.). 600p. (C). 1994. pap. 195.00 (*0-7605-0403-2*) Rector Pr.

Automobile Technician Certification Tests: National Institute for Automotive Service Excellence Exam. 3rd ed. ARCO Editorial Board Staff & Sharp. LC 93-34094. 1994. pap. 16.00 (*0-671-87071-8*, Arco Test) P-H Gen Ref & Trav.

Automobile Technicians Refresher Course, 5 vols., Set. 481p. 1988. 64.95 (*0-685-46967-0*, H M Gousha); audio 99.85 (*0-685-46968-9*, H M Gousha) P-H Gen Ref & Trav.

Automobile Technicians Refresher Course: Automatic Transmissions - Transaxles, Manual Drivetrains & Axles. 93p. 1987. pap. 14.95 (*0-13-032418-3*, H M Gousha) P-H Gen Ref & Trav.

Automobile Technicians Refresher Course: Electrical Systems, Heating & Air Conditioning. 104p. 1987. pap. 14.95 (*0-13-032434-5*, H M Gousha) P-H Gen Ref & Trav.

Automobile Technicians Refresher Course: Engine Performance. 115p. 1987. pap. 14.95 (*0-13-032459-0*, H M Gousha) P-H Gen Ref & Trav.

Automobile Technicians Refresher Course: Engine Repair. 91p. 1987. pap. 14.95 (*0-13-032442-6*, H M Gousha) P-H Gen Ref & Trav.

Automobile Technicians Refresher Course: Suspension & Steering, & Brakes. 78p. 1987. pap. 14.95 (*0-13-032426-4*, H M Gousha) P-H Gen Ref & Trav.

Automobile Technology of the Future. Ulrich Seiffert & Peter Walzer. 242p. 1991. 69.00 (*1-56091-080-1*, R-107) Soc Auto Engineers.

Automobile Theft Investigator: A Learning & Reference Text for the Automobile Theft Investigator, the Police Supervisor, & the Student. Claude W. Cook. (Illus.). 296p. (C). 1987. 53.95x (*0-398-05240-9*) C C Thomas.

***Automobile Transmission Guide, 86-90.** 3rd ed. (Illus.). 600p. (C). 1994. 225.00 (*0-7605-0358-3*) Rector Pr.

***Automobile Transmission Guide, 90-94.** 5th ed. (Illus.). 600p. (C). 1994. 225.00 (*0-7605-0359-1*) Rector Pr.

***Automobile Transmission Parts & Time Guide, 84-92.** 2nd ed. (Illus.). 600p. (C). 1994. 225.00 (*0-7605-0364-8*) Rector Pr.

***Automobile Transmission Parts & Time Guide, 87-94.** 3rd ed. (Illus.). 600p. (C). 1994. 225.00 (*0-7605-0365-6*) Rector Pr.

Automobile Transmission Repair Shops, 1995. American Business Directories Staff. 1995. spiral bd., pap. 1,260.00 (*1-56105-590-5*) Am Busn Direct.

***Automobile Tune Up & Electronics Guide, 89-90, 2 vols., Set.** 6th ed. (Illus.). 1200p. (C). 1994. 295.00 (*0-7605-0397-4*) Rector Pr.

Automobile Under the Blue Eagle: Labor, Management, & the Automobile Manufacturing Code. Sidney Fine. LC 63-14016. 1963. 32.50 (*0-472-32947-2*) U of Mich Pr.

***Automobile Vacuum & Wiring Diagram Guide: Ford - Chrysler 1983-84.** (Illus.). 600p. (C). 1994. 195.00 (*0-7605-0312-5*) Rector Pr.

***Automobile Vacuum & Wiring Diagram Guide: Ford - Chrysler 1985.** (Illus.). 600p. (C). 1994. 195.00 (*0-7605-0314-1*) Rector Pr.

***Automobile Vacuum & Wiring Diagram Guide: Ford - Chrysler 1986.** (Illus.). 600p. (C). 1994. 195.00 (*0-7605-0316-8*) Rector Pr.

***Automobile Vacuum & Wiring Diagram Guide: GM 1983-84.** (Illus.). 600p. (C). 1994. 195.00 (*0-7605-0311-7*) Rector Pr.

***Automobile Vacuum & Wiring Diagram Guide: GM 1985.** (Illus.). 600p. (C). 1994. 195.00 (*0-7605-0313-3*) Rector Pr.

***Automobile Vacuum & Wiring Diagram Guide: GM 1986.** (Illus.). 600p. (C). 1994. 195.00 (*0-7605-0315-X*) Rector Pr.

***Automobile Warranty Law: State & Federal Lemon Rights.** suppl. ed. C. Victoria Woodward. 651p. 1994. 85.00 (*1-55834-064-5*) Michie Butterworth.

Automobile Washing Tokens. H. V. Ford & J. M. Coffee. (Illus.). 208p. 1986. 20.00 (*0-318-21990-5*) Am Vecturist.

Automobile Waste Report. Katie DeBoer. 175p. (Orig.). (C). 1994. pap. text ed. 45.00 (*0-7881-0586-8*) Diane Pub.

***Automobile Wiring Guide: Ford - Chrysler 1987.** (Illus.). 600p. (C). 1994. 195.00 (*0-7605-0318-4*) Rector Pr.

***Automobile Wiring Guide: Ford - Chrysler 1988.** (Illus.). 600p. (C). 1994. 195.00 (*0-7605-0320-6*) Rector Pr.

***Automobile Wiring Guide: Ford - Chrysler 1989.** (Illus.). 600p. (C). 1994. 195.00 (*0-7605-0322-2*) Rector Pr.

***Automobile Wiring Guide: Ford - Chrysler 1990.** (Illus.). 600p. (C). 1994. 195.00 (*0-7605-0324-9*) Rector Pr.

***Automobile Wiring Guide: Ford - Chrysler 1991.** (Illus.). 600p. (C). 1994. 195.00 (*0-7605-0326-5*) Rector Pr.

***Automobile Wiring Guide: Ford - Chrysler 1992.** (Illus.). 600p. (C). 1994. 195.00 (*0-7605-0328-1*) Rector Pr.

***Automobile Wiring Guide: Ford - Chrysler 1993.** (Illus.). 600p. (C). 1994. 195.00 (*0-7605-0330-3*) Rector Pr.

***Automobile Wiring Guide: GM 1987.** (Illus.). 600p. (C). 1994. 195.00 (*0-7605-0317-6*) Rector Pr.

***Automobile Wiring Guide: GM 1988.** (Illus.). 600p. (C). 1994. 195.00 (*0-7605-0319-2*) Rector Pr.

***Automobile Wiring Guide: GM 1989.** (Illus.). 600p. (C). 1994. 195.00 (*0-7605-0321-4*) Rector Pr.

***Automobile Wiring Guide: GM 1990.** (Illus.). 600p. (C). 1994. 195.00 (*0-7605-0323-0*) Rector Pr.

***Automobile Wiring Guide: GM 1991.** (Illus.). 600p. (C). 1994. 195.00 (*0-7605-0325-7*) Rector Pr.

***Automobile Wiring Guide: GM 1992.** (Illus.). 600p. (C). 1994. 195.00 (*0-7605-0327-3*) Rector Pr.

***Automobile Wiring Guide: GM 1993.** (Illus.). 600p. (C). 1994. 195.00 (*0-7605-0329-X*) Rector Pr.

Automobile Workers & the American Dream. 2nd ed. Ely Chinoy. 192p. (C). 1992. pap. 12.95 (*0-252-06263-9*) U of Ill Pr.

***Automobile Year No. 42: 1994-95.** (Illus.). 280p. 1995. 49.95 (*2-88324-035-3*, Pub. by Editions JR SZ) Motorbooks Intl.

Automobile Year Number Thirty-Eight, 1990-1991. 280p. 39.95 (*2-88324-012-4*, 3-AQ-0078) Auto Quarterly.

Automobile Year Number Thirty Seven, 1989-1990. 282p. 1989. 39.95 (*2-88324-006-X*, 3-AQ-0079) Auto Quarterly.

Automobiles. James L. Branton & Jim D. Lovett. (Trial Lawyer's Ser.: Vol. 2). (Illus.). 378p. 1985. ring bd. 135.00 (*1-878337-01-7*) Knowles Law.

Automobiles. J. Cooper. (Traveling Machines Ser.). (J). 1991. 8.95 (*0-86592-495-3*) Rourke Enter.

Automobiles: An Educational Coloring Book. Spizzirri Publishing Co. Staff. Ed. by Linda Spizzirri. (Illus.). 32p. (J). (gr. 1-8). 1981. pap. 1.75 (*0-86545-032-3*) Spizzirri.

Automobiles: Connecting People & Places. Myra H. Immell. LC 93-4553. (Encyclopedia of Discovery & Invention Ser.). (J). (gr. 5-8). 1994. 17.95 (*1-56006-226-6*) Lucent Bks.

***Automobiles & Alcohol: The Deadly Cocktail.** Alyce Schroeder. 60p. (YA). (gr. 7-12). 1994. pap. write for info. (*1-57515-043-3*) PPI Pubng.

***Automobiles & Pollution.** Paul Degobert. 485p. 1995. 95.00 (*1-56091-563-3*, R150) Soc Auto Engineers.

***Automobiles & the Future: Competition, Cooperation, & Change, No. 10.** Ed. by Robert E. Cole. x, 106p. 1983. pap. 9.00 (*0-939512-14-9*) U MI Japan.

Automobiles As an Investment. Stonehouse. 1982. 17.95 (*0-02-606210-0*) Macmillan.

Automobiles of America: Milestones, Pioneers, Roll Call, Highlights. 4th rev. ed. Motor Vehicle Manufacturers Association of the United States Staff. LC 73-19838. 304p. reprint ed. pap. 86.70 (*0-8357-5919-9*, 2031016) Bks Demand.

Automobiles of Distinction: The Imperial Palace Collection, Las Vegas, Nevada. Henry R. Rasmussen. (Illus.). 192p. 1990. 300.00 (*0-87938-461-1*) Motorbooks Intl.

Automobiles of the '50s. Consumer Guide Auto Editors. (Illus.). 96p. 1993. 12.98 (*0-7853-0110-0*, 1013500) Pubns Intl Ltd.

Automobiles of the '60s. Consumer Guide Auto Editors. (Illus.). 96p. 1993. 12.98 (*0-7853-0143-7*, 1002800) Pubns Intl Ltd.

Automobilia. John Gunnell. LC 94-75301. (Automobilia Ser.). (Illus.). 275p. 1994. pap. 19.95 (*0-87341-295-8*) Krause Pubns.

Automobilia of Europe: Reference & Price Guide. Alistair Morris & Gordon Gardiner. (Illus.). 256p. 1992. reprint ed. 49.50 (*1-85149-163-5*) Antique Collect.

Automorphic Forms & Adele Groups. Stephen S. Gelbart. (Annals of Mathematics Studies: No. 83). 280p. 1975. 39.50 (*0-691-08156-5*) Princeton U Pr.

Automorphic Forms & Geometry of Arithmetic Varieties. Ed. by Ki-ichiro Hashimoto. (Advanced Studies in Pure Mathematics: Vol. 15). 530p. 1989. text ed. 140.00 (*0-12-330580-2*) Acad Pr.

Automorphic Forms & Number Theory. Ed. by Ichiro Satake. (Advanced Studies in Pure Mathematics: No. 7). 366p. 1987. 141.00 (*0-444-87940-4*, North Holland) Elsevier.

Automorphic Forms & the Picard Number of an Elliptic Surface, Vol. 5. Peter F. Stiller. (Aspects of Mathematics Ser.). vi, 194p. 1984. pap. 27.00 (*3-528-08587-8*, Pub. by Vieweg & Sohn GW) Ballen Bkslr.

Automorphic Forms of Several Variables: Taniguchi Symposium, Katata, Vol. 46. Ed. by Ichiro Satake et al. (Progress in Mathematics Ser.: Vol. 46). 398p. 1984. 49.50 (*0-8176-3172-0*) Birkhauser.

Automorphic Forms on GL 2, Pt. 2. H. Jacquet. LC 76-108338. (Lecture Notes in Mathematics Ser.: Vol. 278). 142p. 1972. pap. 19.00 (*0-387-05931-8*) Spr-Verlag.

Automorphic Forms on GL (3r R) D. Bump. (Lecture Notes in Mathematics Ser.: Vol. 1083). xi, 184p. 1984. pap. 31.10 (*0-387-13864-1*) Spr-Verlag.

Automorphic Forms on Semisimple Lie Groups. Harish-Chandra. (Lecture Notes in Mathematics Ser.: Vol. 62). 1986. pap. 19.00 (*0-387-04232-6*) Spr-Verlag.

Automorphic Forms, Representations & L-Functions, 2 vols., Pt. 1. Ed. by A. Borel & W. Casselman. LC 78-21184. (Proceedings of Symposia in Pure Mathematics Ser., Humboldt State University, Arcata, CA, July 29-August 16, 1974: Vol. 33). 322p. 1990. 36.00 (*0-8218-1435-4*, PSPUM-33.1) Am Math.

Automorphic Forms, Representations & L-Functions, 2 vols., Pt. 2. Ed. by A. Borel & W. Casselman. LC 78-21184. (Proceedings of Symposia in Pure Mathematics Ser., Humboldt State University, Arcata, CA, July 29-August 16, 1974: Vol. 33). 382p. 1990. pap. 36.00 (*0-8218-1437-0*, PSPUM-33.2) Am Math.

Automorphic Forms, Representations & L-Functions, 2 vols., Set. Ed. by A. Borel & W. Casselman. LC 78-21184. (Proceedings of Symposia in Pure Mathematics Ser., Humboldt State University, Arcata, CA, July 29-August 16, 1974: Vol. 33). 704p. 1990. pap. 60.00 (*0-8218-1474-5*, PSPUM-33) Am Math.

Automorphic Forms, Shimura Varieties, & L-Functions, Vol. 1: Proceedings of a Conference Held at the University of Michigan, Ann Arbor, July 6-16, 1988. Ed. by Laurent Clozel & James S. Milne. (Perspectives in Mathematics Ser.). 438p. 1989. text ed. 73.00 (*0-12-176651-9*) Acad Pr.

An Asterisk (*) at the beginning of an entry indicates that the title is appearing in BIP for the first time.

An Asterisk (*) at the beginning of an entry indicates that the title is appearing in BIP for the first time.

A

Automotive Fundamentals. 3rd ed. Ernest A. Venk & Walter E. Billiet. LC 74-112971. 575p. reprint ed. pap. 163.90 (*0-8357-5924-5*, 2004579) Bks Demand.

Automotive Fundamentals: Text-Laboratory Activities Manual. Lynn Mosher. 160p. (C). 1991. pap. text ed. 14.95 (*0-8403-6780-5*) Kendall-Hunt.

Automotive Giants of America: Men Who Are Making Our Motor Industry. Bertie C. Forbes & Orline D. Foster. LC 72-5603. (Essay Index Reprint Ser.). 1977. reprint ed. 21.95 (*0-8369-2989-6*) Ayer.

Automotive Glassfibre: A Practical Guide to Moulding & Repairing. Dennis Foy. (Illus.). 192p. 1987. pap. 21.95 (*0-947981-19-5*, Pub. by Motor Racing UK) Motorbooks Intl.

Automotive Hand Tools Explained. George Chrestionson. LC 79-730979. 1980. student ed 5.00 (*0-8064-0125-7*, 430); audio 219.00 (*0-8064-0126-5*) Bergwall.

Automotive Heating & Air Conditioning. Tom Birch. LC 94-2467. 352p. 1994. pap. text ed. 42.00 (*0-13-176587-6*) P-H.

Automotive Heating & Cooling. 1986. 19.00 (*0-89883-939-4*, SP668) Soc Auto Engineers.

Automotive History Collection of the Detroit Public Library: A Simplified Guide to Its Holdings, 2 Vols, Set. Detroit Public Library Staff. 1970. lib. bdg. 220.00 (*0-8161-0718-1*, Hall Library) G K Hall.

Automotive Ignition Systems: Diagnosis & Repair. Frank C. Derato. LC 81-8285. 320p. 1982. text ed. 29.95 (*0-07-016501-7*) McGraw.

Automotive Industries in Developing Countries. Jack Baranson. LC 77-85339. (World Bank Staff Occasional Papers: No. 8). 120p. reprint ed. pap. 34.20 (*0-8357-5925-3*, 2021733) Bks Demand.

***Automotive Industry.** 1994. write for info. (*1-879087-39-1*) Assn I M&R.

Automotive Industry in India. Ed. by Hindustan Motors, Ltd. Staff. 1966. 3.75 (*0-910824-14-2*) Kallman.

Automotive Information Systems & Electronic Displays: Recent Developments. 1989. 19.00 (*0-89883-697-2*, SP770) Soc Auto Engineers.

Automotive Literature Index: 1947-1976. Angelo Wallace. 335p. (Orig.). pap. 29.95 (*0-9606804-3-8*) Wallace Pub.

Automotive Literature Index: 1977-1981. Angelo Wallace. 327p. 1982. pap. 29.95 (*0-9606804-4-6*) Wallace Pub.

Automotive Machine Shop. J. F. Reynolds. (C). 1985. text ed. 40.00 (*0-8359-0346-X*, Reston) P-H.

Automotive Maintenance & Repair: A Source Guide. 1991. lib. bdg. 75.00 (*0-8490-4844-3*) Gordon Pr.

Automotive Maintenance Supervisor. Jack Rudman. (Career Examination Ser.: C-2096). 1994. pap. 27.95 (*0-8373-2096-8*) Nat Learn.

Automotive Manual Transmissions & Power Trains. 6th ed. William H. Crouse & Donald L. Anglin. LC 81-17206. (Illus.). 352p. 1983. text ed. 27.95 (*0-07-014776-0*) McGraw.

Automotive Mechanic. Jack Rudman. (Career Examination Ser.: C-1131). 1994. pap. 23.95 (*0-8373-1131-4*) Nat Learn.

Automotive Mechanics. 8th ed. William H. Crouse. LC 79-12845. (Illus.). 1980. text ed. 34.95 (*0-07-014820-1*) McGraw.

Automotive Mechanics. 9th ed. William H. Crouse & Donald L. Anglin. 672p. 1985. text ed. 34.95 (*0-07-014860-0*); 15.95 (*0-07-014871-6*) McGraw.

Automotive Mechanics. 10th ed. William H. Crouse & Donald L. Anglin. LC 92-36588. 1992. write for info. (*0-02-800943-6*) Glencoe.

Automotive Mechanics. 10th ed. William H. Crouse. 1992. 43.15 (*0-07-015013-3*) McGraw.

Automotive Microprocessors Explained. Jim Hannemann. 1984. student ed 8.00 (*0-8064-0203-2*, 481); audio 279.00 (*0-8064-0204-0*) Bergwall.

Automotive Multiplexing. 1987. 19.00 (*0-89883-978-5*, SP707) Soc Auto Engineers.

***Automotive Multiplexing Technology: 1995 International Congress & Exposition Meeting.** 1995. pap. 74.00 (*1-56091-620-6*, SP1070) Soc Auto Engineers.

Automotive Operation & Maintenance. rev. ed. E. Christopher Cone. 300p. 1991. 14.95 (*0-86619-310-3*) Vols Tech Asst.

Automotive Paint Handbook. John Pfanstiehl. LC 92-14868. (Illus.). 176p. 1992. 14.95 (*1-55788-034-4*, HP Books) Berkley Pub.

***Automotive Paints & Coatings.** Ed. by Gordon Fettis. LC 94-45291. 1994. write for info. (*3-527-28637-3*) VCH Pubs.

***Automotive Panic Button: What to Do When You Don't Know What to Do with Your Car!** David D. Solomon. 176p. 1994. pap. 9.95 (*1-880325-10-1*) Borderlnds MD.

Automotive Parts Supervisor. Jack Rudman. (Career Examination Ser.: C-2841). 1994. pap. 27.95 (*0-8373-2841-1*) Nat Learn.

Automotive Pollution Control. Peter Novellino. LC 81-730757. (C). 1982. student ed 7.00 (*0-8064-0157-5*, 447); audio 319.00 (*0-8064-0158-3*) Bergwall.

Automotive Power Train Systems. Jay Webster. LC 80-70124. (Illus.). 304p. reprint ed. pap. 86.70 (*0-8357-8810-5*, 2033291) Bks Demand.

Automotive Power Trains. Frank J. Thiessen & Dales Davis. (C). 1984. pap. text ed. 56.00 (*0-8359-0344-3*) P-H.

Automotive Power Trains. 2nd ed. Sheldon L. Abbott. 256p. 1987. pap. text ed. 23.00 (*0-02-810010-7*); 4.28 (*0-02-810020-4*) Glencoe.

Automotive Preview, Nineteen Ninety. 16p. 1990. 2.95 (*0-685-46969-7*, H M Gousha) P-H Gen Ref & Trav.

Automotive Preview 1985. Chek-Chart Staff. (Illus.). 16p. (C). 1984. pap. text ed. 2.25 (*0-88098-025-7*, H M Gousha) P-H Gen Ref & Trav.

Automotive Principles: Repair & Service, Vol. II. Don Knowles. (Illus.). 400p. 1988. pap. text ed. 19.25 (*0-8359-9378-7*, Reston) P-H.

Automotive Principles: Theory & Fundamentals, Vol. I. Don Knowles. (Illus.). 484p. 1988. text ed. 29.95 (*0-8359-9376-0*, Reston) P-H.

Automotive Principles & Service. 3rd ed. Frank J. Thiessen & Davis N. Dales. 1040p. 1989. text ed. 63.00 (*0-13-053935-X*) P-H.

Automotive Principles & Service. 4th ed. Frank J. Thiessen & Davis N. Dales. LC 93-115. 1993. text ed. 67.00 (*0-13-336561-1*) P-H.

Automotive Radiator Construction & Restoration for Antique & Classic. F. L. Curfman. LC 76-6299. Orig. Title: Manual of Automotive Radiator Construction & Repair. (Illus.). 1976. reprint ed. 6.95 (*0-911160-00-0*) Post Group.

Automotive Radiators Manufactured by the Electroforming Process. University of Michigan Staff. 113p. 1964. 16.95 (*0-317-34497-8*, 37) Intl Copper.

Automotive Rebuilders Hazardous Materials Program Employee Training Manual. Mike Rager. (Illus.). (Orig.). (C). 1989. pap. write for info. (*0-318-65936-0*) Amer Hazmat.

Automotive Reference: A New Approach - to the World of Auto & Related Information. G. J. Davis. 470p. (Orig.). (YA). (gr. 7-12). 1987. 39.95 (*0-937591-01-7*); pap. 24.95 (*0-937591-00-9*) Whitehorse.

Automotive Repair Service: Start & Run a Money-Making Business. Dan Ramsey. LC 93-38576. 1994. pap. text ed. 17.95 (*0-07-051363-5*) TAB Bks.

Automotive Repair Shop Hazardous Materials Program Employee Training Manual. Mike Rager. (Illus.). (Orig.). (C). 1989. pap. write for info. (*0-318-65934-4*) Amer Hazmat.

Automotive Safety: Anatomy, Injury, Testing & Regulation. Jeffrey A. Pike. 184p. 1990. text ed. 79.00 (*1-56091-007-0*, R103) Soc Auto Engineers.

Automotive Science. L. E. Jensen et al. LC 76-3940. (C). 1977. teacher ed 12.00 (*0-8273-1303-9*); pap. 21.95 (*0-8273-1302-0*) Delmar.

Automotive Scrap Recycling: Processes, Prices, & Prospects. James W. Sawyer. LC 74-3101. (Resources for the Future Ser.). (Illus.). 160p. (C). 1974. 17.00 (*0-8018-1620-3*) Johns Hopkins.

Automotive Scrap Recycling: Processes, Prices, & Prospects. James W. Sawyer. LC 74-3101. (Illus.). 160p. reprint ed. pap. 45.60 (*0-8357-5926-1*, 2030220) Bks Demand.

Automotive Sealing. 164p. 1992. pap. 56.00 (*1-56091-238-3*, SP-921) Soc Auto Engineers.

Automotive Seals: An Update. 1989. 19.00 (*0-89883-433-3*, SP776) Soc Auto Engineers.

Automotive Security; Sound; Navigation, Location & Satellite Messaging Systems - Markets, Technologies & Opportunities: 1990-1995 Analysis: Active-Passive-SRVS-Inertial Mapping-RDSS-Loran C-Meteor Scatter-GPS-IVHS-Speakers-Cassette - CD-Radios-EQ's-Amps-Tuners. Dennis M. Zogbi. (Illus.). 180p. 1990. pap. text ed. 995.00 (*1-878218-09-3*) World Info Tech.

Automotive Sensors. M. H. Westbrook & J. D. Turner. (Sensors Ser.). (Illus.). 384p. 1994. 130.00 (*0-7503-0293-3*) IOP Pub.

Automotive Sensors: A Survey on Technology & Markets, No. 67. Richard K. Miller & Terri C. Walker. LC 88-84057. (Survey on Technology & Markets Ser.: No. 67). 50p. 1989. pap. text ed. 200.00 (*1-55865-109-8*) Future Tech Surveys.

Automotive Sensory Systems. Ed. by Christopher Nwagboso. LC 92-47248. (Road Vehicle Automation Ser.). 1993. write for info. (*0-412-45880-2*) Chapman & Hall.

Automotive Service Business: Operation & Management. William H. Crouse. LC 72-666. 1972. text ed. 30.95 (*0-07-014605-5*) McGraw.

Automotive Service Industry in the 1990's. 1988. 19.00 (*0-89883-688-3*, SP761) Soc Auto Engineers.

Automotive Service Management. Frank J. Thiessen. 243p. (C). 1989. text ed. 30.75 (*0-15-504375-7*) SCP.

Automotive Service Marketing: The Complete Guide to Guerrilla Marketing Your Business & Wrenching Customers Away from Your Competitors. Mark Handley & Sal Fariello. Ed. by Vera Fariello. LC 90-91534. (Illus.). 422p. (Orig.). 1990. per. 65.00 (*0-929574-01-X*) SFT Pub.

Automotive Serviceman. Jack Rudman. (Career Examination Ser.: C-65). 1994. pap. 23.95 (*0-8373-0065-7*) Nat Learn.

Automotive Simulation, Ninety-One: 3rd European Symposium, Schliersee, FRG October 28-30, 1991. Ed. by M. R. Heller. (Illus.). x, 250p. 1991. 69.00 (*0-387-54447-X*) Spr-Verlag.

***Automotive Stamping Technology: 1995 International Congress & Exposition Meeting.** 1995. pap. 74.00 (*1-56091-617-6*, SP1067) Soc Auto Engineers.

Automotive Steering & Suspension Systems. William L. Husselbee. 416p. 1988. pap. 26.67 (*0-318-37857-4*) P-H.

Automotive Steering & Suspension Systems: Fundamentals & Service. (Illus.). 220p. 1988. pap. text ed. 24.95 (*0-317-62411-3*) P-H.

Automotive Steering, Suspension & Alignment. James D. Halderman. LC 94-2468. 384p. 1994. pap. text ed. 45.00 (*0-13-845579-1*) P-H.

Automotive Steering, Suspension, & Braking Systems: Principles & Service. Frank J. Thiessen & David N. Dales. (C). 1982. teacher ed write for info. (*0-8359-0292-7*, Reston); pap. text ed. 57.00 (*0-8359-0290-0*, Reston) P-H.

Automotive Steering, Suspension & Wheel Alignment. M. E. Bacon. 128p. 1988. 24.95 (*0-07-079577-0*) McGraw.

Automotive Steering, Suspension, & Wheel Alignment, Set. Chek-Chart Staff. Ed. by Janette E. Kok. LC 92-30385. (C). 1993. text ed. 49.00 (*0-06-500167-2*) HarpCollege.

Automotive Supercharging & Turbo Charging Systems. John D. Humpries. (Illus.). 176p. 1992. pap. 19.95 (*0-87938-657-6*) Motorbooks Intl.

***Automotive Supercharging & Turbocharging Systems.** John Humpries. (Illus.). 160p. 1995. 19.95 (*0-85429-880-0*) Haynes Pubns.

Automotive Suspension & Steering. Sheldon L. Abbott & Ivan D. Hinerman. LC 74-25602. 377p. 1982. teacher ed 4.28 (*0-02-810360-2*); pap. text ed. 25.16 (*0-02-810350-5*) Glencoe.

Automotive Suspension & Steering: Theory & Service. Herbert E. Ellinger & Richard B. Hathaway. 288p. 1988. pap. text ed. 45.00 (*0-13-054123-0*) P-H.

***Automotive Suspension Explained.** Ed. by Kelly Gorham. 19p. Date not set. student ed write for info. (*0-8064-0353-5*, A39) Bergwall.

Automotive Suspension Steering. Sheldon L. Abbott. 1982. 12.95 (*0-02-810110-3*) Macmillan.

Automotive Suspension, Steering & Brakes. Jay Webster. LC 86-11617. 384p. 1987. teacher ed 12.00 (*0-8273-2592-4*); pap. text ed. 32.95 (*0-8273-2591-6*) Delmar.

Automotive Suspensions & Steering Systems. 112p. 1992. pap. 39.00 (*1-56091-234-0*, SP-917) Soc Auto Engineers.

Automotive Suspensions, Steering, Alignment, & Brakes. 5th ed. Walter E. Billiet & Walter Alley. LC 73-80444. (Illus.). 364p. reprint ed. pap. 103.80 (*0-8357-8811-3*, 2033290) Bks Demand.

Automotive Technology. Jack Erjavec & Robert Scharff. 1992. text ed. 50.95 (*0-8273-4142-3*) Delmar.

Automotive Technology: A Systems Approach Computerized Testmaker & Testbank for IBM Computers. Jack Erjavec & Robert Scharff. 1992. 3.5 hd 54.95 (*0-8273-5124-0*); 5.25 hd 54.95 (*0-8273-5125-9*) Delmar.

Automotive Tools Handbook. David H. Jacobs, Jr. LC 92-29761. (Illus.). 160p. 1993. pap. 17.95 (*0-87938-712-2*) Motorbooks Intl.

Automotive Transmission Advancements. 1991. 69.00 (*1-56091-118-2*, SP-854) Soc Auto Engineers.

Automotive Transmissions. 2nd ed. Sheldon L. Abbott. 320p. 1988. teacher ed 4.28 (*0-02-810290-8*); pap. text ed. 19.47 (*0-02-810280-0*) Glencoe.

Automotive Transmissions & Drivelines: Twenty-Seven Papers. 1993. 79.00 (*1-56091-350-9*, SP-965) Soc Auto Engineers.

Automotive Troubleshooting: Glossary. William Carroll. 144p. (Orig.). 1973. pap. 5.00 (*0-910390-18-5*, 118) Auto Bk.

Automotive Tune-up. 2nd ed. William H. Crouse & Donald L. Anglin. LC 82-7320. (Automotive Technology Ser.). 1983. text ed. 28.95 (*0-07-014836-8*) McGraw.

Automotive Tune-up. 3rd ed. William H. Crouse. 1994. pap. 38.50 (*0-02-801856-7*) Glencoe.

***Automotive Undercar: Suspension, Steering & Electronic Systems.** Kalton C. Lahue. LC 94-43216. (West's Automotive Ser.). 1995. spiral bd. write for info. (*0-314-04550-3*) West Pub.

Automotive Upholstery Handbook. Don Taylor. LC 93-7376. (Illus.). 232p. (Orig.). 1993. pap. 19.95 (*1-55561-030-7*) Fisher Bks.

Automotive Window Engraving for Fun & Profit. O. M. Allred. (Illus.). 32p. 1986. pap. 12.95 (*0-936035-00-5*) O M Allred.

Automotive Workbook. Jack Rudman. (Workbook Ser.: No. 2820). 1994. pap. 23.95 (*0-8373-7901-6*) Nat Learn.

Automotive Workplace Guide to EPA & OSHA: Regulations - Sample Programs - Forms. H. Ray Kirk. LC 94-6534. 500p. 1994. ring bd. 89.50 (*1-56759-010-1*) Summers Pr.

Automotive Yearbook. Ed. by Harry A. Stark. 1981. 60.00 (*0-686-35934-8*) Wards Comm.

Automotives Voisin 1919-1958, 2 vols. Pascal Courteult. 1992. Incl. slipcase. 195.00 (*0-904568-72-5*) Motorbooks Intl.

Automotrix Three: Manual de Reparaciones Automotrices. rev. ed. William K. Toboldt. (Illus.). (SPA.). 1983. 50.00 (*0-916628-04-3*) Lineal Pub Co.

Automoviles (Automobiles) J. Cooper. (Spanish Language Books, Set 5: Maquinas de Viaje (Traveling Machines)). (J). 1991. 8.95 (*0-86592-510-0*) Rourke Enter.

AUTONOM 1.0: PC Software for Systematic Names in Organic Chemistry. 150p. 1992. 1,980.00 (*0-387-14111-1*); 980.00 (*0-685-57611-6*) Spr-Verlag.

Autonomation - Automation. Ed. by Esme McTighe. Tr. by Michael Kelsey. (Factory Management Notebook Ser.). (Illus.). 191p. 1991. 125.00 (*1-56327-002-1*) Prod Press.

Autonome Architekur und Partizipatorisches Bauen. Ed. by I. Bohning. 356p. (GER.). (C). 1981. text ed. 55.00 (*0-8176-1260-2*) Birkhauser.

Autonomes und Partnerschaftliches Lernen. Muller et al. 208p. 1989. 24.50 (*3-468-49439-4*) Langenscheidt.

Autonomia: Its Genesis & Early History. Martin Ostwald. (American Classical Studies). 82p. 1982. pap. 15.95 (*0-89130-572-6*, 40 04 11) Scholars Pr GA.

Autonomic & Enteric Ganglia: Transmission & Its Pharmacology. Ed. by Alexander G. Karczmar et al. LC 85-19398. 532p. 1986. 115.00 (*0-306-42039-2*, Plenum Pr) Plenum.

Autonomic Disorders - Disorders of the Spinal Cord & Cauda Equina - Neuropharmacology. Ronald J. Polinsky et al. (Current Opinion in Neurology & Neurosurgery, 1993 Ser.). (Illus.). 162p. (Orig.). 1993. pap. text ed. 49.95 (*1-85922-008-8*) Current Science.

Autonomic Failure: A Textbook of Clinical Disorders of the Autonomic Nervous System. 3rd ed. Ed. by Roger Bannister & Christopher Mathias. (Illus.). 978p. 1992. 175.00 (*0-19-262219-6*) OUP.

Autonomic Failure: A Textbook of Clinical Disorders of the Autonomic Nervous System. 3rd ed. Ed. by Roger Bannister & Christopher J. Mathias. (Illus.). 976p. (C). 1993. reprint ed. pap. 75.00 (*0-19-262218-8*) OUP.

Autonomic Functions in Human Physiology. G. E. Thews & P. Vaupel. Tr. by M. A. Biederman-Thorson. (Springer Study Edition Ser.). (Illus.). 400p. 1984. pap. 34.00 (*0-387-13217-1*) Spr-Verlag.

Autonomic Nervous System. Wilson & Pauwels. 1993. 39.00 (*1-55664-324-1*) Mosby Yr Bk.

Autonomic Nervous System & Exercise. Hilary Green. 212p. 1990. 57.50 (*0-412-32500-4*, A4462) Chapman & Hall.

***Autonomie und Autokratie: Ueber Kants Metaphysik der Sitten.** Peter Koenig. (Quellen und Studien zur Philosophie Ser.: Vol. 36). xii, 243p. (GER.). (C). 1994. lib. bdg. 98.50 (*3-11-014302-X*) De Gruyter.

Autonomisme et Christianisme dans l'Afrique Romaine de Septime Severe a L'invasion Vandale. Jean Paul Brisson. LC 82-45808. (Orthodoxies & Heresies in the Early Church Ser.). 1983. reprint ed. 49.50 (*0-404-62377-8*) AMS Pr.

***Autonomous Agents: From Self-Control to Autonomy.** Alfred R. Mele. 352p. 1995. text ed. 45.00 (*0-19-509454-9*) OUP.

Autonomous Decentralized Systems, 1993 International Symposium. LC 92-75291. 448p. 1993. pap. text ed. 80.00 (*0-8186-3125-2*, 3125) IEEE Comp Soc.

***Autonomous Decentralized Systems, 1995 International Symposium (ISADS '95)** 448p. 1995. pap. text ed. 90.00 (*0-8186-7087-8*, PR07087) IEEE Comp Soc.

Autonomous Histories, Particular Truths: Essays in Honor of John Smail. Ed. by Laurie J. Sears. 300p. 1993. 39.95 (*1-881261-10-7*); pap. 19.95 (*1-881261-11-5*) U Wisc Ctr SE Asian.

Autonomous Image: Cinematic Narration & Humanism. A. J. Prats. LC 81-50182. 192p. (C). 1981. 21.00 (*0-8131-1406-3*) U Pr of Ky.

Autonomous Learning from the Environment. Wei-Min Shen. LC 93-33823. (C). 1995. text ed. write for info. (*0-7167-8265-0*, Computer Sci Pr) W H Freeman.

Autonomous Linear Quadratic Control Problem: Theory & Numerical Solution. Ed. by V. L. Mehrmann et al. (Lecture Notes in Control & Information Sciences Ser.: Vol. 163). (Illus.). 184p. 1991. pap. 33.00 (*0-387-54170-5*) Spr-Verlag.

Autonomous Male of Adam Smith. Stewart Justman. LC 93-9258. (Project for Discourse & Theory Ser.: Vol. 14). 1993. 27.95 (*0-8061-2542-X*) U of Okla Pr.

Autonomous Man. Dean Turner. LC 71-105052. 206p. 1970. 9.95 (*0-8272-0009-9*) Hope Pub Hse.

***Autonomous Man.** Dean Turner. 206p. 1970. 12.95 (*0-8159-5026-8*) Devin.

Autonomous Mobile Robots: Vehicle with Cognitive Control. A. Meystel. (Series in Automation: Vol. 1). 600p. 1991. text ed. 87.00 (*9971-5-0088-4*); pap. text ed. 41.00 (*9971-5-0089-2*) World Scientific Pub.

Autonomous Mobile Robots, Vol. 1: Perception, Vol. 1. S. S. Iyengar & A. Elfes. LC 91-13280. 552p. 1991. 70.00 (*0-8186-9018-6*, 2018) IEEE Comp Soc.

Autonomous Mobile Robots, Vol. 2: Planning, Vol. 2. S. S. Iyengar & A. Elfes. LC 91-13280. 536p. 1991. 70.00 (*0-8186-9116-6*, 2116) IEEE Comp Soc.

Autonomous Region: Poems & Photographs from Tibet. Kathleen Jamie & Sean Smith. (Illus.). 79p. 1993. pap. 16.95 (*1-85224-173-X*, Pub. by Bloodaxe Bks UK) Dufour.

Autonomous Robot Vehicles. Ed. by I. J. Cox & G. T. Wilfong. (Illus.). xxvi, 462p. 1990. 76.00 (*0-387-97240-4*) Spr-Verlag.

Autonomous Self: The Work of John D. Sutherland. Ed. by Jill S. Scharff. LC 93-22563. 480p. 1994. reprint ed. 50.00 (*1-56821-008-6*) Aronson.

Autonomous Technology: Technics-Out-of-Control As a Theme in Political Thought. Langdon Winner. LC 76-40100. 1977. pap. 15.00 (*0-262-73049-9*) MIT Pr.

Autonomous Vehicle Guidance Systems. Richard K. Miller & Terri C. Walker. LC 88-81887. (Survey on Technology & Markets Ser.: No. 90). 50p. 1989. pap. text ed. 200.00 (*1-55865-089-X*) Future Tech Surveys.

Autonomy: An Essay in Philosophical Psychology & Ethics. Lawrence Haworth. LC 85-23806. 224p. 1986. 27.00x (*0-300-03569-1*) Yale U Pr.

***Autonomy: Challenge & - or Solution for the Central-European Minorities.** Ed. by Vilmos Agoston. Tr. by Eva Lengyel et al. 112p. (C). Date not set. pap. 20.00x (*1-882785-07-X*) Matthias Corvinus.

Autonomy & Community: The Royal Manor of Havering, 1200-1500. Marjorie K. McIntosh. (Cambridge Studies in Medieval Life & Thought: No. 5). (Illus.). 320p. 1986. 79.95 (*0-521-32018-6*) Cambridge U Pr.

Autonomy & Dependence in Residential Care: An Evaluation of a Project to Promote Self Determination in a Home for Older People. Ed. by Stella Dixon. 128p. (C). 1991. 59.00 (*0-685-50534-0*, Pub. by Age Concern Eng UK) St Mut.

Autonomy & Interdependence: U. S.-Western European Monetary & Trade Relations, 1958-1984. Thomas L. Ilgen. LC 84-27557. 176p. (C). 1985. 56.00 (*0-8476-7413-4*) Rowman.

Autonomy & Intervention: Parentalism in the Caring Life. John Kultgen. 288p. 1995. 39.95 (*0-19-508531-0*) OUP.

Autonomy & Judaism: The Individual & Community in Jewish Philosophical Thought. Ed. by Daniel H. Frank. LC 91-37943. (Series in Jewish Philosophy). 229p. (C). 1992. 59.50 (*0-7914-1209-1*); pap. 19.95 (*0-7914-1210-5*) State U NY Pr.

Autonomy & Long Term Care. George J. Agich. LC 92-49361. 208p. (C). 1993. 35.00 (*0-19-507495-5*) OUP.

An Asterisk (*) at the beginning of an entry indicates that the title is appearing in BIP for the first time.

An Asterisk (*) at the beginning of an entry indicates that the title is appearing in BIP for the first time.

A

*Autumn Maze: A Scobie Malone Mystery.** Jon Cleary. 1995. 22.00 (*0-688-13697-4*) Morrow.

Autumn Migrations of Selected Species of Ducks at Buckeye Lake, Ohio. Milton B. Trautman. (Biological Notes Ser.: No. 11). 1978. 2.00 (*0-86727-085-3*) Ohio Bio Survey.

*Autumn of Angels.** Karen Hesse. LC 94-4461. 224p. (J). (gr. 5-9). 1995. 15.95 (*0-7868-0087-9*); lib. bdg. 15.89 (*0-7868-2072-1*) Hyprn Child.

Autumn of Central Paris: The Defeat of Town Planning, 1850-1970. Anthony Sutcliffe. LC 70-149125. (Studies in Urban History: No. 1). 408p. reprint ed. pap. 116.30 (*0-8357-5928-8*, 2023839) Bks Demand.

Autumn of Deception. large type ed. Maureen Stephenson. (Linford Romance Library). 320p. 1989. pap. 11.95 (*0-7089-6694-2*, Linford) Ulverscroft.

Autumn of Glory: The Army of Tennessee, 1862-1865. Thomas L. Connelly. LC 70-122353. (Illus.). x, 558p. 1971. 34.95 (*0-8071-0445-0*) La State U Pr.

*Autumn of the Middle Ages.** Johan Huizinga. Tr. by Rodney J. Payton & Ulrich Mammitzsch. 560p. 1995. 39.95 (*0-226-35992-1*) U Ch Pr.

Autumn of the Patriarch. Gabriel Garcia Marquez. 1977. mass mkt. 4.95 (*0-380-01774-1*, Bard) Avon.

*Autumn of the Patriarch.** Gabriel G. Marquez. 288p. 1994. lib. bdg. 29.00 (*0-8095-9137-5*) Borgo Pr.

Autumn of the Patriarch. Gabriel Garcia Marquez. Tr. by Gregory Rabassa. LC 75-30349. 288p. 1991. reprint ed. pap. 12.00 (*0-06-091963-9*, PL) HarpC.

Autumn of the Royal Tar. Bruce Stone. LC 95-6122. (Laura Geringer Book Ser.). 160p. (YA). (gr. 5 up). 1995. lib. bdg. 13.89 (*0-06-021493-7*) HarpC Child Bks.

Autumn of the Royal Tar. Bruce Stone. LC 95-6122. (Laura Geringer Book Ser.). 160p. (YA). (gr. 5 up). 1995. 13.95 (*0-06-021492-9*, HarpT) HarpC Child Bks.

Autumn of the Spring Chicken: Wit & Wisdom for Women in Midlife. Sue P. Thoele. 96p. (Orig.). 1993. 12.95 (*0-943233-47-X*) Conari Press.

Autumn Offerings. Prem Kirpal. 76p. (C). 1989. 50.00 (*81-209-0039-1*, Pub. by Pitambar Pub II) St Mut.

Autumn on the Farm. Janet Fitzgerald. (Science Through the Seasons Ser.). (Illus.). 32p. (J). (gr. 1-3). 1991. 15.95 (*0-237-60222-9*, Pub. by Evans Bros Ltd UK) Trafalgar.

*Autumn Passages: The Ducks Unlimited Waterfowling Anthology.** Ed. by Ducks Unlimited Staff. 320p. 1995. 27.50 (*1-57223-026-6*, WCP) Outlook Pubng.

*Autumn People.** Ray Bradbury. 1994. lib. bdg. 24.95x (*1-56849-434-3*) Buccaneer Bks.

*Autumn People.** White Wolf Staff. (Changeling Ser.). 1995. per., pap. 12.00 (*1-56504-709-5*, 7004) White Wolf.

Autumn Quail. Naguib Mahfouz. 1986. pap. 8.50 (*977-424-107-X*, Pub. by Am Univ Cairo Pr UA) Col U Pr.

Autumn Quail. rev. ed. Naguib Mahfouz. Ed. by John Rodenbeck. Tr. by Roger Allen. 1990. reprint ed. mass mkt. 7.95 (*0-385-26454-2*) Doubleday.

Autumn Quail (Siman wa Khareef) Arabic Novel. Naguib Mahfouz. (ARA.). (J). (gr. 4-7). 1985. 8.95 (*0-86685-162-3*) Intl Bk Ctr.

Autumn Rain. Anita Mills. 384p. (Orig.). 1993. pap. 4.99 (*0-451-40328-2*, Onyx) NAL-Dutton.

Autumn Remembered: Reflections of College Football's Greatest Team. Gary King. Ed. by Charlyce King. LC 87-73386. 300p. (Orig.). (YA). (gr. 9 up). 1988. pap. 12.95 (*0-9619712-0-7*) Red Earth OK.

Autumn Rose. Marjorie Farrell. 224p. 1991. pap. 3.99 (*0-451-16874-7*, Sig) NAL-Dutton.

Autumn Scandals. Martin Pyx. (Victorian Era Ser.). 1989. pap. 4.95 (*0-929654-40-4*, 58) Blue Moon Bks.

*Autumn Sequence.** limited ed. Jan Freeman. (Small Book Ser.). (Illus.). 24p. (Orig.). 1993. pap. 10.00 (*0-9638183-0-9*) Paris Pr MA.

*Autumn Sojourn: (Twenty Four Poems & Three "Interruptions")** Brenda Hillman. 36p. (Orig.). 1994. 70.00 (*0-9632085-7-8*) Em Pr.

Autumn Sonata: Selected Poems of Georg Trakl. Georg Trakl. Tr. by Daniel Simko. 128p. 1989. pap. 9.95 (*0-918825-94-6*) Moyer Bell.

Autumn Songs: Poems on Love, Nature, Beauty, & Life. Robert Navon. LC 82-73411. 96p. (Orig.). 1983. pap. 4.95 (*0-9609866-1-8*) Selene Bks.

Autumn Statement, 1990. Nigel Lawson. 57p. 1990. pap. 22.00 (*0-10-113112-7*, HM7112) UNIPUB.

Autumn Statement, 1992. Nigel Lawson. 57p. 1992. pap. 25.00 (*0-10-120962-2*, HMO9622, Pub. by HMSO UK) UNIPUB.

Autumn Story. Jill Barklem. LC 80-15433. (Brambly Hedge Bks.). (Illus.). 32p. (J). (gr. 1 up). 1986. 8.95 (*0-399-20745-7*, Philomel Bks) Putnam Pub Group.

Autumn Story. Tommaso Landolfi. Tr. by Joachim Neugroschel. LC 88-83031. 145p. 1989. 20.00 (*0-941419-27-4*, Eridanos Library); pap. 11.00 (*0-941419-26-6*, Eridanos Library) Marsilio Pubs.

Autumn Street. Lois Lowry. 192p. (J). (gr. 4-7). 1986. pap. 3.50 (*0-440-40344-8*, YB) Dell.

Autumn Street. Lois Lowry. 160p. (J). (gr. 5 up). 1980. 14.95 (*0-395-27812-0*) HM.

Autumn Tale. David Updike. (Illus.). 40p. (J). (gr. 2 up). 1988. 15.95 (*0-945912-02-1*) Pippin Pr.

Autumn Tiger. Bob Langley. 252p. 1986. 15.95 (*0-8027-0884-6*) Walker & Co.

Autumn Tiger. large type ed. Bob Langley. 480p. 1983. 15.95 (*0-7089-0959-0*) Ulverscroft.

Autumn Trail, No. 30. Bonnie Bryant. (YA). 1993. 3.50 (*0-553-48077-4*) Bantam.

Autumn Warrior: Murray Warmath's Sixty-Five Years in American Football. Mike Wilkinson. LC 92-39021. 1992. write for info. (*0-8087-5262-6*) Burgess MN Intl.

Autumn Wind: A Selection from the Poems of Issa. Tr. by Lewis MacKenzie. LC 83-48874. (Illus.). 126p. (C). 1984. pap. 8.00 (*0-87011-657-6*) Kodansha.

*Autumn Wind & Other Stories.** Tr. & Sel. by Lane Dunlop. 210p. (Orig.). 1994. pap. 9.95 (*0-8048-1921-1*) C E Tuttle.

Autumn Winds. 1989. audio 9.95 (*0-931055-70-9*) LuraMedia.

Autumn Wine. Dolores Dahl. 1990. pap. 12.95 (*0-685-48126-3*) Single Vision.

Autumn Wine: And Other Seasonings. Dolores Dahl. (Illus.). 133p. (Orig.). 1991. pap. 12.95 (*0-9608960-6-6*) Single Vision.

*Autumnal Cadenza: Ballads, Poems, Translations.** Ella Bobrow. 96p. 1995. lib. bdg. 25.00 (*0-8095-4525-X*) Borgo Pr.

Autumnal Equinox. Sibnarayan Ray. (Redbird Ser.). 1975. 10.00 (*0-89253-601-2*); pap. text ed. 4.80 (*0-88253-711-3*) Ind-US Inc.

Autumn's Brightness. Daisy Newman. 251p. 1991. pap. 10.95 (*0-944350-18-6*) Friends United.

Autumns Tender Fire. April Ashmore. 1992. mass mkt. 4.25 (*0-8217-3645-0*) Zebra.

Auvergne & the Massif Central. Rex Grizell. 1989. pap. 16.95 (*0-8442-9936-7*, Passport Bks) NTC Pub Grp.

Auvergne Green Guide. 2nd ed. (FRE.). Date not set. pap. 18.00 (*2-06-700304-6*, 304) Michelin.

*Auvergne Green Guide French Edition.** Michelin Staff. (FRE.). Date not set. pap. 17.95 (*0-7859-7220-X*, 2067003046) Fr & Eur.

Aux Fontaines de Desir; La Petite Infante de Castille. Henry De Montherlant. 248p. (FRE.). 1954. pap. 15.95 (*0-8288-9631-3*, 2070245756) Fr & Eur.

Aux Fontaines du Desir. Henry de Montherlant. 248p. 1954. 4.95 (*0-686-54803-5*) Fr & Eur.

Aux Innocents les Mains Pleines. Andre Maurois. (FRE.). pap. 9.95 (*0-7859-5571-2*) Fr & Eur.

Aux Origines de la Dormition de la Vierge. Michael Van Esbroeck. (Collected Studies Ser.: CS 472). 336p. 1995. 95.00 (*0-86078-454-1*, Pub. by Variorum UK) Ashgate Pub Co.

Aux Sources de la Riviere Kwai. Pierre Boulle. 215p. (FRE.). 1985. 11.95 (*0-7859-1184-7*, 2266015915) Fr & Eur.

AUXAL: Auxological Analysis of Longitudinal Measurements of Human Sature. R. Darrell Bock et al. 1974. 30.00 (*0-89498-036-X*) Sci Ware.

Auxilia of the Roman Imperial Army. G. L. Cheesman. 190p. 1975. pap. 15.00 (*0-89005-096-1*) Ares.

*Auxiliar Biblico Portavoz.** Harold L. Willmington. 1040p. (SPA.). 1995. 34.99 (*0-8254-1874-7*) Kregel.

Auxiliaries. Ed. by Fernando Albornoz. Tr. by Roberto Quiroga. (Rotary Drilling Ser.: Unit I, Lesson 9). (Illus.). 60p. (Orig.). (SPA.). 1983. pap. text ed. 12.00 (*0-88698-037-2*, 2.10922) PETEX.

Auxiliaries. 2nd ed. Ed. by Jodie Leecraft. (Rotary Drilling Ser.: Unit I, Lesson 9). (Illus.). 35p. 1981. pap. text ed. 12.00 (*0-88698-013-5*, 2.10920) PETEX.

Auxiliaries: Canadian Metric Edition. 2nd ed. Ed. by Jodie Leecraft. (Rotary Drilling Ser.: Unit I, Lesson 9). (Illus.). 35p. 1981. pap. text ed. 12.00 (*0-88698-025-9*, 2.10921) PETEX.

Auxiliaries: Cognitive Forces & Grammaticalization. Bernd Heine. (Illus.). 176p. (C). 1993. 55.00 (*0-19-508387-3*) OUP.

Auxiliaries in Health Care: Programs in Developing Countries. N. R. Fendall. LC 79-161655. (Josiah Macy, Jr. Foundation, New York, The Macy Foundation Series on International Problems of Medical Education). 216p. reprint ed. pap. 61.60 (*0-8357-5929-6*, 2019818) Bks Demand.

Auxiliary Cooling: Water Systems. Center for Occupational Research & Development Staff. (EUTEC Power Plant Operator Curriculum Ser.). (Illus.). 24p. (C). 1986. pap. text ed. write for info. (*1-55502-248-0*) CORD Commns.

Auxiliary Materials. W. Espe. LC 64-21217. (Materials of High Vacuum Technology Ser.: Vol. 3). 1968. 222.00 (*0-08-013224-3*, Pub. by Pergamon Repr UK) Franklin.

Auxiliary Police: The Citizen's Approach to Public Safety. Martin A. Greenberg. LC 83-22683. (Contributions in Criminology & Penology Ser.: No. 3). (Illus.). xiv, 231p. 1984. text ed. 55.00 (*0-313-23955-X*, GAU/, Greenwood Pr) Greenwood.

Auxiliary Protective Signaling Systems. (Seventy Ser.). 1993. pap. 32.25 (*0-685-58063-6*, 72-93) Natl Fire Prot.

Auxiliary Reinforcement in Concrete Connections. (PCI Journal Reprints Ser.). 22p. 1968. pap. 5.00 (*0-686-40037-2*, JR105) P-PCI.

Auxiliary Signal Design in Fault Detection & Diagnosis. X. J. Zhang. (Lecture Notes in Control & Information Sciences Ser.: Vol. 134). (Illus.). xii, 213p. 1989. pap. 42.00 (*0-387-51559-3*, 3427) Spr-Verlag.

Auxiliary Teacher. 23.95 (*0-8373-8003-0*, T-3) Nat Learn.

Auxiliary Tip Party Marking Devices. Thomas B. Norling. (ABC Pocket Guide for the Field Ser.). (Illus.). 60p. (Orig.). (C). 1985. pap. 6.95 (*1-56016-036-5*) ABC TeleTraining.

Auyana: Those Who Held onto Home. Sterling Robbins. LC 81-2707. (Anthropological Studies in the Eastern Highlands of New Guinea: No. 6). (Illus.). 274p. 1982. 40.00 (*0-295-95788-3*) U of Wash Pr.

AV Guide see Business

AV Instructional Technology Manual for Independent Study. 6th ed. James V. Brown et al. (Illus.). 208p. (C). 1983. text ed. write for info. (*0-07-008179-4*) McGraw.

AV Market Place, 1994. Ed. by Bowker, R. R., Staff. 1488p. 1994. pap. 139.95 (*0-8352-3419-3*) Bowker.

AV Market Place, 1995. Ed. by Bowker, R. R., Staff. 1500p. 1995. pap. 145.00 (*0-8352-3579-3*) Bowker. "An exhaustive, cross-referenced directory blanketing...the AV industry's manufacturers, producers, distributors, services, techniques & applications."--BACKSTAGE. "You could find a manufacturer & distributor for any AV product you can think of from the information included."--THE BIG REEL. "From suppliers of blank cassettes to film producers, here is a comprehensive & well-indexed classified guide."--THE HUENEFELD REPORT. "Recommended for all libraries in which there is more than a minimum interest in audio-video material."--ACADEMIC LIBRARY BOOK REVIEW. Fully revised & updated, this comprehensive directory is the only tool you need to get in touch with more than 8,750 companies that create, apply, or distribute an extraordinary range of AV equipment & services for business, education, science, & government. Giving you full access to the AV industry--& such developing technologies as multimedia, virtual reality, digital audio, presentation software, & interactive video--this vital reference lets you search: a fast- access index of over 1,350 products & services cross-referenced to companies in the main index. A Products, Services, & Companies Index identifying all firms geographically under separate Audio, Audio-Visual, Computer Systems, Film, Video, Programming, & miscellaneous sections, divided further among specific applications. An alphabetical-by-name Company Directory with complete contact information for every organization listed. ***Publisher Provided Annotation.***

---

*AV Market Place 1996.** Ed. by Bowker, R. R., Staff. 1996. write for info. (*0-8352-3758-3*) Bowker.

AVA. Carole Maso. LC 92-35600. 274p. 1993. 19.95 (*1-56478-029-5*) Dalkey Arch.

*Ava.** Carole Maso. 274p. (Orig.). 1995. pap. 12.95 (*1-56478-074-0*) Dalkey Arch.

Ava: My Story. large type ed. Ava Gardner. LC 91-14687. 521p. 1991. reprint ed. lib. bdg. 21.95 (*1-56054-178-4*) Thorndike Pr.

Ava: My Story. large type ed. Ava Gardner. LC 91-14687. 521p. 1992. pap. 14.95 (*1-56054-979-3*) Thorndike Pr.

Ava: The Autobiography of Ava Gardner. Ava Gardner & Alan Burgess. 1990. 19.95 (*0-685-29540-0*) Bantam.

Ava Gardner: A Bio-Bibliography. Karin J. Fowler. LC 90-3317. (Bio-Bibliographies in the Performing Arts Ser.: No. 14). 256p. 1990. text ed. 39.95 (*0-313-26776-6*, FAB/, Greenwood Pr) Greenwood.

AVA Machine Vision Glossary. Automated Vision Association Staff. 96p. (Orig.). 1985. pap. 9.00 (*0-317-39377-4*) Robot Inst Am.

Avacado Recipes, Etc. 2nd rev. ed. Teri Gordon. LC 88-135675. (Illus.). 136p. 1988. pap. 8.95 (*0-9619870-1-4*) T Gordon Pub.

Avacado Recipes, Etc. 3rd ed. Teri Gordon. LC 88-135675. (Illus.). 136p. 1989. pap. 9.95 (*0-9619870-2-2*) T Gordon Pub.

Avadanacataka: A Century of Edifying Tales Belonging to the Hinayana. Ed. by J. S. Speyer. (Indo-Iranian Reprints Ser.: No. 3). 1958. 101.55 (*90-279-0059-0*) Mouton.

Avadhuta Gita: The Song of the Ever-Free. Dattareya. Tr. by Chetanananda. 138p. 1985. pap. 2.95 (*0-87481-224-0*, Pub. by Advaita Ashrama II) Vedanta Pr.

Avadhuta Gita of Dattatreya. Dattaraya. Tr. by Swami Ashokananḍa. 1978. pap. 4.95 (*0-87481-482-0*, Pub. by Ramakrishna Math II) Vedanta Pr.

Availability. Open Framework Staff. 72p. (C). 1993. pap. text ed. 16.00 (*0-13-630948-8*) P-H.

Availability: Gabriel Marcel & the Phenomenology of Human Openness. Joe McCown. LC 77-22358. (American Academy of Religion. Studies in Religion: No. 14). 94p. reprint ed. pap. 26.80 (*0-7837-5481-7*, 2045246) Bks Demand.

Availability Analysis: A Guide to Efficient Energy Use. rev. ed. Ed. by Michael J. Moran. 260p. 1989. 40.00 (*0-7918-0009-1*, 800091) ASME Pr.

*Availability Engineering & Manufacturing Plant Performance.** Richard G. Lamb. 1995. text ed. 65.00 (*0-13-324112-2*) P-H.

Availability for Work: A Study in Unemployment Compensation. Ralph Altman. LC 68-8935. (Illus.). 350p. 1969. reprint ed. text ed. 65.00 (*0-8371-0004-6*, ALAW, Greenwood Pr) Greenwood.

Availability of Capital in Rural America: Problems & Options. Deborah Markley. (New Alliances for Rural America Ser.). 60p. (Orig.). 1988. pap. text ed. 6.00 (*1-55877-018-6*) Natl Governor.

Availability of Minorities & Women for Professional & Managerial Positions, 1970-1985. Stephen A. Schneider. LC 77-80565. (Manpower & Human Resources Studies: No. 7). 300p. reprint ed. pap. 85.50 (*0-8357-5930-X*, 2025910) Bks Demand.

Availability of Occupational Exposure Data in the European Community. EC Staff. (EUR Ser.: No. 14378). 145p. 1993. pap. 19.00 (*0-685-65427-3*, CE-NA-14378-EN-C, Pub. by Europ Com) UNIPUB.

*Availability of Titanium in Market Economy Countries: A Mineral Availability Appraisal.** Jennifer A. Slatnick. 1994. write for info. (*0-615-00132-7*) US Interior.

Availability of World Energy Resources. D. C. Ion. 355p. 1980. lib. bdg. 63.00 (*0-86010-193-2*) G & T Inc.

Availability of World Energy Resources: First Supplement. D. C. Ion. 112p. (Orig.). 1976. pap. 15.00 (*0-87201-908-X*) Gulf Pub.

Availability, the Problem & the Gift. Robert J. Wicks. LC 85-62868. 144p. (Orig.). 1986. pap. 6.95 (*0-8091-2767-9*) Paulist Pr.

Availability to Ticketing. Carolyn Malone. (Illus.). 135p. (C). 1985. pap. text ed. 21.95 (*0-917063-07-4*) Travel Text.

*Availabilty Method of Energy Conversion.** Kam W. Li. (Combustion: an International Ser.). 352p. 1995. 69.50x (*1-56032-349-3*) Taylor & Francis.

Available Light. Paul Ferrini. (Illus.). (Orig.). 1990. pap. 10.00 (*1-879159-05-8*) Heartways Pr.

Available Light. Marge Piercy. LC 87-40490. 144p. 1988. pap. 12.00 (*0-394-75691-6*) Knopf.

Available Light. Ellen Currie. 1987. reprint ed. pap. 6.95 (*0-317-56210-X*, WSP) PB.

Available Light Photography: How to Shoot Without Flash in All Kinds of Light. Lou Jacobs, Jr. (Illus.). 144p. 1991. pap. 22.50 (*0-8174-3549-2*, Amphoto) Watsn-Guptill.

Available Mind. Carol R. Murphy. LC 73-94186. (Orig.). 1974. pap. 3.00 (*0-87574-193-2*) Pendle Hill.

Available Pay Survey Reports for Other Countries: An Annotated Bibliography. 4th ed. Ed. by Steven Langer. 1995. pap. 160.00 (*0-916506-39-8*) Abbott Langer Assocs.

Available Pay Survey Reports for the U. S. An Annotated Bibliography. 4th ed. Ed. by Steven Langer. 1995. pap. 450.00 (*0-317-55987-7*) Abbott Langer Assocs.

Available Pediatrician: Every Parent's Guide to Common Childhood Illnesses. braille ed. Ralph Berberich & Ann Parker. 454p. 1991. vinyl bd. 36.32 (*1-56956-190-7*, BR7845) W A T Braille.

Available Technologies of the Office of Technology Transfer, U. S. Energy Department. (Illus.). 61p. (Orig.). (C). 1994. pap. text ed. 50.00 (*1-56806-648-1*) Diane Pub.

Availing Prayer. Fay C. Martin. 120p. reprint ed. pap. 1.50 (*0-686-29098-4*) Faith Pub Hse.

Avalanche! Howard Facklam & Margery Facklam. LC 90-45622. (Nature's Disasters Ser.). (Illus.). 48p. (J). (gr. 5-6). 1991. text ed. 12.95 (*0-89686-598-3*, Crstwood Hse) Silver Burdett Pr.

Avalanche. Stephen Kramer. (Nature in Action Ser.). (Illus.). 48p. (J). (gr. 1-4). 1991. lib. bdg. 18.95 (*0-87614-422-9*, Carolrhoda) Lerner Group.

Avalanche: The Kidnaping of Roseta Uvaldo. Zane Grey. 1990. pap. 3.50 (*0-8125-0529-8*) Tor Bks.

Avalanche Awareness: A Practical Guide to Safe Travel in Avalanche Terrain. John Moynier. (Illus.). 32p. (Orig.). 1993. pap. 4.95 (*0-934641-72-2*) Chockstone Pr.

Avalanche Book. rev. ed. Betsy R. Armstrong & Knox Williams. LC 92-53037. (Illus.). 256p. 1992. pap. 16.95 (*1-55591-119-6*) Fulcrum Pub.

*Avalanche Express.** Colin Forbes. 316p. 1977. pap. 12.95 (*0-330-25324-7*, Pub. by Pan Books UK) Trans-Atl Phila.

Avalanche Express. large type ed. Colin Forbes. 1978. 12.00 (*0-7089-0169-7*) Ulverscroft.

Avalanche Handbook. 2nd ed. David McClung & Peter Schaerer. LC 93-2027. (Illus.). 256p. 1993. pap. 19.95 (*0-89886-364-3*) Mountaineers.

Avalanche in the Alps. Betsy Loredo. LC 93-11175. (Explorers Club Ser.). (Illus.). 80p. (Orig.). (J). (gr. 4-6). 1993. lib. bdg. 12.95 (*1-881889-12-2*) Silver Moon.

Avalanche in the Alps see Avalanche in the Alps; Storm at the Shore; Mystery on the Mississippi

*Avalanche in the Alps; Storm at the Shore; Mystery on the Mississippi.** Bd. with Avalanche in the Alps. Betsy Loredo. (Illus.). (J). (gr. 4-6).; Storm at the Shore. Betsy Loredo. (Illus.). (J). (gr. 4-6).; Mystery on the Mississippi. Betsy Loredo. (Illus.). (J). (gr. 4-6). (Explorer Club Ser.). 38.90 (*1-881889-81-5*) Silver Moon.

Avalanche of Anoraks: For People Who Speak Foreign Languages Every Day--Whether They Know It or Not. Robert J. White. LC 94-9851. 1994. pap. 12.50 (*0-517-88131-4*, Crown) Crown Pub Group.

Avalanche of Time: Selected Poems 1964-1984. Alex Gildzen. 112p. 1986. 20.00 (*0-938190-69-5*); pap. 7.95 (*0-938190-68-7*) North Atlantic.

Avalanche Safety for Skiers & Climbers. 2nd enl. rev. ed. Tony Daffern. (Illus.). 192p. 1992. pap. 16.95 (*0-938567-33-0*) Cloudcap.

Avalanche Transit-Time Devices. George I. Haddad. LC 72-77132. (Modern Frontiers in Applied Science Ser.). 602p. reprint ed. pap. 171.60 (*0-8357-5931-8*, 2027164) Bks Demand.

Avalee Des Avales. Rejean Ducharme. (FRE.). 1984. pap. 12.95 (*0-7859-2005-6*, 2070376222) Fr & Eur.

Avalee des Avales, l'Hiver De Force et les Enfantomes De Rejean Ducharme: Une Fiction Mot a Mot et Sa Litterarite. Kenneth W. Meadwell. LC 90-20062. (Canadian Studies: Vol. 11). 284p. (FRE.). 1990. lib. bdg. 89.95 (*0-88946-382-4*) E Mellen.

Avalon. Mary J. Jones. (Orig.). 1991. pap. 9.95 (*0-941483-96-7*) Naiad Pr.

Avalon, Tin Men, & Diner: Three Screenplays. Barry Levinson. 1990. pap. 12.95 (*0-87113-435-7*) Grove-Atltic.

An Asterisk (*) at the beginning of an entry indicates that the title is appearing in BIP for the first time.

Avalovara. Osman Lins. Tr. by Gregory Rabassa. (Texas Pan American Ser.). 344p. 1990. reprint ed. pap. 14.95 (*0-292-70416-X*) U of Tex Pr.

Avalun: Ein Jahrbuch neuer deutscher lyrischer Wortkunst. Ed. by Richard Scheid. 1972. 63.00 (*0-8115-0049-7*) Periodicals Srv.

Avance del Movimiento Revolucionario Require de una Enconada Lucha Contra la Socialdemocracia y el Liquidacionismo. Marxist-Leninist Party, USA Staff. 93p. (SPA.). 1982. pap. 1.00 (*0-86714-023-2*) Marxist-Leninist.

Avances Cientificos Mas Notables Del Siglo XX, Vol. 20. Editorial America, S. A. Staff. Ed. by Maria E. Del Real. (Illus.). 296p. (SPA.). 1990. pap. write for info. (*0-944499-95-3*) Editorial Amer.

Avant-Garde: Russian Architecture. Ed. by Catherine Cooke. (Illus.). 96p. (Orig.). 1991. pap. 19.95 (*0-312-06793-3*, Academy Edits) St Martin.

Avant Garde: The Experimental Theater in France. Leonard C. Pronko. LC 77-26017. (Illus.). 225p. 1978. reprint ed. text ed. 38.50 (*0-313-20096-3*, PRAV, Greenwood Pr) Greenwood.

***Avant-garde & Crisis: The Expressionist Legacy.** Rainer Rumold. 1994. 59.95 (*0-614-03410-8*) Camden Hse.

Avant-Garde & the Landscape: Can They Be Reconciled? Proceedings of the Avant-Garde & the Landscape Conference, University of Minnesota, April 1989. Ed. by Patrick M. Condon & Lance Neckar. (Illus.). 450p. (Orig.). 1990. pap. 42.95 (*0-9625360-0-8*) Landworks Pr.

Avant-Garde Book, 1900-1945. Contrib by Jaroslav Andel. (Illus.). 68p. 1992. pap. 17.50 (*1-56466-023-0*) Archer Fields.

Avant-Garde British Printmaking, 1914-1960. Frances Carey. 1991. pap. 29.95 (*0-486-26763-6*) Dover.

Avant-Garde Film: A Reader of Theory & Criticism. Ed. by P. Adams Sitney. (Illus.). 295p. 1978. pap. 15.00 (*0-911689-08-7*) Anthology Film.

Avant-Garde Film: Motion Studies. Scott MacDonald. LC 92-17446. (Cambridge Film Classics Ser.). (Illus.). 192p. (C). 1993. 47.95 (*0-521-38129-0*); pap. 13.95 (*0-521-38821-X*) Cambridge U Pr.

***Avant-Garde Finds Andy Hardy.** Robert B. Ray. LC 95-13646. (Illus.). 272p. (C). 1996. text ed. 39.95 (*0-674-05537-3*); pap. text ed. 18.95 (*0-674-05538-1*) HUP.

Avant-Garde Florence: From Modernism to Fascism. Walter L Adamson. LC 93-8062. (Studies in Cultural History). 352p. 1993. 42.50 (*0-674-05525-X*) HUP.

Avant-Garde Frontier: Russia Meets the West, 1910-1930. Ed. by Gail H. Roman & Virginia H. Marquardt. LC 92-11323. (Illus.). 320p. 1992. lib. bdg. 49.95 (*0-8130-1157-4*) U Press Fla.

Avant-Garde Gambits, Eighteen Eighty-Eight to Ninety-Three: Gender & the Color of Art History. Griselda Pollock. LC 92-61579. (Walter Neurath Memorial Lecture Ser.). (Illus.). 64p. 1993. 14.95 (*0-500-55025-5*) Thames Hudson.

Avant-Garde in the Eighties. Howard N. Fox. LC 86-34272. (Illus.). 187p. (Orig.). 1987. pap. text ed. 24.95 (*0-87587-138-0*) LA Co Art Mus.

Avant-Garde Jazz Musicians: Performing "Out There" David G. Such. LC 93-3753. (Illus.). 218p. 1993. 29.95 (*0-87745-432-9*); pap. 14.95 (*0-87745-435-3*) U of Iowa Pr.

Avant Garde Theatre: 1892-1992. Christopher D. Innes. LC 92-16204. (Illus.). 256p. 1993. 49.95 (*0-415-06517-8*, A7957, Routledge NY); pap. 15.95 (*0-415-06518-6*, A7961, Routledge NY) Routledge.

Avant-Garde Today: An International Anthology. Ed. by Charles Russell. LC 80-23922. 286p. 1981. 29.95 (*0-252-00851-0*) U of Ill Pr.

Avant-Garde Tradition in Literature. Ed. by Richard Kostelanetz. 424p. 1982. 20.00 (*0-932360-84-X*) Archae Edns.

Avant-Garde Tradition in Literature. Ed. by Richard Kostelanetz. LC 81-86334. 424p. (C). 1982. 34.95x (*0-87975-173-8*); pap. 22.95 (*0-87975-174-6*) Prometheus Bks.

Avant-Gardening: A Guide to One-Upmanship in the Garden. Alan Titchmarsh. 112p. 1987. 14.95 (*0-285-62877-1*, Pub. by Souvenir Pr UK) Intl Spec Bk.

Avant-Gardes Litteraires Au XX Siecle, 2 vols., Set. 1216p. 1984. 300.00 (*0-317-56657-1*, Pub. by Collets UK) Pro-Am Music.

Avant Inke. James M. Dorsey. Ed. by Carolyn Mitchell. (Illus.). 56p. (Orig.). 1993. pap. 8.95 (*1-882362-05-5*) Caro-Lynn Pubn.

Avant-Pop: Fiction for a Daydream Nation. Ed. by Larry McCaffery. (Black Ice Books Ser.). (Illus.). 247p. 1993. pap. 7.00 (*0-932511-72-4*) Fiction Coll.

Avanti! R. Brambilla & A. Crotti. Ed. by J. Owen. (C). 1988. 75.00 (*0-85950-846-3*, Pub. by S Thornes Pubs UK); audio 220.00 (*0-85950-848-X*, Pub. by S Thornes Pubs UK) St Mut.

Avanti! Teacher's Book. G. Bogdanski. Ed. by M. Hirt-Harlass. Tr. by T. Stoletneberg. (C). 1989. 185.00 (*0-85950-847-1*, Pub. by S Thornes Pubs UK) St Mut.

Avantures Du Sr. C. Le Beau, Avocat En Parlement, Ou Voyage Curieux et Nouveau Parmi les Sauvages De L'amerique Septentrionale, 2 vols., Set. Claude Le Beau. (Canadiana Avant 1867 Ser.: No. 16). 1966. 83.10 (*3-10-800086-1*) Mouton.

***Avanzando: Gramatica Espanola y Lectura.** 3rd ed. Sara L. De La Vega & Carmen Salazar. 1994. pap. text ed. write for info. (*0-471-30808-0*) Wiley.

Avanzando: Estrategias Modernas De: Always Advancing: Church Growth. D. Reeves. (SPA.). 5.25 (*84-7645-293-4*, 223361, Pub. by Edit Clie SP) TSELF.

***Avar Cemeteries in County Baranya: (Cemeteries of the Avar Period 567-829 in Hungary 2)** A. Kiss. (Cemeteries of the Avar Period 567-829 in Hungery Ser.). 160p. (C). 1977. 75.00x (*963-05-1008-1*, Pub. by Akad Kiado HU) St Mut.

Avare. Moliere, pseud. 1966. pap. 2.95 (*0-685-11020-6*) Fr & Eur.

***Avare.** Moliere, pseud. 210p. 1969. write for info. (*0-7859-5278-0*) Fr & Eur.

Avare. Moliere. (FRE.). 1986. pap. 10.95 (*0-7859-3130-9*) Fr & Eur.

Avaricious Ardvarks & Other Alphabet Tongue Twisters. Sandy Sheppard. Ed. by Diane Stortz. (Little Deer Bks.). (Illus.). 28p. (J). (ps). 1994. 5.49 (*0-7847-0200-4*, 24-03880) Standard Pub.

***Avars & Ancient Hungarians.** P. Liptak. 208p. (C). 1983. 57.00x (*963-05-2956-4*, Pub. by Akad Kiado HU) St Mut.

Avars & Ancient Hungarians. Pal Liptak. 208p. 1983. 82.50 (*0-685-16982-0*, Pub. by Collets UK) Pro-Am Music.

***Avaryan Rising, 3 vols. in 1.** Judith Tarr. 864p. 1993. 14.58 (*1-56865-069-8*, GuildAmerica) Dblday Bk Music.

Ava's Men: The Private Life of Ava Gardner. large type ed. Jane E. Wayne. 366p. 1991. 11.97 (*1-85089-481-7*, Pub. by ISIS UK) Transaction Pubs.

Avast, Ye Slobs! Alabama Pirate Trivia. Carole Marsh. (Carole Marsh Alabama Bks.). (Illus.). (YA). (gr. 3-12). 1994. lib. bdg. 24.95 (*0-7933-0088-6*); pap. 14.95 (*0-7933-0087-8*); disk 29.95 (*0-7933-0089-4*) Gallopade Pub Group.

Avast, Ye Slobs! Alaska Pirate Trivia. Carole Marsh. (Carole Marsh Alaska Bks.). (Illus.). (YA). (gr. 3-12). 1994. lib. bdg. 24.95 (*0-7933-0112-2*); pap. 14.95 (*0-7933-0111-4*); disk 29.95 (*0-7933-0113-0*) Gallopade Pub Group.

Avast, Ye Slobs! Arizona Pirate Trivia. Carole Marsh. (Carole Marsh Arizona Bks.). (Illus.). (YA). (gr. 3-12). 1994. lib. bdg. 24.95 (*0-7933-0136-X*); pap. 14.95 (*0-7933-0135-1*); disk 29.95 (*0-7933-0137-8*) Gallopade Pub Group.

Avast, Ye Slobs! Arkansas Pirate Trivia. Carole Marsh. (Carole Marsh Arkansas Bks.). (Illus.). (YA). (gr. 3-12). 1994. lib. bdg. 24.95 (*0-7933-0160-2*); pap. 14.95 (*0-7933-0159-9*); disk 29.95 (*0-7933-0161-0*) Gallopade Pub Group.

Avast, Ye Slobs! California Pirate Trivia. Carole Marsh. (Carole Marsh California Bks.). (Illus.). (YA). (gr. 3-12). 1994. lib. bdg. 24.95 (*0-7933-0184-X*); pap. 14.95 (*0-7933-0183-1*); disk 29.95 (*0-7933-0185-8*) Gallopade Pub Group.

Avast, Ye Slobs! Colorado Pirate Trivia. Carole Marsh. (Carole Marsh Colorado Bks.). (Illus.). (YA). (gr. 3-12). 1994. lib. bdg. 24.95 (*0-7933-0208-0*); pap. 14.95 (*0-7933-0207-2*); disk 29.95 (*0-7933-0209-9*) Gallopade Pub Group.

Avast, Ye Slobs! Connecticut Pirate Trivia. Carole Marsh. (Carole Marsh Connecticut Bks.). (Illus.). (YA). (gr. 3-12). 1994. lib. bdg. 24.95 (*0-7933-0232-3*); pap. 14.95 (*0-7933-0231-5*); disk 29.95 (*0-7933-0233-1*) Gallopade Pub Group.

Avast, Ye Slobs! Delaware Pirate Trivia. Carole Marsh. (Carole Marsh Delaware Bks.). (Illus.). (YA). (gr. 3-12). 1994. lib. bdg. 24.95 (*0-7933-0256-0*); pap. 14.95 (*0-7933-0255-2*); disk 29.95 (*0-7933-0257-9*) Gallopade Pub Group.

Avast, Ye Slobs! Florida Pirate Trivia. Carole Marsh. (Carole Marsh Florida Bks.). (Illus.). (YA). (gr. 3-12). 1994. lib. bdg. 24.95 (*0-7933-0304-4*); pap. 14.95 (*0-7933-0303-6*); disk 29.95 (*0-7933-0305-2*) Gallopade Pub Group.

Avast, Ye Slobs! Georgia Pirate Trivia. Carole Marsh. (Carole Marsh Georgia Bks.). (Illus.). (YA). (gr. 3-12). 1994. lib. bdg. 24.95 (*0-7933-0328-1*); pap. 14.95 (*0-7933-0327-3*); disk 29.95 (*0-7933-0329-X*) Gallopade Pub Group.

Avast, Ye Slobs! Hawaii Pirate Trivia. Carole Marsh. (Carole Marsh Hawaii Bks.). (Illus.). (YA). (gr. 3-12). 1994. lib. bdg. 24.95 (*0-7933-0352-4*); pap. 14.95 (*0-7933-0351-6*); disk 29.95 (*0-7933-0353-2*) Gallopade Pub Group.

Avast, Ye Slobs! Idaho Pirate Trivia. Carole Marsh. (Carole Marsh Idaho Bks.). (Illus.). (YA). (gr. 3-12). 1994. lib. bdg. 24.95 (*0-7933-0376-1*); pap. 14.95 (*0-7933-0375-3*); disk 29.95 (*0-7933-0377-X*) Gallopade Pub Group.

Avast, Ye Slobs! Illinois Pirate Trivia. Carole Marsh. (Carole Marsh Illinois Bks.). (Illus.). (YA). (gr. 3-12). 1994. lib. bdg. 24.95 (*0-7933-0400-8*); pap. 14.95 (*0-7933-0399-0*); disk 29.95 (*0-7933-0401-6*) Gallopade Pub Group.

Avast, Ye Slobs! Indiana Pirate Trivia. Carole Marsh. (Carole Marsh Indiana Bks.). (Illus.). (YA). (gr. 3-12). 1994. lib. bdg. 24.95 (*0-7933-0424-5*); pap. 14.95 (*0-7933-0423-7*); disk 29.95 (*0-685-45926-8*) Gallopade Pub Group.

Avast, Ye Slobs! Iowa Private Trivia. Carole Marsh. (Carole Marsh Iowa Bks.). (Illus.). (YA). (gr. 3-12). 1994. lib. bdg. 24.95 (*0-7933-0448-2*); pap. 14.95 (*0-7933-0447-4*); disk 29.95 (*0-7933-0449-0*) Gallopade Pub Group.

Avast, Ye Slobs! Kansas Pirate Trivia. Carole Marsh. (Carole Marsh Kansas Bks.). (Illus.). (YA). (gr. 3-12). 1994. lib. bdg. 24.95 (*0-7933-0472-5*); pap. 14.95 (*0-7933-0471-7*); disk 29.95 (*0-7933-0473-3*) Gallopade Pub Group.

Avast, Ye Slobs! Kentucky Pirate Trivia. Carole Marsh. (Carole Marsh Kentucky Bks.). (Illus.). (J). (gr. 3-8). 1994. lib. bdg. 24.95 (*0-7933-0496-2*); pap. 14.95 (*0-7933-0495-4*); disk 29.95 (*0-685-45938-1*) Gallopade Pub Group.

Avast, Ye Slobs! Louisiana Pirate Trivia. Carole Marsh. (Carole Marsh Louisiana Bks.). (Illus.). (J). (gr. 3-8). 1994. lib. bdg. 24.95 (*0-7933-0520-9*); pap. 14.95 (*0-7933-0519-5*); disk 29.95 (*0-7933-0521-7*) Gallopade Pub Group.

Avast, Ye Slobs! Maine Pirate Trivia. Carole Marsh. (Carole Marsh Maine Bks.). (Illus.). (J). (gr. 3-8). 1994. lib. bdg. 24.95 (*0-7933-0545-4*); pap. 14.95 (*0-7933-0544-6*); disk 29.95 (*0-7933-0546-2*) Gallopade Pub Group.

Avast, Ye Slobs! Maryland Pirate Trivia. Carole Marsh. (Carole Marsh Maryland Bks.). (Illus.). (J). (gr. 3-8). 1994. lib. bdg. 24.95 (*0-7933-0569-1*); pap. 14.95 (*0-7933-0568-3*); disk 29.95 (*0-7933-0570-5*) Gallopade Pub Group.

Avast, Ye Slobs! Massachusetts Pirate Trivia. Carole Marsh. (Carole Marsh Massachusetts Bks.). (Illus.). (J). (gr. 3-8). 1994. lib. bdg. 24.95 (*0-7933-0593-4*); pap. 14.95 (*0-7933-0592-6*); disk 29.95 (*0-7933-0594-2*) Gallopade Pub Group.

Avast, Ye Slobs! Nevada Pirate Trivia. Carole Marsh. (Carole Marsh Nevada Bks.). (Illus.). (J). 1994. lib. bdg. 24.95 (*0-7933-0763-5*); pap. 14.95 (*0-7933-0762-7*); disk 29.95 (*0-7933-0764-3*) Gallopade Pub Group.

Avast, Ye Slobs! New Hampshire Pirate Trivia. Carole Marsh. (Carole Marsh New Hampshire Bks.). (Illus.). (J). 1994. lib. bdg. 24.95 (*0-7933-0787-2*); pap. 14.95 (*0-7933-0786-4*); disk 29.95 (*0-7933-0788-0*) Gallopade Pub Group.

Avast, Ye Slobs! New Jersey Pirate Trivia. Carole Marsh. (Carole Marsh New Jersey Bks.). (Illus.). (J). 1994. lib. bdg. 24.95 (*0-7933-1809-2*); pap. 14.95 (*0-7933-1810-6*); disk 29.95 (*0-7933-1811-4*) Gallopade Pub Group.

Avast, Ye Slobs! New Mexico Pirate Trivia. Carole Marsh. (Carole Marsh New Mexico Bks.). (Illus.). (J). 1994. lib. bdg. 24.95 (*0-7933-0811-9*); pap. 14.95 (*0-7933-0810-0*); disk 29.95 (*0-7933-0812-7*) Gallopade Pub Group.

Avast, Ye Slobs! New York Pirate Trivia. Carole Marsh. (Carole Marsh New York Bks.). (Illus.). (J). 1994. lib. bdg. 24.95 (*0-7933-0835-6*); pap. 14.95 (*0-7933-0834-8*); disk 29.95 (*0-7933-0836-4*) Gallopade Pub Group.

Avast, Ye Slobs! North Carolina Pirate Trivia. Carole Marsh. (Carole Marsh North Carolina Bks.). (Illus.). (J). 1994. lib. bdg. 24.95 (*0-7933-0859-3*); pap. 14.95 (*0-7933-0858-5*); disk 29.95 (*0-7933-0860-7*) Gallopade Pub Group.

Avast, Ye Slobs! North Dakota Pirate Trivia. Carole Marsh. (Carole Marsh North Dakota Bks.). (Illus.). (J). 1994. lib. bdg. 24.95 (*0-7933-0883-6*); pap. 14.95 (*0-7933-0882-8*); disk 29.95 (*0-7933-0884-4*) Gallopade Pub Group.

Avast, Ye Slobs! Ohio Pirate Trivia. Carole Marsh. (Carole Marsh Ohio Bks.). (Illus.). (J). 1994. lib. bdg. 24.95 (*0-7933-0908-5*); pap. 14.95 (*0-7933-0907-7*); disk 29.95 (*0-7933-0909-3*) Gallopade Pub Group.

Avast, Ye Slobs! Oklahoma Pirate Trivia. Carole Marsh. (Carole Marsh Oklahoma Bks.). (Illus.). (J). 1994. lib. bdg. 24.95 (*0-7933-0932-8*); pap. 14.95 (*0-7933-0931-X*); disk 29.95 (*0-7933-0933-6*) Gallopade Pub Group.

Avast, Ye Slobs! Oregon Pirate Trivia. Carole Marsh. (Carole Marsh Oregon Bks.). (Illus.). (J). 1994. lib. bdg. 24.95 (*0-7933-0956-5*); pap. 14.95 (*0-7933-0955-7*); disk 29.95 (*0-685-45979-9*) Gallopade Pub Group.

Avast, Ye Slobs! Pennsylvania Pirate Trivia. Carole Marsh. (Carole Marsh Pennsylvania Bks.). (Illus.). (J). 1994. lib. bdg. 24.95 (*0-7933-0980-8*); pap. 14.95 (*0-7933-0979-4*); disk 29.95 (*0-7933-0981-6*) Gallopade Pub Group.

Avast, Ye Slobs! Rhode Island Pirate Trivia. Carole Marsh. (Carole Marsh Rhode Island Bks.). (Illus.). (J). 1994. lib. bdg. 24.95 (*0-7933-1004-0*); pap. 14.95 (*0-7933-1003-2*); disk 29.95 (*0-7933-1005-9*) Gallopade Pub Group.

Avast, Ye Slobs! South Carolina Pirate Trivia. Carole Marsh. (Carole Marsh South Carolina Bks.). (Illus.). (J). 1994. lib. bdg. 24.95 (*0-7933-1028-8*); pap. 14.95 (*0-7933-1027-X*); disk 29.95 (*0-7933-1029-6*) Gallopade Pub Group.

Avast, Ye Slobs! South Dakota Pirate Trivia. Carole Marsh. (Carole Marsh South Dakota Bks.). (Illus.). (J). 1994. lib. bdg. 24.95 (*0-7933-1052-0*); pap. 14.95 (*0-7933-1051-2*); disk 29.95 (*0-7933-1053-9*) Gallopade Pub Group.

Avast, Ye Slobs! Tennessee Pirate Trivia. Carole Marsh. (Carole Marsh Tennessee Bks.). (Illus.). (J). 1994. lib. bdg. 24.95 (*0-7933-1076-8*); pap. 14.95 (*0-7933-1075-X*); disk 29.95 (*0-7933-1077-6*) Gallopade Pub Group.

Avast, Ye Slobs! Texas Pirate Trivia. Carole Marsh. (Texas Bks.). (Illus.). (J). 1990. lib. bdg. 24.95 (*0-7933-1100-4*); pap. 14.95 (*0-7933-1099-7*); disk 29.95 (*0-685-45953-5*) Gallopade Pub Group.

Avast, Ye Slobs! The Book of Silly Pirate Trivia. Carole Marsh. (Triviatime Ser.). (Illus.). (Orig.). (J). (gr. 1-12). 1994. lib. bdg. 24.95 (*1-55609-281-4*); pap. 14.95 (*0-935326-82-0*) Gallopade Pub Group.

Avast, Ye Slobs! Utah Pirate Trivia. Carole Marsh. (Carole Marsh Utah Bks.). (Illus.). (J). 1994. lib. bdg. 24.95 (*0-7933-1124-1*); pap. 14.95 (*0-7933-1123-3*); disk 29.95 (*0-7933-1125-X*) Gallopade Pub Group.

Avast, Ye Slobs! Vermont Pirate Trivia. Carole Marsh. (Carole Marsh Vermont Bks.). (Illus.). (J). 1994. lib. bdg. 24.95 (*0-7933-1148-9*); pap. 14.95 (*0-685-45958-6*); disk 29.95 (*0-7933-1149-7*) Gallopade Pub Group.

Avast, Ye Slobs! Virginia Pirate Trivia. Carole Marsh. (Carole Marsh Virginia Bks.). (Illus.). (J). 1994. lib. bdg. 24.95 (*0-7933-1172-1*); pap. 14.95 (*0-7933-1171-3*); disk 29.95 (*0-7933-1173-X*) Gallopade Pub Group.

Avast, Ye Slobs! Washington, D.C. Carole Marsh. (Carole Marsh Washington, D.C. Bks.). (Illus.). (YA). (gr. 3-12). 1994. lib. bdg. 24.95 (*0-7933-0280-3*); pap. 14.95 (*0-7933-0279-X*); disk 29.95 (*0-7933-0281-1*) Gallopade Pub Group.

Avast, Ye Slobs! Washington Pirate Trivia. Carole Marsh. (Carole Marsh Washington Bks.). (Illus.). (J). 1994. lib. bdg. 24.95 (*0-7933-1196-9*); pap. 14.95 (*0-7933-1195-0*); disk 29.95 (*0-7933-1197-7*) Gallopade Pub Group.

Avast, Ye Slobs! West Virginia Pirate Trivia. Carole Marsh. (Carole Marsh West Virginia Bks.). (Illus.). (J). 1994. lib. bdg. 24.95 (*0-7933-1220-5*); pap. 14.95 (*0-7933-1219-1*); disk 29.95 (*0-7933-1221-3*) Gallopade Pub Group.

Avast, Ye Slobs! Wisconsin Pirate Trivia. Carole Marsh. (Carole Marsh Wisconsin Bks.). (Illus.). (J). 1994. lib. bdg. 24.95 (*0-7933-1244-2*); pap. 14.95 (*0-7933-1243-4*); disk 29.95 (*0-7933-1245-0*) Gallopade Pub Group.

Avast, Ye Slobs! Wyoming Pirate Trivia. Carole Marsh. (Carole Marsh Wyoming Bks.). (Illus.). (J). 1994. lib. bdg. 24.95 (*0-7933-1268-X*); pap. 14.95 (*0-7933-1267-1*); disk 29.95 (*0-7933-1269-8*) Gallopade Pub Group.

Avast, Ye Slobs!: Michigan Pirate Trivia. Carole Marsh. (Carole Marsh Michigan Bks.). (Illus.). (J). (gr. 3 up). 1994. lib. bdg. 24.95 (*0-7933-0617-5*); pap. 14.95 (*0-7933-0616-7*); disk 29.95 (*0-7933-0618-3*) Gallopade Pub Group.

Avast, Ye Slobs!: Minnesota Pirate Trivia. Carole Marsh. (Carole Marsh Minnesota Bks.). (Illus.). (J). (gr. 3 up). 1994. lib. bdg. 24.95 (*0-7933-0641-8*); pap. 14.95 (*0-7933-0640-X*); disk 29.95 (*0-7933-0642-6*) Gallopade Pub Group.

Avast, Ye Slobs!: Mississippi Pirate Trivia. Carole Marsh. (Carole Marsh Mississippi Bks.). (Illus.). (J). (gr. 3 up). 1994. lib. bdg. 24.95 (*0-7933-0666-3*); pap. 14.95 (*0-7933-0665-5*); disk 29.95 (*0-7933-0667-1*) Gallopade Pub Group.

Avast, Ye Slobs!: Missouri Pirate Trivia. Carole Marsh. (Carole Marsh Missouri Bks.). (Illus.). (J). (gr. 3 up). 1994. lib. bdg. 24.95 (*0-7933-0690-6*); pap. 14.95 (*0-7933-0689-2*); disk 29.95 (*0-7933-0691-4*) Gallopade Pub Group.

Avast, Ye Slobs!: Montana Pirate Trivia. Carole Marsh. (Carole Marsh Montana Bks.). (Illus.). (J). (gr. 3 up). 1994. lib. bdg. 24.95 (*0-7933-0715-5*); pap. 14.95 (*0-7933-0714-7*); disk 29.95 (*0-7933-0716-3*) Gallopade Pub Group.

Avast, Ye Slobs!: Nebraska Pirate Trivia. Carole Marsh. (Carole Marsh Nebraska Bks.). (Illus.). (J). (gr. 3 up). 1994. lib. bdg. 24.95 (*0-7933-0739-2*); pap. 14.95 (*0-7933-0738-4*); disk 29.95 (*0-7933-0740-6*) Gallopade Pub Group.

Avatar. Jean Adriel. 285p. 1972. 9.95 (*0-940700-02-6*); pap. 6.95 (*0-940700-01-8*) Meher Baba Info.

Avatar. Louise Cooper. 1992. mass mkt. 4.99 (*0-8125-0802-5*) Tor Bks.

Avatar & Incarnation: A Comparative Analysis. Prashant Miranda. 1990. 19.50 (*81-85151-42-3*, Pub. by Harman Pub Hse II) S Asia.

Avatar (Incarnation of God) 5.00 (*0-938924-35-4*) Sri Shirdi Sai.

Avatar of the Bowmaster. T. Lynn Neal. LC 92-74369. 304p. 1994. pap. 12.95 (*1-56002-214-0*) Aegina Pr.

Avataras. Annie Besant. 124p. 1983. reprint ed. pap. 5.95 (*0-912181-06-0*) East School Pr.

Avatars of Thrice Great Hermes: An Approach to Romanticism. Ernest L. Tuveson. LC 78-75206. (Illus.). 280p. 1982. 36.50 (*0-8387-2264-4*) Bucknell U Pr.

***Avatars of Vengeance: Japanese Drama & the Soga Literary Tradition.** Laurence R. Kominz. LC 95-2897. (Michigan Monographs in Japanese Studies: No. 13). 1995. write for info. (*0-939512-69-6*) U MI Japan.

AVCA Volleyball Handbook: The Official Handbook of the American Volleyball Coaches' Association. Ed. by Bob Bertucci. LC 87-31240. (Illus.). 352p. 1987. pap. 17.95 (*0-940279-11-8*) Masters Pr IN.

Ave Roma Immortalis. Francis M. Crawford. (Works of Francis Marion Crawford Ser.). 1990. reprint ed. lib. bdg. 79.00 (*0-7812-2565-5*) Rprt Serv.

Avec mon Meilleur Souvenir. Francoise Sagan. (Folio Ser.: No. 1657). 149p. (FRE.). 1987. pap. 6.95 (*2-07-037657-5*) Schoenhof.

Avec Mon Meilleur Souvenir. Francoise Sagan. (FRE.). 1985. pap. 10.95 (*0-8288-3726-0*, F44590) Fr & Eur.

Aveli I Kainy (Canes & Ables) Roman (A Novel) Sergei Djatschenko. LC 90-60636. 293p. (Orig.). (RUS.). 1990. pap. text ed. 18.00 (*0-911971-51-3*) Effect Pub.

Aveline: Life & Dream of the Woman Behind Macrobiotics Today. Aveline Kushi & Alex Jack. LC 87-80492. (Illus.). 240p. 1988. 19.95 (*0-87040-693-0*) Japan Pubns USA.

Aveline Kushi's Complete Guide to Macrobiotic Cooking for Health, Harmony, & Peace. Aveline Kushi. 1988. pap. 15.99 (*0-446-38634-0*) Warner Bks.

Aveline Kushi's Introducing Macrobiotic Cooking. Wendy Esko. (Illus.). 176p. (Orig.). 1987. pap. 14.95 (*0-87040-690-6*) Japan Pubns USA.

Aveline Kushi's Wonderful World of Salads. Aveline Kushi & Wendy Esko. 176p. 1989. pap. 15.95 (*0-87040-785-6*) Japan Pubns USA.

Aven Nelson of Wyoming. Roger L. Williams. LC 83-71133. (Illus.). 419p. reprint ed. pap. 119.50 (*0-8357-5508-8*, 2035123) Bks Demand.

Avenge the Belgrano. Bob Langley. LC 87-34461. 1988. 18.95 (*0-8027-1030-1*) Walker & Co.

Avenge the Belgrano. large type ed. Bob Langley. 1990. 21.95 (*0-7089-2140-X*) Ulverscroft.

***Avenged!** Julie Ellis. 1995. lib. bdg. 19.00 (*0-7278-4748-1*) Severn Hse.

Avenger at War. Barrett Tillman. (Illus.). 128p. 1990. 26.95 (*1-55750-040-1*) Naval Inst Pr.

Avenger from the Sky. J. Judd. (C). 1986. text ed. 115.00 (*0-685-38785-2*, Pub. by Maritime Bks UK) St Mut.

Avengers. Stan Lee & Jack Kirby. (Marvel Masterworks Ser.: Vol. 4). 232p. 1988. 34.95 (*0-87135-479-9*) Marvel Entmnt.

An Asterisk (*) at the beginning of an entry indicates that the title is appearing in BIP for the first time.

553

Avengers. Stan Lee et al. (Marvel Masterworks Ser.: Vol. 9). 210p. 1989. 29.95 (0-87135-595-7) Marvel Entmnt.

Avengers: Emperor Doom. David Michelinie. (Illus.). 640p. 1990. pap. 9.95 (0-87135-256-7) Marvel Entmnt.

Avengers: Too Many Targets. John Peel & Dave Rogers. 192p. (Orig.). 1990. pap. 8.95 (0-312-05003-8) St Martin.

Avengers "New Masters of Evil" 1992. pap. write for info. (0-87135-626-0) Marvel Entmnt.

***Avenging Angel.** David Belbin. (YA). 1994. pap. 3.50 (0-590-48890-2) Scholastic Inc.

Avenging Angel. Frank Rich. 1993. mass mkt. 3.50 (0-373-63607-5, 1-63607-5) Harlequin Bks.

Avenging Liafail. Talbot Mundy. (Tros of Samothrace Ser.: No. 2). 1978. pap. 2.25 (0-89083-378-8) Zebra.

Avenging Saint. Leslie Charteris. 18.95 (0-88411-267-5, Aeonian Pr) Amereon Ltd.

Avenging Storm. Duncan Long. (Night Stalkers Ser.: No. 9). (Orig.). 1992. mass mkt. 3.99 (0-06-100438-3, Harp PBks) HarpC.

Avenging the Maine, a Drunken A. B. & Other Poems. James E. McGirt. LC 73-133160. (Black Heritage Library Collection). 1977. 13.95 (0-8369-8715-2) Ayer.

Avenir De L'homme. Pierre Teilhard De Chardin. (FRE.). 1959. pap. 29.95 (0-7859-1586-9, 202002862X) Fr & Eur.

Avenir Est dans les Oeufs see Theatre

Avenir Havas Media SA & Brunton Curtis Outdoor Advertising Ltd. (Monopolies & Mergers Commission Report Ser.). 113p. 1991. pap. 25.00 (0-10-117372-5, HM2573) UNIPUB.

Aventura de Daniel con los Leones (Daniel's Adventure with the Lions) Hunt & Thorpe. (SPA.). Date not set. 6.99 (1-56063-752-8, 490313) Editorial Unilit.

Aventura de David con el Gigante (David's Adventure with the Giant) Hunt & Thorpe. (SPA.). Date not set. 6.99 (1-56063-751-X, 490312) Editorial Unilit.

Aventura de Estudiar: Programa para Desarrollar Destrezas de Estudio e Informacion en el nivel Elemental e Intermedio. Blanca N. De Ponce. (Illus.). 100p. (Orig.). (SPA.). (J). (gr. 5-9). 1984. write for info. (0-318-64879-2) B Ponce.

Aventura de la Vida (The Adventure of Life) Jean LeLoeuff. Tr. by Luis M. Puebla. (Explorer Ser.). (Illus.). 96p. (SPA.). (J). (gr. 4 up). 1992. lib. bdg. 15.90 (1-56294-177-1) Millbrook Pr.

Aventura de Yolanda; Yolanda's Hike. Tomas R. Gaspar. (Illus.). (ENG & SPA.). (J). (ps-3). 1974. pap. 5.95 (0-938678-03-5) New Seed.

Aventuras: Beginning Spanish. Brenda Stephens. 1989. pap. text ed. 18.45 (0-8013-0005-3, 75671) Longman.

Aventuras a lo Divino: God's Adventures. Irene Burk-Harrell. (SPA.). 3.25 (84-7228-628-2, 360030, Pub. by Edit Clie SP) TSELF.

Aventuras de Amor del Doctor Fonda (la Sombra de Helena) N. Puente-Duany. LC 78-73151. (Coleccion Caniqui Ser.). (Illus.). 1979. pap. 5.95 (0-89729-215-4) Ediciones.

Aventuras de Bartolillo. Efren Quintanilla. (SPA.). 7.95 (84-241-5634-X) E Torres & Sons.

Aventuras de Don Chipote o Cuando los Pericos Mamen. Daniel Venegas. 160p. 1985. 8.00 (0-934770-64-6) Arte Publico.

Aventuras de Don Quijote: Relatos Ilustrados. Miguel de Cervantes Saavedra. (SPA.). 9.00 (84-241-5412-6) E Torres & Sons.

Aventuras de Fe: Adventures of Faith. Arnoldo Canclini. (SPA.). 3.25 (84-7228-213-9, 220059, Pub. by Edit Clie SP) TSELF.

Aventuras De Guerra y Paz: Adventures in War & Peace. Peter Vanwoerden. (SPA.). 2.50 (84-7228-065-9, 220064, Pub. by Edit Clie SP) TSELF.

Aventuras de Tom Sawyer. Mark Twain. (SPA.). 9.00 (84-241-5630-7) E Torres & Sons.

Aventuras en la Oracion. Catherine Marshall. 192p. 1976. 3.95 (0-88113-005-2) Edit Betania.

Aventuras, Inventos y Mixtificaciones De Silvestre Paradox. Pio Baroja. Ed. by E. Inman Fox. (Nueva Austral Ser.: No. 116). (SPA.). 1991. pap. text ed. 24.95x (84-239-1916-1) Elliots Bks.

Aventuras Literarias. 3rd ed. Ana C. Jarvis et al. LC 90-80530. 180p. (SPA.). (C). 1991. pap. text ed. write for info. (0-669-20894-9); Text with free student cassette. pap. text ed. write for info. (0-669-24987-4) Heath.

***Aventuras Literarias.** 4th ed. Ana C. Jarvis et al. 192p. (SPA.). (C). 1995. pap. text ed. write for info. (0-669-33767-6) Heath.

Aventure. Lucien Bodard. (Guerre d'Indochine Ser.: Vol. IV). 544p. (FRE.). 1973. pap. 10.95 (0-7859-1723-3, 2070362981) Fr & Eur.

Aventure de l'Absolu. De Reneville. (Phaenomenologica Ser.: No. 48). 1972. lib. bdg. 80.00 (90-247-1319-6) Kluwer Ac.

Aventure et Passion: Contes et Recits d'Aujourd'hui. Ann Swarbrick et al. (Serie Rouge). (Illus.). 64p. (C). 1994. pap. 5.50 (0-521-44982-0) Cambridge U Pr.

Aventure Litteraire de Joseph Conrad et d'Andre Gide. Walter C. Putnam, III. (Stanford French & Italian Studies: Vol. 67). 276p. (FRE.). 1991. pap. 46.50 (0-915838-83-4) Anma Libri.

Aventure Semiologique. Roland Barthes. (FRE.). 1991. pap. 19.95 (0-7859-2720-4) Fr & Eur.

Aventures D'Alice au Pays des Merveilles. Lewis Carroll. Tr. by Henri Bue. (Illus.). 196p. (FRE.). (J). (gr. 4-8). 1972. reprint ed. pap. 4.95 (0-486-22836-3) Dover.

Aventures de Arthur Gordon Pym. Edgar Allan Poe. (FRE.). 1975. pap. 11.95 (0-7859-4040-5) Fr & Eur.

Aventures de Babar. Laurent de Brunhoff. 18p. (J). 1977. 15.95 (0-686-54134-0) Fr & Eur.

Aventures de Hector, I. Adapt. by Ben Christensen. 1992. pap. 15.95 (0-8384-2550-X) Heinle & Heinle.

Aventures de Hector, II. Adapt. by Ben Christensen. 1992. pap. 15.95 (0-8384-2551-8) Heinle & Heinle.

Aventures de Jerome Bardini. Jean Giraudoux. 1964. pap. 24.95 (0-685-11022-2) Fr & Eur.

***Aventures de Jerome Bardini.** Jean Giraudoux. 221p. 1979. pap. write for info. (0-7859-5258-6) Fr & Eur.

Aventures De L'esprit. Natalie C. Barney. LC 75-12302. (Homosexuality Ser.). (FRE.). 1975. reprint ed. 23.95 (0-405-07394-1) Ayer.

Aventures de Sophie. Paul Claudel. 224p. (FRE.). 1937. pap. 10.95 (0-7859-1113-8, 2070215008) Fr & Eur.

Aventures de Tom Sawyer. Mark Twain, pseud. (Folio - Junior Ser.: No. 449). (Illus.). 296p. (FRE.). (J). (gr. 5-10). 1987. pap. 9.95 (2-07-033449-X) Schoenhof.

Aventures d'Olivier Twist. Charles Dickens. (FRE.). 1973. pap. 11.95 (0-7859-1745-4, 2070363864) Fr & Eur.

Aventures Du Dernier Abencerage. Rene de Chateaubriand et al. 306p. (FRE.). 1978. pap. 13.95 (0-7859-1537-0, 2070370178) Fr & Eur.

Aventures du Dernier Abencerage see Atala

Aventures du Grand Sidonie et du Petit Mederic. Emile Zola. (FRE.). 1976. 26.95 (0-7859-5518-6) Fr & Eur.

Aventures Du Petit Nicholas. Jean-Jacques Sempe & Rene De Goscinny. Ed. by C. Kaplan. 1966. write for info. (0-02-189020-X) Macmillan.

Aventures du Scepticisme: Essai sur l'Evolution Intellectuelle d'Anatole France. Maurice Levaillant. (FRE.). 38.95 (0-8288-9969-X, F59035) Fr & Eur.

Aventures d'un Jeune Homme. John R. Dos Passos. 480p. (FRE.). 1987. pap. 16.95 (0-7859-2234-2, 207037808X) Fr & Eur.

Aventures En Ville. Jean-Pierre Halioua et al. LC 79-63579. (J). (gr. 9-12). 1980. pap. 17.64 (0-395-27833-3) HM.

Aventures Ou la Queste Del Saint Graal: La Mort le Roi Artus. Ed. by H. Oskar Sommer. (Vulgate Version of the Arthurian Romances Ser.: No. 6). reprint ed. 87.50 (0-404-17636-4) AMS Pr.

Aventuriers. Jose Giovanni. 256p. (FRE.). 1974. pap. 10.95 (0-7859-2344-6, 2070365840) Fr & Eur.

Aventuros de Miguel Littin. 6th ed. Gabriel Garcia Marquez. 192p. (SPA.). 1988. pap. 13.95 (0-7859-5021-4) Fr & Eur.

Avenue Bearing the Initial of Christ into the New World: Poems 1946-1964. Galway Kinnell. 1974. pap. 15.95 (0-395-18628-5) HM.

Avenue, Clayton City. C. Eric Lincoln. (Black History Titles Ser.). 1989. mass mkt. 4.99 (0-345-36034-6) Ballantine.

Avenue of Dream. Elyse Nass. 1970. pap. 2.75 (0-8222-0083-X) Dramatists Play.

Avenue of Dreams. Lucy Taylor. 464p. 1990. pap. 5.50 (0-451-16599-3, Sig) NAL-Dutton.

***Avenue of Escape.** Lewis Warsh. 100p. (Orig.). 1995. pap. text ed. 8.00 (0-9645591-0-2) Long News Bks.

Avenue of Ghosts. Mable Renault. 120p. (Orig.). 1988. pap. text ed. 10.00 (0-685-28898-6) Rivendell Hse Ltd.

Avenue of Tears: Selected Poems 1968-1986. Gregg Weinlein. 64p. (Orig.). 1987. 13.95 (0-9617556-3-6); pap. 8.95 (0-9617556-4-4) Kelly Colm Pr.

Avenue of the Americas. James Scully. LC 74-164444. 1971. 5.00 (0-917488-07-5); pap. 2.50 (0-917488-08-3) Ziesing Bros.

Avenues for Articulation: Coordinating Secondary & Postsecondary Programs. 98p. 1986. 9.50 (0-318-21255-2, RD259) Ctr Educ Trng Employ.

Avenues of Involvement. Jarene Robison. Ed. by Gina Howard. 48p. (Orig.). 1993. pap. text ed. 3.95 (1-56309-084-8, New Hope) Womans Mission Union.

Avenues of Love: An Intergenerational Activities Manual. Ed. by Ilene Miller & Jane B. Moore. 66p. (Orig.). 1991. pap. text ed. 10.95 (0-685-57048-7) Geriatric Educ.

Avenues of Participation: Family, Politics & Networks in Urban Quarters of Cairo. Diane Singerman. LC 94-19060. (Studies in Muslim Politics). 1994. 39.50 (0-691-08654-0) Princeton U Pr.

Avenues of Sedimentation of Carbonate Skeletal Sands in Rice Bay, San Salvador, Bahamas. R. Alley et al. (Occasional Paper - 1986: No. 2). 14p. 1986. pap. text ed. 1.50 (0-935909-21-4) Bahamian.

***Avenues ot the Vine.** Michael E. Seckinger, Sr. 320p. 1995. pap. 9.95 (1-56901-885-5) NW Pub.

Avenues to Adulthood: The Origins of the High School & Social Mobility in an American Suburb. Reed Ueda. (Interdisciplinary Perspectives in Modern History Ser.). 325p. 1987. 47.95 (0-521-32770-9) Cambridge U Pr.

Avenues to Progress see California

Average Jones. Samuel H. Adams. LC 75-32731. (Literature of Mystery & Detection Ser.). (Illus.). 1976. reprint ed. 28.95 (0-405-07861-7) Ayer.

Average Nights. Paul Nelson. LC 77-75758. 62p. 1977. per. 3.75 (0-934332-04-5) LEpervier Pr.

Average Workweek as an Economic Indicator. Gerhard Bry. 6.00 (0-405-18756-4, 16470) Ayer.

Average Workweek As an Economic Indicator. Gerhard Bry. (Occasional Papers: No. 69). 127p. 1959. reprint ed. 33.10 (0-87014-383-2) Natl Bur Econ Res.

Averaged Moduli of Smoothness: Applications in Numerical Methods & Approximation. Blagovest Sendov & Vasil A. Popov. LC 88-2434. (Pure & Applied Mathematics Ser.). 200p. 1989. text ed. 110.00 (0-471-91952-7) Wiley.

Averaging in Classical Dynamical Systems. P. Lochak & C. Meunier. (Applied Mathematical Sciences Ser.: Vol. 72). (Illus.). 370p. 1988. pap. 44.00 (0-387-96778-8) Spr-Verlag.

Averaging in Stability Theory: A Study of Resonance Multi-Frequency Systems (piii) M. M. Hapaev. (Mathematics & Its Applications, Soviet Ser.). 296p. (C). 1992. lib. bdg. 145.00 (0-7923-1581-2) Kluwer Ac.

Averaging Methods in Nonlinear Dynamical Systems. J. A. Sanders & F. Verhulst. (Applied Mathematical Sciences Ser.: Vol. 59). (Illus.). 247p. 1985. pap. 54.00 (0-387-96229-8) Spr-Verlag.

Averell-Avery Family: A Record of the Descendants of William & Abigail Averell of Ipswich, Mass., 2 vols., Set. Clara A. Avery. (Illus.). 1094p. 1993. reprint ed. lib. bdg. 159.00 (0-8328-3007-0); reprint ed. pap. 149.00 (0-8328-3008-9) Higginson Bk Co.

Averroes: Epitome of Parva Naturalia. Averroes. Tr. by Harry Blumberg. LC 58-3296. (Medieval Academy Bks.: No. 71). 1961. 30.00 (0-910956-45-6) Medieval Acad.

Averroes: Middle Commentary on Porphyry's Isagoge. Averrois. Ed. by Herbert A. Davidson. LC 68-24427. (Medieval Academy Bks.: No. 79). 1969. 30.00 (0-910956-53-7) Medieval Acad.

Averroes & His Philosophy. Oliver Leaman. (Illus.). 224p. 1988. 55.00 (0-19-826540-9) OUP.

Averroes & the Metaphysics of Causation. Barry S. Kogan. LC 85-2585. 348p. 1985. 74.50 (0-88706-063-3); pap. 24.95 (0-88706-065-X) State U NY Pr.

Averroe's Commentary on Plato's Republic. Ed. by Edwin I. Rosenthal. (University of Cambridge Oriental Publications: No. 1). 1966. 74.95 (0-521-06130-X) Cambridge U Pr.

Averroes Cordubensis Commentarium Magnum in Aristotelis De Anima Libros, Lat. Ed. Averroes. Ed. by F. S. Crawford. LC 53-9617. (Medieval Academy Bks.: No. 59). 1953. 35.00 (0-910956-33-2) Medieval Acad.

Averroes Cordubensis Commentarium Medium et Epitome in Aristotelis De Generatione et Corruptione Libros, Heb Ed. Averrois. Ed. by Samuel Kurland. LC 50-1421. (Medieval Academy Bks.: No. 66). 1958. 30.00 (0-910956-40-5) Medieval Acad.

Averroes Cordubensis Commentarium Medium in Aristotelis De Generatione et Corruptione Libros, Lat. Ed. Averroes. Ed. by F. H. Fobes & Samuel Kurland. LC 50-1421. (Medieval Academy Bks.: No. 65). 1956. 30.00 (0-910956-39-1) Medieval Acad.

Averroes Cordubensis Commentarium Medium in Porphyrii Isagogen et Aristotelis Categorias, Heb. Ed. Averroes. Ed. by Herbert A. Davidson. LC 68-24426. (Medieval Academy Bks.: No. 78). 1969. 30.00 (0-910956-52-9) Medieval Acad.

Averroes Cordubensis Compendia Librorum Aristotelis Qui Parva Naturalia Vocantur. Averroes. Ed. by Harry Blumberg. LC 78-108420. (Medieval Academy Bks.: No. 80). (ARA.). 1972. 30.00 (0-910956-54-5) Medieval Acad.

Averroes Cordubensis Compendia Librorum Aristotelis Qui Parva Naturalia Vocantur, Heb. Ed. Averroes. Ed. by Harry Blumberg. LC 50-1421. (Medieval Academy Bks.: No. 62). 1954. 30.00 (0-910956-36-7) Medieval Acad.

Averroes Cordubensis Compendia Librorum Aristotelis Qui Parva Naturalia Vocantur, Lat. Ed. Averroes. Ed. by E. L. Shields & Harry Blumberg. (Medieval Academy Bks.: No. 54). 1949. 30.00 (0-910956-28-6) Medieval Acad.

Averroes' "De Substantia Orbis" Critical Edition of the Hebrew Text, with English Translation & Commentary. Averroes. Ed. by Arthur Hyman. No. 96. (ENG & HEB.). 1986. 30.00 (0-318-65007-X) Medieval Acad.

Averroes' Destructio Destructionum Philosophiae Algazelis in the Latin Version of Calo Calonymos. Averroes. Ed. by Beatrice H. Zedler. LC 60-10262. 1961. 25.00 (0-87462-421-5) Marquette.

Averroes et l'Averroisme. Ernest Renan. xvi, 486p. 1987. reprint ed. write for info. (3-487-07816-3, Pub. by Georg Olms GW) Lubrecht & Cramer.

Averroe's Middle Commentaries on Aristotle's Categories & De Interpretatione. Tr. by Charles E. Butterworth. LC 82-61359. 192p. 1983. 37.50 (0-691-07276-0) Princeton U Pr.

Averroes' Middle Commentary on Aristole's Categories. Ed. by Mahmoud M Kassem et al. (American Research Center in Egypt, Publications Ser.: Vol. 5). 180p. (Orig.). (ARA & ENG.). 1981. pap. 10.50 (0-936770-04-X, Pub. by Amer Res Ctr Egypt UA) Eisenbrauns.

Averroes' Middle Commentary on Aristole's de Interpretation. Ed. by Mahmoud M. Kassem et al. (American Research Center in Egypt, Publications Ser.: Vol. 6). 147p. (Orig.). (ARA & ENG.). 1981. text ed. 15.00 (0-936770-05-8, Pub. by Amer Res Ctr Egypt UA) Eisenbrauns.

Averroes' Middle Commentary on Aristotle's Poetics. Ed. by C. E. Butterworth & A. A. Haridi. (American Research Center in Egypt, Publications Ser.: No. 9). 152p. (ARA & ENG.). 1986. text ed. 22.50 (0-936770-08-2, Pub. by Amer Res Ctr Egypt UA) Eisenbrauns.

Averroes' Middle Commentary on Aristotle's "Poetics" Tr. by Charles E. Butterworth. LC 85-43272. 160p. 1986. text ed. 32.50 (0-691-07302-3) Princeton U Pr.

Averroes' Middle Commentary on Aristotle's Posterior Analytics. Ed. by M. M. Kassem et al. (American Research Center in Egypt, Publications Ser.: No. 7). 232p. (ARA & ENG.). 1982. pap. text ed. 16.50 (0-936770-07-4, Pub. by Amer Res Ctr Egypt UA) Eisenbrauns.

Averroes' Middle Commentary on Aristotle's Prior Analytics. Ed. by M. M. Kassem et al. (American Research Center in Egypt, Publications Ser.: No. 8). 425p. (ARA & ENG.). 1983. pap. text ed. 19.50 (0-936770-06-6, Pub. by Amer Res Ctr Egypt UA) Eisenbrauns.

Averroes on Aristotle's De Generatione et Corruptione: Middle Commentary & Epitome. Averroes. Tr. by Samuel Kurland. LC 50-1421. (Medieval Academy Bks.: No. 67). 1958. 30.00 (0-910956-41-3) Medieval Acad.

Averroes on the Harmony of Religion & Philosophy. Hourani. (Gibb Memorial New Ser.: Vol. 21). 1976. reprint ed. pap. 60.00 (0-7189-0222-X, Pub. by Aris & Phillips UK) David Brown.

Averroes' Questions in Physics. Ed. by Helen T. Goldstein. (New Synthese Historical Library). 208p. 1990. lib. bdg. 92.00 (0-7923-0997-9) Kluwer Ac.

Averroes Tahafut Al-Tahafut: The Incoherence of the Incoherence, 2 vols. in 1. Tr. by Van den Bergh. (Gibb Memorial New Ser.: Vol. 19). 1978. reprint ed. 60.00 (0-906094-21-6, Pub. by Aris & Phillips UK); reprint ed. Vol. 1 Translation. write for info. (0-318-68522-1, Pub. by Aris & Phillips UK); reprint ed. Vol. 2 Commentary & Notes. write for info. (0-318-68523-X, Pub. by Aris & Phillips UK) David Brown.

Averroes's Middle Commentary on Aristotle's Topics. Ed. by C. E. Butterworth & A. Haridi. (American Research Center in Egypt, Publications Ser.: Vol. 4). 247p. (Orig.). (ARA & ENG.). 1979. pap. 10.50 (0-936770-03-1, Pub. by Amer Res Ctr Egypt UA) Eisenbrauns.

Averroes's Three Short Commentaries on Aristotle's Topic, Rhetoric, & Poetics. Ed. & Tr. by Charles E. Butterworth. LC 75-4900. 206p. 1977. 59.50 (0-87395-208-1) State U NY Pr.

Averse to Beasts: Twenty-Three Reasonless Rhymes. Nick Bantock. Ed. by Annie Barrows. LC 93-37207. (Illus.). 64p. 1994. 16.95 (0-8118-0700-2) Chronicle Bks.

Aversion, Avoidance & Anxiety: Perspectives on Aversively Motivated Behavior. Ed. by T. Archer & L. G. Nilsson. 512p. (C). 1988. text ed. 99.95 (0-8058-0132-4) L Erlbaum Assocs.

Aversive & Non-Aversive Interventions: Controlling Life-Threatening Behavior by the Developmentally Disabled. Ed. by Sandra Harris & Jan Handleman. LC 90-9568. (Behavior Therapy & Behavioral Medicine Ser.: Vol. 25). 216p. 1990. 38.95 (0-8261-7300-4) Springer Pub.

Aversive Stimulation: Proceedings of the Miami Symposium on the Prediction of Behavior, 1967. Miami Symposium on the Prediction of Behavior Staff. Ed. by Marshall R. Jones. LC 68-18946. (Illus.). 1968. 5.95 (0-87024-077-3) U of Miami Pr.

Averting a Latin American Nuclear Arms Race: New Prospects & Challenges for Argentine-Brazil Nuclear Cooperation. Ed. by Paul L. Leventhal & Sharon Tanzer. LC 91-31595. 273p. 1992. text ed. 69.95 (0-312-07277-5) St Martin.

Averting the Apocalypse: Social Movements in India Today. Arthur Bonner. LC 89-28006. 475p. (Orig.). (C). 1990. 55.50 (0-8223-1029-5); pap. 19.95 (0-8223-1048-1) Duke.

***Averting the Old Age Crisis: Policies, to Protect the Old & Promote Growth.** 1994. student ed, disk 14.95 (0-614-04078-7, 13032) World Bank.

***Averting the Old Age Crisis: Policies, to Protect the Old & Promote Growth.** (Policy Research Report Ser.). 630p. (SPA.). 1994. 19.95 (0-8213-2844-1, 12844) World Bank.

Averting the Old Age Crisis: Policies, to Protect the Old & Promote Growth. Estelle James. (Policy Research Report Ser.). 630p. 1994. 19.95 (0-19-520996-6, 60996) World Bank.

Avery Architectural & Fine Arts Library, Columbia University: Avery Index to Architectural Periodicals, Ninth Supplement, 1989. 2nd ed. 525p. 1989. lib. bdg. 410.00 (0-8161-0486-7) G K Hall.

Avery Index to Architectural Periodicals, 15 vols., Set. 2nd ed. Columbia University Editors. 1975. lib. bdg. 1,635.00 (0-8161-1067-0, Hall Library) G K Hall.

Avery Index to Architectural Periodicals: First Supplement. 2nd ed. Columbia University Editors. 1978. lib. bdg. 160.00 (0-8161-0018-7, Hall Library) G K Hall.

Avery Index to Architectural Periodicals: Tenth Supplement, 1989, 3 vols., Set. 2nd ed. Avery Architectural & Fine Arts Library Staff. (Monograph Ser.). 3000p. 1990. lib. bdg. 395.00 (0-8161-0495-6) G K Hall.

Avery Index to Architectural Periodicals: Third Supplement. Columbia University Editors. 1979. lib. bdg. 160.00 (0-8161-0282-1, Hall Library) G K Hall.

Avery Index to Architectural Periodicals: Thirteenth Supplement, 1992, 4 vols., Set. 2nd ed. Avery Architectural & Fine Arts Library Staff. 3000p. 1993. lib. bdg. 450.00 (0-8161-0615-0, Hall Reference) Macmillan.

Avery Index to Architectural Periodicals: 1987, 4 vols. Avery Memorial Library, Columbia University. 2800p. 1988. lib. bdg. 410.00 (0-8161-0460-3, Hall Library) G K Hall.

Avery Index to Architectural Periodicals, Twelfth Supplement: Nineteen-Hundred Ninety-One. 2nd ed. Avery Architectural & Fine Arts Library. 3000p. 1992. text ed. 435.00 (0-8161-0600-2) G K Hall.

Avery Index to Architectural Periodicals, 1979-1982, 3 vols., Set. Columbia University, Avery Architectural & Fine Arts Library Editors. (Library Reference-Supplements Ser.). 1986. lib. bdg. 325.00 (0-8161-0384-4) G K Hall.

Avery Index to Architectural Periodicals, 1983-1984. 275p. 1987. lib. bdg. 410.00 (0-8161-0456-5, Hall Reference) Macmillan.

Avery Index to Architectural Periodicals, 1985, 4 vols., Set. Columbia University, Avery Architectural & Fine Arts Library Editors. (Library Catalogs & Supplements). 3300p. (C). 1986. lib. bdg. 410.00 (0-8161-0447-6, Hall Library) G K Hall.

Avery Index to Architectural Periodicals, 1986, 4 vols. Ed. by Avery Architectural & Fine Arts Library Staff & Columbia University Staff. 2800p. 1987. lib. bdg. 410.00 (0-8161-0457-3, Hall Reference) Macmillan.

An Asterisk (*) at the beginning of an entry indicates that the title is appearing in BIP for the first time.

Avery Memorial - The Wadsworth Atheneum: The First Modern Museum. Eugene R. Gaddis. (Illus.). 69p. 1984. pap. 5.00 (0-918333-00-8) Wadsworth Atheneum.

Avery Notes & Queries: A Quarterly Magazine Devoted to the History of the Groton Averys, No. 1-18. E. M. Avery. (Illus.). 1988. reprint ed. lib. bdg. 47.00 (0-8328-0144-5); reprint ed. pap. 37.00 (0-8328-0145-3) Higginson Bk Co.

Aves. L. Christidis. (Animal Cytogenetics Ser.: Vol. 4: Chordata 3). (Illus.). 116p. 1990. pap. text ed. 54.50 (3-443-26014-4, Pub. by Gebrueder Borntraeger GW) Lubrecht & Cramer.

Aves Hawaiianses: The Birds of Hawaii. Sam Gon. (Illus.). 96p. 1989. boxed 500.00 (1-877690-05-8) Hemmeter Pub.

Aves Hawaiienses: The Birds of the Sandwich Islands. B. Scott Wilson & A. H. Evans. LC 73-17848. (Natural Sciences in America Ser.). (Illus.). 356p. 1979. reprint ed. 34.95 (0-405-05771-7) Ayer.

Aves Migratorias Nearticas En los Neotropicos. John H. Rappole et al. 348p. 1993. 19.00 (0-9638408-0-0) C & RC Nat Zool.

Avesta: Major Portions from the Holy Book of the Magi. Ed. by Ernestine G. Busch. LC 85-90618. 440p. (Orig.). 1985. pap. 17.50 (0-9614750-0-5) E G Busch.

Avesta: The Religious Books of the Parsees. Arthur H. Bleeck. 1974. lib. bdg. 250.00 (0-87968-133-0) Krishna Pr.

Avesta: The Religious Books of the Parsees, from Professor Spiegel's German Translation. Arthur H. Bleeck. 1988. reprint ed. lib. bdg. 59.00 (0-7812-0114-4) Rprt Serv.

Avesta Eschatology: Compared with the Books of Daniel & Revelations. Lawrence H. Mills. LC 74-24644. reprint ed. 29.50 (0-404-12816-5) AMS Pr.

Avesta Grammar in Comparison with Sanskrit, Together with The Avestan Alphabet & Its Transcription. Abraham V. Jackson. LC 77-149387. reprint ed. 49.50 (0-404-09010-9) AMS Pr.

Avesta Reader: First Series. Abraham V. Jackson. LC 70-149388. reprint ed. 21.00 (0-404-09011-7) AMS Pr.

Avesta Set, 2 vols. Ernestine G. Busch. 1990. pap. 26.95 (0-9614750-2-1) E G Busch.

Avestan Symbols & Concepts: Understandings from the Holy Book of the Magi. enl. ed. Ernestine G. Busch. LC 89-90990. 168p. 1989. pap. 9.95 (0-9614750-1-3) E G Busch.

Aveugle au Pistolet. Chester Himes. 373p. (FRE.). 1976. pap. 11.95 (0-7859-2373-X, 2070368181) Fr & Eur.

Aveux et Anathemes. E. M. Cioran. (FRE.). 1986. pap. 13.95 (0-7859-2937-1) Fr & Eur.

Aveux et Anathemes. E. M. Cioran. (Arcades Ser.). 145p. (FRE.). 1987. pap. 15.95 (2-07-070830-6) Schoenhof.

Aveux Infideles. Jacques De Bourbon Busset. (FRE.). 1972. pap. 10.95 (0-7859-2196-6, 207036268X) Fr & Eur.

Avian & Mammalian Wildlife Toxicology - STP 693. Ed. by E. E. Kenaga. 103p. 1979. pap. 16.25 (0-8031-0287-9, 693, 04-693000-48) ASTM.

Avian & Mammalian Wildlife Toxicology: Second Conference - STP 757. Ed. by Lamb & Kenaga. 170p. 1981. pap. 18.50 (0-8031-0759-5, 04-757000-48) ASTM.

***Avian Ark: Tales from a Wild-Bird Hospital.** Kit Chubb. (Illus.). 156p. (Orig.). 1995. pap. 12.00 (1-886913-03-X) Hungry Mind.

***Avian Auditory-Vocal Motor Interfaces, No. 44, No. 4-5.** Ed. by S. E. Brauth & W. S. Hall. (Journal: Brains, Behavior & Evolution: Vol. 44, No. 4-5). (Illus.). 100p. 1994. pap. 47.25 (3-8055-6074-5) S Karger.

Avian Biology, 5 vols., Vol. 1: 1971. Donald S. Farner & James R. King. 1971. Vol. 1, 1971. text ed. 160.00 (0-12-249401-6) Acad Pr.

Avian Biology, 5 vols., Vol. 2: 1972. Donald S. Farner & James R. King. 1972. Vol. 2, 1972. text ed. 160.00 (0-12-249402-4) Acad Pr.

Avian Biology, 5 vols., Vol. 3: 1973. Donald S. Farner & James R. King. 1973. Vol. 3, 1973. text ed. 160.00 (0-12-249403-2) Acad Pr.

Avian Biology, 5 vols., Vol. 4: 1974. Donald S. Farner & James R. King. 1974. Vol. 4, 1974. text ed. 160.00 (0-12-249404-0) Acad Pr.

Avian Biology, 5 vols., Vol. 5: 1975. Donald S. Farner & James R. King. 1975. Vol. 5, 1975. text ed. 160.00 (0-12-249405-9) Acad Pr.

Avian Biology, Vol. 7. Ed. by Donald S. Farner et al. 1983. text ed. 85.00 (0-12-249407-5) Acad Pr.

Avian Biology, Vol. 9. Ed. by Donald S. Farner et al. (Illus.). 368p. 1993. text ed. 60.00 (0-12-249409-1) Acad Pr.

Avian Botulism: An International Perspective. Mel W. Eklund & Vulus R. Dowell, Jr. (Illus.). 428p. 1987. 88.95x (0-398-05311-1) C C Thomas.

Avian Cellular Immunology. Ed. by Sharma. 1990. 167.00 (0-8493-6833-2, SF995) CRC Pr.

Avian Dreamers. Jerry Gildemeister. LC 90-85397. (Illus.). (YA). (gr. 9-12). 1991. 45.00 (0-936376-07-4) Bear Wallow Pub.

Avian Egg: Chemistry & Biology. R. W. Burley & D. Vadehra. 1989. text ed. 138.95 (0-471-84995-2) Wiley.

Avian Embryo: Structural & Functional Development. Alexis L. Romanoff. LC 59-7975. 1323p. reprint ed. pap. 180.00 (0-8357-5932-6, 2051970) Bks Demand.

***Avian Energetics.** Ed. by Cynthia Carey. LC 95-15905. 1995. write for info. (0-412-03701-7) Chapman & Hall.

Avian Energetics. Ed. by Raymond A. Paynter, Jr. (Publications of the Nuttall Ornithological Club: No. 15). (Illus.). 334p. 1974. 17.00 (1-877973-25-4) Nuttall Ornith.

Avian-Exotic Animal Care Guides. R. W. Woerpel & W. J. Rosskopf, Jr. LC 88-83117. 85p. 1988. 35.00 (0-939674-24-6) Am Vet Pubns.

Avian Genetics: A Field & Ecological Approach. Ed. by F. Cooke & P. A. Buckley. 488p. 1987. text ed. 49.00 (0-12-187570-9) Acad Pr.

***Avian Hematology & Cytology.** 2nd ed. Terry W. Campbell. LC 94-36354. (Illus.). 112p. 1995. 62.95 (0-8138-2970-4) Iowa St U Pr.

Avian Hemotology & Cytology. Terry Campbell. LC 87-29714. (Illus.). 110p. (C). 1988. text ed. 57.95 (0-8138-0064-1) Iowa St U Pr.

Avian Histopathology. C. Riddell. (Illus.). (Orig.). 1987. pap. text ed. 26.00 (0-915538-03-2) AAAP PA.

Avian Immunology: Basis & Practice, 2 vols., Set. Ed. by Auli Toivanen & Paavo Toivanen. 1987. 420.00 (0-8493-6767-0, SF995) CRC Pr.

Avian Immunology: Basis & Practice, 2 vols., Vol. I: How It All Began. Ed. by Auli Toivanen & Paavo Toivanen. 272p. 1987. write for info. (0-318-62159-2) CRC Pr.

Avian Immunology: Basis & Practice, 2 vols., Vol. II: Cellular Cooperation in Immunity. Ed. by Auli Toivanen & Paavo Toivanen. 256p. 1987. 128.00 (0-8493-6769-7, CRC Reprint) Franklin.

Avian Incubation. S. Tullett. 304p. 1991. text ed. 175.00 (0-7506-1002-6) Buttrwrth-Heinemann.

Avian Incubation: Egg Temperature, Nest Humidity, & Behavioral Thermoregulation in a Hot Environment. Gilbert S. Grant. 75p. 1982. 9.00 (0-943610-30-3) Am Ornithologists.

Avian Leukosis. Ed. by G. F. De Boer. (Developments in Veterinary Virology Ser.). (C). 1987. lib. bdg. 108.00 (0-89838-872-4) Kluwer Ac.

Avian Medicine: Principles & Application. Ed. by Branson W. Ritchie et al. LC 93-60501. (Illus.). 1384p. (C). 1994. text ed. 175.00 (0-9636996-0-1) Wingers Pub.

***Avian Medicine: Principles & Application.** Ed. by Branson W. Ritchie et al. 1384p. (C). 1994. cd-rom 175.00 (0-9636996-2-8) Wingers Pub.

Avian Medicine & Surgery. B. Coles. (Illus.). 288p. 1986. pap. 45.00 (0-632-01403-2, B-1039-7) Blackwell Pubs.

Avian Osteology. B. Miles Gilbert et al. LC 81-90059. (Illus.). 252p. (Orig.). 1981. pap. 20.00 (0-9611174-1-9) Bone Bks.

Avian Physiology. 4th ed. Ed. by P. D. Sturkie. (Illus.). xiii, 516p. 1986. 96.00 (0-387-96195-X) Spr-Verlag.

Avian Research at the Kalamazoo Nature Center 1970 to 1978. Raymond J. Adams, Jr. (Illus.). 86p. 1982. pap. 5.00 (0-939294-11-7, QL 677-5-A2) Beech Leaf.

Avian Speciation in Tropical South America: With a Systematic Survey of the Toucans (Rampastidae) & Jacamars (Galbulidae) Jurgen Haffer. (Publications of the Nuttall Ornithological Club: No. 14). (Illus.). 390p. (C). 1974. 19.00 (1-877973-24-6) Nuttall Ornith.

Aviaries: A Complete Introduction. Matthew M. Vriends. 1988. pap. 5.95 (0-86622-292-8, CO-004S) TFH Pubns.

***Aviary Slag.** Servin. 1995. pap. text ed. 10.95 (0-932511-92-9) Fiction Coll.

Aviation. (Illus.). 72p. (J). (gr. 6-12). 1968. pap. 1.85 (0-8395-3293-8, 33293) BSA.

Aviation. Wayne M. Dzwonchyk. LC 85-6241. (Army Lineage Series, Center for Military History Publication: No. 60-12). (Illus.). 162p. 1986. 20.00 (0-16-001940-0, S/N 008-029-00135-7) USGPO.

***Aviation.** Lopez. 1995. 27.50 (0-02-860006-1); pap. 18.00 (0-02-860041-X) Macmillan.

Aviation: A Complete Legal Guide. Cliff Roberson. 210p. 1987. 19.95 (0-8306-9414-5, 2414) TAB Bks.

Aviation: A History Through Art. Philip Handleman. 1992. 45.00 (0-943231-55-8) Howell Pr VA.

Aviation: Flight over the Eastern Countries since 1937. Gordon Kinsey. 280p. 1994. 42.00 (0-86138-032-0, Pub. by T Dalton UK) St Mut.

Aviation Accident Law, 3 vols., Set. Lee S. Kreindler. 1963. write for info. (0-8205-1332-6) Bender.

***Aviation Accident Reconstruction & Litigation.** Barnes W. McCormick & Myron P. Papadakis. (Illus.). 800p. 1995. text ed. 99.00 (0-913875-15-5, 5155) Lawyers & Judges.

***Aviation Adventure.** Date not set. pap. 35.00 (1-56997-089-0) Knowldge Adv.

Aviation & Aerospace Almanac. Aviation Daily & Aerospace Daily Staff. 1994. pap. 39.95 (0-07-555121-7) McGraw.

Aviation & Aerospace Almanac. Aviation Daily & Aerospace Daily Staff. 1994. pap. 50.00 (0-07-607068-9) McGraw.

***Aviation & Aerospace Almanac.** Aviation Week Group Newsletter Staff. 1994. pap. text ed. 50.00 (0-07-003047-2) McGraw.

Aviation & Maritime Security Act, 1990, Chap. 31. 68p. 1990. pap. 17.00 (0-10-543190-7, HM9017) UNIPUB.

Aviation & Space Projects for Young Scientists. Ben Millspaugh. 1991. text ed. 16.95 (0-07-157680-0); pap. text ed. 9.95 (0-07-157679-7) McGraw.

Aviation & Space Science Projects. Ben Millspaugh. (J). 1991. 16.95 (0-8306-2157-1); pap. 9.95 (0-8306-2156-3) TAB Bks.

Aviation & the Law. 2nd ed. Laurence E. Gesell. LC 93-70572. (Illus.). 852p. 1993. 49.00 (0-9606874-8-3) Coast Aire.

Aviation & Tourism Policies: Balancing the Benefit. Stephen Wheatcroft. LC 93-46085. (World Tourism Organization Ser.). (Illus.). 160p. 1994. 55.00x (0-415-10987-6, B3986, Routledge NY); pap. 18.95 (0-415-10988-4, B3990, Routledge NY) Routledge.

Aviation Antitrust: The Extraterritorial Application of the United States Antitrust Laws & International Air Transportation. Patricia M. Barlow. LC 87-3795. 1987. 88.00 (90-6544-293-6) Kluwer Law Tax Pubs.

***Aviation Art of Michael Turner.** Michael Turner. (Illus.). 96p. 1995. 49.95 (0-7153-0088-1, Pub. by D & C Pub UK) Sterling.

Aviation Awards of Imperial Germany in World War I & the Men Who Earned Them Vol. IV: The Aviation Awards of Wurttemberg, Vol. 1. Neal W. O'Connor. (Illus.). 288p. (Orig.). (C). 1995. 34.95 (0-9619867-0-0) Fndtn Aviation.

Aviation Careers of Igor Sikorsky. Dorothy Cochrane et al. (Illus.). 216p. 1989. 40.00 (0-295-96842-7); pap. 24.95 (0-295-96916-4) U of Wash Pr.

Aviation Climatology. G. Y. Narovlyanskii. 224p. 1970. text ed. 58.00 (0-7065-0731-2, Pub. by Keter Pub IS) Coronet Bks.

Aviation Consumer Used Aircraft Guide. 2nd ed. Belvoir Publications Staff. (Illus.). 320p. 1989. pap. 24.95 (0-317-67162-6, 2441P) TAB Bks.

Aviation Consumer Used Aircraft Guide. 3rd ed. Belvoir Publications Staff. 1990. pap. 24.95 (0-8306-2441-4, 2441) TAB Bks.

Aviation Consumer Used Aircraft Guide. 3rd exp. ed. Belvoir Publications Staff. 1989. pap. text ed. 24.95 (0-07-155488-2) McGraw.

Aviation Consumer's Used Aircraft Guide. 6th ed. Ed. by Andrew B. Douglas. 888p. 1994. 59.95 (1-879620-18-9) Belvoir Pubns.

Aviation Crossroads - Challenges in a Changing World: Proceedings of the 23rd International Air Transportation Conference. Ed. by William J. Sproule. LC 94-19136. 1994. write for info. (0-7844-0029-6) Am Soc Civil Eng.

Aviation Disasters. David Gero. (Haynes-U. K. Ser.). (Illus.). 208p. 1993. 34.95 (1-85260-379-8) Motorbooks Intl.

Aviation Electronics. 4th ed. Keith W. Bose. LC 92-44735. (Illus.). 384p. 1990. pap. text ed. 24.95 (0-89100-352-5, EA-352) IAP.

Aviation Enforcement for the 90's. 216p. 1990. pap. text ed. 35.00 (1-56986-216-8) Federal Bar.

Aviation for the Private Pilot. L. K. Phillips. 1975. lib. bdg. 250.00 (0-87968-686-3) Gordon Pr.

Aviation Forecasting Methodology: A Special Workshop. (Transportation Research Circular Ser.: No. 348). 92p. 1989. 9.00 (0-685-38560-4) Transport Res Bd.

Aviation Fuel: Thermal Stability Requirements. Ed. by Perry W. Kirklin & Peter David. LC 92-12285. (Special Technical Publication Ser.: No. 1138). (Illus.). 175p. 1992. text ed. 50.00 (0-8031-1431-1, 04-011380-12) ASTM.

Aviation Fundamentals Instructor's Guide. (Illus.). 156p. 1991. pap. text ed. 25.45 (0-88487-157-6, JS414110) Jeppesen Sanderson.

Aviation Fundamentals Textbook. (Illus.). 668p. 1991. text ed. 32.95 (0-88487-154-1, JS314755); pap. 28.45 (0-88487-155-X, JS314766); 9.45 (0-88487-156-8, JS324774) Jeppesen Sanderson.

Aviation Gasoline Production & Control. Charles G. Forbes. (USAF Historical Studies: No. 65). 95p. 1947. pap. text ed. 20.00 (0-89126-146-X) MA-AH Pub.

Aviation Ground Operations Safety Handbook. 3rd ed. National Safety Council, International Air Transport Section, Industrial Division Staff. LC 87-63466. 162p. 1988. pap. 34.95 (0-87912-138-6, 12963-0000) Natl Safety Coun.

Aviation Humor of 1987. Sherm Morgan. LC 87-91286. 128p. (Orig.). (C). 1987. pap. 5.95 (0-944792-00-6) Pendragon TX.

Aviation in Thailand. Edward M. Young. LC 93-40334. (History of Aviation Ser.). 1994. write for info. (1-56098-405-8) Smithsonian.

Aviation in the Cinema. Stephen Pendo. LC 84-14169. 414p. 1985. 35.00 (0-8108-1746-2) Scarecrow.

Aviation in the U. S. Army, 1919-1939. Maurer. (Illus.). 626p. 1987. 29.00 (0-912799-38-2); pap. 29.00 (0-912799-40-4) Off Air Force.

***Aviation Industry Quality Systems: ISO 9000 & the Federal Aviation Regulations.** Michael J. Dreikorn. LC 94-43754. 1995. 60.00 (0-87389-331-X) ASQC Qual Pr.

Aviation Industry Regulation. Harry P. Wolfe & David A. NewMyer. LC 84-13896. (Aviation Management Ser.). 224p. 1985. 29.95 (0-8093-1177-1) S Ill U Pr.

Aviation Instruction & Training. Ed. by Ross A. Telfer. 528p. 1993. 89.95 (1-85742-090-X, Pub. by Ashgate UK) Ashgate Pub Co.

Aviation Instructors Handbook. rev. ed. Federal Aviation Administration Staff. 123p. 1977. reprint ed. pap. text ed. 6.00 (0-939158-03-5) Flightshops.

Aviation Instructor's Handbook. 2nd ed. (Advisory Circular Ser.: No. 60-14). (Illus.). 127p. 1985. reprint ed. pap. 6.00 (0-16-005307-2, S/N 050-011-00072-1) USGPO.

Aviation Instructor's Handbook. FAA Staff. (FAA Reprints Ser.). (Illus.). 1976. reprint ed. pap. text ed. 7.00 (1-56027-003-9, ASA-AC60-14) Av Suppl & Acad.

Aviation Instructor's Handbook (AC 60-14) FAA Department of Transportation Staff. (Illus.). 124p. (Orig.). (C). 1977. reprint ed. pap. text ed. 6.00 (0-941272-02-8) Astro Pubs.

Aviation Insurance. Vera F. Rollo. LC 86-62107. 438p. 1987. lib. bdg. 14.50 (0-917882-22-9) MD Hist Pr.

Aviation Insurance. rev. ed. Adel S. Din. (C). 1989. 850.00 (0-685-33793-6, Pub. by Witherby & Co UK) St Mut.

Aviation Insurance. 2nd ed. Rod D. Margo. 1989. 199.00 (0-406-28811-9, U.K.) Butterworth Legal Pubs.

***Aviation Insurance: Instructor's Manual.** Vera F. Rollo. 97p. 1987. pap. 14.00 (0-614-01409-3) MD Hist Pr.

Aviation Insurance: The Market & Underwriting Practice. Michael Spurway. 96p. 1992. 110.00 (1-85609-025-6, Pub. by Witherby & Co UK) St Mut.

Aviation Insurance Abbreviations, Organizations & Institutions. M. J. Spurway. 72p. 1983. pap. 70.00 (0-900886-77-3, Pub. by Witherby & Co UK) St Mut.

Aviation Law: An Introduction. 3rd ed. Vera F. Rollo. LC 79-64803. 514p. 1994. lib. bdg. 24.50 (0-917882-40-7) MD Hist Pr.

Aviation Law & Claims. Michael Spurway. 96p. (C). 1991. 69.00 (1-85609-031-0, Pub. by Witherby & Co UK) St Mut.

Aviation Law & Regulation, 2 vols. Paul S. Dempsey et al. 930p. 1993. ring bd. 190.00 (0-88063-783-8) Michie Butterworth.

Aviation Law & Regulation: A Framework for the Civil Aviation Industry. Carole Blackshaw. 288p. (C). 1992. 150.00 (0-273-03446-4) Krieger.

Aviation Law and Regulations. Paul S. Dempsey et al. 570p. 1993. student ed. pap. 40.00 (0-685-74656-9) Butterworth Legal Pubs.

Aviation Law for Pilots. 8th ed. S. E. Taylor & H. A. Parmer. (Illus.). 192p. 1992. pap. 39.95 (0-632-03502-1) Blackwell Sci.

Aviation Lawyer's Manual: Representing the Pilot in FAA Enforcement Actions. John S. Yodice. LC 86-61116. 170p. 1986. lib. bdg. 39.95 (0-917882-21-0) MD Hist Pr.

Aviation Litigation. Windle Turley. LC 86-17710. 694p. 1986. text ed. 95.00 (0-07-065403-4) Shepards-McGraw.

Aviation Lore in Faulkner. Robert Harrison. LC 85-17444. (Illus.). viii, 195p. 1985. 65.00x (0-915027-59-3); pap. 27.95x (0-915027-58-5) Benjamins North Am.

Aviation Maintenance Management. Frank King. LC 85-1983. (Aviation Management Ser.). (Illus.). 208p. 1968. text ed. 32.50 (0-8093-1210-7) S Ill U Pr.

***Aviation Maintenance Technician Oral & Practical Exam Guide ASA-OEG-AMT.** Dale Crane. LC 94-33147. (Illus.). 176p. 1994. pap. 9.95 (1-56027-199-X, ASA-OEG-AMT) Av Suppl & Acad.

Aviation Maintenance Technician Series General ASA-AMT-G. Dale Crane. LC 93-1292. (Aviation Maintenance Technician Ser.). (Illus.). 700p. 1993. pap. 34.95 (1-56027-152-3, ASA-AMT-G) Av Suppl & Acad.

Aviation Maintenance Technician Series General ASA-AMT-G. Dale Crane. (Aviation Maintenance Technician Ser.). (Illus.). 980p. 1994. pap. 39.95 (1-56027-153-1, ASA-AMT-A) Av Suppl & Acad.

Aviation Maintenance Technician Series Powerplant. Dale Crane. (Aviation Maintenance Technician Ser.). (Illus.). 1995. pap. 34.95 (1-56027-154-X, ASA-AMT-P) Av Suppl & Acad.

***Aviation Management.** Peggy Baty et al. 528p. (C). 1995. per., pap. text ed. 32.95 (0-7872-0126-X) Kendall-Hunt.

Aviation Mechanic: General Workbook. Dale Crane. 1988. 9.95 (0-940732-70-X, ASA-AC65-9A-WK) Av Suppl & Acad.

Aviation Mechanic Airframe Written Test Book, 1992-94. Federal Aviation Administration Reprint Staff. (Illus.). 131p. 1992. EA-FAA-T-8080-12D. pap. text ed. 6.00 (0-89100-418-1) IAP.

Aviation Mechanic General Question Book. (FAA-T Ser.: No. 8080-10C). (Illus.). 81p. 1989. pap. 4.25 (0-16-005289-0, S/N 050-007-00838-4) USGPO.

Aviation Mechanic General Written Test Book, 1992-94. Federal Aviation Administration Reprint Staff. (Illus.). 96p. 1992. reprint ed. pap. text ed. 5.00 (0-89100-417-3, EA-FAA-T-8080-10D) IAP.

Aviation Mechanic Handbook. Dale Crane. LC 92-34331. 1992. pap. 12.95 (1-56027-132-9, M-HB1) Av Suppl & Acad.

Aviation Mechanic Powerplant Written Test Book, 1992-94. Federal Aviation Administration Reprint Staff. (Illus.). 120p. 1992. reprint ed. pap. text ed. 5.00 (0-89100-416-5, EA-FAA-T-8080-11D) IAP.

***Aviation Medicine.** Ernsting. 756p. 1994. pap. write for info. (0-7506-2275-X, Focal) Buttrwrth-Heinemann.

Aviation Medicine. 3rd ed. Richard M. Harding. Ed. by F. John Mills. (Illus.). 218p. 1993. pap. text ed. 22.00 (0-7279-0814-6, BMJ Pubng Grp) Amer Coll Phys.

***Aviation Meteorology Unscrambled: For VFR & IFR Operations - Certificates & Ratings.** 6th ed. Kenneth B. McCool. LC 95-79659. (Illus.). 625p. (C). Date not set. pap. text ed. write for info. (0-9621387-9-7) K B McCool.

***Aviation Meteorology Unscrambled: For VFR & IFR Operations/Certificated & Ratings.** rev. ed. Kenneth B. McCool. (Illus.). 580p. (C). 1995. pap. text ed. 40.00 (0-9621387-5-4) K B McCool.

***Aviation Programs in the Postsecondary Schools of the United States: 1950 & 1985.** Vera Rollo. 240p. 1990. 50.00 (0-614-01410-7); pap. 40.00 (0-614-01411-5) MD Hist Pr.

Aviation Psychology. Richard S. Jensen. 430p. 1989. pap. text ed. 34.95 (0-566-09059-7, Pub. by Avebury Pub UK) Ashgate Pub Co.

Aviation Psychology. Richard S. Jensen. 430p. 1989. text ed. 76.95 (0-291-39778-6, Pub. by Avebury Pub UK) Ashgate Pub Co.

Aviation Psychology. Stanley N. Roscoe. LC 79-27539. (Illus.). 318p. 1990. reprint ed. pap. text ed. 18.95 (0-8138-1927-X) Iowa St U Pr.

Aviation Psychology in Practice. Ed. by Neil Johnston et al. LC 93-47295. 1994. 59.95 (0-291-39808-1, Pub. by Avebury Technical UK) Ashgate Pub Co.

***Aviation Psychology, Training & Selection Vol. 2: Proceedings of the 21st Conference of the European Association for Aviation Psychology (EEAP)** European Association for Aviation Psychology Staff. Ed. by Neil Johnston et al. 1994. 59.95 (0-291-39819-7) Avebury Technical UK.

Aviation Regulation Study Guide-Workbook (AS 254) Roland Mower. 112p. (C). 1992. pap. text ed. 19.95 (0-8403-8366-5) Kendall-Hunt.

Aviation Regulatory Process. Tony Adamski & Tim Doyle. (C). 1993. pap. text ed. 25.00 (1-881592-49-9) Hayden-McNeil.

A

An Asterisk (*) at the beginning of an entry indicates that the title is appearing in BIP for the first time.

***Aviation Safety & Budgets: Federal Aviation Agency Management Challenges & Foreign Carriers' Compliance with U. S. Safety Regulations.** (Illus.). 61p. (Orig.). (C). 1994. pap. text ed. 35.00x (*0-7881-1000-4*) Diane Pub.

Aviation Safety Challenges in the 1990s: Proceedings of the 44th International Air Safety Seminar, November 11-14, 1991, Singapore. International Air Safety Seminar Staff. LC 80-644006. 270p. reprint ed. pap. 77.00 (*0-7837-3162-0*, 2042819) Bks Demand.

Aviation Safety in the Nineties: Proceedings of the 36th Corporate Aviation Safety Seminar, April 17-19, 1991, White Plains, NY. Corporate Aviation Safety Seminar Staff. LC 83-645693. 228p. reprint ed. pap. 65.00 (*0-7837-3161-2*, 2042820) Bks Demand.

Aviation Safety Programs - A Management Handbook. Richard H. Wood. LC 91-199507. (Illus.). 248p. 1991. pap. text ed. 12.95 (*0-89100-389-4*, EA-389) IAP.

Aviation Safety's Flying Circus. Belvoir Publications Staff. (Illus.). 1989. pap. 14.95 (*0-8306-2421-X*, 2421P) TAB Bks.

***Aviation Security: Development of New Security Technology.** (Illus.). 59p. (Orig.). (C). 1994. pap. text ed. 45.00x (*0-7881-1176-0*) Diane Pub.

***Aviation Security & Terrorism.** 1995. lib. bdg. 251.75 (*0-8490-7551-3*) Gordon Pr.

Aviation Security Problem & Related Technologies: Proceedings of a Conference Held 19-20 July 1992, San Diego, California. Ed. by Wagih H. Makky. LC 92-17417. (Critical Reviews of Optical Science & Technology Ser.: Vol. CR42). 1992. 68.00 (*0-8194-0954-5*); pap. 50.00 (*0-8194-0955-3*) SPIE.

Aviation Terrorism: Historical Survey, Perspectives, & Responses. Jin-Tai Choi. LC 93-15602. 1994. text ed. 69.95 (*0-312-10072-8*) St Martin.

Aviation Tort Law, 3 vols., Set. Stuart M. Speiser & Charles F. Krause. LC 78-55326. 1978. 370.00 (*0-685-59879-9*) Clark Boardman Callaghan.

***Aviation Weather.** Peter F. Lester. LC 95-7862. 1995. write for info. (*0-88487-178-9*) Jeppesen Sanderson.

Aviation Weather. 2nd ed. Federal Aviation Administration Staff. (Pilot Training Ser.). (Illus.). 219p. (C). 1988. reprint ed. pap. 10.50 (*0-89100-160-3*, EA-AC00-6A) IAP.

Aviation Weather. FAA Staff. (FAA Reprints Ser.). (Illus.). 1975. reprint ed. pap. text ed. 11.50 (*1-56027-001-2*, ASA-AC00-6A) Av Suppl & Acad.

***Aviation Weather: For Pilots & Flight Operations Personnel.** (Illus.). 219p. (Orig.). (C). 1994. pap. text ed. 60.00x (*0-7881-1484-0*) Diane Pub.

Aviation Weather: Forces to be Reckoned With. Ed. by Richard Taylor. (Command Decisions Ser.). 240p. 1991. 21.95 (*1-879620-02-2*) Belvoir Pubns.

Aviation Weather & Weather Services. Irvin N. Gleim. LC 93-91537. (Illus.). 442p. (Orig.). 1994. pap. 18.95 (*0-917539-39-7*) Gleim Pubns.

Aviation Weather for Pilots & Flight & Flight Operations Personnel. 1991. lib. bdg. 79.95 (*0-8490-4490-1*) Gordon Pr.

***Aviation Weather for Pilots & Flight Operations Personnel.** 1994. lib. bdg. 260.95 (*0-8490-6437-6*) Gordon Pr.

Aviation Weather for Pilots & Flight Operations Personnel. rev. ed. (Advisory Circular Ser.: No. 00-6A). 235p. 1984. reprint ed. pap. 8.50 (*0-16-005120-7*, S/N 050-007-00283-1) USGPO.

Aviation Weather Services. (Advisory Circular Ser.: No. 00-45C). (Illus.). 127p. 1985. pap. 6.00 (*0-16-005217-3*, S/N 050-007-00705-1) USGPO.

Aviation Weather Services. rev. ed. Federal Aviation Administration Staff & National Oceanic & Atmospheric Administration Staff. 123p. 1985. reprint ed. pap. text ed. 6.00 (*0-939158-02-7*) Flightshops.

Aviation Weather Services. rev. ed. John M. Holley. (Illus.). 139p. 1992. pap. text ed. 7.95 (*0-89100-392-4*, EA-392) IAP.

Aviation Weather Services. FAA Staff. (FAA Reprints Ser.). 1985. reprint ed. pap. text ed. 8.00 (*1-56027-000-4*, ASA-AC00-45) Av Suppl & Acad.

Aviation Weather Services Workbook. rev. ed. John M. Holley. (Illus.). 55p. 1992. 6.00 (*0-89100-403-3*, EA-403) IAP.

Aviation's Golden Age: Portraits from the 1920s & 1930s. Ed. by William M. Leary. LC 89-4753. (Illus.). 232p. 1989. 28.95x (*0-87745-242-3*) U of Iowa Pr.

Aviation's Place in Tomorrow's Business. Earl Reeves. (Airlines History Project Ser.). reprint ed. 35.00 (*0-404-19331-5*) AMS Pr.

Aviators. Robert Rosenbaum. (American Profiles Ser.). (Illus.). 128p. (YA). (gr. 6-12). 1992. lib. bdg. 16.95 (*0-8160-2539-8*) Facts on File.

Aviator's English & French Dictionary. R. G. Wingrove & J. R. Jammes. 285p. (ENG & FRE.). 1986. 95.00 (*0-8288-0013-8*, F126900) Fr & Eur.

Aviator's Field Book. Oswald Boelcke. (Great War Ser.: No. 14). (Illus.). 219p. reprint ed. 29.95 (*0-89839-163-6*) Battery Pr.

Aviator's Guide to Flight Planning. Donald J. Clausing. (Practical Flying Ser.). (Illus.). 224p. 1989. 26.95 (*0-8306-9238-X*, 2438) TAB Bks.

Aviator's Guide to GPS. Bill Clarke. LC 93-44964. 1994. text ed. 29.95 (*0-07-011271-1*); pap. text ed. 17.95 (*0-07-011272-X*) TAB Bks.

Aviator's Guide to Modern Navigation. Donald J. Clausing. (Illus.). 256p. (Orig.). 1987. 28.95 (*0-8306-0208-9*, 2408) TAB Bks.

Aviator's Guide to Navigation. 2nd ed. Donald J. Clausing. (Practical Flying Ser.). 360p. 1992. 28.95 (*0-8306-2171-7*, 3998); pap. 18.95 (*0-8306-2173-3*, 3998) TAB Bks.

Aviators Guide to Navigation. 2nd ed. Donald J. Clausing. 1992. text ed. 28.95 (*0-07-011290-8*); pap. text ed. 18.95 (*0-07-011291-6*) McGraw.

***Aviator's Handbook.** 1995. lib. bdg. 265.99 (*0-8490-6566-6*) Gordon Pr.

***Aviator's Recognition Manual.** 1995. lib. bdg. 275.99 (*0-8490-6567-4*) Gordon Pr.

Avicenna. Lenn E. Goodman. LC 91-40142. (Arabic Thought & Culture Ser.). 256p. 1992. 72.50 (*0-415-01929-X*, A7565); pap. 16.95 (*0-415-07409-6*, A7569) Routledge.

Avicenna & the Aristotelian Tradition: Introduction to Reading Avicenna's Philosophical Works. Dimitri Gutas. (Islamic Philosophy, Theology & Science, Studies & Texts Ser.: Vol. IV). 1988. text ed. 68.75 (*90-04-08500-9*) E J Brill.

Avicenna & the Visionary Recital. Henry Corbin. Tr. by Willard R. Trask. (Bollingen Ser.: No. LXVI). 436p. (C). 1990. pap. text ed. 17.95 (*0-691-01893-6*) Princeton U Pr.

***Avicenna & the Visionary Recital.** Henry Corbin. Tr. by Willard R. Trask. LC 90-41820. (Bollingen Ser.: No. 66). 439p. 1988. reprint ed. pap. 125.20 (*0-7837-8582-8*, 2049397) Bks Demand.

Avicenna, His Life & Works. Soheil M. Afnan. LC 79-8705. 298p. 1980. reprint ed. text ed. 38.50 (*0-313-22198-7*, AFAV, Greenwood Pr) Greenwood.

Avicenna in Renaissance Italy. Nancy G. Siraisi. (Illus.). 520p. 1987. pap. text ed. 65.00 (*0-691-05137-2*) Princeton U Pr.

Avicenna Latinus - Liber Quartus Naturalium: De Actionibus & Passionibus. S. Van Riet. (Avicenna Latinus Ser.: Vol. 7). (FRE & LAT.). 1990. French: v, 37; Latin: vi, 230. 68.75 (*90-6831-246-4*) E J Brill.

Avicenna on Theology. Avicenna. Tr. by Arthur J. Arberry. LC 78-59000. 82p. 1994. reprint ed. 18.00 (*0-88355-676-6*) Hyperion Conn.

Avicennae De Congelatione et Conglutinatione Lapidum. Ed. by E. J. Holmyard & D. C. Mandeville. LC 79-8593. reprint ed. 19.50 (*0-404-18447-2*) AMS Pr.

***Avicenna's Philosophy of Education.** C. George Fry & Jon P. Fry. Date not set. pap. 8.50 (*0-89410-675-9*) Three Continents.

Avicenna's Psychology. Avicenna. Ed. by F. Rahman. LC 79-2848. 127p. 1994. reprint ed. 20.00 (*0-8305-0024-3*) Hyperion Conn.

Aviculture in Australia. Mark Shephard. (Illus.). 380p. 1989. 55.00 (*0-9588106-0-5*) Avian Pubns.

Avidin-Biotin Chemistry: A Handbook. M. Dean Savage et al. LC 91-51199. (Illus.). 513p. (Orig.). 1992. pap. 89.00 (*0-935940-11-1*, 15055) Pierce Chem.

***Avidly Perplexed.** Meg Davis. (Illus.). 48p. (Orig.). 1994. pap. 9.95 (*0-933313-22-5*) SUN Gemini Pr.

Avifauna of British India & Its Dependencies, Set. J. Murray. 1984. reprint ed. 750.00 (*81-7089-020-9*, Pub. by Intl Bk Distr II) St Mut.

Avifauna of the Eastern Highlands of New Guinea. Jared M. Diamond. (Publications of the Nuttall Ornithological Club: No. 12). (Illus.). 438p. (C). 1972. 15.00 (*1-877973-22-X*) Nuttall Ornith.

Avigation & Other Poems. Steven Schmidt. 64p. 1990. pap. 9.95 (*1-877947-19-9*) Padre Prods.

Avila of Saint Teresa: Religious Reform in a Sixteenth-Century City. Jodi Bilinkoff. LC 89-42886. (Illus.). 240p. 1989. 32.95 (*0-8014-2203-5*) Cornell U Pr.

Avila of Saint Teresa: Religious Reform in a Sixteenth-Century City. Jodi Bilinkoff. LC 89-42886. (Illus.). 240p. 1992. pap. 11.95 (*0-8014-8052-3*) Cornell U Pr.

Avioanxiety Becomes Controlled: Now, Fly Without Fear. Jim Remington & Leona Remington. (Illus.). 160p. (Orig.). 1992. 9.95 (*1-879855-01-1*) Inner Marker.

Avioanxiety Becomes Controlled or How to Fly Without Fear: Reducing Fear & Anxiety While Flying on a Commercial Jet Airliner. Jim Remington & Leona Remington. (Illus.). 180p. 1991. audio 49.95 (*1-879855-00-3*) Inner Marker.

Avion de Angela: (Angela's Airplane) Robert Munsch. Tr. by Shirley Langer. (Illus.). 32p. (SPA.). (J). 1991. pap. 5.95 (*1-55037-189-4*, Pub. by Annick CN) Firefly Bks Ltd.

Avion My Uncle Flew. Cyrus Fisher. (J). 1994. 17.75 (*0-8446-6759-5*) Peter Smith.

Avion My Uncle Flew. Cyrus Fisher. (Illus.). 254p. (J). (gr. 5 up). 1993. pap. 4.99 (*0-14-036487-0*, Puffin) Puffin Bks.

Aviones (Airplanes) J. Cooper. (Spanish Language Books, Set 5: Maquinas de Viaje (Traveling Machines)). (J). 1991. 8.95 (*0-86592-507-0*) Rourke Enter.

Avionic System Design. John R. Newport. LC 94-11904. 1994. write for info. (*0-8493-2465-3*) CRC Pr.

***Avionics: Systems & Troubleshooting.** Eiff. 1995. pap. text ed. 41.95 (*0-02-801915-6*) Glencoe.

***Avionics Acronyms & Abbreviations.** Ed. by Avionics Communications Staff. 204p. (C). 1994. pap. 49.00 (*1-885544-01-4*) Avionics Commun.

Avionics Fundamentals. rev. ed. United Airlines Staff. LC 91-23719. (Illus.). 394p. 1987. pap. 24.95 (*0-89100-293-6*, EA-AV) IAP.

Avionics Log. ASA Staff. (Logbook Ser.). 64p. (Orig.). 1992. 5.95 (*1-56027-057-8*, ASA-SA-V) Av Suppl & Acad.

***Avionics Marketing, Airline Edition.** Buckwalter & Chandler Staff. 400p. 1993. pap. 189.00 (*1-885544-04-9*) Avionics Commun.

Avionics Navigation Systems. Ed. by Myron Kayton & Walter Fried. LC 69-13679. 666p. 1969. text ed. 150.00 (*0-471-46180-6*, Wiley-Interscience) Wiley.

Avionics Systems: Operation & Maintenance. James W. Wasson. 370p. 1993. pap. text ed. 32.95 (*0-89100-436-X*, EA-436) IAP.

Avionics,Vol. 1: Every Pilot's Guide to Aviation Electronics. John M. Ferrara. 275p. 1989. pap. 14.75 (*0-911720-24-3*) Aviation.

***Avions Vol. 3: Seconde Guerre Mondiale, France, Allemand, Angleterre.** Enzo Angelucci. 320p. (FRE.). 1978. text ed. 39.95 (*0-7859-7160-2*) Fr & Eur.

***Avions Vol. 4: Seconde Guerre Mondiale, U. S. A., Japan, U. S. S. R.** Enzo Angelucci. 320p. (FRE.). 1978. 39.95 (*0-7859-7161-0*, 2040125450) Fr & Eur.

***Avions Vol. 5: Ere des Engines a Reaction.** Enzo Angelucci. 318p. (FRE.). 1979. 39.95 (*0-7859-7162-9*, 2040125493) Fr & Eur.

***Avions Vol. 6: Aviation Commerciale 1935 a 1960.** Enzo Angelucci. 318p. (FRE.). 1981. 39.95 (*0-7859-7163-7*, 204012781X) Fr & Eur.

Avions, Vol. 1: Des Origines a la Premiere Guerre Mondiale. Jean Anouilh. 320p. (FRE.). 1980. pap. 12.95 (*0-7859-1922-8*, F81860) Fr & Eur.

Avions, Vol. 1: Des Origines a la Premiere Guerre Mondiale. Ed. by Michel Laclotte. 480p. (FRE.). 1984. pap. 32.95 (*0-7859-4828-7*) Fr & Eur.

Avions, Vol. 2: L'Entres Deux Guerres. Enzo Angelucci. (FRE.). 1978. 65.00 (*0-7859-3946-6*) Fr & Eur.

Avis City Road Atlas. 1979. pap. 7.95 (*0-686-52717-8*) Creative Sales.

Avis or the Replete Birdman. Michael Gizzi. (Burning Deck Poetry Ser.). 1979. 15.00 (*0-930900-67-7*); pap. 4.00 (*0-930900-68-5*) Burning Deck.

Aviso de Tormenta. Billy Graham. 1993. pap. 10.99 (*1-56063-376-X*, 498540) Editorial Unilit.

Avitus: Concordantiae in Alcimi Ecdicii Aviti Carmina. Alcimus E. Avitus. Ed. by Johann Ramminger. (Alpha-Omega, Reihe A Ser.: Bd. CIV). 396p. (GER.). 1990. write for info. (*3-487-09179-8*, Pub. by Georg Olms GW) Lubrecht & Cramer.

Avivamiento: Lectures on Revival. Charles G. Finney. (SPA.). 3.25 (*84-7228-816-1*, 220066, Pub. by Edit Clie SP) TSELF.

AVKO Spelling "Difficulty" Dictionary. Don McCabe. Ed. by James E. Webb. 204p. 1988. pap. 19.95 (*1-56400-211-X*) AVKO Educ Res.

AVKO Student Response Book for Sequential Spelling. Don McCabe. 60p. 1980. student ed 5.95 (*1-56400-360-4*) AVKO Educ Res.

***Avkoan Theory: The Complete Volume I. rev. ed. Yecheskiel Zamir. LC 94-90342. (Illus.). 227p. (Orig.). 1994. pap. text ed. 22.00 (*0-9614730-7-X*) Y Z Pubns. Compilation of five titles expounding THE AVKOAN THEORY. Based on the PRINCIPLE OF THE TINIEST PARTICLE (AVKOAN), this title introduces several new perceptions including mass & charge as the only two attributes of matter, co-existence of only two fundamental fields of forces (FFFs), a model termed THE BUBBLE MODEL demonstrating PRECISELY the two FFFs, a new system of particles termed THE SYSTEM OF PRIMARY PARTICLES (PP-SYSTEM), mass & charge as accessary & sufficient for the creation & evolution of matter & the universe, the electron components & its unique configuration, the existence of two types of light rays, etc. This title challenges several prevailing misconceptions concerning energy & temperature (E&T), monopole particle, misinterpretation of Einstein's formula E=mc(2), weak & strong interactions, etc. This title compiles REVISED versions of the following five titles: 1. AVKOAN PRINCIPLE, A PRINCIPLE OF THE TINIEST PARTICLE, (1985) (0-9614730-0-2). 2. ULTIMATENESS & FUNDAMENTAL FORCES, (1987) (0-9614730-6-1). 3. PROBLEMATIC FORCES & NEUTRALIZATION CONUNDRUM, (Not published separately). 4. THE SYSTEM OF PRIMARY PARTICLES, FIRST STEP IN THE SEARCH FOR THE ULTIMATE PARTICLE, (Not published separately). 5. THE COSMIC MEDIUM & THE DUALITY OF LIGHT RAYS, (1994) (0-9614730-9-6). To order: YZ PUBLICATIONS, P.O. BOX 46033, LOS ANGELES, CA 90046. Tel/FAX: (213) 654-9782.**

Publisher Provided Annotation.

Avkoan Theory Vol. I-A: Avkoan Principle-A Principle of the Tiniest Particle, Vol. 1. Yecheskiel Zamir. (Illus.). 51p. (Orig.). 1985. pap. 4.95 (*0-9614730-0-2*) Y Z Pubns.

Avkoan Theory Vol. I-B: Ultimateness & Fundamental Forces, Vol. I, Bk. 2. Yecheskiel Zamir. LC 87-90219. (Avkoan Theory Ser.). 98p. (Orig.). 1987. pap. 7.95 (*0-9614730-6-1*) Y Z Pubns.

Avocado Baby. John Burningham. LC 91-27518. (I Can Read Bk.). (Illus.). 32p. (J). (ps-3). 1994. pap. 4.95 (*0-06-443371-4*, Trophy) HarpC Child Bks.

Avocado Lovers' Cookbook. Joyce Carlisle. LC 85-72111. (Illus.). 144p. (Orig.). 1986. pap. 9.95 (*0-89087-456-5*) Celestial Arts.

Avocado of Death see Snarkout Boys & the Avocado of Death

Avocado Recipes, Etc. Teri Gordon. LC 88-122392. (Illus.). 106p. (Orig.). 1987. pap. 6.95 (*0-9619870-0-6*) T Gordon Pub.

Avocations. William E. Bright. 100p. 1984. pap. 10.00 (*0-911051-12-0*) Plain View.

Avocet. David Hill. 1989. pap. 25.00 (*0-7478-0016-2*, Pub. by Shire UK) St Mut.

Avoid Car Repair: Easy Ways to Keep Your Car Running Great. Jim Gaston. LC 92-75922. (Illus.). 150p. (Orig.). 1993. pap. 17.95 (*1-879699-17-6*) CoNation Pubns.

Avoid Financial Shocks in Your Family's Future. John W. Cochrun. LC 77-77536. (Illus.). 1976. pap. 9.95 (*0-9601050-0-X*) J W Cochrun.

Avoid Immunizations of All Kinds, Legally: Federal Law on Your Side, Military Dispenses, How to Manual & Counseling Guidelines. 1992. pap. 4.50 (*0-916508-03-X*) Happiness Pr.

Avoid Plagorism. Jody Sterling. 8p. (C). 1993. 0.85 (*1-56870-071-7*) RonJon Pub.

***Avoidance & Settlement of Arms Control Disputes: Arms Control & Disarmament Law.** Julie Dahlitz. 239p. 1994. pap. text ed. 35.00 (*92-1-100680-5*) UN.

Avoidance Syndrome: Doing Things Out of Fear. Douglas H. Ruben. 150p. (Orig.). (C). 1993. 22.50 (*0-87527-502-8*) Fireside Bks.

Avoiding & Defending Wrongful Discharge Claims, 2 vols. Stephen P. Pepe & Scott H. Dunham. LC 87-10345. 1990. 210.00 (*0-685-18521-4*) Clark Boardman Callaghan.

Avoiding & Defending Wrongful Discharge Claims. suppl. ed. Stephen P. Pepe & Scott H. Dunham. 1990. write for info. (*0-318-62083-9*) Clark Boardman Callaghan.

Avoiding & Resolving Construction Claims. Barry B. Bramble et al. (Illus.). 240p. 1990. 59.95 (*0-87629-180-9*, 67275) R S Means.

Avoiding & Resolving Disputes During Construction. 82p. 1991. pap. text ed. 14.00 (*0-87262-833-7*) Am Soc Civil Eng.

Avoiding & Surviving Lawsuits: The Executive Guide to Strategic Legal Planning for Business. Marianne M. Jennings & Frank Shipper. LC 88-42791. (Management Ser.). 259p. 1988. 32.95 (*1-55542-123-7*) Jossey-Bass.

***Avoiding Burnout: Managing Time, Space, & People in Early Childhood Education.** Paula J. Bloom. (Illus.). 291p. (C). 1994. pap. text ed. 14.95 (*0-9621894-0-5*) New Horzns Lake Forest.

Avoiding Claims in Building Contracts. Peter J. Lord-Smith & John Dobson. (Architecture Legal Ser.). 181p. 1994. pap. 49.95 (*0-7506-1728-4*) Buttrwrth-Heinemann.

Avoiding Client Grievances. 16p. 1988. pap. 4.95 (*0-685-29732-2*, 720-0001-01) Amer Bar Assn.

Avoiding Common Financial Mistakes. Ron Blue. 24p. 1991. pap. 2.00 (*0-89109-312-5*) NavPress.

Avoiding Common Pilot Errors: An Air Traffic Controller's View. John Stewart. (Practical Flying Ser.). (Illus.). 240p. (Orig.). 1989. 25.95 (*0-8306-1434-6*); pap. 17.95 (*0-8306-2434-1*) TAB Bks.

Avoiding Common Pilot Errors: An Air Traffic Controller's Views. John Stewart. 1989. pap. text ed. 17.95 (*0-07-155395-9*) McGraw.

Avoiding Communication: Shyness, Reticence, & Communication Apprehension. Ed. by John A. Daly & James C. McCroskey. LC 83-27242. (Sage Focus Editions Ser.). (Illus.). 296p. reprint ed. pap. 84.40 (*0-7837-4563-X*, 2044092) Bks Demand.

Avoiding Computer Nightmares. H. H. Hillman. 256p. 1985. pap. text ed. 12.95 (*0-07-028949-2*, BYTE Bks) McGraw.

Avoiding Contract Disputes. Ed. by Thomas G. Poulin. 151p. 1985. 19.00 (*0-87262-484-6*) Am Soc Civil Eng.

***Avoiding Counselor Malpractice.** Robert Crawford. 102p. 1994. 12.95 (*1-55620-130-3*) Am Coun Assn.

Avoiding Cultural Default, & Other Essays. Irwin Shainman. LC 90-25977. 265p. (C). 1991. text ed. 44.95 (*0-8204-1406-9*) P Lang Pubs.

Avoiding Deficiencies, Fines, & Penalties As a Result of Investigations by Licensing Agencies. Ann G. Flores. (Illus.). 103p. (Orig.). (C). 1992. pap. text ed. 10.95 (*1-877735-35-3*, 188) M&H Pub Co TX.

Avoiding Failure of Leachate Collection & Cap Drainage Systems. Jeffrey Bass. LC 86-18191. (Pollution Technology Review Ser.: No. 138). (Illus.). 129p. 1987. 36.00 (*0-8155-1106-X*) Noyes.

Avoiding Inadvertent War: Crisis Management. Ed. by Hilliard Roderick & Ulla Magnusson. (Tom Slick World Peace Ser.). 175p. 1983. 5.00 (*0-89940-005-1*) LBJ Sch Pub Aff.

Avoiding Legal Hassles: What School Administrators Really Need to Know. William A. Streshly & Larry E. Frase. 128p. 1992. pap. 14.95 (*0-8039-6018-2*) Corwin Pr.

***Avoiding Legal Problems in Hiring & Firing: A Handbook for the Video.** 2nd ed. Ed. by Amy L. Greenspan. 112p. 1995. pap. text ed. 14.95 (*1-56759-014-4*) Summers Pr.

***Avoiding Legal Problems in Hiring & Firing in California: A Handbook for the Video.** 2nd ed. Ed. by Amy L. Greenspan. 112p. Date not set. pap. text ed. 14.95 (*1-56759-015-2*) Summers Pr.

Avoiding Liability for Defective Products. Derrick Owles. (C). 1987. 155.00 (*0-685-33792-8*, Pub. by Witherby & Co UK) St Mut.

An Asterisk (*) at the beginning of an entry indicates that the title is appearing in BIP for the first time.

An Asterisk (*) at the beginning of an entry indicates that the title is appearing in BIP for the first time.

A

Awakening. Telester F. Kelly-Powell. (Illus.). (Orig.). 1985. pap. text ed. 4.95 (*0-9614788-0-2*, 111A) Tivoli Pub.
Awakening. James D. Nelson. 1989. pap. 9.95 (*0-8306-9000-X*) TAB Bks.
Awakening. L. J. Smith. (Vampire Diaries Ser.: No. 1). (YA). 1991. mass mkt. 3.99 (*0-06-106097-6*, Harp PBks) HarpC.
Awakening. Lucien Stryk. 1985. pap. 7.95 (*0-8040-0333-5*) Swallow.
Awakening. Yoshiyuki Tomino. (Gundam Mobile Suite Ser.: Vol. 1). 1990. mass mkt. 4.95 (*0-345-35738-8*, Del Rey) Ballantine.
*__Awakening.__ large type ed. Kate Chopin. 230p. 1995. lib. bdg. 20.00 (*0-939495-83-X*) North Bks.
Awakening. 2nd ed. Kate Chopin. (Critical Editions Ser.). (C). 1993. pap. text ed. 6.95 (*0-393-96057-9*) Norton.
Awakening. Kate Chopin. 1992. reprint ed. lib. bdg. 21.95 (*0-89968-270-7*, Lghtyr Pr) Buccaneer Bks.
Awakening. Kate Chopin. 128p. 1993. reprint ed. pap. text ed. 1.00 (*0-486-27786-0*) Dover.
Awakening. Kate Chopin. 1988. reprint ed. lib. bdg. 79.00 (*0-7812-1102-6*) Rprt Serv.
Awakening. Richard W. Heinberg. (Illus.). 10p. 1985. reprint ed. pap. 2.00 (*0-935427-25-2*) Foundation Hse.
Awakening. Mary W. Ovington. LC 70-39096. (Black Heritage Library Collection). 1977. reprint ed. 15.95 (*0-8369-9034-X*) Ayer.
Awakening: A Daily Guide to Conscious Living. Shakti Gawain. 408p. 1993. reprint ed. pap. 8.95 (*1-882591-05-4*) Nataraj Pub.

Awakening: A Holistic Approach to Managing Personal Stress. M. Ellen Stammer. 1992. write for info. (*0-9633657-0-3*) M E Stammer & Assocs.
Combining the best of what is known about self-directed learning & small group educational experiences, AWAKENING is a personalized system of instruction offering ways to explore & enrich the total person, body-mind, psyche (soul) & spirit through meeting one's human needs. Each unit contains text, study guide questions, questions to stimulate small group discussion & individual exercises. Each unit builds upon the previous one guiding the adult learner in the art of self introspection & provides suggestions for meeting one's human needs to manage personal stress. Based on Dr. Stammer's research with women recovering from addiction to alcohol & adult children who are rebuilding shattered lives, this educational approach allows individualized time for in-depth exploration integrating one's life experience with the material presented. Many who have been introduced to AWAKENING agree that it augments the 12-steps of self-help programs. AWAKENING pays particular attention to the women's spiritual process which is different from men's. Table of Contents: Preface. Unit 1: Exploring the Meaning of Stress. Unit 2: The Anatomy of Stress. Unit 3: The Body & Mind Connection. Unit 4: Influence of the Psyche - Introduction to God/ Goddess Archetypes. Unit 5: Having a Spiritual Awakening. Unit 6: Managing The Stress of Transition, Part 1. Unit 7: Managing The Stress of Transition, Part 2. To order contact M.E. Stammer & Associates, Phone: (804) 539-4178.
Publisher Provided Annotation.

---

*__Awakening: A Journal of Personal Transformation.__ Wayne W. Dyer. 160p. (Orig.). 1995. pap. 7.95 (*1-57071-071-6*) Sourcebks.
Awakening: A Novel of Beginnings. Joyce Dyer. (Masterwork Studies). 176p. 1993. text ed. 22.95 (*0-8057-8382-2*, Twayne); pap. 12.95 (*0-8057-8383-0*, Twayne) Macmillan.
Awakening: An Almanac of Lesbian Lore & Vision, Vol. 3. Nett Hart et al. 192p. reprint ed. pap. 8.95 (*0-9615605-4-1*) Word Weavers.
Awakening: An Evolutionary Leap in Human Consciousness. Steven S. Sadleir. 176p. 1993. pap. 12.95 (*1-883544-00-9*) Self Awareness.
*__Awakening: Articles & Stories about Jews & Yeshua (Jesus)__ Des. by Anna Portnov. 104p. (RUS.). 1991. write for info. (*1-880226-01-4*) Lederer Pubns.
*__Awakening: Articles & Stories about Jews & Yeshua (Jesus)__ Des. by Anna Portnov. 104p. 1992. write for info. (*1-880226-09-X*) Lederer Pubns.
Awakening: How One Coach Found Fulfillment in His Job. Will Freeman. 60p. (C). 1988. pap. 9.95 (*0-932741-55-X*) Championship Bks & Vid Prodns.
Awakening: Practical Spirituality. Elizabeth Joy. 53p. (Orig.). 1987. pap. 6.95 (*0-944881-00-9*) E Joy Prodns.
Awakening: Ravenloft Adventure. Lisa Smedman. (Advanced Dungeons & Dragons 2nd Ed. Ser.). 1994. 9.95 (*1-56076-883-5*) TSR Inc.
Awakening a Child from Within. Tara Singh. 1991. 32.95 (*1-55531-254-3*); pap. 16.95 (*1-55531-253-5*) Life Action Pr.
Awakening & Other Stories. K. Chopin. Ed. by L. Leary. LC 79-103399. (Rinehart Editions Ser.). (C). 1970. pap. text ed. 19.75 (*0-03-078395-X*) HB Coll Pubs.
Awakening & Other Stories. Kate Chopin. 1976. 22.95 (*0-8488-0457-0*) Amereon Ltd.
Awakening & Other Stories. Kate Chopin. Ed. by Nina Bayn. 354p. (C). 1981. pap. text ed. write for info. (*0-318-57304-0*) Random.
Awakening & Other Stories. Kate Chopin. 1993. 15.50 (*0-679-42469-5*, Modern Lib) Random.
Awakening & Selected Short Stories. Kate Chopin. 224p. (Orig.). (gr. 9-12). 1985. mass mkt. 4.95 (*0-553-21330-X*, Bantam Classics) Bantam.
Awakening & Selected Short Stories. Kate Chopin. Ed. by Sandra M. Gilbert. (Orig.). 18.00 (*0-8446-6229-1*) Peter Smith.
Awakening & Selected Stories. Kate Chopin. Ed. by Nina Baym. 1981. pap. text ed. write for info. (*0-07-554269-2*) McGraw.
Awakening & Selected Stories. Kate Chopin. LC 80-24429. 416p. 1984. pap. 12.95 (*0-394-60508-X*, Modern Lib) Random.
Awakening & Selected Stories. Kate Chopin. LC 80-24429. (American Library). 320p. 1984. mass mkt. 7.95 (*0-14-039022-7*, Penguin Classics) Viking Penguin.
Awakening & Selected Stories of Kate Chopin. Ed. by Barbara H. Solomon. (Orig.). 1976. pap. 4.95 (*0-451-52448-9*, Sig Classics) NAL-Dutton.
Awakening Arthur! His Return in Our Time. Page Bryant. 208p. 1993. pap. 15.00 (*1-85538-071-4*, Pub. by Aquarian Pr UK) Thorsons SF.
Awakening Earth: Exploring the Dimensions of Human Evolution. Duane Elgin. LC 93-10571. 1993. 23.00 (*0-688-11621-3*) Morrow.
Awakening Edge: New Approaches to Consciousness. Mary V. Hunt. (Illus.). 88p. (Orig.). 1988. pap. 8.95 (*0-910235-08-2*) Prisma Bks.
Awakening Female Power: The Way of the Goddess Warrior. 4th rev. ed. Karen LaPuma & Walt Runkis. LC 89-51331. (Illus.). 240p. (Orig.). 1991. reprint ed. pap. 12.95 (*1-878203-02-9*) SoulSource.
Awakening from a Deep Sleep. Robert Pasick. 288p. 1992. pap. 10.00 (*0-06-250714-1*) Harper SF.
Awakening from Depression: A Mind-Body Approach to Emotional Recovery. Jerome Marmorstein & Nanette Marmorstein. LC 91-27523. 160p. (Orig.). 1992. pap. 9.95 (*0-88007-190-7*) Woodbridge Pr.
Awakening from the American Dream: The Human Rights Movement in the U. S. Assessed During a Crucial Decade, 1960-1970. Paul E. Kraemer. LC 73-78045. (Studies in Religion & Society). 122p. 1973. pap. 12.95 (*0-913348-09-0*) Ctr Sci Study.
Awakening from the Deep Sleep: A Powerful Guide for Courageous Men. rev. ed. Robert Pasick. LC 91-58918. 272p. 1994. pap. 10.00 (*0-06-250650-1*) Harper SF.
Awakening Frontier: Trade & Investment (Plus Economic Trends) in the Sub-Saharan Africa's Burgeoning 500 Million Plus People Marketplace. Jude E. Uba. LC 90-62853. 254p. (Orig.). 1991. 49.95 (*0-9627784-4-3*); pap. 39.95 (*0-9627784-3-5*) Pratt & Hall.
Awakening Heart. Dorothy Mack. 224p. 1993. pap. 3.99 (*0-451-17825-4*, Sig) NAL-Dutton.
Awakening in Time: From Co-Dependence to Co-Creation. Jacquelyn Small. 304p. 1991. pap. 12.95 (*0-553-34955-4*) Bantam.
Awakening in Wales. rev. ed. Jessie Penn-Lewis. 128p. 1993. pap. 4.95 (*0-87508-937-2*) Chr Lit.
Awakening Intuition. Frances E. Vaughan. LC 77-27685. 1979. mass mkt. 9.95 (*0-385-13371-5*, Anchor NY) Doubleday.
Awakening Land. Conrad Richter. 1966. 29.95 (*0-394-41703-8*) Knopf.
Awakening Letters, Vol. 2. Lady Sandys. Ed. by Cynthia Sandys & Rosamond Lehmann. 104p. (Orig.). Date not set. pap. 17.95 (*0-8464-4211-6*) Beekman Pubs.
Awakening Minorities: Continuity & Change. 2nd ed. Ed. by John R. Howard. LC 82-2596. 130p. (C). 1983. 29.95x (*0-87855-468-8*); pap. text ed. 17.95x (*0-87855-911-6*) Transaction Pubs.
Awakening Nightmare. Albert M. Honig. LC 77-189003. 1972. 9.95 (*0-912834-00-5*) Am Faculty Pr.
Awakening Notes. Kay Carey. 74p. (Orig.). (C). 1980. pap. text ed. 3.75 (*0-8220-0218-3*) Cliffs.
Awakening of a Sleeping Giant: Third World Leaders & National Liberation. Thomas E. Hachey & Ralph E. Weber. LC 80-12517. 160p. (C). 1981. pap. text ed. 9.50 (*0-89874-081-9*) Krieger.
Awakening of Adam. Jean Lanier. 1973. pap. 2.25 (*0-913456-63-2*) Interbk Inc.
Awakening of Albion: The Renovation of the Body in the Poetry of William Blake. Thomas R. Frosch. 211p. 1974. 31.95 (*0-8014-0815-6*) Cornell U Pr.
*__Awakening of American Nationalism 1815-1828.__ George Dangerfield. (Illus.). 331p. (C). 1994. pap. text ed. 12.95x (*0-88133-823-0*) Waveland Pr.
Awakening of Faith, Attributed to Asvaghosha. Tr. by Yoshito S. Hakeda. LC 67-13778. 128p. 1974. reprint ed. pap. text ed. 15.00 (*0-231-08336-X*) Col U Pr.
Awakening of Faith in Mahayana. Kevin O'Neil. (Orig.). 1984. pap. 14.95 (*0-685-09623-8*) Crises Res Pr.
Awakening of Faith in the Mahayana & Its Commentary: The Principle & Practice of Mahayana Buddhism. D. T. Suzuki & Dwight Goddard. 253p. 1990. reprint ed. pap. 30.00 (*957-9482-18-7*) Oriental Bk Store.
Awakening of Helena Richie. Margaret W. Deland. LC 78-96881. (Illus.). reprint ed. lib. bdg. 19.00 (*0-8398-0358-3*) Irvington.
Awakening of Hezekiah Jones. John E. Bruce. LC 73-18567. reprint ed. 16.50 (*0-404-11381-8*) AMS Pr.
Awakening of Intelligence. Jiddu Krishnamurti. 1987. pap. 17.00 (*0-06-064834-1*, PL) HarpC.
Awakening of Love: An Experience of Bhakti Yoga. Anup Wing. 153p. (Orig.). 1993. pap. 12.95 (*0-940258-29-3*) Kripalu Pubns.
Awakening of Persia: The Reign of Nasr Al-Din Shah, 1848-1896. A. J. Abraham. 72p. (Orig.). (C). 1993. pap. text ed. 18.95 (*0-9628916-9-X*) Vande Vere.
Awakening of Southern Italy. Margaret Carlyle. LC 85-14821. (Illus.). viii, 147p. 1985. reprint ed. text ed. 52.50 (*0-313-25044-8*, CAAW, Greenwood Pr) Greenwood.
Awakening of St. Augustine, the Anderson Family & the Oldest City: 1821-1924. Thomas Graham. LC 84-154673. (Illus.). 289p. 1979. 25.00 (*0-917553-07-1*); pap. 8.95 (*0-917553-08-X*) St Augustine Hist.
Awakening of the Human Spirit. Hazrat I. Khan. 224p. 1988. pap. 12.95 (*0-930872-35-5*) Omega Pubns NY.
Awakening of the Soviet Union. Geoffrey A. Hosking. 208p. 1990. text ed. 19.95 (*0-674-05550-0*) HUP.
Awakening of the Soviet Union. Geoffrey A. Hosking. 1990. pap. text ed. 10.95 (*0-674-05551-9*) HUP.
Awakening of the West: The Encounter of Buddhism & Western Culture. Stephen Batchelor. 300p. 1994. 30.00 (*0-938077-68-6*); pap. 18.00 (*0-938077-69-4*) Parallax Pr.
Awakening of Western Legal Thought. Max Hamburger. LC 76-79515. 1969. reprint ed. 26.00 (*0-8196-0246-9*) Biblo.
Awakening of Western Legal Thought. Max Hamburger. Tr. by Bernard Miall. LC 74-98763. xxiii, 167p. 1970. reprint ed. text ed. 52.50 (*0-8371-3103-0*, HALT, Greenwood Pr) Greenwood.
Awakening Osiris: The Egyptian Book of the Dead. Tr. & Intro. by Normandi Ellis. LC 88-23224. (Illus.). 227p. (Orig.). 1988. 21.95 (*0-933999-73-9*); pap. 11.95 (*0-933999-74-7*) Phanes Pr.
Awakening Our Self-Healing Body: A Solution to the Health Care Crisis. Arthur M. Baker. LC 93-93516. 306p. (Orig.). 1994. pap. 12.95 (*1-883989-25-6*) Self Hlth Care.
Awakening Palestine. Leon Simon & Leonard Stein. LC 75-6457. (Rise of Jewish Nationalism & the Middle East Ser.). 318p. 1975. reprint ed. 25.85 (*0-88355-342-2*) Hyperion Conn.
Awakening Sacred Dance Through Spirituals & Scripture. Joella Chew. 1987. 3.00 (*0-941500-48-9*) Sharing Co.
Awakening Spirit: Meditations by Women for Women. Ed. by Peg Streep. LC 93-6472. (Illus.). 112p. 1993. 22.50 (*0-670-84887-5*, Viking Studio) Studio Bks.
Awakening Spirits. Tom Brown, Jr. 224p. (Orig.). 1994. pap. 10.00 (*0-425-14140-3*, Berkley Trade) Berkley Pub.
Awakening the Heart: East-West Approaches to Psychotherapy & the Healing Relationship. Ed. by John Welwood. LC 83-42807. (New Science Library). 219p. (Orig.). 1983. pap. 16.00 (*0-394-72182-9*) Shambhala Pubns.
Awakening the Heroes Within: Twelve Archetypes to Help Us Find Ourselves & Transform Our World. Carol S. Pearson. LC 90-55296. 288p. (Orig.). 1991. pap. 16.00 (*0-06-250678-1*) Harper SF.
Awakening the Hidden Storyteller: How to Build a Storytelling Tradition in Your Family. Robin Moore. 1991. pap. 18.00 (*0-87773-599-9*) Shambhala Pubns.
Awakening the Inner Eye: Intuition in Education. Nel Noddings & Paul J. Shore. LC 83-18057. 254p. reprint ed. pap. 72.40 (*0-7837-4628-8*, 2044351) Bks Demand.
Awakening the Life Force: The Philosophy & Psychology of Spontaneous Yoga. Rajarshi Muni. LC 93-40373. (Illus.). 224p. 1994. pap. 15.00 (*0-87542-581-X*) Llewellyn Pubns.
Awakening the Marvelous Powers Within You. Marvin E. Lewis. 345p. 1994. pap. 9.95 (*1-56901-365-9*) NW Pub.
*__Awakening the Mind: Explanations of Basic Buddhist Meditations.__ rev. ed. Geshe N. Wangchen. Orig. Title: Awakeniong the Mind of Enlightenment. (Illus.). 272p. 1995. pap. 14.95 (*0-86171-102-5*) Wisdom MA.
*__Awakening the Mind, Lightening the Heart: Core Teachings of Tibetan Buddhism.__ Dalai Lama. LC 95-11538. (Path to Enlightenment Ser.: Vol. 2). 1995. 17.00 (*0-06-061688-1*) Harper SF.
Awakening the Mind of Enlightenment: Meditations on the Buddhist Path. Geshe N. Wangchen. Ed. by Pauline Poulton & Lydia Muellbauer. (Basic Book - Orange Ser.). (Illus.). 263p. (Orig.). 1987. pap. 12.95 (*0-86171-039-8*, B039) Wisdom MA.
Awakening the Natural Genius of Black Children. Amos N. Wilson. 130p. (Orig.). 1992. pap. 8.95 (*1-879164-01-9*) African World.
Awakening the Poet Within: How to Write 135 Forms, Enter Contests, Win Awards, Get Your Poetry Published & More! Ann Gasser. 168p. 1993. pap. 9.95 (*1-884257-00-3*) AGEE Keyboard.
Awakening the Slower Mind. V. Bruce. 1969. 105.00 (*0-08-006387-X*, Pub. by Pergamon Repr UK) Franklin.
Awakening the Soul. James A. Kitchens. LC 93-34919. 1994. pap. 10.00 (*0-671-87082-3*, Fireside) S&S Trade.
*__Awakening the Warrior Within: Secrets of Personal Safety & Inner Security.__ Dawn Callan. 208p. 1995. pap. 11.95 (*1-882591-20-8*) Nataraj Pub.
Awakening to Community. Rudolf Steiner. Tr. by Marjorie Spock. LC 74-81153. 178p. 1975. 16.95 (*0-910142-61-0*) Anthroposophic.
Awakening to Literacy. Ed. by Hillel Goelman et al. LC 84-727. 240p. 1984. pap. text ed. 22.50 (*0-435-08207-8*) Heinemann.
Awakening to Mission: The Philippine Catholic Church 1964-1981. Pasquale T. Giordano. xv, 276p. (Orig.). (C). 1988. pap. 16.50 (*971-10-0266-3*, Pub. by New Day Pub PH) Cellar.
Awakening to Prayer. Augustine I. Okuma. Tr. by Theresa K. Hiraki & Albert M. Yamato. LC 93-33061. 1994. pap. 8.95 (*0-935216-22-7*) ICS Pubns.
Awakening to the Animal Kingdom. Robert Shapiro & Julie Rapkin. 120p. (Orig.). 1989. pap. 8.95 (*0-945946-02-3*) Cassandra Pr.
Awakening to the Light, Vol. 1: Diaries 1958-1967. Nicholas Hagger. 1994. 30.00 (*1-85230-505-3*) Element MA.
Awakening to the Plant Kingdom. Robert Shapiro & Julie Rapkin. (Illus.). 140p. (Orig.). 1991. pap. 9.95 (*0-945946-12-0*) Cassandra Pr.
Awakening to the Tao. Liu I-Ming. Tr. by Thomas Cleary. LC 88-17478. 96p. (Orig.). 1988. pap. 12.00 (*0-87773-447-X*) Shambhala Pubns.
Awakening to the Truth. Nichiren. Tr. by N. R. Ehara et al. LC 83-45457. Orig. Title: Kaimokusho. 1983. reprint ed. 28.50 (*0-404-20189-X*) AMS Pr.
Awakening to Your Dreams: A Dreamers Handbook. George DeLong. 190p. (Orig.). 1991. pap. 12.95 (*0-9628316-0-3*) New World CA.
Awakening Twenties: A Memoir-History of a Literary Period. Gorham Munson. LC 84-14316. (Illus.). 317p. 1985. 35.00 (*0-8071-1201-1*) La State U Pr.
Awakening Your Child's Natural Genius: Enhancing Your Child's Curiosity, Creativity & Learning Ability. Thomas Armstrong. 288p. 1991. pap. 12.95 (*0-87477-608-2*) J P Tarcher.
Awakening Your Inner Light: Healing Self-Abuse & Reclaiming Your True Identity. Aeoliah Kuthumy. Ed. by Cheryll Melott. (Illus.). 289p. (Orig.). 1992. pap. 14.95 (*0-9633249-3-4*) Helios Rising.
Awakening Your Sexuality: A Guide for Recovering Women & Their Partners. Stephanie S. Covington. LC 92-9999. 1992. pap. 12.00 (*0-06-250191-7*) Harper SF.
Awakening...Eternal Youth, Vibrant Health, Radiant Beauty. Patricia D. Cota-Robles. (Illus.). 176p. (Orig.). 1993. pap. 14.00 (*0-9615287-3-7*) New Age Study Human.
Awakenings. Saranne Dawson. 400p. (Orig.). 1994. pap. 4.99 (*0-505-51921-6*, Love Spell) Dorchester Pub Co.
Awakenings. Thomas Keating. 128p. (Orig.). 1990. pap. 9.95 (*0-8245-1044-5*) Crossroad NY.
Awakenings. Martha J. Ross-Rodgers. LC 93-14401. 180p. 1993. pap. 8.95 (*1-882185-10-2*) Crnrstone Pub.
Awakenings. Oliver Sacks. 21.00 (*0-8446-6277-1*) Peter Smith.
Awakenings. Oliver Sacks. (Illus.). 448p. (C). 1991. reprint ed. lib. bdg. 29.00x (*0-8095-9035-2*) Borgo Pr.
Awakenings. Oliver Sacks. LC 90-4914. (Illus.). 448p. 1990. reprint ed. pap. 10.95 (*0-06-097368-4*, PL) HarpC.
*__Awakenings: A Jewish Woman's Search for Truth.__ Toni L. Brown. 200p. (Orig.). 1993. pap. 12.95 (*1-884052-06-1*) Kochav.
Awakeniong the Mind of Enlightenment see Awakening the Mind: Explanations of Basic Buddhist Meditations
Awara. Gayatri Chatterjee. 1992. 10.00 (*81-224-0421-9*, Pub. by Wiley Eastern II) S Asia.
Awara Messiah: A Biography of Sarat Chandra Chatterjee. Vishnu Prabhakar. (New World Literature Ser.). 1989. 19.50 (*81-7018-564-5*, Pub. by BR Pub II) S Asia.
Award. Lawrence Bantleman. 9.00 (*0-89253-648-9*); 4.80 (*0-89253-649-7*) Ind-US Inc.
Award. Harriet Hinsdale. 1989. pap. 3.95 (*0-8217-2563-7*) Zebra.
Award Certificates for Children's Ministries. Bev Gundersen. (Illus.). 32p. 1991. pap. text ed. 7.99 (*0-87403-789-1*, 14-03069) Standard Pub.
Award Certificates for Special Achievement. Bev Gundersen. (Illus.). 32p. 1991. pap. text ed. 7.99 (*0-87403-788-3*, 14-03068) Standard Pub.
Award Highlights. Stephen Corey et al. (Illus.). (Orig.). 1983. 45.00 (*0-931956-07-2*); pap. 12.00 (*0-931956-08-0*) Water Mark.
Award Living Bible. deluxe ed. 1983. Black Imitation Leather. 7.99 (*0-8423-2287-6*); Black Imitation Leather. 7.99 (*0-8423-2293-0*) Tyndale.
Award Puzzles: Color Zoo. Lois Ehlert. (Caldecott Collection). (J). 1991. 6.95 (*0-938971-66-2*) JTG Nashville.
Award Puzzles: Freight Train. Donald Crews. (Caldecott Collection). (J). 1991. 6.95 (*0-938971-70-0*) JTG Nashville.
Award Puzzles: Frog Went a-Courting. Feodor Rojankovsky. (Caldecott Collection). (J). 1991. 6.95 (*0-938971-69-7*) JTG Nashville.
Award Puzzles: Mufaro's Beautiful Daughters. John Steptoe. (Caldecott Collection). (J). 1991. 6.95 (*0-938971-67-0*) JTG Nashville.
Award Puzzles: Noah's Ark. Peter Spier. (Caldecott Collection). (J). 1990. 6.95 (*0-938971-62-X*) JTG Nashville.
Award Puzzles: Prayer for a Child. Elizabeth Jones. (Caldecott Collection). (J). 1991. 6.95 (*0-938971-64-6*) JTG Nashville.
Award Puzzles: Saint George & the Dragon. Trina S. Hyamm. (Caldecott Collection). (J). 1991. 6.95 (*0-938971-68-9*) JTG Nashville.
Award Puzzles: Song & Dance Man. Stephen Gammell. (Caldecott Collection). (J). 1991. 6.95 (*0-938971-61-1*) JTG Nashville.
Award Puzzles: Sylvester & the Magic Pebble. William Steig. (Caldecott Collection). (J). 1990. 6.95 (*0-938971-60-3*) JTG Nashville.
Award Puzzles: The Caldecott Collection - Alphabatics. Suse MacDonald. (Illus.). 1992. 6.95 (*0-938971-71-9*) JTG Nashville.

An Asterisk (*) at the beginning of an entry indicates that the title is appearing in BIP for the first time.

An Asterisk (*) at the beginning of an entry indicates that the title is appearing in BIP for the first time.

Awesome Chesapeake. David O. Bell. (Illus.). 48p. (J). (gr. 3-8). 1994. 11.95 (*0-87033-457-3*, Tidewtr Pubs) Cornell Maritime.

Awesome Entertainment Records. Stuart A. Kallen. LC 91-73054. (World Records Library). 32p. (J). 1991. lib. bdg. 12.94 (*1-56239-047-3*) Abdo & Dghtrs.

Awesome Experiments! Down to a Science. Steven D. Spangler. Ed. by Elaine M. Myers. (Down to a Science Ser.). (Illus.). 16p. (J). (gr. k-6). 1994. teacher ed, pap. text ed. 14.25 (*0-944943-48-9*, 92227-4) Current Inc.

Awesome Facts to Blow Your Mind. Judith F. Clark. (Facts to Blow Your Mind Ser.). (Illus.). 48p. (Orig.). (J). (gr. 2-6). 1993. pap. 4.95 (*0-8431-3577-8*) Price Stern.

Awesome Foursome. Lyle K. Thadison. 32p. 1994. pap. 5.95 (*0-8059-3447-2*) Dorrance.

Awesome Good Clean Jokes for Kids. Bob Phillips. LC 92-12109. 207p. (J). 1992. mass mkt. 3.99 (*1-56507-062-3*) Harvest Hse.

Awesome Green: The Explosive New Plant Sciences. Carl Tant. LC 93-73250. (Illus.). 192p. (Orig.). 1994. pap. 17.95 (*1-880319-05-5*) Biotech.

Awesome Life Force. (Nikola Tesla Ser.). 1991. lib. bdg. 79.95 (*0-8490-4319-0*) Gordon Pr.

Awesome Life Force. Joseph H. Cater. 479p. 1984. spiral bd. 16.45 (*0-7873-0161-2*) Mokelumne.

***Awesome Neurochemicals: The Essence of Sex.** Carl Tant. LC 95-79488. (Awesome Science of Biology Ser.). (Illus.). 156p. (Orig.). 1995. pap. 15.95 (*1-880319-13-6*) Biotech.

***Awesome Power of Your Attitude: It Can Make You or Break You.** Dale E. Galloway. 211p. 1992. 13.00 (*1-885605-01-3*) Fnd of Hope.

Awesome Profits: From Kitchen Poker Table to Tournament Final Table. George Elias. (Illus.). 384p. (Orig.). 1994. per. 29.95 (*0-9635355-2-8*) Ace Hi Pub.

Awesome Real-Life Bible Devotions for Kids. David C. Cook Publishing Staff. LC 91-18215. (J). (gr. 4-7). 1991. 9.99 (*1-55513-737-7*, Chariot Bks) Chariot Family.

Awesome Sega Genesis Secrets, No. 1. J. Douglas Arnold. (Gaming Mastery Ser.). (Illus.). 256p. (Orig.). (J). 1992. pap. 9.95 (*0-9624676-4-2*, GV1469.3) Sandwich Islands.

Awesome Sega Genesis Secrets, No. 2. J. Douglas Arnold. (Gaming Mastery Ser.). (Illus.). 288p. (Orig.). 1992. pap. 9.95 (*0-9624676-5-0*) Sandwich Islands.

Awesome Sega Genesis Secrets, No. 3. J. Douglas Arnold & Zach Meston. (Gaming Mystery Ser.). (Illus.). 320p. (Orig.). 1993. pap. 11.95 (*0-9624676-3-4*) Sandwich Islands.

Awesome Sega Genesis Secrets 4. Zach Meston & J. Douglas Arnold. (Gaming Mastery Ser.). (Illus.). 352p. (YA). 1994. pap. 11.95 (*0-9624676-2-6*) Sandwich Islands.

***Awesome Sega Genesis Secrets 5.** Sandwich Islands Publishing Staff. Ed. by Zach Meston & J. Douglas Arnold. (Gaming Mastery Ser.). (Illus.). 320p. (Orig.). 1995. pap. 12.95 (*1-884364-05-5*) Sandwich Islands.

Awesome Summer. abr. ed. Kathleen Hof et al. 110p. 1995. pap. 7.95 (*1-56901-403-5*) NW Pub.

Awesome Super Nintendo Secrets. J. Douglas Arnold. (Gaming Mastery Ser.). (Illus.). 320p. (Orig.). 1993. pap. 11.95 (*0-9624676-6-9*) Sandwich Islands.

Awesome Super Nintendo Secrets, No. 2. Zach Meston & J. Douglas Arnold. (Gaming Mastery Ser.). (Illus.). 320p. (Orig.). 1993. pap. 11.95 (*0-9624676-7-7*) Sandwich Islands.

Awesome Super Nintendo Secrets 3. J. Douglas Arnold & Zach Meston. (Gaming Mastery Ser.). 320p. 1994. pap. 11.95 (*0-9624676-8-5*) Sandwich Islands.

***Awesome Super Nintendo Secrets 4.** Sandwich Island Publishing Staff et al. (Gaming Mastery Ser.). (Illus.). 320p. (Orig.). 1994. pap. 12.95 (*1-884364-06-3*) Sandwich Islands.

Awesome Teen. Chris Silkwood & Nancy Levicki. (Illus.). 140p. (Orig.). (YA). (gr. 8-12). 1991. pap. 11.95 (*0-9631318-0-X*) NJL Interests.

Awesomely Gross Jokes. Julius Alvin. 160p. 1991. pap. 3.50 (*0-8217-3613-2*) Zebra.

***Awful Abigail & Why She Changed.** Barbara H. Robbins & Kathryn M. Stahl. (Illus.). 58p. (J). (gr. k-12). 1995. pap. 6.50 (*0-9630060-1-0*) Robbinspring.

Awful America: A Dictionary of 200 Years of European Abuse. Gert Raeithel. Ed. by Reinhold Aman. Tr. by Harry Zohn. LC 76-5698. (Maledicta Press Publications Ser.: Vol.7). Date not set. 15.00 (*0-916500-07-1*) Maledicta.

Awful Disclosures by Marcia Monk of the Hotel Dieu Nunnery of Montreal. Maria Monk & Gerald Grob. LC 76-46089. (Anti-Movements in America Ser.). 1977. lib. bdg. 35.95 (*0-405-09962-2*) Ayer.

Awful Joke Book. Mary Danby. (Funniest Joke Bks.). (Illus.). 96p. (Orig.). 1992. reprint ed. 3.99 (*0-517-07767-1*, Pub. by Wings Bks) Random Hse Value.

Awful Mess Mystery. Adrian Robert. LC 84-8724. (Illus.). 48p. (J). (gr. 2-4). 1985. lib. bdg. 10.89 (*0-8167-0402-3*); pap. text ed. 3.50 (*0-8167-0403-1*) Troll Assocs.

Awful Revolution: The Decline of the Roman Empire in the West. Frank W. Walbank. (Illus.). 165p. reprint ed. pap. 47.10 (*0-8357-4172-9*, 2036946) Bks Demand.

***Awful Thing in the Attic: And Other Scary, True Stories of Ghosts, Strange Disappearances & UFOs.** Brad Steiger. LC 95-15244. 1995. pap. write for info. (*1-880090-17-1*) Galde Pr.

Awfully Big Adventure. Beryl Bainbridge. 224p. 1993. pap. 9.95 (*0-88184-961-8*) Carroll & Graf.

***Awfully Big Adventure.** Beryl Bainbridge. 224p. 1995. pap. 8.95 (*0-7867-0184-6*) Carroll & Graf.

Awfully Short for the Fourth Grade. Elvira Woodruff. LC 89-2082. (Illus.). 112p. (J). (gr. 3-6). 1989. 14.95 (*0-8234-0785-3*) Holiday.

Awfully Short for the Fourth Grade. Elvira Woodruff. (J). 1990. reprint ed. pap. 3.50 (*0-440-40366-9*, Yearling Classics) Dell.

Awit & Corrido: Philippine Metrical Romances. Damiana L. Eugenio. 464p. 1988. text ed. 28.00 (*0-8248-1031-7*, Pub. by U of Philippines Pr) UH Pr.

AWK Programming Language. Alfred V. Aho et al. LC 87-17566. (Computer Science Ser.). (Illus.). 224p. (C). 1988. pap. text ed. 29.25 (*0-201-07981-X*) Addison-Wesley.

Awkward Age. Henry James. Ed. by Ronald Blythe. (Modern Classics Ser.). 1974. mass mkt. 4.95 (*0-14-002451-4*, Penguin Bks) Viking Penguin.

Awkward Age. Henry James. LC 74-158788. (Novels & Tales of Henry James Ser.: Vol. 9). 1971. reprint ed. lib. bdg. 45.00 (*0-678-02809-5*) Kelley.

Awkward Age. Henry James. (BCL1-PS American Literature Ser.). 449p. 1993. reprint ed. lib. bdg. 99.00 (*0-7812-6976-8*) Rprt Serv.

Awkward Dominion: American Political, Economic, & Cultural Relations with Europe 1919-1933. Frank Costigliola. LC 84-45150. 376p. 1984. 45.00 (*0-8014-1679-5*); pap. 16.95 (*0-8014-9505-9*) Cornell U Pr.

Awkward Girl. M. R. Callaghan. (C). 1990. 36.00 (*0-946311-95-1*, Pub. by Attic Pr IE) St Mut.

Awkward Girl. Mary R. Callaghan. (C). 1989. pap. 11.95 (*0-946211-95-7*, Pub. by Attic IE) InBook.

Awkward Partner: Britain in the European Community. Stephen George. 288p. 1994. 55.00 (*0-19-878106-7*); pap. 19.95 (*0-19-878107-5*) OUP.

Awkward Song. Allan Kornblum. LC 80-18370. 57p. 1980. pap. 5.00 (*0-915124-32-7*, Toothpaste) Coffee Hse.

Awkward Warrior: Frank Cousins: His Life & Times. 2nd ed. Geoffrey Goodman. 616p. 1984. pap. 42.50 (*0-85124-417-3*, Pub. by Spokesman Bks UK) Coronet Bks.

Awl-Birds. J. K. Stanford. (Illus.). 1949. 10.00 (*0-8159-5016-0*) Devin.

Awning Marketing Seminar. 91p. 1982. 20.00 (*0-318-01505-6*, 11120) Indus Fabrics.

Awnings & Tents. Ernest Chandler. reprint ed. 50.00 (*0-318-01554-4*, 21040) Indus Fabrics.

***Awntyrs Off Arthure at the Terne Wathelyne: A Critical Edition.** Ed. by Robert J. Gates. 278p. 1969. text ed. 38.95 (*0-8122-7587-X*) U of Pa Pr.

Awo: Ifa & the Theology of Orisha Divination. Fa'lokum Fatunmbi. 1992. 12.95 (*0-942272-24-2*) Original Pubns.

AWP Official Guide to Writing Programs. 6th ed. Ed. by D. W. Fenza & Beth Jarock. 250p. 1992. pap. 15.95 (*0-916685-30-6*) Dustbooks.

Awsome Family Nights. Susan Luke. Date not set. pap. 7.95 (*1-55503-689-9*, 01111639) Covenant Comms.

AWWA Annual Conference Proceedings, Cincinnati, OH, 1990. 2180p. 91.50 (*0-89867-556-1*, 20257) Am Water Wks Assn.

AWWA Annual Conference Proceedings, Denver, CO, 1986. 1842p. 91.50 (*0-89867-367-4*, 20193) Am Water Wks Assn.

AWWA Annual Conference Proceedings, Kansas City, MO, 1987. 2074p. 91.50 (*0-89867-405-0*, 20012) Am Water Wks Assn.

AWWA Annual Conference Proceedings, Los Angeles, CA, 1989. 1756p. 91.50 (*0-89867-487-5*, 20244) Am Water Wks Assn.

AWWA Computer Conference Proceedings, Denver, CO, 1989. 1144p. 75.00 (*0-89867-471-9*, 20243) Am Water Wks Assn.

AWWA Computer Conference Proceedings, Houston, TX, 1991. 1070p. 75.00 (*0-89867-581-2*, 20274) Am Water Wks Assn.

AWWA Distribution System Symposium, Boston, MA, 1988. 160p. 18.50 (*0-89867-453-0*, 20240) Am Water Wks Assn.

AWWA Distribution System Symposium, Dallas, TX, 1989. 252p. 22.00 (*0-89867-501-4*, 20245) Am Water Wks Assn.

AWWA Distribution System Symposium, Los Angeles, CA, 1987. 188p. 19.00 (*0-89867-420-4*, 20021) Am Water Wks Assn.

AWWA Distribution System Symposium, Minneapolis, MN, 1986. 272p. 22.50 (*0-89867-382-8*, 20199) Am Water Wks Assn.

AWWA Distribution System Symposium, Portland, OR, 1990. 408p. 32.00 (*0-89867-553-7*, 20267) Am Water Wks Assn.

AWWA Manuals, 29 vols., Set. (Reference Manual Ser.). (Illus.). 460.00 (*0-685-50831-5*, 30040) Am Water Wks Assn.

AWWA Water Quality Technology Conference, Baltimore, MD, 1987. 1104p. 57.00 (*0-89867-431-X*, 20024) Am Water Wks Assn.

Ax. Ernie Colon. 48p. 1988. 5.95 (*0-87135-490-X*) Marvel Entmnt.

Ax. Ed McBain. 160p. 1977. pap. 4.50 (*0-451-16407-5*, Sig) NAL-Dutton.

Ax. Ed McBain. 1989. pap. 2.95 (*0-451-14599-2*) NAL-Dutton.

Ax Tongue. John M. Bennett. (Illus.). vii, 26p. (Orig.). 1986. pap. 7.98 (*0-935350-16-0*); audio (*0-318-61060-4*) Luna Bisonte.

AX 25: Link-Layer Packet Radio Protocal. 1984. pap. 8.00 (*0-87259-011-9*) Am Radio.

AXA. Donne Avenell & Enrique Romero. (First American Edition Ser.). (Illus.). 64p. 1981. pap. 5.95 (*0-912277-04-1*) K Pierce Inc.

AXA 2. Donne Avenell & Enrique Romero. (First American Edition Ser.). (Illus.). 64p. 1982. pap. 5.95 (*0-912277-05-X*) K Pierce Inc.

AXA 3. Donne Avenell et al. (First American Edition Ser.). (Illus.). 64p. 1983. pap. 5.95 (*0-912277-06-8*) K Pierce Inc.

AXA 4. Donne Avenell et al. (First American Edition Ser.). (Illus.). 64p. 1983. pap. 5.95 (*0-912277-01-7*) K Pierce Inc.

AXA 5. Donne Avenell & Enrique Romero. (First American Edition Ser.). (Illus.). 64p. 1984. pap. 5.95 (*0-912277-21-1*) K Pierce Inc.

AXA 6. Donne Avenell & Enrique Romero. (First American Edition Ser.). (Illus.). 64p. 1984. pap. 5.95 (*0-912277-22-X*) K Pierce Inc.

AXA 7. Donne Avenell & Enrique Romero. (First American Edition Ser.). (Illus.). 64p. 1985. pap. 5.95 (*0-912277-29-7*) K Pierce Inc.

AXA 8. Donne Avenell & Enrique Romero. (First American Edition Ser.). (Illus.). 64p. 1987. reprint ed. pap. 5.95 (*0-912277-35-1*) K Pierce Inc.

AXA 9: The Last AXA. Donne Avenell & Enrique Romero. (First American Edition Ser.). (Illus.). 80p. 1988. reprint ed. pap. 7.95 (*0-912277-36-X*) K Pierce Inc.

Axe. Ludvik Vaculik. Tr. by Marian Sling. (European Classics Ser.). 220p. 1994. reprint ed. pap. 12.95 (*0-8101-1018-0*) Northwestern U Pr.

Axe Handles. Gary Snyder. LC 83-61398. 128p. 1982. pap. 10.00 (*0-86547-120-7*, North Pt Pr) FS&G.

Axe-Monies & Their Relatives. Dorothy Hosler et al. LC 89-17148. (Studies in Pre-Columbian Art & Archaeology: No. 30). (Illus.). 108p. 1990. pap. 28.00 (*0-88402-185-8*, HOAXP, Dumbarton Rsch Lib) Dumbarton Oaks.

Axe Thrower of the Titabawassee. George W. Skinner. (Illus.). 150p. 1989. pap. 10.00 (*0-9620249-2-9*) Broadblade Pr.

Axel. Jean M. Villiers De l'Isle-Adam. Tr. by H. P. Finberg. LC 77-11496. reprint ed. 23.50 (*0-404-16355-6*) AMS Pr.

Axel. Philippe A. Villiers de l'Isle-Adam. Tr. by M. Gaddis Rose. 175p. 1986. reprint ed. pap. 11.95 (*0-948166-05-3*, Pub. by Soho Bk Co UK) Dufour.

Axel Schultes in Bangert Jansen Scholz Schultes. Axel Schultes. 193p. 1993. pap. 54.00 (*0-685-67845-8*, Pub. by W Ernst Sohn) VCH Pubs.

Axelrods Atlas of Freshwater Aquarium Fishes. Herbert Axelrod. 1992. 89.95 (*0-685-62700-4*, H-1077) TFH Pubns.

Axel's Castle: A Study in the Imaginative Literature of 1870-1930. Edmund Wilson. 360p. 1991. pap. 12.95 (*0-02-012871-1*, Collier S&S) S&S Trade.

Axel's Castle: A Study in the Imaginative Literature of 1870-1930. Edmund Wilson. 336p. 1984. reprint ed. pap. 9.95 (*0-393-30194-X*) Norton.

***Axemaker's Gift.** James Burke & Robert Orenstein. LC 95-2146. 1995. write for info. (*0-614-03750-6*, Grosset-Putnam) Putnam Pub Group.

Axeman's Jazz. Julie Smith. (Southern Mysteries Ser.). 1992. mass mkt. 4.99 (*0-8041-0954-0*) Ivy Books.

Axenic Mammalian Cell Reactions. Ed. by George L. Tritsch. LC 70-82153. (Illus.). 427p. reprint ed. pap. 121.70 (*0-7837-0883-1*, 2041189) Bks Demand.

Axes LII. Theodore Enslin. 1981. pap. 1.75 (*0-686-35947-X*) Ziesing Bros.

Axes to Grind. (Illus.). 176p. 1990. pap. 19.95 (*0-8256-1280-2*, AM73404) Music Sales.

Axford - the Axfords of Oxford, NJ: A Genealogy Beginning in 1725. William C. Armstrong. (Illus.). 78p. 1994. reprint ed. lib. bdg. 26.00 (*0-8328-4189-7*); reprint ed. pap. 16.00 (*0-8328-4190-0*) Higginson Bk Co.

***Axford - The Axfords of Oxford, NJ: A Genealogy Beginning in 1725.** Wm. C. Armstrong. (Illus.). 78p. 1994. reprint ed. lib. bdg. 26.00 (*0-8328-4527-2*); reprint ed. pap. 16.00 (*0-8328-4528-0*) Higginson Bk Co.

Axial Flow Fans & Ducts. enl. ed. R. Allan Wallis. LC 91-22967. 476p. 1993. reprint ed. lib. bdg. 79.50 (*0-89464-644-3*) Krieger.

Axial Flow Turbines: Fluid Mechanics & Thermodynamics. J. H. Horlock. LC 73-75589. 286p. 1976. reprint ed. 30.50 (*0-88275-097-6*) Krieger.

Axially Compressed Structures: Stability & Strength. Ed. by R. Narayanan. (Illus.). 316p. 1982. 90.00 (*0-85334-139-7*, I-302-82, Pub. by Elsevier Applied Sci UK) Elsevier.

Axiology: The Science of Values. Archie J. Bahm. LC 80-66405. 168p. 1980. pap. 15.00 (*0-911714-11-1*, World Bks) Bahm.

Axiology: The Science of Values. abr. ed. Archie J. Bahm. LC 84-51726. 84p. 1984. pap. text ed. 3.00 (*0-911714-14-6*, World Bks) Bahm.

Axiom: The Scientific Computation System. Richard D. Jenks & Robert S. Sutor. LC 92-14454. (Illus.). 730p. 1992. 49.00 (*0-387-97855-0*) Spr-Verlag.

Axiomatic Bargaining Game Theory. H. J. Peters. LC 92-21620. (Theory & Decision Library: No. C). 1992. lib. bdg. 112.50 (*0-7923-1873-0*) Kluwer Ac.

Axiomatic Basis for Quantum Mechanics, Vol. 1. G. Ludwig. (Illus.). 240p. 1985. 89.00 (*0-387-13773-4*) Spr-Verlag.

Axiomatic Introduction to Crystallography. Peter Engel. 1986. lib. bdg. 103.00 (*90-277-2339-7*); pap. text ed. 55.50 (*90-277-2341-9*) Kluwer Ac.

Axiomatic Principles of Statistical Science. 2nd ed. V. V. Shvyrkov. LC 93-60151. (Illus.). 204p. (Orig.). 1993. pap. text ed. 37.55 (*0-942004-54-X*) Throwkoff Pr.

Axiomatic Projective Geometry. 2nd rev. ed. A. Heyting. 150p. 1980. 56.50 (*0-444-85431-2*, North Holland) Elsevier.

Axiomatic Set Theory. Paul Bernays. 1991. pap. 6.95 (*0-486-66637-9*) Dover.

Axiomatic Set Theory. Ed. by James E. Baumgartner et al. LC 84-18457. (Contemporary Mathematics Ser.: Vol. 31). 259p. 1989. reprint ed. 36.00 (*0-8218-5026-1*, CONM-31) Am Math.

Axiomatic Set Theory, 2 Vols, Set. Pure Mathematics Symposium Staff. LC 78-125172. (Proceedings of the Symposia in Pure Mathematics Ser.: Vol. 13). 696p. 114.00 (*0-8218-1413-3*, PSPUM-13) Am Math.

Axiomatic Set Theory, 2 Vols, Vol. 1. Pure Mathematics Symposium Staff. LC 78-125172. (Proceedings of the Symposia in Pure Mathematics Ser.: Vol. 13). 474p. 1967. 52.00 (*0-8218-0245-3*, PSPUM-13.1) Am Math.

Axiomatic Set Theory, 2 Vols, Vol. 2. Pure Mathematics Symposium Staff. LC 78-125172. (Proceedings of the Symposia in Pure Mathematics Ser.: Vol. 13). 222p. 1974. 73.00 (*0-8218-0246-1*, PSPUM-13.2) Am Math.

Axiomatic Set Theory of Classes: Impredicative Theories of Classes. R. B. Chuaqui. (Mathematics Studies: Vol. 51). 388p. 1981. 102.75 (*0-444-86178-5*, North Holland) Elsevier.

Axiomatic Theory of Bargaining with a Variable Number of Agents. William Thomson & Terje Lensberg. (Illus.). 230p. 1989. 64.95 (*0-521-34383-6*) Cambridge U Pr.

Axiomatic Theory of Language with Applications to English. Ty Pak. LC 80-12010. (Edward Sapir Monograph Ser. in Language, Culture & Cognition: No. 6). vi, 129p. (Orig.). (C). 1979. pap. 10.00 (*0-933104-08-1*) Jupiter Pr.

Axiomatics & Pragmatics of Conflict Analysis. Paelinck & P. H. Vossen. (Interdisciplinary Studies: Vol. 3). 350p. 1987. text ed. 79.95 (*0-566-05207-5*, Pub. by Avebury Pub UK) Ashgate Pub Co.

Axiomatics of Classical Statistical Mechanics. Rudolf Kurth & I. N. Sneddon. LC 60-8973. (International Series of Monographs on Pure & Applied Mathematics: Vol. 11). 1960. 84.00 (*0-08-009224-1*, Pub. by Pergamon Repr UK) Franklin.

Axiomization of Passage from "Local" Structure to "Global" Object. Paul Feit. LC 92-33858. (Memoirs of the American Mathematical Society Ser.: No. 485). 107p. 1993. 26.00 (*0-8218-2546-1*) Am Math.

Axioms: In Search of a Comprehensive Philosophy of Life. Mounir Murad. (Illus.). 80p. (Orig.). 1992. pap. 7.50 (*0-9633519-6-6*) Murad Pub.

Axioms & Hulls. Donald E. Knuth. Ed. by G. Goos & J. Hartmanis. LC 92-19889. (Lecture Notes in Computer Science Ser.: Vol. 606). ix, 109p. 1992. pap. 30.00 (*0-387-55611-7*) Spr-Verlag.

Axioms & Logics. L. Ron Hubbard. 5.00 (*0-686-30793-3*) Church Scient NY.

Axioms & Quotations of Yosef ben-Jochannan. E. Curtis Alexander. LC 80-70287. 118p. (Orig.). 1980. 10.95 (*0-938818-01-5*) ECA Assoc.

Axioms for Survivors. Lon Nungessor. 128p. (C). 1990. reprint ed. lib. bdg. 23.00x (*0-8095-6568-4*) Borgo Pr.

Axioms of Cooperative Decision-Making. Herve Moulin. (Econometric Society Monographs: No. 15). (Illus.). 300p. 1988. 74.95 (*0-521-36055-2*) Cambridge U Pr.

Axioms of Cooperative Decision-Making. Herve Moulin. (Econometric Society Monographs: No. 15). (Illus.). 400p. (C). 1991. pap. 27.95 (*0-521-42458-5*) Cambridge U Pr.

Axioms of Flight. J. Embree. (Illus.). 190p. 1984. spiral bd. 17.95 (*0-9601062-7-8*) Flight Info.

Axion Esti: English Edition. Odysseus Elytis. Tr. by Edmund Keeley & George Savidis. LC 79-49274. (Poetry Ser.). 104p. (C). 1979. pap. 10.95 (*0-8229-5318-8*) U of Pittsburgh Pr.

Axis: A Quarterly Review of Contemporary Abstract Painting & Sculpture, No. 1-8. Ed. by Myfanwy Evans. LC 68-9236. (Contemporary Art Ser.). (Illus.). 1968. reprint ed. 36.95 (*0-405-00715-9*) Ayer.

Axis & Circumference: The Cylindrical Shape of Plants & Animals. Stephen A. Wainwright. LC 87-21099. (Illus.). 176p. 1988. 29.95x (*0-674-05700-7*) HUP.

Axis Correlation: A Modern Guide to Tonal Colors. rev. ed. Herb Moore. Ed. by Sharon Moore. 72p. (C). (gr. 9-12). 1993. pap. text ed. 15.00 (*0-9635896-0-1*) Moores Music.

Axis Deer in Texas. Ed. by Ernest D. Ables. (Kleberg Studies in Natural Resources). (Illus.). 86p. 1977. pap. 5.95 (*0-89096-196-4*) Tex A&M Univ Pr.

***Axis Forces in Yugoslavia 1941-45.** N. Thomas & K. Mikulan. (Osprey Men-at-Arms Ser.). (Illus.). 48p. 1995. pap. 11.95 (*1-85532-473-3*, Pub. by Osprey UK) Stackpole.

***Axis Navies.** (German Units Ser.). Date not set. 16.00 (*0-614-00590-6*) Valor Pub.

***Axis Two.** Thomas E. Mahon. 580p. 1995. pap. 12.95 (*1-56901-780-8*) NW Pub.

Axisymmetric Fluid-Liquid Interfaces. S. Hartland & R. W. Hartley. 782p. 1976. 174.50 (*0-444-41396-0*) Elsevier.

Axman Cometh. John Farris. 1989. mass mkt. 4.50 (*0-8125-0008-3*) Tor Bks.

Axolotls. Peter W. Scott. (Illus.). 96p. 1981. 9.95 (*0-87666-937-2*, KW-132) TFH Pubns.

Axon. Ed. by Stephen G. Waxman et al. LC 94-9396. 1994. write for info. (*0-19-082931-1*) OUP.

***Axon: Structure, Function, & Pathophysiology.** Ed. by Stephen G. Waxman et al. (Illus.). 865p. 1995. 175.00 (*0-19-508293-1*) OUP.

Axonal Regeneration in the Mammalian Central Nervous System. D. E. Oorschot & D. G. Jones. (Advances in Anatomy, Embryology & Cell Biology Ser.: Vol. 119). (Illus.). 128p. 1990. 58.00 (*0-387-51757-X*) Spr-Verlag.

An Asterisk (*) at the beginning of an entry indicates that the title is appearing in BIP for the first time.

An Asterisk (*) at the beginning of an entry indicates that the title is appearing in BIP for the first time.

561

Azari, Ya Zaban Bastan Azarbaygan: Azari: or The National Language of Azarbaijan. Ahmad Kasravi. LC 93-77135. (Illus.). 96p. (Orig.). (PER.). 1993. pap. 8.95 (*0-936347-31-7*) Iran Bks.

Azarius. Sidney Williams. 1989. mass mkt. 4.50 (*1-55817-229-7*, Pinnacle NY) Windsor NY.

***Azathoth Cycle: 16 Horror Tales Concerning the Ultimate Chaos.** Edward Derby et al. (Call of Cthulhu Fiction Ser.). (Illus.). 256p. (Orig.). Date not set. pap. 10.95 (*1-56882-040-2*) Chaosium.

Azbuka. Nikolas Michka & Vera Michka. (Illus.). 70p. (RUS.). (YA). 1994. write for info. (*1-885024-00-2*) Slavic Christian.

Azbuka Ivana Tedorova, 1578, 2 vols., Set. Ed. by Collet's Holdings, Ltd. Staff. 215p. (RUS.). 1983. 95.00 (*0-317-40833-X*, Pub. by Collets UK) Pro-Am Music.

Azemia see Modern Novel Writing

Azeotropic Data, No. III. Lee H. Horsley. LC 73-75991. (Advances in Chemistry Ser.: No. 116). (Illus.). 638p. reprint ed. pap. 180.00 (*0-7837-6755-2*, 2046384) Bks Demand.

Azerbaijan. (Let's Visit Places & Peoples of the World Ser.). (Illus.). (J). (gr. 5 up). 1988. write for info. (*0-7910-0165-2*) Chelsea Hse.

Azerbaijan. Ed. by Lerner Geography Department Staff. (Then & Now Ser.). (Illus.). 64p. (YA). (gr. 5 up). 1993. lib. bdg. 21.50 (*0-8225-2810-X*, Lerner Publctns) Lerner Group.

Azerbaijan: Economic Review. International Monetary Fund Staff. 94p. 1992. pap. 10.00 (*1-55775-261-3*) Intl Monetary.

Azerbaijan: Ethnicity & Autonomy in Iran after the Second World War. Touraj Atatbaki. 256p. 1993. text ed. 59.50 (*1-85043-640-1*, Pub. by I B Tauris UK) St Martin.

Azerbaijan: From Crisis to Sustained Growth. (Country Study Ser.). 246p. 1993. 19.95 (*0-8213-2672-4*, 12672) World Bank.

Azerbaijan: From Crisis to Sustained Growth. (Country Study Ser.). 256p. (RUS.). 1994. 13.95 (*0-8213-2847-6*, 12847) World Bank.

***Azerbaijan: U. S. Non Profit Aid.** 70p. (Orig.). 1995. pap. 125.00 (*0-7605-1535-2*) Rector Pr.

***Azerbaijan Business Intelligence Handbook.** (Illus.). 70p. (Orig.). 1994. pap. 70.00 (*0-7605-1040-7*) Rector Pr.

Azerbaijan Carpet. Liatif Kerimov. 236p. (C). 1985. 325.00 (*0-685-21943-7*, Pub. by Collets) St Mut.

Azerbaijan Carpet, 2 vols., Vol. 2. Collet's Publishing UK Staff. 304p. (RUS.). 1983. 245.00 (*0-317-57291-1*, Pub. by Collets) St Mut.

Azerbaijan Carpet, 2 vols., Vols. 2-3. Collet's Publishing UK Staff. (RUS.). 1983. Vol. 3, 242 pgs. write for info. (*0-318-61836-2*, Pub. by Collets) St Mut.

Azerbaijan Cookery. Archibald H. Rutledge. 230p. 1986. 12.95 (*0-8285-3799-2*) Firebird NY.

Azerbaijan IMF: Business Risk Overview. Ed. by Lewis B. Sckolnick. 125p. (Orig.). (C). 1994. pap. text ed. 125.00 (*1-57205-664-9*) Rector Pr.

Azerbaijan Legal Texts. Ed. by Lewis B. Sckolnick. 225p. (Orig.). (C). 1994. pap. text ed. 595.00 (*1-57205-433-6*) Rector Pr.

Azerbaijan Miniatures. Ed. by K. Kerimov. (Illus.). 222p. (C). 1980. text ed. 185.00 (*0-685-40240-1*, Pub. by Collets) St Mut.

Azerbaijan-Mosques, Turrets, Palaces. K. Gink & I. Turanszky. 200p. 1979. 80.00 (*0-317-57219-9*, Pub. by Collets UK) St Mut.

Azerbaijan Soviet Encyclopedia. Ed. by Collet's Holdings, Ltd. Staff. 608p. 1982. 115.00 (*0-317-39477-0*, Pub. by Collets UK) St Mut.

Azerbaijani, Colloquial. Kurtulus Oztopcu. 66p. 1994. 9.95 (*0-88432-789-2*); audio 75.00 (*0-88432-788-4*) Audio-Forum.

***Azerbaijani-English Dictionary.** Ed. by Mario Severino et al. 1995. write for info. (*1-881265-18-8*) Dunwoody Pr.

***Azerbaijani Language Course, Set.** 75p. (Orig.). (AZE.). 1994. audio, pap. 175.00 (*0-614-00721-6*) Rector Pr.

Azerbaijani Newspaper Reader. John D. Murphy. LC 93-71726. 113p. 1993. text ed. 42.00 (*1-881265-01-3*); audio 5.00 (*1-881265-04-8*) Dunwoody Pr.

Azerbaijani-Persian Dictionary. Behzad Behzadi. 1145p. 1991. lib. bdg. 45.00 (*0-939214-97-0*) Mazda Pubs.

Azerbaijani Turks: Power & Identity under Russian Rule. Audrey L. Altstadt & Wayne C. Vucinich. (Publication Ser.: No. 410). (Illus.). 334p. (Orig.). (C). 1992. text ed. 38.95 (*0-8179-9181-6*); pap. text ed. 18.95 (*0-8179-9182-4*) Hoover Inst Pr.

Azerbaijany-English, English-Azerbaijany Concise Dictionary. Seville Mamedov. (Concise Dictionaries Ser.). 400p. (Orig.). (AZE & ENG.). 1994. pap. 11.95 (*0-7818-0244-X*) Hippocrene Bks.

Azides & Nitrenes. Eric F. Scriven. 1984. text ed. 179.00 (*0-12-633480-3*) Acad Pr.

Azilian Skeletal Remains from Montardit, France. Ruth O. Sawtell. (HU PMP Ser.: Vol. 11, No. 4). 1931. pap. 10.00 (*0-527-01221-7*) Periodicals Srv.

Azilie of Bordeaux. Mary D. Few. (Illus.). 286p. 1973. 9.95 (*0-914056-01-8*) Carolina Edns.

Aziyade. Pierre Loti. 182p. 1988. pap. 12.95 (*0-7103-0316-5*, Pub. by Kegan Paul Intl UK) Routledge Chapman & Hall.

Aziyade. Pierre Loti. (Folio Ser.: No. 2058). (FRE.). 1990. pap. 12.95 (*2-07-038147-1*) Schoenhof.

Azmat al 'Aql al Muslim: (Crisis in the Muslim Mind) AbdulHamid AbuSulayman. LC 91-38922. (Silsilat al Manhajiyah al Islamiyah Ser.: No. 1). 243p. (Orig.). (ARA.). 1991. pap. 8.00 (*1-56564-015-2*) IIIT VA.

Azmat al Ta'lim al Mu'asir wa Hululuha al Islamiyah: The Contemporary Crisis of Education & Its Islamic Solutions. Z. El-Naggar. (Silsilat Rasa'il Islamiyat al Ma'rifah Ser.: No. 6). 252p. (Orig.). (ARA.). 1989. pap. 5.00 (*1-56564-159-0*) IIIT VA.

Azo Functional Polymers: Functional Group Approach in Macromolecular Design. G. Sudesh Kumar & D. C. Neckers. LC 92-64256. 165p. 1992. text ed. 68.00 (*0-87762-936-6*) Technomic.

Azores Cruising Guide. Gwenda Cornell. (Illus.). 1993. pap. 26.95 (*0-9517486-2-9*, Pub. by World Cruising UK) Bluewater Bks.

Azorin As a Literary Critic. Edward I. Fox. 176p. 1962. 6.00 (*0-318-22341-4*) Hispanic Inst.

Azospirillum - Plant Associations. Ed. by Yaacov Okon. LC 93-26203. 1993. 149.95 (*0-8493-4925-7*, QR82) CRC Pr.

Azospirillum II: Genetics, Physiology, Ecology, Vol. 48. Ed. by W. Klingmuller. (Experientia Supplementa Ser.). 196p. 1984. 41.95 (*3-7643-1576-8*) Birkhauser.

Azosulfones: Versatile Precursors for Aryl Radicals, Aryl Cations, Aryl Anions, Carbenes & Benzynes. M. Kobayashi & N. Kamigata. (Sulfur Report Ser.: Vol. 2, No. 3). 49p. 1982. pap. text ed. 50.00 (*3-7186-0117-6*) Gordon & Breach.

Azote de la Rivalidad Entre Hermanos (The Scourge of Sibling Rivalry) J. Dobson. (SPA.). Date not set. 1.79 (*1-56063-127-9*, 497404) Editorial Unilit.

***Azoth or the Star in the East: Embracing the First Matter of the Magnum Opus, the Evolution of Aphrodite-Urania, the Supernatural Generation of the Son of the Sun, & the Alchemical Transfiguration of Humanity.** Arthur E. Waite. 250p. 1995. pap. 19.95 (*1-56459-480-7*) Kessinger Pub.

Azpeitia (Bacillariophyceae) Related Genera & Promorphology. G. A. Fryxell et al. Ed. by Christiane Anderson. LC 86-10928. (Systematic Botany Monographs: Vol. 13). (Illus.). 74p. 1986. pap. 9.00 (*0-912861-13-4*) Am Soc Plant.

Azrael. Geoffrey Cook. 56p. (Orig.). 1992. pap. text ed. 5.00 (*1-879594-17-X*) Androgyne Bks.

Aztatlan: Prehistoric Mexican Frontier on the Pacific Coast. Carl O. Sauer & Donald Brand. LC 76-43816. (Ibero-Americana Ser.: No. 1). reprint ed. 39.50 (*0-404-15673-8*) AMS Pr.

Aztec. Gary Jennings. 1056p. 1981. mass mkt. 5.95 (*0-380-55889-0*) Avon.

***Aztec.** Gary Jennings. 1994. lib. bdg. 39.95x (*1-56849-410-6*) Buccaneer Bks.

Aztec. Patricia McKissack. LC 84-23142. (New True Bks.). (Illus.). 48p. (J). (gr. k-4). 1985. lib. bdg. 12.90 (*0-516-01936-8*); pap. 4.95 (*0-516-41936-6*) Childrens.

Aztec: The World of Moctezuma. Jane S. Day & Eduardo M. Moctezuma. (Illus.). 96p. (Orig.). 1992. pap. 16.95 (*1-879373-19-X*) R Rinehart.

Aztec & Maya Myths. Karl Taube. (Illus.). 80p. (Orig.). (C). 1994. pap. 9.95 (*0-292-78130-X*) U of Tex Pr.

Aztec & Other Mexican Indian Designs. Caren Caraway. (International Design Library). (Illus.). 48p. (Orig.). 1984. pap. 5.95 (*0-88045-051-7*) Stemmer Hse.

Aztec Art. Esther Pasztory. (Illus.). 336p. 1993. 49.50 (*0-8109-0687-2*) Abrams.

***Aztec Astrology: An Introduction.** Michael Colmer. (Illus.). 128p. 1995. pap. 9.95 (*0-7137-2455-2*, Pub. by Blandford Pr UK) Sterling.

Aztec Chief. Marie de S. Canavarro. 1977. lib. bdg. 59.95 (*0-8490-1464-6*) Gordon Pr.

***Aztec Chronicles: The True History of Christopher Columbus, as Narrated by Quilaztli of Texcoco.** Joseph P. Sanchez. LC 95-4312. 1995. per., pap. 9.95 (*0-89229-030-7*) TQS Pubns.

Aztec City-States. Mary G. Hodge. Ed. by Joyce Marcus. (Memoirs Ser.: No. 18). (Illus.). 166p. (Orig.). 1985. pap. 15.00 (*0-915703-02-5*) U Mich Mus Anthro.

***Aztec Civilization.** Lois Warburton. LC 94-32329. (World History Ser.). (J). 1995. 16.95 (*1-56006-277-0*) Lucent Bks.

Aztec Cosmos. Tomas Filsinger. 32p. (Orig.). 1984. 12.95 (*0-89087-352-6*) Celestial Arts.

***Aztec Empire.** R. Conrad Stein. (Cultures of the Past Ser.). 80p. (J). (gr. 5-8). 1995. lib. bdg. write for info. (*0-7614-0072-9*, Benchmark NY) Marshall Cavendish.

Aztec Empire: The Toltec Resurgence. Nigel Davies. (Civilization of the American Indian Ser.: Vol. 187). (Illus.). 352p. 1987. 45.00 (*0-8061-2098-3*) U of Okla Pr.

Aztec File: A Business Communications Course. A. Jones. (C). 1981. 80.00 (*0-85950-499-9*, Pub. by S Thornes Pubs UK) St Mut.

Aztec Image in Western Thought. Benjamin Keen. LC 74-163952. (Illus.). 570p. 1990. pap. text ed. 22.95 (*0-8135-1572-6*) Rutgers U Pr.

Aztec Image of Self & Society: An Introduction to Nahua Culture. Miguel Leon-Portilla. LC 90-53559. (Illus.). 264p. (C). 1992. lib. bdg. 27.50 (*0-87480-360-8*) U of Utah Pr.

Aztec Imperial Strategies. Frances F. Berdan et al. LC 94-42796. (Illus.). 390p. 1995. write for info. (*0-88402-211-0*, Dumbarton Rsch Lib) Dumbarton Oaks.

Aztec, Inca, & Maya. Elizabeth Baquedano. (Eyewitness Bks.). (Illus.). 64p. (YA). (gr. 5 up). 1993. 16.00 (*0-679-83883-X*) Knopf Bks Yng Read.

Aztec, Inca, & Maya. Elizabeth Baquedano. (Eyewitness Bks.). (Illus.). 64p. (J). (gr. 5 up). 1993. lib. bdg. 15.99 (*0-679-93883-4*) Knopf Bks Yng Read.

Aztec Indians. (Junior Library of American Indians). (Illus.). 80p. (J). (gr. 3-7). 1993. lib. bdg. 14.95 (*0-7910-1658-7*); pap. 6.95 (*0-7910-1963-2*) Chelsea Hse.

Aztec Kings: The Construction of Rulership in Mexica History. Susan D. Gillespie. LC 89-4760. 272p. 1989. 35.00 (*0-8165-1095-4*) U of Ariz Pr.

Aztec Kings: The Construction of Rulership in Mexica History. Susan D. Gillespie. LC 89-4760. (Illus.). 272p. 1992. reprint ed. pap. text ed. 14.95 (*0-8165-1339-2*) U of Ariz Pr.

Aztec Land. Maturin M. Ballou. 1976. lib. bdg. 59.95 (*0-87968-688-X*) Gordon Pr.

Aztec Medicine, Health, & Nutrition. Bernard R. Ortiz De Montellano. LC 89-70142. (Illus.). 310p. (Orig.). (C). 1990. text ed. 40.00 (*0-8135-1562-9*); pap. text ed. 15.00 (*0-8135-1563-7*) Rutgers U Pr.

Aztec, Mixtex, & Zapotec Armies. M. D. Pohl. (Men-at-Arms Ser.: No. 239). (Illus.). 48p. pap. 11.95 (*1-85532-159-9*, 9197, Pub. by Osprey UK) Stackpole.

Aztec Ruins National Monument. Scott Thybony. Ed. by Randolph Jorgan & Ronald J. Foreman. LC 91-67398. (Illus.). 16p. 1992. pap. 2.95 (*1-877856-08-8*) SW Pks Mnmts.

***Aztec Shell.** Jorge Aigla. 84p. (Orig.). 1995. pap. 9.00 (*0-927534-49-5*) Biling Rev-Pr.

Aztec Sorcerers in Seventeenth-Century Mexico: The Treatise on Superstition by Hernando Ruiz de Alarcon. Tr. by Michael D. Coe & Gordon Whittaker. LC 82-81425. (Monographs: No. 7). (Illus.). 329p. (Orig.). 1982. pap. text ed. 21.00 (*0-942041-06-2*) SUNYA Inst Mesoam.

Aztec Stone Sculpture. Intro. by Esther Pasztory. (Illus.). 1976. pap. 4.00 (*0-89192-166-4*, Ctr Inter-Am Rel) Interbk Inc.

Aztec Templo Mayor: Symposium at Dumbarton Oaks, October 8 & 9, 1983. Ed. by Elizabeth H. Boone. LC 86-4539. (Illus.). 520p. 1987. 40.00 (*0-88402-149-1*, BOAT) Dumbarton Oaks.

Aztec Thought & Culture: A Study of the Ancient Nahuatl Mind. Miguel Leon-Portilla. Tr. by Jack E. Davis. LC 63-11019. (Civilization of the American Indian Ser.: Vol. 67). (Illus.). 272p. 1990. reprint ed. pap. 15.95 (*0-8061-2295-1*) U of Okla Pr.

Aztec Warfare: Imperial Expansion & Political Control. Ross Hassig. LC 87-40553. (Civilization of the American Indian Ser.: Vol. 188). (Illus.). 200p. 1988. 35.00 (*0-8061-2121-1*) U of Okla Pr.

Aztec World. Elizabeth H. Boone. LC 94-9830. (Exploring the Ancient World Ser.). 1994. write for info. (*0-89599-040-7*) Smithsonian Bks.

Azteca: The Story of a Jaguar Warrior. Andrea Gaudiano. (Illus.). 80p. (YA). 1992. pap. 7.95 (*1-879373-32-7*) R Rinehart.

Azteca: The Story of a Jaguar Warrior. Andrea Gaudiano. (Illus.). 160p. (ENG & SPA.). (YA). 1992. pap. 14.95 (*1-879373-05-X*) R Rinehart.

Aztecas. Robert Nicholson & Claire Watts. Tr. by Jose R. Araluce. (Raices Ser.). (Illus.). 24p. (SPA.). (J). 1993. 14.95 (*1-56492-091-7*) Laredo.

***Aztecs.** (J). (gr. 5-8). 1990. teacher ed 4.50 (*0-382-24277-7*) Silver Burdett Pr.

Aztecs. Frances F. Berdan. (Indians of North America Ser.). (Illus.). 112p. (YA). (gr. 5 up). 1989. 17.95 (*1-55546-692-3*); pap. 9.95 (*0-7910-0354-X*) Chelsea Hse.

Aztecs. Jacqueline Dineen. LC 91-36169. (Worlds of the Past Ser.). (Illus.). 64p. (J). (gr. 6 up). 1992. text ed. 14.95 (*0-02-730652-6*, Mac Bks Young Read) S&S Childrens.

Aztecs. Peter Hicks. LC 92-44377. (Look into the Past Ser.). 32p. (J). (gr. 4-6). 1993. 14.95 (*1-56847-058-4*) Thomson Lrning.

Aztecs. Fiona MacDonald. (Insights Ser.). (Illus.). 60p. (J). (gr. 4 up). 1993. 15.95 (*0-8120-6377-5*) Barron.

Aztecs. Robert Nicholson. LC 93-29445. (Journey into Civilization Ser.). (Illus.). 32p. (J). (gr. 3-7). 1994. lib. bdg. 14.95 (*0-7910-2701-5*); pap. 7.95 (*0-7910-2725-2*) Chelsea Hse.

***Aztecs.** Pamela Odijk. (Ancient World Ser.). (Illus.). 48p. (J). (gr. 5-8). 1990. pap. 7.95 (*0-382-24262-9*) Silver Burdett Pr.

Aztecs. Pamela Odijk. (Ancient World Ser.). (Illus.). 48p. (J). (gr. 5-8). 1990. lib. bdg. 14.95 (*0-382-09887-0*) Silver Burdett Pr.

Aztecs. Donna A. Shepherd. Ed. by Iris Rosoff. LC 91-28397. (First Bks.). (Illus.). 64p. (J). (gr. 5-8). 1992. lib. bdg. 13.93 (*0-531-20064-7*) Watts.

Aztecs. Donna A. Shepherd. (First Bks.). (Illus.). 64p. (J). (gr. 5-8). 1992. pap. 5.95 (*0-531-15634-6*) Watts.

Aztecs. Ruth Thomson. LC 92-14747. (Craft Topics Ser.). (J). 1993. lib. bdg. 12.95 (*0-531-14245-0*) Watts.

Aztecs. Richard Townsend. LC 91-67301. (Illus.). 224p. 1992. 29.95 (*0-500-02113-9*) Thames Hudson.

Aztecs. Richard Townsend. LC 91-67301. (Illus.). 1993. pap. 14.95 (*0-500-27720-6*) Thames Hudson.

Aztecs. Tim Wood. (See Through History Ser.). (Illus.). 48p. (J). (gr. 3-7). 1992. 14.99 (*0-670-84492-6*) Viking Child Bks.

Aztecs: A History. Nigel Davies. LC 80-12141. (Illus.). 384p. 1980. reprint ed. pap. 19.95 (*0-8061-1691-9*) U of Okla Pr.

Aztecs: An Interpretation. Inga Clendinnen. (Illus.). 325p. (C). 1991. 34.95 (*0-521-40093-7*) Cambridge U Pr.

***Aztecs: An Interpretation.** Inga Clendinnen. (Canto Book Ser.). (Illus.). 414p. (C). 1995. pap. 11.95 (*0-521-48585-1*) Cambridge U Pr.

Aztecs: People of the Sun, Vol. 50. Alfonso Caso. Tr. by Lowell Dunham. LC 58-11603. (Civilization of the American Indian Ser.: No. 50). (Illus.). 144p. 1988. reprint ed. pap. 19.95 (*0-8061-2161-0*) U of Okla Pr.

Aztecs: Reign of Blood & Splendor. Ed. by Dale Brown. (Lost Civilizations Ser.). (Illus.). 168p. 1992. 16.99 (*0-8094-9854-5*); lib. bdg. 19.45 (*0-8094-9855-3*) Time-Life.

Aztecs: Rise & Fall of an Empire. Serge Gruzinski. Tr. by Paul G. Bahn. (Discoveries Ser.). (Illus.). 192p. 1992. pap. 12.95 (*0-8109-2821-3*) Abrams.

Aztecs: Their History, Manners, & Customs. Lucien Biart. 1977. lib. bdg. 59.95 (*0-8490-1466-2*) Gordon Pr.

Aztecs: Their History, Manners & Customs. Lucien Biart. 1976. reprint ed. 59.00 (*0-685-71094-7*, Regency) Scholarly.

Aztecs Activity Book. Penny Bateman. (British Museum Activity Bks.). (Illus.). 16p. (J). 1994. pap. 5.95 (*0-500-27764-8*) Thames Hudson.

Aztecs & Mayas. T. Diven. 1976. lib. bdg. 59.95 (*0-8490-1465-4*) Gordon Pr.

Aztecs & Spaniards: Cortes & the Conquest of Mexico. Albert Marrin. LC 85-28782. (Illus.). 224p. (YA). (gr. 5 up). 1986. text ed. 15.95 (*0-689-31176-1*, Atheneum Bks Young) S&S Childrens.

Aztecs, Maya, & Their Predecessors: Archaeology of Mesoamerica. 3rd ed. Muriel P. Weaver. LC 92-15524. (Illus.). 567p. 1993. text ed. 54.95 (*0-12-739065-0*) Acad Pr.

Aztecs of Central Mexico: An Imperial Society. Frances F. Berdan. 224p. (C). 1982. pap. text ed. 13.50 (*0-03-055736-4*) HB Coll Pubs.

Aztecs Then & Now. Fernando Horcasitas. (Illus.). 168p. 1979. pap. 7.50 (*0-912434-22-8*) Ocelot Pr.

Aztecs Under Spanish Rule: A History of the Indians of the Valley of Mexico, 1519-1810. Charles Gibson. (Illus.). xii, 657p. 1964. 65.00 (*0-8047-0196-2*); pap. 19.95 (*0-8047-0912-2*) Stanford U Pr.

***Aztlan.** FASA Staff. (Shadowrun Ser.). 1995. pap. 18.00 (*1-55560-257-6*) FASA Corp.

Aztlan: Essays on the Chicano Homeland. Ed. by Rudolfo A. Anaya & Francisco Lomeli. LC 89-83942. 248p. 1991. reprint ed. pap. 15.95 (*0-8263-1261-6*) U of NM Pr.

Aztlan y Mexico: Perfiles Literarios e Historicos. Luis Leal. LC 83-71984. 260p. (SPA.). 1985. lib. bdg. 24.00 (*0-916950-46-8*) Biling Rev-Pr.

Aztreonam: New Developments & Current Perspectives. Ed. by J. D. Williams. (Illus.). iv, 108p. 1989. pap. 32.00 (*3-8055-5027-8*) S Karger.

Azubah Nye. Lyle Glazier. 1988. 7.00 (*0-934834-39-3*) White Pine.

Azuki Bean: Botany, Production & Uses. T. Lumpkin & D. McClary. 280p. 1994. 59.50 (*0-85198-765-6*) CAB Intl.

Azul Desesperado. Tula Marti. LC 85-82349. 105p. (Orig.). (SPA.). 1985. pap. 7.95 (*0-89729-387-8*) Ediciones.

Azulin Va a la Escuela (Blue Bug Goes to School) LC 84-23161. (Spanish Blue Bug Bks.). 32p. (ENG & SPA.). (J). (ps-2). 1989. pap. 3.95 (*0-516-53416-5*) Childrens.

Azulin Va a la Escuela (Blue Bug Goes to School) LC 84-23161. (Spanish Blue Bug Bks.). 32p. (ENG & SPA.). (J). (ps-2). 1989. 12.23 (*0-516-33416-6*) Childrens.

Azulin Visita a Mexico (Blue Bug Visits Mexico) Virginia Poulet. LC 89-25420. (Blue Bug Bks.). (Illus.). 32p. (SPA.). (J). (ps-3). 1990. lib. bdg. 11.85 (*0-516-33429-8*); pap. 3.95 (*0-516-53429-7*) Childrens.

Azumaya Algebras, Actions, & Modules Proceedings of a Conference in. Ed. by D. Haile & J. Osterburg. LC 91-41788. (CONM Ser.: Vol. 124). 298p. 1992. 43.00 (*0-8218-5132-2*, CONM-124) Am Math.

Azure Bonds. Kate Novak & Jeff Grubb. LC 88-50057. (Forgotten Realms Finder's Stone Trilogy Ser.: Bk. 1). 352p. (Orig.). 1988. pap. 3.95 (*0-88038-612-6*) TSR Inc.

Azure Bowl: Daughters of a Granite Land Trilogy, Vol. I. Anita Burgh. 448p. 1992. 24.95 (*0-7011-3461-5*, Pub. by Chatto & Windus UK) Trafalgar.

Azure Cities. Romanov et al. LC 72-3284. (Short Story Index Reprint Ser.). 1977. reprint ed. 23.95 (*0-8369-4143-8*) Ayer.

Azure Hearse. Dennis Jackson. Ed. by David Wilde. (Sun Also Sets Ser.). (Illus.). (Orig.). Date not set. pap. text ed. write for info. (*1-882204-03-4*) Wilde Pub.

Azure Scroll. Glenn Malec. 257p. (Orig.). 1991. pap. write for info. (*0-9630657-1-8*) Godolphin Hse.

Azusa Street: The Roots of Modern-Day Pentecost. 2nd ed. Frank Bartleman. LC 80-82806. 188p. 1993. pap. 7.95 (*0-88270-439-7*) Bridge Pub.

Azusa Street & Beyond. Ed. by L. Grant McClung, Jr. LC 86-70742. 245p. 1986. pap. 7.95 (*0-88270-607-1*) Bridge Pub.

Azusa Street till Now. Clara Davis. 144p. 1993. pap. 4.99 (*0-88368-272-9*) Whitaker Hse.

Azusa Street till Now. rev. ed. Clara Davis. 96p. 1989. pap. 3.95 (*0-89274-597-5*) Harrison Hse.

A201 Lab Manual: Exercises in C. Suzanne Menzel. (C). 1993. student ed 14.00 (*1-881592-28-6*) Hayden-McNeil.

A6M Zero. Shigeru Nohara. (Aircraft in Action Ser.). (Illus.). 50p. 1983. 8.95 (*0-89747-141-5*) Squad Sig Pubns.

B

B: Twenty-Nine Letters from Coconut Grove. Sandy Campbell. (Illus.). 1974. 35.00 (*0-917366-03-4*) S Campbell.

B. A. T. S. Jerome McDonough. (Illus.). 56p. (Orig.). 1988. pap. 4.00 (*0-88680-289-X*) I E Clark.

B & B Our Guests for Comfort & Cuisine. Ed. & Intro. by Ron Price. (Illus.). 300p. 1992. spiral bd. 16.95 (*0-9632838-0-4*) OH Bed & Brkfst.

B & C: Mycological Association of M. J. Berkeley & M. A. Curtis. Ronald H. Petersen. (Bibliotheca Mycologica Ser.: No. 72). (Illus.). 120p. 1980. pap. text ed. 19.60 (*3-7682-1258-0*) Lubrecht & Cramer.

B & E. Dave Pedneau. 320p. (Orig.). 1991. mass mkt. 4.95 (*0-345-36420-1*) Ballantine.

B & E Book. Burt Rapp. LC 89-63211. 160p. 1989. pap. text ed. 14.95 (*1-55950-021-2*) Loompanics.

B & G Cartridge Manual. W. A. Bartlett & D. B. Gallatin. 1956. 2.00 (*0-913150-12-6*) Pioneer Pr.

B & O Power. Alvin F. Staufer & Lawrence W. Sagle. LC 64-23536. (Illus.). 352p. 1964. 35.00 (*0-944513-06-9*) Staufer Bks.

An Asterisk (*) at the beginning of an entry indicates that the title is appearing in BIP for the first time.

***B & O Railroad Museum: A Visitor's Guide.** Shawn Cunningham. (Illus.). 112p. (Orig.). 1994. pap. 12.95 (1-886248-00-1) B&O Railrd.

B & O Thunder in the Alleghenies. Deane Mellander. (Carstens Hobby Bks.: No. C-45). (Illus.). 80p. 1983. pap. 12.95 (0-911868-45-3, C45) Carstens Pubns.

B & P A Textbook & a Simulation for Business & Professional Communication. Lawrence W. Huganberg et al. 256p. (C). 1993. spiral bd. 19.95 (0-8403-8933-7) Kendall-Hunt.

B & T Cells in Immune Recognition. Ed. by F. Loor & G. E. Roelants. LC 76-26913. (Illus.). 538p. reprint ed. pap. 153.40 (0-8357-5935-0, 2030511) Bks Demand.

B As in Bravura. Ed. by Stanley Newman. (Expert's Book of Crosswords Ser.). 64p. (Orig.). 1991. pap. 8.00 (0-06-096555-X, PL) HarpC.

B. B. & the Diva. Rupert Kinnard. LC 91-44331. (Illus.). 144p. (Orig.). 1992. pap. 6.95 (1-55583-134-6) Alyson Pubns.

B. B. King: Jazz Musician. Joseph Nazel. (Black American Ser.). (Illus.). 208p. (YA). 1995. 4.95 (0-87067-792-6, Melrose Sq) Holloway.

***B. B. King: King of the Blues.** Cpp Belwin Staff. 1994. pap. 34.95 (0-89898-719-9) CPP Belwin.

B. B. King Anthology. (Illus.). 144p. 1992. pap. 19.95 (0-8256-1317-5, AM85572) Music Sales.

***B. B. World Guide to Television & Film, 1995.** Ed. & Intro. by Donna Witzleben. 1995. pap. 449.00 (0-912920-10-6) North Am Pub Co.

B Book. Stan Berenstain & Janice Berenstain. (Bright & Early Bks.). (Illus.). (J). (ps-1). 1971. lib. bdg. 7.99 (0-394-92324-3) Random Bks Yng Read.

B Book. Brian Randall. LC 93-40927. 96p. 1994. 22.95 (0-446-51801-8) Warner Bks.

B Boron Compounds Vol. II: Boron & Oxygen. 8th ed. Planck, Max, Society for the Advancement of Science, Gmelin Institute for Inorganic Chemistry Staff. (Gmelin Handbuch der Anorganischen Chemie Ser.: Suppl. 4). (Illus.). xvi, 297p. 1993. 1,113.00 (0-387-93673-4) Spr-Verlag.

B Boron Compounds, Vol. IV: Boron & Cl, Br, I, S, Se, Te, Carboranes. 8th ed. (Gmelin Handbook of Inorganic & Organometallic Chemistry Ser.). (Illus.). xx, 323p. 1991. 1,071.00 (0-387-93629-7) Spr-Verlag.

B Boron, Vol. 3b, 4th Supplement: Boron & Nitrogen, Fluorine. (Illus.). xv, 254p. 1992. 914.00 (0-387-93648-3) Spr-Verlag.

B-Boy Blues: A Seriously Sexy, Fiercely Funny, Black-on-Black Love Story. James E. Hardy. 283p. (Orig.). 1994. pap. 10.95 (1-55583-268-7) Alyson Pubns.

B. C. Alive & Well. Johnny Hart. (Illus.). 1983. pap. 1.95 (0-449-12469-X) Fawcett.

B. C. Cave In. Johnny Hart. 128p. 1982. pap. 1.95 (0-449-12371-5, GM) Fawcett.

B. C. Dip in Road. Johnny Hart. (Illus.). 1982. pap. 1.95 (0-449-13678-7) Fawcett.

B. C. Life Goes On. Johnny Hart. (Illus.). 1985. pap. 1.95 (0-449-12649-8); pap. 2.25 (0-449-13043-6) Fawcett.

B. C. Lovers Leap. Johnny Hart. (Illus.). 1985. pap. 2.25 (0-449-12651-X) Fawcett.

B. C. on the Rocks. Johnny Hart. (Illus.). 1985. pap. 1.95 (0-449-13691-4) Fawcett.

B. C. One More Time. Johnny Hart & Brant Parker. 1981. pap. 1.95 (0-449-13646-9, GM) Fawcett.

B. C. Second & Third Letters. Johnny Hart. (Illus.). 1986. pap. 2.25 (0-449-13107-6) Fawcett.

B. C. Truckin' on Down. Johnny Hart. (B.C. Ser.). 1987. pap. 2.95 (0-449-13330-3, GM) Fawcett.

B-Conjecture: Characterization of Chevalley Groups. J. H. Walter. LC 86-3388. (Memoirs of the AMS Ser.: Vol. 61/345). 196p. 1986. text ed. 26.00 (0-8218-2345-0, MEMO 61/345) Am Math.

B. C.'s Own Railroad. Lorraine Harris. 64p. Date not set. pap. 6.95 (0-88839-125-0) Hancock House.

B Decays. Ed. by S. Stone. 500p. (C). 1992. text ed. 127.00 (981-02-0708-5) World Scientific Pub.

B Decays. 2nd rev. ed. Sheldon Stone. 630p. 1994. text ed. 109.00 (981-02-1836-2) World Scientific Pub.

B. E. F. The Whole Story of the Bonus Army. W. W. Waters & William C. White. LC 77-90195. (Mass Violence in America Ser.). (Illus.). 1969. reprint ed. 27.95 (0-405-01340-X) Ayer.

B. E. F. The Whole Story of the Bonus Army. Walter W. Waters. LC 75-125174. reprint ed. 21.50 (0-404-06872-3) AMS Pr.

B-E-S-T Friends. Patricia R. Giff. (New Kids at the Polk Street School Ser.: No. 4). 80p. (Orig.). (J). (gr. k-6). 1988. pap. 3.50 (0-440-40090-2, YB) Dell.

B. F. G. Dahl. Roald Dahl. (Illus.). 1999. pap. 3.95 (0-14-031597-7, Penguin Bks) Viking Penguin.

B. F. Skinner: A Life. Daniel W. Bjork. LC 92-54522. (Illus.). 336p. 1993. 25.00 (0-465-00611-6) Basic.

***B. F. Skinner: A Life.** Daniel W. Bjork. (Illus.). 320p. 1995. pap. 14.00 (0-465-00612-4) Basic.

B. F. Skinner: Controversy & Consensus. Ed. by Sohan Modgil. LC 86-13518. (International Master Minds Challenged Ser.). 400p. 1987. 125.00 (1-85000-026-3, Falmer Pr) Taylor & Francis.

B-Four. Sam Hodges. 288p. 1993. pap. 10.95 (0-312-09246-6) St Martin.

B. G., Vol. 1: The Little Drummer Girl Who Drums for the Sun. George L. Lowe. (Illus.). 21p. (Orig.). (J). (ps). 1988. lib. bdg. 5.00 (0-685-22681-6) G L Lowe.

B-Heterosubstituted, Unsaturated Thioketones: Some Problems of Synthesis & Structure. V. A. Usov & M. G. Voronkov. 46p. 1982. pap. text ed. 50.00 (3-7186-0116-8) Gordon & Breach.

B. I. A. Plate Number Checklist: Plates Numbered 1-20, 000. rev. ed. W. Wallace Cleland. 80p. 1990. pap. text ed. 35.00 (0-930412-18-4) Bureau Issues.

B Is for Baby: Love Letteres. Lisa Jackson. 1994. mass mkt. 3.50 (0-373-09920-7, 1-09920-9) Harlequin Bks.

B Is for Bethlehem: A Christmas Alphabet. Isabel Wilner. LC 89-49481. (Illus.). 32p. (J). (ps up). 1990. 14.00 (0-525-44622-2, DCB) Dutton Child Bks.

***B Is for Bethlehem: A Christmas Alphabet.** Isabel Wilner. (Illus.). 32p. (J). 1995. pap. 4.99 (0-14-055610-9, Puff Unicorn) Puffin Bks.

B Is for Betsy. Carolyn Haywood. LC 85-16381. (Illus.). 159p. (J). (gr. 1-5). 1939. 12.95 (0-15-204975-4, HB Juv Bks) HarBrace.

B Is for Betsy. Carolyn Haywood. 120p. (J). (gr. 2-5). 1990. pap. 3.95 (0-15-204977-0, Odyssey) HarBrace.

B Is for Buffalo. Bud Bouton. (Special Species Ser.). (Illus.). 64p. (J). (gr. 1 up). 1994. 15.95 (1-879244-03-9) Windom Bks.

B Is for Burglar. Sue Grafton. 224p. 1986. pap. 5.99 (0-553-28034-1) Bantam.

B Is for Burglar. Sue Grafton. LC 84-158. 240p. 1985. 21.95 (0-8050-1632-5) H Holt & Co.

B Is for Burglar. braille ed. Sue Grafton. 424p. 1992. vinyl bd. 33.92 (1-56956-042-0, BR8802) W A T Braille.

B Is for Burglar. Sue Grafton. 1994. reprint ed. lib. bdg. 29.95 (1-56849-283-9) Buccaneer Bks.

B. J. & the Language of the Woodland. Alvin N. Deibert. LC 82-24422. (Illus.). 48p. (Orig.). (J). (gr. 2-6). 1983. pap. 7.50 (0-87743-701-7, 353-019, Bellwood Pr) Bahai.

B. J. Crystal Piece. Barbara Johannah. LC 92-54914. 256p. 1993. pap. 24.95 (0-8019-8400-9) Chilton.

B. J.'s Joke Book. Betty J. Bouquet. (Illus.). 74p. (Orig.). 1990. 30.00 (0-937041-80-7); pap. 12.00 (0-937041-81-5) Systems Co.

B-Lymphocyte Differentiation. Ed. by John C. Cambier. 208p. 1986. 100.00 (0-8493-5172-3, QR185, CRC Reprint) Franklin.

B Lymphocytes. G. G. Klaus. (In Focus Ser.). (Illus.). 84p. 1990. pap. 13.95 (0-19-963191-5, IRL Pr) OUP.

B Lymphocytes: Function & Regulation. Ed. by P. Del Guercio & J. M. Cruse. (Contributions to Microbiology & Immunology Ser.: Vol. 11). (Illus.). 310p. 1989. 222.50 (3-8055-4995-4) S Karger.

B Lymphocytes in Human Disease. Ed. by Graham Bird & Jane E. Calvert. (Illus.). 544p. 1988. 98.00 (0-19-261573-4) OUP.

B Lymphocytes Today. J. R. Inglis. 1983. pap. 16.75 (0-444-80454-4) Elsevier.

B. M. Fraeijs De Veubeke Memorial Volume of Selected Papers. M. Geradin. 791p. (C). 1980. lib. bdg. 122.50 (90-286-0900-8) Kluwer Ac.

B. M. O. C. Lars Eighner. (Orig.). 1993. pap. 4.95 (1-56333-077-6) Masquerade.

B-Movie. large type ed. Stan Barstow. 240p. 1988. 15.95 (0-7089-1815-8) Ulverscroft.

B Movie Trivia Quiz. enl. rev. ed. Walter Haan. LC 85-63488. (Illus.). 80p. (Orig.). 1986. pap. 8.95 (0-913337-06-4) Southfarm Pr.

B Movies. Don Miller. 384p. 1987. mass mkt. 4.95 (0-345-34710-2) Ballantine.

B-Movies Blue Book. 40p. pap. 7.50 (0-915195-01-1) Paper Pile.

B, My Name Is Bunny. Norma F. Mazer. (J). (gr. 4-7). 1994. pap. 3.25 (0-590-43895-6) Scholastic Inc.

B-One. Thirteen M - 1979: Metric Screw Threads - M Profile. 40p. 1979. 10.00 (0-685-25547-6, N00046) ASME.

B-P-H - S: Botanico-Periodicum-Huntianum-Supplementum. Ed. & Comp. by G. D. Bridson. 1068p. 1991. text ed. 95.00 (0-913196-54-1) Hunt Inst Botanical.

B. P. Nichol & His Works. Douglas Barbour. 95p. (C). 1992. pap. text ed. 9.95 (1-55022-066-7, Pub. by ECW Press CN) Genl Dist Srvs.

B. R. Ambedkar: His Life, Mission & Vision. V. Chandra Mowli. 144p. 1990. text ed. 22.50 (81-207-1273-0, Pub. by Sterling Pubs II) Apt Bks.

B. R. Ambedkar: Statesman & Constitutionalist. S. R. Bakshi. (C). 1992. 30.00 (0-685-59602-8, Pub. by Anmol II) S Asia.

B. Rugged Books' Prime Material. Susanna Cuyler. (Illus.). 80p. (Orig.). 1993. pap. write for info. (0-9612018-6-X) B Rugged.

B. S. & Live Longer (Beat Stress) Jim Keelan. 1978. 6.00 (0-9606554-2-5) Comm Unltd.

B. S. Bentley's Collection of Oddities & Oddballs Beyond Belief! Albin Sadar. Ed. by Alan Batt. (Illus.). 80p. (Orig.). 1985. pap. 3.95 (0-933477-00-7) Rainbow.

B-Six: The Natural Healer. Alan Gaby. Orig. Title: The Doctor's Guide to Vitamin B6. 272p. 1987. reprint ed. 3.95 (0-87983-434-X) Keats.

***B. Smith's Entertaining & Cooking for Friends.** Barbara Smith & Kathleen Cromwell. LC 94-45991. (Illus.). 1995. 35.00 (1-885183-06-2) Artisan Hse.

B. Traven: A Vision of Mexico. Heidi Zogbaum. LC 91-28235. (Latin American Silhouettes Ser.). 304p. 1992. 24.95 (0-8420-2392-5) Scholarly Res Inc.

B. Traven: Life & Work. Ed. by Ernst Schurer & Philip Jenkins. 350p. 1987. 32.50 (0-271-00382-0) Pa St U Pr.

B. Traven: The Life Behind the Legends. Karl S. Guthke. Tr. by Robert Sprung. LC 90-26277. (Illus.). 478p. 1991. 24.95 (1-55652-132-4); pap. 14.95 (1-55652-131-6) L Hill Bks.

B-Trees for BASIC. 1992. disk 32.50 (0-89496-053-9, Baldar); PC software pkg. disk 20.00 (0-89496-005-9, Baldar); Macintosh software pkg. disk 20.00 (0-89496-006-7, Baldar); UNIX software pkg. disk 20.00 (0-89496-007-5, Baldar) Ross Bks.

B-Trees for BASIC: Create Your Own Lightning-Fast Database. Raymond Robertson. 256p. (C). 1992. disk, pap. text ed. 32.50 (0-89496-008-3, Baldar) Ross Bks.

B Vitamins in Medicine: Proceedings of a Symposium Held in Helsinki, October 1985. J. J. Himberg et al. viii, 181p. 1986. pap. 23.00 (3-528-07975-4, Pub. by Vieweg & Sohn GW) Ballen Bkslr.

B Western Actors Encyclopedia: Facts, Photos & Filmographies for More Than 250 Familiar Faces. Ted Holland. LC 88-42566. (Illus.). 512p. 1988. lib. bdg. 49.95x (0-89950-306-3) McFarland & Co.

***B. Y. High No. 3: Going Home.** Perel Shreiber. (Illus.). 166p. (J). 1994. 9.95 (1-56871-064-X) Targum Pr.

B. Y. High No. 2: Making Her Mark. Perel Schreiber. 160p. (YA). (gr. 7-10). 1994. 9.95 (1-56871-040-2) Targum Pr.

B. Y. Times: Here We Go Again, No. 9. Leah Klein. (J). 1992. pap. 7.95 (0-944070-90-6) Targum Pr.

B. Y. Times: Summer Daze, No. 8. Leah Klein. (J). pap. 7.95 (0-944070-83-3) Targum Pr.

B. Y. Times: The New Kids, No. 10. Leah Klein. (J). 1992. pap. 7.95 (0-944070-91-4) Targum Pr.

***B. Y. Times No. 17: Jen Starts Over.** Leah Klein. (B.Y. Times Ser.). 152p. (J). (gr. 5-9). 1994. pap. 7.95 (1-56871-054-2) Targum Pr.

B. Y. Times Kid Sisters: Running Away, No. 5. Sheryl Prenzlau. (Illus.). 120p. (Orig.). (J). (gr. 2-6). 1993. pap. 5.95 (1-56871-018-6) Targum Pr.

B. Y. Times Kid Sisters: The "I-Can't-Cope-Club", No. 1. Tamar Kamins. (J). 1992. pap. 5.95 (0-944070-84-1) Targum Pr.

B. Y. Times Kid Sisters: The Treehouse Kids, No. 2. Tamar Kamins. (J). 1992. pap. 5.95 (0-944070-92-2) Targum Pr.

***B. Y. Times Kid Sisters No. 10: Giant Steps.** Sheryl Prenelau. (Illus.). 108p. (Orig.). (J). (gr. 3-7). 1994. pap. 6.95 (1-56871-063-1) Targum Pr.

B. Y. Times Kid Sisters No. 6: Teacher's Pet. Sheryl Prenzlau. (Illus.). 115p. (Orig.). (J). (gr. 3-7). 1993. pap. 6.95 (1-56871-025-9) Targum Pr.

B. Y. Times, No. 1: Shani's Scoop. Leah Klein. (J). 1993. pap. 7.95 (0-685-65290-4) Feldheim.

B. Y. Times, No. 10: The New Kids. Leah Klein. (J). 1993. pap. 7.95 (0-685-65299-8) Feldheim.

B. Y. Times, No. 11: Dollars & Sense. Leah Klein. 144p. (J). 1993. pap. 7.95 (1-56871-005-4) Targum Pr.

B. Y. Times, No. 12: Talking It Over. Leah Klein. 149p. (J). 1993. pap. 7.95 (1-56871-010-0) Targum Pr.

B. Y. Times, No. 15: Secrets. Leah Klein. 144p. (J). (gr. 6-8). 1993. pap. 7.95 (1-56871-036-4) Targum Pr.

B. Y. Times, No. 2: Batya's Search. Leah Klein. (J). 1993. pap. 7.95 (0-685-65291-2) Feldheim.

B. Y. Times, No. 3: Twins in Trouble. Leah Klein. (J). 1993. pap. 7.95 (0-685-65292-0) Feldheim.

B. Y. Times, No. 4: War! Leah Klein. (J). 1993. pap. 7.95 (0-685-65293-9) Feldheim.

B. Y. Times, No. 5: Spring Fever. Leah Klein. (J). 1993. pap. 7.95 (0-685-65294-7) Feldheim.

B. Y. Times, No. 6: Party Time. Leah Klein. (J). 1993. pap. 7.95 (0-685-65295-5) Feldheim.

B. Y. Times, No. 7: Changing Times. Leah Klein. (J). 1993. pap. 9.95 (0-685-65296-3) Feldheim.

B. Y. Times, No. 8: Summer Daze. Leah Klein. (J). 1993. pap. 7.95 (0-685-65297-1) Feldheim.

B. Y. Times, No. 9: Here We Go Again. Leah Klein. (J). 1993. pap. 7.95 (0-685-65298-X) Feldheim.

B-1 Bomber. Wayne Wachsmuth. (Detail & Scale Ser.: Vol. 37). (Illus.). 72p. 1990. pap. 10.95 (0-8306-5050-4, 25050) TAB Bks.

***B-2 Bomber: Strategic Utility for the Twenty-First Century.** Colin S. Gray et al. 226p. (C). 1994. pap. text ed. 26.50 (0-8191-9737-8) U Pr of Amer.

***B-2 Bomber: Strategic Utility for the Twenty-First Century.** Colin S. Gray et al. (Illus.). 226p. (C). 1994. lib. bdg. 49.00 (0-8191-9736-X) U Pr of Amer.

B-2 Chronicles: or How Not to Blow It: Or How Not to Butt Heads with the Next Generation. Robert Townsend. LC 94-19874. 208p. 1994. 16.95 (0-89384-266-4) Pfeiffer & Co.

B-2 Story. William B. Scott. (Illus.). 192p. 1991. 18.95 (0-8306-3822-9, 3822, TAB-Aero) TAB Bks.

***B-17 Flying Fortress.** Jeffrey L. Ethell. LC 95-6120. (Enthusiast Color Ser.). (Illus.). 96p. 1995. pap. 12.95 (0-7603-0039-9) Motorbooks Intl.

B-17 Flying Fortress. William N. Hess. (Illus.). 144p. 1994. pap. 24.95 (0-87938-881-1) Motorbooks Intl.

B-17 Flying Fortress. Michael O'Leary. (Osprey Colour Library). (Illus.). 128p. 1992. pap. 15.95 (1-85532-197-1, Pub. by Osprey Pubng Ltd UK) Motorbooks Intl.

B-17 Flying Fortress, Vol. 2, Pt. 1. (Detail & Scale Ser.). (Illus.). 72p. 10.95 (0-8306-8512-X, 25012) TAB Bks.

B-17 Flying Fortress: Part 2. Alwyn T. Lloyd. LC 81-67592. (Detail & Scale Ser.: Vol. 11). (Illus.). 72p. 1983. pap. 8.95 (0-8168-5021-6, 25021, TAB-Aero) TAB Bks.

B-17 Flying Fortress in Color. (Illus.). 32p. 1986. pap. 9.95 (0-89747-180-6, 6561) Squad Sig Pubns.

B-17 Flying Fortress in Detail & Scale: Part 1 (Production Versions) Alwyn T. Lloyd & Terry D. Moore. LC 81-67592. (Detail & Scale Ser.: Vol. 2). (Illus.). 72p. (Orig.). 1981. pap. 8.95 (0-8168-5012-7, 25012, TAB-Aero) TAB Bks.

B-17 Flying Fortress (More Derivatives), Pt. III. Bert Kinzey. (Detail & Scale Ser.: Vol. 20). (Illus.). 72p. (Orig.). pap. 10.95 (0-8168-5029-1, 25029, TAB-Aero) TAB Bks.

B-17 Flying Fortress Nose Art Gallery. John M. Campbell & Donna Campbell. LC 93-1161. 1993. 15.95 (0-87938-747-5) Motorbooks Intl.

B-17 Flying Fortress, Vol. 2: In Detail & Scale. Alwyn T. Lloyd et al. Ed. by Terry Spohn. LC 93-1657. (Illus.). 72p. 1993. pap. 11.95 (0-89024-185-6) Kalmbach.

B-17 in Action. Larry Davis. (In Action Ser.: No. 1063). (Illus.). 58p. 1984. pap. 8.95 (0-89747-152-0) Squad Sig Pubns.

B-17 in Blue: The Flying Fortress in U. S. Navy & U. S. Coast Guard Service. Scott A. Thompson. LC 93-72491. 118p. 1993. pap. 16.95 (0-9637543-3-5) Aero Vintage.

***B-17s over Berlin: Personal Stories from the 95th Bomb Group (H)** Ed. by Ian Hawkins. (World War II Commemorative Ser.). (Illus.). 328p. 1995. pap. 17.95 (0-02-881129-1) Brasseys Inc.

B-17s over Berlin: Personal Stories from the 95th Bomb Group (H). Ed. by Ian L. Hawkins. (Illus.). 328p. 1990. 27.50 (0-08-040569-X) Brasseys Inc.

***B-2 Chronicles: Uncommon Wisdom for Un-Corporate America.** Robert Townsend. LC 95-1247. 208p. 1995. pap. 12.00 (0-399-52160-7, Perigee Bks) Berkley Pub.

B-24 Liberator. Frederick A. Johnsen. LC 93-1160. (Warbird History Ser.). 1993. 24.95 (0-87938-758-0) Motorbooks Intl.

B-24 Liberator in Action. (Illus.). 1987. pap. 8.95 (0-89747-190-3, 1080) Squad Sig Pubns.

B-24 Liberator Legend. Turner Publishing Co. Staff. LC 90-83586. 160p. 1990. 48.00 (0-938021-99-0) Turner Pub KY.

***B-24 Liberator 1935-45.** Martin Bowman. (Illus.). 136p. 1995. 34.95 (1-85260-073-X, Pub. by J H Haynes & Co UK) Motorbooks Intl.

B-24-PB4Y in Combat: The World's Greatest Bomber. Rhodes Arnold. (Illus.). 185p. 1990. 18.00 (0-9619253-3-7) Pima Paisano.

B-25 Mitchell. Steve Pace. 128p. 1994. pap. 19.95 (0-87938-939-7) Motorbooks Intl.

B-25 Mitchell: The Magnificent Medium. Norman L. Avery. LC 92-61209. (Illus.). 200p. (C). 1993. 29.95 (0-9625860-5-6) Phalanx Pub.

B-25 Mitchell in Action. Ernie McDowell & Don Greer. (Aircraft in Action Ser.). (Illus.). 50p. 1984. pap. 8.95 (0-89747-033-8, 1034) Squad Sig Pubns.

B-25s Target Kyusho. Murray A. Bywater. (Illus.). 308p. (C). 1994. 27.50 (0-9639575-0-3) B Twenty Five.

***B-26 Marauder.** Turner Publishing Company Staff. LC 93-60442. 112p. 1993. 48.00 (1-56311-106-3) Turner Pub KY.

B-26 Martin Marauder. (Illus.). 130p. 14.95 (0-87994-005-0) Aviat Pub.

B-29: Pilot's Flight Operating Instructions for the Army Model B-29 Airplanes. (Illus.). 96p. pap. 10.95 (0-317-56108-1) Flying Bks.

B-29 Superfortress. Chester Marshall. LC 93-24759. (Motorbooks International Warbird History Ser.). 1993. 24.95 (0-87938-785-8) Motorbooks Intl.

***B-29 Superfortress.** Turner Publishing Company Staff. LC 94-60016. 112p. 1994. 48.00 (1-56311-133-0) Turner Pub KY.

B-29 Superfortress, Vol. 10, Pt. 1. (Detail & Scale Ser.). (Illus.). 72p. 10.95 (0-8306-8019-5, 25019) TAB Bks.

B-29 Superfortress: Part 1. Alwyn T. Lloyd. LC 83-2789. (Detail & Scale Ser.: Vol. 10). (Illus.). 72p. (Orig.). 1982. pap. 8.95 (0-8168-5019-4, 25019, TAB-Aero) TAB Bks.

B-29 Superfortress Manual. U. S. Air Force Staff. (Illus.). 92p. 1984. pap. 12.95 (0-317-14795-1) Boomerang.

B-36 in Action. Meyers Jacobsen. (Aircraft in Action Ser.). (Illus.). 50p. 1995. pap. 8.95 (0-89747-101-6) Squad Sig Pubns.

***B-36 Peacemaker in Detail & Scale, Vol. 47.** Wachsmuth. 1995. pap. text ed. 11.95 (0-89024-239-9) Kalmbach.

B-47 Stratojet. Bert Kinsey. (Detail & Scale Ser.: Vol. 18). (Illus.). 72p. (Orig.). 1986. pap. 10.95 (0-8168-5023-2, 25023, TAB-Aero) TAB Bks.

B-47 Stratojet. Alwyn T. Lloyd. Ed. by Terry Spohn. LC 93-12806. (Detail & Scale Ser.: Vol. 18). (Illus.). 72p. 1993. reprint ed. pap. 11.95 (0-89024-170-8) Kalmbach.

B-52 Stratofortress in Action. Larry Davis. (Aircraft in Action Ser.). (Illus.). 50p. 1993. pap. 8.95 (0-89747-289-6, 1130) Squad Sig Pubns.

Ba Cao Va Ba Co - Mrs. Fox & Mrs. Stork. Jean De la Fontaine. Tr. by Le Do. (Interlingo Ser.). (Illus.). 19p. (Orig.). (ENG & VIE.). (J). (gr. k-12). 1993. pap. 2.95 (0-922852-25-1) Another Lang Pr.

Ba Ye Zwa. Judy Seidman. LC 77-18421. (Illus.). 1978. 30.00 (0-89608-003-X); pap. 7.50 (0-89608-002-1) South End Pr.

Baa Baa Black Sheep. Pappy Boyington, pseud. 1977. mass mkt. 5.99 (0-553-26350-1) Bantam.

Baa Baa Black Sheep. Pappy Boyington. 16.00 (0-89340-458-00-2) Wilson Pr.

***Baa Baa Black Sheep.** Janovitz. 3.99 (0-517-13660-0) Random Hse Value.

Baa Baa Black Sheep. Marilyn Janovitz. LC 91-71384. (Illus.). 32p. (J). (ps-2). 1991. lib. bdg. 6.89 (1-56282-086-9) Hyprn Child.

Baa, Baa, Black Sheep. Illus. by Moira Kemp. 10p. (J). (ps). 1991. bds. 4.99 (0-525-67331-8, Lodestar Bks) Dutton Child Bks.

Baa, Baa, Black Sheep. Illus. by Moira Kemp. LC 93-18703. 12p. (J). (ps). 1994. 2.99 (0-525-67443-8, Lodestar Bks) Dutton Child Bks.

Baa Baa Black Sheep. Pappy Boyington, pseud. (Military Classics Ser.). 384p. 1989. reprint ed. 22.95 (0-8306-4008-8) TAB Bks.

Baa Baa Book. B. J. Johnson. (Teeny Poppers Ser.). (Illus.). 12p. (J). (ps). 1993. pap. 3.50 (0-671-86530-7, Litl Simon S&S) S&S Childrens.

***Baa Baa Dead Sheep.** Jill Bennett. (YA). 1994. pap. 3.50 (0-590-48507-5) Scholastic Inc.

BAAA. David Macaulay. LC 85-2316. (Illus.). 64p. (J). (gr. 6 up). 1985. 13.95 (0-395-38948-8); pap. 4.95 (0-395-39588-7) HM.

***Baabee.** (J). (ps). Date not set. write for info. (1-881445-01-1) Sandvik Pub.

Baal. Robert R. McCammon. Ed. by Sally Peters. 1988. mass mkt. 5.99 (0-671-77374-0) PB.

B

An Asterisk (*) at the beginning of an entry indicates that the title is appearing in BIP for the first time.

Baal, A Man's A Man, & The Elephant Calf. Bertolt Brecht. Ed. & Tr. by Eric Bentley. Tr. by Martin Esslin. 224p. 1989. pap. 9.95 (0-8021-3159-X) Grove-Atltic.

Baal Babylone. Fernando Arrabal. 172p. pap. 13.95 (0-8288-9021-8, F83452) Fr & Eur.

Baalbek. Friedrich Ragette. LC 80-19626. (Illus.). 128p. 1981. 18.00 (0-8155-5059-6, NP) Noyes.

Baalbek: Ergebnisse der Ausgrabungen & Untersuchungen, 1898-1905, 3 vols., Set. Ed. by Theodor Wiegand. (Illus.). 561p. (GER.). (C). 1973. reprint ed. 1,784.65 (3-11-002370-9) De Gruyter.

Bab: The Herald of the Day of Days. H. M. Balyuzi. 272p. 1973. pap. 19.95 (0-85398-054-3, 7-31-51) G Ronald Pub.

Bab Ballads. W. S. Gilbert. Ed. by James Ellis. LC 77-102668. 376p. 1980. pap. text ed. 15.95 (0-674-05801-1) Belknap Pr.

Bab Ballads, with Which Are Included Songs of a Savoyard. William S. Gilbert. (BCL1-PR English Literature Ser.). 563p. 1992. reprint ed. lib. bdg. 99.00 (0-7812-7532-6) Rprt Serv.

Bab Edh-Dhra: Excavations in the Cemetery Directed by Paul Lapp (1965-67) R. Thomas Schaub & Walter E. Rast. LC 89-7765. (Reports of the Expedition to the Dead Sea Plain, Jordan: Vol. 1). xxv, 598p. 1989. text ed. 75.00 (0-931464-51-X) Eisenbrauns.

Baba a Louis Bakery Bread Book: The Secret Book of the Bread. John McLure. Ed. by Olivia Gay & Kate Mueller. LC 93-78237. (Illus.). 132p. (Orig.). 1993. pap. 13.95 (0-9636892-0-7) B A L Bakery.

Baba Hariram: Saint of Sind. D. H. Butani. (C). 1981. 6.00 (0-8364-2371-2, Pub. by Promilla) S Asia.

Baba Kamma, 2 vols., No. 21. 30.00 (0-910218-71-4) Bennet Pub.

Baba Loved Us, Too: Stories of Meher Baba & His Pets. Mehera J. Irani. Ed. by Davana Brown. LC 89-10132. (Illus.). 155p. (Orig.). 1989. pap. 8.95 (0-913078-66-2) Sheriar Pr.

Baba Mezia, 2 vols. (ENG & HEB.). 30.00 (0-910218-72-2) Bennet Pub.

Baba Nangko. Joan Bettison. LC 93-26225. (Voyages Ser.). (Illus.). (J). 1994. 4.25 (0-383-03733-6) SRA Schl Grp.

Baba Sali. Tr. by Leah Dolinger. 224p. 1986. 16.95 (0-910818-65-7) Judaica Pr.

Baba Yaga. Ernest Small & Blair Lent. (Illus.). 48p. (J). (gr. k-3). 1992. pap. 5.95 (0-395-63037-1, Sandpiper) HM.

Baba Yaga: A Modern Fairy Tale. Linda N. Foster. 32p. (Orig.). 1992. pap. text ed. 4.00 (1-56439-014-4) Ridgeway.

Baba Yaga: A Russian Folktale. Illus. & Ret. by Katya Arnold. LC 92-38199. 32p. (J). (gr. k-3). 1993. 14.95 (1-55858-208-8); lib. bdg. 14.88 (1-55858-209-6) North-South Bks NYC.

Baba Yaga: A Russian Folktale. Eric A. Kimmel. (J). 1993. pap. 5.95 (0-8234-1060-9) Holiday.

Baba Yaga: A Russian Folktale. Illus. by Megan Lloyd. LC 90-39215. 32p. (J). (ps-3). 1991. lib. bdg. 15.95 (0-8234-0854-X) Holiday.

***Baba Yaga: A Russian Folktale.** Margaret Y. Phinney. (Illus.). 40p. (J). (gr. 2-6). Date not set. lib. bdg. 13.95 (1-57255-004-X) Mondo Pubng.

***Baba Yaga: A Russian Folktale.** Margaret Y. Phinney. (Illus.). 40p. (J). (gr. 2-6). Date not set. 25.95 (1-57255-006-6) Mondo Pubng.

Baba Yaga & the Little Girl. Illus. & Ret. by Katya Arnold. LC 93-45752. 32p. (J). (gr. k-3). 1994. 14.95 (1-55858-287-8); lib. bdg. 14.88 (1-55858-288-6) North-South Bks NYC.

Baba Yaga & Vasilisa the Brave. Mayer Marianna. LC 90-38514. (Illus.). 40p. (J). (ps-3). 1994. 16.00 (0-688-08500-8); 15.93 (0-688-08501-6) Morrow Jr Bks.

Baba Yaga's Geese & Other Russian Stories. Bonnie Carev. LC 73-77852. 128p. reprint ed. pap. 36.50 (0-8357-5936-9, 2056225) Bks Demand.

Babaji: Lahiri Mahasay: The Polestar of Kriya. 3rd rev. ed. Satyeswarananda Giri. LC 91-90563. (Biographies Ser.: Vol. II). (Illus.). 232p. 1991. pap. text ed. 15.00 (1-877854-13-1) Sanskrit Classics.

Babaji Vol. 1: The Divine Himalayan Yogi. 3rd rev. ed. Swami Giri Babaji. LC 92-60410. (Illus.). 244p. Date not set. pap. text ed. 20.00 (1-877854-17-4) Sanskrit Classics.

Babaji Vol. 3: Masters of Original Kriya. Swami Giri Babaji. LC 92-61457. (Illus.). 96p. (Orig.). Date not set. pap. text ed. 10.00 (1-877854-18-2) Sanskrit Classics.

***Babaji the Angel of the Lord.** Leonard Orr. 1995. 20.00 (0-945793-18-9) Inspir Univ.

***Babar: Le Livre des Couleurs.** Laurent De Brunhoff. (J). 1985. 24.95 (0-7859-8777-0) Fr & Eur.

Babar a Celesteville. Laurent de Brunhoff. 16p. (J). 1974. 4.95 (0-7859-0678-9, F12062) Fr & Eur.

***Babar a la Ferme.** Jean De Brunhoff & Laurent De Brunhoff. 48p. (J). 1990. 17.95 (0-7859-8778-9) Fr & Eur.

***Babar a la Fete.** Jean De Brunhoff & Laurent De Brunhoff. 48p. (J). 1990. 17.95 (0-7859-8779-7) Fr & Eur.

***Babar a la Fete de Celesteville.** Laurent De Brunhoff. (J). 1975. pap. 17.95 (0-614-02957-0) Fr & Eur.

***Babar a la Maison.** Jean De Brunhoff & Laurent De Brunhoff. 48p. (J). 1990. 17.95 (0-7859-8780-0) Fr & Eur.

Babar a la Mer. Laurent De Brunhoff. (FRE.). (J). (gr. 2-3). 15.95 (0-685-11023-0) Fr & Eur.

***Babar a la Ville.** Jean De Brunhoff & Laurent De Brunhoff. 48p. (J). 1990. 17.95 (0-7859-8781-9) Fr & Eur.

Babar a New York. Laurent De Brunhoff. (Illus.). (FRE.). (J). (gr. 4-6). 1975. bds. 15.95 (0-7859-5281-0, 2010025520) Fr & Eur.

Babar & Father Christmas. Jean De Brunhoff. (Illus.). 40p. (J). (gr. k-3). 1987. 16.95 (0-394-89265-8) Random Bks Yng Read.

Babar & Father Christmas. Jean Debrunhoff. (J). 1949. 10.00 (0-394-80578-X) Random Bks Yng Read.

Babar & Father Christmas - Babar y Papa Noel, Brunhoff/ Jean de. Jean De Brunhoff. (SPA.). (J). 12.95 (84-204-3702-6) Santillana.

Babar & His Children. Jean De Brunhoff. Tr. by Merle Haas. (Illus.). (J). (ps). 1969. 11.00 (0-394-80577-1); lib. bdg. 11.99 (0-394-90577-6) Random Bks Yng Read.

Babar & the Ghost: An Easy-to-Read Version: A Step Two Book. Laurent De Brunhoff. LC 85-11841. (Step into Reading Bks.). (Illus.). 48p. (J). (gr. 1-3). 1986. pap. 3.50 (0-394-87908-2) Random Bks Yng Read.

Babar Artiste Peintre. Laurent De Brunhoff. (FRE.). (J). (gr. 2-3). 1991. 15.95 (0-7859-5285-3, 209201417X) Fr & Eur.

Babar at School. (Babar Board Bks.). (Illus.). 8p. (J). 1991. bds. 3.99 (0-517-05219-9) Random Hse Value.

Babar au Cirque. Jean de Brunhoff. (Illus.). 16p. (J). 1974. 4.95 (0-686-54121-9, FC241) Fr & Eur.

Babar au Cirque. Laurent De Brunhoff. (J). (gr. 2-3). pap. 15.95 (0-685-33966-1, FC241) Fr & Eur.

Babar aux Sports d'Hiver. Laurent de Brunhoff. (Illus.). 20p. (J). 1976. 4.95 (0-7859-0679-7, FC250) Fr & Eur.

Babar Aviateur. Laurent de Brunhoff. 16p. (J). 1974. 4.95 (0-7859-0680-0, M5989) Fr & Eur.

Babar Campeur. Laurent de Brunhoff. 16p. (J). 1974. 4.95 (0-686-54138-3) Fr & Eur.

Babar Chez le Docteur. Laurent De Brunhoff. (FRE.). (J). (gr. 2-3). 15.95 (0-685-28425-5) Fr & Eur.

Babar Compeur. (J). 4.95 (0-685-33973-4) Fr & Eur.

Babar dans l'Ile aux Oiseaux. Laurent de Brunhoff. 29p. (J). 15.95 (0-7859-0681-9, F2002) Fr & Eur.

Babar Eats Lunch. (Babar Board Bks.). (Illus.). 8p. (J). 1991. bds. 3.99 (0-517-05236-9) Random Hse Value.

Babar en Amerique. Laurent de Brunhoff. 23p. (J). 1975. 15.95 (0-686-54140-5) Fr & Eur.

Babar en Ballon. Laurent De Brunhoff. (FRE.). (J). (gr. 2-3). 15.95 (0-685-28422-0) Fr & Eur.

Babar en Famille. Jean de Brunhoff. 26p. (J). 1975. 15.95 (0-7859-0672-X, FC589) Fr & Eur.

***Babar en Foret.** Jean De Brunhoff & Laurent De Brunhoff. 48p. (J). 1990. 17.95 (0-7859-8782-7) Fr & Eur.

Babar en Promenade. Laurent De Brunhoff. (FRE.). (J). (gr. 2-3). 15.95 (0-685-11026-5) Fr & Eur.

***Babar en Vacances.** Jean De Brunhoff & Laurent De Brunhoff. 48p. (J). 1990. 17.95 (0-7859-8783-5) Fr & Eur.

Babar et ce coquin d'Arthur. Laurent De Brunhoff. (Illus.). (FRE.). (J). (gr. 4-6). bds. 15.95 (0-685-11027-3) Fr & Eur.

Babar et la Vieille Dame. (J). (gr. 2-3). pap. 15.95 (0-7859-0614-2, FC254) Fr & Eur.

Babar et le Crocodile. Jean de Brunhoff. 16p. (J). 1975. 4.95 (0-7859-0673-8, FC242) Fr & Eur.

Babar et le Docteur. Laurent de Brunhoff. 16p. (J). 1975. 4.95 (0-686-54141-3) Fr & Eur.

***Babar et le Fantome.** Laurent De Brunhoff. 32p. (J). 1981. pap. 17.95 (0-7859-8784-3) Fr & Eur.

Babar et le Pere Noel. Jean de Brunhoff. 29p. (J). 1975. 15.95 (0-7859-0674-6, FC582) Fr & Eur.

Babar et le Prof. Grifaton. Laurent De Brunhoff. (FRE.). (J). (gr. 2-4). 15.95 (0-685-28434-4) Fr & Eur.

Babar et le Wouly-Wouly. Laurent de Brunhoff. 26p. (J). 15.95 (0-7859-0682-7, M11805) Fr & Eur.

***Babar et les Quatre Voleurs.** Laurent De Brunhoff. 28p. (J). 1979. pap. 17.95 (0-7859-8785-1) Fr & Eur.

***Babar et Moi.** Laurent De Brunhoff. (J). 1987. 24.95 (0-7859-8786-X) Fr & Eur.

Babar et Sa Famille. Laurent de Brunhoff. 26p. (J). 1976. 4.95 (0-686-54143-X) Fr & Eur.

***Babar et Sa Petite Fille Isabelle.** Laurent De Brunhoff. (J). 1988. 24.95 (0-7859-8787-8) Fr & Eur.

***Babar et Ses Amis a la Ferme.** Laurent De Brunhoff. 48p. (J). Date not set. 19.95 (0-7859-8805-X) Fr & Eur.

***Babar et Ses Amis a la Fete.** Laurent De Brunhoff. 48p. (J). Date not set. 19.95 (0-7859-8806-8) Fr & Eur.

***Babar et Ses Amis a la Maison.** Laurent De Brunhoff. 48p. (J). Date not set. 19.95 (0-7859-8804-1) Fr & Eur.

***Babar et Ses Amis a la Ville.** Laurent De Brunhoff. 48p. (J). Date not set. 19.95 (0-7859-8809-2) Fr & Eur.

***Babar et Ses Amis a L'Ecole.** Laurent De Brunhoff. 48p. (J). Date not set. 19.95 (0-7859-8802-5) Fr & Eur.

***Babar et Ses Amis au Spectacle.** Laurent De Brunhoff. 48p. (J). Date not set. 19.95 (0-7859-8803-3) Fr & Eur.

***Babar et Ses Amis en Foret.** Laurent De Brunhoff. 48p. (J). Date not set. 19.95 (0-7859-8811-4) Fr & Eur.

***Babar et Ses Amis en Vacances.** Laurent De Brunhoff. 48p. (J). Date not set. 19.95 (0-7859-8808-4) Fr & Eur.

***Babar et Ses Amis Font les Courses.** Laurent De Brunhoff. 48p. (J). Date not set. 19.95 (0-7859-8810-6) Fr & Eur.

***Babar et Ses Amis Visitent le Royaume.** Laurent De Brunhoff. 48p. (J). Date not set. 19.95 (0-7859-8807-6) Fr & Eur.

Babar et ses Enfants. Laurent De Brunhoff. (FRE.). (J). (gr. 2-3). 15.95 (0-685-28436-0) Fr & Eur.

Babar Fait Du Ski. Laurent De Brunhoff. (FRE.). (J). (gr. 2-3). 14.95 (0-685-11029-X) Fr & Eur.

***Babar Fait Ses Courses.** Jean De Brunhoff & Laurent De Brunhoff. 48p. (J). 1991. 17.95 (0-7859-8788-6) Fr & Eur.

Babar, First of the Moguls. Fernand Grenard. Tr. by Homer White & Richard Glaenzer. LC 70-124236. (Select Bibliographies Reprint Ser.). 1977. reprint ed. 18.95 (0-8369-5424-6) Ayer.

Babar Gets Dressed. (Babar Board Bks.). (Illus.). 8p. (J). 1991. bds. 3.99 (0-517-05220-2) Random Hse Value.

Babar in his Garden. (Babar Board Bks.). (Illus.). 8p. (J). 1991. bds. 3.99 (0-517-05221-0) Random Hse Value.

Babar Jardinier. Laurent De Brunhoff. (FRE.). (J). (gr. 2-3). 15.95 (0-685-11030-3) Fr & Eur.

***Babar le Livre des Chiffres.** Laurent De Brunhoff. (J). 1986. 24.95 (0-7859-8789-4) Fr & Eur.

Babar Learns to Cook. Laurent De Brunhoff. LC 78-11769. (Pictureback Ser.). (Illus.). (J). (ps-3). 1979. 2.25 (0-394-84108-5) Random Bks Yng Read.

***Babar les 500 Premiers Mots.** Laurent De Brunhoff. 48p. (J). Date not set. 19.95 (0-7859-8812-2) Fr & Eur.

Babar Loses His Crown. Laurent De Brunhoff. LC 67-21918. (Illus.). 72p. (J). (gr. k-3). 1967. lib. bdg. 7.99 (0-394-90045-6) Beginner.

Babar-Nama. Ed. by Beveridge. (Gibb Memorial Ser.: Vol. 1). 55.00 (0-7189-0204-1, Pub. by Aris & Phillips UK) David Brown.

Babar on Vacation. (Babar Board Bks.). (Illus.). 8p. (J). 1991. bds. 3.99 (0-517-05222-9) Random Hse Value.

Babar Patissier. Laurent de Brunhoff. 16p. (J). 1975. 4.95 (0-686-54144-8) Fr & Eur.

***Babar Raconte Flore Reporter.** Laurent De Brunhoff. 48p. (J). Date not set. 19.95 (0-7859-8813-0) Fr & Eur.

***Babar Raconte Halte a la Pollution.** Laurent De Brunhoff. 48p. (J). Date not set. 19.95 (0-7859-8816-5) Fr & Eur.

***Babar Raconte la Course a la Lune.** Laurent De Brunhoff. 48p. (J). Date not set. 19.95 (0-7859-8820-3) Fr & Eur.

***Babar Raconte l'Affaire de la Couronne.** Laurent De Brunhoff. 48p. (J). Date not set. 19.95 (0-7859-8818-1) Fr & Eur.

***Babar Raconte l'Arrivee du Bebe Elephant.** Laurent De Brunhoff. 48p. (J). Date not set. 19.95 (0-7859-8815-7) Fr & Eur.

***Babar Raconte le Fantome.** Laurent De Brunhoff. 48p. (J). Date not set. 19.95 (0-7859-8819-X) Fr & Eur.

***Babar Raconte le Meilleur Ami des Elephants.** Laurent De Brunhoff. 48p. (J). Date not set. 19.95 (0-7859-8823-8) Fr & Eur.

***Babar Raconte le Pianiste.** Laurent De Brunhoff. 48p. (J). Date not set. 19.95 (0-7859-8822-X) Fr & Eur.

***Babar Raconte le Plus Beau Cadeau du Monde.** Laurent De Brunhoff. 48p. (J). Date not set. 19.95 (0-7859-8821-1) Fr & Eur.

***Babar Raconte Que la Fete Continue.** Laurent De Brunhoff. 48p. (J). Date not set. 19.95 (0-7859-8824-6) Fr & Eur.

***Babar Raconte un Diner Chez Rataxes.** Laurent De Brunhoff. 48p. (J). Date not set. 19.95 (0-7859-8817-3) Fr & Eur.

***Babar Raconte Zephir Fait le Singe.** Laurent De Brunhoff. 48p. (J). Date not set. 19.95 (0-7859-8814-9) Fr & Eur.

***Babar Retrouve Ses Amis.** Jean De Brunhoff. (J). 1994. pap. 17.95 (0-7859-8790-8) Fr & Eur.

***Babar s'Amuse Avec les Lettres et les Chiffres.** Laurent De Brunhoff. 48p. (J). Date not set. 19.95 (0-614-02959-7) Fr & Eur.

Babar Saves the Day. Laurent De Brunhoff. LC 76-11684. (Pictureback Ser.). (Illus.). (J). (gr. 3-6). 1976. 2.25 (0-394-83341-4) Random Bks Yng Read.

Babar Says Goodnight. (Babar Board Bks.). (Illus.). 8p. (J). 1991. bds. 3.99 (0-517-05235-0) Random Hse Value.

***Babar Sur la Planete Molle.** Laurent De Brunhoff. (J). 1980. pap. 17.95 (0-7859-8791-6) Fr & Eur.

Babar the Boy King. Gail Herman. LC 88-63343. (Babar Mini-Storybooks Ser.). (Illus.). 32p. (Orig.). (J). (ps-3). 1989. pap. text ed. 1.50 (0-394-84533-1) Random Bks Yng Read.

Babar the King. Jean Debrunhoff. (J). 1937. 11.00 (0-394-80580-1); lib. bdg. 11.99 (0-394-90580-6) Random Bks Yng Read.

Babar the King: (El Rey Babar) Jean De Brunhoff. (SPA.). (J). 11.50 (84-204-3038-2) Santillana.

***Babar Visite Son Royaume.** Jean De Brunhoff & Laurent De Brunhoff. 48p. (J). 1991. 17.95 (0-614-02958-9) Fr & Eur.

Babari Masjid. Aslam Abdullah. 60p. 1991. pap. text ed. 3.00 (1-881504-09-3) Minaret Pubns.

Babar's Anniversary Album. Jean De Brunhoff & Laurent De Brunhoff. LC 81-5182. (Illus.). 144p. (J). (ps-3). 1993. 18.00 (0-394-84813-6); lib. bdg. 16.99 (0-394-94813-0) Random Bks Yng Read.

Babar's Bath Book. Laurent De Brunhoff. (Bathtime Bks.). (Illus.). 10p. (J). (ps). 1992. vinyl bd. 3.95 (0-679-83434-6) Random Bks Yng Read.

Babar's Battle. Laurent De Brunhoff. LC 91-53169. (Illus.). 36p. (J). (ps-3). 1992. lib. bdg. 10.99 (0-679-91068-9) Random Bks Yng Read.

Babar's Battle. Laurent De Brunhoff. LC 91-53169. (Illus.). 36p. (J). (ps-3). 1992. 10.00 (0-679-81068-4) Random Bks Yng Read.

Babar's Birthday Surprise. Laurent De Brunhoff. LC 74-123071. (Illus.). 36p. (J). (ps-2). 1970. reprint ed. 12.00 (0-394-80591-7) Random Bks Yng Read.

Babar's Book of Color. Laurent De Brunhoff. LC 84-42737. (Illus.). 36p. (J). (ps-2). 1984. 13.00 (0-394-86896-X); lib. bdg. 10.99 (0-394-96896-4) Random Bks Yng Read.

Babar's Busy Week. Illus. by Laurent De Brunhoff. LC 89-64400. (Chunky Shape Bks.). 22p. (J). (ps). 1990. bds. 2.95 (0-679-80664-4) Random Bks Yng Read.

Babar's Car. Laurent De Brunhoff. (Little Wheel Bks.). (Illus.). 14p. (J). (ps-00). 1992. bds. 3.99 (0-679-83242-4) Random Bks Yng Read.

Babar's Family Album: Five Favorite Stories. Laurent De Brunhoff. LC 90-8748. (Illus.). 112p. (J). (ps-3). 1991. 17.00 (0-679-81167-2) Random Bks Yng Read.

Babar's French & English Word Book. Laurent De Brunhoff. LC 93-27873. (Illus.). 128p. (J). 1994. 16.00 (0-679-83644-6) Random Bks Yng Read.

Babar's French Lessons. Laurent De Brunhoff. (Illus.). (J). (ps). 1963. lib. bdg. 5.99 (0-394-90587-3) Random Bks Yng Read.

Babar's Little Circus Star. Laurent De Brunhoff. LC 87-14149. (Step into Reading Bks.). (Illus.). 32p. (Orig.). (J). (ps-1). 1988. lib. bdg. 7.99 (0-394-98959-7); pap. 3.50 (0-394-88959-2) Random Bks Yng Read.

Babar's Little Girl. Laurent De Brunhoff. LC 68-42962. (Illus.). 36p. (J). (ps-3). 1987. 11.00 (0-394-88689-5) Random Bks Yng Read.

Babar's Little Library: Stories About Earth, About Fire, About Air, About Water, 4 bks. Laurent De Brunhoff. (Illus.). (J). (ps-2). 1992. Set of mini-bks. in slipcase incls. Air, Water, 48 pgs. ea. & Earth & Fire, 32 pgs. ea. 8.99 (0-394-84365-7) Random Bks Yng Read.

Babar's Peekaboo Fair. Laurent De Brunhoff. LC 92-64269. (Peek-a-Boo Board Bks.). (Illus.). 14p. (J). (ps). 1993. bds. 3.99 (0-679-83935-6) Random Bks Yng Read.

Babar's Trunk, 4 bks., Set. Laurent De Brunhoff. Incl. Babar at the Seashore. 1969. (0-318-55395-3); Babar the Gardener. 1969. (0-318-55396-1); Babar Goes Skiing. 1969. (0-318-55397-X); Babar on a Picnic. 1969. (0-318-55398-8); (Illus.). (J). (ps-2). 1969. Set boxed 9.95 (0-394-80585-2) Random Bks Yng Read.

Baba's Grace: Discourses of P. R. Sarkar. Prabhat Rainjan Sarkar. (Illus.). 197p. (Orig.). 1987. reprint ed. pap. 6.95 (0-88476-001-4) Ananda Marga.

Babaylanism in Negros: 1896-1907. Evelyn T. Cullamar. (Illus.). 133p. (Orig.). 1986. pap. 10.00 (971-10-0293-0, Pub. by New Day Pub PH) Cellar.

Babbage: Passages from the Life of a Philosopher. Ed. by Martin Cambepll-Kelly. LC 93-43903. 390p. (Orig.). (C). Date not set. text ed. 18.95 (0-685-70652-4) Rutgers U Pr.

Babbage: Passages from the Life of a Philosopher. Ed. by Martin Campbell-Kelly. LC 93-43903. (C). 1994. pap. 18.95 (0-8135-2066-5) Rutgers U Pr.

Babbitt. Sinclair Lewis. 1976. 22.95 (0-8488-0826-6) Amereon Ltd.

Babbitt. Sinclair Lewis. LC 84-254209. (Book Notes Ser.). 1985. pap. 2.50 (0-8120-3504-6) Barron.

Babbitt. Sinclair Lewis. LC 22-14419. (Modern Classic Ser.). 408p. 1989. 15.95 (0-15-110421-2) HarBrace.

Babbitt. Sinclair Lewis. 1961. pap. 4.95 (0-451-52242-7, Sig Classics) NAL-Dutton.

Babbitt. Sinclair Lewis. 408p. 1987. reprint ed. lib. bdg. 25.95 (0-89966-622-1) Buccaneer Bks.

Babbitt: An American Life. Glen A. Love. LC 92-27096. (Masterwork Studies: No. 105). 105p. 1993. text ed. 21.95 (0-8057-9440-9, Twayne); pap. 12.95 (0-8057-8562-0, Twayne) Macmillan.

Babbitt Family History 1643-1900. William B. Browne. (Illus.). 761p. 1988. reprint ed. lib. bdg. 119.00 (0-8328-0148-8); reprint ed. pap. 109.00 (0-8328-0149-6) Higginson Bk Co.

Babbitt Notes. Gary Carey. 1989. pap. 3.75 (0-8220-0219-1) Cliffs.

Babble. Jonathan Baumbach. LC 76-2876. 117p. 1976. 15.95 (0-914590-26-X); pap. 6.95 (0-914590-27-8) Fiction Coll.

Babble of Ancestral Voices: Shakespeare, Cervantes, & Theobald, No. 73. Ed. by Harriet C. Frazier. (Studies in English Literature). 162p. 1974. text ed. 40.00 (90-279-2692-1) Mouton.

Babcock & Wilcox Cyclone Furnace Vitrification Technology. (Applications Analysis Report). (Illus.). 35p. (Orig.). (C). 1993. pap. text ed. 40.00 (1-56806-669-4) Diane Pub.

Babcock Genealogy. Stephen Babcock. (Illus.). 640p. 1988. reprint ed. lib. bdg. 91.00 (0-8328-0150-X); reprint ed. pap. 81.00 (0-8328-0151-8) Higginson Bk Co.

Babe. Edwards. (J). Date not set. 15.00 (0-06-021811-8, HarpT); lib. bdg. 14.89 (0-06-021812-6, HarpT) HarpC.

Babe: An Iowa Legend. Chuck Offenburger. LC 88-37461. (Illus.). 174p. 1989. 12.95 (0-8138-0269-5) Iowa St U Pr.

BABE: Bay Area's Bachelors Extraordinaire. Darlene Tenes. (Illus.). 48p. (Orig.). 1992. pap. 8.95 (1-881045-00-5) Bay Areas Best.

Babe: Child of Boom & Bust in Old Chicago, Umbilicus Mundi. Alfred De Grazia. 489p. 1992. pap. 22.00 (0-685-59570-6) Metron Pubns.

***Babe: The Gallant Pig.** King. LC 84-11429. 1995. pap. (0-679-87393-7) Random.

Babe: The Gallant Pig. Dick King-Smith. LC 84-11429. (Illus.). 176p. (J). (gr. 3-6). 1993. 13.00 (0-517-55556-5) Crown Bks Yng Read.

Babe: The Legend Comes to Life. Robert W. Creamer. 448p. 1992. pap. 12.00 (0-671-76070-X, Fireside) S&S Trade.

Babe: The Life & Times of Oliver Hardy. John McCabe. 1990. 16.95 (0-8065-1187-7, Citadel Pr) Carol Pub Group.

Babe Didn't Point: And Other Stories about Iowans & Sports. Bill Bryson. Ed. by Michael G. Bryson, Sr. LC 88-9103. (Illus.). 256p. 1989. 21.95 (0-8138-0044-7) Iowa St U Pr.

Babe Didrikson: Athlete of the Century. R. R. Knudson. (Women of Our Time Ser.). (Illus.). 64p. (J). (gr. 2-6). 1986. pap. 4.99 (0-14-032095-4, Puffin) Puffin Bks.

Babe Didrikson Zaharias. Elizabeth Lynn & Matina Horner. (American Women of Achievement Ser.). (Illus.). 112p. (J). (gr. 5 up). 1989. lib. bdg. 17.95 (1-55546-684-2) Chelsea Hse.

Babe Didrikson Zaharias. William R. Sanford & Carl R. Green. LC 91-44870. (Sports Immortals Ser.). (Illus.). 48p. (J). (gr. 5). 1993. text ed. 11.95 (0-89686-736-6, Crstwood Hse) Silver Burdett Pr.

Babe in the Woods. large type ed. Jackie Merritt. (Desire Ser.). 1993. 17.95 (0-373-58804-6, Silhouette Lrg Print); pap. 16.95 (0-373-58904-2, Silhouette Lrg Print) Chivers N Amer.

An Asterisk (*) at the beginning of an entry indicates that the title is appearing in BIP for the first time.

Babe Is Wise: Contemporary Stories by Australian Women. Ed. by Lyn Harwood et al. 313p. 1991. pap. 13.95 (*1-85381-032-0*, Pub. by Virago Pr UK) Trafalgar.

Babe is Wise: Contemporary Stories by Australian Women. Lyn Harwood et al. 313p. (C). 1990. 45.00 (*0-947087-06-0*, Pub. by Pascoe Pub AT) St Mut.

Babe Ruth. Rae Bains. LC 84-2595. (Illus.). 32p. (J). (gr. 3-6). 1985. lib. bdg. 9.49 (*0-8167-0144-X*); pap. text ed. 2.95 (*0-8167-0145-8*) Troll Assocs.

Babe Ruth. Carl R. Green & William R. Sanford. LC 91-21639. (Sports Immortals Ser.). (Illus.). 48p. (J). (gr. 5). 1992. text ed. 11.95 (*0-89686-741-2*, Crstwood Hse) Silver Burdett Pr.

Babe Ruth. Norm Macht. (Baseball Legends Ser.). (Illus.). 64p. (J). (gr. 3 up). 1991. lib. bdg. 14.95 (*0-7910-1189-5*) Chelsea Hse.

Babe Ruth. Richard Rambeck. (Sports Superstars Ser.). (ENG & SPA.). (J). (gr. 2-6). 1992. lib. bdg. 21.36 (*0-89565-962-X*) Childs World.

***Babe Ruth.** Richard Rambeck. (Sports Superstars Ser.). (ENG & SPA.). (J). (gr. 2-6). 1992. lib. bdg. 21.36 (*1-56766-054-1*) Childs World.

Babe Ruth: Classic Sports Shots. Bruce Weber. (J). 1993. pap. 1.25 (*0-590-47018-3*) Scholastic Inc.

Babe Ruth: His Life & Legend. Kal Wagenheim. (Illus.). 288p. (Orig.). 1992. pap. 12.95 (*0-8050-2099-3*, Owl) H Holt & Co.

Babe Ruth: One of Baseball's Greatest. Guernsey Van Riper, Jr. LC 86-10957. (Childhood of Famous Americans Ser.). (Illus.). 192p. (J). (gr. 2-6). 1986. reprint ed. pap. 3.95 (*0-02-042130-3*, Aladdin Paperbacks) S&S Childrens.

***Babe Ruth: Sultan of Swat.** Lois Nicholson. (Illus.). 170p. (YA). (gr. 7-12). 1995. 17.95 (*0-9625427-1-7*) Goodwood Pr.

Babe Ruth, Home Run Hero. Keith Brandt. LC 85-1091. (Illus.). 48p. (J). (gr. 4-6). 1986. lib. bdg. 10.79 (*0-8167-0553-4*); pap. text ed. 3.50 (*0-8167-0554-2*) Troll Assocs.

Babe Ruth-Jackie Robinson. Naunerle C. Farr. (Pendulum Illustrated Biography Ser.). (Illus.). (J). (gr. 4-12). 1979. pap. text ed. 2.95 (*0-88301-359-2*); student ed 1.25 (*0-88301-383-5*) Pendulum Pr.

Babe Ruth Story. Babe Ruth. 1992. pap. 4.99 (*0-451-17492-5*, Sig) NAL-Dutton.

Babe Ruth's Incredible Records & the Forty-Five Players Who Broke Them. John A. Mercurio. 192p. (Orig.). 1993. pap. 5.50 (*1-56171-221-3*, S P I Bks) Sure Sellers.

Babe Ruth's Own Book of Baseball. George H. Ruth. LC 91-38383. xxii, 333p. 1992. reprint ed. 35.00 (*0-8032-3905-X*); reprint ed. pap. 9.95 (*0-8032-8939-1*) U of Nebr Pr.

Babe Signed My Shoe. Ernie Harwell. Ed. by Geoff Upward. LC 94-9249. (Illus.). 240p. 1994. 21.95 (*0-912083-72-7*) Diamond Communications.

***Babe the Gallant Pig: The Movie Storybook.** Korman. 1995. pap. 7.99 (*0-679-87465-8*) Random.

Babel: The Cultural & Linguistic Barriers Between Nations. Ed. by Jerry Payne & Rainer Kolmel. 195p. 1990. pap. text ed. 30.00 (*0-08-037969-9*, Pub. by Aberdeen U Pr) Macmillan.

Babel & Babylon: Spectatorship in American Silent Film. Miriam Hansen. (Illus.). 377p. 1991. 45.00 (*0-674-05830-5*, HANBAB) HUP.

Babel & Babylon: Spectatorship in American Silent Film. Miriam Hansen. 377p. 1994. pap. 19.95 (*0-674-05831-3*) HUP.

***Babel Barbara.** Cristina P. Rossi. Tr. by Decker. (QRL Poetry Book Ser.: Vol. XXXI). 20.00 (*0-614-06448-1*); pap. 10.00 (*0-614-06449-X*) Quarterly Rev.

Babel of the Unconscious: Mother Tongue & Foreign Languages in the Psychoanalytic Dimension. Ed. by J. Amati Mehler et al. 322p. 1993. text ed. 50.00 (*0-8236-0530-2*) Intl Univs Pr.

Babelandia. Demetrio Aguilera-Malta. Tr. by Peter Earle. LC 84-9035. (Contemporary Literature Ser.). (Illus.). 375p. 1985. 19.95 (*0-89603-065-2*) Humana.

Babell. Archibald Pitcairne. LC 75-174208. (Maitland Club, Glasgow. Publications: No. 6). reprint ed. 11.00 (*0-404-52931-3*) AMS Pr.

Babel's Children. J. N. Williamson. 288p. 1990. reprint ed. pap. 3.95 (*0-8439-2888-3*) Dorchester Pub Co.

Babels Hus see House of Babel

Babes & Bullets. Jim Davis. 1989. mass mkt. 5.95 (*0-345-36339-6*, Ballantine Trade) Ballantine.

Babes in Arms. (Vocal Score Ser.). 1981. pap. 35.00 (*0-88188-003-5*, 00312015) H Leonard.

Babes in Arms. (Illus.). 1981. 7.95 (*0-88188-059-0*, 00312014) H Leonard.

Babes in Gangland. Dutton Foster. 28p. 1991. 2.50 (*0-87129-111-8*) Dramatic Pub.

Babes in the Wood. Rick Besoyan. 64p. 1983. pap. 4.95 (*0-88145-011-1*) Broadway Play.

Babes in the Woods. Langley. 1987. pap. 6.95 (*0-930096-90-8*) G Gannett.

Babes in Toyland. James Howe. (Gulliver-HBJ Bk.). (Illus.). 79p. (J). (gr. 3-7). 1988. pap. 9.95 (*0-15-200410-6*) HarBrace.

Babes in Toyland. Mandi McDonald. (Heirloom Collection Ser.). (Illus.). 72p. (J). (gr. 3-7). 1990. 11.95 (*0-88101-100-2*) Unicorn Pub.

Babes in Toyland. John Speirs. (Read with Me Ser.). (Illus.). 32p. (J). (ps-1). 1994. pap. 2.50 (*0-590-48183-5*, Cartwheel) Scholastic Inc.

Babes in Toyland: Christmas Musical. Victor Herbert & Glen MacDonough. Ed. by Ann Smit. 1978. 4.95 (*0-87129-359-5*, B06) Dramatic Pub.

Babes in Toyland: Musical. Victor Herbert. (Orig.). (J). (ps up). 1987. 6.00 (*0-87602-275-1*) Anchorage.

Babes in Toyland: Stage Magic Plays for Children's Theatre. R. Eugene Jackson. (Illus.). 48p. (Orig.). (J). (ps up). 1987. pap. 4.50 (*0-88680-267-9*); 15.00 (*0-88680-268-7*) I E Clark.

Babes in Toyland: The Making & Selling of a Rock & Roll Band. Neal Karlen. 1994. 22.00 (*0-8129-2058-9*, Times Bks) Random.

Babes of the Wild. Gyo Fujikawa. (Illus.). 16p. (J). (ps). 1989. reprint ed. bds. 6.95 (*1-55987-008-7*, Sunny Bks) J B Comns.

Babesiosis of Domestic Animals & Man, Vol. I. Ed. by Miodrag Ristic. 176p. 1988. 152.00 (*0-8493-4908-7*, QR201, CRC Reprint) Franklin.

***Babette Cole's Cats.** Babette Cole. (Illus.). 5p. (J). 1995. 4.95 (*0-446-91067-8*) Warner Bks.

***Babette Cole's Dogs.** Babette Cole. (Illus.). 5p. (J). 1995. 4.95 (*0-446-91068-6*) Warner Bks.

***Babette Cole's Fish.** Babette Cole. (Illus.). 5p. (J). 1995. 4.95 (*0-446-91069-4*) Warner Bks.

***Babette Cole's Ponies.** Babette Cole. (Illus.). 5p. (J). 1995. 4.95 (*0-446-91071-6*) Warner Bks.

Babette's Feast & Other Anecdotes of Destiny. Isak Dinesen. Ed. by Martha Levin. LC 87-51579. 256p. 1988. pap. 6.00 (*0-394-75929-X*, Vin) Random.

Babi Yar: A Document in the Form of a Novel. A. Anatoli. Tr. by David Floyd. LC 78-74649. 1979. reprint ed. lib. bdg. 30.00 (*0-8376-0432-X*) Bentley.

***Babi Yar 1941-1991: A Resource Book & Guide.** Ed. & Comp. by Simon Wiesenthal Center Staff. (Illus.). 64p. (Orig.). 1991. pap. text ed. write for info. (*0-943058-10-4*) S Wiesenthal Ctr.

Babicka. Connie Fox. (Kangaroo Court Ser.: No. 5). (Illus.). 32p. 1986. 3.50 (*0-940381-06-0*) Kangaroo Ct Pub.

Babied, Bullied & Bound: Japanese Youth. John R. Terry. 200p. 1988. pap. 9.95 (*0-933704-71-2*) Dawn Pr.

Babies. Stephanie Calmenson. LC 86-81490. (Golden Sturdy Bks.). (Illus.). 22p. (J). (ps). 1987. write for info. (*0-307-12118-6*, Golden Bks) Western Pub.

***Babies.** Denny. 1995. pap. text ed. 12.95 (*0-9641492-7-3*) Buffalo Hse.

Babies. Illus. by Gyo Fujikawa. (J). (ps). 1963. bds. 4.95 (*0-448-03084-5*, G&D) Putnam Pub Group.

Babies. R. Gee. (Facts of Life Ser.). 48p. (J). (gr. 5-10). 1986. lib. bdg. 13.96 (*0-88110-336-5*); pap. 6.95 (*0-86020-839-7*) EDC.

Babies! Christopher Green. 1994. mass mkt. 5.99 (*0-449-22289-6*) Fawcett.

***Babies.** Jonathan Harvey. 96p. 1995. pap. 11.95 (*0-413-69220-5*, A0739) Heinemann.

Babies. Rachel Isadora. LC 88-18782. (Illus.). (J). (ps up). 1990. 13.95 (*0-688-08031-6*); lib. bdg. 13.88 (*0-688-08032-4*) Greenwillow.

Babies. Anna Lippman. 36p. 1969. 2.50 (*0-87129-154-1*, B10) Dramatic Pub.

Babies: Canada. Moira Kemp & Mathew Kemp. 1992. pap. 5.06 (*0-394-22294-6*) Random.

Babies Aboard. Lindsey Green. 1990. pap. text ed. 11.95 (*0-87742-273-7*) Intl Marine.

Babies Aboard. Lyndsay Green. 1990. pap. text ed. 12.95 (*0-07-156030-0*) McGraw.

Babies All Around. Photos by Laura Dwight. (Baby Photo Board Bks.). (Illus.). 22p. (J). (ps). 1992. bds. 2.95 (*1-56288-184-1*) Checkerboard.

Babies & Other Hazards of Sex. Dave Barry. LC 84-11526. (Illus.). 96p. 1984. 6.95 (*0-87857-666-5*, 10-105-9); pap. 5.95 (*0-87857-510-3*, 10-105-1) Rodale Pr Inc.

Babies & Their Mothers. Donald W. Winnicott. (Illus.). 144p. 1992. pap. 10.53 (*0-201-63269-1*) Addison-Wesley.

Babies & Toddlers. R. Gee. (Parents' Guides Ser.). (Illus.). 48p. 1986. lib. bdg. 13.96 (*0-88110-561-9*); pap. 6.95 (*0-7460-0006-5*) EDC.

Babies First Year. 3.00 (*0-936868-14-7*) Freeland Pubns.

Babies First Year. Deb Mores. 1994. 20.00 (*0-517-59593-1*) Crown Pub Group.

Babies for Beginners. David Brizer. 1994. pap. 9.95 (*0-86316-169-3*) Writers & Readers.

Babies for Sale: The Tennessee Children's Home Adoption Scandal. Linda T. Austin. LC 92-46165. 192p. 1993. text ed. 47.95 (*0-275-94585-5*, C4585, Praeger Pubs) Greenwood.

Babies' Hotel. Mary Hoffman. (Illus.). 32p. (J). (ps-1). 1993. pap. 8.95 (*0-460-88091-8*, J M Dent & Sons) Trafalgar.

Babies in Bottles: Twentieth-Century Visions of Reproductive Technology. Susan M. Squier. LC 94-10154. (Illus.). 285p. (C). 1994. text ed. 48.00 (*0-8135-2116-5*); pap. text ed. 17.00 (*0-8135-2117-3*) Rutgers U Pr.

***Babies Inc. (Bundles of Joy)** Pat Montana. (Sil Romance Ser.). 1995. mass mkt. 2.99 (*0-373-19076-X*, 1-19076-8) Silhouette.

Babies Looking Book: Stimulation for the Newborn to Six Month Old Infant. Sharon K. Hyde. (Illus.). 36p. (J). (ps). 1992. 12.95 (*0-9624349-0-6*) S K Hyde.

Babies of Cockle Bay. Angela McAllister. (Illus.). 32p. (J). (ps-3). 1994. 13.95 (*0-8120-6424-0*); pap. 5.95 (*0-8120-1952-0*) Barron.

Babies on Board. Gina Ferris. 1994. mass mkt. 3.50 (*0-373-09913-4*, 1-09913-4) Harlequin Bks.

Babies on His Mind. Marie Ferrarella. (Silhouette Romance Ser.). 1993. pap. 2.69 (*0-373-08920-1*, 5-08920-6) Silhouette.

Babies on the Doorstep. Raye Morgan. 1994. mass mkt. 2.99 (*0-373-05886-1*, 1-05886-6) Harlequin Bks.

Babies Portraits of Fragile Lives. Illus. & Pref. by Kristine Gunther. 72p. (Orig.). 1986. pap. 8.75 (*0-935399-01-1*) Main St Pub.

Babies Take Us on a Special Journey. Susan S. Florence. (Illus.). 40p. 1987. 6.50 (*0-8378-5108-4*) Gibson.

***Babies with Down Syndrome: A New Parents' Guide.** Stray & Gunderson. 1995. pap. text ed. 14.95 (*0-933149-64-6*) Woodbine House.

Babies with Down Syndrome: A New Parents' Guide. Ed. by Karen Stray-Gundersen. LC 85-52007. 250p. 1986. pap. 14.95 (*0-933149-02-6*) Woodbine House.

Babii Iar: Roman-Dokument. Kuznetsov Anatolii. LC 85-62294. 488p. (RUS.). 1986. reprint ed. 18.00 (*0-911971-16-5*) Effect Pub.

Babilonia, Misterio Religioso: Babylon, Mystery Religion. Ralph Woodrow. (SPA.). 5.00 (*84-599-5994-5*, 220074, Pub. by Edit Clie SP) TSELF.

Babilonia Renace (The Rise of Babylon) Charles Dyer. (SPA.). 1991. 6.99 (*1-56063-082-5*, 498415) Editorial Unilit.

Babine & Carrier Phonology: A Historically Oriented Study. Gillian L. Story. LC 83-51454. (Publications in Linguistics: No. 70). 110p. (Orig.). 1984. fiche 8.00 (*0-88312-401-7*) Summer Instit Ling.

***Baboo & Lion.** Wishing Well Staff. Date not set. 15.99 (*0-88705-752-7*) Joshua Morris.

Baboon: Microbiology, Clinical Chemistry & Some Hematological Aspects. S. S. Kalter. (Primates in Medicine Ser.: Vol. 8). (Illus.). 1973. 57.75 (*3-8055-1442-5*) S Karger.

Baboon Dooley Rock Critic! Baboon Gets Ahead in Life. John Crawford. 248p. (Orig.). 1988. pap. 9.95 (*0-945209-00-2*) Popular Reality.

Baboon in the Nightclub. Kenneth Bernard. LC 93-79280. (Illus.). 72p. (Orig.). 1994. pap. 8.95 (*1-878580-54-X*) Asylum Arts.

Baboon Mothers & Infants. Jeanne Altmann. LC 79-21568. (Illus.). 256p. 1980. 32.00 (*0-674-05856-9*) HUP.

Baboon Mothers & Infants. Jeanne Altmann. LC 79-21568. (Illus.). 256p. 1981. pap. 15.95 (*0-674-05857-7*) HUP.

Baboons. Lynn Stone. (Monkey Discovery Library). (Illus.). 24p. (J). (gr. k-5). 1990. lib. bdg. 11.94 (*0-86593-067-8*); lib. bdg. 8.95 (*0-685-36315-5*) Rourke Corp.

Baboon's Umbrella. Ching. LC 91-7952. (Adventures in Storytelling Ser.). (Illus.). 24p. (J). (ps-3). 1991. lib. bdg. 13.28 (*0-516-05131-8*); pap. 4.95 (*0-516-45131-6*) Childrens.

Babouk. rev. ed. Guy Endore. (Voices of Resistance Ser.). 352p. (YA). (gr. 9-12). 28.00 (*0-85345-759-X*); pap. 9.00 (*0-85345-745-X*) Monthly Rev.

Baboushka & the Three Kings. Ruth Robbins. LC 60-15036. (Illus.). 32p. (J). (ps-3). 1986. pap. 5.95 (*0-395-42647-2*) HM.

Babouvisme apres Babeuf: Societes Secretes et Conspirations Communistes, 1830-1848. Georges Sencier. (History of Political Violence Ser.). (FRE.). 1985. reprint ed. lib. bdg. 50.00 (*0-527-41200-7*) Periodicals Srv.

Babri. James Jacobs. LC 94-11762. (Illus.). 32p. (J). 1994. 15.95 (*0-87905-622-3*) Gibbs Smith Pub.

Babri-Masjid Ramjanambhoomi Controversy. Ashgar A. Engineer. 1990. 30.00 (*81-202-0283-X*, Pub. by Ajanta II) S Asia.

Babrius - Index Mythiamborum Babrii. Ed. by Francisco Garcia & Alfredo R. Lopez. (Alpha-Omega, Reihe A Ser.: Bd. CXVI). vi, 105p. (GER.). 1990. write for info. (*3-487-09353-7*, Pub. by Georg Olms GW) Lubrecht & Cramer.

Babrius & Phaedrus. Babrius. Tr. by B. E. Perry. (Loeb Classical Library: No. 436). 1965. 15.50 (*0-674-99480-9*) HUP.

Babson's Bestiary. Jane F. Babson. LC 90-71155. (Illus.). 32p. (J). (ps-4). 1991. boxed 10.95 (*0-940787-02-4*) Winstead Pr.

Babucha Esta Celosa. Gilles Gauthier & Pierre-Andre Derome. (Primeros Lectores Ser.). (Illus.). 60p. (SPA.). (J). (gr. 5 up). 1994. pap. 5.95 (*958-07-0075-3*) Firefly Bks Ltd.

Babucha Mia, Para Siempre. Gilles Gauthier. (Illus.). 60p. (SPA.). (YA). (gr. 5 up). 1994. pap. 5.95 (*958-07-0079-6*) Firefly Bks Ltd.

***Babuchas de la Mala Suerte.** Yani Canneti. (Illus.). 24p. (J). (gr. 3-5). Date not set. pap. 4.50 (*1-56492-242-1*) Laredo.

Babungo. Willi Schaub. LC 85-14676. (Descriptive Grammars Ser.). 403p. 1985. 72.50 (*0-7099-3352-5*, Pub. by Croom Helm UK) Routledge Chapman & Hall.

Babur: Diarist & Despot. Stephen M. Edwardes. LC 79-180334. reprint ed. 27.50 (*0-404-56246-9*) AMS Pr.

Babur: Founder of the Mughal Empire in India. Mohibbul Hasan. 240p. 1986. 28.00 (*0-8364-1641-4*, Pub. by Manohar II) S Asia.

Babur-Nama in English: Memoirs of Babur, 2 Vols, Set. Babar Emperor of Hindustan. Tr. by Annette S. Beveridge. LC 72-161719. (BCL Ser.: No. I). reprint ed. 137.50 (*0-404-00510-1*) AMS Pr.

Babur-Nama (Memoirs of Babur), Set. Z. M. Ghazi. Tr. by A. S. Beveridge. 1989. reprint ed. 31.50 (*81-85395-07-1*, Pub. by BR Pub II) S Asia.

***Baburnama: Memoirs of Babur, Prince & Emperor.** Ed. by Wheeler M. Thackston, Jr. (Illus.). 472p. 1995. 39.95 (*0-19-509671-1*) OUP.

Babushka: An Old Russian Folktale. Charles Mikolaycak. LC 84-500. (Illus.). 32p. (J). (ps-3). 1984. lib. bdg. 15.95 (*0-8234-0520-6*); pap. 5.95 (*0-8234-0712-8*) Holiday.

Babushka Baba Yaga. Patricia Polacco. LC 92-30361. (Illus.). 32p. (J). 1993. 14.95 (*0-399-22531-5*, Philomel Bks) Putnam Pub Group.

***Babushka's Doll.** Polacco. (J). 1995. pap. 14.95 (*0-689-80255-2*, Aladdin Paperbacks) S&S Childrens.

Babushka's Doll. Patricia Polacco. LC 89-6122. (Illus.). 40p. (J). (ps-1). 1990. pap. 15.00 (*0-671-68343-8*, S&S Bks Young Read) S&S Childrens.

***Babushka's Mother Goose.** Patricia Polacco. LC 94-32332. (J). 1995. write for info. (*0-399-22747-4*, Philomel Bks) Putnam Pub Group.

Baby. LC 91-58213. (What's Inside? Ser.). (Illus.). 24p. (J). (ps-3). 1992. 8.95 (*1-56458-004-0*) Dorling Kindersley.

Baby. (Talkabouts Ser.: No. 735-5). (Illus.). (J). (ps). 3.50 (*0-7214-1121-5*) Ladybird Bks.

Baby. Monica Greenfield. (Illus.). 14p. (J). (ps). 1994. 5.95 (*0-694-00577-0*, Festival) HarpC Child Bks.

Baby. Patricia MacLachlan. LC 93-22117. (J). (gr. 1-8). 1993. 13.95 (*0-385-31133-8*) Delacorte.

Baby. Ellen Parham. 150p. (Orig.). 1992. pap. 12.95 (*0-9630835-1-1*) Whitefield Bks.

Baby. Joseph A. Stirt. LC 92-60566. 314p. 1992. 22.95 (*0-88282-111-3*) New Horizon NJ.

Baby. Nicole Taylor. LC 92-41338. (J). 1993. 16.95 (*0-88682-595-4*) Creative Ed.

Baby. Nicole Taylor. (Illus.). 40p. (YA). (gr. 6 up). 1994. 15.95 (*1-56846-089-9*) Creative Ed.

Baby. 2nd ed. John Burningham. LC 93-24277. (Illus.). 24p. (J). (ps). 1994. 6.95 (*1-56402-334-6*) Candlewick Pr.

Baby? ... Maybe: A Guide to Making the Most Fateful Decision of Your Life. Elizabeth M. Whelan. LC 75-6396. 256p. 1975. 10.95 (*0-672-52096-6*, Bobbs); pap. 6.95 (*0-672-52186-5*, Bobbs) Macmillan.

Baby Aboard. large type ed. Raye Morgan. (Silhouette Desire Ser.). 1994. 17.95 (*0-373-58856-9*, Silhouette Lrg Print) Chivers N Amer.

Baby Album. Nancy Cogan & Roni Akmon. (Illus.). 84p. 1992. 32.95 (*0-926684-03-5*) Eclectic Oregon.

Baby Alicia Is Dying. Lurlene McDaniel. (YA). 1993. pap. 3.50 (*0-553-29605-1*) Bantam.

***Baby & Child Emergency First Aid.** Mitchell Einzig. 1995. pap. 8.00 (*0-671-51976-X*) S&S Trade.

Baby & Child Emergency First-Aid Handbook. Ed. by Mitchell Einzig. (Illus.). 64p. 1992. 13.00 (*0-671-79204-0*) Meadowbrook.

***Baby & Child Emergency First Aid Handbook.** Ed. by Mitchell J. Einzig. 1995. pap. 8.00 (*0-88116-219-1*) Meadowbrook.

Baby & Child Emergency First Aid Handbook: Simple Step-by-Step Instructions for the Most Common Childhood Emergencies. Ed. by Mitchell J. Einzig. LC 92-28339. (Illus.). 96p. 1992. 13.00 (*0-88166-195-3*) Meadowbrook.

Baby & Cottentop. 360p. 1994. pap. 9.95 (*1-56901-205-9*) NW Pub.

Baby & Friends. (Shapshot Soft-to-Touch Bks.). (Illus.). 20p. (J). (ps). 1994. bds. 4.95 (*1-56458-531-X*) Dorling Kindersley.

Baby & I Can Play & Fun with Toddlers. rev. ed. Karen Hendrickson. LC 89-64200. (Getting along Together Ser.). (Illus.). 56p. (J). (ps-3). 1990. lib. bdg. 17.95 (*0-943990-57-2*); pap. 6.95 (*0-943990-56-4*) Parenting Pr.

Baby & Infant Thrift Book. rev. ed. 60p. 1991. pap. text ed. 11.95 (*0-913597-10-4*) Prosperity & Profits.

Baby & Me: The Essential Guide to Pregnancy. Deborah D. Stewart. (Illus.). 144p. 1993. spiral bd., pap. 16.95 (*1-884255-00-0*) Willapa Bay.

***Baby & Me, the Essential Guide to Pregnancy.** 2nd ed. Deborah D. Stewart. (Illus.). 144p. 1995. 16.95 (*1-884255-02-7*) Willapa Bay.

Baby & the Bear. Susan Pearson. (Illus.). (J). (ps-00). 1987. pap. 3.95 (*0-670-81299-4*) Viking Child Bks.

Baby & the Bodyguard. Jule McBride. (American Romance Ser.). 1994. mass mkt. 3.50 (*0-373-16562-5*, 1-16562-0) Harlequin Bks.

Baby & You. Claire Revelli. Ed. by Claire Zion. 320p. (Orig.). 1993. pap. 8.00 (*0-671-77727-0*) PB.

Baby Animals. (Ladybird Stories Ser.). (Illus.). (ARA.). (J). (gr. 1-3). 1987. 3.95 (*0-86685-186-0*) Intl Bk Ctr.

Baby Animals. (Modern Ser.). (Illus.). 24p. (J). (gr. k-2). 1988. 3.95 (*0-87449-500-8*) Modern Pub NYC.

Baby Animals. (Animal Information Ser.). 32p. (J). (ps-1). 1984. pap. 1.25 (*0-8431-1512-2*) Price Stern.

Baby Animals. (Animal Board Bks.). (Illus.). 8p. (J). (ps). 1988. bds. 1.99 (*0-517-66917-X*) Random Hse Value.

***Baby Animals.** Katie Atkinson. (Illus.). (J). 1995. pap. 3.95 (*1-86373-585-2*) IPG Chicago.

Baby Animals. Michael Chinery. LC 93-51048. (Little Library). (Illus.). 32p. (J). (gr. k-2). 1994. 3.95 (*1-85697-501-0*, Kingfisher LKC) LKC.

Baby Animals. Illus. by Gyo Fujikawa. (J). (ps). 1963. bds. 4.95 (*0-448-03083-7*, G&D) Putnam Pub Group.

Baby Animals. Dorling Kindersley. LC 91-27723. (Eye Openers Ser.). (Illus.). 24p. (J). (ps-00). 1992. pap. 7.95 (*0-689-71563-3*, Aladdin Paperbacks) S&S Childrens.

Baby Animals. Susan Kuchalla. LC 81-11434. (Now I Know Ser.). (Illus.). 32p. (J). (gr. k-2). 1982. lib. bdg. 11.59 (*0-89375-666-0*); pap. 2.95 (*0-89375-667-9*) Troll Assocs.

Baby Animals. Joanne Mattern. LC 91-40282. (Illus.). 24p. (J). (gr. 4-7). 1993. pap. text ed. 1.95 (*0-8167-2958-1*) Troll Assocs.

***Baby Animals.** S. Mayes. (Young Nature Ser.). (Illus.). 32p. (J). (ps-1). 1995. pap. 5.95 (*0-7460-1652-2*, Usborne) EDC.

***Baby Animals.** S. Mayes. (Young Nature Ser.). (Illus.). 32p. (J). (ps-1). 1995. lib. bdg. 13.96 (*0-88110-725-5*, Usborne) EDC.

Baby Animals. John Parr. LC 79-62943. (Cloth Bks.). (Illus.). (J). (ps). 1979. 3.50 (*0-394-84244-8*) Random Bks Yng Read.

Baby Animals. Illa Podendorf. LC 81-9938. (New True Bks.). (Illus.). 48p. (J). (gr. k-4). 1981. lib. bdg. 12.90 (*0-516-01605-9*); pap. 4.95 (*0-516-41605-7*) Childrens.

Baby Animals. Richard Roe. LC 85-2223. (Knee-High Bks.). (Illus.). 24p. (J). (ps-1). 1985. 3.95 (*0-394-86956-7*) Random Bks Yng Read.

Baby Animals. Eileen Spinelli. (Childrens' Nature Library). (Illus.). 64p. (J). (gr. k-4). 1992. lib. bdg. 13.75 (*1-878363-80-8*, HTS Bks) Forest Hse.

An Asterisk (*) at the beginning of an entry indicates that the title is appearing in BIP for the first time. 565

B

Baby Animals. John B. Wexo. (Zoobooks Ser.). 24p. (J). (gr. 4). 1989. lib. bdg. 14.95 (0-88682-270-X) Creative Ed.

Baby Animals. Wildlife Education, Ltd. Staff. (Zoobooks Ser.). (Illus.). 20p. (Orig.). (YA). (gr. 5 up). 1981. pap. 2.75 (0-937934-06-2) Wildlife Educ.

Baby Animals. Margaret W. Brown. LC 88-18481. (Illus.). 32p. (J). (ps-1). 1989. reprint ed. 15.00 (0-394-82040-1) Random Bks Yng Read.

Baby Animals. Harry McNaught. LC 75-36462. (Board Bks.). (Illus.). 14p. (J). (ps-1). 1976. reprint ed. bds. 3.95 (0-394-83241-8) Random Bks Yng Read.

Baby Animals, Vol. 2. Wildlife Education, Ltd. Staff. (Zoobooks Ser.). (Illus.). 20p. (Orig.). (J). 1992. 13.95 (0-937934-75-5); pap. 2.75 (0-937934-58-5) Wildlife Educ.

Baby Animals: Bears. Kate Petty. (Illus.). 24p. (J). (ps-3). 1992. pap. 3.95 (0-8120-4964-0) Barron.

Baby Animals: Chimpanzees. Kate Petty. (Illus.). 24p. (J). (ps-3). 1992. pap. 3.95 (0-8120-4965-9) Barron.

Baby Animals: Elephants. Kate Petty. (Illus.). 24p. (J). (ps-3). 1992. pap. 3.95 (0-8120-4966-7) Barron.

Baby Animals: Five Stories of Endangered Species. Derek Hall. LC 91-71861. (Illus.). 64p. (J). (ps up). 1992. 14.95 (1-56402-004-5) Candlewick Pr.

Baby Animals: Five Stories of Endangered Species. Derek Hall. LC 91-71861. (Illus.). 64p. (J). (ps-3). 1994. pap. 7.99 (1-56402-362-1) Candlewick Pr.

Baby Animals: Kittens. Kate Petty. (Illus.). 24p. (J). (ps-3). 1992. pap. 3.95 (0-8120-4967-5) Barron.

Baby Animals: Pandas. Kate Petty. (Illus.). 24p. (J). (ps-3). 1992. pap. 3.95 (0-8120-4968-3) Barron.

Baby Animals: Puppies. Kate Petty. (Illus.). 24p. (J). (ps-3). 1992. pap. 3.95 (0-8120-4969-1) Barron.

Baby Animals: Safe & Sound. Janet McDonnell. LC 89-23978. (Discovery World Ser.). (Illus.). 32p. (J). (ps-2). 1990. lib. bdg. 21.36 (0-89565-554-3) Childs World.

Baby Animals: Seals. Kate Petty. (Illus.). 24p. (J). (ps-3). 1992. pap. 3.95 (0-8120-4970-5) Barron.

Baby Animals: Teacher's Theme Guide. (Wonders! Ser.). (Illus.). (Orig.). 1992. pap. 29.95 (1-56334-156-5) Hampton-Brown.

Baby Animals: Theme Pack - ESL Theme Link Set, Set. (Que Maravilla! Ser.). (Illus.). (Orig.). 1993. pap. 215.00 (1-56334-373-8) Hampton-Brown.

Baby Animals: Tigers. Kate Petty. (Illus.). 24p. (J). (ps-3). 1992. pap. 3.95 (0-8120-4971-3) Barron.

Baby Animals & Their Mothers. (J). 1987. 1.95 (0-8351-1707-3) China Bks.

Baby Animals at Home. (Little Board Books Ser.: No. S851-10). (Illus.). (J). (ps-00). 1989. bds. 3.50 (0-7214-9533-8) Ladybird Bks.

***Baby Animals Board Book.** S. Mayes. (Young Nature Board Book Ser.). (Illus.). 12p. (J). (ps up). 1995. 4.50 (0-7460-1976-9, Usborne) EDC.

Baby Animals Dot-To-Dot Activity Book. Jill Osborne. (J). 1989. pap. 1.25 (0-89375-904-X) Troll Assocs.

Baby Animals Growing Up!, 7 vols., Set. Jane Burton. (Illus.). 384p. (J). (gr. 2-3). 1989. lib. bdg. 120.89 (0-8368-1171-2) Gareth Stevens Inc.

Baby Animals in the Wild. (Little Board Books Ser.: No. S851-12). (Illus.). (J). (ps-00). 1989. bds. 3.50 (0-7214-9535-4) Ladybird Bks.

Baby Animals of the North. Katy Main. (Illus.). 36p. (J). (ps-00). 1992. bds. 9.95 (0-88240-395-8) Alaska Northwest.

Baby Animals on the Farm. (Little Board Books Ser.: No. S851-11). (Illus.). (J). (ps-00). 1989. bds. 3.50 (0-7214-9534-6) Ladybird Bks.

Baby Animals Say Hello. Illus. by Norman Gorbaty. (Cuddle Cloth Bks.). 12p. (J). (ps). 1986. 4.99 (0-394-88241-5) Random Bks Yng Read.

Baby Animals Theme Pack: Level 1. (Que Maravilla! Ser.). (Illus.). (Orig.). (SPA.). 1992. pap. 148.00 (1-56334-192-1) Hampton-Brown.

Baby Animals Theme Pack: Level 1 English. (Wonders! Ser.). (Illus.). (Orig.). (J). (gr. 1-3). 1992. pap. 148.00 (1-56334-075-5) Hampton-Brown.

Baby Animals Two. (Zoobooks Ser.). (J). 1991. lib. bdg. 14.95 (0-88682-418-4) Creative Ed.

Baby Baboon. Mwenye Hadithi. LC 92-56397. (J). 1993. 15.95 (0-316-33729-3) Little.

***Baby Ball Books: Animal Babies.** Time-Life Staff. (Illus.). (J). 1995. pap. text ed. (0-8094-7844-7) Time-Life.

***Baby Ball Books: Animal Colors.** Time-Life Staff. (Illus.). 1995. pap. text ed. (0-8094-7845-5) Time-Life.

***Baby Ball Books: Funny Faces.** Time-Life Staff. (Illus.). 1995. pap. text ed. (0-8094-7842-0) Time-Life.

***Baby Ball Books: Wonderful World.** Time-Life Staff. (Illus.). (J). 1995. pap. text ed. (0-8094-7843-9) Time-Life.

Baby Bargain. Dallas Schulz. (Silhouette Intimate Moments Ser.: No. 377). 1991. mass mkt. 3.25 (0-373-07377-1) Silhouette.

***Baby Bargains: Secrets to Saving 20 to 50 Percent on Baby Furniture, Equipment, Clothes, Toys, Maternity Wear & Much, Much More!** Denise Fields & Alan Fields. 272p. (Orig.). 1994. pap. 11.95 (0-9626556-4-3) Windsor Peak Pr.

Baby Basics: Children's Activities in How Life Begins. Elizabeth R. Picco. LC 92-20519. (Illus.). 1992. write for info. (1-56071-126-4) ETR Assocs.

Baby Basics for New Parents: Quick Answers When You Need Them. Susan Limato. 160p. (Orig.). 1994. mass mkt. 4.99 (0-380-77378-3) Avon.

Baby Battle. Shannon Waverly. 1994. mass mkt. 2.99 (0-373-03316-8, 1-03316-6) Harlequin Bks.

***Baby Be-Bop.** Francesca L. Block. LC 94-44314. (Joanna Cotler Books). 96p. (YA). (gr. 6 up). 1995. 13.95 (0-06-024879-3, HarpT); lib. bdg. 13.89 (0-06-024880-7, HarpT) HarpC Child Bks.

Baby Bear. Patrick Yee. (Illus.). 12p. (J). (ps). 1994. bds. 3.99 (0-670-85288-0) Viking Child Bks.

Baby Bear Cub's Busy Day. Anne Shufflebotham. LC 91-12965. (J). (gr. 3 up). 1991. 5.99 (0-85953-425-1) Childs Play.

Baby Bear Learns Colors. Allen Snolo. (Baby Bear Pop-Ups Ser.). (J). 1988. 3.99 (0-517-65509-8) Random Hse Value.

Baby Bear Learns Numbers. (Baby Bear Pop-Ups Ser.). (J). 1988. 3.99 (0-517-65510-1) Random Hse Value.

Baby Bear Learns Opposites. (Baby Bear Pop-Ups Ser.). (J). 1988. 2.99 (0-517-65511-X) Random Hse Value.

Baby Bear Learns Shapes. (Baby Bear Pop-Ups Ser.). (J). 1988. 3.99 (0-517-65512-8) Random Hse Value.

Baby Bears & How They Grow see Books for Young Explorers

Baby Bear's Bedtime Book. Jane Yolen. LC 89-2161. 29p. (ps-3). 1990. 14.95 (0-15-205120-1) HarBrace.

Baby Bears, Bunnies & Other Little Critters. Ted Menten. 1985. pap. 3.50 (0-486-24782-1) Dover.

Baby Beautiful: A Handbook of Baby Head Shaping. Justine Dobson. LC 94-96024. (Illus.). 320p. (Orig.). 1994. pap. 19.95 (0-9640646-3-4) Heirs Pr.

Baby Beluga. Raffi. LC 89-49367. (Raffi Songs to Read Ser.). (Illus.). 32p. (J). (ps-2). 1990. 14.00 (0-517-57839-5) Crown Bks Yng Read.

Baby Beluga. Raffi. LC 89-49367. (Raffi Songs to Read Ser.). (Illus.). 32p. (J). (ps-2). 1992. pap. 4.99 (0-517-58362-3) Crown Bks Yng Read.

Baby Beluga. Raffi. 1993. pap. 4.99 (0-517-11128-4) Random Hse Value.

***Baby Bible Storybook.** Robin Currie. Ed. by Jeannie Harmon. (Illus.). 48p. (J). (ps). 1994. write for info. (0-7814-0076-7, Chariot Bks) Chariot Family.

***Baby Bird & Chick Carving.** Rosalyn Daisey. (Illus.). 208p. 1994. 49.95 (0-88740-590-8) Schiffer.

Baby Birds. Martina Bonsignori. (Illus.). 18p. (J). (ps-00). 1992. bds. 3.95 (1-56397-153-4) Boyds Mills Pr.

Baby Birds. Mary Rogers. (Cityscapes Ser.). 33p. (J). (ps-00). 1992. pap. text ed. 23.00 (1-56843-003-5); pap. text ed. 4.50 (1-56843-053-1) BGR Pub.

Baby Blessed. Debbie Macomber. 1994. mass mkt. 3.50 (0-373-09895-2, 1-09895-3) Harlequin Bks.

Baby Blue Book, 1994. 1994. pap. 5.00 (0-943716-20-9) Holmes NE.

***Baby Blue Book, 1995.** 1995. pap. 5.00 (0-943716-21-7) Holmes NE.

Baby Blue Cat & the Whole Batch of Cookies. Ainslie Pryor. (Illus.). 32p. (J). (ps-1). 1991. pap. 3.95 (0-14-050770-1, Puffin) Puffin Bks.

Baby Blue Cat Who Said No. Ainslie Pryor. (Illus.). 32p. (J). (ps-1). 1990. pap. 3.95 (0-14-050768-X, Puffin) Puffin Bks.

Baby Blue Cat Who Said No. Ainslie Pryor. LC 87-21026. (Illus.). 32p. (J). (ps-00). 1988. 14.99 (0-670-81780-5) Viking Child Bks.

Baby Blue, 1990. 1990. Minor League Casebook. pap. 5.00 (0-943716-10-1) Holmes NE.

Baby Blue, 1991. 1991. 5.00 (0-943716-14-4) Holmes NE.

Baby Blue, 1992. 1992. pap. 5.00 (0-943716-16-0) Holmes NE.

Baby Blue, 1993. 1993. pap. 5.00 (0-943716-18-7) Holmes NE.

Baby Blues. Kristine Rolofson. 1994. mass mkt. 2.99 (0-373-25594-2, 1-25594-2) Harlequin Bks.

***Baby Blues.** Hope Wurmfeld. 96p. (YA). (gr. 7 up). 1995. pap. 3.99 (0-14-034870-0) Puffin Bks.

Baby Blues: An Adam Joshua Story. Janice L. Smith. LC 93-14492. (Illus.). 96p. (J). (gr. 1-4). 1994. 12.00 (0-06-023642-6, HarpT) HarpC.

Baby Blues: An Adam Joshua Story. Janice L. Smith. LC 93-14492. (Illus.). 96p. (J). (gr. 1-4). 1994. lib. bdg. 11.89 (0-06-023643-4, HarpT) HarpC.

Baby Blues: This Is Going to Be Tougher Than We Thought. Rick Kirkman & Jerry Scott. (Illus.). 128p. (Orig.). 1991. pap. 8.95 (0-8092-3996-5) Contemp Bks.

Baby Bonus. Maggie Simpson. (Superromance Ser.). 1993. mass mkt. 3.50 (0-373-70577-8, 1-70577-1) Harlequin Bks.

Baby Boo. Stephen F. Horan, Sr. (J). 1994. 7.95 (0-533-10753-9) Vantage.

Baby Boo! Illus. by Dana Regan. 12p. (J). (ps). 1992. 5.99 (0-679-81544-9) Random Bks Yng Read.

Baby Book. Kathy Cruickshank. (Golden Super Shape Bks.). (Illus.). (J). (ps-00). 1991. pap. 1.50 (0-307-10029-4, Golden Pr) Western Pub.

Baby Book. Mary Engelbreit. (Illus.). 320p. 1992. 6.95 (0-8362-4602-0) Andrews & McMeel.

Baby Book: Everything You Need to Know About Your Baby - From Birth to Age Two. William M. Sears & Martha Sears. 1993. 40.00 (0-316-77906-7); pap. 19.95 (0-316-77905-9) Little.

Baby Book for... Linda C. Franklin. (Old Fashioned Keepbook Ser.). (Illus.). 96p. 1980. 12.00 (0-934504-03-2) Michel Pub Co.

Baby Book for... Linda Franklin. (Illus.). 96p. 1990. reprint ed. 16.00 (0-685-44911-4) Country Diary.

Baby Book for Grandparents. Bob Cook et al. (Illus.). 40p. 1985. pap. 4.95 (0-916043-02-9) Light Hearted Pub Co.

Baby Books. Chris Hadden et al. 1982. pap. 7.90 (0-941298-06-X) M E Pinkham.

Baby Boom Generation & the Economy. Louise B. Russell. LC 82-70890. (Studies in Social Economics). 183p. 1982. 26.95 (0-8157-7628-4); pap. 9.95 (0-8157-7627-6) Brookings.

Baby Boom Radios, Vol. 1. Sams. 1991. pap. 16.95 (0-7906-1002-7, Prompt Pubns) H W Sams.

Baby Boom Radios, Vol. 2. Sams. 1991. pap. 16.95 (0-7906-1003-5, Prompt Pubns) H W Sams.

Baby Boom Radios, Vol. 3. Sams. 1991. pap. 16.95 (0-7906-1004-3, Prompt Pubns) H W Sams.

Baby Boom Radios, Vol. 4. Sams. 1991. pap. 16.95 (0-7906-1005-1, Prompt Pubns) H W Sams.

Baby Boom Radios, Vol. 5. Sams. 1991. pap. 16.95 (0-7906-1006-X, Prompt Pubns) H W Sams.

Baby Boom Radios, Vol. 6. Sams. 1991. pap. 16.95 (0-7906-1007-8, Prompt Pubns) H W Sams.

***Baby Boomer Blues.** Great Quotations Staff. 366p. (Orig.). 1994. spiral bd., pap. 8.95 (1-56245-167-7) Great Quotations.

***Baby Boomer Games, Identification & Value Guide.** Rick Polizzi. 1995. 24.95 (0-89145-631-7, 3956) Collector Bks.

Baby Boomer Retirement: Sixty-Five Simple Ways to Protect Your Future. Don Silver. LC 94-19422. 208p. (Orig.). 1994. pap. 9.95 (0-944708-65-X) Adams Hall.

Baby Boomer Spirituality: Ten Essential Values of a Generation. Craig K. Miller. LC 91-72143. 192p. 1992. pap. 12.95 (0-88177-106-6, DR106) Discipleship Res.

Baby Boomer Toys & Collectibles. Carol Turpen. LC 92-63109. (Illus.). 204p. (Orig.). 1993. pap. 29.95 (0-88740-495-2) Schiffer.

Baby Boomerang: Catching Baby Boomers As They Return to Church. Doug Murren. Ed. by Earl Roe. LC 90-46029. 200p. 1990. pap. 9.99 (0-8307-1395-6, 5419951) Regal.

Baby Boomers. Paul C. Light. 1988. 19.95 (0-393-02524-1) Norton.

Baby Boomers. Paul C. Light. 1990. pap. 8.95 (0-393-30639-9) Norton.

Baby Bop Discovers Shapes. Stephen White. Ed. by Linda Hartley. LC 93-77867. (Illus.). 14p. (J). (ps-00). 1993. bds. 4.95 (1-57064-010-6) Barney Pub.

Baby Bop Goes to School. Mark Bernthal. Ed. by Linda C. Dowdy. LC 93-74290. (Illus.). 24p. (J). (ps-00). 1994. 4.95 (1-57064-020-3) Barney Pub.

Baby Bop Pretends. Mary A. Dudko & Margie Larsen. Ed. by Linda C. Dowdy. LC 93-74289. (Illus.). 24p. (J). (ps-00). 1994. pap. 2.25 (1-57064-022-X) Barney Pub.

Baby Bop's ABC's. Mark Bernthal. Ed. by Linda Hartley. LC 93-77869. (Illus.). 32p. (J). (ps-00). 1993. pap. 2.25 (1-57064-008-4) Barney Pub.

Baby Bop's Counting Book. Mary A. Dudko & Margie Larsen. Ed. by Linda Hartley. LC 93-77866. 22p. (J). (ps). 1993. reprint ed. bds. 3.95 (1-57064-006-8) Barney Pub.

Baby Bop's Foods. Mary A. Dudko & Margie Larsen. Ed. by Linda C. Dowdy. LC 93-74291. (Illus.). 24p. (J). (ps). 1994. bds. 3.95 (1-57064-014-9) Barney Pub.

Baby Bop's Toys. Kimberly Kearns & Marie O'Brien. Ed. by Linda Hartley. LC 93-77015. (Illus.). 24p. (J). (ps). 1993. bds. 3.95 (1-57064-003-3) Barney Pub.

Baby Born in a Stable. A. H. Kramer-Lampher. LC 65-15145. (Arch Bks.). (J). (gr. k-4). 1965. pap. 1.99 (0-570-06013-3, 59-1118) Concordia.

Baby Born in a Stable: The Christmas Story. Bd. with Secret Journey: Mary & Joseph. (J). (ps-3). 1979. Set audio 6.99 (0-570-08054-1, 59-2105) Concordia.

Baby Breakdown. Ed. by Anne Waldman. LC 73-125999. 1970. 5.00 (0-672-51335-8, Bobbs) Macmillan.

Baby Brendon's Busy Day: A Sexuality Primer. Donna A. Jennings. LC 93-79755. (Illus.). 32p. (J). (ps-00). 1994. 15.95 (0-9638079-0-0) Goose Pond.

Baby Bright Board Books: ABC's. Sia Aryai. (Illus.). (J). 1993. 5.95 (1-56565-049-2) Lowell Hse.

Baby Bright Board Books: Colors. Sia Aryai. (Illus.). (J). 1993. 5.95 (1-56565-050-6) Lowell Hse.

Baby Bright Board Books: Shapes. Sia Aryai. (Illus.). (J). 1993. 5.95 (1-56565-051-4) Lowell Hse.

Baby Bright Board Books: 123's. Sia Aryai. (Illus.). (J). 1993. 5.95 (1-56565-048-4) Lowell Hse.

Baby Brother. John Fitzgerald. LC 93-2803. (J). 1994. write for info. (0-383-03677-1) SRA Schl Grp.

Baby Bubbles. Pam Adams. (J). (gr. 3 up). 1981. 5.95 (0-85953-265-8) Childs Play.

Baby Bubbles. B. J. Johnson. (Teeny Popper Pop-Up Ser.). (J). (ps). 1994. pap. 3.50 (0-671-88606-1, Litl Simon S&S) S&S Childrens.

***Baby Buddy.** Aunt Eeebs. (Illus.). 24p. (Orig.). (J). (ps-2). 1993. pap. write for info. (1-878908-04-9) Rivercrest Indus.

Baby Bug Colors. David A. Carter. (J). (gr. 3 up). 1993. pap. 4.95 (0-671-86875-6, Litl Simon S&S) S&S Childrens.

Baby Bug Counting. David A. Carter. (Illus.). (J). (ps-6). 1993. pap. 4.95 (0-671-86876-4, Litl Simon S&S) S&S Childrens.

Baby Bug In & Out. David A. Carter. (J). (gr. 3 up). 1993. pap. 4.95 (0-671-86630-3, Litl Simon S&S) S&S Childrens.

Baby Bug Opposites. David A. Carter. (Illus.). (J). (ps-6). 1993. pap. 4.95 (0-671-86877-2, Litl Simon S&S) S&S Childrens.

Baby Bunny. Joan W. Anglund. (J). (ps). 1994. 3.95 (0-307-12498-3, Golden Pr) Western Pub.

Baby Bunny. Margaret Hillert. (Illus.). (J). (ps-00). 1981. lib. bdg. 8.99 (0-8136-5064-X, TK2272); pap. 4.79 (0-8136-5564-1, TK2273) Modern Curr.

Baby Bunny Sticker Paper Doll. Carol Munshi. (Illus.). (J). (gr. k-3). 1994. pap. 1.00 (0-486-27925-1) Dover.

Baby Bunny's Day. Elizabeth Worsley. (J). (ps). 1992. bds. 2.50 (0-681-41486-3) Longmeadow Pr.

Baby Bunny's Garden. Elizabeth Worsley. (J). (ps). 1992. bds. 2.50 (0-681-41488-X) Longmeadow Pr.

Baby Bunny's Party. Elizabeth Worsley. (J). (ps). 1992. bds. 2.50 (0-681-41487-1) Longmeadow Pr.

Baby Bunny's Picnic. Elizabeth Worsley. (J). (ps). 1992. bds. 2.50 (0-681-41489-8) Longmeadow Pr.

***Baby Business.** Rebecca Winters. (Romance Ser.). 1995. pap. 2.99 (0-373-03362-1, 1-03362-0) Harlequin Bks.

Baby Bust: A Generation Comes of Age. William Dunn. LC 93-71267. 213p. 1993. pap. 29.95 (0-936889-21-7) American Demo.

Baby Busters: Disillusioned Generation. George Barna. 1994. pap. 9.99 (1-881273-19-9) Northfield Pub.

***Baby by Chance: (New Arrival)** Elda Minger. (American Romance Ser.). 1995. mass mkt. 3.50 (0-373-16584-6, 1-16584-4) Harlequin Bks.

Baby Called John. Penny Frank. (Lion Story Bible Series - New Testament: No. 31). (Illus.). 24p. (J). (ps-3). 3.99 (0-85648-756-2) Lion USA.

Baby Called John see What the Bible Tells Us: Third Series

Baby Care Handbook: A Practical Guide to Infant Care from Birth to 12 Months. Shelby Clark. (Illus.). 112p. (Orig.). 1994. pap. 10.00 (0-9641324-0-0) New Shoes.

***Baby Cat-Face: A Novel.** Ed. by Barry Gifford. LC 95-1148. 192p. 1995. 20.00 (0-15-100183-9) HarBrace.

Baby Challenge: A Handbook on Pregnancy for Women with a Physical Disability. Mukti J. Campion. 208p. 1990. 55.00 (0-415-04858-3, A4693); pap. 14.95 (0-415-04859-1, A4697) Routledge.

***Baby Clown: A Pull-the-Tab Book.** large type ed. Thierry Dedieu. LC 94-78166. (Illus.). 16p. (J). (ps-1). 1995. 12.95 (0-7868-0075-5) Hyprn Child.

Baby, Come Back. Erica Spindler. (Special Edition Ser.). 1994. mass mkt. 3.50 (0-373-09903-7, 1-09903-5) Harlequin Bks.

Baby Comes Home. Debbie Driscoll. LC 91-2414. (Illus.). 40p. (J). (ps-00). 1993. pap. 14.00 (0-671-75540-4, S&S Bks Young Read) S&S Childrens.

Baby Cookbook: Tasty & Nutritious Meals for the Whole Family. rev. ed. Karin Knight. 1992. pap. 13.00 (0-688-10358-8, Quill) Morrow.

***Baby Crafts: Over 25 Projects to Make & Give.** Juliet Moxley. (Illus.). 96p. 1995. 19.95 (0-09-178692-4, Pub. by Ebury Pr UK) Trafalgar.

***Baby Crow.** John A. Rowe. LC 94-18652. (J). (gr. k-3). 1994. 16.95 (1-55858-277-0); 16.88 (1-55858-278-9) North-South Bks NYC.

Baby Daisy's Walk. (Golden Board Bks.). (Illus.). 10p. (J). (ps). 1986. write for info. (0-307-06095-0, Golden Bks) Western Pub.

Baby Days & Lullabye Nights. Illus. by Teresa Ragland. 48p. (J). 1993. 17.95 (0-8249-8619-9, Ideals Child); audio, boxed 24.95 (0-8249-7629-0, Ideals Child) Hambleton-Hill.

Baby Dear: The Sweet Nellie Book of Traditional Advice, Sentiments & Expressions of Endearment from the Past. Pat Ross. (Illus.). 64p. 1993. 8.95 (0-670-84438-1, Viking Studio) Studio Bks.

Baby Di Changes Color. Highlights for Children Staff. (Illus.). (J). (ps-2). 1991. pap. 2.95 (0-87534-332-5) Highlights.

Baby Dino's Busy Day. (Surprise Bks.). (Illus.). 24p. (J). (ps-1). 1988. 6.95 (0-8431-4730-X) Price Stern.

***Baby Dinosaur Board Books.** Time-Life Staff. (Illus.). (J). 1992. bds. (0-8094-7838-2) Time-Life.

Baby Dinosaurs. Helen R. Sattler. LC 83-25631. (Illus.). 40p. (J). (ps-3). 1984. 14.00 (0-688-03817-4); lib. bdg. 13.93 (0-688-03818-2) Lothrop.

Baby Doctor. Perri Klass. 1993. mass mkt. 5.99 (0-8041-0963-X) Ivy Books.

Baby Doctor. Perri Klass. 1992. 21.50 (0-679-40957-2) Random.

Baby Doctor. Peggy Moreland. (Desire Ser.). 1994. mass mkt. 2.99 (0-373-05867-5, 1-05867-6) Silhouette.

Baby Dodds Story. Baby Dodds. LC 91-41646. (Illus.). 144p. 1992. pap. 9.95 (0-8071-1756-0) La State U Pr.

Baby Doll & Tiger Tail. Tennessee Williams. LC 91-6848. 256p. 1991. 23.95 (0-8112-1166-5); pap. 11.95 (0-8112-1167-3, NDP714) New Directions.

Baby Doll Games. Margaret Maron. 208p. 1995. mass mkt. 5.50 (0-446-40418-7, Mysterious Paperbk) Warner Bks.

Baby Doll Games. large type ed. Margaret Maron. (Mystery Ser.). 448p. 1992. 21.95 (0-7089-2775-0) Ulverscroft.

Baby Doll Murders. James O. Causey. LC 88-71696. 160p. reprint ed. pap. 7.95 (0-88739-128-1, Blk Lizard) Creat Arts Bk.

Baby Dolly. Ruby J. Jensen. 1991. mass mkt. 4.99 (0-8217-3598-5) Zebra.

Baby Donald at the Playground. (Golden Board Bks.). (Illus.). 10p. (J). (ps). 1986. write for info. (0-307-06096-9, Golden Bks) Western Pub.

Baby Donald's Busy Play Group. Illus. by Darrell Baker. LC 87-81947. (Golden Sturdy Shape Bks.). 14p. (J). (ps-1). 1988. write for info. (0-307-12316-2) Western Pub.

Baby Dreams of Childless Women. Ed. by Barbara Lloyd McMichael. LC 93-84754. (Illus.). 90p. (Orig.). 1993. pap. 5.95 (0-9636683-0-7) Pacific Cent.

Baby Eats! Homemade Recipes for Healthy, Happy Babies. Lois Smith. 272p. (Orig.). 1994. mass mkt. 4.99 (0-425-14120-9) Berkley Pub.

Baby Elephant's Bedtime. Dick McCue. (Animal Shape Board Bks.). (Illus.). 24p. (J). (ps). 1985. pap. 2.95 (0-671-55853-6, Litl Simon S&S) S&S Childrens.

Baby English: A Dictionary for Interpreting the Secret Language of Babies. Bill Adler, Jr. & Karen Adler. Ed. by Claire Zion. (Illus.). 128p. (Orig.). 1993. pap. 8.00 (0-671-79503-1) PB.

***Baby Face.** Brewer. (Illus.). (J). 1995. mass mkt. 5.50 (0-671-74735-5) PB.

Baby Face: A Mirror Book. Gwynne L. Isaacs & Evelyn C. Mott. LC 93-84221. (Illus.). 14p. (J). (ps). 1994. 4.99 (0-679-84981-5) Random Bks Yng Read.

Baby Face Nelson. Sue Hamilton. Ed. by John Hamilton. LC 89-84922. (America's Most Wanted Ser.). (Illus.). 32p. (J). (gr. 4). 1989. lib. bdg. 11.96 (0-939179-61-X) Abdo & Dghtrs.

566 An Asterisk (*) at the beginning of an entry indicates that the title is appearing in BIP for the first time.

An Asterisk (*) at the beginning of an entry indicates that the title is appearing in BIP for the first time.

567

B

Baby-Sitters Club, Bks. 13-16. Ann M. Martin. (J). (gr. 3-7). 1991. boxed, pap. 13.00 (*0-590-63705-3*) Scholastic Inc.

Baby-Sitters Club, Bks. 17-20. Ann M. Martin. (J). (gr. 3-7). 1991. boxed, pap. 13.00 (*0-590-63704-5*) Scholastic Inc.

Baby-Sitters Club, Bks. 21-24. Ann M. Martin. (J). (gr. 3-7). 1991. boxed, pap. 13.00 (*0-590-63703-7*) Scholastic Inc.

Baby-Sitters Club, Bks. 29-32. Ann M. Martin. (J). (gr. 4-7). 1990. boxed, pap. 13.00 (*0-590-63583-2*) Scholastic Inc.

Baby-Sitters Club, 4 vols., Bks. 33-36. Ann M. Martin. (J). (gr. 4-7). 1990. Boxed set. boxed 13.00 (*0-590-63669-3*) Scholastic Inc.

Baby Sitters Club, Set, No. 2. Ann M. Martin. 1987. Set no. 2. pap. 11.00 (*0-590-63351-1*) Scholastic Inc.

Baby-Sitter's Club, Set, No. 5. Ann M. Martin. (J). (gr. 4 up). 1989. Set no. 5. pap. 11.00 (*0-590-63344-9*) Scholastic Inc.

Baby-Sitters Club, No. 45-48. Ann M. Martin. (J). (gr. 4-7). 1991. boxed, pap. 13.00 (*0-590-63963-3*) Scholastic Inc.

***Baby-Sitters Club, 20 vols., Set.** large type ed. Ann M. Martin. 176p. (J). 1994. lib. bdg. 318.60 (*0-8368-1267-0*) Gareth Stevens Inc.

***Baby-Sitters Club: The Movie.** Scholastic. 1995. pap. (*0-590-54085-8*); pap. (*0-590-60403-1*); pap. (*0-590-60404-X*); pap. (*0-590-60405-8*) Scholastic Inc.

***Baby-Sitters Club - Set 2, 10 vols.** large type ed. Ann M. Martin. 176p. (J). 1994. lib. bdg. 159.30 (*0-8368-1241-7*) Gareth Stevens Inc.

Baby-Sitters Club Guide to Baby-Sitting. Ann M. Martin. (J). (gr. 4-7). 1993. pap. 3.25 (*0-590-47686-6*) Scholastic Inc.

Baby-Sitter's Club, No. 26: Claudia & the Sad Good-Bye. Ann M. Martin. 1989. pap. 3.50 (*0-590-42503-X*) Scholastic Inc.

Baby Sitter's Club, No. 30: Mary Anne & the Great Romance. Ann M. Martin. 1990. pap. 3.50 (*0-590-42498-X*) Scholastic Inc.

Baby-Sitter's Club, No. 32: Kristy & the Secret of Susan. Ann M. Martin. (J). (gr. 4-7). 1990. pap. 3.50 (*0-590-42496-3*) Scholastic Inc.

Baby-Sitter's Club, No. 33: Claudia & the Great Search. Ann M. Martin. (J). (gr. 4-7). 1990. pap. 3.25 (*0-590-42495-5*) Scholastic Inc.

Baby-Sitters Club, No. 50: Dawn's Big Date. Ann M. Martin. (J). (gr. 4-7). 1992. pap. 3.50 (*0-590-44969-9*) Scholastic Inc.

Baby-Sitters Club Notebook. Sonia Black & Pat Brigandi. (Illus.). (J). (gr. 5 up). 1991. pap. 2.50 (*0-590-45074-3*) Scholastic Inc.

Baby-Sitters Club Postcard Book. Ann M. Martin. (J). (gr. 4-7). 1991. pap. 4.95 (*0-590-44783-1*) Scholastic Inc.

Baby-Sitters Club Super Summer Special, Bks. 1-3. Ann M. Martin. (J). (gr. 3-7). 1991. boxed 10.50 (*0-590-63714-2*) Scholastic Inc.

Baby-Sitter's Guide. Nancy Burgeson. LC 91-14959. (Survival Guide Ser.). (Illus.). 32p. (J). (gr. 5-9). 1991. pap. text ed. 1.95 (*0-8167-2467-9*) Troll Assocs.

Baby Sitters Guide by Dennis. Hank Ketcham. (Illus.). 1985. pap. 3.50 (*0-449-12888-1*) Fawcett.

***Baby-Sitters Haunted House.** Ann M. Martin. (Baby-Sitters Club Super Mystery Ser.: No. 1). (J). (gr. 3-7). 1995. pap. 3.99 (*0-590-48311-0*) Scholastic Inc.

Baby-Sitters Little Sister, Bks. 5-8. Ann M. Martin. (J). (gr. 2-4). 1990. boxed 11.00 (*0-590-63593-X*) Scholastic Inc.

Baby-Sitters Little Sister, Bks. 9-12. Ann M. Martin. (J). (gr. 2-4). 1990. boxed, pap. 11.00 (*0-590-63668-5*) Scholastic Inc.

Baby-Sitters Little Sister, Bks. 17-20. Ann M. Martin. (J). 1991. boxed, pap. 11.00 (*0-590-63950-1*) Scholastic Inc.

Baby-Sitters Little Sister: School Scrapbook. Ann M. Martin. (J). (gr. 7-9). 1993. pap. 2.95 (*0-590-47677-7*) Scholastic Inc.

Baby-Sitters Little Sister Boxed Set, 4 bks., Set. Ann M. Martin. (J). 1992. 11.00 (*0-590-66125-6*) Scholastic Inc.

Baby-Sitters Little Sister, No. 24: Karen's School Trip. Ann M. Martin. (J). (gr. 4-7). 1992. pap. 2.95 (*0-590-44859-5*) Scholastic Inc.

Baby-Sitters Little Sister No. 32: Karen's Pumpkin Patch. Ann M. Martin. (Baby-Sitters Club Ser.). (J). 1992. 2.95 (*0-590-45647-4*) Scholastic Inc.

Baby-Sitters Little Sisters: Secret Diary. Ann M. Martin. (J). (gr. 4-7). 1991. pap. 2.50 (*0-590-45010-7*) Scholastic Inc.

Baby-Sitter's Nightmare II. Kate Daniel. (YA). 1994. mass mkt. 3.99 (*0-06-106232-4*, Harp PBks) HarpC.

Baby-Sitters on Board! Ann M. Martin. (Orig.). (YA). (gr. 3-6). 1988. pap. 3.95 (*0-590-44240-6*) Scholastic Inc.

Baby-Sitters Remember. Ann M. Martin. (Baby-Sitters Club Super Special Ser.: no. 11). (J). (gr. 4-7). 1994. pap. 3.95 (*0-590-47015-9*) Scholastic Inc.

Baby-Sitters' Summer Vacation Super Special, No. 2. Ann M. Martin. (J). 1989. pap. 3.95 (*0-590-44239-2*) Scholastic Inc.

Baby-Sitters' Winter Vacation Super Special, No. 3. Ann M. Martin. (J). 1989. pap. 3.95 (*0-590-43973-1*) Scholastic Inc.

***Baby-Sitting Is a Dangerous Job.** Roberts. (J). 1996. pap. 3.95 (*0-689-80657-4*, Mac Bks Young Read) S&S Childrens.

Baby-Sitting Is a Dangerous Job. Willo D. Roberts. 144p. (J). 1987. mass mkt. 3.99 (*0-449-70177-8*, Juniper) Fawcett.

Baby-Sitting Is a Dangerous Job. Willo D. Roberts. LC 84-20445. 168p. (J). (gr. 4-6). 1985. text ed. 14.95 (*0-689-31100-1*, Atheneum Bks Young) S&S Childrens.

Baby Skin: A Leading Dermatologist's Guide to Infant & Childhood Skin Care. Nelson L. Novick. 192p. 1991. pap. 13.00 (*0-517-58422-0*, C P Pubs) Crown Pub Group.

Baby-Snatcher. Susan Terris. 192p. (J). (gr. 5 up). 1985. 14.00 (*0-374-30473-4*) FS&G.

Baby Steps: A Parents' Guide to Understanding During the First Two Years. Claire B. Kopp & Donne L. Bean. LC 93-10365. (C). 1995. text ed. write for info. (*0-7167-2390-5*) W H Freeman.

Baby Steps: A Parents' Guide to Understanding During the First Two Years. Claire B. Kopp & Donne L. Bean. LC 93-10365. (C). 1995. pap. text ed. write for info. (*0-7167-2499-5*) W H Freeman.

Baby Sweet's. Raymond Andrews. LC 88-15344. (Brown Thrasher Bks.). (Illus.). 232p. 1988. reprint ed. pap. 10.95 (*0-8203-1069-7*) U of Ga Pr.

Baby Swim Book. Cinda L. Kochen & Janet McCabe. LC 86-10249. (Illus.). 240p. 1986. pap. 15.95 (*0-88011-312-X*, PKOC0312) Human Kinetics.

Baby Tactics: Parenting Tips That Really Work. Barbara A. Hill. LC 91-24672. (Illus.). 192p. (Orig.). 1991. pap. 8.95 (*0-89529-489-3*) Avery Pub.

Baby Talk. L. E. Blair. (Girl Talk Ser.: No. 21). 128p. (J). (gr. 4-7). 1992. 2.95 (*0-307-22021-4*, 22021) Western Pub.

Baby Talk. Dale Hatcher & Kathleen Lehman. Ed. by Joy Johnson. (Illus.). 24p. 1985. pap. 2.95 (*1-56123-031-6*) Centering Corp.

Baby Talk. Anne Miranda. (Lift-&-Look Flap Bks.). (Illus.). 16p. (J). (ps). 1987. 9.95 (*0-525-44319-3*, 0772-230, DCB) Dutton Child Bks.

***Baby Talk.** Julianna Morris. (Romance Ser.). 1995. mass mkt. 2.99 (*0-373-19097-2*, 1-19097-4) Silhouette.

Baby Talk. Illus. by Erika Stone. (Pudgy Board Bks.). 18p. (J). (ps). 1992. bds. 2.95 (*0-448-40312-9*, G&D) Putnam Pub Group.

***Baby Talk: A Chunky Book.** Hayward. LC 94-67205. 1995. 3.25 (*0-679-85457-6*) Random.

Baby Talk: How to Learn the Language of Infants & Toddlers - & Teach Them to Talk to You, Too. Monica Devine. 1993. mass mkt. 4.99 (*0-425-13984-0*) Berkley Pub.

Baby Talk: The Art of Communicating with Infants & Toddlers. M. Devine. LC 90-28793. (Illus.). 262p. 1991. 21.50 (*0-306-43762-7*, Plenum Insight) Plenum.

Baby Tam Talking to You, Vol. I. Luong S. Hang. 90p. (Orig.). 1992. pap. 5.00 (*0-9633690-1-6*) Vo Vi Frndship.

Baby Tam Talking to You, Vol. II. Luong Si Hang. Ed. by Vuong Thanh Son & William Messick. Tr. by Xuan-Mai Nguyen. 96p. 1994. pap. 6.00 (*0-9633690-3-2*) Vo Vi Frndship.

Baby Times Two. Marie Farrarella. 1994. pap. 2.75 (*0-373-19037-9*, 1-19037-0) Harlequin Bks.

Baby Train: And Other Lusty Urban Legends. Jan H. Brunvand. 352p. 1993. 20.95 (*0-393-03438-0*) Norton.

***Baby Train: And Other Lusty Urban Legends.** Jan H. Brunvand. 1994. pap. 9.98 (*0-393-31208-9*, Norton Paperbks) Norton.

Baby Trap. Jule McBride. (American Romance Ser.). 1994. mass mkt. 3.50 (*0-373-16519-6*, 1-16519-0) Harlequin Bks.

Baby Uggs Are Hatching. Jack Prelutsky. LC 81-7266. (Illus.). 32p. (J). (ps up). 1989. pap. 3.95 (*0-688-09239-X*, Mulberry) Morrow.

Baby Uggs Are Hatching! Jack Prelutsky. LC 81-7266. (Illus.). 32p. (J). (gr. k-3). 1982. 15.00 (*0-688-00922-0*); lib. bdg. 14.93 (*0-688-00923-9*) Greenwillow.

***Baby vs. the Bar.** M. J. Rodgers. 1995. mass mkt. 3.50 (*0-373-22342-0*, 1-22342-9) Harlequin Bks.

Baby Walk. Anne Miranda. (Lift-&-Look Flap Bks.). (Illus.). 14p. (J). (ps). 1988. 8.95 (*0-525-44421-1*, DCB) Dutton Child Bks.

***Baby Wanted.** Cathie Linz. (Montana Mavericks Ser.). 1995. mass mkt. 3.99 (*0-373-50174-9*, 1-50174-1) Harlequin Bks.

Baby Wants the Moon. Sal Murdocca. LC 94-14517. (Illus.). 32p. (J). (ps up). 1994. 15.00 (*0-688-13664-8*); lib. bdg. 14.93 (*0-688-13665-6*) Lothrop.

Baby Whale. Lynn Wilson. (All Aboard Bks.). (Illus.). 32p. (J). (ps-2). 1991. pap. 1.95 (*0-448-40072-3*, G&D) Putnam Pub Group.

Baby Whales Drink Milk. Barbara J. Esbensen. LC 92-30375. (Let's-Read-&-Find-Out Science Bk.: Stage 1). (Illus.). 32p. (J). (ps-1). 1994. 15.00 (*0-06-021551-8*); lib. bdg. 14.89 (*0-06-021552-6*) HarpC Child Bks.

Baby Whales Drink Milk. Barbara J. Esbensen. LC 92-30375. (Let's-Read-&-Find-Out Science Bk.: Stage 2). (Illus.). 32p. (J). (ps-1). 1994. pap. 4.95 (*0-06-445119-4*, Trophy) HarpC Child Bks.

Baby Who Knew Too Much. Georgia A. Johnson. LC 93-91516. 256p. (Orig.). 1993. pap. 7.95 (*0-9626450-2-8*) G A Johnson Pub.

Baby Who Would Not Come Down. Joan Knight. LC 89-3987. (Illus.). 28p. (J). (ps up). 1991. pap. 14.95 (*0-88708-107-X*, Picture Book Studio) S&S Childrens.

Baby Wiggles - Baby Plays. Lizi Boyd. LC 92-50278. (J). (ps). 1992. 8.95 (*1-56305-310-1*) Workman Pub.

Baby Wiggles - Bunny Hop. Liz Boyd. LC 92-50279. (J). (ps). 1992. 8.95 (*1-56305-308-X*) Workman Pub.

Baby Wild Animals. (Baby Animal Padded Photo Board Bks.). (Illus.). 18p. (J). (ps). 1992. bds. 4.50 (*1-56288-306-2*) Checkerboard.

Baby Wish. Myrna Mackenzie. 1994. pap. 2.75 (*0-373-19046-8*, 1-19046-1, Pergamon Pr) Elsevier.

Baby with the Bathwater. Christopher Durang. 1984. pap. 4.75 (*0-8222-0084-8*) Dramatists Play.

Baby, Would I Lie? Donald E. Westlake. 304p. 1994. 19.95 (*0-89296-532-0*) Mysterious Pr.

***Baby, Would I Lie?** Donald E. Westlake. 320p. 1995. mass mkt. 5.99 (*0-446-40342-3*, Mysterious Paperbk) Warner Bks.

***Baby Would I Lie?** large type ed. Donald E. Westlake. 438p. 1994. 20.95 (*0-7862-0343-9*) Thorndike Pr.

***Baby Zoo.** McMillan. (J). 1995. pap. 3.95 (*0-590-44635-5*) Scholastic Inc.

Baby Zoo. Bruce McMillan. 32p. (J). 1992. 13.95 (*0-590-44634-7*, Scholastic Hardcover) Scholastic Inc.

Baby Zoo Animals. (Happytime Ser.: No. S871-1). (Illus.). (J). (ps). pap. 1.25 (*0-7214-9545-1*) Ladybird Bks.

Babycakes. Maupin Armistead. 1994. pap. 12.00 (*0-06-092483-7*, PL) HarpC.

Babydoll. Marilyn Knight. 1988. pap. 3.95 (*0-8217-2530-0*) Zebra.

Babyface. Norma F. Mazer. 176p. (YA). 1991. mass mkt. 3.99 (*0-380-75720-6*, Flare) Avon.

Babyface. Norma F. Mazer. LC 90-6485. 176p. (YA). (gr. 7 up). 1990. 15.00 (*0-688-08752-3*) Morrow Jr Bks.

***Babygetter: And Other Homefolk Tales.** Randee Eddins. (Illus.). 36p. (Orig.). 1994. 6.00 (*0-940880-53-9*) Open Hand.

Babyhood. enl. rev. ed. Penelope Leach. LC 82-48881. 1983. pap. 16.00 (*0-394-71436-9*) Knopf.

Babyland: A Book for Babies. Illus. & Sel. by Jane Dyer. LC 93-4244. (J). 1996. 17.95 (*0-316-19766-1*) Little.

Babylon. Anthony Esler. 320p. 1981. pap. 2.75 (*0-449-24375-3*, Crest) Fawcett.

Babylon. Joan C. Oates. (Ancient Peoples & Places Ser.). (Illus.). 1986. pap. 15.95 (*0-500-27384-7*) Thames Hudson.

Babylon Electrified. A. Bleunard. 1972. 59.95 (*0-87968-690-1*) Gordon Pr.

Babylon Gardens. Timothy Mason. 1993. 4.75 (*0-8222-1369-9*) Dramatists Play.

Babylon Mystery Religion: Ancient & Modern. Ralph Woodrow. (Illus.). 1981. 4.95 (*0-916938-00-X*) R Woodrow.

Babylon or Jerusalem. Jan W. Van Der Hoeven. 196p. (Orig.). 1993. pap. 9.99 (*1-56043-114-8*) Destiny Image.

Babylon Revisited: The Screenplay. F. Scott Fitzgerald. 192p. 1993. pap. 10.95 (*0-88184-968-5*) Carroll & Graf.

Babylon Revisited & Other Stories. F. Scott Fitzgerald. 272p. 1960. pap. 11.00 (*0-684-71757-3*, Scribners) S&S Trade.

Babylon Revisited & Other Stories. F. Scott Fitzgerald. 256p. 1988. pap. 5.95 (*0-02-019980-5*, Collier S&S) S&S Trade.

***Babylon 5 No. 02: Accusations.** Tilton. 1995. mass mkt. (*0-440-22058-0*) Dell.

***Babylonia 689-627 B.C. A Political History.** Grant Frame. 396p. 1992. text ed. 52.25 (*90-6258-069-6*, Pub. by Netherlands Inst NE) Eisenbrauns.

Babylonian Akitu Festival. Svend A. Pallis. LC 78-72756. (Ancient Mesopotamian Texts & Studies). reprint ed. 42.50 (*0-404-18203-8*) AMS Pr.

Babylonian & Assyrian Laws, Contracts, & Letters. C. H. Johns. 1977. lib. bdg. 59.95 (*0-8490-1467-0*) Gordon Pr.

***Babylonian & Assyrian Laws, Contracts & Letters.** C. H. Johns. LC 94-75661. 448p. 1994. 90.00 (*1-56169-096-1*) W W Gaunt.

***Babylonian Archival Texts in the Nies Babylonian Collection.** Gary Beckman. Ed. by Ulla Kasten. (Catalogue of the Babylonian Collections at Yale: No. 2). viii, 173p. (C). 1995. 48.00 (*1-883053-11-0*) CDL Pr.

Babylonian Art. Simon Harcourt-Smith. LC 76-42704. reprint ed. 37.50 (*0-404-15360-7*) AMS Pr.

Babylonian Boundary-Stones & Memorial Tablets in the British Museum, 2 vols., Set. British Museum, Department of Egyptian & Assyrian Antiquities Staff. Ed. by L. W. King. LC 78-72731. (Ancient Mesopotamian Texts & Studies). reprint ed. 65.00 (*0-404-18166-X*) AMS Pr.

Babylonian Business Transactions of the First Millenium B.C. Albert T. Clay. LC 78-63516. (Babylonian Records in the Library of J. Pierpont Morgan: No. I). reprint ed. 27.50 (*0-404-60121-9*) AMS Pr.

***Babylonian Esther Midrash: A Critical Commentary, 3 Vols., Vol. 1: To the End of Esther, Chap. 1.** Eliezer Segal. LC 94-25966. (Brown Judaic Studies: Nos. 291-293). 351p. 1994. 49.95 (*1-55540-996-2*, 140291) Scholars Pr GA.

***Babylonian Esther Midrash: A Critical Commentary, Vol. 2: To the Beginning of Esther, Chap. 5.** Eliezer Segal. LC 94-25966. (Brown Judaic Studies: Nos. 291-293). 391p. 1994. 56.95 (*1-55540-997-0*, 140292) Scholars Pr GA.

***Babylonian Esther Midrash: A Critical Commentary, Vol. 3: Esther, Chap. 5 to End.** Eliezer Segal. LC 94-25966. (Brown Judaic Studies: Nos. 291-293). 337p. 1994. 49.95 (*1-55540-998-9*, 140293) Scholars Pr GA.

Babylonian Expedition of the University of Pennsylvania: Researches & Treatises, Vol. 4. Pennsylvania University, Babylonian Expedition. Ed. by H. V. Hilprecht. LC 18-5954. (Series D: Vol. 4). 355p. reprint ed. pap. 101.20 (*0-8357-5937-7*, 2026653) Bks Demand.

Babylonian Expedition of the University of Pennsylvania: Series D: Researches & Treatises, Vol. 1. Ed. by H. V. Hilprecht. LC 84-5954. 598p. reprint ed. pap. 170.50 (*0-8357-5938-5*, 2052020) Bks Demand.

Babylonian Genesis. 2nd ed. Alexander Heidel. LC 51-822. 1963. pap. text ed. 7.95 (*0-226-32399-4*, P133) U Ch Pr.

Babylonian Historical-Literary Texts. Albert K. Grayson. LC 74-80888. (Toronto Semitic Texts & Studies: No. 3). 127p. reprint ed. pap. 36.20 (*0-8357-5939-3*, 2023626) Bks Demand.

Babylonian Historical Texts Relating to the Capture & Downfall of Babylon. Sidney Smith. xi, 164p. 1975. reprint ed. lib. bdg. 63.70 (*3-487-05615-1*, Pub. by Georg Olms GW) Lubrecht & Cramer.

Babylonian Hymns & Prayers. David V. Myhrman. 1972. 59.95 (*0-87968-691-X*) Gordon Pr.

Babylonian Legal & Business Documents: From the Time of the First Dynasty of Babylon; Chiefly from Nippur. Arno Poebel. (University of Pennsylvania, Babylonian Expedition, Series A: Cuneiform Texts: Vol. 6, Pt. 2). 251p. reprint ed. pap. 71.60 (*0-8357-5940-7*, 2052014) Bks Demand.

Babylonian Life & History. Ernest A. Budge. LC 73-18836. (Illus.). reprint ed. 45.00 (*0-404-11308-7*) AMS Pr.

Babylonian Liturgies. Stephen H. Langdon. LC 78-72746. (Ancient Mesopotamian Texts & Studies). (Illus.). reprint ed. 37.50 (*0-404-18191-0*) AMS Pr.

Babylonian Magic & Sorcery. Leonard W. King. 229p. reprint ed. lib. bdg. 83.20 (*3-487-05616-X*, Pub. by Georg Olms GW) Lubrecht & Cramer.

Babylonian Menologies & the Semitic Calendars. S. Langdon. (British Academy, London, Schweich Lectures on Biblical Archaeology Series, 1930). 1972. reprint ed. pap. 20.00 (*0-8115-1275-4*) Periodicals Srv.

Babylonian Menologies & the Semitic Calendars. Stephen H. Langdon. LC 78-72744. (Ancient Mesopotamian Texts & Studies). reprint ed. 21.50 (*0-404-18192-9*) AMS Pr.

Babylonian Planetary Omens, Enuma Anu Enlil, Tablet 50-51. Erica Reiner & D. Pingree. LC 79-67168. (Bibliotheca Mesopotamica Ser.: Vol. 2, Pt. 2). 100p. (Orig.). 1980. pap. 18.75 (*0-89003-049-9*) Undena Pubns.

Babylonian Planetary Omens, Pt. 2: The Venus Tablet. E. Reiner & D. Pingree. (Bibliotheca Mesopotamica Ser.: Vol. 2-1). 65p. (C). 1975. pap. text ed. 18.75 (*0-89003-010-3*) Undena Pubns.

Babylonian Religion & Mythology. Leonard W. King. LC 73-18854. (Illus.). reprint ed. 38.00 (*0-404-11352-4*) AMS Pr.

Babylonian Texts Relating to the Capture & Downfall of Babylon. Sidney Smith. 1972. 75.00 (*0-87968-692-8*) Gordon Pr.

Babylonian Wisdom. Stephen H. Langdon. 1976. lib. bdg. 34.95 (*0-8490-1468-9*) Gordon Pr.

Babylonian Witchcraft Literature: Case Studies. I. Tzvi Abusch. LC 87-28539. (Brown Judaic Studies). 175p. 1988. 34.95 (*1-55541-191-6*, 14-01-32) Scholars Pr GA.

***Babylonians.** H. W. F. Saggs. LC 94-44288. (Peoples of the Past Ser.). 1995. write for info. (*0-520-20222-8*) U CA Pr.

***Babylonians.** H. W. F. Saggs. LC 95-3386. (Peoples of the Past Ser.: Vol. 1). 1995. write for info. (*0-8061-2765-1*) U of Okla Pr.

Babylonisch-Assyrische Medizin in Texten und Untersuchungen: Erster Teil: Keilschrifttexte, 6 vols. Franz Koecher. Incl. 1. Keilschrifttexte aus Assur. (C). 1964. text ed. 66.70 (*3-11-000111-X*); 2. Keilschrifttexte aus Assur. (C). 1964. text ed. 66.70 (*3-11-000112-8*); 3. Keilschrifttexte aus Assur. (C). 1964. text ed. 66.70 (*3-11-000113-6*); Vol. 4. Keilschrifttexte aus Assur: Teil 4: Babylon, Nippur, Sippar, Uruk und Unbekannter Herkunft. (Illus.). 38p. 1971. text ed. 111.00 (*3-11-001596-X*); Set. Keilschrifttexte aus Ninive 1 und 2. 1980. 352.00 (*3-11-007571-7*); (GER.). (C). write for info. (*0-318-51613-6*) De Gruyter.

Babylonische Breife aus der Zeit der Hammurapidynastic. Arthur Ungnad. LC 78-72771. (Ancient Mesopotamian Texts & Studies). reprint ed. 45.00 (*0-404-18227-5*) AMS Pr.

Babylonische Texte, 5 vols., Set. Ed. by Johann N. Strassmaier. Incl. Vol. 1. Inschriften von Nabuchodnosor. LC 78-72763. 32.50 (*0-404-61451-5*); Vol. 2. Inschriften von Nabonidus. LC 78-72763. 57.50 (*0-404-61452-3*); Vol. 3. Inschriften von Cyrus. LC 78-72763. 30.00 (*0-404-61453-1*); Vol. 4. Inschriften von Cambyses. LC 78-72763. 32.50 (*0-404-61454-X*); Vol. 5. Inschriften von Darius. LC 78-72763. 40.00 (*0-404-61455-8*); LC 78-72763. (Ancient Mesopotamian Texts & Studies). reprint ed. 192.50 (*0-404-61450-7*) AMS Pr.

***Babymaker: Fertility, Fraud & the Fall of Doctor Cecil Jacobson.** Rick Nelson. 1994. mass mkt. 5.99 (*0-553-56162-6*) Bantam.

Baby?...Maybe: A Guide to Making the Most Fateful Decision of Your Life. rev. ed. Elizabeth M. Whelan. LC 79-55437. 256p. 1980. pap. 8.95 (*0-672-52629-8*) Macmillan.

Baby's ABC. Illus. by Bettina Paterson. (So Tall Board Bks.). 18p. (J). 1992. bds. 4.95 (*0-448-40130-4*, G&D) Putnam Pub Group.

Baby's ABC. Photos by Neil Ricklen. (Super Chubby Photo Board Bks.). (Illus.). 24p. (J). 1990. boxed 4.95 (*0-671-69540-1*, Litl Simon S&S) S&S Childrens.

Baby's ABC. Photos by Anita Shevett & Steve Shevett. LC 85-62427. (Chunky Bks.). (Illus.). 28p. (J). (ps). 1986. bds. 2.95 (*0-394-87870-1*) Random Bks Yng Read.

Baby's Album: A Memory Book with Three-Dimensional Illustrations. (Illus.). 28p. 1994. 14.95 (*0-670-85438-7*, Viking Studio) Studio Bks.

Baby's Animal Friends. Photos by Phoebe Dunn. LC 87-61462. (Chunky Bks.). (Illus.). 28p. (J). (ps). 1988. bds. 2.95 (*0-394-89583-5*) Random Bks Yng Read.

Baby's Animal Sounds. (Pudgy Pillow Bks.). (Illus.). 8p. (J). 1989. 3.95 (*0-448-02786-0*, G&D) Putnam Pub Group.

Baby's Baptism: Sacrament of Welcome. Elizabeth Montes & Corinne Hart. (Illus.). 32p. 1990. reprint ed. pap. text ed. 3.60 (*1-55944-019-8*, 9444) Franciscan Comns.

Baby's Bedtime Book. Kay Chorao. LC 84-6067. (Illus.). 64p. (J). (ps). 1984. 15.99 (*0-525-44149-2*, DCB) Dutton Child Bks.

Baby's Bedtime Book. Illus. & Comp. by Kay Chorao. 64p. (J). (ps). 1994. pap. 5.99 (*0-14-055384-3*, Puff Unicorn) Puffin Bks.

B

An Asterisk (*) at the beginning of an entry indicates that the title is appearing in BIP for the first time.

An Asterisk (*) at the beginning of an entry indicates that the title is appearing in BIP for the first time.

569

Baccus Backfill Experiment at the Hades Underground Research Facility at Mol, EUR 14155. B. Neerdael et al. 67p. 1992. pap. 11.00 (*92-826-4397-2*, CD-NA-14155-EN-C, Pub. by Europ Com) UNIPUB.

Bacewicz, Her Life & Works. Judith Rosen. Ed. by Wanda Wilk & Witold Lutoslawski. LC 84-80101. (Polish Music History Ser.: No. 2). (Illus.). 70p. (Orig.). 1984. pap. 10.00 (*0-916545-02-4*, ML 410 B05 R7) Friends of Pol Mus.

Bach. (Masterpieces of Piano Music Ser.). (Illus.). 192p. 1986. pap. 11.95 (*0-8256-2422-3*, AM37219) Music Sales.

Bach. Malcolm Boyd. 1987. 9.95 (*0-394-75277-5*, Vin) Random.

Bach. Tim Dowley. (Illustrated Lives of the Great Composers Ser.). (Illus.). 144p. 1987. pap. 14.95 (*0-7119-0262-3*, OP42480) Omnibus NY.

Bach. Christopher Heddington. LC 93-39719. (Compact Companions Ser.). 1994. pap. 17.50 (*0-671-88788-2*) S&S Trade.

Bach. Ann Rachlin. LC 92-9520. (Famous Children Ser.). (Illus.). (J). 1992. 5.95 (*0-8120-4991-8*) Barron.

Bach: "Mass in B Minor" John Butt. (Cambridge Music Handbooks Ser.). (Illus.). 150p. (C). 1991. pap. 10.95 (*0-521-38716-7*) Cambridge U Pr.

Bach: "The Brandenburg Concertos" Malcolm Boyd. LC 92-39751. (Cambridge Music Handbooks Ser.). (Illus.). 120p. (C). 1993. 29.95 (*0-521-38276-9*); pap. 10.95 (*0-521-38713-2*) Cambridge U Pr.

Bach: A Biography. Charles S. Terry. 1988. reprint ed. lib. bdg. 59.00 (*0-7812-0580-8*) Rprt Serv.

Bach: A Biography. Charles S. Terry. LC 78-181276. 292p. 1962. reprint ed. 49.00 (*0-403-01699-1*) Scholarly.

Bach: Essays on His Life & Music. Christoph Wolff. (Illus.). 461p. 1991. 49.95x (*0-674-05925-5*, WOLBAC) HUP.

Bach: Essays on His Life & Music. Christoph Wolff. 461p. (C). 1994. pap. 24.95x (*0-674-05926-3*) HUP.

Bach: Improvised Ornamentation & Keyboard Cadenzas. Gerhard Krapf. LC 82-61734. 100p. 1982. spiral bd., pap. 17.50 (*0-318-04473-0*) Sacred Music Pr.

Bach: Music Book Index. Eva M. Grew. 239p. 1993. reprint ed. lib. bdg. 79.00 (*0-7812-9586-6*) Rprt Serv.

Bach: Rabbi Joel Sirkes, His Life, Works & Times. Elijah J. Schochet. 19.95 (*0-87306-031-8*) Feldheim.

Bach: The Cantatas & Oratorios, 2 vols. Charles S. Terry. 1990. reprint ed. lib. bdg. 140.00 (*0-7812-9160-7*) Rprt Serv.

Bach: The Conflict Between the Sacred & the Secular. Leo Schrade. LC 73-4331. (Music Reprint Ser.). 1973. reprint ed. lib. bdg. 25.00 (*0-306-70581-8*) Da Capo.

Bach: The Passions, 2 vols. Charles S. Terry. 1990. reprint ed. lib. bdg. 140.00 (*0-7812-9161-5*) Rprt Serv.

Bach & a Catbird. John Fandel. LC 78-61306. pap. 8.50 (*0-87957-006-7*) Roth Pub.

Bach & Handel: The Consummation of the Baroque in Music. Archibald T. Davison & Christoff Wolff. (Music Reprint Ser.). 77p. 1986. reprint ed. 18.50 (*0-306-76258-7*) Da Capo.

Bach & Handel, the Consummation of the Baroque in Music. Archibald T. Davison. LC 51-10950. 84p. reprint ed. pap. 25.00 (*0-8357-5942-3*, 2006011) Bks Demand.

***Bach & the Baroque: European Source Materials from the Baroque & Early Classical Periods with Special Emphasis on the Music of J. S. Bach.** 2nd ed. Anthony Newman. LC 94-5326. 1995. lib. bdg. 48.00 (*0-945193-64-5*); pap. 32.00 (*0-945193-76-9*) Pendragon NY.

Bach, Beethoven, & Brahms for Piano. Maxwell Eckstein. 1935. pap. 9.95 (*0-8256-2009-0*) Music Sales.

Bach, Beethoven & the Boys. D. Barber. (Illus.). 164p. 1986. pap. 13.95 (*0-920151-07-8*, Pub. by Sound & Vision CN) Firefly Bks Ltd.

Bach Cantatas Requiring Limited Resources: A Guide to Editions. William J. Bullock. LC 84-2337. 58p. (C). 1984. lib. bdg. 20.50 (*0-8191-3863-0*) U Pr of Amer.

Bach Chaconne for Solo Violin: A Collection of Views. Ed. by John F Eiche. 11.50 (*0-89917-466-3*) Am String Tchrs.

Bach Chorales for Guitar. Date not set. 14.95 (*1-56222-975-3*, 95050); disk 9.95 (*0-685-75002-7*, 95050IMD); mac hd 9.95 (*0-685-75003-5*, 95050MMD) Mel Bay.

Bach English-Title Index. Ray Reeder. LC 92-37177. (Reference Books in Music: No. 20). viii, 184p. 1993. 33.00 (*0-914913-23-9*) Fallen Leaf.

Bach Family: Seven Generations of Creative Genius. Karl Geiringer. LC 80-12000. (Music Reprint Ser.: 1980). (Illus.). 1981. reprint ed. lib. bdg. 55.00 (*0-306-79596-5*) Da Capo.

***Bach Flower Oracle.** Beate Helm. 1995. 11.75 (*1-885394-10-1*) Bluestar Commun.

Bach Flower Remedies. Edward Bach. LC 79-87679. 1979. pap. 9.95 (*0-87983-193-6*) Keats.

***Bach Flower Remedies.** Weeks. 1995. pap. 9.95 (*0-85207-205-8*) Atrium Pubs.

Bach Flower Remedies for Women. Judy Howard. 1995. pap. 13.95 (*0-85207-261-9*, Pub. by C W Daniel UK) Atrium Pubs.

Bach Flower Remedies for Women. Judy Howard. 192p. Date not set. pap. 20.95 (*0-8464-4210-8*) Beekman Pubs.

Bach Flower Remedies Illustrations & Preparations. Nora Weeks & Victor Bullen. (Illus.). 96p. (Orig.). Date not set. pap. 14.95 (*0-8464-4209-4*) Beekman Pubs.

Bach Flower Remedies Repertory. 16th ed. F. J. Wheeler. 32p. pap. 3.95 (*0-8464-4207-8*) Beekman Pubs.

Bach Flower Remedies Step by Step. Judy Howard. 68p. (Orig.). Date not set. pap. 8.95 (*0-8464-4208-6*) Beekman Pubs.

Bach Flower Remedies to the Rescue. Gregory Vlamis. (Illus.). 176p. 1990. pap. 9.95 (*0-89281-378-4*) Inner Tradit.

Bach Flower Therapy. Mechthild Scheffer. 208p. (Orig.). 1987. pap. 10.95 (*0-89281-239-7*) Inner Tradit.

Bach for Catholics. Edward Schaefer. 1987. 6.95 (*0-912405-36-8*) Pastoral Pr.

Bach for Recorder. Cliff Tobey. 1979. pap. 7.95 (*0-8256-9980-0*, Ariel) Music Sales.

Bach for Three Recorders. Contrib by M. Whitney. 1976. 3.00 (*0-913334-35-9*, CM1039) Consort Music.

Bach: Improvised Ornamentation & Keyboard Cadenzas: An Approach to Creative Performance. Gerhard Krapf. LC 86-61734. (Illus.). 94p. (Orig.). 1983. pap. 17.50 (*0-89328-115-8*, PP103) Lorenz Corp.

Bach Interpretation: Articulation Marks in Primary Sources of J. S. Bach. John Butt. (Cambridge Musical Texts & Monographs). (Illus.). 250p. (C). 1990. 74.95 (*0-521-37239-9*) Cambridge U Pr.

Bach Letters. Ed. by Samuel J. Wesley. LC 81-2078. (Music Reprint Ser.). 60p. 1981. reprint ed. lib. bdg. 19.50 (*0-306-76110-6*) Da Capo.

Bach Manuscripts of Johann Peter Kellner & His Circle: A Case Study in Reception History. Russell Stinson. LC 89-23648. (Sources of Music & Their Interpretation; Duke Studies in Music). 188p. (C). 1990. text ed. 39.50 (*0-8223-1006-6*) Duke.

Bach Organ Book. Homer D. Blanchard. LC 84-62572. (Illus.). 250p. 1985. 45.00 (*0-930112-07-5*) Organ Lit.

***Bach Perspectives, Vol. 1.** Ed. by Russell Stinson. (Illus.). 270p. 1995. text ed. 35.00 (*0-8032-1042-6*) U of Nebr Pr.

Bach Sources in America. Gerhard Herz. (Illus.). 312p. (ENG & GER.). 1991. pap. 50.00 (*3-7618-0724-4*) Univ Rochester Pr.

***Bach Studies, No. 2.** Ed. by Daniel R. Melamed. (Illus.). 304p. (C). 1995. write for info. (*0-521-47067-6*) Cambridge U Pr.

Bach the Borrower. Norman Carrell. LC 79-26050. 396p. 1980. reprint ed. text ed. 35.00 (*0-313-22205-3*, CABB, Greenwood Pr) Greenwood.

Bach to Rock: An Introduction to Famous Composers & Their Music. rev. ed. Rosemary G. Kennedy. (Illus.). 161p. (Orig.). (J). (gr. 4-9). 1989. reprint ed. audio 16.95 (*0-685-45405-3*) Rosemary Corp.

Bach to Rock: An Introduction to Famous Composers & Their Music. 6th rev. ed. Rosemary G. Kennedy. (Illus.). 161p. (Orig.). (J). (gr. 4-9). 1989. reprint ed. 14.95 (*0-685-45404-5*) Rosemary Corp.

***Bachata: Social History of a Dominican Popular Music.** Deborah Pacini-Hernandez. 1995. text ed. 49.95 (*0-615-00084-3*) Temple U Pr.

***Bachata: Social History of a Dominican Popular Music.** Deborah Pacini-Hernandez. (Illus.). (Orig.). (C). 1995. text ed. 49.95 (*1-56639-299-3*); pap. text ed. 18.95 (*1-56639-300-0*) Temple U Pr.

Bachelard: Modern European Philosophy. Mary Tiles. 190p. 1985. 59.95 (*0-521-24803-5*); pap. 21.95 (*0-521-28973-4*) Cambridge U Pr.

Bachelor & the Bobby-Soxer. Sidney Sheldon. 1961. pap. 4.75 (*0-8222-0085-6*) Dramatists Play.

Bachelor at Heart. Roberta Leigh. (Presents Ser.). 1993. mass mkt. 2.99 (*0-373-11568-7*, 1-11568-2) Harlequin Bks.

Bachelor at Heart. large type ed. Roberta Leigh. (Harlequin Ser.). 1993. 18.95 (*0-263-13355-9*, Pub. by Mills & Boon UK) Thorndike Pr.

Bachelor at the Wedding: Wedding Wager. Sandra Steffen. 1994. pap. 2.75 (*0-373-19045-X*, 1-19045-3) Harlequin Bks.

Bachelor Bess: The Homesteading Letters of Elizabeth Corey, 1909-1919. Ed. by Philip L. Gerber. LC 90-36047. (American Land & Life Ser.). (Illus.). 540p. (Orig.). 1990. text ed. 44.95 (*0-87745-302-0*); pap. 17.95 (*0-87745-303-9*) U of Iowa Pr.

***Bachelor Blues.** Carolyn Zane. (Romance Ser.). 1995. mass mkt. 2.99 (*0-373-19093-X*, 1-19093-3) Silhouette.

***Bachelor Bridge: The Amorous Adventures of Jack O'Hearts.** David Bird & Simon Cocheme. 144p. 1995. pap. 13.95 (*0-575-05814-5*, Pub. by V Gollancz UK) Trafalgar.

Bachelor Cure. Pepper Adams. (Silhouette Romance Ser.). 1994. pap. 2.75 (*0-373-19003-4*, 5-19003-8) Harlequin Bks.

Bachelor Cure. Pepper Adams. (Silhouette Romance Ser.). 1994. pap. 2.75 (*0-373-91003-7*, 5-91003-9) Silhouette.

Bachelor Dad. Carole Halston. 1994. mass mkt. 3.50 (*0-373-09915-0*, 1-09915-9) Harlequin Bks.

Bachelor Daddy. Sandra Steffen. (Silhouette Romance Ser.). 1994. pap. 2.75 (*0-373-19028-X*, 1-19028-9) Harlequin Bks.

Bachelor Doctor. large type ed. Marjorie Warby. 368p. 1987. 16.95 (*0-7089-1720-8*) Ulverscroft.

Bachelor Father. Annette Broadrick. (Silhouette Desire Ser.). 1991. pap. 2.79 (*0-373-15159-4*) Silhouette.

Bachelor Father. Karen T. Whittenburg. (American Romance Ser.). 1993. mass mkt. 3.39 (*0-373-16475-0*, 1-16475-5) Harlequin Bks.

Bachelor Father's Cookbook. Carolyn Schlemme. LC 86-51107. (Great American Cookbook Ser.). 160p. 1987. pap. 5.95 (*0-89914-017-3*) Third Party Pub.

Bachelor for Rent. Karen Morrell. 1993. 13.95 (*0-8034-9011-9*) Bouregy.

Bachelor from Bannack. Sally Garrett. (Superromance Ser.). 1993. mass mkt. 3.50 (*0-373-70554-9*, 1-70554-0) Harlequin Bks.

Bachelor Girls. Wendy Wasserstein. LC 90-55682. 224p. 1991. pap. 9.00 (*0-679-73062-1*, Vin) Random.

***Bachelor Husband.** Kate Hoffmann. (Temptation Ser.). 1995. pap. 3.25 (*0-373-25625-6*, 1-25625-4) Harlequin Bks.

Bachelor of Arts. R. K. Narayan. 1980. pap. 10.95 (*0-226-56833-4*) U Ch Pr.

Bachelor of Medicine. large type ed. Alex Stuart. 332p. 1989. 17.95 (*0-7089-1981-2*) Ulverscroft.

Bachelor of the Year. Joseph Baldwin. 33p. 1961. 2.50 (*0-87129-113-4*) Dramatic Pub.

***Bachelor Party.** Paula D. Riggs. (Intimate Moments Ser.). 1995. mass mkt. 3.75 (*0-373-07656-8*, 1-07656-1) Silhouette.

Bachelor Prince. Debbie Macomber. 1994. pap. 2.75 (*0-373-91012-6*, 5-91012-0); pap. 2.75 (*0-373-19012-3*, 5-19012-9) Harlequin Bks.

Bachelor Territory. large type ed. Gloria Bevan. 1991. 17.95 (*0-7451-9941-0*, AH001, Atlantic Lrg Print); pap. 15.95 (*0-7927-0404-5*, AS037, Atlantic Lrg Print) Chivers N Amer.

Bachelorette Party Book. Joni Lord. (Illus.). 80p. (Orig.). 1986. pap. 6.95 (*0-916799-13-1*) Hollow Glen.

Bachelorhood: Tales of the Metropolis. Phillip Lopate. 1989. pap. 8.95 (*0-671-67681-4*) S&S Trade.

Bachelors. Muriel Spark. 208p. (Orig.). 1992. pap. 9.00 (*0-380-71570-8*) Avon.

Bachelors. Henry De Montherlant & Terence Kilmartin. LC 77-10926. 189p. 1977. reprint ed. text ed. 49.75 (*0-8371-9811-9*, MOTB, Greenwood Pr) Greenwood.

Bachelors Anonymous. P. G. Wodehouse. 139p. (C). 1988. pap. 4.95 (*0-88029-279-2*) Marboro Bks.

Bachelor's Banquet. Ed. by Faith Gildenhuys. (Medieval & Renaissance Texts & Studies: Vol. 109). 140p. 1993. 19.00 (*0-86698-159-4*); pap. 8.00 (*0-86698-160-8*) MRTS.

Bachelor's Bible: Staying on Top from a Layman's Perspective. rev. ed. Peter M. Browne & Jill M. Browne. 164p. 1990. reprint ed. pap. 6.95 (*0-9628424-3-5*) PMS Entrps.

***Bachelor's Bride.** Audra Adams. 1995. mass mkt. 3.25 (*0-373-05959-0*, 1-05959-1) Silhouette.

Bachelor's Bride. Stephen Koch. 224p. 1986. 18.95 (*0-7145-2856-0*) M Boyars Pubs.

Bachelor's Christmas & Other Stories. Robert Grant. LC 70-94728. (Short Story Index Reprint Ser.). 1977. 23.95 (*0-8369-3107-6*) Ayer.

***Bachelor's Family.** Jessica Steele. (Romance Ser.). 1995. mass mkt. 2.99 (*0-373-03356-7*, 1-03356-2) Harlequin Bks.

Bachelors Galore. large type ed. Essie Summers. (Romance Ser.). 384p. 1993. 21.95 (*0-7089-2904-4*) Ulverscroft.

Bachelors Hall. 2nd ed. Reginald Underwood. LC 75-12353. (Homosexuality Ser.). 1975. reprint ed. 19.95 (*0-405-07391-7*) Ayer.

Bachelor's Home Companion: A Practical Guide to Keeping House Like a Pig. P. J. O'Rourke. LC 92-38785. 147p. 1993. 16.00 (*0-87113-489-6*) Grove-Atltic.

Bachelor's Japan. rev. ed. Boye De Mente. LC 91-65060. 160p. 1991. pap. 9.95 (*0-8048-1692-1*) C E Tuttle.

Bachelors of Broken Hill. large type ed. Arthur Upfield. 1974. 16.95 (*0-85456-296-6*) Ulverscroft.

Bachelors of Broken Hill: An Inspector Napoleon Bonaparte Mystery. Arthur W. Upfield. 256p. 1984. pap. 6.00 (*0-684-18246-7*, Scribners) S&S Trade.

Bachelor's Travel Log. Mark Koenigil. LC 67-21429. (Illus.). 1968. 7.00 (*0-8315-0067-0*) Speller.

Bachman Books: Four Early Novels. Stephen King. 944p. 1986. pap. 6.99 (*0-451-14736-7*, Sig) NAL-Dutton.

Bach's Brandenburg Concerts. Norman Carrell. 1988. reprint ed. lib. bdg. 59.00 (*0-7812-0749-5*) Rprt Serv.

Bach's Brandenburg Concerts. Norman Carrell. reprint ed. lib. bdg. 59.00 (*0-403-08968-9*) Scholarly.

Bach's Chorales, 3 vols., Set. Charles S. Terry. LC 74-26089. reprint ed. 87.50 (*0-404-13109-3*) AMS Pr.

Bach's Continuo Group: Players & Practices in His Vocal Works. Laurence Dreyfus. (Studies in the History of Music: No. 3). 280p. 1990. pap. 18.95 (*0-674-06030-X*) HUP.

Bach's Fugal Works. Alan E. Dickinson. LC 73-2877. 280p. 1979. reprint ed. text ed. 59.75 (*0-8371-6817-1*, DIBF, Greenwood Pr) Greenwood.

Bach's Orchestra. Charles S. Terry. 1988. reprint ed. lib. bdg. 59.00 (*0-7812-0794-0*) Rprt Serv.

Bach's Orchestra. Charles S. Terry. LC 71-181277. 250p. 1961. reprint ed. 39.00 (*0-403-01700-9*) Scholarly.

Bach's World. Jan Chiapusso. LC 79-20813. (Illus.). 338p. 1980. reprint ed. text ed. 79.50 (*0-313-22139-1*, CHBW, Greenwood Pr) Greenwood.

Bachura Scandal: And Other Stories & Sketches. Jaroslav Hasek. Tr. & Intro. by Alan Menhennet. 1992. pap. 14.95 (*0-946162-41-7*, Pub. by Angel Bks UK) Dufour.

Bacillaria: International Journal for Diatom Research, Vol. 3. Ed. by R. Simonsen. (Illus.). 1980. lib. bdg. 48.00 (*0-17-001891-1*) Lubrecht & Cramer.

Bacillaria: International Journal for Diatom Research, Vol. 5. Ed. by R. Simonsen. (Illus.). 256p. 1982. lib. bdg. 48.00 (*0-686-39500-X*) Lubrecht & Cramer.

Bacillaria: International Journal for Diatom Research, Vol. 6. R. Simonsen. (Illus.). 292p. 1983. lib. bdg. 48.00 (*0-686-40539-0*) Lubrecht & Cramer.

Bacillaria: International Journal for Diatom Research, Vol. 7. R. Simonsen. (Illus.). 200p. 1984. lib. bdg. 48.00 (*0-318-04382-3*) Lubrecht & Cramer.

Bacillariaceae, Epithemiaceae, Surirellaceae. Neue und Wenig Bekannte Taxa, Neue Kombinationen Und Synonyme, Sowie Bemerkungen und und Ergaenzungen zu den Naviculaceae. H. Lange-Bertalot & K. Krammer. (Bibliotheca Diatomologica Ser.: Vol. 15). (Illus.). 272p. (GER.). 1988. lib. bdg. 92.00 (*3-443-57006-2*) Lubrecht & Cramer.

Bacillus. Ed. by Colin R. Harwood. (Biotechnology Handbooks Ser.: Vol. 2). (Illus.). 432p. 1989. 79.50 (*0-306-43137-8*, Plenum Pr) Plenum.

Bacillus Subtilis: Molecular Biology & Industrial Application. Ed. by B. Maruo & Hiroyuki Yoshikawa. (Topics in Secondary Metabolism Ser.: Vol. 1). 268p. 1989. 138.50 (*0-444-98852-1*) Elsevier.

Bacillus Subtilis & Other Gram-positive Bacteria: Biochemistry, Physiology, & Molecular Genetics. Ed. by Abraham L. Sonenshein et al. LC 92-48294. 1000p. 1993. text ed. 125.00 (*1-55581-053-5*) Am Soc Microbio.

Bacillus Thuringiensis, an Environmental Biopesticide: Theory & Practice. Philip F. Entwistle et al. LC 92-27213. 311p. 1993. text ed. 114.95 (*0-471-93306-6*) Wiley.

Bacilly: A Commentary Upon the Art of Proper Singing. Ed. by Austin B. Caswell. (Musical Theorists in Translation Ser.: Vol. 7). 1968. lib. bdg. 67.00 (*0-912024-27-5*) Inst Mediaeval Mus.

Back Almanac. Lanier Publishing Staff. LC 92-25976. 182p. 1992. pap. 14.95 (*0-685-70014-3*) Celestial Arts.

Back-Back & the Lima Bear. Thomas Weck. Ed. by Helen Graves. LC 85-51963. 64p. (J). (gr. 1-6). 1986. 6.95 (*0-938232-97-5*) Winston-Derek.

Back Bay. William Martin. 1992. mass mkt. 5.99 (*0-446-36316-2*) Warner Bks.

***Back Bay: A Living Portrait.** Barbara W. Moore & Gail Weesner. LC 95-67827. (Illus.). 144p. 1995. 35.00 (*0-9632077-2-5*); pap. 25.00 (*0-9632077-3-3*) Centry Hill Pr.

Back Before Day. Reynolds Price. LC 89-62735. 64p. 1989. 25.00 (*0-933598-16-5*) NC Wesleyan Pr.

Back Before the World Turned Nasty. Pauline Mortensen. LC 89-4739. 115p. 1989. 17.95 (*1-55728-104-1*); pap. 8.95 (*1-55728-105-X*) U of Ark Pr.

Back Book. David W. Apts. (Illus.). 42p. (C). 1988. pap. text ed. 6.50 (*0-685-24275-7*) Amer Back School.

Back Care: An Illustrated Guide. Jean Oliver. (Illus.). 192p. 1994. pap. 34.95 (*0-7506-0191-4*) Buttrwrth-Heinemann.

Back Care Basics: A Doctor's Gentle Yoga Program for Back & Neck Pain Relief. Mary P. Schatz. LC 91-78206. (Illus.). 248p. (Orig.). 1992. pap. 19.95 (*0-9627138-2-1*) Rodmell Pr.

Back Country. Gary Snyder. LC 67-23491. (Orig.). 1968. pap. 8.95 (*0-8112-0194-5*, NDP249) New Directions.

Back Country - Two Tales: Mooching Moose & Mumbling Men & Sucker's Teeth. Joe Back. LC 87-82331. (Illus.). 250p. 1987. reprint ed. pap. 9.95 (*1-55566-019-3*) Johnson Bks.

Back Country Roads & Trails, San Diego County. 3rd ed. Jerry Schad. (Illus.). 96p. 1986. pap. 7.95 (*0-911518-46-0*) Touchstone Oregon.

Back Door: Poems. Annie Callan. pap. 7.00 (*0-932264-10-7*) Trask Hse Bks.

Back Door Guest. Lennox Kerr. LC 73-13140. (Foreign Travelers in America, 1810-1935 Ser.). 280p. 1974. reprint ed. 25.95 (*0-405-05462-9*) Ayer.

Back Door to California: The Story of the Mojave River Trail. Clifford J. Walker. Ed. by Patricia J. Keeling. LC 86-62673. (Illus.). 342p. (Orig.). (C). 1986. lib. bdg. 19.95 (*0-918614-04-X*); pap. text ed. 13.95 (*0-918614-03-1*) Mojave Riv Val.

Back Door to Richmond: The Bermuda Hundred Campaign, April-June 1864. William G. Robertson. LC 85-41048. (Illus.). 284p. 1991. pap. 9.95 (*0-8071-1672-6*) La State U Pr.

Back Door to Richmond: The Bermuda Hundred Campaign, April-June 1864. William G. Robertson. LC 85-41048. (Illus.). 288p. 1987. 42.50 (*0-87413-303-3*) U Delaware Pr.

Back Door to the Klondike. Joan Weir. (Illus.). 128p. (Orig.). pap. 9.95 (*0-317-05891-6*, Pub. by Boston Mills Pr CN) Genl Dist Srvs.

Back Door to War: The Roosevelt Foreign Policy 1933-1941. Charles C. Tansill. LC 75-1121. 690p. 1975. reprint ed. text ed. 85.00 (*0-8371-7990-4*, TABD, Greenwood Pr) Greenwood.

Back Down the Line. John Bolton et al. 1991. 29.95 (*1-56060-041-1*); pap. 8.95 (*1-56060-040-3*) Eclipse Bks.

Back Facts. 2nd ed. David W. Apts. (Illus.). 28p. (SPA.). (C). 1981. pap. text ed. 3.50 (*0-685-24276-5*) Amer Back School.

***Back Fire: The CIA's Secret War in Laos & Its Link to War in Vietnam.** Roger Warner. 1995. 25.00 (*0-684-80292-9*) S&S Trade.

***Back Fire: The CIA's Secret War in Laos & Its Links to the Vietnam War.** Roger Warner. LC 95-5758. 1995. write for info. (*0-671-69074-4*) S&S Trade.

Back Fitness the Yoga Way. Kareen Zebroff. (Illus.). 105p. 1989. pap. 14.95 (*0-88976-080-2*) Gordon Soules Bk.

Back from Betrayal: Recovering from His Affairs. Jennifer P. Schneider. 352p. 1990. mass mkt. 4.99 (*0-345-36786-3*) Ballantine.

Back from Hell. Mick Farren. (Car Warriors Ser.: No. 2). 224p. (Orig.). 1993. mass mkt. 4.50 (*0-8125-1990-6*) Tor Bks.

Back from the Brink: A Practical Plan for Privatizing Deposit Insurance & Strengthening Our Banks & Thrifts. Peter J. Wallison. 72p. 1990. pap. 9.75 (*0-8447-7002-7*, AEI Pr) Am Enterprise.

Back from the Dead. Harry Hone. (Illus.). 1978. pap. text ed. write for info. (*0-9601168-2-6*); pap. text ed. write for info. (*0-9601168-3-4*) Am Biog Ctr.

Back from the Deep: The Strange Story of the Sister Subs, Squalus & Sculpin. Carl Lavo. LC 94-25853. (Illus.). 244p. 1994. 27.95 (*1-55750-507-1*) Naval Inst Pr.

Back from the Edge: The American Bison. Lynn M. Stone. LC 90-38385. (Animal Odysseys Ser.). (Illus.). 48p. (J). (gr. 4-6). 1991. lib. bdg. 16.67 (*0-86593-101-1*); lib. bdg. 12.50 (*0-685-59353-3*) Rourke Corp.

Back from the Future: Cuba under Castro. Susan E. Eckstein. LC 93-45884. 1994. 29.95 (*0-691-03445-1*) Princeton U Pr.

An Asterisk (*) at the beginning of an entry indicates that the title is appearing in BIP for the first time.

This self-paced workbook guides the reader step-by-step through five introspective processes for deepening personal & spiritual growth. Based upon the author's NOT WHAT, BUT HOW workshops, this self-directed workbook guides the reader through projection, postures, subpersonalities, disidentification, & centering. The workbook has 18 experiential exercises which focus the reader on HOW s/he is, rather than WHAT s/he does. Six centering exercises & three guided imageries are on the cassette tape accompanying the book. All text is on the right-hand side of the book with ample space for writing left between exercises. The left-hand page is lightly ruled for continued writing as needed. Each introspective process is explained with a minimum of dogma other than advocating freedom from personal conditioning. Order directly from: InnerVision, 9400 Hwy 19W, Bryson City, NC 28713; 800-298-8209. *Publisher Provided Annotation.*

B

*__Back to Basics: An Awareness Primer.__ Nancy Spence. 160p. (YA). (gr. 10 up). 1995. pap. 14.95 (0-9643818-0-X) InnerVis NC.

An Asterisk (*) at the beginning of an entry indicates that the title is appearing in BIP for the first time.

Back to Darwin: The Scientific Case for Deistic Evolution. M. A. Corey. 448p. (Orig.). (C). 1994. lib. bdg. 62.50 (*0-8191-9306-2*); pap. text ed. 37.00 (*0-8191-9307-0*) U Pr of Amer.

Back to Drawing Board. (McGee & Me! Ser.: No. 6). 1990. pap. 4.99 (*0-8423-4111-0*) Tyndale.

Back to Earth: Tommorrow's Environmentalism. Anthony Weston. LC 94-3856. 200p. (C). 1994. text ed. 39.95 (*1-56639-236-5*); pap. text ed. 17.95 (*1-56639-237-3*) Temple U Pr.

Back to Eden. Jethro Kloss. 1981. pap. 5.95 (*0-87904-000-9*) Lust.

Back to Eden. Jethro Kloss. 667p. 1971. reprint ed. spiral bd. 13.75 (*0-7873-0502-2*) Mokelumne.

Back to Eden: A Herbal Guide. Jethro Kloss. 1991. lib. bdg. 89.95 (*0-8490-5117-7*) Gordon Pr.

Back to Eden: Authorized Kloss Family Edition. rev. ed. Jethro Kloss. (Illus.). 7248p. 1984. mass mkt., pap. 6.95 (*0-940676-00-1*) Back to Eden.

Back to Eden: Authorized Kloss Family Edition. rev. ed. Jethro Kloss. (Illus.). 724p. 1985. 16.95 (*0-940676-04-4*); pap. 10.95 (*0-940676-01-X*) Back to Eden.

Back to Eden: The Classic Guide to Herbal Medicine, Natural Foods, & Home Remedies Since 1939. rev. ed. Jethro Kloss & Promise K. Moffet. 940p. 1989. reprint ed. mass mkt., pap. 7.95 (*0-940985-10-1*); reprint ed. pap. 12.95 (*0-940985-09-8*) Back to Eden.

Back to Eden: The Classic Guide to Herbal Medicine, Natural Foods, & Home Remedies Since 1939. 2nd rev. ed. Jethro Kloss & Promise K. Moffet. 940p. 1989. reprint ed. 19.95 (*0-940985-13-6*) Back to Eden.

Back to Eden Cookbook. LC 81-82412. (Illus.). 158p. (Orig.). 1981. pap. 4.25 (*0-940676-03-6*) Back to Eden.

Back to First Principles: U. S. Strategic Forces in the Emerging Environments. David A. Shlapak & David E. Thaler. LC 92-46777. 1993. write for info. (*0-8330-1313-0*, R-4260-AF) Rand Corp.

Back to Forth. Gloria Frym. 1982. per. 7.50 (*0-935724-09-5*) Figures.

Back to Health: A Comprehensive Medical & Nutritional YEAST Control Program. Dennis W. Remington & Barbara W. Higa. (Illus.). 256p. 1986. pap. 9.95 (*0-912547-03-0*, 801-224-9214) Vitality Hse Int Inc.

Back to Home & Duty: Women Between the Wars, 1919-1939. Deidre Beddoe. 250p. (Orig.). 1990. pap. 17.95 (*0-04-440515-4*) Routledge Chapman & Hall.

Back to Kant: The Revival of Kantianism in German Social & Historical Thought, 1860-1914. Thomas E. Willey. LC 77-29215. 232p. reprint ed. pap. 66.20 (*0-7837-3601-0*, 2043466) Bks Demand.

Back to Nature: The Arcadian Myth in Urban America. Peter J. Schmitt. 1990. pap. 13.95 (*0-8018-4013-9*) Johns Hopkins.

Back to Nature in Canoes: A Guide to American Waters. Rainer Esslen. LC 75-39780. (Illus.). 1976. pap. 6.95 (*0-914366-04-1*) Columbia Pub.

Back to Normal: My Back Is Normal. Milton Bowser. Ed. by Alistair MacLean. (Illus.). 120p. (Orig.). 1980. pap. 10.00 (*0-940178-01-X*) Sitare.

Back to One: A Practical Guide for Psychotherapists. Sheldon Kopp. LC 77-608269. 1977. 11.95 (*0-8314-0055-2*) Sci & Behavior.

Back to One: How to Make Good Money as a Hollywood Extra. 5th rev. ed. Cullen G. Chambers. (Illus.). 160p. 1992. pap. 9.95 (*0-9624577-0-1*) C G Chambers.

Back to One: How to Make Good Money As a Hollywood Extra! 7th ed. Cullen G. Chambers. LC 89-92435. (Illus.). 224p. (Orig.). 1994. pap. write for info. (*0-9624577-8-7*, BTO-01) C G Chambers.

Back to Our Roots: Cooking for Control of Sickle Cell Anemia & Cancer Prevention. 2nd rev. ed. Dawud Ujamaa. LC 94-72181. (Illus.). 221p. 1995. pap. 14.95 (*1-884938-01-9*) Al Mai Dah.

***Back to Paul Revere.** Beatrice Gormley. (Travelers Through Time Ser.: No. 02). (J). (gr. 4-7). 1994. pap. 3.25 (*0-590-46227-X*) Scholastic Inc.

***Back to Reality: A Critique of Postmodern Theory in Psychotherapy.** Barbara S. Held. 272p. (C). 1995. 32.00 (*0-393-70192-1*) Norton.

Back to School. Betsy Haynes. (Bone Chillers Ser.: No. 3). (J). (gr. 4-7). 1994. mass mkt. 3.50 (*0-06-106186-7*) HarpC.

Back to School. R. J. Scribbles. (Illus.). 32p. (Orig.). (J). (gr. 2-5). 1992. pap. 12.95 (*0-9632192-0-0*) R J Miller.

Back to School: A College Guide for Returning Students. Ed. by Lauren M. Christman. 200p. (C). 1993. pap. text ed. 19.95 (*1-880344-03-3*) Col Plan Netwk.

Back to School: A College Primer for Adults. LaVerne L. Ludden. 232p. (Orig.). 1995. pap. 14.95 (*1-57112-070-X*, P070X, Park Avenue) JIST Works.

Back to School: A Survival Guide for Parents. Mary A. Bauer. 40p. 1987. pap. 3.95 (*0-317-61668-4*) M A Bauer.

Back to School at My Age? A Guide for Both the Returning Student & the College Administrator. Ed. by Del Witherspoon & Eugenie Nickell. 208p. (Orig.). (C). 1991. lib. bdg. 42.00 (*0-8191-8412-8*); pap. text ed. 21.50 (*0-8191-8413-6*) U Pr of Amer.

Back to School in January. Jeri Carroll et al. (Illus.). 144p. (J). (gr. k-5). 1989. student ed 12.95 (*0-86653-470-9*, GA1067) Good Apple.

Back to School Promotion Audio Package. 1992. pap. 9.98 (*0-425-13653-1*) Berkley Pub.

Back to School with Assertive Discipline. Lee Canter. (Illus.). 174p. 1990. student ed 9.95 (*0-939007-31-2*) Lee Canter & Assocs.

Back to School with Betsy. Carolyn Haywood. LC 85-16380. (Illus.). 176p. (J). (gr. 1-5). 1943. 12.95 (*0-15-205512-6*, HB Juv Bks) HarBrace.

Back to School with Betsy. Carolyn Haywood. 135p. (J). (gr. 2-5). 1990. pap. 3.95 (*0-15-205515-0*, Odyssey) HarBrace.

Back to School with Mom. Jo Hoestlandt. (I Love to Read Collection). (Illus.). 48p. (J). (gr. 3-8). 1990. lib. bdg. 19.93 (*0-89565-815-1*) Childs World.

Back to Sociological Theory: The Construction of Social Orders. Nicos P. Mouzelis. LC 91-9240. 240p. 1991. text ed. 65.00 (*0-312-06175-7*) St Martin.

Back to Sociological Theory: The Construction of Social Orders. Nicos P. Mouzelis. LC 91-9240. 1993. pap. write for info. (*0-312-10361-1*) St Martin.

Back to Square One. Larry Christenson. LC 79-16413. 144p. 1979. pap. 3.99 (*0-87123-025-9*) Bethany Hse.

Back to Square One: Old World Food in a New World Kitchen. Joyce Goldstein. LC 92-8366. 1992. 23.00 (*0-688-10122-4*) Morrow.

Back to the Asylum: The Future of Mental Health Law in the United States. Mary L. Durham & John Q. La Fond. 272p. 1992. 39.95 (*0-19-505520-9*) OUP.

Back to the Barrios: Balikbaryo. Juan M. Flavier. 150p. 1978. 8.50 (*0-942717-02-3*) Intl Inst Rural.

Back to the Barrios (Balikbario) Juan M. Flavier. 1979. pap. 7.50 (*971-10-0316-3*, Pub. by New Day Pub PH) Cellar.

Back to the Basics: The Frontier Schools of Boulder County, Colorado, 1860-1960. Anne Q. Dyni. (Illus.). 160p. (Orig.). 1991. pap. 15.95 (*0-9617799-4-2*) Book Lode.

***Back to the Basics with Practical Faith: A Practical Study for Everyday Faith.** Julian B. Thayer, 3rd. 72p. 1995. pap. 4.95 (*0-9645505-0-4*) Dove Publ NC.

Back to the Batcave. Adam West & Jeff Rovin. 272p. (Orig.). 1994. pap. 12.00 (*0-425-14370-8*, Berkley Trade) Berkley Pub.

Back to the Beanstalk: Enchantment & Reality for Couples. Judith R. Brown. LC 79-89476. (C). 1980. 9.95 (*0-930626-03-6*); pap. 6.95 (*0-930626-04-4*) Psych & Consul Assocs.

Back to the Bible. Harvey Childress. 1980. pap. 3.75 (*0-89137-569-4*) Quality Pubns.

Back to the Blanket. Waterhawk Sorenson. LC 94-60586. 26p. (Orig.). (C). 1994. pap. 5.20 (*1-878142-06-2*) Telstar TX.

Back to the Brink: Proceedings of the Moscow Conference on the Cuban Missile Crisis, January 27-28, 1989. Ed. by Bruce J. Allyn et al. (Occasional Papers Ser.: No. 9). 248p. (Orig.). (C). 1992. lib. bdg. 33.50 (*0-8191-7923-X*); pap. text ed. 19.50 (*0-8191-7924-8*) U Pr of Amer.

Back to the City Movement & the Possibilities of Increasing Racial & Economic Integration. John Michener. 50p. 1978. 3.50 (*0-318-15819-1*) Natl Neighbors.

Back to the Congo. Lieve Joris. Tr. by Stacey Knecht. 256p. 1992. text ed. 22.00 (*0-689-12164-4*, Atheneum S&S) S&S Trade.

Back to the Cross. Watchman Nee. Ed. by Herbert L. Fader. Tr. by Stephen Kaung. 171p. (Orig.). 1988. pap. 4.50 (*0-935008-70-5*) Christian Fellow Pubs.

Back to the Damn Soil. Mary Gubser & Nicholas J. Gubser. LC 86-61319. 160p. 1986. 14.95 (*0-933031-06-8*) Coun Oak Bks.

Back to the Family: Proven Advice on Building a Stronger, Healthier, Happier Family. Raymond N. Guarendi. 272p. 1991. pap. 10.00 (*0-671-74599-9*, Fireside) S&S Trade.

Back to the Father: Sermons from Luke 15. Rick Atchley. 104p. (Orig.). 1994. pap. 6.95 (*1-56794-037-4*, C2299) Star Bible.

Back to the Front: The Unfinished Story in Vietnam. R. P. Kaushik & Susheela Kaushik. 120p. 1979. text ed. 12.50 (*0-86131-188-4*, Pub. by Orient Longman Ltd II) Apt Bks.

Back to the Front: Tourisms of War. Elizabeth Diller & Ricardo Scofidio. (Illus.). 330p. (Orig.). 1994. pap. 29.95 (*1-56898-014-0*) Princeton Arch.

Back to the Future: Modernity, Postmodernity & Locality. Philip Cooke. 192p. 1990. text ed. 39.95 (*0-04-445586-0*) Routledge Chapman & Hall.

***Back to the Future: Tokheim.** Bob Lee. (Gas Pump Ser.: No. 5). (Illus.). 172p. 1993. text ed. 44.95 (*0-9638220-0-4*) Bob Lee.

Back to the Future with God. Uriah Worth. LC 88-62113. 127p. 1989. pap. 6.95 (*1-55523-182-9*) Winston-Derek.

Back to the Galaxy. Ed. by S. S. Holt & F. Verter. (AIP Conference Proceedings Ser.: No. 278). (Illus.). 720p. 1993. text ed. 125.00 (*1-56396-227-6*, AIP Pr) Am Inst Physics.

Back to the Garden: The 'Mal' Texts of Chateaubriand, Senancour & Constant. Michael J. Call. (Stanford French & Italian Studies: No. 52). 144p. (Orig.). 1988. pap. 46.50 (*0-915838-68-0*) Anma Libri.

Back to the Ghetto: Zionism in Retreat. Uri Huppert. 231p. 1988. 26.95 (*0-87975-467-2*) Prometheus Bks.

***Back to the Heart of Youth Work.** Dewey Bertolini. 1994. pap. 9.99 (*1-56476-396-X*, 6-3396, Victor Books) SP Pubns.

Back to the Heart of Youth Work. Dewey M. Bertolini. 228p. 1989. text ed. 16.99 (*0-89693-662-7*, Victor Books) SP Pubns.

Back to the Land. N. W. Walker. (Illus.). pap. 4.95 (*0-89019-063-1*) Norwalk Pr.

Back to the Past. Ethel Tiersky. LC 93-41709. 1994. pap. 7.93 (*0-8092-3687-7*) Contemp Bks.

Back to the Realites: Reflections of a Hungarian Banker. Janos Fekete. 360p. 1982. 120.00 (*0-685-17014-4*, Pub. by Collets UK) Pro-Am Music.

Back to the Rough Ground: Phronesis & Techne in Modern Philosophy & in Aristotle. Joseph Dunne. LC 91-50564. (Revisions: A Series of Books on Ethics: Vol. 11). (C). 1992. text ed. 45.95 (*0-268-00689-X*) U of Notre Dame Pr.

***Back to the Soil: The Jewish Farmers of Clarion, Utah, & Their World.** Robert A. Goldberg. LC 86-13185. (Utah Centennial Ser.: No. 2). 226p. 1986. pap. 64.50 (*0-7837-8559-3*, 2049374) Bks Demand.

Back to the Sources: Reading the Classics. Barry W. Holz. 1986. pap. 13.00 (*0-671-60596-8*) S&S Trade.

Back to the Stone Age. Edgar Rice Burroughs. 256p. 1990. pap. 3.95 (*0-345-36671-9*, Del Rey) Ballantine.

Back to the Time Trap. Keith Laumer. 352p. (Orig.). 1992. mass mkt. 5.99 (*0-671-72127-5*) Baen Bks.

Back to the Trenches: Memoirs of an Educator in Conflict. Paul Treatman. LC 92-34483. (Illus.). 192p. 1993. 20.00 (*0-939713-06-3*) Carriage House.

Back to the Twenties: His Memories of Growing up in Carson City. Jack Curran. LC 94-10587. (Illus.). 1994. 10.95 (*0-935174-41-9*) Tree by River.

Back to the Wind & Waves. Jane Rowley. LC 93-33655. 250p. 1994. 19.95 (*0-944957-19-6*) Rivercross Pub.

Back to Things in Themselves: A Phenomenological Foundation for Classical Realism. Josef Seifert. (Studies in Phenomenological & Classical Realism). 320p. 1986. 29.95 (*0-7102-0711-5*, 07115, RKP) Routledge.

Back to Virtue. Peter Kreeft. LC 92-72114. 195p. 1992. pap. 9.95 (*0-89870-422-7*) Ignatius Pr.

Back to Wholeness. Melanie Jongsma. (Friendship Ser.). (Illus.). 48p. (Orig.). 1993. pap. write for info. (*1-882536-17-7*, A100-0061) Bible League.

Back to Work: Determinants of Women's Successful Re-entry. Eileen Appelbaum. LC 81-8008. 141p. 1981. text ed. 45.00 (*0-86569-076-6*, Auburn Hse) Greenwood.

Back to Work: How to Rejoin the Workforce after an Absence. Laurence Lipsett. 135p. (Orig.). 1993. pap. 15.95 (*0-9637107-0-2*) Curtice Pub.

Back to Work: Testing Reemployment Services for Displaced Workers. Howard S. Bloom. LC 90-12909. 192p. 1990. text ed. 25.00 (*0-88099-097-X*); pap. text ed. 15.00 (*0-88099-098-8*) W E Upjohn.

Back to Work: The Story of PWA. Harold L. Ickes. LC 72-7426. (FDR & the Era of the New Deal Ser.). (Illus.). 276p. 1973. reprint ed. lib. bdg. 39.50 (*0-306-70527-3*) Da Capo.

Back to Your Spiritual Future. Steve Bell. 192p. (Orig.). 1993. pap. 8.99 (*1-56476-205-X*, Victor Books) SP Pubns.

Back Toward the Future: Hints for Interpreting Biblical Prophecy. Walter C. Kaiser, Jr. LC 89-202. 160p. 1989. pap. 8.99 (*0-8010-5499-0*) Baker Bk.

Back Trail of an Old Cowboy. Paul E. Young. Ed. by Nellie S. Yost. LC 82-7096. 235p. reprint ed. pap. 67.00 (*0-7837-1837-3*, 2042038) Bks Demand.

Back Trail; or An Upper Peninsula Boyhood. George E. Christensen. 143p. 1985. 12.50 (*0-933249-00-4*); pap. 7.50 (*0-933249-01-2*) Mid-Peninsula Lib.

Back Trailers from the Middle Border. Hamlin Garland. (Collected Works of Hamlin Garland). 1988. reprint ed. lib. bdg. 79.00 (*0-7812-1251-0*) Rprt Serv.

Back Trailers from the Middle Border see Collected Works of Hamlin Garland

Back-Trailing on the Old Frontiers. H. P. Rabun & W. W. Cheely. 1986. reprint ed. 6.95 (*0-913150-55-X*) Pioneer Pr.

Back Trouble: A New Approach to Prevention & Recovery. Deborah Caplan. (Illus.). 224p. (Orig.). 1987. pap. 12.95 (*0-937404-26-8*) Triad Pub FL.

Back-up Banjo. Janet Davis. 1993. 15.00 (*0-87166-888-2*, 93771); audio 9.98 (*1-56222-602-9*, 93771) Mel Bay.

Back up Girl. Dale Janda. Tr. by Ingram. 260p. 1994. pap. 8.95 (*1-56901-252-0*) NW Pub.

Back-up Pedal Steel Guitar. DeWitt Scott. 1993. 9.95 (*1-56222-424-7*, 94716); audio 9.98 (*1-56222-427-1*, 94716) Mel Bay.

Back-Up Star. Dean Bughes. LC 94-15128. (J). (gr. 1 up). 1995. pap. 4.99 (*0-679-85442-8*, Bullseye Bks) Random Bks Yng Read.

Back-Up Star. Dean Bughes. LC 94-15128. (J). (gr. 1 up). 1995. 4.99 (*0-679-95442-2*, Bullseye Bks) Random Bks Yng Read.

Back Where I Came From. A. J. Liebling. LC 89-38678. 320p. 1990. reprint ed. pap. 11.00 (*0-86547-425-7*, North Pt Pr) FS&G.

Back Yard Angel. Judy Delton. (Illus.). 112p. (J). (gr. 2-5). 1983. 14.95 (*0-395-33883-2*) HM.

Back Yard Attractions. Brigid Gaynor. (Illus.). (J). (ps). 1992. 15.95 (*1-56828-018-1*) Red Jacket Pr.

Back-Yard Mechanic, 3 bks., Set. (Illus.). 224p. 1990. pap. 7.00 (*0-16-009167-5*, S/N 008-070-004) USGPO.

Back-Yard Mechanic, Vol. 1. (Illus.). 57p. 1981. reprint ed. pap. 2.50 (*0-16-002143-X*, S/N 008-070-00374-1) USGPO.

Back-Yard Mechanic, Vol. 2. Don Holt. (Illus.). 75p. 1978. pap. 3.00 (*0-16-002146-4*, S/N 008-070-00406-2) USGPO.

Back-Yard Mechanic, Vol. 3. Ron Lathrop. (Illus.). 92p. 1981. pap. 3.00 (*0-16-002156-1*, S/N 008-070-00463-1) USGPO.

Back Yard Walkin' Training Tips. Allanna L. Jackson. LC 93-74355. (Illus.). 160p. (Orig.). 1993. 65.00 (*0-9639644-0-2*); pap. 18.50 (*0-9639644-1-0*) Four Craftsmen.

Backache. 2nd ed. Ian Macnab & John A. McCulloch. (Illus.). 448p. 1990. 60.00 (*0-683-05352-3*) Williams & Wilkins.

Backache: What Exercises Work. Dava Sobel & Arthur C. Klein. (Illus.). 224p. 1994. 21.95 (*0-312-10933-4*) St Martin.

***Backarc Basins: Tectonics & Magmatism.** Ed. by Brian Taylor. 525p. 1995. 95.00 (*0-306-44937-4*) Plenum.

Backart: On the Flip Side. Danita Rafalovich & Kathryn A. Pellman. (Illus.). 80p. 1991. pap. text ed. 19.95 (*0-942786-10-6*) Leone Pubns.

Backbench Diaries of Richard Crossman. Ed. by Janet Morgan. 1136p. 1981. 55.00 (*0-8419-0686-6*) Holmes & Meier.

Backbench Opinion in the House of Commons, 1945-1955. Hugh B. Berrington. (C). 1973. 118.00 (*0-08-016748-9*, Pub. by Pergamon Repr UK) Franklin.

Backbench Specialization in the House of Commons. David Judge. vii, 243p. 1981. text ed. 59.95 (*0-435-83450-9*) Ashgate Pub Co.

Backboard Battle. Kirk Marshall. (Hoops Ser.: No. 3). 144p. (J). (gr. 4 up). 1989. pap. 4.99 (*0-345-35910-0*) Ballantine.

Backboards & Blackboards. Patricia A. Adler & Peter Adler. 288p. 1991. pap. text ed. 17.50 (*0-231-07307-0*) Col U Pr.

Backboards & Blackboards: College Athletes & Role Engulfment. Peter Adler & Patricia A. Adler. 1990. text ed. 37.00 (*0-231-07306-2*) Col U Pr.

***Backbone.** Mychal Mitchell. 1994. 12.95 (*0-533-10852-7*) Vantage.

Backbone: Short Stories. Carol Bly. LC 84-61733. (Illus.). 126p. (Orig.). (C). 1994. 12.95 (*0-915943-05-0*); pap. 10.95 (*0-915943-36-0*) Milkweed Ed.

Backbone of America. Mark D. Kaufmann. 1992. 2.50 (*0-87129-188-6*, B73) Dramatic Pub.

Backbone of American Passenger Trains: "E" Units. Henry Maywald. (Illus.). 72p. (Orig.). 1988. pap. 25.95 (*0-934088-19-5*) NJ Intl Inc.

Backbone of the King. Marcia Brown. (Illus.). 180p. (J). (gr. 4-8). 1984. reprint ed. 12.95 (*0-8248-0963-7*) UH Pr.

Backcasts: Memories & Recollections of Seventy Years As a Sportsman. John Knowles. LC 92-63249. (Illus.). 200p. (Orig.). 1993. 14.95 (*0-923568-32-8*); pap. 11.95 (*0-923568-28-X*) Wilderness Adventure Bks.

Backcountry. Bob Scott. (Illus.). 24p. (J). (gr. 4-12). 1989. 5.00 (*0-9621201-0-3*) B Scott Bks.

Backcountry Alaska. Ed. by Alaska Geographic Staff. LC 72-92087. (Alaska Geographic Ser.: Vol. 13, No. 2). (Illus.). 1987. pap. 17.95 (*0-88240-177-7*) Alaska Geog Soc.

***Backcountry Brazil.** Alex Bradbury. (Bradt Guides Ser.). (Illus.). 196p. (Orig.). 1994. 17.95 (*1-56440-538-9*) Globe Pequot.

Backcountry Byways. Stewart Green. (Falcon Guide Ser.). (Illus.). 184p. (Orig.). 1991. pap. 9.95 (*1-56044-061-9*) Falcon Pr MT.

Backcountry Classroom. Jack Drury & Bruce Bonney. LC 92-26151. (Illus.). 288p. (Orig.). 1992. pap. 24.99 (*0-934802-18-1*) ICS Bks.

***Backcountry Companion for Denali National Park.** J. Nierenberg. (Illus.). 96p. 1995. pap. 8.95 (*0-930931-03-3*) Alaska Natural.

Backcountry Facilities: Design & Maintenance. R. E. Leonard et al. (Illus.). 224p. 1980. pap. 9.95 (*0-910146-31-4*) AMC Books.

Backcountry First-Aid & Extended Care. 2nd ed. Buck Tilton. 80p. 1994. 3.99 (*0-934802-99-8*) ICS Bks.

***Backcountry Fly Fishing in Salt Water: An Innovative Guide to Some of the Finest & Most Interesting Fishing in Salt Water.** Doug Swisher & Carl Richards. (Illus.). 176p. 1995. 29.95 (*1-55821-328-7*) Lyons & Burford.

Backcountry Handbook: An Illustrated Guide to the Techniques & Joys of the Wilderness Experience. Mother Earth News Editors. 1989. pap. write for info. (*0-671-65795-X*, Fireside) S&S Trade.

***Backcountry Horseman's Guide to Washington.** John Wolcott & Roberta Wolcott. (Falcon Guides Ser.). (Illus.). 224p. 1995. pap. 14.95 (*1-56044-338-3*) Falcon Pr MT.

Backcountry Mexico: A Traveler's Guide & Phrase Book. Bob Burleson & David H. Riskind. (Illus.). 335p. 1986. pap. 14.95 (*0-292-70755-X*) U of Tex Pr.

Backcountry Ranger: In Glacier National Park 1910-1913 the Diaries & Photographs of Norton Pearl. Leslie Lee. LC 94-75921. (Illus.). 264p. (Orig.). 1994. write for info. (*0-9641250-0-5*); text ed. write for info. (*0-9641250-2-1*); lib. bdg. write for info. (*0-9641250-1-3*); pap. write for info. (*0-9641250-3-X*); pap. text ed. write for info. (*0-9641250-4-8*) L Lee Pub.

Backcountry Roads & Trails, San Diego County. 4th rev. ed. Jerry Schad. LC 76-57336. (Illus.). 96p. 1993. pap. 8.95 (*0-9617288-5-X*) Centra Pubns.

Backcountry Skiing: The Sierra Club Guide to Skiing off the Beaten Track. Lito Tejada-Flores. LC 81-8958. (Outdoor Activities Guides Ser.). (Illus.). 288p. 1981. pap. 9.95 (*0-87156-287-1*) Sierra.

Backcountry Skiing in the High Sierra. John Moynier. (Illus.). 200p. (Orig.). 1993. pap. 12.95 (*0-934641-44-7*) Chockstone Pr.

Backdoor to Eugenics. Troy Duster. 1990. 39.95 (*0-415-90154-5*, A3291, Routledge NY); pap. 13.95 (*0-415-90155-3*, Routledge NY) Routledge.

Backdraft. Kirk Mitchell. 1991. pap. 4.50 (*0-425-12879-2*) Berkley Pub.

Backed Against the Sea. Wang Wen-hsing. Tr. by Edward Gunn. (Cornell East Asia Ser.: No. 67). 142p. (Orig.). (C). 1993. 18.00 (*0-939657-86-4*); pap. 11.00 (*0-939657-67-8*, 67) Cornell East Asia Pgm.

Backenstoss Family Association of America: Genealogy. Comp. by Backenstoss Family. 188p. 1993. reprint ed. lib. bdg. 39.50 (*0-8328-3254-5*); reprint ed. pap. 29.50 (*0-8328-3255-3*) Higginson Bk Co.

Backfield in Motion. Peg Schaffer. 78p. (Orig.). 1992. pap. 7.95 (*1-56245-057-3*) Great Quotations.

Backfield Package. Thomas J. Dygard. LC 92-6315. 208p. (YA). (gr. 7 up). 1992. 14.00 (*0-688-11471-7*) Morrow Jr Bks.

Backfield Package. Thomas J. Dygard. LC 93-7721. 208p. (J). (gr. 5 up). 1993. pap. 3.99 (*0-14-036348-3*, Puffin) Puffin Bks.

An Asterisk (*) at the beginning of an entry indicates that the title is appearing in BIP for the first time.

Backfire. Loren Baritz. 408p. 1986. mass mkt. 4.95 (*0-345-33121-4*) Ballantine.

Backfire. Janice Law. (Anna Peters Mystery Ser.). 208p. 1994. 18.95 (*0-312-11474-5*) St Martin.

Backfire. Christopher Newman. 320p. 1990. mass mkt. 5.99 (*0-449-13295-1*, GM) Fawcett.

Backfire. Eric Sauter. 384p. 1993. pap. 4.99 (*0-451-40408-4*, Onyx) NAL-Dutton.

Backfire. large type ed. Clive Egleton. 424p. 1982. 22.95 (*0-7089-0794-6*) Ulverscroft.

***Backfire: The CIA's Biggest Burn.** Ron Ridenour. 179p. 1991. pap. 9.95 (*0-9624975-1-7*) Infoservicios.

Backfire: The Untold Secrets of Self Treatment for Neck & Back Pain. Jan F. Tooke. LC 92-63063. (Illus.). 72p. 1993. pap. 19.95 (*0-9635691-0-4*) Tooke Phys Ther.

Backgammon see Win at Backgammon

Backgammon for People Who Hate to Lose. Tim Holland. 1978. pap. 4.95 (*0-679-14125-1*) McKay.

Backgammon for Winners. Bill Robertie. LC 93-70982. (Illus.). 80p. (Orig.). 1993. pap. 6.95 (*0-940685-42-6*) Cardoza Pub.

***Backgammon for Winners.** 2nd ed. Bill Robertie. (Illus.). 160p. (Orig.). 1995. pap. 9.95 (*0-940685-58-2*) Cardoza Pub.

Backgammon Handbook. Enno Heyken & Martin B. Fischer. (Illus.). 232p. 1991. 34.95 (*1-85223-402-4*, Pub. by Crowood Pr UK) Trafalgar.

Background Actor's Manual. Laurence H. Fitzgerald. 64p. (Orig.). 1987. pap. 6.00 (*0-9622870-4-0*) Fitzgerald CA.

Background Actor's Manual. rev. ed. Laurence H. Fitzgerald. 60p. (Orig.). 1989. pap. 6.00 (*0-685-25933-1*) Fitzgerald CA.

Background & Ceremonies of the Church of Scientology. L. Ron Hubbard. 40.00 (*0-686-30794-1*) Church Scient NY.

Background & Development of Brethren Doctrine, 1650-1987. Dale R. Stoffer. Ed. by William Eberly. (Monograph Ser.). 327p. (C). 1989. 46.00 (*0-936693-22-3*) Brethren Encyclopedia.

Background & Principles: On Words in Color. Caleb Gattegno. 82p. 1962. pap. 2.15 (*0-87825-065-4*) Ed Solutions.

Background Bible Study. Wayne Jackson. 111p. (Orig.). 1986. pap. 4.95 (*0-932859-14-3*) Apologetic Pr.

Background BK - Character Gen: Torg. 1992. 15.00 (*0-87431-328-7*, 20569) West End Games.

Background for Belief. Mark J. Lyons. 74p. (Orig.). 1990. pap. 1.95 (*0-8199-0957-2*, Frncscn Herld) Franciscan Pr.

Background for Domenico Scarlatti, Sixteen Eighty-Five to Seventeen Fifty-Seven. Sacheverell Sitwell. LC 74-107832. (Select Bibliographies Reprint Ser.). 1977. 20.95 (*0-8369-5197-2*) Ayer.

Background for Domenico Scarlatti, Sixteen Eighty-Five to Sixteen Fifty-Seven. Sacheverell Sitwell. LC 74-109845. 163p. 1971. reprint ed. text ed. 35.00 (*0-8371-4335-7*, SIDS, Greenwood Pr) Greenwood.

Background for Domenico Scarlatti, 1685-1757. Sacheverell Sitwell. (Music Book Index Ser.). 168p. 1992. reprint ed. lib. bdg. 69.00 (*0-7812-9486-X*) Rprt Serv.

Background for Glass Collectors. Sylvia Coppen-Gardner. (Illus.). 172p. 1976. 14.95 (*0-7207-0624-6*) Transatl Arts.

Background History of the Coeur D'Alene Indian Reservation. Jerome Peltier. 100p. Date not set. write for info. (*0-318-57414-4*) Ye Galleon.

Background in Tennessee. Evelyn Scott. LC 80-15703. (Tennesseana Editions Ser.). 324p. 1980. reprint ed. 31.00x (*0-87049-297-7*) U of Tenn Pr.

***Background Information.** Malcolm Chalmers & Owen Greene. (Bradford Arms Register Studies). (C). 1995. pap. text ed. 15.00 (*0-8133-2636-2*) Westview.

***Background into the Anzus Pact: Strategy & Diplomacy, 1945-55.** W. David McIntyre. LC 94-31762. 464p. 1995. 65.00 (*0-312-12439-2*) St Martin.

Background Investigations Made Easy by Examining Public Records: Instructional Manual. Maria W. Crago & James D. Crago. 22p. (Orig.). 1985. pap. 6.95 (*0-9616336-0-3*) Invest USA.

Background Issues of Oil Supply Trading in Pacific Island Countries. 44p. 1990. 6.00 (*92-1-119557-8*, 90.II.F.3) UN.

Background Management Guide. Laurence H. Fitzgerald. 49p. (Orig.). 1988. pap. 10.00 (*0-685-25935-8*) Fitzgerald CA.

Background Materials. 281p. 1990. 15.00 (*0-317-05678-6*, P90001EQK); 15.00 (*0-317-05693-X*, P90005EQK) Assn Bay Area.

Background of African Art. Melville J. Herskovits. LC 67-18433. (Cooke-Daniels Lecture Ser., Denver Art Museum). (Illus.). 1945. 22.00 (*0-8196-0201-9*) Biblo.

Background of Ecology: Concept & Theory. Robert P. McIntosh. (Studies in Ecology). 400p. 1986. pap. 29.95 (*0-521-27087-1*) Cambridge U Pr.

Background of English Literature: Classical & Romantic, & Other Collected Essays & Addresses. Herbert J. Grierson. LC 78-2920. 290p. 1978. reprint ed. text ed. 59.75 (*0-313-20306-7*, GRBE, Greenwood Pr) Greenwood.

Background of Modern French Literature. Charles H. Wright. LC 79-37360. (Select Bibliographies Reprint Ser.). 1977. reprint ed. 30.95 (*0-8369-6707-0*) Ayer.

Background of Modern Poetry. Cecil M. Bowra. LC 75-22207. (Studies in Poetry: No. 38). (C). 1975. lib. bdg. 75.00 (*0-8383-2075-9*) M S G Haskell Hse.

Background of Plant Ecology: The Plant Life of the Danube Basin. Henry S. Conard. Ed. by Frank N. Egerton, 3rd. LC 77-74234. (History of Ecology Ser.). 1978. reprint ed. lib. bdg. 21.95 (*0-405-10403-0*) Ayer.

Background of Selective Service, Vol. 1, Pt. 1. United States Selective Service System Staff et al. 1980. 54.95 (*0-405-18744-0*, 15936) Ayer.

Background of Selective Service, Vol. 2, Pts. 1-5. United States Selective Service System Staff et al. 1980. 54.95 (*0-405-18745-9*, 15937) Ayer.

Background of Selective Service, Vol. 2, Pts. 6-10. United States Selective Service System Staff et al. 1979. 54.95 (*0-405-18746-7*, 15938) Ayer.

Background of Selective Service, Vol. 2, Pts. 11-14. United States Selective Service System Staff et al. 1980. 54.95 (*0-405-18747-5*, 15939) Ayer.

Background of Swedish Immigration, 1840-1930. Florence E. Janson. LC 79-129403. (American Immigration Collection Ser. 2). 1979. reprint ed. 36.95 (*0-405-00556-3*) Ayer.

Background of the Epistles. William Fairweather. 427p. lib. bdg. 17.99 (*0-8254-5107-8*) Kregel.

Background of the Gospels. William Fairweather. 486p. lib. bdg. 18.99 (*0-8254-5105-1*) Kregel.

Background of the Gospels. 4th ed. William Fairweather. 464p. 1916. 35.95 (*0-567-02101-7*, Pub. by T & T Clark UK) Bks Intl VA.

Background of the Princess Casamassima. Wesley H. Tilley. LC 61-62688. (University of Florida Humanities Monographs: No. 5). 68p. reprint ed. pap. 25.00 (*0-7837-5008-0*, 2044675) Bks Demand.

Background of the Rebellion of An Lu-Shan. Edwin G. Pulleyblank. LC 82-6200. (London Oriental Ser.). (Illus.). x, 264p. 1982. reprint ed. text ed. 55.00 (*0-313-23549-X*, PUBA, Greenwood Pr) Greenwood.

Background of the Revolution for Mexican Independence. L. E. Fisher. 1976. lib. bdg. 59.95 (*0-8490-1469-7*) Gordon Pr.

Background of Treaty-Making in Western Washington. Barbara Lane. (Treaty Manuscripts Ser.: No. 3). 32p. 15.00 (*0-944253-25-3*) Inst Dev Indian Law.

Background Papers on Chesapeake Bay in Research & Related Matters. Ed. by Chesapeake Research Consortium Staff. pap. 2.00 (*0-943676-14-2*) MD Sea Grant Col.

Background Papers to the Report on the Measurement of International Capital Flows. LC 92-36106. viii, 97p. 1992. pap. 19.50 (*1-55775-320-2*) Intl Monetary.

Background Patterns, Textures & Tints. Clarence Hornung. (Pictorial Archive Ser.). (Illus.). 112p. (Orig.). 1976. pap. 6.95 (*0-486-23260-3*) Dover.

Background Patterns, Textures & Tints: Ninety-Five Plates for Artists & Designers. Clarence P. Hornung. 14.75 (*0-8446-5492-2*) Peter Smith.

Background Readings in Building Library Collections, 1. Ed. by Mary V. Gaver. LC 79-5598. reprint ed. pap. 160.00 (*0-8357-5943-1*, 2051187) Bks Demand.

Background Readings in Building Library Collections, 2. Ed. by Mary V. Gaver. LC 79-5598. 649p. reprint ed. pap. 180.00 (*0-8357-5944-X*) Bks Demand.

Background Research Reports. 199p. 1984. 15.00 (*0-317-05680-8*, P84005EQK) Assn Bay Area.

Background Research Reports. 295p. 1988. 15.00 (*0-317-05682-4*, P88004PLN) Assn Bay Area.

Background Study of the Non-Admitted Insurance Market. J. Ryan. LC 79-93288. 71p. 1980. 25.00 (*0-317-35009-9*) Nat Assn Insu Comm.

Background to Contemporary Greece. Ed. by Marion Sarafis. (C). 1990. lib. bdg. 71.00 (*0-389-20899-X*) B&N Imports.

Background to Danger. Eric Ambler. 280p. 1990. pap. 3.95 (*0-88184-611-2*) Carroll & Graf.

Background to Discovery: Pacific Exploration from Dampier to Cook. Ed. by Derek Howse. 1990. 40.00 (*0-520-06208-6*) U CA Pr.

Background to European Ballet. Peter Brinson. LC 79-7754. (Dance Ser.). (Illus.). 1980. reprint ed. lib. bdg. 23.95 (*0-8369-9279-2*) Ayer.

Background to Glory. John Bakeless. LC 92-10931. (Illus.). vi, 386p. 1992. reprint ed. pap. 12.95 (*0-8032-6105-5*) U of Nebr Pr.

Background to Indian Criminal Law. Tapas K. Banerjee. (C). 1990. 85.00 (*0-89771-189-0*) St Mut.

***Background to Jewish Studies in the Bible & in the Ancient Near East.** Cyrus H. Gordon. 1994. pap. text ed. 7.50x (*0-614-03628-3*) Eisenbrauns.

Background to Modern Science. Ed. by Joseph Needham & Walter Pagel. LC 74-26281. (History, Philosophy & Sociology of Science Ser.). 1975. reprint ed. 21.95 (*0-405-06608-2*) Ayer.

Background to Newton's Principia: A Study of Newton's Dynamical Researches in the Years 1664-84. John Herivel. LC 66-1463. 362p. reprint ed. pap. 103.20 (*0-8357-5945-8*, 2056377) Bks Demand.

Background to Palaeohydrology: A Perspective. Ed. by K. J. Gregory. LC 83-5929. (Wiley-Interscience Publication Ser.). 502p. reprint ed. pap. 143.10 (*0-7837-3224-4*, 2043241) Bks Demand.

Background to Political Geography. G. R. Crone. LC 69-14376. (Illus.). 1967. 13.95 (*0-8023-1202-0*) Dufour.

Background to Prehistory of Yuha Desert Region. Ed. by Philip J. Wilke. (Anthropological Papers: No. 5). (Illus.). 1976. pap. 7.95 (*0-87919-058-2*) Ballena Pr.

Background to Revolution: The Development of Modern Cuba. rev. ed. Robert F. Smith. LC 78-10644. 256p. 1979. reprint ed. pap. 10.95 (*0-88275-773-3*) Krieger.

Background to Technology: Chemistry. Ed. by H. Taylor. (C). 1987. teacher ed 195.00 (*0-85973-062-X*, Pub. by S Thornes Pubs UK) St Mut.

Background to Technology: Physics. Stanley Thornes. (C). 1986. teacher ed 375.00 (*0-85973-061-1*, Pub. by S Thornes Pubs UK) St Mut.

Background to Technology: Pressure, Bk. 3. Ed. by H. Taylor. (C). 1983. 55.00 (*0-685-37698-2*, Pub. by S Thornes Pubs UK) St Mut.

Background to the English Civil War. F. W. Jessup. LC 66-20360. 1966. 88.00 (*0-08-012001-6*, Pub. by Pergamon Repr UK) Franklin.

Background to the Gospel of St. Mark. 2nd ed. Rudolf Steiner. 200p. 1986. pap. 12.95 (*0-88010-145-8*) Anthroposophic.

Backgrounding the News: The Newspaper & the Social Sciences. Sidney Kobre. LC 70-137063. (Illus.). 271p. 1974. reprint ed. text ed. 67.50 (*0-8371-5526-6*, KOBN, Greenwood Pr) Greenwood.

Backgrounds & Preparations for the Roanoke Voyages, 1584-1590. John L. Humber. (America's 400th Anniversary Ser.). (Illus.). xvii, 108p. 1986. pap. 6.00 (*0-86526-208-X*) NC Archives.

Backgrounds for the Bible. Michael P. O'Connor & David N. Freedman. LC 87-13592. xii, 369p. 1987. text ed. 29.50 (*0-931464-30-7*) Eisenbrauns.

Backgrounds of Book Reviewing. H. S. Mallory. 1972. 59.95 (*0-87968-693-6*) Gordon Pr.

Backgrounds of Early Christianity. 2nd ed. Everett Ferguson. (Illus.). 608p. (Orig.). (C). 1993. pap. text ed. 29.99 (*0-8028-0669-4*) Eerdmans.

Backgrounds of Literature. Hamilton W. Mabie. LC 72-111846. (Essay Index Reprint Ser.). 1977. 31.95 (*0-8369-1617-4*) Ayer.

Backgrounds of Selective Service, 2 vols. in four, Set. U. S. Selective Service System Staff. Ed. by Richard H. Kohn. LC 78-22405. (American Military Experience Ser.). 1979. reprint ed. lib. bdg. 218.95 (*0-405-11881-3*) Ayer.

Backgrounds to Communist Thought. James E. Le Rossignol. 1979. 8.75 (*0-8446-2454-3*) Peter Smith.

Backgrounds to David Jones: A Study in Sources & Drafts. Jonathan Miles. xii, 232p. 1990. 40.00 (*0-7083-1051-6*, Pub. by U of Wales UK) Bks Intl VA.

Backgrounds to Restoration & Eighteenth-Century English Literature: An Annotated Bibliographical Guide to Modern Scholarship. Comp. by Robert D. Spector. LC 88-32807. (Bibliographies & Indexes in World Literature Ser.: No. 17). 577p. 1989. text ed. 89.50 (*0-313-24098-1*, SPK) Greenwood.

Backhanded View of the Law: Irreverent Essays on Justice. Mordecai Rosenfeld. LC 91-27013. 1992. 24.95 (*0-918024-90-0*) Ox Bow.

Backing into the Future: The Classical Tradition & Its Renewal. Bernard M. Knox. LC 93-22732. 1994. 25.00 (*0-393-03595-6*) Norton.

***Backlash.** large type ed. Elisabeth Oldfield. (Magna Large Print Ser.). 1994. 18.95 (*0-7505-0667-9*, Pub. by Magna Print Bks) Ulverscroft.

Backlash. large type ed. Bill Reno. (Nightingale Series Large Print Bks.). 295p. (Orig.). 1991. pap. 14.95 (*0-8161-5172-5*, Nightingale) Hall.

Backlash: A Compendium of Lore & Lies (Mostly Lies) Concerning Hunting, Fishing & the Out-of-Doors. Galen Winter. LC 92-93611. 168p. (Orig.). 1993. pap. 12.95 (*0-9635699-0-2*) G Winter.

Backlash: Child Protection under Fire. John E. Myers. 176p. 1994. 38.00 (*0-8039-5403-4*); pap. 17.95 (*0-8039-5404-2*) Sage.

Backlash: The Undeclared War Against American Women. Susan Faludi. 552p. 1991. 24.00 (*0-517-57698-8*, Crown) Crown Pub Group.

Backlash: The Undeclared War Against American Women. Susan Faludi. LC 92-22416. 1992. pap. 12.95 (*0-385-42507-4*, Anchor NY) Doubleday.

Backlashes. Thomas Eveland. Ed. by Kevin McCaney. (Illus.). 160p. (Orig.). 1992. pap. 9.95 (*0-9632298-0-X*) Three E Co.

Backlog Reduction Program in the Supreme Court in New York City: First Interim Evaluation Report. National Center for State Courts. 25p. 1982. 1.50 (*0-685-15459-9*, NERO-103) Natl Ctr St Courts.

Backlund Transformations & Their Applications. C. A. Rogers & William F. Shadwick. LC 81-22783. (Mathematics in Science & Engineering Ser.). 1982. text ed. 106.00 (*0-12-592850-5*) Acad Pr.

Backpack Cookery. Ruth D. Mendenhall. (Illus.). 1974. 2.95 (*0-910856-22-2*) La Siesta.

Backpack Loops & Long Day Trail Hikes in Southern Ohio. Robert H. Ruchhoft. Ed. by Linda Sears. (Illus.). 260p. (Orig.). 1984. pap. text ed. 11.95 (*0-940029-01-4*) Pucelle Pr.

Backpack Techniques. Ruth D. Mendenhall. (Illus.). 1984. 1.95 (*0-910856-24-9*) La Siesta.

Backpacker Magazine's Guide to the Appalachian Trail. Jim Chase. LC 88-28258. (Illus.). 256p. (Orig.). 1989. pap. 14.95 (*0-8117-2237-6*) Stackpole.

***Backpackers: The New Breed.** Alec Goldsmith. 166p. (Orig.). 1995. pap. 12.95 (*0-86470-049-0*, Pub. by Benton-Guy Pub NZ) Seven Hills Bk.

***Backpacker's Africa, East & Southern.** 4th ed. Hilary Bradt. (Bradt Guides Ser.). (Illus.). 342p. 1994. 15.95 (*1-56440-539-7*) Globe Pequot.

***Backpacker's Africa, West & Central.** David Else. (Bradt Guides Ser.). (Illus.). 192p. Date not set. pap. 15.95 (*1-56440-540-0*) Globe Pequot.

Backpacker's Guide to Fly Fishing. R. A. Cordes. 96p. 1992. pap. text ed. 8.95 (*0-9633024-0-X*) Troutbeck Pub.

***Backpacker's Handbook.** Hugh McManners. LC 94-32042. (Illus.). 160p. 1995. 14.95 (*1-56458-852-1*) Dorling Kindersley.

Backpacker's Handbook. Chris Townsend. (Illus.). 384p. 1992. 29.95 (*0-87742-365-2*, 60357); pap. 14.95 (*0-87742-357-1*, 60357) Intl Marine.

Backpacker's Handbook. Chris Townsend. 1992. pap. text ed. 15.95 (*0-07-065242-2*) McGraw.

***Backpacker's Log.** Kenneth Hukari & Scott Griebel. 25p. 1993. 11.95 (*1-884751-02-4*) Wy East Log.

Backpacker's Photography Handbook: How to Take Great Wilderness Pictures While Hiking, Climbing, & Skiing. Charles Campbell. LC 94-9027. (Illus.). 144p. 1994. pap. 19.95 (*0-8174-3609-X*, Amphoto) Watsn-Guptill.

***Backpacker's Songbook.** Ron Middlebrook. (Illus.). 200p. 1994. pap. 5.50 (*0-931759-85-4*) Centerstream Pub.

Backpacking. 80p. 1983. pap. 1.85 (*0-8395-3323-3*, 33323) BSA.

Backpacking. Jimmy Holmes. (All Action Ser.). (Illus.). 48p. (J). (gr. 4 up). 1992. lib. bdg. 17.50 (*0-8225-2479-1*, Lerner Publctns) Lerner Group.

Backpacking. rev. ed. Joel Meier. LC 91-68424. (Illus.). 150p. 1993. reprint ed. pap. 9.95 (*0-915611-53-8*) Sagamore Pub.

Backpacking & Camping in the Developing World. Scott Graham. LC 88-40005. 160p. (Orig.). 1988. pap. 11.95 (*0-89997-091-5*) Wilderness Pr.

***Backpacking & Trekking in Peru & Bolivia.** 6th ed. Hilary Bradt & Petra Schepens. (Illus.). 282p. 1995. pap. 15.95 (*1-56440-613-X*, Pub. by Bradt Pubns UK) Globe Pequot.

Backpacking Basics. 4th ed. Thomas Winnett & Melaine Findling. LC 88-40011. (Illus.). 134p. (Orig.). 1994. pap. 9.95 (*0-89997-172-5*) Wilderness Pr.

Backpacking Death Valley. 2nd ed. Chuck Gebhardt. LC 83-81945. (Illus.). 110p. 1985. pap. 4.50 (*0-685-07646-6*) CWG Creations.

Backpacking Death Valley. 2nd ed. Chuck Gebhardt. LC 83-81945. 92p. 1985. pap. 4.50 (*0-9601410-2-2*) CWG Creations.

***Backpacking in Chile & Argentina.** 3rd ed. Ed. by Clare Hargreaves. (Bradt Guides Ser.). (Illus.). 192p. 1994. 14.95 (*1-56440-535-4*) Globe Pequot.

Backpacking in Michigan. 2nd ed. Pat Allen & Gerald L. DeRuiter. LC 88-27753. (Illus.). 200p. 1989. pap. 14.95 (*0-472-06386-3*) U of Mich Pr.

Backpacking in the Eighties. Bob Wirth. LC 83-13249. 306p. 1983. text ed. 19.95 (*0-13-056747-7*, Parker Publishing Co) P-H.

Backpacking in the Nineties: Tips, Techniques & Secrets. Victoria Logue. LC 92-43314. (Illus.). 1992. pap. 14.95 (*0-89732-163-4*) Menasha Ridge.

Backpacking Made Easy. rev. ed. Michael Abel. LC 75-8529. (Illus.). 128p. 1975. 14.95 (*0-87961-041-7*); pap. 6.95 (*0-87961-040-9*) Naturegraph.

Backpacking, One Step At a Time. Harvey Manning. 1986. pap. 13.00 (*0-394-72939-0*, Vin) Random.

***Backpacking Primer: For the Entire Family.** Lori Saldana. (Outdoor Sports Primer Ser.). (Illus.). 240p. 1995. pap. 15.00 (*1-879415-13-5*) Mtn n Air Bks.

***Backpacking Through Illusions.** Vesna Dye. LC 94-90223. 320p. (Orig.). 1995. pap. 9.95 (*1-56002-472-0*, Univ Edtns) Aegina Pr.

Backpacking with Babies & Small Children. Goldie Silverman. LC 85-41057. 144p. 1986. reprint ed. pap. 9.95 (*0-89997-068-0*) Wilderness Pr.

Backpaddlers Guide to the North Umpqua River, 3 bks., Bk. 1: Soda Springs Dam to Gravel Bin. Ralph Corliss & Richard Chase. (Illus.). 50p. (Orig.). 1990. spiral bd., pap. 6.95 (*1-878947-01-X*) Walk Water.

Backpaddlers Guide to the North Umpqua River, 3 bks., Bk. 2: Gravel Bin to Cable Crossing. Ralph Corliss & Richard Chase. (Illus.). (Orig.). 1990. spiral bd., pap. write for info. (*1-878947-02-8*) Walk Water.

Backpaddlers Guide to the North Umpqua River, 3 bks., Bk. 3: Cable Crossing to Whistlers Bend. Ralph Corliss & Richard Chase. (Illus.). (Orig.). 1990. spiral bd., pap. write for info. (*1-878947-03-6*) Walk Water.

Backpocket Bluegrass Songbook. Wayne Erbsen. (Illus.). 1990. pap. 5.95 (*0-8256-1295-0*, WE10008) Music Sales.

Backpocket Bluegrass Songbook: Words & Music to 40 Classic Bluegrass Tunes. Wayne Erbsen. 56p. 1990. pap. 6.95 (*0-9629327-1-X*) Native Ground.

Backpocket Old-Time Songbook. Wayne Erbsen. (Illus.). 1990. pap. 5.95 (*0-8256-1294-2*, WE10000) Music Sales.

Backpocket Old-Time Songbook: Words & Music to 40 Timeless Mountain Tunes. Wayne Erbsen. 56p. 1990. pap. 6.95 (*0-9629327-0-1*) Native Ground.

Backpower Program. David Imrie. 1990. pap. text ed. 12.95 (*0-471-52879-X*) Wiley.

***Backroad Baja.** Tom Higginbotham & Patti Higginbotham. 120p. Date not set. pap. text ed. 12.95 (*0-9632222-3-6*) Somethins Fishy.

Backroad Wineries of Northern California: A Scenic Tour of California's Country Wineries. Bill Gleeson. LC 93-4407. 128p. 1994. 16.95 (*0-8118-0306-6*) Chronicle Bks.

Backroad Wineries of Southern California: A Scenic Tour of California's Country Wineries. Bill Gleeson. LC 93-31266. 128p. 1994. 16.95 (*0-8118-0335-X*) Chronicle Bks.

Backroads: A Portfolio of Mountain Images. 2nd ed. Randy Ball. 48p. 1992. pap. 6.50 (*0-9631936-0-0*) R Ball Photo.

Backroads & Artism. Guy Beining. LC 79-84873. 1979. pap. 5.00 (*0-931350-05-0*) Moonlight Pubns.

Backroads & Hiking Trails, The Santa Cruz Mountains. Jerry Schad. (Illus.). 80p. (Orig.). pap. 6.95 (*0-911518-54-1*) Touchstone Oregon.

Backroads Explorer: Similkameen & South Okanagan. Murphy Shewchuk. 160p. (Orig.). pap. text ed. 9.95 (*0-88839-205-2*) Hancock House.

Backroads of America. David Cobb. 1992. 14.99 (*0-517-06988-1*) Random Hse Value.

Backroads of America. Ideals Magazine Staff. (Illus.). 1989. 22.95 (*0-8249-4036-9*) Ideals.

***Backroads of Colorado.** Boyd Norton. LC 95-7222. 1995. write for info. (*0-89658-316-3*) Voyageur Pr.

Backroads of Florida. Ann Ruff. 176p. 1992. pap. 9.95 (*0-88415-008-9*) Gulf Pub.

Backroads of Holland: Scenic Excursions by Bike, Car, or Train. Helen Colijn. LC 91-77704. (Illus.). 224p. (Orig.). 1992. pap. 12.95 (*0-933201-48-6*) Bicycle Books.

Backroads of My Memory, Vol. 1. Geri Kisner. 100p. 1990. pap. 7.50 (*1-56770-225-2*) S Scheewe Pubns.

Backroads of My Memory, Vol. 2. Geri Kisner. 100p. 1991. pap. 7.50 (*1-56770-245-7*) S Scheewe Pubns.

B

An Asterisk (*) at the beginning of an entry indicates that the title is appearing in BIP for the first time.

Backroads of New England. B. Howells. 1995. 16.95 (0-88415-143-3) Gulf Pub.

***Backroads of Ontario.** Ron Brown. 256p. 1995. pap. 18.50 (1-55046-166-4, Pub. by Stoddart Publng CN) Pubs Dist MI.

***Backroads of Southern California.** Bob Howells. 200p. 1995. pap. 16.95 (0-88415-146-8) Gulf Pub.

Backroads of Texas. Ed Syers & Larry Hodge. LC 93-15530. 208p. 1993. 14.95 (0-88415-095-X) Gulf Pub.

Backroads to Adventure. H. Glenn Carson. (Illus.). 116p. (Orig.). 1986. pap. 7.95 (0-941620-31-X) Carson Ent.

Backroads Tour: Northern Kentucky Historic Road Tour. Ed. by Billie Cahill et al. (Illus.). 32p. (Orig.). 1992. pap. 5.00 (0-9624673-9-1) Picture This Bks.

Backroads, U. S. A. The Middle Atlantic States. T. J. Glennon. (Illus.). 1988. pap. 10.95 (0-02-032630-0, Collier S&S) S&S Trade.

Backs Against the Wall: Urban-Oriented Colleges & Universities & the Urban Poor & Disadvantaged. Pastora S. J. Cafferty & Gail Spangenberg. LC 82-25124. (Ford Foundation Report Series on Higher Education in the Cities). 76p. (Orig.). 1983. pap. (0-916584-22-4) Ford Found.

Backs of Books, & Other Essays in Librarianship. William W. Bishop. LC 68-54328. (Essay Index Reprint Ser.). 1977. reprint ed. 20.95 (0-8369-0215-7) Ayer.

Backs to the Future: U. S. Government Policy Toward Environmentally Critical Technologies. large type ed. George Heaton & Robert Repetto. 35p. 1992. Large format. pap. 14.95 (0-915825-75-9, HEBTP) World Resources Inst.

Backscattering Spectroscopy. Wei-Kan Chu et al. 1978. text ed. 121.00 (0-12-173850-7) Acad Pr.

***Backseat Buckaroo.** Edward Valfre. LC 94-39597. (Illus.). 48p. (J). (gr. k up). 1995. 14.95 (1-56566-078-1) Thomasson-Grant.

Backshooter. Robert Lake. 1990. pap. 2.95 (0-8217-2875-X) Zebra.

***Backside of Calvary: Where Healing Stained the Cross.** Rod Parsley. 107p. 1991. pap. 5.99 (1-880244-01-2) Wrld Harvest Church.

Backside of Yesterday. Arthelia Brooks. LC 94-71713. (Illus.). 376p. (Orig.). 1994. 25.00 (0-923687-32-7) Celo Valley Bks.

Backslider. 2nd ed. Levi S. Peterson. LC 90-37395. 361p. 1990. pap. 5.95 (1-56085-015-9) Signature Bks.

Backstage at Bunraku: A Behind-the-Scenes Look at Japan's Puppet Theatre. Barbara C. Adachi. (Illus.). 208p. 1985. pap. 25.00 (0-8348-0199-X) Weatherhill.

Backstage at the Grand Old Hatchery. Sue Friddle. (Illus.). (Orig.). Date not set. pap. write for info. (0-9623308-3-3) Anyones Pub.

Backstage at the Metropolitan Opera. Rose Heylbut & Aime Gerber. Ed. by Andrew Farkas. LC 76-29941. (Opera Biographies Ser.). Orig. Title: Backstage at the Opera. (Illus.). 1977. reprint ed. lib. bdg. 31.95 (0-405-09683-6) Ayer.

Backstage at the Opera see Backstage at the Metropolitan Opera

***Backstage Forms.** Paul Carter. 166p. 1990. pap. 15.00 (0-911747-35-4) Broadway Pr.

***Backstage Handbook: An Illustrated Almanac Or Technical Information.** 3rd rev. ed. Paul Carter. (Illus.). 320p. 1995. pap. 15.00 (0-911747-29-X) Broadway Pr.

Backstage in the Big War: A Memoir of World War Two. Kristine Konold. LC 90-83108. 248p. (Orig.). (C). 1991. pap. 14.95 (1-55618-087-X) Brunswick Pub.

Backstage Nurse. large type ed. Jane Converse. 1990. pap. 16.95 (0-7927-0387-1, C0419, Curley Lrg Print) Chivers N Amer.

***Backstage Pass.** Laura Battyanyi-Petose. (Voices Romance Ser.: No. 7). 224p. 1995. mass mkt. 3.99 (0-8217-4879-3) Zebra.

Backstage Pass: A Non-Performer's Guide to Rock 'n Roll, Touring Careers. Eric M. Todd et al. No. 1. 200p. (Orig.). 1989. pap. write for info. (0-318-64806-7) Backstage Pass.

Backstage Passes. Angela Bowie & Patrick Carr. 320p. (Orig.). 1994. mass mkt. 5.99 (0-515-11352-2) Jove Pubns.

Backstage Passes: Life on the Wild Side with David Bowie. Angela Bowie & Patrick Carr. (Illus.). 352p. 1993. 21.95 (0-399-13764-5, Putnam) Putnam Pub Group.

Backstage, Vol. 1: The Essential Source Guide on How to Market & Promote Your Music Contacts. rev. ed. Jaymes Hines. Ed. by Jean Harrison. 162p. 1993. pap. text ed. 29.95 (0-9639255-0-4) Major Bad Artist.

***Backstage with a Ghost.** Joan L. Nixon. LC 94-71793. (Disney Adventures Casebusters Ser.: Bk. 3). (Illus.). 96p. (J). (gr. 2-6). 1995. 13.95 (0-7868-3048-4); pap. 3.95 (0-7868-4025-0) Disney Pr.

Backstage with Actors. Helen Ormsbee. LC 70-84522. (Illus.). 1972. 29.95 (0-405-08830-2) Ayer.

***Backstairs Mission in Moscow: American Autobiography.** Charles Ciliberti. 127p. 1995. lib. bdg. 69.00 (0-7812-8479-1) Rprt Serv.

Backstory: Interviews with Screenwriters of Hollywood's Golden Age. Ed. by Patrick McGilligan. (Illus.). 1986. 40.00 (0-520-05666-3); pap. 15.00 (0-520-05689-2) U CA Pr.

Backstory Two: Interviews with Screenwriters of the 1940s & 1950s. Patrick McGilligan. LC 85-28949. (Illus.). 356p. 1991. 30.00 (0-520-07169-7) U CA Pr.

***Backstreets.** Charles Cross. 1994. pap. 7.99 (0-517-13116-1) Random.

Backstreets: Prostitution, Money, & Love. Cecilie Hoigard & Liv Finstad. 238p. 1992. 35.00 (0-271-00877-6); pap. 14.95 (0-271-00878-4) Pa St U Pr.

Backstreets: Springsteen: The Man & His Music. Charles Cross. 1992. pap. 19.00 (0-517-58929-X, Harmony) Crown Pub Group.

***Backstreets of Desire.** Hanspeter Schneider. 1994. pap. 29.95 (3-7165-0929-9, Pub. by Benteli Verlag SZ) Dist Art Pubs.

Backstretch. Ed. by Harriet H. Randall. 120p. 1989. 14.00 (0-318-16780-8) United Thoroughbred Trnrs.

Backtalk. Robin Becker. LC 81-72094. 74p. (C). 1982. pap. 9.95 (0-914086-36-7) Alicejamesbooks.

Backtalk. Lucy Lippard & Diane Middlebrook. (Illus.). 48p. (Orig.). 1993. pap. write for info. (1-880658-06-2) San Barb CAF.

Backtalk: Women Writers Speak Out. Ed. by Donna Perry. LC 92-41201. (Illus.). 360p. (C). 1993. 24.95 (0-8135-1991-8) Rutgers U Pr.

***Backtalk: Women Writers Speak Out.** Donna Perry. (Illus.). 360p. 1995. pap. 16.95 (0-8135-2199-8) Rutgers U Pr.

Backtrack. Maxine Numes. 1989. pap. 3.95 (0-671-67893-0) PB.

Backtracking. Vern Rutsala. (Poetry Ser.). 66p. (Orig.). 1985. 14.00 (0-934257-01-9); pap. 6.95 (0-934257-00-0) Story Line.

Backtracking: Ancient Art of Southern Idaho. Max G. Pavesic & William Studebaker. (Illus.). 84p. (Orig.). 1993. pap. 19.95 (0-939696-00-2) Idaho Mus Nat Hist.

Backtracking: The Way of a Naturalist. Ted Levin. LC 86-32717. (Illus.). 220p. 1987. pap. 9.95 (0-930031-15-6) Chelsea Green Pub.

Backtracks: Time Travel New Mexico. Ed. by Arnold Vigil. 176p. (Orig.). 1994. pap. 12.95 (0-937206-31-8) New Mexico Mag.

Backtrail. Elizabeth Fackler. LC 93-19980. (Novel of the West Ser.). 238p. 1993. 16.95 (0-87131-716-8) M Evans.

Backtrail. Elizabeth Fackler. 320p. 1994. mass mkt. 4.50 (0-8125-3339-9) Tor Bks.

***Backup Management.** Dorian Cougias. (Network Frontiers Field Manual Ser.). (Illus.). 400p. 1995. pap. write for info. (0-12-192562-5) Acad Pr.

Backup Men. Ross Thomas. 256p. 1992. mass mkt. 5.99 (0-446-40170-6, Mysterious Paperbk) Warner Bks.

***Backus Families of Early New England.** Reno W. Backus. (Illus.). 199p. 1994. reprint ed. lib. bdg. 42.00 (0-8328-4273-7); reprint ed. lib. bdg. 42.50 (0-8328-4398-9); reprint ed. pap. 32.00 (0-8328-4274-5); reprint ed. pap. 32.50 (0-8328-4399-7) Higginson Bk Co.

Backward: An Essay on Indians, Time, & Photography. Will Baker. (Illus.). 420p. 1983. 24.95 (0-938190-13-X) North Atlantic.

Backward Art of Spending Money & Other Essays. Wesley C. Mitchell. vii, 421p. 1964. reprint ed. 39.50 (0-678-00026-3) Kelley.

Backward Boy see Ten Top Stories

Backward Chaining: Teaching Task Performance. Jay Alden. Ed. by Danny G. Langdon. LC 77-25132. (Instructional Design Library). (Illus.). 96p. 1978. 23.95 (0-87778-110-9) Educ Tech Pubns.

Backward, Christian Soldiers? Gary North. 290p. 1984. pap. 5.95 (0-930464-01-X) Inst Christian.

Backward Classes in Contemporary India. Andre Beteille. 125p. 1993. pap. 7.95 (0-19-563035-1) OUP.

Backward Curved Centrifugal Fans in VAV Systems: Selection & Energy Consumption. Ed. by M. J. Holmes. (C). 1976. 40.00 (0-86022-024-9, Pub. by Build Servs Info Assn UK) St Mut.

Backward Glance. Edith Wharton. (Illus.). 1981. text ed. 27.50 (0-684-15983-X, Scribners) S&S Trade.

Backward Glance. Edith Wharton. (Illus.). 424p. 1985. pap. 13.95 (0-684-18381-1, Scribners) S&S Trade.

Backward Glance. Edith Wharton. 1985. 27.50 (0-684-16528-7, Scribners) S&S Trade.

Backward Glance: Los Angeles, 1901-1915. Robert G. Cowan. LC 85-21278. 48p. 1985. reprint ed. lib. bdg. 23.00x (0-89370-866-6) Borgo Pr.

Backward Glances. large type ed. John Gielgud. 269p. 1990. 10.97 (1-85089-410-8, Pub. by ISIS UK) Transaction Pubs.

***Backward Glances: Exploring Italy, Reinterpreting America: 1831-1866.** Leonardo Buonomo. LC 95-10317. 1996. write for info. (0-8386-3649-7) Fairleigh Dickinson.

Backward Glances: Times for Reflection & Distinguished Company. John Gielgud. LC 90-36754. (Illus.). 214p. (Orig.). 1990. pap. 10.95 (0-87910-140-7) Limelight Edns.

Backward Glances I. A. W. Neville. Ed. by Skipper Steely. (Illus.). 320p. 1983. 20.00 (0-915263-25-4) Wright Pr.

Backward Glances II. A. W. Neville. Ed. & Intro. by Skipper Steely. (Illus.). 321p. 1985. 20.00 (0-915263-26-2) Wright Pr.

Backward Glances, Three. A. W. Neville. Ed. by Skipper Steely. (Illus.). 303p. 1985. 20.00 (0-915263-27-0) Wright Pr.

Backward Look: Selected Verse. Clarine C. Gren Fell. (Illus.). 96p. reprint ed. pap. 8.50 (0-9612766-3-0) Gren Fell Read Ctr.

Backward Man. James Wilkey. LC 88-50099. 317p. (Orig.). 1988. pap. 5.95 (0-945719-00-0) Wolfhound FL.

Backward Society. Raymond Frost. LC 73-10735. 246p. 1974. reprint ed. text ed. 59.75 (0-8371-7025-7, FRBS, Greenwood Pr) Greenwood.

Backward Toward Revolution: The Chinese Revolutionary Party. Edward Friedman. LC 73-76095. (Center for Chinese Studies, University of Michigan: No. 3). 1974. pap. 13.00 (0-520-03279-9) U CA Pr.

Backward, Turn Backward: A Study of Books for Children in the Philippines, 1866-1945. Morton J. Netzorg. (Illus.). xx, 246p. 1985. 22.50 (971-08-2402-3, Pub. by Natl Bk Store PH); pap. 15.00 (0-318-18464-8, Pub. by Natl Bk Store PH) Cellar.

Backward, Turn Backward: Recollections of Childhood in Northern Michigan. Beatrice S. Henshaw. (Illus.). 306p. 1986. 18.00 (0-9614344-1-4) Historical Soc MI.

Backwardness & Welfare of Scheduled Castes & Scheduled Tribes in India. P. Hanumantha Rayappa. 1986. 18.00 (81-7024-059-X, Pub. by Ashish II) S Asia.

Backwards & Forwards: A Technical Manual for Reading Plays. David Ball. LC 82-19333. 128p. (Orig.). 1983. pap. 9.95 (0-8093-1110-0) S Ill U Pr.

***Backwards into Battle: A Tail Gunner's Journey in World War II.** Andrew M. Doty. (Illus.). (Orig.). 1995. pap. write for info. (0-9646253-0-X) Tall Tree CA.

Backwards into Delhi. Bunny Knott. LC 89-60941. 300p. (Orig.). 1989. pap. 13.00 (0-910395-52-7) Marlboro Pr.

Backwards Running. Robert K. Stevenson. (Illus.). 1981. pap. 7.95 (0-9606252-0-8) Stevenson Intl.

Backwards Watch. Eric Houghton. LC 91-16951. (Illus.). 32p. (J). (ps-2). 1992. 14.95 (0-531-05968-5); lib. bdg. 14.99 (0-531-08568-6) Orchard Bks Watts.

Backwater. Dorothy M. Richardson. 286p. 1977. reprint ed. lib. bdg. 13.85 (0-89966-154-8) Buccaneer Bks.

BackWhen Ben Again. Johnie B. Sikes. (Tales from the BackWhen Ser.: Bk. 3). 40p. (J). 1992. pap. text ed. 3.95 (0-9633262-3-6) Vitamemoria.

Backwoods America. Charles M. Wilson. LC 35-27064. 1934. reprint ed. 25.00 (0-403-00746-1) Scholarly.

***Backwoods & Along the Seashore: Selections from Henry David Thoreau's Maine Woods & Cape Cod.** Henry Thoreau. Ed. by Peter Turner. LC 94-32675. (Shambhala Pocket Classics Ser.). 1995. pap. 6.00 (1-57062-056-3) Shambhala Pubns.

Backwoods Boy. Horatio Alger, Jr. (Works of Horatio Alger Jr.). 1989. reprint ed. lib. bdg. 79.00 (0-7812-1713-X) Rprt Serv.

Backwoods Ethics: Environmental Issues for Hikers & Campers. 2nd rev. ed. Laura Waterman & Guy Waterman. 280p. 1993. pap. 13.00 (0-88150-257-X) Countryman.

Backwoods Jazz in the Twenties. Raymond F. Meyer. LC 88-64118. 120p. (Orig.). 1989. pap. 9.95 (0-934426-19-8) NAPSAC Reprods.

Backwoods Railroads: Branchlines & Shortlines of Western Oregon. D. C. Jesse Burkhardt. LC 93-42338. (Illus.). 168p. 1994. 45.00 (0-87422-104-8) Wash St U Pr.

Backwoods Surgery & Medicine. Charles S. Moody. (Shorey Lost Arts Ser.). 1974. reprint ed. pap. 3.95 (0-8466-6034-2, U 34) Shorey.

Backwoods to Border. Ed. by Mody C. Boatright & Donald Day. LC 48-18054. (Texas Folklore Society Publications: No. 18). (Illus.). 248p. 1967. reprint ed. 12.95 (0-87074-011-3) UNTX Pr.

Backwoodsman's Year. large type ed. R. W. Poole. 254p. 1991. 10.97 (1-85089-885-5, Pub. by ISIS UK) Transaction Pubs.

***Backwoodsmen: Stockmen & Hunters along a Big Thicket River Valley.** Thad Sitton. LC 95-3681. 1995. write for info. (0-8061-2742-2) U of Okla Pr.

BackWorks: An Illustrated Guide to How Your Back Works & What to Do When It Doesn't. Timothy J. Gray. 185p. 1993. pap. 15.95 (0-9622269-1-2) BookPartners.

Backyard: Adventures for Outdoor Explorers. Imogene Forte. LC 83-80959. (Tabletop Learning Ser.). (Illus.). 80p. (gr. k-6). 1983. pap. text ed. 3.95 (0-86530-091-7, IP 917) Incentive Pubns.

Backyard & Beyond: A Guide for Discovering the Outdoors. Edward Duensing & A. B. Millmoss. (Illus.). 264p. 1992. pap. 14.95 (1-55591-071-8) Fulcrum Pub.

***Backyard Archaeology at the Willis Allen House, 1857-1945.** Bernard A. Paul et al. Ed. by Bonita K. Rubach. (Illus.). 28p. (Orig.). 1994. pap. write for info. (0-913415-08-1) Am Resources.

Backyard Astronomer's Guide. Terence Dickinson & Alan Dyer. Ed. by Barry Estabrook. (Illus.). 288p. 1991. 39.95 (0-921820-11-9, Pub. by Camden Hse CN) Firefly Bks Ltd.

Backyard Attractions. Brigid Gaynor. (Illus.). (J). (ps). 1993. Gift box set of 4 bks., 12p. ea. incl. seed packs. bds. 14.95 (1-56828-043-2) Red Jacket Pr.

Backyard Barbecue & Grill Book. Karen Adler. 144p. (Orig.). 1996. pap. 14.95x (0-925175-18-8) Pig Out Pubns.

Backyard Bear. Jim Murphy. LC 92-15479. (Illus.). 32p. (J). (gr. k-3). 1993. 15.95 (0-590-44375-5) Scholastic Inc.

Backyard Beekeeping. C. N. Smithers. (Illus.). 80p. (Orig.). 1993. pap. 12.95 (0-86417-458-6, Pub. by Kangaroo Pr AT) Seven Hills Bk.

***Backyard Berry Book: A Hands-on Guide to Growing Berries, Brambles, & Vine Fruit in the Home.** Stella Otto. (Illus.). 288p. (Orig.). 1995. pap. 15.95 (0-9634520-6-1) OttoGraphics.

Backyard Biology. Bob De Weese. (Science Mini Unit Intermediate Ser.). (Illus.). 16p. 1994. pap. text ed. 5.95 (1-55799-302-5) Evan-Moor Corp.

***Backyard Bird Song: Eastern & Central North America.** Robert W. Lawson & Richard K. Walton. 32p. 1991. 19.95 (0-395-58416-7) HM.

***Backyard Bird Song: Eastern & Central North America.** Richard K. Walton & Robert W. Lawson. 32p. 1994. cd-rom 19.95 (0-395-71256-4) HM.

Backyard Bird Walk. Lang Elliott. (Bird Walks by Habitat Ser.). (Illus.). 28p. 1993. audio 12.95 (1-878194-07-0) Nature Sound Studio.

Backyard Bird-Watcher: The Classic Guide to Enjoying Wild Birds Outside Your Back Door. George H. Harrison. 1988. pap. 12.00 (0-671-66374-7, Fireside) S&S Trade.

Backyard Birddom. Mary J. Ericson. LC 66-19146. (Illus.). 1974. 5.95 (0-87208-079-X); pap. 3.00 (0-87208-010-2) Island Pr Pubs.

***Backyard Birdfeeding.** John F. Gardner. (Illus.). 64p. 1996. pap. 4.95 (0-8117-2507-3) Stackpole.

Backyard Birds. Jonathan Pine. LC 91-45184. (Nature Study Series: A Trophy Nonfiction Bk.). (Illus.). 48p. (J). (gr. 2-5). 1993. pap. 7.95 (0-06-446150-5, Trophy) HarpC Child Bks.

Backyard Birds: An Enthusiast's Guide to Feeding, Housing, & Fostering Wild Birds. Janann V. Jenner. LC 94-1820. 1994. write for info. (1-56799-058-4, MetroBooks) M Friedman Pub Grp Inc.

***Backyard Birds of Summer.** Carol Lerner. (Illus.). 1996. write for info. (0-688-13600-1); lib. bdg. write for info. (0-688-13601-X) Morrow Jr Bks.

Backyard Birds of Winter. Carol Lerner. LC 94-3036. (Illus.). 48p. (J). 1994. 16.00 (0-688-12819-X); lib. bdg. 15.93 (0-688-12820-3) Morrow Jr Bks.

Backyard Bomber of Pacific Palisades: A Love Story. Martha F. Patterson. LC 84-52475. (Illus.). 237p. 1984. 9.95 (0-9614294-0-2) Seamount Pubns.

Backyard Book: Ideas & Resources for Outdoor Living. Ed. by Tricia Foley. (Illus.). 1988. pap. 24.95 (0-670-81666-3, Viking Studio) Studio Bks.

Backyard Bounty: Pleasures & Treasures from My Own Backyard. Dorothy F. Weber. (Back Porch Bks.: Vol. 2). (Illus.). 64p. (Orig.). 1991. pap. 7.95 (0-9620905-1-4) D F Weber.

Backyard Brickwork: How to Build Walls, Paths, Patios, & Barbecues. Ed. by Mike Lawrence. LC 89-45218. (Illus.). 96p. 1989. pap. 14.95 (0-88266-562-6, Garden Way Pub) Storey Comm Inc.

Backyard Builder: Over One Hundred Fifty Build-It-Yourself Projects for Your Garden, Home & Yard. Ed. by John Warde. LC 93-28710. (Illus.). 1994. 14.99 (0-517-10035-5, Pub. by Wings Bks) Random Hse Value.

Backyard Builder: Over One Hundred Fifty Build-It-Yourself Projects for Your Garden, Home & Yard. Ed. by John Warde. LC 84-24846. (Illus.). 656p. 1985. 21.95 (0-87857-531-6, 14-568-0) Rodale Pr Inc.

Backyard Building Projects. Edward A. Baldwin. 1993. text ed. 25.95 (0-07-157729-7); pap. text ed. 16.95 (0-07-157728-9) McGraw.

Backyard Building Projects. Edward A. Baldwin. (Illus.). 256p. 1993. 25.95 (0-8306-2119-9, 3766); pap. 16.95 (0-8306-2114-8, 3766) TAB Bks.

Backyard Cash Crops: The Source Book for Growing & Marketing Specialty Plants. rev. ed. Craig Wallin. (Illus.). 240p. 1994. pap. 16.95 (0-933239-32-7) Homestead Design.

Backyard Composting: Your Complete Guide to Recycling Yard Clippings. rev. ed. Harmonious Technologies Staff. Ed. by Marialyce Pedersen. (Illus.). 96p. (C). 1995. pap. 6.95 (0-9629768-0-6) Harmonious Tech.

***Backyard Composting: Your Complete Guide to Recycling Yard Clippings.** 2nd expanded rev. ed. Harmonious Technologies Staff. 1995. pap. 6.95 (0-9629768-3-0) Harmonious Tech.

Backyard Design: Making the Most of the Space Around Your House. Jean S. Breskend. (Illus.). 224p. 1991. 32.50 (0-8212-1776-3) Bulfinch Pr.

Backyard Detective: A Guide for Beginning Naturalists. Herbert H. Wong. LC 92-63342. (Illus.). 64p. (Orig.). (J). (gr. k-5). 1993. pap. 7.95 (1-882489-00-4) NatureVision.

Backyard Dragon. Betsy Sterman & Samuel Sterman. LC 92-26292. (Illus.). 192p. (J). (gr. 3-7). 1993. 14.00 (0-06-020783-3); lib. bdg. 13.89 (0-06-020784-1) HarpC Child Bks.

Backyard Explorer Kit. Rona Beame. LC 88-51582. (Illus.). 64p. (J). (gr. k-5). 1989. pap. 10.95 (0-89480-343-3, 1343) Workman Pub.

***Backyard Fish Farming.** Bryant. 1995. pap. 9.95 (0-904727-24-6) Prism Pr.

Backyard Fruits & Berries: Everything You Need to Know About Planting & Growing Fruits & Berries in Your Own Backyard. Miranda Smith. LC 93-50886. 1994. 25.95 (0-87596-638-1) Rodale Pr Inc.

Backyard Games: More Than Fifty Games to Play in Your Own Backyard. A. Cort Sinnes. (Illus.). 128p. 1993. pap. 14.95 (0-8362-4503-2) Andrews & McMeel.

Backyard Ghost. Lynn Cullen. LC 92-24580. 160p. (J). (gr. 4-7). 1993. 13.95 (0-395-64527-1, Clarion Bks) HM.

***Backyard Ghost.** Lynn Cullen. 160p. (J). 1995. reprint ed. pap. 3.50 (0-380-72370-0, Camelot) Avon.

Backyard Homestead, Mini-Farm & Garden Log Book. John Jeavons et al. 224p. (Orig.). 1983. pap. 8.95 (0-89815-093-0) Ten Speed Pr.

Backyard Horseman. Ron Rude. Ed. by Bill Brown. LC 87-11187. (Illus.). 158p. (Orig.). 1987. pap. 15.00 (0-87842-211-0) Mountain Pr.

Backyard Hunter: The Praying Mantis. Bianca Lavies. LC 89-37485. (Illus.). 32p. (J). (gr. 2-5). 1990. 13.95 (0-525-44547-1, DCB) Dutton Child Bks.

***Backyard Hunter: The Praying Mantis.** Bianca Lavies. (Illus.). 32p. (J). (gr. 2-5). 1995. pap. 4.99 (0-14-055494-7, Puff Unicorn) Puffin Bks.

Backyard Insects. Millicent E. Selsam. 40p. (J). (ps-3). 1988. pap. 3.95 (0-590-42256-1) Scholastic Inc.

Backyard Landscaper: Forty Professional Designs for Do-It-Yourselfers. Ireland-Gannon Associates, Inc. Staff. (Illus.). 160p. 1992. pap. 12.95 (0-918894-89-1) Home Planners.

Backyard Livestock: Raising Good Natural Food for Your Family. 2nd enl. rev. ed. Stephen Thomas & George P. Looby. LC 90-15081. (Illus.). 240p. 1990. pap. 15.00 (0-88150-182-4) Countryman.

Backyard Market Gardening: The Entrepreneur's Guide to Selling What You Grow. Andy Lee. LC 90-84585. (Illus.). 352p. (Orig.). 1995. pap. 19.95 (0-9624648-0-5) Good Earth Pubns.

***Backyard Medicine Chest: An Herbal Primer.** Douglas Schar. (Illus.). 144p. (Orig.). 1995. pap. 12.95 (1-880216-28-0) Elliott & Clark.

B

Bacterial Outer Membranes: Biogenesis & Functions. Ed. by Masayori Inouye. LC 79-13999. (Illus.). 544p. reprint ed. pap. 155.10 (0-8357-8904-7, 2056450) Bks Demand.

Bacterial Pathogen Flexibacter Columnaris & Its Epizootiology among Columbia River Fish. C. D. Becker & M. P. Fujihara. (AFS Monograph Ser.: No. 2). 92p. 1978. pap. 10.50 (0-913235-13-X) Am Fisheries Soc.

Bacterial Pathogenesis: A Molecular Approach. Abigail A. Salyers & Dixie D. Whitt. LC 94-1468. (Illus.). 448p. 1994. pap. 44.95 (1-55581-070-5) Am Soc Microbio.

***Bacterial Pathogenesis of Plants & Animals.** J. L. Dangl. Ed. by A. Capron et al. (Currents Topics in Microbiology & Immunology Ser.: Vol. 192). 330p. 1994. 129.00 (0-387-57391-7) Spr-Verlag.

Bacterial Photosynthetic Apparatus As a Photoelectric Transducer. Ed. by V. D. Samuilov. (Physicochemical Biology Reviews Supplement Ser.: Soviet Scientific Reviews, Sect. D, Vol. 2). 136p. 1984. text ed. 207.00 (3-7186-0141-9) Gordon & Breach.

Bacterial Plant Pathology: Cell & Molecular Aspects. David C. Sigee. (Illus.). 300p. (C). 1993. 89.95 (0-521-35064-6) Cambridge U Pr.

Bacterial Plasmids, Vol. 2. K. G. Hardy et al. 456p. 1984. pap. text ed. 69.00 (3-7186-0282-2) Gordon & Breach.

Bacterial Protein Toxins. Ed. by J. E. Alouf et al. (Fems Symposia Ser.). 1984. text ed. 68.00 (0-12-053080-5) Acad Pr.

B

Bacterial Protein Toxins. Paul Falmagne. (Zentralblatt fur Bakteriologie Supplements Ser.: Vol. 15). 398p. 1987. text ed. 145.00 (0-89574-233-0, Pub. by Gustav Fischer Verlag); 125.00 (0-685-55843-6, Pub. by Gustav Fischer Verlag) VCH Pubs.

Bacterial Protein Toxins: Fourth European Workshop, Urbino, July 3-6, 1989. Ed. by R. Rappuoli et al. (International Medical Microbiology Ser.: Supplement 19). 551p. 1990. 95.00 (0-685-48100-X); lib. bdg. 110.00 (0-89574-315-9) G F Verlag.

Bacterial Protein Toxins: Third European Workshop Uberlingen, June 28-July 30, 1987, Vol. 17. Ed. by F. J. Fehrenbach et al. 459p. 1988. pap. text ed. 155.00 (0-89574-260-8, Pub. by Gustav Fischer Verlag); 130.00 (0-685-43983-6, Pub. by Gustav Fischer Verlag) VCH Pubs.

Bacterial Protein Toxins see Microbial Toxins: A Comprehensive Treatise

Bacterial Regrowth in Distribution Systems. 364p. 1988. pap. 31.00 (0-89867-418-2, 90532) Am Water Wks Assn.

Bacterial Rickettsial & Mycotic Diseases, Section A, 2 vols., Set. J. Steele & H. Stoenner. LC 78-10696. (Handbook Series in Zoonoses). 1979. 636.00 (0-8493-2905-1) CRC Pr.

Bacterial Starter Cultures for Food. Ed. by Stanley E. Gilliland. 208p. 1985. 156.00 (0-8493-5686-5, TP456) CRC Pr.

***Bacterial Superantigens: Structure, Function & Therapeutic Potential.** Jacques Thibodeau & Rafick Sekaly. (Molecular Biology Intelligence Unit Ser.). 245p. 1995. write for info. (1-57059-264-0) R G Landes.

Bacterial Systematics. Niall A. Logan. LC 93-26811. (Illus.). 256p. 1994. pap. 32.95 (0-632-03775-X) Blackwell Sci.

Bacterial Transport. Ed. by Barry P. Rosen. LC 78-16191. (Microbiology Ser.: No. 4). 700p. reprint ed. pap. 180.00 (0-7837-3383-6, 2043341) Bks Demand.

Bacterial Vaccine Production. P. D. Walker & W. H. Foster. (Essays in Applied Microbiology Ser.: No. 9). 32p. reprint ed. pap. 25.00 (0-8357-5947-4, 2031943) Bks Demand.

Bacterial Vaccines. Ed. by John B. Robbins et al. LC 86-9523. 589p. 1987. text ed. 115.00 (0-275-92157-3, C2157, Praeger Pubs) Greenwood.

Bacterial Wilt: The Disease & Its Causative Agent, Pseudomonas Solanacearum. Ed. by G. L. Hartman & A. C. Hayward. 270p. 1994. 67.50 (0-85198-875-X) CAB Intl.

Bacteriocins, Microcins, & Lantibiotics. Ed. by Richard James et al. LC 92-26374. (NATO ASI Series H: Cell Biology: Vol. 65). xi, 519p. 1993. 259.00 (0-387-54604-9) Spr-Verlag.

Bacteriocins of Lactic Acid Bacteria. Ed. by Dallas G. Hoover & Larry R. Steenson. (Food Science & Technology Ser.). (Illus.). 275p. 1993. text ed. 85.00 (0-12-355510-8) Acad Pr.

Bacteriofagos. 2nd rev. ed. OAS, General Secretariat, Department of Technological & Scientific Affairs Staff. (Serie de Biologia: No. 12). (Illus.). 102p. (SPA.). (C). 1980. pap. 2.00 (0-8270-1301-9) OAS.

Bacteriologist. Jack Rudman. (Career Examination Ser.: C-80). 1994. pap. 27.95 (0-8373-0080-0) Nat Learn.

Bacteriology. William W. Ford. LC 75-23671. (Clio Medica Ser.: No. 22). (Illus.). reprint ed. 18.00 (0-404-58922-7) AMS Pr.

Bacteriology: A Text & Workbook. Delost. 416p. 1994. pap. 32.95 (0-8016-7853-6) Mosby Yr Bk.

Bacteriology & Immunity for Nurses. 6th ed. Ronald Hare & E. Mary Cooke. (Churchill Livingstone Nursing Text Ser.). (Illus.). 232p. (Orig.). 1984. pap. text ed. 20.00 (0-443-02878-8) Churchill.

Bacteriology of Tuberculosis. Egons Darzins. LC 57-8918. 500p. reprint ed. pap. 142.50 (0-8357-5948-2, 2055853) Bks Demand.

Bacteriology Primer in Air Contamination Control. V. Victor Kingsley. LC 68-82893. 45p. reprint ed. pap. 25.00 (0-8357-5949-0, 2014271) Bks Demand.

Bacteriophage Lambda. Ed. by A. D. Hershey. LC 78-154475. (Cold Spring Harbor Monograph Ser.). 804p. reprint ed. pap. 180.00 (0-7837-6441-3, 2046441) Bks Demand.

Bacteriophage T4. American Society for Microbiology Staff. Ed. by Christopher K. Matthews et al. LC 83-11945. (Illus.). 420p. reprint ed. pap. 119.70 (0-8357-7510-0, 2036002) Bks Demand.

Bacteriophages, Vol. 1. Ed. by R. Calendar. LC 88-9770. (Viruses Ser.). (Illus.). 614p. 1988. 125.00 (0-306-42730-3, Plenum Pr) Plenum.

Bacteriophages, Vol. 2. Ed. by R. Calendar. LC 88-9770. (Viruses Ser.). (Illus.). 778p. 1988. 145.00 (0-306-42853-9, Plenum Pr) Plenum.

Bactria: The History of a Forgotten Empire. Hugh G. Rawlinson. LC 77-93189. reprint ed. 32.50 (0-404-05227-4) AMS Pr.

***Baculovirus Expression Protocols.** Ed. & Intro. by Christopher D. Richardson. LC 94-44674. (Methods in Molecular Biology Ser.: Vol. 39). (Illus.). 432p. 1995. 64.50 (0-89603-272-8) Humana.

Baculovirus Expression System: A Laboratory Guide. L. A. King & R. D. Possee. (Illus.). 192p. (C). 1992. text ed. 65.00 (0-412-37150-2, A6890) Chapman & Hall.

Baculovirus Expression Vectors: A Laboratory Manual. David O'Reilly et al. LC 93-43895. (Illus.). 364p. (C). 1993. 49.95 (0-19-509131-0) OUP.

Baculovirus Expressions Systems & Biopesticides. Ed. by Michael L. Shuler et al. LC 94-17194. 1994. text ed. 85.00 (0-471-06580-3) Wiley-Liss.

Baculum Familliare, a Booke of the Making & Use of a Staffe. John Blagrave. LC 71-26001. (English Experience Ser.: No. 225). 1970. reprint ed. 20.00 (90-221-0225-4) Walter J Johnson.

Baculum in Microtine Rodents. Sydney Anderson. (Museum Ser.: Vol. 12, No. 3). 36p. 1960. pap. 2.00 (0-317-04935-6) U of KS Mus Nat Hist.

Bad. Ed. by Dan Hammer & Isaac Cronin. 240p. 1994. pap. 10.95 (0-7867-0144-7) Carroll & Graf.

Bad Aboriginal Art & Other Essays: Tradition, Media, & Technological Horizons. Eric Michaels. LC 93-5132. (Theory out of Bounds Ser.: No. 3). 296p. 1993. pap. 21.95 (0-8166-2341-4) U of Minn Pr.

Bad Acts & Guilty Minds: Conundrums of the Criminal Law. Leo Katz. LC 87-7035. (Studies in Crime & Justice). 368p. 1987. lib. bdg. 45.00 (0-226-42591-6); pap. text ed. 15.95 (0-226-42592-4) U Ch Pr.

Bad Alchemy. Dionisio D. Martiznez. 80p. 1995. 17.95 (0-393-03733-9) Norton.

Bad Angel. large type ed. Ernest K. Gann. 544p. 1989. 17.95 (0-7089-2025-X) Ulverscroft.

Bad Apple. Anthony Bruno. LC 93-42616. 1994. 21.50 (0-385-30508-7) Delacorte.

Bad Art. Quentin Bell. (Illus.). 320p. 1989. 29.95 (0-226-04203-0) U Ch Pr.

Bad Ass Dogs Don't Do Ballet. Christopher Fitts. LC 92-64162. 96p. (Orig.). 1994. pap. 9.95 (0-9635689-6-5) Storm Grove.

***Bad Astronomy: A Brief History of Bizarre Theories.** Linda Zimmermann. (Illus.). 224p. (Orig.). 1995. pap. 19.95 (0-9645133-0-7) Zimages.

Bad Attitude. Tiffany White. (Temptation Ser.). 1993. mass mkt. 2.99 (0-373-25542-X, 1-25542-1) Harlequin Bks.

Bad Attitude: The Processed World Anthology. Ed. by Chris Carlsson. 1990. 60.00 (0-86091-284-1, Pub. by Verso UK); 19.95 (0-86091-946-3, Pub. by Verso UK) Routledge Chapman & Hall.

Bad August: A Mystery. Daniel Hearn. 224p. 1989. pap. 3.50 (0-380-70665-2) Avon.

Bad Babies' Book of Colors. Tony Bradman. Ed. by Janet Schulman. LC 86-27860. (Illus.). 32p. (J). (ps-2). 1987. 5.95 (0-394-89046-9) Knopf Bks Yng Read.

Bad Babies' Counting Book, Set. Tony Bradman. LC 86-71. (Illus.). 32p. (J). (ps-2). 1986. 4.95 (0-394-88352-7) Knopf Bks Yng Read.

***Bad Back: Coping for Life.** Lucy M. Dobkins. (Illus.). 208p. (Orig.). 1995. pap. 18.95 (1-56554-062-X) Pelican.

Bad Back Book. Jerry Wayne. LC 82-62473. 1983. reprint ed. pap. 8.95 (0-918024-25-0) Ox Bow.

Bad, Bad Bunnies. Judy Delton. (Pee Wee Scouts Ser.: No. 12). (J). (gr. k-6). 1990. pap. 3.25 (0-440-40278-6, YB) Dell.

Bad, Bad Bunny Trouble. Hans Wilhelm. (J). (ps-3). 1994. 3.95 (0-590-47916-4) Scholastic Inc.

***Bad, Bad Day.** Kirsten Hall & Laura Rader. LC 94-39148. (My First Hello Reader Ser.). (Illus.). (J). 1995. write for info. (0-590-25496-0, Cartwheel) Scholastic Inc.

***Bad Bart's Revenge.** Gary Harbo. (If You Want to Succeed, You Have Got to Read! Ser.). (Illus.). 35p. (SPA.). (J). (gr. 1-5). 1995. 8.95 (1-884149-06-5) Kutie Kari Bks.

Bad Bart's Revenge: Advanced Reader. Gary Harbo. (Bad Bart Ser.: Bk. 2). (Illus.). 35p. (J). (gr. 1-4). 1991. text ed. 8.95 (1-884149-03-0) Kutie Kari Bks.

***Bad Behavior.** Ed. & Intro. by Mary Higgins Clark. 320p. 1995. 20.00 (0-15-200179-4, Gulliver Bks) HarBrace.

***Bad Behavior.** Ed. & Intro. by Mary Higgins Clark. 320p. (YA). 1995. pap. 10.00 (0-15-200178-6, Gulliver Bks) HarBrace.

Bad Behavior. Mary Gaitskill. (Contemporaries Ser.). 1989. pap. 10.00 (0-679-72327-7, Vin) Random.

Bad Ben & the Monster. (Scary Stories Ser.: No. S903-2). (J). (gr. k-2). 1990. boxed 3.95 (0-7214-5266-3) Ladybird Bks.

Bad Blood. Hank Edwards. (Judge Ser.: No. 7). (Orig.). 1992. mass mkt. 3.50 (0-06-100389-1, Harp PBks) HarpC.

Bad Blood. Debra Fowler. 352p. 1993. mass mkt. 4.50 (1-55817-750-7, Pinnacle NY) Windsor NY.

Bad Blood. large type ed. Bernard Ashley. (J). (gr. 1-8). 1990. 16.95 (0-7451-1424-5, Galaxy Child Lrg Print) Chivers N Amer.

Bad Blood: A Family Murder in Marin County. Richard M. Levine. 352p. 1983. pap. 4.50 (0-451-15503-3, Sig); pap. 4.99 (0-451-16321-4) NAL-Dutton.

Bad Blood: Militia Abuses in Mindanao, the Philippines. Ed. by Human Rights Watch Staff. 44p. (Orig.). 1992. pap. 5.00 (1-56432-060-X) Hum Rts Watch.

***Bad Blood: The Life & Times of the Horrel Brothers.** Frederick Nolan. LC 94-27503. 1994. 19.95 (0-935269-16-9, Barbed Wire Pr) Western Pubns.

Bad Blood: The Moon Is Full Beware the Beast. Debra Doyle. (YA). 1993. pap. 3.99 (0-425-13953-0) Berkley Pub.

Bad Blood: The Shocking True Story Behind the Menendez Killings. Don Davis. 1994. mass mkt. 4.99 (0-312-95334-8) St Martin.

Bad Blood: The Tuskegee Syphilis Experiment. James H. Jones. LC 92-34818. 1992. pap. 14.95 (0-02-916676-4) Free Pr.

Bad Blood: The Tuskegee Syphilis Experiment. James H. Jones. 300p. 1993. text ed. 24.95 (0-02-916675-6) Free Pr.

***Bad Blood (La Malasangre)** Griselda Gambaro. Tr. by Marguerite Feitlowitz. 1994. 5.00 (0-87129-458-3, B33) Dramatic Pub.

Bad Boats. Laura Jensen. LC 77-71289. (American Poetry Ser.: Vol. 13). 1979. reprint ed. pap. 3.95 (0-912946-40-7) Ecco Pr.

Bad Boy of Music. George Antheil. LC 81-1169. (Illus.). 378p. 1981. lib. bdg. 45.00 (0-306-76084-3) Da Capo.

Bad Boy of Music. George Antheil. LC 90-3331. (Illus.). 378p. 1990. reprint ed. pap. 14.95 (0-573-60604-8) S French Trade.

Bad Boy of Music: Music Book Index. George Antheil. 295p. 1993. reprint ed. lib. bdg. 79.00 (0-7812-9585-8) Rprt Serv.

Bad Boys. 1993. mass mkt. 5.50 (0-373-20094-3, 1-20094-8) Harlequin Bks.

Bad Boys. Allan Baillie. (J). (gr. 4-7). 1994. pap. 2.95 (0-590-48258-0) Scholastic Inc.

***Bad Boys: The Legends of Hockey's Toughest, Meanest Most-Feared Players.** Stan Fischler. (Illus.). 224p. (Orig.). (YA). 1994. pap. 15.95 (1-895629-42-X, Pub. by Warwick Pub CN) Firefly Bks Ltd.

Bad Boys & Tough Tattoos: A Social History of the Tattoo with Gangs, Sailors & Street-Corner Punks, 1950-1965. Samuel M. Steward. LC 90-33832. (Haworth Series in Gay & Lesbian Studies). 204p. 1990. text ed. 10.95 (0-918393-76-0) Harrington Pk.

Bad Boys & Tough Tattoos: A Social History of the Tattoo with Gangs, Sailors & Street-Corner Punks, 1950-1965. Samuel M. Steward & Wardell B. Pomeroy. LC 90-53852. (Gay & Lesbian Studies). 204p. 1990. text ed. 29.95 (1-56024-023-7) Haworth Pr.

Bad Boyz of Rap. (Compact Books ... CBs Ser.). (Illus.). 32p. (J). (gr. 5 up). 1993. pap. 3.95 (0-307-20102-3, 20102, Golden Pr) Western Pub.

Bad Brains. Kathe Koja. 1992. mass mkt. 4.99 (0-440-21114-X) Dell.

***Bad Business.** Dick Hobbs. 200p. 1995. 28.00 (0-19-825848-8) OUP.

Bad Business: A Novel. Nancy Goldstone. (New American Fiction Ser.). 229p. 1992. pap. 9.95 (0-571-12906-4) Faber & Faber.

Bad Business: Short Fictions of Alison Bundy. Alison Bundy. LC 85-5214. (Lost Roads Ser.: No. 27). 56p. (Orig.). 1985. pap. 6.95 (0-918786-31-2) Lost Roads.

Bad Case of the Giggles: Kid's Favorite Funny Poems. Bruce Lansky. 1994. pap. 14.00 (0-671-89982-1) Meadowbrook.

Bad Case of the Giggles: Kid's Favorite Funny Poems. Bruce Lansky. LC 94-3336. (Illus.). (J). 1994. 14.00 (0-88166-213-5, 0671899821) Meadowbrook.

Bad Case of the Sillies. Ray Cunningham. 57p. (Orig.). 1992. pap. 4.95 (0-9631251-2-5) R Cunningham.

***Bad Cats: A Collection of Feline Pranks & Practical Jokes.** Rick Stromoski. (Illus.). 112p. 1995. pap. 5.95 (0-8092-3478-5) Contemp Bks.

Bad Chemistry. Nora Kelly. 256p. 1994. 20.95 (0-312-10934-2) St Martin.

Bad Child's Book of Beasts, 3 bks. Hilaire Belloc. Bd. with More Beasts for Worse Children.; Moral Alphabet. (Illus.). 157p. reprint ed. Set pap. 3.50 (0-486-20749-8) Dover.

Bad Choices: A Look Inside Planned Parenthood. Douglas R. Scott. LC 92-19401. 1992. write for info. (1-880692-02-3) Legacy Comms.

Bad Company. William A. Luckey. 176p. (Orig.). 1991. pap. 3.95 (0-449-14714-2, GM) Fawcett.

***Bad Company: A Stoner McTavish Mystery.** Sarah Dreher. 250p. (Orig.). 1995. 19.95 (0-934678-67-7); pap. 10.95 (0-934678-66-9) New Victoria Pubs.

Bad Company: Drugs, Hollywood & the Cotton Club Murder. Steve Wick. 320p. 1990. 19.95 (0-15-110445-X) HarBrace.

Bad Company: Drugs, Hollywood, & the Cotton Club Murder. Steve Wick. (Illus.). 376p. 1991. mass mkt. 5.99 (0-312-92517-4) St Martin.

Bad Company: The Story of California's Legendary & Actual Stage-Robbers, Bandits, Highwaymen & Outlaws from the Fifties to the Eighties. Joseph H. Jackson. LC 77-7300. (Illus.). xx, 346p. 1977. pap. 9.95 (0-8032-5866-6) U of Nebr Pr.

Bad Dates: Celebrities & Other Talented Types Reveal Their Worst Nights Out. Carole Markin. 256p. 1990. pap. 9.95 (0-8065-1158-3, Citadel Pr) Carol Pub Group.

Bad Day at Black Rock. Michael Niall. 16.95 (0-8488-0107-5, Amereon Hse) Amereon Ltd.

***Bad Day at Riverbend.** LC 95-4154. (J). 1995. 17.95 (0-395-67347-X) HM.

Bad Day Book. Robyn F. Spizman & Tracy Green. LC 93-81149. (Illus.). 80p. 1994. pap. 5.95 (1-56352-145-8) Longstreet Pr Inc.

***Bad Day for Ballet.** Carolyn Keene. Ed. by Anne Greenberg. (Nancy Drew Notebooks Ser.: No. 4). (Illus.). 80p. (Orig.). (J). 1995. pap. 3.50 (0-671-87948-0) PB.

Bad Design. Mitchell. 1995. pap. write for info. (0-442-01733-2) Van Nos Reinhold.

Bad Desire. Gary Devon. 1991. pap. 5.99 (0-451-17098-9, Sig) NAL-Dutton.

***Bad Dog.** G. G. Garth. (YA). 1995. pap. 3.50 (0-553-56730-6) Bantam.

Bad Dog Blues. Bruce Isaacson. (Illus.). 60p. (Orig.). 1988. pap. 4.95 (0-929730-01-1) Zeitgeist Pr.

Bad Dog, George! Sally George. LC 92-34258. (Voyages Ser.). (Illus.). (J). 1993. 4.25 (0-383-03616-X) SRA Schl Grp.

***Bad Dogs: A Collection of Canine Pranks & Practical Jokes.** Rick Stromoski. (Illus.). 112p. 1995. pap. 5.95 (0-8092-3479-3) Contemp Bks.

Bad Dream. Jim Aylesworth. Ed. by Ann Fay. LC 85-685. (Albert Whitman Concept Bks.). (Illus.). 32p. (J). (ps-2). 1985. 11.95 (0-8075-0506-4) A Whitman.

Bad Dreams. Haden-Guest. 1982. 14.95 (0-02-547180-5) Macmillan.

***Bad Dreams.** Kim Newman. 280p. 1995. mass mkt. 4.95 (0-7867-0227-3) Carroll & Graf.

Bad Dreams. R. L. Stine. Ed. by Pat MacDonald. (Fear Street Ser.). 176p. (Orig.). (J). 1994. mass mkt. 3.99 (0-671-78569-9, Archway) PB.

***Bad Dreams, Good Dreams.** Anthology Staff. 192p. 1994. pap. 19.95 (1-885884-13-3) J Avenick.

Bad Dreams of a Good Girl. Susan R. Shreve. LC 92-24593. (Illus.). 96p. (J). (gr. 4 up). 1993. reprint ed. pap. 3.95 (0-688-12113-6, Pub. by Beech Tree Bks) Morrow.

Bad Earth: Environmental Degradation in China. Vaclav Smil. LC 83-14821. 264p. reprint ed. pap. 75.30 (0-8357-2625-8, 2040113) Bks Demand.

Bad English. (Piano-Vocal-Guitar Ser.). 110p. 1990. pap. 14.95 (0-7935-0984-X, 00490345) H Leonard.

Bad Faith. Barry Zalma. 276p. 1993. ring bd. 35.95 (1-884770-06-1) Claimschool.

Bad Faith Actions-Liability & Damages. Stephen S. Ashley. LC 84-28489. 1984. ring bd. 145.00 (0-317-17768-0) Clark Boardman Callaghan.

Bad Faith & Antiblack Racism. Lewis R. Gordon. LC 94-18239. 240p. (C). 1995. pap. 17.50 (0-391-03872-9) Humanities.

Bad Faith & Antiblack Racism. Lewis R. Gordon. LC 94-18239. 240p. (C). 1995. text ed. 45.00 (0-391-03868-0) Humanities.

Bad Faith & Punitive Damages: Annotations to First-Part Insurance Cases, Statutes & Regulations. LC 86-71258. 358p. 1986. ring bd. 59.95 (0-89707-241-3, 519-0054-01) Amer Bar Assn.

Bad Faith & Punitive Damages: First Supplement. LC 89-71258. 198p. 1989. ring bd. 59.95 (0-89707-492-0, 519-0099) Amer Bar Assn.

***Bad Faith, Good Faith & Authenticity in Sartra's Early Philosophy.** Ronald E. Santoni. 256p. (Orig.). (C). 1995. lib. bdg. 49.95 (1-56639-319-1); pap. text ed. 22.95 (1-56639-320-5) Temple U Pr.

Bad for Business. Craig Alpaugh. LC 90-52520. (Orig.). 1985. pap. 5.00 (0-88734-307-4) Players Pr.

Bad-for-You Cookbook. Chris Maynard & Bill Scheller. 1992. pap. 10.00 (0-679-73545-3, Villard Bks) Random.

***Bad Girl.** Leslie Hall. 160p. (Orig.). Date not set. pap. 10.95 (0-88496-401-9) Capra Pr.

Bad Girl Blues. Rex Dancer. LC 93-47452. 1994. 20.00 (0-671-88007-1) S&S Trade.

Bad Girls. Marcia Tucker et al. Ed. by Mimi Young & Melissa Goldstein. (Illus.). 144p. (Orig.). 1994. pap. text ed. 19.95 (0-262-70053-0) New Mus Contemp Art.

***Bad Girls - Good Girls: Women, Sex, & Power in the Nineties.** Ed. by Donna Perry & Nan B. Maglin. (Illus.). 325p. (C). 1996. text ed. 50.00 (0-8135-2250-1); pap. 17.95 (0-8135-2251-X) Rutgers U Pr.

Bad Girls & Dirty Pictures: The Challenge to Reclaim Feminism. Alison Assiter. (C). 1993. pap. text ed. 15.95 (0-7453-0524-5, Pub. by Pluto Pr UK) Westview.

Bad Girls & Dirty Pictures: The Challenge to Reclaim Feminism. Ed. by Alison Assiter & Carol Avedon. 185p. (C). 1993. text ed. 52.50 (0-7453-0523-7, Pub. by Pluto Pr UK) Westview.

Bad Girls Do It! An Encyclopedia. Michael Newton. LC 93-79481. 205p. (Orig.). (C). 1993. pap. 14.95 (1-55950-104-9, 34070) Loompanics.

Bad Girls' Money. Paul. 1993. mass mkt. 4.50 (0-06-108158-2, Harp PBks) HarpC.

Bad Guys. Eugene Bruno. 1989. pap. 3.95 (0-312-91493-8) St Martin.

Bad Guys: A Pictorial History of the Movie Villain. William K. Everson. 1968. pap. 8.95 (0-8065-0198-7, C264, Citadel Pr) Carol Pub Group.

Bad Guys: Women's Tales from the Relationship Front. Brook Hersey. 256p. 1994. pap. 12.95 (0-9638870-0-9) Bishop Bks NY.

Bad Guys & Good Guys: Moral Polarization & Crime. Daniel S. Claster. LC 92-4053. (Contributions in Criminology & Penology Ser.: No. 36). 320p. 1992. text ed. 47.95 (0-313-28489-X, CBY/, Greenwood Pr) Greenwood.

Bad Guys & Psychological Racketeers. Franklin H. Ernst, Jr. 1982. pap. 17.00 (0-916944-25-5) Addressoset.

Bad Guys Don't Have Birthdays: Fantasy Play at Four. Vivian G. Paley. LC 87-21748. x, 118p. 1991. pap. 9.95 (0-226-64496-0) U Ch Pr.

Bad Habits. Lindsay Welsh. (Orig.). 1992. pap. 4.95 (1-56333-068-7) Masquerade.

***Bad Habits, Acting Ed.** rev. ed. Terrence McNally. 1990. pap. 4.75 (0-8222-1435-0) Dramatists Play.

An Asterisk (*) at the beginning of an entry indicates that the title is appearing in BIP for the first time.

Bad Habits: Drinking, Smoking, Taking Drugs, Gambling, Sexual Misbehavior & Swearing in American History. John C. Burnham. (Illus.). 400p. (C). 1992. text ed. 50.00 (*0-8147-1187-1*) NYU Pr.

Bad Habits: Drinking, Smoking, Taking Drugs, Gambling, Sexual Misbehavior & Swearing in American History. John C. Burnham. (Illus.). 385p. 1994. pap. 18.95 (*0-8147-1224-X*) NYU Pr.

***Bad Haircut: Stories of the Seventies.** Tom Perrotta. 256p. (Orig.). 1995. pap. 6.99 (*0-425-14942-0*) Berkley Pub.

Bad Haircut: Stories of the Seventies. Tom Perrotta. LC 93-33687. 197p. (Orig.). 1994. 18.95 (*1-882593-05-7*) Bridge Wrks.

Bad Hand: A Biography of General Ranald S. Mackenzie. Charles M. Robinson. (Illus.). 392p. 1993. 29.95 (*1-880510-00-6*); pap. 17.95 (*1-880510-02-2*) State House Pr.

Bad Hand: A Biography of General Ranald S. Mackenzie. limited ed. Charles M. Robinson. (Illus.). 392p. 1993. 60.00 (*1-880510-01-4*) State House Pr.

***Bad Harvest.** N. Dudley et al. 1995. 19.95 (*1-85383-188-3*, Pub. by Erthscan Pubns UK) Island Pr.

***Bad Housekeeping.** Julie Edelson. 265p. 1995. 21.00 (*1-880909-31-6*) Baskerville.

Bad Infinity: Nine Plays. Mac Wellman. LC 93-1911. (PAJ Bks.). 1994. 45.00 (*0-8018-4687-0*); pap. 15.95 (*0-8018-4688-9*) Johns Hopkins.

Bad Intent: A Maggie MacGowen Mystery. Wendy Hornsby. LC 93-42405. 1994. 18.95 (*0-525-93817-6*, Dutton) NAL-Dutton.

***Bad Intent: A Maggie MacGowen Mystery.** Wendy Hornsby. 384p. 1995. pap. 5.50 (*0-451-18501-3*, Onyx) NAL-Dutton.

***Bad Intentions: The Mike Tyson Story.** rev. ed. Peter Heller. (Illus.). 456p. 1995. pap. 14.95 (*0-306-80669-X*) Da Capo.

Bad Land. Richard E. Braun. LC 70-79736. 1990. pap. 7.50 (*0-912330-08-2*, Inland Bk) Jargon Soc.

Bad Language. Lars Andersson & Peter Trudgill. 160p. 1990. 24.95 (*0-631-17872-4*) Blackwell Pubs.

Bad Little Cricket see Kinder-Fun Insect Series

Bad Love. Jonathan Kellerman. LC 93-26678. 1994. 22.95 (*0-553-08919-6*) Bantam.

***Bad Love.** Jonathan Kellerman. 1994. mass mkt. 6.50 (*0-553-56870-1*) Bantam.

***Bad Luck Boswell.** Hearn. 1995. 15.00 (*0-689-80303-6*) Macmillan.

***Bad Luck Dog.** Warren. 1993. per. 14.95 (*1-55050-047-3*, Pub. by Coteau Bks CN) InBook.

Bad-Mad Boy, Honey Bear & the Magic Water Fall. Virginia Klein. LC 86-27111. 19.95 (*0-933619-11-1*) Hage Pubns.

Bad Man Ballad. Scott R. Sanders. LC 86-2695. 224p. (J). (gr. 6-8). 1986. text ed. 14.95 (*0-02-778230-1*, Bradbury S&S) S&S Childrens.

Bad Man Is Easy to Find. M. J. Verlaine. 256p. 1990. pap. 8.95 (*0-312-05061-5*) St Martin.

Bad Manners. Mame D. Kellogg. 272p. 1995. 21.95 (*0-446-51836-0*) Warner Bks.

Bad Medicine. William Campbell Douglass. 60p. 1994. pap. text ed. 8.95 (*1-885236-00-X*) Second Opinion.

Bad Medicine. Carolyn Keene. (Nancy Drew Files Ser.: No. 35). (Orig.). (YA). (gr. 7 up). 1989. pap. 2.95 (*0-671-64702-4*, Archway) PB.

Bad Medicine. large type ed. Lloyd Madison. (Linford Western Library). 304p. 1986. pap. 11.95 (*0-7089-6282-3*, Linford) Ulverscroft.

Bad Medicine: The Prescription Drug Industry in the Third World. Milton Silverman et al. 348p. (C). 1992. 29.95 (*0-8047-1669-2*) Stanford U Pr.

Bad Men & Bad Towns. Wayne C. Lee. LC 92-17951. (Orig.). 1993. pap. 14.95 (*0-87004-349-8*) Caxton.

***Bad Men Do What Good Men Dream: A Psychiatrist Illuminates the Darker Side of Human Behavior.** Robert I. Simon. 368p. 1995. boxed 22.95 (*0-88048-688-0*, 8688) Am Psychiatric.

Bad Mood Bear. John Richardson. (J). (ps). 1988. 6.95 (*0-8120-5871-2*) Barron.

Bad Mood Bear & the Big Present. John Richarson. (Illus.). 32p. (J). (ps-1). 1994. 13.95 (*0-09-176169-7*, Pub. by Hutchnson UK) Trafalgar.

Bad Moon. Rick Cleveland. 60p. 1992. pap. 5.95 (*1-56850-000-9*) Chicago Plays.

Bad Moon Rising. Dana Ferguson. LC 88-50927. 212p. (Orig.). 1988. pap. 6.95 (*1-55523-165-9*) Winston-Derek.

***Bad Moonlight.** R. L. Stine. (Fear Street Super Chiller Ser.). (J). 1995. mass mkt. 3.99 (*0-671-89424-2*, Archway) PB.

Bad Mouth Christopher. Christopher Sharp. (J). (gr. 1-4). 1980. pap. 4.99 (*0-570-03482-5*, 56-1703) Concordia.

Bad Movies We Love. Edward Margulies & Stephen Rebello. (Illus.). 352p. (Orig.). 1993. pap. 12.00 (*0-452-27005-7*, Plume) NAL-Dutton.

Bad Names for Women. 2nd ed. Hilary Tham. LC 89-50242. 72p. 1989. 10.00 (*0-915380-23-4*) Word Works.

***Bad News Bible: The New Testament.** David Voas. LC 94-43298. 209p. 1995. 25.95 (*0-87975-968-2*) Prometheus Bks.

Bad News Boyfriend, No. 2. Michael J. Pellowski. LC 91-19659. (Riverdale High Ser.). (Illus.). 128p. (YA). (gr. 4-8). 1991. pap. 2.99 (*1-56282-108-3*) Hyprn Child.

Bad News from the Stars. Steve Sneyd. (Doubles Ser.). (Illus.). 88p. 1993. 20.00 (*0-938075-35-7*); pap. 9.95 (*0-938075-36-5*) Ocean View Bks.

Bad News in Bangkok. David B. Smith. Ed. by Gerald Wheeler. LC 92-19353. 1993. pap. 4.95 (*0-8280-0697-0*) Review & Herald.

***Bad News Travels Fast.** Gar A. Haywood. LC 95-7094. 256p. 1995. 21.95 (*0-399-14017-4*, Putnam) Putnam Pub Group.

Bad Night at Dry Creek. large type ed. Cameron Judd. (Linford Western Library). 352p. 1993. pap. 14.95 (*0-7089-7366-3*, Linford) Ulverscroft.

Bad Object: Handling the Negative Therapeutic Reaction in Psychotherapy. Jeffrey Seinfeld. LC 89-15199. 336p. 1990. 42.00 (*0-87668-831-8*) Aronson.

Bad Object: Handling the Negative Therapeutic Reaction in Psychotherapy. Jeffrey Seinfeld. LC 89-15199. 336p. 1993. reprint ed. pap. 35.00x (*1-56821-002-7*) Aronson.

***Bad Objects: Essays Popular & Unpopular.** Naomi Schor. LC 95-15446. 1995. write for info. (*0-8223-1681-1*); pap. write for info. (*0-8223-1693-5*) Duke.

Bad Ol' Boy. Harold Miles. LC 93-2059. 384p. 1993. 22.50 (*0-89603-267-1*) Humana.

Bad: or The Dumbing of America. Paul Fussell, Jr. 208p. 1992. pap. 10.00 (*0-671-79228-8*, Touchstone Bks) S&S Trade.

Bad Penny. (Blue Corner Drama Ser.: No. 2). 1991. pap. 5.95 (*1-55713-123-6*) Sun & Moon CA.

Bad Penny. Susan Fox. (Romance Ser.). 1993. mass mkt. 2.99 (*0-373-03268-4*, 1-03268-9) Harlequin Bks.

***Bad Piece of Luck.** Tom Abrams. LC 94-78598. 128p. (Orig.). 1994. 23.95 (*0-942979-22-2*); pap. 13.00 (*0-942979-23-0*) Livingston U Pr.

Bad Place. Dean Koontz. 432p. 1990. pap. text ed. 6.99 (*0-425-12434-7*) Berkley Pub.

Bad Place. large type ed. Dean R. Koontz. LC 90-42690. 616p. 1990. reprint ed. lib. bdg. 21.95 (*1-56054-044-3*) Thorndike Pr.

Bad Place. large type ed. Dean R. Koontz. LC 90-42690. 616p. 1991. pap. 14.95 (*1-56054-999-8*) Thorndike Pr.

Bad Popes. E. R. Chamberlin. 1987. 17.95 (*0-88029-116-8*) Dorset Pr.

Bad Prescription for the First Amendment: FDA Censorship of Drug Advertising & Promotion. Ed. by Richard T. Kaplar. LC 92-63039. 120p. 1992. 19.95 (*0-937790-48-6*, 4420) Media Institute.

Bad Rap. Franklin W. Dixon. Ed. by Ann Greenberg. (Hardy Boys Casefiles Ser.: No. 73). 160p. (Orig.). (J). (gr. 6 up). 1993. mass mkt. 3.99 (*0-671-73109-2*, Archway) PB.

Bad Record & a Bad Heart. Albert N. Martin. 16p. (Orig.). (C). 1989. pap. 1.25 (*0-9622508-1-3*) Simpson NJ.

Bad Sailing Made Good. Oliver Stewart. (Illus.). 96p. 1973. 20.00 (*0-8464-0165-7*) Beekman Pubs.

***Bad Samaritan.** Barnard. 1995. 21.00 (*0-684-81334-3*, Scribners) S&S Trade.

Bad Samaritans: First World Ethics & Third World Debt. Paul Vallely. 1990. pap. 13.95 (*0-88344-668-5*) Orbis Bks.

Bad Scene. large type ed. Basil Copper. 1991. pap. 13.95 (*0-7089-7021-4*) Ulverscroft.

Bad Science: The Short Life & Hard Times of Cold Fusion. Gary Taubes. LC 91-52693. (Illus.). 304p. 1993. 25.00 (*0-394-58456-2*) Random.

Bad Seed. adapted ed. William March. 1956. pap. 4.75 (*0-8222-0088-0*) Dramatists Play.

Bad Seed. William March. 1993. reprint ed. lib. bdg. 21.95 (*1-56849-107-7*) Buccaneer Bks.

***Bad Sex: A Book of Stories.** Ed. by John Hoyland. 256p. (Orig.). 1994. pap. 12.99 (*1-85242-307-2*) Serpents Tail.

Bad Shakespeare: Revaluations of the Shakespeare Canon. Ed. by Maurice Charney. LC 87-45773. 216p. 1988. 35.00 (*0-8386-3310-2*) Fairleigh Dickinson.

Bad Smoke, Good Body. Clifton Snider. 1979. pap. 2.00 (*0-930090-07-1*) Applezaba.

Bad Spell for the Worst Witch. Jill Murphy. (J). (gr. 4-7). 1991. pap. 3.95 (*0-14-031446-6*, Puffin) Puffin Bks.

Bad Spell for the Worst Witch. large type ed. Jill Murphy. (Illus.). (J). 1993. 16.95 (*0-7451-1809-7*, Galaxy Child Lrg Print) Chivers N Amer.

Bad Spell in Yurt. C. Dale Brittain. 320p. 1991. mass mkt. 5.99 (*0-671-72075-9*) Baen Bks.

Bad Speller's Dictionary. Joseph Kreivsky & Jordon L. Linfield. 1974. 5.00 (*0-394-49199-8*) Random.

Bad Taste Celebrity Jokes. Bella La Balle. 144p. (Orig.). 1993. pap. 4.99 (*1-56171-232-9*, S P I Bks) Sure Sellers.

***Bad Thing.** Orourke. 1995. mass mkt. 4.99 (*0-06-100720-X*, Harp PBks) HarpC.

Bad Times for Good ol'Boys: The Oklahoma County Commissioner Scandal. Harry Holloway & Frank S. Meyers. LC 93-4593. 1993. 24.95 (*0-8061-2548-9*) U of Okla Pr.

Bad Times, Good Friends. Ilse-Margaret Vogel. (YA). 1992. 16.95 (*0-15-205528-2*, HB Juv Bks) HarBrace.

Bad Times, Good News: A Practical Guide to Preparedness & Survival. Bill Yatchman. 118p. (Orig.). 1993. pap. 9.95 (*0-9637664-8-1*) Greentrees.

Bad Times of Irma Baumlein. 2nd ed. Carol R. Brink. LC 91-13976. (Illus.). 144p. (J). (gr. 3-7). 1991. reprint ed. pap. 3.95 (*0-689-71513-7*, Aladdin Paperbacks) S&S Childrens.

Bad Times Primer: A Complete Guide to Survival on a Budget. C. G. Cobb. LC 81-52089. (Illus.). 336p. (Orig.). 1981. pap. 14.95 (*0-9606608-0-1*) Times Pr.

***Bad to the Bone.** Jack Bodine. (Pecos Kid Ser.: No. 6). 1994. pap. 3.50 (*0-06-100657-2*, Harp PBks) HarpC.

Bad to the Bone. Stephen Solomita. 352p. 1992. mass mkt. 4.99 (*0-380-71760-3*) Avon.

Bad Trips. Keath Fraser. LC 90-50618. 384p. 1991. pap. 12.00 (*0-679-72908-9*, Vin) Random.

Bad Trips. Mark Miller. (Encyclopedia of Psychoactive Drugs Ser.: No. 2). (Illus.). 112p. (YA). (gr. 5 up). 1987. lib. bdg. 19.95 (*1-55546-218-9*) Chelsea Hse.

Bad TV: The Very Best of the Very Worst. Craig Nelson. LC 94-14967. 1995. 9.95 (*0-385-31359-4*, Delta) Dell.

Bad War: An Oral History of the Vietnam Conflict. Kim Willenson. 1988. pap. 8.95 (*0-452-26063-9*, Plume) NAL-Dutton.

***Bad Women: The Regulation of Female Sexuality in Early American Cinema.** Janet Staiger. LC 94-46539. 1995. text ed. 49.95 (*0-8166-2624-3*); pap. 18.95 (*0-8166-2625-1*) U of Minn Pr.

Bad Year Economics: Cultural Responses to Risk & Uncertainty. Ed. by Paul Halstead & John O'Shea. (New Directions in Archaeology Ser.). (Illus.). 140p. (C). 1989. 69.95 (*0-521-33021-1*) Cambridge U Pr.

Bad Year for Dragons. John Ryan. LC 89-37279. 28p. (J). (gr. 1-4). 1989. 8.95 (*0-8192-1512-0*) Morehouse Pub.

Bad Year for Tomatoes. John Patrick. 1975. pap. 4.75 (*0-8222-0089-9*) Dramatists Play.

Bada Shanren & Me. Janis Provisor. (Illus.). 16p. 1991. pap. 5.00 (*0-930495-11-X*) San Fran Art Inst.

Badaga-English Dictionary. Paul Hockings & Christiane Pilot-Raichoor. LC 92-19833. (Trends in Linguistics, Documentation Ser.: Vol. 8). xxii, 865p. (C). 1992. lib. bdg. 234.30 (*3-11-012677-X*) Mouton.

Badarian Civilisation & Predynastic Remains Near Badari. Guy Brunton & Gertrude Caton-Thompson. LC 77-86424. (British School of Archaeology in Egypt & Egyptian Research Account. 30th Yr., 1924. Publication Ser.: No. 46). reprint ed. 42.50 (*0-404-16625-3*) AMS Pr.

***Badboy Book of Erotic Poetry.** Ed. by David Laurents. Date not set. mass mkt., pap. 5.95 (*1-56333-382-1*) Masquerade.

Badboy Erotic Library, Vol. I. Ed. by Michael Lowenthal. (Orig.). 1994. pap. text ed. 4.95 (*1-56333-190-X*) Masquerade.

Badboy Erotic Library, Vol. II. Ed. by Michael Lowenthal. (Orig.). 1994. pap. text ed. 4.95 (*1-56333-211-6*) Masquerade.

Badboy Fantasies. (Orig.). 1992. pap. 4.95 (*1-56333-049-0*) Masquerade.

Baden Baden Nineteen Twenty-Five International Chess Tournament. Jimmy Adams. (World's Greatest Chess Tournaments Ser.). (Illus.). 382p. 1991. 45.00 (*0-939433-13-3*) Caissa Edit.

Baden-Powell. Tim Jeal. (Illus.). 670p. 1993. reprint ed. pap. 22.95 (*0-7126-5026-1*, Pub. by Pimlico) Trafalgar.

Baden-Powell: Founder of the Boy Scouts. Pauline Brower. LC 89-33750. (Picture-Story Biographies Ser.). 32p. (J). (gr. 2-4). 1989. lib. bdg. 12.53 (*0-516-04173-8*) Childrens.

Badenheim, Nineteen Thirty-Nine. Aharon Appelfeld. Tr. by Dalya Bilu. LC 80-66192. 160p. 1980. pap. 9.95 (*0-87923-799-6*) Godine.

Bader Reading & Language Inventory. 2nd ed. Lois Bader & Katherine Wiesendanger. 256p. (C). 1994. pap. write for info. (*0-02-305111-6*) Macmillan.

Badge & Buckshot: Lawlessness in Old California. John Boessenecker. LC 87-40209. (Illus.). 1988. 26.95 (*0-8061-2097-5*) U of Okla Pr.

Badge & Buckshot: Lawlessness in Old California. John Boessenecker. LC 87-40209. (C). 1993. pap. 12.95 (*0-8061-2510-1*) U of Okla Pr.

Badge & the Bullet: Police Use of Deadly Force. Peter Scharf & Arnold Binder. LC 83-4106. 268p. 1983. pap. text ed. 16.95 (*0-275-91778-9*, B1778, Praeger Pubs) Greenwood.

Badge & the Bullet: Police Use of Deadly Force. Peter Scharf & Arnold Binder. LC 83-4106. 268p. 1983. text ed. 52.95 (*0-275-91075-X*, C1075, Praeger Pubs) Greenwood.

Badge for Brazos see Aces Wild

Badge of Betrayal. Joe Cantlupe & Lisa Petrillo. 296p. (Orig.). 1991. mass mkt. 4.99 (*0-380-76009-6*) Avon.

Badge of Honor Four: Witness. W. E. B. Griffin. 1992. mass mkt. 5.99 (*0-515-10747-6*) Jove Pubns.

Badge of Honor II: Special Operations. W. E. B. Griffin. 1989. mass mkt. 5.99 (*0-515-10148-6*) Jove Pubns.

Badge of Honor, No. 5: The Assassin. W. E. B. Griffin. 464p. (Orig.). 1993. mass mkt. 6.90 (*0-515-11113-9*) Jove Pubns.

Badge of Honor One: Men in Blue. W. E. B. Griffin. 1988. mass mkt. 6.50 (*0-515-09750-0*) Jove Pubns.

Badge of Honor Three: The Victim. W. E. B. Griffin. 1991. mass mkt. 6.50 (*0-515-10397-7*) Jove Pubns.

Badge of Revenge. Stevan C. Smith. 150p. 1988. per., pap. 7.95 (*0-89697-297-6*) Intl Univ Pr.

Badge of the Assassin. Robert K. Tanenbaum & Philip Rosenberg. 320p. 1990. pap. 5.99 (*0-451-16798-8*, Sig) NAL-Dutton.

Badge of Valor. Joseph A. West. 256p. (Orig.). 1993. mass mkt. 4.99 (*0-425-14014-8*) Berkley Pub.

Badger. Carl R. Green & William R. Sanford. LC 85-19486. (Wildlife Habits & Habitats Ser.). (Illus.). 48p. (J). (gr. 5). 1986. text ed. 12.95 (*0-89686-290-9*, Crstwood Hse) Silver Burdett Pr.

Badger & Her Babies. Curt Jansen et al. (Wildlife Adventure Ser.: Vol. 2). (Orig.). (J). (gr. k-4). pap. write for info. (*0-9614904-2-X*) Adventure Prods.

Badger & the Magic Fan: A Japanese Folktale. Tony Johnston. (Whitebird Bks.). (Illus.). 32p. (J). (ps-3). 1990. 13.95 (*0-399-21945-5*, Putnam) Putnam Pub Group.

Badger, Beano & the Magic Mushroom. Jack Scoltock. (Illus.). 125p. (Orig.). (J). (gr. 2-6). 1990. pap. 8.95 (*0-86327-263-0*, Pub. by Poolbeg Pr IE) Dufour.

Badger Digs. Norm Rockwell. 104p. (Orig.). 1980. pap. 3.95 (*0-9612002-0-0*) Moonlight Press.

Badger Island. Jonathan Guy. 128p. (J). (gr. 5-9). 1994. 18.95 (*1-85681-036-4*, Pub. by J MacRae UK) Trafalgar.

***Badgers.** Lynn Stone. LC 94-46897. (Wild Animals of the Woods Ser.). (J). 1995. write for info. (*1-57103-094-8*) Rourke Pr.

Badgers. Leonid M. Leonov. LC 72-14053. (Soviet Literature in English Translation Ser.). 336p. 1992. reprint ed. 31.50 (*0-88355-008-3*) Hyperion Conn.

Badgers at My Window. large type ed. Phil Drabble. (Non-Governmental Organisations Ser.). 256p. 1992. 21.95 (*0-7089-2710-6*) Ulverscroft.

***Badger's Bring Something Party.** Oram. 1995. (*0-688-14082-3*) Lothrop.

Badger's Illustrated Catalogue of Cast-Iron Architecture. Daniel D. Badger. 144p. 1982. pap. 10.95 (*0-486-24223-4*) Dover.

Badger's Parting Gifts. Susan Varley. LC 83-17500. (Illus.). 32p. (J). (gr. k-3). 1984. 15.00 (*0-688-02699-0*); lib. bdg. 14.93 (*0-688-02703-2*) Lothrop.

Badger's Parting Gifts. Susan Varley. LC 83-17500. (Illus.). 32p. (J). (ps up). 1992. pap. 4.95 (*0-688-11518-7*, Mulberry) Morrow.

Badger's Parting Gifts - Gracias Tejon. Susan Varley. (SPA.). (J). 19.95 (*84-372-6601-7*) Santillana.

***Badges a Guide for the Serious Collector.** 2nd ed. LC 93-90622. (Illus.). 31p. 1993. pap. text ed. 12.95 (*0-9620487-4-7*) Baird-Hedges Pub.

Badges & Battle Honours of HM Ships. Maritime Books Staff. (C). 1986. text ed. 290.00 (*0-907771-26-2*, Pub. by Maritime Bks UK) St Mut.

Badges & Distinctive Branch Insignia of the U. S. Army Quartermaster Corps, 1775-1995. David V. Olson. (Illus.). 60p. (Orig.). 1994. pap. 15.00 (*0-929757-16-5*) Regt QM.

B

Badges & Distinctive Insignia of the Arab Republic of Egypt (A. R. E.) David V. Olson. (Illus.). 50p. 1987. pap. 10.00 (*0-9609690-8-X*) Regt QM.

Badges & Distinctive Insignia of the Israeli Defense Forces (IDF) David V. Olson. (Illus.). 50p. 1986. pap. 10.00 (*0-9609690-7-1*) Regt QM.

Badges & Distinctive Insignia of the Kingdom of Jordan. David V. Olson. (Illus.). 50p. 1987. pap. 10.00 (*0-9609690-5-5*) Regt QM.

Badges & Distinctive Insignia of the Kingdom of Saudi Arabia: Para-Military Forces, Vol. 5. David V. Olson. (Illus.). 50p. 1987. pap. 10.00 (*0-9609690-4-7*) Regt QM.

Badges & Distinctive Insignia of the Kingdom of Saudi Arabia: Royal Saudi Air Force, Vol. 2. David V. Olson. (Illus.). 55p. 1984. pap. 10.00 (*0-9609690-1-2*) Regt QM.

Badges & Distinctive Insignia of the Kingdom of Saudi Arabia: Saudi Arabian Army, Vol. 1. David V. Olson. (Illus.). 192p. 1981. pap. 10.00 (*0-9609690-0-4*) Regt QM.

Badges & Distinctive Insignia of the Multinational Force & Observers (MFO) David V. Olson. (Illus.). 85p. 1986. pap. 15.00 (*0-9609690-6-3*) Regt QM.

Badges & Distinctive Insignia of the Royal Saudi Navy (RSNF), Vol. 4. David V. Olson. (Illus.). 50p. 1985. pap. 10.00 (*0-9609690-2-0*) Regt QM.

Badges & Distinctive Insignia of the Saudi Arabian National Guard (SANG), Vol. 3. D. V. Olson. (Illus.). 50p. (Orig.). 1984. pap. 10.00 (*0-9609690-3-9*) Regt QM.

Badges & Distinctive Insignia of the Syrian Armed Forces. D. V. Olson. (Illus.). 51p. (Orig.). 1989. pap. 10.00 (*0-929757-20-3*) Regt QM.

Badges & Insignia of the Elite Forces. Leroy Thompson. (Illus.). 160p. 1991. 29.95 (*1-85409-129-8*) Sterling.

Badges & Insignia of the Third Reich: 1933-1945. Brian L. Davis. (Illus.). 208p. 1993. pap. 17.95 (*1-85409-179-4*) Sterling.

Badges, Medals & Distinctive Insignia of the United Nations Peace Keeping Forces, 1947-1989. D. V. Olson. (Illus.). 67p. (Orig.). 1989. pap. 15.00 (*0-929757-17-3*) Regt QM.

Badges of Imperial Russia, Including Military, Civil & Religious. S. Andolenko. Tr. by Robert Werlich. (Illus.). 1983. lib. bdg. 50.00 (*0-911200-02-9*) Quaker.

Badges of Law & Order. George Virgines. LC 87-71915. (Illus.). 128p. 1987. 20.00 (*0-936259-06-X*) Cochran Pub.

Badges of the United States Marshals. Raymond Sherrard & George Stumpf. LC 89-61859. (Illus.). (Orig.). (J). 1991. 35.45 (*0-914503-02-2*); pap. 22.45 (*0-914503-03-0*) RHS Ent.

Badinerie. Arcangelo Corelli. 1971. 1.75 (*0-685-51176-6*, CM1010) Consort Music.

Badlands. Steven Grant & Vince Giarrano. (Illus.). 140p. 1993. pap. 13.95 (*1-878574-53-1*) Dark Horse Comics.

Badlands. Richard S. Wheeler. 416p. 1992. mass mkt. 4.99 (*0-8125-1997-3*) Tor Bks.

Badlands: Beauty Carved from Nature. L. Wade. (Doors to America's Past Ser.). (J). 1991. 11.95 (*0-86592-471-6*) Rourke Enter.

Badlands Beyond. large type ed. Norman A. Fox. 289p. 1991. reprint ed. lib. bdg. 15.95 (*1-56054-193-8*) Thorndike Pr.

Badlands Drifter. Dale Oldham. 1979. pap. 1.50 (*0-8439-0629-4*) Dorchester Pub Co.

Badlands Fox. Margaret L. Warren. 160p. (Orig.). 1991. pap. text ed. write for info. (*0-913062-00-6*) Fenwyn Pr.

***Badlands National Park, SD.** Ed. by Trails Illustrated Staff. 1995. 8.99 (*1-56695-003-1*) Trails Illustrated.

Badlands Showdown. large type ed. Chester Allen. (Linford Western Library). 240p. 1987. pap. 8.95 (*0-7089-6348-X*, Linford) Ulverscroft.

Badman. Michael Leonard. 1993. 16.95 (*0-533-10640-0*) Vantage.

Badman's Holiday - The Wind River Kid. Will Cook. 304p. 1994. pap. 4.99 (*0-8439-3614-2*) Dorchester Pub Co.

Badmen. Bill Brooks. 192p. 1992. 18.95 (*0-8027-4129-0*) Walker & Co.

***Badminton.** Steven Boga. (Games Ser.). (Illus.). 96p. 1996. pap. 10.00 (*0-8117-2487-5*) Stackpole.

Badminton. M. L. Johnson & Dewayne J. Johnson. (Illus.). 67p. (Orig.). (C). 1981. pap. text ed. 5.95x (*0-89641-061-7*) American Pr.

Badminton. Roger Mills. (EP Sports Ser.). (Illus.). 1975. 6.95 (*0-7158-0595-9*) Charles River Bks.

An Asterisk (*) at the beginning of an entry indicates that the title is appearing in BIP for the first time. 577

Badminton. Jack Reznik & Ron Byrd. 128p. (C). 1987. pap. 14.00 (0-89787-604-0) Gorsuch Scarisbrick.

Badminton. 3rd ed. James Poole. (Illus.). 162p. (C). 1991. reprint ed. pap. text ed. 8.95 (0-88133-644-0) Waveland Pr.

*Badminton. 4th ed. William A. Grice. (Illus.). 130p. 1994. pap. text ed. 7.95x (0-89641-274-1) American Pr.

Badminton. 7th ed. Margaret V. Bloss & R. Stanton Hales. 144p. 1994. pap. write for info. (0-697-12600-5) Brown & Benchmark.

Badminton: Basic Skills & Drills. Roger Sweeting & Jan Wilson. (Illus.). 179p. (C). 1992. pap. text ed. 14.95 (0-87484-985-3) Mayfield Pub.

*Badminton: The Skills of the Game. Peter Roper. (Illus.). 128p. 1995. pap. 17.95 (1-85223-887-9, Pub. by Crowood Pr UK) Trafalgar.

Badminton Everyone. 2nd ed. Chafin & Turner. 148p. (Orig.). 1988. pap. text ed. 12.95 (0-88725-108-0) Hunter Textbks.

Badminton for Beginners. Ralph Ballou. (Illus.). 112p. (C). 1992. pap. text ed. 14.95x (0-89582-234-2) Morton Pub.

Badminton Handbook. Sandra Stevenson. (Illus.). 40p. pap. 5.95 (0-88839-041-6) Hancock House.

Badminton Made Simple. Edmond Dugas et al. 118p. 1989. pap. 10.95 (0-912855-92-4) E Bowers Pub.

Badminton Today. Tariq Wadood & Karlyne Tan. Ed. by Clyde Perlee. 159p. (C). 1990. pap. text ed. 20.00 (0-314-47596-6) West Pub.

Badr. Mark Dunster. 13p. (Orig.). 1988. pap. 4.00 (0-89642-158-9) Linden Pubs.

Badr al-Din Lu'lu' Atabeg of Mosul, 1211-1259. Douglas Patton. LC 91-27342. (Occasional Papers, Middle East Center Ser.: No. 3). 122p. (C). 1992. pap. text ed. 12.95 (0-295-97156-8) U of Wash Pr.

Baedeker of Chile. Carlos Tornero. 1976. lib. bdg. 59.95 (0-8490-1470-0) Gordon Pr.

Baedeker of the Argentine Republic. Albert B. Martinez. 1976. lib. bdg. 59.95 (0-87968-695-2) Gordon Pr.

Baedeker's Athens. rev. ed. Karl Baedeker. (Baedeker's City Guides Ser.). 1989. pap. 12.95 (0-13-057977-7) P-H.

Baedeker's Bali. Jarrold Printing Staff. 1994. pap. 24.00 (0-671-89692-X, P-H Travel) P-H Gen Ref & Trav.

Baedeker's Belgium. Karl Baedeker. 1993. pap. 23.00 (0-671-87155-2, P-H Travel) P-H Gen Ref & Trav.

Baedeker's Berlin. Jarrold Printing Staff. 1994. pap. 17.00 (0-671-89682-2, P-H Travel) P-H Gen Ref & Trav.

Baedeker's Brussels. (Baedeker's City Guides Ser.). 240p. (Orig.). 1987. pap. 12.95 (0-13-368788-0) P-H.

Baedeker's Canada. (Baedeker's Ser.). (Illus.). 640p. 1993. pap. 24.00 (0-13-061219-7, P-H Travel) P-H Gen Ref & Trav.

Baedeker's China. Jarrold Printing Staff. 1994. pap. 24.00 (0-671-89693-8, P-H Travel) P-H Gen Ref & Trav.

Baedeker's Cologne. (Baedeker's City Guides Ser.). (Illus.). 240p. (Orig.). 1987. pap. 12.95 (0-13-058181-X) P-H.

Baedeker's Copenhagen. (Baedeker's Ser.). (Illus.). 192p. 1992. pap. 17.00 (0-13-059569-1, P-H Travel) P-H Gen Ref & Trav.

Baedeker's Czechoslovakia. Jarrold Printing Staff. 1994. pap. 24.00 (0-671-89687-3, P-H Travel) P-H Gen Ref & Trav.

Baedeker's Denmark. (Baedeker Ser.). (Illus.). (Orig.). 1989. pap. 17.95 (0-13-058124-0) P-H.

Baedeker's Denmark. 2nd ed. Jarrold Printing Staff. 1994. pap. 24.00 (0-671-89688-1, P-H Travel) P-H Gen Ref & Trav.

*Baedeker's Egypt. 1985. 27.50 (0-7153-6392-1) Hippocrene Bks.

Baedeker's Florence. (Baedeker's City Guides Ser.). 240p. (Orig.). 1987. pap. 12.95 (0-13-369505-0) P-H.

Baedeker's Florida. Karl Baedeker. 1993. pap. 23.00 (0-671-84939-5, P-H Travel) P-H Gen Ref & Trav.

Baedeker's France. Jarrold. (Baedeker Travel Guide Ser.). 1994. pap. 24.00 (0-671-89309-2, P-H Travel) P-H Gen Ref & Trav.

Baedeker's Frankfurt. (Baedeker's City Guides Ser.). 240p. (Orig.). 1987. pap. 12.95 (0-13-369570-0) P-H.

Baedeker's Germany. (Baedeker's Ser.). (Illus.). 640p. 1992. pap. 24.00 (0-13-059510-1, P-H Travel) P-H Gen Ref & Trav.

Baedeker's Great Britain. Ed. by Jarrold Staff. (Baedeker's Travel Guide Ser.). (Illus.). 1994. pap. 24.00 (0-671-88006-3, P-H Travel) P-H Gen Ref & Trav.

Baedeker's Greek Islands. Baedeker Staff. 1988. pap. 12.95 (0-13-058132-1) P-H.

Baedekers Guide to Florence. 2nd ed. Baedekers. 1994. pap. 17.00 (0-671-89013-1) P-H.

Baedeker's Guide to the Islands of the Mediterranean. Karl Baedeker. (Baedeker's Travel Ser.). 1984. pap. 17.95 (0-13-056862-7) P-H.

Baedeker's Hamburg. (Baedeker's City Guides Ser.). 240p. (Orig.). 1987. pap. 12.95 (0-13-369687-1) P-H.

Baedeker's Hawaii. (Baedeker's Ser.). (Illus.). 256p. 1992. pap. 23.00 (0-13-061227-8, P-H Travel) P-H Gen Ref & Trav.

Baedeker's Hong Kong. Karl Badeker. 1993. pap. 23.00 (0-671-87131-5, P-H Travel) P-H Gen Ref & Trav.

Baedeker's Hungary. Jarrold Printing Staff. 1994. pap. 24.00 (0-671-89690-3, P-H Travel) P-H Gen Ref & Trav.

Baedeker's Ireland. Jarrold Printing Staff. 1994. pap. 24.00 (0-671-89822-1, P-H Travel) P-H Gen Ref & Trav.

Baedeker's Israel. Karl Baedeker. 1993. pap. 23.00 (0-671-87132-3, P-H Travel) P-H Gen Ref & Trav.

Baedeker's Istanbul. (Baedeker's City Guides Ser.). (Illus.). 240p. (Orig.). 1988. pap. 12.95 (0-13-058207-7) P-H.

Baedeker's Japan. Ed. by Jarrold Staff. (Baedeker's Travel Guide Ser.). (Illus.). 1994. pap. 24.00 (0-671-88005-5, P-H Travel) P-H Gen Ref & Trav.

Baedeker's Lisbon. Karl Baedeker. 1993. pap. 17.00 (0-671-87130-7, P-H Travel) P-H Gen Ref & Trav.

Baedeker's London. Jarrold Printing Staff. 1994. pap. 17.00 (0-671-89821-3, P-H Travel) P-H Gen Ref & Trav.

Baedeker's Madrid. Jarrold Printing Staff. 1994. pap. 17.00 (0-671-89683-0, P-H Travel) P-H Gen Ref & Trav.

Baedeker's Mexico. Ed. by Jarrold Staff. (Baedeker's Travel Guide Ser.). (Illus.). 1994. pap. 24.00 (0-671-87478-0, P-H Travel) P-H Gen Ref & Trav.

Baedeker's Moscow. Jarrold Printing Staff. 1994. pap. 17.00 (0-671-89684-9, P-H Travel) P-H Gen Ref & Trav.

Baedeker's Munich. (Baedeker's City Guides Ser.). 240p. (Orig.). 1987. pap. 12.95 (0-13-370370-3) P-H.

Baedeker's Munich. Jarrold Printing Staff. 1994. pap. 17.00 (0-671-89685-7, P-H Travel) P-H Gen Ref & Trav.

Baedeker's Provence. write for info. (0-318-59686-5) S&S Trade.

Baedeker's Provence - Cote d'Azur. (Baedeker's Ser.). (Illus.). 288p. 1993. pap. 17.00 (0-13-059502-0, P-H Travel) P-H Gen Ref & Trav.

Baedeker's Rhine. Karl Baedeker. (Illus.). 1985. pap. 12.95 (0-13-056466-4) P-H.

Baedeker's Scandinavia. Karl Baedeker. 1993. pap. 23.00 (0-671-87153-6, P-H Travel) P-H Gen Ref & Trav.

Baedeker's Seychelles. (Baedeker's Ser.). (Illus.). 192p. 1992. pap. 17.00 (0-13-059536-5, P-H Travel) P-H Gen Ref & Trav.

Baedeker's Sicily. Karl Baedeker. 1993. pap. 20.00 (0-671-84938-7, P-H Travel) P-H Gen Ref & Trav.

Baedeker's St. Petersburg. Jarrold Printing Staff. 1994. pap. 17.00 (0-671-89691-1, P-H Travel) P-H Gen Ref & Trav.

Baedeker's Stuttgart. (Baedeker's City Guides Ser.). (Illus.). 240p. (Orig.). 1987. pap. 12.95 (0-13-058223-9) P-H.

Baedeker's Thailand. Karl Baedeker. 1993. pap. 23.00 (0-671-87154-4, P-H Travel) P-H Gen Ref & Trav.

Baedeker's Tokyo. rev. ed. (Baedeker's City Guides Ser.). 1989. pap. 12.95 (0-13-058108-9) P-H.

Baedeker's Tunisia. (Baedeker's Ser.). (Illus.). 448p. 1993. pap. 23.00 (0-13-059551-9, P-H Travel) P-H Gen Ref & Trav.

Baedeker's Turkey. Jarrold Printing Staff. 1994. pap. 24.00 (0-671-89686-5, P-H Travel) P-H Gen Ref & Trav.

Baedeker's Turkish Coast. Baedeker Staff. 1989. pap. 12.95 (0-13-058173-9) P-H.

Baedeker's Tuscany. Karl Baedeker. (Illus.). 1985. pap. 12.95 (0-13-056482-6) P-H.

Baedeker's U. S. A. Jarrold Printing Staff. 1994. pap. 24.00 (0-671-89689-X, P-H Travel) P-H Gen Ref & Trav.

Baedeker's U. S. A. Ed. by Karl Baedeker. LC 76-77703. (American Scene Ser.). Orig. Title: The United States with an Excursion into Mexico. (Illus.). 520p. 1971. reprint ed. lib. bdg. 25.00 (0-306-71341-1) Da Capo.

Baedeker's Yugoslavia. Baedeker Staff. (Baedeker Ser.). (Illus.). 280p. 1989. pap. 17.95 (0-13-056184-3) P-H.

Baer: Genealogy of Johannes Baer, 1749-1910. D. M. Bare & R. B. Bare. (Illus.). 288p. 1992. reprint ed. lib. bdg. 54.00 (0-8328-2623-5); reprint ed. pap. 44.00 (0-8328-2624-3) Higginson Bk Co.

Baer-Rings. S. K. Berberian. LC 72-189105. (Grundlehren der Mathematischen Wissenschaften Ser.: Vol. 195). 315p. 1972. 54.00 (0-387-05751-X) Spr-Verlag.

Baffled to Fight Better. Oswald Chambers. 1990. pap. 7.95 (0-87508-304-8) Chr Lit.

Baffled to Fight Better. Oswald Chambers. 1990. 7.99 (0-929239-19-9) Discovery Hse Pubs.

*Baffling Bird Behavior. Mirocha. 1994. pap. 2.99 (0-517-13276-1) Random Hse Value.

Baffling Brain Teasers. Philip J. Carter & Ken A. Russell. (Illus.). 128p. (YA). (gr. 10-12). 1992. pap. 4.95 (0-7063-7090-2, Pub. by Ward Lock UK) Sterling.

Baffling Eyes of Youth. John K. Donohue. LC 74-9578. 251p. 1974. reprint ed. lib. bdg. 22.50 (0-8371-7601-8, DOBY, Greenwood Pr) Greenwood.

Baffling Means: Writings-Drawings. Clark Coolidge & Philip Guston. (Orig.). 1991. 80.00 (1-879645-00-9); pap. 19.95 (1-879645-01-7) Garlic MA.

Baffling Phenomena: And Other Studies in the Philosophy of Knowledge & Valuation. Nicholas Rescher. 188p. (C). 1990. lib. bdg. 46.50 (0-8476-7638-2) Rowman.

Bag Balm & Duct Tape: Tales of a Vermont Doctor. Beach Conger. 272p. 1989. mass mkt. 5.99 (0-449-21793-0, Crest) Fawcett.

Bag Balm & Duct Tape: Tales of a Vermont Doctor. Beach Conger. 224p. 1988. 16.95 (0-316-15258-7) Little.

Bag Full of Pups. Dick Gackenbach. LC 80-23230. 32p. (J). (gr. k-3). 1983. pap. 5.95 (0-89919-179-7, Clarion Bks) HM.

Bag I'm Taking to Grandma's. Shirley Neitzel. LC 94-4115. (Illus.). 32p. (J). 1995. lib. bdg. 14.93 (0-688-12961-7) Greenwillow.

Bag I'm Taking to Grandma's. Shirley Neitzel. LC 94-4115. (Illus.). 32p. (J). (ps up). 1995. 15.00 (0-688-12960-9) Greenwillow.

Bag It! Distinctive Gift Ideas Using Bags! Betsy Broome & Cynthia Cummings. Ed. by Stanley C. Coy. (Illus.). 148p. (Orig.). 1992. pap. 10.95 (1-881459-02-0) Eagle Pr SC.

Bag Lady. Jean-Claude Van Itallie. 1980. pap. 4.75 (0-8222-0090-2) Dramatists Play.

Bag 'o' Diamonds: Poems by Susan Wheeler. Susan Wheeler. LC 93-9955. (Contemporary Poetry Ser.). 88p. (C). 1993. 20.00 (0-8203-1563-X); pap. 9.95 (0-8203-1564-8) U of Ga Pr.

Bag O Games. Donna T. Gamble. 1993. spiral bd. 34.95 (1-55999-399-5) LinguiSystems.

Bag of Bones: Legends of the Wintu Indians of Northern California. Marcelle Masson. LC 66-23398. 130p. (J). (gr. 4 up). 1967. pap. 8.95 (0-911010-26-2) Naturegraph.

Bag of Stories. Edla Van Steen. Tr. & Intro. by David George. LC 91-22902. 174p. 1991. pap. 14.95 (0-935480-54-4) Lat Am Lit Rev Pr.

Bag of Toys. David France. 480p. 1994. mass mkt. 4.99 (0-7860-0034-1) Windsor NY.

Bag of Tricks. Ed. by Jane Sanborn. (Illus.). 125p. (Orig.). 1984. pap. 6.95 (0-910715-02-5) Search Public.

*Bag of Tricks, Vol. II. Jane Sanborn. (Illus.). 121p. 1994. 9.95 (0-910715-09-2) Search Public.

*Bag of Tricks I: Photocopy Handouts for Regular & Substitute ESL Teachers. Paul J. Hamel. (Illus.). 84p. (Orig.). 1990. pap. text ed. 11.95 (0-937354-20-1) Delta Systems.

*Bag of Tricks II: Photocopy Handouts for Regular & Substitute ESL Teachers. Paul J. Hamel. (Illus.). 83p. (Orig.). 1992. pap. text ed. 11.95 (0-937354-77-5) Delta Systems.

Bag O'Tales: A Sourcebook for Story-Tellers. Effie Power. LC 89-62654. 340p. 1990. reprint ed. lib. bdg. 44.00 (1-55888-834-9) Omnigraphics Inc.

*Bag Visitors. Jason L. Perry. LC 95-60149. 112p. 1995. per., pap. 6.95 (0-614-06585-2) TWanda.

Baga. Robert Pinget. Tr. by John Stevenson. 144p. (Orig.). 1985. reprint ed. pap. 9.95 (0-7145-0099-2) Riverrun NY.

Bagages Pour Vancouver. Michel Deon. (Mes Arches De Noe Ser.: Vol. II). 249p. (FRE.). 1987. pap. 11.95 (0-7859-2075-7, 2070378861) Fr & Eur.

Baganda at Home. C. W. Hattersley. (Illus.). 227p. 1968. 40.00 (0-7146-1673-7, Pub. by F Cass Pubs UK) Intl Spec Bk.

Bagarre: (Galiani's Lost Parody) Ed. by Steven L. Kaplan. (International Archives of the History of Ideas Ser.: No. 92). 1979. lib. bdg. 62.00 (90-247-2125-3) Kluwer Ac.

Bagarre De Juillet. Erskine Caldwell. 224p. (FRE.). 1985. pap. 11.95 (0-7859-2008-0, 2070376346) Fr & Eur.

Bagatelle - Guinevere. Nancy Bogen. LC 94-4038. (Illus.). 328p. 1995. 22.95 (0-936726-05-9); pap. 14.95 (0-936726-06-7) Twickenham Pr.

Bagatelles from Passy. Benjamin Franklin. LC 67-28990. 1967. 40.00 (0-87130-005-2) Eakins.

*Bagel Bible. 2nd ed. Marilyn Bagel. LC 95-15386. 1995. write for info. (1-56440-725-X) Globe Pequot.

*Bagel Bible: For Bagel Lovers, the Complete Guide to Great Noshing. Marilyn Bagel & Tom Bagel. LC 92-5790. (Illus.). 192p. (Orig.). 1992. pap. 9.95 (1-56440-096-4) Globe Pequot.

*Bagel Mouse. (J). 3.50 (0-679-86020-7) Random.

*Bagelhead to the Rescue. Michael A. Farber & Anne K. Farber. LC 95-79664. (Illus.). 24p. (Orig.). (J). (ps-3). 1995. audio, pap. write for info. (0-9646094-0-1) KF Classix.

Bagels Are Coming. Arlene Kingston. (Illus.). 40p. (J). (ps up). 1988. pap. 5.95 (0-929934-00-8) Child Time Pubs.

Bagels for Tea. Serita Stevens & Rayanne Moore. 272p. 1993. 18.95 (0-312-09348-9, Pub. by Thomas Dunne Bks) St Martin.

Bagford Ballads, 2 Vols, Set. Ballads Bagford. Ed. by J. W. Ebsworth. (Ballad Society, London. Publications: Nos. 14-17 & 20). (Illus.). reprint ed. 187.50 (0-404-50830-8) AMS Pr.

Bagg Bonanza Farm Heirloom Cookbook. 302p. 1992. lib. bdg. 29.95 (0-9638670-0-8); pap. 19.95 (0-9638670-1-6) Bagg Bonanza.

Baggage Car with Lace Curtains. 2nd ed. Kay Fisher & Bill Fisher. (Illus.). 180p. 1986. 15.95 (0-9603004-2-2); pap. 8.95 (0-9603004-1-4) B & K Fisher.

Baggage to London. Lynn W. Cutler. (Annikins Ser.: No. 13). (Illus.). 24p. (Orig.). (J). (ps-1). 1994. pap. 0.99 (1-55037-345-5, Pub. by Annick CN) Firefly Bks Ltd.

*Bagging Big Bugs: How to Identify, Collect & Display the Largest & Most Colorful Insects of the Rocky Mountain Region. Whitney Cranshaw & Boris Kondratieff. LC 94-34085. 1995. 16.95 (1-55591-178-1) Fulcrum Pub.

Bagging It with Puppets. Gloria Mehrens & Karen Wick. (J). (gr. k-2). 1988. pap. 16.99 (0-8224-0677-2) Fearon Teach Aids.

Baghdad: Metropolis of the Abbasid Caliphate. Gaston Wiet. Tr. by Seymour Feiler. LC 72-123348. (Centers of Civilization Ser.: Vol. 28). (Illus.). 189p. reprint ed. pap. 53.90 (0-8357-9720-1, 2016279) Bks Demand.

Baghdad & Beyond. Baghdad Writers Group. LC 83-63009. (Illus.). 228p. 1985. pap. 13.50 (0-918992-06-0) Middle East Edit.

Baghdad Blues: The Revolution That Brought Saddam Hussein to Power. Sam Greenlee. 186p. 1991. reprint ed. 5.95 (1-879831-02-3) Kayode Pubns.

Baghdad-by-the-Bay. Herb Caen. 288p. 1987. reprint ed. 3.95 (0-89174-047-3) Comstock Edns.

Baghdad During the Abbasid Caliphate: From Contemporary Arabic & Persian Sources. Guy LeStrange. LC 82-25143. xxxi, 381p. 1983. reprint ed. text ed. 99.75 (0-313-23198-2, LEBC, Greenwood Pr) Greenwood.

Baghdad Mission. Sidney Rosen & Dorothy Rosen. LC 93-36965. (J). (gr. 4-7). 1994. 19.95 (0-87614-828-3, Carolrhoda) Lerner Group.

Baghdad Sketches. Freya Stark. 1992. pap. 11.95 (0-910395-81-0) Marlboro Pr.

Baghdad Without a Map: And Other Misadventures in Arabia. Tony Horwitz. 288p. 1992. reprint ed. pap. 10.95 (0-452-26745-5, Plume) NAL-Dutton.

*Bagheria. Dacia Maraini. Tr. by Dick Kitto & Elspeth Spottiswood. 119p. 1995. 30.00 (0-7206-0926-7, Pub. by P Owen Ltd UK) Dufour.

*Bagirmi. Chukwuma Azuonye. LC 94-45818. (Heritage Library of African Peoples). (J). 1995. write for info. (0-8239-1990-0) Rosen Group.

Bagman's Story. Charles Dickens. (Creative's Classic Short Stories Ser.). 48p. (J). (gr. 4 up). 1983. lib. bdg. 13.95 (0-87191-922-2) Creative Ed.

Bagobos: Their Ethnohistory & Acculturation. Heidi K. Gloria. (Illus.). vii, 164p. (Orig.). (C). 1988. pap. 10.75 (971-10-0362-7, Pub. by New Day Pub PH) Cellar.

Bagpipers. George Sand. 395p. 1977. reprint ed. pap. 10.00 (0-915864-45-2) Academy Chi Pubs.

Bags Are Big: A Paper Bag Craft Book. Nancy Renfro. Ed. by Celeste Cromack. (Illus.). 78p. (J). (gr. 1-6). 1983. pap. 14.95 (0-931044-10-3) Renfro Studios.

Bags the Lamb. Wendy Kanno. (Funny Farm Ser.). (Illus.). (J). (gr. k-2). 1984. 7.95 (0-89868-165-0); pap. 2.95 (0-89868-166-9) ARO Pub.

Bagthorpes Abroad: Being the Fifth Part of The Bagthorpe Saga. Helen Cresswell. LC 84-7125. 180p. (J). (gr. 5-9). 1984. text ed. 14.95 (0-02-725390-2, Mac Bks Young Read) S&S Childrens.

Bagthorpes vs. the World: Being the Fourth Part of the Bagthorpe Saga. Helen Cresswell. LC 79-13260. 204p. (J). (gr. 5 up). 1979. lib. bdg. 14.95 (0-02-725420-8, Mac Bks Young Read) S&S Childrens.

Baguazhang: Theory & Applications. Shou-Yu Liang et al. 364p. (Orig.). 1994. pap. 34.95 (0-940871-30-0, B020) YMAA Pubn.

Bah! Humbug? Lorna Balian. (Illus.). 32p. (J). (ps-3). 1988. reprint ed. 7.50 (0-687-37107-4) Humbug Bks.

Bah! Humbug! One Hundred One Reasons to Hate the Holidays. Ron Barrett & Patty Brown. Ed. by Julie Rubenstein. (Illus.). 96p. 1992. pap. 7.00 (0-671-79600-3) PB.

Bah, Humbug! Quotes, Verses, & Stories for the Spiritual Heirs of Ebenezer Scrooge. Ed. by William E. Cole. 160p. 1992. 13.95 (0-312-08279-7, Pub. by Thomas Dunne Bks) St Martin.

Bahadur Shah: The Regent of Nepal (1785-1794 A. D.) B. R. Bajracharya. (C). 1992. 50.00 (0-7855-0172-X, Pub. by Ratna Pustak Bhandar) St Mut.

Bahadur Shah: The Regent of Nepal (1785-1794 A.D.) Bhadra R. Bajracharya. (C). 1992. text ed. 21.00 (81-7041-643-4, Pub. by Anmol II) S Asia.

Bahai. Francis Beckwith. LC 85-20161. 64p. 1985. 3.99 (0-87123-848-9) Bethany Hse.

Baha'i Faith: Its History & Teachings. William M. Miller. LC 74-8745. (Illus.). 444p. 1984. pap. 11.95 (0-87808-137-2) William Carey Lib.

Baha'i Faith in America: Origins, 1892-1900, Vol. 1. Robert H. Stockman. (Illus.). 225p. 1985. 12.95 (0-87743-199-X) Bahai.

*Baha'i Faith in America Vol. 2: Early Expansion 1900-1912. Robert H. Stockman. (Illus.). 400p. 1995. pap. 29.95 (0-85398-388-7) G Ronald Pub.

Baha'i Families: Perspectives, Principles, Practice. Patricia Wilcox. 166p. 1992. pap. 10.95 (0-85398-331-3) G Ronald Pub.

Baha'i Prayers: A Selection of Prayers Revealed by Baha'u'llah, the Bab, & 'Abdu'l-Baha. Baha'u'llah et al. 277p. 1991. 13.95 (0-87743-230-9); pap. 6.95 (0-87743-229-5) Bahai.

Baha'i Teachings: A Resurgent Model of the Universe. (Illus.). 184p. (Orig.). (C). 1990. pap. 13.50 (0-85398-297-X) G Ronald Pub.

Baha'i World: An International Record, 136-40 of the Baha'i Era 1979-83, Vol. XVIII. Universal House of Justice Staff. (Illus.). 1015p. 1987. 51.95 (0-85398-234-1) Bahai.

Baha'i World: An International Record 1954-1963, Vol. XIII. Universal House of Justice Staff. LC 27-5882. (Illus.). 1970. 39.95 (0-87743-042-X, 233-013) Bahai.

Baha'i World: An International Record 1963-1968, Vol. XIV. Universal House of Justice Staff. LC 27-5882. (Illus.). 1974. 19.50 (0-87743-099-3, 233-014) Bahai.

Baha'i World: An International Record 1968-1973, Vol. XV. Universal House of Justice Staff. (Illus.). 1976. 26.50 (0-85398-059-4, 233-015) Bahai.

Baha'i World: An International Record 1973-1976, Vol. XVI. Universal House of Justice Staff. (Illus.). 1979. 24.95 (0-85398-075-6, 233-016) Bahai.

Baha'i World: An International Record 1976-79, Vol. XVII. Universal House of Justice Staff. (Illus.). 1981. 33.95 (0-85398-130-2) Bahai.

Bahais of Iran. Lewis B. Scholnick. (Civil Rights Reporter Ser.). (Illus.). 60p. (Orig.). (C). 1994. pap. 45.00 (1-57205-123-X) Rector Pr.

Bahaism & Its Claims. Samuel G. Wilson. LC 79-131493. reprint ed. 39.50 (0-404-06995-9) AMS Pr.

Bahama Rapture. Jolene Prewit-Parker. (Orig.). 1982. pap. 3.50 (0-8217-1018-4) Zebra.

Bahama Songs & Stories. Charles L. Edwards. 1976. lib. bdg. 59.95 (0-8490-1471-9) Gordon Pr.

Bahama Songs & Stories: A Contribution to Folklore. Charles L. Edwards. LC 09-46. (American Folklore Society Memoirs Ser.: Vol. 3). 1972. reprint ed. 29.00 (0-527-01055-3) Periodicals Srv.

Bahamas. (Insight Guides, Windows on the World Ser.). 1993. pap. 21.95 (0-395-66175-7) HM.

Bahamas. (Insight Pocket Guide Ser.). (Illus.). 108p. 1994. pap. 12.95 (0-395-71056-1) HM.

Bahamas. Paul G. Boultbee. (World Bibliographical Ser.). 1990. lib. bdg. 57.00 (1-85109-102-5) ABC-CLIO.

Bahamas. Patricia E. McCulla. (Places & Peoples of the World Ser.). (Illus.). 104p. (J). (gr. 5 up). 1988. lib. bdg. 14.95 (1-55546-191-3) Chelsea Hse.

Bahamas. Saunders. (Caribbean Guides Ser.). 208p. (Orig.). 1990. pap. 13.95 (0-333-46695-0, 1411) Hunter NJ.

*Bahamas: Commercial Law. 300p. (Orig.). 1994. pap. 295.00 (0-7605-1225-6) Rector Pr.

Bahamas: Consolidated Index of Statutes & Subsidiary Legislation. C. J. Hammett. (West Indian Legislation Indexing Project Ser.). iv, 95p. (Orig.). 1990. pap. text ed. 25.00 (0-317-60927-0, Pub. by UWI Fac Law BB) W W Gaunt.

Bahamas Between Worlds. Dean W. Collinwood. 120p. (Orig.). 1989. pap. 8.95 (0-932265-15-4) White Sound.

An Asterisk (*) at the beginning of an entry indicates that the title is appearing in BIP for the first time.

579

Baja Journey: Reveries of a Sea-Kayaker. Robin Carey. LC 88-18665. 184p. 1989. 29.95 (*0-89096-347-9*); pap. 12.95 (*0-89096-392-4*) Tex A&M Univ Pr.

Baja Love Song. Paul Pierce. (Illus.). 1985. 5.95 (*0-914622-06-4*) Baja Trail.

Baja Mar; the Shallow Seas: A Diver's Guide to the Underwater World of the Bahamas. Rob Palmer. 160p. (C). 1990. 125.00 (*0-907151-82-5*, Pub. by IMMEL Pubng UK) St Mut.

Baja Oklahoma. Dan Jenkins. Ed. by Julie Rubenstein. 1986. mass mkt. 4.99 (*0-671-63927-7*) PB.

Baja Run. Lisbeth Chance. 224p. 1986. 15.95 (*0-8027-0909-5*) Walker & Co.

Baja Run: Racing Fury. Don Smith. LC 75-23412. (Illus.). 32p. (J). (gr. 5-10). 1976. lib. bdg. 10.79 (*0-89375-000-X*) Troll Assocs.

Baja Sea Guide. Leland Lewis. LC 85-173041. (Sea Guide Ser.). (Illus.). 368p. Date not set. reprint ed. 37.50 (*0-688-04314-3*, Hearst Marine Bks) Morrow.

***Baja to Barrow: A Pacific Coast Odyssey.** Erwin Bauer & Peggy Bauer. 160p. 1995. 29.50 (*1-57223-022-3*) Outlook Pubng.

Baja to Patagonia: Latin American Adventures. Larry Rice. (Illus.). 320p. (Orig.). 1993. pap. 15.95 (*1-55591-113-7*) Fulcrum Pub.

Baja Traveler. 2nd ed. Airguide Publications, Inc. Staff. Ed. by Brenda Garcia. LC 86-72692. (Illus.). 368p. 1988. pap. text ed. 24.00 (*0-934754-00-4*) Airguide Pubns.

Bajanellas & Semilinas: Aberdeen University & the Education of Women 1860-1920. Lindy Moore. (SWSS Ser.). (Illus.). 192p. 1991. pap. text ed. 17.90 (*0-08-041202-5*, Pub. by Aberdeen U Pr) Macmillan.

Bajazet. Racine. Tr. by Alan Hollinghurst. (Chatto Playscript Ser.). 64p. 1992. pap. 19.95 (*0-7011-3853-X*, Pub. by Chatto & Windus UK) Trafalgar.

Bajazet. Jean B. Racine. 128p. (FRE.). 1984. pap. 10.95 (*0-7859-1263-0*, 2040160728) Fr & Eur.

Bajazet (Gasparini) see Italian Opera Librettos, Vol. III, 1640-1770

Baje la Guardia! Charles R. Swindoll. Tr. by Juan S. Araujo. 176p. (SPA.). 1987. pap. 4.95 (*0-88113-016-8*) Edit Betania.

Bajo el poder de Poncio Pilato: De Poncio Pilato. Vicente Trezza. LC 93-84979. 278p. (Orig.). (SPA.). 1993. pap. 16.00 (*1-882573-03-X*) Serena Bay.

***Bajo Las Olas.** Kristin J. Pratt. Tr. by Alma F. Ada. (Illus.). 44p. (Orig.). (J). (ps-7). 1995. pap. 7.95 (*1-883220-30-0*) Dawn CA.

Bajo los Efectos de la Poesia. Jose L. Vega. 72p. (SPA.). 1989. pap. 6.95 (*0-8477-0000-3*) U of PR Pr.

Bajo Sus Alas: Under His Wings. Zenobia Bird. (SPA.). 5.95 (*84-7228-018-7*, 220092, Pub. by Edit Clie SP) TSELF.

Bakakai. Witold Gombrowicz. (FRE.). 1990. pap. 11.95 (*0-7859-2599-6*, 2070382982) Fr & Eur.

Bakavi: Change the World I Want to Stay On. Mike Nickerson. (Illus.). 119p. 1992. pap. 12.95 (*0-919970-03-6*) All About Us.

Bakayak Es Rokohaik: Magyarurszagon USA E's Kulfoldon. Arpad Bakay. LC 93-90896. 282p. (HUN.). 1993. 39.95 (*0-9640137-0-3*) A Bakay.

Bake - Face & Other Guava Stories. 2nd ed. Opal P. Adisa et al. Ed. by Xenia Lisanevich. LC 86-7174. (Illus.). 136p. (Orig.). 1987. pap. 7.50 (*0-932716-20-2*) Kelsey St Pr.

Bake-a-Cake Book: Beat the Batter, Measure the Flour, Bake a Cake with the Cakebakers. Illus. by Charlotte Ramel. LC 93-40877. (J). (ps-3). 1994. 16.95 (*0-8118-0693-6*) Chronicle Bks.

Bake a Snake: How to Survive by Your Own Cooking. Gerald R. Hunter & Peggy Hoffmann. LC 81-10293. (Illus.). 68p. (Orig.). (J). (gr. 1-7). 1981. 9.00 (*0-939710-10-2*); pap. 4.75 (*0-939710-09-9*) Meridional Pubns.

Bake & Freeze Desserts: One Hundred Fifty Do-Ahead Cakes, Pies, Tarts, Brownies, Bars, Ice Creams, Terrines & Sorbets. Elinor Klivans. LC 94-7762. 1994. 25.00 (*0-688-12347-3*) Morrow.

***Bake My Brain.** Hume Cronyn. 80p. 1995. lib. bdg. 33.00 (*0-8095-4840-2*) Borgo Pr.

Bake Your Own Bread. Floss Dworkin & Stan Dworkin. 1989. pap. 7.95 (*0-452-26172-4*, Plume) NAL-Dutton.

Bake Your Own Bread. Floss & Stan Dworkin. 1989. pap. 10.95 (*0-452-26464-2*, Plume) NAL-Dutton.

***Baked & Filled Pastas.** Michele A. Jordan. Ed. by Jill Fox. (Williams-Sonoma Pasta Collection Ser.). (Illus.). 128p. 1996. 18.95 (*1-875137-06-8*) Weldon Owen.

***Baked Beads & Beyond: Making Magic with Oven-Bake Clay.** (J). (gr. 3 up). 1995. 11.95 (*0-448-40483-4*, G&D) Putnam Pub Group.

Baked Bean Supper Murders. Virginia Rich. 1984. mass mkt. 4.95 (*0-345-31252-X*) Ballantine.

***Baked Goods (Sweet) Market.** 173p. (Orig.). 1995. pap. 2,295.00 (*0-7605-2205-7*) Rector Pr.

Baked Meats of the Funeral. Charles G. Halpine. (Notable American Authors Ser.). 1992. reprint ed. lib. bdg. 75.00 (*0-7812-2997-9*) Rprt Serv.

Bakelite Jewelry Book. Corinne Davidov & Ginny R. Dawes. (Illus.). 156p. 1988. 45.00 (*0-89659-867-5*) Abbeville Pr.

Baker. Jack Rudman. (Career Examination Ser.: C-1132). 1994. pap. 23.95 (*0-8373-1132-2*) Nat Learn.

Baker & Botts in the Development of Modern Houston. Kenneth J. Lipartito & Joseph A. Pratt. (Illus.). 276p. 1991. 24.95 (*0-292-70782-7*) U of Tex Pr.

***Baker Bible Language Library.** Date not set. pap. 63.49 (*0-614-06485-6*) Baker Bk.

***Baker Bunny: Bookshelf Buddies.** Jerry Smath. (J). (ps-3). 1995. pap. 3.95 (*0-8167-3584-0*) Troll Assocs.

Baker Encyclopedia of Bible Places. John Bimson. (Illus.). 320p. 1994. 29.99 (*0-8010-1093-4*) Baker Bk.

Baker Encyclopedia of Bible Plants: Flowers & Trees, Fruits & Vegetables, Ecology. F. Nigel Hepper. Ed. by J. Gordon Melton. (Illus.). 192p. 1993. reprint ed. 24.99 (*0-8010-4361-1*) Baker Bk.

Baker Encyclopedia of Psychology. Ed. by David G. Benner. LC 85-70713. 1376p. (C). 1985. text ed. 49.99 (*0-8010-0865-4*) Baker Bk.

Baker Encyclopedia of the Bible, 2 vols., Set. Ed. by Walter A. Elwell et al. LC 88-19318. (Illus.). 2000p. 1988. 95.00 (*0-8010-3447-7*) Baker Bk.

***Baker Street: Children of the Night.** Gary Reed & Guy Davis. (Graphic Novel Ser.). (Illus.). 176p. 1993. write for info. (*0-941613-43-7*) Stabur Pr.

***Baker Street: Honour among Punks.** Gary Reed & Guy Davis. (Graphic Novel Ser.). (Illus.). 176p. 1993. write for info. (*0-941613-42-9*) Stabur Pr.

Baker Street By-Ways. James E. Holroyd. 160p. 1994. reprint ed. pap. 8.00 (*1-883402-71-9*) S&S Trade.

Baker Street Irregular: The Unauthorized Biography of Sherlock Holmes. Austin Mitchelson. 1994. 35.00 (*0-88734-905-6*) Players Pr.

Baker Street Puzzles. Tom Bullimore. LC 94-17217. 128p. 1994. pap. 4.95 (*0-8069-0856-4*) Sterling.

Baker Street Reader: Cornerstone Writings about Sherlock Holmes. Ed. by Philip A. Shreffler. LC 83-18350. (Contributions to the Study of Popular Culture Ser.: No. 8). (Illus.). xvi, 212p. 1984. text ed. 47.95 (*0-313-24106-6*, SHR/, Greenwood Pr) Greenwood.

***Baker Street Studies.** H. W. Bell. LC 94-22580. 1995. pap. 8.00 (*1-883402-91-3*) S&S Trade.

***Bakeries by Bicycle: A Guide to Puget Sound's Best Bakeries.** Fred Wert. 192p. (Orig.). 1993. pap. text ed. 10.95 (*1-883195-01-2*) Infinity WA.

Bakerman's ABC's of Adult & Pediatric Drug Therapy. Paul Bakerman & Seymour Bakerman. 1992. pap. text ed. 28.50 (*0-945577-05-2*) Interpret Lab Data.

Bakerman's ABCs of Interpretive Laboratory Data. 3rd ed. Seymour Bakerman. Ed. by Paul Bakerman & Paul Strausbauch. 543p. 1994. 28.50 (*0-945577-06-0*) Interpret Lab Data.

Baker's Bible Atlas. rev. ed. Charles F. Pfeiffer. LC 60-15536. (Illus.). 1961. reprint ed. 24.99 (*0-8010-6930-0*) Baker Bk.

Bakers Bible Atlas Study Guide. Ray Eby. 1977. 5.10 (*0-686-25535-6*); 1.50 (*0-686-31725-4*); 1.80 (*0-686-31726-2*) Rod & Staff.

Baker's Bible Handbook. Ed. by Walter A. Elwell et al. LC 89-6958. 352p. 1989. 14.99 (*0-8010-3203-2*) Baker Bk.

Baker's Biographical Dictionary of Musicians. 7th rev. ed. Nicolas Slonimsky. 2577p. 1984. text ed. write for info. (*0-317-46604-6*) Macmillan.

Baker's Biographical Dictionary of Musicians. 8th ed. Nicolas Slonimsky. 2118p. 1991. text ed. 125.00 (*0-02-872415-1*) Schirmer Bks.

Baker's Biographical Dictionary of Musicians. Theodore Baker. 143p. reprint ed. lib. bdg. 69.00 (*0-7812-9190-9*) Rprt Serv.

***Baker's Biographical Dictionary of 20th Century Music.** Kuhn. 1996. 75.00 (*0-02-871271-4*) Macmillan.

***Baker's Boy.** J. V. Jones. (Book of Words Ser.: Bk. 1). 258p. (Orig.). 1995. pap. 12.99 (*0-446-67097-9*, Aspect) Warner Bks.

***Baker's Boy.** J. V. Jones. (Book of Words Ser.: Bk. 2). 560p. (Orig.). 1996. mass mkt. 5.99 (*0-446-60282-5*, Aspect) Warner Bks.

Baker's Cart, & Other Tales. Gerald W. Bullett. LC 77-125208. (Short Story Index Reprint Ser.). 1977. 20.95 (*0-8369-3575-6*) Ayer.

Baker's Daughter. D. E. Stevenson. 15.95 (*0-8488-1470-3*) Amereon Ltd.

Baker's Daughter. D. E. Stevenson. 321p. 1983. reprint ed. lib. bdg. 16.95 (*0-89966-159-9*) Buccaneer Bks.

Baker's Dictionary. 2nd ed. Albert R. Daniel. 209p. 1971. 32.50 (*0-444-20121-1*, Pub. by Elsevier Applied Sci UK) Elsevier.

***Baker's Dictionary of Rock & Roll.** Helander. 1996. pap. 65.00 (*0-02-871031-2*) Macmillan.

Baker's Dictionary of Theology. Ed. by Everett F. Harrison. LC 60-7333. 566p. 1985. pap. 18.99 (*0-8010-4289-5*) Baker Bk.

Baker's Dozen. Kathleen Norris. LC 71-130068. (Short Story Index Reprint Ser.). 1977. 20.95 (*0-8369-3649-3*) Ayer.

Baker's Dozen. Llewelyn Powys. LC 79-86776. (Essay Index Reprint Ser.). 1977. 19.95 (*0-8369-1153-9*) Ayer.

***Baker's Dozen.** Alicia Schramm. 1995. 16.95 (*0-533-11370-9*) Vantage.

Baker's Dozen: A Colonial American Tale. Heather Forest. (J). (ps-3). 1993. pap. 4.95 (*0-15-205687-4*, HB Juv Bks) HarBrace.

Baker's Dozen: A Colonial American Tale. Illus. by Susan Gaber. 28p. (J). (ps-3). 1988. 14.95 (*0-15-200412-2*, Gulliver Bks) HarBrace.

***Baker's Dozen: A Saint Nicholas Tale.** Illus. by Wendy Edelson. LC 95-2121. (J). 1995. write for info. (*0-689-80298-6*, Atheneum S&S) S&S Trade.

Baker's Dozen: Contemporary Women Poets of Alabama. Ed. by Jerri Beck & Anne George. (Orig.). 1988. pap. 10.00 (*0-945301-03-0*) Druid Pr.

Baker's Dozen: Stars in Their Eyes, No. 4. Aidel Stein. (J). 1992. pap. 7.95 (*0-944070-85-X*) Targum Pr.

Baker's Dozen: The Inside Story, No. 5. Libby Lazewnik. (J). 1992. pap. 7.95 (*0-944070-93-0*) Targum Pr.

Baker's Dozen: Thirteen Short Espionage Novels. Ed. by Martin H. Greenberg & Bill Pronzini. 1985. 9.99 (*0-517-47647-9*) Random Hse Value.

Baker's Dozen: Thirteen Short Science Fiction Novels. Isaac Asimov. 1985. 7.98 (*0-517-47646-0*) Random Hse Value.

***Baker's Dozen No. 12: The Baker Family Circus.** Miriam Rose. 172p. (J). (gr. 6-8). Date not set. pap. 9.95 (*1-56871-062-3*) Targum Pr.

Baker's Dozen Doubled. Mary E. Hopkins. (Illus.). 36p. (Orig.). 1988. 12.95 (*0-929950-00-3*) ME Pubns.

Bakers Dozen, No. 1: On Our Own. Libby Lazewnik. 144p. 1991. 7.95 (*0-944070-34-5*) Targum Pr.

Baker's Dozen, No. 1: On Our Own. Libby Lazewnik. (J). 1993. pap. 7.95 (*0-685-65302-1*) Feldheim.

Baker's Dozen, No. 2: Ghosthunters. Balky Siegel. (J). 1993. pap. 7.95 (*0-685-65303-X*) Feldheim.

Bakers Dozen, No. 2: Ghosthunters! Malky Siegel. 144p. 1992. 7.95 (*0-944070-41-8*) Targum Pr.

Bakers Dozen, No. 3: And the Winner Is. Aidel Stein. 144p. 1992. 7.95 (*0-944070-79-5*) Targum Pr.

Baker's Dozen, No. 3: And the Winner Is... Aidel Stein. (J). 1993. pap. 7.95 (*0-685-65304-8*) Feldheim.

Baker's Dozen, No. 4: Stars in Their Eyes. Aidel Stein. (J). 1993. pap. 7.95 (*0-685-65305-6*) Feldheim.

Baker's Dozen, No. 5: The Inside Story. Libby Lazewnik. (J). 1993. pap. 7.95 (*0-685-65306-4*) Feldheim.

Baker's Dozen, No. 6: Trapped. Libby Lazewnik et al. (J). 1993. pap. 7.95 (*0-685-65307-2*) Feldheim.

Baker's Dozen, No. 6: Trapped! (Super Special) Miriam Zakon. 172p. 1993. pap. 9.95 (*0-944070-94-9*) Targum Pr.

Baker's Dozen, No. 7: Ima Come Home! Aidel Stein. 147p. pap. 7.95 (*1-56871-009-7*) Targum Pr.

Baker's Dozen, No. 8: Hey, Waiter! Emmy Zitter. 136p. 1993. pap. 7.95 (*1-56871-015-1*) Targum Pr.

Baker's Dozen, No. 9: Through Thick & Thin. Debby Garfunkel. 144p. (Orig.). (J). (gr. 4-9). 1993. pap. 7.95 (*1-56871-024-0*) Targum Pr.

Baker's Dozen of Daily Breads & More. Paul M. Novak. LC 89-90838. 64p. (Orig.). 1989. Includes soundsheet (flexidisc) with a recording of "Bread Baker's Stomp" by George Winston. pap. 10.95 (*0-9622472-1-9*) Only Connect.

Baker's Dozen of Daily Breads & More. 2nd ed. Paul M. Novak. LC 91-90205. 64p. (Orig.). 1991. pap. 11.95 (*0-9622472-2-7*) Only Connect.

Baker's Easy Party Cut-up Cakes. (Favorite All Time Recipes Ser.). (Illus.). 96p. 1993. 7.98 (*0-7853-0197-6*, 2019902) Pubns Intl Ltd.

***Bakers Fire.** R. J. Cohn. 480p. Date not set. pap. 12.95 (*0-7610-0268-5*) NW Pub.

Baker's Harmony of the Gospels. Benjamin Davies. (Baker's Paperback Reference Library). 192p. 1983. pap. 7.99 (*0-8010-2928-7*) Baker Bk.

***Baker's Industrial Guide to Hazardous Materials.** Charles J. Baker. LC 93-77536. 330p. 1993. 39.95 (*0-9627052-1-7*) Maltese Ent.

Baker's Maneuvering Card. J. T. Baker. (C). 1987. 35.00 (*0-85174-192-4*, Pub. by Brwn Son Ferg) St Mut.

Baker's Manual. 4th ed. Joseph Amendola. 1993. pap. 29.95 (*0-442-00997-6*) Van Nos Reinhold.

Baker's Ohio School Law Guide, 2 vols., Set. Robert T. Baker & Kimball H. Carey. 1990. 225.00 (*0-87084-074-6*) Anderson Pub Co.

Baker's Ohio School Law Guide, 1981-1990. Robert T. Baker. 225.00 (*0-318-41816-9*) Anderson Pub Co.

Baker's Ohio School Law Guide, 1981-1990. suppl. ed. Robert T. Baker. Suppl. 1988-89. 80.00 (*0-318-41817-7*); Suppl. 1989-90. 90.00 (*0-685-44609-3*); Suppl. 1990-91. 150.00 (*0-685-44610-7*) Anderson Pub Co.

Baker's Ohio School Law Guide, 1981-1990. suppl. ed. Robert T. Baker. 1992. 95.00 (*0-685-54037-5*) Anderson Pub Co.

Baker's Portrait. Michelle Edwards. LC 90-41926. (Illus.). 32p. (J). (gr. k up). 1991. 13.95 (*0-688-09712-X*); lib. bdg. 13.88 (*0-688-09713-8*) Lothrop.

Baker's Position Line Chart. Wilson Ltd. Staff & Imray L. Norie. (C). 1978. 45.00 (*0-685-40425-0*, Pub. by Imray Laurie Norie & Wilson UK) St Mut.

Baker's Principles of Silviculture. 2nd ed. Theodore W. Daniel & John Helms. (Illus.). 1979. text ed. write for info. (*0-07-015297-7*) McGraw.

Baker's Textual & Topical Filing System. deluxe ed. Neal Punt. LC 60-53376. 628p. 1989. reprint ed. 54.95 (*0-945315-15-5*) Northland Bks.

Baker's Wedding Handbook. deluxe ed. Paul E. Engle. (Illus.). 160p. 1994. 15.99 (*0-8010-3225-3*) Baker Bk.

Baker's 1991-92 Handbook of Ohio School Law. Robert T. Baker & Kimball H. Carey. Ed. by Dee Dunn. 544p. 1991. pap. text ed. 47.50 (*0-87084-078-9*) Anderson Pub Co.

***Bakersfield: Heart of the Golden.** Richard C. Bailey. 1985. 22.95 (*0-89781-065-1*) Preferred Mktg.

Bakersfield Vermont: The Way It Was, the Way It Is. Elsie C. Wells. LC 76-10040. (Illus.). 1976. 10.00 (*0-914016-27-X*) Phoenix Pub.

Bakerville the Town That Gold Built. Lorraine Harris. (Illus.). 64p. 1984. pap. 4.95 (*0-88839-152-8*) Hancock House.

Bakery - Bread & Fermented Goods. L. Hanneman. 208p. 1980. 49.95 (*0-434-90708-1*) Buttrwrth-Heinemann.

Bakery - Flour Confectionery. L. Hanneman. 208p. 1981. 49.95 (*0-7506-0447-6*) Buttrwrth-Heinemann.

Bakery Lane Soup Bowl Cookbook. rev. ed. Marge Mitchell & Joan Sedgwick. (Illus.). 128p. 1993. reprint ed. pap. 14.95 (*0-8397-1005-4*) Eriksson.

***Bakery Market.** 500p. (Orig.). 1994. pap. 1,495.00 (*1-57205-893-5*) Rector Pr.

Bakery Materials & Methods. 4th rev. ed. Albert R. Daniel. (Illus.). 464p. 1978. reprint ed. 41.50 (*0-85334-700-X*, Pub. by Elsevier Applied Sci UK) Elsevier.

***Bakery of the Three Whores.** Sibyl James. (Orig.). 1994. pap. text ed. 6.95 (*1-882300-04-1*) Willo Trees.

***Bakery Products (Frozen) Market.** 60p. (Orig.). 1995. pap. 895.00 (*0-7605-2203-0*) Rector Pr.

***Bakery Snacks Market.** 200p. (Orig.). 1995. pap. 2,295.00 (*0-7605-2204-9*) Rector Pr.

Bakery Specialties. A. B. Barrows. (Illus.). vii, 324p. 1985. 66.75 (*0-85334-291-1*, Pub. by Elsevier Applied Sci UK) Elsevier.

Bakery Technology: Nutrition, Packaging, Product Development, QA. Samuel A. Matz. LC 88-33634. (Illus.). 384p. 1989. text ed. 79.00 (*0-942849-03-5*) Pan Tech Intl.

Bakery Technology & Engineering. 3rd ed. Samuel A. Matz. (Illus.). 853p. 1992. text ed. 129.95 (*0-442-30855-8*) Chapman & Hall.

Bakery Technology & Engineering. 3rd ed. Samuel A. Matz. (Illus.). 850p. 1991. text ed. 129.00 (*0-942849-07-8*) Pan Tech Intl.

***Bakhshali Manuscript: An Ancient Indian Mathematical Treatise.** Takao Hayashi. (Groningen Oriental Studies: No. XI). (Illus.). 596p. 1995. lib. bdg. 162.00x (*90-6980-087-X*, Pub. by Egbert Forsten NE) Benjamins North Am.

Bakhtin: Essays & Dialogues on His Work. Ed. by Gary S. Morson. LC 85-24624. xiv, 192p. 1986. lib. bdg. 22.95 (*0-226-54132-0*); pap. text ed. 11.50 (*0-226-54133-9*) U Ch Pr.

Bakhtin & Cultural Theory. Ed. by Ken Hirschkop & David Shepherd. LC 89-30358. 208p. 1989. text ed. 17.50 (*0-7190-2615-6*, Pub. by Manchester Univ Pr UK) St Martin.

***Bakhtin & the Visual Arts.** Deborah J. Haynes. (Cambridge Studies in New Art History & Criticism). (Illus.). 240p. (C). 1995. 70.00 (*0-521-47392-6*) Cambridge U Pr.

***Bakhtin Reader.** Pam Morris. 256p. 1994. pap. 16.95 (*0-340-59267-2*, B3437, Pub. by E Arnold UK) Routledge Chapman & Hall.

***Bakhtin, Stalin & Modern Russian Fiction: Carnival, Dialogism, & History.** M. Keith Booker & Dubravka Juraga. LC 94-24572. (Contributions to the Study of World Literature Ser.: Vol. 58). 200p. 1995. text ed. 49.95 (*0-313-29526-3*, Greenwood Pr) Greenwood.

Bakhtinian Thought: An Introductory Reader. Simon Dentith. LC 94-16524. (Critical Readers in Theory & Practice Ser.). 280p. 1995. 49.95x (*0-415-07751-6*, B3987); pap. 16.95 (*0-415-11899-9*, B4523) Routledge.

***Baking.** Land O Lakes Staff. LC 95-13991. (Land O Lakes Collector Ser.). 128p. 1995. 14.95 (*0-86573-967-6*) Cy De Cosse.

Baking Bread: Old & New Traditions. Beth Hensperger. (Illus.). 164p. 1992. 29.95 (*0-8118-0228-0*); pap. 18.95 (*0-8118-0078-4*) Chronicle Bks.

***Baking Days.** Enid Baron. Ed. by Alice L. Price. (Illus.). 56p. (Orig.). 1994. pap. 9.95 (*0-9641148-0-1*) HCE Pubns.

Baking Ends Meet: Delicious Mouth Watering Meals & Recipes for Around Five Dollars. Alec G. Rhoades & Janet L. Brookshire. Ed. by Holly B. Hogue. (Illus.). 31p. (Orig.). (C). Date not set. student ed 4.99 (*1-881571-00-9*) Letters Etcetera.

Baking for Gift-Giving. Lisa Yockelson. LC 93-16899. (American Baking Classics Ser.). 96p. 1993. 12.50 (*0-06-016750-5*, HarpT) HarpC.

Baking for Health: Wholefood Baking for Better Health. Linda Edwards. (Illus.). 208p. (Orig.). 1988. pap. 8.95 (*0-89529-376-5*) Avery Pub.

Baking for Two: Breads, Cakes, Cookies & Pies. Irol W. Balsley & Larhylia W. Wood. viii, 464p. 1993. 19.95 (*0-931541-48-4*) Mancorp Pub.

***Baking (Home) Market.** 150p. (Orig.). 1995. pap. 2,195.00 (*0-7605-2206-5*) Rector Pr.

Baking in the Sun: Visionary Images from the South. Andy Nasisse & Maude Wahlam. (Illus.). 136p. (Orig.). 1987. pap. 20.00 (*0-936819-03-0*) USL Art Museum.

***Baking in the Sun: Visionary Images from the South.** Maude S. Wahlman & Andy Nasisse. (Illus.). 146p. (Orig.). 1987. 30.00 (*0-614-06299-3*) USL Art Museum.

Baking Projects for Children. Fran Stephens. (Illus.). 128p. (J). (ps-4). lib. bdg. 16.95 (*1-878363-62-X*) Forest Hse.

Baking Projects for Children: Fun Foods to Make with Children from 4 to 10. Fran Stephens. (Projects for Parents Ser.). (Illus.). 128p. (J). (gr. k-5). 1991. pap. 9.95 (*1-878767-10-0*) Murdoch Bks.

Baking Science & Technology, 2 vols. Ernst J. Pyler. (Illus.). 1988. Vol. 1, 588p. write for info. (*1-882005-00-7*); Vol. 2, 757p. write for info. (*1-882005-01-5*) Sosland Pub.

Baking Science & Technology, 2 vols., Set. Ernst J. Pyler. (Illus.). 1988. 78.00 (*1-882005-02-3*) Sosland Pub.

***Baking Soda: Over Five Hundred Fabulous, Fun & Frugal Uses You've Probably Never Thought Of.** Vicki Lansky. (Illus.). 120p. (Orig.). 1995. pap. 6.95 (*0-916773-42-6*) Book Peddlers.

***Baking Soda Bonanza.** Peter A. Ciullo. LC 95-72. 1995. pap. 10.00 (*0-06-095097-8*, PL) HarpC.

Baking Solutions: Helpful Hints for Home Baking. Lyndal Power & Kenneth Power. LC 92-64417. 320p. (Orig.). 1993. pap. 12.95 (*1-880650-12-6*) YCart Pub.

Baking Storybox. (Illus.). (J). (ps). Date not set. bds. 16.95 (*1-56828-053-X*) Red Jacket Pr.

***Baking Technology - Breadmaking.** Wulf Doerry. (Illus.). 250p. (C). Date not set. 49.00 (*1-880877-16-3*) Am Inst Baking.

Baking with Jim Dodge: Simple & Tempting Delights from the American Baker. Jim Dodge & Elaine Ratner. (Illus.). 224p. 1991. 25.00 (*0-671-68100-1*) S&S Trade.

Baking with Yeast with Schmecks Appeal. Edna Staebler. (Schmecks Appeal Cookbook Ser.). (Illus.). 96p. 1991. pap. 9.95 (*0-7710-8278-9*, Pub. by McClelland & Stewart CN) Firefly Bks Ltd.

Baking Without Fat. George Mateljan. Ed. by Jim Burns. (Illus.). 175p. (Orig.). 1993. pap. 9.95 (*0-9633608-1-7*) Hlth Valley Foods.

An Asterisk (*) at the beginning of an entry indicates that the title is appearing in BIP for the first time.

An Asterisk (*) at the beginning of an entry indicates that the title is appearing in BIP for the first time.

581

***Balancing Act: The New Medical Ethics of Medicine's New Economics.** E. Haavi Morreim. 1995. 17.95 (*0-87840-584-4*) Georgetown U Pr.

Balancing Act: The Political Role of the Urban School Superintendent. Barbara L. Jackson. 110p. (C). 1994. lib. bdg. 48.00 (*0-8191-9562-6*); pap. text ed. 19.50 (*0-8191-9563-4*) U Pr of Amer.

Balancing Act: The Republic of Korea Approached 1988. Ralph N. Clough. (Orig.). (C). 1987. pap. text ed. 11.75 (*0-941700-27-5*) JH FPI SAIS.

Balancing Act Nutrition & Weight Guide. Georgia G. Kostas. 1993. pap. 29.95 (*0-9635969-1-8*) Balancing Act.

***Balancing Acts: American Thought & Culture in the 1930's.** Terry A. Cooney. (Twayne's American Thought & Culture Ser.). (Illus.). 288p. 1995. text ed. 27.95x (*0-8057-9060-8*, Twayne); pap. 15.95 (*0-8057-9069-1*, Twayne) Macmillan.

Balancing Acts: Contemporary Stories by Russian Women. Ed. by Helena Goscilo. LC 88-45390. 368p. 1989. 39.95 (*0-253-31134-9*); pap. 17.95 (*0-253-20500-X*, MB-500) Ind U Pr.

Balancing Acts: Essays on the Teaching of Writing in Honor of William F. Irmscher. Ed. by Virginia A. Chappell et al. LC 90-36155. 216p. (C). 1991. 26.50 (*0-8093-1638-2*); pap. 17.95 (*0-8093-1639-0*) S Ill U Pr.

Balancing Acts! Juggling Love, Work, Family & Recreation. Susan S. Stautberg & Marcia L. Worthing. LC 91-60815. 240p. 1992. pap. 12.95 (*0-942361-37-7*) MasterMedia Ltd.

Balancing Acts: Women & the Process of Social Change. Ed. by Patricia L. Johnson. 177p. (C). 1992. pap. text ed. 35.50 (*0-8133-8401-X*) Westview.

Balancing Acts in Personal, Social & Health Education: A Practical Guide for Teachers' Judith Ryder & Lesley Campbell. 320p. (C). 1988. lib. bdg. 55.00 (*0-415-00537-X*, A2468) Routledge.

Balancing Career & Family: Overcoming the Superwoman Syndrome. Marian Thomas. 1991. pap. 7.95 (*1-55852-053-8*) Natl Pr Pubns.

Balancing Economic Growth & Environmental Goals. 160p. 1994. pap. text ed. 25.00 (*1-884032-02-8*) Am Coun Capital.

Balancing Egg: How to Achieve Life's Balance. L. Larry Vegas. (Illus.). 124p. (Orig.). 1993. pap. 6.95 (*0-9641666-0-7*) Eggknowledged.

Balancing Family & Work. Sally Yankhe et al. 1993. 8.00 (*0-911365-34-6*, A261-08482) Home Econ Educ.

Balancing Girl. Berniece Rabe. LC 80-22100. (Unicorn Paperbacks Ser.). (Illus.). 32p. (J). (ps-2). 1988. pap. 4.99 (*0-525-44364-9*, 0382-120, DCB) Dutton Child Bks.

Balancing Home & Career: A Fifty-Minute Program. 4th rev. ed. Pam Conrad. Ed. by Michael Crisp. LC 89-81910. (Fifty-Minute Ser.). (Illus.). 80p. (Orig.). 1990. pap. 9.95 (*1-56052-035-3*) Crisp Pubns.

Balancing Job Satisfaction & Performance: A Guide for Human Resource Professionals. Willa M. Bruce & J. Walton Blackburn. LC 92-15989. 256p. 1992. text ed. 55.00 (*0-89930-658-6*, BBX, Quorum Bks) Greenwood.

Balancing Lifes Demands. rev. ed. J. Grant Howard. 200p. 1994. pap. 8.99 (*0-88070-673-2*, Multnomah Bks) Questar Pubs.

***Balancing Life's Demands: Studies in Coping for Today's Adult Groups.** (LifeTopics Ser.). Date not set. 19.95 (*1-55513-565-X*, 75655) Cook.

Balancing National Security Objectives in an Uncertain World. Aspen Strategy Group Staff. LC 89-34141. (Aspen Strategy Group Reports). 242p. (Orig.). (C). 1989. lib. bdg. 48.00 (*0-8191-7488-2*); pap. text ed. 29.00 (*0-8191-7489-0*) U Pr of Amer.

Balancing Needs of People & Organizations: The Linking Elements Concept. Erwin Rausch. 321p. 1978. 26.50 (*0-87179-274-5*) Didactic Syst.

Balancing of High-Speed Machinery. M. S. Darlow. (Mechanical Engineering Ser.). (Illus.). 185p. 1989. 59.00 (*0-387-96986-1*) Spr-Verlag.

Balancing on an Alp: Ecological Change & Continuity in a Swiss Mountain Community. Robert M. Netting. LC 81-358. (Illus.). 436p. 1981. 64.95 (*0-521-23743-2*) Cambridge U Pr.

Balancing on the Brink of Extinction: The Endangered Species Act & Lessons for the Future. Ed. by Kathryn Kohm. LC 90-5031. 318p. 1991. 34.95 (*1-55963-007-8*); pap. 22.95 (*1-55963-006-X*) Island Pr.

Balancing on the Edge of Nowhere & Forever. Shail K. Ramcharan. 32p. 1991. 6.95 (*0-8059-3192-9*) Dorrance.

***Balancing Oxidation-Reduction Equations Using the Ion-Electron Method.** Marcia Gillette & H. Anthony Neidig. 8p. (C). 1995. 1.25 (*0-614-05700-0*, MISC 458-8) Chem Educ Res.

***Balancing Oxidation-Reduction Equations Using the Oxidation Number Method.** Marcia Gillette & H. Anthony Neidig. 12p. (C). 1995. 1.25 (*0-614-05699-3*, MISC 457-X) Chem Educ Res.

Balancing Pluralism: New Welfare Mixes in Care for the Elderly. Adalbert Evers & Ivan Svetlik. (Public Policy & Social Welfare Ser.: No. 13). 328p. 1993. pap. 33.95 (*1-85628-605-3*, Pub. by Avebury Pub UK) Ashgate Pub Co.

Balancing Pole: A Novel. Ann L. McLaughlin. LC 91-10307. 192p. (Orig.). 1991. pap. 9.95 (*0-936784-90-3*) J Daniel.

***Balancing State Intervention: The Limits of Transatlantic Markets.** Ed. by Roger Benjamin et al. LC 94-23389. 1995. text ed. 49.95 (*0-312-12401-5*) St Martin.

Balancing the Basics: A Handbook for Teachers of Reading (K-8) 2nd ed. Trevor Cairney. 127p. 1990. pap. text ed. 18.50 (*0-86896-545-6*, 00674, Pub. by Ashton Scholastic AT) Heinemann.

Balancing the Body's Energies. rev. ed. Wayne W. Topping. (Illus.). 128p. 1986. student ed 11.95 (*0-935299-04-1*) Topping Inst.

Balancing the Books: Financing American Public Library Service. Urban Libraries Council Staff. Ed. by Jane B. Robbins & Douglas L. Zweizig. LC 92-46918. 168p. 1993. text ed. 30.00 (*0-917846-14-1*, 95519) Highsmith Pr.

Balancing the Christian Life. Charles C. Ryrie. (C). 1969. pap. 8.99 (*0-8024-0452-9*) Moody.

***Balancing the Christian Life: Biblical Principles for Wholesome Living.** Ryrie. 1994. pap. 8.99 (*0-8024-0887-7*) Moody.

Balancing the Christian Life see Equilibrio en la Vida Cristiana

Balancing the Federal Budget: The Cure for U. S. Wealth Dissipation. Ernest J. Oppenheimer. LC 90-62918. 181p. 1991. 20.00 (*0-9603982-6-0*) Pen & Podium.

Balancing the National Interest: U. S. National Security Export Controls & Global Economic Competition. National Academy of Sciences Staff et al. 368p. 1987. 29.95 (*0-309-03738-7*) Natl Acad Pr.

Balancing the Needs of Water Use. J. W. Moore. (Environmental Management Ser.). (Illus.). 310p. 1988. 109.00 (*0-387-96709-5*) Spr-Verlag.

Balancing the News. John Wolcott & Roberta Wolcott. 78p. 1983. pap. 7.50 (*0-931435-02-1*) Features NW.

Balancing the Pairs of Opposites; The Seven Rays & Education; & Other Essays in Esoteric Psychology. Kurt Abraham. (Illus.). 148p. (Orig.). 1993. pap. 9.95 (*0-9609002-5-X*) Lampus Pr.

Balancing the Scales: Managing Biodiversity at the Bioregional Level. large type ed. Kenton R. Miller. 150p. 1993. Large format. pap. 14.95 (*0-915825-85-6*, MIBSP) World Resources Inst.

Balancing the Scales of Opportunity: Ensuring Racial & Ethnic Diversity in the Health Professions. 100p. (Orig.). (C). 1994. pap. text ed. 23.00 (*0-309-05078-2*) Natl Acad Pr.

Balancing Water Demands with Supplies: The Role of Demand Management in a World of Increasing Scarcity. Kenneth D. Frederick. LC 92-28790. (Technical Paper, 0253-7494 Ser.: No. 183). 1992. 7.95 (*0-8213-2206-0*) World Bank.

Balancing Water Demands with Supplies: The Role of Management in a World of Increasing Scarcity. Kenneth D. Frederick. LC 92-38462. (Technical Paper Ser.: No. 189). 81p. 1993. 7.95 (*0-8213-2290-7*, 12290) World Bank.

Balancing Work & Caregiving: For Children, Adults & Elders. Margaret B. Neal et al. (Applications of Family Caregiving Ser.: Vol. 3). (Illus.). 292p. (C). 1993. text ed. 48.00 (*0-8039-4281-8*); pap. text ed. 24.00 (*0-8039-4282-6*) Sage.

Balancing Work & Family Life on Wall Street. Hamilton I. McCubbin & Anne I. Thompson. 224p. (Orig.). 1989. write for info. (*0-8087-7617-7*) Burgess MN Intl.

Balancing Work Responsibilities & Family Needs: The Federal Civil Service Response. U. S. Merit Systems Protection Board Staff. (Illus.). 90p. (Orig.). (C). 1993. pap. text ed. 19.95 (*1-56806-169-2*) Diane Pub.

Balancing Your Budget God's Way. MaryAnn L. Diorio. 29p. (Orig.). 1987. pap. 1.00 (*0-930037-01-4*) Daystar Comm.

Balancing Your Emotions: For Women Who Want Consistency under Stress. Gayle G. Roper. LC 92-30983. 144p. 1992. pap. 7.99 (*0-87788-075-1*) Shaw Pubs.

***Balancing Your Work/Family Responsibilities: A Guide for Employees.** Kathleen J. Papatola. 1993. pap. 3.95 (*1-56246-083-8*, P316) Johnsn Inst.

Balanophoraceae. Bertel Hansen. LC 79-28385. (Flora Neotropica Monograph Ser.: No. 23). (Illus.). 80p. 1980. 10.50 (*0-89327-195-0*) NY Botanical.

Balaton. E. Kajetan. (Illus.). (ENG & GER.). (C). 1989. pap. 40.00 (*0-685-37541-2*, Pub. by Collets) St Mut.

Balaton: A Pocket Guide. T. Sebestyen. 129p. (C). 1991. 35.00 (*0-89771-846-1*, Pub. by Collets) St Mut.

Balaton & Its Environs: Budapest Corvina, 1987. D. Keresztury. (Illus.). 88p. (C). 1987. 90.00 (*0-685-32396-X*, Pub. by Collets UK) Pro-Am Music.

Balberta Project: The Terminal Formative-Early Classic Transition on the Pacific Coast of Guatemala. Ed. by Frederick J Bove et al. Tr. by Jeffrey P. Blick et al. LC 93-2044. (University of Pittsburgh Memoirs in Latin American Archaeology Ser.: No. 6). (Illus.). xviii, 202p. (ENG & SPA.). 1993. pap. 19.00 (*1-877812-08-0*) UPLAAP.

Balboa Firefly. Jack Trolley. 272p. 1994. 19.95 (*0-7867-0117-X*) Carroll & Graf.

***Balboa Park.** Bro Halff. 56p. 1987. pap. 12.95 (*1-885238-02-9*) Simpler Gifts.

***Balboa Park.** Bro Halff. 56p. 1987. 24.95 (*1-885238-03-7*) Simpler Gifts.

BALCA Deskbook. 2nd ed. Ed. by Todd Smyth. 563p. 1992. lib. bdg. 135.00 (*1-878677-41-1*) Amer Immi Law Assn.

BALCA Handbook. Ed. by James Guill & Todd Smyth. 306p. 1990. reprint ed. text ed. 120.00 (*1-878677-15-2*) Amer Immi Law Assn.

***Balch Institute: A Guide to Manuscript & Microfilm Collections.** Monique Bourque & R. Joseph Anderson. (Illus.). 129p. 1992. 15.00 (*0-937437-11-5*) Balch IES Pr.

***Balch Institute: Selections from the Museum Collections of the Research Library of the Balch Institute.** Gail F. Stern & Nancy L. Wygant. LC 92-71103. (Illus.). 91p. 1992. 15.00 (*0-937437-09-3*) Balch IES Pr.

Balcombe: First Book of the Balcombe Family. F. W. Balcomb. 95p. 1993. reprint ed. lib. bdg. 27.00 (*0-8328-3256-1*); reprint ed. pap. 17.00 (*0-8328-3257-X*) Higginson Bk Co.

Balcon. Jean Genet. 1962. write for info. (*0-318-63433-3*) Fr & Eur.

Balcon. Jean Genet. (FRE.). 1979. pap. 10.95 (*0-8288-3644-2*, M5645) Fr & Eur.

Balcon. Jean Genet. (Folio Ser.: No. 1149). 1962. pap. 8.95 (*2-07-037149-2*) Schoenhof.

Balcon see Oeuvres Completes

Balcon De Spetsai. Michel Deon. 256p. (FRE.). 1984. pap. 11.95 (*0-7859-1984-8*, 2070375242) Fr & Eur.

Balcon en Foret. Julien Gracq. 256p. (FRE.). 1990. reprint ed. pap. 38.95 (*0-7859-4599-7*) Fr & Eur.

Balconinny. J. B. Priestley. LC 70-99645. (Essay Index Reprint Ser.). 1977. 23.95 (*0-8369-1426-0*) Ayer.

***Balconville.** Fennario. Date not set. per. 12.95 (*0-88922-145-6*, Pub. by Talonbooks CN) InBook.

Balcony. Jean Genet. Tr. by Bernard Frechtman. 96p. 1985. pap. 8.95 (*0-8021-5034-9*) Grove-Atltic.

Balcony in the Forest. Julien Gracq. Tr. by Richard Howard. 213p. 1987. text ed. 33.50 (*0-231-06672-4*); pap. text ed. 13.00 (*0-231-06673-2*) Col U Pr.

Balcony in the Forest. Julien Gracq. Tr. & Pref. by Richard Howard. (Twentieth-Century Continental Fiction Ser.). 213p. 1989. text ed. 38.50 (*0-231-06642-2*); pap. 12.50 (*0-231-06643-0*) Col U Pr.

Balcony of Europe. Aidan Higgins. 450p. (Orig.). 1982. pap. 13.95 (*0-7145-0103-4*) Riverrun NY.

Balcony over the Fakihani. Liyana Badr. Tr. by P. Clark & C. Tingley. LC 92-23387. (Emerging Voices: New International Fiction Ser.). 144p. 1993. 22.95 (*1-56656-104-3*); pap. 9.95 (*1-56656-107-8*) Interlink Pub.

Balcony People. rev. ed. Joyce L. Heatherley. 72p. 1988. reprint ed. pap. 5.95 (*0-929488-02-4*) Balcony Pub Inc.

Balcony Stories. Grace King. Ed. by Kate Falvey. 1994. 12.95 (*0-8084-0438-5*) NCUP.

Balcony Stories. Grace E. King. LC 68-23722. (Americans in Fiction Ser.). (Illus.). reprint ed. lib. bdg. 19.50 (*0-8398-1055-5*); reprint ed. pap. text ed. 6.95 (*0-89197-669-8*) Irvington.

Balcony Stories. Grace E. King. (BCL1-PS American Literature Ser.). 296p. 1992. reprint ed. lib. bdg. 79.00 (*0-7812-6777-3*) Rprt Serv.

Bald Book: The Complete Book of Hairloss & Regrowth. Walter Klenhard. (Illus.). 200p. (Orig.). 1986. pap. 12.95 (*0-9617051-0-8*) Sci Med Pr.

***Bald Cypress.** C. Brown & G. Montz. 1986. 20.00 (*0-87511-780-5*) Claitors.

Bald Eagle. Jana McConoughey. LC 83-5162. (Wildlife Habits & Habitats Ser.). (Illus.). 48p. (J). (gr. 5). 1983. text ed. 12.95 (*0-89686-218-6*, Crstwood Hse) Silver Burdett Pr.

Bald Eagle: Haunts & Habits of a Wilderness Monarch. Jon M. Gerrard & Gary R. Bortolotti. LC 87-26530. (Nature Bks.). (Illus.). 224p. 1988. pap. 13.95 (*0-87474-451-2*) Smithsonian.

Bald Eagle Magic for Kids. Charlene Gieck. LC 91-50552. (Animal Magic for Kids Ser.). (Illus.). 48p. (J). (gr. 3-4). 1992. lib. bdg. 18.60 (*0-8368-0761-8*) Gareth Stevens Inc.

Bald Eagles. Sandra Lee. (Nature Books Ser.). 32p. (J). (gr. 2-6). 1991. lib. bdg. 22.79 (*0-89565-706-6*) Childs World.

Bald Eagles. Emilie U. Lepthien. LC 88-38055. (New True Bks.). (Illus.). 45p. (J). (gr. k-2). 1989. lib. bdg. 12.90 (*0-516-01160-X*); pap. 4.95 (*0-516-41160-8*) Childrens.

***Bald Eaglets.** Victoria Miles. (Illus.). 24p. (Orig.). (J). (gr. 1-4). 1995. pap. text ed. 5.95 (*1-55143-028-2*) Orca Bk Pubs.

Bald Knobbers: Vigilantes on the Ozarks Frontier. Elmo Ingenthron & Mary Hartman. LC 87-31156. 224p. 1988. 19.95 (*0-88289-694-6*); pap. 10.95 (*0-88289-683-0*) Pelican.

Bald Men Always Come Out on Top. David E. Beswick & Toni Hill. (Illus.). 96p. 1984. pap. 5.95 (*0-9613176-0-4*) Beacon Hill FL.

Bald Soprano see Four Plays

Bald Truth-Hair Transplants-Scalp Reductions-Flaps by Some One Who Had Them All. Bruce M. Waterford. (Illus.). 110p. (Orig.). 1994. pap. 11.95 (*1-57002-006-X*) Univ Publng Hse.

Baldassare Castiglione: The Perfect Courtier, His Life & Letters, 1478-1529, 2 Vols, Set. Julia M. Ady. LC 75-154138. (BCL Ser.: No. I). reprint ed. 87.50 (*0-404-09206-3*) AMS Pr.

Baldassare Donato: Di Baldassara Donato Maestro di Capella della Serenissima Signoria di Venetia in San Marco Il Primo Libro de Motetti a Cinque, a Sei, et Otto Voci Novamente Composti, & dati in Luce, (Venice, Gardano, 1599) Ed. by Richard Sherr. LC 93-48605. (Sixteenth Century Motet Ser.: Vol. 30). 376p. 1994. 106.00 (*0-8240-7930-2*) Garland.

Balderdash. Stephen Cosgrove. (Dreammaker Ser.). (Illus.). 32p. (J). (gr. 3-6). 1991. 14.95 (*1-55868-045-4*) Gr Arts Ctr Pub.

Balderdash. Edward T. Hering. Ed. by James B. Van Treese. 432p. 1994. pap. 12.95 (*1-56901-168-0*) NW Pub.

Balderdash the Brilliant: A Hole-in-the-Page Color Book. Time Life Inc., Staff. Ed. by Neil Kagan. (Early Learning Program Ser.). (Illus.). 56p. (J). (ps-2). 1991. write for info. (*0-8094-9266-0*); lib. bdg. write for info. (*0-8094-9267-9*) Time-Life.

Balding: Hair Loss & Restoration. Gustavo J. Gomez. 160p. 1989. pap. 13.95 (*0-89697-299-2*) Intl Univ Pr.

Baldissare Donato: Il Primo Libro Di Madrigali a Cinque & a Sei Voici (Venice, 1560) Ed. by Jessie A. Owens. LC 90-755248. (Sixteenth Century Madrigal Ser.: Vol. 10). 328p. 1991. 86.00 (*0-8240-5510-1*) Garland.

***Baldness Cure: The Unique Regrowth Programme That Really Works.** Andy Bryant. (Illus.). 116p. 1995. pap. 11.95 (*0-09-178242-2*, Vermillion) Trafalgar.

Baldock: The Excavation of a Pre-Roman Settlement 1968-72. I. M. Stead & Valery Rigby. (Illus.). 436p. 1993. pap. text ed. 55.00 (*0-86299-484-5*) A Sutton Pub.

Baldorioty De Castro. Lidio C. Monclova. (Puerto Rico Ser.). 1979. lib. bdg. 59.95 (*0-8490-2870-1*) Gordon Pr.

***Baldridge Award for Education: How to Measure & Document Quality Improvement.** Jerome S. Arcaro. 320p. (Orig.). 1995. pap. text ed. 39.95 (*1-884015-75-1*) St Lucie Pr.

Baldrige: What It Is, How to Win, & How to Use It to Improve Quality in Your Company. Christopher W. Hart. 1992. text ed. 24.95 (*0-07-026912-2*) McGraw.

Baldrige Award Winning Quality. Mark G. Brown. LC 91-2889. (Illus.). 400p. 1991. pap. text ed. 29.95 (*0-527-91647-1*, 916471) Qual Resc.

Baldrige Award Winning Quality: How to Interpret the Malcolm Baldrige Award Criteria. 2nd ed. Mark G. Brown. LC 92-4133. (Illus.). 430p. 1992. pap. text ed. 32.95 (*0-527-91658-7*, 916587) Qual Resc.

Baldrige Award Winning Quality: How to Interpret the Malcolm Baldrige Award Criteria. 3rd ed. Mark G. Brown. LC 93-19996. (Illus.). 450p. 1993. pap. text ed. 32.95 (*0-527-91722-2*, 917222) Qual Resc.

Baldrige Award Winning Quality: How to Interpret the Malcolm Baldrige Award Criteria. 4th ed. Mark G. Brown. LC 94-2795. (Illus.). 400p. 1994. pap. text ed. 29.95 (*0-527-76250-4*, 762504) Qual Resc.

Baldrige Quality System: The Do-It-Yourself Way to Transform Your Business. Stephen George. 320p. 1992. text ed. 32.95 (*0-471-55798-6*) Wiley.

Bald's Leechbook see Early English Manuscripts in Facsimile

Balduin Mollhausen (1825-1905) America Between Dream & Disillusionment in the Life & Works of a Best-Selling German Author of the 19th Century. Horst Dinkelacker. (American University Studies: Germanic Languages & Literature: Ser. I, Vol. 86). 189p. 1989. 34.50 (*0-8204-1133-7*) P Lang Pubs.

Baldung (Hans) The Graphic Work. Matthias Mende. (Illus.). 336p. (GER.). 1978. 125.00 (*1-55660-168-9*) A Wofsy Fine Arts.

Baldwin: Being Dialogues on Views & Aspirations. Violet Paget. LC 72-291. (Essay Index Reprint Ser.). 1977. reprint ed. 23.95 (*0-8369-2817-2*) Ayer.

Baldwin & the Conservative Party: The Crisis of 1929-31. Stuart Ball. LC 87-22405. 320p. (C). 1988. text ed. 45.00 (*0-300-03961-1*) Yale U Pr.

Baldwin County Alabama Marriages, 1800-1900. Ed. by Dess L. Sangster & Tom Sangster. (Illus.). 160p. (Orig.). 1991. pap. 20.00 (*0-685-48819-5*) Coffeetable.

Baldwin Genealogy, from 1500 to 1881. Charles C. Baldwin. (Illus.). 974p. 1988. reprint ed. lib. bdg. 156.00 (*0-8328-0166-6*); reprint ed. pap. 146.00 (*0-8328-0167-4*) Higginson Bk Co.

Baldwin Genealogy Supplement. Charles C. Baldwin. (Illus.). 498p. 1988. reprint ed. lib. bdg. 78.00 (*0-8328-0168-2*); reprint ed. pap. 68.00 (*0-8328-0169-0*) Higginson Bk Co.

Baldwin Identification Matrix 2. 2nd ed. Alexinia Y. Baldwin. 22p. 1984. pap. 10.00 (*0-89824-125-1*); 12.99 (*0-89824-126-X*) Trillium Pr.

Baldwin Identification Matrix 2. 2nd suppl. ed. Alexinia Y. Baldwin. 22p. 1984. disk 15.00 (*0-89824-153-7*) Trillium Pr.

Baldwin Locomotive Works (BALDWIN) General Catalogue 1915. LC 72-96486. (Illus.). 1972. 9.00 (*0-913556-02-5*); pap. 6.00 (*0-913556-03-3*) Spec Pr NJ.

***Baldwin Locomotive Works, 1831-1915: A Study in American Industrial Practice.** John K. Brown. LC 94-44850. (Studies in Industry & Society). (Illus.). 344p. 1995. text ed. 35.95x (*0-8018-5047-9*) Johns Hopkins.

BALDWIN Logging Locomotives 1913. LC 73-84950. (Illus.). 1973. pap. 4.00 (*0-913556-09-2*) Spec Pr NJ.

BALDWIN Narrow-Gauge Locomotives 1872-1876. LC 73-82229. (Illus.). 1973. 6.00 (*0-913556-35-1*); pap. 4.00 (*0-913556-31-9*) Spec Pr NJ.

Baldwin of Ford: Spirtual Tractates, 2 vols., 1. Tr. & Intro. by David N. Bell. 1986. pap. 20.00 (*0-87907-438-8*, CF38) Cistercian Pubns.

Baldwin of Ford: Spirtual Tractates, 2 vols., 2. Tr. & Intro. by David N. Bell. 1986. write for info. (*0-87907-441-8*, CF41) Cistercian Pubns.

Baldwin of Ford: Spirtual Tractates, 2 vols., Set. Tr. & Intro. by David N. Bell. 1986. 50.00 (*0-685-43512-1*) Cistercian Pubns.

Baldwin Vauclain Compounds 1900. LC 73-82231. (Illus.). 1973. 7.50 (*0-913556-07-6*); pap. 5.00 (*0-913556-08-4*) Spec Pr NJ.

Baldwin's Guide to Inns of the Deep South: Louisiana & Western Mississippi. Jack Baldwin & Winnie Baldwin. LC 93-19971. 256p. 1993. pap. 10.95 (*0-88289-939-2*) Pelican.

Baldwin's Kentucky Practice, 4 vols. Ed. by James M. Baker. 1744p. 1980. 275.00 (*0-8322-0056-5*); 85.00 (*0-685-73602-4*); 85.00 (*0-685-73603-2*) Banks-Baldwin.

Baldwin's Kentucky Revised Statutes Annotated: Official Edition, 9 vols., Set. 12754p. 1975. Nine vol. set. 640.00 (*0-8322-0025-5*); Sixteen vol. set. 740.00 (*0-8322-0282-7*) Banks-Baldwin.

Baldwin's Ohio Civil Practice, 3 vols. James M. Klein et al. 4350p. 1970. 330.00 (*0-8322-0233-9*) Banks-Baldwin.

Baldwin's Ohio Domestic Relations Law, 1 vol. Ed. by Beatrice K. Sowald & Stanley Morganstern. 2040p. 1984. text ed. 190.00 (*0-8322-0080-8*) Banks-Baldwin.

Baldwin's Ohio Legislative Service, 1993. 1994. 295.00 (*0-8322-0401-3*) Banks-Baldwin.

Baldwin's Ohio Revised Code Annotated. 21356p. 1974. Individual titles, write for info. write for info. (*0-318-57645-7*) Banks-Baldwin.

An Asterisk (*) at the beginning of an entry indicates that the title is appearing in BIP for the first time.

Baldwin's Ohio Revised Code Annotated, 31 vols., Set. 21356p. 1974. 1,200.00 (0-8322-0038-7); 1,000.00 (0-8322-0027-1); 125.00 (0-318-57644-9); ring bd. 229.00 (0-685-08023-4) Banks-Baldwin.

Baldwin's Ohio School Law, 3 vols. suppl. ed. Ed. by Jonathan F. Buchter et al. 4274p. 1993. Annual cum. supp. bds. 230.00 (0-8322-0010-7) Banks-Baldwin.

Baldwin's Ohio Tax Law & Rules, 2 vols. 3049p. 1985. 190.00 (0-8322-0017-4) Banks-Baldwin.

Baldwin's Ohio Tax Service. Ed. by Maryann B. Gall. 1993. 165.00 (0-685-60097-1); Combined with Baldwin's Ohio Tax Law & Rules 300.00. write for info. (0-318-69420-4) Banks-Baldwin.

Baldwin's Ohio Township Law, 3 vols. 4th ed. Ed. by William B. Shimp. 2865p. 1984. Incl. Annual Suppl. 200.00 (0-8322-0320-3) Banks-Baldwin.

Bale o' Cotton: The Mechanical Art of Cotton Ginning. Karen G. Britton. LC 92-14229. (Centennial Series of the Association of Former Students: No. 43). (Illus.). 160p. (C). 1992. 27.50 (0-89096-510-2) Tex A&M Univ Pr.

***Balearic Islands.** Photos by Melba Levick. LC 95-15443. (Illus.). 1996. write for info. (0-8118-0659-6) Chronicle Bks.

Balearics. F. Chamberlin. 1976. lib. bdg. 59.95 (0-8490-1473-5) Gordon Pr.

Baleine. Illus. by U. Fuhr & R. Sautai. (Gallimard - Mes Premieres Decouvertes Ser.: No. 26). (FRE.). (J). (ps-1). 1991. 13.95 (2-07-035729-5) Schoenhof.

Balers. Richard K. Miller & Marcia E. Rupnow. LC 90-83888. (Survey on Technology & Markets Ser.: No. 184). 50p. 1991. pap. text ed. 200.00 (1-55865-208-6) Future Tech Surveys.

Balfe: His Life & Work. William A. Barrett. 312p. 1991. reprint ed. lib. bdg. 89.00 (0-7812-9331-6) Rprt Serv.

Balfour Conspiracy. Ian St. James. 1993. mass mkt. 5.50 (0-06-100480-4, Harp PBks) HarpC.

Balfour Conspiracy. large type ed. Ian St. James. 480p. 1984. 15.95 (0-7089-1092-0) Ulverscroft.

Balfour Declaration: An Appral in International Law. W. T. Mallison, Jr. (Information Papers: No. 4). 52p. 1971. pap. text ed. 1.00 (0-937694-20-7) Assn Arab-Amer U Grads.

***Balgo Hills Aboriginal Paintings: Poster Book.** (Illus.). 60p. (Orig.). 1994. pap. 145.00 (0-7605-0487-3) Rector Pr.

Bali. (Insider's Guides Ser.). (Illus.). 224p. (Orig.). 1989. pap. text ed. 15.95 (1-55650-648-1) Hunter NJ.

Bali. (Travel Bug Ser.). (Orig.). 1993. pap. 18.00 (0-671-87914-6) P-H Gen Ref & Trav.

Bali. Patrick R. Booz. (Guidebook Ser.). 1991. pap. 9.95 (962-217-111-7) L A Michaux.

Bali. Kal Muller. 1990. pap. 15.95 (0-8442-9900-6, Passport Bks) NTC Pub Grp.

Bali. Ed. by Eric Oey. 272p. 1991. pap. 37.50 (0-945971-32-X) Periplus.

***Bali.** 3rd ed. Ed. by Eric Oey. 312p. 1995. pap. 19.95 (962-593-028-0) Periplus.

Bali: A Paradise Created. Adrian Vickers. (Illus.). 270p. 1990. pap. 17.95 (0-945971-28-1) Periplus.

Bali: Eiland der Goden. Ed. by Eric Oey. Tr. by Sylvia Pessissiron. (Indonesie Reisbibliotheek Ser.). (Illus.). 272p. (DUT.). 1990. 19.95 (0-945971-17-6) Periplus.

Bali: Rangda & Barong. Jane Belo. LC 84-45517. (American Ethnological Society Monographs: No. 16). 1988. reprint ed. 20.00 (0-404-62915-6) AMS Pr.

Bali: Temple Festival. Jane Belo. LC 84-45521. (American Ethnological Society Monographs: No. 22). 1988. reprint ed. 20.00 (0-404-62921-0) AMS Pr.

Bali: The Emerald Isle. 2nd ed. (Passport's Regional Guides of Indonesia Ser.). (Illus.). 288p. (Orig.). 1993. 17.95 (0-8442-9897-2) NTC Pub Grp.

Bali - Sekala & Niskala: Essays on Society, Tradition, & Craft, Vol. II. rev. ed. Fred B. Eiseman, Jr. Ed. by David Pickell. (Illus.). 416p. 1989. pap. 24.95 (0-945971-05-2) Periplus.

Bali--Sekala & Niskala: Essays on Religion, Ritual & Art, Vol. I. rev. ed. Fred B. Eiseman, Jr. Ed. by David Pickell. (Illus.). 368p. 1989. pap. 24.95 (0-945971-03-6) Periplus.

Bali & Lombok: A Travel Survival Kit. 5th ed. James Lyon & Tony Wheeler. (Illus.). 376p. 1994. pap. 14.95 (0-86442-215-6) Lonely Planet.

Bali Baru. (Insight Guides, Windows on the World Ser.). (Illus.). 350p. 1993. pap. 21.95 (0-395-65991-4) HM.

Bali Island of Grace: A Complete Guide. Suzanne Charle. 1991. pap. 15.95 (0-8442-9693-7, Passport Bks) NTC Pub Grp.

Bali, Lombok. Nelles Verlag. (Nelles Guides Ser.). 1993. pap. 14.95 (3-88618-392-0, Pub. by Nelles Verlag GW) Seven Hills Bk.

Bali to Bahrein. Grant C. Butler. 1969. 12.95 (0-8159-5100-0) Devin.

Balinese. Stephen Lansing. Ed. by George Spindler & Louise Spindler. (Case Studies in Anthropology). (Illus.). 168p. (C). 1995. pap. text ed. write for info. (0-15-500240-6) HB Coll Pubs.

***Balinese Dance in Transition: Kaja & Kelod.** I. Made Bandem & Frederick E. DeBoer. (Illus.). 256p. 1995. 45.00 (967-65-3071-9) OUP.

Balinese Music. Michael Tenzer. (Illus.). 144p. 1992. 25.00 (0-945971-30-3, U of Wash Pr) Periplus.

Balinese Painting. Leland W. Gralapp. (Illus.). 1961. pap. 2.50 (0-916537-27-7, Taylor Museum) CO Springs Fine Arts.

Balinese Paintings. 2nd ed. A. A. Djelantik. (Images of Asia Ser.). (Illus.). 116p. 1990. 19.95 (0-19-588957-6) OUP.

Balinese People: Culture & Character. Gordon D. Jensen & Luh K. Suryani. (Illus.). 184p. 1992. 38.00 (0-19-588557-0) OUP.

Balinese Wajang Koelit & Its Music. Colin McPhee. LC 77-86983. 56p. reprint ed. 29.00 (0-404-16765-9) AMS Pr.

Balinese Worlds. Fredrik Barth. LC 92-18043. (Illus.). 392p. (C). 1993. pap. text ed. 19.95 (0-226-03834-3) U Ch Pr.

Balinese Worlds. Fredrik Barth. LC 92-18043. (Illus.). 392p. (C). 1993. lib. bdg. 55.00 (0-226-03833-5) U Ch Pr.

BALIS Committee Handbook. Ed. by Katharine Scarborough. (Illus.). 63p. (Orig.). 1988. pap. 7.00 (0-685-44286-1) BAL & Info Sys.

Balisand. Joseph Hergesheimer. LC 77-78311. 376p. reprint ed. 52.50 (0-404-15119-1) AMS Pr.

Balisong: The Lethal Art of Filipino Knife Fighting. Sid Campbell et al. (Illus.). 192p. 1986. pap. 12.00 (0-87364-354-2) Paladin Pr.

Balisong Manual. Jeff Imada. (Illus.). 128p. (Orig.). 1984. pap. 11.95 (0-86568-102-3, 519) Unique Pubns.

Balisong Manual. Jeff Imada. 1984. 12.95 (0-938676-04-0) Know Now Pub.

Balkan Babel: Politics, Culture, & Religion in Yugoslavia. Sabrina P. Ramet. 230p. (C). 1992. text ed. 49.95 (0-8133-8184-3) Westview.

Balkan Byzantine Notebook. Carl Sheppard. (Illus.). 101p. (Orig.). 1990. pap. 25.95 (0-9623155-0-8) Carnelian Pr.

Balkan Cinema: Evolution after the Revolution. Michael J. Stoil. Ed. by Diane Kirkpatrick. LC 81-21818. (Studies in Cinema: No. 11). 170p. reprint ed. pap. 48.50 (0-8357-1290-7, 2070212) Bks Demand.

Balkan City, 1400-1900. Nikolai Todorov. LC 82-21836. (Publications on Russia & Eastern Europe of the School of International Studies: No. 12). (Illus.). 672p. 1983. 35.00 (0-295-95897-9) U of Wash Pr.

Balkan Conferences & the Balkan Entente, 1930-1935. Robert J. Kerner. LC 77-110850. 271p. 1970. reprint ed. text ed. 59.75 (0-8371-4517-1, KEBC, Greenwood Pr) Greenwood.

Balkan Cookbook. Vladimir Mirodan. LC 89-35639. 208p. 1989. reprint ed. 17.95 (0-88289-738-1) Pelican.

Balkan Economic History, 1550-1950: From Imperial Borderlands to Developing Nations. John R. Lampe & Marvin R. Jackson. LC 80-8844. (Illus.). 728p. 1982. 39.95 (0-253-30368-0) Ind U Pr.

Balkan Express. Slavenka Drakulic. 176p. 1994. reprint ed. pap. 11.00 (0-06-097608-X, PL) HarpC.

Balkan Express: Fragments from the Other Side of War. Slavenka Drakulic. LC 92-42505. 208p. 1993. 19.95 (0-393-03496-8) Norton.

Balkan Family Structure & European Pattern: Demographic Developments in Ottoman Bulgaria. Maria N. Todoroua. 264p. (C). 1993. 47.00 (1-879383-08-X) Am Univ Pr.

Balkan Ghosts: A Journey Through History. Robert D. Kaplan. 1994. pap. 12.00 (0-679-74981-0, Vin) Random.

Balkan Ghosts: A Journey Through History. Robert D. Kaplan. LC 92-43300. 1993. 22.95 (0-312-08701-2) St Martin.

Balkan Home Life. Lucy M. Garnett. LC 77-87723. (Illus.). 320p. reprint ed. 52.00 (0-404-16580-X) AMS Pr.

Balkan Hours: Travels in the Other Europe. Richard Bassett. (Illus.). 160p. 1991. 29.95 (0-7195-4721-0, Pub. by John Murray UK) Trafalgar.

Balkan Imbroglio: Politics & Security in Southeastern Europe. Daniel N. Nelson. (C). 1991. pap. text ed. 33.50 (0-8133-7956-3) Westview.

Balkan Jewish Communities: Yugoslavia, Bulgaria, Greece, & Turkey. Daniel J. Elazar et al. (Illus.). 208p. (Orig.). (C). 1984. pap. text ed. 24.50 (0-8191-3474-0) U Pr of Amer.

Balkan Politics: International Relations in No Man's Land. Joseph S. Roucek. LC 75-106696. (Illus.). 298p. 1971. reprint ed. text ed. 59.75 (0-8371-3370-X, ROBP, Greenwood Pr) Greenwood.

Balkan Tragedy. rev. ed. Ed. by Laird Archer. 575p. 1983. pap. 51.95 (0-89126-120-6) MA-AH Pub.

Balkan Tragedy: Chaos & Dissolution after the Cold War. Susan L. Woodward. 385p. (C). Date not set. 38.95 (0-8157-9514-9); pap. 16.95x (0-8157-9513-0) Brookings.

Balkan Trial. Frederick W. Moore. LC 75-134826. (Eastern Europe Collection Ser.). 1971. reprint ed. 26.95 (0-405-02768-0) Ayer.

Balkan Trilogy. Olivia Manning. 1982. pap. 9.95 (0-14-005936-9, Penguin Bks) Viking Penguin.

***Balkan Visions: Poetry of the Balkan Nations.** Ed. by B. R. Strahan. (International Anthologies Ser.). (Illus.). 54p. (Orig.). 1995. pap. 6.50 (0-938872-20-6) Black Buzzard.

Balkan Vlachs: A Typological Study. Vatro Murvar. LC 77-87535. reprint ed. 23.50 (0-404-16588-5) AMS Pr.

Balkan Worlds: The First & Last Europe. Traian Stoianovich. LC 94-16917. (Sources & Studies in World History). 454p. 1994. 60.00 (1-56324-032-7); pap. text ed. 24.95 (1-56324-033-5) M E Sharpe.

Balkanization of the West: The Confluence of Postmodernism & Postcommunism. Stjepan G. Mestrovic. LC 94-16377. 240p. 1994. 59.95x (0-415-08754-6, B3805); pap. 18.95 (0-415-08755-4, B3809) Routledge.

Balkans. Nevill Forbes et al. LC 76-121281. (BCL Ser.: I). reprint ed. 52.50 (0-404-02457-2) AMS Pr.

Balkans: Minorities & States in Conflict. 2nd ed. Hugh Poulton. 250p. 1993. 49.95 (1-873194-45-5, Pub. by Minority Rts Pubns UK); pap. 19.95 (1-873194-40-4, Pub. by Minority Rts Pubns UK) Paul & Co Pubs.

Balkans: Rumania, Bulgaria, Serbia & Montenegro. William Miller. LC 72-66. (Select Bibliographies Reprint Ser.). 1977. reprint ed. 30.95 (0-8369-9965-7) Ayer.

Balkans - Minorities. Lewis B. Sckolnick. (Civil Rights Reporter Ser.). (Illus.). 60p. (Orig.). (C). 1994. pap. 45.00 (1-57205-141-8) Rector Pr.

***Balkans Conflicts.** David W. Felder. (Illus.). 114p. 1995. 19.95 (0-910959-17-X, B&G 17H); teacher ed 39.95 (0-910959-37-4, B&G 17T) Felder Bks.

Balkans in International Relations: A Case Study of the Balkans. Branimir M. Jankovic. Tr. by Margot Milosavljevic & Bosko Milosavljevic. LC 87-13023. 256p. 1988. text ed. 55.00 (0-312-01161-X) St Martin.

Balkans in Transition. George W. Hoffman. LC 83-18538. (Searchlight Original Ser.). (Illus.). 124p. 1984. reprint ed. text ed. 49.75 (0-313-24288-7, H0BA, Greenwood Pr) Greenwood.

***Balkin & Davis: Law of Torts.** R. P. Balkin & J. R. Davis. 1015p. 1991. pap. 144.00 (0-409-49554-9, Austral); boxed 216.00 (0-409-49551-4, Austral) Butterworth Legal Pubs.

Ball. Ron Cohen. LC 93-22938. (Illus.). 32p. (J). (gr. k up). 1994. 15.00 (0-688-12390-2); lib. bdg. 14.93 (0-688-12391-0) Lothrop.

Ball: Conquering the Frontiers, a Biography & History of One Branch of the Ball Family. R. H. Ball. (Illus.). 102p. 1994. reprint ed. lib. bdg. 28.50 (0-8328-4191-9); reprint ed. pap. 18.50 (0-8328-4192-7) Higginson Bk Co.

Ball & Roller Bearings. P. S. Houghton. (Illus.). 427p. 1976. 147.75 (0-85334-598-8, Pub. by Elsevier Applied Sci UK) Elsevier.

Ball & Roller Bearings: Theory, Design, & Application. 2nd ed. Paul Eschmann et al. LC 84-13120. (Illus.). 504p. pap. 143.70 (0-8357-4667-4, 2037613) Bks Demand.

***Ball & the Cross.** Gilbert K. Chesterton. LC 95-11742. 1995. pap. write for info. (0-486-28805-6) Dover.

Ball Bearing Lubrication: The Elastohydrodynamics of Elliptical Contacts. Bernard J. Hamrock & Duncan Dowson. LC 81-3006. 414p. 1986. 54.50 (0-471-03553-X) Krieger.

Ball Blue-Ribbon Cookbook. Ed. by Judy Harrold. 188p. 1992. 15.95 (0-89730-229-X, State Fair Bks) Blue-Rib Grp.

Ball Book. Margaret Hillert. (Illus.). (J). (ps-00). 1981. lib. bdg. 8.99 (0-8136-5106-9, TK2158); pap. 4.79 (0-8136-5606-0, TK2159) Modern Curr.

Ball Bounced. Nancy Tafuri. LC 87-37582. (Illus.). 24p. (J). (ps up). 1989. 11.95 (0-688-07871-0) Greenwillow.

***Ball Charles: Charles Ball & American Slavery.** Jane Shuter. LC 94-25546. (J). 1995. lib. bdg. write for info. (0-8114-8281-2) Raintree Steck-V.

Ball Courts & Ceremonial Plazas in the West Indies. Ricardo E. Alegria. (Publications in Anthropology: No. 79). 1983. pap. 12.50 (0-913516-15-5) Yale U Anthro.

Ball Culture Guide: The Encyclopedia of Seed Germination. 2nd ed. Jim Nau. LC 93-31746. (Illus.). 144p. (C). 1993. pap. text ed. 39.00 (1-883052-01-7) Ball Pub.

Ball Family Records: Genealogical Memoirs of Some Ball Families of Great Britain, Ireland, & America. William B. Wright. (Illus.). 284p. 1988. reprint ed. lib. bdg. 52.00 (0-8328-0170-4); reprint ed. pap. 42.00 (0-8328-0171-2) Higginson Bk Co.

Ball Field Guide to Diseases of Greenhouse Ornamentals. Margery Daughtrey & A. R. Chase. LC 91-35939. (Illus.). 224p. (C). 1992. pap., vinyl bd. 67.00 (0-9626796-3-1) Ball Pub.

***Ball Floriculture Dictionary: English-Spanish - Spanish-English: With Spanish Definitions.** Veronica Hoyos de Martens & M. L. Palma De Villarreal. LC 95-12052. 424p. (Orig.). 1995. pap. 86.00 (1-883052-09-2) Ball Pub.

Ball Four. rev. ed. Jim Bouton. 320p. 1990. reprint ed. text ed. 22.95 (0-02-513980-0, Collier S&S); reprint ed. pap. 15.00 (0-02-030665-2, Collier S&S) S&S Trade.

Ball Game. David Packard. LC 92-36008. (Illus.). (J). 1993. 3.95 (0-590-46193-1) Scholastic Inc.

Ball Games. (Games Children Play Ser.). 48p. (J). (gr. 3-8). 1990. 9.95 (1-85435-077-3) Marshall Cavendish.

***Ball Grid Array Technology.** John H. Lau. 1994. text ed. 75.00 (0-07-036608-X) McGraw.

Ball in Criminal Proceedings. Neil Corre. 214p. 1990. 60.00 (1-85190-113-2, Pub. by Tolley Pubng UK) St Mut.

Ball Lightning: A Collection of Soviet Research in English Translation. Donald J. Ritchie. LC 61-15177. 70p. reprint ed. pap. 25.00 (0-8357-5950-4, 2024707) Bks Demand.

Ball Lightning & Bead Lightning: Extreme Forms of Atmospheric Electricity. James D. Barry. LC 79-19017. (Illus.). 308p. 1980. 75.00 (0-306-40272-6, Plenum Pr) Plenum.

Ball Park Numbers: The Year They Did Not Play Ball! David P. Hullinger. 1991. 6.95 (0-533-09486-0) Vantage.

Ball Persons: A Trainer's Manual. Barbara Hultgren. (Illus.). 31p. 1981. 2.25 (0-938822-20-9) USTA.

Ball Pest & Disease Manual. Charles C. Powell & Richard K. Lindquist. LC 91-35855. (Illus.). 332p. (C). 1992. text ed. 58.00 (0-9626796-4-X) Ball Pub.

Ball Player's Career - Cap Anson. Anson. 30.95 (0-8488-1540-8) Amereon Ltd.

***Ball Python Manual.** Philippe De Vosjoli et al. 76p. 1994. pap. text ed. 8.50 (1-882770-28-5) Adv Vivarium.

***Ball Pythons.** Coburn. 1995. pap. text ed. (0-7938-0260-1) TFH Pubns.

Ball RedBook: Greenhouse Growing. 15th ed. Ed. by Vic Ball. LC 91-91994. (Illus.). 802p. (C). 1991. text ed. 60.00 (0-9626796-2-3) Ball Pub.

Ball, Rope, Hoop Activities. rev. ed. Jack Capon. Ed. by Frank Alexander. (Perceptual-Motor Development Ser.: Bk. 2). (Illus.). 54p. 1994. reprint ed. teacher ed 7.00 (0-915256-37-1, 122) Front Row.

Ball Sports. Robert Sandelson. LC 91-21804. (Olympic Sports Ser.). (Illus.). 48p. (J). (gr. 6). 1991. text ed. 13.95 (0-89686-664-5, Crstwood Hse) Silver Burdett Pr.

***Ball-Weight Leverage Bowling.** Ottomar. 1994. 17.95 (0-533-11063-7) Vantage.

Balla (Giacomo) Catalogue of the Work. limited ed. Giovanni Lista. (Illus.). 540p. 1982. Numbered ed. 225.00 (1-55660-165-4) A Wofsy Fine Arts.

Ballad. H. L. Cohen. 1972. 59.95 (0-87968-696-0) Gordon Pr.

Ballad a Jim Fidley. Willard Gellis. 80p. 1985. pap. 7.00 (0-917455-01-0) Big Foot NY.

Ballad & Oral Literature. Ed. by Joseph Harris. (English Studies: No. 17). 317p. (C). 1991. 32.50 (0-674-06045-8) HUP.

Ballad As Narrative: Studies in the Ballad Tradition of England, Scotland, Germany & Denmark. Flemming G. Andersen et al. 162p. (Orig.). 1982. pap. 26.50 (87-7492-392-7, Pub. by Odense Universitets Forlag DK) Coronet Bks.

Ballad As Song. Bertrand H. Bronson. LC 74-84045. (Illus.). 1969. 48.00 (0-520-01399-9) U CA Pr.

Ballad, Bard & Bandage: Saga of Stillman Valley's Theatrical Physician. Anne B. Weyrauch. (Illus.). (Orig.). 1990. pap. 14.95 (1-878924-90-7) Beebe Bks.

Ballad Book. W. Allingham. LC 76-76931. (Granger Index Reprint Ser.). 1977. 21.95 (0-8369-6000-9) Ayer.

Ballad Book. Ed. by Katharine L. Bates. LC 78-103081. (Granger Index Reprint Ser.). 1977. 20.95 (0-8369-6096-3) Ayer.

Ballad Book. Illus. by Georgie Schnobrich. 29p. 1985. pap. 3.50 (0-9615115-1-6) Leaping Hart Pr.

***Ballad by a Different Name: Stories.** Sheila K. Adams. LC 95-8516. 1995. write for info. (0-8078-2243-4); pap. write for info. (0-8078-4536-1) U of NC Pr.

Ballad for Georg Hennig. Victor Paskov. Tr. by Robert Sturm. 144p. 1990. 32.00 (0-7206-0796-5, Pub. by Peter Owen Ltd UK) Dufour.

***Ballad for the New World & Other Stories.** Lawrence Scott. 116p. 1994. pap. 9.95 (0-435-98939-1) Heinemann.

Ballad in Blue. Linda Shaw. 1990. 18.95 (0-7278-4035-5) Severn Hse.

Ballad in Literature. Thomas F. Henderson. LC 68-912. (Studies in Poetry: No. 38). 136p. 1969. reprint ed. 75.00 (0-8383-0664-0) M S G Haskell Hse.

Ballad in Memory. deluxe limited ed. Lisa Cooper. 1991. pap. 75.00 (0-685-56976-4) Chax Pr.

Ballad Matrix: Personality, Milieu, & the Oral Tradition. William B. McCarthy. LC 89-46012. 192p. 1990. 27.95 (0-253-33718-6) Ind U Pr.

Ballad Mongers: Rise of the Modern Folk Song. Oscar Brand. LC 78-60137. 240p. 1979. reprint ed. text ed. 55.00 (0-313-20555-8, BRBM, Greenwood Pr) Greenwood.

Ballad of Another Time. Jose L. Gonzalez. Tr. by Asa Zatz. LC 87-71437. (Fiction & Ser.). 112p. (Orig.). 1987. pap. 7.95 (0-933031-10-6) Coun Oak Bks.

***Ballad of Babe Ruth.** Donald Hall. LC 94-30798. (Illus.). (J). (gr. 1-8). 1995. write for info. (0-15-200273-1) HarBrace.

Ballad of Baby Doe. (Vocal Score Ser.). 1981. pap. 35.00 (0-88188-004-3, 00312019) H Leonard.

Ballad of Belle Dorcas. William H. Hooks. LC 89-2715. (Illus.). 48p. (J). (gr. 2-7). 1990. lib. bdg. 14.99 (0-394-94645-6) Knopf Bks Yng Read.

Ballad of "Big George" Foreman, Vol. 8: The Patriot. James L. Berkman. 4p. (Orig.). 1993. pap. 10.00 (0-943662-14-1, 3-686-021) Runaway Pubns.

Ballad of Bishop Hill. Julie McDonald. LC 85-90372. 1986. 7.95 (0-930942-02-7) Sutherland MA.

Ballad of Daniel Shays. Michael Paulin. (Illus.). 120p. (Orig.). 1986. pap. 12.95 (0-9609404-5-6) J R Greene.

***Ballad of Descent.** Martin Vopenka. Tr. by Ann Bryson. LC 95-8674. (Writings from an Unbound Europe Ser.). 1995. write for info. (0-8101-1252-3) Northwestern U Pr.

***Ballad of Descent.** Martin Vopenka. Tr. by Anna Bryson. LC 95-8674. 1995. pap. text ed. write for info. (0-8101-1253-1) Northwestern U Pr.

Ballad of Gato Guerrero. Manuel Ramos. 192p. 1994. 18.95 (0-312-10935-0, Pub. by Thomas Dunne Bks) St Martin.

Ballad of God & Man: Asa Di Var. Ed. by Sohan Singh. 1984. 9.00 (0-8364-1220-6, Pub. by Nanak Dev Univ IA) S Asia.

Ballad of Harriet Tubman. Sterling Plumpp. (Illus.). (J). 1993. 18.95 (0-88378-062-3) Third World.

Ballad of Love. Frederic Prokosch. LC 74-178787. 311p. 1972. reprint ed. text ed. 38.50 (0-8371-6287-4, PRBL, Greenwood Pr) Greenwood.

***Ballad of Nancy Tyler Reed.** Fred Schlick. 319p. 1995. 16.50 (0-614-07422-3) F Schlick.

***Ballad of Nonose Valley.** J. P. Bernhard. LC 94-68384. 160p. (Orig.). 1995. pap. 8.95 (0-9634913-5-0) Carter Pr.

Ballad of Padre Island, Vol. 1. P. J. Meltabarger. Ed. by Arnold Samuelson & Billie Samuelson. (Illus.). 28p. (Orig.). (J). (gr. 1-5). 1987. pap. text ed. 3.95 (0-923133-00-3) JM Pub.

Ballad of Patty Hearst. Gail Goldsmith. LC 77-94319. (Illus.). 1978. 8.50 (0-9601560-1-1) Forsyth Gall.

Ballad of Peckham Rye. Muriel Spark. 1990. pap. 7.95 (0-380-70936-8) Avon.

Ballad of Reading Gaol. Oscar Wilde. 68p. 1991. pap. 5.00 (1-881355-01-2) Intemprte Stage.

Ballad of Reading Gaol & Other Poems. Oscar Wilde. (Thrift Editions Ser.). 64p. (Orig.). 1992. pap. 1.00 (0-486-27072-6) Dover.

***Ballad of Sara Doom: Myths, Messages, & Markers from The Culture Zone.** Michael O. Harrington. LC 94-41754. (Illus.). 136p. (J). (gr. 7 up). 1995. pap. 14.85 (1-880292-13-0) LangMarc.

Ballad of Sexual Dependency. Photos by Nan Goldin. (Illus.). 140p. (Orig.). 1989. 40.00 (0-89381-236-6) Aperture.

Ballad of Sexual Dependency. Nan Goldin. (Illus.). 140p. (Orig.). 1989. pap. 19.95 (0-89381-339-7) Aperture.

B

An Asterisk (*) at the beginning of an entry indicates that the title is appearing in BIP for the first time. 583

***Ballad of Slick Willy.** Noble L. Crawford. 1994. pap. 2.50 (*0-932364-19-5*) Ann Arbor Bk.

Ballad of the Bible. George F. Haveman. 571p. 1992. pap. 25.00 (*0-9630663-0-7*) G F Haveman.

Ballad of the Bones & Other Poems. Byron H. Reece. LC 85-21338. 96p. 1985. reprint ed. 14.95 (*0-87797-100-5*) Cherokee.

Ballad of the Buried Life. Rudolf Hagelstange. Tr. by Herman Salinger. LC 62-64206. (North Carolina. University. Studies in the Germanic Languages & Literatures: No. 38). reprint ed. 27.00 (*0-404-50938-X*) AMS Pr.

Ballad of the Flim-Flam Man. Guy Owen. LC 84-45411. reprint ed. 29.50 (*0-404-19939-9*) AMS Pr.

Ballad of the Men at Mier: The Black Bean Expedition. Jan E. Seale. (Illus.). 46p. (J). (gr. 4-8). 1986. lib. bdg. 10.95 (*0-936927-14-3*); pap. 7.95 (*0-936927-15-1*) Knowing Pr.

Ballad of the Pirate Queens. Jane Yolen. LC 94-7874. (J). (ps-7). 1995. 15.00 (*0-15-200710-5*) HarBrace.

Ballad of the Sad Cafe. Carson McCullers. 1976. 16.95 (*0-8488-0573-9*) Amereon Ltd.

Ballad of the Sad Cafe. adapted ed. Adapt. by Edward Albee & Carson McCullers. LC 63-23325. 1963. pap. 4.75 (*0-8222-0092-9*) Dramatists Play.

Ballad of the Sad Cafe & Other Stories. Carson McCullers. 160p. 1983. mass mkt. 4.99 (*0-553-27254-3*, Bantam Classics) Bantam.

Ballad of the Sad Young Men. Fran Landesman. LC 81-85724. 64p. 1982. 16.00 (*0-932966-18-7*) Permanent Pr.

Ballad of the West: Seekers of the Fleece. 2nd ed. Bobby Bridger. 156p. reprint ed. pap. 15.00 (*0-9636882-0-0*) Augustine TX.

Ballad of the White Horse. Gilbert K. Chesterton. Ed. by Bernadette Sheridan & J. Totten. (Illus.). (Orig.). 1950. pap. text ed. 12.95 (*0-910334-21-8*) Cath Authors.

Ballad of the White Horse. Gilbert K. Chesterton. Ed. & Intro. by Bernadette Sheridan. (Illus.). 278p. (Orig.). 1993. reprint ed. 22.95 (*0-8187-0183-8*) Harlo Press.

Ballad of the White Horse. Gilbert K. Chesterton. (BCL1-PR English Literature Ser.). 295p. (Orig.). 1992. reprint ed. lib. bdg. 79.00 (*0-7812-7496-6*) Rprt Serv.

Ballad of Tont Lala. deluxe ed. Tom Landry. (Illus.). 32p. (J). (gr. k-8). 6.00 (*0-931108-11-X*) Little Cajun Bks.

Ballad of Tradition. Gordon H. Gerould. LC 74-8734. 311p. 1974. reprint ed. 50.00 (*0-87752-165-4*) Gordian.

Ballad of Twelfth Night & Other Poems. 80p. 1975. pap. 4.00 (*0-685-55369-8*) Cobra Pr.

Ballad of Witches Hill. Jeanne G. Arnold. Ed. by Charles D. Hathaway. (Illus.). 144p. (Orig.). 1988. pap. 8.95 (*0-9620887-0-6*) Media Serv Unltd.

Ballad Opera. Edmond M. Gagey. LC 65-16237. 1972. 23.95 (*0-405-08546-X*) Ayer.

Ballad Poetry of Ireland. Ed. by Charles G. Duffy. LC 72-13882. 256p. 1973. reprint ed. lib. bdg. 50.00 (*0-8201-1116-3*) Schol Facsimiles.

Ballad to an Iowa Farmer & Other Reflections by Clark Mollenhoff. Clark Mollenhoff. LC 91-11279. (Illus.). 116p. 1991. 17.95 (*0-8138-1458-8*) Iowa St U Pr.

Ballade. Ed. by Ann H. Guest. LC 93-16973. (Language of Dance Ser.: No. 5). 1993. text ed. 50.00 (*2-88124-912-4*); pap. text ed. 30.00 (*2-88124-913-2*) Gordon & Breach.

Ballade du Coeur: Poeme Inedit. Charles Peguy. 274p. (FRE.). 1973. pap. 24.95 (*0-7859-1461-7*, 2252015381) Fr & Eur.

Ballads. James L. Berkman. (Illus.). 40p. (Orig.). 1984. pap. 10.00 (*0-943662-04-4*, 164-356) Runaway Pubns.

***Ballads.** Comp. by Jerry Silverman. (Traditional Black Music Ser.). (Illus.). 80p. (YA). (gr. 5 up). 1995. lib. bdg. 15.95 (*0-7910-1829-6*) Chelsea Hse.

Ballads & Ballad Scholarship: An Annotated Bibliography. W. Edson Richmond. LC 84-48017. 328p. 1989. lib. bdg. 46.00 (*0-8240-8932-4*, H499) Garland.

Ballads & Ballast: Traditional Ballads, "Negro" Spirituals, Ancient Myths, & a Few Folk Literature Masterpieces. Charlie Reilly. LC 93-93624. (Illus.). 150p. (Orig.). 1993. pap. 14.50 (*0-9638132-0-X*) A James & Son.

Ballads & Folksongs of the Southwest: More than 600 Titles, Melodies, & Texts Collected in Oklahoma. Ethel Moore & Chauncey O. Moore. 432p. reprint ed. pap. 123.20 (*0-8357-5951-2*, 2007261) Bks Demand.

Ballads & Other Island Things. Marthamarie C. Collman. (Illus.). 104p. (Orig.). (YA). (gr. 9 up). 1992. pap. 8.95 (*0-9631903-0-X*) M R Collman.

Ballads & Other Verses. James T. Fields. (Notable American Authors Ser.). 1992. reprint ed. lib. bdg. 75.00 (*0-7812-2835-2*) Rprt Serv.

Ballads & Songs from Utah. Ed. by Lester A. Hubbard. 497p. reprint ed. pap. 141.70 (*0-8357-5952-0*, 2025279) Bks Demand.

Ballads & Songs of Civil War. Date not set. 19.95 (*1-56222-581-2*, 94734); audio 10.98 (*0-7866-0121-3*, 94734C); cd-rom 15.98 (*0-7866-0122-1*, 94734CD) Mel Bay.

Ballads & Sonnets of Don Javier del Granado. Don J. Del Granado. Tr. & Intro. by Bruce Phenix. 80p. (Orig.). 1991. pap. 2.99 (*0-9628779-1-3*) Invesco LTDA.

Ballads by a Bathroom Baritone. 160p. 1987. pap. 6.95 (*0-939116-17-0*) Frontier OR.

Ballads by a Bathroom Baritone with Some Songs in Search of a Singer. Harold Kaesberg. Ed. by Creative Communications. 128p. (Orig.). 1987. pap. 9.95 (*0-318-22769-X*) H Kaesberg.

Ballads for Little Folk. Alice Cary & Phoebe Cary. LC 73-109136. (Granger Index Reprint Ser.). 1977. 17.95 (*0-8369-6120-X*) Ayer.

Ballads for the Possessed. Harry Smith. LC 86-72830. 84p. (Orig.). 1988. pap. 10.00 (*0-913559-06-7*) Birch Brook Pr.

Ballads for the Possessed. deluxe limited ed. Harry Smith. LC 86-72830. 84p. (Orig.). 1988. pap. 30.00 (*0-318-35188-9*) Birch Brook Pr.

Ballads from an Irish Fireside. Ed. by James N. Healy. 1986. pap. 6.95 (*0-85342-745-3*) Dufour.

Ballads from Manuscripts, 2 vols. Incl. Vol. 1, Pts. 1 & 2. Ballads on the Condition of England in Henry the Eighth's & Edward the Sixth's Reigns. Ed. by F. J. Furnivall. 57.50 (*0-685-73103-0*); Vol. 2, Pt. 1. Poor Man's Pittance. Richard Williams. Ed. by F. J. Furnivall. 57.50 (*0-685-73104-9*); Vol. 2, Pt. 2. Ballads Relating Chiefly to the Reign of Queen Elizabeth. Ed. by W. R. Morfill. 57.50 (*0-685-73105-7*); (Ballad Society Ser.: Nos. 1, 2, 3 & 10). reprint ed. write for info. (*0-318-50529-0*) AMS Pr.

Ballads from Manuscripts, 2 vols., 1. Incl. Vol. 1, Pts. 1 & 2. Ballads on the Condition of England in Henry the Eighth's & Edward the Sixth's Reigns. Ed. by F. J. Furnivall. 57.50 (*0-685-73103-0*); Vol. 2, Pt. 1. Poor Man's Pittance. Richard Williams. Ed. by F. J. Furnivall. 57.50 (*0-685-73104-9*); Vol. 2, Pt. 2. Ballads Relating Chiefly to the Reign of Queen Elizabeth. Ed. by W. R. Morfill. 57.50 (*0-685-73105-7*); (Ballad Society Ser.: Nos. 1, 2, 3 & 10). reprint ed. 57.50 (*0-404-50821-9*) AMS Pr.

Ballads from Manuscripts, 2 vols., 2. Incl. Vol. 1, Pts. 1 & 2. Ballads on the Condition of England in Henry the Eighth's & Edward the Sixth's Reigns. Ed. by F. J. Furnivall. 57.50 (*0-685-73103-0*); Vol. 2, Pt. 1. Poor Man's Pittance. Richard Williams. Ed. by F. J. Furnivall. 57.50 (*0-685-73104-9*); Vol. 2, Pt. 2. Ballads Relating Chiefly to the Reign of Queen Elizabeth. Ed. by W. R. Morfill. 57.50 (*0-685-73105-7*); (Ballad Society Ser.: Nos. 1, 2, 3 & 10). reprint ed. write for info. (*0-404-50822-7*) AMS Pr.

Ballads from Manuscripts, 2 vols., Set. Incl. Vol. 1, Pts. 1 & 2. Ballads on the Condition of England in Henry the Eighth's & Edward the Sixth's Reigns. Ed. by F. J. Furnivall. 57.50 (*0-685-73103-0*); Vol. 2, Pt. 1. Poor Man's Pittance. Richard Williams. Ed. by F. J. Furnivall. 57.50 (*0-685-73104-9*); Vol. 2, Pt. 2. Ballads Relating Chiefly to the Reign of Queen Elizabeth. Ed. by W. R. Morfill. 57.50 (*0-685-73105-7*); (Ballad Society Ser.: Nos. 1, 2, 3 & 10). reprint ed. 115.00 (*0-404-50819-7*) AMS Pr.

Ballads from the English Border. A. C. Swinburne. 1972. 59.95 (*0-87968-697-9*) Gordon Pr.

Ballads from the Pubs of Ireland. Ed. by James N. Healy. (Illus.). 79p. 1988. pap. 6.95 (*0-85342-744-5*, Pub. by Mercier Pr IE) Dufour.

***Ballads Inspired by Lorca-Baladas Inspiradas Por Lorca.** 123p. (ENG & SPA.). 1994. lib. bdg. 29.99 (*1-878382-30-6*) Book Gallery.

Ballads Migrant in New England. Ed. by Helen H. Flanders & Marguerite Olney. LC 68-58825. (Granger Index Reprint Ser.). 1977. 19.95 (*0-8369-6015-7*) Ayer.

Ballads of a Bogman. Sigerson Clifford. 85p. 1993. reprint ed. pap. 10.95 (*1-85635-010-X*, Pub. by Mercier Pr IE) Dufour.

Ballads of American Bravery. Clinton Scollard. LC 75-86803. (Granger Index Reprint Ser.). 1977. 18.95 (*0-8369-6088-2*) Ayer.

Ballads of Books. Ed. by Brander Matthews. LC 77-94814. (Granger Poetry Library). (Illus.). 1978. reprint ed. 16.50 (*0-89609-089-2*) Roth Pub Inc.

Ballads of Madison County. Robert J. Waller. Ed. by Milton Okun. (Illus.). 60p. (Orig.). 1994. pap. 16.95 (*0-89524-803-4*, 02502133) H Leonard.

Ballads of Marco Kraljevic. Tr. by David H. Low. LC 69-10123. (Illus.). 196p. 1968. reprint ed. text ed. 38.50 (*0-8371-0151-4*, LOMK, Greenwood Pr) Greenwood.

Ballads of the Bench & Bar: Idle Lays of the Parliament House. LC 92-71813. 128p. 1992. reprint ed. 35.00 (*0-89941-798-1*, 307540) W S Hein.

Ballads of the Hard Hills. Katharine S. Harrington. 1975. reprint ed. pap. 5.00 (*0-910746-45-1*, BOT01) Hope Farm.

Ballads of the Marathas in English. Henry Acworth. 1972. 59.95 (*0-87968-698-7*) Gordon Pr.

Ballads of the Old West: A Collection of Story Poems. Jean Johenning. 1993. 9.95 (*0-533-10320-7*) Vantage.

Ballads on the Condition of England in Henry the Eighth's & Edward the Sixth's Reigns see Ballads from Manuscripts

Ballads Relating Chiefly to the Reign of Queen Elizabeth see Ballads from Manuscripts

Ballads Without Words: Chopin & the Tradition of the Instrumental Ballade. James Parakilas. LC 91-30216. (Illus.). 358p. 1992. 34.95 (*0-931340-47-0*, Amadeus Pr) Timber.

Ballanger. Trevathan. (Gunsmoke Western Ser.). 12.95 (*0-86220-959-5*, C0500, Gunsmoke) Chivers N Amer.

Ballantine & Sterling California Corporation Laws, 6 vols. 4th suppl. ed. Ed. by Bradbury R. Clark. 50p. 1993. 200.00 (*0-685-67727-3*) Butterworth Legal Pubs.

Ballantine & Sterling California Corporation Laws, 6 vols., Set. 4th ed. Ed. by Ray B. Clark. 1994. ring bd. 1,160.00 (*0-8205-1050-5*) Michie Butterworth.

Ballantine Books: The First Decade. David Aronovitz. 107p. 1987. 16.95 (*0-317-67995-3*) Bailiwick Bks.

***Ballantine House: The Ballantine House & the Decorative Arts Galleries at the Newark Museum.** Ulysses G. Dietz. Ed. by Sheila Schwartz. (Illus.). 80p. (Orig.). 1994. pap. 19.95 (*0-932828-30-2*) Newark Mus.

Ballard Genealogy: The Descendants of Israel Ballard & Alice Fuller. M. G. Dodge. 375p. 1991. reprint ed. lib. bdg. 68.00 (*0-8328-2088-1*); reprint ed. pap. 58.00 (*0-8328-2089-X*) Higginson Bk Co.

Ballard Genealogy: William Ballard (1603-1639) of Lynn, Mass., & William Ballard (1617-1689) of Andover, Mass., & Their Descendants. Charles F. Farlow & Charles H. Pope. 203p. 1988. reprint ed. lib. bdg. 40.00 (*0-8328-0172-0*); reprint ed. pap. 30.00 (*0-8328-0173-9*) Higginson Bk Co.

Balldom. George L. Moreland. 304p. 1989. reprint ed. 35.00 (*0-944786-46-4*) Horton Pub.

Ballena "Blubber" Judy Blume. Tr. by Alma F. Ada. LC 83-2731. 160p. (SPA.). (J). (gr. 4-6). 1983. text ed. 14.95 (*0-02-710940-2*, Bradbury S&S) S&S Childrens.

Ballenas. Norman S. Barrett. LC 90-70885. (Picture Library). (Illus.). 32p. (SPA.). (J). (gr. k-4). 1990. lib. bdg. 12.60 (*0-531-07903-1*) Watts.

Ballentine's Law Dictionary. Ballentine. 1969. text ed. 25.00 (*0-442-01657-3*) Van Nos Reinhold.

Ballentine's Law Dictionary: Legal Assistant Edition. Jack G. Handler. 614p. 1994. pap. text ed. 17.95 (*0-8273-4874-6*) Delmar.

Ballentine's Law Dictionary with Pronunciations. 3rd ed. Ed. by Publisher's Editorial Staff. LC 68-30931. 1429p. 1969. 25.00 (*0-686-14540-2*) Lawyers Cooperative.

***Ballentine's Legal Dictionary & Thesaurus.** Jonathan Lynton. LC 94-33514. 768p. 1994. 32.95 (*0-8273-6526-8*) Delmar.

Ballentine's Thesaurus for Legal Research & Writing. Jonathan S. Lynton. LC 93-13825. (Paralegal Ser.). 401p. 1994. pap. text ed. 19.95 (*0-8273-6208-0*) Delmar.

Ballerina. Edward Stewart. 1989. mass mkt. 4.95 (*0-440-20307-4*) Dell.

Ballerina: A Biography of Violette Verdy. Victoria Huckenpahler. LC 78-9799. (Dance Program Ser.: No. 11). (Illus.). 280p. reprint ed. pap. 79.80 (*0-7837-0829-7*, 2041143) Bks Demand.

Ballerina: My Story. Darci Kistler. Ed. by Ruth Ashby. 128p. (Orig.). (J). 1993. pap. 3.99 (*0-671-64437-8*, Minstrel Bks) PB.

Ballerina Girl. Kirsten Hall. LC 94-12246. (My First Reader Ser.). (Illus.). 28p. (J). (ps-2). 1994. lib. bdg. 10.50 (*0-516-05363-9*); pap. text ed. 3.95 (*0-516-45363-7*) Childrens.

Ballerina Paper Doll. Tom Tierney. (Illus.). (J). (gr. k-3). 1994. pap. 2.95 (*0-486-28060-8*) Dover.

Ballerina Princess. Jan Peck. 18p. (J). (ps-2). 1992. 10.95 (*1-879680-15-7*) About You.

Ballerina Trolls on Their Toes. Nancy E. Krulik. (J). 1993. pap. 2.50 (*0-590-46893-6*) Scholastic Inc.

Ballerinas: From the Court of Louis XIV to Pavlova. Parmenia Migel. (Quality Paperbacks Ser.). (Illus.). 1980. reprint ed. pap. 6.95 (*0-306-80115-9*) Da Capo.

Ballerina's Holiday. Schomer Lichtner. (Illus.). 76p. (Orig.). (J). (gr. 5 up). 1979. pap. 4.95 (*0-941074-04-8*) Lichtner.

***Ballet.** June Ford. (You Can Do It! Ser.). (Illus.). 80p. (Orig.). (J). (ps up). Date not set. pap. 12.95 (*1-56530-068-8*) Summit TX.

Ballet. Serge Lido. 1991. lib. bdg. 15.00 (*0-8288-2636-6*) Fr & Eur.

Ballet. A. Thomas. (Dance Guides Ser.). (Illus.). 48p. (J). (gr. 5 up). 1987. lib. bdg. 14.96 (*0-88110-244-X*); pap. 7.95 (*0-7460-0085-5*) EDC.

Ballet. Kay Tichenor. (Color & Cut-out Bks.). (Illus.). 32p. (Orig.). (J). (gr. 1 up). 1983. pap. 4.50 (*0-8431-1718-4*, Troubador) Price Stern.

Ballet: A Decade of Endeavour. Ed. by A. H. Franks. (Series in Dance). (Illus.). 223p. 1981. reprint ed. lib. bdg. 27.50 (*0-306-76112-2*) Da Capo.

Ballet: An Illustrated History. Mary Clarke & Clement Crisp. (Illus.). 320p. 1993. 35.00 (*0-241-13068-9*, H Hamilton) Viking Penguin.

Ballet: Beyond the Basics. Sandra Noll Hammond. LC 81-84696. (Illus.). 154p. 1982. pap. text ed. 18.95 (*0-87484-522-X*) Mayfield Pub.

Ballet: Bias & Belief. Lincoln Kirstein. LC 82-83628. 458p. 1982. 39.95 (*0-87127-133-8*, Dance Horizons) Princeton Bk Co.

Ballet: The Art Defined. 2nd ed. Louise Frazer. LC 83-62154. 130p. 1984. pap. 8.95 (*0-914447-01-7*) PSI Carmel.

Ballet & Dance. A. Thomas et al. (Dance Guides Ser.). (Illus.). 96p. (J). (gr. 5 up). 1987. pap. 12.95 (*0-7460-0201-7*) EDC.

Ballet & Modern Dance: A Concise History. Susan Au. LC 87-50193. (World of Art Ser.). (Illus.). 200p. (Orig.). (C). 1988. pap. 14.95 (*0-500-20219-2*) Thames Hudson.

Ballet & Modern Dance: A Concise History. 2nd ed. Jack Anderson. (Illus.). 288p. 1992. pap. 16.95 (*0-87127-172-9*, Dance Horizons) Princeton Bk Co.

Ballet Barre Enchainements. Linda A. Crist. LC 94-19033. (Illus.). 200p. (C). 1994. student ed, spiral bd. 19.95 (*0-87127-197-4*) Princeton Bk Co.

Ballet Basics. 3rd ed. Sandra Noll Hammond. 195p. (C). 1993. pap. text ed. 16.95 (*1-55934-134-3*) Mayfield Pub.

Ballet Book. Ginny L. Winter. (Illus.). (J). (gr. 1-5). 1962. 8.95 (*0-8392-3001-X*) Astor-Honor.

Ballet Called Giselle. Cyril W. Beaumont. LC 72-77185. (Illus.). 176p. (Orig.). 1987. reprint ed. pap. 14.95 (*1-85273-004-8*) Princeton Bk Co.

Ballet Center Work. Francoise Martinet. Ed. by Linda A. Crist. (Illus.). 87p. (Orig.). (C). 1988. pap. 12.00 (*0-9620289-0-8*) Crist Pubns.

Ballet Class. Joan Lawson. (Illus.). 126p. 1988. pap. 18.95 (*0-87830-989-6*, A2130, Theatre Arts Bks) Routledge Chapman & Hall.

Ballet-Comique de la Reine Balthazar de Beau Joyeux see Chefs-d'Oeuvres Classiques de l'Opera Francais

Ballet Dancer. Janet Craig. LC 88-10043. (What's It Like to Be a...Ser.). (Illus.). 32p. (J). (gr. k-3). 1989. lib. bdg. 10.89 (*0-8167-1434-7*); pap. text ed. 2.95 (*0-8167-1435-5*) Troll Assocs.

Ballet d'Aujourd'hui of Today. Serge Lido. (Illus.). (ENG & FRE.). 1965. lib. bdg. 9.95 (*0-8288-3984-0*) Fr & Eur.

Ballet des Facheux: Beauchamp's Music for Moliere's Comedy. George Houle. LC 90-751143. (Publications of the Early Music Institute). (Illus.). 64p. 1991. pap. 15.00 (*0-253-32851-9*) Ind U Pr.

***Ballet for Beginners.** Marie-Laure Medova. LC 95-9224. (Illus.). 112p. 1995. 19.95 (*0-8069-3876-5*) Sterling.

Ballet for Charlotte. Varela G. Charbonnet. (J). 1994. 14.95 (*0-8050-3063-8*) H Holt & Co.

Ballet for the Ear: Interviews, Essays, & Reviews. John Logan. Ed. by A. Poulin, Jr. (Poets on Poetry Ser.). 304p. 1983. pap. 13.95 (*0-472-06336-7*) U of Mich Pr.

Ballet Genius. large type ed. G. Freeman & Thorpe E. Freeman. 1990. 21.95 (*0-7089-2314-3*) Ulverscroft.

Ballet in America. George Amberg. LC 82-1476. (Series in Dance). (Illus.). xv, 244p. 1983. reprint ed. lib. bdg. 37.50 (*0-306-76154-8*) Da Capo.

Ballet in Leicester Square: The Alhambra & the Empire 1860-1915. Ivor Guest. (Illus.). 202p. (C). 1992. text ed. 39.95 (*1-85273-034-X*, Pub. by Dance Bks UK) Princeton Bk Co.

Ballet Lesson. Merice Briffa. (C). 1990. pap. 30.00 (*0-908175-98-1*, Pub. by Boolarong Pubns AT) St Mut.

Ballet Music. Denes Agay. (Everybody's Favorite Ser.: Vol. 89). 1953. pap. 9.95 (*0-8256-2089-9*) Music Sales.

Ballet Music. 2nd rev. ed. Humphrey Searle. (Illus.). 10.00 (*0-8446-4814-0*) Peter Smith.

Ballet of Birds. Anna F. Gahr. 16p. (J). (gr. k-6). 1994. pap. text ed. 12.00 (*1-883702-07-0*) Aiello Grp.

Ballet Old & New. Andre Levinson. Tr. by Susan C. Summer. LC 81-70095. 144p. 1982. pap. 15.95 (*0-87127-130-3*, Dance Horizons) Princeton Bk Co.

Ballet or Ballyhoo: The American Careers of Maria Bonfanti, Rita Sangalli, & Giuseppina Morlacchi. Barbara Barker. LC 82-83629. 269p. 1984. 39.95 (*0-685-09496-0*, Dance Horizons) Princeton Bk Co.

Ballet Paintings of Degas. Ariel Books Staff. 1994. 4.95 (*0-8362-3059-0*) Andrews & McMeel.

***Ballet School.** Bobbie Kalman & Petrina Gentile. (Crabapple Ser.). (Illus.). 32p. (J). (ps-3). 1994. lib. bdg. 14.95 (*0-86505-606-4*) Crabtree Pub Co.

***Ballet School.** Bobbie Kalman & Petrina Gentile. (Crabapple Ser.). (Illus.). 32p. (Orig.). (J). (ps-3). 1994. pap. 5.95 (*0-86505-706-0*) Crabtree Pub Co.

Ballet School. Agda Skjerne. Date not set. pap. 14.95 (*0-685-68980-8*, Pub. by Wilhelm Hansen DK) Music Sales.

Ballet School: Katie's Last Class, No. 3. Emily Costello. 1994. mass mkt. 3.50 (*0-06-106214-6*) HarpC.

***Ballet School: Megan's Nutcracker Prince.** Emily Costello. 1994. pap. 3.50 (*0-06-106213-8*) HarpC Child Bks.

Ballet School 1. (Ballet School Ser.: No. 1). 1994. mass mkt. 3.50 (*0-06-106178-6*, Harp PBks) HarpC.

Ballet Shoes. Noel Streatfeild. LC 89-24390. (Illus.). 288p. (J). (gr. 4-9). 1991. 15.00 (*0-679-80105-7*) Random Bks Yng Read.

Ballet Shoes. Noel Streatfeild. LC 89-24390. (Illus.). 288p. (J). (gr. 4-9). 1993. pap. 4.99 (*0-679-84759-6*, Bullseye Bks) Random Bks Yng Read.

Ballet Shoes. Noel Streatfeild. 1993. pap. 4.99 (*0-517-11110-1*) Random Hse Value.

Ballet Steps. enl. rev. ed. Anthony Dufort. LC 89-37078. (Illus.). 176p. (J). (gr. 7 up). 1990. 18.00 (*0-517-57770-4*) Crown Bks Yng Read.

Ballet Technique. Tamara Karsavina. LC 68-28084. (Illus.). 1956. 15.95 (*0-87830-011-2*, Theatre Arts Bks) Routledge Chapman & Hall.

Balletmaker's Handbook. Joan Lawson. (Illus.). 112p. 1991. pap. 18.95 (*0-87830-017-1*, A6219, Theatre Arts Bks) Routledge Chapman & Hall.

Ballets de Monte-Carlo. Georges Detaille. lib. bdg. 24.95 (*0-8288-2635-8*) Fr & Eur.

Ballets de Monte Carlo, 1911-44. Georges Detaille & Mulys. (Illus.). 269p. (FRE.). 1954. lib. bdg. 24.95 (*0-8288-3935-2*) Fr & Eur.

Ballets of Antony Tudor: Studies in Psyche & Satire. Judith Chazin-Bennahum. (Illus.). 336p. 1994. 35.00 (*0-19-507186-7*) OUP.

Ballets Sans Musique. Louis-Ferdinand D. Celine. 1959. pap. 8.95 (*0-7859-0658-4*, F91880) Fr & Eur.

Balling Buddah. John Giorno. pap. 3.50 (*0-686-73476-9*) Kulchur Foun.

***Ballistic Bard: Postcolonial Fictions.** Judie Newman. LC 95-16018. 1995. write for info. (*0-340-53914-3*, Pub. by E Arnold UK); pap. write for info. (*0-340-53915-1*, Pub. by E Arnold UK) Routledge Chapman & Hall.

Ballistic Missile-Carrying Submarines: A Reassessment of Their Contribution to Strategic Stability. Robert D. Glasser. (CISA Working Paper Ser.: No. 68). 28p. (Orig.). Date not set. pap. 10.00 (*0-86682-088-4*) Ctr Intl Relations.

Ballistic Missile Defense. Ed. by Ashton B. Carter & David N. Schwartz. LC 83-24064. 455p. 1984. 38.95 (*0-8157-1312-6*); pap. 16.95 (*0-8157-1311-8*) Brookings.

***Ballistic Missile Defense.** Denoon. (C). 1995. text ed. 55.00 (*0-8133-8912-7*) Westview.

Ballistic Missile Defense. Benson D. Adams. LC 74-165800. (Policy Sciences Book Ser.). 288p. reprint ed. pap. 82.10 (*0-8357-5953-9*, 2007765) Bks Demand.

Ballistic Missile Defense: Evolution & Current Issues. (Illus.). 84p. (Orig.). (C). 1994. pap. text ed. 60.00 (*0-7881-0204-4*) Diane Pub.

Ballistic Missile Proliferation. Aaron Karp. (SIPRI Publication). 200p. 1995. 34.00 (*0-19-829173-6*) OUP.

Ballistic Missiles in Modern Conflict. W. Seth Carus. LC 91-8731. (Washington Papers: No. 146). 112p. 1991. pap. text ed. 11.95 (*0-275-94077-2*, B4077, Praeger Pubs) Greenwood.

An Asterisk (*) at the beginning of an entry indicates that the title is appearing in BIP for the first time.

Ballistic Missiles in the Third World: Threat & Response. W. Seth Carus. LC 90-7567. (Washington Papers: No. 146). 104p. 1990. text ed. 45.00 (*0-275-93749-6*, C3749, Praeger Pubs); pap. text ed. 11.95 (*0-275-93750-X*, B3750, Praeger Pubs) Greenwood.

***Ballistic Science for the Law Enforcement Officer.** Charles G. Wilber. (Illus.). 324p. 1977. pap. 30.95 (*0-398-06496-2*) C C Thomas.

Ballistic Science for the Law Enforcement Officer. Charles G. Wilber. (Illus.). 324p. 1977. 51.95 (*0-398-03579-2*) C C Thomas.

Ballistics in Perspective: A Guide for Weapon Choice in the Hunting of Game in Zimbabwe. rev. ed. Mike LaGrange. Ed. by Nancy Kaytis. 1990. reprint ed. 12.95 (*0-9624807-2-X*) PHS Pub Div.

Ballistics Simulation, Third Conference: Combined with Applied Defense. 166p. 1992. 60.00 (*0-685-66778-2*, SMC92-2) Soc Computer Sim.

Ballistics Simulation Two, 1991. Ed. by Michael J. Chinni. 72p. 1991. pap. 32.00 (*0-911801-90-1*, EMC91-1) Soc Computer Sim.

Ballistics Simulation, 1990. Ed. by Michael J. Chinni. 72p. 1990. pap. 32.00 (*0-911801-69-3*, EMC90-1) Soc Computer Sim.

Ballistocardiographic Methods & Cardiovascular Dynamics: Proceedings of the Ballistocardiography & Cardiovascular Dynamics Congress, 3rd World, 9th European Sofia, 1973. Ballistocardiography & Cardiovascular Dynamics Congress Staff. Ed. by A. Talakov. (Bibliotheca Cardiologica Ser.: No. 33). 300p. 1974. pap. 111.25 (*3-8055-1701-7*) S Karger.

Ballistocardiography - Research & Computer Diagnosis: Proceedings of the Ballistocardiograph Research Society, 16th Annual Meeting, Atlantic City, 1972. Ballistocardiograph Research Society Staff. Ed. by E. K. Franke. (Bibliotheca Cardiologica Ser.: No. 32). (Illus.). 160p. 1973. pap. 33.75 (*3-8055-1376-3*) S Karger.

Ballistocardiography & Cardiac Performance. Abraham Noordergraaf et al. LC 67-27246. 156p. 1967. 8.90 (*0-87527-062-X*) Green.

Ballistocardiography & Cardiovascular Therapy: Proceedings of the World Congress. World Congress on Ballistocardiography & Cardiovascular Dynamics Staff. Ed. by A. Falcao De Freitas. (Bibliotheca Cardiologica Ser.: No. 26). 1970. pap. 76.00 (*3-8055-0033-5*) S Karger.

Ballistocardiography & Clinical Studies: Proceedings of the Ballistocardiograph Research Society, 14th Annual Meeting, Atlantic City, 1970. Ballistocardiograph Research Society Staff. Ed. by W. K. Harrison. (Bibliotheca Cardiologica Ser.: No. 27). 1971. pap. 20.00 (*3-8055-1188-4*) S Karger.

Balloon. Karen Sunde. 96p. 1983. pap. 4.95 (*0-88145-006-5*) Broadway Play.

***Balloon Animals.** Ace Collins. (You Can Do It! Ser.). (Illus.). 80p. (Orig.). (J). (ps up). Date not set. pap. 12.95 (*1-56530-034-3*) Summit TX.

Balloon Animals. Aaron Hsu-Flanders. (Illus.). 96p. (Orig.). 1988. pap. 12.95 (*0-8092-4593-0*) Contemp Bks.

Balloon Book. Roxanne Vallet. (Illus.). 15p. (J). (gr. 1-4). 1992. pap. 11.95 (*1-56606-008-7*) Bradley Mann.

Balloon Buster: Frank Luke of Arizona. Norman S. Hall. LC 70-169420. (Literature & History of Aviation Ser.). 1980. reprint ed. 23.95 (*0-405-03765-1*) Ayer.

Balloon Cartoons: And Other Kid's Favorites. Aaron Hsu-Flanders. 1991. pap. 15.95 (*0-8092-3953-1*) Contemp Bks.

Balloon Catcher. Jerry W. Hardin. 88p. 1992. 8.95 (*1-882446-01-1*); pap. 5.95 (*1-882446-00-3*) I p e Alliance.

Balloon Catcher - Pegabalao: Bi-Lingual Edition. Jerry W. Hardin & Camilo De Andrade. 176p. 1992. 11.95 (*1-882446-03-8*); pap. 9.95 (*1-882446-02-X*) I p e Alliance.

Balloon Catheter Coronary Angioplasty. Paolo Angelini. (Illus.). 384p. 1987. 98.00 (*0-87993-307-0*) Futura Pub.

Balloon Construction: Design Critera, Vol. 1. Robert J. Rechs. (Illus.). 176p. (Orig.). 1987. pap. 35.00 (*0-937568-15-5*, TL 638 R43 V1) Rechs Pubns.

Balloon Construction: Materials & Suppliers, Vol. 2. Robert J. Rechs. (Illus.). 176p. (Orig.). 1987. pap. text ed. 35.00 (*0-937568-16-3*, TL 638 R43 V2) Rechs Pubns.

Balloon Construction: Plans & Construction, Vol. 3. Robert J. Rechs. (Illus.). 176p. (Orig.). 1987. pap. text ed. 35.00 (*0-937568-17-1*, TL 638 R43 V3) Rechs Pubns.

Balloon for Katie Kitten. (Kitten Tales Ser.). (Illus.). 28p. (J). (ps-2). 1992. 3.95 (*0-7214-5308-2*, S915-1) Ladybird Bks.

Balloon Hats & Accessories. Aaron Hsu-Flanders. (Illus.). (Orig.). 1989. pap. 14.95 (*0-8092-4383-0*) Contemp Bks.

Balloon Magic. (Illus.). (J). (ps-2). 1991. lib. bdg. 8.99 (*0-8136-5194-8*); pap. 4.79 (*0-8136-5694-X*) Modern Curr.

***Balloon Magic.** Marvin Hardy. 1985. pap. 5.95 (*0-934126-69-0*) CFI Dist.

Balloon Man. Charlotte Armstrong. 1988. 20.95 (*0-8488-0419-8*) Amereon Ltd.

Balloon Man. Charlotte Armstrong. LC 90-80765. 253p. 1990. reprint ed. pap. 7.95 (*1-55882-068-X*) Intl Polygonics.

Balloon Pins, Vol. 1. Frank Prell. LC 85-71996. (Illus.). 112p. (Orig.). 1985. per. 12.95 (*0-9615189-0-1*) Oxford Promot.

Balloon Post of the Siege of Paris, Eighteen Seventy to Eighteen Seventy-One. Louis Chaintrier. 163p. (ENG.). 12.50 (*0-939429-09-8*) Am Air Mail.

Balloon Ride. Bill Graham. 18p. (J). (ps-2). 1987. 10.95 (*1-879680-02-5*) About You.

Balloon Ride. Evelyn C. Mott. (Illus.). 32p. (J). (ps-1). 1991. 13.95 (*0-8027-8124-1*); lib. bdg. 14.85 (*0-8027-8126-8*) Walker & Co.

Balloon Science. Etta Kaner. (J). (gr. 4-7). 1990. pap. 9.57 (*0-201-52378-7*) Addison-Wesley.

Balloon Science. Etta Kaner. (J). (gr. 4-7). 1993. pap. 9.57 (*0-201-62640-3*) Addison-Wesley.

***Balloon Sculpting: A Fun & Easy Guide to Making Balloon Animals, Toy & Games.** rev. ed. Bruce Fife. (Illus.). 96p. 1994. pap. 9.95 (*0-941599-25-6*) Piccadilly Bks.

Balloon Sculpture. Kay Watts. 1986. pap. 4.95 (*0-87162-442-7*, D1200) Warner Pr.

Balloon Shot. Joe Manchester. 1968. pap. 2.75 (*0-8222-0093-7*) Dramatists Play.

Balloon Technology & Observations. Ed. by W. Reidler & K. M. Torkar. (Advances in Space Research Ser.: Vol. 14). 212p. 1993. pap. 195.00 (*0-08-042473-2*, Pergamon Pr) Elsevier.

Balloon to the Moon: Chronology of New Jersey's Distinguished Aviation History. H. V. Reilly. Ed. by Carol Suplee. (Illus.). 340p. (Orig.). 1992. pap. 29.95 (*0-9632295-0-8*) H V Pubs.

Balloon Voyager. R. Saunders. (Great Adventure Ser.). (Illus.). 32p. (J). (gr. 4 up). 1988. lib. bdg. 17.27 (*0-86592-870-3*); lib. bdg. 12.95 (*0-685-58291-4*) Rourke Corp.

Balloonia. Audrey Wood. LC 90-46602. (Illus.). 32p. (J). (ps-2). 1981. 7.95 (*0-85953-122-8*, Pub. by Childs Play UK); pap. 3.95 (*0-85953-320-4*, Pub. by Childs Play UK) Childs Play.

Ballooning: A Complete Guide to Riding the Winds. Dick Wirth. 1991. 22.50 (*0-679-73116-4*) McKay.

Ballooning: High & Wild. Irene Adler. LC 75-23406. (Illus.). 32p. (J). (gr. 5-10). 1976. lib. bdg. 10.79 (*0-89375-001-8*); pap. 2.95 (*0-89375-017-4*) Troll Assocs.

Ballooning: The Complete Guide to Riding the Winds. Dick Wirth & Jerry Young. LC 80-5281. (Illus.). 168p. 1984. pap. 12.95 (*0-394-72796-7*) Random.

***Ballooning Manual.** R. Howes. 1994. pap. 29.95 (*1-85310-284-9*, Pub. by Airlife Pub Ltd UK) Voyageur Pr.

Balloons. Deborah Chandra. 1990. 12.95 (*0-374-30509-9*) FS&G.

Balloons: And Other Poems. Deborah Chandra. (J). (gr. 4-7). 1993. pap. 3.95 (*0-374-40492-5*) FS&G.

Balloons & Airships. A. Hildebrant. (Illus.). 1976. reprint ed. 21.00 (*0-85409-879-8*) Charles River Bks.

Balloons Are for Chasing. Calvin L. Campbell. (Illus.). 155p. (Orig.). 1985. pap. 5.95 (*0-9615404-0-0*) Zia Enter.

Balloons Are for Chasing. limited ed. Calvin L. Campbell. (Illus.). 155p. (Orig.). 1985. 15.00 (*0-9615404-1-9*) Zia Enter.

Balloons! Candy! Toys! & Other Parables for Storytellers. Daryl Olszewski. LC 85-60241. 104p. (Orig.). 1986. reprint ed. pap. 8.95 (*0-89390-069-9*) Resource Pubns.

Ballot & the Class Struggle. 8th ed. Daniel De Leon. 1971. pap. text ed. 0.50 (*0-935534-04-0*) NY Labor News.

Ballot Clerk. Jack Rudman. (Career Examination Ser.: C-1133). 1994. pap. 23.95 (*0-8373-1133-0*) Nat Learn.

***Ballots: Reconstruction on the Lower Cape Fear.** William M. Evans. 336p. 1995. pap. 19.95 (*0-8203-1731-4*) U of Ga Pr.

Ballots & Bandwagons Series, 3 vols., Set. (Illus.). 128p. (YA). (gr. 5 up). 1991. lib. bdg. 38.85 (*0-382-24313-7*); pap. 23.85 (*0-382-24318-8*) Silver Burdett Pr.

Ballots & Barricades: Class Formation & Republican Politics in France, 1830-1871. Ronald Aminzade. LC 93-18279. (Illus.). 368p. 1993. text ed. 49.50 (*0-691-09479-9*); pap. text ed. 18.95 (*0-691-02871-0*) Princeton U Pr.

Ballots Anyone? How to Run for Office & Win. Foster Furcolo. 270p. 1982. pap. 11.95 (*0-87073-442-3*) Schenkman Bks Inc.

Ballots Before Bullets: The War Referendum Approach to Peace in America, 1914-1941. Ernest C. Bolt. LC 77-680. 227p. reprint ed. pap. 64.70 (*0-8357-3277-0*, 2039500) Bks Demand.

Ballots for Freedom: Antislavery Politics in the United States, 1837-1860. Richard H. Sewell. 400p. 1980. reprint ed. pap. 8.95 (*0-393-00966-1*) Norton.

Ballots of Tumult: A Portrait of Volatility in American Voting. Courtney Brown. (Illus.). 278p. 1991. text ed. 37.50 (*0-472-10250-8*) U of Mich Pr.

Ballou-Wright Automobile Accessories Catalog, 1906. Pref. by Ron Brentano. LC 74-635336. (Illus.). 80p. 1971. pap. 2.95 (*0-87595-028-0*) Oregon Hist.

***Ballpark.** Peter Richmond. 1995. pap. text ed. 12.00 (*0-684-80048-9*, Fireside) S&S Trade.

Ballpark: Camden Yards & the Building of an American Dream. Peter Richmond. (Illus.). 320p. 1993. 23.00 (*0-671-74851-3*) S&S Trade.

Ballparks. Shannon. 50.95 (*0-8488-1561-0*) Amereon Ltd.

Ballparks of North America: A Comprehensive Historical Reference to Baseball Grounds, Yards, & Stadiums, 1845 to Present. Michael Benson. LC 89-45007. 505p. 1989. lib. bdg. 38.50x (*0-89950-367-5*) McFarland & Co.

Ballpoint Bananas & Other Jokes for Kids. Charles Keller. LC 72-7338. (Illus.). 96p. (J). (gr. 3-7). 1976. pap. 5.95 (*0-671-66965-6*, S&S Bks Young Read) S&S Childrens.

Ballroom. Ken Graves & Eva Lipman. LC 89-36395. (Seeing Double Collaborative Book Ser.). 112p. (Orig.). 1989. pap. 18.95 (*0-915943-44-1*) Milkweed Ed.

Ballroom Calypso. (Ballroom Dance Ser.). 1986. lib. bdg. 69.95 (*0-8490-3276-8*) Gordon Pr.

Ballroom Calypso. (Ballroom Dance Ser.). 1985. lib. bdg. 70.00 (*0-87700-775-6*) Revisionist Pr.

***Ballroom Dance - A Step in the Right Direction.** Carol Anne Blazina. (Illus.). (Orig.). Date not set. pap. 9.00 (*0-614-00085-8*) C A Blazina.

Ballroom Dance Games. (Ballroom Dance Ser.). 1986. lib. bdg. 69.95 (*0-8490-3275-X*) Gordon Pr.

Ballroom Dance Games. (Ballroom Dance Ser.). 1985. lib. bdg. 64.50 (*0-87700-774-8*) Revisionist Pr.

***Ballroom Dance Music: A Reference Guide.** 1994. lib. bdg. 255.95 (*0-8490-9068-7*) Gordon Pr.

Ballroom Dance Pack. Walter Laird. LC 93-26744. 1994. 24.95 (*1-56458-483-6*) Dorling Kindersley.

Ballroom Dancer's Handbook. A. H. Franks. (Ballroom Dance Ser.). 1986. lib. bdg. 79.95 (*0-8490-3319-5*) Gordon Pr.

Ballroom Dancer's Handbook. A. H. Franks. (Ballroom Dance Ser.). 1985. lib. bdg. 69.00 (*0-87700-762-4*) Revisionist Pr.

Ballroom Dancing. Phyllis Haylor et al. (Ballroom Dance Ser.). 1986. lib. bdg. 74.95 (*0-8490-3291-1*) Gordon Pr.

Ballroom Dancing. Phyllis Haylor et al. (Ballroom Dance Ser.). 1985. lib. bdg. 250.00 (*0-87700-668-7*) Revisionist Pr.

Ballroom Dancing. Maurice Jay. (Ballroom Dance Ser.). 1986. lib. bdg. 79.95 (*0-8490-3259-8*) Gordon Pr.

Ballroom Dancing. Maurice Jay. (Ballroom Dance Ser.). 1985. lib. bdg. 76.00 (*0-87700-851-5*) Revisionist Pr.

Ballroom Dancing. Alex Moore. (Ballroom Dance Ser.). 1986. lib. bdg. 125.00 (*0-8490-3309-8*) Gordon Pr.

Ballroom Dancing. Alex Moore. (Ballroom Dance Ser.). 1984. lib. bdg. 250.00 (*0-87700-499-4*) Revisionist Pr.

Ballroom Dancing: A Bibliography for Students & Teachers. L. Gordon & H. Gordon. (Bibliographies for Librarians Ser.). 1985. lib. bdg. 79.95 (*0-8490-3244-X*) Gordon Pr.

Ballroom Dancing - Finest of All Hobbies. Doris H. Harker. 1992. 13.95 (*0-533-09621-9*) Vantage.

Ballroom Dancing at the A & P. T. L. Sebastiani. 240p. (Orig.). 1993. pap. 9.95 (*0-9634332-0-2*) Lithodendron.

Ballroom Dancing Diary. Stuart Saunders. (Ballroom Dance Ser.). 1986. lib. bdg. 79.95 (*0-8490-3304-7*) Gordon Pr.

Ballroom Dancing Diary. Stuart Saunders. (Ballroom Dance Ser.). 1985. lib. bdg. 79.95 (*0-87700-872-8*) Revisionist Pr.

Ballroom Dancing Explained. H. S. Rumsey. (Ballroom Dance Ser.). 1985. lib. bdg. 79.95 (*0-87700-656-3*) Revisionist Pr.

Ballroom Dancing Explained. H. St. John Rumsey. (Ballroom Dance Ser.). 1986. lib. bdg. 79.95 (*0-8490-3367-5*) Gordon Pr.

Ballroom Dancing for Teachers. B. White. (Ballroom Dance Ser.). 1986. lib. bdg. 79.95 (*0-8490-3384-5*) Gordon Pr.

Ballroom Dancing for Teachers. B. White. (Ballroom Dance Ser.). 1985. lib. bdg. 250.00 (*0-87700-719-5*) Revisionist Pr.

Ballroom Dancing Made Easy. A. M. Rosanova. (Ballroom Dance Ser.). 1986. lib. bdg. 79.95 (*0-8490-3358-6*) Gordon Pr.

Ballroom Dancing Made Easy. A. M. Rosanova. (Ballroom Dance Ser.). 1985. lib. bdg. 250.00 (*0-87700-685-7*) Revisionist Pr.

Ballroom Dancing Yearbook, 6 vols. (Ballroom Dance Ser.). 1986. lib. bdg. 1,500.00 (*0-8490-3424-8*) Gordon Pr.

Ballroom Dancing Yearbook. (Ballroom Dance Ser.). 1984. lib. bdg. 79.95 (*0-87700-501-X*) Revisionist Pr.

Ballroom Dancing Yearbook, 6 vols. (Ballroom Dance Ser.). 1985. lib. bdg. 600.00 (*0-87700-768-3*) Revisionist Pr.

Ballroom Polka. Earl Atkinson. (Ballroom Dance Ser.). 1983. lib. bdg. 250.00 (*0-87700-476-5*) Revisionist Pr.

Ballroom Studio Guidebook. (Ballroom Dance Ser.). 1986. lib. bdg. 74.95 (*0-8490-3274-1*) Gordon Pr.

Ballroom Studio Guidebook. (Ballroom Dance Ser.). 1985. lib. bdg. 75.00 (*0-87700-773-X*) Revisionist Pr.

Ballroom Teacher Training Manual, 2 Vols. 1984. lib. bdg. 250.00 (*0-87700-505-2*) Revisionist Pr.

Ballroom Teacher Training Manuals. Dance Masters of America. (Ballroom Dance Ser.). 1985. lib. bdg. 76.00 (*0-87700-845-0*) Revisionist Pr.

Ballroom Teacher Training Manuals. Dance Masters of America Staff. (Ballroom Dance Ser.). 1986. lib. bdg. 74.95 (*0-8490-3273-3*) Gordon Pr.

Ballroom Terminology. Earl Atkinson. (Ballroom Dance Ser.). 1986. lib. bdg. 79.95 (*0-8490-3624-0*) Gordon Pr.

Ballroom Terminology. Earl Atkinson. (Ballroom Dance Ser.). 1983. lib. bdg. 250.00 (*0-87700-480-3*) Revisionist Pr.

Ballroom Variations: One Hundred Steps & Combinations with Lesson Plans for 10 Hour Course Class Instruction. Hazel M. Conlon. (Ballroom Dance Ser.). 1986. lib. bdg. 79.95 (*0-8490-3348-9*) Gordon Pr.

Ballroom Variations: One Hundred Steps & Combinations with Lesson Plans for 10 Hour Course Class Instruction. Hazel M. Conlon. (Ballroom Dance Ser.). 1985. lib. bdg. 250.00 (*0-87700-663-6*) Revisionist Pr.

***Balls.** Gorman Bechard. 352p. (Orig.). 1995. pap. 10.95 (*0-452-27294-7*, Plume) NAL-Dutton.

Balls & Strikes: The Money Game in Professional Baseball. Kenneth M. Jennings. LC 89-38009. (Illus.). 283p. 1990. text ed. 35.00 (*0-275-93441-1*, C3441, Praeger Pubs) Greenwood.

Ball's Bluff: A Small Battle & Its Long Shadow. Byron Farwell. LC 90-30049. (Illus.). 232p. (Orig.). 1990. pap. 12.95 (*0-939009-36-6*) EPM Pubns.

Balls of Menzies: Australian Political Songs, 1900-1980. Warren Fahey. (Illus.). 351p. (Orig.). 1990. pap. 19.95 (*0-207-16204-2*) Legacy Books.

Ball's Patent Repeating & Single-loading Firearms. reprint ed. 2.00 (*1-877704-03-2*) Pioneer Pr.

Bally Electronic Pinball Games: Repair Procedures & Module & Component Replacement. rev. ed. Ed. by Frank Adams. (Illus.). 60p. reprint ed. spiral bd. 17.50 (*1-56642-168-3*, R-13) AMR Pub Co.

Bally Machines General Pinball Service Instructions. rev. ed. Ed. by Frank Adams. (Illus.). 58p. reprint ed. spiral bd. 17.50 (*1-56642-169-1*, R-112) AMR Pub Co.

Bally Murphy & the Irish War. Claran De Barold. (C). 1990. pap. text ed. 23.00 (*0-7453-0445-1*, Pub. by Pluto Pr UK) Westview.

Bally Slot Machines: An Illustrated Guide to the 114 Most Popular Ballys Made from 1964-1987. 2nd rev. ed. Marshall Fey. (Illus.). 80p. 1991. 9.95 (*0-9623852-2-0*) Liberty Belle.

Bally Slot Machines: The Complete Service Manual for Electro-Mechanicals 1964-1980. Marshall Fey. (Illus.). 112p. 1993. pap. 19.95 (*0-9623852-5-5*) Liberty Belle.

***Bally Slot Machines: The Complete Service Manual for Series E 1980-1986.** Marshall Fey. (Illus.). 60p. 1995. pap. 19.95 (*0-9623852-3-9*) Liberty Belle.

Bally Variety Bingo Type Pinball, 1954: Operating Instructions & Parts Catalog. rev. ed. Ed. by Frank Adams. (Illus.). 52p. reprint ed. spiral bd. 27.50 (*1-56642-159-4*, R-59) AMR Pub Co.

Ballymaloe Cookbook. Myrtle Allen. (Illus.). 203p. (Orig.). 1984. reprint ed. pap. 15.95 (*0-7171-1339-6*, Pub. by Gill & MacMill IE) Irish Bks Media.

Ballymara Flood: A Tale from Old Ireland. Chad Stuart. LC 94-15162. (Illus.). (J). 1995. write for info. (*0-15-205698-X*) HarBrace.

Ballymurphy & the Irish War. 2nd ed. Ciaran De Baroid. (Illus.). 312p. 1990. reprint ed. pap. 9.95 (*0-937702-12-9*) Irish Bks Media.

***Ballz: The Official Strategy Guide.** Bradygames Staff. 1994. pap. 9.99 (*1-56686-214-0*) Brady Compu Bks.

Balm in Gilead. Sara L. Lightfoot. 1989. pap. 14.42 (*0-201-51807-4*) Addison-Wesley.

***Balm in Gilead: Journey of a Healer.** Sara Lawrence-Lightfoot. (Illus.). 368p. 1995. 13.95 (*0-14-024967-2*, Penguin Bks) Viking Penguin.

Balm in Gilead & Other Plays. Lanford Wilson. Incl. Balm in Gilead. 1965. (*0-318-53361-8*); Home Free. 1965. (*0-318-53362-6*); Ludlow Fair. 1965. (*0-318-53363-4*); (Mermaid Dramabook Ser.). 116p. (Orig.). 1965. Set pap. 9.00 (*0-374-52156-5*, Noonday) FS&G.

Balm of Gilead. rev. ed. Lilian B. Yeomans. 80p. 1973. pap. 2.95 (*0-88243-728-3*, 02-0728) Gospel Pub.

Balmoral. Michael Frayn. 82p. 1988. pap. 8.95 (*0-413-17180-9*, A0016) Heinemann.

Balook. Piers Anthony. (Illus.). 200p. (J). 1990. 24.95 (*0-88733-069-X*) Underwood-Miller.

Balook. deluxe ed. Piers Anthony. (Illus.). 200p. (J). 1990. 75.00 (*0-685-53972-5*) Underwood-Miller.

Balsam Fir, Abies Balsamea (Linnaeus) Miller: A Monographic Review. Egolfs V. Bakuzis & H. L. Hansen. LC 65-17539. (Illus.). 467p. reprint ed. pap. 133.10 (*0-8357-5954-7*, 2033204) Bks Demand.

Balsam Groves of Grandfather Mountain. Shepherd M. Dugger. (Illus.). 1974. 6.00 (*0-686-15218-2*) Puddingstone.

Balsamroot: A Memoir. Mary C. Blew. LC 93-34888. 1994. 21.95 (*0-670-84857-3*, Viking) Viking Penguin.

***Balsamroot: A Memoir.** Mary C. Blew. 1995. pap. 9.95 (*0-14-017624-1*, Penguin Bks) Viking Penguin.

Balseros de la Libertad. Josefina Leyva. 105p. 1992. pap. write for info. (*1-882721-00-4*) Edit Ponce de Leon.

Balta. Paule Constant. 292p. (FRE.). 1986. pap. 11.95 (*0-7859-2053-6*, 2070377830) Fr & Eur.

Baltasar Gracian. Virginia R. Foster. LC 74-19235. (Twayne's World Authors Ser.). 171p. (C). 1975. lib. bdg. 17.95 (*0-8057-2398-6*) Irvington.

Balthasar Hubmaier. Ed. by H. Wayne Pipkin & John H. Yoder. (Classics of the Radical Reformation Ser.: No. 5). 496p. 1989. 49.95 (*0-8361-3103-7*) Herald Pr.

Balthasar Hubmaier: The Leader of the Anabaptists. Henry C. Vedder. LC 79-149670. reprint ed. 45.00 (*0-404-06755-7*) AMS Pr.

Balthasar Hubmaier's Doctrine of the Church. Eddie Mabry. 236p. Date not set. lib. bdg. 32.50 (*0-8191-9472-7*) U Pr of Amer.

Balthazar, Fils De Famille. Francois-Marie Banier. 264p. (FRE.). 1985. pap. 11.95 (*0-7859-2184-2*, 2070704718) Fr & Eur.

Balthus Notebook. Guy Davenport. 1989. 17.95 (*0-88001-234-X*) Ecco Pr.

Balti: A Scheduled Tribe of Jammu & Kashmir. Br Rizvi. 1993. 14.00 (*81-212-0402-X*, Pub. by Gian Publng Hse II) S Asia.

Baltic: A Regional Future? John Fitzmaurice. LC 91-37445. 175p. 1992. text ed. 59.95 (*0-312-07581-2*) St Martin.

Baltic Americans. David Cantor. (Peoples of North America Ser.). (Illus.). 112p. (J). (gr. 5 up). 1991. 17.95 (*0-87754-890-0*) Chelsea Hse.

Baltic & the Outbreak of the Second World War. Ed. by John Hiden & Thomas Lane. (Illus.). 192p. (C). 1992. 54.95 (*0-521-40467-3*) Cambridge U Pr.

Baltic Armorial. P. Glasenapp. (Illus.). 200p. 1980. 130.00 (*0-318-23356-8*) Szwede Slavic.

Baltic Computer Science: Selected Papers. Ed. by J. Barzdins & D. Bjorner. (Lecture Notes in Computer Science Ser.: Vol. 502). x, 619p. 1991. pap. 57.00 (*0-387-54131-4*) Spr-Verlag.

Baltic Countries, 1900-1914: Essays, 2 vols., Set. Ed. by Aleksander Loit. (Studia Baltica Stockholmiensia: No. 5, Vols. 1-2). 787p. (Orig.). (ENG & GER.). 1990. pap. 115.00x (*91-22-01389-X*, Pub. by Almqv & Wiksell SW) Coronet Bks.

***Baltic Crusade.** 2nd enl. rev. ed. William Urban. LC 94-76154. (Illus.). 366p. 1994. 38.50 (*0-929700-10-4*) Lith Res & Studies.

Baltic Dilemma. Edgars Dunsdorfs. 12.50 (*0-8315-0148-0*) Speller.

Baltic Drama: A Handbook & Bibliography. Alfreds Straumanis. LC 81-50710. 720p. (Orig.). 1981. 44.95 (*0-917974-63-8*) Waveland Pr.

B

An Asterisk (*) at the beginning of an entry indicates that the title is appearing in BIP for the first time. 585

Baltic Heritage. S. H. Barkan et al. 1991. boxed 75.00 (*0-89304-952-2*) Cross-Cultrl NY.

Baltic Independence & Russian Empire. Walter C. Clemens, Jr. LC 90-40681. 368p. 1991. pap. 14.95 (*0-312-06499-3*) St Martin.

Baltic Nations: Estonia, Latvia, & Lithuania. Frederick W. Pick. LC 83-45837. reprint ed. 20.00 (*0-404-20202-0*) AMS Pr.

Baltic Nations & Europe: Estonia, Latvia & Lithuania in the Twentieth Century. 2nd rev. ed. John Hiden & Patrick Salmon. LC 94-1889. 232p. (C). 1995. pap. text ed. 19.95 (*0-582-25650-X*, 76876, Pub. by Longman UK) Longman.

Baltic Nations & Europe: Estonia, Latvia & Lithuania in the 20th Century. John Hiden & Patrick Salmon. (Illus.). 224p. (C). 1991. pap. text ed. 25.50 (*0-582-08245-5*, 78922) Longman.

Baltic Odyssey: The Von Rosen Reminiscences & Diary. Ed. by Elvi Whittaker. (Illus.). 294p. (Orig.). 1994. pap. text ed. 21.95 (*1-895176-24-7*, Pub. by Univ Calgary CN) Paul & Co Pubs.

Baltic Oil Shales: Chemistry & Technology. E. Pata. 368p. 1971. text ed. 88.50 (*0-7065-1064-X*, Pub. by Keter Pub IS) Coronet Bks.

Baltic Republics: People to People. Ed. by Jim Haynes. 224p. 1993. pap. 10.95 (*0-939010-30-5*) Zephyr Pr.

Baltic Republics Business Forecaster. Ed. by Lewis B. Sckolnick. 70p. (Orig.). (C). 1994. pap. 675.00 (*1-57205-355-0*) Rector Pr.

Baltic Revolution: Estonia, Latvia, Lithuania & the Path to Independence. Anatol Lieven. (Illus.). 496p. (C). 1994. pap. 15.00 (*0-300-06078-5*) Yale U Pr.

Baltic Sea. Ed. by A. Voipio. (Oceanography Ser.: Vol. 30). 418p. 1981. 161.75 (*0-444-41884-9*) Elsevier.

***Baltic Sea Pilot: Germany, Poland, the Baltic States, Russia, Finland, Sweden & Denmark.** Barry Sheffield & Oz Robinson. (Illus.). 196p. (C). 1992. 69.95 (*0-85288-175-4*, Pub. by Imray Laurie Norie & Wilson UK) Bluewater Bks.

***Baltic Sea Region: Conflict or Cooperation.** Ed. by Christian Wellmann. (Kiel Peace Research Ser.). (C). 1994. pap. text ed. 16.50 (*3-89473-311-X*) Westview.

Baltic Sea Region Environmental Protection: Eastern Perspectives & International Cooperation. Ed. by Mikael Sandberg. (Goteborg Studies of Russia & Eastern Europe). (Illus.). 172p. (Orig.). 1992. pap. 57.50x (*91-22-01507-8*, Pub. by Almqv & Wiksell SW) Coronet Bks.

Baltic States. (Insight Guides, Windows on the World Ser.). (Illus.). 350p. 1993. pap. 21.95 (*0-395-65985-X*) HM.

Baltic States. David C. Flint. LC 92-2240. (Former Soviet States Ser.). (Illus.). 32p. (J). (gr. 4-6). 1992. lib. bdg. 15.40 (*1-56294-310-3*) Millbrook Pr.

Baltic States. Inese A. Smith. (World Bibliographical Ser.). 1993. lib. bdg. 81.50 (*1-85109-196-3*) ABC-CLIO.

Baltic States. Gail B. Stewart. LC 92-40. (Places in the News Ser.). (Illus.). 48p. (J). (gr. 6-7). 1992. text ed. 12.95 (*0-89686-747-1*, Crstwood Hse) Silver Burdett Pr.

Baltic States: A Survey for Further Industrial Cooperation. Ed. by Nordic Council of Ministers Staff. 127p. (Orig.). 1991. pap. 47.50x (*91-7996-381-1*, Pub. by Almqv & Wiksell SW) Coronet Bks.

Baltic States: The National Self-Determination of Estonia, Latvia, & Lithuania. Ed. by Graham Smith. LC 93-45834. 1994. text ed. 45.00 (*0-312-12060-5*) St Martin.

***Baltic States: The Years of Independence: Estonia, Latvia, Lithuania, 1917-1940.** Georg Von Rauch. Tr. by Gerald Onn. LC 94-37552. 1995. write for info. (*0-312-12521-6*) St Martin.

Baltic States & Kaliningrad: A Travel Survival Kit. John Noble & Susan Forsyth. (Illus.). 448p. (Orig.). 1994. pap. 15.95 (*0-86442-183-4*) Lonely Planet.

Baltic States & the End of the Soviet Empire. Kristian Gerner & Stefan Hedlund. LC 93-20390. 224p. 1993. 62.50 (*0-415-07570-X*, B0719) Routledge.

Baltic States & the Great Powers: Foreign Relations, 1938-1940. David M. Crowe. LC 92-24988. 264p. 1992. text ed. 61.00 (*0-8133-0481-4*) Westview.

Baltic States & Weimar Ostpolitik. John Hiden. 1987. 59.95 (*0-521-32037-2*) Cambridge U Pr.

***Baltic States Business Guide.** (Illus.). 225p. (Orig.). 1994. pap. 145.00 (*0-7605-0625-6*) Rector Pr.

Baltic States in Facts, Figures & Maps. Ulf Pauli. (Illus.). 72p. 1994. pap. 8.95 (*1-85756-074-4*, Pub. by Janus Pubng UK) Paul & Co Pubs.

***Baltic States Phrasebook: A Language Survival Kit.** Ed. by Sally Steward. (Illus.). 200p. 1994. pap. 5.95 (*0-86442-300-4*) Lonely Planet.

Baltic States, Years of Dependence, 1940-1992. Romuald J. Misiunas & Rein Taagepera. LC 92-39806. (C). 1993. 45.00 (*0-520-08227-3*); pap. 17.00 (*0-520-08228-1*) U CA Pr.

***Baltic States: Years of Independence: Estonia, Latvia, Lithuania, 1917-1940.** Georg Von Rauch. 265p. 1995. pap. 17.95 (*0-312-12447-3*) St Martin.

Baltic Straits. G. Alexandersson. 1982. lib. bdg. 70.00 (*90-247-2595-X*) Kluwer Ac.

Baltic Teutons: Pioneers of America's Frontier. Myron E. Gruenwald. 100p. (Orig.). 1988. pap. 6.00 (*0-9601536-0-8*) M E Gruenwald.

Baltic Tribunal Against the Soviet Union, July 25 & 26, 1985, Copenhagen. 197p. 1985. 15.00 (*0-685-43554-7*) World Fed Free Latvians.

***Baltic World, 1772-1993: Europe's Nothern Periphery in an Age of Change.** David Kirby. LC 94-22617. 480p. (C). 1996. text ed. 58.95 (*0-582-00408-X*, 76998, Pub. by Longman UK); pap. text ed. 28.95 (*0-582-00409-8*, Pub. by Longman UK) Longman.

Baltics. Tomas Transtromer. 1975. 5.00 (*0-685-56097-X*); pap. 2.50 (*0-685-56099-6*) Oyez.

Baltics. deluxe ed. Tomas Transtromer. 1975. 15.00 (*0-685-56098-8*) Oyez.

Baltimore. Catherine Reef. LC 89-25695. (Downtown America Ser.). (Illus.). 60p. (J). (gr. 3 up). 1990. text ed. 13.95 (*0-87518-427-8*, Dillon Silver Burdett) Silver Burdett Pr.

Baltimore. Catherine Reef. (Illus.). 60p. (J). (gr. 3 up). 1990. write for info. (*0-685-31388-3*, Mac Bks Young Read) S&S Childrens.

Baltimore: A Living Renaissance. Ed. by Lenora H. Nast et al. LC 82-80490. (Illus.). 336p. 1982. 12.95 (*0-942460-00-6*) Hist Balt Soc.

Baltimore: A Portrait. rev. ed. Roger Miller et al. (Illus.). 128p. 1988. 19.95 (*0-911897-15-1*) Image Ltd.

Baltimore: A Portrait. rev. ed. Roger Miller et al. LC 88-81951. (Illus.). 128p. 1988. 34.50 (*0-911897-01-1*) Image Ltd.

Baltimore: A Portrait (An Address Book) Roger Miller. (Illus.). 112p. 1986. 10.95 (*0-911897-03-8*) Image Ltd.

Baltimore: The Building of an American City. Sherry H. Olson. LC 79-21950. (Illus.). 446p. reprint ed. pap. 127.20 (*0-8357-4334-9*, 2037134) Bks Demand.

Baltimore: When She Was What She Used to Be, 1850-1930. Marion E. Warren & Mame Warren. LC 83-48055. (Illus.). 160p. 1983. 29.95 (*0-8018-2994-1*) Johns Hopkins.

Baltimore - Annapolis, 1991-92. 5th ed. Intro. by John J. Russell et al. 640p. 1991. pap. 45.00 (*0-910416-92-3*) Columbia Bks.

Baltimore - Annapolis, 1993-94. 6th ed. Ed. by Buck Downs et al. 650p. 1993. pap. 55.00 (*1-880873-02-8*) Columbia Bks.

Baltimore - Washington Metro Directory, 1993-94: Business & Industry. pap. 95.00 (*1-882893-03-4*) Dalton.

Baltimore Affair. Judson. 1994. 25.00 (*0-465-00626-4*) Basic.

Baltimore Affair. Joyce S. Goldberg. LC 86-4342. (Illus.). 221p. reprint ed. pap. 63.00 (*0-7837-4655-5*, 2044379) Bks Demand.

Baltimore Album Quilts: Historic Notes & Antique Patterns: A Pattern Companion to Baltimore Beauties & Beyond, Vol. I. Elly Sienkiewicz. Ed. by Sayre Van Young. LC 89-82563. (Illus.). 184p. (Orig.). 1990. 29.95 (*0-914881-35-3*); pap. 24.95 (*0-914881-28-0*) C & T Pub.

Baltimore & Its Streetcars. Herbert Harwood, Jr. 1984. pap. 10.95 (*0-915276-44-5*) Quadrant Pr.

Baltimore & Ohio. Ed. by Timothy Jacobs. (Railroad Histories Ser.). (Illus.). 128p. 1989. 14.98 (*0-517-67603-6*, Crescent) Random Hse Value.

Baltimore & Ohio Heritage. John Krause & Ed Christ. (Illus.). 52p. 1991. reprint ed. pap. 7.95 (*0-911868-52-6*, C52) Carstens Pubns.

Baltimore & Ohio in the Civil War: The History of the Baltimore & Ohio Railroad in the Civil War. Festus Summers. (Illus.). 366p. 1993. reprint ed. 30.00 (*1-879664-13-5*); reprint ed. pap. 14.95 (*1-879664-14-3*) Stan Clark Military.

***Baltimore-Annapolis 1995-96: A Comprehensive Directory of the Major Institutions & the People Who Run Them.** Ed. by John J. Russell et al. 650p. 1995. pap. 60.00 (*1-880873-15-X*) Columbia Bks.

Baltimore Beauties & Beyond: Studies in Classic Album Quilt Applique, Vol. II. Elly Sienkiewicz. Ed. by Sayre Van Young. (Illus.). 176p. 1991. 29.95 (*0-914881-40-X*) C & T Pub.

Baltimore Beauties & Beyond, Vol. II: Studies in Classic Album Applique. Elly Sienkiewicz. Ed. by Sayre Van Young. (Illus.). 176p. (Orig.). 1991. pap. 24.95 (*0-914881-34-5*) C & T Pub.

Baltimore Beauties & Beyond, Vol. 1: Studies in Classic Album Quilt Applique. Elly Sienkiewicz. Ed. by Sayre Van Young. LC 89-60479. (Illus.). 176p. (Orig.). 1989. 29.95 (*0-914881-36-1*); pap. 24.95 (*0-914881-23-X*) C & T Pub.

Baltimore Book: New Views of Local History. Ed. by Linda Shopes et al. (Critical Perspectives on the Past Ser.). (Illus.). 288p. (C). 1994. 39.95 (*1-56639-184-9*) Temple U Pr.

Baltimore Bouquets. Mimi Dietrich. LC 92-10358. (Illus.). 72p. 1992. pap. 18.95 (*1-56477-010-9*, B142) That Patchwork.

Baltimore Bride's Quilt Designs. Doreen L. Saunders. LC 93-10728. (Pictorial Archive Ser.). 1993. pap. 3.95 (*0-486-27610-4*) Dover.

Baltimore Captured Memories. Ron Pilling. Ed. by David Miller & Margaritta Finn. LC 88-81952. (Illus.). 72p. 1988. 9.95 (*0-911897-13-5*) Image Ltd.

Baltimore Catechism, No. 1. Baltimore Plenary Council Staff. 1977. reprint ed. pap. 3.00 (*0-89555-010-5*) TAN Bks Pubs.

Baltimore Catechism, No. 2. Baltimore Plenary Council Staff. 1977. reprint ed. pap. 4.00 (*0-89555-008-3*) TAN Bks Pubs.

Baltimore Catechism, No. 3: Cathechism of Christian Doctrine. Baltimore Plenary Council Staff. 1974. reprint ed. pap. 7.00 (*0-89555-007-5*, 147) TAN Bks Pubs.

Baltimore Chefs Book. William Struns. Ed. by R. McMinn. 120p. (Orig.). 1989. pap. text ed. 6.95 (*0-935201-87-4*) Affordable Adven.

Baltimore Clearing House. Charles A. Hales. LC 78-64296. (Johns Hopkins University. Studies in the Social Sciences. Thirtieth Ser. 1912: 27). 368p. 1983. reprint ed. 24.50 (*0-404-61396-9*) AMS Pr.

Baltimore Clipper: Its Origin & Development. Howard I. Chapelle. 240p. 1988. pap. 8.95 (*0-486-25765-7*) Dover.

Baltimore County Design: Administrator's Manual. Janet L. Cyzyk. Ed. by Maryland State Dept. of Education. (Correlates Test to Adult Literacy Ser.). (Illus.). 128p. 1988. student ed, pap. text ed. 3.20 (*0-8428-9500-0*) Cambridge Bk.

Baltimore County Panorama. Richard Parsons & Neal A. Brooks. Ed. by Nancy O. Phillips. LC 88-22953. (Baltimore County Heritage Publications). (Illus.). 375p. 1988. text ed. 29.95 (*0-937076-03-1*) Baltimore Co Pub Lib.

Baltimore Harbor: A Picture History. Robert C. Keith. (Illus.). 1988. 18.95 (*0-9609772-1-X*) Ocean Wrld MD.

Baltimore Harbor: A Picture History. Robert C. Keith. LC 90-63441. (Illus.). 168p. 1991. reprint ed. pap. 16.95 (*0-8018-4204-2*) Johns Hopkins.

Baltimore Harbor: A Picture History, 1985. Robert C. Keith. (Illus.). pap. 14.95 (*0-9609772-0-1*) Ocean Wrld MD.

Baltimore in the Nation, 1789-1861. Gary L. Browne. LC 79-13180. 363p. reprint ed. pap. 103.50 (*0-7837-0311-2*, 2040633) Bks Demand.

Baltimore Orioles. Richard Rambeck. (Baseball: The Great American Game Ser.). 48p. (J). (gr. 4-10). 1992. lib. bdg. 14.95 (*0-88682-451-6*) Creative Ed.

Baltimore Orioles: Forty Years of Magic from 33rd Street to Camden Yards. Ted Patterson. 192p. 1994. 29.95 (*0-87833-865-9*) Taylor Pub.

***Baltimore Orioles: Forty Years of Magic from 33rd Street to Camden Yards; "the Bible of Bird Base..."** Ted Patterson. 1994. 75.00 (*0-87833-873-X*) Taylor Pub.

Baltimore Orioles: Memories & Memorabilia of the Lords of Baltimore. Bruce Chadwick. (Illus.). 1995. 29.95 (*1-55859-862-6*) Abbeville Pr.

Baltimore Streetcars Nineteen Hundred Five to Nineteen Sixty-Three: The Semi-Convertible Era. Bernard J. Sachs et al. (Orig.). 1982. pap. 14.95 (*0-9609638-0-4*) Baltimore Streetcar.

Baltimore Sun, Eighteen Thirty-Seven to Nineteen Eighty-Seven. Harold A. Williams. LC 87-2796. 464p. (Orig.). 1987. 29.50 (*0-8018-3516-X*) Johns Hopkins.

Baltimore Trail Book. rev. ed. Suzanne M. Mittenthal. Ed. by James W. Poultney. LC 82-21216. (Illus.). 176p. (Orig.). 1983. pap. 11.95 (*0-8018-2943-7*) Johns Hopkins.

***Baltimore Unbound: A Strategy for Regional Renewal.** David Rusk. 177p. 1994. pap. 14.95 (*0-8018-5078-9*) Johns Hopkins.

Baltimore Waltz. Paula Vogel. 1992. 4.75 (*0-8222-1359-1*) Dramatists Play.

***Baltimore Waltz: And Other Plays.** Paula Vogel. 300p. (Orig.). 1995. pap. 15.95 (*1-55936-109-3*) Theatre Comm.

***Baltimore's Light Rail.** Hebert Rarwood, Jr. 1995. pap. 15.95 (*0-915276-55-0*) Quadrant Pr.

Baltimore's Loyola, Loyola's Baltimore. Nicholas Varga. 1990. 29.95 (*0-938420-34-8*) MD Hist.

***Baltimore's Past: A Directory of Historical Sources.** Baltimore Archives Network Staff. Ed. by Thomas L. Hollowak et al. (Illus.). iv, 255p. (Orig.). 1995. pap. 15.00 (*1-887124-11-X*) Historyk Pr.

Baluchi Glossary. Mumtaz Ahmad. LC 85-70270. 155p. 1985. text ed. 32.00 (*0-931745-08-X*) Dunwoody Pr.

Baluchi Woven Treasures. Jeff W. Boucher. LC 89-92134. (Illus.). 152p. 1990. 70.00 (*0-9623893-0-7*) J W Boucher.

Baluchis & Pathans. Lewis B. Sckolnick. (Civil Rights Reporter Ser.). (Illus.). 60p. (Orig.). (C). 1994. pap. 45.00 (*1-57205-113-2*) Rector Pr.

Baluchistan (Pakistan) Its Society, Resources & Development. Akhtar H. Siddiqi. 346p. (Orig.). 1991. lib. bdg. 45.00 (*0-8191-8226-5*) U Pr of Amer.

***Baluyut: A Collection of Ninety Portraits.** Butch Baluyut. 96p. Date not set. write for info. (*0-9635453-7-X*); pap. write for info. (*0-9635453-2-9*) B Baluyut.

Balyet. Patricia Wrightson. LC 88-8298. 144p. (J). (gr. 7 up). 1989. text ed. 13.95 (*0-689-50468-3*, McElderry) S&S Childrens.

Balzac. E. Faguet. LC 73-21621. (Studies in French Literature: No. 45). 1974. lib. bdg. 49.95 (*0-8383-1778-2*) M S G Haskell Hse.

Balzac. Andre Maurois. (Illus.). (FRE.). 1976. 49.95 (*0-8288-9740-9*, 2080607464) Fr & Eur.

***Balzac.** Ed. & Intro. by Michael Tilby. LC 94-48738. (Modern Literatures in Perspective Ser.). (C). 1995. text ed. 59.95 (*0-582-08706-6*, Pub. by Longman UK) Longman.

***Balzac.** Ed. & Intro. by Michael Tilby. LC 94-48738. (Modern Literatures in Perspective Ser.). 1995. pap. write for info. (*0-582-08705-8*, Pub. by Longman UK) Longman.

Balzac. Edgar Saltus. LC 71-93190. reprint ed. 34.50 (*0-404-01959-5*) AMS Pr.

Balzac: "Old Goriot" David Bellos. (Landmarks of World Literature Ser.). 1987. pap. 10.95 (*0-521-31634-0*) Cambridge U Pr.

Balzac: "Old Goriot" David Bellos. (Landmarks of World Literature Ser.). 1987. 29.95 (*0-521-32799-7*) Cambridge U Pr.

***Balzac: A Biography.** Graham Robb. (Illus.). 521p. 1994. 57.50x (*0-330-33237-6*, Pub. by Pan Books UK) Trans-Atl Phila.

***Balzac: A Biography.** Graham Robb. (Illus.). 572p. 1995. pap. 15.00 (*0-393-31387-5*, Norton Paperbks) Norton.

Balzac: A Critical Study. Hippolyte A. Taine. Ed. by O'Rourke & Lorenzo. LC 72-8680. (Studies in French Literature: No. 45). 1973. reprint ed. lib. bdg. 75.00 (*0-8383-1670-0*) M S G Haskell Hse.

Balzac: A Life. Graham Robb. LC 94-18614. 1994. 35.00 (*0-393-03679-0*) Norton.

Balzac: Fiction & Melodrama. Christopher Prendergast. LC 78-11267. 205p. 1979. text ed. 32.50 (*0-8419-0457-X*) Holmes & Meier.

Balzac: Selected Short Stories. Honore De Balzac. Ed. & Tr. by Sylvia Raphael. (Classics Ser.). 1977. mass mkt. 8.95 (*0-14-044325-8*, Penguin Classics) Viking Penguin.

Balzac & der Effet de Reel: Eine Untersuchung anhand der Textstufen des Colonel Chabert & des Cure de Village. Joachim Kupper. (Beihefte zu Poetica Ser.: No. 17). 290p. (GER.). 1986. 49.00 (*90-6032-213-4*, Pub. by B R Gruener NE) Benjamins North Am.

Balzac & the Drama of Perspective. Joan Dargan. LC 85-80419. (French Forum Monographs: No. 60). 172p. (Orig.). 1985. pap. 12.95 (*0-917058-61-5*) French Forum.

Balzac Bibliography. W. H. Royce. 1972. 69.95 (*0-87968-699-5*) Gordon Pr.

Balzac et la Recherche de l'Absolu. Fargeau. 32.95 (*0-7859-0616-9*, F56660) Fr & Eur.

Balzac, James & the Realistic Novel. William W. Stowe. LC 82-61388. 224p. 1986. text ed. 35.00x (*0-691-06567-5*); pap. 13.95x (*0-691-10196-5*) Princeton U Pr.

***Balzac, James, & the Realistic Novel.** William W. Stowe. LC 82-61388. Date not set. reprint ed. pap. 63.60 (*0-7837-9454-1*, 2060196) Bks Demand.

Balzacian Montage: Configuring La Comedie Humaine. Allan H. Pasco. (Romance Ser.: No. 65). 192p. 1991. text ed. 45.00 (*0-8020-2776-8*) U of Toronto Pr.

Balzac's Comedy of Words. Martin Kanes. LC 75-2993. 400p. 1975. 45.00 (*0-691-06282-X*) Princeton U Pr.

***Balzac's Comedy of Words.** Martin Kanes. LC 75-2993. reprint ed. pap. 88.40 (*0-7837-9354-5*, 2060096) Bks Demand.

Balzac's Horse & Other Stories. Gert Hofmann. Tr. by Christopher Middleton. LC 87-28923. 200p. 1988. 16.95 (*0-88064-074-X*) Fromm Intl Pub.

Balzac's Letters to His Family. W. S. Hastings. 1972. 59.95 (*0-87968-700-2*) Gordon Pr.

Balzac's Recurrring Characters. Anthony R. Pugh. LC 72-190348. (University of Toronto Romance Ser.: No. 24). 544p. reprint ed. pap. 155.10 (*0-8357-5955-5*, 2029344) Bks Demand.

Balzac's Short Stories. Honore De Balzac. 1991. lib. bdg. 75.00 (*0-8490-4179-1*) Gordon Pr.

Bam, Bam, Bam. Eve Merriam. LC 94-20300. (Illus.). 32p. (J). 1995. 14.95 (*0-8050-3527-3*) H Holt & Co.

Bam! (by Any Means) Grant Dellabough. LC 93-94025. 128p. 1994. pap. 9.95 (*1-56002-360-0*, Univ Edtns) Aegina Pr.

Bama After Bear. Donald F. Staffo. 300p. (Orig.). 1992. pap. 19.95 (*0-943487-40-4*) Sevgo Pr.

Bama & the Bear. 199p. 1983. 19.95 (*0-934126-33-X*) CFI Dist.

Bambi. (FRE.). (J). (gr. 3-8). 13.95 (*0-7859-0613-4*, S26622) Fr & Eur.

Bambi. (Deluxe Golden Sound Story Bks.). (Illus.). 24p. (J). (ps-2). 1991. write for info. (*0-307-74017-X*, Golden Pr) Western Pub.

***Bambi.** (Classics Ser.). 96p. (J). 1989. 6.98 (*1-57082-033-3*) Mouse Works.

Bambi. Walt Disney. (Disney Animated Ser.). 1988. 5.99 (*0-517-66193-4*) Random Hse Value.

***Bambi.** Little Golden Books Staff. (J). Date not set. pap. 1.59 (*0-307-01061-9*, Golden Pr) Western Pub.

Bambi. Felix Salten. (Illus.). (J). (ps up). 1988. mass mkt. 3.99 (*0-671-66607-X*, Minstrel Bks) PB.

Bambi. Felix Salten. LC 90-26533. (Illus.). 160p. (J). (ps up). 1992. pap. 18.00 (*0-671-73937-9*, S&S Bks Young Read) S&S Childrens.

***Bambi.** Walt Disney Company Staff. (FRE.). Date not set. pap. 9.95 (*0-7859-8850-5*) Fr & Eur.

Bambi. Walt Disney Staff. (Penguin-Disney Ser.). 1987. 6.98 (*0-8317-0681-3*) Viking Penguin.

Bambi. Walt Disney Staff. (Penguin-Disney Ser.). (J). (ps-3). 1992. 6.98 (*0-453-03019-X*) Viking Penguin.

Bambi. Felix Salten. 134p. (J). 1981. reprint ed. lib. bdg. 16.95 (*0-89966-358-3*) Buccaneer Bks.

Bambi. Felix Salten. 112p. (J). 1981. reprint ed. lib. bdg. 16.95 (*0-89967-032-6*) Harmony Raine.

Bambi: The New Prince. Illus. by Fred Marvin. LC 93-71377. (Tiny Changing Pictures Bks.). 10p. (J). (ps-00). 1994. 4.95 (*1-56282-601-8*) Disney Pr.

Bambi - Life in the Woods. Felix Salten. (J). 15.95 (*0-8488-1467-3*) Amereon Ltd.

***Bambi En Espanol.** (Spanish Classics Ser.). 96p. (J). 1992. 6.98 (*1-57082-055-4*) Mouse Works.

Bambi Looks for His Forest Friends. Illus. by Alvin S. White Studio Staff. LC 91-73808. (Surprise Lift-the-Flap Ser.). 18p. (J). (ps-00). 1992. 9.95 (*1-56282-074-5*) Disney Pr.

Bambi's Children. Felix Salten. (Illus.). 316p. (YA). 1992. reprint ed. lib. bdg. 21.95 (*0-89966-894-1*) Buccaneer Bks.

Bambo. Gary L. Hargis. LC 90-50349. (Illus.). 392p. (Orig.). (C). 1990. pap. text ed. 13.95 (*0-923568-10-7*) Wilderness Adventure Bks.

Bambo Jordan: An Anthropological Narrative. Bruce T. Williams. (Illus.). 189p. (Orig.). (C). 1994. pap. text ed. 9.50 (*0-88133-790-0*) Waveland Pr.

***Bamboo.** D. Phillip Caron. Ed. & Intro. by Curtis R. McGuirt. (Illus.). 16p. 1994. pap. 4.00 (*1-885799-00-4*) October Release.

Bamboo American. Richard E. Hoffmann. 149p. (Orig.). (C). 1988. pap. 8.75 (*971-10-0366-X*, Pub. by New Day Pub PH) Cellar.

Bamboo & Butterflies: From Refugee to Citizen. JoAn D. Criddle. LC 92-70276. 224p. (Orig.). 1992. pap. 12.95 (*0-9632205-0-0*) East West Bdg.

Bamboo & Cotton. Willard Gellis. (Satan's Suckhole Ser.). 21p. (Orig.). 1991. pap. 3.00 (*0-917455-16-9*) Big Foot NY.

Bamboo & Friends. John Atkinson. LC 88-50844. (Illus.). 104p. (J). (gr. 1-12). 1988. 13.95 (*0-929155-05-X*) Windward Bks.

 An Asterisk (*) at the beginning of an entry indicates that the title is appearing in BIP for the first time.

Bamboo Game. William E. Knight. LC 92-73094. 230p. (Orig.). 1993. pap. 12.00 (0-9636778-0-2) Araluen Pr.

In the corruption plagued Philippines of Ferdinand Marcos, a company under attack by unknown enemies engages a trouble-shooter named Czernik to investigate. Czernik overcomes dangers in Mindanao, Manila & remote mountain areas of Luzon where warlords rule, the military struggles with insurgents & aboriginal tribes that still hunt heads when they can. Knight served in the U.S. Embassy in Manila for four years during the Marcos period & was in Manila when Marcos was overthrown. Library Journal: "fast-paced action adventure...highly recommended for all public libraries." Publishers Weekly: a "convincing story of industrial espionage & intrigue." Rapport magazine: "Knight shocks with scenes of horror when they are least expected." Philippine News: "A dandy read." Filipinas magazine: "Anyone who likes adventure, mysteries & suspense will like THE BAMBOO GAME." Retired U.S. Ambassador Francis Underhill: "A first-class job - fast-paced, cleverly plotted, tough, witty style." An Italian language version will be forthcoming. Order from: Araluen Press, 5000 Park Place, Suite 300, Bethesda, MD 20816-1736; 301-229-8165, FAX 301-229-2246. *Publisher Provided Annotation.*

An Asterisk (*) at the beginning of an entry indicates that the title is appearing in BIP for the first time.

Band of Angels. Julian Thompson. 304p. (YA). (gr. 7 up). 1987. pap. 3.99 (*0-590-43124-2*) Scholastic Inc.

Band of Angels. Robert Penn Warren. LC 55-5814. (Voices of the South Ser.). 375p. 1994. pap. 12.95 (*0-8071-1946-6*) La State U Pr.

Band of Arrogant & United Heroes: The Story of the Royal Shakespeare Co. Production of the Wars of the Roses. Richard Pearson. 168p. (C). 1990. 60.00 (*1-85634-005-8*, Pub. by Excalibur UK) St Mut.

***Band of Brothers.** Jack Bilello. 280p. Date not set. pap. 8.95 (*0-7610-0405-X*) NW Pub.

Band of Brothers. Thomas Fleming. (J). (gr. 8 up). 1988. 13.95 (*0-8027-6740-0*); lib. bdg. 14.85 (*0-8027-6741-9*) Walker & Co.

Band of Brothers. Walter McDonald. LC 89-36088. xvi, 144p. (C). 1989. 16.50 (*0-89672-208-2*); pap. 9.00 (*0-89672-209-0*) Tex Tech Univ Pr.

Band of Brothers. large type ed. Ernest K. Gann. 1980. 12.00 (*0-7089-0400-9*) Ulverscroft.

Band of Brothers: E Company, 506th Regiment, 101st Airborne from Normandy to Hitler's Eagle's Nest. Stephen E. Ambrose. (Illus.). 336p. 1993. pap. 13.00 (*0-671-86736-9*, Touchstone Bks) S&S Trade.

Band of Gold. Christian Zita. 1993. mass mkt. 4.50 (*0-06-108150-7*, Harp PBks) HarpC.

***Band of Prophets: The Vanderbilt Agrarians after Fifty Years.** Ed. by William C. Havard & Walter Sullivan. LC 81-19371. (Southern Literary Studies). 202p. 1982. pap. 57.60 (*0-7837-8520-8*, 2049329) Bks Demand.

***Band Rehearsal Techniques.** Max F. Dalby. 1993. 16.00 (*0-614-01757-2*) Instrumental.

Band Saw Basics. Gene Duginske & Mark Duginske. LC 90-10127. (Basics Ser.). (Illus.). 128p. (Orig.). 1990. pap. 9.95 (*0-8069-7210-6*) Sterling.

Band Saw Book, with Twenty Projects. R. J. De Cristoforo. (Illus.). 288p. (Orig.). 1989. 25.95 (*0-8306-0289-5*) TAB Bks.

Band Structure Engineering in Semiconductor Microstructures. Ed. by R. A. Abram & M. Jaros. (NATO ASI Series B, Physics: Vol. 189). (Illus.). 374p. 1988. 120.00 (*0-306-43080-0*, Plenum Pr) Plenum.

Band Structure of Semiconductors. I. M. Tsidilkovski. Tr. by R. S. Wadhwa. (International Series in the Science of the Solid State: Vol. 19). (Illus.). 407p. 1982. 175.00 (*0-08-021657-9*, Pub. by Pergamon Repr UK) Franklin.

Band Technique: Step by Step Conductor Score. Robert Elledge & Donald Haddad. 208p. 1990. 19.95 (*0-8497-8515-4*, W12F) Kjos.

***Band Technique: Step by Step Conductor Score, Parts.** Robert Elledge & Donald Haddad. 1990. 4.95 (*0-614-03103-6*) Kjos.

***Band Technique: Step by Step Conductor Score, Parts, Percussion.** Robert Elledge & Donald Haddad. 1990. 5.95 (*0-614-03104-4*) Kjos.

Band Theory of Metals. Simon Altmann. (C). 1970. 112.00 (*0-08-015602-9*, Pub. by Pergamon Repr UK) Franklin.

Band Theory of Solids: An Introduction from the Point of View of Symmetry. Simon L. Altmann. (Illus.). 304p. 1994. reprint ed. pap. 29.95 (*0-19-855866-X*) OUP.

Band Three Proteins: Anion Transporters, Binding Proteins, & Senescent Antigenes. Ed. by Ernst Bamberg & Hermann Passow. LC 92-22096. (Progress in Cell Research Ser.: Vol. 2). xvi, 358p. 1992. write for info. (*0-444-89547-7*) Elsevier.

Bandaging & Splinting. (Medical Ser.). 1986. lib. bdg. 79.95 (*0-8490-3568-6*) Gordon Pr.

Bandalars. Sara M. Heiderscheit. (Illus.). 12p. (Orig.). (J). (ps-4). 1988. pap. 3.50 (*0-9620385-0-4*) S Heiderscheit.

Bande a Part. Jacques Perret. (FRE.). 1973. pap. 8.95 (*0-7859-4000-6*) Fr & Eur.

Bande Mataram: Early Political Writings. Sri Aurobindo. 1979. 18.00 (*0-686-85667-8*); pap. 10.00 (*0-89744-900-2*) Auromere.

Bandele's Annual Small Business Guide to African-American Events. Bandele Publications. 150p. (Orig.). 1992. pap. 15.00 (*1-882706-00-5*) Bandele Pubns.

Bandele's Festival Goers' Guide to African-American Events. Bandele Publications. LC 92-75201. 100p. (Orig.). 1992. pap. 8.00 (*1-882706-04-8*) Bandele Pubns.

Bandelier National Monument. Pat Barey. Ed. by T. J. Priehs & Therese Burson. LC 90-60724. (Illus.). 48p. (Orig.). 1990. pap. 7.95 (*0-911408-88-6*) SW Pks Mnmts.

Bandelier National Monument, NM. rev. ed. Ed. by Trails Illustrated Staff. (Illus.). 1994. Folded topographical map. 7.95 (*0-925873-09-8*) Trails Illustrated.

Bandera. Pierre MacOrlan. (FRE.). 1972. pap. 8.95 (*0-7859-3994-6*) Fr & Eur.

Bandera Trail. Ralph H. Compton. 1993. mass mkt. 4.99 (*0-312-95143-4*) St Martin.

***Banderas.** Chris Jueggi. (I Know about Ser.). (Illus.). (J). 1995. pap. 2.50 (*0-528-87397-0*) Rand McNally.

***Banderas-Flags.** (Pequena Biblioteca - Little Library Ser.). (Illus.). 32p. (SPA.). (J). (gr. 1-4). 1995. 2.95 (*1-85697-558-4*, Kingfisher LKC) LKC.

Banderas y Escudos del Mundo (Flags & Coat of Arms of the World) Maria E. Alvarez del Real. (Illus.). 272p. (Orig.). (SPA.). 1986. pap. 7.50 (*0-944499-17-1*) Editorial Amer.

Bandersnatch. Mollie Hardwick. 1994. mass mkt. 4.50 (*0-449-22029-X*) Fawcett.

Bandersnatch. large type ed. Mollie Hardwick. 1991. 21.95 (*0-7089-2534-0*) Ulverscroft.

Bandicoot Run. Manohar Malgonkar. 337p. 1982. 15.00 (*0-86578-134-6*); pap. 6.00 (*0-86578-192-3*) Ind-US Inc.

Bandicotts & Bilbies. Ed. by J. Seebeck et al. 422p. (C). 1991. text ed. 110.00 (*0-949324-33-7*, Pub. by Surrey Beatty & Sons AT) St Mut.

Bandido. Jack Slade. (Lassiter Ser.: No. 2). 192p. 1983. pap. 2.25 (*0-8439-2005-X*) Dorchester Pub Co.

Bandidos: The Varieties of Latin American Banditry. Ed. by Richard W. Slatta. LC 86-12124. (Contributions to Criminology & Penology Ser.: No. 14). 229p. 1987. text ed. 49.95 (*0-313-25301-3*, SBN/, Greenwood Pr) Greenwood.

Banding Together: How Check Offs Will Revolutionize the Consumer Movement. Andrew Sharpless & Sarah Gallup. 44p. 1981. 5.00 (*0-936758-03-1*) Ctr Responsive Law.

Banding Together: The Rise of National Associations in American Higher Education, 1887-1950. Hugh Hawkins. 304p. 1992. text ed. 39.95 (*0-8018-4370-7*) Johns Hopkins.

Bandit. David Alexander. 256p. (Orig.). 1994. mass mkt. 4.99 (*0-380-76860-7*) Avon.

Bandit. Dave Sargent & Pat Sargent. (Animal Pride Ser.). (Illus.). 48p. (Orig.). (J). (gr. k-8). 1993. text ed. 11.95 (*1-56763-048-0*); pap. text ed. 5.95 (*1-56763-049-9*) Ozark Pub.

Bandit: Dossier of a Dangerous Dog. Vicki Hearne. LC 90-56346. 304p. 1992. pap. 12.00 (*0-06-099504-1*, PL) HarpC.

Bandit Bait. large type ed. Marshall Grover. (Linford Western Library). 272p. 1986. pap. 11.95 (*0-7089-6194-0*, Linford) Ulverscroft.

Bandit King: Lampiao of Brazil. Billy J. Chandler. LC 77-99275. 276p. 1978. 24.00 (*0-89096-050-X*); pap. 10.95 (*0-89096-194-8*) Tex A&M Univ Pr.

***Bandit Kings: From Jesse James to Pretty Boy Floyd.** Roger A. Bruns. 256p. 1995. 25.00 (*0-517-59153-7*, Crown) Crown Pub Group.

Bandit of Ashley Downs. Dave Jackson & Neta Jackson. (Trailblazer Bks.). 128p. (Orig.). (J). 1993. pap. 4.99 (*1-55661-270-2*) Bethany Hse.

Bandit of the Black Hills. large type ed. Max Brand. (General Ser.). 348p. 1991. lib. bdg. 18.95 (*0-8161-5078-8*) G K Hall.

Bandit of the Black Hills. Max Brand. reprint ed. lib. bdg. 20.95 (*0-88411-512-7*, Aeonian Pr) Amereon Ltd.

Bandit Wind. Slavko Janevski. Tr. by Charles Simic. (Struga Series of Macedonian Poetry). 80p. (Orig.). 1991. 15.95 (*0-931848-76-8*); pap. 8.95 (*0-931848-77-6*) Dryad Pr.

Bandit Years: A Gathering of Wolves. Mark Dugan. LC 86-30045. (Western Legacy Ser.). (Illus.). 128p. (Orig.). 1987. pap. 10.95 (*0-86534-101-X*) Sunstone Pr.

Banditry, Rebellion & Social Protest in Africa. Ed. by Donald Crummey. LC 85-27352. 404p. (Orig.). 1986. pap. text ed. 27.50 (*0-435-08011-3*) Heinemann.

Bandits. Panait Istrati. Tr. by William A. Drake. LC 72-116956. (Short Story Index Reprint Ser.). 1977. 21.95 (*0-8369-3460-1*) Ayer.

Bandits. Elmore Leonard. 384p. 1988. mass mkt. 5.99 (*0-446-30130-2*, Mysterious Paperbk) Warner Bks.

Bandits. large type ed. Elmore Leonard. 382p. 1987. lib. bdg. 18.95 (*0-8161-4297-1*) G K Hall.

Bandits: Pictorial History of U. S. Navy Adversary & U. S. Air Force Agressor A-C. Dave Parsons & Derk Nelson. (MBI Ser.). (Illus.). 96p. 1993. pap. 14.95 (*0-87938-623-1*) Motorbooks Intl.

Bandits & Bureaucrats: The Ottoman Route of State Centralization. Karen Barkey. LC 94-6099. (Wilder House Series in Politics, History, & Culture). 1994. 35.00x (*0-8014-2944-7*) Cornell U Pr.

Bandit's Blood. Clint Hawkins. (Saddle Tramp Ser.: No. 5). 1993. mass mkt. 3.50 (*0-06-100602-5*, Harp PBks) HarpC.

Bandit's Brazen Kiss. Kay McMahon. 1990. mass mkt. 4.50 (*0-8217-2863-6*) Zebra.

Bandits Embrace. Georgina Gentry. 1989. pap. 3.95 (*0-8217-2596-3*) Zebra.

Bandits in Republican China. Phil Billingsley. LC 87-30518. (Illus.). 400p. 1988. 45.00 (*0-8047-1406-1*) Stanford U Pr.

Bandit's Kiss. Mary L. Rich. (Wildflower Ser.). 336p. (Orig.). 1993. mass mkt. 4.99 (*1-55773-842-4*) Diamond.

Bandits of the Lonesome Ridge. large type ed. Gil Harmon. (Linford Western Library). 288p. 1993. pap. 14.95 (*0-7089-7438-4*, Linford) Ulverscroft.

***Bandits of Whiskey City, No. 2.** Robin Gibson. 1995. 17.95 (*0-8034-9112-3*, 095142) Bouregy.

Bandits, Prophets, & Messiahs: Popular Movements at the Time of Jesus. Richard Horsley. 1988. pap. text ed. 18.00 (*0-86683-993-3*) Harper SF.

Banditti of the Plains. A. S. Mercer. LC 54-5940. (Western Frontier Library: No. 2). (Illus.). 1975. reprint ed. pap. 10.95 (*0-8061-1315-4*) U of Okla Pr.

Banditti of the Rockies. Ed. by Jerome Peltier. 1964. 12.50 (*0-87018-048-7*) Ross.

Bandlet of Righteousness: An Ethiopian Book of the Dead. Tr. by E. A. Wallis-Budge. (COP.). 1984. pap. 5.95 (*0-916411-23-0*, Near Eastern) Holmes Pub.

Bandlet of Righteousness, an Ethiopian Book of the Dead. Lefafa Sedek. Tr. by E. A. Budge. LC 77-87667. (Luzac's Semitic Text & Translation Ser.: No. 19). reprint ed. 27.50 (*0-404-11349-4*) AMS Pr.

B&O Great Photos: A Portfolio. Charles S. Roberts. LC 94-94110. (Illus.). 208p. 1994. 40.00 (*0-934118-21-3*) Barnard Roberts.

Bandora: Its Music & Sources. Lyle Nordstrom. LC 92-19946. (Detroit Studies in Music Bibliography: No. 66). 1992. 30.00 (*0-89990-060-7*) Info Coord.

Bands: The Brass Band Movement in the 19th & 20th Centuries. Ed. by Trevor Herbert. (Popular Music in Britain Ser.). 192p. 1991. 95.00 (*0-335-09703-0*, Open Univ Pr); pap. 36.00 (*0-335-09702-2*, Open Univ Pr) Taylor & Francis.

Bands & Drummer Boys of the Civil War. Arthur Wise & Francis A. Lord. LC 79-14884. (Music Reprint Ser.). 1979. reprint ed. lib. bdg. 39.50 (*0-306-79571-X*) Da Capo.

Bands of America. Harry W. Schwartz. LC 74-23385. (Music Reprint Ser.). (Illus.). 320p. 1975. reprint ed. lib. bdg. 39.50 (*0-306-70672-5*) Da Capo.

Bands of Gold. Angela Benson. 352p. 1994. mass mkt. 4.99 (*0-7860-0072-4*) Windsor NY.

Bandura Cubana: Historia y Poesia. Mercedes Garcia-Turduri. 96p. (Orig.). (SPA.). 1992. pap. text ed. 12.95 (*0-918454-91-3*) Senda Nueva.

Bane in Kennedy's Existence. Bernard M. Bane. LC 66-30557. 169p. 1967. pap. 10.95 (*0-9600164-0-6*) BMB Pub Co.

Bane of the Black Sword. Michael Moorcock. 160p. 1987. pap. 4.99 (*0-441-04885-4*) Ace Bks.

Banff. Shelley S. Sateren. LC 89-33152. (National Parks Ser.). (Illus.). 48p. (J). (gr. 4-5). 1989. text ed. 13.95 (*0-89686-431-6*, Crstwood Hse) Silver Burdett Pr.

Banff & Buchan: An Illustrated Architectural Guide. Charles McKean. (Illus.). 176p. (C). 1990. pap. 35.00x (*1-85158-231-2*, Pub. by Rutland Pr UK) St Mut.

Banff-Cap Workshop on Thermal Field Theory: Proceedings of the 3rd Workshop on Thermal Field Theories. G. Kunstatter. Ed. by F. C. Khanna et al. 552p. 1994. text ed. 112.00 (*981-02-1772-2*) World Scientific Pub.

***Banff National Park - Lake Louise Area, Canada.** 1995. 8.99 (*0-614-07174-7*) Trails Illustrated.

Bang! Rollins. (Illus.). 144p. (Orig.). 1992. reprint ed. pap. 11.00 (*1-880985-03-9*) Two Thirteen Sixty-one.

Bang & Rattle. Sally Hewitt. LC 94-16948. (Get Set-- Go! Ser.). (Illus.). 24p. (J). (ps-3). 1994. lib. bdg. 10.80 (*0-516-07987-5*); pap. 4.95 (*0-516-47987-3*) Childrens.

Bang & Shout. Clara Vulliamy. LC 93-28123. (Illus.). 14p. (J). (ps). 1994. 4.95 (*1-56402-409-1*) Candlewick Pr.

Bang & the Whimper: Apocalypse & Entropy in American Literature. Zbigniew Lewicki. LC 83-12678. (Contributions in American Studies: No. 71). xvii, 135p. 1984. text ed. 45.00 (*0-313-23674-7*, LBW/, Greenwood Pr) Greenwood.

Bang! Bang! A Collection of Stories Intended to Recall Memories of the Nickel Library Days When Boys Were Superhuman & Murder a Fine Art. George Ade. LC 75-160929. (Short Story Index Reprint Ser.). (Illus.). 1977. reprint ed. 13.95 (*0-8369-3908-5*) Ayer.

Bang Book. Thomas Meyer. LC 76-137212. (Illus.). 1971. 12.50 (*0-912330-19-8*, Inland Bk); pap. 7.50 (*0-912330-20-1*, Inland Bk) Jargon Soc.

***Bang Pudding.** Steve Taylor. Ed. by Rob Conrad. (Illus.). 80p. 1995. pap. 9.95 (*0-9644901-0-2*, VAU 254-297) Harlem Lane.

Bang the Drum Slowly. Mark Harris. 1976. 20.95 (*0-8488-1042-2*) Amereon Ltd.

Bang the Drum Slowly. Mark Harris. 1981. reprint ed. lib. bdg. 25.95 (*0-89966-393-1*) Buccaneer Bks.

Bang the Drum Slowly. Mark Harris. LC 83-16922. viii, 243p. 1984. reprint ed. pap. 8.95 (*0-8032-7221-9*, Bison Books) U of Nebr Pr.

***Bang the Drum Slowly: Adapted from the Novel by Mack Harris.** Marc Harris. 1995. pap. 4.75 (*0-8222-1453-9*) Dramatists Play.

Bang: the Evolving Cosmos: Nobel Conference, No. XXVII. Ed. by Richard Fuller. (Illus.). 170p. 1994. lib. bdg. 45.00 (*0-8191-9468-9*); pap. text ed. 18.50 (*0-8191-9469-7*) U Pr of Amer.

Bangalee. Stephen Cosgrove. (Serendipity Bks.). 32p. (J). (gr. 1-4). 1978. pap. 3.95 (*0-8431-0550-X*) Price Stern.

Banged up Angel. Joyce Price. Ed. by M. L. Jones. 192p. (Orig.). (YA). 1993. pap. text ed. 6.95 (*1-882270-07-X*) Old Rugged Cross.

***Banging Book.** Bill Grossman. LC 94-18689. (Illus.). 32p. (J). 1995. lib. bdg. 14.89 (*0-06-024498-4*, Festival) HarpC Child Bks.

***Banging Book.** Bill Grossman. LC 94-18689. (Laura Geringer Bk.). (Illus.). 32p. (J). (ps-1). 1995. 12.95 (*0-06-024497-6*, Festival) HarpC Child Bks.

Bangka Tin & Mentok Pepper: Chinese Settlement on an Indonesian Island. Mary F. Heidhues. 270p. 1992. 52.35 (*981-3016-00-0*, Pub. by Inst SE Asian Studies SI) Ashgate Pub Co.

Bangkok. (Insight Guides Ser.). 1993. pap. 21.95 (*0-395-66267-2*) HM.

Bangkok. (Baedeker's Ser.). (Illus.). 144p. 1992. pap. 17.00 (*0-13-063553-7*, P-H Travel) P-H Gen Ref & Trav.

Bangkok. John Hookin. LC 90-63326. (Thailand Guides Ser.). (Illus.). 142p. 1991. pap. 14.95 (*0-8442-9699-6*, Passport Bks) NTC Pub Grp.

Bangkok. Loren K. Wiseman. (Twilight: Two Thousand Ser.). 104p. (Orig.). (YA). 1991. pap. 12.00 (*1-55878-074-2*) Game Designers.

***Bangkok: City Guide.** 2nd ed. Joe Cummings. (Illus.). 282p. 1995. pap. 9.95 (*0-86442-243-1*) Lonely Planet.

Bangkok: Portrait of a City. Philip Ward. (Travel Bks.: Vol. 3). (Illus.). 1974. pap. 12.50 (*0-902675-44-3*) Oleander Pr.

Bangkok & the Nights of Drunken Stupor. Scott Shaw. LC 89-23884. 104p. (Orig.). 1989. pap. 7.95 (*1-877792-06-3*) Buddha Rose.

***Bangkok Handbook.** 2nd ed. Michael Buckley. (Moon Travel Handbooks Ser.). (Illus.). 300p. (Orig.). 1995. pap. 13.95 (*1-56691-059-5*) Moon Pubns CA.

Bangkok Journal: A Fulbright Year in Thailand. Stephen A. Garrett. LC 85-19621. 281p. 1986. text ed. 19.95 (*0-8093-1275-1*) S Ill U Pr.

***Bangkok Yellow Pages.** (Illus.). 300p. (Orig.). 1994. pap. 295.00 (*0-7605-0699-X*) Rector Pr.

Bangkok, 1992-93. (Frommer's Comprehensive Travel Guide Ser.). (Illus.). 256p. 1991. pap. 13.00 (*0-13-334848-2*, P-H Travel) P-H Gen Ref & Trav.

Bangkok's Backstreets: A Guide to the Pleasures of the World's Most Open City. Bob Todd. 72p. (Orig.). 1986. pap. 9.95 (*0-939597-18-7*) Excogitations.

Bangla-Pak Politics. Shiv Lal. 430p. 1986. 120.00 (*0-317-61939-X*, Pub. by Archives Pubs II) St Mut.

Bangladesh. Donna Bailey & Anna Sproule. LC 90-9652. (Where We Live Ser.). (Illus.). 32p. (J). (gr. 1-4). 1990. lib. bdg. 19.97 (*0-8114-2559-2*) Raintree Steck-V.

***Bangladesh.** Steve Brace. LC 94-27843. (Economically Developing Countries Ser.). (Illus.). 48p. (J). (gr. 6-8). 1995. 15.95 (*1-56847-243-9*) Thomson Lrning.

Bangladesh. Roma Ghosh. (Lands & Peoples of the World Ser.). (Illus.). 88p. 1986. text ed. 12.95 (*0-86590-770-6*, Pub. by Sterling Pubs II) Apt Bks.

Bangladesh. Jason Laure. LC 92-8891. (Enchantment of the World Ser.). (Illus.). 128p. (J). (gr. 5-9). 1992. lib. bdg. 20.55 (*0-516-02609-7*) Childrens.

***Bangladesh.** A. K. Pavithran. LC 70-183008. 122p. 1971. 22.50 (*0-912004-02-9*) W W Gaunt.

Bangladesh: A Travel Survival Kit. 2nd ed. Jon Murray. (Illus.). 168p. 1991. pap. 10.95 (*0-86442-108-7*) Lonely Planet.

Bangladesh: Birth of a Nation. Marta R. Nicholas et al. Ed. by Ward Morehouse. 160p. 1971. pap. 3.50 (*0-88253-201-4*) Ind-US Inc.

Bangladesh: Business Risk Overview. Ed. by Lewis B. Sckolnick. 125p. (Orig.). (C). 1994. pap. text ed. 495.00 (*1-57205-562-6*) Rector Pr.

Bangladesh: Constitutional Quest for Autonomy 1950-1971. Moudud Ahmed. 389p. 1978. pap. 47.50 (*3-515-02908-7*) Coronet Bks.

Bangladesh: Domestic Politics, Vol. 2. Ed. by S. R. Chakravarty & N. V. Narain. xvi, 218p. 1986. 18.00 (*81-7003-068-4*, Pub. by S Asia Pubs II) S Asia.

***Bangladesh: From Stabilization to Growth.** LC 95-13326. (Country Study Ser.). 1995. write for info. (*0-8213-3227-9*) World Bank.

Bangladesh: Origins & Indian Ocean Relations, 1971-75. Dennis Wright. 310p. 1988. pap. text ed. 17.95 (*81-207-0839-3*, Pub. by Sterling Pubs II) Apt Bks.

***Bangladesh: Peasant Migration & the World Capitalist Economy.** Aminul H. Faraizi. (C). 1993. 19.00x (*81-207-1498-9*, Pub. by Sterling Plns Pvt II) S Asia.

Bangladesh: Peasant Migration & the World Capitalist Economy. Amiul H. Faraizi. 1993. 30.00 (*81-207-1499-7*, Pub. by Sterling Pubs II) Apt Bks.

Bangladesh: Problems of Governance. Rahman Sobhan. (Governance in South Asia Ser.). 1993. text ed. 35.00 (*0-685-63384-5*, Pub. by Konark Pubs Pvt Ltd II) Advent Bks Div.

Bangladesh: Reflections on the Water. James J. Novak. LC 92-41794. (Essential Asia Ser.). 1993. 24.95 (*0-253-34121-3*) Ind U Pr.

Bangladesh: Rivers in a Crowded Land. Vimala McClure. LC 88-35911. (Discovering Our Heritage Ser.). (Illus.). 128p. (J). (gr. 5 up). 1989. lib. bdg. 14.95 (*0-87518-404-9*, Dillon Silver Burdett) Silver Burdett Pr.

Bangladesh: Strategies for Enhancing the Role of Women in Economic Development. (Country Study Ser.). 182p. 1990. 10.95 (*0-8213-1630-3*, 11630) World Bank.

Bangladesh: The Nineteen Seventy-Nine Elections. S. R. Chakravarty. (C). 1988. 16.00 (*81-7003-088-9*, Pub. by S Asia Pubs II) S Asia.

Bangladesh: The Strength to Succeed. Jim Monan. (C). 1990. pap. text ed. 21.00 (*0-85598-127-X*, Pub. by Oxfam Pubns UK) St Mut.

Bangladesh: The Test Case for Development. J. Faaland & J. R. Parkinson. 203p. 1977. 19.95 (*0-318-37229-0*) Asia Bk Corp.

Bangladesh: Unlawful Killings & Torture in the Chittagong Hill Tracts. (Illus.). 1986. 5.00 (*0-86210-110-7*) Amnesty Intl USA.

Bangladesh: Whose Ideas, Whose Interests? Geoffrey Wood. 600p. (Orig.). 1994. pap. 37.95 (*1-85339-246-4*, Pub. by Intermed Tech UK) Women Ink.

Bangladesh & the South Asian International System. Dilara Choudhury. 380p. 1992. pap. 19.95 (*0-933511-17-5*); pap. 35.00 (*0-933511-15-9*) Kazi Pubns.

***Bangladesh Business Executive Outlook.** 70p. (Orig.). 1994. pap. 295.00 (*0-7605-1376-7*) Rector Pr.

Bangladesh Business Forecaster. Ed. by Lewis B. Sckolnick. 70p. (Orig.). (C). 1994. pap. 675.00 (*1-57205-334-8*) Rector Pr.

***Bangladesh Business Guide.** 300p. (Orig.). 1994. pap. 395.00 (*0-7605-0589-6*) Rector Pr.

***Bangladesh Business Intelligence Handbook.** (Illus.). 70p. (Orig.). 1994. pap. 295.00 (*0-7605-1008-3*) Rector Pr.

Bangladesh Economy: Some Selected Issues. Ed. by Franklin Vivekananda. 368p. (Orig.). 1989. pap. 127.50x (*91-86702-01-7*, Pub. by Almqv & Wiksell SW) Coronet Bks.

Bangladesh Fertilizer Sector. Yao H. Chuang et al. (Technical Bulletin Ser.: No. T-11). (Illus.). 61p. (Orig.). 1978. pap. 4.00 (*0-88090-010-5*) Intl Fertilizer.

***Bangladesh Foreign Investment.** (Illus.). 70p. (Orig.). 1994. pap. 45.00 (*0-7605-0964-6*) Rector Pr.

Bangladesh: From Mujib to Ershad: An Interpretive Study. Lawrence Ziring. 240p. 1993. 26.00 (*0-19-577420-5*) OUP.

Bangladesh in International Politics: Dilemmas of the Weaker States. Muhammad S. Huq. 300p. (C). 1993. 40.00 (*81-207-1407-5*) Apt Bks.

***Bangladesh under Mujib, Zia & Ershad.** S. R. Chakravarty. (C). 1995. text ed. 30.00 (*81-241-0309-7*, Pub. by Har-Anand Pubns II) S Asia.

Bangladesh Village: Political Conflict & Cohesion. Aminul Islam. (Illus.). 196p. (C). 1987. reprint ed. pap. text ed. 9.95 (*0-88133-297-6*) Waveland Pr.

Bangladesh, Vol. 1: History & Culture. Ed. by S. R. Chakravarty & Virendra Narain. xvi, 220p. 1986. 12.50 (*0-685-58182-9*, Pub. by South Asian Pubs Pvt Ltd II) Nataraj Bks.

Bangladesh, Vol. 1: History & Culture. Ed. by S. R. Chakravarty. 1985. 20.00 (*0-685-12125-9*, Pub. by S Asia Pubs II) S Asia.

An Asterisk (*) at the beginning of an entry indicates that the title is appearing in BIP for the first time.

B

An Asterisk (*) at the beginning of an entry indicates that the title is appearing in BIP for the first time.

***Bank of Fear: A Novel.** large type ed. David Ignatius. LC 94-40719. 576p. 1995. 22.95 (*0-7838-1185-3*, Large Print Bks) Hall.

Bank of Lebanon. Badrud-Din. (C). 1992. text ed. 59.00 (*0-86187-461-7*, Pub. by Pinter Pubs UK) St Martin.

Bank of North Dakota. Alvin S. Tostlebe. LC 74-82241. (Columbia University. Studies in the Social Sciences: No. 254). reprint ed. 21.50 (*0-404-51254-2*) AMS Pr.

Bank of North Dakota: A Monetary Experiment. 1991. lib. bdg. 69.00 (*0-8490-4445-6*) Gordon Pr.

Bank of North Dakota: An Experiment in State Ownership. Rozanne E. Junker. LC 89-1194. 180p. (Orig.). 1989. pap. 9.95 (*0-931832-29-2*) Fithian Pr.

Bank of North Dakota & How Its Model Can Save America from Bankruptcy. 1992. lib. bdg. 75.00 (*0-8490-8736-8*) Gordon Pr.

Bank of the United States. Thomas Benton. 1972. 59.95 (*0-87968-701-0*) Gordon Pr.

Bank Officer's Handbook of Commercial Banking Laws. 6th ed. Milton R. Schroder. 1989. 115.00 (*0-7913-0112-5*) Warren Gorham & Lamont.

Bank Officer's Handbook of Commercial Banking Laws, No. 1. 6th suppl. ed. Milton R. Schroder. 1992. Supplemented semi-annually, write for info. 54.00 (*0-685-56117-8*) Warren Gorham & Lamont.

Bank Officer's Handbook of Commercial Banking Laws, No. 2. 6th suppl. ed. Milton R. Schroder. 1992. 54.00 (*0-685-56118-6*) Warren Gorham & Lamont.

Bank Officer's Handbook of Government Regulations. Stephen K. Huber. 1024p. 1989. boxed 160.00 (*0-7913-0352-7*) Warren Gorham & Lamont.

Bank Officer's Handbook of Government Regulations, No. 1. suppl. ed. Stephen K. Huber. 1024p. 1992. Supplemented semi-annually, write for info. 48.00 (*0-685-56115-1*) Warren Gorham & Lamont.

Bank Officer's Handbook of Government Regulations, No. 2. suppl. ed. Stephen K. Huber. 1024p. 1992. 50.00 (*0-685-56116-X*) Warren Gorham & Lamont.

Bank on It. Sherryl Woods. 240p. (Orig.). 1993. mass mkt. 4.99 (*0-446-36404-5*) Warner Bks.

Bank on It. large type ed. Sherryl Woods. LC 94-17921. 396p. (Orig.). 1994. pap. 17.95 (*0-7862-0264-5*) Thorndike Pr.

Bank Operating Credit Risk: Assessing & Controlling Credit Risk in Bank Operating. Paul F. Mayland. 1993. 60.00 (*1-55738-346-4*) Probus Pub Co.

Bank Operations. New England Banking Institute Staff. 184p. 1991. pap. 30.00 (*0-536-57797-8*) Ginn Pr.

Bank Operations Consolidation Manual: Combining & Streamlining Operations & Systems. Paul A. Carrubba. 1991. 150.00 (*1-55738-305-7*) Probus Pub Co.

Bank Operations Management: Finding & Exploiting Hidden Profit Opportunities Inside Your Bank. Nicholas J. Santoro. 250p. 1992. 55.00 (*1-55738-332-4*) Probus Pub Co.

Bank Planning Models. S. Sunderland. 1990. pap. 68.00 (*0-7121-5621-6*, Pub. by Northcote UK) St Mut.

Bank Policies & Procedures Manual. James A. Grapengeter & Vicki Grapengeter. 368p. 1989. text ed. 79.95 (*0-13-058488-6*) P-H.

Bank President. Daniel I. Lewis & Winnie Lee. (Chief Executive Ser.). 64p. (Orig.). 1984. disk 74.95 (*0-915847-00-0*); pap. 9.95 (*0-915847-02-7*) Lewis Lee Corp.

Bank Productivity: Improvement Techniques. Kent S. Belasco. 1990. 45.00 (*1-55520-168-7*) Probus Pub Co.

Bank Profitability: Financial Statements of Banks - Statistical Supplement 1981-1990. OECD Staff. 194p. (Orig.). (ENG & FRE.). 1992. pap. 37.00 (*92-64-03531-1*) OECD.

Bank Profitability: Financial Statements of Banks 1983-1992. OECD Staff. 190p. (Orig.). 1994. pap. 39.00 (*92-64-04114-1*) OECD.

***Bank Profitability, Financial Statements of Banks, 1984-1993.** 198p. (Orig.). (ENG & FRE.). 1995. pap. 52.00 (*92-64-04363-2*, Pub. by Econ & Coop Dev FR) OECD.

Bank Profitability Statistical Supplement: Financial Statements of Banks 1982-1991. OECD Staff. 200p. (Orig.). 1993. pap. 42.00 (*92-64-03719-5*) OECD.

***Bank Protection Deskbook: Establishing, Managing & Regulating an Effective Security Program.** T. Herbert Stevenson. 297p. 1991. 125.00 (*1-55520-205-5*) Probus Pub Co.

Bank Protection for the Community Bank. T. Herbert Stevenson. 160p. 1989. ring bd. 75.00 (*1-55520-163-6*) Probus Pub Co.

Bank Reconciliation Projects. 3rd ed. Robert J. McCullough & Kenneth Everard. 1987. 7.08 (*0-02-830530-2*) Glencoe.

Bank Records Retention Deskbook: Developing & Managing a Fail-Safe System. T. Herbert Stevenson. 1991. 125.00 (*1-55738-308-1*) Probus Pub Co.

Bank Regulatory Management Deskbook. T. Herbert Stevenson. 1991. 195.00 (*1-55738-309-X*) Probus Pub Co.

***Bank Regulatory Structure: The Federal Republic of Germany.** (Illus.). 52p. (Orig.). (C). 1994. pap. text ed. 50.00x (*0-7881-1083-7*) Diane Pub.

Bank Robber. Giles Tippette. 1993. pap. 4.50 (*0-515-11220-8*) Jove Pubns.

***Bank Robbers.** C. Clark Criscuolo. LC 94-36980. 1995. 21.00 (*0-312-11750-7*) St Martin.

***Bank Sales of Nondeposit Investment Products: A Compliance Guide.** James M. Rockett & Keith D. Ungles. 600p. (Orig.). 1994. pap. 130.00 (*0-8366-0028-2*) Clark Boardman Callaghan.

Bank Secrecy. Cliff E. Cook. Ed. by Mary L. Smith. (Illus.). 292p. 1991. 46.00 (*0-89982-374-2*, 050350) Am Bankers.

Bank Secrecy Act: Exemption Regulations Clarified. Bill Landreth. Ed. by Carolyn Zimmerman. LC 88-70571. (Orig.). 1988. pap. 10.00 (*0-317-91177-5*) Amherst Ent.

Bank Security Desk Reference, No. 2462. rev. suppl. ed. Richard F. Cross. 1991. 58.50 (*0-7913-1074-4*) Warren Gorham & Lamont.

Bank Security Desk Reference, No. 2462. 2nd rev. ed. Richard F. Cross. 1988. 130.00 (*0-7913-0043-9*) Warren Gorham & Lamont.

***Bank Security Documents.** 2nd ed. James R. Lingard. 1993. 175.00 (*0-406-00581-8*, U.K.) Butterworth Legal Pubs.

Bank Security Report. 131.00 (*0-685-69631-6*, BSR) Warren Gorham & Lamont.

Bank Shot. Donald E. Westlake. 192p. 1989. reprint ed. mass mkt. 5.50 (*0-445-40883-9*, Mysterious Paperbk) Warner Bks.

Bank Stock Prices & the Bank Capital Problem. David Durand. (Occasional Papers: No. 54). 86p. 1957. reprint ed. 22.40 (*0-87014-368-9*); reprint ed. mic. film 20.00 (*0-685-61313-5*) Natl Bur Econ Res.

Bank Strategic Management & Marketing. Derek F. Channon. LC 85-201225. 406p. 1986. text ed. 65.95 (*0-471-90383-3*) Wiley.

Bank Strategies for the Nineteen Nineties. Bain et al. 1986. 75.00 (*0-85297-162-1*, Pub. by Inst Bankers UK) St Mut.

Bank Structure of the U. S. S. R. 1992. lib. bdg. 75.00 (*0-8490-8720-1*) Gordon Pr.

Bank Supervision Around the World. Richard Dale. (Report Ser.). 76p. 1982. pap. write for info. (*1-56708-056-1*) Grp of Thirty.

Bank Systems Management: The Project Management Guide to Planning & Implementing Systems. Kent S. Belasco. 1993. 60.00 (*1-55738-380-4*) Probus Pub Co.

Bank Systems Selection Deskbook. Geoffrey H. Wold & Robert F. Shriver. 300p. 1992. 185.00 (*1-55738-324-3*) Probus Pub Co.

***Bank Tax Desk Book, 1995.** 19th ed. Ronald W. Blasi. LC 94-41755. 1995. pap. text ed. 135.00 (*0-471-11303-4*) Wiley.

***Bank Technology Review: A Bank Manager's Guide to New Technology Products, Systems & Applications.** Tom Groenfeldt. 250p. 1995. 37.50 (*1-55738-761-3*) Probus Pub Co.

Bank Teller's Handbook: Everything a Teller Needs to Know to Succeed. 5th ed. Joan G. Grapes. 350p. 1993. pap. 16.95 (*1-55738-347-2*) Probus Pub Co.

Bank Teller's Report. 103.00 (*0-685-70156-5*, BTR) Warren Gorham & Lamont.

Bank Valuation Handbook: A Market-Based Approach to Valuing a Bank. Hazel J. Johnson. 325p. 1992. 75.00 (*1-55738-355-3*) Probus Pub Co.

Bankcard Barometer 91. Robert B. McKinley. 200p. (Orig.). (C). 1991. pap. text ed. 385.00 (*0-943329-72-8*) RAM Res Pub.

Bankcard Barometer 91, No. 1: Cumulative Supplement. rev. ed. Robert B. McKinley. 50p. (C). 1991. pap. text ed. 120.00 (*0-943329-73-6*) RAM Res Pub.

Bankcard Barometer 91, No. 2: Cumulative Supplement. rev. ed. Robert B. McKinley. 50p. (C). 1991. pap. text ed. 120.00 (*0-943329-74-4*) RAM Res Pub.

Bankcard Barometer 91, No. 3: Cumulative Supplement. rev. ed. Robert B. McKinley. 50p. (C). 1991. pap. text ed. 120.00 (*0-943329-75-2*) RAM Res Pub.

Bankcard Barometer 91, No. 4: Cumulative Supplement. rev. ed. Robert B. McKinley. 50p. (C). 1991. pap. text ed. 120.00 (*0-943329-76-0*) RAM Res Pub.

Bankcard Barometer 93. Robert B. McKinley. 1000p. (C). 1993. pap. text ed. 995.00 (*0-943329-80-9*) RAM Res Pub.

Bankcard Business. Michael J. Auriemma & Robert S. Coley. Ed. by Veida Dehmlow. (Illus.). 350p. (C). 1992. pap. text ed. 46.00 (*0-89982-335-1*) Am Bankers.

Banked Fire: Poems: 1929-1976. 2nd ed. George B. Johnston. viii, 24p. 1989. reprint ed. pap. 3.00 (*0-9616760-4-3*, PS3560-0388B3) White Rhino Pr.

Bankei Zen. Ed. by Yoshito Hakeda. Tr. by Peter Haskel. 240p. 1990. pap. 11.95 (*0-8021-3184-0*) Grove-Atltic.

Banken & Borsenrecht der EWG. Diether Hoffmann. 463p. 1990. pap. 53.00 (*0-317-04144-4*, Pub. by Nomos Verlags GW) Intl Bk Import.

Banker. Dick Francis. 1986. mass mkt. 5.95 (*0-449-21199-1*, Crest) Fawcett.

Banker. Cheng Naishan. Tr. & Intro. by Britten Dean. 1993. 19.95 (*0-8351-2492-4*) China Bks.

Banker & the Bear: The Story of a Corner in Lard. Henry K. Webster. LC 68-57559. (Muckrakers Ser.). reprint ed. lib. bdg. 16.00 (*0-8398-2159-X*) Irvington.

Banker or Retailer? R. Reed. (C). 1989. 39.00 (*0-85297-245-8*, Pub. by Inst Bankers UK) St Mut.

Banker Tells You How to Borrow All the Money You'll Ever Need. Ben B. Boothe. 304p. 1993. pap. 12.95 (*0-8092-3719-9*) Contemp Bks.

Banker to the Third World: U. S. Portfolio Investment in Latin America 1900-1986. Barbara Stallings. LC 86-24988. (Studies in International Political Economy: Vol. 18). 450p. 1987. pap. 14.00 (*0-520-06164-0*) U CA Pr.

Banker to the Third World: U. S. Portfolio Investment in Latin America, 1900-1986. Barbara Stallings. LC 86-24988. (Studies in International Political Economy: No. 18). (Illus.). 452p. reprint ed. pap. 128.90 (*0-7837-4678-4*, 2044425) Bks Demand.

Bankers Almanac 1985. Richard B. Miller. (Bankers Reference Ser.). 464p. reprint ed. pap. 132.30 (*0-8357-5962-8*, 2052181) Bks Demand.

Bankers & Beef: An Original Press Anthology. Ed. by Dan C. McCurry & Richard E. Rubenstein. LC 74-30618. (American Farmers & the Rise of Agribusiness Ser.). (Illus.). 1975. reprint ed. 33.95 (*0-405-06763-1*) Ayer.

Bankers & Bureaucrats: The Development of Capital & the Role of the State in Thailand. Kevin Hewison. LC 89-51448. (Monograph Ser: No. 34). xiv, 320p. 30.00 (*0-938692-41-0*); pap. 17.00 (*0-685-58490-9*) Yale U SE Asia.

Bankers & Diplomats in China, 1917-1925: The Anglo-American Relationship. Roberta A. Daver. 324p. 1981. 35.00 (*0-7146-3118-3*, Pub. by F Cass Pubs UK) Intl Spec Bk.

Bankers & Pashas: International Finance & Economic Imperialism in Egypt. David S. Landes. (Illus.). 370p. 1980. pap. 17.50 (*0-674-06165-9*) HUP.

Bankers' & Public Authorities' Management of Risks: Proceedings of the Second International Banking Colloquium Held by the Ecole des Hautes Etudes Commerciales de l'Universite de Lausanne. Ed. by Zuhayr Mikdashi. 225p. 1990. text ed. 49.95 (*0-312-03621-3*) St Martin.

Bankers & Regulators. Intro. by Hans F. Sennholz. iv, 174p. (Orig.). 1993. pap. 14.95 (*0-910614-91-1*) Foun Econ Ed.

Bankers As Brokers: The Complete Guide to Selling Mutual Funds, Annuities & Other Fee-Based Investment Products. Merlin Gackle & Bob Andelman. 1994. 37.50 (*1-55738-702-8*) Probus Pub Co.

Banker's Balances. Leonard L. Watkins. Ed. by Stuart Bruchey. LC 80-1170. (Rise of Commercial Banking Ser.). (Illus.). 1981. reprint ed. lib. bdg. 41.95 (*0-405-13680-3*) Ayer.

Banker's Blood. Bill Rouleau. 1995. pap. 10.95 (*0-9627860-1-2*) Lone Oak MN.

Banker's Confession: A Christian Guide to Getting Out of Debt. Gary Sanseri. 145p. 1991. pap. 9.95 (*1-880045-06-0*) Back Home Indust.

Bankers Conspiracy. Arthur Kitson. 1972. 69.95 (*0-87968-702-9*) Gordon Pr.

Banker's Desk Book. Richard B. Miller. 400p. 1990. text ed. 69.95 (*0-13-058538-6*) P-H.

Bankers Documentary Credits. 3rd ed. F. M. Ventris. 1990. 145.00 (*1-85044-350-5*) Lloyds London Pr.

Banker's Dream: A Fiction - an Argument for the Free Coinage of Silver. Thomas H. Proctor. LC 74-30648. (American Farmers & the Rise of Agribusiness Ser.). 1975. reprint ed. 24.95 (*0-405-06820-4*) Ayer.

Banker's Guide to Better Service, Bigger Profits. A. Lorri Manasse & Claire Schoeppler. 1989. pap. 49.95 (*1-55840-053-2*) Exec Ent Pubns.

Banker's Guide to Loan Participations. 2nd ed. Deborah S. Prutzman. 77p. (C). 1994. 75.00 (*0-89982-376-9*) Am Bankers.

Banker's Guide to New Growth Opportunities. Thomas Thamara. 540p. 1988. text ed. 59.95 (*0-13-056284-X*, Busn) P-H.

Banker's Guide to the Community Reinvestment Act: Case Studies of 33 Institutions. Kevin Kane. 1991. 95.00 (*1-55871-239-9*, BSP191) BNA.

Banker's Handbook. 3rd ed. Ed. by William H. Baughn et al. 1,347p. 1988. text ed. 80.00 (*1-55623-043-5*) Irwin Prof Pubng.

Bankers Handbook for Asia: 1988 Guide to Banks & Finance Companies in Asia Plus 22 Countries of Iran-Arab Region. 12th ed. Ed. by Amitabha Chowdhury. 449p. 1987. 60.00 (*962-7185-01-9*) Am Overseas Bk Co.

Banker's Handbook of Letters & Letter Writing: A Complete Collection of Time-Saving. 3rd ed. Jeffrey L. Seglin. 1992. 65.00 (*1-55738-326-X*) Probus Pub Co.

Bankers in Bolivia: A Study in American Foreign Investment. Margaret C. Marsh. LC 76-99250. reprint ed. 19.75 (*0-404-04190-6*) AMS Pr.

Bankers in the Selling Role: A Consultative Guide to Cross Selling Financial Services. 2nd ed. Linda Richardson. LC 84-11937. 177p. 1984. text ed. 55.00 (*0-471-81005-3*, Wiley-Interscience) Wiley.

Bankers in the Selling Role: A Consultative Guide to Cross-Selling Financial Services. 2nd ed. Linda Richardson. 192p. 1992. pap. text ed. 22.50 (*0-471-57265-9*) Wiley.

Bankers' Lending Techniques. Ed. by R. Rouse. (C). 1989. 125.00 (*0-85297-228-8*, Pub. by Inst Bankers UK) St Mut.

Bankers Letter of the Law. 180.00 (*0-685-69614-6*, BLL) Warren Gorham & Lamont.

Bankers' Liability: Risks & Remedies. Ed. by Dennis Campbell & Rudolf Meroni. LC 93-14368. 1993. write for info. (*90-6433-728-4*) Kluwer Law Tax Pubs.

Bankers Magazine. 105.00 (*0-685-69633-2*, BM) Warren Gorham & Lamont.

Banker's Place. Dorothy B. Ille. LC 92-63253. 82p. (YA). (gr. 6-11). 1993. 7.95 (*1-55523-591-3*) Winston-Derek.

Banker's Portfolio of Model Letters. Fay W. Henry & Donald L. Henry. 610p. 1988. text ed. 59.95 (*0-13-056524-5*, Busn) P-H.

Banker's Real Estate Series, 3 pts. Incl. Advanced Income Property Underwriting. 1990. 285.00 (*0-685-63283-0*); Financial Statement Analysis for Real Estate. 1990. 150.00 (*0-685-63284-9*); Fundamentals of Income Property Underwriting. 1990. 225.00 (*0-685-63285-7*); 1990. Set disk write for info. (*0-318-69953-2*) Am Bankers.

Bankers Remedy of Set Off. Sheelagh McCraken. 300p. 1993. 180.00 (*0-406-00909-0*, UK) Butterworth Legal Pubs.

Banker's Secret. Marc Eisenson. 1990. 14.95 (*0-394-58604-2*, Villard Bks) Random.

Banker's Secret: Your Mortgage Is a Great Investment. Marc Eisenson. 224p. (Orig.). 1989. pap. 9.95 (*0-943973-05-8*) Good Advice Pr.

Banker's Secret Credit Card Software Package (IBM Version) Marc Eisenson. 228p. 1991. disk, pap. 25.00 (*0-943973-09-0*) Good Advice Pr.

Banker's Secret Software Package for Mortgages & Other Loans (IBM Version) rev. ed. Marc Eisenson & Nancy Castleman. 248p. 1991. disk 39.95 (*0-943973-08-2*) Good Advice Pr.

***Banker's Secret Software Package for Mortgages & Other Loans (Macintosh Version)** rev. ed. Marc Eisenson & Nancy Castleman. 248p. 1992. disk 39.95 (*0-943973-10-4*) Good Advice Pr.

Bankers' Services & Lending Handbook. S. Sales & I. Ibbetson. (C). 1989. 50.00 (*0-85297-260-1*, Pub. by Inst Bankers UK) St Mut.

Bankers, Statesmen & Economists. Paul Einzig. LC 67-30185. (Essay Index Reprint Ser.). 1977. 20.95 (*0-8369-0410-9*) Ayer.

Bankers Versus Consumers. G. W. Mallon. 1972. 59.95 (*0-87968-703-7*) Gordon Pr.

Bankers Who Sell: Improving Selling Effectiveness in Banking. Leonard L. Berry et al. LC 84-73198. 1985. 37.50 (*0-87094-629-3*) Irwin Prof Pubng.

Bankim-Tilak-Dayanand. Sri Aurobindo. 49p. 0.50 (*0-317-17425-8*) Auromere.

***Bankimchandra: Essays in Perspective.** Ed. by Sahitya Akademi. (C). 1994. 62.00 (*81-7201-554-2*, Pub. by Sahitya Akademi II) S Asia.

Banking. Charles K. Coe. (Getting the Most from Professional Services Ser.). 20p. (Orig.). 1979. pap. 4.00 (*0-89854-047-X*) U of GA Inst Govt.

Banking. Nancy Dunnan. Ed. by Emily Easton. (Inside Track Library). (Illus.). 128p. (YA). (gr. 12 up). 1990. lib. bdg. 12.95 (*0-382-09917-6*); pap. 5.95 (*0-382-24028-6*) Silver Pr.

Banking. Betty Herzog. (Follet Coping Skills Ser.). 64p. 1988. pap. text ed. 5.50 (*0-8428-2331-X*) Cambridge Bk.

Banking. deluxe ed. Theodore A. Platz, Jr. (Barron's Business Library). 320p. 1991. 14.95 (*0-8120-4542-4*) Barron.

Banking: A Dynamic Business. Don Wright. 1983. 44.95 (*0-8359-0380-X*, Reston) P-H.

***Banking: Establish Your Private International Bank Handbook.** (Illus.). 70p. (Orig.). 1994. pap. 295.00 (*0-7605-0978-6*) Rector Pr.

Banking & Business in South Africa. Ed. by Stuart Jones. LC 87-32245. 256p. 1988. text ed. 45.00 (*0-312-00517-2*) St Martin.

Banking & Credit. Davis Dewey & Martin Shugrue. Ed. by Stuart Bruchey. LC 80-1144. (Rise of Commercial Banking Ser.). (Illus.). 1981. reprint ed. lib. bdg. 49.95 (*0-405-13646-3*) Ayer.

Banking & Credit System of the U. S. S. R. O. Kuschpeta. (Tilburg Studies in Economics: Vol. 18). 1978. lib. bdg. 66.00 (*90-207-0557-1*) Kluwer Ac.

Banking & Debtor-Creditor. Ed. by Will G. Barber. (Texas Court's Charge Ser.: Vol. 5). 370p. 1992. ring bd. 85.00 (*0-409-25683-8*) Michie Butterworth.

Banking & EEC Law: Commentary. Ed. by Martijn Van Empel. (Amsterdam Financial Ser.). 1991. ring bd. 155.00 (*90-6544-952-3*) Kluwer Law Tax Pubs.

Banking & Empire in Iran: The History of the British Bank of the Middle East, Vol. 1. Geoffrey Jones. (Illus.). 406p. 1986. 89.95 (*0-521-32322-3*) Cambridge U Pr.

Banking & Finance - Accounts, Audits & Practice. Dennis W. Cox. 600p. 1993. U.K. text ed. 210.00 (*0-406-00846-9*, U.K.) Butterworth Legal Pubs.

Banking & Finance Collections. Ed. by Jean Deuss. LC 83-26466. (Special Collections Ser.: Vol. 2, No. 3). 164p. 1984. text ed. 49.95 (*0-86656-252-4*) Haworth Pr.

Banking & Finance in Japan: An Introduction to the Tokyo Market. Kazuo Tatewaki. 256p. 1991. 74.50 (*0-415-00992-8*, A4890) Routledge.

Banking & Finance of the People's Republic of China. Jimmy W. Hsu. 250p. (Orig.). 1990. 95.00 (*0-685-30392-6*) Asiatic Corp.

Banking & Finance to 1913. Ed. by Larry E. Schweikart. (Encyclopedia of American Business History & Biography Ser.). 352p. 1990. 85.00 (*0-8160-2193-7*) Facts on File.

Banking & Finance, 1913-1989. Ed. by Larry E. Schweikart. (Encyclopedia of American Business History & Biography Ser.). (Illus.). 352p. 1990. 85.00 (*0-8160-2194-5*) Facts on File.

***Banking & Financial Control in Reforming Planned Economies.** Haiqun Yang. LC 95-14399. 1995. write for info. (*0-312-12724-3*) St Martin.

Banking & Financial Dictionary. E. Assiouly. 338p. (ARA, ENG & FRE.). 1980. pap. 75.00 (*0-8288-0323-4*, M9767) Fr & Eur.

Banking & Financial Institutions Law in a Nutshell. 3rd ed. William A. Lovett. LC 92-18870. (Nutshell Ser.). 470p. (C). 1992. pap. text ed. 18.00 (*0-314-00929-9*) West Pub.

***Banking & Financial Systems in Selected Countries.** Ed. by James R. Gale. LC 94-38439. 228p. 1995. text ed. 89.95 (*0-7734-9143-0*) E Mellen.

Banking & Industrialization in Austria-Hungary: The Role of Banks in the Industrialization of the Czech Crownlands, 1873-1914. Richard L. Rudolph. LC 75-2736. 303p. reprint ed. pap. 86.40 (*0-8357-5963-6*, 2024525) Bks Demand.

Banking & Lending Institution Forms with Commentary. 4th ed. Jacob Reby & James A. Douglas. 1992. 245.00 (*0-685-69634-0*, MBF) Warren Gorham & Lamont.

***Banking & Lending Practice.** 3rd ed. P. M. Weaver. 354p. 1994. pap. 36.00 (*0-949379-18-2*, Pub. by Law Bk Co) W W Gaunt.

Banking & Monetary Statistics: Supplement. Federal Reserve System, U. S. Board of Governors Staff. LC 75-41278. 1976. reprint ed. 82.50 (*0-404-14621-X*) AMS Pr.

Banking & Oil: The History of the British Bank of the Middle East, Vol. 2. Geoffrey Jones. 377p. 1987. 94.95 (*0-521-32323-1*) Cambridge U Pr.

An Asterisk (*) at the beginning of an entry indicates that the title is appearing in BIP for the first time.

Banking & Secured Transactions under the Uniform Commercial Code: Course of Study Transcript. 274p. 1968. pap. 2.50 (*0-317-30889-0*, B384) Am Law Inst.

Banking & Small Business. Derek Hansen. Ed. by Michael Barker. (Studies in State Development Policy: Vol. 12). 113p. (Orig.). (C). 1981. pap. 16.95 (*0-934842-11-6*) CSPA.

Banking & Stock Exchange Six Languages Dictionary. Bobylev. 288p. (ENG, FRE, GER, ITA, RUS & SPA.). 1992. pap. 49.95 (*0-7859-1086-7*, 5870120071) Fr & Eur.

Banking & the Business Cycle: A Study of the Great Depression in the United States. C. A. Phillips et al. LC 70-172226. (Right Wing Individualist Tradition in America Ser.). 1976. reprint ed. 24.95 (*0-405-00435-4*) Ayer.

Banking & the Credit System in Georgia, 1810-1860. Thomas P. Govan. LC 77-14786. (Dissertations in American Economic History Ser.). 1978. 31.95 (*0-405-11036-7*) Ayer.

Banking & the Financial Services Act. W. J. Blair et al. 300p. 1993. boxed 136.00 (*0-406-13520-7*, UK) Butterworth Legal Pubs.

Banking & the Promotion of Technological Development. Nicholas Jequier & Yao-Su Hu. LC 88-6628. 256p. 1989. text ed. 55.00 (*0-312-02085-6*) St Martin.

Banking Around the World: A Treatise on Comparative Banking. J. N. Mongia. 583p. 1982. 35.00 (*0-318-37331-9*) Asia Bk Corp.

Banking Automation, 1970-71, 2 vols. Ed. by Geoffrey W. Dummer et al. 1971. 829.00 (*0-08-016120-0*, Pub. by Pergamon Repr UK) Franklin.

Banking Crimes: Fraud, Money Laundering & Embezzlement. John K. Villa. LC 87-10333. 1987. ring bd. 125.00 (*0-87632-546-0*) Clark Boardman Callaghan.

Banking Crises: Cases & Issues. Ed. by V. Sundararajan & Tomas T. Balino. x, 375p. 1991. 22.50 (*1-55775-187-0*) Intl Monetary.

Banking Crisis: The End of an Epoch. Jules I. Bogen & Marcus Nadler. Ed. by Stuart Bruchey. LC 80-1179. (Rise of Commercial Banking Ser.). 1981. reprint ed. lib. bdg. 20.95 (*0-405-13670-6*) Ayer.

Banking Crisis & Recovery under the Roosevelt Administration. J. F. O'Connor. LC 73-171696. (FDR & the Era of the New Deal Ser.). 168p. 1971. reprint ed. lib. bdg. 27.50 (*0-306-70366-1*) Da Capo.

Banking Crisis of Nineteen Thirty-Three. Susan E. Kennedy. LC 72-91666. 280p. 1973. 30.00 (*0-8131-1285-0*) U Pr of Ky.

***Banking, Currency, & Finance in Europe Between the Wars.** Ed. by Charles Feinstein. (Illus.). 512p. 1995. 75.00 (*0-19-828803-4*) OUP.

Banking, Currency, the Money Trust & War, 3 vols. Charles A. Lindbergh. 1972. 300.00 (*0-87968-704-5*) Gordon Pr.

Banking Dictionary. Hans Klaus. 264p. (ENG & FRE.). 1984. 79.95 (*0-8288-0317-X*, M15030) Fr & Eur.

Banking Dictionary. Hans Klaus. (ENG & SPA.). 1990. lib. bdg. 75.00 (*0-8288-3899-2*, F134020) Fr & Eur.

Banking Dictionary. A. Moriwaki. (ENG & JPN.). 1990. lib. bdg. 85.00 (*0-8288-3900-X*, F117170) Fr & Eur.

Banking Dictionary: English - American German. Ed. by K. Klaus. 1990. 75.00 (*0-7121-5626-7*, Pub. by Northcote UK) St Mut.

Banking Dictionary: English-French. K. Klaus. 1990. pap. 72.00 (*3-258-03340-4*, Pub. by Northcote UK) St Mut.

Banking en Francais: The French Banks of Quebec, 1835-1925. Ronald Rudin. (Social History of Canada Ser.: No. 38). 216p. 1985. 27.50 (*0-8020-2560-9*); pap. 10.95 (*0-8020-6579-1*) U of Toronto Pr.

Banking for People: I. Social Banking & New Poverty, II. Consumer Debts & Unemployment in Europe, National Reports. Ed. by Udo Reifner & Janet Ford. xxxii, 673p. (C). 1992. lib. bdg. 169.25 (*3-11-012675-3*) De Gruyter.

Banking History of Louisiana. Stephen A. Caldwell. Ed. by Stuart Bruchey. LC 80-1137. (Rise of Commercial Banking Ser.). 1981. reprint ed. lib. bdg. 15.95 (*0-405-13637-4*) Ayer.

***Banking in an Unregulated Environment: California 1878-1905.** rev. ed. Lynne P. Doti. LC 95-14436. (Financial Sector of the American Economy Ser.). (Illus.). 184p. 1995. 48.00 (*0-8153-1873-1*) Garland.

Banking in Boston. S. N. Davis. (C). 1989. text ed. 40.00 (*0-902662-64-3*, Pub. by R K Pubns UK); pap. 21.00 (*0-685-65760-4*, Pub. by R K Pubns UK) St Mut.

Banking in California Eighteen Forty-Nine to Nineteen Hundred Ten. Benjamin C. Wright. Ed. by Stuart Bruchey. LC 80-1173. (Rise of Commercial Banking Ser.). (Illus.). 1981. reprint ed. lib. bdg. 20.95 (*0-405-13686-2*) Ayer.

Banking in Europe: The Single Market. Rob Dixon. 160p. 1991. 62.50 (*0-415-05572-5*, A5649); pap. 19.95 (*0-415-05573-3*, A5486) Routledge.

Banking in Europe after 1992. Carlos J. Gonzalez. LC 93-18024. 158p. 1993. 57.95 (*1-85521-362-1*, Pub. by Dartmth Pub UK) Ashgate Pub Co.

Banking in France. Ed. by Christian De Boissier. 192p. 1990. 67.50 (*0-415-01029-2*, A4520) Routledge.

Banking in Frontier Iowa, 1836-1865. Erling A. Erickson. LC 75-146031. 195p. reprint ed. pap. 55.60 (*0-8357-5964-4*, 2029698) Bks Demand.

Banking in Minnesota. T. Harry Gatton & Truman L. Jeffers. (Illus.). 180p. 1989. write for info. (*0-318-64844-X*) MN Bankers Assn.

Banking in Nineteenth-Century Ireland: The Belfast Banks, 1825-1914. Philip G. Ollerenshaw. (Illus.). 275p. 1989. reprint ed. text ed. 27.95 (*0-7190-2277-0*, Pub. by Manchester Univ Pr UK) St Martin.

Banking in Nineteeth-Century Ireland: The Belfast Banks, 1825-1914. Philip G. Ollerenshaw. 288p. 1988. text ed. 75.00 (*0-7190-2276-2*, Pub. by Manchester Univ Pr UK) St Martin.

***Banking in Silence.** 240p. (C). 1994. 225.00 (*0-7605-0879-8*) Rector Pr.

Banking in Switzerland. Ed. by N. Blattner et al. (Studies in Contemporary Economics). vii, 329p. 1993. pap. 67.00 (*0-387-91474-9*) Spr-Verlag.

Banking in the American South from the Age of Jackson to Reconstruction. Larry Schweikart. LC 87-12784. 328p. 1987. text ed. 42.50 (*0-8071-1403-0*) La State U Pr.

Banking in the American West: From the Gold Rush to Deregulation. Lynne P. Doti & Larry Schweikart. LC 91-50302. 336p. 1991. 39.95 (*0-8061-2373-7*) U of Okla Pr.

Banking in the Cayman Islands. Bob Hall & Jami Hall. Ed. by Gary Scott & Merri Scott. 205p. 1992. lib. bdg. 99.00 (*1-884875-19-X*) Adams Carter.

Banking in the European Community after 1992. C. Cowdell. (Occasional Papers Ser.). (C). 1989. 115.00 (*0-85297-302-0*, Pub. by Inst Bankers UK) St Mut.

Banking in the U. S. An Annotated Bibliography. Jean Deuss. LC 90-9069. 174p. 1990. 22.50 (*0-8108-2348-9*) Scarecrow.

Banking in the West. Ed. by Larry Schweikart. (Illus.). 96p. 1984. pap. text ed. 15.00 (*0-89745-051-5*) Sunflower U Pr.

Banking Industry in Turmoil. 1992. lib. bdg. 92.95 (*0-8490-5545-8*) Gordon Pr.

Banking Industry in Turmoil: A Report on the Condition of the United States Banking Industry & the Bank Insurance Fund, Report, Dec. 1990. James R. Barth et al. 204p. 1990. pap. 6.00 (*0-16-028711-1*) USGPO.

Banking Institutions, Bullion Reserves, & Non Legal Tender Note Circulation of the United Kingdom Statistically Investigated. John Dun & Rene Higonnet. Bd. with Bank Deposits in the United Kingdom, 1870-1914. LC 82-48219. LC 82-48219. (Gold, Money, Inflation & Deflation Ser.). 227p. 1983. Set lib. bdg. 22.00 (*0-8240-5229-3*) Garland.

Banking Institutions in Developing Markets, 2 vols., Vol. 1: Building Strong Management & Responding to. Diana McNaughton et al. LC 92-27893. 1992. Vol. 1, Building Strong Management & Responding to Change. 15.95 (*0-8213-2217-6*, 12217) World Bank.

Banking Institutions in Developing Markets, 2 vols., Vol. 2: Interpreting Financial Statements. Diana McNaughton et al. LC 92-27893. 1992. Vol. 2, Interpreting Financial Statements. 15.95 (*0-8213-2218-4*, 12218) World Bank.

Banking Keiretsu. Hazel J. Johnson. 300p. 1993. 32.50 (*1-55738-367-7*) Probus Pub Co.

Banking Law, 12 vols., Set. V. DiLorenzo et al. 1981. ring bd. write for info. (*0-8205-1052-1*) Bender.

Banking Law: Adaptable to Courses Utilizing Macey & Miller's Casebook on Banking Law. Casenote Publishing Co., Inc. Staff et al. (Legal Briefs Ser.). (Orig.). 1994. pap. text ed. write for info. (*0-87457-201-0*, 1610) Casenotes Pub.

Banking Law: Adaptable to Courses Utilizing Symons & White's Casebook on Banking Law. Casenotes Publishing Co., Inc. Staff. Ed. by Norman S. Goldenberg et al. (Legal Briefs Ser.). (Orig.). 1991. pap. text ed. write for info. (*0-87457-153-7*, 1610) Casenotes Pub.

Banking Law & Practice in India. 18th ed. M. L. Tannnan. (C). 1989. 410.00 (*0-685-36535-2*) St Mut.

Banking Law & Regulation, 1989. (Commercial Law & Practice Ser.). 878p. 1989. 17.50 (*0-685-38020-3*, A4-4314) PLI.

***Banking Law & the Financial System in Australia.** 3rd ed. W. S. Weerasooria. pap. 70.00 (*0-409-30407-7*); boxed 94.00 (*0-409-30406-9*) Butterworth Legal Pubs.

Banking Law Anthology, 3 vols., Set. (National Law Anthology Ser.). 3000p. 1992. 299.95 (*0-914250-89-2*) Intl Lib.

Banking Law Anthology, 8 vols., Vol. I-VIII (1983-1994) (National Law Anthology Ser.). 8000p. 1994. Set. 620.00 (*0-914250-71-X*) Intl Lib.

Banking Law Anthology, Vol. VII (1992-1993) Ed. by Allison P. Zabriskie. LC 83-647741. (National Law Anthology Ser.). 1000p. 1993. text ed. 154.95 (*0-914250-91-4*) Intl Lib.

***Banking Law Anthology 1994, Vol. VIII.** Ed. by Allison P. Zabriskie. (National Law Anthology Ser.). 1994. 154.95 (*1-57024-013-2*) Intl Lib.

Banking Law in Australia. Alan Tyree. 1990. pap. 68.00 (*0-409-49436-4*) Butterworth Legal Pubs.

Banking Law in New Zealand. M. Russell. xxxiii, 286p. 1986. pap. 39.00 (*0-455-20658-9*, Pub. by Law Bk Co) W W Gaunt.

***Banking Law in the United States.** Alfred M. Pollard. LC 92-20020. 1994. 60.00 (*0-250-40753-1*) Michie Butterworth.

Banking Law in the United States, 2 vols. 2nd suppl. ed. Alfred M. Pollard et al. LC 92-20020. 1993. 50.00 (*0-685-74451-5*) Butterworth Legal Pubs.

Banking Law in the United States, 2 vols., Set. 2nd ed. Alfred M. Pollard et al. LC 92-20020. 1160p. 1994. ring bd. 185.00 (*0-88063-836-2*) Michie Butterworth.

Banking Law in Theory & Practice (A Comparative Study of English & Indian Law of Banking) S. N. Gupta. (C). 1989. 450.00 (*0-685-44807-X*) St Mut.

Banking Law Journal. Ed. by Gerald T. Dunne. 120.00 (*0-685-69615-4*, BLJ) Warren Gorham & Lamont.

Banking Law Journal: 1947-1992, Vols. 64-110. 3,995.00 (*0-8377-9025-5*) Rothman.

Banking Law Journal Digest: Annual Supplement, 2 vols. 7th ed. Ed. by Banking Law Journal Editori. 1982. 120.00 (*0-685-55627-1*) Warren Gorham & Lamont.

Banking Law Journal Digest: Annual Supplement, 2 vols. 7th suppl. ed. Ed. by Banking Law Journal Editori. 1982. Supplemented semi-annually, write for info. write for info. (*0-318-56375-4*) Warren Gorham & Lamont.

Banking Law Journal Digest: Annual Supplement, No. 1. suppl. ed. Ed. by Patrick J. Hamill. 1992. 50.00 (*0-7913-0969-X*) Warren Gorham & Lamont.

Banking Law Journal Digest: Annual Supplement, No. 2. Ed. by Patrick J. Hamill. 1992. 50.00 (*0-7913-1200-3*) Warren Gorham & Lamont.

Banking Law Manual: Legal Guide to Commercial Banks, Thrift Institutions & Credit Unions. Sherry C. Whitley & Joseph J. Norton. 1983. Looseleaf updates available. ring bd. write for info. (*0-8205-1054-8*) Bender.

Banking Law Reference Guide for National Banks. 2nd ed. Johathan Levin. 250p. 1991. pap. 29.95 (*0-13-093972-2*, 130401) P-H.

Banking Law Reports, Vol. 1. Ed. by Geoffrey M. Hall. 1992. 375.00 (*0-9514449-5-6*, Pub. by Busn & Med UK) St Mut.

Banking Law Series: Private Banking Issues, Federal Legislative Issues, Unexpected Aspects of Real Estate Workouts, Securities Activities of Banking Institutions, Foreign Exchange Activities. (Commercial Law & Practice Ser.). 471p. 1992. pap. text ed. 70.00 (*0-685-56864-4*, A4-4363) PLI.

Banking Law Series 1993: Mergers - Insolvencies - Enforcement Issues - FDICIA Compliance - Collective Investment Vehicles - Derivative Instrument Activities of Banks & Bank Holding Companies. (Commercial Law & Practice Course Handbook Ser.: Vol. 651). 1016p. 1993. 70.00 (*0-685-69701-0*, A4-4411) PLI.

Banking Law, Teaching Materials. 3rd ed. Edward L. Symons, Jr. & James J. White. (American Casebook Ser.). 818p. 1990. text ed. 47.00 (*0-314-78732-1*) West Pub.

Banking Law Teaching Materials, Statutory & Regulatory Supplement To. 3rd ed. Edward L. Symons, Jr. & James J. White. (American Casebook Ser.). 263p. (C). 1992. reprint ed. pap. text ed. 13.50 (*0-314-79887-0*) West Pub.

Banking Law, Teaching Materials, Teacher's Manual to Accompany. 3rd ed. Edward L. Symons, Jr. & James J. White. (American Casebook Ser.). 222p. 1991. pap. text ed. write for info. (*0-314-84677-8*) West Pub.

Banking Laws & Regulations: An Economic Perspective. Nicholas A. Lash. (Illus.). 176p. (C). 1987. pap. text ed. 53.00 (*0-13-055609-2*) P-H.

Banking Laws of Kuwait. Tr. by N. H. Karam. 50p. 1991. 18.00 (*0-86010-139-8*) G & T Inc.

Banking Management: A Guide to More Profitable Banking. James B. Bexley. LC 78-53195. 208p. reprint ed. pap. 59.30 (*0-8357-5965-2*, 2032842) Bks Demand.

Banking Odyssey: The Canara Bank Story. M. V. Kamath. 1991. 75.00 (*0-7069-5830-6*) Advent Bks Div.

Banking on Apartheid: The Financial Links Report. Frwd. by Shridath Ramphal. 96p. 1990. pap. text ed. 15.00 (*0-435-08044-X*, 08044) Heinemann.

Banking on Black Enterprise: The Potential of Emerging Firms for Revitalizing Urban Economics. Timothy Bates. 190p. (C). 1993. lib. bdg. 44.00 (*0-941410-93-5*); pap. text ed. 17.50 (*0-941410-94-3*) Jt Ctr Pol Studies.

Banking on Death: A John Putnam Thatcher Mystery. Emma Lathen. 168p. 1993. reprint ed. pap. 6.95 (*1-883402-06-9*) S&S Trade.

***Banking on Flexibility: A Comparison of Flexible Employment Strategies in the Retail Banking Sector in Britain & France.** Jacqueline O'Reilly. 310p. 1994. 59.95 (*1-85628-549-9*) Ashgate Pub Co.

Banking on Fraud: Drexel, Junk Bonds, & Buyouts. Mary Zey. LC 92-42408. (Social Institutions & Social Change Ser.). 327p. 1993. lib. bdg. 45.95 (*0-202-30465-5*); pap. 22.95 (*0-202-30466-3*) Aldine de Gruyter.

Banking on the Brink: The Troubled Future of American Finance. Roger J. Vaughan & Edward W. Hill. Ed. by Michael Barker. (Washington Post Co. Briefing Bks.). (Illus.). 366p. 1992. 250.00 (*0-9625971-1-2*) Washington Post.

Banking on the Mature Market: A Handbook for Marketing to the 50plus Customer. Michael P. Sullivan & Vicki Thomas. (Illus.). 140p. (Orig.). 1989. 40.00 (*1-55695-000-4*) Bank Mktg Assn.

Banking on the States: The Next Generation of Reinvestment Standards. Robert Stumberg. 170p. 1990. 20.00 (*0-685-56595-5*) CPA Washington.

Banking Operations. M. Hendersonm. 364p. (C). 1987. 50.00 (*0-905435-98-2*) St Mut.

Banking Operations: UK Lending & International Business - Revision Card Pack. Ed. by S. Sales. (C). 1989. 50.00 (*0-85297-251-2*, Pub. by Inst Bankers UK) St Mut.

Banking Policy & Structure: A Comparative Analysis. John S. Wilson. 512p. 1986. 85.00x (*0-8147-9205-7*) NYU Pr.

Banking Policy & the Price Level: An Essay in the Theory of the Trade Cycle. rev. ed. Dennis H. Robertson. LC 50-3461. (Reprints of Economic Classics Ser.). 1989. reprint ed. 25.00 (*0-678-00675-X*) Kelley.

Banking Policy in Japan: American Attempts at Reform During the Occupation. William M. Tsutsui. (Nissan Institute Japanese Studies). 192p. 1988. lib. bdg. 65.00 (*0-415-00003-3*, A2489) Routledge.

***Banking, Politics & Global Finance: American Commercial Banks & Regulatory Change, 1980-1990.** Wolfgang H. Reinicke. (Studies in International Political Economy). 264p. 1995. 59.95 (*1-85898-176-X*, Pub. by E Elgar Pub UK) Ashgate Pub Co.

Banking Principles & Practice. Ray B. Westerfield. Ed. by Stuart Bruchey. LC 80-1171. (Rise of Commercial Banking Ser.). (Illus.). 1981. reprint ed. lib. bdg. 68.95 (*0-405-13683-8*) Ayer.

Banking Problems. A. Piatt Andrew & Frederick I. Kent. Ed. by Stuart Bruchey. LC 80-1178. (Rise of Commercial Banking Ser.). 1981. reprint ed. lib. bdg. 20.95 (*0-405-13631-5*) Ayer.

Banking, Railroads & Industry in Spain: 1829-1874. Gabriel C. Tortella. Ed. by Stuart Bruchey. LC 77-77191. (Dissertations in European Economic History Ser.). (Illus.). 1978. lib. bdg. 59.95 (*0-405-10803-6*) Ayer.

Banking Reform. Ed. by J. Laurence Laughlin, Jr. & Stuart Bruchey. LC 80-1160. (Rise of Commercial Banking Ser.). 1981. reprint ed. lib. bdg. 38.95 (*0-405-13667-6*) Ayer.

Banking Reform: Economic Propellants, Political Impediments. Kenneth E. Scott & Barry R. Weingast. LC 92-29574. (Essays in Public Policy Ser.: No. 34). 1992. 5.00 (*0-8179-5392-2*) Hoover Inst Pr.

***Banking Reform in Central Europe & the Former Soviet Union.** Ed. by Jacek Rostowski. (A Central European University Press Bk.). (Illus.). 256p. 1995. 69.00 (*1-85866-038-6*); pap. 23.00 (*1-85866-039-4*) OUP.

Banking Reform in the CIS. (Illus.). 200p. (C). 1993. pap. 75.00 (*0-934393-39-7*) Rector Pr.

Banking Regulation Act Nineteen Forty-Nine. Vijay Malik. 163p. 1984. 90.00 (*0-317-54836-0*) St Mut.

Banking Regulation Act, 1949: Act No. 10. Ed. by Raghbirlal B. Sethi. (C). 1990. 130.00 (*0-89771-216-1*) St Mut.

Banking Regulation & Supervision: A Comparative Study of the United Kingdom, the United States of America & Japan. Maximilian J. Hall. 320p. 1993. 69.95 (*1-85278-129-7*, Pub. by E Elgar Pub UK) Ashgate Pub Co.

***Banking Regulation Today: The Impact, Issues & Trends.** Hazel J. Johnson. 150p. 1994. 32.50 (*1-55738-711-7*) Probus Pub Co.

Banking Relations: A Guide for Local Government. Rhett D. Harrell & Lisa A. Cole. (Illus.). 100p. 1982. pap. 14.00 (*0-686-84372-X*); pap. 12.00 (*0-686-84373-8*) Municipal.

Banking Scandals: The S & Ls & BCCI. Ed. by Robert E. Long. LC 93-16882. (Reference Shelf Ser.: Vol. 65, No. 3). 1993. 15.00 (*0-8242-0842-0*) Wilson.

Banking Services for the Affluent: A Special Collection from the Journal of Commercial Lending. Ed. by Joan Behr. LC 92-32158. 132p. (Orig.). 1992. pap. 37.00 (*0-936742-90-9*, 36048) Robt Morris Assocs.

Banking Situation in the United States. National Industrial Conference Board Staff. Ed. by Stuart Bruchey. LC 80-1188. (Rise of Commercial Banking Ser.). (Illus.). 1981. reprint ed. lib. bdg. 18.95 (*0-405-13671-4*) Ayer.

Banking Structure in Major Countries. Ed. by George G. Kaufman. (Innovations in Financial Markets & Institutions Ser.). 640p. (C). 1991. lib. bdg. 161.00 (*0-7923-9136-5*) Kluwer Ac.

Banking Supervision - The Regulation of the U. K. Banking Sector under the Banking Act 1987. Graham Penn. 1989. 110.00 (*0-406-13603-3*, U.K.) Butterworth Legal Pubs.

Banking Swindle in America. 1991. lib. bdg. 69.95 (*0-8490-4412-X*) Gordon Pr.

Banking Swindle in America. 1992. lib. bdg. 75.00 (*0-8490-5433-8*) Gordon Pr.

Banking System: Abstract Dimensions for the Next Few Centuries. David Massey & Behzad Yousefzadeh. 64p. (Orig.). 1993. pap. 9.95 (*0-9640970-0-1*) Hillside Pub GA.

Banking System & War Finance. Charles R. Whittlesey. (Occasional Papers: No. 8). 64p. 1943. reprint ed. 20.00 (*0-87014-323-9*); reprint ed. mic. film 20.00 (*0-685-61240-6*) Natl Bur Econ Res.

Banking System in the Countries of the EEC: Institutional & Structural Aspects. S. Mastropasqua. 170p. 1978. lib. bdg. 48.00 (*90-286-0518-5*) Kluwer Ac.

Banking System in Troubled Times: New Issues of Stability & Continuity. Jeremy F. Taylor. LC 88-35683. 203p. 1989. text ed. 55.00 (*0-89930-426-5*, TBM/, Quorum Bks) Greenwood.

Banking System of the State of New York. John Cleaveland & G. S. Hutchinson. Ed. by Stuart Bruchey. LC 80-1181. (Rise of Commercial Banking Ser.). 1981. reprint ed. lib. bdg. 38.95 (*0-405-13642-0*) Ayer.

Banking System of the United States & Its Relation to the Money & Business of the Country. Charles G. Dawes. Ed. by Stuart Bruchey. LC 80-1143. (Rise of Commercial Banking Ser.). 1981. reprint ed. lib. bdg. 15.95 (*0-405-13645-5*) Ayer.

***Banking Technology Competition Handbook.** 125p. (Orig.). 1995. pap. 695.00 (*0-7605-1868-8*) Rector Pr.

Banking Terminology. 3rd rev. ed. American Bankers Association Staff. Ed. by James F. Nielsen. 409p. 1989. pap. text ed. 40.00 (*0-89982-360-2*) Am Bankers.

Banking the Furnace: Restructuring of the Steel Industry in Eight Countries. Trevor Bain. LC 92-18358. 190p. 1992. 25.00 (*0-88099-128-3*); pap. 15.00 (*0-88099-127-5*) W E Upjohn.

Banking Theories in the U. S. Before 1860. Harry E. Miller. LC 78-182194. (Library of Money & Banking History). xi, 240p. 1972. reprint ed. lib. bdg. 35.00 (*0-678-00886-8*) Kelley.

Banking Through the Looking Glass. C. Channon et al. (C). 1989. 40.00 (*0-85297-202-4*, Pub. by Inst Bankers UK) St Mut.

Banking Today. Veronica S. West. (Illus.). 150p. (C). 1993. pap. text ed. 27.00 (*0-89982-318-1*) Am Bankers.

Banking Under Difficulties: Life on the Goldfields of Victoria, New South Wales & New Zealand, Vol. 8. G. O. Preshaw. LC 74-357. (Gold Ser.). 179p. 1974. reprint ed. 23.95 (*0-405-05918-3*) Ayer.

***Banking U.S.A. Market.** 400p. (Orig.). 1994. pap. 2,000.00 (*1-57205-983-4*) Rector Pr.

B

An Asterisk (*) at the beginning of an entry indicates that the title is appearing in BIP for the first time. 591

Banking Vocabulary. L. Vincent. 363p. (ENG & FRE.). 1988. pap. 49.95 (*0-8288-8027-1*) Fr & Eur.

***Banking Without Borders: Challenges & Opportunities in the Era of North America Free Trade & the Emerging Global Marketplace.** Hazel J. Johnson. 225p. 1994. 47.50 (*1-55738-731-1*) Probus Pub Co.

Banking Without Interest. Muhammad N. Siddiqi. 192p. (Orig.). 1983. pap. 6.95 (*0-86037-120-4*, Pub. by Islamic Fnd UK) New Era Publns MI.

Banking Without Interest. M. N. Siddiqui. 12.95 (*0-935782-43-5*) Kazi Pubns.

***Bankline Executive Reports: Banking in the European Union.** Hazel J. Johnson. 150p. 1995. 32.50 (*1-55738-751-6*) Probus Pub Co.

***Bankline Executive Reports: Banking in the Pacific Rim.** Hazel J. Johnson. 150p. 1995. 32.50 (*1-55738-750-8*) Probus Pub Co.

Banknotes & Banking in the Isle of Man. F. Quarmby. 1971. 18.00 (*0-685-51509-5*) S J Durst.

Bankrolling Ballots Update, 1980. Steve Lydenberg. 200p. 1981. 2.95 (*0-87871-016-7*) CEP.

Bankrupt! A Society Living in the Future. James V. McTevia. LC 92-27533. 227p. 1992. 21.95 (*1-879094-18-5*) Momentum Bks.

Bankrupt Education: The Decline of Liberal Education in Canada. Peter C. Emberley & Waller R. Newell. (Toronto Studies in Education). 184p. (C). 1994. 40.00 (*0-8020-0435-0*); pap. 17.95 (*0-8020-7224-0*) U of Toronto Pr.

Bankrupt Law of America: Compared with the Bankrupt Law of England. Thomas Cooper. xx, 399p. 1991. reprint ed. lib. bdg. 75.00 (*0-8377-2019-2*) Rothman.

***Bankruptcy.** (E-Z Legal Guide Ser.). 128p. (Orig.). 1995. pap. text ed. 12.95 (*1-56382-400-0*) E-Z Legal.

***Bankruptcy.** CUNA Staff. 160p. 1995. per., pap. text ed. 8.11 (*0-7872-0968-6*, S400) Kendall-Hunt.

Bankruptcy. David G. Epstein et al. (Hornbook Ser.). 1050p. 1993. text ed. 40.50 (*0-314-01124-2*) West Pub.

Bankruptcy. Journal of Commercial Bank Lending Staff. LC 87-32052. (Special Collection from the Journal of Commercial Bank Lending). 112p. 1987. pap. 37.00 (*0-936742-47-X*, 36033) Robt Morris Assocs.

Bankruptcy. David M. Lira. 184p. 1988. text ed. 29.95 (*0-13-056532-6*, Busn) P-H.

Bankruptcy. Jose Rodriguez. 28p. pap. 2.75 (*0-685-23159-3*, 41,575B) NCLS Inc.

Bankruptcy. W. Tuohey et al. (Illus.). 324p. 1990. pap. 35.00 (*0-685-14621-9*) NJ Inst CLE.

Bankruptcy. 2nd ed. Douglas G. Baird. 1990. 53.00 (*0-316-07681-3*) Little.

Bankruptcy. 2nd ed. Martin A. Frey et al. Ed. by Hannan. 607p. (C). 1992. text ed. 56.00 (*0-314-00191-3*) West Pub.

Bankruptcy, 3 vols. 2nd ed. Robert E. Ginsberg. 900p. 1989. write for info. (*0-318-65473-3*, P05662) P-H.

Bankruptcy. 3rd ed. Robert L. Jordan & William D. Warren. (University Casebook Ser.). 1000p. (C). 1993. text ed. 42.95 (*1-56662-062-7*) Foundation Pr.

Bankruptcy, 1. David G. Epstein et al. LC 92-15823. (Practitioner Treatise Ser.). 1780p. (C). 1992. text ed. write for info. (*0-314-00672-9*) West Pub.

Bankruptcy, 2. David G. Epstein et al. LC 92-15823. (Practitioner Treatise Ser.). 1780p. (C). 1992. text ed. write for info. (*0-314-00681-8*) West Pub.

Bankruptcy, 3. David G. Epstein et al. LC 92-15823. (Practitioner Treatise Ser.). 1780p. (C) 1992. text ed. write for info. (*0-314-00875-6*) West Pub.

Bankruptcy: A Feast for Lawyers. Sol Stein. LC 92-5955. 360p. 1992. pap. 12.95 (*0-87131-702-8*) M Evans.

Bankruptcy: A Study in Comparative Legislation. S. Whitney Dunscomb, Jr. LC 78-82250. (Columbia University. Studies in the Social Sciences: No. 6). reprint ed. 29.50 (*0-404-51006-X*) AMS Pr.

***Bankruptcy: Commentary to the 1994 Suplement.** 3rd ed. Robert J. Jordan & William D. Warren. (University Casebook Ser.). 39p. 1994. pap. text ed. write for info. (*1-56662-226-3*) Foundation Pr.

Bankruptcy: Problem, Process, Reform. David T. Stanley & Marjorie Girth. LC 79-161592. 286p. reprint ed. pap. 81.60 (*0-8357-8812-1*, 2033590) Bks Demand.

Bankruptcy: Text, Statutes, Rules. Robert E. Ginsberg. LC 92-28536. 1992. write for info. (*0-13-024183-0*) Aspen Law.

Bankruptcy: Text, Statutes, Rules. Robert E. Ginsberg. 1989. ring bd. write for info. (*0-13-056615-2*) P-H.

Bankruptcy: Text, Statutes, Rules, Forms, 4 vols. 3rd ed. Robert E. Ginsberg & Robert D. Martin. 4940p. 1992. ring bd. 360.00 (*0-13-291360-7*) Aspen Law.

Bankruptcy: The Law & Practice. Clive Grenville. 566p. 1988. 128.00 (*1-85190-032-2*, Pub. by Tolley Pubng UK) St Mut.

***Bankruptcy: The Solution.** Kevin A. Carey. (Illus.). 325p. (C). 1994. audio 89.99 (*1-886077-05-3*); text ed. 39.99 (*1-886077-03-7*); pap. text ed. 24.99 (*1-886077-04-5*) Cnslting Paralegal.

***Bankruptcy: 1994 Supplement.** 3rd ed. Robert L. Jordan & William D. Warren. (University Casebook Ser.). 129p. 1994. pap. text ed. 7.95 (*1-56662-201-8*) Foundation Pr.

Bankruptcy - Chapter 7: Bankruptcy for Individual. D. C. Schultz. (Illus.). 288p. (Orig.). 1994. pap. 27.95 (*1-879421-00-3*) LawPak.

Bankruptcy - Is It Really Necessary. Jimmy L. Kum & David J. Kum. 352p. 1992. 49.95 (*0-9626817-5-X*) J L Kum.

Bankruptcy - Law & Practice. Christopher Berry & Edward Bailey. 1987. 128.00 (*0-406-52610-9*, U.K.) Butterworth Legal Pubs.

***Bankruptcy Act & Rules.** 2nd ed. 820p. 1995. student ed, pap. 49.00 (*0-455-21310-0*, Pub. by Law Bk Co) W W Gaunt.

***Bankruptcy Administration: Case Receipts Paid to Creditors & Professionals.** (Illus.). 49p. (Orig.). (C). 1995. pap. text ed. 30.00x (*0-7881-1697-5*) Diane Pub.

Bankruptcy Amendments: A Legislative History of the Bankruptcy Judges, United States Trustees & Family Farmer Bankruptcy Act of 1986 Public Law 99-554, 3 vols. Ed. by Eugene M. Wypyski & Bernard D. Reams, Jr. LC 91-71946. 3112p. 1991. lib. bdg. 285.00 (*0-89941-763-9*, 306120) W S Hein.

Bankruptcy & Aviation Law Conference. 272p. (Orig.). 1993. pap. text ed. 45.00 (*1-56986-233-8*) Federal Bar.

Bankruptcy & Collections: The Paralegal Perspective. Darcy Williamson. 366p. (C). 1990. pap. text ed. 30.00 (*0-318-65325-7*) Natl Fed Para.

Bankruptcy & Creditor's Rights. 5th ed. Douglass Boshkoff. (Sum & Substance Ser.). 1989. 17.95 (*0-940366-42-8*) Sum & Substance.

Bankruptcy & Creditors' Rights: Second Edition, Cases & Materials On. 2nd ed. James J. White & Raymond T. Nimmer. LC 92-5651. (American Casebook Ser.). 764p. 1992. text ed. 45.50 (*0-314-00723-7*) West Pub.

Bankruptcy & Debtor-Creditor Law, Cases & Material. Theodore Eisenberg. (University Textbook Ser.). 966p. 1988. pap. text ed. write for info. (*0-88277-705-X*) Foundation Pr.

Bankruptcy & Debtor-Creditor Law, Cases & Material. 2nd ed. Theodore Eisenberg. (University Textbook Ser.). 966p. 1988. text ed. 40.95 (*0-88277-643-6*) Foundation Pr.

Bankruptcy & Distressed Restructurings: Analytical Issues & Investment Opportunities. Ed. by Edward I. Altman. LC 92-12572. 432p. 1992. 55.00 (*1-55623-901-7*) Irwin Prof Pubng.

Bankruptcy & Divorce: Support & Property Division. 2nd ed. Judith K. Fitzgerald & Ramona M. Arena. LC 93-44218. (Family Law Library). 1994. text ed. 118.00 (*0-471-31044-1*) Wiley.

Bankruptcy & Insolvency Accounting, Vol. 1: Practice & Procedure. 5th ed. Grant W. Newton. LC 93-36890. 1994. text ed. 130.00 (*0-471-59834-8*) Wiley.

Bankruptcy & Insolvency Accounting, Vol. 2. 5th ed. Grant W. Newton. LC 93-36890. 1994. Set. text ed. 240.00 (*0-471-59833-X*) Wiley.

Bankruptcy & Insolvency Accounting: Practice & Procedure. 4th ed. Grant W. Newton. 1989. text ed. 200.00 (*0-471-51503-5*); text ed. 105.00 (*0-471-50525-0*); 95.00 (*0-471-50863-2*) Wiley.

Bankruptcy & Insolvency Accounting: Practice & Procedure. 4th suppl. ed. Grant W. Newton. 400p. 1993. 65.00 (*0-685-58445-3*) Wiley.

Bankruptcy & Insolvency Taxation. Grant W. Newton & Gilbert D. Bloom. 576p. 1991. text ed. 110.00 (*0-471-50780-6*) Wiley.

Bankruptcy & Insolvency Taxation. 2nd ed. Grant W. Newton & Gilbert D. Bloom. 720p. 1993. text ed. 135.00 (*0-471-59837-2*) Wiley.

***Bankruptcy & Other Debtor-Creditor Laws in Nutshell.** 5th ed. David G. Epstein. (Nutshell Ser.). 408p. (C). 1995. pap. text ed. 17.00 (*0-314-06537-7*) West Pub.

***Debt: Bankruptcy, Article 9 & Related Laws.** David G. Epstein & Steve H. Nickles. (American Casebook Ser.). 182p. (C). 1994. teacher ed, pap. text ed. write for info. (*0-314-04850-2*) West Pub.

Bankruptcy, Article 9 & Creditors' Remedies: Problems, Cases, Materials. 2nd ed. Arnold B. Cohen. 923p. 1989. 40.00 (*0-87473-448-7*) Michie Butterworth.

Bankruptcy Basics for Small Business. S. Suzanne Walsh. LC 93-48670. (Paralegal Practice Ser.). 1994. ring bd. 75.00 (*0-87632-986-5*) Clark Boardman Callaghan.

***Bankruptcy, Cases & Materials on.** Peter A. Alces & Margaret Howard. (American Casebook Ser.). 704p. 1995. text ed. 45.00 (*0-314-04894-4*) West Pub.

Bankruptcy Citations. Shepard's Citation, Inc. Staff. 1985. 450.00 (*0-685-23123-2*) Shepards-McGraw.

Bankruptcy Citations, 3 vols. 3rd ed. LC 93-7330. 1985. 450.00 (*0-685-64823-0*) Shepards-McGraw.

Bankruptcy Code: Rules & Forms. 1992. lib. bdg. 75.00 (*0-8490-5277-7*) Gordon Pr.

Bankruptcy Code, Rules & Forms Including: Federal Rules of Civil Procedure & Federal Rules of Evidence. 1225p. 1993. pap. text ed. write for info. (*0-314-01981-2*) West Pub.

Bankruptcy Code, Rules & Forms Including Federal Rules of Civil Procedure & Federal Rules of Evidence. 753p. 1994. pap. text ed. write for info. (*0-314-03683-0*) West Pub.

***Bankruptcy Code Rules & Forms Including: Federal Rules of Civil Procedure & Federal Rules of Evidence: 1995 Edition.** 1300p. 1994. pap. text ed. write for info. (*0-314-05625-4*) West Pub.

***Bankruptcy, Code, Rules & Forms, 1995 Supplement.** 75p. (C). 1995. pap. text ed. write for info. (*0-314-06762-0*) West Pub.

Bankruptcy Code, Rules & Official Forms. (Miscellaneous Ser.). 1000p. (C). 1993. pap. text ed. 18.00 (*0-314-02432-8*) West Pub.

Bankruptcy Code, Rules & Official Forms. LC 81-10028. 1981. pap. 40.00 (*0-685-59819-5*) Clark Boardman Callaghan.

***Bankruptcy Code, Rules & Official Forms.** 1079p. (C). 1994. pap. text ed. 18.50 (*0-314-05754-4*) West Pub.

Bankruptcy Concepts: A Desk Reference for Lenders. Bonnie K. Donahue. Ed. by Kathy Tusler & Shelley Geehr. 96p. (Orig.). 1994. pap. 55.00 (*1-57070-003-6*, 32651) Robt Morris Assocs.

Bankruptcy Court Decisions. ring bd. 645.00 (*0-685-38083-1*, 30000) LRP Pubns.

Bankruptcy-Crisis in the Construction Industry, Thursday, January 27, 1983, the New York Hilton, New York, New York. ABA, Forum Committee on the Construction Industry & Fidelity & Surety Law Committee. LC 83-128770. 270p. 1983. 35.00 (*0-685-07625-3*, 557-0008) ABA Prof Educ Pubns.

Bankruptcy Desk Guide, 5 vols., Set. LC 90-62917. 1991. ring bd. 660.00 (*0-685-59821-7*) Clark Boardman Callaghan.

Bankruptcy Desk Reference: Integrated Code & Rules. Jacqueline Varma. LC 93-16965. (Bankruptcy Practice Ser.). 400p. 1993. text ed. 65.00 (*0-07-172473-7*) Shepards-McGraw.

Bankruptcy Deskbook. 2nd ed. Harvey M. Lebowitz. 836p. 1990. text ed. 80.00 (*0-87224-004-5*, A1-1411) PLI.

Bankruptcy Developments for Workout Officers & Lenders Counsel. Robert J. Rosenberg. 758p. 1990. pap. text ed. 17.50 (*0-685-49896-4*, A4-4348) PLI.

Bankruptcy Evidence Manual. Barry Russell. 850p. 1993. pap. text ed. write for info. (*0-314-02223-6*) West Pub.

***Bankruptcy Evidence Manual: 1994-1995 Edition.** Barry Russell. 1000p. 1994. pap. text ed. write for info. (*0-314-04509-0*) West Pub.

Bankruptcy Explained: A Guide for Businesses. Mark S. Summers. 1989. pap. text ed. 16.95 (*0-471-61982-5*) Wiley.

Bankruptcy for Paralegals. Pamela Webster. Ed. by Hannan. 565p. (C). 1991. text ed. 53.25 (*0-314-79871-4*) West Pub.

Bankruptcy Forms. write for info. (*0-318-57330-X*) Anderson Pub Co.

Bankruptcy Forms. Robert D. Martin. 1989. write for info. (*0-318-65474-1*, P05824) P-H.

Bankruptcy, How to Avoid It, How to Use It. George Ritner. write for info. (*0-686-22992-4*) G Ritner.

Bankruptcy in Louisiana. 20p. 1985. pap. 6.00 (*0-317-03731-5*, 37,357B-1) NCLS Inc.

Bankruptcy in United States History. Charles Warren. LC 75-172175. (American Constitutional & Legal History Ser). 196p. 1972. reprint ed. lib. bdg. 25.00 (*0-306-70214-2*) Da Capo.

***Bankruptcy in United States History.** Charles Warren. LC 94-78779. xii, 196p. 1994. reprint ed. 42.00 (*0-89941-907-0*, 308500) W S Hein.

Bankruptcy Investing: How to Profit from Distressed Companies. Hugh Ray & Ben Branch. 286p. 1992. 29.95 (*0-7931-0206-5*, 560840) Dearborn Finan.

Bankruptcy Issues in Matrimonial Cases: A Practical Guide. Ed. by Ronald L. Brown. 638p. 1992. ring bd. 116.00 (*0-13-289075-5*) Aspen Law.

Bankruptcy Issues in Matrimonial Cases: A Practical Guide. Ed. by Ronald L. Brown. LC 92-17146. 1992. 100.00 (*0-13-068701-4*) P-H.

Bankruptcy Kit. Arnold Goldstein. 120p. 1991. 19.95 (*1-56382-143-5*) E-Z Legal.

***Bankruptcy Kit.** 2nd ed. 1996. pap. 19.95 (*0-7931-1518-3*, 5608-4702) Dearborn Finan.

Bankruptcy Kit: A Practical Guide for Overcoming Financial Difficulties & Making a Fresh Start. John Ventura. 178p. 1991. pap. 19.95 (*0-7931-0226-X*, 5608-47) Dearborn Finan.

Bankruptcy Kit, Do It Yourself, Chapter Seven: Valid in all 50 States. Timothy J. Smith. (Illus.). 1991. 24.95 (*0-9625456-3-5*) SJT Enterprises.

Bankruptcy Law. 182p. (Orig.). 1993. pap. text ed. 30.00 (*1-56986-236-2*) Federal Bar.

Bankruptcy Law. Carl Felsenfeld. 275p. 1994. pap. text ed. 13.95 (*1-56542-107-8*) E Law Outlines.

Bankruptcy Law. Ed. by Liz Perris & Kevin Padrick. 1988. write for info. (*0-318-61748-X*) OR Bar CLE.

Bankruptcy Law & Practice: The 1991 Year in Review (a Satellite Program) (Commercial Law & Practice Ser.). 248p. 1992. pap. text ed. 70.00 (*0-685-56862-8*, A4-4362) PLI.

Bankruptcy Law & Practice in Michigan. Patrick E. Mears. LC 87-80722. 552p. 1987. Incl. 1992 cumulative suppl. ring bd. 110.00 (*0-685-22684-0*, 87-007) U MI Law CLE.

Bankruptcy Law & Practice in Michigan. suppl. ed. Patrick E. Mears. LC 87-80722. 552p. 1992. Nineteen Eighty-Eight supp. 60.00 (*0-685-22685-9*, 92-028) U MI Law CLE.

***Bankruptcy Law & Procedure: A Guide for Paralegals, 2 vols., Set.** 3rd ed. Steven N. Berger et al. (Polymer Science & Technology Ser.). 1994. text ed. 150.00 (*0-471-05123-3*) Wiley.

Bankruptcy Law Digest. Elizabeth R. Cohen & Brian O'Neil. 1989. text ed. 125.00 (*0-685-69635-9*, BKLD) Warren Gorham & Lamont.

Bankruptcy Law Digest, No. 2. suppl. ed. Cohen. 592p. 1992. Supplement, 1991-2. 60.00 (*0-7913-1037-X*) Warren Gorham & Lamont.

Bankruptcy Law Digest, No. 2739. suppl. ed. Cohen. 592p. 1989. Supplemented semi-annually. boxed 125.00 (*0-7913-0382-9*) Warren Gorham & Lamont.

Bankruptcy Law Digest, No. 2739. suppl. ed. Cohen. 592p. 1992. Supplement, 1991-1. 54.50 (*0-7913-1181-3*) Warren Gorham & Lamont.

Bankruptcy Law Fundamentals. Richard I. Aaron. LC 83-27535. 1984. ring bd. 145.00 (*0-87632-432-4*) Clark Boardman Callaghan.

Bankruptcy Law Handbook, 2 Vols. 2nd rev. ed. 858p. 1985. pap. text ed. 51.50 (*0-89074-069-0*) Lega Bks.

Bankruptcy Law Letter. Ed. by Charles J. Tabb. 140.00 (*0-685-69636-7*, BKLL) Warren Gorham & Lamont.

Bankruptcy Law Manual. suppl. ed. Benjamin Weintraub & Alan N. Resnick. (Bankruptcy Law Ser.). 1184p. 1992. Supplemented annually, write for info. 50.00 (*0-685-56391-X*) Warren Gorham & Lamont.

Bankruptcy Law Manual. 3rd rev. ed. Benjamin Weintraub & Alan N. Resnick. (Bankruptcy Law Ser.). 1184p. 1992. 125.00 (*0-7913-1002-7*) Warren Gorham & Lamont.

Bankruptcy Litigation, 2 vols., Set. Howard J. Steinberg. LC 89-85752. 1989. 225.00 (*0-685-59824-1*) Clark Boardman Callaghan.

Bankruptcy Litigation & Practice. 2nd ed. Thomas J. Salerno & Brian Sirower. (Bankruptcy Practice Library). 688p. 1993. reprint ed. 138.00 (*0-471-55297-6*); reprint ed. 65.00 (*0-471-58226-3*) Wiley.

Bankruptcy Litigation & Practice. 2nd suppl. ed. Thomas J. Salerno & Brian Sirower. (Bankruptcy Practice Library). 688p. 1990. reprint ed. 45.00 (*0-471-55413-8*) Wiley.

Bankruptcy Litigation & Practice: 1992 Supplement. Thomas J. Salerno & Brian Sirower. 496p. 1992. ring bd. 65.00 (*0-471-57039-7*) Wiley.

Bankruptcy Litigation Manual. Ed. by Michael L. Cook. 725p. 1988. write for info. (*0-318-65475-X*, P05654) P-H.

***Bankruptcy Litigation Manual, 1994-1995.** Ed. by Michael J. Cook. LC 94-40149. 1994. ring bd. write for info. (*0-13-361908-7*) Aspen Law.

Bankruptcy Litigator's Handbook. John S. Hopkins, III. LC 92-56141. 522p. 1993. text ed. 115.00 (*0-8318-0437-8*, B437); pap. text ed. 70.00 (*0-685-66665-4*, B725) Am Law Inst.

Bankruptcy Local Court Rules Service, 4 vols. Fischer. Ed. by Pike & Fischer, Inc. Staff. LC 89-70888. 1989. ring bd. 555.00 (*0-685-30633-X*) Clark Boardman Callaghan.

Bankruptcy: Maneuvering Through the Maze: Maneuvering Through the Maze. S. Suzanne Walsh. LC 93-47230. (Paralegal Practice Ser.). 1994. ring bd. 75.00 (*0-87632-981-4*) Clark Boardman Callaghan.

Bankruptcy of Marriage. V. F. Calverton. LC 76-169403. (Family in America Ser.). 344p. 1977. reprint ed. 29.95 (*0-405-03852-6*) Ayer.

Bankruptcy Practice, 2 vols., Set. 2nd ed. W. Homer Drake, Jr. & A. L. Mullins. 2924p. 1990. text ed. 150.00 (*0-07-172234-3*) Shepards-McGraw.

Bankruptcy Practice & Strategy. Alan N. Resnick et al. 1987. 175.00 (*0-88712-652-9*) Warren Gorham & Lamont.

Bankruptcy Practice & Strategy, No. 1. suppl. ed. Alan N. Resnick et al. 1991. Supplemented annually, write for info. 64.00 (*0-685-56114-3*) Warren Gorham & Lamont.

Bankruptcy Practice Deskbook, 3 vols. suppl. ed. Richard H. Maloy & David D. Bird. 2400p. 1992. Latest supp. 10/92. 47.00 (*1-56257-155-9*) Butterworth Legal Pubs.

Bankruptcy Practice Deskbook, 3 vols., 3. Richard H. Maloy & David D. Bird. 2400p. 1991. 100.00 (*0-88063-730-7*) Butterworth Legal Pubs.

Bankruptcy Practice Deskbook, 3 vols., Set. Richard H. Maloy & David D. Bird. 2400p. 1994. ring bd. 285.00 (*0-88063-779-X*) Michie Butterworth.

Bankruptcy Practice Deskbook, 3 vols., Vols. 1 & 2. Richard H. Maloy & David D. Bird. 2400p. 1991. 205.00 (*0-88063-729-3*) Butterworth Legal Pubs.

Bankruptcy Practice Handbook. Rosemary Williams. LC 83-21070. 1983. ring bd. 145.00 (*0-317-11805-6*) Clark Boardman Callaghan.

Bankruptcy Practice Systems PSL. Joe Lee. LC 79-92367. 1993. ring bd. 112.00 (*0-685-59823-3*) Clark Boardman Callaghan.

Bankruptcy Reform Act of Nineteen Seventy-Eight: Analysis, Legislative History & Selected Bibliography. Mickie A. Voges & Kathy E. Shimpock. (Legal Bibliography Ser.: No. 23). 60p. 1981. 15.00 (*0-935630-06-6*) U of Tex Tarlton Law Lib.

Bankruptcy Reform Amendments: A Legislative History of the Bankruptcy Amendments & Federal Judgeship Act of 1984, Public Law 98-353, 10 vols. Bernard D. Reams, Jr. & Eugene M. Wypyski. LC 91-40244. 1992. 895.00 (*0-89941-783-3*, 307300) W S Hein.

Bankruptcy Reorganization. Martin J. Bienenstock. LC 86-83355. 1318p. 1987. text ed. 108.00 (*0-317-64515-3*, A6-2011) PLI.

Bankruptcy Response Manual for Creditors. 2nd ed. Richard T. Anderson & Brent G. Summers. (Bankruptcy Practice Library). 688p. 1993. text ed. 128.00 (*0-471-59357-5*) Wiley.

Bankruptcy Rules & Forms Handbook, 2 vols. John K. Pearson et al. (Bankruptcy Practice Library: No. 1961). 992p. 1993. disk 125.00 (*0-471-57648-4*); 5.25 hd 125.00 (*0-471-57516-X*) Wiley.

Bankruptcy Rules & Forms Handbook, 2 vols. suppl. ed. John K. Pearson et al. (Bankruptcy Practice Library: No. 1961). 992p. 1993. ring bd. write for info. (*0-471-58712-5*) Wiley.

Bankruptcy Rules & Forms Handbook, 2 vols., 1. suppl. ed. John K. Pearson et al. (Bankruptcy Practice Library: No. 1961). 992p. 1993. ring bd. 116.00 (*0-471-30610-X*) Wiley.

Bankruptcy Rules & Forms Handbook, 2 vols. Set, Vol. 2. John K. Pearson et al. (Bankruptcy Practice Library: No. 1961). 992p. 1992. Set. ring bd. 232.00 (*0-471-55909-1*) Wiley.

Bankruptcy Rules & Forms Handbook, 2 vols., Vol. 2. suppl. ed. John K. Pearson et al. (Bankruptcy Practice Library: No. 1961). 992p. 1993. ring bd. 116.00 (*0-471-30611-8*) Wiley.

Bankruptcy, Second Edition, Teacher's Manual to Accompany Cases & Materials On. James J. White & Raymond T. Nimmer. (American Casebook Ser.). 156p. (C). 1992. pap. text ed. write for info. (*0-314-01377-6*) West Pub.

Bankruptcy Seminar (1988) 230p. 1988. pap. text ed. 10.00 (*1-56986-036-X*) Federal Bar.

Bankruptcy Seminar (1990) 43p. 1990. pap. text ed. 15.00 (*1-56986-037-8*) Federal Bar.

An Asterisk (*) at the beginning of an entry indicates that the title is appearing in BIP for the first time.

Bankruptcy Service - Lawyers Edition, 15 vols., Set. LC 78-71987. 1979. ring bd. 1,525.00 (*0-685-59820-9*) Clark Boardman Callaghan.

Bankruptcy Solution. 2nd ed. Peter F. Geraci. 155p. 1991. pap. text ed. 5.95 (*0-9629413-0-1*) P F Geraci.

Bankruptcy Stays: A Practitioner's Guide to Stays & Release from Stays. Richard S. Ralston. 1989. write for info. (*0-318-66005-9*) Bk Pub Co WA.

Bankruptcy Strategies for Lenders. 2nd ed. Brooke E. Smith et al. LC 92-41580. (Bankruptcy Practice Library). 336p. 1993. text ed. 128.00 (*0-471-59379-6*) Wiley.

***Bankruptcy, Teacher's Manual to Accompany Cases & Materials On.** Peter Alces & Margaret Howard. (America Casebook Ser.). 181p. (C). 1995. pap. text ed. write for info. (*0-314-06753-1*) West Pub.

Bankruptcy Yearbook & Almanac, 1991. Ed. by Christopher McHugh. 270p. (Orig.). 1991. pap. 195.00 (*0-9628991-0-0*) New Gen Research.

Bankruptcy Yearbook & Almanac, 1993. 3rd ed. Ed. by Christopher M. McHugh. 600p. 1993. 145.00 (*0-9628991-2-7*) New Gen Research.

Bankruptcy 1995: The Coming Collapse of America & How to Stop It. Harry E. Figgie, Jr. & Gerald J. Swanson. 1992. 19.95 (*0-316-28205-7*) Little.

Bankruptcy 1995: The Coming Collapse of America & How to Stop It. Harry E. Figgie. 1993. pap. 11.95 (*0-316-28206-5*) Little.

Bankrupting of America: Funny Money & the Federal Budget Deficit. David P. Calleo. (Illus.). 336p. 1992. 22.00 (*0-688-05162-6*) Morrow.

Bankrupting of America: How the Federal Budget Is Impoverishing the Nation. David P. Calleo. 304p. 1993. reprint ed. pap. 12.00 (*0-380-71033-1*) Avon.

***Banks & Bad Debts: Accounting for Loan Losses in International Banking.** Charles Sutcliffe et al. 1995. text ed. 60.00 (*0-471-95317-2*) Wiley.

***Banks & Banking: Federal Regulations, 4 vols., Set.** 1995. lib. bdg. 1,255.95 (*0-8490-6701-4*) Gordon Pr.

Banks & Banking in Michigan. T. H. Hinchman. Ed. by Stuart Bruchey. LC 80-1150. (Rise of Commercial Banking Ser.). 1981. reprint ed. lib. bdg. 18.95 (*0-405-13653-6*) Ayer.

Banks & Money: International & Comparative Finance in History. Ed. by Geoffrey Jones. 198p. 1991. text ed. 35.00 (*0-7146-3444-1*, Pub. by F Cass Pubs UK) Intl Spec Bk.

Banks & Personal Customers. B. Bevan et al. (C). 1989. 40.00 (*0-85297-081-1*, Pub. by Inst Bankers UK) St Mut.

Banks & Personal Customers. Ed. by Institute of Bankers Staff. 1985. 50.00 (*0-317-43724-0*, Pub. by Inst Bankers UK) St Mut.

Banks & Politics During the Progressive Era: The Origins of the Federal Reserve System, 1897-1913. Richard T. McCulley. LC 92-27522. (Financial Sector of the American Economy Ser.). 352p. 1992. 81.00 (*0-8153-0958-9*) Garland.

Banks & Politics in America: From the Revolution to the Civil War. Bray Hammond. 784p. 1991. pap. text ed. 24.95 (*0-691-00553-2*) Princeton U Pr.

Banks & Risk Management. G. Galpin et al. (C). 1989. 40.00 (*0-85297-217-2*, Pub. by Inst Bankers UK) St Mut.

Banks & Society. Ed. by A. Alexander et al. (C). 1989. 50.00 (*0-85297-296-2*, Pub. by Inst Bankers UK) St Mut.

Banks & Technology in the 1980s. Ed. by Institute of Bankers Staff. 1982. 75.00 (*0-85297-067-6*, Pub. by Inst Bankers UK) St Mut.

Banks & the Balance of Payments: Private Lending in the International Adjustment Process. Ed. by Benjamin Cohen. LC 81-1805. 256p. 1981. 53.00 (*0-86598-038-1*) Rowman.

Banks & the Capital Market: An Australian Study. J. O. Perkins & J. Sullivan. (Illus.). 123p. 1972. pap. 9.95 (*0-522-84048-5*) Intl Spec Bk.

Banks & the Public. Ed. by Institute of Bankers Staff. 1985. 44.00 (*0-317-43732-1*, Pub. by Inst Bankers UK) St Mut.

Banks & the Public. Ed. by M. Morse et al. (C). 1989. 40.00 (*0-85297-060-9*, Pub. by Inst Bankers UK) St Mut.

Banks & Their Competitors. R. Rose et al. (C). 1989. 40.00 (*0-85297-057-9*, Pub. by Inst Bankers UK) St Mut.

Banks & Their Customers. Joan F. Garrett. (Oceana's Legal Almanac Series: Law for the Layperson Ser.: No. 3). 104p. (YA). (gr. 9-12). 1995. text ed. 17.50 (*0-379-11194-2*) Oceana.

Banks & Thrifts: Introduction to FDIC-RTC Receivership Law. Warren L. Dennis & Barry S. Zismar. (Commercial Law & Practice Ser.). 585p. 1992. pap. text ed. 70.00 (*0-685-56877-6*, A4-4373) PLI.

Banks & Unions: An Operating Manual for Remaining Non-Union. James B. Clark. Ed. by Harry L. Moore, Jr. 205p. 1984. ring bd. 73.75 (*0-911911-01-4*) S Enright.

Banks As Multinationals. Ed. by Geoffrey Jones. (Comparative & International Business: Modern Histories Ser.). 288p. 1990. 74.00 (*0-415-04245-3*, A4712) Routledge.

Banks, Banking, & Paper Currencies. Richard Hildreth. (Notable American Authors Ser.). 1992. reprint ed. lib. bdg. 75.00 (*0-7812-3124-8*) Rprt Serv.

Banks, Finance & Investment in Germany. Jeremy Edwards & Klaus Fischer. (Illus.). 272p. (C). 1994. 49.95 (*0-521-45348-8*) Cambridge U Pr.

Banks, Liability & Risk. Ross Cranston. 1990. 100.00 (*1-85044-311-4*) Lloyds London Pr.

Banks of the Sea. Kenneth Tindall. LC 86-73235. 224p. 1987. 20.00 (*0-916583-22-8*) Dalkey Arch.

Banks of the Wabash. Robert V. Van Trees. LC 85-73869. 252p. 1986. pap. 5.95 (*0-9616282-0-0*) R Van Trees.

Banks of Your State 1989. 1989. 295.00 (*0-317-93138-5*) Sheshunoff.

Banks or No Banks: The Money Issue in Western Politics, 1832-1865. William G. Shade. LC 72-4229. 329p. reprint ed. pap. 93.80 (*0-7837-3822-6*, 2043642) Bks Demand.

Banks, Thrifts & Insurance Companies: Surviving the 1980s. Alan Gart. LC 84-48440. 160p. 1985. 22.95 (*0-685-09940-7*) Free Pr.

Banks under Stress. OECD Staff. 172p. (Orig.). 1992. pap. 35.00 (*92-64-13631-2*) OECD.

Banks Village Site, Crittenden County, Arkansas. Gregory Perino. Ed. by Carl H. Chapman. (Memoir Ser.: No. 4). (Illus.). 161p. (Orig.). 1966. pap. 4.50 (*0-943414-19-9*) MO Arch Soc.

Bankside. London County Council Staff. LC 78-138274. (London County Council. Survey of London Ser.: No. 22). reprint ed. 84.50 (*0-404-51672-6*) AMS Pr.

Banksters. (Money Reform Ser.). 1994. lib. bdg. 250.00 (*0-8490-5653-5*) Gordon Pr.

Banlieue Sud-Est. Rene Fallet. 384p. (FRE.). 1965. pap. 11.95 (*0-7859-2336-5*, 2070365484) Fr & Eur.

Bannack. Richard Wheeler. (Skye's West Ser.: No. 2). 288p. 1989. pap. 3.95 (*0-8125-1071-2*) Tor Bks.

Bannack: Cradle of Montana. F. Lee Graves. (Illus.). 64p. (Orig.). 1991. pap. 9.95 (*1-56037-003-3*) Am Wrld Geog.

Bannatyne Garlands. Nos. 1-10. Bannatyne Club Staff. LC 79-38498. (Bannatyne Club, Edinburgh. Publications: No. 118). 45.00 (*0-404-52877-5*) AMS Pr.

Bannatyne Manuscript: National Library of Scotland Advocates' MS 1.1.6. Intro. by Denton Fox & William A. Ringler. (Medieval Manuscripts Ser.). 1980. 357.00 (*0-85967-540-8*, Pub. by Scolar Pr UK) Ashgate Pub Co.

Bannatyne Miscellany, 3 vols, Set. Incl. Vol. 1. Ed. by W. Scott. LC 71-144412. (*0-318-50530-4*); Vols. 2-3. Ed. by D. Laing. LC 71-144412. (*0-318-50531-2*); LC 71-144412. (Bannatyne Club, Edinburgh. Publications: No. 19). reprint ed. 151.50 (*0-404-52720-5*) AMS Pr.

Banned! Censorship in the Schools. Donald J. Rogers. LC 87-7736. 128p. (YA). (gr. 5 up). 1987. lib. bdg. 12.98 (*0-671-63708-8*, Julian Messner) Silver Burdett Pr.

Banned Articles of C. Gordon Tether. Gordon C. Tether. 1982. lib. bdg. 69.95 (*0-8490-3230-X*) Gordon Pr.

Banned Books of England & Other Countries: A Study of the Conception of Literary Obscenity. Alec Craig. LC 77-9968. 243p. 1977. reprint ed. text ed. 35.00 (*0-8371-9709-0*, CRBB, Greenwood Pr) Greenwood.

Banned: Classical Erotica: Forty Sensual & Erotic Excerpts from Aristophanes to Whitman - Uncensored. Ed. by Victor Gulotta & Brandon Toropov. 144p. (Orig.). 1992. pap. 5.95 (*1-55850-109-6*) Adams Pubng.

Banned Films: Movies, Censors & the First Amendment. Edward De Grazia & Roger K. Newman. 532p. 1982. 39.95 (*0-8352-1509-1*); pap. 29.95 (*0-8352-1511-3*) Bowker.

Banned in D. C. Photos & Anecdotes from the DC Punk Underground. 3rd ed. Cynthia Connolly et al. Ed. by Lydia Ely. LC 88-92504. 176p. 1994. pap. 16.95 (*0-9620944-0-4*) Sun Dog Propaganda.

Banned in Ireland: Censorship & the Irish Writer. Ed. by Julia Carlson. LC 89-27677. (Illus.). 192p. 1990. pap. 13.95 (*0-8203-1235-5*) U of Ga Pr.

Banned in Pakistan. Fakhar Zaman. (C). 1989. 11.50 (*81-202-0249-X*, Pub. by Ajanta II) S Asia.

Banned in the U. S. A. A Reference Guide to Book Censorship in Schools & Public Libraries. Herbert N. Foerstel. LC 93-29095. 256p. 1994. text ed. 45.00 (*0-313-28517-9*, Greenwood Pr) Greenwood.

Banned Lecture. Aleister Crowley. 1981. reprint ed. pap. 3.50 (*0-935458-99-9*) Thirteenth Hse.

Banneker: A Case Study of Educational Change. John A. Wilson. LC 72-13935. 128p. 1973. 19.95 (*0-88280-005-1*) ETC Pubns.

Banneker: The Afro-American Astronomer. Ed. by Will W. Allen. LC 77-168504. (Black Heritage Library Collection). reprint ed. 10.00 (*0-8369-8858-2*) Ayer.

Banneker the Afro-American Astronomer. W. Allen & D. Murray. 80p. reprint ed. pap. 7.95 (*0-933121-48-2*) Black Classic.

***Banner Book.** Ruth A. Lowery. 96p. 1995. pap. 15.95 (*0-8019-8641-9*) Chilton.

Banner Book. Betty Wolfe. LC 74-80378. (Illus.). 96p. 1974. spiral bd. 8.95 (*0-8192-1173-7*) Morehouse Pub.

Banner Designs for Celebrating Christians. Jane Debor & Linda Isabel. 1984. pap. 5.95 (*0-570-03931-2*, 12-2865) Concordia.

Banner in the Sky. Illus. by Charles Nicholas. (Contemporary Motivators Ser.). (J). (gr. 4-12). 1978. pap. text ed. 2.25 (*0-88301-301-0*) Pendulum Pr.

Banner in the Sky. James R. Ullman. (J). (gr. 7-9). 1980. 2.95 (*0-685-00477-5*, Archway) PB.

Banner in the Sky. James R. Ullman. LC 54-7296. 256p. (YA). (gr. 7 up). 1988. reprint ed. pap. 3.95 (*0-06-447048-2*, Trophy) HarpC Child Bks.

Banner O'Brian. Linda L. Miller. Ed. by Linda Marrow. 1991. mass mkt. 5.99 (*0-671-73766-X*) PB.

***Banner O'Brien.** Miller. 1995. mass mkt. 5.99 (*0-671-53422-X*) PB.

***Banner of David.** J. P. Day. 276p. 1992. pap. 30.00 (*0-86383-754-9*, Pub. by Gomer Pr UK) St Mut.

Banner of Love. Joyce H. Frost. (Wellspring Romance Ser.). 178p. 1989. 5.95 (*0-9614712-5-5*) Wellspring Bks.

Banner Patterns for Worship. Carol J. Harms. (Orig.). 1988. pap. 11.95 (*0-570-04491-X*, 12-3114) Concordia.

Banner Year. Betty Cavanna. LC 87-23692. 224p. (YA). (gr. 7 up). 1987. 12.95 (*0-688-05779-9*) Morrow Jr Bks.

Banner Year. Betty Cavanna. 217p. (J). (gr. 4-7). 1992. pap. 2.50 (*0-8167-1265-4*) Troll Assocs.

Banner Year at Indiana. Bob Hammel. (Illus.). 128p. (C). 1993. pap. 15.95 (*0-253-32687-7*) Ind U Pr.

Bannerman. Jay Flynn. 192p. 1983. pap. 2.25 (*0-8439-2030-0*) Dorchester Pub Co.

Bannerman's Law. John R. Maxim. 1991. pap. 4.99 (*0-553-29326-5*) Bantam.

Banners & Such. Adelaide Ortegel. LC 86-62616. 128p. 1986. pap. 10.95 (*0-89390-092-3*) Resource Pubns.

***Banner's Bonus.** Carole A. Lee. 400p. (Orig.). 1995. mass mkt., pap. text ed. 4.99 (*0-505-52027-3*) Dorchester Pub Co.

Banners for Beginners. Cory Atwood. LC 87-12268. 80p. (Orig.). 1987. pap. 11.95 (*0-8192-1401-9*) Morehouse Pub.

Banners for Worship. Carol J. Harms. (Orig.). 1988. pap. 8.95 (*0-570-04492-8*, 12-3113) Concordia.

Banners in the Air: The Eighth Ohio Volunteers & the Spanish-American War. Curtis V. Hard. Ed. by Robert H. Ferrell. LC 88-12033. (Illus.). 161p. 1988. 22.00 (*0-87338-367-2*) Kent St U Pr.

Banners of Desire. Lorinda Hagen. 1978. pap. 2.25 (*0-8439-0598-0*) Dorchester Pub Co.

Banners of the Champions: An Anthology of Medieval Arabic Poetry from Andalusia & Beyond. Ibn Sa'id al-Maghribi. Tr. by James A. Bellamy & Patricia O. Steiner. 280p. (C). 1989. 20.00 (*0-940639-27-0*) Hispanic Seminary.

Banners, Ribbons & Scrolls: An Archive For Artists & Designers, Five Hundred & Three Copyright-Free Designs. Carol B. Grafton. (Illus.). 96p. (Orig.). 1983. pap. 5.95 (*0-486-24443-1*) Dover.

Banners Unfurled! Pilgrims in Today's World. Ed. by Val Hillsdon-Hutton. (Illus.). (Orig.). 1991. pap. 4.95 (*0-88028-123-5*, 1135) Forward Movement.

Banners with Pizazz: A Step-by-Step Guide. Diane Guelzow. LC 91-40935. (Illus.). 120p. (Orig.). 1992. pap. 15.95 (*0-89390-208-X*) Resource Pubns.

Banners Without Words. Jill Knuth. LC 86-60124. (Illus.). 208p. (Orig.). 1989. pap. 10.95 (*0-89390-075-3*) Resource Pubns.

***Bannertail: The Story of a Gray Squirrel.** Ernest T. Seton. (Illus.). 265p. 1995. pap. 16.95 (*1-885529-08-2*) Stevens Pub.

Banning Branches. Leroy F. Banning. 414p. (Orig.). 1994. pap. text ed. 30.00 (*1-55613-957-8*) Heritage Bk.

Banning Chemical Weapons: The Technical Background. Hugh D. Crone. (Illus.). 120p. (C). 1992. 44.95 (*0-521-41699-X*); pap. 13.95 (*0-521-42711-8*) Cambridge U Pr.

Banning Nuclear Tests: Verification, Compliance, Savings. Betty G. Lall & Paul Brandes. 83p. 1987. pap. 3.00 (*0-87871-053-1*) CEP.

Banning of Corporal Punishment in Child Care, School & Other Educative Settings in the U. S. 8p. 1987. 2.50 (*0-87173-114-2*) ACEI.

Bannisters. Barbara Oaks. LC 86-61475. (Illus.). 200p. (Orig.). (C). 1986. pap. 7.95 (*0-9618582-0-6*) Barbara Oaks.

Bannock. Bernelda Wheeler. LC 92-34255. (Voyages Ser.). (Illus.). (J). 1993. 4.25 (*0-383-03617-8*) SRA Schl Grp.

Bannon. large type ed. Alan Evans. (Linford Mystery Library). 301p. 1989. pap. 11.95 (*0-7089-6643-8*, Linford) Ulverscroft.

Banos de Canela. Juan Arcocha. LC 88-80055. (Coleccion Caniqui Ser.). 119p. (Orig.). (SPA.). 1988. pap. 9.95 (*0-89729-476-9*) Ediciones.

Banquet: Five Short Stories. Rosellen Brown et al. LC 78-56621. (Illus.). 1978. 15.00 (*0-915778-24-6*); 150.00 (*0-915778-23-8*); pap. 8.00 (*0-915778-25-4*) Penmaen Pr.

Banquet Des Leopards. Alphonse Boudard. 288p. (FRE.). 1982. pap. 10.95 (*0-7859-2223-7*, 207037419X) Fr & Eur.

Banquet of Health. Penny Block. (Illus.). 224p. (Orig.). 1994. pap. 17.95 (*1-879260-28-X*) Evanston Pub.

Banquet Years. Roger Shattuck. 1968. pap. 13.00 (*0-394-70415-0*, Vin) Random.

Banquet Years: The Origins of the Avant-Garde in France, 1885 to World War One. rev. ed. Roger Shattuck. LC 79-152213. (Essay Index Reprint Ser.). 1977. reprint ed. 30.95 (*0-8369-2826-1*) Ayer.

Banquet's Wisdom: A Short History of the Theologies of the Lord's Supper. Gary Macy. LC 91-45240. 224p. 1992. pap. 12.95 (*0-8091-3309-1*) Paulist Pr.

Banquetting Stuffe: The Fare & Social Background of the Tudor & Stuart Banquet. Ed. by C. Anne Wilson. (Food & Society in History Today Ser.). (Illus.). 80p. 1989. 22.50 (*0-85224-639-0*, Pub. by Edinburgh U Pr UK) Col U Pr.

Banquetting Stuffe: The Fare & Social Background to the Tudor & Stuart Banquet. Ed. by Anne Wilson. (Illus.). 96p. Date not set. pap. 18.50 (*0-7486-0282-8*, Pub. by Edinburgh U Pr UK) Col U Pr.

Banquiere Des Annees Folles: Marthe Hanau. Dominique Desanti. (FRE.). 1980. pap. 11.95 (*0-7859-1915-5*, 2070371956) Fr & Eur.

Banshee. Margaret Millar. 202p. 1985. reprint ed. pap. 5.95 (*0-930330-14-5*) Intl Polygonics.

Banshee Tide. large type ed. Alice Dwyer-Joyce. 1978. 12.00 (*0-7089-0225-1*) Ulverscroft.

Banshee Train. Odds Bodkin. LC 93-39635. (Illus.). (J). 1995. 14.95 (*0-395-69426-4*, Clarion Bks) HM.

***Banshees, Bugles & Belles: Real Ghosts in Georgia.** Barbara D. Duffey. (Illus.). 150p. (Orig.). 1995. pap. write for info. (*1-883522-08-0*) Rockbridge Pub.

Banshee's Women: Capsized in the Coral Sea. Jeannine Talley. LC 92-60317. (Illus.). 184p. 1992. 21.95 (*0-941300-24-2*); pap. 12.95 (*0-941300-23-4*) Mother Courage.

Bantam - Borland Official Turbo C Plus Plus Object-Oriented Class. David Hu. 640p. 1991. pap. write for info. (*0-553-35442-6*, Random Ref) Random.

Bantam Book of Correct Letter Writing. Lillian E. Watson. 352p. 1983. mass mkt. 4.95 (*0-553-27086-9*, Bantam Classics) Bantam.

Bantam Chickens. Helga Fritzsche. (Illus.). 72p. 1986. pap. 5.95 (*0-8120-3687-5*) Barron.

Bantam College Roget's Thesaurus Dictionary Form. Sidney M. Landau. 1990. mass mkt. 4.99 (*0-553-28769-9*) Bantam.

Bantam Crossword Dictionary. Comp. by Jerome Fried. 1983. mass mkt. 4.99 (*0-553-26375-7*) Bantam.

Bantam Italian Dictionary. Robert C. Melzi. 1984. mass mkt. 5.99 (*0-553-27947-5*) Bantam.

Bantam Library of the Culinary Arts, 4 vols. Jill Norman. 1989. Boxed set. boxed 23.80 (*0-553-30491-7*) Bantam.

Bantam Medical Dictionary. rev. ed. 1982. mass mkt. 6.99 (*0-553-28498-3*) Bantam.

Bantam Model BRC Jeep, 1941 Prototype: TM-10-1205. American Bantam Car Company Staff. Ed. by Dan R. Post. LC 75-185932. (Illus.). 128p. 1971. pap. 12.95 (*0-911160-44-2*) Post Group.

Bantam New College French & English Dictionary. rev. ed. Roger Steiner. 1989. mass mkt. 5.99 (*0-553-27411-2*) Bantam.

Bantam New College German & English Dictionary. Ed. by John C. Traupman. 768p. (Orig.). (ENG & GER.). (gr. 7-12). 1984. mass mkt. 5.99 (*0-553-28088-0*) Bantam.

***Bantam New College Latin & English Dictionary.** enl. rev. ed. John C. Traupman. (ENG & LAT.). 1995. mass mkt. 5.99 (*0-553-57301-2*) Bantam.

Bantam New College Spanish & English Dictionary (Hispanic) Edwin B. Williams. 1982. mass mkt. 4.95 (*0-553-26370-6*) Bantam.

Bantam of the Opera. Mary R. Daheim. 256p. (Orig.). 1993. mass mkt. 4.99 (*0-380-76934-4*) Avon.

Bantam Spanish-English - English-Spanish Dictionary Domesticed. Edwin B. Williams. 1984. mass mkt. 4.95 (*0-553-26714-0*) Bantam.

Bantam Trailer Manual: TM-10-1281. American Bantam Car Co. Staff. (U. S. Army Technical Manual, Jeep Ser.). (Illus.). 1989. reprint ed. pap. 8.00 (*0-910667-21-7*) Northstar Bks.

Bantam Travel Guides. 1988. pap. write for info. (*0-318-63653-0*) Bantam.

***Bantams: The Untold Story of World War I.** Sidney Allinson. (Illus.). 300p. 1995. lib. bdg. 33.00 (*0-8095-4924-7*) Borgo Pr.

Banting: A Biography. rev. ed. Michael Bliss. 336p. 1992. reprint ed. pap. 19.95 (*0-8020-7386-7*) U of Toronto Pr.

Bantu Beliefs & Magic. 2nd ed. C. W. Hobley. (Illus.). 374p. 1967. 35.00 (*0-7146-1009-7*, Pub. by F Cass Pubs UK) Intl Spec Bk.

Bantu, Boer, & Briton: The Making of the South African Native Problem. William M. Macmillan. LC 78-27446. (Illus.). 382p. 1979. reprint ed. text ed. 35.00 (*0-313-20906-5*, MABB, Greenwood Pr) Greenwood.

Bantu Heritage. Henri P. Junod. LC 78-107510. (Illus.). 155p. 1970. reprint ed. text ed. 49.75 (*0-8371-3780-2*, JUB&, Negro U Pr) Greenwood.

Bantu in the City. Ray E. Phillips. LC 74-15080. reprint ed. 49.50 (*0-404-12129-2*) AMS Pr.

Bantu Languages of Africa. Margaret A. Bryan. LC 60-1171. (Handbook of African Languages Ser.: Pt. 4). 191p. reprint ed. pap. 54.50 (*0-8357-3211-8*, 2057082) Bks Demand.

Bantu Languages of Western Equatorial Africa. Malcolm Guthrie. LC 54-1353. (Handbook of African Languages Ser.). 94p. reprint ed. pap. 26.80 (*0-8357-3221-5*, 2057093) Bks Demand.

Bantu of Western Kenya: With Special Reference to the Vugusu & Logoli, 2 vols. in 1. Gunter Wagner. LC 73-20405. 742p. reprint ed. pap. 180.00 (*0-8357-6977-1*, 2039037) Bks Demand.

Bantu Prophets in South Africa. 2nd ed. Bengt Sundkler. LC 61-65161. 385p. reprint ed. pap. 109.80 (*0-8357-3226-6*, 2057121) Bks Demand.

Bantu Tribes of South Africa, 4 vols. in 12 pts., Set. Alfred M. Duggan-Cronin. LC 74-15033. reprint ed. 450.00 (*0-404-12050-4*) AMS Pr.

Banua Toraja: Changing Patterns in Architecture & Symbolism among the Sa'dan Toraja of Sulawesi. Jowa Kis-Jovak et al. (Illus.). 135p. (C). 1991. text ed. 55.00 (*0-7103-0418-8*, A5638, Pub. by Kegan Paul Intl UK) Routledge Chapman & Hall.

Banya. Derek Lambert. 359p. 1992. 24.95 (*1-85619-044-7*, Sinclair-Stevenson) Trafalgar.

Banyan VINES: The Professional Reference. 1200p. 1994. 50.00 (*1-56205-230-6*) New Riders Pub.

Banza. Diane Wolkstein. LC 81-65845. (Pied Piper Bks.). (Illus.). 32p. (J). (ps-3). 1981. 15.99 (*0-8037-0428-3*) Dial Bks Young.

Banza. Diane Wolkstein. LC 81-65845. (Pied Piper Bks.). (Illus.). 32p. (J). (gr. k-2). 1984. pap. 4.95 (*0-8037-0058-X*) Dial Bks Young.

Banzai. F. H. Grautoff. LC 74-15975. (Science Fiction Ser.). (Illus.). 332p. 1975. reprint ed. 26.95 (*0-405-06310-5*) Ayer.

Baphomet. Pierre Klossowski. Tr. by Stephen Sartarelli. LC 88-80808. (Illus.). 216p. 1988. pap. 12.00 (*0-941419-73-8*, Eridanos Library) Marsilio Pubs.

Baptism. William Freburger. 1970. pap. 1.45 (*0-8189-0425-9*) Alba.

Baptism. H. A. Ironside. LC 89-36837. 1989. Pkg. of 5. pap. 12.50 (*0-87213-550-0*); pap. 2.50 (*0-87213-345-1*) Loizeaux.

Baptism. Martin E. Marty. LC 77-78653. 64p. (Orig.). 1977. pap. 6.00 (*0-8006-1317-1*, 1-1317, Fortress Pr) Augsburg Fortress.

Baptism. Karl Rahner. 1979. pap. 4.95 (*0-87193-120-6*) Dimension Bks.

Baptism. C. H. Spurgeon. 1976. pap. 2.00 (*1-56186-403-X*) Pilgrim Pubns.

Baptism. rev. ed. Richard E. Todd. (Wordbook Ser.). (Illus.). 26p. (Orig.). (J). (gr. 2-6). 1993. student ed 2.45 (*0-9605324-1-2*) Crosswalk Res.

An Asterisk (*) at the beginning of an entry indicates that the title is appearing in BIP for the first time.

593

Baptism: A Bible Defense of Believer's Immersion. Philip Mauro. pap. 3.99 (*0-87377-046-3*) GAM Pubns.

Baptism: A Biblical Study. Jack Cottrell. LC 89-43014. (Orig.). 1989. pap. 8.99 (*0-89900-341-9*) College Pr Pub.

Baptism: Christ's Act in the Church. Lawrence H. Stookey. LC 81-17590. 208p. (Orig.). 1982. pap. 13.95 (*0-687-02364-5*) Abingdon.

Baptism: Its Mode & Subjects. Alexander Carson. LC 80-8067. 550p. 1981. pap. 21.99 (*0-8254-2324-4*) Kregel.

Baptism: My Promise to Jesus. Jan Clawson. 24p. (Orig.). (J). (gr. 1-3). 1988. pap. 3.98 (*0-88290-298-9*) Horizon Utah.

***Baptism: The Believer's Wedding Ceremony.** F. LaGard Smith. (Orig.). 1993. pap. 7.99 (*0-89225-422-X*) Gospel Advocate.

Baptism: The Church's Troubled Water. D. L. Norbie. 1985. pap. 2.50 (*0-937396-64-8*) Walterick Pubs.

***Baptism: Who & How? A Study of Sprinkling & Infant Baptism.** Clay Whitehurst. 1995. 10.95 (*0-8062-5195-6*) Carlton.

Baptism: Who Needs It? Robert J. Barnett. 16p. (Orig.). (YA). (gr. 6 up). 1991. pap. text ed. 1.25 (*0-87227-171-4*) Reg Baptist.

Baptism, a Covenant. Gerald F. Mundfrom. (Illus.). 130p. (Orig.). 1985. pap. text ed. 4.00 (*0-9615494-0-8*) Mercy & Truth.

Baptism & Belonging: A Resource for Christian Worship. Keith Watkins. 160p. (Orig.). 1991. pap. 11.99 (*0-8272-0219-9*) Chalice Pr.

Baptism & Change in the Early Middle Ages, c. 200-c. 1150. Peter Cramer. LC 92-17489. (Studies in Medieval Life & Thought, Fourth Ser.: No. 20). 352p. (C). 1993. 59.95 (*0-521-35163-4*) Cambridge U Pr.

***Baptism & Communion.** Debbie Bentley. (Basic Christian Doctrine Ser.: No. 3). 5p. (Orig.). (YA). 1995. pap. 1.00 (*1-885090-02-1*) Cosecha Latina.

Baptism & Confirmation Book. (Illus.). 96p. 1994. 13.95 (*0-09-177876-X*, Pub. by Ebury Pr UK) Trafalgar.

Baptism & Gifts of the Holy Spirit. Merrill F. Unger. LC 74-2931. 192p. (C). 1992. pap. text ed. 8.99 (*0-8024-0467-7*) Moody.

Baptism & Its Influence on Christian Devotion. A. E. Wilder-Smith. 92p. reprint ed. pap. 3.99 (*0-936728-41-8*) Word for Today.

Baptism & Marriage Records of the Reformed Churches of Ghent, West Ghent, Mt. Pleasant, & Stuyvesant Falls, NY, 1775-1899: Reformed Church, Ghent, 1775-1899; Reformed Church of West Ghent, 1843-1899; Reformed Church of Mount Pleasant, Greenport, 1836-1899; Reformed Church, Stuyvesant Falls, 1860-1899. Arthur C. Kelly. LC 73-160685. (Palatine Transcripts Ser.). 172p. 1972. lib. bdg. 32.00 (*1-56012-020-7*) Kinship Rhinebeck.

Baptism & Marriage Records of the Reformed Churches of Upper Red Hook, Tivoli, Mellenville, & Linlithgo, NY, 1766-1899: St. John's Low Dutch Reformed Church, 1785-1898; Red Church, Tivoli, 1766-1813; Reformed Church Mellenville, 1838-1899; Livingston Memorial Reformed Church, Linlithgo, 1859-1899. Arthur C. Kelly. LC 73-179246. (Palatine Transcripts Ser.). 149p. 1973. lib. bdg. 29.00 (*1-56012-021-5*) Kinship Rhinebeck.

Baptism & Marriage Registers of the Old Dutch Church of Kingston, Ulster County, for One Hundred Fifty Years from Their Commencement in 1660. R. R. Hoes. 797p. 1989. reprint ed. lib. bdg. 78.00 (*0-8328-0570-X*) Higginson Bk Co.

Baptism & Related Doctrines. 2nd ed. Omar Gjerness. 54p. 1992. pap. 3.95 (*0-943167-17-5*) Faith & Fellowship Pr.

Baptism & Resurrection: Studies in Pauline Theology Against its Graeco-Roman Background. A. J. Weddernurn. 480p. 1987. lib. bdg. 93.50 (*3-16-145192-9*, Pub. by J C B Mohr GW) Coronet Bks.

Baptism & the Remission of Sins. Ed. by David Fletcher. LC 89-81420. 400p. 1993. reprint ed. pap. 10.99 (*0-89900-369-9*) College Pr Pub.

Baptism & the Restoration Movement. Bob L. Ross. 1979. pap. 1.95 (*1-56186-507-9*) Pilgrim Pubns.

Baptism As Thirty Celebrations. L. Moore. 1990. pap. 3.95 (*0-937032-74-3*) Light&Life Pub Co MN.

***Baptism by Murder.** Jan Maxwell, pseud. 224p. (Orig.). 1995. mass mkt. 4.99 (*0-380-77621-9*) Avon.

***Baptism by the Holy Spirit: God's Gift to All Christians.** Vladimir Sklyarenko. 64p. (Orig.). 1995. pap. 9.95 (*1-881576-41-8*) Providence Hse.

***Baptism in God's Plan.** Oliver F. Fauss. 48p. Date not set. pap. 1.99 (*1-56722-028-2*) Word Aflame.

Baptism in the Holy Spirit. Willard Cantelon. 34p. 1951. pap. 1.00 (*0-88243-692-9*, 02-0692) Gospel Pub.

Baptism in the Holy Spirit. Derek Prince. 1966. pap. 2.95 (*0-934920-07-9*, B-19) Derek Prince.

Baptism in the Holy Spirit: A Re-Examination of the New Testament Teaching on the Gift of the Spirit in Relation to Pentacostalism Today. James D. Dunn. LC 77-3995. 256p. 1977. pap. 14.99 (*0-664-24140-9*, Westminster) Westminster John Knox.

Baptism in the Holy Spirit: A Scriptural Foundation. Francis Martin. 62p. (Orig.). 1986. pap. 3.95 (*0-940535-04-1*, UP105) Franciscan U Pr.

Baptism in the New Testament. George R. Beasley-Murray. 434p. 1973. reprint ed. pap. 17.99 (*0-8028-1493-X*) Eerdmans.

Baptism in the New Testament: The Drama of Decision. Oscar S. Brooks. 280p. 1986. pap. 9.95 (*0-913573-40-X*) Hendrickson MA.

Baptism in Water & Baptism in the Spirit. Philippe Larere. 96p. (Orig.). 1994. pap. text ed. 7.95 (*0-8146-2225-9*) Liturgical Pr.

Baptism into the Holy Spirit. Robert B. Burnette. (Holy Spirit Ser.: Vol. 1). 64p. 1991. pap. 3.95 (*1-881202-09-7*) Anointed Pubns.

***Baptism Is a Beginning: A Four Year Series for Parish & Parents.** rev. ed. Ed. by Victoria M. Tufano. 1994. pap. 5.00 (*1-56854-017-5*, BBNEW) Liturgy Tr Pubns.

Baptism Journal, Boy. Cora Beutler. (Illus.). 28p. (Orig.). (J). 1992. pap. 2.95 (*1-56684-005-8*, Sigma Pub) Pubs Dist Ctr Inc.

Baptism Journal, Girl. Cora R. Beutler. (Illus.). 28p. (Orig.). (YA). 1992. pap. 2.95 (*1-56684-002-3*, Sigma Pub) Pubs Dist Ctr Inc.

Baptism of Desire: Poems. Louise Erdrich. LC 89-45650. 96p. 1991. reprint ed. pap. 11.00 (*0-06-092044-0*, PL) HarpC.

Baptism of Fire. Linda G. De Pauw. 392p. 1993. pap. 14.95 (*0-9634895-0-X*) Minerva Ctr.

Baptism of Fire. large type ed. Stella A. Whitelaw. 296p. 1994. 17.95 (*0-7505-0632-6*, Pub. by Magna Print Bks) Ulverscroft.

Baptism of Fire: The Republican Party in Iowa, 1838-1878. Robert Cook. LC 93-31825. (Illus.). 304p. 1993. text ed. 34.95 (*0-8138-1938-5*) Iowa St U Pr.

Baptism of Howie Cobb. Kenneth Robbins. LC 94-13788. 1994. 13.50 (*0-929925-28-9*) Univ SD Pr.

Baptism of the Holy Ghost. Alan Kitay. LC 87-34657. 144p. (Orig.). 1988. pap. 5.99 (*0-932581-29-3*) Word Aflame.

***Baptism of the Holy Spirit.** Debbie Bentley. (Basic Christian Doctrine Ser.: No. 4). 8p. (Orig.). (YA). 1995. pap. 1.00 (*1-885090-03-X*) Cosecha Latina.

Baptism of the Holy Spirit. Jack Van Impe. 44p. 1984. pap. 2.00 (*0-934803-02-1*) J Van Impe.

Baptism of the Holy Spirit: The Views of A. B. Simpson & His Contemporaries. Richard Gilbertson. LC 93-70746. 340p. (C). 1993. 19.99 (*0-87509-520-8*) Chr Pubns.

***Baptism of Truth: The Mystery of God Revealed.** James Tillman. LC 94-90386. (Illus.). 112p. (Orig.). 1995. pap. 6.95 (*0-9642925-7-2*) Eagle Messenger.

Baptism, Peace & the State in the Reformed & Mennonite Traditions. Ed. by Ross T. Bender & Alan P. Sell. (Calgary Institute for the Humanities Ser.). 264p. (C). 1991. text ed. 35.00 (*0-88920-204-4*, Pub. by Wilfrid Laurier CN) Humanities.

Baptism Record Athens NY, Zion Evangelical Lutheran Church, 1704-1899. Arthur C. Kelly. LC 75-300713. (Palatine Transcripts Ser.). 254p. 1974. lib. bdg. 44.00 (*1-56012-027-4*) Kinship Rhinebeck.

Baptism Record, Linlithgo Reformed Church, Livingston, NY, 1722-1899. Arthur C. Kelly. LC 72-525. (Palatine Transcripts Ser.). 229p. 1968. lib. bdg. 40.00 (*1-56012-004-5*) Kinship Rhinebeck.

Baptism Record of Caughnawaga Reformed Church, Fonda, NY, Now the Reformed Church of Fonda, 1758-1899. Arthur C. Kelly. LC 85-23111. (Palatine Transcripts Ser.). 378p. 1985. lib. bdg. 64.00 (*1-56012-072-X*) Kinship Rhinebeck.

Baptism Record of Gallatin Reformed Church, Gallatinville, NY, 1748-1899: Also Known As: Stissing Church, Dutch Reformed Church of Greenbush, Vedden Church. Arthur C. Kelly. (Palatine Transcripts Ser.). 169p. 1968. lib. bdg. 35.00 (*1-56012-003-7*) Kinship Rhinebeck.

Baptism Record of Gilead Lutheran Church, Brunswick, NY, 1777-1886. Arthur C. Kelly. (Palatine Transcripts Ser.). 242p. 1980. lib. bdg. 43.00 (*1-56012-048-7*) Kinship Rhinebeck.

Baptism Record of Helderburg Reformed Church, Gilderland Center, NY, 1786-1860. Donald A. Keefer. Ed. by Arthur C. Kelly. (Palatine Transcripts Ser.). 172p. 1984. lib. bdg. 33.00 (*1-56012-066-5*) Kinship Rhinebeck.

Baptism Record of Kinderhook Reformed Church, Kinderhook, NY, 1718-1899. Arthur C. Kelly. LC 86-147975. (Palatine Transcripts Ser.). 403p. 1985. lib. bdg. 67.50 (*1-56012-074-6*) Kinship Rhinebeck.

Baptism Record of Reformed Church, Marbletown NY, 1746-1871. Arthur C. Kelly. LC 79-113179. (Palatine Transcripts Ser.). 216p. 1979. lib. bdg. 39.00 (*1-56012-043-6*) Kinship Rhinebeck.

Baptism Record of Reformed Church, Stone Arabia NY, 1739-1899: Also Called: German Reformed Church at Stone Arabia. Arthur C. Kelly. LC 82-142952. (Palatine Transcripts Ser.). 250p. 1982. lib. bdg. 45.00 (*1-56012-055-X*) Kinship Rhinebeck.

Baptism Record of Schenectady Reformed Church, Schenectady NY, 1694-1811. Donald A. Keefer & Arthur C. Kelly. LC 88-132956. (Palatine Transcripts Ser.). 539p. 1987. lib. bdg. 55.00 (*1-56012-080-0*) Kinship Rhinebeck.

Baptism Record of Shokan Reformed Church, Shokan, Ulster County, NY, 1799-1899. Arthur C. Kelly. LC 88-119646. (Palatine Transcripts Ser.). 93p. 1987. lib. bdg. 21.00 (*1-56012-081-9*) Kinship Rhinebeck.

Baptism Record of St. Paul's Lutheran Church, Schoharie, NY, 1728-1899: Schoharie United Presbyterian Church. Arthur C. Kelly. LC 77-368155. (Palatine Transcripts Ser.). 295p. 1977. lib. bdg. 49.00 (*1-56012-034-7*) Kinship Rhinebeck.

Baptism Record of St. Peter's Lutheran Church, Rhinebeck, New York (Called Stone Church), 1733-1899. Arthur C. Kelly. LC 68-6863. (Palatine Transcripts Ser.). 245p. 1968. lib. bdg. 45.00 (*1-56012-001-0*) Kinship Rhinebeck.

Baptism Record of St. Thomas Lutheran Church, Churchtown, NY, 1760-1899: Lutheran Church of Claverack. Arthur C. Kelly. LC 74-12720. (Palatine Transcripts Ser.). 302p. 1969. lib. bdg. 52.00 (*1-56012-008-8*) Kinship Rhinebeck.

Baptism Record of the Reformed Church, Herkimer, NY, 1801-1899. Arthur C. Kelly. LC 83-244834. (Palatine Transcripts Ser.). 211p. 1983. lib. bdg. 38.50 (*1-56012-062-2*) Kinship Rhinebeck.

Baptism Record of the Schoharie Reformed Church, Schoharie, NY, c. 1721. Arthur C. Kelly. LC 77-155044. (Palatine Transcripts Ser.). 256p. 1977. lib. bdg. 45.00 (*1-56012-038-X*) Kinship Rhinebeck.

Baptism Record of Trinity Lutheran Church, Stone Arabia NY, pre-1751-1899. Arthur C. Kelly. LC 82-234223. (Palatine Transcripts Ser.). 319p. 1982. lib. bdg. 55.00 (*1-56012-057-6*) Kinship Rhinebeck.

Baptism Record Reformed Church Coxsackie, NY, 1738-1899. Arthur C. Kelly. LC 76-374227. (Palatine Transcripts Ser.). 202p. 1976. lib. bdg. 37.00 (*1-56012-031-2*) Kinship Rhinebeck.

Baptism Record, Reformed Church West Copake, NY, 1783-1899. Arthur C. Kelly. LC 78-10936. (Palatine Transcripts Ser.). 189p. 1969. lib. bdg. 37.00 (*1-56012-007-X*) Kinship Rhinebeck.

Baptism Record, St. Paul's Lutheran Church of Wurtemburg, Rhinebeck, NY, 1760-1899. Arthur C. Kelly. LC 71-3307. (Palatine Transcripts Ser.). 112p. 1969. lib. bdg. 24.00 (*1-56012-002-9*) Kinship Rhinebeck.

Baptism Record St. Paul's Lutheran Church West Camp, NY, 1708-1899: And Lutheran Chapel Sauqerties, 1844-1851 & Evangelical Lutheran Church of Messiah, Troy 1869. Arthur C. Kelly. LC 76-351661. (Palatine Transcripts Ser.). 105p. 1975. lib. bdg. 22.00 (*1-56012-029-0*) Kinship Rhinebeck.

Baptism Service, Marriage Service, Funeral Rite, Wake & Cemetery Service, Anointing of the Sick, 4 bks., Set. large type ed. pap. 20.00 (*0-317-01850-7*) Cath Guild Blind.

Baptism Sourcebook. Ed. by J. Robert Baker et al. LC 93-4123. (Seasonal Sourcebook Ser.). 224p. 1993. pap. 12.95 (*0-929650-93-X*) Liturgy Tr Pubns.

Baptism with the Holy Spirit. Perry A. Gaspard. 1983. pap. 1.50 (*0-931867-02-9*) Abundant Life Pubns.

Baptism with the Holy Spirit. R. A. Torrey. 96p. 1972. pap. 3.99 (*0-87123-029-1*) Bethany Hse.

Baptismal, Confirmation, Marriage & Death Records: 1860-1952. St. Joseph Catholic Church, Galveston, Texas Staff. 1984. 27.50 (*0-89308-344-5*) Southern Hist Pr.

Baptismal Record of Christ Lutheran Church Germantown, NY, 1746-1899. Arthur C. Kelly. LC 72-171039. (Palatine Transcripts Ser.). 153p. 1972. lib. bdg. 29.00 (*1-56012-019-3*) Kinship Rhinebeck.

Baptismal Record of Eight Episcopal Congregations of Old Rhinebeck, 1816-1899: All Saints Chapel, Upper Red Hook, 1887-1899; Christ's Church, Red Hook, 1854-1899; Church of St. John, Annandale, 1854-1899; Church of the Messiah, Rhinebeck, 1840-1899; St. Paul's Church, Tivoli, 1816-1899. Arthur C. Kelly. LC 72-195484. (Palatine Transcripts Ser.). 181p. 1972. lib. bdg. 34.00 (*1-56012-018-5*) Kinship Rhinebeck.

Baptismal Record of German Flats Reformed Church (Fort Herkimer Reformed Church), 1763-1795; 1811-1848; 1896-1899. Arthur C. Kelly. LC 83-182636. (Palatine Transcripts Ser.). 219p. 1983. lib. bdg. 39.00 (*1-56012-061-4*) Kinship Rhinebeck.

Baptismal Record of Reformed Church, Claverack, NY, 1727-1899. Arthur C. Kelly. LC 70-12703. (Palatine Transcripts Ser.). 443p. 1970. lib. bdg. 72.00 (*1-56012-009-6*) Kinship Rhinebeck.

Baptismal Record of Reformed Church of Germantown, NY, 1729-1898. Arthur C. Kelly. LC 75-12234. (Palatine Transcripts Ser.). 342p. 1969. lib. bdg. 59.00 (*1-56012-005-3*) Kinship Rhinebeck.

Baptismal Record of Reformed Church, Rhinebeck, NY, 1731-1899: Also Called Reformed Church of Rhinebeck Flatts Church of Christ at Rhinebeck Flatts, 1731-1899. Arthur C. Kelly. LC 79-21153. (Palatine Transcripts Ser.). 229p. 1970. lib. bdg. 42.00 (*1-56012-012-6*) Kinship Rhinebeck.

Baptismal Record of Reformed Dutch Church, Hillsdale, NY, 1776-1849: Krum Church, Dutch Church of New Claverack. Arthur C. Kelly. LC 74-15268. (Palatine Transcripts Ser.). 61p. 1970. lib. bdg. 16.00 (*1-56012-010-X*) Kinship Rhinebeck.

Baptismal Record of St. John's Evangelical Lutheran Church, Manorton, NY, 1765-1872: Lutheran Church of Livingston. Arthur C. Kelly. LC 72-177996. (Palatine Transcripts Ser.). 287p. 1971. lib. bdg. 47.00 (*1-56012-017-7*) Kinship Rhinebeck.

Baptismal Record of St. Paul's (Zion's) Lutheran Church, Red Hook, NY, 1730-1899: German Reformed Zion & of Rhinebeck, German Reformed Church of Lower Red Hook, First Lutheran Church of Red Hook. Arthur C. Kelly. LC 78-26776. (Palatine Transcripts Ser.). 301p. 1971. lib. bdg. 52.00 (*1-56012-014-2*) Kinship Rhinebeck.

Baptismal Records of Jerusalem Lutheran & Reformed Church, Berks County, Pennsylvania. John L. Kistler. 62p. 5.75 (*0-915156-07-5*, 23) Natl Genealogical.

Baptismal Regeneration. C. H. Spurgeon. 1970. pap. 2.00 (*1-56186-402-1*) Pilgrim Pubns.

Baptisms & Admission from the Records of First Church in Falmouth (Maine) Comp. by Marquis F. King. (Illus.). 140p. 1990. reprint ed. pap. 13.50 (*1-55613-374-X*) Heritage Bk.

Baptisms, Bk. 4: A Study of the Elementary Principles of Christ. Ed. by Joe Oakley. (First Principles Ser.). 1990. student ed 5.00 (*0-923968-04-0*) Shady Grove Ch Pubns.

Baptisms, Bk. 4: A Study of the Elementary Principles of Christ, Set. Ed. by Joe Oakley. (First Principles Ser.). 1990. 28.00 (*0-318-49990-8*) Shady Grove Ch Pubns.

Baptist Battles: Social Change & Religious Conflict in the Southern Baptist Convention. Nancy T. Ammerman. LC 89-48883. 380p. (Orig.). (C). 1990. text ed. 40.00 (*0-8135-1556-4*); pap. text ed. 14.00 (*0-8135-1557-2*) Rutgers U Pr.

Baptist Beliefs. Edgar Y. Mullins. 1987. pap. 8.50 (*0-8170-1014-9*) Judson.

Baptist Bibliography, Set. Edward C. Starr. Incl. Vol. 1. Authors A. 1947. 13.25 (*0-910056-00-5*); Vol. 2. Authors B-Biloxi. 1952. 16.55 (*0-910056-01-3*); Vol. 3. Authors Bin-Bz. 1953. 21.20 (*0-910056-02-1*); Vol. 4. Authors C-Colby. 1954. 16.55 (*0-910056-03-X*); Vol. 5. Authors Colchester-Cz. 1957. 13.25 (*0-910056-04-8*); Vol. 6. Authors D. 1958. 13.25 (*0-910056-05-6*); Vol. 7. Authors E-Flynt. 1961. 13.25 (*0-910056-06-4*); Vol. 8. Authors Fo-Glazier. 1963. 16.55 (*0-910056-07-2*); Vol. 9. Authors Gleason-Halko. 1964. 16.55 (*0-910056-08-0*); Vol. 10. Authors Hall-Hill, Joseph. 1965. 16.55 (*0-910056-09-9*); Vol. 11. Authors Hill, Kizard. 1966. 13.25 (*0-910056-10-2*); Vol. 12. Authors J. 1967. 13.25 (*0-910056-11-0*); Vol. 13. Authors K-Layton. 1968. 16.55 (*0-910056-12-9*); Vol. 14. Authors Lea-McGuire. 1969. 16.55 (*0-910056-13-7*); Vol. 15. Authors McIlvain-Merrill. 1970. 16.55 (*0-910056-14-5*); Vol. 16. Authors Merrimac-Nevin. 1971. 16.55 (*0-910056-15-3*); Vol. 17. Authors New-Pastors. 1972. 16.55 (*0-910056-16-1*); Vol. 18. Authors Pate-Poynton. 1972. 16.55 (*0-910056-17-X*); Vol. 19. Authors Pra-Rives. 1973. 16.55 (*0-910056-18-8*); Vol. 20. Authors Ro-Sardis. 1974. 13.25 (*0-685-24442-3*); Vol. 21. Authors Sare-Smith, S. 1974. 16.55 (*0-685-24443-1*); Vol. 22. Authors Smith, T.-Steude. 1975. 16.55 (*0-685-24444-X*); Vol. 23. Authors Steven-Torbet. 1976. 16.55 (*0-685-24445-8*); Vol. 24. Authors Torey-Wa. 1976. 16.55 (*0-685-24446-6*); Vol. 25. Authors We-Z. 1976. 21.20 (*0-910056-24-2*); 400.00 (*0-685-00244-6*) Am Baptist.

Baptist Bibliography: Being a Register of the Chief Materials for Babtist History Preserved in Great Britain, Ireland, & the Colonies, 2 vols. in 1. William T. Whitley. 510p. 1984. reprint ed. 102.70 (*3-487-07456-7*, Pub. by Georg Olms GW) Lubrecht & Cramer.

Baptist Church Manual. J. Newton Brown. 38p. 1940. pap. 2.25 (*0-8170-0015-1*) Judson.

Baptist Church Manual. rev. ed. James M. Pendleton. 1966. reprint ed. 12.99 (*0-8054-2510-1*) Broadman.

Baptist Clergy Index 1840-1852. 1988. 40.00 (*0-89593-629-1*) Accelerated Index.

Baptist Confessions of Faith. William L. Lumpkin. (Illus.). 1959. 23.00 (*0-8170-0016-X*) Judson.

Baptist Congregation. Stanley J. Grenz. 128p. 1985. pap. 10.00 (*0-8170-1083-1*) Judson.

Baptist Convictions. Winthrop S. Hudson. 1962. pap. 2.50 (*0-8170-0295-2*) Judson.

Baptist Deacon. Robert E. Naylor. 1955. 11.99 (*0-8054-3501-8*) Broadman.

Baptist Dishes Worth Blessing. Ed. by Judy Bryson. LC 78-631. (Illus.). 300p. 1978. 12.95 (*0-88289-188-X*) Pelican.

Baptist Distinctives: A Pattern for Service. R. Dowd Davis. 64p. (Orig.). 1986. pap. 3.95 (*0-913029-11-4*) Stevens Bk Pr.

Baptist Doctrines & History. D. N. Jackson. 1974. pap. 3.95 (*0-89114-003-4*) Baptist Pub Hse.

Baptist Ecclesiology: An Original Anthology. William H. Allison & W. W. Barnes. Ed. by Edwin S. Gaustad. LC 79-52582. (Baptist Tradition Ser.). 1980. lib. bdg. 23.95 (*0-405-12449-X*) Ayer.

Baptist Heritage. Leon McBeth. LC 86-31667. 1987. 29.99 (*0-8054-6569-3*) Broadman.

Baptist History of the North Pacific Coast. J. C. Baker. Ed. by Edwin S. Gaustad. LC 79-52589. (Baptist Tradition Ser.). (Illus.). 1980. reprint ed. lib. bdg. 53.95 (*0-405-12456-2*) Ayer.

Baptist Hymnal Indices. Wayne L. Hedger. 132p. 1993. pap. 7.95 (*0-9630656-0-2*) Glory Pr.

Baptist Identity: A Study Guide. Terry Hamrick. 40p. (Orig.). 1994. pap. 5.00 (*1-880837-55-2*) Smyth & Helwys.

***Baptist Identity: Four Fragile Freedoms.** Walter Shurden. 152p. (KOR.). 1994. pap. 10.95 (*1-57312-022-7*) Smyth & Helwys.

Baptist Identity: Four Fragile Freedoms. Walter B. Shurden. LC 93-715. 128p. 1993. pap. 9.95 (*1-880837-20-X*) Smyth & Helwys.

Baptist Life & Thought: Sixteen Hundred to Nineteen Eighty. Ed. by William Brackney. 448p. 1983. 16.00 (*0-8170-0959-0*) Judson.

Baptist Manual of Polity & Practice. rev. ed. Norman H. Maring & Winthrop S. Hudson. 1991. 24.00 (*0-8170-1171-4*) Judson.

Baptist Mission Portraits. John A. Moore. 180p. (Orig.). 1994. pap. 11.95 (*1-880837-79-X*) Smyth & Helwys.

Baptist Missions in Nagaland. Joseph Puthenpurakal. 1984. 22.50 (*0-8364-1138-2*, Pub. by Mukhopadhyaya II) S Asia.

Baptist Piety: The Last Will & Testimony of Obadiah Holmes. Edwin S. Gaustad. LC 79-52570. (Baptist Tradition Ser.). 1980. lib. bdg. 19.95 (*0-405-12439-2*) Ayer.

Baptist Piety: The Last Will & Testimony of Obadiah Holmes. Intro. by Edwin S. Gaustad. LC 93-42927. 1994. pap. 12.00 (*0-8170-1204-4*) Judson.

Baptist Roots in America: The Historical Backgrounds of Reformed Baptists in America. Samuel E. Waldron. 54p. (Orig.). 1991. pap. 6.95 (*0-9622508-3-X*) Simpson NJ.

Baptist Succession. D. B. Ray. 1984. reprint ed. 22.00 (*0-317-11348-8*) Church History.

Baptist Successionism: A Crucial Question in Baptist History. James E. McGoldrick. LC 93-5931. (American Theological Library Association Monograph: No. 32). 190p. 1994. 27.50 (*0-8108-2726-3*) Scarecrow.

Baptist Theologians. Timothy George & David Dockery. LC 89-29532. (C). 1992. text ed. 32.99 (*0-8054-6588-X*) Broadman.

Baptist Trailmakers of Michigan. Coe Hayne. 1977. reprint ed. 6.50 (*0-915056-06-2*) Hardscrabble Bks.

An Asterisk (*) at the beginning of an entry indicates that the title is appearing in BIP for the first time.

An Asterisk (*) at the beginning of an entry indicates that the title is appearing in BIP for the first time.

B

Barbara Fealy's Gardens: An Seen & Photographed by Ann Hughes, Dale Jones, & Terry Toedtemeier. Terri Hopkins. (Illus.). 1990. pap. 10.00 (*0-914435-18-3*) Marylhurst Art.

Barbara Frietchie. John Greenleaf Whittier. LC 90-41755. 32p. (J). (gr. 1 up). 1992. 14.00 (*0-688-09829-0*); lib. bdg. 13.93 (*0-688-09830-4*) Greenwillow.

***Barbara Frietchie.** braille ed. John G. Whittier. 25p. 1994. pap. text ed. 2.00 (*1-56956-531-7*, BR9529) W A T Braille.

Barbara Hannah: The Cat, Dog, & Horse Lectures & "The Beyond" Ed. by Dean L. Frantz. 152p. (Orig.). 1992. pap. 14.95 (*0-933029-59-4*) Chiron Pubns.

Barbara Hepworth: A Guide to the Tate Gallery Collection. David F. Jenkins. (Tate Gallery Ser.). (Illus.). 48p. 1982. pap. 10.00 (*0-295-96730-7*) U of Wash Pr.

***Barbara Hepworth: A Memoir.** Margaret Gardiner. (Illus.). 64p. (C). 1994. pap. 15.95 (*0-85331-674-0*, Pub. by Lund Humphries UK) Antique Collect.

***Barbara Hepworth: A Retrospective.** Alan G. Wilkinson & Penelope Curtis. (Illus.). 168p. 1995. pap. 40.00 (*1-85437-141-X*) U of Wash Pr.

Barbara Jordan. Rose Blue & Corinne J. Naden. (Black Americans of Achievement Ser.). (Illus.). 112p. (YA). (gr. 5 up). 1992. lib. bdg. 17.95 (*0-7910-1131-3*) Chelsea Hse.

Barbara Jordan. Norman Kelin. 1993. pap. 3.95 (*0-87067-598-2*, Melrose Sq) Holloway.

***Barbara Jordan.** Diane Patrick-Wexler. LC 95-12611. (Contemporary African Americans Ser.). (J). 1995. write for info. (*0-8172-3976-6*) Raintree Steck-V.

Barbara Jordan: Congresswoman. Linda C. Johnson. (Library of Famous Women). (Illus.). 64p. (J). (gr. 3-7). 1990. lib. bdg. 14.95 (*1-56711-031-2*) Blackbirch.

Barbara Jordan: Congresswomen. Linda C. Johnson. (Library of Famous Women). (Illus.). 64p. (J). (gr. 3-7). 1990. pap. 7.95 (*1-56711-050-9*) Blackbirch.

Barbara Jordan: The Great Lady from Texas. rev. ed. Naurice Roberts. LC 83-23169. (Picture-Story Biographies Ser.). (Illus.). 32p. (J). (gr. 2-5). 1990. lib. bdg. 11.85 (*0-516-03511-8*); pap. 3.95 (*0-516-43511-6*) Childrens.

Barbara Kasten: Works from 1986-1990. Photos by Barbara Kasten. (Illus.). 54p. 1991. 55.00 (*0-9630785-0-X*) Res Art Media.

Barbara Kraus Calorie Guide to Brand Names & Basic Foods. rev. ed. Barbara Kraus. 224p. 1993. pap. 3.50 (*0-451-17385-6*, Sig) NAL-Dutton.

Barbara Kraus Calorie Guide to Brand Names & Basic Foods. rev. ed. Barbara Kraus. 256p. 1994. 3.50 (*0-451-17770-3*, Sig) NAL-Dutton.

Barbara Kraus Calorie Guide, 1988. rev. ed. Barbara Kraus. 1988. pap. 2.75 (*0-317-01379-3*, Sig) NAL-Dutton.

Barbara Kraus Carbohydrate Guide, 1988. Barbara Kraus. 1988. pap. 2.75 (*0-317-01380-7*, Sig) NAL-Dutton.

Barbara Kraus Cholesterol Counter. Barbara Kraus. 128p. (Orig.). 1985. pap. 6.95 (*0-399-51134-2*, Perigree Bks) Berkley Pub.

Barbara Kraus Sodium Guide to Brand Names & Basic Foods. Barbara Kraus. 1983. mass mkt. 6.95 (*0-452-25424-8*, Plume) NAL-Dutton.

***Barbara Lavallee's Painted Ladies: And Other Celebrations.** Illus. by Barbara Lavallee. 80p. 1995. 34.95 (*0-945397-36-4*) Epicenter Pr.

***Barbara Lavallee's Painted Ladies: And Other Celebrations.** Illus. by Barbara Lavallee. 80p. 1995. pap. 22.95 (*0-945397-37-2*) Epicenter Pr.

Barbara Mandrell Story. Charles P. Conn. 1989. 3.95 (*0-318-41967-X*) S&S Trade.

Barbara McClintock. Charlotte Kent. (American Women of Achievement Ser.). (Illus.). 112p. (J). (gr. 5 up). 1991. lib. bdg. 17.95 (*1-55546-666-4*) Chelsea Hse.

***Barbara McClintock: Alone in Her Field.** Deborah Heiligman. (J). (gr. 3-7). 1995. pap. text ed. 4.95 (*0-7167-6548-9*, Sci Am Yng Rdrs) W H Freeman.

Barbara McClintock: Alone in Her Field. Deborah Helligman. LC 94-6542. (J). (gr. 3-7). 1995. text ed. 14.95 (*0-7167-6536-5*, Sci Am Yng Rdrs) W H Freeman.

***Barbara Parks Series.** Barbara Parks. Date not set. 24.98 (*0-679-87019-9*) Random.

Barbara Pentland. Sheila J. Eastman & Tomothy J. McGee. LC 83-171890. (Canadian Composers - Compositeurs Canadiens Ser.: No. 3). 146p. reprint ed. pap. 41.70 (*0-7837-1047-X*, 2041359) Bks Demand.

Barbara Pym. Michael Cotsell. LC 88-4443. (Modern Novelists Ser.). 150p. 1989. text ed. 29.95 (*0-312-02054-6*) St Martin.

Barbara Pym. Robert E. Long. (Literature & Life Ser.). 263p. (C). 1986. 19.95 (*0-8044-2545-0*, F Ungar Bks) Continuum.

Barbara Pym. Jane Nardin. LC 85-774. (English Authors Ser.: No. 406). 1985. text ed. 19.95 (*0-8057-6897-1*, Twayne) Macmillan.

Barbara Pym: A Critical Biography. Anne M. Wyatt-Brown. 232p. (C). 1992. text ed. 29.95 (*0-8262-0820-7*) U of Mo Pr.

Barbara Pym: A Reference Guide. Dale Salwak. (Reference Guides to Literature Ser.). 193p. (C). 1991. text ed. 34.95 (*0-8161-9076-3*, Hall Reference) Macmillan.

Barbara Pym: Writing a Life. Orphia J. Allen. LC 94-18867. 1994. 35.00 (*0-8108-2875-8*) Scarecrow.

Barbara Pym & the Novel of Manners. Annette Weld. 1992. text ed. 45.00 (*0-312-06808-5*) St Martin.

Barbara Taylor Bradford: Three Complete Novels. Barbara Taylor Bradford. LC 92-19641. 1992. 11.99 (*0-517-08470-8*, Pub. by Wings Bks) Random Hse Value.

Barbara Villiers. Alexander Del Mar. 1973. 250.00 (*0-87968-705-3*) Gordon Pr.

Barbara Walker Tarot. Barbara Walker. 48p. 1986. 15.00 (*0-88079-292-2*) US Games Syst.

Barbara Walker's Learn to Knit Afghan Book. Barbara G. Walker. LC 73-10906. (Encore Edition Ser.). (Illus.). 1976. 1.95 (*0-684-16929-0*, Scribners) S&S Trade.

Barbara Walters. Jerry Oppenheimer. 1991. mass mkt. 5.95 (*0-312-92387-2*) St Martin.

Barbara Yochem's Inner Shooting. Barbara Yochem. 128p. 1981. 6.95 (*0-938826-03-4*); pap. 3.95 (*0-938826-02-6*) By By Prods.

Barbara's View: Los Angeles, California. rev. ed. Barbara W. Levy. (Illus.). (Orig.). 1992. pap. 7.50 (*1-882340-08-6*) Barbaras View.

Barbara's View: Miami & South Florida. Barbara W. Levy. (Illus.). 1993. pap. 7.50 (*1-882340-09-4*) Barbaras View.

Barbara's View: Miami & South Florida. rev. ed. Barbara W. Levy. 1994. 7.50 (*1-882340-16-7*) Barbaras View.

***Barbara's View: Miami & South Florida XXI 263-195.** Barbara W. Levy. (Illus.). 1994. pap. 7.50 (*1-882340-17-5*) Barbaras View.

Barbara's View: Milan, Italy. Barbara W. Levy. (Illus.). 1993. reprint ed. pap. 7.50 (*1-882340-14-0*) Barbaras View.

Barbara's View: New York, New York. Barbara W. Levy. (Illus.). 1993. pap. 7.50 (*1-882340-11-6*) Barbaras View.

Barbare en Asie. Henri Michaux. (Imaginaire Ser.). 238p. (FRE.). 1986. pap. 15.95 (*2-07-070622-2*) Schoenhof.

Barbarian Asia & the Greek Experience: From the Archaic Period to the Age of Xenophon. Pericles Georges. LC 93-36319. (Ancient Society & History Ser.). (C). 1994. text ed. 42.50x (*0-8018-4734-6*) Johns Hopkins.

Barbarian Conversion. Richard Fletcher. 1997. 35.00 (*0-8050-2763-7*) H Holt & Co.

***Barbarian Eye: Lord Napier in China, 1834: The Prelude to Hong Kong.** Priscilla Napier. (Illus.). 250p. 1995. 37.00 (*1-85753-116-7*, Pub. by Brasseys UK) Brasseys Inc.

Barbarian in Asia. Henri Michaux. Tr. by Sylvia Beach. LC 86-5362. (Revived Modern Classics Ser.). 192p. 1986. reprint ed. pap. 7.95 (*0-8112-0991-1*, NDP622) New Directions.

Barbarian in the Garden. Zbigniew Herbert. 184p. 1986. pap. 7.95 (*0-15-610681-7*, Harvest Bks) HarBrace.

Barbarian Invasions: Catalyst of a New Order. Ed. by Katherine F. Drew. LC 77-8450. (European Problem Studies). 144p. 1977. reprint ed. pap. text ed. 8.50 (*0-88275-572-2*) Krieger.

Barbarian Invasions: History of the Art of War, Vol. II. Hans Delbruck. (Illus.). 505p. 1990. pap. 16.95 (*0-8032-9200-7*, Bison Books) U of Nebr Pr.

Barbarian Invasions of Italy, 2 vols, Set. Pasquale Villari. Tr. by Linda Villari. LC 70-153607. reprint ed. 22.50 (*0-404-09275-6*) AMS Pr.

Barbarian Play: Plautus' Roman Comedy. William S. Anderson. LC 93-93219. (Robson Classical Lectures Ser.: Vol. 1). 184p. 1994. 50.00 (*0-8020-2815-2*) U of Toronto Pr.

Barbarian Sentiments: Nationalism & Ideology in the Modern Age. William Pfaff. 1989. 19.95 (*0-8090-6665-3*) Hill & Wang.

Barbarian Stories. Naomi M. Mitchison. LC 77-134970. (Short Story Index Reprint Ser.). 1977. 18.95 (*0-8369-3701-5*) Ayer.

Barbarian Temperamental: Toward a Postmodern Critical Theory. Stjepan Mestrovic. LC 92-45836. 1993. write for info. (*0-415-08572-1*, Routledge NY) Routledge.

Barbarian Tides, (1500-600 BC) (Time Frame Ser.). (Illus.). 176p. 1987. lib. bdg. 25.93 (*0-8094-6405-5*) Time-Life.

Barbarian West: Four Hundred to One Thousand. 3rd ed. J. M. Wallace-Hadrill. (Illus.). 181p. 1985. pap. text ed. 19.95 (*0-631-14083-2*) Blackwell Pubs.

Barbarians. Odile Bombarde. LC 87-34092. (Illus.). 38p. (J). (gr. k-5). 1988. 5.95 (*0-944589-10-3*, 103) Young Discovery Lib.

Barbarians: A Soldier's New Guinea Diary. Peter Pinney. (Orig.). 1989. pap. 15.95 (*0-7022-2158-9*, Pub. by Univ Queensland Pr AT) Intl Spec Bk.

Barbarians: Killing Time, Abide with Me, In the City. Barrie Keeffe. 104p. 1981. pap. 8.95 (*0-413-38990-1*, A0017, Pub. by Methuen UK) Heinemann.

Barbarians: Warriors & Wars of the Dark Ages. Tim Newark. (Illus.). 160p. 1988. pap. 16.95 (*0-7137-2042-5*, Pub. by Blandford Pr UK) Sterling.

Barbarians & Bishops: Army, Church, & State in the Age of Arcadius & Chrysostom. J. H. Liebeschuetz. 304p. 1992. pap. 35.00 (*0-19-814073-8*) OUP.

Barbarians & Politics at the Court of Arcadius. Alan Cameron & Jacqueline Long. LC 91-16486. (Transformation of the Classical Heritage Ser.: Vol. XIX). (C). 1992. 55.00 (*0-520-06550-6*) U CA Pr.

Barbarians & Romans: The Birth Struggle of Europe A. D. 400-700. Justine D. Randers-Pehrson. LC 82-20025. 400p. 1993. pap. 14.95 (*0-8061-2511-X*) U of Okla Pr.

Barbarians & Romans: The Birth Struggle of Europe, A.D. 400-700. Justine D. Randers-Pherson. LC 82-20025. (Illus.). 416p. 1983. 37.95 (*0-8061-1818-0*) U of Okla Pr.

Barbarians & Romans, A.D. Four Hundred Eighteen to Five Hundred Eighty-Four: The Techniques of Accommodation. Walter Goffart. (Illus.). 296p. 1987. pap. 18.95 (*0-691-10231-7*) Princeton U Pr.

Barbarians at the Gate. B. Burrough. 1991. pap. 262.80 (*0-06-092073-4*, PL) HarpC.

Barbarians at the Gate: The Fall of RJR Nabisco. Bryan Burrough & John Helyar. LC 89-45635. (Illus.). 544p. 1993. reprint ed. pap. 13.00 (*0-06-092038-6*, PL) HarpC.

Barbarians from the Isle. Sigmund Brouwer. (Winds of Light Ser.: No. 2). 132p. (J). (gr. 5-8). 1992. pap. 4.99 (*0-89693-116-1*) SP Pubns.

Barbarians in Greek Comedy. Timothy Long. LC 85-18363. 328p. (C). 1986. text ed. 29.95 (*0-8093-1248-4*) S Ill U Pr.

Barbarians of Asia: The Peoples of the Steppes from 1600 B.C. Stuart Legg. (Dorset Press Reprints Ser.). (Illus.). 350p. 1990. reprint ed. 19.95 (*0-88029-534-1*) Dorset Pr.

Barbarians of the North: Modern Chihuahua & the Mexican Political System. Manuel A. Machado. (Illus.). 224p. 1993. 19.95 (*0-89015-839-8*) Sunbelt Media.

Barbarian's Quest. Michael Pilla. 392p. (Orig.). 1992. pap. 9.99 (*1-56043-652-2*) Destiny Image.

Barbarians to Bureaucrats: Corporate Life Cycle Strategies. Lawrence M. Miller. 1990. pap. 12.00 (*0-449-90526-8*) Fawcett.

Barbarians Within the Gates of Rome: A Study of Roman Military Policy & the Barbarians, ca. 375-425 A. D. Thomas S. Burns. LC 94-12788. 1994. 35.00 (*0-253-31288-4*) Ind U Pr.

Barbaric Counter-Revolution: Cause & Cure. W. W. Rostow. 140p. 1983. 13.95 (*0-292-70749-5*) U of Tex Pr.

Barbaric Others: A Manifesto of Western Racism. Ziauddin Sardar et al. LC 93-8511. 99p. (C). 1993. text ed. 50.00 (*0-7453-0742-6*, Pub. by Pluto Pr UK); pap. text ed. 13.50 (*0-7453-0743-4*, Pub. by Pluto Pr UK) Westview.

Barbarie a Visage Humaine. B. H. Levy. (FRE.). 1985. pap. 12.95 (*0-7859-3127-9*) Fr & Eur.

Barbarism & Sexual Freedom. Alex. Comfort. LC 76-30586. (Anarchy & Anarchism: No. 99). 1977. lib. bdg. 75.00 (*0-8383-2147-X*) M S G Haskell Hse.

Barbarism of Reason: Max Weber & the Twilight of Enlightenment. Ed. by Asher Horowitz & Terry Maley. 328p. (C). 1994. 60.00 (*0-8020-0558-6*); pap. 24.95 (*0-8020-6980-0*) U of Toronto Pr.

Barbarolexis: Medieval Writing & Sexuality. Alexandre Leupin. Tr. by Kate M. Cooper. LC 89-1999. 272p. 1989. 42.50 (*0-674-06170-5*) HUP.

Barbarossa. Time-Life Books Editors. (Third Reich Ser.). 1990. write for info. (*0-8094-6991-X*); lib. bdg. write for info. (*0-8094-6992-8*) Time-Life.

***Barbarossa: The Axis & the Allies.** Ed. by John Erickson & David Dilks. (Perspectives in Intelligence History Ser.). (Illus.). 256p. 1994. 40.00 (*0-7486-0504-5*, Pub. by Edinburgh U Pr UK) Col U Pr.

Barbarossa: The Russian-German Conflict, 1941-1945. Alan Clark. LC 85-502. (Illus.). 528p. 1985. reprint ed. pap. 13.00 (*0-688-04268-6*, Quill) Morrow.

Barbarossa in Italy: A Verse Translation of the Carmen de Gestis Federici I Imperatoris in Lombardia. Tr. & Intro. by Thomas Carson. LC 94-27071. (Illus.). 232p. (Orig.). 1994. pap. 14.50 (*0-934977-30-5*) Italica Pr.

Barbarous Nights: Legends & Plays. Federico Garcia Lorca. Tr. by Christopher Sawyer-Laucanno. 112p. (Orig.). 1991. pap. 6.95 (*0-87286-257-7*) City Lights.

Barbary & Enlightenment: European Attitudes towards the Maghreb in the 18th Century. Ann Thomson. (Brill's Studies in Intellectual History: Vol. 2). viii, 173p. 1987. 51.00 (*90-04-08273-5*) E J Brill.

***Barbary Baseball: The Pacific Coast League of the 1920s.** R. Scott Mackey. 288p. 1995. pap. 25.95x (*0-7864-0055-2*) McFarland & Co.

Barbary Coast. Herbert Asbury. 1992. reprint ed. lib. bdg. 75.00 (*0-7812-5000-5*) Rprt Serv.

Barbary Coast: Algeria under the Turks. John B. Wolf. (Illus.). 384p. (C). 1982. pap. text ed. 5.95 (*0-393-95201-0*) Norton.

Barbary Coast: An Informal History of the San Francisco Underworld. Herbert Asbury. (Old Town Books Reprints Ser.). (Illus.). 318p. 1990. 19.95 (*0-88029-428-0*) Dorset Pr.

Barbary Corsairs. S. Lane-Poole. 334p. 1984. 200.00 (*1-85077-018-2*, Darf Pubs Ltd) St Mut.

Barbary Legend. Godfrey Fisher. LC 74-9166. (Illus.). 349p. 1982. reprint ed. text ed. 97.50 (*0-8371-7617-4*, AEFIBL, Greenwood Pr) Greenwood.

Barbary Pirates. C. S. Forester. 18.95 (*0-88411-927-0*, Aeonian Pr) Amereon Ltd.

Barbecue: The Fine Art of Charcoal & Gas Outdoor Cooking. Carol D. Brent. LC 77-152731. 1971. 5.95 (*0-88351-005-7*) Test Recipe.

Barbecue Cookbook. Tess Mallos. 1994. 9.99 (*0-517-10251-X*) Random Hse Value.

Barbecue Cookbook. 6th ed. Sunset Magazine & Book Editors. LC 85-81593. 96p. 1986. pap. 8.99 (*0-376-02080-6*) Sunset Menlo Pk.

Barbecue Greats - Memphis Style: Great Restaurants, Great Recipes & Great Personalities. Carolyn Wells. 150p. (Orig.). 1989. pap. 14.95x (*0-925175-03-X*) Pig Out Pubns.

Barbecue, Indoors & Out: Healthful Grilling & Smoking Recipes Included with Instructions for Environmentally Sound Techniques. Linda W. Eckhardt. (Illus.). 176p. 1991. reprint ed. pap. 12.95 (*0-929923-42-1*) Lowell Hse.

Barbecue of the Primitives. Philip Salom. (Poetry Ser.). 75p. (Orig.). 1989. pap. text ed. 12.95 (*0-7022-2221-6*, Pub. by Univ Queensland Pr AT) Intl Spec Bk.

Barbecue on My Mind. Trey Pope. 70p. 1991. pap. 6.95 (*0-9632057-0-6*) Three Pubns.

Barbecue on My Mind: The Thirty Best Barbecue Restaurants in Georgia. Trey Pope. LC 92-15431. 80p. (Orig.). 1992. pap. 7.95 (*0-87797-240-0*) Cherokee.

Barbecue with an International Flavor. Maggie Black. (Illus.). 80p. (Orig.). 1995. pap. 9.95 (*0-572-01215-2*, Pub. by Foulsham UK) Atrium Pubs.

Barbecued Ribs, Smoked Butts. Jeanne Voltz. 1990. 19.95 (*0-394-58293-4*) Knopf.

Barbecuing & Sausage Making Secrets: How to Buy Beef, Pork, Poultry, Lamb, Fish, Seafood & Sausage, Making 95 Percent Fat Free Ground Meats. rev. ed. Charlie Knote & Ruthie Knote. Ed. by John Blue. (Illus.). 312p. 1993. pap. 14.95 (*0-685-63316-0*) Culinary Inst Smoke.

Barbecuing, Grilling & Smoking from the Academy. Ron Clark et al. Ed. by Jill Fox. LC 93-42953. 1994. 11.95 (*1-56426-060-7*, Calif Culinary Acad) Cole Group.

Barbecuing the Weber Covered Way. Carol D. Brent & Betty A. Hughes. LC 72-85084. 1980. 7.95 (*0-88351-002-2*) Test Recipe.

Barbed Wire. Elizabeth Fackler. 176p. 1994. 3.95 (*0-7867-0044-0*) Carroll & Graf.

Barbed Wire. large type ed. Elmer Kelton. (Linford Western Library). 336p. 1987. pap. 11.95 (*0-7089-6425-7*, Linford) Ulverscroft.

Barbed Wire & Mirrors: Essays on New Zealand Prose. 2nd ed. Lawrence Jones. 1990. pap. 22.95 (*0-908569-53-X*, Pub. by U Otago Pr NZ) Intl Spec Bk.

***Barbed-Wire College: Educating German POWs in the United States During World War II.** Ron Robins. LC 94-21161. 1995. 29.95 (*0-691-03700-0*) Princeton U Pr.

Barbed Wit & Malicious Humor. Patrick F. Mahony. 1985. 25.00 (*0-941694-12-7*) Inst Study Man.

Barbedor. Michel Tournier. (Folio - Cadet Rouge Ser.: No. 72). (Illus.). 48p. (FRE.). (J). (gr. 3-7). 1990. pap. 8.95 (*2-07-031172-4*) Schoenhof.

Barbells & Saxophones. David Ritz. 1990. 18.95 (*1-55611-158-4*) D I Fine.

Barbells of the Gods. Mark Cox. 25p. 1988. pap. 3.50 (*0-935331-06-9*) Ampersand RI.

Barbeque! 1985. 11.95 (*0-394-73081-X*) Random.

Barbeque. Leslie Bloom. Ed. by Marian Levine. (Collector's Ser.: Vol. 20). 64p. (Orig.). 1987. pap. 3.49 (*0-942320-26-3*) Am Cooking.

Barbeque. P. Dutery. 36p. (Orig.). 1983. pap. 2.75 (*0-940844-21-4*) Wellspring.

Barbeque & Butterbeans: (And Other Essentials of Life) Delores Ballard. (Orig.). 1992. pap. 7.35 (*0-9618910-1-7*) Jackson Sun.

Barbeque'n with Bobby. Bobby Seale. 192p. 1988. pap. 12.95 (*0-89815-242-9*) Ten Speed Pr.

Barber. Jack Rudman. (Career Examination Ser.: C-1134). 1994. pap. 29.95 (*0-8373-1134-9*) Nat Learn.

Barber, Barber, Shave a Pig. Nina Howard. (Illus.). 16p. (J). (ps-00). 1981. teacher ed 4.95 (*0-917206-13-4*) Children Learn Ctr.

Barber Bear. Bernard Wiseman. LC 86-27594. (Puntown Bks.). (Illus.). 48p. (J). (gr. 1-3). 1987. pap. 11.95 (*0-316-94859-4*) Little.

Barber Genealogy: Descendants of John Barber of Worcester, Massachusetts, 1714-1909. John B. White. 328p. 1994. reprint ed. pap. text ed. 25.00 (*1-55613-959-4*) Heritage Bk.

Barber Genealogy: Section One: Descendants of Thomas Barber of Windsor, Conn. 1614-1909. Section Two: Descendants of John Barber of Worchester, Mass. 1714-1909. William M. Wilson. (Illus.). 826p. 1988. reprint ed. lib. bdg. 113.00 (*0-8328-0182-8*); reprint ed. pap. 103.00 (*0-8328-0183-6*) Higginson Bk Co.

Barber Genealogy, Section I: Descendants of Thomas Barber of Windsor, Connecticut, 1614-1909. John B. White. (Illus.). 494p. 1994. reprint ed. pap. text ed. 30.00 (*1-55613-958-6*) Heritage Bk.

Barber of Kasbeam: Nabokov on Cruelty. Richard Rorty. (Chapbooks in Literature Ser.). 32p. 1988. pap. text ed. 5.00 (*0-9614940-6-9*) Bennington Coll.

Barber of Natchez. Edwin A. Davis & William R. Hogan. LC 54-10885. (Illus.). 278p. 1973. pap. 11.95 (*0-8071-0212-1*) La State U Pr.

Barber of Seville. Pierre-Augustin C. De Beaumarchais. Tr. by Vincent Luciani. Bd. with Marriage of Figaro. (World Classics in Tr. Ser.). (ENG.). 1965. Set pap. 5.95 (*0-685-00706-5*); Bd. with write for info. (*0-8120-0029-3*) Barron.

Barber of Seville. Adapt. by I. E. Clark. (Illus.). 42p. 1968. pap. 10.00 (*0-88680-011-0*); pap. 2.00 (*0-88680-010-2*) I E Clark.

Barber of Seville & Moses. Gioachino Rossini. Ed. by Nicholas John. Tr. by Edward J. Dent et al. LC 85-52162. (English National Opera Guide Series: Bilingual Libretto, Articles: No. 36). (Illus.). 160p. (Orig.). (C). 1986. pap. 9.95 (*0-7145-4080-3*, LIBRETTO, ARTICLES, NO. 36) Riverrun NY.

Barber of Seville & The Marriage of Figaro. Pierre-Augustin C. De Beaumarchais. Tr. by John Wood. (Classics Ser.). 224p. 1964. pap. 8.95 (*0-14-044133-6*, Penguin Classics) Viking Penguin.

Barber Shop Songs. (Illus.). 128p. 1948. pap. 9.95 (*0-8256-2067-8*, AM40270) Music Sales.

Barberian Presidency: Theoretical & Empirical Readings. William D. Pederson. (American University Studies: Political Science: Ser. X, Vol. 14). 265p. (C). 1989. text ed. 37.60 (*0-8204-0693-7*) P Lang Pubs.

Barbers, Cars, & Cigars: Activity Programming for Older Men. Nancy Dezan. 52p. (Orig.). 1992. pap. 7.95 (*1-879633-12-4*) Eldersong.

Barber's Cutting Edge. Gwendolyn Battle-Lavert. LC 94-4013. (J). 1994. 14.95 (*0-89239-127-8*) Childrens Book Pr.

Barber's Trade Union & Other Stories. Mulk R. Anand. 175p. 1983. reprint ed. pap. 3.00 (*0-86578-145-1*) Ind-US Inc.

Barbershopping: Musical & Social Harmony. Ed. by Max Kaplan. LC 92-59053. 1993. 29.50 (*0-8386-3504-0*) Fairleigh Dickinson.

Barbey: The Story of a Pioneer Columbia River Salmon Packer. Roger T. Tetlow & Graham J. Barbey. LC 89-81758. (Illus.). 268p. 1990. 25.00 (*0-8323-0478-6*) Binford Mort.

Barbey D'Aurevilly. Armand B. Chartier. LC 77-8024. (Twayne's World Authors Ser.). 182p. (C). 1977. lib. bdg. 17.95 (*0-8057-6305-8*) Irvington.

Barbican. large type ed. Muriel Howe. 1985. 15.95 (*0-7089-1366-0*) Ulverscroft.

***Barbie.** Golden Western Staff. (J). Date not set. pap. 1.59 (*0-307-02963-8*, Golden Pr) Western Pub.

Barbie. Barbara Slate et al. 96p. (J). 1992. pap. 8.95 (*0-87135-878-6*) Marvel Entmnt.

An Asterisk (*) at the beginning of an entry indicates that the title is appearing in BIP for the first time.

An Asterisk (*) at the beginning of an entry indicates that the title is appearing in BIP for the first time.

597

B

B

Bare Naked Book. Kathy Stinson. 32p. (J). (gr. k-2). 1986. lib. bdg. 14.95 (0-920303-52-8, Pub. by Annick CN); pap. 4.95 (0-920303-53-6, Pub. by Annick CN) Firefly Bks Ltd.

Bare November Days: A Tribute to Ruffed Grouse, King of Upland Birds. George B. Evans et al. LC 92-74034. (Illus.). 136p. 1992. 39.00 (0-924357-26-6, 11150-A) Countrysport Pr.

Bare November Days: A Tribute to Ruffed Grouse, King of Upland Birds. deluxe limited ed. George B. Evans et al. LC 92-74034. (Illus.). 136p. 1992. 95.00 (0-924357-27-4, 11150-B) Countrysport Pr.

Bare Ruined Choirs. R. Morris. (World of Change Ser.). (C). 1987. 40.00 (0-685-47491-7, Pub. by S Thornes Pubs UK) St Mut.

Bare Ruined Choirs: The Fate of a Welsh Abbey. Robert Morris. 52p. (YA). (gr. 11 up). 1987. pap. 7.95 (0-85950-544-8, Pub. by S Thornes UK) Dufour.

Bare Threads: Human Life in the Service of Profit. LC 90-80049. 1991. 9.00 (0-914422-21-9) Glenmary Res Ctr.

***Bare Trees: Zadock Pratt, Master Tanner & the Story of What Happens to the Catskill Mountain Forests.** Patricia E. Millen. (Illus.). 112p. (Orig.). 1995. pap. 11.95 (1-883789-05-2) Blk Dome Pr.

Bareback! One Man's Journey along the Pony Express Trail. Jerry Ellis. LC 93-13538. 1993. 21.95 (0-385-30586-9) Delacorte.

Bareback! One Man's Journey along the Pony Express Trail. large type ed. Jerry Ellis. LC 93-31457. 1994. 21.95 (0-7862-0053-7) Thorndike Pr.

Bareback Beauty. E. J. Hunter. (White Squaw Ser.: No. 20). 1990. pap. 2.95 (0-8217-2929-2) Zebra.

Bareboating. Brian M. Fagan. LC 84-47754. (Illus.). 288p. 1987. text ed. 17.95 (0-87742-173-0) Intl Marine.

Baree: The Story of a Wolf-Dog. James O. Curwood. LC 90-37875. 1990. pap. 7.95 (1-55704-074-5) Newmarket.

Baree, Son of Kazan. James O. Curwood. reprint ed. lib. bdg. 20.95 (0-88411-858-4, Aeonian Pr) Amereon Ltd.

Baree, Son of Kazan. James O. Curwood. 1990. reprint ed. lib. bdg. 18.95 (0-89968-500-5) Buccaneer Bks.

Baree, the Story of a Wolf-Dog. James O. Curwood. LC 90-37875. (Medallion Edition Ser.). 256p. (J). (gr. 3-11). 1992. 18.95 (1-55704-075-3); pap. 3.95 (1-55704-132-6) Newmarket.

***Barefeet & Bandoliers: The Liberation of Ethiopia.** David Shirreff. 304p. 1995. text ed. 39.50 (1-85043-922-2) St Martin.

Barefeet & Bellybuttons: Poems & Activities to Tickle a Child. Patricia Goodrich. (Illus.). 46p. (J). (gr. k-4). 1989. pap. 5.00 (0-9625348-1-1) P Goodrich.

Barefoot. Zaharia Stancu. Ed. by Frank Kirk. LC 68-24278. 1971. lib. bdg. 34.50 (0-8057-5613-2) Irvington.

Barefoot Ballerina. Doris M. Heinzerling. (Illus.). 24p. (J). (gr. k-1). 1993. write for info. (1-879094-40-1) Avonstoke Pr.

Barefoot Book: Economically Appropriate Services for the Rural Poor. Ed. by Marilyn Carr. 128p. (Orig.). 1989. pap. 11.50 (0-942850-17-3) Intermediate Tech.

Barefoot Boy with Cheek. Max Shulman. LC 76-11506. (Illus.). reprint ed. 31.50 (0-404-15296-1) AMS Pr.

Barefoot Bride. Joan Johnston. 1992. mass mkt. 4.99 (0-440-21129-8) Dell.

Barefoot Bride. Rebecca Paisley. 400p. 1990. pap. 3.95 (0-380-76019-3) Avon.

Barefoot Bride. large type ed. Dorothy Cork. (Linford Romance Library). 336p. 1985. pap. 11.95 (0-7089-6067-7) Ulverscroft.

Barefoot Capitalism. Guy Sorman. 300p. 1989. text ed. 40.00 (0-7069-4436-4, Pub. by Vikas II) S Asia.

Barefoot Dancer: The Story of Isadora Duncan. Barbara O'Connor. LC 93-14312. (Trailblazers Ser.). (J). (gr. 4-7). 1994. 17.50 (0-87614-807-0, Carolrhoda) Lerner Group.

Barefoot Doctor's Manual. (Illus.). 1994. reprint ed. lib. bdg. 45.00 (0-7808-0009-5) Omnigraphics Inc.

Barefoot Doctor's Manual: Healing with Medicinal Herbs & Acupuncture, 2 vols., Set. 1984. lib. bdg. 600.00 (0-87700-549-4) Revisionist Pr.

Barefoot Expert: The Interface of Computerized Knowledge Systems & Indigenous Knowledge Systems. Doris M. Schoenhoff. LC 92-40225. (Contributions to the Study of Computer Science Ser.: No. 3). 200p. 1993. text ed. 55.00 (0-313-28821-6, GM8821, Greenwood Pr) Greenwood.

Barefoot Forever. RoseMary Mong. (Illus.). 96p. 1986. 12.95 (0-941974-07-3) Baranski Pub Co.

Barefoot Gen: Life after the Bomb. Keiji Nakazawa. (Barefoot Gen Ser.: Vol. 3). (Illus.). 180p. (Orig.). 1988. 39.95 (0-86571-147-X); pap. 11.95 (0-86571-148-8) New Soc Pubs.

***Barefoot Gen Boxed Set: Vol. 1-2-3-4.** Keiji Nakazawa. 1993. 45.95 (0-86571-290-5) New Soc Pubs.

Barefoot Gen, Vol. 1: A Cartoon Story of Hiroshima. Keiji Nakazawa. (Illus.). 300p. 1987. 39.95 (0-86571-094-5); pap. 14.95 (0-86571-095-3) New Soc Pubs.

Barefoot Gen, Vol. 2: The Day After. Keiji Nakazawa. Tr. by Project Gen Staff & Dadakai. (Illus.). 192p. (Orig.). 1988. 39.95 (0-86571-122-4); pap. 9.95 (0-86571-123-2) New Soc Pubs.

Barefoot Gen, Vol. 4: Out of the Ashes. Keiji Nakazawa. (Illus.). 1993. pap. 39.95 (0-86571-280-8); pap. 12.95 (0-86571-281-6) New Soc Pubs.

Barefoot Hiker. Richard K. Frazine. LC 92-34756. (Orig.). 1993. pap. 7.95 (0-89815-525-8) Ten Speed Pr.

Barefoot in Athens. Maxwell Anderson. 1952. pap. 13.00 (0-8222-0094-5) Dramatists Play.

Barefoot in Babylon. Robert S. Spitz. 1989. pap. 10.95 (0-393-30644-5) Norton.

Barefoot in the Boardroom. Bill Purves. 192p. 1992. pap. 19.95 (1-86373-038-9, Pub. by Allen Unwin AT) Paul & Co Pubs.

Barefoot in the Boardroom: Venture & Misadventure in the People's Republic of China. Bill Purves. 190p. (Orig.). 1992. pap. 14.95 (1-55021-079-3, Pub. by NC Press CN) U of Toronto Pr.

Barefoot in the Palace. John T. Ball. 1985. 6.55 (0-89536-748-3, 5854) CSS OH.

Barefoot in the Park. Neil Simon. 1964. 11.95 (0-394-40515-3) Random.

Barefoot Mailman. Pratt. 220p. 1993. pap. 7.95 (0-912451-32-7) Florida Classics.

Barefoot Mailman. large type ed. Theodore Pratt. 1970. 15.95 (0-85456-010-6) Ulverscroft.

Barefoot Man. Davis Grubb. 1992. pap. 9.00 (0-8217-3653-1) Zebra.

Barefoot Renegade. Ralph Salesky. LC 92-14449. 1992. 14.95 (0-87770-507-0) Ye Galleon.

Barefoot Shiatsu: Whole-Body Approach to Health. Shizuko Yamamoto. 1979. pap. 13.95 (0-87040-439-3) Japan Pubns USA.

Barefoot Shoemaker: Capitalizing on the New Russia. Vladimir Kvint. 256p. 1993. 24.95 (1-55970-182-X) Arcade Pub Inc.

Barefoot Water Skiing: An Illustrated Guide to Learning & Mastering the Sport. Ron Scarpa & Terrence Dorner. Ed. by Jo Robertson. (Illus.). 176p. (Orig.). (YA). (gr. 7 up). 1988. pap. 11.95 (0-944406-01-7) World Pub FL.

***Barely Legal.** Ed. by John Patrick. 512p. (Orig.). 1995. pap. text ed. 14.95 (1-877978-71-X, STARbks Pr) Woldt.

***Barents Region: Cooperation in Arctic Europe.** Olav S. Stokke & Ola Tunander. (Peace Research Institute Ser.). 256p. 1994. 69.95 (0-8039-7897-9) Sage.

***Barf Book.** M. Riskin. 96p. 1994. pap. 5.95 (0-88032-449-X) Ivory Tower Pub.

Barfield Sampler: Poetry & Fiction by Owen Barfield. Owen Barfield. Ed. by Jeanne C. Hunter & Thomas Kranidas. LC 92-30926. 181p. (C). 1993. 49.50 (0-7914-1587-2); pap. 16.95 (0-7914-1588-0) State U NY Pr.

***Bargain.** Patricia Coughlin. (Men Made in America Ser.). 1994. pap. 3.99 (0-373-45189-X, 1-45189-7) Harlequin Bks.

Bargain. Veronica Sattler. (Historical Ser.). 1993. mass mkt. 3.99 (0-373-28791-7, 1-28791-1) Harlequin Bks.

Bargain. large type ed. Mary Munro. 1991. pap. 13.95 (0-7089-6982-8) Ulverscroft.

Bargain: The Story Behind the Thirty Year Honeymoon of GM & UAW. Kathy G. El-Messidi. 141p. 1980. 14.95 (0-8290-2353-4) Irvington.

***Bargain Basement Baby.** Leandra Logan. (Temptation Ser.). 1995. mass mkt. 3.25 (0-373-25635-3, 1-25635-3) Harlequin Bks.

Bargain Beaters: The Handbook for Saving Money in North County & San Diego. Lisa Taliaferro. (Illus.). 120p. (Orig.). Date not set. per. 9.95 (0-9633958-0-7) Bargain Beaters.

Bargain Bride. Rowena Summers. 160p. 1994. 19.00 (0-7278-4531-4) Severn Hse.

***Bargain Bride.** braille ed. Barbara Cartland. 227p. 1991. text ed. 18.16 (1-56956-491-4, BR8348) W A T Braille.

Bargain Chic. Roberta Plutzik. 192p. pap. 7.95 (0-8184-0383-7) Carol Pub Group.

Bargain City: Booking, Betting, & Beating the New Las Vegas. Anthony Curtis. 238p. (Orig.). 1994. pap. 11.95 (0-929712-50-1) Huntington Pr.

***Bargain for Frances.** Laurie Diamond. Ed. by J. Friedland & R. Kessler. (Novel-Ties Ser.). (J). (gr. k-2). 1994. student ed, pap. text ed. 15.95 (1-56982-050-3) Lrn Links.

Bargain for Frances. Russell Hoban. LC 91-12265. (I Can Read Bk.). 64p. (J). (gr. k-3). 1970. 14.95 (0-06-022329-4); lib. bdg. 14.89 (0-06-022330-8) HarpC Child Bks.

Bargain for Frances. Russell Hoban. LC 91-12267. (Trophy I Can Read Bk.). (Illus.). 64p. (J). (gr. k-3). 1978. pap. 3.50 (0-06-444001-X, Trophy) HarpC Child Bks.

Bargain Horses. Gillian Baxter. 138p. (C). 1990. pap. 21.00 (0-85131-561-5, Pub. by J A Allen & Co UK) St Mut.

Bargain Hunters Guide - Atlanta-Athens Area, 1992. Dana McGuinn. (Illus.). 224p. 1992. pap. 8.95 (1-880163-03-9) Firefly Pub.

Bargain Hunters Guide - Georgia & Atlanta: Descriptive Reviews of over 350 Consignment Shops, Outlets, Food, Fleas & Antiques & Entertainment. Dana McGuinn. (Illus.). 245p. 1993. pap. 10.95 (1-880163-04-7) Firefly Pub.

Bargain Hunter's Guide, El Paso - Las Cruces: The Art of Buying Smart. 104p. 1992. pap. 4.95 (0-9633205-0-5) Rich River Pubns.

Bargain Hunting along the Coast of Maine, 1987-88. rev. ed. Barbara McSpadden. (Illus.). 104p. pap. 4.95 (0-9617533-0-7) Thrifty Yankee.

Bargain Hunting in Columbus. Debbie Keri-Brown. 1991. pap. 12.95 (0-9629590-6-5) Lotus Pr OH.

Bargain Hunting in Greater New York: Including the Five Boroughs & the Suburban Discount Malls of New Jersey, Connecticut, & Upstate New York. Richard Laermer. 250p. (Orig.). 1990. pap. 9.95 (1-55958-030-5) Prima Pub.

Bargain Hunting in New Jersey: A Guide. Dolly MacKenzie. (Illus.). 184p. (Orig.). 1988. pap. 7.95 (0-929211-00-6) Directories NJ.

Bargain Seafoods: Cooking the Underutilized Species. R. Marilyn Schmidt. 928p. (Orig.). 1987. pap. 7.95 (0-937996-10-6) Barnegat.

***Bargain Travel Resource Book: How to Save up to 50% on Airfares, Lodging, Dining, Car Rentals, Cruises, & More! Airgares, Lodge.** Suzanne Hogsett. 256p. (Orig.). 1995. pap. 19.95 (1-879265-08-7) Travel Easy.

Bargaining. Myron Lieberman. LC 79-66017. 333p. (Orig.). 1979. pap. 18.95 (0-931028-09-4) Teach-em.

Bargaining: Formal Theories of Negotiation. Ed. by Oran R. Young. LC 72-75493. 420p. 1975. 39.95 (0-252-00273-3) U of Ill Pr.

***Bargaining Across Borders: How to Conduct Business Successfully Anywhere in the World.** Foster. 1995. pap. text ed. 14.95 (0-07-021656-8) McGraw.

Bargaining Across Borders: How to Negotiate Business Successfully Anywhere in the World. Dean A. Foster. 1992. text ed. 26.95 (0-07-021647-9) McGraw.

Bargaining & Markets. Martin J. Osborne & Ariel Rubinstein. (Economic Theory, Econometrics & Mathematical Economics Ser.). 216p. 1990. text ed. 53.00 (0-12-528631-7, AP Prof); pap. text ed. 21.00 (0-12-528632-5, AP Prof) Acad Pr.

Bargaining Behavior. Lawrence E. Fouraker & Sidney Seigel. LC 77-23058. 309p. 1977. reprint ed. text ed. 35.00 (0-8371-9738-4, FOBB, Greenwood Pr) Greenwood.

Bargaining Behavior: An International Study. D. L. Harnett & L. L. Cummings. LC 79-67421. (Illus.). 307p. 1980. text ed. 89.95 (0-931920-14-0) Dame Pubns.

Bargaining Beyond Impasse: Joint Resolution of Public Sector Labor Disputes. Jonathan Brock. LC 81-20652. 279p. 1982. text ed. 49.95 (0-86569-110-X, Auburn Hse) Greenwood.

***Bargaining Book.** 3rd ed. Ralph R. Smith. 141p. (Orig.). 1994. pap. text ed. 12.95 (0-936295-51-1) FPMI Comns.

Bargaining, Communication, & Limited War. Thomas C. Schelling. (Reprint Series in Social Sciences). (C). 1993. reprint ed. pap. text ed. 1.00 (0-8290-2741-6, PS-409) Irvington.

Bargaining for Change. Ed. by B. Towers et al. 1973. 25.00 (0-8464-0167-3) Beekman Pubs.

Bargaining for Change: Union Politics in North America & Europe. Ed. by Miriam Golden & Jonas Pontusson. LC 91-57901. (Illus.). 368p. 1992. 52.50 (0-8014-2647-2); pap. 17.95 (0-8014-9948-8) Cornell U Pr.

Bargaining for Health: Labor Unions, Health Insurance & Medical Care. Raymond Munts. LC 67-13555. 330p. reprint ed. pap. 94.10 (0-8357-5966-0, 2023716) Bks Demand.

Bargaining for Life: A Social History of Tuberculosis, 1876-1938. Barbara Bates. LC 91-40040. (Studies in Health, Illness, & Caregiving). (Illus.). 456p. (Orig.). (C). 1992. pap. text ed. 19.95 (0-8122-1367-X) U of Pa Pr.

Bargaining for National Security: The Postwar Disarmament Negotiations. Lloyd Jensen. Ed. by Charles W. Kegley, Jr. & Donald J. Puchala. (Studies in International Relations). 320p. 1988. text ed. 39.95 (0-87249-529-9) U of SC Pr.

Bargaining for Peace: South Africa & the National Peace Accord. Peter Gastrow. (Orig.). 1995. 19.95 (1-878379-40-2); pap. text ed. 10.95 (1-878379-39-9) US Inst Peace.

Bargaining for Reality: The Construction of Social Relations in a Muslim Community. Lawrence Rosen. LC 84-2501. (Illus.). 264p. 1984. pap. 13.95 (0-226-72611-8) U Ch Pr.

Bargaining Games: A New Approach to Strategic Thinking in Negotiations. J. Keith Murnighan. 1993. pap. 12.00 (0-688-12837-8, Quill) Morrow.

Bargaining Games: A New Approach to Strategic Thinking in Negotiations. Keith Murnighan. 1992. 20.00 (0-688-10905-5) Morrow.

Bargaining in International Conflicts. Charles Lockhart. LC 78-23334. 224p. 1979. text ed. 42.00 (0-231-04560-3) Col U Pr.

Bargaining Manager: Enhancing Organizational Results Through Effective Negotiation. Bernard A. Ramundo. LC 93-32881. 176p. 1994. text ed. 49.95 (0-89930-805-8, Quorum Bks) Greenwood.

Bargaining Power. Roderick Martin. LC 92-13855. (Illus.). 208p. 1992. 49.95 (0-19-827255-3) OUP.

Bargaining, Power, Tactics, & Outcomes. Samuel B. Bacharach & Edward J. Lawler. LC 81-8197. (Jossey-Bass Social & Behavioral Science Ser.). (Illus.). 254p. reprint ed. pap. 72.40 (0-7837-6506-1, 2045618) Bks Demand.

Bargaining under Federalism: Contemporary New York. Sarah F. Liebschutz. LC 90-39852. (SUNY Series in Public Administration). 251p. (C). 1991. 57.50 (0-7914-0634-2); pap. 18.95 (0-7914-0635-0) State U NY Pr.

Bargaining with Incomplete Information. Ed. by Peter B. Linhart et al. (Economic Theory, Econometrics & Mathematical Economics Ser.). (Illus.). 553p. 1992. text ed. 79.00 (0-12-451050-7) Acad Pr.

***Bargaining with the State.** Epstein. 1995. pap. (0-691-00155-3) Princeton U Pr.

Bargaining with the State. Richard A. Epstein. LC 92-46793. 344p. 1993. text ed. 35.00 (0-691-04273-X) Princeton U Pr.

Bargaining with Uncertainty: Decision-Making in Public Health, Technological Safety, & Environmental Policy. Merrie G. Klapp. LC 91-32712. 168p. 1992. text ed. 49.95 (0-86569-046-4, T046, Auburn Hse) Greenwood.

Bargains. Jack Heifner. 1992. pap. 4.75 (0-8222-1299-4) Dramatists Play.

Bargains-by-Mail for Baby & You: Where to Buy for Your Baby, Nursery, Playroom, & Yourself at Mail-Order Wholesale Prices. Dawn Hardy. 608p. (Orig.). 1991. pap. 14.95 (1-55958-112-3) Prima Pub.

Bargains, Deals & Steals: How You Can Save up to 99 Percent on Almost Anything at Hidden Sales & Secret Auctions. Brian G. Marshall. Ed. by Bill Thomas. 160p. (Orig.). 1991. pap. 14.95 (1-878969-21-8) Discovery UT.

Bargains with Fate: Psychological Crises & Conflicts in Shakespeare & His Plays. B. J. Paris. LC 90-28612. (Illus.). 280p. 1991. 24.95 (0-306-43760-0, Plenum Insight) Plenum.

Barge. Dimitris Tsaloumas. (Orig.). 1993. pap. 16.95 (0-7022-2465-0, Pub. by Univ Queensland Pr AT) Intl Spec Bk.

Barge & Minnechaduza Clarendonian Mammalian Faunas of North-Central Nebraska. Sawney D. Webb. LC 72-626952. (University of California Publications in Social Welfare: Vol. 78). (Illus.). 199p. reprint ed. pap. 56.80 (0-8357-5967-9, 2014697) Bks Demand.

Bargello: A Manual of Stitch & Design. large type ed. pap. 15.00 (0-317-01851-5) Cath Guild Blind.

Bargello Book. Frances Salter. 74p. 1993. 24.00 (0-916896-47-1) Lacis Pubns.

Bargello Quilts. Marge Edie. Ed. by Laura Reinstatler. LC 94-18419. (Illus.). 90p. (Orig.). 1994. pap. 19.95 (1-56477-067-2) That Patchwork.

Bargheer's Graphic Work. Detlev Rosenbach. (Illus.). 200p. 1974. 120.00 (0-915346-97-4) A Wofsy Fine Arts.

Barhop U. S. A. One Man's Quest to Find America's Ultimate Bar. Awesome Wells, pseud. (Illus.). 350p. 1989. write for info. (0-318-65880-1) Permanent CA.

Barhop U. S. A., Vol. 1: One Man's Quest to Find America's Ultimate Bar. Awesome Wells. (Illus.). 300p. (Orig.). (C). 1990. pap. 11.95 (0-9624068-0-5) Permanent CA.

Baring Fault. John Stonehouse. LC 86-4861. 448p. 1986. 23.95 (0-7145-4069-2); pap. 11.95 (0-7145-4106-0) Riverrun NY.

Baring Securities Guide to International Finance Reporting. Christopher Nobes. 250p. 1991. 56.95 (0-631-17617-9) Blackwell Pubs.

***Barins-Scottish Children in Photographs.** Iona McGregor & Dorothy Kidd. (Illus.). 152p. (Orig.). 1995. pap. 22.50 (0-948636-65-3, Pub. by Natl Mus Scotland UK) A Schwartz & Co.

Barite. (Metals & Minerals Ser.). 1993. lib. bdg. 250.95 (0-8490-8984-0) Gordon Pr.

Barite. (Metals & Minerals Ser.). 1994. lib. bdg. 250.95 (0-8490-5683-7) Gordon Pr.

***Barite Industry & Resources of Texas.** J. R. Kyle. (Mineral Resource Circular Ser.: No. 85). 1994. 6.50 (0-614-06194-6) Bur Econ Geology.

Barito Isolects of Borneo: A Classification Based on Comparative Reconstruction & Lexicostatistics. Alfred B. Hudson. LC 68-4418. (Cornell University, Southeast Asia Program, Data Paper Ser.: No. 68). 135p. reprint ed. pap. 38.50 (0-8357-5968-7, 2021842) Bks Demand.

Baritone Uke. Date not set. pap. 0.95 (0-87166-537-9, 93757) Mel Bay.

Baritone Uke Chords. Mel Bay. 1993. 3.95 (0-87166-864-5, 93265) Mel Bay.

Bark: The Formation, Characteristics, & Uses of Bark Around the World. Anne E. Prance. LC 92-19569. (Illus.). 176p. 1993. 49.95 (0-88192-262-5) Timber.

Bark Beetles in North American Conifers: A System for the Study of Evolutionary Biology. Ed. by Jeffry B. Mitton & Kareen B. Sturgeon. (Corrie Herring Hooks Ser.: No. 6). (Illus.). 539p. (C). 1982. text ed. 30.00 (0-292-70735-5); pap. 17.50 (0-292-70744-4) U of Tex Pr.

Bark Canoes & Skin Boats of North America. Edwin T. Adney & Howard I. Chappelle. LC 64-62636. (Illus.). 242p. 1993. pap. 24.95 (1-56098-296-9) Smithsonian.

Bark Galianosi: An Armenian-Greek Dictionary of Galen. John A. Greppin. LC 85-29982. (Anatolian & Caucasian Studies Ser.). 1986. 50.00 (0-88206-064-3) Caravan Bks.

Bark Structure: Hardwoods Grown on Southern Pine Sites. Heroki Nanko & Wilfred A. Cote. 1980. pap. 19.95x (0-8156-2234-1) Syracuse U Pr.

Bark Tree. Raymond Queneau. 1991. pap. 11.95 (0-7145-0108-5) Riverrun NY.

Barker: Four Plays. Harley G. Barker. (C). 1993. pap. 13.95 (0-413-67530-0, A0668, Pub. by Methuen UK) Heinemann.

***Barker Bites Back.** Jack Jones. 300p. 1995. pap. 9.95 (1-56901-900-2) NW Pub.

Barker Fairley Portraits. Barker Fairley. 107p. 1981. 999.99 (0-458-95160-9, Pub. by Stoddart Pubng CN) Genl Dist Srvs.

Barker Family. E. F. Barker. 553p. 1992. reprint ed. lib. bdg. 88.50 (0-8328-2303-1); reprint ed. pap. 78.50 (0-8328-2304-X) Higginson Bk Co.

Barker Family of Plymouth Colony & County. Barker Newhall. (Illus.). 102p. 1988. reprint ed. lib. bdg. 29.00 (0-8328-0188-7); reprint ed. pap. 19.00 (0-8328-0189-5) Higginson Bk Co.

Barker-Harland: A Genealogical Study. Marjorie H. Diedrich. LC 89-51151. (Illus.). 318p. 1989. 45.00 (0-9616020-1-5) Genealogic Ent.

***Barker's Crime.** Dick Gackenbach. LC 94-41419. (J). 1996. write for info. (0-15-200628-1) HarBrace.

Barker's Luck, & Other Stories. Bret Harte. LC 70-113668. (Short Story Index Reprint Ser.). 1977. 18.95 (0-8369-3397-4) Ayer.

Barkham Burroughs' Encyclopaedia of Astounding Facts & Useful Information 1889. Barkham Burroughs. Ed. by Miggs Burroughs. (Illus.). 148p. (Orig.). 1983. reprint ed. pap. 8.95 (0-9610994-0-2) Brayden.

Barkham Burrough's Encyclopedia of Astounding Facts & Useful Information. Barkham Burroughs. 1989. 7.99 (0-517-67950-7) Random Hse Value.

Barkhamsted, Connecticut & Its Centennial, 1879. William W. Lee. 178p. 1994. reprint ed. lib. bdg. 29.50 (0-8328-4260-5) Higginson Bk Co.

Barking at a Fox-Fur Coat. Donald Davis. 206p. 1991. 19.95 (0-87483-141-5); pap. 10.95 (0-87483-140-7) August Hse.

Barking at Sunspots & other Poems. Kate Kelly. (Illus.). 144p. (Orig.). 1987. pap. 6.95 (0-918537-01-0) Justin Bks.

Barking Dogs. Robert Irvine. 224p. 1994. 19.95 (0-312-10419-7, Pub. by Thomas Dunne Bks) St Martin.

An Asterisk (*) at the beginning of an entry indicates that the title is appearing in BIP for the first time.

***Barking Ghost.** Stine. (Goosebumps Ser.: No. 32). 1995. pap. (0-590-48344-7) Scholastic Inc.

Barking Man & Other Stories. Madison S. Bell. (Contemporary American Fiction Ser.). 240p. 1991. pap. 8.95 (0-14-014903-1, Penguin Bks) Viking Penguin.

Barking up the Right Tree: Breeding, Rearing & Training the Guide Dogs Way. Derek Freeman. (Illus.). 176p. 1993. 19.95 (0-948955-07-4, Pub. by Ringpr Bks UK) Seven Hills Bk.

Barkley. Syd Hoff. LC 75-6290. (Early I Can Read Bk.). (Illus.). 32p. (J). (gr. k-3). 1975. lib. bdg. 14.89 (0-06-022448-7) HarpC Child Bks.

Barks, Roars & Siren Songs: How Animals Talk to Us & How We Talk Back. Michael Bright. (Illus.). 1991. 17.95 (1-55972-086-7, Birch Ln Pr) Carol Pub Group.

Barksdale Family History & Genealogy. John A. Barksdale. LC 85-71710. 634p. reprint ed. 315.00 (0-916497-63-1); reprint ed. fiche 6.00 (0-916497-62-3) Burnett Micro.

Barksdale Family History & Genealogy: With Collateral Lines. J. A. Barksdale. 634p. 1993. reprint ed. lib. bdg. 105.00 (0-8328-3939-6); reprint ed. pap. 95.00 (0-8328-3940-X) Higginson Bk Co.

Barksdale, No. 21: Home of the Mighty Eighth. David Davies & Mike Vines. (Osprey Colour Superbase Ser.). (Illus.). 128p. 1991. pap. text ed. 15.95 (1-85532-137-8, Pub. by Osprey Pubng Ltd UK) Motorbooks Intl.

Barksdale Stress Control Program Participant's Kit. L. S. Barksdale. (Illus.). 1980. Incl. handbook, participants manual, 3 audio cassette tapes, daily & pocket companions, & additional. pap. 34.95 (0-918588-23-5, 205) Barksdale Foun.

Barksdale Stress Control Program Script for Seminar Instructor. L. S. Barksdale. 91p. 1980. Incl. instructor's script, 4 audio cassette tapes, daily & pocket companions, & additional materials. pap. 80.00 (0-918588-18-9, 204) Barksdale Foun.

Barksdale Stress Control Seminar Instructor's Kit. L. S. Barksdale. (Illus.). 1980. Incl. script, handbook, participants manual, 4 audio cassette tapes, daily & pocket companions, & ad. pap., vinyl bd. 80.00 (0-918588-21-9, 204) Barksdale Foun.

Barlaam & Iosaph. John Damascene. (Loeb Classical Library: No. 34). 676p. 1914. 18.95 (0-674-99038-2) HUP.

Barlaam & Josaphat: A Transcription of MS Egerton 876 with Notes, Glossary, & Comparative Study of the Middle English & Japanese Versions. Keiko Ikegami. LC 91-57958. (Studies in the Middle Ages: No. 21). 1992. 42.50 (0-404-64161-X) AMS Pr.

Barley. D. E. Briggs. 1978. 85.00 (0-412-11870-X, NO. 6043) Chapman & Hall.

Barley. D. C. Rasmusson. 522p. 1985. 40.00 (0-89118-085-0) Am Soc Agron.

Barley: Chemistry & Technology. Ed. by R. S. Bhatty. LC 93-72889. (Illus.). 450p. 1993. 145.00 (0-913250-80-5, BEF 5575) Am Assn Cereal Chem.

Barley: Genetics, Biochemistry, Molecular Biology & Biotechnology. Ed. by P. R. Shewry. (Biotechnology in Agriculture Ser.: No. 5). 600p. 1992. 142.50 (0-85198-725-7) CAB Intl.

Barley & the Bible. James S. Kerr. 96p. pap. 3.95 (0-936369-39-6) Son-Rise Pubns.

Barley Break: An Elizabethan Songbook with Arrangements for the Appalachian Dulcimer. Lorraine L. Hammond. 1992. reprint ed. pap. 10.95 (0-938756-38-9) Yellow Moon.

Barley Genetics, No. 2: Proceedings of the Second International Barley Genetics Symposium. International Barley Genetics Symposium Staff. Ed. by Robert A. Nilan. (Illus.). 638p. reprint ed. pap. 180.00 (0-8357-8034-1, 2034100) Bks Demand.

***Barley Yellow Dwarf: Forty Years of Progress.** C. J. D'Arcy & P. A. Burnett. 408p. 1995. 65.00 (0-89054-167-1) Am Phytopathol Soc.

Barlow Brides. large type ed. Justin Ladd. LC 92-41190. 1993. 14.95 (0-8161-5723-5) G K Hall.

Barlowe's Guide to Extraterrestrials. rev. ed. Wayne D. Barlowe et al. LC 86-40609. (Illus.). 144p. 1987. pap. 12.95 (0-89480-324-7, 1324) Workman Pub.

Barly Fields. Robert Nathan. 1976. 31.95 (0-8488-0099-0, Amereon Hse) Amereon Ltd.

***Barm Bakers Book: Breadmaking with Whole Grain Flours & a Combined Yeast & Lactic Leavening Barm.** Monica Spiker. 186p. 1992. pap. 15.00 (0-9642594-0-0) Hlth Res & Studies.

Barmen Confession: Papers from the Seattle Assembly. Ed. by Hubert G. Locke. LC 86-23874. (Toronto Studies in Theology: Vol. 26). 370p. 1987. lib. bdg. 99.95 (0-88946-770-6) E Mellen.

Barmen Declaration As a Paradigm for a Theology of the American Church. Robert T. Osborn. LC 91-44313. (Toronto Studies in Theology: Vol. 63). 168p. 1992. lib. bdg. 79.95 (0-7734-9472-3) E Mellen.

Barmen Theological Declaration of 1934: The Archeology of a Confessional Text. Rolf Ahlers. LC 86-5186. (Toronto Studies in Theology: Vol. 24). 264p. 1986. lib. bdg. 89.95 (0-88946-768-4) E Mellen.

Barmi: A Mediterranean City Through the Ages. Pilar Comes & Xavier Hernandez. (Illus.). 64p. (J). (gr. 5 up). 1990. 14.95 (0-395-54227-8) HM.

Barn. Avi. LC 94-6920. 112p. (J). (gr. 4-6). 1994. 13.95 (0-531-06861-7); lib. bdg. 13.99 (0-531-08711-5) Orchard Bks Watts.

Barn: The Art of a Working Building. Elric Endersby et al. LC 92-16071. (Illus.). 272p. 1992. 60.00 (0-395-57372-6) HM.

Barn: Vanishing Landmark in North America. Eric Arthur. 1989. 19.98 (0-88486-020-5) Arrowood Pr.

Barn Blind. Jane Smiley. 1993. pap. 12.00 (0-449-90874-7, Columbine) Fawcett.

Barn Dance! Bill Martin, Jr. & John Archambault. LC 86-14225. (Illus.). 32p. (J). (ps-2). 1986. 14.95 (0-8050-0089-5, Bks Young Read) H Holt & Co.

Barn Dance! Bill Martin, Jr. & John Archambault. LC 86-14225. (Illus.). 32p. (J). (ps-2). 1988. pap. 4.95 (0-8050-0799-7, Bks Young Read) H Holt & Co.

Barn Dance Book: Music, Scripts & Figures. 1991. lib. bdg. 79.95 (0-8490-5184-3) Gordon Pr.

Barn Dance Saturday Night: Scripts & Music. 1991. lib. bdg. 79.95 (0-8490-5188-6) Gordon Pr.

Barn Dancin, Country Dancin: Scripts & Music. 1991. lib. bdg. 79.95 (0-8490-5185-1) Gordon Pr.

Barn Fires. Peter Wild. 32p. (Orig.). 1978. pap. 5.00 (0-912449-00-4) Floating Island.

***Barn Full of Tales, 3 bks., Set.** Sherrie S. Fagerstrom. (J). (ps-6). 1995. pap. 16.00 (1-886466-13-0) Wee Folks Pubns.

***Barn Full of Tales Activity Book.** Sherrie S. Fagerstrom. 20p. (J). (ps-6). 1995. pap. 3.00 (1-886466-15-7) Wee Folks Pubns.

Barn House Book: Rhymes, Riddles, & Jokes. Kenneth Brown. (Illus.). (J). Date not set. 12.95 (1-56743-046-5) Amistad Pr.

Barn in the Air. Michael Waters. (Illus.). 26p. (Orig.). 1987. pap. 5.95 (0-942979-00-1) Livingston U Pr.

Barn Kitten, House Kitten. Joy Dueland. (Illus.). (J). (gr. 2-8). 1978. pap. 3.50 (0-931942-00-4) Phunn Pubs.

***Barn on Fire.** H. Amery. (Farmyard Tales Ser.). (Illus.). 16p. (J). (ps). 1989. pap. 3.95 (0-7460-0471-0, Usborne) EDC.

Barn Owl. D. S. Bunn et al. LC 82-72126. (Illus.). 264p. 1982. 32.50 (0-931130-09-3) Harrell Bks.

Barn Owl. Development Education Centre Staff. (Natural History Ser.). 72p. (C). 1991. pap. 75.00 (0-7478-0024-3, Pub. by S Thornes Pubs UK) St Mut.

***Barn Owl.** Mike Read & Jake Allsop. (Illus.). 128p. 1995. 24.95 (0-7137-2349-1, Pub. by Blandford Pr UK) Sterling.

Barn Owl. Iain R. Taylor. 1989. pap. 25.00 (0-685-71516-7, Pub. by Shire UK) St Mut.

Barn Owls. Wolfgang Epple. (Nature Watch Bks.). (Illus.). 48p. (J). (gr. 2-5). 1992. 19.95 (0-87614-742-2, Carolrhoda) Lerner Group.

Barn Owls: Predator-Prey Relationships & Conservation. Iain Taylor. (Illus.). 310p. (C). 1994. 37.95 (0-521-39290-X) Cambridge U Pr.

***Barn Party.** Nancy Tafuri. LC 94-25356. (J). 1995. 14.93 (0-688-04616-9); lib. bdg. 15.00 (0-688-04617-7) Greenwillow.

Barn Swallows. Mark Brisson. (Stories We Tell Ser.). 37p. 1993. pap. 4.00 (1-884983-01-4) Homegrown Bks.

Barna Report 1993-94: How Our Moral & Spiritual Foundations Are Eroding in This Age of Change. George Barna. 1993. pap. 16.99 (0-8307-1641-6, 5422316) Regal.

Barnabas: Encourager & Equipper. Phyllis Vos Wezeman & Colleen A. Wiessner. (Celebrate: A Creative Approach to Bible Study Ser.). 32p. (Orig.). 1989. pap. 5.95 (0-940754-70-3) Ed Ministries.

Barnabas Bear. Donna J. Jones. (Illus.). 32p. (J). (gr. k-5). 1987. pap. 3.50 (0-9617382-1-9) Glacier Pub.

Barnabas Factor. Derek Wood. 159p. 1991. pap. 6.99 (0-8308-5402-9, Pub. by IVP UK) InterVarsity.

Barnabe Riche: His Farewell to Military Profession. Ed. by Donald Beecher. (Medieval & Renaissance Texts & Studies: Vol. 91). 335p. 1992. 28.00 (0-86698-105-5); pap. 12.00 (0-86698-104-7, P9) MRTS.

Barnabetta. Helen R. Martin. 1993. reprint ed. lib. bdg. 89.00 (0-7812-5490-6) Rprt Serv.

Barnaby: The Struggle of a Word Blind Child. Mary L. Murphy. 74p. 1968. pap. 1.95 (0-85225-535-7) Ed Solutions.

Barnaby & the Big Gorilla. Alain Leonard. LC 91-25414. (Illus.). 32p. (J). (ps-3). 1992. 15.00 (0-688-11291-9, Tambourine Bks); lib. bdg. 14.93 (0-688-11292-7, Tambourine Bks) Morrow.

***Barnaby & the Gorilla.** Leonard. (J). 1994. pap. 4.99 (0-517-13486-1) Random Hse Value.

***Barnaby & the Sea.** D-Rok. LC 94-96113. 32p. (J). (gr. k-6). 1995. 15.00 (0-9643620-1-5) High Tide MN.

Barnaby Bear. Margaret Leon. (Illus.). 32p. (J). (ps-8). 1983. 7.95 (0-920806-42-2, Pub. by Penumbra Pr CN) U of Toronto Pr.

Barnaby Brown: Home from Erehwon. Sidney J. Rauch. (Barnaby Brown Bks.: Bk. 5). (Illus.). 80p. (Orig.). (J). (gr. 2-4). 1990. pap. 4.95 (1-55743-162-0) Berrent Pubns.

Barnaby Goes Wild, No. 7. Gary Richmond. (J). (gr. 1-5). 1991. text ed. 6.99 (0-8499-0914-7) Word Inc.

Barnaby Mouse, Detective, & the Mystery of the Big Book. Diane Stortz. LC 93-14425. (Little Deer Bks.). (Illus.). 28p. (J). (ps). 1994. 5.49 (0-7847-0004-4, 24-03870) Standard Pub.

Barnaby Rudge. Charles Dickens. Ed. by G. W. Spence. (English Library). 1974. mass mkt. 6.95 (0-14-043090-3, Penguin Classics) Viking Penguin.

Barnaby Rudge: A Tale of the Riots of 'Eighty see Oxford Illustrated Dickens

Barnaby's Birthday. John Fitzgerald & Lyn Fitzgerald. LC 92-34275. (Voyages Ser.). (Illus.). (J). 1993. 14.00 (0-383-03618-6) SRA Schl Grp.

***Barnaby's Faraway Land.** Wendy W. Rouillard. LC 94-70710. (Illus.). 28p. (J). (ps-4). 1993. pap. 9.95 (0-9642836-0-3) Barnaby Books.

Barnabys First Christmas. A. P. Folmer. (J). 1989. pap. 5.95 (0-590-42892-6) Scholastic Inc.

***Barnaby's Nantucket Coloring Book.** Wendy W. Rouillard. (Illus.). 32p. (J). (ps-4). 1994. pap. 6.95 (0-9642836-1-1) Barnaby Books.

Barnacle Goose. Myrfyn Owen. 1989. pap. 25.00 (0-7478-0053-7, Pub. by Shire UK) St Mut.

Barnacle Parp's New Chain Saw Guide. Ed. by Walter Hall. (Illus.). 288p. (Orig.). 1985. pap. 17.95 (0-938432-25-7) Mother Earth.

Barnard & Michael Gratz: Their Lives & Times. Sidney M. Fish. 270p. 1994. lib. bdg. 36.50 (0-8191-9516-2) U Pr of Amer.

Barnburners. Herbert D. Donovan. LC 73-16337. (Perspectives in American History Ser.: No. 5). (Illus.). 140p. 1974. reprint ed. lib. bdg. 29.50 (0-87991-337-1) Porcupine Pr.

Barnegat Bay Decoys & Gunning Clubs 1880-1920. 2nd ed. Patricia H. Barke. (Illus.). 48p. 1993. reprint ed. pap. text ed. 12.00 (0-941965-04-X) Ocean Cnty Hist.

Barnegat Ways. Alphyn P. Richardson. LC 79-166564. (Short Story Index Reprint Ser.). (Illus.). 1977. reprint ed. 19.95 (0-8369-3994-8) Ayer.

Barnes: Plays One. 2nd ed. Peter Barnes. (Methuen World Dramatists Ser.). 479p. (C). 1990. pap. 12.95 (0-413-62180-4, A0406, Pub. by Methuen UK) Heinemann.

Barnes: Ten Generations of the Barnes Family in Bristol, CT. F. F. Barnes. (Illus.). 280p. 1992. reprint ed. lib. bdg. 62.00 (0-8328-2614-6); reprint ed. pap. 52.00 (0-8328-2615-4) Higginson Bk Co.

Barnes Against the Blackout: Essays Against Interventionism. Harry E. Barnes. 347p. 1991. pap. 13.95 (0-939484-36-6) Inst Hist Rev.

Barnes Family of Boonslick County, Missouri. 2nd ed. Daniel E. Anderson. LC 91-71187. (Illus.). 232p. 1991. pap. 29.00 (0-9614527-2-2) Dan Anderson.

Barnes Family Year Book, Vol. 1. 64p. 1.25 (0-940748-02-9) Conn Hist Soc.

***Barnes Family Year Book Vols. I-III.** Trescott C. Barnes. 157p. 1994. reprint ed. lib. bdg. 35.00 (0-8328-4293-1); reprint ed. pap. 25.00 (0-8328-4294-X) Higginson Bk Co.

Barnes Genealogies, Including a Collection of Ancestral, Genealogical & Family Records & Biological Sketches of Barnes People. George N. Barnes. (Illus.). 226p. 1988. reprint ed. lib. bdg. 44.00 (0-8328-0192-5); reprint ed. pap. 34.00 (0-8328-0193-3) Higginson Bk Co.

Barnes' Notes on the New Testament. Albert Barnes. LC 62-8727. 1776p. 1966. 48.99 (0-8254-2200-0) Kregel.

Barnes' Notes on the Old & New Testaments, 14 vols. Albert Barnes. 1983. 450.00 (0-8010-0834-4) Baker Bk.

Barnes' People II: Seven Duologues. Peter Barnes. LC 83-12718. 58p. (Orig.). 1984. pap. 6.50 (0-435-23065-4, 23065) Heinemann.

Barnes Trilogy: Blasting the Historical Blackout, The Court Historians Versus Revisionism, Revisionism & Brainwashing. Harry E. Barnes. Ed. by Lewis Brandon. 1981. lib. bdg. 600.00 (0-686-73177-8) Revisionist Pr.

Barnese Mountain Dogs. L. Ostermiller. (Illus.). 192p. 1993. 11.95 (0-86622-572-2, KW202) TFH Pubns.

***Barnestorm: The Plays of Peter Barnes.** Bernard F. Dukore. LC 95-4207. (Studies in Modern Drama: Vol. 5). 328p. 1995. 50.00 (0-8153-1134-6, H1654) Garland.

***Barnet & Stubbs' Practical Guide to Writing with Readings.** 7th ed. Barnet & Stubbs. (C). 1995. text ed. 21.75 (0-673-52329-2) HarpCollege.

Barnett Newman. Harold Rosenberg. (Contemporary Artists Ser.). 1994. 75.00 (0-8109-1360-7) Abrams.

Barnett Newman: Selected Writings & Interviews. John P. O'Neill. 1992. pap. 15.00 (0-520-07817-9) U CA Pr.

Barney: Barney (1634) - Hosmer (1635) Family Records. W. F. Adams. (Illus.). 133p. 1991. reprint ed. pap. 21.00 (0-8328-2090-3) Higginson Bk Co.

Barney & Baby Bop: A Tent Too Full. Stephen White. Ed. by Linda Dowdy. LC 93-77870. (Illus.). 24p. (J). (gr. 3-6). 1993. pap. 2.25 (1-57064-009-2) Barney Pub.

***Barney & Baby Bop at the Beach.** Mary A. Dudko. LC 94-79390. (Illus.). 14p. (J). (ps-k). 1995. bds. 7.95 (1-57064-036-X) Barney Pub.

Barney & Baby Bop Follow That Cat! Stephen White. Ed. by Linda C. Dowdy. LC 94-71470. (Seek & Peek Ser.). (Illus.). 14p. (J). (ps-k). 1994. bds. 4.95 (1-57064-017-3) Barney Pub.

***Barney & Baby Bop's Band: A Story about Sharing.** Mark Bernthal. LC 94-79498. (Book & Cassette Ser.). (Illus.). 32p. (Orig.). (J). (ps-3). 1995. pap. 6.95 (1-57064-024-6) Barney Pub.

***Barney Bear Gets Dressed.** Contrib by Rozanne Williams. (Emergent Reader Bks.). 8p. 1995. 1.59 (0-614-06543-7) Creat Teach Pr.

Barney Bipple's Magic Dandelions. Carol Chapman. LC 77-14852. (Illus.). 32p. (J). (ps-3). 1992. pap. 4.99 (0-14-054540-9, Puff Unicorn) Puffin Bks.

Barney Fife's Guide to Life, Love & Self-Defense. Len Oszustowicz et al. LC 93-42332. (Illus.). 167p. 1993. 12.95 (1-56530-103-X) Summit TX.

Barney First Fun. (YA). 1993. pap. 1.95 (0-307-03521-2, Golden Pr) Western Pub.

Barney Goes to the Zoo. Linda C. Dowdy. Ed. by Linda Hartley. LC 93-77868. (Illus.). 18p. (J). (ps-00). 1993. bds. 4.95 (1-57064-011-4) Barney Pub.

Barney Google: An Original Compilation. First Collection of the Complete First Year of the Daily Strip, 1919-1920. Billy De Beck. Ed. by Bill Blackbeard. LC 76-53038. (Classic American Comic Strips Ser.). (Illus.). 1977. 18.00 (0-88355-631-6) Hyperion Conn.

Barney Google & Snuffy Smith: Seventy Five Years of an American Legend. Ed. by Brian Walker. LC 94-9310. (Illus.). 160p. (YA). 1994. pap. 16.95 (0-87816-283-6) Kitchen Sink.

Barney Is Best. Nancy W. Carlstrom. LC 92-30376. (Illus.). 32p. (J). (ps-3). 1994. 15.00 (0-06-022875-X) HarpC Child Bks.

Barney Is Best. Nancy W. Carlstrom. LC 92-30376. (Illus.). 32p. (J). (ps-3). 1994. lib. bdg. 14.89 (0-06-022876-8) HarpC Child Bks.

Barney Is Big. Nicki Weiss. LC 87-8546. (Illus.). 24p. (J). (ps-1). 1988. 11.95 (0-688-07586-X); lib. bdg. 11.88 (0-688-07587-8) Greenwillow.

Barney McCabe see Tommy Scott Young Spins Magical Tales

Barney Says, "Please & Thank You" Stephen White. Ed. by Linda C. Dowdy. LC 93-74288. (Illus.). 24p. (J). (ps-00). 1994. pap. 2.25 (1-57064-023-8) Barney Pub.

***Barney Tales.** Jewel B. Turpin. (Illus.). 1995. 9.95 (0-533-11173-0) Vantage.

Barney the Bear Killer. Pat Sargent. Ed. by Debbie Bowen. (Illus.). 120p. (Orig.). (J). (gr. k-6). 1994. lib. bdg. 19.95 (1-56763-054-5); pap. text ed. 9.95 (1-56763-055-3) Ozark Pub.

Barney the Bus. Ted Fuller. Ed. by Jane Weinberger. LC 88-51276. (Illus.). 48p. (J). (ps-4). 1989. pap. 5.95 (0-932433-49-9) Windswept Hse.

Barney Wigglesworth & the Birthday Surprise. Elspeth C. Murphy. LC 88-4346. (Little Epistles for Kids Ser.). (Illus.). 32p. (J). (ps-2). 1988. 9.99 (1-55513-696-6, Chariot Bks) Chariot Family.

Barney Wigglesworth & the Church Flood. Elspeth C. Murphy. LC 88-5008. (Little Epistles for Kids Ser.). (Illus.). 32p. (J). (ps-2). 1988. 9.99 (1-55513-685-0, Chariot Bks) Chariot Family.

Barney Wigglesworth & the Party That Almost Wasn't. Elspeth C. Murphy. LC 88-4342. (Little Epistles for Kids Ser.). (Illus.). 32p. (J). (ps-2). 1988. 9.99 (1-55513-684-2, Chariot Bks) Chariot Family.

Barney Wigglesworth & the Smallest Christmas Pageant. Elspeth C. Murphy. LC 88-5009. (Little Epistles for Kids Ser.). (Illus.). 32p. (J). (ps-2). 1989. 9.99 (1-55513-686-9, Chariot Bks) Chariot Family.

Barney Years. John D. Rucker. 160p. 1992. 16.95 (1-55971-179-5) NorthWord.

***Barney's Big Balloon.** Mark Bernthal. (Illus.). 24p. (Orig.). (J). (ps-3). 1995. pap. 2.50 (1-57064-044-0) Barney Pub.

Barney's Book of Opposites. Mary A. Dudko & Margie Larsen. LC 94-72000. (Illus.). 20p. (J). (ps-k). 1994. bds. 3.95 (1-57064-016-5) Barney Pub.

Barney's Book on the Olympic Peninsula: A Compendium for Motorists & Hikers of All Major Roads & Trails. Barney Arender. LC 90-91668. (Illus.). 376p. (Orig.). 1991. pap. 18.95 (1-878903-00-4) Nosado Pr.

Barney's Book on the Olympic Peninsula: A Compendium for Motorists & Hikers of All Major Roads & Trails. 2nd ed. Barney Arender. (Illus.). 352p. (Orig.). 1993. pap. 19.95 (1-878903-06-3) Nosado Pr.

Barney's Color Surprise. Mary A. Dudko & Margie Larsen. Ed. by Linda Hartley. LC 93-77865. (Illus.). 18p. (J). (ps). 1993. reprint ed. bds. 3.95 (1-57064-007-6) Barney Pub.

Barney's Farm Animals. Kimberly Kearns & Marie O'Brien. Ed. by Linda Hartley. LC 93-77014. (Illus.). 24p. (J). (ps). 1993. bds. 3.95 (1-57064-002-5) Barney Pub.

Barney's Favorite Mother Goose Rhymes. Stephen White. Ed. by Linda Hartley. LC 93-77864. (Mother Goose Rhymes Ser.: Vol. 2). (Illus.). 32p. (J). (ps-00). 1994. 7.95 (1-57064-012-2) Barney Pub.

Barney's Favorite Mother Goose Rhymes, Vol. 1. Stephen White. Ed. by Linda Hartley. LC 92-76136. (Mother Goose Rhymes Ser.). (Illus.). 32p. (J). (ps-00). 1993. 7.95 (1-57064-001-7) Barney Pub.

***Barney's Friends.** Illus. by June Valentine-Ruppe. 18p. (J). (ps-3). 1995. 4.95 (1-57064-066-1) Barney Pub.

Barney's Hats. Mary A. Dudko & Margie Larsen. Ed. by Linda Hartley. LC 93-77016. 24p. (J). (ps-1). 1993. pap. 2.25 (1-57064-005-X) Barney Pub.

Barney's Horse. Syd Hoff. LC 87-66. (Early I Can Read Bk.). (Illus.). 32p. (J). (ps-3). 1987. lib. bdg. 14.89 (0-06-022450-9) HarpC Child Bks.

Barney's Horse. Syd Hoff. LC 87-66. (Trophy Early I Can Read Bk.). (Illus.). 32p. (J). (ps-2). 1990. pap. 3.50 (0-06-444142-3, Trophy) HarpC Child Bks.

Barney's Imagination Island: Bedtime with Barney. Stephen White. Ed. by Linda C. Dowdy. LC 94-70569. (Illus.). 32p. (J). (ps-3). 1994. 7.95 (1-57064-028-9) Barney Pub.

Barney's Portable Book on the Southeastern Olympic Peninsula: A Small Compendium for Motorists & Hikers of All Major Roads & Trails. Barney Arender. LC 91-90280. (Illus.). 96p. (Orig.). 1991. pap. 8.95 (1-878903-01-2) Nosado Pr.

***Barney's Weather Book.** Mary A. Dudko. LC 94-79379. (Illus.). 22p. (J). (ps-k). 1995. bds. 3.95 (1-57064-037-8) Barney Pub.

Barney's Wonderful Winter Day. Stephen White. LC 94-71999. (Illus.). 32p. (J). (ps-3). 1994. 4.95 (1-57064-027-0) Barney Pub.

***Barney's Wonderful Winter Day.** Stephen White. 32p. (J). 1995. audio, pap. write for info. (1-57064-049-1) Barney Pub.

Barnhart: The Descendants of John & Mariah (Hiveley) Barnhart: a Genealogy of the Ancestors & Descendants of John Barnhart & Mariah Hively of Eastern Ohio to the Present. James K. Raywalt. (Illus.). 109p. 1992. reprint ed. lib. bdg. 29.50 (0-8328-2408-9); reprint ed. pap. 19.50 (0-8328-2409-7) Higginson Bk Co.

***Barnhart Abbreviations Dictionary.** Barnhart. Date not set. text ed. 34.95 (0-471-57146-0) Wiley.

Barnhart Concise Dictionary of Etymologies. Ed. by R. Barnhart. Date not set. 45.00 (0-06-270084-7, Harper Ref) HarpC.

Barnhart Dictionary Companion Index 1982-1985. David K. Barnhart. LC 86-81562. xv, 102p. 1987. 45.00 (0-936368-05-5) Lexik Hse.

Barnhart Dictionary of Etymology. Ed. by Robert K. Barnhart. 1248p. 1988. 64.00 (0-8242-0745-9) Wilson.

Barnhart New Words Concordance. David K. Barnhart. LC 93-80483. vi, 704p. 1994. ring bd. 65.00 (0-936368-07-1) Lexik Hse.

B

An Asterisk (*) at the beginning of an entry indicates that the title is appearing in BIP for the first time.

*__Barnie's Coffee & Tea Company - the Coffee & Tea Lover's Cookbook.__ 96p. 1995. 14.95 (0-8487-4069-6) Oxmoor Hse.

*__Barns.__ Robert Hutchinson. (Illus.). 112p. 1995. 25.95 (1-56313-762-3); pap. 17.95 (1-56313-763-1) BrownTrout Pubs Inc.

*__Barns & Outbuildings of the Lowell Neighborhood.__ Steve Heinzen et al. 60p. 1993. text ed. 99.95 (1-881147-04-5) Lowell Print.

*__Barns & Outbuildings of the Lowell Neighborhood.__ Steve Heinzen et al. 60p. 1993. pap. 10.95 (1-881147-10-X) Lowell Print.

Barns Bluff Camping Equipment Company. 5th ed. Terrie Kroshus. 128p. (C). 1992. Manual practice set. pap. text ed. 19.50 (0-256-11347-5, 38-1346-05) Irwin.

Barns of America. 1991. 14.99 (0-517-05312-8) Random Hse Value.

*__Barns of the Midwest.__ Ed. by Allen G. Noble & Hubert G. Wilhelm. (Illus.). 300p. 1995. text ed. 50.00x (0-8214-1115-2) Ohio U Pr.

*__Barns of the Midwest.__ Ed. by Allen G. Noble & Hubert G. Wilhelm. (Illus.). 300p. 1995. pap. text ed. 25.00x (0-8214-1116-0) Ohio U Pr.

Barns of Wisconsin. Jerold W. Apps. LC 77-5472. (Illus.). 1977. pap. 10.00 (0-915024-14-4) Wl Trails.

Barns of Yesteryear & More. Barbara Brown. (Illus.). 64p. (Orig.). 1993. pap. 8.95 (0-87961-223-1) Naturegraph.

*__Barns on Parade Across America.__ Harold E. Wagner. (Illus.). 96p. (Orig.). (YA). Date not set. 26.95 (0-9637155-0-X); pap. 19.95 (0-614-05276-9) H&O Pioneer.

Barns, Sheds & Outbuildings. Ed. by Byron D. Halsted. LC 76-50020. (Illus.). 1982. reprint ed. 7.95 (0-8289-0293-3) Viking Penguin.

*__Barns, Sheds & Outbuildings: Placement, Design & Construction.__ Byron D. Halstead. LC 76-50020. 238p. 1995. pap. 12.95 (0-911469-12-5) A C Hood.

Barnscapes & More. Donna Bell. 100p. 1990. pap. 7.50 (1-56770-218-X) S Scheewe Pubns.

Barnsdall (Hollyhock) House. (Architecture in Detail Ser.). (Illus.). 60p. 1993. pap. 29.95 (0-7148-2750-9, Pub. by Phaidon Press UK) Chronicle Bks.

Barnsley's Conveyancing Law & Practice. 3rd ed. D. G. Barnsley. 1988. 106.00 (0-406-55634-2, U.K.); pap. 65.00 (0-406-55635-0) Butterworth Legal Pubs.

Barnstormers & Daredevils. K. C. Tessendorf. LC 87-15194. (Illus.). 96p. (J). (gr. 4 up). 1988. text ed. 14.95 (0-689-31346-2, Atheneum Bks Young) S&S Childrens.

Barnstorming. Frank Bacon. (Illus.). 224p. 1987. write for info. (0-914139-04-5) San Jose His Mus Assn.

*__Barnum.__ 1994. pap. 12.95 (1-57007-026-1, XW1641) Astor Bks.

*__Barnum: Prince of Showmen, an Illustrated Biography.__ Philip B. Kunhardt, Jr. & Peter W. Kunhardt. LC 94-42597. (Illus.). 1995. 45.00 (0-679-43574-3) Knopf.

Barnum & Bailey in the Sky: A Collection of Soul Journeys. Arthur K. Pope. (Illus.). 30p. (Orig.). 1991. pap. write for info. (0-9623500-3-6) Ministry Two.

Barnum Memorial Cemetery. 2nd ed. Ed. by Eunice Pines & Eleanor Sabo. (Illus.). 72p. 1987. reprint ed. pap. 8.00 (0-940133-04-0) Kinseeker Pubns.

Barnum's Own Story: Autobiography. Phineas T. Barnum. Ed. by Waldo R. Browne. (Illus.). 1962. 18.75 (0-8446-4001-8) Peter Smith.

Barnwell Addresses, Vol. 1: 1922-1930. LC 74-156610. (Essay Index Reprint Ser.). 1977. reprint ed. 30.95 (0-8369-2342-1) Ayer.

Barnwell County Marriages Seventeen Seventy-Five to Eighteen Seventy-Nine: Implied in Barnwell County, S. C. Probate & Equity Records. rev. ed. Barbara R. Langdon & Shirley P. Langdon. 188p. (Orig.). 1987. reprint ed. pap. text ed. 20.00 (0-938741-01-2) Langdon & Langdon.

Barnyard Animals. (Animal Board Bks.). (Illus.). 8p. (J). (ps). 1991. bds. 1.99 (0-517-66918-8) Random Hse Value.

Barnyard Babies. Joy Evans & Jo E. Moore. (Thematic Resource Unit Ser.). (Illus.). 48p. (J). (ps-1). 1990. pap. text ed. 9.95 (1-55799-169-3) Evan-Moor Corp.

Barnyard Babies: Oink, Baa, Moo, Meow, Neigh, Peep. Time-Life Books Editors. Ed. by Blaine Marshall. (Illus.). 6p. (J). (ps). 1993. 16.95 (0-8094-6692-9) Time-Life.

Barnyard Banter. Denise Fleming. LC 93-11032. (J). 1994. 15.95 (0-8050-1957-X) H Holt & Co.

Barnyard Buddies. Cheryl J. Null & Carol L. Gad. (Illus.). 32p. (J). (gr. 2-6). 1989. pap. 5.95 (1-880171-00-7) Stardom.

Barnyard Buddies in Circus Champions. Cheryl J. Null & Carol L. Gad. (Illus.). 36p. (J). (gr. 2-6). 1990. pap. 5.95 (1-880171-01-5) Stardom.

Barnyard Buddies in Finders Keepers. Cheryl J. Null & Carol L. Gad. (Illus.). 36p. (J). (gr. 2-6). 1992. pap. 5.95 (1-880171-04-X) Stardom.

Barnyard Mystery. Pat Relf & Louise Hanavan. (Little Golden Sound Story Book Ser.). 24p. (J). (ps up). 1992. write for info. (0-307-74801-4, 64801) Western Pub.

Barnyard Tracks. Deborah Duffy. LC 91-72973. (Illus.). 32p. (J). (ps up). 1992. 12.95 (1-878093-66-5) Boyds Mills Pr.

Barnyards & Billygoats. Claudia Nice. 44p. 1982. pap. 6.50 (1-56770-134-5) S Scheewe Pubns.

Barocco. Severo Sarduy. (FRE.). 1991. pap. 16.95 (0-7859-3977-6) Fr & Eur.

Barock und Fruehaufklaerung see Geschichte der Deutschen Poetik

Baroclinic Processes on Continental Shelves. Ed. by C. Mooers. (Coastal & Estuarine Sciences Ser.: Vol. 3). (Illus.). 144p. 1986. 25.00 (0-87590-252-9) Am Geophysical.

Barometer of Modern Reason: On the Philosophies of Current Events. Vincent Descombes. Tr. by Stephen A. Schwartz. LC 92-14531. (Odeon Ser.). 208p. 1993. pap. 19.95 (0-19-507990-6) OUP.

Baron & the Bookseller. June Calvin. 224p. (Orig.). 1994. pap. 3.99 (0-451-18239-1, Sig) NAL-Dutton.

Baron & the Fish. Peter Marginter. Tr. & Aft. by Lowell A. Bangerter. (Studies in Austrian Literature, Culture, & Thought. Translation Ser.). 311p. (Orig.). 1992. pap. 22.00 (0-929497-46-5) Ariadne CA.

Baron Bagge & Count Luna. Alexander Lernet-Holenia. Tr. by Richard Winston et al. LC 88-80805. 240p. 1988. 23.00 (0-941419-20-7, Eridanos Library); pap. 14.00 (0-941419-21-5, Eridanos Library) Marsilio Pubs.

Baron Bean: An Original Compilation, First Collection of the Complete First Year of the Daily Strip, 1916-1917. George Herriman. Ed. by Bill Blackbeard. LC 76-53043. (Classic American Comic Strips Ser.). (Illus.). 1977. 18.00 (0-88355-641-3) Hyperion Conn.

Baron de Fourchevif. Eugene Labiche. (FRE.). pap. 10.95 (0-7859-5349-3) Fr & Eur.

Baron D'Holbach. M. Cushing & W. H. Wickwar. 1972. 59.95 (0-87968-707-X) Gordon Pr.

Baron D'Holbach: A Prelude to the French Revolution. W. H. Wickwar. LC 68-22378. 253p. 1968. reprint ed. 37.50 (0-678-00411-0) Kelley.

Baron Dominique Vivant Denon, 1747-1825: Hedonist & Scholar in a Period of Transition. Judith Nowinski. LC 78-86651. (Illus.). 280p. 1975. 27.50 (0-8386-7470-4) Fairleigh Dickinson.

Baron Friedrich von Hugel & the Debate on Historical Christianity 1902-1905. John A. McGrath. LC 93-396. 380p. 1993. 99.95 (0-7734-9817-6) E Mellen.

Baron in the Trees. Italo Calvino. Tr. by Archibald Colquhoun. LC 76-39704. 217p. 1977. reprint ed. pap. 6.95 (0-15-610680-9, Harvest Bks) HarBrace.

Baron Joseph Eotvos: A Literary Biography. Steven B. Vardy. No. 52. pap. write for info. (0-318-61102-3) Brooklyn Coll Pr.

Baron Joseph Eotvos: A Literary Biography. Steven B. Vardy. (Atlantic Studies on Society in Change). (Illus.). 256p. 1987. text ed. 42.00 (0-88033-111-9, 214) East Eur Quarterly.

Baron Munchausen. 3rd ed. Rudolph E. Raspe. (Dedalus European Fiction Classics Ser.). (Illus.). 287p. Date not set. pap. 11.95 (1-873982-35-6) Hippocrene Bks.

Baron of Grogzwig. Charles Dickens. Ed. by Shirley Greenway. LC 93-18627. (Illus.). (J). (gr. 2-7). 1993. 14.95 (1-879085-81-X) Whsprng Coyote Pr.

Baron on Board. large type ed. John Creasey. LC 91-33571. 274p. 1991. reprint ed. lib. bdg. 18.95 (1-56054-265-9) Thorndike Pr.

Baron, the Logger, the Miner, & Me. John H. Toole. Ed. by William H. Forbis. LC 84-25426. (Illus.). 290p. 1984. pap. 14.95 (0-87842-185-8) Mountain Pr.

Baron Thugut & Austria's Response to the French Revolution. Karl A. Roider, Jr. LC 87-2240. (Illus.). 448p. 1987. text ed. 67.50 (0-691-05135-6) Princeton U Pr.

Baron Trump's Marvellous Underground Journey. Ingersoll Lockwood. 235p. 1972. reprint ed. spiral bd. 10.45 (0-7873-0567-7) Mokelumne.

Baron Von Kodiak, Shirley Temple & Me. Ann Valery. 25.00 (0-8464-0168-1) Beekman Pubs.

Baron Von Mabel's Backpacking. Sheridan Anderson. (Illus.). 96p. 1980. pap. 7.95 (0-89732-123-5) Menasha Ridge.

Baron Von Steuben. Ed. by G. Martin Sleeman. 32p. 1990. pap. 3.95 (0-932052-52-5) North Country.

Baron Von Steuben's Revolutionary War Drill Manual. Frederick W. Von Steuben. 192p. 1985. reprint ed. pap. 4.95 (0-486-24934-4) Dover.

Baronage of England, Or an Historical Account of Our English Nobility, 2 vols., Set. William Dugdale. 1295p. 1977. reprint ed. 323.70 (3-487-06374-3, Pub. by Georg Olms GW) Lubrecht & Cramer.

Barone Di Dolsheim: Libretto by Felice Romani, Music by Giovanni Pacini First Performance Milan, Teatro Alla Scala, 23 September 1818. Giovanni Pacini. LC 89-38889. (Italian Opera 1810-1840 Ser.: Vol. 29). 328p. 1990. 119.00 (0-8240-6578-6) Garland.

*__Baroness of Blood.__ Elaine Bergstrom. (Ravenloft Ser.). 320p. (Orig.). Date not set. pap. 4.95 (0-7869-0146-2) TSR Inc.

Baroness of Harlem. Brett Howard. (Orig.). 1990. pap. 3.50 (0-87067-361-0) Holloway.

Baroness Orczy Collector Guide. Harmony Raine. (Orig.). (C). 1984. pap. 4.95 (0-89966-502-0) Buccaneer Bks.

*__Baronet's Song.__ George MacDonald. 1995. pap. 5.99 (1-55661-580-9) Bethany Hse.

Baronet's Song. abr. rev. ed. George MacDonald. Ed. by Michael Phillips. LC 83-6417. 208p. 1983. pap. 6.99 (0-87123-291-X) Bethany Hse.

Baronia Anglica. Thomas Madox. LC 79-8369. reprint ed. 78.50 (0-404-18358-1) AMS Pr.

Baronial Family in Medieval England: The Clares, 1217-1314. Michael Altschul. LC 78-64244. (Johns Hopkins University. Studies in the Social Sciences. Thirtieth Ser. 1912: 2). reprint ed. 27.00 (0-404-61349-7) AMS Pr.

Baronial Family in Medieval England: The Clares, 1217-1314. Michael Altschul. LC 65-22947. (Johns Hopkins University Studies in Historical & Political Science: Series 83, No. 2). 352p. reprint ed. pap. 100.40 (0-8357-5969-5, 2004926) Bks Demand.

Baronial Opposition to Edward Second: Its Character & Policy. James C. Davies. 644p. 1967. reprint ed. 37.50 (0-7146-1466-1, BHA-01466, Pub. by F Cass Pubs UK) Intl Spec Bk.

Baronies of South Carolina: The South Carolina Historical & Genealogical Magazine. Henry A. Smith. LC 87-26623. (Historical Writings of Henry A. M. Smith: Vol. 1). (Illus.). 224p. 1988. 25.00 (0-87152-424-4) Reprint.

Baron's Apprenticeship. MacDonald George. 1994. pap. 7.99 (1-55661-520-5) Bethany Hse.

Baron's Apprenticeship. George MacDonald & Michael Phillips. LC 86-11734. 250p. 1986. pap. 7.99 (0-87123-655-9) Bethany Hse.

Baron's Bride. large type ed. Marina Oliver. (Linford Romance Library). 1991. pap. 13.95 (0-7089-7107-5, Linford) Ulverscroft.

Barons et Chevaliers dans Raoul de Cambrai: Autopsie d'un Phenomene de Glissement. Francoise Denis. (American University Studies: Romance Languages & Literature: Ser. II, Vol. 114). 267p. (C). 1989. text ed. 39.95 (0-8204-1087-X) P Lang Pubs.

Barons of European Industry. Ed. by Anthony Rowley. LC 74-11193. 169p. 1974. 26.95 (0-8419-0171-6) Holmes & Meier.

Barons of Labor: The San Francisco Building Trades & Union Power in the Progressive Era. Michael Kazin. (Working Class in American History Ser.). 338p. 1987. pap. 11.95 (0-252-06075-X) U of Ill Pr.

Barons of Newport: A Guide to the Gilded Age. Terrence Gavan. (Illus.). 88p. (Orig.). (YA). 1988. pap. 7.50 (0-929249-01-1) Pineapple Pubns.

Barons of the Sky from Early Flight to Strategic Warfare: From Early Flight to Strategic Warfare, the Story of the American Aerospace Industry. Wayne Biddle. LC 92-35232. 368p. 1993. pap. 14.95 (0-8050-2514-6) H Holt & Co.

Barons of the Welsh Frontier: The Corbet, Pantulf, & Fitz Warin Families, 1066-1272. Janet Meisel. LC 80-10273. 251p. reprint ed. pap. 71.60 (0-7837-6886-9, 2046716) Bks Demand.

Baroque. John Martin. LC 76-12059. (Icon Editions Ser.). (Illus.). 288p. 1977. pap. text ed. 15.00i (0-06-430077-3, IN-77, Icon Edns) HarpC.

Baroque: Literature & Culture in Seventeenth Century Europe. Peter N. Skrine. LC 78-15872. 160p. 1979. 27.50 (0-8419-0427-8) Holmes & Meier.

Baroque & Folk Tunes for Recorder. Ed. by Leo Alfassy. pap. 7.95 (0-86001-275-1) Music Sales.

Baroque & Rococo. Germain Bazin. LC 84-51843. (World of Art Ser.). (Illus.). 288p. 1985. pap. 14.95 (0-500-20018-1) Thames Hudson.

Baroque & Rococo Architecture. Henry A. Millon. LC 61-15492. (Great Ages of World Architecture Ser.). (Illus.). 127p. 1961. pap. 10.95 (0-8076-0333-3) Braziller.

Baroque & Rococo Pictorial Imagery: The 1758-60 Hertel Edition of Ripa's Iconologia. Cesare Ripa. 1991. pap. 13.95 (0-486-26595-1) Dover.

Baroque & Romantic Stage Design. Ed. by Janos Scholz. LC 83-45796. (Illus.). 47.50 (0-404-20229-2, ND2885) AMS Pr.

Baroque Architecture. Christian Norberg-Schulz. LC 85-30011. (History of World Architecture Ser.). (Illus.). 220p. 1986. pap. 29.95 (0-8478-0693-6) Rizzoli Intl.

Baroque Architecture. Martin S. Briggs. LC 67-23634. (Architecture & Decorative Art Ser.). 1967. reprint ed. 39.50 (0-306-70960-0) Da Capo.

Baroque Art in Latin America. Damian Bayon et al. (Illus.). 176p. 1992. 50.00 (2-08-013531-7, Pub. by Flammarion) Abbeville Pr.

*__Baroque Baroque: The Culture of Excess.__ Stephen Calloway. (Illus.). 240p. (C). 1994. 49.95 (0-7148-2985-4, Pub. by Phaidon Press UK) Chronicle Bks.

Baroque Beads with Cernit No. 1. Donna Kato. (Illus.). 20p. (Orig.). 1994. pap. 6.95 (1-885669-03-8) Prairie Crft.

Baroque Book Illustration: A Short Survey from the Collection in the Department of Graphic Arts, Harvard College Library. Philip Hofer. LC 51-14003. (Illus.). 192p. reprint ed. pap. 54.80 (0-7837-1707-5, 2057236) Bks Demand.

Baroque Ceiling Paintings in the Churches of Rome, 1600-1750: A Bibliography. Robert England. (Studien Zur Kunstgeschichte Ser.: Vol. 12). x, 142p. 1979. 22.62 (3-487-06954-7, Pub. by Georg Olms GW) Lubrecht & Cramer.

Baroque Chess Openings. Richard Wincor. LC 72-77482. (Illus.). 116p. 1975. reprint ed. pap. 2.95 (0-8065-0503-6, Citadel Pr) Carol Pub Group.

Baroque Clarinet. Albert R. Rice. (Early Music Ser.: No. 13). (Illus.). 216p. 1992. 79.00 (0-19-816188-3) OUP.

Baroque Debut. Contrib by Maurice Whitney. 1975. 3.00 (0-913334-27-8, CM1032) Consort Music.

Baroque et la musique: Essai d'esthetique musicale. Suzanne Clercx. LC 76-43910. reprint ed. 47.50 (0-404-60153-7) AMS Pr.

Baroque Guitar. Frederick Noad. (Illus.). 128p. 1974. pap. 14.95 (0-8256-9951-7, AM35890) Music Sales.

Baroque in Bohemia. Milada Souckova. LC 80-14338. (Michigan Slavic Materials Ser.: No. 17). (Illus.). 1980. pap. 12.00 (0-930042-31-X) Mich Slavic Pubns.

Baroque in Brazil see Colonial Art

Baroque in Central Europe: Places, Architecture, & Art. Manlio Brusatin et al. 290p. 1993. 60.00 (1-56886-000-5) Marsilio Pubs.

Baroque in Slavic Cultures. 352p. (RUS.). 1982. 24.00 (0-317-57221-0, Pub. by Collets UK) St Mut.

Baroque Music. Nicholas Anderson. LC 93-61370. (Illus.). 224p. 1994. 29.95 (0-500-01606-2) Thames Hudson.

Baroque Music. 2nd ed. Claude V. Palisca. (History of Music Ser.). (Illus.). 1981. text ed. 19.95 (0-13-055954-7) P-H.

Baroque Music. 3rd ed. Claude V. Palisca. 1990. pap. text ed. 35.00 (0-13-058496-7, 650102) P-H.

Baroque Music: A Research & Information Guide. John H. Baron. LC 92-19620. (Music Research & Information Guides: Garland Reference Library of the Humanities: Vol. 16, Vol. 871). 600p. 1990. 90.00 (0-8240-4436-3, H871) Garland.

Baroque Music: Style & Performance, A Handbook. Robert Donington. (Illus.). (Orig.). 1982. pap. 14.95 (0-393-30052-8) Norton.

*__Baroque Music Today: Music As Speech, Ways to a New Understanding of Music.__ Nikolaus Harnoncourt. Tr. by Mary O'Neill. 216p. 1995. pap. 14.95 (0-931340-91-8, Amadeus Pr) Timber.

Baroque Narrative of Carlos de Siguenza y Gongora: A New World Paradise. Kathleen Ross. (Studies in Latin American & Iberian Literature: No. 8). 240p. (C). 1994. 54.95 (0-521-45113-2) Cambridge U Pr.

Baroque Organ-Cases of Portugal. Carlos De Azvedo. (Illus.). 130p. (Orig.). 1972. 58.00x (0-913746-23-1) Organ Lit.

Baroque Ornament & Designs. Jacques Stella. (Design Library). 48p. 1987. pap. 3.95 (0-486-25378-3) Dover.

Baroque Painters, Vol. II. (C). 1969. text ed. 20.00 (0-393-02416-4) Norton.

Baroque Painting in Madrid: The Contribution of Claudio Coello. Edward J. Sullivan. LC 86-6939. (Illus.). 312p. 1987. text ed. 58.00 (0-8262-0614-X) U of Mo Pr.

Baroque Painting in Rome. rev. ed. Hermann Voss. Tr. by Thomas Pelzel. (Illus.). 672p. 1995. 125.00 (1-55660-187-5) A Wofsy Fine Arts.

Baroque Period: Masters of the Seventeenth & Eighteenth Century. Denes Agay. (Anthology of Piano Music Ser.: Vol. 1). 232p. 1981. pap. 14.95 (0-8256-8041-7, Yorktown Mus) Music Sales.

*__Baroque Personae.__ Ed. by Rosario Villari. Tr. by Lydia G. Cochrane. LC 94-47217. 1992. lib. bdg. 47.50 (0-226-85636-4); pap. text ed. 18.95 (0-226-85637-2) U Ch Pr.

Baroque Portraiture in Italy: Works from North American Collections. John T. Spike. LC 84-82128. (Illus.). 214p. (Orig.). 1984. pap. 14.95 (0-916758-16-8) Ringling Mus Art.

Baroque Reason: The Aesthetics of Modernity. Christine Buci-Glucksmann & Bryan S. Turner. (Theory, Culture & Society Ser.). 192p. (C). 1994. text ed. 65.00 (0-8039-8975-X); pap. text ed. 19.95 (0-8039-8976-8) Sage.

Baroque Recorder Music. Franz Zeidler. 1993. 3.95 (0-87166-252-3, 93436) Mel Bay.

Baroque Sonatas: For Flute & Guitar. Duncan. 1990. 7.95 (0-685-32138-X, T669) Hansen Ed Mus.

*__Baroque Splendor: The Art of the Hungarian Goldsmith.__ Istvan Fodor et al. 227p. 1994. pap. text ed. write for info. (1-887506-02-0) Bard Grad Ctr.

*__Baroque Splendor: The Art of the Hungarian Goldsmith.__ Magyar Nemzeti Muzeum Curators Staff. (Illus.). 227p. Date not set. pap. 50.00 (0-614-07360-X) Bard Grad Ctr.

Baroque Theatre & Stage Design. Mark S. Weil. LC 82-63080. (Illus.). 40p. 1983. pap. 5.00 (0-936316-04-7) Wash U Gallery.

Baroque Times in Old Mexico: Seventeenth-Century Persons, Places, & Practices. Irving A. Leonard. (Illus.). 1959. pap. 16.95 (0-472-06110-0, 110, Ann Arbor Bks) U of Mich Pr.

Baroque Times in Old Mexico: Seventeenth-Century Persons, Places, & Practices. Irving A. Leonard. LC 80-29256. (Illus.). xi, 260p. 1981. reprint ed. text ed. 59.75 (0-313-22826-4, LEBT, Greenwood Pr) Greenwood.

Baroque Topographies: Literature - History - Philosophy. Ed. by Timothy E. Hampton. (Yale French Studies: No. 80). (Illus.). 288p. (Orig.). (C). 1991. pap. text ed. 17.00 (0-300-05066-6) Yale U Pr.

Baroque Vocal Music II: Italian & Spanish Sacred & Secular Music. Ed. by Kenneth Cooper. (Three Centuries of Music in Score Ser.: Vol. 12). 250p. 1988. lib. bdg. 25.00 (0-8240-0939-8) Garland.

Baroque with That Jazz Feeling. Progris. 1990. 5.95 (0-685-32165-7, K742) Hansen Ed Mus.

Baroreceptor Reflexes: Integrative Functions & Clinical Aspects. Ed. by P. B. Persson & H. R. Kirchheim. xi, 322p. 1991. 149.00 (0-387-53588-8) Spr-Verlag.

Baroreceptors & Hypertension. Ed. by P. Kezdi. 1967. 194.00 (0-08-012488-7, Pub. by Pergamon Repr UK) Franklin.

Barosaurus. William Lindsay. LC 92-52819. (American Museum of Natural History Ser.). (Illus.). 32p. (J). (gr. 3 up). 1993. 12.95 (1-56458-123-3) Dorling Kindersley.

Barozzi: Or, the Venetian Sorceress. Catherine Smith. Ed. by Devendra P. Varma. LC 77-2047. (Gothic Novels III Ser.). 1977. lib. bdg. 42.95 (0-405-10145-7) Ayer.

Barquitos de Papel. Alma F. Ada. (Cuentos con Alma Ser.). (Illus.). 24p. (SPA.). (J). (gr. 3-9). 1993. 16.95 (1-56492-118-2) Laredo.

Barr-Fyke Machines & Postal Markings, 3 vols., Set. Reg Morris & Robert Payne. (Illus.). 116p. 1990. pap. 26.00 (0-9621481-4-8); pap. 26.00 (0-9621481-5-6); pap. 26.00 (0-9621481-6-4) Machine Cancel Soc.

BARR-HASP. 2nd ed. Barr Systems, Inc. Staff. (Illus.). 252p. 1988. pap. text ed. 20.00 (0-938835-07-6) Barr Syst Inc.

BARR-PRINT. Barr Systems, Inc. Staff. 24p. (Orig.). 1987. pap. 10.00 (0-938835-06-8) Barr Syst Inc.

BARR-SNA RJE. Barr Systems, Inc. Staff. 290p. (Orig.). 1988. pap. text ed. 20.00 (0-938835-08-4) Barr Syst Inc.

BARR-TAPE Release 88. 2nd ed. Barr Systems, Inc. Staff. 108p. (Orig.). 1988. pap. text ed. 10.00 (0-938835-11-4) Barr Syst Inc.

BARR-3 Adapter. Barr Systems, Inc. Staff. 24p. (Orig.). 1988. pap. text ed. 10.00 (0-938835-09-2) Barr Syst Inc.

An Asterisk (*) at the beginning of an entry indicates that the title is appearing in BIP for the first time.

An Asterisk (*) at the beginning of an entry indicates that the title is appearing in BIP for the first time.

601

B

B

Barron's Computer Study Program for the SAT. 2nd rev. ed. Allen Lubow et al. 1989. 49.95 (0-318-64978-0) Barron.

Barron's Diccionario Juvenile Illustrado: Ingles para Hispanos. Rupert Livesey & Astrid Proctor. (Illus.). 180p. (J). (gr. 2 up). 1994. 14.95 (0-8120-6457-7) Barron.

***Barron's Finance & Investment Handbook.** 4th ed. John Downes & Jordan E. Goodman. LC 95-10864. 1995. write for info. (0-8120-6465-8) Barron.

Barron's Financial Tables for Better Money Management: Bonds. 2nd ed. Stephen S. Solomon et al. (Financial Guides Ser.). 252p. 1992. pap. 5.95 (0-8120-4995-0) Barron.

Barron's French Idioms. Denoeu et al. 350p. 1991. pap., vinyl bd. 6.95 (0-8120-4635-8) Barron.

Barron's French Vocabulary. Laurie Martin. 256p. 1990. pap. 5.95 (0-8120-4496-7) Barron.

Barron's German Vocabulary. Paul G. Graves. 256p. 1990. spiral bd. 5.95 (0-8120-4497-5) Barron.

Barron's Guide to Financing a Medical School Education. Marguerite J. Dennis. 256p. 1990. pap. 9.95 (0-8120-4297-2) Barron.

Barron's Guide to Financing a Medical School Education. 2nd ed. Marguerite J. Dennis. LC 93-23278. 400p. 1994. pap. 10.95 (0-8120-1858-3) Barron.

Barron's Guide to Graduate Business Schools. 8th ed. Eugene Miller. 1992. pap. 14.95 (0-8120-4863-6) Barron.

Barron's Guide to Law Schools. 10th ed. Barron's Educational Series, Inc. Staff. 362p. 1992. pap. 14.95 (0-8120-4864-4) Barron.

Barron's Guide to Law Schools. 11th ed. Barron's Editors. 360p. 1994. pap. 14.95 (0-8120-1754-4) Barron.

Barron's Guide to Making Investment Decisions. Douglas Sease & John Prestbo. LC 93-23352. 1993. pap. 13.95 (0-13-092909-3); pap. write for info. (0-13-300435-X) P-H.

Barron's Guide to Medical & Dental Schools. 6th ed. Saul Wischnitzer. LC 92-48541. (Illus.). 320p. 1993. pap. 14.95 (0-8120-1631-9) Barron.

***Barron's Guide to Medical & Dental Schools.** 7th ed. Saul Wischnitzer. LC 95-4085. 1995. write for info. (0-8120-9052-7) Barron.

***Barron's Guide to Tax Terms.** D. Larry Crumbley. 1995. pap. 14.95 (0-8120-9373-9) Barron.

***Barron's How to Prepare for Fire Fighter Examinations.** 3rd ed. James J. Murtaugh. LC 94-46425. 1995. write for info. (0-8120-9086-1) Barron.

Barron's How to Prepare for the Air Traffic Controller Exam. James A. Mathews. 416p. 1990. pap. 10.95 (0-8120-3740-5) Barron.

Barron's How to Prepare for the College Board Achievement Test - CBAT: American History & Social Studies. 8th ed. David A. Midgley. 480p. 1990. Metric Converter. pap. 11.95 (0-8120-4376-6) Barron.

Barron's How to Prepare for the College Board Achievement Test - CBAT: Chemistry. 4th ed. Joseph A. Mascetta. 368p. 1990. pap. 10.95 (0-8120-4082-1) Barron.

Barron's How to Prepare for the College Board Achievement Test - CBAT: Mathematics Level I. 5th ed. James J. Rizzuto. Ed. by Howard Dodge. 400p. 1990. pap. 10.95 (0-8120-4396-0) Barron.

***Barron's How to Prepare for the College-Level Examination Program, CLEP, General Examinations.** 7th ed. William C. Doster et al. 1995. write for info. (0-8120-9007-1) Barron.

Barron's How to Prepare for the Graduate Record Examination - GRE: Biology Test. 3rd ed. John A. Snyder & C. Leland Rodgers. 272p. 1989. pap. 11.95 (0-8120-4199-2) Barron.

Barron's How to Prepare for the Graduate Record Examination - GRE: The Psychology Test. 3rd ed. Edward L. Palmer. 272p. 1989. pap. 11.95 (0-8120-4192-5) Barron.

Barron's How to Prepare for the Miller Analogies Test - MAT. 5th ed. Robert J. Sternberg. 176p. 1989. pap. 10.95 (0-8120-4216-6) Barron.

Barron's How to Prepare for the Minimum Competency Examination in Mathematics. Angelo Wieland. LC 80-36732. (gr. 7-12). 1981. pap. text ed. 11.95 (0-8120-2246-7) Barron.

Barron's How to Prepare for the National Council Licensure Examination for Practical Nurses - NCLEX-PN. 2nd ed. Vashti Curlin & Hattie Allen. 432p. 1990. pap. 12.95 (0-8120-4385-5) Barron.

***Barron's How to Prepare for the National Council Licensure Examination for Registered Nurses, NCLEX-RN.** 3rd ed. Sadie Smalls et al. LC 95-13041. 1995. write for info. (0-8120-2824-4) Barron.

***Barron's How to Prepare for the NCLEX-PN.** 3rd rev. ed. Vashti R. Curlin & Hattie L. Allen. LC 94-47443. 1995. write for info. (0-8120-2193-2) Barron.

Barron's How to Prepare for the Regents Competency Examination: Reading. Fredericks & Lipner. (YA). (gr. 11-12). 1982. pap. 12.95 (0-8120-2287-4) Barron.

Barron's How to Prepare for the Regents Competency Examination: Writing. Gersten. (gr. 11-12). 1983. pap. text ed. 10.95 (0-8120-2381-1) Barron.

Barron's How to Prepare for the Test of Standard Written English. Weiner & Green. 1982. pap. 9.95 (0-8120-2095-2) Barron.

Barron's How to Prepare for the U. S. Citizenship Test. 3rd ed. Gladys Alesi. 200p. 1992. pap. 10.95 (0-8120-4826-1) Barron.

Barron's Italian Idioms. R. Hall et al. 350p. 1991. pap., vinyl bd. 6.95 (0-8120-4636-6) Barron.

Barron's Italian Vocabulary. Marcel Danesi. 256p. 1990. spiral bd. 5.95 (0-8120-4471-1) Barron.

Barron's Junior Fact-Finder: An Illustrated Encyclopedia for Children. Jean-Paul Dupre. (Illus.). 296p. (J). (gr. 2-6). 1989. 19.95 (0-8120-6072-5) Barron.

Barron's Junior Illustrated Dictionary - French-English. Jean-Christophe Meyer. (Illus.). 180p. (ENG & FRE.). (J). (gr. 2 up). 1994. 14.95 (0-8120-6458-5) Barron.

Barron's New Student's Concise Encyclopedia. 2nd ed. 1300p. (J). 1993. 29.95 (0-8120-6329-5) Barron.

***Barron's Pass Key to the ACT, American College Testing Program.** 2nd ed. George Ehrenhaft et al. LC 94-35590. 1995. student ed, pap. 6.95 (0-8120-1256-9) Barron.

Barron's Pass Key to the ASVAB. Barron's Test Preparation Staff. (Barron's Pass Key Ser.). 1992. pap. 6.95 (0-8120-1383-2) Barron.

Barron's Pass Key to the GED. Rockowitz et al. (Barron's Pass Key Ser.). 1992. pap. 6.95 (0-8120-1381-6) Barron.

Barron's Pass Key to the GMAT. Jaffe & Hilbert. (Barron's Pass Key Ser.). 1992. pap. 6.95 (0-8120-1380-8) Barron.

Barron's Pass Key to the SAT. Weiner Brownstein & Weiner Green. (Barron's Pass Key Ser.). 1992. pap. 6.95 (0-8120-1382-4) Barron.

Barron's Power Pack: Sequential Mathematics, Course III. Barron's Staff. pap. 9.95 (0-8120-7931-0) Barron.

Barron's Practice Exercises for the TOEFL. 2nd ed. Pamela J. Sharpe. 320p. 1989. pap. 11.95 (0-8120-4275-1) Barron.

Barron's Profiles of American Colleges. 20th ed. Barron's Editors. 1800p. (YA). (gr. 10-12). 1994. pap. 19.95 (0-8120-1752-8) Barron.

Barron's Regents Exams & Answers: Comprehensive Spanish. rev. ed. Ed. by Christopher Kendris & Maxim Newmark. LC 58-31609. 250p. (gr. 10-12). 1992. pap. text ed. 5.95 (0-8120-3193-8) Barron.

Barron's Regents Exams & Answers: French, Level 3. rev. ed. Ed. by Christopher Kendris. LC 58-47141. 250p. (gr. 9-12). 1992. pap. 5.95 (0-8120-3147-4) Barron.

Barron's Regents Exams & Answers: Italian. rev. ed. Ed. by Diego Coscarelli. LC 75-39381. 250p. (gr. 10-12). 1992. pap. text ed. 5.95 (0-8120-3149-0) Barron.

Barron's Regents Exams & Answers Biology. rev. ed. Ed. by Gabrielle I. Edwards. LC 58-19074. 300p. (gr. 9-12). 1992. pap. text ed. 5.95 (0-8120-3197-0) Barron.

Barron's Regents Exams & Answers Chemistry. rev. ed. Ed. by Michael Walsh et al. LC 57-58729. 300p. (gr. 10-12). 1992. pap. text ed. 5.95 (0-8120-3163-6) Barron.

Barron's Regents Exams & Answers Comprehensive English (3 & 4 Years) rev. ed. Ed. by Samuel Kostman. LC 56-35602. 300p. (gr. 9-12). 1992. pap. text ed. 5.95 (0-8120-3191-1) Barron.

Barron's Regents Exams & Answers, Comprehensive Latin. Kenneth J. Larkin. 1992. pap. 5.95 (0-8120-3345-0) Barron.

Barron's Regents Exams & Answers Earth Science. rev. ed. Ed. by David Berey. LC 57-58736. 300p. (gr. 10-12). 1992. pap. text ed. 5.95 (0-8120-3165-2) Barron.

Barron's Regents Exams & Answers Global Studies. Philip Lefton. 160p. 1992. pap. 5.95 (0-8120-4344-8) Barron.

***Barron's Regents Exams & Answers, Spanish Level 3 (Comprehensive Spanish)** Barron's Staff. (SPA.). 1995. pap. text ed. (0-8120-8317-2) Barron.

Barron's Regents Exams & Answers, U. S. History & Government. John McGeehan. 1992. pap. 5.95 (0-8120-3344-2) Barron.

Barron's Regents Power Pack: Global Studies. 1992. pap. 11.95 (0-8120-7674-5) Barron.

Barron's Regents Power Pack: Sequential Mathematics I. pap. 11.95 (0-8120-7671-0) Barron.

Barron's Regents Power Pack: Sequential Mathematics II. pap. 11.95 (0-8120-7672-9) Barron.

Barron's Regents Power Pack: U. S. History & Government. pap. 13.95 (0-8120-7673-7) Barron.

Barron's Russian Grammar. Natalia Lusin. 250p. (RUS.). 1992. pap., vinyl bd. 5.95 (0-8120-4902-0) Barron.

Barron's Russian Verbs. Patricia A. Davis. 322p. 1992. pap. 5.95 (0-8120-4754-0) Barron.

Barron's Spanish Idioms. Saviano & Winget. 350p. 1991. pap., vinyl bd. 6.95 (0-8120-4637-4) Barron.

Barron's Spanish Vocabulary. Julianne Dueber. 256p. 1990. spiral bd. 5.95 (0-8120-4498-3) Barron.

Barron's Talking Business in Korean: Dictionary & Reference for International Business. Un Bok Cheong. 1992. pap. 8.95 (0-8120-3992-0) Barron.

Barron's Top Fifty: An Inside Look at America's Best Colleges. 2nd ed. Ed. by Tom Fischgrund. LC 92-39776. (YA). (gr. 9 up). 1993. pap. 13.95 (0-8120-1447-2) Barron.

***Barron's Top 50: An Inside Look at America's Best Colleges.** 3rd ed. Tom Fischgrund. LC 95-6455. 1995. write for info. (0-8120-9053-5) Barron.

Barros Arana's "Historia Jeneral de Chile" Politics, History & National Identity. Gertrude M. Yeager. LC 80-54161. (Texas Christian University Monographs in History & Culture: No. 15). 188p. 1981. pap. 12.00 (0-912646-71-3) Tex Christian.

Barrow. Mark Raven. LC 86-82477. (Illus.). 191p. 1987. 16.95 (0-9617588-0-5) Huttman Co.

Barrow Family & the Barataria & Lafourche Canal: The Transportation Revolution in Louisiana, 1829-1925. Thomas A. Becnel. LC 88-34070. 208p. 1989. text ed. 30.00 (0-8071-1437-5) La State U Pr.

Barrow Sinister. Elsie Lee. 1989. pap. 2.95 (0-8217-2634-X) Zebra.

Barrows in England & Wales. Leslie V. Grinsell. 1989. pap. 25.00 (0-7478-0052-9, Pub. by Shire UK) St Mut.

Barry: The Bravest Saint Bernard. Lynn Hall. LC 92-1228. (Step into Reading Bks.: Step 4). (Illus.). 48p. (Orig.). (J). (gr. 2-4). 1992. pap. 3.50 (0-679-83054-5) Random Bks Yng Read.

Barry: The Bravest Saint Bernard. Lynn Hall. LC 92-1228. (Step into Reading Bks.: Step 4). (Illus.). 48p. (Orig.). (J). (gr. 2-4). 1992. lib. bdg. 7.99 (0-679-93054-X) Random Bks Yng Read.

***Barry - Barrymore: Records of the Barrys of Co. Cork, from the Earliest to the Present Time, with Pedigrees.** E. Barry. 214p. 1995. reprint ed. lib. bdg. 45.00 (0-8328-4571-X); reprint ed. pap. 35.00 (0-8328-4572-8) Higginson Bk Co.

Barry Album. Peter Nicholson. (Illus.). 48p. (C). 1987. pap. 13.00 (0-317-90464-7, Pub. by Picton UK) St Mut.

Barry Ballister's Fruit & Vegetable Stand. Barry Ballister. (Illus.). 496p. 1990. pap. 15.95 (0-87951-363-2) Overlook Pr.

Barry Ballister's Fruit & Vegetable Stand: A Complete Guide to the Selection, Preparation & Nutrition of Fresh Produce. Barry Ballister. LC 86-43061. (Illus.). 432p. 1987. 19.95 (0-87951-272-5) Overlook Pr.

Barry Bear & the Bad Guys. Margery Cuyler. LC 92-11576. (Illus.). (J). 1993. 14.95 (0-395-59939-3, Clarion Bks) HM.

Barry Bingham: A Man of His Word. Ed. by Samuel W. Thomas. LC 93-18678. (Kentucky Remembered Ser.). (Illus.). 235p. (C). 1993. 25.00 (0-8131-1835-2) U Pr of Ky.

***Barry Bonds.** Richard Rambeck. (Sports Superstars Ser.). (Illus.). 24p. (J). (gr. 2-6). 1995. lib. bdg. 21.36 (1-56766-201-3) Childs World.

Barry Bonds: Baseball's Complete Player. Miles Harvey. LC 93-41053. (Sports Stars Ser.). (Illus.). 48p. (J). (gr. 2-8). 1994. lib. bdg. 11.85 (0-516-04381-1) Childrens.

***Barry Bonds: Baseball's Complete Player.** Miles Harvey. (Sports Stars Ser.). (J). (gr. 3-6). 1994. pap. 3.95 (0-516-44381-X) Childrens.

Barry Edmonds: Photojournalist. Christopher R. Young. LC 86-83177. (Illus.). 27p. (Orig.). 1987. pap. 3.50 (0-939896-08-7) Flint Inst Arts.

Barry Family Records Vol. I: Capt. Charles Barry & His Descendants. L. H. Parker. (Illus.). 148p. 1991. reprint ed. pap. 25.00 (0-685-50980-X) Higginson Bk Co.

Barry Flanagan: Sculpture. LC 90-6194. (Illus.). 32p. 1990. pap. write for info. (1-878283-08-1) PaceWildenstein.

Barry Flanagen: Recent Sculpture. (Illus.). 32p. (Orig.). 1994. pap. write for info. (1-878283-44-8) PaceWildenstein.

***Barry Goldwater & the Shaping of America.** Robert A. Goldberg. LC 94-46848. 1995. write for info. (0-300-06261-3) Yale U Pr.

Barry Gunderson: Ohio Sculptors Two. Heather Hallenburg. (Illus.). 8p. (Orig.). 1986. pap. 1.00 (0-915577-09-7) Taft Museum.

Barry Hannah. Mark Charney. (Twayne's United States Authors Ser.). 115p. (C). 1991. text ed. 21.95 (0-8057-7633-8, Twayne) Macmillan.

Barry Jackson & the London Theatre. George W. Bishop. LC 76-81972. 1972. 24.95 (0-405-08272-X, Pub. by Blom Pubns UK) Ayer.

***Barry Lopez.** Slovic. 1997. text ed. 22.95 (0-8057-4028-7) Macmillan.

Barry Lopez. Peter Wild. LC 84-70252. (Western Writers Ser.: No. 64). 49p. (Orig.). 1984. pap. 3.95 (0-88430-038-2) Boise St U W Writ Ser.

Barry Lyndon. William Makepeace Thackeray. 1982. reprint ed. lib. bdg. 29.95 (0-89966-407-5) Buccaneer Bks.

Barry Moser Engagement Calendar for 1992. Barry Moser. 1991. pap. 12.95 (0-15-610694-9) HarBrace.

Barry Sanders. James R. Rothaus. (Sports Superstars Ser.). 32p. (J). (gr. 2-6). 1991. lib. bdg. 21.36 (0-89565-737-6) Childs World.

Barry Sanders: Football's Rushing Champ. Bill Gutman. LC 92-18165. (Millbrook Sports World Ser.). (Illus.). 48p. (J). (gr. 3-6). 1993. lib. bdg. 13.90 (1-56294-227-1); pap. 5.95 (1-56294-821-0) Millbrook Pr.

Barry Sanders: Lion with a Quiet Roar. Howard Reiser. LC 93-19780. (Sports Stars Ser.). (Illus.). 48p. (J). (gr. 2-8). 1993. lib. bdg. 11.85 (0-516-04377-3); pap. 3.95 (0-516-44377-1) Childrens.

Barry Sanders: Rocket Running Back. Jack Kavanagh. (J). (gr. 4-9). 1994. pap. 4.95 (0-8225-9635-0, Lerner Publctns) Lerner Group.

Barry Sanders: Star Running Back. Nathan Aaseng. LC 93-6173. (Sports Reports Ser.). (Illus.). 104p. (J). (gr. 4-10). 1994. lib. bdg. 17.95 (0-89490-484-1) Enslow Pubs.

Barry's Sister. Lois Metzger. LC 93-7760. 240p. (J). (gr. 5 up). 1993. pap. 4.50 (0-14-036484-6, Puffin) Puffin Bks.

Barry's Sister. Lois Metzger. LC 91-23738. 240p. (J). (gr. 5 up). 1992. text ed. 15.95 (0-689-31521-X, Atheneum Bks Young) S&S Childrens.

***Barrytown Trilogy.** Roddy Doyle. LC 95-12323. 1995. pap. write for info. (0-14-025262-2, Penguin Bks) Viking Penguin.

Bars & Books: How to Successfully Reach & Teach Inmates. Errol C. Sull. Ed. by Catherine Skora. 310p. (Orig.). 1994. write for info. (0-9627558-1-8) Aardvark NY.

***Bars & Taverns.** (Illus.). 188p. 1995. 75.00 (4-7858-0032-1, Pub. by Shotenkenchiku-Sha JA) Bks Nippan.

Bars Coming Near: An Anthology by New Writers in Prison. Ed. by Literacy Volunteers of New York City Staff. (New Writers' Voices Ser.). 64p. (Orig.). 1992. pap. text ed. 3.50 (0-929631-64-1, Signal Hill) New Readers.

Bars of Iron. Ethel M. Dell. 1975. lib. bdg. 21.50 (0-89966-066-5) Buccaneer Bks.

Bars of Iron. Ethel M. Dell. 1976. 25.95 (0-8488-0259-4) Amereon Ltd.

Bars of Santa Clara County: A Beer Drinker's Guide to Silicon Valley. Jay R. Brooks & Karen Knezevich. 296p. (Orig.). 1992. pap. 13.95 (0-9631587-0-8) Zero CA.

Barsac Mission, 2 pts. Jules Verne. Incl. Pt. 1. Into the Niger Bend. 1976. 21.95 (0-88411-911-4); Pt. 2. City in the Sahara. 1976. 18.95 (0-88411-912-2); 1976. reprint ed. write for info. (0-318-50519-3, Aeonian Pr) Amereon Ltd.

Barsaive. 1993. boxed, pap. 25.00 (1-55560-214-2, 6100) FASA Corp.

Barsch Learning Style Inventory. Jeffrey Barsch. 1991. 14.00 (0-87879-905-2) Acad Therapy.

Barsetshire Novels, 6 vols. Incl. Doctor Thorne. Intro. by David Skilton. 672p. 1989. 14.95 (0-19-520812-9); Framley Parsonage. Ed. by P. D. Edwards. 624p. 1989. 14.95 (0-19-520811-0); Last Chronicle of Barset. Ed. by Stephen Gill. 928p. 1989. 14.95 (0-19-520809-9); Barchester Towers. Ed. by Michael Sadleir & Frederick Page. 308p. 1989. 14.95 (0-19-520813-7); 1989. Set. 85.00 (0-19-520814-5) OUP.

Barskii, Iu. P. NA 100 Kletkakh. Ed. by Collet's Holdings, Ltd. Staff. 160p. (RUS.). 1985. 29.00 (0-317-42753-9, Pub. by Collets UK) St Mut.

***Barsotti Symposium in Algebraic Geometry.** Ed. by Valentino Cristante & William Messing. (Perspectives in Mathematics Ser.: Vol. 15). (Illus.). 289p. 1994. text ed. 49.95 (0-12-197270-4) Acad Pr.

Barstow Depots & Harvey Houses. Germaine L. Ramounachou Moon. LC 80-80936. (Illus.). 42p. (Orig.). (C). 1980. pap. text ed. 3.50 (0-918614-02-3) Mojave Riv Val.

Barstow Printer: A Personal Name & Subject Index to the Years 1910-1920. Buckley B. Barrett. LC 84-14550. (West Coast Studies: No. 1). 79p. 1985. lib. bdg. 25.00x (0-89370-840-2); pap. 15.00x (0-89370-940-9) Borgo Pr.

Barsukov Triangle, the Two-Toned Blonde & Other Stories. Ed. by Carl Proffer & Ellendea Proffer. LC 84-387. 360p. 1984. 29.50 (0-88233-805-6) Ardis Pubs.

Bart. 28p. (Orig.). 1982. pap. 5.50 (0-937013-09-9) Potes Poets.

***Bart.** David Roper. (Illus.). 200p. 1995. 34.95 (1-85793-330-3, Pub. by Pavilion UK) Trafalgar.

Bart: A Life of A. Bartlett Giamatti, By Him & About Him. Anthony Valerio. 1991. 19.95 (0-15-110694-0) HarBrace.

Bart: A Life of A. Bartlett Giamatti by Him & About Him. Anthony Valerio. 1993. pap. 10.95 (0-15-610697-3) HarBrace.

***Bart Becomes a Friend.** Gary Harbo. (If You Want to Succeed, You Have Got to Read! Ser.). (Illus.). 33p. (SPA.). (J). (gr. 1-5). 1995. 8.95 (1-884149-08-1) Kutie Kari Bks.

Bart Becomes a Friend: Advanced Reader. Gary Harbo. (Bad Bart Ser.: Bk. 3). (Illus.). 33p. (J). (gr. 1-4). 1992. text ed. 8.95 (1-884149-05-7) Kutie Kari Bks.

Bart Markel Story. Joe Scalzo. (Illus.). 1972. 5.95 (0-393-60019-X) Norton.

Bart Simpson's Guide to Life. Matt Groening. (Illus.). 192p. (Orig.). 1993. pap. 10.00 (0-06-096975-X, PL) HarpC.

Bart Wasserman: North Wall Curving South. Phyllis Plous. (Illus.). 24p. 1985. 10.00 (0-942006-09-7) U of CA Art.

Bartas: His Devine Weekes & Workes. Guillaume D. Du Bartas. LC 65-10398. 1965. reprint ed. lib. bdg. 90.00 (0-8201-1265-8) Schol Facsimiles.

Bartender Poems. Julie Kane. (C). 1990. 35.00 (0-906887-44-5, Pub. by Greville Pr UK) St Mut.

Bartender's Bible. Gary Regan. 1991. 77.70 (0-06-016734-3, HarpT) HarpC.

Bartender's Bible. Gary Regan. 1993. mass mkt. 5.99 (0-06-109220-7, Harp PBks) HarpC.

Bartender's Bible: One Thousand & One Mixed Drinks & Everything You Need to Know to Set up Your Bar. Gary Regan. LC 91-55104. (Illus.). 288p. 1991. 14.95 (0-06-016722-X, HarpT) HarpC.

Bartender's Companion: A Complete Drink Recipe Guide. Robert A. Plotkin. LC 88-9089. (Illus.). 101p. (Orig.). (C). 1988. pap. 10.95 (0-945562-05-5) PSD Pub.

Bartender's Companion: A Complete Drink Recipe Guide. 2nd ed. Ed. by Robert Plotkin. LC 93-83097. (Illus.). (Orig.). 1993. pap. 10.95 (0-945562-11-X) PSD Pub.

Bartender's Favorite Frozen Drinks Guide. 1988. 2.95 (0-685-44001-X, 108) Am Bartenders.

Bartender's Guide on How to Pick-Up Women: With a Special Section for Women Only. Bryan Redfield. (Illus.). 345p. (Orig.). 1990. pap. 19.95 (0-9626455-0-8) New Atlan CA.

Bartenders Standard Manual. Fred Powell. 1988. 5.99 (0-517-29305-6) Random Hse Value.

***Bartending & Cocktail Serving: A Complete Course.** Ken McElligott. (Illus.). 120p. 1994. ring bd. 29.95 (0-9618067-0-2) McElligott Ent.

Barter Associations & Organizations & Businesses: An International Directory. Comp. by Frieda Carrol. LC 83-90672. 200p. 1983. pap. 19.95 (0-911617-54-X, Barter Pub) Prosperity & Profits.

Barter Education, Schools, Workshops, Centers, Etc. A How to Find or Locate Workbook. Ed. by Barter Publishing Staff. 30p. 1985. ring bd. 14.95 (0-911617-10-8, Barter Pub) Prosperity & Profits.

Barter, Exchange & Value: An Anthropological Approach. Ed. by Caroline Humphrey & Stephen Hugh-Jones. (Illus.). 196p. (C). 1992. 54.95 (0-521-40493-2); pap. 16.95 (0-521-40682-X) Cambridge U Pr.

Barter in Panay. Ricaredo Demetillo. 134p. (Orig.). 1984. reprint ed. pap. 7.50 (971-10-0168-3, Pub. by New Day Pub PH) Cellar.

Barter in the World Economy. Bart S. Fisher & Kathleen M. Harte. LC 85-6257. 302p. 1985. text ed. 59.95 (0-275-90100-9, C0100, Praeger Pubs) Greenwood.

An Asterisk (*) at the beginning of an entry indicates that the title is appearing in BIP for the first time.

An Asterisk (*) at the beginning of an entry indicates that the title is appearing in BIP for the first time.

603

Base Stealers. Barden. (Baseball Heroes Ser.). (J). 1991. 12.50 (0-86593-126-7) Rourke Corp.

Base Stock Seminar, Nineteen Eighty Five: Atlanta Hilton Hotel, Atlanta, GA May 23-24. Technical Association of the Pulp & Paper Industry Staff. 55p. reprint ed. pap. 25.00 (0-8357-5971-7, 2025569) Bks Demand.

Base String: The Underworld in Elizabethan Drama. Normand Berlin. 224p. 1975. 26.50 (0-8386-6753-8) Fairleigh Dickinson.

Base Ten Mathematics. Mary Laycock. (J). (gr. 1-9). 1976. pap. 7.95 (0-918932-03-3) Activity Resources.

Base-Ten Response Form. rev. ed. Leonard L. LaPointe. (Illus.). (C). 1991. ring bd. 51.50x (1-879105-28-4, 0212); 32.50 (1-879105-27-6, 0212) Singular Publishing.

Baseball. Ray Broekel. LC 81-38480. (New True Bks.). (Illus.). 48p. (J). (gr. k-4). 1982. lib. bdg. 13.50 (0-516-01081-6) Childrens.

Baseball. Jane Duden. LC 91-7365. (Sportslines Ser.). (Illus.). 48p. (J). (gr. 5). 1991. text ed. 11.95 (0-89686-625-4, Crstwood Hse) Silver Burdett Pr.

Baseball. Bill Gutman. LC 89-7377. (Go for It Ser.). (Illus.). 64p. (J). (gr. 3-8). 1990. lib. bdg. 9.95 (0-942545-84-2) Marshall Cavendish.

*Baseball. Mark Littleton. (Sports Heroes Ser.). 112p. 1995. pap. 5.99 (0-310-49551-2) Zondervan.

*Baseball. Bill Plunkett. (The Summer Olympics Ser.). 32p. (J). (gr. 4-8). 1995. write for info. (1-887068-05-8) Smart Apple.

*Baseball. Michael Ruscoe. 1995. pap. 24.95 (0-88363-700-6) H L Levin.

Baseball. Mark A. Teirstein. LC 93-23271. (How to Play the All-Star Way Ser.). (J). 1993. lib. bdg. 22.13 (0-8114-5776-1) Raintree Steck-V.

Baseball. Ed. by Jim Villani & Rose Sayre. (Pig Iron Ser.: No. 9). (Illus.). 96p. (Orig.). 1981. pap. 5.95 (0-917530-17-9) Pig Iron Pr.

Baseball. rev. ed. Paul Gregory. (Play the Game Ser.). (Illus.). 80p. 1994. pap. 7.95 (0-7137-2441-2, Pub. by Blandford Pr UK) Sterling.

*Baseball: A Book of Quips & Quotes. Ariel Bks. Staff. (Illus.). 80p. 1995. 4.95 (0-8362-3112-0) Andrews & McMeel.

Baseball: A Comprehensive Bibliography. Comp. by Myron J. Smith, Jr. LC 85-43592. 934p. 1986. lib. bdg. 95.00x (0-89950-222-9) McFarland & Co.

Baseball: A Doubleheader Collection of Feats, Facts & Firsts. Sporting News Staff. 1992. 9.98 (0-88365-785-6) Galahad Bks.

Baseball: A Game of Numbers. Michael Sentlowitz & James Thelen. 1988. teacher ed 3.44 (0-318-37367-X); pap. 14.36 (0-201-06816-8) Addison-Wesley.

Baseball: A History of America's Game. Benjamin G. Rader. (Illinois History of Sports Ser.: Vol. 2). (Illus.). 272p. (C). 1993. 24.95 (0-252-01737-4); pap. 11.95 (0-252-06395-3) U of Ill Pr.

Baseball: A Treasury of Art & Literature. Ed. by Michael Ruscoe. (Illus.). 384p. 1993. 75.00 (0-88363-293-4) H L Levin.

Baseball: America's Diamond Mind, 1919-1941. Richard C. Crepeau. LC 79-16237. (Illus.). xii, 228p. 1980. 27.95 (0-8130-0645-7) U Press Fla.

Baseball: An Illustrated History. David Q. Voigt. LC 85-43558. (Illus.). 402p. 1987. 38.50 (0-271-00434-7) Pa St U Pr.

*Baseball: An Illustrated History. David Q. Voigt. LC 85-43558. 402p. 1994. pap. 24.95 (0-271-01448-2) Pa St U Pr.

Baseball: An Illustrated History. Geoffrey C. Ward & Ken Burns. LC 93-39809. (Illus.). 512p. 1994. 60.00 (0-679-40459-7) Knopf.

*Baseball: How to Become a Player. Ward. Date not set. per. 9.95 (0-910137-53-6) Soc Am Baseball Res.

Baseball: Play Like a Pro. Dick Walker. LC 89-27392. (Be the Best! Ser.). (Illus.). 64p. (J). (gr. 4-8). 1990. lib. bdg. 9.79 (0-8167-1927-6); pap. 2.95 (0-8167-1928-4) Troll Assocs.

Baseball: The Early Years. Harold Seymour. (Illus.). 392p. 1989. pap. 13.95 (0-19-505912-3) OUP.

Baseball: The Fan's Game. Mickey Cochrane. (Sabr Reprint Ser.). (Illus.). 189p. 1992. reprint ed. pap. 9.95 (0-910137-47-1) Soc Am Baseball Res.

Baseball: The Golden Age. Harold Seymour. 1971. 24.95 (0-19-501403-0) OUP.

Baseball: The Golden Age. Harold Seymour. (Illus.). 512p. 1989. pap. 14.95 (0-19-505913-1) OUP.

Baseball: The Illustrated History of America's Game. Donald Honig. 1990. 45.00 (0-517-57295-8, Crown) Crown Pub Group.

Baseball: The People's Game. Harold Seymour. (Illus.). 672p. 1990. 24.95 (0-19-503890-8) OUP.

Baseball: The People's Game. Harold Seymour. (Illus.). 672p. 1991. reprint ed. pap. 12.95 (0-19-506907-2) OUP.

Baseball: The Perfect Game. Peter Richmond. LC 91-34778. (Illus.). 128p. 1992. 29.95 (0-8478-1524-2) Rizzoli Intl.

Baseball: The Presidents' Game. William B. Mead & Paul Dickson. LC 92-45077. (Illus.). 225p. 1993. 24.95 (0-918535-16-6) Farragut Pub.

Baseball: The Startling Stories Behind the Records. Jim Benagh. LC 86-30137. (Illus.). 128p. 1988. pap. 4.95 (0-8069-6788-9) Sterling.

BaseBall - America's National Game: The Original Baseball Bible. rev. ed. A. G. Spalding. Ed. by Samm Coombs & Bob West. LC 90-22543. (Illus.). 364p. 1991. pap. 14.95 (0-9622874-1-5) Halo Bks.

Baseball - the Writers' Game. Mike Shannon. LC 91-45278. 1992. 22.95 (0-912083-56-5) Diamond Communications.

Baseball: A Comprehensive Bibliography: 1985-May 1992, Supplement 1. Myron J. Smith, Jr. LC 92-50892. 437p. 1993. lib. bdg. 55.00x (0-89950-799-9) McFarland & Co.

Baseball ABC. Florence C. Mayers. LC 94-1167. (J). 1994. write for info. (0-8109-1938-9) Abrams.

*Baseball Address List, No. 8. Smalling. (Sport Americana Ser.). 1994. pap. 13.95 (0-937424-74-9) Edgewater.

Baseball Almanac, 1993. Consumer Guide Editors. 608p. (Orig.). 1993. pap. 5.99 (0-451-17604-9, Sig) NAL-Dutton.

Baseball Almanac, 1994. Consumer Guide Editors. 672p. (Orig.). 1994. pap. 5.99 (0-451-17913-7, Sig) NAL-Dutton.

*Baseball Almanac, 1995. Consumer Guide Editors Staff. 672p. (Orig.). 1995. pap. 5.99 (0-451-18359-2, Sig) NAL-Dutton.

Baseball America. Donald Honig. 1993. 8.98 (0-88365-817-8) Galahad Bks.

Baseball America's 1989 Almanac. 1989. 7.95 (0-685-22452-X) S&S Trade.

Baseball America's 1995 Almanac. Baseball America Staff. 1995. 12.95 (0-671-88440-9) Baseball Amer.

*Baseball America's 1995 Almanac. Baseball America Staff. 1995. 12.95 (0-671-52504-2) S&S Trade.

Baseball America's 1995 Directory. Baseball America Staff. 1995. 9.95 (0-671-88441-7) Baseball Amer.

*Baseball America's 1995 Directory. Baseball Staff. 1995. pap. 10.95 (0-671-52503-4) S&S Trade.

Baseball Analysis & Reporting System: American League Report. Bill Welch. 340p. 1990. pap. 17.95 (0-929633-03-2) Baseball Analysis.

Baseball Analysis & Reporting System: National League Report. Bill Welch. 300p. 1990. pap. 17.95 (0-929633-04-0) Baseball Analysis.

Baseball Analysis & Reporting System American League Report: Ballpark Edition. Bill Welch & Jeff Moses. (Illus.). 290p. (Orig.). 1989. pap. 12.95 (0-929633-01-6) Baseball Analysis.

Baseball Analysis & Reporting System National League Report: Ballpark Edition. Bill Welch & Jeff Moses. (Illus.). 290p. (Orig.). 1989. pap. 12.95 (0-929633-02-4) Baseball Analysis.

*Baseball & American Culture: A Thematic Bibliography of over 4,500 Works. Donald E. Walker & B. Lee Cooper. LC 94-48267. 232p. 1995. lib. bdg. 39.95 (0-7864-0049-8) McFarland & Co.

Baseball & Benevolence. Mark A. Valenza. LC 93-73299. 389p. (Orig.). 1994. pap. 14.95 (0-9638257-0-4) Bark Pubng.

Baseball & Billions: A Probing Look Inside the Business of Our National Pastime. Andrew Zimbalist. 320p. 1994. pap. 12.00 (0-465-00615-9) Basic.

Baseball & Butterflies. Karen L. Williams. 80p. (J). 1990. 12.95 (0-688-09489-9) Lothrop.

Baseball & Men's Lives: The True Confessions of a Skinny Marink. Robert Mayer. LC 93-26750. 1994. 12.95 (0-385-30926-0, Delta) Dell.

Baseball & Other Poems: A Collection. Louis D. Scalzetto. LC 90-91789. (American Pastime Baseball Poems Ser.). 56p. (Orig.). 1991. reprint ed. pap. 4.50 (1-879008-01-7) L D Scalzetto.

Baseball & Softball. Paul Gregory. (Play the Game Ser.). (Illus.). 80p. (YA). (gr. 10-12). 1992. pap. 6.95 (0-7063-6667-0, Pub. by Ward Lock UK) Sterling.

*Baseball & the American Legal Mind. Ed. by Spencer W. Waller et al. LC 94-39340. 536p. 1995. 75.00 (0-8153-1954-1) Garland.

*Baseball & the American Legal Mind. Ed. by Spencer W. Waller et al. LC 94-39340. 525p. 1995. pap. 19.95 (0-8153-2057-4) Garland.

*Baseball & the Color Line. Tom Gilbert. (African-American Experience Ser.). (Illus.). 176p. (YA). (gr. 7-12). 1995. pap. 9.00 (0-531-15747-4) Watts.

*Baseball & the Color Line. Tom W. Gilbert. (African-American Experience Ser.). (Illus.). (YA). (gr. 7-12). 1995. lib. bdg. 14.98 (0-531-11206-3) Watts.

Baseball & the Game of Ideas: Essays for the Serious Fan. Intro. by Peter C. Bjarkman. (Sporting Life Ser.). 212p. 1993. 30.00 (0-913559-19-9) Birch Brook Pr.

Baseball & the Game of Life. Peter C. Bjarkman. LC 90-50501. 240p. 1991. 10.00 (0-679-73141-5, Vin) Random.

Baseball & the Game of Life: Stories for the Thinking Fan. Ed. by Peter Bjarkman et al. 232p. 1990. 35.00 (0-913559-15-6) Birch Brook Pr.

Baseball & the Pursuit of Innocence: A Fresh Look at the Old Ball Game. Richard Skolnick. LC 93-30794. (Illus.). 272p. 1994. 24.50 (0-89096-559-5); pap. 14.95 (0-89096-612-5) Tex A&M Univ Pr.

Baseball Anecdotes. Daniel Okrent & Steve Wulf. 368p. 1989. 21.95 (0-19-504396-0) OUP.

Baseball Anecdotes. Daniel Okrent & Steve Wulf. 352p. 1993. reprint ed. pap. 13.00 (0-06-273206-4, Harper Ref) HarpC.

Baseball Archaeology: Artifacts of the Great American Game. Photos by Bret Wills. (Illus.). 112p. 1993. 29.95 (0-8118-0365-1); pap. 18.95 (0-8118-0290-6) Chronicle Bks.

Baseball As I Have Known It. Lieb. 1976. 28.95 (0-8488-1549-1) Amereon Ltd.

Baseball Autobiography. Sheed. 1992. pap. 19.45 (0-13-058983-7) P-H.

Baseball Babylon: From the Black Sox to Pete Rose, the Real Stories Behind the Scandals that Rocked the Game. Dan Gutman. (Illus.). 256p. (Orig.). 1992. pap. 11.00 (0-14-016542-8, Viking) Viking Penguin.

Baseball Ballerina. Kathryn Cristaldi. LC 90-20234. (Step into Reading Bks.). (Illus.). 48p. (Orig.). (J). (gr. 1-3). 1992. pap. 3.50 (0-679-81734-4) Random Bks Yng Read.

Baseball Ballerina. Kathryn Cristaldi. LC 90-20234. (Step into Reading Bks.). (Illus.). 48p. (Orig.). (J). (gr. 1-3). 1992. lib. bdg. 7.99 (0-679-91734-9) Random Bks Yng Read.

Baseball Bat. Ski Michaels. LC 85-14065. (Illus.). 48p. (Orig.). (J). (gr. 1-3). 1986. lib. bdg. 10.59 (0-8167-0596-8); pap. text ed. 3.50 (0-8167-0597-6) Troll Assocs.

Baseball Bats for Christmas. Michael Kusugak. (Illus.). 24p. (JPN.). (J). 1993. pap. 5.95 (1-55037-314-5, Pub. by Annick CN) Firefly Bks Ltd.

Baseball Bats for Christmas. Michael A. Kusugak. (Illus.). 24p. (J). (gr. k-3). 1990. 15.95 (1-55037-145-2, Pub. by Annick CN); pap. 5.95 (1-55037-144-4, Pub. by Annick CN) Firefly Bks Ltd.

Baseball Between the Lies: The Hype, Hokum, & Humbug of America's Favorite Pastime. Bob Carroll. 192p. (Orig.). 1994. pap. 12.00 (0-399-51857-6, Perigree Bks) Berkley Pub.

Baseball Between the Lines: Baseball in the '40s & '50s As Told by the Men Who Played It. Donald Honig. LC 93-1609. (Illus.). 252p. 1993. pap. 10.95 (0-8032-7268-5, Bison Books) U of Nebr Pr.

Baseball Bible. rev. ed. Angel Torres. LC 85-130546. (Illus.). 473p. (Orig.). 1985. pap. 14.95 (0-9614110-0-7) A Torres.

Baseball Birthday Party. Annabelle Prager. LC 93-25258. (Illus.). (J). 1995. 3.99 (0-679-84171-7) Random Bks Yng Read.

Baseball Birthday Party. Annabelle Prager. LC 93-25258. (Illus.). (J). 1995. lib. bdg. 9.99 (0-679-94171-1) Random Bks Yng Read.

Baseball Blackbook, 1992: The Winning Edge for Serious Rotisserie. rev. ed. Larry S. Meyers. (Illus.). 225p. 1992. pap. 12.95 (1-55958-141-7) Prima Pub.

Baseball Bloopers. Katy Hall & Lisa Eisenberg. LC 89-62210. (Illus.). 96p. (Orig.). (J). (gr. 2-6). 1991. pap. 2.95 (0-679-80335-1) Random Bks Yng Read.

Baseball Bloopers & Diamond Oddities. Robert Obojski. LC 89-31270. (Illus.). 128p. (YA). 1991. pap. 4.95 (0-8069-6981-4) Sterling.

Baseball Book. Daniel Okrent. pap. write for info. (0-318-61607-6, Penguin Bks) Viking Penguin.

Baseball Book. rev. ed. Ed. by Zander Hollander. LC 90-38060. (Illus.). 192p. (J). (gr. 5 up). 1991. pap. 9.95 (0-679-81055-2) Random Bks Yng Read.

Baseball Book of Why. Dan Schlossberg. 1984. 11.95 (0-8246-0298-6) Jonathan David.

Baseball Book 1990. Bill James. 1990. pap. 12.95 (0-679-72411-7, Villard Bks) Random.

Baseball Book, 1991. Bill James. 1991. 15.00 (0-679-73530-5, Villard Bks); pap. write for info. (0-394-57930-5, Villard Bks) Random.

Baseball, Bouillabaisse & the Best of Class: How to Increase Your Personal Power, Energize Your Team & Astonish Your Customers. Darby Checketts. LC 91-73363. (Illus.). 287p. (Orig.). 1992. pap. 14.95 (0-9618170-1-1) Corner Pro-Dev Pr.

Baseball Brain Teasers: Major League Puzzles. Dom Forker. LC 85-27955. (Illus.). 128p. (Orig.). (J). (gr. 5-9). 1986. pap. 4.95 (0-8069-6284-4) Sterling.

Baseball Business: Pursuing Pennants & Profits in Baltimore. James E. Miller. LC 89-36996. (Illus.). xii, 382p. (C). 1991. reprint ed. 29.95 (0-8078-1876-3); reprint ed. pap. 14.95 (0-8078-4323-7) U of NC Pr.

Baseball by the Numbers: How Statistics are Collected, What They Mean, & How They Reveal the Game. Willie Runquist. 208p. 1994. pap. 24.95 (0-7864-0006-4) McFarland & Co.

*Baseball Card Alphabetical Checklist, No. 6. J. Beckett. (Sport Americana Ser.). 1994. pap. 15.95 (0-937424-73-0) Edgewater.

Baseball Card Conspiracy. Franklin W. Dixon. Ed. by Ellen Winkler. (Hardy Boys Ser.: No. 117). 160p. (Orig.). (J). (gr. 3-6). 1992. pap. 3.99 (0-671-73064-9, Minstrel Bks) PB.

Baseball Card Crazy. Trish Kennedy & Timothy Schodorf. LC 92-14597. 80p. (J). (gr. 4-6). 1993. text ed. 11.95 (0-684-19536-4, C Scribner Sons Young) S&S Childrens.

Baseball Card Fever. Megan Stine & William H. Stine. (Jeffrey & the Fourth Grade Ghost Ser.: Bk. 2). (Illus.). 80p. (J). (gr. 4 up). 1989. pap. 3.95 (0-449-90416-4, Columbine) Fawcett.

Baseball Card Grand Slam Curriculum Activities. Harold Silvani. (Illus.). 30p. (J). (gr. 4-8). 1992. student ed 11.95 (1-878669-52-4) Crea Tea Assocs.

*Baseball Card Price Guide, Vol. 17. J. Beckett. 1995. pap. 19.95 (0-937424-79-X) Edgewater.

Baseball Card Price Guide: 1993 Collector's Edition. Consumer Guide Editors. (Illus.). 608p. (Orig.). 1993. pap. 5.99 (0-451-17607-3, Sig) NAL-Dutton.

Baseball Card Price Guide 1994. Consumer Guide Editors. (Consumer Guide Ser.). 608p. (Orig.). 1994. pap. 5.99 (0-451-17905-6, Sig) NAL-Dutton.

Baseball Card Price Guide 1994. Allan Kaye & Michael McKeever. 720p. (Orig.). 1993. mass mkt. 6.00 (0-380-77235-3, Confident Collect) Avon.

Baseball Card Price Guide 1994: Collector's Edition. Consumer Guide Editors. 336p. (Orig.). 1994. pap. 9.99 (0-451-82273-0, Sig) NAL-Dutton.

*Baseball Card Price Guide, 1995. Consumer Guide Editors Staff. 608p. (Orig.). 1995. pap. 5.99 (0-451-18356-8, Sig) NAL-Dutton.

Baseball Card Price Guide 1995. 2nd ed. Allan Kaye & Michael McKeever. 800p. 1994. pap. 6.00 (0-380-77239-6, Confident Collect) Avon.

*Baseball Card Price Guide 1996. 3rd ed. Allan Kaye & Michael McKeever. 832p. (Orig.). 1995. pap. 5.99 (0-380-78201-4, Confident Collect) Avon.

Baseball Cards of the 50s. Frank Slocum. 1994. 30.00 (0-671-89224-X) S&S Trade.

Baseball Cards of the 60s. Frank Slocum. 1994. 30.00 (0-671-89223-1) S&S Trade.

Baseball Cards, 1991. Consumer Guide Editors. 1991. pap. 6.99 (0-517-05672-0) Random Hse Value.

Baseball Catalog. Dan Schlossberg. pap. 16.95 (0-8246-0361-3) Jonathan David.

Baseball Challenger Quiz Book. David Nemec. 192p. (Orig.). 1991. pap. 3.99 (0-451-16943-3, Sig) NAL-Dutton.

Baseball Champions, 1993: The Toronto Blue Jays. Bob Italia. LC 93-13084. (Year in Sports Ser.). (J). 1993. lib. bdg. 14.96 (1-56239-239-5) Abdo & Dghtrs.

Baseball Champions, 1994: The Toronto Blue Jays. Bob Italia. LC 94-9700. (Year in Sports Ser.). (J). 1994. lib. bdg. 14.96 (1-56239-277-8) Abdo & Dghtrs.

*Baseball Chronicle. Larry Burke & Paul Ladewski. 176p. 1995. 19.98 (0-8317-0680-5) Smithmark.

*Baseball Chronicles. Larry Burke. 1995. 19.98 (0-8317-5153-3) Smithmark.

Baseball Chronicles. Ed. by David Gallen. 416p. 1991. 21.95 (0-88184-694-5) Carroll & Graf.

Baseball Chronicles. Ed. by David Gallen. (Illus.). 416p. 1992. pap. 10.95 (0-88184-815-8) Carroll & Graf.

Baseball Chronicles. David Gallen. 1994. 9.98 (0-88365-851-8) Galahad Bks.

Baseball Chronicles: An Oral History of Baseball Through the Decades. Mike Blake. 336p. (Orig.). 1994. pap. 16.95 (1-55870-350-0) Betterway Bks.

Baseball Classic. Merritt Clifton. 1978. pap. 5.00 (0-686-00579-1) Samisdat.

Baseball Collectibles. Peter Capano. LC 88-64081. (Illus.). 128p. 1989. pap. 14.95 (0-88740-160-0) Schiffer.

Baseball Contest 1990: American League Players. 1990. pap. 8.95 (0-316-08310-0) Little.

Baseball Contest 1990: National League Players. 1990. pap. 8.95 (0-316-08309-7) Little.

Baseball Crosswords. 2nd rev. ed. Mark Roszkowski. LC 94-1718. (Spalding Sports Library). (Illus.). 192p. 1994. pap. 12.95 (0-940279-83-5, Spalding Sports) Masters Pr IN.

Baseball Cyclopedia. Ernest J. Lanigan. 216p. 1988. reprint ed. pap. 12.50 (0-944786-26-X) Horton Pub.

Baseball Days: From the Sandlots to the Show. Bill Littlefield. LC 93-6468. (Illus.). 160p. 1993. 24.95 (0-8212-1955-3) Bulfinch Pr.

Baseball Dream. Rory Real. (Sports Mites Ser.). (Illus.). 32p. (J). (ps-3). 1990. pap. 3.95 (0-8120-4395-2) Barron.

Baseball Encyclopedia. Joseph Raichler. 29.95 (0-02-578970-8) Macmillan.

Baseball Encyclopedia: The Complete & Definitive Record of Major League Baseball. 9th ed. 2857p. 1993. text ed. 55.00 (0-02-579041-2) Macmillan.

Baseball Encyclopedia: The Complete & Official Record of Major League Baseball. 8th ed. Macmillan Staff. 2600p. 1990. text ed. 49.95 (0-02-579040-4) Macmillan.

Baseball Encyclopedia Update, 1994. Macmillan Staff. 224p. 1994. pap. 12.00 (0-02-022649-7, Collier S&S) S&S Trade.

*Baseball Encyclopedia Update, 1995. 1995. pap. 12.00 (0-02-860089-4, J K Lasser) P-H Gen Ref & Trav.

Baseball Fans Guide to Spring Training. Mike Shatzkin. 1990. pap. 9.95 (0-201-51802-3) Addison-Wesley.

Baseball Fan's Resource Guide: A Reference Guide of Baseball Information & Entertainment. Comp. by Art Eaton. (Illus.). 280p. 1994. 25.00 (0-9641037-0-2); pap. 20.00 (0-9641037-1-0) Sambree Baseball.

Baseball Fathers, Baseball Sons: From Orator Jim to Cal, Barry, & Ken, Every One a Player. Larry Ekin. (Illus.). 192p. (Orig.). 1992. pap. 13.95 (1-55870-226-1) Betterway Bks.

*Baseball Fever. Bonnie Ferraro. Ed. by J. Friedland & R. Kessler. (Novel-Ties Ser.). (J). (gr. 3-5). 1995. student ed, pap. text ed. 15.95 (1-56982-298-0) Lrn Links.

Baseball Fever. Johanna Hurwitz. LC 81-5633. (Illus.). 128p. (J). (gr. 4-6). 1981. 15.00 (0-688-00710-4); lib. bdg. 14.93 (0-688-00711-2) Morrow Jr Bks.

Baseball Fever. Johanna Hurwitz. LC 81-5633. (Illus.). 128p. (J). (gr. 3 up). 1991. reprint ed. pap. 3.95 (0-688-10495-9, Pub. by Beech Tree Bks) Morrow.

*Baseball Flyhawk. Matt Christopher. (Illus.). (J). (gr. 3-7). 1995. pap. 3.95 (0-316-14120-8) Little.

Baseball, Football, Daddy & Me. David Friend. (Illus.). 32p. (J). (ps-3). 1992. pap. 3.99 (0-14-050914-3) Puffin Bks.

Baseball for the Love of It. Connor. 1982. 16.95 (0-02-527500-3) Macmillan.

Baseball from a Different Angle. Bob Broeg & William J. Miller, Jr. LC 88-9556. 1989. pap. 12.95 (0-912083-27-1) Diamond Communications.

Baseball from the Ground Up. John Oliviera & Douglas J. DeLisa. (Illus.). 1993. 12.95 (0-533-10411-4) Vantage.

*Baseball Games: Home Versions of the National Pastime, 1860's-1960's. Mark Cooper & Douglas Congdon-Martin. (Illus.). 160p. 1995. 39.95 (0-88740-767-6) Schiffer.

Baseball Goes to War. William B. Mead. LC 84-45528. Orig. Title: Even the Browns. (Illus.). 255p. 1985. reprint ed. pap. 7.95 (0-918535-02-6) Farragut Pub.

Baseball Graphics. John W. Davenport. LC 79-52663. 1979. pap. 7.95 (0-934794-00-6) First Impressions.

*Baseball Guide, 1995: The Almanac of the 1994 Major League & Minor League Seasons. Sporting News Staff. 1995. pap. 13.95 (0-89204-516-7) Sporting News.

Baseball Hall of Fame: The Halls of Fame. Herma Silverstein & Terry J. Dunnahoo. LC 93-6915. (Halls of Fame Ser.). (Illus.). 48p. (J). (gr. 5-6). 1994. text ed. 13.95 (0-89686-849-4, Crstwood Hse) Silver Burdett Pr.

Baseball Hall of Shame, Vol. 4. Bruce Nash & Allan Zullo. 192p. 1991. pap. 8.95 (0-671-74609-X) PB.

Baseball Hall of Shame: Young Fans' Edition. Bruce Nash & Allan Zullo. Ed. by Lisa Clancy. 144p. 1990. pap. 2.99 (0-671-69354-9, Archway) PB.

Baseball Hall of Shame Two: Young Fans' Edition. Bruce Nash & Allan Zullo. Ed. by Lisa Clancy. 144p. (Orig.). (J). 1991. pap. 2.99 (0-671-73533-0, Archway) PB.

An Asterisk (*) at the beginning of an entry indicates that the title is appearing in BIP for the first time.

Baseball Hall of Shame 3: Young Fans' Edition. Bruce Nash & Allan Zullo. Ed. by Lisa Clancy. 144p. (Orig.). (J). 1992. pap. 2.99 (0-671-75355-X) PB.

Baseball Hall of Shame's Funtastic Trivia & Sticker Book. Bruce Nash & Allan Zullo. (Illus.). 24p. (J). (gr. 1 up). 1992. pap. 3.95 (0-671-74439-9, Litl Simon S&S) S&S Childrens.

Baseball Hall of Shame's Warped Record Book. Bruce Nash & Allan Zullo. (Hall of Shame Ser.). 288p. (Orig.). 1991. pap. 8.95 (0-02-029485-9, Collier S&S) S&S Trade.

Baseball Handbook. Fred Reeves. pap. 2.50 (0-87497-246-9) Impress Hse.

Baseball Handbook for Coaches & Players. Jim Depel. LC 75-19308. (Illus.). 96p. 1976. pap. 9.95 (0-684-14265-1, Scribners) S&S Trade.

Baseball Handbook for Coaches & Players. Jim Depel. (Illus.). 96p. 1991. reprint ed. pap. 9.95 (0-02-042861-8, Collier S&S) S&S Trade.

Baseball Heaven. George Atkins. LC 94-75314. (Illus.). 128p. (Orig.). 1994. pap. 14.95 (0-9640266-0-0) Lux Fiat.

Baseball Heroes Series, 8 bks., Set. (J). 1991. 100.00 (0-86593-125-9) Rourke Corp.

Baseball Historical Review. Ed. by L. Robert Davids. (Illus.). 112p. 1981. 6.00 (0-910137-15-3) Soc Am Baseball Res.

Baseball History. Ed. by Peter Levine. (Illus.). 160p. 1990. reprint ed. pap. 14.95 (0-9625132-1-0) Cyberbooks.

Baseball I Gave You All the Best Years of My Life. 5th ed. Ed. by Richard Grossinger & Lisa Conrad. (Illus.). 184p. 1992. pap. 12.95 (1-55643-083-3) North Atlantic.

Baseball in April: And Other Stories. Gary Soto. 111p. (YA). (gr. 7 up). 1990. 14.95 (0-15-205720-X) HarBrace.

Baseball in April & Other Stories. Gary Soto. 137p. (J). (gr. 3-7). 1991. pap. 4.95 (0-15-205721-8, Odyssey) HarBrace.

Baseball in Cincinnati: From Wooden Fences to Astroturf. Ed. by Dottie L. Lewis. (Illus.). 64p. (Orig.). 1988. pap. text ed. 7.50 (0-911497-10-2) Cinc Hist Soc.

Baseball in the Afternoon: Tales from a Bygone Era. Robert Smith. (Illus.). 288p. 1993. 21.00 (0-671-73930-1) S&S Trade.

Baseball in the Fifties: A Decade of Transition. Donald Honig. (Illus.). 256p. 1987. 24.95 (0-517-56578-1) Random Hse Value.

Baseball in the Movies: A Comprehensive Reference, 1915-1991. Hal Erickson. LC 91-42875. 412p. 1992. lib. bdg. 43.50x (0-89950-657-7) McFarland & Co.

Baseball in the Nineteenth Century. Jack Selzer. 24p. 1986. pap. 3.00 (0-910137-24-2) Soc Am Baseball Res.

Baseball in the Thirties: A Decade of Survival. Donald Honig. 1989. 24.95 (0-517-57250-8) Random Hse Value.

Baseball in Vermont, 1887-1935. Merritt Clifton. (Disorganized Baseball Ser.: Vol. II). 44p. 1991. 6.00 (0-317-04127-4) Samisdat.

Baseball in Vermont, 1935-1988. Merritt Clifton. (Disorganized Baseball Ser.: Vol. III). 60p. 1991. 6.00 (0-317-04128-2) Samisdat.

Baseball in 1889: Players vs Owners. Daniel Pearson. LC 92-63282. 234p. (C). 1993. 42.95 (0-87972-618-0); pap. 15.95 (0-87972-619-9) Bowling Green Univ.

***Baseball in 1939: The Watershed Season of the National Pastime.** Lawrence S. Katz. 240p. 1995. pap. 24.95x (0-7864-0056-0) McFarland & Co.

Baseball in '41: A Celebration of the "Best Baseball Season Ever" - in the Year America Went to War. Robert W. Creamer. (Illus.). 352p. 1992. pap. 12.50 (0-14-016943-1, Penguin Bks) Viking Penguin.

Baseball Insight, 1994. Brock Hanke. 1994. pap. 13.95 (0-9625846-5-7) Mad Aztec Pr.

Baseball Legends, 35 vols., Set. Contrib by Earl Weaver. (Illus.). 64p. (J). (gr. 3 up). 1991. lib. bdg. 493.35 (0-7910-1163-1, Am Art Analog) Chelsea Hse.

***Baseball Legends & Lore.** Cantaneo. 1995. 9.98 (0-88365-902-6) Galahad Bks.

Baseball Listener's Guide. Ken Reitz. 90p. (Orig.). 1993. pap. 5.00 (0-9627654-1-4) Xenolith Pr.

Baseball Lives: Men & Women of the Game Talk about Their Jobs, Their Lives, & the National Pastime. Mike Bryan. 364p. 1990. pap. 9.95 (0-449-90510-1, Columbine) Fawcett.

Baseball Market Place. Ed. by Richard A. Lipsey. 320p. 1990. pap. 19.95 (0-685-34606-4) Sportsguide.

***Baseball Megastars 1995.** Weber. (J). 1995. pap. 3.95 (0-590-48673-X) Scholastic Inc.

Baseball Memories: 1900-1909. Mark Okkonen. LC 92-20532. (Illus.). 240p. 1992. 30.00 (0-8069-8728-6) Sterling.

Baseball Memories 1930-1939: A Complete Pictorial History of the "Hall of Fame" Decade. Marc Okkonen. LC 94-20698. (Illus.). 256p. 1994. 24.95 (0-8069-0574-3) Sterling.

Baseball Memories, 1950-1959: An Illustrated Scrapbook of Baseball's Fabulous 50's: All the Players, Managers, Cities & Ballparks. Marc Okkonen. LC 93-4749. (Illus.). 240p. 1993. 30.00 (0-8069-0427-5) Sterling.

Baseball Nicknames: A Dictionary of Origins & Meanings. James K. Skipper, Jr. LC 91-43690. 398p. 1992. lib. bdg. 49.95x (0-89950-684-4) McFarland & Co.

Baseball, 1995. 14th ed. James Beckett. 1994. mass mkt. 6.99 (0-87637-117-9, House of Collect) Ballantine.

Baseball Palace of the World: The Last Year of Comiskey Park. Douglas Bukowski. LC 91-40533. (Illus.). 256p. 1992. 26.00 (0-925065-45-5) Lyceum IL.

Baseball Pals. Matt Christopher. (Illus.). (J). (gr. 4-6). 1990. mass mkt. 3.95 (0-316-14005-8) Little.

Baseball Picture Quiz Book. Bert Sugar & John Grafton. (Illus.). 128p. (Orig.). 1980. pap. 6.95 (0-486-23987-X) Dover.

Baseball Play & Strategy. Fred Reeves. pap. 2.50 (0-87497-244-2) Impress Hse.

Baseball Play & Strategy. 3rd ed. Ethan Allen. LC 81-17177. 458p. (C). 1985. lib. bdg. 19.95 (0-89874-450-4) Krieger.

***Baseball Player Guide A to Z - 1995.** John Benson. 320p. 1995. pap. 17.95 (1-880876-21-3) Diamond Lib.

Baseball Player's Guide to Sports Medicine. Pat Croce. LC 82-83936. (Illus.). 120p. (Orig.). 1987. pap. 11.95 (0-88011-104-6, PCR00104) Human Kinetics.

Baseball Poetry Hotline - The Book. John W. Hart, III. Ed. by Bowerbird Intelligentleman. 120p. (Orig.). 1991. pap. write for info. (0-9623369-4-7) Shelflife.

Baseball Prayers. Robin Rule. 16p. (Orig.). 1990. pap. 3.00 (1-879082-02-0) Rainy Day CA.

Baseball Quizzes. John Grafton. 80p. (Orig.). 1994. pap. text ed. 1.00 (0-486-27855-7) Dover.

Baseball Quotations: The Wisdom & Wisecracks of Players, Manager, Owners, Umpires, Announcers, Writers & Fans on the Great American Pastime. Ed. by David H. Nathan. 1994. mass mkt. 4.99 (0-345-90324-2) Ballantine.

Baseball Quotations: The Wisdom & Wisecracks of Players, Managers, Owners, Umpires, Announcers, Writers & Fans on the Great American Pastime. Ed. by David H. Nathan. LC 90-53512. 1995. mass mkt., pap. 4.99 (0-345-38123-8, Del Rey) Ballantine.

Baseball Quotations: The Wisdom & Wisecracks of Players, Managers, Owners, Umpires, Announcers, Writers & Fans on the Great American Pastime. Comp. by David H. Nathan. LC 90-53512. 231p. 1991. lib. bdg. 27.50x (0-89950-562-7) McFarland & Co.

***Baseball Ratings: The All-Time Best Players at Each Position.** 2nd ed. Charles F. Faber. 272p. 1995. lib. bdg. 27.50 (0-7864-0030-7) McFarland & Co.

Baseball Record Book. Ed. by Pete Palmer & John Thorn. (Official Major League Baseball Bks.). (Illus.). 96p. (J). (gr. 3 up). 1991. pap. 5.95 (0-671-70444-3, Litl Simon S&S) S&S Childrens.

Baseball Records Update, 1993. Lyle Spatz. 1993. pap. 4.95 (0-910137-51-X) Soc Am Baseball Res.

Baseball Research Handbook, 1987. Gerald Tomlinson. 120p. 1987. pap. 6.00 (0-910137-29-3) Soc Am Baseball Res.

Baseball Research Journal, No. 22. Mark Alvarez. 1993. pap. 7.95 (0-910137-54-4) Soc Am Baseball Res.

***Baseball Research Journal No. 23.** Ed. by Alvarez. Date not set. per. 9.95 (0-910137-57-9) Soc Am Baseball Res.

Baseball Research Journal, 1975. 2nd ed. Ed. by L. Robert Davids. (Illus.). 112p. 1983. pap. 3.00 (0-910137-02-1) Soc Am Baseball Res.

Baseball Research Journal, 1976. Incl. 1975 1983. 3.00 (0-685-11681-6); 1975 1983. (0-318-60061-7); 19752nd ed. Ed. by Robert L. Davids. (Illus.). 112p. 1983. pap. 3.00 (0-685-11682-4); 128p. 4.00 (0-685-11683-2); 128p. (0-318-60062-5); 19762nd ed. Ed. by Robert L. Davids. (Illus.). 128p. 1983. pap. 4.00 (0-685-11684-0); 1977144p. 4.00 (0-685-11685-9); 1977144p. (0-318-60063-3); 19772nd ed. Ed. by Robert L. Davids. (Illus.). 144p. 1983. pap. 4.00 (0-685-11686-7); 1978. 116p. 4.00 (0-685-11687-5); 1978. 116p. (0-318-60064-1); 19782nd ed. Ed. by Robert L. Davids. (Illus.). 116p. 1983. pap. 4.00 (0-685-11688-3); 1979 160p. 1983. 5.00 (0-685-11689-1); 19792nd ed. Ed. by Robert L. Davids. (Illus.). 1983. reprint ed. pap. 5.00 (0-685-11690-5); 1980Ed. by Robert L. Davids. (Illus.). 180p. 1980. pap. 5.00 (0-910137-16-1); 1981Ed. by Robert L. Davids. (Illus.). 188p. 1981. 5.00 (0-685-11691-3); 1984Ed. by Clifford Kachline. (Illus.). 88p. 1984. pap. 6.00 (0-685-11693-X); 1985Ed. by Clifford Kachline. (Illus.). 88p. 1985. pap. 6.00 (0-317-36193-7); 1985Ed. by Clifford Kachline. (Illus.). 88p. 1985. pap. 6.00 (0-317-36193-7); 1984Ed. by Clifford Kachline. (Illus.). 88p. 1984. pap. 6.00 (0-685-11693-X); 1979 160p. 1983. 5.00 (0-685-11689-1); 19772nd ed. Ed. by Robert L. Davids. (Illus.). 144p. 1983. pap. 4.00 (0-685-11686-7); 1975 1983. 3.00 (0-685-11681-6); 1975 1983. (0-318-60061-7); 128p. 4.00 (0-685-11680-8); Incl. 3.00 (0-685-11681-6); (0-318-60061-7); pap. 3.00 (0-685-11682-4); 4.00 (0-685-11683-2); (0-318-60062-5); pap. 4.00 (0-685-11684-0); 4.00 (0-685-11685-9); (0-318-60063-3); pap. 4.00 (0-685-11686-7); 4.00 (0-685-11687-5); (0-318-60064-1); pap. 4.00 (0-685-11688-3); 5.00 (0-685-11689-1); reprint ed. pap. 5.00 (0-685-11690-5); pap. 5.00 (0-910137-16-1); 5.00 (0-685-11691-3); pap. 6.00 (0-685-11693-X); pap. 6.00 (0-317-36193-7); pap. 6.00 (0-317-36193-7); pap. 6.00 (0-685-11693-X); 5.00 (0-685-11689-1); pap. 4.00 (0-685-11686-7); 3.00 (0-685-11681-6); (0-318-60061-7); write for info. (0-318-60060-9) Soc Am Baseball Res.

Baseball Research Journal, 1976. 2nd ed. Ed. by L. Robert Davids. (Illus.). 128p. 1983. pap. 4.00 (0-910137-03-X) Soc Am Baseball Res.

Baseball Research Journal, 1977. 144p. 4.00 (0-910137-04-8); write for info. (0-318-60065-X) Soc Am Baseball Res.

Baseball Research Journal, 1978. 2nd ed. Ed. by L. Robert Davids. (Illus.). 116p. 1983. pap. 4.00 (0-910137-05-6) Soc Am Baseball Res.

Baseball Research Journal, 1979. 160p. 1983. 5.00 (0-910137-06-4); write for info. (0-318-60066-8) Soc Am Baseball Res.

Baseball Research Journal, 1981. Ed. by L. Robert Davids. (Illus.). 188p. (Orig.). 1981. 5.00 (0-910137-17-X) Soc Am Baseball Res.

Baseball Research Journal, 1984. Ed. by Clifford Kachline. (Illus.). 88p. (Orig.). 1984. pap. 6.00 (0-910137-10-2) Soc Am Baseball Res.

Baseball Research Journal, 1985. Ed. by Clifford Kachline. (Illus.). 88p. 1986. pap. 6.00 (0-910137-20-X) Soc Am Baseball Res.

Baseball Research Journal, 1987. Ed. by Jim Kaplan. (Illus.). 88p. 1987. pap. 6.00 (0-910137-30-7) Soc Am Baseball Res.

Baseball Research Journal, 1988. Ed. by Jim Kaplan. (Illus.). 88p. 1988. pap. 7.00 (0-910137-34-X) Soc Am Baseball Res.

Baseball Research Journal, 1989. Ed. by Jim Kaplan. 88p. 1989. pap. 8.00 (0-910137-39-0) Soc Am Baseball Res.

Baseball Research Journal, 1990. Ed. by Jim Kaplan. 96p. 1990. pap. 8.00 (0-910137-43-9) Soc Am Baseball Res.

Baseball Research Journal, 1991. Ed. by John B. Holway. 96p. 1991. pap. 8.00 (0-910137-45-5) Soc Am Baseball Res.

Baseball Research Journal, 1992. Ed. by Mark Alvarez. 112p. 1992. pap. 7.95 (0-910137-50-1) Soc Am Baseball Res.

Baseball Rookie Run Down: A Unique Rookie Card-First Card Index: 1991 & 1992. Michael P. Towey. 53p. (Orig.). 1994. pap. 4.95 (0-9635853-4-7) Pop Fly Pub.

Baseball Rookie Run Down, 1992 & 1993, No. 2: A Unique Rookie Card-Subset Card Guide. Michael P. Towey. 66p. (Orig.). 1994. pap. 6.95 (0-9635853-5-5) Pop Fly Pub.

Baseball Rules in Pictures. G. Jacobs & J. R. McCrory. (Illus.). 96p. 1990. pap. 8.95 (0-399-51597-6, Perigree Bks) Berkley Pub.

Baseball Sabermetric 1991. Aztec Mad. 1991. pap. 15.95 (0-9625846-4-9) Mad Aztec Pr.

Baseball Saved Us. Ken Mochizuki. LC 92-73215. (Illus.). 32p. (J). (gr. k up). 1993. 14.95 (1-880000-01-6) Lee & Low Bks.

***Baseball Saved Us.** Ken Mochizuki. (Illus.). 32p. (J). (gr. k up). 1995. pap. 5.95 (1-880000-19-9) Lee & Low Bks.

Baseball Scoop. Dan Greenberg. (Illus.). 32p. (Orig.). (J). (gr. 6-9). 1994. pap. text ed. 1.95 (0-9641208-4-4) Giant Step CA.

Baseball Shorts: 1,000 of the Game's Funniest One-Liners. Glenn Liebman. 240p. 1994. 9.95 (0-8092-3644-3) Contemp Bks.

Baseball Song Book. Addison Lovejoy. 24p. (YA). (gr. 8 up). 1971. 1.95 (0-87884-015-X) Unicorn Ent.

Baseball Sports Cards & Memorabilia, 1995. American Business Directories Staff. 1995. spiral bd., pap. 620.00 (1-56105-591-3) Am Busn Direct.

***Baseball Star.** Fred Arrigg, Jr. LC 95-2414. (Illus.). 32p. (J). (gr. k-3). 1995. lib. bdg. 11.89 (0-8167-3627-8, Whistlstop); pap. text ed. 2.25 (0-8167-3628-6, Whistlstop) Troll Assocs.

Baseball Stars, 1986: Previews & Illustrations. Carol B. Grafton. 1983. pap. 3.50 (0-486-24565-9) Dover.

Baseball Stories for Boys & Girls. Merritt Clifton. 20p. 1982. pap. 1.50 (0-686-37933-0) Samisdat.

Baseball Super Stars. Howard Balzar. (Illus.). 23p. (Orig.). (J). (gr. 1-8). 1990. pap. 2.50 (0-943409-14-4) Marketcom.

Baseball Super Stars. David Gowdey. (Illus.). 64p. (J). (gr. 7-12). 1994. pap. 8.95 (0-448-40544-X, G&D) Putnam Pub Group.

Baseball Super Teams. Bill Gutman. Ed. by Lisa Clancy. 176p. (Orig.). (J). 1992. pap. 2.99 (0-671-74099-7, Archway) PB.

Baseball Superstars. Howard Balzar. (Illus.). 28p. (Orig.). 1987. pap. 2.50 (0-943409-00-4) Marketcom.

Baseball Superstars. Howard Balzar. 29p. (Orig.). (J). 1991. pap. 4.95 (0-943409-18-7) Marketcom.

Baseball Tales: Major League Writers on the National Pastime. Photos by Terry Heffernan. LC 92-56719. (Illus.). 112p. 1993. 14.95 (0-670-84700-3, Viking Studio) Studio Bks.

Baseball Team & Field Management. Fred Reeves. pap. 2.50 (0-87497-245-0) Impress Hse.

Baseball Techniques in Pictures. Michael Brown. (Orig.). 1993. pap. 8.95 (0-399-51798-7, Perigree Bks) Berkley Pub.

Baseball the Beautiful. Marvin Cohen. 1974. 15.00 (0-8256-3030-4); pap. 7.50 (0-8256-3034-7) Ultramarine Pub.

Baseball Thrills Three-D. Ed. by Ray Zone. 32p. (Orig.). 1990. pap. 2.95 (0-925300-03-9) Three-D Zone.

Baseball Through a Knothole. William A. Borst. (Illus.). 120p. (Orig.). 1981. pap. 4.95 (0-940056-05-4) Krank Pr.

Baseball Tips. Dean Hughes & Tom Hughes. LC 92-13406. (Illus.). 96p. (J). (gr. 2-6). 1993. 9.99 (0-679-93642-4); pap. 5.99 (0-679-83642-X) Random Bks Yng Read.

***Baseball Town: A Place Where Yankees Grow.** Bob Whittemore. LC 95-75080. 272p. 1995. 19.95 (0-8338-0218-6); pap. 12.95 (0-8338-0219-4) M Jones.

Baseball Trade Register. Joseph L. Reichler. 1984. 19.95 (0-02-603110-8) Macmillan.

Baseball Treasures: Memorabilia from the National Pastime. Douglas Congdon-Martin & John Kashmanian. LC 92-83775. (Illus.). 256p. 1993. 59.95 (0-88740-492-8) Schiffer.

Baseball Trivia: So You Think You Know Baseball? Robert Alley. LC 94-43. (Spalding Sports Library). 224p. (Orig.). 1994. pap. 12.95 (0-940279-85-1, Spalding Sports) Masters Pr IN.

Baseball Trivia and Fun Book. Bruce Weber. (J). (gr. 4-7). 1993. pap. 2.50 (0-590-47174-0) Scholastic Inc.

Baseball Trivia Book. 1994. pap. 3.50 (0-553-48162-2) Bantam.

Baseball Trivia Book to End All Baseball Trivia Books. Bert R. Sugar. 208p. 1986. 6.95 (0-88191-039-2) Freundlich.

Baseball Uniforms of the Twentieth Century: The Official Major League Baseball Guide. Marc Okkonen. (Illus.). 288p. 1993. pap. 19.95 (0-8069-8491-0) Sterling.

Baseball Vacations: A Guide to Big League Teams, Towns & Tickets. Daniel P. George. (American Travel Themes Ser.). (Illus.). 255p. (Orig.). 1991. pap. 12.95 (1-878446-02-9, BBV-1) Bon A Tirer Pub.

Baseball When the Grass Was Real: Baseball from the Twenties to the Forties, Told by the Men Who Played It. Donald Honig. LC 93-15806. (Illus.). 326p. 1993. pap. 12.95 (0-8032-7267-7, Bison Books) U of Nebr Pr.

Baseball Wit. William Gibson & Harvey Frommer. (Illus.). 216p. 1992. 9.95 (0-685-45429-0, 34507) Interp Mktg Prods.

Baseball Wit & Wisdom. Ed. by David Plaut. LC 91-50911. (Miniature Editions Ser.). (Illus.). 144p. 1992. 4.95 (1-56138-104-7) Running Pr.

Baseball with a Latin Beat: A History of the Latin American Game. Peter C. Bjarkman. 464p. 1994. pap. 28.00 (0-89950-973-8) McFarland & Co.

Baseball Yearbook. R. Dale Turner. (Illus.). 35p. (J). (gr. 2-12). 1991. spiral bd. 9.95 (0-9628939-0-0) SeaWard Graph.

***Baseball '96 Engagement Calendar.** G. Ward & K. Burns. Date not set. pap. write for info. (0-679-76197-7) Random.

***Baseball '96 Wall Calendar.** G. Ward & K. Burns. Date not set. pap. write for info. (0-679-76199-3) Random.

BaseballMath: Grandslam Activities & Projects for Grades 4-8. Christopher Jennison. (Illus.). 100p. (Orig.). 1994. pap. 9.95 (0-673-36122-5) GdYrBks.

Baseball's All-Star Game: A Game-by-Game Guide. Jeff Lenburg. LC 86-2708. 223p. 1986. lib. bdg. 27.50x (0-89950-231-8) McFarland & Co.

Baseball's All-Time Dream Team. John McCarthy, Jr. 240p. (Orig.). 1994. pap. 12.95 (1-55870-329-2) Betterway Bks.

***Baseball's Bad Hops & Lucky Bounces.** Mike Blake. LC 94-32963. 272p. (Orig.). 1995. pap. 15.99 (1-55870-368-3) Betterway Bks.

Baseball's Benchmark Boxscores: Summaries of the Record-Setting Games. Joseph J. Dittmar. LC 89-43648. (Illus.). 240p. 1990. lib. bdg. 29.95x (0-89950-488-4) McFarland & Co.

Baseball's Best: Five True Stories. Andrew Gutelle. LC 89-35413. (Step into Reading Bks.). (Illus.). 48p. (Orig.). (J). (gr. 2-4). 1990. 3.50 (0-394-80983-1); lib. bdg. 7.99 (0-394-90983-6) Random Bks Yng Read.

Baseball's Best Pitchers, 1993. Ralph L. Horton. 100p. 1993. pap. 20.00 (0-944786-90-1) Horton Pub.

***Baseball's Best Short Stories.** Ed. by Paul D. Standohar. 304p. 1995. 20.00 (1-55652-247-9) Chicago Review.

Baseball's Best, 1993. Bob Italia. LC 93-13085. (Year in Sports Ser.). (J). 1993. lib. bdg. 14.96 (1-56239-241-7) Abdo & Dghtrs.

Baseball's Biggest Bloopers: The Games That Got Away. Dan Gutman. LC 92-25933. 160p. 1993. 14.99 (0-670-84603-1) Viking Child Bks.

***Baseball's Biggest Bloopers: The Games That Got Away.** Dan Gutman. 176p. (J). (gr. 3-7). 1995. pap. 3.99 (0-14-037615-1) Puffin Bks.

Baseball's Canadian-American League: A History of Its Inception, Franchises, Participants, Locales, Statistics, Demise & Legacy, 1936-1951. David Pietrusza. LC 89-43627. 236p. 1990. lib. bdg. 38.50x (0-89950-508-2) McFarland & Co.

***Baseball's Dream Teams: The Greatest Players Decade by Decade.** Lloyd Johnson. 1994. 19.99 (0-517-10306-0) Random Hse Value.

Baseball's Even Greater Insults: More of the Game's Most Outrageous & Irreverent Remarks. Kevin Nelson. LC 92-32597. (Illus.). 240p. (Orig.). 1993. pap. 9.00 (0-671-76066-1, Fireside) S&S Trade.

Baseball's Fifty Greatest Games. Bert R. Sugar. 1986. 9.98 (0-671-08346-5) S&S Trade.

Baseball's Fifty Greatest Games. Bert R. Sugar. 200p. 1994. write for info. (0-9640034-0-6) World Pubns.

Baseball's Golden Age: The Photographs of Charles M. Conlon. Neal McCabe & Constance McCabe. LC 93-187. (Illus.). 1993. 29.95 (0-8109-3130-3) Abrams.

Baseball's Great Experiment: Jackie Robinson & His Legacy. Jules Tygiel. (Illus.). 1983. 24.95 (0-19-503300-0) OUP.

Baseball's Great Experiment: Jackie Robinson & His Legacy. Jules Tygiel. (Illus.). 432p. 1993. reprint ed. pap. 10.95 (0-19-507826-8) OUP.

Baseball's Great Moments, 1990 Edition. Joseph Reichler. 1990. 7.98 (0-88365-754-6) Galahad Bks.

Baseball's Great Moments, 1991 Edition. Jack Clary. 1991. 9.98 (0-88365-768-6) Galahad Bks.

***Baseball's Greatest Controversies: Rhubarbs, Hoaxes, Blown Calls, Ruthian Myths, Managers' Miscues & Front-Office Flops.** John G. Robertson. LC 94-48265. 192p. 1995. lib. bdg. 22.50 (0-7864-0107-9) McFarland & Co.

Baseball's Greatest Games. Dan Gutman. LC 93-31504. (Illus.). 160p. (J). (gr. 4-7). 1994. 14.99 (0-670-84604-X) Viking Child Bks.

Baseball's Greatest Hitters. Sydelle A. Kramer. LC 94-16497. (Step into Reading). (Illus.). (J). (gr. 4 up). 1995. pap. 3.99 (0-679-85307-3) Random Bks Yng Read.

Baseball's Greatest Hitters. Sydelle A. Kramer. LC 94-16497. (Step into Reading). (Illus.). (J). (gr. 4 up). 1995. 9.99 (0-679-95307-8) Random Bks Yng Read.

Baseball's Greatest Pitchers. S. A. Kramer. LC 91-27892. (Step into Reading Bks.). (Illus.). 48p. (Orig.). (J). (gr. 2-4). 1992. pap. 3.50 (0-679-82149-X) Random Bks Yng Read.

Baseball's Greatest Pitchers. S. A. Kramer. LC 91-27892. (Step into Reading Bks.). (Illus.). 48p. (Orig.). (J). (gr. 2-4). 1992. lib. bdg. 7.99 (0-679-92149-4) Random Bks Yng Read.

B

An Asterisk (*) at the beginning of an entry indicates that the title is appearing in BIP for the first time. 605

Baseball's Greatest Quotations: From Walt Whitman to Dizzy Dean, Garrison Keillor to Woody Allen, a Treasury of over 5000 Quotations Plus Historical Lore, Notes & Illustrations. Paul Dickson. LC 90-55531. (Illus.). 480p. 1992. reprint ed. pap. 16.00 (0-06-272025-2, E Burlingame Bks) HarpC.

Baseball's Greatest Streaks: The Highs & Lows of Teams, Pitchers & Hitters in the Modern Major Leagues. Allen Lewis. LC 91-51209. 272p. 1992. lib. bdg. 32.50x (0-89950-714-X) McFarland & Co.

Baseball's Greatest Total Hitters. Mark E. Van Overloop. 190p. (Orig.). 1990. pap. 9.95 (0-9626005-0-4) On The Mark.

Baseball's Hall of Fame: Cooperstown, Where the Legends Live Forever. rev. ed. Sporting News Editors. LC 93-9239. 1993. reprint ed. 19.99 (0-517-09277-8) Random Hse Value.

Baseball's Hometown Teams: The Story of the Minor Leagues. Bruce Chadwick. LC 94-9253. 1994. write for info. (1-55859-701-8) Abbeville Pr.

Baseball's Last Golden Age, 1946-1960: The National Pastime in a Time of Glory & Change. J. Ronald Oakley. LC 93-40432. 384p. 1994. pap. 25.95 (0-89950-851-0) McFarland & Co.

Baseball's Pennant Races: A Graphic View. John W. Davenport. LC 81-67611. (Illus.). 1981. 19.95 (0-934794-03-0); pap. 12.95 (0-934794-02-2) First Impressions.

Baseball's Strangest Moments. Robert Obojski. LC 87-33319. (Illus.). 128p. 1989. pap. 4.95 (0-8069-6983-0) Sterling.

Baseballs Ten Greatest Teams. Donald Honig. 1982. 15.95 (0-02-553570-6) Macmillan.

***Baseball's Top One Hundred: The Best Individual Seasons of All Time.** John Benson. 1995. pap. 19.95 (1-880876-01-9) Diamond Lib.

Basel for Visitors. 64p. 1980. pap. 3.75 (0-686-95486-6) Interbk Inc.

Basel Mission Industries in Malabar & South Canara, 1834-1914: A Study of Its Social & Economic Impact. Jaiprakash Raghariah. 1990. 16.50 (81-212-0324-4, Pub. by Gian Publng Hse II) S Asia.

Baseline Fees for Physician Services by Speciality. Innervation Technology Corporation Staff. 1994. Per report, 2 or more. ring bd. write for info. (0-685-70451-3) Hlthcare Mgmt Grp.

Baseline Fees for Physician Services by Speciality. Innervation Technology Corporation Staff. 1995. One speciality, 1 region. ring bd. 95.00 (0-07-600647-6); All specialities, 1 region. ring bd. 495.00 (0-685-74690-9); Electronic, 1 speciality, 1 region. disk, ring bd. 175.00 (0-07-809881-5); Per report, 2 or more. disk, ring bd. write for info. (0-685-70453-X); All specialities, 1 region. disk, ring bd. 795.00 (0-685-70454-8) Hlthcare Mgmt Grp.

***Baseline Sampling for Netware.** Stephen A. Meyer. 512p. 1995. write for info. (0-8493-9446-5, 9446) CRC Pr.

Basement. 1991. pap. 12.95 (0-671-72358-8, Touchstone Bks) S&S Trade.

***Basement: A Novel.** Bari Wood. LC 94-21657. 1995. 17.95 (0-688-13351-7) Morrow.

Basement see Lover

Basement & Foundation. (Fix-It-Yourself Ser.). (Illus.). 144p. 1990. 17.27 (0-8094-6232-X); lib. bdg. 23.27 (0-8094-6233-8) Time-Life.

Basement Baseball Club. Jeffrey Kelly. 1988. pap. 2.95 (0-8167-1819-9) Troll Assocs.

Basement Baseball Club. Jeffrey A. Kelly. LC 86-27545. 160p. (J). (gr. 3-5). 1987. 14.95 (0-395-40774-5) HM.

***Basement Involved Tectonics Foreland Areas.** William G. Brown. (Continuing Education Course Note Ser.: No. 26). (Illus.). iii, 92p. 1984. pap. 15.00 (0-89181-175-3) AAPG.

Basement Membranes. Ed. by S. Shibata. 466p. 1986. 178.00 (0-444-80739-X) Elsevier.

Basement Nukes: The Consequences of Cheap Weapons of Mass Destruction. E. S. Strauss. 1986. lib. bdg. 79.95 (0-8490-3615-1) Gordon Pr.

***Basement Seat to History: Tales of Covering Presidents Nixon, Ford, Carter & Reagan for the Voice of America.** Philomena Jurey. LC 95-76896. (Illus.). 350p. (Orig.). Date not set. pap. write for info. (0-9647015-0-2) Linus Pr.

Basement Stairs. Nola Buck. (Illus.). 16p. (J). (ps-2). 1994. 4.95 (0-694-00649-1, Festival) HarpC Child Bks.

Basement Tectonics, No. 7. Ed. by Robert C. Mason. (C). 1992. lib. bdg. 200.00 (0-7923-1582-0) Kluwer Ac.

Basement Tectonics Eight: Characterization & Comparison of Ancient & Mesozoic Continental Margins, Proceedings of the Eighth International Conference, Butte, Montana, August 8-12, 1988. Ed. by Mervin J. Bartholomew et al. LC 92-41537. (Proceedings of the International Conferences on Basement Tectonics Ser.: Vol. 2). 768p. (C). 1993. lib. bdg. 244.00 (0-7923-2088-3) Kluwer Ac.

Basement Tectonics Nine - Australia & Other Regions: Proceedings of the Ninth International Conference on Basement Tectonics, Held in Canberra, Australia, July, 1990. Ed. by M. J. Rickard. 272p. (C). 1992. lib. bdg. 109.50 (0-7923-1559-6) Kluwer Ac.

***Basement Tectonics 10: Proceedings of the Tenth International Conference on Basement Tectonics, Held in Duluth, Minnesota, U.S.A., August, 1992.** International Conference on Basement Tectonics Staff. Ed. by Richard W. Ojakangas & Albert B. Dickas. LC 95-7865. (Proceedings of the International Conferences on Basement Tectonics Ser.: Vol. 4). 466p. (C). 1995. lib. bdg. 208.00 (0-7923-3429-9) Kluwer Ac.

Basenji Champions, 1945-1981. Jan L. Freund. (Illus.). 152p. 1986. pap. 36.95 (0-940808-17-X) Camino E E & Bk.

Basenji Champions, 1982-1986. Camino E. E. & B. Co. Staff. (Illus.). 95p. 1988. pap. 28.95 (0-940808-60-9) Camino E E & Bk.

Basenji, Dog from the Past. Forrest B. Johnson. Ed. by Chiaki Takeuchi. LC 91-65327. (Illus.). 99p. (C). 1992. text ed. 19.95 (1-882032-00-4) Thousand Autumns Pr.

Basenji Out of Africa to You - A New Look. rev. ed. Susan Coe. 1994. 27.95 (0-944875-42-4) Doral Pub.

Basenji Stacked & Moving. Robert Cole. 188p. 1992. 21.95 (0-920939-00-7) Doral Pub.

Basenjis. Jack Shafer & Bob Mankey. (KW Ser.). (Illus.). 192p. 1989. lib. bdg. 11.95 (0-86622-993-0, KW-118) TFH Pubns.

***Basepaths.** Jerry Klinkowitz. (Poetry & Fiction Ser.). 208p. 1994. 19.95 (0-8018-5092-4) Johns Hopkins.

Bases Abroad: The Global Foreign Military Presence. Robert E. Harkavy. (SIPRI Publication Ser.). (Illus.). 418p. 1989. 79.00 (0-19-829131-0) OUP.

Bases Biblicas De la Etica. J. E. Giles. 1991. reprint ed. 5.50 (0-311-46028-3) Casa Bautista.

Bases Cytologiques & Genetiques de la Sexualite, Vol. 1. Louis E. Gallien. 406p. (FRE.). 1973. text ed. 342.00 (0-677-50540-X) Gordon & Breach.

Bases de la Fe Premilenial. Charles C. Ryrie. Orig. Title: The Basis of the Premillennial Faith. 224p. (SPA.). 1984. pap. 5.25 (0-8254-1626-4) Kregel.

Bases de la Pintura Al Oleo see Basics of Oil Painting

Bases for Science & Technology Promotion in Developing Countries. Hyung Sup Choi. 295p. 1983. text ed. 23.00 (0-685-37899-3, Pub. by APO JA); pap. text ed. 18.50 (0-685-37900-0, 0021, Pub. by APO JA) Qual Resc.

Bases in Banach Spaces I. I. Singer. LC 75-99014. (Grundlehren der Mathematischen Wissenschaften Ser.: Vol. 154). 1970. 119.00 (0-387-04833-2) Spr-Verlag.

Bases in Banach Spaces II. I. Singer. 880p. 1981. 99.00 (0-387-10394-5) Spr-Verlag.

Bases Loaded: Great Baseball of the Twentieth Century, Reading Level 3-5. Mel Cebulash. 1993. 4.25 (0-88336-742-4); audio 12.00 (0-88336-899-4) New Readers.

Bases Loaded...Nobody's Home. Stephen Hicks & Jerry Cohagan. 1990. 8.50 (0-685-68693-0, MP-659) Lillenas.

Bases of Argument: Ideas in Conflict. Craig R. Smith & David M. Hunsaker. LC 72-173978. (Speech Communication Ser.: No. 17). 1972. pap. 4.50 (0-672-61156-2, Bobbs) Macmillan.

Bases of Auditory Brain Stem Evoked Responses. Ed. by Ernest Moore. 481p. 1983. text ed. 54.50 (0-8089-1465-0, 792976, Grune) Saunders.

Bases of Fitness. Edward L. Fox et al. 369p. (C). 1986. pap. write for info. (0-02-339190-1) Macmillan.

Bases of Hearing Sciences. 3rd ed. John D. Durrant & Jean H. Lovrinic. 304p. 1993. text ed. 37.00 (0-683-02737-9) Williams & Wilkins.

Bases of Modern Librarianship. C. M. White. 1964. 63.00 (0-08-010627-7, Pub. by Pergamon Repr UK) Franklin.

Bases of Tantra Sadhana. Parasurama. Tr. by M. P. Pandit. 52p. (SAN.). 1991. reprint ed. 2.00 (0-941524-02-7) Lotus Light.

Bases of Yoga. Sri Aurobindo. LC 93-79795. 108p. 1993. pap. 6.95 (0-941524-77-9) Lotus Light.

Bases of Yoga. Sri Aurobindo. 108p. 1985. pap. 2.75 (81-7058-021-8) Aurobindo Assn.

Bases of Yoga: The Mother's Talks. 251p. (Orig.). 1988. pap. 4.95 (0-317-99971-0, Pub. by Sri Aurob Ashram Trust II) Auromere.

Bases para la Educacion Cristiana. Hayward Armstrong. 190p. (Orig.). 1989. pap. 5.95 (0-311-11048-7) Casa Bautista.

Basestock Coating Manufacture & Technology Seminar, 1990: Hyatt Regency Minneapolis, Minneapolis, MN, November 4-7. Technical Association of the Pulp & Paper Industry Staff. (TAPPI Notes Ser.). 155p. reprint ed. pap. 44.20 (0-8357-3465-X, 2039727) Bks Demand.

***BASF Corp: A Report on the Company's Environmental Policies & Practices.** (Illus.). 34p. (C). 1994. reprint ed. pap. text ed. 200.00x (0-7881-0916-2, Coun on Econ) Diane Pub.

Bashar: Blueprint for Change: A Message from Our Future. Darryl Anka & Luana Ewing. (Illus.). 318p. (Orig.). 1991. pap. 13.95 (1-56284-113-0) New Solutions Pub.

Bashers, Baiters & Bigots: Homophobia in American Society. Ed. by John P. De Cecco. LC 84-19121. 203p. 1985. pap. text ed. 12.95 (0-918393-02-7) Harrington Pk.

Bashful No Longer: An Alaskan Eskimo Ethnohistory, 1778-1988. Wendell H. Oswalt. LC 89-37036. (Civilization of the American Indian Ser.: No. 199). (Illus.). 288p. 1990. 24.95 (0-8061-2256-0) U of Okla Pr.

Basho: The Mystic Dog. Aaron Talsky & David Lane. 64p. (Orig.). 1992. pap. text ed. 4.95 (1-56543-018-2) Mt SA Coll Philos.

Basho & His Interpreters: Selected Hokku with Commentary. Makoto Ueda. LC 91-14035. (Illus.). 472p. 1992. 65.00 (0-8047-1916-0) Stanford U Pr.

***Basho & His Interpreters: Selected Hokku with Commentary.** Makoto Ueda. (Illus.). 468p. (C). 1995. pap. 19.95 (0-8047-2526-8) Stanford U Pr.

***Basho's "Narrow Road" Spring & Autumn Passages.** Matsuo Basho. Tr. by Hiroaki Sato. (Illus.). 152p. (Orig.). 1995. pap. 15.00 (1-880656-20-5, Rock Spring Collect) Stone Bridge Pr.

BASIC. L. Wayne Horn & Michel Boillot. (Illus.). 527p. 1986. Instr's manual. teacher ed, pap. text ed. write for info. (0-314-96635-8) West Pub.

BASIC. John L. Kallas. 252p. (Orig.). (J). (gr. 8-12). 1985. pap. 5.00 (0-89824-167-7); pap. text ed. 14.99 (0-89824-145-6) Trillium Pr.

BASIC. Dean Mackie & David Mackie. (Let's Look At Ser.). (Illus.). 48p. (J). (gr. 1-5). 1985. pap. 3.95 (0-88625-085-4) Durkin Hayes Pub.

BASIC. Timothy Trainor. 1988. pap. text ed. write for info. (0-07-554320-6) McGraw.

BASIC. 2nd ed. Robert L. Albrecht et al. LC 77-14998. (Self-Teaching Guides Ser.). 325p. 1978. pap. text ed. 17.95 (0-471-03500-9) Wiley.

BASIC. 3rd ed. Michel Boillot & L. Wayne Horn. (Illus.). 416p. (C). 1983. pap. text ed. 25.25 (0-314-69636-9) West Pub.

BASIC. 3rd ed. Samuel L. Marateck. 533p. (C). 1986. pap. text ed. 37.25 (0-15-504505-9) Dryden Pr.

BASIC. 4th ed. L. Wayne Horn & Michel Boillot. (Illus.). 527p. 1986. pap. text ed. 48.25 (0-314-93156-2) West Pub.

BASIC: A Hands-on Method. 2nd ed. Herbert D. Peckham. (Illus.). 320p. 1981. pap. text ed. 27.95 (0-07-049160-7, BYTE Bks) McGraw.

BASIC: A Modular Approach. 2nd ed. Robert G. Thompson. 385p. (C). 1985. pap. write for info. (0-675-20280-9, Merrill Pub Co) Macmillan.

BASIC: A Short Self-Instructional Course. Michael Oatey & Carl Payne. 94p. (C). 1984. pap. text ed. 60.00 (0-273-01940-6, Pub. by Pitman Pubng UK) St Mut.

BASIC: A Simplified Structured Approach. 2nd ed. D. Burras et al. 1985. pap. 30.00 (0-8359-0378-8, Reston) P-H.

BASIC: A Structured Approach, IBM Version. 2nd ed. Alfred T. Clark, Jr. 544p. (C). 1990. pap. 38.95 (0-538-10790-1, J79) S-W Pub.

BASIC: An Introduction to Computer Programming. 4th ed. Robert J. Bent & George C. Sethares. LC 89-15835. 416p. (C). 1990. pap. 43.95 (0-534-12642-1) PWS Pubs.

BASIC: An Introduction to Computer Programming Using the BASIC Language. 3rd ed. William F. Sharpe & Nancy L. Jacob. LC 78-72148. (Illus.). 1979. pap. 12.95 (0-02-928390-6) Free Pr.

BASIC: An Introduction to Computer Programming with the Apple. 3rd ed. Robert J. Bent & George C. Sethares. LC 90-44317. 448p. (C). 1991. pap. 35.95 (0-534-14058-0) PWS Pubs.

BASIC: Concepts & Structured Problem Solving. Michel Boillot & Mona Boillot. (Illus.). 560p. 1984. pap. text ed. 32.25 (0-314-77843-8) West Pub.

BASIC: Concepts & Structured Problem-Solving. 2nd ed. Michel Boillot. 442p. (C). 1988. text ed. 48.00 (0-314-65461-5) West Pub.

BASIC: Getting Started. William S. Davis. 69p. 1981. pap. text ed. 8.76 (0-201-03258-9) Addison-Wesley.

BASIC: Programming Fundamentals & Applications. Robert Spear. 416p. (C). 1987. pap. write for info. (0-675-20553-0, Merrill Pub Co) Macmillan.

BASIC: Step-by-Step Programming. Jeffrey B. Morton. (Illus.). 206p. 1977. pap. 21.95 (0-916460-22-3, Matrix Pubs Inc) Weber Systems.

BASIC: The PICK Programming Language. Malcolm Bull. LC 93-673. (Computing Ser.). 1993. write for info. (0-412-46660-0) Chapman & Hall.

***Basic - General Education (CS) Series.** 1994. pap. write for info. (0-8373-6700-X) Nat Learn.

BASIC-A Personal Computer Language. Marvin E. Mundel & David L. Danner. 322p. 1986. pap. 14.00 (92-833-1089-6, 310890, Pub. by APO JA) Qual Resc.

Basic Abstract Algebra. P. B. Bhattacharya et al. 416p. (C). 1994. 69.95 (0-521-46081-6); pap. 29.95 (0-521-46629-6) Cambridge U Pr.

Basic AC Circuits. Stanley R. Fulton & John C. Rawlins. Ed. by Gerald Luecke & C. Battle. LC 80-54793. (Basic Electricity Ser.). (Illus.). 560p. 1986. 29.95 (0-672-27025-0, LCW8168) Sams.

Basic AC Electricity for HVAC. Richard Hunter. (Orig.). 1980. audio 359.00 (0-8064-0338-1); audio 359.00 (0-8064-0340-3) Bergwall.

Basic AC Electricity for HVAC, Pt. 1. Richard Hunter. (Orig.). 1980. student ed, pap. 9.00 (0-8064-0337-3, 833) Bergwall.

Basic AC Electricity for HVAC, Pt. 2. Richard Hunter. (Orig.). 1980. student ed, pap. 9.00 (0-8064-0339-X, 834) Bergwall.

Basic Academics, 10 Modules. (Illus.). 940p. 1982. 295.00 (0-87683-246-X) GP Pub.

Basic Academics, 10 Modules, Set. (Illus.). 940p. 1982. spiral bd. 235.00 (0-87683-224-9) GP Pub.

Basic Accounting. Jeffrey M. Madura. (Illus.). 200p. (C). 1981. pap. text ed. 14.95 (0-916780-16-3) CES.

Basic Accounting. 2nd ed. Calvin Engler. 1969. teacher ed 6.67 (0-672-96018-4, Bobbs); student ed 6.50 (0-672-96019-2, Bobbs); 6.95 (0-672-96020-6, Bobbs); pap. text ed. 8.95 (0-672-96017-6, Bobbs) Macmillan.

Basic Accounting for Attorneys. M. C. Faul et al. 281p. 1987. pap. write for info. (0-7021-1911-3, Pub. by Juta SA) W W Gaunt.

Basic Accounting for Builders. David A. Hughes. LC 84-39199. (Longman Technician Series, Construction & Civil Engineering). 173p. reprint ed. pap. 49.40 (0-8357-2975-3, 2039237) Bks Demand.

Basic Accounting for Churches: A Turn-Key Manual. Jack A. Henry. LC 93-38256. 1994. 10.99 (0-8054-6145-0) Broadman.

Basic Accounting for Hospital Based Non-Financial Managers. Sandra H. Pelfrey. 1992. pap. text ed. 28.95 (0-8273-4894-0) Delmar.

Basic Accounting for Lawyers. 4th ed. Anthony Phillips et al. 268p. 1988. text ed. 94.00 (0-8318-0467-X, B467) Am Law Inst.

Basic Accounting for Small Groups. John Cammack. 64p. (C). 1992. pap. text ed. 21.00 (0-85598-148-2, Pub. by Oxfam Pubns UK) St Mut.

Basic Accounting for the Small Business. 4th ed. Clive G. Cornish. (Business Ser.). 208p. 1992. 7.95 (0-88908-938-8) Self-Counsel Pr.

Basic Accounting for the Small Business: Simple, Foolproof Techniques for Keeping Your Books Straight & Staying Out of Trouble. 9th rev. ed. Clive G. Comish. (Business Ser.). 224p. (C). 1992. Canadian ed. pap. 8.95 (0-88908-998-1) Self-Counsel Pr.

Basic Accounting Practice. 3rd ed. M. W. Glautier et al. (Orig.). 1985. pap. 29.50 (0-273-02426-4, Pub. by Pitman Pub Ltd UK) Trans-Atl Phila.

Basic Acol Bridge Flipper. Ron Klinger. 32p. 1987. pap. 5.95 (0-575-03911-6, Pub. by V Gollancz UK) Trafalgar.

Basic Acoustics. Donald E. Hall. 345p. (C). 1986. text ed. 49.95 (0-06-042611-X) HarpCollege.

Basic Acoustics. Donald E. Hall. LC 92-23278. 368p. (C). 1993. reprint ed. lib. bdg. 61.95 (0-89464-790-3) Krieger.

Basic Acting Techniques. Donald Wait. Keyes. 154p. 1980. pap. 9.95 (0-318-16872-3) World Modeling.

Basic Adolescent Gynecology: An Office Guide. Ed. by Victor C. Strasburger. (Illus.). 270p. 1990. 48.00 (0-683-07947-6) Williams & Wilkins.

Basic Adult Survival English: With Orientation to American Life, Part 1. Robert E. Walsh. (Illus.). 225p. (C). 1984. pap. text ed. 8.95 (0-13-056812-0) P-H.

Basic Adult Survival English: With Orientation to American Life, Part 2. Robert E. Walsh. (Illus.). 144p. (C). 1984. pap. text ed. 8.95 (0-13-056854-6) P-H.

Basic, Advanced Systematic Substitution Training, Set-AS. Russell E. Mason. 1975. pap. 35.00 (0-89533-017-2); Incl. Tape 12. T-13, T-14; H. E. S. T-a SET. write for info. (0-89533-043-1); Notes. write for info. (0-89533-025-3) F I Comm.

Basic Aerobatic Manual. William K. Kershner. LC 86-83134. 110p. (Orig.). (C). 1990. pap. 18.95 (0-8138-0063-3) Iowa St U Pr.

Basic Aerobatics. Geza Szurovy & Mike Goulian. LC 93-38046. 1994. text ed. 29.95 (0-07-062931-5); pap. text ed. 17.95 (0-07-062926-9) TAB Bks.

Basic Aerohemodynamics. 1984. 17.95 (0-930835-03-4) Med Res Assocs.

Basic Air Conditioning. Joe Burgess. Ed. by Kelly Gorham. (Illus.). 24p. Date not set. student ed 7.00 (0-8064-0005-6, A42); audio 329.00 (0-8064-0004-8, A42) Bergwall.

Basic Air Conditioning. Rocco Patella. 1980. student ed 6.00 (0-8064-0333-0, 830); audio 289.00 (0-8064-0334-9) Bergwall.

Basic Air Conditioning & Refrigeration. Meril Taylor & Ervin Easterling. 124p. (C). 1992. 17.76 (1-56870-017-2) RonJon Pub.

Basic Airbrush Painting Techniques. Judy Martin. (Illus.). 128p. (Orig.). 1994. pap. 19.95 (0-89134-585-X) North Light Bks.

Basic Alarm Electronics. John Sanger. (Illus.). 192p. 1988. pap. text ed. 29.95 (0-409-90037-0) Buttrwrth-Heinemann.

Basic Albanian Etymologies. Martin E. Huld. (Illus.). x, 213p. 1984. pap. 19.95 (0-89357-135-0) Slavica.

Basic Algebra. Marilyn Frankenstein. (Illus.). 1979. pap. text ed. write for info. (0-13-056788-4) P-H.

Basic Algebra. Thomas J. McHale & Paul T. Witzke. (Milwaukee Area Technical College Mathematics Ser.). 1971. pap. text ed. 41.95 (0-201-04625-3) Addison-Wesley.

Basic Algebra. 2nd ed. M. N. Manougian. (Illus.). 480p. (C). 1994. text ed. 29.50 (0-931541-32-8) Mancorp Pub.

Basic Algebra. 3rd annot. ed. Jack Barker et al. 846p. (C). 1991. teacher ed write for info. (0-03-054252-9) SCP.

Basic Algebra. 3rd ed. Jack Barker et al. 846p. (C). 1991. pap. text ed. 47.00 (0-03-032219-7) SCP.

Basic Algebra: A Guided Approach. 2nd ed. Robert A. Carman & Marilyn J. Carman. LC 81-11601. 575p. 1982. pap. text ed. 32.00 (0-471-04174-2) P-H.

Basic Algebra for College Students. 2nd ed. Lawrence G. Gilligan et al. LC 84-80415. 402p. (C). 1985. pap. text ed. 23.00 (0-669-05693-6); Instr.'s guide. teacher ed 1.50 (0-669-05695-2) Heath.

Basic Algebra I. 2nd ed. Nathan Jacobson. LC 84-25836. (Illus.). 499p. (C). 1995. text ed. write for info. (0-7167-1480-9) W H Freeman.

Basic Algebra II. 2nd ed. Nathan Jacobson. 688p. (C). 1995. text ed. write for info. (0-7167-1933-9) W H Freeman.

Basic Algebraic Geometry. I. R. Shafarevich. LC 77-6425. (Springer Study Edition Ser.). 1990. pap. 32.00 (0-387-08264-6) Spr-Verlag.

Basic Algebraic Geometry, Vol. 1. 2nd exp. rev. ed. Igor R. Shafarevich. Tr. by Miles Reid. LC 94-11903. (Illus.). 321p. 1994. pap. 45.00 (0-387-54812-2) Spr-Verlag.

Basic Algebraic Geometry, Vol. 2. exp. rev. ed. Igor R. Shafarevich. Tr. by Miles Reid. LC 94-11903. (Illus.). 283p. 1994. pap. 45.00 (0-387-57554-5) Spr-Verlag.

***Basic Allied Health Statistics & Analysis.** Gerda Koch. LC 94-23929. 1996. write for info. (0-8273-5525-4) Delmar.

Basic Alternating Current Control Diagrams. 5th ed. Paul R. Himes. (Illus.). 83p. 1990. reprint ed. 7.95 (0-943876-00-1) Barks Pubns.

Basic Analysis of Regularized Series & Products. Jay Jorgenson & Serge Lang. LC 93-38484. (Lecture Notes in Mathematics Ser.: Vol. 1564). 1993. pap. 23.00 (0-387-57488-3) Spr-Verlag.

Basic Analytic Number Theory. A. A. Karatsuba. Tr. by M. B. Nathanson. (Illus.). 240p. 1992. 79.00 (0-387-53345-1) Spr-Verlag.

Basic Analytical Chemistry. L. Pataki & E. Zapp. (Analytical Chemistry Ser.: Vol. 2). (Illus.). 1981. 191.00 (0-08-023850-5, Pub. by Pergamon Repr UK) Franklin.

Basic Analytical Petrology. Paul C. Ragland. (Illus.). 384p. (C). 1989. pap. text ed. 21.95 (0-19-504535-1) OUP.

B

An Asterisk (*) at the beginning of an entry indicates that the title is appearing in BIP for the first time.

B

An Asterisk (*) at the beginning of an entry indicates that the title is appearing in BIP for the first time.

607

Basic Bible Commentary, Vol. 27: Hebrews. Leonard T. Wolcott. Ed. by Lynne M. Deming. LC 94-10965. 160p. (Orig.). 1994. pap. 4.95 (*0-687-02647-4*) Abingdon.

Basic Bible Commentary, Vol. 28: James; First & Second Peter; First, Second, & Third John; & Jude. Earl S. Johnson, Jr. Ed. by Lynne M. Deming. LC 94-10965. 160p. (Orig.). 1994. pap. 4.95 (*0-687-02648-2*) Abingdon.

Basic Bible Commentary, Vol. 29: Revelation. Robert H. Conn. Ed. by Lynne M. Deming. LC 94-10965. 160p. (Orig.). 1994. pap. 4.95 (*0-687-02649-0*) Abingdon.

Basic Bible Commentary, Vol. 3: Numbers & Deuteronomy. Lynne M. Deming. LC 94-10965. 160p. (Orig.). 1994. pap. 4.95 (*0-687-02622-9*) Abingdon.

Basic Bible Commentary, Vol. 4: Joshua, Judges, & Ruth. Barbara P. Perguson. Ed. by Lynne M. Deming. LC 94-10965. 160p. (Orig.). 1994. pap. 4.95 (*0-687-02623-7*) Abingdon.

Basic Bible Commentary, Vol. 5: First & Second Samuel. Frank Johnson. Ed. by Lynne M. Deming. LC 94-10965. 160p. (Orig.). 1994. pap. 4.95 (*0-687-02624-5*) Abingdon.

B

Basic Bible Commentary, Vol. 6: First & Second Kings. Linda B. Hinton. Ed. by Lynne M. Deming. LC 94-10965. 160p. (Orig.). 1994. pap. 4.95 (*0-687-02625-3*) Abingdon.

Basic Bible Commentary, Vol. 7: First & Second Chronicles. Leonard T. Wolcott. Ed. by Lynne M. Deming. LC 94-10965. 160p. (Orig.). 1994. pap. 4.95 (*0-687-02626-1*) Abingdon.

Basic Bible Commentary, Vol. 8: Ezra, Nehemiah, & Esther. Brady N. Whitehead, Jr. Ed. by Lynne M. Deming. LC 94-10965. 160p. (Orig.). 1994. pap. 4.95 (*0-687-02627-X*) Abingdon.

Basic Bible Commentary, Vol. 9: Job. Gregory M. Weeks. Ed. by Lynne M. Deming. LC 94-10965. 160p. (Orig.). 1994. pap. 4.95 (*0-687-02628-8*) Abingdon.

Basic Bible Dictionary. Velda Matthews & Ray Beard. Ed. by Bob Korth. (Illus.). 128p. (Orig.). (J). (gr. 4-12). 1984. pap. 13.99 (*0-87239-720-3*, 2770) Standard Pub.

Basic Bible Doctrines for Victorious Living. K. A. Whaley. 87p. 1981. pap. 7.95 (*0-686-35778-7*) First Baptist.

Basic Bible Doctrines for Victorious Living. K. A. Whaley. 1981. pap. 7.95 (*0-686-40713-X*) Freedom Univ-FS.

Basic Bible for Real People: Six Key Books of the Bible in One Year of Daily Devotional Readings. Philip D. Long & Beth L. Siefert. 384p. 1991. pap. text ed. 9.95 (*0-9631735-0-2*) E Lib Luth Church.

Basic Bible Interpretation. Roy B. Zuck. 372p. 1991. text ed. 23.99 (*0-89693-819-0*, Victor Books) SP Pubns.

Basic Bible Sermons on Christian Stewardship. J. Alfred Smith. LC 92-12655. 1992. 5.99 (*0-8054-2006-1*) Broadman.

Basic Bible Sermons on Christmas. Chevis F. Horne. (Orig.). 1992. pap. 5.99 (*0-8054-2278-1*) Broadman.

Basic Bible Sermons on Easter. Chevis F. Horne. LC 89-29514. (Orig.). 1990. pap. 5.99 (*0-8054-2271-4*) Broadman.

Basic Bible Sermons on Handling Conflict. Paul W. Powell. 1992. pap. 5.99 (*0-8054-2279-X*) Broadman.

Basic Bible Sermons on Hope. David A. Farmer. 1992. pap. 5.99 (*0-8054-2276-5*) Broadman.

Basic Bible Sermons on John. Herschel H. Hobbs. LC 89-48574. (Orig.). 1990. pap. 5.99 (*0-8054-2272-2*) Broadman.

Basic Bible Sermons on Psalms for Everyday Living. James T. Draper, Jr. (Orig.). 1992. pap. 5.99 (*0-8054-2280-3*) Broadman.

Basic Bible Sermons on Spiritual Living. Stephen B. McSwain. 1992. pap. 5.99 (*0-8054-2274-9*) Broadman.

Basic Bible Sermons on the Cross. W. A. Criswell. LC 89-48573. (Orig.). 1990. pap. 5.99 (*0-8054-2273-0*) Broadman.

Basic Bible Sermons on the Ten Commandments. Jerry Vines. (Orig.). 1992. pap. 5.99 (*0-8054-2281-1*) Broadman.

*__Basic Bible Syllabus.__ Donna R. Fisher. (Illus.). 19p. (YA). 1993. pap. 3.50 (*0-913717-70-3*, 1902) Hewitt Res Fnd.

Basic Bible Truth. Aaron M. Wilson. 195p. 1987. pap. 6.95 (*1-882449-19-3*) Messenger Pub.

Basic Bible Truths Every Believer Should Know. Al Horta. 32p. 1989. pap. 2.95 (*0-88144-148-1*) Christian Pub.

Basic Bible Truths for New Converts. Ralph O. Burns. 30p. 1978. pap. 0.75 (*0-87227-007-6*) Reg Baptist.

Basic Biblical Geography. Denis Baly. LC 86-45206. 80p. 1987. pap. 10.00 (*0-8006-1922-6*, 1-1922, Fortress Pr) Augsburg Fortress.

Basic Biblical Teaching Skills. Dotcy I. Isom, Jr. LC 93-80908. 100p. (Orig.). 1993. pap. text ed. 6.00 (*1-883667-07-0*) Christian Meth.

Basic Bibliography on Experimental Design in Marketing. David M. Gardner & Russell W. Belk. LC 80-19563. (Bibliography Ser.: No. 37). 69p. reprint ed. pap. 25.00 (*0-8357-4759-X*, 2037686) Bks Demand.

Basic Bibliography on Marketing Research, 1974. 3rd ed. American Marketing Association. Ed. by Alain Cousineau et al. LC 74-187908. (American Marketing Association Bibliography Ser.: No. 2). 309p. reprint ed. pap. 88.10 (*0-8357-5973-3*, 2026667) Bks Demand.

*__Basic Biochemical Engineering: Text & Disk with 100 Plus Programs.__ 2nd ed. Henry R. Bungay. (Illus.). 267p. (C). 1993. pap. text ed. 38.00 (*0-9639308-1-8*) BiLine Assocs.

*__Basic Biochemical Laboratory Procedures & Computing.__ R. Cecil Jack. (Topics in Biochemistry Ser.). (Illus.). 384p. (C). 1995. pap. text ed. 29.95 (*0-19-507897-7*) OUP.

Basic Biochemical Methods. 2nd ed. Renee R. Alexander & Joan M. Griffiths. 368p. 1993. pap. text ed. 42.95 (*0-471-56153-3*) Wiley-Liss.

*__Basic Biological Experiences.__ E. William Wischusen. 112p. (C). 1994. 9.56 (*0-8403-9637-6*) Kendall-Hunt.

Basic Biology. 2nd ed. Charles LaRue. (Illus.). 294p. 1992. teacher ed 12.99 (*0-7916-0098-X*); student ed 4.99 (*0-7916-0099-8*); text ed. 19.49 (*0-7916-0097-1*); 9.99 (*0-7916-0107-2*) Media Materials.

*__Basic Biology of Muscles: A Comparative Approach.__ fac. ed. Ed. by Betty M. Twarog et al. LC 82-47510. (Society of General Physiologists Ser.: No. 37). (Illus.). 424p. Date not set. pap. 120.90 (*0-7837-7508-3*, 8247510) Bks Demand.

Basic Biology Questions for GCSE. C. Rouan & B. J. Rouan. (C). 1989. text ed. 60.00 (*0-7487-0057-9*, Pub. by S Thornes Pubs UK) St Mut.

Basic Biomechanics. Hall. 528p. (C). 1990. 41.95 (*0-8016-2087-2*) Mosby Yr Bk.

Basic Biomechanics of the Musculoskeletal System. 2nd ed. Margareta Nordin & Victor H. Frankel. LC 89-2455. (Illus.). 350p. 1989. pap. text ed. 45.00 (*0-8121-1227-X*) Williams & Wilkins.

Basic Biophysics for Biology. Edward K. Yeargers. 202p. 1992. 39.95 (*0-8493-4424-7*, QH505) CRC Pr.

Basic Bioreactor Design. K. Vant'Riet & J. Tramper. 480p. 1991. 170.00 (*0-8247-8446-4*) Dekker.

Basic Biotechnology. J. D. Bulock & B. Kristiansen. 561p. 1987. text ed. 61.00 (*0-12-140752-7*) Acad Pr.

Basic Biotechnology: A Student's Guide. Ed. by P. Prave et al. LC 87-10606. 344p. 1989. pap. text ed. 45.00 (*0-89573-646-2*) VCH Pubs.

Basic Blackjack. Stanford Wong. (Illus.). 224p. (Orig.). 1992. pap. 14.95 (*0-935926-19-4*) Pi Yee Pr.

Basic Blacksmithing: An Introduction to Toolmaking. David Harris & Bernhard Heer. (Illus.). 160p. (Orig.). 1993. pap. 24.95 (*1-85339-195-6*, Pub. by Intermed Tech UK) Women Ink.

Basic Blueprint Reading. John A. Nelson. 1990. text ed. 28.95 (*0-07-157469-7*) McGraw.

Basic Blueprint Reading. John A. Nelson. (Illus.). 256p. 1989. 28.95 (*0-8306-4273-0*); pap. 19.95 (*0-8306-3273-5*) TAB Bks.

Basic Blueprint Reading: Residential. Robert E. Putnam. LC 80-80673. (Illus.). 256p. reprint ed. pap. 73.00 (*0-8357-5974-1*, 2017842) Bks Demand.

Basic Blueprint Reading & Sketching. 5th ed. C. Thomas Olivo et al. (Illus.). 196p. 1988. pap. text ed. 21.95 (*0-8273-3084-7*) Delmar.

Basic Blueprint Reading & Sketching. 6th ed. C. Thomas Olivo et al. LC 92-35367. 199p. 1993. pap. 23.95 (*0-8273-5740-0*) Delmar.

Basic Blueprint Reading & Sketching. 6th ed. C. Thomas Olivo & Thomas P. Olivo. 1993. trans. 99.00 (*0-8273-5924-1*) Delmar.

Basic Blues Guitar. Darryl Winston. (Illus.). 56p. 1993. pap. 4.95 (*0-8256-1366-3*) Music Sales.

*__Basic Boating Skills.__ Katie Hamilton & Gene Hamilton. LC 94-28750. (Illus.). 1995. write for info. (*0-688-13205-7*) Morrow.

Basic Boogie & Blues Guitar. Date not set. 4.95 (*0-87166-820-3*, 93642) Mel Bay.

BASIC Book. 2nd ed. Penny Fanzone & Tom Hankins. Ed. by Carl Diekhans. 608p. (C). 1989. pap. text ed. write for info. (*0-394-39323-6*) Knopf.

Basic Book-Keeping & Accounts. Scheidegger Intl. Schools Ltd. Staff. (C). 1990. 90.00 (*0-7487-0426-4*, Pub. by S Thornes Pubs UK) St Mut.

Basic Book List for Church Libraries. rev. ed. Bernard E. Deitrick. LC 77-4093. 16p. 1991. pap. 4.75 (*0-665-66217-9*) CSLA.

Basic Book List for Church Libraries. 4th rev. ed. Bernard E. Deitrick. LC 77-4093. 16p. 1991. pap. 6.00 (*0-915324-32-6*) CSLA.

Basic Book of Antiques & Collectibles. 3rd ed. George Michael. LC 92-50189. (Illus.). 352p. 1992. pap. 17.95 (*0-87069-649-1*) Chilton.

Basic Book of Fish Keeping. Elizabeth Randolph. 240p. (Orig.). 1990. pap. 3.95 (*0-449-21776-0*) Fawcett.

Basic Book of Organic Gardening. Ed. by Robert Rodale. 384p. 1987. mass mkt. 4.95 (*0-345-34522-3*) Ballantine.

Basic Book of Photography. 2nd rev. ed. Tom Grimm. LC 73-90907. 384p. 1985. pap. 14.95 (*0-452-26096-5*, Plume) NAL-Dutton.

Basic Book of Synonyms & Antonyms. Laurence Urdang. 1985. pap. 4.99 (*0-451-16194-7*, Sig) NAL-Dutton.

Basic Book on Breast Cancer. Kathy C. Folkerts. (Illus.). 128p. (Orig.). 1992. pap. 9.95 (*0-932881-16-5*) Greenpl Bks.

Basic Bookbinding. Arthur W. Lewis. (Illus.). 1952. pap. 3.95 (*0-486-20169-4*) Dover.

Basic Books in the Mass Media: An Annotated, Selected Booklist Covering General Communications, Book Publishing, Broadcasting, Editorial Journalism, Film, Magazines, & Advertising. Eleanor Blum. LC 71-151998. 264p. reprint ed. pap. 75.30 (*0-8357-5975-X*, 2019052) Bks Demand.

Basic Bowl Turning: With Judy Ditmer. Judith A. Ditmer. Ed. by Douglas Congdon-Martin. LC 94-65624. (Illus.). 64p. (Orig.). 1994. pap. 12.95 (*0-88740-627-0*) Schiffer.

Basic Brachot: The All New Shema Is for Real Curriculum. Joel L. Grishaver. (Illus.). (ENG & HEB.). 1988. pap. 5.50 (*0-933873-30-1*) Torah Aura.

Basic Brachot Teacher's Edition. Joel L. Grishaver. (Shema Is for Real Ser.). (Illus.). 128p. (ENG & HEB.). 1988. pap. 5.50 (*0-933873-33-6*) Torah Aura.

Basic Bridge in Three Weeks: The Beginner's 21-Day Guide To Bridge Mastery. Alan Truscott. (Illus.). 224p. 1987. pap. 8.95 (*0-399-51377-9*, Perigree Bks) Berkley Pub.

Basic Buddhism. Kevin O'Neil. 41p. (Orig.). 1981. pap. 5.00 (*0-86627-006-X*) Crises Res Pr.

Basic Buddhist Concepts. Kogen Mizuno. 176p. (Orig.). 1987. pap. 9.95 (*4-333-01203-1*, Pub. by Kosei Pub Co JA) C E Tuttle.

Basic Budget Guide for Small Cities & Counties. rev. ed. Arthur B. Mohor, Jr. 49p. 1985. pap. 6.00 (*0-89854-112-3*) U of GA Inst Govt.

*__Basic Budgeting.__ 64p. 1995. 4.24 (*0-7872-1002-1*, V402) Kendall-Hunt.

Basic Budgeting. 2nd ed. Ewing. (VAP Ser.: No. V402). 64p. 1992. 11.74 (*0-8403-7581-6*) Kendall-Hunt.

*__Basic Budgeting for Churches.__ Jack A. Henry. LC 94-23532. 1995. 10.99 (*0-8054-6175-2*) Broadman.

Basic Budgeting Practices for Librarians. 2nd ed. Richard S. Rounds. LC 93-47476. 180p. 1994. pap. 25.00 (*0-8389-0630-3*) ALA.

Basic Business Bankruptcy Nineteen Ninety-Two. (Commercial Law & Practice Ser.). 227p. 1992. pap. text ed. 70.00 (*0-685-56875-X*, A4-4376) PLI.

Basic Business Communication. 5th ed. Raymond V. Lesikar, Sr. (Business Communication Ser.). (C). 1990. student ed 17.95 (*0-256-08614-1*); text ed. 54.95 (*0-256-08327-4*) Irwin.

*__Basic Business Communication.__ 6th ed. Raymond Lesikar et al. 136p. (C). 1994. student ed, text ed. 19.50 (*0-256-11059-X*) Irwin.

Basic Business Communication. 6th ed. Raymond V. Lesikar, Sr. LC 92-19974. 761p. (C). 1992. text ed. 59.95 (*0-256-10936-2*) Irwin.

*__Basic Business Communication, Canadian.__ Raymond Lesikar et al. 688p. (C). 1993. text ed. 43.75 (*0-256-11690-3*) Irwin.

Basic Business English. Patricia A. Parzych et al. 429p. (C). 1986. pap. text ed. 22.75 (*0-15-504905-4*) HB Coll Pubs.

Basic Business English. 2nd ed. Robert E. Barry. (Illus.). 384p. 1986. pap. text ed. write for info. (*0-13-057225-X*) P-H.

Basic Business Finance. Mel Tainiter. 130p. disk 95.00 (*0-934577-03-X*) Softext Pub.

Basic Business Forecasting. Mel Tainiter. 120p. 1986. disk 95.00 (*0-934577-04-8*) Softext Pub.

Basic Business Graphics. Mel Tainiter. 125p. disk 95.00 (*0-934577-05-6*) Softext Pub.

Basic Business Law. 2nd ed. Charles F. Hemphill, Jr. & Judy A. Long. LC 92-47120. 1993. text ed. write for info. (*0-13-059437-7*) P-H.

Basic Business Library: Core Resources. 3rd ed. Bernard S. Schlessinger. LC 94-22809. 368p. 1994. boxed 39.50 (*0-89774-739-9*) Oryx Pr.

Basic Business Math. Robert L. Dansby. 240p. (C). 1991. pap. text ed. write for info. (*0-13-060971-4*) P-H.

Basic Business Math. Richard Truchon. Ed. by Mike Crisp. LC 89-81953. (Fifty-Minute Ser.). (Illus.). 100p. (Orig.). 1990. pap. 9.95 (*1-56052-024-8*) Crisp Pubns.

*__Basic Business Math & Electronic Calculators.__ Ronald Merchant. 384p. (C). 1995. pap. text ed. 32.95 (*0-89863-189-0*) Star Pub CA.

Basic Business Math & Electronic Calculators. 4th ed. Ronald Merchant. 306p. 1989. pap. text ed. 29.95 (*0-89863-130-0*) Star Pub CA.

Basic Business Mathematics. 4th ed. Gerald Pintel & Jay Diamond. 432p. (C). 1989. pap. text ed. write for info. (*0-13-058728-1*) P-H.

Basic Business Statistics. E. J. Freed. 450p. (C). 1990. text ed. 53.25 (*0-15-504900-3*) Dryden Pr.

Basic Business Statistics. Jarrell. (Illus.). 544p. (C). 1988. Instr.'s manual. teacher ed write for info. (*0-318-62191-6*, H06331); Test bank. teacher ed write for info. (*0-318-62192-4*, H14269) Allyn.

Basic Business Statistics. Bernard J. Landwehr. LC 84-26195. 246p. (C). 1985. lib. bdg. 24.50 (*0-89874-823-2*) Krieger.

Basic Business Statistics. Mel Tainiter. 133p. 1985. disk 95.00 (*0-934577-06-4*) Softext Pub.

Basic Business Statistics. 5th ed. Mark L. Berenson & David M. Levine. 1011p. (C). 1992. text ed. write for info. (*0-13-099540-1*) P-H.

Basic Business Statistics: An Intuitive Approach. Rex Toh & Michael Hu. Ed. by Clyde Perlee. 871p. (C). 1991. text ed. 65.25 (*0-314-74396-0*) West Pub.

Basic Business Statistics: Concepts & Applications. 2nd ed. Mark L. Berenson & David M. Levine. (Illus.). 752p. (C). 1983. student ed 10.95 (*0-685-06112-4*) P-H.

Basic Business Statistics: Concepts & Applications. 3rd ed. Mark L. Berenson et al. (Illus.). 816p. (C). 1987. Wkbk. using minitab. student ed write for info. (*0-13-057779-0*) P-H.

Basic Business Statistics: Concepts & Applications. 6th ed. Mark L. Berenson & David M. Levine. LC 94-12551. 1995. text ed. write for info. (*0-13-303009-1*) P-H.

Basic Business Statistics for Managers. Alan S. Donnahoe. LC 87-24273. (Illus.). 228p. 1988. text ed. 34.95 (*0-471-62939-1*) Wiley.

BASIC Business Subroutines for the Apple II & Apple IIe. Alan G. Porter & Martin G. Rezmer. 160p. 1983. pap. write for info. (*0-201-05663-1*) Addison-Wesley.

Basic Butchering of Livestock & Game: Beef, Veal, Hogs, Lamb, Poultry, Rabbits, Venison. John J. Mettler, Jr. LC 85-70195. (Illus.). 208p. 1986. pap. 11.95 (*0-88266-391-7*, Garden Way Pub) Storey Comm Inc.

Basic C. N. C. Programming. Kenneth J. Laviana. Ed. by E. D. Cormier. 115p. (C). 1983. pap. text ed. 19.95 (*0-912227-00-1*) C E Pub.

Basic Calculations for Chemical & Biological Analyses. J. S. Bassey. 150p. 1993. pap. 43.00 (*0-935584-51-X*) AOAC Intl.

Basic Calculations in Biological Chemistry. Bassey J. Efiok. Ed. by Andrew Philips. (Illus.). 210p. (C). 1991. 23.95 (*0-9629214-0-8*) Intl Spectrum.

Basic Call to Consciousness. rev. ed. Ed. by Akwesasne Notes. LC 91-16048. (Illus.). 128p. 1992. 7.95 (*0-913990-23-X*) Book Pub Co.

Basic Calligraphic Hands. Tom Gourdie et al. (Illus.). 64p. 1986. pap. 5.95 (*0-8008-0667-0*) Taplinger.

Basic Camcorder Guide. rev. ed. Steve Bryant. (Illus.). 128p. 1994. pap. 12.95 (*0-936262-29-X*) Amherst Media.

*__Basic Camp Management: An Introduction to Camp Administration.__ 4th ed. Armand Ball & Beverly Ball. 250p. 1995. per. 19.95 (*0-87603-145-9*) Am Camping.

Basic Canoeing for Pathfinders: A Youth Enrichment Skill. rev. ed. John Malo. Ed. by L. S. Gattis. (Illus.). (Orig.). 1987. pap. 5.00 (*0-936241-17-9*) Cheetah Pub.

Basic Canoeing Workbook. James C. Martini. (Illus.). 98p. (Orig.). 1992. 3.95 (*1-881644-00-6*) P E R Assocs.

Basic Cantonese Cooking. James Rollband. (Illus.). 224p. 1993. reprint ed. pap. 10.95 (*1-880188-45-7*) Bess Pr.

Basic Car Care. (Fix-It-Yourself Ser.). (Illus.). 144p. 1988. 17.27 (*0-8094-6224-9*); lib. bdg. 23.27 (*0-8094-6225-7*) Time-Life.

*__Basic Cardiac Life Support (BCLS) "Quick Reference Guide" in Algorithm Format.__ 2nd ed. Ed. by Jean K. Pals et al. 36p. 1994. pap. text ed. 3.50 (*1-887272-03-8*) Amer Med Pub.

Basic Cardiac Rhythms - Made Easy! Beverly Kempf. (Illus.). 80p. (C). 1992. pap. text ed. 19.95 (*0-9635791-0-X*) Dimensions.

*__Basic Carpentry.__ 1995. pap. 9.99 (*0-376-01580-2*) Sunset Menlo Pk.

Basic Carpentry Illustrated. Ed. by Southern Living Staff. (Southern Living Home Improvement Ser.). (Illus.). 112p. 1992. pap. 8.99 (*0-376-09033-2*) Oxmoor Hse.

Basic Carpentry Illustrated. 2nd rev. ed. Sunset Magazine & Book Editors. LC 84-80610. (Illus.). 112p. 1984. pap. 9.99 (*0-376-01015-0*) Sunset Menlo Pk.

Basic Carpentry Techniques. T. Jeff Williams & Ortho Books Editorial Staff. LC 80-85220. (Illus.). 112p. (Orig.). 1982. pap. 9.95 (*0-917102-95-9*) Ortho Info.

Basic Cartography: For Students & Technicians - Exercise Manual. Ed. by R. W. Anson & F. J. Ormeling, Jr. 288p. 1991. pap. text ed. 45.00 (*1-85166-590-0*) Elsevier.

Basic Cartography for Students & Technicians. 2nd ed. Ed. by R. W. Anson & F. J. Ormeling. LC 93-35427. 1994. text ed. 128.00 (*0-08-042343-4*, Pergamon Pr); pap. text ed. 41.50 (*0-08-042344-2*, Pergamon Pr) Elsevier.

Basic Cases in Constitutional Law. 3rd ed. W. Duane Lockard. 1991. 20.95 (*0-87187-610-8*) Congr Quarterly.

Basic Catechism. Daughters of St Paul. LC 80-149. 1980. pap. 2.95 (*0-8198-0623-4*) Pauline Bks.

Basic Catechism of Christian Doctrine. AMI Press. 1991. 0.25 (*1-56036-022-4*) AMI Pr.

Basic Category Theory for Computer Science. Benjamin C. Pierce. 128p. 1991. pap. 22.00 (*0-262-66071-7*) MIT Pr.

Basic Catholic Beliefs for Today: The Creed Explained. Leonard F. Badia. LC 84-14632. 170p. (Orig.). 1984. pap. 8.95 (*0-8189-0469-0*) Alba.

Basic Catholic Dictionary. Owen O'Sullivan. (C). 1988. 50.00 (*0-685-22279-9*, Pub. by St Paul Pubns UK) St Mut.

*__Basic Cell Culture: A Practical Approach.__ Ed. by J. M. Davis. (Practical Approach Ser.: No. 146). (Illus.). 328p. 1995. pap. text ed. 48.00 (*0-19-963433-5*) OUP.

*__Basic Cell Culture: A Practical Approach.__ Ed. by J. M. Davis. (The Practical Approach Ser.: No. 146). (Illus.). 328p. 1995. spiral bd. 88.00 (*0-19-963434-3*) OUP.

Basic Chemical Principles. Edward I. Peters. 400p. (C). 1988. text ed. 34.75 (*0-03-004809-5*) SCP.

Basic Chemical Safety Principles, Vol. 3. Forum for Scientific Excellence, Inc. Staff. (Practical Guide to Safety Compliance Standards for Medical Facilities Ser.). 100p. 1991. ring bd. 50.00 (*0-87489-586-3*) Med Economics.

Basic Chemical Thermodynamics. 4th ed. E. Brian Smith. (Oxford Chemistry Ser.: No. 35). (Illus.). 180p. (C). 1990. pap. 22.95 (*0-19-855564-4*) OUP.

Basic Chemistry. (Basic Academics Ser.: Module 6). (Illus.). 60p. 1982. spiral bd. 17.50 (*0-87683-230-3*) GP Pub.

Basic Chemistry. Roger D. Barry. LC 74-79831. (Health Occupations Ser.). 1975. 7.50 (*0-672-61377-8*, Bobbs); 3.71 (*0-672-61432-4*, Bobbs); pap. text ed. 13.92 (*0-672-61376-X*, Bobbs) Macmillan.

Basic Chemistry. 2nd ed. Steven S. Zumdahl. 575p. (C). 1993. pap. text ed. write for info. (*0-669-32858-8*); Transparencies. trans. write for info. (*0-318-70078-6*); Instr.'s annotated. write for info. (*0-318-70074-3*); Study guide. write for info. (*0-318-70075-1*); Solutions guide. write for info. (*0-318-70076-X*); Complete solutions guide. write for info. (*0-318-70077-8*); Test item file. write for info. (*0-318-70079-4*) Heath.

Basic Chemistry. 6th ed. G. William Daub & William S. Seese. 710p. (C). 1991. text ed. write for info. (*0-13-059171-8*) P-H.

Basic Chemistry: A Problem Solving Approach. Julien Gendell. Ed. by Conty. LC 92-18201. (Illus.). 550p. (C). 1993. text ed. 57.50 (*0-314-01283-4*); pap. text ed. 50.75 (*0-314-01194-3*) West Pub.

Basic Chemistry: An Introductory Approach - a Self-Teaching Textbook - Workbook. Peggy J. McClure & Arrie F. Boyd. 640p. (C). 1994. per., pap. text ed. 61.95 (*0-8403-8849-7*) Kendall-Hunt.

Basic Chemistry: General, Organic, Biological. Denis M. Callewaert & Julien Genyea. 1980. text ed. 54.95x (*0-87901-130-0*) Worth.

*__Basic Chemistry for Biology.__ Carolyn Chapman. 224p. (C). 1995. spiral bd. write for info. (*0-697-24121-1*) Wm C Brown Pubs.

Basic Chemistry in Microscale. David P. Licata. 30p. 1993. 9.95 (*0-9636095-1-3*) Licatas Edutype.

Basic Chemistry One. Dunmire et al. 160p. (C). 1992. pap. text ed. 10.95 (*0-8403-7873-4*) Kendall-Hunt.

*__Basic Chemometric for Quantitative Analysis.__ Kramer. Date not set. text ed. 39.95 (*0-471-11063-9*) Wiley.

Basic Chess Endings. Reuben Fine. (Illus.). 1979. pap. 17.00 (*0-679-14002-6*, 3, Tarten) McKay.

An Asterisk (*) at the beginning of an entry indicates that the title is appearing in BIP for the first time.

An Asterisk (*) at the beginning of an entry indicates that the title is appearing in BIP for the first time.

Basic Considerations of Christian Baptism: A Nonsectarian Approach to the Important Subject of Christian Baptism. William C. Clearman. 1994. 14.95 (*0-533-10985-X*) Vantage.

Basic Construction BPR. 2nd ed. Mark W. Huth. 1989. 23.95 (*0-8273-3233-5*); teacher ed 12.00 (*0-8273-3234-3*) Delmar.

Basic Construction Management. 3rd ed. Leon Rogers. Ed. by Sharon Lamberton. 80p. 1994. 23.00 (*0-685-74771-9*) Home Builder.

Basic Construction Management: The Superintendent's Job. 2nd ed. Leon Rogers & Jerry Householder. (Illus.). 63p. 1990. pap. 21.00 (*0-86718-342-X*) Home Builder.

***Basic Construction Management: The Superintendent's Job.** 3rd rev. ed. Leon Rogers. LC 95-12274. (Illus.). 96p. 1995. pap. 27.50 (*0-86718-406-X*) Home Builder.

Basic Construction Materials: Methods & Testing. 3rd ed. Charles A. Herubin & Theodore Masotta. (Illus.). 342p. (C). 1986. text ed. 75.00 (*0-8359-0394-X*) P-H.

Basic Construction Materials: Methods & Testing. 4th ed. Theodore W. Marotta & Charles A. Herubin. LC 92-14288. 480p. (C). 1992. text ed. 36.00 (*0-13-059585-3*) P-H.

Basic Construction Math Review: A Manual of Basic Construction Mathematics for Contractor & Tradesman License Exams. Dave Buster. 104p. 1973. pap. 18.95 (*0-935715-06-1*, 0083) Construct Bkstore.

Basic Construction Techniques for Houses & Small Buildings. U. S. Navy, Bureau of Naval Personnel Staff. (Illus.). 568p. 1972. reprint ed. pap. 10.95 (*0-486-20242-9*) Dover.

Basic Construction Techniques for Houses & Small Buildings, 2 vols., Set. 1993. lib. bdg. 627.95 (*0-8490-9008-3*) Gordon Pr.

Basic Construction Techniques for Houses & Small Buildings Simply Explained. Bureau of Naval Personnel Staff. (Illus.). 17.25 (*0-8446-4506-0*) Peter Smith.

Basic Content Analysis. Robert P. Weber. (Quantitative Applications in the Social Sciences Ser.: Vol. 49). (Illus.). 96p. (C). 1990. pap. 9.95 (*0-8039-3863-2*) Sage.

***Basic Continuous Improvement Tools Handbook.** Council for Continuous Improvement Staff. (Illus.). 85p. 1994. pap. text ed. 11.95 (*0-527-76233-4*, 762334) Qual Resc.

Basic Contract Law: Cases On. 5th ed. Melvin A. Eisenberg. (American Casebook Ser.). 1037p. 1991. reprint ed. text ed. 50.00 (*0-314-71858-3*) West Pub.

***Basic Contracts & Checklists for Petroleum Marketing.** Samuel L. Perkins. 1995. 69.95 (*0-9644877-0-5*) Petrol Pub Grp.

Basic Control System Technology. C. J. Chesmond. 1991. pap. 46.95 (*0-442-30386-6*) Chapman & Hall.

Basic Conversational French. 8th ed. Constance K. Knop et al. 604p. (C). 1987. text ed. 45.25 (*0-03-004362-X*) HB Coll Pubs.

Basic Conversations in English, Bk. 2. Robert Lado. (Illus.). 131p. (C). 1993. pap. text ed. 8.95 (*1-879580-54-3*) Lado Intl Pr.

Basic Conversations in English: Book I. Robert Lado. (Illus.). (Orig.). (C). 1992. pap. text ed. 8.95 (*1-879580-50-0*) Lado Intl Pr.

BASIC Cookbook. Ken Tracton. (Illus.). 1978. pap. 5.95 (*0-8306-1055-3*, 1055) TAB Bks.

BASIC Cookbook. 2nd ed. Ken Tracton & Thomas A. Wells. 168p. 1985. 12.95 (*0-8306-0855-9*, 1855) TAB Bks.

Basic Cookery. 3rd ed. Richard Martland & Welsby. 708p. 1993. 23.00 (*0-7506-0532-4*) Buttrwrth-Heinemann.

Basic Cookery: The Process Approach. Ed. by S. Stevenson. (C). 1990. 90.00 (*0-7487-0421-3*, Pub. by S Thornes Pubs UK) St Mut.

***Basic Corporate Law & Business Organizations.** Deborah L. Kutzavich. LC 94-35101. (Legal Studies Ser.). 1994. write for info. (*0-02-801358-1*) Shepards-McGraw.

***Basic Corporate Law & Business Organizations.** Deborah L. Kutzavitch. LC 94-35101. (Legal Studies Ser.). 1994. write for info. (*0-02-801348-4*); student ed write for info. (*0-02-801356-5*); teacher ed write for info. (*0-02-801357-3*) Shepards-McGraw.

Basic Corporate Practice. 2nd ed. George C. Seward & W. John Nauss, Jr. 500p. 1977. 15.00 (*0-317-30786-X*, B129) Am Law Inst.

Basic Corporation Law: Materials-Cases-Text. 3rd ed. Detlev F. Vagts. (University Casebook Ser.). 818p. 1988. text ed. 38.50 (*0-88277-679-7*) Foundation Pr.

Basic Corporation Law: Materials-Cases-Text, Manual for Teachers to Accompany. Detlev F. Vagts. (University Casebook Ser.). 66p. 1990. pap. text ed. write for info. (*0-88277-712-2*) Foundation Pr.

Basic Corporation Law, Materials - Cases - Text: Documentary Supplement. 3rd ed. Detlev F. Vagts. (University Casebook Ser.). 110p. 1988. pap. text ed. 6.95 (*0-88277-701-7*) Foundation Pr.

Basic Cost Engineering. 2nd expanded rev. ed. Humphreys & Wellman. (Cost Engineering Ser.: Vol. 10). 368p. 1987. 59.75 (*0-8247-7630-5*) Dekker.

Basic Country Blues Guitar Solos. Date not set. 4.95 (*1-56222-301-1*, 93411) Mel Bay.

Basic Country Style Guitar. Date not set. 4.95 (*1-56222-817-X*, 95011) Mel Bay.

Basic Course for Reading Attic Greek. Frank J. Groten, Jr. & James K. Finn. LC 85-234367. 284p. (YA). (gr. 9-12). 1990. reprint ed. 19.90 (*0-942573-50-1*) Hill School.

Basic Course Home Economics - Masters. N. Nuffield. (C). 1989. 200.00 (*0-09-145581-2*, Pub. by S Thornes Pubs UK) St Mut.

Basic Course Home Economics - Pupils. Stanley Thornes. (C). 1989. 80.00 (*0-09-145601-0*, Pub. by S Thornes Pubs UK) St Mut.

Basic Course Home Economics - Teacher's Book. Stanley Thornes. (C). 1989. 125.00 (*0-09-145591-X*, Pub. by S Thornes Pubs UK) St Mut.

Basic Course in Algebraic Topology. W. S. Massey. Ed. by J. H. Ewing et al. (Graduate Texts in Mathematics Ser.: Vol. 127). (Illus.). 480p. 1993. 49.95 (*0-387-97430-X*) Spr-Verlag.

Basic Course in American Sign Language. Humphries et al. (Illus.). 288p. 1994. pap. text ed., spiral bd. 27.95 (*0-932666-42-6*) T J Pubs.

Basic Course in American Sign Language. 2nd ed. Humphries et al. (Illus.). 288p. 1994. text ed. 24.95x (*0-932666-43-4*) T J Pubs.

***Basic Course in Arabic.** S. Badawi. (Kitab al Assasi Ser.). 1994. audio 150.00 (*0-86685-641-2*) Intl Bk Ctr.

***Basic Course in Arabic, Bk. 1.** S. Badawi. (Kitab al Assasi Ser.). (ARA.). 1994. 29.95 (*0-86685-638-2*) Intl Bk Ctr.

***Basic Course in Arabic, Bk. 2.** S. Badawi. 1994. 34.95 (*0-86685-639-0*) Intl Bk Ctr.

***Basic Course in Arabic, Bk. 3.** S. Badawi. 1994. 34.95 (*0-86685-640-4*) Intl Bk Ctr.

Basic Course in Civil Procedure, 1993: Supplement to Materials For. 6th ed. Kevin M. Clermont. (University Casebook Ser.). 95p. 1993. pap. text ed. 6.95 (*1-56662-083-X*) Foundation Pr.

Basic Course in Estonian. 3rd rev. ed. Felix Oinas. LC 66-63527. (Uralic & Altaic Ser.: Vol. 54). 393p. 1968. reprint ed. 39.00 (*0-87750-018-5*) Res Inst Inner Asian Studies.

Basic Course in Gulf Arabic. Hamdi Qafisheh. 482p. 1975. 25.00 (*0-86685-048-1*) Intl Bk Ctr.

Basic Course in Gulf Arabic. Hamdi A. Qafisheh. 482p. 1975. pap. 22.95 (*0-8165-0483-0*) U of Ariz Pr.

Basic Course in Manual Communication. Terrence J. O'Rourke. (Illus.). 1973. 11.95 (*0-913072-01-X*) Natl Assn Deaf.

Basic Course in Mongolian. John Hangin. Ed. by John R. Krueger. LC 67-65320. (Uralic & Altaic Ser.: Vol. 73). 208p. 1968. 24.90 (*0-87750-074-6*) Res Inst Inner Asian Studies.

Basic Course in Moroccan Arabic. Richard S. Harrell. (Richard Slade Harrell Arabic Ser.). 395p. 1965. pap. 14.95 (*0-87840-005-2*) Georgetown U Pr.

Basic Course in Moroccan Arabic, Set. Richard S. Harrell. (Richard Slade Harrell Arabic Ser.). 395p. 1965. audio 120.00 (*0-87840-014-1*) Georgetown U Pr.

Basic Course in Statistics. 3rd ed. G. M. Clarke & D. Cooke. LC 92-19729. 451p. 1992. pap. text ed. 36.95 (*0-470-21942-4*) Halsted Pr.

Basic Course in Vegetarian & Vegan Nutrition. George L. Eisman. (Illus.). 152p. 1993. pap. text ed. 18.95 (*0-9614435-0-2*) Diet-Ethics.

Basic Coursebuilding. Maureen Summers. (Threshold Picture Guides Ser.). (Illus.). 24p. (Orig.). 1991. pap. 10.00 (*1-872082-10-6*, Pub. by Threshhold Bks UK) Half Halt Pr.

Basic CPT for the Hospital Coder. J. A. Holloway. 85p. 1983. 35.00 (*0-317-05422-8*) Am Hlth Info.

Basic Crafts. John R. Lindbeck et al. (gr. 7-12). 1979. text ed. 18.60 (*0-02-662430-3*); student ed 5.20 (*0-02-662440-0*) Bennett IL.

Basic Criminal Law. 2nd ed. Allen Z. Gammage & Charles F. Hemphill, Jr. 1979. text ed. 39.95 (*0-07-022756-X*) McGraw.

Basic Criminal Law: Cases & Materials. 3rd ed. George E. Dix & M. Michael Sharlot. 672p. (C). 1987. text ed. 57.50 (*0-314-34733-X*) West Pub.

Basic Criminal Procedure. Stephen A. Saltzburg et al. LC 93-45340. (Black Letter Ser.). 641p. 1993. pap. text ed. 22.50 (*0-314-02734-3*) West Pub.

Basic Criminal Procedure, Cases, Comments & Questions. 7th ed. Yale Kamisar et al. (American Casebook Ser.). 792p. 1990. reprint ed. pap. text ed. 41.00 (*0-314-69124-3*) West Pub.

***Basic Criminal Procedure, Cases, Comments & Questions.** 8th ed. Yale Kamisar et al. (American Casebook Ser.). 859p. 1994. pap. text ed. write for info. (*0-314-04513-9*) West Pub.

Basic Criteria for Indexes. (National Information Standards Ser.). 1984. 14.00 (*0-88738-997-X*, Z39.4) Transaction Pubs.

Basic Crystal Wand Handbook, Vol. 1. John Teal. Ed. by I. G. O. S. Society Staff. LC 93-79379. (Illus.). 61p. (Orig.). 1993. 25.00 (*1-883147-15-8*) Intern Guild ASRS.

Basic Cursive Handwriting. Bearl Brooks. (Handwriting Ser.). 24p. (gr. 2-3). 1979. student ed 5.00 (*0-8209-0270-5*, W-2) ESP.

Basic Cutaneous Surgery: A Primer in Technique. Christopher B. Zachary. (Practical Manuals in Dermatologic Surgery Ser.). (Illus.). 134p. 1991. pap. text ed. 32.00 (*0-443-08660-5*) Churchill.

Basic Darkroom Book: A Complete Guide to Processing & Printing Color & Black-&-White Photographs. Tom Grimm & Michele Grimm. (Orig.). (YA). (gr. 9). 1978. pap. 9.95 (*0-452-25892-8*, Plume) NAL-Dutton.

Basic Darkroom Book: A Complete Guide to Processing & Printing Color & Black-&-White Photographs. rev. ed. Tom Grimm. LC 86-18063. (Illus.). 346p. (Orig.). 1986. pap. 14.95 (*0-452-26019-1*, Plume) NAL-Dutton.

Basic Data Communications. William J. Beyda. 288p. 1989. text ed. 50.67 (*0-13-058421-5*) P-H.

Basic Data Communications: A Comprehensive Overview. William J. Beyda. 384p. 1989. boxed 29.00 (*0-13-092040-1*) P-H.

Basic Data of Plasma Physics: The Fundamental Data on Electrical Discharges in Gases. Sanborn C. Brown. LC 93-27400. (American Vacuum Society Classics Ser.). (Illus.). 336p. 1994. pap. text ed. 35.00 (*1-56396-273-X*, AIP Pr) Am Inst Physics.

Basic Data on Fertility in the Provinces of China, 1940-1982. Ansley J. Coale & Sheng L. Chen. LC 86-32765. (Papers of the East-West Population Institute: No. 104). (Illus.). xviii, 366p. (Orig.). 1987. pap. 5.00 (*0-86638-088-4*) EW Ctr HI.

Basic Data Underlying Clinical Decision Making in Vascular Surgery. Ed. by John M. Porter & Lloyd Taylor. 1994. 75.00 (*0-942219-71-6*) Quality Med Pub.

Basic DC Electricity for HVAC. Richard Hunter. 1980. student ed 9.00 (*0-8064-0335-7*, 832); audio 379.00 (*0-8064-0336-5*) Bergwall.

BASIC Decision Making on the Microcomputer. Peter M. Ginter & Andrew C. Rucks. 475p. (C). 1985. pap. text ed. write for info. (*0-394-33928-2*) Random.

Basic Decompression Theory & Application. B. R. Wienke. 105p. (Orig.). (C). 1991. pap. text ed. 19.95 (*0-941332-17-9*) Best Pub Co.

Basic Democracies & Rural Development in Pakistan. Norman K. Nicholson & Dilawar A. Khan. (Special Series on Rural Local Government: No. 10). 99p. (Orig.). (C). 1974. pap. text ed. 3.50 (*0-86731-096-0*) Cornell CIS RDC.

***Basic Dental Anatomy.** Margaret Dickenson. 175p. (C). 1994. 18.80 (*1-56870-147-0*) RonJon Pub.

Basic Design: Systems, Elements, Applications. John A. Richardson et al. (Illus.). 320p. (C). 1984. pap. text ed. write for info. (*0-13-060186-1*) P-H.

Basic Design & Utilization of Instructional Television. 2nd ed. Kenneth Coffelt & Bob Combs. (Bridges for Ideas Handbook Ser.). 1981. pap. text ed. 6.00 (*0-913648-13-2*) U Tex Austin Film Lib.

Basic Design of Two-Stroke Engines. Gordon P. Blair. 692p. 1990. text ed. 85.00 (*1-56091-008-9*, R104) Soc Auto Engineers.

Basic Desktop Design & Layout. David Collier & Bob Cotton. (Illus.). 160p. 1989. 27.95 (*0-89134-285-0*, 30130) North Light Bks.

***Basic Developing & Printing in Black & White.** Eastman. 1995. pap. text ed. 9.95 (*0-87985-006-X*) Saunders Photo.

***Basic Developing & Printing in Black & White.** rev. ed. Eastman Kodak Company Staff. (Illus.). 72p. (C). Date not set. pap. text ed. write for info. (*0-87985-755-2*, Kodak) Saunders Photo.

Basic Developing, Printing, Enlarging in Color (AE-13) Eastman Kodak Co. Staff. LC 90-85296. (Illus.). 99p. 1992. spiral bd. 12.95 (*0-87985-662-9*) Saunders Photo.

Basic Developmental Screening. 5th ed. R. Illingworth. 1990. pap. 19.95 (*0-632-02905-6*) Blackwell Sci.

Basic Dharma: An Introduction to the Nature of Mind. Ole Nydahl. Ed. by Paul M. Clemens. 32p. 1988. pap. 5.00 (*0-931892-17-1*) B Dolphin Pub.

Basic Dianetics Picture Book: Taken from the Works of L. Ron Hubbard. 1991. pap. 15.00 (*0-88404-727-X*) Bridge Pubns Inc.

Basic Dictionary of Construction. 23th ed. Jose Zurita Ruiz. 248p. (SPA.). 1991. pap. write for info. (*0-7859-4924-0*) Fr & Eur.

Basic Dictionary of English. 2nd ed. G. Capelle. (Illus.). 176p. 1987. pap. text ed. 5.00 (*0-13-058876-8*, 21422) Prentice ESL.

Basic Diemaking. D. Eugene Ostergaard. (Diemaking Ser.). 208p. (Orig.). 1982. pap. 37.95 (*0-910399-34-4*) McGraw.

Basic Diesel Operation & Maintenance. Daniel Ash. LC 84-730280. 1984. student ed 8.00 (*0-8064-0199-0*, 475); audio 239.00 (*0-8064-0200-8*) Bergwall.

BASIC Differential Equations. J. C. Mason & D. C. Stocks. (Basic Ser.). (Illus.). 144p. 1987. pap. text ed. 24.95 (*0-408-01520-9*) Buttrwrth-Heinemann.

Basic Digital Electronics. J. A. Strong. (Illus.). 224p. 1991. pap. 30.95 (*0-442-30832-9*) Chapman & Hall.

Basic Digital Electronics. 2nd ed. Ray Ryan & Lisa A. Doyle. 1990. pap. text ed. 17.95 (*0-07-156112-9*) McGraw.

Basic Digital Electronics. 2nd ed. Ray Ryan. (Illus.). 250p. 1990. pap. 16.95 (*0-8306-3370-7*) TAB Bks.

Basic Digital Electronics: Understanding Number Systems, Boolean Algebra & Logical Circuits. Ray Ryan. LC 74-14326. (Illus.). 1975. pap. 11.95 (*0-8306-3728-1*, 728P) TAB Bks.

***Basic Digital Electronics: With an Emphasis on Practical Design & VSLI.** John R. Burger. (Illus.). (C). 1995. lib. bdg. write for info. (*0-89464-907-8*) Krieger.

Basic Digital Electronics see Digital Electronics

Basic Digital Electronics with MSI Applications. John A. Dempsey. LC 75-9009. 320p. (C). 1976. text ed. write for info. (*0-201-01478-5*) Addison-Wesley.

Basic Digital Photography. Norman Breslow. (Illus.). 212p. 1990. 32.50 (*0-240-80055-9*, Focal) Buttrwrth-Heinemann.

BASIC Digital Signal Processing. G. B. Lockhart. (BASIC Bks.). (Illus.). 160p. 1989. pap. text ed. 24.95 (*0-408-01578-0*) Buttrwrth-Heinemann.

Basic Dilemmas in the Social Sciences. Hubert M. Blalock. LC 83-24590. 184p. reprint ed. pap. 52.50 (*0-7837-6588-6*, 2046153) Bks Demand.

Basic Discipleship. Floyd McClung. LC 92-14863. 192p. 1992. reprint ed. pap. 9.99 (*0-8308-1319-5*) InterVarsity.

BASIC Disk I-O Faster & Better & Other Mysteries. Lewis Rosenfelder. 432p. 1984. 29.95 (*0-936200-09-X*) Blue Cat.

***Basic Diving Physics & Application.** Bruce Wienke. 320p. (C). 1994. 14.95 (*0-941332-41-1*) Best Pub Co.

Basic Doctrines of the Bible. A. Schuetze. 1969. pap. 3.95 (*0-8100-0016-4*, 09N0921) Northwest Pub.

Basic Documents: Including Amendments Adopted up to February 1986. 36th ed. 180p. 1986. pap. 9.00 (*92-4-165036-2*) World Health.

Basic Documents in American History. Richard B. Morris. LC 80-12822. (Anvil Ser.). 194p. 1980. reprint ed. pap. text ed. 10.50 (*0-89874-202-1*) Krieger.

Basic Documents in International Law. 3rd ed. Ed. by Ian Brownlie. 1983. pap. 29.95 (*0-19-876159-7*) OUP.

***Basic Documents in International Law.** 4th ed. Ed. by Ian Brownlie. 430p. 1995. 65.00 (*0-19-876380-8*); pap. 24.95 (*0-19-876381-6*) OUP.

Basic Documents in Iranian Law. Comp. by K. Eftikhar. 1987. 110.00 (*0-946706-35-2*, Pub. by Royston Ltd) St Mut.

Basic Documents in Iraqi Law. 1988. 135.00 (*0-946706-33-6*, Pub. by Royston Ltd) St Mut.

Basic Documents in Medieval History. Norton Downs. LC 92-24092. (Anvil Ser.). 190p. (C). 1992. reprint ed. pap. 12.50 (*0-89464-788-1*) Krieger.

Basic Documents in United States Foreign Policy. Thomas Brockway. (Anvil Ser.). 192p. (Orig.). 1957. reprint ed. pap. 9.50 (*0-685-07014-X*) Krieger.

Basic Documents of African Regional Organizations, 4 vols., Set. Ed. by Louis B. Sohn. LC 72-141326. 1973. 190.00 (*0-379-00361-9*) Oceana.

Basic Documents of American Public Administration since 1950. Ed. by Richard J. Stillman, II. LC 82-11726. 321p. 1983. 36.50 (*0-8419-0818-4*); pap. 16.95 (*0-8419-0819-2*) Holmes & Meier.

Basic Documents of American Public Administration, 1776-1950. Ed. by Frederick C. Mosher. LC 76-13866. 225p. (C). 1976. text ed. 27.95 (*0-8419-0275-5*); pap. 15.95 (*0-8419-0276-3*) Holmes & Meier.

Basic Documents of Asian Regional Organizations, 1974-85, 9 vols., Set. Michael Haas. LC 74-2248. 1984. 430.00 (*0-379-00177-2*) Oceana.

Basic Documents of International Economic Law, 2 vols., Set. American Society of International Law Staff. Ed. by Stephen Zamora & Ronald A. Brand. 1990. 100.00 (*0-685-67167-4*, 5124) Commerce.

Basic Documents of International Economic Law, 2 vols., Set. American Society of International Law Staff. Ed. by Zamora & Brand. 1990. 100.00 (*0-685-66959-9*) Commerce.

Basic Documents of International Relations. Ed. by Frederick H. Hartmann. LC 84-22494. xvi, 312p. 1985. reprint ed. text ed. 69.50 (*0-313-24747-1*, HABD, Greenwood Pr) Greenwood.

Basic Documents of the Seminar on the Acquisition of Latin American Library Materials, 2 pts. Ed. by Sara De Mundo Lo & Jane Garner. (Orig.). 1985. pap. 7.00 (*0-917617-05-3*) SALALM.

Basic Documents on African Affairs. Ed. by Ian Brownlie. 1971. 29.95 (*0-19-876020-5*) OUP.

Basic Documents on Autonomy & Minority Rights. Ed. by Hurst Hannum. LC 92-31347. 1993. lib. bdg. 308.00 (*0-7923-1977-X*) Kluwer Ac.

Basic Documents on Human Rights. 3rd ed. Ed. by Ian Brownlie. 600p. 1993. pap. 35.00 (*0-19-825712-0*) OUP.

***Basic Documents on International Environmental Law.** Alan Boyle & Patricia Birnie. 500p. 1995. pap. text ed. 29.95 (*0-19-876321-2*) OUP.

***Basic Documents on International Environmental Law.** Alan Boyle & Patricia Birnie. 500p. 1995. text ed. 75.00 (*0-19-876320-4*) OUP.

Basic Documents on International Trade Law. Chia-Jui Cheng. LC 85-8804. 1986. lib. bdg. 271.50 (*90-247-3168-2*) Kluwer Ac.

Basic Documents on International Trade Law. rev. ed. Chia-Jui Cheng. (C). 1990. lib. bdg. 270.00 (*1-85333-359-X*) Kluwer Ac.

Basic Documents on the Confederation & Constitution. Richard B. Morris. LC 84-28908. 254p. (C). 1985. reprint ed. pap. 12.50 (*0-89874-839-9*) Krieger.

Basic Documents on United Nations & Related Peace-Keeping Forces. Robert C. Siekmann. LC 85-5094. 1985. lib. bdg. 113.00 (*90-247-3163-1*) Kluwer Ac.

Basic Documents on United Nations & Related Peace-Keeping Forces. Ed. by Robert C. Siekmann. 438p. (C). 1989. lib. bdg. 144.50 (*90-247-3701-X*) Kluwer Ac.

Basic Documents, Vol. 1: 1986 Edition. International Maritime Organization Staff. 1986. text ed. 100.00 (*0-89771-854-2*, Pub. by Intl Maritime Org UK) St Mut.

Basic Dog Training. Miller Watson. (Illus.). 128p. 1989. 9.95 (*0-86622-785-7*, KW-022) TFH Pubns.

Basic Doppler Physics. Hans J. Smith. (Illus.). 136p. (Orig.). (C). 1991. pap. text ed. 39.00 (*0-944838-15-4*) Med Physics Pub.

Basic Double Weave Theory. Sara Farrar. 1980. pap. 8.00 (*1-56659-004-3*) Robin & Russ.

Basic Drafting. John L. Feirer & John R. Lindbeck. (gr. 9-12). 1978. 10.64 (*0-02-662480-X*); pap. 8.56 (*0-02-662470-2*); 6.00 (*0-02-662550-4*) Bennett IL.

Basic Drafting. Frank Pasquale. LC 79-730980. 1980. student ed 6.00 (*0-8064-0283-0*, 720); audio 299.00 (*0-8064-0284-9*) Bergwall.

Basic Drafting. 2nd ed. James H. Earle. 58p. (Orig.). 1985. 7.50 (*0-932702-76-7*); 3.50 (*0-932702-81-3*) Creative Texas.

Basic Drafting II. Frank Pasquale. LC 80-730729. 1981. student ed 6.00 (*0-8064-0285-7*, 721); audio 289.00 (*0-8064-0286-5*) Bergwall.

Basic Drafting III. Bruce Hunter. LC 83-730097. 1983. student ed 8.00 (*0-8064-0287-3*, 722); audio 429.00 (*0-8064-0288-1*) Bergwall.

Basic Drafting Problems. Lawrence E. Gerevas. 1972. pap. 7.30 (*0-672-97612-9*, Bobbs); pap. 5.00 (*0-672-97613-7*, Bobbs) Macmillan.

Basic Drafting Problems. Cecil H. Jensen et al. Ed. by Myrna Breskin. 96p. 1981. pap. text ed. 16.95 (*0-07-032521-9*) McGraw.

An Asterisk (*) at the beginning of an entry indicates that the title is appearing in BIP for the first time.

An Asterisk (*) at the beginning of an entry indicates that the title is appearing in BIP for the first time.

Basic English for Science. Peter Donovan & Oxford University Press, English Language Teaching Development Unit Staff. (Illus.). 1978. teacher ed 11.50 (*0-19-457181-5*); pap. text ed. 8.95 (*0-19-457180-7*) OUP.

Basic English Grammar. Betty S. Azar. (Illus.). 304p. (C). 1983. pap. text ed. 19.50 (*0-13-060434-8*) P-H.

Basic English Grammar. Bonnie L. Walker. (Illus.). 288p. 1990. teacher ed 12.99 (*0-86601-959-6*); student ed 4.99 (*0-7916-0026-2*); text ed. 19.49 (*0-86601-958-8*) Media Materials.

Basic English Review. 3rd ed. Norman Schachter, Jr. & Alfred T. Clark. 1985. pap. 17.95 (*0-538-14240-5*, N24) S-W Pub.

Basic English Revisited. Patrick Sebranek et al. (Illus.). 218p. 1992. pap. text ed. 8.95 (*0-939045-76-1*) Write Source.

Basic English Revisited: A Student Handbook. 5th ed. Patrick Sebranek & Verne Meyer. LC 80-68894. (Illus.). (YA). (gr. 7-12). 1985. text ed. 8.95 (*0-9605312-1-1*); pap. text ed. 7.95 (*0-9605312-0-3*) Write Source.

Basic English Revisited: The Mechanics of Writing. Patrick Sebranek et al. (Illus.). 60p. 1986. student ed 4.95 (*0-939045-00-1*); teacher ed 5.95 (*0-939045-96-6*) Write Source.

Basic English Usage. Michael Swan. 275p. 1985. pap. 11.95 (*0-19-431187-2*) OUP.

Basic English Vocabulary Builder Activity Book: Beginning. Ruth De Jong. 96p. 1993. 5.25 (*0-8442-9010-6*, Natl Textbk); pap. 7.95 (*0-8442-9009-2*, Natl Textbk) NTC Pub Grp.

***Basic English Workbook.** Patricia E. Seraydarian. 224p. (C). 1994. spiral bd. 38.95 (*0-256-15456-2*) Irwin.

***Basic English Workbook.** annot. ed. Patricia E. Seraydarian. 224p. 1995. spiral bd. write for info. (*0-256-18113-6*) Irwin.

***Basic Environmental Engineering: Text & Disk with 100 Plus Programs.** 2nd ed. Henry R. Bungay. (Illus.). 282p. (C). 1992. pap. text ed. 38.00x (*0-9639308-0-X*) BiLine Assocs.

Basic Environmental Problems of Man in Space: Proceedings of the Fifth International Symposium, Washington, D.C., 1973. Ed. by A. Graybiel. 1976. 158.00 (*0-08-021067-8*, Pub. by Pergamon Repr UK) Franklin.

Basic Environmental Toxicology. Ed. by Lorris G. Cockerham & Barbara S. Shane. 680p. 1993. 79.95 (*0-8493-8851-1*, QH545) CRC Pr.

***Basic Enzyme Kinetics.** T. Keleti. 420p. (C). 1986. 144.00x (*963-05-4090-8*, Pub. by Akad Kiado HU) St Mut.

Basic Epidemilgcl Method & Biostat. Randy Page et al. (Life Science Ser.). 350p. (C). 1994. pap. text ed. 35.00 (*0-86720-869-4*) Jones & Bartlett.

Basic Epidemiological Methods & Biostatistics: A Workbook. Slome et al. LC 81-16278. (Health Science Ser.). 350p. (C). 1982. pap. 36.25 (*0-86720-364-1*) Jones & Bartlett.

Basic Equations of Relativistic Physics. Carl A. Zapffe. LC 82-91045. 208p. (Orig.). (C). 1982. pap. 20.00 (*0-9601448-2-X*) C A Zapffe.

Basic Equities of the Palestine Problem. Simon H. Rifkind et al. Ed. by Moshe Davis. LC 77-70736. (America & the Holy Land Ser.). 1977. reprint ed. lib. bdg. 19.95 (*0-405-10279-8*) Ayer.

***Basic ESD Seminar.** (Illus.). 1994. pap. text ed. 100.00 (*1-878303-47-3*, SEM94) EOS ESD.

Basic Esperanto Quick International Understanding in One-Tenth the Time with International Words. Wesley E. Arnold. 104p. (Orig.). 1992. pap. 5.98 (*0-915935-11-2*) W Arnold.

Basic Essentials of Alpine Skiing. Carol Poster. LC 93-29016. (Basic Essentials Ser.). (Illus.). 72p. (Orig.). 1993. pap. 5.99 (*0-934802-40-8*) ICS Bks.

Basic Essentials of Avalanche Safety. Buck Tilton. LC 92-21091. (Basic Essentials Ser.). (Illus.). 72p. (Orig.). 1992. pap. 5.99 (*0-934802-84-X*) ICS Bks.

Basic Essentials of Backpacking. Harry Roberts. LC 88-34802. (Basic Essentials Ser.). (Illus.). 72p. (Orig.). 1989. pap. 5.99 (*0-934802-44-0*) ICS Bks.

Basic Essentials of Bicycle Touring. Michael Nicoson. LC 92-47123. (Basic Essentials Ser.). (Illus.). 72p. (Orig.). 1993. pap. 5.99 (*0-934802-73-4*) ICS Bks.

Basic Essentials of Camping. Cliff Jacobson. LC 88-2693. (Basic Essentials Ser.). (Illus.). 72p. (Orig.). 1988. pap. 5.99 (*0-934802-38-6*) ICS Bks.

Basic Essentials of Canoe Paddling. Harry Roberts. Ed. by Thomas Todd. LC 90-25773. (Basic Essentials Ser.). (Illus.). 72p. (Orig.). 1992. pap. 5.99 (*0-934802-68-8*) ICS Bks.

Basic Essentials of Canoe Poling. Harry Rock. LC 90-26423. (Basic Essentials Ser.). (Illus.). 72p. (Orig.). 1992. pap. 5.99 (*0-934802-36-X*) ICS Bks.

Basic Essentials of Canoeing. Cliff Jacobson. LC 87-36161. (Basic Essentials Ser.). (Illus.). 72p. (Orig.). 1988. pap. 5.99 (*0-934802-39-4*) ICS Bks.

Basic Essentials of Cooking in the Outdoors. Cliff Jacobson. LC 89-35056. (Basic Essentials Ser.). (Illus.). 72p. (Orig.). 1989. pap. 5.99 (*0-934802-46-7*) ICS Bks.

Basic Essentials of Counselling. 1986. 18.95 (*81-207-0065-1*, Pub. by Sterling Pubs II) Apt Bks.

Basic Essentials of Cross-Country Skiing. John Moynier. LC 90-41890. (Basic Essentials Ser.). (Illus.). 72p. (Orig.). 1990. pap. 5.99 (*0-934802-49-1*) ICS Bks.

Basic Essentials of Desert Survival. Dave Ganci. LC 90-25772. (Basic Essentials Ser.). (Illus.). 72p. (Orig.). 1991. pap. 5.99 (*0-934802-67-X*) ICS Bks.

Basic Essentials of Edible Wild Plants & Useful Herbs. Jim Meuninck. LC 88-13354. (Basic Essentials Ser.). (Illus.). 72p. (Orig.). 1988. pap. 5.99 (*0-934802-41-6*) ICS Bks.

Basic Essentials of Hypothermia. William W. Forgey. LC 91-22571. (Basic Essentials Ser.). (Illus.). 72p. (Orig.). 1989. pap. 5.99 (*0-934802-76-9*) ICS Bks.

Basic Essentials of Kayaking Whitewater. Bill Kallner & Donna Jackson. LC 90-31322. (Basic Essentials Ser.). (Illus.). 72p. (Orig.). 1990. pap. 5.99 (*0-934802-54-8*) ICS Bks.

Basic Essentials of Knots for the Outdoors. Cliff Jacobson. LC 89-26850. (Basic Essentials Ser.). (Illus.). 72p. (Orig.). 1990. pap. 5.99 (*0-934802-57-2*) ICS Bks.

Basic Essentials of Map & Compass. Cliff Jacobson. LC 88-22965. (Basic Essentials Ser.). (Illus.). 72p. (Orig.). 1988. pap. 5.99 (*0-934802-42-4*) ICS Bks.

Basic Essentials of Minimizing Impact on the Wilderness. Michael Hodgson. LC 91-22569. (Basic Essentials Ser.). (Illus.). 72p. (Orig.). 1991. pap. 5.99 (*0-934802-78-5*) ICS Bks.

Basic Essentials of Mountain Biking. Michael Strassman. LC 89-37910. (Basic Essentials Ser.). (Illus.). 72p. (Orig.). 1989. pap. 5.99 (*0-934802-47-5*) ICS Bks.

Basic Essentials of Mountaineering. John Moynier. LC 90-26009. (Basic Essentials Ser.). (Illus.). 72p. (Orig.). 1991. pap. 5.99 (*0-934802-65-3*) ICS Bks.

Basic Essentials of Photography Outdoors. Mike Wyatt. LC 90-41497. (Basic Essentials Ser.). (Illus.). 72p. (Orig.). 1991. pap. 5.99 (*0-934802-53-X*) ICS Bks.

Basic Essentials of Rafting. Jib Ellison. LC 90-25771. (Basic Essentials Ser.). (Illus.). 72p. (Orig.). 1991. pap. 5.99 (*0-934802-34-3*) ICS Bks.

Basic Essentials of Rescue from the Backcountry. Buck Tilton. LC 90-26011. (Basic Essentials Ser.). (Illus.). 72p. (Orig.). 1991. pap. 5.99 (*0-934802-69-6*) ICS Bks.

Basic Essentials of Rock Climbing. Michael Strassman. LC 89-36057. (Basic Essentials Ser.). (Illus.). 72p. (Orig.). 1989. pap. 5.99 (*0-934802-45-9*) ICS Bks.

Basic Essentials of Sea Kayaking. Mike Wyatt. LC 90-33354. (Basic Essentials Ser.). (Illus.). 72p. (Orig.). 1990. pap. 5.99 (*0-934802-55-6*) ICS Bks.

Basic Essentials of Snowboarding. John McMullen. LC 91-21207. (Basic Essentials Ser.). (Illus.). 72p. (Orig.). 1991. pap. 5.99 (*0-934802-77-7*) ICS Bks.

Basic Essentials of Solo Canoeing. Cliff Jacobson. LC 90-26010. (Basic Essentials Ser.). (Illus.). 72p. (Orig.). 1991. pap. 5.99 (*0-934802-66-1*) ICS Bks.

Basic Essentials of Survival. James E. Churchill. LC 89-36794. (Basic Essentials Ser.). (Illus.). 72p. (Orig.). 1989. pap. 5.99 (*0-934802-48-3*) ICS Bks.

Basic Essentials of Trailside Shelters. Cliff Jacobson. Ed. by Thomas Todd. LC 92-5191. (Basic Essentials Ser.). (Illus.). 72p. (Orig.). 1992. pap. 5.99 (*0-934802-89-0*) ICS Bks.

Basic Essentials of Weather Forecasting. Michael Hodgson. Ed. by Thomas Todd. LC 92-7829. (Basic Essentials Ser.). (Illus.). 72p. (Orig.). 1992. pap. 5.99 (*0-934802-75-0*) ICS Bks.

Basic Essentials of Women in the Outdoors. Judith Niemi. LC 90-31389. (Basic Essentials Ser.). (Illus.). 72p. (Orig.). 1990. pap. 5.99 (*0-934802-56-4*) ICS Bks.

Basic Estate Administration (1992) Daniel I. Lubetkin. (Illus.). 270p. pap. 35.00 (*0-685-09818-4*) NJ Inst CLE.

Basic Estate Planning. Robert Pinto. (Illus.). 200p. 1992. pap. 35.00 (*0-685-14622-7*) NJ Inst CLE.

***Basic Estate Planning in Florida.** 2nd ed. Florida Bar Legal Education Staff. LC 93-74432. 423p. 1993. ring bd. 85.00 (*0-945979-54-1*, 227) FL Bar Legal Ed.

Basic Etymological Dictionary of Russian Phraseology. N. M. Shanskii. (RUS.). (C). 1987. 40.00 (*0-317-92417-6*, Pub. by Collets UK) Pro-Am Music.

Basic Exercises in Algebra & Trigonometry. J. Richard Lux & Richard S. Pieters. 1979. 8.48 (*0-8013-0068-1*); pap. text ed. 8.22 (*0-88334-122-0*, 76096) Longman.

Basic Exercises in Immunochemistry: A Laboratory Manual. 2nd ed. A. Nowotny. LC 79-14029. (Illus.). 1979. pap. 39.00 (*0-387-09453-9*) Spr-Verlag.

Basic Experimental Microbiology. Ronald M. Atlas et al. 316p. (C). 1986. write for info. (*0-02-304390-3*) Macmillan.

Basic Experiments for General, Organic, & Biological Chemistry. Martha J. Gilleland. 215p. (C). 1982. pap. text ed. 32.25 (*0-314-63239-5*) West Pub.

Basic Experiments in Neuropsychology. Ed. by John L. Bradshaw. 206p. 1987. 117.50 (*0-444-80803-5*); student ed, pap. 56.00 (*0-444-80846-9*) Elsevier.

Basic Exploration Geophysics. 512p. (Orig.). 1988. pap. 21.95 (*0-471-61279-0*) Wiley.

Basic Expoloration Geophysics. Edwin S. Robinson & Cahit Coruh. 562p. 1988. Net. text ed. write for info. (*0-471-87941-X*) Wiley.

Basic Expressions for Trial Lawyers. Robert E. Keeton. 1979. pap. 11.00 (*0-316-48581-0*) Little.

Basic Facilities & Institutions in Policy Studies. Ed. by Stuart Nagel. (C). 1972. pap. 12.00 (*0-918592-01-1*) Pol Studies.

Basic Facts about the United Nations. 178p. 1988. pap. 5.00 (*92-1-100299-0*, E.88.I.3) UN.

Basic Facts about the United Nations. 236p. 1990. 5.00 (*92-1-100420-9*, E.90.I.2) UN.

***Basic Facts about Wisconsin Elementary & Secondary Schools 1994-95.** 204p. 1995. pap. text ed. 18.00 (*1-57337-021-5*) WI Dept Pub Instruct.

Basic Facts for Basic Science. Radovan Zak. 272p. 1991. 31.00 (*0-88167-665-9*) Raven.

Basic Facts on Productivity Change. Solomon Fabricant. (Occasional Papers: No. 63). 61p. 1959. reprint ed. 20.00 (*0-87014-377-8*) Natl Bur Econ Res.

Basic Family Law. Robert Faraguna & Vena Garrett. LC 92-26639. (Legal Studies Ser.). (Illus.). 1993. 36.95 (*0-02-800289-X*) Glencoe.

Basic Family Therapy. 3rd ed. Philip J. Barker. (Illus.). 320p. 1992. pap. 27.50 (*0-19-520947-8*) OUP.

Basic Farm Machinery. 3rd ed. J. M. Shippen et al. (Illus.). 1980. pap. text ed. 22.00 (*0-08-024911-6*, Pergamon Pr) Elsevier.

BASIC Faster & Better & Other Mysteries. Lewis Rosenfelder. (TRS-80 Information Ser.: Vol. 4). (Illus.). 290p. (Orig.). 1981. pap. text ed. 29.95 (*0-936200-03-0*) Blue Cat.

Basic Fault: Therapeutic Aspects of Regression. Michael Balint. LC 79-15682. (Classics in Psychoanalysis Ser.: No. 5). 205p. 1979. reprint ed. 27.95 (*0-87630-219-3*) Brunner-Mazel.

Basic Fault: Therapeutic Aspects of Regression. Michael Balint. 205p. 1992. reprint ed. pap. 14.95 (*0-8101-1025-3*) Northwestern U Pr.

Basic Fears. Manly P. Hall. pap. 4.00 (*0-89314-304-9*) Philos Res.

Basic Federal Income Taxation. 3rd ed. William D. Andrews. LC 84-82457. (C). 1985. 40.95 (*0-316-04228-5*) Little.

Basic Federal Income Taxation: C Corporations, Partnerships, & S Corporations. Samuel C. Thompson, Jr. LC 93-39329. (American Casebook Ser.). 1167p. 1994. text ed. 48.00 (*0-314-02748-3*) West Pub.

***Basic Federal Income Taxation of C Corporations.** Samuel C. Thompson. (American Casebook Ser.). 597p. (C). 1994. pap. text ed. 40.00 (*0-314-03585-0*) West Pub.

***Basic Federal Income Taxation of C Corporations, Teacher's Manual to Accompany.** Samuel Thompson. (American Casebook Ser.). 190p. (C). 1994. pap. text ed. write for info. (*0-314-05936-9*) West Pub.

***Basic Federal Income Taxation of Partnerships & S Corporations.** Samuel C. Thompson. (American Casebook Ser.). 318p. (C). 1994. text ed. 35.00 (*0-314-03546-X*) West Pub.

***Basic Federal Income Taxation of Partnerships & S Corporations, Teacher's Manual To.** Samuel Thompson. (American Casebook Ser.). 70p. (C). 1994. pap. text ed. write for info. (*0-314-05935-0*) West Pub.

Basic Feedback Control Systems: Alternate. 2nd ed. Charles L. Phillips & Royce D. Harbor. 512p. 1990. text ed. 69.00 (*0-13-062845-X*) P-H.

Basic Fiction: The New Writer's Handbook for Creating Fiction that Sells. Duane Unkefer. (Santa Barbara Writers Conference Shop Talk Ser.: Bk. III). 85p. (Orig.). (C). 1991. pap. text ed. 7.95 (*1-880093-02-2*) Charters W.

Basic Figure Drawing Techniques. Ed. by Greg Albert. (Basic Technique Ser.). (Illus.). 128p. 1994. pap. 16.99 (*0-89134-551-5*) North Light Bks.

***Basic Filing for Health Information Management.** Jan Johnson. 70p. 1994. teacher ed 16.00 (*0-8273-6284-6*) Delmar.

Basic Filing for Health Information Management. Jan L. Johnson. LC 93-13902. 1993. 27.95 (*0-8273-5457-6*) Delmar.

Basic Film Technique. Ken Daley. (Media Manuals Ser.). (Illus.). 158p. 1980. pap. 19.95 (*0-240-51016-X*, Focal) Buttrwrth-Heinemann.

Basic Finance, an Introduction to Financial Theory, Practices & Institutions. James R. Bryce. 158p. 1980. pap. text ed. 9.95x (*0-89641-038-2*) American Pr.

Basic Financial Management. William H. Marsh. LC 94-2856. 640p. 1994. 53.95 (*0-538-84170-2*) S-W Pub.

Basic Financial Management. 3rd ed. Arthur J. Keown, II et al. (Illus.). 768p. (C). 1985. pap. text ed. 44.00 (*0-13-060641-3*); student ed 12.95 (*0-685-09121-X*) P-H.

Basic Financial Management. 5th ed. Martin et al. 880p. 1990. text ed. 66.00 (*0-13-060807-6*) P-H.

Basic Financial Management. 6th ed. John D. Martin, II et al. 1008p. 1992. text ed. 66.00 (*0-13-059635-3*) P-H.

Basic Fingerstyle Guitar Method. Hank Mackie & Phil Palermo. 1993. 4.95 (*0-87166-738-X*, 93342) Mel Bay.

Basic First Aid for Horses. Ed. by William E. Jones. (Horse Health & Care Ser.). (Illus.). 1973. pap. 6.95 (*0-912830-04-2*) Printed Horse.

Basic Fishery Science Programs: A Compendium of Microcomputer Programs & Manual Of Operation. S. B. Saila et al. (Developments in Aquaculture & Fisheries Science Ser.: No. 18). 230p. 1988. 72.00 (*0-444-43031-8*) Elsevier.

Basic Fixture Design. Paul D. Campbell. LC 93-33165. 240p. 1994. text ed. 29.95 (*0-8311-3052-0*) Indus Pr.

Basic Flight Physiology. Richard O. Reinhart. 1992. 34.95 (*0-07-051823-8*) McGraw.

Basic Flight Physiology. Richard O. Reinhart. 248p. 1992. 34.95 (*0-8306-3890-3*, 4141) TAB Bks.

Basic Floral Design. Redbook Florist Services Educational Advisory Committee. LC 91-61275. (Encycloflora Ser.). (Illus.). 286p. (Orig.). 1991. pap. text ed. 34.95 (*1-56963-014-3*) Redbk Florist.

Basic Flower. Editorial Staff. (World Textile Collection Ser.: No. 1). (Illus.). 200p. 1992. 42.95 (*4-7636-8091-9*, Pub. by Kyoto Shoin JA) Bks Nippan.

Basic Fluid Power. 2nd ed. Dudley A. Pease & John E. Pippenger. (Illus.). 384p. 1986. text ed. 76.00 (*0-13-061508-0*) P-H.

Basic Fluid System Analysis: With HP-25 & SR-56 Pocket Calculator Programs. G. A. Patterson. LC 76-21585. 95p. 1977. 12.95 (*0-917410-00-9*) Basic Sci Pr.

Basic Fly Fishing. Les Hawkins. (Illus.). 112p. (Orig.). 1993. 23.95 (*0-86417-546-9*, Pub. by Kangaroo Pr AT) Seven Hills Bk.

Basic Fly Tying. Ed Koch & Norm Shires. LC 90-31613. (Illus.). 128p. (Orig.). 1990. pap. 19.95 (*0-8117-2318-6*) Stackpole.

Basic Food & Beverage Cost Control. Jack E. Miller & David K. Hayes. 400p. 1993. Net. text ed. write for info. (*0-471-57918-1*) Wiley.

Basic Food Chemistry. 2nd ed. Frank A. Lee. (Illus.). (C). 1983. text ed. 58.95 (*0-87055-416-6*) AVI.

Basic Food Microbiology. 2nd ed. Banwart. 1989. text ed. 67.95 (*0-442-22120-7*); pap. 32.95 (*0-317-63815-7*) Chapman & Hall.

Basic Food Plant Sanitation Manual. 225p. 1979. pap. 15.00 (*0-318-22937-4*) Am Inst Baking.

Basic Foods. 3rd ed. June C. Gates. 604p. (C). 1987. pap. text ed. 39.25 (*0-03-071463-X*) HB Coll Pubs.

Basic Foodservice Accounting Skillbook. Educational Foundation of the National Restaurant Association Staff. (Management Skills Program Ser.). 37p. (Orig.). 1992. pap. 10.95 (*0-915452-99-5*) Educ Found.

BASIC for Beginners. William E. Conley. (Illus.). 144p. 1982. pap. text ed. 12.95 (*0-89433-141-8*) Petrocelli.

BASIC for Business for the VAX & PDP-11. 2nd ed. Alan J. Parker. (C). 1983. text ed. 30.00 (*0-8359-0358-3*, Reston); pap. text ed. 28.00 (*0-8359-0357-5*, Reston) P-H.

BASIC for DOS. Gary Cornell. 1992. pap. text ed. 21.95 (*0-07-157732-7*) McGraw.

BASIC for DOS. Gary Cornell. 1992. text ed. 31.95 (*0-07-013315-8*) McGraw.

BASIC for IBM-PC Etc. 2nd ed. Bijan Mashaw. 420p. (C). 1990. pap. text ed. 29.95 (*0-934433-06-2*) Am Comp Pr.

BASIC for Students Using the IBM PC. 2nd ed. Michael Trombetta. (Illus.). 512p. (C). 1991. pap. text ed. 41.95 (*0-201-50416-2*) Addison-Wesley.

BASIC for Teachers. Charles Heimler. 128p. 1987. pap. text ed. 20.00 (*0-317-54023-8*) Mitchell Pub.

BASIC for Teachers. Charles H. Heimler et al. 1987. pap. text ed. write for info. (*0-07-554188-2*) McGraw.

BASIC for Teachers. Frank P. Besag & Leonard P. Levine. LC 84-6953. (Illus.). 208p. reprint ed. pap. 59.30 (*0-8357-8473-8*, 2034741) Bks Demand.

BASIC for Technicians. Earl N. Gulledge. LC 84-7659. 352p. (C). 1985. teacher ed 10.00 (*0-8273-2311-5*); pap. text ed. 29.95 (*0-8273-2310-7*) Delmar.

BASIC for the HP 3000. Jesse H. Ruder. LC 85-12044. 240p. reprint ed. pap. 68.40 (*0-7837-2379-2*, 2040065) Bks Demand.

Basic Forensic Psychiatry. 2nd ed. M. Faulk. 352p. 1994. pap. write for info. (*0-632-03321-5*, Pub. by Blckwell Sci Pubns UK) Blackwell Sci.

Basic Forms in Music. Charles W. Walton. LC 73-81046. 226p. 1974. pap. text ed. 17.95 (*0-88284-025-8*) Alfred Pub.

Basic Forms of Prophetic Speech. Claus Westermann. Tr. by Hugh C. White. 240p. (Orig.). 1991. pap. 18.99 (*0-664-25244-3*) Westminster John Knox.

***Basic Formulary for General Practice.** 3rd ed. G. B. Grant et al. (Practical Guides for General Practice Ser.: No. 18). 112p. 1995. pap. 22.95 (*0-19-262492-X*) OUP.

Basic FORTRAN IV Programming. rev. ed. J. J. Healy & D. J. DeBruzzi. 1975. pap. write for info. (*0-201-02827-1*) Addison-Wesley.

Basic Fracture Mechanics. R. N. Smith. Ed. by M. J. Iremonger & P. D. Smith. (Butterworth's Basic Bks.). 160p. 1991. pap. text ed. 24.95 (*0-7506-1489-7*) Buttrwrth-Heinemann.

Basic Framework for Economics. 3rd ed. Richard H. Leftwich & David Gay. 408p. (C). 1987. pap. 28.50 (*0-256-03702-7*) Irwin.

Basic French. (Teach Yourself Ser.). 256p. 1993. pap. 5.95 (*0-8442-3766-3*) NTC Pub Grp.

Basic French. Kate Beeching. 1988. pap. text ed. 19.44 (*0-582-22481-0*, 78060); audio 23.00 (*0-582-22482-9*, 78059) Longman.

Basic French, 3 vols., Set. Theodore Mueller & Henri Niedzielski. Incl. Premiers Pas. (FRE.). 1974. pap. text ed. 4.40 (*0-89197-670-1*); Pratique de la grammaire. (FRE.). 1974. pap. text ed. 8.20 (*0-89197-671-X*); Introduction a la culture. (FRE.). 1974. pap. text ed. 3.10 (*0-89197-672-8*); (FRE.). 1974. Set pap. text ed. 15.70 (*0-89197-673-6*) Irvington.

Basic French Grammar. Gloria Russo & Georges Perla. 259p. (C). 1985. pap. text ed. 19.50 (*0-669-05346-5*) Heath.

Basic French Vocabulary. Heidi A. Spietz. 145p. (Orig.). 1994. pap. 10.95 (*0-929487-70-2*) Am Montessori Consult.

Basic Freshwater Fishing: Step-by-Step Guide to Tackle & Know-How That Catch the Favorite Fish in Your Area. Cliff Hauptman. LC 87-18053. (Illus.). 224p. 1988. pap. 14.95 (*0-8117-2226-0*) Stackpole.

Basic Full Time Training in Business Studies & Languages. FESC. 1985. 45.00 (*0-907659-09-8*) St Mut.

BASIC Fun: Computer Games, Puzzles & Problems Children Can Write. Susan D. Lipscomb & Margaret A. Zuanich. 176p. (J). (gr. k-7). 1982. pap. 2.95 (*0-380-80606-1*, Camelot) Avon.

Basic Fund Accounting Training Package. 3rd ed. 1992. 750.00 (*0-685-62915-5*) NACUBO.

BASIC Game Plans: Computer Games & Puzzles Programmed in BASIC. Ruediger Baumann. 350p. 1988. 26.50 (*0-8176-3366-9*) Birkhauser.

BASIC Games for Your VIC-20 Computer. David D. Busch. 9.95 (*0-89303-910-1*) P-H.

***Basic Gardening: A Handbook for Beginning Gardeners.** Louise Carter. LC 94-37915. (Illus.). 148p. 1995. pap. 9.95 (*1-55591-173-0*) Fulcrum Pub.

***Basic Gardening Skills.** Tim Morehouse. (Illus.). 224p. 1996. pap. 14.95 (*0-8117-2508-1*) Stackpole.

Basic Gas Chromatography-Mass Spectrometry: Principles & Techniques. Francis W. Karasek & R. E. Clement. 202p. 1988. 77.00 (*0-444-42760-0*) Elsevier.

Basic Gastroenterology. 3rd ed. Alan E. Read et al. (Illus.). 558p. (C). 1981. pap. text ed. 44.95 (*0-7236-0551-3*, Pub. by John Wright UK) Buttrwrth-Heinemann.

Basic Genetics. BSCS Staff. 144p. 1990. per. 14.90 (*0-8403-5705-2*) Kendall-Hunt.

Basic Genetics. Hartl & Snyder. 496p. (C). 1988. boxed 40.00 (*0-86720-090-1*) Jones & Bartlett.

An Asterisk (*) at the beginning of an entry indicates that the title is appearing in BIP for the first time.

An Asterisk (*) at the beginning of an entry indicates that the title is appearing in BIP for the first time.

613

Basic Hunter's Guide. rev. ed. Ed. by Earl Shelsby & James Gilford. (Illus.). 280p. (Orig.). 1982. pap. text ed. 14.95 (*0-935998-46-2*) Natl Rifle Assn.

BASIC Hydrodynamics. A. C. Thompson. (Basic Ser.). (Illus.). 176p. 1987. pap. text ed. 21.95 (*0-408-01391-5*) Buttrwrth-Heinemann.

Basic Hypergeometric Series. G. Gasper & M. Rahman. (Encyclopedia of Mathematics & Its Applications Ser.: No. 35). (C). 1990. 74.95 (*0-521-35049-2*) Cambridge U Pr.

Basic Hypergeometric Series & Applications. N. Fine. LC 88-6235. (SURV Ser.: No. 27). 124p. 1989. reprint ed. 49.00 (*0-8218-1524-5*, SURV-27) Am Math.

Basic IC Technology Reference Manual. Ron Bowman. Ed. by William J. McClean & Jim Griffin. (Illus.). 222p. 1993. 195.00 (*1-877750-24-7*) ICE Corp.

Basic ICD-9-CM Coding Handbook. Toula Nicholas & Linda Ertl. 315p. 1992. 42.00 (*0-317-05423-6*) Am Hlth Info.

Basic ICD-9-CM for Physicians' Offices. J. A. Holloway. 53p. 1992. 18.00 (*0-317-05424-4*) Am Hlth Info.

Basic Ideas & Concepts in Nuclear Physics. K. Heyde. (Illus.). 436p. 1994. 160.00 (*0-7503-0300-X*); pap. 49.00 (*0-7503-0301-8*) IOP Pub.

Basic Ideas of Calvinism. 6th ed. Henry H. Meeter. LC 90-33204. 224p. 1990. pap. 12.99 (*0-8010-6269-1*) Baker Bk.

Basic Ideas of Occult Wisdom. Anna K. Winner. LC 75-116528. (Orig.). 1970. pap. 7.95 (*0-8356-0391-1*, Quest) Theos Pub Hse.

Basic Ideas of the Science of Mind. Ernest Holmes. 96p. 1990. reprint ed. pap. 7.95 (*0-87516-623-7*) DeVorss.

BASIC II Advanced, Vol. II. William C. Conley. 1983. pap. 12.95 (*0-685-07399-8*) Petrocelli.

Basic Illinois Government: A Systematic Explanation. 3rd rev. ed. David Kenney & Barbara L. Brown. LC 92-27760. 304p. (C). 1993. pap. 24.95 (*0-8093-1822-9*) S Ill U Pr.

Basic Illustrated Spanish-English Dictionary: Diccionario Basico Ilustrado Espanol-Ingles, 4 vols., Set. Mediterraneo Staff. 1200p. (ENG & SPA.). 1982. 395.00 (*0-8288-2321-9*, S2567) Fr & Eur.

Basic Imaging in Congenital Heart Disease. 3rd ed. Ed. by Leonard Swischuk. (Radiology Ser.). (Illus.). 312p. 1986. text ed. 67.50 (*0-683-08055-5*) Williams & Wilkins.

Basic Immigration Law. (Litigation & Administrative Practice Ser.). 269p. 1992. pap. text ed. 245.00 (*0-685-56927-6*, H4-5129) PLI.

Basic Immigration Law 1993. (Litigation & Administrative Practice Course Handbook, 1983-84 Ser.: Vol. 466). 323p. 1993. 70.00 (*0-685-69740-1*, H4-5176) PLI.

Basic Immunogenetics. 3rd ed. Hugh H. Fudenberg et al. (Illus.). (C). 1984. pap. 19.95 (*0-19-503405-8*) OUP.

Basic Immunology. 2nd ed. Joseph A. Bellanti. (Illus.). 224p. 1985. text ed. 41.95 (*0-7216-1244-X*) Saunders.

***Basic Immunology: Introduction for the Health Sciences.** Gregory Seymour. 152p. 1995. text ed. write for info. (*0-07-452810-6*) Hlth Prof Div.

Basic Improvement Tools, 10 bks., Set. Joiner Associates Inc. Staff. (Navigator Ser.). (Illus.). (Orig.). 1994. write for info. (*0-9622264-7-5*) Joiner Assoc.

Basic Income Tax. 4th ed. Andrews. 1991. 53.00 (*0-316-04232-3*) Little.

Basic Index for a Course in Miracles. Larry Goodman. 1992. pap. 9.00 (*0-9632266-0-6*) Index Miracles.

Basic Industrial Drafting. William P. Spence. 1982. pap. text ed. 15.00 (*0-02-662520-2*); 11.96 (*0-02-662540-7*) Bennett IL.

Basic Industrial Electricity: A Training & Maintenance Manual. Kenneth G. Oliver. 300p. (C). 1990. pap. text ed. 32.95 (*0-8311-3006-7*) Indus Pr.

Basic Industrial Hearing Conservation. David F. Barr & Richard K. Miller. 26.95 (*0-686-74625-2*) Fairmont Pr.

Basic Industrial Hygiene: A Training Manual. Richard S. Brief. 250p. 1975. 25.00 (*0-932627-01-3*) Am Indus Hygiene.

Basic Industrial Instrumentation. Jerry Faulk & Adolph A. Sutko. LC 94-2656. 1994. write for info. (*0-8273-6125-4*) Delmar.

Basic Industrial Mathematics, Metric Edition. Robert M. Johnson & Patricia Tibbits. (Illus.). 1979. text ed. 35.95 (*0-07-032671-1*) McGraw.

Basic Industrial Resources of the U. S. S. R. Theodore Shabad. LC 75-101133. 1969. text ed. 75.00 (*0-231-03077-0*) Col U Pr.

Basic Industries in Texas & Northern Mexico. Texas University Institute of Latin-American Studies Staff. LC 69-19009. (Illus.). 193p. 1970. reprint ed. text ed. 49.75 (*0-8371-1033-5*, TLIM, Greenwood Pr) Greenwood.

Basic Influencing Skills. 1983. 9.95 (*0-917276-03-5*) Microtraining Assocs.

Basic Information Keyboarding Skills: A Collegiate Course. 2nd ed. Jerry W. Robinson et al. (C). 1988. text ed. 26.95 (*0-538-26160-9*, Z16) S-W Pub.

Basic Information You Need to Start & Succeed in Your Own Business. Michael E. Akpan & Juliana M. Akpan. 53p. 1992. pap. write for info. (*0-9634998-1-5*) Ebewos Afr-Am.

Basic Infrared Spectroscopy. J. H. Van der Maas. LC 70-101090. (Illus.). 119p. reprint ed. pap. 34.00 (*0-8357-3057-3*, 2039313) Bks Demand.

Basic Ingredients for Spiritual Growth. LeRoy Eims. (Orig.). 1992. pap. 1.80 (*0-89693-074-2*, Victor Books) SP Pubns.

Basic Injection Molding & Basic Trouble Shooting, 2 vols., Set. rev. ed. William J. Tobin. (Illus.). 127p. 1993. reprint ed. pap. 29.50 (*0-938648-11-X*) T-C Pubns CA.

Basic Injection Molding & Basic Trouble Shooting see Moldeamiento De Inyeccion Basico & Problemas Basico De Disparar

Basic Inorganic Chemistry. 2nd ed. F. Albert Cotton et al. 708p. 1987. Net. text ed. write for info. (*0-471-02969-6*); Net. pap. text ed. 18.95 (*0-471-83701-6*) Wiley.

Basic Inorganic Chemistry. 3rd ed. Albert Cotton et al. LC 94-20754. 1994. text ed. write for info. (*0-471-50532-3*) Wiley.

Basic Instructor Guitar. Jerry Snyder. (Illus.). 96p. (Orig.). (YA). 1993. pap. text ed. 9.95 (*0-89898-570-6*) CPP Belwin.

Basic Instrumentation. 3rd ed. Bruce R. Whalen. (Illus.). 350p. 1983. pap. text ed. 30.00 (*0-88698-003-8*, 1.20030) PETEX.

Basic Instrumentation, Industrial Measurement. Patrick J. O'Higgins. 1966. text ed. 45.95 (*0-07-047649-7*) McGraw.

***Basic Instrumentation Instructor's Guide.** 3rd ed. Bruce Whalen & Annes McCann. (Illus.). 104p. (Orig.). Date not set. teacher ed, pap. text ed. 15.00 (*0-88698-141-7*) PETEX.

Basic Instrumentation Lecture Notes & Study Guide, 2 vols., Vol. 1. 3rd ed. Ralph L. Moore. LC 82-81083. (Illus.). 187p. (Orig.). reprint ed. pap. 53.30 (*0-7837-4884-1*, 2044877) Bks Demand.

Basic Instrumentation Lecture Notes & Study Guide, 2 vols., Vol. 2. Ralph L. Moore. LC 82-81083. (Illus.). 125p. (Orig.). reprint ed. pap. 35.70 (*0-7837-4885-X*, 2044877) Bks Demand.

Basic Instrumentation Lecture Notes & Study Guide: Measurement Fundamentals, Vol. I. rev. ed. Instrument Society of America Staff. Ed. by Ralph L. Moore. (Illus.). 320p. (C). 1984. pap. 31.00 (*0-13-062471-3*) P-H.

Basic Instrumentation Lecture Notes & Study Guide: Process Analyzers & Recorders, Vol. II. rev. ed. Instrument Society of America Staff. Ed. by Ralph L. Moore. (Illus.). 208p. (C). 1984. pap. 31.00 (*0-13-062489-6*) P-H.

***Basic Instrumentation Workbook.** 3rd ed. Bruce Whalen & Annes McCann. 75p. (Orig.). Date not set. pap. text ed. 15.00 (*0-88698-142-5*) PETEX.

Basic Instruments of the OAS. 107p. English. 4.00 (*0-8270-1371-X*); Spanish. 4.00 (*0-8270-1370-1*) OAS.

***Basic Intarsia: With Lucille Crabtree.** Lucille Crabtree. LC 94-37135. (Illus.). 64p. (Orig.). 1995. pap. 12.95 (*0-88740-727-7*) Schiffer.

Basic, Intermediate Systematic Substitution Training, Set-IS. Russell E. Mason. 1973. Incl.: Tape 3, T-10, T-11; Clinical Applications, rev. ed. 1979; Brief Outlines 2, Feeling Training. pap. 35.00 (*0-89533-016-4*) F I Comm.

Basic International Language Quick International Understanding in One-Tenth the Time Using International Words. Wesley E. Arnold. 104p. (Orig.). 1993. pap. 5.98 (*0-915935-12-0*) W Arnold.

Basic Interviewing Skills. Raymond L. Gorden. LC 91-76456. 260p. 1992. pap. 24.00 (*0-87581-358-5*) Peacock Pubs.

Basic Introduction to Health Services Administration: Selected Readings. Ed. by William T. Hall. LC 76-26094. (Illus.). 331p. (C). 1976. pap. text ed. 9.95 (*0-8422-0508-X*) Irvington.

Basic Investors Library Series, 14 vols., Set. Intro. by Paul A. Samuelson. (Illus.). 672p. 1988. lib. bdg. 181.30 (*1-55546-619-2*) Chelsea Hse.

Basic Iris Culture. American Iris Society Staff. (Illus.). 1982. 1.25 (*0-9601242-3-3*) Am Iris.

Basic Is Beautiful: Basic Ecclesial Communities from Third World to First World. Margaret Hebblethwaite. 1993. pap. 15.00 (*0-00-627470-6*, Pub. by Fount UK) Harper SF.

BASIC Is Child's Play: IBM-PCjr Edition. Robert T. Grauer et al. (Illus.). 192p. 1984. pap. text ed. 23.95 (*0-13-058827-X*) P-H.

BASIC Is Child's Play: TRS-80 Edition. Robert T. Grauer et al. (Illus.). 112p. 1984. pap. text ed. 23.95 (*0-13-058801-6*) P-H.

Basic Issues & References in Policy Studies. Ed. by Stuart Nagel. (C). 1972. pap. 12.00 (*0-918592-00-3*) Pol Studies.

Basic Issues in Aesthetics. Marcia M. Eaton. 154p. (C). 1988. pap. 19.95 (*0-534-08256-4*) Intl Thomson.

Basic Issues in Coordinating Family & Child Welfare Programs. Ed. by Charles P. Cella & Rodney Lane. 1964. 39.50 (*0-317-27416-3*) Elliots Bks.

Basic Issues in Hearing: Proceedings of the Eighth International Symposium on Hearing, Groningen. Ed. by H. Duifhuis et al. 470p. 1988. text ed. 72.00 (*0-12-223346-8*) Acad Pr.

Basic Issues in Psychopathology. Ed. by Charles G. Costello. LC 92-48972. 465p. 1993. lib. bdg. 45.00 (*0-89862-139-9*) Guilford Pr.

Basic Issues in Social Sciences. 2nd ed. Ed. by Keshav D. Sharma. 206p. 1994. 17.50 (*0-685-71524-8*) Univ Rescs Pr.

Basic Issues in the Philosophy of Science. Ed. by William R. Shea. LC 76-22198. 1976. pap. text ed. 7.95 (*0-88202-160-5*) Watson Pub Intl.

Basic Italian. 6th annot. rev. ed. Charles Speroni & Carlo L. Golino. Ed. by Julia Price. (Illus.). 512p. (C). 1989. teacher ed 25.90 (*0-03-013593-1*) HB Coll Pubs.

Basic Italian. 6th rev. ed. Charles Speroni & Carlo L. Golino. Ed. by Julia Price. (Illus.). 512p. (C). 1989. text ed. 45.25 (*0-03-013603-2*); audio write for info. (*0-03-023018-7*) HB Coll Pubs.

Basic Italian. 7th ed. Charles Speroni et al. (C). 1993. lib. bdg. 47.00 (*0-03-074991-3*) HB Coll Pubs.

Basic Italian Conversation. Mario Costantino. (Illus.). 280p. 1991. pap. 15.95 (*0-8442-8055-0*, Natl Textbk) NTC Pub Grp.

Basic Italic with an Introduction to Cursive: Book C - Basic Italic. 3rd ed. Barbara Getty & Inga Dubay. (Italic Handwriting Ser.: Bk. C). 60p. 1994. pap. 5.75 (*0-87678-094-X*) PSU CE Pr.

Basic Japanese-Catalan, Catalan-Japanese Dictionary: Diccionari Basic Japones-Catala-Japones. A. Torres. 562p. (CAT & JPN.). 1984. 49.95 (*0-8288-1010-9*, S50354) Fr & Eur.

Basic Japanese Conversation Dictionary: English-Japanese & Japanese-English. Samuel Martin. LC 57-8797. 266p. (ENG & JPN.). 1957. pap. 6.95 (*0-8048-0057-X*) C E Tuttle.

Basic Japanese-English Dictionary. Japan Foundation Staff. LC 92-38748. 976p. 1993. 17.95 (*0-19-864328-4*) OUP.

Basic Japanese-English-Japanese Conversation Dictionary. 50th ed. S. E. Marin. (ENG & JPN.). 1982. pap. 6.95 (*0-8288-1610-7*, M14399) Fr & Eur.

Basic Jewelry Making Techniques. Susan Tolland. 1993. 12.98 (*1-55521-904-7*) Bk Sales Inc.

Basic Jig & Fixture Making for Metalworking Trainees. Herb Harig. 149p. 1982. teacher ed 10.95 (*0-910399-10-7*, 5071); pap. text ed. 14.50 (*0-910399-09-3*, 5070) Natl Tool & Mach.

Basic Judaism. Milton Steinberg. LC 47-30768. 1965. pap. 6.95 (*0-15-610698-1*, Harvest Bks) HarBrace.

Basic Judaism for Young People Vol. 3: God. Naomi Pasachoff. (Basic Judaism Ser.). (J). (gr. 6-7). pap. 8.95 (*0-87441-425-3*); teacher ed, pap. 14.95 (*0-87441-472-5*); student ed, pap. 4.50 (*0-87441-473-3*) Behrman.

Basic Judaism for Young People, Vol. 1: Israel. Naomi Pasachoff. 90p. (J). (gr. 4-5). 1987. By Lesley Silverstone. student ed 4.25 (*0-87441-440-7*); pap. text ed. 7.95 (*0-87441-423-7*) Behrman.

Basic Judaism for Young People, Vol 2: Torah. Naomi Pasachoff. 92p. (J). (gr. 5-6). 1986. By Lois M. Cohn. student ed 4.25 (*0-87441-442-3*); pap. text ed. 7.95 (*0-87441-424-5*) Behrman.

Basic Jumping: Crowood Equestrian Guide. Carol Foster. (Illus.). 96p. 1992. pap. 17.95 (*1-85223-547-0*, Pub. by Crowood Pr UK) Trafalgar.

Basic Kafka. Franz Kafka. Ed. by Erich Heller. 1984. mass mkt. 5.99 (*0-671-53145-X*, WSP) PB.

Basic Karate for College. Daniel H. McGraw. (Illus.). 76p. (C). 1983. pap. text ed. 7.98 (*0-911929-00-2*) Onami Pubns.

Basic Karate Handbook. Fred Neff. LC 75-38471. (Fred Neff's Self-Defense Library). (Illus.). 56p. (J). (gr. 5 up). 1976. lib. bdg. 14.95 (*0-8225-1150-9*, Lerner Publctns) Lerner Group.

***Basic Keelboat: The National Standard for Quality Sailing Instruction.** Monk Henry. Ed. by Mark Smith. (Certification Ser.). (Illus.). 96p. (Orig.). (C). 1995. pap. 14.95 (*1-882502-21-3*) US Sail Assn.

Basic Keyboard Chords. Brimhall. (Keyboard Chords Ser.). 1990. 3.95 (*0-685-32019-7*, P031) Hansen Ed Mus.

Basic Keyboard Skills: An Introduction to Accompaniment Improvisation, Transposition & Modulation, with an Appendix on Sight Reading. William Pelz. LC 80-22820. vii, 173p. 1981. reprint ed. text ed. 38.50 (*0-313-22882-5*, PEBK) Greenwood.

***Basic Keyboarding for the Medical Office Assistant.** Edna J. Moss. LC 94-26242. 312p. 1994. pap. text ed. 24.95 (*0-8273-5798-2*) Delmar.

Basic Knit Sweaters: Step-by-Step. Ondori Publishing Company Staff. (Illus.). 64p. 1986. pap. 11.95 (*0-87040-654-X*) Japan Pubns USA.

Basic Laboratory & Industrial Chemicals. David R. Lide, Jr. 1993. 39.95 (*0-8493-4498-0*, QP64) CRC Pr.

Basic Laboratory Exercises for Physiology I. Edgar J. Cervantes. 96p. 1993. spiral bd. 16.95 (*0-8403-8866-7*) Kendall-Hunt.

Basic Laboratory Principles in General Chemistry with Quantitative Techniques. Bramwell et al. 272p. 1989. spiral bd. 25.95 (*0-8403-5654-4*) Kendall-Hunt.

Basic Laboratory Studies in General Chemistry: With Semimicro Qualitative Analysis. 9th ed. Grace R. Hered. 480p. (C). 1991. pap. text ed. write for info. (*0-669-24432-5*); Instr.'s guide. teacher ed write for info. (*0-669-24433-3*) Heath.

Basic Lace. Nihon Vogue Staff. (Illus.). 1986. pap. 10.95 (*0-87040-651-5*) Japan Pubns USA.

Basic Landscape Techniques. Ed. by Greg Albert & Rachel Wolf. (Basic Technique Ser.). (Illus.). 128p. 1993. pap. 16.95 (*0-89134-464-0*, 30478) North Light Bks.

Basic Latin American Legal Materials 1970-1975. Ed. by Juan F. Aguilar & Armando E. Gonzalez. (American Association of Law Libraries Publications Ser.: No. 13). vi, 106p. 1977. pap. 12.50 (*0-8377-0111-2*) Rothman.

Basic Latin for Plant Taxonomists. A. Baranov. 1971. pap. text ed. 35.00 (*3-7682-0727-7*) Lubrecht & Cramer.

Basic Law & Hong Kong's Future. Wesley-Smith & Chen. 1988. pap. 36.00 (*0-409-99567-3*) Butterworth Legal Pubs.

Basic Law & Hong Kong's Future. Ed. by Peter Wesley-Smith & Albert H. Chen. 400p. 1988. 57.00 (*0-409-99569-X*) Butterworth Legal Pubs.

Basic Law & the Legal Environment of Business. John E. Adamson. LC 94-12327. (Irwin Legal Studies in Business Ser.). 640p. (C). 1994. text ed. 46.95 (*0-256-11302-5*) Irwin.

Basic Law for Allied Health Professions. Michael L. Cowdrey. 368p. 1990. pap. 32.50 (*0-86720-446-X*) Jones & Bartlett.

Basic Law for the Allied Health Professions. Michael L. Cowdrey. LC 83-23390. 300p. (C). 1984. pap. text ed. 27.50 (*0-534-03208-7*) Jones & Bartlett.

***Basic Law for the Allied Health Professions.** 2nd ed. Michael L. Cowdrey & Melinda Drew. LC 94-38115. 1995. 33.75 (*0-86720-710-8*) Jones & Bartlett.

Basic Law of Corporations, Cases, Text & Analyses. J. S. Covington, Jr. LC 89-80347. 643p. 1989. boxed 48.00 (*0-916081-14-1*) J Marshall Pub Co.

Basic Law of Hong Kong: Analysis & Documents. Ed. by Hungdah Chiu. 150p. (Orig.). 1989. pap. 5.00 (*0-942182-91-X*) Occasional Papers.

Basic Law Text: Civil Procedure. Roy L. Brooks. (Winning in Law School Ser.). 200p. (Orig.). (C). 1992. pap. text ed. 12.95 (*0-915667-19-3*) Spectra Pub Co.

Basic Law Text: Criminal Law. Jonathan C. Carlson. (Winning in Law School Ser.). 175p. (Orig.). (C). 1992. pap. text ed. 12.95 (*0-915667-20-7*) Spectra Pub Co.

Basic Law Text: Torts. James M. Dente. (Winning in Law School Ser.: Bk. 6). 199p. (Orig.). 1986. pap. text ed. 12.95 (*0-915667-11-8*) Spectra Pub Co.

Basic Laws on Housing & Community Development. 1986. lib. bdg. 79.95 (*0-8490-3536-8*) Gordon Pr.

Basic Lawyering Skills Training: Participants' Manual. 86p. 1988. 42.00 (*0-685-29759-4*, 44,370) NCLS Inc.

Basic Leader Skills: Handbook for Church Leaders. Richard E. Rusbuldt. 64p. 1981. pap. 9.00 (*0-8170-0920-5*) Judson.

***Basic Learning Skills Bk. II: How Music Can Contribute, Bk. II.** Elizabeth L. Mayer. (Music Makes a Difference Ser.). 12p. 1994. pap. 1.95 (*1-886380-01-5*) Langstaff Vid.

Basic Legal Documents of the Russian Federation. Ed. & Tr. by William E. Butler. (Studies on Socialist Legal Systems. Faculty of Laws. University College, London). 306p. 1992. lib. bdg. 75.00 (*0-379-20308-1*) Oceana.

Basic Legal Documents of the Soviet Legal System. 3rd ed. Ed. & Tr. by William E. Butler. (Studies on Socialist Legal Systems. Faculty of Laws. University College, London). 557p. 1992. lib. bdg. 75.00 (*0-379-20311-1*) Oceana.

Basic Legal Forms. 2nd ed. Marvin Hyman. LC 80-53751. (Forms Ser.). 480p. 1991. 110.00 (*0-7913-0893-6*); Supplemented semi-annually, write for info. write for info. (*0-318-68837-9*) Warren Gorham & Lamont.

Basic Legal Forms for Business. Morris A. Nunes. LC 92-33345. 256p. 1993. disk, pap. 37.50 (*0-471-59279-X*) Wiley.

Basic Legal Research & Writing. Edward A. Nolfi & Pamela R. Tepper. LC 92-25750. (Legal Studies Ser.). 1992. 45.00 (*0-02-801276-3*) Glencoe.

Basic Legal Transactions. Vincent DiLorenzo. (General Law Ser.). 736p. 1985. 110.00 (*0-88712-353-8*) Warren Gorham & Lamont.

Basic Legal Transactions, No. 1. suppl. ed. Vincent DiLorenzo. (General Law Ser.). 736p. 1992. Supplemented semi-annually, write for info. 67.25 (*0-7913-1231-3*) Warren Gorham & Lamont.

Basic Legal Transactions, No. 2. suppl. ed. Vincent DiLorenzo. (General Law Ser.). 736p. 1992. 67.25 (*0-685-55747-2*) Warren Gorham & Lamont.

Basic Lesson Plans for Cosmetology Teacher. 1981. 49.95 (*0-87350-355-4*) Milady Pub.

Basic Lesson Plans for Manicuring. 204p. ring bd. 39.95 (*0-87350-442-9*) Milady Pub.

Basic Lessons in Synergetics. Florence E. Worrell. (Illus.). 90p. (Orig.). 1984. pap. 2.95 (*0-910217-05-X*) Synergetics WV.

Basic Letter & Memo Writing. 3rd ed. Susie J. Vanhuss. 1993. pap. 15.95 (*0-538-61342-4*) S-W Pub.

Basic Library of the World's Greatest Music. Lee Lambert. (Illus.). 155p. (YA). (gr. 7 up). 1988. pap. text ed. 39.00 (*0-9621630-1-5*) L Lambert.

Basic Library of the World's Greatest Music: Musical Learning System. Lee Lambert. (Illus.). 356p. (Orig.). 1990. teacher ed, pap. 29.00 (*0-9621630-0-7*) L Lambert.

Basic Library Skills. 3rd ed. Carolyn Wolf & Richard Wolf. LC 92-51100. (Illus.). 192p. 1993. pap. 19.95 (*0-89950-895-2*) McFarland & Co.

Basic Life Support: Skills Manual. Charles L. Phillips. LC 77-8351. 1977. pap. 14.95 (*0-87618-883-8*) P-H.

Basic Life Support Skills. 2nd ed. Charles L. Phillips. (Illus.). 224p. 1986. pap. text ed. 30.00 (*0-89303-253-0*) P-H.

Basic Lifeguard Textbook. American Red Cross Staff. 1994. 12.50 (*0-8016-7555-3*) Mosby Yr Bk.

Basic Lighting Worktext for Film & Video. Richard K. Ferncase. 109p. 1992. pap. 24.95 (*0-240-80085-0*, Focal) Buttrwrth-Heinemann.

Basic Listening Skills: Strategies, Readings, & Exercises. Allen et al. 168p. 1991. 14.95 (*0-8403-6549-7*) Kendall-Hunt.

Basic Literature of American Public Administration, 1787-1950. Ed. by Frederick C. Mosher. LC 79-28553. 314p. (C). 1981. 34.50 (*0-8419-0574-6*); pap. 15.95 (*0-8419-0575-4*) Holmes & Meier.

Basic Logic. Richard L. Mendelsohn & Lewis M. Schwartz. 320p. (C). 1986. pap. text ed. write for info. (*0-13-062548-5*) P-H.

***Basic Look at WordPerfect 6.0.** Sandra Surman & Eleridge M. James. LC 94-96608. (Illus.). 75p. (Orig.). 1994. pap. 25.00 (*1-886423-00-8*) Basic Look.

***Basic Louisiana Notary Guide, 2 vols., Set.** James D. Johnson, Jr. 1986. 180.00 (*0-87511-760-0*) Claitors.

***Basic Luther.** Martin Luther. LC 95-60058. 1995. pap. 12.95 (*0-87243-213-0*) Templegate.

Basic-ly Communicating: An Activity Approach. 2nd ed. Roy M. Berko et al. 312p. (C). 1989. spiral bd. write for info. (*0-697-04072-0*) Brown & Benchmark.

Basic Machine Shop Theory: All You Need to Know about Tools & Processes. William E. Hardman. 254p. 15.95 (*0-910399-02-6*, 5011); teacher ed, pap. 10.95 (*0-318-17820-6*, 5111) Natl Tool & Mach.

Basic Machine Technology. Thomas C. Olivo. 1980. 21.95 (*0-672-97171-2*, Bobbs) Macmillan.

An Asterisk (*) at the beginning of an entry indicates that the title is appearing in BIP for the first time.

An Asterisk (*) at the beginning of an entry indicates that the title is appearing in BIP for the first time.

615

Basic Matrix Analysis & Synthesis: Applications to Electronic Engineering. G. Zelinger & D. Fry. LC 66-18240. (International Series of Monographs in Electromagnetic Waves: Vol. 36). 1966. 100.00 (*0-08-011590-X*, Pub. by Pergamon Repr UK) Franklin.

BASIC Matrix Methods. John C. Mason. (Basic Ser.). (Illus.). 160p. 1984. pap. 24.95 (*0-408-01390-7*) Buttrwrth-Heinemann.

Basic Meaning in Four Parts. Phil Galgiani. (Illus.). 80p. 1983. pap. 10.00 (*0-939784-05-X*) CEPA Gall.

Basic Measurement Activities. Dorothy Diamond. 72p. (C). 1985. pap. 50.00 (*0-7175-1359-9*, Pub. by S Thornes Pubs UK) St Mut.

Basic Mechanical Drawing. Glen N. Schaeffer & W. E. Burns. 1982. pap. 8.64 (*0-02-827940-9*) Glencoe.

Basic Mechanical Maintenance Procedures at Water & Wastewater Plants. Glenn M. Tillman. (Water & Wastewater Operators Guide Ser.). 96p. 1991. 46.95 (*0-87371-429-6*, TK) Lewis Pubs.

Basic Mechanical Power Transmission. (Principles of Steam Generation Ser.: Module 3). (Illus.). 50p. 1982. spiral bd. 17.50 (*0-87683-253-2*) GP Pub.

BASIC Mechanical Vibrations. A. J. Pretlove. (Basic Ser.). (Illus.). 128p. 1985. pap. text ed. 24.95 (*0-408-01554-3*) Buttrwrth-Heinemann.

Basic Mechanics of Machines. Samuel Doughty. LC 87-23042. 467p. 1988. Net. text ed. write for info. (*0-471-84276-1*) Wiley.

Basic Mechanisms Controlling Term & Preterm Birth. Ed. by Kristof Schwalisz & Robert Garfield. LC 93-37409. (Schering Foundation Workshop Ser.: Vol. 7). 1994. 86.00 (*0-387-57191-4*) Spr-Verlag.

Basic Mechanisms in Fatigue of Materials: Proceedings of the International Colloquium, Brno, Czechoslovakia, 12-14 April, 1988. Ed. by P. Lukas & J. Polak. (Materials Science Monographs: 46). 450p. 1988. 166.75 (*0-444-98926-9*) Elsevier.

Basic Mechanisms in Mucosal Immunology: Journal: Immunologic Research, Vol. 10, Nos. 3-4, 1991. Ed. by M. Zeitz et al. (Illus.). vi, 370p. 1991. pap. 60.00 (*3-8055-5471-0*) S Karger.

Basic Mechanisms in Two-Phase Flow & Heat Transfer: Proceedings of the Symposium, Chicago, 1980. Basic Mechanisms in Two-phase Flow & Heat Transfer Symposium Staff. Ed. by P. H. Rothe & R. T. Lahey. LC 80-69186. 135p. reprint ed. pap. 38.50 (*0-8357-5982-2*, 2024181) Bks Demand.

Basic Mechanisms of Aqueous Corrosion of Nuclear Waste Glasses Task 3, No. EUR 13605. E. Vernaz & J. L. Dussossoy. 98p. 1991. pap. 11.00 (*92-826-2817-5*, CD-NA-13605-EN-C) UNIPUB.

Basic Mechanisms of Headache: Pain Research & Clinical Management, 2, 1988. Ed. by J. Olesen & Lars Edvinsson. 508p. 1988. 192.50 (*0-444-80955-4*) Elsevier.

Basic Mechanisms of Ocular Motility & Their Clinical Implications. Ed. by G. Lennerstrand & Paul Bach-Y-Rita. 1975. 234.00 (*0-08-018885-0*, Pub. by Pergamon Repr UK) Franklin.

Basic Mechanisms of Pediatric Respiratory Disorders: Cellular & Integrative. Chernick. (Illus.). 464p. (C). 1990. 92.00 (*1-55664-137-0*) Mosby Yr Bk.

***Basic Mechanisms of Physiological & Aberrant Lymphoproliferation in the Skin.** Ed. by W. C. Lambert & W. A. Van Vloten. (NATO ASI Series A, Life Sciences: 265). (Illus.). 600p. 1994. 135.00 (*0-306-44736-3*, Plenum Pr) Plenum.

Basic Mechanisms of Solar Activity. Ed. by Vaclav Bumba & Josip Kleczek. (Symposium of the International Astronomical Union Ser.: Vol. 71). 1976. lib. bdg. 149.50 (*90-277-0680-8*); pap. text ed. 89.00 (*90-277-0681-6*) Kluwer Ac.

Basic Mechanisms of the EEG. Ed. by Stephan Zschocke & Erwin-Joseph Speckmann. LC 92-48487. (Brain Dynamics Ser.). (Illus.). xv, 355p. 1993. 99.00 (*0-8176-3596-3*) Birkhauser.

Basic Mechanisms of the Epilepsies: Molecular & Cellular Approaches. Ed. by Antonio V. Delgado-Escueta et al. (Advances in Neurology Ser.: Vol. 44). (Illus.). 1120p. 1986. text ed. 142.50 (*0-88167-152-5*) Raven.

***Basic Media Writing.** Melvin Mencher. 480p. (C). 1995. write for info. (*0-697-27002-5*); pap. write for info. (*0-697-27001-7*) Brown & Benchmark.

Basic Media Writing. 4th ed. Melvin Mencher. 480p. (C). 1993. student ed write for info. (*0-697-08666-6*); pap. text ed. write for info. (*0-697-08664-X*) Brown & Benchmark.

Basic Medical Biochemistry. Dawn B. Marks. (Illus.). 550p. 1995. write for info. (*0-683-05595-X*) Williams & Wilkins.

Basic Medical Endocrinology. 2nd ed. Maurice Goodman. LC 93-25656. (Series in Physiology). 352p. 1994. 69.00 (*0-7817-0106-6*); pap. 38.00 (*0-7817-0105-8*) Raven.

Basic Medical Ethics: A New Approach. Vernon E. Grosvenor. (Orig.). (C). 1993. pap. text ed. 50.00 (*0-9630629-1-3*) Twenty Fst Century.

Basic Medical Laboratory Subjects. Patrick Cuviella & Hugh Woosley. LC 74-18675. (Allied Health Ser.). 1975. pap. write for info. (*0-672-61383-2*) Macmillan.

Basic Medical Laboratory Techniques. 2nd ed. Norma J. Walters et al. LC 85-12885. 412p. 1989. teacher ed 16.00 (*0-8273-3949-6*); pap. text ed. 32.95 (*0-8273-3948-8*) Delmar.

***Basic Medical Laboratory Techniques.** 3rd ed. Norma J. Walters et al. LC 95-9991. (Health & Life Science Ser.). (Illus.). 516p. 1995. pap. 32.95 (*0-8273-6225-0*) Delmar.

***Basic Medical Laboratory Techniques.** 3rd ed. Norma J. Walters et al. LC 95-9991. 1995. write for info. (*0-8273-6228-5*) Delmar.

Basic Medical Microbiology. 3rd ed. Robert F. Boyd & Bryan G. Hoerl. 976p. 1985. 42.50 (*0-316-10441-8*, Little Med Div) Little.

***Basic Medical Microbiology.** 5th ed. Robert F. Boyd. LC 94-24134. 1995. 53.95 (*0-316-10445-0*) Little.

Basic Medical NMR Imaging. Bryan et al. Date not set. pap. 39.95 (*0-8016-0627-6*) Mosby Yr Bk.

Basic Medical-Surgical Nursing. 5th ed. Mildred A. Mason & Grace F. Bates. 915p. 1984. text ed. 36.95 (*0-07-105295-X*); Wkbk. student ed 15.95 (*0-07-105296-8*) Hlth Prof Div.

Basic Medical Techniques & Patient Care for Radiologic Technologists. 4th ed. Lillian S. Torres. LC 92-49543. 1993. text ed. 29.95 (*0-397-54963-6*) Lippincott.

Basic Medical Terminology. J. Patrick Fisher. LC 74-77820. (Allied Health Ser.). 1975. pap. text ed. 14.95 (*0-672-61385-9*, Bobbs); audio 115.50 (*0-672-61387-5*, Bobbs) Macmillan.

Basic Medical Terminology. 2nd ed. J. Patrick Fisher. 288p. 1983. teacher ed write for info. (*0-672-61574-6*); pap. text ed. write for info. (*0-672-61573-8*); audio write for info. (*0-672-61575-4*) Macmillan.

Basic Medical Terminology. 3rd ed. J. Patrick Fisher. 1987. 21.32 (*0-02-685180-6*) Macmillan.

***Basic Medical Terminology Concepts.** 2nd ed. Marilyn W. Wilson. LC 94-45259. 1995. pap. 18.90 (*0-8359-4956-7*) P-H.

Basic Medical Terminology Instructors Guide. Meaus. 1987. 5.84 (*0-02-685470-8*) Macmillan.

Basic Medicine for Emergency Personnel. Roger Evans & Pat Durston. 256p. 1985. pap. text ed. 29.95 (*0-407-00314-2*) Buttrwrth-Heinemann.

Basic Menus & Recipes for Diabetics. Pat Blanchard. Ed. by Sharon K. Boudreaux. 67p. 1989. pap. 7.99 (*0-926423-00-2*) Creole Pub.

Basic Metallurgy. Donald Brown. LC 80-68584. (Mechanical Ser.). (Illus.). 323p. (Orig.). (C). 1981. teacher ed 12.00 (*0-8273-1770-0*); pap. text ed. 29.95 (*0-8273-1769-7*) Delmar.

Basic Metallurgy for Non-Destructive Testing. rev. ed. Ed. by J. L. Taylor. 87p. 1988. 37.50 (*0-903132-18-4*, 1186) Am Soc Nondestructive.

Basic Metalwork. John L. Feirer & John R. Lindbeck. (gr. 9-12). 1978. 10.64 (*0-02-662610-1*); pap. 8.56 (*0-02-662600-4*) Bennett IL.

Basic Meteorology, an Introduction to the Science. L. Moses & John Tomikel. (Illus.). 130p. (C). 1981. pap. text ed. 14.95 (*0-910042-39-X*) Allegheny.

Basic Meteorology Exercise Manual. 3rd ed. Ed. by Carl R. Chelius & Henry J. Frentz. 240p. 1991. spiral bd. 19.95 (*0-8403-6742-2*) Kendall-Hunt.

Basic Methods for Microcomputer-Aided Analysis of Electronic Circuits. M. Bialko et al. LC 94-13684. 1995. pap. text ed. 44.00 (*0-13-061284-7*) P-H.

Basic Methods in Biological X-Ray Microanalysis. Ed. by Om Johari. (Illus.). iv, 284p. (Orig.). 1983. reprint ed. pap. text ed. 22.00 (*0-931288-28-2*) Scanning Microscopy.

Basic Methods in Molecular Biology. 2nd ed. Leonard G. Davis et al. (Illus.). 1994. pap. text ed. 59.95 (*0-8385-0642-9*, A0642-7) Appleton & Lange.

Basic Methods of Evaluative & Action Research. Bangladesh Government, National Institute for Population Research & Training Staff. 166p. 1984. text ed. 15.95 (*0-89914-006-8*) Third Party Pub.

Basic Methods of Policy Analysis & Planning. 2nd ed. Carl V. Patton & David S. Sawicki. 512p. (C). 1993. pap. text ed. write for info. (*0-13-060948-X*) P-H.

Basic Methods of Structural Geology. Stephen Marshak & Gautam Mitra. 446p. (C). 1988. pap. text ed. write for info. (*0-13-065178-8*) P-H.

Basic Methods of Tomography & Inverse Problems. P. C. Sabatier. (Malvern Physics Ser.). (Illus.). 688p. 1987. 140.00 (*0-85274-475-7*) IOP Pub.

Basic Methods, Scales & Fixed Points, Radiation see Temperature: Its Measurement & Control in Science & Industry

Basic Michaelis English-Portuguese, Portuguese-English Dictionary: Dicionario Basico Michaelis Ingles-Portugues-Ingles. Michaelis. 856p. (ENG & POR.). 1985. 75.00 (*0-8288-0493-1*, M9285) Fr & Eur.

Basic Microbiology. Orten C. Skinner. LC 74-78590. (Allied Health Ser.). 1975. pap. 9.50 (*0-672-61390-5*, Bobbs) Macmillan.

Basic Microbiology. 5th ed. Wesley A. Volk & Margaret Wheeler. 704p. (C). 1984. 10.50 (*0-06-046846-7*) HarpCollege.

Basic Microbiology. 6th ed. Wesley A. Volk & Margaret Wheeler. 687p. (C). 1990. text ed. 43.75 (*0-06-046848-3*) HarpCollege.

Basic Microbiology. 7th ed. Wesley A. Volk. (C). 1991. text ed. 69.00 (*0-06-046849-1*) HarpCollege.

Basic Microbiology. 7th ed. Wesley A. Volk. (C). 1992. 20.00 (*0-06-501012-4*) HarpCollege.

Basic Microbiology Dictionary. Jennifer Langlois & David Ashley. (Illus.). 150p. Date not set. lib. bdg. 25.00 (*1-56308-112-1*) Libs Unl.

Basic Microbiology Study Guide. Harry E. Peery & Margaret A. Singer. 288p. 1986. pap. text ed. write for info. (*0-02-304410-1*) Macmillan.

Basic Microbiology Techniques. 3rd ed. Susan G. Kelley & Frederick J. Post. (Illus.). 272p. (C). 1989. 22.95 (*0-89863-116-5*) Star Pub CA.

Basic Microbiology with Application. 3rd ed. Thomas D. Brock et al. (Illus.). 688p. 1986. text ed. write for info. (*0-13-065244-X*) P-H.

Basic Microcomputer Models in Biology. James D. Spain. 368p. (C). 1982. text ed. 35.50 (*0-201-10678-7*) Benjamin-Cummings.

BASIC Microcomputing & Biostatistics. Donald W. Rogers. LC 81-85465. (Contemporary Instrumentation & Analysis Ser.). 304p. 1983. 59.50 (*0-89603-015-6*) Humana.

***Basic Microcurrent Therapy: Acupoint & Body Work Manual.** Carolyn W. Greenlee. Ed. by Dennis L. Greenlee & Thomas W. Wing. (Illus.). 124p. 1995. student ed 35.00 (*1-887400-06-0*) Earthen Vessel Prodns.

Basic Microeconomics. Paul R. Gregory & Roy J. Ruffin. (C). 1988. pap. text ed. 44.00 (*0-673-38043-2*) HarpCollege.

Basic Microwaving. rev. ed. Barbara Methven. LC 87-20082. (Microwave Cooking Library). (Illus.). 160p. 1988. 16.95 (*0-86573-554-9*) Cy De Cosse.

Basic Modelling: Advances & Applications. Ed. by A. G. Dore et al. (Norwegian Pertroleum Society Special Publication Ser.: Vol. 3). 700p. 1993. 200.00 (*0-444-89272-9*) Elsevier.

BASIC Molecular Spectroscopy. P. A. Gorry. LC 85-14992. (Basic Ser.). (Illus.). 160p. 1986. pap. text ed. 24.95 (*0-408-01553-5*) Buttrwrth-Heinemann.

Basic Montessori: Learning Activities for Under-Fives. David Gettman. (Illus.). 240p. 1988. pap. 11.95 (*0-312-01864-9*) St Martin.

Basic Moral Concepts. Robert Spaemann. 96p. 1990. 42.50 (*0-415-04160-0*, A3866); pap. 14.95 (*0-415-02966-X*, A3870) Routledge.

Basic Moral Philosophy. Robert L. Holmes. 244p. (C). 1993. pap. 19.95 (*0-534-19656-X*) Intl Thomson.

***Basic Motorboat Seamanship.** William V. Kielhorn. 164p. (Orig.). 1995. pap. write for info. (*1-885591-68-3*) Morris Pubng.

Basic Movement Activities. rev. ed. Jack Capon. Ed. by Frank Alexander. (Perceptual-Motor Development Ser.: Bk. 1). (Illus.). 27p. 1994. reprint ed. teacher ed 7.00 (*0-915256-36-3*, 121) Front Row.

Basic Movement Exercises. Barbara Mettler. 1973. 18.50 (*0-912536-06-3*) Mettler Studios.

Basic Multivariable Calculus. Jerrold E. Marsden et al. xv, 533p. 1993. write for info. (*3-540-97976-X*) Spr-Verlag.

Basic Multivariable Calculus. Jerrold E. Marsden et al. LC 92-38049. 1993. 49.00 (*0-387-97976-X*) Spr-Verlag.

Basic Music. 6th ed. Robert E. Nye & Bjonnar Bergethon. (Illus.). 256p. (C). 1987. pap. text ed. write for info. (*0-13-065681-X*) P-H.

Basic Music Theory. Charles H. Douglas. Ed. by Wesley M. McKenzie. 1970. pap. 3.95 (*0-910842-01-9*, GE11) Kjos.

Basic Music Work & Play. E. E. Greenleaf. 1964. pap. 1.95 (*0-87511-593-4*) Claitors.

Basic Musicianship: An Introduction to Music Fundamentals with Computer Assistance. Raynold L. Allvin. 180p. (C). 1985. Spiralbound. pap. 33.95 (*0-534-04059-4*) Intl Thomson.

Basic Mutagenicity Tests: UKEMS Recommended Procedures. Ed. by David J. Kirkland. 180p. (C). 1990. 69.95 (*0-521-39347-7*) Cambridge U Pr.

Basic Narcotic Detection Dog Training. Jack Robicheaux & John A. Jons. (Illus.). 52p. (Orig.). 1990. pap. text ed. write for info. (*0-9623099-1-5*) J Jons LA.

***Basic Nature Projects: 120 Fun Explorations.** Priscilla M. Tucker. (Illus.). 256p. 1995. pap. 14.95 (*0-8117-2511-1*) Stackpole.

Basic Needlery Stitches on Mesh Fabrics. Mary A. Beinecke. LC 73-77444. 64p. (Orig.). 1973. pap. 4.50 (*0-486-21713-2*) Dover.

Basic Needs. Clara Cole. (Social Studies Ser.). 24p. (gr. 2-3). 1977. student ed 5.00 (*0-8209-0259-4*, SS-26) ESP.

Basic Needs: A Year with Street Kids in a City School. Julie Landsman. LC 93-16148. 200p. (Orig.). 1993. pap. 12.95 (*0-915943-65-4*) Milkweed Ed.

Basic Needs in Development Planning. M. Hopkins & R. Van der Hoeven. 184p. 1984. text ed. 59.95 (*0-566-00626-X*) Ashgate Pub Co.

Basic Needs Policy Model: A General Equilibrium Analysis with Special Reference to Ecuador - Contribution to Economic Analysis. Ed. by A. Kouwenaar. 175p. 1988. 95.00 (*0-444-70468-X*, North Holland) Elsevier.

Basic Needs, Women & Development: A Survey of Squatters in Lahore, Pakistan. Nasra M. Shah & Muhammad Anwar. xii, 164p. 1986. pap. 6.00 (*0-86638-076-0*) EW Ctr HI.

Basic Negotiation Procedures. (National Contract Management Association Workshop Ser.). 52p. (Orig.). 1991. pap. 10.95 (*0-940343-47-9*) Natl Contract Mgmt.

Basic Network Theory with Computer Applications. Jiri Vlach. 1992. text ed. 62.95 (*0-442-00900-3*) Van Nos Reinhold.

Basic Neuro-Ophthalmology. Bradley K. Farris. 320p. 1991. pap. 39.95 (*0-8016-1600-X*) Mosby Yr Bk.

Basic Neuroanatomy. 2nd ed. Carlton G. Smith. LC 75-31035. 303p. reprint ed. pap. 86.40 (*0-8357-5983-0*, 2056118) Bks Demand.

Basic Neuroanatomy. 3rd ed. Carlton Smith & Direk J. van der Kooy. 1985. pap. text ed. 27.95 (*0-07-105312-3*) McGraw.

Basic Neurochemistry. 3rd ed. George J. Siegel et al. 1981. 39.00 (*0-316-79002-8*) Little.

Basic Neurochemistry: Molecular, Cellular, & Medical Aspects. 5th ed. Ed. by George J. Siegel et al. LC 93-24375. 1104p. 1994. 67.00 (*0-7817-0104-X*); sl. write for info. (*0-7817-0134-1*) Raven.

Basic Neurology. 2nd ed. John Gilroy. 384p. 1990. text ed. 55.00 (*0-07-105271-2*); pap. text ed. 38.00 (*0-07-105272-0*) Hlth Prof Div.

Basic Neurology. 2nd ed. John Gilroy. 384p. (C). 1989. text ed. write for info. (*0-318-36016-0*) Macmillan.

Basic Neurology. 2nd ed. John Gilroy. 1990. text ed. 55.00 (*0-08-040297-6*, Pub. by PPI UK); pap. text ed. 29.50 (*0-08-040301-8*, Pub. by PPI UK) McGraw.

Basic Neuroradiology. Mohammad Sarwar et al. (Illus.). 863p. 1983. 95.00 (*0-87527-230-4*) Green.

Basic Neuroscience: Anatomy & Physiology. 2nd ed. Arthur C. Guyton. (Illus.). 432p. 1991. write for info. (*0-318-68524-8*) Saunders.

Basic Neuroscience for the Health Professions. Elizabeth H. Littell. LC 88-43482. 300p. 1990. 38.00 (*1-55642-053-6*) SLACK Inc.

Basic News Writing. 3rd ed. Melvin Mencher. 512p. (C). 1989. pap. write for info. (*0-697-04284-7*) Brown & Benchmark.

Basic Nonprofit Leadership - Management Concept & Model. William R. Conrad, Jr. (Illus.). 80p. (C). 1992. text ed. 25.00 (*0-945571-02-X*) Voluntary Mgmt Pr.

Basic Notes in Psychiatry. rev. ed. Michael I. Levi. (C). 1992. pap. text ed. 12.50 (*0-7923-8990-5*) Kluwer Ac.

Basic Notes in Psychopharmacology. M. Levi. 64p. (C). 1993. pap. text ed. 10.00 (*0-7923-8806-2*) Kluwer Ac.

Basic Notions in Japanese Social Relations. Toshinao Yoneyama. (Occasional Papers, Institute for Education on Japan: Vol. 1, No. 3). 18p. (C). 1990. reprint ed. pap. 5.00 (*0-9619977-5-3*) Earlham College Pr.

Basic Notions of Condensed Matter Physics, No. 55. P. W. Anderson. (Frontiers in Physics Ser.). 1984. text ed. 51.75 (*0-8053-0220-4*, Adv Bk Prog) Addison-Wesley.

Basic Notions of Condensed Matter Physics, No. 55. P. W. Anderson. (Frontiers in Physics Ser.). (C). 1984. pap. 44.95 (*0-8053-0219-0*, Adv Bk Prog) Addison-Wesley.

Basic Nuclear Engineering. K. Sri Ram. 1990. 32.00 (*81-224-0130-9*, Pub. by Wiley Eastern II) S Asia.

Basic Nuclear Engineering. 4th ed. Arthur R. Foster & Robert L. Wright, Jr. (C). 1982. text ed. 84.00 (*0-205-07886-9*, H78868) P-H.

***Basic Number Theory.** A. Weil. 316p. 1995. pap. 35.00 (*3-540-58655-5*) Spr-Verlag.

Basic Number Theory. 3rd ed. Andre Weil. LC 74-13963. (Grundlehren der Mathematischen Wissenschaften Ser.: Vol. 144). xviii, 325p. 1985. 76.00 (*0-387-06935-6*) Spr-Verlag.

Basic Nursing Procedures. 3rd ed. Grace V. Hornemann. LC 77-94835. (Illus.). 340p. (C). 1980. teacher ed 10.00 (*0-8273-1321-7*); pap. 26.95 (*0-8273-1320-9*) Delmar.

Basic Nursing Skills. Frances Britton. (Illus.). 272p. 1981. pap. text ed. 7.95 (*0-87619-921-X*) P-H.

Basic Nursing Skills & Concepts. Cole. (Illus.). 960p. 1991. pap. 34.95 (*0-8016-5887-X*) Mosby Yr Bk.

Basic Nursing Skills & Concepts Two. Cole. 1996. write for info. (*0-8016-7884-6*) Mosby Yr Bk.

Basic Nursing Theory & Practice, No. 2. Potter & Perry. (Illus.). 1050p. 1990. teacher ed 46.95 (*0-8016-3950-6*) Mosby Yr Bk.

Basic Nursing Three: Theory & Practice. Potter. 1152p. 1994. 47.95 (*0-8016-7876-5*) Mosby Yr Bk.

Basic Nutrition & Diet Therapy. 7th ed. Corinne H. Robinson et al. 544p. (C). 1993. pap. write for info. (*0-02-402502-X*) Macmillan.

Basic Nutrition & Diet Therapy. 9th ed. Sue R. Williams. 486p. 1991. pap. 25.95 (*0-8016-6453-5*) Mosby Yr Bk.

Basic Nutrition in Health & Disease: Including Selection & Care of Food. 7th ed. Phyllis Howe. 450p. 1981. pap. text ed. 37.50 (*0-7216-4796-0*) Saunders.

Basic Nutrition Workbook. Susan Linnenkohl. 160p. (C). 1993. pap. text ed. 14.95 (*0-8403-8388-6*) Kendall-Hunt.

Basic Obstetrics & Gynecology. Norman Gant & F. Gary Cunningham. (Illus.). 450p. (C). 1993. pap. text ed. 34.95 (*0-8385-9633-9*, A9633-7) Appleton & Lange.

Basic Occupational Medicine: A Guide to Developing Delivery Systems. Robert R. Silver. 160p. 1991. 75.00 (*0-8493-4290-2*, RC963) CRC Pr.

Basic of Bead Stringing. 6th rev. ed. David Champion. 48p. 1988. pap. 3.95 (*0-317-93088-5*) Borjay.

Basic of Cleanroom Design. ICE Corporation Staff. (Illus.). 205p. (Orig.). (C). 1988. ring bd. 585.00 (*1-877750-04-2*) ICE Corp.

Basic of Electric Motors. Anthony J. Pansini. 224p. 1989. text ed. 53.00 (*0-13-060070-9*) P-H.

Basic Office Microbiology. Belsey. 1990. 49.95 (*0-87489-455-7*) Med Economics.

Basic Office Systems & Records. Gerard Tavernier. 144p. 1971. 25.00 (*0-8464-0180-0*) Beekman Pubs.

Basic Offset & Presswork. William Levy. LC 80-730005. 1979. student ed 6.00 (*0-8064-0065-X*, 314); audio 139.99 (*0-8064-0066-8*) Bergwall.

Basic Offset Press. John Nagle. 1977. student ed 9.00 (*0-8064-0047-1*, 305); audio 139.00 (*0-8064-0048-X*) Bergwall.

Basic Oil Painting Techniques. Ed. by Greg Albert & Rachel Wolf. (Basic Technique Ser.). (Illus.). 128p. 1993. 16.95 (*0-89134-463-2*, 30477) North Light Bks.

Basic Oil Painting the Van Wyk Way. rev. ed. Helen Van Wyk. Ed. by Herbert Rogoff. Orig. Title: Casselwyk Book on Oil Painting. (Illus.). 134p. 1987. reprint ed. pap. text ed. 14.50 (*0-929552-01-6*) Art Instr Assocs.

Basic Oil Paintings. Bill West. LC 84-90017. (Illus.). 208p. 1985. 24.00 (*0-911614-25-7*) B West.

BASIC on the IBM-PC. Jeffrey G. Bonar. 192p. (C). 1987. Incl. program disk. pap. text ed. 23.00 (*0-15-504918-6*) Dryden Pr.

Basic One- & Two-Dimensional NMR Spectroscopy. enl. ed. Horst Friebolin. Tr. by Jack K. Becconsall. LC 93-782. 1993. write for info. (*3-527-29059-1*) VCH Pubs.

Basic Operational Amplifiers & Linear Integrated Circuits. Thomas L. Floyd. (Illus.). 608p. (C). 1994. pap. text ed. write for info. (*0-02-338641-X*, Merrill Pub Co) Macmillan.

Basic Operative Dentistry Procedures. Bruce Bell & David A. Grainger. LC 72-123419. 419p. reprint ed. pap. 119.50 (*0-8357-3605-9*, 2055997) Bks Demand.

Basic Operator Theory. I. Gohberg & Samuel Goldberg. 304p. (C). 1981. 26.50 (*3-7643-3028-7*) Birkhauser.

Basic Optics & Optical Instruments. U. S. Navy, Bureau of Naval Personnel Staff. (Illus.). 1969. pap. 12.95 (*0-486-22291-8*) Dover.

616

An Asterisk (*) at the beginning of an entry indicates that the title is appearing in BIP for the first time.

An Asterisk (*) at the beginning of an entry indicates that the title is appearing in BIP for the first time.

617

B

Basic Principles of Plasma Physics: A Statistical Approach. Setsuo Ichimaru. (Frontiers in Physics Ser.: No. 41). (Illus.). 352p. (C). 1973. text ed. 29.50 (*0-8053-8752-8*, Adv Bk Prog); pap. 41.95 (*0-8053-8753-6*, Adv Bk Prog) Addison-Wesley.

Basic Principles of Power Electronics. K. Heumann. (Electric Energy Systems & Engineering Ser.). (Illus.). 300p. 1986. 99.00 (*0-387-16138-4*) Spr-Verlag.

Basic Principles of Prayer. Perry A. Gaspard. 1984. pap. 2.00 (*0-931867-07-X*) Abundant Life Pubns.

Basic Principles of Psychoanalysis. A. A. Brill. LC 85-7407. 316p. 1985. reprint ed. pap. text ed. 22.00 (*0-8191-4665-X*) U Pr of Amer.

***Basic Principles of Radiographic Exposure.** 2nd ed. Diane C. De Vos. LC 94-34821. 1995. write for info. (*0-683-02458-2*) Williams & Wilkins.

Basic Principles of Risering. 96p. 1987. pap. 30.00 (*0-317-59845-7*, TE6800) Am Foundrymen.

Basic Principles of Rotational Molding. Paul Bruins. 296p. 1971. text ed. 169.00 (*0-677-14980-8*) Gordon & Breach.

***Basic Principles of Semiconductors.** Irving M. Gottlieb. Date not set. 14.95 (*0-7906-1066-3*) H W Sams.

Basic Principles of Sensory Evaluation: Sponsored by Committee E-18 on Sensory Evaluation of Materials & Products. American Society for Testing & Materials Staff. LC 68-15548. (ASTM Special Technical Publication Ser.: No. 433). (Illus.). 112p. reprint ed. pap. 32.00 (*0-7837-4417-X*, 2044161) Bks Demand.

***Basic Principles of Structural Equation Modelling: An Introduction to LISREL & EQS.** Ralph O. Mueller. LC 95-15043. (Statistics Ser.). 1995. write for info. (*0-387-94516-4*) Spr-Verlag.

Basic Principles of Teaching. Joseph Y. Bello. (Education in Africa Ser.). 183p. reprint ed. pap. 52.20 (*0-8357-5986-5*, 2029643) Bks Demand.

Basic Principles of the Science of Mind. 5th ed. Frederick Bailes. 182p. 1987. reprint ed. pap. 15.95 (*0-87516-404-8*) DeVorss.

Basic Principles of Thermoforming. Ed. by Paul Bruins. LC 75-188122. 294p. 1974. text ed. 169.00 (*0-677-14990-5*) Gordon & Breach.

Basic Principles of Vocational Rehabilitation of the Disabled. 3rd rev. ed. vii, 59p. (Orig.). 1985. pap. 8.00 (*92-2-105130-7*) Intl Labour Office.

Basic Principles to Correct Thinking see Lay Counseling Series

Basic Printmaking Techniques. Bernard Toale. LC 91-73903. (Illus.). 144p. 1992. 26.50 (*0-87192-237-1*) Davis Mass.

Basic Probability. Saeed Ghahramani. 1995. text ed. write for info. (*0-13-065798-0*) P-H.

Basic Probability & Related Topics. Nick White. 1992. 16.50 (*0-536-58256-4*) Ginn Pr.

***Basic Probability Topics Using MATLAB.** Paul E. Pfeiffer. (Bookware Companion Problems Ser.). 160p. 1995. disk, pap. 30.95 (*0-534-94536-8*) PWS Pubs.

BASIC Problem Solving: Structured Programming with Microsoft BASIC. 2nd ed. Penny Fanzone et al. 1989. pap. text ed. write for info. (*0-07-558207-4*) McGraw.

Basic Problems, Concepts, & Techniques. rev. ed. Arch R. Dooley et al. LC 67-30438. 780p. 1968. reprint ed. pap. 180.00 (*0-7837-3438-7*, 2057760) Bks Demand.

Basic Problems of Ethnopsychiatry. George Devereux. Tr. by Basia M. Gulati. LC 79-11104. 1980. reprint ed. lib. bdg. 31.00 (*0-226-14355-4*) U Ch Pr.

Basic Problems of Evidence. 6th ed. Michael M. Martin. 498p. 1988. 105.00 (*0-8318-0525-0*, B525) Am Law Inst.

Basic Problems of Neurolinguistics. A. R. Luria. Tr. by Basil Haigh. (Janua Linguarum, Series Major: No. 73). 1976. text ed. 107.70 (*90-279-3205-0*) Mouton.

Basic Problems of Phenomenology. Martin Heidegger. Tr. & Intro. by Albert Hofstadter. LC 80-8379. (Studies in Phenomenology & Existential Philosophy). 430p. 1982. 45.00 (*0-253-17686-7*); pap. 17.95 (*0-253-20478-X*) Ind U Pr.

***Basic Problems of Phenomenology.** Martin Heidegger. 1982. 45.00 (*0-253-17687-5*) Ind U Pr.

***Basic Problems of State & Society.** Gy Antalffy. 188p. (C). 1974. 35.00x (*963-05-0010-8*, Pub. by Akad Kiado HU) St Mut.

Basic Procedure in Courts & Tribunals. S. Weddle & N. Fridd. 112p. 1989. pap. 39.95 (*0-08-036901-4*, Waterlow) Macmillan.

Basic Procedures in Conducting Survey Research. 4th ed. Isadore Newman. 39p. 1976. pap. text ed. 1.00 (*0-917180-04-6*) I Newman.

Basic Processes see Rorschach's Test

Basic Processes in Helping Relationship. Thomas Wills. 1982. text ed. 65.00 (*0-12-757680-0*) Acad Pr.

Basic Processes in Memory Development. Ed. by Charles J. Brainerd & M. Pressley. (Cognitive Development Ser.). (Illus.). 365p. 1985. 71.00 (*0-387-96064-3*) Spr-Verlag.

Basic Processes in Reading: Visual Word Recognition. Derek Besner & Glyn W. Humphreys. 352p. (C). 1990. text ed. 69.95 (*0-8058-0219-3*); pap. 36.00 (*0-8058-0994-5*) L Erlbaum Assocs.

Basic Processes of Learning, Cognition & Motivation. Stephen M. Cormier. 472p. (C). 1986. text ed. 89.95 (*0-89859-689-0*) L Erlbaum Assocs.

Basic Production Management. 2nd ed. Elwood S. Buffa. LC 74-28396. (Illus.). 697p. reprint ed. pap. 180.00 (*0-8357-5987-3*, 2017836) Bks Demand.

Basic Program Instructor Manual. 2nd ed. Steven L. Mandell. 349p. 1989. pap. text ed. 13.95 (*0-314-57501-4*) West Pub.

BASIC Programming. Heath Company Staff. (Illus.). 564p. 1977. ring bd. 44.95 (*0-87119-083-4*, EC-1100) Heathkit-Zenith Ed.

BASIC Programming. Donald D. Spencer. LC 82-17689. 224p. (YA). (gr. 8 up). 1983. 7.95 (*0-89218-062-5*, NO. 1133) Camelot Pub.

Basic Programming: A Structured Approach. James F. Clark & William O. Drum. 544p. (C). 1983. text ed. write for info. (*0-538-10780-4*, J78) S-W Pub.

BASIC Programming & Applications. C. Joseph Sass. 354p. (C). 1976. write for info. (*0-697-06968-0*) Wm C Brown Pubs.

BASIC Programming Flipper. Eric R. Churchill. 49p. (YA). (gr. 8 up). 1989. 6.25 (*1-878383-10-8*) C Lee Pubns.

Basic Programming for Chemists: An Introduction. Peter C. Jurs et al. 1987. text ed. 74.95 (*0-471-85613-4*) Wiley.

BASIC Programming for Engineers & Technicians. Francis J. Guldner. LC 84-12061. 224p. (C). 1985. pap. text ed. 25.95 (*0-8273-2363-8*) Delmar.

BASIC Programming for Kids. Rosalie S. Ault. LC 83-12773. (Illus.). 192p. (J). (gr. 5 up). 1983. 10.95 (*0-685-06975-3*) HM.

BASIC Programming for Personal Computers. Stair. 544p. (C). 1989. pap. text ed. 38.95 (*0-256-06071-1*) Irwin.

BASIC Programming for the Apple Computer. Robert N. Bateson & Robin D. Raygor. (Illus.). 278p. 1985. Instr's. manual. teacher ed, pap. text ed. write for info. (*0-314-87247-7*) West Pub.

BASIC Programming for the Classroom & Home Teacher. Joan M. Miller et al. 262p. (C). 1982. pap. text ed. 17.95 (*0-8077-2728-8*) Tchrs Coll.

BASIC Programming for the Financial Executive. Thomas Humphrey. LC 78-5670. 295p. reprint ed. pap. 84.10 (*0-8357-5988-1*, 2023144) Bks Demand.

BASIC Programming for the IBM PC. James F. Clark & William O. Drum. 1986. pap. text ed. write for info. (*0-538-10830-4*, J83) S-W Pub.

BASIC Programming for the IBM PC. Robin D. Raygor & Robert N. Bateson. (Illus.). 318p. (Orig.). (C). 1986. text ed. 36.50 (*0-314-93407-3*); teacher ed, pap. text ed. write for info. (*0-314-97148-3*) West Pub.

BASIC Programming for the IBM PC. Gary B. Shelly & Thomas J. Cashman. 450p. 1988. pap. 30.00 (*0-87835-212-0*) Boyd & Fraser.

BASIC Programming for the IBM Personal Computer with Technical Applications. Vincent Kassob. (Illus.). 1984. pap. 21.95 (*0-13-066218-6*) P-H.

BASIC Programming Manual for Business Systems. Ludek J. Strand et al. (C). 1988. pap. text ed. 19.95 (*0-945280-02-5*) Wordwrights Office.

BASIC Programming on the BBC Microcomputer. Neil Cryer & Pat Cryer. xii, 195p. 1982. pap. 11.95 (*0-685-07036-0*) P-H.

BASIC Programming One: Course Code 103-1. Ed. by Catherine Doheny. (Illus.). 112p. (gr. 5). 1989. reprint ed. pap. text ed. 9.95 (*0-917531-45-0*) CES Compu-Tech.

BASIC Programming One: Course Code 103-2. Ed. by Catherine Doheny. (Illus.). 81p. (gr. 5). 1989. reprint ed. pap. text ed. 9.95 (*0-917531-46-9*) CES Compu-Tech.

Basic Programming One: Course Code 303-1. Ed. by Kathy Donald. (Illus.). 106p. 1989. reprint ed. pap. text ed. 9.95 (*0-917531-89-2*) CES Compu-Tech.

BASIC Programming One: Course Code 303-2. rev. ed. Ed. by Kathy McDonald. (Illus.). 78p. (gr. 5). 1989. reprint ed. pap. text ed. 9.95 (*0-917531-90-6*) CES Compu-Tech.

Basic Programming One Teacher Edition: Course Code 103-1. Marcia Harroun. Ed. by Cathy Doheny & Bonnie Schroeder. (Illus.). 130p. 1989. reprint ed. 19.95 (*0-917531-70-1*) CES Compu-Tech.

Basic Programming One Teacher Edition: Course Code 103-2. Marcia Harroun. Ed. by Cathy Doheny. (Illus.). 85p. 1989. reprint ed. 19.95 (*0-917531-71-X*) CES Compu-Tech.

BASIC Programming Solutions for Manufacturing. Society of Manufacturing Engineers Staff. 300p. 1982. 52.00 (*0-13-066332-8*) P-H.

BASIC Programming Solutions for Manufacturing. Jensen E. Nicks. LC 82-137513. (Illus.). 297p. reprint ed. pap. 84.70 (*0-8357-6496-6*, 2035867) Bks Demand.

BASIC Programming Today: A Structured Approach. Steven L. Mandell. (Illus.). 325p. (Orig.). (C). 1986. teacher ed 12.95 (*0-314-96642-0*); pap. text ed. 33.75 (*0-314-93199-6*) West Pub.

BASIC Programming Today: A Structured Approach. 2nd ed. Steven L. Mandell. Ed. by Clyde Perlee. 560p. (Orig.). (C). 1990. pap. text ed. 47.25 (*0-314-47602-4*) West Pub.

BASIC Programming Tools. Steven Holzner. 1990. Incl. 3.5 disk. pap. 44.95 (*0-13-059080-0*) P-H.

BASIC Programming Two: Course Code 393-1. Kim Broadie et al. Ed. by Kathy McDonald. (Illus.). 96p. 1989. reprint ed. pap. text ed. 9.95 (*0-917531-91-4*) CES Compu-Tech.

BASIC Programming Two: Course Code 393-2. Kim Broadie et al. Ed. by Kathy McDonald. (Illus.). 85p. (gr. 6). 1989. reprint ed. pap. text ed. 9.95 (*0-917531-92-2*) CES Compu-Tech.

Basic Programming Two, Teacher Edition: Course Code 193-1. Barbara Koren. (Illus.). 130p. 1989. reprint ed. 19.95 (*0-917531-72-8*) CES Compu-Tech.

Basic Programming Two, Teacher Edition: Course Code 193-2, Grade 6. Barbara Koren. 85p. 1989. reprint ed. 19.95 (*0-917531-73-6*) CES Compu-Tech.

BASIC Programming Visual Masters. Donald D. Spencer. 96p. 1987. pap. 15.95 (*0-89218-107-9*, NO. 3002) Camelot Pub.

BASIC Programming with ProDOS. Apple Computer, Inc. Staff. 1985. write for info. (*0-201-17721-8*) Addison-Wesley.

Basic Programming with Prodos with Disk. 1988. 29.95 (*0-201-17755-2*) Addison-Wesley.

BASIC Programming with Structure & Style. Tom Logsdon. Ed. by Marshall. 589p. (C). 1990. pap. text ed. 50.75 (*0-314-47012-3*) West Pub.

BASIC Programming with the IBM PC. 2nd ed. Peter M. Mears. LC 89-30443. 480p. (C). 1990. pap. 47.95 (*0-534-12156-X*) PWS Pubs.

BASIC Programming 1. Yvonne Mullen & Bonnie Schroeder. (Illus.). 120p. 1989. reprint ed. teacher ed 19.95 (*0-685-45805-9*, T303-1) CES Compu-Tech.

BASIC Programming 1: Lab Pack, Pt. 1. Ed. by Catherine Doheny. 179.95 (*1-56177-032-9*, L103-1) CES Compu-Tech.

Basic Programming 1: Lab Pack, Pt. 1. Yvonne Mullen & Bonnie Schroeder. Ed. by Catherine Doheny. (Illus.). 179.95 (*1-56177-074-4*, L303-1); teacher ed 19.95 (*0-685-45806-7*, T303-1) CES Compu-Tech.

BASIC Programming 1: Lab Pack, Pt. 1, No. 1. Ed. by Catherine Doheny. Apple II 15.95 (*1-56177-030-2*) CES Compu-Tech.

BASIC Programming 1: Lab Pack, Pt. 2. Ed. by Catherine Doheny. (Illus.). Apple II, text ed. 179.95 (*1-56177-033-7*, L103-2) CES Compu-Tech.

Basic Programming 1: Lab Pack, Pt. 2. Yvonne Mullen & Bonnie Schroeder. Ed. by Catherine Doheny. (Illus.). 179.95 (*0-685-45807-5*, L303-2); 19.95 (*1-56177-077-9*, T303-2) CES Compu-Tech.

Basic Programming 1: Lab Pack, Pt. 2, No. 1. Yvonne Mullen & Bonnie Schroeder. Ed. by Catherine Doheny. (Illus.). disk 6.95 (*1-56177-072-8*, D303-1) CES Compu-Tech.

BASIC Programming 1: Lab Pack, Pt. 2, No. 2. Ed. by Catherine Doheny. (Illus.). Apple II 15.95 (*1-56177-031-0*, D103-2) CES Compu-Tech.

Basic Programming 1: Lab Pack, Pt. 2, No. 2. Yvonne Mullen & Bonnie Schroeder. Ed. by Catherine Doheny. (Illus.). disk 6.95 (*1-56177-073-6*, D303-2) CES Compu-Tech.

Basic Programming 2: Lab Pack, Pt. 1. Jeanne Black & Vickie Forker. Ed. by Bonnie Schroeder & Catherine Dohney. (Illus.). 179.95 (*1-56177-080-9*, L393-1); teacher ed 19.95 (*1-56177-082-5*, T393-1) CES Compu-Tech.

BASIC Programming 2: Lab Pack, Pt. 1. Ed. by Catherine Doheny. Apple II, text ed. 179.95 (*1-56177-036-1*, L193-1) CES Compu-Tech.

Basic Programming 2: Lab Pack, Pt. 1, No. 1. Jeanne Black & Vickie Forker. Ed. by Bonnie Schroeder & Catherine Dohney. (Illus.). disk 6.95 (*1-56177-078-7*, D393-1) CES Compu-Tech.

BASIC Programming 2: Lab Pack, Pt. 1, No. 1. Ed. by Catherine Doheny. Apple II 6.95 (*1-56177-034-5*, D193-1) CES Compu-Tech.

Basic Programming 2: Lab Pack, Pt. 1, No. 2. Jeanne Black & Vickie Forker. Ed. by Bonnie Schroeder & Catherine Dohney. (Illus.). disk 6.95 (*1-56177-079-5*, D393-2) CES Compu-Tech.

Basic Programming 2: Lab Pack, Pt. 2. Jeanne Black & Vickie Forker. Ed. by Bonnie. Schroedder & Catherine Doheny. (Illus.). 179.95 (*1-56177-081-7*, L393-2); teacher ed 19.95 (*1-56177-083-3*, TE393-2) CES Compu-Tech.

BASIC Programming 2: Lab Pack, Pt. 2. Ed. by Catherine Doheny. (Illus.). Apple II, text ed. 179.95 (*1-56177-037-X*, L193-2) CES Compu-Tech.

BASIC Programming 2: Lab Pack, Pt. 2, No. 2. Ed. by Catherine Doheny. (Illus.). Apple II 6.95 (*1-56177-035-3*, D193-2) CES Compu-Tech.

BASIC Programs for Chemical Engineering Design. Weber. (Chemical Industries Ser.: Vol. 16). 192p. 1984. 59.75 (*0-8247-7138-9*) Dekker.

Basic Programs for Chemical Engineers. Dennis Wright. LC 85-22712. (Illus.). 350p. 1986. text ed. 49.95 (*0-442-29296-1*) Chapman & Hall.

BASIC Programs for Land Surveying. Peter H. Milne. 420p. 1984. pap. 35.00 (*0-419-13010-1*, NO. 9086, E & FN Spon) Routledge Chapman & Hall.

BASIC Programs for Production & Operations Management. Pricha Pantumsinchai et al. (Illus.). 448p. (C). 1983. pap. 23.33 (*0-685-55652-2*) P-H.

Basic Projects & Plantings for the Garden. Tim Morehouse. LC 92-30915. (Illus.). 192p. (Orig.). 1993. pap. 12.95 (*0-8117-3048-4*) Stackpole.

Basic Projects in Wildlife Watching: Learn More about Wild Birds & Animals Through Your Own First-Hand Experience. Sam Fadala. LC 88-31241. (Illus.). 256p. (Orig.). 1989. pap. 16.95 (*0-8117-2248-1*) Stackpole.

Basic Properties of Ammonium Nitrate Fuel Oil Explosives (ANFO) George B. Clark. Ed. by Jon W. Raese. LC 81-38436. (Colorado School of Mines Quarterly Ser.: Vol. 76, No. 1). (Illus.). 32p. 1981. pap. text ed. 10.00 (*0-686-46975-5*) Colo Sch Mines.

Basic Properties of Semiconductors. Ed. by Peter T. Landsberg & T. S. Moss. LC 92-32392. (Handbook On Semiconductors Ser.: Vol. 1). write for info. (*0-444-88855-1*, North Holland) Elsevier.

Basic Properties of Semiconductors, Set. Ed. by Peter T. Landsberg & T. S. Moss. write for info. (*0-318-70113-8*, North Holland) Elsevier.

Basic Property Law, Teacher's Manual to Accompany. 5th ed. Olin L. Browder et al. (American Casebook Ser.). 369p. (C). 1989. pap. text ed. write for info. (*0-314-67335-0*) West Pub.

Basic Protein & Peptide Protocols. Ed. by John M. Walker. LC 93-48929. (Methods in Molecular Biology Ser.: Vol. 32). (Illus.). 512p. 1994. 89.50 (*0-89603-268-X*); spiral bd. 59.50 (*0-89603-269-8*) Humana.

Basic Psychiatric Nursing. 3rd ed. Susan Irving. LC 77-79396. (Illus.). 1983. pap. text ed. 28.95 (*0-7216-5049-X*) Saunders.

***Basic Psychological Skills for Front-Line Staff of Residential Youth Facilities.** Kenneth France. (Illus.). 212p. 1993. pap. 29.95 (*0-398-06128-9*) C C Thomas.

Basic Psychological Skills for Front-Line Staff of Residential Youth Facilities. Kenneth France. LC 92-37754. (Illus.). 212p. 1993. 45.95 (*0-398-05840-7*) C C Thomas.

Basic Psychology. Henry Gleitman. (Illus.). (C). 1987. Transparencies. student ed, trans. write for info. (*0-393-95594-X*) Norton.

Basic Psychology. Henry Gleitman. (C). 1992. pap. text ed. 16.95 (*0-393-96165-6*) Norton.

Basic Psychology. Henry Gleitman. (C). 1992. Computer test item file avail. student ed, pap. text ed. 15.95 (*0-393-96167-2*) Norton.

***Basic Psychology.** Henry Gleitman. 1995. teacher ed, pap. text ed. write for info. (*0-393-96916-9*) Norton.

***Basic Psychology.** John Jonides & Paul Rozin. 1995. student ed, pap. text ed. write for info. (*0-393-96917-7*) Norton.

Basic Psychology. 2nd ed. Henry Gleitman. (Illus.). (C). 1987. text ed. 43.95 (*0-393-95463-3*) Norton.

Basic Psychology. 3rd ed. Henry Gleitman. (C). 1992. pap. text ed. 49.95 (*0-393-96242-3*) Norton.

Basic Psychopathology: A Programmed Text. 2nd ed. C. W. Johnson et al. (Illus.). 368p. (Orig.). 1981. pap. 21.50 (*0-89335-155-5*) PMA Pub Corp.

Basic Psychopharmacology. Alvin J. Levenson. 131p. 1981. text ed. write for info. (*0-8261-2680-4*); pap. text ed. 21.95 (*0-8261-2681-2*) Springer Pub.

Basic Psychotherapeutics: A Programmed Text. C. W. Johnson et al. 610p. 1980. 29.50 (*0-89335-128-8*) PMA Pub Corp.

Basic Public Speaking. Patricia B. Andrews. (Illus.). 174p. (C). 1991. reprint ed. pap. text ed. 14.50 (*0-8191-8492-6*) U Pr of Amer.

Basic Quality Assurance & Quality Control in the Clinical Laboratory. A. Wayne Bruce. 179p. 1984. 29.95 (*0-316-11252-6*) Little.

Basic Quality Control. G. Vorley & F. Tickle. (Basic Ser.). (Illus.). 160p. 1989. pap. text ed. 19.95 (*0-408-01840-2*) Buttrwrth-Heinemann.

Basic Quality Improvement. Susan Garrity. 304p. 1992. pap. text ed. 39.60 (*0-13-480906-8*) P-H.

***Basic Quality Tool System.** Personal Crafting Staff. 1994. ring bd. 35.00 (*0-87425-973-8*) Human Res Dev Pr.

Basic Quantum Mechanics. J. L. Martin. (Oxford Physics Ser.). (Illus.). 1982. pap. 29.95 (*0-19-851816-1*) OUP.

Basic Quantum Mechanics. 2nd ed. J. M. Cassels. (Illus.). (C). 1995. reprint ed. write for info. (*0-89464-906-X*) Krieger.

Basic Questions in Fatigue, STP 924, Vol. I. Ed. by Jeffrey T. Fong & Richard J. Fields. LC 88-14555. (Special Technical Publication (STP) Ser.). (Illus.). 408p. 1988. text ed. 60.00 (*0-318-40042-1*, 04-924001-30) ASTM.

Basic Questions in Fatigue, STP 924, Vol. II. Ed. by Robert P. Wei & Richard P. Gangloff. LC 88-14555. (Special Technical Publication (STP) Ser.). (Illus.). 336p. 1988. text ed. 50.00 (*0-8031-0925-3*, 04-924002-30) ASTM.

Basic Questions in Paleontology. Otto H. Schindewolf. Ed. by Wolf-Ernst Reif. Tr. by Judith Schaefer. LC 93-10189. (Illus.). 552p. (C). 1993. pap. text ed. 29.95 (*0-226-73835-3*) U Ch Pr.

Basic Questions in Paleontology. Otto H. Schindewolf. Ed. by Wolf-Ernst Reif. Tr. by Judith Schaefer. LC 93-10189. (Illus.). 552p. (C). 1993. lib. bdg. 75.00 (*0-226-73834-5*) U Ch Pr.

Basic Questions of Philosophy: Selected "Problems" of "Logic" Martin Heidegger. Tr. by Richard Rojcewicz & Andre Schuwer. LC 93-30513. (Studies in Continental Thought). 1994. 29.95 (*0-253-32685-0*) Ind U Pr.

Basic R-C Flying. David Boddington. (R-C Handbook Ser.). (Illus.). 64p. 1989. pap. text ed. 10.95 (*0-85242-980-0*, Pub. by Argus Pubs UK) Motorbooks Intl.

Basic Radiation Protection: Principles & Organization. C. W. Easley. 142p. (C). 1969. text ed. 117.00 (*0-677-02080-5*) Gordon & Breach.

Basic Radiation Protection Technology. 3rd ed. Daniel A. Gollnick. (Illus.). 800p. 1994. pap. 75.00 (*0-916339-07-6*, 301) Pacific Rad.

***Basic Radiobiology.** Stephen M. Waldow. (Illus.). 100p. (Orig.). (C). 1994. student ed 28.00 (*1-878045-67-9*) Whittier Pubns.

Basic Radiographic Positioning & Anatomy. G. Bell & David Finlay. (Illus.). 272p. 1984. pap. text ed. 25.50 (*0-7020-0978-4*, Bailliere-Tindall) Saunders.

***Basic Radiology.** Michael Y. Chen et al. 304p. 1995. text ed. 45.00 (*0-07-011148-0*) Hlth Prof Div.

Basic Radiopharmacy C. Lange. 1991. write for info. (*0-8151-5302-3*, Yr Bk Med Pubs) Mosby Yr Bk.

Basic Reader for College Writers. David Daniels et al. 80p. (C). 1989. teacher ed 10.00 (*0-944210-76-7*); pap. text ed. 13.00 (*0-944210-75-9*) Townsend NJ.

Basic Reading. Judith A. Trabert & Jonathan McKallip. Ed. by V. K. Lawson. 1986. Tutor's Video Guide, 51p. pap. text ed. 2.75 (*0-930713-56-7*); Video Trainer's Guide, 70p. pap. text ed. 11.00 (*0-930713-54-0*); Video Module incl. trainer's guide & 6 videocassettes (VHS, Beta, U-Matic). 550.00 (*0-930713-53-2*) Lit Vol Am.

Basic Reading Book, 2 vols., 1. Nancy Stevenson. (Stevenson Language Skills Program Ser.). 168p. (Orig.). 1979. pap. text ed. write for info. (*0-941112-09-8*) Stevnson Lrn.

Basic Reading Book, 2 vols., 2. Nancy Stevenson. (Stevenson Language Skills Program Ser.). 168p. (Orig.). 1979. pap. text ed. write for info. (*0-941112-10-1*) Stevnson Lrn.

Basic Reading Book, 2 vols., Set. Nancy Stevenson. (Stevenson Language Skills Program Ser.). 168p. (Orig.). 1979. pap. text ed. 8.50 (*0-941112-08-X*) Stevnson Lrn.

An Asterisk (*) at the beginning of an entry indicates that the title is appearing in BIP for the first time.

B

An Asterisk (*) at the beginning of an entry indicates that the title is appearing in BIP for the first time.

619

Basic Skills Government Workbook. Fred Justus. (Basic Skills Workbooks). 32p. (gr. 7-12). 1983. 1.98 (*0-8209-0538-0*, SSW-2) ESP.

Basic Skills Handwriting Workbook: Grade 1. Bearl Brooks. (Basic Skills Workbooks). 32p. 1982. teacher ed 1.98 (*0-8209-0370-1*, CHW-1) ESP.

Basic Skills Handwriting Workbook: Grade 2. Bearl Brooks. (Basic Skills Workbooks). 32p. 1982. teacher ed 1.98 (*0-8209-0371-X*, CHW-2) ESP.

Basic Skills Handwriting Workbook: Grade 3. Bearl Brooks. (Basic Skills Workbooks). 32p. 1982. teacher ed 1.98 (*0-8209-0372-8*, CHW-3) ESP.

Basic Skills Health Workbook: Grade 3. Marilyn Hayes. (Basic Skills Workbooks). 32p. 1982. teacher ed 1.98 (*0-686-38397-4*, HW-D) ESP.

Basic Skills Health Workbook: Grade 4. Marilyn Hayes. (Basic Skills Workbooks). 32p. 1982. teacher ed 1.98 (*0-8209-0414-7*, HW-E) ESP.

Basic Skills Health Workbook: Grade 5. Marilyn Hayes. (Basic Skills Workbooks). 32p. 1982. teacher ed 1.98 (*0-8209-0415-5*, HW-F) ESP.

Basic Skills Health Workbook: Grade 6. Jack Houston. (Basic Skills Workbooks). 32p. 1982. teacher ed 1.98 (*0-8209-0416-3*, HW-G) ESP.

Basic Skills Health Workbook: Grade 7. Jack Houston. (Basic Skills Workbooks). 32p. 1982. teacher ed 1.98 (*0-8209-0417-1*, HW-H) ESP.

Basic Skills Health Workbook: Grade 8. Jack Houston. (Basic Skills Workbooks). 32p. 1982. teacher ed 1.98 (*0-8209-0418-X*, HW-I) ESP.

Basic Skills Health Workbook: Grade 9. Jack Houston. (Basic Skills Workbooks). 32p. 1982. teacher ed 1.98 (*0-685-06462-X*, HW-J) ESP.

Basic Skills Healthy Body Workbook. Bearl Brooks. (Basic Skills Workbooks). 32p. (gr. 6-7). 1983. 1.98 (*0-8209-0575-5*, HW-2) ESP.

Basic Skills Holidays Workbook. Dale McMasters. (Basic Skills Workbooks). 32p. (gr. 4-7). 1983. 1.98 (*0-8209-0560-7*, SSW-8) ESP.

Basic Skills How to Study Workbook. Dale McMasters. (Basic Skills Workbooks). 32p. (gr. 5-9). 1983. 1.98 (*0-8209-0534-8*, HSW-1) ESP.

Basic Skills Human Body Workbook: Grade 5. Diana Van Camp. (Basic Skills Workbooks). 32p. 1982. teacher ed 1.98 (*0-8209-0420-1*, HBW-F) ESP.

Basic Skills Human Body Workbook: Grade 8. Diana Van Camp. (Basic Skills Workbooks). 32p. 1982. teacher ed 1.98 (*0-8209-0423-6*, HBW-I) ESP.

Basic Skills Human Workbook: Grade 6. Diana Van Camp. (Basic Skills Workbooks). 32p. 1982. teacher ed 1.98 (*0-8209-0421-X*, HBW-G) ESP.

Basic Skills Human Workbook: Grade 7. Diana Van Camp. (Basic Skills Workbooks). 32p. 1982. teacher ed 1.98 (*0-8209-0422-8*, HBW-H) ESP.

Basic Skills in Getting Around, No. 812542. Eleanor R. Young. (YA). (gr. 7-12). 1991. student ed 9.95 (*0-86703-192-1*) Opportunities Learn.

Basic Skills in Interpreting Laboratory Data. Intro. by Scott L. Traub. 256p. (Orig.). 1992. pap. 55.00 (*1-879907-16-X*) Am Soc Hlth-Syst.

Basic Skills in Kindergarten: Foundations for Formal Learning. Walter B. Barbe et al. (C). 1980. 12.95 (*0-88309-104-6*) Zaner-Bloser.

Basic Skills Learning to Think Workbook. Bearl Brooks. (Basic Skills Workbooks). 32p. (ps-1). 1983. 1.98 (*0-8209-0587-9*, EEW-10) ESP.

Basic Skills Library Workbook. Dale McMasters. (Basic Skills Workbooks). 32p. (gr. 4-7). 1983. 1.98 (*0-686-42990-7*, LW-1) ESP.

Basic Skills Listening for Sounds Workbook. Bearl Brooks. (Basic Skills Workbooks). 32p. (gr. 2-3). 1983. 1.98 (*0-8209-0546-1*, PW-6) ESP.

Basic Skills Listening Skills Workbook. Marlene Whitlock. (Basic Skills Workbooks). 32p. (gr. 2-3). 1983. 1.98 (*0-8209-0589-5*, EEW-12) ESP.

Basic Skills Look, Hear, & Make Words Workbook. Fred Justus. (Basic Skills Workbooks). 32p. (gr. k-1). 1983. 1.98 (*0-8209-0578-X*, EEW-8) ESP.

Basic Skills Map Workbook. Janis Minton. (Basic Skills Workbooks). 32p. (J). (gr. 4-7). 1983. 1.98 (*0-8209-0540-2*, SSW-4) ESP.

Basic Skills Math. Alan K. Garinger. (Basic Skills TV Ser.). 308p. 1990. student ed 8.00 (*0-910475-25-3*) KET.

Basic Skills Mathematics Workbook: Grade 1. Fred Justus. (Basic Skills Workbooks). 32p. (gr. 1). 1982. teacher ed 1.98 (*0-8209-0388-4*, MW-B) ESP.

Basic Skills Mathematics Workbook: Grade 2. Jim Vaughn. (Basic Skills Workbooks). 32p. (gr. 2). 1982. teacher ed 1.98 (*0-8209-0389-2*, MW-C) ESP.

Basic Skills Mathematics Workbook: Grade 3. Jim Vaughn. (Basic Skills Workbooks). 32p. 1982. teacher ed 1.98 (*0-8209-0390-6*, MW-D) ESP.

Basic Skills Mathematics Workbook: Grade 4. Jim Vaughn. (Basic Skills Workbooks). 32p. (gr. 4). teacher ed 1.98 (*0-8209-0391-4*, MW-E) ESP.

Basic Skills Mathematics Workbook: Grade 5. Jim Vaughn. (Basic Skills Workbooks). 32p. (gr. 5). 1982. teacher ed 1.98 (*0-8209-0392-2*, MW-F) ESP.

Basic Skills Mathematics Workbook: Grade 6. Jim Vaughn. (Basic Skills Workbooks). 32p. (gr. 6). teacher ed 1.98 (*0-8209-0393-0*, MW-G) ESP.

Basic Skills Mathematics Workbook: Grade 7. Jim Vaughn. (Basic Skills Workbooks). 32p. (gr. 7). 1982. teacher ed 1.98 (*0-8209-0394-9*, MW-H) ESP.

Basic Skills Mathematics Workbook: Grade 8. Jim Vaughn. (Basic Skills Workbooks). 32p. (gr. 8). 1982. teacher ed 1.98 (*0-8209-0395-7*, MW-I) ESP.

Basic Skills Mathematics Workbook: Grade 9. Jim Vaughn. (Basic Skills Workbooks). 32p. (gr. 9). 1982. teacher ed 1.98 (*0-8209-0396-5*, MW-J) ESP.

Basic Skills Memory Development Workbook. Luther Misenheimer, III. (Basic Skills Workbooks). 32p. (gr. 5-9). 1983. 1.98 (*0-8209-0582-8*, MDW-1) ESP.

Basic Skills Metrics I Workbook. Fred Justus. (Basic Skills Workbooks). 32p. (gr. 3-4). 1983. 1.98 (*0-8209-0571-2*, MW-4) ESP.

Basic Skills Metrics II Workbook. Fred Justus. (Basic Skills Workbooks). 32p. (gr. 4-5). 1983. 1.98 (*0-8209-0572-0*, MW-5) ESP.

Basic Skills Metrics III Workbook. Fred Justus. (Basic Skills Workbooks). 32p. (gr. 5-6). 1983. 1.98 (*0-8209-0573-9*, MW-6) ESP.

Basic Skills Music Workbook. Libby Hobson. (Basic Skills Workbooks). 32p. (gr. 4-7). 1983. 1.98 (*0-8209-0542-9*, MUW-1) ESP.

Basic Skills Music Workbook. Mary Lou Walker. (Basic Skills Workbooks). 32p. (gr. 3-5). 1983. 1.98 (*0-8209-0543-7*, MUW-2) ESP.

Basic Skills Nursery Rhymes Workbook. Carolyn Nelson. (Basic Skills Workbooks). 32p. (gr. k-1). 1983. 1.98 (*0-8209-0565-8*, EEW-6) ESP.

Basic Skills Nutrition Workbook: Grade 2. Diana Van Camp. (Basic Skills Workbooks). 32p. (gr. 2). 1982. teacher ed 1.98 (*0-8209-0408-2*, NW-C) ESP.

Basic Skills Nutrition Workbook: Grade 3. Diana Van Camp. (Basic Skills Workbooks). 32p. (gr. 3). 1982. teacher ed 1.98 (*0-8209-0409-0*, NW-D) ESP.

Basic Skills Nutrition Workbook: Grade 4. Marilyn Hayes. (Basic Skills Workbooks). 32p. (gr. 4). teacher ed 1.98 (*0-8209-0410-4*, NW-E) ESP.

Basic Skills Nutrition Workbook: Grade 5. Marilyn Hayes. (Basic Skills Workbooks). 32p. (gr. 5). teacher ed 1.98 (*0-8209-0411-2*, NW-F) ESP.

Basic Skills Nutrition Workbook: Grade 6. Diana Van Camp. (Basic Skills Workbooks). 32p. (gr. 6). 1982. teacher ed 1.98 (*0-8209-0412-0*, NW-G) ESP.

Basic Skills Outline & Organize Workbook. Martha McFerron. (Basic Skills Workbooks). 32p. (gr. 4-7). 1983. 1.98 (*0-8209-0581-X*, OW-1) ESP.

Basic Skills Parts of Speech Workbook. Marguerite Coe. (Basic Skills Workbooks). 32p. (gr. 5-9). 1983. 1.98 (*0-8209-0547-X*, EW-2) ESP.

Basic Skills Phonics Workbook: Part I. Bearl Brooks. (Basic Skills Workbooks). 32p. (gr. 1-3). 1983. teacher ed 1.98 (*0-8209-0385-X*, PW-1) ESP.

Basic Skills Phonics Workbook: Part II. Bearl Brooks. (Basic Skills Workbooks). 32p. (gr. 1-3). 1982. teacher ed 1.98 (*0-8209-0386-8*, PW-2) ESP.

Basic Skills Phonics Workbook: Part III. Bearl Brooks. (Basic Skills Workbooks). 32p. (gr. 1-3). 1982. teacher ed 1.98 (*0-8209-0387-6*, PW-3) ESP.

Basic Skills Pitch Sight-Reader, Bk. 1a. Burton Kaplan. 175p. (Orig.). 1981. pap. 10.95 (*0-918316-03-0*) Percept Dev Tech.

Basic Skills Punctuation Workbook. Bearl Brooks. (Basic Skills Workbooks). 32p. (gr. 4-7). 1983. 1.98 (*0-8209-0548-8*, EW-4) ESP.

Basic Skills Reading. Alan K. Garinger. (Basic Skills TV Ser.). 284p. 1989. student ed 8.00 (*0-910475-29-6*) KET.

Basic Skills Reading Comprehension Workbook, 4 bks. Bearl Brooks. 128p. (J). 1983. write for info. (*0-318-56924-8*) ESP.

Basic Skills Reading Comprehension Workbook, 4 bks. Bearl Brooks. (Basic Skills Workbooks). 128p. (J). (gr. 1-2). 1983. Grades 1-2. 1.98 (*0-8209-0554-2*, RCW-1) ESP.

Basic Skills Reading Comprehension Workbook, 4 bks. Bearl Brooks. (Basic Skills Workbooks). 128p. (J). (gr. 3-4). 1983. Grades 3-4. 1.98 (*0-8209-0555-0*, RCW-2) ESP.

Basic Skills Reading Comprehension Workbook, 4 bks. Bearl Brooks. (Basic Skills Workbooks). 128p. (J). (gr. 5-6). 1983. Grades 5-6. 1.98 (*0-8209-0556-9*, RCW-3) ESP.

Basic Skills Reading Comprehension Workbook, 4 bks. Bearl Brooks. (Basic Skills Workbooks). 128p. (J). (gr. 7-8). 1983. Grades 7-8. 1.98 (*0-8209-0557-7*, RCW-4) ESP.

Basic Skills Reading Workbook: Grade 1. Lois Roets. (Basic Skills Workbooks). 32p. (gr. 1). 1982. teacher ed 1.98 (*0-8209-0363-9*, RW-B) ESP.

Basic Skills Reading Workbook: Grade 2. Marie-Jose Shaw. (Basic Skills Workbooks). 32p. (gr. 2). 1982. teacher ed 1.98 (*0-8209-0364-7*, RW-C) ESP.

Basic Skills Reading Workbook: Grade 3. Marie-Jose Shaw. (Basic Skills Workbooks). 32p. (J). (gr. 3). 1982. 1.98 (*0-8209-0365-5*, RW-D) ESP.

Basic Skills Reading Workbook: Grade 4. Marie-Jose Shaw. (Basic Skills Workbooks). 32p. (gr. 4). 1982. teacher ed 1.98 (*0-8209-0366-3*, RW-E) ESP.

Basic Skills Reading Workbook: Grade 5. Marie-Jose Shaw. (Basic Skills Workbooks). 32p. (gr. 5). 1982. teacher ed 1.98 (*0-8209-0367-1*, W-F) ESP.

Basic Skills Reading Workbook: Grade 6. Marie-Jose Shaw. (Basic Skills Workbooks). 32p. (gr. 6). 1982. 1.98 (*0-8209-0368-X*, RW-G) ESP.

Basic Skills Reading Workbook: Grade 7. Maie-Jose Shaw. (Basic Skills Workbooks). 32p. (gr. 7). 1982. teacher ed 1.98 (*0-8209-0369-8*, W-H) ESP.

Basic Skills Reading Workbook: Grade 8. Bearl Brooks. (Basic Skills Workbooks). 32p. (gr. 8). 1982. 1.98 (*0-8209-0362-0*, RW-A) ESP.

Basic Skills Reference Materials Workbook. Peggy Yarbro. (Basic Skills Workbooks). 32p. (gr. 4-7). 1983. 1.98 (*0-8209-0579-8*, RMW-1) ESP.

Basic Skills School Newspaper Workbook. Serena K. Bond. (Basic Skills Workbooks). 32p. (gr. 8-12). 1983. 1.98 (*0-8209-0553-4*, SNW-1) ESP.

Basic Skills Science Workbook: Grade 3. Jack Houston. (Basic Skills Workbooks). 32p. (gr. 3). 1982. 1.98 (*0-8209-0402-3*, SW-D) ESP.

Basic Skills Science Workbook: Grade 4. Catherine Patty. (Basic Skills Workbooks). 32p. (gr. 4). 1982. 1.98 (*0-8209-0403-1*, SW-E) ESP.

Basic Skills Science Workbook: Grade 5. Jack Houston. (Basic Skills Workbooks). 32p. (gr. 5). 1982. 1.98 (*0-8209-0404-X*, SW-F) ESP.

Basic Skills Science Workbook: Grade 6. Jack Houston. (Basic Skills Workbooks). 32p. (gr. 6). 1982. 1.98 (*0-8209-0405-8*, SW-G) ESP.

Basic Skills Science Workbook: Grade 7. Jack Houston. (Basic Skills Workbooks). 32p. (gr. 7). 1982. 1.98 (*0-8209-0406-6*, SW-H) ESP.

Basic Skills Science Workbook: Grade 8. (Basic Skills Workbooks). 32p. (gr. 8). 1982. 1.98 (*0-8209-0407-4*, SW-I) ESP.

Basic Skills Seatwork Workbook. Fred Justus. (Basic Skills Workbooks). 32p. (gr. k-1). 1983. 1.98 (*0-8209-0550-X*, EEW-1) ESP.

Basic Skills Seeing Differences Workbook. Marilyn Hayes. (Basic Skills Workbooks). 32p. (gr. k-1). 1983. 1.98 (*0-8209-0588-7*, EEW-11) ESP.

Basic Skills Social Studies Workbook: Grade 3. Catherine Patty. (Basic Skills Workbooks). 32p. (gr. 3). 1982. 1.98 (*0-8209-0398-1*, SSW-D) ESP.

Basic Skills Social Studies Workbook: Grade 4. Catherine Patty. (Basic Skills Workbooks). 32p. (gr. 4). 1982. 1.98 (*0-8209-0399-X*, SSW-E) ESP.

Basic Skills Social Studies Workbook: Grade 5. Marilyn Hayes. (Basic Skills Workbooks). 32p. (gr. 5). 1982. 1.98 (*0-8209-0400-7*, SSW-F) ESP.

Basic Skills Social Studies Workbook: Grade 6. Catherine Patty. (Basic Skills Workbooks). 32p. (gr. 6). 1982. 1.98 (*0-8209-0401-5*, SSW-G) ESP.

Basic Skills Speed Reading Workbook. Luther Misenheimer, III. (Basic Skills Workbooks). 32p. (gr. 5-9). 1983. 1.98 (*0-8209-0583-6*, SRW-1) ESP.

Basic Skills Spelling Tests Workbook, 2 bks. Marie Shaw. 64p. (J). 1983. write for info. (*0-318-56925-6*) ESP.

Basic Skills Spelling Tests Workbook, 2 bks. Marie Shaw. (Basic Skills Workbooks). 64p. (J). (gr. 3-4). 1983. Grades 3-4. 1.98 (*0-8209-0566-6*, STW-1) ESP.

Basic Skills Spelling Tests Workbook, 2 bks. Marie Shaw. (Basic Skills Workbooks). 64p. (J). (gr. 5-6). 1983. Grades 5-6. 1.98 (*0-8209-0567-4*, STW-2) ESP.

Basic Skills Spelling Workbook: Grade 3. Marie-Jose Shaw. (Basic Skills Workbooks). 32p. (gr. 3). 1982. 1.98 (*0-8209-0373-6*, SPW-D) ESP.

Basic Skills Spelling Workbook: Grade 4. Marie-Jose Shaw. (Basic Skills Workbooks). 32p. (gr. 4). 1982. 1.98 (*0-8209-0374-4*, SPW-E) ESP.

Basic Skills Spelling Workbook: Grade 5. Marie-Jose Shaw. (Basic Skills Workbooks). 32p. (gr. 5). 1982. 1.98 (*0-8209-0375-2*, SPW-F) ESP.

Basic Skills Spelling Workbook: Grade 6. Marie-Jose Shaw. (Basic Skills Workbooks). 32p. (gr. 6). 1982. 1.98 (*0-8209-0376-0*, SPW-G) ESP.

Basic Skills Telling Time Workbook. Bearl Brooks. (Basic Skills Workbooks). 32p. (gr. 2-3). 1983. 1.98 (*0-8209-0552-6*, EEW-13) ESP.

Basic Skills Thinking Development Workbook. Catherine Patty. (Basic Skills Workbooks). 32p. (gr. 4-7). 1983. 1.98 (*0-8209-0584-4*, TDW-1) ESP.

Basic Skills Travel & Transportation Workbook. Sharon Smith. (Basic Skills Workbooks). 32p. (gr. 4-7). 1983. 1.98 (*0-8209-0561-5*, SW-9) ESP.

Basic Skills Understanding Instructions Workbook. Janis Minton. (Basic Skills Workbooks). 32p. (gr. 4-7). 1983. 1.98 (*0-8209-0580-1*, IW-1) ESP.

Basic Skills Visual Discrimination Workbook. Fred Justus. (Basic Skills Workbooks). 32p. (gr. 1-2). 1983. 1.98 (*0-8209-0544-5*, PW-4) ESP.

Basic Skills Vocabulary Workbook: Grade 1. Fred Justus. (Basic Skills Workbooks). 32p. (gr. 1). 1982. 1.98 (*0-8209-0377-9*, VW-B) ESP.

Basic Skills Vocabulary Workbook: Grade 2. Marie-Jose Shaw. (Basic Skills Workbooks). 32p. (gr. 2). 1982. 1.98 (*0-8209-0378-7*, VW-C) ESP.

Basic Skills Vocabulary Workbook: Grade 3. Marie-Jose Shaw. (Basic Skills Workbooks). 32p. (gr. 3). 1982. 1.98 (*0-8209-0379-5*, VW-D) ESP.

Basic Skills Vocabulary Workbook: Grade 4. Marie-Jose Shaw. (Basic Skills Workbooks). 32p. (gr. 4). 1982. 1.98 (*0-8209-0380-9*, VW-E) ESP.

Basic Skills Vocabulary Workbook: Grade 5. Marie-Jose Shaw. (Basic Skills Workbooks). 32p. (gr. 5). 1982. 1.98 (*0-8209-0381-7*, VW-F) ESP.

Basic Skills Vocabulary Workbook: Grade 6. Marie-Jose Shaw. (Basic Skills Workbooks). 32p. (gr. 6). 1982. 1.98 (*0-8209-0382-5*, VW-G) ESP.

Basic Skills Vocabulary Workbook: Junior High. James E. Vaughn. (Basic Skills Workbooks). 32p. (gr. 7-9). 1982. 1.98 (*0-8209-0383-3*, VW-H) ESP.

Basic Skills Vocabulary Workbook: Senior High. James E. Vaughn. (Basic Skills Workbooks). 32p. (gr. 9-12). 1982. 1.98 (*0-8209-0384-1*, VW-I) ESP.

Basic Skills with Decimals & Percents. Jerry Howett. 128p. 1988. pap. text ed. 5.50 (*0-8428-2118-X*) Cambridge Bk.

Basic Skills with Fractions. Jerry Howett. 128p. 1988. pap. text ed. 5.50 (*0-8428-2117-1*) Cambridge Bk.

Basic Skills with Math: A General Review. Jerry Howett. 192p. 1988. pap. text ed. 6.75 (*0-8428-2119-8*) Cambridge Bk.

Basic Skills with Whole Numbers. Jerry Howett. 128p. 1988. pap. text ed. 5.50 (*0-8428-2116-3*) Cambridge Bk.

Basic Skills Word Building Workbook. Dale McMasters. (Basic Skills Workbooks). 32p. (gr. 4-7). 1983. 1.98 (*0-8209-0568-2*, WBW-1) ESP.

Basic Skills Word List. 1980. pap. 13.95 (*0-932166-02-4*) IOX Amnt Assocs.

Basic Skills Words We Use Workbook. Marilyn Hayes. (Basic Skills Workbooks). 32p. (J). (gr. k-1). 1983. 1.98 (*0-8209-0577-1*, EEW-7) ESP.

Basic Skills Workbooks: Grade 10. Jim Vaughn. (Basic Skills Workbooks). 32p. (gr. 10). 1982. 1.98 (*0-8209-0397-3*, MW-K) ESP.

Basic Skills World Neighbors Workbook. Bearl Brooks. (Basic Skills Workbooks). 32p. (gr. 4-7). 1983. 1.98 (*0-8209-0558-5*, SSW-6) ESP.

Basic Skills Writing. Alan K. Garinger. (Basic Skills TV Ser.). 198p. 1989. student ed 8.00 (*0-910475-30-X*) KET.

Basic Skills Writing Capital & Small Letters Workbook. Fred Justus. (Basic Skills Workbooks). 32p. (gr. k-1). 1983. 1.98 (*0-8209-0563-1*, EEW-4) ESP.

Basic Skills Written Problems in Math Workbook. Dale McMasters. (Basic Skills Workbooks). 32p. (gr. 3-4). 1983. 1.98 (*0-8209-0574-7*, MW-7) ESP.

Basic Small Business Management. Clifford M. Baumback. (Illus.). 528p. (C). 1983. text ed. write for info. (*0-13-066415-4*) P-H.

Basic Soccer Guide. Bobby Moffat. LC 75-16004. (Illus.). 144p. (Orig.). 1978. pap. 4.95 (*0-89037-060-5*) Anderson World.

Basic Soccer Guide. Bobby Moffat. LC 85-4213. (Orig.). 1985. pap. 8.95 (*0-02-028780-1*, Collier S&S) S&S Trade.

Basic Social Diagnosis for IRRD Planning Conceptual Framework: Case Studies & Some Generalisations. Dov Weintraub & Julia Margulies. 1985. text ed. 64.95 (*0-566-05133-8*, Pub. by Avebury Pub UK) Ashgate Pub Co.

Basic Social Skills for Youth: A Handbook from Boys Town. Father Flanagan's Boys' Home Staff. (Illus.). 38p. (Orig.). (YA). (gr. 6 up). 1992. pap. 5.95 (*0-938510-39-8*, 45-007) Boys Town Pr.

Basic Social Statistics. David Knoke & George Bohrnstedt. LC 90-63041. 384p. 1991. boxed 47.00 (*0-87581-347-X*) Peacock Pubs.

***Basic Social Statistics.** Wilbert M. Leonard, II. 458p. (C). 1994. pap. text ed. 29.95 (*0-87563-509-1*) Stipes.

Basic Social Statistics & Quantitative Research Methods: A Computer-Assisted Introduction. James W. Grimm & Paul R. Wozniak. 493p. (C). 1990. pap. 42.95 (*0-534-12594-8*) Intl Thomson.

Basic Sociology. Gunter W. Remmling & Robert B. Campbell. (Quality Paperback Ser.: No. 229). 384p. 1976. reprint ed. pap. 7.95 (*0-8226-0229-6*) Littlefield.

Basic Soil Mechanics. 2nd ed. Roy Whitlow. 1990. pap. text ed. 59.95 (*0-470-21682-4*) Wiley.

***Basic Soil Mechanics.** 3rd ed. R. Whitlow. LC 95-61. 1995. pap. text ed. 49.95 (*0-470-23499-7*) Wiley.

***Basic Soil Mechanics.** 3rd ed. R. Whitlow. LC 95-61. 1995. write for info. (*0-582-23631-2*, Pub. by Longman UK) Longman.

Basic Solid-State Chemistry Abridged Paper. Anthony R. West. 370p. 1988. pap. text ed. 54.95 (*0-471-91798-2*) Wiley.

Basic Solid-State Electronic Circuit Analysis Through Experimentation. 3rd ed. Lorne MacDonald. 424p. 1992. pap. 23.50 (*0-911908-12-9*) Tech Ed Pr.

Basic Solid-State Electronics, 5 vols. Van Valkenburgh, Nooger & Neville, Inc. Staff. 1982. pap. text ed. 10.50 (*0-8104-0884-8*) Brolet.

Basic Solid-State Electronics. rev. ed. Van Valkenburgh. 1993. pap. 19.95 (*0-7906-1042-6*, Prompt Pubns) H W Sams.

Basic Solid-State Electronics, 5 vols., Set. Van Valkenburgh, Nooger & Neville, Inc. Staff. 1982. 39.95 (*0-8104-0890-2*) Brolet.

Basic Source Readings in the Psychology of Learning. Ed. by Edward Zamble. LC 72-6357. 296p. 1972. pap. text ed. 16.95 (*0-8290-0652-4*) Irvington.

Basic Sources for Family History: Back to Early 1800s. (C). 1987. 30.00 (*0-317-89831-0*, Pub. by Birmingham Midland Soc UK) St Mut.

Basic Sources in Criminal Justice. 1991. lib. bdg. 69.95 (*0-8490-4474-X*) Gordon Pr.

Basic Space Science. Ed. by H. J. Haubold et al. (Conference Proceeding Ser.: No. 245). 352p. 1992. 95.00 (*0-685-60541-8*) Am Inst Physics.

***Basic Space Science.** Ed. by Hans J. Haubold & Lesley I. Onoura. (AIP Conference Proceedings Ser.: No. 320). 324p. 1995. text ed. 115.00x (*1-56396-328-0*) Am Inst Physics.

Basic Spanish. (Teach Yourself Ser.). 192p. 1993. pap. 5.95 (*0-8442-3827-9*) NTC Pub Grp.

Basic Spanish. Joseph W. Barlow. (Illus.). 1939. text ed. 18.50 (*0-89197-044-4*) Irvington.

Basic Spanish Conversation. Juan Kattan-Ibarra. 192p. 1985. pap. 12.95 (*0-8442-7637-5*, Passport Bks) NTC Pub Grp.

Basic Spanish for Elementary Teachers. Marilyn R. Seymann. 240p. 1976. pap. text ed. 24.00 (*0-08-020425-2*, Pergamon Pr) Elsevier.

Basic Spanish for Idiots: An Anti-Textbook. Gene Olson. 64p. 1993. pap. 6.95 (*0-913366-10-2*) Windyridge.

An Asterisk (*) at the beginning of an entry indicates that the title is appearing in BIP for the first time.

Basic Spanish Grammar. 3rd ed. Ana C. Jarvis. Incl. Spanish for Communication. 3rd ed. LC 87-81232. (C). 1988. pap. text ed. 13.50 (*0-669-12245-9*); Spanish for Communication. 3rd ed. LC 87-81232. (ENG & SPA.). (C). 1988. audio 30.00 (*0-669-12246-7*); Spanish for Bus-Finance. 3rd ed. LC 87-81232. (C). 1988. pap. text ed. 13.50 (*0-669-12247-5*); Spanish for Bus-Finance. 3rd ed. LC 87-81232. (ENG & SPA.). (C). 1988. audio 30.00 (*0-669-12248-3*); Spanish For Med-Personnel. 3rd ed. LC 87-81232. (C). 1988. pap. text ed. 13.50 (*0-669-12249-1*); Spanish For Med-Personnel. 3rd ed. LC 87-81232. (ENG & SPA.). (C). 1988. audio 30.00 (*0-669-12250-5*); Spanish for Law Enforcement. 3rd ed. LC 87-81232. (C). 1988. pap. text ed. 13.50 (*0-669-12251-3*); Spanish for Law Enforcement. 3rd ed. LC 87-81232. (ENG & SPA.). (C). 1988. audio 30.00 (*0-669-12253-X*); Spanish for Social Services. 3rd ed. LC 87-81232. (C). 1988. pap. text ed. 13.50 (*0-669-12254-8*); Spanish for Social Services. 3rd ed. LC 87-81232. (ENG & SPA.). (C). 1988. audio 30.00 (*0-685-19283-0*); Spanish for Teachers. 3rd ed. LC 87-81232. (ENG & SPA.). (C). 1988. pap. text ed. 13.50 (*0-669-12256-4*); Spanish for Teachers. 3rd ed. LC 87-81232. (C). 1988. audio 30.00 (*0-669-12257-2*); Getting along in Spanish. 3rd ed. LC 87-81232. (C). 1988. pap. text ed. 13.00 (*0-669-12258-0*); Getting along in Spanish. 3rd ed. LC 87-81232. (ENG & SPA.). (C). 1988. audio 30.00 (*0-669-12259-9*); LC 87-81232. 336p. (Orig.). (ENG & SPA.). (C). 1988. Set pap. text ed. 19.50 (*0-669-12239-4*); Incl. pap. text ed. 13.50 (*0-669-12245-9*); audio 30.00 (*0-669-12246-7*); pap. text ed. 13.50 (*0-669-12247-5*); audio 30.00 (*0-669-12248-3*); pap. text ed. 13.50 (*0-669-12249-1*); audio 30.00 (*0-669-12250-5*); pap. text ed. 13.50 (*0-669-12251-3*); audio 30.00 (*0-669-12253-X*); pap. text ed. 13.50 (*0-669-12254-8*); audio 30.00 (*0-685-19283-0*); pap. text ed. 13.50 (*0-669-12256-4*); audio 30.00 (*0-669-12257-2*); pap. text ed. 13.00 (*0-669-12258-0*); audio 30.00 (*0-669-12259-9*); Cassette program. Set audio 30.00 (*0-669-12241-6*); Incl. pap. text ed. 13.50 (*0-669-12245-9*); audio 30.00 (*0-669-12246-7*); pap. text ed. 13.50 (*0-669-12247-5*); audio 30.00 (*0-669-12248-3*); pap. text ed. 13.50 (*0-669-12249-1*); audio 30.00 (*0-669-12250-5*); pap. text ed. 13.50 (*0-669-12251-3*); audio (*0-669-12253-X*); pap. text ed. 13.50 (*0-669-12254-8*); audio 30.00 (*0-685-19283-0*); pap. text ed. 13.50 (*0-669-12256-4*); audio 30.00 (*0-669-12257-2*); pap. text ed. 13.00 (*0-669-12258-0*); audio 30.00 (*0-669-12259-9*); Tapescript. 2.00 (*0-669-12240-8*); Incl. pap. text ed. 13.50 (*0-669-12245-9*); audio 30.00 (*0-669-12246-7*); pap. text ed. 13.50 (*0-669-12247-5*); audio 30.00 (*0-669-12248-3*); pap. text ed. 13.50 (*0-669-12249-1*); audio 30.00 (*0-669-12250-5*); pap. text ed. 13.50 (*0-669-12251-3*); audio 30.00 (*0-669-12253-X*); pap. text ed. 13.50 (*0-669-12254-8*); audio 30.00 (*0-685-19283-0*); pap. text ed. 13.50 (*0-669-12256-4*); audio 30.00 (*0-669-12257-2*); pap. text ed. 13.00 (*0-669-12258-0*); audio 30.00 (*0-669-12259-9*); IG-TIF. 2.00 (*0-669-12243-2*); Incl. pap. text ed. 13.50 (*0-669-12245-9*); audio 30.00 (*0-669-12246-7*); pap. text ed. 13.50 (*0-669-12247-5*); audio 30.00 (*0-669-12248-3*); pap. text ed. 13.50 (*0-669-12249-1*); audio 30.00 (*0-669-12250-5*); pap. text ed. 13.50 (*0-669-12251-3*); audio 30.00 (*0-669-12253-X*); pap. text ed. 13.50 (*0-669-12254-8*); audio 30.00 (*0-685-19283-0*); pap. text ed. 13.50 (*0-669-12256-4*); audio 30.00 (*0-669-12257-2*); pap. text ed. 13.00 (*0-669-12258-0*); audio 30.00 (*0-669-12259-9*); Demotape. 2.00 (*0-669-12242-4*) Heath.

Basic Spanish Grammar. 4th ed. Ana C. Jarvis et al. 342p. (Orig.). (ENG & SPA.). (C). 1992. pap. text ed. write for info. (*0-669-24286-1*); Instr.'s ed. teacher ed write for info. (*0-669-24287-X*); Testing program. teacher ed write for info. (*0-669-24288-8*); Cassettes. audio write for info. (*0-669-24289-6*); Demo. tape. write for info. (*0-669-24290-X*); Transcript. write for info. (*0-669-24291-8*) Heath.

Basic Spanish Pronounciation. Ralph S. Boggs. (Orig.). (SPA.). (gr. 9-11). 1969. pap. 3.75 (*0-88345-012-7*, 17442); audio 60.00 (*0-685-19785-9*) Prentice ESL.

Basic Speech Communication. Rudolph E. Busby & Randall E. Majors. (C). 1990. pap. text ed. 20.75 (*0-06-041093-0*) HarpCollege.

Basic Speech Communication. LaGuardia Community College Staff. 128p. (C). 1994. spiral bd. 14.36 (*0-8403-8168-9*) Kendall-Hunt.

Basic Spelling: Grade One. Bearl Brooks. (Spelling Ser.). 24p. 1979. student ed 5.00 (*0-8209-0165-2*, SP-1) ESP.

Basic Spelling: Grade Three. Bearl Brooks. (Spelling Ser.). 24p. 1977. student ed 5.00 (*0-8209-0167-9*, SP-3) ESP.

Basic Spelling: Grade Two. Bearl Brooks. (Spelling Ser.). 24p. 1979. student ed 5.00 (*0-8209-0166-0*, SP-2) ESP.

Basic Spiritual Metaphysics. Paul L. Peck. LC 78-61984. 1978. 14.50 (*0-87881-079-X*) Mojave Bks.

Basic Sport Science. Klaus Klausen et al. Tr. by Edmund J. Burke. 1982. pap. 14.95 (*0-932392-11-3*) Mouvement Pubns.

Basic Staff see Organization Executive Course

Basic Stairbuilding. Scott Schuttner. (Illus.). 128p. 1990. pap. text ed. 19.95 (*0-942391-44-6*); VHS, Basic Stairbuilding. vhs 29.95 (*0-942391-32-2*); Beta, Basic Stairbuilding. bmax write for info. (*0-942391-33-0*) Taunton.

Basic Stamp Collecting for Pathfinders: A Youth Enrichment Skill. George Register. (Illus.). 20p. (Orig.). 1987. teacher ed 5.00 (*0-936241-13-6*) Cheetah Pub.

Basic Statistical Analysis. 4th ed. Richard Sprinthall. 1993. text ed. 36.75 (*0-205-15428-X*) Allyn.

Basic Statistical Computing. 2nd ed. D. Cooke et al. LC 92-19688. 178p. 1992. pap. text ed. 37.95 (*0-470-21941-6*) Halsted Pr.

Basic Statistical Computing. 2nd ed. D. Cooke et al. 180p. 1991. pap. 25.00 (*0-340-53919-4*, A6354, Pub. by E Arnold UK) Routledge Chapman & Hall.

Basic Statistical Concepts. 3rd ed. Albert E. Bartz. 621p. (C). 1988. text ed. write for info. (*0-02-306445-5*) Macmillan.

Basic Statistical Methods. 5th ed. N. M. Downie & Robert W. Heath. 384p. (C). 1990. text ed. 33.25 (*0-06-041728-5*) HarpCollege.

Basic Statistical Techniques for Environmental Engineers. 121p. 1984. 30.00 (*0-685-63219-9*) Inst Environ Sci.

Basic Statistics. Jararell. 672p. 1993. 41.95 (*0-8016-7463-8*) Mosby Yr Bk.

Basic Statistics. Stephen Jarrell. 784p. (C). 1993. text ed. write for info. (*0-697-21595-4*); MiniTab wkbk. student ed write for info. (*0-697-21599-7*); Solutions manual. teacher ed write for info. (*0-697-21598-9*) Wm C Brown Pubs.

Basic Statistics. Stephen Jarrell. 784p. (C). 1994. Study guide. student ed write for info. (*0-697-21600-4*) Wm C Brown Pubs.

Basic Statistics. Jack Prins et al. LC 92-41299. (Six Sigma Research Institute Ser.). 1993. write for info. (*0-201-63406-6*) Addison-Wesley.

Basic Statistics. Jack Rudman. (DANTES Ser.: No. 4). 1994. pap. 23.95 (*0-8373-6604-6*) Nat Learn.

***Basic Statistics.** Jack Rudman. (DANTES Ser.: No. 4). 1994. 39.95 (*0-8373-6504-X*) Nat Learn.

Basic Statistics: A Modern Approach. 3rd ed. Morris Hamburg. LC 84-81504. 548p. (C). 1985. text ed. 50.00 (*0-15-505113-X*); 17.50 (*0-15-505114-8*) Dryden Pr.

Basic Statistics: A Primer for the Biomedical Sciences. 2nd ed. Olive J. Dunn. LC 77-9328. (Probability & Mathematical Statistics: Applied Probability & Statistics Section Ser.). 218p. 1977. text ed. 91.95 (*0-471-22744-7*, Wiley-Interscience) Wiley.

Basic Statistics: Tales of Distribution. 5th ed. Chris Spatz. 448p. (C). 1993. text ed. 53.95 (*0-534-19254-8*) Brooks-Cole.

Basic Statistics: Tools for Continuous Improvement. 2nd ed. Mark J. Kiemele & Stephen R. Schmidt. 680p. (C). 1992. text ed. 60.00 (*0-9622176-8-9*) Air Acad Pr.

Basic Statistics: Tools for Continuous Improvement. 3rd ed. Mark J. Kiemele & Stephen R. Schmidt. 850p. (C). 1993. text ed. 59.95 (*1-880156-01-6*) Air Acad Pr.

Basic Statistics: With Applications. Edwin Mansfield. (C). 1986. text ed. 44.95 (*0-393-95393-9*); Instr's. manual & test item file. teacher ed, pap. text ed. write for info. (*0-393-95402-1*); Incl. problems, exercises & case studies. student ed, pap. text ed. 12.95 (*0-393-95396-3*) Norton.

***Basic Statistics for Beginning Researchers.** Mary B. Harris. LC 94-26146. 1994. text ed. write for info. (*0-205-15102-7*) Allyn.

Basic Statistics for Business & Economics. Earl K. Bowen & Martin K. Starr. 1982. text ed. write for info. (*0-07-006725-2*) McGraw.

Basic Statistics for Business & Economics. Douglas A. Lind & Robert D. Mason. LC 93-3530. 528p. (C). 1993. text ed. 60.95 (*0-256-12222-9*) Irwin.

Basic Statistics for Business & Economics. 2nd ed. Leonard J. Kazmier & N. Pohl. 448p. 1984. text ed. write for info. (*0-07-033448-X*) McGraw.

Basic Statistics for High School. 2nd rev. ed. Jack Down. (Illus.). 194p. (Orig.). 1985. pap. text ed. 12.50 (*0-918907-00-4*) Golden Poplar Pr.

Basic Statistics for Laboratories: A Primer for Laboratory Workers. William D. Kelly et al. 192p. 1992. text ed. 44.95 (*0-442-00456-7*) Van Nos Reinhold.

***Basic Statistics for Librarians, 2049999.** 3rd ed. Ian S. Simpson. LC 82-197639. reprint ed. pap. 73.00 (*0-7837-9259-X*) Bks Demand.

Basic Statistics for Non-Math People. 2nd ed. Jack Down. (Illus.). 194p. (Orig.). 1984. pap. text ed. 12.50 (*0-918907-01-2*) Golden Poplar Pr.

Basic Statistics for Nurses. 2nd ed. Rebecca G. Knapp. LC 84-7274. 418p. 1985. pap. text ed. 29.95 (*0-8273-4271-3*) Delmar.

Basic Statistics for the Behavioral Health Sciences. Kaplan. 1986. disk write for info. (*0-318-61513-4*, H86945); 20.00 (*0-685-17401-8*, H86952) Allyn.

Basic Statistics for the Behavioral Sciences. Kenneth Pfeiffer & James N. Olson. LC 80-22778. (C). 1981. text ed. 44.00 (*0-03-049866-X*) HB Coll Pubs.

Basic Statistics for the Behavioral Sciences. 2nd ed. Kenneth D. Hopkins et al. (Illus.). 416p. (C). 1986. text ed. write for info. (*0-13-069402-9*) P-H.

Basic Statistics for the Health Sciences. 2nd ed. Jan W. Kuzma. LC 91-37581. 327p. (C). 1992. text ed. 46.95 (*0-87484-996-9*) Mayfield Pub.

Basic Statistics Minitab Workbook. Jarrell. 192p. 1993. pap. 12.95 (*0-8016-2303-0*) Mosby Yr Bk.

Basic Statistics Study Guide. Jarrell. 192p. 1993. pap. 16.25 (*0-8016-7462-X*) Mosby Yr Bk.

Basic Statistics Using SAS. 2nd ed. Bruce R. Lewis & Richard K. Ford. 148p. (C). 1987. pap. text ed. 28.50 (*0-314-34736-4*) West Pub.

Basic Statistics with Business Applications. Richard C. Clelland et al. LC 72-8057. (Probability & Mathematical Statistics: Applied Probability & Statistics Section Ser.). (Illus.). 703p. (C). reprint ed. pap. 180.00 (*0-8357-9843-7*, 2055099) Bks Demand.

Basic Steel Design. 3rd ed. Bruce G. Johnston et al. (Illus.). 384p. (C). 1985. text ed. 78.00 (*0-13-067737-X*) P-H.

Basic Steps in Planning Nursing Research. 3rd ed. Pamela Brink & Marilyn Wood. 400p. (C). 1988. boxed 38.75 (*0-86720-404-4*) Jones & Bartlett.

Basic Steps in Planning Nursing Research: From Question to Proposal. 4th ed. Pamela J. Brink & Marilynn J. Wood. LC 93-41640. 425p. 1994. text ed. 39.95 (*0-86720-677-2*) Jones & Bartlett.

Basic Steps Toward Community Ministry. Carl S. Dudley. LC 91-72970. 147p. (Orig.). 1991. pap. 11.25 (*1-56699-048-3*, AL127) Alban Inst.

Basic Still Life Techniques. Ed. by Rachel Wolf. (North Light Basic Painting Ser.). 128p. 1994. pap. 16.99 (*0-89134-588-4*) North Light Bks.

Basic Stochastic Process: The Mark Kac Lectures. Reza Iranpour & Paul Chacon. 297p. (C). 1988. write for info. (*0-02-359820-4*) Macmillan.

Basic Story Structure: The Structural Method for English Composition. 3rd ed. Eric Enholm. 1968. 8.50 (*0-685-06810-2*); pap. 7.00 (*0-685-06811-0*) Bayside.

Basic Structural Analysis. B. H. Topping. (Illus.). 160p. 1988. pap. text ed. write for info. (*0-408-01392-3*) Buttrwrth-Heinemann.

Basic Structural Design. K. R. Andrews. (Illus.). 160p. 1988. pap. text ed. 19.95 (*0-408-01589-6*) Buttrwrth-Heinemann.

Basic Structural Detailing. R. Benton. (Illus.). 220p. 1991. pap. 34.95 (*0-87683-617-1*) GP Pub.

Basic Structure & Evolution of Vertebrates, Vol. 1. E. Jarvik. 1981. text ed. 248.00 (*0-12-380801-4*) Acad Pr.

Basic Structure & Evolution of Vertebrates, Vol. 2. E. Jarvik. LC 80-40244. 1981. text ed. 189.00 (*0-12-380802-2*) Acad Pr.

Basic Structure Practice in Russian. Nicholas Maltzoff. 80p. 1991. pap. 12.95 (*0-8442-4260-8*, Passport Bks) NTC Pub Grp.

Basic Structures - American English, Bk. 1: A Textbook for the Learnables. Harris Winitz. (Illus.). 100p. 1990. audio, pap. text ed. 45.00 (*0-939990-60-1*) Intl Linguistics.

Basic Structures - French, Bk. 1: A Textbook for the Learnables. Carmen Waggoner. (Illus.). 127p. (FRE.). (YA). (gr. 7 up). 1991. audio 45.00 (*0-939990-73-3*) Intl Linguistics.

Basic Structures - Spanish, Bk. 1: A Textbook for the Learnables. Harris Winitz. Tr. by Blanca Sagarna. (Illus.). 106p. (YA). (gr. 7 up). 1991. audio, pap. text ed. 45.00 (*0-939990-61-X*) Intl Linguistics.

***Basic Structures, German: A Textbook for the Learnables.** Thorsten Piske & Harris Winitz. 132p. (Orig.). (GER.). 1993. pap. 45.00 (*0-939990-74-1*) Intl Linguistics.

***Basic Structures Hebrew Bk. 1: A Textbook for the Learnables.** Tami Winitz et al. (Illus.). 185p. (Orig.). (HEB.). (YA). (gr. 7 up). 1993. pap. 65.00 (*0-939990-84-9*) Intl Linguistics.

Basic Structures in Japanese. Haruo Aoki et al. 480p. (C). 1984. pap. text ed. 45.00 (*4-469-22062-0*, Asian Human Pr) Jain Pub Co.

Basic Structures of Modern Algebra. Yuri Bahturin. LC 93-11839. (Mathematics & Its Applications Ser.). 434p. (C). 1993. lib. bdg. 182.00 (*0-7923-2459-5*) Kluwer Ac.

Basic Structures of the Head & Neck: A Programmed Instruction in Clinical Anatomy for Dental Professionals. Gretchen M. Reed & Vincent F. Sheppard. LC 75-298. (Illus.). 716p. 1976. pap. text ed. 47.50 (*0-7216-7516-6*) Saunders.

***Basic Structures, Russian Bk. 1: A Textbook for the Learnables.** Vera Korchak & Harris Winitz. 153p. (Orig.). (RUS.). 1993. pap. 60.00 (*0-939990-83-0*) Intl Linguistics.

***Basic Structures, Spanish Bk. 2: A Textbook for The Learnables.** Blanca Sagarna & Harris Winitz. Ed. by Andres Trimino. (Illus.). 362p. (Orig.). (SPA.). (YA). (gr. 7 up). 1993. pap. 59.00 (*0-939990-85-7*) Intl Linguistics.

***Basic Student Charges at Post-Secondary Institutions.** 1994. lib. bdg. 250.00 (*0-8490-5787-6*) Gordon Pr.

Basic Studies in African American History, Book 1. Julia A. Davis. LC 91-65249. (Illus.). 151p. 1993. 16.95 (*1-55523-429-1*) Winston-Derek.

Basic Study & Research. Dale McMasters. (Language Arts Ser.). 24p. (gr. 5-9). 1979. student ed 5.00 (*0-8209-0304-3*, BSR-1) ESP.

Basic Study Manual. L. Ron Hubbard. 268p. 1992. 37.50 (*0-88404-631-1*) Bridge Pubns Inc.

Basic Stuff: Exercise Physiology, No. I. rev. ed. 1987. 7.95 (*0-88314-357-7*) AAHPERD.

Basic Stuff: Humanities, No. I. rev. ed. 1987. 7.95 (*0-88314-361-5*) AAHPERD.

Basic Stuff: In Action, 3 vols., No. II. rev. ed. (J). (gr. k-3). 1987. Grades k-3. 7.95 (*0-88314-364-X*) AAHPERD.

Basic Stuff: In Action, 3 vols., No. II. rev. ed. (J). (gr. 4-8). 1987. Grades 4-8. 7.95 (*0-88314-365-8*) AAHPERD.

Basic Stuff: In Action, 3 vols., No. II. rev. ed. (YA). (gr. 9-12). 1987. Grades 9-12. 7.95 (*0-88314-366-6*) AAHPERD.

Basic Stuff: Kinesiology, No. I. rev. ed. 1987. 7.95 (*0-88314-358-5*) AAHPERD.

Basic Stuff: Motor Development, No. I. rev. ed. 1987. 7.95 (*0-88314-362-3*) AAHPERD.

Basic Stuff: Motor Learning, No. I. rev. ed. 1987. 7.95 (*0-88314-359-3*) AAHPERD.

Basic Stuff: Psycho Social Aspects, No. I. rev. ed. 1987. 7.95 (*0-88314-360-7*) AAHPERD.

Basic Surgery. 4th ed. Ed. by Hiram C. Polk, Jr. et al. LC 92-49686. 1993. 40.00 (*0-942219-29-5*) Quality Med Pub.

***Basic Surgery.** 5th ed. Bernard Gardner & H. Harlan Stone. Ed. by Hiram C. Polk, Jr. et al. 1995. 45.00 (*0-942219-74-0*) Quality Med Pub.

Basic Surgical Exercises Using Swine. M. Michael Swindle. LC 82-24688. 254p. 1983. pap. text ed. 65.00 (*0-275-91415-1*, C1415, Praeger Pubs) Greenwood.

Basic Surgical Instrumentation. Mary F. Smith & Joette Stehn. (Illus.). 256p. 1992. pap. text ed. 30.95 (*0-7216-4211-X*) Saunders.

Basic Surgical Physiology. Frederick W. Preston & John M. Beal. LC 69-13375. (Illus.). 508p. reprint ed. pap. 144.80 (*0-8357-9598-5*, 2013103) Bks Demand.

Basic Surgical Practice. James et al. 1987. 41.00 (*0-8016-2368-5*) Mosby Yr Bk.

Basic Surgical Techniques. 3rd ed. Raymond M. Kirk. (Illus.). 304p. 1989. pap. text ed. 27.95 (*0-443-04004-4*) Churchill.

Basic Survey Computations. Edward G. Zimmerman. (C). 1992. pap. 35.00 (*0-910845-40-9*, 556) Landmark Ent.

Basic Surveying for Technicians. Robert P. Landon. 299p. 1994. text ed. 39.95 (*0-8273-3941-0*) Delmar.

Basic Survival Techniques for Flight Crew & Crewmembers. Jeffrey Hare. (Illus.). 158p. 1984. write for info. (*0-9613179-0-6*) JH Prods.

Basic Swedish: Textbook. Walter Johnson. 279p. 1983. 16.95 (*0-910452-52-0*) Covenant.

***Basic Swedish Grammar.** 3rd ed. Beite. (ENG & SWE.). 1989. 85.00 (*0-7859-7460-1*, 9121015511) Fr & Eur.

Basic Swedish Grammar. 3rd ed. A. M. Beite. 1989. 83.00 (*91-21-01551-1*) IBD Ltd.

***Basic Swimming.** Kiphuth. 1995. (*0-8371-5168-6*) Greenwood.

Basic Swimming Guide. Joseph K. Groscost. LC 75-22501. (Illus.). 101p. 1980. reprint ed. pap. 3.95 (*0-89037-105-9*, Anderson World) Anderson World.

***Basic Symbols of the American Political Tradition.** Willmoore Kendall & George Carey. LC 94-39960. 185p. 1995. pap. 14.95 (*0-8132-0826-2*) Cath U Pr.

***Basic Symbols of the American Political Tradition.** fac. ed. Willmoore Kendall & George W. Carey. LC 76-119112. 169p. 1970. reprint ed. pap. 48.20 (*0-7837-7770-1*, 2047526) Bks Demand.

Basic System Design. D. Downs. (C). 1989. 90.00 (*0-7487-0263-6*, Pub. by S Thornes Pubs UK) St Mut.

Basic Systems Analysis. L. Lee. (C). 1989. 100.00 (*0-09-154091-7*, Pub. by S Thornes Pubs UK) St Mut.

Basic Systems Analysis. Ed. by Don Yeates & Alan Daniels. 380p. (C). 1988. pap. text ed. 120.00 (*0-273-02931-2*, Pub. by Pitman Pubng UK) St Mut.

***Basic Tack.** Vanessa Britton. (Crowood Equestrian Guide Ser.). (Illus.). 96p. 1995. pap. 17.95 (*1-85223-800-3*, Pub. by Crowood Pr UK) Trafalgar.

Basic Tagalog for Foreigners & Non-Tagalogs. Paraluman S. Aspillera. 258p. 1993. pap. 12.95 (*0-8048-1910-6*) C E Tuttle.

Basic Teacher Skills: Handbook for Church School Teachers. Richard E. Rusbuldt. 144p. 1981. pap. 11.00 (*0-8170-0919-1*) Judson.

Basic Teachings of the Great Philosophers. S. E. Frost, Jr. LC 62-15320. 1962. mass mkt. 9.95 (*0-385-03007-X*, C398, Dolp) Doubleday.

Basic Technical College Mathematics. 2nd ed. Leonard Mrachek & Charles Komschilies. 336p. 1993. pap. text ed. write for info. (*0-13-891995-X*) P-H.

Basic Technical Dictionary: French-English-German-Arabic. H. Marei. 363p. (ARA, ENG, FRE & GER.). 1973. lib. bdg. 125.00 (*0-7859-0804-8*, M-9752) Fr & Eur.

Basic Technical Drawing. Phillip Sell. 368p. (C). 1991. write for info. (*0-675-21001-1*, Merrill Pub Co) Macmillan.

Basic Technical English. Jeremy Comfort et al. (Illus.). 1983. teacher ed 9.50 (*0-19-457383-4*); student ed, pap. 10.50 (*0-19-457382-6*) OUP.

Basic Technical Japanese. Edward E. Daub et al. LC 90-50082. 800p. (C). 1990. text ed. 35.00 (*0-299-12730-3*) U of Wis Pr.

Basic Technical Math with Calculus. 4th ed. Allyn J. Washington. (Illus.). 1136p. (C). 1985. teacher ed 9.95 (*0-8053-9551-2*); text ed. 39.95 (*0-8053-9541-5*) Addison-Wesley.

Basic Technical Mathematics. Stuart R. Porter & John F. Ernst. LC 84-8369. 1985. teacher ed write for info. (*0-201-05588-0*); teacher ed write for info. (*0-201-05598-8*); text ed. write for info. (*0-201-05586-4*); student ed write for info. (*0-201-05587-2*) Addison-Wesley.

Basic Technical Mathematics. Stuart R. Porter & John F. Ernst. LC 94-12265. (C). 1995. 46.00 (*0-673-46177-7*) HarpCollege.

Basic Technical Mathematics. Charles R. Wall. 745p. (C). 1986. pap. text ed. 2.25 (*0-15-505132-6*); write for info. (*0-318-60396-9*) SCP.

Basic Technical Mathematics. Allyn J. Washington. LC 77-71469. 864p. 1990. By Zeigler & Brazen. teacher ed 9.95 (*0-685-48378-9*) Addison-Wesley.

Basic Technical Mathematics. 2nd ed. Peter Kuhfittig. LC 88-23222. 695p. (C). 1989. text ed. 55.95 (*0-534-09426-0*) Brooks-Cole.

***Basic Technical Mathematics.** 2nd ed. Porter. (C). 1995. student ed, text ed. 18.50 (*0-673-46376-1*) HarpCollege.

Basic Technical Mathematics. 5th ed. Allyn J. Washington. LC 77-71469. 864p. 1990. student ed 14.95 (*0-685-48379-7*) Addison-Wesley.

Basic Technical Mathematics. 5th ed. Allyn J. Washington. LC 77-71469. 864p. (C). 1990. text ed. 55.95 (*0-8053-8888-5*) Addison-Wesley.

Basic Technical Mathematics. 6th ed. C. Thomas Olivo & Thomas P. Olivo. 694p. 1992. text ed. 38.95 (*0-8273-4666-2*) Delmar.

Basic Technical Mathematics. 6th ed. Allyn J. Washington. LC 94-3041. (C). 1995. text ed. 52.95 (*0-201-60967-3*) Addison-Wesley.

***Basic Technical Mathematics.** 6th ed. Allyn J. Washington. (Illus.). 800p. (C). 1995. text ed. 54.95 (*0-201-54238-2*) Addison-Wesley.

Basic Technical Mathematics Fundamentals. 6th ed. C. Thomas Olivo & Thomas P. Olivo. 384p. 1992. pap. 21.95 (*0-8273-4958-0*) Delmar.

Basic Technical Mathematics Simplified: Instructor's Guide. C. Thomas Olivo. 1992. 12.00 (*0-8273-4642-5*) Delmar.

An Asterisk (*) at the beginning of an entry indicates that the title is appearing in BIP for the first time.

621

Basic Technical Mathematics with Calculus. Stuart R. Porter. Ed. by John F. Ernst. LC 84-9168. 1985. teacher ed write for info. (0-201-05591-0); text ed. 35.16 (0-201-05589-9); Student sol. manual. student ed 13.56 (0-201-05590-2) Addison-Wesley.

***Basic Technical Mathematics with Calculus.** 2nd ed. Ferguson & Seidel. (C). 1995. student ed, text ed. write for info. (0-614-03336-5) HarpCollege.

Basic Technical Mathematics with Calculus. 2nd ed. Peter Kuhfittig. LC 88-23223. 1076p. (C). 1989. boxed, text ed. 65.95 (0-534-10062-7) Brooks-Cole.

Basic Technical Mathematics with Calculus. 2nd ed. Stuart R. Porter & John F. Ernst. LC 94-13873. (C). 1995. 49.00 (0-673-46176-9) HarpCollege.

Basic Technical Mathematics with Calculus. 5th ed. Allyn J. Washington. Ed. by Lisa Moller. 1186p. (C). 1990. teacher ed 8.95 (0-8053-8893-1); text ed. 59.25 (0-8053-8889-3); teacher ed, pap. text ed. 15.00 (0-8053-8891-5) Benjamin-Cummings.

Basic Technical Mathematics with Calculus. 6th ed. Allyn J. Washington. 934p. (C). 1995. text ed. 52.95 (0-201-50173-2) Addison-Wesley.

Basic Technical Physics. Paul E. Tippens. LC 82-7182. 512p. 1983. text ed. 27.95 (0-07-064971-5) McGraw.

Basic Technical Physics. 2nd ed. Paul E. Tippens. 1989. text ed. write for info. (0-07-065040-3) McGraw.

BASIC Technical Systems Simulation. Ed. by A. D. Savic. (Butterworth's Basic Bks.). (Illus.). 160p. 1989. pap. text ed. 24.95 (0-408-01270-6) Buttrwrth-Heinemann.

Basic Technical Writing. (Anthology Ser.). 1991. 25.00 (0-914548-44-1, 108-87) Soc Tech Comm.

Basic Technical Writing. Ed. by Frances J. Sullivan. (Anthology Ser.: No. 7). 1987. 25.00 (0-914548-53-0) Soc Tech Comm.

Basic Techniques, Bk. 1. rev. ed. Linaea Marvell-Mell. Ed. by Lori Stephens. (Skill Builder Ser.). (Illus.). 192p. 1989. reprint ed. student ed 12.95 (1-55552-016-2); reprint ed. audio, pap. 12.95 (0-943920-02-7) Metamorphous Pr.

Basic Techniques, Bk. II. Clifford Wright. Ed. by Lori Stephens. (Skill Builder Ser.). (Illus.). 144p. (Orig.). 1989. pap. 10.95 (1-55552-005-7) Metamorphous Pr.

Basic Techniques for Metal Ceramics. Makoto Yamamoto. (Illus.). 117p. 1990. text ed. 64.00 (4-87417-280-6) Quint Pub Co.

Basic Techniques for the Medical Laboratory. 2nd ed. Jean J. Linne. (Illus.). 1979. text ed. 39.95 (0-07-037948-3) McGraw.

Basic Techniques for Transmission Electron Microscopy. M. A. Hayat. 1985. text ed. 112.00 (0-12-333925-1); pap. text ed. 60.00 (0-12-333926-X) Acad Pr.

Basic Techniques in Clinical Laboratory Science. 3rd ed. Jean J. Linne & Ringsrud. 580p. 1991. 32.95 (0-8016-2864-4) Mosby Yr Bk.

Basic Techniques in Data Communications. 2nd rev. ed. Ralph Glasgal. LC 77-18090. 151p. reprint ed. pap. 43.10 (0-8357-5990-3, 2025052) Bks Demand.

Basic Techniques in Vascular Surgery. Bjorn F. Ericsson. LC 88-71787. (Illus.). 70p. (Orig.). (C). 1988. pap. text ed. 14.95 (0-9620916-0-X) Davis & Geck.

Basic Techniques of Go. 2nd ed. Eight-Dan Haruyama Isamu & Six-Dan Nagahara Yoshiaki. Ed. by Richard Bozulich. (Illus.). 176p. 1992. pap. 13.95 (4-87187-002-2, G2) Ishi Pr Intl.

Basic Techniques of Preparative Organic Chemistry. W. Sabel. 1967. pap. 91.00 (0-08-012307-4, Pub. by Pergamon Repr UK) Franklin.

***Basic Techniques of Psychodynamic Psychotherapy.** Ed. by Michael P. Nichols & Thomas J. Paolino, Jr. 360p. 1995. pap. 30.00 (1-56821-618-1) Aronson.

Basic Telephone Installation. LC 73-85629. (Specialized Ser.). (Illus.). 60p. (Orig.). (C). 1984. pap. text ed. 10.95 (1-56016-021-7) ABC TeleTraining.

Basic Television. 4th ed. Bernard Grob. (C). 1975. text ed. 39.95 (0-07-024927-X) McGraw.

Basic Television: Theory & Servicing-A Text Lab Manual. Electronic Industries Association Staff et al. (Illus.). 1978. pap. text ed. 26.95 (0-07-072752-X) McGraw.

Basic Terminology for Therapeutic Recreation & Other Action Therapies. Scout Lee & Jan Summers. 1990. pap. text ed. 6.80 (0-87563-350-1) Stipes.

Basic Terms of Anatomy & Physiology. 2nd ed. Bruce P. Squires. (Illus.). 184p. 1987. pap. text ed. 23.00 (0-920513-00-X) Saunders.

Basic Terms of Maintenance. Tel-A-Train, Inc. Staff. 1974. student ed 6.50 (1-56355-002-4) Tel-A-Train.

Basic Testing Series, 3 pts. Incl. Fair Use of Selection Tests. Pearn. 12p. (0-318-59479-X); Look at Cognitive Development. Stillman. 12p. (0-318-59480-3); Item Banking. Childs. 12p. (0-318-59481-1); Set. write for info. (0-7005-0485-0) Taylor & Francis.

Basic Tests for Pharmaceutical Substances. 210p. 1986. 20.40 (92-4-154204-7) World Health.

Basic Texas Books: An Annotated Bibliography of Selected Works for a Research Library. rev. ed. John H. Jenkins. (Illus.). xiii, 660p. 1983. 29.95 (0-87611-086-3, VI5-12-8) Tex St Hist Assn.

Basic Text on Administrative Law. 3rd ed. Kenneth C. Davis. LC 71-181451. xvi, 617p. 1972. 19.95 (0-317-00000-4) West Pub.

Basic Text on Insurance Law. Robert E. Keeton. 712p. 1971. 23.95 (0-685-07609-1) West Pub.

Basic Text on Labor Law: Unionization & Collective Bargaining. Robert A. Gorman. (Hornbook Ser.). 914p. 1992. reprint ed. text ed. 33.50 (0-314-31922-0) West Pub.

Basic Textbook of Psychology. Charles A. Heidenreich. 1971. pap. 8.95 (0-9600428-1-4) Heidenreich.

Basic Texts in International Relations: The Evolution of Ideas about International Society. Intro. & Sel. by Evan Luard. LC 91-10832. 300p. (C). 1992. text ed. 49.95 (0-312-06506-X); pap. 19.95 (0-312-06511-6) St Martin.

Basic Texts of FAO. Incl. Vol. 1. , 2 Vols. pap. 6.00 (0-685-12976-4, F53); Vol. 2. , 2 Vols. pap. 5.00 (0-685-43493-1, F54); , 2 Vols. pap. 20.00 (0-685-12978-0, F55); 1974, 2 Vols. pap. 19.00 (0-685-12979-9, F57); 1976, 2 Vols. pap. 19.50 (0-685-12980-2, F58); 1974, 2 Vols. pap. 19.00 (0-685-12979-9, F57); 1976, 2 Vols. pap. 19.50 (0-685-12980-2, F58); Set. Set pap. 19.00 (0-685-12975-6) UNIPUB.

Basic Themes in the Comparative Study of Religion. Cyril G. Williams. LC 92-20929. (Studies in Comparative Religion: Vol. 5). 176p. 1992. text ed. 79.95 (0-7734-9580-0) E Mellen.

Basic Theology. Charles C. Ryrie. 544p. 1986. 26.99 (0-89693-814-X, Victor Books) SP Pubns.

***Basic Theology: Applied.** Ed. by Wesley Willis et al. LC 95-1639. 312p. 1995. 22.99 (1-56476-442-7, 6-3442, Victor Books) SP Pubns.

Basic Theories of Distribution. Benjamin F. Catherwood. LC 71-121454. (Essay Index Reprint Ser.). 1977. 23.95 (0-8369-1700-6) Ayer.

Basic Theory of Algebraic Groups & Line Algebras. G. H. Hochschild. (Graduate Texts in Mathematics Ser.: Vol. 75). 350p. 1981. 49.80 (0-387-90541-3) Spr-Verlag.

Basic Theory of Capitalism: The Forms & Substance of the Capitalist Economy. Makoto Itoh. LC 87-905. 432p. 1987. 69.50 (0-389-20729-2, N8287) B&N Imports.

Basic Theory of Lasers & Masers: A Density Matrix Approach. Jacques Vanier. Ed. by E. W. Montroll et al. (Illus.). 128p. 1971. text ed. 111.00 (0-677-30340-8) Gordon & Breach.

Basic Theory of Music: Programmed Instruction in Intervals, Scales, & Modes. John W. Verrall. (C). 1970. pap. text ed. 6.95 (0-87015-183-5) Pacific Bks.

Basic Theory of Power Series. Jesus M. Ruiz. (Advanced Lectures in Mathematics Ser.). x, 134p. 1993. pap. 26.00 (3-528-06525-7, Pub. by Vieweg & Sohn GW) Ballen Bkslr.

Basic Theory of Psychoanalysis. Robert Waelder. LC 60-8304. 273p. 1964. text ed. 37.50x (0-8236-0460-8); pap. text ed. 24.95 (0-8236-8008-8, 20200) Intl Univs Pr.

Basic Theory of Real Closed Spaces. N. Schwartz. LC 88-8168. (MEMO Ser.: Vol. 77/397). 122p. 1989. pap. 19.00 (0-8218-2460-0, MEMO 77/397) Am Math.

BASIC Theory of Structures. K. R. Andrews. LC 85-4238. (Basic Ser.). (Illus.). 160p. 1985. pap. text ed. 24.95 (0-408-01357-5) Buttrwrth-Heinemann.

Basic Theory of Surface States. Sydney G. Davison & Maria Steslicka. (Monographs on the Physics & Chemistry of Materials). (Illus.). 240p. 1992. 65.00 (0-19-851990-7) OUP.

***Basic Theosophy.** Geoffrey Hodson. 1981. pap. 23.95 (81-7059-171-6) Theos Pub Hse.

***Basic Thermal Science & Engineering for Nuclear Technology Vol. 1: Fundmental Aspects.** Dan Duncan & J. N. Anno. 380p. (C). 1994. pap. text ed. 28.00 (1-57074-190-5) Greyden Pr.

Basic Thermodynamics. Gerald Carrington. LC 93-34952. (Illus.). 400p. (C). 1994. text ed. 59.95 (0-19-851748-3); pap. text ed. 24.95 (0-19-851747-5) OUP.

Basic Thermodynamics: Elements of Energy Systems. Bernhardt G. Skrotzki. 1963. text ed. 45.95 (0-07-057945-8) McGraw.

BASIC Thermodynamics & Heat Transfer. D. H. Bacon. (Basic Ser.). (Illus.). 160p. 1983. pap. text ed. 24.95 (0-408-01312-5) Buttrwrth-Heinemann.

***Basic Thinking: On Beginning at the Beginning in Thinking about Social & Economic Problems.** Wilmer MacNair. 360p. (C). 1995. lib. bdg. 49.00 (0-614-03244-X) U Pr of Amer.

***Basic Thinking: On Beginning at the Beginning in Thinking about Social & Economic Problems.** Wilmer MacNair. LC 94-44029. 1995. write for info. (0-8191-9840-4); pap. write for info. (0-8191-9841-2) U Pr of Amer.

Basic Thinking in Regional Planning. F. B. Gillie. (Publications of the Institute of Social Studies: No. 14). 1967. text ed. 18.50 (90-279-0111-2) Mouton.

Basic TIG & MIG Welding: GTAW & GMAW. 3rd ed. I. H. Griffin et al. LC 83-18844. 128p. (C). 1984. teacher ed 10.00 (0-8273-2130-9); pap. text ed. 17.95 (0-8273-2129-5) Delmar.

Basic Tips on the ACT, American College Testing Assessment Program. 2nd ed. Ehrenhaft et al. 500p. 1991. pap. 6.95 (0-8120-4691-9) Barron.

Basic Tips on the TOEFL. Pamela Sharpe. 192p. (C). (gr. 11-12). 1982. pap. 4.95 (0-8120-2584-9) Barron.

Basic to C Conversion Manual. Robert J. Traister, Sr. (Illus.). 224p. 1987. 22.50 (0-13-058363-4) P-H.

Basic Tools & Equipment for the Oil Field. Jeanette Paxson. (Illus.). 109p. (Orig.). (C). 1982. pap. text ed. 17.00 (0-88698-100-X, 1.80010) PETEX.

Basic Tools of Research. 3rd ed. Philip H. Vitale. 1977. pap. 6.95 (0-8120-0627-5) Barron.

Basic Topics in the Philosophy of Language. Ed. by Robert M. Harnish. LC 93-33484. 1993. pap. text ed. 24.00 (0-13-150509-2) P-H.

Basic Topology. rev. ed. M. A. Armstrong. (Undergraduate Texts in Mathematics Ser.). (Illus.). 250p. 1994. reprint ed. 34.00 (0-387-90839-0) Spr-Verlag.

***Basic Total Selling & Advertising Service - Floorcoverings.** 2nd ed. C. B. Bedell. LC 75-27670. 366p. 1984. spiral bd. 295.00 (0-916014-00-2) BASIC Bedell.

Basic Toxicology: Fundamentals, Target Organs & Risk Assessment. 2nd ed. Frank C. Lu. 376p. 1990. 79.00 (0-89116-894-X); pap. 42.00 (1-56032-080-X) Hemisp Pub.

Basic Traffic Analysis. Roberta Martine. LC 93-8268. 1993. text ed. 76.00 (0-13-335407-5) P-H.

Basic Training. Barbara Ripman. (Crowood Equestrian Guides Ser.). (Illus.). 96p. 1992. pap. 17.95 (1-85223-534-9, Pub. by Crowood Pr UK) Trafalgar.

***Basic Training: Things Every Christian Kid Needs to Know.** (Custom Curriculum Ser.). (Illus.). (J). (gr. 6-9). Date not set. 10.95 (0-7814-5002-0, 85324) Cook.

Basic Training for Horses: English & Western. Eleanor F. Prince & Gaydell M. Collier. 1989. pap. 17.50 (0-385-26238-8) Doubleday.

***Basic Training for Trainers: A Handbook for New Trainers.** Kroehnert. 1995. pap. text ed. 29.95 (0-07-470193-2) McGraw.

***Basic Training in Camera Repair Tape Learning Program.** Edward H. Romney. 122p. 1993. audio 99.00 (1-886996-55-5) Hillcrst Pub.

Basic Training in Journalism. B. J. Hall & B. Henson. LC 68-21102. (Library of Industrial Commercial Education & Training). 1968. 58.00 (0-08-012864-5, Pub. by Pergamon Repr UK) Franklin.

***Basic Training in Mathematics: A Fitness Program for Science Students.** Ramamurti Shankar. LC 95-13532. 360p. 1995. 47.50 (0-306-45035-6, Plenum Pr); pap. 26.50 (0-306-45036-4, Plenum Pr) Plenum.

Basic Trauma Life Support. Alabama ACEP Staff & John E. Campbell. (Illus.). 224p. (C). 1985. teacher ed 17.95 (0-89303-363-4); pap. text ed. 18.95 (0-89303-361-8) P-H.

***Basic Trauma Life Support Access.** James Gargan. 80p. 1995. pap. write for info. (1-887321-00-4) Emerg Trng Assocs.

Basic Trauma Nursing Skills. Linda B. Chitwood. (Illus.). 240p. (Orig.). (C). 1991. pap. text ed. 49.95 (1-878025-27-9) Western Schls.

***Basic Trauma Nursing Skills.** Linda B. Chitwood. 240p. (Orig.). (C). 1994. pap. 49.95 (1-878025-66-X) Western Schls.

Basic Trends of Our Times. Pitirim A. Sorokin. 1964. 19.95 (0-8084-0057-6); pap. 15.95x (0-8084-0058-4) NCUP.

Basic Trilingual Vocabulary of Scientific Psychology. C. Genovard Rossello. 1980. 19.95 (0-8288-1889-4, S37601) Fr & Eur.

Basic Truths of Our Common Faith. Bill Freeman. 65p. (Orig.). 1994. pap. 2.00 (0-914271-54-7) Mnstry Wrd.

***Basic Truths Series, 3 bks.** Incl. Ethel Jenner Rosenberg: The Life & Times of...England's Outstanding Bah'a'i Pioneer Worker. Illus. by Trevor Finch. 32p. (Orig.). 1995. pap. (0-85398-395-X); Ethel Jenner Rosenberg: The Life & Times of...England's Outstanding Bah'a'i Pioneer Worker. Illus. by Trevor Finch. 32p. (Orig.). 1995. pap. (0-85398-396-8); Ethel Jenner Rosenberg: The Life & Times of...England's Outstanding Bah'a'i Pioneer Worker. Robert Weinberg. (Illus.). 350p. (Orig.). 1995. pap. (0-85398-399-2); write for info. (0-85398-397-6) G Ronald Pub.

Basic Truths Series Two. Bambi Betts. (Illus.). 1989. Set incl. What's Fair, 32p., When I Pray, 32p., Nothing Goes Right, 32p. pap. 9.95 (0-85398-286-4) G Ronald Pub.

Basic TV Reporting: Media Manuals. Ivor Yorke. 168p. 1990. pap. 19.95 (0-240-51283-9, Focal) Buttrwrth-Heinemann.

Basic TV Technology. Robert L. Hartwig. (Illus.). 160p. 1989. pap. 19.95 (0-240-80051-6, Focal) Buttrwrth-Heinemann.

***Basic TV Technology: A Media Manual.** 2nd ed. Robert L. Hartwig. (Illus.). 176p. 1995. pap. 19.95 (0-240-80228-4, Focal) Buttrwrth-Heinemann.

Basic Two Phase Flow Modeling in Reactor Safety & Performance: EPRI Workshop Held at Tampa, Fla. 27 Feb.-2 March 1979. Ed. by G. Hetsroni. 170p. 1980. pap. 55.00 (0-08-026160-4, Pergamon Pr) Elsevier.

Basic Types of Pastoral Care & Counseling. Howard Clinebell. LC 83-15590. 464p. 1984. 19.95 (0-687-02492-7) Abingdon.

Basic Typing: A Brief Course. Carol Yacht. 224p. 1979. spiral bd. 18.76 (0-672-97262-X, Bobbs); 3.67 (0-672-97263-8, Bobbs) Macmillan.

Basic Typing Skills. K. Dulmage. 96p. (Orig.). (C). 1986. pap. text ed. 19.95 (0-273-02465-5) Trans-Atl Phila.

Basic Typography: A Design Manual. James Craig. (Illus.). 192p. 1990. pap. 19.95 (0-8230-0451-1, Watsn-Guptill) Watsn-Guptill.

Basic U. S. Government Micrographics Standards & Specifications. 6th ed. U. S. Government Staff & Harry B. Kidd. (Reference Ser.). 530p. 1983. reprint ed. pap. 30.00 (0-89258-089-5, R001) Assn Inform & Image Mgmt.

Basic Understanding for Real Estate Investors. Jimmy L. Kum & David J. Kum. (Technical - Real Estate Ser.). 156p. (gr. 12). 1990. 49.95 (0-9626817-1-7) J L Kum.

Basic Uniform Commercial Code Teaching Materials. 3rd ed. David G. Epstein et al. (American Casebook Ser.). 704p. (C). 1989. reprint ed. text ed. 41.50 (0-314-36437-4) West Pub.

Basic Uniform Commercial Code, 1988 Supplement. 3rd ed. David G. Epstein et al. (American Casebook Ser.). 268p. 1988. Tchr's. ed. teacher ed, pap. text ed. write for info. (0-314-48233-4) West Pub.

Basic United Methodist Beliefs: (An Evangelical View) Ed. by James V. Heidinger, II. LC 86-80014. 128p. 1986. pap. 4.95 (0-917851-01-3) Bristol Hse.

Basic Urogynaecology. Linda Cardozo et al. LC 92-48233. 176p. 1993. 51.50 (0-19-262360-5); pap. 25.95 (0-19-262359-1) OUP.

Basic Urologic Laparoscopy. Arthur I. Sagalowsky & Glenn M. Preminger. LC 93-9570. (Illus.). 160p. 1993. 45.00 (0-87993-563-4) Futura Pub.

Basic Usage, Vocabulary, & Composition. 4th ed. Hulon Willis et al. 396p. (C). 1983. pap. text ed. 22.00 (0-03-062326-X) HB Coll Pubs.

Basic Vacuum Technology. A. Chambers et al. (Illus.). 180p. 1989. 32.00 (0-85274-128-6) IOP Pub.

Basic Values & Ethical Decisions: An Examination of Individualism & Community. Gerry C. Heard. LC 89-27530. 120p. (Orig.). 1990. pap. 12.50 (0-89464-431-9) Krieger.

Basic Values in Law: A Study of the Ethics-Legal Implications of Psychology & Anthropology. Thomas E. Davitt. LC 68-24357. 1968. pap. 15.00 (0-87462-451-7) Marquette.

Basic Values of Western Civilization. Shepard B. Clough. LC 84-27971. xi, 132p. 1985. reprint ed. text ed. 55.00 (0-313-24735-8, CLBV, Greenwood Pr) Greenwood.

Basic Verbal Skills. 2nd ed. Phillip Burnham & Richard Lederer. 243p. (gr. 9-12). 1980. student ed 10.06 (0-88334-130-1, 76104); pap. text ed. 16.32 (0-88334-134-4, 76106) Longman.

Basic Verbal Skills for the Middle School. Phillip Burnham & Richard Lederer. 1976. student ed 18.66 (0-88334-073-9, 76066); 9.15 (0-8013-0071-1, 75735) Longman.

Basic Verbal Skills for the Middle School Grammar & Punctuation Workbook. Phillip Burnham & Richard Lederer. 1976. 5.88 (0-88334-074-7, 76067); student ed 9.15 (0-8013-0072-X, 75736) Longman.

Basic Verities: Prose & Poetry. Charles P. Peguy. Tr. by Ann Green & Julian Green. LC 72-4493. (Essay Index Reprint Ser.). 1977. reprint ed. 21.95 (0-8369-2967-5) Ayer.

Basic Virginia Law for Non-Lawyers: Legal Survival in the Commonwealth of Virginia. Lederer & Posey Staff & Kelley, Gibbs & Reynolds Staff. Ed. by Fredric Lederer. 96p. 1993. pap. 8.95 (0-9615670-3-1, King & Queen Pr) Soc Alu Wm.

Basic Visual Concepts & Principles for Artists, Architects & Designers. Charles Wallschleager & Cynthia Busic-Snyder. 544p. (C). 1992. pap. write for info. (0-697-00651-4) Brown & Benchmark.

Basic Vivid Thinking. Brown Landone. 63p. 1966. reprint ed. spiral bd. 5.50 (0-7873-1254-1) Mokelumne.

Basic VLSI Design: Systems & Circuits. 3rd ed. Doug Pucknell & Kamram Eshraghian. 1994. pap. text ed. 50.00 (0-13-079153-9) P-H.

Basic Vocabulary: American Sign Language for Parents & Children. Terrence J. O'Rourke. 1978. pap. 8.95 (0-932666-00-0) T J Pubs.

Basic Vocabulary & Language Thesaurus for Hearing-Impaired Children. Daniel Ling & Agnes H. Ling. LC 76-52826. 1977. 9.95 (0-88200-078-0, C1437) Alexander Graham.

Basic Vocabulary for Hindi & Urdu. 2nd ed. Ed. by Karine Schomer & Geoffrey G. Reinhard. 194p. (Orig.). (C). 1984. pap. text ed. 27.50 (0-8191-3509-7) U Pr of Amer.

Basic Vocabulary of Marxism: Vocabulario Basico del Marxismo. G. Bekerman. 278p. (SPA.). 1983. pap. 19.95 (0-8288-2265-4, S40317) Fr & Eur.

Basic Vocabulary of Scientific & Technological German. J. Horne. LC 66-16876. 1969. 156.00 (0-08-011671-X, Pub. by Pergamon Repr UK) Franklin.

Basic Vocational Technical Math. 6th ed. Thomas P. Olivo & C. Thomas Olivo. 1992. pap. text ed. 32.95 (0-8273-4641-7) Delmar.

Basic Vocational Technical Mathematics. 5th ed. C. Thomas Olivo. Ed. by Thomas P. Olivo. 448p. (C). teacher ed 12.00 (0-8273-2228-3); text ed. 38.95 (0-8273-2226-7); pap. text ed. 32.95 (0-8273-2225-9) Delmar.

Basic Vocational-Technical Mathematics: Fundamentals Edition. 5th ed. C. Thomas Olivo & Thomas P. Olivo. LC 84-23257. 352p. (C). 1985. pap. text ed. 19.95 (0-8273-2227-5) Delmar.

Basic Water & Waste Water Treatment. T. H. Tebbutt. (Basic Ser.). (Illus.). 160p. 1990. pap. text ed. 24.95 (0-408-70937-5) Buttrwrth-Heinemann.

Basic Water Safety. American Red Cross Staff. 1994. 5.50 (0-8016-7550-2); 5.50 (0-685-65130-4) Mosby Yr Bk.

Basic Water Treatment for Application World-Wide. 2nd ed. George Smethurst. 224p. 1988. 30.00 (0-7277-1331-0) Am Soc Civil Eng.

Basic Water Treatment for Application Worldwide. George Smethurst. (C). 1986. text ed. 185.00 (81-85046-44-1, Scientific) St Mut.

Basic Watercolor Techniques. Ed. by Greg Albert & Rachel Wolf. (Basic Technique Ser.). 128p. 1991. pap. 16.95 (0-89134-387-3, 30331) North Light Bks.

Basic Wave Mechanics: For Coastal & Ocean Engineers. Robert M. Sorensen. LC 93-13309. 284p. 1993. text ed. 74.95 (0-471-55165-1) Wiley.

Basic Ways of Knowing: An Indepth Study of Kumarila's Contribution to Indian Epistemology. G. P. Bhatt. (C). 1989. 31.00 (81-208-0580-1, Pub. by Motilal Banarsidass II) S Asia.

Basic Weight Training see Basic Weight Training for Men & Women

Basic Weight Training for Men & Women. 2nd ed. Thomas D. Fahey. LC 93-577. Orig. Title: Basic Weight Training. 170p. 1994. pap. 13.95 (1-55934-248-X) Mayfield Pub.

***Basic Well Log Analysis for Geologists.** George Asquith & Charles Gibson. (Methods in Exploration: No. 3). (Illus.). vii, 216p. 1982. 36.00 (0-89181-652-6) AAPG.

Basic Wild Edibles for Pathfinders: A Youth Enrichment Skill. Emma L. Tillman. (Illus.). 20p. (Orig.). 1988. pap. 5.00 (0-936241-23-3) Cheetah Pub.

B

An Asterisk (*) at the beginning of an entry indicates that the title is appearing in BIP for the first time.

Basic Wildflowers for Pathfinders: A Youth Enrichment Skill. Emma L. Tillman. (Illus.). 20p. (Orig.). 1987. pap. 5.00 (*0-936241-35-7*) Cheetah Pub.

Basic Wildlife Rehabilitation IAB. rev. ed. Jan White. 150p. 1992. reprint ed. pap. text ed. 25.00 (*1-884196-02-0*) IWRC.

Basic Wildlife Rehabilitation Series, 6 vols., Set. Dale Carlson. (Illus.). 200p. (Orig.). 1994. pap. 37.50 (*1-884158-04-8*) Bick Pub Hse.

Basic Will Drafting, 1992. (Tax Law & Estate Planning Ser.). 245p. 1992. pap. text ed. 70.00 (*0-685-56942-X*, D4-5229) PLI.

Basic Wills Handbook: A Guide to Wisconsin Basic Wills. Michael Klug & Howard Erlanger. 30p. 1985. 12.00 (*0-932622-03-8*) Ctr Public Rep.

Basic Wills, Trusts, & Estates. Edward A. Nolfi. LC 94-13452. (Legal Studies Ser.). 1994. 30.00 (*0-02-801338-7*) Glencoe.

Basic Wire Work for Bead Jewelry. rev. ed. Kate Drew-Wilkinson. Ed. by Colin Haynes. (Kate Drew-Wilkinson's Best Bead Bks.). (Illus.). 100p. 1994. pap. 9.95 (*1-884648-00-2*) Nomad Pr Intl.

***Basic Wiring.** 1995. pap. 9.99 (*0-376-01584-5*) Sunset Menlo Pk.

***Basic Wiring.** Ed. by Time-Life Books Editors. LC 94-32486. (Home Repair & Improvement Ser.). (Illus.). 128p. 1994. write for info. (*0-7835-3862-6*) Time-Life.

Basic Wiring. rev. ed. Creative Homeowner Press Editors & Richard V. Nunn. LC 88-15035. (Illus.). 160p. 1990. pap. 12.95 (*1-880029-36-7*) Creative Homeowner.

Basic Wiring. rev. ed. Time-Life Books Editors. (Home Repair & Improvement Ser.). (Illus.). 128p. (gr. 7 up). 1989. 14.60 (*0-8094-7362-3*); lib. bdg. 20.60 (*0-8094-7363-1*) Time-Life.

Basic Wiring & Electrical Repairs. Cy DeCosse Incorporated Staff. LC 90-42688. (Black & Decker Home Improvement Library). (Illus.). 128p. 1990. 14.95 (*0-86573-714-2*); pap. 12.95 (*0-86573-715-0*) Cy De Cosse.

Basic Wiring Techniques. rev. ed. Steve George & John Lowe. Ed. by Cheryl Smith. LC 92-71349. (Illus.). 112p. 1993. pap. 9.95 (*0-89721-251-7*, UPC05955A) Ortho Info.

***Basic Wood Burning.** Sue Waters. (Illus.). 64p. (Orig.). 1994. pap. text ed. 12.95 (*0-88740-568-1*) Schiffer.

Basic Woodturning: A Layman's Introduction & Guide. S. Blackwell Duncan. (Illus.). 320p. 1986. 24.95 (*0-671-61367-7*) P-H.

Basic Woodturning Techniques. David Regester. (Illus.). 112p. (Orig.). 1993. pap. 14.95 (*1-55870-300-4*) Betterway Bks.

***Basic Woodworking.** 1995. pap. 9.99 (*0-376-01585-3*) Sunset Menlo Pk.

Basic Woodworking. John L. Feirer. (gr. 9-12). 1978. 10.64 (*0-02-662630-6*); pap. 8.56 (*0-02-662620-9*) Bennett IL.

Basic Woodworking Illustrated. Ed. by Southern Living Staff. (Southern Living Home Improvement Ser.). (Illus.). 160p. 1992. pap. 14.99 (*0-376-09042-1*) Oxmoor Hse.

Basic Woodworking Techniques. Roger Holmes. 1993. 12.98 (*1-55521-917-9*) Bk Sales Inc.

Basic Word List. 2nd ed. Samuel C. Brownstein et al. 225p. 1990. pap. 5.95 (*0-8120-4377-4*) Barron.

Basic Word Order: Functional Principles. Russell S. Tomlin. 320p. 1986. 57.50 (*0-7099-2499-2*, Pub. by Croom Helm UK) Routledge Chapman & Hall.

Basic Workbook, 3 Bks., Bk. C. Nancy Stevenson & Janice L. Semple. (Illus.). 107p. (Orig.). 1978. pap. 4.50 (*0-941112-13-6*) Stevnson Lrn.

Basic Workbook, 3 Bks., Bk. A. Nancy Stevenson & Janice L. Semple. (Illus.). 96p. (Orig.). 1978. pap. 4.50 (*0-941112-11-X*) Stevnson Lrn.

Basic Workbook, 3 Bks., Bk. B. Nancy Stevenson & Janice L. Semple. (Illus.). 96p. (Orig.). 1978. pap. 4.50 (*0-941112-12-8*) Stevnson Lrn.

BASIC Workbook for Microcomputers. Donald D. Spencer. (Illus.). 128p. (YA). (gr. 8 up). 1983. pap. 3.95 (*0-89218-069-2*, NO. 1100) Camelot Pub.

Basic Works of Aristotle. Aristotle. Ed. by Richard P. McKeon. 1941. boxed 40.00 (*0-394-41610-4*) Random.

Basic Writer & Reader. Irwin Griggs & Robert Llewellyn. LC 87-33235. 528p. (Orig.). (C). 1988. reprint ed. pap. 19.50 (*0-89464-282-0*) Krieger.

Basic Writer's Book. 2nd ed. Anne Agee & Gary Kline. LC 84-22291. (Illus.). 448p. (C). 1985. pap. text ed. 22.50 (*0-13-066176-7*) P-H.

Basic Writer's Rhetoric. William Herman. 384p. (C). 1988. pap. text ed. 20.75 (*0-03-063334-6*) HB Coll Pubs.

Basic Writing. Joy M. Reid. (Illus.). 208p. (C). 1987. pap. text ed. 17.50 (*0-13-069261-1*) P-H.

Basic Writing: A First Course. Peter Carino. (C). 1990. pap. text ed. 32.50 (*0-673-46232-3*) HarpCollege.

Basic Writing: A Practical Approach. 2nd ed. Sue Lorch. (C). 1987. pap. text ed. 21.50 (*0-673-39278-3*) HarpCollege.

Basic Writing: Process & Product, Cases & Readings. Elizabeth Renfro. 356p. (C). 1985. pap. text ed. 19.75 (*0-03-069773-5*) HB Coll Pubs.

***Basic Writing: Process & Purpose.** 2nd ed. Carino. (C). 1995. text ed. 22.50 (*0-673-99294-2*) HarpCollege.

***Basic Writing: Process & Purpose.** 2nd ed. Peter M. Carino. LC 94-35485. (C). 1995. 7.20 (*0-673-99295-0*) HarpCollege.

Basic Writing: Student Handbook. C. Ruth Sabol. 64p. (C). 1992. 6.95 (*0-8403-7426-7*) Kendall-Hunt.

Basic Writing Book. Joyce Stith. (Orig.). (C). 1987. pap. text ed. 18.75 (*0-673-39314-3*) HarpCollege.

***Basic Writing Book.** Joyce Stith. LC 71-84223. 410p. (Orig.). 1982. reprint ed. pap. 116.90 (*0-7837-8854-1*, 2049562) Bks Demand.

Basic Writing Notebook. Beverly Cohen & Susan Bushnell. 160p. (C). 1994. 18.95 (*0-8403-9200-1*) Kendall-Hunt.

Basic Writing Skills: Capitalization & Punctuation. Mary Gleason & Cynthia Stults. 284p. 1983. spiral bd. 89.00 (*0-574-41516-5*, 512) SRA.

Basic Writing Skills: Sentence Development. Mary Gleason & Cynthia Stults. 228p. 1983. spiral bd. 89.00 (*0-574-41517-3*, 514) SRA.

Basic Writing Skills, Letters & Consumer Complaints: Essential Life Skills. 3rd ed. Carolyn M. Starkey & Norgina W. Penn. 64p. 1994. pap. 6.95 (*0-8442-5173-9*, Natl Textbk) NTC Pub Grp.

***Basic Writing Skills with Readings.** R. Kent Smith et al. 370p. 1995. pap. text ed. 15.00 (*0-944210-70-8*) Townsend NJ.

Basic Writings. 2nd enl. rev. ed. Martin Heidegger. LC 76-9957. 448p. 1993. pap. 15.00 (*0-06-063763-3*) Harper SF.

***Basic Writings: Proslogium; Monologium; Gaunnilo's "In Behalf of the Fool"; Cur Deus Homo.** 2nd ed. St. Anselm. Tr. by Sidney N. Deane. 342p. 1962. pap. 7.00 (*0-87548-109-4*) Open Court.

Basic Writings in the History of Psychology. Robert I. Watson. (Illus.). 1979. pap. text ed. 19.95 (*0-19-502444-3*) OUP.

Basic Writings of Bertrand Russell. Bertrand Russell. Ed. by Robert E. Egner & Lester E. Dennon. (C). 1967. pap. 17.95 (*0-671-20154-9*, Touchstone Bks) S&S Trade.

Basic Writings of C. G. Jung. C. G. Jung. Tr. by R. F. Hull. (Bollingen Ser.). 575p. (C). 1990. pap. text ed. 13.95 (*0-691-01902-9*) Princeton U Pr.

Basic Writings of C. G. Jung. Carl G. Jung. Ed. by Violet S. De Laszlo. LC 59-5910. 1977. 14.95 (*0-394-60419-9*, Modern Lib) Random.

Basic Writings of C. G. Jung. Carl G. Jung. LC 93-17801. 1993. reprint ed. 18.50 (*0-679-60071-X*, Modern Lib) Random.

Basic Writings of Mo Tzu, Hsun Tzu, & Han Fei Tzu. Ed. & Tr. by Burton Watson. LC 67-16170. (Records of Civilization, Sources & Studies: No. 74). 1967. text ed. 21.50 (*0-231-02515-7*) Col U Pr.

Basic Writings of Nietzsche. Ed. & Tr. by Walter Kaufmann. LC 92-50233. 1992. 20.00 (*0-679-60000-0*, Modern Lib) Random.

Basic Writings of Nietzsche. Friedrich Nietzsche. Ed. & Tr. by Walter Kaufmann. LC 68-29392. 1977. 20.00 (*0-394-60406-7*, Modern Lib) Random.

Basic Writings of Saint Augustine, 2 vols. Augustine. Ed. by Whitney J. Oates. 1994p. 1993. reprint ed. text ed. 99.95 (*0-8010-0164-1*) Baker Bk.

Basic Writings of Sigmund Freud. Sigmund Freud. LC 38-27462. 1977. 20.00 (*0-394-60400-8*, Modern Lib) Random.

***Basic Writings of Sigmund Freud.** Sigmund Freud. 1995. 20.00 (*0-679-60166-X*) Random.

Basic Writings on Politics & Philosophy. Friedrich Engels & Karl Marx. LC 59-12053. 1959. 12.95 (*0-385-09420-5*, Anchor NY) Doubleday.

Basic Yields of Bonds, 1926-1947: Their Measurement & Pattern. David Durand & Willis J. Winn. (Technical Papers: No. 6). 48p. 1947. reprint ed. 20.00 (*0-87014-451-0*); reprint ed. mic. film 20.00 (*0-685-61272-4*) Natl Bur Econ Res.

Basic Yields of Corporate Bonds, 1900-1942. David Durand. (Technical Papers: No. 3). 40p. 1942. reprint ed. 20.00 (*0-87014-448-0*); reprint ed. mic. film 20.00 (*0-685-61235-X*) Natl Bur Econ Res.

Basic 1D & 2D NMR Spectroscopy. Horst Friebolin. 344p. 1991. pap. 45.00 (*0-89573-972-0*) VCH Pubs.

Basic 35mm Photo Guide. Craig Alesse. (Illus.). 112p. (Orig.). 1994. 12.95 (*0-936262-02-8*) Amherst Media.

***Basic 35mm Photo Guide.** rev. ed. Craig Alesse. (Orig.). 1994. pap. 12.95 (*0-936262-20-6*) Amherst Media.

BASIC 7.0 for the Commodore 128. Jurgen Huckstadt. Ed. by Susan Dorn. Tr. by Ludwig J. Prazak. 230p. (Orig.). 1987. pap. 19.95 (*0-941689-03-4*) Prog Peripherals.

Basically Academic. Currie. 1991. pap. 18.95 (*0-8384-2911-4*); teacher ed, pap. 10.95 (*0-8384-2912-2*) Heinle & Heinle.

Basically Boys: An Idea Book for Creative Clothing. Barb Griffin. (Illus.). 16p. (Orig.). 1989. pap. 5.00 (*0-937679-02-X*) Sewing Sampler.

***BASICally Newton: Programming for the Newton with NS BASIC.** John Schettino & Liz O'Hara. (Illus.). 375p. 1995. pap. write for info. (*0-12-623955-X*) Acad Pr.

BASICally Speaking: A Beginner's Workbook. Thomas J. Speelhoffer. 1982. 5.25 (*0-318-01169-7*) J W Walch.

Basically Speaking: An Oral History of George Duvivier. Edward Berger. LC 93-28497. (Studies in Jazz: No. 17). (Illus.). 514p. 1993. 59.50 (*0-8108-2691-7*) Scarecrow.

Basically Tender. Arthur W. Knight. (Illus.). 40p. (Orig.). 1991. pap. 6.50 (*0-943557-04-6*) Esoterica Pr.

Basics. James Cavanaugh. (Illus.). 68p. 1989. write for info. (*0-318-64776-1*) CFAOA.

Basics. Ida Fasel. (Illus.). 40p. (Orig.). 1988. pap. 3.50 (*0-934776-07-5*) Bard Pr.

Basics. 2nd ed. John Remling. 1989. text ed. 34.50 (*0-471-61651-6*) P-H.

Basics: A Grammar & Punctuation Workbook. Peter D. Adams. (C). 1988. 28.50 (*0-673-39924-9*) HarpCollege.

Basics: A Guide for Children's Emergencies. John Shufeldt. LC 93-9813. (Illus.). 96p. 1993. pap. 9.95 (*0-942963-35-0*) Distinctive Pub.

Basics: A Guide to the Timex-Sinclair 1000 (2k) H. Mullish. 160p. 1983. pap. text ed. 9.95 (*0-07-044041-7*, BYTE Bks) McGraw.

Basics: A Program Designed to Help You Recognize & Enhance Your Child's Abilities. James J. Cavanaugh. 256p. 1991. 18.95 (*1-55972-085-9*, Birch Ln Pr) Carol Pub Group.

***Basics: A Rhetoric & Handbook.** Sani Buscemi et al. LC 94-29220. 1994. write for info. (*0-07-009405-5*) McGraw.

BASICS: Bridging Vocational & Academic Skills. National Center for Research in Vocational Education Staff. 1987. 198.00 (*0-318-35278-8*, SP 300) Ctr Educ Trng Employ.

Basics: For Peace, Democracy & Social Progress. Gus Hall. LC 80-19720. 360p. (Orig.). 1980. pap. 4.50 (*0-7178-0578-6*) Intl Pubs Co.

Basics: Nailing down What Builds You Up. Mark Littleton. (Illus.). 200p. 1994. pap. 7.99 (*0-87509-549-6*) Chr Pubns.

Basics, Applications & Advanced Techniques. Hallette German. 1990. text ed. 50.95 (*0-442-31867-7*) Van Nos Reinhold.

Basics Book of Frame Relay. Motorola Codex Staff. (Illus.). 176p. 1993. pap. 11.95 (*0-201-56377-0*) Addison-Wesley.

Basics Book of Information Networking. Motorola Codex Staff. 176p. 1992. pap. 15.95 (*0-201-56370-3*) Addison-Wesley.

Basics Book of OSI & Networking Management. Motorola Codex Staff. (Illus.). 96p. 1993. pap. 11.95 (*0-201-56371-1*) Addison-Wesley.

Basics Book of X.25 Packet Switching. Motorola Codex Staff. (Illus.). 80p. 1992. pap. 11.95 (*0-201-56369-X*) Addison-Wesley.

Basics Essentials of First Aid for the Outdoors. William W. Forgey. LC 88-32997. (Basic Essentials Ser.). (Illus.). 72p. (Orig.). 1989. pap. 5.99 (*0-934802-43-2*) ICS Bks.

Basics for Builders: Framing & Rough Carpentry. Scot Simpson. 125p. 1991. 21.95 (*0-87629-251-1*, 67298) R S Means.

Basics for Builders: How to Survive & Prosper in Construction. Thomas N. Frisby. 300p. 1993. pap. 34.95 (*0-87629-342-9*, 67273) R S Means.

***Basics for Builders: Insurance Repair.** 2nd ed. Peter Crosa. Orig. Title: Insurance Repair. 1994. pap. 36.95 (*0-87629-352-6*) R S Means.

Basics for Builders: Plan Reading & Material Takeoff. Wayne DelPico. Ed. by Kevin Foley & Mary Greene. (Illus.). 200p. 1994. pap. 34.95 (*0-87629-348-8*) R S Means.

BASICs for DOS. Gary Cornell. 448p. 1992. 31.95 (*0-8306-2200-4*, Windcrest); pap. 21.95 (*0-8306-2199-7*, Windcrest) TAB Bks.

***Basics for the Fluid Power Mechanic.** John J. Pippenger & Greg P. Gordon. (Illus.). 238p. 1994. 48.00 (*0-929276-04-3*); teacher ed, pap. 6.00 (*0-929276-05-1*) Amalgam Pub Co.

Basics for Writing Your Law Firm Brochure. Susan Raridon. 36p. 1987. pap. 19.95 (*0-89707-347-9*, 511-0223) Amer Bar Assn.

Basics in Listening: Short Tasks for Listening Development. Michael A. Rost & M. Uruno. 71p. 1985. 10.95 (*0-8013-0518-7*, 78364); pap. text ed. 13.50 (*0-8013-0517-9*, 78363); audio 55.00 (*0-8013-0519-5*, 78365) Longman.

Basics in Reading: An Introduction to American Magazines. Edgar J. Boone et al. 115p. 1988. teacher ed 14.95 (*0-8013-0513-6*, 78359); pap. text ed. 13.95 (*0-8013-0514-4*, 78360) Longman.

Basics of a Common Law Practice. W. F. Fish & R. Lockett. 1986. pap. write for info. (*0-406-10240-6*) Butterworth Legal Pubs.

Basics of Acupuncture. G. Stux & B. Pomeranz. (Illus.). xi, 272p. 1988. pap. 19.50 (*0-387-19336-7*) Spr-Verlag.

Basics of Acupuncture. 2nd enl. rev. ed. G. Stux & B. Pomeranz. Tr. by K. A. Sahm. (Illus.). xiii, 291p. 1994. pap. 24.00 (*0-387-53072-X*) Spr-Verlag.

***Basics of Aeromodelling.** Vic Smead. (Illus.). 64p. (Orig.). 1995. pap. 8.95x (*1-85486-113-1*, Pub. by Argus UK) Motorbooks Intl.

Basics of American Politics. 7th ed. Gary Wasserman. (C). 1994. text ed. 19.00 (*0-673-52328-4*) HarpCollege.

Basics of Anesthesia. 3rd ed. Robert K. Stoelting & Ronald D. Miller. LC 94-2905. 1994. 44.95 (*0-443-08962-0*) Churchill.

Basics of Antitrust Policy: A Review of Ten Nations & the European Communities. Roger A. Boner & Reinald Krueger. (Technical Paper Ser.: No. 160). 140p. 1991. 9.95 (*0-8213-1961-2*, 11961) World Bank.

***Basics of Applied Geothermal Engineering.** Ed. by Edward Wehlage. (Illus.). 211p. 1975. text ed. write for info. (*1-877782-13-0*) M&M Assocs.

Basics of Artistic Drawing. LC 93-20813. (Complete Course on Drawing & Painting Ser.). 1994. 21.95 (*0-8120-6387-2*) Barron.

Basics of Artistic Drawing. Jose M. Parramon. (Complete Course on Painting & Drawing Ser.). (Illus.). 128p. 1994. pap. 16.95 (*0-8120-1929-6*) Barron.

Basics of Artistic Painting. LC 93-20837. (Complete Course in Drawing & Painting Ser.). 1994. 21.95 (*0-8120-6388-0*) Barron.

Basics of Artistic Painting. Jose M. Parramon. (Complete Course on Painting & Drawing Ser.). (Illus.). 128p. 1994. pap. 16.95 (*0-8120-1928-8*) Barron.

Basics of Assembly Life. G. Steidl. pap. 3.75 (*0-88172-126-3*) Believers Bkshelf.

Basics of Astrology Series, 3, Vol. 1: Chart Erection. Sehested. LC 73-90440. 192p. 1973. Vol. 1 Chart Erection. 11.00 (*0-9601080-1-7*, S2325-034) Am Fed Astrologers.

Basics of Astrology Series, 3, Vol. 2: Chart Interpretation. Sehested. LC 73-90440. 192p. 1973. Vol. 2 Chart Interpretation. 11.00 (*0-9601080-2-5*) Am Fed Astrologers.

Basics of Astrology Series, 3, Vol. 3: Tables & Reference. Sehested. LC 73-90440. 192p. 1973. Vol. 3 Tables & Reference. 10.00 (*0-9601080-3-3*) Am Fed Astrologers.

Basics of Banking Law, 1991. (Commercial Law & Practice Ser.). 606p. 1991. pap. text ed. 17.50 (*0-685-56856-3*, A4-4352) PLI.

Basics of Bankruptcy & Reorganization, 1992, 2 vols., Set. (Commercial Law & Practice Course Handbook Ser.). 1670p. 1992. pap. 80.00 (*0-685-69386-4*) PLI.

Basics of Bead Stringing. 11th rev. ed. Mel Anderson. (Illus.). 56p. 1993. pap. 4.95 (*0-9615353-0-X*) Borjay.

Basics of Biblical Greek: Grammar. William D. Mounce. 464p. (ENG & GRE.). 1993. Printed caseside. 24.99 (*0-310-59800-1*) Zondervan.

Basics of Biblical Greek: Workbook. William D. Mounce. 242p. (ENG & GRE.). 1993. 12.99 (*0-310-40091-0*) Zondervan.

Basics of Bingo. Avery Cardoza. LC 91-70165. (Basics of Gambling Ser.). (Illus.). 48p. (Orig.). 1991. pap. 2.95 (*0-940685-16-7*, Gambling Res) Cardoza Pub.

Basics of Bonds. Gerald Krefetz. (Making the Most of Your Money Ser.). 167p. (Orig.). 1992. pap. 16.95 (*0-7931-0360-6*, 5608-62) Dearborn Finan.

Basics of Book Marketing for Professional Scholarly Publishers. 1988. write for info. (*0-933636-16-4*) AAP.

Basics of Budgeting. Terry Dickey. Ed. by Michael G. Crisp. LC 91-76241. (Fifty-Minute Ser.). 90p. (Orig.). 1992. pap. 9.95 (*1-56052-134-1*) Crisp Pubns.

Basics of Budgeting. Robert G. Finney. 196p. 1993. pap. 19.95 (*0-8144-7822-0*) AMACOM.

Basics of Business. David Lewis. 288p. (Orig.). 1988. pap. 22.50 (*0-7121-0794-0*, Pub. by Pitman Pub Ltd UK) Trans-Atl Phila.

Basics of Business Writing. Marty Stuckey. (AMA Worksmart Ser.). 120p. (Orig.). 1992. pap. 10.95 (*0-8144-7792-5*) AMACOM.

Basics of Cancer Chemotherapy. 2nd ed. Ellen Carr & Judith Killman. LC 94-60318. (Illus.). 107p. (C). 1993. pap. 39.95 (*1-878025-61-9*) Western Schls.

Basics of Career Counseling. Isaacson. LC 84-21607. 1985. text ed. 49.00 (*0-205-08326-9*, H8326-4) Allyn.

Basics of Chest Film Interpretation. Cynthia Umali. (Illus.). 190p. 1987. 45.95 (*0-316-88739-0*) Little.

Basics of Communication & Coding. William G. Chambers. (Illus.). 1985. 35.00 (*0-19-853195-8*) OUP.

Basics of Community Information Work. 2nd ed. Allan Bunch. 192p. 1993. 45.00 (*1-85604-038-0*, LAP0380, Pub. by Lib Assn Pub UK) UNIPUB.

Basics of Concrete. 52p. 1986. pap. 11.00 (*0-924659-20-3*, 1150) Aberdeen Group.

Basics of Contact Lenses. Jack Hartstein. 112p. 1979. 13.75 (*0-317-94083-X*) Am Acad Ophthal.

***Basics of Creole Cooking.** Tony Chachere. (Illus.). 32p. 1982. pap. 2.95 (*0-9604580-6-9*) Creole Foods.

Basics of Data Management for Information Services. P. G. Underwood & R. J. Hartley. 126p. 1993. 50.00 (*1-85604-052-6*, LAP0526, Pub. by Lib Assn Pub UK) UNIPUB.

Basics of Dermatologic Surgery. 2nd ed. Stegman. 1990. 49.95 (*0-8151-8170-1*, Yr Bk Med Pubs) Mosby Yr Bk.

Basics of Dermatology: A Colour Atlas. Heide M. Heinz. 323p. 1989. lib. bdg. 85.00 (*0-89574-284-5*, Pub. by Gustav Fischer Verlag) VCH Pubs.

Basics of Disco Dancing. Pamela Morton. (Illus.). 56p. 1982. pap. text ed. 5.95x (*0-89641-092-7*) American Pr.

Basics of Drug Education. Albert E. Bedworth & Joseph A. D'Elia. LC 72-94344. 271p. 1973. text ed. 23.95 (*0-89503-027-6*) Baywood Pub.

Basics of Dyeing & Finishing. (Symposium Papers). 204p. 1991. 46.00 (*0-317-53360-6*) AATCC.

Basics of Electricity & Electronics. Matthew Mandl. (Illus.). 448p. 1975. 42.00 (*0-13-060228-0*) P-H.

Basics of Electron Optics. David A. DeWolf. 228p. 1990. text ed. 99.95 (*0-471-52457-3*) Wiley.

Basics of English. Michele G. Miller & Clarice P. Brantley. LC 92-16384. 1993. pap. 16.95 (*0-538-70559-0*) S-W Pub.

Basics of Environmental Law. Lorelie J. Borland. (Real Estate Law & Practice Ser.). 584p. 1991. pap. text ed. 70.00 (*0-685-56944-6*, N4-4556) PLI.

Basics of Environmental Law 1993. (Litigation & Administrative Practice Course Handbook, 1983-84 Ser.: Vol. 459). 663p. 1993. 70.00 (*0-685-69731-2*, H4-5152) PLI.

Basics of Family Support: A Guide for State Planners (& Others) Ed. by Kathy Goetz & Shelley Peck. 132p. 1994. pap. 25.00 (*1-885429-06-1*) Family Resource.

Basics of Finance: Financial Tools for Non-Financial Managers. Bryan E. Milling. LC 90-27684. 208p. 1991. pap. 14.95 (*0-942061-18-7*, Sourcebooks Trade); boxed 24.95 (*0-942061-25-X*, Sourcebooks Trade) Sourcebks.

***Basics of Finance: Financial Tools for Non-Financial Managers.** 2nd ed. Bryan E. Milling. 224p. 1995. pap. 14.95 (*1-57071-055-4*) Sourcebks.

Basics of Foodservice Nutrition Skillbook. Educational Foundation of the National Restaurant Association Staff. (Management Skills Program Ser.). 60p. (Orig.). 1993. pap. 10.95 (*0-915452-06-5*) Educ Found.

Basics of Foodservice Sanitation Skillbook. Educational Foundation of the National Restaurant Association Staff. (Management Skills Program Ser.). 64p. (Orig.). 1992. pap. 10.95 (*0-915452-43-X*) Educ Found.

Basics of Foreign Trade & Exchange. 1994. lib. bdg. 250.75 (*0-8490-5658-6*) Gordon Pr.

Basics of Formatting & WordPerfect 5.1. Judy R. Smith & Susie VanHuss. LC 94-16629. 1995. text ed. 26.95 (*0-538-71115-9*) S-W Pub.

Basics of GMAW-GTAW Welding, Gas Metal Arc Welding, Gas Tungsten Arc Welding. Richard Beard. Ed. by Lois Harrington. 88p. 1992. 10.00 (*0-89606-286-4*, 920); teacher ed 3.00 (*0-89606-297-X*, 920TK); Apple. pap. write for info. (*0-89606-299-6*); disk 40.00 (*0-89606-317-8*); IBM. disk 40.00 (*0-89606-298-8*) Am Assn Voc Materials.

An Asterisk (*) at the beginning of an entry indicates that the title is appearing in BIP for the first time.

***Basics of Gravure Printing.** Frank Robson. (Illus.). (Orig.). 1995. write for info. (1-880290-01-4) Gravure Assn.

Basics of Grounded Theory Analysis: Emergence vs. Forcing. Barney G. Glaser. 129p. 1992. pap. 24.00 (1-884156-00-2) Sociology Pr.

Basics of Group Therapy. Ed. by Harold S. Bernard & K. Roy MacKenzie. LC 94-16964. 224p. 1994. lib. bdg. 25.00 (0-89862-117-8) Guilford Pr.

Basics of Head & Neck Film Interpretation. G. V. Keller. 1989. 53.95 (0-316-48649-3) Little.

***Basics of Histotechnology: H & E Stain.** Frieda Carson. 1992. vhs 135.00 (0-89189-351-2) Am Soc Clinical.

Basics of Horseracing. 2nd ed. Ed. by Whitney L. Cobb. LC 91-72799. (Basics of Gambling Ser.). (Illus.). 64p. (Orig.). 1991. pap. 2.95 (0-940685-20-5, Gambling Res) Cardoza Pub.

Basics of Insect Modeling. Ed. by J. L. Goodenough & J. M. McKinion. LC 92-61514. 232p. 49.00 (0-929355-31-8) Am Soc Ag Eng.

***Basics of Interest Rates.** 1994. lib. bdg. 250.75 (0-8490-5784-1) Gordon Pr.

Basics of Interferometry. P. Hariharan. (Illus.). 213p. 1991. text ed. 39.95 (0-12-325218-0) Acad Pr.

Basics of Investing. Gerald Krefetz. (Making the Most of Your Money Ser.). 196p. (Orig.). 1992. pap. 16.95 (0-7931-0358-4, 5608-60) Dearborn Finan.

Basics of Investing. 4th ed. Benton E. Gup. LC 88-17187. 112p. 1989. teacher ed 15.00 (0-471-62233-8) Wiley.

Basics of Investing. 5th ed. Benton E. Gup. 496p. (C). 1992. Net. text ed. write for info. (0-471-54853-7) Wiley.

Basics of Islamic Culture. S. A. Latif. pap. 4.25 (0-935782-45-1) Kazi Pubns.

Basics of Item Response Theory. Frank B. Baker. LC 85-8623. 131p. (Orig.). 1985. Apple II 37.50 (0-435-08003-2); disk 37.50 (0-435-08020-2); disk 15.00 (0-435-08019-9); Apple II 15.00 (0-435-08005-9) Heinemann.

Basics of Keno. J. Edward Allen. (Basics of Gambling Ser.). (Illus.). 48p. (Orig.). 1985. pap. 2.95 (0-9607618-5-3, Gambling Res) Cardoza Pub.

Basics of Laser Material Processing. Alexander G. Grigoryants. 300p. 1994. 95.00 (0-8493-7534-7) CRC Pr.

Basics of Law Librarianship. Deborah S. Panella. (Haworth Series in Special Librarianship). 136p. (C). 1991. text ed. 32.95 (0-86656-989-8); pap. text ed. 14.95 (0-86656-990-1) Haworth Pr.

Basics of Legal Procedure for Court Reporters. 160p. 16.00 (0-318-15852-3, 185) Natl Shorthand Rptr.

Basics of Library-Based User Services. Kenneth Whittaker. 140p. 1993. 45.00 (1-85604-075-5, LAP0755, Pub. by Lib Assn Pub UK) UNIPUB.

Basics of Lotto - Lottery. Prof. Jones. LC 91-70330. (Basics of Gambling Ser.). (Illus.). 48p. (Orig.). 1991. pap. 2.95 (0-940685-18-3, Gambling Res) Cardoza Pub.

***Basics of Manufacturing.** J. David Viale. Ed. by Philip Gerould. (Fifty-Minute Ser.). (Illus.). 120p. (Orig.). 1995. pap. 9.95 (1-56052-303-4) Crisp Pubns.

***Basics of Model Gliders.** Chas Gardiner. (Illus.). 64p. (Orig.). 1995. pap. 8.95x (1-85486-114-X, Pub. by Argus UK) Motorbooks Intl.

Basics of Model Marine Engines. Alan Hobbs. Ed. by Gerry Yarrish & Laura M. Kidder. (Illus.). 58p. (Orig.). 1992. pap. 12.95 (0-911295-23-2) Air Age.

Basics of Model Rocketry. 2nd ed. Doug Pratt. Ed. by Terry Spohn. LC 92-46672. (RC Performance Ser.: No. 16). (Illus.). 64p. (Orig.). 1993. pap. 8.95 (0-89024-142-2) Kalmbach.

Basics of Music: Opus One. Michael Zinn & Robert Hogenson. 256p. 1987. pap. 28.00 (0-02-873010-0) Schirmer Bks.

Basics of Music: With an Introduction to the Kodaly Method & Its Materials. Robert Culbertson. 96p. (C). 1991. pap. text ed. 14.95 (0-8403-6729-5) Kendall-Hunt.

Basics of Music, Opus No. 1. 2nd ed. Michael Zinn & Robert Hogenson. LC 93-3591. (Illus.). 398p. (C). 1993. Alk. paper. pap. 28.00 (0-02-873012-7) Schirmer Bks.

Basics of Natural Health: Nature & Human Well-Being. P. K. Bhat. 1993. 13.95 (0-8062-4739-8) Carlton.

***Basics of Oil Painting.** Parramon Ediciones Editorial Team. LC 95-12037. (Complete Course on Painting & Drawing Ser.). Orig. Title: Bases de la Pintura Al Oleo. (Illus.). 1995. write for info. (0-8120-9403-4) Barron.

***Basics of Operations Research Analysis in Quality Test & Evaluation.** Donald L. Giadrosich. LC 94-48188. (Education Ser.). 1995. write for info. (1-56347-112-4) AIAA.

Basics of Organizations. G. T. Steadman. 160p. 1988. Australia. pap. 44.00 (0-409-30018-7) Butterworth Legal Pubs.

***Basics of Organizing.** Concept by L. Ron Hubbard. 48p. 1994. pap. 4.00 (0-88404-923-X) Bridge Pubns Inc.

Basics of Paralegal Studies. David Goodrich. 384p. 1991. pap. text ed. 52.00 (0-13-650482-5, 140201) P-H.

Basics of Physical Stratigraphy & Sedimentology. William J. Fritz & Johnnie N. Moore. 371p. 1988. Net. text ed. write for info. (0-471-80235-2) Wiley.

Basics of POLIS (Projective Optimization Land Use Information System) 23p. 1991. 25.00 (0-317-05639-5, P84002PRO); 25.00 (0-317-05640-9, P91007PRO) Assn Bay Area.

Basics of Public Speaking. Hoff et al. 1993. pap. 18.95 (0-685-65896-1) Burgess MN Intl.

Basics of Qualitative Research: Grounded Theory Procedures & Techniques. Anselm Strauss & Juliet Corbin. (Illus.). 272p. (C). 1990. text ed. 45.00 (0-8039-3250-2); pap. text ed. 22.95 (0-8039-3251-0) Sage.

Basics of R-C Scale. Patrick H. Potega. 80p. pap. 11.95 (0-942794-00-1) Model Agency.

Basics of Radio Control Airplanes. L. F. Randolph. Ed. by Richard Uravitch. (Illus.). 80p. 1990. pap. 12.95 (0-911295-10-0) Air Age.

Basics of Radio Control Boat Modeling. John Finch. Ed. by Rick Nacca. (Illus.). 72p. 1988. pap. 12.95 (0-911295-07-0) Air Age.

Basics of Radio Control Cars. Radio Control Car Action Editors. Ed. by Doug Pratt. 52p. 1986. pap. 12.95 (0-911295-03-8) Air Age.

Basics of Radio Control Helicopters. Paul Tradelius. Ed. by Richard Uravitch. (Illus.). 96p. 1989. pap. 12.95 (0-911295-08-9) Air Age.

***Basics of Radio Control Model Cars.** Alan Harman. (Illus.). 64p. (Orig.). 1995. pap. 8.95x (1-85486-115-8, Pub. by Argus UK) Motorbooks Intl.

Basics of Radio Control Power Boat Modeling. 2nd ed. David Thomas. Ed. by Michael Emmerich. (Illus.). (Orig.). 1992. pap. 9.95 (0-89024-132-5) Kalmbach.

Basics of Radio Control Sailplanes. Alan Gornick, Jr. Ed. by Richard Uravitch. (Illus.). 80p. 1989. pap. 12.95 (0-911295-09-7) Air Age.

Basics of RD Books, Vols. 4-7. 120p. 1979. (0-318-62030-8, 0050) Am Lung Assn.

***Basics of Reader's Advisory Work.** Raymond J. Prytherch. LC 87-48257. reprint ed. pap. 32.00 (0-7837-9258-1, 2049998) Bks Demand.

Basics of Reservoir Engineering, Vol. 1. Rene Cosse. 372p. (C). 1993. 310.00 (2-7108-0630-4, Pub. by Edits Technip FR) St Mut.

Basics of Respiratory Therapy: A Laboratory Manual. Frank Sinsheimer. (C). 1983. pap. 20.00 (0-316-79285-3) Little.

Basics of Responsible Alcohol Service Skillbook. Educational Foundation of the National Restaurant Association Staff. (Management Skills Program Ser.). 48p. (Orig.). 1993. pap. 10.95 (0-915452-34-0) Educ Found.

Basics of SCSI. Jan Dedek. 50p. Date not set. pap. text ed. 9.95 (0-9637439-0-2) Ancot Corp.

Basics of Semiotics. John Deely. LC 89-45354. (Advances in Semiotics Ser.). 168p. 1990. 25.00 (0-253-31676-6); pap. 9.95 (0-253-20568-9, MB-568) Ind U Pr.

Basics of Singing. Jan Schmidt. 1986. pap. 16.50 (0-02-872340-6) Macmillan.

Basics of Singing. 2nd ed. Jan Schmidt. (Illus.). 252p. (C). 1989. pap. 29.00 (0-02-872341-4); audio 15.00 (0-02-872342-2); 14.95 (0-02-872343-0) Schirmer Bks.

Basics of Singing. 3rd ed. Jan Schmidt. 304p. 1993. Spiral text. spiral bd. 29.00 (0-02-872337-6) Schirmer Bks.

Basics of Soldering. Armin Rahn. 400p. 1993. text ed. 85.00 (0-471-58471-1) Wiley.

Basics of Speculating. Gerald Krefetz. (Making the Most of Your Money Ser.). 130p. (Orig.). 1992. pap. 16.95 (0-7931-0361-4, 5608-63) Dearborn Finan.

Basics of Sports Betting. Avery Cardoza. LC 91-70115. (Basics of Gambling Ser.). (Illus.). 48p. (Orig.). 1991. pap. 2.95 (0-940685-15-9, Gambling Res) Cardoza Pub.

Basics of Square Dancing. Pamela Morton. (Illus.). 67p. (Orig.). 1981. pap. text ed. 5.95x (0-89641-084-6) American Pr.

Basics of Stocks. Gerald Krefetz. (Making the Most of Your Money Ser.). 152p. (Orig.). 1992. pap. 16.95 (0-7931-0359-2, 5608-61) Dearborn Finan.

Basics of Structural Analysis. Michael R. Botwin & George J. Murnen. LC 85-20540. 282p. (C). 1986. text ed. 32.50x (0-910554-35-8) Engineering.

Basics of Structural Steel Design. 2nd ed. Samuel H. Marcus. 480p. 1981. write for info. (0-8359-0420-2, Reston) P-H.

Basics of Supervision Skills (BOSS) (Kit) Edward E. Hubbard. 72p. 1989. pap. 149.95 (1-883733-14-6) Global Insghts.

Basics of Technical Communicating. B. Edward Cain. LC 88-3325. (Professional Reference Book Ser.). (Illus.). xiii, 200p. 1988. 34.95 (0-8412-1451-4); 24.95 (0-8412-1452-2) Am Chemical.

Basics of the Faith: A Catholic Catechism. Alan Schreck. 378p. (Orig.). 1987. pap. 9.99 (0-89283-307-6) Servant.

Basics of the Faith: A Catholic Catechism. Alan Schreck. 348p. (Orig.). 1989. pap. 23.00 (0-86218-244-1, Pub. by Veritas IE) St Mut.

***Basics of Transesophageal Echocardiography.** Terence D. Rafferty. LC 95-2999. 1995. write for info. (0-443-08922-1) Churchill.

***Basics of Vegetarian Cooking.** Regina Glass. 144p. 1994. 8.95 (0-945383-99-1) Teach Servs.

Basics of Well Construction. 1986. 72.50 (0-89867-351-8, 1841); pap. 6.50 (0-89867-352-6, 1842) Am Water Wks Assn.

Basics of Winning Baccarat. Avery Cardoza. LC 92-81295. (Illus.). 64p. (Orig.). 1992. pap. 3.95 (0-940685-30-2, Gambling Res) Cardoza Pub.

Basics of Winning Blackjack. 2nd ed. J. Edward Allen. LC 92-72054. (Illus.). 64p. 1992. pap. 3.95 (0-940685-24-8, Gambling Res) Cardoza Pub.

Basics of Winning Bridge. 2nd ed. Montgomery Coe. LC 92-74842. (Basics of Winning Ser.). (Illus.). 64p. 1993. pap. 3.95 (0-940685-37-X) Cardoza Pub.

Basics of Winning Chess. 2nd ed. Jacob Cantrell. LC 92-70773. (Illus.). 64p. 1992. pap. 3.95 (0-940685-28-0, Gambling Res) Cardoza Pub.

Basics of Winning Craps. 2nd ed. J. Edward Allen. LC 92-70771. (Illus.). 64p. 1992. pap. 3.95 (0-940685-25-6, Gambling Res) Cardoza Pub.

Basics of Winning Horseracing. 3rd ed. Whitney L. Cobb. LC 94-70606. (Illus.). 64p. 1994. pap. 3.95 (0-940685-49-3) Cardoza Pub.

Basics of Winning Keno. 2nd ed. J. Edward Allen. LC 94-70605. (Illus.). 64p. 1994. pap. 3.95 (0-940685-52-3) Cardoza Pub.

Basics of Winning Lotto-Lottery. 2nd ed. Jones. 64p. 1994. 3.95 (0-940685-46-9) Cardoza Pub.

Basics of Winning Poker. 2nd ed. J. Edward Allen. LC 92-72051. (Illus.). 64p. 1992. pap. 3.95 (0-940685-29-9, Gambling Res) Cardoza Pub.

Basics of Winning Roulette. 2nd ed. J. Edward Allen. LC 92-72053. (Illus.). 64p. 1992. pap. 3.95 (0-940685-26-4, Gambling Res) Cardoza Pub.

Basics of Winning Slots. 2nd ed. J. Edward Allen. LC 92-72052. (Illus.). 64p. 1992. pap. 3.95 (0-940685-27-2, Gambling Res) Cardoza Pub.

Basics of Winning Video Poker. 2nd ed. J. Edward Allen. LC 92-81296. (Illus.). 64p. 1992. pap. 3.95 (0-940685-34-5, Gambling Res) Cardoza Pub.

***Basics of WordPerfect 5.1.** Jan Heck. 50p. (C). 1994. pap. text ed. 9.00 (0-9644132-0-5) Multimed Factory.

Basics of Workers Compensation Law for Legal Assistants. 3rd ed. Therese M. Nichols. 125p. 1991. pap. text ed. 24.95 (1-879563-06-1) Lexicon CA.

***Basics of Writing for Children & Young Adults.** Date not set. pap. text ed. 2.95 (0-89879-584-2) Writers Digest.

Basics to Baby-Sitting. Jodi Hughey. (Illus.). 31p. (Orig.). (J). (gr. 5 up). 1994. pap. 7.95 (1-885419-00-7) Mtn-top Kip.

Basics You Should Know Before Starting Your Own Small Business. Mel Solomon. 1988. 13.95 (0-533-07649-8) Vantage.

Basidiomycetes That Decay Aspen in North America. J. P. Lindsey & R. L. Gilbertson. (Bibliotheca Mycologica Ser.: No. 63). 1978. lib. bdg. 78.00 (3-7682-1193-2) Lubrecht & Cramer.

Basidium & Basidiocarp: Evolution, Cytology, Function & Development. Ed. by K. Wells & E. K. Wells. (Microbiology Ser.). (Illus.). 187p. 1982. 104.00 (0-387-90631-2) Spr-Verlag.

Basil. Wilkie Collins. Ed. by Dorothy Goldman. (World's Classics Ser.). 400p. 1990. pap. 8.95 (0-19-282195-4) OUP.

Basil. Wilkie Collins. 663p. 1992. text ed. 53.04 (1-56956-191-5, BR8436) W A T Braille.

Basil. Janet Hazen. (Illus.). 144p. 1993. 19.95 (0-8118-0170-5) Chronicle Bks.

Basil. Rosy. (J). (ps-3). 1993. 13.95 (0-307-17502-2, Artsts Writrs) Western Pub.

Basil. Wilkie Collins. 352p. 1980. reprint ed. pap. 7.95 (0-486-24015-0) Dover.

Basil Al-Bayati: Recent Works. (Illus.). 132p. 1993. 50.00 (1-85490-170-2, Academy Edits) St Martin.

Basil & Josephine Stories. F. Scott Fitzgerald. (Library of Contemporary Classics). 320p. 1976. pap. 8.95 (0-684-14693-2, Scribners) S&S Trade.

Basil & Josephine Stories. F. Scott Fitzgerald. (Twentieth Century Classics Ser.). 320p. 1987. pap. 6.00 (0-02-019870-1, Collier S&S) S&S Trade.

Basil & Josephine Stories. F. Scott Fitzgerald. 1985. text ed. 20.00 (0-684-18567-9) Macmillan.

Basil & the Pygmy Cats: A Basil of Baker Street Mystery. Eve Titus. (Illus.). (J). (gr. 3-6). 1989. pap. 2.75 (0-671-64119-0, Minstrel Bks) PB.

Basil Broketail. Christopher B. Rowley. 480p. 1992. 5.99 (0-451-45206-2, ROC) NAL-Dutton.

Basil Bunting. Victoria Forde. 300p. 1991. 55.00 (1-85224-047-4, Pub. by Bloodaxe Bks UK); pap. 24.00 (1-85224-048-2, Pub. by Bloodaxe Bks UK) Dufour.

Basil Bunting: Man & Poet. Ed. by Carroll F. Terrell. LC 80-84942. (Man & Poet Ser.). (Illus.). 450p. (Orig.). 1981. 35.00 (0-915032-51-1); pap. 15.95 (0-915032-52-X) Natl Poet Foun.

Basil Hume: Builder of Community. Stephen J. Costelloe. 1989. pap. 22.00 (1-85390-061-3, Pub. by Veritas IE) St Mut.

Basil in Mexico: A Basil of Baker Street Mystery. Eve Titus. (Illus.). 96p. (J). (gr. 3-6). 1990. pap. 2.75 (0-671-64117-4, Minstrel Bks) PB.

Basil in the Wild West: A Basil of Baker Street Mystery. Eve Titus. 86p. (J). 1990. pap. 2.75 (0-671-64118-2, Archway) PB.

Basil Lanneau Gildersleeve. Ed. by Ward W. Briggs & Herbert W. Benario. LC 85-25619. (American Journal of Philology Monographs: No. 1). 128p. 1986. text ed. 25.95x (0-8018-3117-2) Johns Hopkins.

Basil Moore's Lincoln. Ed. by Basil Moore. (Illus.). 100p. 1991. 19.95 (1-878044-02-8) Mayhaven Pub.

Basil of Baker Street. Eve Titus & Paul Galdone. (J). (gr. 3-6). 1958. lib. bdg. 8.95 (0-07-064907-3) McGraw.

Basil of Baker Street. Eve Titus. (Illus.). 1988. pap. 2.50 (0-318-37408-0, Minstrel Bks) PB.

Basil of Caesarea. Philip Rousseau. LC 93-3552. (Transformation of the Classical Heritage Ser.: Vol. 20). 1994. Alk. paper. 55.00 (0-520-08238-9) U CA Pr.

Basil Plant (Tulasi Plant) Worship among the World. Panduranga R. Malyala. (Illus.). 1982. 2.00 (0-938924-06-0) Sri Shirdi Sai.

***Basil Spence in Scotland.** Brian Edwards. 88p. (C). 1994. pap. 35.00x (1-873190-20-4, Pub. by Rutland Pr UK) St Mut.

Basil the Great: Gateway to Paradise. Ed. by Oliver Davies. Tr. by Tim Witherow. 128p. (Orig.). 1992. pap. 7.95 (1-56548-002-3) New City.

Basil Valentine: His Triumphant Chariot of Antimony, with Annotations of Theodore Kirkringius, 1678, Vol. 3. Louis G. Kelly. LC 90-42029. 196p. 1990. 37.00 (0-8240-7134-4, 1242) Garland.

***Basile et les Papillons.** Barbara De Brunhoff. 29p. (J). 1990. 27.95 (0-7859-8792-4) Fr & Eur.

Basile Ler, Empereur De Byzance (867-886) et la Civilisation Byzantine A la Fin Du Ninth Siecle. Albert Vogt. xxxii, 447p. 1973. reprint ed. write for info. (3-487-04920-1, Pub. by Georg Olms GW) Lubrecht & Cramer.

Basileus: The Evidence for Kingship in Geometric Greece. Robert Drews. LC 82-10915. (Yale Classical Monographs: No. 4). 160p. 1983. text ed. 35.00x (0-300-02831-8) Yale U Pr.

Basilian Leaders from Texas. Raphael O'Loughlin. Ed. by J. Whitebird. (Texas-Church History Ser.). (Illus.). 112p. (Orig.). 1992. pap. 20.00 (0-685-50819-6) Wings Pr.

Basilica of St. Mark in Venice Illustrated from the Points of View of Art & History by Venetian Writers. Ed. by Camilo Boito. Tr. by William Scott. 1976. lib. bdg. 125.95 (0-8490-1477-8) Gordon Pr.

Basilica Psalter. Jay Hunstiger. 240p. (Orig.). 1990. spiral bd. 29.95 (0-8146-2007-8) Liturgical Pr.

Basilicorum Libri LX. Ed. by H. J. Scheltema et al. (Series B Volumen VIII Scholia in Libr.: LVIII-LX,16). (Illus.). viii, 3476p. 1983. 163.00 (90-6243-026-0, Pub. by Boumas Boekhuis NE) Benjamins North Am.

Basilicorum Libri LX: Scholia in Librum LX 17-69. Ed. by H. J. Scheltema et al. (Series B: Vol. IX). 500p. (C). 1985. 179.50 (90-6243-037-6, Pub. by Boumas Boekhuis NE) Benjamins North Am.

Basilika In Pompeji: Unter Mitarbeit von Jurgen J. Rasch. Karlfriedrich Ohr. (Denkmaeler Antiker Architektur Ser.: Vol. 17). (Illus.). x, 87p. (GER.). (C). 1991. lib. bdg. 152.35 (3-11-012283-9) De Gruyter.

Basilio. Mark Dunster. 10p. (Orig.). 1991. pap. 4.00 (0-89642-198-8) Linden Pubs.

Basin: Life in a Chinese Province Poems & Translations. Mike O'Connor. 127p. 1989. 15.00 (0-912887-21-4); pap. 10.00 (0-912887-20-6) Empty Bowl.

Basin Analysis & Paleontology of the Paleocene & Eocene Goler Formation, El Paso Mountains California. Ed. by Brett E. Cox. (Illus.). 67p. (Orig.). 1987. pap. 8.00 (1-878861-12-3) Pac Section SEPM.

***Basin Analysis Case Study: The Morrison Formation Grants Uranium Region New Mexico.** Ed. by Christine E. Turner-Peterson et al. (AAPG Studies in Geology: No. 22). (Illus.). vii, 391p. 1986. pap. 42.00 (0-89181-028-5) AAPG.

***Basin Analysis in Petroleum Exploration: A Case Study from the Bekes Basin, Hungary.** Ed. by Paul G. Teleki. LC 94-22321. 344p. (C). 1994. lib. bdg. 145.00 (0-7923-3014-5) Kluwer Ac.

Basin Analysis, Vol. 1: Quantitative Methods. Ed. by Ian Lerche. 562p. 1989. text ed. 160.00 (0-12-444172-6) Acad Pr.

Basin Analysis, Vol. 2: Quantitative Methods. Ian Lerche. (Geology Ser.: Academic Press). 570p. 1990. 115.00 (0-685-31084-1) Acad Pr.

Basin & Range. John McPhee. (Illus.). 216p. (C). 1981. 19.95 (0-374-10914-1) FS&G.

Basin & Range. John McPhee. (Illus.). 216p. (C). 1982. pap. 9.00 (0-374-51690-1) FS&G.

Basin & Range Extensional Tectonics Near the Latitude of Las Vegas, Nevada. Ed. by B. Wernicke. (Memoir Ser.: No. 176). (Illus.). 510p. 1991. 115.00 (0-8137-1176-2) Geol Soc.

Basin City: The First County Seat in the Big Horn Basin. Lylas Skovgard. LC 88-16002. (This Is America Ser.). (Illus.). 146p. 1989. pap. 10.95 (0-914565-37-0, 37-0) Capstan Pubns.

Basin City: The First County Seat in the Big Horn Basin. 2nd rev. ed. Lylas O. Skovgard. LC 89-30208. (This Is America Ser.). (Illus.). 146p. 1989. pap. 10.95 (0-914565-38-9, 38-9) Capstan Pubns.

***Basin Compartments & Seals.** Ed. by Peter J. Ortoleva. (AAPG Memoir Ser.: No. 61). (Illus.). xxxi, 477p. 1995. 149.00 (0-89181-340-3) AAPG.

Basin Formation, Ridge Crest Processes, & Metallogenesis in the North Fiji Basin. Ed. by Loren W. Kroenke & James V. Eade. LC 93-44132. (Circum-Pacific Council for Energy & Mineral Resources Earth Science Ser.: No. 15). 1994. 95.00 (0-387-57372-0) Spr-Verlag.

***Basin Inversion.** Ed. by J. G. Buchanan & P. G. Buchanan. (Geological Society Special Publication Ser.: No. 88). (Illus.). 606p. 1995. 116.00 (1-897799-29-2, Pub. by Geol Soc Pub Hse UK) AAPG.

Basin Machine Operator. Jack Rudman. (Career Examination Ser.: C-2517). 1994. pap. 29.95 (0-8373-2517-X) Nat Learn.

***Basin of Gold: Life in Boise Basin, 1862-1890.** Arthur A. Hart. 84p. 1986. pap. 9.95 (0-9631258-4-2) Historic Idaho.

Basin of Mexico: Ecological Processes in the Evolution of a Civilization. William T. Sanders et al. (Studies in Archaeology). 1979. 44.50 (0-685-41945-2) Acad Pr.

Basin Oil Company: A Comprehensive Problem for Oil & Gas Financial Accounting. Robert L. Grinaker & Della A. Pearson. 56p. 1983. ring bd., pap. 9.50 (0-940966-03-4) UNTX Pro Dev Inst.

***Basin Plateau Aboriginal Sociopolitical Groups.** Julian H. Steward. (Bureau of American Ethnology Bulletins Ser.). 346p. 1995. lib. bdg. write for info. (0-7812-4120-0) Rprt Serv.

Basin Water Treatment for Application World-Wide. George Smethurst. 1986. reprint ed. 100.00 (0-317-62032-0, Scientific) St Mut.

Basing Standard of Need on Median Income. Francis G. Caro & Cynthia B. Green. 25p. (Orig.). 1985. pap. 2.50 (0-88156-023-5) Comm Serv Soc NY.

Basingstoke Past & Present. Robert Brown. (C). 1989. 39.00 (1-85455-007-1, Pub. by Ensign Pubns & Print UK) St Mut.

***Basins of the Rio Grande Rift: Structure, Stratigraphy & Tectonic Setting.** Ed. by G. Randy Keller & Steven M. Cather. LC 94-21616. (Special Papers: Vol. 291). 1994. pap. 72.50 (0-8137-2291-8) Geol Soc.

An Asterisk (*) at the beginning of an entry indicates that the title is appearing in BIP for the first time.

An Asterisk (*) at the beginning of an entry indicates that the title is appearing in BIP for the first time.

***Basketball's Offensive Sets.** Tom Reiter. (Spalding Sports Library). (Illus.). 128p. (Orig.). 1995. pap. 14.95 (*1-57028-038-X*, Spalding Sports) Masters Pr IN.

Basketball's Original Dynasty: The History of the Lakers. Stew Thornley. (Illus.). 120p. (Orig.). 1989. pap. 3.98 (*0-931714-39-7*) Nodin Pr.

Basketball's Origins: Creative Problem-Solving in the Gilded Age. James Naismith. Ed. by Robert Cheney et al. (Illus.). (C). (gr. 7 up). 1976. reprint ed. pap. 1.95 (*0-912934-03-4*) Bear.

Basketball's Stack Offense. Harry L. Harkins. LC 84-3194. 180p. 1984. 19.95 (*0-13-069451-7*, Parker Publishing Co) P-H.

Basketball's Zone Presses: A Complete Coaching Guide. Burrall Paye. 228p. 1983. 19.95 (*0-13-069237-9*, Parker Publishing Co) P-H.

Basketmaker Caves in the Prayer Rock District, Northeastern Arizona. Elizabeth A. Morris. LC 79-20149. (Anthropological Papers: No. 35). 158p. 1980. pap. 14.95 (*0-8165-0499-7*) U of Ariz Pr.

***Basketmaker in Rural Japan.** Louise A. Cort & Nakamura Kenji. LC 94-33582. (Illus.). 160p. 1995. pap. 29.95 (*0-8348-0336-4*) Weatherhill.

Basketmaker's Art: Contemporary Baskets & Their Makers. Ed. by Rob Pulleyn. LC 86-82336. (Illus.). 164p. 1992. pap. 19.95 (*0-937274-63-1*) Lark Books.

Basketmaker's Art: Contemporary Baskets & Their Makers. Rob Pulleyn. (Illus.). 164p. (C). 1991. reprint ed. lib. bdg. 47.00x (*0-8095-7594-9*) Borgo Pr.

Basketmath: For IBM Computers. Robert Cummings. (Illus.). (Orig.). (YA). (gr. 6-12). 1993. pap. 69.00 (*0-9623926-5-0*) Sci Academy Soft.

Basketry. Boy Scouts of America. (Illus.). 32p. (J). (gr. 6-12). 1986. pap. 1.85 (*0-8395-3313-6*, 33313) BSA.

Basketry. Frederick J. Christopher. (Illus.). 1952. pap. 2.95 (*0-486-20677-7*) Dover.

Basketry: Projects from Baskets to Grass Slippers. Hisako Sekijima. (Illus.). 144p. 1991. pap. 17.95 (*4-7700-1525-9*) Kodansha.

Basketry: The Nantucket Tradition. John McGuire. LC 89-83931. (Illus.). 144p. 1990. 24.95 (*0-937274-50-X*) Lark Books.

Basketry: The Shaker Tradition. John McGuire. LC 87-83653. (Illus.). 128p. (Orig.). 1989. 24.95 (*0-937274-46-1*) Lark Books.

Basketry: Tradition in New Form. Bernard Kester. 1982. 4.00 (*0-910663-34-3*) ICA Inc.

Basketry As Metaphor: Arts & Crafts of the Desana Indians of the Northwest Amazon. Gerardo Reichel-Dolmatoff. LC 84-62891. (Occasional Papers of the Museum of Cultural History, Los Angeles: No. 5). (Illus.). 104p. (Orig.). 1985. pap. text ed. 18.00 (*0-930741-03-X*) UCLA Fowler Mus.

Basketry Designs of the Salish Indians. Livingston Farrand. LC 73-3514. (Jesup North Pacific Expedition. Publications: Vol. 1). reprint ed. 22.50 (*0-404-58116-1*) AMS Pr.

Basketry of the Indians of California, 3 vols. Christopher L. Moser. (Illus.). 363p. (Orig.). 1993. Boxed Set. boxed 130.00 (*0-935661-22-0*) Riverside Mus Pr.

Basketry of the Indians of California, 3 vols., Vol. 1: Native American Basketry of Central Califo. Christopher L. Moser. (Illus.). 363p. (Orig.). 1993. pap. 30.00 (*0-935661-12-3*) Riverside Mus Pr.

Basketry of the Indians of California, 3 vols., Vol. 2: Northern California Indian Basketry. Christopher L. Moser. (Illus.). 363p. (Orig.). 1993. Vol. 2, Northern California Indian Basketry. pap. 30.00 (*0-935661-18-2*) Riverside Mus Pr.

Basketry of the Indians of California, 3 vols., Vol. 3: Native American Basketry of Southern Calif. Christopher L. Moser. (Illus.). 363p. (Orig.). 1993. Vol. 3, Native American Basketry of Southern California. pap. 45.00 (*0-935661-20-4*) Riverside Mus Pr.

Basketry of the San Carlos Apache Indians. Helen H. Roberts. LC 72-10331. (American Museum of Natural History Anthropological Papers: Vol. XXXI, Pt. II). (Illus.). 104p. 1985. reprint ed. pap. 10.00 (*0-87380-147-4*) Rio Grande.

Basketry of the Tlingit & the Chilkat Blanket. George T. Emmons. 192p. 1992. pap. text ed. 15.95 (*1-880475-03-0*) Friends of SJM.

Basketry Round Up 1991, No. 1. Ed. by Shereen LaPlantz. (Illus.). 112p. (Orig.). (C). 1990. pap. 18.95 (*0-942002-04-0*) Press LaPlantz.

Basketry Technology: A Guide to Identification & Analysis. James M. Adovasio. LC 77-70388. (Manuals on Archeology Ser.: No. 1). (Illus.). x, 182p. 1977. 18.00 (*0-202-33035-4*) Taraxacum.

Baskets. Nancy Schiffer. LC 84-51185. (Illus.). 176p. 1984. pap. 19.95 (*0-88740-018-3*) Schiffer.

Baskets. Photos by Hans Von Ommeren. LC 94-20425. (Illus.). 1995. write for info. (*0-8109-3136-2*) Abrams.

Baskets - Baskets - Baskets: An Advisory for Collectors. Lew Larason. (Illus.). 8p. (Orig.). 1988. pap. 1.95 (*0-936099-01-1*) Scorpio Pubns.

Baskets & Basket Makers in Southern Appalachia. John R. Irwin. LC 81-86386. (Illus.). 192p. 1982. pap. 14.95 (*0-916838-61-7*) Schiffer.

***Baskets & Basketmaking.** Alastair Heseltine. (C). 1989. pap. 25.00x (*0-85263-611-3*, Pub. by Shire UK) St Mut.

Baskets & Flowers Block Party, Series No. 2. Eleanor Burns. (Illus.). 44p. 1990. 9.95 (*0-922705-31-3*) Quilt Day.

Baskets, Beads, & Black Walnut Owls: Creative Crafts for Ages 9-12. Sarah H. Healton & Kay H. Whiteside. LC 92-41247. (Illus.). (J). (gr. 4-7). 1993. pap. 9.95 (*0-8306-4040-1*) TAB Bks.

Baskets, Beads, & Black Walnut Owls: Creative Crafts for 9-12. Sarah H. Healton & Kay H. Whiteside. 1993. pap. text ed. 9.95 (*0-07-027704-4*) McGraw.

Baskets for Quilters. Betty Boyink. 52p. (Orig.). 1982. pap. 10.00 (*0-9612608-0-7*) B Boyink.

Baskets from Nature's Bounty. Elizabeth Jensen. LC 91-30752. (Illus.). 208p. 1991. 24.95 (*0-934026-69-6*) Interweave.

Baskets in Polynesia. Wendy Arbeit. LC 89-20656. (Illus.). 136p. (Orig.). 1990. pap. 24.95 (*0-8248-1281-6*) UH Pr.

Baskets of Alaska. Arlie Hamar. (Illus.). 64p. 1981. 24.00 (*0-88014-031-3*) Mosaic Pr OH.

Basohli Painting. M. S. Randhawa. 116p. 1981. 49.95 (*0-940500-92-2*, Pub. by Pubns Div II) Asia Bk Corp.

Basque. Mario Saltarelli. (Descriptive Grammars Ser.). 300p. 1988. 82.50 (*0-7099-3353-3*, Pub. by Croom Helm UK) Routledge Chapman & Hall.

Basque & the Boy. John A. Croner. LC 80-15675. 1982. 21.95 (*0-87949-176-0*) Ashley Bks.

Basque-Castilian-Basque Dictionary: Diccionario Euskara-Castellano-Euskara. Kintana X. Hiztegia. 430p. (BAQ & SPA.). 1982. pap. 125.00 (*0-8288-1733-2*, S40698) Fr & Eur.

Basque Cooking & Lore. Darcy Williamson. LC 91-24000. (Illus.). (Orig.). 1991. pap. 10.95 (*0-87004-346-3*) Caxton.

Basque English - English Basque Dictionary. Gorka Aulestia & Linda White. LC 91-44306. (Basque Ser.). 688p. (BAQ & ENG.). (C). 1992. pap. 20.00 (*0-87417-178-4*) U of Nev Pr.

Basque-English Dictionary. Gorka Aulestia. LC 88-32992. (Basque Ser.). (Illus.). 672p. 1989. 50.00 (*0-87417-126-1*) U of Nev Pr.

Basque Grammar: An Introduction to the Language see Basque Language: A Practical Introduction

Basque Hotel. Robert Laxalt. LC 89-4953. (Basque Ser.). 136p. 1993. pap. 15.00 (*0-87417-216-0*) U of Nev Pr.

Basque Insurgents: ETA, 1952-1980. Robert P. Clark. LC 83-40259. (Illus.). 352p. 1984. text ed. 29.50 (*0-299-09650-5*) U of Wis Pr.

Basque Language: A Practical Introduction. Alan R. King. LC 92-40073. (Basque Ser.). Orig. Title: Basque Grammar: An Introduction to the Language. 480p. 1994. 60.00 (*0-87417-155-5*) U of Nev Pr.

Basque Legends. Wentworth Webster. LC 78-63236. (Folktale Ser.). reprint ed. 31.50 (*0-404-16175-8*) AMS Pr.

Basque Nationalism. Stanley G. Payne. LC 75-15698. (Basque Ser.). (Illus.). xii, 304p. 1975. 30.00x (*0-87417-042-7*) U of Nev Pr.

Basque Phase of Spain's First Carlist War. John F. Coverdale. LC 83-43068. (Illus.). 349p. reprint ed. pap. 99.50 (*0-8357-3843-4*, 2036576) Bks Demand.

Basque Phase of Spain's First Carlist War: 1833-1835. John F. Coverdale. LC 83-43068. 312p. 1984. 49.50 (*0-691-05411-8*) Princeton U Pr.

Basque Phonology. Jose I. Hualde. (Theoretical Linguistics Ser.). (Illus.). 240p. 1991. 85.00 (*0-415-05655-1*, A5729) Routledge.

Basque Sheepherders of the American West: A Photographic Documentary. Richard H. Lane & William A. Douglass. LC 85-291. (Basque Book Ser.). (Illus.). 200p. 1985. 40.00 (*0-87417-089-3*) U of Nev Pr.

Basque-Spanish, Spanish-Basque Dictionary: 80 Euskara-Espainiera-Euskara. 2nd ed. X. Hiztegia Kintana. 854p. (BAQ & SPA.). 1984. 39.95 (*0-8288-1114-8*, S40778) Fr & Eur.

Basque Violence: Metaphor & Sacrament. Joseba Zulaika. LC 87-35432. (Illus.). 458p. 1988. 40.00x (*0-87417-132-6*) U of Nev Pr.

Basque Whaling in Labrador in the 16th Century. Jean-Pierre Proulx. (Illus.). 108p. (Orig.). Date not set. pap. 10.70 (*0-660-14819-6*, Pub. by Canada Commun Grp CN) Accents Pubns.

Basques. Roger Collins. 1990. pap. 21.95 (*0-631-17565-2*) Blackwell Pubs.

Basques: The Franco Years & Beyond. Robert P. Clark. LC 79-24926. (Basque Book Ser.). (Illus.). 452p. 1980. 35.00x (*0-87417-057-5*) U of Nev Pr.

Basques & Catalans. Lewis B. Sckolnick. (Civil Rights Reporter Ser.). (Illus.). 60p. (Orig.). (C). 1994. pap. 45.00 (*1-57205-137-X*) Rector Pr.

Basques in the Western United States: A Functional Approach to Determination of Cultural Presence in the Geographical Landscape. Joseph R. Castelli. Ed. by Francesco Cordasco. LC 80-844. (American Ethnic Groups Ser.). 1981. lib. bdg. 23.95 (*0-405-13408-8*) Ayer.

Basques to Bakersfield. Mary G. Paquette. (Illus.). 138p. 1982. 15.00 (*0-943500-00-1*) Kern Historical.

Basquiat Drawings. Jean Michel Basquiat. (Illus.). 176p. 1991. pap. 35.00 (*0-8212-1887-5*) Bulfinch Pr.

Bass, & How to Catch Them. Red Grigsby. 1966. pap. 2.95 (*0-87511-590-X*) Claitors.

Bass & Stogdill's Handbook of Leadership: Theory, Research, & Managerial Applications. 3rd ed. Bernard M. Bass & Ralph M. Stogdill. 1216p. 1990. text ed. 85.00 (*0-02-901500-6*) Free Pr.

Bass Clarinet. Ed. by Bram Wiggins. (Bandstand Junior Album Ser.). Date not set. pap. 5.95 (*0-685-69296-5*, Chester Music) Music Sales.

***Bass Cookbook.** A. D. Livingston. 160p. 1996. pap. 12.95 (*0-8117-2509-X*) Stackpole.

Bass Fever. Bruce Cochran. 96p. 1991. 12.50 (*1-55971-126-4*, 1493); pap. 7.95 (*1-55971-127-2*, 1527) NorthWord.

Bass Fever. Bruce Cochran. 96p. 1994. pap. 7.95 (*1-57223-000-2*) Outlook Pubng.

Bass Fisherman's Bible. 3rd ed. Erwin A. Bauer. 1989. pap. 12.00 (*0-385-24690-0*) Doubleday.

Bass Fishing: Strategy & Tactics. Bill Hornsey. 1967. 3.95 (*0-87511-059-2*) Claitors.

Bass Fishing: Stripers, White Bass, Yellow Bass & Perch. Bob Gooch. LC 75-17965. (Illus.). 159p. 1975. pap. 5.00 (*0-87033-206-6*, Tidewtr Pubs) Cornell Maritime.

Bass Fishing California: Secrets of the Western Pros. 4th ed. Ron Kovach. (Illus.). 240p. 1994. pap. 14.95 (*0-934061-18-1*) Marketscope Bks.

***Bass Fishing Central Alabama: You Can Find & Catch More & Bigger Bass in Central Alabama Lakes.** John E. Phillips. Ed. by Coke Ellington. (Illus.). 160p. (Orig.). 1994. pap. 15.00 (*1-882616-05-7*) Advertiser.

Bass Fishing Facts: Angler's Guide to Bass Lifestyles & Behavior. Larry Larsen. LC 88-91464. (Bass Series Library). (Illus.). 135p. (Orig.). 1989. pap. 9.95 (*0-936513-05-5*, BSL6) Larsens Outdoor.

***Bass Fishing Simplified.** Bob Gooch. (Illus.). 154p. (Orig.). Date not set. pap. text ed. 10.95 (*0-937866-43-1*) Atlantic Pub Co.

Bass Fitness: An Exercise Handbook. (Guitar School Ser.). 72p. 1991. pap. 7.95 (*0-7935-0248-9*, 00660177) H Leonard.

Bass Flies. Dick Stewart. (Illus.). 48p. 1990. 19.95 (*0-936644-03-6*); pap. 12.95 (*0-936644-04-4*) Mtn Pond Pub.

Bass Guide Tips: An Angler's Guide. Larry Larsen. LC 90-63531. (Bass Series Library). (Illus.). 160p. 1991. text ed. 9.95 (*0-936513-10-1*) Larsens Outdoor.

Bass Guitar. Jim Gregory & Harvey Vinson. (Illus.). (Orig.). 1973. pap. 12.95 (*0-8256-4057-1*) Music Sales.

Bass Guitar Chord Chart. Date not set. 2.50 (*0-87166-778-9*, 93297) Mel Bay.

Bass Guitar Chord Chart. Ron Middlebrook. 4p. 1985. pap. 2.50 (*0-931759-01-3*, 286) Centerstream Pub.

Bass Guitar Scale Manual, MFM64. Harvey Vinson. (Illus.). 144p. 1985. pap. 12.95 (*0-8256-4064-4*, AM14796) Music Sales.

Bass Heroes: Styles, Stories & Secrets of 30 Great Bass Players. Ed. by Tom Mulhern. (Illus.). 208p. pap. 17.95 (*0-87930-274-7*) Miller Freeman.

Bass Improvising. Earl Gately. 1993. 8.95 (*0-87166-952-8*, 93491) Mel Bay.

***Bass in Depth.** Bob McNally. (Bob McNally's Complete Bks.). (Illus.). 300p. (Orig.). 1995. pap. text ed. 16.95 (*0-9646265-0-0*) McNally Outdoor Prodns.

Bass Line: The Stories & Photographs of Milt Hinton. Milt Hinton & David G. Berger. LC 87-15338. (Illus.). 344p. 1988. 44.95 (*0-87722-518-4*) Temple U Pr.

Bass Line: The Stories & Photographs of Milt Hinton. Milt Hinton & David Berger. (Illus.). 344p. 1991. pap. 24.95 (*0-87722-681-4*) Temple U Pr.

Bass Lines in Minutes. Kris Berg. (Illus.). 40p. (Orig.). (C). Date not set. pap. 7.95 (*1-56516-035-5*) Houston IN.

Bass Log. Edward Augeri & Dominick Dicicco. 198p. 1993. spiral bd. 19.95 (*0-9639181-0-9*) Edwards Pubng.

***Bass Logic: A Comprehensive Method for Learning Bass.** William H. Edwards & Steve Hodson. (Illus.). 97p. 1994. spiral bd. 19.95 (*0-9624770-3-6*, 40000) Edwards Music Pub.

Bass Lures: Tricks & Techniques. Larry Larsen. LC 87-82758. (Illus.). 128p. (Orig.). 1988. pap. 9.95 (*0-936513-02-0*) Larsens Outdoor.

Bass Marimba Designs. Christopher C. Banta. (Illus.). 312p. (Orig.). (C). 1992. per., pap. text ed. 35.00 (*0-942742-01-X*) CCBANTA.

Bass on the Fly. 2nd rev. ed. A. D. Livingston. LC 93-47194. 1994. pap. text ed. 16.95 (*0-07-038151-8*, Ragged Mntn) McGraw.

***Bass Pro Shops Wildlife Cookbook: A Collection of America's Favorite Game & Fish Recipes.** John Gallaspy. 1995. pap. 14.95 (*1-56530-176-5*) Summit TX.

Bass Pro Strategies. Larry Larsen. LC 87-82757. (Illus.). 128p. (Orig.). 1988. pap. 9.95 (*0-936513-01-2*) Larsens Outdoor.

Bass Reeves: Deputy U. S. Marshal 1875-1902. Mary W. Estes. Ed. by Mary Williamson. 224p. Date not set. 19.95 (*0-89896-307-9*, Harmony House) Larksdale.

Bass Saxophone. Josef Skvorecky. 1994. pap. 12.00 (*0-88001-370-2*) Ecco Pr.

Bass Scales & Modes. William L. Fowler. LC 84-71709. (Illus.). 28p. 1992. pap. text ed. 6.95 (*0-943894-20-4*) Fowler Music.

Bass Viol Technique. Margaret Panofsky. (Educational Ser.: No. 1). (Illus.). xiv, 336p. (Orig.). 1991. pap. text ed. 40.00 (*1-56571-042-8*) PRB Prods.

***Bassanos: Venetian Musicians & Instrument Makers in England, 1531-1665.** David Lasocki & Roger Prior. 324p. 1995. 68.95 (*0-85967-943-8*, Pub. by Scolar Pr UK) Ashgate Pub Co.

Basset Hound. Marcia A. Foy & Anna K. Nicholas. (Illus.). 320p. 1985. text ed. 19.95 (*0-86622-044-5*, PS-815) TFH Pubns.

Basset Hound Champions, 1952-1992. Camino E. E. & B. Co. Staff. (Illus.). 200p. 1996. pap. 36.95 (*1-55893-014-0*) Camino E E & Bk.

Basset Hounds. Diane McCarty & Travis Look. (Illus.). 125p. 1979. 11.95 (*0-86622-809-8*, KW-069) TFH Pubns.

***Basset Hounds.** Diane McCarty. 1994. 11.95 (*0-7938-1088-4*) TFH Pubns.

Bassett - Preston Ancestors: History of Ancestors in America of the Children of Edward M. & Annie Preston Bassett. B. Preston. 359p. 1991. reprint ed. 59.00 (*0-8328-1853-4*); reprint ed. pap. 49.00 (*0-8328-1854-2*) Higginson Bk Co.

Bassett Hall: The Williamsburg Home of Mr. & Mrs. John D. Rockefeller, Jr. Bland Blackford et al. LC 84-17600. (Illus.). 43p. (Orig.). 1984. pap. 3.95 (*0-87935-107-1*) Colonial Williamsburg.

Bassett-Lowke Story. Roland Fuller & Allen Levy. LC 84-71044. (Illus.). 352p. 1984. 29.95 (*0-904568-34-2*) Schiffer.

Bassett Maguire Festschrift: A Tribute to the Man & His Deeds. Ed. by William R. Buck et al. LC 90-25155. (Memoirs Ser.: No. 64). (Illus.). 289p. 1990. pap. 59.75 (*0-89327-362-7*) NY Botanical.

Bassett Women. Grace McClure. LC 85-7143. (Illus.). 270p. 1985. text ed. 25.00 (*0-8040-0876-0*); pap. 9.95 (*0-8040-0877-9*) Swallow.

Bassin' in Michigan. Greg Bolak. (Illus.). 136p. 1992. 22.95 (*1-878005-63-4*); pap. 13.95 (*1-878005-64-2*) Northmont Pub.

Bassin' in New England: A Practical Guide to Productive Black Bass Angling in the Six State Region. William Chauvin & Carl Apperson. LC 85-2800. (Illus.). 175p. (Orig.). 1985. 15.95 (*0-89621-089-8*); pap. 7.95 (*0-89621-090-1*) Nrth Country Pr.

***Bassin' with a Fly Rod: One Fly Rodder's Approach to Serious Bass Fishing.** Jack Ellis. (Illus.). 196p. 1995. 22.95 (*0-936644-21-4*) Lyons & Burford.

Basslines. Joe Hubbard. (Illus.). 48p. pap. 8.95 (*0-7119-0622-X*, AM38795) Music Sales.

Bassoon. Ed. by Bram Wiggins. (Bandstand Junior Album Ser.). Date not set. pap. 5.95 (*0-685-68983-2*, Chester Music) Music Sales.

Bassoon Duets. William Waterhouse. Date not set. pap. 13.95 (*0-685-68984-0*, Chester Music) Music Sales.

Bassoon Reed Making. Mark Popkin & Loren Glickman. 1994. 15.00 (*0-318-37569-9*) Instrumental.

Bassoon Reed Making: A Basic Technique. rev. ed. Christopher Weait. LC 89-8226. 1980. 8.00 (*0-941084-07-8*) McGinnis & Marx.

Bassoon Solos Vol. 1. William Waterhouse. Date not set. pap. 11.95 (*0-685-68985-9*, Chester Music) Music Sales.

Bassoon Solos Vol. 2. William Waterhouse. Date not set. pap. 11.95 (*0-7119-2982-3*, Chester Music) Music Sales.

***Basta! Land & the Zapatista Rebellion in Chiapas.** George A. Collier & Elizabeth L. Quaratiello. 200p. (Orig.). (C). 1994. pap. 12.95x (*0-935028-65-X*) Inst Food & Develop.

***Bastard Feudalism.** Michael Hicks. LC 94-34281. (Medieval World Ser.). 240p. (C). 1996. text ed. 48.95 (*0-582-06091-5*, 76995); pap. text ed. 18.95 (*0-582-06092-3*, 76994) Longman.

Bastard Feudalism & the Law. J. G. Bellamy. 1989. 39.95 (*0-918400-10-4*) Areopagitica.

Bastard Hero in the Novel. Ed. by Margaret B. Goscilo. LC 90-34442. (Studies in Comparative Literature). 264p. 1990. reprint ed. 20.00 (*0-8240-0000-5*) Garland.

Bastard in the Ragged Suit. Herman Spector. LC 76-17183. (Illus.). 1977. bds. 12.50 (*0-912184-03-5*) Synergistic Pr.

Bastard King. Jean Plaidy. 22.95 (*0-8488-0605-0*) Amereon Ltd.

Bastard Out of Carolina. Dorothy Allison. 272p. 1992. 20.00 (*0-525-93425-1*, Dutton) NAL-Dutton.

Bastard Out of Carolina. Dorothy Allison. LC 91-34607. 320p. 1993. pap. 10.95 (*0-452-26957-1*, Plume) NAL-Dutton.

Bastard Prince. Katherine Kurtz. (Heirs of Saint Camber Ser.: Vol. III). 416p. 1994. 22.00 (*0-345-33262-8*, Del Rey) Ballantine.

***Bastard Prince: The Heirs of St. Camber, Vol. 3.** Katherine Kurtz. 1995. pap. 5.99 (*0-345-39177-2*, Del Rey) Ballantine.

Bastards. Bertene Juminer. Ed. by A. James Arnold & Kandioura Drame. Tr. by Keith O. Warner. LC 88-26135. (CARAF Bks.). 239p. 1989. pap. 12.95 (*0-8139-1204-0*) U Pr of Va.

Bastards: Footnotes to History. deluxe ed. Ursule Molinaro. (Treacle Story Ser.: No. 7). (Illus.). 48p. 1979. 8.00 (*0-914232-27-4*) McPherson & Co.

Bastardy & Its Comparative History: Studies in the History of Illegitimacy & Martial Nonconformism. Ed. by Peter Laslett et al. (Studies in Social & Demographic History). (Illus.). 446p. 1980. 47.50 (*0-674-06338-4*) HUP.

***Bastile Day.** Ed Bolme et al. (Cyberpunk Ser.). (Illus.). 48p. (Orig.). 1993. pap. 6.00 (*0-937279-41-2*, CP3261) R Talsorian.

Bastion of Faith. 3rd ed. Avraham Fishelis. 256p. 1980. 9.00 (*0-9605560-1-X*) A Fishelis.

Bastogne: The Story of the First Eight Days. Samuel Lyman & Atwood Marshall. LC 79-18262. reprint ed. 19.95 (*0-89201-060-6*) Zenger Pub.

Bastogne: The Story of the First Eight Days in Which the 101st Airborne Division Was Closed Within the Ring of German Forces. S. L. Marshall et al. (United States Army in Action Series. CMH Pub.: No. 22-2). (Illus.). 273p. 1988. reprint ed. pap. 8.50 (*0-16-001972-9*, S/N 008-029-00170-5) USGPO.

Bastoor. rev. ed. Mehrdad Bahar. Ed. by Ahmad Jabbari. Tr. by Mansoor Alyeshmreni. LC 83-60451. (Illus.). 32p. (J). (gr. 1 up). 1983. reprint ed. pap. 4.95 (*0-939214-17-2*) Mazda Pubs.

Bastrop County, Texas Cemeteries, Vol. 1. Audrey L. Rother. LC 91-75085. 410p. 1991. text ed. 29.98 (*0-9630786-0-7*) A Rother.

Bastrop County, Texas Cemeteries, Vol. 2. Audrey L. Rother. 138p. 1992. text ed. 21.00 (*0-9630786-2-3*) A Rother.

Basutoland: Its Legends & Customs. Minnie Martin. LC 75-88997. 174p. 1969. reprint ed. text ed. 45.00 (*0-8371-1756-9*, MAK&, Negro U Pr) Greenwood.

Basye Family in the U. S. O. Basye. (Illus.). 987p. 1991. reprint ed. lib. bdg. 145.00 (*0-8328-1767-8*); reprint ed. pap. 135.00 (*0-8328-1768-6*) Higginson Bk Co.

Bat. Mary R. Rinehart. 1989. pap. 3.50 (*0-8217-2627-7*) Zebra.

Bat. Zoe Wilmot. LC 93-77342. (Hook a Book Ser.). (J). (ps). 1993. 3.99 (*0-89577-509-3*, Random) RD Assn.

Bat & the Bishop. Robert W. Prichard. LC 89-32719. (Illus.). 128p. (Orig.). 1988. reprint ed. pap. 7.95 (*0-8192-1508-2*) Morehouse Pub.

626

An Asterisk (*) at the beginning of an entry indicates that the title is appearing in BIP for the first time.

Bat Bomb: World War II's Other Secret Weapon. Jack Couffer. LC 92-11888. (Illus.). 284p. 1992. 24.95 (0-292-70790-8) U of Tex Pr.

***Bat Book & See Through Model: Another Idea from Becker & Mayer.** Luann Colombo. (Illus.). 48p. (J). 1995. pap. 14.95 (0-8362-0031-4) Andrews & McMeel.

Bat Boy. Paul Rogers & Emma Rogers. (Illus.). 96p. (J). (gr. 5-8). 1993. pap. 6.95 (0-460-88153-1, J M Dent & Sons) Trafalgar.

Bat Cave Mystery. Carole Marsh. (History Mystery Ser.). (Orig.). (J). (gr. 3-8). 1994. lib. bdg. 24.95 (1-55609-154-0); pap. 14.95 (0-935326-72-3) Gallopade Pub Group.

Bat Chain Puller: Rock & Roll in the Age of Celebrity. Kurt Loder. (Illus.). 320p. 1991. pap. 9.95 (0-312-06301-6) St Martin.

Bat House Builder's Handbook. Merlin D. Tuttle & Donna L. Hensley. (Illus.). 32p. 1995. pap. 6.95 (0-9638248-0-5) Bat Conserv.

Bat in My Pocket: A Memorable Friendship. Amanda Lollar. LC 91-37907. (Illus.). 100p. (Orig.). 1992. pap. 9.95 (0-88496-347-0) Capra Pr.

Bat in My Pocket: A Memorable Friendship. Amanda Lollar. 160p. (Orig.). 1992. reprint ed. lib. bdg. 27.00x (0-8095-4094-0) Borgo Pr.

Bat in the Cave. Helen Riley. LC 89-4469. (Animal Habitats Ser.). (Illus.). 32p. (J). (gr. 4-6). 1989. lib. bdg. 17.27 (0-8368-0112-1) Gareth Stevens Inc.

Bat Masterson. Carl R. Green & William R. Sanford. LC 91-29857. (Outlaws & Lawmen of the Wild West Ser.). (Illus.). 48p. (J). (gr. 4-10). 1992. lib. bdg. 14.95 (0-89490-362-4) Enslow Pubs.

Bat Masterson: The Man & the Legend. Robert K. DeArment. LC 78-21383. (Illus.). 456p. 1989. pap. 15.95 (0-8061-2221-8) U of Okla Pr.

***Bat Mitzvah: A Jewish Girl's Coming of Age.** Barbara D. Godin. (Illus.). 14.99p. (J). (gr. 5-8). 1995. 14.99 (0-670-86034-4) Viking Child Bks.

Bat Poet. Adapt. by Betty Britto. (Illus.). 40p. (Orig.). (J). (gr. 3 up). 1988. pap. 3.00 (0-88680-300-4); 10.00 (0-88680-301-2) I E Clark.

***Bat-Poet.** Randall Jarrell. LC 64-16812. (J). (gr. 4-7). 1995. lib. bdg. 11.89 (0-06-205085-0) HarpC Child Bks.

***Bat-Poet.** Randall Jarrell. LC 94-76271. (Michael di Capua Bks.). (Illus.). 48p. (J). (gr. 3 up). 1995. 12.00 (0-06-205084-2); pap. 4.95 (0-06-205905-X, Trophy) HarpC Child Bks.

***Bat Time.** R. Horowitz. 1994. pap. 4.99 (0-517-13301-6) Random.

Bataan: Our Last Ditch. John W. Whitman. 700p. 1990. 29.95 (0-87052-877-7) Hippocrene Bks.

Bataan & Beyond: Memories of an American POW. John S. Coleman, Jr. LC 78-6365. (Centennial Series of the Association of Former Students: No. 6). (Illus.). 232p. 1991. pap. 12.95 (0-89096-491-2) Tex A&M Univ Pr.

Bataan & Corregidor. Wallace B. Black & Jean F. Blashfield. (World War II 50th Anniversary Ser.). (Illus.). 48p. (J). (gr. 5-6). 1991. text ed. 12.95 (0-89686-557-6, Crstwood Hse) Silver Burdett Pr.

Bataan Diary by Captain Ashton. Paul L. Ashton. LC 85-192945. (Illus.). 463p. (Orig.). 1984. pap. 35.00 (0-9627164-0-5) Ashton Pubns.

Bataan Uncensored. E. B. Miller. 439p. 1991. reprint ed. pap. 13.95 (0-9631642-0-1) Milit Hist Soc MN.

Bataille: Writing the Sacred. Ed. by Carolyn B. Gill. LC 94-13589. (Wawick Studies in European Philosophy Ser.). (Illus.). 256p. 1994. 55.00x (0-415-10122-0, B3493); pap. 16.95 (0-415-10123-9, B3497) Routledge.

Bataille du Silence. Jean Vercors. 349p. (FRE.). 1992. pap. 29.95 (0-7859-1521-4, 2707314145) Fr & Eur.

Bataille, Georges, Erotism: Death & Sensuality. Georges Bataille. Tr. by Mary Dalwood. 288p. (Orig.). 1986. reprint ed. pap. 12.95 (0-87286-190-2) City Lights.

Batailles dans la Montagne. Jean Giono. (FRE.). 1980. pap. 13.95 (0-7859-2351-9, 2070366243) Fr & Eur.

Batailles dans la Montagne. Jean Giono. (Folio Ser.: No. 624). 368p. (FRE.). 1937. 13.95 (2-07-036624-3) Schoenhof.

Batailles dans la Montagne see Oeuvres Romanesques

Bataillon du Ciel. Joseph Kessel. 320p. (FRE.). 1974. pap. 10.95 (0-7859-2354-3, 2070366421) Fr & Eur.

Batak: Peoples of the Island Sumatra. Achim Sibeth. LC 90-71576. (Illus.). 240p. 1991. 45.00 (0-500-97392-X) Thames Hudson.

Batak Cloth & Clothing: A Dynamic Indonesian Tradition. Sandra A. Niessen. (Asia Collection). (Illus.). 148p. 1994. 45.00 (967-65-3040-9) OUP.

Batalla En el Mexico Rural see Struggle for Rural Mexico

Batard. Jack London. Orig. Title: The Faith of Men. (Illus.). 292p. 1987. pap. 6.95 (0-932458-13-0) Star Rover.

Batarde. Violette Leduc. (FRE.). 1964. pap. 49.95 (0-7859-3960-1) Fr & Eur.

Batavia: 1600-1850. Katherine S. Diehl. (Printers & Printing in the East Indies to 1850 Ser.: Vol. I). (Illus.). 445p. 1990. 100.00 (0-89241-390-5) Caratzas.

Batavia Meeting: Proceedings of the 1992 Meeting of the Division of Particles & Fields of the APS, 2 vols., Set. R. Raja & John Yoh. 750p. 1993. text ed. 178.00 (981-02-1323-9) World Scientific Pub.

Batavia Revisited. Thomas A. Mair. (Illus.). 227p. (Orig.). 1990. pap. 12.00 (0-9628268-0-4) Benson Mair & Gosselin.

***Batboy.** Joan Anderson. LC 95-11793. (Illus.). (J). 1996. write for info. (0-525-67511-6, Lodestar Bks) Dutton Child Bks.

Batboy. Mel Cebulash. (Sports Stories Ser.). (Illus.). (J). (gr. 3-8). 1992. lib. bdg. 12.79 (0-89565-882-8) Childs World.

***Batboys & the World of Baseball.** Neil D. Isaacs. LC 94-42700. (Studies in Popular Culture). (Illus.). 288p. 1995. text ed. 42.00 (0-87805-771-4); pap. 16.95 (0-87805-772-2) U Pr of Miss.

Batch Control Systems. T. G. Fisher. (Resources for Measurement & Control Ser.). 400p. 1990. text ed. 70.00 (1-55617-131-5, A131-5) Instru Soc.

Batch File & Macros Quick Reference. Que Development Group Staff. 160p. 1991. pap. 9.95 (0-88022-699-4) Que.

Batch File Hall of Fame. Ronny Richardson. 1992. disk, pap. 34.95 (0-8306-3775-3, Windcrest) TAB Bks.

Batch Files & Beyond: Your Pain to Path PC Power. Dan Gookin. 1993. text ed. 44.95 (0-07-024002-7); pap. text ed. 32.95 (0-07-024003-5) McGraw.

Batch Files & Beyond: Your Path to PC Power. Dan Gookin. LC 93-9593. (Illus.). 529p. 1993. 44.90 (0-8306-4385-0, Windcrest); pap. 32.95 (0-8306-4384-2, Windcrest) TAB Bks.

Batch Files to Go: A Programmer's Library. Charles Ackerman. (Illus.). 304p. 1991. pap. 34.95 (0-8306-3713-3, 3713, Windcrest) TAB Bks.

Batch Files to Go: A Programmer's Library. Ronny Richardson. 1992. pap. 34.95 (0-07-052347-9) McGraw.

Batch Files to Go: A Programmer's Library. Ronny Richardson. 352p. 1992. disk, pap. 34.95 (0-8306-3989-6, Windcrest) TAB Bks.

Batch Process Automation: Theory & Practice. Howard Rosenof & Asish Ghosh. (Illus.). 1987. text ed. 67.95 (0-442-27708-3) Chapman & Hall.

Batchelder, Batcheller: Descendants of Rev. Stephen Bachilar of England, a Leading Non-Conformist Who Settled in the Town of New Hampton, N. H., & Joseph, Henry, Joshua, & John Batcheller of Essex Co., Mass. F. C. Pierce. (Illus.). 623p. 1988. reprint ed. lib. bdg. 103.50 (0-8328-0206-9); reprint ed. pap. 93.50 (0-8328-0207-7) Higginson Bk Co.

Batchelder, Batcheller Genealogy. Frederick C. Pierce. (Illus.). 623p. 1992. reprint ed. pap. 35.00 (1-55613-616-1) Heritage Bk.

Batchelor-Keeper see Virgin Seducer

Batchelor's Delight. Anne Batchelor. (C). 1989. text ed. 50.00 (0-948929-40-5) St Mut.

Batchin' It Specialties: Cooking for "1 or 2" Can Be Fun. rev. ed. Intro. by Peg Bell. LC 88-92429. 198p. (YA). (gr. 8). 1988. spiral bd. 12.95 (0-9621056-0-0) P A Bell Enterps.

Batching in the Glass Industry. Alexis G. Pincus & David H. Davies. LC 81-67427. (Processing in the Glass Industry Ser.). 217p. 1981. 24.95 (0-911993-07-X) Ashlee Pub Co.

Batek Negrito Religion: The World-View & Rituals of a Hunting & Gathering People of Peninsular Malaysia. Kirk M. Endicott. (Illus.). 1979. 55.00 (0-19-823197-0) OUP.

Bat'em in Benjy. C. Friedman. (Middos Ser.). 1993. 6.95 (0-89906-511-2) Mesorah Pubns.

Bateman Blend Weaves. Ed. by Virginia I. Harvey. LC 82-81522. (Guild Monographs: No. 36). (Illus.). 144p. 1982. pap. 16.95 (0-916658-38-4) Shuttle Craft.

***Bates: Pocket Guide to Physical Examination & History Taking.** J. B. Lippincott. 1994. pap. 19.95 (0-397-55057-X) Lippincott.

Bates, Bears & Bunker Hill with a Correction or Two. Edward Deacon. 90p. 1988. reprint ed. lib. bdg. 28.00 (0-8328-0210-7); reprint ed. pap. 18.00 (0-8328-0211-5) Higginson Bk Co.

Bates Method. Peter Mansfield. (Alternative Health Ser.). (Illus.). 166p. (Orig.). 1994. pap. 12.95 (0-8048-3003-7) C E Tuttle.

Bates Method for Better Eyesight Without Glasses. William H. Bates. LC 80-39878. 208p. (Orig.). 1981. pap. 8.95 (0-8050-0241-3, Owl) H Holt & Co.

Batfishing in the Rainforest: Strange Tales of Travel & Fishing. Randy W. White. LC 92-13962. 256p. 1992. pap. 12.95 (0-8050-2229-5, Owl) H Holt & Co.

***Bath.** (Pevensey Heritage Guides Ser.). (Illus.). 112p. 1994. pap. 9.95 (0-907115-59-4) Sterling.

Bath. Pevensey Pr. Staff. (C). 1987. text ed. 100.00 (0-907115-31-4, Pub. by Pevensey UK); pap. text ed. 40.00 (0-907115-32-2, Pub. by Pevensey UK) St Mut.

Bath. Edith Sitwell. 1988. 70.00 (0-317-38772-3, Pub. by Redcliffe Pr Ltd) St Mut.

Bath. Diane Von Furstenberg. LC 93-3626. 1993. 37.50 (0-679-42679-5) Random.

Bath. Edith Sitwell. LC 78-24153. 1980. reprint ed. text ed. 59.75 (0-313-20815-8, SIBT, Greenwood Pr) Greenwood.

Bath. Edith Sitwell. LC 78-14145. (Illus.). 1981. reprint ed. 29.00 (0-88355-818-1) Hyperion Conn.

Bath: History & Guide. Trevor Fawcett & Stephen Bird. (Illus.). 128p. 1994. pap. 16.00 (0-7509-0425-9) A Sutton Pub.

Bath: Profile of a City. Paul Hardy & William Lowndes. 1989. 30.00 (0-317-38775-8, Pub. by Redcliffe Pr Ltd) St Mut.

Ba'th & Syria, 1947-1982, the Evolution of Party & State: From the French Withdrawal to the Era of Hafiz Al-Asad. Robert W. Olson. (Leaders, Politics, & Social Change in the Islamic World Ser.: Vol. 1). 235p. 1982. 19.00 (0-940670-18-6) Kingston Pr.

Ba'th & the Creation of Modern Syria. David Roberts. LC 86-17745. 256p. 1987. text ed. 39.95 (0-312-06948-0) St Martin.

Bath Bramble. Dawn Poore. 1991. pap. 3.50 (0-8217-3547-0) Zebra.

Bath County Kentucky: 1820-1840 Censuses. Rowena Lawson. iv, 67p. (Orig.). 1986. pap. 10.00 (0-917890-88-4) Heritage Bk.

Bath for a Beagle. LC 63-17320. (J). 1989. pap. 1.95 (0-8167-0025-7) Troll Assocs.

Bath-Gymnasium Complex at Sardis. Fikret K. Yegul. (Archaeological Exploration of Sardis Monograph: No. 3). (Illus.). 232p. 1986. 45.00 (0-674-06345-7) HUP.

Bath-Intrigues: In Four Letters to a Friend in London. Eliza Haywood. LC 92-23641. (Augustan Reprints Ser.: No. 236 (1986)). reprint ed. 12.00 (0-404-70236-8, PR3506) AMS Pr.

Bath Mint. L. V. Grinsell. 1973. 5.00 (0-685-51513-3) S J Durst.

***Bath Parish Register (Births, Deaths, Marriages), 1827-1897 & St. Andrews Parish Vestry Book, 1732-1797.** William L. Hopkins. 130p. 1989. lib. bdg. 51.00 (0-8095-8283-X); pap. 24.00 (0-8095-8510-3) Borgo Pr.

Bath Scandal. Joan Smith. (Illus.). 224p. 1991. mass mkt. 3.99 (0-449-21948-8, Crest) Fawcett.

***Bath Scents.** Hayes. 1995. pap. 12.00 (0-207-18230-2) Basic.

Bath Tangle. Georgette Heyer. 1991. mass mkt. 3.99 (0-06-100204-6, Harp PBks) HarpC.

Bath Tangle. large type ed. Georgette Heyer. LC 91-20445. 516p. 1991. reprint ed. lib. bdg. 18.95 (1-56054-201-2) Thorndike Pr.

Bath Tangle. large type ed. Georgette Heyer. LC 91-20445. 516p. 1992. pap. 12.95 (1-56054-949-1) Thorndike Pr.

Ba'th Versus Ba'th: The Conflict Between Syria & Iraq, 1968-1989. Eberhard Kienle. 320p. 1991. text ed. 69.50 (1-85043-192-2, Pub. by I B Tauris UK) St Martin.

***Bathcare Market.** 125p. (Orig.). 1995. pap. 2,195.00 (0-7605-2039-9) Rector Pr.

Bathers. James I. Schempp. 1993. 2.50 (0-87129-216-5, B74) Dramatic Pub.

Bathers. Robert Steiner. LC 79-23084. 1980. pap. 3.95 (0-8112-0753-6, NDP495) New Directions.

Bathers. Lorenzo Thomas. LC 81-52033. 160p. (Orig.). 1981. pap. 5.95 (0-918408-18-0) Reed & Cannon.

Bathers. deluxe limited ed. Robert Steiner. LC 79-23084. 1980. 40.00 (0-8112-0752-8) New Directions.

***Bathers Pavilion Cookbook.** Victoria Alexander. 144p. 1995. 24.95 (0-89815-756-0) Ten Speed Pr.

Bathing Huts. Monique Lange. Tr. by Barbara Beaumont. LC 84-29287. 128p. 1986. 13.95 (0-7145-2821-8) M Boyars Pubs.

Bathroom. Jean-Philippe Toussaint. 1991. 19.95 (0-7145-2880-3) M Boyars Pubs.

Bathroom Humor: Passing Wind, Vol. 1. P. Blud Lambert. LC 88-81771. 200p. (Orig.). 1988. pap. 9.99 (0-317-91202-X) Fulcort Pr.

Bathroom Remodeling. Cy DeCosse Incorporated Staff. LC 93-14916. (Black & Decker Home Improvement Library). 128p. 1993. 14.95 (0-86573-728-2); pap. 12.95 (0-86573-729-0) Cy De Cosse.

Bathroom Remodeling. Leon A. Frechette. 1994. pap. text ed. 15.95 (0-07-015398-1) McGraw.

Bathroom Remodeling. Leon A. Frechette. 1993. pap. 15.95 (0-8306-4479-2) TAB Bks.

Bathroom Remodeling: A Do-It-Yourselfer's Guide. Paul Bianchina. (Illus.). 208p. 1988. 23.95 (0-8306-9001-8, 3001) TAB Bks.

Bathroom Remodeling Handbook. Ed. by Southern Living Staff. (Southern Living Home Improvement Ser.). 128p. 1992. pap. 8.99 (0-376-09023-5) Oxmoor Hse.

***Bathrooms.** Jerry Germer. LC 94-69651. 1995. pap. 12.95 (1-880029-31-6) Creative Homeowner.

Bathrooms. H. Kavet. 64p. 1993. 8.95 (0-88032-359-0) Ivory Tower Pub.

Bathrooms. Mike Lawrence. 1989. 7.98 (1-85368-004-4, Pub. by New Holland Pubs UK) St Mut.

***Bathrooms.** Time-Life Books Editors. (Home Repair & Improvement Ser.). (Illus.). 128p. 1994. write for info. (0-7835-3858-8) Time-Life.

Bathrooms: Planning & Remodeling. Sunset Editors. 112p. 1994. pap. 9.99 (0-376-01294-3) Sunset Menlo Pk.

***Bathrooms: Remodeling Projects.** David H. Jacobs, Jr. LC 94-30231. 1994. pap. text ed. 16.95 (0-07-032405-0) TAB Bks.

***Baths.** Chris C. Madden. LC 95-12991. 1996. write for info. (0-517-59938-4, Clarkson Potter) Crown Bks Yng Read.

Baths of Diocletian. Old Vicarage Publications Staff. 280p. (C). 1982. pap. text ed. 34.00 (0-685-22053-2, Pub. by Old Vicarage UK) St Mut.

Bathsheba. Torgny Lingren. Tr. by Tom Geddes. 250p. 1993. pap. 11.00 (0-00-271271-7, Pub. by HarpC UK) HarpC.

***Bathtime.** (Show Baby Ser.). 12p. (J). 1994. bds. 2.98 (0-86112-855-9) Brimax Bks.

Bathtime. Richardson. (Can You Find Ser.: No. 4). (J). 1994. 2.95 (0-671-89314-9, Litl Simon S&S) S&S Childrens.

***Bathtime.** Roffey. Date not set. pap. 2.99 (0-517-13360-1) Random.

Bathtime. Photos by Stephen Shott. LC 91-11121. (Look at Me Bks.). (Illus.). 12p. (J). (ps). 1991. bds. 4.95 (0-525-44754-7, DCB) Dutton Child Bks.

Bathtime. Maureen Roffey. LC 89-18413. (Illus.). 32p. (J). (ps). 1990. reprint ed. pap. 4.95 (0-689-70808-4, Aladdin Paperbacks) S&S Childrens.

Bathtub Stopper: Tribute to Richard Nixon Former President: Genealogy. B. Stop. (Illus.). 50p. 1994. 25.00 (1-56611-102-1); pap. 15.00 (1-56611-103-X) Jonas.

Bathtubs, Slides, Roller Coaster Rails: Simple Machines That Are Really Inclined Planes. Christopher Lampton. (Gateway Simple Machines Ser.). (Illus.). 32p. (J). (gr. 2-4). 1991. lib. bdg. 13.40 (1-878841-23-8); pap. 4.95 (1-878841-44-0) Millbrook Pr.

***Bathudi & Sounti Tribes: A Bio-Anthropological Profile.** Swaran Singh. (C). 1994. 24.00 (81-212-0466-6, Pub. by Gian Publng Hse II) S Asia.

Bathwater Gang. Jerry Spinelli. (J). (gr. 4-7). 1990. 10.95 (0-316-80720-6) Little.

Bathwater Gang. Jerry Spinelli. (Springboard Bks.). (Illus.). 64p. (J). (gr. 2-4). 1992. mass mkt. 3.95 (0-316-80779-6) Little.

Bathwater Gang Gets down to Business. Jerry Spinelli. (J). (ps-3). 1992. 12.95 (0-316-80808-3) Little.

Bathyal & Abyssal Myodocopid Ostracoda of the Bay of Biscay & Vicinity. Louis S. Kornicker. LC 88-15579. (Smithsonian Contributions to Zoology Ser.: No. 467). 138p. reprint ed. pap. 39.40 (0-8357-6632-2, 2035278) Bks Demand.

Bathymetric Navigation & Charting. Phillip M. Cohen. LC 79-6107. (Navies & Men Ser.). (Illus.). 1980. reprint ed. lib. bdg. 17.95 (0-405-13036-8) Ayer.

Bathymetrical Survey of the Scottish Fresh Water Lochs, Vol. 1. John Murray & Laurence Pullar. Ed. by Frank N. Egerton, 3rd. LC 77-74243. (History of Ecology Ser.). (Illus.). 1978. reprint ed. lib. bdg. 71.95 (0-405-10412-X) Ayer.

Batik. Joy Campbell. (Start a Craft Ser.). 1994. 7.98 (0-7858-0063-8) Bk Sales Inc.

Batik: Fabled Cloth of Java. Inger M. Elliott. (Illus.). 240p. 1984. 75.00 (0-517-55155-1, C P Pubs) Crown Pub Group.

Batik & Tie-Dye. Susie O'Reilly. LC 92-43264. (Arts & Crafts Ser.). 32p. (J). (gr. 4-6). 1993. 14.95 (1-56847-064-9) Thomson Lrning.

Batik & Tie-Dye. Susie O'Reilly. (Arts & Crafts Ser.). (Illus.). 32p. (J). (gr. 4-6). 1995. reprint ed. pap. 5.95 (1-56847-300-1) Thomson Lrning.

Batik & Tie Dye Techniques. rev. ed. Nancy Belfer. Orig. Title: Designing in Batik & Tie Dye. (Illus.). 160p. 1992. reprint ed. pap. 7.95 (0-486-27131-5) Dover.

Batik, Tie Dyeing, Stenciling, Silk Screen, Block Printing: The Hand Decoration of Fabrics. Francis J. Kafka. (Illus.). 198p. 1973. reprint ed. 7.95 (0-486-21401-X) Dover.

***Batilo: Estudios Sobre la Evolucion Estilistica de Melendez Valdes.** John H. Polt. LC 87-7056. (University of California Publications in Entomology: No. 119). 335p. (SPA.). 1987. pap. 95.50 (0-7837-8421-X, 2049223) Bks Demand.

Batisseurs de Ponts. Rudyard Kipling. 240p. (FRE.). 1976. pap. 10.95 (0-7859-2379-9, 2070368599) Fr & Eur.

Batisseurs d'Empire. 4th ed. Boris Vian. (FRE.). 1989. pap. 16.95 (0-7859-1550-8, 2851810235) Fr & Eur.

Batman. Craig S. Gardner. 224p. (Orig.). 1989. mass mkt. 4.95 (0-446-35487-2) Warner Bks.

Batman: A Death in the Family. Jim Starlin. Ed. by Dennis O'Neil. 144p. 1988. pap. 4.95 (0-930289-44-7) DC Comics.

Batman: A Lonely Place of Dying. Marv Wolfman. Ed. by K. C. Carlson. (Illus.). 128p. 1990. pap. 4.95 (0-930289-63-3) DC Comics.

Batman: Almost Got 'Em. (Golden Story Book 'n' Tape Ser.). (Illus.). 32p. (J). (ps-3). Date not set. audio write for info. (0-307-14376-7, 14376) Western Pub.

Batman: Arkham Asylum. Grant Morrison. Ed. by Karen Berger. 128p. 1990. pap. 14.95 (0-930289-56-0) DC Comics.

Batman: Birth of the Demon. Dennis O'Neil. Ed. by Archie Goodwin. 112p. 1993. pap. 12.95 (1-56389-081-X) DC Comics.

Batman: Blind Justice. Sam Hamm. Ed. by Michael Hill. (Illus.). 160p. 1991. pap. 7.50 (1-56389-047-X) DC Comics.

***Batman: Bloodstorm.** D. Moench. Ed. by Denny O'Neil. (Illus.). 96p. Date not set. pap. 12.95 (1-56389-185-9) DC Comics.

***Batman: Bloodstorm.** D. Moench. Ed. by Denny O'Neil. (Illus.). 96p. 1994. 24.95 (1-56389-177-8) DC Comics.

***Batman: Castle of the Bat.** J. C. Harris. Ed. by D. O'Neil. (Illus.). 64p. 1994. pap. 5.95 (1-56389-175-1) DC Comics.

Batman: Collected Legends of the Dark Knight. Ed. by B. Kahan. (Illus.). 160p. (YA). 1994. pap. 12.95 (1-56389-147-6) DC Comics.

Batman: Dark Joker - the Wild. D. Moench. Ed. by D. O'Neil. (Illus.). 96p. (Orig.). 1993. 24.95 (1-56389-111-5) DC Comics.

Batman: Dark Joker - the Wild. D. Moench. Ed. by D. O'Neil. (Illus.). 96p. (Orig.). 1994. pap. 9.95 (1-56389-140-9) DC Comics.

Batman: Exploring the World of Bats. Pringle. (J). 1993. pap. 2.95 (0-590-46128-1) Scholastic Inc.

Batman: Exploring the World of Bats. Laurence Pringle. LC 90-8679. (Illus.). 48p. (J). (gr. 4-6). 1991. text ed. 14.95 (0-684-19232-2, C Scribner Sons Young) S&S Childrens.

***Batman: Faces.** M. Wagner. Ed. by B. Kahan. (Illus.). 96p. 1995. pap. 9.95 (1-56389-126-3) DC Comics.

***Batman: Featuring Two-Face & the Riddler.** Ed. by B. Kahan. (Illus.). 192p. 1995. pap. 12.95 (1-56389-198-0) DC Comics.

***Batman: Forever Movie Adaptation.** D. O'Neil. Ed. by Peterson. (Illus.). 64p. 1995. pap. 5.95 (1-56389-199-9) DC Comics.

Batman: Full Circle. Mike Barr. Ed. by Dennis O'Neil. 64p. 1991. pap. 5.95 (0-930289-98-6) DC Comics.

***Batman: Ghosts, Legend of the Dark Knight Halloween Special.** J. Loeb. Ed. by Goodwin. (Illus.). 48p. 1995. pap. write for info. (1-56389-234-0) DC Comics.

Batman: Gotham by Gaslight. Brian Augustyn. Ed. by Mark Waid. 48p. 1989. pap. 3.95 (0-930289-67-6) DC Comics.

Batman: Holy Terror. Alan Brennert. Ed. by Dennis O'Neil. 48p. 1991. pap. 4.95 (1-56389-018-6) DC Comics.

Batman: Knightfall. Dennis Oneil. 1994. 19.95 (0-553-09673-7) Bantam.

Batman: Knightfall & Beyond. Alan Grant. (J). (gr. 4-7). 1994. mass mkt. 3.99 (0-553-48187-8) Bantam.

An Asterisk (*) at the beginning of an entry indicates that the title is appearing in BIP for the first time.

627

*Batman: KnightsEnd. Moench et al. Ed. by Kahan. (Illus.). 320p. 1995. pap. 14.95 (1-56389-191-3) DC Comics.

Batman: Mask of the Phantasm: M-TV. Andrew Helfer. (J). (gr. 4-7). 1994. pap. 3.99 (0-553-48174-6, Skylark) Bantam.

Batman: Master of the Future. Brian Augustyn. Ed. by Dennis O'Neil. 64p. 1991. pap. 5.95 (1-56389-015-1) DC Comics.

*Batman: Mitefall. A. Grant. Ed. by A. Goodwin. (Illus.). 48p. 1995. pap. 4.95 (1-56389-176-X) DC Comics.

Batman: Night Cries. A. Goodwin & S. Hampton. Ed. by Archie Goodwin. 96p. 1992. pap. 12.95 (1-56389-066-6) DC Comics.

Batman: Plants of Peril. (Golden Story Book 'n' Tape Ser.). (Illus.). 32p. (J). (ps-3). Date not set. write for info. (0-307-14375-9, 14375) Western Pub.

Batman: Prey. Doug Moench. Ed. by Bob Kahan. 136p. 1992. pap. 12.95 (0-930289-68-4) DC Comics.

Batman: Prey. Doug Moench et al. 136p. 1993. 12.99 (0-446-39521-8) Warner Bks.

*Batman: Scar of the Bat. Barretto. Ed. by O'Neil. (Illus.). 48p. Date not set. pap. write for info. (1-56389-231-6) DC Comics.

Batman: Shaman. Dennis O'Neil. Ed. by Bob Kahan. 136p. 1992. pap. 12.95 (1-56389-083-6) DC Comics.

Batman: Shaman. Dennis O'Neil et al. 136p. 1993. 12.99 (0-446-39522-6) Warner Bks.

Batman: Son of the Demon. Mike Barr. Ed. by Dick Giordano. (Illus.). 80p. 1987. pap. 9.95 (0-930289-25-0) DC Comics.

Batman: Sword of Azrael. Dennis O'Neil. Ed. by Bob Kahan. (Illus.). 112p. 1993. pap. 9.95 (1-56389-100-X) DC Comics.

Batman: Tales of the Demon. Dennis O'Neil. Ed. by Paul Levitz et al. (Illus.). 208p. (YA). 1991. pap. 17.95 (0-930289-94-3) DC Comics.

Batman: Tales of the Demon. Frwd. by Sam Hamm. (Illus.). 208p. 1992. reprint ed. pap. 14.99 (0-446-39364-9) Warner Bks.

Batman: Ten Nights of the Beast. J. Starlin. Ed. by B. Kahan. (Illus.). 96p. 1994. pap. 5.95 (1-56389-155-7) DC Comics.

Batman: The Animated Series Pop-up Playbook. DC Comics Staff. (Illus.). (J). (ps-3). 1994. 18.95 (0-316-17788-1) Little.

Batman: The Blue, the Grey & the Bat. Elliot S. Maggin. Ed. by Dennis O'Neil. 64p. 1992. pap. 5.95 (0-930289-75-7) DC Comics.

Batman: The Collected Adventures, Vol. 1. Kelly Puckett & Pasko. Ed. by Bob Kahan. (Illus.). 144p. (YA). 1993. pap. 5.95 (1-56389-098-4) DC Comics.

Batman: The Collected Adventures, Vol. 2. Puckett. Ed. by B. Kahan. (Illus.). 144p. 1994. pap. 5.95 (1-56389-124-7) DC Comics.

Batman: The Cult. Jim Starlin. Ed. by Dan Thorsland & Dennis O'Neil. (Illus.). 208p. 1991. pap. 14.95 (0-930289-85-4) DC Comics.

Batman: The Dailies, 1943-46. deluxe ed. Bob Kane et al. Ed. by Dave Schreiner. (Illus.). 550p. 1991. boxed 60.00 (0-87816-149-X) Kitchen Sink.

Batman: The Dark Knight Returns. Frank Miller et al. 1986. pap. 13.95 (0-446-38505-0) Warner Bks.

Batman: The Dark Night Returns. Frank Miller. Ed. by D. O'Neil & D. Giordano. 200p. 1986. pap. 12.95 (0-930289-13-7) DC Comics.

Batman: The House of Horrors. Andrew Helfer. (J). (ps-3). 1993. pap. 3.50 (0-307-11471-6, Golden Pr) Western Pub.

Batman: The Killing Joke. Alan Moore. Ed. by Dennis O'Neil. 48p. 1988. pap. 3.95 (0-930289-45-5) DC Comics.

*Batman: The Last Angel. Eric Lusterbader. Ed. by D. O'Neil. 96p. 1994. pap. 12.95 (1-56389-156-5) DC Comics.

*Batman: The Last Arkham. Grant. Ed. by Kahan. (Illus.). 112p. 1995. pap. 12.95 (1-56389-190-5) DC Comics.

Batman: The Purrfect Crime. Andrew Helfer. (Golden Look-Look Bks.). (Illus.). (J). (ps-3). 1991. pap. write for info. (0-307-12621-8, Golden Pr) Western Pub.

*Batman: The Riddle Factory. M. Wagner. Ed. by O'Neil. (Illus.). 48p. Date not set. pap. 4.95 (1-56389-196-4) DC Comics.

Batman: The Sunday Classics, 1943-46. Bob Kane et al. Ed. by Dave Schreiner. LC 91-8791. (Illus.). 208p. 1992. pap. 19.95 (0-685-58966-8); bds., boxed 75.00 (0-87816-163-5) Kitchen Sink.

*Batman: The Ultimate Evil. Andrew Vachss. 1995. 19.95 (0-446-51912-X, Aspect) Warner Bks.

*Batman: The Ultimate Evil. Andrew Vachss. 1996. mass mkt. write for info. (0-446-60336-8, Aspect) Warner Bks.

*Batman: Two-Face - Crime & Punishment. M. DeMatteis. Ed. by S. Peterson. (Illus.). 48p. 1995. pap. 4.95 (1-56389-197-2) DC Comics.

Batman: Venom. Dennis O'Neil. Ed. by Bob Kahan. (Illus.). 136p. (YA). 1993. pap. 9.95 (1-56389-101-8) DC Comics.

Batman: Year One. Frank Miller. Ed. by Richard Bruning. 208p. 1988. pap. 9.95 (0-930289-33-1) DC Comics.

Batman: Year One. Frank Miller & David Mazzucchelli. 1988. pap. 10.95 (0-446-38923-4) Warner Bks.

Batman: Year Two. Mike Barr. Ed. by Richard Bruning. 104p. 1990. pap. 9.95 (0-930289-43-9) DC Comics.

Batman: Year Two. Mike W. Barr. 1990. pap. 9.95 (0-446-39191-3) Warner Bks.

Batman Vol. 2: The Dark Knight Archives, Vol. 1. Ed. by M. Hill & B. Kahan. 288p. 1992. 39.95 (1-56389-050-X) DC Comics.

*Batman Vol. 2: The Dark Knight Archives, Vol. 2. Ed. by B. Kahan. (Illus.). 224p. 1995. 59.95 (1-56389-183-2) DC Comics.

Batman - Dracula: Red Rain. Doug Moench. Ed. by Dennis O'Neil. 96p. 1992. pap. 9.95 (1-56389-036-4) DC Comics.

Batman - Green Arrow: The Poison Tomorrow. Dennis O'Neil. Ed. by Archie Goodwin. 64p. 1992. pap. 5.95 (0-930289-15-3) DC Comics.

Batman - Judge Dredd: Judgement on Gotham. John Wagner & Alan Grant. Ed. by Dennis O'Neil. (Illus.). 64p. 1991. pap. 5.95 (1-56389-022-4) DC Comics.

Batman - Judge Dredd: Vendetta in Gotham. Wagner & Grant. Ed. by Dennis O'Neil. (Illus.). 48p. (YA). 1993. pap. 4.95 (1-56389-121-2) DC Comics.

*Batman - Judge Dredd III: The Ultimate Riddle. Grant & Wagner. Ed. by O'Neil. (Illus.). 48p. 1995. pap. 4.95 (1-56389-206-5) DC Comics.

Batman - Punisher: Lake of Fire. D. O'Neil. Ed. by A. Goodwin. (Illus.). 48p. 1994. pap. 4.95 (1-56389-161-1) DC Comics.

Batman - Spawn: War Devil. D. Moench et al. Ed. by D. O'Neil. (Illus.). 48p. 1994. pap. 4.95 (1-56389-144-1) DC Comics.

*Batman Adventures: Mad Love. Dini. Ed. by S. Peterson. (Illus.). 64p. 1995. pap. 4.95 (1-56389-244-8) DC Comics.

Batman & Dracula: Red Rain. Doug Moench et al. 96p. 1992. pap. 9.99 (0-446-39465-3) Warner Bks.

Batman & Houdini: The Devil's Workshop. H. Chaykin & J. F. Moore. Ed. by Dennis O'Neil. (Illus.). 64p. (YA). 1993. pap. 5.95 (1-56389-113-1) DC Comics.

Batman & Me. Bob Kane. 1989. 40.00 (1-56060-016-0); pap. 14.95 (1-56060-017-9) Eclipse Bks.

Batman & the Doomsday Prophecy. Richard Wenk. (Super Powers Ser.: No. 4). (Illus.). (J). (gr. 3-6). 1989. pap. 2.99 (0-671-68312-8, Archway) PB.

*Batman & the Missing Penguins: Golden Super-Duper Shape Book. Colon. (J). 1995. pap. text ed. 4.25 (0-307-10366-8, Golden Pr) Western Pub.

*Batman & the Ninja. Lovitt. (J). 1995. pap. text ed. 2.50 (0-307-12837-7, Golden Pr) Western Pub.

Batman Archives, Vol. 1. Ed. by Mike Gold. 306p. 1990. 39.95 (0-930289-60-9) DC Comics.

Batman Archives, Vol. 2. Bob Kane et al. Ed. by Mike Gold. (Illus.). 288p. (YA). 1991. 49.95 (1-56389-000-3) DC Comics.

Batman Archives, Vol. 3. Bob Kane & Bill Finger. Ed. by Bob Kahan. (Illus.). 224p. (YA). 1994. 39.95 (1-56389-099-2) DC Comics.

Batman: Arkham Asylum. Grant Morrison & David McKeon. 1990. pap. 14.95 (0-446-39189-1) Warner Bks.

Batman Forever. Peter David. 256p. 1995. mass mkt. 5.99 (0-446-60217-5, Warner Vision) Warner Bks.

*Batman Forever. Alan Grant. (Illus.). (J). (gr. 3-7). 1995. pap. 2.95 (0-316-32418-3) Little.

Batman Forever. deluxe ed. (Golden Sound Story Bks.). (Illus.). 24p. (J). (ps up). 1992. write for info. (0-307-74023-4, 64023, Golden Pr) Western Pub.

*Batman Forever Golden Look-Look Book. Helfner. (J). 1995. pap. text ed. 2.50 (0-307-12889-X, Golden Pr) Western Pub.

Batman Gothic. Grant Morrison & Klaus Janson. (Illus.). (Orig.). 1992. pap. 12.99 (0-446-39428-9) Warner Bks.

Batman in Detective Comics: The First Twenty-Five Years of Action Comics Cover. 1993. pap. 10.95 (1-55859-643-7) Abbeville Pr.

Batman: Knightfall, Pt. 1: Broken Bat. D. Moench & C. Dixon. Ed. by Bob Kahan. (Illus.). 288p. (YA). 1993. pap. 12.95 (1-56389-142-5) DC Comics.

Batman: Knightfall, Pt. 2: Who Rules the Night. D. Moench & C. Dixon. Ed. by Bob Kahan. (Illus.). 296p. (YA). 1993. pap. 12.95 (1-56389-148-4) DC Comics.

Batman Returns. Craig S. Gardner. 256p. (Orig.). 1992. mass mkt. 4.99 (0-446-36303-0) Warner Bks.

Batman Returns. Michael Teitelbaum. (Golden Look Look Book Ser.). (Illus.). 24p. (J). (ps-3). 1992. pap. write for info. (0-307-12687-0, 12687, Golden Pr) Western Pub.

Batman Returns: The Movie Storybook. Justine Korman & Ron Fontes. (Golden Favorites Ser.). (Illus.). 48p. (J). (ps-3). 1992. write for info. (0-307-15954-X, 15954, Golden Pr) Western Pub.

Batman Returns: You Write the Script. (J). (ps-3). 1992. pap. 2.95 (0-307-02944-1, Golden Pr) Western Pub.

Batman Role-Playing Game. Jack Barker. 1989. pap. 9.95 (0-923763-08-2) Mayfair Games.

Batman Role-Playing Sourcebook. Mike Stackpole. 1989. pap. 10.00 (0-912771-31-3) Mayfair Games.

Batman, the Dailies, Vol 1: 1943-1944. Bob Kane. Ed. by Peter Poplaski. LC 90-5156. (Batman Ser.). (Illus.). 192p. 1990. pap. 12.95 (0-87816-119-8) Kitchen Sink.

Batman, the Dailies, Vol. 2: 1944-1945. Bob Kane. Ed. by Peter Poplaski. (Batman Ser.). (Illus.). 192p. 1990. pap. 12.95 (0-87816-130-9) Kitchen Sink.

*Batman TV. Golden Western Staff. (J). Date not set. pap. 1.59 (0-307-08238-5, Golden Pr); pap. 1.59 (0-307-08324-1, Golden Pr) Western Pub.

Batman Versus Predator: The Collected Edition. Dave Gibbons. Ed. by Bob Kahan. (Illus.). 128p. (YA). 1992. pap. 5.95 (1-56389-092-5) DC Comics.

Batman, Vol. 3: 1945-1946. Bob Kane. Ed. by Peter Poplaski. LC 90-5156. (Illus.). 192p. 1991. pap. 12.95 (0-87816-147-3) Kitchen Sink.

Batman Vppon Bartholome. Ed. by Jurgen Schafer. (Anglistica & Americana Ser.: No. 161). (Illus.). 441p. 1976. reprint ed. 258.70 (3-487-05919-3, Pub. by Georg Olms GW) Lubrecht & Cramer.

*Batman vs. Predator II: Bloodmatch. Gibbons. Ed. by Kahan. (Illus.). 144p. 1995. pap. write for info. (1-56389-221-9) DC Comics.

Batmania. James Van Hise. 1989. pap. 14.95 (1-55698-252-6) Movie Pubs Servs.

*Batmania Three. Van. 1995. pap. text ed. 16.95 (1-55698-382-4) Movie Pubs Servs.

Batmania Two. James Van Hise. 1992. pap. 14.95 (1-55698-315-8) Movie Pubs Servs.

Baton. Roger L. Lee. LC 59-17691. (Illus.). 98p. 1949. pap. 4.25 (0-913932-14-0) Boosey & Hawkes.

Baton & the Jackboot see Two Worlds of Music

Baton Rouge. David K. Gleason. LC 91-12477. (Illus.). 160p. 1991. 29.95 (0-8071-1715-3) La State U Pr.

Baton Rouge City Court Facilities Program, Baton Rouge, Louisiana. Don Hardenbergh et al. 205p. 1988. 13.00 (0-685-24110-6, SERO-041) Natl Ctr St Courts.

Baton Rouge Hilton Tower: An All Precast Prestressed Systems Building. Prestressed Concrete Institute Staff. (PCI Journal Reprints Ser.). 16p. 1976. pap. 6.00 (0-318-19851-7, JR185) P-PCI.

Baton Twirling: A Complete Illustrated Guide. Doris Wheelus. (Illus.). 144p. (J). (gr. 5 up). 1975. lib. bdg. 13. 95 (0-87460-310-2); pap. 9.95 (0-87460-311-0) Lion Bks.

Batons, Chiffres et Lettres. Raymond Queneau. (Idees Ser.). 384p. (FRE.). 1965. 9.95 (2-07-035070-3) Schoenhof.

Batouala. Rene Maran. LC 87-23642. (African Writers Ser.). (Orig.). 1987. pap. 8.95 (0-435-90135-4) Heinemann.

Batouala. Rene Maran. (Orig.). 1989. reprint ed. lib. bdg. 25.95 (0-89966-640-X) Buccaneer Bks.

Batrachosauria (Anthrosauria) A. L. Panchen. (Encyclopedia of Paleoherpetology Ser.: Pt. 5-A). (Illus.). 1970. pap. text ed. 46.80 (3-437-30111-X) Lubrecht & Cramer.

Batrachosauria (Anthrosauria), Gephyrostegida-Chronlosuchide. R. L. Carroll et al. (Encyclopedia of Paleoherpetology Ser.: Pt. 5-B). (Illus.). 81p. 1972. text ed. 55.20 (3-437-30136-5) Lubrecht & Cramer.

Bats. (Zoobooks Ser.). (J). 1991. lib. bdg. 14.95 (0-88682-337-4) Creative Ed.

*Bats! Melvin Berger. (Ranger Rick Science Spectacular Ser.). 16p. (J). (gr. 2-4). 1996. pap. text ed. 14.95 (1-56784-222-4) Newbridge Comms.

Bats. M. Brock Fenton. (Illus.). 224p. 1992. 45.00 (0-8160-2679-3) Facts on File.

Bats. Michael George. (Nature Books Ser.). 32p. (J). (gr. 2-6). 1991. lib. bdg. 22.79 (0-89565-712-0) Childs World.

Bats. Susan H. Gray. LC 94-10468. (New True Book Ser.). (Illus.). 48p. (J). (gr. k-4). 1994. lib. bdg. 12.90 (0-516-01064-6); pap. 4.95 (0-516-41064-4) Childrens.

Bats. Sylvia A. Johnson. LC 85-15999. (Natural Science Bks.). (Illus.). 48p. (J). (gr. 4 up). 1985. lib. bdg. 19.95 (0-8225-1461-3, Lerner Publctns); pap. 5.95 (0-8225-9500-1, Lerner Publctns) Lerner Group.

Bats. William W. Johnstone. 352p. 1993. mass mkt. 4.50 (0-8217-4190-X) Zebra.

Bats. Cindy Kendall. LC 93-3114. (Dial Nature Notebook Pop-Ups Ser.). (Illus.). 14p. (J). (gr. k up). 1995. pap. 4.95 (0-8037-1272-3) Dial Bks Young.

Bats. Betsy Maestro. LC 93-26153. (Illus.). (J). (gr. 3 up). 1994. 14.95 (0-590-46150-8) Scholastic Inc.

Bats. Richard Mandell. LC 80-83027. 170p. (Orig.). 1981. pap. 4.50 (0-9605008-0-4) Hermes Hse.

Bats. Lynn M. Stone. LC 93-1535. (J). 1993. write for info. (0-86593-293-X) Rourke Corp.

Bats. Wildlife Education, Ltd. Staff. (Zoobooks Ser.). (Illus.). 20p. (J). 1989. 2.75 (0-937934-59-3) Wildlife Educ.

Bats: A Community Perspective. James S. Findley. (Cambridge Studies in Ecology). (Illus.). 200p. (C). 1993. 47.95 (0-521-38054-5) Cambridge U Pr.

*Bats: A Community Perspective. James S. Findley. (Cambridge Studies in Ecology Ser.). (Illus.). 178p. (C). 1995. pap. 19.95 (0-521-47956-8) Cambridge U Pr.

Bats: A Nature-Fact Book. D. J. Arneson. (Nature-Fact Bks.). (Illus.). 32p. (J). 1992. pap. 2.50 (1-56156-147-9) Kidsbks.

Bats! Creatures of the Night. Joyce Milton. LC 92-43198. (All Aboard Reading Ser.). (Illus.). 48p. (J). (ps-1). 1993. 7.99 (0-448-40194-0, G&D); pap. 3.50 (0-448-40193-2, G&D) Putnam Pub Group.

Bats: Mysterious Flyers of the Night. Dee Stuart. LC 93-34304. (J). (gr. 2-5). 1994. 19.95 (0-87614-814-3, Carolrhoda) Lerner Group.

Bats: Mysterious Flyers of the Night. Dee Stuart. (J). (gr. 4-7). 1994. pap. 6.95 (0-87614-631-0, Carolrhoda) Lerner Group.

Bats: Swift Shadows of the Twilight. Ann Cooper. (Wonder Ser.). (Illus.). 64p. (J). (gr. 3-6). 1993. pap. text ed. 7.95 (1-879373-52-1) R Rinehart.

*Bats about Baseball. Jean Little & Claire Mckay. (Illus.). 32p. (J). (ps-3). 1995. 11.99 (0-670-85270-8) Viking Child Bks.

Bats & Other Creatures of the Night. Joyce Milton. (Picturebacks Ser.). (Illus.). 32p. (Orig.). (J). (ps-2). 1994. pap. 2.50 (0-679-86213-7) Random Bks Yng Read.

*Bats, Bugs, & Biodiversity: Adventures in the Amazonian Rain Forest. Susan Goodman. LC 94-35029. (J). (gr. 2-5). 1995. write for info. (0-689-31943-6, Atheneum S&S) S&S Trade.

Bats, Butterflies, & Bugs, Vol. 1. S. Adams Sullivan. (J). (ps-3). 1990. 14.95 (0-316-82185-3, Joy St Bks) Little.

Bats Fly up for Inspector Ghote. H. R. Keating. (Inspector Ghote Mystery). 190p. 1984. pap. 5.95 (0-89733-120-6) Academy Chi Pubs.

Bats in the Basement. Richard Booth. LC 91-51223. (Orig.). 1992. pap. 6.00 (0-88734-249-3) Players Pr.

Bats in the Belfry. Hasler. Date not set. 12.95 (1-55774-025-9) Modan-Adama Bks.

***Bats in the Belfry, by Design. Titus Stauffer. Ed. by John Fremont. LC 95-60010. 478p. (Orig.). 1995. pap. 14.95 (0-9644835-0-5) FreeVoice Pub.**

Soon, we'll spend billions of dollars on genetic engineering. What will we do first: A) build an amusement park, or, B) build weapons of mass destruction? Precedent: Manhattan Project. What gets our money's worth? Did we spend billions on the atom to make an AMUSEMENT PARK? No, we wanted some BANG FOR THE BUCK. Human nature hasn't changed; we still want BANG FOR THE BUCK. Speaking of the Atomic Age...fifty years later, we learn that the government injected plutonium into unknowing, innocent Americans. What will they do secretly, next? This book provides some possible answers. Watch, as creativity becomes monstrosity. Watch, as the desire to save American soldiers turns into genocide. See the dark side of human nature, & how one man finally rebels against the beast within. BATS IN THE BELFRY, BY DESIGN isn't for those who say, "My Country, Right or Wrong" & don't want their thinking challenged. It is for those who care about ideas, freedom & a future for the human race - as well as a few good chuckles & some chills & thrills. To order: Free Voice Publishing, P.O. Box 692168, Houston, TX 77269-2168. Phone: 713-251-5226. ***Publisher Provided Annotation.***

Bats in the Bellfry. Angela Randazzo. 1975. 4.95 (0-87129-360-9, B12) Dramatic Pub.

*Bats of America. fac. ed. Roger W. Barbour & Wayne H. Davis. LC 73-80086. (Illus.). 311p. 1994. pap. 88.70 (0-7837-7587-3, 2047340) Bks Demand.

*Bats of British Columbia. D. W. Nagorsen & R. Mark Brigham. LC 94-153386. (Mammals of British Columbia Ser.: Vol. 1). 164p. 1994. pap. 15.95 (0-7748-0482-3) U BC Pr.

Bats of Egypt. Mazin B. Qumsiyeh. (Special Publications: No. 23). (Illus.). 102p. 1985. 40.00 (0-89672-138-8); pap. 18.00 (0-89672-137-X) Tex Tech Univ Pr.

Bats of Jalisco, Mexico. Larry C. Watkins et al. (Special Publications: No. 1). (Illus.). 44p. (Orig.). 1972. pap. 2.00 (0-89672-026-8) Tex Tech Univ Pr.

Bats of Portugal: Zoogeography & Systematics. Jorge M. Palmeirim. (Miscellaneous Publications: No. 82). (Illus.). 53p. (C). 1990. pap. text ed. 3.25 (0-89338-034-2) U of KS Mus Nat Hist.

Bats of San Salvador Island, Bahamas. Kenneth W. Andersen. (Occasional Paper - 1990: No. 1). (Illus.). 4p. (Orig.). (C). 1990. pap. text ed. 2.00 (0-935909-33-8) Bahamian.

Bats of Texas. David J. Schmidly. LC 90-39108. (W. L. Moody, Jr. Natural History Ser.: No. 11). (Illus.). 224p. 1991. 34.50 (0-89096-403-3); pap. 19.95 (0-89096-450-5) Tex A&M Univ Pr.

Bats of the British Isles. A. A. Wardhaugh. 1989. pap. 25. 00 (0-85263-856-6, Pub. by Shire UK) St Mut.

Bats of the World. Gery L. Graham. 1994. pap. 4.95 (0-307-24080-0, Golden Pr) Western Pub.

Bats on the Bedstead. Norma T. Johnson. 128p. (J). 1988. pap. 2.95 (0-380-70540-0, Camelot) Avon.

Bats Out of Hell. Barry Hannah. LC 93-43692. 400p. 1994. pap. 12.00 (0-8021-3386-X) Grove-Atltic.

Bats Out of Hell. Barry Hannah. LC 92-36629. 320p. 1993. 22.95 (0-395-48883-4) HM.

Bat's Surprise. Gina K. Erickson. (J). (ps-3). 1993. pap. 3.95 (0-8120-1735-8) Barron.

Batsford Book of Chess. Bob Wade. (Illus.). 160p. 1992. 24. 95 (0-7134-6947-1, Pub. by Batsford UK) Trafalgar.

Batsford Book of Curtains & Window Treatments. Angela Fishburn. (Illus.). 120p. 1991. pap. 24.95 (0-7134-6325-2, Pub. by Batsford UK) Trafalgar.

Batsford Book of Sewing. Batsford Staff. (Illus.). 184p. 1990. pap. 22.95 (0-7134-6320-1, Pub. by Batsford UK) Trafalgar.

Batsford Chess Endings. Tisdall W. Speelman. 400p. 1993. pap. 30.00 (0-8050-2947-8) H Holt & Co.

Batsford Chess Openings, No. 2. Gary Kasparov. 416p. 1989. pap. 22.50 (0-02-033991-7, Collier S&S) S&S Trade.

Batsford Chess Openings II. Kasparov. 1994. pap. 30.00 (0-8050-3409-9) H Holt & Co.

Batsford Lace Pattern Pack, Bucks Point. Pamela Nottingham. (Illus.). 1987. 16.95 (0-7134-5451-2) Robin & Russ.

Batsford Second Chess Course. Michael Basman. (Illus.). 80p. 1993. 22.95 (0-7134-6475-5, Pub. by Batsford UK) Trafalgar.

Batson vs. Kentucky's Impact on the Use of Peremptory Challenges in North Carolina Courts. Thomas H. Thornburg. (Special Ser.: No. 7). 39p. (Orig.). (C). 1992. pap. text ed. 9.00 (1-56011-203-4) Institute Government.

Battalion at War: Singapore 1942. Michael Moore. (C). 1989. 59.00 (0-947893-11-3) St Mut.

Battalion Chief-Fire Department. Jack Rudman. (Career Examination Ser.: C-81). 1994. pap. 34.95 (0-8373-0081-9) Nat Learn.

An Asterisk (*) at the beginning of an entry indicates that the title is appearing in BIP for the first time.

***Battalion Level Command and Control at the National Training Center.** Jonathan G. Grossman. LC 94-23264. 1994. write for info. (*0-8330-1580-X*, MR496A) Rand Corp.

***Battalion Reconnaissance Operations at the National Training Center.** Martin Goldsmith. LC 95-16305. 1995. write for info. (*0-8330-1645-8*) Rand Corp.

Battelle Story: Science in the Service of Mankind. George A. Boehm et al. LC 88-3456. (Illus.). 208p. 1986. 10.00 (*0-935470-30-1*) Battelle.

Battenberg & Other Tape Laces: Techniques, Stitches & Designs. abr. ed. Butterick Publishing Co., Staff. (Illus.). 112p. 1988. reprint ed. pap. 6.95 (*0-486-25643-X*) Dover.

Battenberg & Point Lace Book. 2nd ed. Ed. by Nellie C. Brown et al. 64p. 1987. pap. 6.00 (*0-916896-26-9*) Lacis Pubns.

Battenkill. John Merwin. (Illus.). 160p. 1993. 22.95 (*1-55821-208-6*) Lyons & Burford.

Batter My Heart. Gracia F. Ellwood. LC 88-64134. (Orig.). 1988. pap. 3.00 (*0-87574-282-3*) Pendle Hill.

Batter UP! Neil Johnson. 32p. (J). 1992. pap. 3.95 (*0-590-42730-X*) Scholastic Inc.

Batter Up. Jackson Scholz. LC 92-32796. 256p. (J). (gr. 5 up). 1993. 14.00 (*0-688-12485-2*) Morrow Jr Bks.

Batter Up. Jackson Scholz. LC 92-32796. 256p. (J). (gr. 6 up). 1993. pap. 4.95 (*0-688-12158-6*, Pub. by Beech Tree Bks) Morrow.

Batter Up: Humorous Quotes on Baseball. Vern McLellan. 78p. (Orig.). 1993. pap. 7.95 (*1-56245-067-0*) Great Quotations.

Battered: The Abuse of Children. Margaret Jay & Sally Doganis. LC 87-28506. 344p. 1988. text ed. 35.00 (*0-312-01625-5*) St Martin.

Battered & Bruised: All the Women of the Old Testament. Arthur F. Ide. LC 93-21947. (Women in History Ser.: Vol. 20). (Illus.). 460p. (Orig.). 1993. pap. 30.00 (*0-930383-32-X*) Monument Pr.

Battered Bastards. Gordon French. 1979. pap. 1.75 (*0-8439-0631-6*) Dorchester Pub Co.

Battered Bastards of Bastogne. George Koskimaki. (Illus.). 500p. Date not set. 21.00 (*1-877702-04-8*) One Hund First Air.

Battered Child. Ed. by Ray E. Helfer & Ruth S. Kempe. LC 86-19342. (Illus.). 494p. 1988. pap. text ed. 18.95 (*0-226-32632-2*) U Ch Pr.

Battered Child. 4th ed. Ed. by Ray E. Helfer & Ruth S. Kempe. LC 86-19342. (Illus.). 494p. 1987. lib. bdg. 40.00 (*0-226-32631-4*) U Ch Pr.

Battered Child. 4th ed. Ed. by C. Henry Kempe & Ray E. Helfer. 440p. 1987. 37.00 (*0-318-14670-3*, 17); pap. 20.00 (*0-317-01147-2*, 17) Kempe Nat Ctr.

Battered Children & Child Abuse: Proceedings of the CIOMS Round Table Conference, XIXth. Ed. by Z. Bankowski & M. Carballo. 187p. 1986. pap. 12.00 (*92-9036-026-7*) World Health.

***Battered Destinies: Story of Battery D 1861-1865.** 1995. pap. 14.95 (*0-9647203-0-2*) Infotrans Co.

Battered Helpmate. Kathi W. Edwards. (Orig.). (C). 1990. pap. 8.95 (*0-9626945-0-9*) Daffodil Pubns.

Battered Husbands: The Battle of the Sexes Is Running Amuck. Howard Gregory. (Illus.). 128p. (Orig.). 1991. pap. 14.95 (*0-9607086-7-7*) H Gregory.

Battered into Submission: The Tragedy of Wife Abuse in the Christian Home. James Alsdurf & Phyllis Alsdurf. LC 89-15347. 168p. (Orig.). 1989. pap. 9.99 (*0-8308-1263-6*, 1263) InterVarsity.

Battered Jewish Wives: Case Studies in the Response to Rage. Mimi Scarf. LC 87-21946. (Women's Studies: Vol. 2). 264p. 1987. 89.95 (*0-88946-119-8*) E Mellen.

Battered Rich. Steve Bassett. Ed. by Sylvia Ashton. LC 79-15043. 1980. 22.95 (*0-87949-159-0*) Ashley Bks.

***Battered Victory.** William A. Mueller. 330p. 1994. 8.00 (*0-9643960-0-9*) Panhandle Jackie.

Battered Without Bruises. Marlene Wilson & Monty Wilson. 168p. (Orig.). 1987. 12.95 (*0-9618518-0-5*); pap. 7.95 (*0-9618518-1-3*) Omnicorn Prodns.

***Battered Wives.** Del Martin. 1990. mass mkt. 5.99 (*0-671-72761-3*) PB.

Battered Wives. rev. ed. Del Martin. LC 81-12985. 288p. 1981. pap. 12.95 (*0-912078-70-7*) Volcano Pr.

Battered Woman. Lenore Walker. LC 77-11538. 224p. 1980. pap. 12.00 (*0-06-090742-8*, CN-742, PL) HarpC.

Battered Woman & Shelters: The Social Construction of Wife Abuse. Donileen R. Loseke. (SUNY Series in Deviance & Social Control). 216p. (C). 1992. 59.50 (*0-7914-0831-0*); pap. 19.95 (*0-7914-0832-9*) State U NY Pr.

Battered Woman Syndrome. Lenore Walker. LC 84-1324. (Focus on Women Ser.: Vol. 6). 272p. 1984. 29.95 (*0-8261-4320-2*) Springer Pub.

***Battered Woman's Guide to Jumpstart a New Lifestyle. Niki Jansen. LC 94-32895. 1995. pap. 15.95 (*1-885275-34-X*) C J Howie.**
THE BATTERED WOMAN'S GUIDE TO JUMPSTART A NEW LIFESTYLE is a woman's guide for surviving an abusive relationship, shucking a battering situation, educating herself into the job market, & nurturing children to college age. Useful building blocks are: managing stress before it manages her, programmed units about the immune system--defender of the body, & HIV/AIDS, hepatitis; empowering herself, seeing money as just a tool; getting the competitive edge in jobs, & networking. PLUS--marketing herself into a job interview, & where to get help in each of the United States, some territories, & English-speaking countries. Order from: C.J. Howie Company, P.O. Box 27215, Columbus, OH 43227-9998. ***Publisher Provided Annotation.***

Battered Woman's Survival Guide. Jan B. Statman. LC 89-20606. 168p. 1990. 18.95 (*0-87833-718-0*); pap. 9.95 (*0-87833-707-5*) Taylor Pub.

***Battered Woman's Survival Guide: Breaking the Cycle.** rev. ed. Statman. 1995. 18.95 (*0-87833-890-X*); pap. text ed. 9.95 (*0-87833-889-6*) Taylor Pub.

Battered Women: Living with the Enemy. Ann Kosof. (Women Then -- Women Now Ser.). (Illus.). 112p. (YA). (gr. 9-12). 1994. lib. bdg. 14.35 (*0-531-11203-9*) Watts.

***Battered Women: Living with the Enemy.** Anna Kosof. (Women Then - Women Now Ser.). (Illus.). 112p. (YA). (gr. 9-12). 1995. pap. 12.00 (*0-531-15755-5*) Watts.

Battered Women: The Facts. National Center on Women & Family Law Staff. 42p. (Orig.). 1990. pap. text ed. 20.00 (*0-929396-02-2*) Natl Ctr Women & Family Law Inc.

Battered Women & the New Law. Anna Coote & Tess Gill. 1979. 20.00 (*0-317-59362-5*, Pub. by NCCL UK) St Mut.

Battered Women & Their Families: Intervention Strategies & Treatment Programs. Albert Roberts. LC 83-20022. (Social Work Ser.: Vol. 1). 224p. 1984. 25.95 (*0-8261-4590-6*) Springer Pub.

Battered Women As Survivors. Lee A. Hoff. 272p. 1990. pap. 14.95 (*0-415-04395-6*, A4824) Routledge.

Battered Women As Survivors: An Alternative to Treating Learned Helplessness. Edward W. Gondolf & Ellen R. Fisher. 144p. 1988. text ed. 27.95 (*0-669-18166-8*) Free Pr.

Battered Women in Korean Immigrant Families: The Silent Scream. Young I Song. LC 93-33899. (Reference Library of Social Science, Vol. 903, Library of Sociology: Vol. 29). 192p. 1995. 29.00 (*0-8153-1320-9*, SS903) Garland.

Battered Women, Shattered Lives. Kathleen H. Hofeller. LC 82-50377. 125p. (Orig.). 1983. pap. 8.95 (*0-88247-687-4*) R & E Pubs.

Battered Women Who Kill: Psychological Self-Defense As Legal Justification. Charles P. Ewing. LC 86-21323. 192p. 1987. text ed. 32.95 (*0-669-14827-X*) Free Pr.

Battered Women's Directory. 9th ed. Ed. by Betsy Warrior. (Illus.). 283p. (Orig.). 1985. pap. 12.00 (*0-9601544-6-9*) B Warrior.

Battered Women's Directory. 10th ed. Ed. by Betsy Warrior. (Illus.). 283p. (Orig.). 1989. pap. 12.00 (*0-318-41395-7*) B Warrior.

***Batterer: A Psychological Profile.** Donald G. Dutton & Susan K. Golant. 1995. 18.00 (*0-465-03387-3*) Basic.

Batterers Anonymous: Self-Help Counseling for Men Who Batter Women. Jerry M. Goffman. LC 84-73081. 75p. 1984. pap. 9.95 (*0-9612754-0-5*) Batterers Anon.

Batteries & Magnets. H. Amery & A. Littler. (KnowHow Bks.). (Illus.). 32p. (J). (gr. 3-6). 1977. pap. 6.95 (*0-86020-008-6*) EDC.

***Batteries & Magnets.** P. Borton & V. Cave. (How to Make Ser.). (Illus.). 32p. (J). (gr. 2-6). 1995. pap. 5.95 (*0-7460-2083-X*, Usborne) EDC.

***Batteries & Magnets.** P. Borton & V. Cave. (How to Make Ser.). (Illus.). 32p. (J). (gr. 2-6). 1995. lib. bdg. 12.96 (*0-88110-757-3*, Usborne) EDC.

Batteries, Bulbs & Wires. David Glover. LC 92-40215. (Young Discoverers Ser.). 32p. (J). (gr. 1-4). 1993. 10.95 (*1-85697-837-0*, Kingfisher LKC); pap. 5.95 (*1-85697-933-4*, Kingfisher LKC) LKC.

Batteries for Cordless Appliances. Ralph J. Brodd. (Battery Applications Book Ser.). 1987. text ed. 130.00 (*0-471-91611-0*) Wiley.

Batteries for Implantable Biomedical Devices. Ed. by Boone B. Owens. LC 86-582. 380p. 1986. 89.50 (*0-306-42148-8*, Plenum Pr) Plenum.

Batteries, No. 2: Research & Development in Non-Mechanical Electrical Power. Inter Departmental Committe Staff & D. H. Collins. LC 62-22327. 1965. 226.00 (*0-08-010978-0*, Pub. by Pergamon Repr UK) Franklin.

***Batteries Not Included; A Reference, Rarity & Value Guide.** Don Hultzman. (Illus.). 138p. 1994. pap. 22.95 (*0-89689-107-0*) Bks Americana.

Batteries of Life: On the History of Things & Their Perception in Modernity. Christoph Asendorf. Tr. by Don Reneau. LC 92-15011. (Weimar & Now Ser.: Vol. 4). 1993. 35.00 (*0-520-06573-5*) U CA Pr.

Batteries on Ships. Norman E. Bagshaw. LC 82-10954. (Electronic & Electrical Engineering Research Ser.: No. 1). (Illus.). 215p. reprint ed. pap. 61.30 (*0-8357-6035-9*, 2034213) Bks Demand.

Batteries, Vol. 2: Lead-Acid Batteries & Electric Vehicles. Ed. by Karl V. Kordesch. LC 73-82702. (Illus.). 532p. reprint ed. pap. 151.70 (*0-7837-0972-2*, 2041278) Bks Demand.

Battering & Family Therapy: A Feminist Perspective. Marsali Hansen & Michele Harway. (Illus.). 332p. (C). 1993. 49.95 (*0-8039-4320-2*); pap. 24.00 (*0-8039-4321-0*) Sage.

Battering of Women: The Failure of Intervention & the Case for Prevention. Larry L. Tifft. LC 93-18313. 230p. (C). 1993. text ed. 59.00 (*0-8133-1390-2*); pap. text ed. 19.95 (*0-8133-1391-0*) Westview.

Batters & Breadings in Food Processing. Ed. by Karel Kulp & Robert Loewe. LC 90-81317. (Illus.). 267p. 1990. 89.00 (*0-913250-69-4*) Am Assn Cereal Chem.

Battery. Daniel Therriault & Stephen Mellor. 96p. 1983. pap. 4.95 (*0-88145-003-0*) Broadway Play.

***Battery & Ultracapacitor Test Procedures Manuals, Vol. 5.** Idaho National Engineering Laboratory for U. S. Dept. of Energy et al. (Electric Vehicle Information Ser.: Pts. A-B). (Illus.). 92p. 1995. lib. bdg. 135.00x (*0-89934-250-7*, BT932) Busn Tech Info Serv.

***Battery & Ultracapacitor Test Procedures Manuals, Vol. 5.** Idaho National Engineering Laboratory for U. S. Dept. of Energy et al. (Electric Vehicle Information Ser.: Vol. V, Set, Pt. A-B). (Illus.). 92p. 1995. pap. 85.00x (*0-89934-249-3*, BT032) Busn Tech Info Serv.

Battery Book: Five Hundred Ways to Charge Yourself Up. Joey Reiman. LC 93-79668. 96p. 1993. pap. 5.95 (*1-56352-106-7*) Longstreet Pr Inc.

***Battery Book for Your PV Home.** Fowler Solar Electric, Inc. Staff. (The PV Home Series Booklets). (Illus.). 25p. (Orig.). 1991. pap. text ed. 8.00 (*1-879523-02-7*) Fowler Solar.

Battery Book One: Lead Acid Traction Batteries. Ed. by Ken Marsh. LC 81-65733. (Illus.). 72p. (Orig.). 1981. pap. 7.95 (*0-939488-00-0*) Curtis Instruments.

Battery Dealers & Storage, 1995. American Business Directories Staff. 1995. spiral bd., pap. 560.00 (*1-56105-592-1*) Am Busn Direct.

Battery Design & Optimization: Proceedings of the Symposium, Pittsburgh, Pa, 1978. Battery Design & Optimization Symposium Staff. Ed. by Sidney Gross. LC 79-51500. (Electrochemical Society Proceedings Ser.: Vol. 79-1). 493p. reprint ed. pap. 140.60 (*0-8357-5995-4*, 2052059) Bks Demand.

Battery Hazards & Accident Prevention. S. C. Levy & P. Bro. (Illus.). 300p. (C). 1994. 49.50 (*0-306-44758-4*, Plenum Pr) Plenum.

***Battery Market.** 400p. (Orig.). 1994. pap. 1,495.00 (*1-57205-941-9*) Rector Pr.

***Battery Performance, Research & Testing, Set, Pts. A-C.** Ed. by J. A. Bereny. (Electric Vehicle Information Ser.: Vol. I, Pts. A-C). (Illus.). 206p. 1995. lib. bdg. 145.00x (*0-89934-240-X*) Busn Tech Info Serv.

***Battery Performance, Research & Testing Vol. I, Vol. I, Set, Pts. A-C.** J. A. Bereny. (Electric Vehicle Information Ser.: Vol 1, Pts. A-C). (Illus.). 206p. 1995. pap. 95.00x (*0-89934-239-6*) Busn Tech Info Serv.

Battery Point Light & the Tidal Wave of 1964: Includes St. George Reef Light. Bert Webber & Margie Webber. LC 91-373. (Illus.). 96p. (Orig.). 1991. pap. 9.95 (*0-936738-66-9*) Webb Research.

Battery Reconditioning: The Novice's Guide to Becoming a Battery Specialist. Danny R. Edwards. (Illus.). 120p. (Orig.). 1989. pap. 29.95 (*0-9623923-0-8*, 1261) Power Supply.

Battery Reference Book. T. R. Crompton. (Illus.). 528p. 1990. text ed. 195.00 (*0-408-00790-7*) Buttrwrth-Heinemann.

Battery Rodgers. William J. Dickman. 35p. (Orig.). 1980. pap. 7.00 (*0-89126-094-3*) MA-AH Pub.

Battery Technology Handbook. Kiehne. (Electrical Engineering & Electronics Ser.: Vol. 60). 528p. 1989. 165.00 (*0-8247-8180-5*) Dekker.

Battery Toys. Brian Moran. LC 83-51743. (Illus.). 192p. 1984. 29.50 (*0-88740-003-5*) Schiffer.

Battery Wagner: The Siege, the Men Who Fought, & the Casualties. Timothy E. Bradshaw, Jr. 230p. 1993. 29.95 (*0-9639228-0-7*) Palmetto Hist.

Battey: Samson Battey of Rhode Island, the Immigrant Ancestor & His Descendants. H. V. Battey. 400p. 1993. reprint ed. lib. bdg. 69.50 (*0-8328-2816-5*); reprint ed. pap. 59.50 (*0-8328-2817-3*) Higginson Bk Co.

Batting Champs. Bliss. (Baseball Heroes Ser.). (J). 1991. 12.50 (*0-86593-129-1*) Rourke Corp.

Batting One Thousand: Using Baldrige Feedback to Improve Your Business. Randall Willie & Jack Bartholomew. Ed. by Joanne Walker. (AT&T Quality Library). 200p. (Orig.). 1992. pap. 29.95 (*0-932764-23-1*, 500-451) AT&T Customer Info.

Batting One Thousand - Baseball's Leading Hitters: A Tribute to Lou Gehrig. Guy Curato, pseud. LC 88-82916. 124p. (Orig.). (YA). (gr. 9). 1989. pap. write for info. (*0-9621591-0-7*) T Assicurato.

***Battle.** Eyewitness Staff. (J). Date not set. write for info. (*0-679-87333-3*); lib. bdg. write for info. (*0-679-97333-8*) Random.

Battle: Plays, Prose, Poems. Heiner Muller. 176p. 1989. pap. 12.95x (*1-55554-049-X*) PAJ Pubns.

Battle Against Extinction: Native Fish Management in the American West. Ed. by Wendell L. Minckley & James E. Deacon. LC 91-6977. (Illus.). 517p. 1991. 50.00 (*0-8165-1221-3*) U of Ariz Pr.

Battle Against Heart Disease: A Physician Traces the History of Man's Achievements in this Field for the General Reader. P. E. Baldry. LC 75-108098. 200p. reprint ed. pap. 57.00 (*0-8357-5996-2*, 2022434) Bks Demand.

Battle Against Infection. Ed. by Charles B. Clayman. LC 91-42001. (American Medical Association Home Medical Library). (Illus.). 144p. 1992. 16.98 (*0-89577-412-7*) RD Assn.

Battle Against Isolation. Walter Johnson. LC 72-3376. (FDR & the Era of the New Deal Ser.). 270p. 1973. reprint ed. lib. bdg. 35.00 (*0-306-70480-3*) Da Capo.

Battle Against Lord Fear. Louis Anderson. (WildSpace Bks.: No. 2). 1994. pap. 2.95 (*0-7869-0035-0*) TSR Inc.

Battle Against Necros. Louis Anderson. (WildSpace Bks.: No. 1). 1994. pap. 2.95 (*0-7869-0034-2*) TSR Inc.

Battle Against the Draconians. Louis Anderson. (WildSpace Bks.: No. 4). 1994. pap. 2.95 (*0-7869-0037-7*) TSR Inc.

Battle Against the Flayons. Louis Anderson. (WildSpace Bks.: No. 3). 1994. pap. 2.95 (*0-7869-0036-9*) TSR Inc.

Battle Against Unemployment & Inflation. Martin Baily & Arthur M. Okun. (Problems of the Modern Economy Ser.). (Illus.). (C). 1982. pap. text ed. 7.95 (*0-393-95055-7*) Norton.

Battle & the Backlash: The Child Sexual Abuse War. David Hechler. LC 86-45633. 400p. 1989. pap. 10.95 (*0-669-21362-4*) Free Pr.

Battle Angel Alita, Vol. I. Yukito Kishiro. (Illus.). 244p. (Orig.). 1994. pap. 15.95 (*1-56931-003-3*) Viz Commns Inc.

***Battle Angel Alita: Tears of an Angel.** Yukito Kishiro. (Illus.). 1995. pap. 15.95 (*1-56931-049-1*, Viz Comics) Viz Commns Inc.

Battle at Ball's Bluff. Kim B. Holien. Ed. by Stephen W. Sylvia & Michael J. O'Donnell. (Illus.). 170p. 1985. 24.95 (*0-943522-10-2*) Moss Pubns VA.

Battle at Best. S. L. Marshall. (Battery Classics Ser.). (Illus.). 257p. 1988. reprint ed. 22.50 (*0-89839-115-6*) Battery Pr.

***Battle at Bull Run.** William Davis. (Illus.). 336p. 1995. 19.95 (*0-8117-0202-2*) Stackpole.

Battle at Bull Run: A History of the First Major Campaign of the Civil War. William C. Davis. LC 76-42322. (Illus.). xiv, 298p. 1981. pap. 11.95 (*0-8071-0867-7*) La State U Pr.

Battle Babies: The Story of the Ninety-Ninth Infantry Division. 28th ed. Walter E. Lauer. (Illus.). 353p. 1985. 29.95 (*0-89839-089-3*) Battery Pr.

Battle below Giltspur. Cormac MacRaois. (Illus.). 1989. pap. 8.95 (*0-86327-198-7*, Pub. by Wolfhound Pr IE) Dufour.

Battle Blades: A Professional's Guide to Combatd-Fighting Knives. Greg Walker. (Illus.). 168p. 1993. text ed. 30.00 (*0-87364-732-7*) Paladin Pr.

Battle Book: Crucial Conflicts in History from 1469 BC to the Present. Bryan Perrett. 320p. 1993. 24.95 (*1-85409-125-5*) Sterling.

Battle Book: Genealogy of the Battle Family in America. Herbert B. Battle & Lois Yelverton. 768p. 1993. reprint ed. lib. bdg. 109.50 (*0-8328-3606-0*); reprint ed. pap. 99.50 (*0-8328-3607-9*) Higginson Bk Co.

Battle Canyon. Robert T. Hilgardner. LC 86-61648. (Illus.). 110p. (Orig.). 1986. pap. 8.95 (*0-939543-00-1*) Mid-Amer Pub Hse KS.

Battle Chronicles of the Civil War, 6 vols. Ed. by James M. McPherson. (Illus.). 1989. text ed. 150.00 (*0-02-920661-8*) Macmillan.

Battle Circle. Piers Anthony. 544p. 1978. mass mkt. 5.99 (*0-380-01800-4*) Avon.

Battle Creek: The Place Behind the Products: An Illustrated History. Peter J. Schmitt & Larry B. Massie. (Illus.). 136p. 1984. 19.95 (*0-89781-117-8*) Preferred Mktg.

Battle Cry. Leon Uris. 1982. mass mkt. 6.99 (*0-553-25983-0*) Bantam.

Battle Cry, No. 2. Jack McKinney. 1987. mass mkt. 4.95 (*0-345-34134-1*, Del Rey) Ballantine.

Battle Cry of Freedom. James M. McPherson. 1989. pap. 17.50 (*0-345-35942-9*, Ballantine Trade) Ballantine.

Battle Cry of Freedom: New England Emigration Aid Company in the Kansas Crusade. Samuel A. Johnson. LC 77-11619. (Illus.). 357p. 1977. reprint ed. text ed. 59.75 (*0-8371-9813-5*, JOBC, Greenwood Pr) Greenwood.

Battle Cry of Freedom: The Era of the Civil War. James M. McPherson. (History of U.S. Ser.: Vol. VI). (Illus.). 928p. (C). 1988. 39.95 (*0-19-503863-0*) OUP.

***Battle Dice.** Mike Sager. (4001). Date not set. write for info. (*0-614-07186-0*) Thund Castle.

Battle Exhaustion: Soldiers & Psychiatrists in the Canadian Army, 1939-1945. Terry Copp & Bill McAndrew. 280p. (C). 1990. 39.95 (*0-7735-0774-4*, Pub. by McGill CN) U of Toronto Pr.

***Battle Fatigue: The Promise of Rest for Stress-Weary Christians.** Joe B. Brown. LC 94-30988. 1995. 14.99 (*0-8054-6154-X*) Broadman.

***Battle Flag.** Bernard Cornwell. 384p. 1995. 20.00 (*0-06-017634-2*) HarpC.

***Battle Flag.** large type ed. Bernard Cornwell. LC 95-5410. (The Starbuck Chronicles Ser.: Vol. 3). 300p. 1995. 22.95 (*0-7862-0399-4*) Thorndike Pr.

***Battle Flags of Texans in the Confederacy.** Alan K. Sumrall. LC 94-40888. (Illus.). 1995. 29.95 (*0-89015-983-1*, Eakin Pr) Sunbelt Media.

Battle Flags South: Story of the Civil War Navies on Western Waters. James M. Merrill. LC 71-86652. 334p. 1975. 32.50 (*0-8386-7448-8*) Fairleigh Dickinson.

Battle for Alaska Statehood. Ernest Gruening. (Illus.). 122p. 1967. 9.95 (*0-912006-12-9*) U of Alaska Pr.

Battle for An Loc. Paul T. Ringerbach & Peter J. Melly. 102p. 1993. reprint ed. pap. 12.50x (*0-923135-59-6*) Dalley Bk Service.

Battle for Atlanta. (Civil War Ser.). (Illus.). 176p. 1985. 19.93 (*0-8094-4772-X*); lib. bdg. 25.93 (*0-8094-4773-8*) Time-Life.

Battle for Baltimore: 1814. Joseph A. Whitehorne & Carleton Jones. (Illus.). 250p. 1995. 29.95 (*1-877853-23-2*) Nautical & Aviation.

Battle for Batangas: A Philippine Province at War. Glenn A. May. (Illus.). 352p. (C). 1991. text ed. 35.00 (*0-300-04850-5*) Yale U Pr.

Battle for Berlin, Ontario: An Historical Drama. W. R. Chadwick. (Illus.). 192p. (C). 1992. pap. 25.00 (*0-88920-226-5*, Pub. by Wilfrid Laurier CN) Humanities.

Battle for Britain: Citizenship & Ideology in the Second World War. David Morgan & Mary Evans. LC 92-11717. 1993. 62.50 (*0-415-01722-X*, A5913) Routledge.

An Asterisk (*) at the beginning of an entry indicates that the title is appearing in BIP for the first time. 629

Battle for Britain: Thatcher & the New Liberals. Stephen Haseler. 194p. 1990. text ed. 55.00 (*1-85043-148-5*, Pub. by I B Tauris UK) St Martin.

Battle for Burma. Eric D. Smith. LC 78-25679. (Illus.). 190p. 1979. 32.95 (*0-8419-0468-5*) Holmes & Meier.

***Battle for Butte: Mining & Politics on the Northern Frontier, 1864-1906.** Michael P. Malone. LC 95-14591. (Illus.). 281p. (C). 1995. reprint ed. pap. write for info. (*0-917298-34-9*) MT Hist Soc.

Battle for Cassino. Janusz Piekalkiewicz. LC 80-51757. 224p. 1980. 16.95 (*0-672-52667-0*, Bobbs) Macmillan.

Battle for Childhood: Creation of a Russian Myth. Andrew B. Wachtel. LC 89-29961. 274p. 1990. 35.00 (*0-8047-1795-8*) Stanford U Pr.

Battle for Christmas. Stephen Nissenbaum. 1992. write for info. (*0-679-74038-4*); pap. write for info. (*0-679-41223-9*) McKay.

Battle for Coal: Miners & the Politics of Nationalization in France, 1940-1950. Darryl Holter. LC 91-28157. 280p. 1992. 35.00 (*0-87580-167-6*) N Ill U Pr.

Battle for Corporate Control: Shareholder Rights, Stakeholder Interests, & Managerial Responsibilities. Arnold W. Sametz & James L. Bicksler. 240p. 1990. text ed. 52.00 (*1-55623-305-1*) Irwin Prof Pubng.

Battle for Guadalcanal. Samuel B. Griffith. 18.95 (*0-405-13281-6*) Ayer.

Battle for Guadalcanal. Samuel B. Griffith, II. LC 79-90112. (Great War Stories Ser.). (Illus.). 282p. 1979. reprint ed. 24.95 (*0-933852-04-5*) Nautical & Aviation.

Battle for Guatemala: Rebels, Death Squads, & U. S. Power, Vol. 5. Susanne Jonas. (Latin American Perspectives Ser.). (C). 1991. text ed. 57.50 (*0-8133-7462-6*); pap. text ed. 19.95 (*0-8133-0614-0*) Westview.

***Battle for Hell: A Survey & Evaluation of Evangelicals' Growing Attraction to the Doctrine of Annihilationism.** David G. Moore. LC 95-10744. 1995. write for info. (*0-8191-9955-9*) U Pr of Amer.

Battle for Homestead, 1880-1892: Politics, Culture, & Steel. Paul Krause. LC 91-50760. (Series in Social & Labor History). 584p. 1992. 49.95 (*0-8229-3702-6*); pap. 19.95 (*0-8229-5466-4*) U of Pittsburgh Pr.

Battle for Horsetooth Mountain. G. A. Carrington. 1990. mass mkt. 8.95 (*0-440-50314-0*) Dell.

Battle for Human Nature: Science, Morality & Modern Life. Barry Schwartz. 1987. pap. 11.95 (*0-393-30445-0*) Norton.

Battle for Immortality. Lester Sumrall. 120p. (C). 1984. pap. text ed. 10.00 (*0-937580-80-5*) LeSEA Pub Co.

Battle for Investment Survival. Gerald M. Loeb. LC 88-81705. 320p. 1988. reprint ed. pap. text ed. 18.00 (*0-87034-084-0*) Fraser Pub Co.

Battle for Jerusalem. Abraham Rabinovich. 470p. 1987. pap. 17.95 (*0-8276-0285-5*) JPS Phila.

Battle for Khe Sanh. Moyers S. Shore, II. LC 75-603604. (Illus.). 215p. 1977. reprint ed. pap. 7.00 (*0-16-002124-3*, S/N 008-055-00114-5) USGPO.

Battle for Korea: The Associated Press History of the Korean Conflict. Robert J. Dvorchak et al. LC 93-4635. (Illus.). 320p. 1993. 34.95 (*0-938289-30-6*, 7335) Combined Bks.

Battle for Leyte Gulf. (Naval Ser.: No. 3). (Illus.). 244p. 1989. reprint ed. 27.50 (*0-89839-134-2*) Battery Pr.

***Battle for Life.** Jori Schellenberger. (Illus.). 100p. (Orig.). 1994. pap. 8.00 (*1-883893-01-1*) Wine Pr Pub.

***Battle for Manchester City.** Alec Johnson. (Illus.). 187p. 1995. 29.95 (*1-85158-654-7*, Pub. by Mnstream UK) Trafalgar.

Battle for Manila. Lawrence Cortesi. 1984. pap. 3.25 (*0-8217-1334-5*) Zebra.

***Battle for Manila: The Most Devastating Untold Story of World War II.** Richard Connaughton et al. LC 95-11918. 192p. 1995. 24.95 (*0-89141-578-5*) Presidio Pr.

Battle for Moscow. Albert Seaton. (Illus.). 320p. 1993. reprint ed. pap. 12.95 (*0-9627613-2-X*) Sarpedon.

Battle for Moscow: The 1942 Soviet General Staff Study. M. Parrish. (Illus.). 226p. 1989. 45.00 (*0-08-035977-9*) Brasseys Inc.

Battle for Natural Resources. 1983. 10.50 (*0-685-18356-4*) Am Forests.

***Battle for Okinawa.** Hiromichi Yahara. LC 94-43765. 272p. (ENG & JPN.). 1995. text ed. 24.95 (*0-471-12041-3*) Wiley.

Battle for Palembanc. large type ed. Terence Kelly. (Ulverscroft Ser.). (Illus.). 352p. 1994. 21.95 (*0-7089-3011-5*) Ulverscroft.

Battle for Panama: Inside Operation Just Cause. Edward M. Flanagan, Jr. LC 92-14588. (Association of the U. S. Army Book Ser.). 271p. 1993. 25.00 (*0-02-881039-2*) Brasseys Inc.

Battle for Public Opinion: The President, the Press & the Polls During Watergate. Gladys E. Lang & Kurt Lang. 360p. 1983. text ed. 61.00 (*0-231-05548-X*); pap. text ed. 20.00 (*0-231-05549-8*) Col U Pr.

Battle for Rhodesia. Douglas Reed. 1967. 9.95 (*0-8159-5102-7*) Devin.

Battle for Stalingrad: The 1943 Soviet General Staff Study. L. Rotundo. (Illus.). 342p. 1989. 47.00 (*0-08-035974-4*) Brasseys Inc.

Battle for Stock Market Profits. Gerald M. Loeb. LC 70-130483. 1974. 7.95 (*0-671-20751-2*) S&S Trade.

Battle for Tarawa. 12th ed. James R. Stockman. (Elite Unit Ser.). 120p. 1987. 25.00 (*0-89839-104-0*) Battery Pr.

***Battle for the American Church Revisited.** George Kelly. 154p. (Orig.). Date not set. pap. 9.95 (*0-89870-532-0*) Ignatius Pr.

Battle for the Broads. Martin Ewans. 220p. 1992. pap. 48.00 (*0-86138-095-9*, Pub. by T Dalton UK) St Mut.

Battle for the Broads. Martin Ewans. 220p. 1994. 70.00 (*0-86138-092-4*, Pub. by T Dalton UK) St Mut.

Battle for the Buffalo River: A Twentieth-Century Conservation Crisis in the Ozarks. Neil Compton. LC 91-27540. (Illus.). 496p. 1992. 50.00 (*1-55728-235-8*); pap. 30.00 (*1-55728-236-6*) U of Ark Pr.

Battle for the Castle. Elizabeth Winthrop. LC 92-54490. 160p. (J). (gr. 3-7). 1993. 14.95 (*0-8234-1010-2*) Holiday.

Battle for the Castle. Elizabeth Winthrop. 1994. mass mkt. 3.99 (*0-440-40942-X*) Dell.

Battle for the Control of U. S. Broadcasting, 1930-1935. Roberet W. McChesney. LC 92-15440. (C). 1993. 49.95 (*0-19-507174-3*) OUP.

Battle for the Falklands. Max Hastings & Simon Jenkins. (Illus.). 372p. 1984. pap. 13.00 (*0-393-30198-2*) Norton.

Battle for the Falklands, Vol. 1: Land Forces. William Fowler. (Men-at-Arms Ser.: No. 133). (Illus.). 48p. pap. 11.95 (*0-85045-482-4*, 9065, Pub. by Osprey UK) Stackpole.

Battle for the Falklands, Vol. 2: Naval Forces. Adrian English & Anthony Watts. (Men-at-Arms Ser.: No. 134). (Illus.). 48p. pap. 11.95 (*0-85045-492-1*, 9066, Pub. by Osprey UK) Stackpole.

Battle for the Falklands, Vol. 3: Air Forces. Roy Braybrook. (Men-at-Arms Ser.: No. 135). (Illus.). 48p. pap. 11.95 (*0-85045-493-X*, 9067, Pub. by Osprey UK) Stackpole.

Battle for the Fiords: The Forward Maritime Strategy in Action. Eric Grove. LC 90-62894. (Illus.). 128p. 1991. 31.95 (*1-55750-052-5*) Naval Inst Pr.

Battle for the Heartland: The November 1993 Assembly Elections. Arun Kumar. (C). 1994. 19.50 (*81-7167-190-X*, Pub. by Rupa II) S Asia.

Battle for the Mind: You Are Engaged in Battle for the Mind, a Subtle Warfare. Tim LaHaye. LC 82-21453. 1982. student ed, pap. 3.99 (*0-8007-1341-9*) Revell.

Battle for the Mind, a Physiology of Conversion & Brainwashing. William Sargant. LC 73-6261. (Illus.). 263p. 1975. reprint ed. text ed. 65.00 (*0-8371-6899-6*, SABM, Greenwood Pr) Greenwood.

Battle for the Planet of the Apes. David Gerrold. 15.95 (*0-89190-163-9*, Am Repr) Amereon Ltd.

Battle for the Seed. Patricia Morgan. 112p. (Orig.). 1992. pap. 8.99 (*1-56043-099-0*) Destiny Image.

Battle for the Sunlight. 2nd ed. Arvia MacKaye. 62p. 1983. reprint ed. pap. 5.00 (*0-932776-07-8*) Adonis Pr.

Battle for the Ten Hour Day Continues: 1837-1843. LC 72-2519. (British Labour Struggles Before 1850 Ser.). 1974. reprint ed. 23.95 (*0-405-04412-7*) Ayer.

Battle for the Worlds. Harold B. Bullock. Ed. by Jean Anderson. (Tarlian Spiral Ser.: Bk. 1). (Illus.). (J). 1990. 14.95 (*0-9626219-4-3*) Summit TX.

Battle for Ulster: A Study of Internal Security. Tom F. Baldy. 153p. (Orig.). 1987. pap. 3.75 (*0-317-62826-7*, S-N 008-020-01101-1!) US HHS.

Battle for White Russia: The Destruction of Army Group Center, June 1944. G. Niepold. Tr. by Richard E. Simpkin. 287p. 1987. 67.00 (*0-08-033606-X*, Pub. by Brasseys UK) Brasseys Inc.

Battle for Women's Suffrage. Suzanne M. Coil. (Liberty & Justice For All Ser.). (Illus.). 64p. (J). (gr. 5-8). 1995. lib. bdg. 15.98 (*0-8050-2985-0*) TFC Bks NY.

Battle for Yanga. V. Ben Kendrick. LC 80-20643. 127p. 1980. pap. 4.95 (*0-87227-074-2*) Reg Baptist.

Battle for Your Mind. Leslie Parrott. 199p. 1986. pap. 6.95 (*0-8341-1124-1*) Beacon Hill.

Battle Force. (Super Bolan Ser.). 1993. mass mkt. 4.99 (*0-373-61432-2*, 1-61432-0) Harlequin Bks.

Battle from the Start: The Life of Nathan Bedford Forrest. Brian S. Wills. LC 91-58380. (Illus.). 480p. 1993. reprint ed. pap. 16.00 (*0-06-092445-4*, PL) HarpC.

Battle God of the Vikings. Hilda Davidson. (C). 1988. 25.00 (*0-685-37101-8*, Pub. by W Sessions UK) St Mut.

Battle God of the Vikings. Hilda Davidson. (C). 1990. 25.00 (*0-685-37377-0*, Pub. by W Sessions UK) St Mut.

Battle Ground, in & Around: A Pictorial Drama of Early Northwest Pioneer Life. 2nd ed. Louise M. Allworth. LC 75-43292. (Illus.). 400p. 1984. reprint ed. 30.00 (*0-9613899-0-7*) Write Stuff.

Battle Group! German Kampfgruppen Action of World War Two. James Lucas. (Illus.). 224p. 1994. 24.95 (*1-85409-176-X*) Sterling.

Battle History of the First Armored Division. George F. Howe. (Divisional Ser.: No. 11). (Illus.). 1979. reprint ed. 29.95 (*0-89839-025-7*) Battery Pr.

Battle History of the Four Hundred Seventy-Third U. S. Infantry in World War Two. Jack Ramsberger. 22p. 1981. reprint ed. 4.95 (*0-932572-08-1*) Phillips Pubns.

Battle History of the Imperial Japanese Navy: 1941-1945. Paul S. Dull. LC 77-77933. 402p. 1978. 35.00 (*0-87021-097-1*) Naval Inst Pr.

***Battle Honors - U. S. Military Model Show Medal Winners.** Bill Horan & Phil Kessling. (Illus.). 128p. 1995. 24.95 (*1-85915-037-3*, Pub. by Windrow & Green UK) Motorbooks Intl.

Battle Hymn. rev. ed. Dean E. Hess. (Illus.). 249p. 1987. reprint ed. pap. 12.95 (*0-942397-01-0*) Buckeye Aviat Bk.

Battle Hymn of China. Agnes Smedley. LC 74-32113. (China in the 20th Century Ser.). xxiii, 528p. 1975. lib. bdg. 49.50 (*0-306-70693-8*) Da Capo.

Battle in the Ashes. William W. Johnstone. 320p. 1993. mass mkt. 3.99 (*0-8217-4161-6*) Zebra.

Battle in the Bayou Country. Morris Raphael. (Illus.). 199p. (J). (gr. 5-12). 1976. 12.95 (*0-9608866-0-5*) M Raphael.

Battle in the English Channel. Theodore Taylor. (Great Sea Battles of WWII Ser.: Book III). 144p. (Orig.). (YA). (gr. 7 up). 1983. pap. 3.50 (*0-380-85225-X*, Flare) Avon.

Battle in the Irish Sea. 1989. pap. 18.00 (*0-9521432-0-8*, Pub. by Maritime Bks UK) St Mut.

***Battle in the Wilderness: Grant Meets Lee.** Grady McWhiney. (Civil War Campaigns & Commanders Ser.). (Illus.). 132p. (Orig.). 1995. pap. write for info. (*1-886661-00-6*) Ryan Place Pub.

Battle Invisible, & Other Stories. Eleanor C. Reed. LC 71-125236. (Short Story Index Reprint Ser.). 1977. 19.95 (*0-8369-3603-5*) Ayer.

Battle Kings: The History of Tanks. David Jefferis. LC 90-46259. (Wheels Ser.). (Illus.). 32p. (J). (gr. 5-8). 1991. lib. bdg. 13.23 (*0-531-14193-4*) Watts.

Battle Leadership. Adolf Von Schell. 100p. 1987. reprint ed. 2.00 (*0-317-64732-6*) Marine Corps.

Battle Lines: Report of the Twentieth Century Fund Task Force on the Military & the Media. 178p. (Orig.). (C). 1985. pap. text ed. 10.00 (*0-87078-165-0*) TCFP-PPP.

Battle Lost: Romans & Caledonians at Mons Graupius. Gordon S. Maxwell. (Illus.). 112p. 1988. 20.00 (*0-85224-490-8*, Pub. by Edinburgh U Pr UK) Col U Pr.

Battle Maps & Charts of the American Revolution. Henry B. Carrington. LC 74-8018. 96p. 1974. reprint ed. 38.95 (*0-405-05540-4*) Ayer.

Battle Maps & Charts of the American Revolution see Battles of the American Revolution, 1775-1781: Historical & Military Criticism

Battle Mask. Don Pendleton. (Executioner Ser.: No. 3). 1988. pap. 3.50 (*1-55817-026-X*, Pinnacle NY) Windsor NY.

Battle Master: (Drills for Practical Self-Defense) David Elwood. 86p. (Orig.). 1992. student ed 17.00 (*0-9635343-6-X*) Phoenix Karate.

Battle of Agincourt. Jon Nichol. (Resource Units: Middle Ages, 1066-1485 Ser.). (Illus.). 1974. reprint ed. pap. text ed. 12.95 (*0-582-39385-X*) Longman.

Battle of Angels. Tennessee Williams. 1975. pap. 4.75 (*0-8222-0099-6*) Dramatists Play.

Battle of Antietam. Zachary Kent. LC 92-12097. (Cornerstones of Freedom Ser.). (Illus.). 32p. (J). (gr. 3-6). 1992. lib. bdg. 12.30 (*0-516-06657-9*) Childrens.

Battle of Antietam. Zachary Kent. LC 92-12097. (Cornerstones of Freedom Ser.). (Illus.). 32p. (J). (gr. 3-6). 1993. pap. 3.95 (*0-516-46657-7*) Childrens.

Battle of Antietam & the Maryland Campaign of 1862: A Bibliography. D. Scott Hartwig. LC 89-77215. 130p. 1990. text ed. 49.95 (*0-313-28071-1*, HBJ/, Greenwood Pr) Greenwood.

Battle of Atlanta. Dennis A. Walters & Ken Reveill. (Illus.). 32p. (Orig.). (C). 1988. pap. text ed. 3.95 (*0-935031-10-3*) Terrell Missouri.

Battle of Atlanta & the Georgia Campaign. William Key. LC 81-83862. (Illus.). 96p. 1981. 9.95 (*0-931948-22-3*) Peachtree Pubs.

Battle of Ball's Bluff. LC 76-42073. (Civil War Monographs). 1977. pap. 21.00 (*0-527-17575-7*) Periodicals Srv.

Battle of Bataan: A History of the 90 Day Siege & Eventual Surrender of 75,000 Filipino & United States Troops to the Japanese in World War II. Donald J. Young. LC 92-50326. 395p. 1992. lib. bdg. 43.50x (*0-89950-757-3*) McFarland & Co.

Battle of Baton Rouge, Eighteen Sixty-Two. William A. Spedale. 72p. 1985. pap. 7.95 (*0-935545-00-X*) Land & Land.

Battle of Beecher Island & the Indian War of 1867-1869. John H. Monnet. (Illus.). 248p. pap. 17.50 (*0-87081-347-1*) Univ Pr Colo.

Battle of Beirut: Why Israel Invaded Lebanon. Michael Jansen. 142p. 1982. 30.00 (*0-89608-174-5*); pap. 6.50 (*0-89608-173-7*) South End Pr.

Battle of Belmont: Grant Strikes South. Nathaniel C. Hughes, Jr. LC 90-26401. (Illus.). xvii, 310p. (C). 1991. 27.50 (*0-8078-1968-9*) U of NC Pr.

Battle of Big Hole. Ella C. Hathaway. (Shorey Historical Ser.). 14p. reprint ed. pap. 1.95 (*0-8466-0138-9*, S138) Shorey.

Battle of Bosworth. Michael Bennett. (Illus.). 1993. pap. 20.00 (*0-86299-426-8*) A Sutton Pub.

Battle of Bosworth. Michael Bennett. 199p. 1993. pap. 19.95 (*0-312-10320-4*) St Martin.

Battle of Bosworth. Michael J. Bennett. LC 85-14292. 189p. 1985. text ed. 35.00 (*0-312-06972-3*) St Martin.

Battle of Brandywine. Samuel S. Smith. LC 76-9405. (Revolutionary War Bicentennial Ser.). (Illus.). 1976. lib. bdg. 10.95 (*0-912480-12-2*) Freneau.

Battle of Britain. Wallace B. Black & Jean F. Blashfield. LC 90-46579. (World War II 50th Anniversary Ser.). (Illus.). 48p. (J). (gr. 5-6). 1991. text ed. 4.95 (*0-89686-553-3*, Crstwood Hse) Silver Burdett Pr.

***Battle of Britain.** Earle Rice, Jr. LC 95-16224. (Battles of World War II Ser.). (J). 1995. lib. bdg. write for info. (*1-56006-414-5*) Lucent Bks.

***Battle of Britain, Set, Vols. I & II.** Historical Briefs, Inc. Staff. Ed. by Thomas Antonucci & Michael Antonucci. 176p. 1991. pap. 34.95 (*0-89677-027-3*) Hist Briefs.

Battle of Britain: The Greatest Air Battle of World War II. Richard Hough. 1990. pap. 16.95 (*0-393-30734-4*) Norton.

Battle of Britain New Perspectives: Behind the Scenes of the Great Air War. John Ray. (Illus.). 208p. 1994. 24.95 (*1-85409-229-4*) Sterling.

Battle of Brooklyn, 1776. John Gallagher. (Illus.). 248p. 1995. 24.95 (*1-885119-02-X*) Sarpedon.

Battle of Brunanburh. Brunanburh. Ed. by Alistair Campbell. 184p. reprint ed. lib. bdg. 39.00 (*0-403-03315-2*) Scholarly.

Battle of Brunanburh. Alister Campbell. 1988. reprint ed. lib. bdg. 49.00 (*0-7812-0211-6*) Rprt Serv.

Battle of Bull Run. LC 76-41431. (Civil War Monographs). 1972. reprint ed. pap. 21.00 (*0-527-17576-5*) Periodicals Srv.

Battle of Bunker Hill. (Massachusetts Historical Society Picture Books). 32p. 1968. pap. 4.00 (*0-934909-01-6*) Mass Hist Soc.

Battle of Bunker Hill. John R. Elting. LC 75-3540. (Revolutionary War Bicentennial Ser.). (Illus.). 1975. lib. bdg. 16.95 (*0-912480-11-4*) Freneau.

Battle of Bunker's Hill. Hugh H. Brackenridge. (Works of Hugh Henry Brackenridge). 1989. reprint ed. lib. bdg. 79.00 (*0-7812-2044-0*) Rprt Serv.

Battle of Cape Esperance: Encounter at Guadalcanal. Charles Cook. LC 92-4658. (Illus.). 176p. 1992. reprint ed. 26.95 (*1-55750-126-2*) Naval Inst Pr.

Battle of Cedar Creek & the Recaptured Guns. John W. Stevens. 128p. 1987. pap. 10.00 (*0-942211-62-6*) Olde Soldier Bks.

***Battle of Chalk Bluff: An Account of General John S. Marmaduke's Second Missouri Raid.** Jerry Ponder. (Illus.). 202p. (C). 1995. pap. 13.95 (*0-9623922-3-5*) Ponder Bks.

Battle of Chancellorsville. Zachary Kent. LC 94-9486. (Cornerstones of Freedom Ser.). (Illus.). (J). 1994. lib. bdg. 12.30 (*0-516-06679-X*) Childrens.

Battle of Chancellorsville. Zachary Kent. LC 92-11358. (Cornerstones of Freedom Ser.). (Illus.). 260p. (J). 1995. pap. 3.95 (*0-516-46679-8*) Childrens.

Battle of Chateau Thierry - 1918: N. C. Wyeth - Color Lithographic Print. Russell L. Sturzebecker. 1988. 40.00 (*0-9600466-3-1*) Sturzebecker.

***Battle of Chickamauga.** William G. Robertson. (Civil War Ser.). (Illus.). 52p. (Orig.). 1995. pap. 3.95 (*0-915992-77-9*) Eastern Acorn.

Battle of Cloyd's Mountain & the Virginia & Tennessee Railroad Raid. Howard R. McManus. (Virginia Civil War Battles & Leaders Ser.). (Illus.). 107p. 1989. 19.95 (*0-930919-89-0*) H E Howard.

Battle of Cold Harbor. Louis J. Baltz, III. (Virginia Civil War Battles & Leaders Ser.). (Illus.). 282p. 1994. 25.00 (*1-56190-060-5*) H E Howard.

Battle of Cowpens. Kenneth Roberts. 15.95 (*0-89190-967-2*, Am Repr) Amereon Ltd.

***Battle of Cowpens.** Kenneth Roberts. 111p. 1981. pap. 3.50 (*0-915992-05-1*) Eastern Acorn.

Battle of Craney Island: A Matter of Credit. John M. Hallahan. LC 82-60450. (Illus.). 124p. 17.00 (*0-910581-01-0*) W S Dawson.

Battle of Dienbienphu. Jules Roy. 384p. 1984. pap. 10.95 (*0-88184-034-3*) Carroll & Graf.

Battle of Eutaw Springs. William Ioor. (Notable American Authors Ser.). 1992. reprint ed. lib. bdg. 75.00 (*0-7812-3337-2*) Rprt Serv.

Battle of Five Forks. Ed Bearss & Chris Calkins. (Virginia Civil War Battles & Leaders Ser.). (Illus.). 131p. 1985. 19.95 (*0-930919-20-3*) H E Howard.

Battle of Forever. A. E. Van Vogt. LC 78-53319. (Illus.). 1978. reprint ed. 9.95 (*0-931150-01-9*) AC Projects.

Battle of Fort George. rev. ed. Ernest Cruikshank. (Illus.). 56p. 1990. reprint ed. pap. 4.50 (*0-941967-10-7*) Old Fort Niagara Assn.

Battle of Franklin. R. W. Banks. 84p. 1988. 17.50 (*0-89029-065-2*) Morningside Bkshop.

Battle of Franklin. Jacob D. Cox. 351p. 1983. 30.00 (*0-89029-072-5*) Morningside Bkshop.

Battle of Galveston. Tom Townsend. Ed. by Edwin M. Eakin. (Illus.). 80p. (YA). (gr. 9-11). 1990. 10.95 (*0-89015-685-9*); pap. 5.95 (*0-89015-713-8*) Sunbelt Media.

Battle of Gettysburg. Vincent J. Coffey. LC 84-40834. (Turning Points in American History Ser.). (Illus.). 64p. (J). (gr. 5 up). 1985. lib. bdg. 14.95 (*0-382-06830-0*); pap. 7.95 (*0-382-09911-7*) Silver Burdett Pr.

Battle of Gettysburg. LC 63-17320. 1988. 14.95 (*0-8167-1517-3*) Troll Assocs.

Battle of Gettysburg. Alden R. Carter. LC 89-37033. (First Bks.). (Illus.). 1990. lib. bdg. 13.93 (*0-531-10852-X*) Watts.

***Battle of Gettysburg.** Franklin A. Haskell. (Illus.). 160p. 1994. 21.95 (*0-939218-05-4*) Chapman Billies.

Battle of Gettysburg. Neil Johnson. LC 88-30414. (Illus.). 64p. (J). (gr. 5 up). 1989. text ed. 15.95 (*0-02-747831-9*, Four Winds Pr) S&S Childrens.

Battle of Gettysburg. Francis Marshall. 337p. 1987. reprint ed. 30.00 (*0-942211-26-X*) Olde Soldier Bks.

Battle of Glorieta Pass: The Colorado Volunteers in the Civil War. William Whitford. (Illus.). 208p. 1990. reprint ed. pap. 15.00 (*0-87380-171-7*) Rio Grande.

Battle of Groton Heights: A Collection of Narratives, Official Reports, Records, Etc., of the Storming of Ft. Griswold. Charles Allyn. (Illus.). 399p. 1992. reprint ed. lib. bdg. 42.50 (*0-685-61617-7*) Higginson Bk Co.

Battle of Guadalcanal, 11-15 November 1942. LC 93-37891. (Illus.). 1994. reprint ed. 4.50 (*0-945274-22-X*) Naval Hist Ctr.

Battle of Harlem Heights. Henry P. Johnston. LC 79-115990. reprint ed. 36.00 (*0-404-03594-9*) AMS Pr.

Battle of Hastings. Holmes McDougall Editorial Staff. (Illus.). (C). 1988. 35.00 (*0-7157-2138-0*) St Mut.

***Battle of Hastings.** William W. Lace. LC 95-11711. (Battles of the Middle Ages Ser.). (J). 1996. lib. bdg. write for info. (*1-56006-416-1*) Lucent Bks.

***Battle of Hastings: Sources & Interpretations.** Ed. by Stephen Morillo. (Warfare in History: Sources & Interpretations Ser.: vol. 1). (Illus.). 272p. (Orig.). 1995. text ed. 45.00 (*0-85115-593-6*) Boydell & Brewer.

***Battle of Hastings: Sources & Interpretations.** Ed. by Stephen Morillo. (Warfare in History: Sources & Interpretations Ser.: vol. 1). (Illus.). 272p. (Orig.). 1995. pap. text ed. 27.00 (*0-85115-619-3*) Boydell & Brewer.

Battle of Hastings, England & Europe, 1035-1066. Sten Korner. LC 80-2221. reprint ed. 38.00 (*0-404-18765-X*) AMS Pr.

An Asterisk (*) at the beginning of an entry indicates that the title is appearing in BIP for the first time.

Battle of Horseshoe Bend. W. H. Brantley, Jr. (Illus.). 1955. pap. 3.75 (*0-87651-205-8*) Southern U Pr.

Battle of Hubbardton: The American Rebels Stem the Tide. John A. Williams. Ed. by Rebecca Davidson & John P. Dumville. (Illus.). 75p. (Orig.). 1988. pap. 10.00 (*0-9619912-1-6*) VT Div Hist Preservation.

Battle of Human Rights. Cecilia Medina-Quiroga. (C). 1988. lib. bdg. 122.00 (*90-247-3687-0*) Kluwer Ac.

Battle of Iwo Jima & the Men Who Fought There. Turner Publishing Co. Staff. LC 90-71688. 136p. 1990. 55.00 (*0-685-50321-6*) Turner Pub KY.

Battle of Jericho. Penny Frank. (Lion Story Bible Ser.). (Illus.). 24p. (J). (gr. 1 up). 1986. 3.99 (*0-85648-737-6*) Lion USA.

Battle of Jutland. Holloway H. Frost. LC 79-6108. (Navies & Men Ser.). (Illus.). 1980. reprint ed. lib. bdg. 63.95 (*0-405-13037-6*) Ayer.

Battle of Jutland: A Bibliography. Eugene L. Rasor. LC 91-24368. (Bibliographies of Battles & Leaders Ser.: No. 7). 192p. 1991. text ed. 49.95 (*0-313-28124-6*, RJU, Greenwood Pr) Greenwood.

***Battle of Karbala: Marsiya of Anis.** Tr. by David Matthews. (C). 1994. 16.00 (*81-7167-213-2*, Pub. by Rupa II) S Asia.

Battle of Koniggratz: Prussia's Victory over Austria, 1866. Gordon A. Craig. LC 75-35334. (Illus.). 211p. 1976. reprint ed. text ed. 35.00 (*0-8371-8563-7*, CRBK, Greenwood Pr) Greenwood.

Battle of Kosovo. Tr. by John Matthias & Vladeta Vuckovic. LC 87-10061. (Illus.). 76p. 1988. pap. 12.95 (*0-8040-0897-3*) Swallow.

***Battle of Lake Erie.** David Skaggs. 1995. write for info. (*0-614-06309-4*) Nautical & Aviation.

Battle of Lexington & Concord. Neil Johnson. LC 91-22790. (Illus.). 40p. (J). (gr. 4 up). 1992. text ed. 15.95 (*0-02-747841-6*, Four Winds Pr) S&S Childrens.

Battle of Leyte Gulf. Thomas J. Cutler. 288p. 1994. 25.00 (*0-06-016949-4*, HarpT) HarpC.

Battle of Leyte Gulf. Edwin P. Hoyt. 352p. 1987. mass mkt. 4.99 (*0-515-09230-4*) Jove Pubns.

Battle of Little Big Horn. Mari Sandoz. 18.95 (*0-89190-879-X*, Am Repr) Amereon Ltd.

Battle of Little Big Horn, Pt. I. 10.00 (*0-685-71800-X*, J M C & Co) Amereon Ltd.

Battle of Little Big Horn, Pt. II. 10.00 (*0-685-71801-8*, J M C & Co) Amereon Ltd.

Battle of Luke & Longnose. Barbara McClintock. LC 93-12815. (J). 1994. 14.95 (*0-395-65751-2*) HM.

Battle of Lundy's Lane. Donald Graves. LC 93-965. 350p. 1993. 28.95 (*1-877853-22-4*) Nautical & Aviation.

Battle of Maldon. Ed. by E. V. Gordon. (Old English Ser.). 1966. pap. text ed. 4.95 (*0-89197-565-9*) Irvington.

Battle of Maldon. Ed. by D. G. Scragg. (Old & Middle English Text Ser.). 128p. 1988. text ed. 10.95 (*0-7190-0838-7*, Pub. by Manchester Univ Pr UK) St Martin.

Battle of Maldon: A.D. 991. Ed. by D. G. Scragg. 288p. (C). 1991. text ed. 52.95 (*0-631-15987-8*) Blackwell Pubs.

Battle of Maldon: Fiction & Fact. Ed. by Janet Cooper. LC 93-38742. 1993. ring bd. 55.00 (*1-85285-065-5*) Hambledon Press.

Battle of Maldon: Text & Translation. Ed. & Tr. by Bill Griffiths. 96p. (Orig.). 1992. pap. text ed. 14.95 (*0-9516209-0-8*, Pub. by Anglo-Saxon Bks UK) Paul & Co Pubs.

Battle of Maldon & Short Poems from the Saxon Chronicle. Maldon. Ed. by Walter Sedgefield. LC 70-144444. (Belles Lettres Ser., Section I: No. 9). reprint ed. 27.50 (*0-404-53610-7*) AMS Pr.

***Battle of Marathon.** Don Nardo. LC 95-11710. (Battles of the Ancient World Ser.). (J). 1995. lib. bdg. write for info. (*1-56006-412-9*) Lucent Bks.

***Battle of Midway.** Earle Rice, Jr. LC 95-12206. (Battles of World War II Ser.). (J). 1996. lib. bdg. write for info. (*1-56006-415-3*) Lucent Bks.

Battle of Naseby & the Fall of King Charles I. Maurice Ashley. (Illus.). 224p. (C). 1991. text ed. 36.00 (*0-86299-628-7*) A Sutton Pub.

Battle of Naseby & the Fall of King Charles the First. Maurice Ashley. (Illus.). 1993. pap. 19.99 (*0-7509-0376-7*) A Sutton Pub.

Battle of Naseby & the Fall of King Charles the First. Maurice Ashley. (Illus.). 189p. 1993. pap. 19.95 (*0-312-10321-2*) St Martin.

Battle of New Market. William C. Davis. LC 82-18705. (Illus.). xiii, 249p. 1983. pap. 11.95 (*0-8071-1078-7*) La State U Pr.

Battle of New Market. William C. Davis. LC 92-31082. (Illus.). 288p. 1993. 18.95 (*0-8117-0576-5*) Stackpole.

***Battle of Normandy.** David Pietrusza. LC 95-12205. (Battles of World War II Ser.). (J). 1995. lib. bdg. write for info. (*1-56006-413-7*) Lucent Bks.

Battle of Normandy: Falaise Gap. James S. Lucas & James Barker. LC 78-17771. 176p. 1978. 24.50 (*0-8419-0418-9*) Holmes & Meier.

Battle of Pensacola. N. Orwin Rush. (Florida Classics Ser.). (Illus.). 157p. (Orig.). 1981. reprint ed. 9.95 (*0-912451-05-X*); reprint ed. pap. 6.95 (*0-912451-06-8*) Florida Classics.

Battle of Petersburg. LC 76-42075. (Civil War Monographs). 1972. reprint ed. pap. 21.00 (*0-527-17559-5*) Periodicals Srv.

Battle of Princeton. Samuel S. Smith. LC 67-31149. (Revolutionary War Bicentennial Ser.). (Illus.). 1967. lib. bdg. 12.95 (*0-912480-03-3*) Freneau.

***Battle of Sackett's Harbour.** Patrick A. Wilder. LC 94-22932. 1994. 28.95 (*1-877853-27-5*) Nautical & Aviation.

Battle of San Jacinto. James W. Pohl. 40p. 1989. pap. 5.95 (*0-87611-084-7*) Tex St Hist Assn.

Battle of San Pascual: Mini-Play. (Mexican-American Ser.). (J). (gr. 5 up). 1978. 5.00 (*0-89550-308-5*) Stevens & Shea.

Battle of Seven Pines, May 31 - June 1, 1862. Steven H. Newton. (Virginia Civil War Battles & Leaders Ser.). (Illus.). 147p. 1993. 19.95 (*1-56190-048-6*) H E Howard.

***Battle of Stones River.** Peter Cozzens. (Civil War Ser.). (Illus.). 52p. (Orig.). 1995. pap. 3.95 (*0-915992-67-1*) Eastern Acorn.

Battle of Stonington. James T. De Kay. LC 90-6265. (Illus.). 224p. 1990. 27.95 (*0-87021-279-6*) Naval Inst Pr.

***Battle of Tassafaronga.** R. Crenshaw. (Illus.). 224p. 1995. 29.95 (*0-614-06306-X*) Nautical & Aviation.

Battle of the Ages. Lester Sumrall. 64p. (Orig.). 1985. pap. text ed. 1.95 (*0-937580-87-2*) LeSEA Pub Co.

***Battle of the Airfields: Operation Bodenplatte, 1 January 1945.** Norman Franks. (Illus.). 240p. 1995. 29.95 (*1-898697-15-9*, Pub. by Grub St Pubns UK) Seven Hills Bk.

Battle of the Alamo. Ben H. Procter. LC 86-50749. (Illus.). 37p. 1986. pap. 5.95 (*0-87611-081-2*) Tex St Hist Assn.

Battle of the Atlantic. Wallace B. Black & Jean F. Blashfield. LC 91-7989. (World War II 50th Anniversary Ser.). (Illus.). 48p. (J). (gr. 5-6). 1991. text ed. 12.95 (*0-89686-558-4*, Crstwood Hse) Silver Burdett Pr.

***Battle of the Atlantic: The Corvettes & Their Crews: An Oral History.** Chris H. Bailey. (Illus.). 192p. 1995. 28.95 (*1-55750-734-1*) Naval Inst Pr.

Battle of the Atlantic 1939-1945: Proceedings fo the 50th Anniversary International Naval Conference. Ed. by Stephen Howarth & Derek Law. LC 94-66035. 640p. 1994. 49.95 (*1-55750-058-4*) Naval Inst Pr.

Battle of the Bands: Metallica vs. Slayer. pap. 14.95 (*0-89524-751-8*) Cherry Lane.

Battle of the Bands - Guns n' Roses vs. Skid Row. pap. 14.95 (*0-89524-761-5*) Cherry Lane.

Battle of the Bismarck Sea. Lawrence Cortesi. 1977. pap. 1.50 (*0-8439-0510-7*) Dorchester Pub Co.

Battle of the Books. Mary A. Dodge. (Notable American Authors Ser.). 1992. reprint ed. lib. bdg. 75.00 (*0-7812-2659-7*) Rprt Serv.

Battle of the Books: History & Literature in the Augustan Age. Joseph Levine. (Illus.). 448p. 1994. pap. 16.95 (*0-8014-8199-6*) Cornell U Pr.

Battle of the Books: History & Literature in the Augustan Age. Joseph M. Levine. LC 90-55735. (Illus.). 448p. 1991. 42.50 (*0-8014-2537-9*) Cornell U Pr.

Battle of the Books: K-8. Joanne Kelly. (Data Book Ser.). (Illus.). 201p. 1990. pap. text ed. 23.50 (*0-87287-779-5*); disk 25.50 (*0-87287-846-5*); Apple II 25.00 (*0-87287-845-7*); mac hd 26.00 (*0-87287-847-3*) Libs Unl.

Battle of the Books: Literary Censorship in the Public Schools, 1950-1985. Lee Burress. LC 88-30775. (Illus.). 395p. 1989. 42.50 (*0-8108-2151-6*) Scarecrow.

Battle of the Books: What It Takes to Be Educated in America. James Atlas. 160p. 1993. pap. 8.95 (*0-393-31070-1*) Norton.

Battle of the Books in Its Historical Setting. Anne E. Burlingame. LC 68-54230. 1969. reprint ed. 26.00 (*0-8196-0224-8*) Biblo.

***Battle of the Bridges: Community Rivalry in Dawson County, Nebraska.** 3rd ed. Rex German & Russ Czaplewski. Ed. by Bob Wallace. (Illus.). 200p. (C). Date not set. 12.95 (*0-9637898-3-X*); pap. 10.95 (*0-9637898-2-1*) Daw Cnty Hist Mus.

Battle of the Bulge. Wallace B. Black & Jean F. Blashfield. LC 92-1722. (World War II 50th Anniversary Ser.). (Illus.). 48p. (J). (gr. 5-6). 1993. text ed. 12.95 (*0-89686-568-1*, Crstwood Hse) Silver Burdett Pr.

Battle of the Bulge: Hitler's Ardennes Offensive 1944-1945. Danny S. Parker. (Illus.). 320p. 1991. 34.95 (*0-938289-04-7*) Combined Bks.

***Battle of the Bulge: December 1944: A Historical Collage on the Ardennes Offensive, Vol. I The Germans.** Roland Gaul. Tr. by Edward Force. LC 95-67873. (Illus.). 350p. 1995. 35.00 (*0-88740-746-3*) Schiffer.

***Battle of the Bulge: December 1944: A Historical Collage on the Ardennes Offensive, Vol. II The Americans.** Roland Gaul. Tr. by Edward Force. LC 95-67873. (Illus.). 350p. 1995. 35.00 (*0-88740-747-1*) Schiffer.

Battle of the Bulge 50th Anniversary. Turner Publishing Company Staff. LC 90-71723. 136p. 1991. 48.00 (*1-56311-013-X*) Turner Pub KY.

Battle of the Centuries: A List of References. Comp. by Ruth S. Freitag. LC 93-42838. 1994. write for info. (*0-8444-0809-3*) Lib Congress.

Battle of the Class Clowns. Jacqueline A. Ball. (Dino School Ser.). (J). 1990. pap. 2.95 (*0-06-106007-0*, PL) HarpC.

Battle of the Crater. rev. ed. John C. Featherston. Ed. & Intro. by George R. Stewart. LC 87-27585. (Eyewitness Accounts of the Civil War Ser.). (Illus.). 36p. (C). 1987. pap. 10.00 (*0-942301-02-1*) Birm Pub Lib.

Battle of the Dinosaurs. David C. Knight. (Illus.). 96p. (J). (gr. 3-7). 1982. pap. 5.95 (*0-13-069518-1*, Pub. by Treehouse Paperback) P-H.

Battle of the Dinosaurs. George Poppel. 1988. 10.95 (*0-915765-56-X*) Natl Pr Bks.

Battle of the East Coast, Vol. 1: The Defensive. J. P. Foynes. (C). 1991. 59.00 (*0-86138-089-4*, Pub. by T Dalton UK) St Mut.

Battle of the Frogs & Fairford's Flies: Miracles & the Pulp Press During the English Revolution. Jerome Friedman. LC 92-38575. 320p. 1993. text ed. 45.00 (*0-312-09125-7*) St Martin.

Battle of the Frogs & Fairford's Flies: Miracles & the Pulp Press During the English Revolution. Jerome Friedman. 320p. 1993. text ed. 16.95 (*0-312-10170-8*) St Martin.

***Battle of the Generals: The Untold Story of the Falaise Pocket - the Campaign that Should Have Won World War II.** Martin Blumenson. 1995. write for info. (*0-688-14235-4*, Quill) Morrow.

Battle of the Generals: The Untold Story of the Falaise Pocket, the Campaign that Should Have Won World War II. Martin Blumenson. LC 92-31705. 1993. 25.00 (*0-688-11837-2*) Morrow.

Battle of the Gods: The Emerging God of the New Age. Robert A. Morey. 324p. (Orig.). (C). 1989. pap. 9.95 (*0-925703-00-1*) Crown MA.

Battle of the Gods & Giants: The Legacies of Descartes & Gassendi, 1655-1715. Thomas M. Lennon. LC 92-26088. (Studies in Intellectual History & the History of Philosophy). 456p. 1993. 62.50 (*0-691-07400-3*) Princeton U Pr.

Battle of the Ironclads: The Monitor & the Merrimack. Alden R. Carter. LC 93-417. (First Bks.). (Illus.). 64p. (J). (gr. 4-6). 1993. lib. bdg. 13.93 (*0-531-20091-4*) Watts.

Battle of the Little Big Horn. Mari Sandoz. LC 78-8733. (Illus.). 191p. 1978. reprint ed. pap. 7.95 (*0-8032-9100-0*, Bison Books) U of Nebr Pr.

Battle of the Little Bighorn. Mark Henckel. (Highlights in American History Ser.). (Illus.). 32p. (Orig.). (J). (gr. 3-7). 1992. pap. 5.95 (*1-56044-042-2*) Falcon Pr MT.

Battle of the Queens. Jean Plaidy. 384p. 1982. pap. 2.95 (*0-449-24565-9*, Crest) Fawcett.

Battle of the River Plate. Dudley Pope. 296p. 1990. mass mkt. 4.95 (*0-380-71045-5*) Avon.

Battle of the Rosebud: Prelude to the Little Bighorn. Neil C. Mangum. LC 87-50694. (Montana & the West Ser.: Vol. 5). (Illus.). 200p. (C). 1987. 35.00 (*0-912783-11-7*) Upton Sons.

Battle of the Strong. Gilbert Parker. 1976. lib. bdg. 18.50 (*0-89968-078-X*, Lghtyr Pr) Buccaneer Bks.

Battle of the Strong: A Romance of Two Kingdoms. Parker. (Jersey Heritage Editions Ser.). 1991. write for info. (*0-86120-020-9*, Pub. by Aris & Phillips UK) David Brown.

Battle of the Teton Basin. Jason Manning. (High Country Ser.: No. 3). 352p. (Orig.). 1994. pap. 4.50 (*0-451-17829-7*, Sig) NAL-Dutton.

Battle of the Titans: Kasparov - Karpov; New York - Lyon. Raymond Keene. 128p. 1991. pap. 14.95 (*0-02-008351-3*) Macmillan.

Battle of the Washita: The Sheridan-Custer Indian Campaign of 1867-69. Stan Hoig. LC 79-14844. (Illus.). xx, 292p. 1979. reprint ed. 35.00 (*0-8032-2307-2*); reprint ed. pap. 11.95 (*0-8032-7204-9*) U of Nebr Pr.

Battle of the Wilderness. Morris Schaff. 34.00 (*0-8488-1155-0*) Amereon Ltd.

Battle of the Wilderness, May 5-6, 1864. Gordon C. Rhea. LC 93-42110. (Illus.). 520p. 1994. 34.95 (*0-8071-1873-7*) La State U Pr.

Battle of the Wine Dark Sea: The Aegean Sea Campaign, 1940-45. Lew Lind. (Illus.). 192p. 1994. 29.95 (*0-86417-562-0*, Pub. by Kangaroo Pr AT) Seven Hills Bk.

Battle of Tippecanoe. Richard J. Reid. LC 89-155804. (Illus.). 66p. 1988. reprint ed. pap. write for info. (*1-877713-00-7*) R J Reid.

Battle of Trevilian Station: The Civil War's Greatest & Bloodiest All Cavalry Battle, with Eyewitness Memoirs. rev. ed. Walbrook D. Swank. LC 94-14452. (Civil War Heritage Ser.: Vol. IV). (Illus.). 156p. (C). 1994. pap. text ed. 14.99 (*0-942597-68-0*, Burd St Pr) White Mane Pub.

Battle of Wagram. Gilles Lapouge. Tr. by J. Maxwell Brownjohn. 356p. (C). 1988. 19.95 (*0-941533-32-8*) New Amsterdam Bks.

Battle of Wagram. Gilles Lapouge. Tr. by J. Maxwell Brownjohn. 356p. 1990. reprint ed. pap. 12.95 (*1-56131-013-1*) New Amsterdam Bks.

Battle of White Plains. Arthur A. Merrill. (Illus.). (YA). (gr. 7 up). 1976. pap. 3.00 (*0-911894-27-6*) Analysis.

Battle of Wisconsin Heights. Ed. by Crawford B. Thayer. (Black Hawk War Eye-Witness Ser.). (Illus.). 416p. (Orig.). 1983. pap. text ed. 9.95 (*0-9611000-1-X*) Thayer Assocs.

***Battle of Zama.** Don Nardo. LC 95-11760. (Battles of the Ancient World Ser.). (J). 1996. lib. bdg. write for info. (*1-56006-420-X*) Lucent Bks.

Battle off Midway Island. Theodore Taylor. (Great Sea Battles of WWII Ser.: Bk. I). 144p. (Orig.). (YA). (gr. 7 up). 1981. pap. 3.95 (*0-380-78790-3*, Flare) Avon.

Battle over Homework: An Administrator's Guide to Setting Sound & Effective Policies. Harris Cooper. Ed. by Jerry J. Herman & Janice L. Herman. (Roadmaps to Success Ser.). 72p. 1994. pap. 15.00 (*0-8039-6163-4*) Corwin Pr.

Battle-Pieces & Aspects of the War. Herman Melville. LC 60-5042. 1979. reprint ed. lib. bdg. 50.00 (*0-8201-1252-6*) Schol Facsimiles.

***Battle-Pieces & Aspects of the War.** Herman Melville. 282p. 1995. reprint ed. pap. 13.95 (*0-306-80655-X*) Da Capo.

Battle Plan: Equipping the Church for the 90s. Chris Stanton. LC 92-72290. 138p. 1992. pap. 7.99 (*1-56384-034-0*) Huntington Hse.

Battle Poems. Richard O'Connell. 1977. pap. 2.50 (*0-686-17592-1*) Atlantis.

Battle Poems. Richard O'Connell. 1987. pap. 10.00 (*0-318-32928-X*) Atlantis Edns.

Battle Ready: Winning the War with Temptation. 2nd ed. Mark L. Littleton. 1992. pap. 1.80 (*0-89693-577-9*, Victor Books) SP Pubns.

Battle Report: Selected Poems. Harvey Shapiro. LC 66-23924. (Wesleyan Poetry Program Ser.). 80p. reprint ed. pap. 25.00 (*0-7837-0221-3*, 2040529) Bks Demand.

Battle Rock, the Hero's Story: How a Small Canon Done Its Work - a Desperate Encounter of Nine Men with Three Hundred Indians at Port Orford, an Oregon Documentary. Bert Webber & Margie Webber. LC 91-376. (Illus.). 78p. (Orig.). 1992. pap. 8.95 (*0-936738-52-9*) Webb Research.

***Battle Songs of the Second American Revolution.** James E. Norwood. 1996. write for info. (*0-915854-96-1*) Friend Freedom.

Battle Stalin Lost: Memoirs of Yugoslavia 1948-1953. Vladimir Dedijer. 341p. 1978. reprint ed. 57.50 (*0-85124-223-5*, Pub. by Spokesman Bks UK) Coronet Bks.

Battle Stars: Marines & the Quest for Superior Consciousness. William M. Specht, III. LC 85-81005. 216p. (Orig.). 1988. pap. 10.00 (*0-931889-07-3*) Epistemology Pubs.

Battle Station. Ben Bova. 1990. pap. 3.95 (*0-8125-1300-2*) Tor Bks.

Battle Stations: A Grizzly from the Coral Sea (1944) & Peleliu Landing (1945) deluxe ed. Tom Lea. LC 88-19176. (Illus.). 88p. 1988. 30.00 (*0-933841-07-8*) Still Point TX.

Battle Stations! The Homefront World War II. Nan Heacock. LC 92-11857. (Illus.). 152p. 1992. 22.95 (*0-8138-1023-X*) Iowa St U Pr.

Battle Studies: Ancient & Modern Battle. Charles J. Ardant Du Picq. Tr. by John N. Greely & Robert C. Cotton. LC 83-45691. reprint ed. 27.00 (*0-404-20006-0*) AMS Pr.

Battle Tactics of the Western Front: The British Army's Art of Attack, 1916-1918. Paddy Griffith. (Illus.). 304p. 1994. 30.00 (*0-300-05910-8*) Yale U Pr.

Battle Tanks & Support Vehicles. Alan K. Russell. LC 93-36814. (Greenhill Military Manuals Ser.). 160p. 1994. 19.95 (*1-85367-174-6*) Stackpole.

Battle Technology: The Lost Issues. Hilary Ayer. 144p. 1992. pap. 12.95 (*0-9633268-0-5*) Pac Rim CA.

Battle Thunder: The Story of Britain's Artillery. Kenneth Brookes. (Illus.). 256p. 1973. 22.00 (*0-8464-0185-1*) Beekman Pubs.

Battle to Control Broadcast News: Who Owns the First Amendment? Hugh C. Donahue. 240p. 1989. 24.95x (*0-262-04099-9*) MIT Pr.

Battle to Save the Houston. John G. Miller. Ed. by Paul McCarthy. 264p. 1992. reprint ed. mass mkt. 4.99 (*0-671-78621-0*) PB.

Battle to Save the Houston, October 1944 to March 1945. John G. Miller. LC 85-314. (Illus.). 226p. 1985. 24.95 (*0-87021-276-1*) Naval Inst Pr.

Battle to Stay Competitive: Changing the Traditional Workplace: The Delco Moraine NDH Story. Charles R. Birkholz & Jim Villella. LC 90-19195. 110p. 1991. pap. 12.00 (*0-915299-96-8*) Prod Press.

Battle with the Slum. Jacob A. Riis. LC 69-16245. (Criminology, Law Enforcement, & Social Problems Ser.: No. 77). (Illus.). 1969. reprint ed. 14.00 (*0-87585-077-4*) Patterson Smith.

Battle with the Slum: A Ten Years War Rewritten. Jacob A. Riis. (Illus.). 1972. reprint ed. 14.00 (*0-8290-0653-2*) Irvington.

Battle Your Bank. 1992. lib. bdg. 79.00 (*0-8490-5425-7*) Gordon Pr.

Battle Your Bank & Win. 1991. lib. bdg. 69.95 (*0-8490-4471-5*) Gordon Pr.

Battleborn Nevada: Its People, History & Stories. Don Lynch & David Thompson. Ed. by James H. Bean. LC 93-79470. (Illus.). 360p. (YA). (gr. 6 up). 1994. 31.00 (*0-913205-20-6*) Grace Dangberg.

Battlecry. John Barnes. (Time Raider Ser.: No. 605). 1992. mass mkt. 3.50 (*0-373-63605-9*) Harlequin Bks.

Battlecry Forever. Joanna Campbell. (YA). (gr. 7 up). 1992. mass mkt. 3.50 (*0-06-106771-7*, Harp PBks) HarpC.

Battlefield: Farming a Civil War Battleground. Peter Svenson. 256p. 1994. pap. 11.00 (*0-345-38419-9*, Ballantine Trade) Ballantine.

Battlefield: Farming a Civil War Battleground. Peter Svenson. 240p. 1992. 21.95 (*0-571-19798-1*) Faber & Faber.

Battlefield & Classroom: Four Decades with the American Indian, 1867-1904. Richard H. Pratt. Ed. by Robert M. Utley. LC 64-20931. (Yale Western Americana Ser.: Vol. 6). 412p. reprint ed. pap. 117.50 (*0-8357-5997-0*, 2051681) Bks Demand.

Battlefield & Classroom: Four Decades with the American Indian, 1876-1904. Richard H. Pratt. Ed. by Robert M. Utley. LC 86-25019. (Landmark Edition Ser.). xx, 390p. 1987. reprint ed. 35.00 (*0-8032-3679-4*) U of Nebr Pr.

Battlefield Atlas of the American Revolution. Craig L. Symonds. LC 86-63201. (Illus.). 112p. 1986. 22.95 (*0-933852-53-3*) Nautical & Aviation.

Battlefield Atlas of the Civil War. 2nd ed. Craig L. Symonds. LC 83-13325. (Illus.). 130p. 1987. 22.95 (*0-933852-49-5*) Nautical & Aviation.

Battlefield Atlas of the Civil War. 3rd ed. Craig L. Symonds. 115p. 1993. 22.95 (*1-877853-25-9*) Nautical & Aviation.

Battlefield Chaplains: Catholic Priests in World War II. Donald F. Crosby. LC 93-39804. (Modern War Studies). (Illus.). 300p. 1994. 27.50x (*0-7006-0662-9*) U Pr of KS.

***Battlefield Deception.** 1995. lib. bdg. 255.00 (*0-8490-6674-3*) Gordon Pr.

Battlefield Earth. L. Ron Hubbard. 1050p. 1993. pap. 6.99 (*0-88404-681-8*) Bridge Pubns Inc.

Battlefield Nuclear Weapons: Issues & Options. Ed. by Stephen D. Biddle & Peter D. Feaver. LC 89-22275. (Occasional Papers Ser.: No. 5). 170p. (Orig.). (C). 1990. lib. bdg. 43.50 (*0-8191-7604-4*); pap. text ed. 21.00 (*0-8191-7605-2*) U Pr of Amer.

B

Battlefield of the Gods: Aspects of Mexican History, Art & Exploration. P. Kelemen. 1976. lib. bdg. 59.95 (*0-87968-711-8*) Gordon Pr.

***Battlefield Survival & Radioelectronic Combat.** 1995. lib. bdg. 251.95 (*0-8490-6620-4*) Gordon Pr.

Battlefield Walks of the Midlands. David Clark. LC 94-4452. 1994. 20.00 (*0-7509-0258-2*) A Sutton Pub.

Battlefield Weapons Systems & Technology Series, 12 vols., Set. Ed. by R. G. Lee. 2540p. 1985. text ed. 350.00 (*0-08-030003-0*, Pergamon Pr); pap. text ed. 187.00 (*0-08-030526-1*, Pergamon Pr) Elsevier.

Battlefields. Lynn Stone. LC 93-6781. (YA). 1993. write for info. (*0-86625-444-7*) Rourke Pubns.

Battlefields & Burial Grounds: The Indian Struggle to Protect Ancestral Graves & Human Remains in the United States. Roger C. Echo-Hawk & Walter R. Echo-Hawk. LC 92-39893. (YA). (gr. 7 up). 1993. 19.95 (*0-8225-2663-8*, Lerner Publctns) Lerner Group.

***Battlefields & Playgrounds.** Janos Nyiri. Tr. by William Brandon. LC 95-5389. 536p. 1995. 25.00 (*0-374-10918-4*) FS&G.

Battlefields of Britain & Ireland. Howard Green. 1983. pap. 26.50 (*0-09-464520-5*) Trans-Atl Phila.

Battlefields of Germany, from the Outbreak of the Thirty-Years' War. George B. Malleson. LC 68-54798. 360p. 1971. reprint ed. text ed. 38.50 (*0-8371-5017-5*, MABG, Greenwood Pr) Greenwood.

Battlefields of Knowledge. Ed. by Norman Long & Ann Long. LC 92-2785. 370p. 1992. 59.95 (*0-415-07205-0*, A7631); pap. 19.95 (*0-415-07206-9*, A7635) Routledge.

Battlefields of the Civil War. (Illus.). 256p. (Orig.). 1993. pap. 11.95 (*1-55650-603-1*) Hunter NJ.

***Battlefields of the Civil War.** Blair Howard. 288p. (Orig.). 1995. pap. 13.95 (*1-55650-685-6*) Hunter NJ.

Battlefields of the Civil War. James V. Murfin. 1988. 17.99 (*0-517-62371-4*) Random Hse Value.

Battlefields of the Civil War. United States National Park Service Staff. 1979. 30.95 (*0-405-12296-9*) Ayer.

***Battlefields of the Eternal Struggle.** (Vampire Ser.). Date not set. 12.00 (*1-56504-229-8*) White Wolf.

***Battlefields of the First World War: A Travellers Guide.** Tonie Holt & Valmai Holt. (Illus.). 186p. 1995. pap. 15.95 (*1-85793-770-8*, Pub. by Pavilion UK) Trafalgar.

Battlefront Namibia. John Ya-Otto et al. LC 81-7214. 168p. 1981. 12.95 (*0-88208-132-2*); pap. 6.95 (*1-55652-063-8*) L Hill Bks.

Battlefronts of Southern Africa. Colin Legum. LC 87-25481. 1988. 49.50 (*0-8419-1135-5*); pap. 34.50 (*0-8419-1144-4*) Holmes & Meier.

Battleground. Stephen Bates. 1993. 24.00 (*0-671-79358-6*) S&S Trade.

Battleground: Fact & Fantasy in Palestine. Samuel Katz. (Illus.). 322p. 1986. reprint ed. pap. 4.95 (*0-933503-03-2*) Sure Sellers.

Battleground: One Mother's Crusade, the Religious Right, & the Struggle for Our Schools. rev. ed. Stephen Bates. LC 94-17764. 1994. pap. 15.95 (*0-8050-3516-8*) H Holt & Co.

Battleground: The Autobiography of Margaret A. Haley. Margaret A. Haley. Ed. by Robert L. Reid. LC 81-12930. (Illus.). 336p. 1982. 29.95 (*0-252-00913-4*) U of Ill Pr.

Battleground for the Union. William Barney. 448p. (C). 1989. pap. text ed. write for info. (*0-13-069386-3*) P-H.

***Battleground Line of Fire Close Combat.** W. E. B. Griffin. 1995. 11.98 (*0-399-14013-1*) Putnam Pub Group.

Battleground of the Curriculum: Liberal Education & American Experience. W. B. Carnochan. LC 92-40401. 186p. 1993. 35.00 (*0-8047-2147-5*) Stanford U Pr.

***Battleground of the Curriculum: Liberal Education & American Experience.** W. B. Carnochan. 1994. pap. 13.95 (*0-8047-2364-8*) Stanford U Pr.

Battlehymn. Jack McKinney. (Robotech Ser.: No. 4). (Orig.). 1987. mass mkt. 4.95 (*0-345-34137-6*, Del Rey) Ballantine.

Battleplan for the Battlefield. David Benoit & Harold L. Wilmington. (Illus.). 146p. 1990. 49.95 (*0-923105-12-3*) Glory Ministries.

Battles & Battlescenes of World War Two. David G. Chandler. 192p. 1989. text ed. 19.95 (*0-02-897175-2*) Macmillan.

Battles & Enchantments Retold from Early Gaelic Literature. Norreys J. O'Conor. LC 71-124247. (Select Bibliographies Reprint Ser.). 1977. reprint ed. 17.95 (*0-8369-5435-1*) Ayer.

Battles & Leaders of the Civil War. Ed. by Ned Bradford. (Illus.). 640p. 1989. pap. 16.95 (*0-452-01004-7*, Mer) NAL-Dutton.

Battles & Leaders of the Civil War. Ned Bradford. 1988. 9.99 (*0-517-29820-1*) Random Hse Value.

Battles & Leaders of the Civil War, Vol. 1: The Opening Battles. 1985. 12.98 (*0-89009-569-8*) Bk Sales Inc.

Battles & Leaders of the Civil War, Vol. 2: The Struggle Intensifies. 1985. 12.98 (*0-89009-570-1*) Bk Sales Inc.

Battles & Leaders of the Civil War, Vol. 3: The Tide Shifts. 1985. 12.98 (*0-89009-571-X*) Bk Sales Inc.

Battles & Leaders of the Civil War, Vol. 4: Retreat with Honor. 1985. 12.98 (*0-89009-572-8*) Bk Sales Inc.

Battles & Skirmishes of the Great Sioux War, 1876-1877: The Military View. Anno. & Comp. by Jerome A. Greene. LC 93-16433. (C). 1993. 24.95 (*0-8061-2535-7*) U of Okla Pr.

Battle's End & The Three Crosses. Max Brand. 1990. pap. 3.50 (*0-8125-0522-0*) Tor Bks.

Battles for Casino. E. D. Smith. (Battle Standards Ser.). 216p. (C). 1989. reprint ed. lib. bdg. 25.00x (*0-8095-7570-1*) Borgo Pr.

Battles, Hassles, Tantrums & Tears. Susan Beekman & Jeanne Holmes. LC 92-37608. 1993. 12.00 (*0-688-11937-9*) Hearst Bks.

Battles in a New Land: A Sourcebook on Colonial America. Ed. by Carter Smith. LC 91-13940. (American Albums from the Collections of the Library of Congress). (Illus.). 96p. (J). (gr. 5-8). 1991. lib. bdg. 18.90 (*1-56294-034-1*); pap. 5.95 (*1-878841-65-3*) Millbrook Pr.

Battles in the Desert & Other Stories. Jose E. Pacheco. Tr. by Katherine Silver. LC 86-28596. 128p. 1987. 19.95 (*0-8112-1019-7*); pap. 8.95 (*0-8112-1020-0*, NDP637) New Directions.

Battles Lost & Won: Essays from Civil War History. Ed. by John T. Hubbell. LC 75-10045. (Contributions in American History Ser.: No. 45). 289p. 1976. text ed. 29.95 (*0-8371-7959-9*, HCW/, Greenwood Pr) Greenwood.

Battles of Appomattox Station & Appomattox Court House, April 8-9, 1865. Chris M. Calkins. (Illus.). 300p. 1987. 19.95 (*0-930919-46-7*) H E Howard.

Battles of Barnet & Tewkesbury. P. W. Hammond. 210p. 1993. pap. 19.95 (*0-312-10324-7*) St Martin.

Battles of Barnett & Tewksbury. Michael Bennett. (Illus.). 176p. 1993. pap. 19.99 (*0-7509-0374-0*) A Sutton Pub.

Battles of Cape Esperance, 11 October 1942 & Santa Cruz Islands, 26 October 1942. LC 93-37892. (Illus.). 1994. reprint ed. 4.00 (*0-945274-21-1*) Naval Hist Ctr.

Battles of Coral Sea & Midway, 1942: A Selected Bibliography. Myron J. Smith, Jr. LC 91-20673. (Bibliographies of Battles & Leaders Ser.: No. 5). 184p. 1991. text ed. 59.50 (*0-313-28120-3*, SQR, Greenwood Pr) Greenwood.

Battles of Cow Green: A Case Study on Water Resources in Britain. Edward S. Flash, Jr. (Western Societies Papers). 113p. 1981. 11.95 (*0-8014-9635-7*) Cornell U Pr.

Battles of Hastings. Reg Cload. (PECH Pergamon Chess Ser.). (Illus.). 151p. 1991. pap. 19.90 (*0-08-037791-2*, Pub. by CHES UK) Macmillan.

Battles of Life & Death. David Hellerstein. 288p. 1987. mass mkt. 6.95 (*0-446-38422-4*) Warner Bks.

Battles of Peace. Michael L. Lanning. (Orig.). 1992. mass mkt. 4.99 (*0-8041-0609-6*) Ivy Books.

Battles of Saratoga. John R. Elting. LC 77-89325. (Revolutionary War Bicentennial Ser.). (Illus.). 1977. lib. bdg. 19.95 (*0-89180-13-0*) Freneau.

Battles of Savo Island, 9 August 1942 & the Eastern Solomons, 23-25 August 1942. LC 93-37894. (Illus.). 1994. reprint ed. 4.25 (*0-945274-20-3*) Naval Hist Ctr.

Battles of Texas. Joe B. Frantz et al. (Illus.). 190p. 1967. 20.00 (*0-685-50844-7*) Texian.

Battles of the American Revolution, 1775-1781: Historical & Military Criticism, 2 vols in 1. Henry B. Carrington. Incl. Battle Maps & Charts of the American Revolution. LC 67-29047. reprint ed. (*0-318-50788-9*); LC 67-29047. (Eyewitness Accounts of the American Revolution Ser., No. 1). 1968. reprint ed. 31.95 (*0-405-01107-5*) Ayer.

Battles of the British Navy, 2 vols, Set. Joseph Allen. 1977. lib. bdg. 250.00 (*0-8490-1480-8*) Gordon Pr.

Battles of the Prophet of Allah, Vol. 1. Gulzar Ahmad. 290p. (Orig.). 1986. pap. 12.95 (*1-56744-228-5*) Kazi Pubns.

Battles of the Prophet of Allah, Vol. 2. Gulzar Ahmad. 290p. (Orig.). 1986. pap. 12.95 (*1-56744-229-3*) Kazi Pubns.

Battles of the Revolutionary War, 1775-1781. William J. Wood. (Major Battles & Campaigns Ser.: Vol. III). 368p. (C). 1990. 24.95 (*0-945575-03-3*) Algonquin Bks.

***Battles of the Revolutionary War, 1775-1781.** W. J. Wood. Ed. & Intro. by John S. Eisenhower. (Major Battles & Campaigns Ser.). (Illus.). 363p. 1995. reprint ed. pap. 13.95 (*0-306-80617-7*) Da Capo.

Battles of the Scottish Wars of Independence. Andrew Fisher. 200p. (C). 1989. pap. 30.00 (*0-685-65008-1*, Pub. by J Donald) St Mut.

Battles of the Third World War. Larry Bond. Ed. by Marc Miller. (Harpoon Ser.). 49p. (Orig.). 1987. pap. 8.00 (*0-943580-43-9*) Game Designers.

Battles of the Twentieth Century. Chris Bishop. 224p. 1989. 19.99 (*0-517-66221-3*) Random Hse Value.

Battles of World History. W. Marker & H. Helmut. 438p. 1978. 175.00 (*0-317-57279-2*, Pub. by Collets UK) St Mut.

***Battles on the Bench: Conflict Inside the Supreme Court.** Phillip J. Cooper. 224p. (C). 1995. 24.95 (*0-7006-0737-4*) U Pr of KS.

Battles Royal Down North. Norman Duncan. LC 70-125209. (Short Story Index Reprint Ser.). (Illus.). 1977. 19.95 (*0-8369-3576-4*) Ayer.

Battles That Changed the Modern World. Dale Anderson. LC 93-17028. (Twenty Events Ser.). (Illus.). 48p. (J). (gr. 5-7). 1993. lib. bdg. 22.80 (*0-8114-4928-9*) Raintree Steck-V.

Battles with Dragons: Certain Tales of Political Yoga. Eugenia Macer-Story. 180p. (Orig.). 1994. pap. 25.00 (*1-879980-03-7*) Magick Mirror.

Battleship Arizona: An Illustrated History. Paul Stillwell. LC 91-14519. (Illus.). 480p. 1991. 49.95 (*0-87021-023-8*) Naval Inst Pr.

Battleship at War. Ivan Musicant. 376p. 1988. mass mkt. 4.95 (*0-380-70487-0*) Avon.

Battleship Bismarck. Ulrich E. Herzog. LC 89-63850. (Illus.). 160p. 1989. 34.95 (*0-88740-221-6*) Schiffer.

Battleship Bismarck: A Survivor's Story, New & Expanded Edition. Burkard B. Von Mullenheim-Rechberg. Tr. by Jack Sweetman. LC 90-6448. (Illus.). 512p. 1990. 29.95 (*0-87021-027-0*) Naval Inst Pr.

Battleship Building & Party Politics in Germany, 1894-1901: A Cross-section of the Political, Social & Ideological Preconditions of German Imperialism. Eckart Kehr. Ed. by Pauline R. Anderson & Eugene N. Anderson. (Midway Reprint Ser.). 528p. reprint ed. pap. 150.50 (*0-8357-5998-9*, 2024051) Bks Demand.

Battleship Country: The Battle Fleet at Long Beach-San Pedro, California, 1919-1940. Harvey M. Biegel. LC 82-63060. (Illus.). 76p. 1983. 6.95 (*0-933126-30-1*) Pictorial Hist.

Battleship Dreadnought. John Roberts. (Anatomy of the Ship Ser.). (Illus.). 256p. 1993. 36.95 (*1-55750-057-6*) Naval Inst Pr.

Battleship Missouri. Valerie Drogues. LC 93-10423. (Those Daring Machines Ser.). (Illus.). 48p. (J). (gr. 5-6). 1994. text ed. 13.95 (*0-89686-825-7*, Crstwood Hse) Silver Burdett Pr.

***Battleship Missouri: An Illustrated History.** Paul Stillwell. (Illus.). 450p. 1995. 55.00 (*1-55750-780-5*) Naval Inst Pr.

Battleship New Jersey: An Illustrated History. Paul Stillwell. 319p. 1987. 49.95 (*0-87021-029-7*) Naval Inst Pr.

Battleship North Carolina. Ben W. Blee. Ed. by Frank S. Conlon & Amo F. Judd. (Illus.). 100p. 1982. 14.95 (*0-9608538-0-4*); pap. 8.95 (*0-9608538-1-2*) USS North Car.

Battleship Oregon: Bulldog of the Navy. Bert Webber. LC 93-45360. (Illus.). 142p. (Orig.). 1994. pap. 12.95 (*0-936738-79-0*) Webb Research.

Battleship Potemkin. Sergei M. Eisenstein. (Classic Screenplay Ser.). (Illus.). 100p. 1988. pap. 9.95 (*0-571-12559-X*) Faber & Faber.

Battleship Royal Sovereign & Sister Ships. Ed. by S. Smith. (C). 1986. text ed. 130.00 (*0-685-38776-3*, Pub. by Maritime Bks UK) St Mut.

Battleship Sailor. Theodore Mason. LC 81-85440. (Bluejacket Paperback Ser.). 1994. pap. 12.95 (*1-55750-579-9*) Naval Inst Pr.

Battleship Texas. Hugh Power. LC 92-7432. (Centennial Series of the Association of Former Students: No. 45). (Illus.). 166p. 1993. 29.50 (*0-89096-516-1*); pap. 9.95 (*0-89096-519-6*) Tex A&M Univ Pr.

Battleship "Tirpitz" Siegfried Breyer. LC 89-84174. (Illus.). 48p. 1989. pap. 9.95 (*0-88740-184-8*) Schiffer.

Battleship Warspite. Ross Watton. (Anatomy of the Ship Ser.). 120p. 1987. 36.95 (*0-87021-994-4*) Naval Inst Pr.

Battleship Yamato. Janusz Skulski. LC 88-62458. (Anatomy of the Ship Ser.). 192p. 1989. 36.95 (*0-87021-019-X*) Naval Inst Pr.

Battleships. M. Walmer. (Sea Power Library). (Illus.). 48p. (J). (gr. 3-8). 1989. lib. bdg. 18.60 (*0-86625-083-2*) Rourke Corp.

Battleships: Allied Battleships in World War II, Vol. 2. William H. Garzke, Jr. & Robert O. Dulin, Jr. LC 79-90551. (Battleships Ser.). (Illus.). 352p. 1980. 75.00 (*0-87021-100-5*) Naval Inst Pr.

Battleships: Axis & Neutral Battleships in World War II, Vol. 3. William Garzke, Jr. & Robert O. Dulin, Jr. (Battleships Ser.: Vol. 3). (Illus.). 408p. 1985. 75.00 (*0-87021-101-3*) Naval Inst Pr.

Battleships: United States Battleships, 1935-1992, Vol. 1. 2nd rev. ed. William H. Garzke, Jr. & Robert O. Dulin, Jr. LC 93-43601. (Illus.). 404p. 1995. 75.00 (*1-55750-174-2*) Naval Inst Pr.

***Battleships in Action, 2 vols., Set.** H. W. Wilson. (Illus.). 1995. 75.00 (*0-614-06532-1*) Naval Inst Pr.

Battleships in Action, 2 vols., Set. Herbert W. Wilson. 1968. reprint ed. 59.00 (*0-403-00046-7*) Scholarly.

***Battleships in Action, Vol. 1.** H. W. Wilson. (Illus.). 352p. 1995. write for info. (*0-614-06533-X*) Naval Inst Pr.

***Battleships in Action, Vol. 2.** H. W. Wilson. (Illus.). 398p. 1995. write for info. (*1-55750-061-4*) Naval Inst Pr.

Battleships, Sailors & High-Seas Action. C. F. Marley. 94p. 1991. pap. 9.90 (*0-9631610-0-8*) Audubon Hills.

BattleSpace. 1993. pap. 25.00 (*1-55560-208-8*) FASA Corp.

Battlestation. David Drake. Ed. by Bill Fawcett. 272p. (Orig.). 1992. mass mkt. 4.99 (*0-441-04878-1*) Ace Bks.

Battlestation! Star Trek. Diane Carey. (Star Trek Ser.: No. 13). 1991. mass mkt. 4.99 (*0-671-74025-3*) PB.

Battlesystem Arena. Bruce Nesmith. (Advanced Dungeons & Dragons Ser.). 1991. pap. 15.00 (*1-56076-141-5*) TSR Inc.

BattleTech: A Game of Armored Combat. 3rd ed. FASA Staff. 1992. pap. 25.00 (*1-55560-004-2*, 1604) FASA Corp.

***BattleTech: Authorized Strategy Guide.** Bradygames Staff. 1994. pap. 14.99 (*1-56686-208-6*) Brady Compu Bks.

Battletech: Mercenary's Star. William H. Keith, Jr. (Saga of the Gray Death Legion Ser.). 1992. pap. 4.99 (*0-451-45194-5*, ROC) NAL-Dutton.

BattleTech Compendium: The Rules of Warfare. Fasa Corporation Staff. (BattleTech Ser.). (Illus.). 1994. 20.00 (*1-55560-247-9*, 1690) FASA Corp.

Battletech D. R. T. James D. Long. 288p. (Orig.). 1994. pap. 4.99 (*0-451-45366-2*, ROC) NAL-Dutton.

***Battletech Seventeen: I Am Jade Falcon.** Robert Thurston. 288p. (Orig.). 1995. pap. 4.99 (*0-451-45380-8*, ROC) NAL-Dutton.

Battletech Tactical Handbook. Fasa Corporation Staff. (BattleTech Ser.). 1993. pap. 12.00 (*1-55560-212-6*) FASA Corp.

Battletoads Official Battle Book. Steven Schwartz. 1993. pap. 12.95 (*1-55958-469-6*) Prima Pub.

BattleTroops. FASA Staff. (BattleTech Ser.). (Illus.). 1989. pap. 20.00 (*1-55560-097-2*, 1637) FASA Corp.

Battling Anorexia. Anita Haney. (Orig.). 1986. pap. 6.95 (*0-89265-111-3*) Randall Hse.

Battling Bias: The Struggle for Identity & Community on College Campuses. Ruth Sidel. 304p. 1994. 22.95 (*0-670-84112-9*, Viking) Viking Penguin.

***Battling Bias: The Struggle for Identity & Community on College Campuses.** Ruth Sidel. 304p. 1995. pap. 11.95 (*0-14-015831-6*, Penguin Bks) Viking Penguin.

Battling Bluestocking. Amanda Scott. 224p. 1990. pap. 3.50 (*0-451-16437-7*, Sig) NAL-Dutton.

Battling Buzzards: The Odyssey of the 517th Regimental Parachute Combat Team, 1943-1945. Gerald Astor. LC 92-54984. 1993. 23.00 (*1-55611-363-3*) D I Fine.

Battling Dragons: Issues & Controversy in Children's Literature. Lehr. LC 94-31973. (Illus.). 350p. 1995. pap. text ed. 22.50 (*0-435-08828-9*) Heinemann.

***Battling for News: The Rise of the Woman Reporter.** Anne Sebba. (Illus.). 256p. 1995. 45.00 (*0-340-55599-8*, Pub. by Hodder & Stoughton Ltd UK) Trafalgar.

***Battling for Peace: A Memoir.** Shimon Peres. Ed. by David Landau. (Illus.). 350p. 1995. 25.00 (*0-679-43617-0*) Random.

Battling for Profits: How to Win Big on the Marketing Battlefield. Donald W. Hendon. 1987. write for info. (*0-318-59607-5*) S&S Trade.

Battling for the Modern Mind: A Beginner's Chesterton. Thomas C. Peters. LC 94-5963. (Concordia Scholarship Today Ser.). 176p. (Orig.). 1994. pap. 15.99 (*0-570-04664-5*) Concordia.

Battling for the National Parks. George B. Hartzog, Jr. 320p. 1993. reprint ed. pap. 12.95 (*0-918825-95-4*) Moyer Bell.

Battling Malone, Pugiliste. L. Hemon. (FRE.). 1984. pap. 18.95 (*0-7859-3051-5*) Fr & Eur.

Battling Prophet. Arthur W. Upfield. 240p. 1988. pap. 5.00 (*0-02-089691-3*, Collier S&S) S&S Trade.

Battling Prophet. Arthur Upfield. (Napoleon Bonaparte Mysteries Ser.). reprint ed. lib. bdg. 19.95 (*0-89190-551-0*, Rivercity Pr) Amereon Ltd.

Battling Prophet. Arthur W. Upfield. 1994. reprint ed. lib. bdg. 29.95 (*1-56849-352-5*) Buccaneer Bks.

Battling the Federal Gods. Donald H. Kochackis. 1994. pap. text ed. 14.95 (*1-881116-59-X*) Black Forrest Pr.

Battling the Inland Sea: American Political Culture, Public Policy, & the Sacramento Valley, 1850-1986. Robert Kelley. (Latin American Literature & Culture Ser.). 1989. 40.00 (*0-520-06487-9*) U CA Pr.

Battling the Prince of Darkness. Evelyn Christenson. 168p. 1990. teacher ed 5.99 (*0-89693-250-8*); pap. text ed. 8.99 (*0-89693-251-6*); audio 2.80 (*0-89693-240-0*) SP Pubns.

***Battling Wall Street: The Kennedy Presidency.** Donald Gibson. 220p. 1994. pap. text ed. 16.95 (*1-879823-10-1*); 24.95 (*1-879823-09-8*) Sheridan Sq Pr.

Battling with Beasts: Sex in the Life & Letters of St. Paul: The Issue of Homosexuality, Heterosexuality & Bisexuality. Arthur F. Ide. LC 91-28455. (Illus.). 121p. (Orig.). 1991. pap. 12.00 (*0-934667-09-8*) Monument Pr.

Battre la Campagne. Raymond Queneau. 216p. (FRE.). 1968. pap. 10.95 (*0-7859-1336-X*, 2070272974) Fr & Eur.

Batty Riddles. Katy Hall & Lisa Eisenberg. LC 91-20777. (Illus.). 48p. (J). (ps-3). 1993. 11.99 (*0-8037-1217-0*); lib. bdg. 11.89 (*0-8037-1218-9*) Dial Bks Young.

Batu-Khan: A Tale of 13th Century Asia. Vasilii G. Yan. Tr. by L. Britton. LC 75-39019. (Soviet Literature in English Translation Ser.). 320p. 1978. reprint ed. 21.45 (*0-88355-420-8*) Hyperion Conn.

Bau und Entwicklung der Flechtenpycnidien und Ihrer Gonidien. G. Vobis. (Bibliotheca Lichenologica: No. 14). 200p. (GER.). 1981. pap. text ed. 30.00 (*3-7682-1270-X*) Lubrecht & Cramer.

Bau und Funktion des Antheren-Griffel-Komplexes der Compositen. Eva-Maria Thiele. (Dissertationes Botanicae Ser.: Vol. 117). (Illus.). 172p. (GER.). 1988. pap. 45.60 (*3-443-64029-X*) Lubrecht & Cramer.

Baubles, Buttons & Beads: The Heritage of Bohemia. Sibylle Jargstorf. LC 93-85220. (Illus.). 176p. 1993. pap. 29.95 (*0-88740-467-7*) Schiffer.

Baubles, Dangles, & Beads: Stained Glass Jewelry Book. Kay B. Weiner. (Illus.). 15.95 (*0-9625663-2-2*) Eastman Pub.

Baudelaire. Jean-Paul Sartre. (Idees Ser.). 184p. (FRE.). 1988. pap. 10.95 (*0-7859-1358-0*, 2070324931) Fr & Eur.

Baudelaire. Jean-Paul Sartre. Tr. by Martin Turnell. LC 50-6845. 1950. pap. 9.95 (*0-8112-0189-9*, NDP233) New Directions.

Baudelaire. Jean-Paul Sartre. (Folio Essais Ser.). (FRE.). pap. 9.95 (*2-07-032493-1*) Schoenhof.

Baudelaire. Philippe Soupault. LC 77-11486. (Illus.). 144p. reprint ed. 49.50 (*0-404-16346-7*) AMS Pr.

Baudelaire: "Les Fleurs du Mal" F. W. Leakey. (Landmarks of World Literature Ser.). 128p. (C). 1992. 29.95 (*0-521-36116-8*); pap. 10.95 (*0-521-36937-1*) Cambridge U Pr.

Baudelaire: A Fire to Conquer Darkness. Nicole W. Jouve. LC 79-14978. 1980. text ed. 32.50 (*0-312-07005-5*) St Martin.

Baudelaire: A Self-Portrait. Charles P. Baudelaire. Ed. by Lois B. Hyslop & Francis E. Hyslop. LC 78-20447. 1994. reprint ed. 27.00 (*0-88355-827-0*) Hyperion Conn.

Baudelaire: Collected Essays, 1953-1988. F. W. Leakey. (Cambridge Studies in French: No. 30). (Illus.). 320p. (C). 1990. 69.95 (*0-521-32335-5*) Cambridge U Pr.

Baudelaire: Flesh & Spirit. Lewis P. Shanks. LC 74-34363. (Studies in French Literature: No. 45). 1974. lib. bdg. 75.00 (*0-8383-2058-9*) M S G Haskell Hse.

Baudelaire: Heros et Fils: Dualite et Problemes du Travail Dans les Lettres a Sa Mere. Helene Fredrickson. (Stanford French & Italian Studies: No. 8). 138p. 1978. pap. 46.50 (*0-915838-36-2*) Anma Libri.

Baudelaire: Le Fleurs du Mal. Ed. by Starke. (Bristol French Texts Ser.). (FRE.). 1992. 17.95 (*0-685-49968-5*, Pub. by Brstl Class Pr UK) Focus Info Gr.

Baudelaire: Selected Poems. rev. ed. Charles P. Baudelaire. Tr. by Joanna Richardson. (Poets Ser.). 272p. 1975. pap. 8.95 (*0-14-042188-2*, Penguin Classics) Viking Penguin.

Baudelaire: The Life of Charles Baudelaire. Joanna Richardson. 624p. 1994. 35.00 (*0-312-11476-1*) St Martin.

An Asterisk (*) at the beginning of an entry indicates that the title is appearing in BIP for the first time.

Baudelaire & Caricature: From the Comic to an Art of Modernity. Michele Hannoosh. (Illus.). 352p. 1992. 39.50 (0-271-00804-0) Pa St U Pr.

Baudelaire & Intertextuality: Poetry at the Crossroads. Margery A. Evans. (Cambridge Studies in French: No. 38). (Illus.). 236p. (C). 1993. 59.95 (0-521-36508-2) Cambridge U Pr.

Baudelaire & Le Spleen de Paris. J. A. Hiddleston. 160p. 1987. 45.00 (0-19-815839-4); pap. 15.95 (0-19-815845-9) OUP.

Baudelaire & Schizoanalysis: The Socio-Poetics of Modernism. Eugene W. Holland. LC 92-35913. (Cambridge Studies in French: No. 45). 304p. (C). 1993. 64.95 (0-521-41980-8) Cambridge U Pr.

***Baudelaire & the English Tradition.** Patricia Clements. LC 85-42681. reprint ed. pap. 129.20 (0-7837-9319-7, 2060059) Bks Demand.

Baudelaire & the English Tradition: Canonization of the Subversive. Patricia Clements. LC 85-42681. (Illus.). 448p. 1985. text ed. 65.00 (0-691-06649-3) Princeton U Pr.

Baudelaire & the Second Republic: Writing & Revolution. Richard D. Burton. 400p. 1992. 89.00 (0-19-815469-0) OUP.

Baudelaire & the Symbolists. Peter Quennell. LC 72-142689. (Essay Index Reprint Ser.). 1977. reprint ed. 18.95 (0-8369-2423-1) Ayer.

Baudelaire et Hoffmann: Affinites et Influences. Rosemary Lloyd. LC 78-58796. 403p. reprint ed. pap. 114.90 (0-8357-5999-7, 2031683) Bks Demand.

Baudelaire et la Belle aux Cheveux D'or. Albert Feuillerat. 1941. 59.50 (0-686-83483-6) Elliots Bks.

Baudelaire, Man of His Time. Lois B. Hyslop. LC 80-145. 225p. reprint ed. pap. 64.20 (0-7837-3302-X, 2057704) Bks Demand.

Baudelaire Revisited: Forty-One Poems. Kendall E. Lappin. LC 81-90014. (Illus.). 196p. 1981. 11.95 (0-9605710-1-9); pap. 7.95 (0-9605710-0-0) KEL Pubns.

Baudelaire, Rimbaud & Verlaine: Selected Verse & Prose Poems. Charles Baudelaire et al. Ed. by Joseph M. Bernstein. 352p. 1983. reprint ed. pap. 11.95 (0-8065-0196-0, 67, Citadel Pr) Carol Pub Group.

Baudelaire to Beckett: A Century of French Art & Literature. Illus. by William R. Holman. 1976. 25.00 (0-87959-019-X); pap. 17.50 (0-87959-020-3) U of Tex H Ransom Ctr.

Baudelaire's "Argot Plastique" Poetic Caricature & Modernism. Ainslie A. McLees. LC 88-35244. (Illus.). 208p. 1990. 27.50 (0-8203-1151-0) U of Ga Pr.

Baudelaire's Brain. Ivan Arguelles. (Illus.). 56p. (Orig.). 1988. pap. 3.00 (0-945085-08-7) Sub Rosa.

Baudelaire's Paris. Charles P. Baudelaire. 1990. pap. 9.95 (0-948259-97-3) Dufour.

Baudelaire's Prose Poems: The Esthetic, the Ethical, & the Religious in The Parisian Prowler. Edward K. Kaplan. LC 89-27410. 232p. 1990. 35.00 (0-8203-1218-5) U of Ga Pr.

Baudelaire's Voyages: The Poet & His Painters. Jeffrey Coven & Dore Ashton. LC 93-19922. (Illus.). 184p. 1993. 27.95 (0-8212-1999-5) Bulfinch Pr.

Baudha-tarkabhasa of Moksakargupta. Tr. & Notes by B. N. Singh. 134p. 1985. 10.00 (0-685-58183-7, Pub. by Asha Prakashan II) Nataraj Bks.

Baudrillard: A Critical Reader. Ed. by Douglas Kellner. LC 94-1736. (Critical Readers Ser.). 352p. 1994. 54.95 (1-55786-465-9); pap. 21.95 (1-55786-466-7) Blackwell Pubs.

Baudrillard: Critical & Fatal Theory. Mike Gane. 228p. 1991. 49.95 (0-415-03774-3, A5918); pap. 16.95 (0-415-03775-1, A5914) Routledge.

Baudrillard & Signs: Signification Ablaze. Gary Genosko. LC 93-49039. 224p. 1994. 59.95x (0-415-11256-7, B3902); pap. 17.95 (0-415-11257-5, B3906) Routledge.

Baudrillard Live: Selected Interviews. Ed. by Mike Gane. LC 92-26081. 260p. 1993. 49.95 (0-415-07037-6, A9921, Routledge NY); pap. 15.95 (0-415-07038-4, A9925, Routledge NY) Routledge.

Baudrillard's Bestiary: Baudrillard & Culture. Mike Gane. 192p. 1991. 49.95 (0-415-06306-X, A5781); pap. 15.95 (0-415-06307-8, A5785) Routledge.

Bauer Thesis Examined: The Geography of Heresy in the Early Christian Church. Thomas A. Robinson. LC 87-28288. (Studies in the Bible & Early Christianity: Vol. 11). 240p. 1988. lib. bdg. 89.95 (0-88946-611-4) E Mellen.

Bauern-Sensei. Lowell Messerschmidt. 1991. pap. 8.50 (1-55673-311-9, 7762) CSS OH.

Baughman's Handbook of Humor in Education. M. Dale Baughman. 1974. 16.50 (0-13-072504-8) P-H.

Bauhaus. Frank Whitford. LC 83-50527. (World of Art Ser.). (Illus.). 1984. pap. 14.95 (0-500-20193-5) Thames Hudson.

***Bauhaus: A History 1919-1933.** (Illus.). 250p. (C). 1994. 165.00 (0-7605-0427-X) Rector Pr.

***Bauhaus: A History 1919-1933.** (Illus.). 250p. (Orig.). (C). 1994. pap. 125.00 (0-7605-0428-8) Rector Pr.

Bauhaus: Masters & Students by Themselves. Ed. by Frank Whitford. (Illus.). 328p. 1993. 85.00 (0-87951-507-4) Overlook Pr.

Bauhaus & Bauhaus People: Personal Opinions & Recollections of Former Bauhaus Members & Their Contemporaries. rev. ed. Eckhard Neumann. Tr. by Eva Richter & Alba Lorman. LC 92-19324. 1993. text ed. 34.95 (0-442-01279-9) Van Nos Reinhold.

Bauhaus Dessau: Dessau, 1925-6 Walter Gropius. Dennis Sharp. (Illus.). 60p. (C). 1993. pap. 29.95 (0-7148-2779-7, Pub. by Phaidon Press UK) Chronicle Bks.

Bauhaus-Heft. (Bauhaus Ser.). 1990. reprint ed. 70.00 (3-601-00287-6) Periodicals Srv.

***Bauhaus Idea & Bauhaus Politics.** Eva Forgacs. Tr. by John Batki. (Central European University Press Book Ser.). (Illus.). 288p. 1995. 49.00 (1-85866-013-0); pap. 19.95 (1-85866-012-2) OUP.

Bauhaus Sourcebook. Anna Rowland. 1990. text ed. 19.95 (0-442-23903-3) Van Nos Reinhold.

Bauhaus Utopien. (Illus.). 368p. 1988. pap. 60.00 (3-922608-97-3, Pub. by Edition Cantz GW) Dist Art Pubs.

Bauhaus: Weimar, Dessau, Berlin, Chicago. Hans Wingler. (Illus.). 1969. 195.00x (0-262-23033-X); pap. 42.50x (0-262-73047-2) MIT Pr.

Bauhaus: Zeitschrift fur Bau & Gestaltung: Jahren 1-4, Dessau, 1926-1931. 1986. 155.00 (0-8115-0033-0) Periodicals Srv.

Bauhaus 1919-1928. Ed. by Herbert Bayer et al. (Illus.). 224p. 1976. pap. 16.95 (0-87070-240-8, 0-8109-6013-0) Mus of Modern Art.

Bauhaus 1919-1928. Herbert Bayer. 1990. pap. 16.95 (0-8109-6013-3) Abrams.

Bauhaus 1919-1928. Ed. by Herbert Bayer et al. LC 77-169299. (Museum of Modern Art Publications in Reprint). (Illus.). 224p. 1972. reprint ed. 36.95 (0-405-01559-3) Ayer.

Bauls: The Spiritual Vikings. S. C. Chakravarti. 1981. 10.00 (0-8364-0671-0, Pub. by Mukhopadhyaya II) S Asia.

Bauls of Bengal: In Quest for Man of the Heart. R. M. Sarkar. 1990. 32.00 (81-212-0320-1, Pub. by Gian Publng Hse II) S Asia.

Baumback's Guide to Entrepreneurship. Clifford M. Baumback. 1981. 27.95 (0-13-066761-7) P-H.

***Baumgarten Corruption: From Sense to Nonsense in Art & Philosophy.** Robert Dixon. LC 95-3932. 1995. text ed. write for info. (0-7453-0993-3, Pub. by Pluto Pr UK); pap. write for info. (0-7453-0992-5, Pub. by Pluto Pr UK) Westview.

Baumgartner's Bombay. Anita Desai. 1989. 18.95 (0-394-57229-7) Knopf.

Baumgartner's Bombay. Anita Desai. 240p. 1990. pap. 9.00 (0-14-013176-0, Penguin Bks) Viking Penguin.

***Bausch: Photographs by Detlef Erler.** Heiner Muller & Jochen Schmidt. 152p. 1995. 55.00 (3-905514-18-4) Dist Art Pubs.

Baustein 1: Grammatik-Zeichensetzung: Schwerpunkte. Gernot Haeublein et al. (Lehr-und Arbeitsbuch Ser.). 103p. pap. 13.95 (3-468-49821-7); pap. 7.95 (3-468-49822-5) Langenscheidt.

Baustein 2: Telefonieren-Schriftliche Mitteilungen. Gernot Haeublein et al. (Lehr-und Arbeitsbuch Ser.). 79p. pap. 13.95 (3-468-49823-3); audio 20.00 (3-468-84422-0); 7.95 (3-468-49824-1) Langenscheidt.

Baustein 3: Stellensuche-Bewerbung-Kuendigung. Gernot Haeublein et al. 96p. (GER.). 1984. 13.95 (3-468-49825-X); 7.95 (3-468-49826-8); audio 20.00 (3-468-84423-9) Langenscheidt.

Baustein 4: Gespraech-Besprechung-Diskussion. Gernot Haeublein et al. 96p. (GER.). 1985. 13.95 (3-468-49827-6); audio 20.00 (3-468-84424-7) Langenscheidt.

Bautismo. 2nd ed. H. C. Voorehoeve & Gordon H. Bennett. Tr. by Sara Bautista. (Serie Diamante). (Illus.). 36p. (SPA.). 1982. pap. 0.85 (0-942504-06-2) Overcomer Pr.

Bautismo: Sacramento del Pacto de Gracia. Pierre C. Marcel. Tr. by C. Rene Padilla. 288p. (Orig.). (SPA.). 1991. pap. text ed. 10.99 (0-8028-0912-X) Eerdmans.

Bautismo De Su Bebe: Your Baby's Baptism. Redemptorists Pastoral Publication Staff. (Redemptorist Pastoral Publicaitons). 16p. 1994. pap. 2.95 (0-89243-627-1) Liguori Pubns.

Bautismo (The Baptism) Trimar Publishing Staff. (SPA.). Date not set. 1.99 (1-56063-528-2, 498584) Editorial Unilit.

***Bauxite Mines Worldwide.** Errol D. Sehnke. LC 95-13945. (Special Publications). 1995. write for info. (0-615-00711-2) US Geol Survey.

Bavaria. 2nd ed. G. Wood. (Visitor's Guide Ser.). (Illus.). 256p. 1994. pap. 14.95 (0-86190-372-2) Hunter NJ.

***Bavaria & the Alpine Forests.** Rod Bolt. (Cadogan Guides Ser.). (Illus.). 256p. 1995. pap. 14.95 (0-947754-97-0, Pub. by Cadogan Bks UK) Globe Pequot.

Bavaria & the Reich: The Conflict over the Law for the Protection of the Republic. Johannes Mattern. LC 78-64111. (Johns Hopkins University. Studies in the Social Sciences. Thirtieth Ser. 1912: 3). reprint ed. 11.50 (0-404-61226-1) AMS Pr.

Bavaria in the German Confederation, 1820-1848. George S. Werner. 46p. 1977. 35.00 (0-8386-1932-0) Fairleigh Dickinson.

***Bavarian Chronicles Vol. I: The Legacy of Slava.** Julius. (Handjobs by Julius Ser.). 100p. (Orig.). 1994. pap. 20.00 (1-886458-00-6) Avenue Servs.

Bavarian Cooking. Assembled by O. L. Olli Leeb. (Illus.). 171p. 1992. 20.50 (3-921799-85-6, Pub. by Olli Leeb GW) Lubrecht & Cramer.

Bavarian Polka. (Ballroom Dance Ser.). 1985. lib. bdg. 79.00 (0-87700-745-4) Revisionist Pr.

Bavarian Rococo Church: Between Faith & Aestheticism. Karsten Harries. LC 82-11168. 314p. 1983. reprint ed. pap. 89.50 (0-7837-3320-8, 2057724) Bks Demand.

Bavarian Shrine & Other Poems. Eric Ormsby. 62p. (C). 1990. pap. text ed. 12.00 (1-55022-107-8, Pub. by ECW Press CN) Genl Dist Srvs.

Bavarian State Library-Alphabetical Catalogue-Bayerische Staatsbibliothek-Alphabetischer Katalog 1501-1840: BSB-AK 1501-1840 Preliminary Edition-Voraus Ausgabe, Set. (GER.). 1990. lib. bdg. 8,615.00 (3-598-30800-0) U Pubns Amer.

Bavli: An Introduction. Jacob Neusner. (USF Studies in the History of Judaism). 230p. (C). 1992. 59.95 (1-55540-697-1, 240042) Scholars Pr GA.

Bavli & Its Sources: The Question of Tradition in the Case of Tractate Sukkah. Jacob Neusner. LC 87-4665. (Brown Judaic Studies). 226p. 1987. 29.95 (1-55540-117-1, 14-00-85) Scholars Pr GA.

Bavli That Might Have Been: The Tosefta's Theory of Mishnah Commentary Compared with the Bavli's. Jacob Neusner. 215p. 1991. 59.95 (1-55540-575-4, 24 00 18) Scholars Pr GA.

Bavli's Intellectual Character: The Generative Problematic in Bavli Baba Qamma Chapter One & Bavli Shabbat Chapter One. Jacob Neusner. LC 92-33003. (USF Studies in the History of Judaism: Vol. 62). 235p. 1992. 59.95 (1-55540-773-0, 24 00 62) Scholars Pr GA.

Bavli's Massive Miscellanies. Jacob Neusner. (USF Studies in the History of Judaism). 298p. (C). 1992. 64.95 (1-55540-698-X, 240043) Scholars Pr GA.

Bavli's One Statement: The Metapropositional Program of Babylonian Talmud Tractate Zebahim, Chapters 1 & 5. Jacob Neusner. 284p. 1991. 69.95 (1-55540-637-8, 24 00 30) Scholars Pr GA.

Bavli's One Voice. Jacob Neusner. (USF Studies in the History of Judaism). 554p. 1991. 89.95 (1-55540-604-1, 240024) Scholars Pr GA.

Bavli's Primary Discourse: Mishnah Commentary. Jacob Neusner. (USF Studies in the History of Judaism). 190p. (C). 1992. 59.95 (1-55540-689-0, 240038) Scholars Pr GA.

Bavli's Unique Voice, Vol. 3. Jacob Neusner. (USF Studies in the History of Judaism). 311p. 1993. 74.95 (1-55540-841-9, 240073) Scholars Pr GA.

Bavli's Unique Voice, Vol. 4. Jacob Neusner. (USF Studies in the History of Judaism). 342p. 1993. 74.95 (1-55540-863-X, 240076) Scholars Pr GA.

Bavli's Unique Voice, Vol. 5. Jacob Neusner. (USF Studies in the History of Judaism). 226p. 1993. 64.95 (1-55540-864-8, 240077) Scholars Pr GA.

Bavli's Unique Voice, Vol. 6. Jacob Neusner. (USF Studies in the History of Judaism). 276p. 1993. 74.95 (1-55540-865-6, 240078) Scholars Pr GA.

Bavli's Unique Voice, Vol. 7. Jacob Neusner. (USF Studies in the History of Judaism). 315p. 1993. 74.95 (1-55540-866-4, 240079) Scholars Pr GA.

Bavli's Unique Voice: A Systematic Comparison of the Talmud of Babylonia & the Talmud of the Land of Israel, 2 vols., Vol. 1. Jacob Neusner. LC 93-20017. (USF Studies in the History of Judaism: Vols. 71 & 72). 367p. 1993. 79.95 (1-55540-834-6, 24 00 71) Scholars Pr GA.

Bavli's Unique Voice: A Systematic Comparison of the Talmud of Babylonia & the Talmud of the Land of Israel, 2 vols., Vol. 2. Jacob Neusner. LC 93-20017. (USF Studies in the History of Judaism: Vols. 71 & 72). 185p. 1993. 59.95 (1-55540-835-4, 24 00 72) Scholars Pr GA.

Bawdsey: Birth of the Beam. Tr. by Gordon Kinsey. 216p. 1994. 42.00 (0-86138-017-7, Pub. by T Dalton UK) St Mut.

***Bawdy Bride.** Amanda Scott. 352p. 1995. pap. 4.99 (0-7860-0182-8) Windsor NY.

Bawdy House. Kit Dalton. (Buckskin Giant Edition Ser.). 368p. (Orig.). 1994. mass mkt., pap. text ed. 4.99 (0-8439-3657-6) Dorchester Pub Co.

Bax: A Composer & His Time. Lewis Foreman. 534p. 1988. text ed. 79.95 (0-85967-721-4, Pub. by Scolar Pr UK) Ashgate Pub Co.

Baxter. A. S. Humphreys. (Illus.). 139p. 1991. reprint ed. lib. bdg. 32.50 (0-8328-2019-9); reprint ed. pap. 22.50 (0-8328-2020-2) Higginson Bk Co.

Baxter & Koffman: Police, the Constitution & the Community. Ed. by John Baxter & Laurence Koffman. 1985. 54.00 (0-86205-105-3); pap. 27.00 (0-86205-106-1) Butterworth Legal Pubs.

***Baxter Badger's Home.** Doris McClellan. LC 95-9774. (Illus.). 32p. (J). (gr. k up). 1995. 14.95 (1-885777-03-5) Hendrick-Long.

Baxter Bear & Moses Moose. Evariste Bernier. LC 90-61408. (Illus.). 48p. (J). (gr. 1-4). 1990. 12.95 (0-89272-287-8) Down East.

Baxter Black's First Video. Baxter Black. 1991. pap. 24.95 (0-939343-09-6) R Stockman & Coyote.

Baxter Bog Interlude. Arne Bue. Ed. by James B. Van Treese. 300p. 1994. pap. 8.95 (1-56901-072-2) NW Pub.

Baxter Environmental Manual, Vols. I & II. 2006p. 1993. Vol. I: Basic Requirements. write for info. (0-318-70172-3); Vol. II: Regulations & Contracts. write for info. (0-318-70173-1) Interpharm.

Baxter International: A Strategic Analysis of Success in World Markets. Market Intelligence Staff. 249p. 1992. 995.00 (1-56753-285-3) Frost & Sullivan.

Baxter. Memorial of the Baxter Family. J. N. Baxter. 114p. 1991. reprint ed. lib. bdg. 29.00 (0-8328-1987-5); reprint ed. pap. 19.00 (0-8328-1988-3) Higginson Bk Co.

Baxter Trust. J. P. Hailey. LC 87-46277. 256p. 1988. 17.95 (1-55611-090-1) D I Fine.

Baxter's Alaska. Robert Baxter. 1987. 9.95 (0-913384-47-X) Rail-Europe-Baxter.

Baxter's Britrail Guide. Robert Baxter. LC 72-83184. 1987. 9.95 (0-913384-06-2) Rail-Europe-Baxter.

Baxter's Choice. Harrison Arnston. 1988. pap. 3.95 (0-8217-2531-9) Zebra.

Baxter's East Coast Weekend Guide (Williamsburg-Quebec) Robert Baxter. 1987. 9.95 (0-913384-85-2) Rail-Europe-Baxter.

Baxter's Environmental Compliance Manual: Procedures, Checklists, & Forms for Effective Compliance, 3 vols. Baxter Healthcare Corporation Staff et al. Ed. by William R. Blackburn & Verie Sandborg. LC 93-12596. (Environmental Law Ser.). (Illus.). 1993. ring bd. 425.00 (0-87632-907-5) Clark Boardman Callaghan.

***Baxter's Environmental Compliance Manual: Procedures, Checklists, & Forms for Effective Compliance, 3 vols., Set with forms on disk.** Baxter Healthcare Corporation Staff. Ed. by William R. Blackburn & Verie Sandborg. (Environmental Law Ser.). (Illus.). 1993. disk, ring bd. 475.00 (0-614-07302-2) Clark Boardman Callaghan.

Baxter's Eurailpass Travel Guide (All 16 European Countries) Robert Baxter. 1987. 14.95 (0-913384-82-8) Rail-Europe-Baxter.

Baxter's Eurailpass Travel Guide, Vol. 1: Southern & Central Europe. Robert Baxter. 1987. 9.75 (0-913384-80-1) Rail-Europe-Baxter.

Baxter's Eurailpass Travel Guide, Vol. 2: Central & Northern Europe. Robert Baxter. 1987. 9.95 (0-913384-81-X) Rail-Europe-Baxter.

Baxter's Europe (Europe City Guide) Robert Baxter. 1987. 14.95 (0-913384-83-6) Rail-Europe-Baxter.

Baxter's U. S. A. (The U. S. A. by Car, Bus, Train & Plane) Robert Baxter. LC 77-92700. 1981. per. 12.95 (0-913384-44-5) Rail-Europe-Baxter.

Baxter's West Coast Weekend Guide (San Diego-Vancouver) Robert Baxter. 1987. 9.95 (0-913384-84-4) Rail-Europe-Baxter.

Bay. Gilbert C. Klingel. LC 84-47954. (Maryland Paperback Bookshelf Ser.). (Illus.). 1984. pap. 12.95 (0-8018-2536-9) Johns Hopkins.

Bay - Sky. Joel Meyerowitz. (Illus.). 96p. 1993. 50.00 (0-8212-2037-3) Bulfinch Pr.

Bay Area at War: How We Reacted to the Persian Gulf Crisis. Oakland Tribune Staff. 80p. 1991. reprint ed. lib. bdg. 25.00x (0-8095-4956-5) Borgo Pr.

Bay Area at Your Feet. rev. ed. Margot P. Doss. (Illus.). 270p. 1987. pap. 7.95 (0-917583-12-4, Don't Call Frisco) Lexikos.

Bay Area Baby: The Essential Guide to Local Resources for Pregnancy, Childbirth & Parenthood. Paula B. Reynolds & Jenny G. Andrus. LC 87-28445. (Illus.). 324p. (Orig.). 1991. pap. 14.95 (0-944296-05-X) Spirit Pr.

Bay Area Bike Rides. 3rd rev. ed. Ray Hosler. Ed. by Bill LeBlond. LC 94-1051. 180p. 1994. pap. 10.95 (0-8118-0612-X) Chronicle Bks.

Bay Area Blues. Lee Hildebrand. LC 93-84775. (Illus.). 96p. 1993. 25.00 (1-56640-595-5) Pomegranate Calif.

Bay Area Bride Book. Deborah Wood. 240p. 1987. pap. 16.95 (0-937533-03-3) TEC Pubns.

Bay Area Collects: Art from Africa, Oceania, & the Americas. Kathleen Berrin & Thomas K. Seligman. LC 82-71433. (Illus.). 112p. 1982. pap. 7.95 (0-88401-040-6) Fine Arts Mus.

Bay Area Counties, Vol. 5: Public Schools. Lillian S. Clancy. (California Public Schools: How Are They Doing? Ser.). 400p. (Orig.). 1989. pap. 35.95 (0-939580-73-X) CA Schl Surveys.

Bay Area Creative Sourcebook. 1992. 39.95 (0-942454-34-0) Black Bk.

Bay Area Directory. 252p. 1993. 50.00 (0-318-22676-6) Assn Bay Area.

Bay Area Directory. James R. Albin. 208p. 1994. pap. 85.95 (0-916210-94-4) J R Albin.

***Bay Area Dog Lover's Companion: The Inside Scoop on When to Train Your Dog in the Bay Area & Beyond.** 2nd ed. Lyle York & Maria Goodavage. (Illus.). 352p. 1995. pap. 13.95 (0-614-06958-0) Foghorn Pr.

***Bay Area Dog Lover's Companion: The Inside Scoop on Where to Take Your Dog in the Bay Area & Beyond.** 2nd ed. Lyle York & Maria Goodauage. (Illus.). 350p. 1995. pap. 13.95 (0-935701-38-9) Foghorn Pr.

Bay Area Employer Directory, 1988. 1988. write for info. (0-916210-88-X) J R Albin.

Bay Area Employment Agency & Executive Recruiter Directory. James R. Albin. 50p. 1994. 49.95 (0-916210-79-0) J R Albin.

Bay Area Employment Agency & Executive Recruiter Directory, 1989-90 Edition. 49.95 (0-916210-78-2) J R Albin.

Bay Area Figurative Art: 1950-1965. Caroline Jones. 1990. 52.00 (0-520-06841-6); pap. 30.00 (0-520-06842-4) U CA Pr.

Bay Area Green Pages: The Local Handbook for Planet Maintenance. Stephen C. Evans. 1990. pap. 12.95 (0-9627358-0-9) Green Media.

Bay Area Jewish Forum Hagadah. rev. ed. Ed. by Ralph M. Kramer & Philip Schild. (Illus.). 69p. 1985. 13.95 (0-917883-00-4) Benmir Bks.

Bay Area Mountain Bike Trails: Fifty Mountain Bike Trails Throughout the San Francisco Bay Area. Conrad J. Boisvert. (Bay Area Bike Trails Ser.). (Illus.). 160p. (Orig.). 1993. pap. 12.95 (0-9621694-5-5) Penngrove Pubns.

Bay Area Roller Skaters Guide. Sid Campbell & Nelson Warren. (Illus.). 80p. 1985. pap. 28.00 (0-318-04543-5) Gong Prods.

Bay Area Sourcebook 1993. 216p. Date not set. write for info. (0-916098-77-X) Black Bk.

Bay Area 500: Hoover's Guide to the Top San Francisco Area Companies, 1994-1995. Reference Press Editors Staff. 336p. 1994. 24.95 (1-878753-52-5) Ref Press.

Bay Area's Best Restaurants: The San Francisco Chronicle Guide. Patricia Unterman. 352p. 1994. pap. 8.95 (0-8118-0636-7) Chronicle Bks.

Bay At Nice & Wrecked Eggs. David Hare. 96p. 1987. pap. 7.95 (0-571-14694-5) Faber & Faber.

Bay City Blast. Warren Murphy. (Destroyer Ser.: No. 38). 1990. pap. 3.50 (1-55817-443-5, Pinnacle NY) Windsor NY.

Bay Constable. Jack Rudman. (Career Examination Ser.: C-2524). 1994. pap. 27.95 (0-8373-2524-2) Nat Learn.

Bay Constable II. Jack Rudman. (Career Examination Ser.: C-885). 1994. 29.95 (0-8373-0885-2) Nat Learn.

An Asterisk (*) at the beginning of an entry indicates that the title is appearing in BIP for the first time. 633

Bay Country. Tom Horton. LC 87-2756. (Illus.). 256p. 1987. 18.95 (*0-8018-3525-9*) Johns Hopkins.
Bay Country. Tom Horton. (Maryland Paperback Bookshelf Ser.). 248p. (C). 1994. pap. 12.95 (*0-8018-4875-X*) Johns Hopkins.
Bay County, Michigan, Courts' Automation: A Technical Assistance Report. Robert Womack et al. 14p. 1985. 1.00 (*0-685-16648-1*, NERO, T/A-530) Natl Ctr St Courts.
Bay Is the Land. Donna D. De La Torriente. LC 81-84848. (Illus.). 160p. 1982. 12.50 (*0-87881-102-8*) Mojave Bks.
Bay Leaves. 352p. 11.95 (*0-9615014-0-5*) Bay Pubns.
Bay Leaves. Illus. by Nancy Wagner. 323p. reprint ed. spiral bd. 10.95 (*0-918544-83-1*) Bay Pubns.
Bay Management Specialist. Jack Rudman. (Career Examination Ser.: C-1165). 1994. pap. 29.95 (*0-8373-1165-9*) Nat Learn.
Bay of Biscay. Imray Laurie Norie & Wilson Ltd. Staff. (Illus.). (C). 1991. text ed. 80.00 (*0-685-40197-9*, Pub. by Imray Laurie Norie & Wilson UK) St Mut.
Bay of Pigs: A Firsthand Account of the Mission by a U. S. Pilot in Support of the Cuban Invasion Force in 1961. Albert C. Persons. LC 89-13566. 176p. 1990. pap. 21.95x (*0-89950-483-3*) McFarland & Co.
Bay of Pigs: Can of Worms. N. T. Late. 10p. (Orig.). 1994. pap. write for info. (*0-9641448-9-1*) N Late Pub.
***Bay of Sorrows.** Gaylord Fold. 272p. 1995. 21.00 (*0-312-11751-5*, Pub. by Thomas Dunne Bks) St Martin.
Bay of Strangers. large type ed. Lillian Beckwith. 1990. 21.95 (*0-7089-2232-5*) Ulverscroft.
***Bay Shore Park: The Death & Life of an Amusement Park.** Victoria Crenson. LC 94-33633. (Illus.). 40p. (J). (gr. 2 up). 1995. text ed. 16.95 (*0-7167-6580-2*, Sci Am Yng Rdrs) W H Freeman.
***Bay Shrimpers of Texas: Rural Fishermen in a Global Economy.** Robert L. Maril. (Rural America Ser.). (Illus.). 320p. 1995. 35.00x (*0-7006-0703-X*); pap. 17.95 (*0-7006-0704-8*) U Pr of KS.
Bay State Auto Rates: What Are the Driving Forces? Edited Remarks. Pioneer Institute for Public Policy Research Staff. (Dialogue Ser.: No. 2). 25p. (Orig.). 1990. pap. 5.00 (*0-929930-04-5*) Pioneer Inst.
Bay Traditions. Bay Village Women's Club Foundation Staff. Ed. by Gwelda Popp. (Illus.). 238p. 1986. 10.00 (*0-9616678-0-X*) BV Wom Club & Fnd.
Bay Trail Plan: A Recreational Ring around San Francisco Bay. 65p. 1989. 5.00 (*0-317-05694-8*, P89005PLN) Assn Bay Area.
***Bay Tripper Vol. I Eastern Shore: Chesapeake Bay Travel Guide.** Whitey Schmidt. (Illus.). 1995. pap. 12.95 (*0-9613008-1-7*) Hartnett Marian Pr.
Bay View: Pioneer City of the Sound. Eklund. (Occasional Papers: No. 22). 1986. pap. 7.95 (*0-318-23340-1*) WWU CPNS.
Bay Window Bohemia. Oscar Lewis. (Illus.). 248p. 1983. reprint ed. pap. 9.95 (*0-911819-01-0*) Yosemite D.
Baya, 2 vols. Guenter Tessmann. (B. E. Ser.: No. 135). (GER.). 1937. 47.00 (*0-8115-3059-0*) Periodicals Srv.
Bayaderes 'Charles -Simon Catel see Chefs-d'Oeuvres Classiques de l'Opera Francais
Bayard. Joseph Marie Lo Duca. Ed. by Peter C. Bunnell & Robert A. Sobieszek. LC 76-23069. (Sources of Modern Photography Ser.). (Illus.). (FRE.). 1979. reprint ed. lib. bdg. 15.95 (*0-405-09634-8*) Ayer.
Bayard Taylor. Paul C. Wermuth. Ed. by Sylvia E. Bowman. LC 73-2362. (Twayne's United States Authors Ser.). 195p. (C). 1973. lib. bdg. 17.95 (*0-8057-0718-2*) Irvington.
Baybars I of Egypt. Ed. by Syedah F. Sadeque. LC 78-63366. (Crusades & Military Orders Ser.: Second Series). reprint ed. 39.50 (*0-404-17034-X*) AMS Pr.
Bayberry Bluff. Blair Lent. (Illus.). 32p. (J). (gr. k-3). 1992. pap. 4.95 (*0-395-62984-5*, Sandpiper) HM.
Bayerische Gesellschaft fuer Geburtshilfe und Frauenheilkunde, Tagung der Oesterreichischen Gesellschaft fuer Gynaekologie und Geburtshilfe und Jubilaeumstagung, Wuerzburg, May 1987. Ed. by E. Gitsch & E. Reinold. (Journal: Gynaekologische Rundschau: Vol. 27, Suppl. 2, 1987). (Illus.). xii, 368p. 1988. pap. 80.00 (*3-8055-4743-9*) S Karger.
Bayerische Gesellschaft fuer Geburtshilfe und Frauenheilkunde und der Oesterreichischen Gesellschaft fuer Gynaekologie und Geburtshilfe, Jahrestagung, Innsbruck, May, 1989. Ed. by E. Gitsch & E. Reinold. (Journal: Gynaekologische Rundschau: Vol. 29, Suppl. 2, 1989). (Illus.). xiv, 478p. 1989. pap. 136.00 (*3-8055-5104-5*) S Karger.
Bayerische Leibspeisen. Zusammengetragen von O. L. Olli Leeb. (Illus.). 171p. (GER.). 1991. 20.50 (*3-921799-80-5*, Pub. by Olli Leeb GW) Lubrecht & Cramer.
Bayerische Staatsbibliothek Katalog der Geschichtszeitschriften (BSB-Gez) Bavarian State Library Catalogue of Histo Periodical, 2 vols., Set. Ed. by Bayerische Staatsbibliothek Staff. (Zeitschriften der Bayerischen Staatsbibliothek Ser.: Pt. 2). 450p. (ENG & GER.). 1991. lib. bdg. 200.00 (*3-598-22242-4*) U Pubns Amer.
Bayerische Staatsbibliothek, Katalog der Musikdrucke: BSB-Musik, 17 vols., Set. 440p. 1990. lib. bdg. 3,200.00 (*3-598-30560-5*) U Pubns Amer.
Bayerische Staatsbibliothek Katalog der Musikzeitschriften (BSB-MuZ) TeilI-Bd: Bavarian State Library Catalogue of Music Periodicals. Ed. by Bayerische Staatsbibliothek Staff. (Zeitschriften der Bayerischen Staatsbibliothek Ser.). 252p. (GER.). 1990. lib. bdg. 200.00 (*3-598-22241-6*) U Pubns Amer.
Bayern. William W. Connors. (Twenty-Three Hundred AD Ser.). (Illus.). 49p. (Orig.). 1988. pap. 8.00 (*0-943580-74-9*) Game Designers.

Bayes or Bust? A Critical Examination of Bayesian Confirmation Theory. John Earman. (Illus.). 358p. 1992. 37.50 (*0-262-05046-3*) MIT Pr.
Bayes Theory. J. A. Hartigan. (Series in Statistics). (Illus.). 160p. 1983. 35.00 (*0-387-90883-8*) Spr-Verlag.
Bayesian Analysis & Uncertainty in Economic Theory. Richard M. Cyert & Morris H. DeGroot. (Probability & Statistics Ser.). (Illus.). 224p. 1986. 59.00 (*0-8476-7471-1*) Rowman.
Bayesian Analysis in Econometrics & Statistics. Ed. by Arnold Zellner. LC 88-30374. 486p. (C). 1989. reprint ed. lib. bdg. 58.00 (*0-89464-354-1*) Krieger.
Bayesian Analysis in Statistics & Econometrics: Proceedings of the Indo - U. S. Workshops, 1988. Ed. by Prem K. Goel & N. Srinvasa Iyengar. LC 92-11138. (Lecture Notes in Statistics Ser.: Vol. 75). xi, 410p. 1992. 58.00 (*0-387-97863-1*) Spr-Verlag.
Bayesian Analysis of Linear Models. Broemeling. (Statistics: Textbooks & Monographs Ser.: Vol. 60). 472p. 1985. 125.00 (*0-8247-7230-X*) Dekker.
Bayesian Analysis of Time Series & Dynamic Models. Spall. (Statistics: Textbooks & Monographs: Vol. 94). 576p. 1988. 140.00 (*0-8247-7936-3*) Dekker.
Bayesian & Likelihood Methods in Statistics & Econometrics: Essays in Honor George Barnard. Seymour Geisser et al. 1990. 95.00 (*0-444-88376-2*, SBE 7) Elsevier.
Bayesian Approach to Global Optimization: Theory & Applications. Jonas Mockus. (C). 1989. lib. bdg. 134.00 (*0-7923-0115-3*) Kluwer Ac.
Bayesian Choice: A Decision-Theoretic Motivation. Christian P. Robert. LC 94-10781. (Texts in Statistics Ser.). 1994. 49.00 (*0-387-94296-3*) Spr-Verlag.
Bayesian Decision Problems & Makrov Chains. J. J. Martin. LC 74-32489. 216p. 1975. reprint ed. 21.50 (*0-88275-277-4*) Krieger.
Bayesian Estimating & Experimental Design in Linear Regression Models. Jurgen Pilz. LC 87-27515. (Probability & Mathematical Statistics: Applied Probability & Statistics Section Ser.: No. 1345). 296p. 1991. text ed. 79.95 (*0-471-91732-X*) Wiley.
Bayesian Estimation & Experimental Design in Linear Regression Models. Ed. by Collet's Holdings, Ltd. Staff. 1985. 47.00 (*0-317-46580-5*, Pub. by Collets UK) Pro-Am Music.
Bayesian Forecasting & Dynamic Models. M. West & J. Harrison. (Series in Statistics). (Illus.). 705p. 1989. 56.00 (*0-387-97025-8*, 2928) Spr-Verlag.
Bayesian Full Information Analysis of Simultaneous Equation Models Using Integration by Monte Carlo. L. Bauwens. (Lecture Notes in Economics & Mathematical Systems Ser.: Vol. 232). vi, 114p. 1984. pap. 30.00 (*0-387-13384-4*) Spr-Verlag.
Bayesian Implementation. Thomas R. Palfrey & Sanjay Srivastava. Ed. by A. Postlewaite. LC 92-32494. (Fundamentals of Pure & Applied Economics Ser.: Vol. 53). 1993. pap. text ed. 22.00 (*3-7186-5314-1*) Gordon & Breach.
Bayesian Inference & Decision Techniques: Essays in Honor of Bruno de Finetti. Ed. by Prem K. Goel & A. Zellner. (Studies in Bayesian Econometrics: Vol. 6). 300p. 1986. 80.00 (*0-444-87712-6*, North Holland) Elsevier.
Bayesian Inference in Statistical Analysis. George E. Box & George C. Tiao. (Classics Library). 1992. pap. text ed. 46.95 (*0-471-57428-7*) Wiley.
Bayesian Inference with Geodetic Applications. K. R. Koch. Ed. by S. Bhattacharji et al. (Lecture Notes in Earth Sciences Ser.: Vol. 31). ix, 198p. 1990. pap. 31.00 (*0-387-53080-0*) Spr-Verlag.
***Bayesian Infern.** Ed. by Nicholas G. Polson & George C. Tiao. (International Library of Critical Writings in Econometrics: Vol. 7). 800p. 1995. 239.95 (*1-85278-668-X*, Pub. by E Elgar Pub UK) Ashgate Pub Co.
Bayesian Methodology for Verifying Recommendations to Minimize Asphalt Pavement Distress. (National Cooperative Highway Research Program Report Ser.: No. 213). 52p. 1979. 6.00 (*0-309-03006-4*) Transport Res Bd.
***Bayesian Methods & Ethics in a Clinical Trial Design.** Ed. by Joseph B. Kadane. LC 95-14352. (Series in Probability & Mathematical Statistics: Applied Probability & Statistics Ser.). 1995. write for info. (*0-471-84680-5*) Wiley.
Bayesian Methods in Reliability. Ed. by P. Sander & R. Badoux. 232p. (C). 1991. lib. bdg. 93.00 (*0-7923-1414-X*) Kluwer Ac.
Bayesian Modeling of Uncertainty in Low-Level Vision. Richard Szeliski. (C). 1989. lib. bdg. 69.50 (*0-7923-9039-3*) Kluwer Ac.
Bayesian Models in Economic Theory. Ed. by M. Boyer & R. E Kihlstrom. (Studies in Bayesian Econometrics: Vol. 5). 320p. 1984. 89.75 (*0-444-86502-0*, I-544-83, North Holland) Elsevier.
Bayesian Reliability Analysis. Harry F. Martz & Ray A. Waller. LC 89-6172. 768p. (C). 1991. reprint ed. lib. bdg. 69.50 (*0-89464-395-9*) Krieger.
Bayesian Spectrum Analysis & Parameter Estimation. G. L. Bretthorst. (Lecture Notes in Statistics Ser.: Vol. 48). xii, 209p. 1988. pap. 36.00 (*0-387-96871-7*) Spr-Verlag.
Bayesian Statistical Inference. Gudmund R. Iversen. LC 84-50890. (Quantitative Applications in the Social Sciences Ser.: Vol. 43). 80p. 1984. pap. 9.95 (*0-8039-2328-7*) Sage.
Bayesian Statistics: An Introduction. Peter M. Lee. 294p. 1992. pap. text ed. 34.95 (*0-470-21961-0*) Halsted Pr.
Bayesian Statistics: Principles, Models & Applications. James S. Press. LC 88-5407. (Probability & Mathematical Statistics Ser.). 237p. 1989. text ed. 69.95 (*0-471-63729-7*) Wiley.

Bayesian Statistics, A Review. D. V. Lindley. (CBMS-NSF Regional Conference Ser.: No. 2). v, 83p. (Orig.). 1972. reprint ed. pap. text ed. 16.00 (*0-89871-002-2*) Soc Indus-Appl Math.
Bayesian Statistics in Actuarial Science: With Emphasis on Credibility. Stuart A. Klugman. (S. S. Huebner International Ser.). 256p. (C). 1992. lib. bdg. 69.95 (*0-7923-9212-4*) Huebner Foun Insur.
Bayesian Statistics Two: Proceedings of the Second Valencia International Meeting on Bayesian Statistics, 6-10 Sept., 1983. Ed. by J. M. Bernardo et al. 770p. 1985. 177.25 (*0-444-87746-0*, North Holland) Elsevier.
Bayesian Statistics 3. Ed. by J. M. Bernardo et al. (Illus.). 824p. 1989. 125.00 (*0-19-852220-7*) OUP.
Bayesian Statistics 4: Proceedings of the Fourth Valencia International Meeting. Ed. by J. O. Berger & J. M. Bernardo. 880p. 1992. 95.00 (*0-19-852266-5*) OUP.
Bayesian Theory. Jose M. Bernardo & Adrian F. M. Smith. LC 93-37554. (Probability & Mathematical Statistics Ser.). 586p. 1994. text ed. 84.95 (*0-471-92416-4*) Wiley.
Bayeux Tapestry. Wolfgang Grape. (Illus.). 184p. 1994. pap. 29.95 (*3-7913-1365-7*, Pub. by Prestel) TeNeues.
Bayeux Tapestry: A Critical, Annotated Bibliography with Cross-References & Summary Outlines of Scholarship: 1729-1988. Richard D. Wissolik. LC 88-21377. (Scholars Bibliography Ser.: No. 1). vi, 78p. (Orig.). 1989. pap. text ed. 12.50 (*0-929914-00-7*) Eadmer Pr.
Bayeux Tapestry: A Critical, Annotated Bibliography with Cross-References & Summary Outlines of Scholarship: 1729-1988. 2nd rev. ed. Richard D. Wissolik. LC 90-82880. (Scholars Bibliography Ser.: No. 3). xii, 74p. (Orig.). 1990. pap. text ed. 18.50 (*0-929914-08-2*) Eadmer Pr.
Bayeux Tapestry: History & Bibliography. Shirley A. Brown. 320p. 1989. 79.00 (*0-85115-509-X*) Boydell & Brewer.
BayKeeper. Glenn Lawson. 340p. (Orig.). 1993. pap. 12.95 (*0-9620439-5-8*) ZAK Bks.
Bayla & the SleepStone. Bridget Schmidt. (J). (ps-3). 1992. pap. 14.99 (*0-9634525-0-9*) Bayla Prods.
***Bayles Families of Long Island & N. J., & Their Descendants; Also Ancestors of James Bayles & Julia Halsey Day.** H. G. Bayles & F. P. Bayles. 270p. 1994. reprint ed. lib. bdg. 52.00 (*0-8328-4295-8*); reprint ed. pap. 42.00 (*0-614-01338-0*) Higginson Bk Co.
Bayley: The Bailleuls of Flanders & Bayleys of Willow Hall. F. Bayley. 272p. 1992. reprint ed. lib. bdg. 53.00 (*0-8328-2629-4*); reprint ed. pap. 43.00 (*0-8328-2630-8*) Higginson Bk Co.
Baylis Family of Virginia: With Supplements on the Chunn, Fawcett, Hawkins & Turner Families & a Baylis Family in England. W. B. Blum & William Blum, Sr. (Illus.). 669p. 1993. reprint ed. lib. bdg. 109.00 (*0-8328-3641-9*); reprint ed. pap. 99.00 (*0-8328-3642-7*) Higginson Bk Co.
***Baynes Clan No. 1: Montana Horseman.** John S. McCord. 256p. (Orig.). 1995. pap. text ed. 4.99 (*0-515-11532-0*) Jove Pubns.
***Baynes Clan No. 2: Texas Comebacker.** John S. McCord. 256p. (Orig.). 1995. pap. text ed. 4.99 (*0-515-11585-1*) Jove Pubns.
***Baynes Clan No. 3: Wyoming Giant.** John S. McCord. 256p. 1995. pap. text ed. 6.50 (*0-515-11651-3*) Jove Pubns.
Bayocean; The Oregon Town That Fell into the Sea: (Documentary - Coastal Erosion) Bert Webber & Margie Webber. LC 89-9067. (Illus.). 208p. (Orig.). 1989. 24.95 (*0-936738-40-5*) Webb Research.
Bayocean; The Oregon Town That Fell into the Sea: (Documentary - Coastal Erosion) Bert Webber & Margie Webber. LC 89-9067. (Illus.). 208p. (Orig.). 1992. pap. 12.95 (*0-936738-37-5*) Webb Research.

Bayonet! Forward: My Civil War Reminiscences. Joshua L. Chamberlain. (Illus.). 328p. 1994. 25.00 (*1-879664-21-6*); pap. 14.95 (*1-879664-22-4*) Stan Clark Military. BAYONET! FORWARD: MY CIVIL WAR REMINISCENCES by Joshua Lawrence Chamberlain is a compilation of the General's most substantial Civil War addresses & writings. This collection contains chapters on the campaigns of Fredericksburg, Gettysburg, Petersburg, the White Oak Road, Five Forks, Appomattox, as well as Chamberlain's personal account of the surrender of the Confederate Army & the Grand Review of the Army of the Potomac. As a prominent member of the Fifth Army Corps, Chamberlain's reminiscences also serve as a history of that Corps' service from Fredericksburg through the end of the war at Appomattox. Also contained in this informative assemblage are appendices including official battle reports of the Gettysburg & Appomattox campaigns, a moving account of the last salute to the Army of Northern Virginia, monument dedication exercises on the Gettysburg Battlefield, & a stirring memorial address on the life of President Abraham Lincoln. BAYONET! FORWARD is further enhanced with photographs, maps, a bibliography, index & full color covers. Anyone interested in General Joshua Lawrence Chamberlain, the Fifth Army Corps or the American Civil War, will find this reading insightful & entertaining. A masterful publishing event. Order from: Stan Clark Military Books, 915 Fairview Ave., Gettysburg, PA 17325, (717) 337-1728. ***Publisher Provided Annotation.***

Bayonets Before Bullets: The Imperial Russian Army, 1861-1914. Bruce W. Menning. LC 92-8233. (Indiana-Michigan Series in Russian & East European Studies). (Illus.). 416p. (C). 1992. 35.00 (*0-253-33745-3*) Ind U Pr.
Bayonets from Janzen's Notebook. Jerry Janzen. (Illus.). 512p. 1991. reprint ed. 30.00 (*0-9619789-1-0*) Cedar Ridge Pubns.
Bayonets in the Streets. 2nd rev. ed. Comp. by Robin Higham. 268p. 1989. pap. 11.95 (*0-89745-096-5*) Sunflower U Pr.
***Bayonets of the Remington Cartridge Period.** Jerry L. Janzen. LC 93-72412. (Illus.). 196p. 1994. 39.95 (*0-9619789-2-9*) Cedar Ridge Pubns.
Bayonets of the Republic: Motivation & Tactics in the Army of Revolutionary France, 1791-94. John A. Lynn. LC 83-9093. 368p. 1984. 29.95 (*0-252-01091-4*) U of Ill Pr.
Bayonets to Lhasa. Peter Fleming. (Oxford Asia Paperbacks Ser.). 345p. 1986. pap. 9.95 (*0-19-583862-9*) OUP.
Bayonets to Lhasa. Peter Fleming. LC 73-16737. (Illus.). 319p. (C). 1974. reprint ed. text ed. 35.00 (*0-8371-7216-0*, FLBL, Greenwood Pr) Greenwood.
Bayou. Pamela Jekel. 1991. 20.00 (*0-8217-3490-3*) Zebra.
Bayou. Pamela Jekel. 1992. mass mkt. 5.99 (*0-8217-3740-6*) Zebra.
Bayou Bill's Best Stories: Most of Them True. Bill Scifres. LC 89-78533. (Illus.). 216p. 1990. 19.95 (*0-253-35059-X*); pap. 12.95 (*0-253-20596-4*, MB-596) Ind U Pr.
Bayou Boy. Lars Eighner. (Orig.). 1993. pap. 4.95 (*1-56333-084-9*) Masquerade.
Bayou Bride. Bobbi Smith. 448p. 1991. mass mkt. 4.50 (*0-8217-3311-7*) Zebra.
Bayou Cookbook: Creole Cooking from the Plantation Country & New Orleans. Thomas Holmes, Jr. (Illus.). 185p. 1983. spiral bd. 10.95 (*0-88289-417-X*) Pelican.
Bayou Cuisine. St. Stephen's Episcopal Church Staff. 438p. 1970. 14.95 (*0-9606490-0-X*) Starr-Toof.
Bayou Folk. Kate Chopin. 1974. lib. bdg. 250.00 (*0-87968-712-6*) Gordon Pr.
Bayou Folk see Collected Works of Kate Chopin
Bayou Midnight. Emilie Richards. 1994. 3.59 (*0-373-45168-7*) Silhouette.
Bayou Passion. Jane Archer. 1991. mass mkt. 4.50 (*0-8217-3469-5*) Zebra.
Bayou Road. Mignon G. Eberhart. 1976. 19.95 (*0-88411-297-7*, Aeonian Pr) Amereon Ltd.
Bayou Suzette. Lois Lenski. 1976. 18.95 (*0-8488-4049-6*) Amereon Ltd.
Bayou Suzette. Lois Lenski. 250p. 1991. reprint ed. lib. bdg. 19.95 (*0-89966-852-6*) Buccaneer Bks.
Bayou Triste: A Story of Louisiana. Josephine H. Nicholls. LC 72-1516. (Black Heritage Library Collection). 1977. reprint ed. 26.95 (*0-8369-9040-4*) Ayer.
Bayram al-Tunisi's Egypt. Booth. 1991. 97.50 (*0-86372-088-9*, Pub. by Ithaca UK) Paul & Co Pubs.
Bayreuth: A History of the Wagner Festival. Frederic Spotts. LC 93-36805. (Illus.). 336p. (C). 1994. 35.00 (*0-300-05777-6*) Yale U Pr.
Bayreuth: The Early Years; an Account of the Wagner Festival, 1876-1914 As Seen by Celebrated Visitors & Participants. Ed. by Robert Hartford. (Illus.). 288p. 1981. 34.95 (*0-521-23822-6*) Cambridge U Pr.
Bays Are Sere Followed by Interior Monologue. Edouard Dujardin. 160p. (FRE.). 1991. text ed. 37.50 (*1-870352-70-X*, Pub. by Libris UK) Paul & Co Pubs.
Bayside Guide to Weather on the Chesapeake. Mark E. Jacoby. pap. 5.95 (*0-943676-19-3*) MD Sea Grant Col.
Bayside Impressions: Maryland's Eastern Shore & the Chesapeake Bay. deluxe limited ed. James Drake Iams & William L. Thompson. LC 83-40047. (Illus.). 153p. 1984. 125.00 (*0-87033-321-6*, Tidewtr Pubs) Cornell Maritime.
Bayside Madness. Beth Cruise. LC 91-46070. (Saved by the Bell Ser.: No. 1). 144p. (Orig.). (YA). (gr. 5 up). 1992. pap. 2.95 (*0-02-042775-1*, Collier Bks Young) S&S Childrens.
Baysville: Poems. John Donlan. 63p. (Orig.). 1993. pap. 12.95 (*0-88784-540-1*, Pub. by Hse of Anansi Pr CN) Genl Dist Srvs.
Bayswater Brasserie Book of Food. Tony Papas & Hamash Keith. (Illus.). 192p. 1990. reprint ed. 24.95 (*0-89815-367-0*) Ten Speed Pr.
Bayt-al-Maqdis Pt. I: Abd al-Malik's Jerusalem. Julian Raby & Jeremy Johns. (Studies in Islamic Art: Vol. IX). (Illus.). 176p. 1993. 55.00 (*0-19-728017-X*) OUP.
Bayt-al-Maqdis Pt. II: Abd al-Malik's Jerusalem. Julian Raby & Jeremy Johns. (Oxford Studies in Islamic Art: No. IX). (Illus.). 160p. 1995. 45.00 (*0-19-728018-8*) OUP.
Baytown Phases of the Cairo Lowland of Southeast Missouri, Vol. 36. J. Raymond Williams & Robert T. Bray. (Missouri Archaeologist Ser.). (Illus.). 109p. (Orig.). 1974. pap. 4.00 (*0-943414-53-9*) MO Arch Soc.

An Asterisk (*) at the beginning of an entry indicates that the title is appearing in BIP for the first time.

An Asterisk (*) at the beginning of an entry indicates that the title is appearing in BIP for the first time.

Be Available: Leaders Guide. Lin Johnson. 64p. (Orig.). 1994. pap. 5.99 (*1-56476-320-X*, Victor Books) SP Pubns.

Be Aware. Be Safe: Difficult Terms Translated into Cambodian, Lao, Chinese & Vietnamese. Debbie Wong & Scott Wittet. Tr. by Lenhi Truong et al. (Illus.). 34p. (Orig.). 1987. pap. 1.50 (*0-941953-08-4*) KCSA Res Ctr.

Be Beautiful from Your Head to Your Feet. Carlita Faxton. 52p. (Orig.). 1994. pap. write for info. (*0-9636553-4-5*) C Faxton.

Be Beryllium. 8th ed. (Gmelin Handbook of Inorganic & Organometallic Chemistry Ser.: Supplement Vol. A2). (Illus.). xiv, 276p. 1991. 906.00 (*0-387-93626-2*) Spr-Verlag.

Be Beryllium, Suppl. Vol. A, Pt. 3. (Gmelin Handbook of Inorganic & Organometallic Chemistry Ser.). (Illus.). xvi, 277p. 1993. 1,044.00 (*0-387-93674-2*) Spr-Verlag.

Be Blessed in What You Do: The Unity of Christian Ethics & Spirituality. Michael K. Duffey. 160p. 1988. pap. 8.95 (*0-8091-2960-4*) Paulist Pr.

Be-Bop, Re-Bop. Xam W. Cartier. 1990. mass mkt. 4.95 (*0-345-36764-2*) Ballantine.

Be Buried in the Rain. Barbara Michaels. 50p. 1987. mass mkt. 6.50 (*0-425-09634-3*) Berkley Pub.

Be Careful. Harry Bornstein. (Signed English Ser.). (Illus.). 32p. (J). (ps-3). 1976. pap. 5.50 (*0-913580-55-4*) Gallaudet Univ Pr.

Be Careful in Florida. Frances W. Hall. (Illus.). 1979. pap. 1.95 (*0-8200-9906-6*) Great Outdoors.

Be Careful, Little Antelope. Claude Clement. LC 93-2950. (Little Animal Adventures Ser.). (Illus.). 22p. (J). (ps-3). 1993. 5.98 (*0-89577-504-2*, Readers Digest Kids) RD Assn.

Be Careful, Mr. Frumble! Richard Scarry. LC 89-43154. (Pictureback Ser.). (Illus.). 24p. (Orig.). (J). (ps-2). 1990. pap. 2.25 (*0-679-80566-4*) Random Bks Yng Read.

Be Careful What You Dream (It Might Come True) Lynne Norris. LC 84-29619. 200p. (Orig.). 1985. pap. 7.95 (*0-933380-43-7*) Olive Pr Pubns.

Be Careful What You Wish For. R. L. Stine. (J). (gr. 3 up). 1993. pap. 3.50 (*0-590-49447-3*) Scholastic Inc.

Be Challenged! rev. ed. Warren Wiersbe. LC 82-12404. (J). (gr. 7). 1982. pap. 4.50 (*0-8024-1080-4*) Moody.

Be Comforted. Warren Wiersbe. 168p. 1992. pap. 7.99 (*0-89693-797-6*, Victor Books) SP Pubns.

Be Committed. Warren W. Wiersbe. LC 92-34114. 168p. (Orig.). 1993. pap. 7.99 (*1-56476-067-7*, Victor Books) SP Pubns.

***Be Committed Leaders Guide.** Scripture Press Staff. Date not set. pap. 5.99 (*1-56476-068-5*, Victor Books) SP Pubns.

***Be Committed Leaders Guide.** Scripture Press Staff. 1994. pap. 5.99 (*1-56476-157-6*, Victor Books) SP Pubns.

Be Compassionate. Warren W. Wiersbe. 156p. 1988. pap. 7.99 (*0-89693-591-4*, Victor Books) SP Pubns.

***Be Compassionate Leaders Guide.** Warren W. Wiersbe. 1989. pap. 5.99 (*0-89693-592-2*, Victor Books) SP Pubns.

Be Complete. Warren Wiersbe. 160p. 1981. pap. 7.99 (*0-89693-726-7*, Victor Books) SP Pubns.

***Be Complete Leaders Guide.** Warren W. Wiersbe. 1988. pap. 5.99 (*0-88207-401-6*) SP Pubns.

Be Confident. Warren W. Wiersbe. 176p. 1982. pap. 7.99 (*0-89693-728-3*, Victor Books) SP Pubns.

***Be Confident Leaders Guide.** Warren W. Wiersbe. 1988. pap. 5.99 (*0-88207-435-0*) SP Pubns.

Be Courageous. Billy J. Daugherty. 32p. (Orig.). 1993. pap. 0.50 (*1-56267-075-1*) Victory Ctr OK.

Be Courageous. Warren W. Wiersbe. 156p. 1989. pap. 7.99 (*0-89693-665-1*) SP Pubns.

***Be Courageous Leaders Guide.** Warren Wiersbe. 1989. pap. 5.99 (*0-89693-666-X*) SP Pubns.

Be Daring. Warren W. Wiersbe. 156p. 1988. pap. text ed. 7.99 (*0-89693-447-0*, Victor Books) SP Pubns.

***Be Daring Leaders Guide.** Warren W. Wiersbe. 1989. pap. 5.99 (*0-89693-448-9*, Victor Books) SP Pubns.

***Be Decisive.** Warren Wiersbe. 1995. 7.99 (*1-56476-489-3*, 6-3489, Victor Books) SP Pubns.

***Be Decisive LG.** 72p. 1995. pap. 5.99 (*1-56476-490-7*, 6-3490, Victor Books) SP Pubns.

Be Determined. Warren Wiersbe. LC 92-13327. (Orig.). 1992. pap. 7.99 (*0-89693-071-8*, Victor Books) SP Pubns.

***Be Determined Leaders Guide.** Scripture Press Staff. Date not set. pap. 5.99 (*0-89693-072-6*, Victor Books) SP Pubns.

Be Diligent. Warren W. Wiersbe. 156p. 1987. pap. 7.99 (*0-89693-356-3*, Victor Books) SP Pubns.

***Be Dilligent Leaders Guide.** Warren W. Wiersbe. 1989. pap. 5.99 (*0-89693-962-6*, Victor Books) SP Pubns.

Be Dynamic: Acts 1-12. Warren W. Wiersbe. 168p. 1987. pap. 7.99 (*0-89693-358-X*, Victor Books) SP Pubns.

***Be Dynamic Leaders Guide.** Warren W. Wiersbe. 1989. pap. 5.99 (*0-89693-959-6*, Victor Books) SP Pubns.

Be Encouraged. Warren W. Wiersbe. 156p. 1984. pap. 7.99 (*0-88207-620-5*, Victor Books) SP Pubns.

***Be Encouraged Leaders Guide.** Warren Wiersbe. 1988. pap. 5.99 (*0-88207-848-8*) SP Pubns.

Be Ever Hopeful, Hannalee. Patricia Beatty. LC 88-21581. 208p. (J). (gr. 5-9). 1988. 13.00 (*0-688-07502-9*) Morrow Jr Bks.

Be Ever Hopeful Hannalee. Patricia Beatty. 216p. (J). (gr. 5-9). 1990. pap. 2.95 (*0-8167-2259-5*) Troll Assocs.

Be Expert with Map & Compass: The Complete Orienteering Handbook. Bjorn Kellstrom. LC 93-28827. (Illus.). 240p. 1994. pap. 17.00 (*0-02-029265-1*, Collier S&S) S&S Trade.

Be Expert with Map & Compass: The Orienteering Handbook. rev. ed. Bjorn Kjellstrom. LC 76-12550. (Illus.). 176p. 1976. pap. 14.95 (*0-684-14270-8*, SL595, Scribners) S&S Trade.

Be Fair: An Equal Opportunities Resource Manual. Comp. by Cabinet Office Staff. 224p. (C). 1987. 150.00 (*0-85292-390-2*, Pub. by IPM Hse UK) St Mut.

Be Faithful. Warren W. Wiersbe. 1981. pap. 7.99 (*0-89693-685-6*, Victor Books) SP Pubns.

***Be Faithful Leaders Guide.** Wiersbe. 1989. pap. 5.99 (*0-89693-686-4*) SP Pubns.

Be Fertile & Increase, Fill the Earth & Master It: The Ancient & Medieval Career of a Biblical Text. Jeremy Cohen. LC 89-7149. 392p. 1989. 54.50 (*0-8014-2307-4*) Cornell U Pr.

Be Fertile & Increase, Fill the Earth & Master It: The Ancient & Medieval Career of a Biblical Text. Jeremy Cohen. LC 89-7149. 392p. 1992. pap. 16.95 (*0-8014-8053-1*) Cornell U Pr.

Be Filled Now. Roy Hession. 1989. pap. 1.95 (*0-87508-235-1*) Chr Lit.

Be Filled with the Fullness of God: Living with the Indwelling Trinity. George A. Maloney. 144p. (Orig.). 1993. pap. 8.95 (*1-56548-024-4*) New City.

Be Free. Warren W. Wiersbe. LC 74-33824. 160p. 1975. pap. 7.99 (*0-89693-733-X*, Victor Books) SP Pubns.

***Be Free Leaders Guide.** Warren W. Wiersbe. 1988. pap. 5.99 (*0-88207-938-7*, Victor Books) SP Pubns.

Be Friends of God: Spiritual Reading from Gregory the Great. LC 90-35274. 203p. 1990. pap. 10.95 (*1-56101-009-X*) Cowley Pubns.

Be Fruitful & Multiply. Ed. by Richard V. Grazi. 1994. 19.95 (*0-87306-677-4*) Feldheim.

***Be Fruitful & Multiply.** J. W. Matlock, Sr. 1994. 10.95 (*0-533-10920-5*) Vantage.

Be Gentle with Yourself: You Have a Right to be Happy! Ruth Boyer. LC 81-85421. 125p. 1982. pap. 8.95 (*0-88247-656-4*) R & E Pubs.

Be Gentle with Yourself: Your Feelings & the Bad Guys. Ruth Boyer. LC 81-85503. 125p. 1982. pap. 8.95 (*0-88247-657-2*) R & E Pubs.

***Be Glad & Rejoice.** Date not set. 8.99 (*0-310-96494-6*) Zondervan.

Be Good, Sweet Maid: An Anthology of Women & Literature. Ed. by Janet Todd. LC 81-1461. 174p. (C). 1981. 32.50 (*0-8419-0692-0*); pap. 19.50 (*0-8419-0702-1*) Holmes & Meier.

Be Good to Each Other: An Open Letter on Marriage. Lowell Erdahl & Carol Erdahl. LC 91-6334. 96p. 1991. pap. 7.99 (*0-8066-2541-4*, 9-2541, Augsburg) Augsburg Fortress.

Be Good to Eddie Lee. Virginia Fleming. (Illus.). 32p. (J). (ps-3). 1993. lib. bdg. 14.95 (*0-399-21993-5*, Philomel Bks) Putnam Pub Group.

Be Good to Your Back. William Evans. 1989. write for info. (*0-9619258-2-5*) Clearwtr Pools Pub Co.

Be-Good-to-Your-Body Therapy. Steve Ilg. LC 92-73686. (Illus.). 76p. 1992. pap. 3.95 (*0-87029-255-2*) Abbey.

Be-Good-to-Your-Marriage Therapy. Kass Dotterweich. LC 89-82665. (Illus.). 68p. (Orig.). 1990. pap. 3.95 (*0-87029-224-2*, 20205-1) Abbey.

Be Good to Yourself. Darwin Gross. (Illus.). 208p. (Orig.). 1988. pap. text ed. 4.95 (*0-931689-12-0*) D Gross.

Be Good to Yourself. John MacKenzie. (Illus.). 156p. 1981. pap. 9.95 (*0-89496-026-1*) Ross Bks.

Be-Good-to-Yourself Therapy. Cherry Hartman. LC 87-72436. (Illus.). 78p. (Orig.). 1987. pap. text ed. 3.95 (*0-87029-209-9*) Abbey.

Be Good to Yourself Therapy. Cherry Hartman. 1992. 10.95 (*0-87029-243-9*) Abbey.

Be-Good-to-Yourself Therapy. Cherry Hartman. (Illus.). 80p. (Orig.). 1992. reprint ed. mass mkt. 4.50 (*0-446-39394-0*) Warner Bks.

***Be Happier Starting Now: A Medical Doctor Explores the Fascinating Field of Happiness.** Ray Sahelian. LC 93-92796. 200p. (Orig.). 1995. pap. 12.00 (*0-9639755-6-0*) Be Happier Pr.

Be Happy. Mariarosa Guerrini. 132p. (C). 1991. 40.00 (*0-85439-409-5*, Pub. by St Paul Pubns UK) St Mut.

Be Happy Attitudes. 1987. pap. 11.00 (*0-394-29852-7*) Random.

Be-Happy Attitudes. Robert Schuller. 231p. 1987. pap. 4.99 (*0-8499-4177-6*) Word Inc.

***Be-Happy Attitudes.** Robert Schuller. 1994. 4.99 (*0-8499-5097-X*) Word Inc.

Be (Happy) Attitudes. Robert H. Schuller. 240p. 1987. mass mkt. 5.50 (*0-553-26458-3*) Bantam.

Be Happy Not Sad, 2 bks., Set. Kristeen Gough. (J). (ps-3). 1989. Children's storybook in sign language, 16p. pap. 7.50 (*0-916708-19-5*); Colorbook, 16p. pap. write for info. (*0-916708-20-9*) Modern Signs.

Be Healed. Marilyn Hickey. 235p. (Orig.). pap. write for info. (*1-56441-021-8*) M Hickey Min.

Be Heart Smart: The HCF Way to a Healthy Heart. James W. Anderson. (Illus.). 120p. (Orig.). 1989. pap. 5.95 (*0-922859-00-0*) HCF NRF.

Be Here Now. (Illus.). 380p. 1971. 13.13 (*0-517-54305-2*, Harmony) Crown Pub Group.

Be Holy. Warren Wiersbe. (Be Ser.). 168p. (Orig.). 1994. teacher ed 5.99 (*1-56476-336-6*, Victor Books); pap. 7.99 (*1-56476-335-8*, Victor Books) SP Pubns.

Be Hopeful. Warren W. Wiersbe. 1982. pap. 7.99 (*0-89693-737-2*, Victor Books) SP Pubns.

***Be Hopeful Leaders Guide.** Warren W. Wiersbe. 1988. pap. 5.99 (*0-88207-545-4*) SP Pubns.

***Be I Whole.** Gita Brown. 225p. 1995. 16.95 (*1-878448-66-8*) MacMurray & Beck.

Be in Health. Alan Rabe. 288p. (C). 1993. pap. text ed. 19.95 (*0-8403-8387-8*) Kendall-Hunt.

Be It Ever So Humble. Virgie V. Jones. LC 83-90176. (Illus.). 108p. 1983. 17.50 (*0-9600890-3-9*) Morris-Burt Pr.

Be Joyful: A Practical Study of Philippians. Warren W. Wiersbe. LC 74-76328. 130p. 1974. pap. 7.99 (*0-89693-739-9*, Victor Books) SP Pubns.

***Be Joyful Leaders Guide.** Warren W. Wiersbe. 1988. pap. 2.99 (*0-88207-918-2*) SP Pubns.

Be Jubilant My Feet: African American Abolitionists in the American Missionary Association, 1839-1861. Clara M. DeBoer. LC 93-33226. (Studies in African American History & Culture). (Illus.). 288p. 1993. 67.00 (*0-8153-1592-9*) Garland.

Be Jubilant, My Heart. Elizabeth Richman. LC 93-10926. 1993. 9.95 (*1-56233-039-X*) Star Song TN.

***Be Jubilant My Heart.** Elizabeth Richman. 1994. pap. 7.99 (*1-56233-301-1*, Star Song Contemp) Star Song TN.

Be Just & Fear. abr. ed. Pat Olive. 266p. 1994. pap. 8.95 (*1-56901-388-8*) NW-Pub.

Be Kind to Your Mother (Earth) Douglas Love. (Illus.). 64p. (J). (gr. 3 up). 1994. pap. 3.50 (*0-694-00654-8*, Festival) HarpC Child Bks.

Be King of the Mountain. Ralph G. Bryant. 1988. pap. 4.75 (*0-89137-820-0*) Quality Pubns.

Be Like the Sun & Shine. Vicki Evans. (Illus.). 32p. (ENG, FRE & SPA.). (J). (ps-5). 1993. pap. 9.00 (*0-9636367-0-7*) V Evans.

Be Likeminded - One to Another. Daniel Andersen. 24p. (Orig.). 1992. pap. 2.50 (*1-880573-04-0*) Grace WI.

Be Loyal. Warren Wiersbe. LC 79-92552. Orig. Title: Meet Your King. 216p. 1980. pap. 7.99 (*0-89693-313-X*, Victor Books) SP Pubns.

***Be Loyal Leaders Guide.** Warren W. Wiersbe. 1988. pap. 5.99 (*0-89693-949-9*, Victor Books) SP Pubns.

Be Mature. Warren W. Wiersbe. LC 78-52558. 176p. 1978. pap. 7.99 (*0-89693-754-2*, Victor Books) SP Pubns.

***Be Mature Leaders Guide.** Warren Wiersbe. 1988. pap. 5.99 (*0-88207-985-9*, Victor Books) SP Pubns.

Be Mine. Jane McFann. (J). (gr. 12 up). 1994. pap. 3.25 (*0-590-46690-9*) Scholastic Inc.

Be Mine. Che Rudko. (Press-Out Fun Ser.). (Illus.). 16p. (J). 1994. write for info. (*0-307-12925-X*, Golden Bks) Western Pub.

***Be Mine, Valentine; To Have It All; Cupid's Task; Only with the Heart, 4 vols. in 1.** Vicki Lewis et al. (Romance Digest Ser.: Vol. 4, No. 4). 1995. pap. 2.75 (*0-373-82722-9*, 1-82722-9) Harlequin Bks.

Be My Baby. Kay Wilding. (American Romance Ser.). 1994. mass mkt. 3.50 (*0-373-16530-7*, 1-16530-7) Harlequin Bks.

Be My Baby: How I Survived Mascara, Miniskirts, & Madness or My Life as a Fabulous Ronette. Ronnie Spector & Vince Waldron. 1990. 19.95 (*0-517-57499-3*, Harmony) Crown Pub Group.

Be My Daddy. Lamar Dodson. (J). 1992. 12.95 (*0-533-10200-6*) Vantage.

Be My Friend. Gloria Garcia. LC 90-49243. (J). (ps). 1990. 9.95 (*0-85953-421-9*) Childs Play.

Be My Friend. Anna Ross. LC 89-24389. (Sesame Street Toddler Bks.). (Illus.). 24p. (J). (ps). 1991. 3.95 (*0-394-85496-9*) Random Bks Yng Read.

Be My Guest: Sermons on the Lord's Supper. C. Thomas Hilton. 1991. pap. 7.95 (*0-687-02822-1*) Abingdon.

Be My Valentine. M. J. Carr. (J). (ps-3). 1992. pap. 2.50 (*0-590-45131-6*) Scholastic Inc.

Be My Valentine, Charlie Brown. Charles M. Schulz. 1985. pap. 1.95 (*0-590-10348-2*) Scholastic Inc.

Be Myself: Memoirs of a Bridgebuilder. Warren Wiersbe. (Illus.). 224p. 1994. 15.99 (*1-56476-333-1*, Victor Books) SP Pubns.

Be Nice but Firm: A Down-to-Earth Approach to Child Management. Walter M. Block. LC 92-53193. 300p. 1992. 13.95 (*1-878208-12-8*) Guild Pr IN.

Be Nice, I'm Dead. Aramashot Babayan. LC 89-77564. (Illus.). 130p. (Orig.). 1990. pap. 8.00 (*0-934728-22-4*) D O A C.

Be Nice to Marilyn. Ida Luttrell. LC 91-25879. (Illus.). 32p. (J). (ps-3). 1992. text ed. 13.95 (*0-689-31716-6*, Atheneum Bks Young) S&S Childrens.

Be Nice to Spiders. Margaret B. Graham. LC 67-17101. (Illus.). 32p. (J). (gr. k-3). 1967. lib. bdg. 14.89 (*0-06-022073-2*) HarpC Child Bks.

Be Not Afraid. Jean Vanier. 160p. 1975. pap. 12.95 (*0-8091-1885-8*) Paulist Pr.

Be Not Afraid: Words of Hope & Promise. large type ed. Alanson B. Houghton. (Large Print Inspirational Ser.). 96p. 1988. pap. 6.95 (*0-8027-2612-7*) Walker & Co.

Be Not Deceived. W. W. Crouch. 1992. pap. 7.95 (*1-55673-474-3*, 7924) CSS OH.

Be Obedient. Warren Wiersbe. 156p. 1991. pap. text ed. 7.99 (*0-89693-875-1*, Victor Books) SP Pubns.

Be of Good Cheer. Marvin J. Ashton. LC 87-22357. 107p. 1987. 8.95 (*0-87579-106-9*) Deseret Bk.

Be of Good Cheer. Marvin J. Ashton. LC 87-22357. vii, 107p. 1994. pap. 6.95 (*0-87579-837-3*) Deseret Bk.

Be of Good Cheer. rev. ed. John C. Seville. 64p. 1990. pap. 0.75 (*0-88028-112-X*, 626) Forward Movement.

Be on Fire for the Lord. Billy J. Daugherty. (Orig.). 1991. pap. 0.50 (*1-56267-008-5*) Victory Ctr OK.

Be Organized for College: A Basic Study Guide. Nathalie Marshall-Nadel. 82p. 1995. pap. text ed. 19.95 (*0-9632383-3-7*) Intl Mgmt FL.

Be Our Guest: Cooking with Missouri's Innkeepers. Tracy Winters & Phyllis Winters. LC 93-60337. (Illus.). 96p. (Orig.). 1993. pap. 9.95 (*0-9625329-7-5*) Winters IN.

Be Past Participle Construction in Spoken English: With Special Emphasis on the Passive. Ed. by S. Granger. (Linguistic Ser.: Vol. 49). 390p. 1983. 79.50 (*0-444-86744-9*, I-255-83, North Holland) Elsevier.

Be Patient. Warren Wiersbe. (Be Ser.). 168p. 1991. pap. 7.99 (*0-89693-896-4*); teacher ed, pap. 5.99 (*0-89693-897-2*) SP Pubns.

Be Patient - I'm Not Perfect Yet. Juanita Purcell. (Women's Ser.). 120p. (Orig.). 1993. pap. 5.95 (*0-87227-178-1*) Reg Baptist.

Be Patient, Abdul. Dolores Sandoval. LC 93-34224. 32p. (J). Date not set. text ed. 14.95 (*0-689-50607-4*, McElderry) S&S Childrens.

Be Patient, Little Chick. Claude Clement. LC 93-2951. (Little Animal Adventures Ser.). (Illus.). 22p. (J). (ps-3). 1993. 5.98 (*0-89577-503-4*, Readers Digest Kids) RD Assn.

Be Patient, Little Chick. Patricia Jensen. (J). (ps-3). 1994. 6.99 (*0-89577-580-8*, Readers Digest Kids) RD Assn.

Be Perfect. 2nd ed. Tr. by Man Chong Fung. 160p. (CHI.). 1982. pap. write for info. (*0-941598-03-9*) Living Spring Pubns.

Be Positive. Miriam Moss. LC 92-26717. (Staying Healthy Ser.). (Illus.). 32p. (J). (gr. 6). 1993. text ed. 13.95 (*0-89686-786-2*, Crstwood Hse) Silver Burdett Pr.

Be Proud of All You've Achieved: Poems on the Meaning of Success. Ed. by Blue Mountain Arts Staff. LC 94-1656. 1994. pap. 7.95 (*0-88396-374-4*) Blue Mtn Pr CO.

Be Ready. Warren W. Wiersbe. LC 78-65555. 175p. 1979. pap. 7.99 (*0-89693-773-9*, Victor Books) SP Pubns.

Be Ready, Be Safe for Earthquakes: A Child's Guide to Preparedness. Libby Lafferty & Tina Lafferty. (Illus.). 32p. (Orig.). (J). (gr. k-4). 1994. pap. text ed. 3.50 (*0-9641072-0-1*) Lafferty & Assocs.

***Be Ready Leaders Guide.** Warren W. Wiersbe. 1988. pap. 5.99 (*0-88207-997-2*, Victor Books) SP Pubns.

Be Real. Warren W. Wiersbe. LC 72-77014. 190p. 1972. pap. 7.99 (*0-89693-774-7*, Victor Books) SP Pubns.

***Be Real Leaders Guide.** Warren W. Wiersbe. 1988. pap. 2.99 (*0-88207-902-6*) SP Pubns.

Be Reasonable: Selected Quotations for Inquiring Minds; An Authoritative Reference Guide. John George. Ed. by Laird Wilcox. LC 93-34704. 361p. 1994. 32.95 (*0-87975-867-8*) Prometheus Bks.

Be Reconciled! Ed. by Seamus O'Bryne. 113p. 1989. pap. 30.00 (*0-86217-235-7*, Pub. by Veritas IE) St Mut.

Be Rich. Robert Collier. 1985. pap. 3.95 (*0-912576-05-7*) R Collier.

Be Rich. Warren W. Wiersbe. LC 76-6833. 175p. 1976. pap. 7.99 (*0-89693-775-5*, Victor Books) SP Pubns.

Be Rich! Robert Collier. 46p. reprint ed. spiral bd. 3.50 (*0-7873-1078-6*) Mokelumne.

Be Rich: The Science of Getting What You Want. 1993. lib. bdg. 259.95 (*0-8490-8908-5*) Gordon Pr.

***Be Rich Leaders Guide.** Warren W. Wiersbe. 1988. pap. 5.99 (*0-88207-948-4*, Victor Books) SP Pubns.

Be Rich or Poor - the Choice Is Yours. Claude R. Dunbar. 1993. 17.95 (*0-533-10528-5*) Vantage.

Be Right. Warren W. Wiersbe. LC 77-154327. 175p. 1977. pap. 7.99 (*0-89693-778-X*, Victor Books) SP Pubns.

***Be Right Leaders Guide.** Warren Wiersbe. 1988. pap. 5.99 (*0-88207-963-8*, Victor Books) SP Pubns.

Be Safe in a Dangerous World. Vernon Howard. 1981. pap. 1.50 (*0-911203-04-4*) New Life.

Be Satisfied. Warren Wiersbe. 156p. 1990. pap. 7.99 (*0-89693-796-8*) SP Pubns.

Be Seated: A Book About Chairs. James C. Giblin. LC 92-25073. (Illus.). 144p. (J). (gr. 3-7). 1993. lib. bdg. 14.89 (*0-06-021538-0*) HarpC Child Bks.

Be Sexy after Sixty. Claude O. Vann, Jr. 150p. 1993. text ed. 15.95 (*0-9636542-0-9*) VanMar Pub.

Be Sick Well: A Healthy Approach to Chronic Illness. Jeff Kane. 188p. (Orig.). 1991. 19.95 (*1-879237-09-1*); pap. 11.95 (*1-879237-08-3*) New Harbinger.

***Be Skillful.** Warren W. Wiersbe. LC 94-38286. (Proverbs Ser.). 168p. 1995. pap. 7.99 (*1-56476-430-3*, 6-3430, Victor Books) SP Pubns.

***Be Skillful LGA.** Gary Wilde. 72p. 1995. pap. 5.99 (*1-56476-458-3*, 6-3458, Victor Books) SP Pubns.

Be Slim & Healthy see Mantegase Delgado Y Sano

Be Somebody! A Practical Philosophy for All Times. Warren F. Hannas. LC 80-81396. (Illus.). 165p. 1980. 12.00 (*0-936888-01-6*) King Authors Court.

Be Somebody Be Yourself Greetings for the Fax Machine, Etc. Alpha Pyramis Staff. 50p. 1992. ring bd. 16.95 (*0-913597-37-6*) Prosperity & Profits.

Be Somebody, Be Yourself Letterheads to Duplicate & Use. Center for Self-Sufficiency Staff. Ed. by A. C. Doyle. 1992. pap. text ed. 25.95 (*0-910811-74-1*) Ctr Self Suff.

Be Somebody Be Yourself Poetry, Bk. 1. rev. ed. Poet's Workshop Staff. 11p. (YA). (gr. 7-12). 1994. pap. 4.50 (*0-913597-98-8*) Prosperity & Profits.

Be Somebody! Learning Facilitator. Warren F. Hannas. (Illus.). 60p. 1979. pap. 4.75 (*0-936888-00-8*) King Authors Court.

***Be Still & Know...** Denis Duncan. (C). 1994. pap. 24.95 (*0-85305-332-4*, Pub. by J Arthur Ltd UK) St Mut.

Be Still & Know. Millie Stamm. 384p. 1981. pap. 10.99 (*0-310-32991-4*, 10844P) Zondervan.

Be Still & Know: A Study in the Life of Prayer. Michael Ramsey. LC 83-4765. 120p. (Orig.). 1993. reprint ed. pap. 9.95 (*1-56101-083-9*) Cowley Pubns.

Be Still & Know That I Am God. Wanda J. Pence. 1988. pap. 6.25 (*0-89137-332-2*) Quality Pubns.

Be Still & Listen. Samuel V. White. LC 86-51344. 142p. 1987. 7.95 (*1-55523-066-0*) Winston-Derek.

Be Still My Beating Heart: A Titillating Pictorial of Art Throughout the Ages. Benjamin Darling. 1990. 15.95 (*0-942139-11-9*) Tale Weaver.

***Be Still My Heart.** Jennings J. Thompson. 176p. 1995. pap. 8.00 (*1-57087-134-5*) Prof Pr NC.

Be Still My Soul. Elizabeth Urch. (C). 1990. pap. 35.00 (*0-85305-173-9*, Pub. by J Arthur Ltd UK) St Mut.

***Be Still My Soul: Resting in the Greatness of God & His Love for You.** Martyn L. Jones. 200p. 1995. 8.99 (*0-89283-888-4*, Vine Bks) Servant.

Be Street Smart - Be Safe: Raising Safety Minded Children. Nily Glaser. LC 93-80451. (Library Edition Ser.). (Illus.). 72p. (Orig.). (J). (gr. k-6). 1994. pap. 9.95 (*0-9632663-3-0*) Gan Pub.

An Asterisk (*) at the beginning of an entry indicates that the title is appearing in BIP for the first time.

Be Street Smart - Be Safe: Raising Safety Minded Children. Nily Glaser. LC 93-80451. (Illus.). 96p. (Orig.). (J). (gr. k-6). 1994. pap. 9.95 (0-9632663-2-2) Gan Pub.

Be Strong. Warren W. Wiersbe. LC 93-3197. 168p. (Orig.). 1993. pap. 7.99 (1-56476-122-3, Victor Books) SP Pubns.

Be Strong: Strength Training for Muscular Fitness for Men & Women. Wayne L. Westcott. 150p. 1993. pap. write for info. (0-697-13073-8) Brown & Benchmark.

Be Strong & Courageous (Joshua) Leader's Guide. (New Horizons Bible Study Ser.). 47p. 1986. pap. 2.35 (0-89367-112-6) Light & Life.

Be Strong & Courageous (Joshua) Student Guide. (New Horizons Bible Study Ser.). 64p. (Orig.). 1986. pap. 2.95 (0-89367-111-8) Light & Life.

***Be Strong & of Good Courage.** Jack R. Christianson. 1994. write for info. (0-88494-957-5) Bookcraft Inc.

Be Strong in the Lord. Billy J. Daugherty. 32p. (Orig.). 1993. pap. 0.50 (1-56267-080-8) Victory Ctr OK.

***Be Strong Leaders Guide.** Warren Wiersbe. Date not set. pap. 5.99 (1-56476-198-3, Victor Books) SP Pubns.

Be Sure to Close Your Eyes. Hugh Hood. 192p. Date not set. 24.95 (0-88784-165-1, Pub. by Hse of Anansi Pr CN) Genl Dist Srvs.

Be Sure Your Child Learns to Read. James Carroll & Barbara Overton. 160p. 1976. pap. 1.95 (0-89826-000-0) Natl Paperback.

Be Tender with My Love. Mary Hopkins. (Illus.). 108p. (Orig.). 1982. pap. 7.95 (0-938292-05-6) Being Bks.

Be Thankful for Your Troubles. Robert R. Updegraff & Stan Fraydas. (Illus.). 14p. (Orig.). 1980. reprint ed. pap. 1.00 (0-9613203-2-X) Updegraff.

Be the Best: A Focus on Individual Responsibility for Achieving. Best, Inc. Staff & Harvey Alston. 160p. 1994. per., pap. text ed. 16.95 (0-8403-9374-1) Kendall-Hunt.

Be the Best: Do It Easy, Do It Now. Uriah J. Fields. LC 83-71413. 255p. 1983. per. 9.95 (0-938844-10-5) Am Mutuality.

Be the Best You Can Be. Kirby Puckett. (Illus.). 40p. (J). Date not set. 14.95 (0-931674-20-4) Waldman Hse Pr.

Be the Boss: Start & Run Your Own Service Business. Sandi Wilson. 272p. 1986. mass mkt. 4.50 (0-380-75237-9) Avon.

Be the Boss! The Must-Have Book for Anyone Starting Their Own Business. 1994. pap. 19.95 (0-9625075-3-9) Lemonade Kids.

Be the Boss II: Running a Successful Service Business. Sandi Wilson. 256p. 1993. mass mkt. 4.99 (0-380-76614-0) Avon.

Be the Good News - In Living the Full Life. Henry R. Rust. 1990. 5.95 (0-940754-87-8, 3551) Ed Ministries.

Be the Hero of Your Own Life Story. Shane Barker. 1994. pap. 6.95 (0-88494-922-2) Bookcraft Inc.

***Be the Leader You Were.** LeRoy Eims. 132p. 1996. pap. 8.99 (1-56476-513-X, 6-3513) SP Pubns.

Be the Leader You Were Meant to Be. Leroy Eims. LC 75-5392. 132p. 1975. pap. 7.99 (0-88207-723-6, Victor Books) SP Pubns.

***Be the Leader You Were Meant to Be.** LeRoy Eims. Tr. by Samuel Kao. 242p. (CHI.). 1985. pap. 5.50 (1-56582-025-8) Christ Renew Min.

Be the Master of Your Relationship: The Woman's Training Manual. Gail Brakie & Yvette Chisom-Chapman. (Illus.). 120p. (Orig.). 1993. pap. 10.00 (0-9639617-0-5) Love Advisors.

Be Thou an Example. Gordon B. Hinckley. LC 81-15109. 144p. 1981. 9.95 (0-87747-899-6) Deseret Bk.

***Be Thou My Vision: Daily Inspiration from the Greatest Hymns of All Time.** John Fischer. 380p. 1995. pap. 12.99 (0-89283-924-4, Vine Bks) Servant.

Be Thou Present: Prayers, Litanies, & Hymns for Christian Worship. Peggy Haymes. 112p. (Orig.). 1994. pap. 10.95 (1-880837-90-0) Smyth & Helwys.

Be Transformed. Warren W. Wiersbe. 156p. 1986. pap. 7.99 (0-89693-352-0, Victor Books) SP Pubns.

***Be Transformed Leaders Guide.** Warren W. Wierbe. 1988. pap. 5.99 (0-89693-965-0, Victor Books) SP Pubns.

Be True to Your Future. Elwood N. Chapman. Ed. by Michael G. Crisp. LC 87-73559. (Illus.). 256p. 1988. pap. 15.95 (0-931961-47-5) Crisp Pubns.

Be True to Your School. Bob Greene. 352p. 1988. mass mkt. 4.99 (0-345-35394-3) Ballantine.

Be True to Yourself: I Don't Want to Be a Lion Anymore. braille ed. Trenna Daniells. (One to Grow On! Ser.). (Illus.). 11p. (Orig.). (J). (gr. 1). 1992. vinyl bd. 10.95 (1-56956-001-3, BI0003) W A T Braille.

Be True to Yourself: I Don't Want to Be a Lion Anymore. braille ed. Trenna Daniells. (One to Grow On! Ser.). (Illus.). (Orig.). (J). (gr. 2). 1992. vinyl bd. 10.95 (1-56956-026-9, BI0003) W A T Braille.

Be Upright with a Wright, 2 bks., Bk. 1. Esther G. Houghtalen & Laura C. Uhl. (Wright Genealogy Ser.). 138p. 1989. text ed. 25.00 (0-943240-00-X) UHLs Pub.

Be Upright with a Wright, 2 bks., Bk. 2: Supplement. Esther G. Houghtalen & Laura C. Uhl. (Wright Genealogy Ser.). 1989. pap. text ed. 10.00 (0-943240-01-8) UHLs Pub.

Be Upright with a Wright, 2 bks., Set. Esther G. Houghtalen & Laura C. Uhl. (Wright Genealogy Ser.). 1989. write for info. (0-943240-02-6) UHLs Pub.

Be Victorious. Warren W. Wiersbe. 156p. 1985. pap. 7.99 (0-89693-547-7, Victor Books) SP Pubns.

***Be Victorious Leaders Guide.** Warren W. Wiersbe. 1988. pap. 5.99 (0-89693-839-5, Victor Books) SP Pubns.

***Be Well, Beware.** Jessie Haas. (J). 1996. write for info. (0-614-05167-3) Greenwillow.

Be Well...Stay Well! Joan A. Friedrich. 164p. (Orig.). 1989. pap. 9.95 (0-87983-478-1) Keats.

Be What You Are: Love. John W. Adams. 96p. 1983. pap. 6.95 (0-9602166-0-X) Golden Key.

Be Who You Are. Jean Klein. 1990. pap. 11.95 (1-85230-103-1, Pub. by Element Bks UK) Element MA.

Be Wise. Wiersbe. 1983. 7.99 (0-89693-304-0, Victor Books) SP Pubns.

***Be Wise Leaders Guide.** Warren W. Wiersbe. 1988. pap. 5.99 (0-88207-847-X, Victor Books) SP Pubns.

Be with Me. Mike Chernuk. 1986. pap. 5.00 (0-932298-49-4) Tri-State Pr Corp.

Be WorkWise: Retooling Your Work for the 21st Century. Mildred L. Culp. LC 94-94116. (Illus.). 85p. (Orig.). 1994. pap. 8.95 (0-9640712-5-8) Exec Direct.

Be-Yaar Vysoka. Daniel Strauss. 24p. (Orig.). (HEB.). 1982. pap. 3.50 (0-9608338-1-1) D Strauss.

Be Ye Fruitful. Ira Hearne. 147p. 1986. pap. 3.95 (0-910068-68-2) Am Christian.

Be Ye Holy: The Call to Christian Separation. Fred Moritz. LC 93-50169. 1994. pap. 8.95 (0-89084-737-1) Bob Jones Univ Pr.

Be Ye Transformed. Elizabeth S. Turner. LC 69-17411. 286p. 1969. 9.95 (0-87159-008-5) Unity Bks.

Be Young & Flexible after Thirty, Forty, Fifty, Sixty.... Ruth Bender. 1976. spiral bd. 5.95 (0-917434-01-3) Ruben Pub.

Be Your Age. Mary Orr & Reginald Denham. 1953. pap. 13.00 (0-8222-1301-X) Dramatists Play.

Be Your Best: Personal Effectiveness in Your Life & Your Relationships. rev. ed. Linda Adams & Elinor Lenz. 240p. 1989. pap. 9.95 (0-399-51563-1, Perigree Bks) Berkley Pub.

Be Your Best Self. Thomas S. Monson. LC 79-54782. 209p. 1979. 9.95 (0-87747-787-6) Deseret Bk.

Be Your Mate's Best Friend. Stephen Bly & Janet Bly. (Illus.). (Orig.). 1989. pap. 6.99 (0-8024-3576-9) Moody.

Be Your Own Architect. Gene B. Williams. (Illus.). 288p. 1990. 26.95 (0-8306-8336-4, 3336); pap. 16.95 (0-8306-3336-7) TAB Bks.

Be Your Own Astrologer. 4th ed. Diane Martin. (Illus.). 1987. pap. 9.95 (0-931485-27-4) Scriptorium Pr.

Be Your Own Best Friend: How to Achieve Greater Self-Esteem, Health, & Happiness. Louis Proto. 176p. 1994. reprint ed. pap. text ed. 4.99 (0-425-14296-5) Berkley Pub.

***Be Your Own Boss for $100 or Less.** Date not set. pap. text ed. 39.95 (0-9627132-0-1) Edwards TX.

Be Your Own Contractor! James M. Shepherd. LC 92-29670. 315p. (Orig.). 1993. pap. 24.95 (0-7931-0496-3, 4105-1201) Dearborn Trade.

Be Your Own Detective. Richard Cummings. (YA). (gr. 7 up). 1980. 7.95 (0-679-20682-5) McKay.

Be Your Own Detective: How to Find Out Anything about Just about Anybody. Greg Fallis & Ruth Greenberg. LC 89-23676. 252p. 1989. pap. 9.95 (0-87131-579-3) M Evans.

Be Your Own Dick: Private Investigating Made Easy. John Q. Newman. LC 92-70018. 113p. (Orig.). 1992. pap. 12.00 (1-55950-083-2, 55090) Loompanics.

Be Your Own Doctor: A Positive Guide to Natural Living. 2nd ed. Ann Wigmore. 200p. 1982. pap. 3.95 (0-89529-193-2) Avery Pub.

Be Your Own Doctor by Using Natural Methods. Stan Malstrom. (Tree of Knowledge Ser.: No. 4). 34p. pap. 3.95 (0-913923-37-0) Woodland UT.

Be Your Own Equalizer: How to Fight the System & Win. Victor Santoro. 104p. 1990. pap. 10.00 (0-87364-551-0) Paladin Pr.

Be Your Own Financial Planner: Total Money Management in 30 Days. Dorlene V. Shane. LC 86-11005. 264p. 1987. pap. text ed. 17.95 (0-471-84534-5) Wiley.

Be Your Own Guru. Betty Bethards. 123p. 1988. pap. 12.95 (0-918915-19-8) Inner Light Found.

Be Your Own Guru. Sri S. Chakravarti. 1971. pap. 2.50 (0-685-58384-8) Ranney Pubns.

***Be Your Own Headhunter.** P. Dickson & S. Tiersten. 1995. 16.00 (0-679-76193-4) Random.

***Be Your Own House Contractor: How to Save 25 Percent Without Lifting a Hammer.** 3rd ed. Carl Heldmann. 144p. 1995. pap. 12.95 (0-88266-266-X, Storey Pub) Storey Comm Inc.

Be Your Own Lawyer Videos: Chapter Seven Bankruptcy. John A. Cimino. 1992. Incl. video, guide & forms. write for info. (1-879833-07-7) Be Own Lawyer.

***Be Your Own Literary Agent.** Martin Levin. 256p. 1995. 16.95 (0-89815-766-8) Ten Speed Pr.

Be Your Own Management Consultant: The Manager's Guide to Internal Consulting. Mark Pinder & Stuart McAdam. (Financial Times Management Ser.). 232p. 1994. 75.00x (0-273-60466-X, Pub. by Pitman Pubng UK) St Mut.

Be Your Own Map Expert. Barbara Taylor. LC 93-31692. 48p. (J). 1994. 16.95 (0-8069-0664-2) Sterling.

Be Your Own Music Critic. Ed. by Robert E. Simon. LC 70-134135. (Essay Index Reprint Ser.). 1977. 23.95 (0-8369-2095-3) Ayer.

Be Your Own Napoleon. William Seymour. 1988. 6.99 (0-517-66556-5) Random Hse Value.

Be Your Own Psychic. Doris T. Patterson & Violet M. Shelley. 81p. 1975. pap. 4.95 (0-87604-079-2) ARE Pr.

***Be Your Own Therapist: Whoever You Hire Is Just Your Assistant.** Thayer White. LC 94-69007. (Illus.). 282p. (Orig.). 1995. pap. 12.95 (0-9643375-8-4) Purple Paradox.

Be Your Own Undertaker. A. R. Bowman. (Illus.). 56p. 1992. pap. 10.00 (0-87364-697-5) Paladin Pr.

Bea & Mr. Jones. Amy Schwartz. LC 81-18041. (Illus.). 32p. (J). (ps-2). 1982. text ed. 13.95 (0-02-781430-0, Bradbury S&S) S&S Childrens.

Bea & Mr. Jones. Amy Schwartz. LC 93-20572. (Illus.). 32p. (J). (gr. k-2). 1994. reprint ed. pap. 3.95 (0-689-71796-2, Aladdin Paperbacks) S&S Childrens.

BEA Projections to 2040: A Review of Economic Analysis (BEA) Projections of Population, Employment, & Income. (Electronic Bulletin Board Ser.). 1991. 7.00 (0-318-40067-7) U VA Ctr Pub Serv.

BEA Regional Projections to Two Thousand Forty, Vol. 1: States. 144p. 1990. per., pap. 7.50 (0-16-024174-X, S/N 003-010-001) USGPO.

BEA Regional Projections to Two Thousand Forty, Vol. 2: Metropolitan Statistical Areas. 352p. 1990. per., pap. 17.00 (0-16-027310-2, S/N 003-010-002) USGPO.

BEA Regional Projections to Two Thousand Forty, Vol. 3: BEA Economic Areas. 199p. 1990. per., pap. 10.00 (0-16-027824-4, S/N 003-010-002) USGPO.

Beach. Elve F. De Hieronymis. LC 92-72119. (J). (ps). 1992. 4.50 (1-56397-204-2) Boyds Mills Pr.

Beach. Francis H. Wise. Ed. & Illus. by Joyce M. Wise. (Learn to Read Ser.: No. 14). 21p. (J). (ps-1). 1983. pap. 1.50 (0-915766-63-9) Wise Pub.

Beach: The Rev. John Beach & His Descendants. R. D. Beach & R. D. Gibbons. 397p. 1991. reprint ed. lib. bdg. 71.00 (0-8328-2092-X); reprint ed. pap. 61.00 (0-8328-2093-8) Higginson Bk Co.

***Beach Affair.** Barbara Johnson. 192p. 1995. pap. 10.95 (1-56280-090-6) Naiad Pr.

Beach & Nearshore Sediments & Processes. Ed. by Richard A. Davis, Jr. (Reprint Ser.: No. 12). 288p. 1987. pap. 19.50 (0-918985-66-8) SEPM.

Beach at Cleone. Toby Lurie. 80p. 1983. pap. 4.95 (0-930090-20-9) Applezaba.

Beach at Falesa. 2nd ed. Dylan Thomas. LC 83-42963. 132p. (C). 1983. pap. 7.95 (0-8128-6205-8, Scrbrough Hse) Madison Bks UPA.

***Beach Baby.** Karen Leabo. (Desire Ser.). 1995. mass mkt. 3.25 (0-373-05922-1, 1-05922-9) Silhouette.

Beach Ball. Peter Sis. LC 89-2076. (Illus.). 24p. (J). (ps). 1990. 12.95 (0-688-09181-4); lib. bdg. 12.88 (0-688-09182-2) Greenwillow.

Beach Ball - Left, Right. Bruce McMillan. LC 91-32802. (Illus.). 32p. (J). (ps-3). 1992. lib. bdg. 14.95 (0-8234-0946-5) Holiday.

Beach Banquet. Tom Rice. Ed. by Dale Swant. (Illus.). 64p. (Orig.). 1983. pap. 2.95 (0-943470-01-3) Daisy Bks.

Beach Blanket Burglary. Carla Tedrow. (Patti Pinkerton Mystery Stories Ser.: No. 2). (J). (gr. 2-6). 1993. pap. 3.95 (1-56969-178-9) FamilyVision.

***Beach Blanket Psycho.** Golden. 1995. mass mkt. 3.99 (0-553-56706-3) Bantam.

Beach Book & Beach Bucket. Karen Dawe. LC 87-40648. (Illus.). (J). (gr. k-5). 1988. pap. 7.95 (0-89480-590-8, 1590) Workman Pub.

Beach Bountiful: Southeast: The Family Primer for Beaches from Nags Head, North Carolina to Melbourne, Florida. Carol M. Williams. LC 93-83639. (Illus.). 160p. 1993. 14.95 (0-9636114-4-5) Pegasus Medallion.

Beach Boys. Mark Ribowsky & Bill Feinberg. (Illus.). 240p. 1986. 17.45 (0-671-53013-5); pap. 7.95 (0-671-54135-8) S&S Trade.

Beach Boys: Southern California Pastoral. rev. ed. Bruce Golden & Paul D. Seldis. LC 90-2538. (Woodstock Series: Popular Music of Today: Vol. 1). 104p. (Orig.). 1991. pap. 15.00x (0-89370-459-8) Borgo Pr.

Beach Boys: Southern California Pastoral. 2nd rev. ed. Bruce Golden & Paul D. Seldis. LC 90-2538. (Woodstock Series: Popular Music of Today: Vol. 1). 104p. (Orig.). 1991. lib. bdg. 25.00x (0-89370-359-1) Borgo Pr.

***Beach Boys Compilation Vol. 1.** Cpp Belwin Staff. 1993. pap. 19.95 (0-89898-688-5) CPP Belwin.

***Beach Bunny.** Jennifer Selby. LC 95-10685. (J). 1996. write for info. (0-15-200840-3) HarBrace.

Beach Colors & Beach Creatures. Elizabeth Gregory. (Illus.). (J). 1981. 6.95 (0-933184-17-4); pap. 5.50 (0-933184-18-2) Flame Intl.

Beach Cruising. Douglas Alvord. 192p. 1991. pap. 15.95 (0-87742-973-1) Intl Marine.

Beach Cruising. Douglas Alvord. 1991. pap. 15.95 (0-07-157978-8) McGraw.

Beach Day. Douglas Florian. LC 89-1933. (Illus.). 32p. (J). (ps up). 1990. 12.95 (0-688-09104-0); lib. bdg. 12.88 (0-688-09105-9) Greenwillow.

Beach Day. Helen Oxenbury. LC 81-69273. (Illus.). 14p. (J). (ps-00). 1991. bds. 3.95 (0-8037-0992-7) Dial Bks Young.

***Beach Feet.** Lynn Reiser. LC 95-12208. (Illus.). 32p. (J). 1996. write for info. (0-688-14400-4); lib. bdg. write for info. (0-688-14401-2) Greenwillow.

Beach for the Birds. Bruce McMillan. LC 92-10920. (Illus.). 32p. (J). (gr. 2-5). 1993. 15.95 (0-395-64050-4) HM.

Beach Fun Stickers. Jill Dubin. (Illus.). (J). (gr. k-3). 1993. pap. 1.00 (0-486-27682-1) Dover.

Beach Glass. John Gabel. (Cleveland Poets Ser.: No. 22). 29p. (Orig.). 1979. pap. 2.50 (0-914946-18-8) Cleveland St Univ Poetry Ctr.

Beach Grass. Oliver Eldridge. 72p. 1992. 12.00 (0-9634194-0-4) O Eldridge.

Beach House. R. L. Stine. 224p. (YA). (gr. 7 up). 1992. pap. 3.50 (0-590-45386-6, Point) Scholastic Inc.

Beach House Seven. Paul Roadarmel. 320p. 1988. pap. 4.50 (0-373-97077-3) Harlequin Bks.

Beach Houses from Malibu to Laguna. Elizabeth McMillian. LC 93-38144. 208p. 1994. 50.00 (0-8478-1802-0) Rizzoli Intl.

Beach in Maine. Suzanne Jacob. (Prose Ser.: No. 20). 52p. 1994. pap. 8.00 (0-920717-77-2) Guernica Editions.

Beach-la-Mar, the Jargon or Trade Speech of the Western Pacific. William Churchill. LC 75-32806. reprint ed. 34.50 (0-404-14110-2) AMS Pr.

Beach-la-Mar to Bislama: The Emergence of a Natural Language in Vanuatu. Terry Crowley. (Oxford Studies in Language Contact). (Illus.). 448p. 1990. 110.00 (0-19-824893-8) OUP.

Beach Money. Preston Pairo. 208p. 1991. 18.95 (0-8027-5786-3) Walker & Co.

***Beach Music.** Pat Conroy. 1995. 27.50 (0-385-41304-1, N A Talese); 29.95 (0-385-47578-0, N A Talese) Doubleday.

Beach Nourishment: Theory & Practice. Robert G. Dean. (Advanced Series in Ocean Engineering). 300p. 1995. text ed. 86.00 (981-02-1547-9); pap. text ed. 43.00 (981-02-1548-7) World Scientific Pub.

Beach Nourishment Engineering & Management Considerations. Ed. by Donald K. Stauble & Nicholas C. Kraus. LC 93-2248. (Coastlines of the World Ser.). 256p. 1993. 25.00 (0-87262-965-1) Am Soc Civil Eng.

Beach of Dreams. large type ed. Newlyn Nash. (Linford Romance Library). 288p. 1989. pap. 11.95 (0-7089-6665-9, Linford) Ulverscroft.

Beach of Falesa. Robert Louis Stevenson. Ed. by Barry Menikoff. LC 87-60216. 108p. (Orig.). 1987. pap. 9.95 (0-8047-1399-5) Stanford U Pr.

***Beach Party.** Applegate. (Ocean City Ser.: No. 10). 1995. mass mkt. 3.99 (0-06-106300-2, Harp PBks) HarpC.

Beach Party. R. L. Stine. (YA). 1990. pap. 3.50 (0-590-43278-8, Point) Scholastic Inc.

Beach Party with Alexis. Sarita Johnson-Calvo. (Illus.). 32p. (Orig.). (J). (gr. k-3). 1993. student ed 2.95 (1-55583-230-X) Alyson Pubns.

Beach Plum Jelly - Rose Hip Jam & Other Favorites. R. Marilyn Schmidt. 36p. (Orig.). 1993. pap. 5.95 (0-937996-25-4) Pine Barrens Pr.

Beach Realities. Judith Daniels. (Voices Romance Ser.: No. 5). 224p. 1994. mass mkt. 3.50 (0-8217-4765-7) Zebra.

Beach Ride. Bonnie Bryant. (Saddle Club Ser.: No. 6). (J). (gr. 4-7). 1993. pap. 3.50 (0-553-48073-1) Bantam.

Beach Seiners. Edith Patten. 1986. pap. 3.00 (0-942396-38-3) Blackberry ME.

Beach Supervisor. Jack Rudman. (Career Examination Ser.: C-836). 1994. pap. 29.95 (0-8373-0836-4) Nat Learn.

Beach Troop of the Gombe. Timothy W. Ransom. LC 77-92573. (Illus.). 319p. 1979. 46.50 (0-8387-1704-7) Bucknell U Pr.

Beach Walking in San Diego County. William Carroll. LC 91-73239. (Exploring San Diego County Ser.). (Illus.). 144p. (Orig.). 1992. pap. 10.00 (0-910390-33-9, Coda Pubns) Auto Bk.

Beacham's Guide to Environmental Issues & Sources, 5 vols., Set. Ed. by Charles J. Moseley et al. LC 92-42027. 1993. 240.00 (0-933833-31-8) Beacham Pub.

Beacham's Guide to Key Lobbyists: An Analysis of Their Issues & Impact. Ed. by Walton Beacham. LC 89-380. 658p. 1989. lib. bdg. 95.00 (0-933833-13-X) Beacham Pub.

Beacham's Guide to Literature for Young Adults, 3 vols., Set. Ed. by Kirk Beetz. (Illus.). 1544p. 1989. lib. bdg. 189.00 (0-933833-11-3) Beacham Pub.

Beacham's Guide to Literature for Young Adults, 3 vols., Set. Ed. by Kirk Beetz. (Illus.). 1800p. 1994. lib. bdg. 189.00 (0-933833-32-6) Beacham Pub.

Beacham's Guide to Literature for Young Adults, Vol. 4. Ed. by Kirk Beetz & Suzanne Niemeyer. (Illus.). 568p. 1990. 63.00 (0-933833-16-4) Beacham Pub.

Beacham's Guide to Literature for Young Adults, Vol. 5. Ed. by Kirk Beetz. (Illus.). 610p. 1991. lib. bdg. 63.00 (0-933833-25-3) Beacham Pub.

Beacham's Marketing Reference, 2 vols., Set. Ed. by Walton Beacham et al. LC 86-20271. 1045p. (C). 1986. lib. bdg. 69.00 (0-933833-03-2) Beacham Pub.

Beacham's Popular Fiction in America: 1950-1986, 4 vols., Set. Ed. by Walton Beacham. LC 86-25857. 1574p. (C). 1987. lib. bdg. 149.00 (0-933833-10-5) Beacham Pub.

Beacham's Popular Fiction Update, 1991, 2 vols., Set. Ed. by Walton Beacham. 1440p. 1991. lib. bdg. 159.00 (0-933833-26-1) Beacham Pub.

Beachcombers. John Light. LC 91-38130. (Light Reading Ser.). (J). (gr. 4 up). 1991. 2.95 (0-85953-502-9) Childs Play.

Beachcombers All: Exploring the New England Seashore. Ron Rood. LC 90-5817. (Illus.). 128p. (Orig.). 1990. pap. 9.95 (0-933050-80-1) New Eng Pr VT.

Beachcomber's Botany. Loren C. Petry. LC 68-26716. (Illus.). 160p. 1975. pap. 12.95 (0-85699-119-8) Chatham Pr.

Beachcomber's Companion. Ted Wesemann. (Illus.). 128p. 1991. 14.95 (0-85699-145-7) Chatham Pr.

Beachcomber's Field Guide to Shells. Idaz Greenberg. (Illus.). 1985. 5.50 (0-913008-16-8) Seahawk Pr.

***Beachcomber's Guide: From Cape Cod to Cape Hatteras.** Henry Keatts. LC 95-12534. (Illus.). 300p. 1995. 18.95 (0-88415-130-1) Gulf Pub.

Beachcomber's Guide to California Marine Life. Thomas M. Niesen. LC 93-29207. (Illus.). 180p. 1994. pap. 16.95 (0-88415-075-5) Gulf Pub.

Beachcomber's Guide to Florida Marine Life. William S. Alevizon. LC 94-17568. 184p. 1994. 12.95 (0-88415-128-X) Gulf Pub.

Beachcomber's Guide to Gulf Coast Marine Life: Florida, Alabama, Mississippi, Louisiana, Texas. 2nd ed. Nick Fotheringham & S. L. Brunemeister. (Illus.). 144p. 1989. pap. 12.95 (0-87201-186-0) Gulf Pub.

Beachcomber's Handbook. Warren Merkitch. 1984. 4.00 (0-89316-605-7) Exanimo Pr.

Beachcomber's Handbook of Seafood Cookery. Hugh Zachary. LC 71-88673. (Illus.). 208p. 1981. 8.95 (0-910244-55-3) Blair.

Beachcombing & Beachcrafting. Anne W. Dodd. Ed. by Julius M. Wilensky. LC 89-50754. (Illus.). 144p. (Orig.). 1989. pap. 12.95 (0-918752-10-8) Wescott Cove.

B

An Asterisk (*) at the beginning of an entry indicates that the title is appearing in BIP for the first time. 637

Beachcombing & Camping along the Northwest Coast. Bert Webber & Margie Webber. (Illus.). 190p. 1978. 12.50 (0-87770-192-X); pap. 8.95 (0-87770-162-8) Ye Galleon.

Beachcombing Between Tides. Wesley M. Farmer. (Illus.). 24p. 1992. 4.25 (0-937772-04-6) W M Farmer.

***Beachcombing for a Shipwrecked God.** Joe Coomer. 304p. Date not set. 22.95 (1-55597-228-4) Graywolf.

Beachcombing for Beginners. Norman Hickin. 1976. reprint ed. pap. 2.00 (0-87980-315-0) Wilshire.

Beachcombing for Japanese Glass Floats. 4th ed. Amos L. Wood. LC 84-72155. (Illus.). 272p. 1991. reprint ed. 24.95 (0-8323-0437-9); reprint ed. pap. 14.95 (0-8323-0438-7) Binford Mort.

Beachcombing the Pacific. Amos L. Wood. LC 87-60203. (Illus.). 225p. 1987. pap. 9.95 (0-88740-097-3) Schiffer.

Beachcraft Bonanza. Brian J. Heinz. LC 86-2272. (Illus.). 96p. (Orig.). 1986. pap. 8.95 (0-936335-00-9) Ballyhoo Bks.

Beachcrafts Too. Brian J. Heinz. LC 87-35232. (Illus.). 112p. (Orig.). (J). 1988. pap. 9.95 (0-936335-01-7) Ballyhoo Bks.

Beachcruising & Coastal Camping. Ida Little & Michael Walsh. Ed. by Julius M. Wiiensky. LC 92-60226. (Illus.). 352p. 1992. pap. 17.95 (0-918752-15-9) Wescott Cove.

Beached Boats. Jenny Joseph & Robert Mitchell. (Illus.). 59p. (Orig.). 1991. pap. 17.95 (1-870612-61-2, Pub. by Enitha Pr UK); 75.00 (1-870612-66-3, Pub. by Enitha Pr UK) Dufour.

Beaches. Iris R. Dart. 1986. mass mkt. 5.99 (0-553-27746-4) Bantam.

Beaches Are for Kids! An Activity Book for Kids. Bobbi Salts. (Illus.). 32p. (J). (gr. 1-6). 1990. pap. 2.95 (0-929526-09-0) Double B Pubns.

Beaches Are Moving: The Drowning of America's Shoreline. Wallace Kaufman & Orrin Pilkey, Jr. LC 83-1761. (Living with the Shore Ser.). (Illus.). 326p. 1983. pap. 14.95 (0-8223-0574-7) Duke.

Beaches II: I'll Be There. Iris R. Dart. 384p. 1992. mass mkt. 5.99 (0-446-36327-8) Warner Bks.

Beaches of Baja. Walt Wheelock. (Illus.). 1985. 4.50 (0-910856-28-1) La Siesta.

Beaches of Kaua'i & Ni'ihau. John R. Clark. LC 89-36116. (Illus.). 144p. (Orig.). 1990. pap. 12.95 (0-8248-1260-3) UH Pr.

Beaches of Maui County. rev. ed. John R. Clark. LC 89-4794. (Kolowalu Bks.). (Illus.). 168p. 1989. pap. 12.95 (0-8248-1246-8) UH Pr.

Beaches of O'ahu. John R. Clark. LC 77-8244. (Illus.). 210p. (Orig.). 1977. pap. 14.95 (0-8248-0510-0) UH Pr.

Beaches of the Big Island. John R. Clark. LC 85-13971. (Illus.). 204p. 1985. pap. 12.95 (0-8248-0976-9) UH Pr.

Beaches of Thule. Jean Laude. Tr. by David Cloutier. LC 84-48261. (Modern Poets in Translation Ser.: Vol. III). Orig. Title: Les Plages de Thule. ix, 57p. (Orig.). (C). 1985. 15.00 (0-916426-09-2); pap. 6.95 (0-916426-10-6) KOSMOS.

Beachhead. C. E. Case. 1983. pap. 3.95 (0-8217-1219-5) Zebra.

Beachhead. Jack Williamson. 368p. 1993. mass mkt. 4.99 (0-8125-1308-8) Tor Bks.

***Beachheads: Alabama to Anzio: 45th Division.** Charles M. Kirkpatrick. (Illus.). 201p. (Orig.). 1994. pap. text ed. 8.95 (0-945301-11-1) Druid Pr.

Beachheads in Space. Grey. 1983. 14.95 (0-02-545590-7) Macmillan.

Beachmen. David Higgins. 280p. (C). 1994. 54.00x (0-86138-047-9, Pub. by T Dalton UK) St Mut.

Beachside Entries-Specific Ghosts. Peter Weltner. LC 89-83340. (Five Fingers Book Ser.: No. 2). (Illus.). 100p. (Orig.). 1989. pap. 6.00 (0-9618409-4-3) Five Fingers.

Beachy Head & Other Poems. Charlotte Smith. LC 93-7015. 1993. 50.00 (0-8201-1468-5) Schol Facsimiles.

Beachy Head to Boulogne & le Havre. Imray Laurie Norie & Wilson Ltd. Staff. (Illus.). (C). 1989. text ed. 60.00 (0-685-40226-6, Pub. by Imray Laurie Norie & Wilson UK) St Mut.

Beacon. Fazil H. Daglarca. Ed. by Stanley H. Barkan & Talat S. Halman. (Review Turkish Writers Chapbook Ser.: No. 1). 48p. 1989. 15.00 (0-89304-275-7); 15.00 (0-89304-277-3); pap. 5.00 (0-89304-276-5); pap. 5.00 (0-89304-278-1) Cross-Cultrl NY.

Beacon Across the Prairie. William C. Hunter. LC 61-63838. (Illus.). 309p. 1961. 5.50 (0-911042-05-9) N Dak Inst.

Beacon at Alexandria. Gillian Bradshaw. LC 86-3017. (Hera Ser.). 376p. 1994. pap. 14.00 (1-56947-010-3) Soho Press.

Beacon Bible Expositions, 12 vols., Set. Ed. by William Greathouse et al. 1985. 125.00 (0-8341-0323-0) Beacon Hill.

Beacon Bible Expositions Vol. 2: Mark. A. Elwood Sanner et al. 255p. 1978. 12.50 (0-8341-0313-3) Beacon Hill.

Beacon Bible Expositions Vol. 3: Luke. Reuben Welch. Ed. by William M. Greathouse & Willard H. Taylor. 223p. 1974. 12.50 (0-8341-0314-1) Beacon Hill.

Beacon Bible Expositions Vol. 4: John. Samuel Young. Ed. by William M. Greathouse & Willard H. Taylor. 196p. 1979. 12.50 (0-8341-0315-X) Beacon Hill.

Beacon Bible Expositions Vol. 5: Acts. Arnold E. Airhart. Ed. by William M. Greathouse & Willard H. Taylor. (Beacon Bible Exposition Ser.). 196p. 1977. 12.50 (0-8341-0316-8) Beacon Hill.

Beacon Bible Expositions Vol. 6: Romans. Willam M. Greathouse. Ed. by Willard H. Taylor. (Beacon Bible Exposition Ser.). 224p. 1975. 12.50 (0-8341-0317-6) Beacon Hill.

Beacon Bible Expositions Vol. 7: Corinthians. Oscar F. Reed. Ed. by William M. Greathouse & Willard H. Taylor. 298p. 1976. 12.50 (0-8341-0318-4) Beacon Hill.

Beacon Bible Expositions Vol. 8: Galatians-Ephesians. Willard H. Taylor. 228p. 1981. 12.50 (0-8341-0734-1) Beacon Hill.

Beacon Bible Expositions Vol. 9: Philippians, Colossians, Philemon. John A. Knight. Ed. by William H. Greathouse. 300p. 1985. 12.50 (0-8341-0320-6) Beacon Hill.

Beacon Bible Expositions Vol. 10: Thessalonians, Timothy, Titus. Sydney Martin. Ed. by William M Greathouse & Willard H. Taylor. 247p. 1977. 12.50 (0-8341-0321-4) Beacon Hill.

Beacon Bible Expositions Vol. 11: Hebrews, James, Peter. W. T. Purkiser. Ed. by William M. Greathouse & Willard H. Taylor. 232p. 1974. 12.50 (0-8341-0322-2) Beacon Hill.

Beacon Bible Expositions Vol. 12: John, Jude, Revelation. T. E. Martin. Ed. by M. Greathouse. 282p. 1983. 12.50 (0-8341-0809-7) Beacon Hill.

Beacon Bible Expositions, Vol. 1: Matthew. William E. McCumber et al. (Beacon Bible Exposition Ser.). 223p. 1975. 12.50 (0-8341-0312-5) Beacon Hill.

***Beacon Book of Essays by Contemporary American Women.** Wendy Martin. 336p. (C). 1996. pap. 26.00 (0-8070-6346-0) Beacon Pr.

Beacon Book of Quotations by Women. Rosalie Maggio. LC 92-4697. 416p. 1993. 25.00 (0-8070-6764-4) Beacon Pr.

Beacon Book of Quotations by Women. Rosalie Maggio. LC 92-4697. 400p. 1994. pap. 15.00 (0-8070-6765-2) Beacon Pr.

Beacon City: An Urban Land Use Simulation. 2nd ed. Louis A. Iozzi. (Preparing for Tomorrow's World Ser.). 246p. 1992. reprint ed. teacher ed 90.00 (0-944584-24-1) Sopris.

Beacon Dictionary of Theology. Ed. by Richard S. Taylor. 559p. 1984. 29.95 (0-8341-0811-9) Beacon Hill.

Beacon Guide to New England Houses of Worship: An Architectural Companion. G. E. Kidder Smith. LC 89-31276. (Illus.). 187p. (Orig.). 1989. pap. 9.95 (0-8070-5101-2, BP827) Beacon Pr.

Beacon Handbook, 2 Vols. 2nd ed. Perrin. (C). 1990. pap. 7.16 (0-395-52688-4) HM.

Beacon Handbook, 2 Vols. 2nd ed. Perrin. (C). 1990. 89.56 (0-395-52987-5) HM.

Beacon Hill: A Living Portrait. Barbara W. Moore & Gail Weesner. 120p. 1992. 30.00 (0-9632077-0-9); pap. 20.00 (0-9632077-1-7) Centry Hill Pr.

Beacon Light. Raghavan Iyer. (Sangam Texts Ser.). 124p. 1984. pap. 8.75 (0-88695-021-X) Concord Grove.

Beacon Lights, Bks. I-IV: True Tales for Children, 2 vol. set. Abdul Waheed Khan. 32p. (J). (gr. 1-6). 1985. pap. 6.50 (1-56744-222-6) Kazi Pubns.

Beacon Lights of Grace: Twelve Biographical Vignettes. Richard E. Day. LC 71-148210. (Biography Index Reprint Ser.). 1977. 19.95 (0-8369-8057-3) Ayer.

Beacon Lights of Patriotism. Henry B. Carrington. LC 74-133068. (Granger Index Reprint Ser.). 1977. 25.95 (0-8369-6196-X) Ayer.

Beacon of Gold. large type ed. Helga Moray. 483p. 1989. 17.95 (0-7089-1979-0) Ulverscroft.

***Beacon of Mosquito Inlet: A History of the Ponce de Leon Inlet Lighthouse.** Thomas W. Taylor. LC 93-94110. (Illus.). 56p. (Orig.). (YA). (gr. 8-8). 1993. pap. 8.95 (1-885853-00-9) T W Taylor.

Beacon Small-Group Bible Studies, Acts, Pt, I: The Spirit-Filled Church. Alfred F. Harper. 96p. 1982. pap. 3.95 (0-8341-0800-3) Beacon Hill.

Beacon Small-Group Bible Studies, Acts, Pt. II: The Continuing Mission of the Church. Lebron Fairbanks. Ed. by Earl C. Wolf. 96p. (Orig.). 1985. pap. 3.95 (0-8341-0947-6) Beacon Hill.

Beacon Small Group Bible Studies, Amos-Haggai. Glen Van Dyne. 64p. (Orig.). 1988. pap. 3.95 (0-8341-1247-7) Beacon Hill.

Beacon Small-Group Bible Studies, Daniel: Daring to Live by Faith. Harold DeMott. Ed. by Earl C. Wolf. 76p. (Orig.). 1985. pap. 3.95 (0-8341-0962-X) Beacon Hill.

Beacon Small-Group Bible Studies, Deuteronomy: Words to Live By. Clayton Bonar. Ed. by Earl C. Wolf. 100p. (Orig.). 1986. pap. 3.95 (0-8341-0959-X) Beacon Hill.

Beacon Small-Group Bible Studies, Ecclesiastes: "Faith or Futility?" Evelyn A. Stenbock. Ed. by Earl C. Wolf. 83p. (Orig.). 1986. pap. 3.95 (0-8341-0964-6) Beacon Hill.

Beacon Small-Group Bible Studies, Ephesians. Gene Van Note. 88p. (Orig.). 1981. pap. 3.95 (0-8341-0722-8) Beacon Hill.

Beacon Small-Group Bible Studies: Exodus: "Set Free" Earl C. Wolf. 86p. (Orig.). 1984. pap. 3.95 (0-8341-0887-9) Beacon Hill.

Beacon Small-Group Bible Studies, Ezra-Nehemiah: God's Faithfulness & Man's Obedience. C. Neil Strait. Ed. by Earl C. Wolf. 72p. (Orig.). 1985. pap. 3.95 (0-8341-0927-1) Beacon Hill.

Beacon Small-Group Bible Studies, Genesis, Pt. II: God's Hand in History. Ken Bible. Ed. by Earl C. Wolf. 72p. (Orig.). 1986. pap. 3.95 (0-8341-1108-X) Beacon Hill.

Beacon Small-Group Bible Studies, Gospel of John, Pt. II: That You Might Have Life. Charles Shaver. Ed. by Earl C. Wolf. 64p. (Orig.). 1983. pap. 3.95 (0-8341-0881-X) Beacon Hill.

Beacon Small-Group Bible Studies, Hebrews: He is Here at Last. Gene Van Note. 64p. (Orig.). 1980. pap. 3.95 (0-8341-0623-X) Beacon Hill.

Beacon Small-Group Bible Studies, Hosea: The Triumph of God. Hugh Gorman. 88p. (Orig.). 1984. pap. 3.95 (0-8341-0914-X) Beacon Hill.

Beacon Small-Group Bible Studies, I & II Peter: A Faith for Testing Times. J. Grant Swank, Jr. 80p. 1982. pap. 3.95 (0-8341-0790-2) Beacon Hill.

Beacon Small-Group Bible Studies, I & II Samuel: David-A Man after God's Own Heart" A. F. Harper. Ed. by Earl C. Wolf. 102p. (Orig.). 1985. pap. 3.95 (0-8341-0934-4) Beacon Hill.

Beacon Small-Group Bible Studies, I & II Thessalonians: The Distinguishing Marks of a Christian. Bill Nielson. 56p. 1981. pap. 3.95 (0-8341-0738-4) Beacon Hill.

Beacon Small-Group Bible Studies, I & II Timothy, Titus: Being Christian in Today's World. Jerry Hull. 72p. 1980. pap. 3.95 (0-8341-0622-1) Beacon Hill.

Beacon Small-Group Bible Studies, I Corinthians, Living As a Responsible Christian. Beacon Hill Staff. 60p. 1982. pap. 3.95 (0-8341-0755-4) Beacon Hill.

Beacon Small-Group Bible Studies, I, II & III John: Everybody Ought to Know. Earl C. Wolf. 80p. 1982. pap. 3.95 (0-8341-0791-0) Beacon Hill.

Beacon Small-Group Bible Studies, II Corinthians, Galatians: Reckless Freedom, Responsible Living. Stephen M. Miller. Ed. by Earl C. Wolf. 96p. (Orig.). 1985. pap. 3.95 (0-8341-0957-3) Beacon Hill.

Beacon Small-Group Bible Studies, Isaiah: Preparing the Way of the Lord. Robert Branson. Ed. by Earl C. Wolf. 96p. (Orig.). 1985. pap. 3.95 (0-8341-0961-1) Beacon Hill.

Beacon Small-Group Bible Studies, James: Does God Want Faith or Obedience. A. F. Harper. 80p. (Orig.). 1980. pap. 3.95 (0-8341-0625-6) Beacon Hill.

Beacon Small-Group Bible Studies: Jeremiah, Lamentations: God's Unfailing Love. Winn O. Allison. Ed. by Earl C. Wolf. 96p. (Orig.). 1986. pap. text ed. 3.95 (0-8341-1106-3) Beacon Hill.

Beacon Small-Group Bible Studies, Job: The Trial & Triumph of Faith. David G. Grosse. Ed. by Earl C. Wolf. 88p. (Orig.). 1986. pap. 3.95 (0-8341-1109-8) Beacon Hill.

Beacon Small Group Bible Studies, Joel-Jonah. Bill Manning. 76p. (Orig.). 1987. pap. 3.95 (0-8341-1207-8) Beacon Hill.

Beacon Small-Group Bible Studies, John: That All Might Believe, Vol. 1. Charles Shaver. 68p. (Orig.). 1980. pap. 3.95 (0-8341-0651-5) Beacon Hill.

Beacon Small-Group Bible Studies, Joshua: Never a Dull Moment. Glen Van Dyne. Ed. by Earl C. Wolf. 80p. 1986. pap. 3.95 (0-8341-1098-9) Beacon Hill.

Beacon Small-Group Bible Studies, Luke: Good News for All of Us, Vol. 1. Jerry Hull. 72p. (Orig.). 1980. pap. 3.95 (0-8341-0657-4) Beacon Hill.

Beacon Small-Group Bible Studies, Luke: Lessons on Discipleship, Vol. 2. Sherrill Munn. 68p. (Orig.). 1981. pap. 3.95 (0-8341-0689-2) Beacon Hill.

Beacon Small-Group Bible Studies, Mark: Getting in on the Action. Jim Spruce. 80p. (Orig.). 1980. pap. 3.95 (0-8341-0650-7) Beacon Hill.

Beacon Small Group Bible Studies, Matthew, Part 2: Come & Learn from Me. Frank Carver. Ed. by Earl Wolf. 84p. 1986. pap. 3.95 (0-8341-1076-8) Beacon Hill.

Beacon Small-Group Bible Studies, Matthew, Vol. I: To Be a Disciple. Frank Carver. Ed. by Earl C. Wolf. (Beacon Small-Group Bible Study Ser.). 88p. (Orig.). 1984. pap. 3.95 (0-8341-0870-4) Beacon Hill.

Beacon Small-Group Bible Studies, Micah-Obadiah: What Does the Lord Require? Wesley D. Tracy. Ed. by Earl C. Wolf. 96p. (Orig.). 1985. pap. 3.95 (0-8341-0963-8) Beacon Hill.

Beacon Small Group Bible Studies, Nahum-Habakkuk. Ivan A. Beals. 80p. (Orig.). 1988. pap. 3.95 (0-8341-1214-0) Beacon Hill.

Beacon Small-Group Bible Studies, Philippians, Colossians, Experiencing His Peace. LeBron Fairbanks. 100p. 1982. pap. 3.95 (0-8341-0778-3) Beacon Hill.

Beacon Small-Group Bible Studies, Proverbs: Wisdom for Today's Challenges. Carlton D. Hansen. 80p. (Orig.). 1984. pap. 3.95 (0-8341-0905-0) Beacon Hill.

Beacon Small-Group Bible Studies: Psalms: Keeping the Heart Aglow. Ivan A. Beals. 96p. (Orig.). 1984. pap. 3.95 (0-8341-0885-2) Beacon Hill.

Beacon Small-Group Bible Studies, Romans: More than Conquerors. John M. Nielson. Ed. by Earl C. Wolf. 88p. (Orig.). 1985. pap. 3.95 (0-8341-0944-1) Beacon Hill.

Beacon Small-Group Bible Studies, Ruth-Esther: Faith That Risks All. Frances Simpson. Ed. by Earl C. Wolf. 96p. (Orig.). 1985. pap. 3.95 (0-8341-0941-7) Beacon Hill.

Beacon Small Group Bible Studies, Zehariah-Malachi: Prisoners of Hope. John B. Nielson. 80p. (Orig.). 1986. pap. 3.95 (0-8341-1100-4) Beacon Hill.

***Beacons: Great Teachers of the Georgetown School of Foreign Service.** Ed. by Margery B. Thompson. LC 94-32604. (Illus.). 208p. (Orig.). 1994. pap. text ed. 15.00 (0-934742-77-4, GU Schl Foreign) Geo U Inst Dplmcy.

Beacons along a Naturalist's Trail: California Naturalists & Innovators. Paul F. Covel. LC 87-34691. (Illus.). xii, 153p. (Orig.). 1988. pap. 10.95 (0-931430-01-1) Western Interp.

Beacons for Youth. rev. ed. Leslie Wilcox. 1967. pap. 1.99 (0-685-70960-4) Schmul Pub Co.

Beacons Imaging Within - As Promises. John Perlman. (Chapbook Ser.). 25p. (Orig.). 1990. pap. 4.00 (0-945112-08-4) Generator Pr.

***Beacons in the Night: With the OSS & Tito's Partisans in Wartime Yugoslavia.** Franklin Lindsay. (Illus.). 428p. 1995. pap. 14.95 (0-8047-2588-8) Stanford U Pr.

Beacons in the Night: With the OSS & Tito's Partisans in Wartime Yugoslavia. Franklin Lindsay. LC 92-36774. (Illus.). 428p. (C). 1995. 45.00x (0-8047-2123-8) Stanford U Pr.

***Beacons of Hope: An Early History of Cape Otway & King Island Lighthouses.** 2nd ed. Donald Walker. 144p. 1991. pap. 60.00 (0-614-04021-3, Pub. by Deakin Univ AT) St Mut.

***Beacons of Light: Ecclesiastical Writers Cited in the Catechism.** Louis Miller. 64p. 1995. pap. 4.95 (0-89243-784-7) Liguori Pubns.

Beacons of Light: Lighthouses. Gail Gibbons. LC 89-33884. (Illus.). 32p. (J). (gr. 1 up). 1990. 16.00 (0-688-07379-4); lib. bdg. 15.93 (0-688-07380-8) Morrow Jr Bks.

Bead Dazzled. Geri Weitzman. (J). (gr. 4-7). 1994. pap. 6.95 (0-8167-3469-0) Troll Assocs.

Bead Directory: Everything You Need to Bead. 2nd ed. Linda Benmour. 202p. 1993. pap. 14.95 (1-883153-10-7) Artstone Pr.

Bead Directory: The Most Comprehensive Collection of Bead Sources Available! 3rd ed. Linda Benmour. Ed. by Milton Firestone & Alice Scherer. (Illus.). 304p. (Orig.). 1995. pap. 18.95 (1-883153-18-2) Artstone Pr.

Bead Embroidery. Valerie Campbell-Harding & Pamela Watts. (Illus.). 124p. 1993. 35.00 (0-916896-50-1) Lacis Pubns.

Bead Embroidery. Joan Edwards. (Illus.). 192p. (C). 1992. pap. 20.00 (0-916896-44-7) Lacis Pubns.

Bead It! A Complete Jewelry Kit. Lara R. Bergen. (Illus.). 24p. (J). (gr. 3 up). 1994. pap. 13.95 (0-448-40499-0, G&D) Putnam Pub Group.

***Bead Jewelry.** Stephany Tomalin. (Workstations Ser.). (Illus.). 48p. (J). (gr. 4 up). 1995. pap. 21.95 (0-8431-3760-6) Price Stern.

Bead Primer. Elizabeth Harris. (Illus.). 36p. (Orig.). 1987. pap. 7.00 (0-9618396-0-0) Bead Mus.

Bead Setting Diamonds: With Pave Applications. Robert R. Wooding. Ed. by Robert A. Wainscot. LC 85-73051. (Illus.). 208p. 1985. 29.95 (0-9613545-2-6) Dry Ridge.

Bead Talk. Peggy Crisman & Shirley Worley. (Illus.). 201p. (YA). 1994. pap. text ed. 8.95 (0-9635501-0-1) Beads Unique.

Bead Work. Ed. by Jules Kliot & Kaethe Kliot. 56p. 1984. pap. 6.00 (0-916896-21-8) Lacis Pubns.

Bead Workbook Designer Pages to Color. Illus. by Z. Susanne Aikman. 16p. (Orig.). 1991. pap. 2.95 (0-9629155-1-3) Morning Flower.

***Beaded Amulet Purses: A Source of Instruction & Inspiration.** Nicolette Stessin. Ed. by Mardi Rhodes. (Illus.). 72p. 1994. reprint ed. pap. 18.95 (0-9641865-0-0) Beadwrld Pubng.

***Beaded Animals in Jewelry.** Letty Lammens & Els Scholte. 56p. 1994. pap. 14.00 (0-916896-61-7) Lacis Pubns.

Beaded Birds of the Four Seasons: Charted for Counted Beadwork & Counted Cross-Stitch. Carol Krob. 12p. 1986. 5.98 (0-88290-278-4) Horizon Utah.

Beaded Clothing Techniques. rev. ed. Therese Spears. (Illus.). 20p. (Orig.). 1989. pap. 6.00 (0-318-50071-X) Promenade Pub.

Beaded Dream Catchers. Mary R. Musgrove. (Illus.). 4p. 1993. pap. 3.95 (0-932255-05-1) Promenade Pub.

Beaded Earrings. rev. ed. Therese Spears. (Illus.). 20p. 1988. pap. 4.00 (0-318-50072-8) Promenade Pub.

Beaded Images: Intricate Beaded Jewelry Using Brick Stitch. Barbara Elbe. Ed. by Denise Knight. LC 94-72285. (Illus.). 72p. (Orig.). 1995. per. 9.95 (0-943604-46-X) Eagles View.

***Beaded Images: Intricate Beaded Jewelry Using Brick Stitch, Bk. 2.** Barbara Elbe. Ed. by Denise Knight & Monte Smith. (Illus.). 72p. (Orig.). 1995. pap. 9.95 (0-943604-49-4) Eagles View.

***Beading.** Tubbs. 1995. write for info. (0-517-88468-2) Random Hse Value.

Beading & Bonding in Ribbon Embroidery. Joyce Randall. (Illus.). 56p. 1994. 14.95 (0-86417-563-9, Pub. by Kangaroo Pr AT) Seven Hills Bk.

Beading Book. Julia Jones. 144p. 1993. 30.00 (0-916896-48-X) Lacis Pubns.

***Beading Necklaces with Ani Afshar.** Ani Afshar. LC 94-46707. (Illus.). 64p. (Orig.). 1995. pap. 12.95 (0-88740-735-8) Schiffer.

Beads. Jo Moody. (Keepsake Crafts Ser.). 1995. pap. 9.99 (0-376-04258-3) Sunset Menlo Pk.

Beads: Make Your Own Unique Jewelry. Stefany Tomalin. (Illus.). 128p. 1995. pap. 14.95 (0-7153-9838-5, Pub. by D & C Pub UK) Sterling.

Beads & Beadwork of East & South Africa. Margaret Carey. 1989. pap. 25.00 (0-85263-797-7, Pub. by Shire UK) St Mut.

Beads & Beadwork of the American Indian. rev. ed. Ed. by Monte Smith & F J. Dockstader. LC 75-16030. (Illus.). 184p. 1985. reprint ed. per., pap. text ed. 9.95 (0-943604-08-7) Eagles View.

Beads & Beadwork of West & Central Africa. Margaret Carey. 1989. pap. 25.00 (0-7478-0100-2, Pub. by Shire UK) St Mut.

Beads & Cabochons: How to Create Fashion Earrings & Jewelry. Patricia Lyman. Ed. by Denise Knight. LC 90-86227. (Illus.). 92p. (Orig.). 1992. per., pap. 9.95 (0-943604-32-X) Eagles View.

Beads & Threads: A New Technique for Fiber Jewelry. Diane Fitzgerald & Helen Banes. Ed. by Seymour Bress. (Illus.). 144p. 1993. 37.95 (0-9620543-5-6) Flower Valley Pr.

***Beads & Threads: A New Technique for Fiber Jewelry.** Diane Fitzgerald. 1994. pap. 24.95 (0-9620543-6-4) Flower Valley Pr.

***Beads, Badges, & Bangles.** Clare Beaton. (Fun to Do Ser.). (Illus.). 32p. (J). 1995. lib. bdg. write for info. (1-887238-00-X) Fitzgerald.

Beads of the World. Peter Francis, Jr. LC 93-87060. (Illus.). 1994. pap. 19.95 (0-88740-559-2) Schiffer.

Beads, The Art of Stringing. Genie Ragan. (Illus.). 58p. (Orig.). 1986. pap. text ed. 3.95 (0-935182-44-6) Gem Guides Bk.

Beads to Buckskins. Peggy S. Henry. 100p. 1992. pap. text ed. 10.95 (1-881646-00-9) Beads to Buckskins.

An Asterisk (*) at the beginning of an entry indicates that the title is appearing in BIP for the first time.

An Asterisk (*) at the beginning of an entry indicates that the title is appearing in BIP for the first time.

639

***Bear & the Mountain: Themes: Bears, Flowers, Friendship.** Jean Warren. (Nature Ser.). (Illus.). 32p. (J). 1995. 12.95 (*0-614-06900-9*, WPH 1906); pap. 5.95 (*0-614-06901-7*, WPH 1905) Totline Bks.

Bear at the Gate: Chinese Policy Making under Soviet Pressure. Harold C. Hinton. LC 78-187517. (AEI Hoover Policy Studies: No. 1). 120p. reprint ed. pap. 34.20 (*0-8357-3604-0*, 2017132) Bks Demand.

Bear Attacks: Their Causes & Avoidance. Stephen Herrero. (Illus.). 292p. 1988. reprint ed. pap. 14.95 (*0-941130-82-7*) Lyons & Burford.

***Bear Bones & Feathers.** Halfe. 1994. per. 9.95 (*1-55050-055-4*, Pub. by Coteau Bks CN) InBook.

Bear Brigade. Comp. by Jocelyn Stevenson. (Illus.). 64p. (J). (gr. 3-5). 1992. pap. 11.95 (*1-85158-400-5*, Pub. by Mnstream UK) Trafalgar.

Bear Bryant: Football's Winning Coach. Simpson E. Smith. LC 83-40404. (Illus.). 128p. (J). (gr. 7 up). 1984. 11.95 (*0-8027-6526-2*) Walker & Co.

***Bear Bryant: What Made Him a Winner.** V. Delbert Reed. (Illus.). 210p. 1995. 29.95 (*1-885219-01-6*) Vision AL.

Bear Bryant on Winning Football. Paul Bryant. 240p. 1983. 18.95 (*0-13-071274-4*); pap. 7.95 (*0-13-071266-3*) P-H.

***Bear Buys a Car.** Stephen Wyllie. LC 94-25901. (Illus.). (J). 1995. 13.95 (*0-8037-1840-3*) Dial Bks Young.

Bear Called Paddington. Michael Bond. (Illus.). 128p. (J). (gr. 1-5). 1960. 14.95 (*0-395-06636-0*) HM.

Bear Called Paddington see Hilarious Adventures of Paddington

Bear Called Snorty & Other Stories. Ronald F. Ayres. 1994. 7.95 (*0-8062-4891-2*) Carlton.

Bear Child. Daria Jennings. LC 90-55246. 138p. (Orig.). 1991. pap. 4.00 (*1-56002-055-5*) Aegina Pr.

Bear Child's Book of Special Days. Anne Rockwell. LC 89-1633. (Illus.). 32p. (J). (ps-1). 1989. 12.95 (*0-525-44508-0*, DCB) Dutton Child Bks.

Bear Crossing. Kell Robertson. Ed. & Illus. by Steven Jacobsen. 33p. 1990. pap. text ed. 4.00 (*0-9625349-0-0*) Guerilla Poetics.

Bear Crossings: An Anthology of North American Poets. Ed. by Anne Newman & Julie Suk. 124p. 1983. pap. 6.95 (*0-917990-08-0*) New South Co.

Bear Cub Scout Action Book. 64p. 1981. pap. 2.15 (*0-8395-3903-7*, 33903) BSA.

Bear Cub Scout Book. rev. ed. 256p. (gr. 3). 1984. 3.50 (*0-8395-3228-8*, 33228) BSA.

Bear Cubs. Illus. by Pat Paris. (Baby Animal Pop-Up Bks.). 10p. (J). (ps). 1989. 4.95 (*0-8120-5987-5*) Barron.

***Bear Cub's Adventure.** Lee Roddy. 132p. (J). 1996. pap. 4.99 (*1-56476-503-2*, 6-3503) SP Pubns.

***Bear Dance.** Zimmer. 1995. pap. text ed. 9.99 (*0-9639882-4-7*) Goodfellow Pr.

***Bear Dancing: The Story of a Most Remarkable Bear Indeed.** Will Green. LC 93-93799. (Illus.). 64p. (Orig.). (J). 1994. pap. 7.75 (*1-56002-329-5*, Univ Edtns) Aegina Pr.

***Bear Days.** Marilynn Barr. (Illus.). 48p. 1993. teacher ed, pap. 5.95 (*0-87827-955-5*, MM 1976) Evan-Moor Corp.

Bear Days. Marilynn G. Barr. (Illus.). 48p. (J). (ps-1). 1993. pap. 5.95 (*1-878279-55-6*) Monday Morning Bks.

Bear Detectives. Stan Berenstain & Janice Berenstain. LC 75-1603. (Illus.). 48p. (J). (gr. k-3). 1975. 6.95 (*0-394-83127-6*) Beginner.

Bear Detectives. Stan Berenstain & Janice Berenstain. LC 75-1603. (Illus.). 48p. (J). (gr. k-3). 1975. lib. bdg. 7.99 (*0-394-93127-0*) Beginner.

Bear E. Bear. large type ed. Susan Straight. LC 94-19306. (Illus.). 32p. (J). (ps-2). 1995. 14.95 (*1-56282-526-7*); lib. bdg. 14.89 (*1-56282-527-5*) Hyprn Child.

Bear Essentials. Patricia Rex. (J). (ps-00). 1988. pap. 9.99 (*0-8224-0697-7*) Fearon Teach Aids.

***Bear Family.** Bett. (J). 1994. pap. 3.99 (*0-517-13487-X*) Random Hse Value.

Bear Family. Dieter Betz. LC 91-42698. (Illus.). 60p. (J). (gr. 2-6). 1992. 15.00 (*0-688-11647-7*, Tambourine Bks); lib. bdg. 14.93 (*0-688-11648-5*, Tambourine Bks) Morrow.

Bear Flag. Cecelia Holland. 480p. 1992. mass mkt. 5.99 (*1-55817-635-7*, Pinnacle NY) Windsor NY.

Bear for All Seasons. Fuchs. 32p. (J). 1995. 14.95 (*0-8050-2139-6*) H Holt & Co.

Bear for Christmas. Holly Keller. LC 85-12645. (Illus.). 32p. (J). (ps-3). 1986. 11.75 (*0-688-05988-0*); lib. bdg. 11.88 (*0-688-05989-9*) Greenwillow.

***Bear for Miguel.** Elaine M. Alphin. LC 94-36723. (I Can Read Bks.). (Illus.). (J). 1996. 14.00 (*0-06-024521-2*); lib. bdg. 13.89 (*0-06-024522-0*) HarpC Child Bks.

Bear Fruit in Plenty: Economic Lessons of the Supreme Economist. Hank Monrobey. (Illus.). 200p. (Orig.). 1990. write for info. (*0-9623564-4-1*); pap. text ed. write for info. (*0-9623564-3-3*) H Monrobey & Assocs.

Bear Grease, Builders & Bandits: The Men & Women of Wichita's Past. Beccy Tanner. 152p. 1991. pap. 15.95 (*1-880652-09-9*) Wichita Eagle.

Bear Guardian. Peter Leschak. (Illus.). 184p. 1990. 9.95 (*0-87839-061-8*) North Star.

Bear Heads & Fish Tales. Alan Liere. (Illus.). 144p. (Orig.). 1989. pap. 9.95 (*0-916771-05-9*) Alaska Angler.

Bear Heads & Fish Tales. Alan Liere. Ed. by Christopher M. Batin. LC 88-70823. (Illus.). 140p. (Orig.). 1990. pap. 9.95 (*0-916771-25-3*, SK33.L5) Alaska Angler.

Bear Hug. Jerome Doolittle. Ed. by Bill Grose. 240p. 1993. mass mkt. 4.99 (*0-671-74569-7*) PB.

Bear Hug. Sylvia Tasher. 350p. 1990. 19.95 (*0-937557-10-2*) Litarvan Lit.

Bear Hugs, 4 bks. (Illus.). (J). (ps up). 1993. Boxed set. boxed 19.95 (*1-56402-203-X*) Candlewick Pr.

Bear Hugs. Kathleen Hague. LC 88-28458. (Illus.). 64p. (J). (ps-2). 1992. pap. 4.95 (*0-8050-2344-5*, Bks Young Read) H Holt & Co.

***Bear Hugs for Accepting Change: Positive Activities That Help Children Cope with Change in Their Lives.** Patty Claycomb. Ed. by Gayle Bittinger & Jean Warren. (Bear Hugs Ser.). (Illus.). 24p. (Orig.). 1996. pap. 3.95 (*1-57029-042-3*) Warren Pub Hse.

***Bear Hugs for Being Afraid: Positive Activities for Easing Common Childhood Fears.** Patty Claycomb. Ed. by Gayle Bittinger & Jean Warren. (Bear Hugs Ser.). (Illus.). 24p. (Orig.). 1995. pap. 3.95 (*1-57029-038-5*) Warren Pub Hse.

***Bear Hugs for Being Healthy: Positive Activities That Foster Healthful Attitudes & Behaviors.** Patty Claycomb. Ed. by Gayle Bittinger & Jean Warren. (Bear Hugs Ser.). (Illus.). 24p. (Orig.). 1996. pap. 3.95 (*1-57029-040-7*) Warren Pub Hse.

***Bear Hugs for Being Responsible: Positive Activities That Foster Responsible Attitudes.** Patty Claycomb. Ed. by Gayle Bittinger & Jean Warren. (Bear Hugs Ser.). (Illus.). 24p. (Orig.). 1995. pap. 3.95 (*1-57029-039-3*) Warren Pub Hse.

***Bear Hugs for Circle Time.** Patty Claycomb. (Bear Hugs Ser.). (Illus.). 24p. (J). (ps). 1994. pap. 3.95 (*1-57029-011-3*, WPH 2503) Warren Pub Hse.

***Bear Hugs for Getting Along: Positive Activities Encourage Cooperation & Sharing.** Totline Staff. Ed. by Gayle Bittinger & Jean Warren. (Bear Hugs Ser.). (Illus.). 24p. (Orig.). 1996. pap. 3.95 (*1-57029-036-9*) Warren Pub Hse.

***Bear Hugs for Remembering the Rules.** Patty Claycomb. (Bear Hugs Ser.). (Illus.). 24p. (J). (ps). 1994. pap. 3.95 (*1-57029-009-1*, WPH 2501) Warren Pub Hse.

***Bear Hugs for Respecting Others: Positive Activities That Inspire Respect & Appreciation for One Another.** Totline Staff. Ed. by Gayle Bittinger & Jean Warren. (Bear Hugs Ser.). (Illus.). 24p. (Orig.). 1996. pap. 3.95 (*1-57029-043-1*) Warren Pub Hse.

***Bear Hugs for Saving the Earth: Positive Activities That Encourage Respect for Our Earth.** Patty Claycomb. Ed. by Gayle Bittinger & Jean Warren. (Bear Hugs Ser.). (Illus.). 24p. (Orig.). 1995. pap. 3.95 (*1-57029-035-0*) Warren Pub Hse.

***Bear Hugs for Saying Goodbye.** Patty Claycomb. (Bear Hugs Ser.). (Illus.). 24p. (J). (ps). 1994. pap. 3.95 (*1-57029-014-8*, WPH 2506) Warren Pub Hse.

***Bear Hugs for Self Esteem: Positive Activities That Affirm Confidence & Self Worth.** Totline Staff. Ed. by Gayle Bittinger & Jean Warren. (Bear Hugs Ser.). (Illus.). 24p. (Orig.). 1995. pap. 3.95 (*1-57029-037-7*) Warren Pub Hse.

***Bear Hugs for Staying in Line.** Patty Claycomb. (Bear Hugs Ser.). (Illus.). 24p. (J). (ps). 1994. pap. 3.95 (*1-57029-010-5*, WPH 2502) Warren Pub Hse.

***Bear Hugs for Time Out.** Patty Claycomb. (Bear Hugs Ser.). (Illus.). 24p. (J). (ps). 1994. 3.95 (*1-57029-013-X*, WPH 2505) Warren Pub Hse.

***Bear Hugs for Transition Time.** Patty Claycomb. (Bear Hugs Ser.). (Illus.). 24p. (J). (ps). 1994. 3.95 (*1-57029-012-1*, WPH 2504) Warren Pub Hse.

***Bear Hugs for Welcoming Children: Positive Activities That Make Children Feel at Ease in the Classroom.** Patty Claycomb. Ed. by Gayle Bittinger & Jean Warren. (Bear Hugs Ser.). (Illus.). 24p. (Orig.). 1996. pap. 3.95 (*1-57029-041-5*) Warren Pub Hse.

Bear Hunting with the Politburo: The Real Story of Doing Business in the New Russia. A. Craig Copetas. 288p. 1993. pap. 12.00 (*0-671-79721-2*, Touchstone Bks) S&S Trade.

Bear in Mind: A Book of Bear Poems. Illus. by William Pene Du Bois. 32p. (J). (ps-3). 1991. pap. 4.99 (*0-14-050799-X*, Puffin) Puffin Bks.

Bear in the Air. Leslie Williams. LC 80-10290. (Illus.). 28p. (J). (gr. k up). 1980. 7.95 (*0-916144-54-2*) Stemmer Hse.

Bear in the Chair. Stephanie Mellen. LC 94-75065. (Illus.). 50p. (J). (gr. k-2). 1994. pap. 6.95 (*0-9637414-1-1*) Meltec.

Bear Knife: And Other American Indian Tales. Ruth-Inge Heinze. LC 93-33089. (Illus.). 176p. (Orig.). 1994. pap. 19.95 (*0-9626184-9-7*, Bramble Bks) Bramble Co.

Bear Knife: And Other American Indian Tales. Ruth-Inge Heinze. 1993. pap. 19.95 (*0-9621684-9-1*) G K Scott Pub.

Bear Magic. Chris Cahill. LC 89-61636. (Rhyme-Fingerplay-Puppet Book Ser.). (Illus.). 12p. (J). (ps-1). 1990. bds. 5.95 (*1-877779-00-8*) Schneider Educational.

Bear Meat 'n' Honey: An Oral History of the Sabinal Canyon, Vol. I. Ed. & Illus. by Greg Walton. LC 90-82305. 240p. 1990. 14.95 (*0-9627318-0-3*) Onion Creek Pr.

Bear Memorabilia: Reference & Price Guide. Dee Hockenberry. (Illus.). 192p. 1992. pap. 12.95 (*0-87588-392-3*) Hobby Hse.

Bear Named Song: The Gift of a Lifetime. Kimberly A. Shope. (Illus.). 32p. (J). 1992. 11.99 (*0-87403-865-0*, 24-03565) Standard Pub.

Bear Needs Help! Rita Schlachter. LC 81-14052. (Illus.). 48p. (Orig.). (J). (gr. 1-3). 1986. lib. bdg. 10.59 (*0-8167-0600-X*); pap. text ed. 3.50 (*0-8167-0601-8*) Troll Assocs.

Bear Next Door. Ginnie Hofmann. (Picturebacks Ser.). (Illus.). 32p. (Orig.). (J). (ps-3). 1992. pap. 0.49 (*0-679-83893-7*) Random Bks Yng Read.

Bear Next Door. Ida Luttrell. LC 90-4153. (I Can Read Bk.). (Illus.). 64p. (J). (gr. k-3). 1991. lib. bdg. 11.89 (*0-06-024024-5*) HarpC Child Bks.

Bear Next Door: Story & Pictures. Ginnie Hofmann. LC 93-616. (Pictureback Ser.). (Illus.). (J). (ps-3). 1994. 2.50 (*0-679-83957-7*) Random Bks Yng Read.

Bear Nobody Wanted. Allan Ahlberg. (Illus.). 144p. (J). (gr. 3-7). 1993. 15.00 (*0-670-83982-5*) Viking Child Bks.

Bear Notes. James Roberts. 86p. (Orig.). 1986. pap. text ed. 4.50 (*0-8220-0222-1*) Cliffs.

Bear on the Moon. Joanne Ryder. LC 89-13133. (Illus.). 32p. (J). (gr. 1 up). 1991. 16.00 (*0-688-08109-6*); lib. bdg. 15.93 (*0-688-08110-X*) Morrow Jr Bks.

***Bear Out There.** Joanne Ryder. (Illus.). (J). (gr. 2-3). 1995. 15.00 (*0-689-31780-8*, Atheneum Bks Young) S&S Childrens.

***Bear Party.** William P. Du Bois. (Illus.). (Orig.). (J). (gr. k-3). 1991. audio, pap. 14.95 (*0-87499-195-1*) Live Oak Media.

Bear Party. William P. Du Bois. (Orig.). (J). (ps-1). 1987. pap. 3.99 (*0-14-050793-0*, Puffin) Puffin Bks.

***Bear Party, 4 bks., Set.** William P. Du Bois. (Illus.). (Orig.). (J). (gr. k-3). 1991. audio, pap. 29.95 (*0-87499-197-8*) Live Oak Media.

***Bear Paw Horses.** large type ed. Will Henry. 1995. pap. 15.95 (*0-7838-1121-7*) Hall.

***Bear Paws & Crystal Spires.** Ruth Huffman. 44p. 1994. pap. 8.95 (*0-9644289-3-8*) R & R Impress.

Bear Photo Album: Teddies Frolic Through the Seasons. Dee Hockenberry. (Illus.). 96p. 1988. 19.95 (*0-87588-358-3*) Hobby Hse.

***Bear Play.** Miela Ford. LC 94-25739. (Illus.). 24p. (J). (ps up). 1995. 15.00 (*0-688-13832-2*); lib. bdg. 14.93 (*0-688-13833-0*) Greenwillow.

***Bear Princess.** Ed. by Barbara D. Goldin. LC 95-7538. (Illus.). (J). 1996. write for info. (*0-15-200684-2*, Gulliver Bks) HarBrace.

Bear Raid. limited ed. Ken Follett. LC 90-45282. 160p. 1990. reprint ed. 75.00 (*0-922890-68-4*) Armchair Detective.

Bear Raid. Ken Follett. LC 90-45282. 160p. 1990. reprint ed. 17.95 (*0-922890-66-8*); reprint ed. 25.00 (*0-922890-67-6*) Armchair Detective.

Bear Record Book. Peggy Rosamond. 48p. 1983. 16.95 (*0-87588-195-5*, 2402) Hobby Hse.

Bear Record Book Refill Set. Peggy Rosamonds. 24p. 1984. ring bd. 3.95 (*0-87588-196-3*, 2403) Hobby Hse.

Bear River Massacre. Newell Hart. (Illus.). 300p. (C). 1982. 35.00 (*0-941462-01-3*) Cache Valley.

***Bear Santa Claus Forgot.** Diana Kimpton. LC 94-37247. (Illus.). (J). 1995. write for info. (*0-590-26564-4*, Cartwheel) Scholastic Inc.

Bear Scouts. Stan Berenstain & Janice Berenstain. LC 67-21919. (Illus.). 72p. (J). (gr. k-3). 1967. 6.95 (*0-394-80046-X*) Beginner.

Bear Shadow. Frank Asch. (YA). (gr. 6 up). 1992. pap. 19.95 (*0-590-72736-2*) Scholastic Inc.

Bear Shadow. Frank Asch. LC 82-18250. (Illus.). 32p. (J). (ps-2). 1988. pap. 14.00 (*0-671-66279-1*, S&S Bks Young Read); pap. 4.95 (*0-671-66866-8*, S&S Bks Young Read) S&S Childrens.

Bear Sleep Soup. Jasper Tomkins. (Orig.). (J). (ps-3). 1991. pap. 7.95 (*0-671-75278-2*, Green Tiger S&S) S&S Childrens.

Bear Songs: A Woman's Journey to Personal Power. Sally Seed. Ed. by Rini Price. LC 90-92286. (Illus.). 117p. (Orig.). 1991. pap. 10.95 (*0-9631054-0-X*) White Cloud.

Bear-Star My Name. Bettina T. Barrett. LC 89-32680. 76p. (Orig.). 1989. pap. 7.50 (*0-931832-32-2*) Fithian Pr.

Bear That Heard Crying. Natalie Kinsey-Warnock & Helen Kinsey. (Illus.). 32p. (J). (ps-3). 1993. 13.99 (*0-525-65103-9*, Cobblehill Bks) Dutton Child Bks.

Bear That Turned White & Other Native Tales. Maurine Grammer. LC 90-53590. (Illus.). 104p. (Orig.). (J). (gr. 4 up). 1991. pap. 11.95 (*0-87358-515-1*) Northland AZ.

Bear That Was Chicken. Ane Weber et al. (Land of Pleasant Dreams Ser.). (Illus.). 26p. (J). (ps up). 1986. Book & Cassette. 7.95 (*1-55578-101-2*) Worlds Wonder.

Bear That Wasn't. Frank Tashlin. (Illus.). v, 51p. (J). (gr. 4 up). 1946. pap. 2.50 (*0-486-20939-3*) Dover.

Bear, the Cubs, & the Eagle: Soviet Bloc Interventionism in the Third World & the U. S. Response. Bertil Duner. 209p. 1987. text ed. 52.95 (*0-566-05631-3*, Pub. by Dartmth Pub UK) Ashgate Pub Co.

Bear Tribe's Self Reliance Book. rev. ed. Sun Bear et al. 1977. pap. 6.95 (*0-943404-00-2*) Bear Tribe.

Bear under the Stairs. Helen Cooper. LC 92-23840. (J). (ps-2). 1993. 12.99 (*0-8037-1279-0*) Dial Bks Young.

Bear Up: Bear Ways to Cope with Lifes Bumps & Surprises. Jane Noland & Mimi Noland. LC 93-27109. (Illus.). 72p. 1993. pap. 6.95 (*0-89638-323-7*) Hazelden.

***Bear-Walker: And Other Tales.** Basil H. Johnston. (Illus.). 64p. (C). Date not set. 19.95 (*0-88854-415-4*, Pub. by Royal Ont Mus CN) U of Toronto Pr.

***Bear Went over the Mountain.** Rozanne Williams. (Emergent Reader Bks.). 8p. 1994. 1.59 (*0-916119-51-3*) Creat Teach Pr.

Bear Went over the Mountain: Tall Tales of American Animals. Ed. by Robert B. Downs. 1995. reprint ed. 40.00 (*1-55888-931-0*) Omnigraphics Inc.

Bear Who Came To Stay. Allen Woodman & David Kirby. LC 92-7799. (Illus.). 40p. (J). (ps-3). 1994. text ed. 14.95 (*0-02-793397-0*, Bradbury S&S) S&S Childrens.

Bear Who Couldn't Do Anything. Dina Anastasia. (Teddy Bear Tales Ser.: No. S897-4). (J). (ps-2). 1989. boxed, pap. text ed. 3.95 (*0-7214-5227-2*) Ladybird Bks.

***Bear Who Went to the Ballet.** Jean Richardson. (J). 1995. 14.95 (*0-7894-0318-8*, 5-70668) Dorling Kindersley.

***Bear Whose Bones Were Jezebel Jones.** Bill Grossman. LC 94-31907. (J). 1996. write for info. (*0-8037-1742-3*); lib. bdg. write for info. (*0-8037-1743-1*) Dial Bks Young.

Bear with Me: Story & Coloring Book Adjusting to Life with a New Baby. Illus. by Mary M. Young. 16p. (J). (ps-3). 1989. pap. 7.95 (*0-943114-20-9*, CB100) Childbirth Graphics.

Bear, Your Manners Are Showing. Kathleen A. Meyer. Ed. by Shirley Beegle. (Happy Day Bks.). (Illus.). 24p. (J). (ps-3). 1994. reprint ed. pap. 1.89 (*0-7847-0251-9*) Standard Pub.

Bearables: Parables of Bear Wisdom for Everyday Living. Jane Noland & Mimi Noland. (Illus.). 72p. (Orig.). 1993. pap. 6.95 (*0-89638-298-2*) Hazelden.

Bearables of Bernie Bear. Verna Larson. Ed. by Debra S. Pappas. (Illus.). 30p. (Orig.). (J). 1994. pap. 8.95 (*1-56550-022-9*) Vis Bks Intl.

Beard of Prometheus. Mokwugo Okoye. 220p. 1985. 35.00 (*0-317-39407-X*, Pub. by A H S Ltd UK) St Mut.

Beard of Prometheus. Mokwugo Okoye. 220p. 1987. 35.00 (*0-7223-9988-X*, Pub. by A H S Ltd UK) St Mut.

Beard on Birds. James Beard. 1989. pap. 10.95 (*0-446-39032-1*) Warner Bks.

***Beard on Bread.** James Beard. 1995. pap. 15.00 (*0-679-75504-7*) Knopf.

Beard on Bread. James A. Beard. 1981. mass mkt. 5.99 (*0-345-29550-1*) Ballantine.

***Beard on Pasta.** James Beard. LC 94-21596. (Illus.). 1994. pap. 8.99 (*0-517-11927-7*, Pub. by Wings Bks) Random.

Beardance. Will Hobbs. LC 92-44874. 208p. (J). (gr. 5-9). 1993. text ed. 14.95 (*0-689-31867-7*, Atheneum Bks Young) S&S Childrens.

***Beardance.** Will Hobbs. 208p. (J). (gr. 7 up). 1995. pap. 3.99 (*0-380-72317-4*, Camelot) Avon.

***Bearded Collie.** Charlotte Laning. (Illus.). 188p. (SWE.). 1995. 40.00 (*0-9644628-1-8*) C Laning.

Bearded Collie. Chris Walkowicz. Ed. by William W. Denlinger & R. Annabel Rathman. LC 87-13713. (Breed Bks.). (Illus.). 1987. 29.95 (*0-87714-123-1*) Denlingers.

Bearded Collie Champions, 1977-1986. Camino E. E. & B. Co. Staff. (Illus.). 110p. 1988. pap. 36.95 (*0-940808-69-2*) Camino E E & Bk.

Bearded Collies. Carol Gold. (Illus.). 192p. 1990. lib. bdg. 11.95 (*0-86622-570-6*, KW200) TFH Pubns.

Bearded Ladies. Kate Grenville. 168p. 1985. pap. 14.95 (*0-7022-1716-6*) Intl Spec Bk.

***Bearded Lion Who Roars: Simba Mandefu Mabe.** Elise Dallemagne-Cookson. (J). 288p. (Orig.). 1995. pap. 12.95 (*1-56474-115-X*) Fithian Pr.

Bearded Mother. Anne Halley. LC 79-4020. 60p. 1979. lib. bdg. 15.00 (*0-87023-271-1*); pap. 8.95 (*0-87023-282-7*) U of Mass Pr.

***Beardless Warriors.** Richard Matheson. 1994. lib. bdg. 24.95x (*1-56849-431-9*) Buccaneer Bks.

Beards & Wings. Alexis Rotella. 40p. 1985. pap. text ed. 6.00x (*0-917951-01-8*) White Peony.

Beard's Massage. 3rd ed. Elizabeth C. Wood & Paul Becker. 208p. 1981. pap. text ed. 35.50 (*0-7216-9592-2*) Saunders.

Beardsley. Aileen Reid. 112p. 1994. 14.98 (*0-8317-6114-8*) Smithmark.

Beardsley Limner & Some Contemporaries: Postrevolutionary Portraiture in New England, 1785-1805. Christine S. Schloss. LC 72-91465. (Abby Aldrich Rockefeller Folk Art Collection Catalog Ser). (Illus.). 48p. (Orig.). 1972. pap. 1.99 (*0-87935-005-9*) Colonial Williamsburg.

Beardsley Period. Osbert Burdett. LC 75-79196. 1969. reprint ed. 46.00 (*0-8154-0297-X*) Cooper Sq.

Beardsley Period: An Essay in Perspective. Osbert Burdett. 1971. reprint ed. 6.00 (*0-403-00881-6*) Scholarly.

Beardsley Period: An Essay in Perspective. Osbert Burdett. (BCL1-PR English Literature Ser.). 302p. 1992. reprint ed. lib. bdg. 89.00 (*0-7812-7047-2*) Rprt Serv.

Beardstown Ladies' Commonsense Investment Guide: How We Beat the Stock Market & How You Can, Too. Beardstown Ladies' Investment Club Staff & Leslie Whitaker. (Illus.). 256p. 1995. 19.95 (*0-7868-6043-X*) Hyperion.

***Beardstown Ladies' Stitch-in-Time Guide to Growing Your Nest Egg: Step-by-Step Planning for a Comfortable Financial Future.** Beardstown Ladies' Investment Club Staff & Robin Dellabough. (Illus.). 272p. 1996. 19.95 (*0-7868-6192-4*) Hyperion.

Bearer of a Million Dreams: The Biography of the Statue of Liberty. Frank Spiering. LC 85-24084. (Illus.). 288p. 1986. 16.95 (*0-915463-35-0*) Green Hill.

***Bearer of the Pipe.** Don Coldsmith. 1995. 21.95 (*0-385-47030-4*) Doubleday.

Bearer of Tradition: Dwight Stump, Basketmaker. Rosemary O. Joyce. LC 88-29644. (Illus.). 256p. 1990. 34.95 (*0-8203-1148-0*) U of Ga Pr.

Bearers of Blackness. Hazel Clayton-Harrison. LC 86-83352. 60p. (Orig.). 1987. pap. 5.00 (*0-940248-29-8*) Guild Pr.

Bearers of Meaning: The Classical Orders in Antiquity, the Middle Ages, & the Renaissance. John Onians. (Illus.). 400p. (Orig.). 1990. 85.00 (*0-691-04043-5*); pap. text ed. 27.50 (*0-691-00219-3*) Princeton U Pr.

Bearers of Memories, Vol. II. Dee Hockenberry. (Illus.). 32p. (Orig.). 1989. spiral bd. 5.95 (*0-87588-342-7*, 3822) Hobby Hse.

Bearers of Memories I. Dee Hockenberry. (Illus.). 32p. (C). 1989. spiral bd. 5.95 (*0-87588-338-9*, 3727) Hobby Hse.

***Bearers of the Mysteries: A Guide to the Local Church.** Intro. by Fred Saato. (Illus.). 128p. (Orig.). 1988. pap. 6.95 (*1-56125-014-7*) Educ Services.

Bearers of the Sun. Chris Foster. 200p. (Orig.). 1987. pap. 7.95 (*0-969034l-2-1*, B3) Foundation Hse.

Beargrass, a History. Lawrence J. Fleenor, Jr. 135p. 1992. 29.95 (*0-9632918-0-7*) L J Fleenor.

Bearhead: A Russian Folktale. Illus. by Charles Mikolaycak. LC 91-55026. 32p. (J). (ps-3). 1991. lib. bdg. 15.95 (*0-8234-0902-3*) Holiday.

Bearheart: The Heirship Chronicles. Gerald Vizenor. Orig. Title: Darkness in St. Louis, Bearheart. 268p. 1990. reprint ed. text ed. 29.95 (*0-8166-1851-8*); reprint ed. pap. 12.95 (*0-8166-1852-6*) U of Minn Pr.

Bearing an Hourglass. Piers Anthony. (Incarnations of Immortality Ser.: Bk. 2). 384p. (Orig.). 1985. mass mkt. 5.95 (*0-345-31315-1*, Del Rey) Ballantine.

An Asterisk (*) at the beginning of an entry indicates that the title is appearing in BIP for the first time.

640

Bearing & Seal Design in Nuclear Power Machinery: Proceedings of the Symposium on Lubrication in Nuclear Applications, Miami Beach, Florida, June 5-7, 1967. Ed. by Ralph A. Burton. LC 67-27785. 539p. reprint ed. pap. 153.70 (*0-8357-7084-2*, 2016809) Bks Demand.

***Bearing (Antifriction) Market.** 400p. (Orig.). 1994. pap. 1, 495.00 (*1-57205-913-3*) Rector Pr.

Bearing Capacity of Building Foundations. A. Myslivec & Z. Kysela. (Developments in Geotechnical Engineering Ser.: Vol. 21). 1978. 97.50 (*0-444-99794-6*) Elsevier.

Bearing Capacity of Soils. American Society of Civil Engineers. LC 94-243. (Technical Engineering & Design Guides As Adapted from the U. S. Army Corps of Engineers Ser.: No. 7). 1994. pap. 32.00 (*0-87262-997-X*, ASCE Press) Am Soc Civil Eng.

Bearing Design - Historical Aspects, Present Technology, & Future Problems: Presented at the International Conference on Bearing Design, Historical Aspects, Present Technology, & Future Problems, Century 2--Emerging Technology Conferences, San Francisco, California, August 18-21, 1980. International Conference on Bearing Design Staff. Ed. by W. J. Anderson. LC 80-66044. (Illus.). 220p. reprint ed. pap. 62.70 (*0-8357-2829-3*, 2039065) Bks Demand.

Bearing Dreams, Shaping Visions: Asian Pacific American Perspectives. Ed. by Linda A. Revilla et al. LC 93-1862. (Association for Asian American Studies Ser.). 284p. 1993. pap. 30.00 (*0-87422-099-8*) Wash St U Pr.

Bearing Fruit: Sermons for Children. Harold Steindam. LC 94-35080. (Illus.). 136p. (Orig.). 1994. pap. 9.95 (*0-8298-1013-7*) Pilgrim OH.

Bearing Gifts. Aimee Thurlo. (Intrigue Ser.). 1994. mass mkt. 2.99 (*0-373-22304-8*, 1-22304-9) Harlequin Bks.

Bearing Gifts. deluxe ed. Jascha Kessler. (Treacle Story Ser.: No. 9). (Illus.). 48p. 1979. 8.00 (*0-914232-31-2*) McPherson & Co.

Bearing Influence & Representation in Rotor Dynamics Analysis. W. Shapiro & J. H. Rumbarger. LC 72-92595. (Flexible Rotor-Bearing System Dynamics Ser.: Vol. 2). (Illus.). 27p. reprint ed. pap. 25.00 (*0-8357-7085-0*, 2011329) Bks Demand.

***Bearing Meaning: The Language of Birth.** Robbie P. Kahn & Levin M. Pfeufer. LC 94-42159. (Illus.). 1995. text ed. write for info. (*0-252-02171-1*) U of Ill Pr.

Bearing of Basic Research on Clinical Otolaryngology. Ed. by C. R. Pfaltz et al. (Advances in Oto-Rhino-Laryngology Ser.: Vol. 46). (Illus.). x, 182p. 1991. 149. 00 (*3-8055-5338-2*) S Karger.

Bearing of Certain Personality Factors Other Than Intelligence on Academic Success: Study of Tests Made at Teacher's College, Columbia University. Henry T. Tyler. LC 78-177693. (Columbia University. Teachers College. Contributions to Education Ser.: No. 468). reprint ed. 37.50 (*0-404-55468-7*) AMS Pr.

Bearing Our Sorrows: Christian Reflections for Courage, Hope, & Healing. Mary E. Ashcroft & Holly B. Elliott. LC 93-34181. 208p. 1994. 15.00 (*0-06-060311-9*) Harper SF.

Bearing Precious Seed: A Guide to Visitation Ministries. James F. Dersham. 27p. 1985. pap. 1.95 (*0-87227-106-4*, RBP5135) Reg Baptist.

Bearing Steels: The Rating of Nonmetallic Inclusion-STP 575. 228p. 1975. 22.25 (*0-8031-0289-5*, 04-575000-02) ASTM.

Bearing the Bad News: Contemporary American Literature & Culture. Sanford Pinsker. LC 90-35570. 195p. 1990. 25.95 (*0-87745-292-X*) U of Iowa Pr.

Bearing the Cross: Martin Luther King, Jr. & the Southern Christian Leadership Conference. David J. Garrow. LC 87-50419. 800p. 1987. pap. 18.00 (*0-394-75623-1*, Vin) Random.

Bearing the Dead: The British Culture of Mourning from the Enlightenment to Victoria. Esther Schor. LC 94-11753. (Literature in History Ser.). 1994. 35.00 (*0-691-03396-X*) Princeton U Pr.

Bearing the Unbearable: Yiddish & Polish Poetry in the Ghettos & Concentration Camps. Frieda W. Aaron. LC 89-11593. (Modern Jewish Literature & Culture Ser.). 242p. 1990. 39.50 (*0-7914-0247-9*) State U NY Pr.

Bearing the Word: Language & Female Experience in Nineteenth-Century Women's Writing. Margaret Homans. LC 85-20960. xiv, 326p. (C). 1989. pap. text ed. 14.95 (*0-226-35106-8*) U Ch Pr.

Bearing Witness. Bob Hicok. 54p. (Orig.). 1991. pap. 4.75 (*1-56439-001-2*) Ridgeway.

Bearing Witness: Gay Men's Health Crisis & the Politics of AIDS. Philip M. Kayal. LC 92-40293. 275p. (C). 1993. pap. text ed. 19.95 (*0-8133-1729-0*) Westview.

***Bearing Witness: Liberation & the Nuremberg Trials.** Stuart A. Kallen. LC 94-26391. (Holocaust Ser.). (YA). 1994. lib. bdg. 13.99 (*1-56239-354-5*) Abdo & Dghtrs.

Bearing Witness: Quaker Process & a Culture of Peace. Gray Cox. LC 85-61133. 32p. (Orig.). 1985. pap. 3.00 (*0-87574-262-9*) Pendle Hill.

Bearing Witness: Selections from African-American Autobiography in the Twentieth Century. Ed. by Henry L. Gates, Jr. LC 90-52538. 400p. 1991. pap. 16.00 (*0-679-73520-8*) Pantheon.

Bearing Witness: Selections from 150 Years of African-American Autobiography. Ed. by Henry L. Gates, Jr. LC 90-52538. 494p. 1991. 16.00 (*0-394-58522-4*) Pantheon.

***Bearing Witness: Sexual Harassment & Beyond.** Celia Morris. 1995. pap. 12.95 (*0-316-58423-1*) Little.

Bearing Witness: Sexual Harassment & Beyond - Everywoman's Story. Celia Morris. 1994. 21.95 (*0-316-58422-3*) Little.

***Bearing Witness: Stories of the Holocaust.** Sel. by Hazel Rochman & Darlene Z. McCampbell. LC 95-13352. 144p. (YA). (gr. 7 up). 1995. 15.95 (*0-531-09488-X*); lib. bdg. 15.99 (*0-531-08788-3*) Orchard Bks Watts.

***Bearing Witness: The Holocaust, America & the Jews.** Henry L. Feingold. LC 95-15862. 300p. 1995. 39.95 (*0-8156-2669-X*); pap. 16.95 (*0-8156-2670-3*) Syracuse U Pr.

Bearing Witness to the Holocaust, 1939-1989. Ed. by Alan L. Berger. LC 91-28678. (Symposium Ser.: Vol. 31). (Illus.). 376p. 1991. lib. bdg. 99.95 (*0-7734-9644-0*) E Mellen.

Bearings. M. J. Neale. (Tribology Handbooks Ser.). (Illus.). 180p. 1993. pap. write for info. (*0-7506-0979-6*) Buttrwrth-Heinemann.

Bearings. Ed. by M. J. Neale. LC 93-10932. (Tribology Handbook). 180p. 1993. 39.00 (*1-56091-393-2*, R-131) Soc Auto Engineers.

Bearings: Faculty Architecture in North America. 80p. (Orig.). 1991. pap. 5.95 (*1-878271-28-8*) Princeton Arch.

Bearings & Lubrication: A Mechanical Designers' Workbook. Joseph E. Shigley & Charles R. Mischke. 1990. pap. text ed. 31.95 (*0-07-056928-2*) McGraw.

Bearings & Seals. rev. ed. Ed. by Deere & Company Staff. (Fundamentals of Service Ser.). (Illus.). 118p. 1992. Slide set. sl. 118.95 (*0-685-45882-2*, FOS5405S) Deere & Co.
Helps students understand bearings & seals & service them with speed & skill. Covers all types. Explains bearing loads, friction, "crush," & other concepts. Explains maintenance of bearings - cleaning, lubrication, adjustment, & repair. Explains use of gaskets, oil seals, sealing rings, & others. Tells how to care for seals, both static & dynamic types. "Test Yourself" questions & answers help participants review important facts. CONTENTS: Bearings - basic theory, types of bearings, plain bearings (bushings), ball bearings, roller bearings, needle bearings, maintenance & repair, & diagnosing failures. Seals - basic principles, static & dynamic seals, oil seals, sealing rings, gaskets, sealants & failures & repair. ***Publisher Provided Annotation.***

Bearings & Seals. 5th rev. ed. Ed. by Deere & Company Staff. (Fundamentals of Service Ser.). (Illus.). 96p. 1992. pap. text ed. 12.95 (*0-86691-144-8*, FOS5405B) Deere & Co.
Helps students understand bearings & seals & service them with speed & skill. Covers all types. Explains bearing loads, friction, "crush," & other concepts. Explains maintenance of bearings - cleaning, lubrication, adjustment, & repair. Explains use of gaskets, oil seals, sealing rings, & others. Tells how to care for seals, both static & dynamic types. "Test Yourself" questions & answers help participants review important facts. CONTENTS: Bearings - basic theory, types of bearings, plain bearings (bushings), ball bearings, roller bearings, needle bearings, maintenance & repair, & diagnosing failures. Seals - basic principles, static & dynamic seals, oil seals, sealing rings, gaskets, sealants & failures & repair. ***Publisher Provided Annotation.***

Bearings: Plain, Ball & Roller - U. S. Manufacturers & Selected Distributors: 1992 Competitive Analysis. Kimberly McGowan. 1993. pap. text ed. 2,400.00 (*1-878218-38-7*) World Info Tech.

Bearly Any Fat: Low Fat, Low Sugar, Low Salt Cookbook. Sheri Dunn. (Illus.). 162p. (Orig.). 1988. pap. 8.95 (*0-9620860-0-2*) S Dunn.

Bearly Any Fat Too. Sheri Dunn. 192p. 1993. pap. text ed. 9.95 (*0-9620860-1-0*) S Dunn.

Bearly There at All. Ron Krueger et al. (Land of Pleasant Dreams Ser.). (Illus.). 26p. (J). (ps up). 1986. Incl. cass. 7.95 (*1-55578-106-3*) Worlds Wonder.

Bearly There at All. Ron Krueger et al. (Tell Me a Story Ser.). (Illus.). 26p. (J). (ps up). 1988. audio 7.95 (*1-55578-912-9*) Worlds Wonder.

Bearman: Exploring the World of Black Bears. Laurence Pringle. LC 89-5890. (Illus.). 48p. (J). (gr. 5-7). 1989. text ed. 13.95 (*0-684-19094-X*, C Scribner Sons Young) S&S Childrens.

Bearman: Exploring the World of Black Bears. braille ed. Laurence Pringle. (Illus.). 49p. (J). 1992. Braille. vinyl bd. 3.92 (*1-56956-351-9*, BR8735) W A T Braille.

Bears. Donna Bailey. LC 89-22015. (Animal World Ser.). (Illus.). 32p. (J). (gr. 1-4). 1990. lib. bdg. 19.97 (*0-8114-2633-5*); pap. 3.95 (*0-8114-4614-X*) Raintree Steck-V.

Bears. Laura Bour. (First Discovery Bks.). (Illus.). (J). (ps). 1992. bds. 10.95 (*0-590-45270-3*, 038, Cartwheel) Scholastic Inc.

Bears. Alfred Brockman. (J). (ps-3). 1989. pap. 1.95 (*0-8167-1541-6*) Troll Assocs.

Bears. Donald Dewey. LC 94-9538. 1994. pap. write for info. (*1-56799-105-X*, Friedman-Fairfax) M Friedman Pub Grp Inc.

Bears. Robert Elman. (Illus.). 144p. 1992. 14.98 (*0-681-41589-4*) Longmeadow Pr.

Bears. Gabriele. (J). 1985. pap. 1.95 (*0-911211-68-3*) Penny Lane Pubns.

Bears. Helen Gilks. LC 92-37693. (Illus.). 32p. (J). (gr. 2-4). 1993. 15.95 (*0-395-66899-9*) Ticknor & Flds Bks Yng Read.

***Bears.** Casey Horton. (Endangered! Ser.). 32p. (J). (gr. 3-5). 1995. lib. bdg. write for info. (*0-7614-0211-X*, Benchmark NY) Marshall Cavendish.

***Bears.** Bobbie Kalman & Tammy Everts. LC 94-27536. (Crabapples Ser). (Illus.). 32p. (J). (ps-3). 1994. lib. bdg. 14.95 (*0-86505-612-9*); pap. 5.95 (*0-86505-712-5*) Crabtree Pub Co.

Bears. Krauss. (J). 1993. pap. 19.95 (*0-590-71703-0*) Scholastic Inc.

Bears. Susan Kuchalla. LC 81-11368. (Now I Know Ser.). (Illus.). 32p. (J). (gr. k-2). 1982. lib. bdg. 11.59 (*0-89375-674-1*); pap. 2.95 (*0-89375-675-X*) Troll Assocs.

Bears. Joanne Mattern. LC 92-20176. (Illus.). 24p. (J). (gr. 4-7). 1992. pap. 1.95 (*0-8167-2952-2*) Troll Assocs.

Bears. Mark Rosenthal. LC 82-17910. (New True Bks.). (Illus.). 48p. (J). (gr. k-4). 1983. lib. bdg. 12.90 (*0-516-01675-X*); pap. 4.95 (*0-516-41675-8*) Childrens.

Bears. Jim Rothaus. (Zoobooks Ser.). 24p. (J). (gr. 3). 1991. lib. bdg. 14.95 (*0-88682-221-1*) Creative Ed.

Bears. Ian Stirling. (Wildlife Library). (Illus.). 64p. (J). (gr. 3-6). 1995. 14.95 (*0-87156-574-9*) Sierra.

***Bears.** Ian Stirling. (Wildlife Library). (Illus.). 64p. (J). (gr. 3-6). 1995. 7.95 (*0-87156-441-6*) Sierra.

Bears. Lynn Stone. (North American Animal Discovery Library). (Illus.). 24p. (J). (gr. k-5). 1990. lib. bdg. 11.94 (*0-86593-042-2*); lib. bdg. 8.95 (*0-685-46449-0*) Rourke Corp.

Bears. Lynn Stone. LC 92-34487. (Predators Ser.). (J). 1993. 12.67 (*0-86625-438-2*); 9.50 (*0-685-66262-4*) Rourke Pubns.

Bears. Ed. by John B. Wexo. (Zoobooks Ser.). (Illus.). 20p. (Orig.). 1982. pap. 2.75 (*0-937934-07-0*, Benchmark NY) Marshall Cavendish.

***Bears, 6 vols., Set.** Casey Horton. (Endangered! Ser). (J). (gr. 3-5). 1995. lib. bdg. write for info. (*0-7614-0210-1*, Benchmark NY) Marshall Cavendish.

***Bears: A Global Look at Bears in the Wild.** Joni P. Hunt. Ed. by Vicki Leon. LC 94-30911. (Close up: A Focus on Nature Ser.). (Illus.). 48p. (YA). (gr. 5 up). 1994. lib. bdg. 14.95 (*0-382-24872-4*); pap. 7.95 (*0-382-24873-2*) Silver Burdett Pr.

***Bears: A Seventy-Five-Year Celebration.** Richard Whittingham. 1994. 39.95 (*0-87833-082-8*) Taylor Pub.

***Bears: A Seventy-Five-Year Celebration.** limited ed. Richard Whittingham. 1994. 75.00 (*0-87833-083-6*) Taylor Pub.

Bears: A Thematic Unit. Kathy Hofer. (Thematic Units Ser.). (Illus.). 80p. (gr. 1-3). 1990. student ed 8.95 (*1-55734-267-9*) Tchr Create Mat.

Bears: Art, Legend, History. Giorgio Coppin. LC 92-30655. (Bulfinch Library of Collectibles). 1993. 14.95 (*0-8212-2005-5*) Little.

Bears: Majestic Creatures of the Wild. Ed. by Ian Stirling. (Illus.). 240p. 1993. 40.00 (*0-87596-552-0*) Rodale Pr Inc.

Bears: Monarchs of the Northern Wilderness. Wayne Lynch. LC 93-666. (Illus.). 256p. 1993. 40.00 (*0-89886-372-4*) Mountaineers.

***Bears: Their Biology & Management.** Ed. by James Claar & Paul Schullery. (Illus.). 586p. 1993. pap. text ed. 45.00 (*0-944740-04-9*) Intl Assn Bear Res.

***Bears: Their Biology & Management.** Ed. by Laura Darling & W. R. Archiband. (Illus.). 448p. 1990. pap. text ed. 46.00 (*0-944740-03-0*) Intl Assn Bear Res.

Bears: Their Biology & Management. Ed. by Peter Zager. (Illus.). 224p. (Orig.). (C). 1986. pap. text ed. 30.00 (*0-944740-00-6*) Intl Assn Bear Res.

Bears: Their Biology & Management. Ed. by Peter Zager. (Illus.). 390p. (Orig.). (C). 1987. pap. text ed. 35.00 (*0-944740-01-4*) Intl Assn Bear Res.

Bears: Their Life & Behavior. Photos by Art Wolfe. (Illus.). 224p. 1992. 40.00 (*0-517-58498-0*, Crown) Crown Pub Group.

Bear's Adventure. Brian Wildsmith. LC 81-18814. (Illus.). 32p. (J). (ps-2). 1982. 9.95 (*0-394-85295-8*) Pantheon.

Bear's Adventure in Alphabet Town. Janet McDonnell. LC 91-20543. (Read Around Alphabet Town Ser.). (Illus.). 32p. (J). (ps-2). 1992. lib. bdg. 11.85 (*0-516-05402-3*) Childrens.

***Bears & Dinosaurs Make Friends.** Sangamon State University Preschoolers. (Wee Write Bks.: No. 3). (Illus.). 23p. (J). (ps-2). 1994. 17.95 (*1-884987-12-5*) WeWrite.

***Bears & Dinosaurs Make Friends.** Sangamon State University Preschoolers. (Wee Write Bks.: No. 3). (Illus.). 23p. (J). (ps-2). 1994. pap. 7.95 (*1-884987-13-3*) WeWrite.

***Bears & Dinosaurs Make Friends, Big Bk.** Sangamon State Univ. Preschoolers. (Wee Write Bks.: No. 3). (Illus.). 23p. (J). (ps-2). 1994. 32.95 (*1-884987-14-1*) WeWrite.

Bears & Men: A Gathering. William Mills. LC 86-7855. (Illus.). 168p. 1986. 24.95 (*0-912697-41-5*) Algonquin Bks.

Bears & Their Forest Cousins. Annemarie Schmidt & Christian R. Schmidt. LC 91-9428. (Animal Families Ser.). (Illus.). 32p. (J). (gr. 4-6). 1991. lib. bdg. 18.60 (*0-8368-0684-0*) Gareth Stevens Inc.

Bear's Assurance in Poetics. Sheila R. Hill. (Illus.). 12p. (Orig.). pap. 2.45 (*0-9624486-2-1*) S R Hill.

Bears at Work. Richard Hefter. LC 83-2192. (Stickybear Bks.). (Illus.). 32p. (J). (ps-1). 1983. 5.95 (*0-911787-00-3*) Optimum Res Inc.

***Bears at Work: An A to Z of Bearable Jobs.** Gage Taylor. LC 94-32764. (J). (gr. 1-4). 1995. 12.95 (*0-8118-0844-0*) Chronicle Bks.

Bears' Autumn. Keizaburo Tejima. Tr. by Susan Matsui. LC 91-17118. (Illus.). 42p. (J). (gr. 1-4). 1991. 12.95 (*0-671-74981-1*, Green Tiger S&S) S&S Childrens.

Bears Away from Home. Richard Hefter. LC 83-4149. (Stickybear Bks.). (Illus.). (J). (gr. 3-6). 1983. 5.95 (*0-911787-05-4*) Optimum Res Inc.

Bear's Bargain. Frank Asch. (Big Book Ser.). (J). (ps-3). 1992. pap. 19.95 (*0-590-72698-6*) Scholastic Inc.

Bear's Bargain. Frank Asch. LC 85-6355. (Illus.). (J). (ps-2). 1985. pap. 14.00 (*0-671-66690-8*, S&S Bks Young Read) S&S Childrens.

Bear's Bargain. Frank Asch. LC 85-6355. (Illus.). (J). (ps-2). 1989. pap. 4.95 (*0-671-67838-8*, S&S Bks Young Read) S&S Childrens.

***Bears, Bears & More Bears.** Jackie Morris. LC 94-42980. (J). 1995. write for info. (*0-8120-6516-6*); pap. write for info. (*0-8120-9349-6*) Barron.

Bears, Bears & More Bears. Ed Radlauer. (Ed Radlauer Bks.). (Illus.). 32p. (J). (ps-4). 1991. lib. bdg. 10.95 (*1-878363-34-4*) Forest Hse.

Bears, Bears, & More Bears: A Teacher's Resource Book of Bears. Patricia A. Welsh. 42p. 1989. pap. text ed. 7.95 (*1-884620-05-1*) PAW Prods.

Bears Bears Bears. Jo E. Moore & Leslie Tryon. (Illus.). 48p. (J). (gr. k-1). 1988. pap. 8.95 (*1-55799-130-8*) Evan-Moor Corp.

Bears, Bears, Bears. Illus. by Karen L. Schmidt. 96p. (J). (ps-2). 1990. pap. 14.95 (*0-671-69631-9*, S&S Bks Young Read) S&S Childrens.

***Bears, Bears, Everywhere.** Luella Connelly. (Emergent Reader Bks.). 16p. 1994. 2.49 (*0-916119-60-2*) Creat Teach Pr.

Bears, Bears Everywhere. Rita Milios. (Rookie Reader Ser.). (J). (ps-2). 1988. lib. bdg. 10.35 (*0-516-02085-4*); pap. 2.95 (*0-516-42085-2*) Childrens.

Bear's Bicycle. Emilie W. McLeod. (Illus.). 32p. (J). (gr. k-3). 1975. lib. bdg. 14.95 (*0-316-56203-3*, Joy St Bks) Little.

Bear's Bicycle. Emilie W. McLeod. (Illus.). 32p. (J). (gr. k-3). 1986. mass mkt. 5.95 (*0-316-56206-8*, Joy St Bks) Little.

Bear's Bicycle. Emilie W. McLeod. (Illus.). (J). (gr. 1-3). 1986. audio 22.95 (*0-87499-025-4*); audio, pap. 14.95 (*0-87499-023-8*) Live Oak Media.

Bear's Bicycle, 4 bks., Set. Emilie W. McLeod. (Illus.). (J). (gr. 1-3). 1986. audio, pap. 33.95 (*0-87499-024-6*) Live Oak Media.

Bears, Big & Little. Pierre Pfeffer. Tr. by Vicki Bogard. LC 89-8883. (Young Discovery Library). (Illus.). 38p. (J). (gr. k-5). 1989. 5.95 (*0-944589-23-5*, 023) Young Discovery Lib.

Bears' Blitz: And Other Sports Stories. Highlights for Children Staff. LC 90-85908. (Illus.). 96p. (J). (gr. 3-7). 1992. pap. 2.95 (*1-878093-29-0*) Boyds Mills Pr.

Bear's Boat. Burton Marks. (Go-Along Book Ser.). (Illus.). 10p. (J). (ps-3). 1993. 4.99 (*0-89577-516-6*, Random) RD Assn.

Bear's Busy Year: A Book about Seasons. Marcia Leonard. LC 89-4946. (Illus.). 24p. (J). (gr. k-2). 1990. lib. bdg. 9.59 (*0-8167-1720-6*); pap. text ed. 2.50 (*0-8167-1721-4*) Troll Assocs.

Bears, Buttons, & Bananas: Nine Thematic Units That Explore Popular Products. Robert Young & Rebecca Smith. (Illus.). 80p. (J). (gr. k-3). 1994. 9.95 (*0-86653-824-0*, GA1516) Good Apple.

Bears' Christmas. Stan Berenstain & Janice Berenstain. LC 79-117542. (Illus.). 72p. (J). (gr. k-3). 1987. 6.95 (*0-394-80090-7*) Beginner.

Bear's Christmas Surprise. Elizabeth Winthrop. LC 90-26414. (Illus.). 32p. (J). (ps-3). 1991. lib. bdg. 14.95 (*0-8234-0888-4*) Holiday.

***Bear's Curiosity Book: An Adventure in Early Learning.** David Howgrave-Graham. (Illus.). 48p. (J). (ps). 1995. 9.95 (*0-89577-681-2*, Readers Digest Kids) RD Assn.

Bears Dancing in the Northern Air. Christiane J. Kyle. (Series of Younger Poets). 72p. (Orig.). (C). 1991. text ed. 17.00 (*0-300-05007-0*); pap. text ed. 10.00 (*0-300-05008-9*) Yale U Pr.

Bear's Designs Unlimited, Vol. I. Beverly Wirtzfeld. 60p. (J). (gr. 4-10). Date not set. ring bd. 4.95 (*0-9638473-0-9*) Bears Designs.

Bears Discover Fire & Other Stories. Terry Bisson. 1995. write for info. (*0-312-85411-0*); pap. 12.95 (*0-312-89035-4*) Orb NYC.

Bears Everywhere: An Integrated Unit. Kathy Rogers. (Primary Thematic Units Ser.). (Illus.). 96p. (Orig.). 1993. pap. 12.95 (*0-944459-78-1*) ECS Lrn Systs.

Bears for All Seasons. Rosemary Volpp. 96p. 1989. 19.95 (*0-87588-348-6*) Hobby Hse.

Bears for Breakfast: The Thiessen Family Adventures. Nan Doerksen. (Kinderbook Ser.). 34p. (J). (ps-00). 1983. pap. 2.50 (*0-919797-07-5*) Kindred Prods.

Bears for Kids. Jeff Fair. 48p. (J). 1991. 14.95 (*1-55971-119-1*); pap. 6.95 (*1-55971-134-5*) NorthWord.

Bear's Guide to Earning College Degrees Non-Traditionally. 11th ed. John Bear. LC 91-71685. 304p. 1994. lib. bdg. 23.95 (*0-9629312-0-9*) C & B Pub.

B

An Asterisk (*) at the beginning of an entry indicates that the title is appearing in BIP for the first time. 641

***Bear's Guide to Earning College Degrees Non-Traditionally.** 12th ed. John Bear. 1995. pap. 27.95 (*0-89815-699-8*) Ten Speed Pr.

***Bear's Guide to Earning College Degrees Nontraditionally.** 12th ed. John Bear & Mariah Bear. LC 95-67362. 336p. 1995. pap. 27.95 (*0-9629312-3-3*) C & B Pub.

Bears' House. Marilyn Sachs. 80p. (J). (gr. 3-7). 1989. pap. 2.99 (*0-380-70582-6*, Camelot) Avon.

Bear's Hug: Christian Belief & the Soviet State, 1917-86. Gerald Buss. LC 87-19639. 223p. reprint ed. pap. 63.60 (*0-8357-4359-4*, 2037187) Bks Demand.

Bears in My Kitchen: An Exclusive Collection of Black Bear Recipes. Carol V. Suddendorf. LC 88-141979. 131p. (Orig.). 1988. pap. 7.95 (*0-9620852-0-0*) C Suddendorf.

Bears in Pairs. Niki Yektai. LC 86-18828. (Illus.). 32p. (J). (ps-k). 1987. text ed. 14.95 (*0-02-793691-0*, Bradbury S&S) S&S Childrens.

Bears in Pairs. Niki Yektai. LC 91-229. (Illus.). 32p. (J). (ps). 1991. reprint ed. pap. 4.95 (*0-689-71500-5*, Aladdin Paperbacks) S&S Childrens.

Bears in the Forest. Karen Wallace. LC 93-39668. (Read & Wonder Ser.). (Illus.). 32p. (J). (ps up). 1994. 14.95 (*1-56402-336-2*) Candlewick Pr.

Bears in the Night. Stan Berenstain & Janice Berenstain. (Bright & Early Bks.). (Illus.). (J). (ps-1). 1971. 7.99 (*0-394-82286-2*); lib. bdg. 9.99 (*0-394-92286-7*) Random Bks Yng Read.

Bears in Toyland. 4.98 (*0-317-38610-7*) Gick.

***Bears Learn & Play Everyday.** Wishing Well Staff. Date not set. 5.99 (*0-88705-775-6*) Joshua Morris.

Bear's New House. Annie Cobb. (Going Places Ser.). (Illus.). 32p. (J). (gr. k-3). 1991. 4.95 (*0-671-70397-8*); lib. bdg. 6.95 (*0-671-70393-5*) Silver Pr.

Bears of Blue River. Charles Major. LC 91-95522. (Library of Indiana Classics). (Illus.). 288p. 1984. 20.00 (*0-253-10590-0*); pap. 8.95 (*0-253-20330-9*, MB-330) Ind U Pr.

Bears of Blue River. Charles Major. reprint ed. lib. bdg. 21.95 (*0-88411-094-X*, Aeonian Pr) Amereon Ltd.

***Bears of Paris.** Miles D. Moore. LC 95-61228. 80p. (Orig.). 1996. pap. 10.00 (*0-915380-32-3*) Word Works.

Bears of the World. Terry Domico. (Illus.). 208p. 1988. 29.95 (*0-8160-1536-8*) Facts on File.

Bears of Yellowstone. Paul D. Schullery. LC 79-65734. (Illus.). 180p. (Orig.). 1980. 12.95 (*0-934948-01-1*); pap. 5.95 (*0-934948-00-3*) Yellowstone Assn.

Bears of Yellowstone. 3rd ed. Paul Schullery. LC 91-78168. (Illus.). 332p. (Orig.). 1992. 25.00 (*0-9623333-9-5*); pap. 12.50 (*1-881019-00-4*) High Plns WY.

Bears on Hemlock Mountain. Alice Dalgliesh. LC 52-11023. (Illus.). 64p. (J). 1981. pap. 3.95 (*0-689-70497-6*, Aladdin Paperbacks) S&S Childrens.

Bears on Hemlock Mountain. 2nd ed. Alice Dalgliesh. LC 91-40166. (Illus.). 64p. (J). (gr. 1-3). 1992. reprint ed. pap. 3.95 (*0-689-71604-4*, Aladdin Paperbacks) S&S Childrens.

Bears on Hemlock Mountain. Alice Dalgliesh. LC 89-27651. (Illus.). 64p. (J). (gr. 1-4). 1990. reprint ed. text ed. 13.95 (*0-684-19169-5*, C Scribner Sons Young) S&S Childrens.

Bears on Stairs: A Beginner's Book of Rhymes. Muriel Kalish & Lionel Kalish. LC 92-10144. (Illus.). 12p. (J). (ps-1). 1993. 7.95 (*0-590-44918-4*) Scholastic Inc.

Bears on Wheels. Stan Berenstain & Janice Berenstain. LC 72-77840. (Bright & Early Bks.). (Illus.). (J). (ps-1). 1969. 6.95 (*0-394-80967-X*); lib. bdg. 9.99 (*0-394-90967-4*) Random Bks Yng Read.

Bear's Paw Quilt. Jean Wells. Ed. by Barbara K. Kuhn & Joyce E. Lytle. (Patchwork Quilts Made Easy Ser.: No. II). (Illus.). 24p. 1994. pap. 8.95 (*0-914881-73-6*, CT174) C & T Pub.

Bears' Picnic. Stan Berenstain & Janice Berenstain. LC 66-10156. (Illus.). 72p. (J). (gr. k-3). 1966. 6.95 (*0-394-80041-9*); lib. bdg. 7.99 (*0-394-90041-3*) Beginner.

Bears, Pirates & Silver Lace. Anne B. Fisher. (Illus.). 146p. (J). (gr. 3-7). 1975. pap. 5.95 (*0-8323-0255-4*) Binford Mort.

Bears Repeating. Terry Michaud & Doris Michaud. (Illus.). 96p. 1985. 14.95 (*0-87588-263-3*, 3119) Hobby Hse.

***Bears to Barely Bears: A Theme Unit about Alaskan Bears.** Jane Niebergall. (Alaskan Teaching Unit Ser.). (Illus.). 71p. (Orig.). (C). 1990. teacher ed, pap. 9.95 (*1-870511-21-2*) Circumpolar Pr.

***Bears to Carve with Dale Power: With Dale Power.** Dale Power. LC 94-23248. (Illus.). 64p. (Orig.). 1995. pap. 12.95 (*0-88740-719-6*) Schiffer.

Bear's Toothache. David McPhail. (Illus.). 32p. (J). (gr. k-3). 1972. lib. bdg. 14.95 (*0-316-56312-9*, Joy St Bks) Little.

Bear's Toothache. David McPhail. (Illus.). (J). (ps-3). 1988. mass mkt. 5.95 (*0-316-56325-0*, Joy St Bks) Little.

Bear's Toothache. David McPhail. (Illus.). (J). (gr. k-2). 1986. reprint ed. audio 22.95 (*0-87499-081-5*); reprint ed. audio, pap. 14.95 (*0-87499-080-7*) Live Oak Media.

Bear's Toothache, 4 bks., Set. David McPhail. (Illus.). (J). (gr. k-2). 1986. reprint ed. audio, pap. 33.95 (*0-87499-082-3*) Live Oak Media.

***Bears Upstairs.** Jane B. Moncure. LC 87-11715. (Magic Castle Readers Ser.). (Illus.). 32p. (ENG & SPA.). (J). (ps-2). 1987. pap. 14.95 (*0-89565-927-1*) Childs World.

Bears Upstairs. Jane B. Moncure. LC 87-11715. (Magic Castle Readers Ser.). (Illus.). 32p. (ENG & SPA.). (J). (ps-2). 1987. lib. bdg. 21.36 (*0-89565-373-7*) Childs World.

Bears' Vacation. Stan Berenstain & Janice Berenstain. LC 68-28460. (Illus.). 72p. (J). (gr. k-3). 1968. 6.95 (*0-394-80052-4*) Beginner.

Bear's Walk. Alma F. Ada. (ESL Theme Links Ser.). (Illus.). (Orig.). 1993. ring bd. 99.50 (*1-56334-288-X*); audio 10.50 (*1-56334-286-3*); 35.00 (*1-56334-287-1*) Hampton-Brown.

Bears We Know. Brenda Silsbe. (Annick Press Ser.: Series 8). (Illus.). 24p. (Orig.). (J). (ps-2). 1989. pap. 0.99 (*1-55037-048-0*, Pub. by Annick CN) Firefly Bks Ltd.

***Bear's World: Remedy for the Blues.** Barry Newman. (Illus.). (Orig.). 1994. pap. 9.95 (*0-9642844-4-8*) Chubby Bear.

Bearsted: A Biography of Marcus Samuel, First Viscount Bearsted & Founder of "Shell" Transport & Trading Company. Robert Henriques. LC 73-122071. (Illus.). xi, 676p. 1970. reprint ed. 49.50 (*0-678-03163-0*) Kelley.

Bearstone. Will Hobbs. 160p. (J). (gr. 5). 1991. pap. 3.50 (*0-380-71249-0*, Camelot) Avon.

Bearstone. Will Hobbs. LC 89-6641. 160p. (J). (gr. 6-9). 1989. text ed. 14.95 (*0-689-31496-5*, Atheneum Bks Young) S&S Childrens.

Beartooth Country: Montana's Absaroka & Beartooth Mountains. rev. ed. Robert Anderson. (Montana Geographic Ser.: No. 7). (Illus.). 112p. 1994. pap. 17.95 (*1-56037-065-3*) Am Wrld Geog.

Beartooth Fishing Guide. Pat Marcusson. LC 85-80382. (Falcon Guide Ser.). (Illus.). 144p. (Orig.). 1985. pap. 7.95 (*0-934318-33-6*) Falcon Pr MT.

Beary, Beary, Quite Contrary. Rosanna Graf & Virginia Graf. (Illus.). (Orig.). (J). Date not set. pap. 9.50 (*1-882788-02-8*) VanGar Pubs.

Bearymore. Don Freeman. (Picture Puffins Ser.). (Illus.). (J). (ps-3). 1979. pap. 4.99 (*0-14-050279-3*, Puffin) Puffin Bks.

Bearymore. Don Freeman. LC 76-94. (Illus.). 40p. (J). (gr. k-3). 1976. 14.95 (*0-670-15174-2*) Viking Child Bks.

Bea's Four Bears. Martha Weston. (Illus.). 32p. (J). (ps-00). 1992. 9.95 (*0-395-57791-8*, Clarion Bks) HM.

Beast. Alice Bartels. (Illus.). 32p. (J). (ps-2). 1990. 14.95 (*1-55037-101-0*, Pub. by Annick CN); pap. 5.95 (*1-55037-102-9*, Pub. by Annick CN) Firefly Bks Ltd.

Beast. Peter Benchley. 1991. 21.00 (*0-679-40355-8*) Random.

Beast. Peter Benchley. 1992. mass mkt. 5.99 (*0-449-22089-3*, Crest) Fawcett.

Beast. Jonathan Fast. 1982. pap. 2.95 (*0-345-29896-9*) Ballantine.

Beast. Susan Meddaugh. (Illus.). 32p. (J). (gr. k-3). 1985. pap. 3.95 (*0-317-18511-X*) HM.

Beast. Walter J. Sheldon. (Orig.). 1980. pap. 1.95 (*0-449-14327-9*, GM) Fawcett.

Beast. R. L. Stine. Ed. by Pat MacDonald. 128p. (Orig.). (J). 1994. mass mkt. 3.99 (*0-671-88055-1*, Minstrel Bks) PB.

Beast. A. E. Van Vogt. 224p. 1992. pap. 3.95 (*0-88184-883-2*) Carroll & Graf.

Beast. James G. White & Marie A. White. 368p. (Orig.). 1994. pap. 4.50 (*0-8439-3618-5*) Dorchester Pub Co.

Beast. Margaret Wild. LC 93-34596. (YA). 1995. 13.95 (*0-590-47158-9*) Scholastic Inc.

Beast. large type ed. Peter Benchley. (General Ser.). 432p. 1993. pap. 16.95 (*0-8161-5447-3*) G K Hall.

Beast. large type ed. Peter Benchley. (General Ser.). 389p. 1992. text ed. 20.95 (*0-8161-5422-8*, Large Print Bks) Hall.

Beast & Animals in Decorative Woodcuts of the Renaissance. Conrad Gesner. Ed. by Carol B. Grafton. (Illus.). 64p. (Orig.). 1983. pap. 4.95 (*0-486-24430-X*) Dover.

Beast & Behemoths: Prehistoric Creatures in the Movies. Roy Kinnard. LC 87-23424. (Illus.). 193p. 1988. 25.00 (*0-8108-2062-5*) Scarecrow.

***Beast & Man: The Roots of Human Nature.** Mary Midgley. LC 95-7506. 1995. 15.95 (*0-415-12740-8*) Routledge.

***Beast & Man: The Roots of the Human Nature.** Mary Midgley. 400p. 1995. pap. 17.95 (*0-415-10445-9*, C0560) Routledge.

Beast & the Babysitter. Kathleen Stevens. LC 88-42917. (Illus.). 32p. (J). (gr. 2-3). 1989. lib. bdg. 18.60 (*1-55532-929-2*) Gareth Stevens Inc.

***Beast & the Boy.** Masssimo Mostacchi & Monica Miceli. LC 94-44060. Orig. Title: Marcolino und das Monster. (Illus.). 32p. (J). (gr. k-3). 1995. 14.95 (*1-55858-443-9*); lib. bdg. 14.88 (*1-55858-444-7*) North-South Bks NYC.

Beast & the Halloween Horror. Patricia R. Giff. (Kids of the Polk Street School Ser.: No. 13). (Orig.). (J). (gr. k-6). 1990. pap. 3.50 (*0-440-40335-9*, YB) Dell.

Beast & the Kansas Bed & Breakfast. Carole Marsh. (Carole Marsh Kansas Bks.). (J). (gr. 3-12). 1994. 24.95 (*1-55609-371-3*); pap. 14.95 (*1-55609-372-1*); disk 29.95 (*1-55609-373-X*) Gallopade Pub Group.

Beast at Work. (Phoenix Journals). 238p. 1993. pap. 7.95 (*1-56935-006-X*) Phoenix Source.

Beast Feast. Douglas Florian. LC 93-10720. (J). (ps-3). 1994. 14.95 (*0-15-295178-4*) HarBrace.

Beast Forms see Beastmorfs

Beast from the Bottomless Pit. Gordon Lindsay. (Revelation Ser.: Vol. 10). 1962. 1.95 (*0-89985-043-X*) Christ for the Nations.

Beast from the Sea. Bill Hallsted. LC 88-51960. 180p. 1989. pap. 6.95 (*1-55523-220-5*) Winston-Derek.

Beast in Me & Other Animals. James Thurber. reprint ed. lib. bdg. 23.95 (*0-89190-265-1*, Rivercity Pr) Amereon Ltd.

Beast in Me & Other Animals: A Collection of Pieces & Drawings about Human Beings & Less Alarming Creatures. James Thurber. LC 73-5563. (Illus.). 340p. 1973. reprint ed. pap. 5.95 (*0-15-610850-X*, Harvest Bks) HarBrace.

Beast in Ms. Rooney's Room. Patricia R. Giff. (Kids of the Polk Street School Ser.: No. 1). 80p. (Orig.). (J). (gr. 1-4). 1984. pap. 3.50 (*0-440-40485-1*, YB) Dell.

Beast in Ms. Rooney's Room see Kids of the Polk Street School

Beast in the Bathroom. Chris Huntley. (Illus.). 32p. (J). (ps). 1991. write for info. (*0-9616679-2-3*) Aquarelle Pr.

Beast in the Bathtub. Kathleen Stevens. LC 85-12691. (Illus.). 32p. (J). (gr. 2-3). 1985. lib. bdg. 18.60 (*0-918831-15-6*) Gareth Stevens Inc.

Beast in the Boudoir: Petkeeping in Nineteenth-Century Paris. Kathleen Kete. LC 93-32265. 1994. 30.00 (*0-520-07101-8*) U CA Pr.

***Beast in the Boudoir: Petkeeping in Nineteenth-Century Paris.** Kathleen Kete. 1995. pap. write for info. (*0-520-20339-9*) U CA Pr.

Beast in the Jungle see Altar of the Dead

Beast in the Jungle & Other Stories. Henry James. LC 92-38681. 112p. 1993. reprint ed. pap. 1.00 (*0-486-27552-3*) Dover.

Beast in the Temple. James G. Stuart. 199p. 1988. 49.00 (*0-317-20326-6*, Pub. by Stuart Titles Ltd UK); pap. 29.00 (*0-85335-254-2*, Pub. by Stuart Titles Ltd UK) St Mut.

Beast in View. Margaret Millar. LC 83-80874. 251p. 1983. reprint ed. pap. 4.95 (*0-930330-07-2*) Intl Polygonics.

Beast Is a Wolf with Brown Fire. Barry Wallenstein. (New Poets of America Ser.: No. 2). 1977. pap. 7.00 (*0-918526-08-6*) BOA Edns.

Beast Must Die. large type ed. Blake. 1991. pap. 15.95 (*0-7927-0253-0*, C0435, Atlantic Lrg Print) Chivers N Amer.

Beast of Burden. Aaron Travis. (Orig.). 1993. pap. text ed. 4.95 (*1-56333-105-5*) Masquerade.

Beast of Exmoor: And Other Mystery Predators of Britain. Di Francis. (Illus.). 192p. 1994. pap. 17.95 (*0-224-03665-3*, Pub. by Jonathan Cape UK) Trafalgar.

Beast of Heaven. Victor Kelleher. LC 83-21736. 205p. 1987. pap. 14.95 (*0-7022-2033-7*, Pub. by Univ Queensland Pr AT) Intl Spec Bk.

***Beast of Heaven.** Victor Kelleher. (YA). 1995. 12.95 (*0-7022-2802-8*, Pub. by Univ Queensland Pr AT) Intl Spec Bk.

***Beast of Heaven.** Victor Kelleher. 220p. 1995. pap. 16.95 (*0-7022-2831-1*, Pub. by Univ Queensland Pr AT) Intl Spec Bk.

Beast of Monsieur Racine. Tomi Ungerer. LC 74-149216. (Illus.). 32p. (J). (ps-3). 1971. 15.95 (*0-374-30640-0*) FS&G.

Beast of Monsieur Racine. Tomi Ungerer. (Sunburst Ser.). (Illus.). 32p. (J). (ps up). 1986. pap. 5.95 (*0-374-40570-0*) FS&G.

Beast of Property see Revolutionaire Kriegswissenschaft

Beast of Revelation. Kenneth L. Gentry, Jr. 209p. 1989. pap. 8.95 (*0-930464-21-4*) Inst Christian.

Beast of the Alabama Bed & Breakfast. Carole Marsh. (Carole Marsh Alabama Bks.). (Illus.). (YA). (gr. 3-12). 1994. lib. bdg. 24.95 (*0-7933-1332-5*); pap. 14.95 (*0-7933-1331-7*); disk 29.95 (*0-7933-1330-9*) Gallopade Pub Group.

Beast of the Apocalypse: Risible Irreverencies from the Pages of Books & Religion. 128p. 1990. 8.95 (*0-9628212-0-9*) B & R Pr.

Beast of the Arizona Bed & Breakfast. Carole Marsh. (Carole Marsh Arizona Bks.). (Illus.). (YA). (gr. 3-12). 1994. lib. bdg. 24.95 (*0-7933-1365-1*); pap. 14.95 (*0-7933-1366-X*); disk 29.95 (*0-7933-1367-8*) Gallopade Pub Group.

Beast of the Arkansas Bed & Breakfast. Carole Marsh. (Carole Marsh Arkansas Bks.). (Illus.). (YA). (gr. 3-12). 1994. lib. bdg. 24.95 (*0-7933-1381-3*); pap. 14.95 (*0-7933-1382-1*); disk 29.95 (*0-7933-1383-X*) Gallopade Pub Group.

Beast of the Colorado Bed & Breakfast. Carole Marsh. (Carole Marsh Colorado Bks.). (Illus.). (YA). (gr. 3-12). 1994. lib. bdg. 24.95 (*0-7933-1413-5*); pap. 14.95 (*0-7933-1414-3*); disk 29.95 (*0-7933-1415-1*) Gallopade Pub Group.

Beast of the Connecticut Bed & Breakfast. Carole Marsh. (Carole Marsh Connecticut Bks.). (Illus.). (YA). (gr. 3-12). 1994. lib. bdg. 24.95 (*0-7933-1429-1*); pap. 14.95 (*0-7933-1430-5*); disk 29.95 (*0-7933-1431-3*) Gallopade Pub Group.

Beast of the Delaware Bed & Breakfast. Carole Marsh. (Carole Marsh Delaware Bks.). (Illus.). (YA). (gr. 3-12). 1994. lib. bdg. 24.95 (*0-7933-1447-X*); pap. 14.95 (*0-7933-1448-8*); disk 29.95 (*0-7933-1449-6*) Gallopade Pub Group.

Beast of the East. Alvin M. Shifflett. 112p. 1992. pap. 6.95 (*0-914984-41-1*) Starburst.

Beast of the Florida Bed & Breakfast. Carole Marsh. (Carole Marsh Florida Bks.). (Illus.). (YA). (gr. 3-12). 1994. lib. bdg. 24.95 (*0-7933-1493-X*); pap. 14.95 (*0-7933-1494-1*); disk 29.95 (*0-7933-1495-X*) Gallopade Pub Group.

Beast of the Georgia Bed & Breakfast. Carole Marsh. (Carole Marsh Georgia Bks.). (Illus.). (YA). (gr. 3-12). 1994. lib. bdg. 24.95 (*0-7933-1512-3*); pap. 14.95 (*0-7933-1513-1*); disk 29.95 (*0-7933-1514-X*) Gallopade Pub Group.

Beast of the Haitian Hills. Philippe Thoby-Marcelin & Pierre Marcelin. Tr. by Peter C. Rhodes. 176p. reprint ed. pap. 6.95 (*0-87286-189-9*) City Lights.

Beast of the Hawaii Bed & Breakfast. Carole Marsh. (Carole Marsh Hawaii Bks.). (Illus.). (YA). (gr. 3-12). 1994. lib. bdg. 24.95 (*0-7933-1531-X*); pap. 14.95 (*0-7933-1532-8*); disk 29.95 (*0-7933-1533-6*) Gallopade Pub Group.

Beast of the Idaho Bed & Breakfast. Carole Marsh. (Carole Marsh Idaho Bks.). (Illus.). (YA). (gr. 3-12). 1994. lib. bdg. 24.95 (*0-7933-1550-6*); pap. 14.95 (*0-7933-1551-4*); disk 29.95 (*0-7933-1552-2*) Gallopade Pub Group.

Beast of the Illinois Bed & Breakfast. Carole Marsh. (Carole Marsh Illinois Bks.). (Illus.). (YA). (gr. 3-12). 1994. lib. bdg. 24.95 (*0-7933-1590-5*); pap. 14.95 (*0-7933-1591-3*); disk 29.95 (*0-7933-1592-1*) Gallopade Pub Group.

Beast of the Indiana Bed & Breakfast. Carole Marsh. (Carole Marsh Indiana Bks.). (Illus.). (YA). (gr. 3-12). 1994. lib. bdg. 24.95 (*0-7933-1609-X*); pap. 14.95 (*0-7933-1610-3*); disk 29.95 (*0-7933-1611-1*) Gallopade Pub Group.

Beast of the Iowa Bed & Breakfast. Carole Marsh. (Carole Marsh Iowa Bks.). (Illus.). (YA). (gr. 3-12). 1994. lib. bdg. 24.95 (*0-7933-1628-6*); pap. 14.95 (*0-7933-1629-4*); disk 29.95 (*0-7933-1630-8*) Gallopade Pub Group.

Beast of the Kentucky Bed & Breakfast. Carole Marsh. (Carole Marsh Kentucky Bks.). (Illus.). (J). (gr. 3-8). 1994. lib. bdg. 24.95 (*0-7933-1650-2*); pap. 14.95 (*0-7933-1651-0*); disk 29.95 (*0-7933-1652-9*) Gallopade Pub Group.

Beast of the Louisiana Bed & Breakfast. Carole Marsh. (Carole Marsh Louisiana Bks.). (Illus.). (J). (gr. 3-8). 1994. lib. bdg. 24.95 (*0-7933-1669-3*); pap. 14.95 (*0-7933-1670-7*); disk 29.95 (*0-7933-1671-5*) Gallopade Pub Group.

Beast of the Maine Bed & Breakfast. Carole Marsh. (Carole Marsh Maine Bks.). (Illus.). (J). (gr. 3-8). 1994. lib. bdg. 24.95 (*0-7933-1681-2*); pap. 14.95 (*0-7933-1682-0*); write for info. (*0-7933-1683-9*) Gallopade Pub Group.

Beast of the Maryland Bed & Breakfast. Carole Marsh. (Carole Marsh Maryland Bks.). (Illus.). (J). (gr. 3-8). 1994. lib. bdg. 24.95 (*0-7933-1690-1*); pap. 14.95 (*0-7933-1691-X*); disk 29.95 (*0-7933-1692-8*) Gallopade Pub Group.

Beast of the Massachusetts Bed & Breakfast. Carole Marsh. (Carole Marsh Massachusetts Bks.). (Illus.). (J). (gr. 3-8). 1994. lib. bdg. 24.95 (*0-7933-1699-5*); pap. 14.95 (*0-7933-1700-2*); disk 29.95 (*0-7933-1701-0*) Gallopade Pub Group.

Beast of the Michigan Bed & Breakfast. Carole Marsh. (Carole Marsh Michigan Bks.). (Illus.). (J). (gr. 3 up). 1994. lib. bdg. 24.95 (*0-7933-1708-8*); pap. 14.95 (*0-7933-1709-6*); disk 29.95 (*0-7933-1710-X*) Gallopade Pub Group.

Beast of the Minnesota Bed & Breakfast. Carole Marsh. (Minnesota Bks.). (Illus.). (J). (gr. 3 up). 1994. lib. bdg. 24.95 (*0-7933-1714-2*); pap. 14.95 (*0-7933-1715-0*); disk 29.95 (*0-7933-1716-9*) Gallopade Pub Group.

Beast of the Mississippi Bed & Breakfast. Carole Marsh. (Mississippi Bks.). (Illus.). (J). (gr. 3 up). 1994. lib. bdg. 24.95 (*0-7933-0644-2*); pap. 14.95 (*0-7933-1726-6*); disk 29.95 (*0-7933-1727-4*) Gallopade Pub Group.

Beast of the Missouri Bed & Breakfast. Carole Marsh. (Missouri Bks.). (Illus.). (J). (gr. 3 up). 1994. lib. bdg. 24.95 (*0-7933-1734-7*); pap. 14.95 (*0-7933-1735-5*); disk 29.95 (*0-685-45946-2*) Gallopade Pub Group.

Beast of the Montana Bed & Breakfast. Carole Marsh. (Montana Bks.). (Illus.). (J). (gr. 3 up). 1994. lib. bdg. 24.95 (*0-7933-1743-6*); pap. 14.95 (*0-7933-1744-4*); disk 29.95 (*0-7933-1745-2*) Gallopade Pub Group.

Beast of the Nebraska Bed & Breakfast. Carole Marsh. (Carole Marsh Nebraska Bks.). (Illus.). (J). (gr. 3 up). 1994. lib. bdg. 24.95 (*0-7933-1752-5*); pap. 14.95 (*0-7933-1753-3*); disk 29.95 (*0-7933-1754-1*) Gallopade Pub Group.

Beast of the Nevada Bed & Breakfast. Carole Marsh. (Carole Marsh Nevada Bks.). (Illus.). (J). 1994. lib. bdg. 24.95 (*0-7933-1761-4*); pap. 14.95 (*0-7933-1762-2*); disk 29.95 (*0-7933-1763-0*) Gallopade Pub Group.

Beast of the New Hampshire Bed & Breakfast. Carole Marsh. (Carole Marsh New Hampshire Bks.). (Illus.). (J). 1994. lib. bdg. 24.95 (*0-7933-1770-3*); pap. 14.95 (*0-7933-1771-1*); disk 29.95 (*0-7933-1772-X*) Gallopade Pub Group.

Beast of the New Jersey Bed & Breakfast. Carole Marsh. (Carole Marsh New Jersey Bks.). (Illus.). (J). 1994. lib. bdg. 24.95 (*0-7933-1779-7*); pap. 14.95 (*0-7933-1780-0*); disk 29.95 (*0-7933-1781-9*) Gallopade Pub Group.

Beast of the New Mexico Bed & Breakfast. Carole Marsh. (Carole Marsh New Mexico Bks.). (Illus.). (J). 1994. lib. bdg. 24.95 (*0-7933-1812-2*); pap. 14.95 (*0-7933-1813-0*); disk 29.95 (*0-7933-1814-9*) Gallopade Pub Group.

Beast of the New York Bed & Breakfast. Carole Marsh. (Carole Marsh New York Bks.). (Illus.). (J). 1994. lib. bdg. 24.95 (*0-7933-1821-1*); pap. 14.95 (*0-7933-1822-X*); disk 29.95 (*0-7933-1823-8*) Gallopade Pub Group.

Beast of the North Dakota Bed & Breakfast. Carole Marsh. (Carole Marsh North Dakota Bks.). (Illus.). (J). 1994. lib. bdg. 24.95 (*0-7933-1839-4*); pap. 14.95 (*0-7933-1840-8*); disk 29.95 (*0-7933-1841-6*) Gallopade Pub Group.

Beast of the Ohio Bed & Breakfast. Carole Marsh. (Carole Marsh Ohio Bks.). (Illus.). (J). 1994. lib. bdg. 24.95 (*0-7933-0905-0*); pap. 14.95 (*0-7933-1848-3*); disk 29.95 (*0-7933-1849-1*) Gallopade Pub Group.

Beast of the Oklahoma Bed & Breakfast. Carole Marsh. (Carole Marsh Oklahoma Bks.). (Illus.). (J). 1994. lib. bdg. 24.95 (*0-7933-1869-6*); pap. 14.95 (*0-7933-1870-X*); disk 29.95 (*0-7933-1871-8*) Gallopade Pub Group.

Beast of the Oregon Bed & Breakfast. Carole Marsh. (Carole Marsh Oregon Bks.). (Illus.). (J). 1994. lib. bdg. 24.95 (*0-7933-1901-3*); pap. 14.95 (*0-7933-1902-1*); disk 29.95 (*0-7933-1903-X*) Gallopade Pub Group.

Beast of the Pennsylvania Bed & Breakfast. Carole Marsh. (Carole Marsh Pennsylvania Bks.). (Illus.). (J). 1994. lib. bdg. 24.95 (*0-7933-1933-1*); pap. 14.95 (*0-7933-1934-X*); disk 29.95 (*0-7933-1935-8*) Gallopade Pub Group.

Beast of the Revelation: The Antichrist Network. Kingdom Quotes Staff. Date not set. pap. write for info. (*0-930179-22-6*) Johns Enter.

An Asterisk (*) at the beginning of an entry indicates that the title is appearing in BIP for the first time.

B

An Asterisk (*) at the beginning of an entry indicates that the title is appearing in BIP for the first time.

643

Beating Bully O'Brien. Karen Mueller. (J). (gr. 3-7). 1991. pap. 2.95 (*0-380-75935-7*, Camelot) Avon.

Beating Burnout: The Survival Guide for the 90s. 2nd ed. Peter M. Mcgugan. Ed. by Irene Hickman. (Illus.). 224p. 1991. pap. write for info. (*0-9694312-0-1*) Potentls Pr.

Beating Cancer with Nutrition. Patrick Quillin & Noreen Quillin. 272p. (Orig.). 1995. pap. 14.95 (*0-9638372-0-6*) Nutrit Times.

Beating Caro-Kann. Vassilios Kotronias. (Batsford Chess Library Ser.). 1994. pap. 16.95 (*0-8050-3284-3*) H Holt & Co.

Beating Depression. A. John Rush. LC 84-13564. (Illus.). 155p. reprint ed. pap. 44.20 (*0-8357-4248-2*, 2037037) Bks Demand.

Beating Fantasies. Ed. by Bernard D. Fine et al. Bd. with Regressive Ego Psychoanalysis. LC 65-18383. (C). LC 65-18383. (Kris Study Group Monograph: No. 1). 103p. (C). 1966. Set text ed. 25.00 (*0-8236-0480-2*) Intl Univs Pr.

Beating International Terrorism: An Action Strategy for Preemption & Punishment. 1991. lib. bdg. 69.00 (*0-8490-4223-2*) Gordon Pr.

Beating International Terrorism: An Action Strategy for Preemption & Punishment. Stephen Sloan. 63p. (Orig.). (C). 1992. pap. text ed. 19.95 (*1-56806-104-8*) Diane Pub.

Beating Japan: How Hundreds of American Companies Are Beating Japan Now - & What Your Company Can Learn from Their Strategies & Successes. Francis McInerney & Sean White. 352p. 1994. pap. 12.95 (*0-452-27223-8*, Plume-Truman Talley Bks) NAL-Dutton.

***Beating Job Burnout.** Paul Stevens. Ed. by Sarah Kennedy. 1995. 16.95 (*0-8442-4450-3*, VGM Career Bks) NTC Pub Grp.

***Beating Job Burnout.** Paul Stevens. Ed. by Sarah Kennedy. (Orig.). 1995. pap. 12.95 (*0-8442-4474-0*, VGM Career Bks) NTC Pub Grp.

Beating Job Burnout: How to Transform Work Pressure into Productivity. rev. ed. Beverly Potter. (Illus.). 302p. 1994. pap. 12.95 (*0-914171-69-0*) Ronin Pub.

Beating Mediocrity: Six Habits of the Highly Effective Christian. John Guest. (John Guest Accelerated Growth Ser.). 176p. 1993. pap. 9.99 (*0-8010-3851-0*) Baker Bk.

***Beating Menopause & Early Ovarian Failure with the Help of One Natural Ingredient.** Julia Elliott. 1995. 9.95 (*0-8062-5238-3*) Carlton.

***Beating Murphy's Law: The Amazing Science of Risk.** Bob Berger. 1994. pap. 11.95 (*0-385-31317-9*, Delta) Dell.

Beating of Wings. Gertrude Rubin. Ed. by Carol Spelius. 96p. (Orig.). 1991. pap. 8.95 (*0-941363-09-0*) Lake Shore Pub.

Beating Sea & Changeless Bar. Jacob Lazarre. LC 79-86149. (Short Story Index Reprint Ser.). 1977. 17.95 (*0-8369-3053-3*) Ayer.

Beating Tantra at Its Own Game: Spiritual Sexuality. Arthur Lytle. LC 89-81551. 200p. (Orig.). 1990. pap. 12.95 (*0-941404-89-7*) New Falcon Pubns.

Beating the Adoption Game. rev. ed. Cynthia Martin. 544p. 1988. pap. 13.95 (*0-15-610930-1*) HarBrace.

Beating the Age Game: Redefining Retirement. Jack Ballard & Phoebe Ballard. LC 93-19494. 1993. 12.95 (*0-942361-79-2*) MasterMedia Ltd.

***Beating the Anti-Sicilians.** Joe Gallagher. (Batsford Chess Library Ser.). 176p. 1994. pap. 20.95 (*0-8050-3575-3*) H Holt & Co.

Beating the Bureaucrats: How to Get All You Earned from Social Security, Vol. 2. Gene E. Nelson. 1990. pap. 14.95 (*0-9623810-3-9*) White Plume Pr.

Beating the Bushes: Selected Essays, 1941-1970. John C. Ransom. LC 79-159738. (New Directions Bks.). 186p. reprint ed. pap. 53.10 (*0-8357-7086-9*, 2026174) Bks Demand.

Beating the Chemical Cop-Out. Charles Dickson. Ed. by Becky Nelson. 22p. (Orig.). (YA). (gr. 7-12). 1992. pap. text ed. 1.95 (*1-56309-036-8*, Wrld Changers Res) Womans Mission Union.

Beating the Clock: A Guide to Maturing Successfully. Frank B. Minirth et al. (Life Enrichment Ser.). 1986. pap. 3.99 (*0-8010-6205-5*) Baker Bk.

Beating the College Blues. Paul Grayson & Philip Meilman. 192p. 1992. lib. bdg. 19.95 (*0-8160-2455-3*) Facts on File.

Beating the College Blues: A Student's Guide to Coping with the Emotional Ups & Downs of College Life. Paul Grayson & Philip Meilman. 192p. 1992. pap. 12.95 (*0-8160-2832-X*) Facts on File.

Beating the Competition: A Practical Guide to Benchmarking. Kaiser Associates, Inc. Staff. 175p. 1992. 155.00 (*1-56365-018-5*) Wash Res.

Beating the Competition: One Hundred Fifty Ways to Win New Customers for Your Small Business. Tait Trussell. LC 92-28459. 144p. (Orig.). 1992. pap. 10.95 (*0-8191-8617-1*) Madison Bks UPA.

Beating the Devil Out of Them: Corporal Punishment in American Families. Murray A. Straus. 352p. 1994. text ed. 24.95 (*0-02-931730-4*) Free Pr.

Beating the Dow: A High Return, Low-Risk Method for Investing in the Dow Jones Industrial Stocks with As Little As 5,000 Dollars. Michael O'Higgins & John Downes. LC 89-46551. 288p. 1992. reprint ed. pap. 13.00 (*0-06-098404-X*, PL) HarpC.

Beating the Drum. Josephine Paker. LC 92-5164. (Millbrook Arts Library). (Illus.). 48p. (J). (gr. 2-6). 1992. lib. bdg. 14.40 (*1-56294-093-7*) Millbrook Pr.

Beating the Food Giants. Paul A. Stitt. 288p. (Orig.). 1993. pap. 9.95 (*0-939956-06-3*) Natural Pr.

Beating the French. Gary Lane. (Batsford Chess Library Ser.). 144p. 1994. pap. 16.95 (*0-8050-3292-4*) H Holt & Co.

Beating the Grunfeld. Anatoly Karpov. (Batsford Chess Library). 192p. 1993. pap. 19.95 (*0-8050-2632-0*, Owl) H Holt & Co.

Beating the Marriage Odds: When You Are Smart, Single, & over Thirty-Five. Barbara Lovenheim. LC 90-37647. 256p. 1990. 17.95 (*0-688-08426-5*) Morrow.

Beating the Odds. Deborah Gordon. (Orig.). 1992. mass mkt. 4.99 (*0-06-104071-1*, Harp PBks) HarpC.

Beating the Odds. large type ed. Janet Bode. 165p. 1993. reprint ed. lib. bdg. 15.95 (*1-56054-591-7*) Thorndike Pr.

Beating the Odds: A Mini Autobiography. Elbert R. Moses. (Illus.). 50p. (Orig.). (YA). 1992. pap. text ed. 3.95 (*0-922484-03-1*) Poligion Pub.

Beating the Odds: Four Stories. 38p. 1990. 5.00 (*0-317-05355-8*) NASBE.

***Beating the Odds: How the Poor Get to College.** Arthur Levine & Jana Nidiffer. LC 95-9137. (Higher & Adult Education Ser.). 1995. 27.95 (*0-7879-0132-6*) Jossey-Bass.

Beating the Odds: Overcoming Life's Trials. Frank Minirth et al. (Life Enrichment Ser.). 128p. (Orig.). 1987. pap. 5.99 (*0-8010-6217-9*) Baker Bk.

Beating the Odds: Stories of Unexpected Achievers. Janet Bode. LC 91-14215. (Non-Fiction Ser.). 144p. (YA). (gr. 9-12). 1991. lib. bdg. 15.33 (*0-531-10985-2*) Watts.

Beating the Odds: Ten Smart Steps to Small Business Success. Scott A. Clark. 283p. 1992. pap. 15.95 (*0-8144-7811-5*) AMACOM.

Beating the Odds Against Breast & Ovarian Cancer: Reducing Your Hereditary Risk. Mary M. Kemeny & Paula Dranov. LC 91-39411. (Illus.). 216p. 1992. pap. 7.64 (*0-201-57783-6*) Addison-Wesley.

Beating the Odds Against Heart Disease & High Cholesterol: Reducing Your Hereditary Risk. C. Richard Conti & Diana Tonnessen. (Illus.). 160p. 1992. pap. 7.64 (*0-201-57782-8*) Addison-Wesley.

Beating the Odds; Alternative Treatments That Have Worked Miracles Against Cancer. Albert Marchetti. 1990. mass mkt. 4.95 (*0-312-92236-1*) St Martin.

***Beating the Odds in Small Business: The New Entrepreneur's Bible.** Tom Culley. 304p. 1995. pap. 13.95 (*0-7867-0262-1*) Carroll & Graf.

***Beating the Odds on the North Pacific: A Guide to Fishing Safety.** 2nd ed. Ed. by Susan Jensen. (Marine Advisory Bulletin Ser.: No. 41). 250p. 1994. ring bd. 12.00 (*1-56612-025-X*) AK Sea Grant CP.

Beating the Radar Rap. 2nd rev. ed. Dale Smith & John Tomerlin. LC 89-81940. (Illus.). 160p. 1990. pap. 14.95 (*0-933893-89-2*) Bonus Books.

Beating the Sicilian Two: A Complete New Repertoire for White. John Nunn. (Illus.). 160p. 1990. pap. 12.95 (*0-7134-6445-3*, Pub. by Batsford UK) Trafalgar.

Beating the Stock Market. R. W. McNeel. LC 63-22594. 1963. reprint ed. 12.00 (*0-87034-008-5*) Fraser Pub Co.

Beating the Street: The Best-Selling Author of One Up on Wall Street Shows You How to Pick Winning Stocks & Mutual Funds. Peter Lynch & John Rothchild. 320p. 1993. 23.00 (*0-671-75915-9*) S&S Trade.

Beating the Street: The Best-Selling Author of (One up on Wall Street) Shows You How to Pick Winning Stocks & Mutual Funds. Peter Lynch & John Rothchild. 1994. pap. 12.50 (*0-671-89163-4*, Fireside) S&S Trade.

Beating the System: The Underground Economy. Carl P. Simon & Ann D. Witte. LC 81-12846. 304p. 1982. text ed. 55.00 (*0-86569-105-3*, Auburn Hse) Greenwood.

Beating the Term Paper Deadline: A Student Guide to Getting Help at the Library - in Record Time. Laura Windsor. 24p. (Orig.). (J). (ps-12). 1990. 4.75 (*0-918734-34-7*) Reymont.

***Beating the Tough Times: How to Win Your Financial & Personal Battles.** Dennis M. Powers. 250p. 1995. pap. 18.95 (*0-306-45082-8*, Plenum Pr) Plenum.

Beating the Wheel: The System That's Won More Than 6 Million Dollars - From Las Vegas to Monte Carlo. Russell T. Barnhart. (Illus.). 320p. 1992. pap. 15.95 (*0-8184-0553-8*, L Stuart) Carol Pub Group.

Beating the Wild Tattoo. Lynne Youngs. 1993. pap. 5.95 (*1-56201-037-9*) Blue Moon Bks.

***Beating Time: A Musician's Memoir.** Harry E. Dickson. (Illus.). 208p. 1995. 21.95 (*1-55553-229-2*) NE U Pr.

***Beating to Windward: A Voyage in the Gloucester Daily Times Through the Stormy Years from 1967 to 1973.** Joseph Garland. (Illus.). 147p. (Orig.). 1994. pap. 14.95 (*0-9625660-1-2*) Curious Traveller Pr.

Beating Wife-Beating. Lee H. Bowker. LC 82-48603. 176p. 1983. text ed. 35.00 (*0-669-06345-2*) Free Pr.

Beating Your Competition Through Quality. Owen. 144p. 1989. 39.75 (*0-8247-8065-5*) Dekker.

Beatitudes. Bernard Haring. (C). 1988. 39.00 (*0-85439-130-4*, Pub. by St Paul Pubns UK) St Mut.

Beatitudes. C. H. Spurgeon. 1978. pap. 3.95 (*1-56186-214-2*) Pilgrim Pubns.

Beatitudes. Thomas Watson. 307p. 1981. kivar 13.95 (*0-85151-035-3*) Banner of Truth.

***Beatitudes: A Quest for Understanding.** Norman Gidney. 220p. (Orig.). 1995. pap. write for info. (*1-885591-82-9*) Morris Pubng.

Beatitudes: Attitudes for a Better Future. George Drew. 63p. (Orig.). 1980. pap. 7.95 (*0-940754-03-7*) Ed Ministries.

Beatitudes: Pattern for Christian Living. Helen C. Swift. LC 90-41241. 96p. (Orig.). 1990. pap. 4.95 (*0-8189-0592-1*) Alba.

Beatitudes: Soundings in Christian Traditions. Simon Tugwell. 192p. 1980. 10.95 (*0-87243-140-1*) Templegate.

Beatitudes: Their Inner Meaning. J. Donald Walters. 70p. (Orig.). 1989. pap. 4.95 (*0-916124-54-1*, CCP18) Crystal Clarity.

Beatitudes: To Evangelize As Jesus Did. Segundo Galilea. Tr. by Robert R. Barr. LC 83-19342. 112p. (Orig.). reprint ed. pap. 32.00 (*0-7837-6414-6*, 2046394) Bks Demand.

***Beatitudes & the Lord's Prayer.** Arthur W. Pink. 144p. 1995. reprint ed. pap. 7.99 (*0-8010-7142-9*) Baker Bk.

Beatitudes Bestilaes De Balthazar B. J. P. Donleavy. 587p. (FRE.). 1977. pap. 12.95 (*0-7859-1864-7*, 2070369870) Fr & Eur.

Beatitudes, for a Cappella SATB Chorus & SATB Soloists. Brian Banks. (University Choral Ser.: No. 1). 14p. 1992. 2.50 (*1-56571-062-2*, UC001) PRB Prods.

Beatitudes in Context. Dennis Hamm. (Zacchaeus Studies: New Testament). 120p. (Orig.). 1990. pap. 7.95 (*0-8146-5676-5*) Liturgical Pr.

Beatle Dreams & Other Stories. Guillermo Samperio. Ed. by Yvette E. Miller. Tr. by L. Howard Quackenbush & Russell M. Cluff. LC 92-21225. 150p. 1994. pap. 15.95 (*0-935480-60-9*) Lat Am Lit Rev Pr.

Beatle Myth: The British Invasion of American Popular Music, 1956-1969. Michael B. Kelly. LC 90-53500. (Illus.). 231p. 1991. lib. bdg. 28.50x (*0-89950-579-1*) McFarland & Co.

Beatle Poems. Howard A. DeWitt. (Illus.). 60p. (Orig.). 1987. pap. 6.95 (*0-938840-06-1*) Horizon Bks CA.

***Beatle! The Pete Best Story.** Best & Doncaster. Date not set. per. 14.95 (*0-85965-077-4*, Pub. by Plexus Pub UK) InBook.

***BeatleCraze: Memories & Memorobilia.** Richard Buskin. 1994. pap. 12.99 (*0-517-12046-1*) Random Hse Value.

Beatlefan: The Authoritative Publication of Record for Fans of the Beatles, Vols. 1 & 2. (Rock & Roll Reference Ser.: No. 18). (Illus.). 306p. 1985. 34.50 (*0-87650-199-4*) Popular Culture.

Beatles. Ariel Books Staff. (Illus.). 80p. 1993. 4.95 (*0-8362-3046-9*) Andrews & McMeel.

***Beatles.** Jon Ewing. (CD Bks.). (Illus.). 120p. 1994. pap. 7.99 (*1-886894-13-2*, MBS Paperbk) Mus Bk Servs.

***Beatles.** Allan Kozinn. (20th-Century Composers Ser.). (Illus.). 240p. (Orig.). 1995. pap. 19.95 (*0-7148-3203-0*, Pub. by Phaidon Press UK) Chronicle Bks.

Beatles. L. Loewen. (Profiles in Music Ser.). (Illus.). 112p. (J). (gr. 5 up). 1989. lib. bdg. 18.60 (*0-86592-610-7*); lib. bdg. 13.95 (*0-685-58616-2*) Rourke Corp.

Beatles. Michael Stern et al. 144p. 1993. pap. 17.95 (*0-89145-532-9*, 3428) Collector Bks.

***Beatles.** John A. Taylor. 64p. 1994. write for info. (*1-57215-030-0*) World Pubns.

Beatles. Bill Yenne. 1994. 9.98 (*0-681-00576-9*) Longmeadow Pr.

Beatles: A Bio-Bibliography. William McKeen. LC 89-2219. (Popular Culture Bio-Bibliographies Ser.). 200p. 1989. text ed. 42.95 (*0-313-25993-3*, MBE/, Greenwood Pr) Greenwood.

Beatles: A Celebration. Geoffrey Gilliano. 1992. 19.98 (*1-55521-794-X*) Bk Sales Inc.

Beatles: A Musical Revolution. Terence J. O'Grady. LC 82-21288. (Music Ser.). (Illus.). 208p. 1983. text ed. 20.95 (*0-8057-9453-0*, Twayne) Macmillan.

***Beatles: An Illustrated Diary.** Fulpen. (Illus.). Date not set. per. 14.95 (*0-85965-070-7*, Pub. by Plexus Pub UK) InBook.

Beatles: In the Beginning. Harry Benson. (Illus.). 128p. 1993. 24.95 (*0-87663-642-3*) Universe.

Beatles: In the Beginning. Harry Benson. (Illus.). 128p. 1994. pap. 15.95 (*0-87663-788-8*) Universe.

Beatles: In Their Own Words. Comp. by Miles. (Illus.). 128p. 1978. pap. 15.95 (*0-86001-540-8*, OP40419) Omnibus NY.

Beatles: The Ultimate Recording Guide. Allen Wiener. (Illus.). 1992. 35.00 (*0-8160-2511-8*) Facts on File.

***Beatles: The Ultimate Recording Guide.** 3rd rev. ed. Allen J. Wiener. LC 94-29085. 1994. pap. 15.00 (*1-55850-414-1*) Adams Pubng.

Beatles: Untold Tales. Howard A. DeWitt. (Illus.). 272p. 1994. reprint ed. pap. text ed. 14.95 (*0-938840-03-7*) Horizon Bks CA.

Beatles after the Break-Up: In Their Own Words. David Bennahum. (Illus.). 96p. 1991. pap. 15.95 (*0-7119-2558-5*, OP46424) Omnibus NY.

Beatles Again. Harry Castleman & Walter Podrazik. LC 77-92320. (Rock & Roll Reference Ser.: No. 2). 280p. 1977. 32.00 (*0-87650-089-0*) Popular Culture.

Beatles Album: Thirty Years of Music & Memorabilia. Geoffrey Giuliano. LC 91-50152. (Illus.). 256p. 1991. 29.95 (*0-670-84118-8*, Viking Studio) Studio Bks.

Beatles Album: Thirty Years of Music & Memorabilia. Geoffrey Giuliano. (Illus.). 256p. 1994. 16.95 (*0-14-023777-1*, Viking Studio) Studio Bks.

Beatles at the Beeb: The Story of Their Radio Career, 1962-1965. Kevin Howlett. (Rock & Roll Remembrances Ser.: No. 5). (Illus.). 144p. 1983. 28.50 (*0-87650-168-4*) Popular Culture.

Beatles Ballads. (Illus.). 88p. (Orig.). 1994. pap. 14.95 (*0-7935-3351-1*, HL00308236) H Leonard.

Beatles Bass Book. (Bass Recorded Versions Ser.). 80p. (Orig.). 1990. pap. 14.95 (*0-7935-0332-9*, HL00660103) H Leonard.

Beatles Best. 512p. 1987. pap. 27.95 (*0-88188-613-0*, HL 00356223) H Leonard.

Beatles Complete Scores. (Illus.). 1136p. 1994. 59.95 (*0-7935-1832-6*, 00673228) H Leonard.

Beatles Day by Day. Mark Lewisohn. 1990. pap. 9.95 (*0-517-57750-X*, Harmony) Crown Pub Group.

Beatles Down Under: The 1964 Australia & New Zealand Tour. Glenn A. Baker. (Rock & Roll Remembrances Ser.: No. 7). (Illus.). 130p. 1985. reprint ed. 28.50 (*0-87650-186-2*) Popular Culture.

Beatles' England: There Are Places I'll Remember. David Bacon & Norman Maslov. LC 81-82555. (Illus.). 144p. 1982. pap. 12.95 (*0-9606736-1-X*) Nine Hundred-Ten Pr.

Beatles Fake Book. Ed. by Todd Lowry. 176p. 1987. pap. 25.00 (*0-88188-757-9*, 00240069) H Leonard.

Beatles First Four Albums from Originals. 1987. pap. 18.95 (*0-88188-623-8*, 00356233) H Leonard.

Beatles Forever. Tim Schaffner & Nicholas Schaffner. (Illus.). 1994. 14.98 (*1-56731-008-7*, MJF Bks) Fine Comms.

Beatles Forever. Helen Spencer. 1991. 9.99 (*0-517-35771-2*) Random Hse Value.

Beatles Guitar Book. (Guitar Recorded Versions Ser.). 88p. (Orig.). 1990. pap. 18.95 (*0-7935-0299-3*, HL00660140) H Leonard.

Beatles Illustrated Lyrics. Ed. by Alan Aldridge. (Illus.). 272p. 1991. pap. 27.95 (*0-395-59426-X*) HM.

Beatles Japanese Record Guide. Jason Anjoorian. LC 93-91865. (Illus.). 228p. (Orig.). 1994. pap. 29.95 (*0-9640079-0-8*) Jason Pr MA.

Beatles London. Mark Lewisohn et al. (Illus.). 144p. 1994. pap. 10.95 (*0-312-11184-3*) St Martin.

Beatles Memorabilia Price Guide. Jeff Augsburger et al. LC 88-70713. (Illus.). 256p. 1988. pap. 19.95 (*0-929207-00-9*) Branyan Pr.

Beatles Memorabilia Price Guide. 2nd ed. Jeff Augsburger et al. (Illus.). 240p. 1993. pap. 24.95 (*0-87069-697-1*, Wallace-Hmestead) Chilton.

Beatles Price Guide for American Records: The Definitive Reference for Their Records, Tapes, & Compact Discs. 3rd ed. Perry Cox & Joe Lindsay. 284p. 40.00 (*0-9617347-3-6*); pap. 25.00 (*0-9617347-4-4*) BIODISC.

Beatles Reader: A Selection of Contemporary Views, News & Reviews of the Beatles in Their Heyday. Charles P. Neises. LC 84-60267. (Rock & Roll Remembrances Ser.: No. 6). 232p. 1991. reprint ed. 28.50 (*1-56075-024-3*) Popular Culture.

Beatles Recording Sessions. Mark Lewisohn. 1990. pap. 20.00 (*0-517-58182-5*, Harmony) Crown Pub Group.

Beatles: Recording Sessions: The Official Abbey Road Studio Session Notes, 1962-1970. Mark Lewisohn. (Illus.). 204p. 1989. 27.50 (*0-517-57066-1*, Harmony) Crown Pub Group.

***Beatles with Lacan: Rock-n-Roll As Requiem for the Modern Age.** Henry W. Sullivan. LC 94-36301. (Sociocriticism Ser.: Vol. 4). 232p. (C). 1995. pap. text ed. 29.95 (*0-8204-2183-9*) P Lang Pubs.

Beatlesongs. William J. Dowlding. 1989. pap. 12.95 (*0-671-68229-6*, Fireside) S&S Trade.

Beatrice. Arthur Schnitzler. Tr. by Agnes Jacques. LC 72-175440. reprint ed. 37.50 (*0-404-05612-1*) AMS Pr.

Beatrice: From Buildup Through Breakup. Neil R. Gazel. (Illus.). 272p. 1990. 27.95 (*0-252-01729-3*) U of Ill Pr.

***Beatrice & Some Back Burner Recipes.** Betty Ryder. LC 93-95022. (Illus.). 112p. (Orig.). 1994. pap. 8.00 (*1-56002-406-2*, Univ Edtns) Aegina Pr.

Beatrice Cenci. Irene M. Mitchell. LC 90-22598. (American University Studies: History: Ser. IX, Vol. 104). 236p. (C). 1991. text ed. 46.95 (*0-8204-1525-1*) P Lang Pubs.

Beatrice Cuming, Nineteen Hundred Three to Nineteen Seventy-Four. William Bendig et al. (Illus.). 28p. (Orig.). 1990. write for info. (*0-318-66809-2*) Lyman Allyn.

Beatrice D'Este: Duchess of Milan, 1475-1497; a Study of the Renaissance. Julia Cartwright. LC 73-38345. (Select Bibliographies Reprint Ser.). 1977. 24.95 (*0-8369-6762-3*) Ayer.

Beatrice D'Este, Duchess of Milan, 1475-1497. Julia M. Ady. LC 71-154137. reprint ed. 43.50 (*0-404-09204-7*) AMS Pr.

Beatrice du Congo. Bernard B. Dadie. 148p. (FRE.). 1971. pap. 27.95 (*0-7859-4883-X*) Fr & Eur.

Beatrice Goes to Brighton. Marion Chesney. 1992. mass mkt. 3.99 (*0-312-92794-0*) St Martin.

Beatrice Goes to Brighton. large type ed. Marion Chesney. LC 92-41194. (Nightingale Ser.). 1993. 14.95 (*0-8161-5546-1*) G K Hall.

Beatrice Hereford's Monologues. Beatrice Hereford. 80p. 1937. 5.00 (*0-573-60064-3*) French.

***Beatrice Mandelman, Taos Modernist.** Richard Hobbs. LC 94-18705. (Illus.). 200p. 1995. 60.00x (*0-8263-1603-4*); pap. 29.95 (*0-8263-1604-2*) U of NM Pr.

Beatrice of Nazareth in Her Context, Vol. 1. Roger DeGanck. (Cistercian Studies: No. 121). 341p. 1991. 28.95 (*0-87907-421-3*); pap. 12.95 (*0-87907-721-2*) Cistercian Pubns.

Beatrice of Nazareth in Her Context, Vol. 2: Towards Unification with God. Roger DeGanck. (Cistercian Studies: No. 122). 262p. 1991. 28.95 (*0-87907-422-1*); pap. 12.95 (*0-87907-622-4*) Cistercian Pubns.

***Beatrice Ojakanga Light Baking Book.** Beatrice Ojakanga. Date not set. write for info. (*0-517-70134-0*) Random.

Beatrice Ojakangas' Great Holiday Baking Book. Beatrice A. Ojakangas. 1994. 25.00 (*0-517-59330-0*, Clarkson Potter) Crown Bks Yng Read.

Beatrice Trum Hunter's Baking Sampler see Family Whole Grain Baking Book

Beatrice Webb: A Life. Carole Seymour-Jones. (Illus.). 384p. 1992. 30.00 (*1-56663-001-0*) I R Dee.

Beatrice Webb's American Diary, Eighteen Ninety-Eight. Ed. by David Shannon. (Illus.). 198p. 1963. 17.50 (*0-299-02851-8*) U of Wis Pr.

Beatrice Witherspoon. Emma Burton. (Heritage Reprint Ser.). 1970. 11.25 (*0-8309-0023-3*) Herald Hse.

Beatrice Wood Retrospective. California State University, Fullerton Staff. (Illus.). 48p. (Orig.). 1983. pap. 12.00 (*0-935314-23-7*) CSU Art Gallery.

Beatrix. Honore De Balzac. 1962. write for info. (*0-318-63434-1*); pap. 11.95 (*0-8288-9337-3*) Fr & Eur.

An Asterisk (*) at the beginning of an entry indicates that the title is appearing in BIP for the first time.

An Asterisk (*) at the beginning of an entry indicates that the title is appearing in BIP for the first time.

645

Beautiful Flowers of Kashmir, Vols. 1-2. Ed. by E. Blatter. (C). 1984. 125.00 (0-317-92342-0, Scientific) St Mut.

Beautiful Flowers of Kashmir, Vols. 1-2. E. Blatter. 1984. reprint ed. 375.00 (81-7089-011-X, Pub. by Intl Bk Distr II) St Mut.

Beautiful Garden & Other Bible Tales. Elma E. Levinger. (Illus.). (J). (gr. 3-5). 6.95 (0-8197-0253-6) Bloch.

Beautiful Gardens: Guide to over Eighty Botanical Gardens Arboretums & More. Eric A. Johnson. LC 90-85370. 1991. pap. 12.95 (0-9628236-0-0) Ironwood AZ.

*__Beautiful Gardens with Less Water.__ John Patrick. (Lothian Austalian Garden Ser.). (Illus.). 64p. (Orig.). 1995. pap. 9.95 (0-85091-657-7, Pub. by Lothian Pub AT) Seven Hills Bk.

Beautiful Girl. Alice Adams. 1987. pap. 3.95 (0-449-21412-5, Crest) Fawcett.

Beautiful Imperialist: China Perceives America, 1972-1990. David Shambaugh. (Illus.). 350p. 1991. text ed. 42.50 (0-691-07864-5) Princeton U Pr.

Beautiful Imperialist: China Perceives America, 1972-1990. David Shambaugh. (Illus.). 350p. 1993. pap. text ed. 17.95 (0-691-02486-3) Princeton U Pr.

Beautiful in Music. Edward Hanslick. Tr. by Gustav Cohen & Morris Weitz. LC 57-14627. 1957. pap. 3.95 (0-672-60211-3, LLA45, Bobbs) Macmillan.

Beautiful in Music: A Contribution to the Revisal of Musical Aesthetics. rev. ed. Eduard Hanslick. Tr. by Gustav Cohen. LC 74-1362. (Music Ser.). 174p. 1974. reprint ed. lib. bdg. 29.50 (0-306-70649-0) Da Capo.

Beautiful Ireland. (Illus.). 150p. (Orig.). 1990. pap. 15.95 (0-7171-1772-3, Pub. by Gill & MacMill IE) Irish Bks Media.

Beautiful Japan: A Kodansha Postcard Book. Kodansha International Staff. Ed. by Ogawa & Pocknell. (Illus.). 56p. 1993. pap. 8.00 (4-7700-1673-5) Kodansha.

Beautiful Joe. Marshall Saunders. 19.95 (0-8488-1152-6) Amereon Ltd.

Beautiful Joe. abr. rev. ed. Quinn Currie. (Illus.). 72p. (J). (gr. k-8). 1990. reprint ed. pap. 10.95 (0-9623072-1-1) S Ink WA.

Beautiful Joe: An Autobiography, the Original 1894 Edition. Marshall Saunders. 1994. 24.95 (1-55709-303-2) Applewood.

Beautiful Junk. Karen Brackett & Rosie Manley. (J). (gr. 1-6). 1990. pap. 11.99 (0-8224-0626-8) Fearon Teach Aids.

Beautiful Junk II. Karen Brackett & Rosie Manley. 1992. pap. 11.99 (0-86653-937-9) Fearon Teach Aids.

Beautiful Just! large type ed. Lillian Beckwith. Bd. with Bruach Blend. 1989. 12.00 (0-7089-0348-7) Ulverscroft.

Beautiful Kyoto. Ed. by Ogawa & Katayama. (Postcard Book Ser.). (Illus.). 56p. 1994. 8.00 (4-7700-1674-3) Kodansha.

Beautiful Lace. Nihon Vogue Staff. LC 81-84803. (Illus.). 82p. 1982. pap. 11.95 (0-87040-504-7) Japan Pubns USA.

Beautiful Land: A Story of the Oklahoma Land Rush. Nancy Antle. (Illus.). 64p. (J). (gr. 2-6). 1994. 12.99 (0-670-85304-6) Viking Child Bks.

Beautiful Land: Palestine: Historical, Geographical & Pictorial. John Fulton. Ed. by Moshe Davis. LC 77-70694. (America & the Holy Land Ser.). (Illus.). 1977. reprint ed. lib. bdg. 57.95 (0-405-10248-8) Ayer.

Beautiful Land & Seascapes, No. 1. Anton Gutknecht. (How to Draw & Paint Ser.). (Illus.). 32p. (Orig.). 1989. pap. 5.95 (0-929261-41-0, HT180) W Foster Pub.

Beautiful Land & Seascapes, No. 2. Anton Gutknecht. (How to Draw & Paint Ser.). (Illus.). 32p. (Orig.). 1989. pap. 5.95 (0-929261-44-5, HT198) W Foster Pub.

*__Beautiful Loot: Russia's Treasure Troves of Stolen Art from World War II.__ A. Konstantin & G. Koslov. 1995. 25.00 (0-679-44389-4) Random.

Beautiful Losers. Leonard Cohen. Date not set. pap. write for info. (0-679-75287-0) Random.

Beautiful Losers. Leonard Cohen. LC 93-10916. 1993. pap. 11.00 (0-679-74825-3, Vin) Random.

Beautiful Losers: Essays on the Failure of American Conservatism. Samuel Francis. LC 93-15848. 256p. 1993. 37.50 (0-8262-0907-6) U of Mo Pr.

Beautiful Losers: Essays on the Failure of American Conservatism. Samuel Francis. 256p. 1994. pap. 16.95 (0-8262-0976-9) U of Mo Pr.

Beautiful Machine: Rivers & the Republican Plan, 1755-1825. John Seelye. (Illus.). 448p. 1991. 45.00 (0-19-504551-3) OUP.

Beautiful Memories of Days Gone By. Ronald W. Taylor. (Orig.). 1991. pap. 7.95 (0-9624777-3-7) Green & White Pub.

Beautiful Merchandise: Prostitution in China, 1860-1936. Ed. by Sue Gronewold. LC 82-6049. (Women & History Ser.: No. 1). 114p. 1982. text ed. 32.95 (0-86656-134-X) Haworth Pr.

Beautiful Merchandise: Prostitution in China 1860-1936. Sue Gronewold. LC 85-7672. 114p. 1985. reprint ed. pap. 9.95 (0-918393-15-9) Harrington Pk.

Beautiful Mexico. V. Quinn. 1976. lib. bdg. 69.95 (0-8490-1481-6) Gordon Pr.

Beautiful Moon of No Shadow. Poems. Susan Ludvigson. LC 86-21073. 50p. 1987. text ed. 13.95 (0-8071-1378-6) La State U Pr.

Beautiful Mrs. Seidenman. Andrzei Szczypiorski. LC 90-50184. (Vintage International Ser.). 208p. 1991. 9.95 (0-679-73214-4, Vin) Random.

Beautiful Music. James Magorian. LC 88-71142. (Illus.). 12p. (J). (gr. 2-5). 1988. pap. 3.00 (0-930674-25-1) Black Oak.

Beautiful Must Be the Mountains. Norman Blanchard. LC 87-71720. 75p. (Orig.). 1988. pap. 6.00 (0-916383-38-5) Aegina Pr.

Beautiful Nails. (Illus.). 64p. 1993. spiral bd. 5.98 (1-56173-733-X, 3613900) Pubns Intl Ltd.

Beautiful New England. Bill Harris. 1986. 17.99 (0-517-61395-6) Random Hse Value.

*__Beautiful, Novel, & Strange: Aesthetics & Heterodoxy.__ Ronald Paulson. (Illus.). 304p. 1995. text ed. 39.95x (0-8018-5171-8) Johns Hopkins.

Beautiful Nubian Baby: A Book of Memoirs for Baby's First Six Years. Malaika Adero. (Illus.). 1991. write for info. (1-879831-04-X) Kayode Pubns.

Beautiful Old Houses of Quebec. P. Roy Wilson & Jean Palardy. LC 75-8501. 125p. reprint ed. pap. 35.70 (0-8357-7088-5, 2026402) Bks Demand.

Beautiful Origami. Zubal Ayture-Scheele. LC 90-9735. (Illus.). 80p. 1990. 21.95 (0-8069-7381-1); pap. 10.95 (0-8069-7382-X) Sterling.

Beautiful Ornament of the Three Visions. Ngorchen K. Lhundrub. Ed. by Lobsand Dagpa & Jay Goldbert. 232p. 1991. pap. 12.95 (0-937938-99-8) Snow Lion Pubns.

Beautiful Painted Arrow. Rael. 1992. pap. 12.95 (1-85230-310-7) Element MA.

*__Beautiful Paiute Girl.__ F. C. Scrivner. 1995. 15.95 (0-8062-5293-6) Carlton.

Beautiful Pearl. Nancy Whitelaw. Ed. by Kathleen Tucker. LC 90-28761. (Illus.). 32p. (J). (gr. 2-5). 1991. 13.95 (0-8075-0599-4) A Whitman.

Beautiful Phantoms: Selected Poems, 1968-1980. Barry Gifford. 100p. (Orig.). 1981. pap. 5.00 (0-939180-00-6) Tombouctou.

Beautiful Philosophy of Life. R. Swinburne Clymer. 1986. reprint ed. spiral bd. 13.75 (0-7873-1135-9) Mokelumne.

Beautiful Philosophy of Life as Taught by the Grand Lama in the Temple of Lasa, Tibet: Lessons in the 49 Degrees. Ed. by R. Swinburne Clymer. (Tibetan Buddhism Ser.). 1991. lib. bdg. 79.95 (0-8490-5171-1) Gordon Pr.

Beautiful Place to Die. Philip R. Craig. 224p. 1991. mass mkt. 4.99 (0-380-71155-9) Avon.

Beautiful Poems on Jesus. Comp. by Basil Miller. LC 68-58826. (Granger Index Reprint Ser.). 1977. 19.95 (0-8369-6029-7) Ayer.

Beautiful Rio De Janeiro. A. Bell. 1976. lib. bdg. 69.95 (0-8490-1482-4) Gordon Pr.

Beautiful Road Home: Living in the Knowledge That You Are Spirit. White Eagle. 96p. (Orig.). 1992. pap. 9.95 (0-85487-088-1, Pub. by White Eagl Pub Trust UK) DeVorss.

Beautiful Room Empty. Edmund White. 1989. mass mkt. 4.95 (0-345-35151-7) Ballantine.

*__Beautiful Room Is Empty.__ Edmund White. 1995. pap. write for info. (0-614-03326-8) Ballantine.

Beautiful Room Is Empty. Edmund White. 1994. pap. 11.00 (0-679-75540-3, Vin) Random.

Beautiful Roses. NK Lawn & Garden Co. Staff. (NK Lawn & Garden Step-by-Step Visual Guides Ser.). (Illus.). 80p. (Orig.). 1992. pap. 6.95 (0-380-76663-9) Avon.

Beautiful Roses. NK Lawn & Garden Staff. (Step-by-Step Visual Guide Ser.). 80p. 1991. pap. 7.95 (1-880281-01-5) NK Lawn & Garden.

*__Beautiful San Diego.__ Josiah Sand. (Illus.). 24p. (Orig.). 1994. pap. 2.95 (1-878505-07-6) Road Runner Card.

Beautiful Senoritas & Other Plays. Dolores Prida. Ed. by Judith Weiss. LC 90-1239. 180p. (Orig.). 1994. pap. 11.00 (1-55885-026-0) Arte Publico.

Beautiful Shirt. Donald Revell. LC 94-20492. 80p. 1994. 22.50 (0-8195-2216-3, Wesleyan Univ Pr); pap. 10.95 (0-8195-1219-2, Wesleyan Univ Pr) U Pr of New Eng.

Beautiful Side of Death. Floyd C. McElveen. (Orig.). 1988. 3.95 (0-9620963-0-X) Inst Rel Rsch.

Beautiful Side of Evil. Johanna Michaelsen. LC 82-82240. 224p. (Orig.). 1982. pap. 8.99 (0-89081-322-1) Harvest Hse.

*__Beautiful Simplicity: The Journey into a Hidden Reality, 2.__ (Illus.). 157p. (Orig.). 1994. pap. 12.95 (0-916337-06-5) Thundbird Pub.

*__Beautiful Soul: Aesthetic Morality in the Eighteenth Century.__ Robert E. Norton. 336p. 1995. 35.00x (0-8014-3050-X) Cornell U Pr.

Beautiful Soup: A Novel for the Twenty-First Century. Harvey Jacobs. 265p. (Orig.). 1992. 12.95 (0-9634185-0-5) Celadon Pr.

Beautiful Sublime: The Making of "Paradise Lost," 1701-1734. Leslie E. Moore. 256p. 1990. 29.50 (0-8047-1632-3) Stanford U Pr.

Beautiful Swimmers: Waterman, Crabs & the Chesapeake Bay. William W. Warner. (Illus.). 1977. mass mkt. 6.95 (0-14-004405-1, Penguin Bks) Viking Penguin.

Beautiful Swimmers: Watermen, Crabs, & the Chesapeake Bay. William W. Warner. 1994. pap. 13.95 (0-316-92335-4) Little.

Beautiful, the Sublime, & the Picturesque: British Influences on American Landscape Painting. Joseph D. Ketner, II & Michael J. Tammenga. LC 83-51827. (Illus.). 76p. 1984. pap. 8.00 (0-936316-05-5) Wash U Gallery.

Beautiful Theories: The Spectacle of Discourse in Contemporary Criticism. Elizabeth W. Bruss. LC 81-48178. 528p. (C). 1982. text ed. 55.00 (0-8018-2670-5) Johns Hopkins.

Beautiful Things to Make for Baby. Mark Publishing Staff. 1991. pap. 8.95 (0-937769-21-5) Mark Inc CA.

Beautiful Things to Make for Baby. Ed. by Sunset Editors. 80p. 1993. pap. 9.99 (0-376-04295-8) Sunset Menlo Pk.

Beautiful Things to Make for Brides: Clever Ideas for a Perfect Wedding. Mark Publishing Staff. 1991. pap. 8.95 (0-937769-18-5) Mark Inc CA.

Beautiful Thoughts from French & Italian Authors. C. T. Ramage. 1972. 70.00 (0-87968-713-4) Gordon Pr.

Beautiful Thoughts from German & Spanish Authors. C. T. Ramage. 1972. 70.00 (0-87968-714-2) Gordon Pr.

Beautiful Thoughts from Greek Authors. Crawford T. Ramage. 1973. 69.95 (0-87968-715-0) Gordon Pr.

Beautiful Ways Songs. (J). (gr. k-6). pap. 0.50 (0-686-29099-2) Faith Pub Hse.

*__Beautiful Wedding Decorations & Gifts on a Small Budget.__ Diane Warner. LC 95-15217. (Illus.). 176p. (Orig.). 1995. pap. 12.99 (1-55870-393-4) Betterway Bks.

Beautiful Weddings Without a Hitch: Understanding Bridal Contracts. 2nd ed. Kristina Garvin. Ed. by William Kathios. LC 89-51194. (Illus.). 20p. reprint ed. pap. 5.95 (0-685-58461-5) Weatherford Pubns.

Beautiful Woman Without Mercy: The King of the Scarecrows. Steven Culbert. LC 92-75409. 235p. 1993. 18.00 (1-880909-03-0) Baskerville.

Beautiful Wreaths. (Illus.). 64p. 1993. spiral bd. 5.98 (1-56173-743-7, 3614700) Pubns Intl Ltd.

Beautifully Old. Ed. by Frank Dituri. (Illus.). 72p. (Orig.). 1984. pap. text ed. write for info. (0-910463-04-2) Edit Heliodor.

Beauty. Manoje Basu. Tr. by Sachindra L. Ghosh. 103p. 1969. pap. 1.80 (0-88253-011-9) Ind-US Inc.

Beauty. Brian D'Amato. 1993. mass mkt. 5.99 (0-440-21282-0) Dell.

Beauty. Mark Dunster. 10p. (Orig.). 1990. pap. 4.00 (0-89642-185-6) Linden Pubs.

Beauty. Sheri S. Tepper. 1992. mass mkt. 5.99 (0-553-29527-6, Spectra) Bantam.

Beauty. Bill Wallace. LC 88-6422. 192p. (J). (gr. 3-7). 1988. 14.95 (0-8234-0715-2) Holiday.

Beauty: A Retelling of the Story of Beauty & the Beast. Robin McKinley. LC 77-25636. 256p. (YA). (gr. 7-9). 1978. 16.00 (0-06-024149-7); lib. bdg. 15.89 (0-06-024150-0) HarpC Child Bks.

Beauty: A Retelling of the Story of Beauty & the Beast. Robin McKinley. LC 77-25636. (Trophy Bk.). 256p. (J). (gr. 5 up). 1993. pap. 4.95 (0-06-440477-3, Trophy) HarpC Child Bks.

Beauty: The Value of Values. Frederick Turner. (C). 1992. text ed. 20.00 (0-8139-1357-8) U Pr of Va.

*__Beauty & Beast - Mrs. Potts Story.__ Told to Little Golden Books Staff. (J). Date not set. 1.59 (0-307-30120-6, Golden Pr) Western Pub.

Beauty & Belief: Aesthetics & Religion in Victorian Literature. Hilary Fraser. 306p. 1986. 69.95 (0-521-30767-8) Cambridge U Pr.

Beauty & Cancer: A Woman's Guide to Looking Great While Experiencing the Side Effects of Cancer Therapy. Diane D. Noyes & Peggy Mellody. LC 88-71039. (Illus.). 200p. (Orig.). 1988. pap. 12.95 (0-929482-01-8) AC Press.

Beauty & Cancer: Looking & Feeling Your Best. Diane D. Noyes & Peggy Mellody. LC 92-14254. (Illus.). 192p. 1992. pap. 12.95 (0-87833-809-8) Taylor Pub.

Beauty & Critique. Ed. by Richard Milazzo. LC 82-50165. 176p. (Orig.). 1983. pap. text ed. 8.00 (0-939858-01-0) T S L Pr.

Beauty & Fitness with "Saved by the Bell" Jessica Vitkus. LC 91-42583. (Illus.). 64p. (Orig.). (J). (gr. 5 up). 1992. pap. 6.95 (0-02-045425-2, Collier Bks Young) S&S Childrens.

Beauty & Good Properties of Women As Also Their Vices & Evil Conditions. Calisto & Melebea. LC 70-133640. (Tudor Facsimile Texts. Old English Plays Ser.: No. 10). reprint ed. 49.50 (0-404-53310-8) AMS Pr.

Beauty & Health Through Yoga Relaxation. Swami Jyotir Maya Nanda. (Illus.). 1976. pap. 3.95 (0-934664-02-1) Yoga Res Foun.

Beauty & Holiness: The Dialogue Between Aesthetics & Religion. James A. Martin, Jr. (Illus.). 269p. 1990. text ed. 32.50 (0-691-07357-0) Princeton U Pr.

Beauty & Human Nature: Elements of Psychological Aesthetics. Albert R. Chandler. LC 75-3110. reprint ed. 26.00 (0-404-59106-X) AMS Pr.

Beauty & Revelation in the Thought of Saint Augustine. Carol Harrison. (Oxford Theological Monographs). (Illus.). 304p. 1992. 65.00 (0-19-826342-2) OUP.

*__Beauty & Sadness.__ Kawabata. Date not set. write for info. (0-679-76105-5) Random Hse Value.

Beauty & Sadness. Yasunari Kawabata. Tr. by Howard Hibbett. (Perigee Japanese Library). 224p. 1981. pap. 9.95 (0-399-50529-6, Perigee Bks) Berkley Pub.

Beauty & Sensibility in the Thought of Jonathan Edwards: An Essay in Aesthetics & Theological Ethics. Roland A. Delattre. LC 68-13902. 254p. reprint ed. pap. 72.40 (0-8357-8701-X, 2033705) Bks Demand.

Beauty & the Beast. (Recorder Fun! Ser.). (Illus.). 24p. (J). (gr. 3 up). 1992. Incl. songbk. & recorder. 9.95 (0-7935-1501-7, 00710359); Incl. xylotone. 14.95 (0-7935-1502-5, 00824005) H Leonard.

Beauty & the Beast. (Harmonica Fun! Ser.). (Illus.). (J). 1993. spiral bd. 9.95 (0-7935-1771-0, 00850122) H Leonard.

Beauty & the Beast. (Piano Fun! Ser.). (Illus.). 1993. pap. 19.95 (0-7935-2810-0, HL00826001) H Leonard.

Beauty & the Beast. (Favorite Fairy Tales Ser.). (Illus.). 24p. (J). 1993. 4.98 (1-56173-917-0) Pubns Intl Ltd.

Beauty & the Beast. (Play - a - Sound Ser.). (Illus.). 24p. (J). 1993. 12.98 (0-7853-0134-8); write for info. (0-7853-0107-0) Pubns Intl Ltd.

Beauty & the Beast. (Favorite Fairy Tales Ser.). (J). 1991. 5.99 (0-517-05419-1) Random Hse Value.

*__Beauty & the Beast.__ (Little Library). 8p. (J). 1994. 4.98 (0-8317-5525-3) Smithmark.

*__Beauty & the Beast.__ Illus. by Sheilah Beckett. LC 95-14521. (Little Activity Bks.). (J). 1995. pap. write for info. (0-486-28824-2) Dover.

Beauty & the Beast. Jan Brett. LC 88-16965. (Illus.). 48p. (J). (gr. 1-7). 1989. 15.95 (0-89919-497-4, Clarion Bks) HM.

Beauty & the Beast. Jan Brett. (J). (ps-3). 1990. pap. 5.95 (0-395-55702-X, Clarion Bks) HM.

Beauty & the Beast. Jan Carr. (Illus.). 32p. (J). (ps-3). 1993. pap. 2.50 (0-590-46451-5, Cartwheel) Scholastic Inc.

Beauty & the Beast. Illus. by David Chestnutt. LC 78-54959. (Pictureback Ser.). 32p. (Orig.). (J). (gr. k-4). 1991. pap. 2.25 (0-394-83954-4) Random Bks Yng Read.

Beauty & the Beast. Fred Crump, Jr. (Illus.). 44p. (J). (gr. k-2). 1991. pap. 6.95 (1-55523-379-1) Winston-Derek.

Beauty & the Beast. David Curland. (Language-Film Study Guide Ser.). 52p. (Orig.). (gr. 9-12). 1984. pap. text ed. 4.95 (0-913349-02-X) Public Media Inc.

Beauty & the Beast. Audrey Daly. (Favorite Tales Ser.). (Illus.). 28p. (J). 1994. 2.99 (0-7214-5453-4) Ladybird Bks.

Beauty & the Beast. Patricia Daniels. LC 79-28433. (Fairy Tales Ser.). (Illus.). 24p. (J). (gr. k-5). 1980. lib. bdg. 9.95 (0-8393-0258-4) Raintree Steck-V.

Beauty & the Beast. Ret. by Patricia Daniels. LC 79-28433. (Fairy Tale Clippers Ser.). (Illus.). 24p. (J). (gr. k-5). 1981. audio, lib. bdg. 29.28 (0-8172-1833-5); audio 14.00 (0-685-09554-1) Raintree Steck-V.

Beauty & the Beast. Madame De Beaumont. (Talking Mother Goose Ser.). (Illus.). 26p. (J). (ps). 1987. Packaged with pre-programmed audio cass. tape. 9.95 (0-934323-66-6) Alchemy Comms.

*__Beauty & the Beast.__ Edens. (J). Date not set. 14.95 (0-671-75198-0, S&S Bks Young Read) S&S Childrens.

Beauty & the Beast. Illus. & Ret. by Mordicai Gerstein. 48p. (J). (ps-2). 1989. audio 17.95 (0-525-44511-0, DCB) Dutton Child Bks.

*__Beauty & the Beast.__ Golden Western Staff. (J). Date not set. pap. 1.95 (0-307-02992-1, Golden Pr) Western Pub.

Beauty & the Beast. Warren Graves. 1982. pap. 4.75 (0-8222-0100-3) Dramatists Play.

Beauty & the Beast. Illus. by Michael Hague. LC 83-5495. 80p. (J). (gr. 2-4). 1988. pap. 6.95 (0-8050-0948-5, Bks Young Read) H Holt & Co.

Beauty & the Beast. Ret. by Deborah Hautzig. LC 93-34694. (Step into Reading Bks.: Step 3). (J). 1995. 3.99 (0-679-85296-4); lib. bdg. 9.99 (0-679-95296-9) Random Bks Yng Read.

Beauty & the Beast. Illus. & Ret. by Carol Heyer. LC 89-7624. 32p. (J). (ps-3). 1989. 13.95 (0-8249-8359-9, Ideals Child) Hambleton-Hill.

Beauty & the Beast. Illus. & Ret. by Carol Heyer. 32p. (J). (ps-3). 1992. per., pap. 5.95 (0-8249-8579-6, Ideals Child) Hambleton-Hill.

Beauty & the Beast. Hannah Howell. 448p. (Orig.). 1992. pap. 4.50 (0-8439-3324-0) Dorchester Pub Co.

Beauty & the Beast. Warwick Hutton. LC 84-48441. (Illus.). 32p. (J). 1985. text ed. 14.95 (0-689-50316-4, McElderry) S&S Childrens.

*__Beauty & the Beast.__ Illus. by Jaime Diaz Studios Staff. (Look & Find Ser.). 24p. (J). (gr. k-6). 1995. lib. bdg. 12.95 (1-56674-093-2) Forest Hse.

Beauty & the Beast. Marie Leprince de Beaumont. Tr. by Richard Howard. (Illus.). 48p. (J). (gr. 1-5). 1990. pap. 14.95 (0-671-70720-5, S&S Bks Young Read) S&S Childrens.

*__Beauty & the Beast.__ Little Golden Books Staff. (J). Date not set. 1.59 (0-307-00644-1, Golden Pr) Western Pub.

Beauty & the Beast. Joseph MacLeod. LC 74-30346. (Studies in Comparative Literature: No. 35). 1974. lib. bdg. 53.95 (0-8383-1884-3) M S G Haskell Hse.

Beauty & the Beast. Madame de Villeneuve. (Creative's Collection of Fairy Tales). (Illus.). 48p. (J). (gr. 4 up). 1984. lib. bdg. 13.95 (0-87191-946-X) Creative Ed.

Beauty & the Beast. Paul Mantell & Avery Hart. (X-Men Picturebacks Ser.). (Illus.). 24p. (Orig.). (J). (ps-3). 1995. pap. 2.50 (0-679-86931-X) Random Bks Yng Read.

Beauty & the Beast. Robert Mathias. (J). 1991. 4.99 (0-517-06693-9) Random Hse Value.

Beauty & the Beast. Marianna Mayer. LC 78-54679. (Illus.). 48p. (J). (gr. k up). 1984. text ed. 15.95 (0-02-765270-X, Four Winds Pr) S&S Childrens.

Beauty & the Beast. Ed McBain. 224p. 1994. mass mkt. 5.99 (0-446-60131-4) Warner Bks.

Beauty & the Beast. Ed McBain, pseud. 256p. 1992. mass mkt. 3.99 (1-55817-662-4, Pinnacle NY) Windsor NY.

Beauty & the Beast. Illus. by Karen Milone. LC 81-612. 32p. (J). (gr. k-4). 1981. lib. bdg. 9.79 (0-89375-464-1); pap. text ed. 2.50 (0-89375-465-X) Troll Assocs.

Beauty & the Beast. Charles Moore. LC 90-26307. (Illus.). 32p. (J). 1991. 17.95 (0-8478-1368-1) Rizzoli Intl.

Beauty & the Beast. Illus. by Burgandy Nilles & Sam Thiewes. (Favorite Fairy Tales Ser.). 24p. (J). 1993. lib. bdg. 10.95 (1-56674-061-4, HTS Bks) Forest Hse.

Beauty & the Beast. Arthur Quiller-Couch. (Illus.). 64p. 1991. 6.99 (0-517-06630-0, Pub. by Gramercy) Random Hse Value.

Beauty & the Beast. Illus. by Ruth Sanderson. 32p. (J). (ps-3). 1992. 6.95 (0-8362-4919-4) Andrews & McMeel.

*__Beauty & the Beast.__ Slate. 1995. pap. (0-7851-0102-0) Marvel Entmnt.

Beauty & the Beast. Bayard Taylor. LC 72-76930. (American Fiction Reprint Ser.). 1977. 18.95 (0-8369-7009-8) Ayer.

*__Beauty & the Beast.__ Walt Disney Company Staff. (FRE.). Date not set. pap. 9.95 (0-7859-8844-0) Fr & Eur.

Beauty & the Beast. Nancy Willard. (Illus.). (J). 1992. 19.95 (0-15-206052-9, HB Juv Bks) HarBrace.

Beauty & the Beast. abr. ed. Ed. & Intro. by Cooper Edens. LC 88-81988. (Illus.). 48p. (YA). (gr. 9-12). 1991. 14.95 (0-88138-115-2, Green Tiger S&S) S&S Childrens.

Beauty & the Beast. William Glennon. 57p. 1964. reprint ed. 3.45 (0-87129-053-7, B64) Dramatic Pub.

Beauty & the Beast. Marianna Mayer. LC 87-1095. (Illus.). 48p. (J). (ps up). 1987. reprint ed. pap. 5.95 (0-689-71151-4, Aladdin Paperbacks) S&S Childrens.

Beauty & the Beast, Bk. 2. Wendy Pini. 1990. pap. 5.95 (0-915419-75-0) First Pub IL.

*__Beauty & the Beast: A Celebration of the Broadway Musical.__ Don Frantz. (Illus.). 160p. 1995. 35.00 (0-7868-6179-7) Hyperion.

An Asterisk (*) at the beginning of an entry indicates that the title is appearing in BIP for the first time.

An Asterisk (*) at the beginning of an entry indicates that the title is appearing in BIP for the first time.

647

***Beauty vs. the Beast.** M. J. Rodgers. (Intrigue Ser.). 1995. mass mkt. 3.50 (0-373-22335-8, 1-22335-3) Harlequin Bks.

Beauty Wars. Carol Conroy. 136p. 1992. pap. 9.95 (0-393-30851-0) Norton.

Beauty, Wealth, & Power: Jewels & Ornaments of Asia. Asian Art Museum of San Francisco Curatorial Staff. (Illus.). 64p. 1992. pap. 17.50 (0-295-97201-7) U of Wash Pr.

Beauty Works: How to Look Ten Years Younger. Arline Usden. 128p. (C). 1990. 59.00 (1-85283-286-X, Pub. by Boxtree Ltd UK) St Mut.

Beautyful Ones Are Not Yet Born. Ayi K. Armah. (African Writers Ser.). 183p. (Orig.). (C). 1989. pap. 9.95 (0-435-90540-6) Heinemann.

Beauty's Punishment. A. N. Roquelaure. 1984. pap. 10.95 (0-452-26662-9, Plume) NAL-Dutton.

Beauty's Release. A. N. Roquelaure. 1985. pap. 10.95 (0-452-26663-7, Plume) NAL-Dutton.

Beauvais Cathedral: Architecture of Transcendence. Stephen Murray. (Illus.). 352p. (C). 1989. text ed. 65.00 (0-691-04236-5) Princeton U Pr.

Beaux Arch Eighty-Nine: An Exposition of Recent Architecture on Long Island. Alastair Gordon. LC 89-84780. (Illus.). 120p. (Orig.). 1989. pap. 10.00 (0-685-26594-3) Hampton Day.

Beaux-Arts Architecture in New York: A Photographic Guide. Edmund V. Gillon & Henry H. Reed. (Illus.). 96p. (Orig.). 1988. pap. 8.95 (0-486-25698-7) Dover.

Beaux-Arts Medal in America: Catalogue of the Exhibition Held at the American Numismatic Society, September 26, 1987-April 16, 1988. Barbara A. Baxter. (Illus.). 92p. 1987. 25.00 (0-89722-221-0) Am Numismatic.

Beaux-Arts Tradition in French Architecture. Donald D. Egbert. Ed. by David Van Zanten. LC 79-23798. (Illus.). 220p. 1980. 65.00 (0-691-03943-7); pap. 21.95x (0-691-10106-X) Princeton U Pr.

Beaux Messieurs de Bois-Dore. George Sand. 380p. (FRE.). 1976. pap. 17.95 (0-7859-1450-1, 2226003959) Fr & Eur.

Beaux Messieurs de Bois-Dore, 2 vols. George Sand. 269p. (FRE.). 1990. pap. 24.95 (0-7859-1658-X, 2903950407) Fr & Eur.

Beaux Messieurs de Bois-Dore, 2 vols., Set. George Sand. 237p. (FRE.). 1990. pap. 24.95 (0-7859-1659-8, 2903950415) Fr & Eur.

***Beaux of Beyley Dell.** Dorothea Donley. 256p. 1995. mass mkt. 3.99 (0-8217-4913-7) Zebra.

Beaux Quartiers. Louis Aragon. (Folio Ser.: No. 241). 624p. (FRE.). 1965. pap. 13.95 (2-07-036241-8) Schoenhof.

Beaux Quartiers (Le Monde Reel) Louis Aragon. (Monde Reel Ser.). 640p. (FRE.). 1989. reprint ed. pap. 17.95 (0-7859-1714-4, 2070362418) Fr & Eur.

Beaux' Strategem. George Farquhar. Ed. by Michael Cordner. (New Mermaid Ser.). (C). 1980. pap. text ed. 6.95 (0-393-90007-X) Norton.

Beaux' Strategem. George Farquhar. Ed. by Charles N. Fifer. LC 77-89834. (Regents Restoration Drama Ser.). 181p. reprint ed. pap. 51.60 (0-8357-4104-4, 2036870) Bks Demand.

Beaux Strategem see Restoration Plays

Beauzee's Grammaire Generale: Theory & Methodology. Barrie E. Bartlett. LC 74-81133. (Janua Linguarum, Series Major: No. 82). 202p. 1975. text ed. 80.00 (90-279-3433-9) Mouton.

Beaver. Paula Z. Hogan. LC 79-13305. (Life Cycles Bks.). (Illus.). 32p. (J). (gr. 1-4). 1979. lib. bdg. 19.97 (0-8172-1502-6) Raintree Steck-V.

Beaver. Paula Z. Hogan. LC 79-13305. (Life Cycles Clippers Ser.). (Illus.). 32p. (J). (gr. 1-4). 1981. audio, lib. bdg. 29.28 (0-8172-1848-3) Raintree Steck-V.

Beaver. Margaret Lane. LC 81-67074. (Illus.). 32p. (J). (gr. k-4). 1981. 13.99 (0-8037-0624-3) Dial Bks Young.

Beaver. Margaret Lane. (Illus.). 32p. (J). (gr. k-4). 1993. pap. 4.99 (0-14-054925-0, Puff Pied Piper) Puffin Bks.

Beaver. Jerolyn Nentl. LC 83-5323. (Wildlife Habits & Habitats Ser.). (Illus.). 48p. (J). (gr. 5). 1983. text ed. 12.95 (0-89686-219-4, Crstwood Hse) Silver Burdett Pr.

Beaver. Hope Ryden. (Illus.). 64p. (J). 1992. pap. 9.95 (1-55821-142-X) Lyons & Burford.

Beaver, Reading Level 3-4. Dalmais. (World Animal Library). (Illus.). 28p. (J). (gr. 2-5). 1983. lib. bdg. 16.67 (0-86592-859-2) Rourke Corp.

Beaver at Long Pond. William T. George & Lindsay B. George. LC 87-281. (Illus.). 24p. (J). (ps-3). 1988. 14.00 (0-688-07106-6); lib. bdg. 13.88 (0-688-07107-4) Greenwillow.

Beaver Ball at the Bug Club. Mike Craver. (Illus.). 32p. (J). (ps-3). 1992. bds. 12.00 (0-374-30662-1) FS&G.

Beaver Bites Back? American Popular Culture in Canada. Ed. by David H. Flaherty & Frank E. Manning. 368p. 1993. 49.95 (0-7735-1119-9, Pub. by McGill CN); pap. 19.95 (0-7735-1120-2, Pub. by McGill CN) U of Toronto Pr.

Beaver Boys. Bonnie Pryor. LC 90-38515. (Illus.). 40p. (J). (ps up). 1992. 15.00 (0-688-08702-7); lib. bdg. 14.93 (0-688-08703-5) Morrow Jr Bks.

Beaver County Church History Data Base. Mark H. Welchley. 143p. 1993. pap. 11.00 (1-55856-139-0) Closson Pr.

Beaver County, PA Cemeteries, Vol. 1. Beaver County Research Center Staff & Closson Press Staff. 85p. 1982. pap. text ed. 11.00 (0-933227-54-X) Closson Pr.

Beaver County, PA Cemeteries, Vol. 2. Beaver County Research Center Staff & Closson Press Staff. 109p. per., pap. text ed. 11.00 (0-933227-53-1) Closson Pr.

Beaver County, PA Cemeteries, Vol. 4. Beaver County Research Center Staff & Closson Press Staff. 58p. per., pap. text ed. 11.00 (0-933227-27-2) Closson Pr.

Beaver County, PA WB Index. Bob Closson & Mary Closson. 39p. 1988. pap. text ed. 9.50 (1-55856-002-5) Closson Pr.

Beaver County, Pennsylvania Marriages 1830-1873. Mark Welchley. 99p. (Orig.). per. 11.00 (0-933227-34-5) Closson Pr.

Beaver Family Book. Sybille Kalas & Klaus Kalas. Tr. by Patricia Crampton. LC 87-13914. (Illus.). (J). (gr. k up). 1991. pap. 15.95 (0-88708-050-2, Picture Book Studio) S&S Childrens.

Beaver Gets Lost. Ariane Chottin. LC 91-40651. (Little Animal Adventures Ser.). (Illus.). 24p. (J). (ps-3). 1992. 6.99 (0-89577-419-4, Random) RD Assn.

Beaver Men: Spearheads of Empire. Mari Sandoz. LC 77-14081. (Illus.). xvi, 343p. 1978. pap. 9.95 (0-8032-5884-4, Bison Books) U of Nebr Pr.

***Beaver, PA.** Historical Briefs, Inc. Staff. Ed. by Thomas Antonucci & Michael Antonucci. 176p. 1992. pap. 14.95 (0-614-03685-2) Hist Briefs.

Beaver, PA: Argus Genealogical Gleanings, 1830-1858. Mark H. Welchley. 130p. 1986. pap. text ed. 11.00 (0-933227-49-3) Closson Pr.

Beaver Stream. Marilyn F. Holmer. LC 94-1768. (Smithsonian Wild Heritage Collection). (Illus.). 32p. (J). (gr. k-3). 1994. audio 16.95 (1-56899-060-X); audio 39.95 (1-56899-062-6); audio 25.95 (1-56899-061-8); audio write for info. (1-56899-063-4) Soundprints.

Beaver Stream. Marilyn F. Holmer. LC 94-1768. (Smithsonian Wild Heritage Collection). (Illus.). 32p. (J). (gr. k-3). 1994. 11.95 (1-56899-059-6) Soundprints.

Beaver Tails & Dorsal Fins: Wild Meat Recipes. rev. ed. G. Lamont Burley. (Illus.). 55p. 1984. pap. 6.00 (0-9615949-0-X) Beaver Tails.

Beaver Towers. large type ed. Nigel Hinton. (Illus.). (J). (gr. 1-8). 1994. 16.95 (0-7451-2224-8, Galaxy Child Lrg Print) Chivers N Amer.

Beavers. Theresa Desmond. LC 94-8512. (Illus.). (J). 1995. write for info. (0-590-47083-3) Scholastic Inc.

Beavers. Emilie U. Lepthien. LC 92-14909. (New True Book Ser.). (Illus.). 48p. (J). (gr. k-4). 1992. lib. bdg. 12.90 (0-516-01131-6) Childrens.

Beavers. Emilie U. Lepthien. (New True Bks.). (Illus.). 48p. (J). (gr. k-4). 1993. pap. 4.95 (0-516-41131-4) Childrens.

Beavers. Peter Murray. (Nature Books Ser.). (J). (gr. 2-6). 1992. lib. bdg. 22.79 (0-89565-844-5) Childs World.

Beavers. Lynn Stone. (North American Animal Discovery Library). (Illus.). 24p. (J). (gr. k-5). 1990. lib. bdg. 11.94 (0-86593-041-4); lib. bdg. 8.95 (0-685-36338-4) Rourke Corp.

Beavers Beware! (J). 1992. pap. 3.99 (0-553-35386-1) Bantam.

Beavers, Water, Wildlife & History. Earl L. Hilfiker. LC 90-12698. (Illus.). 198p. 1991. 24.95 (1-55787-067-5, NY73069, Windswept Books); pap. 14.95 (1-55787-068-3, NY73070, Windswept Books) Hrt of the Lakes.

Beaversprite: My Years Building an Animal Sanctuary. 2nd ed. Dorothy Richards & Hope S. Buyukmichi. LC 77-24150. (Illus.). 192p. 1984. 14.95 (0-932334-66-0, NY73053); pap. 9.95 (0-932334-67-9, NY73054) Hrt of the Lakes.

Beavis & Butt-Head: Greatest Hits. Mike Lackey. 96p. 1994. pap. 12.95 (0-7851-0030-X) Marvel Entmnt.

***Beavis & Butt-Head No. 2: Trashcan Edition.** Mike Lackey. 96p. 1994. pap. 12.95 (0-7851-0048-2) Marvel Entmnt.

***Beavis & Butt-Head No. 3: Holidazed & Confused.** Guy M. Graham. 96p. 1995. pap. 12.95 (0-7851-0069-5) Marvel Entmnt.

Beavis & Butthead Tips That Don't Suck. 1994. pap. 9.95 (1-56686-194-2) Brady Compu Bks.

Beazley Addenda: Additional References to ABV, ARV2 & Paralipomena. 2nd ed. Ed. by Thomas H. Carpenter. (British Academy Ser.). 536p. 1989. 85.00 (0-19-726069-1) OUP.

Beazley & Oxford. Ed. by Donna Kurtz. (Illus.). 1986. pap. 9.95 (0-947816-10-0, Pub. by Univ Comm Archeology UK) David Brown.

Bebe Daisy Sal a Pasar. (SPA.). (J). (ps-3). 1993. pap. 2.95 (0-307-96095-1, Golden Pr) Western Pub.

Bebe de los Osos Berenstain: (The Berenstain Bears' New Baby) Stan Berenstain & Janice Berenstain. Tr. by Pilar De Cuenca & Ines Alvarez. LC 81-12193. (Bilingual Picturebacks Ser.). (Illus.). 32p. (Orig.). (SPA.). (J). (ps-3). 1982. pap. 2.50 (0-394-85144-7) Random Bks Yng Read.

Bebe de los Osos Berenstain: (The Berenstain Bears' New Baby) Stan Berenstain & Janice Berenstain. Tr. by Pilar De Cuenca & Ines Alvarez. LC 81-12193. (Bilingual Picturebacks Ser.). (Illus.). 32p. (Orig.). (SPA.). (J). (ps-3). 1982. lib. bdg. 5.99 (0-394-95144-1) Random Bks Yng Read.

Bebe Donald en el Parque. (SPA.). (J). (ps-3). 1993. pap. 2.95 (0-307-96096-X, Golden Pr) Western Pub.

Bebe Donald Juega en Grupo. (SPA.). (J). (ps-3). 1993. pap. 4.95 (0-307-72316-X, Golden Pr) Western Pub.

Bebe Mickey - Juega a Las Escondillas. (SPA.). (J). (ps-3). 1993. pap. 2.95 (0-307-96097-8, Golden Pr) Western Pub.

Beber en Supropio Pozo: En el Itinerario Espiritual de un Pueblo see We Drink from Our Own Wells: The Spiritual Journey of a People

***Bebo & the Band.** Manuel P. Garcia. 77p. 1993. pap. text ed. 4.95 (1-885901-05-4) Presbyters Peartree.

Bebop: The Music & Its Players. Thomas Owens. LC 93-32504. (Illus.). 336p. 1995. 25.00 (0-19-505287-0) OUP.

Bebop in Nothingness. Francis Davis. 1995. text ed. 25.00 (0-02-870471-1) Schirmer Bks.

Bebop Revolution in Words & Music. Ed. by Dave Oliphant. (Illus.). 227p. 1994. pap. 20.00 (0-87959-131-5) U of Tex H Ransom Ctr.

***Bebop to the Boolean Boogie: An Unconventional Guide to Electronics Fundamentals, Components & Processes.** Clive Maxfield. 460p. 1995. pap. 35.00 (1-878707-22-1) HighText.

Becalmed. Joris-Karl Huysmans. Tr. by Terry Hale. 128p. (Orig.). 1993. pap. 13.99 (0-947757-30-9) Serpents Tail.

Becalmed in the Mullet Latitudes: Al Burt's Florida. Al Burt. Ed. by Val Martin. LC 83-81677. 350p. (Orig.). 1983. pap. 10.95 (0-912451-10-6) Florida Classics.

Because. Gary Geiser. LC 88-50833. (Illus.). 72p. (J). (gr. 3-5). 1988. pap. 6.95 (1-55523-164-0) Winston-Derek.

Because a Little Bug Went Ka-Choo! Rosetta Stone. LC 75-1605. (Illus.). 48p. (J). (gr. k-3). 1975. 6.95 (0-394-83130-6) Beginner.

Because God Loves Us. Susan Bachman. 1988. pap. 2.75 (0-89137-056-0) Quality Pubns.

Because God Said So. (Bible Adventure Bks.). (J). (gr. 4-6). 1990. 1.55 (0-89636-114-4, JB 3B) Accent CO.

Because I Am Human. Leo F. Buscaglia. LC 72-92809. 72p. 1972. 5.95 (0-913590-06-1) SLACK Inc.

***Because I Can't Do Standup.** Lynda H. Miller. 60p. 1995. pap. 7.95 (1-56901-700-X) NW Pub.

Because I Care. Bill Gillespie. 24p. (Orig.). (J). 1985. pap. 5.95 (0-940859-01-7) Snd Dollar Pub.

Because I Care. large type ed. Joan Mandover. (Linford Romance Library). 1990. pap. 12.95 (0-7089-6823-6) Ulverscroft.

Because I Live Here: The Theory & Practice of Vita-Erg Ward Therapy with Deteriorated Psychotic Women. S. R. Slavson. LC 70-125477. 374p. 1970. text ed. 42.50 (0-8236-0490-X) Intl Univs Pr.

***Because I Love You.** Hap Corbett. 160p. Date not set. pap. 7.95 (0-7610-0247-2) NW Pub.

***Because I Love You.** Patricia E. Leach. 193p. 1994. 19.95 (0-9642323-0-8) Garnet Hse Pub.

Because I Love You. Comp. by Anna E. Mack. LC 77-121931. (Granger Index Reprint Ser.). 1977. 19.95 (0-8369-6172-2) Ayer.

Because I Love You. Lee Witte. 147p. (Orig.). 1993. pap. 26.95 (1-880994-13-5) Mt Olive Coll Pr.

Because I Was Flesh. Edward Dahlberg. LC 64-10079. 1964. 9.95 (0-8112-0029-9, NDP227) New Directions.

Because I'm the Mother, That's Why: Mostly True Confessions of Modern Motherhood. Stephanie Pierson. LC 93-5917. (Illus.). 1994. 16.95 (0-385-31096-X) Delacorte.

Because It Is Bitter, & Because It Is My Heart. Joyce Carol Oates. 416p. 1991. pap. 11.95 (0-452-26581-9, Plume) NAL-Dutton.

Because Love Welcomed Me. Jackina Stark. LC 91-77276. 165p. (Orig.). 1992. pap. text ed. 6.99 (0-89900-408-3) College Pr Pub.

Because of August. Joe E. Pierce. LC 81-81920. 200p. (Orig.). 1981. pap. 6.95 (0-913244-54-6) Hapi Pr.

Because of Christmas. Morcus Bach. (Illus.). 192p. 1986. pap. 8.00 (0-940581-00-0) Fellowship Spirit.

Because of Francie. Karen R. Smith. 224p. (Orig.). 1993. pap. 2.95 (1-56597-086-1, Kismet) Meteor Pub.

Because of Jesus. 2nd ed. Kenneth Hagin, Jr. 1979. 1.95 (0-89276-701-4) Hagin Ministries.

Because of Love: My Life & Art with Meher Baba. Rano Gayley. Ed. by Ann Conlon. LC 83-9845. (Illus.). 132p. 1983. 25.00 (0-913078-45-X) Sheriar Pr.

Because of Stephen. Grace L. Hill. 1976. 18.95 (0-89190-018-7) Amereon Ltd.

***Because of Stephen.** Grace L. Hill. (Grace Livingston Hill Ser.: No. 96). 200p. 1994. pap. 4.99 (0-8423-1320-6) Tyndale.

Because of Stephen. Grace L. Hill. 1976. reprint ed. lib. bdg. 18.95 (0-685-00318-3, Rivercity Pr) Amereon Ltd.

Because of Stephen. Grace L. Hill. 1990. reprint ed. lib. bdg. 17.95 (0-89968-521-8) Buccaneer Bks.

Because of the Cross. Fayne Bass & Stanley Sherman. 64p. 1993. 1.25 (0-940999-79-X, B0019) Star Bible.

Because of the Lockwoods. large type ed. Dorothy Whipple. 528p. 1983. 15.95 (0-7089-0953-1) Ulverscroft.

Because of the Sand Witches There. Mary Q. Steele. LC 75-5932. (Illus.). 192p. (J). (gr. 3-7). 1975. 11.75 (0-688-80001-7); lib. bdg. 11.88 (0-688-84001-9) Greenwillow.

Because of Their Faith: CALVAC & Religious Opposition to the Vietnam War. Mitchell K. Hall. (Columbia Studies in Contemporary American History). 264p. 1990. text ed. 39.50 (0-231-07140-X) Col U Pr.

***Because of Thomas.** Sara Tatham. LC 94-39817. (J). 1995. pap. write for info. (0-89084-794-0) Bob Jones Univ Pr.

Because of Women. M. S. Dipoko. (African Writers Ser.). 178p. 1969. pap. 8.95 (0-435-90057-9) Heinemann.

Because of You. Micki Brown. 1993. mass mkt. 4.99 (0-312-92960-9) St Martin.

Because She's My Friend. Harriet Sirof. LC 92-46426. 192p. (J). (gr. 5-9). 1993. text ed. 14.95 (0-689-31844-8, Atheneum Bks Young) S&S Childrens.

Because Somebody Prayed: Miracles in Nazarene Missions. Lorraine O. Schultz. 92p. 1994. pap. write for info. (0-8341-1522-0) Beacon Hill.

***Because the Brain Can Be Talked into Anything: Poems.** Jan Richman. LC 94-37532. 64p. 1995. text ed. 15.95 (0-8071-1993-8); pap. 8.95 (0-8071-1994-6) La State U Pr.

Because the Night. James Ellroy. 240p. 1987. mass mkt. 4.99 (0-380-70063-8) Avon.

Because the Sea Is Black: Poems. Blaga Dimitrova. Tr. by Niko Boris & Heather McHugh. LC 88-21961. (Wesleyan Poetry in Translation Ser.). 78p. 1989. pap. 10.95 (0-8195-1167-6, Wesleyan Univ Pr) U Pr of New Eng.

Because Their Hearts Were Pure: or The Secret of the Mine. Cary Morland. 1952. pap. 4.75 (0-8222-0102-X) Dramatists Play.

Because There Is Hope. large type ed. Jan Tempest. 432p. 1988. 17.95 (0-7089-1874-3) Ulverscroft.

Because They Chose the Plan of God: The Story of the Bulhoek Massacre. Robert Edgar. (History Workshop Topic Ser.: No. 1). (Illus.). 41p. (C). 1988. pap. 8.95 (0-86975-331-2, Pub. by Ravan Pr ZA) Ohio U Pr.

Because They Endured: Being a History of the Clark-Sanders Ancestors of Middle TN & Their Descendents. Ed. by Gentrace Associates Staff. LC 85-81496. (Illus.). 390p. 1986. 46.00 (0-936065-00-1); 45.00 (0-685-12046-5) Gentrace Assocs.

Because They Were Jews: A History of Antisemitism. Meyer Weinberg. LC 86-15013. (Contributions to the Study of World History Ser.: No. 4). 300p. 1986. text ed. 59.95 (0-313-25606-3, WBJ/, Greenwood Pr) Greenwood.

Because We Believe: A Session-by-Session Plan for Your Parish RCIA Using Believing in Jesus. Rick Voell & Carol Rottier. 92p. 1986. 7.95 (0-86716-074-8) St Anthony Mess Pr.

***Because We Dream.** Claire Ottenstein & Violette Newton. LC 94-70819. (Illus.). 68p. 1994. lib. bdg. 8.00 (1-878149-25-3) Counterpoint Pub.

Because We're All in This Together: The Case for a National Long Term Care Insurance Policy. Robert M. Ball & Thomas N. Bethell. (Illus.). 119p. 1989. pap. 10.00 (0-685-35416-4) Fam USA Found.

***Because We're Queers: The Life & Crimes of Kenneth Halliwell & Joe Orton.** Shepherd. Date not set. 15.00 (0-85449-090-6, Pub. by Gay Mens Pr UK) InBook.

Because You Asked Me: Inspirational Poems. Peggy Conyers. 1984. 6.95 (0-916620-74-3) Portals Pr.

Because You Listen, Lord. Barbara B. Heerema. 64p. (Orig.). 1992. per., pap. 5.95 (0-9627852-0-2) Windmill FL.

Because You Talk: Anthology of Bay Area Poets. LC 76-15563. 1976. pap. 6.95 (0-916518-06-X) Other Voices Literary Society Inc.

Because You Want to Write: A Workbook for Women. Pearlie McNeill. 238p. 1992. pap. 17.95 (1-85727-030-4, Pub. by Scarlet Pr UK) InBook.

Because You Want to Write: A Workbook for Women. Pearlie McNeill. 238p. 1993. 49.95 (1-85727-035-5) InBook.

***Because Your Clients Don't Live in a Vacuum: Treating Adults Within Family & Other Systems.** Ed. by Anne M. Christner. 1994. 49.95 (1-884937-06-3) Manisses Communs.

***Because You're Mine.** Nan Ryan. 384p. (Orig.). 1995. mass mkt. 5.50 (0-451-40595-1, Topaz) NAL-Dutton.

Because You're My Friend. Illus. by Flavia. 32p. 1993. 6.95 (0-8362-4700-0) Andrews & McMeel.

Becauseway. Wesley Burrowes. (New Abbey Theatre Ser.). 1983. pap. 2.95 (0-912262-74-5) Proscenium.

Becca: (Musical) Wendy Kesselman. 61p. (J). 1988. 6.00 (0-87602-277-8) Anchorage.

***Becca & Sue Make Two.** Sandra Haines. (Illus.). 32p. (Orig.). (J). 1995. pap. 6.99 (1-885101-15-5) Writers Pr Srv.

Becca Backward, Becca Frontward: A Book of Concept Pairs. Bruce McMillan. LC 86-7221. (Illus.). 32p. (J). (ps-1). 1986. 16.00 (0-688-06282-2); lib. bdg. 15.93 (0-688-06283-0) Lothrop.

Becca Bumbum Bunny, Vol. 3: Tails with a Moral. Sandi Z. Griffin. (YEA US Ser.). (Illus.). 28p. (J). (ps-2). 1993. write for info. (1-883838-03-7) S Z Griffin.

Becca's Independence. Judith Stafford. (Regency Romance Ser.). 1993. mass mkt. 2.99 (0-373-31197-4, 1-31197-6) Harlequin Bks.

Becca's Story. James D. Forman. LC 92-1375. 192p. (YA). (gr. 7 up). 1992. text ed. 14.95 (0-684-19332-9, C Scribner Sons Young) S&S Childrens.

Bech Is Back. John Updike. LC 82-161. (Illus.). 224p. 1982. 25.00 (0-394-52806-9) Knopf.

Bechamp Blood & Its Third Anatomical Element. reprint ed. spiral bd. 22.50 (0-7873-1163-4) Mokelumne.

Bechamp or Pasteur? A Lost Chapter in the History of Biology. E. Douglas Hume. 301p. 1989. reprint ed. spiral bd. 16.50 (0-7873-1128-6) Mokelumne.

Bechamp or Pasteur: The Myth of Pasteur's Germ Theory. E. Douglas Hume. 1991. lib. bdg. 250.00 (0-87700-928-7) Revisionist Pr.

Bechet's Disease. Ed. by Goro Inaba. 587p. 1983. 100.00 (0-86008-322-5, Pub. by U of Tokyo JA) Col U Pr.

Bechol Levavcha: With All Your Heart, 2 vols., Set. Harvey J. Fields. (Illus.). (gr. 7-9). 1977. 12.00 (0-8074-0197-8, 142611) UAHC.

Bechuanaland Protectorate. Anthony Sillery. LC 83-1756. xii, 236p. (C). 1983. reprint ed. text ed. 55.00 (0-313-23970-3, SIBE, Greenwood Pr) Greenwood.

Beck & Braithwaite's Invertebrate Zoology: A Laboratory Manual. 4th ed. Robert L. Wallace et al. 475p. (C). 1989. pap. write for info. (0-02-307763-8) Macmillan.

Becker-Shaffer's Diagnosis & Therapy of the Glaucoma. Hoskins & Stamper. 780p. 1994. 110.00 (0-8016-7726-2) Mosby Yr Bk.

Becker-Shaffers Diagnosis & Therapy of the Glaucomas. Hoskins & Kass. (Illus.). 688p. 1989. 105.00 (0-8016-2453-3) Mosby Yr Bk.

Becker the Counterfeiter. G. F. Hill. 111p. 1979. 20.00 (0-916710-52-1) Obol Intl.

Becket. Jean Anouilh. 1960. pap. 7.95 (0-399-51354-X, Perigree Bks) Berkley Pub.

Becket, Anouilh: Critical Monographs in English. 64p. 1993. pap. 32.00 (0-85261-251-6, Pub. by Univ of Glasgow UK) St Mut.

Becket ou, l'Honneur de Dieu. Jean Anouilh. (Folio Ser.: No. 191). (FRE.). 1973. pap. 8.95 (0-685-11038-9, 1716) Schoenhof.

An Asterisk (*) at the beginning of an entry indicates that the title is appearing in BIP for the first time.

Becket Ou l'Honneur De Dieu. Jean Anouilh. 160p. (FRE.). 1972. pap. 10.95 (*0-7859-1709-8*, 2070361918) Fr & Eur.

Beckett - Beckett: The Classic Study of a Modern Genius. Vivian Mercier. 256p. 1995. pap. 12.95 (*0-285-63010-5*, Pub. by Souvenir UK) Atrium Pubs.

Beckett Actor: Jack MacGowran, Beginning to End. Jordan R. Young. LC 87-22069. (Illus.). 208p. (Orig.). 1988. 24.95 (*0-940410-82-6*, Moonstone Pr) Past Times.

Beckett & Babel: An Investigation into the Status of the Bilingual Work. Brian T. Fitch. (Romance Ser.: No. 57). 256p. 1988. 35.00 (*0-8020-5778-0*) U of Toronto Pr.

Beckett & Joyce: Friendship & Fiction. Barbara R. Gluck. LC 76-50290. 225p. 1979. 32.50 (*0-8387-2060-9*) Bucknell U Pr.

Beckett & Myth: An Archetypal Approach. Mary A. Doll. 128p. 1988. 29.95x (*0-8156-2447-6*) Syracuse U Pr.

Beckett & the Voice of Species: A Study of the Prose Fiction. Eric P. Levy. 145p. 1980. 44.00 (*0-389-20004-2*, 06781) B&N Imports.

Beckett & Zen: A Study of Dilemma in the Novels of Samuel Beckett. Paul Foster. LC 88-40563. (East-West Book - Grey Ser.). 296p. (Orig.). 1989. pap. 18.95 (*0-86171-059-2*) Wisdom MA.

Beckett at Eighty: Beckett in Context. Ed. by Enoch Brater. LC 85-21523. 192p. 1986. 25.00 (*0-19-504001-5*) OUP.

Beckett in Performance. Jonathan Kalb. (Illus.). 288p. (C). 1917. pap. 18.95 (*0-521-42379-1*) Cambridge U Pr.

Beckett in Performance. Jonathan Kalb. (Illus.). (C). 1989. 54.95 (*0-521-36549-X*) Cambridge U Pr.

Beckett in the Theatre: The Author As Practical Playwright & Director. Dougald McMillan & Martha Fehsenfeld. LC 86-13813. (Illus.). 352p. 1989. pap. 19.95 (*0-7145-4151-6*) Riverrun NY.

Beckett Studies Reader, 1976-1991. Ed. by S. E. Gontarski. LC 92-39423. 240p. 1993. lib. bdg. 34.95 (*0-8130-1197-3*) U Press Fla.

Beckett Translating: Translating Beckett. Ed. by Alan W. Friedman et al. LC 86-43032. 280p. 1987. 30.00 (*0-271-00480-0*) Pa St U Pr.

Beckett's Critical Complicity: Carnival, Contestation & Tradition. Sylvie D. Henning. LC 88-15569. 240p. 1988. 26.00 (*0-8131-1664-3*) U Pr of Ky.

***Beckett's Dying Words.** Christopher Ricks. 224p. 1995. pap. 12.95 (*0-19-282407-4*) OUP.

Beckett's Dying Words: The Clarendon Lectures, 1990. Christopher Ricks. LC 92-47234. 224p. (C). 1993. 28.00 (*0-19-812358-2*) OUP.

Beckett's Fiction: In Different Words. Leslie Hill. (Cambridge Studies in French: No. 29). 224p. (C). 1990. 54.95 (*0-521-35645-8*) Cambridge U Pr.

Beckett's Game: Self & Language in the Trilogy. Jean Y. Toyama. LC 90-46468. (American University Studies: Romance Languages & Literature: Ser. II, Vol. 157). 141p. (C). 1991. text ed. 31.95 (*0-8204-1398-4*) P Lang Pubs.

Beckett's Theaters: Interpretations for Performance. Sidney Homan. LC 83-45918. (Illus.). 256p. 1984. 38.50 (*0-8387-5064-8*) Bucknell U Pr.

Beckford Don. large type ed. Richard Haley. (Dales Mystery Ser.). 267p. 1992. pap. 16.95 (*1-85389-348-X*, Pub. by Magna Print Bks) Ulverscroft.

Beckley, Descendants of Richard Beckley of Wethersfield, Conn. C. B. Sheppard. (Illus.). 406p. 1991. reprint ed. lib. bdg. 71.50 (*0-8328-1983-2*); reprint ed. pap. 61.50 (*0-8328-1984-0*) Higginson Bk Co.

Beckmann. Stephen Lackner. (Masters of Art Ser.). (Illus.). 128p. 1991. 22.95 (*0-8109-3109-5*) Abrams.

***Beckoning.** Virginia Coffman. 1994. reprint ed. lib. bdg. 20.00 (*0-7278-4661-2*) Severn Hse.

Beckoning: A Story of Love. Nora S. McNab. 261p. 1990. pap. 11.95 (*0-942323-09-2*) N Amer Heritage Pr.

Beckoning Dream. Evelyn Berckman. 18.95 (*0-88411-269-1*, Aeonian Pr) Amereon Ltd.

Beckoning Fairground: Notes of a British Exile in Lotus Land. Ian Whitcomb. 1993. pap. 11.95 (*1-879395-04-5*) CA Classics Bks.

Beckoning Flame. Jessica Hart. (Romance Ser.). 1994. mass mkt. 2.99 (*0-373-03302-8*, 1-03302-6) Harlequin Bks.

***Beckoning Ghost.** Catherine Kohman. 400p. 1995. mass mkt. 4.99 (*0-505-52039-7*) Dorchester Pub Co.

Beckoning Hands from the Near Beyond. J. C. Grumbine. 101p. 1993. spiral bd. 5.50 (*0-7873-0358-5*) Mokelumne.

Beckoning Path: Lessons of a Lifelong Garden. Photos by Ted Nierenberg. (Illus.). 108p. 1993. 35.00 (*0-89381-544-6*) Aperture.

Beckoning Shore. large type ed. E. V. Timms. 624p. 1983. 21.95 (*0-7089-1049-1*) Ulverscroft.

Beckoning the Bold. Rafe Gibbs. LC 76-16212. 266p. 1976. pap. 8.95 (*0-89301-031-6*) U of Idaho Pr.

Beckoning Trails. Emilie Loring. 1976. reprint ed. lib. bdg. 19.95 (*0-88411-351-5*, Aeonian Pr) Amereon Ltd.

Beckonings. Gwendolyn Brooks. (YA). (gr. 12). 1975. pap. 5.00 (*0-910296-37-5*) Broadside Pr.

***Beck's Theory & Principles of Pleading in Civil Actions.** 5th ed. I. Isaacs. 358p. 1982. pap. 139.00 (*0-409-01236-X*, Sa) Butterworth Legal Pubs.

Beckwith: Additional Beckwith Notes, Including Avery, Ely, Gilbert, Holmes, Lee, Smith, Southerland, Wightman & Williams Families. F. W. Beckwith. 49p. 1993. reprint ed. lib. bdg. 20.00 (*0-8328-3762-8*); reprint ed. pap. 10.00 (*0-8328-3763-6*) Higginson Bk Co.

Beckwith Notes, Nos. 1-6: Marvin Beckwith & His Wife Abigail Clark; Their Colonial Ancestors & Desc., with Some Notes on Allied Families. 378p. 1993. reprint ed. lib. bdg. 67.00 (*0-8328-3760-1*); reprint ed. pap. 57.00 (*0-8328-3761-X*) Higginson Bk Co.

Beckwiths. Paul Beckwith. 384p. 1988. reprint ed. lib. bdg. 69.50 (*0-8328-0222-0*); reprint ed. pap. 59.50 (*0-8328-0223-9*) Higginson Bk Co.

***Becky & Benny Thank God.** Howard Bogot. (Illus.). 20p. (J). 1995. write for info. (*0-88123-065-0*) Central Conf.

Becky & Her Friends. Rolando Hinojosa. LC 89-35418. (Klail City Death Trip Ser.). 160p. 1990. 9.50 (*1-55885-006-6*) Arte Publico.

Becky Blackley Songbook. Ed. by Becky Blackley. (Illus.). 36p. 1986. pap. 6.95 (*0-912827-10-6*) I A D Pubns.

***Becky, Boys, & Ballet.** Emily Costello. (Ballet School Ser.: No. 5). (J). (gr. 4-7). 1994. pap. 3.50 (*0-06-106274-X*) HarpC Child Bks.

Becky Garcia. Elspeth C. Murphy. LC 86-8877. (Apple Street Church Ser.). 108p. (J). (gr. 3-7). 1986. pap. 4.99 (*1-55513-029-1*, Chariot Bks) Chariot Family.

Becky Makes a Wish. Sean Kelly. (Shining Time Station Classics Ser.). 40p. (J). (ps-3). 1993. pap. 5.95 (*1-884336-03-5*) Qual Family.

***Becky Sharp.** Ed. by Harold Bloom. (Major Literary Characters Ser.). 224p. Date not set. 29.95 (*0-7910-0946-7*) Chelsea Hse.

***Becky Tirabassi.** Becky Tirabassi. (Today's Heroes Ser.). 96p. 1994. pap. 4.99 (*0-310-49651-9*) Zondervan.

Becky's Braces. Pamela Barrett. (J). 1993. 7.75 (*0-8062-4689-8*) Carlton.

Becky's Brainstorm. Elaine L. Schulte. LC 92-15202. (Twelve Candles Club Ser.: Bk. 1). 144p. (Orig.). (J). (gr. 3-7). 1992. pap. 4.99 (*1-55661-250-8*) Bethany Hse.

Becky's Christmas. Tasha Tudor. LC 91-61679. (Illus.). 46p. (J). (gr. 3 up). 25.00 (*0-9621753-5-8*) Jenny Wren Pr.

Becky's Island. Elizabeth Ogilvie. reprint ed. lib. bdg. 18.95 (*0-88411-326-4*, Aeonian Pr) Amereon Ltd.

Become a Bird & Fly! Michael E. Ross. LC 91-36562. (Illus.). 32p. (J). (gr. k up). 1992. lib. bdg. 15.90 (*1-56294-074-0*) Millbrook Pr.

Become a More Positive Person: Three Practical Skills to Improve Your Self Esteem. Shirley Brackett. (Illus.). 72p. 1991. pap. text ed. 10.00 (*0-9628250-0-X*) Relationship Trg.

Become a Non-Smoker. 3.00 (*0-686-40905-1*, SR11) Transitions.

Become a Non Smoker. 1985. 5.95 (*0-409-49204-3*, Pub. by Buttrwrth Can Acad CN) Buttrwrth-Heinemann.

Become a Nontaxpayer & Save. Floyd Wright. 116p. 1990. pap. write for info. (*1-881923-12-6*) Grass Val Realty.

Become a Nontaxpayer & Save. rev. ed. Floyd Wright. 205p. 1992. pap. write for info. (*1-881923-13-4*) Grass Val Realty.

Become a Successful Consultant: Manage & Market Your Skills Effectively. Raymond Hebson. 96p. 1995. 15.95 (*0-572-01500-3*, Pub. by Foulsham UK) Atrium Pubs.

Become a Super Salesperson. 3.00 (*0-686-40907-8*, SR13) Transitions.

Become a Top Consultant: How the Experts Do It. Ronald Tepper. LC 85-12066. 264p. 1987. text ed. 21.95 (*0-471-81706-6*); pap. text ed. 14.95 (*0-471-85938-9*) Wiley.

Become Like Jesus. James McKeever. 408p. 1984. write for info. (*0-86694-101-0*); pap. 6.95 (*0-86694-100-2*) Omega Pubns OR.

Become Rich & Loved. Dorutu H. Riscuta. Ed. by Elletro Productions Staff. LC 93-12862. 120p. (Orig.). 1993. pap. 6.95 (*1-56875-040-4*) R & E Pubs.

Become "Streetwise" A Woman's Guide to Personal Safety. Arthur Cohen. (Illus.). 1988. pap. text ed. 9.50 (*0-685-23074-0*) Target Consult Intl.

Become Streetwise! A Woman's Guide to Personal Safety. Arthur Cohen. (Illus.). 132p. 1993. pap. 11.95 (*0-922759-01-4*) Target Consult Intl.

***Become the Arrow.** Byron Ferguson. Ed. by Glenn Helgeland. LC 92-83909. (On Target Ser.). (Illus.). 116p. 1994. pap. 12.95 (*0-913305-09-X*) Target Comm.

***Become What You Are.** Alan Watts. LC 94-36155. (Shambhala Pocket Classics Ser.). 1995. pap. 6.00 (*1-57062-091-1*) Shambhala Pubns.

Become Younger. 2nd ed. N. W. Walker. (Illus.). 204p. 1975. pap. 5.95 (*0-89019-051-8*) Norwalk Pr.

Becoming. Blaine Yorgason & Brenton Yorgason. LC 86-70295. xiv, 162p. 1986. pap. 8.95 (*0-87579-643-5*) Deseret Bk.

***Becoming.** Charlotte V. Allen. 1994. reprint ed. lib. bdg. 20.00 (*0-7278-4659-0*) Severn Hse.

Becoming: Basic Considerations for a Psychology of Personality. Gordon W. Allport. (Terry Lecture Ser.). (C). 1960. pap. 9.00 (*0-300-00002-2*, Y20) Yale U Pr.

Becoming a Basketball Player: Individual Drills. Hal Wissel. (Illus.). 119p. 1990. pap. 14.95 (*1-878915-00-2*) Basketball World.

Becoming a Better Friend. Melodie M. Davis. LC 88-19455. 160p. (Orig.). 1988. pap. 6.99 (*1-55661-001-7*) Bethany Hse.

Becoming a Better Grandparent: Strengthening the Family. Robert D. Strom & Shirley Strom. (Grandparent Education Project Ser.). 104p. (C). 1991. pap. text ed. 19.95 (*0-8039-4508-6*) Sage.

Becoming a Better Grandparent: Viewpoints on Strengthening the Family. Robert D. Strom & Shirley K. Strom. (Grandparent Education Project Ser.). 180p. (C). 1991. pap. text ed. 19.95 (*0-8039-4509-4*) Sage.

Becoming a Brother: A Child Learns about Life, Family & Self. Morton J. Mendelson. (Illus.). 272p. 1993. pap. 9.95x (*0-262-63146-6*) MIT Pr.

Becoming a Care Supervisor. Clive Curtis & Jane Metcalf. LC 92-34226. (Skills for Caring Ser.). 1992. 12.00 (*0-443-04621-2*) Churchill.

Becoming a Catechist: Ways to Outfox Teenage Skepticism. William J. O'Malley. LC 92-14192. 208p. 1992. pap. 9.95 (*0-8091-3323-7*) Paulist Pr.

Becoming a Catholic Christian. Ed. by William J. Reedy. 198p. pap. 10.80 (*0-8215-9326-9*) Sadlier.

Becoming a Catholic Christian: A Pilgrim's Guide to the Rite of Christian Initiation of Adults. Julia Upton. 88p. (Orig.). 1993. pap. 9.95 (*1-56929-003-2*) Pastoral Pr.

Becoming a Celestial Person in a Telestial World. Allan Burgess. 9.95 (*0-88494-752-1*) Bookcraft Inc.

Becoming a Chef. A. Dornenburg. 1993. pap. 29.95 (*0-442-01513-5*) Van Nos Reinhold.

Becoming a Christian. Harold Odor & Ruth Odor. (Illus.). 16p. (J). (gr. 3-7). 1985. 0.99 (*0-87239-901-X*, 3301) Standard Pub.

Becoming a Christian Person. Robert E. Lauder. 124p. (Orig.). 1984. pap. 6.95 (*0-914544-58-6*) Living Flame Pr.

Becoming a Citizen: Adopting a New Home. Fred Bratman. LC 92-24061. (Good Citizenship Library). (Illus.). 48p. (J). (gr. 5-6). 1992. lib. bdg. 22.13 (*0-8114-7354-6*) Raintree Steck-V.

Becoming a Civilian Family. Ralph Blanchard. (Family Forum Library). 16p. 1994. 1.95 (*1-56688-164-1*) Bur For At-Risk.

Becoming a Clinical Psychologist. Robert H. Woody & Malcolm H. Robertson. 343p. 1988. 47.50 (*0-8236-0491-8*, BN#00491) Intl Univs Pr.

Becoming a Computer Animator with CD-ROM. Mike Morrison. 1994. pap. 39.99 (*0-672-30463-5*) Sams.

Becoming a Computer Artist. Chad M. Little. 1994. disk, pap. 39.95 (*0-672-30397-3*) Sams.

Becoming a Computer Musician. Jeffrey H. Bowen. (Illus.). 400p. (Orig.). 1994. Incl. CD-ROM. pap. 38.00 (*0-672-30513-5*) Sams.

Becoming a Constant Object in Psychotherapy with the Borderline Patient. Charles Cohen & Vance Sherwood. LC 90-14556. 336p. 1991. 45.00x (*0-87668-613-7*) Aronson.

Becoming a Contagious Christian. 2nd abr. rev. ed. Bill Hybels & Mark Mittelberg. 240p. 1994. 18.99 (*0-310-48500-2*) Zondervan.

Becoming a Courageous Manager: Overcoming Career Problems of New Managers. Ross A. Webber. 1991. boxed 24.95 (*0-13-086372-6*) P-H.

Becoming a Critical Teacher Through Reflection & Research. Leonard Kochendorfer. LC 93-23714. (Interactive Resources Ser.). 1994. write for info. (*0-8106-3352-3*) NEA.

Becoming a Critical Thinker: A User-Friendly Manual. Sherry Diestler. LC 92-40153. (Illus.). 250p. (Orig.). (C). 1994. pap. write for info. (*0-02-328772-1*) Macmillan.

***Becoming a Critically Reflective Teacher.** Stephen Brookfield. LC 95-12699. (Higher & Adult Education Ser.). 1995. 31.95 (*0-7879-0131-8*) Jossey-Bass.

Becoming a Designer: Leading Design Professionals Talk Candidly about What It Takes to Get Started & Succeed As a Graphic Designer. Mark Isaacson. Ed. by Karen Buffenbarger. LC 89-82320. 102p. (C). 1989. pap. text ed. 16.95 (*0-9622576-0-5*) Impact Studio.

Becoming a Disciple of Christ: A Monk of Marmion Abbey. 1984. pap. 8.95 (*0-87193-195-8*) Dimension Bks.

Becoming a Doctor: A Journey of Initiation in Medical School. Melvin Konner. 412p. 1988. pap. 12.95 (*0-14-011116-6*, Penguin Bks) Viking Penguin.

Becoming a Dynamic Youth Leader: A Guide for Equipping Volunteer Youth Workers. Larry Maxwell. Ed. by Cindy G. Spear. 208p. (Orig.). 1993. pap. 9.95 (*0-941005-88-7*) Chrch Grwth VA.

Becoming a Family Physician. Ed. by M. Little et al. (Illus.). 288p. 1989. 54.00 (*0-387-96949-7*, 2588) Spr-Verlag.

Becoming a Family Therapist: Developing an Integrated Approach to Working with Families. Charles H. Kramer. LC 80-11322. 322p. 1980. 34.95 (*0-87705-470-3*) Human Sci Pr.

Becoming a Father. Charles Lewis. LC 86-2635. 192p. 1986. 90.00 (*0-335-15128-0*, Open Univ Pr); pap. 32.00 (*0-335-15127-2*, Open Univ Pr) Taylor & Francis.

***Becoming a Father.** Ed. by Jerrold L. Shapiro et al. LC 94-39952. (Focus on Men Ser.). 384p. 1995. write for info. (*0-8261-8400-6*) Springer Pub.

Becoming a Father: How to Nurture & Enjoy Your Family. William Sears. (Growing Family Ser.). (Illus.). 242p. 1986. pap. 8.95 (*0-912500-21-2*) La Leche.

Becoming a French Aristocrat: The Education of the Court Nobility, 1580-1715. Mark Motley. 262p. (C). 1990. text ed. 45.00 (*0-691-05547-5*) Princeton U Pr.

***Becoming a Friend to the Creation: Earthcare Leaven for Friends & Friends' Meetings.** Ed. by Lisa L. Gould. (Illus.). 130p. (Orig.). 1994. pap. 12.00 (*1-881083-01-2*) Fr Comm Unity.

Becoming a Friend with an International Student. 1990. write for info. (*0-318-68801-8*) Intl Students Inc.

Becoming a Friendly Helper: A Handbook for Student Facilitators. Robert D. Myrick & Robert P. Bowman. Ed. by Don L. Sorenson. LC 81-82899. (Illus.). 120p. (Orig.). (gr. 5-6). 1981. pap. 5.95 (*0-932796-08-7*) Ed Media Corp.

Becoming a Fundraiser: The Principles & Practice of Library Development. Victoria Steele & Stephen D. Elder. LC 92-11940. 139p. (C). 1992. pap. text ed. 25.00 (*0-8389-0589-7*) ALA.

Becoming a Giving Church. Herbert Mather. LC 85-72879. 56p. (Orig.). 1985. pap. 4.95 (*0-88177-023-X*, DR023) Discipleship Res.

Becoming a Good Doctor: The Place of Virtue & Character in Medical Ethics. James F. Drane. LC 88-61721. 226p. (Orig.). 1988. pap. 14.95 (*1-55612-209-8*) Sheed & Ward MO.

Becoming a Great Moose Hunter. Richard Hackenberg. (Illus.). 112p. (Orig.). 1988. pap. 8.95 (*0-936608-74-9*) F Amato Pubns.

Becoming a Helper. 2nd ed. Gerald Corey & Marianne Corey. 365p. (Orig.). (C). 1993. pap. 28.95 (*0-534-19440-0*) Brooks-Cole.

Becoming a Heroine: Reading about Women in Novels. Rachel M. Brownstein. 1994. pap. 14.95 (*0-231-10000-0*) Col U Pr.

***Becoming a Heroine: Reading about Women in Novels.** Rachel M. Brownstein. (Gender & Culture Ser.). 1994. write for info. (*0-231-00000-6*) Col U Pr.

Becoming a Historian: A Survival Manual for Women & Men, 1991. rev. ed. Melanie Gustafson. 108p. 1991. 8.00 (*0-87229-047-6*) Am Hist Assn.

Becoming a Jew. Maurice Lamm. 500p. 1991. 25.00 (*0-8246-0350-8*) Jonathan David.

Becoming a Kwoma: Teaching & Learning in a New Guinea Tribe. John W. Whiting. LC 75-35163. reprint ed. 20.50 (*0-404-14178-1*) AMS Pr.

Becoming a Lawyer: A Humanistic Perspective on Legal Education, Professionalism. Elizabeth Dvorkin et al. LC 80-6225. 211p. (C). 1993. reprint ed. pap. text ed. 17.50 (*0-8299-2126-5*) West Pub.

Becoming a Lawyer: Individual Choice & Responsibility in the Practice of Law, Teacher's Manual to Accompany. Howard Lesnick. (American Casebook Ser.). 100p. (C). 1992. pap. text ed. write for info. (*0-314-01332-6*) West Pub.

Becoming a Learning Organization. J. Swieringa & A. F. Wierdsma. LC 92-33912. (C). 1993. pap. text ed. 23.75 (*0-201-62753-1*) Addison-Wesley.

Becoming a Man: A Celebration of Sexuality, Responsibility & the Christian Young Man. Donald Joy. Ed. by Ron Durham. LC 90-44045. 120p. (Orig.). 1990. pap. 7.99 (*0-8307-1392-1*, 5419943) Regal.

Becoming a Man: Basic Information, Guidance, & Attitudes on Sex for Boys. William J. Bausch. LC 87-51569. 324p. (Orig.). (YA). (gr. 5-12). 1988. pap. 9.95 (*0-89622-357-4*) Twenty-Third.

Becoming a Man: Half a Life Story. Monette. 1992. 19.95 (*0-15-111519-2*) HarBrace.

Becoming a Man: Half a Life Story. Paul Monette. LC 92-54661. 288p. 1993. reprint ed. pap. 12.00 (*0-06-250724-9*) Harper SF.

Becoming a Manager: How New Managers Master the Challenges of Leadership. Linda A. Hill. 336p. 1993. pap. 12.00 (*0-14-017920-8*, Penguin Bks) Viking Penguin.

Becoming a Manager: Mastery of a New Identity. Linda A. Hill. LC 91-40612. 352p. 1992. 22.95 (*0-87584-302-6*) Harvard Busn.

Becoming a Manager: Mastery of New Identity. Linda A. Hill. 1992. text ed. 22.95 (*0-07-103313-0*) McGraw.

Becoming a Marihuana User. Howard S. Becker. (Reprint Series in Sociology). (C). 1993. reprint ed. pap. text ed. 1.00 (*0-8290-2619-3*, S-9) Irvington.

Becoming a Master Counselor: Introduction to the Profession. Richard H. Byrne. LC 94-19530. 1995. text ed. 49.95 (*0-534-25110-2*) Brooks-Cole.

Becoming a Master Manager: A Competency Framework. Robert E. Quinn et al. Ed. by Michael P. Thompson & Michael R. McGrath. 345p. 1990. Net. pap. text ed. write for info. (*0-471-51577-9*) Wiley.

Becoming a Master Student. 5th ed. David B. Ellis. LC 85-61906. (Illus.). 344p. 1986. pap. 19.95 (*0-942456-06-8*) Breakthrgh Enter.

Becoming a Master Student. 5th suppl. ed. David B. Ellis. LC 85-61906. (Illus.). 135p. 1986. 7.35 (*0-942456-08-4*) Breakthrgh Enter.

Becoming a Master Student. 6th ed. David B. Ellis. LC 91-70102. (Illus.). 350p. (C). 1991. pap. text ed. 19.95 (*0-942456-10-6*) Breakthrgh Enter.

***Becoming a Master Student, 7 Vols.** 7th ed. David B. Ellis. 384p. (C). 1993. pap. 25.96 (*0-395-69293-8*) HM.

Becoming a Master Student Course Manual. David B. Ellis. LC 85-61906. (Illus.). 200p. 1985. 38.00 (*0-942456-07-6*) Breakthrgh Enter.

Becoming a Mental Math Wizard. Jerry Lucas. LC 91-19472. (Illus.). 192p. (Orig.). (YA). (gr. 12 up). 1991. pap. 8.95 (*1-55870-216-4*) Shoe Tree Pr.

Becoming a Midwife. Carolyn Steiger. (Illus.). 188p. (Orig.). (C). 1987. per., pap. text ed. 24.95 (*0-9619239-0-3*) Hoogan Hse.

Becoming a Mighty Voice: Conflict & Change in the United Furniture Workers of America. Daniel B. Cornfield. LC 89-70192. 320p. 1990. 35.00 (*0-87154-200-5*) Russell Sage.

Becoming a Minister. Thomas C. Oden. (Classical Pastoral Care Ser.). 192p. 1994. reprint ed. pap. 10.99 (*0-8010-6763-4*) Baker Bk.

Becoming a Minister in the African Methodist Episcopal Church. Maurice Wilson. (Illus.). (Orig.). 1988. pap. write for info. (*0-929386-02-7*) AMEC Sunday Schl Union.

***Becoming a Modern Contemplative: A Psychospiritual Model for Personal Growth.** Richard B. Patterson. LC 94-37758. 106p. 1995. pap. 11.95 (*0-8294-0814-2*, Campion Bks) Loyola Univ Pr.

Becoming a Mother. T. Seidman. 1987. pap. 3.50 (*0-449-21568-7*) Fawcett.

***Becoming a Mother: Research on Maternal Role Identity from Rubin to the Present.** Ramona T. Mercer. LC 95-2601. (Focus on Women Ser.: Vol. 18). (Illus.). 352p. 1995. write for info. (*0-8261-8970-9*) Springer Pub.

Becoming a New Person: Twelve Steps to Christian Growth. Philip St. Romain. LC 83-82855. 96p. 1984. pap. 3.95 (*0-89243-200-4*) Liguori Pubns.

Becoming a Parent. Hemsoth et al. Ed. by Therese A. Zak. LC 79-18187. (Lifeworks Ser.). 1980. text ed. 13.96 (*0-07-060911-X*) McGraw.

Becoming a Person. Ed. by Martin Woodhead et al. (Child Development in Social Context Ser.). 320p. 1991. 72.00 (*0-415-05828-7*, A5454); pap. 18.95 (*0-415-05829-5*, A5458) Routledge.

An Asterisk (*) at the beginning of an entry indicates that the title is appearing in BIP for the first time.

***Becoming a Physician: Students, Medicine, & National Cultures, 1750-1945.** Thomas N. Bonner. 416p. 1995. 39.95 (*0-19-506298-1*) OUP.

Becoming a Poet. David Kalstone et al. 420p. 1991. pap. 12.95 (*0-374-52276-6*, Noonday) FS&G.

Becoming a Poet: Elizabeth Bishop with Marianne Moore & Robert Lowell. David Kalstone. 420p. 1989. 22.50 (*0-374-10960-5*) FS&G.

***Becoming a Political Pain in the Ass.** Thomas F. Metzger. (Illus.). 176p. (Orig.). 1995. pap. 12.95 (*0-931892-99-6*) B Dolphin Pub.

***Becoming a Practical Mystic: The Practice of Focused Spiritual Intent.** Jacquelyn Small. LC 95-8591. 1995. pap. 8.00 (*0-06-255274-0*, Hazelden SF) Harper SF.

***Becoming a Practical Mystic: The Practice of Focused Spiritual Intent.** Jacquelyn Small. LC 95-3415. 1995. 6.00 (*0-89486-989-2*) Hazelden.

Becoming a Principal: The Challenges of Beginning Leadership. Forrest W. Parkay & Gene E. Hall. 432p. (C). 1991. text ed. 63.00 (*0-205-13180-8*) Allyn.

Becoming a Profession: The History of Art Therapy in Britain 1940-82. Diane Waller. 240p. (C). 1991. text ed. 55.00 (*0-415-02581-8*, A5156) Routledge.

Becoming a Professional Counselor: Preparing for Certification & Comprehensive Exams. Sheri A. Wallace & Michael D. Lewis. (Illus.). 136p. (C). 1990. pap. text ed. 22.95 (*0-8039-3565-X*) Sage.

Becoming a Professional Genealogist. Nancy E. Carlberg. 250p. (Orig.). 1991. pap. 20.00 (*0-944878-13-X*) Carlberg Pr.

***Becoming a Professional Leader: Becoming a Professional Leader.** Ed. & Intro. by Johanna K. Lemlech. LC 94-29653. (Leadership Policy Reseach Ser.). (Illus.). 240p. (C). 1995. 24.95x (*0-590-49334-5*) Scholastic Inc.

Becoming a Professional Pilot. Robert Mark. LC 93-32866. 1993. text ed. 27.95 (*0-07-040485-2*) TAB Bks.

Becoming a Professional Pilot. Robert Mark. 1994. pap. 17.95 (*0-8306-4146-7*); pap. text ed. 17.95 (*0-07-040486-0*) TAB Bks.

Becoming a Psychoanalyst: A Study of Psychoanalytic Supervision. Pref. by Robert S. Wallerstein. LC 81-8337. (Monograph of the Supervision Study Group of the Committee on Psychoanalytic Education). xiii, 351p. (C). 1981. text ed. 42.50x (*0-8236-0492-6*) Intl Univs Pr.

Becoming a Psychotherapist. Jacquelin Goldman. (Illus.). 140p. 1976. 25.95x (*0-398-03497-4*) C C Thomas.

***Becoming a Psychotherapist.** Jacquelin Goldman. (Illus.). 140p. 1976. pap. 13.95 (*0-398-06354-0*) C C Thomas.

Becoming a Psychotherapist: A Clinical Primer. Rosemary M. Balsam & Alan Balsam. LC 83-24301. xxii, 338p. (C). 1984. pap. text ed. 15.95 (*0-226-03636-7*) U Ch Pr.

***Becoming a Public Relations Writer: A Writing Process Workbook for the Profession.** Ronald D. Smith. LC 95-3936. (C). 1995. pap. write for info. (*0-673-99529-1*, Harper Ref) HarpC.

Becoming a Reader: A Developmental Approach to Reading Instruction. Michael P. O'Donnell & Margo Wood. 300p. (C). 1991. pap. text ed. write for info. (*0-205-12826-2*) Allyn.

Becoming a Reader: The Experience of Fiction from Childhood to Adulthood. J. A. Appleyard. 280p. (C). 1991. 39.95 (*0-521-38364-1*) Cambridge U Pr.

Becoming a Reader: The Experience of Fiction from Childhood to Adulthood. J. A. Appleyard. 228p. (C). 1994. pap. 14.95 (*0-521-46756-X*) Cambridge U Pr.

***Becoming a Real Estate Professional.** Shawn J. Murphy. 1995. pap. 19.95 (*0-533-11243-5*) Vantage.

Becoming a Reflective Educator: How to Build a Culture of Inquiry in the Schools. John W. Brubacher et al. 160p. 1993. text ed. 38.00 (*0-8039-6094-8*); pap. text ed. 18.00 (*0-8039-6095-6*) Corwin Pr.

***Becoming a School Board Member.** Lee G. Bolman et al. 88p. 1995. pap. 15.00 (*0-8039-6224-X*) Corwin Pr.

Becoming a Scientist in Mexico: The Challenge of Creating a Scientific Community in an Underdeveloped Country. Jacqueline Fortes & Larissa A. Lomnitz. Tr. by Alan P. Hynds. LC 93-15760. (Illus.). 240p. (C). 1994. 35.00 (*0-271-01018-5*) Pa St U Pr.

Becoming a Secondary Headteacher. Julia Evetts. (Teacher Development Ser.). 124p. 1994. 60.00 (*0-304-32672-0*); pap. 17.95 (*0-304-32670-4*) Cassell.

Becoming a Secondary School Science Teacher. 5th ed. Leslie W. Trowbridge & Rodger Bybee. 512p. (C). 1990. pap. write for info. (*0-675-21166-2*, Merrill Pub Co) Macmillan.

Becoming a Self Before God: Critical Transformations. Romney M. Moseley. 1991. pap. 13.95 (*0-687-02504-4*) Abingdon.

Becoming a Sexual Person. 2nd ed. Robert T. Francoeur & Anna K. Francoeur. 768p. (C). 1990. write for info. (*0-02-339220-7*) Macmillan.

Becoming a Sexual Person. 2nd ed. Robert T. Francoeur & Anna K. Francoeur. 240p. (C). 1991. student ed, pap. write for info. (*0-02-339224-X*) Macmillan.

Becoming a Sexually Intimate Person. James R. Barbour. Ed. by Diane Parker. LC 93-24214. 250p. 1993. pap. 12.95 (*1-56875-042-0*) R & E Pubs.

Becoming a Skilled Reader. Jane Oakhill & Alan Garnham. (Illus.). 240p. 1988. pap. text ed. 21.95 (*0-631-15776-X*) Blackwell Pubs.

Becoming a Stepfamily: Patterns of Development in Remarried Families. Patricia L. Papernow. LC 93-21716. (Social & Behavioral Science Ser.). 448p. 1993. 30.95 (*1-55542-551-8*) Jossey-Bass.

Becoming a Stretcher Bearer: Lifting One Another in Times of Need with the Gifts of Encouragement & Support. Michael Slater. Ed. by Earl Roe. LC 89-38821. 198p. 1989. pap. 7.99 (*0-8307-1377-8*, 5419927) Regal.

***Becoming a Student of Teaching: Methodologies for Exploring Self & School Context.** Robert V. Bullough, Jr. & Andrew Gitlin. LC 94-28785. (Critical Education Practice Ser.: Vol. 2). 288p. 1994. 43.00 (*0-8153-0916-3*, SS853); pap. 18.95 (*0-8153-1624-0*) Garland.

Becoming a Successful Student. 2nd ed. Laraine M. Flemming & Judith Leet. LC 93-32728. (C). 1993. text ed. 20.75 (*0-673-46831-3*) HarpCollege.

***Becoming a Teacher.** Gary Borich. (Teacher's Library: No. 7). 140p. 1995. 75.00x (*0-7507-0264-8*, Falmer Pr); pap. 23.95x (*0-7507-0265-6*, Falmer Pr) Taylor & Francis.

Becoming a Teacher. Deborah Meier. (DeGarmo Lecture Ser.: No. 16). 1991. 3.00 (*0-685-51004-2*) Soc Profs Ed.

Becoming a Teacher: A Practical & Political School Survival Guide. Robin Grusko & Judy Kramer. Ed. by Warren Lewis. LC 93-5409. (Illus.). 140p. (Orig.). 1993. pap. 14.95 (*0-927516-37-3*, EDINFO Pr) ERIC-REC.

Becoming a Teacher: Accepting the Challenge of a Profession. Forrest W. Parkay & Beverly Hardcastle. 560p. 1990. text ed. 47.00 (*0-205-11910-7*, H19102); teacher ed, trans. write for info. (*0-318-66360-0*, H19110) Allyn.

Becoming a Teacher: Accepting the Challenge of a Profession. 2nd ed. Forrest W. Parkay & Beverly H. Stanford. 576p. (C). 1993. text ed. 47.00 (*0-205-13327-4*) Allyn.

***Becoming a Teacher: Accepting the Challenge of a Profession.** 3rd ed. Forrest W. Parkay & Beverly H. Stanford. LC 94-28853. 1994. text ed. write for info. (*0-205-16293-2*) Allyn.

Becoming a Teacher Leader: From Isolation to Collaboration. Lee G. Bolman & Terrence E. Deal. 96p. 1993. pap. text ed. 15.00 (*0-8039-6087-5*) Corwin Pr.

Becoming a Teacher of Young Children. 3rd ed. Margaret Lay-Dopyera. 416p. (C). 1989. text ed. 31.95 (*0-07-555547-6*) McGraw.

Becoming a Teacher of Young Children. 4th ed. Margaret Lay-Dopyera & John Dopyera. 1990. teacher ed 10.95 (*0-07-036776-0*); text ed. write for info. (*0-07-036775-2*) McGraw.

Becoming a Teacher of Young Children. 5th ed. Margaret Lay-Dopyera & John Dopyera. LC 92-14951. 1992. text ed. write for info. (*0-07-036777-9*) McGraw.

Becoming a Technical Leader: An Organic Problem-Solving Approach. Gerald M. Weinberg. LC 86-71049. (Illus.). 304p. (Orig.). 1986. pap. 30.00 (*0-932633-02-1*) Dorset Hse Pub Co.

Becoming a Thinking Christian. John B. Cobb, Jr. LC 93-14951. 144p. (Orig.). 1993. pap. 9.95 (*0-687-28752-9*) Abingdon.

Becoming a Treasured Teacher. Jody Capehart. (Orig.). 1992. pap. 7.99 (*0-89693-979-0*, Victor Books) SP Pubns.

Becoming a Vessel of Honor. Rebecca Brown. 304p. 1993. pap. 10.99 (*0-88368-322-9*) Whitaker Hse.

Becoming a Vessel of Honor - Como llegar a Ser una Vasija para Honra. Rebecca Brown. 304p. (SPA.). 1993. pap. 9.99 (*0-88368-317-2*) Whitaker Hse.

Becoming a Whole Language School: The Fair Oaks Story. Ed. by Lois B. Bird. LC 89-3094. 151p. (Orig.). (C). 1989. pap. text ed. 14.95 (*0-913461-15-6*) R Owen Pubs.

Becoming a Winner in the Classroom. Rotella & Coop. 53p. Incl. 3 cass. 34.50 (*0-88432-233-5*, S01830) Audio-Forum.

***Becoming a Woman: And Other Essays in 19th & 20th Century Feminist History.** Sally Alexander. 318p. 1995. 45.00 (*0-8147-0635-5*); pap. 17.95 (*0-8147-0636-3*) NYU Pr.

Becoming a Woman: Basic Information, Guidance, & Attitudes on Sex for Girls. Valerie R. Dillon. LC 89-52154. 160p. 1990. pap. 7.95 (*0-89622-433-3*) Twenty-Third.

Becoming a Woman of Excellence. C. Heald. 114p. 1986. pap. 6.00 (*0-89109-066-5*) NavPress.

Becoming a Woman of Freedom. Cynthia Heald. 108p. (Orig.). 1992. pap. 6.00 (*0-89109-675-2*) NavPress.

***Becoming a Woman of God: Day by Day.** Ronda De Sola Chervin & Eileen Spotts. 365p. (YA). 1995. pap. 8.95 (*1-887582-04-5*) Chiaro Oscuro Pr.

Becoming a Woman of Purpose. Cynthia Heald. 120p. (Orig.). 1994. pap. 6.00 (*0-89109-790-2*) NavPress.

Becoming a Woman of Strength: Fourteen Life Challenges for Women & the Men Who Love Them. Ruth R. Barton. LC 94-12458. 240p. 1994. pap. 9.99 (*0-87788-063-8*) Shaw Pubs.

Becoming a Woman Through Romance. Linda K. Christian-Smith. 256p. 1990. 42.50 (*0-415-90103-0*, A3105, Routledge NY); pap. 14.95 (*0-415-90104-9*, A3109, Routledge NY) Routledge.

Becoming a Worker. Kathryn M. Borman & Jane Reisman. LC 86-1083. 296p. 1986. text ed. 39.50 (*0-89391-314-6*) Ablex Pub.

Becoming a Writer. Dorothea Brande. LC 80-53146. 192p. 1981. pap. 7.95 (*0-87477-164-1*) J P Tarcher.

Becoming a Writer: Developing Academic Writing Skills. R. Wong et al. (Illus.). 1987. pap. text ed. 13.95 (*0-582-90722-5*, 75235) Longman.

Becoming a Zion People. Lindon Robison. Tr. by Ingram. 1992. pap. 6.95 (*1-880416-22-0*) NW Pub.

Becoming Adult, Becoming Christian: Adult Development & Christian Faith. James W. Fowler. LC 83-48987. 144p. 1984. 18.00 (*0-06-062841-3*) Harper SF.

Becoming Alcoholic: Alcoholics Anonymous & the Reality of Alcoholism. David R. Rudy. LC 85-11750. 192p. 1986. 19.95 (*0-8093-1244-1*); pap. 12.95 (*0-8093-1245-X*) S Ill U Pr.

Becoming Alien. Rebecca Ore. 1989. pap. 3.95 (*0-8125-0313-9*) Tor Bks.

Becoming American: An Ethnic History. Thomas J. Archdeacon. LC 82-48691. 320p. 1984. 19.95 (*0-02-900830-1*); pap. 13.95 (*0-02-900980-4*) Free Pr.

Becoming American: The Early Arab Immigrant Experience. Alixa Naff. LC 92-33848. 392p. 1993. pap. 16.95 (*0-8093-1896-2*) S Ill U Pr.

Becoming American Women: Clothing & the Jewish Immigrant Experience. Barbara A. Schreier. LC 93-40708. 1994. pap. write for info. (*0-913820-19-9*) Chicago Hist.

Becoming Americans: Asian Sojourners, Immigrants & Refugees in the Western United States. Tricia Knoll. LC 82-4539. (Illus.). 354p. 1982. 22.50 (*0-9602664-3-7*) Coast to Coast.

***Becoming an "A" Student.** Harriet Whyte. 176p. (C). 1994. per., pap. text ed. 25.95 (*0-8403-9730-5*) Kendall-Hunt.

Becoming an "A" Student. 2nd ed. Harriet L. Whyte. 176p. 1991. per. 25.95 (*0-8403-7144-6*) Kendall-Hunt.

***Becoming an Academic Writer: A Modern Rhetoric.** Joseph M. Moxley. 384p. 1994. pap. text ed. write for info. (*0-669-24496-1*) Heath.

Becoming an Achiever: A Student Guide. Carolyn Coil. (Illus.). 96p. (YA). (gr. 5 up). 1993. pap. 9.95 (*1-880505-07-X*) Pieces of Lrning.

Becoming an Adult. Gordon D. Jensen. Ed. by J. J. Head. LC 83-70599. (Carolina Biology Readers Ser.: No. 145). (Illus.). 16p. (gr. 7 up). 1984. pap. 2.75 (*0-89278-345-1*, 45-9745) Carolina Biological.

Becoming an Adult Child of an Alcoholic. Tony D. Crespi. 172p. (C). 1990. text ed. 36.95x (*0-398-05682-X*) C C Thomas.

***Becoming An Adult Child of an Alcoholic.** Tony D. Crespi. 172p. (C). 1990. pap. 19.95x (*0-398-06079-7*) C C Thomas.

Becoming an Agent: Patterns & Dynamics for Shaping Your Life. Larry Cochran & Joan Laub. 186p. 1993. 49.50 (*0-7914-1719-0*); pap. 16.95 (*0-7914-1720-4*) State U NY Pr.

Becoming an Airline Pilot. Jeff Griffin. 1990. pap. text ed. 12.95 (*0-07-155597-8*) McGraw.

Becoming an Airline Pilot. Jeff W. Griffin. 1990. pap. 12.95 (*0-8306-8449-2*) TAB Bks.

Becoming an American. Randolph N. Levy. 1993. pap. 17.95 (*0-533-10372-X*) Vantage.

***Becoming an Ascended Master: Entering Realms of Spirit.** Jeremiah. 275p. (Orig.). 1995. pap. 12.95 (*0-9639053-6-8*) Univ Truth Pr.

Becoming an Effective Classroom Manager. Bob Steere. LC 87-9907. 215p. 1988. 74.50 (*0-88706-620-8*); pap. 24.95 (*0-88706-621-6*) State U NY Pr.

Becoming an Effective Leader. Donald H. Weiss. LC 93-4119. (Successful Office Skills Ser.). 64p. 1993. 4.00 (*0-8144-7816-6*) AMACOM.

Becoming an Effective Rider: Developing Your Mind & Body for Balance & Unity. Cherry Hill. Ed. by Deborah Burns & Pam Art. LC 91-55078. (Illus.). 192p. 1991. pap. 14.95 (*0-88266-688-6*, Garden Way Pub) Storey Comm Inc.

Becoming an Effective Tutor. Lynda Myers. Ed. by Phil Gerould. LC 89-82096. (Fifty-Minute Ser.). 80p. (Orig.). 1990. pap. 9.95 (*1-56052-028-0*) Crisp Pubns.

Becoming an Entrepreneur in Your Own Setting. rev. ed. Kathy K. Helm. (Study Kit Ser.). Orig. Title: Starting a Private Practice. 50p. 1990. Incl. 2 60-min. audiocassettes. spiral bd. 70.65 (*0-88091-084-4*, 1303-SK3) Am Dietetic Assn.

Becoming an Ex: The Process of Role Exit. Helen R. F. Ebaugh. (Illus.). 272p. 1988. pap. text ed. 11.95 (*0-226-18070-0*) U Ch Pr.

***Becoming an Indispensable Employee in a Disposable World.** Neal Whitten. LC 94-40711. 272p. 1994. 19.95 (*0-89384-269-9*) Pfeiffer & Co.

Becoming an Industrialized Nation: ROC Development of Taiwan. Yuan Li Wu. LC 85-9413. 154p. 1985. text ed. 49.95 (*0-275-90238-2*, C0238, Praeger Pubs) Greenwood.

Becoming Anabaptist. J. Denny Weaver. LC 86-33650. 176p. (Orig.). 1987. pap. 14.95 (*0-8361-3434-6*) Herald Pr.

Becoming & Being Old: Sociological Approaches to Later Life. Ed. by Bill Bytheway et al. 208p. (C). 1989. 18.95 (*0-8039-8171-6*); text ed. 45.00 (*0-8039-8170-8*) Sage.

Becoming & Belonging: A Practical Design for Confirmation. Ed. by William R. Myers. LC 93-23349. 184p. 1993. pap. 12.95 (*0-8298-0942-2*) Pilgrim OH.

Becoming & Bonding: Contemporary Feminism & Popular Fiction by American Women Writers. Katherine B. Payant. LC 92-39268. (Contributions in Women's Studies: No. 134). 256p. 1993. text ed. 52.95 (*0-313-28574-8*, PWC/) Greenwood.

Becoming Assertive. Herman. 1978. pap. 33.75 (*0-442-23259-4*) Jones & Bartlett.

Becoming at Home in the World. Kenneth W. Phifer. 191p. 1992. pap. text ed. 14.95 (*0-9634955-0-X*) Castellio Pr.

Becoming Attached: Unfolding the Mystery of the Infant-Mother Bond & Its Impact on Later Life. Robert Karen. 512p. 1995. pap. 13.99 (*0-446-67101-0*) Warner Bks.

Becoming Aware: A Human Relations Workbook. 4th ed. Velma Walker & Lynn Brokaw. 464p. 1992. per. 27.95 (*0-8403-6741-4*) Kendall-Hunt.

Becoming Aware of the Logos. Georg Kuhlewind. LC 85-23126. 195p. (Orig.). 1985. pap. 9.95 (*0-940262-09-6*) Lindisfarne Pr.

***Becoming Ballet.** Jonelle Toriseva. LC 95-6299. (J). 1995. 14.00 (*0-689-80289-7*, S&S Bks Young Read) S&S Childrens.

Becoming Bamboo: Western & Eastern Explorations of the Meaning of Life. Robert E. Carter. 248p. 1992. 29.95 (*0-7735-0884-8*, Pub. by McGill CN) U of Toronto Pr.

Becoming Benjamin Franklin: The Autobiography & the Life. Ormond Seavey. LC 87-43125. 280p. 1988. lib. bdg. 27.50 (*0-271-00627-7*) Pa St U Pr.

Becoming Best Friends. Jane E. Leon. 1993. mass mkt. 4.99 (*0-425-13956-5*) Berkley Pub.

Becoming Best Friends: Building a Loving Relationship Between Your Pet & Your Child. Jane E. Leon. 1991. pap. 8.95 (*0-9625043-2-7*) Pecos Pr.

***Becoming Better Leaders: The Challenge of Improving Student Learning.** Gordon A. Donaldson, Jr. & George F. Marnik. (Illus.). 176p. 1995. 38.00 (*0-8039-6181-2*); pap. 18.00 (*0-8039-6182-0*) Corwin Pr.

Becoming Better Parents. Maurice Balson. (C). 1990. 65.00 (*0-86431-076-5*, Pub. by Aust Coun Educ Res AT) St Mut.

Becoming Bilingual: A Guide to Language Learning. Donald N. Larson & William A. Smalley. LC 84-15383. 450p. 1984. reprint ed. pap. text ed. 34.00 (*0-8191-4246-8*) U Pr of Amer.

Becoming Black American: Haitians & American Institutions in Evanston, Illinois. Tekle M. Woldemikael. LC 88-84001. (Immigrant Communities & Ethnic Minorities in the U. S. & Canada Ser.: No. 54). 1989. 47.50 (*0-404-19464-8*) AMS Pr.

Becoming Brave: The Path to Native American Manhood. Laine Thom. (Illus.). 120p. 1992. 29.95 (*0-8118-0219-1*); pap. 18.95 (*0-8118-0163-2*) Chronicle Bks.

Becoming Bread: Meditations on Loving & Transformation. Gunilla Norris. LC 92-19259. (Illus.). 96p. 1993. 15.00 (*0-517-59168-5*, Bell Tower) Crown Pub Group.

Becoming Brothers. Arthur Waskow & Howard Waskow. LC 93-16701. 250p. 1993. text ed. 22.95 (*0-02-933997-9*) Free Pr.

Becoming Browning: The Poems & Plays of Robert Browning, 1833-1846. Clyde de L. Ryals. LC 83-4140. 305p. 1983. 42.50 (*0-8142-0352-3*) Ohio St U Pr.

Becoming Canonical in American Poetry. Timothy Morris. LC 94-12411. 1995. write for info. (*0-252-02136-3*); pap. write for info. (*0-252-06428-3*) U of Ill Pr.

Becoming Catholic, Even If You Happen to Be One. Gerard Weber & James J. Killgallon. LC 79-89875. 1980. pap. 6.95 (*0-914070-13-4*, 105) ACTA Pubns.

Becoming Children of God: John's Gospel & Radical Discipleship. J. Howard-Brook. LC 94-21927. (Bible & Liberation Ser.). 480p. (Orig.). 1994. pap. 21.95 (*0-88344-983-8*) Orbis Bks.

Becoming Christian. Ed. by Bill J. Leonard. 252p. (Orig.). 1990. pap. 16.99 (*0-664-25119-6*) Westminster John Knox.

Becoming Clerical Workers. Linda Valli. (Critical Social Thought Ser.). 257p. (C). 1986. text ed. 37.50 (*0-7102-0336-5*, 03365, RKP) Routledge.

Becoming Comprehensive: Case Histories. Ed. by E. Halsall. (C). 1970. 127.00 (*0-08-015820-X*, Pub. by Pergamon Repr UK) Franklin.

Becoming Coyote. Wayne Ude. LC 80-27152. 165p. (Orig.). 1979. pap. 9.00 (*0-89924-031-3*) Lynx Hse.

Becoming Critical: Education, Knowledge & Action Research. Wilford Carr & Stephen Kemmis. 240p. 1986. pap. 32.50 (*1-85000-090-5*, Falmer Pr) Taylor & Francis.

Becoming Critical: Education, Knowledge & Action Research. Wilfred Carr & Stephen Kemmis. 249p. (C). 1990. pap. 56.00x (*0-7300-0437-6*, ECT432, Pub. by Deakin Univ AT) St Mut.

Becoming Culturally Competent in the United Kingdom. Stephen M. Hennessy & Alan Goldman. 152p. 1993. student ed 109.00 (*0-9630772-6-0*) Leader Scottsdale.

Becoming Doctors: The Professionalization of Medical Students. Jaber F. Gubrium et al. (Contemporary Ethnographic Studies). 1987. 73.25 (*0-89232-718-9*) Jai Pr.

Becoming Excellent Students Today: Academic Organizer. Linda M. Schroeder. 102p. (YA). (gr. 9-12). Date not set. pap. text ed. 6.95 (*1-883583-01-2*) Gratitude Pub.

Becoming Excellent Students Today: Assignment Planner. Linda M. Schroeder. 102p. (J). (gr. 5-8). 1993. pap. text ed. 6.95 (*1-883583-00-4*) Gratitude Pub.

Becoming Excellent Students Today: Study & Learning Improvement Program. Linda M. Schroeder. 56p. 1992. Tchr's. Manual Grade 5th-12th. teacher ed, pap. text ed. write for info. (*1-883583-03-9*) Gratitude Pub.

Becoming Female: Perspectives on Development. Ed. by Clarie B. Kopp. LC 79-9970. (Women in Context Ser.). (Illus.). 488p. 1979. 69.50 (*0-306-40229-7*, Plenum Pr) Plenum.

Becoming Financially Sound in an Unsound World. Greg Roy & Richard Caron. (Illus.). 240p. (Orig.). 1992. pap. 14.95 (*1-55870-253-9*) Betterway Bks.

Becoming Fire: Experience the Presence of Jesus Every Day. Jeanie Miley. LC 93-11922. 272p. (Orig.). 1993. pap. 9.99 (*0-8007-5479-4*) Revell.

Becoming Free: A Biblically Oriented Haggadah for Passover: The Permanent Relevance of the Ancient Lesson. Howard S. Rubenstein & Judith S. Rubenstein. LC 93-73663. 200p. (J). 1993. pap. 9.95 (*0-9638886-0-9*) Granite Hills Pr.

Becoming Free: The Struggle for Human Development. William L. Ewens. LC 84-13872. 328p. (C). 1984. 40.00 (*0-8420-2208-2*); pap. text ed. 16.95 (*0-8420-2233-3*) Scholarly Res Inc.

Becoming Friends. Jeff Johnson. (Discovering Program Ser.). (Illus.). 74p. (Orig.). 1990. teacher ed 6.00 (*0-88489-207-7*); text ed. 2.80 (*0-88489-206-9*) St Marys.

Becoming Friends, What Friends Believe. Dorothy Barratt et al. (Illus.). 78p. (J). (gr. 5-6). 1990. teacher ed 19.95 (*0-943701-16-3*) George Fox Pr.

Becoming Gershona. Nava Semel. Tr. by Seymour Simckes. LC 92-20306. 160p. (J). (gr. 5 up). 1992. reprint ed. pap. 4.50 (*0-14-036071-9*) Puffin Bks.

***Becoming God's Peacemakers.** Suella L. Gerber et al. LC 92-70568. (Illus.). 174p. (J). (gr. 3-8). 1992. pap. 29.95 (*0-87303-183-0*) Faith & Life.

An Asterisk (*) at the beginning of an entry indicates that the title is appearing in BIP for the first time.

An Asterisk (*) at the beginning of an entry indicates that the title is appearing in BIP for the first time.

Bed & Breakfast U. S. A., 1991. Betty Rundback. (Illus.). 768p. 1991. pap. 12.95 (*0-452-26571-1*, Plume) NAL-Dutton.

Bed & Breakfast U. S. A., 1992. Betty Rundback. Ed. by Peggy Ackerman. (Illus.). 720p. (Orig.). 1992. pap. 14.00 (*0-452-26747-1*, Plume) NAL-Dutton.

Bed & Breakfast U. S. A. 1993. Betty Rundback. LC 86-649303. (Illus.). 752p. (Orig.). 1993. pap. 14.00 (*0-452-26926-1*, Plume) NAL-Dutton.

***Bed & Breakfast U. S. A. 1995.** Betty Rundback & Peggy Ackerman. 784p. (Orig.). 1995. pap. 15.95 (*0-452-27369-2*, Plume) NAL-Dutton.

Bed & Breakfast Ultramanager. Janet K. Strong. 1985. 79.95 (*0-9614578-2-1*) B & B Prod.

Bed & Breakfast, 1994. Betty Rundback. (Illus.). 784p. (Orig.). 1994. pap. 13.95 (*0-452-27126-6*, Plume) NAL-Dutton.

***Bed & Breakfasts: Audit Technique Guides.** (IRS Tax Audit Information Ser.). 40p. 1994. pap. 8.50 (*1-57402-105-2*) Athena Info Mgt.

Bed & Breakfasts & Country Inns: Mid-Atlantic Region: Delightful Places to Stay & Great Things to Do When You Get There. 2nd ed. 1993. pap. 15.00 (*0-679-02562-6*) Fodors Travel.

Bed & Breakfasts & Country Inns: New England: Delightful Places to Stay & Great Things to Do When You Get There. 2nd ed. 1993. pap. 15.00 (*0-679-02563-4*) Fodors Travel.

Bed & Breakfasts & Country Inns: The Official Guide to American Historic Inns. 4th ed. Tim Sakach & Deborah Sakach. pap. 14.95 (*0-9615481-4-2*) American Hist.

Bed & Breakfasts & Country Inns - The Southwest: Delightful Places to Stay & Great Things to Do When You Get There. 1994. pap. 15.00 (*0-679-02565-0*) Fodors Travel.

Bed & Breakfasts & Country Inns & Other Weekend Pleasures: Upper Great Lakes Region. Fodor Staff. 1993. pap. 15.00 (*0-679-02354-2*) Fodors Travel.

Bed & Breakfasts & Country Inns of New England. 2nd ed. Deborah Patton. 1991. pap. 12.95 (*0-89909-225-X*, 80-650-3) Yankee Bks.

Bed & Breakfasts & Country Inns of New England. 3rd ed. Deborah Patton. LC 93-1287. (Travel Guide Ser.). (Illus.). 256p. 1993. pap. 12.95 (*0-89909-367-1*) Yankee Bks.

***Bed & Breakfasts of Montana, Wyoming, Idaho, South Dakota Directory, 1993-94.** Paula Deigert. (Illus.). 34p. (Orig.). 1993. pap. text ed. write for info. (*0-9625887-3-3*) B & B Western Ad.

Bed Bouncers. Kimberley Knutson. LC 94-14410. (J). 1995. text ed. 14.95 (*0-02-743507-5*) Macmillan.

***Bed Bouncers.** Kimberley Knutson. (Illus.). (J). (ps-3). 1995. 14.00 (*0-02-750871-4*, Mac Bks Young Read) S&S Childrens.

Bed, Breakfast & Bike - Mid-Atlantic: A Cycling Guide to Country Inns. Alex May & Nancy May. LC 92-60539. (Illus.). 256p. (Orig.). 1992. pap. 12.95 (*0-933855-06-0*) White Meadow.

Bed, Breakfast & Bike - Northern California: A Cycling Guide to Country Inns. Naomi Bloom. LC 94-60242. (Illus.). 230p. (Orig.). 1994. pap. 14.95 (*0-933855-07-9*) White Meadow.

Bed, Breakfast & Bike New England: A Cycling Guide to Country Inns. Alex May & Nancy May. LC 91-65376. (Illus.). 205p. (Orig.). 1991. pap. 12.95 (*0-933855-05-2*) White Meadow.

Bed Bugs. Taylor McCafferty. Ed. by Jane Chelius. 256p. (Orig.). 1993. mass mkt. 5.50 (*0-671-75468-8*) PB.

Bed by the Window. M. Scott Peck. 1991. pap. 12.95 (*0-553-35387-X*) Bantam.

Bed Called Home: Life in the Migrant Labor Hostels of Cape Town. Mamphela Ramphele. LC 93-19117. (Illus.). 176p. (Orig.). (C). 1993. pap. text ed. 21.95 (*0-8214-1063-6*) Ohio U Pr.

Bed for the Wind. Roger B. Goodman. 1990. pap. 4.95 (*0-671-69443-X*) S&S Trade.

Bed Hangings: A Treatise on Fabrics & Styles in the Curtaining of Beds, 1650-1850. Abbott L. Cummings. LC 94-28239. (Illus.). 74p. (C). 1994. reprint ed. pap. 13.95 (*0-87451-972-1*) U Pr of New Eng.

Bed-Knob & Broomstick. Mary Norton. 229p. (J). (gr. 3-7). 1990. pap. 3.95 (*0-15-206231-9*, Odyssey) HarBrace.

Bed-Knob & Broomstick. large type ed. Mary Norton. 296p. (J). (gr. 3-7). 1989. 14.95 (*0-8161-4786-8*, Large Print Bks) Hall.

Bed-Load Transport: Theory & Practice. K. Stelczer. LC 80-54288. 1981. 25.00 (*0-918334-39-X*) WRP.

Bed 'N Breakfast Directory, 1984-1985. 3rd ed. Gail R. Parker. 56p. 1984. pap. 3.95 (*0-910115-01-X*) PS Pubns.

Bed Number Ten. Sue Baier & Mary Z. Schomaker. 302p. 1989. pap. 15.95 (*0-8493-4270-8*, RC416) CRC Pr.

***Bed of Coals: Poems by Joe Hutchison.** Joe Hutchison. 72p. Date not set. 12.50 (*0-87081-374-9*) Univ Pr Colo.

***Bed of Honor.** Alf J. Mapp, Jr. 480p. 1995. pap. 12.95 (*1-56901-717-4*) NW Pub.

Bed of Lists. Elizabeth Robinson. Ed. by Rena Rosenwasser & Patricia Dienstfrey. LC 90-39994. 48p. (Orig.). (C). 1990. pap. text ed. 8.00 (*0-932716-25-3*) Kelsey St Pr.

***Bed of Roses.** Suzanne Simmons. 384p. (Orig.). 1995. mass mkt. 4.99 (*0-451-40519-6*, Topaz) NAL-Dutton.

Bed of Roses: Premier. Elyn Day. (Silhouette Special Edition Ser.). 1993. mass mkt. 3.50 (*0-373-09846-4*, 5-09846-2) Silhouette.

Bed of Spices. Barbara Samuel. 1993. mass mkt. 4.50 (*0-06-108078-0*, Harp PBks) HarpC.

Bed-Time-Story. Jill Robinson. 272p. 1979. pap. 1.95 (*0-449-24064-9*, Crest) Fawcett.

Bed-Trick in English Renaissance Drama: Explorations in Gender, Sexuality, & Power. Marliss C. Desens. LC 92-50885. 1994. write for info. (*0-87413-476-5*) U Delaware Pr.

Bed Wetting: Cause & Correction. Stanley M. Heston. 146p. 1987. text ed. 29.95 (*0-9620473-0-9*) Med Info Internatl.

Bed-Wetting: Origins & Treatment. rev. ed. Warren B. Baller. 300p. 1975. 56.00 (*0-08-017859-6*, Pub. by Pergamon Repr UK) Franklin.

Beda Venerablis: Opera Historica, 2 vols., Set. J. Stevenson. (English Historical Society Publication Ser.: Vol. 1). 1972. reprint ed. 83.00 (*0-8115-1514-9*) Periodicals Srv.

Bedae Opera De Temporibus. Beda. Ed. by C. W. Jones. (Medieval Academy Bks.: No. 41). 1966. reprint ed. 25.00 (*0-910956-17-0*) Medieval Acad.

***Bedazzled.** Rita Rainville. (Desire Ser.). 1995. pap. 3.25 (*0-373-05918-3*, 1-05918-7) Silhouette.

Bedbug & Selected Poetry. Vladimir Mayakovsky. Ed. by Patricia Blake. Tr. by Max Hayward & George Reavey. LC 75-10805. 320p. 1975. reprint ed. pap. 12.95 (*0-253-20189-6*, MB-189) Ind U Pr.

***Bedbugs' Night Dance & Other Hopi Sexual Tales: Mumuspi'yyungqa Tuutuwutsi.** Ed. & Tr. by Ekkehart Malotki. 224p. (C). 1995. text ed. 35.00 (*0-8032-3190-3*) U of Nebr Pr.

***Bedders, Bulldogs & Bedells: A Cambridge Glossary.** Frank Stubbings. (Illus.). 136p. (C). 1995. pap. 14.95 (*0-521-47978-9*) Cambridge U Pr.

Bedding Plant Expert. D. G. Hessayon. (Expert Ser.). (Illus.). 128p. 1995. pap. 10.95 (*0-903505-34-7*, Pub. by Expert Bks UK) Sterling.

Bedding Plants. Graham Rice. (Royal Horticultural Society - Wisley Handbooks Ser.). (Illus.). 64p. 1993. pap. 5.95 (*0-304-32025-0*, Pub. by Cassell UK) Sterling.

Bedding Plants: Prolonging Shelf Performance: Postproduction Care & Handling. Allan M. Armitage. LC 92-45175. (Postproduction Ser.). (Illus.). 80p. (Orig.). (C). 1993. pap. 37.00 (*0-9626796-6-6*) Ball Pub.

Bedding Plants IV: A Manual on the Culture of Bedding Plants as a Greenhouse Crop. 4th ed. Ed. by E. Jay Holcomb. LC 94-19177. (Illus.). 452p. 1994. per., pap. 55.00 (*1-883052-05-X*) Ball Pub.

Beddy Bye. B. J. Johnson. (Teeny Poppers Ser.). (Illus.). 12p. (J). (ps). 1993. pap. 3.50 (*0-671-86533-1*, Litl Simon S&S) S&S Childrens.

Bede: On the Tabernacle. Tr. & Intro. by Arthur G. Holder. (Translated Texts for Historians Ser.). 224p. (Orig.). 1994. pap. text ed. 17.95 (*0-85323-378-0*, Pub. by Liverpool Univ Pr UK) U of Pa Pr.

Bede & His World: The Jarrow Lectures, 1958-1993. Intro. by Michael Lapidge. (Illus.). 1000p. 1994. 245.00 (*0-86078-449-5*, Pub. by Variorum UK) Ashgate Pub Co.

Bede Jarrett: Letters. 1991. write for info. (*0-318-68824-7*, Pub. by Dominican Sources UK) Parable.

Bede, the Schools, & the Computus, 2 vol. set. Charles W. Jones. Ed. by Wesley M. Stevens. LC 94-5126. (Collected Studies). 1024p. 1994. 245.00 (*0-86078-413-4*, Pub. by Variorum UK) Ashgate Pub Co.

Bede the Venerable. George H. Brown. (Twayne's English Authors Ser.). 144p. 1987. text ed. 22.95 (*0-8057-6940-4*, TEAS 443, Twayne) Macmillan.

Bede's Ecclesiastical History of the English People. rev. ed. Bede. Ed. by Bertram Colgrave & Roger Mynors. Tr. by Roger Mynors. 696p. 1993. 110.00 (*0-19-822173-8*) OUP.

Bede's Ecclesiastical History of the English People: A Historical Commentary. Ed. by J. M. Wallace-Hadrill. (Oxford Medieval Texts Ser.). 336p. 1988. pap. 75.00 (*0-19-822269-6*) OUP.

Bede's Ecclesiastical History of the English People: A Historical Commentary. J. M. Wallace-Hadrill. LC 92-38131. (Oxford Medieval Texts Ser.). 1993. pap. 14.95 (*0-19-822174-6*, Clarendon Pr) OUP.

Bede's Historia Ecclesiastica. Bede. Ed. by F. W. Garforth. (Illus.). 158p. (LAT.). (C). 1988. reprint ed. pap. 11.00 (*0-86516-218-2*) Bolchazy-Carducci.

Bedeutu ng des Entwicklungsbeqriffs fuer Menschenbild und Dichtungstheorie bei Gottfried Benn. Gerlinde F. Miller. (New York University Ottendorfer Ser.: Vol. 29). 291p. 1988. text ed. 47.80 (*0-8204-0835-2*) P Lang Pubs.

Bedeutung der Wundererzaehlungen fuer die Christologie des Markusevangeliums. Dietrich-Alex Koch. (Beiheft 42 zur Zeitschrift fuer die Neuetestamentliche Wissenschaft Ser.). 217p. (C). 1975. 119.25 (*3-11-004783-7*) De Gruyter.

Bedeutung von Anatomischen und Physiologischen Eigenschaften und Ihrer Interaktionen fuer die Trockenanpassung und Oekologische Stabilitaet bei Sukkulenten. T. Helbsing. (Dissertationes Botanicae Ser.: Vol. 138). (Illus.). 256p. (GER.). 1989. pap. text ed. 64.00 (*0-685-29612-1*, Pub. by Gebruder Borntraeger GW) Lubrecht & Cramer.

Bedeutungsworterbuch. (Duden Ser.: Vol. 10). 797p. 1985. 29.95 (*3-411-20911-9*, Pub. by Bibliogr Inst Brockhaus GW) Langenscheidt.

***Bedeviled.** Bronwyn Williams. 384p. (Orig.). 1995. pap. 4.99 (*0-451-40456-4*, Topaz) NAL-Dutton.

Bedeviled Baron. Sarah Eagle. 208p. (Orig.). 1994. pap. 3.99 (*0-515-11281-X*) Jove Pubns.

Bedford: The Commercial Vehicle for all Purposes. Leslie Geary. (Illus.). 148p. 1991. 40.00 (*0-86025-437-2*, Pub. by Ian Henry Pubns UK) Empire Pub Srvs.

***Bedford & Fulton Counties, Pennsylvania: An Inventory of Historic Engineering & Industrial Sites.** Scott Brown et al. Ed. by Kim E. Wallace. 1994. write for info. (*0-615-00067-3*) US Interior.

***Bedford Basics: A Workbook for Writers.** 2nd ed. Diana Hacker & Wanda Van Goor. 432p. 1994. pap. text ed. 12.00 (*0-312-08681-4*) St Martin.

Bedford Catalog. William Smyth. 1986. pap. 18.95 (*0-943396-10-7*) Willmann-Bell.

Bedford Connection: Varsity Sporting Goods. (Accounting Connection Ser.). (C). 1991. write for info. (*0-538-81689-9*, AB65A8H81) S-W Pub.

***Bedford Contextual Companion to Ralph Ellison's Invisible Man.** Eric Sundquist. 192p. (C). 1995. pap. text ed. 6.65 (*0-312-10081-7*, Bedford Bks) St Martin.

***Bedford County: Virginia Index to Wills from 1754 to 1830.** 16p. 1994. lib. bdg. 20.00 (*0-8095-8273-2*); pap. 5.00 (*0-8095-8511-1*) Borgo Pr.

***Bedford County: Virginia Publick Claims.** Janice L. Abercrombie & Richard Slatten. (Virginia Publick Claims Ser.). ix, 64p. 1991. pap. 8.00x (*0-8095-8512-X*) Borgo Pr.

Bedford County: Virginia Publick Claims. Janice L. Abercrombie & Richard Slatten. (Virginia Publick Claims Ser.). ix, 64p. (C). 1991. reprint ed. lib. bdg. 23.00x (*0-8095-8305-4*) Borgo Pr.

Bedford County PA: Unrecorded Bible Records. Comp. by Margaret A. Spielman. 38p. 1987. per., pap. 5.00 (*0-933227-71-X*) Closson Pr.

Bedford County, PA Archives, Vol. I. Ed. by James B. Whisker. 133p. 1985. pap. text ed. 16.00 (*0-933227-12-4*) Closson Pr.

Bedford County, PA Archives, Vol. II. Ed. by James B. Whisker. 1985. pap. text ed. 16.00 (*0-933227-17-5*) Closson Pr.

Bedford County, PA Archives, Vol. III. James B. Whisker. 1986. per., pap. text ed. 16.00 (*0-933227-57-4*) Closson Pr.

Bedford County, PA Archives, Vol. IV. Ed. by James B. Whisker. 127p. 1988. pap. text ed. 16.00 (*0-933227-32-9*) Closson Pr.

Bedford County, PA Archives, Vol. 7. James B. Whisker. 151p. 1994. pap. 16.00 (*1-55856-163-3*) Closson Pr.

Bedford County, PA Archives, Vol. 6: Bedford Records, Births, Marriages, & Partitions 1850-1870. Kenneth T. McFarland. 227p. 1994. pap. 16.00 (*1-55856-158-7*) Closson Pr.

Bedford County (PA) Courthouse Facility Improvement Plan. National Center for State Courts Staff. 42p. 1982. 2.52 (*0-685-15348-7*, NERO-121) Natl Ctr St Courts.

Bedford County, PA in the American Revolution. Ed. by James B. Whisker. 219p. 1985. lib. bdg. 22.00 (*0-933227-16-7*) Closson Pr.

Bedford County, Pa. Marriage Records, Oct. 1885 - April 1890. Comp. by Michael Hengst. 221p. 1989. pap. text ed. 24.95 (*1-55856-020-3*) Closson Pr.

Bedford County Pennsylvania Rifle Book. Whisker. 1985. pap. 15.00 (*0-317-15140-1*) Gun Room.

Bedford County Rifle & Its Makers. 2nd ed. Calvin Hetrick. (Illus.). 41p. 1975. pap. 10.00 (*0-87387-071-9*) Shumway.

***Bedford County, Virginia Deeds, 1761-1766.** T.L.C. Genealogy Staff. LC 91-75274. 92p. 1991. spiral bd., pap. 11.00 (*1-886633-43-6*) TLC Genealogy.

Bedford Forrest & His Critter Company. Andrew N. Lytle. 402p. (Orig.). 1984. reprint ed. 60.00 (*0-918450-16-0*) C Elder.

Bedford Forrest & His Critter Company. Andrew N. Lytle. (Southern Classics Ser.). 405p. (Orig.). 1992. reprint ed. pap. 12.95 (*1-879941-09-0*) J S Sanders.

Bedford Forrest, the Confederate's Greatest Cavalryman. Eric W. Sheppard. (Illus.). 320p. 1988. 30.00 (*0-89029-062-8*) Morningside Bkshop.

Bedford Guide for College Writers: With Reader & Research Manual. 3rd ed. X. J. Kennedy et al. LC 92-52514. 750p. (C). 1993. pap. text ed. 20.50 (*0-312-06550-7*, Bedford Bks) St Martin.

Bedford Guide for College Writers: With Reader, Research Manual, & Handbook. 3rd ed. X. J. Kennedy et al. LC 92-52526. 950p. (C). 1993. pap. text ed. 23.50 (*0-312-06549-3*, Bedford Bks) St Martin.

Bedford Guide to College. Kennedy Kennedy. 1992. pap. 14.95 (*0-312-07116-7*) St Martin.

***Bedford Guide to Teaching Writing in the Disciplines: An Instructor's Desk Reference.** Rebecca M. Howard & Sandra Jamieson. 304p. 1994. pap. text ed. 8.00 (*0-312-10666-1*, Bedford Bks) St Martin.

Bedford Guide to the Research Process. 2nd ed. Jean Johnson. LC 90-71611. 432p. (C). 1991. pap. text ed. 10.00 (*0-312-03466-0*) St Martin.

***Bedford Handbook for Writers.** 4th ed. Diana Hacker. 800p. 1994. pap. text ed. 16.50 (*0-312-07529-4*); pap. text ed. 18.00 (*0-312-07530-8*) St Martin.

Bedford Hours. Jane Backhouse. (Medieval Manuscripts from the British Library). (Illus.). 64p. (Orig.). 1991. pap. 18.95 (*1-56131-021-2*) New Amsterdam Bks.

Bedford Introduction to Drama. 2nd ed. Lee A. Jacobus. LC 92-52513. (Illus.). 1435p. (Orig.). (C). 1992. pap. text ed. 28.00 (*0-312-06655-4*, Bedford Bks) St Martin.

Bedford Introduction to Literature. Michael Meyer. 1992. 19.95 (*0-312-07115-9*) St Martin.

Bedford Introduction to Literature. 3rd ed. Michael Meyer. LC 92-52518. 2122p. (C). 1993. pap. text ed. 28.00 (*0-312-06546-9*, Bedford Bks) St Martin.

Bedford Introduction to Literature. 3rd ed. Michael Meyer. LC 92-52518. 2122p. (C). 1993. pap. text ed. 8.50 (*0-312-07833-1*, Bedford Bks) St Martin.

Bedford Reader. 4th ed. X. J. Kennedy et al. LC 89-63907. 864p. (C). 1991. pap. text ed. 0.72 (*0-312-03586-1*, Bedford Bks) St Martin.

***Bedford Reader.** 5th ed. X. J. Kennedy et al. 784p. 1994. pap. text ed. 18.00 (*0-312-08637-7*) St Martin.

Bedford Row. large type ed. Claire Rayner. (Orig.). 1991. 21.95 (*0-7089-2557-X*) Ulverscroft.

Bedford Square: An Architectural Study. Andrew Byrne. LC 89-48598. (Illus.). 160p. (C). 1990. text ed. 70.00 (*0-485-11386-4*, Pub. by Athlone Pr UK) Humanities.

Bedford to Berlin & Beyond: QL: the Forces Favorite 4x4. Robert Coates. (Illus.). 112p. 1994. 29.95 (*0-948358-05-X*, Pub. by Motor Racing UK) Motorbooks Intl.

Bedfordshire Family of Laces. Jennifer Fisher. (Illus.). 144p. 1991. 24.95 (*0-86417-328-8*, Pub. by Kangaroo Pr AT) Seven Hills Bk.

Bedfordshire Lace Patterns. Margaret Turner. 1986. pap. 19.50 (*0-903585-21-9*) Robin & Russ.

Bedhaya Court Dances of Central Java: A Mataram Tradition of Ritual Art. Clara Brakel-Papenhuyzen. LC 91-17941. (Illus.). xvi, 349p. 1992. 91.50 (*90-04-09424-5*) E J Brill.

Bedienungsprozesse. Gennadi P. Klimow & Dieter Konig. (Mathematische Reihe Ser.: No. 68). (Illus.). 256p. (GER.). 1980. 52.50 (*0-8176-1049-9*) Birkhauser.

Bedini's Free Energy Generator. 1987. 5.50 (*0-914119-01-X*) Tesla Bk Co.

Bedlam: A Year in the Life of a Mental Hospital. Dominick Bosco. 288p. 1992. 19.95 (*1-55972-113-8*, Birch Ln Pr) Carol Pub Group.

Bedlam: Greed, Profiteering & Fraud in a Mental Health System Gone Crazy. Joseph Sharkey. 320p. 1994. 22.95 (*0-312-10421-9*, Pub. by Thomas Dunne Bks) St Martin.

Bedlam: Short Stories. John Domini. LC 81-71002. 136p. (Orig.). 1981. pap. 6.95 (*0-931362-03-2*) SDSU Press.

Bedlam Boyz. Ellen Guon. Orig. Title: Healer's Crusade. 304p. 1993. mass mkt. 4.99 (*0-671-72177-1*) Baen Bks.

Bedlam Patterns: Love & the Idea of Madness in Poe's Fiction. Richard Benton. 1979. pap. 2.75 (*0-910556-13-X*) Enoch Pratt.

Bedlam Without Bars. George H. Tucker. 1991. pap. 9.95 (*1-878901-23-0*) Hampton Roads Pub Co.

Bedlington Terriers. Elinor E. Young. (KW Ser.). (Illus.). 192p. 1992. text ed. 11.95 (*0-86622-593-5*) TFH Pubns.

Bedouin. John King. LC 92-16506. (Threatened Cultures Ser.). (Illus.). 48p. (J). (gr. 5-6). 1992. lib. bdg. 22.80 (*0-8114-2304-2*) Raintree Steck-V.

Bedouin. Fred Rendell & Arnold Bell. (C). 1989. 30.00 (*1-85098-069-1*, Pub. by Jordanhill College UK) St Mut.

***Bedouin: Nomads of the Desert.** Alan Keohane. (Illus.). 176p. 1995. 45.00 (*1-85626-106-9*, Pub. by C Kyle) Trafalgar.

Bedouin Hornbook. Nathaniel Mackey. LC 86-1471. (From a Broken Bottle Traces of Perfume Still Emanate Ser.: No. 1). 216p. (Orig.). reprint ed. pap. 61.60 (*0-7837-6485-5*, 2046512) Bks Demand.

Bedouin Jewellery in Saudi Arabia. Heather C. Ross. (Illus.). 128p. 1990. 50.00 (*2-88373-002-4*, Pub. by Arabesque Comm SZ) Empire Pub Srvs.

Bedouin Life in the Egyptian Wilderness. Joseph J. Hobbs. (Illus.). 207p. 1989. pap. 11.95 (*0-292-70789-4*) U of Tex Pr.

Bedouin Love, Law & Legend, Dealing Exclusively with the Badu of Beersheba. Arif Al-Arif. LC 79-180318. (Mid-East Studies). (Illus.). reprint ed. 37.50 (*0-404-56213-2*) AMS Pr.

Bedouin of Cyrenaica: Studies in Personal & Corporate Power. Emrys Peters. Ed. by Jack Goody & Emanuel Marx. (Cambridge Studies in Social & Cultural Anthropology: No. 72). (Illus.). 320p. (C). 1991. 64.95 (*0-521-38561-X*) Cambridge U Pr.

Bedouin of Northern Arabia: The Traditions of Al Dhafir. Bruce Ingham. (Illus.). 180p. 1986. 45.00 (*0-7103-0093-X*, 0093X, Pub. by Kegan Paul Intl UK) Routledge Chapman & Hall.

Bedouin of the Sinai. Paola Crociani. (Illus.). 128p. 1994. 45.00 (*1-873938-48-9*, Pub. by Garnet Pubng Ltd UK) Paul & Co Pubs.

Bedouin Poetry from Sinai & the Negev: Mirror of a Culture. Clinton Bailey. (Illus.). 504p. 1991. 125.00 (*0-19-826547-6*) OUP.

Bedouin Tribes of the Euphrates, 2 vols. in 1. Anne Blunt. (Illus.). xxviii, 629p. reprint ed. write for info. (*0-318-71490-6*, Pub. by Georg Olms GW) Lubrecht & Cramer.

Bedouin Village: A Study of a Saudi Arabian People in Transition. Ed. by Motoko Katakura. 189p. 1977. 29.50 (*0-86008-176-1*, Pub. by U of Tokyo JA) Col U Pr.

Bedouin, Village, & Urban Arabic: An Ecolinguistic Study. Frederic J. Cadora. LC 92-10032. (Studies in Semitic Languages & Linguistics: Vol. 18). 168p. 1992. 51.50 (*90-04-09627-2*) E J Brill.

Bedouins. James G. Huneker. LC 72-6579. (Illus.). reprint ed. 39.50 (*0-404-10526-2*) AMS Pr.

Bedouins. James G. Huneker. (BCL1-PS American Literature Ser.). 271p. 1992. reprint ed. lib. bdg. 79.00 (*0-7812-6747-1*) Rprt Serv.

***Bedouins & the Desert: Aspects of Nomadic Life in the Arab East.** Jibrail S. Jabbur. Ed. by Suhayl J. Jabbur & Lawrence I. Conrad. Tr. by Lawrence I. Conrad. (SUNY Series Near Eastern Studies). (Illus.). 696p. 1995. text ed. 29.50x (*0-7914-2851-6*) State U NY Pr.

Bedouins of Arabia. Thierry Mauger. (Illus.). 139p. 1990. 45.00 (*0-7103-0366-1*, A4185, Pub. by Kegan Paul Intl UK) Routledge Chapman & Hall.

Bedouins of Qatar. Klaus Ferdinand. LC 92-82026. (Carlsberg Nomad Ser.). (Illus.). 416p. 1993. 50.00 (*0-500-01573-2*) Thames Hudson.

Bedpan Commando: The Story of a Combat Nurse During World War II. 2nd ed. June Wandrey. LC 89-81460. (Illus.). 234p. 1991. reprint ed. 14.00 (*0-9625555-0-9*) Elmore Pub.

Bedrest Before Baby: What's a Mother to Do? A Survival Handbook for High Risk Moms. Patricia D. Isennock. LC 92-80763. 104p. (Orig.). 1992. pap. 12.95 (*0-9632392-5-2*) Mustard Seed.

***Bedrest Before Baby: What's a Mother to Do? A Survival Handbook for High Risk Moms.** 2nd ed. Patricia D. Isennock. 112p. (Orig.). Date not set. pap. 12.95 (*0-9632392-6-0*) Mustard Seed.

An Asterisk (*) at the beginning of an entry indicates that the title is appearing in BIP for the first time.

An Asterisk (*) at the beginning of an entry indicates that the title is appearing in BIP for the first time.

653

Beef Production, Science & Economics, Application & Reality. D. Porter Price. LC 81-51944. (Illus.). 358p. 1985. 32.00 (*0-9606246-0-0*); pap. text ed. 24.95 (*0-9606246-3-5*) SWI.

Beef Stew. Barbara Brenner. LC 89-36769. (Step into Reading Bks.). (Illus.). 32p. (J). (ps-1). 1990. lib. bdg. 7.99 (*0-394-95046-1*); pap. 3.50 (*0-394-85046-7*) Random Bks Yng Read.

Beef Usage Attitudes & Opportunities in Foodservice & Customer Markets. GMA Research Corporation Staff. Ed. by Mary M. Adolf. (Illus.). 250p. (Orig.). 1984. pap. 185.00 (*0-88700-003-7*) Natl Live Stock.

***Beef, Veal, Lamb, & Pork.** Knapp. 1994. 7.99 (*0-517-13596-5*) Random Hse Value.

Beefcake Bazaar. Cork Millner. LC 90-52519. (Orig.). 1984. pap. 6.00 (*0-88734-208-6*) Players Pr.

Beefin' Up: Daily Feed for Amazing Grazing. Mark R. Littleton. Ed. by Liz Heaney. LC 89-29297. 181p. (Orig.). (YA). (gr. 7-12). 1990. pap. 8.99 (*0-88070-317-2*, Gold & Honey) Questar Pubs.

Beef...with Love. Jeannine B. Browning. 1994. pap. write for info. (*0-9627729-9-2*) J B Browning.

Beehive. Andy Hoffman. 219p. 1992. pap. 16.00 (*1-877946-35-4*) Permanent Pr.

Beeinflussing von Pilzlichen Stoffwechselleistungen und Fermentationsprozessen durch Sporotrichum Pulverulentum (Novobranova) Pleurotus Ostreatus ((Jacq. Ex Fr.) Kumm) und Trichoderma Viride (Pers. ex S. F. Gray) bei Variationen des Kohlenstoff-und Stickstoffbangbotes. Anne Traulich. (Dissertationes Botanicae Ser.: Vol. 118). (Illus.). 177p. (GER.). (C). 1988. pap. text ed. 53.00 (*3-443-64030-3*) Lubrecht & Cramer.

Beekeeper Ugli, Bk. One. Donald H. Cox, Sr. LC 88-70542. (Illus.). 56p. 1988. pap. write for info. (*0-9620307-0-8*) D H Cox.

Beekeeper Ugli, Bk. Two: My Visit to Li'l Pinch. Donald H. Cox, Sr. LC 88-70543. (Illus.). 60p. 1988. pap. write for info. (*0-9620307-1-6*) D H Cox.

Beekeeper's Apprentice: On the Segregation of the Queen. Laurie R. King. 336p. 1994. 21.95 (*0-312-10423-5*, Pub. by Thomas Dunne Bks) St Martin.

Beekeeper's Handbook. Diana Sammataro & Alphonse Avitabile. 131p. (Orig.). 1981. reprint ed. pap. 10.95 (*0-684-17331-X*, Scribners) S&S Trade.

Beekeeper's Year. Sylvia A. Johnson. LC 93-10199. (Illus.). (J). 1994. 14.95 (*0-316-46745-6*) Little.

Beekeeping. Boy Scouts of America. (Illus.). 56p. (J). (gr. 6-12). 1983. pap. 1.85 (*0-8395-3362-4*, 33362) BSA.

Beekeeping: A Practical Guide. Richard E. Bonney. Ed. by Sandra Webb. LC 92-56145. (Illus.). 192p. 1993. pap. 16.95 (*0-88266-861-7*, Garden Way Pub) Storey Comm Inc.

Beekeeping: An Owner's Manual. Werner Melzer. 1989. pap. 5.95 (*0-8120-4089-9*) Barron.

Beekeeping: Nine Lectures on Bees. Rudolf Steiner. Tr. by Marna Pease & Carl A. Meier. LC 64-8530. 104p. 1988. pap. 12.00 (*0-89345-246-7*, Steinerbks) Garber Comm.

Beekeeping As a Hobby. E. F. Phillips. (Shorey Lost Arts Ser.). 40p. reprint ed. pap. 1.95 (*0-8466-6039-3*, U39) Shorey.

Beekeeping Guide. rev. ed. Harlan H. Attfield. (Illus.). 45p. 1989. 7.25 (*0-86619-154-2*); French, 37p. 7.25 (*0-86619-140-2*) Vols Tech Asst.

Beekeeping in Africa. Stephen O. Adjare. (Agricultural Services Bulletin Ser.: No. 68-6). 140p. 1990. pap. 12.00 (*92-5-102794-3*, F7943) UNIPUB.

Beekeeping in California. Eric C. Mussen. LC 87-71574. (Illus.). 72p. (Orig.). 1987. pap. 3.50 (*0-931876-79-6*, 21422) ANR Pubns CA.

Beekeeping Questions & Answers. Dadant & Sons Inc. LC 77-80061. (Illus.). (C). 1978. 9.96 (*0-915698-04-8*) Dadant & Sons.

Beekman: Distinguished Families in America Descended from Wilhelmus Beekman & Jan Tomasse Van Dyke. W. B. Aitken. (Illus.). 264p. 1992. reprint ed. lib. bdg. 52.00 (*0-8328-2631-6*); reprint ed. pap. 42.00 (*0-8328-2632-4*) Higginson Bk Co.

Beekmantown, New York: Forest Frontier to Farm Community. Philip L. White. LC 78-26558. (Illus.). 398p. reprint ed. pap. 113.50 (*0-8357-4282-2*, 2037081) Bks Demand.

Beelzebub's Tales to His Grandson, 3 vols. in 1. G. I. Gurdjieff. 1964. pap. 30.00 (*0-525-47351-3*, Dutton) NAL-Dutton.

Beelzebub's Tales to His Grandson. G. I. Gurdjieff. (All & Everything, First Ser.). 1248p. 1993. 50.00 (*0-670-84125-0*, Viking) Viking Penguin.

Been Down So Long It Looks Like up to Me. Richard Farina. 1983. pap. 11.95 (*0-14-006536-9*, Penguin Bks) Viking Penguin.

***Been Down So Long It Looks Like Up to Me.** Richard Farina. 352p. 1995. 11.95 (*0-14-018930-0*, Penguin Classics) Viking Penguin.

Been in the Storm So Long: A Meditation Manual. Ed. by Mark Morrison-Reed & Jacqui James. 53p. 1991. 6.00 (*1-55896-202-6*, Skinner Hse Bks) Unitarian Univ.

Been in the Storm So Long: The Aftermath of Slavery. Leon F. Litwack. LC 80-11073. 672p. 1980. pap. 15.96 (*0-394-74398-9*, Vin) Random.

Been Taken. Roger Hedden. 1991. pap. 4.75 (*0-8222-0103-8*) Dramatists Play.

Been There. Done That. Now What? Ed Young. 256p. 1994. 18.99 (*0-8054-6158-2*, 4261-58) Broadman.

***Been to Yesterdays: Poems of a Life.** Lee B. Hopkins. LC 94-73320. 64p. (J). (gr. 5-8). 1995. 14.95 (*1-56397-467-3*, Wordsong) Boyds Mills Pr.

Beep-Bap-Zap-Jack. Alta M. Rymer. LC 74-20428. (Tales of Planet Artembo Ser.: Bk. 1). (Illus.). 48p. (J). (gr. 5-7). 1974. 20.00 (*0-9600792-0-3*) Rymer Bks.

Beep, Beep. Barbara Gregorich. Ed. by Joan Hoffman. (Start to Read! Ser.). (Illus.). 16p. (Orig.). (J). (gr. k-2). 1984. pap. 2.25 (*0-88743-007-4*, 06007) Sch Zone Pub Co.

Beep, Beep. Barbara Gregorich. Ed. by Joan Hoffman. (Start to Read! Trade Edition Ser.). (Illus.). 32p. (Orig.). (J). (gr. k-2). 1992. pap. 3.95 (*0-88743-405-3*, 06057) Sch Zone Pub Co.

Beepers: Twenty-One Electronics Projects for the Timex-Sinclair 1000. Susan B. Adams & Gordon Rockmaker. 128p. 1979. pap. 11.95 (*0-685-08641-0*, BYTE Bks) McGraw.

Beepers: Twenty-One Electronics Projects for the Timex-Sinclair 1000 & 1500. Gordon Rockmaker & Susan B. Adams. 112p. 1984. pap. text ed. 8.95 (*0-685-09096-5*) McGraw.

Beeple. Alan Cullen. (J). 1968. 5.00 (*0-87602-108-9*) Anchorage.

Beer: A Connoisseur's Guide to the World's Best. Christopher Finch. (Illus.). 176p. 1989. 29.95 (*0-89659-913-2*) Abbeville Pr.

***Beer Across America: A Regional Guide to Brewpubs & Microbreweries.** Marty Nachel. (Illus.). 192p. 1995. pap. 14.95 (*0-88266-902-8*, Storey Pub) Storey Comm Inc.

Beer Advertising Openers: A Pictorial Guide. Donald Bull. LC 77-94261. (Illus.). 1978. pap. 8.95 (*0-9601190-4-3*) Bullworks.

Beer & Brewing Vol. 6: AHA. Ed. by Virginia Thomas. (Illus.). 250p. 1986. 20.95 (*0-937381-02-0*) Brewers Pubns.

Beer & Brewing Vol. 7: AHA. Comp. by American Homebrewers Association Staff. (Illus.). 237p. 1987. 20.95 (*0-937381-07-1*) Brewers Pubns.

Beer & Brewing Vol. 8: AHA. (Illus.). 229p. 1988. pap. 21.95 (*0-937381-11-X*) Brewers Pubns.

Beer & Brewing Vol. 9: AHA. (Illus.). 250p. 1989. 21.95 (*0-937381-15-2*) Brewers Pubns.

Beer & Brewing Vol. 10: AHA. (Illus.). 198p. 1990. pap. 21.95 (*0-937381-21-7*) Brewers Pubns.

Beer & Brewing in the Inland Northwest, 1850 to 1950. Herman W. Ronnenberg. Ed. by Louie W. Allebery. LC 92-16284. (Northwest Folklife Ser.). (Illus.). 240p. 1993. pap. 26.95 (*0-89301-162-2*) U of Idaho Pr.

Beer & Whiskey League. David Nemec. 256p. 1994. 27.95 (*1-55821-285-X*) Lyons & Burford.

Beer & Wine Production: Analysis, Characterization, & Technological Advances. Ed. by Barry H. Gump & David J. Pruett. LC 93-24349. (Symposium Ser.: No. 536). (Illus.). 280p. 1993. 59.95 (*0-8412-2714-4*) Am Chemical.

Beer & Wine Production: Analysis, Characterization, & Technological Advances. Barry H. Gump & David J. Pruett. LC 93-24349. (ACS Symposium Ser.: No. 536). 275p. 1994. pap. 24.95 (*0-8412-2724-1*) Am Chemical.

Beer Barons. abr. ed. Anthony Degiusti. 420p. 1994. pap. 12.95 (*1-56901-324-1*) NW Pub.

***Beer Basics: A Quick & Easy Guide.** Peter LaFrance. LC 94-49717. 1995. pap. text ed. 12.95 (*0-471-11936-9*) Wiley.

Beer, Bed & Breakfast. 4th ed. Roger Protz. (Illus.). 260p. 1993. pap. 10.95 (*0-86051-785-3*, Robson-Parkwest) Parkwest Pubns.

Beer Can by The Highway: Essays on What's "American" about America. John A. Kouwenhoven. LC 87-46303. (Illus.). 264p. 1988. reprint ed. text ed. 38.00 (*0-8018-3667-0*); reprint ed. pap. 13.95x (*0-8018-3653-0*) Johns Hopkins.

Beer Can Collectors Bible. Jack Martells. 1979. pap. 7.95 (*0-394-28918-8*, Ballantine Trade) Ballantine.

Beer Cans, Bullets, Things & Pieces. Arthur Pfister. 1972. pap. 2.00 (*0-910296-29-4*) Broadside Pr.

Beer Cuisine: A Cookbook for Beer Lovers. Jay Harlow. LC 91-14928. (Illus.). 120p. (Orig.). 1991. pap. 16.95 (*0-9627345-2-7*, Astolat Bks) Harlow & Ratner.

***Beer Directory: An International Guide.** Ed. by Heather Wood. 224p. 1995. pap. 12.95 (*0-88266-903-6*, Storey Pub) Storey Comm Inc.

Beer Drinker's Dream Diet. Elwin Law. (Illus.). 90p. 1991. pap. text ed. 7.95 (*0-9631321-4-8*) Winnstead Pub.

***Beer Drinkers Guide to Australia & New Zealand.** James D. Robertson. (Illus.). 80p. 1994. per. 9.95 (*0-9635332-6-6*) Bosak Pub.

Beer Drinker's Guide to Munich. 3rd rev. ed. Larry Hawthorne. LC 92-71254. (Illus.). 208p. (Orig.). 1995. pap. 11.95 (*0-9628555-0-2*) Freizeit Pubs.

Beer Drinkers Guide to Southern Germany. James D. Robertson. (Illus.). 96p. 1994. per. 9.95 (*0-9635332-3-1*) Bosak Pub.

Beer Enthusiast's Guide: Tasting & Judging Brews from Around the World. Gregg Smith. LC 93-14117. (Illus.). 144p. 1994. pap. 12.95 (*0-88266-838-2*, Storey Pub) Storey Comm Inc.

Beer Explorer's Logbook: A Record of Great Beers. Victoria Thomas. 128p. (Orig.). 1994. pap. 8.95 (*0-943289-01-7*) Passport Adventure.

***Beer Fear.** Jeff Gilbert. Ed. by Grant Alden. (Illus.). 334p. (Orig.). 1995. pap. 9.99 (*0-9646781-0-1*) Hairball Pr.

Beer Games 2: The Exploitative Sequel. expanded rev. ed. Andy Griscom et al. LC 94-32647. (Illus.). 144p. 1994. pap. 8.95 (*0-914457-67-5*) Mustang Pub.

***Beer Here: A Traveler's Guide to American Brewpubs & Microbreweries.** Stuart A. Kallen. (Illus.). 416p. 1995. pap. 16.95 (*0-8065-1639-9*, Citadel Pr) Carol Pub Group.

Beer in the Snooker Club. Waguih Ghali. LC 87-20372. 220p. (C). 1987. 15.95 (*0-941533-09-3*) New Amsterdam Bks.

Beer in the Snooker Club. Waguih Ghali. 220p. (C). 1989. reprint ed. pap. 9.95 (*0-941533-81-6*) New Amsterdam Bks.

Beer, Its History & Its Economic Value As a National Beverage. Frederick W. Salem. LC 72-5072. (Technology & Society Ser.). (Illus.). 292p. 1975. reprint ed. 21.95 (*0-405-04722-3*) Ayer.

Beer Labels of the World. Bill Yenne. (Illus.). 128p. 1993. 12.98 (*1-55521-857-1*) Bk Sales Inc.

Beer Labels of the World. Bill Yenne. 1993. 12.98 (*1-55521-958-6*) Bk Sales Inc.

Beer Log. James D. Robertson. (Illus.). 408p. ring bd. 37.50 (*0-9635332-0-7*) Bosak Pub.

***Beer Log.** James D. Robertson. (Illus.). 384p. 1995. pap. 39.75 (*0-9635332-5-8*) Bosak Pub.

***Beer Log 1993 Update.** James D. Robertson. (Illus.). 182p. 1994. ring bd. 16.00 (*0-9635332-1-5*) Bosak Pub.

***Beer Log 1994 Update.** James D. Robertson. (Illus.). Date not set. ring bd. 16.00 (*0-9635332-2-3*) Bosak Pub.

Beer Lover's Rating Guide. Robert Klein. Ed. by Suzanne Rafer. (Illus.). 352p. (Orig.). 1994. pap. 7.95 (*1-56305-682-8*) Workman Pub.

***Beer Market.** 400p. (Orig.). 1994. pap. 1,595.00 (*1-57205-890-0*) Rector Pr.

***Beer Market International Handbook.** (Illus.). 420p. (Orig.). 1994. pap. 8,900.00 (*0-7605-0947-6*) Rector Pr.

***Beer Market Mexico.** 200p. (Orig.). 1995. pap. 4,995.00 (*0-7605-2162-X*) Rector Pr.

***Beer Market U. S. A.** 345p. (Orig.). 1995. pap. 1,595.00 (*0-7605-2161-1*) Rector Pr.

***Beer Market 1994 (Jobsons)** 172p. (Orig.). 1995. pap. 695.00 (*0-7605-2158-1*) Rector Pr.

Beer Stein Book: Illustrated Catalog, Current Prices, Collector's Information: A 400 Year History. Gary Kirsner & Jim Gruhl. Ed. by Beth Kirsner. 416p. 1990. 39.95 (*0-9614130-3-4*) Glentiques.

Beer Supply Agreements. William Elland. 300p. 1991. U.K. pap. 170.00 (*0-406-04519-4*) Butterworth Legal Pubs.

Beer Trucks: A Photographic Salute. Michael C. Hennech & Doug Pierson. (Illus.). 128p. (Orig.). 1992. pap. 14.95 (*1-881301-03-6*) Ale Pub.

Beercans on the Side of the Road: The Story of Henry the Hitchhiker. Ken Wachsberger. xii, 244p. (Orig.). 1988. pap. 8.95 (*0-945531-00-1*) Azenphony Pr.

***Beers & Coolers.** Manfred Moll. Date not set. 155.00 (*1-898298-09-2*) Spr-Verlag.

Beers Atlas Ulster County, 1875. Orange County Genealogical Society Staff. 80p. 1986. lib. bdg. 30.00 (*0-685-12121-6*) Orange County Genealog.

Beer's History of Green County: New York with Biographical Sketches of Its Prominent Men. 1983. reprint ed. 56.00 (*0-910746-29-X*, BHO01) Hope Farm.

***Beer's Law Study.** David P. Dingledy. Ed. by H. A. Neidig. (Modular Laboratory Program in Chemistry Ser.). 12p. (C). 1989. pap. text ed. 1.25x (*0-87540-358-1*) Chem Educ Res.

Beers of North America. Bill Yenne. (Illus.). 208p. 1992. 12.98 (*0-681-41595-9*) Longmeadow Pr.

Beers of North America. rev. ed. Bill Yenne. (Illus.). 208p. 1990. 18.95 (*0-8317-0723-2*, Crescent) Random Hse Value.

***Beers of the World.** Bill Yenne. 1994. 19.98 (*0-7858-0020-4*) Bk Sales Inc.

Beersheba Springs: A History. Margaret B. Coppinger et al. 167p. 1983. pap. 12.00 (*0-9613156-1-X*) Herschel Gower.

Beertown Blazes. 2nd rev. ed. R. L. Nailen & James S. Haight. 1982. 20.00 (*0-932476-01-5*) Renaiss Bks.

***Bees.** James E. Gerholdt. LC 95-5444. (Incredible Insects Ser.). (J). 1995. lib. bdg. 13.99 (*1-56239-483-5*) Abdo & Dghtrs.

Bees: For Fun & Profit. Mark Bryant. (Illus.). (Orig.). 1992. 3.95 (*0-9626811-1-3*) Hummngbrd OH.

Bees & Beekeeping: Science, Practice, & World Resources. Eva Crane. LC 89-17477. (Illus.). 640p. 1990. 110.00 (*0-8014-2429-1*) Cornell U Pr.

Bees & the Law. Murray Loring. LC 80-66362. 128p. (C). 1981. 8.96 (*0-915698-07-2*) Dadant & Sons.

Bees, Ants & Wasps: A Key to Genera of the British Aculeates. Pat Willmer. (Illus.). 28p. (Orig.). 1985. pap. 9.99x (*0-916422-58-5*) Mad River.

Bees as Superorganisms: An Evolutionary Reality. Robin F. Moritz & Edward E. Southwick. LC 92-14560. (Illus.). 304p. 1992. 129.00 (*3-540-54821-1*); 129.00 (*0-387-54821-1*) Spr-Verlag.

Bees, Birds & Butterflies in Lace. Edna Sutton & Mary Moseley. (Illus.). 96p. 1991. 34.95 (*0-7134-6365-1*, Pub. by Batsford UK) Trafalgar.

Bees Dance & Whales Sing: The Mysteries of Animal Communication. Margery Facklam. (Illus.). 48p. (J). (gr. 3-6). 1992. 14.95 (*0-87156-573-0*) Sierra.

Bees Don't Get Arthritis. Fred Malone. (Illus.). 179p. 1992. pap. 13.95 (*0-914960-60-1*) Academy Bks.

Bee's Flight: A Potpourri of Ideas. Bernice P. Grebner et al. 166p. 1991. pap. 11.95 (*0-9626273-1-3*) Grebner Bks Pub.

Bees in Wet Weather. Barbara Drake. Ed. by Brian Browning & Joe Dionne. (Illus.). 30p. 1992. pap. 12.00 (*0-945950-07-1*) Canoe Pr MI.

Bees Learn to Read. Francis Wise. 1986. 1.50 (*0-915766-35-3*) Wise Pub.

***Bees of Passion.** Dan Kantak. (Illus.). 72p. 1995. pap. 11.00 (*0-9646195-1-2*) Plumeria Pr.

Bees of the Eastern United States, 2 vols., Set. T. B. Mitchell. 1960. 20.00 (*0-910914-05-2*) J Johnson.

Bees of the New Genus Ctenoceratina in Africa South of the Sahara (Hymenoptera: Apoides) Howell V. Daly. (Publications in Entomology: Vol. 108). 80p. 1988. pap. 17.00 (*0-520-09725-4*) U CA Pr.

Bees of the World. Christopher O'Toole & Anthony Raw. (Of the World Ser.). (Illus.). 192p. 1992. lib. bdg. 25.95 (*0-8160-1992-4*) Facts on File.

Bee's Sneeze. Ellis Nadler. LC 92-32470. (Illus.). 32p. (J). (ps-1). 1993. pap. 12.00 (*0-671-86575-7*, S&S Bks Young Read) S&S Childrens.

Bees, Wasps, & Ants. George S. Fichter. (Junior Guides Ser.). (Illus.). 36p. (J). (gr. k-3). 1993. 4.95 (*0-307-11434-1*, 11434, Golden Pr) Western Pub.

Beeson Genealogy. Jasper L. Beeson. 144p. 1994. reprint ed. lib. bdg. 35.00 (*0-8328-4195-1*); reprint ed. pap. 25.00 (*0-8328-4196-X*) Higginson Bk Co.

***Beeson Genealogy.** Jasper L. Beeson. 144p. 1994. reprint ed. lib. bdg. 35.00 (*0-8328-4549-3*); reprint ed. pap. 25.00 (*0-8328-4550-7*) Higginson Bk Co.

Beestys' Journey, 20 Vols., Vol. 1. Yolanda L. Salazar. (Illus.). 36p. (J). (gr. 3 up). 1989. write for info. (*0-318-65111-4*) ADAPT Pub Co.

Beestys' What Color Is... Yolanda L. Salazar. (Illus.). 10p. (J). (ps). 1989. 7.95 (*0-317-94002-3*) ADAPT Pub Co.

Beesty's What Shape Is... Yolanda L. Salazar. (Illus.). 10p. (J). (ps). 1989. 7.95 (*0-317-94001-5*) ADAPT Pub Co.

Beestys' What Time Is... Yolanda L. Salazar. (Illus.). 10p. (J). (ps). 1989. 7.95 (*0-317-94003-1*) ADAPT Pub Co.

Beeswax Crafting. Robert Berthold, Jr. Ed. by Larence J. Connor. LC 93-19562. 1993. 17.95 (*1-878075-02-0*) Wicwas Pr.

Beet Queen. Louise Erdrich. 320p. 1989. pap. 10.95 (*0-553-34723-3*) Bantam.

Beet Queen. Louise Erdrich. LC 86-4788. 352p. 1986. 16.95 (*0-8050-0058-5*) H Holt & Co.

Beethoven. (Portraits of Greatness Ser.: No. I). (ENG.). 1987. pap. 12.50 (*0-918367-04-2*) Elite.

Beethoven. (Masterpieces of Piano Music Ser.). (Illus.). 192p. 1986. pap. 11.95 (*0-8256-2418-5*, AM37177) Music Sales.

Beethoven. Vincent D'Indy. Tr. by Theodore Baker. LC 74-107808. (Select Bibliographies Reprint Ser.). 1977. 20.95 (*0-8369-5184-0*) Ayer.

Beethoven. Steven Johnson. LC 93-39720. (Compact Companions Ser.). 1994. pap. 17.50 (*0-671-88789-0*) S&S Trade.

Beethoven. William Kinderman. LC 94-4813. 1995. 35.00 (*0-520-08796-8*) U CA Pr.

Beethoven. L. Loewen. (Profiles in Music Ser.). (Illus.). 112p. (J). (gr. 5 up). 1989. lib. bdg. 18.60 (*0-86592-609-3*); lib. bdg. 13.95 (*0-685-58617-0*) Rourke Corp.

Beethoven. Ates Orga. (Illustrated Lives of the Great Composers Ser.). (Illus.). 176p. 1987. pap. 14.95 (*0-7119-0251-8*, OP42373) Omnibus NY.

Beethoven. Anne Rachlin. (Famous Children Ser.). (Illus.). 24p. (J). (gr. k-3). 1994. pap. 5.95 (*0-8120-1996-2*) Barron.

Beethoven. Romain Rolland. LC 76-95077. (Select Bibliographies Reprint Ser.). 1977. 29.95 (*0-8369-5077-1*) Ayer.

Beethoven. Maynard Solomon. LC 77-5242. (Illus.). 416p. 1979. pap. 16.00 (*0-02-872240-X*) Schirmer Bks.

Beethoven. Robert Tine. 96p. (Orig.). 1992. pap. 4.50 (*0-425-13648-5*) Berkley Pub.

Beethoven. W. Turner. 1972. lib. bdg. 59.95 (*0-87968-716-9*) Gordon Pr.

Beethoven. Paul Bekker. Tr. by M. M. Bozman. LC 75-175938. (BCL Ser. I). (Illus.). 1972. reprint ed. 42.50 (*0-404-00728-7*) AMS Pr.

Beethoven. Paul Bekker. 391p. 1990. reprint ed. lib. bdg. 79.00 (*0-7812-9042-2*) Rprt Serv.

Beethoven. Romain Rolland. Ed. by A. Eaglefield Hull. Tr. by B. Constanace Hull. 244p. 1990. reprint ed. lib. bdg. 69.00 (*0-7812-9046-5*) Rprt Serv.

Beethoven: "Missa Solemnis" William Drabkin. (Cambridge Music Handbooks Ser.). (Illus.). 150p. (C). 1991. pap. 10.95 (*0-521-37831-1*) Cambridge U Pr.

Beethoven: A Critical Biography. Vincent D'Indy. LC 72-125054. (Music Ser.). (Illus.). 1970. reprint ed. lib. bdg. 22.50 (*0-306-70019-0*) Da Capo.

Beethoven: A Critical Biography. Vincent D'Indy. 127p. 1990. reprint ed. lib. bdg. 59.00 (*0-7812-9043-0*) Rprt Serv.

Beethoven: His Life, Work & World. H. C. Landon. LC 92-64271. (Illus.). 248p. 1993. 40.00 (*0-500-01540-6*) Thames Hudson.

Beethoven: His Spiritual Development. John W. Sullivan. 1960. pap. 8.00 (*0-394-70100-3*, Vin) Random.

Beethoven: Impressions by His Contemporaries. Ed. by Oscar G. Sonneck. 1926. pap. 4.95 (*0-486-21770-1*) Dover.

Beethoven: Les Grandes Epoques Creatices. Romain Rolland. 1520p. (FRE.). 1992. reprint ed. 115.00 (*0-7859-5440-6*) Fr & Eur.

Beethoven: Letters, Journals, & Conversations. Ed. & Tr. by Michael Hamburger. LC 83-72975. (Illus.). 282p. 1992. pap. 14.95 (*0-500-27324-3*) Thames Hudson.

Beethoven: Letters, Journals & Conversations. Ludwig Van Beethoven. Ed. by Michael Hamburger. LC 77-13799. 282p. 1978. reprint ed. text ed. 47.50 (*0-8371-9899-2*, BELJ, Greenwood Pr) Greenwood.

Beethoven: Music Book Index. Donald F. Tovey. 138p. 1993. reprint ed. lib. bdg. 69.00 (*0-7812-9573-4*) Rprt Serv.

***Beethoven: Pastoral Symphony.** David W. Jones. (Cambridge Music Handbooks Ser.). (Illus.). 108p. (C). 1995. write for info. (*0-521-45074-8*); pap. write for info. (*0-521-45684-3*) Cambridge U Pr.

Beethoven: Studies in the Creative Process. Lewis Lockwood. (Illus.). 283p. (C). 1992. 45.00 (*0-674-06362-7*) HUP.

Beethoven: Symphony No. Five in C Minor. Ludwig Van Beethoven. Ed. by Elliot Forbes. LC 73-98890. (Critical Scores Ser.). (C). 1971. pap. text ed. 10.95 (*0-393-09893-1*) Norton.

654

An Asterisk (*) at the beginning of an entry indicates that the title is appearing in BIP for the first time.

B

An Asterisk (*) at the beginning of an entry indicates that the title is appearing in BIP for the first time.

655

***Before Biology: Animal Morphology & the German Universities, 1800-1900.** Lynn K. Nyhart. LC 95-3227. (Science & Its Conceptual Foundations Ser.). 1995. lib. bdg. 75.00 (0-226-61086-1); pap. text ed. 24.95 (0-226-61088-8) U Ch Pr.

Before Birth: Prenatal Testing for Genetic Disease. Elena O. Nightingale & Melissa Goodman. (Illus.). 128p. 1990. 27.00 (0-674-06390-2); pap. text ed. 9.95 (0-674-06391-0) HUP.

Before Birth, Beyond Death. Connie R. Taylor. LC 87-82117. 64p. (J). (gr. 4-6). 1987. pap. 7.98 (0-88290-315-2) Horizon Utah.

Before Book One: Listening Activities for Prebeginning Students of English. 2nd ed. John R. Boyd & Mary A. Boyd. 112p. (C). 1991. pap. text ed. 8.95 (0-13-068289-6, 640104) P-H.

Before Book One: Teacher's Manual. John R. Boyd & Mary A. Boyd. (Illus.). 30p. (gr. 9-12). 1987. pap. text ed. 5.75 (0-13-072554-4, 20660) Prentice ESL.

Before Brecht: Four German Plays. Ed. by Eric Bentley. LC 85-15623. (Eric Bentley's Dramatic Repertoire Ser.). (Illus.). 272p. (Orig.). 1985. 24.95 (1-55783-009-6); pap. 8.95 (1-55783-010-X) Applause Theatre Bk Pubs.

Before Burnout: Balanced Living for Busy People. Frank Minirth. 1989. pap. 8.99 (0-8024-0879-6) Moody.

Before Calculus: Functions, Graphs, & Analytic Geometry. 3rd ed. Louis Leithold. LC 93-34084. (C). 1994. 42.00 (0-673-46911-5) HarpCollege.

Before Caligari: German Cinema, 1895-1920. Ed. by Paolo C. Usai & Lorenzo Codelli. 520p. 1991. 75.00 (0-299-97075-2) U of Wis Pr.

Before Calling the Doctor. Phyllis Speight. (C). 1976. pap. 6.95 (0-8464-0994-1) Beekman Pubs.

Before College Book for Women: Protecting Yourself from Campus Crime. Donna L. Betancourt. LC 93-91066. (Illus.). 127p. (Orig.). Date not set. pap. 12.95 (0-9639693-0-7) D Betancourt.

Before Color Prejudice: The Ancient View of Blacks. Frank M. Snowden, Jr. (Illus.). 224p. 1991. pap. 15.95x (0-674-06381-3, SNOBEX) HUP.

Before Columbus. Muriel Batherman. (Illus.). 32p. (J). (gr. k-3). 1990. pap. 5.95 (0-395-54954-X) HM.

Before Columbus: Exploration & Colonization from the Mediterranean to the Atlantic, 1229-1492. Felipe Fernandez-Armesto. LC 87-10764. (Middle Ages Ser.). 294p. (C). 1987. pap. text ed. 17.95 (0-8122-1412-9) U of Pa Pr.

Before Columbus Foundation Fiction Anthology: Selections from the American Book Awards 1980-1990. Ed. by Ishmael Reed et al. 400p. 1991. 22.95 (0-393-03055-5); pap. 14.95 (0-393-30832-4) Norton.

Before Columbus Foundation Poetry Anthology: Selections from the American Book Awards 1980-1990. Ed. by Ishmael Reed et al. 320p. 1991. 22.95 (0-393-03056-3); pap. 14.95 (0-393-30833-2) Norton.

Before Command: An Economic History of Russia From Emancipation to the First Five - Year Plan. Paul R. Gregory. LC 93-39139. 1994. 35.00 (0-691-04265-9) Princeton U Pr.

Before Copyright: The French Book-Privilege System 1498-1526. Elizabeth Armstrong. (Cambridge Studies in Publishing & Printing History). (Illus.). 328p. (C). 1990. 74.95 (0-521-37408-1) Cambridge U Pr.

Before Creation. Joseph Donahue. 60p. (Orig.). 1989. pap. text ed. 5.00 (0-9622390-1-1) Central Park.

Before Disaster Strikes: Developing an Emergency Procedures Manual. Illus. by Maureen Smith. 168p. (Orig.). (C). 1990. pap. text ed. 85.00 (0-944298-49-4); vhs (0-944298-50-8) Inst Real Estate.

Before Disaster Strikes: Prevention, Planning, & Recovery: Caring for Your Personal Collections in the Event of Disaster. Priscilla O. Lawrence. LC 92-37511. 1992. pap. 6.95 (0-917860-32-2) Historic New Orleans.

Before Elvis, There Was Nothing. Ed. by Patrick Higgins. (Illus.). 96p. 1994. pap. 11.95 (0-7867-0145-5) Carroll & Graf.

***Before Equal Suffrage: Women in Partisan Politics from Colonial Times to 1920.** Robert J. Dinkin. LC 95-19321. (Contributions in Women's Studies). 1995. text ed. write for info. (0-313-29482-8, Greenwood Pr) Greenwood.

Before European Hegemony: The World System A.D. 1250-1350. Janet L. Abu-Lughod. (Illus.). 464p. 1991. reprint ed. pap. 17.95 (0-19-506774-6) OUP.

Before First Grade: The Early Training Project for Culturally Disadvantaged Children. Susan W. Gray. LC 66-24872. (Early Childhood Education Ser.). (Illus.). 128p. reprint ed. pap. 36.50 (0-8357-7090-7, 2030158) Bks Demand.

Before France & Germany: The Creation & Transformation of the Merovingian World. Patrick J. Geary. (Illus.). 272p. 1988. pap. 15.95 (0-19-504458-4) OUP.

Before Freedom: Forty-Eight Oral Histories of Former North & South Carolina Slaves. Ed. by Belinda Hurmence. 224p. 1990. pap. 5.99 (0-451-62781-4, Ment) NAL-Dutton.

Before Freedom & After. Ansar Harvani. (Illus.). 220p. 1989. 21.00 (81-212-0284-1, Pub. by Gian Publng Hse II) S Asia.

Before Freedom Came: African-American Life in the Antebellum South. Ed. by Edward D. Campbell, Jr. & Kym S. Rice. (Illus.). 300p. 1991. pap. 19.95 (0-8139-1332-2) U Pr of Va.

Before Freedom When I Just Can Remember. Ed. by Belinda Hurmence. LC 89-243. (Illus.). 135p. (Orig.). 1988. pap. 8.95 (0-89587-069-X) Blair.

Before Freud: Neurasthenia & the American Medical Community, 1870-1910. F. G. Gosling. LC 87-6038. (Illus.). 214p. 1988. 24.95 (0-252-01406-5) U of Ill Pr.

Before Golda: Manya Shochat: A Biography. Rachel Y. Ben-Zvi. Tr. by Sandra Shurin. LC 88-14522. (Illus.). 250p. (Orig.). 1989. reprint ed. pap. 9.00 (0-685-23476-2) Biblio NY.

Before He Takes You Out: The Safe Dating Guide for the 90's. Scott Lindquist. LC 89-51783. 172p. 1989. pap. 9.95 (0-9623779-0-2) Vigal Pubs.

Before He Wakes: A True Story of Money, Marriage, Sex, & Murder. Jerry Bledsoe. (Illus.). 352p. 1994. 22.95 (0-525-93826-5) NAL-Dutton.

Before Head Start: The Iowa Station & America's Children. Hamilton Cravens. LC 92-44806. xx, 328p. 1993. 39.95 (0-8078-2092-X) U of NC Pr.

***Before Hearsay.** David Hough. 192p. 1995. pap. write for info. (0-201-60761-1) Addison-Wesley.

Before His Eyes: Essays in Honor of Stanley Kauffmann. Ed. by Bert Cardullo. (Illus.). 198p. (Orig.). (C). 1987. lib. bdg. 44.00 (0-8191-5636-1); pap. text ed. 22.50 (0-8191-5637-X) U Pr of Amer.

Before Hollywood: Turn-of-the-Century American Film. Jay Leyda et al. (Illus.). 172p. (Orig.). 1987. pap. 25.00 (0-917418-81-6) Am Fed Arts.

Before I Die. Ruth Peterson. 32p. 1987. pap. 0.75 (0-88144-095-7) Christian Pub.

Before I Die: A Creative Legacy. Therese Donath. (Illus.). 148p. 1989. 22.95 (0-87975-518-0) Prometheus Bks.

Before I Get Old: The Story of the Who. Dave Marsh. (Illus.). 592p. 1983. pap. 10.95 (0-312-07155-8) St Martin.

***Before I Give You Away.** William Coleman. 192p. 1995. 11.99 (1-55661-487-X) Bethany Hse.

Before I Go Out on the Road. Grace Butcher. (Cleveland Poets Ser.: No. 20). (Orig.). 1979. pap. 6.00 (0-914946-15-3) Cleveland St Univ Poetry Ctr.

Before I Go to Sleep. Thomas Hood. (Illus.). 32p. (J). (ps-3). 1990. 14.95 (0-399-21638-3, Putnam) Putnam Pub Group.

Before I Go to Sleep. Thomas Hood. (Sandcastle Ser.). (Illus.). 32p. (J). (ps-1). 1992. pap. 4.95 (0-399-22440-8, Putnam) Putnam Pub Group.

Before I Go to Sleep: A Collection of Bible Stories, Poems & Prayers for Children. Ann Pilling. LC 89-7816. (Illus.). 96p. (J). 1990. lib. bdg. 15.99 (0-517-58019-5) Crown Bks Yng Read.

Before I Wake. Alan Kaufman. 47p. (Orig.). 1991. pap. 4.95 (1-879665-11-5) Cyborg Prods.

Before I Wake. Peggy Moore. 160p. 1991. per. 7.95 (0-8187-0136-6) Harlo Press.

Before I Wake. Steven Spruill. 1993. mass mkt. 4.99 (0-312-92896-3) St Martin.

Before I Wake. large type ed. Steven Spruill. LC 92-18923. 539p. 1992. reprint ed. lib. bdg. 17.95 (1-56054-497-X) Thorndike Pr.

Before I Wake...& Other Tales by Detroiters. Detroit Black Writers Guild Staff. LC 91-70953. (Illus.). 160p. 1991. pap. 7.95 (0-9613078-7-0) Detroit Black.

Before I Was Born. Carolyn Nystrom. Ed. by Stan Jones & Brenna Jones. (God's Design for Sex Ser.: Bk. 2). (Illus.). 48p. 1995. pap. 9.00 (0-89109-844-5, NavPr) NavPress.

Before I Was I: Psychoanalysis & the Imagination. Ed. by Enid Balint et al. LC 92-49564. 190p. 1992. lib. bdg. 29.95 (0-89862-258-1) Guilford Pr.

Before Infallibility: Liberal Catholicism in Biedermeier Vienna. Adam Bunnell. LC 88-45618. 240p. 1990. 37.50 (0-8386-3344-7) Fairleigh Dickinson.

Before It Hits Home. Cheryl L. West. 1993. 4.75 (0-8222-1322-2) Dramatists Play.

Before It Is Too Late. Sheila A. Jeter & Frankie L. Jeter. 84p. 1986. pap. 5.00 (0-9617447-0-7) Twelve Gates Pubns.

Before It Vanishes. Robert Pack. 85p. 1989. pap. 9.95 (0-87923-813-5) Godine.

Before It's Too Late: A Scientist's Case for Nuclear Energy. Bernard L. Cohen. LC 83-11083. 308p. 1983. 18.95 (0-306-41425-2, Plenum Pr) Plenum.

Before It's Too Late: Employee Involvement . . . An Idea Whose Time Has Come. Peter B. Grazier. Ed. by Irene Frankel. (Illus.). 174p. (Orig.). 1989. pap. 13.95 (0-9622232-0-4) Teambuilding.

***Before It's Too Late: Helping Women in Controlling or Abusive Relationships.** Robert J. Ackerman & Susan Pickering. 200p. (Orig.). 1995. pap. 9.95 (1-55874-345-6, 3456) Health Comm.

Before It's Too Late: The Child Guidance Movement in the United States, 1922-1945. Margo Horn. LC 88-33709. (American Civilization Ser.). 260p. (C). 1989. 34.95 (0-87722-589-3) Temple U Pr.

Before It's Too Late: Why Some Kids Get into Trouble--& What Parents Can Do about It. Stanton E. Samenow. (Illus.). 288p. 1989. 23.00 (0-8129-1646-8, Times Bks) Random.

Before It's Too Late: Working with Substance Abuse in the Family. David C. Treadway. 1989. 23.95 (0-393-70068-2) Norton.

***Before Knossos: Arthur Evans' Travels in the Balkans & Crete.** Ann Brown. (Illus.). 112p. 1995. 19.95 (1-85444-030-6, 0306, Pub. by Ashmolean Mus UK); pap. 15.95 (1-85444-029-2, 0292, Pub. by Ashmolean Mus UK) A Schwartz & Co.

Before Lascaux. White. 1993. 75.00 (0-8493-8883-X, GN772) CRC Pr.

Before Lewis & Clark: Documents Illustrating the History of the Missouri, 1785-1804, Vol. II. Ed. by A. P. Nasatir. LC 89-25080. (Illus.). xvi, 478p. 1990. reprint ed. 42.50 (0-8032-3321-3); reprint ed. pap. 12.95 (0-8032-8362-8) U of Nebr Pr.

Before Lewis & Clark: Documents Illustrating the History of the Missouri, 1785-1804, Vol. II, Vol. I. Ed. by A. P. Nasatir. LC 89-25080. (Illus.). xxii, 375p. 1990. reprint ed. 42.50 (0-8032-3320-5); reprint ed. pap. 11.95 (0-8032-8361-X) U of Nebr Pr.

Before Lift-Off: The Making of a Space Shuttle Crew. Henry S. Cooper, Jr. LC 87-2761. (New Series in NASA History). (Illus.). 288p. 1987. 34.95x (0-8018-3524-0) Johns Hopkins.

Before Lunch. Angela Thirkell. (Barsetshire Novels Ser.). 336p. 1988. pap. 5.95 (0-88184-397-0) Carroll & Graf.

Before Man in Michigan. R. Ray Baker. 1936. 12.50 (0-911586-52-0) Wahr.

Before Mickey: The Animated Film, 1898-1928. Donald Crafton. (Illus.). xx, 416p. 1993. pap. 15.95 (0-226-11667-0) U Ch Pr.

Before Midnight. Rex Stout. 1993. pap. 4.99 (0-685-65925-9) Bantam.

Before Midnight. large type ed. Rex Stout. LC 94-7342. 267p. 1994. pap. 15.95 (0-8161-5985-8) Hall.

Before My Eyes: Film Criticism & Comment. Stanley Kauffmann. LC 82-9774. (Quality Paperbacks Ser.). (Illus.). 460p. 1982. reprint ed. pap. 9.95 (0-306-80179-5) Da Capo.

Before My Time. Niccolo Tucci. 638p. 1991. reprint ed. pap. 12.95 (1-55921-055-9) Moyer Bell.

Before Newton: The Life & Times of Isaac Barrow. Ed. by Mordechai Feingold. (Illus.). 368p. (C). 1990. 64.95 (0-521-30694-9) Cambridge U Pr.

Before Night Falls: A Memoir. Reinaldo Arenas. Tr. by Dolores M. Koch. 336p. 1994. reprint ed. pap. 11.95 (0-14-015765-4, Penguin Bks) Viking Penguin.

Before Nomination: Our Primary Problems. Ed. by George Grassmuck. 146p. 1985. pap. 12.25 (0-8447-2259-6) Am Enterprise.

Before Novels: The Cultural Contexts of Eighteenth Century English Fiction. J. Paul Hunter. 448p. 1992. pap. 13.95 (0-393-30861-8) Norton.

Before Our Eyes. Joan Alden. LC 93-30089. 153p. (Orig.). 1993. 18.95 (1-56341-034-6); pap. 8.95 (1-56341-033-8) Firebrand Bks.

Before Our Eyes. Lawrence Joseph. 1993. 18.00 (0-374-11009-3) FS&G.

Before Our Eyes. Lawrence Joseph. 1994. pap. 8.00 (0-374-52404-1) FS&G.

Before Pastoral: Theocritus & the Ancient Tradition of Bucolic Poetry. David M. Halperin. LC 82-10879. 296p. 1983. text ed. 40.00x (0-300-02582-3) Yale U Pr.

Before Reading: Narrative Conventions & the Politics of Interpretation. Peter J. Rabinowitz. LC 87-47602. 272p. (C). 1987. 35.95 (0-8014-2010-5); pap. 13.95 (0-8014-9472-9) Cornell U Pr.

Before Recollection. Ann Lauterbach. 80p. 1987. text ed. 21.95 (0-691-06698-1); pap. text ed. 9.95 (0-691-01437-X) Princeton U Pr.

Before Reforms: Human Rights in the Warsaw Pact States, 1972-1988. Ed. by Georg Brunner. LC 90-37865. 540p. 1991. text ed. 55.00 (0-312-05203-0) St Martin.

Before Revelation: The Boundaries of Muslim Moral Thought. A. Kevin Reinhart. LC 94-13372. (SUNY Series in Middle Eastern Studies). 267p. 1995. text ed. 59.50 (0-7914-2289-5); pap. 19.95 (0-7914-2290-9) State U NY Pr.

Before Rockne at Notre Dame. Chet Grant. LC 78-12487. (Illus.). 1978. 19.95 (0-89651-050-6) B L Pub.

Before Sexuality: The Construction of Erotic Experience in the Ancient Greek World. Ed. by David M. Halperin et al. (Illus.). 545p. 1991. pap. 19.95 (0-691-00221-5) Princeton U Pr.

Before She Met Me. Julian Barnes. LC 92-50091. 1992. 10.00 (0-679-73609-3, Vin) Random.

Before Silent Spring: Pesticides in Pre-DDT America. James Whorton et al. LC 74-2984. 316p. 1975. 45.00 (0-691-08139-5) Princeton U Pr.

Before Social Anthropology: Essays on the History of British Anthropology. Ed. by James Urry. (Studies in Anthropology & History). 1993. text ed. 48.00 (3-7186-5292-7) Gordon & Breach.

Before Stalinism: The Rise & Fall of Soviet Democracy. Samuel Farber. 275p. 1990. 55.00 (0-86091-315-5, A4993, Pub. by Verso UK); pap. 17.95 (0-86091-530-1, A4997, Pub. by Verso UK) Routledge Chapman & Hall.

Before Stanislavsky: American Professional Acting Schools & Acting Theory, 1875-1925. James H. McTeague. LC 93-26669. 1993. 39.50 (0-8108-2657-7) Scarecrow.

Before Stonewall: The Making of a Gay & Lesbian Community. Andrea Weiss & Greta Schiller. LC 88-9111. (Illus.). 96p. 1988. pap. 7.95 (0-941483-20-7) Naiad Pr.

***Before Sunrise.** Linklater. 1995. pap. 13.95 (0-312-13345-6) St Martin.

Before Tennessee: The Southwest Territory, 1790-1796: A Narrative History of the Territory of the United States South of the River Ohio. Walter T. Durham. (Illus.). 327p. 1990. 24.95 (0-9627696-0-6) Rocky Mt Hist Assn.

Before the Anasazi. Larry Agenbroad. 32p. 1990. 6.95 (0-89734-101-5, PL61-2) Mus Northern Ariz.

***Before the Apple Drops: 15 Essays on Dinosaur Education.** Enoch Haga. LC 94-96376. (Illus.). xii, 142p. (Orig.). 1994. 30.00 (1-885794-03-7); pap. 20.00 (1-885794-04-5) E Haga Pub.

Before the Basics: Creating Conversations with Children. Beverley J. Bos. LC 82-74059. (Illus.). 1978. pap. 12.50 (0-931540-01-1) Turn the Page.

Before the Beginning. Patricia C. Groth. LC 84-71323. (Illus.). 84p. 1984. pap. 8.00 (0-9610346-4-5) Belle Mead Pr.

Before the Beginning: Cosmology Explained. George F. Ellis. LC 92-43668. (Briefings Ser.). 1993. 14.95 (0-685-63326-8) M Boyars Pubs.

Before the Beginning of Time. Jacob Meyerowitz. LC 93-86657. (Illus.). 336p. 1994. 35.00 (0-9607034-1-1) RRP Pub.

Before the Bell Rings. Gregory Stricherz. Ed. by Roger E. Olsen. (Illus.). 78p. 1982. pap. text ed. 10.72 (0-13-068297-7) Alemany Pr.

Before the Best Interests of the Child. Joseph Goldstein et al. LC 79-64249. 1980. text ed. 22.95 (0-02-912220-1) Free Pr.

Before the Best Interests of the Child, Vol. 2. Joseph Goldstein. 1986. pap. 13.95 (0-02-912390-9) Free Pr.

Before the Black Death: Studies in the "Crisis" of the Early Fourteenth Century. Ed. by Bruce M. Campbell. (Illus.). 240p. (C). 1993. text ed. 24.95 (0-7190-3927-4, Pub. by Manchester Univ Pr UK) St Martin.

Before the Blood Tribunal see Three Against Hitler

Before the Blueprint: Science Center Buildings. Peter Anderson. (Illus.). 96p. 1991. spiral bd. 22.00 (0-944040-27-6) AST Ctrs.

Before the Box Boats. A. W. Kinghorn. 232p. 1987. 49.00 (0-85937-297-9, Pub. by K Mason Pubns Ltd UK) St Mut.

Before the Brave. Kenneth Patchen. LC 74-3035. (Studies in Poetry: No. 38). 1974. lib. bdg. 75.00 (0-8383-2062-7) M S G Haskell Hse.

***Before the Bridge: Reminiscences.** Phillip J. Wingate. LC 84-26694. reprint ed. pap. 62.20 (0-7837-9073-2, 2049822) Bks Demand.

Before the Bulldozer: The Nambiquara Indians & the World Bank. David Price. LC 89-6065. 212p. 1989. 18.95 (0-932020-67-4) Seven Locks Pr.

Before the Bulldozers Came. Edgar Prescott. (Orig.). 1985. pap. 3.00 (0-936563-05-2) Signpost.

Before the Burning. Elaine Woodruff. LC 93-46258. 64p. 1994. pap. 12.95 (0-7734-2718-X, Mellen Poetry Pr) E Mellen.

Before the Civil Rights Revolution: The Old Courts & Individual Rights. John Braeman. LC 87-32291. (Contributions in Legal Studies: No. 41). 225p. 1988. text ed. 55.00 (0-313-26205-5, BCY/, Greenwood Pr) Greenwood.

Before the Cock Crows Twice: Why the Churches Have Fallen. Harland H. Hay. 135p. (Orig.). 1994. pap. 9.95 (0-9639204-2-1) Aquarian Pubns.

Before the Communist Revolution. Stuart A. Kallen. Ed. by Rosemary Wallner. LC 92-13472. (Rise & Fall of the Soviet Union Ser.). (J). 1992. lib. bdg. 13.99 (1-56239-100-3) Abdo & Dghtrs.

Before the Computer: IBM, NCR, Burroughs, & Remington Rand & the Industry They Created, 1865-1956. James W. Cortada. LC 92-25399. (Studies in Business & Technology). (Illus.). 392p. 1993. text ed. 59.50 (0-691-04807-X) Princeton U Pr.

Before the Convention: Religion & the Founders. M. Susan Power. LC 84-12004. 268p. (Orig.). 1984. pap. text ed. 23.00 (0-8191-4134-8) U Pr of Amer.

Before the Convention: Strategies & Choices in Presidential Nomination Campaigns. John H. Aldrich. LC 79-27752. (Illus.). xiv, 258p. 1980. lib. bdg. 25.00 (0-226-01269-7) U Ch Pr.

Before the Curfew & Other Poems. Oliver W. Holmes. (Notable American Authors Ser.). 1992. reprint ed. lib. bdg. 75.00 (0-7812-3165-5) Rprt Serv.

Before the Darkness Falls. Eugenia Price. LC 87-556. 480p. 1987. 17.95 (0-385-23068-0) Doubleday.

Before the Darkness Falls. Eugenia Price. 1980. pap. 6.99 (0-515-10538-4) Jove Pubns.

Before the Dawn. Joseph Altsheler. 1976. lib. bdg. 21.95 (0-89968-000-3, Lghtyr Pr) Buccaneer Bks.

Before the Dawn. Joseph A. Altsheler. 20.95 (0-8488-1234-4) Amereon Ltd.

Before the Dawn. Mickey Block. 1990. mass mkt. 4.99 (0-671-72607-2) PB.

Before the Dawn. Toson Shimazaki. Tr. by William E. Naff. LC 87-5046. 816p. 1987. 30.00 (0-8248-0914-9); pap. 19.95 (0-8248-1164-X) UH Pr.

Before the Dawn. Joseph Altsheler. 1990. reprint ed. lib. bdg. 18.95 (0-89968-456-4) Buccaneer Bks.

Before the Dawn. E. T. Bell, pseud. LC 74-16522. (Science Fiction Ser.). 247p. 1975. reprint ed. 21.95 (0-405-06314-8) Ayer.

***Before the Deluge: Parisian Society in the Reign of Louis the Sixteenth.** Evelyn Farr. 216p. 1994. 33.00 (0-7206-0893-7, Pub. by P Owen Ltd UK) Dufour.

Before the Devil Knows You're Dead: Irish Blessings, Toasts & Curses. Ed. by Padraic O'Farrell. 117p. 1993. pap. 11.95 (1-85635-033-9, Pub. by Mercier Pr IE) Dufour.

Before the Dinosaurs. Miriam Schlein. LC 93-25781. (J). 1994. 14.95 (0-590-47910-5) Scholastic Inc.

Before the Divorce, Read This! M. A. Butcher. (Illus.). 48p. (Orig.). 1984. pap. text ed. 5.00 (0-9622939-0-3) Yamoo Pubs.

Before the Dome: Baseball in Minnesota When the Grass Was Real. David Anderson. 188p. 1993. pap. 12.95 (0-931714-50-8) Nodin Pr.

Before the Earth Arose. J. Dobracyynski. 267p. 1981. 6.25 (0-8199-0783-9, Frncscn Herld) Franciscan Pr.

***Before the Echo: Essays on Nature.** Pete Dunne. LC 94-22910. (Corrie Herring Hooks Ser.). (Illus.). 152p. 1995. 19.95 (0-292-71578-1) U of Tex Pr.

***Before the End of the Day.** Michael Malus. 1995. pap. 15.95 (1-55065-055-6) InBook.

Before the Ending of the Day. Norman Pittenger. LC 84-62373. 110p. 1985. pap. 6.95 (0-8192-1365-9) Morehouse Pub.

Before the European Challenge: The Great Civilizations of Asia & the Middle East. Jaroslav Krejci. LC 89-11594. 348p. 1990. 59.50 (0-7914-0168-5); pap. 19.95 (0-7914-0169-3) State U NY Pr.

Before the Face of God: A Daily Guide for Living from the Book of Romans, Vol. 1. R. C. Sproul. LC 92-31634. 488p. 1992. 22.99 (0-8010-8340-0) Baker Bk.

Before the Face of God: A Daily Guide for Living from the Gospel of Luke, Vol. 2. R. C. Sproul. LC 92-31634. 560p. 1993. lib. bdg. 22.99 (0-8010-8358-3) Baker Bk.

An Asterisk (*) at the beginning of an entry indicates that the title is appearing in BIP for the first time.

An Asterisk (*) at the beginning of an entry indicates that the title is appearing in BIP for the first time.

657

Beggar. Naguib Mahfouz. Tr. by Kristin W. Henry. 1987. pap. 10.50 (*977-424-135-5*, Pub. by Am Univ Cairo Pr UA) Col U Pr.

Beggar. Naguib Mahfouz. 1990. mass mkt. 7.95 (*0-385-26456-9*) Doubleday.

Beggar: Al Shahad. Nagib Mahfouz. (ARA.). 1985. pap. 8.95 (*0-86685-151-8*) Intl Bk Ctr.

Beggar: Meditations & Prayers on the Supreme Lord. Swami Krenapada. 150p. 1994. pap. 10.00 (*1-885414-00-5*) Hari-Nama Pr.

***Beggar at Damascus Gate.** Yasimine Zahran. 155p. (Orig.). 1995. pap. 12.95 (*0-942996-24-0*) Post Apollo Pr.

Beggar at the Banquet: The Story of Dr. Woo Jun Hong. Ed. by Donald B. Sheley. LC 81-13971. (Illus.). 178p. (Orig.). pap. 7.95 (*0-88289-306-8*) Pelican.

Beggar in Jerusalem. Elie Wiesel. 1989. pap. 14.00 (*0-8052-0897-6*) Schocken.

Beggar in the Street. Dorothea E. Hammond. 700p. (Orig.). 1983. pap. 14.95 (*0-942874-02-1*) Hammond Records.

Beggar King. Dan Hamilton. LC 93-19200. (Tales of the Forgotten God Ser.: Bk. 1). (Illus.). 156p. (Orig.). 1993. pap. 7.99 (*0-8308-1671-2*, 1671) InterVarsity.

Beggar Maid. Alice Munro. (Fiction Ser.). 224p. 1984. mass mkt. 6.95 (*0-14-006011-1*, Penguin Bks) Viking Penguin.

Beggar Maid. Alice Munro. 1991. 10.00 (*0-679-73271-3*) McKay.

Beggar on Horseback. Sylvia Thorpe. 1977. pap. 1.50 (*0-449-23091-0*, Crest) Fawcett.

Beggar Queen. Lloyd Alexander. (J). (gr. 6-12). 1985. pap. 3.99 (*0-440-90548-6*, LFL) Dell.

Beggar T. Bear: The History, Significance, Manufacture, Promotion, Identification Guide, Photographs & Current Values of the American Teddy Bear Circa 1903-1945. Marguerite J. Cantine. (Illus.). 64p. 1981. pap. 5.95 (*0-940548-00-3*) Cantine & Kilpatrick.

Beggar Your Neighbours: Apartheid Power in Southern Africa. Joseph Hanlon. LC 86-45581. (Illus.). 364p. 1986. 35.00 (*0-253-33131-5*) Ind U Pr.

Beggars & Choosers. Nancy Kress. 320p. 1994. 22.95 (*0-312-85749-7*) Tor Bks.

***Beggars & Choosers.** Nancy Kress. 1996. pap. 4.99 (*0-614-05522-9*) Tor Bks.

Beggars Ape. Richard Niccols. LC 37-5555. 1980. reprint ed. 50.00 (*0-8201-1178-3*) Schol Facsimiles.

Beggars, Beasts & Easter Fire: Stories of Early Saints. Carol Greene. Ed. by Robert Klausmeier. LC 92-31408. (Illus.). 128p. (J). (gr. 3-6). 1993. 15.95 (*0-7459-2221-X*) Lion USA.

Beggars Bible: An Illustrated Historical Fiction of John Wycliffe for the 9-14 Age-Group. Louise A. Vernon. LC 77-131534. (Illus.). 128p. (J). (gr. 4-9). 1971. 5.95 (*0-8361-1732-8*) Herald Pr.

Beggar's Bowl: Parables & Short Stories for Spiritual Pondering. James L. Henderschedt et al. LC 94-94544. (Illus.). 70p. 1994. pap. 5.95 (*0-9641778-0-3*) Faith Jrny.

Beggar's Choice. Jerry Kennealy. 256p. 1994. 20.95 (*0-312-11478-8*, Pub. by Thomas Dunne Bks) St Martin.

Beggar's Choice. Patricia Wentworth. 20.95 (*0-8488-1217-4*) Amereon Ltd.

Beggar's Choice. Patricia Wentworth. 256p. 1990. mass mkt. 4.50 (*0-446-35909-2*) Warner Bks.

Beggar's Cup. Eric Blau. LC 93-18365. 1993. 23.00 (*0-679-42557-8*) Knopf.

Beggar's Gulch. large type ed. Cameron Judd. 212p. (Orig.). 1991. reprint ed. lib. bdg. 16.95 (*1-56054-106-7*) Thorndike Pr.

Beggar's Handbook. M. T. Pockets. 39p. 1989. pap. text ed. 5.95 (*1-55950-012-3*) Loompanics.

Beggars in Spain. Nancy Kress. 448p. 1994. mass mkt. 4.99 (*0-380-71877-4*, AvoNova) Avon.

Beggars in Spain: A Novel. Nancy Kress. LC 92-25070. 1993. 23.00 (*0-688-12189-6*) Morrow.

Beggars in the House of Plenty. John P. Shanley. 1992. pap. 4.75 (*0-8222-1300-1*) Dramatists Play.

Beggar's Knife. Rodrigo Rey-Rosa. Tr. by Paul Bowles. 112p. (Orig.). 1985. 12.95 (*0-87286-166-X*); pap. 5.95 (*0-87286-164-3*) City Lights.

Beggars of Life. Jim Tully. 1993. reprint ed. lib. bdg. 89.00 (*0-7812-5409-4*) Rprt Serv.

Beggars on Golden Stools: Report on Latin America. Peter Schmid. Tr. by Mervyn Savill. LC 74-20278. (Illus.). 327p. 1975. reprint ed. text ed. 59.75 (*0-8371-7853-3*, SCGS, Greenwood Pr) Greenwood.

Beggar's Opera. John Gay. 128p. 1987. mass mkt. 7.95 (*0-14-043220-5*, Penguin Classics) Viking Penguin.

Beggar's Opera. John Gay. Ed. by Edgar V. Roberts. LC 68-21878. (Regents Restoration Drama Ser.). (Illus.). xxx, 238p. 1969. pap. 7.95 (*0-8032-5361-3*) U of Nebr Pr.

***Beggar's Opera.** John Gay. 1994. 6.00 (*0-88734-283-3*) Players Pr.

Beggar's Opera: Its Predecessors & Successors. Frank Kidson. LC 72-109760. 109p. 1971. reprint ed. text ed. 38.50 (*0-8371-4250-4*, KIBE, Greenwood Pr) Greenwood.

Beggar's Opera & Companion Pieces. John Gay. Ed. by C. F. Burgess. (Crofts Classics Ser.). 136p. 1966. pap. text ed. write for info. (*0-88295-037-1*) Harlan Davidson.

Beggars Opera & Other Eighteenth Century Plays. John Gay et al. Ed. by David W. Lindsay. 472p. 1993. pap. 5.95 (*0-460-87314-8*, Everyman's Classic Lib) C E Tuttle.

Beggars' Ride. Theresa Nelson. LC 90-52515. 256p. (YA). (gr. 6 up). 1992. 15.95 (*0-531-05896-4*); lib. bdg. 15.99 (*0-531-08496-5*) Orchard Bks Watts.

Beggar's Ride. Theresa Nelson. (YA). 1994. mass mkt. 3.99 (*0-440-21887-X*) Dell.

Beggar's Strike. Aminata S. Fall. (African Classics Ser.). (C). 1981. pap. text ed. 9.95 (*0-582-00243-5*) Longman.

Beggarstaff Poster. Colin Campbell. (Illus.). 128p. 1993. 24.95 (*1-55859-545-7*, Cross Riv Pr) Abbeville Pr.

Begging for More. 1991. pap. 4.50 (*0-8216-5087-4*, Univ Books) Carol Pub Group.

Begging Pardon & Favor: Ritual & Political Order in Early Medieval France. Geoffrey Koziol. LC 91-55073. (Illus.). 480p. 1992. 46.50 (*0-8014-2369-4*) Cornell U Pr.

Begging the Question: Circular Reasoning As a Tactic of Argumentation. Douglas N. Walton. LC 90-24984. (Contributions in Philosophy Ser.: No. 48). 360p. 1991. text ed. 59.95 (*0-313-27596-3*, WAJ/, Greenwood Pr) Greenwood.

***Begin a Portrait.** Harry Hurwitz. 1994. 24.95 (*0-910250-27-8*); pap. 19.95 (*0-910250-28-6*) Bnai Brith Intl.

Begin-Again Land. Clara M. Hobbs. (J). 1993. 10.95 (*0-533-10386-X*) Vantage.

Begin at Start: Some Thoughts on Personal Liberation & World Change. Su Negrin. LC 72-87031. (Illus.). 176p. (Orig.). 1972. 15.95 (*0-87810-520-4*); pap. 7.95 (*0-87810-020-2*) Times Change.

Begin at the Beginning. John R. Boyd & Mary A. Boyd. 80p. (Orig.). 1988. teacher ed 2.95 (*0-933759-12-6*); pap. text ed. 3.95 (*0-933759-11-8*); audio 29.95 (*0-933759-13-4*) Abaca Bks.

Begin at the Beginning. Amy Schwartz. LC 82-48257. (Illus.). 32p. (J). (ps-3). 1983. lib. bdg. 13.89 (*0-06-025228-6*) HarpC Child Bks.

Begin at the Beginning. Amy Schwartz. LC 82-48257. (Trophy Picture Bk.). (Illus.). 32p. (J). (gr. k-3). 1984. pap. 4.95 (*0-06-443060-X*, Trophy) HarpC Child Bks.

Begin at the Beginning with Books: Curriculum & Guide. Ann Wilmshurst. Ed. by Penny Markey. (Illus.). 1992. ring bd. 28.00 (*0-9627818-1-9*) Cnty of Los Angeles Public Library.

Begin Basic Budget - Saving Shopping Spending: A Budget Seminar Workbook. 2nd rev. ed. Dolores E. Washington. (C). 1991. reprint ed. student ed 5.00 (*0-9623123-2-0*) DEW Educational.

Begin Basic Budget Saving Shopping Spending, Vol. I. Dolores E. Washington. 13p. (YA). (gr. 11 up). 1989. student ed 2.50 (*0-685-26101-8*) DEW Educational.

Begin Bridge with Reese. Terence Reese. 1979. pap. 4.50 (*0-451-16292-7*, Sig) NAL-Dutton.

Begin Chess. David B. Pritchard. 160p. 1987. pap. 2.95 (*0-451-14723-5*, Sig) NAL-Dutton.

Begin Chess. D. B. Ritchard. 1987. pap. 3.95 (*0-451-16518-7*, Sig) NAL-Dutton.

Begin Chess. 2nd ed. David B. Pritchard. 168p. 1992. pap. 4.99 (*0-451-17438-0*, Sig) NAL-Dutton.

Begin Here: The Forgotten Conditions of Teaching & Learning. Jacques Barzun. Ed. by Morris Philipson. 232p. 1991. 24.95 (*0-226-03846-7*) U Ch Pr.

Begin Here: The Forgotten Conditions of Teaching & Learning. Jacques Barzun. Ed. by Morris Philipson. LC 90-25877. 234p. 1992. pap. 12.95 (*0-226-03847-5*) U Ch Pr.

Begin in English Vol. II: Vocabulary - Expanding Short Stories for Launched Beginners, Vol. I. Judith Bailey & Joan Ashkenas. LC 87-81968. (Illus.). 112p. (Orig.). 1992. pap. text ed. 9.95 (*0-943327-04-0*) JAG Pubns.

Begin It Now. Susan Hayward. 1989. 15.95 (*0-9590439-1-8*) In-Tune Bks.

***Begin the Beloved Words: Greek Lyric Poetry.** Melisa Gough et al. 96p. 1994. pap. 9.95 (*0-9630069-2-4*) Whi Stone.

Begin the Harp. N. Calthorpe. Date not set. 19.75 (*0-685-75005-1*, 95182WW) Mel Bay.

Begin to Exit Here: A Novel of the Wayward Press. John Welter. Ed. by Robert A. Rubin. 308p. 1992. 16.95 (*0-945575-51-3*) Algonquin Bks.

Begin to Keep Bees. Franklin H. Carrier. (Illus.). 234p. 1981. text ed. 17.25 (*0-9607550-0-4*) Carriers Bees.

Begin Two A. William Caxton. LC 72-5980. (English Experience Ser.: No. 508). 1973. reprint ed. 61.00 (*90-221-0508-3*) Walter J Johnson.

Begin with Phonics. Suzanne Kirsten. Ed. by Betsey Kahn. LC 81-85695. (Illus.). 80p. (Orig.). (J). (gr. 1-4). 1982. pap. 4.95 (*0-89709-033-0*) Liberty Pub.

Begin with Prayer: Prayers & Devotional Outlines for Church Meetings. Kenneth W. Rogahn. 112p. 1985. 7.95 (*0-570-03962-2*, 15-2178) Concordia.

Begin with Sadat. Wim Malgo. 2.95 (*0-937422-17-7*) Midnight Call.

Beginnende Photographie im Spiegel von Tageszeintungen und Tagebuchern. Erich Stenger. Ed. by Peter C. Bunnell & Robert A. Sobieszek. LC 76-23049. (Sources of Modern Photography Ser.). (Illus.). (GER.). 1979. reprint ed. lib. bdg. 15.95 (*0-405-09610-0*) Ayer.

Beginner in Water Color, Oil, & China Painting, 3 bks. D. M. Campana. (Illus.). 3.50 (*0-939608-30-8*) Campana Art.

Beginners ABC Bible Memory Book. C. Spencer Morris & V. Gilbert Beers. 287p. (Orig.). (J). (ps-3). 1988. 12.99 (*0-945564-41-4*, Gold & Honey) Questar Pubs.

Beginner's Ancestor Research Kit. Philip Breck. 96p. 1990. ring bd., pap. 8.95 (*1-55867-019-X*) Bristol Pub Ent CA.

Beginner's Approach to Using Microsoft Windows. Al Schroeder et al. LC 93-1475. (Illus.). 272p. (Orig.). (C). 1994. pap. write for info. (*0-02-408001-2*) Macmillan.

Beginner's Astrology Course, Dimensions into Self-Discovery. Carol Hemingway. 148p. 1990. 16.00 (*0-685-47914-5*, H3117-014) Am Fed Astrologers.

***Beginners Bible: My Favorite Bible Stories.** Karyn Henley. (A Kid-Friendly Inspirational Ser.). (Illus.). 1995. 10.99 (*0-679-87638-3*) Random Bks Yng Read.

***Beginners Bible: Tales of Virtue.** Carolyn N. Baker. (A Kid-Friendly Inspirational Ser.). (Illus.). 1995. 8.99 (*0-679-87637-5*) Random Bks Yng Read.

Beginner's Bible: Timeless Children's Stories. Karyn Henley. (Illus.). 528p. (J). (ps-3). 1989. 16.99 (*0-945564-31-7*, Gold & Honey) Questar Pubs.

***Beginner's Bible for Toddlers.** Illus. by Danny B. Dalby. LC 95-12627. (J). 1995. write for info. (*0-8499-1198-2*) Word Pub.

Beginners Bible Questions & Answer Book. Ben Alex & Mack Thomas. (Illus.). 384p. (Orig.). (J). (ps-5). 1992. 14.99 (*0-945564-21-X*, Gold & Honey) Questar Pubs.

Beginner's Book of Magic. Francis J. Rigney. (Illus.). (J). (gr. 6 up). 1963. 9.95 (*0-8159-5103-5*) Devin.

Beginner's Book of TEX. R. Seroul & S. Levy. xii, 282p. 1992. pap. 29.95 (*0-387-97562-4*) Spr-Verlag.

Beginner's Book, Vol. 1: The Holy Ground Discourse. Tisziji Munoz. 127p. (Orig.). (C). 1981. pap. 15.00 (*0-945174-00-4*) Illum Soc Pubns.

Beginners Book, Vol. 2: Satsang Talks & Readings. Tizsiji Munoz. 169p. (Orig.). (C). 1987. pap. text ed. 15.00 (*0-945174-01-2*) Illum Soc Pubns.

Beginners Bookshelf, 8 vols. (J). (ps-3). 79.95 (*0-685-09844-3*) Ency Brit Inc.

***Beginner's Brazilian Portuguese.** Eliane Taddei. (Beginner's Language Ser.). 200p. (Orig.). (POR.). 1995. pap. 9.95 (*0-7818-0338-1*) Hippocrene Bks.

***Beginner's Brazilian Portuguese, Set.** Eliane Taddei. (Beginner's Language Ser.). (Orig.). (POR.). 1995. digital audio 12.95 (*0-7818-0339-X*) Hippocrene Bks.

Beginner's Bulgarian. Mariana Raykov. (Eurolingua Beginner's Languages Ser.). 200p. 1994. pap. 7.95 (*0-7818-0300-4*) Hippocrene Bks.

Beginner's Course in Topology. D. B. Fuks & V. A. Rokhlin. Tr. by A. Iacob. (Universitext Ser.). (Illus.). xi, 519p. 1984. pap. 64.00 (*0-387-13577-4*) Spr-Verlag.

Beginner's Course of Polish. W. Bisko et al. 326p. 1966. audio, pap. 17.50 (*83-214-0058-2*) IBD Ltd.

***Beginner's Course of Polish.** W. Bisko et al. 326p. 1966. audio 17.50 (*0-88431-158-9*) IBD Ltd.

Beginner's Course of Polish. Waclaw Bisko et al. 329p. (ENG & POL.). 1979. pap. 14.95 (*0-8288-4722-3*, M9130) Fr & Eur.

Beginner's Course of Polish Book & Cassettes. W. Bisko & S. Karolak. 328p. (C). 1988. 90.00 (*0-89771-844-5*, Pub. by Collets) St Mut.

Beginner's Czech. (Language Ser.). 250p. (Orig.). (CZE & ENG.). 1994. pap. 9.95 (*0-7818-0231-8*) Hippocrene Bks.

Beginner's Devotional. Stephen T. Barclift. (Illus.). 384p. (Orig.). 1991. 14.99 (*0-945564-28-7*, Gold & Honey) Questar Pubs.

Beginner's Dictionary of American English Usage. P. H. Collin et al. (Illus.). 288p. 1986. text ed. 9.95 (*0-8325-0440-8*, Natl Textbk); pap. 5.95 (*0-8325-0439-4*, Natl Textbk) NTC Pub Grp.

Beginner's Dictionary of American English Usage. P. H. Collin. 1994. pap. 5.95 (*0-8442-0439-0*) NTC Pub Grp.

Beginners' Dictionary of Chinese-Japanese Characters & Compounds. Arthur Rose-Innes. (CHI & JPN.). 1977. reprint ed. pap. 11.95 (*0-486-23467-3*) Dover.

Beginner's Dictionary of Prayerbook Hebrew. Ethelyn Simon & Irene Resnikoff. 80p. (Orig.). 1989. pap. 14.95 (*0-939144-13-1*) EKS Pub Co.

Beginner's Dog Obedience. rev. ed. Carol Sigona. (Illus.). 49p. (Orig.). reprint ed. pap. text ed. 5.00 (*0-9602056-1-6*) C Sigona.

Beginner's Esperanto. Joseph Conroy. (Beginner's Language Ser.). 250p. (Orig.). (ENG & ESP.). 1994. pap. 14.95 (*0-685-70169-7*) Hippocrene Bks.

Beginner's Faith in Things Unseen. John Hay. LC 94-8410. (Concord Library). 176p. 1994. 22.00 (*0-8070-8532-4*) Beacon Pr.

Beginner's Fingerpicking Guitar Workshop. Stefan Grossman. 1985. pap. 10.95 (*0-89898-359-2*) CPP Belwin.

Beginners Fishing. Steve Starling. (Lothian Australian Fishing Guides Ser.). (Illus.). 96p. (Orig.). 1995. pap. 5.95 (*0-85091-606-2*, Pub. by Lothian Pub AT) Seven Hills Bk.

Beginner's French Dictionary. H. Davies. (Beginner's Language Dictionaries Ser.). (Illus.). 128p. (J). 1989. lib. bdg. 16.96 (*0-88110-346-2*); pap. 10.95 (*0-7460-0016-2*) EDC.

Beginner's German Dictionary. H. Davies. (Beginner's Language Dictionaries Ser.). (Illus.). 128p. 1989. lib. bdg. 16.96 (*0-88110-347-0*); pap. 10.95 (*0-7460-0018-9*) EDC.

Beginner's Glossary to a Course in Miracles. 1992. pap. text ed. 10.00 (*0-9633394-0-0*) One Miracle.

***Beginner's Golf Only.** Edward W. Eckhardt. Ed. by Christopher Card. (Illus.). 70p. (Orig.). (J). 1995. pap. 22.50 (*1-886759-01-4*) IntroTech.

Beginner's Grammar of the Greek New Testament. William H. Davis. 1923. text ed. 17.00 (*0-06-061710-1*) Harper SF.

***Beginner's Guide.** Wizards of the Coast Inc. Staff. (Magic: The Gathering Ser.). 1994. pap. 12.00 (*0-06-105317-1*, Prism Bks) P-H.

***Beginner's Guide: Microsoft Dos 5.0-6.2 - Microsoft Windows 3.1.** Dave McKay. 1995. write for info. (*1-881023-89-3*) Inst Publishing.

***Beginner's Guide: Quicken-QuickBook-TurboTax.** Dave McKay. 1995. write for info. (*1-881023-91-5*) Inst Publishing.

***Beginner's Guide: Windows '95.** Dave McKay. 1995. write for info. (*1-881023-90-7*) Inst Publishing.

***Beginner's Guide for Law Students.** Duard Kleyn & Frans Viljoen. 316p. 1995. pap. 32.00 (*0-7021-3366-3*, Pub. by Juta SA) W W Gaunt.

Beginner's Guide to Aikido. Joseph Billingiere & Larry Reynosa. (Illus.). 123p. (Orig.). (C). 1989. pap. 10.95 (*0-9625269-0-8*) R & B Pub.

Beginner's Guide to Amateur Astronomy: An Owner's Manual for the Night Sky from the Publishers of Astronomy Magazine. David J. Eicher. Ed. by Michael Emmerich. LC 92-41663. (Astronomy Library: No. 7). (Illus.). 176p. (Orig.). 1993. pap. 19.95 (*0-913135-18-6*) Kalmbach.

Beginner's Guide to Amateur Radio. American Radio Relay League Inc., Staff. (Illus.). 208p. 1982. pap. 17.00 (*0-13-072140-9*) P-H.

Beginner's Guide to American Bonsai. Jerald P. Stowell. LC 77-15372. (Illus.). 140p. 1987. pap. 19.00 (*0-87011-802-1*) Kodansha.

Beginner's Guide to Aquariums. (Illus.). 64p. 1993. spiral bd. 5.98 (*1-56173-289-3*, 3611600) Pubns Intl Ltd.

Beginner's Guide to Attracting Birds to Your Backyard. (Illus.). 64p. 1993. spiral bd. 5.98 (*1-56173-261-3*, 3611300) Pubns Intl Ltd.

Beginners Guide to Ayurvedic Medicine: How an Ancient Medical Tradition Can Transform Your Health. Vivek Shanbhag. 50p. (Orig.). 1994. pap. 3.50 (*0-87983-604-0*) Keats.

Beginner's Guide to Baseball Card Collecting: A Step-by-Step Guide for the Young Collector. Casey Childress & Linda McKenzie. LC 88-90757. (Illus.). 46p. (Orig.). (J). (gr. 4-8). 1990. reprint ed. vinyl bd. 7.95 (*0-9620167-0-5*) C Mack Pub.

Beginner's Guide to Bettas. W. L. Whitern. (Beginner's Guide Ser.). (Illus.). 64p. 1986. 3.95 (*0-86622-318-5*, T-118) TFH Pubns.

Beginner's Guide to Birdwatching. (Illus.). 64p. 1993. spiral bd. 5.98 (*1-56173-101-3*, 3610600) Pubns Intl Ltd.

Beginner's Guide to Budgerigars. Anmarie Barrie. (Beginner's Guide Ser.). (Illus.). 64p. 1986. 3.95 (*0-86622-300-2*, T-101) TFH Pubns.

Beginner's Guide to Canaries. Norton Marsden. (Beginner's Guide Ser.). (Illus.). 64p. 1986. 3.95 (*0-86622-301-0*, T-102) TFH Pubns.

Beginner's Guide to Car Maintenance, Fault-finding & Repair. Denis Rea & Rodney Jacques. 1987. pap. 26.95 (*0-434-90898-3*) Buttrwrth-Heinemann.

Beginner's Guide to Cockatiels. Anmarie Barrie. (Beginner's Guide Ser.). (Illus.). 64p. 1986. 3.95 (*0-86622-302-9*, T-103) TFH Pubns.

Beginner's Guide to Cockatoos. Anmarie Barrie. (Beginner's Guide Ser.). (Illus.). 61p. 1986. 3.95 (*0-86622-308-8*, T-115) TFH Pubns.

Beginner's Guide to Computers: Everything You Need to Know about the New Technology. Robin Bradbeer et al. (Illus.). 208p. 1982. pap. 10.53 (*0-201-11209-4*) Addison-Wesley.

Beginner's Guide to Constructing the Universe: The Mathematical Archetypes of Nature, Art, & Science. Michael S. Schneider. LC 92-56222. (Illus.). 224p. 1994. 30.00 (*0-06-016939-7*, HarpT) HarpC.

Beginner's Guide to Converted Coaches. Larry Plachno. (Illus.). 120p. 1992. pap. 15.00 (*0-933449-13-5*) Transport Trails.

Beginner's Guide to Doberman Pinschers. Bernadette E. Winkler. (Beginner's Guide Ser.). (Illus.). 64p. 1986. 3.95 (*0-86622-323-1*, T-123) TFH Pubns.

Beginner's Guide to Easy Horo Const. Marwayne Leipzig. 1978. 6.00 (*0-86690-211-2*, L1273-014) Am Fed Astrologers.

***Beginner's Guide to Family History Research.** 2nd ed. Desmond W. Allen & Carolyn E. Billingsley. 52p. 1994. pap. 6.95 (*1-56546-059-6*) Arkansas Res.

Beginners' Guide to Family Preparedness - Food Storage, Back to Basics & Survival Facts. Rosalie Mason. LC 77-79750. (Illus.). 160p. 1977. pap. 10.98 (*0-88290-082-X*) Horizon Utah.

Beginner's Guide to Figure Drawing. Viv Levy. 1993. 12.98 (*1-55521-854-7*) Bk Sales Inc.

Beginners Guide to Flight Instruction. 2nd ed. John L. Nelson. (Practical Flying Ser.). (Illus.). 208p. 1989. pap. 15.95 (*0-8306-2443-0*) TAB Bks.

Beginner's Guide to Freehand Decorative Painting. Jackie Shaw. (Illus.). 64p. (Orig.). 1987. pap. 8.95 (*0-941284-40-9*) J Shaw Studio.

Beginner's Guide to French. Ed. by Susannah Bradley. (FunFax Ser.). (Illus.). 48p. (J). (gr. 3-6). 1992. pap. 2.95 (*1-56680-004-8*) Mad Hatter Pub.

Beginner's Guide to German Shepherd. Franklin Steinitz. (Beginner's Guide Ser.). (Illus.). 61p. 1986. 3.95 (*0-86622-314-2*, T-111) TFH Pubns.

Beginners Guide to Getting Published. LC 94-11186. 1994. pap. 16.99 (*0-89879-672-5*) Writers Digest.

Beginner's Guide to Goldfish. Anmaire Barrie. (Beginner's Guide Ser.). (Illus.). 64p. 1986. 3.95 (*0-86622-303-7*, T-104) TFH Pubns.

Beginner's Guide to Golf: How to Get Started... & Have Fun Doing It. Larry Dennis. LC 93-85975. 120p. 1993. pap. 9.95 (*0-9638647-0-X*) Natl Golf.

Beginner's Guide to Great Golf for Women. Vern Juergens & Rhonda Glenn. LC 93-42903. (Illus.). 168p. 1994. pap. 11.95 (*0-87833-853-5*) Taylor Pub.

Beginner's Guide to Guinea Pigs. Tom Willkie. (Beginner's Guide Ser.). (Illus.). 64p. 1986. 3.95 (*0-86622-304-5*, T-105) TFH Pubns.

Beginner's Guide to Guppies. Carroll Friswold. (Beginner's Guide Ser.). (Illus.). 64p. 1986. 3.95 (*0-86622-317-7*, T-117) TFH Pubns.

Beginner's Guide to Hamsters. Jay Stephens. (Beginner's Guide Ser.). (Illus.). 64p. 1986. 3.95 (*0-86622-305-3*, T-106) TFH Pubns.

Beginners Guide to Hispanic Genealogy. Norma P. Flores & Patsy Ludwig. LC 93-85298. (Illus.). 80p. (Orig.). 1993. pap. 10.95 (*0-936029-31-5*) Western Bk Journ.

Beginner's Guide to Horseback Riding. Sheila Wall. 1974. pap. 5.00 (*0-87980-284-7*) Wilshire.

Beginner's Guide to Hunting & Trapping Secrets. Duane R. Lund. 1988. 8.95 (*0-934860-52-1*) Adventure Pubns.

An Asterisk (*) at the beginning of an entry indicates that the title is appearing in BIP for the first time.

An Asterisk (*) at the beginning of an entry indicates that the title is appearing in BIP for the first time.

659

Beginning Again: More Hors D'oeuvres for Cooks Who Love in the Beginning. braille ed. Rockdale Temple Sisterhood Staff. (Illus.). 200p. (Orig.). 1981. Braille ed. pap. write for info. (*0-318-55537-9*) Rockdale Ridge.

*__Beginning Again: People & Nature in the New Millennium.__ David Ehrenfeld. 232p. 1995. pap. 10.95 (*0-19-509637-1*) OUP.

Beginning Again: People & Nature in the New Millennium. David W. Ehrenfeld. 232p. 1993. 22.00 (*0-19-507812-8*) OUP.

*__Beginning Again: SIDS Families Share Their Hopes, Dreams, Fears, & Joy.__ Deborah R. Gemmill. 80p. (Orig.). 1995. pap. 10.95 (*0-9630341-1-1*) Beachcomber.

Beginning Again 1911-1918. Leonard Woolf. 1992. 19.75 (*0-8446-6515-0*) Peter Smith.

Beginning Algebra. Patricia J. Cass & Elizabeth R. O'Connor. LC 93-25648. 1994. pap. 50.95 (*0-534-92623-1*) PWS Pubs.

Beginning Algebra. Dennis T. Christy & Robert Rosenfeld. 496p. (C). 1993. text ed. write for info. (*0-697-12588-2*); Study Guide. student ed write for info. (*0-697-12590-4*) Wm C Brown Pubs.

Beginning Algebra. James W. Hall. (C). 1992. text ed. 53.95 (*0-534-92781-5*) PWS Pubs.

Beginning Algebra. Margaret L. Liall et al. (C). 1991. 21.00 (*0-673-46461-X*); 18.50 (*0-673-46460-1*) HarpCollege.

Beginning Algebra. Robert G. Marcucci & Harold L. Schoen. (C). 1990. 90.36 (*0-395-52954-9*) HM.

Beginning Algebra. K. Elayn Martin-Gay. 560p. (C). 1992. text ed. write for info. (*0-13-073784-4*) P-H.

Beginning Algebra. K. Elayn Martin-Gay. LC 92-33973. 1993. write for info. (*0-13-086778-0*) P-H.

Beginning Algebra. J. Louis Nanney & John L. Cable. 512p. (C). 1991. student ed write for info. (*0-697-12086-4*) Wm C Brown Pubs.

Beginning Algebra. J. Louis Nanney & John L. Cable. 512p. (C). 1991. pap. write for info. (*0-697-11652-2*) Wm C Brown Pubs.

Beginning Algebra. Dennis Weltman & Gilbert Perez. 486p. (C). 1990. text ed. 46.95 (*0-534-11778-3*) PWS Pubs.

*__Beginning Algebra.__ 2nd ed. James W. Hall. LC 94-31431. 608p. 1995. text ed. 50.95 (*0-534-94038-2*) PWS Pubs.

Beginning Algebra. 2nd ed. Dennis Weltman & Gilbert Perez. LC 93-5842. 1994. text ed. 53.95 (*0-534-93762-4*) PWS Pubs.

Beginning Algebra. 3rd ed. R. David Gustafson & Peter D. Frisk. LC 91-3767. 608p. (C). 1992. text ed. 49.95 (*0-534-16392-0*) Brooks-Cole.

Beginning Algebra. 3rd ed. James Streeter et al. LC 92-11715. 1992. teacher ed write for info. (*0-07-063020-8*); pap. text ed. write for info. (*0-07-031718-6*) McGraw.

*__Beginning Algebra.__ 3rd ed. John Tobey & Jeffrey Slater. LC 94-21954. 1994. pap. text ed. 50.67 (*0-13-299900-5*) P-H.

*__Beginning Algebra.__ 4th ed. R. David Gustafson & Peter D. Frisk. LC 94-29956. 500p. (YA). (gr. 7 up). 1995. text ed. 50.95 (*0-534-24618-4*) Brooks-Cole.

Beginning Algebra. 4th ed. M. A. Munem & W. Tschirhart. 404p. (C). 1988. text ed. 48.95x (*0-87901-378-8*); student ed 11.95x (*0-87901-380-X*) Worth.

Beginning Algebra. 5th ed. Alfonse Gobran. 528p. (C). 1991. text ed. 53.95 (*0-534-92443-3*) PWS Pubs.

Beginning Algebra. 5th ed. Margaret L. Lial & Charles D. Miller. (C). 1987. text ed. 32.25 (*0-673-18808-6*) HarpCollege.

Beginning Algebra. 6th ed. Margaret L. Liall et al. (C). 1991. text ed. 57.50 (*0-673-46459-8*) HarpCollege.

*__Beginning Algebra.__ 7th ed. Margaret L. Lial et al. LC 95-9797. (C). 1995. write for info. (*0-673-99139-3*) HarpCollege.

Beginning Algebra: A Modular Approach, 8 Vols., 1. Irving Drooyan & William Wooton. LC 75-29776. reprint ed. pap. 20.00 (*0-8357-7092-3*, 2012437) Bks Demand.

Beginning Algebra: A Modular Approach, 8 Vols., 2. Irving Drooyan & William Wooton. LC 75-29776. 104p. reprint ed. pap. 29.70 (*0-8357-7093-1*) Bks Demand.

Beginning Algebra: A Modular Approach, 8 Vols., 3. Irving Drooyan & William Wooton. LC 75-29776. 97p. reprint ed. pap. 27.70 (*0-8357-7094-X*) Bks Demand.

Beginning Algebra: A Modular Approach, 8 Vols., 4. Irving Drooyan & William Wooton. LC 75-29776. 81p. reprint ed. pap. 25.00 (*0-8357-7095-8*) Bks Demand.

Beginning Algebra: A Modular Approach, 8 Vols., 5. Irving Drooyan & William Wooton. LC 75-29776. 143p. reprint ed. pap. 40.80 (*0-8357-7096-6*) Bks Demand.

Beginning Algebra: A Modular Approach, 8 Vols., 6. Irving Drooyan & William Wooton. LC 75-29776. 143p. reprint ed. pap. 40.80 (*0-8357-7097-4*) Bks Demand.

Beginning Algebra: A Modular Approach, 8 Vols., 7. Irving Drooyan & William Wooton. LC 75-29776. 82p. reprint ed. pap. 25.00 (*0-8357-7098-2*) Bks Demand.

Beginning Algebra: A Modular Approach, 8 Vols., 8. Irving Drooyan & William Wooton. LC 75-29776. 106p. reprint ed. pap. 30.30 (*0-8357-7099-0*) Bks Demand.

Beginning Algebra: A Text - Workbook. Charles P. McKeague. 542p. (C). 1989. student ed, teacher ed write for info. (*0-318-66683-9*) SCP.

Beginning Algebra: A Text - Workbook. 3rd ed. Charles P. McKeague. 542p. (C). 1989. teacher ed 5.25 (*0-15-505235-7*); teacher ed 3.00 (*0-15-505236-5*); pap. text ed. 43.00 (*0-15-505234-9*); disk write for info. (*0-318-66681-2*); disk write for info. (*0-318-66682-0*); 22.75 (*0-15-555254-6*) SCP.

Beginning Algebra: An Individualized Approach. Irving Drooyan & William Wooton. LC 78-625. 420p. 1978. text ed. 44.50 (*0-471-03877-6*) P-H.

Beginning Algebra: With Applications. 2nd ed. Linda L. Exley & Vincent K. Smith. LC 93-36451. 1993. student ed, text ed. write for info. (*0-13-067257-2*) P-H.

Beginning Algebra & Geometry. Patricia Juelg. 928p. (C). 1991. pap. write for info. (*0-02-361501-X*) Dellen Pub.

Beginning Algebra & Geometry, Student's Solutions Manual. Patricia Juelg. 528p. (C). 1992. pap. write for info. (*0-02-323827-5*) Dellen Pub.

Beginning Algebra & Problem Solving. 2nd ed. Alan Wise. 802p. (C). 1989. pap. text ed. 43.00 (*0-15-505345-0*); disk, vhs write for info. (*0-318-64936-5*); disk write for info. (*0-318-64935-7*); 7.50 (*0-15-505346-9*) SCP.

Beginning Algebra for College Students. 4th ed. Karl J. Smith & Patrick J. Boyle. 400p. (C). 1990. text ed. 50.95 (*0-534-12354-6*) Brooks-Cole.

Beginning Algebra Form B. 2nd ed. James Streeter et al. 624p. 1991. pap. text ed. write for info. (*0-07-062622-7*) McGraw.

Beginning Algebra with Applications. Richard N. Aufmann & Vernon C. Barker. (C). 1986. 3.50 (*0-685-43437-0*) HM.

Beginning Algebra with Applications. 2nd annot. ed. Richard N. Aufmann et al. LC 88-81319. 480p. 1988. Incl. study guide, computor tutor sets. teacher ed 15.16 (*0-318-36877-3*) HM.

Beginning Algebra with Applications. 2nd ed. Richard N. Aufmann et al. LC 88-81319. 480p. 1988. Instr's. manual with test program. teacher ed 38.36 (*0-318-36878-1*) HM.

Beginning Algebra with Applications, 3 Vols. 3rd ed. Richard N. Aufmann & Vernon C. Barker. (C). 1992. text ed. 51.56 (*0-395-58883-9*) HM.

Beginning Algebra with Fundamentals. Patricia J. Cass & Elizabeth R. O'Connor. LC 93-25646. 1994. pap. 49.95 (*0-534-92622-3*) PWS Pubs.

Beginning an Academic Medical Career: Research, Writing, Speaking. Reginald Tsang & William Oh. LC 92-74264. (Illus.). (Orig.). 1993. pap. text ed. 9.95 (*1-56053-064-2*) Hanley & Belfus.

Beginning & Development of Doctrine in the New Church. Theodore Pitcairn. 64p. 1968. pap. 3.25 (*1-883270-09-X*) Swedenborg Assn.

*__Beginning & End of Snow.__ Yves Bonnefoy. Tr. by Sapinkopf. (QRL Poetry Book Ser.: Vol. XXXI). 20.00 (*0-614-06452-X*); pap. 10.00 (*0-614-06453-8*) Quarterly Rev.

*__Beginning & Intermediate Algebra.__ Margaret L. Lial et al. LC 95-9796. (C). 1995. write for info. (*0-673-99857-6*) HarpCollege.

Beginning & Now: Cosmology & Cosmogany for Intellectuals & Philistines. Lugoe. 1993. 11.95 (*0-533-10679-6*) Vantage.

Beginning & the End. Naguib Mahfouz. (ARA.). 1985. pap. 8.95 (*0-86685-153-4*) Intl Bk Ctr.

Beginning & the End. Naguib Mahfouz. 1989. mass mkt. 10.00 (*0-385-26458-5*) Doubleday.

Beginning & the End. Nikolai A. Berdiaev. Tr. by Reginald M. French. LC 76-6083. 256p. 1976. reprint ed. text ed. 59.75 (*0-8371-8837-7*, BEBE, Greenwood Pr) Greenwood.

Beginning & the End: Collected Poems. Alister Kershaw. (Illus.). 96p. 1983. 35.00 (*0-930126-12-2*) Typographeum.

Beginning & the End of the SS: Lords of the Inner Circle, Vol. I. Dahk Knox. 120p. 1993. 15.95 (*1-881116-06-9*) Black Forrest Pr.

Beginning Anew. Lyle Pointer. (Christian Living Ser.). 27p. (Orig.). 1987. pap. 2.50 (*0-8341-1189-6*) Beacon Hill.

Beginning at Williams Monument. Heman Chase. LC 81-3605. (Illus.). 72p. 1981. pap. 6.95 (*0-87233-060-5*) Bauhan.

Beginning Backgammon. Tim Holland. LC 73-84051. 1974. pap. 4.95 (*0-679-14038-7*) McKay.

*__Beginning Ballet: From the Classroom to the Stage.__ 2nd ed. Joan Lawson. (Illus.). 1994. pap. 16.95 (*0-87830-056-2*, B4551) Routledge.

*__Beginning Baseball.__ Don Geng. (Beginning Sports Ser.). Orig. Title: Fundamental Baseball. (Illus.). (J). 1995. write for info. (*0-8225-3505-X*, Lerner Publctns) Lerner Group.

Beginning BASIC for the Commodore 64. Steven L. Mandell. (Illus.). 160p. (Orig.). 1985. pap. text ed. 33.75 (*0-314-85264-6*) West Pub.

*__Beginning Basic Sight Word Fractions.__ 1981. pap. text ed. 2.00 (*0-938256-87-4*) Sch Zone Pub Co.

Beginning Bass Scales. Peter Pickow. (Illus.). 48p. 1992. pap. 4.95 (*0-8256-1342-6*, AM87482) Music Sales.

Beginning Bass Solos. Earl Gately. 1993. 4.95 (*1-56222-603-7*, 93772) Mel Bay.

Beginning Behavioral Research: A Conceptual Primer. Ralph L. Rosnow & Robert Rosenthal. (Illus.). 528p. (C). 1993. text ed. write for info. (*0-02-403781-8*) Macmillan.

*__Beginning Behavioral Research: A Conceptual Primer.__ 2nd ed. Ralph L. Rosnow & Robert Rosenthal. LC 95-10444. 1995. text ed. write for info. (*0-13-436916-5*) P-H.

Beginning Bluegrass Guitar. Russ Barenberg. (Illus.). 64p. 1989. pap. 9.95 (*0-8256-2368-5*, AM35213) Music Sales.

Beginning Blues - Rock Harmonica. Warren Ham. (Illus.). 24p. 1990. audio. pap. 14.95 (*0-8256-1154-7*, AM67471) Music Sales.

Beginning Blues Guitar. Arlen Roth. LC 75-32888. (Illus.). (Orig.). 1976. pap. 9.95 (*0-8256-2350-2*) Music Sales.

Beginning Blues Guitar. Jerry Silverman. (Illus.). 64p. pap. 12.95 (*0-8256-0009-X*, OK63461, Oak) Music Sales.

Beginning Blues Harp. Don Baker. (Illus.). 48p. audio, pap. 14.95 (*0-7119-2507-0*, AM78977) Music Sales.

Beginning Blues Piano. Eric Kriss. 1977. pap. 9.95 (*0-8256-2353-7*) Music Sales.

Beginning Bonsai: The Gentle Art of Japanese Miniature Tree Growing. Larry Student & Shirley Student. (Illus.). 48p. (Orig.). 1993. pap. 9.95 (*0-8048-1729-4*) C E Tuttle.

Beginning Book of Letters & Consonant Sounds. Sylvia Foust. (J). (gr. k-2). 1986. pap. 6.99 (*0-8224-0692-6*) Fearon Teach Aids.

Beginning Book of Vowel Sounds. Sylvia Foust. (J). (gr. k-2). 1986. pap. 6.99 (*0-8224-0693-4*) Fearon Teach Aids.

Beginning Book Reporting. Elaine Prizzi & Jeanne Hoffmann. LC 83-63175. (J). (gr. 2-5). 1984. pap. 12.99 (*0-8224-2175-5*) Fearon Teach Aids.

Beginning Bridge. Alan Hiron & Maureen Hiron. 114p. 1992. pap. 15.95 (*1-85223-351-6*, Pub. by Crowood Pr UK) Trafalgar.

Beginning Bridge Complete. Michael Penick. 176p. 1991. pap. 8.95 (*0-910791-06-6*) Devyn Pr.

Beginning Bridge Quizzes. Michael Penick. 1989. pap. 6.95 (*0-910791-67-8*) Devyn Pr.

Beginning Broadcast Newswriting: A Self-Instructional Learning Experience. 3rd ed. K. Tim Wulfemeyer. LC 92-47477. 96p. (C). 1993. pap. text ed. 12.95 (*0-8138-0211-3*) Iowa St U Pr.

Beginning Burmese. William S. Cornyn & D. Haigh Roop. LC 66-21513. (Yale Linguistic Ser.). 525p. reprint ed. pap. 149.70 (*0-8357-7100-8*, 2011091) Bks Demand.

Beginning Cadkey Light. Leonard O. Nasman. 240p. (Orig.). Date not set. pap. text ed. 29.95 (*1-880544-12-1*) Micro Educ.

Beginning Cadkey 6. Leonard O. Nasman. (Illus.). 440p. (C). 1993. pap. 36.95 (*1-880544-18-0*, CAD6-1) Micro Educ.

Beginning Cebuano, 2 pts., Pt. 1. John U. Wolff. LC 65-22474. (Yale Linguistic Ser.: No. 9). 712p. reprint ed. pap. 180.00 (*0-8357-8036-8*, 2033926) Bks Demand.

Beginning Cebuano, Pt. 2. John Wolff. LC 65-22474. (Linguistic Ser.). (C). 1968. pap. text ed. 16.00 (*0-300-00260-2*) Yale U Pr.

Beginning Cebuano, 2 pts., Pt. 2. John U. Wolff. LC 65-22474. (Yale Linguistic Ser.: No. 9). 712p. reprint ed. pap. 148.80 (*0-8357-8037-6*, 2033926) Bks Demand.

Beginning Census Research. Nancy E. Carlberg. 160p. (Orig.). 1991. pap. 15.00 (*0-944878-14-8*) Carlberg Pr.

Beginning Ceramics. rev. ed. Dale Swant. 68p. 1994. pap. 4.95 (*0-916809-72-2*) Scott Pubns MI.

Beginning Charts, Graphs & Diagrams. John Carratello & Patty Carratello. (Illus.). 80p. (Orig.). (gr. 2-4). 1990. student ed 8.95 (*1-55734-168-0*) Tchr Create Mat.

Beginning Chemistry: A Workbook to Use in the Laboratory. 6th ed. Elizabeth Rogers & Iris Stoval. 1994. pap. 9.80 (*0-87563-499-0*) Stipes.

*__Beginning Cherokee.__ Ruth B. Holmes & Betty S. Smith. 332p. Date not set. audio, text ed. 44.95 (*0-88432-726-4*, AFCK10) Audio-Forum.

Beginning Cherokee. 2nd ed. Ruth B. Holmes & Betty S. Smith. LC 76-16498. (Illus.). 346p. 1978. pap. 21.95 (*0-8061-1463-0*) U of Okla Pr.

Beginning Chess: Over Three Hundred Elementary Problems for Players New to the Game. Bruce Pandolfini. LC 93-9693. (Illus.). 256p. (Orig.). 1993. pap. 12.00 (*0-671-79501-5*, Fireside) S&S Trade.

Beginning Chess Play. Bill Robertie. LC 94-70604. (Illus.). 144p. 1994. pap. 8.95 (*0-940685-50-7*) Cardoza Pub.

Beginning Child Psychiatry. Paul L. Adams & Ivan Fras. LC 87-32587. 624p. 1988. 54.95 (*0-87630-493-5*) Brunner-Mazel.

Beginning Chinese. rev. ed. John Defrancis. LC 76-5099. (Yale Linguistic Ser.). 1976. pap. text ed. 27.50 (*0-300-02058-9*) Yale U Pr.

Beginning Chinese Reader, 2 pts., 2. 2nd ed. John DeFrancis. LC 76-5103. 1977. pap. 27.50 (*0-300-02061-9*) Yale U Pr.

Beginning Chinese Reader, 2 pts., Pt. I. 2nd ed. John DeFrancis. LC 76-5103. 1977. text ed. 55.00 (*0-300-02056-2*) Yale U Pr.

Beginning Chinese Reader, 2 pts., Pt. II. 2nd ed. John DeFrancis. LC 76-5103. 1977. 55.00 (*0-300-02057-0*) Yale U Pr.

Beginning Chinese Reader, 2 pts., Vol I, Pts. I & II. 2nd ed. John DeFrancis. LC 76-5103. 1977. pap. 27.50 (*0-300-02060-0*) Yale U Pr.

Beginning Chinese Readers: Supplementary Materials, 2 vols., Set. Pauline Chang et al. (PALI Language Text Ser.). 280p. (C). 1987. pap. text ed. 9.50 (*0-8248-1115-1*) UH Pr.

Beginning Clerical Worker. Jack Rudman. (Career Examination Ser.: No. C-3505). 1994. 19.95 (*0-8373-3505-1*) Nat Learn.

Beginning Clerical Worker: Account Clerk - Audit Clerk - Statistical Clerk - File Clerk - Payroll Clerk - Receptionist. 11th ed. John C. Czukor. 304p. 1989. pap. 12.00 (*0-13-068206-3*, Arco Test) P-H Gen Ref & Trav.

Beginning Consultant Training Program, 3 vols. 117p. student ed 40.00 (*0-685-43377-3*) NAPC.

Beginning Consultant Training Program, 3 vols., Set. 117p. 225.00 (*0-317-35010-2*) NAPC.

Beginning Country Fiddle. Marilyn Bos. (Illus.). 96p. pap. 14.95 (*0-8256-0294-7*, OK64725, Oak) Music Sales.

Beginning Country Guitar Handbook. Dix Bruce. 1993. 7.95 (*1-56222-106-X*, 94330); audio 16.95 (*0-685-64321-2*, 94330); audio 9.98 (*1-56222-173-6*, 94330) Mel Bay.

Beginning Course in Spanish. Juan A. Baldor. 375p. (Orig.). (C). 1990. pap. text ed. 24.95 (*0-9625897-0-5*) DonMar Pub.

Beginning Creator's Copyright Manuals. Howard P. Killough. 192p. 1988. per. 14.00 (*0-8187-0110-2*) Harlo Press.

Beginning Curricula A, B & Affixes Used in Signing Exact English. Gerilee Gustason. 124p. (Orig.). 1983. student ed, pap. text ed. 12.95 (*0-916708-09-8*) Modern Signs.

Beginning Danish Research. Nancy E. Carlberg & Norma S. Keating. 160p. (Orig.). 1991. pap. 20.00 (*0-944878-18-0*) Carlberg Pr.

Beginning DataCAD. Leonard O. Nasman. LC 91-66358. 165p. (C). 1991. pap. 29.95 (*1-880544-00-8*) Micro Educ.

Beginning dBASE IV. Fritz H. Grupe. 128p. (C). 1990. spiral bd. write for info. (*0-697-11795-2*) Bus & Educ Tech.

Beginning dBASE IV for Windows. Fritz H. Grupe. 112p. 1997. write for info. (*0-697-17137-X*) Bus & Educ Tech.

Beginning Dobro. Stacy Phillips. (Illus.). 56p. pap. 4.95 (*0-8256-1123-7*, AM67497) Music Sales.

Beginning DOS for Nontechnical Business Users. Gordon Kimbell. 1993. pap. 11.95 (*1-56052-212-7*) Crisp Pubns.

Beginning Early: Adult Responsibilities to Gifted Young Children. Jamie C. Smith. 1985. pap. 9.99 (*0-89824-151-0*) Trillium Pr.

Beginning Electronic Fabrication. 2nd ed. J. A. Markum & M. P. Silva. (Illus.). 160p. 1986. pap. text ed. 8.50 (*0-911908-07-2*) Tech Ed Pr.

Beginning English Day by Day. Michael Roddy. 224p. 1991. pap. text ed. 16.00 (*0-87879-907-9*) Acad Therapy.

Beginning English Research. Nancy E. Carlberg. 175p. 1993. pap. 15.00 (*0-944878-26-1*) Carlberg Pr.

Beginning Entrepreneur. John Matthews. LC 93-1466. 1994. 12.95 (*0-8442-4141-5*, VGM Career Bks) NTC Pub Grp.

Beginning Equal: A Manual about Non-Sexist Childrearing for Infants & Toddlers. Ed. by Merle Froschel & Barbara Sprung. Tr. by Victoria Ortiz. 241p. (Orig.). 1983. pap. 9.75 (*0-9605828-4-3*) Women's Action.

Beginning Excel for Nontechnical Business Users. William Amadio. 1993. pap. 11.95 (*1-56052-215-1*) Crisp Pubns.

Beginning Excel 3.0: IBM Version. Fritz H. Grupe & William A. Newman. 144p. (C). 1992. spiral bd. write for info. (*0-697-12096-1*) Bus & Educ Tech.

*__Beginning Farming: And What Makes a Sheep Tick.__ Lowell Christensen. (Illus.). 144p. (Orig.). 1994. pap. 9.00 (*0-9642483-0-1*) Pinon Pr NM.

Beginning Fiddle. Stacy Phillips. (Illus.). 64p. 1990. pap. 4.95 (*0-8256-2541-6*, AM26329) Music Sales.

Beginning Film Maker's Guide to Directing. Renee Harmon. LC 92-5536. 197p. 1992. 24.95 (*0-8027-1219-3*); pap. 14.95 (*0-8027-7384-2*) Walker & Co.

Beginning Filmmaker's Business Guide: Financial, Legal, Marketing, & Distribution Basics of Making Movies. Renee Harmon. LC 93-10977. 200p. (Orig.). 1994. pap. 14.95 (*0-8027-7409-1*) Walker & Co.

Beginning Fingerstyle Blues Guitar. Arnie Berle & Mark Galbo. (Illus.). 1993. pap. 14.95 (*0-8256-2556-4*) Music Sales.

Beginning Folk Guitar. Jerry Silverman. (Illus.). 96p. 1964. pap. 12.95 (*0-8256-0015-4*, 000015, Oak) Music Sales.

Beginning Folksinger: A Self Instruction Method for Learning to Play the Six String Guitar. Andrew F. Jensen. 81p. (Orig.). 1991. pap. 19.95 (*0-9630350-0-2*) A F Jensen.

Beginning FORTH. rev. ed. Paul M. Chirlian. 220p. (Orig.). 1983. pap. 21.95 (*0-916460-36-3*, Matrix Pubs Inc) Weber Systems.

Beginning FoxBase for Windows. Fritz H. Grupe. 112p. 1997. write for info. (*0-697-17138-8*) Bus & Educ Tech.

Beginning French Bilingual Dictionary. 2nd rev. ed. Gladys C. Lipton. 368p. 1989. pap. 5.95 (*0-8120-4273-5*) Barron.

Beginning French for Preschoolers: A Montessori Handbook. Rachel Adler-Golden & Debbie Gordon. LC 80-83136. (Illus.). 85p. 1980. pap. 12.95 (*0-915676-04-4*) Ed Sys Pub.

*__Beginning from the Middle: A Collection of Fiction, Poetry, & Essays by the Kansas City Writers' Group.__ Illus. by Sophia Myers. 128p. (Orig.). 1994. pap. 9.95 (*0-9644170-0-6*) Whispering Prairie.

Beginning Geography. Jo E. Moore & Joy Evans. (Geography Mini-Unit Ser.). (Illus.). 16p. (J). (gr. k-2). 1992. pap. text ed. 5.95 (*1-55799-219-3*) Evan-Moor Corp.

Beginning Geography, Vol. 2: Landforms & Bodies of Water. Jo E. Moore. (Illus.). 16p. (J). (gr. k-2). 1993. pap. text ed. 5.95 (*1-55799-253-3*) Evan-Moor Corp.

Beginning Geography, Vol. 3: Continents & Oceans. Jo E. Moore. (Illus.). 16p. (J). (gr. k-2). 1993. pap. text ed. 5.95 (*1-55799-254-1*) Evan-Moor Corp.

Beginning German. Jack Rudman. (DANTES Ser.: No. 5). 1994. pap. 23.95 (*0-8373-6605-4*) Nat Learn.

*__Beginning German.__ Jack Rudman. (DANTES Ser.: No. 5). 1994. 39.95 (*0-8373-6505-8*) Nat Learn.

Beginning German: A Way to Self-Awareness. Guenter G. Pfister. (Illus.). 383p. (C). 1989. text ed. 28.80 (*0-87563-302-1*) Stipes.

*__Beginning Golf.__ Julie Jensen. (Beginning Sports Ser.). (Illus.). 64p. (J). (gr. 2-5). 1995. lib. bdg. 19.95 (*0-8225-3504-1*) Lerner Group.

Beginning Golf. 2nd ed. Robert Gensemer. (Illus.). 144p. (C). 1994. pap. text ed. 14.95x (*0-89582-264-4*) Morton Pub.

Beginning Greek: A Functional Approach. Stephen W. Paine. (YA). (gr. 9 up). 1961. 24.95 (*0-19-501013-2*) OUP.

Beginning Guitar. Artie Traum. (Illus.). 64p. 1985. pap. 4.95 (*0-8256-2332-4*, AM36997) Music Sales.

*__Beginning Gymnastics.__ Julie Jensen & Linda Wallenberg. LC 95-7677. (Illus.). (J). 1995. write for info. (*0-8225-3503-3*, Lerner Publctns) Lerner Group.

Beginning Hittite. Warren H. Held, Jr. et al. (Illus.). ix, 218p. (Orig.). 1988. pap. 19.95 (*0-89357-184-9*) Slavica.

An Asterisk (*) at the beginning of an entry indicates that the title is appearing in BIP for the first time.

An Asterisk (*) at the beginning of an entry indicates that the title is appearing in BIP for the first time.

661

Beginning Secondary School Teacher's Guide: Some Problems & Suggested Solutions. Melvin Keene. LC 85-9074. 256p. 1985. reprint ed. pap. text ed. 19.50 (0-8191-4668-4) U Pr of Amer.

Beginning Skills for Casework Practice with Families: A Laboratory Manual. Diane De Anda. 1991. 9.95 (0-88247-850-8) R & E Pubs.

Beginning Skills for Casework Practice with Families: A Student Manual. Diane De Anda. 1991. 9.95 (0-88247-851-6) R & E Pubs.

Beginning Slide Guitar. Mark Hanson. (Illus.). 40p. 1991. pap. 4.95 (0-8256-1319-1, AM85593) Music Sales.

Beginning Slovak. Oscar E. Swan & Sylvia Galova-Lorinc. (Illus.). xlviii, 522p. (Orig.). (C). 1990. pap. text ed. 24.95 (0-89357-214-4) Slavica.

***Beginning Soccer.** Julie Jensen. (Beginning Sports Ser.). (Illus.). 64p. (J). (gr. 2-5). 1995. lib. bdg. 19.95 (0-8225-3501-7) Lerner Group.

Beginning Songwriter's Answer Book. rev. ed. Paul Zollo. 128p. (Orig.). 1993. pap. 16.95 (0-89879-561-3) Writers Digest.

Beginning Sounds. Bearl Brooks. (Early Education Ser.). 24p. (ps-1). 1978. 5.00 (0-8209-0204-7, K-6) ESP.

Beginning Sounds. Barbara Gregorich. Ed. by Joan Hoffman. (Get Ready! Bks.). (Illus.). 32p. (J). (ps). 1983. student ed 1.99 (0-938256-54-8) Sch Zone Pub Co.

Beginning Spanish. Jack Rudman. (DANTES Ser.: No. 6). 1994. pap. 23.95 (0-8373-6606-2) Nat Learn.

***Beginning Spanish.** Jack Rudman. (DANTE Ser.: No. 6). 1994. 39.95 (0-8373-6506-6) Nat Learn.

Beginning Spanish. 6th ed. DaSilva. 1987. text ed. 48.95 (0-8384-3493-2); student ed, pap. 29.95 (0-8384-3498-3) Heinle & Heinle.

Beginning Spanish: A Teacher's Manual: Comprehension Based Activities for the Learnables, Book One. Constance Bouwman et al. (Illus.). 163p. (YA). (gr. 7 up). 1989. pap. text ed. 28.00 (0-939990-78-4) Intl Linguistics.

Beginning Spanish Bilingual Dictionary. 2nd rev. ed. Gladys C. Lipton & Olivia Munoz. 400p. 1989. pap. 5.95 (0-8120-4274-3) Barron.

Beginning Spanish for Teachers of Hispanic Students. Pamela Sharpe. 1994. pap. 29.95 (0-8120-8118-8) Barron.

***Beginning Spanish Grammar I, 2 vols., Vol I, 160 pgs.** Intro. by DiAnne Krumm. (Orig.). (C). Date not set. student ed, pap. 9.32 (0-9634303-0-0) Dickens CA.

***Beginning Spanish Grammar I, 2 vols., Vol. I, 160 pgs.** 2nd ed. Intro. by DiAnne Krumm. (Orig.). (C). Date not set. student ed, pap. 9.32 (0-9634303-2-7) Dickens CA.

***Beginning Spanish Grammar II, 2 vols., Vol. II, 140 pgs.** Intro. by DiAnne Krumm. (Orig.). (C). Date not set. student ed, pap. 9.32 (0-9634303-1-9) Dickens CA.

***Beginning Spanish Grammar II, 2 vols., Vol. II, 140 pgs.** 2nd ed. Intro. by DiAnne Krumm. (Orig.). (C). Date not set. student ed, pap. 9.32 (0-9634303-3-5) Dickens CA.

Beginning Speed Practice for Machine Shorthand. (C). reprint ed. pap. 10.95 (0-685-31742-0); reprint ed. pap. text ed. 8.95 (0-685-31743-9) Stenograph Corp.

Beginning Spiritual Direction. David E. Rosage. 170p. (Orig.). 1994. pap. 7.99 (0-89283-759-4, Charis) Servant.

Beginning Standard Chinese. Helen T. Lin. 188p. (Orig.). (C). 1992. pap. 15.95 (0-8351-1940-8) China Bks.

Beginning Statistics. Gene Zirkel & Robert Rosenfeld. 320p. 28.50 (0-930745-14-0) Williams Bk Co.

Beginning Statistics: A to Z. William Mendenhall. 525p. (C). 1993. text ed. 51.95 (0-534-19122-3) Intl Thomson.

Beginning Statistics Within a Research Context. Lowell D. Groninger. 384p. (C). 1989. text ed. 53.00 (0-06-042528-8) HarpCollege.

Beginning Structured COBOL. Edward J. Coburn. 571p. (C). 1988. pap. text ed. 39.00 (0-15-505370-1); Instr's. manual, incl. transparency masters. pap. text ed. 28.75 (0-15-505371-X) Dryden Pr.

Beginning Structured COBOL. Edward J. Coburn. 571p. (C). 1988. Four Program disks 5.25" for IBM PC & true compatibles. 19.00 (0-15-505372-8) Dryden Pr.

Beginning Structured COBOL. Khan. 544p. (C). 1990. pap. write for info. (0-675-21174-3, Merrill Pub Co) Macmillan.

Beginning Swedish Research. Nancy E. Carlberg. LC 89-156347. 150p. (Orig.). 1989. pap. 15.00 (0-944878-05-9) Carlberg Pr.

Beginning Swimming. Robert A. Oliver & Dewayne J. Johnson. (Illus.). 52p. (C). 1982. pap. text ed. 5.95x (0-89641-075-7) American Pr.

Beginning Syntax. Linda Thomas. LC 92-39658. 192p. 1993. 34.95 (0-631-18827-4); pap. 14.95 (0-631-18826-6) Blackwell Pubs.

Beginning Synthesizer. Helen Casabona et al. Ed. by Tom Darter. LC 86-10765. (Keyboard Magazine Library for Electronic Musicians). (Illus.). 96p. 1986. pap. 12.95 (0-88284-353-2, 2606) Alfred Pub.

Beginning Tagalog: A Course for Speakers of English. Ed. by J. Donald Bowen. LC 65-25321. (Orig.). 1965. pap. 35.00 (0-520-00156-7) U CA Pr.

***Beginning Tai Chi.** Tri Dang. (Illus.). 64p. (Orig.). 1994. pap. 9.95 (0-8048-2001-5) C E Tuttle.

Beginning Tai Ji. Al Huang. LC 88-62843. 1989. pap. 14.95 (0-89087-556-1) Celestial Arts.

Beginning Teacher's Resource Handbook. Jane E. Bluestein. 407p. (Orig.). 1982. pap. 24.95 (0-915817-00-4) ISS Pubns.

Beginning Teacher's Resource Handbook. rev. ed. Jane E. Bluestein. 407p. (Orig.). 1983. pap. 18.75 (0-915817-12-8) ISS Pubns.

Beginning Teaching: An Introduction to Early Years Education. Anne D. Cockburn et al. 128p. 1992. pap. 23.00 (1-85396-162-0, Pub. by Paul Chapman UK) Taylor & Francis.

Beginning Teaching: Professional Development & Probation in Scotland. Bryan Peck & Ted Archer. (C). 1989. 35.00 (1-85098-140-X, Pub. by Jordanhill College UK) St Mut.

***Beginning Teaching, Beginning Learning in Primary Education.** Ed. by Janet Moyles. LC 95-1199. 1995. write for info. (0-335-19436-2, Open Univ Pr); pap. write for info. (0-335-19435-4, Open Univ Pr) Taylor & Francis.

Beginning Technical Mathematics Made Easy. David Brianza. 1990. text ed. 15.95 (0-07-156255-9) McGraw.

Beginning Technical Mathematics Made Easy. David Brianza. (Illus.). 140p. 1989. 14.95 (0-8306-7383-0); pap. 8.95 (0-8306-3383-9) TAB Bks.

***Beginning Television Studio Production Manual.** Thomas A. Young & Kathryn E. Young. (Illus.). 28p. (Orig.). (C). 1995. pap. text ed. 20.00 (0-9647170-0-X) Young Media.

***Beginning Tennis.** Julie Jensen. LC 94-21107. (Beginning Sports Ser.). (Illus.). 64p. (J). (gr. 2-5). 1994. lib. bdg. 19.95 (0-8225-3500-9, Lerner Publctns) Lerner Group.

***Beginning the Bible.** Joseph O'Hanlon. 122p. 1994. pap. 29.00 (0-85439-496-6, Pub. by St Paul Pubns UK) St Mut.

Beginning the Christian Life. Russell Krabill. 216p. 1988. Pgs. 216. teacher ed 6.95 (0-8361-3459-1); Pgs. 160. student ed, pap. 6.95 (0-8361-3458-3) Herald Pr.

***Beginning the Good News: A Narrative Approach.** Francis J. Moloney. 176p. (Orig.). 1995. pap. text ed. 9.95 (0-8146-2265-8, Liturg Pr Bks) Liturgical Pr.

Beginning the Novel. Peter Porosky. LC 94-8397. 128p. (Orig.). 1994. lib. bdg. 39.50 (0-8191-9501-4); pap. text ed. 18.50 (0-8191-9502-2) U Pr of Amer.

Beginning the Walk: A Tool for Developing Your Preschooler's Faith. Mary A. Burt. (Illus.). 184p. (Orig.). 1994. pap. 19.95 (0-9641134-0-6) Prods With A Purpose.

***Beginning Theory: An Introduction to Literary & Cultural Theory.** Peter Barry. LC 94-43136. 1995. text ed. write for info. (0-7190-4325-5, Pub. by Manchester Univ Pr UK); text ed. write for info. (0-7190-4326-3, Pub. by Manchester Univ Pr UK) St Martin.

Beginning to Add. Liz Jonson & Emery Silliman. Ed. by Judith E. Nayer. (Learn Today for Tomorrow Ser.). (Illus.). 32p. (J). (gr. k-1). 1991. student ed 1.95 (1-878624-55-5) McClanahan Bk.

Beginning to Add: Step Ahead Plus Workbook. (J). (ps-3). 1993. pap. 3.50 (0-307-03670-7, Golden Bks) Western Pub.

Beginning to Heal. Ellen Bass. 1994. mass mkt. 5.99 (0-06-109246-0, Harp PBks) HarpC.

Beginning to Heal: The First Book for Survivors of Child Sexual Abuse. Ellen Bass & Laura Davis. 112p. 1993. pap. 10.00 (0-06-096927-X, PL) HarpC.

Beginning to Learn About Series, Set. (Illus.). 32p. (J). (gr. k-3). 1989. lib. bdg. 256.68 (0-8172-1391-0) Raintree Steck-V.

Beginning to Pray. Anthony Bloom. LC 70-169613. 128p. 1982. pap. 5.95 (0-8091-1509-3) Paulist Pr.

Beginning to Pray. large type ed. Anthony Bloom. (Large Print Inspirational Ser.). 160p. 1986. pap. 8.95 (0-8027-2517-1) Walker & Co.

Beginning to Pray: Prayer for Young People & Those Who Would Like to Start Again. Thomas O'Caoimh. 112p. (Orig.). 1992. pap. 8.95 (1-85607-055-7, Pub. by Columba Pr IE) Twenty-Third.

Beginning to Pray in Old Age. Intro. by Susan Coupland & Paul Wessinger. LC 85-17075. (Parish Life Sourcebooks Ser.: Vol. II). xiv, 80p. 1985. reprint ed. pap. 6.95 (0-936384-29-8) Cowley Pubns.

Beginning to Read. Beth A. Wise. Ed. by Judith E. Nayer. (Learn Today for Tomorrow Ser.). (Illus.). 32p. (J). (gr. k-1). 1991. student ed 1.95 (1-878624-62-8) McClanahan Bk.

Beginning to Read: Thinking & Learning about Print. Marilyn J. Adams. (Illus.). 504p. 1994. pap. 18.50 (0-262-51076-6, Bradford Bks) MIT Pr.

Beginning to Read the Fathers. Boniface Ramsey. 288p. (Orig.). 1985. pap. 15.95 (0-8091-2691-5) Paulist Pr.

Beginning to See. 8th ed. Sujata. LC 81-4681. (Illus.). 144p. 1989. pap. 7.95 (0-89087-575-8) Celestial Arts.

Beginning to See the Light: Sex, Hope, & Rock-&-Roll. 2nd ed. Ellen Willis. LC 91-50822. 359p. (C). 1992. pap. 15.95 (0-8195-6255-6, Wesleyan Univ Pr) U Pr of New Eng.

Beginning to Spell: A Study of First-Grade Children. Rebecca Treiman. (Illus.). 384p. 1992. 49.95 (0-19-506219-1) OUP.

Beginning to Subtract. Karen Evans. Ed. by Judith E. Nayer. (Learn Today for Tomorrow Ser.). (Illus.). 32p. (J). (gr. k-1). 1991. student ed 1.95 (1-878624-56-3) McClanahan Bk.

Beginning to Teach. Judy-Arin Krupp et al. LC 94-8860. (Keeping Afloat Ser.). 16p. (Orig.). 1994. pap. 1.50 (0-912099-20-8) Kappa Delta Pi.

***Beginning to Teach: Breaking Down Walls of Teacher Isolation.** Nancy F. Dana & Allan S. Vann. (Beginning to Teach Booklet Ser.). 16p. (Orig.). 1995. pap. 1.50 (0-912099-21-6, KDP #172) Kappa Delta Pi.

Beginning to Teach: Primary Teaching Explained. Clare Marlow. 144p. 1994. pap. 23.00 (1-85346-259-4) Taylor & Francis.

***Beginning Tonal Dictation.** Thomas L. Durham. 323p. (Orig.). (C). 1994. pap. text ed. 22.95x (0-88133-797-8) Waveland Pr.

Beginning Underwater Photography. 5th ed. Jim Church & Cathy Church. (Illus.). 96p. 1987. pap. 9.95 (0-9616093-1-1) J-C Church.

Beginning Unix. M. Joy. 1994. pap. 27.50 (0-412-57660-0, Blackie & Son-Chapman NY) Routledge Chapman & Hall.

Beginning Unix Comands: A Reference Card for Unix Novices. Belinda Frazier. 4p. Date not set. pap. 0.30 (0-916151-67-0) Specialized Sys.

***Beginning Volleyball.** Julie Jensen. LC 94-29509. (Beginning Sports Ser.). (Illus.). 64p. (J). (gr. 2-5). 1995. lib. bdg. 19.95 (0-8225-3502-5, Lerner Publctns) Lerner Group.

Beginning Weight Training. Vincent P. Lombardi. 256p. (C). 1989. pap. write for info. (0-697-05496-9) Brown & Benchmark.

Beginning Weight Training. Phillip A. Sienna. 263p. (C). 1989. pap. text ed. write for info. (0-697-14826-2) Brown & Benchmark.

***Beginning Weight Training: Something for Everyone.** Christine O. Wells. (Illus.). 110p. (Orig.). (C). 1993. pap. text ed. 7.95x (0-89641-257-1) American Pr.

Beginning Weight Training for Young Athletes. William J. Maitland. (Illus.). 84p. (YA). (gr. 7 up). 1987. pap. 9.95 (0-936759-00-3) Maitland Enter.

Beginning Well: Framing Fictions in Late Middle English Poetry. Judith M. Davidoff. LC 83-49344. 248p. 1988. 35.00 (0-685-16465-9) Fairleigh Dickinson.

Beginning Well: Framing Fictions in Late Middle English Poetry. Judith M. Davidoff. 1989. 38.50 (0-8386-3208-4) Fairleigh Dickinson.

***Beginning Welsh Research.** Annie Lloyd. 155p. 1993. 15.00 (0-9644567-0-2) A Lloyd.

Beginning Where I Am: Meditations for Young People. Godfrey Holmes. 1991. pap. 5.95 (0-687-85069-X) Abingdon.

Beginning Wicca. Judith DeFrain et al. Ed. by Ken Johnson & Arielweehawk. (Illus.). 100p. (Orig.). 1988. pap. text ed. 13.00 (0-9619008-4-9) Eye Cat.

***Beginning with AND: New & Selected Poems.** Alberta Turner. Ed. by Larry Smith. (Midwest Writers Ser.). 160p. (Orig.). (C). Date not set. pap. 9.95 (0-933087-33-0) Bottom Dog Pr.

Beginning with Awareness. Verena Tsuchudin. (Illus.). 164p. 1991. write for info. (0-443-04290-X); student ed 96.00 (0-443-04292-6) Churchill.

Beginning with Books: Library Programming for Infants, Toddlers, & Preschoolers. Nancy DeSalvo. LC 92-14858. (Illus.). xiii, 186p. (C). 1993. pap. 27.50 (0-208-02318-6, Lib Prof Pubns) Shoe String.

Beginning with Budgerigars. Anne R. Streeter. 1986. 9.95 (0-86622-127-1, PS-839) TFH Pubns.

Beginning with C: An Introduction to Professional Programming. Ron House. LC 93-41049. 1994. pap. 43.95 (0-534-94122-2) PWS Pubs.

Beginning with Christ. H. L. Heijkoop. pap. 4.25 (0-88172-082-8) Believers Bkshelf.

Beginning with Christ. rev. ed. NAVI Staff. 1980. pap. 10.00 (0-89109-159-9) NavPress.

Beginning with Cockatiels. Anne R. Streeter. (Illus.). 128p. 1989. 9.95 (0-86622-696-6, PS-838) TFH Pubns.

Beginning with LOGO: Terrapin Version. Steve Tipps & Glen Bull. (Illus.). 256p. (C). 1986. pap. text ed. 47.00 (0-13-071739-8) P-H.

***Beginning with Mary: Women of the Gospels in Portrait.** fac. ed. Thomas J. Carlisle. 118p. (Orig.). 1986. reprint ed. pap. 33.70 (0-7837-7947-X, 2047703) Bks Demand.

Beginning with My Streets: Essays & Recollections. Czeslaw Milosz. Tr. by Madeline G. Levine. 288p. 1992. 30.00 (0-374-11010-7) FS&G.

Beginning with O. Olga Broumas. LC 76-49697. (Younger Poets Ser.). 1977. 17.00 (0-300-02106-2); pap. 10.00 (0-300-02111-9) Yale U Pr.

Beginning with Ourselves in Practice, Theory & Human Affairs. David E. Hunt. (Illus.). 182p. 1987. text ed. 24.95 (0-914797-33-6); pap. text ed. 17.95 (0-914797-34-4) Brookline Bks.

Beginning with Poems. Ed. by Reuben A. Brower et al. (Orig.). (C). 1966. pap. text ed. 12.95 (0-393-09509-6) Norton.

Beginning with Poems. Ed. by Reuben A. Brower et al. (Orig.). (C). 1966. text ed. 17.95 (0-393-09685-8) Norton.

Beginning with Snakes. Richard F. Stratton. (Illus.). 96p. 1989. 9.95 (0-86622-782-2, KW-127) TFH Pubns.

Beginning with the Pre-Socratics. Merrill Ring. LC 86-63292. 166p. (C). 1987. pap. text ed. 18.95 (0-87484-791-5) Mayfield Pub.

Beginning with Tropicals. Diane Schofield. pap. 3.95 (0-87666-165-7, M-523) TFH Pubns.

Beginning Woodwind Class Method. 4th ed. Frederick W. Westphal. 224p. 1984. spiral bd. write for info. (0-697-03565-4) Brown & Benchmark.

Beginning Woodwork. John L. Feirer. 1984. text ed. 14.60 (0-02-662640-3) Bennett IL.

Beginning WordPerfect 5.0. Fritz H. Grupe & Arthur R. Broten. 128p. (C). 1990. spiral bd. write for info. (0-697-11059-1) Bus & Educ Tech.

Beginning WordPerfect 5.1. Fritz H. Grupe. 148p. (C). 1991. spiral bd. write for info. (0-697-10791-4) Bus & Educ Tech.

Beginning WordPerfect 5.1 for Nontechnical Business Users. Mark Workman. 1993. pap. 11.95 (1-56052-214-3) Crisp Pubns.

Beginning WordPerfect 6.0. Fritz H. Grupe. 160p. 1997. write for info. (0-697-21206-8) Bus & Educ Tech.

Beginning WordPerfect 6.0 for DOS. O'Donell et al. 1994. pap. text ed. write for info. (0-07-070387-6) McGraw.

Beginning Writer's Answer Book. rev. ed. Writer's Digest Staff & Kirk Polking. LC 93-18462. 336p. 1994. pap. 16.99 (0-89879-599-0) Writers Digest.

***Beginning Writers in the Zone of Proximal Development.** Elizabeth Petrick-Steward. 288p. 1993. pap. 29.95 (0-8058-1866-9) L Erlbaum Assocs.

Beginning Writers in the Zone of Proximal Development. Elizabeth Petrick-Steward. 288p. 1993. text ed. 75.00 (0-8058-1302-0) L Erlbaum Assocs.

Beginning Writers Manual: Spelling Checker, Grammar Rules & Suggested Topics. Edward Fry & Elizabeth Sakiey. Ed. by Reta Holmback. 128p. (Orig.). 1993. pap. 14.95 (0-87673-024-1) Laguna Bch Ed.

Beginning Writing. John Nicholls et al. (English, Language & Education Ser.). 128p. 1990. pap. 27.00 (0-335-09224-1, Open Univ Pr) Taylor & Francis.

***Beginning Your Enneagram Journey.** Loretta Brady. 132p. (Orig.). 1994. pap. 14.95 (0-88347-284-8, 7284) Thomas More.

Beginning Your Familiy History in Great Britain. 4th rev. ed. George Pelling. (Illus.). 64p. 1989. 7.50 (0-8063-1253-X, 4560) Genealog Pub.

Beginning Your Family History. (C). 1987. 30.00 (0-317-89879-5, Pub. by Birmingham Midland Soc UK) St Mut.

***Beginning Your Marriage.** 8th ed. John L. Thomas. LC 94-70380. (Illus.). 192p. (Orig.). 1994. pap. 4.50 (0-915388-24-3, 150) ACTA Pubns.

Beginning Your Marriage see Camino Hacia el Amor

Beginning Youth. Brown Landone. 62p. 1966. reprint ed. spiral bd. 5.50 (0-7873-1130-8) Mokelumne.

Beginnings. Dwight L. Grubbs. 1994. pap. 12.95 (1-55673-586-3, 7985) CSS OH.

Beginnings. Prabhu Guptara. 8.00 (0-89253-689-6); 4.80 (0-89253-690-X) Ind-US Inc.

Beginnings. Katherine Hershey. (Illus.). 51p. (J). (gr. k-6). 1979. pap. text ed. 9.45 (1-55976-004-4) CEF Press.

Beginnings. Carol L. Pearson. 6.95 (0-88494-561-8) Bookcraft Inc.

Beginnings. Laura Phillips. 224p. (Orig.). 1992. pap. 2.95 (1-56597-025-X, Kismet) Meteor Pub.

Beginnings. Grace Sandness. 78p. (Orig.). 1980. pap. write for info. (0-318-60920-7) Mini-World Pubns.

Beginnings: A Rhetoric & Handbook. William J. Kelly. (Illus.). 704p. (Orig.). (C). 1992. pap. write for info. (0-02-363470-7) Macmillan.

Beginnings: Egypt & Assyria. Warren R. Dawson. LC 75-23650. (Clio Medica Ser.: No. 1). reprint ed. 9.50 (0-404-58901-4) AMS Pr.

Beginnings: How Families Came to Be. Virginia L. Kroll. LC 93-29594. (Illus.). (J). 1994. write for info. (0-8075-0602-8) A Whitman.

Beginnings: Intention & Method. Edward W. Said. LC 84-17044. (Morningside Bk.). 431p. 1985. reprint ed. text ed. 48.50 (0-231-05936-1); reprint ed. pap. text ed. 16.50 (0-231-05937-X) Col U Pr.

Beginnings: Louis I. Kahn's Philosophy of Architecture. Alexandra Tyng. LC 83-6799. (Wiley-Interscience Publication Ser.). 214p. reprint ed. pap. 61.00 (0-7837-2380-6, 2040066) Bks Demand.

Beginnings: Monologues of the Stars. Ed. by Eric Kraus. Date not set. pap. 11.95 (1-880399-55-5) Smith & Kraus.

***Beginnings: Our First Five Hundred Years.** Gerald Bastien. 182p. (Orig.). 1994. pap. 7.99 (1-56043-809-6) Destiny Image.

Beginnings: Physical Therapy & the APTA. Eugene Michels. (Illus.). 1979. pap. 6.00 (0-912452-03-X) Am Phys Therapy Assn.

Beginnings: Teaching & Learning in the Kindergarten. Ron Benson. LC 93-20194. 155p. 1993. pap. text ed. 19.95 (1-878450-54-9) R Owen Pubs.

***Beginnings: The Sacred Design.** Bonnie Gaunt. LC 95-79654. (Illus.). 224p. (Orig.). 1995. pap. 12.00 (0-9602688-4-7) B Gaunt.

Beginnings: The Social & Affective Development of Black Children. Ed. by Margaret B. Spencer et al. 350p. (C). 1985. pap. 34.50 (0-8058-0228-2) L Erlbaum Assocs.

Beginnings: The Story of Origins, of Mankind, Life, the Earth, the Universe. Isaac Asimov. 1989. mass mkt. 5.99 (0-425-11586-0) Berkley Pub.

Beginnings: Word & Spirit in Conversion. Paul Helm. 133p. (Orig.). 1986. pap. 7.50 (0-85151-470-7) Banner of Truth.

Beginnings & Beyond: Foundations in Early Childhood Education. 3rd ed. Ann M. Gordon & Kathryn W. Browne. LC 92-24557. 580p. 1993. text ed. 39.95 (0-8273-4930-0) Delmar.

Beginnings & Beyond Instructor's Guide. 3rd ed. Ann Gordon & Kathryn W. Browne. 90p. 1993. teacher ed 14.00 (0-8273-4931-9) Delmar.

***Beginnings & Endings.** Henry Pluckrose. LC 94-44515. (New Look Ser.). (Illus.). (J). 1995. write for info. (0-516-08236-1) Childrens.

Beginnings & Endings: Creative Warmups & Closure Activities. Michele Barca & Kate Cobb. 145p. 1994. pap. 34.95 (0-87425-249-0) Human Res Dev Pr.

Beginnings & Other Poems. C. J. Stevens. LC 89-515642. 80p. (Orig.). 1990. text ed. 12.95 (0-9623934-2-8); pap. text ed. 8.95 (0-9623934-3-6) J Wade.

Beginnings & the Renaissance see St. James Reference Guide to English Literature

Beginning's End. Shaykh F. Haeri. 224p. 1987. 39.50 (0-7103-0220-7, Routledge NY); pap. 16.95 (0-7103-0221-5, 02215, Routledge NY) Routledge Chapman & Hall.

***Beginnings Endings & Somewhere-in-Between.** Judy Clouston. 68p. 1992. pap. 6.95 (1-884754-14-7) Potpourri Pubns.

Beginnings: From Creation Until Abraham see Torah Anthology: Meam Lo'ez

Beginnings I. Linda A. Ferreira. (Express English Ser.). 1985. pap. 12.95 (0-8384-2789-8, Newbury); teacher ed, pap. 14.95 (0-8384-3051-1, Newbury); audio 15.00 (0-8384-3050-3, Newbury) Heinle & Heinle.

Beginnings in Classical Literature. Ed. by Francis M. Dunn & Thomas Cole. (Yale Classical Studies: No. 29). 258p. (C). 1992. 64.95 (0-521-41319-2) Cambridge U Pr.

***Beginnings in Drama.** E. Martin Browne. 32p. (Orig.). 1994. pap. 4.00 (0-88734-909-9) Empire Pub Srvs.

An Asterisk (*) at the beginning of an entry indicates that the title is appearing in BIP for the first time.

An Asterisk (*) at the beginning of an entry indicates that the title is appearing in BIP for the first time.

663

Behavior & Design Criteria for Bond in Reinforced Concrete: Report for Distribution to the Reinforced Concrete Research Council of the American Society of Civil Engineers. Emory L. Kemp & Jah-Chi Wang. 456p. reprint ed. pap. 130.00 (*0-8357-7104-0*, 2022638) Bks Demand.

Behavior & Design of Aluminum Structures. LC 92-22257. 1992. text ed. 47.00 (*0-07-056478-7*) McGraw.

Behavior & Design of Prestressed Concrete Beams with Large Web Openings. Prestressed Concrete Institute Staff. (PCI Journal Reprints Ser.). 32p. 1985. pap. 7.00 (*0-318-19855-X*, JR193) P-PCI.

Behavior & Design of Steel Structures. N. Trahair & M. A. Bradford. (Illus.). 420p. 1988. pap. text ed. 39.95 (*0-412-29480-X*) Chapman & Hall.

Behavior & Determination of Volatile Organic Compounds in Soil: Literature. 1994. lib. bdg. 250.00 (*0-8490-8591-8*) Gordon Pr.

Behavior & Development in Fragile X Syndrome. Elisabeth Dykens et al. (Developmental Clinical Psychology & Psychiatry Ser.: Vol. 28). (Illus.). 112p. (C). 1993. text ed. 37.00 (*0-8039-4887-5*); pap. text ed. 16.95 (*0-8039-4888-3*) Sage.

Behavior & Ecology of the African Buffalo. M. J. Mloszewski. LC 82-1153. (Illus.). 280p. 1983. 64.95 (*0-521-24478-1*) Cambridge U Pr.

Behavior & Environment: Psychological & Geographical Approaches. Ed. by Tommy Garling & Reginald G. Golledge. LC 92-44318. (Advances in Psychology Ser.: Vol. 96). 1993. write for info. (*0-444-89698-8*, North Holland) Elsevier.

Behavior & Evolution. Anne Roe & George G. Simpson. LC 58-11260. 567p. reprint ed. pap. 161.60 (*0-8357-7105-9*, 2003070) Bks Demand.

Behavior & Evolution of Birds. Douglas Mock. (C). 1995. text ed. write for info. (*0-7167-2237-2*) W H Freeman.

Behavior & Handling of Ships. Henry H. Hooyer. LC 83-71312. 140p. 1983. text ed. 17.50 (*0-87033-306-2*) Cornell Maritime.

Behavior & Immunity. Alan J. Husband. 200p. 1991. 79.95 (*0-8493-0199-8*, QP56) CRC Pr.

Behavior & Instructional Management: An Ecological Approach. William H. Evans et al. (Illus.). 350p. 1989. teacher ed write for info. (*0-318-63894-0*, H19300); pap. text ed. 35.00 (*0-205-11929-8*, H19292) Allyn.

Behavior & Its Causes: Philosophical Foundations of Operant Psychology. Terry L. Smith. (Studies in Cognitive Systems). 292p. (C). 1994. lib. bdg. 95.00 (*0-7923-2815-9*) Kluwer Ac.

Behavior & Medicine. Wedding. (Illus.). 592p. 1991. pap. 37.95 (*0-8016-5509-9*) Mosby Yr Bk.

*__Behavior & Medicine.__ 2nd ed. Ed. by Danny Wedding. LC 94-24593. 1995. write for info. (*0-8151-9142-1*) Mosby Yr Bk.

Behavior & Mind: The Roots of Modern Psychology. Howard Rachlin. LC 92-47398. (Illus.). 176p. 1994. 35.00 (*0-19-507979-5*) OUP.

*__Behavior & Misbehavior: A Teacher's Guide to Discipline.__ James L. Hymes, Jr. 96p. 1995. reprint ed. pap. text ed. 14.95 (*0-940139-33-2*) Consortium RI.

Behavior & Motivation: Index of Modern Information. Uriel Rottlevy. LC 90-31679. 150p. 1990. 39.50 (*1-55914-140-9*); pap. 34.50 (*1-55914-141-7*) ABBE Pubs Assn.

Behavior & Physiology of Pinnipeds. Ed. by Richard J. Harrison. LC 68-58514. 425p. reprint ed. pap. 121.20 (*0-8357-7106-7*, 2055685) Bks Demand.

Behavior & Properties of Refractory Metals. T. E. Tietz & J. W. Wilson. ix, 419p. 1965. 52.50 (*0-8047-0162-8*) Stanford U Pr.

*__Behavior & Properties of Refractory Metals.__ fac. ed. Thomas E. Tietz & J. W. Wilson. LC 63-10737. (Illus.). 111p. 1965. reprint ed. pap. 30.00 (*0-7837-7909-7*, 2047665) Bks Demand.

Behavior & Taxonomy of the Epicauta Maculata Group (Coleoptera, Meloidae) John D. Pinto. LC 79-27381. (University of California Publications in Social Welfare: No. 89). (Illus.). 117p. reprint ed. pap. 33.40 (*0-8357-7107-5*, 2031584) Bks Demand.

Behavior & the Menstrual Cycle. Ed. by Richard C. Friedman. (Sexual Behavior Ser.: Vol. 1). (Illus.). 480p. 1982. 140.00 (*0-8247-1852-6*) Dekker.

Behavior & the Natural Environment. Ed. by Irwin Altman & Joachim F. Wohlwill. LC 83-7285. (Human Behavior & Environment Ser.: Vol. 6). (Illus.). 346p. 1983. 65.00 (*0-306-41099-0*, Plenum Pr) Plenum.

Behavior-Based Safety Process. T. Krause. 1990. text ed. 69.95 (*0-442-00227-0*) Van Nos Reinhold.

Behavior, Bias, & Handicaps: Labeling the Emotionally Disturbed Child. Judy Kugelmass. 260p. 1986. 39.95x (*0-88738-114-6*) Transaction Pubs.

Behavior Change in the Classroom: Self-Management Interventions. Edward S. Shapiro & Christine L. Cole. LC 93-42172. (School Practitioner Ser.). 1994. lib. bdg. 25.00 (*0-89862-366-9*) Guilford Pubns.

Behavior Changes Resulting from a Study of Communicable Diseases: An Evaluation of the Effects of Learning on Certain Actions of High School Pupils. John Urban. LC 75-177687. (Columbia University. Teachers College. Contributions to Education Ser.: No. 896). reprint ed. 37.50 (*0-404-55896-8*) AMS Pr.

Behavior, Culture, & Conflict in World Politics. Ed. by William Zimmerman & Harold K. Jacobson. 320p. (C). 1993. text ed. 49.50 (*0-472-10453-5*) U of Mich Pr.

*__Behavior Cycle As a Framework for Dynamic Psychotherapy.__ Joseph Jacob. 296p. (C). 1995. text ed. write for info. (*0-89876-217-0*) Gardner Pr.

Behavior Description Interview. D. Janz. 1985. text ed. 35.60 (*0-205-08597-0*) Allyn.

Behavior Development in Infants: A Survey of the Literature on Prenatal & Postnatal Activity 1920-1932. Evelyn Dewey. LC 72-343. (Body Movement Perspectives in Research Ser.). 334p. 1973. reprint ed. 24.95 (*0-405-03142-4*) Ayer.

Behavior Difficulties of Children As Perceived & Judged by Parents, Teachers, & Children Themselves, Vol. 25. William E. Griffiths. LC 75-142313. (Illus.). xxi, 116p. 1970. reprint ed. text ed. 45.00 (*0-8371-8080-5*, CWGB, Greenwood Pr) Greenwood.

Behavior Disorders: Theory & Practice. 2nd ed. Margaret C. Coleman. 544p. (C). 1991. text ed. 47.00 (*0-205-13206-5*) Allyn.

Behavior Disorders in Childhood. 2nd ed. Rita Wicks-Nelson & Allan C. Israel. 1991. text ed. 32.00 (*0-13-084070-X*, 670203) P-H.

Behavior Disorders in Children. 3rd ed. Harvey F. Clarizio & George F. McCoy. 724p. (C). 1990. text ed. 57.50 (*0-06-041304-2*) HarpCollege.

Behavior Disorders in Infants, Children, & Adolescents. Ed. by John M. Reisman. 400p. (C). 1986. pap. text ed. write for info. (*0-07-553909-8*) McGraw.

Behavior Disorders of Adolescence: Research, Intervention, & Policy in Clinical & School Settings. Ed. by R. J. McMahon & R. DeV. Peters. LC 91-1957. (Illus.). 224p. 1991. 75.00 (*0-306-43813-5*, Plenum Pr) Plenum.

Behavior Disorders of Children & Adolescents. Douglas Cullinhan et al. (Illus.). 384p. 1983. text ed. write for info. (*0-13-072041-0*) P-H.

Behavior Disorders of Children & Adolescents: Assessment, Etiology & Intervention. 2nd ed. Marilyn T. Erickson. 416p. 1992. text ed. 58.00 (*0-13-095043-2*) P-H.

*__Behavior Genetic Approaches in Behavioral Medicine.__ Ed. by J. Rick Turner et al. (Perspectives on Individual Differences Ser.). 260p. 1995. 45.00 (*0-306-44969-2*) Plenum.

Behavior Guide to African Mammals. Richard Estes. LC 89-4877. (Illus.). 660p. 1990. 75.00 (*0-520-05831-3*) U CA Pr.

Behavior Guide to African Mammals. Richard Estes. 1992. pap. 22.50 (*0-520-08085-8*) U CA Pr.

Behavior, Health, & Environmental Stress. Ed. by Sheldon Cohen et al. 294p. 1986. 39.50 (*0-306-42138-0*, Plenum Pr) Plenum.

Behavior in Excess: An Examination of the Volitional Disorders. Ed. by S. Joseph Mule. LC 81-65506. (Illus.). 480p. 1981. text ed. 45.00 (*0-02-922220-6*) Free Pr.

Behavior in Mind & Body by Choice: Index of New Information with Authors & Subjects. American Health Research Institute Staff. LC 92-54229. 180p. 1992. 44.50 (*1-55914-606-0*); pap. 39.50 (*1-55914-607-9*) ABBE Pubs Assn.

Behavior in Organizations. David D. Van Fleet. (C). 1991. write for info. (*0-395-55432-2*); student ed write for info. (*0-395-55433-0*) HM Soft Schl Col Div.

Behavior in Organizations. 5th ed. James B. Lau & A. B. Shani. 704p. (C). 1991. pap. text ed. 39.95 (*0-256-08701-6*, 08-1107-05) Irwin.

Behavior in Organizations: A Systems Approach to Managing. 2nd ed. Edgar F. Huse & James L. Bowditch. LC 76-9329. (Illus.). 1977. text ed. write for info. (*0-201-02965-0*) Addison-Wesley.

*__Behavior in Organizations: An Experiential Approach.__ 6th rev. ed. Abraham B. Shani & James B. Lau. LC 95-14431. 576p. (C). 1995. 39.95 (*0-256-14115-0*) Irwin.

Behavior in Organizations: Understanding & Managing the Human Side of Work. 3rd ed. Robert A. Baron & Jerald Greenberg. 608p. 1989. teacher ed write for info. (*0-318-66365-1*, H21629); student ed 18.00 (*0-685-29833-7*, H21652); write for info. (*0-318-66366-X*, H22197); write for info. (*0-318-66367-8*, 21637) Allyn.

*__Behavior in Organizations: Understanding & Managing the Human Side of Work.__ 5th ed. Jerald Greenberg & Robert A. Baron. LC 94-22355. 1994. text ed. write for info. (*0-205-16176-6*) Allyn.

Behavior in Public Places: Notes on the Social Organization of Gatherings. Erving Goffman. LC 62-11850. 1966. 19.95 (*0-02-911930-8*); pap. 14.95 (*0-02-911940-5*) Free Pr.

Behavior in Public Places: Notes on the Social Organization of Gatherings. Erving Goffman. LC 80-19005. viii, 248p. 1980. reprint ed. text ed. 35.00 (*0-313-22390-4*, GOBP, Greenwood Pr) Greenwood.

Behavior in Small Groups. Alfred D. Benjamin. LC 77-73213. (C). 1978. pap. 27.16 (*0-395-25447-7*) HM.

Behavior Management: A Practical Approach for Educators. 6th ed. Thomas M. Shea & James E. Walker. LC 94-4471. 395p. (C). 1995. pap. write for info. (*0-02-423871-6*, Merrill Pub Co) Macmillan.

Behavior Management: Applications for Teachers & Parents. Thomas J. Zirpoli & Kristine J. Melloy. (Illus.). 464p. (Orig.). (C). 1993. pap. write for info. (*0-02-431725-X*) Macmillan.

Behavior Management: Practical Approach for Educators. 5th ed. James E. Walker. 352p. (C). 1990. pap. write for info. (*0-675-21385-1*, Merrill Pub Co) Macmillan.

Behavior Management: Strategies & Techniques. Susan K. Peterson & Henry A. Tenenbaum. LC 86-9113. 84p. (Orig.). (C). 1986. lib. bdg. 35.50 (*0-8191-5361-3*); pap. 14.50 (*0-8191-5362-1*) U Pr of Amer.

Behavior Management in Juvenile Justice Facilities Correspondence Course. American Correspondence Association Staff. 266p. (Orig.). 1993. pap. 60.00 (*0-929310-82-9*, 160) Am Correctional.

Behavior Management in K-6 Classrooms. Karen Malm. 128p. 1992. 11.95 (*0-8106-0365-9*) NEA.

Behavior Management in the School Library Media Center. Ed. by Thomas L. Hart. LC 85-11206. 176p. reprint ed. pap. 50.20 (*0-7837-5914-2*, 2045713) Bks Demand.

Behavior Management in the Schools: Principles & Procedures. 2nd ed. Richard M. Wielkiewicz. 1994. text ed. 39.95 (*0-205-16458-7*); pap. text ed. 29.95 (*0-205-16459-5*) Allyn.

Behavior, Mimetic Songs & Song Dialects, & Relationships of the Parasitic Indigobirds (Vidua) of Africa. Robert B. Payne. 333p. 1973. 12.50 (*0-943610-11-7*) Am Ornithologists.

Behavior Mismatch: How to Manage Problem Employees Whose Actions Don't Match Your Expectations. Rebecca B. Mann. LC 93-24873. 176p. 1993. 19.95 (*0-8144-5121-7*) AMACOM.

Behavior Modeling Training: Principles & Applications. Phillip J. Decker & Barry R. Nathan. LC 84-18155. 256p. 1985. text ed. 42.95 (*0-275-90084-3*, C0084, Praeger Pubs) Greenwood.

Behavior Models: Specifying User's Expectations. James A. Kowal. 365p. 1991. text ed. 55.00 (*0-13-292715-2*, 270109) P-H.

Behavior Modification. 2nd ed. (What Research Says to the Teacher Ser.). 1985. 3.95 (*0-8106-1065-5*) NEA.

Behavior Modification: An Empirical Approach to Self-Control. John A. Glover & Albert L. Gary. LC 79-88. 208p. 1979. 26.95 (*0-88229-298-6*) Nelson-Hall.

Behavior Modification: Behavioral Approaches to Human Problems. William H. Redd et al. 1978. text ed. write for info. (*0-394-32134-0*) Random.

Behavior Modification: Contributions to Education. Ed. by Sidney W. Bijou & Roberto Ruiz. LC 80-278780. 352p. 1981. text ed. 69.95 (*0-89859-051-5*) L Erlbaum Assocs.

Behavior Modification: Handbook of Assessment, Intervention, & Evaluation. Eileen D. Gambrill. LC 76-50700. (Jossey-Bass Behavioral Science Ser.). 1253p. reprint ed. pap. 180.00 (*0-7837-0169-1*, 2040466) Bks Demand.

*__Behavior Modification: HP 612.__ California College for Health Sciences Staff. 346p. (C). 1992. student ed, spiral bd. write for info. (*0-933195-68-0*) Allied Hlth Pubns.

Behavior Modification: Principles & Clinical Applications. 2nd ed. Ed. by W. Stewart Agras. 307p. 1978. 20.00 (*0-316-02031-1*) Little.

Behavior Modification: The Scientific Way to Self Control. William C. Budd. LC 73-79774. 1973. 10.95 (*0-87212-027-9*) Libra.

Behavior Modification: Thinking & Test-Taking for Academic & Personal Success. Small & Brantley. 176p. (C). 1991. pap. text ed. 26.95 (*0-8403-7042-3*) Kendall-Hunt.

Behavior Modification: What It Is & How to Do It. 4th ed. Garry L. Martin & Joseph Pear. 528p. (C). 1991. pap. text ed. write for info. (*0-13-067166-5*) P-H.

Behavior Modification & Special Education: Perspectives & Trends. Ed. by Lee H. Swanson. (Illus.). 288p. (C). 1978. text ed. 29.50 (*0-8422-5300-9*) Irvington.

Behavior Modification & the Child: An Annotated Bibliography. Hazel B. Benson. LC 79-7358. (Contemporary Problems of Childhood Ser.: No. 3). 398p. 1979. text ed. 49.95 (*0-313-21489-1*, BBM/, Greenwood Pr) Greenwood.

Behavior Modification & What It Is & How to Do It. 3rd ed. Garry L. Martin & Joseph Pear. (Illus.). 576p. 1988. pap. text ed. 42.33 (*0-13-072315-0*) P-H.

Behavior Modification for Exceptional Children & Youth. Marcia D. Smith. 320p. 1992. 39.50 (*1-56372-042-6*) PRO-ED.

*__Behavior Modification for Exceptional Children & Youth.__ Marcia D. Smith. LC 94-40045. 1995. write for info. (*0-89079-652-1*) PRO-ED.

Behavior Modification for the Classroom Teacher. 2nd ed. Saul Axelrod. (Illus.). 272p. (C). 1983. text ed. write for info. (*0-07-002572-X*) McGraw.

Behavior Modification in a Rehabilitation Facility. Richard M. Sanders. LC 75-5866. (Illus.). 127p. 1975. pap. 3.95 (*0-8093-0719-7*) S Ill U Pr.

Behavior Modification in Applied Settings. 4th ed. Alan E. Kazdin. 382p. (C). 1989. pap. 29.95 (*0-534-11116-5*) Brooks-Cole.

Behavior Modification in Applied Settings. 5th ed. Alan E. Kazdin. LC 93-27397. 1994. pap. 29.95 (*0-534-21786-9*) Brooks-Cole.

Behavior Modification in Black Populations: Psychosocial Issues & Empirical Findings. Ed. by Samuel M. Turner & Russell T. Jones. LC 82-3746. 348p. 1982. 54.50 (*0-306-40867-8*, Plenum Pr) Plenum.

Behavior Modification in Business & Industry: A Selected Bibliography. Dolores Rescigno. (CPL Bibliographies Ser.: No. 140). 58p. 1984. 14.00 (*0-86602-140-X*) Coun Plan Librarians.

Behavior Modification in the Human Services: A Systematic Introduction to Concepts & Applications. 3rd ed. Sandra S. Sundel & Martin Sundel. (Illus.). 428p. (C). 1993. text ed. 55.00 (*0-8039-3415-7*); pap. text ed. 27.50 (*0-8039-3416-5*) Sage.

Behavior Modification in Therapeutic Recreation: An Introductory Learning Manual. John Dattilo & William D. Murphy. LC 87-51016. 174p. 1987. pap. text ed. 19.95 (*0-910251-21-5*) Venture Pub PA.

Behavior Modification of the Mentally Retarded. 2nd ed. Ed. by Travis Thompson & John Grabowski. (Illus.). 1977. pap. text ed. 19.95 (*0-19-502053-7*) OUP.

Behavior Modification Techniques for the Special Educator. Ed. by Stanley A. Winters & Eunice Cox. LC 72-86203. 309p. (C). 1972. pap. text ed. 12.95 (*0-8290-0654-0*) Irvington.

Behavior Modification with the Severely & Profoundly Retarded: Research & Application. Ed. by Thomas L. Whitman et al. LC 82-22720. (Monograph). 1983. text ed. 58.00 (*0-12-747280-0*) Acad Pr.

Behavior Modification with Women. Ed. by Elaine A. Blechman. LC 82-15655. 560p. reprint ed. pap. 159.60 (*0-7837-0687-1*, 2041020) Bks Demand.

Behavior-Modifying Chemicals for Insect Management. Ridgway et al. 760p. 1990. 250.00 (*0-8247-8156-2*) Dekker.

Behavior Neurology. Orrin Devinsky. LC 92-49804. (One Hundred Maxims in Neurology Ser.). 1992. 35.95 (*0-8016-7280-5*) Mosby Yr Bk.

Behavior Observation & Measurement. Ellsworth Community College Staff. Ed. by Michael Davis. (RATES Ser.: No. 5). (Illus.). 56p. (Orig.). 1983. pap. 3.00 (*0-916671-41-0*) Material Dev.

Behavior of Attendants see Critical Behaviors in Psychiatric-Mental Health Nursing: Monograph

Behavior of Blood & Its Components at Interface, Vol. 283. Ed. by Leo Vroman & Edward F. Leonard. (Annals Ser.). 1977. 43.00 (*0-89072-029-0*) NY Acad Sci.

Behavior of Captive Wild Animals. Ed. by Hal Markowitz & Victor Stevens. LC 77-18156. (Illus.). 320p. 1978. text ed. 35.95 (*0-88229-385-0*) Nelson-Hall.

Behavior of Communicating: An Ethnological Approach. W. John Smith. 557p. 1980. pap. 17.95 (*0-674-06466-6*) HUP.

Behavior of Concrete under Temperature Extremes. American Concrete Institute Staff. LC 73-85854. (American Concrete Institute Publication Ser.: No. SP-39). (Illus.). 214p. reprint ed. pap. 61.00 (*0-8357-7109-1*, 2004296) Bks Demand.

Behavior of Deep Foundations - STP 670. 610p. 1979. pap. 49.50 (*0-8031-0291-7*, 670, 04-670000-38) ASTM.

Behavior of Dense Media under High Dynamic Pressures. ICC Staff. 576p. 1968. text ed. 406.00 (*0-677-13710-9*) Gordon & Breach.

Behavior of Distant Maximal Geodesics in Finitely Connected Complete 2-Dimensional Riemannian Manifolds. Takashi Shioya. LC 93-48484. (Memoirs of the American Mathematical Society Ser.: No. 517). 1994. pap. 31.00 (*0-8218-2578-X*) Am Math.

Behavior of Gonadectomized Rhesus Monkeys. J. D. Loy et al. (Contributions to Primatology Ser.: Vol. 20). (Illus.). viii, 144p. 1983. 53.00 (*3-8055-3795-6*) S Karger.

Behavior of Income Shares: Selected Theoretical & Empirical Issues. (Studies in Income & Wealth: No. 27). 404p. 1964. reprint ed. 105.10 (*0-87014-183-X*) Natl Bur Econ Res.

Behavior of Industrial Prices. George J. Stigler & James K. Kindahl. (General Ser.: No. 90). 220p. 1970. text ed. 57.20 (*0-87014-216-X*) Natl Bur Econ Res.

Behavior of Industrial Prices. George J. Stigler & James K. Kindahl. LC 79-121003. (National Bureau of Economic Research. General Ser.: No. 90). 220p. reprint ed. pap. 62.70 (*0-8357-3239-8*, 2057133) Bks Demand.

Behavior of Industrial Work Groups: Prediction & Control. Leonard R. Sayles. Ed. by Leon Stein. LC 77-70530. (Work Ser.). 1977. reprint ed. lib. bdg. 19.95 (*0-405-10198-8*) Ayer.

Behavior of Insonated Metals see Radiation Damage: Proceedings of CISM, Department for Mechanics of Defamable Bodies, Univ. of Vienna, 1970

Behavior of Interest Rates: A Progress Report. Joseph W. Conard. (General Ser.: No. 81). 159p. 1966. 41.40 (*0-87014-081-7*) Natl Bur Econ Res.

Behavior of Interest Rates: A Progress Report. Joseph W. Conard. LC 66-22745. (National Bureau of Economic Research. General Ser.: No. 81). 159p. reprint ed. pap. 45.40 (*0-8357-3240-1*, 2057134) Bks Demand.

Behavior of Joints in High Temperature Materials. Ed. by T. G. Gooch et al. (Illus.). 272p. 1983. 74.00 (*0-85334-187-7*, Pub. by Elsevier Applied Sci UK) Elsevier.

Behavior of Law. Donald Black. 1980. reprint ed. pap. text ed. 33.00 (*0-12-102652-3*) Acad Pr.

Behavior of Macromolecules. H. J. Cantow et al. (Advances in Polymer Science Ser.: Vol. 46). (Illus.). 170p. 1982. 66.00 (*0-387-11640-0*) Spr-Verlag.

Behavior of Marine Animals, Vol. 3: Cetaceans. Howard E. Winn & Bori L. Olla. LC 79-167675. 458p. 1979. 89.50 (*0-306-37573-7*, Plenum Pr) Plenum.

Behavior of Marine Animals, Vol. 4: Marine Birds. Ed. by Howard E. Winn et al. LC 79-167675. 532p. 1980. 95.00 (*0-306-37574-5*, Plenum Pr) Plenum.

Behavior of Marine Animals, Vol. 5: Shorebirds: Breeding Behavior & Population. Ed. by Joanna Burger & Bori L. Olla. LC 79-167675. 452p. 1984. 95.00 (*0-306-41590-9*, Plenum Pr) Plenum.

Behavior of Marine Animals, Vol. 6: Shorebirds: Migration & Foraging Behavior. Ed. by Joanna Burger & Bori L. Olla. LC 79-167675. 344p. 1984. 85.00 (*0-306-41591-7*, Plenum Pr) Plenum.

Behavior of Metal Structures: Research to Practice. Ed. by W. J. Hall & M. P. Gaus. 240p. 1983. pap. 24.00 (*0-87262-364-5*) Am Soc Civil Eng.

Behavior of Money: Exploratory Studies. James W. Angell. LC 75-85140. (Reprints of Economic Classics Ser.). 1969. reprint ed. 27.50 (*0-678-00525-7*) Kelley.

*__Behavior of Non-Oil Commodity Prices.__ Eduardo Borensztein et al. LC 94-33965. (Occassional Papers: 112). 1994. 15.00 (*1-55775-412-8*) Intl Monetary.

Behavior of Nonlinear Vibrating Systems, Vol. I: Fundamental Concepts & Methods; Applications to Single Degree-of-Freedom Systems, 2 vols. Wanda Szemplinska. (C). 1990. lib. bdg. 115.50 (*0-7923-0368-7*) Kluwer Ac.

Behavior of Nonlinear Vibrating Systems, Vol. I: Fundamental Concepts & Methods; Applications to Single Degree-of-Freedom Systems, 2 vols., Set. Wanda Szemplinska. (C). 1990. 169.00 (*0-685-31780-3*) Kluwer Ac.

Behavior of Penguins: Adapted to Ice & Tropics. Dietland Muller-Schwarze. LC 83-18020. (Animal Behavior Ser.). (Illus.). 193p. 1985. 64.50 (*0-87395-866-7*); pap. 22.95 (*0-87395-867-5*) State U NY Pr.

An Asterisk (*) at the beginning of an entry indicates that the title is appearing in BIP for the first time.

B

An Asterisk (*) at the beginning of an entry indicates that the title is appearing in BIP for the first time.

Behavioral Ecology of the Komodo Monitor. Walter Auffenberg. LC 80-26683. (Illus.). x, 406p. 1981. 59.95 (*0-8130-0621-X*) U Press Fla.

Behavioral Economics. James Allison. LC 83-8058. 240p. 1983. text ed. 49.95 (*0-275-90935-2*, C0935, Praeger Pubs) Greenwood.

Behavioral Effects of Nicotine: Proceedings of the International Workshop, Zurich, September 15-17, 1976. Ed. by K. Baettig. (Illus.). 1977. 39.25 (*3-8055-2763-2*) S Karger.

Behavioral Embryology see Studies on the Development of Behavior & the Nervous System

Behavioral Emergencies: A Field Guide for EMT's & Paramedics. Ellen L. Bassuk et al. 1983. teacher ed write for info. (*0-316-08331-3*); pap. text ed. 16.00 (*0-316-08330-5*) Little.

Behavioral Endocrinology. Ed. by Jill B. Becker. (Illus.). 688p. 1992. 68.00 (*0-262-02342-3*); pap. 39.95 (*0-262-52171-7*) MIT Pr.

Behavioral Energetics: The Cost of Survival in Vertebrates. Ed. by Wayne P. Aspey & Sheldon I. Lustick. LC 82-12512. (Biosciences Colloquia Ser.: No. 6). 312p. 1983. 42.50 (*0-8142-0332-9*) Ohio St U Pr.

*__Behavioral Engineering Through Safety Training: The B. E. S. T. Approach.__ James P. Kohn. (Illus.). 212p. 1982. pap. 25.95 (*0-398-06210-2*) C C Thomas.

Behavioral Engineering Through Safety Training: The B. E. S. T. Approach. James P. Kohn. (Illus.). 202p. (C). 1988. text ed. 42.95x (*0-398-05434-7*) C C Thomas.

Behavioral Evolution & Integrative Levels. Ed. by Gary Greenberg & Ethel Tobach. (T. C. Scneirla Conference Ser.: Vol. 1). 320p. (C). 1984. text ed. 69.95 (*0-89859-363-8*) L Erlbaum Assocs.

Behavioral Expression & Biosocial Bases of Sensation Seeking. Marvin Zuckerman. LC 93-40276. (Illus.). 560p. (C). 1994. 64.95 (*0-521-43200-6*); pap. 32.95 (*0-521-43770-9*) Cambridge U Pr.

Behavioral Family Intervention. Matthew R. Sanders. 1992. pap. 25.95 (*0-685-64776-5*) Allyn.

Behavioral Family Intervention. Matthew R. Sanders & Mark R. Dadds. (Practitioner Guidebook Ser.). 256p. 1992. text ed. 34.95 (*0-205-14600-7*, Longwood Div); pap. text ed. 25.95 (*0-205-14599-X*, Longwood Div) Allyn.

Behavioral Family Therapy. Ed. by Bruce A. Thyer. (Illus.). 266p. 1989. text ed. 57.95 (*0-398-05561-0*) C C Thomas.

*__Behavioral Family Therapy.__ Ed. by Bruce A. Thyer. (Illus.). 266p. 1989. pap. 35.95 (*0-398-06461-X*) C C Thomas.

Behavioral Family Therapy for Psychiatric Disorders. Kim T. Mueser & Shirley M. Glynn. 1994. text ed. 39.95 (*0-205-16653-9*, Longwood Div) Allyn.

Behavioral Foundations of Community Emergency Response Planning. Ronald W. Perry & Michael K. Lindell. (Illus.). 630p. 1992. 75.00 (*0-89116-620-3*) Hemisp Pub.

Behavioral Foundations of System Development. 2nd ed. David Meister. LC 83-19964. 392p. 1985. 49.50 (*0-89874-703-1*) Krieger.

Behavioral Genetics. Research & Education Association Staff. LC 82-80748. (Illus.). 224p. (C). 1982. text ed. 13. 30 (*0-87891-537-0*) Res & Educ.

Behavioral Genetics: A Primer. 2nd ed. Robert Plomin et al. (Psychology Ser.). 416p. (C). 1995. text ed. 39.95 (*0-7167-2056-6*) W H Freeman.

*__Behavioral Group Practice Performance Characteristics: The Council of Behavioral Group Practices Benchmarking Study.__ Allen S. Daniels et al. (Managed Behavioral Healthcare Library). 1995. pap. 45.00 (*1-887452-00-1*) CentraLink.

*__Behavioral Health Services Handbook.__ 300p. (Orig.). 1995. pap. 295.00 (*0-7605-1900-5*) Rector Pr.

*__Behavioral High-Risk Paradigm in Psychopathology.__ Ed. by Gregory A. Miller. LC 95-6678. (Series in Psychopathology). (Illus.). 304p. 1995. 98.00 (*0-387-94504-0*) Spr-Verlag.

*__Behavioral Human Resource Management.__ Robert B. Bowin. 110p. (C). 1992. pap. text ed. 20.00x (*0-9628796-0-6*) Bjorklund Pub.

Behavioral Individuality in Early Childhood. Alexander Thomas et al. 150p. reprint ed. pap. 42.80 (*0-8357-7113-X*, 2010287) Bks Demand.

Behavioral Instruction: An Evaluative Review. Kent R. Johnson & Robert S. Ruskin. LC 77-9258. 198p. reprint ed. pap. 56.50 (*0-7837-0483-6*, 2040807) Bks Demand.

*__Behavioral Intervention As First Line Treatment.__ David A. Smith. (Geriatric Psychopathology Ser.). 75p. 1995. pap. 39.95 (*1-884937-20-9*) Manisses Communs.

Behavioral Intervention in Human Problems. Ed. by Henry C. Rickard. LC 76-112398. 434p. 1972. 181.00 (*0-08-016327-0*, Pub. by Pergamon Repr UK) Franklin.

Behavioral Intervention Techniques in Drug Abuse Treatment. 1986. lib. bdg. 79.95 (*0-8490-3521-X*) Gordon Pr.

Behavioral Interventions with Brain-Injured Children. A. MacNeill Horton, Jr. LC 93-41064. (Critical Issues in Neuropsychology Ser.). 216p. 1994. 34.50 (*0-306-44438-0*, Plenum Pr) Plenum.

Behavioral Issues in Autism. Ed. by Eric Schopler & Gary B. Mesibov. (Current Issues in Autism Ser.). (Illus.). 314p. (C). 1994. 45.00 (*0-306-44600-6*, Plenum Pr) Plenum.

Behavioral Learning Systems Approach to Instruction: Analysis & Synthesis. Don Stewart. LC 75-13673. (Instruction As a Humanizing Science Ser.: Vol. 2). 564p. 1975. 18.95 (*0-913448-08-7*); pap. 14.95 (*0-913448-09-5*) SLATE Servs.

Behavioral Management of Obesity. Ed. by Jean Storlie & Henry A. Jordan. LC 87-22619. (LaCrosse Exercise & Health Ser.). (C). 1988. reprint ed. text ed. 35.00 (*0-87322-908-8*, BSTO0908) Human Kinetics.

Behavioral Management of the Cardiac Patient. D. G. Byrne. Ed. by Glenn R. Caddy. LC 87-1324. (Developments in Clinical Psychology Ser.: Vol. 7). 208p. 1987. text ed. 39.50 (*0-89391-386-3*) Ablex Pub.

Behavioral Measures of Neurotoxicity. National Research Council, U. S. National Committee for the International Union of Psychological Science Staff. 452p. 1990. 42.50 (*0-309-04047-7*) Natl Acad Pr.

Behavioral Mechanisms in Ecology. Douglass H. Morse. LC 80-12130. 391p. 1980. 40.00 (*0-674-06460-7*) HUP.

Behavioral Mechanisms in Ecology. Douglass H. Morse. LC 80-12130. 391p. 1982. pap. 16.95 (*0-674-06461-5*) HUP.

Behavioral Mechanisms in Evolutionary Biology. Ed. by Leslie A. Real. LC 94-14131. 1994. lib. bdg. 80.00 (*0-226-70595-1*); pap. text ed. 29.95 (*0-226-70597-8*) U Ch Pr.

Behavioral Medicine. Eldon Tunks. (Practitioner Guidebook Ser.). (C). 1991. 31.95 (*0-205-14485-3*, H4485, Longwood Div); pap. 21.95 (*0-205-14484-5*, H4484, Longwood Div) Allyn.

Behavioral Medicine: Assessment & Treatment Strategies. Ed. by Daniel M. Doleys et al. LC 81-23376. 648p. (C). 1982. 90.00 (*0-306-40841-4*, Plenum Pr) Plenum.

Behavioral Medicine: Psychological Treatment of Somatic Disorder. Ed. by A. A. Kaptein et al. 1990. text ed. 106.95 (*0-471-92410-5*) Wiley.

Behavioral Medicine: Work, Stress & Health. Ed. by W. Doyle Gentry et al. (NATO Advanced Science Institutes Series C: Mathematical & Physical Sciences). 1986. lib. bdg. 135.50 (*90-247-3264-6*) Kluwer Ac.

Behavioral Medicine Vol. 1: International Perspectives. Don G. Byrne & Glenn R. Caddy. 480p. (C). 1991. text ed. 69.50 (*0-89391-620-X*) Ablex Pub.

Behavioral Medicine Vol. 2: International Perspectives. Don G. Byrne & Glenn R. Caddy. 432p. (C). 1992. text ed. 69.50 (*0-89391-680-3*) Ablex Pub.

Behavioral Medicine & Developmental Disabilities. Ed. by J. K. Luiselli. (Disorders of Human Learning, Behavior, & Communication Ser.). (Illus.). 235p. 1989. 68.00 (*0-387-96875-X*) Spr-Verlag.

*__Behavioral Medicine Approaches to Coronary Heart Disease Prevention.__ Ed. by Kristina Orth-Gomer & Neil Schneiderman. LC 95-2986. 280p. 1995. text ed. 55.00 (*0-8058-1820-0*) L Erlbaum Assocs.

Behavioral Medicine, Biofeedback, & Behavioral Approaches in Psychosomatic Medicine. Ed. by H. Leigh. (Journal: Psychotherapy & Psychosomatics: Vol. 36, No. 3-4, 1981). (Illus.). 122p. 1982. pap. 48.00 (*3-8055-3521-X*) S Karger.

*__Behavioral Medicine in Cardiovascular Disorders.__ fac. ed. Ed. by Thomas Elbert et al. LC 87-21068. (Wiley Medical Publication Ser.). (Illus.). 340p. 1994. pap. 96. 90 (*0-7837-7652-7*, 2047405) Bks Demand.

Behavioral Medicine, Stress Management & Biofeedback. George D. Fuller. (Orig.). 1980. sl. 275.00 (*0-686-27973-5*); pap. 225.00 (*0-686-27972-7*) Biofeed Pr.

Behavioral Medicine, Vol. 3: International Perspectives. Don G. Byrne & Glenn R. Caddy. (Developments in Clinical Psychology Ser.). 464p. (C). 1994. text ed. 5.90 (*0-89391-744-3*) Ablex Pub.

Behavioral Medicine with the Developmentally Disabled. Ed. by Dennis C. Russo & J. H. Kedesdy. LC 88-17953. (Illus.). 308p. 1988. 49.50 (*0-306-42884-9*, Plenum Pr) Plenum.

Behavioral Methods in Social Welfare: Helping Children, Adults, & Families in Community Settings. Ed. by Steven P. Schinke. LC 80-66479. (Modern Applications of Social Work Ser.). 386p. 1981. lib. bdg. 44.95 (*0-202-36026-1*) Aldine de Gruyter.

Behavioral Modelling in Geography & Planning. Ed. by Reginald G. Golledge & Harry Timmermans. 544p. 1988. lib. bdg. 111.50 (*0-7099-3853-5*, A1759) Routledge Chapman & Hall.

Behavioral Models & the Analysis of Drug Action: Proceedings of the Oholio Conference, 27th, Israel, March 28-31, 1982. Spiegelstein. 498p. 1982. 161.75 (*0-444-42125-4*) Elsevier.

Behavioral Neurology. 3rd ed. Jonathan H. Pincus & Gary J. Tucker. (Illus.). 1985. pap. text ed. 19.95 (*0-19-503555-0*) OUP.

Behavioral Neurology: A Practical Approach. Howard S. Kirshner. (Clinical Neurology & Neurosurgery Monographs). (Illus.). 230p. 1985. text ed. 39.95 (*0-443-08410-6*) Churchill.

*__Behavioral Neurology & Neuropsychology.__ Todd E. Feinberg & Martha Farah. (Illus.). 752p. 1996. text ed. 79.00 (*0-07-020361-X*) Hlth Prof Div.

*__Behavioral Neurology of Movement Disorders.__ William J. Weiner & Anthony E. Lang. (Advances in Neurology Ser.: Vol. 65). 368p. 1995. 110.00 (*0-7817-0174-0*) Raven.

Behavioral Neuroscience, Vol. II. Ed. by A. Sahgal. (Practical Approach Ser.: No. 129). (Illus.). 244p. 1993. 79.00 (*0-19-963458-0*); pap. 44.00 (*0-19-963457-2*) OUP.

Behavioral Neuroscience: An Introduction. Carl W. Cotman & James L. McGaugh. LC 79-50214. 1980. text ed. 83.00 (*0-12-191650-2*) Acad Pr.

Behavioral Objectives: Evaluation in Nursing. 3rd ed. Dorothy Reilly & Marilyn Oermann. 278p. 1990. 22.95 (*0-88737-500-6*) Natl League Nurse.

Behavioral Objectives: The Position of the Pendulum. Ed. by Miriam B. Kapfer. LC 77-25988. (Illus.). 200p. 1978. 34.95 (*0-87778-125-7*) Educ Tech Pubns.

Behavioral Objectives for Learning Disabilities (BOLD) 2nd ed. Joyce DeWolfe & Sharon Herman. 192p. (Orig.). (C). 1992. text ed. 44.50 (*0-87562-071-X*) Spec Child.

Behavioral Objectives in Curriculum Development: Selected Readings & Bibliography. Ed. by Miriam B. Kapfer. LC 77-122809. 414p. 1971. 37.95 (*0-87778-001-3*) Educ Tech Pubns.

Behavioral Observations in Cardiovascular Research. A. D. Appels. 200p. 1991. 29.00 (*90-265-1036-5*, Pub. by Swets Pub Serv NE) Taylor & Francis.

Behavioral Pediatrics. Ed. by Donald E. Greydanus & Mark L. Wolraich. (Illus.). xxi, 471p. 1991. 98.00 (*0-387-97547-0*) Spr-Verlag.

Behavioral Pediatrics: Research & Practice. Dennis C. Russo et al. LC 82-3799. 432p. 1982. 65.00 (*0-306-40961-5*, Plenum Pr) Plenum.

Behavioral Pharmacology of 5-HT. P. Duphar et al. 528p. (C). 1991. text ed. 89.95 (*0-8058-0135-9*) L Erlbaum Assocs.

Behavioral Police Management. Harry W. More & W. Fred Wegener. (Illus.). 576p. (C). 1992. teacher ed write for info. (*0-318-69531-6*); text ed. write for info. (*0-02-383350-5*) Macmillan.

Behavioral Primatology: Advances in Research & Theory, Vol. 1. Ed. by A. M. Schrier. 208p. 1977. 39.95 (*0-89859-139-2*) L Erlbaum Assocs.

Behavioral Psychotherapy. Marks. 133p. 1986. 23.95 (*0-7236-0875-X*, Pub. by John Wright UK) Buttrwrth-Heinemann.

Behavioral Psychotherapy. Richards. 1990. 38.95 (*0-433-02526-3*) Buttrwrth-Heinemann.

Behavioral Regulators of Behavior in Primates. Ed. by C. R. Carpenter. LC 72-3602. (Illus.). 303p. 1974. 40.00 (*0-8387-1099-9*) Bucknell U Pr.

Behavioral Relaxation Training. Poppen. (Practitioner Guidebook Ser.). (C). 1988. pap. 25.95 (*0-205-14457-8*, H4457, Longwood Div) Allyn.

Behavioral Research: A Conceptual Approach. Frederick N. Kerlinger. 336p. (C). 1979. text ed. 42.75 (*0-03-013331-9*) HB Coll Pubs.

Behavioral Science. 2nd ed. Fadem. (Board Review Ser.). 1994. 19.95 (*0-685-75157-0*) Williams & Wilkins.

Behavioral Science. 2nd ed. Fedem. (National Medical Ser.). 1990. 25.00 (*0-685-75164-3*) Williams & Wilkins.

Behavioral Science. 2nd ed. Jerry M. Wiener. (National Medical Ser.). (Illus.). 287p. 1991. 24.00 (*0-683-06202-6*) Williams & Wilkins.

Behavioral Science: Concepts & Management Application. Harold M. Rush. (Studies in Personnel Policy: No. 216). 174p. (Orig.). 1969. pap. text ed. 40.00 (*0-8237-0003-8*) Conference Bd.

Behavioral Science & Human Factors in Power Plant Applications. Catherine D. Gaddy et al. 137p. reprint ed. pap. 39.10 (*0-8357-7114-8*, 2029777) Bks Demand.

Behavioral Science BRS. 2nd ed. Barbara Fadem. 1994. pap. 19.95 (*0-683-02953-3*) Williams & Wilkins.

Behavioral Science for Social Workers. Ed. by Edwin J. Thomas. LC 67-10837. 1967. text ed. 22.95 (*0-02-932480-7*) Free Pr.

Behavioral Science for Students. Frederick Sierles. 560p. 1993. 28.00 (*0-683-07730-9*) Williams & Wilkins.

Behavioral Science for the Boreds. 3rd ed. Frederick S. Sierles. (Illus.). 146p. (Orig.). 1993. pap. text ed. 14.95 (*0-940780-19-4*) MedMaster.

Behavioral Science in Family Medicine. Comp. by STFM Task Force on Behavioral Science. 118p. 1979. 15.50 (*0-942295-00-5*) Soc Tchrs Fam Med.

Behavioral Science in Family Medicine: A Program for Second & Third Year Family Medicine Residents Ser. rev. ed. Howard F. Stein. Ed. by Willam D. Grant. (Illus.). 94p. (C). 1986. pap. 15.00 (*0-9617230-1-7*) Univ Health Ctr.

Behavioral Sciences. R. S. Krug & A. R. Cass. (Oklahoma Notes Ser.). (Illus.). 128p. (C). 1988. pap. 15.95 (*0-387-96333-2*) Spr-Verlag.

Behavioral Sciences. 2nd ed. R. S. Krug & A. R. Cass. (Oklahoma Notes Ser.). (Illus.). xiii, 281p. 1991. pap. 18. 95 (*0-387-96967-5*) Spr-Verlag.

Behavioral Sciences. 2nd ed. Robert E. Pieroni. (Medical Examination Review Ser.). 248p. 1989. pap. 18.00 (*0-444-01049-1*) Elsevier.

Behavioral Sciences. 3rd ed. R. S. Krug. (Oklahoma Notes Ser.). (Illus.). 272p. 1994. 17.95 (*0-387-97782-1*) Spr-Verlag.

*__Behavioral Sciences.__ 4th ed. Ronald S. Krug & Alvah R. Cass. LC 94-25309. (Oklahoma Notes Ser.). 1995. write for info. (*0-387-94393-5*) Spr-Verlag.

Behavioral Sciences: PreTest Self-Assessment & Review. 6th ed. Evan G. Pattishall, Jr. (Basic Sciences PreTest Ser.). (Illus.). 264p. 1993. pap. text ed. 16.95 (*0-07-051996-X*) Hlth Prof Div.

*__Behavioral Sciences: PreTest Self-Assessment & Review.__ 7th ed. Ed. by Evan G. Pattishall, Jr. LC 95-5754. 1995. pap. text ed. 16.95 (*0-07-052084-4*) McGraw.

Behavioral Sciences: Research & Subject Analysis with Reference Bibliography. Clayton R. Mellows. LC 85-48099. 150p. 1987. 44.50 (*0-88164-470-6*); pap. 39.50 (*0-88164-471-4*) ABBE Pubs Assn.

Behavioral Sciences & the Mass Media. Ed. by Frederick T. Yu. LC 68-25421. 270p. 1968. 34.95 (*0-87154-983-2*) Russell Sage.

Behavioral Sciences for Nurses. Jack Rudman. (College Level Examination Ser.: CLEP-39). 1994. 39.95 (*0-8373-5389-0*); pap. 23.95 (*0-8373-5339-4*) Nat Learn.

Behavioral Sciences in Psychiatry. 3rd ed. (National Medical Ser.). Date not set. 25.00 (*0-685-75165-1*) Williams & Wilkins.

Behavioral Sciences in Psychiatry. 3rd ed. Jerry M. Wiener & Nancy Breslin. LC 93-23682. (National Medical Series for Independent Study). 1994. pap. 26.00 (*0-683-06203-4*) Williams & Wilkins.

Behavioral Simulation Methods in Tax Policy Analysis. Martin Feldstein. LC 82-21766. (National Bureau of Economic Research Project Report Ser.). (C). 1983. lib. bdg. 52.00 (*0-226-24084-3*) U Ch Pr.

Behavioral Social Work. John S. Wodarski & Dennis Bagarozzi. LC 78-26356. 335p. 1979. 45.95 (*0-87705-375-8*); pap. 20.95 (*0-87705-395-2*) Human Sci Pr.

Behavioral Sociology: The Experimental Analysis of Social Process. Robert L. Burgess. Ed. by Don Bushell, Jr. LC 79-90821. (Illus.). 1972. text ed. 67.00 (*0-231-03203-X*); pap. text ed. 25.50 (*0-231-08673-3*) Col U Pr.

Behavioral Statistics: An Introduction to the Basic Methods of Analysis & Persuasion. Donald V. Huard. 112p. (C). 1992. pap. text ed. 12.95 (*0-8403-7408-9*) Kendall-Hunt.

Behavioral Statistics: Logic & Methods. Richard B. Darlington & Patricia M. Carlson. 640p. 1987. text ed. 32.95 (*0-02-907860-1*) Free Pr.

Behavioral Statistics in Action. Mark Vernoy & Judith Vernoy. 410p. (C). 1992. text ed. 53.95 (*0-534-16086-7*) Brooks-Cole.

Behavioral Supervision: Practical Ways to Change Unsatisfactory Behavior & Increase Productivity. Les Donaldson. LC 79-25100. 1980. pap. 17.95 (*0-201-01473-4*) Addison-Wesley.

Behavioral Systems. Robert L. Morasky. LC 82-12334. 192p. 1982. text ed. 45.00 (*0-275-90863-1*, C0863, Praeger Pubs) Greenwood.

Behavioral Teratogenesis & Behavioral Mutagenesis: A Primer in Abnormal Development. E. W. Abel. (Illus.). 254p. 1989. 39.50 (*0-306-43053-3*, Plenum Pr) Plenum.

Behavioral Teratology: A Bibliography to the Study of Birth Defects of the Mind. Ernest L. Abel. LC 85-21946. xv, 206p. 1985. text ed. 55.00 (*0-313-25066-9*, ABT/, Greenwood Pr) Greenwood.

Behavioral Theories & Treatment of Anxiety. Ed. by Samuel M. Turner. 454p. 1984. 75.00 (*0-306-41593-3*, Plenum Pr) Plenum.

Behavioral Theory in Sociology: Essays in Honor of George C. Homans. Ed. by Robert L. Hamblin & John Kunkel. LC 76-1776. 546p. 1976. 49.95x (*0-87855-149-2*) Transaction Pubs.

Behavioral Theory of Labor Negotiations: An Analysis of a Social Interaction System. 2nd ed. Richard E. Walton & Robert B. McKersie. LC 91-3561. 492p. 1991. pap. 23.95 (*0-87546-179-4*) ILR Pr.

Behavioral Treatment of Alcoholism. P. M. Miller. 1976. 88.00 (*0-08-019519-9*, Pub. by Pergamon Repr UK) Franklin.

Behavioral Treatment of Obsessional States. H. R. Beech & M. Vaughan. LC 78-4552. 197p. reprint ed. pap. 56.20 (*0-8357-4317-9*, 2037116) Bks Demand.

Behavioral Treatment of Psychotic Illness. Ed. by William DiScipio. LC 73-18292. 240p. 1974. 35.95 (*0-87705-131-3*) Human Sci Pr.

Behavioral Treatments for Drug Abuse & Dependence, 2 vols., Set. 1994. lib. bdg. 350.00 (*0-8490-8606-X*) Gordon Pr.

Behavioral Treatments of Obesity: A Practical Handbook. Ed. by John P. Foreyt. 1977. 215.00 (*0-08-019902-X*, Pub. by Pergamon Repr UK) Franklin.

*__Behavioral Types & the Art of Patient Management.__ Stephen Prather et al. Ed. by Gregg Rogers. 212p. 1995. text ed. 39.95 (*1-57066-031-X*) Practice Mgmt Info.

Behavioral Variation: Case Study of a Malagasy Lemur. Alison F. Richard. LC 76-19837. (Illus.). 213p. 1978. 37. 50 (*0-8387-1965-1*) Bucknell U Pr.

Behavioral Vision Approach for Persons with Physical Disabilities. William V. Padula. Ed. by Sally M. Corngold. (Illus.). 208p. (C). 1988. 49.50 (*0-943599-04-0*) OEPF.

Behaviorally Disordered? Assessment for Identification & Instruction. Bob Algozzine et al. 36p. 1991. 8.90 (*0-86586-198-6*, P339) Coun Exc Child.

Behaviordyne InHouse Software User's Guide. Roger W. Sward. 40p. (Orig.). 1992. pap. 20.00 (*1-879858-02-9*) Behaviordyne.

Behaviorism. John Staddon. 1993. pap. 9.95 (*0-7156-2488-1*, Pub. by Duckworth UK) Focus Info Gr.

Behaviorism: A Conceptual Reconstruction. Gerald Zuriff. LC 84-12664. 416p. 1986. text ed. 54.00 (*0-231-05912-4*) Col U Pr.

Behaviorism & Christianity. Gordon H. Clark. Ed. & Intro. by John W. Robbins. 106p. (Orig.). 1982. pap. 5.95 (*0-940931-04-4*) Trinity Found.

Behaviorism & Logical Positivism: A Reassessment of the Alliance. Laurence D. Smith. 412p. 1986. 47.50 (*0-8047-1301-4*); pap. 15.95 (*0-8047-1520-3*) Stanford U Pr.

Behaviorism, Neobehaviorism & Cognitivism in Learning Theory: Historical & Contemporary Perspectives. Abram Amsel. 116p. 1988. 24.95 (*0-8058-0332-7*) L Erlbaum Assocs.

Behaviorism, Science, & Human Nature. Barry Schwartz & Hugh Lacey. (Illus.). (C). 1982. pap. text ed. 18.95 (*0-393-95197-9*) Norton.

Behaviorists' Misconduct in Science. Ed. by Akhter Ahsen. 200p. (C). 1990. pap. text ed. 25.00 (*0-913412-21-X*) Brandon Hse.

Behaviour. Donald E. Broadbent. LC 86-4661. 215p. 1986. reprint ed. text ed. 55.00 (*0-313-25216-5*, BBEH, Greenwood Pr) Greenwood.

Behaviour Analysis in Theory & Practice: Contributions & Controversies. Ed. by D. E. Blackman & H. Lejeune. 360p. 1990. text ed. 69.95 (*0-86377-144-0*) L Erlbaum Assocs.

Behaviour & Evolution. Ed. by P. J. Slater & T. R. Halliday. (Illus.). 256p. (C). 1994. 59.95 (*0-521-41858-5*); pap. 24.95 (*0-521-42923-4*) Cambridge U Pr.

An Asterisk (*) at the beginning of an entry indicates that the title is appearing in BIP for the first time.

An Asterisk (*) at the beginning of an entry indicates that the title is appearing in BIP for the first time.

Behind the Blue & Gray: The Soldier's Life in the Civil War. Delia Ray. (Young Readers' History of the Civil War Ser.). (Illus.). 112p. (J). (gr. 5-9). 1991. 16.99 (0-525-67333-4, Lodestar Bks) Dutton Child Bks.

Behind the Border. Nina Kossman. LC 93-48617. (J). 1994. 14.00 (0-688-13494-7) Lothrop.

Behind the Chutes: The Mystique of the Rodeo Cowboy. Rosamond Norbury. LC 92-34662. 128p. 1993. 17.00 (0-87842-287-0) Mountain Pr.

Behind the Chutes at Cheyenne Frontier Days: Your Pocket Guide to Rodeo. Avis Acton. Ed. by Cindy Garretson-Weibel. (Illus.). 112p. (Orig.). (YA). (gr. 6 up). 1991. pap. 7.95 (0-9627412-0-5) ABC Pub.

Behind the Cloud. Emilie Loring. reprint ed. lib. bdg. 17.95 (0-88411-367-1, Aeonian Pr) Amereon Ltd.

Behind the Couch: Revelations of a Psychoanalyst. rev. ed. Herbert Strean. 240p. 1991. pap. 11.95 (0-8245-1290-1) Crossroad NY.

***Behind the Courtyard Door: The Daily Life of Tribeswomen in Northern Morocco.** Ursula K. Hart. (Illus.). 196p. (Orig.). 1994. pap. 11.95 (0-938864-18-1) Ipswich Pr.

Behind the Covers: Interviews with Authors & Illustrators of Books for Children & Young Adults. Jim Roginski. 261p. 1989. lib. bdg. 27.50 (0-87287-627-6) Libs Unl.

Behind the Covers: Interviews with Authors & Illustrators of Books for Children & Young Adults, Vol. 1. Jim Roginski. LC 85-18129. 249p. 1985. lib. bdg. 23.50 (0-87287-506-7) Libs Unl.

Behind the Crimson Blind. Carter Dickson. 1989. pap. 3.50 (0-8217-2607-2) Zebra.

Behind the Crimson Blind. Carter Dickson & John K. Melling. (Black Dagger Crime Ser.). 280p. 1990. reprint ed. text ed. 16.50 (0-86220-768-1, Black Dagger) Chivers N Amer.

Behind the Curtain. Christian Thee. Ed. by Anne Kostick. (Illus.). 16p. 1994. 17.95 (1-56305-525-2) Workman Pub.

Behind the Curtains. Carmen M. Gaite. Tr. by Frances M. Lopez-Morillas. 288p. 1990. text ed. 30.00 (0-231-06888-3) Col U Pr.

Behind the Dark Pines. Martha Young. LC 72-4641. (Black Heritage Library Collection). (Illus.). 1977. reprint ed. 25.95 (0-8369-9133-8) Ayer.

Behind the Day. Mary Kennedy. 1972. 6.95 (0-910664-18-8) Gotham.

Behind the Diffusion Curve: Theoretical & Applied Contributions to the Microeconomics of Technology Adoption. Paul A. David. (Underground Classics in Economics Ser.). 150p. (C). 1995. pap. text ed. 22.50 (0-8133-7483-9) Westview.

Behind the Disappearances: Argentina's Dirty War Against Human Rights & the United Nations. Iain Guest. LC 90-35689. (Pennsylvania Studies in Human Rights). (Illus.). 624p. (C). 1990. text ed. 49.95 (0-8122-8204-3); pap. 19.95 (0-8122-1313-0) U of Pa Pr.

Behind the Dolphin Smile. Richard O'Barry & Keith Coulburn. (Illus.). 296p. 1989. 17.95 (0-912697-79-2) Algonquin Bks.

Behind the Door. Giorgio Bassani. Tr. by William Weaver. LC 75-29308. (Helen & Kurt Wolff Bk.). 150p. 1976. reprint ed. pap. 3.95 (0-15-611685-5, Harvest Bks) HarBrace.

Behind the Door of Delusion. Marle Woodson. 192p. 1994. 19.95 (0-87081-314-5); pap. 12.95 (0-87081-315-3) Univ Pr Colo.

Behind the Eight Ball. Linda Berman. 1992. pap. 11.95 (0-13-117581-5) P-H.

Behind the Eight-Ball: A Guide for Families of Gamblers. Linda Berman & Mary-Ellen Siegel. (Fireside - Parkside Recovery Book Ser.). 224p. 1992. pap. 10.00 (0-671-76711-9, Fireside) S&S Trade.

Behind the Essenes: History & Ideology in the Dead Sea Scrolls. Philip R. Davies. LC 87-9714. (Brown Judaic Studies). 150p. 1987. 25.95 (1-55540-140-6, 14-00-94) Scholars Pr GA.

Behind the Eurocentric Veils: The Search for African Realities. Clinton M. Jean. LC 91-22685. 136p. (C). 1992. text ed. 20.00 (0-87023-757-8) U of Mass Pr.

Behind the Eye. Donald M. MacKay. Ed. by Valerie MacKay. (Illus.). 288p. 1990. 24.95 (0-631-17332-3) Blackwell Pubs.

Behind the Eyes: Eight German Artists. Georg Jappe et al. LC 85-26143. (Illus.). 147p. (Orig.). 1986. pap. 14.95 (0-317-46704-2) San Fran MOMA.

Behind the Factory Walls: Decision Making in Soviet & U. S. Enterprises. Ed. by Paul R. Lawrence & Charalambos A. Vlachoutsicos. 1990. text ed. 29.95 (0-07-103247-9) McGraw.

Behind the Family Mask: Therapeutic Change in Rigid Family Systems. Maurizio Andolfi et al. LC 82-22817. 176p. 1983. pap. 21.50 (0-87630-574-5) Brunner-Mazel.

Behind the Figures. 1991. 14.95 (0-911703-35-7) CDS Assocs.

Behind the Front Line of the Civil War: Political Parties & Social Movements in Russia, 1918-1922. Vladimir N. Brovkin. 1994. 55.00 (0-691-03278-5) Princeton U Pr.

Behind the Front Page: Organizational Self-Renewal in a Metropolitan Newspaper. Chris Argyris. LC 73-22558. (Jossey-Bass Behavioral Science Ser.). 325p. reprint ed. pap. 92.70 (0-8357-4695-X, 2052350) Bks Demand.

Behind the Front Panel: The Design & Development of 1920's Radios. David Rutland. LC 94-60507. (Illus.). 186p. (Orig.). 1994. pap. 18.95 (1-885391-00-5) Wren Pubs.

Behind the Frontlines: Journey into Afro-Britain. Ferdinand Dennis. 216p. 1989. pap. 11.95 (0-575-04327-X, Pub. by V Gollancz UK) Trafalgar.

Behind the Geometrical Method: A Reading of Spinoza's Ethics. Edwin Curley. 148p. 1988. text ed. 35.00 (0-691-07322-8); pap. text ed. 12.95 (0-691-02037-X) Princeton U Pr.

Behind the Glory: The Grafs of Ostfriesland. Mildred Fielder. (Illus.). 388p. (Orig.). 1994. pap. 19.50 (0-9620162-4-1) M Fielder.

***Behind the Gold Curtain: Fifty Years in the Metropolitan Opera Orchestra.** David Berkowitz & Dolores Soyer. LC 95-76145. 190p. 1995. 28.95 (0-913559-29-6); pap. 15.95 (0-913559-30-X) Birch Brook Pr.

Behind the Gospels. Henry J. Cadbury. LC 68-8591. (Orig.). 1968. pap. 3.00 (0-87574-160-6) Pendle Hill.

Behind the Great Wall: A Post-Jungian Approach to Kafkaesque Literature. James Whitlark. LC 90-55830. 288p. 1992. 46.50 (0-8386-3427-3) Fairleigh Dickinson.

***Behind the Greencard: How to Legally Live, Work, & Conduct Business in the United States.** 2nd ed. Gerald Kaiser. 400p. 1995. 69.95 (0-9646304-6-X); pap. text ed. 39.95 (0-9646304-0-0) Glden Door Pub.

Behind the Headlines. Thomas Fleming. (American History Series for Young People). (J). (gr. 5 up). 1989. 14.95 (0-8027-6890-3); lib. bdg. 15.85 (0-8027-6891-1) Walker & Co.

Behind the Ice Curtain. Dina Gable. LC 92-71177. 500p. 1992. 21.95 (1-56062-127-3) CIS Comm.

Behind the Intifada: Labor & Women's Movements in the Occupied Territories. Joost R. Hiltermann. (Illus.). 283p. 1992. text ed. 39.50 (0-691-07869-6) Princeton U Pr.

Behind the Intifada: Labor & Women's Movements in the Occupied Territories. Joost R. Hiltermann. (Near East Studies). (Illus.). 282p. 1993. pap. text ed. 15.95 (0-691-02480-4) Princeton U Pr.

Behind the Iron Curtain. Joseph S. Roucek & Kenneth Lottich. 631p. 1986. 10.00 (0-317-52987-0) Noontide.

Behind the Iron Curtain: The Story of John Visser. A. H. Barbee. 75p. 1985. reprint ed. pap. 5.95 (0-89084-280-9) Bob Jones Univ Pr.

Behind the Japanese Bow: An In-Depth Guide to Understanding & Predicting Japanese Behavior. Boye De Mente. 200p. 1993. pap. 14.95 (0-8442-8491-2, Passport Bks) NTC Pub Grp.

Behind the Jester's Mask: Canadian Editorial Cartoons about Dominant & Minority Groups 1960-1979. Raymond N. Morris. 230p. 1989. text ed. 40.00 (0-8020-5806-X) U of Toronto Pr.

Behind the King's Kitchen Door. Ed. by Carol Ra. LC 91-66056. (Illus.). 56p. (J). (gr. 5 up). 1992. 18.95 (1-56397-024-4, Wordsong) Boyds Mills Pr.

Behind the Line: An Inquiry into Drawing. Thomas Sokolowski. (Illus.). 24p. 1988. 8.00 (0-934483-10-8) Gal Assn NY.

Behind the Lines. Isabelle Holland. LC 93-2576. (Illus.). 240p. (YA). (gr. 7 up). 1994. 13.95 (0-590-45113-8, Scholastic Hardcover) Scholastic Inc.

Behind the Lines: A Sourcebook on the Civil War. Ed. by Carter Smith. LC 92-16662. (American Albums from the Collections of the Library of Congress). (Illus.). 96p. (J). (gr. 5-8). 1993. lib. bdg. 18.90 (1-56294-265-4) Millbrook Pr.

Behind the Lines: Case Studies in Investigative Reporting. Ed. by Robert H. Russell & Margaret J. Patterson. 350p. 1986. text ed. 37.00 (0-231-06058-0) Col U Pr.

Behind the Lines: East London Labour Nineteen Fourteen to Nineteen Nineteen. Julia Bush. (Illus.). 254p. 1984. 40.00 (0-85036-304-7, Merlin Pr); pap. 18.95 (0-85036-306-3, Merlin Pr) Dufour.

***Behind the Lines: From North Africa to Germany During World War II.** Frederic R. Convery. 225p. 1995. pap. write for info. (0-614-04793-5) Red-Apple Pub.

Behind the Lines: Gender & the Two World Wars. Margaret R. Higonnet. LC 86-28102. 336p. (C). 1989. pap. 14.00 (0-300-04429-1) Yale U Pr.

Behind the Lines: Inside the "New" New York Times. Edwin Diamond. LC 93-14744. 1994. 24.00 (0-679-41877-6, Villard Bks) Random.

Behind the Locked Door. Paul McCusker. (Adventures in Odyssey Ser.: No. 4). (J). (gr. 3-7). 1993. pap. 4.99 (1-56179-133-4) Focus Family.

Behind the Lodge Door: Church, State & Freemasonry in America. Paul Fisher. LC 91-66415. 362p. 1991. reprint ed. pap. 15.00 (0-89555-450-X) TAN Bks Pubs.

Behind the Mask. Ian Buruma. 1985. pap. 12.00 (0-452-01054-3, Mer) NAL-Dutton.

Behind the Mask. Jabiya Dragonsun. Ed. by Zulma Gonzalez-Parker. (Orig.). 1989. pap. 5.00 (0-685-28956-7) Heartfelt Pr.

Behind the Mask. Kim Larabee. LC 88-83327. 200p. (Orig.). 1989. pap. 6.95 (1-55583-151-6) Alyson Pubns.

Behind the Mask. Dave Pallone & Alan Steinberg. (Illus.). 352p. 1991. pap. 5.99 (0-451-17029-6, Sig) NAL-Dutton.

Behind the Mask. Bari Rolfe. LC 77-76975. (Illus.). 66p. 1977. pap. 6.50 (0-932456-01-4) Personabks.

Behind the Mask: Kierkegaard's Pseudonymic Treatment of Lessing in the Concluding Unscientific Postscript. Michelle Stott. LC 92-54945. (C). 1993. 29.50 (0-8387-5246-2) Bucknell U Pr.

Behind the Mask: On Sexual Demons, Sacred Mothers, Transvestites, Gangsters & Other Japanese Cultural Heroes. Ian Buruma. 1985. pap. 8.95 (0-452-00738-0, Mer) NAL-Dutton.

***Behind the Mask: The Ian Young Goaltending Method.** I. Young & C. Gudgeon. (Illus.). 112p. (Orig.). (J). (gr. 4-8). 1993. pap. 14.95 (0-919591-93-0, Pub. by Polestar Bk Pubs CN) Orca Bk Pubs.

Behind the Mask of Adolescent Satanism. Joyce A. Mercer. LC 91-72991. (Illus.). 160p. 1991. pap. 9.95 (0-925190-22-5) Fairview Press.

***Behind the Mask of Chivalry: The Making of the Second Ku Klux Klan.** Nancy K. MacLean. (Illus.). 336p. 1995. pap. 13.95 (0-19-509836-6) OUP.

Behind the Mask of Chivalry: The Making of the Second Ku Klux Klan in a Georgia Town. Nancy K. MacLean. LC 93-27548. 336p. 1994. 30.00 (0-19-507234-0) OUP.

Behind the Mask of Innocence: Sex, Violence, Crime: Films of Social Conscience in the Silent. Kevin Brownlow. 1992. pap. 25.00 (0-520-07626-5) U CA Pr.

Behind the Mask of Innocence: Sex, Violence, Prejudice, Crime: Films of Social Conscience in the Silent Era. Kevin Brownlow. (Illus.). 579p. 1990. 50.00 (0-394-57747-7) Knopf.

Behind the Mask of Tutankhamen. large type ed. Barry Wynne. (Illus.). 368p. 1987. 16.95 (0-7089-1676-7) Ulverscroft.

Behind the Masks: Personality Disorders in Religious Behavior. Wayne E. Oates. LC 87-8221. 140p. (Orig.). 1987. pap. 10.99 (0-664-24028-3, Westminster) Westminster John Knox.

Behind the Masks - Tras las Mascaras. Wayne E. Oates. Tr. by Alicia Zorzoli. 144p. (SPA.). 1989. pap. 5.95 (0-311-46116-6) Casa Bautista.

Behind the Masks of God: An Essay Toward Comparative Theology. Robert C. Neville. LC 90-36353. 200p. (C). 1991. 49.50 (0-7914-0578-8); pap. 16.95 (0-7914-0579-6) State U NY Pr.

Behind the Masonic Curtain: The Soviet Attack on Masonry. George Moshinsky. (Illus.). 61p. (Orig.). 1986. pap. 6.95 (0-938103-00-8) ZZYZX Pub.

***Behind the Mass: A Sequel to "Let Holy Mass be Your Life"** Albert J. Shamon. Ed. by Joe Kindel. LC 95-67168. 80p. (Orig.). 1995. pap. 3.50 (1-877678-34-1) Riehle Found.

Behind the Mirror: A Search for a Natural History of Human Knowledge. Konrad Lorenz. Tr. by Ronald Taylor. LC 78-6031. (Helen & Kurt Wolff Bk.). (Illus.). 1978. pap. 7.95 (0-15-611776-2, Harvest Bks) HarBrace.

Behind the Mirror: A Search for a Natural History of Human Knowledge. Konrad Lorenz. 19.00 (0-8446-6212-7) Peter Smith.

Behind the Monocle, & Other Stories. Joseph S. Fletcher. LC 72-122698. (Short Story Index Reprint Ser.). 1977. 19.95 (0-8369-3531-4) Ayer.

Behind the Motion-Picture Screen. Austin C. Lescarboura. LC 75-174878. (Illus.). 1972. reprint ed. 30.95 (0-405-08742-X, Pub. by Blom Pubns UK) Ayer.

Behind the Mountains. Oliver LaFarge. 188p. 1994. reprint ed. pap. 12.00 (0-912880-07-4) Charles Pub.

Behind the Mule: Race & Class in African-American Politics. Michael C. Dawson. LC 93-44088. 1994. 35.00 (0-691-08770-9) Princeton U Pr.

Behind the Myth: Yasser Arafat & the Palestinian Revolution. Andrew Gowers & Tony Walker. LC 91-25963. (Illus.). 464p. 1992. 24.95 (0-940793-86-5, Olive Branch Pr) Interlink Pub.

***Behind the Myth of European Union: Prospects for Cohesion.** Ed. by Ash Amin & John Tomaney. LC 95-5185. 1995. write for info. (0-415-12552-9); pap. write for info. (0-415-13078-6) Routledge.

Behind the Numbers: U. S. Trade in the World Economy. Panel on Foreign Trade Statistics Staff & National Research Council Staff. Ed. by Anne Y. Kester. 312p. 1992. 29.95 (0-309-04590-8) Natl Acad Pr.

Behind the One-Way Mirror: Advances in the Practice of Strategic Therapy. Cloe Madanes. LC 83-49266. (Social & Behavioral Science Ser.). 213p. 1984. 27.95x (0-87589-599-9) Jossey-Bass.

***Behind the One-Way Mirror: Psychotherapy & Children.** Katharine D. Fishman. LC 95-5446. 1995. 27.50 (0-553-07886-0) Bantam.

Behind the Oscar: The Secret History of the Academy Awards. Anthony Holden. (Illus.). 672p. 1994. pap. 14.95 (0-452-27131-2, Plume) NAL-Dutton.

Behind the Painting & Other Stories. Siburapha, pseud. Tr. & Intro. by David Smyth. (Illus.). 150p. 1990. pap. 12.95 (0-19-588962-2) OUP.

Behind the Phantom's Mask: A Serial. Roger Ebert. (Illus.). 256p. 1993. pap. 9.95 (0-8362-8021-0) Andrews & McMeel.

Behind the Play-Doh Curtain: A Year in My Life as A Preschool Teacher. Patti G. Wollman. LC 94-8583. 1994. text ed. 22.00 (0-684-19665-4, Scribners) S&S Trade.

Behind the Playground Walls: Sexual Abuse in Preschools. Jill Waterman et al. LC 91-35420. 300p. 1993. lib. bdg. 30.00 (0-89862-523-8) Guilford Pr.

Behind the Poem: A Teacher's View of Children Writing. Robert Hull. 256p. 1988. pap. text ed. 16.95 (0-415-00701-1, A2058) Routledge.

Behind the Poison Cloud: Union Carbide's Bhopal Massacre. Larry Everest. LC 85-26863. 192p. 1986. 21.95 (0-916650-26-X); pap. 8.95 (0-916650-25-1) Banner Pr.

Behind the Postmodern Facade: Architectural Change in Late Twentieth-Century America. Magali S. Larson. LC 92-25694. 1993. 35.00 (0-520-08135-8) U CA Pr.

***Behind the Postmodern Facade: Architectural Change in Late Twentieth-Century America.** Magali S. Larson. (Illus.). 319p. 1995. pap. 15.00 (0-520-20161-2) U CA Pr.

Behind the Prison Fence. R. Winn Henderson. 95p. 1992. pap. 8.95 (0-9634173-2-0) Hugos Pr.

***Behind the Question: Listen for Success in Job Interviews.** Barbara B. Nixon. 1995. 18.95 (0-614-05150-9); 18.95 (0-614-05418-4) SPECTRA Inc.

Behind the Scene, Pt. 2. Douglas Reed. 1976. Part 2 of Far & Wide. pap. 6.95 (0-911038-41-8) Noontide.

Behind the Scenes. 1984. write for info. (0-915279-02-9) Miss Botan.

Behind the Scenes. Rudy Behlmer. LC 89-84945. (Illus.). 340p. 1989. pap. 14.95 (0-573-60600-5) S French Trade.

Behind the Scenes. Chelsea Brooks. LC 93-7628. (California Edition Ser.). (Illus.). 64p. (J). (gr. 5 up). 1993. pap. 7.95 (0-02-041650-4, Collier Bks Young) S&S Childrens.

Behind the Scenes. Michael Pollard. LC 94-6385. (Arts Library). (Illus.). 48p. (J). (gr. 2-6). 1994. lib. bdg. 14.40 (1-56294-394-4) Millbrook Pr.

Behind the Scenes. Douglas Reed. 1982. lib. bdg. 75.00 (0-87700-433-1) Revisionist Pr.

***Behind the Scenes: A Canadian Scene Book.** Ed. by Mary Ross & Ron Cameron. 124p. 1990. pap. text ed. 17.00 (0-88924-194-5, Pub. by Simon & Pierre Pub CN) Empire Pub Srvs.

***Behind the Scenes: A Canadian Scene Book.** Walter Williamson. 176p. 1987. pap. text ed. 17.00 (0-8027-6703-6, Pub. by Simon & Pierre Pub CN) Empire Pub Srvs.

Behind the Scenes: An Inside Look at the Selective College Admission Process. 10th ed. Edward B. Wall. 1994. 4.00 (0-945981-89-9) Octameron Assocs.

***Behind the Scenes: In South Dakota.** Joyce L. Vander Lugt. LC 94-61724. (Illus.). 248p. (Orig.). Date not set. pap. 12.95 (0-9643769-0-3) ThinkPrint Pub.

Behind the Scenes: Or, Thirty Years a Slave, & Four Years in the White House. Elizabeth H. Keckley. (Schomburg Library of Nineteenth-Century Black Women Writers). 414p. 1988. reprint ed. 27.00 (0-19-505259-5) OUP.

Behind the Scenes: Or, Thirty Years a Slave, & Four Years in the White House. Elizabeth H. Keckley. (Schomburg Library of Nineteenth-Century Black Women Writers). 414p. 1989. reprint ed. pap. 12.95 (0-19-506084-9) OUP.

***Behind the Scenes: The Politics of a Constitutional Convention.** fac. ed. Philip G. Schrag. LC 84-21120. (Illus.). 312p. 1985. reprint ed. pap. 89.00 (0-7837-7784-1, 2047539) Bks Demand.

Behind the Scenes: Thirty Years a Slave & Four Years in the White House. Elizabeth H. Keckley. (American Biography Ser.). 371p. 1991. reprint ed. lib. bdg. 79.00 (0-7812-8227-6) Rprt Serv.

Behind the Scenes: Yeats, Horniman, & the Struggle for the Abbey Theater. Adrian Frazier. 1990. 30.00 (0-520-06549-2) U CA Pr.

***Behind the Scenes Vol. 2: A Canadian Scene Book.** Ed. by Mary Ross & Ron Cameron. 124p. 1990. pap. text ed. 17.00 (0-88924-196-1, Pub. by Simon & Pierre Pub CN) Empire Pub Srvs.

Behind the Scenes at "Saved by the Bell" An Inside Look at TV's Hottest Teen Show. Beth Cruise. LC 91-27599. (Illus.). 64p. (Orig.). (J). (gr. 5 up). 1992. pap. 6.95 (0-02-042778-6, Collier Bks Young) S&S Childrens.

Behind the Scenes at Sega: The Making of a Video Game. Nic Lavroff. 1994. pap. 14.95 (1-55958-525-0) Prima Pub.

***Behind the Scenes at the Ballet: Rehearsing & Performing the Sleeping Beauty.** Photos & Text by Leslie E. Spatt. (Illus.). 48p. (J). (gr. 3-7). 1995. 13.99 (0-670-86162-6) Viking Child Bks.

***Behind the Scenes at the Casa: Sketches.** Betsy B. Bromfield. 80p. (Orig.). 1995. pap. 10.00 (1-56474-134-6) Fithian Pr.

Behind the Scenes at the Dynamic Community Library: Simplifying Technical Services in the Small Library. Beth W. Fox. LC 90-31351. 190p. (C). 1990. pap. text ed. 25.00 (0-8389-0531-5, 0531-5) ALA.

Behind the Scenes at the Local News. Robert S. Goald. LC 93-44166. 1994. 10.95 (0-240-80453-8, Focal) Buttrwrth-Heinemann.

Behind the Scenes at the Local News. Robert S. Goald. 224p. 1994. vhs 14.95 (0-240-80153-9, Focal); pap., vhs 149.00 (0-240-80155-5, Focal) Buttrwrth-Heinemann.

Behind the Scenes in American Government: Personalities & Politics. Ed. by Peter Woll. LC 93-2596. (C). 1993. 17.75 (0-673-52325-X) HarpCollege.

Behind the Scenes in Washington. James D. McCabe, Jr. LC 73-19158. (Politics & People Ser.). (Illus.). 548p. 1974. reprint ed. 41.95 (0-405-05880-2) Ayer.

Behind the Scenes of Home Alone 2: Lost in New York. Jordan Horowitz. (J). 1992. 3.95 (0-590-45720-9) Scholastic Inc.

Behind the Scenes of International Finance. Paul Einzig. Ed. by Mira Wilkins. LC 78-3912. (International Finance Ser.). 1979. reprint ed. lib. bdg. 19.95 (0-405-11216-5) Ayer.

Behind the Scenes of the Comedie Francaise. Arsene Houssaye. LC 78-81210. 1972. 30.95 (0-405-08640-7, Pub. by Blom Pubns UK) Ayer.

Behind the Scenes of the New Testament. Paul Barnett. LC 90-45492. 247p. (Orig.). 1991. pap. 11.99 (0-8308-1329-2, 1329) InterVarsity.

Behind the Scenes of the Third Reich Diplomacy. Herman Rozanov. 196p. 1984. pap. 30.00 (0-317-53846-2, Pub. by Collets UK) Pro-Am Music.

Behind the Scenes or Thirty Years a Slave, & Four Years in the White House. Elizabeth H. Keckley. LC 68-29006. (American Negro: His History & Literature, Ser. No. 1). 1968. reprint ed. 27.95 (0-405-01824-X) Ayer.

Behind the Scenes with Edwin Booth. Katherine Goodale. LC 76-87121. (Illus.). 328p. 1972. 26.95 (0-405-08564-8, Pub. by Blom Pubns UK) Ayer.

Behind the Scenes with the Mediums. 5th rev. ed. David P. Abbott. 340p. 1971. reprint ed. spiral bd. 11.00 (0-7873-0014-4) Mokelumne.

Behind the Scenes with the Metaphysicians. Arthur Corey. 1968. 10.95 (0-87516-014-X) DeVorss.

Behind the Screen: Five Video Artists. Contrib by Peter F. Spooner. (Illus.). 32p. 1990. 8.00 (0-945558-10-4) ISU Univ Galls.

Behind the Screen: The American Museum of the Moving Image Guide to Who Does What in Motion Pictures & Television. David Draigh. (Illus.). 144p. 1988. spiral bd. 7.95 (0-89659-955-8) Abbeville Pr.

An Asterisk (*) at the beginning of an entry indicates that the title is appearing in BIP for the first time.

Behind the Screen see Scoop

Behind the Screen Guide to Who Does What in Motion Pictures & Television. David Draigh. Ed. by Georgette M. Hasiotis. (Illus.). (Orig.). 1988. write for info. (*0-318-62753-1*) Amer Mus Moving Image.

Behind the Screens: Nursing Somology & the Problem of the Body. Jocalyn Lawler. 264p. 1991. pap. text ed. 24.00 (*0-443-04444-9*) Churchill.

Behind the Screens: Nursing, Somology, & the Problem of the Body. Jocalyn Lawler. LC 93-9933. 1993. write for info. (*0-8053-4070-X*) Benjamin-Cummings.

Behind the Screens: Nursing, Somology, & the Problem of the Body. Jocalyn Lawler. LC 93-9933. (C). 1993. pap. text ed. 22.75 (*0-8053-4090-4*) Benjamin-Cummings.

Behind the Screens: The Structure of British Television in the Nineties. Ed. by Stuart Hood. 224p. (C). 1994. pap. 19.95 (*0-85315-774-X*, Pub. by Lawrence & Wishart UK) Humanities.

Behind the Secret Window: A Memoir of a Hidden Childhood. Nelly Toll. (Illus.). 160p. (J). (gr. 5 up). 1993. 17.00 (*0-8037-1362-2*) Dial Bks Young.

Behind the Sheltering Bomb. Noel F. Parrish. Ed. by Richard H. Kohn. LC 78-22415. (American Military Experience Ser.). 1980. lib. bdg. 24.95 (*0-405-11889-9*) Ayer.

Behind the Silicon Curtain: The Seductions of Work in a Lonely Era. Dennis Hayes. LC 88-35624. 200p. 1989. 30.00 (*0-89608-351-9*); pap. 10.00 (*0-89608-350-0*) South End Pr.

Behind the Spanish Lens: Spanish Cinema under Fascism & Democracy. Peter Besas. LC 85-22874. (Illus.). 291p. (Orig.). 1985. 26.00 (*0-912869-06-2*) Arden Pr.

Behind the State Capitol; or, Cincinnati Pike. John Wieners. 125p. 1975. 100.00 (*0-686-10663-6*) Good Gay.

Behind the Tears - I Can See the Light. Jeanette Vetro. LC 92-93328. 153p. (Orig.). 1992. pap. text ed. 9.95 (*0-9631411-0-4*) J Vetro.

Behind the Telephone Debates. Carol Weinhaus & Anthony Oettinger. LC 87-19459. (Communication & Information Science Ser.). 272p. 1988. text ed. 59.50 (*0-89391-452-5*) Ablex Pub.

Behind the Therapists' Notes: Fears, Feelings & Hopes. Theodore C. Kent. LC 92-72426. 352p. 1993. pap. 12.95 (*0-87212-256-5*) Libra.

Behind the Three Stooges: The White Brothers: Conversations with David N. Bruskin. rev. ed. Ed. by David N. Bruskin. LC 93-72187. (Oral History Ser.). 368p. 1993. pap. 16.95 (*1-882766-00-8*) Dirs Guild Am.

Behind the Throne: Servants of Power to Imperial Presidents, 1898-1968. Ed. by Thomas McCormick & Walter LaFeber. LC 93-18754. 288p. (C). 1993. text ed. 45.50 (*0-299-13740-6*) U of Wis Pr.

Behind the Tiananmen Massacre: Social, Political & Economic Ferment in China. Chu-Yuan Cheng. 256p. 1990. text ed. 47.50 (*0-8133-1047-4*) Westview.

***Behind the Times: Inside the New "New York Times"** Edwin Diamond. vi, 441p. 1995. pap. 16.95 (*0-226-14472-0*) U Ch Pr.

Behind the Trail of Broken Treaties: An Indian Declaration of Independence. Vine Deloria, Jr. 310p. 1985. reprint ed. pap. 12.95 (*0-292-70754-1*) U of Tex Pr.

Behind the Tree of Peace: A Sociological Analysis of Iroquois Warfare. George S. Snyderman. LC 76-43838. reprint ed. 34.50 (*0-404-15692-4*) AMS Pr.

Behind the Tube: A History of Broadcasting Technology & Business. Andrew F. Inglis. (Illus.). 548p. 1990. 44.95 (*0-240-80043-5*, Focal) Buttrwrth-Heinemann.

Behind the U. S. Invasion of Somalia: Statements of the Workers League. (Illus.). 88p. (Orig.). (C). 1993. pap. 4.00 (*0-929087-61-5*) Labor Pubns Inc.

Behind the Uprising: Israelis, Jordanians, & Palestinians. Yossi Melman & Dan Raviv. LC 89-7486. (Contributions in Political Science Ser.: No. 238). 264p. 1989. text ed. 55.00 (*0-313-26787-1*, MBU/, Greenwood Pr) Greenwood.

Behind the Urals: An American Worker in Russia's City of Steel. enl. ed. John Scott. LC 88-46214. (Illus.). 334p. 1989. 29.95 (*0-253-35125-1*); pap. 10.95 (*0-253-20536-0*, MB-536) Ind U Pr.

Behind the Urals: An American Worker in Russia's City of Steel. John Scott. LC 70-115583. (Russia Observed Ser.). (Illus.). 1971. reprint ed. 18.95 (*0-405-03137-8*) Ayer.

Behind the Veil: Ceremonies, Customs & Colour. 2nd ed. Shaista Suhrawardy Ikramullah. (Illus.). 220p. 1994. 27.00 (*0-19-577419-1*) OUP.

Behind the Veil in Arabia: Women in Oman. Unni Wikan. LC 81-18622. (Illus.). xiv, 314p. 1991. reprint ed. pap. 14.95 (*0-226-89683-8*) U Ch Pr.

Behind the Veil of Economics: Essays in the Worldly Philosophy. Robert L. Heilbroner. LC 87-20392. 1989. pap. 7.95 (*0-393-30577-5*) Norton.

Behind the Veils of Death & Sleep. Gladys Mayer. 1973. lib. bdg. 250.00 (*0-87968-541-7*) Krishna Pr.

Behind the Wall. Richard Huff. 1994. pap. 12.95 (*1-56625-011-0*) Bonus Books.

Behind the Wall: An American in East Germany, 1988-89. Paul Gleye. LC 90-28575. 256p. (C). 1991. 24.95 (*0-8093-1743-5*) S Ill U Pr.

Behind the Wall: The Inner Life of Communist Germany. Hans J. Maaz. Date not set. 27.50 (*0-393-03364-3*) Norton.

Behind the Wall of China. Joelle Busuttil. (Young Discovery Library). (Illus.). 40p. (J). (gr. k-5). 1993. lib. bdg. 9.95 (*1-56674-057-6*, HTS Bks) Forest Hse.

Behind the Wall of China. Joelle Busuttil. Tr. by Vicki Bogard. LC 92-969. (Illus.). (J). (gr. k-5). 1992. 5.95 (*0-944589-42-1*) Young Discovery Lib.

Behind the Wall of Respect: Experiments in Heroin Addiction Control in Chicago Neighborhoods. Patrick H Hughes. LC 76-25640. 1977. 10.95 (*0-226-35930-1*) U Ch Pr.

Behind the Wall Street Curtain. Edward J. Dies. LC 73-86745. (Essay Index Reprint Ser.). 1977. 19.95 (*0-8369-1178-4*) Ayer.

Behind the Walls of Terra. Philip Jose Farmer. 1993. reprint ed. lib. bdg. 18.95 (*0-89968-400-9*, Lghtyr Pr) Buccaneer Bks.

Behind the Watchtower Curtain. David A. Reed. 160p. (Orig.). 1989. pap. write for info. (*0-925703-08-7*) Crown MA.

Behind the Wheel. Raymond A. Montgomery. (J). 1992. pap. 3.25 (*0-553-29401-6*) Bantam.

***Behind the Wheel at Chrysler: The Iacocca Legacy.** Doron P. Levin. 1995. 25.00 (*0-15-111703-9*) HarBrace.

Behind the White Screen. Sotiris Spatharis. Tr. by Leslie Finer & Mario Rinvolucri. LC 73-88906. 1976. 10.95 (*0-87376-022-0*) Red Dust.

Behind These Mountains, 3 vols., Set. Mona L. Vanek. (Illus.). 310p. (J). 1986. pap. 16.95 (*0-940151-00-6*) Statesman Exam.

Behind These Mountains, Vol. III: The Fabulous Valley in the Foothills of the Rockies. Mona L. Vanek. (Illus.). 288p. (Orig.). (C). 1991. pap. 19.95 (*0-940151-22-7*) Statesman Exam.

Behind These Mountains, Vol. 2: God's Country in the United States of America. Mona L. Vanek. (Illus.). 220p. (Orig.). (C). 1991. pap. 19.95 (*0-940151-21-9*) Statesman Exam.

Behind This Mortal Bone: Poems. Janet P. Piper. 160p. 1990. 16.95 (*0-944266-07-X*) Maecenas Pr.

Behind Those Garden Walls in Historic Savannah. Louisa F. Wood. LC 83-103942. (Illus.). 80p. 1982. pap. text ed. 7.75 (*0-9610106-1-4*) Historic Sav.

Behind World Revolution: The Strange Career of Nesta H. Webster, Vol. 1. Richard M. Gilman. LC 82-90685. (Illus.). 128p. 1982. pap. 7.95 (*0-910087-00-8*) Insights Bks.

Behinderte Kind. H. J. Roelli. Ed. by A. Anderhalden. (Paediatrische Fortbildungskurse fuer die Praxis Ser.: Vol. 56). (Illus.). vi, 110p. 1982. pap. 42.50 (*3-8055-3493-0*) S Karger.

Behnisch & Partners. (Illus.). 288p. 1992. pap. 49.50 (*3-922608-53-1*, Pub. by Edition Cantz GW) Dist Art Pubs.

Behold! Spot-the-Difference Bible Stories. Wendy Madgwick. LC 93-5506. (Illus.). 48p. (J). (gr. k-3). 1994. 12.00 (*0-679-85333-2*) Random Bks Yng Read.

Behold a Cry. Alden Bland. LC 73-18554. reprint ed. 37.50 (*0-404-11369-9*) AMS Pr.

Behold, a Greater Than Soloman. Alvin E. Wagner. LC 89-27471. 144p. 1989. pap. 14.95 (*0-685-29066-2*) Evan Lutheran.

Behold, a Mystery! Joan Smith. 256p. 1994. 20.95 (*0-312-10424-3*, Pub. by Thomas Dunne Bks) St Martin.

***Behold, a Mystery!** Joan Smith. 1995. mass mkt. 4.99 (*0-449-22176-8*) Fawcett.

Behold a Pale Horse. William Cooper. 499p. (Orig.). 1991. pap. 25.00 (*0-929385-22-5*) Light Tech Comns Servs.

Behold, He Cometh. Howard B. Rand. 1955. 5.00 (*0-685-08798-0*) Destiny.

Behold, Here's Poison. large type ed. Georgette Heyer. LC 91-44212. 411p. 1992. lib. bdg. 18.95 (*1-56054-278-0*) Thorndike Pr.

Behold, Here's Poison. Georgette Heyer. reprint ed. lib. bdg. 22.95 (*0-89190-639-8*, Rivercity Pr) Amereon Ltd.

Behold I Come Quickly. Marie B. Hall. 1985. pap. 10.00 (*0-938760-13-0*) Veritat Found.

***Behold, I Come Quickly: The Last Days & Beyond.** Hoyt W. Brewster, Jr. LC 94-22203. xxi, 246p. 1994. 14.95 (*0-87579-865-9*) Deseret Bk.

Behold, I Make All Things New. Rene Querido & Hilmar Moore. 1990. 10.95 (*0-945803-07-9*) R Steiner Col Pubns.

Behold I Show You a Mystery. C. W. Mabie. LC 80-82229. 150p. (Orig.). 1980. pap. 4.95 (*0-9601416-5-0*) J C Print.

***Behold, Jesus Is Coming! Revelation.** Kay Arthur & David Arthur. (International Inductive Study Ser.). (Orig.). 1995. pap. 4.99 (*1-56507-318-5*) Harvest Hse.

Behold Man. Lennart Nilsson. LC 73-14087. (Illus.). 1978. 29.95 (*0-316-60751-7*) Little.

Behold Our Land. Russell Lord. LC 74-2395. (FDR & the Era of the New Deal Ser.). 309p. 1974. reprint ed. lib. bdg. 39.50 (*0-306-70593-1*) Da Capo.

Behold That Star: A Christmas Anthology: A Collection of Fifteen Christmas Stories. 3rd ed. Ed. by Society of Brothers Staff. LC 67-25968. (Illus.). 368p. (J). (gr. 4 up). 1966. 17.00 (*0-87486-003-2*) Plough.

Behold the Beauty of the Lord: Praying with Icons. Henri J. Nouwen. LC 86-72698. (Illus.). 80p. (Orig.). 1987. spiral bd. 8.95 (*0-87793-356-1*) Ave Maria.

***Behold the Child.** Avery. 25.00 (*0-370-31952-4*) Ballantine.

***Behold the Child: American Children & Their Books, 1621-1922.** Gillian Avery. LC 94-29832. (Illus.). 239p. 1994. text ed. 29.95x (*0-8018-5066-5*) Johns Hopkins.

***Behold the Golfer.** Great Quotations Staff. 64p. 1995. 5.95 (*1-56245-215-0*) Great Quotations.

Behold the Lamb of God. F. Von Kietzell. 6.95 (*0-88172-136-0*) Believers Bkshelf.

Behold the Lamb of God. J. Reuben Clark, Jr. LC 91-18679. (Classics in Mormon Literature Ser.). 382p. 1991. reprint ed. 12.95 (*0-87579-536-6*) Deseret Bk.

***Behold! the Lamb of God: An Easter Passover Seder Service for Christians.** John Dan. (Illus.). 64p. (Orig.). 1995. pap. 3.95 (*1-884898-05-X*) Eden Pubng NV.

Behold, the Land. Helen Fine. (Illus.). 280p. (J). (gr. 4-6). 1978. pap. 8.95 (*0-8074-0129-3*, 127270) UAHC.

Behold the Man. Robert McKewin. pap. 9.95 (*0-910924-95-3*) Macalester.

Behold the Man. Michael Moorcock. 150p. 1987. pap. 2.95 (*0-88184-369-5*) Carroll & Graf.

Behold the Man: Exalting the Christ of Easter. Joseph Linn. 1989. 5.25 (*0-8341-9204-7*, ME-40); audio 10.98 (*0-685-68617-5*, BCTA-9112C) Lillenas.

Behold the Man: Re-Reading Gospels, Re-Humanizing Jesus. Scott McCormick, Jr. 180p. (C). 1994. 19.95 (*0-8264-0680-7*) Continuum.

Behold the Man: Seven Meditations on the Passion, Death & Resurrection of Jesus. Judy Marley. (Illus.). 48p. (Orig.). 1990. pap. 3.50 (*0-9623410-2-9*) Resurrection.

Behold the Mighty Wurlitzer: The History of the Theatre Pipe Organ. John W. Landon. LC 83-5557. (Contributions to the Study of Popular Culture Ser.: No. 6). xv, 231p. 1983. text ed. 55.00 (*0-313-23827-8*, LPO/, Greenwood Pr) Greenwood.

Behold the Nazarite Woman. Joy Haney. LC 90-30639. (Illus.). 96p. (Orig.). (YA). 1990. pap. 5.99 (*0-932581-63-3*) Word Aflame.

Behold the People: R. C. Hickman's Photographs of Black Dallas, 1949-1961. R. C. Hickman. LC 94-2947. (Barker Texas History Center Ser.: No. 3). (Illus.). 1994. 29.95 (*0-87611-136-3*) Tex St Hist Assn.

Behold the Pierced One. Joseph C. Ratzinger. LC 86-80103. 128p. 1986. pap. 9.95 (*0-89870-087-6*) Ignatius Pr.

Behold! the Polish-Americans. Joseph A. Wytrwal. LC 77-88476. 1977. 15.00 (*0-686-65640-7*) Endurance.

Behold the Spirit. Alan W. Watts. 288p. 1972. pap. 9.00 (*0-394-71761-9*, Vin) Random.

Behold! The Third Day Cometh. Alberta Hawse. 1957. 4.25 (*0-685-68679-5*, ME-3) Lillenas.

Behold, Thy Handmaid. Chris McQuay. 208p. (Orig.). (C). 1992. pap. 7.95 (*0-9619761-1-X*) Chris Life Ctr.

***Behold Thy Mother.** (Illus.). 80p. 1995. 9.95 (*1-57036-233-5*) Turner Pub GA.

Behold, We Knew It Not. Jonathan Berman. 350p. (Orig.). 1989. pap. write for info. (*0-318-64792-3*) JMPS Pubs.

Behold Your God. Agnes Sanford. pap. 9.95 (*0-910924-63-5*) Macalester.

***Beholden.** Pat Warren. (Orig.). 1996. mass mkt. write for info. (*0-446-60084-9*) Warner Bks.

Beholder's Eye. John Wheatcroft. LC 87-628. 280p. 1987. 17.95 (*0-8453-4724-1*, Cornwall Bks) Assoc Univ Prs.

***Beholding & Becoming.** Jerry Coulter. LC 94-69043. 140p. (Orig.). 1995. pap. 7.95 (*0-940232-51-0*) Seedsowers.

Beholding God in Many Faces. Holly B. Elliott. Ed. by Carl Koch. 87p. (Orig.). 1993. pap. 5.95 (*0-88489-310-3*) St Marys.

Beholdings. Poems. Betty Adcock. LC 87-33247. 55p. 1988. text ed. 13.95 (*0-8071-1465-0*); pap. 6.95 (*0-8071-1466-9*) La State U Pr.

Bei Aller Bruderlichen Liebe. . . The Letters of Sophie Tieck to Her Brother Friedrich. Ed. by James Trainer. (Quellen und Forschungen zur Sprach und Kulturgeschichte der Germanischen Voelker Ser.: NF 97 (221)). viii, 314p. (C). 1991. lib. bdg. 144.65 (*3-11-012354-1*) De Gruyter.

Bei Mir Bist Du Schon: Story of Sholom Secunda. Victoria Secunda. 1986. 12.00 (*0-913660-15-9*) Magic Cir Pr CT.

Beiderbecke Connection. 2nd large type ed. Alan Plater. 273p. 1993. 22.95 (*1-85695-360-2*, Pub. by ISIS UK) Transaction Pubs.

Beijing. (Insight Guides Ser.). 1993. pap. 21.95 (*0-395-66297-4*) HM.

Beijing. Victor Sit. (World Cities Ser.). 224p. 1994. text ed. 49.95 (*0-470-22015-5*) Halsted Pr.

***Beijing.** Victor Sit. (World Cities Ser.). Date not set. text ed. 54.95 (*0-471-94983-3*) Wiley.

Beijing. 2nd ed. (China Guides Ser.). (Illus.). 1992. 14.95 (*0-8442-9808-5*, Passport Bks) NTC Pub Grp.

Beijing: City Guide. Robert Storey. (Illus.). 280p. (Orig.). 1994. pap. 9.95 (*0-86442-206-7*) Lonely Planet.

Beijing: The New Forbidden City. Skya Gardner-Abbate. LC 90-72130. (Orig.). 1991. pap. 14.95 (*0-9628620-0-2*) SW Acpncture.

Beijing, Hanoi & the Overseas Chinese. Pao-min Chang. LC 82-2641. (China Research Monographs: No. 24). 1982. pap. 3.50 (*0-912966-50-5*) IEAS.

Beijing Lectures in Harmonic Analysis. Ed. by E. M. Stein. LC 85-43314. (Annals of Mathematics Studies: No. 112). (Illus.). 650p. 1986. pap. text ed. 35.00 (*0-691-08419-X*) Princeton U Pr.

Beijing (Peking) Restaurant Guide. John E. Felber. 24p. 1981. pap. 3.00 (*0-910794-11-1*) Intl Intertrade.

Beijing Photos. Bethsabee Sussman & Roland Sussman. (Illus.). 1987. 39.95 (*0-915361-97-3*) Modan-Adama Bks.

Beijing Real Estate Report, 1988. 50.00 (*0-318-37571-0*) Natl Coun US-China.

Beijing Spring 1989: An Outsider's Inside Account. David J. Firestein. LC 90-91861. (Illus.). 240p. (Orig.). (C). 1990. pap. 9.95 (*0-9627219-6-4*) Banner TX.

Beijing Spring, 1989: Confrontation & Conflict: the Basic Documents. Ed. by Michel Oksenberg et al. LC 90-8077. 448p. (C). 1990. 57.95 (*0-87332-683-0*); pap. text ed. 20.95 (*0-87332-684-9*) M E Sharpe.

Beijing Street Voices: The Poetry & Politics of China's Democracy Movement. David S. Goodman. (Illus.). 208p. 1984. pap. 9.95 (*0-7145-2703-3*) M Boyars Pubs.

Beijing Summit to Normalize Sino-Soviet Relations. Coit D. Blacker & Brian A. Davenport. (Pew Case Studies in International Affairs). 50p. (C). 1994. pap. text ed. 2.50 (*1-56927-357-X*) Geo U Inst Dplmcy.

Beijinger in New York. Glen Cao. 256p. 1993. 14.95 (*0-8351-2526-2*) China Bks.

Beijingwalks: Six Intimate Walking Tours. Don Cohn. (Illus.). 280p. 1992. pap. 15.95 (*0-8050-2105-1*, Owl) H Holt & Co.

Beilinson's Conjectures on Special Values of L-Functions. Ed. by M. Rapoport et al. (Perspectives in Mathematics Ser.: Vol. 4). 373p. 1988. text ed. 79.00 (*0-12-581120-9*) Acad Pr.

Beilis Transcripts: The Anti-Semitic Trial That Shook the World. Ezekiel Leikin. LC 92-39643. 280p. 1993. 25.00 (*0-87668-179-8*) Aronson.

Beilstein: Centennial Index - Generalregister. 4th ed. Ed. by Beilstein-Institut fur Literature der Organischen Chemie Staff & R. Luckenbach. (Handbook of Organic Chemistry Ser.: Vol. 28, Pt. 2). iv, 1419p. 1991. 684.00 (*0-387-54048-2*) Spr-Verlag.

Beilstein: Centennial Index - Generalregister. 4th ed. Ed. by R. Luckenbach. (Handbook of Organic Chemistry Ser.: Vol. 28, Pts. 3-6). 1991. 642.00 (*0-685-74382-9*) Spr-Verlag.

Beilstein: Centennial Index - Generalregister, Vol. 28, Pt. 3: Benzol-Bz. 4th ed. Ed. by R. Luckenbach. (Handbook of Organic Chemistry Ser.: Vol. 28, Pts. 3-6). iv, 1483p. 1991. 684.00 (*0-387-54082-2*) Spr-Verlag.

Beilstein: Centennial Index - Generalregister, Vol. 28, Pt. 4: D-F. Ed. by R. Luckenbach. (Handbook of Organic Chemistry Ser.: Vol. 28, Pts. 3-6). 1600p. 1991. 684.00 (*0-387-54085-7*) Spr-Verlag.

Beilstein: Centennial Index - Generalregister, Vol. 28, Pt. 6: G-I. 4th ed. Ed. by R. Luckenbach. (Handbook of Organic Chemistry Ser.: Vol. 28, Pts. 3-6). 1600p. 1991. 684.00 (*0-387-54086-5*) Spr-Verlag.

Beilstein: Centennial Index - Generalregister: General Formula Index - General-Formelregister, Vol. 29, Pt. 4. 4th ed. Comp. by Beilstein-Institut fur Literatur der Organischen Chemie Staff. (Handbook of Organic Chemistry Ser.). 1280p. 1992. 721.00 (*0-387-55572-2*) Spr-Verlag.

Beilstein: Centennial Index - Generalregister: General Formula Index - General-Formelregister, Vol. 29, Pt. 5. 4th ed. Comp. by Beilstein-Institut fur Literatur der Organischen Chemie Staff. (Handbook of Organic Chemistry Ser.). 1280p. 1992. 721.00 (*0-387-55573-0*) Spr-Verlag.

Beilstein: Compound-Name Index for Vols. 20-22: E-Pq. 4th ed. Ed. by R. Luckenbach. (Handbook of Organic Chemistry: Supplementary Ser.). iv, 976p. 1992. 1,149.00 (*0-387-54625-1*) Spr-Verlag.

Beilstein: Compound-Name Index for Vols. 20-22: Pr-Z. 4th ed. Ed. by R. Luckenbach. (Handbook of Organic Chemistry: Supplementary Ser.). 1000p. 1992. 1,163.00 (*0-387-54626-X*) Spr-Verlag.

Beilstein: Heterocyclic Compounds, Vols. 23 - 25. 861p. 1993. 2,218.00 (*0-387-56115-3*) Spr-Verlag.

Beilstein Handbook of Organic Chemistry: Centennial Index - Generalregister, 3 pts., Vol. 28, Pt. 8: P - Propanol. 4th ed. Comp. by Beilstein-Institut fur Literature der Organischen Chemie Staff. iv, 1401p. 1991. 684.00 (*0-387-54088-1*) Spr-Verlag.

Beilstein Handbook of Organic Chemistry: Centennial Index - Generalregister, 3 pts., Vol. 28, Pt. 9: Propanon. 4th ed. Comp. by Beilstein-Institut fur Literature der Organischen Chemie Staff. 1600p. 1991. 684.00 (*0-387-54089-X*) Spr-Verlag.

Beilstein Handbook of Organic Chemistry: Centennial Index - Generalregister, 3 pts., Vol. 28, Pt. 10: S-Z. 4th ed. Comp. by Beilstein-Institut fur Literature der Organischen Chemie Staff. 1600p. 1991. Vol. 28, Pt. 10: S - Z, 1600p. 684.00 (*0-387-54090-3*) Spr-Verlag.

Beilstein Handbook of Organic Chemistry: Formula Index for Vols. 20-22. 4th ed. Ed. by R. Luckenbach. (Supplementary Series 5). iv, 859p. 1993. 945.00 (*0-387-56103-X*) Spr-Verlag.

Beilstein Handbook of Organic Chemistry: Heterocyclic Compounds. Beilstein-Institut fur Literatur der Organischen Chemie. Ed. by R. Luckenbach. (Fifth Supplementary Ser.: Vol. 25, Pt. 17). (Illus.). 74p. 1993. 1,950.00 (*0-387-56116-1*) Spr-Verlag.

Beilstein Handbook of Organic Chemistry: Heterocyclic Compounds. Beilstein-Institut fur Literatur der Organischen Chemie. Ed. by R. Luckenbach. (Fifth Supplementary Ser.: Vol. 25, Pt. 18). 820p. 1993. 1,791.00 (*0-387-56117-X*) Spr-Verlag.

Beilstein Handbook of Organic Chemistry: Heterocyclic Compounds. 4th ed. Ed. by R. Luckenbach. (Fifth Supplementary Ser.: Vol. 26, Pt. I). lxxxvi, 772p. 1993. 2,400.00 (*0-387-56118-8*) Spr-Verlag.

Beilstein Handbook of Organic Chemistry: Heterocyclic Compounds, Pt. 15. 4th ed. Comp. by Beilstein-Institut fur Literatur der Organischen Chemie. (Supplementary Series 5: Vol. 25). xxii, 807p. 1993. 2,138.00 (*0-387-56114-5*) Spr-Verlag.

Beilstein, Handbook of Organic Chemistry, Vol. 28, Pt. 1: Centennial Index - Generalregister, General Compound-Name Index - General-Sachregister. 4th ed. Ed. by R. Luckenbach. 1600p. 1991. 684.00 (*0-387-54047-4*) Spr-Verlag.

Beilstein-Leitfaden: Eine Anleitung Zur Benutzung Von Beilsteins Handbuch der Organischen Chemie. Beilstein Institute for Literature of Organic Chemistry Staff. 56p. 1975. pap. 465.00 (*0-387-07431-7*) Spr-Verlag.

Beilstein Online Database: Implementation, Content, & Retrieval. Ed. by Stephen R. Heller. LC 90-41494. (Symposium Ser.: No. 436). (Illus.). 155p. 1990. 39.95 (*0-8412-1862-5*) Am Chemical.

Beilstein's Index. F. Giese. 225p. 1986. pap. 39.00 (*0-387-16142-2*) Spr-Verlag.

Bein' Green. Joe Raposo. (Sing-a-Song Storybooks Ser.). (Illus.). 24p. (J). 1993. 9.95 (*0-7935-1680-3*, 00183008) H Leonard.

Bein' with You This Way. W. Nikola-Lisa. LC 93-5164. (Illus.). 32p. (J). (gr. k-3). 1994. 14.95 (*1-880000-05-9*) Lee & Low Bks.

An Asterisk (*) at the beginning of an entry indicates that the title is appearing in BIP for the first time. 669

***Bein' with You This Way.** W. Nikola-Lisa. LC 93-5164. (Illus.). 32p. (J). (ps up). 1995. pap. 5.95 (*1-880000-26-1*) Lee & Low Bks.

Beinecke Lesser Antilles Collection at Hamilton College: A Catalogue of Books, Manuscripts, Prints, Maps, & Drawings, 1521-1860. Samuel J. Hough & Penelope R. O. Hough. LC 94-4285. (Illus.). 424p. 1994. lib. bdg. 150.00 (*0-8130-1292-9*) U Press Fla.

Beinecke Rare Book & Manuscript Library: A Guide to Its Collections. rev. ed. Beinecke Rare Book-Manuscript Library Staff. Ed. by Christa Sammons. LC 94-14511. (Illus.). 1994. pap. write for info. (*0-8457-3127-0*) Yale U Lib.

***Being.** John W. Malenda. 35p. (Orig.). 1995. pap. 3.50 (*1-886482-01-2*) Guiding Lght.

Being. Michael Redfinn. 368p. (Orig.). 1988. pap. 3.95 (*0-8439-2643-0*) Dorchester Pub Co.

Being: Guide to a New Way. Sunlight. LC 88-81372. (Illus.). 79p. (Orig.). 1988. pap. 5.95 (*0-929151-03-8*) Earth Bks.

***Being: The Metamorphosis of Consciousness.** Cary R. Mangum & Ralph W. Garvis. (Illus.). 162p. (Orig.). 1992. pap. 12.95 (*1-879337-00-2*) Garrett Pub.

Being - Being Happy - Being Gay: Pathways to a Rewarding Life for Lesbians & Gay Men. Bert Herrman. LC 89-81744. 128p. (Orig.). 1990. pap. 8.00 (*0-9624751-0-6*) Alamo Sq Pr.

Being a Black Republican It's Not Easy. Edward R. Tiller. (Illus.). 128p. (Orig.). 1994. pap. text ed. 17.95 (*0-9616671-8-4*) Tiller Pubng.

Being a Blessing: Fifty-Four Ways You Can Help People Living with AIDS. Harris R. Goldstein. 160p. (Orig.). 1994. pap. 13.95 (*1-881283-08-9*) Alef Design.

Being a Boss. Cheryl Reimold. (Clear & Simple Ser.). (Orig.). 1995. pap. 8.95 (*0-440-50595-X*, Dell Trade Pbks) Dell.

Being a Boy. Paxton Davis. LC 88-22224. 253p. 1988. 16. 95 (*0-89587-065-7*) Blair.

***Being a Boy Again: Autobiography & the American Boy Book.** Marcia Jacobson. LC 94-14510. 200p. 1995. 29. 95 (*0-8173-0764-8*) U of Ala Pr.

Being a Buddhist. Peggy Morgan. (Looking into World Religions Ser.). (Illus.). 72p. (YA). (gr. 7-10). 1989. 19. 95 (*0-7134-6015-6*, Pub. by Batsford UK) Trafalgar.

Being a Character: Psychoanalysis & Self Experience. Christopher Bollas. LC 92-6213. 304p. 1992. 30.00 (*0-8090-2662-7*) Brunner-Mazel.

Being a Character: Psychoanalysis & Self Experience. Christopher Bollas. 1992. 30.00 (*0-8090-2862-X*) Hill & Wang.

Being a Character: Psychoanalysis & Self-Experience. Christopher Bollas. 1994. pap. 11.00 (*0-8090-1569-2*) Hill & Wang.

Being a Christian. David Walters. (Illus.). 40p. (Orig.). (J). (gr. 2-10). Date not set. student ed write for info. (*0-9629559-2-2*) Good News Min.

Being a Christian. Washington T. Gladden. LC 72-4168. (Select Bibliographies Reprint Ser.). 1977. reprint ed. 17. 95 (*0-8369-6880-8*) Ayer.

Being a Christian at School. William Coleman. 48p. (Orig.). 1994. pap. 2.99 (*1-56476-291-2*, Victor Books) SP Pubns.

Being a Christian at School: Leaders Guide. William Coleman. 96p. (Orig.). 1994. pap. 4.99 (*1-56476-282-3*, Victor Books) SP Pubns.

Being a Christian Friend. Kristen J. Ingram. 112p. 1985. pap. 9.00 (*0-8170-1084-X*) Judson.

Being a Counselor: Directions & Challenges. Jeannette A. Brown & Robert H. Pate, Jr. LC 82-20764. (Psychology Ser.). 450p. (C). 1983. text ed. 37.95 (*0-534-01261-2*) Brooks-Cole.

Being a Dog Is a Full-Time Job: A Peanuts Collection. Charles Schulz. 1994. pap. 8.95 (*0-8362-1746-2*) Andrews & McMeel.

Being a Father: Family, Work & Self. Mothering Magazine Editors. (Illus.). 176p. (Orig.). 1990. pap. 12.95 (*0-945465-69-6*) John Muir.

Being a Food Service Worker. Hospital Research & Educational Trust of the AHA Staff. (Illus.). 1967. pap. 13.95 (*0-87618-046-2*) P-H.

Being a Food Service Worker: Student Manual. (Food Service Workers Ser.). 276p. 1967. 13.95 (*0-685-18409-9*, 9775) Hosp Res & Educ.

Being a Gentleman: A Resource for Men. Glenn Pickering. LC 93-9723. 192p. 1993. pap. 12.95 (*0-938586-75-0*) Whole Person.

Being a Green Mother. Piers Anthony. (Incarnations of Immortality Ser.: Bk. 5). 1988. mass mkt. 5.95 (*0-345-32223-1*, Del Rey) Ballantine.

Being a Happy Millionaire: How to Do It. Charley Love. 227p. (Orig.). 1993. pap. text ed. 9.95 (*1-883978-01-7*, Loveseed Pr) Loveseed Revel.

Being a Health Unit Coordinator. Kay Cox. LC 83-15824. (Illus.). 368p. (C). 1984. teacher ed 9.95 (*0-89303-329-4*); pap. text ed. 19.95 (*0-89303-236-0*) P-H.

Being a Health Unit Coordinator. 3rd ed. Kay Cox. 384p. 1990. pap. 25.65 (*0-89303-103-8*) P-H.

Being a Homemaker: Home Health Aide. Elana Zucker. LC 81-21770. (Illus.). 320p. 1982. teacher ed 11.95 (*0-685-04207-3*); student ed 7.95 (*0-89303-230-1*); pap. text ed. 18.95 (*0-89303-113-5*) P-H.

Being a Homemaker: Home Health Aide. 2nd ed. Elana Zucker. 352p. 1988. pap. text ed. 25.00 (*0-89303-091-0*) P-H.

Being a Homemaker: Home Health Aide. 3rd ed. Elena Zucker. 1991. pap. 21.25 (*0-89303-087-2*, 740102) P-H.

Being a Homemaker-Home Health Aide. Julie K. Wernig & Barbara Baranishyn. 192p. (C). 1985. teacher ed, pap. 11.95 (*0-89303-460-6*) P-H.

Being a Housekeeping Aide. Hospital Research & Educational Trust of the AHA Staff. (Illus.). 1968. pap. 16.95 (*0-87618-048-9*) P-H.

Being a Housekeeping Aide: Student Manual. 320p. 1967. 11.95 (*0-685-43353-6*, 585785) Hosp Res & Educ.

Being a Housekeeping Aide in a Nursing Home: Employee Workbook. (Illus.). 88p. 8.50 (*0-318-12741-5*, 901-001077) Am Health Care Assn.

Being a Lawyer: Individual Choice & Responsibility in the Practice of Law. Howard Lesnick. LC 92-16679. (American Casebook Ser.). 500p. (C). 1992. pap. text ed. 29.00 (*0-314-00916-7*) West Pub.

Being a Long-Term Care Nursing Assistant. 3rd ed. ON Health Care Systems Staff et al. 416p. 1991. pap. 23.50 (*0-89303-101-1*) P-H.

***Being a Long-Term Care Nursing Assistant.** 4th ed. Connie Will-Black & Judith B. Eighmy. LC 95-15489. 1995. write for info. (*0-89303-000-7*) P-H.

Being a Man: A Guide to the New Masculinity. Matthew McKay & Patrick Fanning. 260p. (Orig.). 1992. text ed. 29.95 (*1-879237-41-5*); pap. text ed. 12.95 (*1-879237-40-7*) New Harbinger.

Being a Medical Admitting Clerk. Linda Barber & Ruth Garwood. 144p. 1994. pap. 16.50 (*0-89303-072-4*) P-H.

Being a Medical Information Coder. Laurie Dodson. 304p. 1992. pap. 21.75 (*0-89303-084-8*) P-H.

Being a Medical Insurance Clerk. Linda Barber & Derbish. 240p. 1994. pap. 19.75 (*0-89303-223-9*) P-H.

Being a Medical Records Clerk. Kathy McMiller. 224p. (C). 1991. 23.10 (*0-89303-807-5*, 740504) P-H.

Being a Medical Transcriptionist. Norma L. Morrow. 208p. 1991. pap. 19.80 (*0-89303-082-1*) P-H.

Being a Minister's Wife...& Being Yourself. Nancy Pannell. (Orig.). 1993. pap. 8.99 (*0-8054-5359-8*) Broadman.

Being a Minor Writer. Gail Gilliland. LC 94-10562. 282p. 1994. 24.95x (*0-87745-473-6*); pap. 12.95 (*0-87745-486-8*) U of Iowa Pr.

Being a Nursing Assistant. 3rd ed. Rose Schniedman et al. LC 81-10113. (Illus.). 496p. 1981. teacher ed 8.95 (*0-89303-059-7*); student ed 6.95 (*0-89303-049-X*); pap. text ed. 16.95 (*0-89303-027-9*) P-H.

***Being a Nursing Assistant.** 6th ed. Rose B. Schiedman et al. LC 94-40683. (Nurses' Aides Ser.). 1994. pap. 23.50 (*0-8359-4902-8*) P-H.

Being a Nursing Assistant. 6th ed. Rose Schniedman et al. 640p. 1991. pap. 21.00 (*0-89303-115-1*) P-H.

Being a Parent: Unchanging Values in a Changing World. Ed. by David K. Bernhardt. LC 74-484635. 202p. reprint ed. pap. 57.60 (*0-8357-7117-2*, 2023594) Bks Demand.

Being a Philosopher: The History of a Practice. David W. Hamlyn. LC 91-40390. 224p. 1992. 29.95 (*0-415-02968-6*, A6939) Routledge.

Being a Priest Today. Donald J. Goergen. 206p. 1992. pap. text ed. 9.95 (*0-8146-5032-5*) Liturgical Pr.

Being a Roman Citizen. Jane F. Gardner. LC 92-29382. 256p. 1993. 49.95 (*0-415-00154-4*, B0336, Routledge NY) Routledge.

Being a Single Parent see Single Parenting

Being a Successful Teacher. Janet Bluestein. (J). (gr. k-6). 1988. pap. 26.99 (*0-8224-6791-7*) Fearon Teach Aids.

Being a Teacher: A Positive Approach to Change & Stress. Guy Claxton. 224p. 1989. text ed. 55.00 (*0-304-31822-1*); pap. text ed. 18.95 (*0-304-31824-8*) Cassell.

Being a Terrific Teen in Troubled Times. Allan Burgess & Max Molgard. 1994. pap. 7.95 (*0-88494-917-6*) Bookcraft Inc.

Being a Twin, Having a Twin. Maxine B. Rosenberg. LC 84-17159. (Illus.). 48p. (J). (gr. 1-4). 1985. lib. bdg. 11. 88 (*0-688-04329-1*) Lothrop.

Being a Ward Clerk: Student Manual. 247p. 1967. 9.95 (*0-87914-013-5*, 9780) Hosp Res & Educ.

Being a Widow. Lynn Caine. 264p. 1990. pap. 10.95 (*0-14-013025-X*, Penguin Bks) Viking Penguin.

Being a Wild, Wonderful Woman for God. Becky Tirabassi. 208p. 1994. pap. 15.99 (*0-310-44250-8*) Zondervan.

***Being a Wild, Wonderful Woman for God.** Becky Tirabassi. 1994. 12.99 (*0-310-24538-9*) Zondervan.

Being a Woman: Fulfilling Your Femininity & Finding Love. Toni Grant. 256p. (Orig.). 1989. mass mkt. 4.99 (*0-380-70698-9*) Avon.

Being a Woman: Fulfilling Your Feminity & Finding Love. Toni Grant. LC 87-9667. 224p. 1988. 17.95 (*0-394-55497-3*) Random.

Being about Music: The Collected Writings of Benjamin Boretz & J. K. Randall. Benjamin Boretz & J. K. Randall. LC 91-90391. 350p. 1994. write for info. (*0-9629865-3-4*) Open Space NY.

Being Adolescent: Conflict & Growth in the Teenage Years. Mihaly Csikszentmihalyi & Reed Larson. LC 83-45253. (Illus.). 352p. 1986. pap. text ed. 18.00 (*0-465-00645-0*) Basic.

Being Adopted. Stephanie Herbert. (Illus.). 24p. (J). 1991. 12.95 (*0-87868-478-6*) Child Welfare.

Being Adopted. Maxine B. Rosenberg. LC 83-17522. (Illus.). 48p. (J). (gr. 1-4). 1984. 16.00 (*0-688-02672-9*); lib. bdg. 15.93 (*0-688-02673-7*) Lothrop.

Being Adopted: The Lifelong Search for Self. David M. Brodzinsky et al. LC 92-38103. 1993. pap. 12.95 (*0-385-41426-9*, Anchor NY) Doubleday.

Being Alive on Land: Proceedings of the International Symposium on Adaptations to Terrestrial Environment, Held in Halkidiki, Greece, 1982. Ed. by N. S. Margaris et al. (Tasks for Vegetation Science Ser.). 334p. 1984. 72.00 (*0-318-01972-8*) Kluwer Ac.

Being an Actor. Simon Callow. 224p. 1988. pap. 9.95 (*0-8021-3123-9*) Grove-Atltic.

Being an Actor. Simon Callow. (Illus.). 208p. 1986. 13.95 (*0-312-07276-7*) St Martin.

Being an American. William O. Douglas. LC 77-134071. (Essay Index Reprint Ser.). 1977. reprint ed. 18.95 (*0-8369-2223-9*) Ayer.

Being an Artist. Lew Lehrman. (Illus.). 144p. 1992. 29.95 (*0-89134-429-2*, 30409) North Light Bks.

Being an Effective Teacher. Robert G. Davidson. 20p. 1987. pap. 5.50 (*0-940754-42-8*) Ed Ministries.

Being an Entrepreneur in Alabama. Anthony Brogdon. Ed. by James Brogdon. 1991. pap. 12.95 (*1-879036-04-5*) Multi Concepts.

Being an Entrepreneur in California. Anthony Brogdon. Ed. by James Brogdon. 1991. pap. text ed. 12.95 (*0-9622538-6-3*) Multi Concepts.

Being an Entrepreneur in Colorado. Anthony Brogdon. Ed. by James Brogdon. 1991. pap. 12.95 (*1-879036-03-7*) Multi Concepts.

Being an Entrepreneur in Florida. Anthony Brogdon. Ed. by James Brogdon. 110p. (Orig.). (C). 1991. pap. 12.95 (*1-879036-00-2*) Multi Concepts.

Being an Entrepreneur in Georgia. Anthony Brogdon. Ed. by James Brogdon. 180p. (C). 1989. 12.95 (*0-9622538-0-4*) Multi Concepts.

Being an Entrepreneur in Illinois. Anthony Brogdon. 110p. (C). 1991. pap. 12.95 (*0-9622538-4-7*) Multi Concepts.

Being an Entrepreneur in Louisiana. Anthony Brogdon. Ed. by James Brogdon. 1991. pap. 12.95 (*1-879036-02-9*) Multi Concepts.

Being an Entrepreneur in Maryland. Anthony Brogdon. Ed. by James Brogdon. 1991. pap. 12.95 (*0-9622538-9-8*) Multi Concepts.

Being an Entrepreneur in Michigan. Anthony Brogdon. Ed. by James Brogdon. 110p. (Orig.). (C). 1991. pap. 12.95 (*0-9622538-3-9*) Multi Concepts.

Being an Entrepreneur in Minnesota. Anthony Brogdon. Ed. by James Brogdon. 1991. pap. 12.95 (*1-879036-05-3*) Multi Concepts.

Being an Entrepreneur in New Jersey. Anthony Brogdon. Ed. by James Brogdon. 1991. pap. 12.95 (*1-879036-08-8*) Multi Concepts.

Being an Entrepreneur in New York. Anthony Brogdon. Ed. by James Brogdon. 1991. pap. 12.95 (*0-9622538-8-X*) Multi Concepts.

Being an Entrepreneur in Ohio. Anthony Brogdon. Ed. by James Brogdon. (Illus.). 110p. (Orig.). (C). 1991. pap. 12.95 (*0-9622538-5-5*) Multi Concepts.

Being an Entrepreneur in Pennsylvania. Anthony Brogdon. Ed. by James Brogdon. 1991. pap. 12.95 (*1-879036-07-X*) Multi Concepts.

Being an Entrepreneur in Texas. Anthony Brogdon. Ed. by James Brogdon. 1991. pap. 12.95 (*1-879036-01-0*) Multi Concepts.

Being an Entrepreneur in Washington, D. C. Anthony Brogdon. Ed. by James Brogdon. 1991. pap. 12.95 (*0-9622538-7-1*) Multi Concepts.

Being & Becoming. Anne King & Sandra Kurtinitis. 1024p. (C). 1987. pap. text ed. write for info. (*0-07-555050-4*) McGraw.

Being & Becoming: A Critique of Post-Modernism, No. 44. F. F. Centore. LC 90-45070. 304p. 1991. text ed. 59.95 (*0-313-27616-1*, CBM, Greenwood Pr) Greenwood.

Being & Becoming Indian. James A. Clifton. 1988. 32.95 (*0-256-06254-4*) Dorsey.

Being & Becoming Indian: Biographical Studies of North American Frontiers. James A. Clifton. (Illus.). 337p. (C). 1993. reprint ed. pap. text ed. 14.95 (*0-88133-735-8*) Waveland Pr.

Being & Becoming Old see Perspectives on Aging & Human Development Series

Being & Becoming or the Passing of Spirit. Fenwicke L. Holmes. 50p. 1993. pap. 4.00 (*0-89540-263-7*, SB-263) Sun Pub.

Being & Belonging: Group, Intergroup, & Gestalt. Gaie Houston. LC 93-3472. (Series in Psychotherapy & Counselling). 220p. 1994. text ed. 42.95 (*0-471-93548-4*) Wiley.

Being & Breakfast. Marti Duncan. 1975. 1.00 (*0-686-71049-5*) Windless Orchard.

***Being & Caring: A Journey to Self.** Victor Daniels & Laurence J. Horowitz. (C). 1984. teacher ed, pap. text ed. write for info. (*0-87484-759-1*) Mayfield Pub.

Being & Caring: A Journey to Self. 2nd ed. Victor Daniels & Laurence J. Horowitz. LC 84-60885. 371p. 1984. pap. text ed. 31.95 (*0-87484-544-0*) Mayfield Pub.

Being & Circumstance: Notes Toward a Conditional Art. Robert Irwin. LC 85-81088. (Illus.). 157p. (Orig.). 1985. 35.00 (*0-932499-06-6*); pap. 19.50 (*0-932499-07-4*) Lapis Pr.

Being & Doing: A Workbook for Actors. Eric Morris. 190p. 1990. pap. text ed. 12.95 (*0-9629709-0-5*) Ermor Enter.

Being & Existence in Kierkegaard's Pseudonymous Works. John W. Elrod. LC 74-25615. 279p. reprint ed. pap. 79. 60 (*0-8357-6037-5*, 2034284) Bks Demand.

Being & God: Introduction to the Philosophy of Being & to Natural Theology. George P. Klubertanz & Maurice R. Holloway. LC 63-15359. 1963. 39.50 (*0-89197-045-2*); pap. text ed. 19.95 (*0-89197-674-4*) Irvington.

Being & Goodness: The Concept of Good in Metaphysics & Philosophical Theology. Ed. by Scott MacDonald. LC 90-55197. 336p. 1991. 46.95 (*0-8014-2312-0*); pap. 15.95 (*0-8014-9779-5*) Cornell U Pr.

Being & Idea: Development of Some Themes in Spinoza & Hegel. Leslie Armour. (Philos. Texte und Studien Ser.: Vol. 26). 185p. 1992. 25.87 (*3-487-09513-0*, Pub. by Georg Olms GW) Lubrecht & Cramer.

Being & Idea: Developments of Some Themes in Spinoza & Hegel. Leslie Armour. (Philos. Texte und Studien Ser.: Vol. 26). 185p. 1992. pap. text ed. 27.95 (*0-685-66951-3*, Pub. by Georg Olms GW) Lubrecht & Cramer.

Being & Loving. rev. ed. Althea Horner. LC 90-33413. 184p. 1990. 25.00 (*0-87668-774-5*) Aronson.

Being & Nothingness. Jean-Paul Sartre. Tr. & Intro. by Hazel E. Barnes. 1993. pap. 14.00 (*0-671-86780-6*, WSP) PB.

Being & Order: The Metaphysics of Thomas Aquinas in Historical Perspective. Andrew N. Woznicki. (American University Studies: Philosophy: Ser. V, Vol. 16). 340p. (C). 1989. text ed. 51.00 (*0-8204-0919-7*) P Lang Pubs.

***Being & Other Realities.** Paul Weiss. 390p. 1995. pap. text ed. 21.95 (*0-8126-9293-4*) Open Court.

Being & Race: Black Writing since Nineteen Seventy. Charles Johnson. LC 86-46405. 144p. 1988. 20.00 (*0-253-31165-9*); pap. 7.95 (*0-253-20537-9*, MB-537) Ind U Pr.

Being & the Between: Metaphysics & Transcendence. William Desmond. LC 94-8840. (SUNY Series in Philosophy). 576p. 1995. text ed. 74.50 (*0-7914-2271-2*); pap. text ed. 24.95 (*0-7914-2272-0*) State U NY Pr.

Being & the Meaning of Life, Bk. 3: Diamond Heart. A. H. Almaas. 211p. (Orig.). 1990. pap. 12.00 (*0-936713-05-4*) Diamond Bks CA.

Being & the Messiah: The Message of St. John. Jose P. Miranda. LC 77-5388. Orig. Title: El Ser y el Mesias. 255p. (Orig.). reprint ed. pap. 72.70 (*0-8357-8816-4*, 2033467) Bks Demand.

Being & Time. Martin Heidegger. LC 72-78334. 1962. text ed. 27.00 (*0-06-063850-8*) Harper SF.

***Being & Time: A Translation of Sein und Zeit.** Martin Heidegger. Tr. by Joan Stambaugh. (SUNY Series in Chinese Philosophy & Culture). 576p. (C). 1995. text ed. 57.50x (*0-7914-2677-7*); pap. text ed. 18.95x (*0-7914-2678-5*) State U NY Pr.

***Being & Value: Toward a Constructive Postmodern Metaphysics.** Frederick Ferre. (Constructive Postmodern Thought Ser.). 448p. 1995. text ed. 74.50 (*0-7914-2755-2*); pap. text ed. 24.95x (*0-7914-2756-0*) State U NY Pr.

Being & Vibration. Joseph Rael. LC 92-72320. (Illus.). 185p. 1993. pap. 14.95 (*0-933031-72-6*) Coun Oak Bks.

Being & Will: An Essay in Philosophical Theology. John Burbidge. LC 76-45934. 214p. reprint ed. pap. 61.00 (*0-8357-9484-9*, 2013527) Bks Demand.

Being Antinova. Eleanor Antin. LC 83-72104. (Illus.). 88p. 1983. pap. 10.00 (*0-937122-11-4*) Astro Artz.

Being Antinova. limited ed. Eleanor Antin. LC 83-72104. (Illus.). 88p. 1983. 25.00 (*0-937122-12-2*) Astro Artz.

Being As Communion: Studies in Personhood & the Church. John D. Zizioulas. LC 85-2134. (Contemporary Greek Theologians Ser.: No. 4). 269p. (Orig.). 1985. pap. 14.95 (*0-88141-029-2*) St Vladimirs.

Being at Leisure - Playing at Life: A Guide to Health & Joyful Living. Bruno H. Geba. LC 84-82403. (Illus.). 192p. 1985. 19.95 (*0-932057-01-2*); pap. 14.95 (*0-932057-00-4*) Leisure Sci Sys.

Being Bad for the Baby-Sitter. Richard Tulloch. (J). (gr. 4-7). 1994. pap. 2.95 (*0-590-46061-7*) Scholastic Inc.

Being Beautiful. Ed. by Katherine Isaac. LC 86-73252. 300p. 1987. pap. 10.00 (*0-936758-20-1*) Ctr Responsive Law.

Being Big. Liddell & Cathcart. (NFS Canada). (J). (ps-3). 1994. pap. 5.95 (*0-929005-60-0*, Pub. by Second Story Pr CN) InBook.

Being Big. Liddell & Cathcart. (NFS Canada). (J). (ps-3). 1995. 12.95 (*0-929005-62-7*, Pub. by Second Story Pr CN) InBook.

***Being Bilingual Is Fun!** Claudia Schwalm. 32p. (J). (ps-4). 1995. lib. bdg. 15.95 (*1-57371-012-1*) Cult Connect.

Being Born. Sheila Kitzinger. (Illus.). (J). (ps-1). 1992. pap. 11.95 (*0-399-22225-1*, Putnam) Putnam Pub Group.

***Being Brett: Chronicle of a Daughter's Death.** Douglas Hobbie. LC 95-13280. 1996. write for info. (*0-8050-2520-0*, J Macrae Bks) H Holt & Co.

Being Bright Is Not Enough: The Unwritten Rules of Doctoral Study. Peggy Hawley. LC 92-43857. (Illus.). 174p. 1993. pap. 31.95 (*0-398-05848-2*) C C Thomas.

Being Bullied. Kate Petty. (Playground Ser.). (Illus.). 24p. (J). (ps-2). 1991. pap. 4.95 (*0-8120-4661-7*) Barron.

Being Called to Care. Mary E. Lashley et al. LC 93-7296. 215p. 1994. 59.50 (*0-7914-1839-1*); pap. 19.95 (*0-7914-1840-5*) State U NY Pr.

Being Catholic. Michael Carotta. (Discovering Program Ser.). (Illus.). 74p. (Orig.). 1989. teacher ed 6.00 (*0-88489-189-5*); text ed. 2.80 (*0-88489-188-7*) St Marys.

Being Catholic: Believing, Living, Praying. Michael Pennock. LC 93-73883. (Friendship in the Lord Ser.). (Illus.). 232p. (Orig.). (YA). (gr. 10-12). 1994. teacher ed, pap. 15.95 (*0-87793-528-9*); pap. text ed. 11.95 (*0-87793-527-0*) Ave Maria.

Being Catholic: Commonweal from the Seventies to the Nineties. Rodger Van Allen. LC 92-40701. 224p. 1993. pap. 12.95 (*0-8294-0744-8*) Loyola Univ Pr.

Being Changed by Cross-Cultural Encounters: The Anthropology of Extraordinary Experience. Ed. by David E. Young & Jean-Guy Goulet. 300p. 1994. 34.95 (*1-55111-032-6*); pap. 21.95 (*1-55111-040-7*) Broadview Pr.

Being Christian: A United Methodist Vision for the Christian Life. Jerry L. Mercer. LC 93-72074. 104p. 1993. pap. 9.95 (*0-88177-125-2*, DR125) Discipleship Res.

Being Christian Today: An American Conversation. Ed. by Richard J. Neuhaus & George Weigel. 310p. (C). 1992. 24.95 (*0-89633-164-4*) Ethics & Public Policy.

Being Clergy, Staying Human: Taking Our Stand in the River. Dorothy McRae-McMahon. LC 92-72457. (Orig.). 1992. pap. 10.95 (*1-56699-061-0*, AL135) Alban Inst.

Being Colloquial in Esperanto. David K. Jordan. 278p. (Orig.). (ENG & ESP.). (C). 1992. pap. text ed. 18.50 (*0-8191-8646-5*) U Pr of Amer.

B

An Asterisk (*) at the beginning of an entry indicates that the title is appearing in BIP for the first time.

An Asterisk (*) at the beginning of a an entry indicates that the title is appearing in BIP for the first time.

671

*Beirut Blues. Hanan Al-Shaykh. LC 94-40939. (ARA & ENG.). 1995. 21.95 (0-385-47381-8, Anchor NY) Doubleday.

Beirut Diary: A Husband Held Hostage & a Wife Determined to Set Him Free. Sis Levin. LC 89-19750. 239p. 1989. 14.99 (0-8308-1716-6, 1716, Saltshaker Bk) InterVarsity.

Beirut Fragments: A War Memoir. Jean S. Makdisi. LC 89-26533. 256p. 1990. 19.95 (0-89255-150-X) Persea Bks.

Beirut Fragments: A War Memoir. Jean S. Makdisi. LC 89-26533. 256p. 1991. reprint ed. pap. 9.95 (0-89255-164-X) Persea Bks.

Beirut Nineteen Eighty-Four: A Population & Health Profile. Ed. by Huda G. Zurayk & Haroutune K. Armenian. 288p. 1985. text ed. 30.00 (0-8156-6076-6, Am U Beirut) Syracuse U Pr.

Beirut of Tomorrow: Planning for Reconstruction. Ed. by Friedrich Ragette. (Illus.). 142p. 1983. pap. text ed. 9.95 (0-8156-6069-3, Am U Beirut) Syracuse U Pr.

Beirut Outtakes: A TV Correspondent's Portrait of America's Encounter with Terror. Larry Pintak. 368p. 1989. text ed. 24.95 (0-669-19512-X); pap. 12.95 (0-669-21361-6) Free Pr.

*Beirut '75. Ghada Samman. Tr. by Nancy N. Roberts. LC 95-13545. 1995. write for info. (1-55728-383-4); pap. write for info. (1-55728-382-6) U of Ark Pr.

Beis Halevi - Shemos. Yosef D. Soloveichik. 1991. 14.95 (0-685-53657-2) Feldheim.

Beis Halevi, Bk. II: Shemos (Exodus) Rav Y. Soloveichik. Tr. by Yisrael I. Herczeg. 216p. 1991. write for info. (0-944070-29-9) Targum Pr.

Beisbol. John Krich. (Spectator Ser.). 1990. pap. 9.95 (0-685-46177-7) P-H.

Beisbol: Latin Americans & the Grand Old Game. Michael M. Oleksak & Mary A. Oleksak. LC 91-10697. (Illus.). 320p. 1991. 22.95 (0-940279-35-5) Masters Pr IN.

Beisbol Es Nuestro Juego (Baseball's Our Game) Joan Downing. Tr. by Lada Kratky. LC 82-4418. (Spanish Easy Reading Bks.). (Illus.). 32p. (SPA.). (J). (gr. k-3). 1984. pap. 3.95 (0-516-53402-5) Childrens.

*Beisbol Nos Salvo. Ken Mochizuki. Tr. by Tomas Gonzalez. LC 94-32517. (Illus.). 32p. (SPA.). (J). (gr. k up). 1995. 14.95 (1-880000-21-0); pap. 5.95 (1-880000-22-9) Lee & Low Bks.

Beispiel und Vorbild der Vorfahren. Karl Jost. Ed. by Gregory Vlastos. LC 78-19366. (Morals & Law in Ancient Greece Ser.). (GER & GRE.). 1979. reprint ed. lib. bdg. 18.00 (0-685-96158-3) Ayer.

Beit El-Wali Temple of Ramesses Second. Herbert Ricke et al. LC 67-18437. (Oriental Institute Nubian Expedition Publications: Vol. 1). (Illus.). 1967. lib. bdg. 30.00 (0-226-62365-3, OINE1) U Ch Pr.

*Beit Hashoah: Museum of Tolerance. Simon Wiesenthal Center Staff. (Illus.). 48p. (Orig.). 1993. pap. 9.24 (0-943058-16-3) S Wiesenthal Ctr.

Beitraege zur Entstehung & Entwicklung der Stadt Brandenburg im Mittelalter. Ed. by Winfried Schich. (Veroeffenlichungen der Historischen Kommission zu Berlin Ser.: Band 84). (Illus.). xx, 379p. (GER.). (C). 1993. lib. bdg. 96.00 (3-11-013983-9) Mouton.

Beitraege zur gesamtwirtschaftlichen Allokation: Staatl. Allokations-Politik im Marktwiss. System, Vol. 4. Ed. by Eberhard Wille. 257p. (GER.). 1983. 46.90 (3-8204-7692-X) P Lang Pubs.

Beitraege Zur Geschichte der Deutschen Romantischen Oper Zwischen Spohrs Faust und Wagners Lohengrin. Siegfried Goslich. LC 80-2281. reprint ed. 31.50 (0-404-18846-X) AMS Pr.

Beitraege zur Geschichte und Interpretation der Philosophie Kants. Gerhard Lehmann. (C). 1969. 107.70 (3-11-002561-2) De Gruyter.

Beitraege zur Geschichte von Text & Sprache des Alten Testaments Gesammelte Aufsaetze. Rudolph Meyer. (Beiheft zur Zeitschrift fuer die Alttestamentliche Wissenschaft Ser.: Bd 209). viii, 259p. (GER.). (C). 1993. lib. bdg. 129.25 (3-11-013695-3) De Gruyter.

Beitraege zur Kenntnis der arctischen Diatomeen. P. T. Cleve & A. Grunow. 121p. 1976. reprint ed. pap. text ed. 54.00 (3-87429-101-4) Koeltz Sci Bks.

Beitraege zur Kenntnis der Flechtenflora des Himalaya. VII Die Gattungen Caloplaca, Fulgensis, und Ioplaca: (Mit Englischem Bestimmungsschluessel) J. Poelt & Erika Hinteregger. (Bibliotheca Lichenologica Ser.: Vol. 50). (Illus.). 247p. (GER.). 1993. pap. text ed. 78.50 (3-443-58029-7, Pub. by Cramer-Borntraeger GW) Lubrecht & Cramer.

Beitraege zur Kenntnis der Meeresalgen von Neapel, zugleich mikrophotographischer Atlas. Georg Funk. (Pubbl. d. Stazione Zool. di Napoli). (Illus.). 178p. (GER.). 1978. reprint ed. lib. bdg. 84.00 (3-87429-146-4) Koeltz Sci Bks.

Beitraege zur Lichenologie: Festschrift J. Poelt. Ed. by H. Hertel & Oberwinkler. (Nova Hedwigia Beiheft Ser.: No. 79). (Illus.). 900p. (ENG, FRE & GER.). 1985. lib. bdg. 125.00 (3-7682-5479-8) Lubrecht & Cramer.

Beitraege zur Orchideenkunde von Colombia. R. Schlechter. (Feddes Repertorium Ser.: Beiheft 27). 183p. (GER.). 1980. reprint ed. lib. bdg. 74.00 (3-87429-182-0) Koeltz Sci Bks.

Beitraege zur Orchideenkunde von Zentralamerika, 2 vols. in 1. R. Schlechter. (Feddes Repertorium Ser.: Beiheft 17 & 18). 402p. (GER.). 1980. reprint ed. lib. bdg. 123.00 (3-87429-181-2) Koeltz Sci Bks.

Beitraege zur Syntaxonomie und Chorologie des Kalk-Buchenwaldes im Ausseralpinen Deutschland. Reiner Suck. (Dissertationes Botanicae Ser.: Vol. 175). (Illus.). 214p. (GER.). 1991. pap. text ed. 67.10 (3-443-64087-7, Pub. by Cramer-Borntraeger GW) Lubrecht & Cramer.

Beitrag zur Kenntnis der Desmidiaceen des Banado Cruces, Provinz Valdivia, Chile. Monika Durrschmidt. (Bibliotheca Phycologica Ser.: No. 73). (Illus.). 138p. 1985. pap. text ed. 36.00 (3-7682-1430-3) Lubrecht & Cramer.

Beitrage Zu Aristoteles' Poetik. Johannes Vahlen & Hermann Schone. viii, 362p. 1965. reprint ed. write for info. (0-318-71057-9, Pub. by Georg Olms GW) Lubrecht & Cramer.

Beitrage zue Genaueren Kenntnis der Attischen Gerichtssprache aus den Zehn Rednern & Die Schuldenerbfoige im Attischen Recht, 2 vols. in one. Konrad Schodorf & Edwin Demisch. Ed. by Gregory Vlastos. LC 78-14617. (Morals & Law in Ancient Greece Ser.). (GER & GRE.). 1979. reprint ed. lib. bdg. 18.95 (0-405-11592-X) Ayer.

Beitrage Zum Griechischen Liebesroman. Hans Gartner. Bd. 20. write for info. (0-318-70810-8, Pub. by Georg Olms GW) Lubrecht & Cramer.

Beitrage Zum Griechischen Liebesroman. Hans Gartner. (Olms GW Studien: Bd. 20). xii, 478p. (GER.). 1984. write for info. (3-487-07497-4, Pub. by Georg Olms GW) Lubrecht & Cramer.

*Beitrage Zum Verfassungrecht der Kirche. Winfried Aymans. (Kanonistische Studien und Texte). vi, 300p. 1992. lib. bdg. 95.00x (90-6032-324-6) Benjamins North Am.

Beitrage Zur Erganzung Des Jocher'schen Allgemeinen Gelehrten-Lexikon's und Des Meusel'schen Lexikon's der von 1750 Bis 1800 Verstorbenen Deutschen Schriftsteller, 3 vols. in 1. Karl A. Hennicke. 320p. 1969. reprint ed. write for info. (0-318-70767-5, Pub. by Georg Olms GW) Lubrecht & Cramer.

Beitrage Zur Geschichte Beider Rechte Im Mittelalter, Bd. I: Zur Geschichte der Popularen Literatur des Romiscshen Kanonischen Rechts (Mehr Nicht Erschienen) Emil Seckel. xx, 539p. 1967. reprint ed. write for info. (0-318-71280-6, Pub. by Georg Olms GW) Lubrecht & Cramer.

Beitrage Zur Geschichte Der Christlich-Lateinischen Poesie. Carl Weymann. xii, 308p. 1975. reprint ed. write for info. (3-487-05346-2, Pub. by Georg Olms GW) Lubrecht & Cramer.

Beitrage zur Geschichte der Kabbala. Adolph Jellinek. Ed. by Steven Katz. LC 79-7138. (Jewish Philosophy, Mysticism & History of Ideas Ser.). 1980. reprint ed. lib. bdg. 18.95 (0-405-12264-0) Ayer.

Beitrage zur Geschichte der Kunst im Sudeten und Karpathenraum: Vols. 1-7, Brno, 1938-1943. 1972. pap. 180.00 (0-8115-1549-4) Periodicals Srv.

Beitrage zur Geschichte der Philosophie. Manuel Joel. Ed. by Steven Katz. LC 79-7140. (Jewish Philosophy, Mysticism & History of Ideas Ser.). 1980. reprint ed. lib. bdg. 56.95 (0-405-12266-7) Ayer.

Beitrage Zur Geschichte und Litteratur der Italienischen Gelehrtenrenaissance. Theodor Klette. v, 350p. 1970. reprint ed. write for info. (0-318-71262-8, Pub. by Georg Olms GW); reprint ed. write for info. (0-318-71601-1, Pub. by Georg Olms GW) Lubrecht & Cramer.

Beitrage zur Geschicte Agyptens unter Dem Islam, 2 vols. in 1. Carl H. Becker. LC 77-10579. (Studies in Islamic History: No. 5). 198p. 1978. reprint ed. lib. bdg. 35.00 (0-87991-454-8) Porcupine Pr.

Beitrage Zur Griechischen Inschriftenkunde. Adolf Wilhelm. (Sonderschriften des Osterreichischen Archaologischen Instituts in Wein Ser.: Vol. VII). 379p. (GER.). 1990. reprint ed. write for info. (3-487-09212-3, Pub. by Georg Olms GW) Lubrecht & Cramer.

Beitrage Zur Historischen Syntax der Griechischen Sprache. Ed. by M. Schanz. vi, 371p. 1976. reprint ed. write for info. (3-487-05574-0, Pub. by Georg Olms GW) Lubrecht & Cramer.

Beitrage Zur Kenntnis der Poesie der Alten Araber. Theodor Noldeke. xxiv, 244p. 1967. reprint ed. write for info. (0-318-71540-6, Pub. by Georg Olms GW) Lubrecht & Cramer.

Beitrage zur Kenntnis des Gewerbes im Hellenistischen Agypten. Theodor Reil. Ed. by Moses Finley. LC 79-5001. (Ancient Economic History Ser.). (GER.). 1979. reprint ed. lib. bdg. 21.95 (0-405-12390-6) Ayer.

Beitrage Zur Kritik und Erklarung Des Plautus. Peter Langen. iv, 348p. (GER.). 1973. reprint ed. write for info. (3-487-04991-0, Pub. by Georg Olms GW) Lubrecht & Cramer.

Beitrage Zur Kunde der Lateinischen Literatur Des Mittelalters. Jacob Werner. 227p. 1979. reprint ed. write for info. (3-487-06732-3, Pub. by Georg Olms GW) Lubrecht & Cramer.

Beitrage zur Linguistik. Probleme der Sprachwissenschaft Staff. (Janua Linguarum, Ser. Minor: No. 118). 1971. pap. text ed. 64.60 (90-279-1797-3) Mouton.

Beitrage Zur Quellenkritik der Naturgeschichte Des Plinius. Friedrich Munzer. xii, 432p. 1988. write for info. (3-615-00040-4, Pub. by Georg Olms GW) Lubrecht & Cramer.

Beitrage Zur Syntax Epikurs. Hans Widmann. (Tubinger Beitrage Zur Altertumswissenschaft Ser.: No. 24). xv, 266p. 1974. reprint ed. write for info. (3-487-05455-8, Pub. by Georg Olms GW) Lubrecht & Cramer.

Beizvogel. Al G. Gassani. (Illus.). iv, 276p. 1988. write for info. (3-487-09020-1, Pub. by Georg Olms GW) Lubrecht & Cramer.

Beka Lamb. Zee Edgell. (Caribbean Writers Ser.). 172p. (Orig.). (C). 1986. pap. 9.95 (0-435-98844-1) Heinemann.

Bekoroth, 1 vol. (ENG & HEB.). 18.00 (0-910218-82-X) Bennet Pub.

Bektashi Order of Dervishes. John K. Birge. LC 77-87662. reprint ed. 35.00 (0-404-16400-5) AMS Pr.

Bel Air. Katherine Stone. 1990. mass mkt. 4.95 (0-8217-2979-9) Zebra.

Bel-Air Bambi & the Mall Rats. Richard Peck. LC 92-29377. (J). 1993. 15.95 (0-385-30823-X) Delacorte.

*Bel-Air Bambi & the Mall Rats. Richard Peck. (YA). 1995. pap. 3.99 (0-440-21925-6) Dell.

Bel-Air Book of Southern California Food & Entertaining. Norman Kolpas & George Mahaffey. (Illus.). 160p. 1991. 50.00 (0-517-58414-X, Crown) Crown Pub Group.

Bel Ami. Guy De Maupassant. Ed. by Deliasement. write for info. (0-318-63435-X) Fr & Eur.

Bel Ami. Guy De Maupassant. Ed. by Delaisement. (Folio Ser.: No. 865). (FRE.). 9.95 (2-07-036865-3) Schoenhof.

Bel Ami. Guy De Maupassant. Tr. by Douglas Parmee. (Classics Ser.). 408p. 1975. mass mkt. 9.95 (0-14-044315-0, Penguin Classics) Viking Penguin.

Bel Canto: Principles & Practices. Cornelius L. Reid. LC 76-368704. 1950. reprint ed. pap. 6.95 (0-915282-01-1) J Patelson Mus.

Bel Canto: The Teaching of the Classical Italian Song-Schools, Its Decline & Restoration. Lucie Manen. (Illus.). 88p. 1987. pap. 22.95 (0-19-317109-0) OUP.

Bel Canto: Theoretical & Practical Vocal Method. Mathilde Marchesi. 1970. reprint ed. pap. text ed. 8.95 (0-486-22315-9) Dover.

Bel Canto & Its Golden Age. Phillip A. Duey. (Music Reprint Ser.: 1980). 1980. reprint ed. lib. bdg. 32.50 (0-306-76021-5) Da Capo.

*Bel Canto Operas: A Guide to the Operas of Rossini, Bellini, & Donizetti. Charles Osborne. 378p. 1994. pap. 19.95 (0-931340-84-5, Amadeus Pr) Timber.

Bela Balazs: The Man & the Artist. Joseph Zsuffa. LC 85-8589. (Illus.). 604p. 1988. 55.00x (0-520-05545-4) U CA Pr.

Bela Banerjee, Bringing Health to India's Villages: Bringing Health to India's Villages. LaVonne G. Platt. LC 87-51688. (Illus.). xi, 178p. (Orig.). 1995. pap. 11.95 (0-945530-00-5) Wordsworth KS.

*Bela Bartok. Kenneth Chalmers. (20th Century Composers Ser.). (Illus.). 240p. (Orig.). (C). 1995. pap. 19.95 (0-7148-3164-6, Pub. by Phaidon Press UK) Chronicle Bks.

Bela Bartok. Emil Haraszti. 1988. reprint ed. lib. bdg. 75.00 (0-7812-0267-1) Rprt Serv.

Bela Bartok: An Analysis of His Music. Erno Lendvai. 1991. 16.95 (0-912483-33-4) Pro-Am Music.

*Bela Bartok: Composition, Concepts, & Autograph Sources. Laszlo Somfai. LC 95-6043. (Ernest Bloch Lectures: No. 9). 1996. write for info. (0-520-08485-3) U CA Pr.

Bela Bartok: His Life in Pictures & Documents. 2nd ed. Ferenc Bonis. Tr. by Lili Halay et al. (Illus.). 288p. 1989. reprint ed. 35.00 (0-912483-24-5) Pro-Am Music.

Bela Bartok: The Man & His Work. T. Talian. 281p. (C). 1988. 80.00 (0-569-22357-1, Pub. by Collets) St Mut.

Bela Bartok, a Complete Catalogue of His Published Works. LC 75-24263. (Illus.). 40p. 1970. pap. 10.50 (0-913932-37-X) Boosey & Hawkes.

*Bela Bartok's Folk Music Research in Turkey. A. A. Saygun. Ed. by L. Vikar. 430p. (C). 1976. 108.00x (963-05-0377-8, Pub. by Akad Kiado HU) St Mut.

Bela Juhos: Selected Papers. Ed. by Gerhard Frey. Tr. by Paul Foulkes. LC 76-17019. (Vienna Circle Collection Ser: No. 7). 1976. lib. bdg. 112.50 (90-277-0686-7); pap. text ed. 63.00 (90-277-0687-5) Kluwer Ac.

Bela Kalman Bibliographie. Zersammeugestellt Von Antol Kiss. (Arcadie Bibliographia Vixorum Exuditorom Ser.: Vol. 12). 100p. 1993. 24.00 (0-931922-49-6) Eurolingua.

Bela Kalmoni Bibliographie. Zvsammengestellt Von Antal Kiss. (Arcadie Bibliographia Vixorum Exuditorum Ser.: Fasc 12). 100p. 24.00 (0-685-70235-9) Eurolingua.

Bela Keredy: A Hungarian Odyssey. Andrew Kevey. LC 91-9826. (Illus.). 384p. (Orig.). 1991. pap. 11.95 (0-931832-83-7) Fithian Pr.

Belaia Gvardiia. Mikhail Bulgakov. Ed. by Ellendea Proffer. (Sobranie Sochineii Ser.: Vol. 4). 280p. (RUS.). 1989. lib. bdg. 25.00 (0-88233-992-3) Ardis Pubs.

Belarmino & Apolonio. Ramon Perez De Ayala. Tr. by Murray Baumgarten & Gabriel Berns. 1971. pap. 10.00 (0-520-04958-6) U CA Pr.

Belarus. Ed. by Lerner Geography Department Staff. (Then & Now Ser.). (Illus.). 64p. (YA). (gr. 5 up). 1993. lib. bdg. 21.50 (0-8225-2811-8, Lerner Publctns) Lerner Group.

Belarus: At the Crossroads in History. Jan Zaprudnik. LC 92-42923. (Series on the Post-Soviet Republics). 278p. 1993. text ed. 59.00 (0-8133-1339-2) Westview.

Belarus: At the Crossroads in History. Jan Zaprudnik. LC 92-42923. (Series on the Post-Soviet Republics). 278p. (C). 1993. pap. text ed. 19.95 (0-8133-1794-0) Westview.

Belarus: Economic Review. International Monetary Fund Staff. 76p. 1992. pap. 10.00 (1-55775-249-4) Intl Monetary.

*Belarus: U. S. Non Profit Aid. 70p. (Orig.). 1995. pap. 125.00 (0-7605-1536-0) Rector Pr.

Belarus IMF: Business Risk Overview. Ed. by Lewis B. Sckolnick. 125p. (Orig.). (C). 1994. pap. text ed. 125.00 (1-57205-668-1) Rector Pr.

Belarus Secret. John Loftus. Ed. by Nathan Miller. LC 82-48483. (Illus.). 196p. 1982. 18.95 (0-394-52292-3) Knopf.

Belarus, Ukraine, & Moldava. Kelvin Gosnell. LC 92-2241. (Former Soviet States Ser.). (Illus.). 32p. (J). (gr. 4-6). 1992. lib. bdg. 15.40 (1-56294-306-5) Millbrook Pr.

*Belated Bride. Charlotte Moore. (Romance Ser.). 1995. mass mkt. 2.99 (0-373-19088-3, 1-19088-3) Silhouette.

Belated Census of Earliest Settlers of Cape Girardeau County, Missouri. William J. Gammon. 70p. 6.75 (0-915156-18-0, 18) Natl Genealogical.

Belated Feudalism: Labor, the Law & Liberal Development in the United States. Karen Orren. 260p. (C). 1992. 59.95 (0-521-41039-8); pap. 17.95 (0-521-42254-X) Cambridge U Pr.

Belated Modernity & Aesthetic Culture: Inventing National Literature. Gregory Jusdanis. (Theory & History of Literature Ser.: Vol. 81). 208p. (C). 1991. text ed. 39.95 (0-8166-1980-8); pap. text ed. 14.95 (0-8166-1981-6) U of Minn Pr.

Belated Revenge. Robert M. Bird. (Works of Robert Montgomery Bird). 1989. reprint ed. lib. bdg. 79.00 (0-7812-1994-9) Rprt Serv.

Belated Travelers: Orientalism in the Age of Colonial Dissolution. Ali Behdad. (Post-Contemporary Interventions Ser.). (Illus.). 208p. 1994. lib. bdg. 44.95 (0-8223-1454-1); pap. text ed. 15.95 (0-8223-1471-1) Duke.

Belbin Team-Roles Package. Meredith Belbin. LC 94-65595. 72p. 1994. ring bd. 295.00 (0-88390-442-X) Pfeiffer & Co.

Belchamber. Howard O. Sturgis. LC 75-41266. reprint ed. 18.00 (0-404-14613-9) AMS Pr.

Belchamber Scandal. large type ed. Frances Murray. 448p. 1986. 15.95 (0-7089-1558-2) Ulverscroft.

Belcher Brothers & Co.'s Eighteen Sixty Price List of Boxwood & Ivory Rules. Ed. by Kenneth D. Roberts. (Illus.). 40p. 1982. reprint ed. pap. text ed. 5.00 (1-879335-06-9) Astragal Pr.

Belchite - South Bronx: A Trans-Cultural & Trans-Historical Landscape. Francesc Torres. Tr. by Simon Saad L' Hoeste. (Illus.). 160p. (ENG & SPA.). 1988. 25.00 (0-929597-00-1) UMass Univ Gallery.

Beldan's Fire. Midori Snyder. 384p. 1993. mass mkt. 4.99 (0-8125-0913-7) Tor Bks.

Belding H. Scribner Festschrift. Ed. by C. M. Kjellstrand. (Journal: Nephron: Vol. 33, No. 2). (Illus.). 96p. 1983. pap. 64.00 (3-8055-3675-5) S Karger.

Beldonald Holbein see Daisy Miller

Beleaguered City. Margaret Oliphant. (BCL1-PR English Literature Ser.). 267p. 1992. reprint ed. lib. bdg. 79.00 (0-7812-7610-1) Rprt Serv.

Beleaguered City. Margaret O. Oliphant. LC 79-98862. 267p. 1970. reprint ed. text ed. 55.00 (0-8371-3137-5, OLBC, Greenwood Pr) Greenwood.

Beleaguered City: Richmond, 1861-1865. Alfred H. Bill. LC 80-16702. (Illus.). xiv, 313p. 1980. reprint ed. text ed. 52.50 (0-313-22568-0, BIBE, Greenwood Pr) Greenwood.

*Beleaguered City: The Vicksburg Campaign, Dec. 1862-July 1863. Shelby Foote. LC 95-6789. Orig. Title: Originally Published as Part of Vol. 2 of the Civil War, a Narrative. 1995. write for info. (0-679-60170-8, Modern Lib) Random.

Beleaguered Presidency. Aaron Wildavsky. 325p. (C). 1991. 39.95 (0-88738-401-3) Transaction Pubs.

Beleaguered Presidency. Aaron Wildavsky. 325p. (C). 1994. pap. 21.95 (1-56000-754-0) Transaction Pubs.

Belehrung und Verkuendigung: Schriften zur deutschen Literatur vom Mittelalter bis zur Neuzeit. Friedrich-Wilhelm Wentzlaff-Eggebert. Ed. by Manfred Dick & Gerhard Kaiser. 344p. (C). 1975. 181.55 (3-11-005714-X) De Gruyter.

Belels Images? La Femmer Rompue, Baeuvoir: Critical Monographs in English. Terry Keefe. 88p. 1993. pap. 32.00 (0-85261-269-9, Pub. by Univ of Glasgow UK) St Mut.

Belfast. Jonathan Bardon. 1983. 40.00 (0-85640-272-9) Dufour.

Belfast: An Illustrated History. Jonathan Bardon. (Illus.). 322p. 1982. 34.00 (0-685-25869-6, Pub. by Blackstaff Pr IE) Dufour.

Belfast: From Loyalty to Rebellion. Goldring. (C). 1991. pap. 17.50 (0-85315-728-6, Pub. by Lawrence & Wishart UK) Humanities.

Belfast: Portraits of a City. Robert Johnstone. (Illus.). 166p. 1991. 39.95 (0-7126-3744-3, Pub. by Barrie & Jenkins) Trafalgar.

Belfast: The Making of the City. J. C. Beckett et al. (Illus.). 192p. 1988. pap. 17.95 (0-86281-119-8, Pub. by Appletree Pr IE) Irish Bks Media.

Belfast-Beirut: A Tale of Two Cities. Alternative Museum Staff. LC 89-82083. (Illus.). (Orig.). (C). 1990. pap. 8.00 (0-932075-28-2) Alternative Mus.

Belfast Confetti. Ciaran Carson. LC 89-40527. 100p. 1989. 13.95 (0-916390-41-1); pap. 8.95 (0-916390-40-3) Wake Forest.

Belfast Cookery Book. Margaret Bates. 222p. 1967. reprint ed. pap. 124.00 (0-08-018952-0, Pub. by Pergamon Repr UK) Franklin.

Belfast Diary: War as a Way of Life. John Conroy. LC 87-47539. 218p. 1987. pap. 12.95 (0-8070-0205-4) Beacon Pr.

*Belfast Diary: War As a Way of Life. John Conroy. LC 94-41937. 240p. 1995. pap. 12.00 (0-8070-0217-8) Beacon Pr.

Belfast English & Standard English: Dialect Variation & Parameter Setting. Alison Henry. 160p. 1995. 49.95 (0-19-508291-5); pap. 24.95 (0-19-508292-3) OUP.

Belfast in the Thirties: An Oral History. Ronnie Munck & Bill Rolston. LC 85-18395. 256p. 1987. text ed. 39.95 (0-312-07424-7) St Martin.

Belfast Lough to Crinan & Islay. Imray Laurie Norie & Wilson Ltd. Staff. (C). 1989. text ed. 70.00 (0-685-40203-7, Pub. by Imray Laurie Norie & Wilson UK) St Mut.

Belfast Stories. Sam McAughtry. 157p. 1993. pap. 10.95 (0-85640-520-5, Pub. by Blackstaff Pr IE) Dufour.

Belfast Woman. Mary Beckett. 112p. 1980. pap. 8.95 (0-905169-85-9, Pub. by Poolbeg Pr IE) Dufour.

*Belfer Bar Mitzvah. Gloria T. Pushker. (Illus.). 32p. (J). (gr. 3-5). 1995. 14.95 (1-56554-095-6) Pelican.

An Asterisk (*) at the beginning of an entry indicates that the title is appearing in BIP for the first time.

An Asterisk (*) at the beginning of an entry indicates that the title is appearing in BIP for the first time.

Believer As Citizen: John Courtney Murray in a New Context. Thomas Hughson. LC 93-4655. (Isaac Hecker Studies in Religion & American Culture). 208p. 1993. pap. 14.95 (*0-8091-3412-8*) Paulist Pr.

Believer in Exile. Spong. Date not set. 18.00 (*0-06-067532-2*, HarpT) HarpC.

Believers. Rebecca C. Jones. 144p. (YA). (gr. 6 up). 1989. 13.95 (*1-55970-035-1*) Arcade Pub Inc.

Believers. Intro. by Al Young. 234p. (Orig.). (C). 1993. pap. 8.95 (*0-933277-07-5*) Ploughshares.

Believers. Janice H. Giles. LC 88-27901. 232p. 1989. reprint ed. pap. 15.00 (*0-8131-0189-1*) U Pr of Ky.

Believers: Spiritual Leaders of the World. Elizabeth Goldman. (Profiles Ser.). (Illus.). 240p. (J). (gr. 4 up). 1995. lib. bdg. 30.00 (*0-19-508240-0*) OUP.

Believer's Absolute Surrender. Andrew Murray. LC 85-447. 150p. 1985. pap. 5.99 (*0-87123-827-6*) Bethany Hse.

Believer's Armor. John MacArthur, Jr. (John MacArthur's Bible Studies). 1986. pap. 6.99 (*0-8024-5092-X*) Moody.

Believer's Authority. 2nd ed. Kenneth E. Hagin. 1985. pap. 3.95 (*0-89276-406-6*) Hagin Ministries.

Believer's Baptism for Children of the Church. Marlin Jeschke. LC 82-23406. 160p. (Orig.). 1983. pap. 7.95 (*0-8361-3318-8*) Herald Pr.

Believer's Bible Commentary New Testament. Ed. by William MacDonald & Arthur Farstad. 1205p. 1989. 24.95 (*0-945681-00-3*) A & O Pr.

Believer's Call to Commitment. Andrew Murray. LC 83-3819. 101p. 1983. reprint ed. pap. 5.99 (*0-87123-289-8*) Bethany Hse.

Believers' Church. Donald F. Durnbaugh. LC 85-7599. 328p. (Orig.). 1985. reprint ed. pap. 15.95 (*0-8361-1271-7*) Herald Pr.

Believer's Daily Renewal. Andrew Murray. LC 81-6143. 125p. 1981. pap. 5.99 (*0-87123-147-6*) Bethany Hse.

Believer's First Bible Course. William W. Orr. (Basic Bible Ser.). 48p. reprint ed. pap. 3.50 (*0-944412-00-9*) Glad Tid.

***Believer's Foundation Study Guide.** Patricia Williams. Ed. by Dewilda M. Williams. 50p. (Orig.). 1995. pap. 7.95 (*1-886493-02-2*) NBC Study Pub.

Believer's Full Blessing of Pentecost. Andrew Murray. LC 84-12301. 112p. 1984. reprint ed. pap. 5.99 (*0-87123-597-8*) Bethany Hse.

Believer's Guide to Hebrews. Jerry Vines. LC 93-22331. (Orig.). 1993. pap. 14.99 (*0-87213-896-8*) Loizeaux.

Believer's Guide to Spiritual Warfare: Wising Up to Satan's Influence in Your World. Thomas B. White. 200p. (Orig.). 1990. pap. 8.99 (*0-89283-680-6*, Vine Bks) Servant.

Believer's Guide to Worship. Chris Bowater. (Orig.). 1993. pap. 13.95 (*0-85476-351-1*) Trans-Atl Phila.

Believer's Handbook. Gerard Berghoef & Lester DeKoster. LC 82-72686. 295p. 1982. 18.95 (*0-934874-03-4*); pap. 12.95 (*0-934874-05-0*) Chr Lib Pr.

Believers in America: Poems about Americans of Asian & Pacific Island Descent. Steve Izuki. LC 94-5081. (Many Voices, One Song Ser.). (Illus.). 48p. (J). (gr. 3-6). 1994. lib. bdg. 15.45 (*0-516-05152-0*); pap. 7.95 (*0-516-45152-9*) Childrens.

Believer's New Covenant. Andrew Murray. LC 83-21408. 128p. 1983. reprint ed. pap. 5.99 (*0-87123-406-8*) Bethany Hse.

Believer's New Life. Andrew Murray. LC 83-3006. 208p. 1984. pap. 6.99 (*0-87123-431-9*) Bethany Hse.

Believers of Beguilers: Old Testament Women. Sara Buswell. 1993. pap. 4.99 (*0-8010-1046-2*) Baker Bk.

***Believer's Prayer Life.** Andrew Murray. Tr. by CRM Staff. 187p. (CHI.). 1991. pap. 5.00 (*1-56582-033-9*) Christ Renew Min.

Believer's Prayer Life. rev. ed. Andrew Murray. LC 83-12254. (Andrew Murray Prayer Library). 141p. 1983. pap. 5.99 (*0-87123-277-4*) Bethany Hse.

Believer's Road: A Journey Through Luke. Bruce Van Blair. 310p. 1990. pap. 15.00 (*0-685-29068-9*) Mercer Isl Ch Christ.

Believers School of Healing Study Guide. Jason Guerrero. 125p. Date not set. pap. text ed. write for info. (*0-940487-12-8*) Jubilee CA.

Believer's School of Prayer. rev. ed. Andrew Murray. LC 82-4401. 201p. 1982. pap. 6.99 (*0-87123-195-6*) Bethany Hse.

Believer's Secret of a Perfect Heart. Andrew Murray. LC 83-22490. 176p. 1984. reprint ed. pap. 5.99 (*0-87123-425-4*) Bethany Hse.

Believer's Secret of Christian Love. Andrew Murray & Jonathan Edwards. Ed. by L. G. Parkhurst, Jr. 144p. (Orig.). 1990. pap. 5.99 (*1-55661-129-3*) Bethany Hse.

Believer's Secret of Holiness. Andrew Murray. LC 84-2973. 208p. 1984. reprint ed. pap. 6.99 (*0-87123-432-7*) Bethany Hse.

Believer's Secret of Intercession. Andrew Murray & Charles Spurgeon. Ed. by L. G. Parkhurst. LC 87-34145. 160p. (Orig.). (C). 1988. pap. 5.99 (*0-87123-992-2*) Bethany Hse.

Believer's Secret of Living Like Christ. Andrew Murray. LC 85-26683. 176p. (Orig.). 1985. pap. 6.99 (*0-87123-445-9*) Bethany Hse.

Believer's Secret of Obedience. Andrew Murray. LC 82-14603. (Andrew Murray Christian Maturity Library). 88p. 1982. reprint ed. pap. 5.99 (*0-87123-279-0*) Bethany Hse.

Believer's Secret of Spiritual Power. rev. ed. Andrew Murray & Charles G. Finney. Ed. by L. G. Parkhurst. LC 87-16838. 160p. 1987. pap. 5.99 (*0-87123-983-3*) Bethany Hse.

Believer's Secret of the Abiding Presence. rev. ed. Andrew Murray et al. LC 86-28307. (Andrew Murray Devotional Library). 144p. 1987. pap. 5.99 (*0-87123-899-3*) Bethany Hse.

Believer's Secret of the Master's Indwelling. rev. ed. Andrew Murray. LC 86-6814. 192p. 1986. pap. 6.99 (*0-87123-653-2*, 210653) Bethany Hse.

Believer's Secret of Waiting on God. Andrew Murray. LC 85-32068. 169p. 1986. pap. 5.99 (*0-87123-886-1*) Bethany Hse.

Believer's Security: Conditional or Unconditional? Daniel D. Corner. (Illus.). 128p. (Orig.). 1994. pap. 8.95 (*0-9639076-5-4*) Reed & Witting.

Believers' Topical Bible. Derwin B. Stewart. 560p. 1990. KJV. 18.95 (*1-56229-100-9*); New International Version. 18.95 (*1-56229-101-7*); Spanish RVR. 14.95 (*1-56229-102-5*) Pneuma Life Pub.

Believer's Tree of Life. Albert J. Wahlie. Ed. by Shmuel Ben Menachem. (Illus.). 105p. (Orig.). 1986. pap. 6.95 (*0-9616488-0-5*) Alef Bet Comns.

***Believer's Way of Life Vol. 2: Selections of Bible Readings for Daily Devotions.** Comp. by Melvin J. Loewen. xviii, 365p. 1994. pap. 9.95 (*0-9640876-1-8*) Heritageclassics.

Believing: Understanding the Creed. Gerald O'Collins et al. 1991. pap. 8.95 (*0-8091-3282-6*) Paulist Pr.

Believing Bible Study. 2nd ed. Edward F. Hills. (Illus.). 258p. 1991. reprint ed. pap. 14.95 (*0-915923-01-7*) Christian Res Pr.

Believing Christ: The Parable of the Bicycle & Other Good News. Stephen E. Robinson. LC 92-20924. 131p. 1992. 11.95 (*0-87579-634-6*) Deseret Bk.

Believing Everything: An Anthology of New Writing. Kate Green et al. Ed. by Mary Logue & Laurence Sutin. LC 79-91217. (Illus.). 160p. (Orig.). 1980. pap. 4.95 (*0-930100-06-9*) Holy Cow.

Believing Heart. Bruce C. Hafen. LC 90-43781. 126p. 1990. reprint ed. 10.95 (*0-87579-419-X*) Deseret Bk.

Believing Humanism: My Testament, 1902-1965. 2nd ed. Martin Buber. LC 90-32330. 264p. (C). 1990. pap. 15.00 (*0-391-03654-8*) Humanities.

***Believing in Democracy: Philadelphia II.** Don Kemner. 275p. (Orig.). 1995. pap. 14.95 (*0-9644031-0-2*) One World CA.

Believing in God: A Philosophical Essay. Gareth Moore. 300p. 1989. 37.95 (*0-567-09498-7*, Pub. by T & T Clark UK) Bks Intl VA.

Believing in God: Statements on Faith & Reason. Ed L. Miller. LC 92-41719. (Illus.). 220p. (Orig.). (C). 1997. pap. write for info. (*0-02-381192-7*) Macmillan.

***Believing in Jesus: A Popular Overview of the Catholic Faith.** 3rd ed. Leonard Foley. 232p. (Orig.). 1994. 6.95 (*0-86716-217-1*) St Anthony Mess Pr.

Believing in Miracles: (Mr. Right, Inc., under the Mistletoe) Linda Varner. (Sil Romance Ser.). 1994. pap. 2.75 (*0-373-19051-4*, 1-19051-1) Silhouette.

Believing in Myself: Self-Esteem: Daily Meditations. Earnie Larsen & Carol L. Hegarty. 384p. 1991. pap. 9.00 (*0-671-76616-3*, Fireside) S&S Trade.

Believing in Ourselves: The Wisdom of Women. (Illus.). 80p. 1992. 4.95 (*0-8362-3015-9*) Andrews & McMeel.

***Believing in the Future: Toward a Missiology of Western Culture.** David J. Bosch. Ed. by Alan Neely et al. LC 95-16093. (Christian Mission & Modern Culture Ser.). 60p. (Orig.). 1995. pap. 7.00 (*1-56338-117-6*) TPI PA.

Believing in the Wind. Mark Raney. 235p. 1981. 10.00 (*0-933272-02-2*) Hurricane Co.

Believing in Yourself, Reading Level 2. Elaine Goley. (Learn the Value Ser.: Set II). (Illus.). 32p. (J). (gr. 1-4). 1989. 11.95 (*0-685-58777-0*); lib. bdg. 15.94 (*0-86592-398-1*) Rourke Corp.

***Believing Is Seeing: Attitudes & Assumptions That Affect Learning about Development.** Carrol Joy. 64p. (C). 1990. pap. 8.00 (*0-614-02988-0*) Amer Forum.

Believing Is Seeing: Creating the Culture of Art. Mary A. Staniszewski. LC 94-1449. 320p. 1995. 14.95 (*0-14-016824-9*, Penguin Bks) Viking Penguin.

Believing Jew: The Selected Writings. Milton Steinberg. LC 76-152215. (Essay Index Reprint Ser.). 1977. reprint ed. 20.95 (*0-8369-2256-5*) Ayer.

Believing Our Beliefs: Preaching on the Foundations & Evidence for New Life. Stephen F. Olford. (Stephen Olford Biblical Preaching Library). 112p. 1991. pap. 6.99 (*0-8010-6720-0*) Baker Bk.

Believing Skeptics: American Political Intellectuals, 1945-1964. Robert B. Fowler. LC 77-87967. (Contributions in Political Science Ser.: No. 5). 317p. 1978. text ed. 59.95 (*0-313-20026-2*, FAP/, Greenwood Pr) Greenwood.

***Believing Sophie.** Hazel J. Hutchins. LC 95-3124. (Illus.). (J). 1995. write for info. (*0-8075-0625-7*) A Whitman.

***Believing the Articles of Faith.** Elaine Cannon. 1994. pap. write for info. (*0-88494-958-3*) Bookcraft Inc.

Believing the Bible. David Winter. LC 82-62582. 116p. (Orig.). 1983. reprint ed. pap. 5.95 (*0-8192-1325-X*) Morehouse Pub.

Believing the Truth. Anne De Graaf. (Illus.). 32p. (J). 1989. 4.95 (*0-310-52770-8*) Zondervan.

Believing Three Ways in One God: A Reading of the Apostles' Creed. Nicholas Lash. LC 92-33909. (C). 1993. text ed. 21.95 (*0-268-00691-1*) U of Notre Dame Pr.

Believing Three Ways in One God: A Reading of the Apostles' Creed. Nicholas Lash. LC 92-33903. (C). 1993. pap. text ed. 12.95 (*0-268-00692-X*) U of Notre Dame Pr.

Believing Today: Jew & Christian in Conversation. Leon Klenicki & Richard J. Neuhaus. LC 88-13934. 116p. reprint ed. pap. 33.10 (*0-7837-0518-2*, 2040842) Bks Demand.

Believing Truth about the Church. Harold Cooper. (Illus.). 80p. (J). (gr. 8-9). 1975. P. 64. teacher ed 1.50 (*0-89114-071-9*); pap. 3.50 (*0-89114-070-0*) Baptist Pub Hse.

Belinda. Pamela Allen. (Illus.). 32p. (J). (ps-3). 1993. 13.99 (*0-670-84372-5*) Viking Child Bks.

Belinda. Maria Edgeworth. Ed. by Eilean Ni Chuilleanain. 512p. 1993. pap. 9.95 (*0-460-87228-1*, Everyman's Classic Lib) C E Tuttle.

Belinda. Maria Edgeworth. LC 93-42825. (World's Classics Ser.). 484p. 1994. pap. 11.95 (*0-19-283123-2*) OUP.

Belinda. Anne Rice. Ed. by Anne Rampling. 512p. 1988. pap. text ed. 6.99 (*0-515-09355-6*) Jove Pubns.

Belinda: A Novel. Rhoda Broughton. LC 78-108463. 460p. 1884. 39.00 (*0-403-00448-9*) Scholarly.

Belinda Goes to Bath. large type ed. Marion Chesney. 232p. 1992. pap. 14.95 (*0-8161-5375-2*, Nightingale) Hall.

Belinda, or, the Rivals. A. S. Holmes. (Found Bks.: No. 2). 122p. (Orig.). 1975. pap. 4.95 (*0-88784-333-6*, Pub. by Hse of Anansi Pr CN) Genl Dist Srvs.

Belinda's Bouquet. Leslea Newman. (Illus.). 24p. (J). (gr. k-3). 1991. 6.95 (*1-55583-154-0*) Alyson Pubns.

Belinda's Hurricane. Elizabeth Winthrop. LC 84-8028. (Illus.). 64p. (J). (gr. 1-4). 1984. 10.95 (*0-525-44106-9*, DCB) Dutton Child Bks.

Belinskij & Russian Literary Criticism: The Heritage of Organic Aesthetics. Victor Terras. LC 73-2050. 316p. 1974. 40.00 (*0-299-06350-X*) U of Wis Pr.

Belizaire the Cajun. Glen Pitre. Ed. by Dean Shapiro. LC 88-9820. 1988. 13.95 (*0-88289-711-X*); pap. 7.95 (*0-88289-671-7*) Pelican.

Belize. (Insight Guide Ser.). (Illus.). 350p. 1994. pap. 21.95 (*0-395-71053-7*) HM.

***Belize.** Alex Bradbury. (Bradt Guides Ser.). (Illus.). 200p. 1994. 15.95 (*1-56440-532-X*) Globe Pequot.

***Belize.** Carlos Miller. 450p. Date not set. pap. 12.95 (*0-7610-0223-5*) NW Pub.

Belize. 2nd ed. Peggy Wright. (World Bibliographical Ser.). 1994. lib. bdg. 75.00 (*1-85109-132-7*) ABC-CLIO.

Belize: A Natural Destination. Richard Mahler & Steele Wotkyns. 288p. (Orig.). 1991. pap. 16.95 (*1-56261-011-2*) John Muir.

Belize: A Natural Destination. 2nd ed. Richard Mahler & Steele Wotkyns. LC 93-22122. (Natural Destination Ser.). (Illus.). 304p. (Orig.). 1993. pap. 16.95 (*1-56261-141-0*) John Muir.

Belize: Case Study for Democracy in Central America. Julio A. Fernandez. 120p. 1989. text ed. 55.95 (*0-566-05721-2*, Pub. by Dartmth Pub UK) Ashgate Pub Co.

Belize: Consolidated Index of Statutes & Subsidiary Legislation. Ed. by C. J. Hammett. (West Indian Legislation Indexing Project Ser.). vii, 82p. (Orig.). 1991. pap. text ed. 25.00 (*0-685-14453-4*, Pub. by UWI Fac Law BB) W W Gaunt.

Belize: The Uncut Gem. Ed. by Judith H. Eckert. (Illus.). 128p. 1989. write for info. (*0-318-63769-3*) Worldwide Images.

Belize Guide. 6th rev. ed. Paul Glassman. (Passport Press Travel Guides Ser.). 320p. 1993. pap. 13.95 (*1-883323-04-5*) Open Rd Pub.

Belize Guide: Description & Travel. 5th ed. Paul Glassman. LC 90-91877. (Illus.). 288p. 1992. pap. 12.95 (*0-930016-15-7*) Passport Pr.

Belize Handbook. 2nd ed. Chicki Mallan. LC 92-21235. 263p. (Orig.). 1993. pap. 13.95 (*0-918373-95-6*) Moon Pubns CA.

***Belize Handbook.** 3rd ed. Chicki Mallan. (Moon Travel Handbooks Ser.). (Illus.). 268p. (Orig.). 1995. pap. 14.95 (*1-56691-030-7*) Moon Pubns CA.

Belize-Land by the Carib Sea. Sadie Schrock. (J). (gr. 3). 1991. 2.95 (*0-87813-539-1*) Christian Light.

Belize Retirement Guide: How to Live in a Tropical Paradise on 350 Dollars a Month. 2nd ed. Bill Gray & Claire Gray. (Illus.). 1992. pap. 14.95 (*1-880862-45-X*) Preview Pub.

Belize Retirement Guide: How to Live in a Tropical Paradise on 350 Dollars a Month. 3rd rev. ed. Bill Gray & Claire Gray. (Illus.). 144p. 1995. pap. 19.95 (*1-880862-46-8*, 0782181) Preview Pub.

***Belize Tax Law.** 150p. (C). 1994. pap. 295.00 (*0-7605-0081-9*) Rector Pr.

Belizean Rain Forest: The Community Baboon Sanctuary. 2nd ed. Robert H. Horwich & Jonathan Lyon. (Illus.). 420p. Date not set. pap. 14.95 (*0-9637982-0-0*) Orang-Utan Pr.

Bell. Iris Murdoch. 342p. 1987. pap. 10.95 (*0-14-001688-0*, Penguin Bks) Viking Penguin.

Bell: Alexander Graham Bell & the Conquest of Solitude. Robert V. Bruce. LC 89-22951. (Illus.). 576p. 1990. 47.50 (*0-8014-2419-4*); pap. 17.95 (*0-8014-9691-8*) Cornell U Pr.

Bell AH-1 Cobra. Mike Verier. (Osprey Air Combat Ser.). (Illus.). 200p. 1990. pap. 14.98 (*0-85045-934-6*, Pub. by Osprey Pubng Ltd UK) Motorbooks Intl.

Bell Aircraft since Nineteen Thirty-Five. A. J. Pelletier. (Putnam Aviation Ser.). (Illus.). 288p. 1992. 47.95 (*1-55750-056-8*) Naval Inst Pr.

Bell & Baldwin, Their Development of Aerodomes & Hydrodomes at Baddeck, Nova Scotia. John H. Parkin. LC 65-1207. 619p. reprint ed. pap. 176.50 (*0-8357-7122-9*, 2014333) Bks Demand.

Bell & the Drum: Shih Ching as Formulaic Poetry in an Oral Tradition. Shan Yeh. LC 73-76104. (Illus.). 165p. reprint ed. pap. 47.10 (*0-8357-7123-7*, 2029069) Bks Demand.

Bell & Us. Patrick Comiskey. 64p. (Orig.). 1988. pap. 7.00 (*0-945926-02-2*) Paradigm RI.

Bell & Us. deluxe ed. Patrick Comiskey. 64p. (Orig.). 1988. pap. 12.00 (*0-945926-03-0*) Paradigm RI.

Bell Antonio. Vitaliano Brancati. 1256p. 1994. pap. 13.00 (*0-00-271327-6*, Pub. by HarpC UK) HarpC.

Bell, Book & Candle. John Van Druten. 1951. pap. 4.75 (*0-8222-0104-6*) Dramatists Play.

Bell Branch. large type ed. Lucy Walker. 448p. 1983. 15.95 (*0-7089-1050-5*) Ulverscroft.

Bell Buckle Years. Charlotte Barr. LC 92-12352. 1992. pap. 8.95 (*0-918518-93-8*) Iris Pr.

***Bell County, Kentucky.** Turner Publishing Company Staff. LC 93-61859. 360p. 1994. 48.00 (*1-56311-128-4*) Turner Pub KY.

Bell Curve: The Reshaping of American Life by Differences in Intelligence. Richard J. Herrnstein & Charles Murray. 1994. 30.00 (*0-02-914673-9*) Free Pr.

***Bell Curve Debate: History, Documents, Opinions.** Russell Jacoby & Glauberman. 1995. pap. 15.00 (*0-8129-2587-4*, Times Bks) Random.

***Bell Curve Wars: Race, Intelligence & the Future of America.** Ed. by Steven Fraser. LC 95-1880. 176p. 1995. pap. 10.00 (*0-465-00693-0*) Basic.

***Bell Curve Wars: Race, Intelligence, & the Future of America.** Ed. by Steven Fraser. 1995. 25.00 (*0-465-00692-2*) Basic.

Bell Eight. Rick Lyon. (New Poets of America Ser.). 1994. pap. 12.50 (*1-880238-09-8*) BOA Edns.

Bell for Adano. John R. Hersey. 1944. 22.95 (*0-394-41660-0*) Knopf.

Bell for Adano. large type ed. John Hersey. LC 91-28615. 386p. 1991. lib. bdg. 19.95 (*1-56054-266-7*) Thorndike Pr.

Bell for Adano. John Hersey. LC 87-45943. 300p. 1991. reprint ed. lib. bdg. 22.95 (*0-89966-845-3*) Buccaneer Bks.

Bell for Adano. John Hersey. LC 87-45943. 288p. 1988. reprint ed. pap. 11.00 (*0-394-75695-9*, Vin) Random.

Bell in the Fog & Other Stories. Gertrude Atherton. 1972. reprint ed. 28.00 (*0-8422-8003-0*) Irvington.

Bell Jar. Sylvia Plath. 224p. 1983. mass mkt. 5.99 (*0-553-27835-5*, Bantam Classics) Bantam.

Bell Jar. Sylvia Plath. 300p. 1991. reprint ed. lib. bdg. 25.95 (*0-89966-815-1*) Buccaneer Bks.

Bell Jar: A Novel of the Fifties. Linda Wagner-Martin. 128p. 1992. pap. 12.95 (*0-8057-8561-2*, Twayne) Macmillan.

Bell Jar Notes. Jean Inness. 78p. (Orig.). (C). 1984. pap. 4.50 (*0-8220-0226-4*) Cliffs.

***Bell Keeper: The Story of Sophia & the Massacre of the Indians at Gnadenhutten, Ohio, in 1781.** Marilyn W. Seguin. Ed. by Adolpho Caso. (Illus.). 76p. (Orig.). (J). (gr. 3-9). 1995. pap. 12.95 (*0-8283-2009-8*) Branden Pub Co.

Bell Notes. Arthur M. Young. (Illus.). 205p. 1984. reprint ed. pap. 10.95 (*0-9609850-4-2*) Rob Briggs.

Bell of Africa. W. D. Bell. (Illus.). 236p. 1960. 35.00 (*0-87556-135-7*) Saifer.

Bell of Africa. W. D. Bell. (Illus.). 236p. 1989. 24.95 (*0-940143-26-7*) Safari Pr.

Bell of St. Patrick Called the Clog an Edachta. William Reeves. 1991. reprint ed. pap. 5.95 (*0-89979-055-0*) British Am Bks.

Bell of Time. Charles Angoff. 1966. 4.00 (*0-87141-018-4*) Manyland.

Bell Operating Companies Exchange Service Telephone Rates. 509p. 1994. ring bd. 47.50 (*0-317-01647-4*) NARUC.

Bell Operating Companies' Long Distance Message Telephone Rates. 306p. 1994. 30.00 (*0-317-01613-X*) NARUC.

Bell or a Hook. Peter Fortunato. LC 77-22186. 45p. 1977. 3.50 (*0-87886-087-8*, Greenfld Rev Pr) Greenfld Rev Lit.

Bell P-63 Kingcobra. (Illus.). 52p. 1974. pap. 9.25 (*0-87994-036-0*) Aviat Pub.

Bell Pull Finishing. Mary-Dick Digges. (Illus.). 32p. (Orig.). 1988. pap. 9.95 (*0-929339-01-0*) Embroidery Research Pr Inc.

Bell Ranch: Cattle Ranching in the Southwest, 1824-1947. David Remley. LC 92-23474. (Illus.). 409p. 1993. 42.50x (*0-8263-1399-X*) U of NM Pr.

***Bell Rang in Uniontown: The First Hundred Years of Aracta & Its Methodist Church, 1850-1950.** Gayle Karshner. LC 94-30765. 1994. write for info. (*0-89865-915-9*) Donning Co.

Bell Ringer & Other Stories. Abelardo S. Albis. 103p. (Orig.). (C). 1982. pap. 5.75 (*0-686-37572-6*, Pub. by New Day Pub PH) Cellar.

Bell-Ringer of Angel's Etc. Bret Harte. LC 72-12500. (Short Story Index Reprint Ser.). 1977. reprint ed. 29.95 (*0-8369-4236-1*) Ayer.

Bell Rings at Four: A Black Teacher's Chronicle of Change. Dorothy R. Robinson. LC 78-61472. (Illus.). 1979. 15.50 (*0-89052-024-0*) Madrona Pr.

***Bell Sports Corporation Report.** 60p. (Orig.). 1995. pap. 295.00 (*0-7605-2101-8*) Rector Pr.

Bell System & Regional Business: The Telephone in the South, 1877-1920. Kenneth Lipartito. LC 89-32037. (AT&T Series in Telephone History). (Illus.). 304p. 1989. text ed. 42.50x (*0-8018-3797-9*) Johns Hopkins.

Bell Telephone: The Deposition of Alexander Graham Bell in the Suit Brought by the United States to Annul the Bell Patents. Alexander G. Bell. LC 74-4665. (Telecommunications Ser.). (Illus.). 480p. 1974. reprint ed. 36.95 (*0-405-06032-7*) Ayer.

Bell Tidings. Dorothy M. Anthony. (Illus.). 52p. 1987. 9.95 (*0-9607944-4-1*) D M Anthony.

Bell Tolls at Mousehaven Manor. Mary D. Kwitz. (J). (gr. 4-7). 1993. pap. 3.25 (*0-590-43841-7*) Scholastic Inc.

Bell-Tower see Piazza Tales

Bell X-15 (NASA) (Illus.). 1974. pap. 3.00 (*0-87994-003-4*) Aviat Pub.

Bella: Collection Diamant. Jean Giraudoux. (FRE.). 1959. 11.95 (*0-8288-9796-4*, F103940) Fr & Eur.

***Bella Addormentata Nel Bosco.** Tr. by DigiPro Staff. (Comes to Life Bks.). 16p. (ITA.). (J). (ps-2). 1994. write for info. (*1-883366-98-4*) YES Ent.

An Asterisk (*) at the beginning of an entry indicates that the title is appearing in BIP for the first time.

Bella Arabella. Liza Fosburgh. LC 85-42809. (Illus.). 112p. (J). (gr. 4-7). 1986. text ed. 13.95 (*0-02-735430-X*, Four Winds Pr) S&S Childrens.

Bella Bella Tales. Ed. by Franz Boas. LC 34-11630. (American Folklore Society Memoirs Ser.: Vol. 25). 1972. reprint ed. 25.00 (*0-527-01077-4*) Periodicals Srv.

Bella Bella Texts. Franz Boas. (Columbia University. Contributions to Anthropology Ser.: No. 5). reprint ed. 32.50 (*0-404-50555-4*) AMS Pr.

Bella B.'s Fantasy & Other Stories. Raymond Jean. Ed. by Richard Mandell. Tr. by Juliette Dickstein. LC 86-80690. Orig. Title: Un Fantasme de Bella B. et Autres Recits. 144p. (Orig.). 1987. pap. 6.00 (*0-9605008-3-9*) Hermes Hse.

Bella Coola Indians, Vols. 1 & 2. 2nd ed. T. F. McIlwraith. 1536p. 1992. 125.00 (*0-8020-2820-9*); pap. 60.00 (*0-8020-7692-0*) U of Toronto Pr.

***Bella Durmiente.** (Illus.). (SPA.). (J). 1995. pap. 2.95 (*0-486-28192-2*) Dover.

***Bella Durmiente.** Tr. by DigiPro Staff. (Comes to Life Bks.). 16p. (SPA.). (J). (ps-2). 1994. write for info. (*1-57234-010-X*) YES Ent.

Bella Europa. Pietro Attinasi. 71p. 1989. pap. 10.00 (*0-89304-516-0*) Cross-Cultrl NY.

***Bella Europa.** Pietro Attinasi. 71p. 1989. 20.00 (*0-89304-517-9*) Cross-Cultrl NY.

Bella Figura: A Choice. Ed. by Rose Romano. 192p. (Orig.). 1993. pap. 8.95 (*1-883112-00-1*) Malafemmina.

Bella Malmaridada. Lope De Vega. Ed. by Donald McGrady et al. 206p. 1986. pap. 32.00 (*84-599-1505-0*) Biblio Siglo.

Bella Pittura: The Art of the Gandolfi. Ed. by Mimi Cazort. 80p. 1993. pap. 24.95 (*0-88884-629-0*, Pub. by Natl Gallery CN) U Ch Pr.

Bella Vista: Avec: Trois, Six, Neuf. Sidonie-Gabrielle Colette. (FRE.). 1974. pap. 11.95 (*0-8288-9137-0*, M3321) Fr & Eur.

***Bella y la Bestia - Beauty & the Beast.** (Spanish Classics Ser.). 96p. (J). 1992. 6.98 (*1-57082-054-6*) Mouse Works.

Bella y la Bestia (Beauty & the Beast) Walt Disney Staff. (Penguin-Disney Ser.). (SPA.). (J). (ps-3). 1992. 6.98 (*0-453-03016-5*) Viking Penguin.

Belladonna. Michael Stewart. 1993. mass mkt. 5.50 (*0-06-109065-4*, Harp PBks) HarpC.

Bellagio Meeting on Vitamin A Deficiency & Childhood Mortality: Proceedings of "Public Health Significance of Vitamin A Deficiency & Its Control" Keith P. West, Jr. LC 93-10308. (Illus.). 74p. (Orig.). 1993. pap. 14.50 (*0-915173-21-2*) Helen Keller Intl.

Bellaire Guide to Controlling TV Commercial Cost. 2nd ed. Arthur Bellaire. LC 82-72510. 160p. 1982. 34.95 (*0-8442-3075-8*, Crain Bks) NTC Pub Grp.

Bellairs Collection. Leonard Harrow. 39.95 (*0-905906-53-5*, Pub. by Scorpion Pub UK) Interlink Pub.

Bellamy Solution: The Way Out. T. M. Anthony. 141p. (Orig.). 1982. pap. 5.95 (*0-88286-153-0*) C H Kerr.

Bellanca C. F. The Emergence of the Cabin Monoplane in the United States. Jay P. Spenser. LC 81-607557. (Famous Aircraft of the National Air & Space Museum Ser.: No. 6). (Illus.). 96p. 1982. pap. 12.95 (*0-87474-881-X*, SPEBP) Smithsonian.

Bellbird in a Flame Tree: The Twelve Days of Christmas. Kilmeny Niland. LC 90-25869. 32p. (J). (ps-3). 1991. 12.95 (*0-688-10797-4*, Tambourine Bks); lib. bdg. 12.88 (*0-688-10798-2*, Tambourine Bks) Morrow.

Bellbirds Calling. large type ed. Anthea Edgcome. (Linford Romance Library). 1991. pap. 13.95 (*0-7089-7098-2*) Ulverscroft.

Bellboy: A Muletrain Journey. Margaret S. McClain. LC 89-61681. (Illus.). 154p. (J). (gr. 5 up). 1990. 14.95 (*0-9622468-1-6*) NM Pub Co.

Bellcore Technical Work Efforts. 89p. 1992. 25.00 (*0-317-05190-3*) NARUC.

Belle Americaine. Barbara Keller. 1990. mass mkt. 4.50 (*0-06-100094-9*, Harp PBks) HarpC.

***Belle au Bois Dormant.** Tr. by DigiPro Staff. (Comes to Life Bks.). 16p. (FRE.). (J). (ps-2). 1994. write for info. (*1-883366-68-2*) YES Ent.

Belle Bachem: The Complete Work, 1935-1986. Ulrike Gartner. 412p. (GER.). 1986. 150.00 (*1-55660-109-3*) A Wofsy Fine Arts.

***Belle, Bella Byleo Russia.** Jeffrey Essman. 1992. 13.00 (*0-8222-1437-7*) Dramatists Play.

Belle Boyd in Camp & Prison. Belle Boyd. (American Biography Ser.). 448p. 1991. reprint ed. lib. bdg. 89.00 (*0-7812-8034-6*) Rprt Serv.

Belle Captive. Alain Robbe-Grillet. (Illus.). (FRE.). 1976. 95.00 (*0-7859-5558-5*) Fr & Eur.

Belle Captive: A Novel. Alain Robbe-Grillet & Rene Magritte. Tr. by Ben Stoltzfus. LC 94-17127. 1995. 35.00 (*0-520-05916-6*) U CA Pr.

***Belle Case la Follette 1859-1931: A Resource Guide.** Jocelyn Riley. 114p. 1995. 20.00 (*1-877933-05-8*) Her Own Words.

Belle Dame sans Merci & the Aesthetics of Romanticism. Barbara Fass. LC 73-8365. 312p. reprint ed. pap. 89.00 (*0-7837-3616-9*, 2043482) Bks Demand.

Belle Dame sans Mercy. Alain Chartier. 127p. 1949. 19.95 (*0-8288-7476-X*) Fr & Eur.

Belle de Jour. Luis Bunuel. (Illus.). 160p. 1988. pap. 9.95 (*0-571-12560-3*) Faber & Faber.

Belle de Jour. Joseph Kessel. 192p. (FRE.). 1989. pap. 10.95 (*0-7859-2629-1*, 207036125X) Fr & Eur.

Belle de Jour. Joseph Kessel. (Folio Ser.: No. 125). (FRE.). 1989. pap. 6.95 (*2-07-036125-X*) Schoenhof.

Belle de Seigneur. A. Cohen. (FRE.). 1986. 110.00 (*0-8288-3464-4*, F73582) Fr & Eur.

Belle du Seigneur. Albert Cohen. (Gallimard Ser.). (FRE.). 1968. pap. 44.95 (*2-07-026917-5*) Schoenhof.

Belle-Duck at the Peabody. Dean F. Wells. (Illus.). 48p. (J). (ps-8). 1984. 9.95 (*0-916242-24-2*) Yoknapatawpha.

***Belle En Het Beest - Beauty & the Beast.** Adapt. by Sarah Harris. (Comes to Life Bks.). 16p. (DUT & ENG.). (J). (ps-2). 1995. write for info. (*1-57234-036-3*) YES Ent.

Belle Epoque. Frwd. by Emile Langui. (Illus.). 1970. pap. 8.50 (*0-88397-016-3*) Art Srvc Intl.

Belle Epoque of Surgery: The Life & Times of Theodor Billroth, 2 vols., Set. enl. rev. ed. Karel B. Absolon. Orig. Title: The Surgeon's Surgeon. (Illus.). 312p. (Orig.). (C). 1995. text ed. 59.50 (*0-930329-64-3*) KABEL Pubs.

Belle Epoque, Varietes. Boris Vian. (FRE.). 1987. pap. 15.95 (*0-7859-3197-X*, 2264010290) Fr & Eur.

Belle et la Bete. De Leprince de Beaumont. (Folio - Cadet Bleu Ser.: No. 188). (Illus.). 87p. (FRE.). (J). (gr. 1-5). 1989. pap. 11.95 (*2-07-031188-0*) Schoenhof.

***Belle et la Bete - Beauty & the Beast.** Adapt. by Sarah Harris. (Comes to Life Bks.). 16p. (ENG & FRE.). (J). (ps-2). 1995. write for info. (*1-57234-045-2*) YES Ent.

Belle Gunness: The Lady Bluebeard. Janet L. Langlois. LC 84-43172. (Illus.). 188p. 1985. 24.95 (*0-253-31157-8*) Ind U Pr.

Belle Haven. large type ed. Juliet Fitzgerald. (General Ser.). 310p. 1991. text ed. 18.95 (*0-8161-5195-4*, Large Print Bks) Hall.

Belle Highwalking: The Narrative of a Cheyenne Woman. Ed. by Katherine Weist. (Indian Culture Ser.). (J). (gr. 5 up). 1979. pap. 6.95 (*0-89992-075-6*) Coun India Ed.

Belle Jenny. Theophile Gautier. (FRE.). 1976. 29.95 (*0-8288-9983-5*, F62920) Fr & Eur.

Belle Mentalite, Snoopy. Charles M. Schulz. (Peanuts Ser.). (FRE.). (J). 1985. 4.95 (*0-8288-4526-3*) Fr & Eur.

Belle Methode Ou l'Art De Bien Chanter. Jean Millet. LC 71-126600. (Music Ser.). 76p. 1973. reprint ed. lib. bdg. 21.50 (*0-306-70044-1*) Da Capo.

Belle Moskowitz: Feminine Politics & the Exercise of Power in the Age of Alfred E. Smith. Elisabeth I. Perry. (Illus.). 304p. 1987. 29.95 (*0-19-504426-6*) OUP.

Belle Moskowitz: Feminine Politics & the Exercise of Power in the Age of Alfred E. Smith. Elisabeth I. Perry. 1992. pap. 15.95 (*0-415-90545-1*, A6798, Routledge NY) Routledge.

Belle-Nivernaise, & Other Stories. Alphonse Daudet. LC 77-130056. (Short Story Index Reprint Ser.). 1977. 17.95 (*0-8369-3643-4*) Ayer.

Belle of Nauvoo. Becky Paget. Date not set. pap. 8.95 (*1-55503-690-2*, 01111698) Covenant Comms.

Belle of the Ball. Joan Overfield. 224p. (Orig.). 1993. mass mkt. 3.99 (*0-380-76923-9*) Avon.

Belle of the Belfast City & Did You Hear the One about the Irishman. Christina Reid. (Methuen New Theatrescripts Ser.). 89p. (Orig.). (C). 1989. pap. 9.95 (*0-413-61480-8*, A0374, Pub. by Methuen UK) Heinemann.

Belle of the Fifties: Memoirs of Mrs. Virginia Clay of Alabama. Ed. by Ada Sterling. LC 79-84187. (American Scene Ser.). 1969. reprint ed. lib. bdg. 45.00 (*0-306-71395-0*) Da Capo.

***Belle Prater's Boy.** Ruth White. LC 94-43625. (J). 1995. 15.00 (*0-374-30668-0*) FS&G.

Belle Scott: Or, Liberty Overthrown. LC 70-138332. (Black Heritage Library Collection). 1977. 22.95 (*0-8369-8724-1*) Ayer.

Belle Starr. Carl R. Green & William R. Sanford. LC 91-22310. (Outlaws & Lawmen of the Wild West Ser.). (Illus.). 48p. (J). (gr. 4-10). 1992. lib. bdg. 14.95 (*0-89490-363-2*) Enslow Pubs.

Belle Starr & Her Times: The Literature, the Facts, & the Legends. Glenn Shirley. LC 81-14683. (Illus.). 336p. (YA). (gr. 10 up). 1990. pap. 13.95 (*0-8061-2276-5*) U of Okla Pr.

Belle Vie. Iouri Kazakov. 246p. (FRE.). 1979. pap. 10.95 (*0-7859-2422-1*, 2070371344) Fr & Eur.

Belle Wolfienne, 6 vols. in 2, Set. Jean H. Formey. (Wolff, Christian, Materialien und Dokumente Ser.: Vol. III, No. 16). 1282p. 1983. reprint ed. write for info. (*3-487-07313-7*, Pub. by Georg Olms GW) Lubrecht & Cramer.

Belle Zoa; Or, the Insurrection of Haiti. Frances H. Pratt. LC 72-1820. (Black Heritage Library Collection). 1977. reprint ed. 15.95 (*0-8369-9049-8*) Ayer.

Belled Buzzards, Hucksters & Grieving Spectres: Strange & True Tales of the Appalachian Mountains. Gary Carden & Nina Anderson. Ed. by Jerry Bledsoe. LC 94-70669. (Illus.). 160p. (Orig.). 1994. pap. 13.95 (*1-878086-28-6*) Down Home NC.

Belleek: The Complete Collector's Guide & Illustrated Reference. 2nd ed. Richard K. Degenhardt. (Illus.). 256p. 1993. 60.00 (*0-87069-698-X*) Chilton.

Belleek-Irish Porcelain: An Illustrated Guide to Over 2000 Pieces. Marion Langham. 1993. 79.95 (*1-870948-77-7*, Pub. by Quiller Pr UK) St Mut.

Bellefleur. Joyce Carol Oates. 1991. pap. 15.95 (*0-452-26794-3*, Plume) NAL-Dutton.

Bellefontaine: A Historical Narrative. Carole Owen. (Illus.). 70p. (Orig.). 1989. pap. write for info. (*0-9624102-1-7*) Canyon Ranch.

Bellefontaine: An Historical Narrative. Carole Owen. (Illus.). 120p. (Orig.). 1989. 14.95 (*0-685-28881-1*) Canyon Ranch.

Bellefonte Collects: Exhibition Catalogue. Ed. by Olga K. Preisner. (Illus.). 54p. 1989. pap. 10.00 (*0-911209-40-9*) Palmer Mus Art.

Bellerophon. Jean-Baptiste Lully. Ed. by Theodore De Lajarte. (Chefs-d'oeuvre classiques de l'opera francaise Ser.: Vol. 19). (Illus.). 318p. (FRE.). 1970. reprint ed. pap. 35.00 (*0-8450-1119-7*) Broude.

Belles, Beaux & Brains of the Sixties. Thomas C. De Leon. LC 74-3937. (Women in America Ser.). (Illus.). 476p. 1974. reprint ed. 40.95 (*0-405-06084-X*) Ayer.

Belle's Daughter. large type ed. Joan Hessayon. 1991. 21.95 (*0-7089-2519-7*) Ulverscroft.

Belles Images. Simone De Beauvoir. (Folio Ser.: No. 243). (FRE.). 1966. pap. 6.95 (*2-07-036243-4*) Schoenhof.

Belles Images. Simone De Beauvoir. (FRE.). 1972. pap. 10.95 (*0-8288-3621-3*, F85660) Fr & Eur.

***Belle's Journey.** Marilynn Reynolds. (Illus.). 32p. (Orig.). (J). (gr. 1-4). 1994. pap. 6.95 (*1-55143-021-5*) Orca Bk Pubs.

Belles Lettres, Ser. I: Poems of Love. Mark Pilipski. LC 92-62379. 50p. 1993. pap. write for info. (*1-882965-00-0*) Markov Pr.

Belles Lettres, Ser. II: The Marriage of Mark & Marianne. Mark Pilipski. LC 92-62382. 50p. 1993. pap. write for info. (*1-882965-01-9*) Markov Pr.

Belles Lettres, Ser. III: The Vision. Mark Pilipski. LC 92-62391. 50p. 1993. pap. write for info. (*1-882965-02-7*) Markov Pr.

Belles Lettres, Ser. IV: Four Roles for Three Characters. Mark Pilipski. LC 92-62380. 50p. (J). (gr. k-8). 1993. pap. write for info. (*1-882965-03-5*) Markov Pr.

Belles Lettres Series, Sections One & Two: Old & Middle English Literature, 13 vols., Set. reprint ed. 398.50 (*0-404-53600-X*) AMS Pr.

Belles Lisses Poires de France. Pef. (Folio - Cadet Bleu Ser.: No. 216). 56p. (FRE.). (J). (gr. 1-5). 1990. pap. 8.95 (*2-07-031216-X*) Schoenhof.

Belles of the Ballpark. Diana S. Helmer. LC 92-12683. (Illus.). 96p. (J). (gr. 7 up). 1993. lib. bdg. 15.90 (*1-56294-230-1*) Millbrook Pr.

Belles on Their Toes. Frank B. Gilbreth, Jr. & Ernestine G. Carey. 240p. 1984. mass mkt. 3.99 (*0-553-25605-X*) Bantam.

Belles Saisons: A Colette Scrapbook. Robert Phelps. (Illus.). 304p. 1978. 15.00 (*0-374-11030-1*) FS&G.

Belle's Surprise Party. (Pop-up Pals Ser.). 10p. (J). 1994. 6.98 (*1-57082-142-9*) Mouse Works.

Belleville: Jean Belleville the Huguenot, His Descendants. Paul B. Taylor. 610p. 1992. reprint ed. lib. bdg. 99.00 (*0-8328-2360-0*); reprint ed. pap. 89.00 (*0-8328-2361-9*) Higginson Bk Co.

***Bellevue - Stratford Hotel.** Roger S. Lucas. 66p. 1994. pap. 9.00 (*1-887287-02-7*) Res Rev Pubns.

Bellevue & the New Eastside. Bob Welch. 1989. 32.95 (*0-89781-331-6*) Preferred Mktg.

***Bellfounding.** Trevor S. Jenning. (C). 1989. pap. 25.00x (*0-85263-911-2*, Pub. by Shire UK) St Mut.

Belli for Your Malpractice Defense. 2nd ed. Melvin M. Belli, Sr. & John Carlova. 256p. 1989. boxed 49.95 (*0-87489-550-2*) Med Economics.

Bellievre & Villeroy: Power in France under Henry III & Henry IV. Edmund H. Dickerman. LC 70-127365. 212p. reprint ed. 60.50 (*0-8357-7124-5*, 2027502) Bks Demand.

Belligerence. Andrei Codrescu. LC 91-14096. 79p. (Orig.). 1991. pap. 8.95 (*0-918273-85-4*) Coffee Hse.

Belligerent Miss Boynton. Kasey Michaels. 224p. (Orig.). 1982. pap. 2.95 (*0-380-77073-3*) Avon.

Belling the Cat: And Other Aesop's Fables. Tom Paxton. LC 89-39851. (Illus.). 40p. (J). (ps up). 1990. 13.95 (*0-688-08158-4*); lib. bdg. 13.88 (*0-688-08159-2*) Morrow Jr Bks.

***Belling the Old Grey Cat: A Read-with-Me Story for Grown-Ups & Others, Vol. 3.** David P. Williams & Helen C. Williams. (Read-with-Me Mouse Stories Ser.). (Illus.). 15p. (J). 1993. pap. 4.00 (*1-886058-03-2*) D P Williams.

Bellingham Theatre Guild & Shelley's "The Cenci" Hicks & Clark. 1986. pap. 4.95 (*0-317-89456-0*) WWU CPNS.

Bellini. Mario Pasi. (Portraits of Greatness Ser.). (Illus.). 80p. 1989. text ed. 17.50 (*0-918367-33-6*); pap. text ed. 12.50 (*0-918367-32-8*) Elite.

Bellmaker. Brian Jacques. LC 94-9730. (J). (gr. 1 up). 1994. 17.95 (*0-399-22805-5*, Philomel Bks) Putnam Pub Group.

Bellmakers. large type ed. Jean Chapman. (General Ser.). 544p. 1993. 21.95 (*0-7089-2819-6*) Ulverscroft.

Bellman Continuum. Ed. by R. S. Roth. 892p. 1987. text ed. 114.00 (*9971-5-0090-6*) World Scientific Pub.

Bello & Bolivar: Poetry & Politics in the Spanish American Revolution. Antonio Cussen. (Cambridge Studies in Latin American & Iberian Literature: No. 6). 200p. (C). 1992. 54.95 (*0-521-41248-X*) Cambridge U Pr.

Bellona Island Beliefs & Rituals. Torben Monberg. LC 90-20224. (Pacific Islands Monograph Ser.: No. 9). (Illus.). 480p. 1991. text ed. 42.00 (*0-8248-1147-X*) UH Pr.

Bellows Genealogy: John Bellows, the Boy Emigrant of 1635 & His Descendants. Thomas B. Peck. (Illus.). 673p. 1988. reprint ed. lib. bdg. 93.50 (*0-8328-0230-1*); reprint ed. pap. 83.50 (*0-8328-0231-X*) Higginson Bk Co.

Bellringer. Ruth Laurene. LC 74-75851. (Illus.). 1974. 30.00 (*0-933652-08-9*) Domjan Studio.

Bells. Thomas B. Aldrich. (Works of Thomas Bailey Aldrich). 1989. reprint ed. lib. bdg. 79.00 (*0-685-27611-2*) Rprt Serv.

Bells: Donald Lipski. Jan Riley. Ed. by Victoria Robinson. (Illus.). 36p. 1991. pap. 60.00x (*0-917562-59-3*) Contemp Arts.

Bells: Donald Lipski. limited ed. Jan Riley. Ed. by Victoria Robinson. (Illus.). 36p. 1991. 300.00x (*0-685-59430-0*) Contemp Arts.

Bells Alaska Travel Guide. 432p. 1992. 11.95 (*1-880840-00-6*) Bells AK Trvl.

Bell's Alaska Travel Guide. 34th ed. Ed. by Timothy J. Bell. 432p. 1994. 8.95 (*1-880840-02-2*) Bells AK Trvl.

***Bells Alaska Travel Guide: 1995 Edition.** rev. ed. Ed. by Timothy J. Bell. 432p. 1995. write for info. (*1-880840-03-0*) Bells AK Trvl.

Bells & Bell-Founding. J. Llewellyn. (Illus.). 57p. 1987. reprint ed. pap. 25.00 (*0-87556-696-0*) Saifer.

Bells & Pomegranates. C. Paul Willis. 210p. 1991. pap. 8.99 (*1-56043-047-8*) Destiny Image.

Bells Are Ringing. (Vocal Score Ser.). 1981. pap. 35.00 (*0-88188-005-1*, 00312038) H Leonard.

Bell's British Theatre, Seventeen Seventy-Six to Seventeen Eighty-One, 21 vols. Ed. by John Bell. (Illus.). 1977. reprint ed. write for info. (*0-318-50532-0*) AMS Pr.

Bell's British Theatre, Seventeen Seventy-Six to Seventeen Eighty-One, 21 vols., Set. Ed. by John Bell. LC 76-44551. (Illus.). 1977. reprint ed. 1,207.50 (*0-404-00800-3*) AMS Pr.

Bell's Electric Speaking Telephone: Its Invention, Construction, Application, Modification & History. George B. Prescott. LC 72-5069. (Technology & Society Ser.). (Illus.). 536p. 1977. reprint ed. 42.95 (*0-405-04718-5*) Ayer.

Bells in Australia. J. D. Keating. LC 79-670594. 1979. 27.50 (*0-522-84163-5*) Intl Spec Bk.

Bells of Agony. Autran Dourado. Tr. by John M. Parker. LC 88-51686. 236p. 1989. 30.00 (*0-7206-0681-0*, Pub. by P Owen Ltd UK) Dufour.

Bells of Autumn. large type ed. Ted Willis. (General Ser.). 464p. 1993. 21.95 (*0-7089-2888-9*) Ulverscroft.

Bells of Christmas. Virginia Hamilton. 59p. (J). (ps up). 1989. 17.95 (*0-15-206450-8*) HarBrace.

Bells of Conquest. Daughters of St. Paul. LC 68-28105. (Encounter Ser.). (J). (gr. 3-7). 1987. 3.00 (*0-8198-0228-X*); pap. 2.00 (*0-8198-1109-2*) Pauline Bks.

Bells of Dis. Helen Adam. (Morning Coffee Chapbook Ser.). (Illus.). 18p. (Orig.). 1985. pap. 10.00 (*0-915124-92-0*) Coffee Hse.

Bells of Freedom. Dorothy G. Butters. (Illus.). (J). (gr. 4-8). 1984. 15.50 (*0-8446-6162-7*) Peter Smith.

***Bells of I Can.** Slightly Off Center Writers Group Staff. (Orig.). 1995. pap. 8.95 (*1-56721-108-9*) Twnty-Fifth Cent Pr.

***Bells of Lake Superior.** Dayton Hyde. LC 94-71022. (Illus.). 104p. (YA). (gr. 5 up). 1995. 12.95 (*1-56397-188-7*, Wordsong) Boyds Mills Pr.

Bells of Lombardy. Lucien Stryk. LC 86-8548. (Illus.). 64p. 1986. 15.00 (*0-87580-127-7*) N Ill U Pr.

Bells of Nagasaki. Takashi Nagai. Ed. by Shaw. 118p. 1994. pap. 9.00 (*4-7700-1845-2*) Kodansha.

Bells of Russia: History & Technology. Edwards V. Williams. LC 85-3453. (Illus.). 273p. 1985. text ed. 75.00 (*0-691-09131-5*) Princeton U Pr.

***Bells of San Filipo.** Max Brand. 240p. 1995. mass mkt. 3.99 (*0-8439-3819-6*) Dorchester Pub Co.

***Bells of the Kremlin: An Experience in Communism.** fac. ed. Arvo Tuominen. Ed. by Piltti Heiskanen. Tr. by Lily Leino. LC 82-17647. (Illus.). 367p. 1983. reprint ed. pap. 104.60 (*0-7837-8100-8*, 2047904) Bks Demand.

Bells of Victory: The Pitt-Newcastle Ministry & the Conduct of the Seven Years' War, 1757-1762. Richard Middleton. 251p. 1985. 69.95 (*0-521-26546-0*) Cambridge U Pr.

Bells of Worship. Contrib by Glena M. Kratzer. 1980. 7.95 (*0-685-68375-3*, MB-493) Lillenas.

Bells on Their Toes. Frank B. Gilbreth. 1976. 23.95 (*0-8488-0800-2*) Amereon Ltd.

***Bell's Orofacial Pains.** 5th ed. Jeffrey P. Okeson. LC 95-1313. 500p. 1995. text ed. 68.00 (*0-86715-293-1*) Quint Pub Co.

Bells Tell Stories. Dorothy M. Warren. (Illus.). 80p. (Orig.). 1988. pap. 5.50 (*0-685-31979-2*) D M Warren.

Bells, Their History, Legends, Making, & Uses. Satis N. Coleman. LC 70-109722. (Illus.). ix, 462p. 1971. reprint ed. text ed. 38.50 (*0-8371-4212-1*, COBE, Greenwood Pr) Greenwood.

Bells, Their History, Legends, Making & Uses. Satis N. Coleman. 462p. 1990. reprint ed. lib. bdg. 89.00 (*0-7812-9112-7*) Rprt Serv.

Bell's Theorem. Matthias Schultheiss. Ed. by Bernd Metz. Tr. by Tom Leighton. (Illus.). 48p. 1987. pap. 10.95 (*0-87416-037-5*) Catalan Communs.

Bell's Theorem & the Foundations of Modern Physics: International Conference. Alwyn Van Der Merwe et al. 500p. 1993. text ed. 109.00 (*981-02-1088-4*) World Scientific Pub.

Bell's Theorem, No. 2: The Connection. Matthias Schultheiss. Ed. & Tr. by Bernd Metz. (Illus.). 48p. (Orig.). 1989. pap. 10.95 (*0-87416-062-6*) Catalan Communs.

Bell's Theorem (Three) Contact. Matthias Schultheiss. Tr. by Bernd Metz. (Illus.). 49p. (Orig.). 1989. pap. 10.95 (*0-87416-074-X*) Catalan Communs.

Bellsong for Sarah Raines. Bettie Cannon. LC 87-4299. 192p. (YA). (gr. 7 up). 1987. text ed. 14.95 (*0-684-18839-2*, C Scribner Sons Young) S&S Childrens.

Bellum Africanum. Ed. by Rudolf Schneider. vii, 157p. 1962. write for info. (*3-296-10700-2*, Pub. by Georg Olms GW) Lubrecht & Cramer.

Bellum Alexandrinum. Ed. by Rudolf Schneider. vii, 65p. 1962. write for info. (*3-296-10800-9*, Pub. by Georg Olms GW) Lubrecht & Cramer.

Bellwood. Elisabeth Ogilvie. 1976. 18.95 (*0-8488-1118-6*) Amereon Ltd.

Bellwood Treasure. Lillian Lincoln. 1987. pap. 2.50 (*0-449-21187-8*) Fawcett.

Belly & Its Power: The Liberation of the Natural Energy Center in Man. Allan Saltzman. LC 87-50038. (Illus.). 120p. (Orig.). 1987. pap. 8.95 (*0-941821-00-5*) Yoga Tools.

Belly Button Brigade. Mimi Tate. (J). 1974. pap. 2.25 (*0-685-47446-1*, BBB01) Quality Pubns.

An Asterisk (*) at the beginning of an entry indicates that the title is appearing in BIP for the first time.

Belly Dancer in the Barrel of Oil. Rebecca Newman. LC 84-90336. 1984. 10.00 (*0-87212-177-1*) Libra.

Belly Laughs! Food Jokes & Riddles. Charles Keller. LC 89-28201. (Illus.). 32p. (J). (gr. k-3). 1990. pap. 13.95 (*0-671-70068-5*, S&S Bks Young Read); pap. 5.95 (*0-671-70069-3*, S&S Bks Young Read) S&S Childrens.

***Belly of Paris.** Emile Zola. (Classics Ser.: No. 70). 336p. (Orig.). 1995. pap. 14.95 (*1-55713-066-3*) Sun & Moon CA.

Belly of the Wolf. R. A. MacAvoy. LC 93-22924. 1994. 20.00 (*0-688-09601-8*) Morrow.

Belly Song & Other Poems. Etheridge Knight. LC 72-90098. 50p. (Orig.). (YA). (gr. 12 up). 1973. pap. 5.00 (*0-910296-88-X*) Broadside Pr.

Bellyache Road, (An Excerpt from the Tarnish on the Golden Years) Nona K. Carver. (Illus.). 24p. (Orig.). 1994. pap. 7.00 (*0-9641195-3-6*) Carver Cntry.

Bellybuttons Are Navels. Mark Schoen. (Illus.). 40p. (J). (ps-00). 1990. 12.95 (*0-8290-2409-3*) Irvington.

Bellybuttons Are Navels. Mark Schoen. (Young Readers Ser.). (Illus.). 44p. (J). (ps-3). 1990. reprint ed. 17.95 (*0-87975-585-7*) Prometheus Bks.

Bellydancer. Lee. (NFS Canada Ser.). Date not set. pap. 14.95 (*0-88974-039-9*, Pub. by Press Gang CN) InBook.

Belly's Deli. R. L. Shafner & Eric J. Weisberg. LC 92-44636. (In the State of Punsylvania Ser.). (YA). (gr. 5 up). 1993. 13.50 (*0-8225-2101-6*, Lerner Publctns) Lerner Group.

Belmont Avenue Social Club. Bruce Graham. 1993. 4.75 (*0-8222-1323-0*) Dramatists Play.

Belmont, Massachusetts: The Architecture & Development of the Town of Homes. Belmont Historic District Commission Project Staff. (Illus.). 120p. 1984. write for info. (*0-318-57643-0*) Belmont Hist Dist Comm.

Belmont Murders. L. J. Best. 1991. pap. 13.95 (*0-87949-353-4*) Ashley Bks.

Belmont Square, No. 9. large type ed. Margaret Erskine. 1991. 21.95 (*0-7089-2514-6*) Ulverscroft.

Belmont und Constanze see Alceste

***Belo Horizonte.** Richard B. Abbott. LC 94-79311. 186p. (Orig.). 1995. pap. 14.95 (*1-882897-01-3*) Lost Coast.

Belomor: An Account of the Construction of the New Canal Between the White Sea & the Baltic Sea. Ed. by Maksim Gorkii. LC 75-37339. (Russian Studies). 1977. reprint ed. lib. bdg. 30.25 (*0-88355-432-1*) Hyperion Conn.

Belonging. Mary A. McElmurry. (Illus.). 64p. (J). (gr. 2-8). 1983. student ed 8.95 (*0-9607366-0-3*, GA 492) Good Apple.

Belonging. Clairr O'Connor. 224p. (Orig.). (C). 1991. pap. 13.99 (*1-85594-014-0*, Pub. by Attic IE) InBook.

Belonging. Larraine Segil. 416p. (Orig.). 1994. pap. 4.99 (*0-451-18110-7*, Sig) NAL-Dutton.

***Belonging.** Nancy Thayer. 336p. 1995. 22.95 (*0-312-13026-0*) St Martin.

Belonging. Maureen Wartski. (Orig.). (J). (gr. 7 up). 1993. mass mkt. 3.99 (*0-449-70419-X*, Juniper) Fawcett.

Belonging. Virginia M. Scott. LC 85-31135. 176p. (YA). (gr. 7-12). 1987. reprint ed. pap. 2.95 (*0-930323-33-5*) Gallaudet Univ Pr.

***Belonging: A Guidebook to Overcome Loneliness.** William R. Brassell. LC 94-67042. (Orig.). Date not set. pap. 13.95 (*1-879237-76-8*) New Harbinger.

***Belonging: A Guidebook to Overcome Loneliness.** William R. Brassell. LC 94-67042. 200p. (Orig.). Date not set. text ed. 24.95 (*1-879237-77-6*) New Harbinger.

Belonging: Bonds of Healing & Recovery. Dennis Linn et al. LC 92-29855. 288p. 1993. pap. 9.95 (*0-8091-3365-2*) Paulist Pr.

Belonging: Self & Social Discovery for Children of All Ages. Jayne Derencenzi & Susan Pendergast. (Illus.). 265p. (Orig.). 1988. 19.95 (*0-9623822-0-5*) Belonging.

Belonging: The Meaning & Future of Canadian Citizenship. Ed. by William Kaplan. 400p. 1993. 55.00 (*0-7735-0985-2*, Pub. by McGill CN); pap. 24.95 (*0-7735-0987-9*, Pub. by McGill CN) U of Toronto Pr.

Belonging - A Guide for Group Facilitators: Self & Social Discovery for Children of All Ages. Jayne Devencenzi & Susan Pendergast. (Illus.). (Orig.). 1988. pap. text ed. 19.95 (*0-685-28128-0*) Belonging.

Belonging! Adventures in Church Membership. Donald N. Bastian. 1990. pap. 4.95 (*0-685-37876-4*) Light & Life.

Belonging & Alienation: Religious Foundations for the Human Future. Ed. by Philip Hefner & W. Widick Schroeder. LC 75-30254. (Studies in Religion & Society). 200p. 1976. 28.95 (*0-913348-07-4*); pap. 17.95 (*0-913348-08-2*) Ctr Sci Study.

Belonging Heart. Bruce C. Hafen & Marie Hafen. LC 93-40451. xviii, 345p. 1994. 13.95 (*0-87579-827-6*) Deseret Bk.

Belonging in America: Reading Between the Lines. Constance Perin. LC 87-40371. (New Directions in Anthropological Writing Ser.). 320p. (C). 1988. pap. 30.00 (*0-299-11580-1*) U of Wis Pr.

Belonging in America: Reading Between the Lines. Constance Perin. LC 87-40371. (New Directions in Anthropological Writing Ser.). 320p. 1990. pap. 13.95 (*0-299-11584-4*) U of Wis Pr.

Belonging in the Two Berlins: Kin, State, Nation. John Borneman. (Cambridge Studies in Social & Cultural Anthropology: No. 86). (Illus.). 368p. (C). 1992. 69.95 (*0-521-41589-6*); pap. 22.95 (*0-521-42715-0*) Cambridge U Pr.

Belonging to America: Equal Citizenship & the Constitution. Kenneth L. Karst. LC 88-23438. 304p. (C). 1989. 37.00 (*0-300-04322-8*) Yale U Pr.

Belonging to America: Equal Citizenship & the Constitution. Kenneth Karst. 304p. (C). 1991. reprint ed. pap. text ed. 18.00 (*0-300-05028-3*) Yale U Pr.

Belonging to God: A Commentary on "A Brief Statement of Faith" William C. Placher & David Willis-Watkins. 224p. (Orig.). 1992. pap. 9.99 (*0-664-25296-6*) Westminster John Knox.

Belonging to Others: Cultural Construction of Womanhood among Muslims in a Village in Bangladesh. Jitka Kotalova. (Uppsala Studies in Cultural Anthropology: No. 19). 252p. (Orig.). 1993. pap. 55.50x (*91-554-3105-4*, Pub. by Uppsala Universitet SW) Coronet Bks.

Belonging to the Universe: Explorations on the Frontiers of Science & Spirituality. Fritjof Capra et al. LC 90-56454. 240p. 1992. reprint ed. pap. 10.00 (*0-06-250195-X*) Harper SF.

Belorussian National Dress: Belaruskae Narodnae Adzenne. Mikhass Romaniouk. (BEL, ENG, FRE, GER, RUS & SPA.). 1981. 143.00 (*0-317-57297-0*, Pub. by Collets UK) St Mut.

Belorussian Painting XII - XVIII Centuries. Ed. by Collet's Holdings, Ltd. Staff. 316p. 1985. 110.00 (*0-317-39479-7*, Pub. by Collets UK) St Mut.

Belourussian SSSR: Facts & Figures. Ed. by Collet's Holdings, Ltd. Staff. 64p. 1984. 45.00 (*0-317-42759-8*, Pub. by Collets UK) St Mut.

Belousov-Zhabotinskii Reaction. J. J. Tyson. Ed. by S. A. Levin. (Lecture Notes in Biomathematics Ser.: Vol. 10). 1976. pap. 22.00 (*0-387-07792-8*) Spr-Verlag.

Beloved. Phoebe Conn. 512p. 1994. mass mkt. 4.99 (*0-8217-4770-3*) Zebra.

Beloved. P. C. Kuttykrishnan. Tr. by R. R. Menon. 194p. 1975. pap. 2.80 (*0-88253-696-6*) Ind-US Inc.

Beloved. Toni Morrison. LC 87-46157. 288p. 1987. 27.50 (*0-394-53597-9*) Knopf.

Beloved. Toni Morrison. 1988. pap. 10.95 (*0-452-26446-4*, Plume) NAL-Dutton.

Beloved. Toni Morrison. 1991. pap. 5.99 (*0-451-15659-5*) NAL-Dutton.

Beloved. David Schloss. 64p. 1973. pap. 6.00 (*0-912592-14-1*) Ashland Poetry.

Beloved. Bertrice Small. 480p. (Orig.). 1985. mass mkt. 4.99 (*0-345-32785-3*) Ballantine.

Beloved. Antoinette Stockenberg. 1993. mass mkt. 4.99 (*0-440-21330-4*) Dell.

Beloved. John Updike. 50p. 1982. write for info. (*0-686-86291-0*) Lord John.

Beloved. deluxe limited ed. John Updike. 50p. 1982. 60.00 (*0-935716-15-7*) Lord John.

Beloved: From God's Heart to Yours. Kay Arthur. LC 94-10728. 1994. 16.99 (*1-56507-198-0*) Harvest Hse.

Beloved: Reflections on the Path of Love. Kahlil Gibran. Tr. by John Walbridge. (Illus.). 132p. 1994. 17.00 (*1-883991-05-6*) Whte Cloud Pr.

Beloved: The Life & Work of Meher Baba. rev. ed. Naosherwan Anzar. LC 83-13540. (Illus.). 160p. 1983. 18.00 (*0-913078-50-6*); pap. 12.00 (*0-913078-47-6*) Sheriar Pr.

Beloved & Darling Child. Ed. by Agatha Rann. 256p. 1991. 40.00 (*0-86299-880-8*) A Sutton Pub.

Beloved & God: The Story of Hadrian & Antinous. Royston Lambert. 352p. reprint ed. pap. 9.95 (*0-8216-2003-7*) Carol Pub Group.

Beloved Avenger. Mary Brendan. 1991. mass mkt. 4.50 (*0-8217-3584-5*) Zebra.

Beloved Avenger. Joan Van Nuys. 400p. (Orig.). 1989. pap. 3.95 (*0-380-75878-4*) Avon.

***Beloved Baby.** Michaela Davis. 1995. 18.00 (*0-671-52269-8*) PB.

***Beloved Beast: Poems.** Dennis Finnell. LC 94-29149. 88p. 1995. pap. 11.95 (*0-8203-1708-X*) U of Ga Pr.

Beloved Betrayal. Carol Finch. 512p. 1988. pap. 3.95 (*0-8217-2346-4*) Zebra.

Beloved Bondage. Katharine Kincaid. 448p. 1993. mass mkt. 4.50 (*0-8217-4059-8*) Zebra.

Beloved Coast & Suffolk Sandlings. R. A. Whitehead. 224p. 1994. 60.00 (*0-86138-075-4*, Pub. by T Dalton UK) St Mut.

Beloved Community: The Cultural Criticism of Randolph Bourne, Van Wyck Brooks, Waldo Frank, & Lewis Mumford. Casey N. Blake. LC 90-50013. (Cultural Studies of the United States). (Illus.). xvi, 365p. (C). 1990. 37.50 (*0-8078-1935-2*); pap. 13.95 (*0-8078-4296-6*) U of NC Pr.

***Beloved Deceiver.** Joan Van Nuys. 384p. (Orig.). 1994. mass mkt. 4.50 (*0-380-77208-6*) Avon.

***Beloved Disciple.** James Charlesworth. (C). 1995. write for info. (*1-56338-135-4*) TPI PA.

Beloved Disciple: A Witness Against Anti-Semitism. Philip S. Kaufman. 72p. (Orig.). 1991. pap. text ed. 4.95 (*0-8146-2067-1*) Liturgical Pr.

Beloved Disciple: His Name, His Story, His Thought: Two Studies from the Gospel of John. Vernard Eller. LC 87-16772. (Illus.). 134p. reprint ed. pap. 38.20 (*0-8357-4362-4*, 2037190) Bks Demand.

Beloved Embrace. 1991. mass mkt. 4.50 (*0-8217-2941-1*) Zebra.

Beloved Enchantress. Joan Van Nuys. 448p. (Orig.). 1990. pap. 3.95 (*0-8439-2889-1*) Dorchester Pub Co.

***Beloved Enemies: Our Need for Opponents.** David P. Barash. 309p. (C). 1994. 25.95 (*0-87975-908-9*) Prometheus Bks.

Beloved Enemy. Al Lacy. (Battles of Destiny Ser.: No. 3). 320p. 1994. pap. 4.99 (*0-88070-626-0*, Multnomah Bks) Questar Pubs.

Beloved Enemy. Maura Seger. 1992. mass mkt. 4.99 (*0-06-104081-9*, Harp PBks) HarpC.

Beloved Enemy. large type ed. Dawn Stacey. (Dales Romance Ser.). 155p. 1992. pap. 16.95 (*1-85389-312-9*, Dales) Ulverscroft.

Beloved Enemy: A Novel. Ellen Jones. LC 93-42290. 1994. 23.00 (*0-671-87279-6*) S&S Trade.

***Beloved Exile.** Parke Godwin. 432p. (Orig.). 1994. mass mkt. 5.50 (*0-380-77553-0*, AvoNova) Avon.

Beloved Exiles. large type ed. Agnes N. Keith. 1979. 15.95 (*0-7089-0385-1*) Ulverscroft.

***Beloved Honor.** Mallory Burgess. 384p. 1995. mass mkt. 4.99 (*0-8217-4968-4*) Windsor NY.

***Beloved Image: The Drama of W. B. Yeats 1965-1939.** Nancy A. Watanabe. 432p. (C). 1995. 62.50 (*0-9645278-0-4*) Lit Comparatist.

Beloved Infidel. Dean Young. LC 91-50823. (Wesleyan Poetry Ser.). 72p. (C). 1992. 22.50 (*0-8195-2201-5*, Wesleyan Univ Pr); pap. 10.95 (*0-8195-1204-4*, Wesleyan Univ Pr) U Pr of New Eng.

Beloved Intruder. Joan Van Nuys. 400p. (Orig.). 1992. mass mkt. 4.50 (*0-380-76476-8*) Avon.

Beloved Intruder. large type ed. Jocelyn Griffin. 464p. 1983. 15.95 (*0-7089-0930-2*) Ulverscroft.

Beloved Invader. Eugenia Price. 1977. mass mkt. 4.99 (*0-553-26909-7*) Bantam.

Beloved Invader. large type ed. Eugenia Price. LC 91-15592. 456p. 1991. reprint ed. lib. bdg. 20.95 (*1-56054-182-2*) Thorndike Pr.

Beloved Kathe Kruse Yesterday & Today. Lydia Richter. 112p. 1991. pap. 12.95 (*0-87588-210-2*) Hobby Hse.

Beloved Knight. Mallory Burgess. 448p. 1993. mass mkt. 4.50 (*0-8217-4324-4*) Zebra.

Beloved Madison: A Pictorial Tour of Indiana's Historic Madison. Robert E. Snodgrass. LC 90-63137. (Illus.). 175p. 1991. 34.50 (*0-9628086-0-1*) Jefferson Hist Soc.

Beloved Mother: The Story of Nancy Ward. Charlotte J. Ellington. (Illus.). 200p. 1994. 14.95 (*0-932807-92-5*) Overmountain Pr.

Beloved Notes. Mary Robinson. 1993. pap. 4.50 (*0-8220-0227-2*) Cliffs.

Beloved of the Sky: Essays & Photographs on Clearcutting. Ed. by John Ellison. LC 92-72432. (Turning Point Ser.). (Illus.). 272p. (Orig.). 1993. pap. 14.95 (*0-913089-38-9*) Broken Moon.

Beloved One: Words of Hope for the Divorced. Marie Shropshire. (Orig.). 1990. pap. 4.00 (*0-915541-81-5*) Star Bks Inc.

Beloved Outlaw. Linda Benjamin. 464p. 1986. pap. 3.95 (*0-8217-1944-0*) Zebra.

Beloved Paradise. Johanna Hailey. 496p. 1987. pap. 3.95 (*0-8217-2014-7*) Zebra.

Beloved People. large type ed. Denise Robertson. 671p. 1994. 19.95 (*0-7505-0615-6*, Pub. by Magna Print Bks) Ulverscroft.

Beloved Pirate. Casey Stuart. 512p. 1988. pap. 3.95 (*0-8217-2348-0*) Zebra.

Beloved Pretender. Joan Van Nuys. 384p. (Orig.). 1993. mass mkt. 4.50 (*0-380-77207-8*) Avon.

Beloved Pretender. large type ed. Julia A. Ashwell. (Linford Romance Library). 272p. 1992. pap. 14.95 (*0-7089-7191-1*, Linford) Ulverscroft.

Beloved Prisoner. large type ed. Catherine Dillon. 430p. 1980. 12.00 (*0-7089-0557-9*) Ulverscroft.

Beloved Prophet: The Love Letters of Kahlil Gibran & Mary Haskell & Her Private Journal. Ed. by Virginia Hilu. 1972. 30.00 (*0-394-43298-3*) Knopf.

Beloved Rivals. Danice Allen. 352p. (Orig.). 1993. mass mkt. 4.99 (*1-55773-840-8*) Diamond.

Beloved Rogue. Deana James. 448p. 1994. mass mkt. 5.99 (*0-8217-4682-0*) Zebra.

Beloved Rogue. Penelope Williamson. 368p. 1988. pap. 3.95 (*0-380-75528-9*) Avon.

Beloved Savage. Sandra Bishop. 1990. mass mkt. 4.25 (*0-8217-3134-3*) Zebra.

Beloved Scoundrel. Iris Johansen. 1994. 5.99 (*0-553-29945-X*, Fanfare) Bantam.

Beloved Scoundrel. Penelope Neri. 1983. pap. 3.75 (*0-8217-1259-4*) Zebra.

Beloved Scoundrel. Clarissa Ross. 1980. pap. 1.95 (*0-8439-0710-X*) Dorchester Pub Co.

Beloved Scoundrel. large type ed. Iris Johansen. LC 94-2189. 497p. 1994. reprint ed. 21.95 (*0-8161-5964-5*) Hall.

Beloved St. Anne. Matt Christopher. LC 92-56932. (Illus.). 69p. (YA). (gr. 6-11). 1993. pap. 6.95 (*1-55523-569-7*) Winston-Derek.

***Beloved Stranger.** Christina Cordaire. 192p. (Orig.). 1995. pap. text ed. 4.50 (*0-515-11550-9*) Jove Pubns.

Beloved Stranger. Grace L. Hill. 19.95 (*0-89190-066-7*, Am Repr) Amereon Ltd.

Beloved Stranger. large type ed. Elizabeth Oldfield. (Magna Romance Ser.). 1992. 17.95 (*0-7505-0401-3*, Pub. by Magna Print Bks) Ulverscroft.

Beloved Stranger, No. 44. Grace L. Hill. 1992. pap. 4.99 (*0-8423-0303-0*) Tyndale.

Beloved Stranger; Summer Storm, 2 bks. in 1. Joan Wolf. 352p. 1994. pap. 3.99 (*0-451-18251-0*, Sig) NAL-Dutton.

Beloved Unbeliever: Loving Your Husband into the Faith. Jo Berry. 176p. (Orig.). 1981. pap. 9.99 (*0-310-42621-9*, 11215P) Zondervan.

Beloved Viking. Betty Brooks. 448p. 1994. mass mkt. 4.50 (*0-8217-4460-7*) Zebra.

Beloved Warrior. Deborah James. 320p. (Orig.). 1993. mass mkt. 4.99 (*0-425-13717-1*) Berkley Pub.

Beloved Wide Spot. Nona Freeman. 1990. 9.95 (*0-685-60162-5*) Nonas Bk Sales.

Beloved Widespot. Nona Freeman. Ed. by Nell Perry. LC 89-86051. 286p. 1989. pap. 9.95 (*1-878366-00-9*) Nonas Bk Sales.

Beloved Woman. Deborah Smith. 1991. mass mkt. 4.50 (*0-553-28759-1*) Bantam.

Beloved World. Eugenia Price. 1991. mass mkt. 10.00 (*0-385-41716-0*) Doubleday.

Below Devil's Gap. Louise B. James. (Illus.). 240p. 1984. 19.95 (*0-934188-09-2*) Evans Pubns.

Below Replacement Fertility in Industrial Societies: Causes, Consequences, Politics. Kingsley Davis et al. Ed. by Hoover Institution Staff The. 450p. 1987. 69.95 (*0-521-34324-0*) Cambridge U Pr.

Below-Replacement Fertility in Industrialized Societies: Causes, Consequences, Policies - Supplement to Population & Development Review, Vol. 12. Ed. by Kingsley Davis et al. LC 87-2458. 1987. pap. 12.00 (*0-87834-056-4*) Population Coun.

Below Suspicion. John D. Carr. (Library of Crime Classics). 186p. 1986. pap. 4.95 (*0-930330-50-1*) Intl Polygonics.

Below the Belt. Addie Bell. Ed. by Gwen Costa. (Illus.). 1993. 13.95 (*0-87949-360-7*) Ashley Bks.

Below the Belt. Endel Markowitz. 78p. T.V. Shooting Script. write for info. (*0-318-56910-8*) Haymark.

Below the Belt: Cartoons from the Syracuse Herald Journal, Herald American. Frank Cammuso. (Illus.). 144p. 1993. pap. 9.95 (*0-925168-26-2*) North Country.

Below the Belt: Cartoons from the Syracuse Herald Journal, Herald American. Frank Cammuso. LC 93-37909. 1993. write for info. (*0-9629159-5-5*) Pine Tree NY.

Below the Belt & Other Stories. Phil Andros. LC 92-4773. 128p. (Orig.). 1992. reprint ed. pap. 7.95 (*1-55583-220-2*, Perineum Pr) Alyson Pubns.

***Below the Green Pond.** Humphrey. 1995. pap. text ed. (*0-8114-3745-0*) Raintree Steck-V.

***Below the Green Pond.** Paul Humphrey. LC 94-28573. (Read All About It, Science, Level B Ser.). (Illus.). (J). 1995. lib. bdg. write for info. (*0-8114-5739-7*) Raintree Steck-V.

Below the James Lies Dixie. Park Rouse, Jr. (Illus.). 1968. pap. 7.50 (*0-87517-048-X*) Dietz.

Below the Line: Living Poor in America. Eugene Richards & Christiane Bird. 224p. (Orig.). 1987. 132.00 (*0-89043-062-4*); pap. 20.00 (*0-89043-061-6*) Consumer Reports.

Below-the-Line-Promotion. John Wilmshurst. (Professional Development Ser.). (Illus.). 399p. 1993. pap. 29.95 (*0-7506-0548-0*) Buttrwrth-Heinemann.

Below-the-Line Publicity. Wilmhurst. 1991. write for info. (*0-434-92285-4*) Buttrwrth-Heinemann.

Below the Magic Mountain: A Social History of Tuberculosis in Twentieth Century Britain. Linda Bryder. (Oxford Historical Monographs). (Illus.). 320p. 1988. pap. 65.00 (*0-19-822947-X*) OUP.

Below the Root. Zilpha K. Snyder. 244p. (J). (gr. 5 up). 1992. pap. 3.50 (*0-440-21266-9*, LFL) Dell.

Below the Summit. Joseph V. Torres-Metzgar. LC 76-41036. 1976. pap. 5.00 (*0-89229-005-6*) TQS Pubns.

Below the Surface. Milt McLeod. Ed. by Michael Sofranko. (New Texas Poetry Sampler Ser.: No. 6). 28p. (Orig.). 1992. 10.00 (*0-930324-25-0*) Wings Pr.

***Below the Surface.** Anne S. Parry. 1994. 10.00 (*0-207-18043-1*, Pub. by Angus & Robertson AT) HarpC.

Below Two Skies. Timothy Houghton. LC 92-18156. 80p. (Orig.). 1993. pap. 11.95 (*0-914061-30-5*) Orchises Pr.

***Belowground Responses to Rising Atmospheric CO2 - Implications for Plants, Soil Biota & Ecosystem Processes: Proceedings of a Workshop Held May 29-June 2, 1993, University of Michigan Biological Station, Pellston, Michigan.** Ed. by Peter S. Curtis et al. LC 94-46911. (Developments in Plant & Soil Sciences Ser.: Vol. 60). 1995. lib. bdg. 89.00 (*0-7923-2901-5*) Kluwer Ac.

Belshazzar's Feast: For Baritone Solo, Mixed Choir, & Orchestra. William Walton. 1978. boxed 250.00 (*0-19-338463-9*) OUP.

Belt Conveyors for Bulk Materials. 3rd ed. 346p. 1988. 95.00 (*0-318-35062-9*) Conveyor Equip Mfrs.

Belt Selection & Application for Engineers. Erickson. (Mechanical Engineering Ser.: Vol. 58). 496p. 1987. 160.00 (*0-8247-7353-5*) Dekker.

Belt Up. Norman Thelwell. (Illus.). 128p. 1990. pap. 8.95 (*0-417-01090-7*, Pub. by Methuen London UK) Trafalgar.

***Beltane at Aphelion: Longer Poems.** John Matthias. 203p. 1995. text ed. 32.95x (*0-8040-0983-X*) Swallow.

Beltenebros: De la Naturaleza y Figuracion Fronteriza De la Poesia. Jose Bergamin. 77p. (C). 1969. 3.75 (*0-8477-3112-X*); pap. 3.00 (*0-8477-3113-8*) U of PR Pr.

Belton Estate. Anthony Trollope. Ed. & Intro. by John Halperin. (World's Classics Ser.). 480p. 1986. pap. 8.95 (*0-19-281725-6*) OUP.

Belton Estate. Anthony Trollope. 448p. 1994. pap. 8.95 (*0-14-043819-X*, Penguin Classics) Viking Penguin.

Belton Estate. Anthony Trollope. LC 85-8773. (Literature Ser.). 396p. 1985. reprint ed. pap. 7.50 (*0-486-24815-1*) Dover.

Belton House. National Trust Staff. (Illus.). 96p. 1991. pap. 10.95 (*0-7078-0113-3*, Pub. by Natl Trust UK) Trafalgar.

Belton Systems, Seventeen Fifty-Eight & Seventeen Eighty-Four to Eighty-Six: America's First Repeating Firearms. Robert Held. LC 86-62143. (Illus.). 93p. 1986. pap. 20.00 (*0-917218-25-6*) A Mowbray.

Beltrami Fields in Chiral Media: Contemporary Chemical Physics Ser. Akhlesh Lakhtakia. 556p. 1994. text ed. 86.00 (*981-02-1403-0*) World Scientific Pub.

Beltran: Basque Sheepman of the American West. Beltran Paris. LC 79-20311. (Basque Ser.). (Illus.). 208p. 1988. reprint ed. pap. 16.95 (*0-87417-144-X*) U of Nev Pr.

Beltravia. Evan J. Wright. LC 93-60440. 224p. 1993. 14.92 (*0-9636656-0-X*) Wright-Reading.

Belts & Chains. 5th rev. ed. Ed. by Deere & Company Staff. (Fundamentals of Service Ser.). (Illus.). 72p. 1994. pap. text ed. 10.95 (*0-86691-199-5*, FOS5305B); Slide set. sl. 79.95

An Asterisk (*) at the beginning of an entry indicates that the title is appearing in BIP for the first time.

B

An Asterisk (*) at the beginning of an entry indicates that the title is appearing in BIP for the first time.

677

Ben McCulloch & the Frontier Military Tradition. Thomas W. Cutrer. LC 92-50812. (Civil War America Ser.). (Illus.). xiv, 402p. 1993. 34.95 (*0-8078-2076-8*) U of NC Pr.

Ben Messick. James R. Lafferty, Sr. LC 89-92682. (Illus.). 96p. 1993. 70.00 (*1-883246-01-6*); pap. 45.00 (*1-883246-02-4*) Eclectic Gal.

Ben Messick. deluxe limited ed. James R. Lafferty, Sr. LC 89-92682. (Illus.). 96p. 1993. boxed 350.00 (*1-883246-00-8*) Eclectic Gal.

Ben Myer's Tales. Morton Leeds. (Illus.). 136p. (Orig.). 1988. pap. 4.95 (*0-317-90584-8*) Lone Oak Pr.

Ben Nevis & Its Observatory. Picton Publishing Staff. (Illus.). (C). 1987. 30.00 (*0-317-90420-5*, Pub. by Picton UK) St Mut.

Ben Nicholson. Jeremy Lewison. LC 91-11556. (Illus.). 128p. 1991. 24.95 (*0-8478-1395-9*) Rizzoli Intl.

***Ben Nicholson.** Jeremy Lewison. 277p. 1994. pap. 60.00 (*1-85437-130-4*) U of Wash Pr.

Ben Nicholson. Norbert Lynton. (Illus.). 472p. (C). 1993. reprint ed. 125.00 (*0-7148-2813-0*, Pub. by Phaidon Press UK) Chronicle Bks.

Ben Nicholson: Fifty Years of His Art. Steven A. Nash. LC 78-62949. (Illus.). 1978. 14.00 (*0-914782-21-5*) Buffalo Acad.

Ben Nighthorse Campbell: Cheyenne Chief-U. S. Senate. Christopher E. Henry. (North American Indians of Achievement Ser.). (Illus.). 1994. 18.95 (*0-7910-2046-0*, Am Art Analog) Chelsea Hse.

***Ben Nighthorse Campbell, Senator & Artist.** Nuchi Nashoba. (Illus.). (J). (gr. 1-4). 1995. lib. bdg. 9.95 (*0-8136-5757-1*); pap. 4.95 (*0-8136-5763-6*) Modern Curr.

Ben of Colonial Newport. Sandra MacDonald. (Geronimo Pack Ser.). 8p. (J). (gr. k-2). 1993. pap. write for info. (*1-882563-08-5*) Lamont Bks.

Ben O'Wulf: The Canine of a Thousand Faces. Kirstie A. Rothauge. LC 93-93771. (Illus.). 72p. (Orig.). 1994. pap. 7.00 (*1-56002-306-6*, Univ Edtns) Aegina Pr.

Ben Pepper. Margaret Sidney. (YA). 1992. reprint ed. lib. bdg. 25.95 (*0-89966-969-7*) Buccaneer Bks.

Ben Shahn. Frances K. Pohl. LC 93-24781. (Illus.). 168p. 1993. 50.00 (*1-56640-313-8*); pap. 35.00 (*1-56640-312-X*) Pomegranate Calif.

Ben Shahn: New Deal Artist in a Cold War Climate, 1947-1954. Frances K. Pohl. LC 88-39304. (American Studies Ser.). (Illus.). 250p. 1989. 24.95 (*0-292-75537-6*); pap. 14.95 (*0-292-75538-4*) U of Tex Pr.

Ben Shahn: The Passion of Sacco & Vanzetti. Martin H. Bush. LC 68-54903. (Illus.). 1969. 24.95 (*0-8156-8047-3*) Syracuse U Pr.

Ben Shahn: Voices & Visions. Alma King. LC 81-14432. (Illus.). 96p. 1981. 25.00 (*0-86534-004-8*) Santa Fe E Gallery.

***Ben Shahn & the Task of Photography in Thirties America.** Susan H. Edwards. (Illus.). 32p. (Orig.). Date not set. pap. 8.00 (*1-885998-02-3*) Hunter College.

Ben Shahn, Photographer. Ed. by Margaret R. Weiss. LC 77-75271. (Photography Ser.). 1973. reprint ed. lib. bdg. 25.00 (*0-306-71312-8*) Da Capo.

Ben Sira's View of Women: A Literary Analysis. Warren C. Trenchard. LC 82-16755. (Brown Judaic Studies: No. 38). 352p. (C). 1982. pap. 16.75 (*0-89130-593-9*, 14-00-38) Scholars Pr GA.

Ben Snipes: Northwest Cattle King. 5th ed. Roscoe Sheller. LC 57-13209. (Illus.). 218p. 1987. pap. 9.95 (*0-8323-0250-3*) Binford Mort.

Ben Unleashed. John Troy. (Illus.). 96p. 1988. 12.50 (*0-932558-46-1*) Willow Creek Pr.

Benabarre: The Modernization of a Spanish Village. Richard A. Barrett. (Illus.). 110p. (C). 1986. reprint ed. pap. text ed. 8.50 (*0-88133-241-0*) Waveland Pr.

Benaki see **Greek Museums**

Benami Transaction (Prohibition) Act, 1988 with Loophole; Locunae & Remedies. D. K. Gupta. (C). 1989. 150.00 (*0-685-27900-6*) St Mut.

Benami Transactions. Nathuni Lal. (C). 1990. 125.00 (*0-89771-268-4*) St Mut.

Benard Cells & Taylor Vortices. E. L. Koschmieder. LC 92-11009. (Monographs on Mechanics & Applied Mathematics). (Illus.). 288p. (C). 1993. 69.95 (*0-521-40204-2*) Cambridge U Pr.

Benares. Anita Ganeri. LC 93-72036. (Holy Spirit Minibooks Ser.). (Illus.). 48p. (J). (gr. 5 up). 1993. text ed. 13.95 (*0-87518-573-8*, Dillon Silver Burdett) Silver Burdett Pr.

Benares: The Sacred City of the Hindus. M. A. Sherring. 1990. reprint ed. 16.00 (*81-85418-68-3*, Pub. by Low Price II) S Asia.

Benavides' Memorial of Sixteen Thirty. Tr. by Peter Forrestal. (Documentary Ser.). (Illus.). 1954. 30.00 (*0-88382-001-3*) AAFH.

Benazir Bhutto: Prime Minister. Elizabeth Bouchard. (Library of Famous Women). (Illus.). 64p. (J). (gr. 3-7). 1992. lib. bdg. 14.95 (*1-56711-027-4*) Blackbirch.

Bench & Bar: Reminiscences of One of the Last of an Ancient Race. Serjeant Robinson. (Illus.). xi, 327p. 1988. reprint ed. lib. bdg. 32.50 (*0-8377-2537-2*) Rothman.

Bench & Bar of Colonial Easton. H. J. Steele. 14p. (Orig.). 1931. pap. 3.00 (*1-877701-01-7*) NCH&GS.

Bench & Bar of Other Lands. William L. Burdick. LC 39-32691. xii, 652p. 1982. reprint ed. lib. bdg. 47.50 (*0-89941-163-0*, 302090) W S Hein.

Bench & Bar of the Commonwealth of Massachusetts, 2 vols, Set. William Davis. (American Constitutional & Legal History Ser). 1299p. 1974. reprint ed. lib. bdg. 145.00 (*0-306-70612-1*) Da Capo.

***Bench & Bar of the South & Southwest.** Henry S. Foote. LC 94-79744. 274p. 1994. 45.00 (*0-89941-914-3*, 308550) W S Hein.

Bench & Bureaucracy: The Public Career of Sir Julius Caesar, 1580-1636. L. M. Hill. LC 87-7043. 336p. 1988. 39.50 (*0-8047-1417-7*) Stanford U Pr.

Bench & Me: Teaching & Learning Medicine. J. Willis Hurst. LC 92-1517. (Illus.). 112p. 1992. pap. 19.95 (*0-89640-223-1*) Igaku-Shoin.

Bench & the Bar, 2 vols. James Grant. 1985. reprint ed. Vol. 1, 315p & Vol. 2, 308p. lib. bdg. 55.00 (*0-8377-0619-X*) Rothman.

Bench Book for Trial Judges - New York. suppl. ed. Committee of the Association of Justices of the State of New York Staff. 1993. Suppl. 1993. 28.00 (*0-317-03808-7*) Lawyers Cooperative.

Bench Coaching: Offensive Strategy. Mel Hankinson. 60p. (Orig.). 1983. pap. 8.95 (*0-89279-062-8*) Championship Bks & Vid Prodns.

Bench Coaching Defensive Strategy. Mel Hankinson. 142p. (Orig.). 1993. pap. 14.95 (*1-56404-053-4*) Championship Bks & Vid Prodns.

Bench-Scale Production, Characterization & Application of Polyaluminum Sulfate. 66p. 1988. pap. 12.50 (*0-89867-463-8*, 90540) Am Water Wks Assn.

Bench-Top Orthodontics. Harvey Lawson & Joan Blazucki. (Illus.). 140p. 1990. pap. text ed. 38.00 (*0-86715-233-8*) Quint Pub Co.

Bench Warrants: Their Insurance, Service, & Review. National Center for State Courts Staff. (Paul Reardon Ser.). 28p. 1981. 1.68 (*0-685-15151-4*, PRS-025) Natl Ctr St Courts.

Bench Workout. Nancy Burstein. 1991. mass mkt. 7.95 (*0-446-39246-4*) Warner Bks.

***Benchbook: Anecdotes from the Lighter Side of the Law.** fac. ed. Jerry L. Hayes. LC 87-2065. (Illus.). 114p. 1994. pap. 32.50 (*0-7837-7628-4*, 2047380) Bks Demand.

Benchbook Planning Manual: With Civil & Criminal Law Model Outlines. National Conference of State Trial Judges Judical Benchbook Committee. LC 84-72182. 82p. 1985. pap. 10.00 (*0-89707-153-0*, 484-0003) Amer Bar Assn.

Benched! David Halecroft. (Alden All Stars Ser.). 128p. (J). (gr. 3-7). 1992. pap. 2.99 (*0-14-036038-7*) Puffin Bks.

Benchley Beside Himself. Robert Benchley. (Illus.). 1976. reprint ed. lib. bdg. 20.95 (*0-88411-307-8*, Aeonian Pr) Amereon Ltd.

Benchley Lost & Found. Robert Benchley. 18.95 (*0-89190-498-0*, Am Repr) Amereon Ltd.

Benchley Lost & Found. Robert Benchley. LC 78-88786. (Illus.). 183p. 1970. reprint ed. pap. 4.95 (*0-486-22410-4*) Dover.

***Benchley on Crime.** Robert Benchley. Ed. by Robert Lopresti. 1995. write for info. (*0-89296-576-2*) Mysterious Pr.

Benchley or Else. Robert Benchley. (Illus.). 1976. reprint ed. lib. bdg. 21.95 (*0-88411-306-X*, Aeonian Pr) Amereon Ltd.

Benchley Roundup. Robert Benchley. 23.95 (*0-8488-0915-7*) Amereon Ltd.

Benchley Roundup: A Selection by Nathaniel Benchley of His Favorites. Robert Benchley. LC 83-5111. (Illus.). xii, 334p. 1983. pap. 17.95 (*0-226-04218-9*) U Ch Pr.

Benchmark: Anthology of Contemporary Illinois Poetry. Ed. by James McGowan & Lynn DeVore. LC 88-60183. 331p. 1988. pap. 11.95 (*0-935153-09-8*) Stormline Pr.

Benchmark & Blaze: The Emergence of William Everson. Ed. by Lee Bartlett. LC 78-27137. 292p. 1979. lib. bdg. 22.50 (*0-8108-1198-7*) Scarecrow.

Benchmark Cases for Computer Programs for Pressure Vessel Components Based on BS 5500: 1988. EEMUA Staff. (C). 1988. 90.00 (*0-685-25180-2*, Pub. by EEMUA UK) St Mut.

***Benchmark for Reporting on Chemicals at Industrial Facilities.** Frances H. Irwin et al. LC 95-12147. 1995. pap. write for info. (*0-89164-144-0*) World Wildlife Fund.

Benchmark Handbook for Database & Transaction Processing Systems. 2nd ed. Intro. by Jim Gray. 592p. (C). 1993. text ed. 64.95 (*1-55860-292-5*) Morgan Kaufmann.

Benchmark Ohio, 1989. Ed. by William J. Shkurti & John Bartle. 170p. 1989. pap. 15.00 (*0-8142-0495-3*) Ohio St U Pr.

Benchmark Ohio, 1991. Ed. by William Shkurti & John Bartle. (Illus.). 304p. 1991. pap. text ed. 18.95 (*0-8142-0526-7*) Ohio St U Pr.

Benchmark Problems for Heat Transfer Codes. Ed. by B. Blackwell & D. W. Pepper. (HTD Ser.: Vol. 222). 96p. 1992. 30.00 (*0-7918-1065-8*, G00709) ASME.

Benchmark Problems for the Validation of Eddy Current Computer Codes. Ed. by Larry Turner. (Illus.). 110p. (Orig.). (C). 1990. 49.50 (*0-907383-53-X*, Pub. by J & J Sci Pubs UK) Bks Intl VA.

***Benchmarking.** Rolstadas. 1995. (*0-412-62680-2*) Chapman & Hall.

***Benchmarking: A Managers Care.** Meredith Bolon & Amy Weber. (Monograph Ser.). 104p. 1995. pap. 12.95 (*0-944533-44-2*) Coopers Total Qlty.

Benchmarking: A Practitioner's Guide for Becoming & Staying Best of the Best. Gerald J. Balm. 125p. 1992. pap. 19.95 (*0-9632167-0-8*) Quality & Prod Mgt.

Benchmarking: A Signpost to Excellence in Quality & Productivity. Bengt Karlof & Svante Ostblom. Tr. by Alan J. Gilderson. LC 93-5131. 1994. text ed. 49.95 (*0-471-94180-8*) Wiley.

Benchmarking: A Tool for Continuous Improvement. C. J. McNair & Kathleen H. Leibfried. LC 93-61001. 344p. (C). 1993. pap. 18.00 (*0-939246-53-8*) Oliver Wight.

Benchmarking: Adding Distinctive Value to Every Aspect of Your Business. Carol J. McNair. 1992. 29.00 (*0-88730-548-2*) Harper Busn.

***Benchmarking: Finding & Using Best Practices.** James G. Patterson. Ed. by Philip Gerould. (50-Minute Ser.). (Illus.). 100p. (Orig.). 1995. pap. 9.95 (*1-56052-356-5*) Crisp Pubns.

Benchmarking: Focus on World-Class Practices. Kathleen Mallette & Joann Tomlinson. Ed. by Susan Serritella. (AT&T Quality Library). 126p. (Orig.). 1992. pap. 29.95 (*0-932764-24-X*, 500-454) AT&T Customer Info.

Benchmarking: The Search for Industry Best Practices That Lead to Superior Performance. Robert C. Camp. (Illus.). 299p. 1989. 34.95 (*0-87389-058-2*, H0575) ASQC Qual Pr.

Benchmarking: The Search for Industry Best Practices That Lead to Superior Performance. Robert C. Camp. (Illus.). 320p. 1989. text ed. 34.95 (*0-527-91635-8*, 916358) Qual Resc.

Benchmarking Book. Michael J. Spendolini. 224p. 1993. 26.95 (*0-8144-5077-6*) AMACOM.

Benchmarking Book. Michael J. Spendolini. 209p. 1994. pap. 17.95 (*0-8144-7866-2*) AMACOM.

Benchmarking Customer Satisfaction in the Help Desk Industry: A Help Desk Institute White Paper. Peter J. Ziek & Fred Schrecengost. Ed. by Patrick Baltema et al. (Illus.). (Orig.). (C). Date not set. pap. write for info. (*1-57125-001-8*) Help Desk Inst.

Benchmarking Customer Service. Glen Peters. (Financial Times Management Ser.). 256p. 1995. 67.50x (*0-273-61069-4*, Pub. by Pitman Pub Ltd UK) Trans-Atl Phila.

Benchmarking for Best Practices. Christopher E. Bogan. 1994. text ed. 24.95 (*0-07-006375-3*) McGraw.

Benchmarking for Competitive Advantage. Tony Bendell et al. (Financial Times Management Ser.). 224p. 1993. 75.00x (*0-273-60168-7*, Pub. by Pitman Pub Ltd UK) Trans-Atl Phila.

Benchmarking For Competitive Advantage. Robert J. Boxwell. 1994. text ed. 34.95 (*0-07-006899-2*) McGraw.

***Benchmarking for Effective Network Management.** Kornel Terplan. LC 95-6614. 1995. text ed. 55.00 (*0-07-063638-9*) TAB Bks.

***Benchmarking for Facility Management Workbook.** Earnie Leake & John L. Stanley. 108p. (Orig.). 1994. pap. 150.00 (*1-883176-05-0*, 146050) Intl Facility Mgmt Assn.

Benchmarking Global Manufacturing: Understanding International Suppliers, Customers, & Competitors. Jeffrey G. Miller et al. (APICS Ser.). 443p. 1994. 47.50 (*1-55623-674-3*) Irwin Prof Pubng.

***Benchmarking in Health Care: A Collaborative Approach.** Robert G. Gift & Doug Mosel. LC 94-22781. 191p. 1994. 49.00 (*1-55648-125-X*, 16907) AHPI.

Benchmarking Management Guide. American Productivity & Quality Center Staff. (Illus.). 255p. 1993. 40.00 (*1-56327-045-5*) Prod Press.

***Benchmarking Purchasing in the Semiconductor Industry with Sigma Barometers.** Henry A. Malec. Ed. by Carol Ketchum. 22p. (Orig.). (C). 1991. pap. text ed. 20.00 (*0-945968-09-4*) Ctr Advanced Purchasing.

Benchmarking Staff Performance: How Staff Departments Can Enhance Their Value to the Customer. Jac Fitz-enz. LC 93-27747. (Management Ser.). 223p. 1993. 28.95 (*1-55542-573-9*) Jossey-Bass.

Benchmarking Strategies for Healthcare Management. Mark T. Czarnecki. LC 94-18369. 1994. Loose leaf. ring bd. 249.00 (*0-8342-0604-8*, S153) Aspen Pub.

Benchmarking Workbook: Adapting Best Practices for Performance Improvement. Gregory H. Watson. (Illus.). 169p. 1992. 30.00 (*1-56327-033-1*) Prod Press.

Benchmarks. Henry J. Friendly. LC 67-12149. 334p. reprint ed. pap. 95.20 (*0-8357-7127-X*, 2020063) Bks Demand.

Benchmarks: Alternative Methods in Toxicology. Ed. by M. A. Mehlman. LC 88-63539. 220p. 1989. 55.00 (*0-911131-19-0*) Princeton Sci Pubs.

Benchmarks: G[illegible] Bookshelf. Algis Budrys. LC 84-10518. 380p. 1985. 19.95 (*0-8093-1187-9*) S Ill U Pr.

***Benchmarks: Great Constitutional Controversies in the Supreme Court.** Ed. by Terry Eastland. 152p. 1995. 17.99 (*0-8028-3771-9*) Eerdmans.

Benchmarks for Designing Workers' Compensation Medical Fee Schedules. Stacey M. Eccleston et al. LC 93-35599. 1993. 50.00 (*0-935149-42-2*) Workers Comp Res Inst.

***Benchmarks for Designing Workers' Compensation Medical Fee Schedules: 1994-1995.** Philip L. Burstein. 1994. 50.00 (*0-935149-50-3*) Workers Comp Res Inst.

***Benchmarks for Job Analysis: A Guide for Functional Job Analysis (FJA) Scales.** Sidney A. Fine & Maury Getkate. (Applied Psychology Ser.). 350p. 1995. 70.00 (*0-8058-1813-8*); pap. 40.00 (*0-8058-1814-6*) L Erlbaum Assocs.

Benchmarks for Science Literacy. American Association for the Advancement of Science Staff. 448p. 1994. 21.95 (*0-19-508986-3*) OUP.

Benchmarks for Science Literacy: Science for All Americans Set. American Association for the Advancement of Science Staff. 1994. 32.50 (*0-19-509110-8*) OUP.

Benchmarks for Science Literacy on Disk: MS-DOS Version. American Association for the Advancement of Science Staff. (Illus.). 1994. reprint ed. 24.95 (*0-19-509399-2*) OUP.

***Benchmarks II.** International Facility Management Association Staff. (Research Reports Ser.: No. 13). (Illus.). 64p. (Orig.). 1994. pap. 100.00 (*1-883176-00-X*, 146011) Intl Facility Mgmt Assn.

Benchmarks in Time & Culture: An Introduction to the History & Methodology of Syro-Palestinian Archaeology. Ed. by Joel F. Drinkard, Jr. et al. LC 87-20513. (Society of Biblical Literature Ser.). 500p. 1988. pap. 31.95 (*1-55540-173-2*) Scholars Pr GA.

Benchmarks of Quality in the Church. Gustave Rath & Norman Shawchuck. 144p. (Orig.). 1994. pap. 14.95 (*0-687-34912-5*) Abingdon.

Benchtop Electronics Reference Manual. 2nd ed. Victor F. Veley. (Illus.). 816p. 1990. 39.95 (*0-8306-7414-4*, 3414); pap. 29.95 (*0-8306-3414-2*) TAB Bks.

Benchtop Electronics Reference Manual. 3rd ed. Victor F. Veley. LC 93-44634. (Orig.). 1994. text ed. 54.95 (*0-07-067376-4*) TAB Bks.

Benchwork. Robert G. Dixon. LC 80-66607. (Machine Trades-Machine Shop Ser.). (Illus.). 211p. 1981. teacher ed 12.00 (*0-8273-1744-1*); pap. text ed. 19.95 (*0-8273-1743-3*) Delmar.

Bend Backward for Better Reception. David Gianatasio. 30p. (Orig.). 1992. pap. 3.00 (*0-926935-69-0*) Runaway Spoon.

Bend in Central Oregon. 2nd ed. Raymond R. Hatton. LC 78-63256. (Illus.). 160p. 1986. pap. 9.95 (*0-8323-0316-X*) Binford Mort.

Bend in the Ganges. Monohar Malgonkar. 382p. (C). 1981. reprint ed. pap. 4.00 (*0-88253-772-5*) Ind-US Inc.

Bend in the River. V. S. Naipaul. 1992. 21.00 (*0-8446-6631-9*) Peter Smith.

Bend in the River. V. S. Naipaul. (International Ser.). 1989. pap. 10.00 (*0-679-72202-5*, Vin) Random.

Bend in the River. V. S. Naipaul. 1980. pap. 5.95 (*0-394-74314-8*) Random.

Bend in the River: A Prehistory & Contact Period History, Lowell, Dracut, Chelmsford, Tyngsborough & Dunstable (Nashua, NH), Massachusetts 17,000 BP to AD1700. John Pendergast. (Illus.). xvii, 92p. (Orig.). 1991. pap. text ed. 14.95 (*0-9629338-0-5*) Merrimack River.

Bend Like the Bamboo. Eleanor H. Murray. 91p. (Orig.). (YA). (gr. 9-12). 1982. pap. 8.95 (*1-879313-02-2*) Murrays Leprechaun Bks.

Bend Sinister. Vladimir Nabokov. LC 89-40559. (Vintage International Ser.). 256p. 1990. pap. 13.00 (*0-679-72727-2*, Vin) Random.

Bend This Heart. Jonis Agee. LC 89-7100. 130p. (Orig.). 1989. pap. 9.95 (*0-918273-51-X*) Coffee Hse.

Bend Toward Asia. Tom Sexton. 68p. (Orig.). (C). 1993. pap. 9.95 (*0-9634000-3-7*) Salmon Run.

Bendable Siege Poems. Albert Mohilio. 14p. 1991. 3.00 (*0-87376-068-9*) Red Dust.

Bendecidos Para Bendecir - Blessed to Be a Blessing: Teologia de la Mision - Biblical Theology of Mission. W. Douglas Smith. 384p. (Orig.). (SPA.). 1992. pap. 8.65 (*0-311-29011-6*) Casa Bautista.

Bendemolena see **Cat Who Wore a Pot on Her Head**

Bender. Paul Scott. 320p. 1986. pap. 3.95 (*0-88184-231-1*) Carroll & Graf.

Bender Gestalt Screening for Brain Dysfunction. Patricia Lacks. (Personality Processes Ser.: No. 223). 223p. 1984. text ed. 64.95 (*0-471-88046-9*, Wiley-Interscience) Wiley.

Bender Visual Motor Gestalt Test for Children: A Manual. Aileen Clawson. LC 79-57294. (Illus.). 92p. 1962. pap. 39.50x (*0-87424-035-2*, W-35) Western Psych.

Benders: Keepers of the Devil's Inn. Fern M. Wood. (Illus.). 120p. (Orig.). 1992. pap. 7.95 (*0-9606922-1-5*) F M Wood.

Bender's Anatomy: Charts. Houts & Bloodhart. 1962. Desk edition. write for info. (*0-8205-1066-1*) Bender.

Bender's Anatomy Charts. Marshall Houts. (Illus.). 1962. Courtroom edition. write for info. (*0-8205-1065-3*) Bender.

Bender's Federal Practice Forms, 16 vols. Louis R. Frumer et al. 1957. ring bd. write for info. (*0-8205-1090-4*) Bender.

Bender's Federal Practice Manual, 2 vols. I. Hall & Marvin Waxner. 1948. Updates available. ring bd. write for info. (*0-8205-1100-5*) Bender.

Bender's Federal Tax Forms. Matthew Bender's Tax Staff. 1990. write for info. (*0-8205-1367-9*) Bender.

Bender's Federal Tax Service, 20 vols. 1989. write for info. (*0-8205-1067-X*) Bender.

Bender's Florida Forms: Pleadings, 14 vols. Richard H. Maloy & Wilbur S. McDuff. 1968. write for info. (*0-8205-1101-3*) Bender.

Bender's Forms for the Civil Practice, 32 vols. Louis R. Frumer & Oscar L. Warren. 1963. ring bd. write for info. (*0-8205-1075-0*) Bender.

Bender's Forms for the Consolidated Laws of New York, 53 vols., Set. Bender's Editorial Staff et al. 1930. write for info. (*0-8205-1070-X*) Bender.

Bender's Forms of Discovery, 20 vols., Set. Bender's Editorial Staff. LC 63-3100. 1963. ring bd. write for info. (*0-8205-1103-X*) Bender.

Bender's Forms of Pleading, 22 vols. Oscar L. Warren & Gloria C. Markuson. 1946. Updates available. ring bd. write for info. (*0-8205-1120-X*) Bender.

Bender's Immigration & Nationality Pamphlet. 1987. write for info. (*0-8205-1466-7*) Bender.

***Benders in Kansas.** John T. James. (Illus.). 196p. 1995. write for info. (*1-882355-04-0*); pap. write for info. (*1-882355-05-9*) Mostly Bks Pub.

Bender's INS Regulation Service. 1989. write for info. (*0-8205-1695-3*) Bender.

Bender's Master Federal Tax Handbook. 1989. write for info. (*0-8205-1601-5*) Bender.

Bender's New York Evidence: CPLR, 7 vols. Louis R. Frumer & Elliot Bisking. 1962. Updates available. ring bd. write for info. (*0-8205-1108-0*) Bender.

Bender's Payroll Tax Guide. Bender's Tax Staff & Marcus Jason. 1982. Annual. write for info. (*0-8205-1539-6*) Bender.

Bender's Tax Return Manual. Bender's Tax Staff. 1973. write for info. (*0-8205-1121-8*) Bender.

Bendiceme, Ultima: Bless Me, Ultima. Rudolfo Anaya. Tr. by Alicia Smithers. 320p. (SPA.). 1994. mass mkt. 5.50 (*0-446-60177-2*) Warner Bks.

An Asterisk (*) at the beginning of an entry indicates that the title is appearing in BIP for the first time.

An Asterisk (*) at the beginning of an entry indicates that the title is appearing in BIP for the first time.

Beneficiary. Barbara Konig. Tr. by Roslyn Theobald. 120p. 1993. 19.95 (0-8101-1105-5) Northwestern U Pr.

Beneficiary Book. Martin Kuritz et al. 1992. ring bd. 30.00 (0-9637228-0-8) Active Insights.

***Beneficiation of Mineral Fines: Problems & Research Needs: Report of Workshop Organized by Columbia University & Held at Sterling Forest, New York, August 27-29, 1978.** fac. ed. Ed. by P. Somasundaran & N. Arbiter. LC 79-91945. (Illus.). 414p. 1979. reprint ed. pap. 118.00 (0-7837-7861-9, 2047620) Bks Demand.

Beneficiation of Phosphate: Theory & Practice. Ed. by H. El-Shall et al. LC 93-84489. (Illus.). 481p. 1993. 85.00 (0-87335-119-3, 119-3) SMM&E Inc.

Beneficios De la Lectura De la Biblia: Benefits of Bible Reading. Arthur Pink. (SPA.). 4.25 (84-7228-621-5, 220095, Pub. by Edit Clie SP) TSELF.

Beneficios y Beneficiarios: Una Introduccion a la Estimacion de los Efectos Distributivos en el Analisis Costo Beneficio. Elio Londero. 312p. 1987. write for info. (0-940602-24-5) IADB.

Benefit - Cost Analysis: Theory & Policy. Zerbe & Dively. (C). 1993. text ed. 66.50 (0-673-18066-2) HarpCollege.

***Benefit Adjuster.** (Career Examination Ser.: Series 1). Date not set. pap. 27.95 (0-8373-3694-5) Nat Learn.

Benefit Communications: Enhancing the Employer's Investment. Victor S. Barocas. (Report Ser.: No. 1035). (Illus.). 52p. (Orig.). 1993. pap. text ed. 100.00 (0-8237-0507-2) Conference Bd.

Benefit-Cost Analyses of Social Regulation: Case Studies from the Council on Wage & Price Stability. Ed. by James C. Miller, III & Bruce Yandle. LC 79-876. 183p. reprint ed. pap. 52.20 (0-8357-4436-1, 2037270) Bks Demand.

Benefit-Cost Analysis for Water System Planning. Ed. by Charles W. Howe. LC 72-182565. (Water Resources Monograph Ser.: Vol. 2). (Illus.). 114p. 1971. pap. 10.00 (0-87590-302-9) Am Geophysical.

Benefit-Cost Analysis of Alternative Library Delivery Systems. Hu Teh-Wei et al. LC 74-5989. (Contributions in Librarianship & Information Science Ser.: No. 13). 256p. 1975. text ed. 55.00 (0-8371-7528-3, HUA/, Greenwood Pr) Greenwood.

Benefit-Cost Analysis of Data Used to Allocate Funds. B. P. Spencer. (Lecture Notes in Statistics Ser.: Vol. 3). 296p. 1980. pap. 45.00 (0-387-90511-1) Spr-Verlag.

Benefit-Cost Model for the Seismic Rehabilitation of Buildings, Vol. 1: A User's Manual. (Illus.). 130p. (Orig.). (C). 1993. pap. text ed. 40.00 (1-56806-996-0) Diane Pub.

Benefit-Cost Model for the Seismic Rehabilitation of Buildings, Vol. 2: Supporting Documentation. (Illus.). 125p. (Orig.). (C). 1993. pap. text ed. 40.00 (1-56806-997-9) Diane Pub.

Benefit Design: Clinical Preventive Services. 1994. lib. bdg. 250.00 (0-8490-8544-6) Gordon Pr.

Benefit Design: Patient Cost-Sharing, Background Paper. 1994. lib. bdg. 250.00 (0-8490-8545-4) Gordon Pr.

Benefit Design in Health Care Reform: Clinical Preventive Services. (Illus.). 95p. (Orig.). (C). 1994. pap. text ed. 40.00 (0-7881-0757-7) Diane Pub.

Benefit Design in Health Care Reform: Patient Cost-Sharing. (Illus.). 65p. (Orig.). (C). 1994. pap. text ed. 30.00 (0-7881-0756-9) Diane Pub.

Benefit Designs for the C Corporation. A. S. Feksenfeld. Date not set. 39.50 (1-56461-041-1, 46140) Rough Notes.

Benefit Designs for the S Corporation. A. S. Fehsenfeld. 1993. 29.50 (1-56461-040-3, 46130) Rough Notes.

Benefit Increases & System Utilization: The Connecticut Experience. John A. Gardner. 1991. 25.00 (0-935149-31-7, WC-91-5) Workers Comp Res Inst.

Benefit Plans Disputes: Arbitration Case Stories. Morris Stone. 92p. 1976. pap. 3.50 (0-685-25770-3) Am Arbitration.

Benefit Plans in Higher Education. Francis P. King & Thomas J. Cook. LC 79-28751. (Illus.). 1980. text ed. 66.00 (0-231-04914-5) Col U Pr.

Benefit Your Business. James F. Schwoob. LC 89-90862. (Illus.). (Orig.). 1989. pap. 16.95 (0-9622483-0-4) Single-Knight.

Benefiting from Basic Education in Developing Countries: A Review of Research on the External Efficiency of Educational Investments. Thomas O. Eisemon. LC 87-23829. (Special Studies in Comparative Education: No. 20). 78p. 1987. pap. text ed. 10.00 (0-937033-10-3) SUNY GSE Pub.

Benefits & Beneficiaries: An Introduction to Estimating Distributional Effects in Cost-Benefit Analysis. Elio Londero. 304p. 1987. write for info. (0-940602-23-7) IADB.

Benefits & Burdens: A Report on the West Bank & Gaza Strip Economies Since 1967. Brian Van Arkadie. LC 76-57443. 1977. pap. text ed. 3.75 (0-87003-006-X) Carnegie Endow.

***Benefits & Compensation Strategies: 1995.** (Illus.). 300p. (Orig.). 1994. pap. 495.00 (0-7605-0975-1) Rector Pr.

Benefits & Costs of Import Substitution in India: Microeconomic Study. Anne O. Krueger. LC 74-81752. 154p. reprint ed. pap. 43.90 (0-8357-7128-8, 2055887) Bks Demand.

Benefits & Risks of Knowledge-Based Systems. Council for Science & Society Staff. 88p. 1989. pap. 14.95 (0-19-854743-9) OUP.

Benefits, Costs & Cycles in Workers Compensation. Ed. by Philip S. Borba & David Appel. (S. S. Huebner International Ser.). (C). 1990. lib. bdg. 53.00 (0-7923-9037-7) Huebner Foun Insur.

Benefits Estimates & Environment Decision-Making. OECD Staff. 64p. (Orig.). 1992. pap. 14.00 (92-64-13751-3) OECD.

Benefits in Medical Care Programs. Avedis Donabedian. 432p. 1990. 45.00 (0-674-06580-8) HUP.

***Benefits of Brain-Based Art in Schools: A New Look at the Role of Art in Education.** Ken Renshaw & Joyce Renshaw. LC 94-21286. (Illus.). 115p. 1994. pap. 21.95 (0-614-04750-1) Constellation Pr.

Benefits of Computer-Aided Design & Manufacture-Clothing & Textiles. Design Council Staff. (C). 1992. pap. text ed. 125.00 (0-85072-307-8) St Mut.

Benefits of Different Transport Modes: Round Table, No. 93. OECD Staff. 105p. (Orig.). 1994. pap. 18.00 (92-821-1189-X) OECD.

Benefits of Doubt. Felix Pollak. 200p. 1988. 15.95 (0-944024-04-1) Spoon Riv Poetry.

Benefits of Doubt: A Comparative Study of the Unemployment Benefit Schemes & Reintegration Opportunities of Great Britain, France, the Federal Republic of Germany & the Netherlands. F. Pennings. 512p. 1991. pap. 79.00 (90-6544-512-9) Kluwer Law Tax Pubs.

Benefits of Environmental Improvement: Theory & Practice. A. Myrick Freeman. LC 78-20532. (Resources for the Future Ser.). 272p. 1979. text ed. 23.00 (0-8018-2163-0); pap. text ed. 9.95 (0-8018-2195-9) Johns Hopkins.

Benefits of Exercise: The Evidence. P. H. Fentem et al. 320p. 1990. text ed. 90.00 (0-7190-2430-7, Pub. by Manchester Univ Pr UK) St Martin.

Benefits of Exercise & Physical Fitness: The Continuing Plan. S. Mikielle Chatman. (Fat Chance Series Book Group: No. 12). 50p. 1992. pap. 3.99 (1-881146-13-8) Fat Chance.

Benefits of Famine: A Political Economy of Famine & Relief in Southwestern Sudan, 1983-1989. David Keen. LC 93-34900. 1994. 47.50 (0-691-03423-0) Princeton U Pr.

Benefits of Free Trade: East Asia & Latin America. OECD Staff. 228p. (Orig.). 1994. pap. 49.00 (92-64-14110-3) OECD.

Benefits of Leisure. Ed. by B. L. Driver et al. LC 91-67118. 483p. 1991. 31.95 (0-910251-48-7) Venture Pub PA.

Benefits of Old Age: Social Welfare Policy for the Elderly. Elizabeth A. Kutza. LC 80-24241. 176p. (C). 1981. pap. text ed. 8.00 (0-226-46566-7) U Ch Pr.

Benefits of Psychotherapy. Mary L. Smith et al. LC 80-11610. 285p. reprint ed. pap. 81.30 (0-8357-7129-6, 2025628) Bks Demand.

***Benefits of Recreation Research Update (1991-1994)** Judy M. Sefton & W. Kerry Mummery. LC 95-60644. 40p. (C). 1995. pap. text ed. 12.95 (0-910251-75-4, BRU80) Venture Pub PA.

Benefits of Righteousness. Robert D. Shackelford. 73p. (Orig.). (YA). (gr. 9-12). 1988. pap. 3.95 (0-9618308-2-4) R Shackelford.

Benefits of Slavery: The New Proslavery Argument. Ed. by John D. Smith. LC 92-27189. (Anti-Black Thought, 1863-1925 Ser.: Vol. 4). 400p. 1993. 62.00 (0-8153-0976-7) Garland.

Benefits of Therapeutic Recreation: A Consensus View. Coyle et al. 424p. (C). 1993. pap. text ed. 32.00 (1-882883-06-3) Idyll Arbor.

***Benefits of Timeshare Ownership: Results from a Nationwide Survey of Timeshare Owners.** (Industry Issues Ser.). 59p. 1992. 75.00 (0-614-04625-4, 21300) ARDA.

Benefits Review Board Reporters: Black Lung Reporter, 3 vols. Bender's Editorial Staff. 1980. write for info. (0-8205-1144-7) Bender.

Benefits Review Board Reporters: Longshore, 3 vols. Bender's Editorial Staff. 1974. Updates available. write for info. (0-8205-1135-8) Bender.

Benefits Review, Tax & Legal Occupations. (Career Examination Ser.: No. C-3552). 1994. 23.95 (0-8373-3552-3) Nat Learn.

***Benefits Study.** ATA National Accounting & Finance Council Staff. 1995. pap. 150.00 (0-88711-273-0) Am Trucking Assns.

Benefits Today. BNA's Business & Human Resources Services Staff. 1984. ring bd. 480.00 (0-685-14344-9) BNA.

Benelux: An Economic Geography of Belgium, the Netherlands, & Luxembourg. R. C. Riley & Gregory Ashworth. LC 74-84586. (Illus.). 258p. 1975. 30.00 (0-8419-0174-0) Holmes & Meier.

***Benelux Red Guide.** Michelin Staff. 1994. 24.95 (0-7859-7164-5, 2060060494) Fr & Eur.

***Benelux Red Guide.** Michelin Staff. 1995. 24.00 (2-06-006059-1, 605) Michelin.

Benet's Reader's Encyclopedia: The Classic & Only Encyclopedia of World Literature in a Single Volume. 3rd ed. LC 87-45022. 1091p. 1987. 45.00 (0-06-181088-6, Harper Ref) HarpC.

Benet's Reader's Encyclopedia of American Literature. Ed. by George Perkins et al. LC 91-55001. 1056p. 1991. 45.00 (0-06-270027-8, Harper Ref) HarpC.

***Benevent Treasure.** P. Wentworth. Date not set. pap. 3.99 (0-517-13221-4) Random.

Benevent Treasure. Patricia Wentworth. 1976. reprint ed. lib. bdg. 21.95 (0-88411-731-6, Aeonian Pr) Amereon Ltd.

Benevent Treasure: A Miss Silver Mystery. Patricia Wentworth. LC 92-52678. 1992. pap. 8.00 (0-06-092336-9, PL) HarpC.

Beneventan Chant. Thomas F. Kelly. (Cambridge Studies in Music). (Illus.). (C). 1989. 94.95 (0-521-34310-0) Cambridge U Pr.

Benevolence among Slaveholders: Assisting the Poor in Charleston, 1670-1860. Barbara L. Bellows. LC 93-18057. 272p. (C). 1993. text ed. 29.95 (0-8071-1833-8) La State U Pr.

Benevolence & Betrayal: Five Italian Jewish Families under Fascism. Alexander Stille. (Illus.). 368p. 1993. pap. 12.50 (0-14-017715-9, Penguin Bks) Viking Penguin.

***Benevolence & Blasphemy: Memoirs of a Contemporary Art Collector.** J. Robert Orton, Jr. LC 95-60520. 288p. (Orig.). 1995. pap. 13.95 (1-885983-05-0) Turtle Point Pr.

Benevolent Assimilation: The American Conquest of the Philippines, 1899-1903. Stuart C. Miller. LC 82-1957. 342p. 1984. reprint ed. pap. 17.00 (0-300-03081-9, Y-488) Yale U Pr.

***Benevolent Conspiracies: The Role of Enabling Technologies in Reframing the Welfare of Nations. The Case of SDI, Sematech & Eureka.** Helmut Wilke et al. LC 95-3267. (Studies in Organization: No. 62). 367p. 1995. lib. bdg. 129.25 (3-11-014485-9) De Gruyter.

Benevolent Deity: Ebenezer Gay & the Rise of Rational Religion in New England, 1669-1787. Robert J. Wilson, III. LC 83-3657. (Illus.). 320p. 1984. 41.95x (0-8122-7891-7) U of Pa Pr.

Benevolent Dictators see Advertising's Benevolent Dictators

Benevolent Living: Tracing the Roots of Motivation to God. Richard Hazelett & Dean Turner. LC 89-11197. (Illus.). 448p. 1990. 19.95 (0-932727-32-8) Hope Pub Hse.

Benevolent Man: A Life of Ralph Allen of Bath. Benjamin Boyce. LC 67-11667. (Illus.). 318p. reprint ed. pap. 90.70 (0-7837-1675-3, 2057207) Bks Demand.

Benevolent Repression: Social Control & the American Reformatory-Prison Movement. Alexander W. Pisciotta. LC 93-41515. 1994. 35.00 (0-8147-6623-4) NYU Pr.

***Bengal: Communities, Development, & States.** Ed. by Sekhar Bandyopadhyay. (C). 1994. text ed. 30.00 (81-7304-089-3, Pub. by Manohar II) S Asia.

Bengal: Imperial Gazetteer of India. 1985. reprint ed. 76.00 (0-8364-1339-3, Pub. by Usha II) S Asia.

Bengal: The British Bridgehead. P. J. Marshall. (New Cambridge History of India Ser.: II: 2). (Illus.). 200p. 1988. 44.95 (0-521-25330-6) Cambridge U Pr.

Bengal: The Nationalist Movement, 1876-1940. Leonard A. Gordon. LC 73-12974. 407p. 1974. text ed. 56.00 (0-231-03753-8) Col U Pr.

***Bengal Cats: Everything about Purchase, Care, Nutrition, Breeding, Diseases, & Behavior.** Dan Rice. (Complete Pet Owner's Manual Ser.). (Illus.). 1995. write for info. (0-8120-9243-0) Barron.

Bengal Cavalry Regiments 1857-1914. R. G. Harris. (Men-at-Arms Ser.: No. 91). (Illus.). 48p. pap. 11.95 (0-85045-308-9, 9213, Pub. by Osprey UK) Stackpole.

Bengal Divided: Hindu Communalism & Partition, 1932-1947. Joya Chatterji. (Cambridge South Asian Studies: No. 57). (Illus.). 376p. (C). 1995. 59.95 (0-521-41128-9) Cambridge U Pr.

Bengal Fairy Tales. F. B. Bradley-Birt. 1976. lib. bdg. 59.95 (0-8490-1487-5) Gordon Pr.

Bengal in Seventeen Fifty-Six to Seventeen Fifty-Seven: A Selection of Public & Private Papers Dealing with the Affairs of the British in Bengal During the Reign of Siraj-Uddaula, 3 Vols, Set. Samuel C. Hill. LC 70-180684. reprint ed. 92.50 (0-404-03310-5) AMS Pr.

Bengal in the Sixteenth Century A. D. J. N. Dasgupta. 1989. reprint ed. 26.00 (81-85326-11-8) S Asia.

Bengal Monitor. Walter Auffenberg. LC 94-3869. (Illus.). 592p. 1994. lib. bdg. 79.95 (0-8130-1295-3) U Press Fla.

Bengal Native Army to Year Eighteen Ninety-Five: A Sketch of the Services. G. F. Cardew. (Illus.). 576p. 1971. reprint ed. 10.00 (0-88065-025-7, Messers Today & Tomorrow) Scholarly Pubns.

Bengal Nights. Mircea Eliade. Tr. by Catherine Spencer. LC 93-1489. (ENG & FRE.). 1994. 22.50 (0-226-20418-9) U Ch Pr.

***Bengal Nights: A Novel.** Mircea Eliade. Tr. by Catherine Spencer. 184p. 1995. pap. 9.95 (0-226-20419-7) U Ch Pr.

Bengal, Nineteen Twenty to Forty-Seven: The Land Question. Partha Chatterjee. 1985. 18.50 (0-8364-1305-9, Pub. by KP Bagchi IA) S Asia.

Bengal Peasant Life. Lal B. Day. LC 76-44747. reprint ed. 37.50 (0-404-15946-X) AMS Pr.

Bengal Rubies. Lisa Bingham. Ed. by Carolyn Tolley. 288p. (Orig.). 1993. mass mkt. 5.50 (0-671-77095-0) PB.

Bengal Tiger. Jeannie Ebner. Tr. & Aft. by Lowell A. Bangerter. (Studies in Austrian Literature, Culture, & Thought. Translation Ser.). 101p. (Orig.). 1992. pap. 12.50 (0-929497-54-6) Ariadne CA.

Bengal under Akbar & Jahangir: An Introductory Study in Social History. Tapan Raychaudhuri. 275p. 1969. text ed. 25.00 (0-685-43637-3) Coronet Bks.

Bengala: or Some Time Ago. Mary T. Vidal. Ed. by Susan McKernan. (Colonial Text Ser.). 445p. 1990. pap. 29.95 (0-86840-028-9, Pub. by New South Wales Univ Pr AT) Intl Spec Bk.

Bengali Complete Course. 1994. audio 25.95 (0-8442-3851-1, NTC Busn Bks) NTC Pub Grp.

Bengali-English. 2nd ed. S. Biswas. 932p. 1987. 30.00 (0-88431-106-6) IBD Ltd.

Bengali-English Dictionary. (BEN.). 27.50 (0-87557-109-3) Saphrograph.

***Bengali English Dictionary.** Sahitya Samsad. 1074p. (BEN & ENG.). 1995. 24.95 (0-7818-0372-1) Hippocrene Bks.

Bengali Household Tales. W. McCulloch. LC 78-63211. (Folktale Ser.). reprint ed. 28.00 (0-404-16146-4) AMS Pr.

Bengali Language Handbook. Punya S. Ray et al. LC 66-29717. (Language Handbook Ser.). 155p. reprint ed. pap. 44.20 (0-8357-3357-2, 2039594) Bks Demand.

Bengali Literature. Jyotish C. Ghosh. LC 78-3657. (BCL Ser.: II). reprint ed. 29.50 (0-404-14545-0) AMS Pr.

Bengali Muslim Thought 1818-1947. Pradip K. Lahiri. (C). 1991. 14.00 (81-7074-067-3, Pub. by KP Bagchi IA) S Asia.

Bengali Muslims: A Study in Their Politicization. Chandiprasad Sarkar. (C). 1991. 22.50 (81-7074-096-7, Pub. by KP Bagchi IA) S Asia.

***Bengali Phrasebook.** Bimal Maity. (Illus.). 200p. 1995. pap. 5.95 (0-86442-312-8) Lonely Planet.

Bengali Poems on Calcutta. Samir Dasgupta. 1973. 15.00 (0-88253-324-X); pap. text ed. 6.75 (0-88253-795-4) Ind-US Inc.

Bengali Women. Manisha Roy. LC 92-14268. (Illus.). xviii, 206p. 1992. pap. text ed. 12.95 (0-226-73043-3) U Ch Pr.

Bengal's Contribution to Sanskrit Literature & Studies in Bengal Vaisnavism. S. K. De. 150p. 1974. reprint ed. 10.00 (0-88065-047-8, Messers Today & Tomorrow) Scholarly Pubns.

Benham Book of Palmistry, Complete Book. William G. Benham. 654p. (Orig.). 1991. 14.95 (0-87877-137-9) Newcastle Pub.

BenHur: A Classic Story of Revenge & Redemption. Lew Wallace. Ed. by James S. Bell, Jr. (Christian Epics Ser.). 504p. 1993. pap. 11.99 (0-8024-7101-3) Moody.

Beni the Bashful Beaver. Grandma Marian, pseud. LC 87-71490. (Illus.). 32p. (J). 1988. 6.95 (0-9614989-1-9) Banmar Inc.

Benia Krik: A Film Novel. Isaak E. Babel. Tr. by Ivor Montagu & Sergei Nalbandov. LC 72-90292. (Soviet Literature in English Translation Ser.). 95p. 1976. reprint ed. 15.00 (0-88355-000-8) Hyperion Conn.

Benicia Belle. large type ed. Larry J. Martin. LC 92-32527. (General Ser.). 316p. 1993. 19.95 (0-8161-5609-3) G K Hall.

Benighted Mexico. Randolph W. Smith. 1976. lib. bdg. 59.95 (0-87968-721-5) Gordon Pr.

Benign & Malignant Bone Disease. Ed. by J. H. McKillop & I. Fogelman. (Illus.). 160p. 1991. text ed. 30.00 (0-443-04436-8) Churchill.

Benign & Malignant Lymphadenopathies: A Guide to Clinical & Laboratory Diagnosis. Ed. by Gerassimos A. Pangalis & Aaron Polliack. LC 92-49470. 1993. text ed. 95.00 (3-7186-5232-3) Gordon & Breach.

Benign Breast Disorders & Diseases. Hughes et al. (Illus.). 230p. 1989. text ed. 93.95 (0-7020-1290-4, Bailliere-Tindall) Saunders.

***Benign by Design: Alternative Synthetic Design for Pollution Prevention.** Ed. by Paul T. Anastas & Carol A. Farris. LC 94-38830. (Symposium Ser.: No. 577). (Illus.). 208p. 1994. 59.95 (0-8412-3053-6) Am Chemical.

***Benign Cerebral Glioma, Vol. I.** Ed. by Michael L. Apuzzo. 275p. 1995. 90.00 (1-879284-31-6) Am Assn Neuro.

Benign Crucifixion. E. Robert Bayley, Jr. LC 90-55260. 276p. (Orig.). 1991. pap. 10.00 (1-56002-069-5) Aegina Pr.

Benign Diseases of the Vulva & Vagina. 3rd ed. Ed. by Kaufman. 494p. 1989. 99.00 (0-8151-4974-3, Yr Bk Med Pubs) Mosby Yr Bk.

Benign Diseases of the Vulva & Vagina. 4th ed. Kaufman. 510p. 1994. 95.00 (0-8016-6836-0) Mosby Yr Bk.

Benign Localized & Generalized Epilepsies of Early Childhood. Ed. by R. Degen & F. E. Dreifuss. LC 92-10111. (Epilepsy Research Ser.: Supplement No. 6). 1992. 236.25 (0-444-81266-0) Elsevier.

Benign Postreproductive Gynecology Surgery. Ed. by Marvin H. Grody. LC 93-40645. 480p. 1995. text ed. 69.00 (0-07-105460-X) Hlth Prof Div.

***Benign Prostatic Hyperplasia.** 1995. lib. bdg. 251.95 (0-8490-6847-9) Gordon Pr.

Benign Prostatic Hyperplasia. Ed. by K. H. Kurth & Donald W. Newling. LC 94-5991. (Progress in Clinical & Biological Research Ser.: Vol. 386). 1994. text ed. 125.00 (0-471-30355-0) Wiley.

Benign Prostatic Hyperplasia: Conservative & Operative Management. Ed. by G. Jakse et al. LC 92-49308. 1993. 98.00 (0-387-55424-6) Spr-Verlag.

Benign Prostatic Hyperplasia: Innovations in the Maanagement. Ed. by Z. Petrovich & L. Baert. LC 94-527. (Illus.). 384p. 1994. 129.00 (0-387-56628-7) Spr-Verlag.

Benign Prostatic Hypertrophy. Ed. by F. Hinman, Jr. (Illus.). 1056p. 1983. 193.00 (0-387-90779-3) Spr-Verlag.

***Benign Prostatic Hypertrophy.** David G. Williams. 26p. 1992. pap. 14.95 (0-944649-11-4) Mtn Home Pub.

Benign Reality. Harvey Jackins. LC 81-51519. (Orig.). 1981. 19.00 (0-911214-77-1); pap. 16.00 (0-911214-76-3) Rational Isl.

Benign Structures of the Bile Ducts. Galperin et al. 1987. 60.00 (0-8236-0494-2, BN#00494) Intl Univs Pr.

Benign to Malignant Progression in Cervical Squamous Epithelium. Robert L. Ehrmann. LC 93-31971. (Illus.). 280p. 1994. 95.00 (0-89640-241-X) Igaku-Shoin.

Benign Tumors in the Third Ventricle of the Brain: Diagnosis & Treatment. Walter E. Dandy. (Illus.). 1970. reprint ed. 25.00 (0-87266-037-0) Argosy.

Benigna Machiavelli. Charlotte P. Gilman. LC 93-72625. (Illus.). 178p. (Orig.). 1993. pap. 7.95 (0-942208-18-8) Bandanna Bks.

Benin. (Let's Visit Places & Peoples of the World Ser.). (Illus.). (J). (gr. 5 up). 1989. 14.95 (0-7910-0143-1) Chelsea Hse.

***Benin: Lords of the River.** Philip Koslow. (Kingdoms of Africa Ser.). (Illus.). 64p. (J). (gr. 3 up). 1995. 14.95 (0-7910-3133-0); pap. 7.95 (0-7910-3134-9) Chelsea Hse.

Benin: Political Imprisonment & Torture. 1988. 2.00 (0-685-23305-7) Amnesty Intl USA.

Benin: Royal Art of Africa. Ed. by Armand Duchateau. (Illus.). 136p. 1994. 50.00 (3-7913-1368-1, Pub. by Prestel) TeNeues.

680

An Asterisk (*) at the beginning of an entry indicates that the title is appearing in BIP for the first time.

Benjamin Henry Latrobe & Moncure Robinson: The Engineer As Agent of Technological Transfer. Ed. by Barbara Benson. (Illus.). 72p. 1975. pap. 1.25 (*0-914650-07-6*) Hagley Museum.

Benjamin Henry Latrobe & the Development of Internal Improvements in the New Republic, 1796-1820. Lee W. Formwalt. 1981. 38.95 (*0-405-14080-0*) Ayer.

Benjamin Holt & Caterpillar: Tracks & Combines. Reynold M. Wik. LC 84-72594. 130p. (Orig.). 1984. pap. 18.95 (*0-916150-66-6*, HO984) Am Soc Ag Eng.

Benjamin Jarnes. J. S. Bernstein. LC 78-110707. (Twayne's World Authors Ser.). 1985. lib. bdg. 17.95 (*0-8057-2464-8*) Irvington.

Benjamin John. Kelly Cherry. Ed. by Robert Bixby. 36p. 1993. pap. 6.00 (*1-882983-01-7*) March Street Pr.

Benjamin Katz: Photographs. (Illus.). 180p. 1990. 25.00 (*3-89322-164-6*, Pub. by Edition Cantz GW) Dist Art Pubs.

Benjamin Kidd: Portrait of a Social Darwinist. D. P. Crook. LC 83-19009. 280p. 1984. 79.95 (*0-521-25804-9*) Cambridge U Pr.

Benjamin Lemasters of Nicholas County, West Virginia: His Ancestors, His War Service, His Descendants. Ronald V. Hardway. 138p. 1994. pap. 14.95 (*0-9640644-0-5*) R V Hardway.

Benjamin Levy: La Familia, Memories & Reflections. Ori Z. Soltes. (Illus.). (Orig.). Date not set. pap. text ed. write for info. (*1-881456-09-9*) B B K Natl Jew Mus.

Benjamin Logan: Kentucky Frontiersman. Charles G. Talbert. LC 62-13458. 332p. 1989. reprint ed. 12.50 (*0-935680-22-5*) Kentucke Imprints.

Benjamin Lundy & the Struggle for Negro Freedom. Merton L. Dillon. LC 66-15473. 293p. reprint ed. pap. 83.60 (*0-8357-9663-9*, 2015497) Bks Demand.

Benjamin O. Davis, Jr., American: An Autobiography. Benjamin O. Davis, Jr. (Illus.). 1991. 24.95 (*0-87474-742-2*) Smithsonian.

Benjamin of Tudela: Travels in the Middle Ages. limited ed. Michael A. Signer. Tr. by M. N. Adler. LC 83-50186. (Illus.). 176p. 1987. reprint ed. 30.00 (*0-934710-06-6*) J Simon.

Benjamin of Tudela: Travels in the Middle Ages. Michael A. Signer. Tr. by M. N. Adler. LC 83-50186. (Illus.). 176p. 1987. reprint ed. 20.00 (*0-934710-07-4*) J Simon.

Benjamin Parrott, c1795-1839, & Lewis Stover 1781-1850-60, of Overton County, Tennessee & Their Descendants. Ed. by Mary W. Kelsey et al. 133p. 1978. 25.00 (*0-9613308-3-X*) M P Kelsey.

Benjamin Peirce: Father of Pure Mathematics in America. An Original Anthology. Ed. by I. Bernard Cohen. LC 79-7981. (Three Centuries of Science in America Ser.). (Illus.). 1980. lib. bdg. 35.95 (*0-405-12563-1*) Ayer.

Benjamin Peirce & the U. S. Coast Survey. V. F. Lenzen. (Illus.). 1968. 5.00 (*0-911302-06-9*) San Francisco Pr.

Benjamin Peret. J. H. Matthews. LC 74-30229. (Twayne's World Authors Ser.). 176p. (C). 1975. lib. bdg. 17.95 (*0-8057-2691-8*) Irvington.

Benjamin R. Tucker: A Reader. (Anarchist Studies). 1994. lib. bdg. 250.95 (*0-8490-8942-5*) Gordon Pr.

Benjamin R. Tucker & the Champions of Liberty: A Centenary Anthology. Ed. by Michael E. Coughlin et al. LC 86-11647. (Illus.). 228p. (Orig.). 1986. 15.00 (*0-9602574-4-6*); pap. 7.95 (*0-9602574-5-4*) M E Coughlin.

Benjamin Rush: Revolutionary Gadfly. David F. Hawke. LC 70-145859. 1971. 24.50 (*0-672-51599-7*) Irvington.

Benjamin Rush, Physician & Citizen, 1746-1813. Nathan G. Goodman. 1993. reprint ed. lib. bdg. 89.00 (*0-7812-5462-0*) Rprt Serv.

Benjamin Rush's Lectures on the Mind. Benjamin Rush. Ed. by Eric T. Carlson et al. LC 80-70300. (American Philosophical Society, Memoirs Ser.: No. 144). 755p. reprint ed. pap. 180.00 (*0-7837-2682-1*, 2043059) Bks Demand.

***Benjamin Short: A Migrant with a Mission.** Wilsie Short. 138p. Date not set. pap. 24.95 (*0-86840-102-1*, Pub. by New South Wales Univ Pr AT) Intl Spec Bk.

Benjamin Silliman: A Life in the Young Republic. Chandos M. Brown. 363p. (C). 1989. text ed. 45.00 (*0-691-08533-1*) Princeton U Pr.

Benjamin Silliman & His Circle. Ed. by Leonard G. Wilson. 1979. 20.00 (*0-88202-173-7*) Watson Pub Intl.

Benjamin Strong: Central Banker. Lester V. Chandler. Ed. by Mira Wilkins. LC 78-3903. (International Finance Ser.). 1979. reprint ed. lib. bdg. 46.95 (*0-405-11208-4*) Ayer.

Benjamin Tabart's Juvenile Library: A Bibliography of Books for Children, Published, Written, Edited, & Sold by Mr. Tabart 1801-1820. Marjorie Moon. (Illus.). 180p. 1990. lib. bdg. 36.00 (*0-906795-89-3*) Oak Knoll.

Benjamin Tallmadge: Revolutionary Soldier & American Businessman. Charles S. Hall. LC 43-2318. reprint ed. 20.00 (*0-404-03028-9*) AMS Pr.

Benjamin, the Littlest Brother. Zev Paamoni. (Shulsinger Biblical Ser.). (Illus.). (J). (gr. 5-10). 1970. 3.00 (*0-914080-28-8*) Shulsinger Sales.

Benjamin the Waggoner. William Wordsworth. Ed. by Paul Betz. LC 79-25800. (Cornell Wordsworth Ser.). (Illus.). 368p. 1981. 69.50 (*0-8014-1270-6*) Cornell U Pr.

Benjamin Thompson-Count Rumford: Count Rumford Nature of Heat. S. C. Brown & D. Ter Haar, pseud. LC 66-28414. (Men of Physics Ser.). 1967. 95.00 (*0-08-012179-9*, Pub. by Pergamon Repr UK) Franklin.

Benjamin Vaughan, Seventeen Fifty-One to Eighteen Thirty-Five: The Life of an Anglo-American Intellectual. Craig Murray. 1981. 66.95 (*0-405-14101-7*) Ayer.

Benjamin Visits the Jungle. F. A. Hasenau. LC 82-81827. (Illus.). (J). (gr. k-2). 1982. 6.00 (*0-913042-14-5*) Holland Hse Pr.

Benjamin Waterhouse, M. D., First Professor of the Theory & Practice of Physics at Harvard & Introducer of Cowpox Vaccination into America. J. Worth Estes. Incl. Concordance of Dr. Waterhouse's Horus Siccus. 1974. (*0-318-51871-6*); (Boston Medical Library Studies). (Illus.). 55p. 1974. 3.50 (*0-686-00002-1*) F A Countway.

Benjamin West: American Painter at the English Court. LC 88-36584. 1989. pap. 19.95 (*0-912298-64-2*) Baltimore Mus.

Benjamin West: The Context of His Life's Work with Particular Attention to Paintings with Religious Subject Matter. John Dillenberger. LC 76-42004. 239p. 1977. write for info. (*0-911536-65-5*) Trinity U Pr.

Benjamin West Drawings from the Historical Society of Pennsylvania, (Exhibition Catalogue) 1,987th ed. Randy Ploog. (Illus.). 66p. (Orig.). 1987. pap. 7.50 (*0-911209-36-0*) Palmer Mus Art.

Benjamin West, His Life & Work. Henry Jackson. 1993. reprint ed. lib. bdg. 89.00 (*0-7812-5472-8*) Rprt Serv.

Benjamin Wisner Bacon: Pioneer in American Biblical Criticism. Roy A. Harrisville. LC 76-16178. (Studies in American Biblical Scholarship Ser.: No. 2). 143p. reprint ed. pap. 40.80 (*0-7837-5450-7*, 2045215) Bks Demand.

Benjamin's Balloon. Alan Baker. (Illus.). 32p. (J). 1990. 12.95 (*0-688-09744-8*) Lothrop.

Benjamin's Barn. Reeve Lindbergh. (Illus.). 32p. (J). (ps-3). 1990. 13.95 (*0-8037-0613-8*) Dial Bks Young.

Benjamin's Barn. Reeve Lindbergh. (Illus.). 24p. (J). (ps-3). 1994. pap. 5.99 (*0-14-050863-5*, Puff Pied Piper) Puffin Bks.

***Benjamin's Basket.** Robyn Wild. (Illus.). (J). (ps-4). Date not set. 12.95 (*0-944576-17-6*) Rocky River Pubs.

***Benjamin's Beach Trip.** Diane Ohanesian. LC 95-61142. (Illus.). 24p. (Orig.). (J). Date not set. pap. write for info. (*0-9641089-3-3*) VanderWyk & Burnham.

Benjamin's Bugs. Mary Morgan. LC 93-22911. (Illus.). 44p. (J). (ps-1). 1994. text ed. 12.95 (*0-02-767450-9*, Bradbury S&S) S&S Childrens.

Benjamin's Crossing. Jay Parini. 1995. 23.00 (*0-8050-3180-4*) H Holt & Co.

Benjamin's Ground: New Readings of Walter Benjamin. Ed. by Rainer Nagele. LC 88-14300. 190p. 1988. reprint ed. 27.95 (*0-8143-2040-6*); reprint ed. pap. 15.95 (*0-8143-2041-4*) Wayne St U Pr.

Benjamin's Portrait. Alan Baker. LC 86-10396. (Illus.). 32p. (J). (ps-2). 1987. lib. bdg. 11.93 (*0-688-06878-2*) Lothrop.

Benjamin's Three Hundred Sixty-Five Birthdays. 2nd ed. Judi Barrett. LC 92-2497. (Illus.). 40p. (J). (ps-1). 1992. text ed. 13.95 (*0-689-31791-3*, Atheneum Bks Young) S&S Childrens.

***Benjamin's 365 Birthdays.** Judi Barrett. (Illus.). (J). (gr. k-3). 1993. audio 22.95 (*0-87499-310-5*); audio, pap. 14.95 (*0-87499-309-1*) Live Oak Media.

Benjamin's 365 Birthdays. 2nd ed. Judi Barrett. LC 92-2497. (Illus.). 40p. (J). (ps-1). 1992. reprint ed. pap. 4.95 (*0-689-71635-4*, Aladdin Paperbacks) S&S Childrens.

***Benjamin's 365 Birthdays, 4 bks., Set.** Judi Barrett. (Illus.). (J). (gr. k-3). 1993. audio, pap. 31.95 (*0-87499-311-3*) Live Oak Media.

Benja's Girl. Isabel Brogan. Ed. & Illus. by Kathleen Murphy. (Saga of the Dead Sea Scrolls Ser.: Bk. 6). 140p. 1991. pap. text ed. 15.00 (*0-9620092-4-5*) Pine Isl Pr.

Benji Bear's Adventure in the Thunderstorm. Ingrid Shelton. (Kinderbook Ser.). 31p. (J). (ps-00). 1984. pap. 2.50 (*0-919797-09-1*) Kindred Prods.

Benji Bear's Race. Ingrid Shelton. (Kinderbook Ser.). (Illus.). 35p. (Orig.). (J). (ps-2). 1992. pap. 2.50 (*0-919797-74-1*) Kindred Prods.

Benji Bear's Surprise Day. Ingrid Shelton. (Kinderbook Ser.). 30p. (J). (ps-00). 1986. pap. 2.50 (*0-919797-54-7*) Kindred Prods.

Benji Lopez: A Picaresque Tale of Puerto Rican Emigration & Return. Barry B. Levin. 202p. 1987. boxed 28.95 (*0-465-00653-1*) Transaction Pubs.

Benjie's Fun Time with Numbers. Doris-Marie Smith. (Illus.). 16p. (J). (ps-00). pap. 3.95 (*0-8059-3341-7*) Dorrance.

Benji's Book of ABC. (J). (ps). 1976. bds. 5.50 (*0-904494-12-8*, Brimax Bks) Borden.

Benji's Book of One, Two, Three. 1977. 5.50 (*0-904494-34-9*, Brimax Bks) Borden.

Benji's Rainbow Book. 1977. 5.50 (*0-904494-87-X*) Borden.

Benjy: A Ferocious Fairy Tale. Edwin O'Conner. LC 88-46131. (Pocket Paragon Ser.). (Illus.). 128p. (J). (gr. 4-7). 1995. pap. 11.95 (*0-87923-795-3*) Godine.

Benjy the Football Hero. Jean Van Leeuwen. LC 84-21459. (Illus.). 192p. (J). (gr. 2-6). 1985. lib. bdg. 11.89 (*0-8037-0190-X*) Dial Bks Young.

Benjy's Bible Trails. Chaya Burstein. LC 90-25421. (Illus.). 32p. (J). (gr. 1-5). 1992. pap. 3.95 (*0-929371-27-5*) Kar Ben.

Benjy's New Home. Bonnie Scherer. LC 89-60806. (Illus.). 7p. (J). 1989. pap. 1.50 (*0-9622421-0-1*) B Scherer.

Benjy's Room. E. Van Hansel. (Middos Ser.). (J). 6.95 (*0-89906-991-6*) Mesorah Pubns.

Benko Gambit! Jon Edwards. (ChessBase University Power Play! Ser.). (Illus.). 64p. (Orig.). 1993. pap. 10.95 (*1-883358-04-3*) R&D Pub NJ.

Benmussa: Three Plays, Includes: Singular Life of Albert Nobbs, Appearances, & Death of Ivan Illich. Simone Benmussa. Tr. by Barbara Wright & Donald Watson. (Illus.). 200p. (Orig.). 1997. pap. 13.95 (*0-7145-4156-7*) Riverrun NY.

Benn Gottfried: Konkordanz Zur Lyrik Gottfried Benns. Ed. by James K. Lyon & Craig Inglis. (Alpha-Omega, Reihe D Ser.). 524p. 1971. write for info. (*3-487-04037-9*, Pub. by Georg Olms GW) Lubrecht & Cramer.

Bennett: A Texas Family. Becki B. Schwarz. 200p. 1991. text ed. write for info. (*0-9630902-0-8*) Lazy E Pr.

Bennett Cerf's Book of Riddles. Bennett A. Cerf. LC 60-13492. (Illus.). 72p. (J). (gr. 1-2). 1960. 6.95 (*0-394-80015-X*); lib. bdg. 7.99 (*0-394-90015-4*) Beginner.

Bennett Law of Eighteen Eighty-Nine: Education & Politics in Wisconsin. Robert J. Ulrich. Ed. by Francesco Cordasco. LC 80-902. (American Ethnic Groups Ser.). 1981. lib. bdg. 60.95 (*0-405-13462-2*) Ayer.

Bennett, Wells & Conrad: Narrative in Transition. Linda R. Anderson. LC 87-312. 248p. 1988. text ed. 35.00 (*0-312-00743-4*) St Martin.

Bennetton: Formula 1. Chris Bennett. (Osprey Motor Sport Ser.). (Illus.). 128p. 1994. pap. 15.95 (*1-85532-421-0*, Pub. by Osprey Pubng Ltd UK) Motorbooks Intl.

Bennett's Angel. Barton A. Midwood. Ed. by George Plimpton. 224p. 1989. 17.95 (*0-945167-15-6*) British Amer Pub.

Bennett's Cosmetic Formulary. H. Bennett. 1992. 75.00 (*0-8206-0340-6*) Chem Pub.

***Bennett's Guide to Jury Selection & Trial Dynamics: California Civil Litigation.** Cathy E. Bennett. Ed. by Robert B. Hirschhorn. 1994. pap. text ed. write for info. (*0-314-05113-9*) West Pub.

***Bennett's Guide to Jury Selection & Trial Dynamics: California Criminal Litigation.** Cathy E Bennett & Robert B. Hirschhorn. (C). 1994. pap. text ed. write for info. (*0-314-05114-7*) West Pub.

Bennett's Guide to Jury Selection & Trial Dynamics in Civil & Criminal Litigation CLE Edition. Cathy E. Bennett & Robert B. Mirschhorn. 220p. 1993. pap. text ed. write for info. (*0-314-02270-8*) West Pub.

Bennett's "New York Herald" & the Rise of the Popular Press. James L. Crouthamel. (New York State Bks.). 224p. 1989. text ed. 34.95x (*0-8156-2461-1*) Syracuse U Pr.

***Bennett's Ophthalmic Prescription Work.** 3rd ed. Kelvin G. Wakefield. LC 94-29015. 1995. 49.95 (*0-7506-1748-9*) Buttrwrth-Heinemann.

Bennett's Small House Catalog, 1920. Ray H. Bennett Lumber Co., Inc. Staff. LC 93-40012. (Illus.). 80p. 1993. reprint ed. pap. text ed. 8.95 (*0-486-27809-3*) Dover.

Bennett's Welcome. Inglis Fletcher. 1990. reprint ed. lib. bdg. 25.95 (*0-89968-503-X*) Buccaneer Bks.

Bennett's Welcome. Inglis Fletcher. (Albemarle Ser.). 451p. 1976. reprint ed. lib. bdg. 27.95 (*0-89244-001-5*) Queens Hse-Focus Serv.

Bennigan's Do-It-Yourself Bar Book. Myke Gorecki & Carol St. George. (Illus.). (Orig.). 1989. pap. 12.95 (*0-9623461-0-1*) S & A Restaurants.

Bennington's Battle Monument: Massive & Lofty. Tyler Resch. 64p. 1994. pap. 9.95 (*1-884592-00-7*) Beech Seal Pr.

Benny: King of Swing. Benny Goodman. (Quality Paperbacks Ser.). (Illus.). 208p. 1987. reprint ed. pap. 14.95 (*0-306-80289-9*) Da Capo.

***Benny & the Bodybuilder.** Shirley A. Fischer. (Illus.). 32p. 1994. 14.95 (*1-883939-03-8*) Nickel Pr AL.

***Benny & the Bodybuilder.** Shirley A. Fischer. (Illus.). 32p. (J). (gr. k-3). 1994. pap. 7.95 (*1-883939-05-4*) Nickel Pr AL.

Benny & the Crazy Contest. Cheryl Zach. LC 90-43903. (Illus.). 80p. (J). (gr. 2-6). 1991. text ed. 12.95 (*0-02-793705-4*, Bradbury S&S) S&S Childrens.

Benny & the No-Good Teacher. Cheryl Zach. LC 91-30588. (Illus.). 80p. (J). (gr. 2-6). 1992. text ed. 12.95 (*0-02-793706-2*, Bradbury S&S) S&S Childrens.

Benny Andersen: Selected Poems. Benny Andersen. Tr. by Alexander Taylor. LC 75-3477. (Lockert Library of Poetry in Translation). 150p. 1975. pap. 8.95 (*0-691-01319-5*) Princeton U Pr.

Benny Anderson: A Critical Study. Leonie Marx. LC 83-12945. (Contributions to the Study of World Literature Ser.: No. 1). xvii, 161p. 1983. text ed. 45.00 (*0-313-24168-6*, MAN/, Greenwood Pr) Greenwood.

Benny Bakes a Cake. Eve Rice. LC 80-17313. (Illus.). 32p. (J). (gr. k-3). 1981. write for info. (*0-688-80312-1*); lib. bdg. write for info. (*0-688-84312-3*) Greenwillow.

Benny Bakes a Cake. Eve Rice. LC 80-17313. 32p. (J). (ps-3). 1993. 14.00 (*0-688-11579-9*); lib. bdg. 13.93 (*0-688-11580-2*) Greenwillow.

Benny Bakes a Cake. Eve Rice. LC 92-33053. (Illus.). 32p. (J). (ps up). 1993. pap. 4.95 (*0-688-07814-1*, Mulberry) Morrow.

Benny Bear Believes for A Healing. Susan Tate. (Petal Pals Ser.). (Illus.). (Orig.). (J). (gr. k-3). 1993. pap. 3.99 (*1-884395-00-7*) Clear Blue Sky.

Benny, Bernie, Betye, Noah & John. Howard Smith. (Illus.). 20p. 1971. 1.00 (*0-915478-24-2*) Galleries Coll.

Benny Carter: A Life in American Music, 2 vols. Morroe Berger et al. No. 1. 877p. 1982. Vol. I, Biography, 456p. write for info. (*0-318-56802-0*); Vol. II, Discography, Filmography, & Bibliography, iv, 421p. write for info. (*0-318-56803-9*) Scarecrow.

Benny Carter: A Life in American Music, 2 vols., Set. Morroe Berger et al. LC 82-10634. (Studies in Jazz: No. 1). 877p. 1982. 49.50 (*0-8108-1580-X*) Scarecrow.

***Benny Eats a Pumpkin.** Matthew V. Smith. (Illus.). 17p. (J). (gr. k-4). 1995. pap. 9.95 (*1-56606-032-X*) Bradley Mann.

Benny Goodman: Listen to His Legacy. Russell D. Connor. LC 87-32069. (Studies in Jazz: No. 6). (Illus.). 409p. 1988. 57.50 (*0-8108-2095-1*) Scarecrow.

Benny Goodman & the Swing Era. James L. Collier. (Illus.). 432p. 1989. 30.00 (*0-19-505278-7*) OUP.

Benny Goodman & the Swing Era. James L. Collier. (Illus.). 432p. 1991. reprint ed. pap. 10.95 (*0-19-506776-2*, 7356) OUP.

Benny Goodman for Bb Clarinet, MFM201. Stan Ayeroff. (Illus.). 64p. 1980. pap. 10.95 (*0-8256-4201-9*, AM29307) Music Sales.

Benny Hill Story. large type ed. John Smith. 296p. 1989. reprint ed. lib. bdg. 9.97 (*1-85089-326-8*, Pub. by ISIS UK) Transaction Pubs.

Benny the Breakdown Truck. Willy Smax. LC 93-50048. (Illus.). 64p. (J). (gr. k-4). 1994. 16.00 (*0-517-59921-X*) Crown Bks Yng Read.

Benny, the Lazy Beaver. George W. Fisk. LC 90-45200. (Illus.). 32p. (J). 1991. 10.99 (*0-9620507-1-7*) Cosmic Concepts Pr.

Benny Uncovers a Mystery. Gertrude C. Warner. (Boxcar Children Mysteries Ser.: No. 19). (J). (gr. 2-7). 1991. 10.95 (*0-8075-0644-3*); pap. 3.50 (*0-8075-0645-1*) A Whitman.

Benny's Baby Brother. Shirley Simon. Ed. by Barbara Gregorich. (Start to Read! Ser.). (Illus.). 16p. (Orig.). (J). (gr. k-2). 1985. pap. 2.25 (*0-88743-016-3*, 06016) Sch Zone Pub Co.

Benny's Bad Day. Michael J. Pellowski. LC 85-14016. (Illus.). 48p. (Orig.). (J). (gr. 1-3). 1986. lib. bdg. 10.59 (*0-8167-0620-4*); pap. text ed. 3.50 (*0-8167-0621-2*) Troll Assocs.

Benny's Hat. Dirk Walbrecker. (Illus.). 28p. (J). (ps-1). 1991. 9.95 (*1-56182-028-8*) Atomium Bks.

***Benny's Island: A Novel.** Patrick O'Flaherty. 64p. 1995. pap. 9.95 (*1-55081-102-9*) Paul & Co Pubs.

***Benny's Pennies.** Brisson. 1995. pap. 4.99 (*0-440-41016-9*) Bantam.

Benny's Pennies. Pat Brisson. (J). (gr. 4 up). 1993. pap. 14.95 (*0-385-41602-4*) Doubleday.

Beno Eckmann - Selecta. B. Eckmann. xii, 835p. 1987. 169.00 (*0-387-17518-0*) Spr-Verlag.

Benoits see Family Stories

***Benozzo Gozzoli.** Cristina A. Luchinat. Tr. by Christopher Evans. (Library of Great Masters). (Illus.). 80p. (Orig.). 1995. pap. 12.99 (*1-878351-47-8*) Riverside NY.

Benozzo Gozzoli. Hugh Stokes. LC 75-41264. reprint ed. 32.50 (*0-404-14612-0*) AMS Pr.

Ben's ABC Day. Terry Berger. LC 81-13754. (Illus.). 32p. (J). (gr. k-3). 1982. lib. bdg. 14.93 (*0-688-00882-8*) Lothrop.

Ben's Book of Virtues: Ben Franklin's Simple Plan for Success & Happiness. LC 94-17180. (Illus.). 32p. (J). (gr. k up). 1994. 9.95 (*0-943545-03-X*) New Hope Pr.

Ben's Dream. Chris Van Allsburg. (Illus.). 32p. (J). (gr. 2 up). 1982. 15.95 (*0-395-32084-4*) HM.

Ben's Exit. Paul Trachtenberg. 128p. (Orig.). 1993. pap. 7.00 (*0-916156-91-5*) Cherry Valley.

Ben's Gift: Reading Level 3. Cynthia Barnett. (Sundown Fiction Collection). 64p. 1993. 3.75 (*0-88336-210-4*); audio 13.50 (*0-88336-221-X*); audio 10.50 (*0-88336-255-4*) New Readers.

Ben's in Love. Katherine Applegate. (Boyfriends & Girlfriends Ser.: No. 4). (YA). 1994. mass mkt. 3.99 (*0-06-106183-2*, Harp PBks) HarpC.

***Ben's Revolution.** Elliot Ring. 170p. Date not set. pap. 7.95 (*0-7610-0225-1*) NW Pub.

Ben's Secret. Sandra Allen & Eric Dlugokinski. 28p. (J). (gr. k-6). 1992. pap. 9.95 (*1-882801-00-8*) Feelings Factory.

Ben's Snow Song. H. Hutchins. (Illus.). 24p. (J). (ps-8). 1987. 12.95 (*0-920303-91-9*, Pub. by Annick CN); pap. 4.95 (*0-920303-90-0*, Pub. by Annick CN) Firefly Bks Ltd.

Ben's Story: A Deaf Child's Right to Sign. Lorraine Fletcher. LC 88-24741. (Illus.). 267p. 1988. reprint ed. pap. 7.95 (*0-930323-47-5*) Gallaudet Univ Pr.

Ben's Trumpet. Rachel Isadora. LC 78-12885. (Illus.). 32p. (J). (gr. k-3). 1979. 14.00 (*0-688-80194-3*) Greenwillow.

Ben's Trumpet. Rachel Isadora. LC 79-12885. (Illus.). 32p. (J). (ps up). 1991. reprint ed. pap. 4.95 (*0-688-10988-8*, Mulberry) Morrow.

Ben's Wayne. Levi Miller. LC 89-32436. 168p. 1989. 14.95 (*0-934672-77-6*) Good Bks PA.

Ben's Wayne. Levi Miller. LC 89-32436. 168p. 1992. pap. 9.95 (*1-56148-061-4*) Good Bks PA.

Benselars Greek-German Dictionary: Benselers Griechisch-Deutsches Woerterbuch. 18th ed. A. Kaegi & A. Clausing. 887p. (GER & GRE.). 1985. 75.00 (*0-8288-0508-3*, F67112) Fr & Eur.

Benserade & His Ballets de Cour. Charles I. Silin. LC 76-43940. (Music & Theatre in France in the 17th & 18th Centuries Ser.). reprint ed. 52.50 (*0-404-60195-2*) AMS Pr.

Benson & Hedges British Theatre Yearbook, 1992. David Lemmon. (Illus.). 376p. 1993. pap. 34.95 (*0-233-98780-0*, Pub. by A Deutsch UK) Trafalgar.

Benson & Pernoll's Handbook of Obstetrics & Gynecology. 9th ed. Ralph C. Benson & Martin L. Pernoll. (Illus.). 832p. 1994. pap. text ed. 29.00 (*0-07-105405-7*) Hlth Prof Div.

Benson Family of Newport, RI: With an Appendix Concerning the Bensons in America of English Descendants. W. P. Garrison. 65p. 1991. reprint ed. pap. 13.00 (*0-8328-1745-7*) Higginson Bk Co.

Benson, Frank W. American Impressionist. Faith A. Bedford. LC 94-4638. 240p. 1994. 50.00 (*0-8478-1609-5*) Rizzoli Intl.

Benson Murder Case. S. S. Van Dine. reprint ed. lib. bdg. 22.95 (*0-89190-511-1*, Rivercity Pr) Amereon Ltd.

***Bent & Battered Rotors.** Wayne Mutza. (Aircraft Specials Ser.). (Illus.). 56p. 1993. pap. 9.95 (*0-89747-306-X*) Squad Sig Pubns.

Bent & Battered Winds, Vol. 2: USAAF - USAF. Larry Davis. (Specials Ser.). (Illus.). 80p. 1989. pap. 9.95 (*0-89747-219-5*, 6049) Squad Sig Pubns.

682

An Asterisk (*) at the beginning of an entry indicates that the title is appearing in BIP for the first time.

B

B

Berdan's U. S. Sharpshooters. Charles A. Stevens. (Facsimile Ser.: No. 7). (Illus.). 597p. 1984. reprint ed. 30.00 (*0-89029-013-X*) Morningside Bkshop.

Berdine Un-Theory of Evolution: And Other Scientific Studies Including Hunting, Fishing & Sex. William C. Berdine. LC 91-90760. 248p. 1992. 19.95 (*0-9631802-0-7*) Berdine.

Berean. John H. Noyes. LC 74-83431. (Religion in America, Ser. 1). 1974. reprint ed. 35.95 (*0-405-00256-4*) Ayer.

***Berea's First 125 Years, 1855-1980.** fac. ed. Elisabeth S. Peck & Emily A. Smith. LC 82-6955. (Illus.). 308p. 1994. pap. 87.80 (*0-7837-7596-2*, 2047349) Bks Demand.

Bereaved: Coping with Loss. Ian Knox. (Orig.). 1994. pap. 18.95 (*0-85476-379-1*) Trans-Atl Phila.

Bereaved Child: Analysis, Education, & Treatment - An Abstracted Bibliography. Gillian S. Mace et al. LC 81-8637. 292p. 1981. 95.00 (*0-306-65197-1*, IFI-Plenum) Plenum.

***Bereaved Children & Teens: A Support Guide for Parents & Professionals.** rev. ed. Ed. by Earl A. Grollman. LC 94-40338. 256p. 1995. 25.00 (*0-8070-2306-X*) Beacon Pr.

Bereaved Parent. Harriet S. Schiff. 1978. pap. 10.00 (*0-14-005043-4*, Penguin Bks) Viking Penguin.

Bereavement. 2nd ed. Colin M. Parkes. 1987. text ed. 37.50x (*0-8236-0481-0*) Intl Univs Pr.

Bereavement: Counseling the Grieving Throughout the Life Cycle. David A. Crenshaw. 180p. 1995. pap. 12.95 (*0-8245-1291-X*) Crossroad NY.

Bereavement: Its Psychological Aspects. Ed. by Bernard Schoenberg et al. LC 75-16422. 368p. 1975. text ed. 52.00 (*0-231-03974-3*) Col U Pr.

Bereavement: Reactions, Consequences, & Care. National Research Council. 312p. 1984. pap. 29.95 (*0-309-03438-8*) Natl Acad Pr.

Bereavement & Adaptation: A Comparative Study of the Aftermath of Death. Marc Cleiren. LC 92-26136. 296p. 1992. 27.50 (*1-56032-279-9*) Hemisp Pub.

***Bereavement & Grief: Supporting Older People Through Loss.** Steve Scrutton. 192p. 1995. pap. 29.95 (*1-56593-391-5*, 0825) Singular Publishing.

Bereavement & Health: The Psychological & Physical Consequences of Partner Loss. Wolfgang Stroebe & Margaret S. Stroebe. (Illus.). 288p. 1987. 64.95 (*0-521-24470-6*); pap. 19.95 (*0-521-28710-3*) Cambridge U Pr.

***Bereavement & Support: Healing in a Group Environment.** Marylou Hughes. 224p. 1995. 49.00x (*1-56032-370-1*); pap. 24.50x (*1-56032-371-X*) Taylor & Francis.

Bereavement Care: A Look at Hospice & Community Based Services. Ed. by Jane M. Kirschling & Stephen Fleming. LC 89-11038. (Hospice Journal Ser.: Vol. 5, No. 1). (Illus.). 129p. 1989. text ed. 32.95 (*0-86656-944-8*) Haworth Pr.

Bereavement Counseling: A Multidisciplinary Handbook. Ed. by B. Mark Schoenberg. LC 79-7471. (Illus.). 266p. 1980. text ed. 59.95 (*0-313-21434-4*, SBR/, Greenwood Pr) Greenwood.

Bereavement in Childbearing. Rosemary Mander. LC 94-13658. (Illus.). 240p. 1994. pap. 19.95 (*0-632-03826-8*, Pub. by Blckwell Sci Pubns UK) Blackwell Sci.

Bereavement of Physical Disability: Recommitment to Life, Health & Function. Ed. by John A. Downey et al. 1982. 20.95 (*0-405-14214-5*) Ayer.

Bereavement Support Group Program for Children: Leader Manual. Beth Haasl & Jean Marrocha. 95p. (Orig.). 1990. pap. text ed. 10.95 (*1-55959-011-4*) Accel Devel.

Bereavement Support Group Program for Children: Participant Workbook. Beth Haasl & Jean Marrocha. 39p. (Orig.). (J). (ps-8). 1990. 6.95 (*1-55959-012-2*) Accel Devel.

Bereavements. James B. Hall. 108p. 1991. 19.95 (*0-934257-62-0*); pap. 14.95 (*0-934257-63-9*) Story Line.

Bereavements. Richard Lortz. 22.00 (*0-932966-08-X*) Permanent Pr.

Berechenbare Vernunft: Kalkul und Rationalismus Im 17. Jahrhundert. Sybille Kramer. x, 431p. (GER.). (C). 1991. lib. bdg. 140.00 (*3-11-012106-9*) De Gruyter.

***Bereft of Reason: On the Decline of Social Thoughts & Prospects for Its Renewal.** Halton Eugene. LC 94-28377. (Illus.). 288p. 1994. pap. 16.95 (*0-226-31462-6*) U Ch Pr.

Bereft of Reason: On the Decline of Social Thoughts & Prospects for Its Renewal. Eugene Halton. LC 94-28377. (Illus.). 288p. 1995. 31.50 (*0-226-31461-8*) U Ch Pr.

Bereishes-Genesis, 3 vols. Meir Zlotowitz. Incl. Vol. 1. Bereishes-Noah. 416p. 1977. 15.95 (*0-89906-350-0*); Vol. 1. Bereishes-Noah. 416p. 1977. pap. 12.95 (*0-89906-351-9*); Vol. 2. Lech Lecha-Vayeira. 480p. 1978. 16.95 (*0-89906-352-7*); Vol. 2. Lech Lecha-Vayeira. 480p. 1978. pap. 13.95 (*0-89906-353-5*); (ArtScroll Tanach Ser.). write for info. (*0-318-54305-2*) Mesorah Pubns.

Bereishes-Noah see Bereishes-Genesis

Bereishis: Genesis: A New Translation with a Commentary Anthologized from Rabbinic Sources, 2 vols., Set. Meir Zlotowitz. (ArtScroll Tanach Ser.). 2336p. 1986. 64.95 (*0-89906-362-4*) Mesorah Pubns.

Bereits Lieferbar, Band 5: Hessen A-L. (GER.). Date not set. write for info. (*0-318-70548-6*, Pub. by Georg Olms GW) Lubrecht & Cramer.

Berelson on Population. Ed. by J. A. Ross & W. P. Mauldin. (Illus.). 345p. 1988. 44.00 (*0-387-96716-8*) Spr-Verlag.

Berengar & the Reform of the Sacramental System. Allan J. Macdonald. 444p. 1977. reprint ed. lib. bdg. 30.00 (*0-915172-25-9*) Richwood Pub.

Berengario da Carpi, on Fracture of the Skull or Cranium. L. R. Lind. LC 90-55267. (Transactions Ser.: Vol. 80, Pt. 4). (Illus.). 164p. (C). 1990. pap. 20.00 (*0-87169-804-8*, T804-LIL) Am Philos.

Berenice. Jean B. Racine. 224p. (FRE.). 1991. pap. 10.95 (*0-7859-1259-2*, 2038714037) Fr & Eur.

Berenice Abbott: Photographs. Berenice Abbott. LC 89-21993. (Illus.). 176p. 1990. reprint ed. pap. 24.95 (*0-87474-211-0*) Smithsonian.

Berenice Abbott, Photographer: A Modern Vision. Berenice Abbott. (Illus.). 96p. (Orig.). 1989. pap. 14.95 (*0-87104-420-X*) NY Pub Lib.

***Berenson & the Connoisseurship of Italian Painting.** David A. Brown. (Illus.). 208p. 1995. 24.95 (*1-883145-04-X*) Ursus Press.

Berenson Archive: An Inventory of Correspondence Compiled on the Centenary of the Birth of Bernard Berenson, 1865-1959. Nicky Mariano. Ed. by Bernard Berenson. LC 65-28597. (Illus.). 134p. 1965. 19.00 (*0-674-06750-9*) HUP.

Berenstain Bears: Family Tree House. Stan Berenstain & Jan Berenstain. (Pop-Up Sound-Up Bks.). 2p. (J). (ps-2). 1993. write for info. (*1-883366-06-2*) YES Ent.

Berenstain Bears: No Girls Allowed. Stan Berenstain & Janice Berenstain. LC 85-18246. (First Time Bks.). (Illus.). 32p. (J). (ps-1). 1986. pap. 2.50 (*0-394-87331-9*) Random Bks Yng Read.

Berenstain Bears Accept No Substitutes. Stan Berenstain & Jan Berenstain. (Big Chapter Bks.). (Illus.). 112p. (Orig.). (J). (gr. 2-6). 1993. lib. bdg. 7.99 (*0-679-94035-9*) Random Bks Yng Read.

Berenstain Bears Accept No Substitutes. Stan Berenstain & Janice Berenstain. (Big Chapter Bks.). (Illus.). 112p. (Orig.). (J). (gr. 2-6). 1993. pap. 2.99 (*0-679-84035-4*) Random Bks Yng Read.

Berenstain Bears' Almanac. Stan Berenstain & Janice Berenstain. LC 73-2298. (Bear Facts Library). (Illus.). 72p. (J). (ps-4). 1984. pap. 6.99 (*0-394-86601-0*) Random Bks Yng Read.

Berenstain Bears & Mama's New Job. Stan Berenstain & Janice Berenstain. LC 84-4787. (First Time Bks.). (Illus.). 32p. (J). (ps-1). 1984. lib. bdg. 5.99 (*0-394-96881-6*); pap. 2.25 (*0-394-86881-1*) Random Bks Yng Read.

***Berenstain Bears & Media Madness.** Stan Berenstain & Jan Berenstain. LC 94-40741. (Big Chapter Bks.). (J). 1995. lib. bdg. 7.99 (*0-679-96664-1*); pap. text ed. 3.50 (*0-679-86664-7*) Random.

Berenstain Bears & the Bad Dream. Stan Berenstain & Janice Berenstain. LC 87-27295. (First Time Bks.). (Illus.). 32p. (J). (ps-1). 1988. lib. bdg. 5.99 (*0-394-97341-0*); pap. 2.50 (*0-394-87341-6*) Random Bks Yng Read.

Berenstain Bears & the Bad Dream. Stan Berenstain & Jan Berenstain. (Berenstain Bears First Time Book & Cassette Library). (Illus.). 32p. (J). (ps-1). 1992. audio 6.95 (*0-679-82761-7*) Random Bks Yng Read.

Berenstain Bears & the Bad Habit. Stan Berenstain & Janice Berenstain. LC 86-3205. (First Time Bks.). (Illus.). 32p. (J). (ps-1). 1987. lib. bdg. 5.99 (*0-394-97340-2*); pap. 2.25 (*0-394-87340-8*) Random Bks Yng Read.

Berenstain Bears & the Big Election. Stan Berenstain & Janice Berenstain. LC 83-62399. (Berenstain Bears Mini-Storybooks). (Illus.). 32p. (J). (ps-3). 1984. pap. 1.50 (*0-394-86542-1*) Random Bks Yng Read.

Berenstain Bears & the Big Road Race. Stan Berenstain & Janice Berenstain. LC 87-4581. (First Time Readers Ser.). (Illus.). 32p. (J). (gr. k-3). 1987. lib. bdg. 5.99 (*0-394-99134-6*); pap. 2.50 (*0-394-89134-1*) Random Bks Yng Read.

Berenstain Bears & the Bully. Stan Berenstain & Janice Berenstain. (First Time Bks.). (Illus.). 32p. (J). (ps-3). 1993. lib. bdg. 5.99 (*0-679-94805-8*) Random Bks Yng Read.

Berenstain Bears & the Bully. Stan Berenstain & Janice Berenstain. (First Time Bks.). (Illus.). 32p. (J). (ps-3). 1993. pap. 2.50 (*0-679-84805-3*) Random Bks Yng Read.

Berenstain Bears & the Dinosaurs. Stan Berenstain & Janice Berenstain. LC 84-60384. (Berenstain Bears Mini-Storybooks). (Illus.). 32p. (J). (ps-3). 1984. pap. 1.50 (*0-394-86883-8*) Random Bks Yng Read.

Berenstain Bears & the Double Dare. Stan Berenstain & Janice Berenstain. LC 87-27296. (First Time Bks.). (Illus.). 32p. (J). (ps-1). 1988. pap. 2.25 (*0-394-89748-X*) Random Bks Yng Read.

Berenstain Bears & the Double Dare. Stan Berenstain & Janice Berenstain. LC 87-27296. (First Time Bks.). (Illus.). 32p. (J). (ps-1). 1988. lib. bdg. 5.99 (*0-394-99748-4*) Random Bks Yng Read.

Berenstain Bears & the Dress Code. Stan Berenstain & Jan Berenstain. (Berenstain Bears Big Chapter Bks.). (Illus.). 112p. (Orig.). (J). (gr. 2-6). 1994. lib. bdg. 3.50 (*0-679-86665-5*); pap. 7.99 (*0-679-96665-X*) Random Bks Yng Read.

Berenstain Bears & the Drug Free Zone. Stan Berenstain & Jan Berenstain. LC 92-31604. (Berenstain Bears Big Chapter Bks.). (Illus.). 112p. (Orig.). (J). (gr. 2-6). 1993. lib. bdg. 7.99 (*0-679-93612-2*) Random Bks Yng Read.

Berenstain Bears & the Drug Free Zone. Stan Berenstain & Janice Berenstain. LC 92-31604. (Berenstain Bears Big Chapter Bks.). (Illus.). 112p. (Orig.). (J). (gr. 2-6). 1993. pap. 3.50 (*0-679-83612-8*) Random Bks Yng Read.

Berenstain Bears & the Female Fullback. Stan Berenstain & Janice Berenstain. (Big Chapter Bks.). (Illus.). 112p. (Orig.). (J). (gr. 2-6). 1993. lib. bdg. 7.99 (*0-679-93611-4*); pap. 2.99 (*0-679-83611-X*) Random Bks Yng Read.

Berenstain Bears & the Galloping Ghost. Stan Berenstain & Janice Berenstain. (Berenstain Bears Big Chapter Bks.). (Illus.). 112p. (Orig.). (J). (gr. 2-6). 1994. 7.99 (*0-679-95815-0*) Random Bks Yng Read.

Berenstain Bears & the Galloping Ghost. Stan Berenstain & Janice Berenstain. (Berenstain Bears Big Chapter Bks.). (Illus.). 112p. (Orig.). (J). (gr. 2-6). 1994. pap. 2.99 (*0-679-85815-6*) Random Bks Yng Read.

Berenstain Bears & the Ghost of the Forest. Stan Berenstain & Janice Berenstain. LC 88-42586. (First Time Readers Ser.). (Illus.). 32p. (Orig.). (J). (gr. k-3). 1988. 2.50 (*0-394-80565-8*) Random Bks Yng Read.

Berenstain Bears & the Ghost of the Forest. Stan Berenstain & Janice Berenstain. LC 88-42586. (First Time Readers Ser.). (Illus.). 32p. (Orig.). (J). (gr. k-3). 1988. lib. bdg. 5.99 (*0-394-90565-2*) Random Bks Yng Read.

Berenstain Bears & the Giddy Grandma. Stan Berenstain & Jan Berenstain. (Berenstain Bears Big Chapter Bks.). (Illus.). 112p. (Orig.). (J). (gr. 2-6). 1994. pap. 3.50 (*0-679-85814-8*) Random Bks Yng Read.

Berenstain Bears & the Giddy Grandma. Stan Berenstain & Jan Berenstain. (Berenstain Bears Big Chapter Bks.). (Illus.). 112p. (Orig.). (J). (gr. 2-6). 1994. lib. bdg. 7.99 (*0-679-95814-2*) Random Bks Yng Read.

Berenstain Bears & The Green-Eyed Monster. Stan Berenstain & Jan Berenstain. LC 93-50109. (First Time Books Ser.). (Illus.). (J). (gr. 1 up). 1995. 6.99 (*0-679-96434-7*) Random Bks Yng Read.

***Berenstain Bears & The Green-Eyed Monster.** Stan Berenstain & Jan Berenstain. (First Time Bks.). (Illus.). (J). 1995. pap. 2.50 (*0-679-86434-2*) Random Bks Yng Read.

Berenstain Bears & the In-Crowd. Stan Berenstain & Janice Berenstain. LC 88-32095. (First Time Bks.). (Illus.). 32p. (Orig.). (J). (ps-1). 1989. pap. 2.50 (*0-394-83013-X*) Random Bks Yng Read.

Berenstain Bears & the Messy Room. Stan Berenstain & Janice Berenstain. Ed. by Sharon Lerner. (First Time Bks.). (Illus.). 32p. (J). (ps-2). 1983. pap. 2.50 (*0-394-85639-2*) Random Bks Yng Read.

Berenstain Bears & the Messy Room. Stan Berenstain & Janice Berenstain. Ed. by Sharon Lerner. (First Time Bks.). (Illus.). 32p. (J). (ps-2). 1983. lib. bdg. 5.99 (*0-394-95639-7*) Random Bks Yng Read.

Berenstain Bears & the Messy Room see Berenstain Bears' Take-Along Library

Berenstain Bears & the Missing Dinosaur Bone. Stan Berenstain & Janice Berenstain. LC 79-3458. (Beginner Bks.). (Illus.). 48p. (J). (ps-3). 1980. 7.99 (*0-394-84447-5*); lib. bdg. 7.99 (*0-394-94447-X*) Beginner.

Berenstain Bears & the Missing Honey. Stan Berenstain & Janice Berenstain. LC 87-4549. (First Time Readers Ser.). (Illus.). 32p. (J). (ps-3). 1987. lib. bdg. 5.99 (*0-394-99133-8*); pap. 2.25 (*0-394-89133-3*) Random Bks Yng Read.

Berenstain Bears & the Nerdy Nephew. Stan Berenstain & Janice Berenstain. LC 92-32564. (Berenstain Bears Big Chapter Bks.). (Illus.). 112p. (Orig.). (J). (gr. 2-6). 1993. lib. bdg. 7.99 (*0-679-93610-6*); pap. 2.99 (*0-679-83610-1*) Random Bks Yng Read.

Berenstain Bears & the New Girl in Town. Stan Berenstain & Janice Berenstain. LC 92-32570. (Berenstain Bears Big Chapter Bks.). (Illus.). 112p. (Orig.). (J). (gr. 2-6). 1993. lib. bdg. 7.99 (*0-679-93613-0*); pap. 2.99 (*0-679-83613-6*) Random Bks Yng Read.

Berenstain Bears & the Prize Pumpkin. Stan Berenstain & Janice Berenstain. LC 90-32865. (First Time Bks.). (Illus.). 32p. (Orig.). (J). (ps-1). 1990. lib. bdg. 5.99 (*0-679-90847-1*); pap. 2.25 (*0-679-80847-7*) Random Bks Yng Read.

Berenstain Bears & the Red-Handed Thief. Stan Berenstain & Janice Berenstain. (Big Chapter Bks.). (Illus.). 112p. (Orig.). (J). (gr. 2-6). 1993. lib. bdg. 7.99 (*0-679-94033-2*); pap. 3.50 (*0-679-84033-8*) Random Bks Yng Read.

Berenstain Bears & the School Scandal Sheet. Stan Berenstain & Janice Berenstain. (Berenstain Bears Big Chapter Bks.). (Illus.). 112p. (Orig.). (J). (gr. 2-6). 1994. lib. bdg. 7.99 (*0-679-95812-6*); pap. 2.99 (*0-679-85812-1*) Random Bks Yng Read.

***Berenstain Bears & the Showdown at Chainsaw Gap.** Stan Berenstain & Jan Berenstain. LC 95-8472. (Big Chapter Book Ser.). (J). 1995. write for info. (*0-679-97571-3*); pap. 3.50 (*0-679-87571-9*) Random.

Berenstain Bears & the Sitter. Stan Berenstain & Janice Berenstain. LC 81-50046. (Berenstain Bears First Time Bks.). (Illus.). 32p. (J). (ps-1). 1981. pap. 2.50 (*0-394-84837-3*) Random Bks Yng Read.

Berenstain Bears & the Sitter. Stan Berenstain & Janice Berenstain. LC 81-50046. (Berenstain Bears First Time Bks.). (Illus.). 32p. (J). (ps-1). 1981. lib. bdg. 5.99 (*0-394-94837-8*) Random Bks Yng Read.

Berenstain Bears & the Sitter. Stan Berenstain & Janice Berenstain. (First Time Book & Puppet Packages Ser.). (Illus.). 32p. (J). (ps-1). 1987. 2.95 (*0-394-88890-1*) Random Bks Yng Read.

Berenstain Bears & the Sitter see Berenstain Bears' Take-Along Library

Berenstain Bears & the Slumber Party. Stan Berenstain & Janice Berenstain. LC 89-35223. (First Time Bks.). (Illus.). 32p. (Orig.). (J). 1990. lib. bdg. 5.99 (*0-679-90419-0*); pap. 2.25 (*0-679-80419-6*) Random Bks Yng Read.

Berenstain Bears & the Spooky Old Tree. Stan Berenstain & Janice Berenstain. LC 77-93771. (Bright & Early Bks.). (Illus.). (J). (ps-2). 1978. 6.95 (*0-394-83910-2*) Random Bks Yng Read.

Berenstain Bears & the Spooky Old Tree. Stan Berenstain & Janice Berenstain. LC 77-93771. (Bright & Early Bks.). (Illus.). (J). (ps-2). 1978. lib. bdg. 7.99 (*0-394-93910-7*) Random Bks Yng Read.

Berenstain Bears & the Trouble with Friends. Stan Berenstain & Janice Berenstain. LC 85-30165. (First Time Bks.). (Illus.). 32p. (J). (ps-1). 1987. pap. 2.50 (*0-394-87339-4*) Random Bks Yng Read.

Berenstain Bears & the Trouble with Friends. Stan Berenstain & Janice Berenstain. LC 85-30165. (First Time Bks.). (Illus.). 32p. (J). (ps-1). 1987. lib. bdg. 5.99 (*0-394-97339-9*) Random Bks Yng Read.

Berenstain Bears & the Trouble with Grownups. Stan Berenstain & Janice Berenstain. LC 91-27430. (First Time Bks.). (Illus.). 32p. (Orig.). (J). (ps-1). 1992. lib. bdg. 5.99 (*0-679-93000-0*); pap. 2.25 (*0-679-83000-6*) Random Bks Yng Read.

Berenstain Bears & the Truth. Stan Berenstain & Janice Berenstain. LC 83-3304. (First Time Bks.). (Illus.). 32p. (J). (ps-00). 1983. lib. bdg. 5.99 (*0-394-95640-0*); pap. 2.50 (*0-394-85640-6*) Random Bks Yng Read.

Berenstain Bears & the Week at Grandma's. Stan Berenstain & Janice Berenstain. LC 85-25743. (First Time Bks.). (J). (ps-1). 1986. lib. bdg. 5.99 (*0-394-97335-6*); pap. 2.50 (*0-394-87335-1*) Random Bks Yng Read.

Berenstain Bears & the Wheelchair Commando. Stan Berenstain & Janice Berenstain. (Big Chapter Bks.). (Illus.). 112p. (Orig.). (J). (gr. 2-6). 1993. lib. bdg. 7.99 (*0-679-94034-0*); pap. 2.99 (*0-679-84034-6*) Random Bks Yng Read.

Berenstain Bears & the Wild, Wild Honey. Stan Berenstain & Janice Berenstain. LC 83-60057. (Berenstain Bears Mini-Storybooks). (Illus.). 32p. (J). (ps). 1983. pap. 1.50 (*0-394-85924-3*) Random Bks Yng Read.

Berenstain Bears & Too Much Birthday. Stan Berenstain & Janice Berenstain. LC 85-14529. (First Time Bks.). (Illus.). 32p. (J). (ps-1). 1986. pap. 2.50 (*0-394-87332-7*) Random Bks Yng Read.

Berenstain Bears & Too Much Junk Food. Stan Berenstain & Janice Berenstain. Ed. by Sharon Lerner. LC 84-40393. (First Time Bks.). (Illus.). 32p. (J). (ps-2). 1985. lib. bdg. 5.99 (*0-394-97217-1*); pap. 2.50 (*0-394-87217-7*) Random Bks Yng Read.

Berenstain Bears & Too Much Pressure. Stan Berenstain & Janice Berenstain. LC 92-6544. (First Time Bks.). (Illus.). 32p. (Orig.). (J). (ps-1). 1992. pap. 2.50 (*0-679-83671-3*) Random Bks Yng Read.

Berenstain Bears & Too Much Pressure. Stan Berenstain & Janice Berenstain. LC 92-6544. (First Time Bks.). (Illus.). 32p. (Orig.). (J). (ps-1). 1992. lib. bdg. 5.99 (*0-679-93671-8*) Random Bks Yng Read.

***Berenstain Bears & Too Much Teasing.** Stan Berenstain & Jan Berenstain. LC 95-1634. (First Time Bks.). (J). 1995. 2.99 (*0-679-87706-1*); lib. bdg. write for info. (*0-679-97706-6*) Random.

Berenstain Bears & Too Much TV. Stan Berenstain & Janice Berenstain. LC 83-22887. (First Time Bks.). (Illus.). (J). (gr. 3-6). 1984. lib. bdg. 5.99 (*0-394-96570-1*); pap. 2.50 (*0-394-86570-7*) Random Bks Yng Read.

Berenstain Bears & Too Much TV. Stan Berenstain & Janice Berenstain. (Berenstain Bears First Time Book & Cassette Library). (Illus.). (J). (ps-1). 1989. audio 6.95 (*0-394-82894-1*) Random Bks Yng Read.

Berenstain Bears & Too Much TV see Berenstain Bears' Take-Along Library

Berenstain Bears & Too Much Vacation. Stan Berenstain & Janice Berenstain. LC 88-32094. (First Time Bks.). (Illus.). 32p. (Orig.). (J). (ps-1). 1989. pap. 2.50 (*0-394-83014-8*) Random Bks Yng Read.

Berenstain Bears & Too Much Vacation. Stan Berenstain & Janice Berenstain. LC 88-32094. (Berenstain Bears First Time Book & Cassette Library). (Illus.). 32p. (Orig.). (J). (ps-1). 1990. reprint ed. Includes audio cassette. pap. 6.95 (*0-679-80311-4*) Random Bks Yng Read.

Berenstain Bears Are a Family. Stan Berenstain & Janice Berenstain. LC 90-63082. (First First Time Bks.). (Illus.). 24p. (Orig.). (J). (ps). 1991. 2.95 (*0-679-80746-2*) Random Bks Yng Read.

Berenstain Bears at Camp Crush. Stan Berenstain & Janice Berenstain. (Berenstain Bears Big Chapter Bks.). (Illus.). 112p. (Orig.). (J). (gr. 2-6). 1994. 7.99 (*0-679-96028-7*) Random Bks Yng Read.

Berenstain Bears at Camp Crush. Stan Berenstain & Janice Berenstain. (Berenstain Bears Big Chapter Bks.). (Illus.). 112p. (Orig.). (J). (gr. 2-6). 1994. pap. 2.99 (*0-679-86028-2*) Random Bks Yng Read.

Berenstain Bears at the Super-Duper Market. Stan Berenstain & Janice Berenstain. LC 90-63080. (First First Time Bks.). (Illus.). 24p. (Orig.). (J). (ps). 1991. 2.95 (*0-679-80748-9*) Random Bks Yng Read.

Berenstain Bears' Bath Book. Stan Berenstain & Janice Berenstain. (Bathtime Bks.). (Illus.). 10p. (J). (ps). 1985. vinyl bd. 3.95 (*0-394-87116-2*) Random Bks Yng Read.

Berenstain Bears' Big Rummage Sale. Stan Berenstain & Jan Berenstain. (Golden Sound Story Book - Deluxe Edition Ser.). 24p. (J). (ps up). 1992. write for info. (*0-307-74020-X*, 64020) Western Pub.

Berenstain Bears Blaze a Trail. Stan Berenstain & Janice Berenstain. LC 87-4552. (First Time Readers Ser.). (Illus.). 32p. (J). (ps-1). 1987. lib. bdg. 5.99 (*0-394-99132-X*); pap. 2.25 (*0-394-89132-5*) Random Bks Yng Read.

***Berenstain Bears Cook-It.** Berenstain. (J). write for info. (*0-679-87316-3*) Random.

***Berenstain Bears Count Their Blessings.** Stan Berenstain & Jan Berenstain. LC 95-1629. (First Time Bks.). (Illus.). (J). 1995. 2.99 (*0-679-87707-X*); lib. bdg. write for info. (*0-679-97707-4*) Random.

An Asterisk (*) at the beginning of an entry indicates that the title is appearing in BIP for the first time.

An Asterisk (*) at the beginning of an entry indicates that the title is appearing in BIP for the first time.

685

Bering's Search for the Strait: The First Kamchatka Expedition 1725-1730. Evgenii G. Kushnarev. Tr. by E. A. Crownhart-Vaughan. (North Pacific Studies: No. 15). (Illus.). 252p. 1990. 24.95 (*0-87595-224-0*) Oregon Hist.

Bering's Voyages: The Reports From Russia. Gerhard F. Muller. Ed. & Tr. by Carol Urness. LC 86-51585. (Rasmuson Library Historical Translation Ser.: Vol. III). (Illus.). 221p. (Orig.). 1986. pap. 15.00 (*0-912006-22-6*) U of Alaska Pr.

Beringsford Experiment. Marvin R. Wilson, Jr. (Orig.). 1984. pap. 5.00 (*0-88734-309-0*) Players Pr.

Berio. David Osmond-Smith. (Oxford Studies of Composers: No. 20). (Illus.). 176p. 1991. 49.95 (*0-19-315478-1*); pap. 21.00 (*0-19-315455-2*) OUP.

Berit Milah in the Reform Context. Ed. by Lewis M. Bartl. 246p. 1990. 30.00 (*0-8216-5082-3*, 381631) UAHC.

Berji Kristin: Tales from the Garbage Hills. Latife Tekin. Tr. by Ruth Christie & Saliha Paker. 176p. 1993. 21.95 (*0-7145-2944-3*) M Boyars Pubs.

Berkeley. G. Dawes Hicks. LC 88-15279. (Philosophy of George Berkeley Ser.). 358p. 1988. 30.00 (*0-8240-2441-9*) Garland.

Berkeley: An Interpretation. Kenneth P. Winkler. 336p. 1989. 69.00 (*0-19-824907-1*) OUP.

Berkeley: An Interpretation. Kenneth P. Winkler. 336p. 1994. reprint ed. pap. 18.95 (*0-19-823509-7*) OUP.

Berkeley: An Introduction. Jonathan Dancy. LC 86-31038. 200p. 1987. pap. text ed. 21.95 (*0-631-15509-0*) Blackwell Pubs.

Berkeley: Critical & Interpretive Essays. Ed. by Colin M. Turbayne. LC 82-1967. 352p. reprint ed. pap. 100.40 (*0-7837-2912-X*, 2057542) Bks Demand.

Berkeley: The Central Arguments. A. C. Grayling. 232p. 1986. 36.95 (*0-8126-9037-0*) Open Court.

Berkeley: The Philosophy of Immaterialism. Ed. by George Pitcher. (Philosophy of George Berkeley Ser.). 397p. 1988. lib. bdg. 35.00 (*0-8240-2443-5*) Garland.

Berkeley-Ames Workshop on Nonlinear Problems in Control & Fluid Mechanics, Pt. B. L. R. Hunt & C. F. Martin. (LIE Groups B Ser.: Vol. 2). 450p. 1984. 57.00 (*0-915692-37-6*, 991600150) Math Sci Pr.

Berkeley & Malebranche: A Study in the Origins of Berkeley's Thought. Ed. by George Pitcher. (Philosophy of George Berkeley Ser.). 248p. 1989. lib. bdg. 25.00 (*0-8240-2442-7*) Garland.

Berkeley at War: The Nineteen Sixties. W. J. Rorabaugh. 336p. 1990. pap. 11.95 (*0-19-506667-7*) OUP.

Berkeley Barb: Social Control of an Underground Newsroom. Arthur Seeger. 176p. (C). 1984. text ed. 26.50 (*0-8290-1379-2*) Irvington.

Berkeley Barb: Social Control of an Underground Newsroom. Arthur Seeger. 176p. (C). 1987. reprint ed. pap. text ed. 12.95 (*0-8290-2151-5*) Irvington.

***Berkeley Conference on Dutch Linguistics: Dutch Linguistics in a Changing Europe.** Ed. by Thomas F. Shannon & Johan P. Snapper. (Publications of the American Association for Netherlandic Studies: Vol. 8). 190p. (Orig.). (C). 1995. lib. bdg. 32.50 (*0-8191-9744-0*) U Pr of Amer.

Berkeley Conference on Dutch Linguistics: Issues & Controversies. Ed. by Thomas F. Shannon & Johan P. Snapper. 224p. (C). 1991. lib. bdg. 46.00 (*0-8191-8338-5*) U Pr of Amer.

Berkeley Conference on Dutch Literature, 1987: New Perspectives on the Modern Period. Ed. by Johan P. Snapper et al. LC 88-38849. (Publications of the American Association for Netherlandic Studies: Vol. 2). 180p. (C). 1989. lib. bdg. 35.00 (*0-8191-7325-8*, Amer Assn Netherlandic Studies) U Pr of Amer.

Berkeley Conference on Dutch Literature 1991: Europe 1991: Dutch Literature in an International Context. Ed. by Johan P. Snapper & Thomas F. Shannon. 232p. (C). 1993. lib. bdg. 46.50 (*0-8191-8942-1*, Amer Assn Netherlandic Studies) U Pr of Amer.

***Berkeley County: Virginia Publick Claims.** Janice L. Abercrombie & Richard Slatten. (Virginia Publick Claims Ser.). ix, 30p. (C). 1991. pap. 5.00x (*0-8095-8513-8*) Borgo Pr.

Berkeley County: Virginia Publick Claims. Janice L. Abercrombie & Richard Slatten. (Virginia Publick Claims Ser.). ix, 30p. (C). 1991. reprint ed. lib. bdg. 20.00 (*0-8095-8306-2*) Borgo Pr.

Berkeley: Eastern Europe: On the Loose. 2nd ed. 1993. pap. 17.50 (*0-679-02595-2*) Fodors Travel.

Berkeley Guide On the Loose in Europe 1995. Berkeley Staff. (Berkeley Travel Guides Ser.). (Illus.). 1994. pap. 18.95 (*0-679-02641-X*) Fodors Travel.

***Berkeley Guide to California '96.** Berkeley Travel Staff. 1995. pap. 17.50 (*0-679-02978-8*) Fodors Travel.

Berkeley Guide to Central America. 1993. pap. 16.50 (*0-679-02441-7*) Fodors Travel.

***Berkeley Guide to Central America.** 2nd ed. Berkeley Travel Staff. 1996. pap. 17.95 (*0-679-02979-6*) Fodors Travel.

***Berkeley Guide to Eastern Europe.** 3rd ed. Berkeley Travel Staff. 1996. pap. 18.50 (*0-679-02980-X*) Fodors Travel.

Berkeley Guide to Employment for New College Graduates. Ed. by James I. Briggs & Robert B. Nelson. LC 84-51136. 256p. (Orig.). (C). 1984. pap. 7.95 (*0-89815-136-8*) Ten Speed Pr.

***Berkeley Guide to Europe '96.** Berkeley Travel Staff. 1996. pap. 19.95 (*0-679-02981-8*) Fodors Travel.

***Berkeley Guide to France '96.** Berkeley Travel Staff. 1996. pap. 17.95 (*0-679-02982-6*) Fodors Travel.

***Berkeley Guide to Germany & Austria '96.** Berkeley Travel Staff. 1996. pap. 18.50 (*0-679-02983-4*) Fodors Travel.

***Berkeley Guide to Great Britain '96.** Berkeley Travel Staff. 1996. pap. 17.95 (*0-679-02984-2*) Fodors Travel.

Berkeley Guide to Italy, 1995. Berkeley Travel Staff. (Berkeley Guides Ser.). (Illus.). 1994. pap. 16.95 (*0-679-02640-1*) Fodors Travel.

***Berkeley Guide to Italy '96.** Berkeley Travel Staff. 1996. pap. 17.95 (*0-679-02985-0*) Fodors Travel.

***Berkeley Guide to London '96.** Berkeley Travel Staff. 1995. pap. 12.00 (*0-679-02986-9*) Fodors Travel.

***Berkeley Guide to Mexico '96.** Berkeley Travel Staff. 1995. pap. 17.95 (*0-679-02987-7*) Fodors Travel.

***Berkeley Guide to Paris '96.** Berkeley Travel Staff. 1995. pap. 12.00 (*0-679-02988-5*) Fodors Travel.

***Berkeley Guide to San Francisco '96.** Berkeley Travel Staff. 1995. pap. 12.95 (*0-679-02989-3*) Fodors Travel.

Berkeley Guide to the Pacific Northwest & Alaska. Berkeley Staff. 1992. 15.50 (*0-679-02225-2*) Fodors Travel.

Berkeley Inside-Out. Don Pitcher. (Illus.). 384p. (Orig.). 1989. pap. 12.95 (*0-930588-33-9*) Heyday Bks.

Berkeley Inside-Out. Don Pitcher & Malcolm Margolin. 384p. (Orig.). 1991. reprint ed. lib. bdg. 33.00x (*0-8095-4967-0*) Borgo Pr.

***Berkeley Lectures on Sikhism.** Harbans Singh. (C). 1995. 14.00x (*81-7304-067-2*, Pub. by Abhinav II) S Asia.

Berkeley Love & War Songs. Ralph Moreno. 75p. 1957. pap. 4.00 (*0-317-57830-8*) Hartmus Pr.

Berkeley Manuscript. Ed. & Tr. by Oliver B. Ellsworth. LC 84-7470. (Greek & Latin Music Theory Ser.). (Illus.). x, 317p. 1984. 35.00 (*0-8032-1808-7*) U of Nebr Pr.

Berkeley on Abstraction & Abstract Ideas. Ed. by Willis Doney & George Pitcher. (Philosophy of George Berkeley Ser.). 265p. 1989. lib. bdg. 30.00 (*0-8240-2446-X*) Garland.

Berkeley Physics Course, 5 vols. Incl. Vol. 1. Mechanics. 2nd ed. 1973. text ed. (*0-07-004880-0*); Vol. 3. Waves. 1968. text ed. (*0-07-004860-6*); Vol. 4. Quantum Physics. 1970. text ed. (*0-07-004861-4*); Vol. 5. Statistical Physics. 1967. text ed. (*0-07-004862-2*); write for info. (*0-318-54183-1*) McGraw.

Berkeley Physics Course: Electricity & Magnetism, Vol. 2. 2nd ed. E. M. Purcell. 1985. text ed. write for info. (*0-07-004908-4*) McGraw.

Berkeley Poets Cooperative Anthology, 1970-1980. Ed. by Berkeley Poets Cooperative Staff. 256p. 1980. pap. 6.95 (*0-917658-12-4*) BPW & P.

Berkeley Symposia on Mathematical Statistics & Probability: Proceedings of the Sixth Symposium, Vols. 1-6. Incl. Vol. 2. Probability Theory, Pt. 1. Berkeley Symposia Staff. Ed. by Lucien M. Le Cam et al. 1972. 70.00 (*0-520-02184-3*); Vol. 4. Contributions to Biology & the Problems of Health. Berkeley Symposia Staff. Ed. by Lucien M. Le Cam et al. 1973. 54.50 (*0-520-02187-8*); Vol. 6. Effects of Pollution on Health. Berkeley Symposia Staff. Ed. by Lucien M. Le Cam et al. 1972. 65.00 (*0-520-02189-4*); write for info. (*0-318-56012-7*) U CA Pr.

Berkeley, the First Seventy-Five Years. Writers' Program, California Staff. LC 73-3596. (American Guide Ser.). reprint ed. 24.50 (*0-404-57901-9*) AMS Pr.

Berkeley Through Bifocals. LaRue M. Evans. (Illus.). 303p. (Orig.). 1988. 9.95 (*0-9619360-0-2*) Marksman Pr.

Berkeley Unix: A Simple & Comprehensive Guide. James Wilson. 234p. 1991. Net. pap. text ed. write for info. (*0-471-61582-X*) Wiley.

Berkeley UNIX Environment. 2nd ed. R. Nigel Horspool. 400p. 1992. pap. text ed. 42.00 (*0-13-089368-4*) P-H.

Berkeley's American Sojourn. Benjamin Rand. LC 75-3329. reprint ed. 8.50 (*0-404-59323-2*) AMS Pr.

Berkeley's Analysis of Perception. George J. Stack. LC 90-23674. 184p. (C). 1991. text ed. 30.95 (*0-8204-1528-6*) P Lang Pubs.

Berkeley's Argument. C. D. Broad. LC 75-1069. (Studies in Philosophy: No. 40). 1975. lib. bdg. 59.95 (*0-8383-0113-4*) M S G Haskell Hse.

Berkeley's Doctrine of Notions: A Reconstruction Based on His Theory of Meaning. Daniel E. Flage. 240p. 1986. text ed. 39.95 (*0-312-00208-4*) St Martin.

***Berkeley's France '95: On the Loose.** Fodors Staff. (Berkeley Guides Ser.). 1995. 16.95 (*0-679-02779-3*) Fodors Travel.

***Berkeley's Metaphysics: Structural, Interpretive, & Critical Essays.** Ed. by Robert G. Muehlmann. 288p. 1995. 45.00 (*0-271-01427-X*) Pa St U Pr.

Berkeleys of Barn Elms. Frances C. Young. LC 64-8496. (Illus.). 141p. reprint ed. pap. 40.20 (*0-8357-7140-7*, 2050368) Bks Demand.

Berkeley's Ontology. Robert G. Muehlmann. LC 92-17820. 320p. 1992. lib. bdg. 37.95 (*0-87220-146-5*) Hackett Pub.

Berkeley's Philosophical Writings. George Berkeley. Ed. by David M. Armstrong. (Orig.). 1965. pap. 6.95 (*0-02-064170-2*, Collier S&S) S&S Trade.

Berkeley's Philosophy of Mathematics. Douglas M. Jesseph. LC 92-43495. (Science & Its Conceptual Foundations Ser.). (Illus.). 384p. (C). 1993. lib. bdg. 57.50 (*0-226-39897-8*); pap. text ed. 19.95 (*0-226-39898-6*) U Ch Pr.

Berkeley's Revolution in Vision. Margaret Atherton. LC 89-49632. (Illus.). 264p. 1990. 35.00 (*0-8014-2358-9*) Cornell U Pr.

Berkeley's Theory of Vision: A Critical Examination of Bishop Berkeley's Essay Towards a New Theory of Vision. Ed. by George Pitcher. (Philosophy of George Berkeley Ser.). 128p. 1989. reprint ed. lib. bdg. 20.00 (*0-8240-2448-6*) Garland.

Berkley. (Phytopathological Classics Ser.). 108p. 1948. 15.00 (*0-89054-009-8*) Am Phytopathol Soc.

Berkouwer's Doctrine of Election: Balance or Imbalance? Alvin L. Baker. 1981. pap. 5.99 (*0-87552-119-3*) Presby & Reformed.

Berks Authors Collection, Vol. 1. Ed. by Chet Hagan. 120p. 1994. 30.00 (*0-9639079-1-3*); pap. 12.50 (*0-9639079-0-5*) Frnds Reading-Berks.

Berks County: The Green Diamond of Pennsylvania. James L. Holton. (Illus.). 176p. 1993. 27.95 (*0-89781-463-0*) Preferred Mktg.

Berks County Pa. Archives, 1767. Comp. by Katharine F. Dix. 33p. 1989. pap. text ed. 6.00 (*1-55856-016-5*) Closson Pr.

Berks County Pa. Archives, 1784. Ed. by Katharine F. Dix. 95p. 1989. pap. text ed. 8.00 (*1-55856-015-7*) Closson Pr.

***Berks the Bizarre.** Charles J. Adams, 3rd. 1995. 10.95 (*1-880683-06-7*) Exeter Hse.

Berkshire & Texas Type: North American Steam Locomotives. Jack W. Farrell. Ed. by Pacific Fast Mail Staff. 191p. 1988. 39.95 (*0-915713-15-2*) Pac Fast Mail.

Berkshire Anthology. Ed. by Gerald Hausman & David Silverstein. 176p. (Orig.). 1972. pap. 10.00 (*0-912846-01-1*) Bookstore Pr.

Berkshire Bands: A Pictorial Review from 1884 to 1984. Alan B. Grieve. (Illus.). 250p. 1992. pap. 20.00 (*0-9633376-1-0*) P Drozd Grap Art.

Berkshire-Bennington Locater. Asia W. Davenport. 112p. 1988. pap. 10.95 (*0-934794-05-7*) First Impressions.

Berkshire Book. rev. ed. Jonathan Sternfield. 1994. pap. 16.95 (*0-936399-60-0*) Berkshire Hse.

Berkshire Cottages: A Vanishing Era. Carole Owens. (Illus.). 240p. (Orig.). 1984. pap. 27.95 (*0-918343-00-3*) Cottage Pr.

Berkshire Further off the Trail. Bernard A. Drew. (Illus.). 56p. 1992. pap. 7.50 (*0-941583-19-8*) Attic Rev Pr.

Berkshire Hills. Ed. by Writers of the Works Progress Administration. (Illus.). 390p. 1987. reprint ed. pap. 14.95 (*1-55553-012-5*) NE U Pr.

Berkshire of One Hundred Years Ago. David Buxton. LC 92-21444. 1992. 36.00 (*0-7509-0217-5*) A Sutton Pub.

***Berkshire Reader.** Richard Nunley. 1995. pap. 16.95 (*0-936399-63-5*) Berkshire Hse.

Berkshire Reader: Writings from New England's Secluded Paradise. Richard Nunley. (Illus.). 1992. 29.95 (*0-936399-33-3*) Berkshire Hse.

Berkshire Seasons of Celebration. Ed. by Sam Bittman & Steven A. Satullo. (Illus.). 108p. 1982. 25.00 (*0-910931-01-1*); pap. 15.00 (*0-910931-00-3*) Either-or Pr.

Berkshire Superlatives: One Thousand-One Firsts & Lasts, Biggests, & Smallests, Tallests & Shortests. Bernard A. Drew. 32p. 1993. pap. 5.00 (*0-941583-20-1*) Attic Rev Pr.

Berkshire Tower. Rebecca H. Duncan. Ed. by James B. Van Treese. 520p. 1994. pap. 9.95 (*1-56901-090-0*) NW Pub.

Berkshire Victuals. Intro. by Janet P. Cook. (Illus.). 202p. (Orig.). 1993. pap. 19.95 (*0-9639206-0-X*) Berkshire Cnty Hist.

***Berkshires.** Bill Binzen. 1995. 24.95 (*0-936399-67-8*) Berkshire Hse.

Berkshires: A History & Guide. John Miller. pap. write for info. (*0-318-58334-8*) Random.

Berkshires - Collected Works of Federal Writers Project, Vol. 4. Federal Writers Project Staff. 1991. reprint ed. lib. bdg. 98.00 (*0-7812-5629-1*) Rprt Serv.

Berl: The Biography of a Socialist Zionist; Berl Katznelson, 1887-1944. Anita Shapira. LC 84-7008. (Illus.). 416p. 1985. 64.95 (*0-521-25618-6*) Cambridge U Pr.

Berlin. Eleanor H. Ayer. LC 91-29721. (Cities at War Ser.). (Illus.). 96p. (J). (gr. 6 up). 1992. text ed. 14.95 (*0-02-707800-0*, Mac Bks Young Read) S&S Childrens.

Berlin. Ed. by Alan Balfour. (World Cities Ser.: No. 3). (Illus.). 400p. 1994. 95.00 (*1-85490-374-8*, Academy Edits) St Martin.

Berlin. Beazley. (American Express Pocket Travel Guides Ser.). (Illus.). 1994. pap. 14.00 (*0-671-86826-8*, P-H Travel) P-H Gen Ref & Trav.

Berlin. Mitchell Beazley & Derek Blyth. (American Express Pocket Travel Guides Ser.). (Illus.). 152p. 1992. pap. 13.00 (*0-13-028747-4*, P-H Travel) P-H Gen Ref & Trav.

Berlin. Berlitz Editors. (Berlitz Pocket Guides Ser.). 1994. pap. 7.95 (*2-8315-2558-6*) Berlitz.

Berlin. Beth Reiber. (Frommer's Walking Tours Ser.). (Illus.). 176p. 1993. pap. 12.00 (*0-671-79837-5*, P-H Travel) P-H Gen Ref & Trav.

Berlin. A. Reiche. Date not set. 25.00 (*0-06-018212-1*, HarpT); pap. 12.95 (*0-06-098112-1*) HarpC.

Berlin. Richard Steins. (Great Cities Library). (Illus.). 64p. (J). (gr. 3-7). 1991. lib. bdg. 14.95 (*1-56711-019-3*) Blackbirch.

Berlin. Ian Wallace. (World Bibliographical Ser.). 1993. lib. bdg. 68.50 (*1-85109-142-4*) ABC-CLIO.

***Berlin.** 3rd ed. Frommer Staff. (Frommer's Travel Guides Ser.). 1995. pap. 12.95 (*0-02-860046-0*) Macmillan.

***Berlin: Berlin.** 2nd ed. (Travellers Guides Ser.). (Illus.). 320p. 1994. pap. 11.95 (*2-8315-1721-4*) Berlitz.

Berlin: Cadogan City Guides. Andrew Gumbel. LC 91-15789. 224p. 1991. pap. 14.95 (*0-87106-238-0*) Globe Pequot.

Berlin: Capital of the New Germany. Gordon M. McLachlan. 1994. pap. 16.95 (*0-8442-9674-0*, Passport Bks) NTC Pub Grp.

Berlin: Culture & Metropolis. Ed. by Charles W. Haxthausen & Heidrun Suhr. (Illus.). 256p. 1990. text ed. 24.95 (*0-8166-1860-7*) U of Minn Pr.

Berlin: Development of Its Government & Administration. Elmer Plischke. LC 70-98789. 257p. 1970. reprint ed. text ed. 59.75 (*0-8371-3024-7*, PLB, Greenwood Pr) Greenwood.

Berlin: From Symbol of Confrontation to Keystone of Stability. James S. Sutterlin & David Klein. LC 89-33974. 243p. 1989. text ed. 55.00 (*0-275-93259-1*, C3259, Praeger Pubs) Greenwood.

Berlin: Hostage for the West. John Mander. LC 79-9953. (Illus.). 124p. 1979. reprint ed. text ed. 49.75 (*0-313-20996-0*, MABE, Greenwood Pr) Greenwood.

Berlin: Prestel Guide. Ed. by Joachim Fait. (Illus.). 192p. (Orig.). 1992. pap. 19.95 (*3-7913-1183-2*, Pub. by Prestel) TeNeues.

Berlin: Spatial Structure of a Divided City. T. H. Elkins & B. Hofmeister. (Illus.). 240p. 1988. text ed. 70.00 (*0-416-92220-1*, A1951) Routledge Chapman & Hall.

Berlin: The Politics of Order. Alan Balfour. LC 90-344704. (Illus.). 269p. 1990. 39.95 (*0-8478-1271-5*) Rizzoli Intl.

Berlin: The Red Room & White Beer. Robert J. Hellman. LC 90-11299. 230p. 1991. 28.00 (*0-89410-667-8*); pap. 15.00 (*0-89410-668-6*) Three Continents.

Berlin - New York: Like & Unlike: Essays on Architecture & Art from 1870 to the Present. Ed. by Josef P. Kleihues. LC 92-37372. (Illus.). 496p. 1994. 85.00 (*0-8478-1657-5*) Rizzoli Intl.

Berlin Airlift. Scott Westerfeld. (Turning Points in American History Ser.). (Illus.). 64p. (J). (gr. 5 up). 1989. lib. bdg. 14.95 (*0-382-09833-1*); pap. 7.95 (*0-382-09852-8*) Silver Burdett Pr.

Berlin Alert: The Memoirs & Reports of Truman Smith. Ed. by Robert Hessen. LC 83-22621. (Publication Series: Archival Documentaries: No. 289). xx, 172p. 1984. 7.98 (*0-8179-7891-7*); pap. 3.98 (*0-8179-7892-5*) Hoover Inst Pr.

Berlin Alexanderplatz. Alfred Doblin. 640p. (FRE.). 1981. pap. 13.95 (*0-7859-1925-2*, 2070372391) Fr & Eur.

Berlin Alexanderplatz: The Story of Franz Biberkopf. Alfred Doblin. Tr. by Eugene Jolas. 500p. 1984. pap. text ed. 15.95 (*0-8044-6121-X*, F Ungar Bks) Continuum.

Berlin & Potsdam. rev. ed. Comp. by Nelles Verlag. (Nelles Guides Ser.). (Illus.). 256p. 1992. pap. 14.95 (*3-88618-381-5*, Pub. by Nelles Verlag GW) Seven Hills Bk.

***Berlin & Potsdam: Nelles Guide.** rev. ed. (Nelles Guides Ser.). (Illus.). 256p. 1995. pap. 14.95 (*3-88618-043-3*, Pub. by Nelles Verlag GW) Seven Hills Bk.

Berlin Base. Bailey et al. Date not set. write for info. (*0-517-59808-6*) Crown Pub Group.

Berlin Before the Wall: A Foreign Student's Diary with Sketches. Hsi-Huey Liang. (Illus.). 258p. 1990. 29.95 (*0-415-90168-5*, A4290, Routledge NY) Routledge.

Berlin! Berlin! Its Culture, Its Times. Michael Farr. (Illus.). 216p. 1993. 29.95 (*1-85626-064-X*) Trafalgar.

***Berlin-Bibliographie.** 1996. write for info. (*3-598-23432-5*) K G Saur.

Berlin-Bibliographie bis 1960: In der Senatsbibliothek Berlin. Ed. by Hans Zopf & Gerd Heinrich. (Veroeffentlichungen der Historischen Kommission zu Berlin, Band 67, Beitraege zu Inflation und Wiederaufbau in Deutschland und Europa 1914-1924: Vol. 15). (C). 1965. 142.35 (*3-11-000902-1*) De Gruyter.

Berlin Blind. large type ed. Alan Scholefield. (Adventure Suspense Ser.). 400p. 1993. 21.95 (*0-7089-2919-2*) Ulverscroft.

Berlin Blockade: A Study in Cold War Politics. W. Phillips Davison. Ed. by Harriet Zuckerman & Robert K. Merton. LC 79-8992. (Dissertations on Sociology Ser.). (Illus.). 1980. reprint ed. lib. bdg. 44.95 (*0-405-12963-7*) Ayer.

***Berlin by Night.** White Wolf Staff. (Vampire). Date not set. per., pap. 15.00 (*1-56504-075-9*, 2214) White Wolf.

Berlin Cabaret. Peter Jelavich. LC 93-16096. (Studies in Cultural History: Vol. 9). 336p. 1993. 42.50 (*0-674-06761-4*) HUP.

Berlin Calling: American Broadcasters in Service to the Third Reich. John C. Edwards. LC 90-20841. 288p. 1991. text ed. 35.00 (*0-275-93905-7*, C3905, Praeger Pubs) Greenwood.

Berlin Church Records, Somerset County, PA. Comp. by E. C. Saylor. 195p. 1989. pap. text ed. 19.95 (*0-933227-82-5*) Closson Pr.

***Berlin Commentary on Martianus Capella's de Nutpiis Philologiae et Mercurii, Book I.** Ed. by Haijo J. Westra. LC 94-33781. (Mittelateinische Studien und Texte: Bd. 20). 1994. write for info. (*90-04-10170-5*) E J Brill.

Berlin Confidential. Christoph Amberger. 222p. 1990. 12.95 (*0-945332-21-1*) Agora Inc MD.

Berlin Crisis of 1961: Soviet-American Relations & the Struggle for Power in the Kremlin, June-November, 1961. Robert M. Slusser. LC 72-4025. 527p. reprint ed. pap. 150.20 (*0-8357-8039-2*, 2034127) Bks Demand.

Berlin Crisis of 1961: Soviet-American Relations & the Struggle for Power in the Kremlin, June-November, 1961. Robert M. Slusser. LC 72-4025. 525p. (C). 1973. 68.00x (*0-8018-1404-9*) Johns Hopkins.

Berlin Crisis, 1958-1962: Guide & Index, 2 vols., Set. National Security Archive Staff & Chadwyck-Healey Staff. Ed. by Laurence Chang. (Making of U. S. Policy Ser.). (Illus.). 1992. 900.00 (*0-89887-096-8*) Chadwyck-Healey.

***Berlin Dada, Berlin Revolution.** Simon Alaric. 1996. pap. 15.00 (*1-899438-17-3*, Pub. by Porcupine Bks UK) Humanities.

Berlin, Deutsche Staatsbibliothek, MS L.215. Alexander Silbiger. LC 88-752438. (Seventeenth Century Keyboard Music Ser.: Vol. 7). 402p. 1989. 35.00 (*0-8240-8006-8*) Garland.

Berlin Diaries, 1940-45. Marie Vassiltchikov. LC 87-45932. (Illus.). 400p. 1988. reprint ed. pap. 12.00 (*0-394-75777-7*, Vin) Random.

Berlin Diary: The Journal of a Foreign Correspondent, 1934-1941. William L. Shirer. 1988. pap. 17.95 (*0-316-78704-3*) Little.

***Berlin Diptychon.** Bill Barrette & John Yau. (Illus.). 96p. (Orig.). 1995. pap. 19.95 (*0-943221-23-4*) Timken Pubs.

An Asterisk (*) at the beginning of an entry indicates that the title is appearing in BIP for the first time.

An Asterisk (*) at the beginning of an entry indicates that the title is appearing in BIP for the first time.

Bernard Brodie & the Foundations of American Nuclear Strategy. Barry H. Steiner. LC 90-22618. (Modern War Studies). xvi, 368p. 1991. 40.00 (0-7006-0441-3) U Pr of KS.

Bernard Clayton's Complete Book of Cooks: Cooking with 101 Home Cooks & Chefs Throughout the Country & 250 of Their Best Recipes. LC 92-15637. 1993. 25.00 (0-671-67290-8) S&S Trade.

Bernard Delicieux et l'Inquisition Albigeoise, 1300-1320. Barthelemy Haureau. LC 78-63180. (Heresies of the Early Christian & Medieval Era Ser.: Second Ser.). reprint ed. 45.00 (0-404-16223-1) AMS Pr.

Bernard DeVoto. Orlan Sawey. LC 69-18502. (Twayne's United States Authors Ser.). 1969. lib. bdg. 17.95 (0-89197-675-2) Irvington.

Bernard E. Harkness Seedlist Handbook. 2nd ed. Comp. by Mabel G. Harkness. LC 92-21121. 520p. 1993. pap. 29.95 (0-88192-226-9) Timber.

Bernard Foy's Third Castling. Lars Gustafsson. Tr. by Yvonne L. Sandstroem. LC 88-17968. 416p. 1988. 19.95 (0-8112-1086-3) New Directions.

Bernard H. Breslauer Collection of Manuscript Illuminations. William M. Voelkle & Roger S. Wieck. Ed. by Maria F. Saffiotti. LC 92-50519. (Illus.). 254p. 1994. pap. 49.95 (0-87598-095-3) Pierpont Morgan.

Bernard Herrmann: Film Music & Narrative. Graham D. Bruce. Ed. by Diane Kirkpatrick. LC 85-16336. (Studies in Cinema: No. 38). 256p. reprint ed. pap. 69.20 (0-8357-1966-9) Bks Demand.

Bernard Langlais, Sculptor. Pat Reef. LC 84-81337. (Illus.). 48p. (J). (gr. 3-7). 1985. pap. 9.95 (0-933858-06-X) Kennebec River.

Bernard-Lazare: Antisemitism & the Problem of Jewish Identity in the Late Nineteenth-Century France. Nelly Wilson. LC 77-82524. 360p. reprint ed. pap. 102.60 (0-8357-7142-3, 2031745) Bks Demand.

Bernard Leach. Bernard Leach. 1966. boxed 300.00 (0-685-45126-7) R S Barnes.

Bernard Leach, Hamada & Their Circle: From the Wingfield Digby Collection. Tony Birks & Cornelia W. Digby. (Illus.). 192p. 1992. pap. 29.95 (0-9517700-4-7, Pub. by Marston Hse UK) Seven Hills Bk.

Bernard Lonergan's Philosophy of God. Bernard J. Tyrrell. LC 73-22205. 216p. reprint ed. pap. 61.60 (0-8357-7143-1, 2022063) Bks Demand.

Bernard M. Baruch: Speculator & Statesman. Blythe F. Finke. Ed. by D. Steve Rahmas. LC 78-190249. (Outstanding Personalities Ser.: No. 32). 32p. (Orig.). (J). (gr. 7-12). 1972. lib. bdg. 4.95 (0-87157-532-9) SamHar Pr.

Bernard Malamud. Intro. by Harold Bloom. (Modern Critical Views Ser.). 231p. 1986. 29.95 (0-87754-674-6) Chelsea Hse.

Bernard Malamud. Sidney Richman. (United States Authors Ser.: No. 109). 1966. text ed. 19.95 (0-8057-0472-8, Twayne) Macmillan.

Bernard Malamud: A Collection of Critical Essays. Ed. by Joyce Field & Leslie Field. (Twentieth Century Views Ser.). 192p. 1975. 12.95 (0-13-548032-9, Spectrum Bks) P-H.

Bernard Malamud: A Descriptive Bibliography. Rita N. Kosofsky. LC 90-19915. (Bibliographies & Indexes in American Literature Ser.: No. 13). 296p. 1991. text ed. 55.00 (0-313-27694-3, KBF/, Greenwood Pr) Greenwood.

Bernard Malamud: A Study of the Short Fiction. Robert Solotaroff. (Twayne's Studies in Short Fiction: No. 8). 240p. 1989. text ed. 22.95 (0-8057-8316-4, Twayne) Macmillan.

Bernard Malamud: An Annotated Checklist. Rita N. Kosofsky. LC 75-626236. (Serif Series: Bibliographies & Checklists: No. 7). 77p. reprint ed. pap. 25.00 (0-7837-0571-9, 2040915) Bks Demand.

Bernard Malamud Revisited. Edward A. Abramson. (Twayne's United States Authors Ser.). 160p. 1993. text ed. 22.95 (0-8057-7641-9, Twayne) Macmillan.

Bernard Maybeck: Visionary Architect. Sally B. Woodbridge. LC 92-12633. (Illus.). 248p. 1992. 55.00 (1-55859-280-6) Abbeville Pr.

Bernard Meadows: Sculpture & Drawings. Alan Bowness. (British Sculptors & Sculpture Ser.: Vol. IV). (Illus.). 160p. (C). 1994. 75.00 (0-85331-644-9, Pub. by Lund Humphries UK) Antique Collect.

Bernard Meninsky. John R. Taylor. 128p. (C). 1989. 90.00 (0-685-38648-1, Pub. by Redcliffe Pr Ltd) St Mut.

Bernard of Clairvaux. Richars D. Storrs. 1973. 150.00 (0-87968-723-1) Gordon Pr.

***Bernard of Clairvaux: A Saint's Life in Word & Image.** M. Basil Pennington & Yael Katzir. LC 93-83255. (Illus.). 256p. 1994. 29.95 (0-87973-467-1, 467) Our Sunday Visitor.

Bernard of Clairvaux: Consideration: Advice to a Pope. Tr. by John D. Anderson & Elizabeth T. Kennan. LC 75-27953. (Cistercian Fathers Ser.: No. 37). 1976. 5.00 (0-87907-137-0) Cistercian Pubns.

Bernard of Clairvaux: Five Books on Consideration - Advice to a Pope. 1989. pap. 9.95 (0-318-41663-8) Cistercian Pubns.

Bernard of Clairvaux: Man, Monk, Mystic. Michael Casey. 123p. 1991. audio, pap. 49.95 (0-87907-199-0) Cistercian Pubns.

Bernard of Clairvaux: On Loving God. Tr. by Robert Walton. 1993. pap. write for info. (0-318-70014-X) Cistercian Pubns.

Bernard of Clairvaux: Parables (Parabolae) Bernard. Tr. by Michael Casey. (Cistercian Studies: No. 55A). (Illus.). 112p. 1991. write for info. (0-87907-155-9) Cistercian Pubns.

Bernard of Clairvaux: Selected Writings. Tr. & Frwd. by G. R. Evans. (Classics of Western Spirituality Ser.). 352p. 1987. 19.95 (0-8091-0398-2); pap. 14.95 (0-8091-2917-5) Paulist Pr.

Bernard of Clairvaux: Sermons for the Summer Seasons, Liturgical Sermons 3. Bernard. Tr. by Beverly Kienzle. (Cistercian Fathers Ser.: No. 53). 256p. write for info. (0-87907-153-2); pap. write for info. (0-87907-453-1) Cistercian Pubns.

Bernard of Clairvaux: Sermons I on Conversion; Lenten Sermons on the Psalm "He Who Dwells" Bernard Of Clairvaux. Tr. by Marie-Bernard Said. (Cistercian Fathers Ser.: No. 25). (LAT.). 1982. 25.95 (0-87907-125-7); pap. 7.00 (0-87907-925-8) Cistercian Pubns.

Bernard of Clairvaux: Sermons on the Song of Songs, Vol. III. Tr. by Kilian Walsh & Irene Edmonds. (Cistercian Fathers Ser.: No. 31). 1979. 15.95 (0-87907-131-1); pap. 5.00 (0-87907-931-2) Cistercian Pubns.

Bernard of Clairvaux: Sermons on the Song of Songs, Vol. IV. Bernard Of Clairvaux. Tr. by Irene Edmonds & Jean Leclercq. (Cistercian Fathers Ser.: N0. 40). 1980. 15.95 (0-87907-140-0) Cistercian Pubns.

Bernard of Clairvaux: Studies Presented to Dom Jean Leclercq. LC 73-8099. (Cistercian Studies: No. 23). 1973. 5.50 (0-87907-823-5) Cistercian Pubns.

Bernard of Clairvaux: The Irishman. Tr. by Robert T. Mayer. LC 78-768. (Cistercian Fathers Ser.). 1978. 7.95 (0-685-87078-2); pap. 4.00 (0-87907-910-X) Cistercian Pubns.

Bernard of Clairvaux & the Cistercian Spirit. LC 76-15487. (Cistercian Studies: No. 16). (Illus.). 1976. 10.95 (0-87907-816-2) Cistercian Pubns.

***Bernard of Clairvaux & the Shape of Monastic Thought: Broken Dreams.** M. B. Pranger. LC 94-3716. (Studies in Intellectual History Ser.: 56). 1994. 85.75 (90-04-10055-5) E J Brill.

Bernard of Clairvaux on the Song of Songs, Vol. I. Tr. by Kilian Walsh. (Cistercian Fathers Ser.: No. 4). pap. 5.00 (0-87907-104-4) Cistercian Pubns.

Bernard of Clairvaux on the Song of Songs, Vol. II. Bernard of Clairvaux. Tr. by Kilian Walsh. (Cistercian Fathers Ser.: No. 7). pap. 5.00 (0-87907-707-7) Cistercian Pubns.

Bernard of Clairvaux, Treatises II: The Steps of Humility & Pride, on Loving God. LC 74-7147. (Cistercian Fathers Ser.: No. 13). 1974. reprint ed. pap. 5.00 (0-87907-713-1) Cistercian Pubns.

Bernard of Clairvaux, Treatises III: On Grace & Free Choice, in Praise of the New Knighthood. Tr. by Daniel O'Donovan. (Cistercian Studies: No. 3). 1977. 10.95 (0-87907-119-2); pap. 4.95 (0-87907-719-0) Cistercian Pubns.

***Bernard of Hollywood Pin-ups: Blondes!** Ed. by Susan Bernard. (Illus.). 60p. 1995. 6.95 (0-446-91003-1) Warner Bks.

***Bernard of Hollywood Pin-ups: Brunettes!** Ed. by Susan Bernard. (Illus.). 60p. 1995. 6.95 (0-446-91004-X) Warner Bks.

***Bernard of Hollywood Pin-ups: Redheads!** Susan Bernard. (Illus.). 60p. 1995. 6.95 (0-446-91005-8) Warner Bks.

Bernard of Hollywood's Marilyn. Photos by Bruno Bernard. LC 92-41317. 1993. 29.95 (0-312-08882-5) St Martin.

Bernard on His Own. Syd Hoff. LC 92-21770. (Illus.). 32p. (J). (gr. k-3). 1993. 14.95 (0-395-65226-X, Clarion Bks) HM.

Bernard Quesnay. Andre Maurois. 1963. pap. 17.50 (0-685-11045-1) Fr & Eur.

Bernard Quesnay. Andre Maurois. 192p. (FRE.). 1973. pap. 10.95 (0-7859-0109-4, M3757) Fr & Eur.

Bernard Romans: Forgotten Patriot of the American Revolution, Military Engineer & Cartographer of West Point & the Hudson Valley. Lincoln Diamant. LC 85-5421. (Illus.). 160p. 1985. 15.95 (0-916346-56-0) Harbor Hill Bks.

Bernard Shaw. Edward Shanks. LC 74-6481. (George Bernard Shaw Ser., No. 92). (C). 1974. lib. bdg. 33.95 (0-8383-1955-6) M S G Haskell Hse.

Bernard Shaw. 2nd ed. Holbrook Jackson. LC 71-124239. (Select Bibliographies Reprint Ser.). 1977. reprint ed. 20.95 (0-8369-5427-0) Ayer.

Bernard Shaw: A Chronicle. Robert F. Rattray. LC 74-30342. (George Bernard Shaw Ser.: No. 92). 1974. lib. bdg. 52.95 (0-8383-1892-4) M S G Haskell Hse.

Bernard Shaw: A Critical View. Nicholas Grene. LC 83-24547. 188p. 1984. text ed. 39.95 (0-312-07661-4) St Martin.

Bernard Shaw: A Guide to Research. Stanley Weintraub. 160p. 1992. text ed. 35.00 (0-271-00831-8) Pa St U Pr.

Bernard Shaw: A Psychological Study. A. Daniel Dervin. LC 73-8301. 350p. 1975. 36.50 (0-8387-1418-8) Bucknell U Pr.

Bernard Shaw: The Darker Side. Arnold Silver. LC 79-92454. (Illus.). 368p. 1982. 42.50 (0-8047-1091-0) Stanford U Pr.

Bernard Shaw: The Diaries, 1885-1897, 2 vols. Ed. by Stanley Weintraub. LC 84-625360. 1241p. 1986. text ed. 100.00 (0-271-00386-3) Pa St U Pr.

Bernard Shaw: The Search for Love, Vol. I. Michael Holroyd. LC 89-40603. 528p. 1990. pap. 15.95 (0-679-72505-9, Vin) Random.

***Bernard Shaw Vol. 3: Lure.** M. Holroyd. 1994. pap. 9.99 (0-517-13035-1) Random.

Bernard Shaw & Mrs. Patrick Campbell: Their Correspondence. George Bernard Shaw. Ed. by Alan Dent. LC 83-45801. reprint ed. 36.50 (0-404-20233-0, PR5366) AMS Pr.

Bernard Shaw & the Art of Drama. Charles A. Berst. LC 73-180884. 363p. reprint ed. pap. 103.50 (0-8357-6038-3, 2034426) Bks Demand.

Bernard Shaw, Frank Harris, & Oscar Wilde. Robert H. Sherard. LC 74-30469. (English Literature Ser.: No. 33). 1974. lib. bdg. 75.00 (0-8383-2019-8) M S G Haskell Hse.

Bernard Shaw II: The Pursuit of Power 1898-1918. Michael Holroyd. LC 88-42660. (Illus.). 496p. 1989. 24.95 (0-394-57553-9) Random.

Bernard Shaw on the London Art Scene, 1885-1950. Stanley Weintraub. LC 88-43442. 494p. 1990. lib. bdg. 50.00 (0-271-00665-X) Pa St U Pr.

Bernard Shaw, Vol. Two: The Pursuit of Power. Michael Holroyd. LC 89-40603. 464p. 1991. pap. 16.00 (0-679-73132-6, Vin) Random.

Bernard Shaw, Vol. 1: The Search for Love, 1856-1898. Michael Holroyd. LC 88-2660. (Illus.). 496p. 1988. 24.95 (0-394-52577-9) Random.

Bernard Shaw, Vols. 3 & 4: The Lure of Fantasy, 1918-1951, the Last Laugh, 1950-1991. Michael Holroyd. LC 88-42660. 1993. pap. 18.00 (0-679-72507-5, Vin) Random.

Bernard Shaw's 'An Unsocial Socialist' Robert Hogan. (Adaptations Ser.). 1978. 6.95 (0-685-04178-6); pap. 2.95 (0-912262-54-0) Proscenium.

Bernard Shaw's "Arms & the Man" A Composite Production Book. Comp. by Bernard F. Dukore. LC 80-29681. (Special Issues Ser.). (Illus.). 214p. 1982. 23.95 (0-8093-1017-1) S Ill U Pr.

Bernard Shaw's Book Reviews. Brian Tyson. 608p. 1991. 65.00 (0-271-00721-4) Pa St U Pr.

Bernard Shaw's Letters to Siegfried Trebitsch. Ed. by Samuel A. Weiss. LC 84-40329. (Illus.). 512p. 1986. 52.50 (0-8047-1257-3) Stanford U Pr.

Bernard Shaw's Marxian Romance. Paul A. Hummert. LC 75-144815. 243p. reprint ed. pap. 69.30 (0-7837-6026-4, 2045838) Bks Demand.

Bernard Shaw's Nondramatic Literary Criticism. Bernard Shaw. Ed. by Stanley Weintraub. LC 70-149739. (Regents Critics Ser.). 274p. reprint ed. pap. 78.10 (0-7837-1392-4, 2041573) Bks Demand.

Bernard Shaw's Plays: Major Barbara, Heartbreak House, Saint Joan, Too True to Be Good. George Bernard Shaw. Ed. by Warren S. Smith. (Critical Editions Ser.). (C). 1970. pap. text ed. 12.95 (0-393-09942-3) Norton.

Bernard Siegfried Albinus (1697-1770) on Human Nature: Anatomical & Physiological Ideas in 18th Century Leiden. H. Punt. (Illus.). 226p. 1983. lib. bdg. 97.50 (90-6078-088-4, Pub. by B M Israel NE) Coronet Bks.

Bernard Spilsbury: His Life & Cases. Browne & Tullett. (Reprints Ser.). 464p. 1989. 24.95 (0-88029-307-1) Dorset Pr.

Bernard Stern. Pierre Restany. (Illus.). 200p. 1990. 60.00 (0-312-04923-4) St Martin.

Bernard Stern. Antoine Stern et al. (Academy Editions Ser.). (Illus.). 96p. 1981. 35.00 (0-312-07670-3) St Martin.

Bernard Stevens & His Music: A Symposium. Comp. by Bertha Stevens. 1990. 23.95 (0-912483-20-2) Pro-Am Music.

Bernard Venet. Kyoichi Tsuzuki. (Art Random Ser.: No. 52). (Illus.). 48p. 1991. 32.95 (4-7636-8550-3, Pub. by Kyoto Shoin JA) Bks Nippan.

Bernard Wlete's Fundamental Theological Approach to Christology. Anthony J. Godzieba. LC 93-15512. (Am. Univ. Studies, VII: Vol. 160). 213p. (C). 1994. text ed. 41.95 (0-8204-2218-5) P Lang Pubs.

Bernardin de Saint-Pierre ou le Triomphe de Flore. Jean-Jacques Simon. 160p. (FRE.). 1968. pap. 14.95 (0-7859-5548-8) Fr & Eur.

Bernardine. Mary Chase. 1954. pap. 4.75 (0-8222-0105-4) Dramatists Play.

Bernardino Ochino: Seven Dialogues. Tr. by Rita Belladonna. (Medieval & Renaissance Texts & Studies: Vol. CRR3). 144p. 1985. pap. 10.00 (0-919473-63-6, Centre Reform Renaiss Stu) MRTS.

***Bernardo Bertolucci.** Claretta Tonetti. LC 95-10642. (Twayne's Filmmakers Ser.). 1995. write for info. (0-8057-9313-5, Twayne) Macmillan.

***Bernardo Bertolucci.** Claretta Tonetti. LC 95-10642. (Twayne's Filmmakers Ser.). 1995. pap. write for info. (0-8057-9336-4, Twayne) Macmillan.

Bernardo de Galvez. Frank De Varona. LC 89-38079. (Hispanic Stories Ser.). (Illus.). 32p. (ENG & SPA.). (J). (gr. 4-5). 1991. lib. bdg. 19.97 (0-8172-3379-2) Raintree Steck-V.

***Bernardo De Galvez.** Devarona. (J). 1995. pap. text ed. (0-8114-6756-2) Raintree Steck-V.

Bernardo de Galvez: Hero of the American Revolution. Lorenzo G. LaFarelle. 92p. 1992. 14.95 (0-89015-849-5) Sunbelt Media.

Bernardo de Galvez in Louisiana: 1776-1783. 2nd ed. John W. Caughey. LC 72-86562. 290p. 1972. reprint ed. 25.00 (0-911116-78-8) Pelican.

Bernardo's Revenge & Other Western Yarns. Zane Grey. Ed. by J. E. Clauss. 1976. lib. bdg. 20.95 (0-89190-751-3, Rivercity Pr) Amereon Ltd.

Bernard's Nautical Star Chart. Brown, Son & Ferguson Ltd. Staff. (C). 1987. 36.00 (0-85174-559-8, Pub. by Brwn Son Ferg) St Mut.

Bernardus Magister. Ed. by John R. Sommerfeldt. (Cistercian Studies: No. 135). 1992. write for info. (0-87907-635-6); pap. write for info. (0-87907-735-2) Cistercian Pubns.

Bernarr Macfadden: A Study in Success. Clement Wood. (American Newspapermen 1790-1933 Ser.). 316p. 1974. reprint ed. 25.00 (0-8464-0001-4) Beekman Pubs.

Bernd & Hilla Becher: Pennsylvania Coal Mine Tipples. Bernd Becher & Hilla Becher. (Illus.). 136p. 1993. 45.00 (0-944521-23-1) Dia Ctr Arts.

Bernd Degen Discus: A Reference Book. Bernd Degen. (Illus.). 128p. 1991. text ed. 29.95 (0-86622-545-5, TS-163) TFH Pubns.

Bernd Koberling. (Illus.). 120p. 1992. 55.00 (3-89322-219-7, Pub. by Edition Cantz GW) Dist Art Pubs.

***Bernd Koberling: Paintings 1991-1993.** Eckart Britsch. (Illus.). 90p. Date not set. 55.00 (3-928762-19-2) Dist Art Pubs.

Berne Convention for the Protection of Literary & Artistic Works, 3 Pts. Incl. Pt. 1. 1970. (0-318-60518-X, WIPO24); Pt. 2. 1970. (0-318-60519-8, WIPO25); Pt. 3. 1977. (0-318-60520-1, WIPO26); Suppl. 1. 1968. 16.50 (0-685-99314-0, WIPO5); Suppl. 2. 1972 (Paris Act) 1972. 7.50 (0-685-99315-9, WIPO7); Suppl. 3. 1973. 1973. 7.50 (0-685-99316-7, WIPO8); Suppl. 4. 1975. 1975. 7.50 (0-685-99317-5, WIPO9); Suppl. 4. 1975. 1975. 7.50 (0-685-99317-5, WIPO9); Suppl. 3. 1973. 1973. 7.50 (0-685-99316-7, WIPO8); write for info. (0-318-60517-1); Incl. Pt. 1. (0-318-60518-X, WIPO24); Pt. 2. (0-318-60519-8, WIPO25); Pt. 3. (0-318-60520-1, WIPO26); Suppl. 1. 16.50 (0-685-99314-0, WIPO5); Suppl. 2. 7.50 (0-685-99315-9, WIPO7); Suppl. 3. 7.50 (0-685-99316-7, WIPO8); Suppl. 4. 7.50 (0-685-99317-5, WIPO9); Suppl. 4. 7.50 (0-685-99317-5, WIPO9); Suppl. 3. 7.50 (0-685-99316-7, WIPO8); write for info. (0-318-62064-2) UNIPUB.

Bernese Anabaptists: And Their American Descendants. 2nd ed. Delbert L. Gratz. (Illus.). 219p. 1994. 18.95 (1-883294-14-2) Olde Sprgfld.

***Bernese & Other Mountain Dogs: Bernese, Greater Swiss, Appenzellers, & Entlebuchers: Everything about Purchase, Care, Nutrition, Breeding, Behavior, & Training.** Gerd Ludwig & Christine Steimer. Tr. by Elizabeth D. Crawford. LC 94-49012. (Complete Pet Owner's Manual Ser.). (Illus.). 1995. write for info. (0-8120-9135-3) Barron.

Bernhard Eduard Fernow: A Story of North American Forestry. Andrew D. Rodgers, III. 640p. 1991. reprint ed. text ed. 21.95 (0-89030-047-X) Duke.

***Bernhard Guttman: An American Impressionist.** Percy North. LC 95-15263. 1995. write for info. (1-55859-611-9) Abbeville Pr.

Bernhard von Breydenbach & His Journey to the Holy Land 1483-4: A Bibliography. Hugh W. Davies. (Illus.). xxxii, 47p. 1968. reprint ed. text ed. 72.50 (0-317-55849-8, Pub. by B De Graaf NE) Coronet Bks.

Bernhardt & the Theatre of Her Time. Ed. by Eric Salmon. LC 83-1439. (Contributions in Drama & Theatre Studies: No. 6). (Illus.). x, 287p. 1984. text ed. 55.00 (0-313-23755-7, SAL/, Greenwood Pr) Greenwood.

Bernhardt Hamlet: A Synergetic View of Nineteenth-Century Theatre & Culture. Gerda Taranow. LC 93-32954. (Artists & Issues in the Theatre Ser.: Vol. 4). 1994. write for info. (0-8204-2335-1) P Lang Pubs.

Bernhardt, Terry, Duse: The Actress in Her Time. John Stokes et al. (Illus.). 200p. 1988. 49.95 (0-521-25615-1) Cambridge U Pr.

Bernhardt's Edge. Collin Wilcox. 1991. pap. 3.95 (0-8125-1148-4) Tor Bks.

Bernheim's New Studies in Hypnotism. Hippolyte Bernheim. Ed. by Richard S. Sandor. (Illus.). xix, 407p. (C). 1980. text ed. 50.00 (0-8236-0496-9) Intl Univs Pr.

Berni Wrightson: A Look Back. limited ed. Illus. by Berni Wrightson. 360p. 1991. reprint ed. 125.00 (0-88733-129-7); reprint ed. pap. 34.95 (0-88733-128-9) Underwood-Miller.

***Bernice Bobs Her Hair.** F. Scott Fitzgerald. 1982. 3.00 (0-87129-577-6, B50) Dramatic Pub.

Bernice Pauahi Bishop Museum of Polynesian Ethnology & Natural History, Honolulu Memoirs: 1899-1949, Set. 1972. write for info. (0-527-01624-1) Periodicals Srv.

Bernie & the Bessledorf Ghost. Phyllis R. Naylor. 144p. (J). 1992. pap. 3.50 (0-380-71351-9, Camelot) Avon.

Bernie & the Bessledorf Ghost. Phyllis R. Naylor. LC 88-29389. (Bessledorf Mysteries Ser.). 144p. (J). (gr. 3-7). 1990. text ed. 13.95 (0-689-31499-X, Atheneum Bks Young) S&S Childrens.

***Bernie Drives a Truck.** Radford. LC 91-58718. (J). 1995. pap. text ed. 4.99 (1-56402-488-1) Candlewick Pr.

Bernie, the Saint. Francis H. Wise & Joyce M. Wise. (Dr. Wise Learn to Read Ser.: No. 20). (Illus.). 21p. (Orig.). (J). (gr. 1). 1980. pap. 1.50 (0-915766-41-8) Wise Pub.

***Bernie Wrightson's Frankenstein: Or the Modern Prometheus.** 2nd ed. Mary W. Shelley. 200p. (YA). (gr. 7 up). 1995. 24.95 (0-88733-194-7) C F Miller.

***Bernie Wrightson's Frankenstein: Or the Modern Prometheus.** 2nd ed. Mary Wollstonecraft Shelley. 200p. (YA). (gr. 7 up). 1995. pap. 15.95 (0-88733-193-9) Underwood-Miller.

Bernie's Safe Ideas. Eric Berg. LC 93-8905. (J). 1993. write for info. (1-56071-324-0) ETR Assocs.

Bernini. Howard Hibbard. (Illus.). (Orig.). 1966. pap. 7.95 (0-14-020701-5, Penguin Bks) Viking Penguin.

Bernini. Charles Scribner, III. (Masters of Art Ser.). (Illus.). 128p. 1991. 22.95 (0-8109-3111-7) Abrams.

Bernini: Flights of Love, the Art of Devotion. Giovanni Careri. Tr. by Linda Lappin. (Illus.). 160p. 1995. pap. text ed. 16.95 (0-226-09273-9) U Ch Pr.

Bernini: Flights of Love, the Art of Devotion. Giovanni Careri. Tr. by Linda Lappin. (Illus.). 160p. 1995. lib. bdg. 39.95 (0-226-09272-0) U Ch Pr.

Bernini & the Idealization of Death: The Blessed Ludovica Albertoni & the Altieri Chapel. Shelley Perlove. LC 89-16336. (Illus.). 152p. 1990. lib. bdg. 32.50 (0-271-00684-6) Pa St U Pr.

Bernini Bust. Iain Pears. LC 94-14514. 1994. 20.00 (0-15-111830-2) HarBrace.

***Bernini Bust.** Iain Pears. 1995. write for info. (0-7862-0367-6) Thorndike Pr.

Bernini in France: An Episode in Seventeenth-Century History. Cecil Gould. LC 81-47998. (Illus.). 192p. 1982. 39.95 (0-691-03994-1) Princeton U Pr.

An Asterisk (*) at the beginning of an entry indicates that the title is appearing in BIP for the first time.

Bernique Longley: A Retrospective. Alma S. King. LC 82-6025. (Illus.). 80p. (Orig.). 1983. pap. 20.00 (0-941430-03-0) Santa Fe E Gallery.

Bernisches Mammasymposium: Festschrift fuer Max Berger Mammasymposium, Bern, September 1987. Ed. by E. Dreher. (Journal: Gynaekologische Rundschau: Vol. 28, Suppl. 1, 1988). (Illus.). vi, 94p. 1988. pap. 28.00 (3-8055-4832-X) S Karger.

Bernot on Breezes. Jean-Yves Bernot. (Illus.). 111p. 1994. pap. 16.95 (1-85310-372-1) Voyageur Pr.

Bernoulli Society, U. S. S. R. Proceedings of the First World Congress, 1986, 2 vols., Set. Ed. by Yu. V. Prohorov & V. V. Sazonov. 1690p. 1987. lib. bdg. 400.00 (90-6764-103-0, Pub. by VSP NE) Coronet Bks.

Bernoulli's Book. B. K. Hixson. 52p. 1991. pap. text ed. 13.99 (1-57156-002-5) Wild Goose UT.

Bernstein on Broadway. pap. 19.95 (0-911320-00-8, XH1201) Astor Bks.

Bernstein on Broadway. (Leonard Bernstein Ser.). 19.95 (0-685-61547-2, XH1201) Boosey & Hawkes.

Bernstein Polynomials. 2nd ed. George G. Lorentz. x, 132p. 1985. text ed. 14.95 (0-8284-0323-6) Chelsea Pub.

Bernstein Polynomials. G. G. Lorentz. LC 55-527. (Mathematical Expositions Ser.: No. 8). 140p. reprint ed. pap. 39.90 (0-8357-7144-X, 2051966) Bks Demand.

Bernstein Projections: A Metaphysical Comedy. Victor Chaney. LC 90-92086. 256p. (Orig.). 1991. pap. 5.95 (0-9628586-0-9) V Chaney.

Bernstein's Reverse Dictionary. 2nd ed. Theodore M. Bernstein. LC 85-40847. 320p. 1988. 19.95 (0-8129-1593-3, Times Bks) Random.

Berossos und die Babylonisch-Hellenistissche Literatur. Paul Schnabel. 275p. 1968. reprint ed. write for info. (0-318-70824-8, Pub. by Georg Olms GW) Lubrecht & Cramer.

*__Berreyesa: The Rape of the Mexican Land Grant, Rancho Canada de Capay.__ Eftimeos Salonites. LC 94-96533. 350p. 1994. 49.95 (0-9638225-0-0) Mission Bell.

Berried Treasures Cookbook. rev. ed. Elaine K. Jauman. (Illus.). 128p. 1985. pap. 4.95 (0-9609282-3-5) Kitchen Treas.

Berries. Robert Berkley. 1990. pap. 16.95 (0-671-69019-1, Fireside) S&S Trade.

Berries: A Country Garden Cookbook. Sharon Kramis. 1994. 14.95 (0-00-255344-9) Collins SF.

Berries for the Queen. Janet Noonan & Jacquelyn Calvert. LC 92-32336. (J). (ps-2). 1994. 8.99 (0-7814-0903-9, Chariot Bks) Chariot Family.

Berries Goodman. Emily C. Neville. LC 65-19485. (Trophy Bk.). (J). (gr. 5-9). 1975. pap. 3.95 (0-06-440072-7, Trophy) HarpC Child Bks.

Berries Goodman. Emily C. Neville. (J). (gr. 5-9). 1992. 18.50 (0-8446-6584-3) Peter Smith.

Berries on the Hill: Cookbook. Nettie B. Atwood. LC 87-91506. 448p. 1987. 12.50 (0-9618721-0-1) Nettie B Atwood.

Berringer House Cookie Collection. Berringer. 1991. pap. 12.95 (0-89716-372-9) P B Pubng.

Berry & Bailey: Personal Insolvency - Law & Practice. 2nd ed. Christopher Berry & Edward Bailey. 731p. 1992. 156.00 (0-406-15711-1, UK) Butterworth Legal Pubs.

Berry & Kohn's Introduction to Operating Room Technique. 5th ed. L. J. Atkinson & M. J. Kohn. 1978. text ed. 34.95 (0-07-002540-1) McGraw.

Berry & Kohn's Introduction to Operating Room Techniques. 6th ed. L. J. Atkinson & M. J. Kohn. 640p. 1986. text ed. 37.95 (0-07-002541-X) McGraw.

Berry & Kohn's Operating Room Technique. 7th ed. Lucy J. Atkinson. 734p. 1991. pap. 40.95 (0-8016-6048-3) Mosby Yr Bk.

Berry Benson's Civil War Book: Memoirs of a Confederate Scout & Sharpshooter. Ed. by Susan W. Benson. LC 92-27349. (Illus.). 215p. 1993. 19.95 (0-8203-1487-0) U of Ga Pr.

Berry Finder: A Guide to Native Plants with Fleshy Fruits for Eastern North America. Dorcas S. Miller. 62p. 1986. pap. 2.50 (0-912550-14-7) Nature Study.

Berry-Limousin Green Guide. 2nd ed. (FRE.). Date not set. pap. 18.00 (2-06-700305-4, 305) Michelin.

*__Berry-Limousin Green Guide French Edition.__ Michelin Staff. (FRE.). Date not set. pap. 17.95 (0-7859-7221-8, 2067003054) Fr & Eur.

Berry Patch. Ruth Balckett et al. Ed. by Kathey Shreves. (Illus.). 104p. (C). 1981. spiral bd. 5.95 (0-940158-02-7) Zucchini Patch.

Berry Woman's Children. Dale De Armond. LC 84-29760. (Illus.). 40p. (J). (gr. 1 up). 1985. 15.00 (0-688-05814-0); lib. bdg. 14.93 (0-688-05815-9) Greenwillow.

Berryhill Family History. Virginia T. Brittain. (Illus.). 338p. 1982. reprint ed. 25.00 (0-89308-293-7, FH 16) Southern Hist Pr.

Berryman & Lowell: The Art of Losing. Steven Matterson. LC 87-1824. 144p. 1987. 49.00 (0-389-20730-6, N8288) B&N Imports.

Berrymans' Building Claims Cases. Paul Taylor & Dianna Holtham. 1993. U.K. 158.00 (0-406-16507-6) Butterworth Legal Pubs.

Berryman's Understanding: Reflections on the Poetry of John Berryman. Ed. by Harry Thomas. 280p. 1988. 37.50 (1-55553-027-3) NE U Pr.

*__Berserk! Vol. 1.__ Graham Chester. 1995. mass mkt. 5.50 (0-312-95442-5) St Martin.

Berserker Kill. Fred Saberhagen. 448p. 1993. 24.95 (0-312-85266-5) Tor Bks.

Berserker Kill. Fred Saberhagen. 448p. 1995. mass mkt. 5.99 (0-8125-5059-5) Tor Bks.

Berserker Throne. Fred Saberhagen. 320p. 1991. reprint ed. pap. 3.95 (0-8125-1402-5) Tor Bks.

Berserker Wars. Fred Saberhagen. 400p. 1994. pap. 4.99 (0-8125-3643-6) Tor Bks.

*__Berserker's House.__ Lisa Maxwell. 256p. (Orig.). 1995. pap. text ed. 4.99 (0-441-00199-8) Ace Bks.

Berserker's Planet. Fred Saberhagen. 1991. mass mkt. 3.99 (0-8125-0981-1) Tor Bks.

Bert. Mary A. Skulavik. (Illus.). 32p. (J). (ps-3). 1990. 13.95 (0-8027-6962-4); lib. bdg. 14.85 (0-8027-6963-2) Walker & Co.

Bert & Ernie on the Go. Illus. by Tom Cooke. LC 80-54574. (Sesame Street Pop up Ser.: No. 15). 16p. (J). (ps-2). 1981. 8.99 (0-394-84869-1) Random Bks Yng Read.

Bert & the Magic Lamp & Other Good-Night Stories. Michaela Muntean. (Big Golden Book Ser.). (Illus.). 24p. (J). (ps-1). 1989. write for info. (0-307-12073-2, Golden Bks) Western Pub.

Bert & the Missing Mop Mix-Up. Sarah Roberts. LC 82-22971. (Sesame Street Start-to-Read Bks.). (Illus.). 40p. (J). (gr. k-2). 1983. 4.95 (0-394-85752-6) Random Bks Yng Read.

Bert Brecht. Willy Haas. LC 68-31450. (Literature & Life Ser.). 192p. (C). 1970. 19.95 (0-8044-2323-7, F Ungar Bks) Continuum.

Bert Breen's Barn. Walter D. Edmonds. (New York Classics Ser.). 280p. (YA). 1991. reprint ed. pap. 9.95 (0-8156-0255-3) Syracuse U Pr.

Bert Clarke, Typographer: A Catalogue of an Exhibition of Selected Works. Notes by Bert Clarke. (Illus.). 85p. (Orig.). 1987. pap. 16.95 (0-87104-297-5) NY Pub Lib.

Bert Combs the Politician: An Oral History. Ed. by George W. Robinson. LC 90-19970. (Kentucky Remembered: An Oral History Ser.). 240p. 1991. text ed. 30.00 (0-8131-1740-2) U Pr of Ky.

Bert Geer Phillips & the Taos Art Colony. Julie Schimmel & Robert R. White. LC 93-5082. (Illus.). 377p. 1994. 55.00 (0-8263-1444-9) U of NM Pr.

Bert Greene's Kitchen: A Book of Memories & Recipes. Bert Greene. LC 92-50931. 1993. 19.95 (0-89480-765-X, 1765) Workman Pub.

Bert Williams: A Biography of the Pioneer Black Comedian. Eric L. Smith. LC 91-50947. 316p. 1992. lib. bdg. 41.50x (0-89950-695-X) McFarland & Co.

Bert Williams, Son of Laughter. Ed. by Mabel Rowland. LC 72-84693. 218p. 1969. reprint ed. text ed. 52.50 (0-8371-1667-8, ROW&, Negro U Pr) Greenwood.

Bert y la Lampara Magica. (SPA.). (J). (ps-3). 1993. pap. 4.95 (0-307-52073-0, Golden Pr) Western Pub.

Berta Benz & the Motorwagen. Mindy Bingham. (Illus.). 48p. (J). (gr. 1-6). 1992. 14.95 (0-911655-38-7) Advocacy Pr.

Berta Broadfoot & Pepin the Short: A Merovingian Romance. Barbara Goldberg. LC 86-50181. (Illus.). 72p. (Orig.). 1986. pap. 15.00 (0-915380-20-X) Word Works.

*__Bertelsmann Lexikon Astronomie.__ Bertelsmann. 348p. (GER.). 1993. 95.00 (0-7859-8429-1, 3570016129) Fr & Eur.

*__Bertelsmann Lexikon der Abkurzungen.__ Heinz Koblischke. 700p. (GER.). 1994. 75.00 (0-7859-8427-5, 3570016048) Fr & Eur.

*__Bertelsmann Lexikon Deutsche Autoren, 5 vols.__ Walther Killy. 2080p. (GER.). 1994. 95.00 (0-7859-8687-1, 357010530x) Fr & Eur.

*__Bertelsmann Lexikon Geschichte.__ Bertelsmann. 830p. (GER.). 1991. 95.00 (0-7859-8433-X, 3570071901) Fr & Eur.

*__Bertelsmann Lexikon Informatik, EDV, Computertechnik.__ Bertelsmann. 480p. (GER.). 1993. write for info. (0-7859-8428-3, 3570016110) Fr & Eur.

*__Bertelsmann Lexikon Wirtschaft.__ Bertelsmann. 815p. (GER.). 1992. 95.00 (0-7859-8686-3, 357007191x) Fr & Eur.

Bertha Knight Landes of Seattle: Big-city Mayor. Sandra Haarsager. LC 93-29485. (Illus.). 352p. 1994. 28.95 (0-8061-2592-6) U of Okla Pr.

Bertha Lum. Mary E. Okeefe-Gravalos & Carol Pulin. (American Printmakers Ser.). 1991. pap. 19.95 (1-56098-008-7) Smithsonian.

Bertha, the Bartender's Beautiful Baby. Charles George. 1960. pap. 4.75 (0-8222-0106-2) Dramatists Play.

*__Bertha Von Suttner's Die Waffen Nieder! Moral Literature in the Tradition of Harriet Beecher Stowe's Uncle Tom's Cabin.__ Regina Braker. LC 94-3633. (Austrian Culture: 16). 1995. write for info. (0-8204-2626-1) P Lang Pubs.

Bertha's Christmas Vision: An Autumn Sheaf. Horatio Alger, Jr. (Illus.). 248p. 1978. reprint ed. 24.00 (0-686-35748-5) G K Westgard.

Bertha's Garden. Elisabeth Dyjak. LC 93-28594. (Illus.). (J). 1995. 12.95 (0-395-68715-2) HM.

Berthe Morisot. Kathleen Adler & Tamar Garb. LC 86-47971. (Illus.). 128p. 1987. 38.95 (0-8014-2038-5) Cornell U Pr.

*__Berthe Morisot.__ Kathleen Adler & Tamar Garb. (Illus.). 128p. 1995. pap. 24.95 (0-7148-3479-3, Pub. by Phaidon Press UK) Chronicle Bks.

Berthe Morisot. Anne Higonnet. LC 92-36278. (Rizzoli Art Ser.). (Illus.). 24p. 1993. pap. 7.95 (0-8478-1646-X) Rizzoli Intl.

*__Berthe Morisot.__ Anne Higonnet. LC 94-31157. 1995. pap. 13.00 (0-520-20156-6) U CA Pr.

Berthe Morisot: Correspondence. Ed. by Denis Rouart. Tr. by Betty W. Hubbard. 272p. pap. 9.95 (0-918825-62-8) Moyer Bell.

Berthe Morisot's Images of Women. Anne Higonnet. (Illus.). 311p. 1992. 49.95 (0-674-06798-3) HUP.

Berthe Morisot's Images of Women. Anne Higonnet. 311p. 1994. pap. 19.95 (0-674-06799-1) HUP.

Berthold Lowenfeld on Blindness & Blind People. Berthold Lowenfeld. LC 81-3520. 254p. 1981. pap. 21.95 (0-89128-101-0) Am Foun Blind.

Bertie & Alix. large type ed. Graham Fisher & Heather Fisher. (Shadows of the Crown Ser.). 1975. 15.95 (0-85456-603-1) Ulverscroft.

Bertie & the Crime of Passion. Peter Lovesey. 256p. 1995. 19.95 (0-89296-550-9) Mysterious Pr.

*__Bertie & the Crime of Passion.__ Peter Lovesey. 240p. 1995. mass mkt. 5.50 (0-446-40368-7, Mysterious Paperbk) Warner Bks.

*__Bertie & the Crime of Passion.__ large type ed. Peter Lovesey. LC 95-5405. (Large Print Book Ser.). 1995. pap. 20.95 (1-56895-099-3) Wheeler Pub.

Bertie & the Seven Bodies. Peter Lovesey. 208p. 1990. 16.95 (0-89296-399-9) Mysterious Pr.

Bertie & the Seven Bodies. large type ed. Peter Lovesey. LC 90-40509. 398p. 1990. reprint ed. lib. bdg. 19.95 (1-56054-038-9) Thorndike Pr.

Bertie & the Tinman. Peter Lovesey. 1988. 15.95 (0-89296-196-1) Mysterious Pr.

Bertie County: A Brief History. Alan D. Watson. (Illus.). vii, 91p. (Orig.). 1982. pap. 5.00 (0-86526-194-6) NC Archives.

*__Bertie County, North Carolina Marriage Bonds & Certificates, 1759-1866.__ Francis T. Ingmire. 74p. 1994. lib. bdg. 27.00 (0-8095-8010-1); pap. 9.50 (0-8095-8514-6) Borgo Pr.

Bertie of Thame: Edwardian Ambassador. Keith A. Hamilton. (Royal Historical Society: Studies in History: No. 60). 446p. (C). 1990. 71.00 (0-86193-217-X) Boydell & Brewer.

*__Bertie the Bus & Thomas the Tank Engine.__ Awdry. LC 94-66490. 1995. 4.50 (0-679-86996-4) Random.

Bertie the Bus Wheel Book. W. Awdry. (Little Wheel Bks.). (Illus.). 14p. (J). (ps-00). 1993. 4.99 (0-679-84469-4) Random Bks Yng Read.

Bertie Wooster Sees It Through. P. G. Wodehouse. 16.95 (0-8488-0671-9) Amereon Ltd.

*__Bertil Ohlin: Critical Assessments, 4 vols., Set.__ Ed. by John C. Wood. (Critical Assessments of Leading Economists Ser.). 1995. 695.00 (0-415-07492-4, C0370) Routledge.

Bertil Ohlin, 1899-1979. Ed. by Mark Blaug. (Pioneers in Economics Ser.: Vol. 43). 208p. 1992. 77.95 (1-85278-507-1, Pub. by E Elgar Pub UK) Ashgate Pub Co.

Bertoldo di Giovanni, Sculptor of the Medici Household: Critical Reappraisal & Catalogue Raisonne. James D. Draper. (Illus.). 320p. (C). 1992. 75.00 (0-8262-0819-3) U of Mo Pr.

Bertolet: Genealogical History of the Bertolet Family; the Descendents of Jean Bertolet. D. H. Bertolet. (Illus.). 260p. 1991. reprint ed. lib. bdg. 51.00 (0-8328-1871-2); reprint ed. pap. 41.00 (0-8328-1872-0) Higginson Bk Co.

Bertolt Brecht. Martin Esslin. LC 74-76246. (Columbia Essays on Modern Writers Ser.: No. 42). 48p. 1969. pap. text ed. 7.50 (0-231-02962-4, MW42) Col U Pr.

Bertolt Brecht. Ronald Speirs. Ed. by Bruce King & Adele King. (Modern Dramatists Ser.). 203p. 1992. pap. 11.95 (0-333-29207-3) St Martin.

Bertolt Brecht: Chaos, According to Plan. John Fuegi. (Directors in Perspective Ser.). (Illus.). 220p. 1987. pap. 21.95 (0-521-28245-4) Cambridge U Pr.

Bertolt Brecht: Dialectics, Poetry, Politics. Peter Brooker. 240p. 1988. lib. bdg. 57.50 (0-7099-5015-2, Pub. by Croom Helm UK) Routledge Chapman & Hall.

Bertolt Brecht: His Life, His Art, & His Times. Frederic Ewen. 1969. reprint ed. pap. 15.95 (0-8065-0194-4, Citadel Pr) Carol Pub Group.

*__Bertolt Brecht: Journals 1934-1955.__ Bertolt Brecht. 576p. 1995. pap. 22.95 (0-415-91282-2, C0606) Routledge.

Bertolt Brecht & Rudyard Kipling: A Marxist's Imperialist. James K. Lyon. LC 73-94231. (Studies in General & Comparative Literature: No. 3). 138p. 1975. pap. text ed. 50.70 (90-279-3411-8) Mouton.

Bertolt Brecht & the Theory of Media. Roswitha Mueller. LC 88-33805. (Modern German Culture & Literature Ser.). (Illus.). xiv, 149p. 1989. 30.00 (0-8032-3132-6) U of Nebr Pr.

Bertolt Brecht, "Cahiers du Cinema", & Contemporary Film Theory. George P. Lellis. Ed. by Diane Kirkpatrick. LC 82-2051. (Studies in Cinema: No. 13). 208p. reprint ed. 59.00 (0-8357-1300-8, 2070332) Bks Demand.

Bertolt Brecht in America. James K. Lyon. LC 80-7543. (Illus.). 440p. (Orig.). 1980. reprint ed. pap. 16.95x (0-691-01394-2) Princeton U Pr.

Bertolt Brecht, Journals 1934 to 1955. Bertolt Brecht. 1993. 39.95 (0-415-90837-X, Pub. by Tavistock UK) Routledge Chapman & Hall.

Bertolt Brecht Short Stories, 1921-1946. Ed. by John Willett & Ralph Manheim. Tr. by Yvonne Knapp. 1983. 14.95 (0-413-37050-X, NO. 3765) Routledge.

Bertolt Brecht's Art of Dissemblance. Tony Calabro. LC 90-5995. 125p. 1990. 25.00 (0-89341-606-1, Longwood Academic) Hollowbrook.

Bertolt Brecht's Berlin: A Scrapbook of the Twenties. Wolf Von Eckardt & Sander L. Gilman. LC 93-8468. (Illus.). xxxiv, 172p. 1993. pap. 25.00 (0-8032-9612-6, Bison Books) U of Nebr Pr.

Bertolucci's Dream Loom: A Psychoanalytic Study of Cinema. T. Jefferson Kline. LC 86-25038. (Illus.). 216p. 1987. lib. bdg. 27.50x (0-87023-569-9) U of Mass Pr.

Bertolucci's 1900: A Narrative & Historical Analysis. Robert Burgoyne. LC 90-12355. (Contemporary Film & Television Ser.). (Illus.). 184p. (C). 1991. text ed. 19.95 (0-8143-2083-X) Wayne St U Pr.

Bertone. Luciano Greggio. (Illus.). 416p. 100.00 (88-7911-066-7, Pub. by Giorgio Nada Editore IT) Howell Pr VA.

Bertram. Charles R. Maturin. LC 92-36902. 110p. 1992. reprint ed. 40.00 (1-85477-120-5, Pub. by Woodstock Bks UK) Cassell.

Bertram Cope's Year. Henry B. Fuller. LC 78-63987. (Gay Experience Ser.). reprint ed. 26.00 (0-404-61506-6) AMS Pr.

Bertram Grosvenor Goodhue, Architect & Master of Many Arts. Ed. by Charles H. Whitaker. LC 76-22484. (Architecture & Decorative Art Ser.). (Illus.). 1976. 95.00 (0-306-70826-4) Da Capo.

Bertrams. Anthony Trollope. Ed. by Geoffrey Harvey. (World's Classics Ser.). 632p. 1991. pap. 10.95 (0-19-282645-X) OUP.

Bertrams, 3 vols. Anthony Trollope. Ed. by N. John Hall. LC 80-1877. (Selected Works of Anthony Trollope Ser.). 1981. reprint ed. lib. bdg. 115.95 (0-405-14130-0) Ayer.

Bertrams. Anthony Trollope. 487p. 1986. reprint ed. pap. 9.95 (0-486-25119-5) Dover.

*__Bertram's Journal Vol. I.__ Kalb. 1991. 5.00 (0-614-04725-0) Royal Fireworks.

Bertrams (1859) Anthony Trollope. 496p. 1993. 8.95 (0-14-043807-6, Penguin Classics) Viking Penguin.

Bertrand & the Mehkqoverse. 64p. (Orig.). (C). 1989. lib. bdg. 15.00 (0-941720-64-0); pap. text ed. 8.00 (0-941720-65-9) Slough Pr TX.

Bertrand Barere: A Reluctant Terrorist. Leo Gershoy. LC 61-11848. 481p. reprint ed. pap. 137.10 (0-8357-9494-6, 2011476) Bks Demand.

Bertrand Meets the Fox & the Owl: Essays in the Theory of Price Competition. M. Canoy. (Tinbergen Institute Ser.). 189p. 1993. pap. 25.00 (90-5170-198-5, Pub. by Thesis Pubs NE) IBD Ltd.

Bertrand Russell. Alfred J. Ayer. 168p. 1988. pap. 12.95 (0-226-03343-0) U Ch Pr.

Bertrand Russell. Paul G. Kuntz. (English Authors Ser.: No. 421). 1986. text ed. 19.95 (0-8057-6916-1, Twayne) Macmillan.

Bertrand Russell. Bertrand Russell. Ed. by Ann Redpath. (Living Philosophies Ser.). (Illus.). 32p. (YA). (gr. 9 up). 1986. lib. bdg. 12.95 (0-88682-012-X) Creative Ed.

Bertrand Russell: A Political Life. Alan Ryan. 240p. 1993. pap. 12.95 (0-19-508634-1) OUP.

Bertrand Russell & the Origins of the Set-Theoretic 'Paradoxes' Alejandro R. Garciadiego. LC 92-35528. xxix, 264p. 1992. 77.50 (0-8176-2669-7) Birkhauser.

Bertrand Russell & Trinity: A College Controversy of the Last War. Godfrey H. Hardy. Ed. by Walter P. Metzger. LC 76-56697. (Academic Profession Ser.). 1977. reprint ed. lib. bdg. 17.95 (0-405-10022-1) Ayer.

Bertrand Russell Case. John Dewey & Horace M. Kallen. LC 78-37289. (Civil Liberties in American History Ser.). 228p. 1972. reprint ed. lib. bdg. 29.00 (0-306-70426-9) Da Capo.

Bertrand Russell Dictionary of Mind, Morals, & Matter. Ed. by Lester E. Denonn. LC 92-39508. 1993. reprint ed. 9.95 (0-8065-1400-0, Citadel Pr) Carol Pub Group.

Bertrand Russell on Ethics, Sex, & Marriage. Ed. by Al Seckel. LC 87-60825. (Great Books in Philosophy). 348p. (Orig.). 1987. pap. 18.95 (0-87975-400-1) Prometheus Bks.

Bertrand Russell on God & Religion. Ed. by Al Seckel. (Great Books in Philosophy). 350p. 1991. pap. 18.95 (0-87975-323-4) Prometheus Bks.

Bertrand Russell Speaks His Mind. Bertrand Russell. LC 74-3626. (Illus.). 173p. 1974. reprint ed. text ed. 35.00 (0-8371-7445-7, RUBR, Greenwood Pr) Greenwood.

Bertrand Russell's Best. Bertrand Russell. Ed. by Robert E. Egner. (Orig.). 1958. pap. 3.95 (0-451-62508-0, ME2223, Ment) NAL-Dutton.

Bertrand Russell's Dialogue with His Contemporaries. Elizabeth R. Eames. LC 88-31125. 320p. (C). 1989. 34.95 (0-8093-1516-5) S Ill U Pr.

Bertrand Russell's Philosophy of Logical Atomism. Wayne A. Patterson. LC 91-17584. (American University Studies: Philosophy: Ser. V, Vol. 89). 364p. 1993. 29.95 (0-8204-1235-X) P Lang Pubs.

Bert's Little Bedtime Story: A Sesame Street Book. K. K. Ross. LC 89-64283. (Chunky Tales Ser.). (Illus.). 28p. (J). (ps). 1991. bds. 3.25 (0-679-80757-8) Random Bks Yng Read.

Bert's Little Garden: A Sesame Street Book. Illus. by Tom Cooke. LC 90-61311. (Chunky Shape Bks.). 22p. (J). (ps). 1991. bds. 2.95 (0-679-81061-7) Random Bks Yng Read.

Beruehrungsfreie Nierensteinzertruemmerung durch extrakorporal erzeugte, fokussierte Stosswellen. Charles Chaussy et al. (Beitraege zur Urologie Ser.: Vol. 2). vi, 94p. 1980. pap. 40.00 (3-8055-1901-X) S Karger.

*__Berufleben, Bk. 1.__ Peter Kowallik et al. (German Language Ser.). (Illus.). 56p. (Orig.). (GER.). (YA). (gr. 7 up). 1993. pap. 22.00 (0-939990-87-3) Intl Linguistics.

Beruhmte Platon-Edition, 3 vols. Henricus Stephanus. 2141p. (GER.). reprint ed. write for info. (0-318-70536-2, Pub. by Georg Olms GW) Lubrecht & Cramer.

Berulle & the French School: Selected Writings. Ed. by William M. Thompson. Tr. by Lowell M. Glendon. (Classics of Western Spirituality Ser.). 1989. 19.95 (0-8091-0426-1); pap. 14.95 (0-8091-3080-7) Paulist Pr.

*__Bery Fine Rooster.__ Michael Walker. (Amazing English Ser.: Little Bks., Level A). (J). 1995. pap. write for info. (0-201-85341-8) Addison-Wesley.

Beryl. John Sinkankas & Peter G. Read. (Gemmology Bks.). (Illus.). 248p. 1986. text ed. 39.95 (0-408-01543-8) Buttrwrth-Heinemann.

Beryllium. (Metals & Minerals Ser.). 1993. lib. bdg. 250.95 (0-8490-8982-4) Gordon Pr.

Beryllium. A. V. Novoselova & L. R. Batsanova. (Analytical Chemistry of the Elements Ser.). 233p. 1970. text ed. 60.00 (0-7065-0742-8, Pub. by Keter Pub IS) Coronet Bks.

Beryllium. George E. Darwin & J. H. Buddery. (Metallurgy of the Rarer Metals Ser.: No. 7). 402p. reprint ed. pap. 114.60 (0-8357-7145-8, 2025761) Bks Demand.

B

An Asterisk (*) at the beginning of an entry indicates that the title is appearing in BIP for the first time. 689

***Beryllium, Cadmium, Mercury, & Exposures in the Glass Manufacturing Industry.** Ed. by World Health Organization Staff. (IARC Monographs on the Evaluation of Carcinogenic Risk of Chemicals to Man). 444p. 1993. 67.50 (92-832-1258-4) World Health.

Beryllium Oxide. Ed. by R. Smith & J. Howe. 1964. write for info. (0-317-17784-2) Elsevier.

Beryllium Science & Technology, 2 vols., Vol. 1. Ed. by D. Webster et al. LC 78-20778. (Illus.). 348p. 1979. 75.00 (0-306-40106-1, Plenum Pr) Plenum.

Beryllium Science & Technology, 2 vols., Vol. 2. Ed. by D. Webster et al. LC 78-20778. (Illus.). 458p. 1979. 85.00 (0-306-40136-3, Plenum Pr) Plenum.

Beryllium Technology: Proceedings, Philadelphia, Pennsylvania, October 15-17, 1964, 2 Vols. Ed. by L. M. Schetky & Henry A. Johnson. LC 65-27854. (Metallurgical Society Conference Ser.: Vol. 33). 1286p. reprint ed. pap. 180.00 (0-8357-7146-6, 2001521) Bks Demand.

Beryl's Box. Lisa Taylor. LC 92-44990. (Illus.). 32p. (J). (ps-2). 1993. 12.95 (0-8120-6355-4); pap. 5.95 (0-8120-1673-4) Barron.

Beryn: The Tale of Beryn. Ed. by F. J. Furnivall & W. B. Stone. (EETS, ES Ser.: No. 105). 1972. reprint ed. 35.00 (0-527-00307-7) Periodicals Srv.

Besa: The Life of Shenoute. Tr. & Intro. by David N. Bell. (Cistercian Studies: No. 73). 1983. pap. 11.95 (0-87907-873-1) Cistercian Pubns.

Besame Mucho. Pedro Usabiaga. (Illus.). (Orig.). 1992. pap. 34.95 (3-924163-69-3, Pub. by Bruno Gmunder GW) InBook.

Besant's History of London: Edwardian London, Vol. 3. Village Press Editorial Board Staff. (C). 1989. 95.00 (1-85540-013-8, Pub. by Village Pr UK) St Mut.

Besant's History of London: Edwardian London, Vol. 4. Village Press Editorial Board Staff. (C). 1989. 95.00 (1-85540-014-6, Pub. by Village Pr UK) St Mut.

Besant's History of London: Roman Saxons & Normans. Village Press Editorial Board Staff. (C). 1989. 95.00 (1-85540-003-0, Pub. by Village Pr UK) St Mut.

Besant's History of London: The Eighteenth Century, Vol. I. Village Press Editorial Board Staff. (C). 1990. 95.00 (1-85540-006-5, Pub. by Village Pr UK) St Mut.

Besant's History of London: The Eighteenth Century, Vol. II. Village Press Editorial Board Staff. (C). 1990. 95.00 (1-85540-007-3, Pub. by Village Pr UK) St Mut.

Besant's History of London: The Stuarts. Village Press Editorial Board Staff. (C). 1989. 95.00 (1-85540-002-2, Pub. by Village Pr UK) St Mut.

Besant's History of London: The Tudors. Village Press Editorial Board Staff. (C). 1989. 95.00 (1-85540-001-4, Pub. by Village Pr UK) St Mut.

Beschaffenheit Des Grundwassers, 1990. 2nd ed. Georg Matthes. (Lehrbuch der Hydrobiologie Ser.: Vol. 2). (Illus.). 498p. (GER.). 1990. text ed. 97.50 (3-443-01007-5, Pub. by Gebrueder Borntraeger GW) Lubrecht & Cramer.

Bescherelle 1: La Conjugaison 12,000 Verbes. Ed. by Bescherelle. 175p. (FRE.). 1990. 12.95 (2-218-01660-5) Hatier Pub.

Bescherelle 2: L'Orthographe pour Tous. Ed. by Bescherelle. (Hatier Ser.). 253p. (FRE.). 1990. 15.95 (2-218-02470-5) Hatier Pub.

Bescherelle 3: La Grammaire pour Tous. Ed. by Bescherelle. (Hatier Ser.). 351p. (FRE.). 1990. 16.95 (2-218-02471-3) Hatier Pub.

***Beschreiben und Deuten Im der Archaologie Des Alten Orients: Festschrift Fur Ruth Mayer-Opificius Mit Beitragen von Freunden und Schulern.** Ed. by Manfried Dietrich & Oswald Loretz. (Altertumskunde Des Vorderen Orients Ser.: Vol. 4). xvii, 354p. (ACE & GER.). 1994. text ed. 72.00x (3-927120-18-9, Pub. by UGARIT GW) Eisenbrauns.

Beschreibendes und Kritisches Verzeichnis der Werke der Hervorragendsten Hollandischen Maler des XVIIJh, 3 vols., Set. C. Hofstede De Groot. (Catalogue Raisonne of the Works of the Most Eminent Dutch Painters of the Seventeenth Century). 180p. 1976. lib. bdg. 590.00 (0-85964-027-2) Chadwyck-Healey.

Beschreibendes und Kritisches Verzeichnis der Werke der Hervorragendsten Hollandischen Maler des XVIIJh, Vols. 9 & 10. C. Hofstede De Groot. (Catalogue Raisonne of the Works of the Most Eminent Dutch Painters of the Seventeenth Century). 180p. 1976. lib. bdg. 190.00 (0-85964-025-6) Chadwyck-Healey.

Beschworungen Aus Fara und Ebla. Manfred Krebernik. (Texte und Studien Zur Orientalistik Ser.: Vol. 2). xvi, 385p. 1984. write for info. (3-487-07479-6, Pub. by Georg Olms GW) Lubrecht & Cramer.

Besedi S Williamom Shekspirom: Dialogs with William Shakespeare. Roman Gershgorin. 254p. (Orig.). (RUS.). 1992. pap. 3.00 (1-881910-01-6) Adventure NY.

Beseiged Culture: Czechoslovakia Ten Years after Helsinki. Helsinki Watch Staff & Foundation 77 Foundation Staff. 300p. 1985. 10.00 (0-938579-97-5, Fund Free Exp) Hum Rts Watch.

Besely Clon (Merry Elephant) Alexsandr Ostrovsky. (Illus.). 32p. (Orig.). (RUS.). (J). 1991. pap. 14.95 (0-934393-22-2) Rector Pr.

Be'Sha'ah Tovah: The Complete Clinical & Halachic Guide to Pregnancy & Childbirth. Baruch Finkelstein & Michal Finkelstein. LC 93-9493. 1993. 26.95 (0-87306-629-4) Feldheim.

Beside Every Great Dad. Ken R. Canfield & Nancy L. Swihart. LC 92-43412. 1993. 8.99 (0-8423-1103-3) Tyndale.

Beside Herself. Sarah Daniels. (Women's Playhouse Plays Ser.). 73p. (Orig.). 1990. pap. 9.95 (0-413-62400-5, A0460, Pub. by Methuen UK) Heinemann.

Beside Herself: Pocahontas to Patty Hearst. Pamela W. Hadas. LC 82-49003. 240p. 1983. 14.95 (0-394-52993-6) Knopf.

Beside Old Hearth-Stones. Abram E. Brown. (Illus.). 412p. 1990. reprint ed. pap. 27.50 (1-55613-332-4) Heritage Bk.

Beside Ourselves: Our Hidden Personality in Everyday Life. Naomi L. Quenk. LC 93-4373. 292p. 1993. pap. 14.95 (0-89106-062-6) Consulting Psychol.

Beside Still Waters. Maria L. Fargion. Tr. by Iole F. Magri. LC 91-47653. (Illus.). 367p. 1992. text ed. 25.00 (0-913993-15-8) Paideia MA.

Beside Still Waters. Millie Stamm. 1990. pap. 9.99 (0-310-33062-9) Zondervan.

Beside the Bonnie Brier Bush. Ian MacLaren. 1976. 21.95 (0-8488-0290-X) Amereon Ltd.

Beside the Bonnie Brier Bush. Ian MacLaren. 224p. 1992. reprint ed. lib. bdg. 16.95 (0-89966-891-7) Buccaneer Bks.

Beside the Fire: A Collection of Irish Gaelic Folk Stories. Douglas Hyde. LC 78-67719. (Folktale Ser.). reprint ed. 28.00 (0-404-16096-4) AMS Pr.

Beside the Ocean of Time. George M. Brown. 224p. 1994. 24.95 (0-7195-5368-7, Pub. by John Murray UK) Trafalgar.

Beside the Seaside & Other Tales. Roy Kerridge. (C). 1986. 80.00 (0-9502723-2-9, Pub. by Brynmill Pr Ltd UK) St Mut.

***Beside the Still Water.** Carrie F. Goss. Ed. by Old Time Publications Staff. LC 89-91560. Date not set. 11.00 (0-9622285-1-6) C F Goss.

Beside the Still Waters. Willa Fogle. 1979. pap. 5.95 (0-87516-282-7) DeVorss.

Beside the Waters of the Buffalo: A History of Milligan College to 1941. Cynthia A. Cornwell. LC 88-63934. (Illus.). 225p. 1989. 20.00 (0-9621740-0-9) Milligan Coll Hist Proj.

Besides, the Wench Is Dead. Robert Ullin. 1993. reprint ed. lib. bdg. 89.00 (0-7812-3848-X) Rprt Serv.

***Besieged.** Laurel Ames. 1995. mass mkt. 4.50 (0-373-28889-1, 1-28889-3) Harlequin Bks.

Besieged. Charlotte Lamb. (Presents Ser.). 1992. pap. 2.89 (0-373-11498-2, 1-11498-2) Harlequin Bks.

Besieged: A Doctor's Story of Life & Death in Beirut. Chris Giannou. LC 91-6690. (Illus.). 288p. 1991. 29.95 (0-940793-80-6, Olive Branch Pr); pap. 12.95 (0-940793-75-X, Olive Branch Pr) Interlink Pub.

Besieged: The World War II Ordeal of Malta, 1940-1942. Charles A. Jellison. LC 84-40305. (Illus.). 302p. reprint ed. pap. 86.10 (0-8357-6517-2, 2035888) Bks Demand.

Besieged Bedfellows: Israel & the Land of Apartheid. Benjamin M. Joseph. LC 86-17723. (Contributions in Political Science Ser.: No. 199). 184p. 1988. text ed. 37. 95 (0-313-25461-3, JBB/, Greenwood Pr) Greenwood.

***Besieging the Castle of Ladies.** Thomas M. Greene. LC 94-40662. (Occasional Papers, Center for Medieval & Early Renaissance Studies: Vol. 4). 44p. 1995. pap. 6.00 (0-86698-145-4, CM4) MRTS.

Besler Florilegium: Plants of the Four Seasons. Comment & Intro. by Gerard G. Aymonin. (Illus.). 544p. 1989. 195.00 (0-8109-1174-4) Abrams.

Besnard (Albert) Catalogue Raisonne of the Graphic Work. Louis Godefroy. (Illus.). 280p. (FRE.). 1969. reprint ed. 125.00 (1-55660-036-4) A Wofsy Fine Arts.

Beso de la Mujer Arana. Manuel Puig. (SPA.). 1994. pap. 11.00 (0-679-75545-4, Vin) Random.

Beso de la Mujer Arana. 12th ed. Manuel Puig. 287p. (SPA.). 1992. pap. 14.95 (0-7859-0562-6, 843223026X) Fr & Eur.

Beso De la Mujer Arana see Kiss of the Spider Woman

Besoin de Voir Clair. Jules Romains. 256p. (FRE.). 1958. pap. 10.95 (0-7859-1394-7, 2080505890) Fr & Eur.

Bespangled, Painted & Embroidered: Decorated Masonic Aprons in America, 1790-1850. Barbara Franco. (Illus.). 124p. (Orig.). (C). 1980. pap. text ed. 7.00 (0-9621107-6-0) Scottish Rite Masonic Mus.

Bespoken Mile. large type ed. March Cost. 782p. 1974. 15. 95 (0-85456-272-9) Ulverscroft.

Bess Collection. Junior Service League of Independence, Missouri Staff. (Illus.). 372p. 1993. 17.95 (0-9615328-0-7) JSL Indep MO.

Bess Streeter Aldrich. Abigail A. Martin. LC 92-52529. (Western Writers Ser.: No. 104). (Illus.). 46p. (Orig.). 1992. pap. 3.95 (0-88430-103-6) Boise St U W Writ Ser.

***Bess Streeter Aldrich.** Carol M. Petersen. (Illus.). 232p. 1995. text ed. 35.00 (0-8032-3700-6) U of Nebr Pr.

Bess Streeter Aldrich Treasury. Bess S. Aldrich. 320p. reprint ed. lib. bdg. 31.95 (0-88411-263-2, Aeonian Pr) Amereon Ltd.

***Bess W. Truman.** Margaret Truman. (Illus.). 445p. 1994. reprint ed. pap. 6.95 (0-915992-69-8) Eastern Acorn.

Bessarabia & Bukovina: The Soviet-Romanian Territorial Dispute. Nicholas Dima. (East European Monographs: No. 110). 173p. 1983. text ed. 30.00 (0-88033-003-1) East Eur Quarterly.

Bessarabian Knight. Immanuel Weiss & George F. Wieland. 149p. 1991. pap. 15.50 (0-914222-23-6) Am Hist Soc Ger.

Bessemer: A Sociological Perspective of a Chicano Barrio. Irene I. Blea. LC 87-45778. (Immigrant Communities & Ethnic Minorities in the U. S. & Canada Ser.: No. 13). (Illus.). 1991. 49.50 (0-404-19423-0) AMS Pr.

***Bessemer & Lake Erie RR in Color.** Robert Lorenzo & Nate Clark, Jr. (Illus.). 128p. 1994. 49.95 (1-878887-34-3) Morning NJ.

Besseres Deutsch 1. und 2. Klasse: Teil A: Wortschatz und Ausdrucksschulung. (Mentor Lernspass Ser.). 80p. 1989. 13.95 (3-580-63111-X) Langenscheidt.

Besseres Deutsch 1. und 2. Klasse: Teil B: Rechtschreibung und Grammatik. (Mentor Lernspass Ser.). 80p. 1989. 13.95 (3-580-63112-8) Langenscheidt.

Besseres Deutsch 1. und 2. Klasse: Teil C: Leseubungen und Sprachspiele. (Mentor Lernspass Ser.). 80p. 1989. 13.95 (3-580-63113-6) Langenscheidt.

Besseres Deutsch 3. und 4. Klasse: Teil A: Wortschatz und Ausdrucksschulung. (Mentor Lernspass Ser.). 80p. 1989. 13.95 (3-580-63116-0) Langenscheidt.

Besseres Deutsch 3. und 4. Klasse: Teil B: Rechtschreibung und Grammatik. (Mentor Lernspass Ser.). 80p. 1989. 13.95 (3-580-63117-9) Langenscheidt.

Besseres Deutsch 3. und 4. Klasse: Teil C: Textverstandis und Sprachspiele. (Mentor Lernspass Ser.). 80p. 1989. 13.95 (3-580-63118-7) Langenscheidt.

Bessie. Chris Albertson. LC 79-163353. 253p. 1974. pap. 8.95 (0-8128-1700-1, Scrbrough Hse) Madison Bks UPA.

Bessie Blue Killer: A Hobart LIndsey - Marvia Plum Mystery. Richard A. Lupoff. 304p. 1994. 20.95 (0-312-10425-1) St Martin.

Bessie Coleman: The Brownskin Lady Bird. Elizabeth A. H. Freydberg. LC 93-44882. (Studies in African American History & Culture). 156p. 1994. 42.00 (0-8153-1461-2) Garland.

Bessie Coleman: Writer. LaVerne C. Johnson. LC 92-35255. (Empak Heritage Kids: An Empak "Black History" Publication Ser.). (Illus.). (J). 1992. 3.95 (0-922162-95-6) Empak Pub.

Bessie Smith Companion. Edward Brooks. (Roots of Jazz Ser.). x, 250p. 1983. lib. bdg. 27.50 (0-306-76202-1) Da Capo.

***Bessie Smith Songbook.** Hal Leonard Publishing Staff. 152p. 1994. pap. 16.95 (0-7935-3273-6, HL00308232) H Leonard.

***Bess's Log Cabin Quilt.** D. Anne Love. (Illus.). 88p. (J). (gr. 2-6). 1995. 14.95 (0-8234-1178-8) Holiday.

Best: From the Interior Design Hall of Fame. John C. Aves. LC 92-27941. (Illus.). 240p. 1993. pap. 20.00 (0-9624596-8-2) Vitae Pub.

Best: From the Interior Design Hall of Fame. John C. Aves. LC 92-27941. 240p. 1993. 47.50 (0-9624596-6-6) Vitae Pub.

Best: High-Low Books for Reluctant Readers. Marianne L. Pilla. (Libraries Unlimited Data Bks.). 100p. 1990. pap. text ed. 12.50 (0-87287-532-6); disk 16.50 (0-87287-775-2); Apple II 16.00 (0-87287-780-9); mac hd 17.00 (0-87287-790-6) Libs Unl.

Best: Self-Esteem Activities for the Elementary Grades. Terry Akin et al. (Illus.). 224p. (Orig.). 1990. teacher ed, pap. 24.95 (0-9625486-2-6) Innerchoice Pub.

Best Adventure of the Puzzle Squad. U. S. Kids Editorial Staff. (Illus.). 48p. (J). (gr. k-6). Date not set. student ed 6.95 (1-885453-75-2) Chldrns Better Hlth.

Best American Card Games: A Deal of Fresh Excitement for Every Player. David Duncan. 128p. 1995. pap. 8.95 (0-572-01542-9, Pub. by Foulsham UK) Atrium Pubs.

Best American Erotica. Bright. 256p. 1993. text ed. 27.50 (0-684-19627-1, Scribners) S&S Trade.

Best American Erotica 1993. Ed. by Susie Bright. 256p. 1993. pap. 12.00 (0-02-079262-X, Collier S&S) S&S Trade.

Best American Erotica, 1994. Ed. by Susie Bright. 1994. pap. 12.00 (0-671-89942-2, Touchstone Bks) S&S Trade.

Best American Essays. Ed. by John R. Howard. LC 73-86761. (Essay Index Reprint Ser.). 1977. 23.95 (0-8369-1140-7) Ayer.

Best American Essays, 1986. Ed. by Elizabeth Hardwick & Robert Atwan. 1987. 15.95 (0-317-53357-6); pap. 8.95 (0-317-53358-4) HM.

Best American Essays 1989. Ed. by Geoffrey Wolff & Robert Atwan. 1989. 17.95 (0-685-30571-6); pap. 8.95 (0-685-30572-4) HM.

Best American Essays 1991. Ed. by Justin E. Kaplan & Robert Atwan. 1991. 19.95 (0-685-54943-7, 6-92402); pap. 9.95 (0-685-54944-5, 6-92401) HM.

Best American Essays, 1992. Ed. by Susan Sontag & Robert Atwan. 352p. 1992. pap. 11.95 (0-395-59936-9) HM.

Best American Essays, 1993. Joseph Epstein. 378p. 1993. pap. 12.95 (0-395-63648-5) HM.

Best American Essays, 1994. Ed. by Tracy Kidder & Robert Atwan. 382p. 1994. 24.95 (0-395-69254-7); pap. 11.95 (0-395-69253-9) HM.

***Best American Freethought Letters to Editor, 1990-1995.** Ed. by Edward M. Buckner & Stephen Kilbride. 100p. 1996. pap. 12.00 (1-887392-05-X) Atl Freethought Soc.

Best American Humor, 1994. Moshe Waldoks. 1994. pap. 11.00 (0-671-89940-6, Touchstone Bks) S&S Trade.

Best American Made Products: A Handbook for Consumers & Exporters. 1991. lib. bdg. 69.95 (0-8490-4232-1) Gordon Pr.

Best American Plays. Ed. by John Gassner & Clive Barnes. (Sixth Ser. 1963-1967). 32.95 (0-88411-639-5, Aeonian Pr) Amereon Ltd.

Best American Plays: Fifth Series, 1958-1963. Ed. & Intro. by John Gassner. Incl. Touch of the Poet. 1983. (0-318-51491-5); Night of the Iguana. 1983. (0-318-51492-3); Who's Afraid of Virginia Woolf? 1983. (0-318-51493-1); Rope Dancers. 1983. (0-318-51494-X); Look Homeward Angel. 1983. (0-318-51495-8); All the Way Home. 1983. (0-318-51496-6); Silent Night, Lonely Night. 1983. (0-318-51497-4); Two for the Seesaw. 1983. (0-318-51498-2); Mary, Mary. 1983. (0-318-51499-0); Thousand Clowns. 1983. (0-318-51500-8); Cave Dwellers. 1983. (0-318-51501-6); Oh, Dad, Poor Dad, Mama's Hung You in the Closet and I'm Feelin So Sad. 1983. (0-318-51502-4); Gideon. 1983. (0-318-51503-2); J. B. 1983. (0-318-51504-0); Best Man. 1983. (0-318-51505-9); Orpheus Descending. 1983. (0-318-51506-7); Dark at the Top of the Stairs. 1983. (0-318-51507-5); 704p. 1983. 19.95 (0-517-50860-5, Crown) Crown Pub Group.

Best American Plays: Fourth Series, 1952-1957. Ed. & Intro. by John Gassner. Incl. I Am a Camera. 1958. (0-318-51508-3); Cat on a Hot Tin Roof. 1958. (0-318-51509-1); Rose Tattoo. 1958. (0-318-51510-5); Moon for the Misbegotten. 1958. (0-318-51511-3); Hatful of Rain. 1958. (0-318-51512-1); Picnic. 1958. (0-318-51513-X); Bus Stop. 1958. (0-318-51514-8); Tea & Sympathy. 1958. (0-318-51515-6); View from the Bridge. 1958. (0-318-51516-4); Crucible. 1958. (0-318-51517-2); Inherit the Wind. 1958. (0-318-51518-0); Caine Mutiny Court-Martial. 1958. (0-318-51519-9); Fourposter. 1958. (0-318-51520-2); Seven Year Itch. 1958. (0-318-51521-0); Matchmaker. 1958. (0-318-51522-9); No Time for Sergeants. 1958. (0-318-51523-7); Solid Gold Cadillac. 1958. (0-318-51524-5); 672p. 1958. 35.00 (0-517-50436-7, Crown) Crown Pub Group.

Best American Plays: Seventh Series. Ed. by Clive Barnes. LC 57-12830. 640p. 1975. 35.00 (0-517-51387-0, Crown) Crown Pub Group.

Best American Plays: Sixth Series, 1963-1967. Ed. by John Gassner & Clive Barnes. 700p. 1971. 35.00 (0-517-50951-2, Crown) Crown Pub Group.

Best American Plays: Third Series, 1945-51. Intro. by John Gassner. Incl. Death of a Salesman. 1987. (0-318-51525-3); Streetcar Named Desire. 1987. (0-318-51526-1); Detective Story. 1987. (0-318-51527-X); Member of the Wedding. 1987. (0-318-51528-8); Bell, Book & Candle. 1987. (0-318-51529-6); Moon Is Blue. 1987. (0-318-51530-X); Mister Roberts. 1987. (0-318-51531-8); State of the Union. 1987. (0-318-51532-6); Anne of the Thousand Days. 1987. (0-318-51533-4); Iceman Cometh. 1987. (0-318-51534-2); Come Back, Little Sheba. 1987. (0-318-51535-0); Billy Budd. 1987. (0-318-51536-9); Darkness at Noon. 1987. (0-318-51537-7); Summer & Smoke. 1987. (0-318-51538-5); All My Sons. 1987. (0-318-51539-3); Medea. 1987. (0-318-51540-7); Autumn Garden. 1987. (0-318-51541-5); 736p. 1987. 35. 00 (0-517-50950-4, Crown) Crown Pub Group.

Best American Plays, 1983-1992. Clive Barnes. 1993. 40.00 (0-517-57452-7, Crown) Crown Pub Group.

Best American Plays, 1983-1992. Ed. by Clive Barnes. (John Gassner Best Plays Ser.: Ninth Ser.). 1993. 35.00 (0-685-63464-7) Random.

Best American Poetry, 1989. David Lehman. 272p. 1989. pap. 9.95 (0-02-044182-7) Macmillan.

Best American Poetry, 1990. Intro. by Jorie Graham. 304p. 1990. pap. 11.00 (0-02-032785-4, Collier S&S) S&S Trade.

Best American Poetry, 1991. Intro. by Mark Strand. 288p. 1991. text ed. 27.95 (0-684-19311-6, Scribners); pap. 12. 95 (0-02-069844-5, Collier S&S) S&S Trade.

Best American Poetry, 1992. Ed. by Charles Simic & David Lehman. 352p. 1992. text ed. 25.00 (0-684-19501-1, Scribners); pap. 13.00 (0-02-069845-3, Scribners) S&S Trade.

Best American Poetry, 1993. David Lehman & Louise Gluck. 288p. 1993. pap. 13.00 (0-02-069846-1, Scribners) S&S Trade.

Best American Poetry, 1994. Ed. by A. R. Ammons. 1994. 26.00 (0-671-51004-5); pap. 13.00 (0-671-89948-1, Touchstone Bks) S&S Trade.

Best American Screen Plays Two. Ed. by Sam Thomas. LC 90-2423. 612p. 1990. 35.00 (0-517-57463-2, Crown) Crown Pub Group.

Best American Screenplays. Ed. by Sam Thomas. LC 85-17091. 544p. 1985. pap. 35.00 (0-517-55542-5, Crown) Crown Pub Group.

***Best American Screenplays: 3 Complete Screenplays.** Sam Thomas. 1995. 50.00 (0-517-59104-9, Crown) Crown Pub Group.

Best American Short Plays of 1990. Ed. by Howard Stein & Glenn Young. 209p. 1991. 24.95 (1-55783-084-3); pap. 12.95 (1-55783-085-1) Applause Theatre Bk Pubs.

***Best American Short Plays 1990-1992.** Ed. by Howard Stein & Glenn Young. 1993. 17.99 (1-56865-011-6, GuildAmerica) Dblday Bk Music.

Best American Short Plays 1991-1992. Ed. by Howard Stein & Glenn Young. (Best American Short Plays Ser.). 304p. 1991. 25.95 (1-55783-112-2); pap. 12.95 (1-55783-113-0) Applause Theatre Bk Pubs.

Best American Short Plays 1992-1993: The Theatre Annual since 1937. Billy Aronson et al. (Best Short Plays Ser.). 352p. 1993. 29.95 (1-55783-167-X); pap. 14.95 (1-55783-166-1) Applause Theatre Bk Pubs.

***Best American Short Plays, 1992-1994, 2 vols. in 1.** Howard Stein & Glenn Young. 1995. 19.99 (1-56865-144-9, GuildAmerica) Dblday Bk Music.

***Best American Short Plays 1993-1994.** Ed. by Howard Stein & Glenn Young. (Best American Short Plays Ser.). 352p. (Orig.). 1995. pap. 14.95 (1-55783-199-8) Applause Theatre Bk Pubs.

***Best American Short Plays 1993-1994.** Ed. by Howard Stein & Glenn Young. (Best American Short Plays Ser.). 352p. (Orig.). 1995. 29.95 (1-55783-200-5) Applause Theatre Bk Pubs.

Best American Short Stories & the Yearbook of the American Short Story. (BCL1-PS American Literature Ser.). 1992. reprint ed. lib. bdg. 79.00 (0-7812-6655-6) Rprt Serv.

Best American Short Stories 1980-89. Intro. by Shannon Ravenel. 384p. 1990. pap. 10.95 (0-395-52223-4) HM.

Best American Short Stories, 1986. 71th ed. Ed. by Raymond Carver & Shannon Ravenel. 1987. 15.95 (0-317-53355-X); pap. 8.95 (0-317-53356-8) HM.

Best American Short Stories 1991. Ed. by Richard Ford & Shannon Ravenel. 1991. 19.95 (0-685-54941-0, 6-80129); pap. 9.95 (0-685-54942-9, 6-80128) HM.

Best American Short Stories, 1993. Louise Erdrich. 1993. pap. 11.95 (0-395-63627-2) HM.

690

An Asterisk (*) at the beginning of an entry indicates that the title is appearing in BIP for the first time.

B

Best Concords: Polyphonic Music in Thirteenth-Century Britain. Nicky Losseff. LC 93-45595. (Outstanding Dissertations in Music from British Universities Ser.). 328p. 1994. 72.00 (*0-8153-1710-7*) Garland.

Best Congress Money Can Buy. Philip Stern. LC 87-43116. 196p. 1988. 18.95 (*0-394-56628-9*) Pantheon.

Best Contemporary Women's Humor. Ed. by Roz Warren. 317p. 1994. pap. 12.95 (*0-89594-694-7*) Crossing Pr.

Best Cookin' in the Country. Tom Wiecks. LC 79-91262. (Illus.). (Orig.). 1979. pap. 6.95 (*0-935566-00-7*) Grey Heron.

Best Country Songs Ever. rev. ed. (Best Ever Ser.). 256p. 1991. pap. 16.95 (*0-7935-0636-0*, 00359135) H Leonard.

Best Country Songs Ever: Seventy-Nine All-Time Hits. rev. ed. (EZ Play Today Ser.). 216p. (Orig.). 1992. pap. 16.95 (*0-7935-0496-1*, 00101540) H Leonard.

Best Covered & Kettle Grills Cookbook Ever. Melanie Barnard. 224p. 1994. 16.95 (*0-06-017091-3*, HarpT) HarpC.

Best Crime Stories of the Nineteenth Century. Ed. by Isaac Asimov et al. LC 87-30581. 284p. 1988. 16.95 (*0-934878-99-4*, Dembner NY) Barricade Bks.

Best Crossword Puzzles. Troll Associates Staff. (J). (gr. 4-7). 1992. pap. 1.95 (*0-8167-2804-6*) Troll Assocs.

Best Day Ever: The Story of Jesus. Marilyn Lashbrook. LC 90-63764. (Me Too! Readers Ser.). (Illus.). (J). (gr. k-3). 1991. 5.95 (*0-86606-444-3*, 875) Roper Pr.

B

Best Day Hikes of the California Northwest. Art Bernstein. (Illus.). 224p. (Orig.). 1991. pap. 13.50 (*1-879415-02-X*) Mtn n Air Bks.

Best Deals for New Wheels. Edward Roop. 144p. (Orig.). 1992. pap. 3.99 (*0-425-13473-3*) Berkley Pub.

Best Defense. Alan M. Dershowitz. LC 82-40426. (Illus.). 464p. 1983. pap. 14.00 (*0-394-71380-X*, Vin) Random.

Best Defense. Kate Wilhelm. Date not set. pap. 6.99 (*0-449-22314-0*) Fawcett.

Best Defense. Kate Wilhelm. 352p. 1994. 21.95 (*0-312-10937-7*) St Martin.

Best Defense: Policy Alternatives for U. S. Nuclear Security from the 1950s to the 1990s. David Goldfischer. LC 92-56778. (Cornell Studies in Security Affairs). 304p. 1993. 42.95 (*0-8014-2570-0*) Cornell U Pr.

Best Destiny. Diane Carey. Ed. by Kevin Ripin. (Star Trek Ser.). 416p. 1993. reprint ed. mass mkt. 5.99 (*0-671-79588-0*) PB.

Best Detective Fiction: A Guide from Godwin to the Present. Melvyn Barnes. LC 75-22344. 121p. 1975. 18.95 (*0-208-01376-8*) Boulevard.

Best Detective Stories of Agatha Christie. Agatha Christie. (Bridge Ser.). 136p. (Orig.). (YA). 1986. pap. text ed. 5.95 (*0-582-54087-9*) Longman.

Best Directory of Recruiters - Print Only: Executive Recruiters, Agencies Consultants. Thomas P. Gove. (Illus.). 1040p. (Orig.). 1994. pap. text ed. 29.95 (*0-9636121-1-5*) Gove Pub Co.

***Best Directory of Recruiters, Agencies & Consultants. Thomas P. Gove. Ed. by Stephen P. Alborghetti. (Illus.). 1040p. 1996. pap. 39.99 (*0-9636121-2-3*); cd-rom 69.99 (*0-9636121-3-1*) Gove Pub Co. The most comprehensive publication of its type available in print & electronic media. THE BEST DIRECTORY OF RECRUITERS (tm) IS NOT ANOTHER HOW TO FIND A JOB publication. Only facts are printed; professionals concentrating in specific areas of expertise, how recruiters work & how recruiters expect individuals & companies to work with them, entry level through senior management, United States & International. Over 6,000 Recruiter Firms, Employment & Management Consulting Companies with over 30,000 specific job speciality Recruiters are listed. Information listed: Company, contact name, address, recruiter job search specialty, contingency or retained, telephone/FAX & INTERNET numbers where applicable in 100 sections, 1,040 pages, sorted by Job Specialty & Location. Several category examples: Hi-Technology, Medical, Engineering, Construction, Administration, Retail, Wholesale, International, Finance, Manufacturing. Author: Thomas P. Gove, Senior Executive, President/CEO of The Original Resume Company(c), a national Resume Marketing Company & Gove Publishing. Mr. Gove has a hi-tech, sales & marketing & recruiter background, start-ups to boardroom environments. THE BEST DIRECTORY data base is available with 3.5 computer disk CD/ROM with mail merge letters included in most popular WINDOWS word processing programs for mass mailings, IBM/Macintosh compatible. Ordering/Distribution: Gove Publishing Co., MA, 508 957 6600. FAX 508 957 6605 E-Mail OrigResume@AOL.COM.** *Publisher Provided Annotation.*

Best Directory of Recruiters, Agencies, Consultants. Thomas P. Gove. (Illus.). 500p. 1993. pap. 69.95 (*0-9636121-0-7*) Gove Pub Co.

Best Dives of the Caribbean. Joyce Huber & John Huber. (Illus.). 380p. (Orig.). 1994. pap. 15.95 (*1-55650-644-9*) Hunter NJ.

Best Dives of the Western Hemisphere. Jon Huber & Joyce Huber. (Adventure Guides Ser.). (Illus.). 320p. (Orig.). 1990. pap. 17.95 (*1-55650-250-8*) Hunter NJ.

Best Divisions for Knowledge of the Regions. Al-Muqaddasi. Tr. by Basil Collins. 464p. 1994. 100.00 (*1-873938-14-4*, Pub. by Garnet Pubng Ltd UK) Paul & Co Pubs.

Best Dr. Thorndyke Detective Stories. R. Austin Freeman. Ed. by E. F. Bleiler. 274p. 1973. pap. 4.95 (*0-486-20388-3*) Dover.

Best Doctors in America 1992-1993. Ed. by Steven Naifeh & Gregory W. Smith. 500p. 1992. lib. bdg. 65.00 (*0-913391-05-0*) Woodward-White.

***Best Doctors in America 1994-1995.** Steven Naifeh & Gregory W. Smith. Ed. by Lucienne P. Stec et al. 1130p. (C). Date not set. 76.00 (*0-614-04589-4*) Woodward-White.

Best Dog Stories. Lesley O'Mara. 256p. 1991. reprint ed. 8.99 (*0-517-06498-7*) Random Hse Value.

Best-Dressed Bear. Mary Blocksma. LC 84-9565. (Just One More Ser.). (Illus.). 24p. (J). (ps-2). 1984. pap. text ed. 4.50 (*0-516-41585-9*) Childrens.

Best Easy Listening Songs Ever. (EZ Play Today Ser.). 336p. (J). (gr. 5 up). 1986. 15.95 (*0-7935-0972-6*, 00101542) H Leonard.

Best Easy Listening Songs Ever. rev. ed. Hal Leonard Publishing Staff. (Best Ever Ser.). 208p. 1992. pap. 15.95 (*0-7935-0867-3*, 00359193) H Leonard.

Best Editorial Cartoons of the Year: 1974 Edition. Ed. by Charles Brooks. LC 74-3807. (Illus.). 160p. (Orig.). 1974. 17.95 (*0-88289-027-1*) Pelican.

Best Editorial Cartoons of the Year: 1975 Edition. Ed. by Charles Brooks. LC 74-29707. (Best Editorial Cartoons Ser.). (Illus.). 160p. 1975. 17.95 (*0-88289-077-8*) Pelican.

Best Editorial Cartoons of the Year: 1976 Edition. Ed. by Charles Brooks. LC 74-29707. (Best Editorial Cartoons Ser.). (Illus.). 160p. (J). 1976. 17.95 (*0-88289-122-7*) Pelican.

Best Editorial Cartoons of the Year: 1977 Edition. Ed. by Charles Brooks. LC 74-29707. (Best Editorial Cartoons Ser.). (Illus.). (J). 1977. 17.95 (*0-88289-170-7*) Pelican.

Best Editorial Cartoons of the Year: 1980 Edition. Ed. by Charles Brooks. LC 73-643645. (Illus.). 160p. (Orig.). 1980. 17.95 (*0-88289-264-9*) Pelican.

Best Editorial Cartoons of the Year: 1981 Edition. Ed. by Charles Brooks. LC 73-643645. (Best Editorial Cartoons of the Year Ser.: Vol. 9). (Illus.). 160p. 1981. pap. 13.95 (*0-88289-281-9*) Pelican.

Best Editorial Cartoons of the Year: 1982 Edition. Ed. by Charles Brooks. LC 73-643645. (Illus.). 160p. (Orig.). 1982. pap. 13.95 (*0-88289-319-X*) Pelican.

Bést Editorial Cartoons of the Year: 1984 Edition. 12th ed. Ed. by Charles Brooks. LC 73-643645. (Illus.). 160p. (Orig.). 1984. pap. 13.95 (*0-88289-445-5*) Pelican.

Best Editorial Cartoons of the Year: 1985 Edition. Ed. by Charles Brooks. LC 73-643645. (Best Editorial Cartoons of the Year Ser.). (Illus.). 160p. 1985. pap. 13.95 (*0-88289-478-1*) Pelican.

Best Editorial Cartoons of the Year: 1986 Edition. Ed. by Charles Brooks. 1986. pap. 13.95 (*0-88289-605-9*) Pelican.

Best Editorial Cartoons of the Year: 1987 Edition. Ed. by Charles Brooks. (Illus.). 160p. (Orig.). 1987. pap. 13.95 (*0-88289-638-5*) Pelican.

Best Editorial Cartoons of the Year: 1989 Edition. Ed. by Charles Brooks. (Illus.). 160p. (Orig.). 1989. pap. 13.95 (*0-88289-731-4*) Pelican.

Best Editorial Cartoons of the Year: 1990 Edition. Ed. by Charles Brooks. (Illus.). 176p. (Orig.). 1990. pap. 13.95 (*0-88289-781-0*) Pelican.

Best Editorial Cartoons of the Year: 1991 Edition. Ed. by Charles Brooks. (Illus.). 176p. (Orig.). 1991. pap. 13.95 (*0-88289-837-X*) Pelican.

Best Editorial Cartoons of the Year: 1992 Edition. Ed. by Charles Brooks. (Illus.). 176p. 1992. pap. 13.95 (*0-88289-910-4*) Pelican.

Best Editorial Cartoons of the Year: 1993 Edition. Ed. by Charles Brooks. 192p. 1993. pap. 13.95 (*0-88289-968-6*) Pelican.

Best Editorial Cartoons of the Year: 1994 Edition. Ed. by Charles Brooks. LC 74-29707. (Best Editorial Cartoons Ser.). (Illus.). 192p. 1994. pap. 13.95 (*1-56554-011-5*) Pelican.

***Best Editorial Cartoons of the Year: 1995 Edition.** Ed. by Charles Brooks. (Illus.). 208p. 1995. 14.95 (*1-56554-117-0*) Pelican.

Best Efforts. Kenny Moore. LC 80-2057. 199p. 1992. reprint ed. pap. 12.95 (*0-915297-10-8*, BES) Cedarwinds.

Best Elizabethan Plays. Ed. by William R. Thayer. LC 76-111114. (Play Anthology Reprint Ser.). 1977. 31.95 (*0-8369-8207-X*) Ayer.

Best Encyclopedias: A Guide to General & Specialized Encyclopedias. 2nd ed. Kenneth F. Kister. 512p. 1994. 42.50 (*0-89774-744-5*) Oryx Pr.

Best Enemies. Kathleen Leverich. LC 88-19150. (Illus.). (J). (gr. 1 up). 1989. 10.95 (*0-688-08316-1*) Greenwillow.

Best Enemies. Kathleen Leverich. LC 88-19150. (Illus.). 80p. (J). (gr. 1-4). 1990. reprint ed. pap. 3.50 (*0-679-80156-1*) Knopf Bks Yng Read.

Best Enemies Again. Kathleen Leverich. LC 90-30303. (Illus.). 96p. (J). (gr. 2 up). 1991. 12.95 (*0-688-09440-6*) Greenwillow.

***Best Enemies Forever.** Kathleen Leverich. LC 94-26790. (Illus.). (J). 1995. 14.00 (*0-688-13963-9*) Greenwillow.

Best Enemy Money Can Buy. Anthony C. Sutton. 288p. (Orig.). 1986. 16.95 (*0-937765-00-7*); pap. 12.95 (*0-937765-01-5*) Liberty Hse Pr.

Best English see Needed Words

Best English Short Stories, No. IV. Ed. by Giles Gordon & David Hughes. 308p. 1993. pap. 10.95 (*0-393-31028-0*) Norton.

Best English Short Stories I. Giles Gordon. 1991. pap. 10.95 (*0-393-30782-4*) Norton.

Best English Short Stories II. Ed. by Giles Gordon & David Hughes. 352p. 1992. pap. 10.95 (*0-393-30877-4*) Norton.

Best English Short Stories III. Ed. by Giles Gordon & David Hughes. 320p. 1992. pap. 10.95 (*0-393-30978-9*) Norton.

Best English Short Stories V. Ed. by Giles Gordon & David Hughes. 352p. 1994. 22.00 (*0-393-03580-8*) Norton.

Best English Short Stories, 1989. large type ed. Ed. by G. Gordon & D. Hughes. 1991. 21.95 (*0-7089-2403-4*) Ulverscroft.

Best Engravings. Skip Whitson. (Illus.). 128p. 1975. 25.00 (*0-89540-015-4*, SB-015); pap. 15.00 (*0-89540-014-6*, SB-014) Sun Pub.

***Best Entrepreneurial Businesses for You to Start Part-Time or Full-Time.** Glenn Desmond & Monica Faulkner. LC 95-1373. 1995. text ed. 34.95 (*0-471-11812-5*); pap. text ed. 16.95 (*0-471-11813-3*) Wiley.

Best European Travel Tips: 1991 Edition. John Whitman. LC 88-37983. 274p. 1991. pap. 8.00 (*0-88166-147-3*) Meadowbrook.

Best European Travel Tips, 1994-1995. John Whitman. 288p. (Orig.). 1994. pap. 14.00 (*0-06-273267-6*, Harper Ref) HarpC.

Best-Ever Book of Dog & Cat Names. Leslie Garisto & Peg Streep. 192p. 1988. pap. 7.95 (*0-8050-0775-X*) H Holt & Co.

***Best Ever Cat Names.** Walker. 1995. 6.98 (*0-88365-892-5*) Galahad Bks.

Best Ever Costume Party. Kaffa. (J). 1992. pap. 6.95 (*0-590-46958-4*) Scholastic Inc.

Best-Ever Good-Bye Party. Amy Hest. LC 88-13208. (Illus.). 32p. (J). (gr. k up). 1989. 13.95 (*0-688-07325-5*); lib. bdg. 13.88 (*0-688-07326-3*) Morrow Jr Bks.

Best-Ever Guide to the Monterey Peninsula & Carmel Area. Thom Akeman. (Illus.). 192p. (Orig.). 1994. pap. 14.95 (*0-9623209-2-7*) Kaskaskia Pr.

Best Ever Kids' Book of Lists. Eugenie Allen. 128p. (Orig.). (YA). 1991. pap. 2.95 (*0-380-76357-5*, Camelot) Avon.

Best Ever Paper Airplane Book & Kit. (Illus.). 96p. 1994. 24.95 (*0-8069-0904-8*, Pub. by Tamos Bks CN) Sterling.

Best Ever Paper Airplanes. Norman Schmidt. LC 93-39122. (Illus.). 96p. (J). (gr. 4 up). 1994. 19.95 (*1-895569-20-6*, Pub. by Tamos Bks CN) Sterling.

***Best Ever Paper Airplanes.** Norman Schmidt. (Illus.). 96p. 1995. pap. 12.95 (*1-895569-42-7*, Pub. by Tamos Bks CN) Sterling.

Best Ever Pressure Cooker Cookbook. J. Boswell. (Illus.). 1994. 16.95 (*0-06-017092-1*, HarpT) HarpC.

Best Ever Writing Models. Nancy Polette. (Illus.). 124p. (J). (gr. 4-9). 1989. pap. 12.95 (*0-913839-78-7*) Bk Lures.

Best Evidence. David S. Lifton. 1981. 19.95 (*0-02-571870-3*) Macmillan.

Best Evidence: Disguise & Deception in the Assassination of John F. Kennedy. David S. Lifton. 1992. pap. 6.99 (*0-451-17573-5*, Sig) NAL-Dutton.

Best Face of All. Wilesse Comissiong. 1991. pap. 5.95 (*0-913543-19-5*) African Am Imag.

Best Fake Book Ever: Bb Edition. (Ultimate Fake Book Ser.). 768p. 1991. pap. 39.95 (*0-7935-0350-7*, 00240083) H Leonard.

Best Fake Book Ever: Eb Edition. (Ultimate Fake Book Ser.). 768p. 1991. pap. 39.95 (*0-7935-0351-5*, 00240084) H Leonard.

Best Fake Book Ever - Over 1000 Songs: For Piano, Vocal, Guitar, Electronic Keyboards, & All "C" Instruments. (Fake Book Ser.). 768p. (Orig.). 1990. pap. 39.95 (*0-7935-0021-4*, 00290239) H Leonard.

Best Family Videos: For the Discriminating Viewer. Quentin J. Schultze. 1994. pap. 5.99 (*1-881273-21-0*) Northfield Pub.

***Best Fed Dog in America: Canine Cuisine, Dog Culture, Facts & Merriment.** Ellen Goss. 1995. pap. 8.95 (*1-885623-09-7*) Owl Bay Pubs.

Best Festivals Mid-Atlantic: Over Two Hundred Fifty Festivals from New York State to Virginia. Dale Adams. 240p. (Orig.). 1992. pap. 13.00 (*0-88150-222-7*) Countryman.

Best Festivals of North America: A Performing Arts Guide. 3rd ed. Carol Spivack & Richard A. Weinstock. Orig. Title: Best Festivals of North America: A Practical Guide to Festival-Vacations. 208p. 1989. pap. 10.95 (*0-916401-08-1*) Printwheel.

Best Festivals of North America: A Practical Guide to Festival-Vacations see Best Festivals of North America: A Performing Arts Guide

Best Fiction of Rudyard Kipling. Rudyard Kipling. 1989. pap. 12.95 (*0-385-26091-1*) Doubleday.

***Best 50 Buttermilk Recipes.** Christie Katona & Thomas Katona. (Best 50 Ser.). 80p. (Orig.). 1995. pap. 4.95 (*1-55867-115-3*) Bristol Pub Ent CA.

***Best 50 Crepe Recipes.** Coleen Simmons & Bob Simmons. (Best 50 Ser.). 80p. (Orig.). 1995. pap. 4.95 (*1-55867-113-7*) Bristol Pub Ent CA.

***Best 50 Dips.** Joanna White. (Best 50 Ser.). 80p. (Orig.). 1995. pap. 4.95 (*1-55867-110-2*) Bristol Pub Ent CA.

***Best 50 Salsas.** Christie Katona & Thomas Katona. (Best 50 Ser.). 72p. (Orig.). 1995. pap. 4.95 (*1-55867-112-9*) Bristol Pub Ent CA.

***Best 50 Shortbreads.** Barbara Karoff. (Best 50 Ser.). 80p. (Orig.). 1995. pap. 4.95 (*1-55867-111-0*) Bristol Pub Ent CA.

***Best 50 Smoothies.** Joanna White. (Best 50 Ser.). 72p. (Orig.). 1995. pap. 4.95 (*1-55867-114-5*) Bristol Pub Ent CA.

Best Fight. Anne Schlieper. Ed. by Judith Mathews. (Illus.). 64p. (J). (gr. 3-7). 1994. lib. bdg. 10.95 (*0-8075-0662-1*) A Whitman.

***Best Film Scenes & Monologues of the Year, 1994.** Jocelyn Beard. 1995. pap. 14.95 (*1-880399-24-5*) Smith & Kraus.

Best Financial Advertising, No. 1. Ed. by David E. Carter. LC 79-50633. (Illus.). 1979. 35.00 (*0-910158-56-8*) Art Dir.

Best Financial Advertising, No. 2. David E. Carter. LC 79-50633. (Illus.). 424p. 1981. 35.00 (*0-910158-74-6*) Art Dir.

Best Financial Advertising, No. 3. David E. Carter. LC 79-50633. (Best Financial Advertising Ser.). 400p. 1984. 35.00 (*0-88108-013-6*) Art Dir.

Best Financial Advertising, No. 4. David E. Carter. 1986. 39.50 (*0-88108-032-2*) Art Dir.

Best Fine Woodworking Lathes & Turning Techniques. 1991. pap. 14.95 (*1-56158-021-X*) Taunton.

Best Football in Texas! Victor Rios, Jr. 1994. pap. 12.95 (*0-533-10851-9*) Vantage.

***Best for Last.** Stephanie Howard. (Romance Ser.). 1995. mass mkt. 2.99 (*0-373-03373-7*, 1-03373-7) Harlequin Bks.

Best for Me. Becki Trueblood. (J). 1991. pap. 4.99 (*0-8163-1050-5*) Pacific Pr Pub Assn.

Best for Our Kids: Exemplary Elementary Guidance & Counseling Programs. Martin Gerstein & Marilyn Lichtman. 1990. 17.95 (*1-55620-066-8*) Am Coun Assn.

***Best Free Historic Attractions in Oregon & Washington.** KiKi Canniff. LC 95-15283. (Northwest Free Ser.: Vol. 1). (Illus.). 1995. write for info. (*0-941361-08-X*) KITwo Enter.

Best Free Historic Attractions in Oregon & Washington, Vol. 1: Favorite Freebies. KiKi Canniff. LC 92-14405. (Illus.). 192p. (Orig.). 1992. pap. 10.95 (*0-941361-01-2*) KITwo Enter.

Best Friend. R. L. Stine. Ed. by Patricia McDonald. (Fear Street Ser.: No. 17). 160p. (Orig.). (YA). (gr. 7 up). 1992. mass mkt. 3.99 (*0-671-73866-6*, Archway) PB.

Best Friend. G. Walton Williams & John Kollock. (J). 1991. 10.95 (*0-87844-098-4*); pap. 6.95 (*0-87844-103-4*) Sandlapper Pub Co.

Best Friend Game. Francine Pascal. (Unicorn Club Ser.: No. 3). (J). (gr. 4-7). 1994. pap. 3.50 (*0-553-48210-6*) Bantam.

Best Friend Insurance. Beatrice Gormley. (Illus.). 160p. (J). (gr. 3-7). 1985. pap. 2.50 (*0-380-69854-4*, Camelot) Avon.

Best Friend Insurance. Beatrice Gormley. LC 83-5713. (Illus.). 160p. (J). (gr. 3-6). 1983. 10.95 (*0-525-44066-6*, DCB) Dutton Child Bks.

Best Friend Is Forever. Ed. by Robin Andrews. LC 92-271. (Illus.). 64p. 1992. 16.95 (*0-88396-357-4*) Blue Mtn Pr CO.

Best Friends. Molly Albright. LC 87-13874. (Two of a Kind Ser.). (Illus.). 96p. (J). (gr. 3-6). 1988. lib. bdg. 9.89 (*0-8167-1151-8*); pap. text ed. 2.95 (*0-8167-1152-6*) Troll Assocs.

Best Friends. Antoinette Becker & Eisabeth Reuter. (J). (gr. 1-4). 1993. 12.95 (*0-943706-18-1*) Pitspopany.

Best Friends. Miriam Cohen. LC 70-146620. (Illus.). 32p. (J). (ps-1). 1971. text ed. 13.95 (*0-02-722800-2*, Mac Bks Young Read) S&S Childrens.

Best Friends. Etienne Delessert. LC 93-27461. (Yok-Yok Ser.). (Illus.). 32p. (J). (gr. 1-8). 1994. lib. bdg. 10.95 (*0-88682-639-X*, 97927-098) Creative Ed.

Best Friends. Ed. by Lee B. Hopkins. LC 85-45257. (Charlotte Zolotow Bk.). (Illus.). 48p. (J). (gr. k-4). 1986. lib. bdg. 14.89 (*0-06-022562-9*) HarpC Child Bks.

Best Friends. Steven Kellogg. LC 85-15971. (Illus.). 32p. (J). (ps-3). 1986. 14.99 (*0-8037-0099-7*); lib. bdg. 13.89 (*0-8037-0101-2*) Dial Bks Young.

Best Friends. Steven Kellogg. Ed. by Phyllis J. Fogelman. LC 85-15971. (Illus.). 32p. (J). (ps-3). 1990. pap. 4.99 (*0-8037-0829-7*) Dial Bks Young.

Best Friends. Penny J. Mann. (Miss Penny's Adventures Ser.: No. 1). 48p. 1993. pap. 5.00 (*0-9638742-0-9*) Good News Express.

Best Friends. Francine Pascal. (Sweet Valley Twins Ser.: No. 1). 112p. (Orig.). (YA). (gr. 7-12). 1986. 3.25 (*0-553-15655-1*, Skylark) Bantam.

Best Friends. Dave Sargent. (Illus.). 48p. (Orig.). (J). (gr. k-8). 1993. text ed. 11.95 (*1-56763-056-1*); pap. text ed. 5.95 (*1-56763-057-X*) Ozark Pub.

***Best Friends.** Lynda Trent. 480p. 1995. mass mkt. 4.99 (*0-8217-4801-7*) Zebra.

Best Friends. large type ed. Jamie Suzanne. (Sweet Valley Twins Ser.: No. 1). 104p. (YA). (gr. 7-12). 1990. reprint ed. 9.95 (*1-55905-064-0*) Grey Castle.

Best Friends. Miriam Cohen. LC 89-31266. (Illus.). 32p. (J). (ps-1). 1989. reprint ed. pap. 3.95 (*0-689-71334-7*, Aladdin Paperbacks) S&S Childrens.

Best Friends: A Pictorial Celebration by the Winners of the Parade - Kodak National Photo Contest. Intro. by Walter Anderson. (Illus.). 144p. 1991. 24.95 (*0-8264-0534-7*) Continuum.

692

An Asterisk (*) at the beginning of an entry indicates that the title is appearing in BIP for the first time.

B

An Asterisk (*) at the beginning of an entry indicates that the title is appearing in BIP for the first time.

693

Best Joke Book for Kids, No. 2. Joan Eckstein & Joyce Gleit. (Illus.). 64p. (J). (gr. 3 up). 1987. pap. 2.99 (*0-380-75209-3*, Camelot) Avon.

Best Joke Book for Kids, No. 3. Joan Eckstein & Joyce Gleit. 64p. (J). 1990. pap. 3.50 (*0-380-75872-5*, Camelot) Avon.

Best Joke Book for Kids, No. 4. Joan Eckstein & Joyce Gleit. 64p. (J). 1991. pap. 3.50 (*0-380-76263-3*, Camelot) Avon.

Best Jokes & Riddles. Ed. by Anna Pansini. LC 89-20324. (Illus.). 48p. (J). (gr. 2-6). 1990. lib. bdg. 8.59 (*0-8167-1917-9*); pap. text ed. 2.50 (*0-8167-1918-7*) Troll Assocs.

Best Jokes from Talk Radio. Bill Wattenburg. 144p. 1993. 10.00 (*0-913136-10-7*) Montgomery St Pr.

Best Judo. Isao Inokuma & Nobuyuki Sato. LC 79-84656. (Illus.). 256p. 1987. pap. 24.00 (*0-87011-786-6*) Kodansha.

Best Jumbo Paper Aircraft. Campbell Morris. LC 92-40581. (Illus.). 32p. (Orig.). 1993. pap. 6.95 (*0-399-51801-0*, Perigree Bks) Berkley Pub.

Best Karate, Vol 11: Goiushiho, Sho, Meikyo. Masatoshi Nakayama. LC 77-74829. (Best Karate Ser.). (Illus.). 1990. pap. 15.00 (*0-87011-758-0*) Kodansha.

Best Karate: Bassai Sho, Kaiku Sho Chintei. Nakayama. LC 77-74829. (Best Karate Ser.: Vol. 9). (Illus.). 1986. pap. 15.00 (*0-87011-680-0*) Kodansha.

Best Karate: Comprehensive. Masatoshi Nakayama. LC 77-74829. (Best Karate Ser.: Vol. 1). (Illus.). 1977. pap. 15.00 (*0-87011-317-8*) Kodansha.

Best Karate: Fundamentals. Masatoshi Nakayama. LC 77-74829. (Best Karate Ser.: Vol. 2). (Illus.). 1978. pap. 15.00 (*0-87011-324-0*) Kodansha.

Best Karate: Kata: Bassai & Kanku. Masatoshi Nakayama. LC 77-74829. (Best Karate Ser.: Vol. 6). (Illus.). (Orig.). 1980. pap. 15.00 (*0-87011-383-6*) Kodansha.

Best Karate: Kata: Gankaku, Jion. Masatoshi Nakayama. LC 77-74829. (Best Karate Ser.: Vol. 8). (Illus.). 144p. (Orig.). 1981. pap. 15.00 (*0-87011-402-6*) Kodansha.

Best Karate: Kata: Heian & Tekki. Masatoshi Nakayama. LC 77-74829. (Best Karate Ser.: Vol. 5). 1979. pap. 15.00 (*0-87011-379-8*) Kodansha.

Best Karate: Kata: Jutte, Hangetsu, Empi. Masatoshi Nakayama. LC 77-74829. (Best Karate Ser.: Vol. 7). (Illus.). 144p. 1981. pap. 15.00 (*0-87011-390-9*) Kodansha.

Best Karate: Kumite 1. Masatoshi Nakayama. LC 77-74829. (Best Karate Ser.: Vol. 3). (Illus.). 1978. pap. 15.00 (*0-87011-332-1*) Kodansha.

Best Karate: Kumite 2. Masatoshi Nakayama. LC 77-74829. (Best Karate Ser.: Vol. 4). (Illus.). 1979. pap. 15.00 (*0-87011-359-3*) Kodansha.

Best-Kept Secret. Emily Rodda. 112p. (J). (gr. 5). 1991. reprint ed. pap. 2.95 (*0-380-75870-9*, Camelot) Avon.

Best Kept Secret: Sexual Abuse of Children. Florence Rush. 1992. pap. 9.95 (*0-07-158192-8*) McGraw.

Best-Kept Secret: Sexual Abuse of Children. Florence Rush. 238p. 1991. pap. 9.95 (*0-8306-3907-1*) TAB Bks.

Best Kept Secret of the New Rich. Steven A. Houseman. (Illus.). 150p. (Orig.). 1987. pap. 6.95 (*0-915451-07-7*) New Start Pubns.

Best Kept Secret on Wall Street: How to Invest in Convertible Securities Like the Pros. Wayne F. Nelson. LC 93-21502. 193p. 1993. 24.95 (*0-7931-0720-2*, 560887) Dearborn Finan.

Best Kept Secrets. Sandra Brown. 432p. 1989. mass mkt. 6.50 (*0-446-35393-0*) Warner Bks.

***Best Kept Secrets.** large type ed. Sandra Brown. LC 94-22715. 1995. 21.95 (*1-56054-790-1*) Thorndike Pr.

Best Kept Secrets: Of Chocolate Drinks & Life. Antoinette Y. Trainer. Ed. by Elsie Washington. 100p. 1989. write for info. (*0-9621966-0-6*) Starbud Pr.

***Best Kind of Loving: A Black Woman's Guide to Finding Intimacy.** Gwendolyn G. Grant. 288p. 1995. 22.00 (*0-06-017088-3*) HarpC.

Best Known Latin Songs. rev. ed. (Piano-Vocal-Guitar Ser.). 144p. 1993. pap. text ed. 15.95 (*0-7935-1942-X*, 00311600) H Leonard.

Best Known Works. Nathaniel Hawthorne. Incl. Scarlet Letter. LC 70-37548. (*0-318-50789-7*); House of the Seven Gables. LC 70-37548. (*0-318-50790-0*); Best of Twice-Told Tales. LC 70-37548. (*0-318-50791-9*); LC 70-37548. (Short Story Index Reprint Ser.). 1977. reprint ed. 34.95 (*0-8369-4107-1*) Ayer.

Best Known Works, Vol. 1. Anton P. Chekhov. LC 72-5899. (Short Story Index Reprint Ser.). 1977. reprint ed. 36.95 (*0-8369-4198-5*) Ayer.

Best Laid Plans. William Rouse. LC 94-16433. 228p. 1994. write for info. (*0-13-300054-0*) P-H.

Best Laid Plans. Alan Weiss. 1994. 22.50 (*0-910924-98-8*) Macalester.

Best-Laid Plans. large type ed. Vanessa Gray. LC 92-43475. (Orig.). 1993. 21.95 (*0-7927-1568-3*, Curley Lrg Print); pap. 19.95 (*0-7927-1567-5*, Curley Lrg Print) Chivers N Amer.

Best Laid Plans: A Study of Student Development in an Experimental College Program. Robert F. Suczek. LC 72-5891. (Jossey-Bass Higher Education Ser.). 208p. reprint ed. pap. 59.30 (*0-8357-9297-8*, 2013953) Bks Demand.

Best-Laid Plans of Jonah Twist. Natalie Honeycutt. 128p. (J). (gr. 2). 1990. pap. 2.95 (*0-380-70762-4*, Camelot) Avon.

Best-Laid Plans of Jonah Twist. Natalie Honeycutt. LC 88-7288. 128p. (J). (gr. 3-5). 1988. text ed. 13.95 (*0-02-744850-9*, Bradbury S&S) S&S Childrens.

Best Laid Schemes: The Psychology of the Emotions. Keith Oatley. (Studies in Emotion & Social Interaction). (Illus.). 496p. (C). 1992. 74.95 (*0-521-41037-1*); pap. 34.95 (*0-521-42387-2*) Cambridge U Pr.

Best Laugh Last. John B. Rosenman. LC 81-12990. 218p. 1983. reprint ed. pap. 6.95 (*0-914232-62-2*) McPherson & Co.

Best Law Schools: In-Depth Profiles of 40 Top Schools by a Trusted Admissions Expert! Thomas H. Martinson. 304p. 1993. pap. 17.00 (*0-671-84858-5*, Arco Test) P-H Gen Ref & Trav.

Best Lawyers in America: Directory of Experts, 1990. Ed. by Steven Naifeh & Gregory W. Smith. 275p. 1990. lib. bdg. 80.00 (*0-913391-07-7*) Woodward-White.

Best Lawyers in America: Directory of Experts, 1992. 2nd ed. Gregory W. Smith. Ed. by Steven Naifeh. 375p. 1992. lib. bdg. 90.00 (*0-913391-08-5*) Woodward-White.

Best Lawyers in America: 1989-1990. 3rd ed. Steven Naifeh & Gregory W. Smith. 720p. 1989. lib. bdg. 89.00 (*0-913391-03-4*) Woodward-White.

Best Lawyers in America: 1991-1992. 4th ed. Steven Naifeh & Gregory White Smith. 1000p. 1991. lib. bdg. 95.00 (*0-913391-04-2*) Woodward-White.

Best Lawyers in America, 1993-1994. 5th ed. Ed. by Steven Naifeh & Gregory W. Smith. 1000p. 1993. write for info. (*0-913391-09-3*) Woodward-White.

***Best Lawyers in America 1995-1996: 1995 - 1996.** Steven Naifeh & Gregory W. Smith. Ed. by Christopher J. Greame et al. (Biennial Ser.). 1313p. (C). Date not set. 88.00 (*0-913391-11-5*) Woodward-White.

Best Left As Indians: Native-White Relations in the Yukon Territory, 1840-1973. Ken S. Coates. (McGill-Queen's Studies in Ethnic History). 1991. text ed. 49.95 (*0-7735-0780-9*, Pub. by McGill CN) U of Toronto Pr.

Best Left as Indians: Native-White Relations in the Yukon Territory, 1840-1973. Ken S. Coates. 384p. 1993. pap. 19.95 (*0-7735-1100-8*, Pub. by McGill CN) U of Toronto Pr.

Best Lessons of a Chess Coach. Sunil Weeramantry & Ed Eusebi. LC 93-1375. 1994. pap. 14.00 (*0-8129-2265-4*, Times Bks) Random.

Best Little Bachelor Book in Texas. Goldstein. 1980. pap. 4.95 (*0-934180-03-2*) Money Business.

Best Little Book of One-Liners. Henny Youngman. LC 92-53813. (Miniature Editions Ser.). (Illus.). 96p. 1992. 4.95 (*1-56138-180-2*) Running Pr.

Best Little Boy in the World. John Reid. 1986. mass mkt. 4.95 (*0-345-34361-1*) Ballantine.

Best Little Boy in the World. John Reid. 256p. 1993. pap. 9.00 (*0-345-38176-9*, Ballantine Trade) Ballantine.

Best Little Escape Stories. C. Brian Kelly. 220p. (Orig.). Date not set. pap. write for info. (*0-9624875-1-1*) Montpelier Pub.

***Best Little Game in Town.** Jack M. Harrison. 100p. (Orig.). 1995. pap. 8.95 (*0-9645816-0-4*) Rebel Enter.

Best Little Girl in the World. Steven Levenkron. 1989. mass mkt. 5.99 (*0-446-35865-7*) Warner Bks.

Best Little Hors d'oeuvres in Kansas. Betty M. May. (Illus.). 81p. (Orig.). 1987. pap. 9.95 (*0-9619522-0-2*) B M May.

Best Little Monkeys in the World. Natalie Standiford. LC 86-15425. (Step into Reading Bks.: Bk. 2). (Illus.). 48p. (J). (gr. 1-3). 1987. 3.50 (*0-394-88616-X*); lib. bdg. 7.99 (*0-394-98616-4*) Random Bks Yng Read.

Best Little Party Book Ever! Kathleen M. Johnson. LC 84-52165. (Illus.). 200p. (Orig.). 1985. pap. 9.95 (*0-9614700-0-3*) Willow Run Pub.

Best Little Stories from the Civil War. C. Brian Kelly & Ingrid Smyer. (Best Little Stories From Ser.). (Illus.). 250p. 1995. pap. 14.50 (*0-9624875-7-0*) Montpelier Pub.

Best Little Stories from the White House. C. Brian Kelly. (Best Little Stories Ser.). 215p. 1989. pap. 10.95 (*0-9624875-3-8*) Montpelier Pub.

Best Little Stories from the White House. C. Brian Kelly. (Best Little Stories Ser.). 242p. 1993. pap. 12.95 (*0-9624875-4-6*) Montpelier Pub.

Best Little Stories from World War II. C. Brian Kelly. (Best Little Stories Ser.). (Illus.). 216p. (Orig.). 1993. pap. 10.95 (*0-9624875-0-3*) Montpelier Pub.

Best Love Songs Ever. rev. ed. (Best Ever Ser.). (Illus.). 248p. 1991. pap. 17.95 (*0-7935-1004-X*, HL00359198) H Leonard.

Best Loved Bible Stories. Ed. by Jeannie Harmon. LC 89-463. 168p. (ps-2). 1989. 13.99 (*1-55513-242-1*, Chariot Bks) Chariot Family.

Best Loved Bible Stories. Ed. by Dave Jackson & Neta Jackson. (J). 1993. pap. 9.99 (*0-7814-0136-4*, Bible Discovery) Chariot Family.

Best Loved Classics, 10 vols. 1985. 82.50 (*0-911156-49-6*) Bern Porter.

Best-Loved Classics: Sleeping Beauty. 1989. 2.98 (*0-671-06599-8*) S&S Trade.

Best-Loved Contemporary Poems. Ed. by Eddie-Lou Cole. 39.95 (*0-317-29086-X*) World Poetry Pr.

Best Loved Dog Stories of Albert Payson Terhune. A. P. Terhune. 22.95 (*0-89190-363-1*, Am Repr) Amereon Ltd.

Best-Loved Doll. Rebecca Caudill. LC 92-898. (Illus.). 64p. (J). (ps-2). 1992. 12.95 (*0-8050-2103-5*, Bks Young Read) H Holt & Co.

Best-Loved Fairy Tales Treasury: Snow White; The Three Little Pigs; Beauty & the Beast; Hansel & Gretel; Puss in Boots; Goldilocks & the Three Bears, 6 bks., Set. (Illus.). 24p. (J). 1993. boxed 9.98 (*0-7853-0072-4*) Pubns Intl Ltd.

Best Loved Folktales of the World. Ed. by Joanna Cole. LC 81-43288. (Anchor Folktale Library). 816p. 1983. pap. 14.95 (*0-385-18949-4*, Anchor NY) Doubleday.

Best Loved Poems in Large Print. large type ed. Ed. by Virginia S. Reiser. (General Ser.). 1983. 21.95 (*0-8161-3575-4*, Large Print Bks) Hall.

Best Loved Poems of Korea: Selected for Foreigners. Tr. by Chang-soo Koh. LC 83-81485. 128p. 1984. 14.50 (*0-930878-35-3*) Hollym Intl.

Best Loved Poems of the American People. Ed. by Hazel Felleman. 1936. pap. 17.95 (*0-385-00019-7*) Doubleday.

Best Loved Poems to Read: Again & Again. Mary S. Laurence. (Second Ser.). 1989. 9.98 (*0-88365-726-0*) Galahad Bks.

Best Loved Poems to Read Again & Again. Mary S. Laurence. 1989. 9.98 (*0-88365-714-7*) Galahad Bks.

Best Loved Poems to Read Again & Again, 2 vols. Mary S. Laurence. 1990. boxed 19.98 (*0-88365-760-0*) Galahad Bks.

***Best Loved Saints.** Date not set. 4.95 (*0-89942-160-1*) Catholic Bk Pub.

Best-Loved Stories at the National Storytelling Festival. Comp. by National Association for the Preservation & Perpetuation of Storytelling Staff. 224p. 1991. pap. 14.95 (*1-879991-00-4*, Natl Storytell) Natl Assn Preserv & Perpet Storytelling.

Best-Loved Tales of Peter Rabbit: Benjamin Bunny; The Flopsy Bunnies; Ginger & Pickles; Squirrel Nutkin; Tom Kitten; Two Bad Mice, 6 bks., Set. (Illus.). 24p. (J). 1993. boxed 9.98 (*0-7853-0071-6*) Pubns Intl Ltd.

***Best Low-Fat, No-Sugar Bread Machine Cookbook Ever.** Madge Rosenberg. 1995. 16.95 (*0-06-017174-X*) HarpC.

Best Mac Tips Ever. Steve Michel & Dale Coleman. 1993. pap. text ed. 19.95 (*0-07-881968-7*) McGraw.

Best Made Plans. Leigh Michaels. (Romance Ser.: No. 214). 1992. pap. 2.89 (*0-373-03214-5*) Harlequin Bks.

Best Magazine Articles: 1988. Ed. by Thomas Fensch. 216p. (C). 1989. pap. 22.50 (*0-8058-0468-4*) L Erlbaum Assocs.

***Best Magazine Publication Design No. 29.** Rockport Publishers Staff. 1995. 49.99 (*1-56496-152-4*) Rockport Pubs.

***Best Maine Stories.** Ed. by S. Phippen et al. LC 94-5391. 320p. 1994. pap. 11.95 (*0-89272-351-3*) Down East.

***Best Man.** Phoebe Gallant. 512p. 1995. pap. 4.99 (*0-8217-5044-5*) Zebra.

Best Man. Gore Vidal. 1962. pap. 4.75 (*0-8222-0107-0*) Dramatists Play.

***Best Man.** Shannon Waverly. 1995. mass mkt. 2.99 (*0-373-03380-X*, 1-03380-2) Harlequin Bks.

Best Man. Grace L. Hill. reprint ed. lib. bdg. 21.95 (*0-89190-035-7*, Rivercity Pr) Amereon Ltd.

Best Man. Paul Reidinger. LC 88-83328. 176p. 1989. reprint ed. pap. 7.95 (*1-55583-149-4*) Alyson Pubns.

Best Man, No. 7. Grace L. Hill. 1989. pap. 4.99 (*0-8423-0371-5*) Tyndale.

Best Man: A Screen Adaptation of the Original Play, Directed by Franklin Schaffner. Gore Vidal. Ed. by George P. Garrett et al. LC 71-135273. (Film Scripts Ser.). 1989. pap. text ed. 19.95 (*0-89197-676-0*) Irvington.

Best Man: Selections from the First Three Years of MAN! Magazine. Ed. by Sharon Adams. 130p. 1992. pap. 12.50 (*0-9633927-3-5*) Mandala TX.

Best Man for the Job: A Story about the Meaning of Father's Day. Louise Mandrell & Ace Collins. (Illus.). 32p. (J). (gr. 1-4). 1993. 12.95 (*1-56530-039-4*) Summit TX.

Best Man to Die. Ruth Rendell. 208p. 1987. mass mkt. 4.95 (*0-345-34530-4*) Ballantine.

Best Man to Die. Ruth Rendell. 18.95 (*0-89190-887-0*) Yestermorrow.

Best Man to Die. Ruth Rendell. 18.95 (*0-685-71740-2*) Yestermorrow.

Best Management Practices for Florida Golf Courses: Greens Construction, Water, Fertilizing, Cultural Practices & Pest Management. (Illus.). 184p. 1995. pap. 16.00 (*0-916287-06-8*) Univ Fla Food.

Best Management Resources: Developing Management Skills: A Self-Directed Approach, Bk. 2. Gerald De Jaager. LC 84-51544. 373p. (C). 1985. 80.00 (*0-916001-01-6*) Seiler-Doar.

Best Manners Book Ever. Randall Mehew & Karen Mehew. (Virtue & Values Ser.). (Illus.). 68p. (J). 1990. pap. text ed. 5.95 (*0-929985-55-9*) Jackman Pubng.

Best Man's Organiser. Christopher Hobson. 128p. (Orig.). 1993. pap. 13.95 (*0-572-01864-9*, Pub. by W Foulsham UK) Trans-Atl Phila.

Best Man's Passport. Scott Vandame. 40p. 1993. 8.00 (*0-9634411-6-7*) Auguste Pr.

***Best Maritime Short Stories.** Ed. by George Peabody. (Illus.). 232p. 1995. pap. 14.95 (*0-88780-068-8*) Formac Dist Ltd.

Best Mathematical Puzzles of Sam Loyd. Sam Loyd. Ed. by Martin Gardner. 1959. pap. 4.50 (*0-486-20498-7*) Dover.

Best Medicine. Janet L. Walters. 480p. 1993. mass mkt. 4.50 (*0-8217-4220-5*) Zebra.

Best Medicine: How to Choose the Top Doctors, the Top Hospitals, & the Top Treatments. Robert Arnot. 1993. pap. 14.38 (*0-201-62478-8*) Addison-Wesley.

Best Men's Stage Monologues of 1990. Ed. by Jocelyn A. Beard. LC 90-91798. 74p. (Orig.). 1991. pap. 8.95 (*0-9622722-2-1*) Smith & Kraus.

Best Men's Stage Monologues of 1991. Ed. by Jocelyn A. Beard. 96p. 1992. 8.95 (*1-880399-02-4*) Smith & Kraus.

Best Men's Stage Monologues of 1992. Ed. by Jocelyn A. Beard. 82p. 1993. pap. 8.95 (*1-880399-11-3*) Smith & Kraus.

Best Men's Stage Monologues of 1993. Ed. by Jocelyn A. Beard. (Monologue Audition Ser.). 100p. 1993. pap. 8.95 (*1-880399-43-1*) Smith & Kraus.

***Best Men's Stage Monologues of 1994.** Jocelyn Beard. 1995. pap. 8.95 (*1-880399-64-4*) Smith & Kraus.

***Best Men's Stage Monologues of 1995.** Ed. by Jocelyn A. Beard. (Annual Best Monologues Ser.). 112p. 1995. 8.95 (*1-880399-70-9*) Smith & Kraus.

Best Methods for the Analysis of Change: Recent Advances, Unanswered Questions, Future Directions. Ed. by Linda M. Collins & John L. Horn. 375p. (Orig.). (C). 1991. 40.00 (*1-55798-113-2*) Am Psychol.

***Best Mexican & Central American Travel Tips.** John Whitman. LC 94-25950. 400p. (Orig.). 1994. pap. 14.00 (*0-06-273268-4*, PL) HarpC.

Best Mistake Ever! A Step Two Book. Richard Scarry. LC 84-2029. (Step into Reading Bks.). (Illus.). 48p. (J). (ps-2). 1984. pap. 3.50 (*0-394-86816-1*) Random Bks Yng Read.

Best Motion Pictures of Nineteen Thirty-Nine to Forty: Year Book of Motion Pictures. Jerry Wald & Richard Macaulay. 1975. lib. bdg. 300.00 (*0-87968-241-8*) Gordon Pr.

Best Moving Pictures Nineteen Twenty-Two to Nineteen Twenty-Three. Robert E. Sherwood. 1974. 250.00 (*0-87700-136-7*) Revisionist Pr.

Best Music for High School Band: A Selective Repertoire Guide for High School Bands & Wind Ensembles. Thomas L. Dvorak et al. Ed. by Bob Margolis. (Orig.). (C). 1993. pap. write for info. (*0-931329-03-5*, BMHSB) Manhattan Beach.

Best Music for Young Band: A Selective Guide to the Young Band-Young Wind Ensemble Repertoire. Thomas L. Dvorak et al. Ed. by Bob Margolis. 52p. (Orig.). 1986. pap. 19.95 (*0-931329-02-7*, 31) Manhattan Beach.

Best Mysteries of Isaac Asimov. Isaac Asimov. 416p. 1987. mass mkt. 5.95 (*0-449-13287-0*, GM) Fawcett.

Best Name for Your Baby: A Creative Guide to Proper Nomenclature. Barbara Binswanger & Lisbeth Mark. 256p. (Orig.). 1990. pap. 9.95 (*0-8050-0877-2*, Owl) H Holt & Co.

***Best Nature Writing of Joseph Wood Krutch.** Frwd. by Edward Lenders. (Illus.). 392p. 1995. pap. 17.95 (*0-87480-480-9*) U of Utah Pr.

Best-Natured Man: Sir Samuel Garth, Physician & Poet. John F. Sena. LC 85-48009. (Studies in the Eighteenth Century: No. 9). 1986. 39.50 (*0-404-61475-2*) AMS Pr.

Best Nest. P. D. Eastman. LC 68-28459. (Illus.). 72p. (J). (gr. k-3). 1968. lib. bdg. 7.99 (*0-394-90051-0*) Beginner.

Best Nest. Philip D. Eastman. LC 68-28459. (Illus.). 72p. (J). (gr. k-3). 1968. 6.95 (*0-394-80051-6*) Beginner.

Best New America Logo. Ed. by Gerry Rosentswieg. (Illus.). 211p. 1994. 37.50 (*0-942604-34-2*) Madison Square.

***Best New Animation Design.** Date not set. 34.99 (*1-56496-166-4*) Rockport Pubs.

Best New Chicano Literature 1986. Ed. by Julian Palley. 84p. 1986. pap. 8.00 (*0-916950-66-2*) Biling Rev-Pr.

Best New Chicano Literature, 1989. Ed. by Julian Palley. 126p. 1989. pap. 9.00 (*0-927534-01-0*) Biling Rev-Pr.

Best New Horror. Ed. by Stephen Jones & Ramsey Campbell. 416p. 1991. pap. 10.95 (*0-88184-762-3*) Carroll & Graf.

Best New Horror, No. 2. Ed. by Stephen Jones & Ramsey Campbell. 464p. 1993. pap. 11.95 (*0-88184-921-9*) Carroll & Graf.

Best New Horror, No. 3. Stephen Jones & Ramsey Campbell. 464p. 1992. 21.00 (*0-88184-858-1*) Carroll & Graf.

***Best New Horror, No. 6.** 480p. 1995. pap. 11.95 (*0-7867-0277-X*) Carroll & Graf.

Best New Horror Five. Ed. by Stephen Jones & Ramsey Campbell. 512p. 1995. pap. 9.95 (*0-7867-0155-2*) Carroll & Graf.

Best New Horror Four. Ed. by Stephen Jones & Ramsey Campbell. 512p. 1993. 21.95 (*0-7867-0004-1*) Carroll & Graf.

Best New Horror Three. Ed. by Stephen Jones & Ramsey Campbell. 448p. 1994. pap. 11.95 (*0-7867-0028-9*) Carroll & Graf.

Best Newspaper Writing 1985. Ed. by Roy P. Clark & Don Fry. LC 80-646604. (Illus.). 283p. 1985. pap. 7.95 (*0-935742-10-7*) Poynter Inst.

Best Newspaper Writing 1986. Ed. by Don Fry. LC 80-646604. 294p. 1986. pap. 7.95 (*0-935742-12-3*) Poynter Inst.

Best Newspaper Writing 1987. Ed. by Don Fry. LC 80-646604. 396p. 1987. pap. 9.95 (*0-935742-14-X*) Poynter Inst.

Best Newspaper Writing, 1993. Don Fry. (Illus.). 280p. 1993. pap. 11.95 (*1-56625-029-3*) Bonus Books.

***Best Newspaper Writing 1994: Winners of the American Society of Newspaper Editors Distinguished.** Christopher Scanlan. 1994. pap. 12.95 (*1-56625-014-5*) Bonus Books.

Best Nightmare on Earth: A Life in Haiti. Herbert Gold. 320p. 1992. pap. 12.00 (*0-671-75516-1*, Touchstone Bks) S&S Trade.

Best Nine Hundred Numbers. 1991. pap. 3.50 (*0-312-92496-8*) St Martin.

Best Nonfranchise Business Opportunities: The Smart Entrepreneur's Guide to Dealerships, License Agreements, Distributorships, & More. Andrew J. Sherman & Donna T. Cavanagh. LC 92-34838. 416p. 1993. pap. 19.95 (*0-8050-2208-2*, Owl) H Holt & Co.

Best Novellas of Medieval Germany. Tr. by J. W. Thomas. LC 83-70284. (Studies in German Literature, Linguistics & Culture: Vol. 17). (Illus.). 104p. 1983. 29.00 (*0-938100-10-6*) Camden Hse.

Best Novels & Stories of Eugene Manlove Rhodes. Eugene M. Rhodes. Ed. by Frank V. Dearing. LC 87-12466. xxiv, 552p. 1987. reprint ed. pap. 14.95 (*0-8032-8928-6*) U of Nebr Pr.

Best of A. B. Simpson. A. B. Simpson. LC 86-72008. 1987. pap. 6.99 (*0-87509-314-0*) Chr Pubns.

Best of A. W. Tozer. A. W. Tozer. (Best Ser.). 1978. pap. 7.99 (*0-8010-8899-2*) Baker Bk.

An Asterisk (*) at the beginning of an entry indicates that the title is appearing in BIP for the first time.

Best of A. W. Tozer. W. Wiersbe. 249p. 1979. pap. 7.99 (0-87509-458-9) Chr Pubns.

***Best of A. W. Tozer.** A. W. Tozer. Ed. by Warren W. Wiersbe. 256p. 1995. reprint ed. pap. 7.99 (0-8010-5265-3) Baker Bk.

***Best of A. W. Tozer, Vol. 2.** A. W. Tozer. Ed. & Intro. by Warren W. Wiersbe. 296p. 1995. reprint ed. pap. 9.99 (0-8010-5253-X) Baker Bk.

Best of Abbie Hoffman: Selections from "Revolution for the Hell of It", "Woodstock Nation", "Steal This Book" & New Writings. Abbie Hoffman. LC 89-23585. (Illus.). 421p. 1990. 21.95 (0-941423-27-1); 14.95 (0-941423-42-5) FWEW.

Best of AC-DC. (Illus.). 48p. 1988. pap. 11.95 (0-8256-1200-4, AM72851) Music Sales.

Best of AC-DC: Guitar Tablature Edition. (Illus.). 136p. 1990. pap. 17.95 (0-8256-2582-3, AM76688) Music Sales.

Best of Admiral Burke. Arleigh Burke. Ed. by Douglass H. Hubbard. (Orig.). 1987. pap. 2.00 (0-934841-13-6) Adm Nimitz Foun.

Best of Aerosmith. (Piano-Vocal-Guitar Personality Folio Ser.). 112p. (Orig.). 1991. pap. 16.95 (0-7935-0099-0, 00490410) H Leonard.

Best of Aesop's Fables. Margaret G. Clark. (J). (ps-4). 1990. 16.95 (0-316-14499-1, Joy St Bks) Little.

***Best of AFN, Vol. III.** Ed. by John M. Drewes & Dorothy J. Drewes. (Illus.). 200p. (Orig.). 1995. pap. 19.95 (0-929931-11-4) Amer Fireworks.

Best of AFN Two. John M. Drewes. (Illus.). 200p. (Orig.). 1990. pap. 19.95 (0-929931-06-8) Amer Fireworks.

***Best of Aixtra Vol. 1.** IBM Staff. 1995. pap. text ed. 40.00 (0-13-328626-6) P-H.

***Best of Al Green.** Ed. by Carol Cuellar. 76p. (Orig.). 1995. pap. text ed. 14.95 (0-89724-517-2) Warner Brothers.

Best of Alabama. Lee Sentell. 344p. (Orig.). 1993. pap. 14. 95 (1-878561-16-2) Seacoast AL.

Best of Alaska: The Art of Jon Van Zyle. Carol A. Phillips. LC 89-1574. (Illus.). 80p. 1990. 29.95 (0-945397-06-2); pap. 19.95 (0-945397-07-0) Epicenter Pr.

Best of Alexander Maclaren. Alexander Maclaren. Ed. by Gaius G. Atkins. LC 74-179733. (Biography Index Reprint Ser.). 1977. reprint ed. 17.95 (0-8369-8101-4) Ayer.

Best of All. Elizabeth Carlson. 320p. 1993. mass mkt. 3.99 (0-8217-4055-5) Zebra.

***Best of All Family Baking.** Caroline Best. 1995. pap. 16.95 (0-9635257-4-3) Mt Ivy Pr.

Best of All Is Jesus. Alger Fitch. (C). 1991. pap. 9.99 (0-89900-389-3) College Pr Pub.

Best of All Main Dish Salads. Caroline Best. 1993. pap. 16. 95 (0-9635257-1-9) Mt Ivy Pr.

Best of All Possible Worlds: Romances & Tales, Vol. 1. Francois-Marie de Voltaire. LC 72-3277. (Short Story Index Reprint Ser.). 1977. reprint ed. 23.95 (0-8369-4165-9) Ayer.

Best of Aloha. Ed. by Paul Turley. (Illus.). 194p. 1990. 34. 95 (0-89610-167-3) Island Heritage.

Best of America. Capalbo & Washburn. (Illus.). 256p. 1995. 19.98 (0-8317-1758-0) Smithmark.

Best of American Machinist Magazine, Jan-Jun 1909. American Machinist Magazine Staff. 1985. reprint ed. pap. 9.95 (0-917914-26-0) Lindsay Pubns.

Best of American Machinist Magazine, July-December, 1909. 1986. reprint ed. pap. 9.95 (0-917914-42-2) Lindsay Pubns.

Best of American Music Awards. Ed. by Milton Okun. pap. 19.95 (0-89524-669-4) Cherry Lane.

Best of Amish Cooking. Phyllis P. Good. LC 88-82138. (Color Plates Ser.). 224p. 1988. 19.95 (0-934672-70-9) Good Bks PA.

Best of AMJ Maintenance Tips. IAP, Inc. Staff. LC 90-108619. (Illus.). 184p. (C). 1989. pap. 12.95 (0-89100-341-X, EA-341) IAP.

Best of Andrew Murray. Andrew Murray. (Best Ser.). 256p. 1991. reprint ed. pap. 7.99 (0-8010-6281-0) Baker Bk.

***Best of Apples.** 46p. 1995. write for info. (1-57215-043-2) World Pubns.

Best of Archi Work Details 1: Exteriors. Boyne & Wright. 1987. pap. 52.95 (0-85139-766-2, Butterwrth Archit) Buttrwrth-Heinemann.

Best of Archi Work Details 2: Interiors. Boyne & Wright. 1982. pap. 52.95 (0-85139-767-0, Butterwrth Archit) Buttrwrth-Heinemann.

Best of Arizona: A Witty, Definitive & Remarkably Useful Guide to the Grand Canyon State. rev. ed. Ed. by Don W. Martin & Betty W. Martin. (Best of...Ser.: No. 3). (Illus.). 336p. 1993. pap. 12.95 (0-942053-07-9) Pine Cone Pr CA.

Best of Arizona: Chef's Recipes from Arizona's Favorite Resorts & Restaurants. Marjorie Scaffidi. (Illus.). 289p. (Orig.). 1995. pap. 14.95 (0-918080-45-2, 20989) Treas Chest Bks.

Best of Ascent: Twenty-Five Years of the Mountaineering Experience. Ed. by Steve Roper & Allen Steck. LC 92-24722. (Illus.). 416p. 1993. 25.00 (0-87156-517-X) Sierra.

Best of Audio Video Interiors. Roman Beyer & Chirs Esse. 240p. 1990. 39.95 (0-9627922-0-9) CRB Pub.

Best of Auditory Skills. Andrea Lazzari et al. 1993. 19.95 (1-55999-390-1) LinguiSystems.

Best of B. C. Lake Fishing. Karl Bruhn. 296p. 1993. pap. 14.95 (1-878175-28-9) F Amato Pubns.

Best of Babcock. Havilah Babcock. LC 70-117281. 275p. 1985. reprint ed. 19.95 (0-936075-10-4) Gunnerman Pr.

Best of Bach. Joseph Castle. 1993. 3.95 (1-56222-134-5, 93453) Mel Bay.

Best of Bad Faulkner. Wells. 1991. pap. 8.95 (0-15-611850-5, Harvest Bks) HarBrace.

Best of Bad Hemingway, Vol. I. Ed. by Harry's Bar & Grill Staff. 1991. pap. 8.95 (0-15-611866-1, Harvest Bks) HarBrace.

Best of Bad Hemingway: Choice Entries from the Harry's Bar & American Grill Imitation Hemingway Competition. Intro. by George Plimpton. (Illus.). 163p. 1989. pap. 8.95 (0-15-611861-0) HarBrace.

Best of Baking. 1989. 17.99 (0-517-65591-8) Random Hse Value.

Best of Bamboo Ridge. Ed. by Eric Chock & Darrell Lum. LC 83-73232. 325p. (YA). (gr. 9-12). 1986. pap. 9.00 (0-910043-07-8) Bamboo Ridge Pr.

Best of Barbara Ray. Barbara Ray. 160p. 1989. write for info. (0-318-65419-9) Rayve Prodns.

Best of Beer & Brewing Vols. 1-5: AHA, 5 vols., Vols. 1-5. Ed. by American Homebrewers Association Staff. (Illus.). 260p. 1987. 17.95 (0-937381-05-5) Brewers Pubns.

Best of Beetle Bailey. Mort Walker. (Illus.). 240p. pap. 9.95 (0-685-10111-8) Comicana.

Best of Ben, 5 booklets, Set. Ben Feldman. 1981. 10.95 (0-87863-205-0, 2418-04) Dearborn Finan.

***Best of Bible Pathway: Bible Pathway Devotional, Vol. I.** John A. Hash. (Illus.). 336p. 1990. 12.00 (1-879595-00-1) Bible Path Minist.

***Best of Bible Pathway Vol. I.** John A. Hash. Ed. by Barney E. Bell & Benjamin Wallace. 350p. (Orig.). 1993. pap. 8.95 (1-879595-02-8) Bible Path Minist.

Best of Bible Trivia I: Kings, Criminals, Saints & Sinners. J. Stephen Lang. 1990. pap. 4.99 (0-8423-0464-9) Tyndale.

Best of Bible Trivia II: Palaces, Poisons, Feasts & Beasts. J. Stephen Lang. 176p. 1990. pap. 3.95 (0-8423-0465-7) Tyndale.

Best of Bible Trivia III: Angels, Demons, Scrolls, & Scribes. Stephen J. Lang. 1991. pap. 3.95 (0-8423-0466-5) Tyndale.

Best of Bill. 48p. 1960. pap. 2.00 (0-933685-02-5) A A Grapevine.

Best of Bill Nye's Humor. Bill Nye. Ed. by Louis Hasley. (Masterworks of Literature Ser.). 1972. 18.95 (0-8084-0343-5); pap. 14.95x (0-8084-0344-3) NCUP.

Best of Bits & Pieces. Ed. by Arthur F. Lenehan. 300p. Date not set. 29.95 (0-910187-08-8) Economics Pr.

***Best of Bizarro Vol. II.** Dan Piraro. 1994. pap. 9.95 (0-8118-0771-1) Chronicle Bks.

Best of Bizzaro. Dan Piraro. (Illus.). 144p. 1992. pap. 9.95 (0-8118-0276-0) Chronicle Bks.

Best of Black Sabbath. (Illus.). 48p. 1981. pap. 11.95 (0-86001-931-4, AM28911) Music Sales.

Best of Bloopers. Kermit Schafer. 18.95 (0-89190-214-7, Am Repr) Amereon Ltd.

Best of Blueberries. R. Marilyn Schmidt. 76p. (Orig.). 1993. pap. 7.95 (0-937996-20-3) Pine Barrens Pr.

Best of Blues: The Essential Guide. Roger St. Pierre. 1993. 9.95 (0-00-255337-6) Collins SF.

Best of Blues Guitar. Fred Sokolow. 1993. 5.95 (0-87166-283-3, 94138); audio 14.95 (0-685-74546-5, 94138); audio 9.98 (0-87166-282-5, 94138) Mel Bay.

Best of Bombeck. Erma Bombeck. 1987. 9.98 (0-88365-721-X) Galahad Bks.

Best of Borneo Travel. Comp. & Intro. by Victor T. King. (Illus.). 338p. 1993. pap. 16.95 (0-19-588603-8) OUP.

Best of Both Worlds. Rod Parsley. 32p. (Orig.). 1986. pap. 0.75 (0-88144-083-3) Christian Pub.

Best of Both Worlds: Winning Government Funding for Commercial Product Development under the Small Business Innovation Research Program. John H. Sangster & Barbara C. Sangster. (Illus.). xiii, 245p. 1994. 64.95 (0-9640102-1-6); pap. 49.95 (0-9640102-0-8) SPHINX Tech.

***Best of Boulder Climbs.** Richard Rossiter. (Illus.). 180p. (Orig.). 1992. pap. 15.00 (0-934641-26-9) Chockstone Pr.

Best of Bragg. Addison Bragg. Ed. by Richard J. Wesnick. (Illus.). (Orig.). 1985. pap. 9.95 (0-913311-01-4) Unicorn Comm.

***Best of Brat Attack.** Fish. (Orig.). 1995. pap. 12.95 (1-56333-349-X) Masquerade.

***Best of Breads: From Amish & Mennonite Kitchens.** 1995. pap. text ed. 1.95 (1-56148-158-0) Good Bks PA.

Best of Britain's Countryside: Northern England & Scotland. Bill North & Gwen North. LC 90-5455. (Two-Week Traveler Ser.). 272p. (Orig.). 1990. pap. 12. 95 (0-89886-205-1) Mountaineers.

Best of Britain's Countryside: Southern England, a Driving & Walking Itinerary. Bill North & Gwen North. LC 90-48755. (Illus.). 272p. 1991. pap. 12.95 (0-89886-264-7) Mountaineers.

Best of Britain's Countryside: The Heart of England & Wales: a Driving & Walking Itinerary. Bill North & Gwen North. LC 92-41891. (Two-Week Traveler Ser.). 256p. (Orig.). 1993. pap. 12.95 (0-89886-341-4) Mountaineers.

Best of British Architecture, 1980-2000. Noel Moffett. LC 92-40841. 1992. write for info. (0-419-17240-8, E & FN Spon); write for info. (0-442-31640-2, E & FN Spon) Routledge Chapman & Hall.

Best of British Bikes. Jim Reynolds. (Illus.). 160p. 1991. 27.95 (1-85260-033-0, Pub. by Thorsons UK) Motorbooks Intl.

Best of British Pluck: The Boy's Own Paper 1879-1967. Philip Warner. (Illus.). 1976. 25.00 (0-8464-0190-8) Beekman Pubs.

Best of Broadside: A Humorous Look at Life in the Navy. Jeff Bacon. LC 92-72180. (Illus.). 96p. (Orig.). 1992. pap. 7.95 (1-881651-11-8) Deep Water VA.

Best of Broadway for Vocal Duets. (Chappell Education Ser.). 64p. 1984. 7.95 (0-88188-339-5, 00312032) H Leonard.

Best of Broadway Today. (Coates Easy Piano Arrangements Ser.). 60p. pap. 9.95 (0-89724-041-3) Warner Brothers.

***Best of Brochure Design.** Date not set. pap. 34.99 (1-56496-123-0) Rockport Pubs.

Best of Brochure Design. Rockport Publsihers Editors. (Illus.). 256p. 1992. 49.99 (1-56496-004-8, 30455) Rockport Pubs.

Best of Brochure Design, No. 2. 192p. 1994. 39.99 (1-56496-092-7) Rockport Pubs.

***Best of Bugialli.** Giuliano Bugialli. 1994. 22.50 (1-55670-384-8) Stewart Tabori & Chang.

Best of Bulk Solids Handling: Bulk Handling in Open Pit Mines & Quarries. 320p. 1986. text ed. 36.00 (0-87849-065-5, Pub. by Trans Tech GW) LPS Dist Ctr.

Best of Bulk Solids Handling: Bulk Port Development Design & Operation. 464p. 1986. text ed. 48.00 (0-87849-067-1, Pub. by Trans Tech GW) LPS Dist Ctr.

Best of Bulk Solids Handling: Continuous Ship Unloading & Self-Unloading Vessels. 272p. 1986. text ed. 36.00 (0-87849-062-0, Pub. by Trans Tech GW) LPS Dist Ctr.

Best of Bulk Solids Handling: Conveyor Belt Technology. 464p. 1986. text ed. 48.00 (0-87849-068-X, Pub. by Trans Tech GW) LPS Dist Ctr.

Best of Bulk Solids Handling: Hydraulic Conveying & Slurry Pipeline Technology. 240p. 1986. text ed. 36.00 (0-87849-064-7, Pub. by Trans Tech GW) LPS Dist Ctr.

Best of Bulk Solids Handling: Mechanical Conveying, Transporting & Feeding. 288p. 1986. text ed. 36.00 (0-87849-066-3, Pub. by Trans Tech GW) LPS Dist Ctr.

Best of Bulk Solids Handling: Pneumatic Conveying of Bulk & Powder. 240p. 1986. text ed. 36.00 (0-87849-063-9, Pub. by Trans Tech GW) LPS Dist Ctr.

Best of Bulk Solids Handling: Sampling, Weighing & Proportioning of Bulk Materials. 256p. 1986. text ed. 36.00 (0-87849-069-8, Pub. by Trans Tech GW) LPS Dist Ctr.

Best of Bulk Solids Handling: Silos, Hoppers, Bins & Bunkers for Storing Bulk Materials. 480p. 1986. text ed. 48.00 (0-87849-060-4, Pub. by Trans Tech GW) LPS Dist Ctr.

Best of Bulletin Board: Of Simple Pleasures, Cute Kids, Dumb Customers, the Kindness of... St. Paul Pioneer Press Staff. 1994. pap. 8.95 (0-8362-8060-1) Andrews & McMeel.

Best of Business Card Design. Rockport Book Staff. 160p. 1994. 34.99 (1-56496-045-5, 30583) Rockport Pubs.

Best of Business Humor. Nancy Wittington. 78p. (Orig.). 1993. pap. 7.95 (1-56245-043-3) Great Quotations.

Best of BYTE: Two Decades on the Leading Edge. Jay Rande. 1993. pap. text ed. 24.95 (0-07-051344-9) McGraw.

Best of C. H. Spurgeon. C. H. Spurgeon. 256p. 1986. pap. 7.99 (0-8010-8267-6) Baker Bk.

Best of C. L. Moore. C. L. Moore. 384p. (Orig.). 1980. pap. 2.25 (0-345-28952-8) Ballantine.

Best of C. L. Moore. C. L. Moore. (Orig.). 1993. reprint ed. lib. bdg. 18.95 (0-89968-354-1, Lghtyr Pr) Buccaneer Bks.

Best of C. L. S. Out of Print Volumes. 1988. 10.00 (0-318-35426-8) Chicago Ling.

Best of Cajun-Creole Recipes. Theresa Millang. 1992. pap. 5.95 (0-934860-93-9) Adventure Pubns.

***Best of Cakes: From Amish & Mennonite Kitchens.** 1995. pap. text ed. 1.95 (1-56148-159-9) Good Bks PA.

Best of California. 1994. 14.95 (0-00-255478-X) Collins SF.

Best of California Rocketry, No. 1, 4-81, 7-81, 10-81, 1-82, 4-82. 128p. 15.00 (0-912468-20-3, TBO #1); lib. bdg. 19.95 (0-912468-39-4, TBO #2) CA Rocketry.

Best of Canadian Theatre Review. Ed. by Alan Filewod. 768p. 1992. 27.50 (0-8020-6812-X) U of Toronto Pr.

***Best of Candies: From Amish & Mennonite Kitchen.** 1995. pap. text ed. 1.95 (1-56148-164-5) Good Bks PA.

***Best of Case Studies in Technical Training.** Ed. by Patricia A. Galagan & Ellen S. Carnevale. LC 94-71336. (Best of Ser.). 120p. 1994. pap. 25.00 (1-56286-005-4) Am Soc Train & Devel.

***Best of Casseroles: From Amish & Mennonite Kitchens.** 1995. pap. text ed. 1.95 (1-56148-154-8) Good Bks PA.

Best of Catherine Marshall. Catherine Marshall. Ed. by Leonard E. LeSourd. LC 93-1606. 352p. 1993. 14.99 (0-8007-9209-2) Chosen Bks.

***Best of Catherine Marshall.** large type ed. Ed. by Leonard E. LeSourd. LC 94-42713. Date not set. pap. 14.95 (0-8027-2687-9) Walker & Co.

***Best of Catherine Marshall: Her Intimate Life.** Ed. by Leonard E. LeSourd. 352p. 1995. reprint ed. pap. 9.00 (0-380-72383-2) Avon.

Best of CD-ROM Professional: Timeless Tips & Practical Advice. Ed. by Nancy K. Herther. (Illus.). 272p. 1992. 34.95 (0-910965-04-8) Online.

***Best of Central California: Main Roads & Side Trips.** Bob Carter & Mike Jaynes. 320p. (Orig.). 1994. pap. 14.95 (1-881409-10-4) Jhnstn Assocs.

Best of Challenge, 3 vols. Incl. Vol. 1. Articles from the Dec. 1965 Through May-June 1970 Issues. American Alliance for Health, Physical Education, Recreation & Dance Staff. pap. 4.95 (0-88314-032-2, 245-25124); Vol. 2. Articles from the Sept.-Oct. 1970 Through May-June 1973 Issues. American Alliance for Health, Physical Education, Recreation & Dance Staff. pap. 4.95 (0-88314-033-0, 245-25562); Vol. 3. Articles from the Sept. 73 Through May 76 Issues. American Alliance for Health, Physical Education, Recreation & Dance Staff. pap. 4.95 (0-88314-034-9); Set pap. write for info. (0-318-50146-5) AAHPERD.

Best of Chevy Hot Line. Ed. by John Thawley. (Illus.). 96p. (Orig.). Date not set. pap. text ed. 10.95 (0-936834-24-2) S S Autosports.

***Best of Chicago.** 2nd ed. Andre Gayot. 1995. pap. 18.00 (1-881066-14-2) Gault Millau.

Best of Chief Executive. Ed. by J. P. Donlon. 450p. 1992. 27.00 (1-55623-781-2) Irwin Prof Pubng.

Best of Children's Books, 1964-1978. 1992. lib. bdg. 79.95 (0-8490-8777-5) Gordon Pr.

Best of Chili Recipes. Theresa Millang. 1993. spiral bd., pap. 5.95 (0-934860-08-4) Adventure Pubns.

Best of China: A Cookbook. Evie Righter & Grace Young. LC 92-17592. 1992. 14.95 (0-00-255149-7) Collins SF.

***Best of Chocolate.** 46p. 1995. write for info. (1-57215-046-7) World Pubns.

Best of Chocolate. Mary Goodbody & Brooke Dojny. 1994. 14.95 (0-00-255254-X) Collins SF.

Best of Ciarcia's Cellar. Steve Ciarcia. 1992. text ed. 40.00 (0-07-011019-0) McGraw.

Best of Ciarcia's Circuit Cellar. Steve Ciarcia. 1992. pap. text ed. 24.95 (0-07-011025-5) McGraw.

Best of Clarence Day. Clarence Day. 27.95 (0-88411-528-3, Aeonian Pr) Amereon Ltd.

***Best of Clay Pot Cooking.** Dana Jacobi. LC 95-10823. (Illus.). 1995. 14.95 (0-00-225051-9) Collins SF.

***Best of Coal-Surface Mining.** (Illus.). 194p. 1995. pap. write for info. (0-929531-29-9) MacLn Hunter Pub.

Best of Coffee: A Cookbook. Sandra Gluck. LC 94-17338. (Illus.). 1994. 14.95 (0-00-255476-3) Collins SF.

Best of Cole Porter. 160p. 1992. pap. 14.95 (0-7935-1517-3, 00311577) H Leonard.

***Best of Collectible Dinnerware: With Values.** Jo Cunningham. LC 95-8474. (Books for Collectors). (Illus.). 192p. 1995. 29.95 (0-88740-833-8) Schiffer.

Best of College Photography, 1992. 256p. 1992. text ed. 50. 00 (0-685-60652-X) Serbin Commns.

Best of Colorado's Summer Skiing. Floyd Wright. LC 89-83401. (Illus.). 88p. (Orig.). (C). 1990. 10.95 (0-9623988-0-2) Colo Ski Pubns.

Best of Colored Pencil. Rockport Press Staff. (Illus.). 160p. 1993. 24.99 (1-56496-049-8, 30503) Rockport Pubs.

***Best of Colored Pencil: Box Set.** Date not set. 39.99 (1-56496-129-X) Rockport Pubs.

Best of Colored Pencil 2. 160p. 1994. 24.99 (1-56496-108-7) Rockport Pubs.

Best of Conejo: The Community Resource Guide. Anne LaBelle. 200p. (Orig.). 1992. pap. 9.95 (0-9634949-0-2) Labelle.

***Best of Contemporary Folk.** Ed. by Milton Okun. (Illus.). 120p. (Orig.). (YA). 1995. pap. 17.95 (0-89524-861-1, HL02502122) Cherry Lane.

***Best of Cookies: From Amish & Mennonite Kitchens.** 1995. pap. text ed. 1.95 (1-56148-155-6) Good Bks PA.

Best of Corvette News. Ed. by Karl Ludvigsen. LC 76-20955. 656p. 1976. 39.95 (0-915038-07-2, 3-AQ-0011) Auto Quarterly.

Best of Costume Jewelry. Nancy Schiffer. LC 89-84169. (Illus.). 160p. 1990. pap. 29.95 (0-88740-223-2) Schiffer.

Best of Count Basie. (Jazz Masters Series for Guitar). 40p. (Orig.). pap. 9.95 (0-89724-066-9) Warner Brothers.

Best of Country: The Essential Guide. Stacy Harris. 1993. 9.95 (0-00-255335-X) Collins SF.

Best of Country Cooking. Ed. by Linda Piepenbrink. LC 93-83133. 292p. 1993. 24.98 (0-89821-106-9) Reiman Pubns.

Best of Country Guitar. (Best of...for Guitar Ser.). 128p. (Orig.). 1993. pap. 14.95 (0-89724-108-8) Warner Brothers.

Best of Country Guitar Solos. Tommy Flint. 1993. 5.95 (0-87166-575-1, 94336); audio 9.98 (0-87166-993-5, 94336) Mel Bay.

Best of Country Songs. Brimhall. 1990. 4.95 (0-685-32046-4, H441) Hansen Ed Mus.

Best of Crazyhorse: Thirty Years of Poetry & Fiction. Ed. by David Jauss. LC 89-20642. 494p. 1990. 24.95 (1-55728-164-5); pap. 14.95 (1-55728-165-3) U of Ark Pr.

***Best of Crocus Coulee.** Betty Kilgour. (Illus.). 91p. (Orig.). 1986. pap. 9.95 (0-920490-54-9) Temeron Bks.

***Best of Crosby, Stills, Nash & Young for Guitar.** (Best of.. .for Guitar Ser.). 32p. (Orig.). 1994. pap. 12.95 (0-89724-184-3) Warner Brothers.

Best of Dark Horse Presents, Vol. 1. Ed. by Randy Stradley. (Illus.). 128p. 1989. ring bd. 5.95 (1-878574-06-X) Dark Horse Comics.

Best of Dark Horse Presents, Vol. 2. Ed. by Randy Stradley. (Illus.). 112p. 1990. pap. 8.95 (1-56971-002-3) Dark Horse Comics.

Best of Dark Horse Presents, Vol. 3. Ed. by Randy Stradley & Kij Johnson. (Illus.). 144p. 1993. pap. 12.95 (1-878574-81-7) Dark Horse Comics.

Best of David Bowie for Guitar. (Best of...for Guitar Ser.). 60p. (Orig.). pap. 12.95 (0-89724-053-7) Warner Brothers.

Best of Davie Napier. Davie Napier. 272p. (Orig.). 1992. pap. 9.95 (0-687-02827-2) Abingdon.

Best of Daytripping & Dining in Southern New England & Nearby New York. enl. rev. ed. Betsy Wittemann & Nancy Webster. LC 85-51326. (Daytripping & Dining Ser.). (Illus.). 186p. 1989. pap. 9.95 (0-934260-66-4) Wood Pond.

Best of Dear Abby. 2nd ed. Abigail Van Buren. 252p. 1989. pap. 9.95 (0-8362-6241-7) Andrews & McMeel.

Best of Dear Bureaucrat: The Selected Letters of Peter Bollen. Peter D. Bollen. LC 88-82942. (Illus.). 128p. (Orig.). 1988. pap. 6.95 (0-9611350-2-6) Highland Hillside.

Best of Defoe's Review: Proceedings of the Symposium, Boston, Nov. 30-Dec. 2, 1977. Syrian Hamster in Toxicology & Carcinogenesis Research Symposium Staff. Ed. by William L. Payne. LC 73-128233. (Essay Index Reprint Ser.). 1977. 23.95 (0-8369-1873-8) Ayer.

Best of Dell Crossword Puzzles, No. 3. 1993. mass mkt. 9.99 (0-440-50540-2) Dell.

Best of Dell Crosswords. 1990. mass mkt. 9.99 (0-440-50277-2) Dell.

B

An Asterisk (*) at the beginning of an entry indicates that the title is appearing in BIP for the first time. 695

Best of Deming. Ed. by Ron McCoy. 175p. reprint ed. pap. 6.00 (*0-945320-37-X*) SPC Pr.

Best of Dental Humor. Ed. by Stephen T. Sonis & Gerald Shklar. (Illus.). 250p. 1995. 32.00 (*1-56053-067-7*) Hanley & Belfus.

***Best of Desserts: From Amish & Mennonite Kitchens.** 1995. pap. text ed. 1.95 (*1-56148-161-0*) Good Bks PA.

***Best of Dick Idol's Whitetail World: Hunting the Four Periods of the Rut.** Dick Idol. Ed. by Gordon Whittington. LC 95-60952. 288p. 1995. 29.95 (*0-9633315-1-5*) Venture Pr MT.

Best of Disney. 80p. (J). 1985. pap. 10.95 (*0-88188-580-0*, 00359192) H Leonard.

Best of Doll Reader, No. IV. 4th ed. Virginia Heyerdahl. (Illus.). 192p. 1991. pap. 14.95 (*0-87588-374-5*) Hobby Hse.

Best of Doll Reader, Vol. I. Ed. by Virginia A. Heyerdahl. 212p. 1980. pap. 14.95 (*0-87588-187-4*, 204) Hobby Hse.

Best of Dwight L. Moody. Dwight L. Moody. (Best Ser.). 249p. 1991. pap. 7.99 (*0-8010-6216-0*) Baker Bk.

Best of E. E. Doc Smith. E. E. Smith. 285p. 1975. 25.00 (*0-297-77004-7*) Ultramarine Pub.

Best of E. M. Bounds on Prayer. E. M. Bounds. (Best Ser.). 232p. 1986. pap. 7.99 (*0-8010-0935-9*) Baker Bk.

***Best of Eagles for Guitar.** (Best of...Ser.). 68p. (Orig.). 1994. pap. 12.95 (*0-89724-170-3*) Warner Brothers.

Best of East Texas, 1. Bob Bowman. 1991. 12.95 (*1-878096-13-3*) Best E TX Pubs.

Best of East Texas, 2. Bob Bowman. 1991. 13.95 (*1-878096-14-1*) Best E TX Pubs.

Best of East Texas, 3. Bob Bowman. 1991. 14.95 (*1-878096-15-X*) Best E TX Pubs.

Best of Eddie Kantar. 214p. 1989. 13.95 (*0-940257-03-3*) Granovetter Bks.

Best of Edward Abbey. Edward Abbey. LC 87-23568. (Illus.). 400p. 1988. pap. 12.00 (*0-87156-786-5*) Sierra.

Best of Elektor Audio. Elektor Electronics Editors. (Illus.). 96p. (Orig.). 1993. pap. 16.95 (*1-882580-02-8*) Audio Amateur.

Best of Elvis. Cindy Hazer & Mike Freeman. 288p. 1994. mass mkt. 4.99 (*0-7860-0026-0*) Windsor NY.

Best of Elvis: Recollections of a Great Humanitarian. Mike Freeman & Cindy Hazen. LC 92-60186. 1992. pap. 12.95 (*0-9632274-0-8*) Memphis Explor.

Best of Elvis Collectibles. Steve Templeton et al. (Illus.). 129p. 1992. pap. 19.95 (*0-932807-77-1*) Overmountain Pr.

Best of Enemies. Carolyn Keene. Ed. by Ann Greenberg. (Nancy Drew & Hardy Boys Supermystery Ser.). 224p. (Orig.). (J). 1991. mass mkt. 3.99 (*0-671-67465-X*, Archway) PB.

Best of Enemies: Israel & Trans-Jordan in the 1948 War. Uri Bar-Joseph. 224p. 1986. 37.50 (*0-7146-3211-2*, Pub. by F Cass Pubs UK) Intl Spec Bk.

Best of Enterprise Incidents: The Magazine for Star Trek Fans. James Van Hise. 1990. pap. 9.95 (*1-55698-231-3*) Movie Pubs Servs.

Best of Eric Clapton: Piano, Vocal, Guitar. 112p. (Orig.). 1993. pap. 15.95 (*0-7935-2388-5*, HL00308182) H Leonard.

Best of Ernie Bushmillers Nancy. Brian Walker. LC 88-71457. (Illus.). 240p. pap. 10.95 (*0-318-41167-9*) Comicana.

Best of Ethan Allen. Ethan Allen. 116p. 1992. write for info. (*1-56541-225-7*); pap. write for info. (*1-56541-224-9*) Chalidze.

Best of Everything. Jana Ellis. LC 88-12380. (Merivale Mall Ser.). 160p. (YA). (gr. 7 up). 1988. pap. text ed. 2.50 (*0-8167-1356-1*) Troll Assocs.

Best of Everything. Rona Jaffe. 1976. reprint ed. lib. bdg. 28.95 (*0-89966-130-0*) Buccaneer Bks.

Best of Family Circle Cookbook. Family Circle Editors. Ed. by Diane Mogelever. LC 85-4465. 1985. 19.95 (*0-933585-00-4*) Family Circle Bks.

Best of Father Brown. G. K. Chesterton. Ed. by H. R. Keating. 310p. 1993. pap. 7.95 (*0-460-87395-4*, Everyman's Classic Lib) C E Tuttle.

***Best of Father Quotations.** Helen Exley. (Best of Quotations Ser.). (Illus.). 60p. Date not set. 6.99 (*1-85015-609-3*) Exley Giftbooks.

Best of Fiction Forum, Five. Ed. by John C. Brainerd. 40p. (Orig.). 1991. pap. 4.58 (*0-685-48277-4*) Dayspring Pr.

Best of Fiction Forum, Four. Ed. by John C. Brainerd. 40p. (Orig.). 1991. pap. 4.58 (*0-685-48276-6*) Dayspring Pr.

Best of Fiction Forum, One. Ed. by John C. Brainerd. 40p. (Orig.). 1991. pap. 4.58 (*0-685-48273-1*) Dayspring Pr.

Best of Fiction Forum, Three. Ed. by John C. Brainerd. 40p. (Orig.). 1991. pap. 4.58 (*0-685-48275-8*) Dayspring Pr.

Best of Fiction Forum, Two. Ed. by John C. Brainerd. 40p. (Orig.). 1991. pap. 4.58 (*0-685-48274-X*) Dayspring Pr.

***Best of Field & Stream: 100 Years of Great Writing From America's Premier Sporting Magazine.** Ed. by J. I. Merrit et al. LC 94-37855. (Illus.). 352p. 1995. 25.00 (*1-55821-288-4*) Lyons & Burford.

Best of Fifty. Intro. by Katherine Hanna. LC 77-70784. (Illus.). 84p. (Orig.). 1977. pap. 3.00 (*0-915577-00-3*) Taft Museum.

Best of Fine Gardening: Great Gardens. Fine Gardening Magazine Editors Staff. LC 93-41877. 1994. pap. 14.95 (*1-56158-078-3*) Taunton.

Best of Fine Gardening: Perennials. Fine Gardening Staff. LC 93-3150. 1993. pap. 14.95 (*1-56158-054-6*) Taunton.

Best of Fine Gardening: Shrubs & Trees. Fine Gardening Staff. LC 93-3134. 1993. pap. 14.95 (*1-56158-055-4*) Taunton.

Best of Fine Woodworking: Finishes & Finishing Techniques. 1991. pap. 14.95 (*1-56158-003-1*) Taunton.

Best of Fine Woodworking: Joinery Techniques. Fine Woodworking Magazine Editors. Ed. by Helen Albert. 1993. pap. text ed. write for info. (*1-56158-060-0*) Taunton.

Best of Fine Woodworking: Modern Furniture Projects. Fine Woodworking Magazine Editors. Ed. by John Kelsey. 128p. 1991. pap. 14.95 (*0-942391-91-8*) Taunton.

Best of Fine Woodworking: Modern Woodworking Techniques. Fine Woodworking Magazine Editors. Ed. by John Kelsey. 128p. 1991. pap. 14.95 (*0-942391-92-6*) Taunton.

Best of Fine Woodworking: Router Projects & Techniques. Fine Woodworking Magazine Editors. 1992. pap. 14.95 (*1-56158-002-3*) Taunton.

Best of Fine Woodworking: Small Woodworking Projects. Fine Woodworking Magazine Editors. 1992. pap. 14.95 (*1-56158-018-X*) Taunton.

Best of Fine Woodworking: The Small Wood Shop. Fine Woodworking Magazine Editors. Ed. by Helen Albert. 1993. pap. text ed. write for info. (*1-56158-061-9*) Taunton.

Best of Fine Woodworking: Traditional Furniture Projects. Fine Woodworking Magazine Editors. Ed. by John Kelsey. 128p. 1991. pap. 14.95 (*0-942391-93-4*) Taunton.

Best of Fine Woodworking: Traditional Woodworking Techniques. Fine Woodworking Magazine Editors. Ed. by John Kelsey. 128p. 1991. pap. 14.95 (*0-942391-94-2*) Taunton.

Best of Fine Woodworking Bench Tools. Fine Woodworking Magazine Editors. Ed. by Andrew Schultz. 128p. 1990. pap. text ed. 14.95 (*0-942391-84-5*) Taunton.

Best of Fine Woodworking Power Saws & Planers. Fine Woodworking Magazine Editors. Ed. by Andrew Schultz. 128p. 1990. pap. 14.95 (*0-942391-83-7*) Taunton.

Best of Finnish Americana. Mike Karni. 1994. pap. 14.95 (*1-57216-003-9*) Penfield.

Best of Fisher: Twenty-Eight Years of Editorial Cartoons from Faubus to Clinton. George Fisher. LC 92-23222. (Illus.). 288p. 1993. 24.95 (*1-55728-268-4*); pap. 14.95 (*1-55728-269-2*) U of Ark Pr.

Best of Florida. Andre Gayot. 1993. pap. 17.00 (*1-881066-07-X*) Gault Millau.

Best of Folk & Rock Guitar. (Best of...for Guitar Ser.). 128p. (Orig.). 1993. pap. 14.95 (*0-89724-106-1*) Warner Brothers.

Best of Folk-Pop-Rock. Brimhall. 1990. 4.95 (*0-685-32045-6*, H443) Hansen Ed Mus.

Best of Food & Wine. LC 83-26634. (Illus.). 240p. 1984. 19.95 (*0-916103-00-5*) Am Express Food.

Best of France: A Cookbook. Ed. by Evie Righter. (Best of Ser.). 96p. 1992. 14.95 (*0-00-255086-5*) Collins SF.

Best of France, '94-'95. 6th ed. Andre Gayot. 1994. pap. 20.00 (*1-881066-09-6*) Gault Millau.

***Best of France, 95-96.** 7th ed. Andre Gayot. 1995. 20.00 (*1-881066-18-5*) Gault Millau.

***Best of Free Spirit: Five Years of Award-Winning News & Views on Growing Up.** Free Spirit Editors Staff. (Illus.). 276p. (Orig.). (YA). (gr. 5 up). 1995. pap. 23.95 (*0-915793-91-1*) Free Spirit Pub.

Best of "Freedom after Fifty" Dorothy Kostka. 1976. pap. text ed. 4.50 (*0-87315-065-1*) Golden Bell.

***Best of Fresh Hot Bread II.** Ed. by Waverley Writers Staff. 68p. (Orig.). 1994. pap. 6.47 (*0-9627007-3-8*) Monday Pr CA.

Best of Friends. (Jataka Tales Ser.). (Illus.). 32p. (Orig.). (J). (gr. 1-5). 1989. 15.95 (*0-89800-186-2*); pap. 7.95 (*0-89800-187-0*) Dharma Pub.

***Best of Friends.** Andrews & McMeel Staff. 1994. 6.95 (*0-8362-4724-8*) Andrews & McMeel.

Best of Friends. James Elward. 1970. pap. 4.75 (*0-8222-0108-9*) Dramatists Play.

Best of Friends. Debbie Hansen. 168p. (Orig.). 1993. pap. 5.95 (*1-56245-070-0*) Great Quotations.

Best of Friends. Nancy Lindquist. 1991. pap. 4.99 (*0-8024-1081-2*) Moody.

***Best of Friends.** Pamela Prince. 1994. pap. 5.99 (*0-517-13137-4*) Random.

Best of Friends. Dee Reiser & Teresa Dormer. LC 85-90457. 168p. (Orig.). 1985. pap. 9.95 (*0-9615950-5-1*) Best Friends.

Best of Friends. Alan Thornhill. 1989. 7.50 (*0-551-01395-8*, Pub. by Marshall Pickering) Grosvenor USA.

Best of Friends. Susan Walley. Ed. by Elizabeth Lyall. (Light Line Ser.). (Illus.). 156p. (Orig.). (J). (gr. 4-8). 1980. pap. 5.95 (*0-89084-486-0*) Bob Jones Univ Pr.

Best of Friends. 2nd ed. Teresa Dormer & Dee Reiser. 168p. 1987. pap. 9.95 (*0-9615950-4-3*) Best Friends.

Best of Friends: A Cookbook. Friends of the Maitland Public Library Staff. Ed. by Mary J. Coltan. (Illus.). 254p. (Orig.). 1984. pap. 10.00 (*0-9614036-0-8*) Maitland Lib.

Best of Friends: Adventures with Goldens & Other Family Members. Richard S. Jackson. (Illus.). 64p. (Orig.). 1994. pap. 8.95 (*1-56474-090-0*) Fithian Pr.

Best of Friends: Sixth Grade Can Really Kill You; Sixth Grade Sleepover; Sixth Grade Secrets; & A Really Popular Girl. (J). (gr. 2-6). 1989. boxed 11.00 (*0-590-63454-2*) Scholastic Inc.

Best of Friends, Etc. Cookbook: Easy & Elegant for People-on-the-Go. 2nd ed. Darlene G. Skees. (Illus.). 272p. 1987. spiral bd. 13.95 (*0-9619158-0-3*) Rembrandt MT.

Best of Friends, the Worst of Enemies. Eva Margolies. 1987. 4.50 (*0-317-61573-4*) PB.

Best of Friends, Too! Cookbook, Vol. 2: Town & Country Cuisine for People on the Go. Darlene G. Skees. LC 90-91505. (Illus.). 352p. 1990. spiral bd. 13.95 (*0-9619158-1-1*) Rembrandt MT.

Best of Friends, Vol. 3: Festive Occasions: Festive Cooking for People-on-the-Go. Darlene G. Skees. LC 93-92726. (Illus.). 350p. 1993. spiral bd. 13.95 (*0-9619158-2-X*) Rembrandt MT.

Best of G. Campbell Morgan. G. Campbell Morgan. Ed. by Ralph G. Turnbull. (Best Ser.). 232p. 1991. reprint ed. pap. 7.99 (*0-8010-6282-9*) Baker Bk.

BEST of Games That Come Alive! Jerry D. Poppen. (Illus.). 235p. (Orig.). (C). 1990. pap. text ed. 15.00 (*0-9608868-4-2*) Action Prods.

Best of Garth Brooks. Garth Brooks. Ed. by Carol Cuellar & Aaron Stang. 116p. (Orig.). (YA). 1992. pap. text ed. 16.95 (*0-89898-633-8*) CPP Belwin.

***Best of Garth Brooks: Greatest Hits Tabulation.** Cpp Belwin Staff. 1993. pap. 16.95 (*0-89898-632-X*) CPP Belwin.

Best of Gauntlet. Ed. by Barry Hoffman. (Orig.). 1994. pap. 12.95 (*1-56333-202-7*) Masquerade.

Best of General Information. Andrea Lazzari et al. 1993. 19.95 (*1-55999-391-X*) LinguiSystems.

Best of George Ade. Ed. by A. L. Lazarus. LC 84-43170. (Illus.). 280p. 1985. 17.95 (*0-253-10609-5*) Ind U Pr.

***Best of George Benson.** (Piano-Vocal-Guitar Ser.). 80p. 1994. 14.95 (*0-7935-2395-8*) H Leonard.

***Best of Germany.** 2nd ed. Andre Gayot. 1995. 20.00 (*1-881066-15-0*) Gault Millau.

Best of Gil Thorp. Ed. by Matt Shaughnessy. 200p. (Orig.). 1985. pap. 10.95 (*0-930099-02-8*) Take Five Pubs.

Best of Gil Thorp, Vol. 2. Jack Berrill. Ed. by Matt Shaughnessy. (Illus.). 256p. (Orig.). 1988. pap. 16.95 (*0-930099-03-6*) Take Five Pubs.

***Best of Gil Thorp Vol. 3, Vol. 3.** Jack Berrill. 256p. 1989. pap. 19.95 (*0-930099-04-4*) Take Five Pubs.

Best of Gilbert & Sullivan. (Illus.). 256p. 1981. pap. 14.95 (*0-88188-169-4*, 00312177) H Leonard.

Best of Gimmicks & Gadgets. 122p. 1990. spiral bd. 24.50 (*0-89867-524-3*) Am Water Wks Assn.

Best of Go Graphics. Ed. by Larry W. Wood. (Compuserve Directories Ser.: Bk. 1). (Illus.). 550p. (Orig.). 1992. pap. 12.50 (*1-881257-00-2*) PRC Database.

Best of Go Graphics. Ed. by Larry W. Wood. (Compuserve Directories Ser.: Bk. 2). (Illus.). 608p. (Orig.). 1992. pap. 16.00 (*1-881257-01-0*) PRC Database.

Best of Gottlieb's Bottom Line: A Practical Profit Guide for Today's Food Service Operator. Leon Gottlieb. LC 80-16535. 1980. pap. 21.95 (*0-912016-39-6*) Lebhar Friedman.

Best of Gourmet, Vol. 1. Gourmet Magazine Editors. LC 85-24458. (Illus.). 320p. 1986. 24.95 (*0-394-55258-X*) Random.

Best of Gourmet, Vol. 2. Gourmet Magazine Editors. LC 85-24458. (Illus.). 320p. 1987. 24.95 (*0-394-56039-6*) Random.

Best of Gourmet, Vol. 3. Gourmet Magazine Editors. LC 87-640167. (Illus.). 320p. 1988. 24.95 (*0-394-56955-5*) Random.

Best of Gourmet, Vol. 4. Gourmet Magazine Editors. 1989. 24.95 (*0-394-57529-6*) Random.

Best of Gourmet, Vol. 5. Gourmet Magazine Editors. (Illus.). 336p. 1990. 24.95 (*0-394-58321-3*) Random.

Best of Gourmet, Vol. VI. Gourmet Magazine Staff. 1991. 27.45 (*0-679-40068-0*) Random.

Best of Gourmet, Vol. 7. Gourmet Magazine Staff. 1992. 27.50 (*0-679-41204-2*) McKay.

Best of Gourmet: Featuring the Flavors of China. 1994. 28.00 (*0-679-43347-3*) Random.

Best of Gourmet: Featuring the Flavors of Italy. Gourmet Magazine Editors. LC 92-36723. 336p. 1993. 28.00 (*0-679-42364-8*) Random.

***Best of Gourmet: Flavor Mexico.** Gourmet Magazine Editors. 1995. 28.00 (*0-679-44146-8*) Random.

Best of Gourmet Recipes for Two. Beatrice Ojakangas. 1993. pap. 5.95 (*0-934860-99-8*) Adventure Pubns.

***Best of Grand Canyon Nature Notes.** Ed. by Susan Lamb. 168p. 1994. pap. 11.95 (*0-938216-49-X*) GCNHA.

Best of Granta Reportage. Ed. by Bill Buford. 448p. 1994. pap. 11.95 (*0-14-014071-9*, Penguin Bks) Viking Penguin.

Best of Granta Travel. 1992. pap. 12.00 (*0-14-014041-7*, Penguin Bks) Viking Penguin.

***Best of Grateful Dead for Guitar.** 92p. (Orig.). 1994. pap. 12.95 (*0-89724-264-5*) Warner Brothers.

Best of Gravestone Humor. Louis S. Schafer. LC 89-49402. (Illus.). 128p. (Orig.). (J). (gr. 4 up). 1990. pap. 5.95 (*0-8069-7274-2*) Sterling.

***Best of Guns n' Roses for Easy Guitar.** 61p. Date not set. pap. 12.95 (*0-89524-891-3*, 02506875) Cherry Lane.

***Best of Guns 'n Roses (Vocal - Guitar)** 79p. (Orig.). (YA). 1994. pap. write for info. (*0-89524-845-X*, 02502126) Cherry Lane.

Best of H. E. Bates. H. E. Bates. LC 76-167441. (Short Story Index Reprint Ser.). 1977. reprint ed. 37.95 (*0-8369-3967-0*) Ayer.

Best of H. P. Lovecraft: Bloodcurdling Tales of Horror & the Macabre. H. P. Lovecraft. 304p. 1987. pap. 10.00 (*0-345-35080-4*) Ballantine.

Best of Hagar. Dik Browne. LC 85-72413. (Illus.). 240p. pap. 10.95 (*0-03-005599-7*) Comicana.

Best of Hair Trigger. 2nd rev. ed. Intro. by John Schultz. 500p. 1992. pap. 8.95 (*0-932026-31-1*) Columbia College Chi.

Best of Hank Williams. (Piano-Vocal-Guitar Personality Folio Ser.). 96p. (Orig.). 1990. pap. 12.95 (*0-7935-0087-X*, 00490475) H Leonard.

Best of Hank Williams, Jr., No. 371. (Easy ABC Music for All Keyboards Ser.). 64p. 1990. pap. 4.95 (*0-7935-0210-1*, HL00001337) H Leonard.

***Best of Hawaii.** 2nd ed. Andre Gayot. 1994. pap. 18.00 (*1-881066-13-4*) Gault Millau.

Best of Hawaii. 2nd rev. ed. Jocelyn K. Fujii. LC 93-13711. 1994. 16.00 (*0-517-88001-6*, Crown) Crown Pub Group.

Best of Hawthorne. Ed. by Mark Van Doren. LC 51-9259. 444p. reprint ed. pap. 126.60 (*0-8357-9845-3*, 2012525) Bks Demand.

Best of Healthy Exchanges Food Newsletter. JoAnna M. Lund. (Illus.). 180p. (Orig.). 1993. 11.50 (*0-9635632-1-1*) Hlthy Exchange.

***Best of Heart-Y Cooking.** Diana Helfand. (Illus.). 96p. (Orig.). 1995. pap. 12.95 (*1-886229-09-0*) Hawaiian Resources.

***Best of Hearts.** 10th aniversary ed. Lighten Up Enterprises Staff. 1994. pap. 6.50 (*1-879127-30-X*) Lighten Up Enter.

Best of Herb Caen: 1960-1975. Herb Caen. Ed. by Irene Mecchi. 240p. 1991. 18.95 (*0-8118-0020-2*) Chronicle Bks.

Best of Herman. Jim Unger. (Illus.). 208p. (Orig.). 1993. pap. 10.95 (*0-8362-1727-6*) Andrews & McMeel.

Best of Herman Sourdough. Watland-Johanson. 1991. 4.95 (*0-934860-66-1*) Adventure Pubns.

Best of Herman Sourdough Giftpack. Adventure Staff. 1991. 9.95 (*0-934860-67-X*) Adventure Pubns.

Best of Heydays: A Warm & Witty Hooray! for Yesterday & Today. Ed Hayes. LC 92-28022. 224p. 1992. pap. 9.95 (*0-939009-65-X*) EPM Pubns.

Best of Hi & Lois. Mort Walker & Dik Browne. LC 86-81210. (Illus.). 240p. pap. 10.95 (*0-318-41166-0*) Comicana.

Best of Hill & Valley. Illus. by Boyd Carr et al. 1985. pap. write for info. (*0-943461-00-6*) Hill & Valley Pub.

Best of Honey Giftpack. Adventure Staff. 1991. 9.95 (*0-934860-69-6*) Adventure Pubns.

Best of Honey Recipes. Beatrice Ojakangas. 1991. 5.95 (*0-934860-68-8*) Adventure Pubns.

Best of Hot Tip Harry. Ed. by David Cohn. LC 92-43874. 282p. 1993. disk, pap. 29.95 (*0-929870-14-X*) Advanstar Commns.

Best of How to Win at Nintendo Games. Jeff Rovin. 1992. mass mkt. 5.99 (*0-312-92874-2*) St Martin.

Best of Huey Lewis & the News: Piano - Vocal. Ed. by Milton Okun. (Illus.). 158p. (Orig.). 1990. pap. text ed. 17.95 (*0-89524-341-5*) Cherry Lane.

Best of Human Events: Fifty Years of Conservative Thought & Action. Ed. by Thomas Winter & Renatti Dupont. LC 93-77299. 304p. 1994. 34.95 (*1-56384-018-9*) Huntington Hse.

Best of Humanism. Ed. by Roger E. Greeley. LC 87-43317. 224p. (Orig.). 1987. 19.95 (*0-87975-381-1*) Prometheus Bks.

Best of Huntsville, '90s Edition. Mike Kaylor. Ed. by Michael R. Kaylor & Jennifer W. Kaylor. (Illus.). 200p. 1992. 15.95 (*0-916039-06-4*); pap. text ed. 9.95 (*0-916039-07-2*) Kaylor Christ Co.

Best of Ice Cream. Beverly Cox & Malvina Kinard. 1994. 14.95 (*0-00-255253-1*) Collins SF.

Best of Ideals. Ideals Magazine Staff. (Illus.). 1989. 22.95 (*0-8249-4037-7*) Ideals.

Best of India. Balraj Khanna. LC 93-8401. (Illus.). 1993. 14.95 (*0-00-255223-X*) Collins SF.

Best of India. Paige Palmer. LC 86-25304. 196p. 1987. pap. 7.95 (*0-87576-128-3*) Pilot Bks.

Best of Instauration 1976. Ed. by Wilmot Robertson. 117p. 1980. pap. 10.00 (*0-914576-11-9*) Howard Allen.

Best of Instauration 1977. Ed. by Wilmot Robertson. 127p. 1982. pap. 10.00 (*0-914576-19-4*) Howard Allen.

Best of Instauration 1978. Ed. by Wilmot Robertson. 119p. 1986. pap. 12.00 (*0-914576-20-8*) Howard Allen.

Best of Intentions. Sandra S. Yamate. LC 93-45794. (Illus.). (J). 1994. 12.95 (*1-879965-09-7*) Polychrome Pub.

Best of Intentions: And Other Stories. Artie Shaw. LC 89-1585. 168p. (Orig.). 1989. pap. 9.95 (*0-936784-74-1*) J Daniel.

Best of International Self-Promotion. Supon Phornirunlit. 1993. 45.00 (*0-942604-32-6*) Madison Square.

Best of Iron-on Transfers. Joni Prittie. (Illus.). 87p. 1990. 9.95 (*0-937769-53-3*) Mark Inc CA.

***Best of Italian Regional Cookbook.** Carla Capalbo. (Illus.). 128p. 1995. 14.98 (*0-8317-0744-5*) Smithmark.

***Best of Italy.** Andre Gayot. 1995. 20.00 (*1-881066-16-9*) Gault Millau.

Best of Italy: A Cookbook. Ed. by Evie Righter. (Best of Ser.). 96p. 1992. 14.95 (*0-00-255085-7*) Collins SF.

Best of It's Simple: Easy Recipes for Todays Lifestyles & Tastes. Ann Heller. Ed. by Kate Lawson. (Illus.). 147p. 1992. pap. text ed. 9.95 (*0-9616347-6-6*) Dayton Newspapers.

Best of J. E. Coleman: Clockmaker. Orville R. Hagans. 1979. 30.00 (*0-918845-02-5*) Am Watchmakers.

***Best of J. L. Bolar.** Jerry L. Bolar. 120p. (Orig.). 1995. pap. write for info. (*1-57502-031-9*) Morris Pub.

Best of Jack Vance. Jack Vance. 1993. reprint ed. lib. bdg. 18.95 (*0-89968-379-7*, Lghtyr Pr) Buccaneer Bks.

***Best of Jackson Browne, Eagles & Neil Young for Guitar.** 96p. (Orig.). 1994. pap. 12.95 (*0-89724-423-0*) Warner Brothers.

Best of Jake Winkman. Don Von Elsner. LC 84-223821. 117p. 1981. pap. 5.95 (*0-939460-16-5*) Devyn Pr.

Best of James H. Schmitz. James Schmitz. Ed. by Mark Olson. LC 91-61064. (Illus.). 243p. 1991. 18.95 (*0-915368-46-3*) New Eng SF Assoc.

Best of James Herriot. James Herriot. (Illus.). 504p. 1983. 26.95 (*0-312-07716-5*) St Martin.

Best of James Herriot. deluxe ed. James Herriot. (Illus.). 504p. 1983. Signed, gilt-edged, leather, limited ed. of five hundred copies. 300.00 (*0-312-07718-1*) St Martin.

Best of James Whitcomb Riley. James W. Riley. Ed. by Donald C. Manlove. LC 82-47958. (Illus.). 224p. 1982. 17.95 (*0-253-10610-9*); pap. 8.95 (*0-253-20299-X*, MB-299) Ind U Pr.

***Best of Jams: From Amish & Mennonite Kitchens.** 1995. pap. text ed. 1.95 (*1-56148-163-7*) Good Bks PA.

An Asterisk (*) at the beginning of an entry indicates that the title is appearing in BIP for the first time.

Best of Jazz: The Essential Guide. Martin Gayford. 1993. 9.95 (*0-00-255339-2*) Collins SF.

Best of Jazz Score. Ed. by Roy Pellett. (Illus.). 160p. 1994. 17.95 (*0-563-36326-6*, BBC-Parkwest) Parkwest Pubns.

Best of "Jelly Roll" Morton. (Piano Solos Ser.). 48p. (Orig.). 1993. pap. 7.95 (*0-7935-2063-0*, 00292023) H Leonard.

Best of Jim Fisher. James J. Fisher. Ed. by Roger O'Connor. 154p. 1992. 24.95 (*1-882355-00-8*); pap. 14.95 (*1-882355-01-6*) Mostly Bks Pub.

Best of Joan Hohl: The Tawny Gold Man - Morning Rose, Evening Savage. Amii Lorin, pseud. 382p. 1989. reprint ed. pap. 3.95 (*0-8439-2738-0*) Dorchester Pub Co.

Best of Joan Hohl Writing As Amii Lorin Snowbound Weekend - Gambler's Love. Joan Hohl. 368p. 1989. reprint ed. pap. 3.95 (*0-8439-2726-7*) Dorchester Pub Co.

Best of John Axe. John Axe. (Illus.). 192p. (Orig.). 1991. pap. 14.95 (*0-87588-373-7*) Hobby Hse.

***Best of John Denver for Easy Guitar.** Ed. by Milton Okun. 64p. (YA). Date not set. pap. 9.95 (*0-89524-913-8*) Cherry Lane.

***Best of John Denver for Easy Piano.** Ed. by Milton Okun. 63p. Date not set. pap. 9.95 (*0-89524-910-3*) Cherry Lane.

Best of John Henry Jowett. John H. Jowett. Ed. by Gerald Kennedy. LC 79-179729. (Biography Index Reprint Ser.). 1977. reprint ed. 18.95 (*0-8369-8097-2*) Ayer.

Best of Jones & Schmidt. (Illus.). 182p. 1991. 14.95 (*0-7935-0024-9*, HL00490285) H Leonard.

Best of Judson Cornwall: Anthology of Judson's Writings for the Last Twenty-Five Years. Judson Cornwall. 180p. (Orig.). 1992. pap. 7.95 (*0-88270-655-1*) Bridge Pub.

Best of Just Cross Stitch. Oxmoor Staff. 1994. pap. 14.95 (*0-8487-1421-0*) Oxmoor Hse.

Best of Kin Hubbard: Abe Martin's Sayings & Wisecracks, Abe's Neighbors, His Almanack, Comic Drawings. Kin Hubbard. Ed. by David S. Hawes. LC 84-47704. 154p. 1984. reprint ed. pap. 43.90 (*0-7837-3712-2*, 2057890) Bks Demand.

Best of Knife World, Vol. 2. Knife World Publications Staff. LC 81-168825. (Illus.). 224p. 1984. pap. 6.95 (*0-940362-07-4*) Knife World.

***Best of Koltavowski.** George Koltavowski. Ed. by Tom Dorsch. LC 95-75438. (Orig.). Date not set. pap. write for info. (*1-886040-15-X*) Hypermodern Pr.

Best of K'tonton. Sadie R. Weilerstein. LC 80-20177. (Illus.). 96p. (J). (gr. 1 up). 1980. pap. 9.95 (*0-8276-0187-5*) JPS Phila.

Best of Larry Alcala's Mang Ambo, Bk. 2. Larry Alcala. (Illus.). 66p. (Orig.). 1993. pap. 6.75 (*971-10-0523-9*, Pub. by New Day Pub PH) Cellar.

***Best of Larry King Live: The Greatest Interviews.** Sel. by Larry King. LC 95-22. 1995. 10.95 (*1-57036-208-4*) Turner Pub GA.

***Best of Latin American Short Stories - A Bilingual Edition: Los Mejores Cuentos Hispanoamericanos.** Anthony Ramierz. Ed. by Bernard H. Hamel. 114p. (Orig.). 1994. spiral bd., pap. 10.95 (*1-886835-02-0*) Bilingual Bk Pr.

Best of Lawrence Green. Ed. by Maureen Barnes. 400p. (C). 1986. 49.00 (*0-317-89987-2*) St Mut.

***Best of Lemmons.** 46p. 1995. write for info. (*1-57215-044-0*) World Pubns.

Best of Lenny Kravitz. Ed. by Milton Okun. 1994. pap. 12.95 (*0-89524-829-8*) Cherry Lane.

Best of Lenny Kravitz for Guitar. 1994. pap. 17.95 (*0-89524-811-5*) Cherry Lane.

Best of Lenotre: Glorious Desserts from France's Finest Pastry Maker. Gaston Lenotre. Tr. by Philip Hyman & Mary Hyman. 1983. pap. 14.95 (*0-8120-2450-8*) Barron.

Best of Lester Del Rey. Lester Del Rey. (Del Rey Bk.). 384p. 1986. pap. 5.99 (*0-345-32933-3*) Ballantine.

Best of Lewis Carroll. Lewis Carroll. (J). 1992. 7.98 (*0-89009-700-3*) Bk Sales Inc.

Best of Life. Life Magazine Editors. 1988. 19.99 (*0-517-61940-7*) Random Hse Value.

Best of Life. Ed. by David E. Scherman. 1976. pap. 14.95 (*0-380-00187-X*) Avon.

***Best of Lindsay Welsh.** Lindsay Welsh. (Orig.). 1995. mass mkt., pap. 5.95 (*1-56333-368-6*) Masquerade.

Best of Little Spouse on the Prairie. Lana Robinson. 1993. pap. 9.95 (*0-9636248-0-6*) Bedford Hse.

Best of Live Steam: Nineteen Sixty-Six to Nineteen Seventy-One, Vol. 1. Ed. by Joe D. Rice. LC 85-51037. (Illus.). 176p. 1985. 26.95 (*0-914104-08-X*) Wildwood Pubns MI.

***Best of Local Angle.** Bruce Greeley. 48p. 1993. pap. 7.95 (*1-881147-07-X*) Lowell Print.

Best of London: Over One Thousand Frank & Witty Reviews of Restaurants, Hotels, Nightspots, Shops. Andre Gayot. 1994. pap. 20.00 (*1-881066-11-8*) Gault Millau.

Best of Lord Krishna's Cuisine. abr. ed. Yamuna Devi. Ed. by Joshua M. Greene & Philip Gallelli. Orig. Title: Lord Krishna's Cuisine: The Art of Indian Vegetarian Cooking. (Illus.). 256p. 1991. pap. 12.95 (*0-89647-029-6*) Bala Bks.

Best of Lord Krishna's Cuisine: Favorite Recipes from "The Art of Indian Vegetarian Cooking" Yamuna Devi. 256p. (Orig.). 1991. pap. 12.95 (*0-452-26683-1*, Plume) NAL-Dutton.

Best of Los Angeles. (Gault Millau Ser.). 450p. 1992. pap. 17.00 (*0-13-089475-3*, P-H Travel) P-H Gen Ref & Trav.

Best of Los Angeles & Southern California. 4th ed. Ed. by Andre Gayot et al. LC 92-40137. 1992. 18.00 (*1-881066-01-0*) Gault Millau.

***Best of Mable.** Edwin Purviance. 100p. 1995. pap. text ed. 4.00 (*0-9620694-4-2*) E & M Purviance.

Best of Madonna, No. 362. (Easy ABC Music for All Keyboards Ser.). 64p. 1990. pap. 5.95 (*0-7935-0195-4*, HL00001427) H Leonard.

Best of Maine Railroads. Ron Johnson. (Illus.). 144p. 1985. pap. 14.95 (*0-9615157-0-8*) Four Hun Svty RR.

Best of Mang Ambo. Larry Alcala. (Illus.). 132p. (Orig.). 1989. pap. 6.50 (*971-10-0372-4*, Pub. by New Day Pub PH) Cellar.

Best of Marco Island. Van B. Hooper & Joan S. Hooper. (Illus.). 144p. (Orig.). 1991. pap. 5.95 (*1-879685-01-9*) Hooper Pub FL.

Best of Marion Zimmer Bradley. Marion Zimmer Bradley. Ed. by Martin H. Greenberg. 365p. 1991. 18.95 (*0-685-47743-6*) Mapes Monde.

Best of Marion Zimmer Bradley's Fantasy Magazine. Ed. by Marion Zimmer Bradley. 256p. (Orig.). 1994. mass mkt. 4.99 (*0-446-60140-3*, Aspect) Warner Bks.

***Best of Marion Zimmer Bradley's Fantasy Magazine, Vol. II.** Ed. by Marion Zimmer Bradley & Elisabeth Waters. 256p. (Orig.). 1995. mass mkt. 5.99 (*0-446-60192-6*, Aspect) Warner Bks.

***Best of Marty Robbins.** Ed. by Carol Cuellar. (Legendary Performers Ser.). 84p. (Orig.). (YA). 1995. pap. text ed. 13.95 (*0-89724-523-7*) Warner Brothers.

Best of Martyn Lloyd-Jones. D. Martyn Lloyd-Jones. Ed. by Christopher Catherwood. 144p. (Orig.). 1993. pap. 9.99 (*0-8010-5686-1*) Baker Bk.

***Best of Marv Taylor.** Marv Taylor. 178p. 1994. pap. 22.95 (*0-9645155-1-2*) Belly Boat Pub.

Best of Marvel Comics, Vol. 1. 260p. 1987. 19.95 (*0-87135-292-3*) Marvel Entmnt.

***Best of Marvel 1994.** Mark Gruenwald. 240p. 1994. pap. 12.95 (*0-7851-0071-7*) Marvel Entmnt.

Best of Mary Love. Mary Love. (Orig.). 1993. pap. text ed. 4.95 (*1-56333-099-7*) Masquerade.

Best of Maui: Sports, Recreation, Dining, & Shopping. Ed. by Joe Harabin. (Illus.). 1995. 12.00 (*1-884364-20-9*) Sandwich Islands.

Best of Maui: Sports, Recreation, Shopping, Dining. Ed. by Joe Harabin. (Illus.). 1990. text ed. 7.95 (*0-9624676-1-8*) Sandwich Islands.

Best of Me. M. E. Slack. Ed. by Ceil Cleveland. 136p. 1991. 12.95 (*0-9630675-9-1*) Mill Pond NY.

***Best of Meats: From Amish & Mennonite Kitchens.** 1995. pap. text ed. 1.95 (*1-56148-162-9*) Good Bks PA.

Best of Medical Humor. Intro. by Howard J. Bennett. LC 90-85031. (Illus.). 249p. 1991. text ed. 31.00 (*1-56053-003-0*) Hanley & Belfus.

Best of Meister Eckhart. Meister Eckhart. Ed. by Halcyon Backhouse. LC 92-29381. 144p. (Orig.). 1993. reprint ed. pap. 10.95 (*0-8245-1262-6*) Crossroad NY.

Best of Mennonite Fellowship Meals. Phyllis P. Good & Louise Stoltzfus. LC 91-74051. 304p. 1991. pap. 11.95 (*1-56148-048-7*) Good Bks PA.

Best of Metal: The Essential Guide. Paul Elliott & Jon Hotten. 1993. 9.95 (*0-00-255336-8*) Collins SF.

Best of Metal Guitar. 128p. (Orig.). 1993. pap. 14.95 (*0-89724-107-X*) Warner Brothers.

Best of Mexico: A Cookbook. Evie Righter. LC 92-19622. (Illus.). 96p. 1992. 14.95 (*0-00-255148-9*) Collins SF.

Best of MGM. Elizabeth M. Montgomery. 1993. 15.98 (*1-55521-953-5*) Bk Sales Inc.

Best of Michael Franks for Guitar. (Best of...for Guitar Ser.). 56p. (Orig.). pap. 12.95 (*0-89724-036-7*) Warner Brothers.

***Best of Michael Rosen: Poetry for Kids.** Michael Rosen. (Illus.). 150p. (Orig.). (J). (gr. 1-5). 1995. pap. 15.95 (*0-614-03292-X*, Wetlands Pr) RDR Bks.

Best of Mick Mayoh: Poems of Australia. Boolarong Publications Staff. 143p. (C). 1990. 48.00 (*0-7316-7609-2*, Pub. by Boolarong Pubns AT) St Mut.

Best of Mignery. Herb Mignery. Ed. by Cornhuskers Press Staff. LC 85-70978. 1985. pap. text ed. 15.95 (*0-933909-01-2*) Cornhusker Pr.

Best of Mike Grenby: A Year-Round Guide to Managing Your Money. Mike Grenby. (Financial Ser.). (Illus.). 208p. (Orig.). 1989. Canadian ed. pap. 7.95 (*0-88908-880-2*) Self-Counsel Pr.

Best of Miniature Quilts. Chitra Publications Staff. Ed. by Joanne Nolt & Janice Johnson. LC 94-3825. (Illus.). 40p. (Orig.). 1994. pap. 9.95 (*0-9622565-5-2*) Chariot Pub PA.

Best of Model Railroading Track Plans. Ed. & Illus. by Robert Schleicher. LC 83-82161. 96p. 1983. pap. text ed. 6.50 (*0-9612692-0-0*) Rocky Mntn Pub Co.

Best of Montreal & Quebec City: A Guide to the Places, Peoples, & Pleasures of French Canada. Martin Kevan. (Illus.). 320p. 1992. pap. 14.00 (*0-517-58230-9*, Crown) Crown Pub Group.

***Best of Mother Goose.** (Tell Tale Theater Pop-up Bks. & Story Tape). (Illus.). 12p. 1995. digital audio, pap. 12.95 (*1-56138-502-6*) Running Pr.

Best of Mr. Punch: The Humorous Writings of Douglas Jerrold. Douglas W. Jerrold. Ed. by Richard Kelly. LC 73-111045. (Illus.). 412p. reprint ed. pap. 117.50 (*0-8357-6541-5*, 2035904) Bks Demand.

Best of My Very Own Recipes. Adventure Publications Staff. 1992. pap. 5.95 (*0-934860-92-0*) Adventure Pubns.

Best of Names. Ed. by Kelsie B. Harder. (International Library of Names). 400p. text ed. write for info. (*0-8290-1220-6*) Irvington.

***Best of Nature Quotations.** Helen Exley. (Best of Quotations Ser.). (Illus.). 60p. Date not set. 6.99 (*1-85015-526-7*) Exley Giftbooks.

Best of Nell: A Selection of Writings Over 14 Years. Nell McCafferty. 128p. (C). 1987. pap. 9.99 (*0-946211-06-X*, Pub. by Attic IE) InBook.

Best of Neon. Vilma Barr. (Illus.). 256p. 1991. 49.99 (*0-935603-60-3*, 30385) Rockport Pubs.

Best of Nevada: A Witty, Definitive & Remarkably Useful Guide to Las Vegas, Reno-Tahoe & Beyond. Ed. by Don W. Martin & Betty W. Martin. (Best of...Ser.: No. 5). (Illus.). 352p. (Orig.). 1992. pap. 12.95 (*0-942053-13-3*) Pine Cone Pr CA.

Best of New England Humor...Or Pretty Darn Close. Jim Brunelle. 256p. 1990. pap. 12.95 (*0-89909-226-8*, 80-550-3) Yankee Bks.

Best of New Orleans. 1994. 14.95 (*0-00-255477-1*) Collins SF.

Best of New York, 1994. 5th ed. Andre Gayot. 1994. pap. 18.00 (*1-881066-06-1*) Gault Millau.

Best of Newspaper Design. 12th ed. Society of Newspaper Design Staff. 224p. 1991. 39.95 (*1-878107-01-1*) Madison Square.

Best of Newspaper Design, No. 13. Comp. by Society of Newspaper Design Staff. (Illus.). 256p. 1992. 49.99 (*1-56496-027-7*, 30465) Rockport Pubs.

Best of Newspaper Design, No. 15. Society of Newspaper Design Staff. 256p. 1994. 49.99 (*1-56496-062-5*, 30557) Rockport Pubs.

***Best of Newspaper Design: Society of Publication Designers.** 16th ed. 256p. 1995. 49.99 (*1-56496-202-4*) Rockport Pubs.

***Best of Newspaper Design No. 15.** Date not set. 49.99 (*1-56496-149-4*) Rockport Pubs.

Best of Newspaper Design, 1984-1985: Society of Newspaper Design Annual Awards Competition. 6th ed. (Illus.). 304p. 1986. 39.95 (*0-89730-172-2*) Blue-Rib Grp.

Best of Nineteen-Eighty. Ed. by Arnold Perrin. 32p. (Orig.). 1981. pap. 2.95 (*0-939736-20-9*) Wings ME.

Best of Ninety-Niner, Vol. I. Ninety Niner Home Computer Magazine Editors. (Illus.). 360p. (Orig.). 1984. pap. 19.95 (*0-933094-11-6*) Emerald Pub.

Best of Nitty Gritty. Ed. by Laura Wilson. (Illus.). 192p. (Orig.). 1987. pap. 6.95 (*0-911954-86-4*) Bristol Pub Ent CA.

Best of Northern Italian Cooking. Hedy Giusti-Lanham & Andrea Dodi. 366p. (Orig.). 1994. pap. 14.95 (*0-8120-1122-8*) Barron.

Best of Nursing Humor. Ed. by Colleen Kenefick & Amy Young. (Illus.). 200p. 1993. text ed. 25.00 (*1-56053-062-6*) Hanley & Belfus.

Best of O. Henry. O. Henry. LC 91-58651. (Literary Classics Ser.). 176p. 1992. 5.98 (*1-56138-111-X*) Courage Bks.

Best of O. Henry. O. Henry. 234p. 1993. pap. text ed. 5.95 (*0-460-87339-3*, Everyman's Classic Lib) C E Tuttle.

Best of O. Henry. William S. Porter. (Illustrated Classics Collection 3). 64p. 1994. pap. 3.60 (*1-56103-540-8*) Lake Pub Co.

Best of O. Henry. abr. ed. William S. Porter. Ed. by John N. Fago. (Now Age Illustrated III Ser.). (Illus.). (J). (gr. 4-12). 1977. pap. 2.95 (*0-88301-268-5*) Pendulum Pr.

Best of O. Henry: Student Activity Book. Marcia Sohl & Gerald Dackerman. (Now Age Illustrated Ser.). (Illus.). (gr. 4-12). 1976. student ed 1.25 (*0-88301-292-8*) Pendulum Pr.

Best of O. Henry Readalong. William S. Porter. (Illustrated Classics Collection 3). 64p. 1994. audio, pap. 13.50 (*1-56103-542-4*) Lake Pub Co.

Best of Off Broadway: Eight Contemporary Obie-Winning Plays. Ed. by Ross Wetzsteon. 656p. (Orig.). 1994. pap. 6.99 (*0-451-62865-9*, Ment) NAL-Dutton.

Best of Old Dorp, Bk. I. Larry Hart. (Illus.). 284p. (Orig.). Date not set. pap. text ed. 16.50 (*0-932035-10-8*) Old Dorp Bks.

Best of Old Times Not Forgotten. Sammie J. Rhodes. LC 91-90544. 210p. 1991. pap. 11.95 (*0-9630257-0-8*) Cty Rhodes.

Best of Ontario. Mary MacPherson. 240p. 1994. pap. 19.95 (*1-55111-052-0*) Broadview Pr.

Best of OPL: Five Years of the One-Person Library. Guy St. Clair & Andrew Berner. 147p. 1990. 34.50 (*0-87111-357-0*) SLA.

Best of Orange County, California: A Guide to Scenic, Recreational & Historical Attractions. Gregory Lee. LC 93-24671. (Illus.). 304p. (Orig.). 1993. pap. 12.95 (*1-881409-05-8*) Jhnstn Assocs.

***Best of Oranges.** 46p. 1995. write for info. (*1-57215-041-6*) World Pubns.

Best of Orygun: Or, Learning How to Say Oregon So Everyone Won't Think You're from New Jersey. James Cloutier. LC 86-62944. (Illus.). 254p. 1986. pap. 7.95 (*0-918966-10-8*) Image West.

Best of Out of My Treasure. Don E. Boatman. 370p. (Orig.). 1990. pap. 6.95 (*0-89900-358-3*) College Pr Pub.

***Best of Painted Furniture.** Florence De Dampierre. LC 86-43192. (Illus.). 200p. 1995. pap. 29.95 (*0-8478-1886-1*) Rizzoli Intl.

Best of Pamela Sargent. Pamela Sargent. Ed. by Martin H. Greenberg. 322p. 1987. pap. 9.00 (*0-89733-241-5*) Academy Chi Pubs.

Best of Pancake & Waffle Giftpack. Adventure Staff. 1990. 17.95 (*0-934860-60-2*) Adventure Pubns.

Best of Pancake & Waffle Recipes. Beatrice Ojakangas. 102p. (Orig.). 1990. pap. 5.95 (*0-934860-59-9*) Adventure Pubns.

Best of Paris, 1994. 5th ed. Andre Gayot. 1994. pap. 20.00 (*1-881066-08-8*) Gault Millau.

***Best of Paris, 95.** 6th ed. Andre Gayot. 1995. 20.00 (*1-881066-17-7*) Gault Millau.

Best of Patsy Cline. (Piano-Vocal-Guitar Ser.). 80p. (Orig.). 1991. pap. 10.95 (*0-7935-0100-8*, 00490431) H Leonard.

***Best of Paula Vaughan.** Oxmoor Staff. 1994. 29.95 (*0-942237-49-8*) Leisure AR.

Best of Peaceful Easy Feeling. 1992. pap. 16.95 (*0-943351-46-4*, XW1507) Astor Bks.

Best of People & the Other Animals. abr. rev. ed. W. J. Resla. 200p. 1988. reprint ed. 14.00 (*0-318-35260-5*) Grant Dahlstrom.

Best of People & the Other Animals. W. J. Resla. Ed. by Elva Marshall. 200p. 1988. reprint ed. 14.00 (*0-9620682-0-9*) W J Resla.

***Best of Performance Support in the Workplace.** Ed. by Patricia A. Galagan & Ellen S. Carnevale. LC 94-71337. (Best of Ser.). 114p. 1994. pap. 25.00 (*1-56286-007-0*) Am Soc Train & Devel.

Best of Peter Marshall. Ed. by Catherine Marshall. LC 83-7341. 340p. 1988. reprint ed. pap. 11.99 (*0-8007-9123-1*) Chosen Bks.

Best of Photojournalism: Nineteen Newspaper & Magazine Pictures of the Year. Ed. by National Press Photographers Association Staff & University of Missouri School of Journalism Staff. (Illus.). 256p. (Orig.). 1994. pap. 21.95 (*1-56138-412-7*) Running Pr.

Best of Photojournalism, No. 18: Newspaper & Magazine Pictures of the Years. Ed. by National Press Photographers Association Staff & Universith of Missouri School of Journalism Staff. (Best of Photojournalism Ser.). (Illus.). 256p. (Orig.). 1993. pap. 21.95 (*1-56138-296-5*) Running Pr.

***Best of Pies: From Amish & Mennonite Kitchens.** 1995. pap. text ed. 1.95 (*1-56148-153-X*) Good Bks PA.

Best of Planning. Intro. by Melvin R. Levin. LC 88-83721. (Illus.). 614p. (Orig.). 1989. lib. bdg. 45.00 (*0-918286-59-X*); pap. text ed. 29.95 (*0-918286-60-3*) Planners Pr.

Best of Playboar. Thomas Hagey. (Illus.). 56p. 1988. pap. 8.95 (*1-55824-067-5*) Day Dream SBCA.

Best of Plays & Players, Vol. 2. Ed. by Peter Roberts. (Illus.). 272p. 1989. pap. 25.95 (*0-413-53720-X*, A0494, Pub. by Methuen UK) Heinemann.

Best of Plays & Players: 1969-1983, Vol. 2. Ed. by Peter Roberts. (Illus.). 272p. 1989. 31.95 (*0-413-62150-2*, A0391, Pub. by Methuen UK) Heinemann.

Best of Plays & Players, Vol. I: 1953-1968. Ed. by Peter Roberts. (Illus.). 253p. 1988. 29.95 (*0-413-52960-6*, A0022) Heinemann.

Best of Plays & Players, Vol. One: 1953-1968. Illus. by Zoe Dominic. 254p. (Orig.). 1990. pap. 11.95 (*0-413-52970-3*, A0392, Pub. by Methuen UK) Heinemann.

Best of Plimpton. George Plimpton. 1991. pap. 12.95 (*0-87113-503-5*) Grove-Atltic.

Best of Poe. Edgar Allan Poe. (Illustrated Classics Collection 3). 64p. 1994. pap. 3.60 (*1-56103-543-2*) Lake Pub Co.

Best of Poe. abr. ed. Edgar Allan Poe. Ed. by Naunerle Farr. (Now Age Illustrated III Ser.). (Illus.). (J). (gr. 4-12). 1977. pap. text ed. 2.95 (*0-88301-269-3*) Pendulum Pr.

Best of Poe: Student Activity Book. Marcia Sohl & Gerald Dackerman. (Now Age Illustrated Ser.). (Illus.). (gr. 4-12). 1976. student ed 1.25 (*0-88301-293-6*) Pendulum Pr.

Best of Poe Readalong. Edgar Allan Poe. (Illustrated Classics Collection 3). 64p. 1994. audio, pap. 13.50 (*1-56103-545-9*) Lake Pub Co.

Best of Poet's Forum, Five. Ed. by John C. Brainerd. 40p. (Orig.). 1991. pap. 4.58 (*0-685-48300-2*) Dayspring Pr.

Best of Poet's Forum, Four. Ed. by John C. Brainerd. 40p. (Orig.). 1991. pap. 4.58 (*0-685-48299-5*) Dayspring Pr.

Best of Poet's Forum, One. Ed. by John C. Brainerd. 40p. (Orig.). 1991. pap. 4.58 (*0-685-48297-9*) Dayspring Pr.

Best of Poet's Forum, Six. Ed. by John C. Brainerd. 40p. (Orig.). 1991. pap. 4.58 (*0-685-48301-0*) Dayspring Pr.

Best of Poet's Forum, Three. Ed. by John C. Brainerd. 40p. (Orig.). 1991. pap. 4.58 (*0-9624641-5-5*) Dayspring Pr.

Best of Poet's Forum, Two. Ed. by John C. Brainerd. 40p. (Orig.). 1991. pap. 4.58 (*0-685-48298-7*) Dayspring Pr.

Best of Polish Cooking. Karen West. 1989. 6.99 (*0-517-68631-7*) Random Hse Value.

Best of Polish Cooking. rev. ed. Karen West. (Polish Interest Ser.). 205p. 1991. pap. 8.95 (*0-87052-123-3*) Hippocrene Bks.

Best of Pop Waltzes. Brimhall. 1990. 4.95 (*0-685-32043-X*, H440) Hansen Ed Mus.

Best of Pope. Alexander Pope. (BCL1-PR English Literature Ser.). 467p. 1992. reprint ed. lib. bdg. 99.00 (*0-7812-7393-5*) Rprt Serv.

***Best of Popular Christmas Music.** Cpp Belwin Staff. 1994. pap. 12.95 (*0-7604-0017-2*) CPP Belwin.

Best of Portals of Prayer. Rudolph F. Norden. 384p. 1990. 19.99 (*0-570-03083-8*, 06-1198) Concordia.

Best of Practical Pointers. Ed. by Susan Grosse. (Illus.). 323p. (Orig.). 1989. pap. text ed. 13.95 (*0-88314-437-9*) AAHPERD.

Best of Primary Education? A Sociological Study of Junior Middle Schools. Ronald A. King. 200p. 1989. 50.00 (*1-85000-602-4*, Falmer Pr); pap. 28.00 (*1-85000-603-2*, Falmer Pr) Taylor & Francis.

Best of Problem Solving. Andrea Lazzari et al. 1993. 19.95 (*1-55999-393-6*) LinguiSystems.

Best of Psychology Today. Paul Chance. 350p. (C). 1990. pap. text ed. write for info. (*0-07-557138-2*); pap. text ed. write for info. (*0-07-010509-X*) McGraw.

Best of Pugad Baboy. Pol Medina, Jr. (Tagalog Ser.). (Illus.). 78p. (Orig.). 1991. pap. 6.25 (*971-10-0440-2*, Pub. by New Day Pub PH) Cellar.

Best of Pulphouse. Ed. by Kristine K. Rusch. 352p. 1992. pap. 13.95 (*0-685-56691-9*) St Martin.

Best of Pulphouse: The Hardback Magazine. Kristine K. Rusch. 1992. pap. 13.95 (*0-312-08317-3*) St Martin.

Best of Pupung. Tonton Young. (Illus.). 76p. (Orig.). (TAG.). 1993. pap. 6.75 (*971-10-0526-3*, Pub. by New Day Pub PH) Cellar.

B

An Asterisk (*) at the beginning of an entry indicates that the title is appearing in BIP for the first time. 697

Best of Quick 'n Easy Cookin', 1986-87. Ed. by Zeta Overgard. 82p. 1987. pap. 6.95 (*0-9618379-0-X*) Parkside Pubns.

Best of Quick 'n Easy Cookin', 1988-89. Ed. by Zeta Overgard. 124p. 1989. pap. 6.95 (*0-9618379-1-8*) Parkside Pubns.

Best of Quiet Riot (Guitar - Vocal) Ed. by Mark Phillips. (Illus.). 63p. (Orig.). 1990. pap. text ed. 12.95 (*0-89524-381-4*) Cherry Lane.

Best of Quincy Scott. Hugh Scott. LC 80-83078. (Illus.). 208p. 1980. pap. 7.95 (*0-87595-087-6*) Oregon Hist.

***Best of Quintana.** Patricia Quintana. LC 94-45985. (Illus.). 128p. 1995. 22.50 (*1-55670-409-7*) Stewart Tabori & Chang.

Best of R. A. Torrey. R. A. Torrey. (Best Ser.). 254p. (Orig.). 1991. reprint ed. pap. 7.99 (*0-8010-8897-6*) Baker Bk.

Best of Ragtime Piano. Max Morath. pap. 8.95 (*0-89524-749-6*) Cherry Lane.

Best of Ralph McGill. Selected Columns. Comp. by Michael Strickland et al. LC 80-66816. (Illus.). 240p. 1980. bds. 12.50 (*0-87797-052-1*) Cherokee.

Best of Rated-X: Eight Classic Tales for Adults Only. Helga. (Illus.). 110p. 1991. pap. 9.95 (*1-56398-013-4*) Malibu Graphics.

Best of Reba McEntire: Twenty-Two of Her Greatest Hits. (Piano-Vocal-Guitar Ser.). 112p. (Orig.). 1992. pap. 14.95 (*0-7935-1194-1*, 00308123) H Leonard.

Best of Research Windows. Betty Collis. 108p. 1990. 12.95 (*0-924667-66-4*) Intl Society Tech Educ.

Best of Resurgence: A Selection of the First Twenty-Five Years. Ed. by John Button. 384p. (Orig.). 1992. pap. 17.95 (*1-870098-27-7*, Pub. by Green Bks UK) Seven Hills Bk.

Best of Richard Marx. Ed. by Milton Okun. 63p. (YA). 1994. per., pap. 12.95 (*0-89524-828-X*, 02502136) Cherry Lane.

Best of Rilke: Seventy-Two Form-True Verse Translations with Facing Originals, Commentary, & Compact Biography. Rainer Maria Rilke. LC 88-40345. 213p. 1989. pap. 12.95 (*0-87451-461-4*) U Pr of New Eng.

Best of RMM. Robert M. Miller. LC 86-73111. (Illus.). 239p. 1987. 26.50 (*0-939674-18-1*) Am Vet Pubns.

Best of Roald Dahl. Roald Dahl. 1978. pap. 10.95 (*0-394-72549-2*) Random.

Best of Roald Dahl. Roald Dahl. LC 89-40287. 1990. pap. 14.00 (*0-679-72991-7*, Vin) Random.

Best of "Rob Wagner's Script" Ed. by Anthony Slide. LC 85-2315. 183p. 1985. 20.00 (*0-8108-1810-8*) Scarecrow.

Best of Robert Heinlein. Robert Heinlein. reprint ed. lib. bdg. 23.95 (*0-685-00356-6*, Aeonian Pr); reprint ed. write for info. (*0-88411-884-3*, Aeonian Pr) Amereon Ltd.

Best of Robert Ingersoll: Selections from His Writings & Speeches. rev. ed. Ed. by Roger E. Greeley. LC 77-90495. 175p. 1982. pap. 18.95 (*0-87975-209-2*) Prometheus Bks.

Best of Robert Service. Robert Service. 19.95 (*0-89190-928-1*, Am Repr) Amereon Ltd.

Best of Robert Service. Robert Service. (Robert Service Ser.). 1989. 8.95 (*0-399-55008-9*) Putnam Pub Group.

Best of Robert Service. Robert Service. LC 89-43594. (Illus.). 200p. 1990. 19.95 (*0-89471-813-4*) Running Pr.

Best of Rock: The Essential Guide. Alan Clayson. 1993. 9.95 (*0-00-255338-4*) Collins SF.

Best of Rodgers & Hammerstein. (Piano-Vocal Ser.). 112p. (Orig.). 1994. pap. 12.95 (*0-7935-2842-9*, 00308210) H Leonard.

Best of Rodgers & Hart. (Piano-Vocal Ser.). 112p. (Orig.). 1993. pap. text ed. 12.95 (*0-7935-2865-8*, 00308211) H Leonard.

Best of Roxette. Ed. by Milton Okun. 1994. pap. 12.95 (*0-89524-827-1*) Cherry Lane.

Best of Rumpole. John Mortimer. 288p. 1994. reprint ed. pap. 10.95 (*0-14-017684-5*, Penguin Bks) Viking Penguin.

Best of Runner's World Complete Runner, Vol. 2. (Illus.). 464p. 1982. 14.95 (*0-89037-078-8*) Anderson World.

Best of Russian Cooking. Alexandra Kropotkin. (International Cookbook Classics Ser.). 270p. 1993. reprint ed. pap. 9.95 (*0-7818-0131-1*) Hippocrene Bks.

Best of Sabine R. Ulibarri: Selected Stories. Intro. by Dick Gerdes. LC 93-12714. (Paso por Aqui Series on the Nuevomexicano Literary Heritage). 527p. (C). 1993. 32.50 (*0-8263-1457-0*) U of NM Pr.

Best of Sacred Music. Brimhall. 1990. 4.95 (*0-685-32047-2*, H446) Hansen Ed Mus.

***Best of Sail Trim.** Ed. by Charles Mason. (Illus.). 288p. Date not set. pap. 25.00 (*0-7136-3594-0*) Sheridan.

Best of Saki. Saki. 1977. pap. 10.00 (*0-14-004484-1*, Penguin Bks) Viking Penguin.

Best of Saki. Saki. 17.95 (*0-89190-115-9*, Am Repr) Amereon Ltd.

Best of Saki. Saki. Ed. by Martin Stephen. 300p. 1993. pap. 5.95 (*0-460-87340-7*, Everyman's Classic Lib) C E Tuttle.

Best of Saki. Munro Saki. 196p. 1993. 18.95 (*1-56723-087-3*) Yestermorrow.

***Best of Salads: From Amish & Mennonite Kitchens.** 1995. pap. text ed. 1.95 (*1-56148-157-2*) Good Bks PA.

Best of San Francisco: An Insider's Guide. 3rd expanded rev. ed. Don Martin & Betty Martin. Ed. by Bill LeBlond. 208p. 1994. pap. 10.95 (*0-8118-0611-1*) Chronicle Bks.

Best of San Francisco & Northern California. 3rd ed. Andre Gayot. 1993. pap. 18.00 (*1-881066-04-5*) Gault Millau.

Best of Sanibel & Captiva Islands. Van B. Hooper & Joan S. Hooper. (Illus.). 144p. (Orig.). 1991. pap. 5.95 (*1-879685-00-0*) Hooper Pub FL.

Best of Sanibel-Captiva Islands Restaurants & Recipes. 208p. 1992. 14.95 (*0-9634228-0-4*) Sanibel-Captiva.

***Best of Santa Barbara: Independent Reader's Poll.** (Illus.). 96p. (Orig.). 1994. pap. 7.99 (*0-9644465-0-2*) Snta Barbara Indep.

Best of Scanfest: An Authentic Treasury of Scandinavian Recipes & Proverbs. Ed. by Cheryl Long. 1992. pap. 14.95 (*0-914667-13-0*) Culinary Arts Ltd.

Best of Schleicher. William F. Schleicher. 242p. (Orig.). 1984. pap. 19.95 (*0-933931-06-9*) Hitchcock Pub.

Best of Schools. Jean-Marie Besset. Tr. by Mark O'Donnell. (New French Plays Ser.). 92p. (Orig.). 1992. pap. 7.95 (*0-913745-34-0*) Ubu Repertory.

Best of Schultz: Easy Piano. Pamela Schultz & Robert Schultz. 64p. (Orig.) (YA). 1992. pap. text ed. 8.95 (*0-89898-647-8*) CPP Belwin.

Best of Screen Printing. Ed. by Blount & Co. Staff. (Design Sourcebook Ser.). (Illus.). 240p. 1989. 49.99 (*0-935603-17-4*, 30140) Rockport Pubs.

Best of Sears Collectibles, Nineteen Five to Nineteen Ten. Sears, Roebuck & Company Staff et al. 1976. 15.95 (*0-405-06688-0*, 19379) Ayer.

Best of Seasons: The 1944 St. Louis Cardinals & St. Louis Browns. Bill Borst. 272p. 1994. pap. 22.95x (*0-89950-974-6*) McFarland & Co.

***Best of Seasons Menu Cookbook.** Schultz. 1992. pap. text ed. 12.95 (*0-88995-065-2*, Pub. by Red Deer CN) BookWorld Dist.

Best of Set: Discipline. Llyn Richards & Peter Jeffery. (C). 1990. 59.00 (*0-86431-000-5*, Pub. by Aust Coun Educ Res AT) St Mut.

Best of Set: Junior Classes. Llyn Richards & Peter Jeffery. (C). 1992. 60.00 (*0-86431-222-9*, Pub. by Aust Coun Educ Res AT) St Mut.

Best of Set: Writing. Llyn Richards et al. (C). 1990. 70.00 (*0-685-67426-6*, Pub. by Aust Coun Educ Res AT) St Mut.

Best of Sewing with Nancy. LC 93-84933. 144p. 1993. pap. 19.95 (*0-8487-1180-7*) Oxmoor Hse.

Best of Shadowland. Ed. by Anna K. Sterling. LC 87-4747. 224p. 1987. 25.00 (*0-8108-1990-2*) Scarecrow.

Best of Shaker Cooking. Ed. by Amy B. Miller & Persis W. Fuller. LC 92-30875. 482p. 1993. reprint ed. pap. 12.00 (*0-02-035045-7*, Collier S&S) S&S Trade.

Best of Sherlock Holmes. Arthur Conan Doyle. Ed. by H. R. Keating. 384p. 1993. pap. 8.95 (*0-460-87368-7*, Everyman's Classic Lib) C E Tuttle.

Best of Sholom Aleichem. large type ed. Ed. by Irving Howe & Ruth R. Wisse. (Large Print Jewish Classics Ser.). 1991. pap. 14.95 (*0-8027-2645-3*) Walker & Co.

Best of Simple. Langston Hughes. (Illus.). 245p. (J). (gr. 4-6). 1990. pap. 9.95 (*0-374-52133-6*, Noonday) FS&G.

Best of Simple. Langston Hughes. LC 83-46025. (Classics of Modern American Humor Ser.). (Illus.). reprint ed. 29.00 (*0-404-19936-4*) AMS Pr.

Best of Six Hundred & Six Aggie Jokes: A Collection of the Best of Six Volumes of Aggie Jokes & Their Descendents. Illus. by Bob Taylor. 176p. (Orig.). 1976. write for info. (*0-945430-00-0*) Gigem Pr.

Best of Skin Two. Ed. by Tim Woodward. (Orig.). 1993. pap. 12.95 (*1-56333-130-6*) Masquerade.

Best of Slavic Cooking. Alojzije Kapetanovic & Ruzica Kapetanovic. LC 81-71605. 276p. 1982. 13.89 (*0-910164-04-5*); pap. 7.95 (*0-910164-06-1*) Assoc Bk Pubs.

Best of Soul: The Essential Guide. Ralph Tee. 1993. 9.95 (*0-00-255340-6*) Collins SF.

***Best of Soundgarden for Bass.** 72p. (Orig.). (YA). Date not set. pap. 16.95 (*0-89524-904-9*) Cherry Lane.

***Best of Soundgarden for Guitar.** 88p. (Orig.). (YA). Date not set. pap. 19.95 (*0-89524-903-0*, 02501250) Cherry Lane.

***Best of Soups: From Amish & Mennonite Kitchens.** 1995. pap. text ed. 1.95 (*1-56148-156-4*) Good Bks PA.

Best of Sources, Vol. 1. Ed. by Michael Williams. (Illus.). (Orig.). 1993. pap. 49.95 (*0-916974-16-2*, 191) NAUI.

Best of Southern Cooking. Ideals Magazine Staff. 1988. pap. 3.95 (*0-8249-3075-4*) Ideals.

Best of Southern Italian Cooking. J. C. Grasso. 1984. 19.95 (*0-8120-5483-0*) Barron.

Best of Southern Italian Cooking. J. C. Grasso. 196p. 1994. pap. 12.95 (*0-8120-1990-3*) Barron.

Best of Southern Rose, Vol. I. Ed. by Joan Cissom. (Illus.). 150p. (Orig.). 1989. pap. 12.50 (*0-929560-02-7*) Southern Rose Prodns.

Best of Soviet Semiconductor Physics & Technology, 1987-1988. Ed. by Mikhail Levinshtein. 360p. 1991. 95.00 (*0-88318-782-5*); pap. 45.00 (*0-88318-783-3*) Am Inst Physics.

Best of Soviet Semiconductor Physics & Technology (1989-1990) M. Levinshtein. 900p. 1995. text ed. 109.00 (*981-02-1579-7*) World Scientific Pub.

Best of Spain: A Cookbook. Evie Righter & Alicia Saacs. LC 92-36631. (Illus.). 1993. 14.95 (*0-00-255207-8*) Collins SF.

Best of Spicy Tales. Ed. by Tom Mason. 104p. 1990. pap. 9.95 (*0-944735-71-1*) Malibu Graphics.

Best of Spitball. Shannon. 20.95 (*0-8488-1563-7*) Amereon Ltd.

Best of Standish Chowders Soup. Marjorie Standish. 1987. pap. 4.50 (*0-930096-94-0*) G Gannett.

Best of Standish Seafood. Marjorie Standish. (Illus.). 62p. 1984. pap. 4.50 (*0-930096-61-4*) G Gannett.

Best of Star Trek. Mike Barr et al. Ed. by Bob Greenberger et al. (Illus.). 240p. (YA). 1991. pap. 19.95 (*1-56389-009-7*) DC Comics.

Best of Star Trek: The Next Generation. Friedman & DeLancie. Ed. by B. Kahan. (Illus.). 192p. (YA). 1994. pap. 19.95 (*1-56389-125-5*) DC Comics.

Best of Steve Wariner. Ed. by Milton Okun. pap. 14.95 (*0-89524-672-4*) Cherry Lane.

Best of Store Designs 2. (Illus.). 256p. 49.95 (*0-87102-145-5*, 60-7677) Natl Ret Merch.

Best of Storylines: Story for the Whole Family. Hanoch Teller. (Illus.). 224p. (YA). (gr. 2-12). 1991. 14.95 (*0-9614772-9-6*) NYC Pub Co.

***Best of Strawberries.** 46p. 1995. write for info. (*1-57215-042-4*) World Pubns.

***Best of "Strickly Speaking" Ethics Readings & Study Materials for Life Insurance & Financial Services Professionals.** Ed. by Burke A. Christensen & Ken Cooper. 135p. (Orig.). (C). 1995. pap. text ed. 9.95 (*0-943590-69-8*) Amer College.

Best of Success: A Treasury of Success Ideas. Ed. by Mac Anderson. 77p. (Orig.). 1988. pap. 7.50 (*1-880461-13-7*) Celebrat Excell.

Best of Success: A Treasury of Success Ideas. 2nd deluxe ed. Ed. by Mac Anderson. 1988. 49.95 (*1-880461-15-3*) Celebrat Excell.

Best of Success: A Treasury of Success Ideas. 2nd ed. Ed. by Mac Anderson. 1988. 34.95 (*1-880461-14-5*) Celebrat Excell.

***Best of Summer Fruits.** 46p. 1995. write for info. (*1-57215-045-9*) World Pubns.

***Best of Sunset Low-Fat Cook Book.** 1994. 29.95 (*0-376-02654-5*) Sunset Menlo Pk.

***Best of Sunset Low-Fat Cook Book.** Sunset Books Staff. 1994. pap. 17.95 (*0-376-02655-3*) Sunset Menlo Pk.

***Best of Teams the Worst of Teams: A Major League Baseball Statistical Reference, 1903-1994.** Russell O. Wright. 192p. 1995. lib. bdg. 29.95 (*0-7864-0011-0*) McFarland & Co.

Best of Tech Tips. Ed. by Steve Smith. (Illus.). 80p. (Orig.). Date not set. pap. text ed. 10.95 (*0-936834-15-3*) S S Autosports.

***Best of Technology in Training.** Ed. by Patricia A. Galagan & Ellen S. Carnevale. LC 94-71335. (Best of Ser.). 88p. 1994. pap. 25.00 (*1-56286-006-2*) Am Soc Train & Devel.

***Best of Ted Nugent for Guitar.** 52p. (Orig.). 1994. pap. 12.95 (*0-89724-235-1*) Warner Brothers.

Best of Teddy Bear & Friends: Magazine Articles. Hobby House Press Staff & Carolyn Cook. (Illus.). 192p. 1992. pap. 14.95 (*0-87588-391-5*) Hobby Hse.

Best of Texas Festivals. Ann Ruff. LC 85-23722. (Illus.). 100p. (Orig.). 1986. pap. 9.95 (*0-88415-863-2*, Lone Star Bks) Gulf Pub.

Best of Thailand: A Cookbook. Evie Righter & Grace Young. LC 92-37715. (Illus.). 1993. 14.95 (*0-00-255206-X*) Collins SF.

Best of the Achaeans: Concepts of the Hero in Archaic Greek Poetry. Gregory Nagy. LC 79-9907. 416p. 1981. pap. 15.95 (*0-8018-2388-9*) Johns Hopkins.

Best of the Alaska Bed & Breakfast. Carole Marsh. (Carole Marsh Alaska Bks.). (Illus.). (YA). (gr. 3-12). 1994. lib. bdg. 24.95 (*0-7933-1349-X*); pap. 14.95 (*0-7933-1350-3*); disk 29.95 (*0-7933-1351-1*) Gallopade Pub Group.

Best of the Appalachian Trail: Overnight Hikes. Frank Logue & Victoria Logue. (Illus.). 242p. 1994. pap. 12.95 (*0-89732-139-1*) Menasha Ridge.

Best of the Appalachian Trail, Day Hikes. Frank Logue & Victoria Logue. (Illus.). 198p. 1994. pap. 12.95 (*0-89732-138-3*) Menasha Ridge.

Best of the Argonauts: The Redefinition of the Epic Hero in Book One of the Apollonius' Argonautica. James J. Clauss. (C). 1993. 35.00 (*0-520-07925-6*) U CA Pr.

Best of the Badboys. Ed. by Michael Lowenthal. (Orig.). 1995. pap. 12.95 (*1-56333-233-7*) Masquerade.

Best of the Bay Area for You & Your Child: Where to Shop, What to Do & Where to Find Help. Susan D. Waldman. (Illus.). 269p. (Orig.). 1989. pap. 12.95 (*0-929892-00-3*) Firestone Pr.

***Best of the Beach: The Complete Outdoors & Travel Guide to the Alabama & NW Florida Coasts.** Thomas E. Bailey. 192p. (Orig.). 1994. pap. 9.95 (*1-878561-28-6*) Seacoast AL.

Best of the Best. Jimmy Houston & Ricky Green. Ed. by John Scott. (Illus.). 48p. (Orig.). (C). 1984. pap. 3.95 (*0-945270-22-4*) J Houston.

Best of the Best. Satoh Kohshin. 1993. pap. 75.00 (*0-929279-92-1*, Cadence Bks) Viz Commns Inc.

Best of the Best. Ed. by Mark Phillips. (Easy Guitar Ser.). (Illus.). 63p. (Orig.). 1990. pap. text ed. 10.95 (*0-89524-368-7*) Cherry Lane.

Best of the Best: Notable New Jersey Restaurants. Sherie Schmauder. (Orig.). 1992. pap. 5.50 (*0-9625060-2-8*) J J Fox Pubns.

Best of the Best: The Oustanding Yachts of Sparkman & Stephens Design. Francis Kinney. (Illus.). 1989. 50.00 (*0-393-02495-4*) Norton.

Best of the Best: Twelve Great Bible Chapters. D. Arthur Delafield. LC 94-3928. 1994. pap. 8.95 (*0-8163-1229-X*) Pacific Pr Pub Assn.

Best of the Best from Alabama: Selected Recipes from Alabama's Favorite Cookbooks. Ed. by Gwen McKee & Barbara Moseley. LC 89-60781. (Illus.). 288p. (Orig.). 1989. pap. 14.95 (*0-937552-28-3*) Quail Ridge.

Best of the Best from Arkansas: Selected Recipes from Arkansas' Favorite Cookbooks. Ed. by Gwen McKee & Barbara Moseley. LC 92-12155. (Best of the Best State Cookbook Ser.). (Illus.). 288p. (Orig.). 1992. pap. 14.95 (*0-937552-43-7*) Quail Ridge.

Best of the Best from Florida: Selected Recipes from Florida's Favorite Cookbooks. Ed. by Gwen McKee & Barbara Moseley. (Illus.). 288p. (Orig.). 1986. pap. 14.95 (*0-937552-16-X*) Quail Ridge.

Best of the Best from Georgia: Selected Recipes from Georgia's Favorite Cookbooks. Ed. by Gwen McKee & Barbara Moseley. LC 89-10205. (Illus.). 336p. (Orig.). 1989. pap. 14.95 (*0-937552-30-5*) Quail Ridge.

***Best of the Best from Illinois: Selected Recipes from Illinois' Favorite Cookbooks.** Ed. by Gwen McKee & Barbara Moseley. (Best of the Best Ser.). (Illus.). 288p. (Orig.). 1995. pap. 14.95 (*0-937552-58-5*) Quail Ridge.

***Best of the Best from Indiana: Selected Recipes from Indiana's Favorite Cookbooks.** Ed. by Gwen McKee & Barbara Moseley. (Best of the Best Ser.). (Illus.). 288p. (Orig.). 1995. pap. 14.95 (*0-937552-57-7*) Quail Ridge.

Best of the Best from Kentucky: Selected Recipes from Kentucky's Favorite Cookbooks. Ed. by Gwen McKee & Barbara Moseley. LC 88-90826. (Illus.). 288p. (Orig.). 1988. pap. 14.95 (*0-937552-27-5*) Quail Ridge.

Best of the Best from Louisiana: Selected Recipes from Louisiana's Favorite Cookbooks. Ed. by Gwen McKee & Barbara Moseley. (Best of the Best Ser.). (Illus.). 288p. (Orig.). 1984. pap. 14.95 (*0-937552-13-5*) Quail Ridge.

Best of the Best from Mississippi: Selected Recipes from Mississippi's Favorite Cookbooks. rev. ed. Ed. by Barbara Moseley. (Best of the Best Ser.). (Illus.). 288p. 1987. pap. 14.95 (*0-937552-19-4*) Quail Ridge.

Best of the Best from Missouri: Selected Recipes from Missouri's Favorite Cookbooks. Ed. by Gwen McKee & Barbara Moseley. LC 92-25259. (Best of the Best State Cookbook Ser.). (Illus.). 288p. (Orig.). 1992. pap. 14.95 (*0-937552-44-5*) Quail Ridge.

Best of the Best from New England: Selected Recipes from the Favorite Cookbooks of Rhode Island, Massachusetts, Connecticut, Vermont, New Hampshire & Maine. Ed. by Gwen McKee & Barbara Moseley. LC 94-5578. (Illus.). 368p. (Orig.). 1994. pap. 16.95 (*0-937552-50-X*) Quail Ridge.

Best of the Best from North Carolina: Selected Recipes from North Carolina's Favorite Cookbooks. Ed. by Gwen McKee & Barbara Moseley. LC 90-45535. (Illus.). 536p. (Orig.). 1990. pap. 14.95 (*0-937552-38-0*) Quail Ridge.

Best of the Best from Pennsylvania: Selected Recipes from Pennsylvania's Favorite Cookbooks. Ed. by Gwen McKee & Barbara Moseley. (Best of the Best State Cookbook Ser.). (Illus.). 320p. 1993. ring bd. 14.95 (*0-937552-47-X*) Quail Ridge.

Best of the Best from South Carolina: Selected Recipes from South Carolina's Favorite Cookbooks. Ed. by Gwen McKee & Barbara Moseley. LC 90-42214. (Illus.). 288p. (Orig.). 1990. pap. 14.95 (*0-937552-39-9*) Quail Ridge.

Best of the Best from Tennessee: Selected Recipes from Tennessee's Favorite Cookbooks. Ed. by Barbara Moseley. (Best of the Best Ser.). (Illus.). 288p. (Orig.). 1987. pap. 14.95 (*0-937552-20-8*) Quail Ridge.

Best of the Best from Texas: Selected Recipes from Texas' Favorite Cookbooks. Ed. by Gwen McKee & Barbara Moseley. (Illus.). 352p. (Orig.). 1985. pap. 14.95 (*0-937552-14-3*) Quail Ridge.

Best of the Best from Texas: Selected Recipes from Texas' Favorite Cookbooks. Ed. by Gwen McKee & Barbara Moseley. (Best of the Best Ser.). (Illus.). 352p. (Orig.). 1989. 16.95 (*0-937552-34-8*) Quail Ridge.

Best of the Best from Virginia: Selected Recipes from Virginia's Favorite Cookbooks. Ed. by Gwen McKee & Barbara Moseley. LC 91-23169. (Best of the Best State Cookbook Ser.). (Illus.). 320p. 1991. pap. 14.95 (*0-937552-41-0*) Quail Ridge.

Best of the Best of Trek II. Ed. by Walter Irwin & G. B. Love. 400p. 1992. 12.00 (*0-451-45159-7*, ROC) NAL-Dutton.

***Best of the Better Cookery Cookbook.** Gloria Pitzer. (Illus.). 120p. 1995. reprint ed. pap. write for info. (*1-886138-05-2*) G Pitzers.

Best of the Big South Fork National River & Recreation Area: A Hiker's Guide to Trails & Attractions. Russ Manning & Sondra Jamieson. (Tag-Along Bks.). (Illus.). 92p. (Orig.). 1989. pap. 4.95 (*0-9625122-0-6*) Mtn Laurel Pl.

Best of the Big South Fork National River & Recreation Area: A Hiker's Guide to Trails & Attractions. 2nd ed. Russ Manning & Sondra Jamieson. (Tag-Along Bks.). (Illus.). 112p. (Orig.). 1990. pap. 6.95 (*0-9625122-4-9*) Mtn Laurel Pl.

Best of the Book & Cook: Great Menus & Recipes by America's Most Talented Cookbook Authors. Phyllis Stein-Novack. 250p. (Orig.). 1990. pap. 12.95 (*0-940159-07-4*) Camino Bks.

***Best of the British Virgin Islands.** Pamela Acheson. LC 94-61892. 128p. (Orig.). 1994. pap. 12.95 (*0-9639905-5-1*) Two Thous-Three Assocs.

Best of the Bushel. Junior League of Charlottesville, Inc. Staff. LC 76-8648. 108p. 1987. pap. 10.00 (*0-9615013-1-6*) Jr Charlottesville.

Best of the California Bed & Breakfast. Carole Marsh. (Carole Marsh California Bks.). (Illus.). (YA). (gr. 3-12). 1994. lib. bdg. 24.95 (*0-7933-1397-X*); pap. 14.95 (*0-7933-1398-8*); disk 29.95 (*0-7933-1399-6*) Gallopade Pub Group.

Best of the Caribbean: Handbook Companion. William G. Van Arsdale. (Travel Guides Ser.: Vol. 1). (Illus.). 132p. (Orig.). 1986. pap. 6.95 (*0-939005-01-8*) Van Arsdale Video.

Best of the Caribbean: Handbook Companion. William G. Van Arsdale. (Travel Guides Ser.: Vol. 2). (Illus.). 130p. (Orig.). 1987. pap. 6.95 (*0-939005-03-4*) Van Arsdale Video.

Best of the "Carolina Senior Citizen" Ed. by David George. (Illus.). 144p. (Orig.). 1993. pap. 8.95 (*1-56664-002-4*, Land Sky Bks) WorldComm.

Best of the Carrot Recipes. Helen O. Dandar & Emil B. Dandar. (Illus.). 102p. (Orig.). 1992. pap. text ed. 8.95 (*0-9620818-5-X*) Sterling Specialty.

An Asterisk (*) at the beginning of an entry indicates that the title is appearing in BIP for the first time.

B

An Asterisk (*) at the beginning of an entry indicates that the title is appearing in BIP for the first time.

B

***Best of Wheeling.** Junior League of Wheeling Inc. Staff. 1994. 15.95 (0-87197-404-5) Favorite Recipes.

***Best of Whitney Houston for Guitar.** (Best of...for Guitar Ser.). 68p. (Orig.). 1994. pap. 12.95 (0-89724-154-1) Warner Brothers.

Best of Wild Rice Recipes. Beatrice Ojakangas. 1989. 5.95 (0-934860-56-4); 13.95 (0-934860-58-0) Adventure Pubns.

Best of Wild Rice Recipes. Beatrice Ojakangas. 1991. Gift Pack, Hand-Picked, incl. rice & wood crate. 17.95 (0-934860-71-8) Adventure Pubns.

Best of Will Rogers. Bryan Sterling. LC 90-45768. (Illus.). 252p. 1990. pap. 9.95 (0-87131-631-5) M Evans.

***Best of Will Rogers.** Bryan B. Sterling. (Illus.). 256p. 1995. reprint ed. 7.98 (1-56731-078-8, MJF Bks) Fine Comms.

Best of Willie Nelson for Guitar. (Best of...for Guitar Ser.). 48p. (Orig.). Date not set. pap. 12.95 (0-89724-115-0) Warner Brothers.

***Best of Wind: Works from Twenty-Two Years of Wind Magazine.** Ed. by Quentin R. Howard et al. 220p. (Orig.). 1994. pap. 11.95 (0-9636545-0-0) Wind Pubns.

***Best of Wood Series Bk. 3.** Wood Staff. 160p. 1994. 21.95 (0-696-02583-3) Meredith Bks.

Best of Woodsmoke: A Manual of Primitive Outdoor Skills. Ed. by Richard Jamison. LC 82-81292. 240p. 1982. 16.98 (0-88290-203-2, 4031) Horizon Utah.

Best of Word Finding. Andrea Lazzari et al. 1993. 19.95 (1-55999-392-8) LinguiSystems.

***Best of Writers at Work 1994.** Northwest Publishing Staff. 1994. pap. 12.95 (1-56901-696-8) NW Pub.

Best of Wyoming. Catherine E. Mealey. xvi, 203p. 1990. pap. 12.95 (0-9627054-0-3) Meadowlark Wy.

Best of Yank, the Army Weekly. 1980. 48.95 (0-405-13289-1) Ayer.

Best of Your Personal Finance: Money Management Tips from the Nationally Syndicated Radio Program & Newspaper Column. Charles Ross. 164p. (Orig.). 1991. pap. text ed. 12.95 (0-9629100-0-7) FMS Pub.

Best of Zane Grey, Outdoorsman: Hunting & Fishing Tales. Comp. by George Reiger. LC 91-35932. (Classics of American Sport Ser.). (Illus.). 368p. 1992. pap. 16.95 (0-8117-2599-5) Stackpole.

Best of ZZ Top for Bass Guitar. Ed. by Carol Cuellar & Aarm Stang. (Orig.). (YA). Date not set. pap. text ed. 18.95 (0-89898-769-5) CPP Belwin.

Best of 1960-1964. Joel Whitburn. (Billboard Songbook Ser.). (Illus.). 312p. 1991. 19.95 (0-88188-822-2, 00490013) H Leonard.

***Best of 50's & 60's - Trumpet.** (Instrumental Magic Ser.). 48p. (Orig.). 1994. pap. 8.95 (0-89724-189-4) Warner Brothers.

***Best of 90's Country Music.** Cpp Belwin Staff. 1994. pap. 16.95 (0-89898-900-0) CPP Belwin.

***Best of 90's Popular Music.** Cpp Belwin Staff. 1994. pap. 16.95 (0-89898-899-3) CPP Belwin.

Best Old Farmers Almanac. Yankee Publishing Inc. Date not set. pap. 7.99 (0-517-11222-1) Random Hse Value.

Best on Quality, 4 bks., Set. H. J. Zeller. (C). 1988. text ed. 124.50 (1-56990-121-X) Hanser-Gardner.

***Best on Quality, Vol. 5.** Ed. by John D. Hromi. 1995. 43.00 (0-87389-286-0) ASQC Qual Pr.

***Best on Quality, Vol. 6.** Ed. by John D. Hromi. 1995. 43.00 (0-87389-343-3) ASQC Qual Pr.

Best on Quality, Vol. 1: Targets, Improvement, Systems. H. J. Zeller. 295p. (C). 1988. text ed. 28.00 (1-56990-042-6) Hanser-Gardner.

Best on Quality, Vol. 2: Targets, Improvement, Systems. H. J. Zeller. 365p. (C). 1989. text ed. 42.00 (1-56990-041-8) Hanser-Gardner.

Best on Quality, Vol. 3: Targets, Improvements, Systems. H. J. Zeller. 317p. (C). 1990. text ed. 48.00 (1-56990-040-X) Hanser-Gardner.

Best on Quality, Vol. 4: Targets, Improvements, Systems. H. J. Zeller. 280p. (C). 1991. text ed. 48.00 (1-56990-039-6) Hanser-Gardner.

Best One-Act Plays from Los Angeles: Actors' Theatre-Los Angeles Theatre Centre. Jim Goeghan et al. Ed. by Joseph S. Kierland. (Illus.). 144p. (Orig.). 1985. 16.95 (0-915572-79-6); pap. 7.95 (0-915572-78-8) Panjandrum.

***Best One-Act Plays of 1958-59.** Ed. by Hugh Miller. 255p. 1960. 14.95 (0-910278-83-0) Boulevard.

Best One Hundred Twenty-Five Low-Fat Fish & Seafood Dishes. Susann Geiskopf-Hadler & Mindy Toomay. LC 92-39919. 350p. (Orig.). 1993. pap. 14.95 (1-55958-302-9) Prima Pub.

Best One Hundred Twenty-Five Meatless Italian Dishes. Susann Geiskipf-Hadler & Mindy Toomay. LC 94-21791. 1994. write for info. (1-55958-560-9) Prima Pub.

Best One Hundred Twenty-Five Meatless Main Dishes. Mindy Toomay & Susann Geiskopf-Hadler. (Illus.). 256p. (Orig.). 1992. pap. 12.95 (1-55958-227-8) Prima Pub.

Best 125 Meatless Pasta Dishes. Mindy Toomay & Susan Geiskopf-Hadler. (Illus.). 250p. (Orig.). 1991. pap. 12.95 (1-55958-145-X) Prima Pub.

Best 125 Vegetable Dishes. Mindy Toomay & Susann Geiskopf-Hadler. (Illus.). 256p. (Orig.). 1993. pap. 14.95 (1-55958-359-2) Prima Pub.

Best One Thousand One WordPerfect Tips Ever. Mary Campbell. 1993. disk, pap. text ed. 39.95 (0-07-881819-2) Osborne-McGraw.

Best 'OTC' Drugs for Self-Care: A Guide for Using Over-the-Counter (OTC) Drugs to Relieve Common Symptoms & Treat Disease. David O. Thueson. LC 92-74273. 240p. (Orig.). 1993. pap. 9.95 (0-9634507-3-5) Abat Pathos.

Best Paper Aircraft. Campbell Morris. (Illus.). 64p. (Orig.). 1986. pap. 7.95 (0-399-51301-9, Perigree Bks) Berkley Pub.

Best Parent - Both Parents. David L. Levy. 1993. 9.95 (1-878901-56-7) Hampton Roads Pub Co.

Best Party Book. Penny Warner. 1992. pap. 7.00 (0-671-78049-2) S&S Trade.

Best Party Book: 1001 Creative Ideas for Fun Parties. Penny Warner. LC 92-8115. (Illus.). 217p. 1992. pap. 8.00 (0-88166-188-0) Meadowbrook.

***Best Pathfinder Walks.** Brian Conduit. (Ordnance Survey Pathfinder Guides Ser.). (Illus.). 120p. (Orig.). 1995. 24.95 (0-7117-0813-4, Pub. by Jarrold Pub UK) Seven Hills Bk.

Best Peanut Butter Sandwich in the Whole World. Bill McLean. (Illus.). 28p. (J). (ps-2). 1990. pap. 4.95 (0-88753-207-1, Pub. by Black Moss Pr CN) Firefly Bks Ltd.

Best Performance by a Patsy. Stan Cutler. 336p. 1993. pap. 4.50 (0-451-40359-2, Onyx) NAL-Dutton.

Best Pet Name Book Ever. Wayne Eldridge. 208p. 1990. pap. 6.95 (0-8120-4258-1) Barron.

Best Pets Yet. Gina C. Erickson & Kelli C. Foster. (Get Ready...Get Set...Read! Ser.). (Illus.). 24p. (J). (ps-2). 1992. pap. 3.50 (0-8120-4857-1) Barron.

Best Pizza Is Made at Home. Donna R. German. (Illus.). 176p. (Orig.). 1994. pap. 8.95 (1-55867-094-7, Nitty Gritty Ckbks) Bristol Pub Ent CA.

***Best Places to Bed & Breakfast in Ontario: A Selective Guide.** Janette Higgins. (Illus.). 172p. (Orig.). 1995. pap. 17.95 (0-921516-03-7) Firefly Bks Ltd.

Best Places to Go: A Family Destination Guide. Nan Jeffrey. (Illus.). 350p. (Orig.). 1994. pap. 14.95 (0-935701-75-3) Foghorn Pr.

Best Places to Kiss in & Around New York City: A Romantic Travel Guide. 3rd ed. Sheree Bykofsky. Ed. by Miriam Bulmer. (Best Places to Kiss Ser.). Orig. Title: The Best Places to Kiss in New York City. 300p. 1993. pap. 12.95 (1-877988-10-3) Beginning Pr.

Best Places to Kiss in Hawaii: A Romantic Travel Guide. Paula Begoun & Stephanie Bell. Ed. by Miriam Bulmer. (Best Places to Kiss Ser.). 200p. (Orig.). 1993. pap. 10.95 (1-877988-08-1) Beginning Pr.

Best Places to Kiss in New England: A Romantic Travel Guide. Pamela Hegarty. Ed. by Miriam Bulmer. (Best Places to Kiss Ser.). 400p. (Orig.). 1993. pap. 13.95 (1-877988-02-2) Beginning Pr.

Best Places to Kiss in New York City see Best Places to Kiss in & Around New York City: A Romantic Travel Guide

Best Places to Kiss in Northern California: A Romantic Travel Guide. 3rd ed. Stephanie C. Bell & Elizabeth Janda. Ed. by Miriam Bulmer. (Best Places to Kiss Ser.). 300p. 1994. pap. 12.95 (1-877988-12-X) Beginning Pr.

Best Places to Kiss in Southern California: A Romantic Travel Guide. 3rd ed. Caroline O'Connell & Debra Brada. Ed. by Miriam Bulmer. (Best Places to Kiss Ser.). 300p. 1994. pap. 12.95 (1-877988-13-8) Beginning Pr.

Best Places to Kiss in the Northwest: A Romantic Travel Guide. Paula Begoun & Stephanie Bell. 1993. 12.95 (1-877988-07-3) Beginning Pr.

Best Places to Kiss in the Northwest: A Romantic Travel Guide. 5th ed. Paula Begoun et al. Ed. by Miriam Bulmer. (Best Places to Kiss Ser.). 340p. 1994. pap. text ed. 13.95 (1-877988-14-6) Beginning Pr.

Best Places to Meet Good Men. Ellen Lederman. 352p. (Orig.). 1991. pap. 12.95 (1-55958-106-9) Prima Pub.

Best Places to Photograph North American Wildlife. Mark Warner. LC 92-39905. (Illus.). 192p. (Orig.). 1993. pap. 18.95 (0-8174-3556-5, Amphoto) Watsn-Guptill.

Best Places to Stay in America's Cities. 2nd ed. Bruce Shaw. 400p. 1992. pap. 14.95 (0-395-62226-3) HM.

Best Places to Stay in California. 3rd ed. Marilyn McFarlane. 1994. pap. 16.95 (0-395-65569-2) HM.

Best Places to Stay in Florida. 3rd rev. ed. Christine Davidson. (Best Places to Stay Ser.). (Illus.). 400p. 1994. pap. 16.95 (0-395-66615-5) HM.

Best Places to Stay in Hawaii. 3rd ed. Bill Jamison. 1993. pap. 14.95 (0-395-62227-1) HM.

Best Places to Stay in Mexico. 2nd ed. Bill Jamison. 1993. pap. 14.95 (0-395-62228-X) HM.

Best Places to Stay in New England. 5th ed. Christina Tree. 1994. pap. 16.95 (0-395-65570-6) HM.

***Best Places to Stay in South America.** Alex Newton. (Illus.). 288p. (Orig.). 1995. pap. 14.95 (1-55650-696-1) Hunter NJ.

Best Places to Stay in the Caribbean. 3rd rev. ed. Bill Janison & Cheryl A. Janison. (Best Places to Stay Ser.). (Illus.). 480p. 1994. pap. 16.95 (0-395-66617-1) HM.

Best Places to Stay in the Mid-Atlantic States. 2nd rev. ed. Dana N. Foley. (Best Places to Stay Ser.). (Illus.). 400p. 1994. pap. 16.95 (0-395-66616-3) HM.

Best Places to Stay in the Midwest. 2nd rev. ed. John Monaghan. (Best Places to Stay Ser.). (Illus.). 352p. 1994. pap. 16.95 (0-395-66618-X) HM.

Best Places to Stay in the Pacific Northwest. 3rd ed. Marilyn McFarlane. (Best Places to Stay Ser.). (Illus.). 512p. 1993. pap. 14.95 (0-395-62229-8) HM.

***Best Places to Stay in the Pacific Northwest.** 4th ed. Marilyn McFarlane. (Best Places to Stay Ser.). 1995. pap. 16.95 (0-395-70008-6) HM.

Best Places to Stay in the Rocky Mountain Region. 2nd rev. ed. Roger Cox. (Best Places to Stay Ser.). (Illus.). 352p. 1994. pap. 16.95 (0-395-66619-8) HM.

Best Places to Stay in the South. 2nd ed. Carol Timblin. 1994. pap. 16.95 (0-395-65568-4) HM.

Best Places to Stay in the Southwest. 3rd ed. Anne E. Wright. (Illus.). 400p. 1993. pap. 14.95 (0-395-62230-1) HM.

***Best Places to Stay in the Southwest.** 4th ed. Anne E. Wright. (Best Places to Stay Ser.). 1995. pap. 16.95 (0-395-70009-4) HM.

***Best Plants for New Mexico Gardens & Landscapes: Keyed to Cities & Regions in New Mexico & Adjacent Areas.** Baker H. Morrow. (Illus.). 300p. 1995. pap. 24.95 (0-8263-1595-X) U of NM Pr.

Best Plays. Anton P. Chekhov. Tr. by Stark Young. LC 56-8837. 1966. pap. 3.95 (0-685-06607-X, Modern Lib) Random.

Best Plays of Albert Innaurato: Coming of Age in Soho, Gemini, Transformation of Benno Blimpie. Albert Innaurato. (JH Play Script Ser.). 192p. (Orig.). 1987. pap. 7.95 (0-914017-14-4) Gay Pr NY.

Best Plays of Phillip Massinger: With Critical Biographical Essay & Notes, 2 vols., Set. Ed. by Arthur Symons. 1988. reprint ed. lib. bdg. 59.00 (0-7812-0793-2) Rprt Serv.

Best Plays of Phillip Massinger: With Critical Biographical Essay & Notes, 2 vols., Set. Ed. by Arthur Symons. LC 72-108511. 1970. reprint ed. 35.00 (0-403-00219-2) Scholarly.

Best Plays of Richard Steele. Richard Steele. Ed. by G. A. Aitken. 1981. reprint ed. 39.00 (0-403-00043-2) Scholarly.

Best Plays of the Modern American Theatre: Second Series, 1939-1946. Ed. & Intro. by John Gassner. Incl. Glass Menagerie. 1983. (0-318-51542-3); Time of Your Life. 1983. (0-318-51543-1); I Remember Mama. 1983. (0-318-51544-X); Life with Father. 1983. (0-318-51545-8); Born Yesterday. 1983. (0-318-51546-6); Voice of the Turtle. 1983. (0-318-51547-4); Male Animal. 1983. (0-318-51548-2); Man Who Came to Dinner. 1983. (0-318-51549-0); Dream Girl. 1983. (0-318-51550-4); Philadelphia Story. 1983. (0-318-51551-2); Arsenic & Old Lace. 1983. (0-318-51552-0); Hasty Heart. 1983. (0-318-51553-9); Home of the Brave. 1983. (0-318-51554-7); Tomorrow the World. 1983. (0-318-51555-5); Watch on the Rhine. 1983. (0-318-51556-3); Patriots. 1983. (0-318-51557-1); Abe Lincoln in Illinois. 1983. (0-318-51558-X); 768p. 1983. 23.95 (0-517-50948-2, Crown) Crown Pub Group.

Best Plays of the Old Dramatists. Richard Steele. LC 77-131605. 32.00 (0-685-47626-X) Scholarly.

Best Plays of 1919-1920. Ed. by Burns Mantle. LC 75-19860. (Best Plays Series). 1978. 30.95 (0-405-09168-0) Ayer.

Best Plays of 1928-1929. Ed. by Burns Mantle. LC 75-19860. (Best Plays Series). 1976. 30.95 (0-405-09169-9) Ayer.

Best Plays of 1929-1930. Ed. by Burns Mantle. LC 75-19860. (Best Plays Series). 1975. 30.95 (0-405-09170-2) Ayer.

Best Plays of 1930-1931. Ed. by Burns Mantle. LC 75-19860. (Best Plays Series). 1977. 30.95 (0-405-09171-0) Ayer.

Best Plays of 1932-1933. LC 75-19860. (Best Plays Series). 1975. 27.95 (0-405-07647-9) Ayer.

Best Plays of 1938-1939. Ed. by Burns Mantle. LC 75-19860. (Best Plays Series). 1977. 30.95 (0-405-09174-5) Ayer.

Best Plays of 1987-1988. Ed. by Otis L Guernsey, Jr. & Jeffrey Sweet. (Burns Mantle Theater Yearbook Ser.). (Illus.). 606p. 1989. 35.95 (1-55783-040-1) Applause Theatre Bk Pubs.

Best Plays of 1988-1989. 70th ed. Ed. by Otis L. Guernsey, Jr. & Jeffrey Sweet. (Burns Mantle Theater Yearbook Ser.). 680p. 1989. 36.95 (1-55783-056-8); pap. 18.95 (1-55783-057-6) Applause Theatre Bk Pubs.

Best Plays of 1989-1990. Ed. by Otis L. Guernsey, Jr. & Jeffrey Sweet. (Burns Mantle Theater Yearbook Ser.). (Illus.). 672p. 1990. 37.95 (1-55783-091-6); pap. 19.95 (1-55783-090-8) Applause Theatre Bk Pubs.

Best Plays Series, 44 vols., Set. LC 75-19860. 1976. 1,270.00 (0-405-07637-1) Ayer.

Best Plays 1919-1967. 1,270.00 (0-685-43148-7, 408) Ayer.

Best Plays, 1963-1964. 1981. 30.95 (0-405-13215-8) Ayer.

Best Plays, 1964-1965. 1981. 30.95 (0-405-13216-6) Ayer.

Best Plays, 1966-1967. 1981. 30.95 (0-405-13217-4) Ayer.

***Best Poems & the Book of Five Makings.** Ivor Gurney. 192p. 1995. pap. 18.95 (1-85754-200-2) Paul & Co Pubs.

Best Poems of Roy Rajacic. Roy Rajacic. Ed. by Djuro Maljkovic-Petkovic & Katarina Kostic. (Illus.). 80p. (Orig.). 1982. 7.95 (0-943898-00-5); pap. 6.95 (0-943898-01-3) Gospic Realty.

Best Poems of 1922. Thomas Moult. LC 78-74821. (Granger Poetry Library). (Illus.). 1979. reprint ed. 15.00 (0-89609-140-6) Roth Pub Inc.

Best Poems of 1923. Ed. by Thomas Moult. LC 78-74822. (Granger Poetry Library). (Illus.). 1979. reprint ed. 15.00 (0-89609-141-4) Roth Pub Inc.

Best Poems of 1923. Ed. by Leonard A. Strong. LC 70-39360. (Granger Index Reprint Ser.). 1977. reprint ed. 19.95 (0-8369-6354-7) Ayer.

Best Poems of 1924. Ed. by Thomas Moult. LC 79-50845. (Granger Poetry Library). (Illus.). 1979. reprint ed. 15.00 (0-89609-163-5) Roth Pub Inc.

Best Poems of 1926. Ed. by Thomas Moult. LC 79-50846. (Granger Poetry Library). (Illus.). 1979. reprint ed. 15.00 (0-89609-164-3) Roth Pub Inc.

Best Poems of 1930. Ed. by Thomas Moult. LC 77-94819. (Granger Poetry Library). (Illus.). 1978. reprint ed. 15.00 (0-89609-090-6) Roth Pub Inc.

Best Poems of 1931. Ed. by Thomas Moult. LC 78-73492. (Granger Poetry Library). (Illus.). 1979. reprint ed. 15.00 (0-89609-118-X) Roth Pub Inc.

Best Poems of 1932. Ed. by Thomas Moult. LC 78-73493. (Granger Poetry Library). (Illus.). 1979. reprint ed. 15.00 (0-89609-119-8) Roth Pub Inc.

Best Poems of 1958: Borestone Mountain Poetry Awards 1959, Vol. 11. Ed. by Borestone Mountain Poetry Awards Staff. LC 49-49262. 1959. 12.95 (0-87015-095-2) Pacific Bks.

Best Poems of 1960: Borestone Mountain Poetry Awards 1961, Vol. 13. Ed. by Borestone Mountain Poetry Awards Staff. LC 49-49262. 1961. 12.95 (0-87015-105-3); pap. 7.95 (0-87015-106-1) Pacific Bks.

Best Poems of 1963: Borestone Mountain Poetry Awards 1964, Vol. 16. Ed. by Borestone Mountain Poetry Awards Staff. LC 49-49262. 1964. 12.95 (0-87015-126-6); pap. 7.95 (0-87015-127-4) Pacific Bks.

Best Poems of 1964: Borestone Mountain Poetry Awards 1965, Vol. 17. Ed. by Borestone Mountain Poetry Awards Staff. LC 49-49262. 1965. 12.95 (0-87015-142-8) Pacific Bks.

Best Poems of 1966: Borestone Mountain Poetry Awards 1967, Vol. 19. Ed. by Borestone Mountain Poetry Awards Staff. LC 49-49262. 1967. 12.95 (0-87015-157-6) Pacific Bks.

Best Poems of 1967: Borestone Mountain Poetry Awards, 1968, Vol. 20. Ed. by Borestone Mountain Poetry Awards Staff. LC 49-49262. 1968. 12.95 (0-87015-171-1) Pacific Bks.

Best Poems of 1968: Borestone Mountain Poetry Awards 1969, Vol. 21. Ed. by Borestone Mountain Poetry Awards Staff. LC 49-49262. 1969. 12.95 (0-87015-179-7) Pacific Bks.

Best Poems of 1969: Borestone Mountain Poetry Awards 1970, Vol. 22. Ed. by Borestone Mountain Poetry Awards Staff. LC 49-49262. 1970. 12.95 (0-87015-186-X) Pacific Bks.

Best Poems of 1970: Borestone Mountain Poetry Awards 1971, Vol. 23. Ed. by Borestone Mountain Poetry Awards Staff. LC 49-49262. 1971. 12.95 (0-87015-195-9) Pacific Bks.

Best Poems of 1971: Borestone Mountain Poetry Awards 1972, Vol 24. Ed. by Borestone Mountain Poetry Awards Staff. LC 49-49262. 1972. 12.95 (0-87015-200-9) Pacific Bks.

Best Poems of 1972: Borestone Mountain Poetry Awards 1973, Vol. 25. Ed. by Borestone Mountain Poetry Awards Staff. LC 49-49262. 1973. 12.95 (0-87015-208-4) Pacific Bks.

Best Poems of 1973: Borestone Mountain Poetry Awards 1974, Vol. 26. Ed. by Borestone Mountain Poetry Awards Staff. LC 49-49262. 1974. 12.95 (0-87015-217-3) Pacific Bks.

Best Poems of 1974: Borestone Mountain Poetry Awards 1975, Vol. 27. Ed. by Borestone Mountain Poetry Awards Staff. LC 49-49262. 1975. 12.95 (0-87015-219-X) Pacific Bks.

Best Poems of 1975: Borestone Mountain Poetry Awards 1976, Vol. 28. Ed. by Borestone Mountain Poetry Awards Staff. LC 49-49262. 1976. 12.95 (0-87015-223-8) Pacific Bks.

Best Poems of 1976: Borestone Mountain Poetry Awards 1977, Vol.29. Ed. by Borestone Mountain Poetry Awards Staff. LC 49-49262. 1977. 12.95 (0-87015-227-0) Pacific Bks.

***Best Poems of 1995.** Ed. by Caroline Sullivan & Cynthia Stevens. 1500p. 1995. 69.95 (1-56167-260-2) Nat Lib Poetry.

***Best Police in the World: An Oral Police of English Policing from the 1930s to the 1960s.** Barbara Weinberger. (Illus.). 240p. 1995. 68.95 (1-85928-223-7, Pub. by Scolar Pr UK) Ashgate Pub Co.

Best Practice: New Standards for Teaching & Learning in America's Schools. Steve Zemelman et al. LC 92-47034. 252p. (C). 1993. pap. text ed. 19.00 (0-435-08788-6, 08788) Heinemann.

***Best Practice in Music Therapy: Utilizing Group Percussion Strategies for Promoting Volunteerism in the Well Older Adult.** Barbara L. Reuer & Barbara Crowe. 88p. (Orig.). 1995. pap. text ed. 25.00 (1-879167-08-5) SDSU Univ Ctr on Aging.

Best Practices for Moving Seed Technoloy: New Approaches to Doing Business. Jitendra P. Srivastava & Steven Jaffee. LC 93-14541. (Technical Paper, 0253-7494 Ser.: No. 213). 47p. 1993. 6.95 (0-8213-2506-X, 12506) World Bank.

***Best Practices for the Learner-Centered Classroom: A Collection of Articles by Robin Fogarty.** Robin Fogarty. LC 95-75387. 304p. (J). (gr. k up). 1995. pap. 19.95 (0-932935-93-1) IRI-Skylght.

Best Practices I: The Classroom As an Assessment Arena, 2. Ed. by Katharine G. Butler. LC 93-36264. (Topics in Language Disorders Ser.). 240p. 1994. pap. 30.00 (0-8342-0586-6, 20586) Aspen Pub.

Best Practices II: The Classroom As an Intervention Context. Ed. by Katharine G. Butler. LC 93-36264. (Topics in Language Disorders Ser.). 240p. 1994. 30.00 (0-8342-0587-4, 20587) Aspen Pub.

Best Practices in Assessment for School & Clinical Settings. Ed. by Booney Vance. LC 91-75519. 555p. 1993. lib. bdg. 49.50 (0-88422-114-8) Clinical Psych.

Best Practices in Assisted Living: Innovations in Design, Management & Financing. Victor Reginer et al. (Illus.). 166p. (Orig.). (C). 1991. 18.00 (1-881010-25-2) USC Andrus Geron.

Best Practices in European Innovation Development. 105p. 1989. 35.00 (0-317-05040-0) Natl Coun Econ Dev.

***Best Practices in Reengineering: What Works & What Doesn't in the Reengineering Process.** David K. Carr. 1995. text ed. 29.95 (0-07-011224-X) McGraw.

Best Practices in School Psychology II. Ed. by Alex Thomas & Jeff Grimes. 1048p. 1990. pap. text ed. 42.00 (0-932955-11-8) Natl Assn Psych.

Best Practices in School Psychology III. rev. ed. Ed. by Alex Thomas & Jeff Grimes. 1296p. 1995. pap. text ed. 80.00 (0-932955-99-1) Natl Assn Psych.

Best Practices in Trade Policy Reform. Ed. by Vinod Thomas & John Nash. (World Bank Publication Ser.). 240p. 1991. 24.95 (0-19-520871-4, 60871) OUP.

Best Practices in U. S. Innovation Development, Vols. I & II. 146p. 1989. 45.00 (0-317-05512-7) Natl Coun Econ Dev.

An Asterisk (*) at the beginning of an entry indicates that the title is appearing in BIP for the first time.

An Asterisk (*) at the beginning of an entry indicates that the title is appearing in BIP for the first time.

701

Best Sports Stories, 1953. Irving T. Marsh. 1980. 25.95 (*0-405-12031-1*) Ayer.
Best Sports Stories, 1954. Irving T. Marsh. 1980. 25.95 (*0-405-12030-3*) Ayer.
Best Sports Stories, 1955. Irving T. Marsh. 1980. 25.95 (*0-405-12029-X*) Ayer.
Best Sports Stories, 1956. Irving T. Marsh. 1980. 25.95 (*0-405-12028-1*) Ayer.
Best Sports Stories, 1958. Irving T. Marsh. 1980. 25.95 (*0-405-12026-5*) Ayer.
Best Sports Stories, 1959. Irving T. Marsh. 1980. 25.95 (*0-405-12025-7*) Ayer.
Best Sports Stories, 1960. Irving T. Marsh. 1980. 25.95 (*0-405-12074-5*) Ayer.
Best Sports Stories, 1961. Irving T. Marsh. 1980. 25.95 (*0-405-12073-7*) Ayer.
Best Sports Stories, 1962. Irving T. Marsh. 1980. 25.95 (*0-405-12072-9*) Ayer.
Best Sports Stories, 1963. Irving T. Marsh. 1980. 25.95 (*0-405-12071-0*) Ayer.
Best Sports Stories, 1964. Irving T. Marsh. 1980. 25.95 (*0-405-12070-2*) Ayer.
Best Sports Stories, 1965. Irving T. Marsh. 1980. 25.95 (*0-405-12069-9*) Ayer.
Best Sports Stories, 1966. Irving T. Marsh. 1980. 25.95 (*0-405-12068-0*) Ayer.
Best Sports Stories, 1967. Irving T. Marsh. 1980. 25.95 (*0-405-12067-2*) Ayer.
Best Sports Stories, 1968. Irving T. Marsh. 1980. 25.95 (*0-405-12066-4*) Ayer.
Best Sports Stories, 1969. Irving T. Marsh. 1980. 25.95 (*0-405-12065-6*) Ayer.
Best Sports Stories, 1970. Irving T. Marsh. 1980. 25.95 (*0-405-12064-8*) Ayer.
Best Sports Stories, 1973. Irving T. Marsh. 1980. 25.95 (*0-405-12061-3*) Ayer.
Best Sports Stories, 1974. Irving T. Marsh. 1980. 25.95 (*0-405-12060-5*) Ayer.
Best Sports Stories, 1975. Irving T. Marsh. 1980. 25.95 (*0-405-12059-1*) Ayer.
Best Sports Stories, 1976. Irving T. Marsh. 1980. 25.95 (*0-405-12058-3*) Ayer.
Best Sports Stories, 1977. Irving T. Marsh & Edward Ehre. 1980. 25.95 (*0-405-12871-1*) Ayer.
Best Sports Stories, 1978. Irving T. Marsh. 1980. 25.95 (*0-405-12872-X*) Ayer.
***Best Spot Illustration.** Date not set. 24.99 (*1-56496-116-8*) Rockport Pubs.
Best Stage Scenes for Men from the Nineteen Eighties. Ed. by Jocelyn A. Beard & Kristin Graham. (Scene Study Ser.). 214p. 1991. pap. 8.95 (*0-9622722-8-0*) Smith & Kraus.
Best Stage Scenes for Women from the Nineteen Eighties. Ed. by Jocelyn A. Beard & Kristin Graham. (Scene Study Ser.). 220p. 1991. pap. 8.95 (*0-9622722-7-2*) Smith & Kraus.
Best Stage Scenes of 1992. Ed. by Jocelyn A. Beard. (Scene Study Ser.). 202p. 1993. pap. 11.95 (*1-880399-18-0*) Smith & Kraus.
Best Stage Scenes of 1993. Ed. by Jocelyn A. Beard. (Monologue Audition Ser.). 256p. 1993. pap. 11.95 (*1-880399-44-X*) Smith & Kraus.
***Best Stage Scenes of 1994.** Jocelyn Beard. 1995. pap. 11. 95 (*1-880399-66-0*) Smith & Kraus.
***Best Stage Scenes of 1995.** Ed. by Jocelyn A. Beard. (Scene Anthologies Ser.). 256p. 1996. 11.95 (*1-57525-015-2*) Smith & Kraus.
Best Standards Ever, Vol. 1: A-L. rev. ed. (Best Ever Ser.). 224p. (Orig.). 1991. pap. 15.95 (*0-7935-1123-2*, 00359231) H Leonard.
Best Standards Ever, Vol. 2: M-Z. rev. ed. (Best Ever Ser.). 232p. 1991. pap. 15.95 (*0-7935-1124-0*, 00359232) H Leonard.
***Best Stocks to Trade for 1995: Windows of Time for Trading Profits.** William F. Eng. 208p. 1985. pap. text ed. 44.95 (*1-886375-50-X*) J W Martin.
Best Stories, 2 vols. in 1. Sarah O. Jewett. 16.25 (*0-8446-1248-0*) Peter Smith.
Best Stories, 2 vols., Set. Sara O. Jewett. (BCL1-PS American Literature Ser.). 1992. reprint ed. lib. bdg. 150.00 (*0-7812-6774-9*) Rprt Serv.
Best Stories from Guideposts. 480p. (Orig.). 1987. pap. 8.99 (*0-8423-0340-5*) Tyndale.
Best Stories from New Writers. Ed. by Linda S. Sanders. 198p. 1989. 16.95 (*0-89879-367-X*) Writers Digest.
Best Stories from the Best Book: And Thou Shalt Teach Them Diligently Unto Thy Children. J. Edson White. (Pioneer Ser.). (Illus.). 160p. (YA). (gr. 5 up). 1990. reprint ed. pap. 8.95 (*0-945460-06-6*) Upward Way.
***Best Stories from the Texas Storytelling Festival.** Ed. by Finley Stewart. (American Storytelling Ser.). 240p. 1995. text ed. 25.00 (*0-87483-404-X*) August Hse.
***Best Stories from the Texas Storytelling Festival.** Ed. by Finley Stewart. (American Storytelling Ser.). 240p. 1995. pap. text ed. 15.00 (*0-87483-405-8*) August Hse.
Best Stories of Heroism I Know. John C. Minot. 1977. 20. 95 (*0-8369-4231-0*, 6042) Ayer.
Best Stories of Mary E. Wilkins. Mary E. Wilkins Freeman. 1988. reprint ed. lib. bdg. 79.00 (*0-7812-0042-3*) Rprt Serv.
Best Stories of Mary E. Wilkins Freeman. Mary E. Wilkins Freeman. Ed. by Henry W. Lanier. LC 70-145023. 1971. reprint ed. 69.00 (*0-403-00970-7*) Scholarly.
Best Stories of Paul Laurence Dunbar. Paul L. Dunbar. Ed. by B. Brawley. (Notable American Authors Ser.). 1992. reprint ed. lib. bdg. 75.00 (*0-7812-2715-1*) Rprt Serv.
Best Stories of Walter de la Mare. Walter De la Mare. 400p. (Orig.). 1983. pap. 9.95 (*0-571-13076-3*) Faber & Faber.
Best Stories of Wilbur Daniel Steele. Wilbur D. Steele. LC 75-36513. 469p. 1976. reprint ed. text ed. 37.50 (*0-8371-8637-4*, STWS, Greenwood Pr) Greenwood.
Best Story about Jesus. Sheila S. Coleman. (Happy Day Bks.). 32p. (J). (gr. k-2). 1989. 2.50 (*0-87403-602-X*, 3862) Standard Pub.
***Best Summer Ever: A Parents' Guide.** Joan Bergstrom. LC 94-42376. 112p. (J). (gr. 1-7). 1995. pap. 9.95 (*1-883672-22-8*) Tricycle Pr.
Best Supernatural Tales of Arthur Conan Doyle. Arthur Conan Doyle. Ed. by E. F. Bleiler. LC 78-66710. (Illus.). 256p. 1979. pap. 6.95 (*0-486-23725-7*) Dover.
Best System: Basic Recordkeeping for a Small Business. Thomas P. Duffy. LC 84-70087. 116p. 1984. 35.00 (*0-916115-00-3*) Challenge Pub Co.
Best Tales of Hoffmann. E. T. Hoffmann. Ed. by E. F. Bleiler. (Illus.). (Orig.). (YA). (gr. 9-12). 1963. pap. 8.95 (*0-486-21793-0*) Dover.
Best Tales of Hoffmann. E. T. Hoffmann. Ed. & Intro. by E. F. Bleiler. (Orig.). 20.00 (*0-8446-2262-1*) Peter Smith.
Best Talk in Town. Scott Young & Margaret Hogan. (Illus.). 280p. 1979. 13.95 (*0-7720-1257-1*, Pub. by Stoddart Pubng CN) Genl Dist Srvs.
Best Teacher in the World. Bernice Chardiet & Grace Maccarone. (School Friends Ser.). (Illus.). 32p. (J). (ps-2). 1991. reprint ed. 2.50 (*0-590-43307-5*) Scholastic Inc.
Best Teacher "Stuff" from Nancy L. Johnson. Nancy L. Johnson. (Illus.). 96p. (J). (gr. k-8). 1993. pap. 10.95 (*1-880505-06-1*) Pieces of Lrning.
Best Test Design. Benjamin D. Wright & Mark H. Stone. LC 79-88489. (Illus.). (C). 1979. pap. 25.00 (*0-941938-00-X*) Mesa Pr.
***Best Test Preparation for CLEP: General Examinations.** Research & Education Association Staff. 1008p. 1995. pap. text ed. 17.95 (*0-87891-901-5*) Res & Educ.
Best-Tested Recipes of Hawaii: Hawaiiana. Margaret Stone. LC 84-146717. (Hawaiiana Ser.). (Illus.). 63p. (Orig.). 1984. pap. 4.95 (*0-941351-05-X*) Aloha.
Best Thanksgiving Book. Patricia Whitehead. LC 84-8831. (ABC Adventures Ser.). (Illus.). 32p. (J). (gr. k-2). 1985. lib. bdg. 11.59 (*0-8167-0371-X*); pap. text ed. 2.95 (*0-8167-0372-8*) Troll Assocs.
Best Thanksgiving Ever. Francine Pascal. (Sweet Valley Kids Ser.: No. 34). (J). (ps-3). 1992. 2.99 (*0-553-48007-3*) Bantam.
***Best the Country Affords: Vermont Furniture 1765-1850.** Kenneth J. Zogry. Ed. by Philip Zea. (Illus.). 176p. Date not set. 50.00 (*0-614-04159-7*); pap. 32.00 (*0-614-04158-9*) Benni Mus.
Best There Ever Was: The History of the Heisman Memorial Trophy & the Men Who Made It Famous. Mike Bynum. (Illus.). 288p. 1992. text ed. 35.00 (*1-878839-05-5*) Gridiron Football.
Best Thing about Easter. Christine H. Tangvald. (Happy Day Ser.). (Illus.). 28p. (J). (ps). 1993. lib. bdg. 5.49 (*0-7847-0035-4*, 24-03825) Standard Pub.
Best Thing in Life Is a Friend. Ed. by Susan P. Schutz. LC 86-73019. (Illus.). 64p. (Orig.). 1987. pap. 7.95 (*0-88396-249-7*) Blue Mtn Pr CO.
***Best Thing of All.** Pat Thomson. (Illus.). 32p. (J). (ps-1). 1995. pap. 8.95 (*0-575-05997-4*, Pub. by V Gollancz UK) Trafalgar.
Best Things about Dolls. Joan B. Hecht. (Illus.). 16p. (J). (ps-3). 1987. pap. 4.95 (*0-931271-08-8*) Hi Plains Pr.
***Best Things in Life.** Rita C. Estrada. (Western Lovers Ser.). 1995. mass mkt. 3.99 (*0-373-88515-6*, 1-88515-1) Harlequin Bks.
Best Things in Life. Peter Kreeft. LC 84-6697. 190p. (Orig.). 1984. pap. 10.99 (*0-87784-922-6*, 922) InterVarsity.
***Best Things in Life: Two Hundred Thirty-Six Things about Cleveland.** Ed. by Christopher Johnston. 144p. (Orig.). 1994. pap. 5.95 (*0-9631738-8-X*) Gray & Co Pubs.
Best Time. Elaine M. Starkman. (Illus.). 50p. (Orig.). 1992. pap. 6.95 (*0-9601254-4-2*) Sheer Pr.
Best Time I Ever Had Was at Uncle Ben's. abr. ed. A. G. Strickland. 230p. 1995. pap. 8.95 (*1-56901-462-0*) NW Pub.
Best Time of Your Life. Edward Ethell. LC 86-91880. (Illus.). 64p. (Orig.). 1987. pap. 10.00 (*0-9617984-0-8*) E O Ethell.
Best Times to See the Greatest Wonders of the West. Dean Spieth. 92p. 1994. pap. 6.95 (*0-9639514-0-8*) Glacier Photo.
Best Tobacco Cartoons of All Time. C. J. Phillips. Ed. by Mike Gurian & Brad Hemeon. (Illus.). 80p. 1992. pap. 5.95 (*0-9621639-9-5*) Grand Natl Pr.
Best TOEFL Test Book. Nancy Stanley. 300p. (C). 1984. audio write for info. (*0-201-16470-1*); pap. text ed. write for info. (*0-201-16471-X*) Addison-Wesley.
Best TOEFL Test Book. rev. ed. Nancy Stanley. (College ESOL Ser.). 320p. 1987. pap. text ed. 12.95 (*0-201-15422-6*) Addison-Wesley.
Best TOEFL Test Book, No. I. Nancy Stanley. 300p. (C). 1984. audio write for info. (*0-201-16472-8*) Addison-Wesley.
Best TOEFL Test Book, No. II. Nancy Stanley. 300p. (C). 1984. audio write for info. (*0-201-16473-6*) Addison-Wesley.
Best Town in the World. Byrd Baylor. LC 83-9033. (Illus.). 32p. (J). (gr. 1-3). 1983. text ed. 14.95 (*0-684-18035-9*, C Scribner Sons Young) S&S Childrens.
Best Town in the World. Byrd Baylor. LC 86-3381. (Illus.). 32p. (J). (gr. 1-3). 1986. reprint ed. pap. 3.95 (*0-689-71086-0*, Aladdin Paperbacks) S&S Childrens.
***Best Toys, Books & Videos for Kids, 1995: A Guide to One Thousand Plus Kid-Tested, Classic & New Products for Ages 0-10.** Joanne Oppenheim & Stephanie Oppenheim. (Illus.). 352p. (Orig.). 1994. pap. 12.00 (*0-06-273315-X*, Harper Ref) HarpC.
***Best Toys, Books and Videos for Kids 1996.** Joanne Oppenheim & Stephanie Oppenheim. (Illus.). 384p. 1995. pap. 13.00 (*0-06-273379-6*) HarpC.
***Best Trade of All.** Bourque. 1995. pap. text ed. (*0-8114-8401-7*) Raintree Steck-V.
Best Trade of All. Nina Bourque. LC 83-7352. (Imagination Bks.). (Illus.). 32p. (J). (gr. 3-6). 1983. 14.65 (*0-940742-33-0*) Raintree Steck-V.
Best Trade of All. Nina Bourque. LC 83-7352. (Imagination Clippers Ser.). (Illus.). 32p. (J). (gr. 3-6). 1984. audio, lib. bdg. 27.99 (*0-8172-2280-4*); audio 14.00 (*0-317-19659-6*) Raintree Steck-V.
Best Travel Activity Book Ever. 1991. pap. 5.95 (*0-528-80378-6*) Rand McNally.
***Best Travel Activity Book Ever!** Rand McNally Staff. (Backseat Bks.). (Illus.). 320p. (J). (gr. 1-6). 1994. pap. 3.95 (*0-528-81410-9*) Rand McNally.
Best Travel Guide To: Yellowstone & Teton National Park Including Jackson Hole Wyoming. Joy M. Johnson. LC 93-60623. (Illus.). 210p. (Orig.). 1993. pap. 12.95 (*1-880782-14-6*) Spirit Dance.
Best Treatment. Isadore Rosenfeld. 1992. mass mkt. 5.99 (*0-553-29879-8*) Bantam.
Best Treatment. large type ed. Isadore Rosenfeld. LC 92-32815. (General Ser.). 1993. 22.95 (*0-8161-5657-3*) G K Hall.
Best Trick of All. Nora Dale. (Real Readers Ser.: Level Red). (Illus.). 32p. (J). (gr. 1-4). 1989. lib. bdg. 19.97 (*0-8172-3505-1*); pap. 3.95 (*0-8114-6700-7*) Raintree Steck-V.
Best True Ghost Stories of the Twentieth Century. David C. Knight. LC 83-23075. (Illus.). 64p. (J). (gr. 3-7). 1984. pap. 11.95 (*0-671-66556-1*) S&S Trade.
Best True Ghost Stories of the 20th Century. David C. Knight. (YA). 1987. pap. 5.95 (*0-671-66557-X*) S&S Trade.
Best Type of Girl: A History of Girls' Independent Schools. Gillian Avery. (Illus.). 424p. 1991. 45.00 (*0-233-98642-1*, Pub. by A Deutsch UK) Trafalgar.
Best Unix Tips Ever. Kenneth H. Rosen. 1994. pap. text ed. 29.95 (*0-07-881924-5*) Osborne-McGraw.
***Best Use of Landscape Items in Architectural Rendering.** Ed. by Akira Ryu. (Illus.). 144p. 1995. pap. text ed. 36. 95 (*4-7661-0771-3*, Pub. by Graphic Sha JA) Bks Nippan.
Best Uses for Your Computer. Gus Venditto. (Illus.). (Orig.). 1994. pap. 16.95 (*1-56276-261-3*) Ziff-Davis.
***Best Vacation? An Ego Trip!** Marykay Gaines. Ed. by Rosemary Garner. Date not set. pap. text ed. write for info. (*0-9641822-3-8*) O W L Press.
Best Vacation Rentals: Caribbean. Philip Lief Staff. 1991. pap. 17.95 (*0-13-928227-0*) P-H.
Best Vacation Rentals: Europe. Philip Lief Staff. 1991. pap. 17.95 (*0-13-928219-X*) P-H.
Best Valentine Book. Patricia Whitehead. LC 84-8829. (ABC Adventures Ser.). (Illus.). 32p. (J). (gr. k-2). 1985. lib. bdg. 11.59 (*0-8167-0369-8*); pap. text ed. 2.95 (*0-8167-0370-1*) Troll Assocs.
Best Valentine in the World. Marjorie W. Sharmat. LC 81-13345. (Illus.). 32p. (J). (ps-3). 1982. lib. bdg. 14.95 (*0-8234-0440-4*) Holiday.
Best Videos for Children & Young Adults. Jennifer J. Gallant. 185p. 1990. lib. bdg. 45.00 (*0-87436-561-9*) ABC-CLIO.
Best War at the Time. Clarence Lininger. 10.95 (*0-8315-0068-9*) Speller.
Best War Ever: America & World War II. Michael C. Adams. LC 93-4364. (American Moment Ser.). (Illus.). 208p. (C). 1993. text ed. 38.95 (*0-8018-4696-X*); pap. text ed. 12.95 (*0-8018-4697-8*) Johns Hopkins.
Best Way Out Is Within. Gale L. Finger. Ed. by Margaret Thompson et al. 96p. (Orig.). 1990. pap. 7.95 (*0-9622707-2-5*) Zivah Pubs.
Best Way to Destroy a Ship: The Evidence of European Naval Operations in World War II. Tweed W. Ross, Jr. 219p. (Orig.). 1980. pap. 27.95 (*0-89126-069-2*) MA-AH Pub.
***Best Way to Lose.** Janet Dailey. 1993. mass mkt. 5.99 (*0-671-87499-3*) PB.
Best Way to Plan Your Day. Edward R. Dayton & Ted W. Engstrom. 96p. 1989. pap. 2.99 (*0-8423-0373-1*) Tyndale.
***Best Way to See a Shark.** Allan Fowler. LC 94-36347. (Rookie Read-About Science Ser.). 32p. (J). (ps-2). 1995. lib. bdg. 11.93 (*0-516-06032-5*) Childrens.
Best Way to Train Your Gun Dog: The Delmar Smith Method. Bill Tarrant. 1977. 18.00 (*0-679-50750-7*) McKay.
Best We Can Be. (Manned Flight Awareness Ser.). (Illus.). 24p. (Orig.). 1989. pap. 2.00 (*0-16-004244-5*, S/N 033-000-010) USGPO.
Best We Can Do Is Forgive. Joe Forte. (Illus.). 128p. (Orig.). 1989. pap. 15.00 (*0-9624755-0-5*) Ashleigh Face Pr.
Best Wedding Shower Book: A Complete Guide for Party Planners. Courtney Cooke. LC 87-5599. 128p. 1987. pap. 5.00 (*0-88166-096-5*) Meadowbrook.
***Best Western Stores of Ed Gorman.** large type ed. Ed. by Bill Pronzini & Martin H. Greenberg. 205p. 1995. 17.95 (*0-7838-1283-3*) Hall.
Best Western Stories of Bill Pronzini. Bill Pronzini. Ed. by Martin M. Greenberg. LC 89-21778. (Best Western Stories Ser.). 200p. 1990. 24.95 (*0-8040-0932-5*) Swallow.
Best Western Stories of Bill Pronzini. Bill Pronzini. LC 89-21778. (Best Western Stories of...Ser.). 200p. 1991. pap. 14.95 (*0-8040-0933-3*) Swallow.
Best Western Stories of Bill Pronzini. large type ed. Bill Pronzini. Ed. by Martin H. Greenberg. (Nightingale Ser.). 287p. 1991. pap. 14.95 (*0-8161-5115-6*, Nightingale) Hall.
Best Western Stories of Ed Gorman. Ed Gorman. Ed. by Bill Pronzini & Martin H. Greenberg. LC 92-15421. (Western Writers Ser.). 160p. (C). 1992. 26.95 (*0-8040-0959-7*) Swallow.
Best Western Stories of Frank Bonham. Frank Bonham. Ed. by Bill Pronzini & Martin H. Greenberg. LC 89-11263. (Western Writers Ser.). 288p. 1989. 24.95 (*0-8040-0929-5*); pap. 15.95 (*0-8040-0930-9*) Swallow.
Best Western Stories of John Jakes. John Jakes. Ed. by Bill Pronzini & Martin H. Greenberg. LC 90-49427. (Western Writers Ser.). 291p. 1991. pap. 14.95 (*0-8214-0983-2*) Ohio U Pr.
Best Western Stories of Les Savage, Jr. Les Savage, Jr. Ed. by Bill Pronzini & Martin H. Greenberg. (Western Writers Ser.). 248p. 1991. 29.95 (*0-8040-0950-3*, Ohio U Ctr Intl) Ohio U Pr.
Best Western Stories of Lewis B. Patten. large type ed. Ed. by Bill Pronzini & Martin Greenberg. 336p. 1989. pap. 13.95 (*0-8161-4781-7*, Large Print Bks) Hall.
Best Western Stories of Lewis Patten. Lewis Patten. Ed. by Bill Pronzini & Martin H. Greenberg. LC 86-26144. (Western Writers Ser.). 180p. 1989. reprint ed. pap. 12. 95 (*0-8040-0925-2*) Swallow.
Best Western Stories of Loren D. Estleman. Loren D. Estleman. Ed. by Bill Pronzini. LC 88-38733. (Best Western Stories Ser.). 135p. 1990. 22.95 (*0-8040-0911-2*); pap. 11.95 (*0-8040-0912-0*) Swallow.
Best Western Stories of Ryerson Johnson. Ryerson Johnson. Ed. by Bill Pronzini & Martin H. Greenberg. LC 90-33709. (Western Writers Ser.). 246p. 1990. 24.95 (*0-8040-0937-6*) Swallow.
***Best Western Stories of Ryerson Johnson.** large type ed. Ed. by Bill Pronzini & Martin H. Greenberg. 283p. 1995. reprint ed. pap. 18.95 (*0-7838-1381-3*) Hall.
Best Western Stories of Steve Frazee. Steve Frazee. Ed. by Bill Pronzini. LC 83-18052. (Best Western Stories Ser.). 294p. 1989. reprint ed. pap. 12.95 (*0-8040-0914-7*) Swallow.
Best Western Stories of Wayne D. Overholser. Wayne D. Overholser. Ed. by Bill Pronzini & Martin H. Greenberg. LC 83-20111. (Best Western Stories Ser.). 220p. 1989. reprint ed. pap. 12.95 (*0-8040-0913-9*) Swallow.
Best Wine Buys for Ten Dollars Or Less: A Guide for the Frugal Connoisseur. Barbara Ensrud. 1991. 9.95 (*0-679-73918-1*, Villard Bks) Random.
Best Wisconsin Bike Trips. Phil Van Valkenberg. 80p. 1985. pap. 9.95 (*0-915024-29-2*) WI Trails.
Best Wishes. Cynthia Rylant. LC 92-7796. (Meet the Author Ser.). (Illus.). 32p. (J). (gr. 2-5). 1992. 13.95 (*1-878450-20-4*) R Owen Pubs.
***Best Wishes, Joe Brady.** Mary P. Osborne. (YA). 1994. pap. 4.99 (*0-679-84650-6*, Bullseye Bks) Random Bks Yng Read.
Best Wishes, Joe Brady. Mary P. Osborne. 192p. (YA). (gr. 7 up). 1994. pap. 4.99 (*0-679-84560-7*, Bullseye Bks) Random Bks Yng Read.
Best Witches. Jane Yolen. (Illus.). 48p. (J). (gr. k-4). 1989. 14.95 (*0-399-21539-5*, Putnam) Putnam Pub Group.
***Best Witness: The Mermelstein Case & the Controversy on Historical Revisionism.** 1994. lib. bdg. write for info. (*0-8490-9071-7*) Gordon Pr.
Best Women's Stage Monologues of 1990. Ed. by Jocelyn A. Beard. LC 90-91799. 86p. (Orig.). 1991. pap. 8.95 (*0-9622722-1-3*) Smith & Kraus.
Best Women's Stage Monologues of 1991. Ed. by Jocelyn A. Beard. 98p. (Orig.). 1991. pap. 8.95 (*1-880399-01-6*) Smith & Kraus.
Best Women's Stage Monologues of 1992. Ed. by Jocelyn A. Beard. 88p. 1993. pap. 8.95 (*1-880399-10-5*) Smith & Kraus.
Best Women's Stage Monologues of 1993. Ed. by Jocelyn A. Beard. (Monologue Audition Ser.). 104p. 1993. pap. 8.95 (*1-880399-42-3*) Smith & Kraus.
***Best Women's Stage Monologues of 1994.** Jocelyn Beard. 1995. pap. 8.95 (*1-880399-65-2*) Smith & Kraus.
***Best Women's Stage Monologues of 1995.** Ed. by Jocelyn A. Beard. (Annual Best Monologues Ser.). 112p. 1996. 8.95 (*1-880399-62-8*) Smith & Kraus.
Best Word Book. Richard Scarry. (FRE.). (J). (gr. 3-8). 14. 95 (*0-685-28441-7*) Fr & Eur.
Best Works of Aubrey Beardsley. Aubrey Beardsley. 1990. pap. 7.95 (*0-486-26273-1*) Dover.
Best, Worst & Most Unusual. Bruce Felton. 1994. 10.98 (*0-88365-861-5*) Galahad Bks.
***Best Worst Day.** Bonnie B. Graves. LC 94-43189. (Illus.). (J). 1996. write for info. (*0-7868-0167-0*); lib. bdg. write for info. (*0-7868-2139-6*) Hyprn Child.
Best Writing on Writing. Ed. by Jack Heffron. 208p. (Orig.). 1994. pap. 16.99 (*1-884910-01-7*) Story Pr Ohio.
Best Years. Lucina B. Moxley. LC 91-58047. 510p. 1991. pap. 16.95 (*1-878208-10-1*) Guild Pr IN.
Best Years of the Century: Richard Watson Gilder, Scribner's Monthly, & the Century Magazine, 1870-1909. Arthur John. LC 80-25841. (Illus.). 305p. 1981. 29.95 (*0-252-00857-X*) U of Ill Pr.
Best Years of Their Lives: A Resource Guide for Teenagers in Crisis. Stephanie Zvirin. LC 92-5575. 150p. (C). 1992. pap. text ed. 22.00 (*0-8389-0586-2*) ALA.
Best You Can Be: A Woman's Guide to Personal Growth. Dorothy E. Watts. LC 93-17358. 1993. pap. 7.95 (*0-8280-0722-5*) Review & Herald.
Best You Can Do Is Forgive. Joseph R. Forte & Joe Forte. (Illus.). 128p. (Orig.). 1989. pap. 15.00 (*0-685-29457-9*) Ashleigh Face Pr.
***Best 50 Apple Recipes.** Joanna White. (Best 50 Ser.). 80p. (Orig.). 1995. pap. 4.95 (*1-55867-126-9*) Bristol Pub Ent CA.
***Best 50 Biscotti Recipes.** Barbara Karoff. (Best 50 Ser.). 80p. (Orig.). 1995. pap. 4.95 (*1-55867-129-3*) Bristol Pub Ent CA.

An Asterisk (*) at the beginning of an entry indicates that the title is appearing in BIP for the first time.

***Best 50 Chicken Breast Recipes.** Joanna White. (Best 50 Ser.). 80p. (Orig.). 1995. pap. 4.95 (*1-55867-125-0*) Bristol Pub Ent CA.

***Best 50 Chili Recipes.** Tom Katona & Christie Katona. (Best 50 Ser.). 80p. (Orig.). 1995. pap. 4.95 (*1-55867-130-7*) Bristol Pub Ent CA.

***Best 50 Mushroom Recipes.** Barbara Karoff. (Best 50 Ser.). 80p. (Orig.). 1995. pap. 4.95 (*1-55867-128-5*) Bristol Pub Ent CA.

***Best 50 Shrimp & Prawn Recipes.** Tom Katona & Christie Katona. (Best 50 Ser.). 80p. (Orig.). 1995. pap. 4.95 (*1-55867-127-7*) Bristol Pub Ent CA.

Bestaires. Henry de Montherlant. (FRE.). 1972. pap. 10.95 (*0-8288-3714-7*, F115680) Fr & Eur.

Bestandskatalog: Archiv-und Internationale Dokumentationsstelle fur das Blinden-und Sehbeeintrentwesen. Ed. by Deutsche Blindenstudienstalt Staff & Lahn Marburg. xii, 759p. (GER.). 1987. lib. bdg. 150.00 (*3-598-10641-6*) K G Saur.

Besteuerung und Innenfinanzierung. Wolfgang Lichy. (C). 1967. 67.70 (*3-11-000911-0*) De Gruyter.

Bestfeeding. Mary Renfrew et al. LC 89-920. 1989. pap. 12. 95 (*0-89087-571-5*) Celestial Arts.

Bestia. Ed. by Benjamin Bennani. (Yearbook of the Beast Fable Society Ser.: Vol. 4). 120p. 1992. pap. 55.00x (*1-5619-475-7*) Benjamins North Am.

Bestiaire Celeste. Henri De Montherlant. 13.95 (*0-8288-9630-5*, F115680) Fr & Eur.

Bestiaires. Henry De Montherlant. 332p. (FRE.). 1972. pap. 10.95 (*0-7859-1629-6*, 2070362698) Fr & Eur.

Bestializing the Human Female. Margot Sims. LC 82-61146. (Illus.). 140p. 1982. pap. 6.00 (*0-89608-150-8*) South End Pr.

Bestiare. Guillaume de Normandie. LC 73-180441. reprint ed. 55.00 (*0-404-56615-4*) AMS Pr.

Bestiary. Boynton Merrill, Jr. LC 75-3549. (Illus.). 72p. 1976. 10.00 (*0-8131-1329-6*) U Pr of Ky.

Bestiary. S. Mitchell. Date not set. 25.00 (*0-06-016918-4*, HarpT) HarpC.

Bestiary. Richard Wilbur. 1993. 25.00 (*0-679-42875-5*) Pantheon.

Bestiary: Being an English Version of the Bodlian Library, Oxford, MS Bodley 764. Tr. by Richard Barber. (Illus.). 208p. (C). 1993. text ed. 63.00 (*0-85115-329-1*) Boydell & Brewer.

Bestiary of Bridge. James J. Kilpatrick. (Illus.). 128p. 1986. ring bd. 9.95 (*0-8362-7930-1*) Andrews & McMeel.

Bestiary of Christ. Louis Charbonneau-Lassay. Tr. & Abr. by D. M. Dooling. (Illus.). 496p. 1992. pap. 16.00 (*0-14-019449-5*, Arkana) Viking Penguin.

Bestiary of Christ. abr. ed. Louis Charbonneau-Lassay. Tr. & Intro. by D. M. Dooling. (Illus.). 496p. 1991. 29.95 (*0-930407-18-0*) Parabola Bks.

Bestiary of Discontent: Bestiario dos Descontentos. Miguelanxo Murado. Tr. by Carys Evans-Corrales. LC 93-32609. (Hispanic Literature Ser.: Vol. 21). (Illus.). 144p. 1993. 69.95 (*0-7734-9338-7*) E Mellen.

Bestimmungsschluessel Europaeischer Flechten. J. Poelt. (Illus.). 1969. pap. 56.00 (*3-7682-0159-7*) Lubrecht & Cramer.

Bestimmungsschluessel Europaeischer Flechten. J. Poelt & A. Vezda. (Bibliotheca Lichenologica Ser.: No. 9, suppl. I). 1977. lib. bdg. 32.50 (*3-7682-1162-2*) Lubrecht & Cramer.

Bestimmungsschluessel Europaeischer Flechten, Suppl. II. J. Poelt & A. Vezda. (Bibliotheca Lichenologica Ser.: No. 16). 390p. (GER.). 1981. text ed. 52.00 (*3-7682-1312-9*) Lubrecht & Cramer.

Best's Advance Company Reports. (Property-Casualty & Life-Health Editions Ser.). 1994. 20.00 (*0-685-65175-4*) A M Best.

Best's Agents Guide to Life Insurance Companies. Best, A. M., Staff. 550p. 1994. 95.00 (*0-685-11479-1*) A M Best.

Best's Aggregates & Averages: Life-Health Edition. Best, A. M., Staff. 75p. 1994. pap. 95.00 (*0-685-43288-2*) A M Best.

Best's Aggregates & Averages: Property-Casualty Edition. Best, A. M., Staff. 300p. 1994. pap. 285.00 (*0-685-11471-6*) A M Best.

Best's Directory of Recommended Insurance Adjusters. Best, A. M., Staff. 1000p. 1994. 65.00 (*0-317-07371-0*) A M Best.

Best's Directory of Recommended Insurance Attorneys. Best, A. M., Staff. 2500p. 1994. 75.00 (*0-317-07366-4*) A M Best.

Best's Experience by State (by Line) Best, A. M., Staff. 1994. ring bd. write for info. (*0-318-59847-5*); audio, cd-rom write for info. (*0-318-59848-5*) A M Best.

Best's Flitcraft Compend. Best, A. M., Staff. 1994. 55.00 (*0-317-53406-8*) A M Best.

Best's Insurance Management Reports. (Property-Casualty & Life-Health Editions Ser.). 1994. 390.00 (*0-317-53409-2*) A M Best.

Best's Insurance Reports. Best, A. M., Staff. (Property-Casualty & Life-Health Editions Ser.). 2000p. 1994. 600. 00 (*0-317-53402-5*); cd-rom write for info. (*0-318-59845-0*) A M Best.

Best's Insurance Reports - International. 1994. 600.00 (*0-317-53398-3*) A M Best.

Best's Key Rating Guide. Best, A. M., Staff. (Property-Casualty & Life-Health Editions Ser.). 1994. 95.00 (*0-317-53393-2*) A M Best.

Best's Key Rating Guide Supplement. (Property-Casualty & Life-Health Editions Ser.). 1994. 120.00 (*0-685-17512-X*) A M Best.

Best's Loss Control Engineering Manual. A. M. Best Staff. 1994. 295.00 (*0-685-62527-3*) A M Best.

Best's Market Guide, Vol. I: Corporate Stocks. Best, A. M., Staff. 700p. 1994. 500.00 (*0-317-53411-4*) A M Best.

Best's Market Guide, Vol. II: Corporate Bonds. Best, A. M., Staff. 1200p. 1994. 625.00 (*0-685-11480-5*) A M Best.

Best's Market Guide, Vol. III: Municipal Bonds. Best, A. M., Staff. 1200p. 1994. 625.00 (*0-685-11481-3*) A M Best.

Best's Retirement Income Guide. 1994. 65.00 (*0-317-53404-1*) A M Best.

Best's Safety Directory. Best, A. M., Staff. 1800p. 1994. pap. 45.00 (*0-685-43285-8*) A M Best.

Best's Underwriting Guide. A. M. Best Staff. 1994. 295.00 (*0-685-62526-5*) A M Best.

Besuch der Alten Dame. Friedrich Durrenmatt. Ed. by Paul K. Ackermann. LC 60-3863. (GER.). (C). (gr. 11-12). 1960. pap. 21.16 (*0-395-04089-2*) HM.

Besuch der Alten Dame, Durrenmatt: Critical Monographs in English. Sydney G. Donald. 90p. 1993. pap. 32.00 (*0-85261-342-3*, Pub. by Univ of Glasgow UK) St Mut.

Bet a Million! the Story of John W. Gates. Lloyd Wendt & Herman Kogan. Ed. by Stuart Bruchey. LC 80-1349. (Railroads Ser.). (Illus.). 1981. reprint ed. lib. bdg. 33.95 (*0-405-13821-0*) Ayer.

***Bet Against the House.** Catherine Dain. 224p. (Orig.). 1995. pap. text ed. 4.99 (*0-425-14580-8*, Prime Crime) Berkley Pub.

Bet Din - the Jewish People's Court: A Teacher's Guide. Joel L. Grishaver. 70p. 1987. pap. 10.00 (*0-933873-38-7*) Torah Aura.

Bet Din Student Casebook: The Jewish People's Court. Joel L. Grishaver. (Illus.). 32p. 1987. pap. text ed. 3.95 (*0-933873-11-5*) Torah Aura.

Bet Low: Paintings & Drawings 1945-1985. 28p. 1985. 30. 00 (*0-906474-49-3*, Pub. by Third Eye Centre UK) St Mut.

Bet Man. Ira J. Wise. (Illus.). 96p. (J). (gr. 1-2). 1991. 4.95 (*0-933873-55-7*) Torah Aura.

Bet on Cowboys, Not Horses: A Technological Breakthrough for Employee Selection. Brooks Mitchell. Ed. by T. J. Ross & Mary Ross. LC 93-60890. (Illus.). 181p. 1994. 19.95 (*0-9634940-2-3*) York Pub.

Bet on It! Book of South Dakota Trivia, a Jackpot of Amazing Facts about the State That Rand McNally Forgot. Stephen C. Bakken. LC 92-40905. 1992. 12.95 (*0-944287-09-3*) Ex Machina.

Bet on It! The Ultimate Guide to Nevada. Mary Jane Edwards & Greg Edwards. LC 90-50863. (Illus.). 208p. (Orig.). 1992. pap. 10.95 (*0-914457-44-6*) Mustang Pub.

Bet on Your Golf Game! An Indispensable Guide for Betting on the Golf Course. Ralph Monti. LC 93-74488. (Illus.). 160p. 1994. pap. 7.95 (*1-884490-20-4*) Fortune Media.

Bet Sbaar Hakavonot. R. Issac Luria. (HEB.). 1983. write for info. (*0-924457-48-1*) Res Ctr Kabbalah.

Bet They'll Miss Us When We're Gone: Stories. Marianne Wiggins. LC 89-46130. 192p. 1992. reprint ed. pap. 10. 00 (*0-06-092164-1*, PL) HarpC.

Bet You Can! Science Possibilities to Fool You. Vicki Cobb & Kathy Darling. (Illus.). 112p. (J). (gr. 3-7). 1983. pap. 3.99 (*0-380-82180-X*, Camelot) Avon.

Bet You Can: Science Possibilities to Fool You. Vicki Cobb. (Illus.). 112p. (J). 1990. 12.95 (*0-688-09865-7*) Lothrop.

***Bet You Can't!** Diana G. Gallagher. (Orig.). (J). (gr. 3-6). 1995. pap. 3.50 (*0-671-53300-2*, Minstrel Bks) PB.

Bet You Can't! Science Impossibilities to Fool You. Vicki Cobb & Kathy Darling. LC 79-9254. (Illus.). 128p. (J). (gr. 5 up). 1980. 15.00 (*0-688-41905-4*); lib. bdg. 14.93 (*0-688-51905-9*) Lothrop.

Bet You Can't: Science Impossibilities to Fool You. Vicki Cobb & Kathy Darling. (Illus.). 128p. (J). (gr. 3-7). 1983. pap. 3.99 (*0-380-54502-0*, Camelot) Avon.

Beta: A Novel. Esther R. Olmstead. 1994. 15.95 (*0-533-10771-7*) Vantage.

Beta-Adrenergic Receptors. Intro. by John P. Perkins. LC 90-15616. (Receptors Ser.). (Illus.). 416p. 1991. 109.50 (*0-89603-173-X*) Humana.

Beta-Adrenoceptors: Molecular Biology, Biochemistry & Pharmacology. Ed. by R. R. Ruffolo. (Progress in Basic & Clinical Pharmacology Ser.: Vol. 7). (Illus.). x, 240p. 1991. 196.00 (*3-8055-5366-8*) S Karger.

Beta Adrenoceptors in Asthma. Ed. by John Morley. (Perspectives in Asthma Ser.). 1984. text ed. 69.00 (*0-12-506440-3*) Acad Pr.

Beta Agonists in the Treatment of Asthma. Ed. by J. F. Costello & R. D. Mann. LC 92-49662. 170p. 1992. 68. 00 (*1-85070-438-4*) Prthnon Pub.

Beta Alpha Psi, from Omega to Zeta Omega: The Making of a Comprehensive Accounting Fraternity, 1946-1984. Terry K. Sheldahl. Ed. by Richard P. Brief. (Accounting Thought & Practice Ser.). 775p. 1987. lib. bdg. 25.00 (*0-8240-7855-1*) Garland.

***Beta-Aluminas & Beta Batteries: Proceedings of the International Workshop, Druzhba, Bugaria, May 1991.** International Workshop Staff. Ed. by G. Staikov. (Key Engineering Materials Ser.: Vols. 59-60). 408p. 1991. text ed. 136.00 (*0-87849-549-5*) LPS Dist Ctr.

Beta, Bene & the Peripheral Diaspora (Black Hebrews in the Diaspora) James H. Boykin. LC 90-92967. 96p. (Orig.). (C). 1990. pap. 5.00 (*0-9603342-9-7*) Boykin.

Beta-Blockers & Cardiac Arrhythmias. Ed. by Deedwania. (Fundamental & Clinical Cardiology Ser.: Vol. 5). 336p. 1992. 150.00 (*0-8247-8450-2*) Dekker.

Beta Blockers in Clinical Practice. 2nd ed. J. M. Cruickshank. 1994. 295.00 (*0-443-04522-4*) Churchill.

Beta-Blockers in the Elderly. Ed. by E. Lang. (Illus.). 107p. 1982. pap. 32.00 (*0-387-11682-6*) Spr-Verlag.

***Beta Blockers in the Treatment of Cardiovascular Disease.** Ed. by John B. Kostis & Eugene A. De Felice. LC 83-42985. (Illus.). Date not set. reprint ed. pap. 90.40 (*0-7837-9563-7*, 2060312) Bks Demand.

Beta-Blockers in the Treatment of Hypertension in the 90s: Experience with Tertatolol. Ed. by K. Oenen & C. Diehm. (Journal: Cardiology: Vol. 83, Suppl. 1, 1993). (Illus.). iv, 72p. 1993. pap. 21.75 (*3-8055-5869-4*) S Karger.

Beta-Carotene. Richard A. Passwater. Ed. by Earl Mindell. (Good Health Guide Ser.). 32p. 1984. pap. 2.50 (*0-87983-363-7*) Keats.

Beta-Carotene: Biological Properties & Applications. Dimitrov. 1989. pap. 4.95 (*0-87983-445-5*) Keats.

Beta Carotene: How It Can Help You to Better Health. Caroline Wheater. 128p. (Orig.). 1991. pap. 6.95 (*0-7225-2445-5*) Thorsons SF.

Beta-Carotene & Carotenoids: Index of New Information & Medical Research Bible. Ramsey B. Gottlieb. 150p. 1994. 44.50 (*0-7883-0138-1*); pap. 39.50 (*0-7883-0139-X*) ABBE Pubs Assn.

Beta Decay of Hyperons. A. Garcia & P. Kielanowski. (Lecture Notes in Physics Ser.: Vol. 222). viii, 173p. 1985. pap. 20.00 (*0-387-15184-2*) Spr-Verlag.

Beta-Homotopy Equivalences Have Alpha Cross Sections. Luis Montejano et al. LC 82-20616. (Memoirs Ser.: No. 41/274). 37p. 1982. pap. 16.00 (*0-8218-2274-8*, MEMO 41/274) Am Math.

Beta Israel (Falasha) in Ethiopia: From Earliest Times to the Twentieth Century. Steven Kaplan. 341p. (C). 1992. text ed. 55.00 (*0-8147-4625-X*); pap. 17.95 (*0-8147-2617-8*) NYU Pr.

***Beta Israel (Falasha) in Ethiopia: From Earliest Times to the Twentieth Century.** Steven Kaplan. 341p. (C). 1992. pap. 19.50 (*0-8147-4664-0*) NYU Pr.

Beta Mathematics Handbook: Concepts, Theorems, Methods, Algorithms, Formulas, Graphs, Tables. 2nd ed. Lennart Rade & Bertil Westergren. 1992. 39.95 (*0-8493-7758-7*, QA) CRC Pr.

Beta Titanium Alloys in the 1990's: Proceedings. Ed. by Eylon D et al. 535p. 1993. 68.00 (*0-87339-200-0*) Minerals Metals.

Beta Two-Microglobulin: Its Significance in Clinical Medicine. Ed. by M. D. Poulik. (Journal: Vox Sanguinis: Vol. 38, No. 6). (Illus.). 1980. pap. 26.50 (*3-8055-1560-X*) S Karger.

***Beta 3-Adrenergic Agonism: A New Concept in Human Pharmacotherapy.** Ed. by Daniel E. Goldberg & William H. Frishman. (Illus.). 208p. 1994. 35.00 (*0-87993-601-0*) Futura Pub.

Betania, Venezuela, Apparitions: Mary, Virgin, Mother, Reconciler of All People. Margaret C. Sims. 139p. 1992. 9.00 (*0-9639504-9-5*) Medugorje Messengers.

Betarezeptoren in der Kardiologie - Probleme aus klinischer Sicht: Proceedings of the Symposium, 1st, Bad Krozingen, October, 1977. Oberrheinisches Kardiologen Symposium Staff. Ed. by H. Roskamm. (Cardiology Journal: Vol. 63, Suppl. 1). (Illus.). (FRE & GER.). 1978. 13.00 (*3-8055-2870-1*) S Karger.

Betcha Ain't: Poems from Attica. Ed. by Celes Tisdale. 1974. 5.00 (*0-910296-19-7*); pap. 2.50 (*0-685-00858-4*) Broadside Pr.

Betcha Can't Read Just One. Ed. by Alan D. Foster. 256p. (Orig.). 1993. mass mkt. 4.99 (*0-441-24883-7*) Ace Bks.

Bete. David Hirson. 1992. pap. 4.75 (*0-8222-0621-8*) Dramatists Play.

Bete Humaine. Emile Zola. 1953. write for info. (*0-318-63436-8*) Fr & Eur.

Bete Humaine. Emile Zola. Ed. by Henri Mitterand. 502p. 1977. 4.95 (*0-686-55769-7*) Fr & Eur.

Bete Humaine. Emile Zola. (Folio Ser.: No. 948). (FRE.). 1953. 9.95 (*2-07-036948-X*) Schoenhof.

Bete Humaine. Emile Zola. Tr. by Leonard W. Tancock. (Classics Ser.). 1977. mass mkt. 9.95 (*0-14-044327-4*, Penguin Classics) Viking Penguin.

Bete Quaternaire. Renee Massip. (FRE.). 1981. pap. 11.95 (*0-7859-4145-2*) Fr & Eur.

Betech 85. Ed. by C. A. Brebbia & B. J. Noye. (BETECH Ser.: Vol. 1). 298p. 1985. 88.00 (*0-931215-07-2*) Computational Mech MA.

BETECH 86. Ed. by J. J. Connor & C. A. Brebbia. (BETECH Ser.: Vol. 2). 828p. 1986. 130.00 (*0-931215-30-7*) Computational Mech MA.

Beteiligung der Arbeitnehmer am Produktivvermogen: Grachter Symposion vom 8 und 9 Marz 1984. Ed. by Hersausgegeben Von Gert Lassmann & Eberhard Schwark. x, 204p. (GER.). 1985. 60.00 (*3-11-010290-0*) De Gruyter.

Betel-Chewing Equipment of East New Guinea. Harry Beran. 1989. pap. 25.00 (*0-85263-969-4*, Pub. by Shire UK) St Mut.

Betel Chewing Traditions in South-East Asia. Dawn F. Rooney. LC 93-400. (Images of Asia Ser.). (Illus.). 104p. 1994. 16.95 (*0-19-588620-8*) OUP.

Betel Cutters: From the Samuel Eilenberg Collection. Henry Brownrigg. LC 89-50633. (Illus.). 160p. 1992. 35. 00 (*0-500-97376-8*) Thames Hudson.

Beth: The Little Girl of Pine Knoll. Gerald Hausman. LC 74-82228. (Illus.). 32p. (J). (gr. 6 up). 1974. 15.00 (*0-912846-08-9*) Bookstore Pr.

***Beth & the Barbarian: Presents Plus.** Miranda Lee. (Presents Ser.). 1995. pap. 2.99 (*0-373-11711-6*, 1-11711-8) Harlequin Bks.

Beth Bauer's Enjoy China More or How to Relate to the Chinese People. Beth C. Bauer. (Beth Bauer's Ser.). (Illus.). 232p. (Orig.). (C). 1988. reprint ed. pap. 14.95 (*0-937133-01-9*) Cain Lockhart.

Beth El Story: With a History of the Jews in Michigan Before 1850 & Three Hundred Years in America. Irving I. Katz & Jacob R. Marcus. LC 55-7560. (Illus.). 256p. reprint ed. pap. 73.00 (*0-7837-3584-7*, 2043444) Bks Demand.

Beth Henley: Four Plays. LC 92-4075. 264p. (C). 1992. pap. 15.95 (*0-435-08612-X*) Heinemann.

Beth Henley: Monologues for Women. Beth Henley. 64p. 1992. pap. 7.95 (*0-940669-20-X*) Dramaline Pubns.

Beth Neilsen Chapman - "You Hold the Key" (Personality Folio Ser.). 64p. (Orig.). 1994. pap. 19.95 (*0-89724-099-5*) Warner Brothers.

Beth Russell's Traditional Needlepoint. Beth Russell. LC 92-17581. (Illus.). 128p. 1992. 25.00 (*0-89577-446-1*, Random) RD Assn.

Beth Tartan's Cook Book. 3rd ed. Beth Tartan. 197p. 1981. spiral bd. 6.00 (*0-686-11593-7*) TarPar.

Beth Tartan's North Carolina & Old Salem Cookery. 8th ed. Elizabeth Sparks. 269p. 1980. 7.95 (*0-686-11592-9*) TarPar.

Bethany: A Story of the Old South. Thomas E. Watson. LC 72-4596. (Black Heritage Library Collection). 1977. reprint ed. 25.95 (*0-8369-9131-1*) Ayer.

Bethany Ann: A Mother's Difficult Choice. Ann M. Martin. 98p. 1991. pap. 6.95 (*1-880153-36-X*) AmericaWORKS.

Bethany in Kansas: The History of a College. Emory K. Lindquist. LC 75-18910. (Illus.). 320p. 1975. 5.00 (*0-916030-03-2*) Bethany Coll KS.

Bethany Learns about Giving. Vicky Billings. 1989. pap. 3.50 (*0-89137-057-9*) Quality Pubns.

Bethany Learns about Prayer. Vicky Billings. 1990. pap. 3.50 (*0-89137-063-3*) Quality Pubns.

Bethany Learns about the Lord's Supper. Vicky Billings. 1988. pap. 3.50 (*0-89137-053-6*) Quality Pubns.

***Bethany Learns about the Preaching of the Gospel.** Vicky Billings. Date not set. pap. text ed. 3.50 (*0-89137-067-6*) Quality Pubns.

Bethany Parallel Commentary on the New Testament. Matthew Henry et al. 1500p. 1983. 49.99 (*0-87123-474-2*) Bethany Hse.

Bethany Parallel Commentary on the Old Testament. Matthew Henry et al. 1500p. 1985. 59.99 (*0-87123-617-6*) Bethany Hse.

Bethany's Sin. Robert R. McCammon. Ed. by Sally Peters. 1988. mass mkt. 5.99 (*0-671-73775-9*) PB.

Bethel & Aurora. Robert J. Hendricks. LC 75-134380. reprint ed. 55.00 (*0-404-08428-1*) AMS Pr.

Bethel to Sharpsburg, 2 vols., Set. Daniel H. Hill, Jr. (Illus.). 1993. reprint ed. 60.00 (*1-56837-046-6*) Broadfoot.

***Bethesda, a Social History.** William M. Offutt. (Illus.). 784p. (Orig.). 1995. pap. 25.00 (*0-9643819-0-7*) Innovat Game.

***Bethesda System for Reporting Cervical Vaginal Cytologic Diagnoses.** R. J. Kurman. Ed. by D. Solomon. 60p. 1994. 60.00 (*0-387-92120-6*) Spr-Verlag.

Bethesda System for Reporting Cervical Vaginal Cytologic Diagnoses: Definitions, Criteria & Explanatory Notes for Terminology & Specimen Adequacy. Robert Kurman et al. LC 93-31572. 88p. 1994. pap. 25.00 (*0-387-94077-4*) Spr-Verlag.

Bethesden Road. Sheldon Webster. Ed. by Richard S. Danbury, III. (Illus.). 176p. (Orig.). 1995. pap. 8.95 (*0-89754-094-8*) Dan River Pr.

Bethlehem. Federick W. Faber. LC 78-66306. 1978. reprint ed. pap. 16.50 (*0-89555-080-6*) TAN Bks Pubs.

Bethlehem Bach Choir: An Historical & Interpretive Sketch, No. 248. Raymond Walters. LC 77-135726. reprint ed. 52.50 (*0-404-07200-3*) AMS Pr.

Bethlehem Diary. Floyd I. Brewer. Ed. by Teresa A. Buckley. (Illus.). 1994. 19.00 (*0-9635402-1-1*) Town Beth Bicent.

Bethlehem in Broad Daylight. Mark Doty. LC 89-46188. 1991. pap. 10.95 (*0-87923-848-8*) Godine.

Bethlehem Mystery. Clarence M. Wagner. (Orig.). 1981. 3.50 (*0-937498-03-3*) Tru-Faith.

Bethlehem Oil Mill Seventeen Forty-Five to Nineteen Thirty-Four: German Technology in Early Pennsylvania. Carter Litchfield et al. LC 82-61069. (Illus.). 128p. 1984. 25.00 (*0-917526-02-3*) Olearius Edns.

Bethlehem on the Lehigh. Ralph Schwarz. (Illus.). 96p. 1991. pap. 15.00 (*0-9631444-1-3*) Lehigh Valley Comm.

Bethlehem Revisited. Douglas V. Steere. LC 65-26995. (Orig.). 1965. pap. 3.00 (*0-87574-144-4*) Pendle Hill.

Bethlehem Revisited: A Bicentennial Story, 1793-1993. 501p. 1993. text ed. 29.00 (*0-9635402-0-3*) Town Beth Bicent.

Bethlehem Road. Anne Perry. 320p. 1991. mass mkt. 5.99 (*0-449-45316-2*, Crest) Fawcett.

Bethlehem Road. Anne Perry. 1991. mass mkt. 5.99 (*0-449-21914-3*) Fawcett.

Bethlehem Steel Corporation: A History from Origin to World War I. W. Bruce Drinkhouse. 19p. (Orig.). 1969. pap. text ed. 3.00 (*1-877701-06-8*) NCH&GS.

Bethlehem Steelmaker: My Ninety Years in Life's Loop. Edmund F. Martin & David J. Morrison. 168p. 1992. 19.98 (*0-9635251-0-7*) BMS Pr.

Bethnal Inheritance. Martha Whitfield. (Orig.). 1981. pap. 2.95 (*0-89083-857-7*) Zebra.

***Bethsaida Excavations Project Text & Studies Vol. 1: Bethsaida: A City by the North Shore of the Sea of Galilee.** Ed. by Richard A. Freund & Rami Arav. LC 94-41015. 1995. write for info. (*0-943549-30-2*) TJU Pr.

Bethune on Bass. John Bethune. (Illus.). 88p. 1993. 32.50 (*0-86417-511-6*, Pub. by Kangaroo Pr AT) Seven Hills Bk.

Bethy & the Mouse. Donald C. Bakely. LC 85-70634. (Illus.). 1985. 10.95 (*0-87303-111-3*) Faith & Life.

Bethylidae of America North of Mexico. Howard E. Evans. (Memoir Ser.: No. 27). (Illus.). 332p. 1978. 45.00 (*1-56665-025-9*) Assoc Pubs FL.

Betray Not My Passion. Sylvie F. Sommerfield. 1984. pap. 3.95 (*0-8217-1466-X*) Zebra.

Betrayal. Merritt Clifton. 1980. 2.50 (*0-686-26981-0*) Samisdat.

Betrayal. Janice Harrell. (Secret Diaries Ser.: No. 02). (YA). 1994. pap. 3.95 (*0-590-47712-9*) Scholastic Inc.

B

An Asterisk (*) at the beginning of an entry indicates that the title is appearing in BIP for the first time.

B

Betrayal. Hunter. 1994. mass mkt. 5.99 (0-671-89153-7) PB.

Betrayal. Janice Kaiser. (Temptation Ser.). 1993. mass mkt. 2.99 (0-373-25562-4, 1-25562-9) Harlequin Bks.

*Betrayal. Susan Lewis. 1994. pap. 5.99 (0-06-100561-4, Harp PBks) HarpC.

Betrayal. Harold Pinter. 1980. pap. 2.75 (0-8222-0109-7) Dramatists Play.

Betrayal. Harold Pinter. 144p. 1988. pap. 9.95 (0-8021-3080-1) Grove-Atltic.

Betrayal. R. L. Stine. (Fear Street Ser.: No. 1). 176p. (Orig.). (YA). (gr. 6-9). 1993. mass mkt. 3.99 (0-671-86831-4, Archway) PB.

Betrayal. Lois Tilton. Ed. by Kevin Ryan. (Star Trek: Deep Space Nine Ser.: No. 6). 288p. (Orig.). 1994. mass mkt. 5.50 (0-671-88117-5) PB.

*Betrayal: Employee Relations at Dupont, 1981-1994. Edward E. Dent. LC 95-14896. 1995. pap. write for info. (1-55618-152-3) Brunswick Pub.

Betrayal: Michael Dukakis & the Struggle to Save Historic Prowse Farm. Harvey B. Robbins. (Illus.). 112p. 1988. 12.95 (0-89803-161-3) Green Hill.

Betrayal: The Shattering Sex Discrimination Case of Silver vs. Pacific Press Publishing Association. Merikay McLeod. LC 84-62638. 356p. (Orig.). 1985. pap. 10.00 (0-9614230-0-5) Mars Hill Pubns.

*Betrayal: The Story of Aldrich Ames, An American Spy. Lewis & Johnson Weiner Staff. 1995. 25.00 (0-679-44050-X) Random.

Betrayal: The Two Parties Against the People. Walter Karp. 1993. pap. 6.95 (1-882206-03-7) Argonaut Pr.

Betrayal: The Untold Story of the Kurt Waldheim Investigation & Cover-Up. Eli Rosenbaum & William Hoffer. (Illus.). 576p. 1993. 25.95 (0-312-08219-3, Pub. by Thomas Dunne Bks) St Martin.

Betrayal & Betrayers: The Sociology of Treachery. Malin Akerstrom. 196p. (C). 1990. 37.95 (0-88738-358-0) Transaction Pubs.

Betrayal at Blackcrest. large type ed. Jennifer Wilde. 344p. 1993. 21.95 (0-7505-0142-1, Pub. by Magna Print Bks) Ulverscroft.

Betrayal at Krondor: Offical Strategy Guide. Bernard H. Yee. 1994. pap. 19.95 (1-55958-549-8) Prima Pub.

Betrayal at Pearl Harbor: How Churchill Lured Roosevelt into World War II. James Rusbridger & Eric Nave. (Illus.). 304p. 1992. pap. 12.00 (0-671-79231-8, Touchstone Bks) S&S Trade.

Betrayal at Pearl Harbor: How Churchill Lured Roosevelt into World War II. James Rusbridger & Eric Nave. (Illus.). 303p. 19.95 (0-685-52042-0) Summit Bks.

Betrayal by Any Other Name: An Honest Appraisal of Black & Hispanic American Leadership over the Last 100 Years. Khalid A. Al-Mansour. 800p. (Orig.). (C). 1993. pap. 29.95 (1-883136-14-8) First Afr Arabian.

Betrayal from Within: Joseph Avenol, Secretary-General of the League of Nations, 1933-1940. James Barros. LC 75-81413. 301p. reprint ed. pap. 85.80 (0-8357-7147-4, 2021978) Bks Demand.

Betrayal in Bali. large type ed. Sally Wentworth. 1992. 18.95 (0-7451-8378-6, Atlantic Lrg Print); pap. 16.95 (0-7927-1119-X, Atlantic Lrg Print) Chivers N Amer.

Betrayal in Mexico: A True Story of Romance & Adventure in the Early Days of Exotic Puerto Vallarta. Louis E. Bittrich & Theresia J. Lewis. LC 94-4054. 1994. 14.95 (1-56875-072-2) R & E Pubs.

Betrayal in Psychotherapy & Its Antidotes: Challenges for Patient & Therapist. Intro. by E. Mark Stern. LC 92-45159. (Psychotherapy Patient Ser.: Vol. 8, Nos. 3-4). 186p. 1993. lib. bdg. 24.95 (1-56024-448-8) Haworth Pr.

*Betrayal in Tombstone. Ray Hogan. 1995. 15.95 (0-7451-4634-1) Chivers N Amer.

Betrayal of Canada. Mel Hurtig. (Illus.). 366p. 1991. 24.95 (0-7737-2542-3, Pub. by Stoddart Pubng CN) Genl Dist Srvs.

Betrayal of Canada. Mel Hurtig. 1992. pap. 16.95 (0-7737-5541-1, Pub. by Stoddart Pubng CN) Genl Dist Srvs.

Betrayal of Christ by the Churches. John M. Murry. 1972. 59.95 (0-87968-724-X) Gordon Pr.

Betrayal of God: Ideological Conflict in Job. David Penchansky. (Literary Currents in Biblical Interpretation Ser.). 128p. (Orig.). 1990. pap. 11.99 (0-664-25132-3) Westminster John Knox.

Betrayal of Health: The Impact of Nutrition, Environment, & Lifestyle on Illness in America. Joseph D. Beasley. 1991. 22.50 (0-8129-1897-5) Random.

Betrayal of Innocence: Incest & Its Devastation. Susan Foward & Craig Buck. 198p. 1978. 8.50 (0-318-17073-6) Kempe Nat Ctr.

Betrayal of Innocence: Incest & Its Devastation. rev. ed. Susan Forward & Craig Buck. 208p. 1988. pap. 10.00 (0-14-011002-X, Penguin Bks) Viking Penguin.

Betrayal of Krishna: Vicissitudes of a Great Myth. Krishna Chaitanya. (C). 1991. 42.50 (81-85120-39-0, Pub. by Clarion II) S Asia.

Betrayal of Liliuokalani: Last Queen of Hawaii, 1838-1917. Helena G. Allen. 432p. 1991. reprint ed. 6.95 (0-935180-89-3) Mutual Pub HI.

Betrayal of Love. large type ed. Diana Hamilton. 1990. reprint ed. lib. bdg. 18.95 (0-263-12262-X, Pub. by Mills & Boon UK) Thorndike Pr.

Betrayal of Marx. Ed. by Frederick L. Bender. 16.50 (0-8446-5158-3) Peter Smith.

*Betrayal of Means, Means of Betrayal: Contemporary Art & the Photographic Experience. Alison D. Nordstrom. 27p. 1992. pap. text ed. 10.00 (1-887040-01-3) SE Mus Photo.

Betrayal of Richard the Third. V. B. Lamb. (Illus.). 160p. (C). 1990. pap. 14.00 (0-86299-778-X) A Sutton Pub.

Betrayal of the Body. Alexander Lowen. 288p. 1969. pap. 6.95 (0-02-077300-5, Collier S&S) S&S Trade.

Betrayal of the Poor: The Transformation of Community Action. Stephen M. Rose. LC 76-178829. 199p. 1972. pap. text ed. 15.95 (0-87073-285-4) Schenkman Bks Inc.

*Betrayal of Trust. Vernon Coleman. 1995. pap. 12.95 (0-9521492-3-0) InBook.

Betrayal of Trust: "Clergy Abuse of Children" Annie L. Gaylor. 92p. (Orig.). 1989. pap. 10.00 (0-318-42494-0) Freedom Rel Found.

*Betrayal of Trust: Sex & Power in Professional Relationships. Joel Friedman & Marcia M. Boumil. LC 94-28004. 142p. 1995. text ed. 21.95 (0-275-95029-8, Praeger Pubs) Greenwood.

*Betrayal of Trust: Sexual Misconduct in the Pastorate. Stanley J. Grenz & Roy D. Bell. 192p. (Orig.). 1995. pap. text ed. 10.99 (0-8308-1857-X, 1857) InterVarsity.

*Betrayal on Sky Mountain. Margaret H. Van Damm. LC 94-90156. 136p. (Orig.). 1995. pap. 8.00 (1-56002-457-7, Univ Edtns) Aegina Pr.

Betrayals. Brian Freemantle. 1991. mass mkt. 4.95 (0-8125-8257-8) Tor Bks.

Betrayals. Christiane Heggan. 416p. (Orig.). 1994. pap. 4.99 (0-451-40508-0, Onyx) NAL-Dutton.

*Betrayals. Charles Palliser. LC 94-22769. 1995. 23.00 (0-345-36959-9) Ballantine.

Betrayals. Anne Harrell. 1991. reprint ed. 19.95 (0-7278-4216-1) Severn Hse.

Betrayals: Fort William Henry & the "Massacre" Ian K. Steele. (Illus.). 272p. 1990. 28.00 (0-19-505893-3) OUP.

Betrayals: Fort William Henry & the "Massacre" Ian K. Steele. (Illus.). 272p. 1993. reprint ed. pap. 10.95 (0-19-508426-8) OUP.

Betrayals of the Body Politic: The Literary Commitments of Nadine Gordimer. Andrew V. Ettin. LC 92-27675. 1993. 26.50 (0-8139-1430-2) U Pr of Va.

Betrayed. Anne Mather. (Presents Ser.). 1992. pap. 2.89 (0-373-11492-3, 1-11492-5) Harlequin Bks.

Betrayed. Stan Telchin. LC 81-10043. 140p. 1982. pap. 7.99 (0-8007-9068-5) Chosen Bks.

Betrayed. large type ed. Anne Mather. 1992. reprint ed. lib. bdg. 18.95 (0-263-12892-X, Pub. by Mills & Boon UK) Thorndike Pr.

Betrayed: Northpoint. Judith McWilliams. (Historical Ser.). 1994. mass mkt. 3.99 (0-373-28849-2, 1-28849-7) Harlequin Bks.

Betrayed & Soldout. Eugene Berniak. (Illus.). 203p. (Orig.). 1993. pap. 19.95 (0-9639748-0-7) E H Berniak.

Betrayed by F. Scott Fitzgerald. Ron Carlson. 224p. 1984. reprint ed. pap. 6.95 (0-393-30168-0) Norton.

*Betrayed by Love. Diana Palmer. (Western Lovers Ser.). 1995. mass mkt. 3.99 (0-373-88501-6, 1-88501-1) Harlequin Bks.

*Betrayed by Rita Hayworth. Manuel Puig. 224p. 1996. pap. 11.00 (0-393-31384-0, Norton Paperbks) Norton.

Betrayed Confidence: Seven Series of Dogear Wryde Postcards. Edward Gorey. LC 91-68194. (Illus.). 192p. (Orig.). 1992. pap. 12.95 (0-940160-52-8) Parnassus Imprints.

*Betrayed in Paradise. Marie Murphy. Ed. by Jon Robertson. 240p. 1995. pap. 14.95 (0-87604-345-7, 417) ARE Pr.

Betrayers. Phyllis Schlafly & Chester Ward. 1968. 1.00 (0-934640-01-7) Pere Marquette.

Betrayer's Fortune. Dave Jackson. (J). (gr. 4-7). 1994. pap. 4.99 (1-55661-467-5) Bethany Hse.

Betrayers of the Profession: Lawyering at the End of the Twentieth Century. Sol M. Linowitz & Martin Mayer. LC 93-31995. 320p. 1994. text ed. 25.00 (0-684-19416-3, Scribners) S&S Trade.

Betraying the Bishops: How the Pastoral Letter on War & Peace Is Being Taught. Matthew F. Murphy & John C. O'Connor. LC 87-32932. 146p. (Orig.). (C). 1988. lib. bdg. 33.50 (0-89633-121-0); pap. text ed. 14.25 (0-89633-122-9) Ethics & Public Policy.

Betraying the National Interest. Frances M. Lappe & Rachel Schurmann. (Food First Bks.). 160p. 1987. 18.95 (0-8021-0012-0); pap. 8.95 (0-8021-3027-5) Inst Food & Develop.

Betrekkeningen see Cross Roads, Vol. 1: The Netherlands

Betrothal. Arnette Lamb. Ed. by Carolyn Tolley. 384p. (Orig.). 1992. mass mkt. 5.50 (0-671-73002-9, Pocket Star Bks) PB.

Betrothal. Lanford Wilson. 1986. pap. 4.75 (0-8222-0110-0) Dramatists Play.

Betrothal. large type ed. Arnette Lamb. LC 92-27928. 521p. (Orig.). 1992. reprint ed. lib. bdg. 17.95 (1-56054-546-1) Thorndike Pr.

Betrothal see Blue Bird

Betrothal of Elypholate, & Other Tales of the Pennsylvania Dutch. Helen R. Martin. LC 76-128739. (Short Story Index Reprint Ser.). (Illus.). 1977. 19.95 (0-8369-3630-2) Ayer.

Betrothed. Alessandro Manzoni. Tr. by Bruce Penman. (Classics Ser.). 720p. 1984. pap. 11.95 (0-14-044274-X, Penguin Classics) Viking Penguin.

*Bets & Scams: A Novel of the Art World. Gary Schwartz. 208p. 1996. 22.95 (0-7145-3008-5) M Boyars Pubs.

Bet's on, Lizzie Bingman! Rhea B. Ross. (YA). 1992. pap. 4.95 (0-395-64375-9) HM.

Bets You Can't Lose. Patrick B. Sullivan. (Illus.). 1979. pap. 2.95 (0-8431-0535-6) Putnam Pub Group.

Betsie's Secret. J. H. Taylor. 266p. (C). 1989. 35.00 (0-7223-2251-8, Pub. by A H S Ltd UK) St Mut.

Betsy. Robbins. 1993. mass mkt. 5.99 (0-671-87483-7) PB.

Betsy & Billy. Carolyn Haywood. LC 41-51926. (Illus.). 119p. (J). (gr. 1-5). 1941. 12.95 (0-15-206765-5, HB Juv Bks) HarBrace.

Betsy & Billy. Carolyn Haywood. LC 41-51926. 119p. (J). (gr. 2-5). 1990. pap. 3.95 (0-15-206768-X) HarBrace.

Betsy & Joe. Maud H. Lovelace. LC 48-8096. (Illus.). 256p. (YA). (gr. 5 up). 1948. 14.95 (0-690-13378-2, Crowell Jr Bks) HarpC Child Bks.

*Betsy & Joe. Maud H. Lovelace. LC 48-8096. (Trophy Bk.). (Illus.). 288p. (J). (gr. 4-7). 1995. pap. 4.95 (0-06-440546-X, Trophy) HarpC Child Bks.

Betsy & Tacy Go Downtown. Maud H. Lovelace. LC 43-51264. (Illus.). 192p. (J). (gr. 2-5). 1966. lib. bdg. 14.89 (0-690-13450-9, Crowell Jr Bks) HarpC Child Bks.

Betsy & Tacy Go Downtown. Maud H. Lovelace. LC 43-51264. (Trophy Bk.). (Illus.). 192p. (J). (gr. 2-5). 1979. pap. 3.95 (0-06-440098-0, Trophy) HarpC Child Bks.

Betsy & Tacy Go over the Big Hill. Maud H. Lovelace. LC 42-23557. (Illus.). 176p. (J). (gr. 2-5). 1966. lib. bdg. 14.89 (0-690-13521-1, Crowell Jr Bks) HarpC Child Bks.

Betsy & Tacy Go over the Big Hill. Maud H. Lovelace. LC 42-23557. (Trophy Bk.). (Illus.). 176p. (J). (gr. 2-5). 1979. pap. 3.95 (0-06-440099-9, Trophy) HarpC Child Bks.

Betsy & the Boys. Carolyn Haywood. LC 45-35133. 140p. (J). (gr. 1-5). 1945. 12.95 (0-15-206944-5, HB Juv Bks) HarBrace.

Betsy & the Boys. Carolyn Haywood. 140p. (J). (gr. 2-5). 1990. pap. 3.95 (0-15-206947-X) HarBrace.

Betsy Ashton's Guide to Living on Your Own for the Very First Time. Betsy Ashton. 1988. pap. 12.95 (0-316-05409-7) Little.

Betsy in Spite of Herself. Maud H. Lovelace. LC 46-11995. (Trophy Bk.). (Illus.). 288p. (J). (gr. 4-7). 1980. pap. 3.95 (0-06-440111-1, Trophy) HarpC Child Bks.

Betsy Ross. Sally Hille. 48p. 1979. 24.00 (0-88014-015-1) Mosaic Pr OH.

Betsy Ross. Alexandra Wallner. LC 93-3559. (Illus.). 32p. (J). (ps-3). 1994. lib. bdg. 15.95 (0-8234-1071-4) Holiday.

Betsy Ross: Designer of Our Flag. Ann Weil. LC 86-10775. (Childhood of Famous Americans Ser.). (Illus.). 192p. (J). (gr. 2 up). 1986. reprint ed. pap. 3.95 (0-02-042120-6, Aladdin Paperbacks) S&S Childrens.

Betsy Ross, Little Rebel. Ethlyn Walkington. LC 89-25774. 140p. (Orig.). (J). (gr. 4-6). 1990. pap. 8.95 (0-944350-13-5) Friends United.

Betsy-Tacy. Maud H. Lovelace. LC 40-30965. (Illus.). 128p. (J). (gr. 2-5). 1966. lib. bdg. 14.89 (0-690-13805-9, Crowell Jr Bks) HarpC Child Bks.

Betsy-Tacy. Maud H. Lovelace. LC 40-30965. (Trophy Bk.). (Illus.). 128p. (J). (gr. 2-5). 1979. pap. 3.95 (0-06-440096-4, Trophy) HarpC Child Bks.

*Betsy-Tacy. Maud H. Lovelace. LC 40-30965. (Illus.). 128p. (J). (gr. 2-5). 1994. 9.95 (0-06-024415-1) HarpC Child Bks.

Betsy-Tacy & Tib. Maud H. Lovelace. LC 41-18714. (Illus.). 144p. (J). (gr. 2-5). 1966. lib. bdg. 14.89 (0-690-13876-8, Crowell Jr Bks) HarpC Child Bks.

Betsy-Tacy & Tib. Maud H. Lovelace. LC 41-18714. (Trophy Bk.). (Illus.). 144p. (J). (gr. 2-5). 1979. pap. 3.95 (0-06-440097-2, Trophy) HarpC Child Bks.

*Betsy-Tacy & Tib. Maud H. Lovelace. (Illus.). 144p. (J). (gr. 2-5). 1994. 9.95 (0-06-024416-X) HarpC Child Bks.

Betsy-Tacy Companion: A Biography of Maud Hart Lovelace. Sharla S. Whalen. LC 91-66704. (Illus.). 514p. 1995. 39.95 (0-9630783-0-5) Portalington.

*Betsy-Tacy in Deep Valley: People & Places. Carlienne A. Frisch. (Illus.). 58p. (Orig.). 1985. pap. 3.50 (0-9645628-0-4) FMVRL.

*Betsy-Tacy Treasury. Maud H. Lovelace. LC 94-25063. (Illus.). (J). (gr. 1-8). 1994. 5.50 (0-06-024919-6) HarpC.

Betsy the Babysitter. (J). 1989. pap. 1.95 (0-8167-0026-5) Troll Assocs.

Betsy Was a Junior: A Betsy - Tacy High School Story. Maud H. Lovelace. LC 46-11995. (Illus.). 248p. (YA). (gr. 5 up). 1947. 14.95 (0-690-13946-2) HarpC Child Bks.

*Betsy Was a Junior: A Betsy - Tacy High School Story. Maud H. Lovelace. LC 46-11995. (Trophy Bk.). (Illus.). 288p. (J). (gr. 4-7). 1995. pap. 4.95 (0-06-440547-8, Trophy) HarpC Child Bks.

Betsy's Breads. rev. ed. Betsy Oppenneer. (Illus.). 70p. (YA). (gr. 8 up). 1991. pap. 7.95 (0-9627665-2-6) Breadworks.

Betsy's Buddies. Harvey Kurtzman & Sarah Downs. Ed. by Helle Nielsen. (Illus.). 48p. 1987. 15.95 (0-87816-029-9) Kitchen Sink.

Betsy's Busy Summer. Carolyn Haywood. LC 56-7894. (Illus.). (J). (gr. 3-7). 1956. lib. bdg. 15.93 (0-688-31087-7) Morrow Jr Bks.

Betsy's Butter. Reed Bond. (Read-with-Me Ser.). (Illus.). 16p. (Orig.). (J). (gr. 1-3). 1992. pap. 4.50 (0-9631992-1-8) Bonding Place.

Betsy's Riddles. Abbie Dee & Annie Scott. (Emergent Reader Ser.). 11p. (J). (ps-1). 1991. pap. text ed. 21.00 (1-56843-035-3); pap. text ed. 4.25 (1-56843-083-3) BGR Pub.

Betsy's Wedding. Maud H. Lovelace. LC 55-11108. (Illus.). 241p. (J). (gr. 5 up). 1955. 14.95 (0-690-13733-8, Crowell Jr Bks) HarpC Child Bks.

Betsy's Winterhouse. Carolyn Haywood. LC 55-8453. (Illus.). 192p. (J). (gr. 3-7). 1958. lib. bdg. 14.00 (0-688-31090-7) Morrow Jr Bks.

Bettas. Marshall Ostrow. (Illus.). 96p. 1980. 9.95 (0-86622-745-8, KW-052) TFH Pubns.

Bettas, Gouramis & Other Anabantoids. Jorg Vierke. Tr. by John Coborn. (Illus.). 192p. 1988. lib. bdg. 19.95 (0-86622-897-7, TS-104) TFH Pubns.

Bette. Charles Higham. 1981. 13.95 (0-02-551500-4) Macmillan.

*Bette: An Intimate Biography of Bette Midler. George Mair. (Illus.). 368p. 1995. 22.50 (1-55972-272-X, Birch Ln Pr) Carol Pub Group.

Bette Bao Lord: Novelist & Chinese Voice for Change. Mary V. Fox. LC 92-36805. (People of Distinction Ser.). (Illus.). 152p. (J). (gr. 4 up). 1993. pap. 5.95 (0-516-43291-5) Childrens.

Bette Davis: A Biography. Barbara Leaming. 1993. mass mkt. 5.99 (0-345-38272-2) Ballantine.

Bette Davis: An Intimate Memoir. Roy Moseley. 1990. 18.95 (1-55611-218-1) D I Fine.

Bette Davis: Film Star. Gene Brown. (Library of Famous Women). (Illus.). 64p. (J). (gr. 3-7). 1990. lib. bdg. 14.95 (1-56711-028-2) Blackbirch.

Bette Davis Murder Case. George Baxt. 196p. 1994. 18.95 (0-312-10939-3) St Martin.

Bette Midler Greatest Hits. Cpp Belwin Staff. 1993. pap. 14.95 (0-89898-668-0) CPP Belwin.

*Bettelheim. Sutton. 1995. 27.00 (0-465-00635-3) Basic.

Bettelheim Memorial Album. Leslie Konnyu. (Illus.). (ENG, HUN & JPN.). 1989. 15.00 (0-911862-23-4); pap. 10.00 (0-318-65926-3) Hungarian Rev.

Better a Dinner of Herbs: A Novel by Byron Herbert Reece. Byron H. Reece. LC 92-22952. (Brown Thrasher Bks.). 240p. 1992. reprint ed. pap. 14.95 (0-8203-1489-7) U of Ga Pr.

Better a Shield Than a Sword: Perspectives on Defense & Technology. Edward Teller. 225p. 1987. text ed. 29.95 (0-02-932461-0) Free Pr.

Better All the Time: A Young Person's Recovery Workbook. Donald Scherling. 30p. (Orig.). (YA). 1989. student ed, pap. 7.95 (0-942421-12-4) Hazelden.

Better & Better. Betty Weider. (Six Weeks to a Better Body Any Age Ser.). 1993. pap. 12.95 (0-440-50313-2) Dell.

*Better Angel. Forman Brown. (Illus.). 222p. 1995. pap. 9.95 (1-55583-284-9) Alyson Pubns.

Better Answer: Homemaker-Home Health Aide Services for the Person with Developmental Disabilities & Family. Community Guide, 1983. 5.50 (0-318-03443-3); Handbook for the Aide, 1981. 20.00 (0-318-03445-X) Natl Homecaring.

Better Answer: Homemaker-Home Health Aide Services for the Person with Developmental Disabilities & Family. 1981. Instruction Manual, 1981. teacher ed, pap. text ed. 5.95 (0-318-03444-1) Natl Homecaring.

Better Baby Care: A Book for Family Day Care Providers. rev. ed. M. Nash et al. 164p. 1993. pap. text ed. 15.95 (1-884093-03-5) Chldrns Fnd.

Better Baby Care: A Training Course for Family Day Care Providers. L. Eggbeer et al. 60p. 1988. teacher ed 175.00 (1-884093-00-0) Chldrns Fnd.

Better Back Book: Simple Exercises for the Prevention & Care of Back Pain. Constance A. Bean. LC 88-12925. 216p. 1990. pap. 7.95 (0-688-10003-1, Quill) Morrow.

Better Backgammon. Tim Holland. LC 74-82267. 128p. 1979. pap. 4.95 (0-679-14126-X) McKay.

Better BASIC for the Apple. J. N. Hume & B. C. Holt. 1983. pap. 27.00 (0-8359-0466-0, Reston) P-H.

Better Bed & Breakfast Inns. Jim Franklin. LC 93-81011. (Illus.). 256p. (Orig.). 1994. pap. 14.95 (0-943972-31-0) Homestead WY.

Better Beer & How to Brew It. M. R. Reese. LC 81-7003. (Illus.). 128p. 1981. pap. 9.95 (0-88266-257-0, Garden Way Pub) Storey Comm Inc.

Better Bidding with Bergen, Vol. I: Uncontested Auctions. Marty Bergen. LC 86-159457. 199p. 1986. pap. 11.95 (0-939460-32-7, 1701) Devyn Pr.

Better Bidding with Bergen, Vol. II: Competitive Auctions. Marty Bergen. LC 86-159457. 149p. 1986. pap. 9.95 (0-939460-33-5, 1702) Devyn Pr.

Better Blackjack. Robert M. Charlton. (Illus.). 36p. (Orig.). 1986. 4.95 (0-9617552-0-2, TXU247597) Charlton Hi Tech.

Better Bodies after Thirty-Five: A Commonsense Approach to Healthful Living. Irving A. Beychok. LC 91-10232. 175p. (Orig.). 1991. pap. 9.95 (0-938179-28-4) Mills Sanderson.

*Better Bodies for Beauties: The Fitness Manual for Glamorous Women. Michael D. Fifrick. LC 94-94514. (Illus.). 224p. (Orig.). (YA). 1995. pap. 29.95 (0-9642287-9-3) FitFoxPress.

Better Body Management. Stormie Omartian. LC 93-23876. 1993. 10.95 (0-917143-25-6) Sparrow TN.

Better Book for Getting Hired: How to Write a Great Resume, Sell Yourself in the Interview. 3rd ed. Robert P. Downe. (Reference Ser.). 200p. 1993. pap. 12.95 (0-88908-762-8) Self-Counsel Pr.

Better Born Lucky. W. Frank Cottrell. 416p. 1984. 59.00 (0-7212-0689-1, Pub. by Regency Press) St Mut.

Better Born Lucky Than Rich. Eddie Lovejoy. (C). 1989. 39.00 (0-86303-322-9) St Mut.

Better Boss in Multicultural Organizations: A Guide to Success Using Transactional Analysis. Muriel James. (Illus.). 176p. (Orig.). 1991. pap. 10.95 (1-879369-00-1) Marshall Lafayette.

*Better Breakfast, Better Learning. 1994. pap. 0.24 (0-8011-1148-X) Calif Education.

Better Breathing Through Harmonica: The Large Print Method. David Harp. 1994. pap. 8.95 (0-918321-51-4) Musical Idiot.

Better Broaching Operations. Ed. by Edward W. Kokmeyer. LC 83-51470. (Manufacturing Update Ser.). (Illus.). 250p. reprint ed. pap. 71.30 (0-8357-6494-X, 2035865) Bks Demand.

Better Brochures, Catalogs & Mailing Pieces. Jane Maas. (Illus.). 128p. 1984. pap. 7.95 (0-312-07731-9) St Martin.

Better Building: Your Money's Worth in Design, Construction & Maintenance. R. S. Beri. 1990. text ed. 27.50 (0-86311-130-0, Pub. by Orient Longman Ltd II) Apt Bks.

Better Bulletin Boards. rev. ed. Cheryl A. Anderson. (Bridges for Ideas Handbook Ser.). 1981. pap. text ed. 6.00 (0-913648-10-8) U Tex Austin Film Lib.

An Asterisk (*) at the beginning of an entry indicates that the title is appearing in BIP for the first time.

An Asterisk (*) at the beginning of an entry indicates that the title is appearing in BIP for the first time.

B

Better Paragraphs, Plus. 6th ed. John Ostrom & William Cook. 208p. (C). 1990. pap. text ed. 14.50 (0-06-044973-X) HarpCollege.

Better Parent Conferences: A Manual for School Psychologists. Paula S. Wise. 46p. 1986. student ed 8.00 (0-932955-02-9) Natl Assn Psych.

Better Parts of a Life. Robert S. Lancaster. (Illus.). 249p. (Orig.). 1990. pap. 14.95 (0-9627687-1-5) Proctors Hall Pr.

Better Parts of a Life. Robert S. Lancaster. (Orig.). 1990. pap. 14.95 (0-918769-33-7) Univ South Pr.

Better Photos. Gladys J. Peterson. 96p. 1994. pap. text ed. 10.95 (1-884752-06-3) D C Cook Fnd.

Better Place. Barbara Hall. 1994. 21.00 (0-671-78422-6) S&S Trade.

*Better Place to Live. Philip Langdon. 1995. pap. 14.00 (0-06-097661-6, PL) HarpC.

Better Place to Live: Reshaping the American Suburb. Philip Langdon. LC 93-42348. (Illus.). 288p. 1994. text ed. 29.95 (0-87023-914-7) U of Mass Pr.

Better Products Faster: Practical Uses for Knowledge Based Systems in Manufacturing. William H. Verduin. 220p. 1994. text ed. 40.00 (0-7863-0113-9) Irwin Prof Pubng.

Better Quality: An Illustrated History of the Lisk Manufacturing Company. Lynda M. Hotra. LC 87-62462. (Business & Technology Ser.). (Illus.). 158p. 1987. pap. text ed. 25.00 (0-318-39967-9) Ont Cty Hist Soc.

Better Quality of Work Life Through Productivity. Intl. Productivity Congress Staff. 320p. 1993. pap. text ed. 30.00 (92-833-2118-9, Pub. by APO JA) Qual Resc.

Better Reason: A Handbook for Critical Thinking, Reading Comprehension & Test Mastery. J. Evans Alloway & Jerry Weisbrodt. LC 88-146057. 160p. 1988. student ed 8.95 (0-945623-00-3) ESI Pubns.

Better Red: The Writing & Resistance of Tillie Olsen & Meridel Le Sueur. Constance Coiner. (Illus.). 304p. 1995. 45.00 (0-19-505695-7) OUP.

Better Resumes for Attorneys & Paralegals. Adele B. Lewis & David A. Saltman. 1986. pap. 9.95 (0-8120-3649-2) Barron.

Better Resumes for Executives & Professionals. 2nd ed. Robert F. Wilson. 1991. pap. 11.95 (0-8120-4629-3) Barron.

Better Resumes for Sales & Marketing Personnel. Adele B. Lewis. 176p. 1985. pap. 11.95 (0-8120-2981-X) Barron.

***Better Resumes in 3 Easy Steps. 2nd ed. Ben T. Field & Paul K. MacLeod. 50p. 1995. pap. text ed. 12.95 (0-9645808-0-2) F&W Pub. BETTER RESUMES IN 3 EASY STEPS shows you the new & professional way of the nineties to write resumes that are effective! BETTER RESUMES is the first (Feb. 1995) in a new series of Job Search manuals by Ben T. Field & Paul MacLeod written in clear, concise language. Jam-packed in fifty pages, the information is about what employers want & how you can be sure the employer will read your resume. According to experts, employers spend less than twenty seconds scanning a resume to determine whether to read it. This book shows you how to write a resume that employers will read, how to write an effective cover letter plus a new idea to increase response from employers. The book comes with a computer disk with formats for ten resumes, four cover letters, & the response form. Marvin Walberg, nationally known Job Search Consultant & syndicated columnist wrote in his review that "BETTER RESUMES is for everyone & that it will benefit all job searchers & anyone preparing resumes for others, whether as a favor or as a profession". The book retails for 12.95. Quantity discounts are available. MC/Visa accepted. Contact: Elizabeth Field at F & W Publishing, 871 S. Boeke Rd., Evansville, Indiana 47714 or call 1-800-977-9332; FAX 1-812-479-0499.** *Publisher Provided Annotation.*

Better Roller Skating. Richard Arnold. 89p. (C). 1984. 59.00 (0-7182-1479-X, Pub. by Elm Pubns UK) St Mut.

*Better Runs: 25 Years Worth of Lessons for Running Farther & Faster. Joe Henderson. LC 95-14571. 280p. (Orig.). 1995. pap. 14.95 (0-87322-866-9, PHEN0866) Human Kinetics.

Better Safe Than Provocative. Marie-Louise Van Muijen. 250p. 1993. pap. text ed. 35.00 (90-5383-180-0, Pub. by VU Univ Pr NE) Paul & Co Pubs.

Better Safe Than Sorry Book: A Family Guide for Sexual Assault Prevention. Sol Gordon. (Young Readers Ser.). 44p. (J). (ps-3). 1992. pap. 8.95 (0-87975-768-X) Prometheus Bks.

Better Said & Clearly Written: An Annotated Guide to Business Communication Sources, Skills & Samples. Comp. by Sandra E. Belanger. LC 89-17227. (Bibliographies & Indexes in Mass Media & Communications Ser.: No. 3). 216p. 1989. text ed. 45.00 (0-313-26641-7, BBF/) Greenwood.

Better Sampling: Concepts, Techniques & Evaluation. Y. P. Aggarwal. 112p. 1988. text ed. 15.95 (81-207-0875-X, Pub. by Sterling Pubs II) Apt Bks.

Better School: Who Says So? Robert E. Mason. (Occasional Paper: No. 9). 1976. pap. 3.00 (0-933669-12-7) Soc Profs Ed.

Better Schooling for the Children of Poverty: Alternatives to Conventional Wisdom. Ed. by Michael S. Knapp & Patrick Shields. LC 92-60678. 1991. 33.00 (0-8211-1022-5); text ed. write for info. (0-685-54308-0) McCutchan.

Better Schools: A Values Perspective on Education. Clive Beck. 220p. 1989. 65.00 (1-85000-622-9, Falmer Pr); pap. 33.00 (1-85000-623-7, Falmer Pr) Taylor & Francis.

Better Scientific & Technical Writing. Morris I. Bolsky & AT&T Bell Labortories Staff. 156p. 1988. pap. 14.95 (0-13-074253-8) P-H.

Better Sentence. Colette Dollarhide. 200p. (C). 1987. pap. text ed. 13.95 (0-935920-36-6, Ntl Pubs Blck) P-H.

*Better Sentence Writing in Thirty Minutes a Day. Diana Campbell. 224p. (Orig.). (YA). 1995. pap. 8.99 (1-56414-203-5) Career Pr Inc.

Better Services for Older People. Chris Payne. (C). 1989. 70.00 (0-7855-0086-3, Pub. by Natl Inst Soc Work) St Mut.

Better Services for Older People. Chris Payne. (C). 1989. 65.00 (0-902789-60-0, Pub. by Natl Inst Soc Work) St Mut.

*Better Sex Diet: The 6-Week Low-Fat Prescription for Increased Sexual Vitality, Potency & Health. Lynn Fischer & Jennifer Douglas. 256p. (Orig.). 1996. pap. 14.95 (1-879326-27-2) Living Planet Pr.

Better Sex Through Chemistry: A Guide to the New Prosexual Drugs & Nutrients. John Morgenthaler et al. 240p. 1995. 14.95 (0-9627418-2-5, Smart Pubns) Hlth Freedom.

Better Shape Up. Ann Rosen. (Illus.). 32p. 1984. pap. 6.00 (0-318-35556-6) Visual Studies.

Better Shortwave Reception. 5th ed. William I. Orr & Stuart D. Cowan. LC 57-14916. (Illus.). 160p. 1957. 9.95 (0-933616-05-8) Radio Pubns.

Better Shot. K. Davies. (Illus.). 136p. 1992. 37.50 (0-940143-78-X) Safari Pr.

Better Shot. Ken Davies. 1992. 38.00 (1-870948-64-5, Pub. by Quiller Pr UK) St Mut.

Better Sort. Henry James. LC 75-110201. (Short Story Index Reprint Ser.). 1977. 23.95 (0-8369-3352-4) Ayer.

Better Soybean Recipes. Mary L. Jones. 1964. pap. 2.95 (0-911080-13-9) Outdoor Pict.

Better Speech Can Be Fun: F Book; L Book; R Book; S Book; & TH Book. Goldberg & Braslow. 1973. text ed. 1.50 (0-317-05958-0) Expression.

Better Speeches in Ten Simple Steps. James W. Robinson. 1989. pap. 7.95 (0-914629-86-7) Prima Pub.

*Better Speeches in Ten Simple Steps. 2nd rev. ed. James Robinson. LC 94-39592. 1995. 9.95 (1-55958-691-5) Prima Pub.

Better Spelling: Fourteen Steps to Spelling Improvement. 3rd ed. James I. Brown & Thomas E. Pearsall. 132p. (C). 1990. pap. text ed. 12.50 (0-669-07653-8) Heath.

Better Spelling: Fourteen Steps to Spelling Improvement. 4th ed. James I. Brown & Thomas E. Pearsall. 157p. (C). 1992. pap. text ed. write for info. (0-669-28198-0) Heath.

*Better Spelling in Thirty Minutes a Day. Robert W. Emery. Ed. by Harry H. Croby. 224p. (Orig.). (YA). 1995. pap. 8.99 (1-56414-202-7) Career Pr Inc.

Better Sport Skating: The Key to Improved Performance. Richard Arnold. 96p. (C). 1982. 59.00 (0-7182-1468-4, Pub. by Elm Pubns UK) St Mut.

Better Start. Ed. by Fred M. Hechinger. 228p. 1986. 16.95 (0-8027-0897-8); pap. 10.95 (0-8027-7300-1) Walker & Co.

Better Strangers. large type ed. Delia Ellis. 1991. 21.95 (0-7089-2499-9) Ulverscroft.

*Better Takeoffs & Landings. Michael C. Love. LC 95-13583. 1995. write for info. (0-07-038805-9); pap. write for info. (0-07-038806-7) TAB Bks.

Better Teaching, More Learning: Strategies for Success in Post-Secondary Settings. James Davis. LC 93-9809. (American Council on Education-Oryx Press Series on Higher Education). 392p. 1993. 35.00 (0-89774-813-1) Oryx Pr.

Better Teaching Through Better Measurement. Gerald S. Hanna. 576p. (C). 1993. lib. bdg. write for info. (0-15-500099-3); Computerized test bank, IBM 3.5. 14.50 (0-15-500835-8); Computerized test bank, Mac. 14.50 (0-15-500574-X) HB Coll Pubs.

Better Than a Brother. Edith McCall. (Illus.). 1988. 13.95 (0-8027-6782-6); 14.85 (0-8027-6783-4) Walker & Co.

*Better Than a Lemonade Stand: Business Ideas for Kids. Daryl Bernstein. (Kid's Books by Kids Ser.). (Illus.). (J). (gr. 2-10). 1992. 14.95 (1-885223-15-3) Beyond Words Pub.

Better Than a Lemonade Stand: Business Ideas for Kids. Daryl Bernstein. (Kid's Books by Kids Ser.). (Illus.). (J). (gr. 2-10). 1992. pap. 8.95 (0-941831-75-2) Beyond Words Pub.

Better Than Book Reports. Scholastic Books Staff. 1993. pap. 14.95 (0-590-49213-6) Scholastic Inc.

Better Than Gold. George M. Adams. LC 79-167301. (Essay Index Reprint Ser.). 1977. reprint ed. 20.95 (0-8369-2632-3) Ayer.

Better Than Gold & Silver. Sandra Mackey. 1975. pap. 6.25 (0-89137-407-8) Quality Pubns.

Better Than Mom's Cookbook. Janet E. Talbert & Lisa J. Talbert. 107p. (Orig.). 1993. pap. 10.00 (0-9638345-0-9) J Talbert.

Better Than Money: Tales to Treasure for a Lifetime. Joe McHugh. LC 91-70909. (Illus.). 125p. (J). (gr. 1-8). 1991. 11.95 (0-9619943-1-2) Catalpa Pr.

Better Than Nice & Other Unconventional Prayers. Frederick Ohler. 120p. 1989. 14.00 (0-664-21880-6) Westminster John Knox.

Better Than One. Damon Knight & Kate Wilhelm. LC 79-89652. xiv, 76p. 1980. 3.00 (0-9603146-0-1) MA Convent Fandom.

Better Than Our Best - Women of Valor in American History. Arlene Ferman et al. (Illus.). 150p. (Orig.). (YA). (gr. 6-9). 1990. pap. 9.95 (0-8283-1941-3) Branden Pub Co.

Better Than Plowing & Other Personal Essays. James M. Buchanan. LC 91-44417. (Illus.). 200p. 1992. 23.95 (0-226-07816-7) U Ch Pr.

Better Than Riches. Frederick D. Pile. 116p. (C). 1989. text ed. 65.00 (1-85821-005-4, Pub. by Pentland Pr UK) St Mut.

Better Than Rivers of Oil. Gerald Gerbrandt. LC 85-81305. (Faith & Life Bible Studies). 78p. (Orig.). 1985. pap. 4.95 (0-87303-105-9) Faith & Life.

Better Than School: One Family's Declaration of Independence. Nancy Wallace. LC 83-11333. (Illus.). 256p. 1983. pap. write for info. (0-943914-04-3) Larson Pubns.

Better Than Second Best: Love & Work in the Life of Helen Magill. Glenn C. Altschuler. LC 89-5041. (Women in American History Ser.). (Illus.). 200p. 1990. 29.95 (0-252-01669-6) U of Ill Pr.

Better Than Sex. Hunter S. Thompson. 1993. write for info. (0-679-40695-6) McKay.

*Better than Sex. Hunter S. Thompson. 272p. 1995. pap. 12.95 (0-345-39635-9) Ballantine.

Better Than Sex: Fear & Loathing on the Campaign Trail, 1992. Hunter S. Thompson. 304p. 1993. 23.00 (0-679-42447-4) Random.

Better Than the Sons of Kings. Patricia A. Quinn. (Studies in History & Culture: Vol. 2). 265p. (C). 1989. text ed. 59.00 (0-8204-0472-1) P Lang Pubs.

Better Than the Truth. Jana Ellis. LC 88-15881. (Merivale Mall Ser.). 160p. (YA). (gr. 7 up). 1988. pap. text ed. 2.50 (0-8167-1362-6) Troll Assocs.

Better Than Wine. Ruth S. Fajfr. 1970. pap. 1.99 (1-56632-088-7) Revival Lit.

Better Things to Do. Milton Jordan. Bd. with Lights & Shadows. (Ohio Writers Ser.: No. 3). (Illus.). 36p. (Orig.). 1985. Set pap. 4.00 (0-933087-03-9) Bottom Dog Pr.

Better Think Twice about It: And Twelve Other Stories. Luigi Pirandello. (Short Story Index Reprint Ser.). 1977. reprint ed. 29.95 (0-8369-4269-8) Ayer.

Better Time to Be: Utopian Attitudes to Society among Sydney Anglicans, 1885 to 1914. William J. Lawton. 220p. 1990. pap. 24.95 (0-86840-068-8, Pub. by New South Wales Univ Pr AT) Intl Spec Bk.

Better Times. Barrie Keeffe. (Methuen New Theatrescripts Ser.). 44p. 1985. pap. 8.95 (0-413-59670-2, A0030) Heinemann.

*Better Times Than These. Winston Groom. 1994. mass mkt. 5.99 (0-671-52266-3) PB.

Better to Eat You. Charlotte Armstrong. 1992. pap. 3.50 (0-8217-3696-5) Zebra.

*Better to See You. Urias. 1993. per. 10.95 (0-920953-59-X, Pub. by Cormorant Bks CN) InBook.

Better Translation for Better Communication: A Survey of the Translation Market, Present & Future, Prepared for the Commission of the European Communities, Directorate-General Information Market & Innovation. Commission of the European Communities, Luxembourg. (Commission of the European Communities Ser.). 200p. 1983. 90.00 (0-08-030534-2, Pub. by Pergamon Repr UK) Franklin.

Better Understanding Learning Disabilities: New Views from Research & Their Implications for Education & Public Policies. Ed. by G. Reid Lyon et al. 304p. (C). 1993. boxed 35.00 (1-55766-116-2) P H Brookes.

Better Video Images. Ed. by Jeffrey Friedman. 400p. 1989. pap. 35.00 (0-940690-15-2) Soc Motion Pic & TV Engrs.

Better Way: Achieving Total Quality. Roger L. Kirkham. LC 92-70749. (Illus.). 145p. (Orig.). 1992. pap. 8.95 (0-9632349-0-0) Am Trng Alliance.

Better Way (Hebrews) (New Horizons Bible Study Ser.). 68p. (Orig.). 1986. teacher ed 2.35 (0-89367-104-5); student ed, pap. 2.95 (0-89367-103-7) Light & Life.

Better Way to Drink: Moderation & Control of Problem Drinking. Roger E. Vogler & Wayne R. Bartz. 208p. 1985. reprint ed. write for info. (0-934986-17-7); reprint ed. pap. 11.95 (0-934986-16-9) New Harbinger.

Better Way to Live. large type ed. Og Mandino. 176p. 1992. pap. 14.95 (0-8161-5234-9) G K Hall.

Better Way to Live: For the First Time, Og Mandino Shares His Personal Success Story. Og Mandino. 1991. mass mkt. 5.50 (0-553-28674-9) Bantam.

Better Way to Make Money. Burton H. Pugh. (Illus.). 1987. 25.00 (0-939093-09-X) Lambert Gann Pub.

*Better Woman. Sylvia Durant. 35p. (Orig.). 1993. pap. write for info. (0-9641133-1-7) Pocket Perks.

Better World. Harvey Jackins. LC 92-19434. 1992. 16.00 (0-913937-63-0); pap. 13.00 (0-913937-64-9) Rational Isl.

Better World: Stalinism & the American Intellectuals. William L. O'Neill. 464p. 1989. pap. 21.95 (0-88738-631-8) Transaction Pubs.

Better World, a Better You. Louis E. Tice. 1989. 23.95 (0-13-073479-9) P-H.

Better World for Our Children: Rebuilding American Family Values. Benjamin M. Spock. 1994. 22.95 (1-882605-12-8) Natl Pr Bks.

Better World Shopping: What to Buy & Where to Buy Products for the New Age. 1992. lib. bdg. 76.95 (0-8490-5281-5) Gordon Pr.

Better Writing: From Paragraph to Essay. Gene Stanford & Marie N. Smith. LC 80-142. 190p. (Orig.). (C). 1980. pap. text ed. 21.50 (0-03-051161-5) HB Coll Pubs.

Bettering Our Condition: Work, Workers, & Ethics in British & German Economic Thought. Philip J. Chmielewski. LC 92-13304. (American University Studies: Philosophy: Ser. V, Vol. 137). 299p. (C). 1993. text ed. 49.95 (0-8204-1851-X) P Lang Pubs.

Betti: Corruzione Al Palazzo di Giustizia. Ed. by Vincent Luciani. (C). 1980. pap. 8.95 (0-913298-20-4) S F Vanni.

*Bettie Page: Queen of Hearts. Jim Silke. (Illus.). 96p. 1995. pap. 19.95 (1-56971-124-0) Dark Horse Comics.

*Bettie Page: The Life of a Pin-Up Legend. Karen Essex et al. (Illus.). 288p. 1995. 40.00 (1-881649-62-8) Genl Pub Grp.

Bettina Brentano-von Arnim: Gender & Politics. Ed. by Elke Frederiksen & Katherine R. Goodman. (Kritik: German Literary Theory & Cultural Studies). (Illus.). 472p. 1995. text ed. 39.95 (0-8143-2516-5) Wayne St U Pr.

Bettina the Ballerina. (Golden Story Book 'n Tape Ser.). (Illus.). 24p. (J). (ps-3). 1991. write for info. (0-307-14165-9, 14165) Western Pub.

Bettine von Arnim & the Politics of Romantic Conversation. Edith Waldstein. LC 87-70868. (Studies in German Literature, Linguistics & Culture: vol. 33). (Illus.). 150p. 1988. 29.00 (0-938100-54-8) Camden Hse.

Betting & Gambling. 60p. 1981. 120.00 (0-686-71950-6, Pub. by Euromonitor Pubns UK) St Mut.

Betting Cheap Claimers. Stanford Wong. (Illus.). 190p. (Orig.). 1992. pap. 14.95 (0-935926-16-X) Pi Yee Pr.

Betting Gaming & Lotteries. Kerry Barker & David Hamilton. 235p. 1993. 84.00 (1-85190-186-8, Pub. by Tolley Pubng UK) St Mut.

Betting Horses to Win. Les Conklin. 1980. pap. 7.00 (0-87980-265-0) Wilshire.

Betting on Ideas: Wars, Invention, Inflation. Reuven Brenner. LC 85-8750. (Illus.). xii, 248p. 1986. 32.00 (0-226-07400-5) U Ch Pr.

Betting on Ideas: Wars, Invention, Inflation. Reuven Brenner. LC 85-8750. (Illus.). xii, 248p. 1989. pap. text ed. 12.95 (0-226-07401-3) U Ch Pr.

Betting on Love. Ann Patrick. 224p. (Orig.). 1993. pap. 2.95 (1-56597-010-X, Kismet) Meteor Pub.

Betting on Theories. Patrick Maher. LC 92-13817. (Studies in Probability, Induction & Decision Theory). 384p. (C). 1993. 54.95 (0-521-41850-X) Cambridge U Pr.

Betting on Yourself. Robert Anthony. 1991. pap. 8.95 (0-425-13038-X, Berkley Trade) Berkley Pub.

Betting Thoroughbreds: A Professional's Guide for the Horseplayer. rev. ed. Steven Davidowitz. (Illus.). 1983. pap. 8.95 (0-525-48237-7, Dutton) NAL-Dutton.

Betting Thoroughbreds: A Professional's Guide for the Horseplayer. 2nd rev. ed. Steven Davidowitz. 288p. 1994. pap. 9.95 (0-452-27042-1, Plume) NAL-Dutton.

*Betting Thoroughbreds: A Professional's Guide for the Horseplayer. 2nd rev. ed. Steven Davidowitz. LC 94-34539. (Illus.). 352p. 1995. 29.95 (0-525-93951-2, Dutton) NAL-Dutton.

Betting to Win on Sports. Wayne A. Root & Wilbur Cross. 1989. pap. 8.95 (0-685-28265-1) Bantam.

Bettmann: The Picture Man. Otto L. Bettmann. Ed. by Norman Sheffield, Jr. LC 92-10639. (Illus.). 192p. 1992. 32.95 (0-8130-1153-1) U Press Fla.

Bettmann Archive Illustrated History of the Civil War, 1861-1865. David E. Roth. (Illus.). 256p. 1992. 24.98 (0-8317-0775-5) Smithmark.

Bettmann Portable Archive. David Greenstein & Katherine G. Bang. (Illus.). 336p. 1993. 29.95 (0-9638093-9-3) Bettmann.

Bettor's Guide to Harness Racing: A New Guide to Successful Handicapping. Ronald Roblin. 1979. 9.95 (0-8065-0645-8, Citadel Pr) Carol Pub Group.

Betty. Georges Simenon. (FRE.). 1992. pap. 11.95 (0-7859-3255-0, 2266049801) Fr & Eur.

Betty Alden. Jane G. Austin. (Works of Jane (Goodin) Austin). 1989. reprint ed. lib. bdg. 79.00 (0-7812-1833-0) Rprt Serv.

Betty & Pansy's Severe Queer Review of San Francisco. 2nd ed. John Orcutt. (Illus.). 1992. pap. text ed. 8.95 (0-9633048-0-1) Bedpan Prods.

Betty & Pansy's Severe Queer Review of San Francisco, No. 3. 3rd ed. Betty & Pansy. (Illus.). 153p. 1993. pap. 9.95 (0-9633048-1-X) Bedpan Prods.

Betty Bear's Birthday. Gyo Fujikawa. (Illus.). 16p. (J). (ps). 1989. reprint ed. bds. 6.95 (1-55987-011-7, Sunny Bks) J B Comns.

Betty Bonnet Paper Dolls in Full Color. Sheila Young. (J). 1982. pap. 3.95 (0-486-24415-6) Dover.

Betty Book. Stewart E. White. 288p. 1988. reprint ed. pap. 9.95 (0-89804-151-1) Ariel GA.

Betty Boop's Big Break. Joshua Quagmire. Ed. by Byron Erickson. (Illus.). 48p. (Orig.). 1990. pap. 5.95 (0-915419-49-1) First Pub IL.

Betty Boop's Hollywood Chronicles. Illus. by Max Fleischer. 1990. mass mkt. 5.95 (0-380-76072-X) Avon.

Betty Comden & Adolph Green: A Bio-Bibliography. Alice M. Robinson. LC 93-21050. (Bio-Bibliographies in the Performing Arts Ser.: No. 45). 384p. 1993. text ed. 59.95 (0-313-27659-5, Greenwood Pr) Greenwood.

Betty Crocker International Cookbook. Ed. by Betty Crocker Staff. 1994. pap. 19.00 (0-671-88763-7, B Crocker Ckbks) P-H Gen Ref & Trav.

An Asterisk (*) at the beginning of an entry indicates that the title is appearing in BIP for the first time.

Betty Crocker New Choices Cookbook. LC 92-41048. 1993. 23.00 (*0-671-86767-9*, B Crocker Ckbks) P-H Gen Ref & Trav.

Betty Crocker's American Country Cooking. General Mills Staff. Ed. by Elisabeth Scharlatt. LC 87-42642. (Illus.). 96p. 1987. 9.95 (*0-394-56302-6*) Random.

Betty Crocker's Best Barbecue Recipes. LC 92-34873. 1993. 8.00 (*0-671-86517-X*, B Crocker Ckbks) P-H Gen Ref & Trav.

Betty Crocker's Best Breakfasts & Brunches. LC 93-32577. 1994. 8.00 (*0-671-88772-6*, B Crocker Ckbks) P-H Gen Ref & Trav.

***Betty Crocker's Boys & Girls Baking.** LC 94-24258. (J). 1995. 15.00 (*0-671-52284-1*) Macmillan.

Betty Crocker's Boys & Girls Microwave Cookbook. Betty Crocker Editors. 160p. (J). 1992. pap. 15.00 (*0-13-085549-9*, B Crocker Ckbks) P-H Gen Ref & Trav.

***Betty Crocker's Bread Machine Cookbook.** LC 95-4973. 1995. 8.00 (*0-02-860367-2*) Macmillan.

Betty Crocker's Casual Country Cooking. LC 92-32344. 1993. 16.00 (*0-671-79923-1*, B Crocker Ckbks) P-H Gen Ref & Trav.

***Betty Crocker's Complete Pasta Cookbook.** LC 95-12564. 1995. write for info. (*0-02-860374-5*) Macmillan.

Betty Crocker's Cookbook. Betty Crocker Editors. 752p. 1987. mass mkt. 7.99 (*0-553-26660-8*) Bantam.

Betty Crocker's Cookbook. 7th ed. Betty Crocker. 1993. pap. 14.00 (*0-671-85039-3*, B Crocker Ckbks) P-H Gen Ref & Trav.

Betty Crocker's Cookbook: Fortieth Anniversary Edition. Betty Crocker Editors. (Illus.). 432p. 1991. pap. 14.00 (*0-13-094269-3*, B Crocker Ckbks); ring bd. 22.00 (*0-13-073768-2*, B Crocker Ckbks) P-H Gen Ref & Trav.

Betty Crocker's Cookbook: Special Holiday Edition, 2 bks., Set. Betty Crocker Editors. (Illus.). 1992. pap. 25.00 (*0-13-068503-8*, B Crocker Ckbks) P-H Gen Ref & Trav.

Betty Crocker's Cookbook with Microwave. 7th ed. Betty Crocker. 1993. 18.00 (*0-671-88540-5*) P-H.

Betty Crocker's Cooking for Two. LC 93-34241. 1994. 12.00 (*0-671-88827-7*, B Crocker Ckbks) P-H Gen Ref & Trav.

***Betty Crocker's Cooking with Kids.** LC 94-24259. 1995. 15.00 (*0-671-52283-3*) Macmillan.

***Betty Crocker's Creative Cookies.** LC 95-4981. 1995. 8.00 (*0-02-860366-4*) Macmillan.

Betty Crocker's Do-Ahead Cookbook. Betty Crocker Editorial Staff. (Illus.). 1994. 18.00 (*0-671-50124-0*, B Crocker Ckbks) P-H Gen Ref & Trav.

***Betty Crocker's Do Ahead Cookbook.** Betty Crocker. 1995. 18.00 (*0-02-860030-4*, B Crocker Ckbks) P-H Gen Ref & Trav.

***Betty Crocker's Easy Low Fat Cooking.** Betty Crocker. 1995. pap. 15.00 (*0-02-860086-X*, B Crocker Ckbks) P-H Gen Ref & Trav.

***Betty Crocker's Easy Mexican Cooking.** Betty Crocker. LC 94-42663. 1995. 15.00 (*0-02-860359-1*) Macmillan.

Betty Crocker's Eat & Lose Weight. Betty Crocker Editors. (Illus.). 1990. 20.00 (*0-13-074303-8*, B Crocker Ckbks) P-H Gen Ref & Trav.

***Betty Crocker's Fabulous Fish & Seafood.** Betty Crocker Staff. LC 94-37683. 1996. 25.00 (*0-02-860281-1*, B Crocker Ckbks) P-H Gen Ref & Trav.

Betty Crocker's Great Chicken Recipes. LC 92-25398. 1993. 8.00 (*0-671-84689-2*, B Crocker Ckbks) P-H Gen Ref & Trav.

Betty Crocker's Great Main Dishes Without Meat. LC 93-4528. (Illus.). 1994. 14.00 (*0-671-88251-1*) P-H.

Betty Crocker's Holiday Baking. LC 92-46360. 1994. 8.00 (*0-671-06961-6*, B Crocker Ckbks) P-H Gen Ref & Trav.

Betty Crocker's Holiday Baking. Betty Crocker Editors. 1993. 8.00 (*0-671-86961-2*, B Crocker Ckbks) P-H Gen Ref & Trav.

Betty Crocker's It's Chicken Cookbook. LC 93-44974. 1994. 16.00 (*0-671-89243-6*) P-H.

Betty Crocker's Low-Calorie Cooking. LC 92-25397. 1993. 8.00 (*0-671-84690-6*, B Crocker Ckbks) P-H Gen Ref & Trav.

Betty Crocker's Low-Fat Cooking. LC 93-38096. 1994. 8.00 (*0-671-88771-8*, B Crocker Ckbks) P-H Gen Ref & Trav.

Betty Crocker's Low Fat, Low Cholesterol Cookbook. Ed. by Betty Crocker Editors. 1991. 18.00 (*0-671-86752-0*, B Crocker Ckbks) P-H Gen Ref & Trav.

Betty Crocker's Mexican Made Easy. LC 92-25395. 1993. 8.00 (*0-671-84691-4*, B Crocker Ckbks) P-H Gen Ref & Trav.

Betty Crocker's Microwave Cookbook. (Illus.). 384p. 1990. pap. 19.95 (*0-13-073859-X*, B Crocker Ckbks) P-H Gen Ref & Trav.

Betty Crocker's Microwave Cooking. (Illus.). 288p. 1991. 7.99 (*0-517-05368-3*) Random Hse Value.

Betty Crocker's Microwaving for One or Two. 1985. 12.95 (*0-394-53593-6*) Random.

Betty Crocker's New Boys & Girls Cookbook. (Illus.). 144p. (J). 1990. spiral bd. 11.00 (*0-13-083262-6*, B Crocker Ckbks) P-H Gen Ref & Trav.

Betty Crocker's New Cake Decorating. rev. ed. Betty Crocker Staff. LC 93-51020. 1994. 15.00 (*0-671-89748-9*, B Crocker Ckbks) P-H Gen Ref & Trav.

Betty Crocker's New Chinese Cookbook. Betty Crocker Editors. (Illus.). 144p. 1990. 15.00 (*0-13-083254-5*, B Crocker Ckbks) P-H Gen Ref & Trav.

***Betty Crocker's New Choices for Pasta, Grains & Beans: Great Ideas for Healthy Meals.** Crocker. 1995. 18.00 (*0-02-860362-1*, B Crocker Ckbks) P-H Gen Ref & Trav.

***Betty Crocker's New Choices for Pasta, Grains & Beans Cookbook.** Betty Crocker. 1995. 16.00 (*0-671-52285-X*) Macmillan.

***Betty Crocker's New Choices for Two.** LC 95-4980. 1995. 18.00 (*0-02-860368-0*) Macmillan.

Betty Crocker's New Christmas Cookbook. LC 92-35119. 1993. 18.00 (*0-671-79927-4*, B Crocker Ckbks) P-H Gen Ref & Trav.

Betty Crocker's New Microwaving for One or Two. Betty Crocker Editors. (Illus.). 128p. 1990. 14.95 (*0-13-073685-6*) P-H.

Betty Crocker's New Microwaving for One or Two. large type ed. Betty Crocker. LC 90-45452. 1990. reprint ed. lib. bdg. 18.95 (*1-56054-033-8*) Thorndike Pr.

Betty Crocker's One-Dish Main Meals. LC 93-6073. 1994. 12.00 (*0-671-88331-3*) P-H.

Betty Crocker's One Hundred Twenty-Five Low-Calorie Main Dishes. Betty Crocker Editors. (Illus.). 144p. 1992. pap. 14.00 (*0-13-085531-6*, B Crocker Ckbks) P-H Gen Ref & Trav.

Betty Crocker's Pasta Favorites. LC 92-34872. 1993. 8.00 (*0-671-86516-1*, B Crocker Ckbks) P-H Gen Ref & Trav.

Betty Crocker's Quick Dinners. LC 92-25396. 1993. 8.00 (*0-671-84692-2*, B Crocker Ckbks) P-H Gen Ref & Trav.

***Betty Crocker's Sensational Salads.** Betty Crocker Cookbooks Staff. LC 94-36647. 1995. pap. 20.00 (*0-02-860280-3*, B Crocker Ckbks) P-H Gen Ref & Trav.

Betty Crocker's Sizzling Stir-Fries. LC 93-32578. 1994. 8.00 (*0-671-88773-4*, B Crocker Ckbks) P-H Gen Ref & Trav.

Betty Crocker's Soups & Stews. LC 92-44793. 1993. 8.00 (*0-671-86960-4*, B Crocker Ckbks) P-H Gen Ref & Trav.

Betty Crocker's Ultimate Cookie Book. Betty Crocker Editors. (Illus.). 208p. 1992. 18.00 (*0-13-084492-6*, B Crocker Ckbks) P-H Gen Ref & Trav.

Betty Crocker's Vegetarian Cookbook. LC 93-36694. 1994. 8.00 (*0-671-88770-X*, B Crocker Ckbks) P-H Gen Ref & Trav.

Betty Elizabeth Brown: A Keepsake Book. Illus. by Connie Ross. 32p. (J). (ps up). 1992. pap. 2.75 (*1-878893-26-2*) Telcraft Bks.

Betty Feezor's Carolina Recipes, Vol. I. Betty Feezor. 331p. 1964. pap. 8.50 (*0-915605-01-5*) B Feezor Bks.

Betty Feezor's Carolina Recipes, Vol. II. Betty Feezor. 328p. 1974. pap. 7.50 (*0-915605-02-3*) B Feezor Bks.

Betty Feezor's Carolina Recipes, Vol. III. Bob Feezor. 288p. 1984. pap. 8.50 (*0-915605-04-X*) B Feezor Bks.

Betty Friedan. Justine Blau. (American Women of Achievement Ser.). (Illus.). 112p. (J). (gr. 5 up). 1990. lib. bdg. 17.95 (*1-55546-653-2*) Chelsea Hse.

Betty Friedan. Susan Taylor-Boyd. LC 90-9691. (People Who Have Helped the World Ser.). (Illus.). 64p. (J). (gr. 5-6). 1990. lib. bdg. 21.26 (*0-8368-0104-0*) Gareth Stevens Inc.

Betty Friedan: Fighter for Women's Rights. Sondra Henry & Emily Taitz. LC 89-23582. (Contemporary Women Ser.). (Illus.). 128p. (J). (gr. 6 up). 1990. lib. bdg. 17.95 (*0-89490-292-X*) Enslow Pubs.

Betty Grable: A Bio-Bibliography. Larry Billman. LC 93-17579. 328p. 1993. text ed. 45.00 (*0-313-28156-4*, Greenwood Pr) Greenwood.

***Betty Grable: The Girl with the Million Dollar Legs.** Tom McGee. LC 94-31145. 1994. 29.95 (*1-879511-15-0*); pap. 19.95 (*1-879511-18-5*) Vestal.

Betty Groff's Pennsylvania Dutch Cookbook. Betty Groff. 1994. 9.98 (*0-88365-852-6*) Galahad Bks.

***Betty Hahn: Photography or Maybe Not.** Steve Yates. LC 95-4358. (Illus.). 208p. 1995. 80.00 (*0-8263-1601-8*); pap. 39.95 (*0-8263-1602-6*) U of NM Pr.

Betty Husney's Cook Book with Love. Betty Husney. 49p. 1989. text ed. 9.95 (*0-685-26565-X*); pap. 9.95 (*0-685-26566-8*) B Husney.

***Betty Mitchell.** Kenneth Dyba. (Illus.). 186p. 1986. 19.95 (*0-920490-63-8*) Temeron Bks.

Betty Neuman: The Neuman Systems Model. Karen S. Reed. (Notes on Nursing Theories Ser.: Vol. 11). (Illus.). 64p. (C). 1993. text ed. 18.95 (*0-8039-4861-1*); pap. text ed. 8.95 (*0-8039-4862-X*) Sage.

Betty Page Captured Jungle Girl 3-D. Ray Zone & Pizz Staff. (Illus.). 24p. (Orig.). 1990. pap. text ed. 3.95 (*0-925300-02-0*) Three-D Zone.

Betty Page Confidential. Stan Corwin Productions Staff. (Illus.). 128p. (Orig.). 1994. pap. 13.95 (*0-312-10940-7*) St Martin.

Betty Page 3-D Picture Book. Ed. by Ray Zone. (Illus.). 32p. (Orig.). 1989. pap. 3.95 (*0-925300-01-2*) Three-D Zone.

Betty Parsons: Artist - Dealer - Collector. Lee Hall. (Illus.). 192p. 1991. 45.00 (*0-8109-3712-3*) Abrams.

Betty Rosbottom's Cooking School Cookbook. Betty Rosbottom. LC 87-42746. 416p. 1987. 19.95 (*0-89480-526-6*, 1526); pap. 10.95 (*0-89480-525-8*, 1525) Workman Pub.

Betty-San. Michiko Yamamoto. Ed. by Shaw. Tr. by Geraldine Harcourt. LC 82-48786. (Illus.). 148p. 1992. pap. 7.00 (*0-87011-736-X*) Kodansha.

Betty Talmadge's Lovejoy Plantation Cookbook. Betty Talmadge. LC 83-61917. (Illus.). 166p. 1983. pap. 12.95 (*0-931948-44-4*) Peachtree Pubs.

***Betty the Yeti.** Jon Klein. 1995. pap. 4.75 (*0-8222-1455-5*) Dramatists Play.

Betty Zane. Zane Gray. 1978. pap. 1.75 (*0-89083-363-X*) Zebra.

Betty Zane. Zane Grey. 1992. mass mkt. 3.99 (*0-06-100523-1*, Harp PBks) HarpC.

Betty Zane. Zane Grey. 1976. reprint ed. lib. bdg. 22.95 (*0-89190-752-1*, Rivercity Pr) Amereon Ltd.

Betty Zane. Zane Grey. 1990. reprint ed. lib. bdg. 29.95x (*0-89968-510-2*) Buccaneer Bks.

Betty Zane. Zane Grey. 1993. reprint ed. lib. bdg. 89.00 (*0-7812-5368-3*) Rprt Serv.

***Betty Zane: The Authorized Edition.** Zane Grey. 296p. (C). 1995. pap. 12.00 (*0-8032-7057-7*, Bison Books) U of Nebr Pr.

Betty's Bright Idea. Harriet Beecher Stowe. LC 72-37562. (Short Story Index Reprint Ser.). 1977. reprint ed. 17.95 (*0-8369-4121-7*) Ayer.

Betty's Not Well Today. Gus Clarke. (Illus.). 32p. (J). (ps-00). 1994. 16.95 (*0-86264-433-X*, Pub. by Andersen Pr UK) Trafalgar.

Betty's Secret & Other Stories by Grandmother Lois. Mary M. Landis. 181p. 1972. 5.60 (*0-686-05593-4*) Rod & Staff.

Between. J. W. Curry & Steven Smith. (Illus.). 30p. (Orig.). 1989. pap. 3.00 (*0-926935-12-7*) Runaway Spoon.

***Between: A Novel.** Tananarive Due. LC 95-2415. 1995. 22.00 (*0-06-017250-9*, HarpT) HarpC.

Between: Selected Poems of Agnes Nemes Nagy. Tr. by Hugh Maxton. (C). 1988. pap. 15.00 (*0-948268-39-5*, Pub. by Dedalus Pr IE) St Mut.

Between a Dream & a Cup of Coffee. Peter Cherches. LC 87-42544. 48p. 1987. pap. 4.00 (*0-87376-054-9*) Red Dust.

***Between a Rock & a Hard Place.** Alden R. Carter. LC 94-39803. 1995. write for info. (*0-590-48684-5*) Scholastic Inc.

Between a Rock & a Heart Place. Rick Wilson. 63p. 1990. 25.00 (*0-916379-51-5*) Scripta.

Between Action & Cut: Five American Directors. Ed. by Frank Thompson. LC 84-23540. 320p. 1985. 27.50 (*0-8108-1744-6*) Scarecrow.

Between Actor & Critic: Selected Letters of Edwin Booth & William Winter. Daniel Watermeier. LC 72-113012. (Illus.). 1971. 47.50 (*0-691-06193-9*) Princeton U Pr.

***Between Actor & Critic: Selected Letters of Edwin Booth & William Winter.** Edwin Booth. Ed. & Intro. by Daniel J. Watermeier. LC 72-113012. Date not set. reprint ed. pap. 100.10 (*0-7837-9472-X*, 2060214) Bks Demand.

Between Adolescents & Parent. Moshe Smilansky. 304p. (C). 1991. 29.95 (*0-9625963-4-5*) Psychosocial & Educ Pubns.

***Between Affluence & Rebellion: The Work of Thomas Brasch in the Interface Between East & West.** Margrit Frolich. LC 94-24569. (DDR-Studien & East German Studies: Vol. 9). 1995. write for info. (*0-8204-2575-3*) P Lang Pubs.

Between Analyst & Patient: New Dimensions in Countertransference & Tranference. Ed. by Helen C. Meyers. 280p. 1986. text ed. 32.50 (*0-88163-043-8*) Analytic Pr.

Between Angels. Stephen Dunn. 1990. pap. 8.95 (*0-393-30658-5*) Norton.

Between Angels. Stephen Dunn. 1990. 15.95 (*0-685-46181-5*) Norton.

Between Animal & Man. Michael W. Fox. LC 85-12574. 224p. 1986. reprint ed. lib. bdg. 21.50 (*0-89874-827-5*) Krieger.

Between Art & Science: Essays in Psychotherapy & Psychiatry. Jeremy Holmes. LC 92-2377. 240p. 1993. 59.95 (*0-685-59408-4*, B0220, Tavistock); pap. 18.95 (*0-415-08308-7*, B0224, Tavistock) Routledge.

***Between Artists: Twelve Contemporary American Artists Interview Twelve Contemporary American.** Ed. by William S. Bartman & Rodney Sappington. (Explores the Work of Artists in Mid-Career Ser.). (Illus.). 240p. (Orig.). 1995. pap. text ed. 18.00 (*0-923183-16-7*) ART Pr CA.

***Between Artists: Twelve Contemporary American Artists Interview Twelve Contemporary American Artists.** Ed. by Rodney Sappington & William S. Bartman. (Illus.). 250p. 1995. write for info. (*0-614-02591-5*) ART Pr CA.

Between Athens & Berlin: The Theological Education Debate. David H. Kelsey. 232p. (Orig.). 1993. pap. 14.99 (*0-8028-0672-4*) Eerdmans.

Between Author & Reader: A Psychoanalytic Approach to Writing & Reading. Stanley J. Coen. LC 93-24579. (Psychoanalysis & Culture Ser.). 210p. (C). 1994. 65.00 (*0-231-07356-9*); pap. 17.50 (*0-231-07357-7*) Col U Pr.

Between Autumn & Spring. Herman M. Ward. 76p. 1983. pap. 5.00 (*0-9610346-3-7*) Belle Mead Pr.

Between Bailout & Breakdown: A Modular Approach to Latin America's Debt Crisis. William Guttman. (Significant Issues Ser.). 56p. (Orig.). 1989. pap. 6.95 (*0-89206-132-4*) CSI Studies.

Between Bands & States. Ed. by Susan A. Gregg. LC 90-61288. (Center for Archaeological Investigations Research Paper Ser.: No. 9). (Illus.). xix, 450p. (Orig.). 1991. pap. 30.00 (*0-88104-072-X*) Center Archaeo.

Between Basti Dwellers & Bureaucrats: Lessons in Squatter Settlement Upgrading in Karachi. Ed. by J. J. Van Der Linden et al. (Illus.). 330p. 1983. 134.00 (*0-08-027971-6*, Pub. by Pergamon Repr UK) Franklin.

Between Battles & Ballots: Israeli Military in Politics. Yoram Peri. (Cambridge Middle East Library: No. 1). 368p. 1983. 69.95 (*0-521-24414-5*) Cambridge U Pr.

Between Berlin & Slobodka: Jewish Transition Figure from Eastern Europe. Hiller Goldberg. 400p. 1989. 29.50 (*0-88125-142-9*); pap. 14.95 (*0-88125-300-6*) Ktav.

Between Biology & Medicine: The Formation of Intermediary Metabolism. Frederic L. Holmes. LC 91-62712. 115p. 1992. pap. text ed. 18.00 (*0-918102-18-9*) U Cal Hist Sci Tech.

Between Births. Gauri Deshpande. 1975. 8.00 (*0-88253-508-0*); pap. text ed. 4.00 (*0-88253-507-2*) Ind-US Inc.

Between Black & White. Henry H. Proctor. LC 79-173611. (Black Heritage Library Collection). 1977. reprint ed. 20.95 (*0-8369-8903-1*) Ayer.

Between Black & White: Race, Politics, & the Free Coloreds in Jamaica, 1792-1865. Gad J. Heuman. LC 80-661. (Contributions in Comparative Colonial Studies: No. 5). (Illus.). xiii, 231p. 1981. text ed. 55.00 (*0-313-20984-7*, HBW/, Greenwood Pr) Greenwood.

Between Blake & Nietzsche: The Reality of Culture. Harvey Birenbaum. LC 91-58182. 184p. 1992. 32.50 (*0-8387-5222-5*) Bucknell U Pr.

Between Boards: New Thoughts on Old Books. Leona Rostenberg & Madeleine B. Stern. 240p. 1989. pap. 18.00 (*0-929246-02-0*) Modoc Pr.

Between Borders: Essays on Mexicana - Chicana History. Ed. by Adelaida Del Castillo. (Mujer Latina Ser.). (Illus.). 560p. (C). 1990. pap. 45.00 (*0-915745-14-3*) Floricanto Pr.

Between Borders: Pedagogy & the Politics of Cultural Studies. Ed. by Henry A. Giroux & Peter McLaren. 256p. 1993. 49.95 (*0-415-90777-2*, B0622, Routledge NY); pap. 15.95 (*0-415-90778-0*, B0626, Routledge NY) Routledge.

Between Brothers & Sisters. Adele Faber & Elaine Mazlish. 192p. 1991. pap. 9.95 (*0-380-71250-4*) Avon.

Between Budapest & Jerusalem, Vol. 3: The Patai Letters, 1933-1938. Raphael Patai. LC 91-51097. (Illus.). 320p. (C). 1992. 29.95 (*0-87480-384-5*) U of Utah Pr.

Between Caesar & Jesus. George D. Herron. LC 75-324. (Radical Tradition in America Ser.). 278p. 1975. reprint ed. 24.00 (*0-88355-227-2*) Hyperion Conn.

Between Capitalism & Democracy: Educational Policy & the Crisis of the Welfare State. Svi Shapiro. LC 89-37674. (Critical Studies in Education). 208p. 1990. text ed. 49.95 (*0-89789-150-3*, H150, Bergin & Garvey); pap. text ed. 14.95 (*0-89789-149-X*, G149, Bergin & Garvey) Greenwood.

Between Center & Periphery: Grassroots Politicians in Italy & France. Sidney G. Tarrow. LC 76-26642. 288p. reprint ed. pap. 82.10 (*0-7837-4548-6*, 2080337) Bks Demand.

***Between Christ & Caesar: Classic & Contemporary Texts on Church & State.** Ed. by Charles Villa-Vicencio. LC 86-16514. 295p. 1986. reprint ed. pap. 84.10 (*0-7837-8096-6*, 2047850) Bks Demand.

Between Christ & Satan. Kurt E. Koch. LC 79-160690. 192p. 1972. pap. 5.99 (*0-8254-3003-8*) Kregel.

Between Church & State: The Lives of Four French Prelates in the Late Middle Ages. Bernard Guenee. Tr. by Arthur Goldhammer. LC 90-35045. 456p. 1990. 39.95 (*0-226-31032-9*) U Ch Pr.

Between Churchill & Stalin: The Soviet Union, Great Britain, & the Origins of the Grand Alliance. Stephen M. Miner. LC 88-4828. xi, 320p. (C). 1988. 39.95 (*0-8078-1796-1*) U of NC Pr.

***Between Churchill & Stalin: The Soviet Union, Great Britain, & the Origins of the Grand Alliance.** Steven M. Miner. LC 88-4828. reprint ed. pap. 95.00 (*0-7837-9015-5*, 2049767) Bks Demand.

Between Citizen & City: Neighborhood Organizations & Urban Politics in Cincinnati. John C. Thomas. LC 86-7726. (Studies in Government & Public Policy). xii, 196p. 1986. 25.00 (*0-7006-0303-4*) U Pr of KS.

Between Civil & Religious Law: The Plight of the Agunah in American Society. Irving A. Breitowitz. LC 92-551. (Contributions in Legal Studies: No. 70). 448p. 1993. text ed. 59.95 (*0-313-28471-7*, BZC, Greenwood Pr) Greenwood.

Between Civilization & Barbarism: Women, Nation, & Literary Culture in Modern Argentina. Francine Masiello. LC 91-45603. (Engendering Latin America Ser.: Vol. 2). x, 246p. 1992. 40.00 (*0-8032-3158-X*) U of Nebr Pr.

Between Class & Nation: The Formation of the Jewish Working Class in the Period before Israel's Statehood. Amir Ben-Porat. LC 85-27281. (Contributions in Labor History Ser.). 255p. 1986. text ed. 55.00 (*0-313-25127-4*, BPB/, Greenwood Pr) Greenwood.

Between Classes: Faculty Life at Truman High. Charles E. Bruckerhoff. 160p. (C). 1991. text ed. 32.95 (*0-685-54184-3*); pap. text ed. 17.95 (*0-8077-3075-0*) Tchrs Coll.

Between Client & Community: A Study in Responsibility in Social Case Work. Bertha C. Reynolds. LC 82-81785. (NASW Classics Ser.). 128p. 1982. reprint ed. pap. text ed. 8.95 (*0-87101-102-6*) Natl Assn Soc Wkrs.

Between Commitment & Disillusion: The Obstructed Path & The Sea Change, 1930-1965. H. Stuart Hughes. LC 87-16841. 608p. 1987. text ed. 40.00 (*0-8195-5136-8*, Wesleyan Univ Pr); pap. 19.95 (*0-8195-6193-2*, Wesleyan Univ Pr) U Pr of New Eng.

Between Communication & Information. Ed. by Jorge R. Schement & Brent D. Ruben. (Information & Behavior Ser.: Vol. 4). 450p. 1992. text ed. 54.95 (*1-56000-037-6*) Transaction Pubs.

Between Concord & Plymouth: The Transcendentalists & the Watsons. L. D. Geller. (Illus.). 1973. 6.00 (*0-685-42210-0*) Thoreau Found.

Between Copernicus & Galileo: Christoph Clavius & the Collapse of Ptolemaic Cosmology. James M. Lattis. LC 94-8675. 1994. lib. bdg. 54.00 (*0-226-46927-1*); pap. text ed. 22.50 (*0-226-46929-8*) U Ch Pr.

Between Craft & Class: Skilled Workers & Factory Politics in the United States & Britain, 1890-1922. Jeffrey Haydu. 292p. 1991. reprint ed. pap. 14.00 (*0-520-07664-8*) U CA Pr.

Between Crown & Swastika: The Impact of the Radical Right on the Afrikaner Nationalist Movement in the Fascist Era. Patrick J. Furlong. LC 89-11944. (Illus.). 368p. 1991. text ed. 45.00 (*0-8195-5229-1*, Wesleyan Univ Pr) U Pr of New Eng.

Between Culture & Fantasy: A New Guinea Highlands Mythology. Gillian Gillison. LC 92-31119. (Illus.). 390p. 1993. lib. bdg. 60.00 (*0-226-29380-7*); pap. text ed. 22.50 (*0-226-29381-5*) U Ch Pr.

Between Culture & Politics: Intellectuals in Modern Society. Ron Eyerman. Ed. by Sue Leigh. 220p. 1994. 39.95 (*0-7456-0904-X*) Blackwell Pubs.

B

An Asterisk (*) at the beginning of an entry indicates that the title is appearing in BIP for the first time.

707

***Between Culture & Tradition: The Dialectics of Modern Jewish Religion & Identity.** David H. Ellenson. LC 94-29538. (South-Florida-Rochester-Saint-Louis Studies on Religion & Social Order: Vol. 10). 1994. 74.95 (0-7885-0015-5, 245010) Scholars Pr GA.

Between Cultures. Pratima Bowes. 230p. 1987. 24.00 (0-317-59369-2, Pub. by Allied II) S Asia.

Between Darkness & Darkness. Rolf Aggestam. Tr. by Lars Nordstrom & Erland Anderson. 85p. 1989. pap. 15.00 (0-915986-24-8) Prescott St Pr.

Between Darkness & Dawn: A Saga of the Hehalutz. Abraham Thomi. LC 85-73455. (Illus.). 350p. 1986. 19.95 (0-8197-0501-2) Bloch.

Between Dawn & the Wind: Selected Poetry by Anna Frajlich. Anna Frajlich. Tr. & Intro. by Regina Grol-Prokopczyk. (Illus.). 120p. (Orig.). (C). 1991. pap. text ed. 9.95 (0-924047-04-6) Host Pubns.

Between Death & Life. Dolores Cannon. 206p. 1993. pap. 14.00 (0-9632776-5-0) Ozark Mountn.

Between Deep Valley & the Great World: Maud Hart Lovelace in Minneapolis. Amy Dolnick. 38p. 1993. pap. 10.00 (0-9640846-0-0) M H Lovelace.

Between Desert & River: Hohokam Settlement & Land Use in the Los Robles Community. Christian E. Downum. LC 92-44964. (Anthropological Papers: No. 57). (Illus.). 140p. (Orig.). 1993. 12.95 (0-8165-1375-9) U of Ariz Pr.

Between Desert & Sea. Martin Bates. (C). 1988. 25.00 (0-904524-50-7, Pub. by Rivelin Grapheme Pr) St Mut.

Between Desire & Consumption. I. E. Steele. 1979. pap. 3.00 (0-9603092-0-9) Pulp.

Between Desire & Consumption. deluxe ed. I. E. Steele. 1979. 4.00 (0-9603092-2-5) Pulp.

***Between Duality: The Art of Transcendence.** Laurence Galian. (Illus.). 160p. (Orig.). 1995. pap. 12.95 (1-56184-076-9) New Falcon Pubns.

Between Dusk & Dawn. Val Daniels. 1994. mass mkt. 3.50 (0-373-27042-9, 1-27042-0) Harlequin Bks.

Between Dying & Birth. Robert S. Bachelder. 1983. 6.25 (0-89536-623-1, 0236) CSS OH.

***Between Earth & Angels.** Douglas S. Johnson. (Illus.). 40p. (Orig.). 1995. pap. text ed. 6.95 (1-56315-039-5) Sterling Hse.

Between Earth & Paradise. Mike Tomkies. (Illus.). 224p. 1992. 29.95 (0-224-02880-4, Pub. by Jonathan Cape UK) Trafalgar.

***Between Earth & Sky.** Cagim. 7.99 (0-517-13771-2) Random Hse Value.

Between Earth & Sky. Kenneth W. Canipe. 48p. (Orig.). 1986. pap. 3.00 (0-9616329-0-9) K W Canipe.

Between Earth & Sky: How CFCs Changed Our World & Threatened the Ozone Layer. Seth Cagin & Philip Dray. LC 92-50472. (Illus.). 512p. 1993. 30.00 (0-679-42052-5) Pantheon.

***Between Earth & Sky: Legends of Native American Sacred Places.** Joseph Bruchac. LC 95-10862. (J). 1996. write for info. (0-15-200042-9) HarBrace.

Between Earth & Sky: Poets of the Cowboy West. Anne H. Widmark et al. 288p. 1995. 30.00 (0-393-03736-3) Norton.

***Between Earthquakes & Volcanoes: Markets, State, & Revolution in Central America.** Carlos M. Vilas. Tr. by Ted Kuster. (Illus.). 300p. (Orig.). (C). 1994. text ed. 36.00 (0-85345-902-9) Monthly Rev.

***Between Earthquakes & Volcanoes: Markets, State, & Revolution in Central America.** Carlos M. Vilas. Tr. by Ted Kuster. (Illus.). (Orig.). (C). 1994. pap. text ed. 18.00 (0-85345-903-7) Monthly Rev.

Between East & West: Across the Borderlands of Europe. Anne Applebaum. LC 94-5091. 1994. 24.00 (0-679-42150-5) Pantheon.

Between East & West: Finland in International Politics, 1944-1947. Tuomo Polvinen. Ed. by D. G. Kirby & Peter Herring. Tr. by Peter Herring. LC 85-20863. (Nordic Ser.: Vol. 13). (Illus.). 374p. 1986. text ed. 44.95 (0-8166-1459-8) U of Minn Pr.

Between East & West: Israel's Foreign Policy Orientation, 1948-1956. Uri Bialer. (London School of Economics Monographs in International Studies). 296p. (C). 1990. 59.95 (0-521-36249-0) Cambridge U Pr.

Between East & West: Trieste, the United States & the Cold War, 1941-1954. Roberto G. Rabel. LC 87-31775. xvii, 222p. (C). 1988. lib. bdg. 36.95 (0-8223-0831-2) Duke.

Between East & West: The Balkan & Mediterranean Worlds: Material Culture & Mentalities: Land, Sea & Destiny, Vol. 4. Traian Stoianovich. (Illus.). 160p. (ENG & FRE.). 1993. text ed. 95.00 (0-89241-507-X) Caratzas.

Between East & West The Balkan & Mediterrean Worlds: Economies & Societies: Land, Lords, States, & Middlemen, Vol. 1. Traian Stoianovich. (Illus.). 178p. (ENG & FRE.). (C). 1992. text ed. 85.00 (0-89241-501-0) Caratzas.

Between East & West The Balkan & Mediterrean Worlds: Economies & Societies: Traders, Towns, & Households, Vol. 2. Traian Stoianovich. (Illus.). 204p. (ENG & FRE.). (C). 1992. text ed. 85.00 (0-89241-502-9) Caratzas.

Between East & West: The Balkan & Mediterrean Worlds: Material Culture & Mentalites: Power & Ideology, Vol. 3. Traian Stoianovich. (Illus.). 160p. (ENG & FRE.). 1993. text ed. 95.00 (0-89241-506-1) Caratzas.

Between Education & Schooling: Outline of a Diachronic Curriculum Theory. Ulf P. Lundgren. 73p. (C). 1991. pap. 48.00x (0-7300-1242-5, ECS802, Pub. by Deakin Univ AT) St Mut.

Between Europe & America: The Canadian Tradition in Fiction. T. D. Maclulich. 266p. (C). 1988. text ed. 25.00 (0-920763-96-0, Pub. by ECW Press CN); pap. text ed. 15.00 (0-920763-95-2, Pub. by ECW Press CN) Genl Dist Srvs.

Between Exile & Return: S. Y. Agnon & the Drama of Writing. Anne G. Hoffman. LC 90-35371. (Modern Jewish Literature & Culture Ser.). 246p. (C). 1991. 64.50 (0-7914-0540-0); pap. 21.95 (0-7914-0541-9) State U NY Pr.

Between Existentialism & Marxism: Sartre on Philosophy, Politics, Psychology & the Arts. Jean-Paul Sartre. 1983. pap. 15.00 (0-394-71584-5) Pantheon.

Between Experience & Metaphysics: Philosophical Problems of the Evolution of Science. Stefan Amsterdamski. Tr. by P. Michalowski. LC 75-2184. (Boston Studies in the Philosophy of Science: No. 35). xviii, 193p. 1975. lib. bdg. 62.00 (90-277-0568-2); pap. text ed. 36.50 (90-277-0580-1) Kluwer Ac.

Between Fact & Fiction: Essays on Post-Mao Chinese Literature & Society. Kam Louie. 150p. (C). 1990. pap. text ed. 18.00 (0-9590735-6-6, Pub. by Wild Peony Pty AT) UH Pr.

Between Faith & Criticism: Evangelicals, Scholarship, & the Bible in America. 2nd ed. Mark A. Noll. LC 91-11037. 288p. 1991. pap. text ed. 13.99 (0-8010-6785-5) Baker Bk.

Between Fantoine & Agapa. Robert Pinget. Tr. by Barbara Wright. LC 82-60911. (Illus.). 83p. 1983. 8.95 (0-87376-040-9) Red Dust.

Between Father & Child: How to Become the Kind of Father You Want to Be. Ronald F. Levant. 256p. 1991. pap. 10.00 (0-14-015261-X, Penguin Bks) Viking Penguin.

Between Fear & Hope: A Decade of Peace Activism. Ed. by Sonia Shah. 290p. (Orig.). 1992. pap. 17.95 (1-879175-10-X) Fortkamp.

Between Fear & Hope: Jewish Youth in the Third Reich. Werner T. Angress. Tr. by Christine Granger. (Illus.). 200p. 1988. text ed. 32.00 (0-231-06598-1) Col U Pr.

Between Feminism & Labor: The Significance of the Comparable Worth Movement. Linda M. Blum. LC 90-37561. 215p. 1991. 35.00 (0-520-07032-1); pap. 13.00 (0-520-07259-6) U CA Pr.

Between Feminism & Psychoanalysis. Ed. by Teresa Brennan. 224p. 1989. 55.00 (0-415-01489-1, A3333); pap. 15.95 (0-415-01490-5, A3337) Routledge.

Between Field & Cooking Pot: The Political Economy of Marketwomen in Peru. Florence E. Babb. (Sourcebooks in Anthropology: No. 15). (Illus.). 259p. 1989. text ed. 30.00x (0-292-70775-4); pap. 14.95 (0-292-70776-2) U of Tex Pr.

Between Fire & Ice: The Science of Heat. David Darling. LC 91-40966. (Experiment! Ser.). (Illus.). 60p. (J). (gr. 5 up). 1992. text ed. 13.95 (0-87518-501-0, Dillon Silver Burdett) Silver Burdett Pr.

Between Fixity & Flux: A Study of the Concept of Poetry in the Criticism of T. S. Eliot. Mary C. Costello. LC 47-5815. 128p. reprint ed. pap. 36.50 (0-8357-7149-0, 2029521) Bks Demand.

Between Flops: A Biography of Preston Sturges. James Curtis. LC 84-7129. (Illus.). 339p. 1984. reprint ed. pap. 16.95 (0-87910-027-3) Limelight Edns.

Between Fontane & Tucholsky: Literary Criticism & the Public Sphere in Imperial Germany. Russell A. Berman. LC 83-9371. (New York University Ottendorfer Ser.: Vol. 17). 176p. (Orig.). (C). 1983. pap. text ed. 18.40 (0-8204-0012-2) P Lang Pubs.

Between Fordism & Flexibility: The Automobile Industry & Its Workers. Ed. by Jonathan Zeitlin & Stephen Tolliday. 344p. 1992. pap. 22.95 (0-85496-312-X) Berg Pubs.

Between Form & Freedom: A Practical Guide to the Teenage Years. Betty Staley. 288p. 1990. pap. 14.95 (1-869890-08-6, 1290, Pub. by Hawthorn Press UK) Anthroposophic.

Between France & Germany: The Jews of Alsace-Lorraine, 1871-1918. Vicki Caron. LC 88-2131. 296p. 1988. 37.50 (0-8047-1443-6) Stanford U Pr.

Between Freiburg & Frankfurt: Toward a Critical Ontology. Fred Dallmayr. LC 91-15780. 256p. (C). 1991. text ed. 35.00 (0-87023-764-0) U of Mass Pr.

Between Friends. Lynne Gerard. (Illus.). 48p. 1994. 8.95 (0-8378-7609-5) Gibson.

Between Friends. Kate Green. (Fossil Family Tales Ser.). (Illus.). 32p. (J). (gr. 1-4). 1992. lib. bdg. 22.79 (0-89565-780-5) Childs World.

Between Friends. Gillian E. Hanscombe. 178p. (Orig.). 1982. pap. 7.95 (0-932870-22-8) Alyson Pubns.

Between Friends. Mickey Pearlman. 1994. pap. 13.95 (0-395-65784-9, HoughtonT) HM.

Between Friends. large type ed. Kathleen Rowntree. (Ulverscroft Ser.). 592p. 1994. 21.95 (0-7089-3027-1) Ulverscroft.

Between Friends. large type ed. Candace Spencer. (Desire Ser.). 1993. 17.95 (0-373-58810-0, Silhouette Lrg Print); pap. 16.95 (0-373-58910-7, Silhouette Lrg Print) Chivers N Amer.

Between Friends: Discourses of Power & Desire in the Machiavelli-Vettori Letters of 1513-1515. John M. Najemy. LC 93-9737. 392p. 1993. text ed. 39.50 (0-691-03262-9) Princeton U Pr.

Between Friends: The Correspondence of Hannah Arendt & Mary McCarthy, 1949-1975. Hannah Arendt & Mary McCarthy. Ed. by Carol Brightman. LC 93-47425. 412p. Date not set. 34.95 (0-15-100112-X) HarBrace.

Between Genealogy & Epistemology: Psychology, Politics, & Knowledge in the Thought of Michel Foucault. Todd May. LC 92-29112. 144p. (C). 1993. 27.50 (0-271-00905-5) Pa St U Pr.

Between Give & Take: A Clinical Guide to Contextual Therapy. Ivan Boszormenyi-Nagy & Barbara R. Krasner. LC 86-2219. 450p. 1986. 44.95 (0-87630-418-8) Brunner-Mazel.

***Between Globalism & Nationalism: Socialist Register 1994.** Ed. by Ralph Miliband & Leo Panitch. 288p. (Orig.). (C). 1994. pap. text ed. 18.00 (0-85345-907-X, Pub. by Merlin UK) Monthly Rev.

Between God & Beast: An Examination of Amos Oz's Prose. Avraham Balaban. 272p. (C). 1993. 35.00 (0-271-00851-2) Pa St U Pr.

Between God & Gold: Protestant Evangelicalism & the Industrial Revolution, 1820-1914. Robert A. Wauzzinski. LC 91-58959. 272p. (C). 1993. 39.50 (0-8386-3481-8) Fairleigh Dickinson.

Between God & Man, an Interpretation of Judaism. Abraham J. Heschel. 1965. pap. 12.95 (0-02-914510-4) Free Pr.

Between God & the Party: Religion & Politics in Revolutionary Cuba. John M. Kirk. LC 87-16006. 256p. 1989. 27.95 (0-8130-0879-4); pap. 18.95 (0-8130-0909-X) U Press Fla.

Between God, the Dead, & the Wild: Chamba Interpretations of Ritual & Religion. Richard Fardon. LC 90-63714. (Illus.). 288p. (C). 1991. 40.00 (1-56098-044-3) Smithsonian.

Between Good & Evil: Polarities of Power. William Gray. LC 88-37510. (Llewellyn's New World Magic Ser.). 272p. (Orig.). 1989. pap. 9.95 (0-87542-273-X) Llewellyn Pubns.

Between Greene Leaves. Greene County Homemakers Extension Association Staff. (Illus.). 256p. (Orig.). 1984. pap. 7.95 (0-9613043-0-8) Greene Coun Home Ext Assn.

Between Hashemites & Zionists: The Struggle for Palestine, 1908-1988. Martin Sicker. LC 88-32834. 176p. 1989. 34.50 (0-8419-1176-2) Holmes & Meier.

***Between Heart & Mind.** Cynthia D. Osbourne. 12p. (Orig.). 1995. pap. write for info. (1-885206-16-X, Iliad Pr) Cader Pubng.

Between Heaven & Charing Cross: The Life of Francis Thompson. Brigid Boardman. LC 87-37243. (C). 1988. text ed. 45.00 (0-300-04143-8) Yale U Pr.

Between Heaven & Earth. Notes by Paul Moss. (Illus.). 160p. 1988. 49.95 (0-89815-280-1) Ten Speed Pr.

Between Heaven & Earth. Franz V. Werfel. LC 71-128333. (Essay Index Reprint Ser.). 1977. 20.95 (0-8369-2086-4) Ayer.

Between Heaven & Earth: A Guide to Chinese Medicine. Harriet Beinfield & Efrem Korngold. 448p. 1992. pap. 14.00 (0-345-37974-8) Ballantine.

Between Heaven & Earth: A Guide to Heaven & Earth. Efrem Korngold. 1991. 19.50 (0-345-35943-7, Ballantine Trade) Ballantine.

Between Heaven & Earth: Recipes for Living & Loving. Laura A. Huxley. LC 90-80706. 336p. 1991. reprint ed. pap. 12.00 (0-937611-87-5, 120) Hay House.

Between Heaven & Hell. Peter Kreeft. LC 82-8975. 115p. (Orig.). 1982. pap. 8.99 (0-87784-389-9, 389) InterVarsity.

Between Heaven & Hell: The Myth of Siberia in Russian Culture. Ed. by Galya Diment & Yurl Slezkine. LC 92-23337. 1993. text ed. 39.95 (0-312-06072-6) St Martin.

Between Hell & Reason: Essays from the Resistance Newspaper, "Combat" 1944-1947. Albert Camus. Tr. by Alexandre De Gramont. LC 87-21331. 189p. 1991. text ed. 35.00 (0-8195-5188-0, Wesleyan Univ Pr); pap. 14.95 (0-8195-5189-9, Wesleyan Univ Pr) U Pr of New Eng.

Between Hello & Goodbye. Jean Craig. Ed. by Julie Rubenstein. 416p. 1992. reprint ed. mass mkt. 5.99 (0-671-75039-9) PB.

Between Hermeneutics & Science: An Essay on the Epistemology of Psychoanalysis. Carlo Strenger. (Psychological Issues Monograph: No. 59). 250p. 1991. 30.00 (0-8236-6181-4) Intl Univs Pr.

Between High Tides: Poems. Daisy Aldan. (C). 1978. pap. 9.95 (0-913152-00-5) Folder Edns.

Between History & Literature. Lionel Gossman. 416p. 1990. 47.00 (0-674-06815-7) HUP.

Between History & Memory. Ed. by M. N. Bourguet et al. 1990. text ed. 51.00 (3-7186-5067-3) Gordon & Breach.

Between History & Method: Disputes about the Rationality of Science (Miedzy Historia a Metoda) Stefan Amsterdamski. Tr. by Olga Amsterdamska & Gene M. Moore. LC 92-18172. 240p. (C). 1992. lib. bdg. 89.00 (0-7923-1941-9) Kluwer Ac.

Between Home & Heaven: Contemporary American Landscape Photography. Contrib by Mary Foresta et al. LC 91-33448. (Illus.). 176p. 1992. 50.00 (0-8263-1363-9); pap. 2.00 (0-8263-1364-7) U of NM Pr.

Between Home & Nursing Home: The Board & Care Alternative. Ivy M. Down & Lorraine Schnurr. (Golden Age Bks.). 216p. (Orig.). (C). 1990. 21.95 (0-87975-619-5); pap. 15.95 (0-87975-620-9) Prometheus Bks.

Between Honesty & Hope: Documents from & about the Church in Latin America. Peruvian Bishops' Commission for Social Action. LC 78-143185. (Maryknoll Documentation Ser.). 271p. reprint ed. pap. 77.30 (0-8357-7150-4, 2025116) Bks Demand.

Between Husbands & Wives. Ed. by Lois L. Kaufman. (Illus.). 48p. 1992. 7.99 (0-88088-047-3) Peter Pauper.

Between Husbands & Wives: Communication in Marriage. Mary A. Fitzpatrick. (Series in Interpersonal Communication: Vol. 7). 320p. (C). 1988. text ed. 49.95 (0-8039-2618-9); pap. text ed. 24.00 (0-8039-2619-7) Sage.

***Between Ideology & Real Politics: Woodrow Wilson & the Russian Revolution, 1917-1921.** Georg Schild. LC 94-46927. (Study of World History: No. 51). 192p. 1995. text ed. 49.95 (0-313-29570-0, Greenwood Pr) Greenwood.

Between Indian & White Words: The Cultural Broker. Ed. by Margaret C. Szasz. LC 93-41717. (Illus.). 448p. 1994. 45.00 (0-8061-2595-0) U of Okla Pr.

Between Innocence & Peace: Favourite Poems of Ireland. Ed. by Brendan Kennelly. 196p. 1993. pap. 18.95 (1-85635-040-1, Pub. by Mercier Pr IE) Dufour.

***Between Inquiry & Advocacy: A Critique of the Pragmatic Foundation of Academic Public Policy.** E. Robert Statham. LC 95-1308. 120p. (C). 1995. text ed. 20.00 (0-9635752-6-0) Pkway Pubs.

Between Islam & Christendom: Travellers, Facts & Legends in the Middle Ages & the Renaissance. (Collected Studies: No. CS175). 326p. (C). 1983. reprint ed. lib. bdg. 87.50 (0-86078-123-2, Pub. by Variorum UK) Ashgate Pub Co.

***Between Jerusalem & Athens: Ethical Perspectives on Culture, Religion, & Psychotherapy.** Alvin C. Dueck. (Christian Explorations in Psychology Ser.). 240p. (Orig.). 1995. pap. 14.99 (0-8010-2008-5) Baker Bk.

Between Jerusalem & Benares: Comparative Studies in Judaism & Hinduism. Ed. by Hananya Goodman. LC 92-47229. 344p. (C). 1994. 57.50 (0-7914-1715-8); pap. 18.95 (0-7914-1716-6) State U NY Pr.

***Between Justice & Beauty: Race, Planning, & the Failure of Urban Policy in Washington, D. C.** Howard Gillette, Jr. LC 94-45938. (Illus.). 256p. 1995. 32.95 (0-8018-5069-X) Johns Hopkins.

Between Kant & Kabbalah: An Introduction to Isaac Breuer's Philosophy of Judaism. Alan L. Mittleman. LC 89-34101. (SUNY Series in Judaica Hermeneutics, Mysticism, & Religion). 227p. 1990. 59.50 (0-7914-0239-8); pap. 19.95 (0-7914-0240-1) State U NY Pr.

Between Kinship & the State: Social Security & Law in Developing Countries. Franz Von Benda-Beckmann et al. (Law Ser.). viii, 496p. (Orig.). (C). 1988. pap. 129.25 (90-6765-380-2) Mouton.

Between Known Men & Visible Saints: A Study of Sixteenth Century English Dissent. M. T. Pearse. LC 94-16045. 1995. write for info. (0-8386-3563-6) Fairleigh Dickinson.

Between Labor & Capital. Ed. by Pat Walker. LC 78-78359. (Political Controversies Ser.). 337p. 1979. pap. 12.00 (0-89608-037-4) South End Pr.

***Between Labor & Management.** Clara H. Friedman. (Oral History Ser.). 1995. pap. 15.95 (0-8057-9116-7, Twayne) Macmillan.

Between Labor & Management. Clara H. Friedman. (Twayne's Oral History Ser.). 200p. 1995. text ed. 24.95 (0-8057-9101-9, Twayne) Macmillan.

Between Labor & Management: An Oral History of European Migration to America. Clara H. Friedman. (Oral History Ser.: No. 12). 281p. 1995. lib. bdg. 28.95x (0-8057-9109-4, Twayne) Macmillan.

Between Landscapes. Wailim Yip. 32p. (Orig.). 1994. pap. 6.00 (0-938631-24-1) Pennywhistle Pr.

***Between Language & Silence: The Novels of Virginia Woolf.** fac. ed. Howard M. Harper. LC 81-20779. 350p. 1982. reprint ed. pap. 99.80 (0-7837-7738-8, 2047494) Bks Demand.

Between Languages: The Uncooperative Text in Early Welsh & Old English Nature Poetry. Sarah L. Higley. 304p. (C). 1993. 45.00 (0-271-00876-8) Pa St U Pr.

Between Languages & Cultures: Translation & Cross-Cultural Texts. Ed. by Anuradha Dingwaney & Carol Maier. (Pittsburgh Series in Composition, Literacy, & Culture). (Illus.). 352p. (C). 1994. 49.95 (0-8229-3858-8); pap. 19.95 (0-8229-5541-5) U of Pittsburgh Pr.

Between Life & Death. Nathalie Sarraute. Tr. by Maria Jolas. 1980. 14.95 (0-7145-0122-0) Riverrun NY.

***Between Life & Death: History of Jewish Life in Wartime Poland 1939-1944.** Ben A. Soifer. 420p. 1995. 35.00 (1-85756-240-2); pap. 18.95 (1-85756-241-0) Paul & Co Pubs.

Between Literature & Science: The Rise of Sociology. Wolf Lepenies. Tr. by R. J. Hollingdale. (Cambridge Ideas in Context Ser.). 392p. 1988. pap. 22.95 (0-521-33810-7) Cambridge U Pr.

Between Little Rock & a Hard Place. Tommi A. Mecca. 1993. pap. 9.95 (0-9635289-3-9) Williams OR.

Between Love & Hate: A Guide to Civilized Divorce. L. Gold. (Illus.). 345p. 1992. 24.95 (0-306-44132-2, Plenum Pr) Plenum.

Between Love & Madness Lies the Shoe Department. Cathy Guisewite. (Illus.). 1992. reprint ed. mass mkt. 3.99 (0-449-22037-0, Crest) Fawcett.

***Between Lovers.** Fran C. Goodman. Ed. by Bob Hansmann. 200p. Date not set. 10.95 (0-9643473-1-8) Francie PR.

Between Madison & Palmetto. Jacqueline Woodson. LC 92-38783. (J). (gr. 1-6). 1993. 13.95 (0-385-30906-6) Delacorte.

***Between Madison & Palmetto.** Jacqueline Woodson. (J). (gr. 4-7). 1995. pap. 3.50 (0-440-41062-2) Dell.

Between Man & Beast: True Tales & Observations of the Animal Kingdom. Gilbert Phelps. 1989. 7.99 (0-517-69038-1) Random Hse Value.

Between Man & His Fellow Man. C. B. Chavel. 64p. 1980. pap. 3.50 (0-88328-030-2) Shilo Pub Hse.

Between Man & Man. 2nd ed. Martin Buber. Tr. by Ronald G. Smith. LC 85-6702. 229p. 1985. pap. 12.00 (0-02-084210-4, Collier S&S) S&S Trade.

Between Mare & Foal see Farnam Horse Library Series

Between Marginalism & Marxism: The Economic Sociology of J. A. Schumpeter. Thomas B. Bottomore. LC 92-32885. 160p. 1993. text ed. 39.95 (0-312-09105-2) St Martin.

Between Markets & Politics: Co-Operatives in Sweden. Victor A. Pestoff. (C). 1991. pap. text ed. 59.50 (0-8133-8294-7) Westview.

An Asterisk (*) at the beginning of an entry indicates that the title is appearing in BIP for the first time.

An Asterisk (*) at the beginning of an entry indicates that the title is appearing in BIP for the first time.

Between the Creeks: Recollections of Northeast Texas. Katharine Gust & Deborah Brown. (Illus.). 1976. 12.50 (0-88426-048-8) Encino Pr.

Between the Danube & the Caucasus. G. Kara. 374p. (C). 1987. 240.00 (0-569-09013-X, Pub. by Collets UK) Pro-Am Music.

Between the Devil & the Deep Blue Sea: Merchant Seamen, Pirates & the Anglo-American Maritime World, 1700-1750. Marcus Rediker. LC 87-6304. (Illus.). 340p. 1987. 44.95 (0-521-30342-7) Cambridge U Pr.

Between the Devil & the Deep Blue Sea: Merchant Seamen, Pirates, & the Anglo-American Maritime World, 1700-1750. Marcus Rediker. (Canto Book Ser.). (Illus.). 352p. (C). 1993. pap. 11.95 (0-521-45720-3) Cambridge U Pr.

Between the Double Eagle & the Crescent, No. 348: The Republic of Dubrovnik & the Origins of the Eastern Question. Zdenko Zlatar. 350p. 1992. text ed. 49.00 (0-88033-245-X) Col U Pr.

***Between the Eagle & the Sun: Traces of Japan.** Ihab Hassan. LC 95-13544. 1996. write for info. (0-8173-0819-9) U of Ala Pr.

Between the Earth & Sun. Eleanor Farjeon. (J). Date not set. 15.00 (0-06-020795-7, HarpT) HarpC.

Between the Enemy & Texas: Parsons's Texas Cavalry in the Civil War. Anne J. Bailey. LC 88-31194. (Illus.). 358p. 1989. 25.95 (0-87565-034-1) Tex Christian.

Between the Fields & the City: Women, Work, & Family in Russia, 1861-1914. Barbara A. Engel. LC 93-31191. 304p. (C). 1994. 59.95 (0-521-44236-2) Cambridge U Pr.

Between the Flags. B. H. Friedman. 1990. text ed. 18.95 (0-932511-29-5); pap. text ed. 8.95 (0-932511-30-9) Fiction Coll.

Between the Floating Mist: Poems of Ryokan. Ryokan. Tr. by Maloney & Oshiro. 96p. (Orig.). 1992. pap. 12.00 (1-877800-01-5) Springhse Editions.

Between the Generations: A Jewish Dialogue. Samuel H. Dresner. LC 79-172413. 80p. 1971. pap. 1.75 (0-87677-042-1) Hartmore.

Between the Guns: Children As a Zone of Peace. Varindra T. Vittachi. (Illus.). 128p. 1994. pap. 11.95 (0-340-60231-7, Pub. by H & S UK) Trafalgar.

Between the Hammer & the Anvil? Chinese & Russian Policies in Outer Mongolia, 1911-1921. Thomas E. Ewing. LC 80-52924. (Uralic & Altaic Ser.: Vol. 138). 300p. 1980. 22.00 (0-933070-06-3) Res Inst Inner Asian Studies.

***Between the Heartbeats: Fiction, Poetry, & Memoirs by Nurses.** Ed. by Cortney Davis & Judy Schaefer. 256p. 1995. text ed. 27.95x (0-87745-516-3); pap. 14.95x (0-87745-517-1) U of Iowa Pr.

Between the Hills & the Sea. K. B. Gilden. LC 89-15651. (Literature of American Labor Ser.). 568p. 1989. pap. 15.95 (0-87546-154-9) ILR Pr.

Between the Human & the Divine: The Political Thought of Simone Weil. Mary G. Dietz. LC 87-20569. 224p. 1988. 53.00 (0-8476-7574-2); pap. 21.00 (0-8476-7575-0) Rowman.

***Between the Lamb & the Lion: A New View of Jesus in the Book of Revelation, from the Cross to His Coming.** Clifford Goldstein. LC 94-27807. 1995. pap. 8.95 (0-8163-1238-9) Pacific Pr Pub Assn.

Between the Landscape & Its Other. Paul Vanderbilt. (Illus.). 160p. (C). 1993. text ed. 50.00 (0-8018-4258-1) Johns Hopkins.

***Between the Levees: A Collection of Mississippi Delta Rice Recipes.** Delta Rice Promotions Staff. 237p. 1994. 12.00 (0-9642126-0-9) Delta Rice Promot.

Between the Library & the Laboratory: The Language of Chemistry in Eighteenth-Century France. Wilda C. Anderson. LC 84-47942. 1985. text ed. 32.00 (0-8018-3229-2) Johns Hopkins.

Between the Lines. Anna Gottlieb. LC 92-70691. 420p. 1992. 21.95 (1-56062-115-X); pap. write for info. (1-56062-116-8) CIS Comm.

Between the Lines. Jayne A. Krentz. 1993. mass mkt. 4.50 (0-373-83270-2, 1-83270-8) Harlequin Bks.

***Between the Lines.** Jayne A. Krentz. (Mira Bks.). 1995. pap. 4.99 (1-55166-066-0, 1-66066-1, Mira Bks) Harlequin Bks.

Between the Lines. Alan W. Wootton. (C). 1989. 60.00 (0-947934-28-6, Pub. by Bridge Pubns UK); pap. 45.00 (0-947934-27-8, Pub. by Bridge Pubns UK) St Mut.

Between the Lines. Jean Zukowski-Faust et al. 264p. (C). 1983. pap. text ed. 20.50 (0-03-059601-7) HB Coll Pubs.

Between the Lines: (Reflections of a Family Physician) B. Lewis Barnett, Jr. (Orig.). (C). 1989. pap. 14.95 (0-942295-17-X) Soc Tchrs Fam Med.

Between the Lines: An Anthology by Pacific-Asian Lesbians of Santa Cruz, California. Ed. by Cristy Chung et al. 56p. (Orig.). 1987. pap. 6.00 (0-9622819-0-5) Dancing Bird.

Between the Lines: International Short Stories of War. Ed. by Pauletta J. Otis & Steven A. Kaplan. LC 94-650. 384p. (C). 1994. 26.95 (0-87081-328-5); pap. 14.95 (0-87081-329-3) Univ Pr Colo.

Between the Lines: Interpreting Welfare Rights. R. Shep Melnick. 344p. (C). 1994. 36.95 (0-8157-5664-X); pap. 16.95 (0-8157-5663-1) Brookings.

Between the Lines: Letters Between Undocumented Mexican & Central American Immigrants. Larry Siems. 1994. pap. 15.00 (0-88001-347-8) Ecco Pr.

Between the Lines: Letters Between Undocumented Mexican & Latin American Immigrants & Their Families & Friends. Intro. by Larry Siems. 320p. 1992. 24.95 (0-88001-277-3) Ecco Pr.

***Between the Lines: Letters Between Undocumented Mexican & Latin American Immigrants & Their Families & Friends.** Larry Siems. 335p. 1995. pap. 19.95 (0-8165-1552-2) U of Ariz Pr.

Between the Lines: One Athlete's Struggle to Escape the Nightmare of Addiction. Steve Howe & Jim Greenfield. LC 89-2795. 288p. 1989. 17.95 (0-940279-25-8) Masters Pr IN.

***Between the Lines: Parable Acrostics & Other Revelations.** Thomas A. Young. 64p. (Orig.). 1995. pap. 5.95 (1-883893-05-4) Wine Pr Pub.

Between the Lines: Understanding Yourself & Others Through Handwriting Analysis. Reed Hayes. (Illus.). 208p. (Orig.). 1993. pap. 12.95 (0-89281-371-7, Destiny Bks) Inner Tradit.

Between the Nanticoke & the Choptank: An Architectural History of Dorchester County, Maryland. Ed. by Christopher Weeks. LC 83-48684. (Illus.). 352p. (Orig.). 1984. pap. 16.95 (0-8018-3045-1) Johns Hopkins.

Between the Norm & the Exception: The Frankfurt School & the Rule of Law. William E. Scheuerman. 328p. 1994. 37.50x (0-262-19351-5) MIT Pr.

Between the Old World & the New: Being Studies in Literary Personality from Goethe & Balzac to Anatole France & Thomas Hardy. Mary P. Willcocks. LC 67-28772. (Essay Index Reprint Ser.). 1977. 21.95 (0-8369-0999-2) Ayer.

Between the One & the Many: An Introduction to Comparative Literature. Claudio Guillen. Tr. by Cola Franzen. LC 92-16810. (Studies in Comparative Literature: No. 43). 1993. write for info. (0-674-06860-2) HUP.

Between the Question & the Word: Poems. J. D. Sedgwick. Ed. by David Sedgwick. (Illus.). 48p. 1994. pap. 9.95 (0-9639627-0-1) J D Sedgwick.

Between the Rivers: A History of Early Calaveras County, California. 2nd ed. O. Henry Mace. (Illus.). 159p. 1993. pap. 24.95 (0-938121-05-7) Cenotto Pubns.

Between the Rivers: A History of United Methodism in Iowa. John Nye. LC 86-80106. (Illus.). 350p. 1986. 12.95 (0-9616298-0-0); pap. 10.95 (0-9616298-1-9) IA Conf Com Arch.

Between the Rivers: A West Carroll Chronicle. Florence S. McKoin. 1971. 12.50 (0-87511-082-7) Claitors.

Between the Rivers: History of the Land Between the Lakes. Betty J. Wallace. (Miscellaneous Publication Ser.: No. 8). (Illus.). 297p. (Orig.). 1992. pap. 8.00 (1-880617-01-3) APSU Ctr Fld Bio.

Between the Rivers: Itinerant Painters from the Connecticut to the Hudson. Colleen C. Heslip. LC 90-31330. (Illus.). 95p. 1990. pap. 18.95 (0-931102-28-6) S & F Clark Art.

Between the Rock & a Hard Place: Adventuring into the Life of Jesus of Nazareth. James S. Woodroof. 179p. (Orig.). 1989. pap. 6.95 (0-9622649-0-3) Bible Hse.

Between the Rock & Hard Places. Eldon Weisheit. 160p. (Orig.). 1992. pap. 8.99 (0-570-04571-1) Concordia.

Between the Sea & Home. Almitra David. LC 93-7200. 112p. (Orig.). 1993. lib. bdg. 21.95 (0-933377-23-1); pap. 10.95 (0-933377-22-3) Eighth Mount Pr.

***Between the Sexes.** Elliott Erwitt. 1994. 29.95 (0-393-03676-6) Norton.

Between the Sexes: Foundations for a Christian Ethics of Sexuality. Lisa S. Cahill. LC 84-48717. 160p. 1985. pap. 11.00 (0-8006-1834-3, 1-1834, Fortress Pr) Augsburg Fortress.

Between the Shadows: New & Selected Works. Herman Taube. LC 85-13005. 1986. 15.95 (0-931848-71-7) Dryad Pr.

Between the Sign & the Gaze. Herman Rapaport. (Illus.). 312p. 1993. 41.50 (0-8014-2898-X); pap. 16.95 (0-8014-8133-3) Cornell U Pr.

Between the Stars. Time-Life Books Editors. (Voyage Through the Universe Ser.). 144p. 1990. write for info. (0-8094-6895-6); lib. bdg. write for info. (0-8094-6896-4) Time-Life.

Between the Strokes of Night. Charles Sheffield. 352p. 1985. mass mkt. 4.99 (0-671-55977-X) Baen Bks.

Between the Sun, the Moon & Me. Colin West. (Illus.). 32p. (J). (ps-2). 1992. 15.95 (0-09-173644-7, Pub. by Hutchinson UK) Trafalgar.

Between the Testaments. D. S. Russell. LC 77-74742. 182p. 1960. pap. 10.00 (0-8006-1856-4, 1-1856, Fortress Pr) Augsburg Fortress.

***Between the Thorns.** Libby Lazewnik. (Illus.). 526p. 1994. 21.95 (1-56871-057-7) Targum Pr.

Between the Thorns: Windcarver Songs of Appalachia. M. Ray Allen. Ed. by Joseph D. Adams. LC 91-61028. xii, 68p. (Orig.). 1991. pap. 5.00 (1-880016-06-0) Road Pubs.

***Between the Thunder & the Sun.** Vincent Sheean. (American Autobiography Ser.). 428p. 1995. reprint ed. lib. bdg. 99.00 (0-7812-8637-9) Rprt Serv.

Between the Tides see Seashore Life Between the Tides

Between the Times: The Travail of the Protestant Establishment in America, 1900-1960. Ed. by William R. Hutchison. (Studies in Religion & American Public Life). (Illus.). 320p. (C). 1989. 69.95 (0-521-36168-0) Cambridge U Pr.

Between the Times: The Travail of the Protestant Establishment in America, 1900-1960. Ed. by William R. Hutchison. (Studies in Religion & American Public Life). (Illus.). 320p. (C). 1990. pap. 17.95 (0-521-40601-3) Cambridge U Pr.

Between the Two World Wars. Philip Steele. LC 94-10692. (Food & Feasts). (J). (gr. 3 up). 1994. text ed. 14.95 (0-02-726322-3, New Dscvry Bks) Silver Burdett Pr.

Between the Wars: America, Nineteen Nineteen to Nineteen Forty-One, 2 Vols. 2nd ed. David A. Shannon. LC 78-69558. (Illus.). (C). 1979. pap. 28.76 (0-395-26535-5) HM.

Between the Wars: Essays & Letters. Aldous Huxley. Ed. by David Bradshaw. 288p. 1994. 26.00 (1-56663-055-X) I R Dee.

Between the Wars: 1919-39: the Cartoonist's Vision. Roy Douglas. (Illus.). 352p. 1992. 29.95 (0-415-04497-9, A6635) Routledge.

Between the Woods & the Water. Patrick L. Fermor. (Illus.). 248p. 1987. pap. 11.00 (0-14-009430-X, Penguin Bks) Viking Penguin.

Between the Word, Hidden Meanings in What People Say. Gerard I. Nierenberg. 1985. 9.95 (0-671-60662-X) S&S Trade.

Between the Worlds: Poems, 1983-1988. Constance Hunting. 96p. (Orig.). 1990. pap. 8.95 (0-913006-43-2) Puckerbrush.

***Between the Worlds: Witchcraft & the Tree of Life: a Program of Spiritual Development.** Stuart Myers. (Illus.). 256p. 1995. pap. 17.95 (0-87542-480-5) Llewellyn Pubns.

Between Theater & Anthropology. Richard Schechner. LC 84-5197. (Illus.). 356p. 1985. pap. 20.95 (0-8122-1225-8) U of Pa Pr.

Between Therapists: The Processing of Transference - Countertransference Material. Arthur Robbins. 227p. (C). 1988. 38.95 (0-89885-373-7) Human Sci Pr.

***Between Thought.** Reed. 4.99 (0-517-13654-6) Random Hse Value.

Between Time & Eternity: The Essentials of Judaism. Jacob Neusner. 196p. (C). 1975. pap. 21.95 (0-8221-0160-2) Intl Thomson.

***Between Time & Terror.** Ed. by Robert Weinberg et al. 352p. (Orig.). 1995. mass mkt., pap. 4.99 (0-451-45452-9, ROC) NAL-Dutton.

Between Today & Tomorrow. Esther Weakley. 44p. 1987. 4.50 (0-910347-07-7) Chatham Comm Inc.

Between Totalitarianism & Pluralism. Ed. by Alexander Dallin. LC 91-48457. (Articles on Russian & Soviet History, 1500-1991 Ser.: Vol. 9). 456p. 1992. 84.00 (0-8153-0566-4) Garland.

Between Totalitarianism & Postmodernity: A Thesis Eleven Reader. John Rundell. Ed. by Peter Beilharz et al. (Illus.). 276p. 1992. 14.95 (0-262-52179-2) MIT Pr.

Between Towns: Poems. Laurie Kutchins. LC 92-31518. 96p. 1993. 16.50 (0-89672-296-1) Tex Tech Univ Pr.

Between Tradition & Modernity: Wang Tao & Reform in Late Ch'ing China. Paul A. Cohen. LC 87-13606. (East Asian Monographs: No. 133). 347p. 1987. reprint ed. pap. 18.00 (0-674-06876-9) HUP.

***Between Tradition & Modernity: Zhitlowski, Dubnow, Ahad Ha-Am, & the Shaping of Modern Jewish Identity.** David Weinberg. (New Perspectives, Jewish Life & Thought Ser.). 376p. 1995. text ed. 35.00 (0-8419-1355-2) Holmes & Meier.

Between Tradition & Revolution: The Hegelian Transformation of Political Philosophy. Manfred Riedel. LC 83-20885. 210p. 1984. 74.95 (0-521-25644-5) Cambridge U Pr.

***Between Transcendence & Nihilism: Species-Ontology in the Ludwig Feuerbach.** Larry Johnston. LC 94-22409. (Studies in European Thought: Vol. 12). 1995. write for info. (0-8204-2616-4) P Lang Pubs.

Between Troy & Florence: Poems & Translations. Frank Salvidio. (New Poets Ser.: No. 4). (Illus.). 72p. (Orig.). 1989. pap. 10.00 (0-933806-57-4) Black Swan CT.

Between Tsar & People: Educated Society & the Quest for Public Identity in Late Imperial Russia. Ed. by Edith W. Clowes et al. 367p. 1991. text ed. 69.50 (0-691-03153-3); pap. text ed. 18.95 (0-691-00851-5) Princeton U Pr.

Between Two Absolutes: Public Opinion & the Politics of Abortion. Elizabeth A. Cook et al. LC 92-25268. 1992. text ed. 54.50 (0-8133-8286-6) Westview.

Between Two Absolutes: Public Opinion & the Politics of Abortion. Elizabeth A. Cook et al. LC 92-25268. (C). 1992. pap. text ed. 17.95 (0-8133-8287-4) Westview.

Between Two Abysses, Pt. 1. Samuel Lewin. Tr. by Joseph Leftwich. LC 85-22377. (Trilogy Ser.). 224p. 1988. 12.95 (0-8453-4795-0, Cornwall Bks) Assoc Univ Prs.

Between Two Abysses: A Trilogy, 3 pts. Samuel Lewin. Tr. by Joseph Leftwich. Boxed Set. boxed 29.50 (0-318-36511-1, Cornwall Bks); Pt. 3: Shining Through the Clouds. write for info. (0-318-63293-4, Cornwall Bks) Assoc Univ Prs.

Between Two Abysses: A Trilogy, 3 vols. Samuel Lewin. Tr. by Joseph Leftwich. 1988. Boxed set. boxed 29.50 (0-8453-4818-3, Cornwall Bks) Assoc Univ Prs.

Between Two Abysses: A Trilogy, 3 pts., Pt. 1: Between Two Abysses. Samuel Lewin. Tr. by Joseph Leftwich. 12.95 (0-318-36512-X, Cornwall Bks) Assoc Univ Prs.

Between Two Ages: America's Role in the Technetronic Era. Zbigniew K. Brzezinski. LC 82-15867. xvii, 334p. 1982. reprint ed. text ed. 45.00 (0-313-23498-1, BRZB, Greenwood Pr) Greenwood.

Between Two Amnesties: Former Political Prisoners & Exiles in the Roman Revolution of 1848. Leopold G. Glueckert & O. Carm. LC 91-12408. (Modern European History Ser.). 176p. 1991. 48.00 (0-8240-2540-7) Garland.

Between Two Armies in the Ixil Towns of Guatemala. David Stoll. LC 93-22046. 383p. (C). 1993. 47.50 (0-231-08182-0); pap. 17.50 (0-231-08183-9) Col U Pr.

Between Two Cultures: An Introduction to Economic History. Carlo M. Cipolla. 1991. 19.95 (0-393-02977-8) Norton.

Between Two Cultures: An Introduction to Economic History. Carlo M. Cipolla. 224p. 1992. pap. 10.95 (0-393-30816-2) Norton.

Between Two Cultures: Kiowa Art from Fort Marion. Moira F. Harris. LC 89-60217. (Illus.). 148p. 1989. 39.95 (0-9617767-3-0) Pogo Pr.

Between Two Cultures: The Life of an American-Mexican, as Told to John J. Poggie, Jr. Ramon Gonzales. LC 72-84765. 112p. reprint ed. pap. 32.00 (0-8357-8592-0, 2034964) Bks Demand.

Between Two Cultures: The Vietnamese in America. Alan B. Henkin & Liem Thanh Nguyen. LC 80-69333. 125p. 1981. per. 9.95 (0-86548-039-7) R & E Pubs.

Between Two Earthquakes - Entre Dos Terremotos: Cultural Property in Seismic Zones - Los Bienes Culturales en Zonas Sismicas. Bernard M. Feilden. (Illus.). 108p. 1987. pap. 12.00 (0-89236-128-X) J P Getty Trust.

Between Two Fires. Pamela Edgar. 384p. 1994. 26.95 (1-85797-098-5) Trafalgar.

Between Two Fires: Black Soldiers in the Civil War. Joyce Hansen. LC 92-37381. (African-American Experience Ser.). (Illus.). 160p. (YA). (gr. 9-12). 1993. lib. bdg. 14.98 (0-531-11151-2) Watts.

Between Two Fires: Black Soldiers in the Civil War. Joyce Hansen. (African-American Experience Ser.). (Illus.). (YA). (gr. 7-12). 1993. pap. 6.95 (0-531-15676-1) Watts.

Between Two Fires: Europe's Path in the 1930s. (Illus.). 1990. 22.50 (0-393-02751-1) Norton.

Between Two Fires: Europe's Path in the 1930s. David C. Large. 1991. pap. 15.95 (0-393-30757-3) Norton.

***Between Two Fires: The Tragedy of American Indians in the Civil War.** Laurence M. Hauptman. LC 94-42217. 1995. 25.00 (0-02-914180-X) Free Pr.

Between Two Fires: Towards an Understanding of Jawaharlal Nehru's Foreign Policy, Vol. 1. Iqbal Singh. 1993. 37.50 (0-86311-388-5, Pub. by Orient Longman Ltd II) Apt Bks.

Between Two Gardens: Reflections on Sexuality & Religious Experience. James B. Nelson. LC 83-11119. 208p. (Orig.). 1983. pap. 12.95 (0-8298-0681-4) Pilgrim OH.

Between Two Islands: Dominican International Migration. Sherri Grasmuck & Patricia R. Pessar. LC 90-50924. 280p. 1991. 40.00 (0-520-07149-2); pap. 15.00 (0-520-07150-6) U CA Pr.

Between Two People: Exercises Toward Intimacy. Mark E. Johnson et al. 225p. (C). 1993. pap. text ed. 30.95 (1-55620-107-9, 72127) Am Coun Assn.

Between Two Rivers: Poems by Ten North Jersey Poets. Ed. by William J. Higginson & Penny Harter. 48p. (Orig.). 1981. pap. 3.95 (0-89120-015-0) From Here.

Between Two Rivers: Selected Poems. Maurice Kenny. 1987. pap. 10.00 (0-934834-73-3) White Pine.

Between Two Seasons. I. J. Boodhoo. LC 93-36168. (Longman Caribbean Writers Ser.). (C). 1994. pap. text ed. 9.95 (0-582-22869-7) Longman.

Between Two Tanpuras. Vamanrao H. Deshpande. (C). 1989. 32.50 (0-86132-226-6) S Asia.

***Between Two Towers: The Drawings of the School of Miami.** Vincent Scully et al. (Illus.). 208p. (Orig.). 1995. pap. 40.00 (1-885254-07-5) Monacelli Pr.

Between Two Wars. John Golby et al. (War, Peace & Social Change Series: Europe, 1900-1955). 240p. 1990. 90.00 (0-335-09309-4, Open Univ Pr); pap. 32.00 (0-335-09308-6, Open Univ Pr) Taylor & Francis.

Between Two Wars. Henry W. Nevinson. 1972. 69.95 (0-87968-725-8) Gordon Pr.

Between Two Wars, 2 vols., Set. Porter Sargent. 1975. lib. bdg. 600.00 (0-87700-220-7) Revisionist Pr.

Between Two Wars: The Story of Pope Pius XI. Robin Anderson. 1978. 3.95 (0-8199-0687-5, Frncscn Herld) Franciscan Pr.

Between Two Wars, Eighteen Sixty-One to Nineteen Twenty-One: Being Memories, Opinion & Letters Received by James Mark Baldwin, 2 vols., Set. James M. Baldwin. LC 75-3020. reprint ed. 72.50 (0-404-59013-6) AMS Pr.

Between Two Waters: Literary Transculturation in Latin America. Silvia Spitta. LC 93-11346. (Illus.). 200p. (C). 1995. 27.50 (0-89263-321-2) Rice Univ.

Between Two Worlds. Sandra Brand. LC 82-60204. 128p. 1982. pap. 8.95 (0-88400-084-2) Shengold.

Between Two Worlds. Monique R. High. 356p. 1989. 19.95 (1-55611-139-8) D I Fine.

Between Two Worlds. Joan Lingard. 192p. (J). (gr. 7 up). 1993. pap. 4.50 (0-14-036505-2, Puffin) Puffin Bks.

Between Two Worlds. Maisie Masco. 1993. mass mkt. 5.50 (0-06-100623-8, Harp PBks) HarpC.

Between Two Worlds. Milton H. Nothdurft. 1985. 9.00 (0-9615415-0-4) Mtn Valley Pub.

Between Two Worlds. Americo Paredes. LC 90-38832. 144p. (Orig.). 1991. pap. 7.00 (1-55885-022-8) Arte Publico.

Between Two Worlds. Candice F. Ransom. (J). (gr. 4-7). 1994. pap. 3.25 (0-590-45755-1) Scholastic Inc.

Between Two Worlds. Sarah Sargent. LC 93-24533. (J). 1995. 13.95 (0-395-66425-X) Ticknor & Flds Bks Yng Read.

Between Two Worlds. Simone Schwarz-Bart. Tr. by Barbara Bray. (Caribbean Writers Ser.). 212p. 1992. pap. 8.95 (0-435-98929-4) Heinemann.

Between Two Worlds. Frederick Wiedemann. LC 85-40773. 200p. (Orig.). 1986. pap. 6.95 (0-8356-0602-3, Quest) Theos Pub Hse.

Between Two Worlds. Monique R. High. 528p. 1991. reprint ed. pap. 4.95 (0-8439-3061-6) Dorchester Pub Co.

Between Two Worlds: A History of German-Jewish Writers. Lothar Kahn & Donald D. Hook. LC 93-7676. 304p. (C). 1993. text ed. 42.95 (0-8138-1233-X) Iowa St U Pr.

Between Two Worlds: A Story about Pearl Buck. Barbara Mitchell. (Creative Minds Ser.). (Illus.). 56p. (J). (gr. 3-6). 1988. lib. bdg. 15.95 (0-87614-332-X, Carolrhoda) Lerner Group.

***Between Two Worlds: Autobiography of a Child Survivor of the Holocaust.** R. Gabriele Silten. 176p. (Orig.). Date not set. pap. 10.95 (1-56474-126-5) Fithian Pr.

An Asterisk (*) at the beginning of an entry indicates that the title is appearing in BIP for the first time.

Between Two Worlds: Black Students in an Urban Community College. Lois Weis. (Critical Social Thought Ser.). 224p. 1985. 18.95 (0-7100-9980-0, 99800, RKP) Routledge.

Between Two Worlds: Children from the Soviet Union in Israel. Ed. by Tamar R. Horowitz. LC 86-11071. 240p. (Orig.). (C). 1986. pap. text ed. 24.00 (0-8191-5455-5) U Pr of Amer.

Between Two Worlds: Choices for Grown Children of Jewish-Christian Parents. Leslie Goodman-Malmuth & Robin Margolis. Ed. by Denise Silvestro. (Orig.). 1992. pap. 10.00 (0-671-70007-3) PB.

Between Two Worlds: Ethnographic Essays on American Jewry. Ed. by Jack Kugelmass. LC 88-47735. (Anthropology of Contemporary Issues Ser.). 352p. 1988. 42.50 (0-8014-2084-9); pap. 15.95 (0-8014-9408-7) Cornell U Pr.

Between Two Worlds: Ireland Since Independence. Brian Girvin. 240p. (C). 1989. text ed. 50.50 (0-389-20876-0) B&N Imports.

Between Two Worlds: Modern Wives in a Traditional Setting. Stella R. Quah. 66p. 1988. pap. 10.00 (9971-988-85-2, Pub. by Inst SE Asian Studies SI) Ashgate Pub Co.

Between Two Worlds: Realism, Idealism, & the Future of American Foreign Policy. David Callahan. 224p. 1994. 25.00 (0-06-018213-X, HarpT) HarpC.

Between Two Worlds: Science, the Environmental Movement & Policy Choice. Lynton K. Caldwell. (Environmental Policy Ser.: No. 1). 232p. (C). 1992. pap. 21.95 (0-521-33743-7) Cambridge U Pr.

Between Two Worlds: The American Novel in the Nineteen Sixties. Sanford Pinsker. LC 79-64168. 139p. 1980. 7.50 (0-87875-169-6) Whitston Pub.

***Between Two Worlds: The Construction of the Ottoman State.** Cemal Kafadar. LC 94-21024. 1995. 40.00 (0-520-08807-7) U CA Pr.

Between Two Worlds: The Human Side of Development. Donnamarie West. LC 90-33104. 192p. (Orig.). 1990. pap. 16.95 (0-933662-88-2) Intercult Pr.

Between Two Worlds: The Message of Ramtha. Ronald G. Kaufmann. LC 87-154806. 125p. (Orig.). 1987. pap. 9.95 (0-940539-06-3) Heridonius.

Between Two Worlds: The World Bank's Next Decade. Ed. by Richard E. Feinberg. (U. S. Third World Policy Perspectives Ser.: No. 7). 208p. 1986. 32.95 (0-88738-123-5); pap. 17.95 (0-88738-665-2) Transaction Pubs.

Between Two Worlds - Messages Found in an Oxygen Bottle. Terry Carr & Bob Shaw. LC 86-61272. 171p. 1986. 15.00 (0-915368-33-1) New Eng SF Assoc.

Between Two Worlds an Intellectual Biography of Premchand. Geetanjali Pandey. (C). 1989. 25.00 (81-85054-59-2, Pub. by Manohar II) S Asia.

Between Two Worlds: Eighteen Twenty see Byron's Letters & Journals

Between Underdevelopment & Revolution: A Latin American Perspective. Rodolfo Stavenhagen. 1981. 18.00 (0-8364-0700-8, Pub. by Abhinav II) S Asia.

Between Understanding & Misunderstanding: Problems & Prospects for International Cultural Exchange. Ed. by Yasushi Sugiyama. LC 90-34317. (Contributions to the Study of Education Ser.: No. 41). 208p. 1990. text ed. 49.95 (0-313-27436-3, SGU/, Greenwood Pr) Greenwood.

Between Universalism & Skepticism: Ethics As Social Artifact. Michael Philips. 224p. 1994. 35.00 (0-19-508646-5) OUP.

Between Us - Time. Adela Popescu. (Illus.). (Orig.). 1993. pap. 25.00 (0-9619930-6-5) Moonfall Pr VA.

Between Us-Between the Lines. Joseph D. Adams. LC 88-92385. xii, 156p. (Orig.). 1989. pap. 9.95 (1-880016-00-1) Road Pubs.

Between Us Friends. John M. Larsen. LC 83-61454. 112p. 1983. pap. 7.95 (0-89390-050-8) Resource Pubns.

***Between Voice & Silence: Women & Girls, Race & Relationship.** Ed. by Jill Taylor et al. 240p. (C). 1995. 22.00 (0-674-06879-3) HUP.

Between Walden & the Whirlwind see Finding Focus in a Whirlwind World

Between War & Peace: The Potsdam Conference. Herbert Feis. LC 83-12966. viii, 367p. 1983. reprint ed. text ed. 52.50 (0-313-24219-4, FBWP, Greenwood Pr) Greenwood.

Between Washington & Jerusalem: A Reporter's Notebook. Wolf Blitzer. (Illus.). 259p. 1985. 24.95 (0-19-503708-1) OUP.

Between Water & Heaven: Carl Milles' Search for American Commissions. Elisabeth Liden. (Illus.). 128p. 1986. 46.50x (91-22-00815-2, Pub. by Almqv & Wiksell SW) Coronet Bks.

Between Whiles. Helen H. Jackson. (Notable American Authors Ser.). 1992. reprint ed. lib. bdg. 75.00 (0-7812-3361-5) Rprt Serv.

Between Women. Luise Eichenbaum & Susie Orbach. 1988. 17.95 (0-317-66626-6) Viking Penguin.

Between Women: Biographers, Novelists, Critics, Teachers, & Artists Write about Their Work on Women. Ed. by Carol Ascher et al. LC 93-13009. 500p. 1993. reprint ed. Alk. paper. pap. 17.95 (0-415-90770-5, B0658, Routledge NY) Routledge.

Between Women: Domestics & Their Employers. Judith Rollins. LC 85-8022. (Labor & Social Change Ser.). 256p. 1985. pap. 17.95 (0-87722-491-9) Temple U Pr.

Between Women: Love, Envy, & Competition in Women's Friendships. Luise Eichenbaum & Susie Orbach. 240p. 1989. pap. 11.00 (0-14-008980-2, Penguin Bks) Viking Penguin.

***Between Women of God: Passing on the Convictions of Our Hearts, the Passion of Our Lives.** Donna Otto. (Orig.). 1995. pap. 8.99 (1-56507-365-7) Harvest Hse.

Between Work & Social Citizenship. Ed. by Jon E. Kolberg. LC 90-32225. (Comparative Public Policy Analysis Ser.). 220p. 1992. 51.95 (0-87332-652-0) M E Sharpe.

Between Worlds: A Reader, Rhetoric, & Handbook. Ed. by Melinda Barth. LC 94-9459. (C). 1994. 21.50 (0-673-46884-4) HarpCollege.

Between Worlds: A Study of the Plays of John Webster. Dena Goldberg. 136p. (C). 1987. text ed. 28.50 (0-88920-953-7, Pub. by Wilfrid Laurier CN) Humanities.

Between Worlds: Access to Second Language Acquisition. Freeman. LC 94-15010. 424p. 1994. pap. text ed. 23.50 (0-435-08819-X) Heinemann.

Between Worlds: Contemporary Asian-American Plays. Ping Chong et al. LC 90-10821. 272p. (Orig.). 1989. pap. 13.95 (1-55936-004-6) Theatre Comm.

Between Worlds: Contemporary Mexican Photography. Ed. by Trisha Ziff. 144p. 1990. pap. 30.00 (1-56131-003-4) New Amsterdam Bks.

Between Worlds: Interpreters, Guides, & Survivors. Frances Karttunen. LC 93-8366. (Illus.). 360p. (C). 1994. 24.95 (0-8135-2030-4) Rutgers U Pr.

Between Worlds: New & Selected Poems. John Gill. 1993. text ed. 20.00 (0-914610-75-9); pap. 12.00 (0-914610-74-0) Hanging Loose.

Between Worlds: The Life & Thought of Rabbi David ben Judah Messer Leon. Hava Tirosh-Rothschild. LC 89-26341. (SUNY Series in Judaica: Hermeneutics, Mysticism, & Religion). 385p. (C). 1991. 74.50 (0-7914-0447-1); pap. 24.95 (0-7914-0448-X) State U NY Pr.

Between Worlds: The Literary Dilemma of Ursula K. Le Guin. 2nd ed. George E. Slusser. (Milford Ser.: Popular Writers of Today: Vol. 3). 160p. Date not set. lib. bdg. write for info. (0-89370-122-X); pap. write for info. (0-89370-222-6) Borgo Pr.

Between Worlds: Women Writers of Chinese Ancestry. Amy Ling. (Athene Ser.). 292p. 1990. text ed. 37.50 (0-08-037464-6, Pub. by PPI UK); pap. text ed. 16.95 (0-08-037463-8, Pub. by PPI UK) Elsevier.

Between Worlds: Women Writers of Chinese Ancestry. Amy Ling. (Athene Ser.). 232p. (C). 1990. text ed. 37.50 (0-8077-6237-7); pap. text ed. 16.95 (0-8077-6238-5) Tchrs Coll.

Between Yafeth & Shem: On the Relationship Between Jewish & General Philosophy. Ze'ev Levy. (American University Studies: Philosophy: Ser. V, Vol. 21). 253p. 1987. text ed. 40.90 (0-8204-0373-3) P Lang Pubs.

Between You & Me. Meeka Muse. 101p. 1992. pap. 10.00 (0-9639774-0-7) Meeka Muse.

Between Your House & Mine: The Letters of Lorine Neidecker to Cid Corman, 1960-1970. Lisa P. Faranda. LC 86-24188. x, 261p. 1986. 31.95 (0-8223-0669-7) Duke.

Betweenness of Place: Towards a Geography of Modernity. J. Nicholas Entrikin. LC 90-32418. 224p. 1991. text ed. 38.50 (0-8018-4083-X); pap. text ed. 13.95 (0-8018-4084-8) Johns Hopkins.

Betwene Ernest & Game: The Literary Artistry of the Confessio Amantis. Alexandra H. Olsen. LC 89-133292. (American University Studies: English Language & Literature: Ser. IV, Vol. 110). 130p. 1990. text ed. 31.50 (0-8204-1141-8) P Lang Pubs.

Betwixt & Between: Patterns of Masculine & Feminine Initiation. Ed. by Louise C. Mahdi et al. LC 86-31271. (Reality of the Psyche Ser.). 528p. 1987. 39.95 (0-8126-9047-8); pap. 18.95 (0-8126-9048-6) Open Court.

Betwixt Heaven & Charing Cross. Martin Burrell. LC 68-16916. (Essay Index Reprint Ser.). 1977. 20.95 (0-8369-0266-1) Ayer.

Betwixt Jest & Earnest: Marprelate, Milton, Marvell, Swift & the Decorum of Religious Ridicule. Raymond A. Anselment. LC 79-12498. 215p. reprint ed. pap. 61.30 (0-8357-7152-0, 2026446) Bks Demand.

***Betye Saar: Personal Icons.** Lizzetta Le-Falle-Collins. Ed. by Kristen Gladsky. 28p. (Orig.). (C). 1995. 10.00 (1-882603-01-X) Mid Am Arts.

Betye Saar: Secret Heart. Fresno Art Museum Staff. (Illus.). 48p. 1993. pap. 20.00 (0-932325-31-9) Fresno Arts Mus.

Betz Handbook of Industrial Water Conditioning. 9th ed. A. M. Agree et al. LC 91-61770. 448p. 1991. 70.00 (0-913641-00-6) Betz Labs.

***Betz MCAT Diagnostic Test.** 1995. 29.95 (0-941406-64-4) Betz Pub Co Inc.

Beulah. Augusta J. Evans. LC 91-44959. (Library of Southern Civilization). 440p. (C). 1992. text ed. 45.00 (0-8071-1749-8); pap. text ed. 16.95 (0-8071-1750-1) La State U Pr.

Beulah: A Biography of the Mineral King Valley of California. Louise Jackson. (Great West & Indian Ser.: Vol. 50). (Illus.). 1987. 26.95 (0-87026-065-0) Westernlore.

Beulah Land. Harold L. Davis. LC 75-136062. 314p. 1971. reprint ed. text ed. 35.00 (0-8371-5212-7, DABL, Greenwood Pr) Greenwood.

Be'ur S'tumot B'Rashi: Interpretation of Difficult Passages in Rashi (Hebrew) Vol.: 4: Deuteronomy. Pinchas Doron. 472p. (HEB.). (C). 1994. 19.95 (0-87203-141-1) Hermon.

Beutel's Brannan Negotiable Instruments Law: The Negotiable Instruments Law Annotated, Together with Discussions of Interpretation, Bills of Exchange Act, Statutory Variations, Comparative Tables, Commissioners' Notes, etc., Set. 7th ed. Joseph D. Brannan & Frederick K. Beutel. LC 74-92297. xiii, 1628p. 1971. reprint ed. text ed. 195.00 (0-8371-3076-X, BRNI) Greenwood.

Beuve De Hanstone: The Romance of Sir Beves of Hamtoun. Ed. by Eugene Koelbing. (EETS, ES Ser.: No. 46, 48, 65). 1972. reprint ed. 63.00 (0-527-00255-0) Periodicals Srv.

Beuys, Klein, Rothko: Transformation & Prophecy. Anne Seymour. (Illus.). 88p. 1987. 30.00 (0-947564-12-8, Pub. by A D'Offay Gallery UK) Dist Art Pubs.

***Bev Doolittle.** Text by Elise Maclay. LC 95-15087. 1995. write for info. (0-553-10104-8) Bantam.

***Bev Doolittle: New Magic.** Elise Maclay. LC 95-15256. 1995. write for info. (0-86713-026-1) Greenw Pr Ltd.

Bevels & Jewels Stained Glass Pattern Book: 83 Designs for Workable Projects. Ed Sibbett, Jr. (Stained Glass Ser.). 64p. 1985. pap. 4.95 (0-486-24844-5) Dover.

***Beverage Acquisitions Market U. S. A. 1994.** 400p. (Orig.). 1995. pap. 2,495.00 (0-7605-2150-6) Rector Pr.

***Beverage Container Market.** 151p. (Orig.). 1995. pap. 2,900.00 (0-7605-2149-2) Rector Pr.

Beverage Control Inspector. Jack Rudman. (Career Examination Ser.: C-83). 1994. pap. 23.95 (0-8373-0083-5) Nat Learn.

Beverage Control Investigator. Jack Rudman. (Career Examination Ser.: C-918). 1994. pap. 23.95 (0-8373-0918-2) Nat Learn.

***Beverage Corporations Environmental Report.** 133p. (Orig.). 1995. pap. 1,000.00 (0-7605-2139-5) Rector Pr.

Beverage Journal Guide to Maryland Taverns, Clubs & Bars: One Hundred One of the Most Interesting Water Holes from Deep Creek Lake to Ocean City. Michael L. Spaur. (Illus.). 144p. (Orig.). 1992. pap. 8.95 (1-881675-00-9) Beverage Jrnl.

Beverage Management Instructor's Manual. M. Coltman. 1989. text ed. 20.95 (0-442-23540-2) Van Nos Reinhold.

***Beverage (New Age) Market.** 150p. (Orig.). 1995. pap. 2,195.00 (0-7605-2143-3) Rector Pr.

Beverage Sales & Service. 2nd ed. Brian Julyan. 200p. 1991. pap. 24.95 (0-7506-0105-1) Buttrwrth-Heinemann.

***Beverage (Sport) Market.** 150p. (Orig.). 1995. pap. 2,195.00 (0-7605-2144-1) Rector Pr.

Beverages: Three-Language Technical Dictionary. Neumann-Duscha. 424p. (ENG, FRE & GER.). 1986. 225.00 (0-8288-7915-X) Fr & Eur.

Beverages, Drinks & Juices: Medical Research Reference Analysis with Bibliography. Charlene P. Singh. LC 84-45987. 150p. 1987. 39.50 (0-88164-296-7); pap. 34.50 (0-88164-297-5) ABBE Pubs Assn.

***Beverages (Hot) Market.** 400p. (Orig.). 1994. pap. 1,295.00 (1-57205-880-3) Rector Pr.

Beveridge & Social Security: An International Retrospective. Ed. by John Hills et al. (Illus.). 246p. 1994. 55.00 (0-19-828806-9) OUP.

Beverley - A Visitor's Guide. Ed. by Highgate Publications (Beverley) Ltd. Staff. (C). 1989. text ed. 35.00 (0-948929-28-6) St Mut.

Beverley Arms: The Story of a Hotel. John Markham. (C). 1989. text ed. 35.00 (0-948929-00-6) St Mut.

Beverley Tucker: Heart over Head in the Old South. Robert J. Brugger. LC 77-16294. (Johns Hopkins University Studies in Historical & Political Science: Ser. 96, No. 2). 322p. reprint ed. pap. 91.80 (0-8357-7153-9, 2025834) Bks Demand.

Beverly Center. Ryan Woodward. 480p. (Orig.). 1985. pap. 3.95 (0-8439-2267-2) Dorchester Pub Co.

Beverly Clearly: She Makes Reading Fun. Patricia S. Martin. (Reaching Your Goal Bks.). (Illus.). 24p. (J). (gr. 1-4). 1987. 10.95 (0-685-67568-8); lib. bdg. 14.60 (0-86592-171-7) Rourke Corp.

Beverly Cleary. Julie Berg. LC 93-12958. (Young at Heart Ser.). (YA). (gr. 6 up). 1993. lib. bdg. 13.99 (1-56239-222-0) Abdo & Dghtrs.

***Beverly Cleary.** Susan Onion. (Favorite Authors Ser.). (Illus.). 1994. 10.95 (1-55734-457-4) Tchr Create Mat.

Beverly Cleary. Pat Pflieger. (Twayne's United States Authors Ser.: No. 572). 232p. (C). 1991. text ed. 20.95 (0-8057-7613-3, Twayne) Macmillan.

Beverly Cleary, 4 vols., Set. Beverly Cleary. (J). (gr. 4-7). 1991. boxed, pap. 14.00 (0-380-71719-0, Camelot) Avon.

Beverly Halstead -- His Life, Vol. 18. A. S William. (Halstead Memorial Ser.: Vol 18, Pt. 1). 1993. pap. text ed. 245.00 (2-88124-905-1) Gordon & Breach.

***Beverly Hillbillies.** Paul Henning. 1968. 5.00 (0-87129-411-7, B16) Dramatic Pub.

Beverly Hillbillies. Todd Strasser. 1993. mass mkt. 5.99 (0-06-100710-2, Harp PBks) HarpC.

Beverly Hillbillies. Stephen Cox. LC 92-56266. (Illus.). 256p. (Orig.). 1993. reprint ed. pap. 12.00 (0-06-097565-2, PL) HarpC.

Beverly Hills. Pat Booth. 416p. 1990. mass mkt. 5.99 (0-345-35217-3) Ballantine.

Beverly Hills: An Illustrated History. Genevieve Davis. (Illus.). 208p. (YA). (gr. 7 up). 1988. 36.95 (0-89781-238-7) Preferred Mktg.

Beverly Hills Diet. Judy Mazel. 1981. 10.95 (0-02-582600-X) Macmillan.

***Beverly Hills Diet.** Judy Mazel. 1994. reprint ed. lib. bdg. 24.95x (1-56849-542-0) Buccaneer Bks.

Beverly Hills Diet Lifetime. Judy Mazel. 1982. 13.95 (0-02-582630-1) Macmillan.

Beverly Hills International Party Planner. Jan Roberts. 1994. 29.95 (0-9634398-9-8); pap. 19.95 (0-9634398-4-7) J Roberts Pubns.

Beverly Hills Organizer's House Book: The Ultimate Household Organizing Guide & Workbook. Linda Koopersmith. (Illus.). 123p. (Orig.). Date not set. student ed. 19.95 (0-9639672-6-6) Bev Hills Org.

Beverly Hills 90210. Daniel Cohen. (YA). 1991. pap. 3.99 (0-671-77052-7) S&S Trade.

Beverly Hills, 90210. Mel Gilden. (YA). 1991. mass mkt. 3.99 (0-06-100417-0, Harp PBks) HarpC.

Beverly Hills 90210. Rosemary Wallner. LC 92-16789. (TV's Hottest Teens Ser.). (YA). 1992. lib. bdg. 12.94 (1-56239-139-9) Abdo & Dghtrs.

Beverly Hills, 90210, No. 1. Mel Gilden. (YA). 1994. pap. 1.99 (0-06-106230-8, Harp PBks) HarpC.

Beverly Hills, 90210: 'Tis the Season. Mel Gilden. (YA). 1992. mass mkt. 3.99 (0-06-106786-5, Harp PBks) HarpC.

Beverly Hills, 90210: Exposed. M. J. Davis. (YA). 1991. mass mkt. 4.50 (0-06-106137-9, Harp PBks) HarpC.

Beverly Hills, 90210: Fantasies. K. T. Smith. (YA). 1992. mass mkt. 3.99 (0-06-106727-X, Harp PBks) HarpC.

Beverly Hills, 90210: Graduation Day. Mel Gilden. (YA). 1994. mass mkt. 3.99 (0-06-106208-1, Harp PBks) HarpC.

Beverly Hills, 90210: No Secrets. Mel Gilden. (YA). (gr. 7 up). 1992. mass mkt. 3.99 (0-06-106136-0, Harp PBks) HarpC.

Beverly Hills, 90210: Where the Boys Are, No. 8. Mel Gilden. (YA). (gr. 9-12). 1993. mass mkt. 3.99 (0-06-106145-X, Harp PBks) HarpC.

Beverly Hills, 90210: Which Way to the Beach? Mel Gilden. (YA). 1992. mass mkt. 3.99 (0-06-106768-7, Harp PBks) HarpC.

Beverly Hills, 90210 Fun Book. Venice L. Holmes, Jr. 64p. (Orig.). (YA). (gr. 7-12). 1994. pap. 3.95 (0-9638305-8-9) New King Pub.

Beverly Hills, 90210 Guide. Venice Holmes, Jr. LC 93-92734. 112p. (Orig.). 1993. pap. 7.95 (0-9638305-9-7) New King Pub.

Beverly Malibu. Katherine V. Forrest. (Kate Delafield Mystery Ser.). 288p. 1991. reprint ed. pap. 10.95 (0-941483-48-7) Naiad Pr.

Beverly of Graustark. George B. McCutcheon. 1976. lib. bdg. 16.25 (0-89968-057-7, Lghtyr Pr) Buccaneer Bks.

Beverly Pepper: Sculpture in Place. Rosalind Krauss. LC 86-7931. (Illus.). 176p. 1986. 59.95 (0-89659-667-2) Abbeville Pr.

Beverly Pepper, Small Scale Sculpture & Drawings. Ed. by Gayle Maxon. LC 89-83479. (Illus.). 21p. 1989. 8.00 (0-935037-28-4) G Peters Gallery.

Beverly Semmes. (C). 1993. 5.00 (0-88454-069-3) U of Pa Contemp Art.

Beverly Sills: Opera Singer. Bridget Paolucci. LC 89-17324. (American Women of Achievement Ser.). (Illus.). 112p. (YA). (gr. 5 up). 1990. 17.95 (1-55546-677-X) Chelsea Hse.

Bevier Family in America. Kenneth C Hasbrouck. 287p. 1970. 32.00 (0-318-14363-1) Huguenot Hist.

Bevin & Co. Patricia Strauss. LC 71-128317. (Essay Index Reprint Ser.). 1977. 21.95 (0-8369-1896-7) Ayer.

Bevolkerung der Griechisch-Romischen Welt. Julius Beloch. Ed. by Moses Finley. LC 79-4962. (Ancient Economic History Ser.). (GER.). 1979. reprint ed. lib. bdg. 48.95 (0-405-12349-3) Ayer.

Bevy of Baskets. 4th ed. Sandra L. Jordan & Carole H. Wells. (Illus.). 192p. 1989. pap. 12.00 (0-318-50007-8) Crafters Pr.

Bevy of Beasts: The Enchanting Animals of Borneo, Belize & Beyond. Edward Mendell. 144p. 1995. 50.00 (0-9515863-1-9, Pub. by Mendell Pubng UK) Atrium Pubs.

Bevy of Embellishments. 2nd ed. Beth Karjala. 1990. 8.95 (0-932394-19-1) Dos Tejedoras.

Bewaltigung der Katastrophe: Untersuchungen zu Ausgewahlten Fremdvolkersprüchen im Ezechielbuch. Friedrich Fechter. (Beiheft zur Zeitschrift fuer die Alttestamentliche Wissenschaft Ser.: Bd. 208). x, 350p. (GER.). (C). 1992. lib. bdg. 110.80 (3-11-013642-2) De Gruyter.

Beware. B. Hayes. (Bone Chillers Ser.: No. 1). 1994. mass mkt. 3.50 (0-06-106176-X, Harp PBks) HarpC.

Beware America! Charles R. Taylor. Orig. Title: A Message to the President. (Illus.). 48p. (Orig.). 1983. pap. 3.50 (0-937682-06-3) Today Bible.

Beware Anarchist - A Life for Freedon: An Autobiography. Intro. by Theo Waldinger. 248p. (Orig.). 1992. pap. 15.00 (0-88286-215-4) C H Kerr.

Beware! Be Wise. Bettie Crosson. 130p. (Orig.). 1984. pap. 4.95 (0-87508-148-7) Chr Lit.

Beware Beware. Susan Hill. LC 92-54960. (Illus.). 32p. (J). (ps up). 1993. 14.95 (1-56402-245-5) Candlewick Pr.

Beware! Beware! A Witch Won't Share. Ida DaLage. (Old Witch Bks.). (Illus.). 48p. (J). (gr. k-4). 1991. reprint ed. lib. bdg. 12.95 (0-7910-1473-8) Chelsea Hse.

Beware: Children in Peril. Rexella Van Impe. 40p. 1984. pap. 2.00 (0-934803-13-7) J Van Impe.

Beware Dawn! Ann M. Martin. (Baby-Sitters Club Mystery Ser.: No. 2). 160p. (J). 1991. pap. 3.50 (0-590-44085-3) Scholastic Inc.

Beware! Ducks Crossing. Uriel Ofek. Tr. by David Kriss. (Hippy Ser.). (Illus.). 24p. (Orig.). (J). (ps). 1992. pap. text ed. 3.00 (1-56134-145-2) Dushkin Pub.

Beware Falling Tortoises. Sheenagh Pugh. LC 87-60981. 64p. 1987. pap. 10.95 (0-907476-70-8, Pub. by Poetry Wales Pr UK) Dufour.

Beware Familiar Spirits. John Mulholland. LC 75-7388. (Perspectives in Psychical Research Ser.). 1975. reprint ed. 29.95 (0-405-07036-5) Ayer.

Beware Lest You Entertain Angels Unaware: A Biblical Study of the Angelic Realm. Gregory Gaines. LC 93-90104. (Illus.). 250p. 1993. pap. 19.95 (0-9635991-0-0) Gaines Pub.

***Beware! Museum Bears.** Jacqueline Karas. (Illus.). 20p. (J). 1994. 15.95 (0-8167-3338-4) BridgeWater.

Beware of Boys. Tony Blundell. LC 90-24299. (Illus.). 32p. (J). (ps up). 1992. 15.00 (0-688-10924-1); lib. bdg. 14.93 (0-688-10925-X) Greenwillow.

Beware of Imitations see Absolutely Mad Inventions

An Asterisk (*) at the beginning of an entry indicates that the title is appearing in BIP for the first time. 711

B

***Beware of Kissing Lizard Lips.** Phyllis Shalant. 160p. (YA). (gr. 5 up). 1995. 13.99 (*0-525-45199-4*) Dutton Child Bks.

Beware of the Aunts! Pat Thomson. LC 90-28928. (Illus.). 32p. (J). (gr. k-3). 1992. text ed. 14.95 (*0-689-50538-8*, McElderry) S&S Childrens.

Beware of the Concision. Harley W. Cline. 96p. (Orig.). 1994. pap. 6.99 (*1-56043-805-3*) Destiny Image.

***Beware of the Dog.** Peter Corris. 1995. pap. 4.99 (*0-440-21753-9*) Dell.

Beware of the Ice. Penelope Rosemont & Enrico Baj. (Illus.). 64p. 1992. pap. 12.00 (*0-941194-29-9*) Black Swan Pr.

Beware of the Leaven of the Pharisees. David Chadwell. 1987. pap. 6.50 (*0-89137-566-X*) Quality Pubns.

Beware of the Mouse. Leonard Wibberley. LC 78-14993. (Illus.). 189p. 1978. reprint ed. lib. bdg. 29.00x (*0-89370-126-2*); reprint ed. pap. 19.00x (*0-89370-226-9*) Borgo Pr.

Beware of the Wolves. Ruth W. Schuler. (Illus.). 24p. (Orig.). (C). 1982. pap. 2.50 (*0-910083-07-X*) Heritage Trails.

Beware of Those Who Ask for Feedback. Richard A. Moran. 1994. pap. 6.00 (*0-88730-710-8*) Harper Busn.

Beware of Trains & Other Stories. Edmund Crispin. 1976. 18.95 (*0-8488-0469-4*) Amereon Ltd.

***Beware of Your Next Door Neighbor & Other Stories for Children by Children.** Ed. by Virginia L. Graf. (Stories for Children by Children Ser.). (Illus.). 288p. (Orig.). (J). (gr. 3-8). 1995. pap. 10.50 (*1-882788-04-4*) VanGar Pubs.

Beware Soul Brother. Chinua Achebe. (African Writers Ser.). 68p. (C). 1972. pap. 8.95 (*0-435-90120-6*) Heinemann.

Beware the Babysitter. Francine Pascal. (Sweet Valley High Ser.: No. 99). (YA). 1993. pap. 3.50 (*0-553-29856-9*) Bantam.

Beware the Barking Bumblebees: And Forty-Three More Nature Talks. Robert H. Neill. Ed. by Ellen Rolfes. (Something to Talk about Ser.). 96p. (J). (gr. k-6). 1993. spiral bd. 5.95 (*1-879958-18-X*) Tradery Hse.

Beware the Brindlebeast. Anita Riggio. LC 93-70875. (Illus.). 32p. (J). (ps-1). 1994. 14.95 (*1-56397-133-X*) Boyds Mills Pr.

Beware the Cat: The First English Novel. William Baldwin. LC 88-13057. (Illus.). 156p. reprint ed. pap. 44.50 (*0-7837-6673-4*, 2046289) Bks Demand.

Beware the First Drink! The Washington Temperance Movement & Alcoholics Anonymous. Leonard Blumberg. LC 90-19639. 304p. (Orig.). 1991. pap. 12.95 (*0-934125-22-8*) Glen Abbey Bks.

Beware the Fish. Gordon Korman. (Illus.). (Orig.). (J). (gr. 4-7). 1991. pap. 3.25 (*0-590-44205-8*, Apple Paperbacks) Scholastic Inc.

***Beware the God Who Smiles.** Larry Townsend. 1995. pap. text ed. 5.95 (*1-56333-321-X*) Masquerade.

Beware the Mare. Jessie Haas. LC 92-14505. (Illus.). 64p. (J). (gr. 2 up). 1993. 13.00 (*0-688-11762-7*) Greenwillow.

Beware the Naked Man Who Offers You His Shirt. Harvey Mackay. 416p. 1991. mass mkt. 5.95 (*0-8041-0583-9*) Ivy Books.

Beware the People Weeping: Public Opinion & the Assassination of Abraham Lincoln. Thomas R. Turner. LC 81-14252. (Illus.). 312p. 1982. pap. 11.95 (*0-8071-1722-6*) La State U Pr.

Beware the Pretenders see Cuidado con los Falaces!

***Beware the Ravens, Aunt Morbelia.** Joan D. Carris. LC 94-25654. (J). (gr. 1-8). 1995. 14.95 (*0-316-12961-5*) Little.

Beware the Sirens. Bill Burns. 80p. 1992. 10.95 (*1-56167-079-0*) Noble Hse MD.

Beware the Slippery Slope: Notes Toward the Definition of Justifiable Intervention. Ernst B. Haas. (Policy Papers in International Affairs: No. 42). 43p. 1993. pap. write for info. (*0-87725-542-3*) U of Cal IAS.

***Beware the Snake's Venom.** McMurtry. (Choose Your Own Nightmare Ser.: No. 2). (J). 1995. pap. 3.50 (*0-553-48230-0*) Bantam.

Beware the Talking Cure: Psychotherapy May Be Hazardous to Your Mental Health. Terence Campbell. 265p. (Orig.). 1994. pap. 14.95 (*0-89777-147-8*, Upton Bks) Sirs Inc.

Beware the Wolfman: Super Thriller Ed. Francine Pascal. (Sweet Valley High Ser.: No. 106). (YA). 1994. mass mkt. 3.99 (*0-553-56234-7*) Bantam.

***Beware Wet Paint: Designs by Alan Fletcher.** Jeremy Myerson. (Illus.). 266p. 1995. 55.00 (*0-7148-3354-1*, Pub. by Phaidon Press UK) Chronicle Bks.

Beware...the Song Shark! Shad O'Shea. (Illus.). 400p. (Orig.). 1990. pap. write for info. (*0-918243-01-7*) Positive Feedback Comns.

Bewegungsgruppen der Kristallographie. 2nd rev. ed. J. J. Burckhardt. (Mineralogisch-Geotechnische Reihe Ser.: No. 2). 209p. (GER.). 1980. 58.00 (*0-8176-0058-2*) Birkhauser.

Beweismass und Beweislast im Zivilprozess. Dieter Leipold. (Schriftenreihe der Juristischen Gesellschaft zu Berlin Ser.: Heft 93). 26p. (GER.). 1985. pap. 13.85 (*3-11-010580-2*) De Gruyter.

Bewildered. Jennifer Greene. 1994. mass mkt. 2.99 (*0-373-05861-6*, 5-05861-5) Harlequin Bks.

***Bewitched.** Constance O. Flannery. 400p. 1995. pap. 5.99 (*0-8217-4960-9*) Zebra.

Bewitching. Jill Barnett. 480p. (Orig.). 1993. mass mkt. 5.99 (*0-671-77863-3*, Pocket Star Bks) PB.

Bewitching. Carla Neggers. (Temptation Ser.). 1993. mass mkt. 2.99 (*0-373-25552-7*, 1-25552-0) Harlequin Bks.

***Bewitching.** Gloria D. Skinner. 384p. 1995. mass mkt. 4.99 (*0-8217-4807-6*) Windsor NY.

***Bewitching.** large type ed. Jill Barnett. 657p. 1995. reprint ed. 20.95 (*0-7862-0500-8*) Hall.

***Bewitching Familiar.** Caroline Burnes. 1995. mass mkt. 3.50 (*0-373-22343-9*, 1-22343-7) Harlequin Bks.

Bewitching Imposter. large type ed. Rowena Tenet. (Historical Romance Ser.). 304p. 1992. 21.95 (*0-7089-2652-5*) Ulverscroft.

Bewitching Kisses. Rainy Kirkland. 384p. 1991. mass mkt. 4.25 (*0-8217-3435-0*) Zebra.

***Bewitching Lord Winterton.** Marilyn Clay. 224p. 1995. pap. 3.99 (*0-8217-5082-8*) Zebra.

Bewitching Minx. Janis Laden. 512p. 1993. mass mkt. 3.99 (*0-8217-4233-7*) Zebra.

Bewitching of Alison Allbright. Alan Davidson. 160p. (YA). (gr. 5-9). 1991. pap. 3.95 (*0-14-032520-4*, Puffin) Puffin Bks.

***Bewitching Women, Pious Men: Gender & Body Politics in Southeast Asia.** Ed. by Aihwa Ong & Michael Peletz. LC 94-22740. 1995. 45.00 (*0-520-08860-3*); pap. 16.00 (*0-520-08861-1*) U CA Pr.

Bewusstseinsfeld. Aron Gurwitsch. Tr. by Werner D. Froehlich. LC 74-81087. (Phaenomenologisch-Psychologische Forschungen Ser.: Vol. 1). 1974. 142.30 (*3-11-002334-2*) De Gruyter.

Bexar Archives, 1717-1836: A Name Guide. Comp. by Adan Benavides, Jr. 1195p. 1989. text ed. 70.00 (*0-292-70772-X*) U of Tex Pr.

***Beyer on Speed.** Andrew Beyer. 1995. pap. 12.95 (*0-395-73523-8*) HM.

Beyer on Speed: New Strategies for Racetrack Betting. Andrew Beyer. LC 93-24036. 1993. 22.95 (*0-395-67390-9*) HM.

***Beyerlein Beginnings.** Ed. by Douglas Beyerlein. 117p. (C). 1989. pap. text ed. 18.00 (*0-9623312-0-1*) D Beyerlein.

Beyers Naude: Pilgrimage of Faith. Colleen Ryan. 248p. (C). 1990. 49.95 (*0-86543-193-0*); pap. 9.95 (*0-86543-190-6*) Africa World.

Beyers Naude: Pilgrimage of Faith. Colleen Ryan. (Illus.). 248p. 1990. pap. 19.99 (*0-8028-0531-0*) Eerdmans.

***Beyers Naude: Pilgrimage of Faith.** Colleen Ryan. LC 90-82835. (Illus.). 246p. 1990. reprint ed. pap. 70.20 (*0-7837-8092-3*, 2047846) Bks Demand.

Beyond. D. B. Harper. 1994. 14.95 (*0-533-10764-4*) Vantage.

Beyond. Jose D. Sigaud. 36p. 1993. 5.95 (*0-8059-3415-4*) Dorrance.

***Beyond: Journey Towards.** R. Stone. 1994. pap. 3.99 (*0-517-13386-5*) Random.

Beyond a Boundary. C. L. James. LC 93-17398. 291p. 1993. pap. 14.95 (*0-8223-1383-9*) Duke.

Beyond a Christian Commonwealth: The Protestant Quarrel with the American Republic, 1830-1860. Mark Y. Hanley. LC 93-8467. xii, 210p. (C). 1994. 34.95 (*0-8078-2121-7*) U of NC Pr.

Beyond a Dream: An Instructor's Guide for Small Business Exploration. Judy M. Balogh et al. 228p. 1985. 25.00 (*0-318-17848-6*, LT 68) Ctr Educ Trng Employ.

Beyond a Dream Deferred: Multicultural Education & the Politics of Excellence. Ed. by Becky W. Thompson & Sangeeta Tyagi. LC 93-15603. 302p. 1993. text ed. 44.95 (*0-8166-2267-1*); pap. 17.95 (*0-8166-2269-8*) U of Minn Pr.

Beyond a Reasonable Doubt. Nathan Mayer. (Orig.). 1992. 4.95 (*0-87129-166-5*, B71) Dramatic Pub.

Beyond a Reasonable Doubt? The Original Trial of Caryl Chessman. William M. Kunstler. LC 73-8155. (Illus.). 304p. 1973. reprint ed. text ed. 35.00 (*0-8371-6951-8*, CHBR, Greenwood Pr) Greenwood.

Beyond a Reasonable Doubt - Thirteen Lessons on Christian Evidences. Herbert C. Casteel. 202p. (Orig.). 1990. pap. 8.99 (*0-89900-351-6*) College Pr Pub.

Beyond a Sleeping Prairie. Howard Norskog. 40p. (Orig.). 1994. pap. 6.00 (*0-9625171-3-5*) H L Norskog.

Beyond a Technology's Promise: An Examination of Children's Educational Computing at Home. Joseph B. Giacquinta et al. LC 93-20444. 1994. 49.95 (*0-521-40447-9*); pap. 16.95 (*0-521-40784-2*) Cambridge U Pr.

Beyond Abortion: A Chronicle of Fetal Experimentation. Suzanne M. Rini. LC 92-82133. 197p. 1993. reprint ed. pap. 10.00 (*0-89555-487-9*) TAN Bks Pubs.

***Beyond Abstraction: Knowledge, Universality & the Dialectical Method.** Mike McKenna. 1996. pap. 19.50 (*1-899438-19-X*, Pub. by Porcupine Bks UK) Humanities.

Beyond Absurdity: The Philosophy of Albert Camus. Robert C. Trundle & R. Puligandla. (Illus.). 124p. (Orig.). 1986. lib. bdg. 47.00 (*0-8191-5225-0*); pap. text ed. 19.50 (*0-8191-5226-9*) U Pr of Amer.

Beyond Acceptance. Carolyn W. Griffin. 1990. pap. 9.95 (*0-312-04993-5*) St Martin.

Beyond Accommodation: Ethical Feminism, Deconstruction, & the Law. Drucilla Cornell. (Thinking Gender Ser.). 240p. 1991. 45.00 (*0-415-90105-7*, A2804, Routledge NY); pap. 14.95 (*0-415-90106-5*, A2808, Routledge NY) Routledge.

Beyond Addiction: A Step-by-Step Guide to the Spiritual Principles of Addiction & Recovery. Ray Geide. LC 90-85263. (Illus.). 232p. (Orig.). 1991. pap. 7.95 (*0-9628012-0-8*) Dexter KS.

Beyond Addictions, Beyond Boundaries: The Defiant Power of the Human Spirit. Ed. by Shirley Burton & Leo Kiley. (Illus.). 220p. (Orig.). 1986. pap. text ed. 10.95 (*1-55796-000-3*) Brookridge Pub.

Beyond Adjustment: The Asian Experience. Ed. by Paul Streeten. xii, 274p. 1988. pap. 15.00 (*1-55775-000-9*) Intl Monetary.

Beyond Adjustment: The Asian Experience. Ed. by Paul Streeten. LC 87-36163. 286p. reprint ed. pap. 81.60 (*0-8357-7154-7*, 2032121) Bks Demand.

Beyond Adolescence: Problem Behavior & Young Adult Development. Richard Jessor et al. (Illus.). 272p. (C). 1992. 44.95 (*0-521-39417-1*) Cambridge U Pr.

Beyond Adolescence: Problem Behavior & Young Adult Development. Richard Jessor et al. 312p. (C). 1994. pap. 16.95 (*0-521-46758-6*) Cambridge U Pr.

Beyond Adversary Democracy. Jane J. Mansbridge. xiv, 412p. 1983. pap. text ed. 16.95 (*0-226-50355-0*) U Ch Pr.

Beyond Aerobics: Optimal Fitness Through Recreational Sports. Kenneth Forsythe & Neil Feineman. write for info. (*0-318-59576-1*) S&S Trade.

Beyond Aesthetics: Artists of Conscience. Alternative Museum Staff. LC 90-55615. (Illus.). (Orig.). 1991. pap. 10.00 (*0-932075-33-9*) Alternative Mus.

Beyond Aesthetics: Confrontations with Poststructuralism & Postmodernism. Stuart Sim. LC 92-94833. 181p. 1992. 45.00 (*0-8020-2951-5*); pap. 16.95 (*0-8020-7777-3*) U of Toronto Pr.

***Beyond Affairs.** James Vaughan & Peggy Vaughan. 212p. 1980. 5.95 (*0-936390-01-8*) Dialog Pr.

Beyond Affection: An Autobiography by Peter Kavanagh. Peter Kavanagh. 224p. 1977. 50.00 (*0-914612-06-9*) Kavanagh.

Beyond Afghanistan: The Emerging U. S. - Pakistan Relations. Ed. by Leo E. Rose & Kamal Matinuddin. LC 89-81688. (Research Papers & Policy Studies). 336p. (Orig.). (C). 1990. pap. text ed. 20.00 (*1-55729-017-2*) IEAS.

Beyond Agenda Setting: Information Subsidies & Public Policy. Oscar H. Gandy, Jr. LC 82-13823. (Communication & Information Science Ser.). 272p. 1982. text ed. 55.00 (*0-89391-096-1*); pap. text ed. 27.50 (*0-89391-194-1*) Ablex Pub.

Beyond Agendas: New Directions in Communication Research. Ed. by Philip Gaunt. LC 93-12978. (Contributions to the Study of Mass Media & Communications Ser.: No. 43). 248p. 1993. text ed. 55.00 (*0-313-28863-1*, GM8863, Greenwood Pr) Greenwood.

Beyond Alcoholism: Alcohol & Public Health Policy. Dan E. Beauchamp. 240p. 1982. pap. 18.95 (*0-87722-286-X*) Temple U Pr.

Beyond Alfalfa Sprouts & Cheese: The Healthy Meatless Cookbook: A Practical Guide with More Than 125 Easy-to-Prepare Recipes Using Ingredients Found in Virtually Any Grocery Store. Judy Gilliard & Joy Kirkpatrick. 220p. 1993. pap. 12.95 (*1-56561-020-2*) Chronimed.

***Beyond Alienation: Political Essays on the West.** George Melnyk. 122p. (Orig.). 1993. pap. text ed. 13.95x (*1-55059-060-X*) Temeron Bks.

Beyond All Belief: Science, Religion & Reality. Peter Lemesurier. (Illus.). 222p. 1990. 19.95 (*0-906540-41-0*) Element MA.

***Beyond All Cost.** Thomas Gardiner. 49p. (Orig.). 1994. pap. 4.00 (*1-57514-108-6*, 1162) Encore Perform Pub.

***Beyond All Reason: The Crime That Shocked the World - The Story of Two British Ten-Year-Old.** David J. Smith. 1995. 21.95 (*1-55611-439-7*) D I Fine.

Beyond All Reason: Wide Open Spaces. Judith Duncan. (Silhouette Intimate Moments Ser.). 1993. mass mkt. 3.50 (*0-373-07536-7*, 5-07536-1) Silhouette.

Beyond Alliance: Israel in U. S. Foreign Policy. Camille Mansour. LC 93-28046. 1994. 37.50 (*0-231-08492-7*) Col U Pr.

***Beyond Alliance: Israel in U. S. Foreign Policy.** Camille Mansour. 340p. 1994. 37.50 (*0-614-02727-6*) Inst Palestine.

Beyond Altruism: Social Welfare Policy in American Society. Willard C. Richan. LC 86-29437. (Administration in Social Work Ser.: Supp. No. 3). 238p. 1987. 39.95 (*0-86656-633-3*) Haworth Pr.

Beyond Amazement: New Essays on John Ashbery. Ed. by David Lehman. LC 79-6850. 312p. 1980. 42.50 (*0-8014-1235-8*); pap. 17.95 (*0-8014-9183-5*) Cornell U Pr.

***Beyond Ambedkar: Essays on Dalits in India.** Nandu Ram. (C). 1995. 44.00 (*81-241-0239-2*, Pub. by Har-Anand Pubns II) S Asia.

Beyond Ambition: How Driven Managers Can Lead Better & Live Better. Robert E. Kaplan et al. LC 91-12695. (Management Ser.). 293p. 1991. 29.95 (*1-55542-315-9*) Jossey-Bass.

Beyond Analytical Philosophy: Doing Justice to What We Know. Hao Wang. 288p. 1988. pap. 12.50 (*0-262-73080-4*, Bradford Bks) MIT Pr.

Beyond Androcentrism: New Essays on Women & Religion. Rita M. Gross. LC 77-13312. (American Academy of Religion. Aids for the Study of Religion Ser.: No. 6). 354p. reprint ed. pap. 100.90 (*0-7837-5434-5*, 2045199) Bks Demand.

Beyond Anger: A Study of Juvenal's Third Book of Satires. Susan H. Braund. (Cambridge Classical Studies). 320p. 1989. 49.95 (*0-521-35637-7*) Cambridge U Pr.

Beyond Anger: On Being a Feminist in the Church. Carolyn Osiek. LC 85-62936. 96p. 1985. pap. 7.95 (*0-8091-2777-6*) Paulist Pr.

Beyond Anger & Pity. Lester Sumrall. Ed. by Helen Hoosier. 81p. (Orig.). 1988. pap. text ed. 1.95 (*0-937580-21-X*) LeSEA Pub Co.

***Beyond Animal Rights: A Feminist Caring Ethic for the Treatment of Animals.** Adams. Ed. by Donovan. 192p. 1996. 22.95 (*0-8264-0836-2*) Continuum.

Beyond Another Door. Sonia Levitin. (YA). 1994. mass mkt. 3.99 (*0-449-70425-4*, Juniper) Fawcett.

Beyond Anthropology: Society & the Other. Bernard McGrane. 176p. 1989. text ed. 31.00 (*0-231-06684-8*) Col U Pr.

Beyond Anthropology: Society & the Other. Bernard McGrane. 176p. (C). 1992. pap. 15.00 (*0-231-06685-6*) Col U Pr.

Beyond Antibiotics: Fifty (or So) Ways to Boost Immunity. 2nd rev. ed. Michael Schmidt et al. LC 93-42356. 328p. 1994. 16.95 (*1-55643-180-5*) North Atlantic.

Beyond Any Reasonable Doubt: A Book of Irish Murder Trials. rev. ed. Kenneth E. Deale. 256p. 1990. pap. 13.95 (*0-7171-1811-8*, Pub. by Gill & MacMill IE) Irish Bks Media.

Beyond Apartheid. Robert Fine. (C). 1991. pap. text ed. 22.00 (*0-7453-0572-5*, Pub. by Pluto Pr UK) Westview.

Beyond Apartheid: Human Resources for a New South Africa. Commonwealth Expert Group Staff. 133p. 1991. pap. 17.50 (*0-435-08069-5*, 08069) Heinemann.

Beyond Apartheid: Labour & Liberation in South Africa. Robert Fine et al. 338p. (C). 1991. text ed. 66.50 (*0-7453-0045-6*, Pub. by Pluto Pr UK) Westview.

Beyond Apollo. Barry Malzberg. 1989. pap. 3.50 (*0-88184-551-5*) Carroll & Graf.

Beyond Appearances: Moving from Fear to Faith. Ed. by Kathleen Juline. 372p. (Orig.). 1990. pap. 12.95 (*0-917849-10-8*, 0555) Sci of Mind.

Beyond Appearances: Stories from the Kabbalistic Ethical Writings. Aryeh Wineman. 184p. 1988. 21.95 (*0-8276-0307-X*) JPS Phila.

Beyond Ararat: A Journey Through East Turkey. large type ed. Bettina Selby. (Charnwood Ser.). (Illus.). 352p. 1994. 25.95 (*0-7089-8756-7*, Charnwood) Ulverscroft.

Beyond Arbitration: Designing Alternatives to Securities Litigation. Ralph C. Ferrara & Danny Ertel. 600p. 1991. boxed 105.00 (*0-88063-713-7*) Michie Butterworth.

Beyond Armageddon. Ed. by Walter M. Miller, Jr. & Martin H. Greenberg. LC 85-80625. 387p. 1986. pap. 3.95 (*0-917657-96-9*) D I Fine.

***"Beyond Ascension"** Joshua D. Stone. 280p. (Orig.). 1995. pap. 14.95 (*0-929385-73-X*) Light Tech Comns Servs.

Beyond Assertive Discipline: Humanistic Classroom Management. Albert Eglash. LC 80-50440. (Beyond Assertion Training Ser.: "Dont Step on My Castle!"). (Illus.). 100p. 1981. pap. 30.00 (*0-935320-18-0*) San Luis Quest.

Beyond Assistance: Report of the IEWS Task Force on Western Assistance to Transition in the Czech & Slovak Federal Republic, Hungary, & Poland. Krzysztof Ners et al. LC 92-18010. 1992. 12.85 (*0-913449-32-6*) Inst EW Stud.

***Beyond Atlanta.** Lincoln S. Bates. 160p. 1995. pap. text ed. 12.95 (*0-943734-27-4*) Ocean Tree Bks.

Beyond Authority: How to Play to Win by the New Ethics. Clifford Kaeser. LC 82-4020. 143p. 1984. pap. 12.95 (*0-87949-222-8*) Ashley Bks.

Beyond Aztlan: Ethnic Autonomy in Comparative Perspective. Mario Barrera. LC 88-5432. 221p. 1988. text ed. 49.95 (*0-275-92923-X*, C2923, Praeger Pubs) Greenwood.

Beyond Aztlan: Ethnic Autonomy in Comparative Perspective. Mario Barrera. LC 88-5432. 212p. (C). 1990. reprint ed. pap. text ed. 10.95 (*0-268-00688-1*) U of Notre Dame Pr.

Beyond B., M., & D. A Guide to Collecting & Publishing Family History. Kit Lane. LC 90-60630. 52p. (Orig.). 1990. pap. 3.84 (*1-877703-18-4*) Pavilion Pr.

Beyond Baby Fat: Weight-Loss Plans for Children & Teenagers. Frances S. Goulart. 1989. pap. 3.95 (*0-425-11616-6*) Berkley Pub.

Beyond Baby M. Ed. by D. Bartels et al. LC 89-49394. (Contemporary Issues in Biomedicine, Ethics, & Society Ser.). 304p. 1990. 34.50 (*0-89603-166-7*) Humana.

Beyond Backache: A Personal Guide to Back & Neck Pain Relief. Michael M. Livingston. LC 87-92101. 1988. 12.95 (*0-87212-212-3*) Libra.

Beyond Ballyhoo: Motion Picture Promotion & Gimmicks. Mark T. McGee. LC 89-42731. 253p. 1989. lib. bdg. 32.50 (*0-89950-435-3*) McFarland & Co.

Beyond Banquets, Plaques & Pins: Creative Ways to Recognize Volunteers & Staff. Sue Vineyard. (Illus.). 1989. pap. text ed. 7.00 (*0-911029-01-X*) Heritage Arts.

Beyond Baptism: A Guide for New Converts. Elaine Cannon. 1994. 10.95 (*0-88494-911-7*) Bookcraft Inc.

Beyond Basic Dog Training. 2nd ed. Diane L. Bauman. (Illus.). 256p. 1991. 22.95 (*0-87605-410-6*) Howell Bk.

Beyond Basic Dog Training Workbook. Diane Baumann et al. (Illus.). 216p. 1994. pap. 14.95 (*0-931866-74-X*) Alpine Pubns.

Beyond Basic Photography: A Technical Manual. Henry Horenstein. (Illus.). 1977. pap. 19.95 (*0-316-37312-5*) Little.

Beyond Basic Textiles. Allen C. Cohen. (Illus.). 350p. (C). 1982. ring bd. 22.50 (*0-87005-407-4*) Fairchild.

Beyond Basic Turning: Off-Center Coopered & Laminated Work. Jack Cox. LC 93-27393. (Illus.). 256p. 1993. pap. 28.95 (*0-941936-25-2*) Linden Pub Fresno.

Beyond Basics: A Developmental Reading Program. (Nine Book Ser.). (Illus.). 216p. (Orig.). (YA). (gr. 10). 1987. teacher ed 17.00 (*0-89061-444-X*); pap. text ed. 11.95 (*0-89061-435-0*) Jamestown Pubs.

Beyond Basics: A Developmental Reading Program. (Nine Book Ser.). (Illus.). 216p. (Orig.). (YA). (gr. 11). 1987. 11.95 (*0-89061-436-9*); teacher ed 17.00 (*0-89061-445-8*) Jamestown Pubs.

Beyond Basics: A Developmental Reading Program. (Nine Book Ser.). (Illus.). 216p. (Orig.). (YA). (gr. 12). 1987. teacher ed 17.00 (*0-89061-446-6*); pap. text ed. 11.95 (*0-89061-437-7*) Jamestown Pubs.

Beyond Basics: A Developmental Reading Program. (Nine Book Ser.). (Illus.). 216p. (Orig.). (J). (gr. 4). 1987. teacher ed 17.00 (*0-89061-438-5*); pap. text ed. 11.95 (*0-89061-429-6*) Jamestown Pubs.

An Asterisk (*) at the beginning of an entry indicates that the title is appearing in BIP for the first time.

An Asterisk (*) at the beginning of an entry indicates that the title is appearing in BIP for the first time.

Beyond Constructive Engagement: United States Foreign Policy Toward Africa. Ed. by Elliott P. Skinner. LC 86-4899. 282p. 1986. pap. 10.95 (*0-88702-210-3*) Washington Inst Pr.

Beyond Containment: Reconstructing European Security. Kim E. Spiezio. LC 94-20271. 158p. 1994. lib. bdg. 36.50 (*1-55587-451-7*) Lynne Rienner.

Beyond Containment & Division: Western Cooperation from a Post-Totalitarian Perspective. Franz A. Von Geusau. LC 92-34732. 1992. lib. bdg. 160.00 (*0-7923-2014-X*) Kluwer Ac.

Beyond Control? Schools & Suspension. Rob Grunsell. (Chameleon Education Ser.). 148p. (Orig.). 1981. pap. 4.95 (*0-906495-23-7*) Writers & Readers.

Beyond Countertransference: The Therapist's Subjectivity in the Therapeutic Process. Joseph Natterson. LC 90-14542. 256p. 1991. 30.00 (*0-87668-558-0*) Aronson.

***Beyond Courage.** Teresa Lucero. 1994. pap. text ed. 13.95 (*1-881116-42-5*) Black Forrest Pr.

Beyond Courage: One Regiment Against Japan, 1941-1945. Dorothy Cave. LC 91-68402. (Illus.). 448p. 1992. 22.95 (*0-9622940-7-1*) Yucca Tree Pr.

***Beyond Courage: One Regiment Against Japan, 1941-1945.** rev. ed. Dorothy Cave. (Illus.). 448p. 1995. pap. 18.95 (*1-881325-14-8*) Yucca Tree Pr.

Beyond Courage: Shipwrecked & Adrift, One Family Fights to Survive. Robert Aros & Rob Ternan. Ed. by Paul Buchanan. (Illus.). 272p. 1994. 22.95 (*0-9638704-0-8*); pap. 15.95 (*0-9638704-1-6*) Shore Pubng.

Beyond Crime Lab: New Science of Investigation. Jon Zonderman. 205p. 1990. text ed. 29.95 (*0-471-62296-6*) Wiley.

Beyond Crisis: Development Issues in Uganda. Ed. by Paul D. Wiebe & Cole P. Dodge. 158p. 1987. pap. 15.00 (*0-918456-60-6*, Crossroads) African Studies Assn.

Beyond Crisis: Our National Health in the 1990s. Ed. by Nancy F. McKenzie. 608p. (Orig.). 1994. pap. 19.95 (*0-452-01108-6*, Mer) NAL-Dutton.

Beyond Cuba: Latin America Takes Charge of Its Future. Ed. by Luigi R. Einaudi. LC 73-8644. 250p. 1973. pap. 18.00 (*0-8448-0266-2*, Crane Russak) Taylor & Francis.

Beyond Culture. Edward T. Hall. 1992. 20.00 (*0-8446-6551-7*) Peter Smith.

Beyond Culture. Lionel Trilling. LC 79-11660. 256p. 1978. 10.95 (*0-15-111987-2*) HarBrace.

Beyond Culture. Edward T. Hall. LC 74-3550. 1977. reprint ed. mass mkt. 9.95 (*0-385-12474-0*, Anchor NY) Doubleday.

Beyond Culture Wars: Is America a Mission Field or a Battlefield? Michael S. Horton. 1994. 16.99 (*0-8024-0893-1*) Moody.

Beyond Curry: Quick & Easy Indian Cooking Featuring Cuisine from Maharashtra State. Hemalata C. Dandekar. LC 82-74367. (Special Publication Ser.: No. 3). (Illus.). 162p. (Orig.). 1983. pap. 14.95 (*0-89148-026-9*) Ctr S&SE Asian.

Beyond Customer Service. Richard Gerson. Ed. by W. Philip Gerould. LC 91-72653. (Fifty-Minute Ser.). (Illus.). 90p. (Orig.). 1992. pap. 9.95 (*1-56052-115-5*) Crisp Pubns.

***Beyond Dark Hills: A Personal History.** 3rd ed. Jesse H. Stuart. Ed. by John H. Spurlock. 1995. 20.00 (*0-945084-53-6*) J Stuart Found.

Beyond Death. F. R. Ansari. pap. 1.00 (*0-935782-48-6*) Kazi Pubns.

Beyond Death. C. J. Baker. 1977. pap. 3.25 (*0-87813-953-2*) Christian Light.

Beyond Death: The Gates of Consciousness. Stanislav Grof & Christina Grof. (Art & Imagination Ser.). (Illus.). 1980. pap. 14.95 (*0-500-81019-2*) Thames Hudson.

Beyond Death: The Undiscover'd Country. Howard Murphet. 240p. (Orig.). (C). 1990. pap. 9.95 (*0-8356-0654-6*, Quest) Theos Pub Hse.

***Beyond Death: Theological & Philosphical Reflections on Life After Death.** Ed. by Dan Cohn-Sherbok & Christopher Lewis. LC 94-34880. 1995. write for info. (*0-312-12482-1*); pap. write for info. (*0-312-12483-X*) St Martin.

Beyond Death & Exile: The Spanish Republicans in France, 1939-1955. Louis Stein. LC 79-12797. (Illus.). 326p. 1979. reprint ed. pap. 93.00 (*0-7837-6093-0*, 2059139) Bks Demand.

Beyond Death & Taxes: Old Questions, New Answers, a Guide to the New Estate Planning. Gregory J. Englund. (Warrior Ser.). 78p. 1993. write for info. (*0-9636401-0-0*) Est Plan Pr.

Beyond Death's Door. Richard Paget. LC 78-14485. 1979. 22.95 (*0-87949-113-2*) Ashley Bks.

Beyond Death's Door. Maurice Rawlings. 1991. mass mkt. 4.99 (*0-553-22970-2*) Bantam.

Beyond Death's Door. Brent Top & Wendy Top. 1993. 12.95 (*0-88494-895-1*) Bookcraft Inc.

Beyond Debate: A Paper on Televised Presidential Debates. Joel L. Swerdlow. 89p. (Orig.). (C). 1984. pap. 6.00 (*0-87078-153-7*) TCFP-PPP.

Beyond Deconstruction: The Uses & Abuses of Literary Theory. Howard Felperin. 230p. 1987. pap. 17.95 (*0-19-812896-7*) OUP.

Beyond Deduction: Ampliative Aspects of Philosophical Reflection. Frederick L. Will. 288p. 1988. text ed. 32.50 (*0-415-00177-3*) Routledge.

Beyond Deficiency: New Views on the Function & Health Effects of Vitamins. Ed. by Howerde E. Sauberlich & Lawrence J. Machlin. LC 92-30616. (Annals Ser.: Vol. 669). 1992. write for info. (*0-89766-749-2*); pap. write for info. (*0-89766-750-6*) NY Acad Sci.

Beyond Definition: New Writing from Gay & Lesbian San Francisco. Ed. by Marci Blackman & Trebor Healey. 168p. (Orig.). 1994. pap. 10.95 (*0-916397-30-0*) Manic D Pr.

Beyond Depression. Canale. 1992. pap. 12.95 (*1-85230-341-7*) Element MA.

***Beyond Desert Storm.** Norman Mathers. 1993. pap. 9.95 (*0-916573-96-6*) LIFETIME.

Beyond Desert Storm: Hope for Days Ahead. Norman W. Mathers. (Illus.). 96p. 1993. pap. 12.95 (*0-9634654-0-6*) ATS Pubns.

Beyond Deserving. Sandra Scofield. LC 92-53546. 320p. 1992. pap. 10.95 (*0-452-26907-5*, Plume) NAL-Dutton.

Beyond Deserving. Sandra Scofield. LC 90-53328. 310p. 1991. 22.00 (*1-877946-07-9*) Permanent Pr.

Beyond Desire. Thea Devine. 448p. 1993. mass mkt. 4.99 (*0-8217-4215-9*) Zebra.

***Beyond Despair.** Donald Finkel. 42p. (Orig.). 1994. pap. 6.95 (*0-9643009-1-5*) Garlic Pr MO.

Beyond Despair: Three Lectures & a Conversation with Philip Roth. Aharon Appelfeld. Tr. by Jeffrey M. Green. LC 93-34763. 128p. 1994. 17.50 (*0-88064-150-9*) Fromm Intl Pub.

Beyond Deterrence: From Power Politics to World Public Order. Joseph A. Mikus. (American University Studies: Political Science: Ser. X, Vol. 15). 219p. (C). 1988. text ed. 33.00 (*0-8204-0699-6*) P Lang Pubs.

***Beyond Development Cooperation: Toward a New Era of Global & Human Security.** Fauzya Moore. 78p. 1994. pap. 19.95 (*0-88936-714-0*, IDRC7140, Pub. by IDRC CN) UNIPUB.

Beyond Dichotomy: An Integrative Model of Teacher Education. U. Hanke. (Illus.). 230p. 1993. text ed. 44.00 (*0-88937-056-7*) Hogrefe & Huber Pubs.

Beyond Dieting: Psychoeducational Interventions for Chronically Obese Women - A Non-Dieting Approach. Donna Ciliska. LC 90-1533. (Eating Disorders Monograph Ser.: No. 5). (Illus.). 192p. 1990. 28.95 (*0-87630-583-4*) Brunner-Mazel.

Beyond Dieting, Creating a Life without Shame, Guilt or Deprivation. Christopher Wilde & Janet A. Van Burger. 171p. 1993. pap. text ed. 19.95 (*0-9637551-0-2*) Beyond Diet Am.

***Beyond Difference.** Al Condeluci. 340p. 1995. pap. text ed. 29.95 (*1-878205-14-5*) GR Press.

Beyond Diplomacy: First Interim Report of the Atlantic Council's Special Committee on Intergovernmental Organization & Reorganization. 87p. 1975. 4.50 (*0-317-33690-8*) Atl Coun US.

***Beyond Disappointment...Hope.** Phillip R. Stout. 72p. 1994. per., pap. 4.95 (*0-8341-1530-1*) Beacon Hill.

Beyond Discipline: Parenting That Lasts a Lifetime. Edward R. Christophersen. LC 90-50485. 152p. (Orig.). 1990. pap. 9.95 (*0-933701-48-9*) Westport Pubs.

Beyond Dispute: The Invention of Team Syntegrity. Stafford Beer. LC 94-2439. (Managerial Cybernetics of Organization Ser.). 1994. text ed. 49.95 (*0-471-94451-3*) Wiley.

Beyond Dissent: Essays in Institutional Economics. Philip A. Klein. (Studies in Institutional Economics). 344p. 1994. text ed. 50.00 (*1-56324-321-0*); pap. text ed. 22.50 (*1-56324-322-9*) M E Sharpe.

Beyond Distance Teaching, Towards Open Learning. Ed. by Vivien E. Hodgson et al. 220p. 1987. 95.00 (*0-335-15603-7*, Open Univ Pr) Taylor & Francis.

***Beyond Document: Essays on Nonfiction Film.** Ed. by Charles Warren. (Illus.). 320p. (C). 1995. 45.00 (*0-8195-5287-9*, Wesleyan Univ Pr); pap. 16.95 (*0-8195-6290-4*, Wesleyan Univ Pr) U Pr of New Eng.

Beyond Domestication: Subsistence Archaeology & Social Complexity in Ancient Europe. Ed. by Graeme Barker & Clive Gamble. (Studies in Archaeology). 1985. text ed. 109.00 (*0-12-078840-3*) Acad Pr.

Beyond Domination: New Perspectives on Women & Philosophy. Ed. by Carol Gould. LC 83-10894. (New Feminist Perspectives Ser.). 344p. (C). 1984. pap. text ed. 23.25 (*0-8476-7236-0*) Rowman.

Beyond Doubt: A Devotional Response to Questions of Faith. Cornelius Plantinga, Jr. LC 80-10647. (Illus.). 256p. (Orig.). 1980. pap. text ed. 11.95 (*0-933140-12-6*); teacher ed, pap. text ed. 8.50 (*0-933140-61-4*) CRC Pubns.

***Beyond Dreams.** Marilyn Reynolds. (True-to-Life Series from Hamilton High). (Illus.). 192p. (Orig.). (YA). (gr. 7-13). 1995. 15.95 (*1-885356-00-5*); pap. 8.95 (*1-885356-01-3*) Morning Glory.

***Beyond Dreams & Beasts: Computers & the Culture of Simulation.** Sherry Turkle. 1995. 25.00 (*0-684-80353-4*) S&S Trade.

Beyond Dreams of Rescue: Poems. Mary-Ella Holst. LC 92-60934. 80p. 1992. pap. 10.95 (*0-9633273-0-5*) Wind Rose Pr.

Beyond Drill & Practice: Expanding the Computer Mainstream. Susan J. Russell et al. 120p. 1989. 10.00 (*0-86586-190-0*, P333) Coun Exc Child.

Beyond Drugs. Stanley Einstein. LC 73-7940. 1975. 126.00 (*0-08-017767-0*, Pub. by Pergamon Repr UK) Franklin.

Beyond Earth's Boundaries: Human Exploration of the Solar System in the 21st Century, 1988 Annual Report to the Administrator. (Illus.). 51p. (Orig.). 1989. pap. 4.25 (*0-16-004251-8*, S/N 033-000-01045-1) USGPO.

Beyond East & West: Problems in Liturgical Understanding. Robert Taft. (NPM Studies in Church Music & Liturgy). 203p. 1984. pap. 11.95 (*0-912405-13-9*) Pastoral Pr.

Beyond East-West Confrontation: Searching for a New Security Structure in Europe. Armand Clesse & Lothar Ruhl. 640p. 1990. 61.00 (*3-7890-2211-X*, Pub. by Nomos Verlags GW) Intl Bk Import.

***Beyond Economic Liberalization in Africa: Structural Adjustment & the Alternatives.** Ed. by Kidane Mengisteab & Ikubolajeh Logan. (Illus.). 320p. (C). 1995. text ed. 59.95 (*1-85649-293-1*, Pub. by Zed Books UK) Humanities.

***Beyond Economic Liberalization in Africa: Structural Adjustment & the Alternatives.** Ed. by Kidane Mengisteab & Ikubolajeh Logan. (Illus.). 320p. (C). 1995. pap. 25.00 (*1-85649-294-X*, Pub. by Zed Books UK) Humanities.

Beyond Economic Man: A New Approach to Micro-Economic Theory. Harvey Leibenstein. (Illus.). 302p. 1980. pap. 14.50 (*0-674-06892-0*) HUP.

Beyond Economic Man: Feminist Theory & Economics. Ed. by Marianne A. Ferber & Julie A. Nelson. LC 92-40149. 160p. (C). 1993. pap. text ed. 12.95 (*0-226-24201-3*) U Ch Pr.

Beyond Eden. Catherine Coulter. 448p. 1993. pap. 5.99 (*0-451-40339-8*, Onyx) NAL-Dutton.

***Beyond Eden.** Lyle P. Earney. 320p. Date not set. pap. 9.95 (*0-7610-0262-6*) NW Pub.

Beyond Eden. J. M. Morgan. 1992. mass mkt. 4.99 (*1-55817-602-0*, Pinnacle NY) Windsor NY.

Beyond Education: A New Perspective on Society's Management of Learning. Alan M. Thomas. LC 90-48584. (Higher & Adult Education Ser.). 221p. 1991. 32.95 (*1-55542-311-6*) Jossey-Bass.

Beyond Ego Psychology. Rubin Blanck & Gertrude Blanck. LC 85-21356. 248p. 1986. text ed. 31.50 (*0-231-06266-4*) Col U Pr.

Beyond Egotism: The Fiction of James Joyce, Virginia Woolf & D. H. Lawrence. Robert Kiely. LC 80-14231. 244p. 1980. 32.00 (*0-674-06896-3*) HUP.

Beyond Eighteen Forty-Eight: Readings in the Modern Chicano Historical Experience. Michael R. Ornelas. 336p. (C). 1993. per., pap. text ed. 28.95 (*0-8403-8818-7*) Kendall-Hunt.

***Beyond Einstein: The Cosmic Quest for the Theory of the Universe.** rev. ed. Micho Kaku & Jennifer T. Thompson. LC 95-1815. 1995. pap. write for info. (*0-385-47781-3*, Anchor NY) Doubleday.

Beyond Empire & Revolution: Militarization & Consolidation in the Third World. Irving L. Horowitz. 1982. 29.95 (*0-19-502931-3*) OUP.

Beyond Employment: Time, Work & the Informal Economy. Claire Offe & Rolf G. Heinze. Tr. by Alan Braley. 248p. 1992. 44.95 (*0-87722-951-1*) Temple U Pr.

Beyond Enchantment: German Idealism & English Romantic Poetry. Mark Kipperman. LC 86-3368. 254p. 1986. text ed. 41.95 (*0-8122-8024-5*) U of Pa Pr.

Beyond Endearment. Dorothy P. O'Neill. 1993. 13.95 (*0-8034-9037-2*) Bouregy.

Beyond Endurance. Djavad Zamanzadeh. 304p. (Orig.). (ENG & PER.). 1990. pap. 9.00 (*0-936347-07-4*) Iran Bks.

Beyond Entitlement: The Social Obligations of Citizenship. Lawrence M. Mead. 336p. (C). 1985. 29.95 (*0-02-920890-4*) Free Pr.

Beyond Entrepreneurship: Turning Your Business into an Enduring Great Company. James C. Collins & William C. Lazier. 1992. 19.95 (*0-13-085366-6*, Busn) P-H.

Beyond Environmental Crisis: From Technocrat to Planetary Person. Alan R. Drengson. (American University Studies: Philosophy: Ser. V, Vol. 74). 259p. (C). 1989. text ed. 38.70 (*0-8204-0871-9*) P Lang Pubs.

Beyond Equality: Labor & the Radical Republicans, 1862-1872. David Montgomery. LC 80-24434. 552p. 1981. reprint ed. pap. 15.95 (*0-252-00869-3*) U of Ill Pr.

Beyond Equality & Difference: Citizenship, Feminist Politics & Female Subjectivity. Ed. by Gisela Bock & Susan James. 288p. 1992. 49.95 (*0-415-07988-8*, A7944); pap. 16.95 (*0-415-07989-6*, A7948) Routledge.

Beyond Establishment: Protestant Establishment in a Post-Protestant Age. Ed. by Jackson W. Carroll & Wade C. Roof. LC 92-30370. 304p. (Orig.). 1993. pap. 19.99 (*0-664-25396-2*) Westminster John Knox.

Beyond Eternity: The Spiritual World of Ryukyu. Rokuro Takayasu. Tr. & Pref. by Christopher A. Reichl. LC 92-46334. 1993. write for info. (*0-9618793-5-1*) Reichl Pr.

Beyond Ethnicity: Consent & Descent in American Culture. Werner Sollors. (Illus.). 1987. pap. 18.95 (*0-19-505193-9*) OUP.

Beyond Ethnocentrism: A Reconstruction of Marx's Concept of Science. Charles McKelvey. LC 90-45602. (Contributions in Sociology Ser.: No. 94). 232p. 1991. text ed. 59.95 (*0-313-27420-7*, MBD, Greenwood Pr) Greenwood.

Beyond European Civilization: Marxism, Process Philosophy & the Environment. Arran Gare. 240p. 1994. pap. 29.95 (*0-646-14856-7*, Pub. by White Horse Pr UK) Paul & Co Pubs.

Beyond Everest. Patrick Morrow. (Illus.). 176p. 1986. pap. 19.95 (*0-920656-46-3*) Firefly Bks Ltd.

Beyond Evolution. Wilbur A. Jasson. LC 84-52700. (Illus.). 141p. 1986. 14.95 (*0-9614464-0-4*); pap. 8.95 (*0-9614464-1-2*) Sarasota Sci.

Beyond Experience. 2nd rev. ed. Theodore Gochenour. LC 93-34374. 196p. 1993. reprint ed. pap. 17.95 (*1-877864-24-2*) Intercult Pr.

Beyond Experience: Metaphysical Theories & Philosophical Constraints. Norman Swartz. 448p. 1991. 50.00 (*0-8020-2783-0*); pap. 19.95 (*0-8020-6832-4*) U of Toronto Pr.

Beyond Experience: The Experiential Approach to Cross-Cultural Education. Ed. by Donald Batchelder & Elizabeth G. Warner. LC 77-82854. (Intercultural Exchange Ser.). 196p. 1977. reprint ed. pap. text ed. 9.00 (*0-936141-00-X*) Experiment Pr.

Beyond Experts: A Guide for Citizen Group Training. Duane Dale et al. LC 79-64419. (Orig.). (C). 1979. pap. 7.00 (*0-934210-07-1*) Devlp Commy.

Beyond Explanation: Religious Dimensions in Cultural Anthropology. Mark K. Taylor. LC 85-13770. x, 262p. 1985. text ed. 26.95 (*0-86554-165-5*, MUP-H155) Mercer Univ Pr.

Beyond Fact: Nonfiction for Children & Young People. Jo Carr. LC 82-1601. 237p. reprint ed. pap. 67.60 (*0-8357-7156-3*, 2025609) Bks Demand.

***Beyond Fair Chase: The Ethic & Tradition of Hunting.** Jim Posewitz. 1994. 17.95 (*1-56044-302-2*) Falcon Pr MT.

Beyond Fair Chase: The Ethic & Tradition of the Hunt. Jim Posewitz. LC 94-10052. 128p. (Orig.). 1994. pap. 5.95 (*1-56044-283-2*) Falcon Pr MT.

***Beyond Faith & Infidelity: The Sufi Poetry & Teachings of Mahmud Shabistari.** Leonard Lewisohn. (Sufi Ser.: No. 5). 220p. (C). 1995. pap. 19.95 (*0-7007-0343-8*, Pub. by Curzon Pr UK) Humanities.

Beyond Fantasy. Ed. by William M. Merrill. 215p. 16.95 (*0-9618391-0-4*) Inland Pub.

Beyond Farmer First: Rural People's Knowledge, Agricultural Research & Extension Practice. Ed. by Ian Scoones & John Thompson. 288p. (Orig.). 1994. text ed. 28.50 (*1-85339-237-5*, Pub. by Intermed Tech UK); pap. 7.95 (*1-85339-250-2*, Pub. by Intermed Tech UK) Women Ink.

Beyond Feelings: A Guide to Critical Thinking. 3rd ed. Vincent R. Ruggiero. 190p. (C). 1990. pap. text ed. 19.95 (*0-87484-950-0*) Mayfield Pub.

Beyond Feelings: A Guide to Critical Thinking. 4th ed. Vincent R. Ruggiero. LC 94-8839. 248p. (C). 1994. pap. 19.95 (*1-55934-357-5*) Mayfield Pub.

Beyond Female Masochism. Frigga Haug. 256p. 1991. 54.95 (*0-86091-358-9*, A6408, Pub. by Verso UK); pap. 16.95 (*0-86091-562-X*, A6412, Pub. by Verso UK) Routledge Chapman & Hall.

Beyond Feminism: Towards a Dialogue on Difference. Cornelius F. Murphy. LC 93-47404. 300p. (C). 1995. 24.95 (*0-8132-0806-8*); pap. 14.95 (*0-8132-0807-6*) Cath U Pr.

Beyond Feminist Aesthetics: Feminist Literature & Social Change. Rita Felski. LC 88-34460. 240p. 1989. pap. 13.50 (*0-674-06895-5*) HUP.

Beyond Fido: The Definitive Guide to Naming Your Pet. Tom Torriglia & Tami Kesler. 96p. 1991. pap. text ed. 4.95 (*0-9630459-0-3*) Pet Proj.

Beyond First Aid. Peter R. Hewett. (Illus.). 256p. (Orig.). 1992. pap. text ed. 36.00 (*0-443-04579-8*) Churchill.

Beyond Flexible Scheduling: A Workshop Guide. Nancy L. Dobrot & Rosemary McCawley. 75p. 1992. pap. 20.00 (*0-931510-44-9*) Hi Willow.

Beyond Flexner: Medical Education in the Twentieth Century. Ed. by Barbara M. Barzansky & Norman Gevitz. LC 91-24333. (Contributions in Medical Studies: No. 34). 264p. 1992. text ed. 55.00 (*0-313-25984-4*, BMU, Greenwood Pr) Greenwood.

***Beyond Forever.** Rosalyn Alsobrook. 400p. 1995. mass mkt. 4.99 (*0-8217-4963-3*) Windsor NY.

Beyond Forgiveness: The Healing Touch of Church Discipline. Don Baker. LC 84-3417. 102p. 1984. 8.99 (*0-88070-054-8*, Multnomah Bks) Questar Pubs.

Beyond Form Criticism: Essays in Old Testament Literary Criticism. Ed. by Paul R. House. LC 92-29701. (Sources for Biblical & Theological Study Ser.: Bk. 2). xvi, 448p. 1992. text ed. 32.50 (*0-931464-65-X*) Eisenbrauns.

Beyond Formal Operations: Late Adolescent & Adult Cognitive Development. Francis A. Richards & Cheryl Armon. Ed. by Michael L. Commons. LC 83-21142. 494p. 1984. text ed. 55.00 (*0-275-91139-X*, C1139, Praeger Pubs) Greenwood.

Beyond Formal Operations Vol. 2: Adolescent & Adult Development Models. Ed. by Michael L. Commons et al. LC 88-27425. 362p. 1989. text ed. 59.95 (*0-275-92748-2*, C2748, Praeger Pubs) Greenwood.

Beyond Formalism: Literary Essays, 1958-1970. Geoffrey H. Hartman. LC 79-115371. 412p. reprint ed. pap. 117.50 (*0-8357-8040-6*, 2033746) Bks Demand.

Beyond Formalism: Naming & Necessity for Human Beings. Jay F. Rosenberg. LC 93-12691. 256p. 1994. 44.95 (*1-56639-118-0*) Temple U Pr.

Beyond Formula: American Film Genres. Stanley J. Solomon. (Illus.). 310p. (Orig.). (C). 1976. pap. text ed. 20.00 (*0-15-505400-7*) HB Coll Pubs.

Beyond Forty Percent: Record Setting Recycling & Composting Programs. Institute for Local Self-Reliance Staff. LC 90-19181. 1991. pap. 25.00 (*1-55963-073-6*) Island Pr.

Beyond Forty Percent: Record Setting Recycling & Composting Programs. Institute for Local Self-Reliance Staff. LC 90-19181. 1991. 39.95 (*1-55963-074-4*) Island Pr.

Beyond Free Markets: The Revival of Activist Economics. Marc Levinson. LC 87-45775. 224p. 1990. pap. 12.95 (*0-669-16973-0*) Free Pr.

Beyond Free Trade: Firms, Government & Global Competition. Ed. by David B. Yoffie. 1993. text ed. 45.00 (*0-07-103416-1*) McGraw.

Beyond Free Trade: Firms, Governments, & Global Competition. Ed. by David B. Yoffie. LC 92-29834. 496p. 1993. 45.00 (*0-87584-344-1*) Harvard Busn.

Beyond Free Trade & Protectionism: The Public Interest in a U. S. Auto Policy. Daniel Luria. 30p. 1990. 10.00 (*0-944826-08-3*) Economic Policy Inst.

Beyond Frontiers: Islam & Contemporary Needs. Ed. by M. Wyn-Davies & A. Pasha. 224p. 1989. text ed. 80.00 (*0-7201-2039-X*, Mansell Pub) Cassell.

Beyond Fundamentalism. James Barr. LC 84-12029. 206p. 1984. pap. 10.99 (*0-664-24620-6*, Westminster) Westminster John Knox.

Beyond Futility. 2nd ed. David Hubbard. Tr. by Beer-Shiba Semarians. 106p. (CHI.). 1982. pap. write for info. (*0-941598-02-0*) Living Spring Pubns.

Beyond Futility: The Filipino as Critic. Isagani R. Cruz. LC 84-169203. vii, 96p. (Orig.). (C). 1984. pap. 6.50 (*971-10-0160-8*, Pub. by New Day Pub PH) Cellar.

An Asterisk (*) at the beginning of an entry indicates that the title is appearing in BIP for the first time.

An Asterisk (*) at the beginning of an entry indicates that the title is appearing in BIP for the first time.

715

Beyond Mechanization: Work & Technology in a Post-Industrial Age. Larry Hirschhorn. (Illus.). 216p. 1986. pap. 12.95 (*0-262-58081-0*) MIT Pr.

Beyond Media: New Approaches to Mass Communication. rev. ed. Ed. by Richard W. Budd & Brent D. Ruben. 320p. (C). 1988. pap. 18.95 (*0-88738-698-9*) Transaction Pubs.

Beyond Medicare: Achieving Long-Term Care Security. Malvin Schechter. LC 93-14558. (Health-Management Ser.). 175p. 1993. 34.95 (*1-55542-583-6*) Jossey-Bass.

Beyond Mendel's Garden: Biotechnology in the Service of World Agriculture, No. 1. Gabrielle J. Persley. (Biotechnology in Agriculture Ser.). 176p. (Orig.). 1990. pap. text ed. 24.50 (*0-85198-682-X*) CAB Intl.

Beyond Metafiction: Self-Consciousness in Soviet Literature. David Shepherd. LC 92-12479. 225p. 1992. 59.00 (*0-19-815666-9*, Clarendon Pr) OUP.

Beyond Metaphor: The Theory of Tropes in Anthropology. James W. Fernandez. 312p. 1991. 39.50 (*0-8047-1940-3*); pap. 13.95 (*0-685-47785-1*) Stanford U Pr.

Beyond Metaphysics? The Hermeneutic Circle in Contemporary Philosophy. John Llewelyn. LC 84-4638. 256p. (C). 1989. pap. 18.50 (*0-391-03619-X*) Humanities.

Beyond Method: Strategies for Social Research. Ed. by Gareth Morgan. 424p. 1983. 49.95 (*0-8039-1973-5*); pap. 22.50 (*0-8039-2078-4*) Sage.

Beyond Methodology: Feminist Scholarship as Lived Research. Ed. by Mary M. Fonow & Judith A. Cook. LC 90-43508. (Illus.). 318p. 1991. 37.50 (*0-253-32345-2*); pap. 14.95 (*0-253-20629-4*, MB-629) Ind U Pr.

Beyond Methodology: Second Language Teaching & Communities. Mary Ashworth. (New Directions in Language Teaching Ser.). 152p. 1986. 39.95 (*0-521-26665-3*); pap. 15.95 (*0-521-31991-9*) Cambridge U Pr.

Beyond MFN: Trade with China & American Interests. James R. Lilley & Wendell L. Willkie, III. LC 94-8228. 192p. (Orig.). 1994. 29.95 (*0-8447-3856-5*, AEI Pr); pap. 12.95 (*0-8447-3857-3*, AEI Pr) Am Enterprise.

Beyond Mind. W. E. Mons. LC 84-52292. 256p. (Orig.). 1985. pap. 8.95 (*0-87728-633-7*) Weiser.

Beyond Mind Games: The Marketing Power of Psychographics. Rebecca Piirto. LC 91-58121. 263p. (C). 1991. 34.50 (*0-936889-08-X*) American Demo.

Beyond Mind Games: The Marketing Power of Psychographics. Rebecca Piirto. LC 91-58121. 263p. (C). 1992. pap. 29.95 (*0-936889-10-1*) American Demo.

Beyond Mind Games: The Marketing Power of Psychographics. abr. ed. Rebecca Piirto. (Maro Business Reviews Ser.). 52p. 1993. pap. 7.95 (*0-9627362-1-X*); audio 19.95 (*0-9627362-2-8*) Maro Comns.

Beyond Minimalism: Beckett's Late Style in the Theatre. Enoch Brater. 224p. 1987. 49.95 (*0-19-504167-4*) OUP.

Beyond Minimalism, George Waterman Collection. Daniel Robbins. LC 78-105670. (Illus.). 1969. 2.00 (*0-911517-21-9*) Mus of Art RI.

Beyond Modernism: Essays on Art from the '70s & '80s. Kim Levin. LC 87-45637. (Illus.). 258p. 1989. pap. 15.00 (*0-06-430176-1*, IN-176, Icon Edns) HarpC.

Beyond Modernity: Reflections of a Post-Modern Catholic. George W. Rutler. LC 86-82636. 227p. (Orig.). 1986. pap. 12.95 (*0-89870-135-X*) Ignatius Pr.

Beyond Modularity: A Developmental Perspective on Cognitive Science. Annette Karmiloff-Smith. (Bradford Learning Development & Conceptual Change Ser.). (Illus.). 290p. 1992. 37.50 (*0-262-11169-1*, Bradford Bks) MIT Pr.

***Beyond Modularity: A Developmental Perspective on Cognitive Science.** Annette Karmiloff-Smith. (Learning, Development, & Conceptual Change Ser.). (Illus.). 256p. 1995. reprint ed. pap. 12.50x (*0-262-61114-7*, Bradford Bks) MIT Pr.

Beyond Monogamy: Recent Studies of Sexual Alternatives in Marriage. Ed. by James R. Smith & Lynn G. Smith. LC 73-19345. 348p. reprint ed. pap. 99.20 (*0-8357-7160-1*, 2025874) Bks Demand.

Beyond Monopoly: Lawyers, State Crisis & Professional Empowerment. Terence C. Halliday. LC 86-30867. xx, 396p. 1987. 29.95 (*0-226-31389-1*) U Ch Pr.

Beyond Monopoly Capitalism & Monopoly Socialism: Distributive Justice in a Competitive Society. Guy C. Ankerl. 108p. 1978. 21.95 (*0-87073-938-7*) Transaction Pubs.

Beyond Morality. Richard Garner. LC 93-7399. (Ethics & Action Ser.). 384p. (C). 1993. 49.95 (*1-56639-076-1*); pap. 22.95 (*1-56639-108-3*) Temple U Pr.

Beyond Mormonism: An Elder's Story. James R. Spencer. LC 84-9633. 180p. 1984. pap. 8.99 (*0-8007-9076-6*) Chosen Bks.

Beyond Mortal Boundaries. Annalee Skarin. 342p. 1972. pap. 6.95 (*0-87516-089-1*) DeVorss.

***Beyond Motivation: Waking up the Knowing Within.** Debra Whiddon. Ed. by Wendy Lackritz & Laura Jacobus. 165p. (Orig.). 1994. pap. text ed. 14.95 (*1-886112-00-2*) Antares.

***Beyond Multicultural Education: International Perspectives.** Ed. & Intro. by Kogila A. Moodley. 318p. (Orig.). (C). 1992. pap. text ed. 18.95x (*1-55059-029-4*) Temeron Bks.

Beyond Multinationalism: Management Policy & Bargaining Relationships in International Companies. Jairus Banahi. 200p. (C). 1990. text ed. 25.00 (*0-8039-9637-3*) Sage.

Beyond Murder: The Inside Account of the Gainesville Student Murders. John Philpin & John Donnelly. 416p. (Orig.). 1994. pap. 4.99 (*0-451-40409-2*, Onyx) NAL-Dutton.

Beyond My Canopy. James W. Miller. Ed. by Ken Asher. LC 80-82869. 64p. (Orig.). 1980. write for info. (*0-9620151-0-5*); pap. write for info. (*0-9620151-1-3*) J W Miller.

Beyond My Expectation: A Personal Chronicle. Guy R. Lyle. LC 81-5071. 244p. 1981. 20.00 (*0-8108-1426-9*) Scarecrow.

Beyond My Fear. Tomi Keitlen. Orig. Title: Dearest It's Time. 340p. Date not set. pap. 16.95 (*0-9630485-3-8*) In Print.

***Beyond My Fear.** Tomi Keitlen. (Illus.). Date not set. pap. write for info. (*1-886966-03-6*) In Print.

***Beyond My Wildest Dreams: Diary of a UFO Abductee.** Kim Carlsberg. (Illus.). 288p. (Orig.). 1995. pap. 25.00 (*1-879181-25-8*) Bear & Co.

***Beyond NAFTA: The Western Hemisphere Interface.** Dobell & Neufeld. 1994. per. 12.95 (*0-88982-131-3*, Pub. by Oolichan Bks CN) InBook.

Beyond Naive Belief: The Bible & Adult Catholic Faith. Paul E. Dinter. 320p. 1994. 9.95 (*0-8245-1421-1*) Crossroad NY.

Beyond Nakedness. Paul Ableman. (Illus.). 112p. (C). 1986. reprint ed. pap. 16.95 (*0-910550-56-5*) Elysium.

Beyond Nakedness & Shame: The Case for Nudity, 2 vols., Set. 1991. lib. bdg. 500.00 (*0-8490-4606-8*) Gordon Pr.

Beyond Names for Things: Young Children's Acquisition of Verbs. Ed. by Michael Tomasello & William E. Merriman. 424p. 1994. text ed. 79.95 (*0-8058-1250-4*) L Erlbaum Assocs.

Beyond National Sovereignty: International Communications in the 1990s. Kaarle Nordenstreng & Herbert I. Schiller. Ed. by Brenda Dervin. (Communication & Information Science Ser.). 483p. (C). 1993. text ed. 85.00 (*0-89391-959-4*); pap. text ed. 39.95 (*0-89391-960-8*) Ablex Pub.

Beyond Nationalism: A Social & Political History of the Habsburg Officer Corps, 1848-1918. Istvan Deak. (Illus.). 304p. 1990. 19.95 (*0-19-504505-X*) OUP.

Beyond Nationalization: The Labor Problems of British Coal. George B. Baldwin. LC 55-10966. (Wertheim Publications in Industrial Relations). (Illus.). 346p. 1955. 24.95 (*0-674-06900-5*) HUP.

***Beyond NATO: Staying Out of Europe's Wars.** Ted G. Carpenter. LC 94-23704. 1994. 18.95 (*1-882577-16-7*); pap. write for info. (*1-882577-17-5*) Cato Inst.

Beyond Natural Selection. Robert Wesson. (Illus.). 617p. 1991. 37.50 (*0-262-23161-1*, Bradford Bks) MIT Pr.

Beyond Natural Selection. Robert Wesson. (Illus.). 376p. (C). 1993. pap. 17.00 (*0-262-73102-9*, Bradford Bks) MIT Pr.

Beyond Naturalism: A New Realism in American Theatre. William W. Demastes. LC 88-17787. (Contributions in Drama & Theatre Studies: No. 27). 182p. 1988. text ed. 45.00 (*0-313-26320-5*, DBN/, Greenwood Pr) Greenwood.

Beyond Negative Thinking: Breaking the Cycle of Depressing & Anxious Thoughts. Joseph T. Martorano & John P. Kildahl. (Illus.). 314p. 1989. 20.95 (*0-306-43196-3*, Plenum Insight) Plenum.

Beyond Negative Thinking: Reclaiming Your Life Through Optimism. Joseph T. Martorano & John P. Kildahl. 224p. 1992. mass mkt. 4.99 (*0-380-71606-2*) Avon.

Beyond Negotiation. C. Carlisel & P. Parker. 188p. (C). 1989. 180.00 (*0-685-39926-5*, Inst Pur & Supply) St Mut.

Beyond Negotiation: Redeeming Customer-Supplier Relationships. John A. Carlisle & Robert C. Parker. 1989. text ed. 47.50 (*0-471-92203-X*) Wiley.

Beyond Neutrality: A Christian Critique of the Media. John Bluck. LC 80-505714. (Illus.). 70p. reprint ed. pap. 25.00 (*0-7837-5997-5*, 2045807) Bks Demand.

Beyond New Testament Theology. Heikki Raisanen. LC 89-48393. 224p. (Orig.). (C). 1990. pap. 14.95 (*0-334-01907-9*) TPI PA.

Beyond News of the Weird. Chuck Shepherd et al. (Illus.). 224p. 1991. pap. 8.00 (*0-452-26716-1*, Plume) NAL-Dutton.

Beyond Newton. Dewey B. Larson. LC 63-22695. (Illus.). 1964. 15.00 (*0-913138-03-7*) North Pacific.

Beyond Nihilism: Nietzsche As Edifying Philosopher. Nimrod Aloni. 216p. (C). 1992. lib. bdg. 40.00 (*0-8191-8431-4*) U Pr of Amer.

Beyond Nihilism: Nietzsche Without Masks. Ofelia Schutte. LC 83-9240. xvi, 234p. 1986. pap. text ed. 10.95 (*0-226-74141-9*) U Ch Pr.

Beyond NIMBY: Hazardous Waste Siting in Canada & the United States. Barry G. Rabe. LC 94-19039. 199p. (C). 1994. 34.95x (*0-8157-7308-0*); pap. 14.95x (*0-8157-7307-2*) Brookings.

Beyond Nineteen Ninety-Two: U. S. Strategy Toward the European Community. Ed. by William E. Brock et al. (CSIS Panel Report). 64p. (Orig.). 1990. pap. text ed. 10.95 (*0-89206-152-9*) CSI Studies.

Beyond Normal Cognition: An Evaluative & Methodological Study of the Mental Content of Certain Trance Phenomena. John F. Thomas. LC 75-7405. (Perspectives in Psychical Research Ser.). 1975. reprint ed. 28.95 (*0-405-06992-8*) Ayer.

Beyond Nuclear Thinking. Robert W. Malcolmson. 168p. (C). 1990. text ed. 37.95 (*0-7735-0784-1*, Pub. by McGill CN); pap. text ed. 17.95 (*0-7735-0802-3*, Pub. by McGill CN) U of Toronto Pr.

Beyond Numeracy. John A. Paulos. 1992. pap. 12.00 (*0-679-73807-X*, Vin) Random.

Beyond Numeracy: An Uncommon Dictionary of Mathematics. John A. Paulos. 1991. 21.50 (*0-394-58640-9*) Knopf.

Beyond Numeracy: Ruminations of a Numbers Man. John A. Paulos. 1991. 22.00 (*0-685-48163-8*) Knopf.

***Beyond O. J. Race, Sex & Class Lessons for America.** Earl O. Hutchinson. LC 95-76059. 240p. 1996. 19.95 (*1-881032-12-4*); pap. 17.95 (*1-881032-07-8*) Middle Passage.

Beyond Objectivism & Relativism: Science, Hermeneutics, & Praxis. Richard J. Bernstein. LC 83-12439. 320p. (Orig.). 1983. pap. 17.95 (*0-8122-1165-0*) U of Pa Pr.

Beyond Obsession. Richard Hammer. 392p. 1993. mass mkt. 5.50 (*0-380-71037-4*) Avon.

Beyond Oil: The Threat to Food & Fuel in the Coming Decades. John Gever et al. (Illus.). 312p. 1991. pap. 17.50 (*0-87081-242-4*) Univ Pr Colo.

Beyond Oil: Unity & Development in the Gulf. Muhammad Rumaihi. pap. 9.95 (*0-86356-032-6*, Pub. by Saqi Bks UK) Interlink Pub.

Beyond O.K. - Psychogenic Tools Relating to Health of Body & Mind. Win Wenger. (Psychegenic Library of Experiential Protocols). (Illus.). (Orig.). (C). 1980. pap. 10.00 (*0-931865-01-8*) Psychegenics.

***Beyond Ontological Blackness: An Essay on African American Religious & Cultural Criticism.** Anderson. 176p. 1995. 19.95 (*0-8264-0865-6*) Continuum.

Beyond Oppression: Feminist Theory & Political Strategy. M. E. Hawkesworth. 288p. 1993. pap. text ed. 14.95 (*0-8264-0591-6*) Continuum.

Beyond Optimizing: A Study of Rational Choice. Michael Slote. LC 88-24522. 208p. 1989. 32.00x (*0-674-06918-8*) HUP.

Beyond Our Ghettos: Gay Theology in Ecological Perspective. J. Michael Clark. LC 93-4196. 128p. (Orig.). (C). 1993. pap. 9.95 (*0-8298-0959-7*) Pilgrim OH.

Beyond Our Means: How Reckless Borrowing Now Threatens to Overwhelm Us. Alfred L. Malabre, Jr. LC 87-45931. 192p. 1988. pap. 6.95 (*0-394-75816-1*, Vin) Random.

Beyond Our Selves. Catherine Marshall. (Catherine Marshall Library). 286p. 1994. reprint ed. pap. 8.99 (*0-8007-9089-8*) Revell.

Beyond Our Solar System. Fred Justus. (Science Ser.). 24p. (gr. 8). 1976. student ed. 5.00 (*0-8209-0146-6*, S-8) ESP.

Beyond Ourselves. Catherine Marshall. 272p. 1976. mass mkt. 4.99 (*0-380-00246-9*) Avon.

Beyond Ourselves. Catherine Marshall. 272p. 1994. pap. 8.00 (*0-380-72202-X*) Avon.

Beyond Outlining: New Approaches to Rhetorical Form. Betty Cain. 218p. (C). 1991. lib. bdg. 42.00 (*0-8191-8415-2*); pap. text ed. 18.50 (*0-8191-8416-0*) U Pr of Amer.

Beyond Painting: And Other Writings by the Artist & His Friends. Max Ernst. LC 83-45752. reprint ed. 57.50 (*0-404-20090-7*) AMS Pr.

Beyond Palmistry: The Art & Science of Modern Hand Analysis. Beverly Jaegers. 224p. (Orig.). 1992. mass mkt. 5.50 (*0-425-13403-2*) Berkley Pub.

Beyond Paper: The Official Guide to Adobe Acrobat. Adobe Systems Staff & Patrick Ames. LC 93-78061. (Illus.). 127p. (Orig.). 1993. pap. text ed. 16.95 (*1-56830-050-6*) Adobe Calif.

Beyond Paradise: Encounters in Hawaii Where the Tour Bus Never Runs. Peter S. Adler. LC 93-13728. 1993. pap. 16.00 (*1-881987-01-9*) Ox Bow.

Beyond Parsley. Junior League of Kansas City, Mo., Inc. Staff. (Illus.). 260p. 1984. 24.50 (*0-9607076-1-1*) Jr League KC.

Beyond Participative Management: Toward Total Employee Empowerment for Quality. G. Ronald Gilbert & Ardel E. Nelson. LC 91-11429. 264p. 1991. text ed. 55.00 (*0-89930-612-8*, GBF/, Quorum Bks) Greenwood.

Beyond Partnership: Strategies for Innovation & Lean Supply. Richard Lamming. LC 92-38797. (Manufacturing Practitioner Ser.). 1993. pap. text ed. 36.95 (*0-13-143785-2*) P-H.

Beyond Patching: Faith & Feminism in the Catholic Church. Sandra M. Schneiders. LC 90-46866. 1991. pap. 8.95 (*0-8091-3215-X*) Paulist Pr.

Beyond Patient Satisfaction: Building Patient Loyalty. R. Scott MacStravic. LC 91-7086. 279p. 1991. text ed. 42.00 (*0-910701-70-9*, 0905) Health Admin Pr.

Beyond Patriarchy: The Images of Family in Jesus. Diane Jacobs-Malina. LC 93-24501. 208p. (Orig.). 1993. pap. 13.95 (*0-8091-3421-7*) Paulist Pr.

Beyond Patronage & Exploitation: Changing Relations in South Gujarat. Jan Breman. (India Paperbacks Ser.). 424p. 1994. pap. 12.95 (*0-19-563087-4*) OUP.

***Beyond Patterns: The Psychology of Health & Excellence, Bk. 7.** Rose A. Parvin. 288p. 1995. lib. bdg. 15.00 (*1-885917-06-6*) Univrsl Pubng.

Beyond PC: Toward a Politics of Understanding. Patricia Aufderheide. 256p. 1992. pap. 10.00 (*1-55597-164-4*) Graywolf.

Beyond Peace. Richard Nixon. 1994. 23.00 (*0-679-43323-6*) Random.

***Beyond Peanut Butter & Jelly Sandwiches.** Cheryl Kirsch. 350p. 1995. pap. 9.95 (*1-56901-814-6*) NW Pub.

Beyond Pedigrees: Getting Organized to Make the Most of Your Research. Beverly D. Whitaker. 104p. 1993. pap. 12.95 (*0-916489-52-3*) Ancestry.

Beyond Pendulum Power: Entering the Energy World. Greg Nielsen. LC 88-70068. (Illus.). 153p. (Orig.). 1988. pap. 9.95 (*0-9619917-0-4*) Conscious Bks.

Beyond Perestroika. Ernest Mandel. 300p. 1988. 60.00 (*0-86091-223-X*, Pub. by Verso UK); pap. 18.95 (*0-86091-935-8*, Pub. by Verso UK) Routledge Chapman & Hall.

Beyond Perestroika: Challenges & Choices Facing Gorbachev. Ed. by Manohar L. Sondhi. (C). 1989. 18.00 (*81-7017-254-3*, Pub. by Abhinav II) S Asia.

Beyond Perestroika: The Future of Gorbachev's U. S. S. R. rev. ed. Ernest Mandel. Tr. by Gus Fagan. 300p. 1991. 64.95 (*0-86091-339-2*, A6355, Pub. by Verso UK); pap. 18.95 (*0-86091-549-2*, A6359, Pub. by Verso UK) Routledge Chapman & Hall.

Beyond Persuasion: Organizational Efficiency & Presidential Power. Matthew R. Kerbel. LC 90-42324. (Presidency: Contemporary Issues Ser.). 214p. (C). 1991. 59.50 (*0-7914-0693-8*); pap. 19.95 (*0-7914-0694-6*) State U NY Pr.

Beyond Pesticides: Biological Approaches to Pest Management in California. J. Patrick Madden et al. LC 92-61146. (Illus.). 220p. 1992. pap. 14.00 (*1-879906-10-4*, 3354) ANR Pubns CA.

Beyond-Physics: A Velocity Theory. Alexander Arzoumanian. LC 91-67797. 100p. (C). 1992. 12.95 (*0-9601206-2-9*) Persepolis NJ.

Beyond Piaget: A Philosophical Psychology. Jean-Claude Brief. (C). 1983. text ed. 18.95 (*0-8077-2739-3*) Tchrs Coll.

Beyond Picture Books. 2nd ed. Ed. by Bowker, R. R., Staff. 450p. 1995. 47.00 (*0-8352-3519-X*) Bowker. "...an outstanding sourcebook for librarians, educators, & parents...Highly recommended..."--ACADEMIC LIBRARY BOOK REVIEW. Encourage reading skills from the earliest age with this welcome companion to Bowker's classic A TO ZOO. The more than 2,500 first readers profiled all feature lively interaction of text & illustration, & present themes of interest to young children. Each entry offers a brief plot synopsis, critical evaluation, & comments about the illustrations; title, author, & illustrator information; details on publisher, series, & subjects; & more. A special list of 200 outstanding first readers makes collection development easy. There are five indexes: subject, title, illustrator, series, & reading level. ***Publisher Provided Annotation.***

Beyond Picture Books: A Guide to First Readers. Barbara Barstow & Judith Riggle. 354p. 1989. 43.00 (*0-8352-2515-1*) Bowker.

***Beyond Piety: Critical Essays on the Visual Arts, 1986-1993.** Jeremy Gilbert-Rolfe. (Cambridge Studies in New Art History & Criticism). (Illus.). 450p. (C). 1995. 80.00 (*0-521-46055-7*); pap. 29.95 (*0-521-46611-3*) Cambridge U Pr.

***Beyond Pink & Blue: Exploring Our Stereotypes of Sexuality & Gender.** Tracey Robinson-Harris & Ritch C. Sowin-Williams. 80p. 1994. 19.00 (*1-55896-322-7*) Unitarian Univ.

Beyond Playing Church. Michael Slaughter. 199p. (Orig.). 1993. pap. 9.95 (*0-917851-78-1*) Bristol Hse.

Beyond Polarization: Emerging Strategies for Reconciling Community & the Environment. Kirk Johnson. 59p. (Orig.). (C). 1993. pap. text ed. 25.00x (*1-56806-415-2*) Diane Pub.

Beyond Policy & Language Choice: An Analysis of Texts in Four Instructional Contexts in East Africa. Dennis M. Mbuyi. LC 87-6362. (Special Studies in Comparative Education: No. 18). 1987. pap. text ed. 10.00 (*0-937033-08-1*) SUNY GSE Pubns.

Beyond Polite Japanese: A Dictionary of Japanese Slang & Colloquialisms. Akihiko Yonekawa. (Power Japanese Ser.). 128p. (Orig.). 1993. pap. 10.00 (*4-7700-1539-9*) Kodansha.

Beyond Political Correctness: Are There Limits to This Lunacy? Thibodaux. LC 94-76352. 1994. pap. 9.99 (*1-56384-066-9*) Huntington Hse.

***Beyond Political Correctness: Toward the Inclusive University.** Ed. by Stephen Richer & Lorna Weir. 232p. 1995. pap. 17.95 (*0-8020-6010-2*) U of Toronto Pr.

Beyond Political Independence: Zambia's Development Predicament in the 1980's. Ed. by Klaas Woldring. xi, 252p. 1985. 75.40 (*3-11-009951-9*) Mouton.

Beyond Politics. Christopher H. Dawson. LC 74-111825. (Essay Index Reprint Ser.). 1977. 17.95 (*0-8369-1603-4*) Ayer.

***Beyond Politics: Markets, Welfare, & the Failure of Bureaucracy.** William C. Mitchell. (C). 1994. pap. text ed. 19.95 (*0-8133-2208-1*) Westview.

***Beyond Politics: Markets, Welfare, & the Failure of Bureaucracy.** William C. Mitchell. (C). 1994. text ed. 55.00 (*0-8133-2207-3*) Westview.

***Beyond Politics: The Meta-Historical View.** Solange Hertz. (Illus.). 236p. (Orig.). 1995. pap. 12.50 (*1-883511-06-2*) Veritas Pr CA.

Beyond Port & Prejudice: Charles Lloyd of Oxford, 1784-1829. William J. Baker. LC 76-24243. 1981. 20.00 (*0-89101-032-7*) U Maine Pr.

Beyond Positive Thinking: Core Beliefs & Identity. Henry M. Esposito. 90p. 1992. pap. 8.95 (*0-9631665-0-6*) Success Cnslt.

Beyond Positive Thinking: Putting Your Thoughts into Action. Arnold Fox & Barry Fox. Ed. by Dan Olmos. LC 91-71697. 256p. (Orig.). 1991. pap. 10.00 (*1-56170-020-7*, 134) Hay House.

716

An Asterisk (*) at the beginning of an entry indicates that the title is appearing in BIP for the first time.

Beyond Positivism: Critical Reflections on International Relations. Claire T. Sjolander & Wayne S. Cox. LC 93-33324. 206p. 1994. lib. bdg. 36.00 (*1-55587-483-5*) Lynne Rienner.

Beyond Positivism: Economic Methodology in the Twentieth Century. Bruce J. Caldwell. 288p. 1984. pap. text ed. 18.95 (*0-04-330342-0*) Routledge Chapman & Hall.

Beyond Positivism: Economic Methodology in the Twentieth Century. 2nd rev. ed. Bruce Caldwell. LC 93-48811. 304p. 1994. pap. 19.95 (*0-415-10911-6*, B3703, Routledge NY) Routledge.

Beyond Postmodern Politics: Selves, Community, & a Politics of Difference. Honi F. Haber. LC 93-48108. 1994. 49.95 (*0-415-90822-1*, Routledge NY); pap. 15.95 (*0-415-90823-X*, Routledge NY) Routledge.

***Beyond Poverty & Affluence: Toward an Economy of Care.** Bob Goudzwaard & Harry De Lange. Ed. & Tr. by Mark Vander Vennen. 160p. 1994. pap. 14.99 (*0-8028-0827-1*) Eerdmans.

Beyond Power: On Women, Men & Morals. Marilyn French. 1986. pap. 14.00 (*0-345-33405-1*, Ballantine Trade) Ballantine.

Beyond Prejudice. Toru Matsumoto. Ed. by Roger Daniels. LC 78-54826. (Asian Experience in North America Ser.). 1979. reprint ed. lib. bdg. 15.95 (*0-405-11283-1*) Ayer.

***Beyond Prejudice: The Moral Significance of Human & Nonhuman Animals.** Evelyn B. Pluhar. LC 95-865. 1995. write for info. (*0-8223-1634-X*); pap. write for info. (*0-08-223164-8*) Duke.

Beyond Preservation: Restoring & Inventing Landscapes. A. Dwight Baldwin, Jr. et al. 256p. 1993. text ed. 44.95 (*0-8166-2346-5*); pap. 16.95 (*0-8166-2347-3*) U of Minn Pr.

Beyond Prison Walls: The Jeris Bragan Story. Jeris E. Bragan. LC 93-12995. 1993. 16.95 (*0-8280-0716-0*) Review & Herald.

Beyond Pritikin. Ann L. Gittleman & John M. Desgrey. 240p. 1989. mass mkt. 5.99 (*0-553-27512-7*) Bantam.

Beyond Privatization: The Tools of Government Action. Ed. by Lester M. Salamon & Michael S. Lund. LC 88-27948. 284p. (Orig.). 1989. lib. bdg. 57.00 (*0-87766-455-2*); pap. text ed. 24.00 (*0-87766-454-4*) Urban Inst.

Beyond Problem Solving & Comprehension. Arthur Whimbey & Jack Lockhead. (Illus.). (C). 1984. teacher ed write for info. (*0-89859-740-4*); pap. text ed. 14.95 (*0-89859-742-0*) L Erlbaum Assocs.

***Beyond Programming: To a New Era of Design.** Bruce I. Blum. (Johns Hopkins Applied Physics Laboratory Series in Science & Engineering). (Illus.). 256p. 1995. 29.95 (*0-19-509160-4*) OUP.

Beyond Progress & Development. J. Berting & W. Blockmans. 110p. 1987. text ed. 59.95 (*0-566-05397-7*, Pub. by Avebury Pub UK) Ashgate Pub Co.

Beyond Prophecies & Predictions. Moira Timms. (Orig.). 1993. mass mkt. 5.99 (*0-345-36475-9*) Ballantine.

***Beyond Prospecting: Waking up the Natural Flow of Business.** Debra Whiddon. Ed. by Wendy Lackritz & Charles Munro. 180p. (Orig.). 1995. pap. text ed. 14.95 (*1-886112-04-5*) Antares.

***Beyond Prozac.** Michael Norden. 1995. 22.00 (*0-06-039151-0*, HarpT) HarpC.

Beyond Psychology. Otto Rank. pap. text ed. 6.95 (*0-486-20485-5*) Dover.

***Beyond Psychology: Letters & Journals, 1934-1939.** Wilhelm Reich. Ed. & Intro. by Mary B. Higgins. LC 94-14721. 1994. 25.00 (*0-374-11247-9*) FS&G.

Beyond Public Education. Myron Lieberman. LC 80-25571. 272p. 1985. text ed. 49.95 (*0-275-92039-9*, C2039, Praeger Pubs) Greenwood.

***Beyond Punishment.** Louis J. Marx. 200p. Date not set. pap. 8.95 (*0-7610-0426-2*) NW Pub.

Beyond Punishment: A New View on the Rehabilitation of Criminal Offenders. Edgardo Rotman. LC 89-37996. (Contributions in Criminology & Penology Ser.: No. 26). 229p. 1990. text ed. 55.00 (*0-313-26493-7*, RCI/, Greenwood Pr) Greenwood.

Beyond Punjab. Prakash Tandon. 215p. 1971. pap. 3.00 (*0-88253-731-8*) Ind-US Inc.

Beyond Putting the Toilet Seat Down: Four Hundred & Twenty-Three Real Comments from Men & Women. Jack York. 1992. pap. 83.40 (*0-9634739-1-3*) Armchair Pr.

Beyond Putting the Toilet Seat Down: Four Hundred Twenty-Three Real Comments from Men & Women about Their Relationships. Jack York & Brian Krueger. LC 92-74490. 224p. 1993. pap. 6.95 (*0-9634739-0-5*) Armchair Pr.

Beyond Quality. Jerry Bowles & Joshua Hammond. 256p. 1992. pap. 9.00 (*0-425-13408-3*) Berkley Pub.

***Beyond Quality: An Agenda for Improving Manufacturing Capabilities in Developing Countries.** Steven R. Wilson et al. 224p. 1995. 63.95 (*1-85898-120-4*, Pub. by E Elgar Pub UK) Ashgate Pub Co.

Beyond Quality Circles: The Path to Profits. Robert C. Wood. Ed. by Irving L. Blackman. (Special Report Ser.: No. 120). 37p. 1983. pap. 23.00 (*0-916181-21-9*) Blackman Kallick Bartelstein.

***Beyond Quebec: Taking Stock of Canada.** Ed. by Kenneth McRoberts. 464p. 1995. 44.95 (*0-7735-1301-9*) U of Toronto Pr.

***Beyond Quebec: Taking Stock of Canada.** Ed. by Kenneth McRoberts. 464p. 1995. pap. 22.95 (*0-7735-1314-0*) U of Toronto Pr.

Beyond Quick Fixes: Control Your Irresistible Urges Before They Control You. Georgia Witkin. 1991. pap. 4.95 (*0-425-12608-0*) Berkley Pub.

Beyond Race & Gender: Unleashing the Power of Your Total Work Force by Managing Diversity. R. Roosevelt Thomas, Jr. 208p. 1992. pap. 15.95 (*0-8144-7807-7*) AMACOM.

Beyond Rage: Mastering Unavoidable Health Changes. rev. ed. JoAnn LeMaistre. LC 93-36467. 208p. 1993. 24.95 (*0-931712-11-4*); audio 12.95 (*0-931712-12-2*) Alpine Guild.

***Beyond Ragnarok.** Mickey Z. Reichert. (Renshai Chronicles Ser.: Vol. 1). 688p. 1995. 21.95 (*0-88677-658-9*) DAW Bks.

Beyond Ramen Noodles: How to Feed Yourself When You Don't Have the Time, the Space, or the Equipment, & You Can't Afford to Eat Every Meal Out. Ima G. Maum, pseud. (Illus.). 132p. (Orig.). 1993. pap. 9.95 (*1-883770-00-9*, El Moro Pr) El Moro Pub.

Beyond Rational Management: Mastering the Paradoxes & Competing Demands of High Performance. Robert E. Quinn. LC 87-46339. (Management Ser.). 221p. 1988. 28.95x (*1-55542-075-3*) Jossey-Bass.

Beyond Rational Management: Mastering the Paradoxes & Competing Demands of High Performance. Robert E. Quinn. LC 87-46339. (Management Ser.). 221p. 1991. pap. 19.00 (*1-55542-377-9*) Jossey-Bass.

***Beyond Raton.** Paul Fontaine. Date not set. pap. write for info. (*1-885766-19-X*) Brand Cross.

Beyond Reagan. Paul Duke et al. LC 86-1508. 338p. 1986. pap. 9.95 (*0-446-37019-3*) Warner Bks.

Beyond Reaganomics: A Further Inquiry into the Poverty of Economics. Charles K. Wilber & Kenneth P. Jameson. LC 89-40745. (C). 1991. pap. text ed. 12.95 (*0-268-00686-5*) U of Notre Dame Pr.

Beyond Realism: Turgenev's Poetics of Secular Salvation. Elizabeth C. Allen. LC 91-19405. 288p. 1992. 37.50 (*0-8047-1873-3*) Stanford U Pr.

Beyond Realism & Marxism: Critical Theory & International Relations. Andrew Linklater. LC 89-32801. 212p. 1990. text ed. 49.95 (*0-312-03249-8*) St Martin.

Beyond Reality: The Role Unseen Dimensions Play in Our Lives. D. Scott Rogo. 1990. pap. 12.95 (*0-85030-886-0*) Thorsons SF.

Beyond Reason. Ken Englade. 1990. mass mkt. 4.95 (*0-312-92346-5*) St Martin.

Beyond Reason. John R. Rose. 432p. 1993. pap. 19.95 (*1-881170-03-9*) Rose Pub OR.

***Beyond Reason: A Factual Account of Possible Contact with the Supernatural.** Peter Jackson. 1995. 15.95 (*0-533-11422-5*) Vantage.

Beyond Reason: Essays on the Philosophy of Paul Feyerabend. Ed. by Gonzalo Munevar. 548p. (C). 1991. lib. bdg. 161.50 (*0-7923-1272-4*) Kluwer Ac.

Beyond Reasonable Doubt & Probable Cause: Historical Perspectives on the Anglo-American Law of Evidence. Barbara J. Shapiro. LC 92-5314. 352p. 1991. 42.50 (*0-520-07286-3*); pap. 15.00 (*0-520-08451-9*) U CA Pr.

Beyond Recognition: Representation, Power, & Culture. Craig Owens. 1992. 30.00 (*0-520-07739-3*) U CA Pr.

***Beyond Recognition: Representation, Power, & Culture.** Craig Owens. LC 92-5314. 1994. pap. 15.00 (*0-520-07740-7*) U CA Pr.

Beyond Recrimination: Perspectives on U. S. Taiwan Trade Tensions. Jimmy W. Wheeler & Perry L. Wood. 237p. (Orig.). 1987. pap. text ed. 25.00 (*1-55813-001-2*) Hudson Instit IN.

Beyond Reductionism. Theodore R. Malloch. 290p. 1983. text ed. 29.50 (*0-8290-1292-3*) Irvington.

***Beyond Reengineering: How the 21st Century Corporation Will Change our Work & Our Lives.** Michael Hammer. 1995. 25.00 (*0-88730-729-9*) Harper Busn.

***Beyond Regrets.** Guy Doud. 200p. 1996. 15.99 (*1-56476-386-2*, 6-3386, Victor Books) SP Pubns.

Beyond Regulation: The Informal Economy in Latin America. Ed. by Victor E. Tokman. LC 92-14361. 296p. 1992. lib. bdg. 40.00 (*1-55587-318-9*) Lynne Rienner.

Beyond Rejection: The Church, Homosexuality, & Hope. Don Baker. LC 85-8789. 95p. 1985. pap. 2.99 (*0-88070-340-7*, Multnomah Bks) Questar Pubs.

Beyond Relationships: Cultural Fantasy. Angela Barnett. 73p. 1993. write for info. (*0-925421-32-4*) Amer Intercultural.

Beyond Relativism: Science & Human Values. Roger D. Masters. LC 93-16925. (Illus.). 262p. 1993. 24.95 (*0-87451-634-X*) U Pr of New Eng.

***Beyond Relativity.** Niels Engle & Morten Engel. (Illus.). 160p. (C). 1994. pap. text ed. write for info. (*0-9641607-0-6*) Engel.

Beyond Relevancy: A Book for Teachers of the Future. Michael C. Giammatteo. (Illus.). (C). 1973. pap. 16.95 (*0-918428-09-2*) Sylvan Inst.

Beyond Representation: Chinese Painting & Calligraphy, 8th-14th Century. Wen C. Fong. (Illus.). 576p. (C). 1992. text ed. 85.00x (*0-300-05701-6*) Yale U Pr.

Beyond Reproach: Ethical Restrictions on the Extrajudicial Activities of State & Federal Judges. Steven Lubet. LC 84-45429. 66p. (Orig.). 1984. pap. 6.95 (*0-938870-35-1*, 8578) Am Judicature.

Beyond Rescue: New Poems. Lee Rossi. 72p. (Orig.). 1991. pap. 7.95 (*0-941017-19-2*) Bombshelter Pr.

Beyond Results: Still More Observations of a Chiropractic Advocate. William D. Esteb. 240p. 1994. pap. text ed. 24.95 (*0-9631711-2-7*) Back Talk Systs.

***Beyond Retention: A Study of Retention Rates, Practices, & Successful Alternatives in California - Summary Report.** (Illus.). 16p. 1993. pap. 4.25 (*0-8011-1079-3*) Calif Education.

Beyond Retention: A Survival Guide for the Regular Classroom Teacher. H. Wayne Light & Pam Morrison. Ed. by Betty L. Kratoville. (Illus.). 112p. (Orig.). 1990. pap. text ed. 15.00 (*0-87879-900-1*) Acad Therapy.

Beyond Revolution: A New Theory of Social Movements. Daniel A. Foss & Ralph W. Larkin. LC 85-20157. (Critical Perspectives in Social Theory Ser.). 192p. 1986. text ed. 45.00 (*0-89789-077-9*, Bergin & Garvey); pap. text ed. 14.95 (*0-89789-087-6*, Bergin & Garvey) Greenwood.

***Beyond Revolution: The Guide to Complete Political & Social Reform.** Phil Menges. 260p. (Orig.). 1994. pap. 14.95 (*0-9643663-0-4*) Outside NY.

Beyond Rhetoric: Fundamental Issues in Adult Literacy Education. Ed. by Thomas Valentine. (Orig.). 1994. write for info. (*0-89464-691-5*) Krieger.

***Beyond Rhetoric & Realism in Economics: Towards a Reformulation of Methodology.** Thomas A. Boylan & Paschal F. O'Gorman. LC 94-39813. (Economics As Social Theory Ser.). 340p. 1995. 59.95x (*0-415-08220-X*, C0290) Routledge.

***Beyond Rhetoric & Realism in Economics: Towards a Reformulation of Methodology.** Thomas A. Boylan & Paschal F. O'Gorman. (Economics As Social Theory Ser.). 340p. 1995. pap. 24.95 (*0-415-12513-8*, C0422) Routledge.

***Beyond Rio: The Environmental Issue & Sustainable Livelihoods in the Third World.** Ed. by Iftikhar Ahmed & Jacobus A. Doeleman. LC 95-13883. (ILO Ser.). 1995. write for info. (*0-312-12712-X*) St Martin.

Beyond Risk: Conversation with Climbers. Nicholas O'Connell. LC 93-22723. (Illus.). 256p. 1993. 19.95 (*0-89886-296-5*) Mountaineers.

Beyond Romanticism: New Approaches to Texts & Contexts. Ed. by Stephen Copley & John Whale. 272p. (Orig.). 1992. 77.50 (*0-415-05200-9*, A6074); pap. 16.95 (*0-415-05201-7*, A6078) Routledge.

Beyond Romanticism: Tuckerman's Life & Poetry. Eugene England. LC 90-24401. 314p. (C). 1991. 49.50 (*0-7914-0791-8*) State U NY Pr.

Beyond Rope & Fence. David Grew. 18.95 (*0-88411-658-1*, Amereon Hse) Amereon Ltd.

Beyond Safaris: A Guide to Building People-to-People Ties with Africa. Kevin Danaher. LC 91-70803. 1991. 39.95 (*0-86543-204-X*); pap. 12.95 (*0-86543-205-8*) Africa World.

Beyond Safe Boundaries. Margaret Sacks. (J). (gr. 4 up). 1990. pap. 4.99 (*0-14-034407-1*, Puffin) Puffin Bks.

Beyond Safe Places: Trusting God Through Life's Risks. Ruth Senter. LC 92-23899. 1992. 8.99 (*0-87788-084-0*) Shaw Pubs.

***Beyond Salvation.** Bob Currier. Ed. by Marge Ellison. 48p. 1995. pap. 8.00 (*0-8059-3667-X*) Dorrance.

Beyond Sambation: Selected Essays & Editorials, 1928-1955. A. M. Klein. Ed. by M. W. Steinberg & Usher Kaplan. (Collected Works of A. M. Klein). 1982. 35.00 (*0-8020-5566-4*) U of Toronto Pr.

Beyond Samosir: Recent Studies of the Batak Peoples of Sumatra. Ed. by Rita S. Kipp & Richard D. Kipp. LC 83-2248. (Papers in International Studies: Southeast Asia Ser.: No. 62). 164p. reprint ed. pap. 46.80 (*0-7837-6477-4*, 2046482) Bks Demand.

Beyond Sanctions: Reorienting U. S. Policy on Southern Africa. Michael Clough. (Critical Issues 1988 Ser.: No. 3). 32p. 1988. pap. 3.95 (*0-87609-033-1*) Coun Foreign.

***Beyond Sanity & Madness: The Way of Zen Master Dogen.** Dennis G. Merzel. 176p. (Orig.). 1994. pap. 14.95 (*0-8048-3035-5*) C E Tuttle.

Beyond Sarah & Sam: An Enlightened Guide to Jewish Baby Naming. Linda Rosenkrantz & Pamela R. Satran. 128p. (Orig.). 1992. pap. 8.95 (*0-312-06904-9*) St Martin.

Beyond Saru. T. A. Roberts. Ed. by Nancy Chirich. 264p. (Orig.). 1993. pap. 12.95 (*0-912761-38-5*) Cliffhanger Pr.

Beyond Schools: Education for Economic, Social & Personal Development. Ed. by Horace B. Reed & Elizabeth L. Loughran. LC 84-70668. (Illus.). 253p. (C). 1984. pap. text ed. 15.00 (*0-934210-10-1*) Devlp Commy.

Beyond Schools: Education for Economic, Social & Personal Development. Ed. by Horace B. Reed & Elizabeth L. Loughran. (Illus.). 266p. 1985. reprint ed. pap. text ed. 27.00 (*0-8191-5174-2*) U Pr of Amer.

Beyond Security: Private Perceptions among Arabs & Israelis. John E. Mroz. LC 80-82857. (Illus.). 230p. 1981. text ed. 46.00 (*0-08-027517-6*, Pergamon Pr); pap. text ed. 20.00 (*0-08-027516-8*, Pergamon Pr) Elsevier.

Beyond Security: Private Perceptions among Arabs & Israelis. John E. Mroz. 200p. 1980. 23.00 (*0-685-11730-8*); pap. 9.95 (*0-937722-00-6*) Intl Peace.

Beyond Seduction: A Return to Biblical Christianity. Dave Hunt. LC 86-80987. 1987. pap. 9.99 (*0-89081-558-5*) Harvest Hse.

Beyond Seeing & Hearing: Teaching Geography to Sensory Impaired Children - An Integrated Based Curriculum. Sona K. Andrews et al. (Pathways in Geography Ser.: No. 2). (Illus.). 62p. (Orig.). 1991. pap. text ed. 7.00 (*0-9627379-4-1*) NCFGE.

Beyond Self-Esteem: Developing a Genuine Sense of Human Value. Nancy E. Curry & Carl N. Johnson. LC 90-62662. (Research Monograph Ser.: No. 4). (Illus.). 177p. (Orig.). 1990. pap. text ed. 8.00 (*0-935989-39-0*, NAEYC #143) Natl Assn Child Ed.

Beyond Self-Help Housing. Ed. by Kosta Mathey. (Illus.). 432p. 1992. text ed. 90.00 (*0-7201-2047-0*, Mansell Pub) Cassell.

Beyond Self-Interest. Ed. by Jane J. Mansbridge. LC 89-38629. 332p. 1990. pap. text ed. 16.95 (*0-226-50360-7*) U Ch Pr.

Beyond Selling. Ed Reese. LC 87-63208. 1988. 19.95 (*0-916990-19-2*) META Pubns.

Beyond Separate Spheres: Intellectual Roots of Modern Feminism. Rosalind Rosenberg. LC 81-15967. (Illus.). 1983. pap. 15.00 (*0-300-03092-4*, Y-464) Yale U Pr.

***Beyond Separateness.** Schmitt. (C). 1995. pap. text ed. 14.95 (*0-8133-1250-7*) Westview.

Beyond Separateness: The Social Nature of Human Beings - Their Anatomy, Knowledge & Power. Richard Schmitt. 236p. (C). 1995. text ed. 48.50 (*0-8133-1224-8*) Westview.

Beyond Servanthood: Christianity & the Liberation of Women. Susan N. Dunfee. LC 88-27856. 192p. (Orig.). (C). 1989. lib. bdg. 38.00 (*0-8191-7223-5*); pap. text ed. 22.50 (*0-8191-7224-3*) U Pr of Amer.

Beyond Severe Disability: A Functional Bibliography. Lois S. Rood & Karen Faison. 32p. (Orig.). 1985. pap. 2.50 (*1-55719-014-3*) U NE CPAR.

Beyond Severe Disability: Models & Strategies for Change. Lois S. Rood. 43p. (Orig.). 1983. pap. 3.15 (*1-55719-006-2*) U NE CPAR.

Beyond Severe Disability: National Approaches & Networking Guide. Floyd T. Waterman et al. 305p. (Orig.). 1985. pap. 9.95 (*1-55719-018-6*) U NE CPAR.

Beyond Severe Disability: Nebraska Services Guide. Lois S. Rood. 38p. (Orig.). 1985. pap. 3.15 (*1-55719-013-5*) U NE CPAR.

Beyond Severe Disability: The Challenge of Private Enterprise. Lois S. Rood & Carole M. Davis. 38p. (Orig.). 1985. pap. 3.15 (*1-55719-015-1*) U NE CPAR.

Beyond Sex see **Tantric Sex**

Beyond Sex Roles: A Guide for the Study of Female Roles in the Bible. Gilbert G. Bilezikian. LC 84-73199. 264p. 1985. pap. 12.99 (*0-8010-0885-9*) Baker Bk.

Beyond Sexual Abuse: Therapy with Women Who Were Childhood Victims. Jehu. (Methods in Psychotherapy Ser.). 384p. 1988. text ed. 76.95 (*0-471-91913-6*) Wiley.

Beyond Sexuality: Feminism, Men's Liberation, Gender & Power, Sexuality, Class & Economics. Anslim. (Illus.). 115p. (Orig.). 1992. pap. 10.00 (*0-948984-24-4*, Pub. by Phoenix Pr UK) AK Pr Dist.

Beyond Shannon & Sean: An Enlightened Guide to Irish Baby Naming. Linda Rosenkrantz & Pamela R. Satran. 128p. 1992. pap. 8.95 (*0-312-06905-7*) St Martin.

Beyond Shyness: How to Conquer Social Anxieties. Jonathan Berent & Amy Lemley. 256p. 1993. 21.00 (*0-671-74137-3*) S&S Trade.

Beyond Shyness: How to Conquer Social Anxieties. Jonathan Berent. 1994. pap. 11.00 (*0-671-88525-1*, Fireside) S&S Trade.

Beyond Siberia. large type ed. Christina Dodwell. 1993. 39.95 (*0-7066-1027-X*, Pub. by Remploy Pr CN) St Mut.

Beyond Silenced Voices: Class, Race, & Gender in United States Schools. Ed. by Lois Weis & Michelle Fine. LC 91-46125. (SUNY Series, Frontiers in Education). 437p. (C). 1993. 59.50 (*0-7914-1285-7*); pap. 19.95 (*0-7914-1286-5*) State U NY Pr.

***Beyond Singleness.** Helena Wilkinson. Date not set. pap. 8.99 (*0-551-02902-1*) Zondervan.

***Beyond Skepticism: All the Way to Enlightenment.** Stephen H. Martin. 160p. (Orig.). 1995. pap. 11.95 (*0-9646601-4-8*) Oaklea Pr.

Beyond Socialist Realism: Soviet Fiction Since Ivan Denisovich. Geoffrey Hosking. LC 78-31891. 260p. (C). 1980. 45.00 (*0-8419-0484-7*) Holmes & Meier.

Beyond Southern Skies: Radio Astronomy & the Parkes Telescope. Peter Robertson. (Illus.). 336p. (C). 1992. 75.00 (*0-521-41408-3*) Cambridge U Pr.

***Beyond Sovereignty: Territory & Political Economy in the Twenty-First Century.** David J. Elkins. 288p. 1995. 50.00 (*0-8020-2940-X*); pap. 18.95 (*0-8020-7768-4*) U of Toronto Pr.

Beyond Sovereignty: The Challenge of Global Policy. Marvin S. Soroos. (Studies in International Relations). 398p. (Orig.). 1986. text ed. 39.95 (*0-87249-474-8*); pap. text ed. 21.95 (*0-87249-478-0*) U of SC Pr.

***Beyond Soviet Studies.** Ed. by Daniel Orlovsky. 400p. (Orig.). 1995. pap. text ed. 24.95x (*0-943875-69-2*) Johns Hopkins.

Beyond Sovietology: Essays in Politics & History. Ed. by Susan G. Solomon. LC 93-22211. (Contemporary Soviet - Post-Soviet Politics Ser.). 264p. 1993. 62.95 (*1-56324-221-4*) M E Sharpe.

Beyond Space. Pascal P. Parente. 1977. reprint ed. pap. 7.00 (*0-89555-053-9*) TAN Bks Pubs.

***Beyond Space & Time.** Dewey B. Larson. 385p. 1995. 30.00 (*0-913138-12-6*) North Pacific.

Beyond Spaceship Earth: Environmental Ethics & the Solar System. Ed. by Eugene C. Hargrove. (Illus.). 336p. (C). 1992. reprint ed. pap. 14.95 (*0-9626807-1-0*) Environ Ethics Bks.

Beyond Spinoff: Military & Commercial Technologies in a Changing World. John A. Alic et al. LC 91-36175. 448p. 1992. 35.00 (*0-87584-318-2*) Harvard Busn.

Beyond Spinoff: Military & Commercial Technologies in a Changing World. John A. Alic et al. 1992. text ed. 35.00 (*0-07-103365-3*) McGraw.

Beyond Spoon River: The Legacy of Edgar Lee Masters. Ronald Primeau. 230p. (C). 1981. text ed. 22.50 (*0-292-70731-2*) U of Tex Pr.

Beyond Spoon River: The Legacy of Edgar Lee Masters. Ronald Primeau. LC 80-25825. (Dan Danciger Publication Ser.). 231p. reprint ed. pap. 65.90 (*0-7837-5193-1*, 2044927) Bks Demand.

Beyond Sportdiving: Exploring the Deepwater Shipwrecks of the Atlantic. Brad Sheard. 208p. 1992. pap. 14.95 (*0-89732-105-7*) Menasha Ridge.

Beyond Spring: Tzu Poems of the Sung Dynasty. Tr. by Julie Landau. (Translations from the Asian Classics Ser.). 1994. write for info. (*0-231-09678-X*) Col U Pr.

Beyond Stalinism: Communist Political Evolution. Ed. by Ronald J. Hill. LC 92-12866. 180p. 1992. text ed. 29.50 (*0-7146-3463-8*, Pub. by F Cass Pubs UK) Intl Spec Bk.

An Asterisk (*) at the beginning of an entry indicates that the title is appearing in BIP for the first time.

Beyond Standardized Testing: Assessing Authentic Academic Achievement in the Secondary School. Doug A. Archbald & Fred M. Newmann. 73p. (Orig.). (C). 1988. pap. 9.00 (*0-88210-214-1*) Natl Assn Principals.

Beyond Star Wars. William F. Dankenbring. LC 78-60520. 1978. 10.95 (*0-917182-07-3*) Triumph Pub.

Beyond Status Offender Deinstitutionalization: Public Child Welfare Services for Troubled Adolescents in the 80's. George Thomas et al. 181p. 1980. 6.00 (*0-318-16341-1*, B4) Regional Inst Social Welfare.

Beyond Stereotypes: The Critical Analysis of Chicana Literature. Ed. by Maria Herrera-Sobek. LC 84-73316. 152p. 1985. 24.00 (*0-916950-54-9*); pap. 15.00 (*0-916950-55-7*) Biling Rev-Pr.

Beyond Stonehenge. Gerald S. Hawkins. (Reprints Ser.). 320p. 1989. 24.95 (*0-88029-295-4*) Dorset Pr.

Beyond Storybooks: Young Children & the Shared Book Experience. Judith P. Slaughter. LC 92-32773. 176p. 1993. pap. 15.00 (*0-87207-377-7*) Intl Reading.

Beyond Strategic Planning: How to Involve Nonprofit Boards in Growth & Change. Douglas C. Eadie. (Nonprofit Governance Ser.: No. 51). 23p. (Orig.). (C). 1993. pap. text ed. 14.00 (*0-925299-28-6*) Natl Ctr Nonprofit.

Beyond Structural Adjustment in Africa: The Political Economy of Sustainable & Democratic Development. Ed. by Julius E. Nyang'oro & Timothy M. Shaw. LC 91-47087. 192p. 1992. text ed. 49.95 (*0-275-94221-X*, C4221, Praeger Pubs) Greenwood.

B

Beyond Student Teaching. Ellen L. Kronowitz. 218p. (Orig.). (C). 1992. pap. text ed. 27.95 (*0-8013-0609-4*, 78542) Longman.

Beyond Subjective Morality: Ethical Reasoning & Political Philosophy. James S. Fishkin. LC 83-14701. 224p. 1986. 40.00x (*0-300-03048-7*); pap. 14.00x (*0-300-03625-6*, Y-569) Yale U Pr.

Beyond Subsistence: Plains Archaeology & the Postprocessual Critique. Ed. by Philip Duke & Michael C. Wilson. LC 94-11820. 320p. 1995. pap. 29.95 (*0-8173-0760-5*) U of Ala Pr.

Beyond Success: Corporations & Their Critics in the 1990s. James W. Kuhn & Donald W. Shriver, Jr. (Ruffin Series in Business Ethics). 352p. 1991. 38.00 (*0-19-506433-X*) OUP.

Beyond Success: How Volunteer Service Can Help You Begin Making a Life Instead of Just a Living. John F. Raynolds, III & Eleanor Raynolds. 1989. 19.95 (*0-942361-04-0*); pap. 9.95 (*0-942361-14-8*) MasterMedia Ltd.

***Beyond Success: The 15 Secrets of a Winning Life!** Brian D. Biro. (Illus.). 368p. 1995. 24.00 (*0-9647453-0-5*) Pygmalion MT.

***Beyond Success: The 15 Secrets to a Winning Life!** Brian D. Biro. (Illus.). 368p. 1995. pap. text ed. 14.00 (*0-9647453-1-3*) Pygmalion MT.

Beyond Success & Failure: Ways to Emotional Maturity. rev. ed. Willard Beecher & Marguerite Beecher. LC 66-24877. 230p. 1986. reprint ed. pap. 9.95 (*0-87516-569-9*) Beecher Found.
In BEYOND SUCCESS & FAILURE, the Beechers do not offer any panaceas, nor do they provide you with elaborate programs & disciplines. But they do help you to find your own direction & your own abilities to handle any & all confronting problems. They show how you can find your own center of gravity inside yourself & begin to know the satisfaction that flows from using your own talents & living as a responsible adult. Their book is dedicated to Dr. Alfred Adler, founder of Individual Psychology, who was their teacher the last years of his life, during which time he gave them their first understanding of human behavior. The Beechers state that there are eight concepts which rule the lives of all adults. They encourage each to use to the awakening touch of self-reliance to shape its parts & aspects. Only those who are self-reliant emotionally & physically can function as adult human beings able to cooperate with other adults, because life demands that we be useful & productive, or as Adler said, to "be a help & not a burden." TO ORDER CONTACT- Beecher Foundation, P.O. Box 833027, Richardson, TX 75083 DeVorss & Co., P.O. Box 550, Marina del Ray, CA 90294. ***Publisher Provided Annotation.***

Beyond Suffrage: Women in the New Deal. Susan Ware. LC 80-25265. (Illus.). 216p. 1981. 32.00 (*0-674-06921-8*) HUP.

Beyond Suffrage: Women in the New Deal. Susan Ware. 216p. 1987. pap. 12.95 (*0-674-06922-6*) HUP.

Beyond Summer. Karen Young. (Superromance Ser.: No. 472). 1991. mass mkt. 3.29 (*0-373-70472-0*) Harlequin Bks.

Beyond Superfailure: America's Toxics Policy for the 1990s. Daniel Mazmanian & David Morell. 278p. (C). 1992. pap. text ed. 20.95 (*0-8133-1467-4*) Westview.

Beyond Superfailure: America's Toxics Policy for the 1990s. Daniel Mazmanian & David Morell. 278p. 1992. text ed. 61.00 (*0-8133-1466-6*) Westview.

***Beyond Superfund: Voluntary Industrial Cleanup.** (State Legislative Reports Ser.: Vol. 19, No. 14). 5p. 1994. 5.00 (*1-55516-382-3*, 7302-1914) Natl Conf State Legis.

Beyond Superpower Rivalry: Latin America & the Third World. Ed. by John F. Weeks. 320p. 1991. text ed. 50.00x (*0-8147-9235-9*) NYU Pr.

Beyond Superstructuralism. Richard Harland. LC 92-31425. 224p. 1993. 49.95 (*0-415-06358-2*, A7834, Routledge NY); pap. 16.95 (*0-415-06359-0*, A7838, Routledge NY) Routledge.

Beyond Surrender. Joyce Myrus. 1988. pap. 3.95 (*0-8217-2525-4*) Zebra.

Beyond Survival. Gerald Coffee. 1991. mass mkt. 4.99 (*0-425-12442-8*) Berkley Pub.

Beyond Survival. Walter S. Smitson. (Illus.). 160p. (Orig.). 1988. pap. 10.00 (*0-910487-18-9*) Royalty Pub.

Beyond Survival: A Guide for the Business Owner & His Family. Leon A. Danco. LC 74-29583. (Illus.). 1975. 19.95 (*0-9603614-0-5*) Ctr Family Busn.

Beyond Survival: A Writing Journey for Healing Childhood Sexual Abuse. Maureen Brady. 256p. 1992. pap. 16.00 (*0-89486-809-8*, 5163A) Hazelden.

***Beyond Survival: Creating Prosperity Through People.** Robert B. Blaha. 184p. 1995. 19.95 (*1-880156-04-0*) Air Acad Pr.

Beyond Survival: New Directions for the Disarmament Movement. Ed. by Michael Albert & David Dellinger. 365p. 1983. pap. 12.00 (*0-89608-175-3*) South End Pr.

Beyond Survival: The New Testament Solution for Adult Children of Alcoholics. Nancy Curtis. 1990. 10.95 (*1-877717-01-0*) Accord Bks.

Beyond Survival: The Seven Dimensions of Life. Keith Conning. 180p. 1993. 9.95 (*0-8059-3338-7*) Dorrance.

***Beyond Survival: Wage Labor & Capital in the Late Twentieth Century.** Ed. by Cyrus Bina et al. (Labor & Human Resources Ser.). 320p. 1995. 55.00 (*1-56324-515-9*) M E Sharpe.

***Beyond Survival: Wage Labor & Capital in the Late Twentieth Century.** Ed. by Cyrus Bina et al. (Labor & Human Resources Ser.). 320p. 1995. pap. text ed. 24.95 (*1-56324-516-7*) M E Sharpe.

***Beyond Survival to Victory: A Practical Guide for Victorious Christian Living.** Leon C. Price. 96p. 1993. pap. 6.00 (*0-9637311-0-6*) Evergreen AL.

Beyond Symbolism: Textual History & the Future of Reading. Kevin Newmark. LC 91-55056. 256p. 1991. 34.95 (*0-8014-2577-8*) Cornell U Pr.

Beyond Sympathy: What to Say & Do for Someone Suffering an Injury, Illness or Loss. 2nd ed. Janice H. Lord. 192p. (C). 1990. reprint ed. lib. bdg. 31.00x (*0-8095-5904-8*) Borgo Pr.

Beyond Sympathy: What to Say & Do for Someone Suffering an Injury, Illness or Loss. 2nd ed. Janice H. Lord. Ed. by Eugene D. Wheeler. LC 88-61044. 192p. 1989. pap. 11.95 (*0-934793-21-2*) Pathfinder CA.

Beyond Symptom Suppression: Improving Long-Term Outcomes of Schizophrenia. Committee on Psychopathology Staff. Ed. by Group for the Advancement of Psychiatry Staff. LC 91-26231. 125p. 1992. text ed. 27.50 (*0-87318-202-2*) Am Psychiatric.

Beyond Tacos: Mexican Cuisine. Regina Akers & Herb Weiner. 68p. 1984. pap. 7.50 (*0-937383-00-7*) Kitchen Wisdom.

Beyond Teaching & Learning: Ways to Profoundly Improve the Experience & Results of Learning. 2nd ed. Win Wenger. (Compendium of Enhanced Learning Techniques Ser.). (Illus.). 315p. (Orig.). (C). 1992. pap. text ed. 29.95 (*0-931865-04-2*) Psychegenics.

***Beyond Technique: An Individualized Approach to Psychotherapy.** Lawrence LeShan. 1996. 30.00 (*1-56821-550-9*) Aronson.

***Beyond Telling.** Jewel Mogan. LC 94-39166. 173p. 1995. 19.95 (*0-86538-082-1*) Ontario Rev NJ.

Beyond Terman: Contemporary Longitudinal Studies of Giftedness & Talent. Ed. by Rena F. Subotnik & Karen D. Arnold. LC 93-25250. 1993. 65.25 (*1-56750-082-X*); pap. 24.50 (*1-56750-011-0*) Ablex Pub.

Beyond Terminal Cancer. Jay Van Rensselaer. 1994. 16.95 (*0-533-10885-3*) Vantage.

Beyond Terror. Barbara Siegal & Scott Siegal. Ed. by Patricia MacDonald. (Ghostworld Ser.). 160p. (Orig.). (J). 1991. pap. 3.50 (*0-671-70904-6*, Archway) PB.

Beyond Terrorism. Jenny Hocking. 192p. 1993. pap. text ed. 19.95 (*1-86373-360-4*, Pub. by Allen Unwin AT) Paul & Co Pubs.

***Beyond Terrorism: New Hope for Kashmir.** Salman Khurshid. (C). 1995. 15.00x (*81-7476-019-9*, Pub. by UBS Pubs Dist II) S Asia.

***Beyond Testing: Towards a Theory of Educational Assessment.** Caroline Gipps. LC 94-27621. 202p. 1994. 75.00x (*0-7507-0328-8*, Falmer Pr); pap. 29.00x (*0-7507-0329-6*, Falmer Pr) Taylor & Francis.

***Beyond Textuality: Asceticism & Violence in Anthropological Interpretation.** Ed. by Gilles Bibeau & Ellen Corin. (Approaches to Semiotics Ser.: No. 120). xiv, 364p. (C). 1994. lib. bdg. 136.95 (*3-11-013889-1*) Mouton.

Beyond That Further Hill. Macdonald Carey. 121p. (Orig.). 1989. pap. 9.95 (*0-87249-621-X*) U of SC Pr.

Beyond Thatcherism: Social Policy, Politics & Society. Ed. by Phillip Brown. 192p. 1989. pap. 29.00 (*0-335-09903-3*, Open Univ Pr) Taylor & Francis.

***Beyond the Absolute Limit.** Stan Kellner. (Illus.). 224p. 1995. pap. 14.95 (*0-9644175-0-2*) Yes I Can.

Beyond the Acropolis: A Rural Greek Past. Tjeerd H. Van Andel & Curtis N. Runnels. (Illus.). 236p. 1995. 39.50x (*0-8047-1389-8*) Stanford U Pr.

***Beyond the Acropolis: A Rural Greek Past.** Tjeerd H. Van Andel & Curtis N. Runnels. (Illus.). 236p. 1995. pap. 14.95 (*0-8047-2621-3*) Stanford U Pr.

Beyond the Adirondacks: The Story of St. Regis Paper Company. Eleanor Amigo & Mark Neuffer. LC 80-1798. (Contributions in Economics & Economic History Ser.: No. 35). (Illus.). xi, 219p. 1980. text ed. 55.00 (*0-313-22735-7*, AFN/, Greenwood Pr) Greenwood.

Beyond the Aegean. Elia Kazan. 1994. 25.00 (*0-679-42565-9*) Knopf.

Beyond the Age of Waste: A Report to the Club of Rome. 2nd ed. D. Gabor et al. LC 80-41614. (Illus.). 265p. 1981. text ed. 108.00 (*0-08-027303-3*, Pub. by Pergamon Repr UK) Franklin.

***Beyond the Amber Waves of Grain: An Examination of Social & Economic Restructuring in the Heartland.** Paul Lasley et al. (Rural Studies Ser.). 256p. (C). 1995. pap. text ed. 39.95 (*0-8133-8930-5*) Westview.

Beyond the American Housing Dream: Accommodation to the 1980s. Kenneth R. Tremblay, Jr. & Don A. Dillman. LC 83-9269. (Illus.). 166p. (C). 1983. 52.00 (*0-8191-3478-3*); pap. text ed. 24.50 (*0-8191-3479-1*) U Pr of Amer.

Beyond the American Revolution: Explorations in the History of American Radicalism. Ed. by Alfred F. Young. LC 92-42367. 377p. (C). 1993. lib. bdg. 35.00 (*0-87580-176-5*); pap. text ed. 15.00 (*0-87580-557-4*) N Ill U Pr.

Beyond the Ancient Cities. Jose Maria Merino. Tr. by Helen Lane. LC 93-35482. (J). 1994. 16.00 (*0-374-34307-1*) FS&G.

Beyond the Angry Black. Ed. by John A. Williams. LC 66-28491. 198p. 1966. 32.50 (*0-8154-0260-0*) Cooper Sq.

Beyond the Arab-Israeli Settlement: New Directions for U. S. Policy in the Middle East. R. K. Ramazani. LC 77-87564. (Foreign Policy Reports). 69p. 1977. 11.95 (*0-89549-006-4*) Inst Foreign Policy Anal.

Beyond the Archipelago: Selected Poems. Muhammad H. Salleh. (Monographs in International Studies, Southeast Asia Ser.: No. 93). 247p. (Orig.). (MAY.). (C). 1994. pap. text ed. 20.00 (*0-89680-181-0*) Ohio U Pr.

Beyond the Art Gallery. Picton Publishing (Chippenham) Ltd. Staff. (C). 1987. 50.00 (*0-948251-08-5*, Pub. by Picton UK) St Mut.

Beyond the Ashes: Cases of Reincarnation from the Holocaust. Yonassan Gershom. Ed. by Jon Robertson. 317p. (Orig.). 1992. pap. 11.95 (*0-87604-293-0*, 374) ARE Pr.

Beyond the Aspen Grove. Ann Zwinger. LC 87-34274. 345p. 1988. reprint ed. pap. 16.95 (*0-8165-1054-7*) U of Ariz Pr.

Beyond the Astral Planes. Solitaire Parke. (Larger World Trilogy Ser.). (Illus.). 245p. (C). 1994. text ed. 21.95 (*1-885431-00-7*) Gray Wolf Prods.

Beyond the Bake Sale: An Educator's Guide to Working with Parents & Citizens. National Committee for Citizens in Education. 160p. 1986. 10.95 (*0-934460-22-1*) NCCE.

***Beyond the Balance Sheet: The Integration of Work, Personal & Family Life.** Business Executives for Economic Justice. 48p. (Orig.). 1994. pap. 3.95 (*0-87946-100-4*) ACTA Pubns.

Beyond the Ballot Box: A Social History of the Boston Irish, 1845-1917. Dennis P. Ryan. LC 89-5157. (Illus.). 176p. (Orig.). (C). 1989. reprint ed. pap. 12.95x (*0-87023-683-0*) U of Mass Pr.

Beyond the Barricades: South Africa in the 1980s. (Illus.). 126p. (Orig.). 1989. pap. 24.95 (*0-89381-375-3*) Aperture.

Beyond the Barricades: The Sixties Generation Grows Up. Jack Whalen & Richard Flacks. 324p. 1990. pap. 18.95 (*0-87722-707-1*) Temple U Pr.

***Beyond the Barrier: Book of Worlds.** (Mage). Date not set. 20.00 (*1-56504-434-7*) White Wolf.

Beyond the Barrier: The Story of Byrd's First Expedition to Antarctica. Eugene Rodgers. LC 89-28450. 320p. 1990. 25.95 (*0-87021-022-X*) Naval Inst Pr.

Beyond the Barriers Toward Two Thousand A. D. 8.00 (*0-942511-39-5*) OICJ.

Beyond the Bars: A Journey of Faith in the Modern World. Stephen C. Mahowald. 128p. (Orig.). 1989. pap. 6.95 (*0-685-25936-6*) Goals Unlimited.

Beyond the Bars: The Zoo Dilemma. Ed. by Virginia McKenna et al. 208p. (C). 1988. reprint ed. lib. bdg. 31.00x (*0-8095-7076-9*) Borgo Pr.

Beyond the Basics: A Text for Advanced Legal Writing. Mary B. Ray & Barbara J. Cox. 427p. 1993. reprint ed. pap. text ed. 22.00 (*0-314-85410-X*) West Pub.

Beyond the Basics: A Text for Advanced Legal Writing. Mary B. Ray & Barbara J. Cox. 375p. (C). 1993. reprint ed. teacher ed, pap. text ed. write for info. (*0-314-92269-5*) West Pub.

Beyond the Basics: Innovative Techniques for Nature Photography. George D. Lepp. 156p. 1993. pap. 32.95 (*0-9637313-0-0*) Lepp & Assocs.

***Beyond the Basics: Maintaining & Optimizing Netware Three Servers.** Edward Liebing. (Illus.). 360p. (Orig.). 1995. pap. 29.95 (*0-9645751-0-8*) SevenL Pr.

Beyond the Basics (Concepts in Advanced Meteorology for Aviation) Preliminary Edition. John Holley. 128p. (C). 1994. 16.95 (*0-8403-9278-8*) Kendall-Hunt.

Beyond the Basics of Reengineering: Survival Tactics for the '90s. Industrial Engineering & Management Press Staff. (Illus.). 237p. 1994. 29.95 (*0-89806-138-5*) Ind Eng Mgmt Pr.

***Beyond the Basics of Reengineering: Survival Tactics for the 90's.** Institute of Industrial Engineers Staff. 250p. 1994. text ed. 29.95 (*0-527-76257-1*, 762571) Qual Resc.

Beyond the Basilica: Christians & Muslims in Nazareth. Chad F. Emmett. (Illus.). 336p. 1994. pap. text ed. 22.00 (*0-226-20711-0*) U Ch Pr.

Beyond the Bay. Illus. by Paul Brent. 352p. 1985. 13.95 (*0-9615014-1-3*) Bay Pubns.

Beyond the Beachhead: The Twenty-Ninth Infantry Division in Normandy. Joseph Balkoski. LC 88-21903. (Illus.). 320p. 1989. 19.95 (*0-8117-0221-9*) Stackpole.

Beyond the Beauty Strip: Saving What's Left of Our Forests. Mitch Lansky. (Illus.). 400p. (Orig.). 1992. 35.00 (*0-88448-103-4*); pap. 19.95 (*0-88448-094-1*) Tilbury Hse.

Beyond the Beginning: A Reader in English. Mary M. Church et al. 128p. (C). 1990. pap. text ed. 11.25 (*0-13-068164-4*) P-H.

Beyond the Beltway: Engaging the Public in U.S. Foreign Policy. Ed. by Daniel Yankelovich & I. M. Destler. 288p. 1994. 28.00 (*0-393-03598-0*) Norton.

Beyond the Bend. Gretta P. Gossett. (Illus.). 502p. 1980. 19.95 (*0-87770-213-6*) Ye Galleon.

Beyond the Bend in the River: African Labor in Eastern Zaire, 1865-1940. David Northrup. (Monographs in International Studies, Africa Ser.: No. 52). 195p. 1988. pap. text ed. 15.00 (*0-89680-151-9*, Ohio U Ctr Intl) Ohio U Pr.

Beyond the Best Interests of the Child. Joseph Goldstein et al. LC 79-7630. 1980. 19.95 (*0-02-912200-7*); pap. 9.95 (*0-02-912190-6*) Free Pr.

Beyond the Best Interests of the Child. Joseph Goldstein et al. 1984. pap. 13.95 (*0-02-912360-7*) Free Pr.

Beyond the Big Bang: Ancient Myth & the Science of Continuous Creation. Paul LaViolette. (Illus.). 288p. 1995. 29.95 (*0-89281-457-8*) Inner Tradit.

Beyond the Big Bang - Quantum Cosmologies & God. Willem Drees. LC 90-38498. 344p. 1990. 44.95 (*0-8126-9117-2*); pap. 19.95 (*0-8126-9118-0*) Open Court.

Beyond the Bilingual Classroom: Literacy Acquisition among Peruvian Amazon Communities. LC 93-60646. (Publications in Linguistics: No. 117). x, 162p. 1993. pap. 18.00 (*0-88312-615-X*); fiche 12.00 (*0-88312-911-6*) Summer Instit Ling.

Beyond the Billable Hour: An Anthology of Alternative Billing Methods. 227p. 1989. pap. 79.95 (*0-89707-428-9*, 511-0260) Amer Bar Assn.

***Beyond the Biomass: Compositional & Functional Analysis of Soil Microbial Communities.** Ed. by K. Ritz et al. 1994. text ed. 95.00 (*0-471-95096-3*) Wiley.

Beyond the Bird Feeder: The Habits & Behavior of Feeding Station Birds When They Are Not at Your Feeder. John V. Dennis. LC 81-47491. (Illus.). 224p. 1981. 25.00 (*0-394-50890-4*) Knopf.

Beyond the Black Ocean: A Story of Social Revolution. Thomas McGrady. LC 75-154450. (Utopian Literature Ser.). 1976. reprint ed. 25.95 (*0-405-03532-2*) Ayer.

Beyond the Blank Page. Michael Hogan. 1993. 15.70 (*0-536-58376-5*) Ginn Pr.

Beyond the Blast Furnace. Amit Chatterjee. LC 93-13331. 1993. 195.00 (*0-8493-6676-3*, TN706) CRC Pr.

Beyond the Blue Event Horizon, No. 2. Frederik Pohl. 1987. mass mkt. 4.95 (*0-345-35046-4*, Del Rey) Ballantine.

Beyond the Blue Horizon: Myths & Legends of the Sun, Moon, Stars, & Planets. Edwin C. Krupp. (Illus.). 400p. 1992. 18.95 (*0-19-507800-4*) OUP.

Beyond the Blue Mountains. Jane W. Joyce. LC 92-71663. (Illus.). 112p. (Orig.). 1992. pap. 10.50 (*0-917788-52-4*) Gnomon Pr.

Beyond the Blue Ridge. Paul W. Olson. (Illus.). (Orig.). 1990. pap. write for info. (*1-879077-50-7*) Olson Pub Co.

Beyond the Boardwalk. Rod McKuen. 1976. 5.95 (*0-910368-01-5*); 12.50 (*0-686-14426-0*); pap. 3.95 (*0-686-14427-9*) Cheval Bks.

Beyond the Body. Wilma Wake. 304p. 1983. pap. 2.95 (*0-8439-2036-X*) Dorchester Pub Co.

Beyond the Body: An Investigation of Out-of-the-Body Experiences. Susan J. Blackmore. (Illus.). 256p. 1992. pap. 13.00 (*0-89733-344-6*) Academy Chi Pubs.

Beyond the Bomb, Living Without Nuclear Weapons: A Field Guide to Alternative Strategies for Building a Stable Peace. Mark Sommer. (Illus.). (Orig.). 1986. pap. 7.95 (*0-936391-00-6*); pap. text ed. 7.95 (*0-936391-01-4*) Expro Pr.

Beyond the Book: Extending MARC for Subject Access. Ed. by Toni Petersen & Pat Molholt. (Professional Librarian Ser.). 230p. 1990. text ed. 39.95 (*0-8161-1924-4*, Hall Reference); pap. 27.50 (*0-8161-1925-2*, Hall Reference) Macmillan.

Beyond the Books: Reflections on Learning & Teaching. Francis R. Hart. 1989. pap. 18.95 (*0-8142-0520-8*) Ohio St U Pr.

Beyond the Booze Battle. Ruth Maxwell. 1988. mass mkt. 4.95 (*0-345-35474-5*) Ballantine.

Beyond the Border: A New Age in Latin American Women's Fiction. Ed. by Nora Erro-Peralta & Caridad Silva-Nunez. 320p. (Orig.). (C). 1991. 24.95 (*0-939416-42-5*); pap. 12.95 (*0-939416-43-3*) Cleis Pr.

Beyond the Border: Mexico & the U. S. Today. Peter Baird & Ed McCaughan. (Illus.). 205p. 1979. pap. 5.95 (*0-916024-37-7*) NA Cong Lat Am.

Beyond the Bottom Line. William Lawrence. 1994. pap. 9.99 (*0-8024-1082-0*) Moody.

***Beyond the Bottom Line: A Painless Look at Finance & Accounting for the Nonfinancial Executive.** Charles A. Alessandrini & I. Gregg Van Wert. Ed. by Robert F. Guder. (The Practical Executive's Bookshelf Ser.). 146p. 1995. 14.95 (*0-910187-09-6*) Economics Pr.

Beyond the Bottom Line: Advanced Financial Knowledge for Managers. Alan Warner. 231p. 1992. 39.95 (*0-566-07265-3*, Pub. by Gower UK) Ashgate Pub Co.

Beyond the Bottom Line: How Business Leaders Are Turning Principles into Profits. Tad Tuleja. LC 84-1571. 240p. reprint ed. pap. 68.40 (*0-7837-2673-2*, 2043044) Bks Demand.

An Asterisk (*) at the beginning of an entry indicates that the title is appearing in BIP for the first time.

B

Beyond the Great South Wall: The Secret of the Antarctic. Frank Savile. reprint ed. spiral bd. 13.20 (*0-7873-0741-6*) Mokelumne.

***Beyond the Great Story: History As Text & Discourse.** Robert F. Berkhofer, Jr. LC 95-2005. (Illus.). 392p. (C). 1995. text ed. 39.95 (*0-674-06907-2*) Belknap Pr.

***Beyond the Great Wall: Urban Form & Transformation on the Chinese Frontiers.** Piper R. Gaubatz. LC 95-2555. 1996. write for info. (*0-8047-2399-0*) Stanford U Pr.

Beyond the Green Revolution: New Approaches for Third World Agriculture. Edward C. Wolf. LC 86-51251. (Worldwatch Papers). 48p. (Orig.). 1986. pap. 5.00 (*0-916468-74-7*) Worldwatch Inst.

Beyond the Guru. Y. P. Dhawan. 227p. 1980. pap. 3.25 (*0-86578-060-9*) Ind-US Inc.

Beyond the Gutenberg Galaxy: Microcomputers & the Emergence of Post-Typographic Culture. Eugene F. Provenzo. LC 86-1938. 128p. (Orig.). reprint ed. pap. 36.50 (*0-7837-4629-6*, 2044352) Bks Demand.

Beyond the Hero: Classic Stories of Men in Search of Soul. Allan B. Chinen. LC 92-31732. 304p. 1993. 21.95 (*0-87477-737-2*) J P Tarcher.

Beyond the Hidden Pain of Abortion. Patricia A. Bigliardi. 236p. 1994. pap. 9.95 (*1-56616-011-1*) Aglow Communs.

***Beyond the Hill: A Directory of Congress from 1984 to 1993 Where Have All the Members Gone?** Rebecca Borders & C. C. Dockery. 232p. (Orig.). (C). 1995. lib. bdg. 46.50 (*0-8191-9819-6*); pap. text ed. 19.50 (*0-8191-9820-X*) U Pr of Amer.

Beyond the Himalayas. M. MacDonald-Bayne. 1973. 250.00 (*0-87968-063-6*) Gordon Pr.

Beyond the Hoppo Ryodo: Japanese-Soviet-American Relations in the 1990s. Ed. by Jo D. Jacob. (Special Analysis Ser.). 60p. (C). 1991. pap. text ed. 9.75 (*0-8447-7009-4*, AEI Pr) Am Enterprise.

***Beyond the Horizon.** Amma Darko. (African Writers Ser.). 1995. pap. 9.95 (*0-435-90990-8*, 90990) Heinemann.

***Beyond the Horizon.** Valerie Hearder. Ed. by Barbara Koncak-Kuhn. (Illus.). 80p. 1995. pap. text ed. 21.95 (*1-57120-001-0*, 10123) C & T Pub.

Beyond the Horizon. Connie Mason. 448p. (Orig.). 1990. pap. 4.50 (*0-8439-3029-2*) Dorchester Pub Co.

***Beyond the Horizon.** Connie Mason. (Women West Ser.). 448p. 1995. mass mkt., pap. text ed. 5.99 (*0-8439-3798-X*) Dorchester Pub Co.

Beyond the Horizon. Eugene O'Neill. 1948. pap. 4.75 (*0-8222-0112-7*) Dramatists Play.

***Beyond the Horizon.** Eugene O'Neill. 1994. lib. bdg. 21.95x (*1-56849-514-5*) Buccaneer Bks.

Beyond the Horizon: A Pathologist's Life. Joseph Song. 1994. 18.95 (*0-533-10992-2*) Vantage.

Beyond the Horizon: Adventures in Faraway Lands. Ed. by Toni Eugene. (Special Publications Series 26: No. 4). (Illus.). 1992. 12.95 (*0-87044-831-5*) Natl Geog.

***Beyond the Horizon: Combat Aircraft of the Next Century.** Philip Handleman. (Illus.). 160p. 1994. 19.95 (*0-87938-963-X*) Motorbooks Intl.

Beyond the Horizon: Overcoming the Fear of Death. Charles G. Branz. 64p. 1991. 4.95 (*0-9629500-0-9*) C G Branz Min.

Beyond the Horizon of the Pacific. Yasuhiro Nakasone. (CISA Working Paper Ser.: No. 63). 21p. (Orig.). Date not set. pap. 10.00 (*0-86682-080-9*) Ctr Intl Relations.

Beyond the Horizons, 6 vols., Set. (J). (gr. 4-7). 1994. lib. bdg. 95.76 (*0-8114-7257-4*) Raintree Steck-V.

Beyond the Hot Seat: Gestalt Approaches to Group. Ed. by Ruth Ronall. 272p. 1994. reprint ed. pap. 20.00 (*0-939266-13-X*) Gestalt Journal.

Beyond the Hotline: Controlling a Nuclear Crisis. William L. Ury & Richard Smoke. 87p. (Orig.). 1984. pap. 4.00 (*0-9613615-0-6*, TX 1-333-518) Nuclear Project.

Beyond the Hundredth Meridian: John Wesley Powell & the Second Opening of the West. Wallace Stegner. (Illus.). 464p. 1992. pap. 12.95 (*0-14-015994-0*, Penguin Bks) Viking Penguin.

Beyond the Hype: Illusion & Reality in Real Estate Sales, Why 95 Percent of the Agents are Doomed to Failure & How the Successful Ones Destroy Their Lives. Pat Lawrence. 284p. (Orig.). 1991. pap. 19.95 (*0-9630082-0-X*) Hazelhurst.

Beyond the Hype: Rediscovering the Essence of Management. Robert Eccles. 1994. pap. text ed. 14.95 (*0-07-103588-5*) McGraw.

Beyond the Hype: Rediscovering the Essence of Management. Robert G. Eccles et al. LC 92-18707. 304p. 1992. 29.95 (*0-87584-331-X*) Harvard Busn.

Beyond the Hype: Rediscovering the Essence of Management. Robert G. Eccles. 1994. pap. 14.95 (*0-87584-506-1*) Harvard Busn.

Beyond the Hype: Rediscovering the Essence of Management. Robert G. Eccles, Jr. & Nittin Nohria. 1992. text ed. 24.95 (*0-07-103381-5*) McGraw.

Beyond the Icefall: Australian Everest Expedition. Sorrel Wilby. (Illus.). 160p. 1989. 35.00 (*0-938567-16-0*) Cloudcap.

Beyond the Impasse? Robison B. James & David S. Dockery. (Orig.). 1992. pap. 15.99 (*0-8054-6036-5*) Broadman.

***Beyond the Impasse: New Directions in Development Theory.** Schuurman. 1993. pap. 22.50 (*1-85649-210-9*, Pub. by Zed Books UK) Humanities.

Beyond the Impasse: New Directions in Development Theory. Ed. by Frans J. Schuurman. 256p. 1993. pap. 22.50 (*1-85649-501-9*, Pub. by Zed Books UK) Humanities.

Beyond the Impasse: New Directions in Development Theory. Ed. by Frans J. Schuurman. 256p. (C). 1993. text ed. 55.00 (*1-85649-209-5*, Pub. by Zed Books UK) Humanities.

Beyond the Individual: Environmental Approaches & Prevention. Ed. by Abraham Wandersman & Robert Hess. LC 85-14154. (Prevention in Human Services Ser.: Vol. 4, Nos. 1-2). 211p. 1985. text ed. 39.95 (*0-86656-391-1*) Haworth Pr.

Beyond the INF Treaty: Arms, Arms Control, & the Atlantic Alliance. Richard N. Haass. LC 88-5583. (Occasional Papers Ser.: No. 3). 78p. (Orig.). (C). 1988. lib. bdg. 29.00 (*0-8191-6941-2*, HU Ctr Sci); pap. text ed. 9.00 (*0-8191-6942-0*, HU Ctr Sci) U Pr of Amer.

Beyond the Informal Sector: Including the Excluded in Developing Countries. Ed. by Jerry Jenkins. (Sequoia Seminar Publication). 250p. (C). 1988. 29.95 (*1-55815-039-0*); pap. 12.95 (*1-55815-038-2*) ICS Pr.

Beyond the Information Given: Studies in the Psychology of Knowing. Jerome S. Bruner. Ed. by Jeremy M. Anglin. (Illus.). (C). 1973. pap. text ed. 10.95 (*0-393-09363-8*) Norton.

***Beyond the Information Systems Outsourcing Bandwagon: Downsizing, Rightsizing, Outsourcing...Insourcing?** Mary C. Lacity & Rudy Hirschheim. LC 95-12057. (Information Systems Ser.). 1995. text ed. 55.00 (*0-471-95822-0*) Wiley.

Beyond the Inner & the Outer: Wittgenstein's Philosophy of Psychology. Michel Ter Hark. Tr. by Anthony P. Runia. (Synthese Library: No. 214). 356p. 1990. lib. bdg. 102.50 (*0-7923-0850-6*) Kluwer Ac.

Beyond the Inner City. David Byrne. 176p. 1989. 90.00 (*0-335-15872-2*, Open Univ Pr); pap. 34.00 (*0-335-15871-4*, Open Univ Pr) Taylor & Francis.

***Beyond the Innocence of Childhood: Helping Children & Adolescents Cope with Threat to Their Lives, Dying, Death & Bereavement, 3 vols., Set.** Ed. by David Adams & Ellie Deveau. 1995. write for info. (*0-614-03979-7*) Baywood Pub.

***Beyond the Innocence of Childhood: Helping Children & Adolescents Cope with Threat to Their Lives, Dying, Death & Bereavement, 3 vols., Set.** Ed. by David W. Adams & Ellie J. Deveau. (Death, Value & Meaning Ser.). (C). 1995. text ed. write for info. (*0-614-02642-3*) Baywood Pub.

***Beyond the Innocence of Childhood: Helping Children & Adolescents Cope with Threat to Their Lives, Dying, Death & Bereavement, 3 vols., Set.** Ed. by David W. Adams & Ellie J. Deveau. (Death, Value & Meaning Ser.). (C). 1995. pap. text ed. write for info. (*0-614-02643-1*) Baywood Pub.

Beyond the Inverted Pyramid: Effective Writing for Newspapers, Magazines, & Specialized Publications. George Kennedy et al. LC 92-50036. 276p. (C). 1992. pap. text ed. 25.00 (*0-312-04058-X*) St Martin.

Beyond the Iran-Contra Crisis: The Shape of U. S. Anti-Terrorism Policy in the Post-Reagan Era. Ed. by Neil C. Livingston & Terrell E. Arnold. LC 87-45376. (Issues in Low-Intensity Conflict Ser.). 352p. 1988. text ed. 45.00 (*0-669-16466-6*); pap. 19.95 (*0-669-16467-4*) Free Pr.

Beyond the Ivory Tower: Social Responsibilities of the Modern University. Derek C. Bok. LC 81-20278. 328p. 1982. 29.95 (*0-674-06899-8*) HUP.

Beyond the Ivory Tower: Social Responsibilities of the Modern University. Derek C. Bok. LC 81-20278. 328p. 1984. pap. text ed. 10.95 (*0-674-06898-X*) HUP.

Beyond the Ivy Wall: Ten Essential Steps to Graduate School Admission. Howard Greene & Robert Minton. 288p. (Orig.). 1989. pap. 13.95 (*0-316-32684-4*) Little.

Beyond the Khyber Pass: The Road to British Disaster in the First Afghan War. John H. Waller. 1990. 24.95 (*0-394-56934-2*) Random.

Beyond the Khyber Pass: The Road to British Disaster in the First Afghan War. John H. Waller. LC 92-24008. 365p. 1993. pap. 17.95 (*0-292-79073-2*) U of Tex Pr.

Beyond the Killing Fields. Kari R. Hall & Dith Pran. (Illus.). 216p. 1992. 40.00 (*0-89381-504-7*); pap. 29.95 (*0-89381-505-5*) Aperture.

Beyond the Killing Fields: Voices of Nine Cambodian Survivors. Usha Welaratna. LC 92-28557. 300p. (C). 1993. 37.50 (*0-8047-2139-4*) Stanford U Pr.

***Beyond the Killing Fields: Voices of Nine Cambodian Survivors in America.** Usha Welaratna. 1994. pap. 14.95 (*0-8047-2372-9*) Stanford U Pr.

***Beyond the Killing Tree: A Journey of Discovery.** Stephen Reynolds. Ed. by Don Graydon. (Illus.). 192p. 1995. 19.95 (*0-945397-42-9*) Epicenter Pr.

***Beyond the Killing Tree: A Wildlife Officer's Journey of Discovery from the Desert Southwest to the Alaska Bush.** Stephen Reynolds. (Illus.). 192p. 1995. write for info. (*0-614-04392-1*) Epicenter Pr.

Beyond the Known. rev. ed. Roy Masters. Ed. by Dorothy Baker. LC 88-83553. 255p. (Orig.). 1989. reprint ed. pap. text ed. 12.95 (*0-933900-03-1*) Foun Human Under.

Beyond the Known: The Real Meaning of the Martial Arts. Tri T. Dang. 152p. 1993. pap. 12.95 (*0-8048-1891-6*) C E Tuttle.

Beyond the Laboratory: Scientists As Political Activists in 1930s America. Peter J. Kuznick. LC 87-5098. vi, 345p. 1987. 29.95 (*0-226-46583-7*) U Ch Pr.

Beyond the Laboratory: Scientists As Political Activists in 1930s America. Peter J. Kuznick. LC 87-5098. vi, 345p. 1989. pap. text ed. 14.95 (*0-226-46584-5*) U Ch Pr.

Beyond the Lagoon: A Biography of Charles Melville Scammon. Lyndall B. Landauer. LC 85-81389. 1986. 19.95 (*0-933185-00-6*) Ransom Dist Co.

Beyond the Land Itself: Views of Nature in Canada & the United States. Marcia Kline. LC 77-114407. (Essays in History & Literature Ser.). 83p. 1970. pap. 12.00 (*0-674-06915-3*) HUP.

Beyond the Land of Hattamala & Scandal in Fairyland. Badal Sircar. (C). 1992. pap. text ed. 5.00 (*81-7046-091-3*, Pub. by Seagull Bks II) S Asia.

Beyond the Language Classroom: A Guide for Teachers. Margaret B. Cassidy et al. (Intercultural Exchange Ser.). 146p. 1986. reprint ed. pap. text ed. 11.00 (*0-936141-02-6*) Experiment Pr.

Beyond the Law. Franklin W. Dixon. Ed. by Anne Greenberg. (Hardy Boys Casefiles Ser.: No. 55). 160p. (Orig.). (J). 1991. pap. 3.50 (*0-671-73091-6*, Archway) PB.

Beyond the Law: Lawyers & Business in Canada 1830 to 1930. Wilton. 512p. 1990. 63.00 (*0-409-89777-9*) Butterworth Legal Pubs.

Beyond the Law: The Religious & Ethical Meaning of the Lawyer's Vocation. James A. Pike. LC 73-10754. 102p. 1973. reprint ed. text ed. 35.00 (*0-8371-7021-4*, PIBL, Greenwood Pr) Greenwood.

Beyond the Legal Frontier: Knights of the Order of Tria Capita. Edward L. Teague. LC 92-91044. (Illus.). 62p. (Orig.). 1991. write for info. (*0-9635145-0-4*); teacher ed write for info. (*0-9635145-5-5*); student ed write for info. (*0-9635145-6-3*); write for info. (*0-9635145-7-1*); text ed. write for info. (*0-9635145-2-0*); lib. bdg. write for info. (*0-9635145-1-2*); pap. write for info. (*0-9635145-3-9*); pap. text ed. write for info. (*0-9635145-4-7*); write for info. (*0-9635145-8-X*) KOTO Tria Capita.

Beyond the Liberal Consensus: A Political History of the United States since 1965. Iwan W. Morgan. LC 93-44098. 1994. write for info. (*0-312-10747-1*); pap. 18.95 (*0-312-12015-X*) St Martin.

***Beyond the Light.** P. M. Atwater. 352p. 1995. mass mkt. 5.50 (*0-380-72540-1*) Avon.

Beyond the Light: What Isn't Being Said about the Near-Death Experience. P. M. Atwater. LC 93-42169. 1994. 16.95 (*1-55972-229-0*) Carol Pub Group.

Beyond the Lighthouse. Clarice Albritton. LC 77-83447. (Illus.). 1978. pap. 4.25 (*0-87516-243-6*) DeVorss.

Beyond the Limit. Irina Ratushinskaya. Tr. by Frances P. Brent & Carol Avins. 121p. (ENG & RUS.). 1987. pap. 10.95 (*0-8101-0749-X*) Northwestern U Pr.

***Beyond the Limits.** Donella H. Meadows et al. 300p. 1992. 19.95 (*0-614-02997-X*) Amer Forum.

Beyond the Limits: A Law Enforcement Guide to Speed Enforcement. 114p. (Orig.). (C). 1994. pap. text ed. 40.00 (*0-7881-0749-6*) Diane Pub.

Beyond the Limits: A Self Portrait of Myasthenia Gravis. Clete Gress. (Illus.). 104p. (Orig.). 1994. pap. 10.00 (*0-9641276-0-1*) Palette Pubng.

Beyond the Limits: A Woman's Triumph on Everest. Stacy Allison & Peter Carlin. 1993. 21.95 (*0-316-03468-1*) Little.

Beyond the Limits: Confronting Global Collapse, Envisioning a Sustainable Future. Donella H. Meadows et al. (Illus.). 320p. 1993. reprint ed. pap. 16.95 (*0-930031-62-8*) Chelsea Green Pub.

Beyond the Limits: Flight Enters the Computer Age. Paul Ceruzzi. (Illus.). 200p. (Orig.). 1989. 42.50x (*0-262-03143-4*); pap. 19.95 (*0-262-53082-1*) MIT Pr.

***Beyond the Limits of Thought.** Graham Priest. 287p. (C). 1995. 54.95 (*0-521-45420-4*) Cambridge U Pr.

Beyond the Looking Glass: Extraordinary Works of Fairy Tale & Fantasy. Ed. by Jonathan Cott. LC 84-22675. (Illus.). 519p. 1985. 22.50 (*0-87951-995-9*) Overlook Pr.

Beyond the Looking Glass: Extraordinary Works of Fairy Tale & Fantasy. Ed. by Jonathan Cott. (Illus.). 519p. 1988. pap. 10.95 (*0-87951-238-5*) Overlook Pr.

Beyond the Loom: Keys to Understanding Early Southwestern Weaving. Ann Hedlund. LC 90-4126. 112p. (Orig.). 1990. reprint ed. pap. 9.95 (*1-55566-064-9*) Johnson Bks.

Beyond the Love Game. Robert Scheid. LC 79-53839. 144p. (Orig.). 1980. pap. text ed. 7.95 (*0-89087-254-6*) Celestial Arts.

Beyond the Magic Circle: The Role of Intimacy in Business. Brian R. Smith & Myrna M. Milani. LC 88-275523. (Illus.). (Orig.). 1989. pap. 12.50 (*0-943290-07-4*) Fainshaw Pr.

Beyond the Magic Sphere. Gail Jarrow. LC 94-6884. (J). 1994. 15.95 (*0-15-200193-X*) HarBrace.

Beyond the Magpie: A Selection of Winning Entries from Four Years - 1987, 1988, 1989, 1990 - of the West Virginia Writers, Inc. Annual Awards Competition. West Virginia Writers, Inc., Staff & Patricia McClure. Ed. by Helen Carper. 147p. (Orig.). 1991. pap. 9.40 (*0-941092-23-2*) Mtn St Pr.

Beyond the Mainstream: A Search for Alternatives. Raymond Frye. LC 93-91037. 118p. 1994. pap. 10.00 (*0-9639988-0-3*) R Frye.

Beyond the Market & the State: New Direction. Severyn T. Bruyn & James Meehan. LC 86-30065. (Labor & Social Change Ser.). 272p. 1987. 37.95 (*0-87722-484-6*) Temple U Pr.

Beyond the Marketplace: Rethinking Economy & Society. Ed. by Roger Friedland & A. F. Robertson. LC 89-77722. (Sociology & Economics: Controversy & Integration Ser.). (Illus.). 371p. (Orig.). 1990. lib. bdg. 59.95 (*0-202-30370-5*); pap. text ed. 31.95 (*0-202-30371-3*) Aldine de Gruyter.

***Beyond the Marriage Fantasy.** Beaver. 1995. mass mkt. 5.50 (*0-06-100866-4*, Harp PBks) HarpC.

Beyond the Martyrs: A Social History of Chicago's Anarchists, 1870-1900. Bruce C. Nelson. (Class & Culture Ser.). 352p. (C). 1988. text ed. 40.00 (*0-8135-1344-8*); pap. text ed. 15.00 (*0-8135-1345-6*) Rutgers U Pr.

Beyond the Mask: Edward Gordon Craig, Movement, & the Actor. Irene Eynat-Confino. LC 86-31569. 254p. 1987. text ed. 29.95 (*0-8093-1372-3*) S Ill U Pr.

***Beyond the Mask: The Ian Young Goal Tending Method, Advanced Techniques, BK. II.** I. Young & C. Gudgeon. 120p. (Orig.). 1993. pap. 14.95 (*0-919591-82-5*, Pub. by Polestar Bk Pubs CN) Orca Bk Pubs.

***Beyond the Masks: Race, Gender & Subjectivity.** Amina Mama. LC 95-8479. (Critical Psychology Ser.). 1995. write for info. (*0-415-03543-0*); pap. write for info. (*0-415-03544-9*) Routledge.

Beyond the Melting Pot: The Negroes, Puerto Ricans, Jews, Italians, & Irish of New York City. 2nd rev. ed. Nathan Glazer & Daniel P. Moynihan. (C). 1970. pap. 16.00 (*0-262-57022-X*) MIT Pr.

Beyond the Metafictional Mode: Directions in the Modern Spanish Novel. Robert C. Spires. LC 84-7565. 168p. 1984. 18.00 (*0-8131-1520-5*) U Pr of Ky.

***Beyond the Metafictional Mode: Directions in the Modern Spanish Novel.** Robert C. Spires. LC 84-7565. (Studies in Romance Languages: No. 30). reprint ed. pap. 47.10 (*0-7837-9586-6*, 2060335) Bks Demand.

Beyond the Minarets. Kellsye M. Finnie. 192p. 1993. text ed. 4.95 (*0-87508-969-0*) Chr Lit.

Beyond the Mind. David Frawley. 180p. 1993. pap. 12.95 (*1-878423-14-2*) Morson Pub.

Beyond the Miracle of the Market: The Political Economy of Agrarian Development in Kenya. Robert H. Bates. (Political Economy of Institutions & Decisions Ser.: No. 4). (Illus.). 230p. (C). 1989. 54.95 (*0-521-34257-0*) Cambridge U Pr.

Beyond the Miracle of the Market: The Political Economy of Agrarian Development in Kenya. Robert H. Bates. (Political Economy of Institutions & Decisions Ser.: No. 4). (Illus.). 230p. (C). 1992. pap. 18.95 (*0-521-43792-X*) Cambridge U Pr.

Beyond the Mirror: Reflections on Death & Life. Henri M. Nouwen. 80p. 1991. reprint ed. pap. 5.95 (*0-8245-1130-1*) Crossroad NY.

Beyond the Mirrors: The Study of the Mental & Spiritual Aspects of Horsemanship. Jill K. Hassler. Ed. by Jane Bartholomew. (Illus.). 126p. (Orig.). 1991. 19.95 (*0-9632562-0-3*); pap. 14.95 (*0-9632562-1-1*) Goals Unltd.

Beyond the Model T: The Other Ventures of Henry Ford. Ford R. Bryan. LC 89-27663. (Great Lakes Bks.). (Illus.). 204p. (C). 1990. 39.95 (*0-8143-2236-0*); pap. 24.95 (*0-8143-2237-9*) Wayne St U Pr.

***Beyond the Modern Medical Horizon: Are Allergens Synomymous with Carcinogens?** Elinor L. Brown. 1994. write for info. (*0-614-04689-0*) Midwest Pub NE.

***Beyond the Modern Medical Horizon: Cancer Prevention & Pretentious Cancer Therapies.** Elinor L. Brown. 1994. write for info. (*0-614-04690-4*) Midwest Pub NE.

Beyond the Modern Mind: The Spiritual & Ethical Challenge of the Environmental Crisis. Douglas C. Bowman. LC 90-31914. 144p. (Orig.). (C). 1990. pap. 10.95 (*0-8298-0847-7*) Pilgrim OH.

Beyond the Mogollon Rim. Romer Z. Grey. 1994. 14.95 (*0-7451-4587-6*, Gunsmoke) Chivers N Amer.

Beyond the Monitor Model: Comments on Current Theory & Practice in 2nd Language Acquisition. Ronald M. Barasch & C. Vaughan James. 1993. pap. 22.95 (*0-8384-3967-5*) Heinle & Heinle.

Beyond the Moon: Festschrift Luther Dittmer. Ed. by Bryan Gillingham & Paul Merkley. (Wissenschaftliche Abhandlungen-Musicological Studies: Vol. 53). 414p. (ENG & GER.). 1990. 80.00 (*0-931902-65-7*) Inst Mediaeval Mus.

Beyond the Moongate. Agnes N. Johnston. LC 86-45961. (Illus.). 102p. (Orig.). (YA). (gr. 7-12). 1987. per., pap. 7.00 (*0-916418-64-2*) Lotus.

Beyond the Moons: Spelljammer. David Cook. LC 90-71504. (Cloakmaster Cycle Ser.: No. 1). (Illus.). 320p. (Orig.). 1991. pap. 4.95 (*1-56076-153-9*) TSR Inc.

Beyond the Mosque: Christians Within Muslin Community. Phil Parshall. 256p. 1991. pap. 10.99 (*0-8010-7089-9*) Baker Bk.

Beyond the Mountain. Elizabeth Arthur. LC 92-39955. (Discovery Ser.). 224p. 1993. 11.00 (*1-55597-171-7*) Graywolf.

Beyond the Mountains. Kenneth Rexroth. LC 51-9631. 192p. 1974. pap. 3.25 (*0-8112-0552-5*, NDP384) New Directions.

***Beyond the Mountains, More Mountains: Haiti Faces the Future.** Ed. by EPICA-Voices for Haiti Staff. (Illus.). 48p. 1994. pap. 3.50 (*0-918346-15-0*) EPICA.

***Beyond the Multifibre Arrangement: Third World Competition & Restructuring Europe's Textile Industry.** Navaretti et al. 250p. (Orig.). 1995. pap. 32.00 (*92-64-14326-2*, Pub. by Econ & Coop Dev FR) OECD.

Beyond the Myth: The Story of Joan of Arc. Polly S. Brooks. LC 89-37327. (Illus.). 192p. (YA). (gr. 7 up). 1990. lib. bdg. 15.89 (*0-397-32423-5*, Lipp Jr Bks) HarpC Child Bks.

Beyond the Myth of Dominance: An Alternative to a Violent Society. Edwin McMahon. LC 92-38036. 288p. (Orig.). 1993. pap. 16.95 (*1-55612-563-1*) Sheed & Ward MO.

Beyond the Myths & Magic of Mentoring: How to Facilitate an Effective Mentoring Program. Margo Murray. LC 90-25580. (Management Ser.). 236p. 1991. 29.95 (*1-55542-333-7*) Jossey-Bass.

Beyond the Nation-State: Functionalism & International Organization. Ernst B. Haas. LC 64-21999. x, 595p. 1964. 62.50 (*0-8047-0186-5*); pap. 19.95 (*0-8047-0187-3*) Stanford U Pr.

Beyond the Natural Body: An Archaeology of Sex Hormones. Nelly Oudshoorn. LC 94-4945. 240p. 1994. 55.00x (*0-415-09190-X*, A9978); pap. 16.95 (*0-415-09191-8*, A9982) Routledge.

Beyond the Neat Houses Cheaptalk Built. T. S. Wallace. LC 89-80389. 64p. (Orig.). pap. 5.95 (*0-943512-14-X*) Linwood Pub.

An Asterisk (*) at the beginning of an entry indicates that the title is appearing in BIP for the first time.

Beyond the Neighborhood Unit: Residential Environments & Public Policy. Tridib Banerjee & William Baer. LC 84-11619. (Environment, Development, & Public Policy: Public Policy & Social Services Ser.). 270p. 1984. 65.00 (*0-306-41555-0*, Plenum Pr) Plenum.

Beyond the Nerves: The Effectiveness of Acupuncture. Robert Tien Huang. 176p. (Orig.). 1994. pap. write for info. (*0-9640207-0-X*) EO Acupuncture.

Beyond the New Morality: The Responsibilities of Freedom. rev. ed. Germain Grisez & Russell Shaw. LC 80-18293. 240p. (C). 1980. pap. 7.95 (*0-268-00665-2*) U of Notre Dame Pr.

Beyond the New Morality: The Responsibilities of Freedom. 3rd ed. Germain Grisez & Russell B. Shaw. LC 88-4805. (C). 1988. text ed. 19.95 (*0-268-00678-4*); pap. text ed. 10.95 (*0-268-00679-2*) U of Notre Dame Pr.

***Beyond the New Right.** 208p. 1995. pap. 16.95 (*0-415-10706-7*, B4000) Routledge.

Beyond the New Right: Markets, Government, & the Common Environment. John Gray. LC 92-40306. 224p. 1993. 34.50 (*0-415-09297-3*, B0725, Routledge NY) Routledge.

Beyond the News: Sexual Abuse. Ed. by Jerry L. Holsopple. 1993. 19.95 (*1-877736-15-5*) MB Missions.

Beyond the Nonformal Fashion: Towards Educational Revolution in Tanzania. Arthur L. Gillette. 312p. (Orig.). 1977. pap. text ed. 6.00 (*0-932288-47-2*) Ctr Intl Ed U of MA.

Beyond the North-South Stalemate. Roger D. Hansen. LC 78-10607. 348p. (C). 1979. pap. 5.95 (*0-07-026049-4*) Overseas Dev Council.

Beyond the North Wind. Gillian Bradshaw. LC 92-9671. 192p. (J). (gr. 5 up). 1993. 14.00 (*0-688-11357-5*) Greenwillow.

Beyond the Nouveau Roman: Essays on the Contemporary French Novel. Ed. by Michael Tilby. LC 89-35886. (French Studies). 267p. 1990. 49.95 (*0-85496-611-0*) Berg Pubs.

Beyond the Numbers: A Reader on Population & Consumption Issues. Ed. by Laurie A. Mazur. LC 94-75842. 1994. text ed. 40.00 (*1-55963-298-4*); pap. text ed. 19.95 (*1-55963-299-2*) Island Pr.

Beyond the Obvious with SAS Screen Control Language. 347p. 1994. 28.95 (*1-55544-600-0*, 55073) SAS Inst.

Beyond the Occult: A Twenty Year Investigation into the Paranormal. Colin Wilson. 1989. 21.95 (*0-88184-520-5*) Carroll & Graf.

Beyond the Occult: A Twenty Year Investigation into the Paranormal. Colin Wilson. 381p. 1991. pap. 11.95 (*0-88184-650-3*) Carroll & Graf.

Beyond the Oil Era? Arab Mineral Resources & Alternative Development. M. R. Khawlie. 142p. 1990. text ed. 80.00 (*0-7201-2040-3*, Mansell Pub) Cassell.

Beyond the Old Frontier. George B. Grinnell. (Illus.). 374p. 1976. reprint ed. 24.00 (*0-87928-069-7*) Corner Hse.

Beyond the Open Classroom: Toward Informal Education. Lorraine L. Morgan et al. LC 80-69235. 1981. 10.50 (*0-86548-050-8*) R & E Pubs.

Beyond the Open Door. Andrew Lansdown. (J). (gr. 4-7). 1993. pap. 2.95 (*0-590-47160-0*) Scholastic Inc.

Beyond the Open Door. Kathryn P. Cross. LC 77-170212. (Jossey-Bass Series in Higher Education). 220p. reprint ed. pap. 62.70 (*0-8357-4938-X*, 2037868) Bks Demand.

Beyond the Open Door: A Citizens Guide to Increasing Public Access to Local School Boards. Nancy Berla & Susan Hlesciak Hall. Ed. by Chrissie Bamber. LC 89-62855. 120p. 1989. pap. 10.00 (*0-934460-33-7*) NCCE.

Beyond the Open Door: Contemporary Painting from the People's Republic of China. Richard E. Strassberg & Waldemar A. Nielsen. LC 87-60823. (Illus.). 76p. 1987. pap. 16.95 (*0-295-96566-5*) U of Wash Pr.

Beyond the Open Door: Contemporary Paintings from the People's Republic of China. Richard E. Strassberg & Waldemar A. Nielsen. (Illus.). 76p. 1987. pap. 16.95 (*0-685-66765-0*) Pacific Asia.

Beyond the Outsider. Colin Wilson. 256p. 1991. pap. 8.95 (*0-88184-704-6*) Carroll & Graf.

Beyond the Paddle. Garrett Conover. 112p. (Orig.). 1991. pap. 17.95 (*0-88448-066-6*) Tilbury Hse.

Beyond the Pale. Ed. by Robin Sheiner. 112p. (C). 1990. 30.00 (*0-947087-22-2*, Pub. by Pascoe Pub AT) St Mut.

Beyond the Pale: Essays on the History of Colonial South Africa. Robert Ross. LC 92-56910. (Illus.). 284p. 1993. 50.00 (*0-8195-5258-5*, Wesleyan Univ Pr) U Pr of New Eng.

Beyond the Pale: White Women, Racism & History. Vron Ware. (Questions for Feminism Ser.). (Illus.). 280p. 1991. 59.95 (*0-86091-336-8*, A6418, Pub. by Verso UK); pap. 16.95 (*0-86091-552-2*, A6422, Pub. by Verso UK) Routledge Chapman & Hall.

Beyond the Parent: The Role of Other Adults in Children's Lives. Ed. by Robert Pianta. LC 85-644581. (New Directions for Child Development Ser.: No. CD 57). 110p. 1992. 17.95 (*1-55542-732-4*) Jossey-Bass.

Beyond the Pattern: A Guide to Creative Sewing & Design with Knit Fabrics. Virginia P. Allen. LC 73-91225. 1973. lib. bdg. 15.95 (*0-686-09885-4*); pap. 9.95 (*0-686-09884-6*) Spinning Spool.

***Beyond the Pattern: Great Sewing Techniques for Clothing.** Threads Editors Staff. LC 94-37378. 1995. 15.95 (*1-56158-094-5*) Taunton.

Beyond the Pavement. Albert Drake. LC 80-53525. 175p. 1981. 9.95 (*0-917976-10-X*, White Ewe Pr) Thunder Baas Pr.

Beyond the Pay-Packet: Proven Techniques for Leading, Motivating, & Inspiring Salespeople to Achieve Success. John Lidstone. LC 92-21880. 1992. 24.95 (*0-07-707697-4*) McGraw.

Beyond the Pearly Gates. George L. Cavanaugh. 128p. (Orig.). 1989. pap. 5.95 (*0-945767-01-3*) Write Place.

Beyond the Petroleum Age: Designing a Solar Economy. Christopher Flavin & Nicholas Lenssen. 70p. (Orig.). 1990. pap. 5.00 (*1-878071-01-7*) Worldwatch Inst.

Beyond the Pits. Rae S. Stewart. (Orig.). 1991. pap. 3.50 (*0-87067-343-2*) Holloway.

Beyond the Plane: American Constructions, 1930-1965. Ed. by Jennifer Toher. (Illus.). 112p. (Orig.). 1983. pap. 15.00 (*0-938766-02-3*) NJ State Mus.

Beyond the Plane: The Relief Paintings of Judith Rothschild. Richard H. Axsom. LC 92-12136. (Illus.). 104p. 1992. 45.00 (*1-55595-077-9*) Hudson Hills.

Beyond the Pleasure Principle. Sigmund Freud. Ed. & Tr. by James Strachey. 96p. 1990. reprint ed. pap. 5.95 (*0-393-00769-3*) Norton.

Beyond the Politics of Place: New Directions in Community Organizing in the 1990s. Gary Delgado. 99p. (Orig.). 1994. pap. 16.00 (*0-9636725-1-7*) Appl Res Ctr.

Beyond the Poseidon Adventure. Paul Gallico. 20.95 (*0-88411-568-2*, Aeonian Pr) Amereon Ltd.

Beyond the Post-Modern Mind. 2nd ed. Huston Smith. LC 89-40175. 218p. 1989. pap. 9.95 (*0-8356-0647-3*, Quest) Theos Pub Hse.

Beyond the Power Struggle: Dealing with Conflict in Love & Work. Susan M. Campbell. LC 84-11846. 256p. (Orig.). 1984. pap. 8.95 (*0-915166-46-1*) Impact Pubs CA.

Beyond the "Primitive" Religions of Nonliterate Peoples. Sam D. Gill. (Illus.). 200p. (C). 1981. pap. text ed. 19.33 (*0-13-076034-X*) P-H.

Beyond the Promised Land. Glenn Frankel. 1994. 24.00 (*0-671-79649-6*) S&S Trade.

Beyond the Protective State: The Political Economy of Australia's Manufacturing Industry Policy. M. Ann Capling & Brian Galligan. LC 92-17349. (Illus.). 256p. (C). 1993. 59.95 (*0-521-41626-4*); pap. write for info. (*0-521-42629-4*) Cambridge U Pr.

***Beyond the Provinces: Literary Canada at Century's End.** David Staines. (F. E. L. Priestley Memorial Lectures in the History of Ideas). 144p. 1995. 45.00 (*0-8020-0652-3*); pap. 14.95 (*0-8020-7606-8*) U of Toronto Pr.

***Beyond the Psychoanalytic Dyad: Developmental Semiotics in Freud, Peirce, & Lacan.** John P. Muller. LC 95-14600. 1995. write for info. (*0-415-91068-4*, Routledge NY); pap. write for info. (*0-415-91069-2*, Routledge NY) Routledge.

Beyond the Public-Domestic Dichotomy: Contempory Perspectives on Women's Public Lives. Janet Sharistanian. LC 86-29408. (Contributions in Women's Studies: No. 78). 221p. 1987. text ed. 49.95 (*0-313-25768-X*, SB, Greenwood Pr) Greenwood.

***Beyond the Pyramids: Egyptian Regional Art from the Museo Egizio, Turin.** Ed. by Gay Robins. (EUMILOP Ser.: No. 4). (Illus.). 95p. 1995. pap. text ed. 24.95 (*0-9638169-2-6*) M C Carlos Mus.

Beyond the Quantum Paradox: Probability Riddles... Quantum Riddles... Other Riddles... Lazar Mayants. LC 94-1214. 102p. 1994. write for info. (*0-7484-0206-3*, Pub. by Tay Francis Ltd UK); pap. 49.50 (*0-7484-0207-1*, Pub. by Tay Francis Ltd UK) Taylor & Francis.

Beyond the Quick Fix: Managing Five Tracks to Organizational Success. Ralph H. Kilmann. LC 84-47988. (Management Ser.). 322p. 1984. 32.95 (*0-87589-620-0*) Jossey-Bass.

Beyond the Rainbow. Jeff Jordan. LC 92-91128. 254p. (Orig.). 1994. pap. 12.95 (*1-56002-253-1*, Univ Edtns) Aegina Pr.

Beyond the Rainbow. Jeff Jordan. 183p. (Orig.). 1991. pap. 20.96 (*0-685-48260-X*) Dayspring Pr.

Beyond the Rainbow: A Guide for Parents of Children with Dyslexia & Other Learning Disabilities. Patricia Dodds et al. 1991. pap. write for info. (*0-9636054-0-2*) Educ Intervent.

Beyond the Ranges. Consuelo A. Seoane. 9.95 (*0-8315-0069-7*) Speller.

***Beyond the Rat Race.** Glen S. Martin. LC 95-6451. 1995. write for info. (*0-8054-6151-5*) Broadman.

***Beyond the Rat Race.** Arthur G. Gish. LC 73-9336. reprint ed. pap. 54.80 (*0-7837-9058-9*, 2049809) Bks Demand.

***Beyond the Red Notebook: Essays on Paul Auster.** Ed. by Dennis Barone. LC 95-13881. (Penn Studies in Contemporary American Fiction). 225p. 1995. text ed. 36.95 (*0-8122-3317-4*); pap. text ed. 17.95 (*0-8122-1556-7*) U of Pa Pr.

Beyond the Red Pony: A Reader's Companion to Steinbeck's Complete Short Stories. R. S. Hughes. LC 86-31567. (Illus.). 184p. 1987. 22.50 (*0-8108-1970-8*) Scarecrow.

Beyond the Red, White, & Blue: A Student's Introduction to American Studies. Lewis Carlson & James M. Ferreira. 480p. (C). 1993. per., pap. text ed. 43.95 (*0-8403-8816-0*) Kendall-Hunt.

Beyond the Relaxation Response. Herbert Benson & William Proctor. 192p. 1985. mass mkt. 4.99 (*0-425-08183-4*) Berkley Pub.

Beyond the Ridge. Paul Goble. LC 87-33113. (Illus.). 32p. (J). (ps-3). 1989. text ed. 14.95 (*0-02-736581-6*, Bradbury S&S) S&S Childrens.

Beyond the Ridge. Paul Goble. LC 92-39786. (Illus.). 32p. (J). (gr. k-3). 1993. reprint ed. pap. 4.95 (*0-689-71731-8*, Aladdin Paperbacks) S&S Childrens.

Beyond the Ring: The Role of Boxing in American Society. Jeffrey T. Sammons. LC 87-19041. (Sport & Society Ser.). (Illus.). 376p. 1988. 34.95 (*0-252-01473-1*); pap. 14.95 (*0-252-06145-4*) U of Ill Pr.

Beyond the Rising Sun: Nationalism in Contemporary Japan. Bruce Stronach. LC 94-19577. 208p. 1995. text ed. 59.95 (*0-275-95005-0*, Praeger Pubs); pap. text ed. 17.95 (*0-275-95035-2*, Praeger Pubs) Greenwood.

Beyond the River. Robert Elmer. (J). (gr. 4-7). 1994. pap. 5.99 (*1-55661-375-X*) Bethany Hse.

Beyond the River. Gilbert Morris & Bobby Funderburtk. 288p. 1994. pap. 8.95 (*0-914984-51-9*) Starburst.

***Beyond the River: A Novel.** Michael Fillerup. 1995. pap. 14.95 (*1-56085-068-X*) Signature Bks.

Beyond the Rivers: An Anthology of Twentieth Century Paraguayan Poetry. Ed. by Charles R. Carlisle. LC 77-3497. text ed. 10.00 (*0-914476-73-4*); pap. 5.00 (*0-914476-64-5*) Thorp Springs.

Beyond the Rockies: A Narrative History of Idaho. Ronald K. Fisher. LC 89-83506. (Illus.). (J). (gr. 4-9). 1993. text ed. 14.85 (*0-941734-00-5*) Alpha Om ID.

Beyond the Rocky Mountains, Report on the Territory of Oregon. Caleb Cushing. 210p. Date not set. write for info. (*0-87770-442-2*); pap. 14.95 (*0-685-38681-3*) Ye Galleon.

Beyond the Rodney King Story: An Investigation of Police Conduct in Minority Communities. National Association for the Advancement of Colored People Staff et al. 224p. 1994. text ed. 24.95 (*1-55553-202-0*) NE U Pr.

Beyond the Rope's End. Robert E. Ross. LC 81-83846. (Illus.). 180p. (Orig.). 1982. pap. 12.95 (*0-9607312-0-2*) Priority Proj.

***Beyond the Ruins.** Marco Micone. Tr. by Jill MacDougall. (Drama Ser.: No. 10). 78p. 1995. 10.00 (*0-920717-86-1*) Guernica Editions.

Beyond the Ruling Class: Strategic Elites in Modern Society. Suzanne Keller. 368p. (C). 1991. pap. 21.95 (*1-56000-550-5*) Transaction Pubs.

Beyond the Ruling Class: Strategic Elites in Modern Society. Suzanne I. Keller. Ed. by Lewis A. Coser & Walter W. Powell. LC 79-7000. (Perennial Works in Sociology Ser.). 1980. reprint ed. lib. bdg. 31.95 (*0-405-12099-0*) Ayer.

Beyond the Safe Zone. Robert Silverberg. 576p. 1987. mass mkt. 5.95 (*0-446-30173-6*) Warner Bks.

Beyond the Safe Zone: Collected Short Fiction of Robert Silverberg. Robert Silverberg. LC 85-81169. 437p. 1986. 18.95 (*0-917657-60-8*) D I Fine.

Beyond the Salt II Failure. John F. Lehman & Seymour Weiss. LC 81-2874. 224p. 1981. text ed. 49.95 (*0-275-90667-1*, C0667, Praeger Pubs) Greenwood.

Beyond the Schoolhouse Gate: Free Speech & the Inculcation of Values. Robert W. Lane. LC 94-16430. 224p. (C). 1994. text ed. 49.95 (*1-56639-274-8*) Temple U Pr.

Beyond the Schoolhouse Gate: Free Speech & the Inculcation of Values. Robert W. Lane. LC 94-16430. 224p. (C). 1995. pap. text ed. 17.95 (*1-56639-275-6*) Temple U Pr.

Beyond The Schools. American Assoc. of School Administrators Staff & National School Boards Assoc. Staff. 1991. 2.50 (*0-87652-160-X*, 021-00313) Am Assn Sch Admin.

Beyond the Sea of Ice: The First Americans, Bk. 1. William Sarabande. 336p. 1987. pap. 5.99 (*0-553-26889-9*) Bantam.

Beyond the Second Sex: New Directions in the Anthropology of Gender. Ed. by Peggy R. Sanday & Ruth Gallagher Goodenough. LC 90-30497. 358p. (C). 1990. pap. text ed. 18.95 (*0-8122-1303-3*) U of Pa Pr.

Beyond the Secular Mind: A Jewish Response to the Problems of Modernity. Paul Eidelberg. LC 88-34732. (Contributions in Philosophy Ser.: No. 38). 194p. 1989. text ed. 49.95 (*0-313-26663-8*, EBS/, Greenwood Pr) Greenwood.

Beyond the Self: Wittgenstein, Heidegger & the Limits of Language. Paul Standish. (Series in Philosophy). 283p. 1992. 68.95 (*1-85628-271-6*, Pub. by Avebury Pub UK) Ashgate Pub Co.

Beyond the Shame: Understanding & Treating the Child Molester. James A. Kitchens. 120p. (Orig.). (C). 1991. pap. 7.95 (*0-9624469-0-4*) Ads-Co.

Beyond the Silvered Pane. James Marciniak & Steven Marciniak. (Illus.). 1978. 5.95 (*0-940244-08-X*) Flying Buffalo.

Beyond the Single Vision: Henry James, Michel Butor, Uwe Johnson. 2nd ed. Marianne Hirsch. LC 81-68414. 205p. 1981. 16.95 (*0-917786-21-1*) Summa Pubns.

Beyond the Site: Regional Studies in the Aegean Area. Ed. by P. Nick Kardulias. (Illus.). 448p. (Orig.). (C). 1994. lib. bdg. 57.50 (*0-8191-9632-0*); pap. text ed. 38.50 (*0-8191-9633-9*) U Pr of Amer.

***Beyond the Smile.** Kate S. Watkins. 96p. 1995. pap. 9.95 (*1-881576-60-4*) Providence Hse.

Beyond the Society Threat: Rethinking American Security Policy in a New Era. Ed. by William Zimmerman. (Illus.). 300p. (C). 1992. text ed. 39.50 (*0-472-10341-5*) U of Mich Pr.

Beyond the Sociology of Agrarian Transformation: Economy & Society in Zambia, Nepal & Zanzibar. Melsome Nelson-Richards. Ed. by K. Ishwaran. LC 87-20931. (Monographs & Theoretical Studies in Sociology & Anthropology in Honour of Nels Anderson: Vol. 20). (Illus.). v, 141p. (Orig.). 1988. pap. 34.50 (*90-04-08282-4*) E J Brill.

Beyond the Sociology of Conflict. David Binns. LC 77-82860. 1978. text ed. 26.00 (*0-312-07784-X*) St Martin.

Beyond the Solar System: One Hundred Best Deep-Sky Objects for Amateur Astronomers. David Eicher. Ed. by Michael Emmerich. (Illus.). 80p. (Orig.). 1992. pap. 12.95 (*0-913135-10-0*) Kalmbach.

Beyond the Song. 2nd ed. Miljenko Kovacicek. 40p. (Orig.). 1991. pap. 6.00 (*1-880286-00-9*) Singular Speech Pr.

Beyond the Sound of Cannon: Military Strategy in the 1990s. Richard J. Meinhold. LC 91-50943. 200p. 1992. lib. bdg. 32.50x (*0-89950-697-6*) McFarland & Co.

Beyond the Sound of Guns. Emilie Loring. reprint ed. lib. bdg. 21.95 (*0-88411-361-2*, Aeonian Pr) Amereon Ltd.

Beyond the Soviet Threat: The U. S. Army in a Post Cold War Environment. James B. Motley. (Low Intensity Conflict Ser.). 224p. 1991. text ed. 39.95 (*0-669-24986-6*) Free Pr.

Beyond the "SP" Label: Improving the Spelling of Learning Disabled & Basic Writers. Patricia J. McAlexander et al. LC 92-11633. 90p. 1992. 12.95 (*0-8141-0289-1*) NCTE.

Beyond the Spring: Cordelia Stanwood of Birdsacre. rev. ed. Chandler S. Richmond. LC 88-83667. (Illus.). 176p. (Orig.). 1989. pap. 12.95 (*0-932448-03-8*) Latona Pr.

Beyond the Spring: Cordelia Stanwood of Birdsacre. 2nd rev. ed. Chandler S. Richmond. LC 88-83667. (Illus.). 176p. (Orig.). 1989. 24.95 (*0-932448-02-X*) Latona Pr.

Beyond the Staff of Life: The Wheatless, Dairyless Cookbook. Kief Adler. LC 76-43076. 80p. (Orig.). 1976. 13.95 (*0-87961-076-X*); pap. 5.95 (*0-87961-075-1*) Naturegraph.

Beyond the Standard Model II. Ed. by K. A. Milton et al. 400p. (C). 1991. text ed. 118.00 (*981-02-0569-4*) World Scientific Pub.

Beyond the Standard Model III. S. Godfrey & P. Kalyniak. 400p. 1993. text ed. 121.00 (*981-02-1164-3*) World Scientific Pub.

Beyond the Stars. David W. Ross. 528p. 1991. mass mkt. 5.95 (*0-380-71471-X*) Avon.

Beyond the Stars: Stock Characters in American Popular Culture. Ed. by Paul Loukides & Linda K. Fuller. LC 89-82334. (Illus.). 245p. (C). 1990. lib. bdg. 40.95 (*0-87972-479-X*); pap. 19.95 (*0-87972-480-3*) Bowling Green Univ.

***Beyond the Stars No. 145: Camfield.** Barbara Cartland. 176p. (Orig.). 1995. pap. text ed. 3.99 (*0-515-11706-4*) Jove Pubns.

***Beyond the Stars - the Memoirs of Sergei Eisenstein: Selected Works, Vol. IV.** Ed. by Richard Taylor. (Illus.). 992p. Date not set. text ed. 75.00 (*0-85170-460-3*) Ind U Pr.

Beyond the Stars, Beyond the Heavens: A Book of Lines, Sayings & Verses of Love. Mark Edgeworth. LC 78-56835. 1980. 10.95 (*0-87212-103-8*) Libra.

Beyond the Stars Four: Locales in American Popular Film. Ed. by Paul Loukides & Linda Fuller. LC 89-82334. 280p. (C). 1993. 39.95 (*0-87972-588-5*); pap. 18.95 (*0-87972-589-3*) Bowling Green Univ.

Beyond the Stars Two: Plot Conventions in American Popular Film. Paul Loukides & Linda K. Fuller. LC 89-82334. 225p. (C). 1991. lib. bdg. 39.95 (*0-87972-517-6*); pap. text ed. 18.95 (*0-87972-518-4*) Bowling Green Univ.

***Beyond the State: An Introductory Critique.** John Hoffman. 240p. (C). 1995. text ed. write for info. (*0-7456-1180-X*, Pub. by Polity Pr UK); pap. text ed. write for info. (*0-7458-1181-7*, Pub. by Polity Pr UK) Blackwell Pubs.

Beyond the Status Quo: Policy Proposals for America. Ed. by David Boaz & Edward H. Crane. 292p. 1985. 5.00 (*0-932790-46-1*); pap. 3.00 (*0-932790-49-6*) Cato Inst.

Beyond the Steady State: A Revival of Growth Theory. Ed. by Joseph Halevi et al. LC 91-10319. 372p. 1992. text ed. 65.00 (*0-312-06505-1*) St Martin.

Beyond the Storm. Carol A. Osley. (Orig.). 1985. write for info. (*0-910119-13-9*) SOCO Pubns.

Beyond the Storm: A Gulf Crisis Reader. Ed. by Phyllis Bennis & Michel Moushabeck. LC 91-22095. (Illus.). 480p. (C). 1991. 29.95 (*0-940793-87-3*); pap. 14.95 (*0-940793-82-2*) Interlink Pub.

Beyond the Storm: True Story of Jack McWilliams. W. R. Morris. 200p. Date not set. 14.95 (*0-9634779-7-8*) Cherokee Pr.

Beyond the Stream: Islam & Society in a West African Town. Robert Launay. (Comparative Studies on Muslim Societies: No. 15). (C). 1992. 38.00 (*0-520-07718-0*) U CA Pr.

Beyond the Street: A Handbook for EMS Leadership & Management. Jay Fitch. Ed. by Keith Griffiths & Valla Howell. LC 87-82161. (Illus.). 325p. 1987. text ed. 29.95 (*0-936174-04-8*) Jems Comm.

Beyond the Structuralist Myth of Ecriture. R. Champagne. 1977. 51.55 (*90-279-3166-6*) Mouton.

Beyond the Subconscious: The Ultimate Mind Game. Chuck Francis. 320p. (Orig.). 1988. pap. 12.95 (*0-9620761-0-4*) Imagin Store.

Beyond the Sublime Porte. Barnette Miller. LC 79-111774. reprint ed. 62.50 (*0-404-04329-1*) AMS Pr.

Beyond the Summerhouse. Constance Hunting. 1976. pap. 3.50 (*0-913006-10-6*) Puckerbrush.

Beyond the Sun: The Next Step Forward Is a Scientifically Designed, Moneyless Society. Ray Kelly. (Illus.). 204p. (Orig.). 1992. pap. 9.95 (*0-910303-33-9*) Writers Pub Serv.

Beyond the Sunrise. Mary Balogh. 384p. (Orig.). 1992. pap. 4.99 (*0-451-40342-8*, Onyx) NAL-Dutton.

Beyond the Sunset. Louise Hurren. 392p. (C). 1988. 35.00 (*0-7212-0714-6*, Pub. by Regency Press) St Mut.

Beyond the Superconscious Mind. Avadhutika A. Acarya. (Illus.). 102p. (Orig.). 1989. pap. 6.00 (*0-88476-004-9*) Ananda Marga.

Beyond the Superconscious Mind. Ananda Mitra. (Illus.). 96p. (Orig.). 1991. reprint ed. pap. 6.00 (*0-945934-06-8*) New Wrld Lib.

Beyond the Supernatural. Randy McCall & Kevin Siembieda. Ed. by Alex Marciniszyn & Florence Siembieda. (Illus.). 256p. (Orig.). (YA). (gr. 8 up). 1988. pap. 19.95 (*0-916211-18-5*, 700) Palladium Bks.

B

An Asterisk (*) at the beginning of an entry indicates that the title is appearing in BIP for the first time.

Beyond the Symbiotic Orbit: Advances in Separation - Individuation - Essays in Honor of Selma Kramer, M. D. Ed. by Salman Akhtar & Henri Parens. 374p. 1991. 45.00 (*0-88163-109-4*) Analytic Pr.

Beyond the Tanabata Bridge: A Textile Journey in Japan. Seattle Art Museum Staff. (Illus.). 196p. (Orig.). 1992. pap. 29.95 (*0-932216-40-4*) Seattle Art.

Beyond the Tanabata Bridge: Traditional Japanese Textiles. William Rathbun. LC 93-60436. (Illus.). 208p. 1993. 45.00 (*0-500-01586-4*) Thames Hudson.

Beyond the Technology Race: An Analysis of Technology Policy in Seven Industrial Countries. A. J. Roobeek. 268p. 1990. 92.50 (*0-444-88637-0*) Elsevier.

Beyond the Tenure Track: Fifteen Months in the Life of an English Professor. James Phelan. 1991. 45.00 (*0-8142-0535-6*); pap. 17.50 (*0-8142-0546-1*) Ohio St U Pr.

Beyond the Texas Rainbow. Leona Karr. 1989. pap. 3.95 (*0-8217-2817-2*) Zebra.

Beyond the Text: A Holistic Approach to Liturgy. Lawrence Hoffman. LC 85-45886. (Jewish Literature & Culture Ser.). (Illus.). 224p. 1987. 35.00 (*0-253-31199-3*); pap. 9.95 (*0-253-20538-7*, MB-538) Ind U Pr.

Beyond the Text: Contemporary Writing on Distance Education. Terry Evans & Bruce King. 264p. (C). 1991. pap. 76.50x (*0-949823-19-8*, Pub. by Deakin Univ AT) St Mut.

Beyond the Therapeutic Community: Social Learning & Social Psychiatry. Maxwell Jones. LC 68-13913. 172p. reprint ed. pap. 49.10 (*0-8357-8041-4*, 2033774) Bks Demand.

Beyond the Thin Line. Robert Gard. LC 92-7951. 1992. 17.95 (*1-879483-06-8*) Prairie Oak Pr.

Beyond the Third Dimension: Geometry, Computer Graphics & Higher Dimensions. Thomas F. Banchoff. (Illus.). (C). 1995. text ed. write for info. (*0-7167-5025-2*) W H Freeman.

***Beyond the Third Rail with Monte Ballough & His Camera.** Doris B. Osterwald. (Illus.). 216p. 1994. 44.95 (*0-931788-40-4*) Western Guideways.

Beyond the Thirty-Second Spot: Enhancing the Media's Role in Congressional Campaigns. Paul S. Hoff & Ken Bernstein. 156p. (Orig.). (C). 1988. pap. text ed. 17.75 (*0-939715-11-2*) Ctr Politics.

Beyond the Three: The Material World in American Popular Film. Ed. by Paul Loukides & Linda K. Fuller. LC 89-82334. 245p. 1993. 35.95 (*0-87972-622-9*); pap. 13.95 (*0-87972-623-7*) Bowling Green Univ.

Beyond the Threshold: Families Caring for Their Children Who Have Significant Developmental Disabilities. Kathleen McKaig et al. LC 89-105211. 62p. (Orig.). 1986. pap. text ed. 6.00 (*0-88156-044-8*) Comm Serv Soc NY.

Beyond the Timberline: The Trials & Triumphs of a Black Entrepreneur. T. M. Alexander, Sr. LC 92-71604. (Illus.). 268p. 1992. 17.95 (*1-878647-08-3*) Duncan & Duncan.

Beyond the Tomb. H. M. Riggle. 288p. 5.00 (*0-686-29100-X*) Faith Pub Hse.

Beyond the Tower: London for Return Travellers. Joan Cornblath. LC 93-81356. (Illus.). 210p. (Orig.). 1994. pap. 10.95 (*0-9640203-0-0*) J Cornblath.

***Beyond the Traditional Family: New Choices, New Voices.** Betty Polisar & Rita K. Spina. 224p. 1995. write for info. (*0-8261-9030-8*) Springer Pub.

Beyond the Trail. Lily Bear. 318p. 1993. 9.15 (*0-317-05264-0*) Rod & Staff.

Beyond the Transistor: 133 Electronics Projects. Rufus P. Turner & Brinton L. Rutherford. (Illus.). 170p. 1987. 16.95 (*0-8306-7887-5*, 2887) TAB Bks.

Beyond the Tunnel: The Arts & Aging in America. Joan Hart. LC 91-38480. (Illus.). 128p. (Orig.). 1992. pap. 9.95 (*0-9630825-0-7*) Museum One.

Beyond the Tunnel of History. Jacques Darras & Daniel Snowman. LC 90-34702. 136p. (C). 1990. reprint ed. text ed. 22.95 (*0-472-10208-7*) U of Mich Pr.

Beyond the Twelve Steps: Roadmap to a New Life. Lynn Grabborn. 240p. 1992. pap. 12.95 (*0-89254-021-4*) Nicolas-Hays.

Beyond the Twin Deficits: A Trade Strategy for the 1990s. Robert A. Blecker. LC 92-9033. (Economic Policy Institute Ser.). 296p. 1992. 51.95 (*1-56324-090-4*); pap. text ed. 22.95 (*1-56324-091-2*) M E Sharpe.

Beyond the Two Cultures: Essays on Science, Technology, & Literature. Ed. by Joseph W. Slade & Judith Y. Lee. LC 88-30711. (Illus.). 322p. 1990. text ed. 34.95 (*0-8138-0162-1*) Iowa St U Pr.

***Beyond the Two Party System: Political Representation, Economic Competitiveness & Australian Politics.** Ian Marsh. (Reshaping Australian Institutions Ser.: No. 1). (Illus.). 448p. (C). 1995. write for info. (*0-521-46223-1*) Cambridge U Pr.

Beyond the Typewriter: Gender, Class, & the Origins of Modern American Office Work, 1900-1930. Sharon H. Strom. (Women in American History Ser.). (Illus.). 464p. 1992. 47.50 (*0-252-01806-0*) U of Ill Pr.

***Beyond the Typewriter: Gender, Class, & the Origins of Modern American Office Work, 1900-1930.** Sharon H. Strom. 1994. pap. 14.95 (*0-252-06425-9*) U of Ill Pr.

Beyond the Unconscious: Essays of Henri F. Ellenberger in the History of Psychiatry. Ed. by Mark S. Micale. Tr. by Francoise Dubor. 488p. 1993. text ed. 49.50 (*0-691-08550-1*) Princeton U Pr.

Beyond the Uniform: A Career & Family Transition Guide for Veterans & Federal Employees. W. Dean Lee. 224p. 1991. pap. text ed. 14.95 (*0-471-54620-8*) Wiley.

Beyond the Urban Fringe: Land Use Issues of Nonmetropolitan America. Ed. by Rutherford H. Platt & George Macinko. LC 83-3518. 432p. reprint ed. pap. 123.20 (*0-7837-2926-X*, 2057528) Bks Demand.

Beyond the Veil. Georgie Gregory. 52p. 1992. pap. 9.95 (*1-882185-03-X*) Crnrstone Pub.

Beyond the Veil. Boyce Mouton. 158p. 1987. pap. 5.99 (*0-89900-314-1*) College Pr Pub.

***Beyond the Veil.** Lee Nelson. 142p. 1994. pap. 10.95 (*1-55517-166-4*) CFI Dist.

***Beyond the Veil, No. II.** Lee Nelson. 163p. 1995. pap. 10.95 (*1-55517-172-9*) CFI Dist.

***Beyond the Veil, No. III.** Lee Nelson. 151p. 1994. pap. 10.95 (*1-55517-165-6*) CFI Dist.

***Beyond the Veil: A Journey into the Hidden Truths & Exploited Myths of America's Most Misunderstood Industry: Network Marketing.** Leonard W. Clements. 156p. 1995. pap. 12.95 (*0-9646186-0-5*) Marketwave.

Beyond the Veil: Male-Female Dynamics in Modern Muslim Society. rev. ed. Fatima Mernissi. LC 86-46034. 224p. 1987. 25.00 (*0-253-31162-4*); pap. 8.95 (*0-253-20423-2*, MB-423) Ind U Pr.

Beyond the Veil: Posthumous Work of Paschal Beverly Randolph. Paschal B. Randolph. reprint ed. spiral bd. 8.80 (*0-7873-0696-7*) Mokelumne.

Beyond the Veil of Stars. Robert Reed. 352p. 1994. 21.95 (*0-312-85730-6*) Tor Bks.

Beyond the Veil of Stars. Robert Reed. 320p. 1995. mass mkt. 4.99 (*0-8125-2406-3*) Tor Bks.

Beyond the Velvet Underground. Dave Thompson. (Illus.). 96p. 1989. pap. 16.95 (*0-7119-1691-8*, OP45087) Omnibus NY.

Beyond the Verse: Talmudic Readings & Lectures. Emmanuel Levinas. Tr. by Gary D. Mole. LC 94-8618. 1994. 27.95 (*0-253-33288-5*) Ind U Pr.

Beyond the "Vietnam Syndrome" U. S. Interventionism in the 1980's. Michael T. Klare. (Illus.). 137p. (Orig.). (C). 1981. pap. 4.95 (*0-89758-027-3*) Inst Policy Stud.

Beyond the View. W. Calder. (Illus.). 176p. 1981. pap. 24.95 (*0-909605-26-2*, Pub. by Inkata Pr AT) Intl Spec Bk.

Beyond the Village Gate: Cookbook. Parmadale Christmas Committee. (Illus.). 320p. 1985. 11.95 (*0-9615123-0-X*) Parmadale.

***Beyond the Visible: Yaakov Agam & Jewish Art.** Tr. by Sayako Aragaki. 1995. pap. text ed. write for info. (*965-229-113-7*, Pub. by Gefen Pub Hse IS) Gefen Bks.

Beyond the Vision: Essays on American Indian Culture. William K. Powers. LC 87-40218. (Civilization of the American Indian Ser.: Vol. 184). (Illus.). 256p. 1987. 35.00 (*0-8061-2091-6*) U of Okla Pr.

Beyond the Vote: Canadian Women & Politics. Ed. by Linda Kealey & Joan Sangster. 452p. 1989. 45.00 (*0-8020-2677-X*); pap. 19.95 (*0-8020-6650-X*) U of Toronto Pr.

Beyond the Wall. J. J. Maloney. 1973. per. 3.00 (*0-912678-05-4*, Greenfld Rev Pr) Greenfld Rev Lit.

Beyond the Wall. Norbert Weinberg. LC 78-60648. 1978. 7.95 (*0-8197-0462-8*) Bloch.

Beyond the Wall: Adventures in the North of Arthur's Britain. Tom Rogan et al. Ed. by Sam Shirley. (Pendragon Roleplaying Ser.). (Illus.). 128p. (Orig.). 1995. pap. 12.95 (*1-56882-026-7*, 2717) Chaosium.

Beyond the Wall: Essays from the Outside. Edward Abbey. LC 83-18346. 224p. 1984. pap. 11.95 (*0-8050-0820-9*, Owl) H Holt & Co.

Beyond the Wall: Germany's Road to Unification. Elizabeth Pond. 367p. (C). 1993. 28.95x (*0-8157-7154-1*); pap. 16.95x (*0-8157-7155-X*) Brookings.

***Beyond the Wall of Resistance: Unconventional Strategies That Build Support for Change.** Rick Maurer. (Illus.). 208p. 1995. 24.95 (*1-885167-07-5*) Bard & Stephen.

Beyond the Wall of Tears. K. Martin Aul. (Illus.). 1984. 7.95 (*0-940244-18-7*) Flying Buffalo.

Beyond the Walls: A Congregation Guide for Lifestyle Relational Evangelism. James Hollis. LC 93-71177. 144p. 1993. pap. 11.95 (*0-88177-124-4*, DR124) Discipleship Res.

Beyond the War on Drugs: Overcoming a Failed Public Policy. Steven Wisotsky. 279p. (C). 1990. reprint ed. pap. 19.95 (*0-87975-587-3*) Prometheus Bks.

***Beyond the Warming: The Hazards of Climate Prediction in the Age of Chaos.** Antony Milne. (Illus.). 192p. (Orig.). (C). 1995. pap. 14.95 (*1-85327-098-9*, Pub. by Prism Pr UK) Atrium Pubs.

Beyond the Waste Land: A Study of the American Novel in the Nineteen-Sixties. Raymond M. Olderman. LC 73-182210. 269p. reprint ed. pap. 76.70 (*0-8357-8042-2*, 2033848) Bks Demand.

Beyond the Welfare State: An Examination of Basic Incomes in a Market Economy. Samuel Brittan & Steven Webb. (David Hume Papers: No. 17). 78p. 1990. pap. text ed. 14.00 (*0-08-040915-6*, Pub. by Aberdeen U Pr) Macmillan.

Beyond the Welfare State: Economic Planning & Its International Implications. Gunnar Myrdal. LC 82-15819. xiii, 287p. 1982. reprint ed. text ed. 38.50 (*0-313-23697-6*, MYBW, Greenwood Pr) Greenwood.

Beyond the Welfare State? The New Political Economy of Welfare. Christopher Pierson. 260p. 1991. text ed. 35.00 (*0-271-00820-2*); pap. text ed. 14.95 (*0-271-00821-0*) Pa St U Pr.

Beyond the Western Tradition: Readings in Moral & Political Philosophy. Daniel Bonevac et al. LC 91-33102. 372p. (C). 1992. pap. text ed. 19.95 (*1-55934-075-4*) Mayfield Pub.

Beyond the Winning Streak: Using Conscious Creation to Consistently Win at Life. Lynda M. Dahl. LC 92-39769. 208p. (Orig.). 1993. pap. 11.95 (*0-9634629-0-3*) WindSong WA.

***Beyond the Word: Reconstructing Sense in the Joyce Era of Technology, Culture, & Communication.** Donald F. Theall. (Theory - Culture Ser.). 360p. (C). 1995. 50.00 (*0-8020-0630-2*) U of Toronto Pr.

Beyond the Word: The Multiple Gestures of Tradition. Sitakant Mahapatra. (C). 1993. 14.00 (*81-208-1108-9*, Pub. by Motilal Banarsidass II) S Asia.

Beyond the Word: The World of Mime. Stephan Niedzialkowski & Jonathan Winslow. LC 93-3164. 116p. 1993. pap. 12.95 (*1-879094-23-1*) Momentum Bks.

Beyond the Written Word: Oral Aspects of Scripture in the History of Religion. William A. Graham. 375p. 1988. 59.95 (*0-521-33176-5*) Cambridge U Pr.

Beyond the Written Word: Oral Aspects of Scripture in the History of Religion. William A. Graham. 320p. (C). 1993. pap. 21.95 (*0-521-44820-4*) Cambridge U Pr.

***Beyond the Yellow Star to America.** Inge Auerbacher. (Illus.). 224p. (Orig.). (YA). 1995. lib. bdg. 19.99 (*0-88092-253-2*); pap. 7.99 (*0-88092-252-4*) Royal Fireworks.

Beyond the Zone System. 3rd ed. Phil Davis. LC 93-17818. (Illus.). 224p. 1993. pap. 30.00 (*0-240-80193-8*, Focal) Buttrwrth-Heinemann.

Beyond Their Dreams. Mildred J. Nash. LC 89-37565. 104p. (Orig.). 1989. pap. 5.95 (*0-936015-16-0*) Pocahontas Pr.

Beyond Theological Tourism: Mentoring As a Grassroots Approach to Theological Education. Ed. by Susan B. Thistlethwaite & George F. Cairns. LC 94-31784. 182p. (Orig.). 1994. pap. 19.95 (*0-88344-965-X*) Orbis Bks.

Beyond Theology: The Art of Godmanship. Alan W. Watts. 1973. pap. 5.95 (*0-394-71923-9*, Vin) Random.

Beyond Theory: Eighteenth-Century German Literature & the Poetics of Irony. Benjamin Bennett. LC 92-46530. (Illus.). 376p. (C). 1993. 42.50 (*0-8014-2841-6*) Cornell U Pr.

Beyond Therapy. Anne W. Schaef. 368p. 1992. pap. 12.00 (*0-06-250716-8*) Harper SF.

***Beyond Therapy, Beyond.** Schaif. Date not set. pap. 5.99 (*0-517-13255-9*) Random.

Beyond Therapy, Beyond Science: A New Model for Healing the Whole Person. Anne W. Schaef. 368p. 1994. pap. 14.00 (*0-06-250833-4*) Harper SF.

Beyond There Be Demons. J. G. Hontz. LC 93-93948. 168p. (Orig.). 1994. pap. 9.00 (*1-56002-356-2*, Univ Edtns) Aegina Pr.

***Beyond There Be Dragons.** Kimberly T. Fried. 280p. 1996. pap. 8.95 (*0-7610-0494-7*) NW Pub.

Beyond This Darkness. Linn Creighton. 176p. (Orig.). 1993. pap. 7.95 (*0-8361-3642-X*) Herald Pr.

Beyond This Horizon. Robert A. Heinlein. 1960. pap. 3.50 (*0-317-00243-0*, Sig) NAL-Dutton.

Beyond This Place. A. J. Cronin. 1976. 23.95 (*0-88411-525-9*) Amereon Ltd.

Beyond This Place. A. J. Cronin. 320p. 1984. reprint ed. 16.45i (*0-316-16195-0*) Little.

Beyond This Point Are Monsters. Margaret Millar. 213p. pap. 4.95 (*0-930330-31-5*) Intl Polygonics.

***Beyond This Reality: A Personal Account of the Near Death Experience.** Grace Bubulka. 114p. (Orig.). 1995. pap. 11.95 (*1-884995-03-9*) Word Dancer.

Beyond Those Mountains. Dick Thiessen. 148p. (Orig.). 1993. pap. 6.95 (*0-919797-46-6*) Kindred Prods.

Beyond Time: The Art of Alfred Van Loen. Eleanor Flomenhaft. (Illus.). 146p. (Orig.). 1993. 50.00 (*1-883269-01-6*); pap. 34.95 (*1-883269-00-8*) Sunstorm Arts.

Beyond Time Management: Organizing the Organization. Jane E. Allen. 144p. 1986. 14.95 (*0-201-15793-4*) Addison-Wesley.

Beyond Today. Pearl J. Ray. 288p. (Orig.). (C). 1986. pap. 6.95 (*0-9616405-0-2*) Harvest Age.

Beyond Today's Energy Crisis. Ed. by Kenneth W. Tolo. (Symposia Ser.). 142p. 1975. pap. 3.00 (*0-89940-412-X*) LBJ Sch Pub Aff.

***Beyond Tokenism: Parents As Partners in Literacy.** Trevor H. Cairney & Lynne Munsie. LC 94-31882. 95p. 1995. pap. text ed. 15.00 (*0-435-08832-7*) Heinemann.

Beyond Tomorrow. Fern Michaels. 1994. mass mkt. 4.50 (*0-373-48302-3*, 5-48302-9) Silhouette.

Beyond Tomorrow. Billy O. Urfer. 107p. (Orig.). 1981. pap. 2.95 (*0-9604306-0-1*, 501U) Urfer.

Beyond Tomorrow: Strategic Planning for Churches. Robert Johnson-Smith, II. 100p. 1994. student ed 59.95 (*0-9640699-0-3*) ATAP Communs.

Beyond Tomorrow: Trends & Prospects in Medical Science. LC 77-24824. 150p. 1977. pap. 2.95 (*0-87470-023-X*) Rockefeller.

Beyond Tomorrow, a Rational Utopia. Burnham P. Beckwith. 188p. (C). 1986. reprint ed. 9.00 (*0-9603262-5-1*) Beckwith.

Beyond Tools. Chris Bigum. 67p. (C). 1987. 30.00 (*0-7300-0523-2*, Pub. by Deakin Univ AT) St Mut.

Beyond Total Quality Management: Toward the Emerging Paradigm. Greg Bounds. 1993. text ed. write for info. (*0-07-006678-7*) McGraw.

Beyond TQM. Robert L. Flood. LC 93-12004. 275p. 1993. text ed. 49.95 (*0-471-93967-6*) Wiley.

***Beyond TQM: Making World Class Performance a Reality.** Michael Joyce. (Financial Times Management Ser.). 275p. (C). 1995. 57.50x (*0-273-61081-3*, Pub. by Pitman Pub Ltd UK) Trans-Atl Phila.

Beyond Trade Friction: Japan-U. S. Economic Relations. Ed. by Ryuzo Sato & Julianne Nelson. (Illus.). 225p. (C). 1989. 44.95 (*0-521-36467-1*) Cambridge U Pr.

Beyond Tradition: Contemporary Indian Art & Its Evolution. Photos by Jerry Jacka. LC 88-60922. (Illus.). 216p. 1988. 55.00 (*0-87358-471-6*) Northland AZ.

Beyond Tradition: Contemporary Indian Art & Its Evolution. Lois E. Jacka. LC 88-60922. (Illus.). 216p. 1991. reprint ed. pap. 35.00 (*0-87358-520-8*) Northland AZ.

Beyond Tradition: Transcripts of the First National Symposium on Non-Traditional Casting. Ed. by Harry Newman & Clinton T. Davis. (Illus.). 122p. (Orig.). 1988. pap. 15.00 (*0-927340-00-3*) Non-Traditional.

***Beyond Traditional Job Development: The Art of Creating Opportunity.** Denise Bissonnette. LC 94-21858. 1994. 29.95 (*0-942071-29-8*) M Wright & Assocs.

***Beyond Traditional Peacekeeping.** Donald C. Daniel & Bradd C. Hayes. 1995. write for info. (*0-312-12512-7*) St Martin.

Beyond Traditional Tenure: A Guide to Sound Policies & Practices. Richard Chait & Andrew T. Ford. LC 81-23606. (Jossey-Bass Series in Higher Education). 317p. reprint ed. pap. 90.40 (*0-8357-4935-5*, 2037865) Bks Demand.

Beyond Traffic Safety. J. Peter Rothe. 366p. (C). 1993. text ed. 39.95 (*1-56000-095-3*) Transaction Pubs.

Beyond Tragedy: Essays on the Christian Interpretation of History. Reinhold Niebuhr. 1979. pap. text ed. write for info. (*0-684-16410-8*, SL38, Scribners) S&S Trade.

Beyond Tragedy: Essays on the Christian Interpretation of History. Reinhold Niebuhr. LC 76-167397. (Essay Index Reprint Ser.). 1977. reprint ed. 26.95 (*0-8369-2437-1*) Ayer.

Beyond Tragedy: Structure & Experience in Shakespeare's Romances. Robert W. Uphaus. LC 80-5184. 160p. 1981. 16.00 (*0-8131-1441-1*) U Pr of Ky.

Beyond Training: How Athletes Enhance Performance Legally & Illegally. 2nd ed. Melvin H. Williams. LC 88-14801. (Illus.). 232p. (Orig.). 1989. pap. 13.95 (*0-88011-336-7*, PWIL0336) Human Kinetics.

Beyond Transference: When the Therapist's Real Life Intrudes. Ed. by Judith H. Gold & John C. Nemiah. LC 92-7053. 192p. 1992. text ed. 27.50 (*0-88048-361-X*) Am Psychiatric.

***Beyond Translation: Essays Towards a Modern Philosophy.** A. L. Becker. LC 94-47089. 1995. 49.50 (*0-472-10573-6*) U of Mich Pr.

***Beyond Trauma: Cultural & Societal Dynamics.** Ed. by R. J. Kleber et al. (Stress & Coping Ser.). (Illus.). 325p. (C). 1995. write for info. (*0-306-45058-5*, Plenum Pr) Plenum.

Beyond Trinity. Bernard J. Cooke. LC 70-81373. (Aquinas Lectures). 1969. 10.00 (*0-87462-134-8*) Marquette.

***Beyond Trout: A Flyfishing Guide.** Barry Reynolds & John Berryman. (Illus.). 176p. (Orig.). 1995. 23.00 (*1-55566-155-6*); pap. 16.95 (*1-55566-156-4*) Johnson Bks.

Beyond Turmoil: A Guide to Renewal Through Deep Personal Change. Alice Mack. 176p. 1992. pap. 12.95 (*0-9632450-7-4*) Connexions.

Beyond TV: Activities for Using Video with Children. Martha Dewing. 140p. 1990. pap. text ed. 45.00 (*0-87436-601-1*) ABC-CLIO.

Beyond TV Dinners: Three Levels of Recipes for Visually Handicapped Cooks. large type ed. P. Canter et al. 214p. 1979. reprint ed. 30.69 (*0-317-01874-4*, 4-02470-00) Am Printing Hse.

Beyond Two Thousand: A Minimum Model for the Global Future. Rob Matthews. (Illus.). 230p. (Orig.). (C). 1989. pap. 16.00 (*0-9622962-0-1*) Global Dynamics.

Beyond Two Thousand: The Future of Direct Marketing: 28 of the World's Leading Experts Predict the Changes Which Will Impact You, Your Job, & Your Company. Comp. by Jerry I. Reitman. LC 93-42158. 1994. 34.95 (*0-8442-3450-8*, NTC Busn Bks) NTC Pub Grp.

Beyond Two Thousand One: The Light Age. Glen Hiemstra. (Illus.). 300p. 1990. 18.95 (*0-317-91190-2*) Lincoln Global Prodns.

***Beyond Uhura: Star Trek & Other Memories.** Nichelle Nichols. 336p. Date not set. pap. text ed. 5.99 (*1-57297-011-1*) Blvd Books.

Beyond Uhura: Star Trek & Other Memories. Nichelle Nichols. 320p. 1995. 22.95 (*0-399-13993-1*) Putnam Pub Group.

Beyond Ujamaa in Tanzania: Underdevelopment & an Uncaptured Peasantry. Goran Hyden. LC 79-65773. 1980. pap. 16.00 (*0-520-04017-1*) U CA Pr.

Beyond Underdevelopment: Structural Constraints of the Development of Productive Forces among the Jok Gor, the Sudan. Salah E. Ibrahim. (Bergen Studies in Social Anthropology: No. 22). 223p. 1993. reprint ed. text ed. 13.95 (*0-936508-75-2*, Pub. by Bergen Univ Dept Social Anthro NO) Barber Pr.

Beyond Understanding: The Complete Guide to Princess Louisa Inlet, Chatterbox Falls & Jervis Inlet. William H. Schweizer. (Illus.). 300p. 1989. 19.95 (*0-925244-01-5*); pap. 19.95 (*0-925244-00-7*) EOS Pub.

Beyond Universals in Cognitive Development. David H. Feldman. LC 79-24338. (Publications for the Advancement of Theory & History in Psychology, the PATH Ser.). (Illus.). 204p. 1980. 39.50 (*0-89391-029-5*) Ablex Pub.

Beyond Universals in Cognitive Development. David H. Feldman. LC 94-16334. 224p. 1994. pap. 22.50 (*1-56750-032-3*) Ablex Pub.

Beyond Universals in Cognitive Development. 2nd ed. David H. Feldman. LC 94-16334. 224p. 1994. 47.50 (*1-56750-031-5*) Ablex Pub.

Beyond Universities: A New Republic of the Intellect. Douglas Hague. 86p. (C). 1991. text ed. 59.95 (*0-255-36244-7*, Pub. by Inst Economic Affairs UK) St Mut.

Beyond Urban Bias. Ed. by Ashutosh Varshney. LC 93-24138. (Illus.). 258p. 1993. text ed. 37.50 (*0-7146-4511-7*, Pub. by F Cass Pubs UK) Intl Spec Bk.

Beyond Urban Bias in Africa: Urbanization in an Era of Structural Adjustment. Charles M. Becker et al. LC 93-32405. 296p. (C). 1994. 60.00 (*0-435-08091-1*, 08091); pap. 27.50 (*0-435-08093-8*, 08093) Heinemann.

An Asterisk (*) at the beginning of an entry indicates that the title is appearing in BIP for the first time.

Beyond Utility: Liberal Education for a Technological Age. Athanasios Moulakis. LC 93-27212. 184p. 1994. 21.95 (*0-8262-0929-7*) U of Mo Pr.

***Beyond Utopia: Science, Values, & the Citizen.** John C. Honey. 1995. 17.95 (*0-533-11404-7*) Vantage.

Beyond Valor. Frank Geron. 352p. 1984. pap. 3.50 (*0-8217-1425-2*) Zebra.

Beyond Vaneck Phreaking. John J. Williams. Ed. by Laurie Williams. (Illus.). 54p. 1992. pap. 29.00 (*0-934274-33-9*) Consumertronics.

Beyond Velikovsky: The History of a Public Controversy. Henry H. Bauer. LC 83-17935. 368p. 1984. 29.95 (*0-252-01104-X*) U of Ill Pr.

Beyond Vengenance. J. L. Bouma. 192p. 1986. reprint ed. pap. 2.25 (*0-8439-2326-1*) Dorchester Pub Co.

Beyond Victim: You Can Overcome Childhood Abuse ... Even Sexual Abuse! Martha Baldwin. LC 88-4673. 328p. (Orig.). 1988. pap. 16.95 (*0-935834-68-0*) Rainbow Books.

***Beyond Victimhood: Embrace the Future.** Tom Fitzgerald. LC 95-120. 1995. 10.95 (*0-925190-42-X*) Fairview Press.

Beyond Victory. Ed. by Ruth N. Anshen. LC 75-156605. (Essay Index Reprint Ser.). 1977. reprint ed. 20.95 (*0-8369-2303-0*) Ayer.

Beyond Vision: One Hundred Historic Scientific Photographs. Jon Darius. LC 84-4405. (Illus.). 224p. 1984. 39.95 (*0-19-853245-8*) OUP.

Beyond Wage Slavery. Ken Coates. 170p. 1977. 42.50 (*0-85124-176-X*, Pub. by Spokesman Bks UK) Coronet Bks.

Beyond Walls & Wars: Art, Politics, & Multiculturalism. Ed. by Kim Levin. LC 91-68502. 1993. pap. text ed. 15.50 (*1-877675-11-3*) Midmarch Arts-WAN.

Beyond Walras, Keynes & Marx. Kaoru Yamaguchi. (Synthesis in Economic Theory Toward a New Social Design Ser.). 346p. (C). 1989. text ed. 43.50 (*0-8204-0762-3*) P Lang Pubs.

Beyond Washington: An Association Guide to Shaping a State Government Affairs Program. Ed. by Jared O. Blum. (Orig.). 1990. pap. 20.00 (*0-88034-042-8*) Am Soc Assn Execs.

Beyond Welfare: A Symposium on Earnings- & Asset-Based Welfare Reform. Ed. by Empowerment Network Foundation Staff. LC 94-5167. 1994. write for info. (*1-55815-352-7*) ICS Pr.

Beyond Welfare: New Approaches to the Problem of Poverty in America. Ed. by Harrell R. Rodgers, Jr. LC 87-28876. 184p. 1988. pap. text ed. 25.95 (*0-87332-461-7*) M E Sharpe.

***Beyond Westphalia? State Sovereignty & International Invention.** Ed. by Gene M. Lyons & Michael Mastanduno. 360p. 1994. text ed. 48.50x (*0-8018-4953-5*); pap. text ed. 16.95x (*0-8018-4954-3*) Johns Hopkins.

Beyond Wilderness. Ed. by Charles Hagen. 80p. 1990. pap. 18.50 (*0-89381-456-3*) Aperture.

Beyond Winning. Keshavan Nair. LC 87-62803. 105p. (Orig.). 1988. 14.95 (*0-945150-19-9*); pap. 9.95 (*0-945150-22-9*) Paradox AZ.

Beyond Winning: Group Centered Games & Sports. Larry Rowen. (J). (gr. 2-6). 1990. pap. 9.99 (*0-8224-3380-X*) Fearon Teach Aids.

Beyond Winning: The Timeless Wisdom of Great Philosopher Coaches. Gary M. Walton. LC 91-23761. (Illus.). 208p. (Orig.). 1992. pap. text ed. 13.95 (*0-88011-453-3*, PWAL0453) Human Kinetics.

Beyond Within. Bobbi. 96p. 1984. 8.95 (*0-9626608-2-5*) Magik NY.

Beyond Within. Sri Chinmoy. 525p. 1985. pap. 10.95 (*0-88497-115-5*) Aum Pubns.

Beyond Within. Alphonse Goettmann & Rachel Goettmann. Tr. by Theodore J. Nottingham & Rebecca Nottingham. LC 92-73338. 138p. 1992. pap. 8.95 (*0-87029-247-1*) Abbey.

Beyond Words. Norman W. Evans & Mark O. James. 275p. (C). 1989. pap. text ed. 19.50 (*0-13-074048-9*) P-H.

Beyond Words. Sri Swami Satchidanada. Ed. by Lester Alexander. LC 76-29896. (Illus.). 190p. 1977. pap. 9.95 (*0-03-016911-9*) Integral Yoga Pubns.

Beyond Words: A Lexicon of Metaphysical Thought. Paula B. Slater & Barbara Sinor. (Illus.). 272p. (Orig.). 1993. per. 15.95 (*0-944202-05-5*) Harbin Springs.

Beyond Words: Images from America's Concentration Camps. Deborah Gesensway & Mindy Roseman. LC 86-29088. (Illus.). 192p. 1987. 39.95 (*0-8014-1919-0*); pap. 21.95 (*0-8014-9522-9*) Cornell U Pr.

Beyond Words: Movement Observation & Analysis. Carol-Lynne Moore & Kaoru Yamamoto. 320p. (C). 1988. text ed. 58.00 (*2-88124-250-2*); pap. text ed. 30.00 (*2-88124-251-0*); teacher ed. pap. text ed. 25.00 (*2-88124-252-9*); vhs 247.00 (*2-88124-313-4*); vhs 257.00 (*2-88124-315-0*) Gordon & Breach.

Beyond Words: Picture Books for Older Readers & Writers. Ed. by Susan Benedict & Lenore Carlisle. LC 92-11964. 144p. 1992. pap. text ed. 18.00 (*0-435-08710-X*, 08710) Heinemann.

***Beyond Words: Sign Language Stories for Hand & Voice.** Valerie Marsh. (Illus.). 80p. (J). (ps-5). 1995. student ed 10.95 (*0-917846-49-4*, 33902, Alleyside) Highsmith Pr.

Beyond Words: The Story of Sensitivity Training & the Encounter Movement. Kurt W. Back. LC 73-182935. 266p. (Orig.). 1972. 45.00 (*0-87154-077-0*) Russell Sage.

Beyond Words: The Story of Sensitivity Training & the Encounter Movement. Kurt W. Back. 285p. (Orig.). 1987. pap. 21.95 (*0-87855-677-X*) Transaction Pubs.

Beyond Words: Unlocking the Secret to Communicating. Patricia St. John. Ed. by Dorothy Seymour. 288p. 1994. pap. 13.95 (*0-913299-96-0*) Stillpoint.

Beyond Words: Writing Poems with Children. Judith Steinbergh & Elizabeth McKim. 136p. 1983. pap. 9.95 (*0-931694-13-2*) Wampeter Pr.

Beyond Words & Thoughts. Joel S. Goldsmith. 6.00 (*0-8216-0041-9*, Univ Bks) Carol Pub Group.

Beyond Words & Thoughts. Joel S. Goldsmith. 200p. 1974. reprint ed. pap. 7.95 (*0-8065-0447-1*, Citadel Pr) Carol Pub Group.

Beyond Words, Writing Poems with Children: A Guide for Parents & Teachers. rev. ed. Elizabeth McKim & Judith W. Steinbergh. LC 82-70442. 152p. 1992. reprint ed. pap. text ed. 14.95 (*0-944941-03-6*) Talking Stone Pr.

***Beyond Work-Family Programs: Confronting & Resolving the Underlying Causes of Work-Personal Life Conflict.** Joan R. Kofodimos. 58p. 1995. pap. text ed. 25.00 (*1-882197-05-4*) Ctr Creat Leader.

***Beyond Workplace Two Thousand: Essential Strategies for the New American Corporation.** Joseph H. Boyett. 368p. 1995. 24.95 (*0-525-93782-X*, Dutton) NAL-Dutton.

Beyond X's & O's. Jack Hutslar. 1985. 8.95 (*0-318-18990-9*) No Amer Youth.

Beyond Yiddishkeit: The Struggle for Jewish Identity in a Reform Synagogue. Frida K. Furman. LC 94-18415. 168p. (C). reprint ed. pap. text ed. 18.00 (*0-8191-9507-3*) U Pr of Amer.

Beyond Yin & Yang. George Ulett. (Illus.). 172p. 1992. pap. 22.50 (*0-87527-490-0*) Green.

Beyond Your Command. Ralph Pape. 1988. pap. 4.75 (*0-8222-0113-5*) Dramatists Play.

Beyond Your Wedding Day. Jack Quesnell. 209p. (Orig.). 1986. pap. 7.95 (*0-317-40176-9*) Family Visions.

***Beyond Your Wildest Dreams: Daring to Risk with God Student Journal.** Randy Petersen & Byron Emmert. (1994 50-Day Spiritual Adventure Ser.). (Illus.). 80p. (Orig.). (YA). (gr. 7-12). 1993. student ed, pap. text ed. 4.99 (*1-879050-15-3*) Chapel of Air.

***Beyond Your Wildest Dreams: Daring to Risk with God, Student Leader's Guide.** Byron Emmert. (1994 50-Day Spiritual Adventure Ser.). (Illus.). 32p. (Orig.). (YA). (gr. 7-12). 1993. student ed, pap. text ed. 4.99 (*1-879050-21-8*) Chapel of Air.

Beyond Yugoslavia: Politics, Economics, & Culture in a Shattered Community. Ed. by Sabrina P. Ramet. (Eastern Europe After Communism Ser.). 484p. (C). 1995. text ed. 49.95 (*0-8133-7953-9*) Westview.

Beyond Zero: The Russian Avant-Garde, 1915-1932 Art, Architecture, & Design. Catherine Cooke. 1992. 85.00 (*0-89207-095-1*) S R Guggenheim.

Beyond 1492: Encounters in Colonial North America. James Axtell. (Illus.). 400p. 1992. pap. 17.95 (*0-19-508033-5*) OUP.

Beyond "1984" The Future of Library Technical Services. Ed. by Peter Gellatly. LC 83-17166. (Technical Services Quarterly Ser.: Vol. 1, Nos. 1/2). 265p. 1984. text ed. 49.95 (*0-86656-275-3*) Haworth Pr.

Beyond 911: A New Era for Policing. Malcolm K. Sparrow et al. LC 90-80239. 269p. 1992. reprint ed. pap. 15.00 (*0-465-00676-0*) Basic.

Beyondism: Religion from Science. Raymond B. Cattell. LC 87-17885. 336p. 1987. text ed. 55.00 (*0-275-92431-9*, C2431, Praeger Pubs) Greenwood.

Beytrag Zum Jocherischen Gelehrtenlexikon. Ernst C. Hauber. 48p. 1968. reprint ed. write for info. (*0-318-70766-7*, Pub. by Georg Olms GW) Lubrecht & Cramer.

Beytrage Zur Historie der Gelehrtheit, Worinnen die Geschichte der Gelehrten Unserer Zeiten Beschrieben Werden, 2 vols., Set. Johann C. Strodtmann. reprint ed. write for info. (*0-318-71904-5*, Pub. by Georg Olms GW) Lubrecht & Cramer.

Bez Rossii. Arsenij Nesmelov. (Illus.). 480p. (Orig.). 1990. 35.00 (*1-878445-57-X*) Antiquary CT.

Bezae Codex Cantabrigiensis: Being an Exact Copy, in Ordinary Type of the Celebrated Uncial Graeco-Latin Manuscript of the Four Gospels & Acts of the Apostles. Theodore Beza. Ed. by Frederick H. Scrivener. LC 78-4144. (Pittsburgh Reprint Ser.: No. 5). 1978. pap. 30.00 (*0-915138-39-5*) Pickwick.

Bezah, 1 vol. (ENG & HEB.). 15.00 (*0-910218-60-9*) Bennet Pub.

Bezalel: The Evolution of a Heritage - the Paintings of Aharona Reiner & Sculptures of Danny Kafr. (Illus.). (Orig.). Date not set. pap. text ed. write for info. (*1-881456-10-2*) B B K Natl Jew Mus.

Bezeichnungen fuer den Boettcher im niederdeutschen Sprachbereich. Ulrich Witte. (European University Studies: German Language & Literature: Ser. 1, Vol. 539). xii, 489p. (GER.). 1982. 68.45 (*3-8204-6288-0*) P Lang Pubs.

Bezeichnungen Fur Himmelsrichtungen in Den Finnisch Ugrischen Sprachen. Erzebet Beothy. LC 67-63037. (Uralic & Altaic Ser.: Vol. 84). 241p. 1967. pap. text ed. 14.00 (*0-87750-033-9*) Res Inst Inner Asian Studies.

Bezeichnungen fur Soziale Stande, Schichten & Gruppen in den Leges Barbarorum. Gabriele Von Olberg. (Volkssprachigen Worter der Leges Barbarorum; Teil 2 - Arbeiten zur Fruhmittelalterforschung Ser.: Band 11). vi, 335p. (GER.). (C). 1991. lib. bdg. 152.35 (*3-11-012218-9*) De Gruyter.

Bezeugung von Ciceros Schrift "De Re Publica" Eberhard Heck. Bd. 4. xi, 298p. (GER.). 1966. write for info. (*0-318-70611-3*, Pub. by Georg Olms GW) Lubrecht & Cramer.

Bezeugung Von Ciceros Schrift De Re Publica. Eberhard Heck. Bd. IV. xi, 298p. 1966. write for info. (*0-318-71141-9*, Pub. by Georg Olms GW) Lubrecht & Cramer.

Beziehung der Fruhchristlichen Sittenlehre Zur Ethik der Stoa. Johannes Stelzenberger. xx, 525p. 1989. reprint ed. write for info. (*3-487-09148-8*, Pub. by Georg Olms GW) Lubrecht & Cramer.

Beziehungen Zwischen Vegetation, Boden-wasser, Mikroklima und Energiehaushalt von Feuchtwiesen Unter Besonderer Beruecksichtigung der Evatranspiration. M. O. Rosset. (Dissertationes Botanicae Ser.: Vol. 159). (Illus.). 244p. (GER.). 1990. pap. text ed. 76.00 (*3-443-64071-0*, Pub. by Cramer-Borntraeger GW) Lubrecht & Cramer.

BE2 in Action. Peter Cooksley. (Aircraft in Action Ser.). (Illus.). 50p. 1992. pap. 8.95 (*0-89747-275-6*, 1123) Squad Sig Pubns.

BF 109 Aces of North Africa & the Mediterranean. Jerry Scutts. (Illus.). 96p. 1994. pap. 12.95 (*1-85532-448-2*, Pub. by Osprey Pubng Ltd UK) Motorbooks Intl.

Bf 110 Zerstorer in Action. Jerry Campbell. (Aircraft in Action Ser.). (Illus.). 50p. 1977. pap. 8.95 (*0-89747-029-X*, 1030) Squad Sig Pubns.

BFG. Roald Dahl. LC 93-22605. (Children's Classics Ser.). (J). 1993. 13.95 (*0-679-42813-5*, Everymans Lib) Knopf.

BFG. Roald Dahl. LC 85-566. (Illus.). 221p. (J). (gr. 1 up). 1982. 16.00 (*0-374-30469-6*) FS&G.

BFG. Roald Dahl. (Illus.). (J). 1989. pap. 4.99 (*0-14-034019-X*, Puffin) Puffin Bks.

BFI Companion to the Western. Ed. by Edward Buscombe. (Quality Paperbacks Ser.). (Illus.). 432p. 1991. pap. 26.95 (*0-306-80440-9*) Da Capo.

***BGMI CD-ROM 95 IBM Single User Version.** Ed. by Barbara McNeil. (Global Access: BGMI Ser.). 1994. 1,250.00 (*0-8103-6197-3*) Gale.

BGS Short Communications Eight. (British Geological Survey - BSG Reports: Vol. 19, No. 2). (Illus.). 1988. pap. 7.00 (*0-11-884429-6*, HM3221, Pub. by HMSO UK) UNIPUB.

BG128 Medical Savings Accounts (Medical IRA's) An Idea Whose Time Has Come. John C. Goodman & Gerald Musgrave. 1993. 5.00 (*1-56808-011-5*) Natl Ctr Pol.

BG129 Managed Competition. Merrill Matthews. Date not set. 5.00 (*0-685-67208-5*) Natl Ctr Pol.

BHA, Bibliography of the History of Art, Bibliographie d'Histoire de L'Art, 4 vols., Set. Getty Art History Information Program (AHIP) Staff & Institute de l'Information Scientifique et Technique-CNRS (INIST) Staff. 1992. 325.00 (*0-685-45791-5*) J P Getty Trust.

Bhabani Bhattacharya: A Stylistic Analysis of His Novels. Nathan M. Aston. (C). 1994. 20.00 (*81-207-1342-7*, Pub. by Sterling Plns Pvt II) S Asia.

Bhabani Bhattacharya: His Vision & Themes. K. K. Sharma. 1980. 10.00 (*0-8364-0584-6*, Pub. by Abhinav II) S Asia.

Bhadramayakara-Vyakarana. Konstanty Regamey. 1990. reprint ed. 19.00 (*81-208-0761-8*, Pub. by Motilal Banarsidass II) S Asia.

Bhadresvar: The Oldest Islamic Monuments in India. Mehrdad Shokoohy. (Studies in Islamic Art & Architecture Supplements to Muqarnas: Vol. II). (Illus.). 123p. 1988. text ed. 41.25 (*90-04-08341-3*) E J Brill.

Bhagat Singh: Patriot & Martyr. S. R. Bakshi. (C). 1990. 42.00 (*0-685-33288-8*, Pub. by Anmol II) S Asia.

Bhagat Singh & His Thought. Hansraj Rahbar. 1990. 23.50 (*81-85445-07-9*, Pub. by Usha II) S Asia.

Bhagavad. Mark Dunster. 9p. (Orig.). 1993. pap. 4.00 (*0-89642-215-1*) Linden Pubs.

Bhagavad - Gita: A New Translation & Commentary, Chapters 1-6. Maharishi Mahesh Yogi. 373p. 1967. 18.95 (*0-89186-000-2*); 5.00 (*0-89186-002-9*) Age Enlight Pr.

***Bhagavad Gita.** Besant. 1994. 11.50 (*0-8356-7051-1*, Quest) Theos Pub Hse.

Bhagavad Gita. Antonio T. De Nicolas. 156p. (Orig.). 1990. pap. 12.50 (*0-89254-018-4*) Nicolas-Hays.

Bhagavad Gita. Tr. by Eknath Easwaran. LC 85-10637. 240p. 1985. 18.00 (*0-915132-36-2*); pap. 9.95 (*0-915132-35-4*) Nilgiri Pr.

Bhagavad Gita. Tr. by Gita-Swarupananda. 435p. (ENG & SAN.). 1982. pap. 4.50 (*0-87481-064-7*) Vedanta Pr.

Bhagavad Gita. Tr. & Intro. by W. J. Johnson. LC 93-40558. (World's Classics Ser.). 120p. 1994. pap. 5.95 (*0-19-282952-1*) OUP.

Bhagavad Gita. Juan Mascaro. 1962. mass mkt. 7.95 (*0-14-044121-2*, Penguin Classics) Viking Penguin.

Bhagavad-Gita. Tr. & Intro. by Barbara S. Miller. 176p. (Orig.). 1986. mass mkt. 4.50 (*0-553-21365-2*, Bantam Classics) Bantam.

Bhagavad-Gita. Chaman Nahal. 64p. (C). 1989. 60.00 (*81-209-0753-7*, Pub. by Pitambar Pub II); pap. 20.00 (*81-209-0032-4*, Pub. by Pitambar Pub II) St Mut.

Bhagavad-Gita. Chaman Nahal. 1990. 60.00 (*81-209-0753-1*, Pub. by Pitambar Pub II) St Mut.

Bhagavad Gita. Tr. by Swami Nikhilananda. LC 44-33674. 404p. 1944. 14.50 (*0-911206-09-4*) Ramakrishna.

Bhagavad Gita. Yogi Ramacharaka. 184p. 1978. 6.00 (*0-318-37175-8*) Asia Bk Corp.

Bhagavad Gita. Yogi Ramacharaka. 9.00 (*0-911662-10-3*) Yoga.

Bhagavad Gita. Tr. by Haroutiun T. Saraydarian. LC 74-11759. 1974. 10.00 (*0-911794-36-0*); pap. 8.00 (*0-911794-37-9*) Aqua Educ.

Bhagavad Gita. Tr. by Shri Purohit Swami. 168p. 1994. pap. 6.00 (*0-87773-975-7*, Sham Pocket Class) Shambhala Pubns.

Bhagavad Gita. Tr. by Swamii Gambhirananda & Shankara. 826p. (Orig.). 1989. pap. 8.95 (*0-87481-231-3*, Pub. by Advaita Ashrama II) Vedanta Pr.

Bhagavad-Gita. Ed. by Robert C. Zaehner. 492p. 1973. pap. 14.95 (*0-19-501666-1*) OUP.

Bhagavad Gita. rev. ed. Winthrop Sargeant. LC 83-18287. (Cultural Perspectives Ser.). 739p. 1984. pap. 16.95 (*0-87395-830-6*) State U NY Pr.

Bhagavad Gita. 7th ed. Annie Besant. 1983. 5.95 (*0-8356-7001-5*) Theos Pub Hse.

Bhagavad Gita. Tr. by Franklin Edgerton. 218p. 1972. reprint ed. pap. text ed. 12.00 (*0-674-06925-0*) HUP.

Bhagavad Gita. Ed. by N. V. Thadani. 164p. 1990. reprint ed. Centenary edition. 20.00 (*0-317-99930-3*, Pub. by M Manoharial II) Coronet Bks.

Bhagavad Gita: A New Translation with Commentary. David White. (American University Studies: Theology & Religion: Ser. VII, Vol. 39). 246p. (C). 1989. text ed. 42.50 (*0-8204-0527-2*) P Lang Pubs.

Bhagavad Gita: A Philosophical System. Hasmukh Raval. (Illus.). 112p. 1990. 15.00 (*0-87527-484-6*) Green.

Bhagavad Gita: A Scripture for the Future. Tr. & Intro. by Sachin K. Majumdar. LC 91-21423. 272p. (Orig.). 1992. 45.00 (*0-89581-885-X*, Asian Human Pr); pap. 15.00 (*0-89581-896-5*, Asian Human Pr) Jain Pub Co.

Bhagavad Gita: A Sublime Hymn of Yoga Composed by the Ancient Seer Vyasa. Tr. by Nataraja Guru. (C). 1993. text ed. 28.50 (*81-246-0010-4*, Pub. by DK Pubs Dist II) S Asia.

Bhagavad Gita: A Translation & Commentary. Ed. by Santosh K. Ganguli. LC 91-71704. 310p. (Orig.). (C). 1991. pap. 13.95 (*0-945510-06-3*) Intl Info Assocs.

Bhagavad Gita: An Exegetical Commentary. Robert Minor. 1982. 38.00 (*0-8364-0817-9*); text ed. 18.50 (*0-8364-0862-4*) S Asia.

Bhagavad Gita: An Interpretation. Mohandas K. Gandhi. Ed. by Narahari D. Parikh. 309p. (Orig.). (C). 1984. pap. 10.00 (*0-934676-65-8*) Greenlf Bks.

Bhagavad Gita: An Introduction. Georg Feuerstein. LC 82-42702. 191p. 1983. reprint ed. pap. 7.95 (*0-8356-0575-2*, Quest) Theos Pub Hse.

Bhagavad Gita: Economic Development & Management. A. K. Srivastava. 1980. 14.00 (*0-8364-0592-7*) S Asia.

Bhagavad Gita: Interpretation of Sriyukteswar. Swami S. Giri. (Illus.). 334p. (Orig.). 1991. pap. 20.00 (*1-877854-12-3*) Sanskrit Classics.

Bhagavad Gita: Interpretations of Lahiri Mahasay. Satyeswarananda Giri. LC 91-66548. (Complete Works of Lahiri Mahasay: Vol. II). (Illus.). 192p. (Orig.). 1991. pap. text ed. 15.00 (*1-877854-16-6*) Sanskrit Classics.

Bhagavad-Gita: Krishna's Counsel in Time of War. Tr. by Barbara S. Miller. LC 86-13725. (Illus.). 176p. 1986. text ed. 28.00 (*0-231-06468-3*) Col U Pr.

Bhagavad-Gita: Krishna's Counsel in Time of War. Barbara S. Miller. 1991. mass mkt. 9.00 (*0-553-35340-3*) Bantam.

Bhagavad-Gita: Recension with Essays. William Q. Judge. LC 70-92964. 238p. 1978. reprint ed. 12.00 (*0-911500-27-8*); reprint ed. pap. 7.00 (*0-911500-28-6*) Theos U Pr.

Bhagavad-Gita: The Book of Devotion Dialogue Between Krishna, Lord of Devotion, & Arjuna, Prince of India. Tr. & Intro. by William Q. Judge. xviii, 133p. 1930. reprint ed. 4.00 (*0-938998-09-9*) Theosophy.

Bhagavad Gita: The Divine Message, 2 vols., Set. Swami Abhedananda. 1969. 25.95 (*0-87481-625-4*) Vedanta Pr.

Bhagavad Gita: The Journey Through Life to Enlightenment. Swami Savitripriya. 200p. (Orig.). Date not set. pap. 13.95 (*1-879722-03-8*) New Life Bks.

Bhagavad Gita: The Song of God. Tr. by Gita-Prabhavananda & Christopher Isherwood. 192p. 1993. 9.95 (*0-87481-008-6*); pap. 7.95 (*0-87481-043-4*) Vedanta Pr.

Bhagavad Gita: The Song of God. 2nd ed. Goswami Kriyananda. (Illus.). 137p. reprint ed. pap. text ed. 5.95 (*0-9613099-3-8*) Temple Kriya Yoga.

Bhagavad Gita: Thus Sang Lord Krishna. Satguru S. Keshavadas. (Illus.). 104p. (Orig.). 1975. pap. 8.00 (*0-685-51013-1*) Vishwa.

Bhagavad Gita: Translated with Introduction & Notes. 2nd rev. ed. Tr. by B. Srinivasa Murthy. LC 90-82501. 156p. 1991. 11.95 (*0-941910-05-9*) Long Beach Pubns.

Bhagavad Gita: Translation & Commentary. Richard Gotshalk. xvi, 245p. 1986. 19.00 (*81-208-0006-0*, Pub. by Motilal Banarsidass II) S Asia.

Bhagavad Gita: With Text, Translation & Commentary by Sri Sankaracharya. Sri Sankaracharya. Tr. by Alladi M. Sastri. 534p. 1989. 19.95 (*0-910261-03-2*, Pub. by Samata Bks II); pap. 17.95 (*0-910261-04-0*, Pub. by Samata Bks II) Lotus Light.

Bhagavad Gita & Its Message: With Text, Translation & Sri Aurobindo's Commentary. Sri Aurobindo. Ed. by Anilbaran Roy. LC 94-75589. 325p. (Orig.). 1994. pap. 14.95 (*0-941524-78-7*) Lotus Light.

Bhagavad Gita As It Is. (Illus.). 904p. 1991. 10.95 (*0-89213-123-3*) Bhaktivedanta.

Bhagavad-gita As It Is. 1042p. 1989. vinyl bd. 10.95 (*0-89213-268-X*) Bhaktivedanta.

Bhagavad-Gita As It Is. A. C. Prabhupada. 904p. 1988. 19.95 (*0-318-37155-3*) Asia Bk Corp.

Bhagavad Gita As It Is. Bhaktivedanta Swami. 1990. 5.95 (*0-89213-134-9*) Bhaktivedanta.

Bhagavad Gita for Daily Living, Set. 1984. SET. 82.00 (*0-915132-06-0*); SET. pap. 52.00 (*0-915132-20-6*) Nilgiri Pr.

Bhagavad Gita for Daily Living Vol. I: The End of Sorrow. Eknath Easwaran. LC 74-20130. 425p. 1975. 30.00 (*0-915132-03-6*); pap. 19.95 (*0-915132-17-6*) Nilgiri Pr.

Bhagavad Gita for Daily Living Vol. II: Like a Thousand Suns. Eknath Easwaran. LC 79-1448. 512p. 1979. 30.00 (*0-915132-04-4*); pap. 19.95 (*0-915132-18-4*) Nilgiri Pr.

Bhagavad Gita for Daily Living Vol. III: To Love Is to Know Me. Eknath Easwaran. LC 79-1448. 512p. 1984. 30.00 (*0-915132-05-2*); pap. 19.95 (*0-915132-19-2*) Nilgiri Pr.

Bhagavad Gita in Light of Sri Aurobindo. Sri Aurobindo. Ed. by Maheshwar. 1979. 10.00 (*0-89744-902-9*); pap. 7.25 (*0-89744-903-7*) Auromere.

Bhagavad Gita (Pocket Edition) Tr. by Swami Nikhilananda. LC 44-33674. 256p. 1944. 10.50 (*0-911206-10-8*) Ramakrishna.

B

An Asterisk (*) at the beginning of an entry indicates that the title is appearing in BIP for the first time. 723

Bhagavad Gita, Srimad: The Scripture of Mankind. Tr. by Swami Tapasyananda. (ENG & SAN.). 1985. Pocket edition. pap. 3.95 (*0-87481-533-9*, Pub. by Ramakrishna Math II) Vedanta Pr.

Bhagavad-Gita, Srimad see Srimad-Bhagavad-Gita

Bhagavad Gita, Srimad Bhasya of Sri Sankaracarya. Gita. Tr. by A. G. Warrier. 652p. (Orig.). (C). 1984. pap. 8.95 (*0-87481-525-8*, Pub. by Ramakrishna Math II) Vedanta Pr.

Bhagavad Gita, Srimad, with the Gloss of Sridhara Swami. Tr. by Gita-Vireshwarananda. (ENG & SAN.). 1989. pap. 5.95 (*0-87481-575-4*, Pub. by Ramakrishna Math II) Vedanta Pr.

Bhagavad Gita with the Uttara Gita. Ed. by Raghavan Iyer. (Pythagorean Sangha Ser.). 416p. 1986. pap. 19.75 (*0-88695-041-4*) Concord Grove.

Bhagavadgeeta-Bible-Khuran (Krishna-Jesus Mohammad) Panduranga R. Malyala. Date not set. 3.99 (*0-938924-04-4*) Sri Shirdi Sai.

Bhagavadgita. Tr. by Edwin Arnold. LC 93-1448. (Thrift Editions Ser.). 112p. 1993. pap. 1.00 (*0-486-27782-8*) Dover.

Bhagavadgita. Pref. by M. K. Gandhi. LC 86-71762. 14.50 (*0-86516-179-8*) Bolchazy-Carducci.

Bhagavadgita: The Song of God. Tr. by Ramanand Prasad. LC 88-72192. 144p. (Orig.). 1988. pap. 4.95 (*0-9621099-1-6*) Gita Pr W.

Bhagavadgita: Translated into English Verse. N. V. Thadani. 1990. 19.00 (*0-685-37838-1*, Pub. by Munshiram Manoharial II) S Asia.

Bhagavadgita & Jivana Yoga. R. N. Vyas. 1986. 14.00 (*81-7017-203-9*, Pub. by Abhinav II) S Asia.

Bhagavadgita in the Mahabharata: A Bilingual Edition. Ed. by J. A. Van Buitenen. LC 79-13021. 184p. 1981. lib. bdg. 19.00 (*0-226-84660-1*); pap. text ed. 9.95 (*0-226-84662-8*) U Ch Pr.

***Bhagavan Sri Sathya Sai Baba, My Divine Teacher.** Curth Orefjaerd. (C). 1995. 14.00x (*81-208-1269-7*, Pub. by Motilal Banarsidass II); pap. 14.00x (*81-208-1270-0*, Pub. by Motilal Banarsidass II) S Asia.

***Bhagavata-Glimpses Glorious.** C. L. Dhody. (C). 1994. 36.00x (*81-85880-46-8*, Pub. by Print Hse II) St Mut.

Bhagavata Purana, Pt. I. Tr. by G. V. Tagare. (Ancient Indian Tradition & Mythology Ser.: Vol. 7). 1986. 26.00 (*81-208-0096-6*, Pub. by Motilal Banarsidass II) S Asia.

Bhagavata Purana, Pt. III. Tr. by G. V. Tagare. (Ancient Indian Tradition & Mythology Ser.: Vol. 9). 1987. 26.00 (*81-208-0313-2*, Pub. by Motilal Banarsidass II) S Asia.

Bhagavata Purana, Pt. IV. Tr. by G. V. Tagare. (Ancient Indian Tradition & Mythology Ser.: Vol. 10). 1988. 26.00 (*81-208-0342-6*, Pub. by Motilal Banarsidass II) S Asia.

Bhagavata Purana, Pt. V. G. V. Tagare. (Ancient Indian Tradition & Mythology Ser.: Vol. 11). 1989. 26.00 (*81-208-0343-4*, Pub. by Motilal Banarsidass II) S Asia.

Bhagavata Purana: An Illustrated Oriya Palmleaf Manuscript. Ed. by P. K. Mishra. (Illus.). 60p. 1987. 32.50 (*81-7017-219-5*, Pub. by Abhinav II) S Asia.

Bhagavata Purana: Mytho-Social Study. S. S. Dange. LC 84-900334. 1984. 28.50 (*0-685-08432-9*, Pub. by Ajanta II) S Asia.

Bhagavata, Srimad, 4. Bhagavatam. Tr. by Swami Tapasyananda. 1983. 21.00 (*0-87481-519-3*, Pub. by Ramakrishna Math II) Vedanta Pr.

Bhagavata, Srimad, Vol. 1. Bhagavatam. Tr. by Swami Tapasyananda. 455p. 1983. 21.00 (*0-87481-516-9*, Pub. by Ramakrishna Math II) Vedanta Pr.

Bhagavata, Srimad, Vol. 2. Bhagavatam. Tr. by Swami Tapasyananda. 492p. 1983. 21.00 (*0-87481-517-7*, Pub. by Ramakrishna Math II) Vedanta Pr.

Bhagavata, Srimad, Vol. 3. Bhagavatam. Tr. by Swami Tapasyananda. 447p. 1983. 21.00 (*0-87481-518-5*, Pub. by Ramakrishna Math II) Vedanta Pr.

Bhagavatam, Srimad: The Wisdom of God. Bhagavatam. 1979. pap. 5.95 (*0-87481-490-1*, Pub. by Ramakrishna Math II) Vedanta Pr.

Bhagavatam, Srimad: The Wisdom of God. Swami Prabhavananda. 1978. reprint ed. 5.95 (*0-87481-483-9*) Vedanta Pr.

Bhagita Vidhi: (Law of Partnership in Hindi) 3rd ed. Ed. by Avtar Singh. (HIN.). (C). 1988. 22.00 (*0-685-39592-8*) St Mut.

Bhagita Vidhi (Law of Partnership in India) Avtar Singh. 1979. 30.00 (*0-317-57658-5*) St Mut.

Bhagwadgita. N. S. Subrahmanian. 79p. 1980. 6.95 (*0-7069-0920-8*) Asia Bk Corp.

Bhagwan Shree Rajneesh: The Most Dangerous Man since Jesus Christ. Sue Appleton. 91p. (Orig.). 1987. pap. text ed. 4.95 (*3-89338-001-9*, Pub. by Rebel Hse GW) Osho Chidvilas.

Bhai Vir Singh. G. S. Khosla. 1984. 15.00 (*0-8364-1230-3*, Pub. by Heritage IA) S Asia.

Bhakapur Nepal - Building Today in a Historical Context. G. Scheiblor. 1991. 175.00 (*0-7855-0302-1*, Pub. by Ratna Pustak Bhandar) St Mut.

Bhaktapur Nepal - Building Today in a Historical Context. G. Scheiblor. (C). 1991. text ed. 90.00 (*0-7855-0129-0*, Pub. by Ratna Pustak Bhandar) St Mut.

Bhakti & the Bhakti Movement: A New Perspective. Krishna Sharma. (Study in the History of Ideas). 360p. 1987. text ed. 45.00 (*81-215-0029-X*) Coronet Bks.

Bhakti Ratnavali: An Anthology from the Bhagavata. Vishnu Puri. Tr. by Bhagavatam. 256p. 1980. 5.95 (*0-87481-499-5*, Pub. by Ramakrishna Math II) Vedanta Pr.

Bhakti-Ratnavali: With the Commentary of Visnu Puri. Bhagavatapurana Puranas. LC 73-3794. (Sacred Books of the Hindus: No. 7 Pt.3). reprint ed. 25.00 (*0-404-57835-7*) AMS Pr.

Bhakti Religion in North India: Community Identity & Political Action. Ed. by David N. Lorenzen. LC 93-41538. (SUNY Series in Religious Studies). 304p. (C). 1994. 59.50 (*0-7914-2025-6*); pap. 19.95 (*0-7914-2026-4*) State U NY Pr.

Bhakti Sect of Vallabhacarya. Richard Barz. (C). 1992. reprint ed. 24.00 (*81-215-0576-3*, Pub. by Munshiram Manoharial II) S Asia.

Bhakti Studies. Ed. by G. M. Bailey & I. Kesarcodi-Watson. 353p. 1992. text ed. 40.00 (*81-207-0835-0*, Pub. by Sterling Pubs II) Apt Bks.

Bhakti Sutras of Narada. Narada. Tr. & Intro. by Nandalal Sinha. LC 73-3792. (Sacred Books of the Hindus: No. 7, Pt. 1). reprint ed. 17.50 (*0-404-57807-1*) AMS Pr.

Bhakti Yoga. Yogi Bhikshu. 9.00 (*0-911662-21-9*) Yoga.

Bhakti Yoga: The Yoga of Love & Devotion. Swami Vivekananda. 1922. pap. 1.95 (*0-87481-157-0*, Pub. by Advaita Ashrama II) Vedanta Pr.

***Bhaminivilasa.** E. V. Dadape & D. G. Apte. (C). 1994. reprint ed. 17.00x (*81-208-1170-4*, Pub. by Motilal Banarsidass II) S Asia.

Bhangai: A Sweeper Caste. Shyamlal. (C). 1992. 17.50 (*81-7154-550-5*, Pub. by Popular Prakashan II) S Asia.

Bhangra Dance: Poems, Nineteen Sixty-Seven to Nineteen Seventy. Gail D. Chiarello. 1970. pap. 2.00 (*0-685-04665-6*) Oyez.

Bharadvajas in Ancient India. Thaneswar Sarmah. (C). 1991. 18.50 (*81-208-0639-5*, Pub. by Motilal Banarsidass II) S Asia.

Bharat Ka Samvidhan: (Constitution of India), 2 vols., Set. Mahavir Singh. (HIN.). (C). 1987. 150.00 (*0-685-37439-4*) St Mut.

Bharat Ka Samvidhan (Constitution of India in Hindi), 2 vols. Mahavir Singh. 627p. 1985. 225.00 (*0-685-73861-2*) St Mut.

Bharat Ka Samvidhan, 1987: With Supplement (Constitution of India in Hindi), 2 vols., Set. Mahavir Singh. (HIN.). (C). 1990. 175.00 (*0-685-39770-X*) St Mut.

***Bharata: Love & Justice in the Ramayana.** Anantanand Rambachan. 76p. (Orig.). 1993. pap. 5.00 (*0-9634164-3-X*) Vijnana Pubns.

Bharata Natyam Dancer. 2nd ed. G. S. Sharat Chandra. (Redbird Ser.). 1976. 8.00 (*0-89253-129-0*); 4.80 (*0-89253-140-1*) Ind-US Inc.

Bharata Natyam in Cultural Perspective. George Kliger. (C). 1993. 28.00 (*81-7304-034-6*, Pub. by Manohar II) S Asia.

Bharata Sindhi Rashmi: (A Working Summary in England of the Epic of That Name Prepared by the Author. Vinayak K. Gokak. (New World Literature Ser.: No. 57). (C). 1992. pap. 8.00 (*81-7018-721-4*, Pub. by BR Pub II) S Asia.

Bharatavarsha: An Account of Early India with Special Emphasis on Social & Economic Aspects. Arun Bhattacharjee. 212p. (C). 1988. 27.00 (*81-7024-169-3*, Pub. by Ashish II) S Asia.

***Bharati Mukherjee.** Fakrul Alam. LC 95-10832. (Twayne's United States Authors Ser.: Vol. 653). 1995. 26.95 (*0-8057-3997-1*, Twayne) Macmillan.

Bharati Mukherjee: Critical Perspectives, Vol. 1663. Emmanuel S. Nelson. LC 93-18145. 256p. 1993. 38.00 (*0-8153-1173-7*, H1663) Garland.

Bharatiya Dand Sanhita, Eighteen Sixty. K. Chaturvedi. 816p. (HIN.). 1982. 150.00 (*0-317-54757-7*) St Mut.

Bharatiya Jana Sangh: Organization & Ideology. Geeta Puri. 292p. 1980. 24.95 (*0-940500-26-4*) Asia Bk Corp.

Bharatiya Sakshya Adhiniyam. K. K. Singh. 352p. 1979. 54.00 (*0-317-57666-6*); pap. 38.00 (*0-317-57667-4*) St Mut.

Bharatiya Sakshya Adhiniyam. 2nd ed. K. K. Singh. (C). 1979. 30.00 (*0-685-39708-4*) St Mut.

Bhargava's Concise Hindi-English Dictionary. 6th ed. R. C. Pathak. 1040p. 1981. 22.95 (*0-8288-1744-8*, M9437) Fr & Eur.

Bhartiya Dand Sanhita, 1860: (Indian Penal Code, 1860, in Hindi) with Supplement. Ed. by M. Chaturvedi. (HIN.). (C). 1987. 55.00 (*0-685-39590-1*) St Mut.

Bhartriji - Immortal Yogi of Two Thousand Years. Leonard Orr. 1990. 12.00 (*0-945793-05-7*) Inspir Univ.

Bhatkhande's Contribution to Music: A Historical Perspective. Sobhana Nayar. (C). 1989. 32.00 (*0-86132-238-X*, Pub. by Popular Prakashan II) S Asia.

Bhavabhiti's Malatimadhva with the Commentary of Jagaddhara. Tr. by M. R. Kali. 1983. reprint ed. 11.50 (*0-8364-2625-8*, Pub. by Motilal Banarsidass II) S Asia.

Bhavanarayana Temples: An Epigraphical & Architectural Study. Avadhanula V. Babu. (C). 1991. 94.00 (*81-85067-68-6*, Pub. by Sundeep Prakashan II) S Asia.

Bheesma. T. R. Narayana. (Illus.). (J). (gr. 1-8). 1979. pap. 3.00 (*0-89744-151-6*) Auromere.

Bhikshugita: The Mendicant's Song. Saint Eknath. Tr. by Justin E. Abbott & Swami Tapasyananda. 193p. 1989. 9.95 (*0-910261-10-5*, Pub. by Samata Bks II) Lotus Light.

Bhilsa Topes; or Buddhist Monuments of Central India. Alexander Cunningham. LC 78-72401. reprint ed. 47.50 (*0-404-17263-6*) AMS Pr.

***Bhimsen Joshi: A Biography.** Mahan Nadkarni. (C). 1995. 22.50x (*81-7223-126-1*, Pub. by Indus Pub II) S Asia.

Bhojpuri Grammar. Shaligram Shukla. LC 81-13172. 332p. reprint ed. pap. 94.70 (*0-7837-6339-5*, 2046051) Bks Demand.

Bhopal: Anatomy of a Crisis. Paul Shrivastava. 176p. 1992. pap. 29.95 (*1-85396-192-2*, Pub. by Paul Chapman UK) Taylor & Francis.

Bhopal: Its Setting, Responsibility & Challenge. Ed. by Sidney C. Sufrin. 1985. 13.50 (*0-8364-1508-6*, Pub. by Ajanta II) S Asia.

Bhopal: The Inside Story - Carbide Workers Speak Out on the World's Worst Industrial Disaster. T. R. Chouhan et al. 212p. (Orig.). 1994. pap. 15.00 (*0-945257-22-8*) Apex Pr.

Bhopal Chemical Leak. Arthur Diamond. LC 90-6011. (World Disasters Ser.). (Illus.). 64p. (J). (gr. 5-8). 1990. lib. bdg. 14.95 (*1-56006-009-3*) Lucent Bks.

Bhopal Tragedy: What Really Happened & What It Means for American Workers & Communities at Risk. Ward Morehouse & Arun Subramaniam. (Illus.). 190p. 1986. pap. 13.50 (*0-936876-47-6*) LRIS.

Bhowani Junction. John Masters. 450p. 1987. pap. 4.50 (*0-88184-310-5*) Carroll & Graf.

Bhowani Junction. large type ed. John Masters. 576p. 1983. 21.95 (*0-7089-1056-4*) Ulverscroft.

Bhrigu Nandi Nadi. R. G. Rao. (C). 1991. reprint ed. text ed. 24.00 (*0-8364-2878-1*, Pub. by Ranjan Pubs II) S Asia.

Bhsai Course Companion. Jo French. 160p. 1990. pap. 40.00 (*0-85131-500-3*, Pub. by J A Allen & Co UK) St Mut.

Bhutan. Ramesh C. Dogra. (World Bibliographical Ser.). 1991. lib. bdg. 49.50 (*1-85109-128-9*) ABC-CLIO.

Bhutan. Leila M. Foster. LC 88-37375. (Enchantment of the World Ser.). (Illus.). 128p. (J). (gr. 5-9). 1989. lib. bdg. 21.53 (*0-516-02709-3*) Childrens.

Bhutan. Francoise Pommeret. LC 90-63329. (India Guides Ser.). (Illus.). 277p. 1993. reprint ed. pap. 14.95 (*0-8442-9924-3*, Passport Bks) NTC Pub Grp.

***Bhutan: A Movement in Exile.** D. N. Dhakal & Christopher Strawn. xxviii, 631p. 1994. 39.00x (*81-85693-41-2*, Pub. by Nirala Pubns II) Nataraj Bks.

Bhutan: A Physical & Cultural Geography. Pradyumna P. Karan. LC 67-17842. 125p. reprint ed. pap. 35.70 (*0-8357-7162-8*, 2030054) Bks Demand.

Bhutan: Environment, Culture & Development Strategy. P. P. Karan. 1990. 29.00 (*81-7076-027-5*, Pub. by Intellectual II) S Asia.

Bhutan: Ethnic Identity & National Dilemma. A. C. Sinha. (Sociological Publications in Honour of Dr. K. Ishwaran: Vol. 10). xxii, 258p. 1991. text ed. 37.50 (*81-85047-82-0*, Pub. by Reliance Pub Hse II) Apt Bks.

Bhutan: Problems & Policies. H. N. Misra. 1988. 27.00 (*0-8364-2311-9*, Heritage) S Asia.

Bhutanese Newspaper Reader. Stuart H. Buck. LC 88-70866. 274p. 1988. 39.00 (*0-931745-41-1*) Dunwoody Pr.

Bhutto: A Political Biography. Salmaan Taseer. 208p. 1980. 19.95 (*0-318-37225-8*) Asia Bk Corp.

Bi Any Other Name: Bisexual People Speak Out. Ed. by Loraine Hutchins & Lani Kaahumanu. LC 90-45816. 416p. (Orig.). 1991. pap. 11.95 (*1-55583-174-5*) Alyson Pubns.

Bi-Centenary Memorial of Jeremiah Carter Who Came to the Provence of Pennsylvania in 1682, a Historic-Genealogy of His Descendents down to the Present. T. M. Potts. (Illus.). 304p. 1989. reprint ed. lib. bdg. 59.00 (*0-8328-0372-3*); reprint ed. pap. 49.00 (*0-8328-0373-1*) Higginson Bk Co.

***Bi-Cultural Critical Essays on Shakespeare.** Joo-Hyon Kim. 128p. (Orig.). (C). 1995. pap. text ed. 27.00 (*0-85991-418-6*, DS Brewer) Boydell & Brewer.

Bi-Lingual Education in the Western Isles, Scotland 1975-81. John Murray & Catherine Morrison. 1985. 65.00 (*0-86152-036-X*, Pub. by Acair Ltd UK) St Mut.

Bi-Literal Cypher of Sir Francis Bacon. Elizabeth W. Gallup. LC 76-135731. (Illus.). reprint ed. 49.50 (*0-404-02669-9*) AMS Pr.

Bi-Polar: Foundations of Productivity. J. W. Thomas & T. J. Thomas. LC 91-143775. (Illus.). 335p. 1995. reprint ed. 25.00 (*0-9637450-0-X*) Inst Fnd Trning.

Bi-Ranchers, Bi-Mates. Bill Lee. 176p. (Orig.). 1991. pap. 9.95 (*1-879194-02-3*) GLB Pubs.

Bi-Sexual Man: Evolution of the Sexes. Buzzacott & Wymore. 83p. 1966. reprint ed. spiral bd. 8.25 (*0-7873-0137-X*) Mokelumne.

Bi-State Bicycle Tours: Tour Book. 3rd ed. Ed. by Bill Houghton. 138p. 1989. pap. 10.00 (*0-9630129-0-8*) Am Youth Hostels.

BIA Index: Decisions Reporter. Ed. by Immigration Appeals Board Staff. 578p. 1988. ring bd. 85.00 (*0-685-50635-5*) Amer Immi Law Assn.

BIA Index: Decisions Reporter. Ed. by Immigration Appeals Board Staff. 194p. 1989. ring bd. 105.00 (*0-685-50634-7*) Amer Immi Law Assn.

BIA Index: Decisions Reporter. Ed. by Immigration Appeals Board Staff. 283p. 1990. ring bd. 125.00 (*1-878677-09-8*); ring bd. 105.00 (*0-685-50633-9*) Amer Immi Law Assn.

Biafra. Ed. by Peter Schwab. LC 73-140967. 156p. reprint ed. pap. 44.50 (*0-8357-7163-6*, 2006282) Bks Demand.

Biafra Goodbye. Herbert Gold. (Orig.). 1970. pap. 8.00 (*0-685-04864-0*) Twowindows Pr.

Biafra War: Nigeria & the Aftermath. Herbert Ekwe-Ekwe. LC 90-21372. (African Studies: Vol. 17). 148p. 1991. lib. bdg. 69.95 (*0-88946-235-6*) E Mellen.

***Biafran Ideology: An African Critique of the Present World Systems.** Chukwudi Okeke Maduno. 115p. 1994. pap. text ed. write for info. (*0-9644596-1-2*) Ekumeku Commun.

Biagio Rossetti: Libellus De Rudimenis Muscices. Ed. by Albert Seay. (Critical Texts Ser.: No. 12). iv, 94p. (LAT.). (C). 1981. pap. text ed. 7.50 (*0-933894-11-2*) Colo Coll Music.

Bianca. Joan Phipson. LC 88-13192. 176p. (YA). (gr. 7 up). 1988. text ed. 14.95 (*0-689-50448-9*, McElderry) S&S Childrens.

Bianca & Roja. Hesba Brinsmead. (Illus.). 112p. (Orig.). (J). (gr. 2-6). 1993. pap. 7.95 (*1-86373-082-6*, Pub. by Allen & Unwin Aust Pty AT) IPG Chicago.

Bianchi of Thirteen Hundred Ninety-Nine: Popular Devotion in Late Medieval Italy. Daniel E. Bornstein. (Illus.). 248p. 1994. 32.50 (*0-8014-2910-2*) Cornell U Pr.

***Biannual Book of Brass Models.** Carl K. Middlebrooks. 122p. 1995. pap. write for info. (*0-9646066-0-7*) CMC Pub VA.

Bias Against Agriculture: Trade & Macroeconomic Policies in Developing Countries. Romeo M. Bautista & Alberto Valdes. 340p. 1993. pap. 24.95 (*1-55815-245-8*) ICS Pr.

Bias Crime: American Law Enforcement & Legal Responses. 2nd rev. ed. Ed. by Robert J. Kelly. LC 92-39895. 1993. 18.00 (*0-942511-58-1*) OICJ.

Bias for Hope: Essays on Development & Latin America. Albert O. Hirschman. LC 77-140531. (Illus.). reprint ed. pap. 73.00 (*0-8357-9078-9*, 2016762) Bks Demand.

Bias-Free Word Finder: A Dictionary of Non-Discriminatory Language. Rosalie Maggio. 294p. 1992. pap. 16.00 (*0-8070-6003-8*) Beacon Pr.

Bias in Human Reasoning: Causes & Consquences. Ed. by B. T. Evans. 160p. 1990. text ed. 39.95 (*0-86377-106-8*); pap. 22.50 (*0-86377-156-4*) L Erlbaum Assocs.

***Bias in Local Government: Law & Policy.** G. C. Kelly. 1995. pap. write for info. (*0-409-31011-5*, Austral) Butterworth Legal Pubs.

Bias in Mental Testing. Arthur R. Jensen. LC 79-7583. (Illus.). 1980. text ed. 35.00 (*0-02-916430-3*) Free Pr.

Bias in Psychotherapy. Joan Murray & Paul R. Abramson. 398p. 1983. text ed. 65.00 (*0-275-91050-4*, C1050, Praeger Pubs) Greenwood.

Bias in Quantifying Judgments. E. C. Poulton. 328p. 1989. 69.95 (*0-86377-105-X*) L Erlbaum Assocs.

Bias Issues in Teacher Certification Testing. Ed. by R. G. Allan et al. 184p. 1988. 36.00 (*0-8058-0080-8*) L Erlbaum Assocs.

Bias-Motivated Crimes. (Illus.). 118p. (Orig.). (C). 1994. pap. text ed. 31.95 (*1-56806-144-7*) Diane Pub.

***Bias Square Miniatures.** Christine Carlson. Ed. by Christine Barnes. (Illus.). 80p. (Orig.). 1995. pap. 18.95 (*1-56477-099-0*, B216) That Patchwork.

Biases of Management. Barbara W. Carroll. LC 93-7408. (Organizational Behaviour & Management Ser.). 1993. write for info. (*0-415-10196-4*) Routledge.

Biathanatos, John Donne, II. Ed. by Ernest W. Sullivan. LC 80-66387. 352p. 1984. 47.50 (*0-87413-175-8*) U Delaware Pr.

Biathanatos. John Donne. Ed. by Robert Kastenbaum. LC 76-19567. (Death & Dying Ser.). 1977. reprint ed. lib. bdg. 25.95 (*0-405-09563-5*) Ayer.

Biathlon. Arthur E. Stegen. (Illus.). 144p. 30.00 (*0-317-35230-X*, ASB16130) Natl Rifle Assn.

Biaxial & Uniaxial Capacity of Rectangular Columns. 31p. 1967. pap. 6.40 (*0-89312-005-7*, EB031D) Portland Cement.

Bib - Triv: Profundities, Banalities & Trivialities in Libraryland. Frederick Duda. LC 92-53507. (Illus.). 128p. 1992. pap. 18.95x (*0-89950-725-5*) McFarland & Co.

Bib & Tucker. Joan Abell. (Illus.). 50p. (Orig.). (J). (gr. 1-3). 1994. 23.00 (*1-56611-087-4*); pap. 15.00 (*1-56611-088-2*) Jonas.

BIB Television Programming Source Books - 1991, 4 vols. rev. ed. Ed. by Heidi Holland. 4000p. 1991. Vol. 1, Films A-L. write for info. (*0-912920-61-0*); Vol. 2, Films M-Z. write for info. (*0-912920-62-9*); Vol. 3, Film Packages. write for info. (*0-912920-63-7*) North Am Pub Co.

BIB Television Programming Source Books - 1991, 4 vols., Set. rev. ed. Ed. by Heidi Holland. 4000p. 1991. pap. 725.00 (*0-912920-60-2*) North Am Pub Co.

BIB Television Programming Source Books - 1991, 4 vols., Vol. 4: Series. rev. ed. Ed. by Heidi Holland. 4000p. 1991. Vol. 4, Series. pap. 330.00 (*0-912920-64-5*) North Am Pub Co.

BIB Television Programming Source Books - 1991, 4 vols., Vols. 1 & 2. rev. ed. Ed. by Heidi Holland. 4000p. 1991. pap. 440.00 (*0-685-54315-3*) North Am Pub Co.

BIB Television Programming Source Books, 1992-93: Films A-L; Films M-Z; Film Packages; Series, 4 vols. rev. ed. Ed. by Heidi Holland. 2900p. 1992. pap. 745.00 (*0-912920-68-8*) North Am Pub Co.

BIB Television Programming Source Books, 1992-93 Vol. 1: Films A-L. rev. ed. Ed. by Heidi Holland. 725p. 1992. pap. 455.00 (*0-912920-69-6*) North Am Pub Co.

BIB Television Programming Source Books, 1992-93 Vol. 2: Films M-Z. rev. ed. Ed. by Heidi Holland. 725p. 1992. pap. 455.00 (*0-912920-70-X*) North Am Pub Co.

BIB Television Programming Source Books, 1992-93 Vol. 3: Film Packages. rev. ed. Ed. by Heidi Holland. 725p. 1992. pap. 455.00 (*0-912920-71-8*) North Am Pub Co.

BIB Television Programming Source Books, 1992-93 Vol. 4: Series. rev. ed. Ed. by Heidi Holland. 725p. 1992. pap. 345.00 (*0-912920-72-6*) North Am Pub Co.

BIB Television Programming Source Books, 1993-94, Set. rev. ed. Ed. by Heidi Holland. 1993. pap. 745.00 (*0-912920-80-7*) North Am Pub Co.

BIB Television Programming Source Books, 1993-94, Vol. 4: Series. rev. ed. Ed. by Heidi Holland. 700p. 1993. Vol. 4 Series, 700p. pap. 345.00 (*0-912920-79-3*) North Am Pub Co.

BIB Television Programming Source Books, 1993-94, Vols. 1-3. rev. ed. Ed. by Heidi Holland. 1993. pap. 455.00 (*0-685-65417-6*) North Am Pub Co.

BIB Television Programming Source Books, 1993-94, Vols. 1-4. rev. ed. Ed. by Heidi Holland. 1993. Vol. 1: Films A-L, 700p. write for info. (*0-912920-76-9*); Vol. 2: Films M-Z, 700p. write for info. (*0-912920-77-7*); Vol. 3: Film Packages, 600p. write for info. (*0-912920-78-5*) North Am Pub Co.

***BIB Television Programming Source Books, 1994-1995, 4 vols., Set.** Ed. & Intro. by Donna Witzleben. 1994. pap. text ed. 795.00 (*0-912920-88-2*) North Am Pub Co.

724

An Asterisk (*) at the beginning of an entry indicates that the title is appearing in BIP for the first time.

An Asterisk (*) at the beginning of an entry indicates that the title is appearing in BIP for the first time.

725

Bible-Centered Crosswords. Donovan A. Epp. 1989. pap. 3.99 (0-8010-3201-6) Baker Bk.

Bible-Centered Object Sermons for Children. C. W. Bess & Roy E. DeBand. (Object Lesson Ser.). 128p. 1985. pap. 4.99 (0-8010-0886-7) Baker Bk.

Bible Characters. Ernest A. Clevenger, Jr. (Bible Drill Flash Cards Flipbook Ser.). (J). (gr. 3 up). 1994. pap. 5.00 (0-88428-018-7) Parchment Pr.

Bible Characters from the Old & New Testaments. Alexander Whyte. LC 90-36547. 920p. 1990. pap. 22.99 (0-8254-3980-9) Kregel.

Bible Children Puzzles. Nancy Persaud. (Bible Baffler Ser.). 48p. (J). (gr. 3 up). 1990. 7.95 (0-86653-534-9, SS891, Shining Star Pubns) Good Apple.

Bible Christmas Puzzles. William Schlegl. (Bible Baffler Ser.). (Illus.). 48p. (J). (gr. 3 up). 1987. pap. 7.95 (0-86653-409-1, SS 884, Shining Star Pubns) Good Apple.

Bible Chronology & the Scientific Method. Eugene W. Faulstich. (Illus.). 98p. (C). 1990. pap. 19.95 (0-940887-04-5) Chrono Bks.

Bible, Church & God. William McCarthy. 50.00 (0-936128-46-1) De Young Pr.

Bible, Church & God. 2nd ed. William McCarthy. LC 70-169211. (Atheist Viewpoint Ser.). (Illus.). 736p. 1972. reprint ed. 45.95 (0-405-03805-4) Ayer.

Bible Class Commentaries, 6 vols. Henry T. Mahan. Incl. Romans. 1984. pap. (0-85234-184-9); 1st & 2nd Corinthians. 1984. pap. (0-85234-194-6); Galatians Thru Colossians. 1984. pap. (0-85234-210-1); 1st & 2nd Thessalonians; 1st & 2nd Timothy. 1984. pap. (0-85234-185-7); Hebrews & James. 1984. pap. (0-85234-187-3); Titus, Philemon, & 1st & 2nd Peter Thru Jude. 1984. pap. (0-85234-211-X); 1984. Set pap. 4.95 (0-685-74589-9) Pilgrim Pubns.

Bible Class Commentaries, 6 vols., Set. Henry T. Mahan. Incl. Romans. 1984. pap. (0-85234-184-9); 1st & 2nd Corinthians. 1984. pap. (0-85234-194-6); Galatians Thru Colossians. 1984. pap. (0-85234-210-1); 1st & 2nd Thessalonians; 1st & 2nd Timothy. 1984. pap. (0-85234-185-7); Hebrews & James. 1984. pap. (0-85234-187-3); Titus, Philemon, & 1st & 2nd Peter Thru Jude. 1984. pap. (0-85234-211-X); 1984. Set pap. 29.95 (0-85234-215-2) Pilgrim Pubns.

Bible Codes & Messages. William Schlegl. (Bible Baffler Ser.). (Illus.). 48p. (J). (gr. 3 up). 1989. 7.95 (0-86653-479-2, SS887, Shining Star Pubns) Good Apple.

Bible Communism: A Compilation from the Annual Reports & Other Publications of the Oneida Association & Its Branches. Oneida Community Staff. LC 72-2978. reprint ed. 27.50 (0-404-10742-7) AMS Pr.

Bible Concordance. pap. 5.95 (1-55748-227-6) Barbour & Co.

Bible Condensed: Written in Current American. Gene H. Mouw. Ed. by Lynne A. Mouw. LC 89-92099. 144p. (Orig.). (C). 1989. pap. 8.95 (0-9624551-0-5) Mouw.

Bible Contradicts Itself. John Bowden. 36p. (C). 1982. reprint ed. 4.00 (0-911826-46-7, 5040) Am Atheist.

Bible Count & Color. Mary Backman. 1992. pap. 2.75 (0-89137-065-X) Quality Pubns.

***Bible Country.** Woodrow Kroll. 1992. 24.99 (0-8474-1455-8) Back to Bible.

Bible Crafts for Holidays. Susan Stegenga. (Bible Craft Ser.). (Illus.). 96p. (J). (gr. k-6). 1994. 9.95 (0-86653-770-8, SS3803, Shining Star Pubns) Good Apple.

Bible Crafts from Recycled Materials. Cathy Falk. (Bible Craft Ser.). (Illus.). 96p. (J). (gr. k-6). 1994. 9.95 (0-86653-772-4, SS3805, Shining Star Pubns) Good Apple.

Bible Crossword Fun. Linda Krein. (Bible Baffler Ser.). 48p. (J). (gr. 3 up). 1990. 7.95 (0-86653-547-0, SS892, Shining Star Pubns) Good Apple.

Bible Crossword Puzzle Book. S. K. Davis. (Quiz & Puzzle Bks.). (J). (gr. k-3). 1969. pap. 4.99 (0-8010-2812-4) Baker Bk.

Bible Crosswords. Linda Krein. (Bible Baffler Ser.). 48p. (J). (gr. 3 up). 1986. student ed 7.95 (0-86653-366-4, SS 881, Shining Star Pubns) Good Apple.

Bible Dates Itself. Arthur Earle. LC 73-88548. 1974. 12.50 (0-9600788-1-9) A Earle.

Bible, Day by Day. John Kersten. 1990. pap. 4.95 (0-89942-150-4) Catholic Bk Pub.

Bible Days Are Here Again. Gordon Lindsay. 1960. per. 5.95 (0-89985-194-0) Christ for the Nations.

Bible de la Sagesse Bantoue: Choix d'Aphorismes, Devinettes et Mots d'Espirts du Cameroun et du Gabon. Dika Akwa. (B. E. Ser.: No. 128). (FRE.). 1955. 18.00 (0-8115-3055-8) Periodicals Srv.

Bible de Mace de la Charite, VI: Evangiles, Actes des Apostres. J. R. Smeets & Q. I. Mok. (Leidse Romanistische Reeks Ser.: Vol. 10). vii, 328p. 1986. pap. 64.00 (90-04-07711-1) E J Brill.

Bible Defence of Slavery. Josiah Priest & W. S. Brown. LC 74-92439. 1851. 95.00 (0-403-00171-4) Scholarly.

Bible Defence of Slavery. W. S. Brown & Josiah Priest. 1988. reprint ed. lib. bdg. 95.00 (0-7812-0387-2) Rprt Serv.

Bible Dictionary. pap. 5.95 (1-55748-165-2) Barbour & Co.

Bible Dictionary: A First Reference Book. Etta Wilson & Sally L. Jones. (Illus.). 24p. (J). (gr. 3-5). 1993. text ed. 10.99 (0-7847-0079-6, 24-03619) Standard Pub.

Bible Dictionary: Dizionario Biblico. J. L. McKenzie. 1062p. (ITA.). 1981. 75.00 (0-8288-2315-4, M7640) Fr & Eur.

Bible Dictionary for Young Readers. William N. McElrath. LC 65-15604. (Illus.). (J). (gr. 4-6). 1965. 12.99 (0-8054-4404-1, 4244-04) Broadman.

Bible Difficulties & Seeming Contradictions. William F. Arndt. 1987. pap. 9.95 (0-570-04470-7, 12-3081) Concordia.

Bible Difficulties Solved: Answers to More Than 500 Baffling Questions from Genesis to Revelation. Larry Richards. LC 92-598. 416p. 1993. 15.99 (0-8007-1681-7) Revell.

Bible Digest Treasures. deluxe ed. Herschel B. Dean. (Illus.). 414p. 1988. 19.95 (0-944035-00-0) LaMar Pub.

Bible Discovery Collection: Animals. (Illus.). 64p. (J). (gr. 4-6). 1992. 12.99 (0-8423-1006-1) Tyndale.

Bible Doctrines. P. C. Nelson. LC 81-82738. 128p. (YA). (gr. 9-12). 1981. pap. 2.95 (0-88243-479-9, 02-0479) Gospel Pub.

Bible Doctrines: A Pentecostal Perspective. enl. rev. ed. Ed. by William W. Menzies & Stanley H. Horton. LC 92-43219. 304p. 1993. 19.95 (0-88243-318-0) Gospel Pub.

Bible Double Trouble Puzzles. Shirley Beegle. (Illus.). 64p. (J). (gr. 5 up). 1992. student ed 6.99 (0-87403-671-2, 28-02791) Standard Pub.

Bible Dramas for Older Boys & Girls. Sarah W. Miller. LC 75-95409. (J). (gr. 3-6). 1970. pap. 4.99 (0-8054-7506-0) Broadman.

Bible Easter Puzzles. Richard Latta. (Bible Baffler Ser.). 48p. (J). (gr. 3 up). 1988. 7.95 (0-86653-427-X, SS885, Shining Star Pubns) Good Apple.

***Bible Encyclopedia: A First Reference Book.** Etta Wilson & Sally L. Jones. (Illus.). 24p. (J). (gr. 3-5). 1995. 11.99 (0-7847-3442-9, 24-03654) Standard Pub.

Bible Explorer's Guide. John Phillips. LC 86-18565. 320p. 1987. pap. 11.99 (0-87213-682-5) Loizeaux.

Bible Exposition Commentary, 2 vols. Warren W. Wiersbe. 1400p. 1989. 62.99 (0-89693-659-7); 32.99 (0-685-74052-8) SP Pubns.

Bible Exposition Commentary, 2 vols., 1. Warren W. Wiersbe. 1400p. 1989. write for info. (1-56476-030-8) SP Pubns.

Bible Exposition Commentary, 2 vols., 2. Warren W. Wiersbe. 1400p. 1989. write for info. (1-56476-031-6) SP Pubns.

Bible Expounded with Understanding. Mack L. Shelton. 1993. 26.95 (0-8062-4543-3) Carlton.

Bible Fact or Fiction? Earl Robinson. 1992. pap. 4.99 (0-88019-296-8) Schmul Pub Co.

Bible Faith Study Course. 2nd ed. Kenneth E. Hagin. 1991. pap. 8.95 (0-89276-083-4) Hagin Ministries.

Bible Favorites Activity Book. Michael D. Rhoda. Ed. by Jonna Gress. (Illus.). 6p. (J). (ps-5). 1993. pap. 8.25 (0-944943-41-1, 22656-1) Current Inc.

Bible Folding Stories: Old Testament Stories & Paperfolding Together As One. Christine P. Kallevig. LC 93-85089. (Illus.). 80p. 1993. pap. write for info. (0-9628769-4-1) Storytime Ink.

Bible for Americans. Ed. by Serge Procopius. 103p. (Orig.). 1991. pap. 11.81 (0-685-48278-2) Dayspring Pr.

Bible for Beginning Readers. (Illus.). (J). (gr. 3 up). 1991. text ed. 9.99 (0-8499-0917-1) Word Inc.

Bible for Busy People. Mark D. Berrier, Jr. LC 93-36082. 130p. (Orig.). 1993. pap. 8.95 (1-55622-032-4, Seaside Pr) Wordware Pub.

Bible for Children. B. Hadaway. 1988. 9.99 (0-517-37641-5) Random Hse Value.

***Bible for Children.** Wangerin. 1995. 9.97 (1-57122-076-3) Nickel Pr.

Bible for Children. Walter Wangerin, Jr. (Illus.). 416p. (J). (ps up). 1987. pap. 14.95 (1-56288-187-6) Checkerboard.

Bible for Ethics: Juan Luis Segundo & First-World Ethics. Anthony J. Tambasco. LC 80-6253. 286p. (Orig.). 1981. pap. text ed. 23.00 (0-8191-1557-6) U Pr of Amer.

Bible for Little Hearts. Ed. by Livingstone Corporation Staff. LC 94-9694. (J). (gr. k up). 1995. 8.99 (0-8423-1306-0) Tyndale.

Bible for Today's Family: New Testament Contemporary English Version. 758p. (Orig.). 1993. 5.95 (0-8146-2296-8) Liturgical Pr.

***Bible for Tots.** Tyndale House Publishers Staff. LC 94-43716. (J). 1995. text ed. write for info. (0-8423-1323-0) Tyndale.

Bible for Young People. Daughters of St. Paul. 142p. (J). (gr. 4 up). 1988. pap. 5.00 (0-8198-0212-3) Pauline Bks.

Bible Fun Book, No. 8. Steve Crain. (Bethany House Activity Bks.). 32p. (Orig.). (J). (gr. k-4). 1981. pap. 1.19 (0-87123-772-5) Bethany Hse.

Bible Fun Book: Puzzles, Riddles, Magic, & More. David A. Adler. (Fun-to-Do Bks.). (Illus.). (Orig.). (J). (gr. 1-5). 1979. pap. 3.95 (0-88482-769-0) Hebrew Pub.

Bible Game, 1. Donna B. Smith et al. (Easy Does It Ser.: Nos. 1 & 2). 1990. pap. 6.50 (0-89137-061-7) Quality Pubns.

Bible Game, 2. Donna B. Smith et al. (Easy Does It Ser.: Nos. 1 & 2). 1990. pap. 6.50 (0-89137-062-5) Quality Pubns.

Bible Game & Workbook. Jacqueline J. Pliskin. 96p. (J). 1990. pap. 5.95 (0-944007-84-8) Sure Sellers.

Bible Game Book see Bible Games & Activities

Bible Games & Activities. Ronald F. Keeler. (Game & Party Bks.). Orig. Title: The Bible Game Book. 96p. 1982. reprint ed. pap. 4.99 (0-8010-5489-3) Baker Bk.

Bible Gems. Ivor C. Powell. LC 86-27525. 176p. 1987. pap. 8.99 (0-8254-3527-7) Kregel.

Bible Gems: New International Version. 1993. text ed. 4.99 (0-310-96258-7) Zondervan.

Bible Gems of Comfort. Zondervan Staff. 1994. 4.99 (0-310-96273-0) Zondervan.

Bible Gems of Faith. Zondervan Staff. (Tiny Treasures Ser.). 1994. 4.99 (0-310-96274-9) Zondervan.

Bible Gems of Joy. Zondervan Staff. (Tiny Treasures Ser.). 1994. 4.99 (0-310-96272-2) Zondervan.

Bible Gems of Love. Zondervan Staff. (Tiny Treasures Ser.). 1994. 4.99 (0-310-96271-4) Zondervan.

Bible Goes to Kruka Town. T. Eugene Oody. (Illus.). 74p. (Orig.). 1994. pap. 5.00 (0-9640888-0-0) T E Oody.

Bible Group: An Owner's Manual. William Riley. 154p. 1989. pap. 22.00 (0-86217-098-2, Pub. by Veritas IE) St Mut.

Bible Guide: A Reader's Companion to the Bible. LC 93-85518. (Gem Ser.). (Illus.). 320p. (Orig.). (YA). 1994. pap. 5.95 (1-56138-379-1) Running Pr.

Bible Guidebook. William N. McElrath. LC 72-79174. 144p. (J). (gr. 3-6). 1972. 12.99 (0-8054-4410-6) Broadman.

Bible Handbook. G. W. Foote. 1991. lib. bdg. 75.00 (0-87700-982-1) Revisionist Pr.

Bible Handbook. rev. ed. G. W. Foote & W. P. Ball. 372p. 1986. pap. 9.00 (0-910309-26-4, 5008) Am Atheist.

Bible Handbook: For Freethinkers & Inquiring Christians. 11th ed. Ed. by G. W. Foote & W. P. Ball. LC 71-161330. (Atheist Viewpoint Ser.). 176p. 1976. reprint ed. 23.95 (0-405-03797-X) Ayer.

Bible Handwork Ideas for Twos & Threes. Joy Averitt & Donna Smith. 1983. pap. 3.95 (0-89137-613-5) Quality Pubns.

Bible Has the Answer. Henry M Morris. 1971. pap. 11.99 (0-8010-5905-4) Baker Bk.

Bible Has the Answer. rev. ed. Henry M. Morris & Martin Clark. LC 76-20206. 408p. 1987. pap. 10.95 (0-89051-018-0) Master Bks.

Bible Heroes: Joseph, Esther, Mary & Peter. Paul Woods. (Active Bible Curriculum Ser.). (Illus.). 48p. 1992. pap. 9.99 (1-55945-137-8) Group Pub.

Bible Heroes: Stories for Children Ages One to Six. Louise A. Randall. LC 87-82112. 56p. (J). (ps). 1988. pap. 4.98 (0-88290-316-0) Horizon Utah.

Bible Heroes I Can Be. Ann Eisenberg. LC 89-48188. (Illus.). 24p. (J). (ps). 1990. 12.95 (0-929371-09-7); pap. 4.95 (0-929371-10-0) Kar Ben.

Bible Highways. Ivor Powell. LC 85-8097. 176p. 1985. pap. 8.99 (0-8254-3521-8) Kregel.

Bible History. Ed. by Richard Grunze. (WELS Lutheran Elementary Schools' Religion Curriculum Ser.). (Illus.). 556p. (gr. 5-6). 1984. 11.95 (0-938272-14-4) WELS Board.

Bible History. Ignatius Schuster. Ed. by H. J. Heck. Tr. by Philip Schumacher. (Illus.). (J). (gr. 6-8). 1974. reprint ed. pap. 10.00 (0-89555-006-7) TAN Bks Pubs.

Bible History: Teachers' Manual. Richard Grunze. 228p. 1985. ring bd., vinyl bd. 12.95 (0-938272-15-2) WELS Board.

Bible History Commentary: Old Testament. Werner H. Franzmann. LC 80-53145. (Illus.). 616p. 1981. 19.95 (0-938272-04-7) WELS Board.

Bible History Commentary-New Testament, 2 vols., Set. Werner H. Franzmann. (Illus.). 1546p. (C). 1989. 28.97 (0-685-26585-4); text ed. 39.95 (0-938272-06-3) WELS Board.

Bible History Commentary-New Testament, Vol. 3. Werner H. Franzmann. (Illus.). 764p. (C). 1989. 28.97 (0-685-44672-7); text ed. 39.95 (0-938272-02-0) WELS Board.

Bible History-New Testament, Vol. 2. Werner H. Franzmann. (Illus.). 782p. (C). 1989. 28.97 (0-685-26587-0); text ed. 39.95 (0-938272-05-5) WELS Board.

***Bible History Old Testament.** Alfred Edersheim. 1056p. 1995. 29.95 (1-56563-165-X) Hendrickson MA.

Bible History Overview: Old Testament. Gary Olsby. (Orig.). 1989. pap. 13.99 (0-89900-440-7); student ed 5.99 (0-89900-441-5) College Pr Pub.

Bible History Overview - New Testament. Gary Olsby. 1991. student ed 5.99 (0-89900-443-1); student ed, pap. 13.99 (0-89900-442-3) College Pr Pub.

Bible II: How to Get to Heaven. Ed. by New World Foundation Staff. 630p. (Orig.). (C). 1991. pap. 14.95 (1-879964-00-7) New World TX.

Bible Illuminated. Swami Bhaktipada. LC 94-8030. (Illuminated Scriptures of the World Ser.). 1994. write for info. (0-932215-33-5) Palace Pub.

Bible Illustrated for Little Children. Ella K. Lindvall. (Illus.). (J). (ps-2). 1991. text ed. 9.99 (0-8024-0569-X) Moody.

Bible Illustration. Johann U. Krause. (Printed Sources of Western Art Ser.). (Illus.). 50p. (GER.). 1981. reprint ed. pap. 50.00 (0-915346-54-0) A Wofsy Fine Arts.

Bible in a Nutshell. Dale Pritchard. LC 94-11993. 80p. (Orig.). 1995. 7.00 (0-87573-029-9) Jain Pub Co.

Bible in America: Essays in Cultural History. Ed. by Nathan O. Hatch & Mark A. Noll. LC 81-18751. 1982. pap. 7.95 (0-19-503100-8) OUP.

Bible in American Education. Ed. by David Barr & Nicholas Piediscalzi. LC 81-14436. (Society of Biblical Literature the Bible in American Culture Ser.). (C). 1982. 21.95 (0-89130-538-6, 061205) Scholars Pr GA.

Bible in American Law, Politics, & Political Rhetoric. Ed. by James T. Johnson. LC 83-16327. (Bible in American Culture Ser.). (C). 1984. pap. 21.95 (0-89130-652-8, 06 12 04) Scholars Pr GA.

Bible in Aramaic: Based on Old Manuscripts & Printed Texts, 4 vols. in 5 pts. Ed. by Alexander Sperber. 1992. reprint ed. Vol. I, xxii, 357p. write for info. (0-318-69001-2); reprint ed. Vol. II, x, 331p. write for info. (0-318-69002-0); reprint ed. Vol. III, xi, 505p. write for info. (0-318-69003-9); reprint ed. Vol. IVa, lviii, 205p. write for info. (0-318-69004-7); reprint ed. Vol. IVb, xv, 417p. write for info. (0-318-69005-5) E J Brill.

Bible in Aramaic: Based on Old Manuscripts & Printed Texts, 4 vols. in 5 pts., Set. Ed. by Alexander Sperber. LC 91-39374. 1992. reprint ed. pap. 271.50 (90-04-09580-2) E J Brill.

Bible in Art: Old Testament. Richard Muhlberger. 1991. 19.99 (0-517-03746-7) Random Hse Value.

***Bible in Christian Education.** Iris V. Cully. LC 95-3486. 1995. write for info. (0-8006-2806-3, Fortress Pr) Augsburg Fortress.

Bible in Church & Synagogue Libraries. William H. Gentz. (Guide Ser.: No. 16). 26p. 1989. pap. 7.25 (0-915324-27-X) CSLA.

Bible in Court: The Method of Legal Inquiry Applied to the Study of the Scriptures. Joseph E. Sagebeer. xiv, 201p. 1988. reprint ed. lib. bdg. 25.00 (0-8377-2620-4) Rothman.

Bible in Early English Literature. David C. Fowler. LC 76-7786. (Illus.). 274p. 1976. 22.50 (0-295-95438-8) U of Wash Pr.

Bible in English Drama: An Annotated Bibliography. rev. ed. Edward D. Coleman. 1969. 35.00 (0-87068-034-X) Ktav.

Bible in English Literature. E. W. Wock. 1972. 250.00 (0-87968-727-4) Gordon Pr.

Bible in Faith & Life: As Taught by James M. Gray. James G. Gray. Ed. by Joel A. Carpenter. LC 88-5826. (Fundamentalism in American Religion, 1880-1950 Ser.: Vol. 18). 592p. 1988. 20.00 (0-8240-5019-3) Garland.

***Bible in History.** Thomas Thompson. Date not set. pap. write for info. (0-679-44167-0); pap. write for info. (0-679-76195-0) Random.

Bible in Human Transformation: Towards a New Paradigm for Biblical Study. Walter Wink. LC 73-79047. 96p. (Orig.). 1980. pap. 8.00 (0-8006-1034-2, 1-1034, Fortress Pr) Augsburg Fortress.

Bible in India. Louis Jacolliot. 324p. 1992. pap. 26.00 (0-89540-211-4, SB-211) Sun Pub.

Bible in Its Ancient & English Version. Ed. by Henry W. Robinson. LC 76-109832. 337p. 1970. text ed. 59.75 (0-8371-4323-3, ROBI, Greenwood Pr) Greenwood.

Bible in Middle English Literature. David C. Fowler. LC 84-7453. (Illus.). 336p. 1984. 30.00 (0-295-96130-9) U of Wash Pr.

Bible in Pictures for Little Eyes. Kenneth N. Taylor. (Illus.). (J). (ps-2). 1956. 14.99 (0-8024-0595-9) Moody.

Bible in Pictures for Little Eyes. Kent Taylor. (J). (gr. 2 up). Date not set. 18.99 (0-8024-0685-8) Moody.

Bible in Pictures for Little Eyes see Biblia en Cuadros para Ninos

Bible in Pocket, Gun in Hand: The Story of Frontier Religion. Ross Phares. LC 64-11375. viii, 182p. 1971. pap. 8.95 (0-8032-5725-2, Bison Books) U of Nebr Pr.

Bible in Public Schools. 2nd ed. Johann B. Stallo et al. LC 67-27464. (Law, Politics & History Ser.). 1967. reprint ed. lib. bdg. 39.50 (0-306-70963-5) Da Capo.

Bible in Scottish Life & Literature. David Wright et al. (C). 1989. pap. text ed. 49.00 (0-7152-0629-X) St Mut.

Bible in Scottish Life & Literature. David F. Wright et al. 244p. (C). 1992. pap. 59.00 (0-685-60692-9, Pub. by St Andrew UK) St Mut.

Bible in Shakespeare. William Burgess. 1972. 79.95 (0-87968-728-2) Gordon Pr.

Bible in Shakespeare. William Burgess. LC 68-24900. (Studies in Shakespeare: No. 24). 1969. reprint ed. lib. bdg. 75.00 (0-8383-0921-6) M S G Haskell Hse.

Bible in Stained Glass. Sonia Halliday & Laura Lushington. (Illus.). 160p. 1991. 39.95 (0-8192-1552-X) Morehouse Pub.

Bible in the Churches: How Various Christians Interpret the Scriptures. 2nd rev. ed. Ed. by Kenneth Hagan. (Studies in Theology). 1994. pap. 20.00 (0-87462-628-5) Marquette.

Bible in the Early Church. Ed. by Everett Ferguson. LC 92-42825. (Studies in Early Christianity: Vol. 3). 400p. 1993. 63.00 (0-8153-1063-3) Garland.

Bible in the Early Middle Ages. Robert McNally. (Reprints & Translations Ser.). (C). 1986. reprint ed. pap. 15.95 (0-89130-912-8, 00-07-14) Scholars Pr GA.

Bible in the Latin West. Margaret T. Gibson. LC 92-56862. (Mediaeval Book Ser.: Vol. 1). (C). 1993. text ed. 26.95 (0-268-00693-8) U of Notre Dame Pr.

Bible in the Light of Cuneiform Literature: Scripture in Context III. Ed. by William W. Hallo et al. LC 90-43132. (Ancient Near Eastern Texts & Studies: Vol. 8). 504p. 1990. lib. bdg. 119.95 (0-88946-219-4) E Mellen.

Bible in the Lilly Library. Joel Silver. (Illus.). 56p. 1991. pap. 10.00 (1-879598-03-5) IN Univ Lilly Library.

Bible in the Medieval World: Essays in Memory of Beryl Smalley. Ed. by Katherine Walsh & Diana Wood. (Studies in Church History: Subsidia 4). 352p. 1985. 42.95 (0-631-14275-4) Blackwell Pubs.

Bible in the Middle Ages: Its Influence on Literature & Art. Ed. by Bernard S. Levy. (Medieval & Renaissance Texts & Studies: Vol. 89). 224p. 1992. 25.00 (0-86698-101-2, MR89) MRTS.

Bible in the Modern World. James Barr. LC 90-31632. 208p. (C). 1990. pap. text ed. 12.95 (0-334-00113-7) TPI PA.

Bible in the Pulpit: The Renewal of Biblical Preaching. Leander E. Keck. LC 77-12015. 1978. pap. 12.95 (0-687-03160-5) Abingdon.

Bible in the Sixteenth Century. Ed. by David C. Steinmetz. LC 89-27910. (Duke Monographs in Medieval & Renaissance Studies: No. 11). 269p. (C). 1990. text ed. 34.50 (0-8223-1012-0) Duke.

Bible in the Syropalestinian Version, Pt.1: Pentateuch & Prophets. Ed. by M. H. Goshen-Gottstein. 111p. 1973. text ed. 30.00 (0-685-74246-6, Pub. by Magnes Press IS) Eisenbrauns.

Bible in the Twenty-First Century. Ed. by Howard C. Kee. LC 92-34043. 1993. 10.95 (1-56338-047-1) TPI PA.

Bible in the Wesleyan Heritage. Mack B. Stokes. LC 80-23636. 96p. (Orig.). 1981. pap. 4.95 (0-687-03100-1) Abingdon.

Bible in the Works of Thomas More, 2 vols., Set. Germain Marc'hadour. 1098p. 1969. text ed. 167.50 (90-6004-107-0, Pub. by B De Graaf NE) Coronet Bks.

An Asterisk (*) at the beginning of an entry indicates that the title is appearing in BIP for the first time.

B

An Asterisk (*) at the beginning of an entry indicates that the title is appearing in BIP for the first time.

Bible Records, Barbour County, Ala., Vol. 1. Helen S. Foley. 80p. 1983. reprint ed. pap. 10.00 (0-89308-180-9) Southern Hist Pr.

Bible Records, Barbour County, Ala., Vol. 2. Helen S. Foley. 84p. 1983. reprint ed. pap. 10.00 (0-89308-181-7) Southern Hist Pr.

Bible Records of Sharlot Hall Museum & Archives, Prescott, AZ. Dora M. Whiteside. 26p. (Orig.). 1983. pap. 3.50 (0-938353-00-4) D M Whiteside.

Bible References of John Ruskin. M. Gibbs & E. Gibbs. 1973. 59.95 (0-87968-729-0) Gordon Pr.

Bible Research - Revised. Ken Malmin. (Illus.). 202p. 1976. pap. 13.95 (0-914936-71-9) Bible Temple.

Bible Revisited: Collected Essays. George Savitt. (Illus.). 200p. (Orig.). 1990. 16.95 (0-87961-214-2); pap. 8.95 (0-87961-215-0) Naturegraph.

Bible Riddles of Birds & Beasts & Creeping Things. Lydia Regehr. (Illus.). 36p. (Orig.). (J). (gr. 7-12). 1982. pap. 1.25 (0-89323-030-8) Bible Memory.

Bible-Ryrie Study Bible, New American Standard. Nas. 1986. 35.99 (0-8024-7425-X) Moody.

Bible Says: A Look at Opposing Claims. Thomas M. Scheets. LC 88-62605. 64p. (Orig.). (YA). 1989. pap. 4.95 (1-55612-239-X) Sheed & Ward MO.

Bible Scenes: Joshua to Solomon. Star J. Beiner. LC 88-70868. 235p. 1988. pap. text ed. 9.75 (0-86705-022-5) A R E Pub.

***Bible, Science & Creation.** Henry Morris. 1991. pap. 1.99 (0-8474-0868-X) Back to Bible.

Bible-Scofield Reference Bible, King James Version (180) Kjv. 1968. 34.95 (0-19-527161-0) OUP.

Bible Secret of Divine Health. Gordon Lindsay. 1960. 1.95 (0-89985-023-5) Christ for the Nations.

Bible Selections for Reading Practice. (Mongolia Society Special Papers: Issue No. 10). 1988. pap. 5.00 (0-910980-30-6) Mongolia.

Bible-Sermon Companion. Colleen Lucas. Date not set. pap. text ed. write for info. (0-9634547-0-6) Lucas Assocs.

Bible Seven, History Zero. A. P. McIntyre. LC 88-51390. 154p. 1989. 9.95 (1-55523-201-9) Winston-Derek.

Bible Smuggler. Louise A. Vernon. LC 67-15994. (Illus.). 138p. (J). (gr. 4-9). 1967. pap. 5.95 (0-8361-1557-0) Herald Pr.

Bible Societies, American Missionaries & the National Revival of Bulgaria. James F. Clarke. LC 71-135841. (Eastern Europe Collection Ser.). 1971. 23.95 (0-405-02783-4) Ayer.

Bible Speaks. Illus. by Hawkes. 128p. (CHI & ENG.). 1989. pap. 0.75 (0-932221-19-X) Christ Action.

Bible Speaks. rev. ed. Connelly L. Graham. (Illus.). 64p. 1988. pap. 0.35 (0-932221-13-0) Christ Action.

Bible Speaks, 3 Vols., Set. Hella Taubes. 203p. (J). (gr. k-4). 1965. 19.95 (0-900689-35-8) Soncino Pr.

Bible Speaks: La Biblia Habla. rev. ed. Connelly L. Graham. (Illus.). 64p. (SPA.). 1988. pap. 0.35 (0-932221-14-9) Christ Action.

Bible Speaks on Aging. Frank Stagg. LC 81-66092. 1981. pap. 6.99 (0-8054-5292-3) Broadman.

Bible Speaks to Children. Gail Linam. LC 88-7529. (Orig.). 1989. pap. 4.99 (0-8054-4931-0) Broadman.

Bible Speaks to Me about My Church. Leslie Parrott. 111p. (Orig.). 1987. pap. 5.95 (0-8341-1213-2) Beacon Hill.

Bible Speaks to Me about My Service & Mission. Phyllis H. Perkins. 128p. 1990. pap. 5.95 (0-8341-1359-7) Beacon Hill.

Bible Speaks to Me about My Witness. Charles Shaver. 125p. 1992. pap. 7.95 (0-8341-1404-6) Beacon Hill.

Bible Speaks to Our Times: The Christian's Victory in Christ. Alan Redpath. (Alan Redpath Library). 124p. 1993. reprint ed. pap. 9.99 (0-8007-5492-1) Revell.

Bible Speaks to You. Robert M. Brown. LC 84-19578. 324p. (C). 1985. pap. 12.99 (0-664-24597-8, Westminster) Westminster John Knox.

Bible Speaks Today Series, 31 bks., Set. 1991. pap. 384.99 (0-87784-925-0, 925) InterVarsity.

Bible Stories. William Anthony. LC 77-71655. (Illus.). (Orig.). 1978. pap. 7.50 (0-912330-25-2, Inland Bk) Jargon Soc.

Bible Stories. John Barrett. (Illus.). 32p. (J). (gr. k-4). 1992. pap. 19.95 (1-882954-04-1) Aspen Press.

***Bible Stories.** Illus. by Janusz Grabianski. 256p. (YA). (gr. 3 up). 1995. pap. 12.95 (1-56294-689-7) Millbrook Pr.

***Bible Stories: A Treasury for Young Readers.** Ret. by Jane P. Resnick. (Illus.). 1995. pap. 9.98 (1-56138-485-2) Running Pr.

Bible Stories: Four of the Greatest Tales Ever Told. LC 93-85528. (Illus.). 128p. (J). 1994. 4.95 (1-56138-376-7) Running Pr.

Bible Stories: From the Old & New Testament. Leo Pavlat. (J). (gr. 1 up). 1994. 12.98 (0-7858-0013-1) Bk Sales Inc.

Bible Stories & Activities for Children. (J). 1991. pap. 5.95 (0-687-03183-4) Abingdon.

Bible Stories & Celebrations: Learning Center. Irene Handberg. 128p. 1992. teacher ed write for info. (1-56831-551-1) Lrning Connect.

Bible Stories & Celebrations: Learning Center, Set. Irene Handberg. 128p. 1992. write for info. (1-56831-510-4) Lrning Connect.

***Bible Stories for Children.** 224p. (J). 1994. 9.98 (0-86112-854-0) Brimax Bks.

Bible Stories for Children. Geoffrey Horn & Arthur Cavanaugh. LC 79-27811. (Illus.). 336p. (J). (gr. 1-5). 1980. text ed. 14.95 (0-02-554060-2, Mac Bks Young Read) S&S Childrens.

Bible Stories for Little Children, Bk. 1. rev. ed. Betty R. Hollender. (Illus.). 80p. (Orig.). (J). (gr. 1-3). 1985. pap. text ed. 6.00 (0-8074-0309-1, 103100) UAHC.

Bible Stories for Little Children, Vol. 2. rev. ed. Betty R. Hollender. (Illus.). 80p. (Orig.). (J). (gr. 1-3). 1987. pap. text ed. 6.00 (0-8074-0324-5, 103101) UAHC.

Bible Stories for Little Children, Vol. 3. rev. ed. Betty R. Hollender. (Illus.). 80p. (Orig.). (J). (gr. 1-3). 1988. pap. text ed. 6.00 (0-8074-0416-0, 103102) UAHC.

Bible Stories for Little Children, Vol. 4. rev. ed. Betty R. Hollender. (Illus.). 80p. (Orig.). (J). (gr. 1-3). 1989. pap. text ed. 6.00 (0-8074-0418-7, 103103) UAHC.

Bible Stories from the Old Testament. P. Hunt. (Illus.). (J). (gr. k-5). 4.98 (0-517-43909-3) Random Hse Value.

Bible Stories of the Old Testament. Christos Kondeatis. (J). (ps-6). 1993. pap. 18.00 (0-671-87573-6, S&S Bks Young Read) S&S Childrens.

Bible Stories to Read & Color. (Illus.). 388p. (J). (ps-4). pap. 9.95 (1-55748-069-9) Barbour & Co.

Bible Stories You Never Heard Before. William R. Phillippe. LC 87-11618. ix, 155p. (Orig.). 1989. pap. 9.95 (0-940473-06-2) Wm Caxton.

Bible Story. Philip Turner. (Illus.). 142p. (J). 1987. 19.95 (0-19-273104-1) OUP.

Bible Story. Philip Turner. (Illus.). 142p. (J). (gr. k up). 1989. pap. 10.95 (0-19-273160-2) OUP.

Bible Story Activity Book. Jacqueline J. Pliskin. (Illus.). 96p. (J). (gr. 1-4). 1990. pap. 5.95 (0-944007-67-8) Sure Sellers.

Bible Story Balloon Sculpture. Kay Watts. 1990. pap. 6.95 (0-87162-584-9, D1250) Warner Pr.

Bible Story Bulletin Boards. Mary McMillan. (Bulletin Board Ser.). 96p. (J). (ps-3). 1988. 10.95 (0-86653-430-X, SS1828, Shining Star Pubns) Good Apple.

Bible Story Clip & Copy Patterns. Corbin Hillam. (Bible Clip & Copy Ser.). (Illus.). 96p. (J). (ps-3). 1992. 10.95 (0-86653-693-0, SS2823, Shining Star Pubns) Good Apple.

Bible Story Crafts. Kathleen S. Yawger. (Teacher Helper Ser.). 96p. (J). (ps-5). 1991. 10.95 (0-86653-637-X, SS1895, Shining Star Pubns) Good Apple.

***Bible Story Crafts & Projects Children Love.** Ed. by Jody Brolsma. (Illus.). 112p. 1995. pap. 14.99 (1-55945-698-1) Group Pub.

Bible Story Hour see Child Horizons

Bible Story Library. Turner Hodges. 1963. 12.95 (0-672-23099-2, Audel) Macmillan.

Bible Storybook. Georgie Adams. LC 93-40682. (J). 1995. 15.99 (0-8037-1760-1) Dial Bks Young.

Bible Students? Duane Magnani. 1983. 11.95 (1-883858-03-8) Witness CA.

Bible Studies. G. Adolf Deissmann. 400p. 1988. reprint ed. 19.95 (0-943575-08-7) Hendrickson MA.

Bible Studies for New Believers. Wendell Heatwole. 1988. pap. 2.95 (0-87813-529-4) Christian Light.

Bible Studies for Senior Citizens. Mary K. Klim. 91p. 1986. pap. 5.95 (0-932910-59-9) Potentials Development.

Bible Studies on World Evangelization & the Simple Lifestyle. Harvie M. Conn. 1981. pap. 1.50 (0-87552-208-4) Presby & Reformed.

Bible Studies Series. Frances Easter. (Studies in Luke: Vol. I). 1985. pap. 4.50 (0-8309-0424-7) Herald Hse.

Bible Studies Series. Frances Easter. (Studies in Luke: Vol. II). 1985. pap. 4.50 (0-8309-0430-1) Herald Hse.

Bible Study. Frances Easter. (Studies in Acts: vol. I). 1986. pap. 4.50 (0-8309-0436-0) Herald Hse.

***Bible Study Companion Set, 5 vols., Set.** E. G. White. 2418p. (Orig.). (C). 1993. pap. 39.95 (1-883012-58-9) Remnant Pubns.

Bible Study Course of the New Treatment. Dallas I. S. D. Staff. (YA). 1993. reprint ed. pap. 4.95 (0-925279-28-5) Wallbuilders.

Bible Study Guide for All Ages: For Classes, Study Groups, & Family Devotionals, 4 vols. Donald Baker & Mary Baker. (Illus.). 200p. 1985. 19.95 (0-685-72469-7) BSG Printing.

Bible Study Guide for All Ages: For Classes, Study Groups, & Family Devotionals, 4 vols., Set. Donald Baker & Mary Baker. (Illus.). 200p. 1985. ring bd. 69.95 (1-879614-00-6) BSG Printing.

Bible Study Guide for All Ages: For Classes, Study Groups, & Family Devotionals, 4 vols., Unit 1. Donald Baker & Mary Baker. (Illus.). 200p. 1981. 19.95 (1-879614-01-4) BSG Printing.

Bible Study Guide for All Ages: For Classes, Study Groups, & Family Devotionals, 4 vols., Unit 2. Donald Baker & Mary Baker. (Illus.). 200p. 1982. 19.95 (1-879614-02-2) BSG Printing.

Bible Study Guide for All Ages: For Classes, Study Groups, & Family Devotionals, 4 vols., Unit 3. Donald Baker & Mary Baker. (Illus.). 200p. 1983. 19.95 (1-879614-03-0) BSG Printing.

Bible Study Guide for All Ages: For Classes, Study Groups, & Family Devotionals, 4 vols., Unit 4. Donald Baker & Mary Baker. (Illus.). 200p. 1985. 19.95 (1-879614-04-9) BSG Printing.

Bible-Study King James Version. Bible. 1986. 35.99 (0-8024-7421-7) Moody.

Bible-Study New King James Version: Ryrie-Brown. Nkjv. 1986. 35.99 (0-8024-7375-X) Moody.

Bible Study Notebook. 1987. 4.99 (0-529-06373-5) World Bible.

Bible Study Notes, Vol. 1. Anita S. Dole. Ed. by William R. Woofenden. LC 76-24081. 1978. Vol 1. lib. bdg. write for info. (0-917426-01-0) Am New Church Sunday.

Bible Study Notes, Vol. 2. Anita S. Dole. Ed. by William R. Woofenden. LC 76-24081. 1978. lib. bdg. write for info. (0-917426-02-9) Am New Church Sunday.

Bible Study Notes, Vol. 3. Anita S. Dole. Ed. by William R. Woofenden. LC 76-24081. 1978. lib. bdg. write for info. (0-917426-03-7) Am New Church Sunday.

Bible Study Notes, Vol. 4. Anita S. Dole. Ed. by William R. Woofenden. LC 76-24081. 1979. write for info. (0-917426-04-5) Am New Church Sunday.

Bible Study Notes, Vol. 5. Anita S. Dole. Ed. by William R. Woofenden. LC 76-24081. 1979. write for info. (0-917426-05-3) Am New Church Sunday.

Bible Study Notes, Vol. 6. Anita S. Dole. Ed. by William R. Woofenden. LC 76-24081. 1979. write for info. (0-917426-06-1) Am New Church Sunday.

Bible Study Notes, Vols. 1-3. Anita S. Dole. Ed. by William R. Woofenden. LC 76-24081. 1978. lib. bdg. write for info. (0-685-92171-9) Am New Church Sunday.

Bible Study Skills: Teacher's Guide. Joel Fredrich. 6.50 (0-8100-0394-5) WELS Board.

***Bible Study That Works.** rev. ed. David L. Thompson. 128p. (C). 1994. pap. 6.95 (0-916035-61-1) Evangel Indiana.

Bible Summarized Handbook. Keith L. Brooks. 1990. pap. 9.99 (0-529-06935-0) World Bible.

Bible Surprises. Barbara Lockwood & Marilyn McAuley. LC 87-71384. (Peek & Find Ser.). (J). (ps). 1992. bds. 4.99 (1-55513-120-4, Chariot Bks) Chariot Family.

Bible Symbols of the Bible in Pictures. Frank Beard. (J). 1985. pap. 7.99 (0-88019-170-8) Schmul Pub Co.

***Bible Talks for Fun & Prophet.** David Schmeling. 116p. 1994. pap. 7.99 (1-884553-53-2) Discipleshp.

Bible Teacher Time Savers. Rebecca Daniel. (Helping Hand Ser.). 48p. (J). (gr. k-5). 1984. student ed 7.95 (0-86653-235-8, SS 817, Shining Star Pubns) Good Apple.

***Bible Teaches Me.** Kathy Downs. Ed. by Karen Brewer. (Children's Bible Study Ser.). (Illus.). 320p. (Orig.). 1995. teacher ed, pap. 26.99 (0-7847-0362-0, 13-42034) Standard Pub.

Bible-Teaching Ideas That Work. Betty B. Robertson. (Illus.). 56p. 1989. pap. 5.95 (0-8341-1313-9) Beacon Hill.

Bible Tells Me So. Victor P Wierwille. LC 70-176281. (Studies in Abundant Living: Vol. 1). 202p. 1971. 8.95 (0-910068-10-0) Am Christian.

Bible Tells Me So: The Beginner's Guide to Loving & Understanding God's Word. Mack Thomas. (J). (gr. k-5). 1992. 12.99 (0-945564-20-1, Gold & Honey) Questar Pubs.

***Bible Tells Me So: Uses & Abuses of Holy Scripture.** Jim Hill & Rand Cheadle. LC 94-41097. 1995. 12.00 (0-385-47695-7, Anchor NY) Doubleday.

Bible Tells Them So: The Discourse of Protestant Fundamentalism. Kathleen C. Boone. LC 88-7270. 139p. 1988. 59.50 (0-88706-894-4); pap. 19.95 (0-88706-895-2) State U NY Pr.

Bible Tells Us So: Twelve Short Chapters on Major Themes of the Bible. R. B. Kuiper. 1978. pap. 5.95 (0-85151-001-9) Banner of Truth.

Bible Text Cyclopedia see Compact Topical Bible

Bible That Was Lost & Is Found. 4th ed. John Bigelow. LC 78-65549. 74p. 1979. pap. 1.95 (0-87785-159-X) Swedenborg.

Bible, the Christian & Jehovah's Witnesses. Gordon Lewis. 1966. pap. 2.99 (0-87552-324-2) Presby & Reformed.

Bible, the Christian & Latter Day Saints. Gordon Lewis. 1966. pap. 2.99 (0-87552-325-0) Presby & Reformed.

Bible, the Christian & Seventh Day Adventists. Gordon Lewis. 1966. pap. 2.99 (0-87552-326-9) Presby & Reformed.

***Bible, the Church, & Authority: The Canon of the Christian Bible in History & Theology.** Joseph T. Lienhard. (Orig.). 1995. pap. text ed. write for info. (0-8146-5536-X, M Glazier) Liturgical Pr.

Bible, the Church, & the Poor. Boff & Pixley. Tr. by Paul Burns. (Theology & Liberation Ser.). Orig. Title: Opcas Pelos Pobres. 286p. 1989. 39.95 (0-88344-614-6); pap. 16.95 (0-88344-599-9) Orbis Bks.

Bible the Qur'an & Science. Maurice Bucaille. 1990. 10.00 (0-685-66736-7, 9) Tahrike Tarsile Quran.

Bible the Quran & the Science. Maurice Bucaille. pap. 14.50 (0-935782-49-4) Kazi Pubns.

Bible, The Story of a Book. Manly P. Hall. 1985. pap. 5.00 (0-89314-818-0) Philos Res.

***Bible, the Supernatural & the Jews.** McCandlish Phillips. 368p. 1995. pap. 10.99 (0-88965-115-9, Pub. by Horizon Books CN) Chr Pubns.

***Bible Thoughts.** Joseph Caryl. Ed. by Ingram Cobbin. 252p. 1995. 22.95 (1-877611-95-6) Soli Deo Gloria.

Bible Through Asian Eyes. Masao Takenaka & Ron O'Grady. (Orig.). 1991. 35.00 (0-377-00226-7); pap. 25.00 (0-377-00225-9) Friendship Pr.

Bible Through Pictures. Charles M. Stewart. 1989. 6.99 (0-517-68238-9) Random Hse Value.

Bible-Time Nursery Rhyme Book. Emily Hunter. 96p. (J). 1988. 12.99 (0-89081-404-X) Harvest Hse.

***Bible Time Travelers Spinner Game.** Greg Holder. (Illus.). 10p. (J). (gr. k-5). 1995. 7.99 (0-7847-0389-2, 28-02656) Standard Pub.

***Bible Time with God Compact Edition.** deluxe ed. Bible Staff. 1992. 27.99 (0-8499-5008-2) Word Inc.

***Bible Timeline Workbook: A Step-by-Step Learning Guide for Those Who Think that the Old Testament is Too Difficult to Piece Together.** Eric J. Ellis. (Illus.). 240p. (YA). (gr. 9 up). 1994. pap. 12.95x (1-886001-01-4); spiral bd. 12.95x (1-886001-02-2); trans. 10.00x (1-886001-00-6) Crnstone Pr.

Bible Times. Deborah Manley. (It's Fun Finding out about Ser.). 48p. (J). 1990. 4.99 (0-517-69616-9) Random Hse Value.

Bible Times Crafts for Kids. Comp. by Neva Hickerson. LC 92-31344. 1993. 12.99 (0-8307-1596-7) Regal.

***Bible Tour Guide: A 365 Spiritual Journey.** Kevin C. Rudolph. LC 94-66386. (Illus.). 379p. 1994. 18.00 (0-927577-01-1) Rich Pub Co.

Bible Translation & the Spread of the Church: The Last 200 Years. Ed. by Philip C. Stine. LC 90-46957. (Studies in Christian Mission: No. 2). xii, 154p. 1992. reprint ed. 48.75 (90-04-09331-1) E J Brill.

Bible Translation Controversy. Wayne Jackson. (That You May Believe Ser.). 20p. (Orig.). 1985. pap. 1.50 (0-932859-01-1) Apologetic Pr.

Bible Translations. Commission Christian Lit. 1981. pap. 0.79 (0-8100-0132-2, 04N1212) Northwest Pub.

Bible Translations: A History Through Source Documents. Roland H. Worth, Jr. LC 91-52513. 205p. 1992. lib. bdg. 38.50x (0-89950-537-6) McFarland & Co.

Bible Trivia. William Schlegl. (Bible Baffler Ser.). 48p. (J). (gr. 3 up). 1986. student ed 7.95 (0-86653-368-0, SS 883, Shining Star Pubns) Good Apple.

Bible Truths. Alva J. McClain. 1981. pap. 1.75 (0-88469-013-X) BMH Bks.

Bible Truths Unmasked. Finis J. Dake, Sr. 114p. 1987. 8.95 (1-55829-029-X) Dake Bible.

Bible Truths with Shakespearian Parallels. 6th ed. James Buchan Brown. LC 74-19106. reprint ed. 37.50 (0-404-01136-5) AMS Pr.

Bible Unmasked. Joseph Lewis. 1991. lib. bdg. 69.95 (0-8490-4272-0) Gordon Pr.

Bible Unmasked. Joseph Lewis. 236p. 1975. reprint ed. spiral bd. 6.60 (0-7873-0557-X) Mokelumne.

Bible Unmasked, Vol. I. Joseph Lewis. 122p. 1990. pap. text ed. 13.00 (0-916157-37-7) African Islam Miss Pubns.

Bible Unmasked, Vol. II. Joseph Lewis. 120p. 1990. pap. text ed. 13.00 (0-916157-38-5) African Islam Miss Pubns.

Bible Update: A New Look at Some Basic Church Doctrine. A. B. Student. LC 92-70564. 148p. (Orig.). 1992. pap. 4.95 (0-9632172-6-7) ABS Bks.

***Bible Verse Coloring Book.** Illus. by Elaine Cole. 32p. (J). (gr. 1-6). 1994. pap. 2.80 (1-883426-00-6) Chldrns Outrch.

Bible Verses in Verse. Boris Randolph. LC 80-67992. 144p. 1980. pap. 3.95 (0-87516-424-2) DeVorss.

***Bible, Violence, & the Sacred: Liberation from the Myth of Sanctioned Violence.** James G Williams. 304p. 1995. pap. 16.00 (1-56338-116-8) TPI PA.

Bible Visual Resource Book. Illus. by Hugh Claycombe. LC 89-36764. 288p. 1989. 19.99 (0-8307-1368-9, 5203057) Regal.

Bible Walk. John M. Nielson & Otis Skillings. (J). 1980. 5.25 (0-685-68193-9, MB-492); audio 10.98 (0-685-68194-7, TA-9016C); 6.00 (0-685-68195-5, L-9016C) Lillenas.

Bible Way of the Cross for Children. Gwen Costello. (Illus.). 32p. (Orig.). (J). (gr. 4-6). 1988. pap. 1.95 (0-89622-353-1) Twenty-Third.

Bible Way to Receive the Holy Spirit. Kenneth E. Hagin. 1981. pap. 0.75 (0-89276-255-1) Hagin Ministries.

Bible Windows. Ivor Powell. LC 85-8103. 180p. 1985. pap. 8.99 (0-8254-3522-6) Kregel.

Bible Wisdom for Fathers. Gary Wilde. 1993. 5.99 (0-7814-0074-0, LifeJourney) Chariot Family.

Bible Wisdom for Mothers. Gary Wilde. 1993. 5.99 (0-7814-0073-2, LifeJourney) Chariot Family.

Bible Wisdom for New Parents. Ed. by Gary Wilde. 1993. pap. 5.99 (0-7814-0149-6, LifeJourney) Chariot Family.

***Bible Wisdom for Newlyweds.** Wilde. 1995. pap. 5.99 (0-7814-0145-3, LifeJourney) Chariot Family.

Bible Wisdom for Parents. Gary Wilde. 1993. 5.99 (0-7814-0071-6, LifeJourney) Chariot Family.

Bible Wisdom for Parents of Teens. Ed. by Gary Wilde. 1993. pap. 5.99 (0-7814-0148-8, LifeJourney) Chariot Family.

Bible Wisdom for Single Parents. Gary Wilde. 1993. 5.99 (0-7814-0072-4, LifeJourney) Chariot Family.

Bible Without Illusions. R. P. Hanson & A. T. Hanson. LC 89-37907. 160p. (Orig.). (C). 1990. pap. text ed. 11.95 (0-334-00101-3) TPI PA.

Bible Women Speak to Us Today. Mary E. Jensen. LC 83-70507. 128p. (Orig.). 1983. pap. 9.99 (0-8066-2013-7, 10-0708, Augsburg) Augsburg Fortress.

Bible Word Fun. Karen Layton & Ron Layton. (Bible Baffler Ser.). 48p. (J). (gr. 3 up). 1986. student ed 7.95 (0-86653-367-2, SS 882, Shining Star Pubns) Good Apple.

Bible Word Play. Karen Layton & Ron Layton. (Bible Baffler Ser.). (Illus.). 48p. (J). (gr. 3 up). 1989. 7.95 (0-86653-472-5, SS888, Shining Star Pubns) Good Apple.

Bible Word Search. William C. Gordon. (Quiz & Puzzle Bks.). 112p. 1983. pap. 4.99 (0-8010-3679-8) Baker Bk.

Bible Word Search Old Testament. Doug Shipman & Sandy Shipman. (Bible Baffler Ser.). (Illus.). 48p. (J). (gr. 3 up). 1994. 6.95 (0-86653-774-0, SS3807, Shining Star Pubns) Good Apple.

Bible Word-Search Puzzles: Glimpses of Christ. Howard Annable. (Illus.). 48p. 1990. pap. 3.99 (0-87403-729-8, 28-02776) Standard Pub.

Bible Word-Search Puzzles: Glimpses of Paul. Howard Annable. (Illus.). 48p. 1990. pap. 3.99 (0-87403-730-1, 28-02777) Standard Pub.

Bible Words Crossword Puzzles, No. 3. Marvin Kananen. 120p. (Orig.). 1990. pap. 4.99 (0-8010-5289-0) Baker Bk.

Bible Words Crossword Puzzles, No. 4. Marvin Kananen. (Quiz & Puzzle Bks.). 120p. (Orig.). 1991. pap. 4.99 (0-8010-5296-3) Baker Bk.

***Bible Words Crossword Puzzles No. 5: Based on the New International Version.** Marvin Kananen. 120p. (Orig.). 1995. pap. 4.99 (0-8010-5042-1) Baker Bk.

Bible Words Crossword Puzzles 1. Marvin Kananen. (Quiz & Puzzle Bks.). 128p. 1988. pap. 4.99 (0-8010-5491-5) Baker Bk.

Bible Words Crossword Puzzles 2. Marvin Kananen. 1989. pap. 4.99 (0-8010-5275-0) Baker Bk.

An Asterisk (*) at the beginning of an entry indicates that the title is appearing in BIP for the first time.

An Asterisk (*) at the beginning of an entry indicates that the title is appearing in BIP for the first time.

729

Biblical Exegesis & Church Doctrine. Raymond E. Brown. 176p. (Orig.). 1986. pap. 10.95 (*0-8091-2750-4*) Paulist Pr.

Biblical Explanation of the Church's Covenant: Preaching from the Covenant. J. R. Mosley, Sr. 1990. pap. text ed. write for info. (*0-9627958-2-8*) J R Mosleys Pr.

Biblical Exposition. Robert Whitelaw. pap. 1.49 (*0-87377-111-7*) GAM Pubns.

Biblical Expositor: The Living Theme of the Great Book. Ed. by Carl F. Henry. 1332p. 1994. reprint ed. 95.00 (*0-8010-0890-5*) Baker Bk.

Biblical Facts. Robert Whitelaw. pap. 1.49 (*0-87377-094-3*) GAM Pubns.

Biblical Faith & Natural Theology: The Gifford Lectures for 1991, Delivered in the University of Edinburgh. James Barr. LC 92-14219. 256p. 1993. 49.95 (*0-19-826205-1*, Clarendon Pr) OUP.

***Biblical Faith & Natural Theology: The Gifford Lectures for 1991: Delivered in the University of Edinburgh.** James Barr. 256p. 1995. pap. 18.95 (*0-19-826376-7*) OUP.

Biblical Favorites. Jim Lewis. LC 85-50948. 134p. (Orig.). 1985. pap. 7.95 (*0-942482-08-5*) Unity Church Denver.

***Biblical Flood: A Case Study of the Church's Response to Extrabiblical Evidence.** Davis A. Young. LC 95-1899. 334p. (Orig.). 1995. pap. 19.99 (*0-8028-0719-4*) Eerdmans.

Biblical Foundations & a Method for Doing Christian Ethics. Elton M. Eenigenburg. Ed. by Susan Eenigenburg. LC 93-26374. 180p. (C). 1993. lib. bdg. 38.50 (*0-8191-9283-X*) U Pr of Amer.

Biblical Foundations for Mission. Donald Senior & Carroll Stuhlmueller. LC 82-22430. 384p. (Orig.). 1983. pap. 19.95 (*0-88344-047-4*) Orbis Bks.

Biblical Foundations for Mission. Donald Senior & Carroll Stuhlmueller. LC 82-22430. 383p. (Orig.). reprint ed. pap. 109.20 (*0-8357-4051-X*, 2036741) Bks Demand.

Biblical Foundations for Small Group Ministry: An Integrational Approach. Gareth W. Icenogle. LC 93-32390. 395p. (Orig.). 1994. pap. 15.99 (*0-8308-1771-9*, 1771) InterVarsity.

Biblical Graphics. Roger C. Reeds. 1977. 6.95 (*0-89265-058-3*); pap. 5.95 (*0-89265-042-7*) Randall Hse.

Biblical Greek Language & Linguistics: Open Questions in Current Research. Ed. by Porter & Carson. 280p. 1993. 35.00 (*1-85075-390-3*, Pub. by Sheffield Acad UK) CUP Services.

Biblical Hapax Legomena in the Light of Akkadian & Ugaritic: Society of Biblical Literature. Harold R. Cohen. LC 77-13422. (Dissertation Ser.: No. 37). 201p. reprint ed. pap. 57.30 (*0-8357-9565-9*, 2017528) Bks Demand.

Biblical Healing: Hebrew & Christian Roots. Frank C. Darling. 274p. (Orig.). 1989. pap. 10.95 (*0-9622504-0-6*) F C Darling.

Biblical Healing for Modern Medicine: Choosing Life & Health: Or Disease & Death. Franklin E. Payne, Jr. LC 93-71420. 240p. (Orig.). 1993. pap. 12.95 (*0-9629876-1-1*) Covenant Enter.

Biblical Hebrew. Harvey E. Finley & Charles D. Isbell. 231p. 1975. pap. text ed. 13.95 (*0-8341-0350-8*) Beacon Hill.

Biblical Hebrew: An Analytical Introduction. Winfred P. Lehmann et al. LC 94-15418. (Berkeley Models of Grammars Ser.: Vol. 3). 1994. write for info. (*0-8204-2283-5*) P Lang Pubs.

Biblical Hebrew: An Introductory Grammar. Page H. Kelley. viii, 450p. (Orig.). 1992. pap. 29.99 (*0-8028-0598-1*) Eerdmans.

***Biblical Hebrew & Discourse Linguistics.** Ed. by Robert L. Bergen. 540p. 1994. pap. text ed. 40.00 (*1-55671-007-0*) Summer Instit Ling.

Biblical Hebrew for Beginners. Bonnie P. Kittel. LC 88-28077. 456p. (C). 1989. text ed. 35.00 (*0-300-04394-5*); audio 12.00 (*0-300-04395-3*) Yale U Pr.

Biblical Hebrew Grammar. D. Waylon Bailey & John O. Strange. LC 85-60960. 240p. 1985. 24.00 (*0-914520-23-7*) Insight Pr.

Biblical Hebrew Step by Step: A Significant Breakthrough for Learning Biblical Hebrew. Menahem Mansoor. 1978. pap. 13.99 (*0-8010-6041-9*); audio 7.99 (*0-8010-6074-5*) Baker Bk.

Biblical Hebrew Step by Step II: Readings from the Book of Genesis. Menahem Mansoor. 230p. (Orig.). (C). 1984. pap. 13.99 (*0-8010-6151-2*); audio 7.99 (*0-8010-6198-9*) Baker Bk.

Biblical Hebrew Workbook: An Inductive Study for Beginners. A. Vanlier Hunter. LC 88-5519. 246p. (C). 1988. student ed 21.75 (*0-8191-5715-5*) U Pr of Amer.

Biblical Herem: A Window on Israel's Religious Experience. Philip Stern. (Brown Judaic Studies). 258p. 1991. 59.95 (*1-55540-552-5*, 140211) Scholars Pr GA.

Biblical Heritage of American Democracy. A. I. Katsch. pap. 11.95 (*0-87068-488-4*) Ktav.

Biblical Hermeneutics: An Introduction. Duncan S. Ferguson. LC 85-45456. 204p. 1986. pap. 15.99 (*0-8042-0050-5*, John Knox) Westminster John Knox.

Biblical Hermeneutics: Toward a Theory of Reading as the Production of Meaning. J. Severino Croatto. Tr. by Robert R. Barr. LC 87-12314. 96p. (Orig.). (ENG.). 1987. pap. 14.95 (*0-88344-582-4*) Orbis Bks.

Biblical Hermeneutics & Black Theology in South Africa. Itumeleng J. Mosala. 1989. pap. 14.99 (*0-8028-0372-5*) Eerdmans.

Biblical Hermeneutics in Historical Perspective. Paula Fredriksen et al. Ed. by Mark S. Burrows & Paul Rorem. 368p. 1991. 29.99 (*0-8028-3693-3*) Eerdmans.

***Biblical Hermeneutics of Liberation: Modes of Reading the Bible in the South African Context.** Gerald West. LC 94-43953. (Bible & Liberation Ser.). 250p. (Orig.). 1995. pap. 19.95 (*1-57075-020-3*) Orbis Bks.

Biblical Hermeneutics. Gerhard Maier. Tr. by Robert W. Yarbrough. LC 93-42342. 560p. (Orig.). 1994. pap. 22.00 (*0-89107-767-7*) Crossway Bks.

Biblical Higher Criticism & the Defense of Infallibilism in 19th Century Britain. Nigel de S. Cameron. LC 87-7924. (Texts & Studies in Religion: Vol. 33). 440p. 1987. lib. bdg. 109.95 (*0-88946-821-4*) E Mellen.

Biblical History & the Quest for Maturity. John S. Peale. LC 85-5067. (Symposium Ser.: Vol. 15). 120p. 1985. lib. bdg. 59.95 (*0-88946-706-4*) E Mellen.

Biblical Humanist. John H. Nichols. (Orig.). 1989. pap. 30.00 (*0-685-29796-9*) Unitarian Soc WH.

Biblical Humanist Companion. John H. Nichols. 157p. (Orig.). 1989. pap. 30.00 (*0-9624948-0-1*) Unitarian Soc WH.

Biblical Illustrator, 23 vols., Set. Ed. by Joseph S. Exell. LC 54-11086. (Illus.). 34860p. 1988. reprint ed. 950.00 (*0-8010-3280-6*) Baker Bk.

***Biblical Imagery for God.** Christina Bucher. 95p. 1995. pap. 4.95 (*0-87178-093-3*) Brethren.

Biblical Images. Adin Steinsaltz. LC 94-579. 304p. 1994. 30.00 (*1-56821-178-3*) Aronson.

Biblical Influences in Shakespeare's Great Tragedies. Peter Milward. LC 86-45543. 224p. 1987. 20.00 (*0-253-31198-5*) Ind U Pr.

Biblical Interleaves in Prose & Verse. Albert S. Newton. 56p. 1987. pap. 1.95 (*0-88028-070-0*, 901) Forward Movement.

Biblical Interpretation. Robert Morgan & John Barton. 352p. (C). 1988. 62.00 (*0-19-213256-3*); pap. text ed. 19.95 (*0-19-213257-1*) OUP.

Biblical Interpretation. Joseph W. Trigg. (Father's of the Church Ser.: Vol. 9). 1988. 19.95 (*0-8146-5349-9*); pap. 19.95 (*0-8146-5339-1*) Liturgical Pr.

Biblical Interpretation: An Integrated Approach. W. Randolph Tate. 256p. 1991. pap. 14.95 (*0-943575-50-8*) Hendrickson MA.

Biblical Interpretation: Principles & Practice. Ed. by F. Furman Kearley et al. LC 85-73721. 336p. 1986. pap. 12.99 (*0-8010-5472-9*) Baker Bk.

Biblical Interpretation & Christian Ethics. J. I. McDonald. LC 93-16555. (New Studies in Christian Ethics: No. 2). 260p. (C). 1994. 59.95 (*0-521-43059-3*) Cambridge U Pr.

Biblical Interpretation & the Church: Text & Context. Ed. by D. A. Carson. LC 93-20337. 240p. (Orig.). 1988. pap. 14.99 (*0-8010-2528-1*) Baker Bk.

Biblical Interpretation in Ancient Israel. Michael Fishbane. (Illus.). 640p. 1989. pap. 29.95 (*0-19-826699-5*) OUP.

Biblical Interpretation in Crisis: The Ratzinger Conference on Bible & Church, Vol. 9. Ed. by Richard J. Neuhaus. (Encounter Ser.). 1989. pap. 10.99 (*0-8028-0209-5*) Eerdmans.

Biblical Interpretation in the Book of Jubilees. John C. Endres. Ed. by Robert J. Karris. LC 86-6845. (Catholic Biblical Quarterly Monographs: no. 18). 284p. (Orig.). 1987. pap. 8.50 (*0-915170-17-5*) Catholic Bibl Assn.

Biblical Interpretation in the Early Church. Ed. & Tr. by Karlfried Froehlich. LC 84-47922. (Sources of Early Christian Thought Ser.). 128p. 1985. pap. 11.00 (*0-8006-1414-3*, 1-1414, Fortress Pr) Augsburg Fortress.

Biblical Interpretation in the Early Church: An Historical Introduction to Patristic Exegesis. Manlio Simonetti. Ed. by Anders Bergquist et al. Tr. by John A. Hughes. 168p. 1994. text ed. 33.95 (*0-567-09557-6*, Pub. by T & T Clark UK) Bks Intl VA.

Biblical Interpretation in the Gnostic Gospel of Truth from Nag Hammadi. Jacqueline A. Williams. LC 86-3831. (Society of Biblical Literature Dissertation Ser.). 228p. 1988. pap. 14.95 (*0-89130-877-6*) Scholars Pr GA.

Biblical Interpretation Then & Now: Contemporary Hermeneutics in the Light of the Early Church. David S. Dockery. LC 91-44120. 272p. 1992. pap. 14.99 (*0-8010-3010-2*) Baker Bk.

Biblical Interpretation Today. Gerhard F. Hasel. Ed. by Frank B. Holbrook. 137p. (Orig.). 1985. pap. 4.95 (*0-925675-06-7*) BRI DC.

Biblical Israel: A People's History. Jorge Pixley. LC 92-38146. 176p. (Orig.). 1992. pap. 10.00 (*0-8006-2551-X*, 1-2551, Fortress Pr) Augsburg Fortress.

Biblical Israel: State & People. Benjamin Mazar. Ed. by Shmuel Ahituv. 175p. 1992. text ed. 25.00 (*0-685-72549-9*, Pub. by Magnes Press IS) Eisenbrauns.

Biblical Lands: The Making of the Past. P. R. Moorey. (Illus.). 160p. (gr. 8 up). 1991. pap. 16.95 (*0-87226-247-2*) P Bedrick Bks.

Biblical Law Bibliography. John W. Welch. LC 90-35690. (Toronto Studies in Theology: Vol. 51). 348p. 1990. lib. bdg. 99.95 (*0-88946-891-5*) E Mellen.

Biblical Lovemaking: A Study of the Song of Solomon. Arnold G. Fruchtenbaum. 70p. 1983. pap. 5.00 (*0-914863-03-7*) Ariel Ministries.

***Biblical Manual: "The History of Doctrine in the New Testament.** Ernest L. Martin. (Illus.). (Orig.). (YA). (gr. 10). Date not set. pap. write for info. (*0-945657-76-5*) Acad Scriptural Knowledge.

Biblical Meditations for Advent & the Christmas Season. Carroll Stuhlmueller. LC 80-82083. (Biblical Meditations Ser.: Vol. 3). 288p. (Orig.). 1980. pap. 4.95 (*0-8091-2318-5*) Paulist Pr.

Biblical Meditations for Lent. rev. ed. Carroll Stuhlmueller. LC 77-91366. 190p. 1978. pap. 7.95 (*0-8091-2089-5*) Paulist Pr.

Biblical Meditations for Ordinary Time, Pt. II: Weeks 10-22. Carroll Stuhlmueller. 416p. (Orig.). 1984. Pt. II, Weeks 10-22. pap. 8.95 (*0-8091-2645-1*) Paulist Pr.

Biblical Meditations for Ordinary Time, Pt. III: Weeks 23-34. Carroll Stuhlmueller. 416p. (Orig.). 1984. Pt. III, Weeks 23-34. pap. 8.95 (*0-8091-2648-6*) Paulist Pr.

Biblical Meditations for Ordinary Time: Pt. I, Weeks 1-9. Carroll Stuhlmueller. 320p. (Orig.). 1984. pap. 8.95 (*0-8091-2644-3*) Paulist Pr.

Biblical Meditations for the Easter Season. Carroll C. Stuhmueller. LC 80-81030. 256p. 1980. pap. 6.95 (*0-8091-2283-9*) Paulist Pr.

Biblical-Missiological Exploration of the Cross-Cultural Dimensions in Luke - Acts. Harold E. Dollar. LC 92-44979. 448p. 1993. text ed. 109.95 (*0-7734-2212-9*) E Mellen.

Biblical Mormonism: Refuting Evangelical Criticisms of LDS Theology. Richard R. Hopkins. 288p. 1994. 18.98 (*0-88290-482-5*, 1041) Horizon Utah.

Biblical Mosaic. Ed. by Robert Polzin & Eugene Rothman. (Masoretic Studies). 1982. pap. 15.95 (*0-89130-692-7*, 06 06 10) Scholars Pr GA.

Biblical Narrative in the Philosophy of Paul Ricoeur: A Study in Hermeneutics & Theology. Kevin J. Vanhoozer. 296p. (C). 1990. 69.95 (*0-521-34425-5*) Cambridge U Pr.

Biblical Numerology. John J. Davis. LC 68-19207. (Orig.). 1968. pap. 6.99 (*0-8010-2813-2*) Baker Bk.

Biblical Origins of Modern Secular Culture. Willis B. Glover. LC 84-14868. xx, 300p. 1984. 23.95 (*0-86554-138-8*, MUP-H129) Mercer Univ Pr.

***Biblical Outliner for Teachers & Preachers.** Willie Tolison. 1994. pap. text ed. 8.95 (*0-89137-143-5*) Quality Pubns.

***Biblical Pacifism: A Peace Church Perspective.** fac. ed. Dale W. Brown. LC 85-30636. 224p. 1994. pap. 63.90 (*0-7837-7341-2*, 2047294) Bks Demand.

Biblical Pattern for Divine Healing. 1979. pap. 1.50 (*0-88469-108-X*) BMH Bks.

Biblical Patterns in Modern Literature. Ed. by David H. Hirsch & Nehama Aschkenasy. (Brown Judiac Studies: No. 77). 252p. (C). 1985. pap. 18.95 (*0-89130-814-8*) Scholars Pr GA.

Biblical Performances for Early Childhood. Comp. by Rebecca Daniel. (Christian On-Stage Ser.). 96p. (J). (ps-1). 1990. 10.95 (*0-86653-548-9*, SS1872, Shining Star Pubns) Good Apple.

Biblical Performances for Vacation Bible School. Judith Schera et al. (Christian On-Stage Ser.). 96p. (J). (gr. 1-8). 1991. 10.95 (*0-86653-578-0*, Shining Star Pubns) Good Apple.

Biblical Perspective on Alcoholism. Darryl R. Sletten. LC 93-61291. 98p. 1994. pap. 7.95 (*1-55523-658-8*) Winston-Derek.

Biblical Perspectives on Evangelism: Living in a Three-Storied Universe. Walter Brueggemann. 160p. (C). 1993. pap. text ed. 12.95 (*0-687-41233-1*) Abingdon.

Biblical Pictures of Bread. Steven Swanson. 1985. 4.15 (*0-89536-718-1*, 5802) CSS OH.

Biblical Plants: A Guide to the Rodef Shalom Biblical Botanical Garden. Irene Jacob. (Illus.). 60p. (Orig.). 1990. reprint ed. pap. 5.00 (*0-929699-01-7*) Rodef Shalom Pr.

Biblical Poetry Through Medieval Jewish Eyes. Adele Berlin. LC 90-26773. (Indiana Studies in Biblical Literature). 228p. 1991. 29.95 (*0-253-31176-4*) Ind U Pr.

Biblical Preaching: How to Find & Remove the Barriers. Richard C. White. 144p. (Orig.). 1988. pap. 9.99 (*0-8272-0217-2*) Chalice Pr.

Biblical Preaching: The Development & Delivery of Expository Messages. Haddon Robinson. LC 80-66776. 1980. 14.99 (*0-8010-7700-1*) Baker Bk.

Biblical Preaching for Today's World. Lloyd M. Perry. LC 73-7471. 256p. (C). 1973. 19.99 (*0-8024-0715-3*) Moody.

Biblical Preaching for Today's World see Predicacion Biblica para el Mundo Actual

Biblical Preaching on the Death of Jesus. William A. Beardslee et al. 256p. 1989. pap. 15.95 (*0-687-03446-9*) Abingdon.

Biblical Principles: Issues of Importance to Godly Christians. Rus Walton. 370p. 1984. 5.95 (*0-317-39815-6*) Plymouth Rock Found.

Biblical Principles & Business: The Foundations. Richard C. Chewning. LC 88-63590. 312p. (Orig.). 1989. pap. 25.00 (*0-89109-556-X*) NavPress.

Biblical Principles & Business: The Practice. Richard C. Chewning. LC 90-60918. 300p. 1990. pap. 25.00 (*0-89109-294-3*) NavPress.

Biblical Principles & Economics: The Foundations. Richard C. Chewning. LC 89-62168. 324p. 1990. pap. 25.00 (*0-89109-560-8*) NavPress.

Biblical Principles & Public Policy: The Practice. Richard C. Chewning. LC 90-61784. (Christians in the Marketplace Ser.: Vol. 4). 332p. (Orig.). 1991. pap. 25.00 (*0-89109-299-4*) NavPress.

Biblical Principles for Business Workbook. Larry Burkett. (Christian Financial Concepts Ser.). 66p. 1989. 7.00 (*1-56427-102-1*) Christian Fin Concepts.

Biblical Principles for New Christians. John Hedgepeth. 1989. 2.50 (*0-911866-09-4*) LifeSprings Res.

Biblical Principles of Church Growth. Kenneth C. Fleming. 1993. pap. 6.95 (*0-937396-95-8*) Walterick Pubs.

***Biblical Principles of Success: A Practical Guide for Living.** Arthur L. Mackey. 1993. pap. 8.00 (*0-927936-47-X*) Vincom Inc.

***Biblical Proclamation for Africa Today.** Zwomunondiita Kurewa. 128p. (Orig.). 1995. pap. 19.95 (*0-687-01444-1*) Abingdon.

***Biblical Prophets in Byzantine Palestine: Reassessing the Lives of the Prophets.** David Satran. LC 94-37300. (Studia in Veteris Testamenti Pseudepigrapha Ser.: Vol. 11). 1994. write for info. (*90-04-10234-5*) E J Brill.

***Biblical Prophets, Seers, & the New Apocalypticism: Rightly Explaining the Word of Truth.** Milton P. Brown. 100p. 1995. pap. 14.95 (*0-7734-2424-5*) E Mellen.

Biblical Prose Prayer: As a Window to the Popular Religion of Ancient Israel. Moshe Greenberg. LC 83-47662. 78p. 1983. pap. 11.00 (*0-520-05012-6*) U CA Pr.

Biblical Psychology. Oswald Chambers. 1982. pap. 5.95 (*0-551-05208-2*) Chr Lit.

Biblical Psychology of Learning. Ruth Beechick. 160p. (Orig.). (C). 1982. pap. 7.95 (*0-685-00100-8*); write for info. (*0-89636-083-0*) Accent CO.

Biblical Puppet Performances. J. Scherra et al. (Christian On-Stage Ser.). 96p. (J). (ps-8). 1990. 10.95 (*0-86653-549-7*, SS1873, Shining Star Pubns) Good Apple.

Biblical Quotations. Ed. by Jennifer Speake. LC 83-1511. 221p. reprint ed. pap. 63.00 (*0-7837-1097-6*, 2041629) Bks Demand.

Biblical Quotations in Middle English Literature, 2 vols. Mary W. Smyth. 1972. 105.00 (*0-87968-730-4*) Gordon Pr.

Biblical Quotations in Old English Prose Writers. Albert S. Cook. 1972. 59.95 (*0-87968-731-2*) Gordon Pr.

Biblical References in Shakespeare's Comedies. Naseeb Shaheen. LC 91-51137. 264p. 1993. 39.50 (*0-87413-457-9*) U Delaware Pr.

Biblical References in Shakespeare's History Plays. Naseeb Shaheen. LC 87-40703. 256p. 1989. 38.50 (*0-87413-341-6*) U Delaware Pr.

Biblical References in Shakespeare's Tragedies. Naseeb Shaheen. LC 85-40636. 248p. 1987. 35.00 (*0-87413-293-2*) U Delaware Pr.

Biblical Reflections on Crises Facing the Church. Raymond E. Brown. LC 75-19861. 132p. 1975. pap. 8.95 (*0-8091-1891-2*) Paulist Pr.

Biblical Religion & the Search for Ultimate Reality. Paul Tillich. LC 55-5149. 1964. pap. text ed. 6.95 (*0-226-80341-4*) U Ch Pr.

Biblical Researches in Palestine: Mount Sinai & Arabia Petraea: A Journal of Travels in the Year 1838, 3 vols, 1. Edward Robinson. Ed. by Moshe Davis. LC 77-70738. (America & the Holy Land Ser.). 1977. reprint ed. lib. bdg. 58.95 (*0-405-10282-8*) Ayer.

Biblical Researches in Palestine: Mount Sinai & Arabia Petraea: A Journal of Travels in the Year 1838, 3 vols, 2. Edward Robinson. Ed. by Moshe Davis. LC 77-70738. (America & the Holy Land Ser.). 1977. reprint ed. lib. bdg. 58.95 (*0-405-10283-6*) Ayer.

Biblical Researches in Palestine: Mount Sinai & Arabia Petraea: A Journal of Travels in the Year 1838, 3 vols, 3. Edward Robinson. Ed. by Moshe Davis. LC 77-70738. (America & the Holy Land Ser.). 1977. reprint ed. lib. bdg. 58.95 (*0-405-10284-4*) Ayer.

Biblical Researches in Palestine: Mount Sinai & Arabia Petraea: A Journal of Travels in the Year 1838, 3 vols, Set. Edward Robinson. Ed. by Moshe Davis. LC 77-70738. (America & the Holy Land Ser.). 1977. reprint ed. lib. bdg. 173.95 (*0-405-10281-X*) Ayer.

Biblical Resources for Holiness Preaching Vol. 1: From Text to Sermon. Ed. by H. Ray Dunning & Neil B. Wiseman. 466p. 1990. 32.95 (*0-8341-1339-2*) Beacon Hill.

Biblical Resources for Holiness Preaching Vol. 2: From Text to Sermon. H. Ray Dunning. 358p. 1993. boxed 32.95 (*0-8341-1465-8*, 75378) Beacon Hill.

***Biblical Resources for Ministry: A Bibliography Useful for Teaching & Preaching in the Church.** 2nd enl. rev. ed. David R. Bauer. 144p. 1995. pap. 7.95 (*0-916035-62-X*) Evangel Indiana.

Biblical Return. Robert Whitelaw. pap. 1.49 (*0-87377-095-1*) GAM Pubns.

Biblical Revelation & Inspiration. Harold S. Bender. 1959. reprint ed. pap. 1.45 (*0-8361-1322-5*) Herald Pr.

Biblical Rhythms in Biography. Diether Lauenstein. 126p. 1990. pap. 8.95 (*0-86315-001-2*, 732, Pub. by Floris Books UK) Anthroposophic.

Biblical Separation: The Struggle for a Pure Church. Ernest D. Pickering. LC 78-26840. 259p. 1979. pap. 7.95 (*0-87227-069-6*) Reg Baptist.

Biblical Sermons: How Twelve Preachers Apply the Principles of Biblical Preaching. Ed. by Haddon W. Robinson. LC 89-428. 224p. 1989. 16.99 (*0-8010-7751-6*) Baker Bk.

Biblical Sexuality & the Battle for Science. F. Earle Fox. LC 88-80409. 208p. (Orig.). (YA). 1988. pap. 7.00 (*0-945778-00-7*) Emmaus Ministries.

Biblical Social Values & Their Meaning: A Handbook. John J. Pilch & Bruce J. Malina. LC 93-26041. 1993. 19.95 (*1-56563-004-1*) Hendrickson MA.

Biblical Sound & Sense: Poetic Sound Patterns in Proverbs 10-29. Thomas P. McCreesh. (JSOT Supplement Ser.: No. 128). 175p. (C). 1991. 22.50 (*1-85075-326-1*, Pub. by Sheffield Acad UK) CUP Services.

Biblical Spirituality of the Heart. Jan G. Bovenmars. LC 91-7738. 230p. (Orig.). 1991. pap. 12.95 (*0-8189-0584-0*) Alba.

Biblical Standard for Evangelists. Billy Graham. LC 84-51639. 144p. 1984. pap. 5.95 (*0-89066-057-3*) World Wide Pubs.

Biblical Stewardship. Alfred Martin. LC 91-150. 1992. reprint ed. pap. 7.99 (*0-87213-645-0*) Loizeaux.

Biblical Strategies for a Community in Crisis: What African Americans Can Do. Ed. by Colleen Birchett. 255p. (Orig.). 1992. teacher ed 4.95 (*0-940955-20-2*); pap. text ed. 5.95 (*0-940955-19-9*) Urban Ministries.

Biblical Structuralism: Method & Subjectivity in the Study of Ancient Texts. Robert M. Polzin. LC 76-15895. (Semeia Supplements Ser.). (Illus.). 224p. reprint ed. pap. 63.90 (*0-7837-5413-2*, 2045177) Bks Demand.

Biblical Studies: Meeting Ground of Jews & Christians. Ed. by Lawrence Boadt et al. LC 80-82812. (Stimulus Book Ser.). 232p. (Orig.). 1981. pap. 7.95 (*0-8091-2344-4*) Paulist Pr.

An Asterisk (*) at the beginning of an entry indicates that the title is appearing in BIP for the first time.

An Asterisk (*) at the beginning of an entry indicates that the title is appearing in BIP for the first time.

731

Bibliographic Guide to Black Studies: 1985, Vol. 1. Ed. by New York Public Library Staff. 1985. lib. bdg. 115.00 (*0-8161-7019-3*, Biblio Guides) G K Hall.

Bibliographic Guide to Black Studies: 1987. Schomburg Center for Research in Black Culture. 217p. 1988. lib. bdg. 140.00 (*0-8161-7053-3*, Hall Library) G K Hall.

Bibliographic Guide to Black Studies: 1989. New York Public Library Staff. 400p. (C). 1989. Catalog. lib. bdg. 150.00 (*0-8161-7110-6*, Hall Reference) Macmillan.

Bibliographic Guide to Black Studies: 1991. New York Public Library Schomburg Collection of Negro Literature & History Staff. (Bibliographic Guides Ser.). 545p. 1992. text ed. 160.00 (*0-8161-7153-X*) G K Hall.

***Bibliographic Guide to Black Studies: 1993.** New York Public Library Staff. 399p. 1994. 170.00 (*0-7838-2068-2*, Biblio Guides) G K Hall.

***Bibliographic Guide to Business & Economics, 3 Vols.** New York Public Library Staff. 1816p. 1994. 575.00 (*0-7838-2069-0*, Biblio Guides) G K Hall.

Bibliographic Guide to Business & Economics, 1987. New York Public Library Staff. 2256p. 1988. lib. bdg. 520.00 (*0-8161-7086-X*, Hall Reference) Macmillan.

Bibliographic Guide to Business & Economics, 1989, 3 vols., Set. New York Public Library Staff. (C). 1990. lib. bdg. 540.00 (*0-8161-7117-3*, Hall Reference) Macmillan.

Bibliographic Guide to Business & Economics, 1991, 3 vols., Vol. 3. New York Public Library Staff & Library of Congress Staff. (Bibliographic Guides Ser.). 1560p. 1992. text ed. 550.00 (*0-8161-7154-8*) G K Hall.

***Bibliographic Guide to Business & Economics, 1994 Vol. 1.** New York Public Library Staff. (Reference Library). 1995. 210.00 (*0-7838-2166-2*) G K Hall.

***Bibliographic Guide to Business & Economics, 1994 Vol. 2.** New York Public Library Staff. (Reference Library). 1995. 210.00 (*0-7838-2167-0*) G K Hall.

Bibliographic Guide to Caribbean Mass Communication. John A. Lent. LC 92-19373. (Bibliographies & Indexes in Mass Media & Communications Ser.: No. 5). 320p. 1992. text ed. 65.00 (*0-313-28210-2*, LBM, Greenwood Pr) Greenwood.

Bibliographic Guide to Computer Science, 1987. 200p. 1988. lib. bdg. 165.00 (*0-8161-7070-3*, Hall Library) G K Hall.

Bibliographic Guide to Computer Science, 1988. Massachusetts Institute of Technology Staff & Stanford University Staff. 250p. 1989. lib. bdg. 165.00 (*0-8161-7099-1*, Hall Reference) Macmillan.

Bibliographic Guide to Computer Science, 1989. MIT Staff & Stanford University Staff. 250p. 1990. lib. bdg. 150.00 (*0-8161-7130-0*, Hall Reference) Macmillan.

Bibliographic Guide to Computer Science, 1991. (Bibliographic Guides Ser.). 250p. 1992. text ed. 175.00 (*0-8161-7155-6*) G K Hall.

Bibliographic Guide to Conference Publications, 1991, 2 vols. Research Libraries of the New York Public Library Staff & Library of Congress Staff. (Bibliographic Guides Ser.). 1031p. 1992. text ed. 325.00 (*0-8161-7156-4*) G K Hall.

***Bibliographic Guide to Conference Publications, 1993, 2 Vols.** New York Public Library Staff. Incl. Vol. 1. Bibliographic Guide to Conference Publications, 1993. 640p. 1994. 170.00 (*0-7838-2074-7*, Biblio Guides); 340.00 (*0-7838-2073-9*, Biblio Guides) G K Hall.

***Bibliographic Guide to Conference Publications, 1994, 2 vols.** New York Public Library Staff. Incl. Bibliographic Guide to Conference Publications, 1994 Vol. 1. 1995. 185.00 (*0-7838-2170-0*); Bibliographic Guide to Conference Publications, 1994 Vol. 2. 1995. 185.00 (*0-7838-2171-9*); 365.00 (*0-7838-2169-7*) G K Hall.

Bibliographic Guide to Conference Publications, 1984, 2 vols., Set. Bibliographic Guide Editors. 1984. lib. bdg. 225.00 (*0-8161-7003-7*, Hall Reference) Macmillan.

Bibliographic Guide to Conference Publications, 1987. New York Public Library Staff. 1392p. 1988. lib. bdg. 300.00 (*0-8161-7096-7*, Hall Reference) Macmillan.

Bibliographic Guide to Conference Publications, 1988. New York Public Library Staff. (Bibliographic Guides Ser.). 1235p. 1989. lib. bdg. 300.00 (*0-8161-7073-8*, Hall Reference) Macmillan.

Bibliographic Guide to Conference Publications, 1989. New York Public Library Staff. 1200p. (C). 1989. lib. bdg. 310.00 (*0-8161-7111-4*, Hall Reference) Macmillan.

Bibliographic Guide to Dance, 1990. New York Public Library Staff. (Bibliographic Guides Ser.). 1150p. 1991. lib. bdg. 360.00 (*0-8161-7136-X*) G K Hall.

Bibliographic Guide to Dance, 1991, 3 vols., Set. Comp. by New York Public Library Staff. (Bibliographic Guides Ser.). 1800p. 1992. text ed. 450.00 (*0-8161-7157-2*) G K Hall.

***Bibliographic Guide to Dance, 1993, 3 Vols.** New York Public Library Staff. Incl. Bibliographic Guide to Dance, 1993, Vol. 1. 686p. 1994. 160.00 (*0-7838-2077-1*, Biblio Guides); 480.00 (*0-7838-2076-3*, Biblio Guides) G K Hall.

***Bibliographic Guide to Dance, 1994, 3 vols.** New York Public Library Staff. Incl. Bibliographic Guide to Dance, 1994 Vol. 1. 1995. 170.00 (*0-7838-2173-5*); Bibliographic Guide to Dance, 1994 Vol. 2. 1995. 170.00 (*0-7838-2174-3*); Bibliographic Guide to Dance, 1994 Vol. 3. 1995. 170.00 (*0-7838-2175-1*); 510.00 (*0-7838-2172-7*) G K Hall.

Bibliographic Guide to East Asian Studies, 1989. New York Public Library Staff. (Monograph Ser.). 350p. (C). 1990. lib. bdg. 160.00 (*0-8161-7126-2*) G K Hall.

Bibliographic Guide to East Asian Studies, 1990. LC Marc Tapes Staff & Oriental Division of the New York Public Library Staff. (Bibliographic Guides Ser.). 350p. (C). 1991. lib. bdg. 165.00 (*0-8161-7137-8*) G K Hall.

Bibliographic Guide to East Asian Studies, 1991. Comp. by New York Public Library Staff & Library of Congress Staff. (Bibliographic Guides Ser.). 600p. 1992. text ed. 175.00 (*0-8161-7158-0*) G K Hall.

***Bibliographic Guide to East Asian Studies, 1993.** New York Public Library Staff. 432p. 1994. 185.00 (*0-7838-2080-1*, Biblio Guides) G K Hall.

***Bibliographic Guide to East Asian Studies, 1994.** New York Public Library Staff. 1995. 200.00 (*0-7838-2176-X*) G K Hall.

Bibliographic Guide to Education: 1984. Bibliographic Guide Editors. (Bibliographic Guides Ser.). (C). 1985. lib. bdg. 225.00 (*0-8161-7005-3*) G K Hall.

Bibliographic Guide to Education: 1987. 470p. 1988. lib. bdg. 275.00 (*0-8161-7067-3*, Hall Library) G K Hall.

Bibliographic Guide to Education: 1990. Columbia University Teachers College OCLC Tapes Staff & New York Public Library OCLC Tapes Staff. (Bibliographic Guides Ser.). 625p. (C). 1991. lib. bdg. 285.00 (*0-8161-7138-6*) G K Hall.

***Bibliographic Guide to Education, 1993.** New York Public Library Staff. 432p. 1994. 315.00 (*0-7838-2081-X*, Biblio Guides) G K Hall.

***Bibliographic Guide to Education 1994.** New York Public Library Staff. 1995. 335.00 (*0-7838-2177-8*) G K Hall.

Bibliographic Guide to Educational Research. 3rd ed. Dorothea M. Berry. LC 90-48184. 508p. 1990. 49.50 (*0-8108-2343-8*) Scarecrow.

Bibliographic Guide to Gabriel Garcia Marquez, 1979-1985. Ed. by Nelly Sfeir De Gonzalez. LC 86-371. (Bibliographies & Indexes in World Literature Ser.: No. 7). 198p. 1986. text ed. 65.00 (*0-313-25248-3*, FBG/) Greenwood.

Bibliographic Guide to Gabriel Garcia Marquez, 1986-1992. Nelly S. De Gonzalez. LC 93-45321. (Bibliographies and Indexes in World Literature Ser.: Vol. 42). 464p. 1994. text ed. 89.50 (*0-313-28832-1*, Greenwood Pr) Greenwood.

***Bibliographic Guide to Goverment Publications, 1993 - U.S., 2 Vols.** New York Public Library Staff. 944p. 1994. 520.00 (*0-7838-2086-0*, Biblio Guides) G K Hall.

Bibliographic Guide to Government Publications - U. S. 1982, 2 vols., Set. Bibliographic Guide Editors. 1983. lib. bdg. 340.00 (*0-8161-6973-X*, Hall Reference) Macmillan.

Bibliographic Guide to Government Publications - U. S. 1983, 2 vols., Set. Bibliographic Guide Editors. 980p. 1984. lib. bdg. 350.00 (*0-8161-6994-2*) G K Hall.

Bibliographic Guide to Government Publications - U. S. 1987. New York Public Library Staff. 1448p. 1988. lib. bdg. 435.00 (*0-8161-7089-4*, Hall Reference) Macmillan.

Bibliographic Guide to Government Publications - U. S. 1988. New York Public Library Staff. 1175p. 1989. lib. bdg. 455.00 (*0-8161-7102-5*, Hall Reference) Macmillan.

Bibliographic Guide to Government Publications - U. S. 1989, 2 vols. 1295p. 1990. lib. bdg. 470.00 (*0-8161-7119-X*) G K Hall.

Bibliographic Guide to Government Publications - U. S. 1990, 2 vols., Set. Research Library of the New York Public Library & the Library of Congress MARC Tapes Staff. (Bibliographic Guides Ser.). 1415p. 1991. lib. bdg. 475.00 (*0-8161-7140-8*) G K Hall.

Bibliographic Guide to Government Publications - Foreign: 1983, 2 vols., Set. New York Public Library Staff. 1195p. 1984. lib. bdg. 350.00 (*0-8161-6995-0*, Hall Reference) Macmillan.

Bibliographic Guide to Government Publications - Foreign: 1988. New York Public Library Staff. 1720p. 1989. lib. bdg. 505.00 (*0-8161-7103-3*, Hall Reference) Macmillan.

Bibliographic Guide to Government Publications - Foreign: 1989, 2 vols., Set. 1320p. 1990. lib. bdg. 520.00 (*0-8161-7120-3*) G K Hall.

Bibliographic Guide to Government Publications - Foreign: 1990, 2 vols., Set. Research Libraries of the New York Public Library & the Library of Congress MARC Tapes Staff. (Bibliographic Guides Ser.). 1600p. 1991. lib. bdg. 525.00 (*0-8161-7139-4*) G K Hall.

Bibliographic Guide to Government Publications-Foreign: 1987. New York Public Library Staff. 1808p. 1988. lib. bdg. 495.00 (*0-8161-7090-8*, Hall Reference) Macmillan.

***Bibliographic Guide to Government Publications, 1993 - Foriegn, 2 Vols.** New York Public Library Staff. 1664p. 1994. 575.00 (*0-7838-2083-6*, Biblio Guides) G K Hall.

***Bibliographic Guide to Government Publications 1994 Vol. 1: Foreign.** New York Public Library Staff. 1995. 300.00 (*0-7838-2180-8*) G K Hall.

***Bibliographic Guide to Government Publications, 1994 Vol. 1: U. S.** New York Public Library Staff. 1995. 275.00 (*0-7838-2183-2*) G K Hall.

***Bibliographic Guide to Government Publications 1994 Vol. 2: Foreign.** New York Public Library Staff. 1995. 300.00 (*0-7838-2181-6*) G K Hall.

***Bibliographic Guide to Government Publications, 1994 Vol. 2: U. S.** New York Public Library Staff. 1995. 275.00 (*0-7838-2184-0*) G K Hall.

***Bibliographic Guide to Latin American Studies, 2 Vols.** New York Public Library Staff. 1668p. 1994. 550.00 (*0-7838-2089-5*, Biblio Guides) G K Hall.

Bibliographic Guide to Latin American Studies: 1987. New York Public Library Staff & University of Texas Austin Staff. 2048p. 1988. lib. bdg. 520.00 (*0-8161-7083-5*, Hall Reference) Macmillan.

Bibliographic Guide to Latin American Studies: 1990. University of Texas Library, Austin, Nettie Lee Benson Latin American Collection Staff & Library of Congress Staff. (Bibliographic Guides Ser.). 1660p. 1991. lib. bdg. 485.00 (*0-8161-7141-6*, Hall Reference) Macmillan.

Bibliographic Guide to Latin American Studies: 1991, 2 vols., Set. (Bibliographic Guides Ser.). 1992. text ed. 500.00 (*0-8161-7162-9*) G K Hall.

***Bibliographic Guide to Latin American Studies, 1994 Vol. 1.** New York Public Library Staff. 1995. 290.00 (*0-7838-2186-7*) G K Hall.

***Bibliographic Guide to Latin American Studies, 1994 Vol. 2.** New York Public Library Staff. 1995. 290.00 (*0-7838-2187-5*) G K Hall.

Bibliographic Guide to Law: 1987. New York Public Library Staff. 1544p. 1988. lib. bdg. 315.00 (*0-8161-7095-9*, Hall Reference) Macmillan.

Bibliographic Guide to Law: 1989. 1096p. 1989. lib. bdg. 325.00 (*0-8161-7112-2*) G K Hall.

Bibliographic Guide to Law: 1991, 2 vols., Vol. 2. Library of Congress Staff. (Bibliographic Guides Ser.). 1053p. 1992. text ed. 340.00 (*0-8161-7163-7*) G K Hall.

***Bibliographic Guide to Law 1994 Vol. 1.** New York Public Library Staff. 1995. 190.00 (*0-7838-2189-1*) G K Hall.

***Bibliographic Guide to Law 1994 Vol. 2.** New York Public Library Staff. 1995. 190.00 (*0-7838-2190-5*) G K Hall.

Bibliographic Guide to Maps & Atlases, 1985. Ed. by New York Public Library Staff. 1986. lib. bdg. 225.00 (*0-8161-7027-4*, Hall Reference) Macmillan.

Bibliographic Guide to Maps & Atlases, 1987. New York Public Library Staff. 880p. 1988. lib. bdg. 300.00 (*0-8161-7085-1*, Hall Reference) Macmillan.

Bibliographic Guide to Maps & Atlases, 1988. New York Public Library Staff & Library of Congress Staff. 675p. 1989. lib. bdg. 300.00 (*0-8161-7105-X*, Hall Reference) Macmillan.

Bibliographic Guide to Maps & Atlases, 1989. (Illus.). 740p. 1989. lib. bdg. 300.00 (*0-8161-7121-1*, Hall Reference) Macmillan.

Bibliographic Guide to Maps & Atlases, 1990. New York Public Library Map Division & the Geography & Map Division of the Library of Congress Staff. (Bibliographic Guides Ser.). 770p. 1991. lib. bdg. 300.00 (*0-8161-7143-2*) G K Hall.

***Bibliographic Guide to Maps & Atlases, 1993.** New York Public Library Staff. 535p. 1994. 325.00 (*0-7838-2095-X*, Biblio Guides) G K Hall.

Bibliographic Guide to Materials on Greeks in the United States: 1890-1968. Michael M. Cutsumbis. LC 74-130283. 100p. 1970. 9.95 (*0-913256-02-1*) Ctr Migration.

Bibliographic Guide to Microform Publications. New York Public Library Staff. (Bibliographic Guides Ser.). 600p. (C). 1990. lib. bdg. 250.00 (*0-8161-7129-7*) G K Hall.

Bibliographic Guide to Microform Publications. New York Public Library Staff. (Bibliographic Guides Ser.). 600p. 1989. lib. bdg. 250.00 (*0-8161-7106-8*, Hall Reference) Macmillan.

Bibliographic Guide to Microform Publications: 1987. 650p. 1988. lib. bdg. 235.00 (*0-8161-7078-9*, Hall Library) G K Hall.

Bibliographic Guide to Microform Publications: 1990. LC Marc Tapes Staff & New York Public Library Staff. (Bibliographic Guides Ser.). 600p. (C). 1991. lib. bdg. 250.00 (*0-8161-7144-0*) G K Hall.

Bibliographic Guide to Microform Publications, 1991. (Bibliographic Guides Ser.). 600p. 1992. text ed. 260.00 (*0-8161-7165-3*) G K Hall.

***Bibliographic Guide to Microform Publications, 1993.** New York Public Library Staff. 535p. 1994. 275.00 (*0-7838-2096-8*, Biblio Guides) G K Hall.

Bibliographic Guide to Middle Eastern Studies, 1991. Comp. by New York Public Library Staff & Library of Congress Staff. (Bibliographic Guides Ser.). 500p. 1992. text ed. 195.00 (*0-8161-7172-6*) G K Hall.

***Bibliographic Guide to Middle Eastern Studies, 1993.** New York Public Library Staff. 497p. 1994. 195.00 (*0-7838-2097-6*, Biblio Guides) G K Hall.

***Bibliographic Guide to Middle Eastern Studies 1994.** New York Public Library Staff. 1995. 205.00 (*0-7838-2192-1*) G K Hall.

Bibliographic Guide to Middle Eastern Studies, 1990 Edition. New York Public Library Staff. (Bibliographic Guides Ser.). 800p. 1991. text ed. 195.00 (*0-8161-7151-3*) G K Hall.

Bibliographic Guide to Music, 1984. Bibliographic Guide Editors. (Bibliographic Guides Ser.). 1984. lib. bdg. 175.00 (*0-8161-7011-8*) G K Hall.

Bibliographic Guide to Music, 1987. New York Public Library Staff. 752p. 1988. lib. bdg. 205.00 (*0-8161-7093-2*, Hall Reference) Macmillan.

Bibliographic Guide to Music, 1988. New York Public Library Staff. (Bibliographic Guides Ser.). 690p. 1989. lib. bdg. 205.00 (*0-8161-7075-4*, Hall Reference) Macmillan.

Bibliographic Guide to Music, 1989. 551p. 1990. lib. bdg. 210.00 (*0-8161-7113-0*, Hall Reference) Macmillan.

Bibliographic Guide to Music, 1990. large type ed. New York Public Library, Music Div. Staff. 792p. 1991. 210.00 (*0-8161-7146-7*, Hall Reference) Macmillan.

Bibliographic Guide to Music, 1991. American Music Center Staff et al. (Bibliographic Guides Ser.). 600p. 1992. text ed. 225.00 (*0-8161-7167-X*) G K Hall.

***Bibliographic Guide to Music, 1993.** New York Public Library Staff. 767p. 1994. 235.00 (*0-7838-2098-4*, Biblio Guides) G K Hall.

Bibliographic Guide to Neuroenzyme Literature. Dorothy J. Hoijer. LC 72-102211. 330p. reprint ed. pap. 94.10 (*0-8357-7166-0*, 2024704) Bks Demand.

Bibliographic Guide to North American History: 1984. Bibliographic Guide Editors. (Bibliographic Guides Ser.). 1985. lib. bdg. 225.00 (*0-8161-7012-6*, Hall Reference) Macmillan.

Bibliographic Guide to North American History: 1986. 760p. 1987. lib. bdg. 260.00 (*0-8161-7047-9*, Hall Library) G K Hall.

Bibliographic Guide to North American History: 1987. New York Public Library Staff. 768p. 1988. lib. bdg. 275.00 (*0-8161-7092-4*, Hall Reference) Macmillan.

Bibliographic Guide to North American History: 1989. New York Public Library Staff. (C). 1990. lib. bdg. 290.00 (*0-8161-7118-1*, Hall Reference) Macmillan.

Bibliographic Guide to North American History: 1990. Research Libraries of the New York Public Library & The Library of Congress Staff. (Bibliographic Guides Ser.). 740p. 1991. lib. bdg. 290.00 (*0-8161-7145-9*) G K Hall.

***Bibliographic Guide to North American History: 1993.** New York Public Library Staff. 808p. 1994. 315.00 (*0-7838-2099-2*, Biblio Guides) G K Hall.

Bibliographic Guide to Psychology: 1985, Vol. 1. (New York Public Library). 1985. lib. bdg. 155.00 (*0-8161-7030-4*) G K Hall.

Bibliographic Guide to Psychology: 1987. New York Public Library Staff. 152p. 1988. lib. bdg. 175.00 (*0-8161-7094-0*, Hall Reference) Macmillan.

Bibliographic Guide to Psychology: 1989. New York Public Library Staff. 150p. 1989. lib. bdg. 190.00 (*0-8161-7114-9*) G K Hall.

***Bibliographic Guide to Psychology: 1993.** New York Public Library Staff. 224p. 1994. 195.00 (*0-7838-2100-X*, Biblio Guides) G K Hall.

Bibliographic Guide to Refrigeration, 1965-1968: Guide Bibliographique du Froid. 260.00 (*0-08-006557-0*, Pub. by Pergamon Repr UK) Franklin.

Bibliographic Guide to Soviet & East European Studies: 1987. New York Public Library Staff. 2360p. 1988. lib. bdg. 545.00 (*0-8161-7091-6*, Hall Reference) Macmillan.

Bibliographic Guide to Soviet & East European Studies: 1989, 3 vols. 3010p. 1990. lib. bdg. 580.00 (*0-8161-7123-8*, Hall Reference) Macmillan.

Bibliographic Guide to Soviet & East European Studies: 1990, 3 vols., Set. Research Libraries of the New York Public Library & the Library of Congress MARC Tapes Staff. (Bibliographic Guides Ser.). 2980p. 1991. lib. bdg. 580.00 (*0-8161-7148-3*) G K Hall.

***Bibliographic Guide to Soviet & East European Studies 1994 Vol. 1.** New York Public Library Staff. 1995. 220.00 (*0-7838-2197-2*) G K Hall.

***Bibliographic Guide to Soviet & East European Studies 1994 Vol. 2.** New York Public Library Staff. 1995. 220.00 (*0-7838-2198-0*) G K Hall.

***Bibliographic Guide to Soviet & East European Studies 1994 Vol. 3.** New York Public Library Staff. 1995. 220.00 (*0-7838-2199-9*) G K Hall.

Bibliographic Guide to Spanish Diplomatic History: Fourteen Sixty to Nineteen Seventy-Seven. Comp. by James W. Cortada. LC 77-4565. 390p. 1977. text ed. 59.95 (*0-8371-9685-X*, CBG/, Greenwood Pr) Greenwood.

Bibliographic Guide to Technology: 1983, 2 vols., Set. 1984. lib. bdg. 260.00 (*0-8161-6999-3*, Biblio Guides) G K Hall.

Bibliographic Guide to Technology: 1987. New York Public Library Staff. 1080p. 1988. lib. bdg. 360.00 (*0-8161-7088-6*, Hall Reference) Macmillan.

Bibliographic Guide to Technology: 1989. 790p. 1990. lib. bdg. 250.00 (*0-8161-7122-X*) G K Hall.

Bibliographic Guide to Technology: 1990, 2 vols., Set. New York Public Library & Library of Congress MARC Tapes Staff. (Bibliographic Guides Ser.). 1020p. 1991. lib. bdg. 350.00 (*0-8161-7150-5*) G K Hall.

***Bibliographic Guide to Technology 1994 Vol. 1.** New York Public Library Staff. 1995. 180.00 (*0-7838-2201-4*) G K Hall.

***Bibliographic Guide to Technology 1994 Vol. 2.** New York Public Library Staff. 1995. 180.00 (*0-7838-2202-2*) G K Hall.

Bibliographic Guide to the Environment, 1991. Comp. by New York Public Library Staff & Library of Congress Staff. (Bibliographic Guides Ser.). 250p. 1992. text ed. 165.00 (*0-8161-7222-6*) G K Hall.

***Bibliographic Guide to the Environment 1994.** New York Public Library Staff. 1995. 185.00 (*0-7838-2178-6*) G K Hall.

Bibliographic Guide to the History of Computing, Computers & the Information Processing Industry. Comp. by James W. Cortada. LC 90-3093. (Bibliographies & Indexes in Science & Technology Ser.: No. 6). 672p. 1990. text ed. 95.00 (*0-313-26810-X*, CBF, Greenwood Pr) Greenwood.

***Bibliographic Guide to the Law, 1993, 2 Vols.** Incl. Vol. 1. Bibliographic Guide to the Law, 1993. 686p. 1994. 180.00 (*0-7838-2093-3*, Biblio Guides); Vol. 2. Bibliographic Guide to the Law. 453p. 1994. 180.00 (*0-7838-2094-1*, Biblio Guides); 360.00 (*0-7838-2092-5*, Biblio Guides) G K Hall.

Bibliographic Guide to the Literature of Contemporary American Poetry, 1970-1975. Phillis Gershator. LC 76-41812. 1976. 20.00 (*0-8108-0987-7*) Scarecrow.

Bibliographic Guide to Theater Arts: 1989. New York Public Library Staff. (Bibliographic Guides Ser.). 200p. (C). 1989. lib. bdg. 200.00 (*0-8161-7115-7*, Hall Reference) Macmillan.

Bibliographic Guide to Theatre Arts: 1984. 1984. lib. bdg. 155.00 (*0-8161-7016-9*, Biblio Guides) G K Hall.

Bibliographic Guide to Theatre Arts: 1987. New York Public Library Staff. 264p. 1988. lib. bdg. 190.00 (*0-8161-7084-3*, Hall Reference) Macmillan.

Bibliographic Guide to Theatre Arts: 1990. large type ed. New York Public Library, Research Libraries Staff. 244p. 1991. 185.00 (*0-8161-7149-1*, Hall Reference) Macmillan.

Bibliographic Guide to Theatre Arts: 1991. New York Public Library Theatre & Drama Collections Staff & Library of Congress Staff. (Bibliographic Guides Ser.). 203p. 1992. text ed. 195.00 (*0-8161-7170-X*) G K Hall.

***Bibliographic Guide to Theatre Arts 1994.** New York Public Library Staff. 1995. 205.00 (*0-7838-2203-0*) G K Hall.

An Asterisk (*) at the beginning of an entry indicates that the title is appearing in BIP for the first time.

Bibliographic Guides to Computer Science: 1990. Ed. by Massachusetts Institute of Technology Library Staff & Stanford University Library Staff. (Bibliographic Guides Ser.). 250p. (C). 1991. lib. bdg. 165.00 (*0-8161-7134-3*) G K Hall.

***Bibliographic History of the Book: An Annotated Guide to the Literature.** annot. ed. Joseph Rosenblum. LC 95-5327. (History of the Book Ser.: No. 3). 439p. 1995. 55.00 (*0-8108-3009-4*) Scarecrow.

Bibliographic Index, 1956-1968. 250.00 (*0-685-22233-0*) Wilson.

Bibliographic Index, 1969-1990. 205.00 (*0-318-57944-8*) Wilson.

Bibliographic Index, 1991-94. 205.00 (*0-318-57945-6*) Wilson.

Bibliographic Index of Health Education Periodicals (BIHEP) Vol. 2, 1981 Cumulative Edition. William J. Bailey & Stephen J. Guynn. 650p. 1982. lib. bdg. 75.00 (*0-941636-01-1*) IN U Dept Health.

Bibliographic Index of Health Education Periodicals (BIHEP) 1980 Cumulative Edition. William J. Bailey & J. Guynn. 428p. 1982. lib. bdg. 75.00 (*0-941636-00-3*) IN U Dept Health.

Bibliographic Index to Romance Philology, Vols. 1-25. Mark G. Littlefield. LC 73-76118. 274p. reprint ed. pap. 78.10 (*0-8357-7167-9*, 2031537) Bks Demand.

Bibliographic Information Interchange. 1985. 12.00 (*0-88738-998-8*, Z30.2) Transaction Pubs.

Bibliographic Instruction: A Handbook. Beverly Renford & Linnea Hendrickson. LC 80-12300. 192p. 1980. 29.95 (*0-918212-24-3*) Neal-Schuman.

Bibliographic Instruction: The Second Generation. Constance A. Mellon. 204p. 1987. lib. bdg. 29.50 (*0-87287-563-6*) Libs Unl.

Bibliographic Instruction - Course Handbook: A Skills & Concepts Approach to the Undergraduate Research Methodology, Credit Course - For College & University Personnel. Helen R. Wheeler. LC 88-14003. (Illus.). 632p. 1988. 62.50 (*0-8108-2131-1*) Scarecrow.

Bibliographic Instruction & Computer Database Searching. Ed. by Teresa B. Mensching & Keith J. Stanger. (Library Orientation Ser.: No. 17). 173p. 1988. pap. 35.00 (*0-87650-251-6*) Pierian.

Bibliographic Instruction & the Learning Process: Theory, Style & Motivation. Carolyn A. Kirkendall. LC 84-60638. (Library Orientation Ser.: No. 14). 180p. 1984. 25.00 (*0-87650-182-X*) Pierian.

Bibliographic Instruction in Practice: A Tribute of the Legacy of Evan Ira Farber. Ed. by Larry Hardesty et al. (Library Orientation Ser.: No. 24). 166p. 1993. pap. 35.00 (*0-87650-328-8*) Pierian.

Bibliographic Overview of Housing in Developing Countries: Annotated, Nos. 1225-1227. Donald R. Mackenzie & Erna W. Kerst. 1977. 12.50 (*0-686-19686-4*) CPL Biblios.

Bibliographic Record & Information Technology. 2nd ed. Ronald Hagler. LC 90-45317. 331p. (C). 1991. text ed. 44.00 (*0-8389-0554-4*, 0554-4) ALA.

Bibliographic References. (National Information Standards Ser.). 1977. 30.00 (*0-88738-974-0*, Z30.20) Transaction Pubs.

Bibliographic Services Throughout the World. Ed. by Marcelle Beaudiquez. Incl. 1970-1974. 419p. 1977. 14.00 (*92-3-101394-7*, U817, UNESCO); 1975-1979462p. 1985. pap. 5.00 (*92-3-101982-1*, U1406, UNESCO); (Documentation, Libraries & Archives Bibliographies & Reference Works). write for info. (*0-318-60638-0*) UNIPUB.

Bibliographic Sketch of Herman Melville. J. E. Smith. 1973. 35.00 (*0-87968-734-7*) Gordon Pr.

Bibliographica Cartographica 1989. Ed. by Lothar Zogner. (International Documentation of Cartographical Literature Ser.: Vol. 16). 260p. 1990. pap. 70.00 (*3-598-20632-1*) K G Saur.

Bibliographica Textilia Historiae - A General Bibliography on the History of Textiles. Ed. by Center for Social Research on Old Textiles Staff. (Art, Craft, Technique, Industry & Commerce Ser.). (Illus.). 300p. 1995. pap. 60.00 (*0-88477-038-9*) Intl General.

Bibliographical Account of Catholic Bibles, Testaments & Other Portions of Scripture Translated from the Latin Vulgate. John D. Shea. 1980. lib. bdg. 49.95 (*0-8490-3114-1*) Gordon Pr.

Bibliographical Account of English Theatrical Literature from Earliest Times to the Present Day. R. W. Lowe. 1972. 59.95 (*0-87968-735-5*) Gordon Pr.

Bibliographical & Critical Account of the Rarest Books in the English Language, 4 Vols. J. Payne Collier. reprint ed. 17.50 (*0-685-73106-5*) AMS Pr.

Bibliographical & Critical Account of the Rarest Books in the English Language, 4 Vols, 1. J. Payne Collier. reprint ed. 86.25 (*0-404-01721-5*) AMS Pr.

Bibliographical & Critical Account of the Rarest Books in the English Language, 4 Vols, 2. J. Payne Collier. reprint ed. 86.25 (*0-404-01722-3*) AMS Pr.

Bibliographical & Critical Account of the Rarest Books in the English Language, 4 Vols, 3. J. Payne Collier. reprint ed. 86.25 (*0-404-01723-1*) AMS Pr.

Bibliographical & Critical Account of the Rarest Books in the English Language, 4 Vols, 4. J. Payne Collier. reprint ed. 86.25 (*0-404-01724-X*) AMS Pr.

Bibliographical & Critical Account of the Rarest Books in the English Language, 4 Vols, Set. J. Payne Collier. reprint ed. 345.00 (*0-404-01720-7*) AMS Pr.

Bibliographical & Pictorial Curriculum Guide to Egypt: From Abu Simbel to the Egyptian Museum of Antiquities. Mwalimu I. Mwadilifu. LC 89-81781. (Monograph Ser.: No. 5). 64p. 1989. 4.95 (*0-938818-20-1*, Alkebulan Hist Res Soc) ECA Assoc.

Bibliographical, Antiquarian, & Picturesque Tour in France & Germany, 3 Vols, Set. 2nd ed. Thomas F. Dibdin. LC 76-111768. reprint ed. 195.00 (*0-404-02130-1*) AMS Pr.

Bibliographical Catalogue of Seventeenth-Century German Books Published in Holland. J. Bruckner. (Anglica Germanica Ser.: No. 13). 1971. text ed. 124.60 (*90-279-1706-X*) Mouton.

Bibliographical Companion. Roy Stokes. LC 88-34831. 308p. 1989. 29.50 (*0-8108-2175-3*) Scarecrow.

Bibliographical Essay on the History of the Society of Jesus. William V. Bangert. Ed. by George E. Ganss. LC 76-12667. (Studies on Jesuit Topics Series IV: No. 6). xvi, 75p. 1976. pap. 1.50 (*0-912422-16-5*) Inst Jesuit.

Bibliographical Essays: A Tribute to Wilberforce Eames. LC 67-23178. (Essay Index Reprint Ser.). 1977. 34.95 (*0-8369-0209-2*) Ayer.

Bibliographical Foundations of French Historical Studies. Ed. by Lawrence J. McCrank. LC 91-25540. (Primary Sources & Original Works). (Illus.). 245p. 1991. lib. bdg. 39.95 (*1-56024-150-0*) Haworth Pr.

Bibliographical Ghost Revisits His Old Haunts. Frank Francis. LC 72-619563. (Bibliographical Monograph: No. 5). (Illus.). 1972. 10.00 (*0-87959-046-7*) U of Tex H Ransom Ctr.

Bibliographical Guide to African-American Women Writers. Comp. by Casper LeRoy Jordan. LC 93-6561. (Bibliographies & Indexes in Afro-American & African Studies: Vol. 31). 416p. 1993. text ed. 65.00 (*0-313-27633-1*, JBG/, Greenwood Pr) Greenwood.

Bibliographical Guide to Black Studies Programs in the United States: An Annotated Bibliography. Lenwood G. Davis & George Hill. LC 85-12722. (Bibliographies & Indexes in Afro-American & African Studies: No. 6). xvii, 120p. 1985. text ed. 45.00 (*0-313-23328-4*, DBS/) Greenwood.

Bibliographical Guide to Iran: The Middle East Library Committee Guide. Ed. by L. P. Elwell-Sutton. LC 82-22748. 488p. (C). 1983. text ed. 53.50 (*0-389-20339-4*, N7180) B&N Imports.

Bibliographical Guide to Japanese Research on the Chinese Economy, 1958-1970. W. P. Hall. LC 71-184106. (East Asian Monographs: No. 46). 114p. 1972. pap. 11.00 (*0-674-06985-4*) HUP.

Bibliographical Guide to Self-Disclosure Literature Nineteen Fifty-Six to Nineteen Seventy-Six. Carolyn J. Moss. LC 77-89643. 219p. 1978. 15.00 (*0-87875-132-7*) Whitston Pub.

Bibliographical Guide to Spanish American Literature: Twentieth-Century Sources. Comp. by Walter Rela. LC 88-15443. (Bibliographies & Indexes in World Literature Ser.: No. 13). 400p. 1988. text ed. 65.00 (*0-313-25861-9*, RBG/, Greenwood Pr) Greenwood.

Bibliographical Guide to the Study of Southern Literature. Ed. by Louis D. Rubin, Jr. LC 69-17627. (Southern Literary Studies). 375p. reprint ed. pap. 106.90 (*0-8357-7168-7*, 2019591) Bks Demand.

Bibliographical Guide to the Study of the Literature of the U. S. A. 5th enl. rev. ed. Ed. by Clarence Gohdes & Sanford E. Marovitz. LC 84-1677. xv, 256p. 1984. lib. bdg. 37.00 (*0-8223-0592-5*) Duke.

Bibliographical Guide to the Study of Western American Literature. Richard W. Etulain. LC 82-8579. xviii, 317p. 1982. 35.00 (*0-8032-1801-X*) U of Nebr Pr.

***Bibliographical Guide to the Study of Western American Literature.** 2nd ed. Ed. by Richard W. Etulain & N. Jill Howard. 464p. 1995. 39.95x (*0-8263-1644-1*) Free Spirit Pub.

Bibliographical Guide to the Works of William Inge 1913-1973. Ed. by Arthur F. McClure & C. David Rice. LC 91-30669. (Studies in American Literature: Vol. 14). 180p. 1991. lib. bdg. 79.95 (*0-7734-9688-2*) E Mellen.

Bibliographical Handbook of American Music. D. W. Krummel. LC 87-20597. (Music in American Life Ser.). 288p. 1988. 29.95 (*0-252-01450-2*) U of Ill Pr.

Bibliographical History of Economics. Arnold Heertje. Date not set. write for info. (*0-930405-59-5*) Norman SF.

Bibliographical History of Electricity & Magnetism. Ed. by Paul F. Mottelay. LC 74-26277. (History, Philosophy & Sociology of Science Ser.). (Illus.). 1975. reprint ed. 52.95 (*0-405-06605-8*) Ayer.

Bibliographical Index of Five English Mystics: Richard Rolle, Julian of Norwich, The Author of the Cloud of Unknowing, Walter Hilton, Margery Kempe. Comp. by Michael E. Sawyer. LC 73-110788. 1978. 10.00 (*0-931222-09-5*) Pitts Theolog.

Bibliographical Introduction to Seventy-Five Modern American Authors. Gary Lepper. 1975. 30.00 (*0-685-56280-8*) SPD-Small Pr Dist.

Bibliographical Inventory to the Early Music in the Newberry Library, Chicago, Illinois. Newberry Library, Chicago Staff. Ed. by Donald W. Krummel. 1978. lib. bdg. 85.00 (*0-8161-0042-X*, Hall Library) G K Hall.

Bibliographical List of Plays in the French Language, Seventeen Hundred to Seventeen Eighty-Nine. Clarence D. Brenner. LC 76-43909. (Music & Theatre in France in the 17th & 18th Centuries Ser.). reprint ed. 64.50 (*0-404-60152-9*) AMS Pr.

Bibliographical List of Works Illustrative of the Dialect of Northumberland. R. O. Heslop. (English Dialect Society Publications Ser.: No. 80). 1972. reprint ed. pap. 15.00 (*0-8115-0498-0*) Periodicals Srv.

Bibliographical List of Works That Have Been Published, or Are Known to Exist in Ms. Illustrative of the Various Dialects of English. Ed. by W. W. Skeat & J. H. Nodal. (English Dialect Society Publications Ser.: Nos. 2, 8, 18). 1972. reprint ed. pap. 20.00 (*0-8115-0435-2*) Periodicals Srv.

Bibliographical Manual. 3rd ed. John W. Spargo. 295p. 1956. 5.00 (*0-87532-075-9*) Hendricks House.

Bibliographical Manual for the Student of Criminology. 1991. lib. bdg. 69.95 (*0-8490-4500-2*) Gordon Pr.

Bibliographical Notes. Halldor Hermannsson. LC 43-13095. (Islandica Ser.: Vol. 29). 1972. 15.00 (*0-527-00359-X*) Periodicals Srv.

***Bibliographical Review of Colloid Transport Through the Geosphere, No. EUR 15481.** European Commission Staff. 100p. 1994. pap. 16.00 (*92-826-8485-7*, CDNA15481ENC, Pub. by Europ Com) UNIPUB.

Bibliographical Society of America 1904 to 1979: A Retrospective Collection. 557p. (C). 1980. 20.00 (*0-914930-08-7*) Biblio Soc Am.

Bibliographical Study of Shakespeare. Percy Simpson. Bd. with Standard Descriptions of Printed Books (Oxford Bibliographic Society Ser.: Vol. 1, Pt. 1). 1972. reprint ed. Set pap. 13.00 (*0-8115-1225-8*) Periodicals Srv.

Bibliographical Study of the Writings of Joaquin Costa (1846-1911) George G. Cheyne. (Serie A: Monografias, XXIV). (Illus.). 189p. (Orig.). (C). 1972. pap. 36.00 (*0-900411-36-8*, Pub. by Tamesis Bks Ltd UK) Boydell & Brewer.

Bibliographical Study of William Blake's Notebook. Bunsho Jugaku. LC 78-118007. (Studies in Blake: No. 3). 1970. reprint ed. lib. bdg. 59.95 (*0-8383-1064-8*) M S G Haskell Hse.

Bibliographical Supplement to Liberty of Conscience. Helena R. Costa. 105p. 1986. pap. 10.00 (*0-916617-03-3*) J C Brown.

Bibliographical Survey of Contemporary Sources for the Economic & Social History of the World War. Mildred E. Bulkley. 1922. 200.00 (*0-686-83490-9*) Elliots Bks.

Bibliographical Survey of Secondary Literature on Military Expenditures. 39p. 1990. 10.00 (*0-685-39197-3*, GV.89.0.14) UN.

Bibliographie. Bartsch Eberhard. 280p. (GER.). 1989. lib. bdg. 16.00 (*3-598-10878-8*) K G Saur.

Bibliographie: Bachtrag 1961-1966. Rainald Stromeyer. (Veroeffentlichungen der Historischen Kommission zu Berlin, Band 67, Beitraege zu Inflation und Wiederaufbau in Deutschland und Europa 1914-1924: Vol. 43). 400p. (GER.). (C). 1973. 76.95x (*3-11-004060-3*) De Gruyter.

Bibliographie Bildende Kunst: Deutschsprachige Hochschulschriften & Veroffentlichungen Ausserhalb des Buchandels 1966-1980, 6 vols., Set. Ed. by Irene Butt et al. 440p. (GER.). 1992. lib. bdg. 1,135.00 (*3-598-22380-3*) K G Saur.

Bibliographie Ceramique Depuis Le XVIe Siecle. J. F. Champfleury. xv, 352p. 1981. reprint ed. lib. bdg. 76.70 (*3-487-07058-8*, Pub. by Georg Olms GW) Lubrecht & Cramer.

Bibliographie Courante d'Articles de Periodiques Posterieurs a 1944 sur les Problemes Politiques, Economiques et Sociaux, 2 vols., Set. Fondation Nationale des Sciences Politiques, Paris, France Staff. 1972. Fourth suppl., 1972, 2 vols. lib. bdg. 250.00 (*0-8161-1056-5*, Hall Library) G K Hall.

Bibliographie Courante d'Articles de Periodiques Posterieurs a 1944 sur les Problemes Politiques, Economiques et Sociaux, 17 Vols, Set. Fondation Nationale des Sciences Politiques, Paris, France Staff. 1972. lib. bdg. 1,850.00 (*0-8161-0769-6*, Hall Library) G K Hall.

Bibliographie Courante d'Articles de Periodiques Posterieurs a 1944 sur les Problemes Politiques, Economiques et Sociaux, 2 vols., Set. suppl. ed. Fondation Nationale des Sciences Politiques, Paris, France Staff. 1969. First suppl., 1969, 2 vols. lib. bdg. 250.00 (*0-8161-0803-X*, Hall Library) G K Hall.

Bibliographie Courante d'Articles de Periodiques Posterieurs a 1944 sur les Problemes Politiques, Economiques et Sociaux, 2 vols., Set. suppl. ed. Fondation Nationale des Sciences Politiques, Paris, France Staff. 1970. Second suppl., 1970, 2 vols. lib. bdg. 250.00 (*0-8161-0917-6*, Hall Library) G K Hall.

Bibliographie Courante d'Articles de Periodiques Posterieurs a 1944 sur les Problemes Politiques, Economiques et Sociaux, 2 vols., Set. suppl. ed. Fondation Nationale des Sciences Politiques, Paris, France Staff. 1971. Third suppl., 1971, 2 vols. lib. bdg. 250.00 (*0-8161-0981-8*, Hall Library) G K Hall.

Bibliographie Courante d'Articles de Periodiques Posterieurs a 1944 Sur les Problemes Politiques, Economiques et Sociaux: Seventh Supplement, 2 vols, Set. Fondation Nationale des Sciences Politiques, Paris, France Staff. 1976. lib. bdg. 250.00 (*0-8161-0035-7*, Hall Library) G K Hall.

Bibliographie Courante d'Articles de Periodiques Posterieurs a, 1944 Sur les Problems, Economiques et Sociaux, Fifth Supplement, 2 vols., Set. Fondation Nationale des Sciences Politiques, Paris, France Staff. 1345p. 1973. lib. bdg. 250.00 (*0-8161-1122-7*, Hall Library) G K Hall.

Bibliographie Courante D'Articles De Periodiques Posterieurs a 1944 Sur les Problems Poliiques, Economiques, et Sociaux, Suppl 6, 2 vols., Set. Fondation Nationale des Sciences Politiques, Paris, France Staff. 1974. lib. bdg. 250.00 (*0-8161-1171-5*, Hall Library) G K Hall.

Bibliographie Courante D'Articles De Periodiques Posterieurs a 1944 Sur les Problems Politiques, Economiques et Sociaux: Dixieme Supplement, 2 vols., Set. Fondation Nationale des Sciences Politiques, Paris, France Staff. (Library Catalogs-Bib. Guides). Orig. Title: Index to Post-1944 Periodical Articles on Political Economic & Social Problems - Tenth Supplement. 1979. lib. bdg. 320.00 (*0-8161-0298-8*, Hall Library) G K Hall.

Bibliographie Critique d'Origene: Supplement, No. I. H. Crozel. 1982. pap. text ed. 148.00 (*90-247-2704-9*) Kluwer Ac.

Bibliographie d'Aristote. M. Schwab. (Classical Studies Ser.). (FRE.). reprint ed. lib. bdg. 47.50 (*0-697-00047-8*) Irvington.

Bibliographie Darstellende Kunst & Musik: Deutschsprachige Hochschulschriften & Veroffentlichungen Ausserhalb des Buchhandels 1966-1980, 3 vols., Set. Ed. by Margarethe Wolf. (GER.). 1992. lib. bdg. 475.00 (*3-598-21950-4*) K G Saur.

Bibliographie Darstellende Kunst & Musik: Deutschsprachige Hochschulschriften & Veroffentlichungen Ausserhalb des Buchhandels 1966-1980, 3 vols., Vol. 1. Ed. by Margarethe Wolf. 470p. (GER.). 1992. lib. bdg. write for info. (*3-598-21951-2*) K G Saur.

Bibliographie Darstellende Kunst & Musik: Deutschsprachige Hochschulschriften & Veroffentlichungen Ausserhalb des Buchhandels 1966-1980, 3 vols., Vol. 2. Ed. by Margarethe Wolf. 470p. (GER.). 1992. lib. bdg. write for info. (*3-598-21952-0*) K G Saur.

Bibliographie Darstellende Kunst & Musik: Deutschsprachige Hochschulschriften & Veroffentlichungen Ausserhalb des Buchhandels 1966-1980, 3 vols., Vol. 3. Ed. by Margarethe Wolf. 470p. (GER.). 1992. lib. bdg. write for info. (*3-598-21953-9*) K G Saur.

Bibliographie de la Critique Sur Emile Zola, 1971-1980. David Baguley. 242p. (FRE.). 1982. 40.00 (*0-8020-2456-4*) U of Toronto Pr.

Bibliographie de la Litterature Francaise du Dix-Huitieme Siecle: Vol. 2, E-Q. Cioranesco. 690p. (FRE.). 1969. lib. bdg. 79.95 (*0-7859-3637-8*, 2222011981) Fr & Eur.

Bibliographie de la Litterature Francaise du XVIIe Siecle, 3 vols., Tome 1: A-C. Cioranesco. (FRE.). Tome 1, A-C. 54.95 (*0-8288-9104-4*, F125000) Fr & Eur.

Bibliographie de la Litterature Francaise du XVIIe Siecle, 3 vols., Tome 2: D-M. Cioranesco. (FRE.). Tome 2, D-M. 74.95 (*0-8288-9105-2*, F125001) Fr & Eur.

Bibliographie de la Litterature Francaise du XVIIe Siecle, Tome 3: N-Z, Tables. 2nd ed. Cioranesco. 724p. (FRE.). 1969. 79.95 (*0-7859-4619-5*) Fr & Eur.

Bibliographie de la Litterature Francaise du XVIIe Siecle, Vol. 3: N-Z. Jean Cocteau. 147p. (FRE.). 1983. pap. write for info. (*0-318-72615-7*) Fr & Eur.

Bibliographie de la Litterature Francaise du XVIIIe Siecle, 3 tomes. Cioranesco. 772p. (FRE.). 1969. 79.95 (*0-318-72614-9*) Fr & Eur.

Bibliographie de la Litterature Francaise du XVIIIe Siecle, 3 tomes. Cioranesco. (FRE.). 1970. Tome 1, A-D. write for info. (*0-318-51933-X*) Fr & Eur.

Bibliographie de la Litterature Francaise du XVIIIe Siecle, 3 tomes, Tome 3, R-Z. Cioranesco. 704p. (FRE.). 1970. 79.95 (*0-7859-3638-6*) Fr & Eur.

Bibliographie de la Litterature Francaise du 18eme Siecle, Vol. 1: A-D. Paul Claudel. 285p. (FRE.). 1986. pap. 29.95 (*0-7859-4715-9*) Fr & Eur.

Bibliographie de la Litterature Francaise du 18eme Siecle, Vol. 3: R-Z. Jean Genet. (FRE.). 1953. pap. 59.95 (*0-7859-0564-2*, F101954) Fr & Eur.

Bibliographie de la Litterature Francaise (1940-1948) Drevet. write for info. (*0-8288-7715-7*, F12520) Fr & Eur.

Bibliographie de la Peninsule du Quebec-Labrador, 2 Vols, Set. Universite Laval, Centre d'Etudes Nordiques, Quebec Staff. 1970. lib. bdg. 220.00 (*0-8161-0758-0*, Hall Library) G K Hall.

Bibliographie de la Philosophie. Institut International de Philosophie Staff. Incl. 19551956. 150.00 (*0-7859-5286-1*); 19571958. 59.95 (*0-7859-5287-X*); 19581959. 125.00 (*0-7859-5288-8*); 19591960. 125.00 (*0-7859-5289-6*); 19621963. 125.00 (*0-7859-5290-X*); 19631964. 150.00 (*0-7859-5291-8*); 1964150.00 (*0-7859-5547-X*); 19651966. 150.00 (*0-7859-5292-6*); 19681969. 150.00 (*0-7859-5293-4*); 19691970. 150.00 (*0-7859-5294-2*); 19701971. 150.00 (*0-7859-5295-0*); 19711972. 150.00 (*0-7859-5296-9*); 19721973. 125.00 (*0-7859-5297-7*); 19731974. 150.00 (*0-7859-5298-5*); 19751976. 150.00 (*0-7859-5299-3*); 19771978. 150.00 (*0-7859-5300-0*); Dictionnaire des Philosophes6.50 (*0-685-33994-7*); 1964150.00 (*0-7859-5547-X*); write for info. (*0-318-51934-8*) Fr & Eur.

Bibliographie de l'histoire de Paris pendant la Revolution francaise, 5 vols., Set. Maurice Tourneux. LC 76-177568. reprint ed. 450.00 (*0-404-07540-1*) AMS Pr.

Bibliographie der Almanache, Kalender un Taschenbucher. Hans Kohring. 175p. 1929. write for info. (*0-318-71835-9*, Pub. by Georg Olms GW) Lubrecht & Cramer.

***Bibliographie der Autobiographien: Selbstzeugnisse, Einnerungen, Tagebucher und Briefe deutschsprachiger Arzte, Vol. 4.** Jens Jessen. 630p. 1995. write for info. (*3-598-10862-1*) K G Saur.

Bibliographie der Autobiographien, Band 3: Selbstzeugnisse, Erinnerungen, Tagebucher und Briefe Deutscher Mathematiker, Naturwissenschaftler und Techniker. Jens Jessen. 371p. (GER.). 1989. lib. bdg. 54.00 (*3-598-10675-0*) K G Saur.

Bibliographie der Autobiographien, Vol. 2: Selbstzeugnisse, Erinnerungen, Tgebucher, und Briefe deutscher Geisteswissenschaftler. Jens Jessen. 256p. 1987. lib. bdg. 60.00 (*3-598-10674-2*) K G Saur.

Bibliographie der Deutschen und der Niederlaendischen Jagdliteratur von 1480 bis 1850. Kurt Lindner. (Illus.). (C). 1977. 384.60 (*3-11-006640-8*) De Gruyter.

Bibliographie der Deutschen Universitaten. Wilhelm Erman & Ewald Horn. xlvi, 2385p. 1965. reprint ed. write for info. (*0-318-71776-X*, Pub. by Georg Olms GW) Lubrecht & Cramer.

Bibliographie der Deutschsprachigen Lyrikanthologien, 1840-1914, 2 vols. Ed. by Gunter Hantzschel. 695p. 1991. lib. bdg. 320.00 (*3-598-10838-9*) K G Saur.

B

An Asterisk (*) at the beginning of an entry indicates that the title is appearing in BIP for the first time.

Bibliographie der Freimaurerischen Literatur, 3 vols. August Wolfstieg. 1992. reprint ed. write for info. (*3-487-00770-3*, Pub. by Georg Olms GW) Lubrecht & Cramer.

Bibliographie der Griechischen Vers-Inschriften. Gerhard Pfohl. 62p. (GER.). 1964. write for info. (*0-318-70446-3*, Pub. by Georg Olms GW); write for info. (*0-318-71855-3*, Pub. by Georg Olms GW) Lubrecht & Cramer.

Bibliographie Der Griechischen Vers-Inschriften. Gerhard Pfohl. 62p. 1964. write for info. (*0-318-70996-1*, Pub. by Georg Olms GW) Lubrecht & Cramer.

Bibliographie der Inquisition. Emile V. Vekene. 323p. 1963. write for info. (*0-318-71871-5*, Pub. by Georg Olms GW) Lubrecht & Cramer.

Bibliographie der Klassischen Alterthumswissenschaften. Ernst W. Hubner. xiii, 434p. 1973. reprint ed. write for info. (*3-487-04737-3*, Pub. by Georg Olms GW) Lubrecht & Cramer.

Bibliographie der Musik-Druckwerke Bis 1700. Emil Bohn. vii, 450p. 1969. reprint ed. write for info. (*0-318-71745-X*, Pub. by Georg Olms GW) Lubrecht & Cramer.

Bibliographie der Musik-Sammelwerke des 16 und 17: Jahrhunderts. Robert Eitner. ix, 964p. 1977. reprint ed. write for info. (*3-487-00403-8*, Pub. by Georg Olms GW) Lubrecht & Cramer.

Bibliographie der Psychologischen Literatur des 16 Jahrhunderts. Hermann Schuling. Vol. IV. 320p. 1967. write for info. (*0-318-71864-2*, Pub. by Georg Olms GW) Lubrecht & Cramer.

Bibliographie der Schriften Schleiermachers Nebst Einer Zusammenstellung und Datierung Seiner Gedruckten Predigten: Bearbeitet Von Wichmann Von Meding. Ed. by Hermann Fischer. (Schleiermacger Archiv Ser.: No. 9). viii, 367p. (GER.). (C). 1992. lib. bdg. 113.85 (*3-11-013555-8*) De Gruyter.

Bibliographie der sowjetischen Philosophie, 7 vols. Incl. Voprosy Filosophie, 1947-1956. Thomas J. Blakeley. 75p. 1960. lib. bdg. 42.50 (*90-277-0044-3*); Buecher, 1947-1956, Buecher und Aufsaetze, 1957-1958, Namenverzeichnis 1947-1958. 109p. 1960. lib. bdg. 47.00 (*90-277-0045-1*); Buecher und Aufsaetze, 1959-1960. 73p. 1962. lib. bdg. 42.50 (*90-277-0046-X*); Ergaenzungen, Supplement, 1947-1960. 158p. 1963. lib. bdg. 51.50 (*90-277-0047-8*); Register, Indices 1947-1960. 144p. 1964. lib. bdg. 47.00 (*90-277-0048-6*); Buecher und Aufsaetze 1961-1963. 195p. 1968. lib. bdg. 56.50 (*90-277-0049-4*); Buecher und Aufsaetze 1964-1966. 311p. 1968. lib. bdg. 84.00 (*90-277-0050-8*); (Sovietica Ser.). (GER.). write for info. (*0-318-53997-7*) Kluwer Ac.

***Bibliographie der Tamschriften 1933-1945.** Heinz Gittig. 256p. 1995. write for info. (*3-598-11224-6*) K G Saur.

Bibliographie der Veroffentlichungen von S. B. Liljegren. Ed. by Roland Arnold. (Essays & Studies on English Language & Literature: Vol. 16). 1972. reprint ed. pap. 15.00 (*0-8115-0214-7*) Periodicals Srv.

Bibliographie des Auteurs Modernes de Langue Francaise, 1801-1972: Montfort, Montherlant, Vol. 20. Georges Place et al. 299p. (FRE.). 1973. 150.00 (*0-7859-5387-6*) Fr & Eur.

Bibliographie des Bibliographies Musicales. Michel Brenet, pseud. LC 73-125065. (Music Ser.). 1971. reprint ed. lib. bdg. 29.50 (*0-306-70002-6*) Da Capo.

Bibliographie des Deutschen Volksliedes in Bohmen. Gustav Jungbauer. (Volkskundliche Quellen Ser.: No. VIII). xlvii, 576p. 1976. reprint ed. write for info. (*3-487-05766-2*, Pub. by Georg Olms GW) Lubrecht & Cramer.

Bibliographie des Ecrits d'Andre Gide Depuis 1891 Jusqu'a Sa Mort. Naville. (FRE.). 15.95 (*0-8288-9780-8*, F102790) Fr & Eur.

Bibliographie des Judischen Schrifttums in Deutschland, 1933-43. Henry Wassermann. Ed. by Leo Baeck Institut Staff et al. xxv, 166p. (GER.). 1989. lib. bdg. 82.00 (*3-598-10750-1*) K G Saur.

Bibliographie des Napoleonischen Zeitalters Einschlieslich der Vereinigten Staaten von Nordamerika, 2 vols. in 1, Set. Friedrich M. Kircheisen. xlviii, 620p. 1977. reprint ed. write for info. (*3-487-06298-4*, Pub. by Georg Olms GW) Lubrecht & Cramer.

Bibliographie Des Ouvrages Illustres Du Nineteenth Siecle. Jules Brivois. (Principalement Des Livres A Gravures Sur Bois Ser.). xiv, 468p. 1974. reprint ed. write for info. (*3-487-05419-1*, Pub. by Georg Olms GW) Lubrecht & Cramer.

Bibliographie des Ouvrages Relatifs a l'Afrigue et a l'Arabie. Jean Gay. 1977. reprint ed. 45.95 (*0-518-19000-5*) Ayer.

Bibliographie des Ouvrages Relatifs a l'Amour, aux Femmes, au Mariage, et des Livres Facetieux, Pantagrueliques, Scatalogiques, Satyriques, 4 vols. Jules Gay. xv, 2302p. reprint ed. write for info. (*0-318-71342-X*, Pub. by Georg Olms GW) Lubrecht & Cramer.

Bibliographie Des Principales Editions Originales D'Ecrivains Francaise Du Fifteenth Au Eighteenth Siecle. Jules Le Petit. viii, 583p. 1969. reprint ed. write for info. (*3-487-04174-X*, Pub. by Georg Olms GW) Lubrecht & Cramer.

Bibliographie Des Regions Du Senegal. L. Porges. 1977. 159.25 (*90-279-7544-2*) Mouton.

Bibliographie Deutscher Uebersetzungen aus dem Franzosischen, 1700-1948: Baden-Baden, 6 vols. Hans Fromm. (RUS.). 1953. 390.00 (*0-8115-3754-4*) Periodicals Srv.

Bibliographie d'Historie Litteraire Francaise, Vol. 10, 1972. Otto Klapp. 696p. 1973. pap. 250.00 (*0-7859-4878-3*) Fr & Eur.

Bibliographie Generals Des Ecrits De Louis-Claude de Saint-Martin, Vol. IV. Robert Amadou. 300p. write for info. (*0-318-71425-6*, Pub. by Georg Olms GW) Lubrecht & Cramer.

Bibliographie Henri Focillon. Louis Grodecki. LC 62-16232. (Yale Publications in the History of Art: No. 15). 134p. reprint ed. pap. 38.20 (*0-8357-7169-5*, 2022001) Bks Demand.

Bibliographie Historique et Critique De la Presse Periodique Francaise. Eugene Hatin. cxix, 660p. 1965. reprint ed. write for info. (*0-318-71349-7*, Pub. by Georg Olms GW) Lubrecht & Cramer.

Bibliographie Historique et Critique de la Presse Periodique Francaise. Eugene Hatin. cxix, 660p. 1965. reprint ed. write for info. (*0-318-71796-4*, Pub. by Georg Olms GW) Lubrecht & Cramer.

Bibliographie II der Veroffentlichungen von S. B. Liljegren. Ed. by Roland Arnold. (Essays & Studies on English Language & Literature: Vol. 22). 1972. reprint ed. pap. 15.00 (*0-8115-0220-1*) Periodicals Srv.

Bibliographie III der Veroffentlichungen von S. B. Liljegren. Ed. by Roland Arnold. (Essays & Studies on English Language & Literature: Vol. 26). 1972. reprint ed. pap. 15.00 (*0-8115-0224-4*) Periodicals Srv.

Bibliographie Linguistique de l'Annee 1986: Linguistic Bibliography for the year 1986. Ed. by Mark Janse et al. (C). 1988. lib. bdg. 322.50 (*90-247-3775-3*) Kluwer Ac.

Bibliographie Linguistique de L'Annee, 1987: Linguistic Bibliography for the Year, 1987. Ed. by Mark Janse & Sijmen Tol. (C). 1990. lib. bdg. 317.50 (*0-7923-0509-4*) Kluwer Ac.

Bibliographie Linguistique de l'Annee, 1988 - Linguistic Bibliography for the Year 1988: Et Complement des Annees Precedentes - & Supplement for Previous Years. Ed. by Mark Janse & Sijmen Tol. (C). 1990. lib. bdg. 348.50 (*0-7923-0936-7*) Kluwer Ac.

Bibliographie Linguistique de l'Annee 1989 - Linguistic Bibliography for the Year 1989: Et Complement des Annees Precedantes - & Supplement for Previous Years. Ed. by Mark Janse & Sijmen Tol. 1328p. (C). 1992. lib. bdg. 372.00 (*0-7923-1378-X*) Kluwer Ac.

Bibliographie Linguistique de l'Annee 1991 - Linguistic Bibliography for the Year 1991. Ed. by Mark Janse. (LIBI Yearbook Ser.). 1312p. (C). 1994. lib. bdg. 400.00 (*0-7923-2387-4*) Kluwer Ac.

Bibliographie Linguistique 1939-1975. Ed. by Permanent International Committee on Linguistics Staff. 1986. lib. bdg. 0.01 (*90-247-3320-0*) Kluwer Ac.

Bibliographie Medizin: Deutschsprachige Hochschulschriften & VerNffentlichungen Ausserhalb des Buchhandels 1966-1980, 34 vols. Ed. by Irene Butt & Monika Eichler. 420p. (GER.). 1993. lib. bdg. 4,730.00 (*3-598-22499-0*) K G Saur.

Bibliographie Methodique et Raisonnee Des Beaux- Arts. Ernest Vinet. xx, 288p. 1967. reprint ed. write for info. (*0-318-71445-0*, Pub. by Georg Olms GW) Lubrecht & Cramer.

Bibliographie Methodique et Raisonnee des Beaux-Arts, 2 pts. in 1. Ernest Vinet. xx, 288p. 1967. reprint ed. write for info. (*0-318-71872-3*, Pub. by Georg Olms GW) Lubrecht & Cramer.

Bibliographie Psychologie: Deutschsprachige Hochschulschriften & Veroffentlichungen Ausserhalb des Buchhandels 1966 bis 1980, 2 vols., Set. Ed. by Monika Eichler & Margarethe Wolf. (GER.). 1992. lib. bdg. 250.00 (*3-598-21927-X*) K G Saur.

Bibliographie Psychologie: Deutschsprachige Hochschulschriften & Veroffentligchungen Ausserhalb des Buchhandels 1966 bis 1980, 2 vols., Vol. 1. Ed. by Monika Eichler & Margarethe Wolf. 416p. (GER.). 1992. lib. bdg. write for info. (*3-598-21928-8*) K G Saur.

Bibliographie Psychologie: Deutschsprachige Hochschulschriften & Veroffentligchungen Ausserhalb des Buchhandels 1966 bis 1980, 2 vols., Vol. 2. Ed. by Monika Eichler & Margarethe Wolf. 416p. (GER.). 1992. lib. bdg. write for info. (*3-598-21929-6*) K G Saur.

Bibliographie Religion und Philosophie: Deutschsprachige Hochschulschriften & Veroffentlichungen Ausserhalb des Buchhandels 1966-1980, 5 vols. Ed. by Irene Butt & Monika Eichler. 2091p. (GER.). 1993. lib. bdg. 925.00 (*3-598-22485-0*) K G Saur.

Bibliographie Seiner Werke. Samuel J. Agnon. Ed. by Werner Martin. xi, 118p. 1980. write for info. (*3-487-06972-5*, Pub. by Georg Olms GW) Lubrecht & Cramer.

Bibliographie Seiner Werke. Paul Heyse. Ed. by Werner Martin. (Bibliographien Zur Deutschen Literature Ser.: Vol. 3). xviii, 189p. 1978. write for info. (*3-487-06573-8*, Pub. by Georg Olms GW) Lubrecht & Cramer.

Bibliographie Seiner Werke. Eduard Reinacher. (Bibliographien Zur Deutschen Literature Ser.: Vol. 4). lii, 272p. 1984. write for info. (*3-487-07598-9*, Pub. by Georg Olms GW) Lubrecht & Cramer.

Bibliographie Seiner Werke. Alexander Solschenizyn. Ed. by Werner Martin. 184p. 1977. write for info. (*3-487-06429-4*, Pub. by Georg Olms GW) Lubrecht & Cramer.

Bibliographie Sport & Freizeit: Deutschsprachige Hochhschulschriften & Veroffentlichungen Ausserhalb des Buchhandels 1966-1980, 2 vols., Set. Ed. by Monika Eichler & Margarethe Wolf. (GER.). 1991. lib. bdg. 255.00 (*3-598-21955-5*) K G Saur.

Bibliographie Sport & Freizeit: Deutschsprachige Hochhschulschriften & Veroffentlichungen Ausserhalb des Buchhandels 1966-1980, 2 vols., Vol. 1. Ed. by Monika Eichler & Margarethe Wolf. 424p. (GER.). 1991. lib. bdg. write for info. (*3-598-21956-3*) K G Saur.

Bibliographie Sport & Freizeit: Deutschsprachige Hochhschulschriften & Veroffentlichungen Ausserhalb des Buchhandels 1966-1980, 2 vols., Vol. 2. Ed. by Monika Eichler & Margarethe Wolf. 424p. (GER.). 1991. lib. bdg. write for info. (*3-598-21957-1*) K G Saur.

Bibliographie Sprach und Literatur: Deutschsprachige Hochschulschriften & Veroffentlichungen Ausserhalb des Buchhandels 1966-1980, 8 vols., Set. Ed. by Irene Butt & Monika Eichler. 430p. (GER.). 1992. lib. bdg. 1,650.00 (*3-598-22470-2*) K G Saur.

Bibliographie Ueber Vermehrung, Kultur und Mykorrhiza Terrestrischer Orchideen. Michael Weinert. 224p. 1989. pap. 67.00 (*3-87429-301-7*) Koeltz Sci Bks.

Bibliographie und Berichte: Festschrift fur Werner Schochow, dem Langjahreigen Redakteur der Bibliographischen Berichte. Ed. by Hartmut V. Walravens. 299p. (GER.). 1990. lib. bdg. 75.00 (*3-598-10907-5*) K G Saur.

Bibliographie Veterinarmedizin: Deutschsprachige Hochschulschriften & Veroffentlichungen Ausserhalb des Buchhandels 1966-1980, 3 vols., Set. Ed. by Irene Butt & Monika Eichler. 330p. (GER.). 1992. lib. bdg. 295.00 (*3-598-22494-X*) K G Saur.

Bibliographie Zur alteuropaeischen Religionsgeschichte, Vol. 1: 1954 bis 1964 Literatur zu den antiken Rand- und Nachfolgekulturen im aussermediterranen Europa unter besonderer Beruecksichtigung der nichtchristlichen Religionen. Ed. by Peter Buchholz. (Arbeitem zur Fruehmittelalterforschung Ser.: Vol. 2). (C). 1967. 60.80 (*3-11-000373-2*) De Gruyter.

Bibliographie zur Entwicklung des Fernsehens - Bibliography on the Development of Television: Fernsehsysteme & Programmgeschichte in den U. S. A., Gro Britannien & der Bundesrepublik Deutschland - Television Systems & Programme Development in the U. S. A., Gr. Britain & FRG. Peter Ludes. 241p. (GER.). 1990. lib. bdg. 45.00 (*3-598-10973-3*) K G Saur.

Bibliographie Zur Geschichte der Chinesischen Literatur. Eugen Feifel. 489p. 1992. write for info. (*3-487-09438-X*, Pub. by Georg Olms GW) Lubrecht & Cramer.

Bibliographie Zur Geschichte des Deutschen Kirchenliedes Im XVI Jahrhundert. Philipp Wackernagel. x, 718p. 1987. reprint ed. write for info. (*3-487-00096-2*, Pub. by Georg Olms GW) Lubrecht & Cramer.

Bibliographie zur Geschichte des Pietismus, Vol. 1, Die Werke der Wuerttembergischen Pietisten. Ed. by G. Maelzer. 415p. (C). 1972. 104.60 (*3-11-002219-2*) De Gruyter.

Bibliographie zur Geschichte des Weines: 2 mit all Supplementen kumulierte und aktualisierte Auflage. Ed. by E. V. Gesellschaft des Weines. 480p. 1988. lib. bdg. 190.00 (*3-598-10748-X*) K G Saur.

Bibliographie zur Geschichte und Theologie des Augustiner Eremiten Ordens bis zum Beginn der Reformation. Ed. by Egon Gindele. (Spaetmittelalter und Reformation Ser.: Texte und Untersuchungen, Vol. 1). 1977. text ed. 192.30 (*3-11-004949-X*) De Gruyter.

Bibliographie Zur Linguistischen Gesprachsforschung. Stefan Mayer & Michael Weber. (Germanistische Linguistik Ser.). 216p. 1983. write for info. (*3-487-07399-4*, Pub. by Georg Olms GW) Lubrecht & Cramer.

Bibliographie zur Zeitgeschichte: 1981-1989. Ed. by Instituts fur Zeitgeschichte Munchen Staff. (Bibliographie zur Zeitgeschichte 1953-1980 Ser.: Band 4). 609p. (GER.). 1991. lib. bdg. 225.00 (*3-598-10924-5*) K G Saur.

Bibliographie zur Zeitgeschichte, 1953 to 1989, 3 vols. Ed. by Thilo Vogelsang et al. 1991. lib. bdg. 300.00 (*3-598-10420-0*) K G Saur.

Bibliographies: Their Aims & Methods. D. Krummel. 202p. 1984. text ed. 27.50 (*0-7201-1687-2*, Mansell Pub) Cassell.

Bibliographies for Accounting Historians. R. H. Parker. Ed. by Richard P. Brief. LC 80-1462. (Dimensions of Accounting Theory & Practice Ser.). 1980. lib. bdg. 37.95 (*0-405-13484-3*) Ayer.

Bibliographies for African Studies, 1970-1986. Comp. by Yvette Scheven. 637p. 1988. Cumulative volume. lib. bdg. 125.00 (*0-905450-33-7*, Pub. by H Zell Pubs UK) Bowker-Saur.

***Bibliographies for African Studies 1987-1993.** Ed. by Yvette Scheven & Phyllis Bischof. 198p. 1994. 70.00 (*1-873836-51-1*, Pub. by H Zell Pubs UK) Bowker-Saur.

Bibliographies for Biblical Research: The Gospel of John. Ed. & Comp. by Watson E. Mills. LC 93-30864. (New Testament Ser.: Vol. IV). 436p. Date not set. text ed. 129.95 (*0-7734-2357-5*) E Mellen.

***Bibliographies for Biblical Research: The Gospel of John.** Comp. by Watson E. Mills. LC 93-30864. (New Testament Ser.: Vol. IV). 436p. Date not set. text ed. 169.95 (*0-7734-2400-8*) E Mellen.

***Bibliographies for Biblical Research: The Gospel of Luke.** Comp. by Watson E. Mills. LC 93-30864. (New Testament Series: The Gospel of Luke: Vol. III). 416p. Date not set. text ed. 129.95 (*0-7734-2385-0*) E Mellen.

***Bibliographies for Biblical Research: The Gospel of Luke.** Comp. by Watson E. Mills. LC 93-30864. (New Testament Series: The Gospel of Luke: Vol. III). 416p. Date not set. text ed. 169.95 (*0-7734-2402-4*) E Mellen.

Bibliographies for Biblical Research: The Gospel of Mark. Ed. & Comp. by Watson E. Mills. LC 93-30864. (New Testament Ser.: Vol. II). 552p. 1994. text ed. 129.95 (*0-7734-2349-4*, Mellen Biblical Pr) E Mellen.

***Bibliographies for Biblical Research: The Gospel of Mark.** Comp. by Watson E. Mills. LC 93-30864. (New Testament Ser.: Vol. II). 552p. 1994. text ed. 169.95 (*0-7734-2398-2*) E Mellen.

Bibliographies for Biblical Research: The Gospel of Matthew. Ed. & Comp. by Watson E. Mills. LC 93-30864. (New Testament Ser.: Vol. I). 304p. 1993. text ed. 169.95 (*0-7734-2347-8*, Mellen Biblical Pr) E Mellen.

***Bibliographies for Biblical Research: The Gospel of Matthew.** Ed. by Watson E. Mills. LC 93-30864. (New Testament Ser.: Vol. I). 304p. 1993. text ed. 129.95 (*0-7734-2396-6*) E Mellen.

Bibliographies Generales see Sources du Travail Bibliographique

Bibliographies in American History, 1942 to 1978, 2 vols., Set. Henry P. Beers. Ed. by Research Publications, Inc. Staff. LC 81-68886. 978p. 1982. text ed. 290.00 (*0-89235-038-5*) Res Pubns CT.

Bibliographies in Criminal Justice. 1991. lib. bdg. 64.95 (*0-8490-4473-1*) Gordon Pr.

Bibliographies of Behavioral Science Literature. Steven R. Poole et al. 55p. 1983. 5.00 (*0-942295-01-3*, A) Soc Tchrs Fam Med.

***Bibliographies of New England History No. 9: Additions to 1994.** Ed. by Roger Parks. (Bibliographies of New England History Ser.). 324p. 1995. text ed. 40.00 (*0-87451-714-1*) U Pr of New Eng.

Bibliographies of Studies in Victorian Literature, for the ten Years 1955-1964. Ed. by Robert C. Slack. LC 79-8839. reprint ed. 67.50 (*0-404-18033-7*) AMS Pr.

Bibliographies of Studies in Victorian Literature, for the Ten Years 1965-1974. Ed. by Ronald E. Freeman. LC 79-8838. 1981. 67.50 (*0-404-18032-9*) AMS Pr.

Bibliographies of Studies in Victorian Literature for the Ten Years 1975-1984. Ed. & Contrib by Richard C. Tobias. LC 90-10316. (Studies in the Nineteenth Century: No. 11). 1991. 94.50 (*0-404-61491-4*) AMS Pr.

Bibliographies of the Languages of the North American Indians, 9 Pts. in 3 Vols, Set. James C. Pilling. LC 76-174200. reprint ed. 125.00 (*0-404-07390-5*) AMS Pr.

Bibliographies of Works on Playing Cards & Gaming. Incl. Bibliography of Works in English on Playing Cards & Gaming. Frederic Jessel. LC 77-129310. 1972. reprint ed. (*0-318-54970-0*); Bibliography of Card Games & of the History of Playing Cards. Norton T. Horr. LC 77-129310. 1972. reprint ed. (*0-318-54971-9*); LC 77-129310. (Criminology, Law Enforcement, & Social Problems Ser.: No. 132). 1972. 35.00 (*0-87585-132-0*) Patterson Smith.

Bibliographies on Plato. Constantin Ritter. LC 78-66617. (Ancient Philosophy Ser.). 906p. 1980. lib. bdg. 29.00 (*0-8240-9590-1*) Garland.

Bibliographies on Tourism & Related Subjects: An Annotated Sourcebook. J. Jafari et al. 81p. 1988. pap. text ed. 25.00 (*0-89478-007-7*) U CO Busn Res Div.

Bibliographies Specialisees; Sciences Humaines see Sources du Travail Bibliographique

Bibliographies to Supplement the New Variorum Editions of Shakespeare, Set. Incl. Life & Death of King Richard II. Comp. by Matthew W. Black & G. Harold Metz. ix, 31p. 1977. pap. 10.00 (*0-87352-281-8*); Henry the Fourth, Part One. Comp. by Michael Kiernan. xi, 15p. 1977. pap. 10.00 (*0-87352-279-6*); Henry the Fourth, Part Two. Comp. by M. A. Shaaber. ix, 18p. 1977. pap. 10.00 (*0-87352-280-X*); Tragedy of Julius Caesar. Comp. by John W. Velz. x, 58p. 1977. pap. 10.00 (*0-87352-282-6*); 1977. Set spiral bd. 35.00 (*0-87352-283-4*) Modern Lang.

Bibliographische Grundbegriffe und Fachtermini. K. Simon. 150p. (GER.). 1973. 45.00 (*0-8288-6231-1*, M-7309) Fr & Eur.

Bibliographisches Handbuch der Philologischen Literatur der Deutschen. Johann S. Ersch. 1029p. 1974. reprint ed. write for info. (*3-487-05260-1*, Pub. by Georg Olms GW) Lubrecht & Cramer.

Bibliographisches Handbuch Uber die Theoretische und Praktische Literatur Fur Hebraische Sprachkunde. Moritz Steinschneider. xxxvi, 295p. 1976. reprint ed. write for info. (*3-487-05684-4*, Pub. by Georg Olms GW) Lubrecht & Cramer.

Bibliographisches Notizen Uber Ludwig van Beethoven. Franz G. Wegeler. 1972. reprint ed. write for info. (*3-487-04495-1*, Pub. by Georg Olms GW) Lubrecht & Cramer.

Bibliography. Bonnie Gurewitsch. (Bibliography Ser.). 27p. (Orig.). 1981. pap. 3.00 (*0-9609970-0-8*) Mus Jew Heritage.

***Bibliography.** Girja Kumar & Krishan Kumar. (C). 1993. 26.00x (*0-7069-7004-7*, Pub. by Vikas II) S Asia.

Bibliography. 2nd rev. ed. Asghar Ali & Krishan Kumar. (C). 1980. text ed. 22.50 (*0-7069-0738-8*, Pub. by Vikas II) S Asia.

Bibliography. 11th ed. Ed. by George A. Johnson. LC 81-69977. 109p. 1987. pap. 7.50 (*0-685-69212-4*) Am Prod & Inventory.

Bibliography: Current State & Future Trends. Ed. by Robert B. Downs & Frances B. Jenkins. LC 67-21851. (Illinois Contributions to Librarianship Ser.: No. 8). 619p. reprint ed. pap. 176.50 (*0-8357-7172-5*, 2019015) Bks Demand.

Bibliography: Social Networks, Social Planning & Community Needs, No. 1135. Robyn McClelland. 1976. 5.00 (*0-686-20409-3*) CPL Biblios.

Bibliography: State Appellate Court Workload & Delay. National Center for State Courts Staff. 73p. 1979. 4.38 (*0-685-16910-3*, NERO-038) Natl Ctr St Courts.

Bibliography: State Appellate Court Workload & Delay; 1979-82. National Center for State Courts Staff. 13p. 1983. 0.78 (*0-685-16911-1*, NCSC-030) Natl Ctr St Courts.

Bibliography No. 1: Bibliographies of American Notables. Clyde N. Wilson & John C. Calhoun. LC 90-6508. 184p. 1990. text ed. 55.00 (*0-313-28081-9*, WBB/, Greenwood Pr) Greenwood.

An Asterisk (*) at the beginning of an entry indicates that the title is appearing in BIP for the first time.

Bibliography a Philatelic Literature on the French Colonies, Protectorates, & Overseas Territories, Vol. 1. Robert G. Stone. 110p. 1981. pap. 5.00 (*0-318-40121-5*) Am Philatelic Society.

Bibliography & Book Production. R. Astbury & R. Robinson. LC 66-30623. (Commonwealth & International Library). 1967. 116.00 (*0-08-012328-7*, Pub. by Pergamon Repr UK); 116.00 (*0-08-012329-5*, Pub. by Pergamon Repr UK) Franklin.

Bibliography & Catalogue of the Fossil Vertebrata of North America. Oliver P. Hay. LC 73-17823. (Natural Sciences in America Ser.). 872p. 1974. reprint ed. 64.95 (*0-405-05741-5*) Ayer.

Bibliography & Cross-Reference of Weed-Crop Interference & Corp Losses Due to Weeds. J. M. Chandler et al. 142p. 1987. pap. 12.00 (*0-911733-09-4*) Weed Sci Soc.

Bibliography & Documentation in Health Sciences: Medical Analysis Index with Reference Bibliography. Andrew S. Zunotto. 150p. 1987. 39.50 (*0-88164-362-9*); pap. 34.50 (*0-88164-363-7*) ABBE Pubs Assn.

Bibliography & Documentation in Health Sciences: Medical Analysis Index with Reference Bibliography. rev. ed. Andrew S. Zunotto. LC 92-31213. 150p. 1992. 49.50 (*1-55914-898-5*); pap. 39.50 (*1-55914-899-3*) ABBE Pubs Assn.

Bibliography & Footnotes: A Style Manual for Students & Writers. 3rd enl. rev. ed. Peyton Hurt. Ed. by Mary L. Richmond. (Illus.). (C). 1968. pap. 14.00 (*0-520-00589-9*) U CA Pr.

Bibliography & Index of Colorado Geology, 1875 to 1975. American Geological Institute Staff. (Bulletin Ser.: No. 37). 488p. 1976. 7.50 (*1-884216-02-1*); pap. 3.50 (*1-884216-03-X*) Colo Geol Survey.

Bibliography & Index of Colorado Geology: 1981-1982. American Geological Institute Staff. (Information Ser.: No. 19). 111p. (Orig.). 1983. pap. 2.00 (*1-884216-17-X*) Colo Geol Survey.

Bibliography & Index of Colorado Geology, 1983. American Geological Institute Staff. (Information Ser.: No. 21). 127p. (Orig.). 1983. pap. 5.00 (*1-884216-18-8*) Colo Geol Survey.

Bibliography & Index of Colorado Geology, 1984-1989. American Geological Institute Staff. (Information Ser.: No. 30). 584p. (Orig.). 1990. pap. 12.00 (*1-884216-22-6*) Colo Geol Survey.

Bibliography & Index of English Verse Printed, 1476-1558. William A. Ringler. 448p. 1989. text ed. 200.00 (*0-7201-1892-1*, Mansell Pub) Cassell.

Bibliography & Index of Mainland Southeast Asian Languages & Linguistics. Franklin E. Huffman. LC 85-52119. 672p. 1986. text ed. 50.00 (*0-300-03679-5*) Yale U Pr.

Bibliography & Index of North American Carboniferous Brachiopoda 1898-1968. John L. Carter & Ruth C. Carter. LC 74-129146. (Geological Society of America Ser.: No. 128). 392p. reprint ed. pap. 111.80 (*0-8357-7170-9*, 2025460) Bks Demand.

Bibliography & Index of Paleozoic Crinoids, Nineteen Sixty-Nine to Nineteen Seventy-Three. G. D. Webster. LC 77-76475. (Microform Publication: No. 8). 1977. mic. film 1.25 (*0-8137-6008-9*) Geol Soc.

Bibliography & Index of Paleozoic Crinoids, 1942-1968. Gary D. Webster. LC 73-76885. (Geological Society of America, Memoir Ser.: No. 137). 353p. reprint ed. pap. 100.70 (*0-8357-7171-7*, 2023737) Bks Demand.

Bibliography & Index of Texas Geology. Incl. 1933-1950 R. M. Girard. 238p. 1959. 1.50 (*0-318-12074-7*); 1951-1960 E. T. Moore & M. D. Brown. 575p. 1979. reprint ed. 11.00 (*0-318-12075-5*); 1961-1974 E. T. Moore. 446p. 1985. reprint ed. 15.00 (*0-318-12076-3*); 1975-1980 Amanda R. Masterson. 334p. 1981. 8.00 (*0-318-12077-1*); (Publication Ser.: No. 5910). write for info. (*0-318-59436-6*) Bur Econ Geology.

Bibliography & Index of Texas Geology, 1981-1985. A. R. Masterson & Lana Dieterich. (Bibliography Ser.). 463p. 1990. 25.00 (*0-317-03129-5*) Bur Econ Geology.

Bibliography & Index of the Work of Eugenio Maria De Hostos. Ed. by Adolfo De Hostos. (Puerto Rico Ser.). 1979. lib. bdg. 99.75 (*0-8490-2873-6*) Gordon Pr.

Bibliography & Keyword-in-Context Index of the Ceratopogonidae (Diptera) from Seventeen Fifty-Eight to Nineteen Seventy-Three. William R. Atchley et al. 300p. (Orig.). 1975. pap. 4.00 (*0-89672-052-7*) Tex Tech Univ Pr.

Bibliography & Reading: A Festschrift in Honour of Ronald Staveley. Ed. by Ia McIlwaine et al. LC 82-21489. 180p. 1983. 25.00 (*0-8108-1601-6*) Scarecrow.

Bibliography & Reel Index: A Guide to the Microfilm Edition of U. S. Decennial Census Publications, 1790-1970. LC 75-33819. 276p. 1975. 65.00 (*0-89235-003-2*) Res Pubns CT.

Bibliography & Resource Guide on Alcohol & Other Drugs for Social Work Educators. 1991. lib. bdg. 76.00 (*0-8490-5047-2*) Gordon Pr.

Bibliography & Sourcebook on Seventh-day Adventists' Work with Soyfoods, Vegetarianism, & Wheat Gluten: Detailed Information on 835 Published Documents (Bibliographic), 602 Commercial Food Products, 207 Unpublished Archival Documents, 158 Original Interviews (Many Full Text) & Overviews. Ed. by Akiko Aoyagi. (Bibliographies & Sourcebooks on Soya Ser.). 407p. (Orig.). 1992. spiral bd. 122.00 (*0-933332-78-5*) Soyfoods Center.

***Bibliography & Species Citation Index of World Literature on Rotifera in the John J. Gallagher Collection.** John J. Gallagher et al. (Special Publications of CMNH Ser.: 19). 132p. (Orig.). 1994. pap. 12.00x (*0-911239-45-6*) Carnegie Mus.

Bibliography & Various Readings, George Meredith. Arundell J. Esdaile. LC 72-4494. (Studies in George Meredith: No. 21). 1972. reprint ed. lib. bdg. 56.95 (*0-8383-1511-9*) M S G Haskell Hse.

Bibliography & Vocabulary of the Akan (Twifante) Language of Ghana. Dennis Warren. (African Ser.: No. 6). 1976. pap. text ed. 20.00 (*0-87750-184-X*) Res Inst Inner Asian Studies.

Bibliography for Medieval & Renaissance Musical Manuscript Research: Secondary Materials at the Alcuin Library & the Hill Monastic Manuscript Library, St. John's University, Collegeville, Minnesota. Peter G. Jeffery. vi, 68p. (Orig.). 1980. pap. text ed. 3.00 (*0-940250-76-4*) Hill Monastic.

Bibliography for Teachers of Social Studies. Raymond Ducharme, Jr. et al. LC 68-18106. (Social Studies Sources). 43p. reprint ed. pap. 25.00 (*0-8357-7173-3*, 2026007) Bks Demand.

Bibliography for the Gospel of Mark: 1954-1980. Hugh M. Humphrey. LC 81-18717. (Studies in the Bible & Early Christianity: Vol. 1). 176p. 1982. lib. bdg. 79.95 (*0-88946-916-4*) E Mellen.

Bibliography for the Housing of Children with AIDS. Theresa Cameron. LC 92-10380. (CPL Bibliographies Ser.: No. 278). 1992. 18.00 (*0-86602-278-3*) Coun Plan Librarians.

Bibliography for the Study of African Politics. Comp. by Eric Siegel. Incl. Vol. 3. 1983. 18.00 (*0-918456-47-9*); write for info. (*0-317-31360-6*) African Studies Assn.

Bibliography for the Study of Natural Resource & Environmental Conflict. Michael T. Lesnick & James E. Crowfoot. (CPL Bibliographies Ser.: No. 64). 55p. 1981. 8.00 (*0-86602-064-0*) Coun Plan Librarians.

Bibliography for Training in Child & Adolescent Mental Health. 3rd ed. Ed. by Irving N. Berlin & Bennett L. Leventhal. LC 91-11973. 608p. 1991. 32.50x (*0-8263-1275-6*) U of NM Pr.

Bibliography. History of a Tradition. Liugi Balsamo. Tr. by William A. Pettas. 1990. 45.00 (*0-9600094-2-6*) B M Rosenthal Inc.

Bibliography of Abridgments, Digests, Dictionaries & Indexes of English Law to the Year Eighteen Hundred. John D. Cowley. LC 79-54119. (Illus.). 196p. 1979. reprint ed. lib. bdg. 105.00 (*0-912004-15-0*) W W Gaunt.

***Bibliography of Abstracts & Compilations of Virginia City & County Records.** Robert Vernon. vi, 107p. 1993. lib. bdg. 33.00 (*0-8095-8271-6*) Borgo Pr.

Bibliography of Actuopalynology: 1671-1966. O. Hulshof & A. Manten. 1971. 39.00 (*0-317-17785-0*) Elsevier.

Bibliography of Adult Education: A Source Book. Ed. by Peter G. Haywood. (C). 1983. 50.00 (*0-902031-68-6*, Pub. by Univ Nottingham UK) St Mut.

Bibliography of Adult Teaching Psychology & Research: A Source Book. Comp. by Peter Haywood. (C). 1981. text ed. 40.00 (*0-685-44252-7*, Pub. by Univ Nottingham UK) St Mut.

Bibliography of Adventure: Mundy, Burroughs, Rohmer, Haggard. rev. ed. Ed. by Bradford M. Day et al. LC 77-84282. (Lost Race & Adult Fantasy Ser.). 1978. lib. bdg. 19.95 (*0-405-11019-7*) Ayer.

Bibliography of Aeronautics. Paul Brockett. 1966. reprint ed. 85.00 (*1-55888-932-9*) Omnigraphics Inc.

Bibliography of Africa: Conference Proceedings, 1967. James D. Pearson. Ed. by Ruth Jones. 362p. 1970. 45.00 (*0-7146-2394-6*, Pub. by F Cass Pubs UK) Intl Spec Bk.

Bibliography of African American Family History at the Newberry Library. David T. Thackery. 54p. 1993. 3.50 (*0-911028-53-6*) Newberry.

Bibliography of African Ecology: A Geographically & Topically Classified List of Books & Articles. Ed. by Dilwyn J. Rogers. LC 78-19935. (Special Bibliographic Ser.: No. 6). 499p. 1979. text ed. 105.00 (*0-313-20552-3*, RAE/, Greenwood Pr) Greenwood.

Bibliography of African Language Texts in the Collections of the School of Oriental & African Studies, University of London to 1963. Ed. by Valerie Sanders. LC 93-33750. 448p. 1993. 105.00 (*1-873836-31-7*, Pub. by H Zell Pubs UK) Bowker-Saur.

Bibliography of African Women Writers & Journalists. Brenda Berrian. LC 84-52276. (Illus.). 1985. 25.00 (*0-89410-226-5*); pap. 15.00 (*0-89410-227-3*) Three Continents.

Bibliography of Africana. Hans E. Panofsky. LC 72-823. (Contributions in Librarianship & Information Science Ser.: No. 11). 350p. 1975. text ed. 59.95 (*0-8371-6391-9*, PAA/, Greenwood Pr) Greenwood.

Bibliography of Africana in the Lilly Library. Ed. by Jean I. Gosebrink. 76p. 1977. pap. 4.00 (*0-941934-26-8*) Indiana Africa.

Bibliography of Agricultural Meteorology. Ed. by Jen Y. Wang & Gerald L. Barger. LC 61-12212. 685p. reprint ed. pap. 180.00 (*0-8357-7174-1*, 2023710) Bks Demand.

Bibliography of Agriculture Annual Cumulation, 1990, 2 vols. Ed. by Oryx Press Staff. 1991. Pt. 1, 1920p. write for info. (*0-89774-634-1*); Pt. 2, 2128p. write for info. (*0-89774-635-X*) Oryx Pr.

Bibliography of Agriculture in the Virgin Islands, Including the Danish West Indies: Origins to 1987. Arnold Highfield. (Illus.). 136p. (Orig.). (C). 1992. write for info. (*0-9628909-1-X*) U VI CES.

Bibliography of Agriculture, 1986: Cumulation, 2 pts. 1987. write for info. (*0-318-61552-5*) Oryx Pr.

Bibliography of Alaskan Aviation, 1940-1984. Dale Stirling. LC 84-80776. (Heritage North Reference Publication: No. 4). (Orig.). spiral bd., pap. 5.00 (*0-913905-00-3*) Heritage N Pr.

Bibliography of American Children's Books Printed Prior to 1821. D'Alte Welch. LC 77-163898. 1972. 60.00 (*0-8271-7133-1*, U Pr of Va) Am Antiquarian.

Bibliography of American Cookery Books 1742-1860. Eleanor Lowenstein. 132p. 1972. 18.00 (*0-912296-02-X*, U Pr of Va) Am Antiquarian.

Bibliography of American County Histories. P. William Filby. 449p. 1987. reprint ed. 24.95 (*0-8063-1126-6*, 1825) Genealog Pub.

***Bibliography of American Demographic History: The Literature from 1984 to 1994.** David R. Gerhan. LC 94-42117. (Bibliographies & Indexes in American History Ser.: No. 30). 368p. 1995. text ed. 79.50 (*0-313-26677-8*, Greenwood Pr) Greenwood.

Bibliography of American Directories Through 1860. Dorothea N. Spear. LC 77-28204. 389p. 1978. reprint ed. text ed. 65.00 (*0-313-20251-6*, SPBA, Greenwood Pr) Greenwood.

Bibliography of American Editions of Robinson Crusoe to 1830. Clarence S. Brigham. 1958. pap. 3.00 (*0-912296-21-6*, Am Antiquarian) Am Antiquarian.

Bibliography of American Educational History: An Annotated & Classified Guide. Ed. by Francesco Cordasco & William W. Brickman. LC 74-29140. (Studies in Education: No. 3). 47.50 (*0-404-12661-8*) AMS Pr.

Bibliography of American Ethnology. 350p. 1976. 25.00 (*0-686-62438-6*) B Klein Pubns.

Bibliography of American Historical Societies. A. P. Griffin. 1972. 59.95 (*0-87968-736-3*) Gordon Pr.

Bibliography of American Immigration History. Ed. by George Washington University Staff. LC 77-3477. 1978. reprint ed. lib. bdg. 57.50 (*0-678-00748-9*) Kelley.

Bibliography of American Imprints to 1991, 92 vols. 1992. write for info. (*3-598-33340-4*) U Pubns Amer.

Bibliography of American Literature, 7 vols. Comp. by Jacob Blanck. Incl. Vol. 4. Nathaniel Hawthorne to Joseph Holt Ingraham. LC 54-5283. xxii, 495p. 1963. 85.00x (*0-300-00313-7*); Vol. 5. Washington Irving to Henry Wadsworth Longfellow. LC 54-5283. xxii, 1969p. 1969. 85.00x (*0-300-01099-0*); Vol. 7. James Kirke Paulding to Frank Richard Stockton. LC 54-5283. 700p. 1983. text ed. 85.00x (*0-300-02636-6*); LC 54-5283. (Illus.). write for info. (*0-318-56510-2*) Yale U Pr.

Bibliography of American Literature, Vol. 8. Jacob Blanck. LC 54-5283. 576p. (C). 1990. text ed. 85.00x (*0-300-03839-9*) Yale U Pr.

***Bibliography of American Literature: A Selective Index.** Michael Winship & Philip B. Eppard. 452p. (C). 1994. text ed. 70.00x (*1-55591-951-0*, North Amer Pr) Fulcrum Pub.

Bibliography of American Literature, Vol. 9: Edward Noyes Westcott to Elinor Wylie. Ed. by Michael Winship. (Illus.). 548p. 1991. 85.00x (*0-300-05141-7*) Yale U Pr.

Bibliography of American Poetry, Sixteen Fifty to Eighteen-Twenty, 2 vols. in 1. O. Wegelin. 18.00 (*0-8446-1469-6*) Peter Smith.

Bibliography of American Publications on East Central Europe, 1945-1957. Robert F. Byrnes. LC 69-106305. (Indiana University Publications Russian & East European: Vol. 12). 243p. reprint ed. pap. 69.30 (*0-8357-7175-X*, 2050954) Bks Demand.

Bibliography of Ancient Ephesus. Richard E. Oster. LC 87-12617. (American Theological Library Association Monograph: No. 19). 181p. 1987. 25.00 (*0-8108-1996-1*) Scarecrow.

Bibliography of Antislavery in America. Dwight L. Dumond. LC 61-9306. 130p. reprint ed. pap. 37.10 (*0-8357-7176-8*, 2051081) Bks Demand.

Bibliography of Appraisal Literature, 1981-1986. 71p. 1987. 14.50 (*0-911780-86-6*) Appraisal Inst.

Bibliography of Appraisal Literature, 1987. 9p. 1988. 5.00 (*0-685-30542-2*) Appraisal Inst.

Bibliography of Appraisal Literature, 1988. 19p. 1989. 5.00 (*0-685-30543-0*) Appraisal Inst.

Bibliography of Arizona Ornithology. Anders H. Anderson. LC 76-163008. 241p. (Orig.). 1972. pap. 10.95 (*0-8165-0313-3*) U of Ariz Pr.

Bibliography of Arms Control Verification. David Scrivener & Michael Sheeham. LC 89-23838. 145p. 1990. text ed. 55.95 (*1-85521-044-4*, Pub. by Dartmth Pub UK) Ashgate Pub Co.

Bibliography of Arthur Machen. Adrian Goldstone & Wesley D. Sweetser. LC 72-6469. (English Literature Ser.: No. 33). 180p. 1972. reprint ed. lib. bdg. 75.00 (*0-8383-1614-X*) M S G Haskell Hse.

Bibliography of Arthur Waley. Francis A. Johns. LC 87-18706. 220p. (C). 1988. text ed. 70.00 (*0-485-11344-9*, Pub. by Athlone Pr UK) Humanities.

Bibliography of Articles & Papers on North American Indian Art. Anne D. Harding & Patricia Bolling. 1980. lib. bdg. 75.00 (*0-8490-3115-X*) Gordon Pr.

Bibliography of Articles on Iqbal. Malik Mueen Azhar. 64p. (Orig.). 1985. pap. 7.95 (*1-56744-233-1*) Kazi Pubns.

Bibliography of Articles on the Danish West Indies & the United States Virgin Islands in the New York Times 1867-1975. Ed. by Arnold R. Highfield. LC 78-622684. (Caribbean Research Institute Occasional Paper Ser.: No. 1). 218p. reprint ed. pap. 62.20 (*0-7837-4902-3*, 2044567) Bks Demand.

Bibliography of Asian Studies, Nineteen Seventy-seven. Ed. by Estrella S. Bryant et al. 732p. reprint ed. pap. 180.00 (*0-8357-7177-6*, 2014786) Bks Demand.

Bibliography of A.U.B. Faculty Publications, Eighteen Sixty-Six to Nineteen Sixty-Six. Ed. by Suha Tamim. 1967. 24.95 (*0-8156-6005-7*, Am U Beirut) Syracuse U Pr.

***Bibliography of Australian Multicultural Writers.** Sneja Gunew et al. 291p. 1992. pap. 90.00 (*0-7300-1503-3*, Pub. by Deakin Univ AT) St Mut.

Bibliography of Australian Poetry: 1935-55. Sue Murray & Monash University Staff. 274p. 1991. 45.00 (*1-875589-00-7*) D W Thorpe.

Bibliography of Australian Women's Literature, 1795-1990. Debra Adelaide. 880p. 1991. 55.00 (*0-909532-90-7*) D W Thorpe.

***Bibliography of Aviation Medicine.** Ebbe C. Hoff & John F. Fulton. 1942. 250.00 (*0-614-00149-8*) Elliots Bks.

***Bibliography of Aviation Medicine.** Ebbe C. Hoff & John F. Fulton. 1942. 250.00 (*0-614-00254-0*) Elliots Bks.

Bibliography of Bagpipe Music. Roderick D. Cannon. 296p. (C). 1989. 45.00 (*0-85976-024-3*, Pub. by J Donald) St Mut.

Bibliography of Balzac Criticism 1930-1990. Comp. by Mark W. Waggoner. LC 90-80420. 300p. (Orig.). (C). 1990. pap. 50.00 (*0-9625770-0-6*) French Rsch Pubns.

Bibliography of Bertrand Russell, 2 vols., 1. Kenneth Blackwell & Harry Roja. LC 94-5168. 1994. write for info. (*0-415-10487-4*) Routledge.

Bibliography of Bertrand Russell, 2 vols., 2. Kenneth Blackwell & Harry Roja. LC 94-5168. 1994. write for info. (*0-415-11086-6*) Routledge.

***Bibliography of Bertrand Russell, 3 vols., Set.** Ed. by Kenneth Blackwell. (Collected Papers of Bertrand Russell). (Illus.). 1504p. 1994. 455.00 (*0-415-11644-9*, B4525) Routledge.

Bibliography of Bibliographies in Aesthetics. Allan Shields. 80p. 1974. pap. 14.50 (*0-916304-16-7*) SDSU Press.

Bibliography of Bibliographies in American Literature. Charles H. Nilon. LC 73-103542. 495p. reprint ed. pap. 141.10 (*0-8357-7178-4*, 2013299) Bks Demand.

Bibliography of Bibliographies of the Languages of the World, Vol. II. Rudolph C. Troike. (Library & Information Sources in Linguistics: No. 19). Date not set. write for info. (*90-272-3744-1*) Benjamins North Am.

Bibliography of Bibliographies of the Languages of the World Vol. 1: General & Indo-European Languages of Europe. Comp. by Rudolf C. Troike. LC 90-426. (Library & Information Sources in Linguistics: Vol. 19). xxii, 473p. 1990. 118.00x (*90-272-3743-3*) Benjamins North Am.

Bibliography of Bioethics, 9 vols., 6. Ed. by Leroy Walters. LC 75-4140. 1978. 70.00 (*0-8103-0987-4*) Gale.

Bibliography of Bioethics, 9 vols., Vol. 1. Ed. by Leroy Walters. LC 75-4140. 256p. 1978. 70.00 (*0-8103-0978-5*) Gale.

Bibliography of Bioethics, 9 vols., Vol. 3. Ed. by Leroy Walters. LC 75-4140. 1977. 70.00 (*0-8103-6864-1*) Gale.

Bibliography of Bioethics, Vol. 7. Ed. by Leroy Walters. 375p. 1981. 80.00 (*0-02-933770-4*) Free Pr.

Bibliography of Bioethics, 9 vols., Vol. 7. Ed. by Leroy Walters. LC 75-4140. 1981. 70.00 (*0-685-01815-6*) Gale.

Bibliography of Bioethics, Vol. 10. Ed. by LeRoy Walters & Tamar J. Kahn. xi, 387p. 1984. text ed. 60.00 (*0-9614448-0-0*) Geo U Kennedy Inst.

Bibliography of Bioethics, Vol. 11. Ed. by LeRoy Walters & Tamar J. Kahn. xi, 444p. 1985. text ed. 60.00 (*0-9614448-1-9*) Geo U Kennedy Inst.

Bibliography of Bioethics, Vol. 13. Ed. by LeRoy Walters & Tamar J. Kahn. 619p. 1987. 60.00 (*0-9614448-3-5*) Geo U Kennedy Inst.

Bibliography of Bioethics, Vol. 14. Ed. by LeRoy Walters & Tamar J. Kahn. 579p. 1988. 60.00 (*0-9614448-4-3*) Geo U Kennedy Inst.

Bibliography of Bioethics, Vol. 15. Ed. by LeRoy Walters & Tamar J. Kahn. 601p. 1989. 60.00 (*0-9614448-5-1*) Geo U Kennedy Inst.

Bibliography of Bioethics, Vol. 16. Ed. by LeRoy Walters & Tamar J. Kahn. 1990. 60.00 (*0-9614448-6-X*) Geo U Kennedy Inst.

Bibliography of Bioethics, Vol. 17. Ed. by LeRoy Walters & Tamar J. Kahn. 669p. 1991. 60.00 (*0-9614448-7-8*) Geo U Kennedy Inst.

***Bibliography of Bioethics, Vol. 18.** Ed. by Leroy Walters & Tamar J. Kahn. 627p. 1992. 60.00 (*0-9614448-8-6*) Geo U Kennedy Inst.

***Bibliography of Bioethics, Vol. 19.** Ed. by Leroy Walters & Tamar J. Kahn. 771p. 1993. 60.00 (*0-9614448-9-4*) Geo U Kennedy Inst.

***Bibliography of Bioethics, Vol. 20.** Ed. by Leroy Walters & Tamar J. Kahn. 811p. 1994. 60.00 (*1-883913-00-4*) Geo U Kennedy Inst.

Bibliography of Black Music: Afro-American Idioms, Vol. 2. Dominique-Rene De Lerma. LC 80-24681. (Encyclopedia of Black Music Ser.). 240p. 1981. text ed. 65.00 (*0-313-23144-3*, DBI/02, Greenwood Pr) Greenwood.

Bibliography of Black Music: Geographical Studies, Vol. 3. Dominique-Rene de Lerma. LC 80-24681. (Encyclopedia of Black Music Ser.). xiv, 284p. 1982. text ed. 65.00 (*0-313-23510-4*, DBI/03, Greenwood Pr) Greenwood.

Bibliography of Black Music: Reference Materials, Vol. 1. Dominique-Rene De Lerma. LC 80-24681. (Encyclopedia of Black Music Ser.). xv, 124p. 1981. text ed. 55.00 (*0-313-21340-2*, DBI/01, Greenwood Pr) Greenwood.

Bibliography of Black Music: Theory, Education, & Related Studies, Vol. 4. Dominique-Rene De Lerma. LC 80-24681. (Encyclopedia of Black Music Ser.). xiv, 254p. 1984. text ed. 65.00 (*0-313-24229-1*, DBI/04, Greenwood Pr) Greenwood.

Bibliography of Bookplate Literature. Ed. by George W. Fuller. LC 72-178635. 1971. reprint ed. 48.00 (*1-55888-933-7*) Omnigraphics Inc.

Bibliography of Books for Children, 1988-89. Ed. by Helen Shelton. LC 89-345. 112p. (J). (ps-6). 1989. 15.00 (*0-87173-118-5*) ACEI.

Bibliography of Books on Music & Collections of Music. Harold Gleason & Albert T. Luper. 471p. 1990. reprint ed. lib. bdg. 99.00 (*0-7812-9282-4*) Rprt Serv.

An Asterisk (*) at the beginning of an entry indicates that the title is appearing in BIP for the first time.

Bibliography of British Business Histories. Francis Goodall. 500p. 1987. text ed. 95.50 (*0-566-05307-1*, Pub. by Gower UK) Ashgate Pub Co.

Bibliography of British History, 1851-1914. Ed. by Henry J. Hanham. 1976. 160.00 (*0-19-822389-7*) OUP.

Bibliography of British Industrial Relations. George S. Bain & G. B. Woolven. LC 76-53516. 689p. reprint ed. pap. 180.00 (*0-8357-7179-2*, 2030578) Bks Demand.

Bibliography of British Industrial Relations, 1971-1979. George S. Bain & John D. Bennett. 258p. 1985. 74.95 (*0-521-26699-8*) Cambridge U Pr.

Bibliography of British Literary Bibliographies. 2nd ed. Trevor H. Howard-Hill. (Index to British Literary Bibliography Ser.: Vol. I). (Illus.). 912p. 1988. 160.00 (*0-19-818184-1*) OUP.

Bibliography of British Theological Literature 1850-1940. Ed. by Dikran Y. Hadidian. LC 85-26839. (Bibliographia Tripotamopolitana Ser.: No. 12). (Illus.). 500p. 1985. pap. 35.00 (*0-931222-11-7*) Pitts Theolog.

Bibliography of Business Ethics, 1971-1975. Donald G. Jones. LC 76-52486. 227p. reprint ed. pap. 64.70 (*0-8357-8043-0*, 2033972) Bks Demand.

Bibliography of Business Ethics, 1976-1980. Ed. by Donald G. Jones & Helen Troy. LC 81-16003. (Publications of the Colgate Darden Graduate School of Business Administration, University of Virginia). 220p. 1982. 20.00 (*0-8139-0921-X*) U Pr of Va.

Bibliography of Business Ethics, 1981-1985: University of Virginia. Ed. by Donald G. Jones & Patricia Bennett. LC 86-23545. (Mellen Studies in Business: Vol. 2). 304p. 1986. lib. bdg. 99.95 (*0-88946-154-6*) E Mellen.

Bibliography of Butterflies, Vol. 124. G. Lamas et al. (Atlas of Neotropical Lepidoptera Ser.). 1995. 42.95 (*0-945417-31-4*) Sci Pubs.

Bibliography of Cameroon. Mark Delancey & Virginia Delancey. LC 75-1165. (African Bibliography Ser.: Vol. 4). 675p. 1975. 45.00 (*0-8419-0167-8*, Africana) Holmes & Meier.

Bibliography of Canadian Bibliographies. 3rd ed. Comp. by Ernie Ingles. 1178p. 1994. 150.00 (*0-8020-2837-3*) U of Toronto Pr.

Bibliography of Canadian Bibliographies. Bibliographie des bibliographies Canadiennes. Raymond Tanghe. LC 60-4415. 216p. reprint ed. pap. 61.60 (*0-8357-6392-7*, 2035748) Bks Demand.

Bibliography of Canadiana Published in Great Britain, 1519-1763. Freda F. Waldon. Ed. by W. F. Morley. 535p. (C). 1990. text ed. 170.00 (*1-55022-087-X*, Pub. by ECW Press CN) Genl Dist Srvs.

Bibliography of Card Games & of the History of Playing Cards see Bibliographies of Works on Playing Cards & Gaming

Bibliography of Carlyle. Richard Shepherd. LC 70-116801. (Reference Ser.: No. 44). 1970. reprint ed. lib. bdg. 53.95 (*0-8383-1043-5*) M S G Haskell Hse.

Bibliography of Cartography, 5 vols., Set. Library of Congress, Washington, D. C., Geography & Map Division Staff. 1973. lib. bdg. 615.00 (*0-8161-1008-5*, Hall Library) G K Hall.

Bibliography of Cartography, First Supplement. Library of Congress, Washington, D. C., Geography & Map Division Staff. 1980. lib. bdg. 285.00 (*0-8161-0259-7*, Hall Library) G K Hall.

Bibliography of Cello Ensemble Music. Claude Kenneson. LC 73-79444. (Detroit Studies in Music Bibliography: No. 31). 59p. 1974. pap. 6.00 (*0-911772-60-X*) Info Coord.

Bibliography of Ceramics & Glass. Ed. by Larry L. Hench & B. A. McEldowney. LC 67-7492. 120p. 1976. 5.00 (*0-916094-17-0*, BIBLCG) Am Ceramic.

Bibliography of Child Language. Werner F. Leopold. LC 71-128944. (Northwestern Humanities Ser.: No. 28). reprint ed. 27.50 (*0-404-50728-X*) AMS Pr.

Bibliography of Child Psychiatry & Child Mental Health: With a Selected List of Films. Ed. by Irving N. Berlin. LC 74-11813. 508p. 1976. 44.95 (*0-87705-244-1*) Human Sci Pr.

Bibliography of Child Study. Louis N. Wilson. LC 74-21433. (Classics in Child Development Ser.). 360p. 1975. reprint ed. 31.95 (*0-405-06482-9*) Ayer.

Bibliography of Chinese Government Serials: 1880-1949. Comp. by Julia Tung. LC 79-2456. 146p. (Orig.). 1979. pap. 9.95 (*0-8179-4242-4*) Hoover Inst Pr.

Bibliography of Chinese-Language Materials on the People's Communes. Wei-Yi Ma. LC 82-14617. (Michigan Monographs in Chinese Studies: No. 44). xxviii, 301p. (C). 1982. pap. text ed. 11.00 (*0-89264-044-8*) Ctr Chinese Studies.

Bibliography of Chinese Social History. E-Tu Zen Sun. 1952. 3.00 (*0-88710-004-X*) Yale Far Eastern Pubns.

Bibliography of Christian Worship. Bard Thompson. LC 88-38650. (American Theological Library Association Monograph: No. 25). 830p. 1989. 79.50 (*0-8108-2154-0*) Scarecrow.

Bibliography of Circum-Pacific Plutonism. Ed. by W. S. Pitcher & L. Aguirre. (Microform Publication: No. 12). 1982. 1.50 (*0-8137-6012-7*) Geol Soc.

Bibliography of Coin Hoards of Great Britain & Ireland, Fifteen Hundred to Nineteen Sixty-Seven. I. D. Brown & M. Dolley. 1977. 20.00 (*0-685-51521-4*) S J Durst.

Bibliography of Collective Bargaining in Hospitals & Related Facilities, 2 vols. William A. Rothman. Incl. Vol. 1. 1959-1968. 1970. 6.95 (*0-87736-301-3*); Vol. 2. 1969-1971. 1970. 7.95 (*0-87736-320-X*); 1970. write for info. (*0-318-56089-5*) U of Mich Inst Labor.

Bibliography of Collective Bargaining in Hospitals & Related Facilities, 1972-1974. William A. Rothman. LC 76-21690. (ILR Bibliography Ser.: No. 14). 164p. 1976. pap. 1.00 (*0-87546-287-1*) ILR Pr.

***Bibliography of Colon Classification 1930-1993.** M. P. Satija & Amnik Singh. 129p. (C). 1994. 30.00x (*81-85880-29-8*, Pub. by Print Hse II) St Mut.

Bibliography of Colorado Mining History. Arthur Smith, Jr. 46p. (Orig.). 1993. pap. 9.95 (*0-928693-09-0*) L R Ream.

Bibliography of Comedias Sueltas in the University of Toronto Library. Toronto University Library Staff. 159p. reprint ed. pap. 45.40 (*0-8357-7180-6*, 2051854) Bks Demand.

Bibliography of Commissions of Enquiry & Other Government-Sponsored Reports on the Commonwealth Caribbean, 1900-1975. Audrey Roberts. (Bibliography & Reference Ser.: No. 14). 89p. (Orig.). 1985. pap. 17.50 (*0-917617-06-1*) SALALM.

Bibliography of Commonwealth Law Reports. Ed. by Wallace Breem & Sally Phillips. 320p. 1991. text ed. 110.00 (*0-7201-2023-3*, Mansell Pub) Cassell.

Bibliography of Comparative Adult Education: A Source Book. Peter Haywood. (C). 1981. text ed. 42.00 (*0-685-22135-0*, Pub. by Univ Nottingham UK) St Mut.

Bibliography of Comparative Religious Ethics. Ed. by John Carmen & Mark Juergensmeyer. 864p. (C). 1991. 115.00 (*0-521-34448-4*) Cambridge U Pr.

***Bibliography of Completed Research on Administration of Physical Education & Athletics 1971-1982.** John A. Baker & Mary S. Collins. Ed. by Earle F. Zeigler. (Monograph Series on Sport & Physical Education Management). 77p. (C). 1995. pap. text ed. 5.80 (*0-87563-562-8*) Stipes.

***Bibliography of Computed Research & Scholarly Endeavor Relating to Management in the Allied Professions (1980-1990 Inclusive)** John A. Baker & Jean Zarriello. Ed. by Earle F. Zeigler. (Monograph Series on Sport & Physical Education Management). 47p. (C). 1995. pap. text ed. 5.60 (*0-87563-565-2*) Stipes.

Bibliography of Computer-Aided Language Learning. Vance Stevens et al. LC 86-17450. (Studies in Education: No. 6). 1986. 32.50 (*0-404-12666-9*) AMS Pr.

Bibliography of Computer Music. Sandra L. Tjepkema. LC 81-2967. 294p. 1981. text ed. 39.95 (*0-87745-110-9*) U of Iowa Pr.

Bibliography of Conifers: Selected Literature on Taxonomy & Related Disciplines Etc. Aljos Farjon. (Regnum Vegetabile Ser.: Vol. 122). 124p. 1990. lib. bdg. 101.00 (*3-87429-306-8*) Koeltz Sci Bks.

Bibliography of Conjuring Periodicals in English, 1791-1983. James B. Alfredson & George Daily. (Illus.). 425p. 1986. text ed. 45.00 (*0-916638-37-5*) Meyerbooks.

Bibliography of Contemporary American Fiction, 1945-1988: An Annotated Checklist. William McPheron. 190p. 1989. text ed. 42.95 (*0-313-27702-8*) Greenwood.

Bibliography of Contemporary American Poetry, 1945-1985. William McPheron. 72p. 1986. text ed. 42.95 (*0-313-27703-6*) Greenwood.

Bibliography of Contemporary Art in Latin America: Books, Articles & Exhibition Catalogs in the Tulane University Library, 1950-1980. Comp. by Monica E. Kupfer. x, 97p. (Orig.). 1983. pap. 7.00 (*0-9603212-5-X*) Tulane SE Arch.

Bibliography of Cookery Books Published 1875-1914. E. Driver. 752p. 1989. text ed. 140.00 (*0-907325-41-6*) Cassell.

Bibliography of Corrosion by Chlorine, TPC 4, 2 vols., Set. 2nd ed. LC 85-60226. 131p. 1987. 33.00 (*0-915567-08-3*) NACE Intl.

Bibliography of Costume. Hilaire Hiler & Meyer Hiler. LC 66-12285. 1972. reprint ed. 36.95 (*0-405-08614-8*) Ayer.

Bibliography of Crime & Criminal Justice: Nineteen Thirty-Two to Nineteen Thirty-Seven. Ed. by Dorothy C. Culver. LC 69-16227. (Criminology, Law Enforcement, & Social Problems Ser.: No. 100). 1969. reprint ed. 30.00 (*0-87585-100-2*) Patterson Smith.

Bibliography of Crime & Criminal Justice: Nineteen Twenty-Seven to Nineteen Thirty-One. Dorothy C. Culver. LC 69-16228. (Criminology, Law Enforcement, & Social Problems Ser.: No. 99). 1969. reprint ed. 30.00 (*0-87585-099-5*) Patterson Smith.

Bibliography of Criminal Law: General Principles. A. Rabie. 96p. 1987. pap. 16.00 (*0-7021-1852-4*, Pub. by Juta SA) W W Gaunt.

Bibliography of Critical Legal Studies. Theoretical Studies Committee. write for info. (*0-318-61182-1*) Natl Lawyers Guild.

Bibliography of Criticism of Contemporary Chicano Literature. Ernestina N. Eger. (Chicano Studies Library Publications: No. 5). 295p. (Orig.). 1982. pap. 16.50 (*0-685-05653-8*) Chicano Stud Lib.

Bibliography of Cuban Mass Communications. John A. Lent. LC 92-24462. (Bibliographies & Indexes in Mass Media & Communications Ser.: No. 6). 384p. 1992. text ed. 69.50 (*0-313-28455-5*, LBN, Greenwood Pr) Greenwood.

Bibliography of Culinary History: Food Resources in Eastern Massachusetts. Ed. by Patricia M. Kelly. 450p. 1988. lib. bdg. 80.00 (*0-8161-0455-7*, Hall Library) G K Hall.

Bibliography of D. H. Lawrence. 2nd ed. Warren Roberts. LC 81-10149. 644p. reprint ed. pap. 180.00 (*0-8357-7181-4*, 2024582) Bks Demand.

Bibliography of Dancing. Ed. by Paul Magriel. LC 65-16242. (Illus.). 1972. 20.95 (*0-405-08776-4*) Ayer.

Bibliography of Dancing. Cyril W. Beaumont. LC 63-23181. 1978. reprint ed. 23.95 (*0-405-08247-9*, Pub. by Blom Pubns UK) Ayer.

Bibliography of Death, Grief, & Bereavement II, 1975-1980. Comp. by Robert Fulton. LC 81-1368. 239p. 1980. lib. bdg. 30.95 (*0-405-14212-9*) Ayer.

Bibliography of Design in Britain, 1851-1970. Anthony J. Coulson. 292p. (C). 1979. text ed. 90.00 (*0-85072-091-5*) St Mut.

Bibliography of Discographies Vol. II: Jazz. Daniel Allen. 239p. 1981. 40.00 (*0-8352-1342-0*) Bowker.

Bibliography of Doctoral Dissertations & Masters' Theses on Conflict, 1975-86. Ed. by M. Afzalur Rahim. 17p. (C). 1987. 5.00 (*0-9623337-0-0*) Intl ACM.

Bibliography of Doctoral Dissertations & Masters' Theses on Conflict, 1975-89. 2nd ed. Ed. by M. Afzalur Rahim & Sanda Kaufman. 46p. (C). 1989. 10.00 (*0-9623337-1-9*) Intl ACM.

Bibliography of Domesday Book. David Bates. 224p. 1986. 63.00 (*0-85115-433-6*) Boydell & Brewer.

Bibliography of E. M. Forster. 2nd ed. B. J. Kirkpatrick. (Soho Bibliographies Ser.). 320p. 1986. 84.00 (*0-19-818191-4*) OUP.

Bibliography of Early American Architecture: Writings on Architecture Constructed Before 1860 in Eastern & Central U. S. Frank J. Roos, Jr. LC 68-24624. (Illus.). 399p. reprint ed. pap. 113.80 (*0-8357-9665-5*, 2014984) Bks Demand.

Bibliography of Early American Fiction, Seventeen Seventy-Four to Eighteen Thirty. O. Wegelin. 10.75 (*0-8446-1470-X*) Peter Smith.

Bibliography of Early American Law, 5 Vols. Ed. by Morris L. Cohen. 1988. lib. bdg. write for info. (*0-527-18573-6*) Kraus Intl.

Bibliography of Early English Law Books. Joseph H. Beale. LC 26-16217. viii, 304p. 1993. reprint ed. lib. bdg. 50.00 (*0-89941-351-X*, 502180) W S Hein.

Bibliography of Early Modern Algebra, Fifteen Hundred to Eighteen Hundred. Comp. by Robin E. Rider. LC 81-51030. (Berkeley Papers in History of Science: No. 7). 150p. (Orig.). 1982. pap. 8.00 (*0-918102-08-1*) U Cal Hist Sci Tech.

Bibliography of Early Secular American Music: Eighteenth Century. 3rd ed. Oscar G. Sonneck. LC 64-18992. (Music Reprint Ser.). 1964. reprint ed. lib. bdg. 75.00 (*0-306-70902-3*) Da Capo.

Bibliography of Early Secular American Music (18th Century) Oscar G. Sonneck. 617p. 1993. reprint ed. lib. bdg. 109.00 (*0-7812-9698-6*) Rprt Serv.

Bibliography of Eastern Asiatic Botany: Supplement 1. E. D. Merrill & E. H. Walker. 1960. 45.00 (*0-934454-11-6*) Lubrecht & Cramer.

Bibliography of Ecclesiastical History of the French Revolution. Charles A. Gliozzo. LC 73-154506. (Bibliographia Tripotamopolitana Ser.: No. 6). 1972. 8.00 (*0-931222-05-2*) Pitts Theolog.

Bibliography of Editions of the Writings of Benjamin Constant to 1833, Vol. 10. C. P. Courtney. 267p. 1981. write for info. (*0-318-60067-6*) Modern Humanities Res.

Bibliography of Editions, Translations, & Commentary on Xenophon's Socratic Writings 1600-Present. Comp. by Donald R. Morrison. 120p. 1988. 15.00 (*0-935225-02-1*) Mathesis Pubns.

Bibliography of Education in the Caribbean. Ed. by V. O. Alcala. 1976. lib. bdg. 59.95 (*0-8490-1498-0*) Gordon Pr.

Bibliography of Edward Carpenter. Edward Carpenter. 1972. 59.95 (*0-87968-737-1*) Gordon Pr.

Bibliography of Edward Dahlberg. Illus. by William Holman. LC 75-633117. (Tower Bibliographical Ser.: No. 8). 1971. 15.00 (*0-87959-037-8*) U of Tex H Ransom Ctr.

Bibliography of Eighteenth Century English Literature. Frederic Ewen. LC 68-25310. (Reference Ser.: No. 44). 1969. reprint ed. lib. bdg. 40.95 (*0-8383-0937-2*) M S G Haskell Hse.

Bibliography of Electronic Music. Lowell M. Cross. LC 67-2573. 136p. reprint ed. pap. 38.80 (*0-8357-7182-2*, 2014178) Bks Demand.

Bibliography of Electrophoretic Studies of Biochemical Variation in Natural Vertebrate Populations. M. W. Smith et al. LC 82-62007. 105p. 1982. 19.95 (*0-89672-106-X*); pap. 8.00 (*0-89672-105-1*); ring bd. 5.00 (*0-89672-104-3*) Tex Tech Univ Pr.

Bibliography of English Language Works on the Babi & Baha'i Faiths 1844-1985. Comp. by William P. Collins. 550p. 1991. 65.00 (*0-85398-315-1*) G Ronald Pub.

Bibliography of English Translations from Medieval Sources, 1943-1968. Comp. by Mary A. Ferguson. LC 73-7751. (Records of Civilization, Sources & Studies: No. 88). 244p. 1974. text ed. 50.00 (*0-231-03435-0*) Col U Pr.

Bibliography of Epictetus. W. A. Oldfather. 177p. 1952. 20.00 (*0-685-02325-7*) Holmes.

Bibliography of Ethnobotany. S. K. Jain et al. (Botanical Survey of India Ser.). 157p. 1984. text ed. 20.00 (*0-945345-58-5*, Pub. by Mahendra Pal Singh II) Lubrecht & Cramer.

***Bibliography of Ethnographic Films.** Rolf Husmann. (Gottingen Cultural Studies). (C). 1994. pap. text ed. 28.00 (*3-89473-352-7*) Westview.

Bibliography of European Economic & Social History. 2nd ed. Derek H. Aldcroft & Richard Rodger. 304p. 1993. text ed. 69.95 (*0-7190-3492-2*, Pub. by Manchester Univ Pr UK) St Martin.

Bibliography of Evelyn Waugh. Ed. by Paul A. Doyle et al. 500p. 1986. 35.00 (*0-87875-313-3*) Whitston Pub.

Bibliography of Extractive Industries Accounting 1960-1982. Ed. by Charles E. Boynton, IV & Alan D. Campbell. LC 84-80466. 147p. 1984. pap. 14.95 (*0-940966-05-0*) UNTX Pro Dev Inst.

Bibliography of F. C. S. Schiller. Herbert L. Searles & Allan Shields. 106p. 1968. pap. 14.50 (*0-916304-06-X*) SDSU Press.

Bibliography of Fatigue Materials Component & Structure 1838-1950. J. Mann. LC 71-102401. 1970. 136.00 (*0-08-006754-9*, Pub. by Pergamon Repr UK) Franklin.

Bibliography of Feminist Criticism - Bibliographie de la Critique Feminist. Ed. by Barbara Godard. 200p. (C). 1987. text ed. 30.00 (*0-920763-97-9*, Pub. by ECW Press CN) Genl Dist Srvs.

Bibliography of Fifteenth Century Literature, with Special Reference to the History of English Culture. Lena L. Tucker. 1974. lib. bdg. 49.95 (*0-87968-738-X*) Gordon Pr.

Bibliography of Finance. Ed. by Richard A. Brealey & Helen Edwards. (Illus.). 864p. 1991. 90.00 (*0-262-02319-9*) MIT Pr.

Bibliography of Firework Books: Works on Recreative Fireworks from the Sixteenth to the Twentieth Century. Chris Philip. (Illus.). xxx, 170p. 1988. reprint ed. text ed. 14.95 (*0-685-44318-3*); reprint ed. write for info. (*0-929931-00-9*) Amer Fireworks.

Bibliography of Florida Archaeology Through 1980 - Index to Bibliography of Florida Archaeology Through 1980. Gregory Toole et al. (Florida Archaeology Ser.: No. 1). 235p. 1986. pap. 8.00 (*0-923308-01-6*) FL Bur Archaeol.

Bibliography of Florida, Vol. 1: 1507-1845. James A. Servies & Lana D. Servies. LC 93-77633. xxiv, 424p. 1993. lib. bdg. 165.00 (*0-9636370-0-2*) Kng & Queen Bks.

Bibliography of Folklore, 1905-1907. Comp. by Northcote W. Thomas. (Folk-Lore Society, London Monographs: Vol. 57A-C). 1972. reprint ed. pap. 15.00 (*0-8115-0526-X*) Periodicals Srv.

Bibliography of Forest Botany in Japan: 1940-1963. Ed. by Satoru Kurata. 146p. 1966. 20.00 (*0-86008-025-0*, Pub. by U of Tokyo JA) Col U Pr.

Bibliography of Forth References. 3rd rev. ed. Ed. by Thea Martin. 1987. pap. 15.00 (*0-914593-06-4*) Inst Appl Forth.

Bibliography of Fossil Vertebrates. Ed. by Joseph T. Gregory et al. LC 80-70567. 624p. (Orig.). 1985. pap. text ed. 115.00 (*0-918799-01-5*) Soc Vertebrate.

Bibliography of Fossil Vertebrates, Exclusive of North America, 1509-1927. Alfred S. Romer et al. LC 63-1118. (Geological Society of America, Memoir Ser.: No. 87, Vol. 2). 779p. reprint ed. pap. 180.00 (*0-8357-7183-0*, 2031792) Bks Demand.

Bibliography of Fossil Vertebrates, 1949-1953. Charles L. Camp & H. J. Allison. LC 61-65012. (Geological Society of America, Memoir Ser.: No. 84). 570p. reprint ed. 162.50 (*0-8357-7184-9*, 2031790) Bks Demand.

Bibliography of Fossil Vertebrates, 1954-1958. Charles L. Camp et al. LC 64-19064. (Geological Society of America, Memoir Ser.: No. 92). 675p. reprint ed. pap. 180.00 (*0-8357-7185-7*, 2031796) Bks Demand.

Bibliography of Fossil Vertebrates, 1959-1963. Charles L. Camp et al. LC 68-54218. (Geological Society of America, Memoir Ser.: No. 117). 688p. reprint ed. pap. 180.00 (*0-8357-7186-5*, 2031816) Bks Demand.

Bibliography of Fossil Vertebrates, 1964-1968. Charles L. Camp et al. LC 79-190170. (Geological Society of America, Memoir Ser.: No. 134). 1183p. reprint ed. pap. 180.00 (*0-8357-7187-3*, 2025028) Bks Demand.

Bibliography of Fossil Vertebrates, 1969-1972. (Geological Society of America, Memoir Ser.: No. 141). 782p. reprint ed. pap. 180.00 (*0-8357-7188-1*, 2007185) Bks Demand.

Bibliography of Fossil Vertebrates, 1973-1977. Ed. by J. A. Bacskai et al. LC 80-70567. (Bibliography of Fossil Vertebrates Ser.). 576p. 1983. pap. 240.00 (*0-913312-68-1*) Am Geol.

Bibliography of Fossil Vertebrates, 1978. Joseph T. Gregory et al. LC 80-70567. 381p. 1981. pap. 95.00 (*0-913312-52-5*) Am Geol.

Bibliography of Fossil Vertebrates, 1980. Ed. by Laurie J. Bryant. LC 80-70567. 471p. 1983. pap. 115.00 (*0-913312-69-X*) Am Geol.

Bibliography of Fossil Vertebrates, 1981. Ed. by Joseph T. Gregory et al. LC 80-70567. 576p. (Orig.). 1984. pap. text ed. 115.00 (*0-918799-00-7*) Soc Vertebrate.

Bibliography of Fund Raising & Philanthropy. 2nd ed. National Catholic Development Conference Staff. LC 82-81523. 76p. 1982. 22.50 (*0-9603196-1-1*) Natl Cath Dev.

Bibliography of Gas Meters & Metering. 58p. 1970. pap. 3.00 (*0-318-12590-0*, X12270) Am Gas Assn.

Bibliography of Geographical Thought: Bibliographies & Indexes in Geography, No. 1. Comp. by Catherine L. Brown & James O. Wheeler. LC 89-25958. 520p. 1989. text ed. 89.50 (*0-313-26899-1*, BBJ/, Greenwood Pr) Greenwood.

Bibliography of Geography. Chauncy D. Harris. LC 76-1910. (University of Chicago, Department of Geography, Research Paper Ser.: Vol. 179). 288p. reprint ed. pap. 82.10 (*0-8357-7189-X*, 2032474) Bks Demand.

Bibliography of Geography Pt. I: Introduction to General Aids. Chauncy D. Harris. LC 76-1910. (Research Papers Ser.: No. 179). 288p. 1976. pap. 12.00 (*0-89065-086-1*) U Chicago Comm Geo.

Bibliography of Geography Pt. II: Regional: The United States of America, Vol. 1. Chauncy D. Harris. LC 76-1910. (Research Papers Ser.: No. 206). 178p. 1984. pap. 12.00 (*0-89065-112-4*) U Chicago Comm Geo.

Bibliography of Geoscience Theses of the United States & Canada, 3 vols., Set. LC 92-44740. 3500p. 1992. text ed. 325.00 (*0-922152-18-7*) Am Geol.

Bibliography of Geothermal Reports in Colorado. Richard H. Pearl et al. (Bulletin Ser.: No. 44). 24p. (Orig.). 1981. pap. 1.00 (*1-884216-06-4*) Colo Geol Survey.

Bibliography of German Expressionism: Catalog of the Library of the Robert Gore Rifkind Center for German Expressionist Studies at the Los Angeles County Museum of Art. Rifkind Center Staff. 500p. (C). 1990. lib. bdg. 165.00 (*0-8161-0494-8*) G K Hall.

Bibliography of German Studies, 1945-1971: Germany under Allied Occupation, Federal Republic of Germany. Gisela Hersch. LC 72-79903. (Indiana University Institute of German Studies Publications Ser.). 621p. reprint ed. pap. 177.00 (*0-8357-7190-3*, 2050074) Bks Demand.

An Asterisk (*) at the beginning of an entry indicates that the title is appearing in BIP for the first time.

Bibliography of Ghana, 1930-1961. Albert F. Johnson. LC 64-17304. 224p. reprint ed. pap. 63.90 (*0-8357-7191-1*, 2006907) Bks Demand.

***Bibliography of Giambattista Vico: Works in English (1884-1994)** 196p. 1994. 37.00 (*0-912632-97-6*) Philos Document.

Bibliography of Graham Greene. Neil Brennan & A. R. Redway. (Soho Bibliographies Ser.). (Illus.). 380p. 1996. 90.00 (*0-19-818187-6*) OUP.

Bibliography of Growth Management Sources. Timothy Beatley. LC 85-31369. (CPL Bibliographies Ser.: No. 166). write for info. (*0-86602-166-3*) Coun Plan Librarians.

Bibliography of Henry Miller. Maxine Renken. LC 72-4735. (American Literature Ser.: No. 49). 1972. reprint ed. lib. bdg. 75.00 (*0-8383-1592-5*) M S G Haskell Hse.

Bibliography of Henry Vaughan. A. Marilla. LC 72-6142. (English Literature Ser.: No. 33). 1972. reprint ed. lib. bdg. 39.95 (*0-8383-1598-4*) M S G Haskell Hse.

Bibliography of Historical Economics to 1980. Ed. by Donald N. McCloskey & George K. Hersh, Jr. 1991. 64. 95 (*0-521-40327-8*) Cambridge U Pr.

Bibliography of Historical Writings Published in Great Britain & the Empire: Nineteen Forty to Nineteen Forty-Five. Louis B. Frewer. LC 74-12628. 346p. 1974. reprint ed. text ed. 65.00 (*0-8371-7735-9*, FRHW, Greenwood Pr) Greenwood.

Bibliography of Holy Land Sites Pt. 1: Compiled in Honor of Dr. Nelson Glueck. Eleanor K. Vogel. 96p. 1982. reprint ed. pap. text ed. 5.00 (*0-87820-626-4*) Am Sch Orient Res.

Bibliography of Holy Land Sites, 1970-1981, Pt. 2. Eleanor K. Vogel & Brooks Holtzclaw. 92p. 1982. pap. text ed. 5.00 (*0-87820-625-6*) Am Sch Orient Res.

Bibliography of Hong Kong Marine Science: 1842-1990. Comp. by Brian Morton. 148p. (C). 1990. pap. text ed. 69.00 (*962-209-275-6*, Pub. by Hong Kong U Pr HK) St Mut.

Bibliography of Human Behavior. Comp. by Hiram Caton. LC 93-3066. (Bibliographies & Indexes in Anthropology Ser.: No. 7). 600p. 1993. Alk. paper. text ed. 95.00 (*0-313-27897-0*, CBJ) Greenwood.

Bibliography of Hydrogenation, Margarine & Shortening: 601 References from 1869 to 1990, Extensively Annotated. Ed. by Akiko Aoyagi. (Bibliographies of Soya Ser.). 139p. 1990. spiral bd., pap. 70.00 (*0-933332-71-8*) Soyfoods Center.

Bibliography of Iain Crichton Smith. Ed. by Grant F. Wilson. 226p. 1991. pap. text ed. 17.95 (*0-08-036599-X*, Pub. by Aberdeen U Pr) Macmillan.

Bibliography of Ichneumonidae (Parasitic Hymenoptera), 1970-1990. Virendra Gupta & Santosh Gupta. (Memoir Ser.: No. 48). 364p. 1991. 50.00 (*1-56665-047-X*) Assoc Pubs FL.

Bibliography of ICPE: 1985-1986. Comp. by Matjaz Musek et al. 139p. 1987. pap. 20.00 (*92-9038-103-5*, Pub. by Intl Ctr Pub Ent XV) Kumarian Pr.

Bibliography of ICPE: 1987-1989. Ed. by Zdravka Pejova & Alenka Subic. 1990. 20.00 (*92-9038-105-1*, Pub. by Intl Ctr Pub Ent XV) Kumarian Pr.

Bibliography of Illinois Archaeology. Gwen P. Bennett. (Scientific Papers: Vol. XXI). xii, 356p. (Orig.). 1985. pap. text ed. 10.00 (*0-89792-105-4*) Ill St Museum.

Bibliography of Illinois Imprints, 1814-58. Cecil K. Byrd. LC 65-24423. 627p. reprint ed. pap. 178.70 (*0-8357-7192-X*, 2024086) Bks Demand.

Bibliography of Important Tilapias for Aquaculture: (Pisces: Cichlidae) Peter Schoenen. (Bibliographies Ser.: No. 3). 336p. (Orig.). 1983. pap. 32.50 (*0-89955-376-1*, Pub. by ICLARM PH) Intl Spec Bk.

Bibliography of Important Tilapias (Pisces: Cichlidae) for Aquaculture. Peter Schoenen. (Bibliographies Ser.: 6). 99p. 1985. pap. 15.00 (*971-10-2219-2*, Pub. by ICLARM PH) Intl Spec Bk.

Bibliography of Indian Law Periodical Articles, 1980-1991. Ed. by Delores A. Jorgensen & Barbara B. Heisinger. LC 92-70678. xviii, 50p. 1992. 45.00 (*0-89941-788-4*, 307470) W S Hein.

Bibliography of Indonesian Peoples & Cultures. 2nd rev. ed. Raymond Kennedy. Ed. by Thomas W. Maretzki & H. T. Fischer. LC 62-20539. (Behavior Science Bibliographies Ser.). 229p. reprint ed. pap. 65.30 (*0-8357-7193-8*, 2021751) Bks Demand.

Bibliography of Industrial Relations in the Railroad Industry. James O. Morris. LC 75-8878. (ILR Bibliography Ser.: No. 12). 172p. 1975. 1.00 (*0-87546-058-5*) ILR Pr.

Bibliography of Industrial Utilization of Soybeans: 1,587 References from A. D. 980 to 1989. Ed. by Akiko Aoyagi. (Bibliographies of Soya Ser.). 236p. 1989. spiral bd. 118.00 (*0-933332-58-0*) Soyfoods Center.

Bibliography of Information Technology: An Annotated Critical Bibliography of English Language Sources Since 1980. 319p. 1989. text ed. 74.95 (*1-85278-040-1*, Pub. by E Elgar Pub UK) Ashgate Pub Co.

Bibliography of Insurance History. 2nd ed. Humbert O. Nelli & Soga Ewedemi. LC 76-6938. (Research Monograph: No. 70). 120p. 1976. spiral bd. 19.95 (*0-88406-106-X*) GA St U Busn Pr.

Bibliography of Integrated Science & Mathematics Teaching & Learning Literature. Donna F. Berlin. (Topics for Teachers Ser.). 64p. (Orig.). (C). 1991. pap. text ed. 7.50 (*0-912047-10-0*) Sch Sci Math.

Bibliography of Irish Trials & Other Legal Proceedings. Paul O'Higgins. 1986. U.K. text ed. 111.00 (*0-86205-080-4*) Butterworth Legal Pubs.

Bibliography of Isaac Bashevis Singer 1924-1949. David N. Miller. LC 83-47647. 315p. (Orig.). (C). 1984. pap. text ed. 28.95 (*0-8204-0002-5*) P Lang Pubs.

***Bibliography of Islamic Central Asia, Pts. I - IV.** (Uralic & Altaic Ser.: Vol. 160). 1995. write for info. (*0-933070-35-7*) Ind U Res Inst.

***Bibliography of Islamic Law, 1980-1993.** Laila A. Zwaini & Rudolph Peters. Vol. 19. 1994. 65.75 (*90-04-10009-1*) E J Brill.

Bibliography of Ismailism. Nagib Tajdin. LC 85-26960. 1986. 25.00 (*0-88206-063-5*) Caravan Bks.

Bibliography of Issues Relating to Women in the Judiciary. National Center for State Courts Staff. 59p. 1982. write for info. (*0-318-61325-5*, NCSC-029) Natl Ctr St Courts.

Bibliography of Izaack Walton's Lives see Charles Viner's General Abridgement of Law & Equity

Bibliography of James Joyce: Eighteen Eighty-Two to Nineteen Forty-One. John J. Slocum. LC 70-138182. 195p. 1971. reprint ed. text ed. 49.75 (*0-8371-5639-4*, SLJJ, Greenwood Pr) Greenwood.

Bibliography of James T. Farrell's Writings, 1921-1957. Edgar M. Branch. LC 58-10532. 148p. reprint ed. pap. 42.20 (*0-8357-7194-6*, 2051184) Bks Demand.

Bibliography of James Whitcomb Riley. Anthony Russo & Dorothy Russo. LC 72-1267. (American Literature Ser.: No. 49). 351p. 1972. reprint ed. lib. bdg. 69.95 (*0-8383-1418-X*) M S G Haskell Hse.

Bibliography of Jazz. Alan P. Merriam. LC 75-127282. (Roots of Jazz Ser.). 1970. reprint ed. lib. bdg. 22.50 (*0-306-70036-0*) Da Capo.

Bibliography of Jewish Bibliographies. 2nd enl. ed. S. Shunami. 1969. 50.00 (*0-87068-882-0*) Ktav.

Bibliography of Jewish Education in the United States. Comp. by Norman Drachler. LC 93-47221. Date not set. write for info. (*0-8143-2353-7*) Wayne St U Pr.

Bibliography of Jewish Instrumental Music. National Jewish Welfare Board Staff. 60p. 1993. reprint ed. lib. bdg. 69.00 (*0-7812-9686-2*) Rprt Serv.

Bibliography of Jewish Numismatics, 1966. L. A. Mayer. 15.00 (*0-87068-796-4*) Ktav.

Bibliography of Jewish Vocal Music. National Jewish Welfare Board Staff. 66p. 1993. reprint ed. lib. bdg. 69. 00 (*0-7812-9687-0*) Rprt Serv.

Bibliography of John Bale. Davis W. Pennar. Bd. with Rump Songs H. F. Brooks.; Notes on Serialization & Competitive Publishing. P. B. Cove. (Oxford Bibliography Society Ser.: Vol. 5, Pt. 4). 1972. reprint ed. Set pap. 13.00 (*0-8115-1240-1*) Periodicals Srv.

Bibliography of John Brown. Donald D. Eddy. 210p. 1971. 7.50 (*0-914930-01-X*) Biblio Soc Am.

Bibliography of John Masefield. Charles H. Simmons. LC 30-33082. reprint ed. 20.00 (*0-404-06005-6*) AMS Pr.

Bibliography of Judaic Cultures, Nos. 749-750. Ed. by Joel M. Halpern. 1975. 8.00 (*0-686-20342-9*) CPL Biblios.

Bibliography of Jurisprudence. 3rd ed. R. W. Dias. 1979. 46.00 (*0-406-57428-6*, U.K.) Butterworth Legal Pubs.

Bibliography of Katherine Mansfield. B. J. Kirkpatrick. (Soho Bibliographies Ser.). (Illus.). 424p. 1990. 95.00 (*0-19-818401-8*) OUP.

Bibliography of Kentucky History. John W. Coleman. LC 49-11965. 534p. reprint ed. pap. 152.20 (*0-8357-7195-4*, 2001468) Bks Demand.

Bibliography of Koji-Grains & - Or Soybeans Cultured with Aspergillus Oryzae: 535 References from 700 B.C.-1993. annot. ed. Ed. by Akiko Aoyagi. LC 93-33474. 151p. 1993. spiral bd. 46.00 (*0-933332-83-1*) Soyfoods Center.

Bibliography of Ladakh. Bray. 1988. 39.95 (*0-85668-435-X*, Pub. by Aris & Phillips UK) David Brown.

Bibliography of Land-Locked States. Ed. by Martin I. Glassner. 1985. lib. bdg. 110.00 (*90-247-3261-1*) Kluwer Ac.

Bibliography of Language Arts Materials for Native North Americans, 1975-76. G. Edward Evans & Karin Abbey. (American Indian Bibliographic Ser.). 153p. 1979. pap. 5.00 (*0-935626-14-X*) U Cal AISC.

Bibliography of Latin America & the Caribbean: The Hilton Library. Ronald Hilton. LC 79-25777. 679p. 1980. 39. 50 (*0-8108-1275-4*) Scarecrow.

Bibliography of Latin American & Caribbean Bibliographies: Annual Report 1992-1993. Gayle A. Williams. (Bibliography & Reference Ser.: No. 34). iii, 81p. (Orig.). 1993. pap. 22.00 (*0-917617-40-1*) SALALM.

***Bibliography of Latin American & Caribbean Bibliographies: Annual Report, 1993-1994.** Gayle A. Williams. (Bibliography & Reference Ser.: No. 35). i, 110p. (Orig.). 1994. pap. 26.00 (*0-917617-42-8*) SALALM.

Bibliography of Latin American & Caribbean Bibliographies, Annual Report, 1991-1992. Comp. by Lionel V. Lorona. (Bibliography & Reference Ser.: No. 31). 59p. (Orig.). 1992. pap. 20.00 (*0-917617-34-7*) SALALM.

Bibliography of Latin American & Caribbean Bibliographies, 1985-1989, Supplement No. 5: Social Sciences & Humanities. Ed. by Lionel V. Lorona. 330p. 1993. 39.50 (*0-8108-2702-6*) Scarecrow.

Bibliography of Latin American & Caribbean Bibliographies, 1987-1988. Ed. by Lionel V. Lorona. (Bibliography & Reference Ser.: No. 23). (Orig.). 1988. pap. 15.00 (*0-917617-20-7*) SALALM.

Bibliography of Latin American & Caribbean Bibliographies, 1988-1989. Ed. by Lionel V. Lorona. (Bibliography & Reference Ser.: No. 25). 1989. 17.50 (*0-917617-23-1*) SALALM.

Bibliography of Latin American & Caribbean Bibliographies, 1989-1990. Lionel V. Lorona. (Bibliography & Reference Ser.: No. 27). viii, 48p. (Orig.). 1990. pap. 17.50 (*0-917617-27-4*) SALALM.

Bibliography of Latin American & Caribbean Bibliographies, 1990-1991. Lionel V. Lorona. (Bibliography & Reference Ser.: No. 30). 125p. 1992. pap. 21.50 (*0-917617-29-0*) SALALM.

Bibliography of Latin American Bibliographies. 2nd ed. Cecil K. Jones. LC 69-13955. 307p. 1970. reprint ed. text ed. 65.00 (*0-8371-1160-9*, JOBL, Greenwood Pr) Greenwood.

Bibliography of Latin American Bibliographies: Social Sciences & Humanities, Supplement No. 2 to Arthur E. Gropp's A Bibliography of Latin American Bibliographies, Vol. 1. Ed. by Daniel R. Cordeiro. LC 78-11935. 1979. lib. bdg. 29.50 (*0-8108-1170-7*) Scarecrow.

Bibliography of Latin American Bibliographies, 1975 - 1979: Social Sciences & Humanities. Ed. by Haydee Piedracueva. LC 82-651. (Bibliography of Latin American Bibliographies Ser.: Supplement 3). 329p. 1982. 35.00 (*0-8108-1524-9*) Scarecrow.

Bibliography of Latin American Bibliographies, 1980-1984: Social Sciences & Humanities, Supplement to Arthur E. Gropp's a Bibliography of Latin American Bibliographies, No. 4. Ed. by Lionel V. Lorona. LC 86-22093. 239p. 1987. 29.50 (*0-8108-1941-4*) Scarecrow.

Bibliography of Latin American Folk Music. U. S. Library of Congress, Music Division Staff. LC 72-1794. reprint ed. 29.50 (*0-404-08305-6*) AMS Pr.

Bibliography of Law & Economics. Ed. by Boudewijn Bouckaert. 684p. (C). 1992. lib. bdg. 187.50 (*0-7923-1645-2*) Kluwer Ac.

Bibliography of Lecithin: 683 References from 1793 to 1990, Extensively Annotated. Ed. by Akiko Aoyagi. (Bibliographies of Soya Ser.). 133p. (Orig.). 1990. spiral bd., pap. 67.00 (*0-933332-70-X*) Soyfoods Center.

Bibliography of Librarianship. Margaret Burton & Marion Vosburgh. 1976. lib. bdg. 59.95 (*0-8490-1499-9*) Gordon Pr.

Bibliography of Limited & Signed Editions in Literature, Twentieth Century American Authors. 1,973th ed. Larry Dingman. 1973. 15.00 (*0-87018-069-X*) Ross.

Bibliography of Loyalist Source Material in the United States, Canada & Great Britain. Ed. by Gregory Palmer. LC 80-19682. 1073p. 1982. text ed. 195.00 (*0-313-28103-3*, PBE/, Greenwood Pr) Greenwood.

Bibliography of Malawi. John B. Webster et al. (Foreign & Comparative Studies Program, Eastern Africa Ser.: No. 1). 161p. 1965. pap. 7.00 (*0-686-70994-2*) Syracuse U Foreign Comp.

Bibliography of Marketing Research Methods. 3rd ed. John R. Dickinson. 1072p. 1990. text ed. 75.00 (*0-669-21697-6*) Free Pr.

Bibliography of Materials on Missouri Basin Development. Virginia C. Westfall. 1950. 5.00 (*1-55614-022-3*) U of SD Gov Res Bur.

Bibliography of Mathematical Works Printed in America Through Eighteen Fifty: Reprinted with Supplement & Second Supplement to the Bibliography. Louis C. Karpinski. Ed. by I. Bernard Cohen. LC 79-7971. (Three Centuries of Science in America Ser.). (Illus.). 1980. reprint ed. lib. bdg. 66.95 (*0-405-12553-4*) Ayer.

Bibliography of Matrix Isolation Spectroscopy 1954-1985. David W. Ball et al. LC 87-60695. 643p. 1988. text ed. 50.00 (*0-89263-266-6*) Rice Univ.

Bibliography of Mayan Languages & Linguistics. Lyle Campbell et al. (Monographs: No. 3). 182p. (Orig.). 1978. pap. text ed. 10.00 (*0-942041-02-X*) SUNYA Inst Mesoam.

Bibliography of McClelland & Stewart Imprints. Ed. by Charlotte Stewart-Murphy et al. 500p. (C). 1993. text ed. 75.00 (*1-55022-171-X*, Pub. by ECW Press CN) Genl Dist Srvs.

Bibliography of Media Management & Economics. 2nd ed. Rita M. Du Charme. 131p. (C). 1988. pap. text ed. 12.00 (*0-944866-01-8*) Media Mgmt & Econ.

Bibliography of Medical & Biomedical Biography. 2nd ed. Leslie T. Morton & Robert J. Moore. LC 94-8284. 1994. 99.95 (*0-85967-981-0*, Pub. by Scolar Pr UK) Ashgate Pub Co.

Bibliography of Meteorology see International Bibliography of Meteorology: From the Beginning of Printing to 1889

Bibliography of Mexican American History. Comp. by Matt S. Meier. LC 83-18585. x, 500p. 1984. text ed. 69. 50 (*0-313-23776-X*, MBI/, Greenwood Pr) Greenwood.

***Bibliography of Meyer Schapiro.** Ed. by Lillian M. Schapiro. (Illus.). 104p. 1995. write for info. (*0-8076-1387-8*) Braziller.

Bibliography of Microelectronics & Electronics Packaging & Interconnecting References, 1986-89. John F. Graves, III. 500p. 1990. 44.95 (*0-9617152-1-9*) Technology Seminars.

Bibliography of Micronesia. Fujio Uchinomi. Tr. by Mitsuno Fukuda. LC 52-7596. 170p. reprint ed. pap. 48. 50 (*0-8357-7196-2*, 2000093) Bks Demand.

Bibliography of Military Name Lists from Pre-1675 to 1900: A Guide to Genealogical Research. Lois Horowitz. LC 88-3053. 1118p. 1990. 99.50 (*0-8108-2166-4*) Scarecrow.

Bibliography of Minnesota Geology, 1951-1980. G. B. Morey et al. (Bulletin: No. 46). 1981. 10.00 (*0-934938-01-6*) Minn Geol Surv.

Bibliography of Minnesota Geology, 1981-1985. Lynn Swanson et al. (Bulletin: 47). 1987. 10.00 (*0-934938-02-4*) Minn Geol Surv.

Bibliography of Miso & Soybean Chiang: 1,604 References from A.D. 535 to 1989. Ed. by Akiko Aoyagi. (Bibliographies of Soya Ser.). 227p. (Orig.). 1989. spiral bd. 113.00 (*0-933332-52-1*) Soyfoods Center.

Bibliography of Modern Hebrew Literature in English Translation. Yohai Goell. 132p. 1968. boxed 34.95x (*0-87855-187-5*) Transaction Pubs.

Bibliography of Modern History. Ed. by John Roach. LC 67-11528. 412p. reprint ed. pap. 117.50 (*0-8357-7197-0*, 2051466) Bks Demand.

Bibliography of Modern Icelandic Literature in Translation: Including Works Written by Icelanders in Other Languages. Comp. by P. M. Mitchell & Kenneth H. Ober. LC 74-19751. (Islandica Ser.: Vol. XL). 324p. 1975. 69.50 (*0-8014-0897-0*) Cornell U Pr.

Bibliography of Modern Icelandic Literature in Translation: Supplement 1971-1980. Kenneth H. Ober. LC 89-46232. (Islandica Ser.: No. 47). 325p. 1990. 44.50 (*0-8014-2475-5*) Cornell U Pr.

Bibliography of Modern Irish & Anglo-Irish Literature. Frank L. Kersnowski et al. LC 75-43274. (Checklists in the Humanities & Education Ser.). 173p. reprint ed. pap. 49.40 (*0-8357-6349-8*, 2035624) Bks Demand.

Bibliography of Modern Irish Drama, 1899-1970. E. H. Mikhail. LC 72-1373. 63p. 1972. 25.00 (*0-295-95229-6*) U of Wash Pr.

Bibliography of Mono- & Multilingual Dictionaries & Glossaries of Technical Terms Used in Geography As Well As in Related Natural & Social Sciences. Ed. by Emil Meynen. 266p. (Orig.). 1974. pap. 58.50 (*3-515-01846-8*) Coronet Bks.

Bibliography of Morphology Nineteen Sixty-Nineteen Eighty-Five. Ed. by Robert Beard & Bogdan Szymanek. LC 87-34172. (Library & Information Sources in Linguistics: Vol. 18). xiv, 193p. 1988. 38.00x (*90-272-3742-5*) Benjamins North Am.

Bibliography of Mughal India: Fifteen Twenty-Six to Seventeen Hundred Seven. Sri A. Sharma. LC 77-10597. (Studies in Islamic History Ser.). ix, 206p. 1978. reprint ed. lib. bdg. 35.00 (*0-87991-467-X*) Porcupine Pr.

Bibliography of Multivariate Statistical Analysis. T. W. Anderson et al. LC 76-54249. 652p. 1977. reprint ed. lib. bdg. 49.50 (*0-88275-477-7*) Krieger.

Bibliography of Municipal Problems & City Conditions. Robert C. Brooks. LC 78-112527. (Rise of Urban America Ser.). 1973. reprint ed. 25.95 (*0-405-02439-8*) Ayer.

***Bibliography of Municipal Solid Waste Management Alternatives.** 103p. (Orig.). (C). 1995. pap. text ed. 35. 00x (*0-7881-1532-4*) Diane Pub.

Bibliography of Museum & Art Gallery Publications & Audio Visual Aids in Great Britain & Ireland, 1979-80. Ed. by Michael Roulstone. 1980. lib. bdg. 100.00 (*0-85964-097-3*) Chadwyck-Healey.

Bibliography of Museum Studies. 11th ed. Simon J. Knell. LC 94-8279. 248p. 1994. 69.95 (*1-85928-061-7*, Pub. by Scolar Pr UK) Ashgate Pub Co.

Bibliography of Mutualism & Individualist Anarchism. B. Chaim. 1979. lib. bdg. 42.95 (*0-686-25748-0*) Mutualist Pr.

Bibliography of Neale Books & Biography of Walter Neale Publisher. Robert J. Krick. 520p. 1977. 25.00 (*0-89029-301-5*) Morningside Bkshop.

Bibliography of Nepalese Language & Linguistics. S. Toba. (C). 1991. 35.00 (*0-7855-0174-6*, Pub. by Ratna Pustak Bhandar) St Mut.

Bibliography of Netherlandic (Dutch, Flemish) Dictionaries: An Exhaustive Bibliography of Netherlandic Dictionaries from the Outset of Printing to the Present Day. Comp. by Frans M. Claes. xvi, 314p. (C). 1980. 68.00 (*3-262-02024-9*) Benjamins North Am.

Bibliography of New Orleans Imprints, 1764-1864. Florence M. Jumonville. LC 89-11166. (Illus.). xl, 760p. 1989. 59.95 (*0-917860-25-X*) Historic New Orleans.

Bibliography of New Religious Movements in Primal Societies, Vol. 6. Ed. by Harold W. Turner. (G. K. Hall Reference Ser.). 300p. 1993. text ed. 45.00 (*0-8161-9089-5*, Hall Reference) Macmillan.

Bibliography of New Religious Movements in Primal Societies: Latin America, Vol. 5. Harold W. Turner. 203p. (C). 1991. text ed. 45.00 (*0-8161-7929-8*, Hall Reference) Macmillan.

Bibliography of New Religious Movements, Vol. 3: Oceana. Harold W. Turner. (Religion Ser.). 450p. (C). 1990. text ed. 45.00 (*0-8161-8984-6*, Hall Reference) Macmillan.

Bibliography of New Religious Movements, Vol. 4: Europe & Asia. Harold W. Turner. 296p. 1990. text ed. 45.00 (*0-8161-7930-1*, Hall Reference) Macmillan.

Bibliography of New York State Communities. 3rd ed. Harold Nestler. 312p. 1990. pap. 20.00 (*1-55613-330-8*) Heritage Bk.

Bibliography of Newfoundland, Vols. 1 & 2. Ed. by Anne Alexander. 1449p. 1986. text ed. 200.00 (*0-8020-2402-5*) U of Toronto Pr.

Bibliography of Nineteen Seventy-Eight Publications of University Bureaus of Business & Economic Research, Vols. 23. Ed. by Stanley J. Kloc et al. 286p. 1979. 12.50 (*0-318-13493-4*) Assn U Busn & Econ Res.

Bibliography of Nineteen-Seventy Five Publications of University Bureaus Business & Economic Research, Vol. 20. Ed. by Dennis R. Leyden et al. 209p. 1976. 7.50 (*0-318-13494-2*) Assn U Busn & Econ Res.

Bibliography of Nineteen-Seventy Nine Publications of University Bureaus of Business & Economic Research, Vols. 24. Ed. by Stanley J. Kloc et al. 304p. 1980. 12.50 (*0-318-13495-0*) Assn U Busn & Econ Res.

Bibliography of Nineteen Seventy-Seven Publications of University Bureaus of Business & Economic Research, Vols. 22. Ed. by Dennis R. Leyden et al. 264p. 1978. 12.50 (*0-318-13496-9*) Assn U Busn & Econ Res.

Bibliography of Nineteen Seventy-Six Publications of University Bureaus of Business & Economic Research, Vol. 21. Ed. by Dennis R. Leyden et al. 258p. 1977. 12. 50 (*0-318-13497-7*) Assn U Busn & Econ Res.

Bibliography of Nineteenth-Century American Piano Music: With Location Sources & Composer Biography-Index. John Gillespie & Anna Gillespie. LC 84-8993. (Music Reference Collection Ser.: No. 2). xiii, 358p. 1984. text ed. 69.50 (*0-313-24097-3*, GNP/) Greenwood.

B

Bibliography of Nineteenth Century British Topographical Books with Steel Engravings. M. Holloway. 1989. pap. 50.00 (*0-87556-641-3*) Saifer.

Bibliography of Nineteenth-Century Legal Literature. Ed. by J. N. Adams & M. I. Davies. 3000p. (C). 1993. lib. bdg. 2,195.00 (*0-907977-42-1*) Chadwyck-Healey.

Bibliography of Noise for 1965-1970. LC 72-87107. xxx, 375p. 1973. 17.00 (*0-87875-029-0*) Whitston Pub.

Bibliography of Noise for 1971. LC 72-87107. 150p. 1973. 10.00 (*0-87875-031-2*) Whitston Pub.

Bibliography of Noise for 1972. LC 72-87107. xvii, 126p. 1974. 10.00 (*0-87875-054-1*) Whitston Pub.

Bibliography of Noise for 1973. LC 72-87107. 1975. 10.00 (*0-87875-055-X*) Whitston Pub.

Bibliography of Noise for 1974. LC 72-82107. 1976. 10.00 (*0-87875-078-9*) Whitston Pub.

Bibliography of Noise for 1975. LC 72-87107. 171p. 1977. 10.00 (*0-87875-099-1*) Whitston Pub.

Bibliography of Noise for 1976. LC 72-87107. 202p. 1978. 12.50 (*0-87875-128-9*) Whitston Pub.

Bibliography of Noise for 1977-1981. LC 72-87107. (Bibliography of Noise Ser.). 177p. 1983. 22.50 (*0-87875-177-7*) Whitston Pub.

Bibliography of Non-Euclidean Geometry. 2nd ed. Duncan Y. Sommerville. LC 72-113150. 1960. text ed. 29.50 (*0-8284-0175-6*) Chelsea Pub.

Bibliography of Nonparametric Statistics. I. Richard Savage. LC 62-11403. 294p. reprint ed. pap. 83.80 (*0-7837-5941-X*, 2045740) Bks Demand.

Bibliography of Nonsexist Supplementary Books (K-12) Northwest Regional Educational Laboratory, Center for Sex Equity Staff. LC 83-42838. 120p. 1984. pap. 32.50 (*0-89774-101-3*) Oryx Pr.

Bibliography of North American Gasteromycetes I: Phalales. W. R. Burk. 200p. 1981. pap. text ed. 30.00 (*3-7682-1262-9*) Lubrecht & Cramer.

Bibliography of North American Indian Mental Health. Comp. by Dianne R. Kelso & Carolyn L. Attneave. LC 81-800. (Illus.). 404p. 1981. text ed. 55.00 (*0-313-22930-9*, KEB/, Greenwood Pr) Greenwood.

Bibliography of North Carolina, 1589-1956. Comp. by Mary L. Thornton. LC 73-441. 597p. 1973. reprint ed. text ed. 38.50 (*0-8371-6765-5*, THNC, Greenwood Pr) Greenwood.

Bibliography of Nursing Literature 1859-1960: With an Historical Introduction. Ed. by Alice M. Thompson. LC 68-141603. 152p. reprint ed. pap. 43.40 (*0-7837-7008-1*, 2046822) Bks Demand.

Bibliography of Nursing Literature, 1961-1970. Ed. by Alice M. Thompson. LC 75-311186. 237p. reprint ed. pap. 67.60 (*0-7837-7009-X*, 2046823) Bks Demand.

Bibliography of Ohio Botany. Ethel M. Miller. (Bulletin Ser.: No. 27). 1932. 3.00 (*0-86727-026-8*) Ohio Bio Survey.

Bibliography of Ohio Zoology. Herbert Osborn. (Bulletin Ser.: No. 23). 1930. 2.00 (*0-86727-022-5*) Ohio Bio Survey.

Bibliography of Old Catalan Texts. Beatrice J. Concheff. (Bibliographical Ser.: No. 5). xii, 176p. 1985. 15.00 (*0-942260-66-X*) Hispanic Seminary.

Bibliography of Old French Lyrics. Robert W. Linker. LC 79-11948. (Romance Monographs: No. 31). 1979. 52.00 (*84-499-2809-5*) Romance.

Bibliography of Old Norse-Icelandic Romances. Comp. by Marianne E. Kalinke & P. M. Mitchell. LC 84-45810. (Islandica Ser.). 192p. (C). 1985. 39.95 (*0-8014-1681-7*) Cornell U Pr.

Bibliography of Old Time Saddlemakers. Mark L. Nelson. 98p. (Orig.). 1992. pap. 20.00 (*0-9632094-1-8*) Nelson Pub.

Bibliography of Oliver Wendell Holmes. Thomas F. Currier. Ed. by Eleanor M. Tilton. LC 53-11420. 708p. reprint ed. pap. 180.00 (*0-8357-7198-9*, 2050257) Bks Demand.

Bibliography of Onchocerciasis. R. Muller. 292p. (Orig.). 1987. pap. text ed. 69.00 (*0-85198-604-8*) CAB Intl.

Bibliography of or about Theador Billroth: And His Pupils. Karel B. Absolon. (Illus.). 68p. (C). pap. 10.50 (*0-685-71326-1*) KABEL Pubs.

Bibliography of or about Theador Billroth: And His Pupils. Karel B. Absolon. (Illus.). 68p. (C). 1994. pap. text ed. 12.50 (*0-930329-73-2*) KABEL Pubs.

***Bibliography of Organization Development Literature.** Ed. by Glenn H. Varney & Allan K. Foss. LC 94-78876. 157p. 1994. reprint ed. pap. 20.00 (*1-56286-013-5*) Am Soc Train & Devel.

Bibliography of Original Meaning of the United States Constitution. 1990. lib. bdg. 79.00 (*0-8490-4045-0*) Gordon Pr.

Bibliography of Oscar Wilde, 2 vols. Stuart Mason. LC 75-184647. (Reference Ser.: No. 44). 607p. 1972. reprint ed. lib. bdg. 150.00 (*0-8383-1378-7*) M S G Haskell Hse.

Bibliography of Pacific Area Maps. Clifford H. Macfadden. LC 75-30119. (International Research Series of the Institute of Pacific Relations). 1976. reprint ed. 22.50 (*0-404-59542-1*) AMS Pr.

Bibliography of Pamphlets Relating to Calvin Coolidge. J. R. Greene. (Illus.). 50p. (Orig.). (C). 1989. pap. 9.95 (*0-9609404-8-0*) J R Greene.

Bibliography of Pennsylvania History: A Supplement. Carol Wall. LC 77-624218. 252p. 1976. 8.95 (*0-911124-90-X*) Pa Hist & Mus.

Bibliography of Periodical Literature in Musicology & Allied Fields, No. 1 & 2. D. H. Daugherty et al. LC 71-177974. 148p. 1971. reprint ed. lib. bdg. 39.50 (*0-306-70413-7*) Da Capo.

Bibliography of Periodicals on the Quality of Working Life. (Conditions of Work Digest Ser.: Vol. 2, No. 1). x, 88p. 1983. pap. 12.00 (*92-2-103475-5*) Intl Labour Office.

Bibliography of Persia. Arnold T. Wilson. 1976. lib. bdg. 59.95 (*0-8490-1500-6*) Gordon Pr.

Bibliography of Petroleum Dictionaries. Charles M. Stacy. 35p. (Orig.). 1984. 9.75 (*0-916409-00-7*) Specialized Intl Biblio.

Bibliography of Philippine Linguistics & Minor Languages: With Annotations & Indices Based on Works in the Library of Cornell University. Jack H. Ward. LC 73-161419. (Cornell University, Southeast Asia Program, Data Paper Ser.: No. 83). 555p. reprint ed. pap. 158.20 (*0-8357-3674-1*, 2036399) Bks Demand.

Bibliography of Philosophical Bibliographies. Ed. by Herbert Guerry. LC 77-71862. 332p. 1977. text ed. 69.50 (*0-8371-9542-X*, GUC/, Greenwood Pr) Greenwood.

Bibliography of Picaresque Literature: Supplement. Joseph L. Laurenti. LC 79-8635. 1981. 32.50 (*0-404-18018-3*) AMS Pr.

Bibliography of Planned Languages (Excluding Esperanto) Richard K. Harrison. LC 92-90270. 60p. (Orig.). 1992. pap. write for info. (*0-9633073-0-4*) R K Harrison.

Bibliography of Plant Viruses & Index to Research. Ed. by Helen P. Beale. LC 73-3200. 1495p. 1976. text ed. 172.00 (*0-231-03763-5*) Col U Pr.

Bibliography of Printed Items Relating to the City of Lincoln. Comp. by D. Mary Short. (Lincoln Record Society Ser.: No. 79). 480p. 1990. 39.00 (*0-901503-52-5*) Boydell & Brewer.

Bibliography of Programmed Instruction & Computer-Assisted Instruction. Ed. & Comp. by Taher A. Razik. LC 76-125875. (Educational Technology Bibliography Ser.: Vol.1). 288p. 1971. 34.95 (*0-87778-013-7*) Educ Tech Pubns.

Bibliography of Psychological & Experimental Aesthetics, Eighteen Sixty-Four to Nineteen Thirty-Seven. Albert R. Chandler & Edward N. Barnhart. LC 75-3111. reprint ed. 45.00 (*0-404-59107-8*) AMS Pr.

Bibliography of PTSM Literature: Update No. 1. 16p. 1985. 20.00 (*0-86688-086-0*, PTSM-750) Joint Comm Hlthcare.

***Bibliography of Publications: Technical Department, Africa Region, July 1987 to April 1994.** Ed. by P. C. Mohan. (Technical Paper Ser.: No. 255). 54p. 1994. 6.95 (*0-8213-2972-3*, 12972) World Bank.

Bibliography of Publications: Technical Department, Africa Region, July 1987 to December 1992. Ed. by P. C. Mohan. (Technical Paper Ser.: No. 218). 48p. 1993. 6.95 (*0-8213-2513-2*, 12513) World Bank.

Bibliography of Publications by the Faculty, Staff, & Students of the University of California, 1876-1980, on Grapes, Wines & Related Subjects. Ed. by Herman J. Phaff. (UC Publications in Catalogs & Bibliographies: Vol. 2). 1986. 45.00 (*0-520-09702-5*) U CA Pr.

Bibliography of Publications on Old English Literature to the End of 1972: The Collection of E. E. Ericson. Stanley B. Greenfeld & Fred C. Robinson. LC 78-4989. 461p. reprint ed. pap. 131.40 (*0-8357-7199-7*, 2056139) Bks Demand.

Bibliography of Publications Prepared by U. S. Geological Survey Personnel under Cooperative Programs with the U. S. Department of Energy, 1957-1991, with Emphasis on Nuclear Testing Programs. Ed. by V. M. Glanzman. 83p. (Orig.). (C). 1993. pap. text ed. 30.00 (*1-56806-491-8*) Diane Pub.

Bibliography of Published Articles on American Presbyterianism, 1901-1980. Comp. by Harold M. Parker, Jr. LC 85-7987. (Bibliographies & Indexes in Religious Studies: No. 4). xv, 261p. 1985. text ed. 55.00 (*0-313-24544-4*, PBP/, Greenwood Pr) Greenwood.

Bibliography of Published Genealogical Source Records, Prince George's County, MD. rev. ed. Ed. by Jean A. Sargent. 28p. 1988. pap. 2.00 (*0-318-35306-7*) Prince Georges County Gen Soc.

Bibliography of Published Genealogical Sources, Prince Georges's County, Maryland. rev. ed. Ed. by Jean A. Sargent. 1986. 2.00 (*0-685-10510-5*) Prince Georges County Gen Soc.

Bibliography of Published Research of the World Employment Programme. 9th ed. (International Labour Bibliography Ser.: No. 9). xi, 129p. 1991. 14.00 (*92-2-107746-2*) Intl Labour Office.

***Bibliography of Published Studies Using the Child Behavior Checklist & Related Materials, 1994.** rev. ed. Jill S. Brown & Thomas M. Achenbach. 120p. 1994. disk 40.00 (*0-938565-35-4*) U of VT Psych.

***Bibliography of Published Studies Using the Child Behavior Checklist & Related Materials, 1994.** rev. ed. Jill S. Brown & Thomas M. Achenbach. 125p. 1995. pap. text ed. 45.00 (*0-938565-37-0*) U of VT Psych.

Bibliography of Published Works by Kenneth E. Boulding. Vivian L. Wilson. LC 82-74149. 118p. reprint ed. pap. 33.70 (*0-8357-5530-4*, 2035143) Bks Demand.

Bibliography of Quabbin Valley History. J. R. Greene. 44p. (Orig.). 1992. pap. 10.00 (*0-9609404-9-9*) J R Greene.

***Bibliography of Quantitative Linguistics.** Reinhard Kohler & Christiane Hoffman. LC 95-15252. (Library & Information Sources in Linguistics: No. 25). 800p. 1995. lib. bdg. 135.00 (*1-55619-255-X*) Benjamins North Am.

Bibliography of Quantitative Studies on Science & Its History. Roger Hahn. LC 79-65637. (Berkeley Papers in History of Science: No. 3). (Orig.). 1980. pap. 5.00 (*0-918102-04-9*) U Cal Hist Sci Tech.

Bibliography of Quincy Wright, 1890-1970: Professor of International Law, University of Chicago, 1931-1956. Comp. by Louise Wright. LC 78-110788. 1974. 8.00 (*0-931222-08-7*) Pitts Theolog.

Bibliography of Recreational Mathematics, Vol. 2. William L. Schaaf. LC 73-12168. 1970. pap. 6.00 (*0-87353-022-5*) NCTM.

Bibliography of References to Rice Field Aquatic Fauna, Their Ecology & Rice-Fish Culture. C. H. Fernando & Constantine Herbert. Ed. by Herman S. Forest. 1993. 2.00 (*1-883641-01-2*) St U NY Geneseo.

Bibliography of Religion in the South. Charles H. Lippy. LC 85-13575. xvi, 498p. 1985. text ed. 49.95 (*0-86554-161-2*, MUP-H151) Mercer Univ Pr.

Bibliography of Repeat Photography for Evaluating Landscape Change. Garry F. Rogers et al. LC 84-23437. (Illus.). 215p. reprint ed. pap. 61.30 (*0-7837-6867-2*, 2046697) Bks Demand.

Bibliography of Research in Library & Information Science in India. Vijay Pathak & L. S. Ramaiah. 1986. 18.00 (*0-8364-1827-1*, Pub. by Indian Doc Serv II) S Asia.

Bibliography of Research Studies in Music Education, 1932-48. Music Education Research Council Staff. 119p. 1993. reprint ed. lib. bdg. 69.00 (*0-7812-9685-4*) Rprt Serv.

Bibliography of Riddles. A. Taylor. 1972. 59.95 (*0-87968-739-8*) Gordon Pr.

Bibliography of Robert Bridges. McKay. 1972. 59.95 (*0-87968-740-1*) Gordon Pr.

Bibliography of Robert Bridges. George L. McKay. LC 33-31729. reprint ed. 9.00 (*0-404-04132-9*) AMS Pr.

Bibliography of Rockbursts 1900-1979, Pt. I. I. M. Petukhov & I. M. Batugina. 308p. (C). 1991. text ed. 135.00 (*90-6191-177-X*, Pub. by A A Balkema NE) Ashgate Pub Co.

Bibliography of Salon Criticism from the July Monarchy to the Second Republic, 1831-1851, Vol. 2. Ed. by Neil McWilliam. (Studies in the History of Art). 300p. (C). 1991. 15.00 (*0-521-40091-0*) Cambridge U Pr.

Bibliography of Salon Criticism in Paris from the Ancien Regime to the Restoration, 1699-1827, Vol. 1. Ed. by Neil McWilliam. (Studies in the History of Art). 275p. (C). 1991. 15.00 (*0-521-34634-7*) Cambridge U Pr.

Bibliography of Salvation Army Literature in English, 1865-1987: Mightier than the Sword. R. G. Moyles. LC 88-8964. (Texts & Studies in Religion: Vol. 38). 250p. 1988. lib. bdg. 89.95 (*0-88946-827-3*) E Mellen.

Bibliography of Samuel Johnson. With Johnson Bibliography, a Supplement to Courtney. William P. Courtney & David N. Smith. Ed. by R. W. Chapman. 256p. 1984. reprint ed. 55.00 (*0-938768-11-5*) Oak Knoll.

Bibliography of Schlicht Functions. S. D. Bernardi. 363p. 1982. 15.00 (*0-936166-09-6*) Polygonal Pub.

Bibliography of Scholarly Literature on Colonial Louisiana & New France. Carl A. Brasseaux & Glenn R. Conrad. 430p. (C). 1992. text ed. 20.00 (*0-940984-73-3*) U of SW LA Ctr LA Studies.

Bibliography of Scholarship on Plautus. J. D. Hughes. 154p. 1975. pap. text ed. 42.00 (*0-317-54429-2*, Pub. by A M Hakkert SP) Coronet Bks.

Bibliography of Seeds. Ed. by Lela V. Barton. LC 66-20492. 858p. 1967. text ed. 127.50 (*0-231-02937-3*) Col U Pr.

Bibliography of Selected Computer Security Publications. 1992. lib. bdg. 88.95 (*0-8490-5542-3*) Gordon Pr.

Bibliography of Selected Contemporary Rhode Island Authors. Jeanne L. Richardson. Ed. by Carolyn M. Schneider. 33p. 1984. pap. 2.00 (*0-917012-70-4*) RI Pubns Soc.

Bibliography of Selected Topics in Economic Development Literature, 1987-1993. Ed. by Ronald J. Swager. 138p. (Orig.). 1994. pap. 45.00 (*0-9616567-6-X*) Amer Econ Dev Council.

Bibliography of Semiological & Structural Studies of Religion. Alfred M. Johnson. LC 79-110955. 1979. 10.00 (*0-931222-10-9*) Pitts Theolog.

Bibliography of Semiotics, 1975-1985, 2 vols., 1. Ed. by Viktoria Eschbach-Szabo. LC 86-26830. (Library & Information Sources in Linguistics: Vol. 16). 950p. 1986. 162.00 (*90-272-3740-9*) Benjamins North Am.

Bibliography of Semiotics, 1975-1985, 2 vols., 2. Ed. by Viktoria Eschbach-Szabo. LC 86-26830. (Library & Information Sources in Linguistics: Vol. 16). 950p. 1986. 227.00 (*90-272-3741-7*) Benjamins North Am.

Bibliography of Semiotics, 1975-1985, 2 vols., Set. Ed. by Viktoria Eschbach-Szabo. LC 86-26830. (Library & Information Sources in Linguistics: Vol. 16). 950p. 1986. 227.00 (*90-272-3739-5*) Benjamins North Am.

Bibliography of Seventeenth-Century French Prose Fiction. Ralph W. Baldner. LC 67-28711. xiv, 197p. 1967. 37.50 (*0-87352-016-5*, Z0030) Modern Lang.

Bibliography of Sex Rites & Customs. Roger Goodland. LC 72-9839. reprint ed. 42.50 (*0-404-57445-9*) AMS Pr.

Bibliography of Sierra Leone, Nineteen Twenty-Five to Nineteen Sixty-Seven. Geoffrey J. Williams. LC 74-80858. (African Bibliography Ser.: Vol. 1). 216p. 1971. 32.50 (*0-8419-0022-1*, Africana) Holmes & Meier.

Bibliography of Skiing Studies. 8th ed. Charles R. Goeldner & Andy Dudiak. 139p. 1989. pap. text ed. 25.00 (*0-89478-009-3*) U CO Busn Res Div.

Bibliography of Slavic Mythology. Mark Kulikowski. 137p. 1989. 19.95 (*0-89357-203-9*) Slavica.

Bibliography of Social Networks, Nos. 1170-1171. Linton C. Freeman. 1976. 12.50 (*0-686-20415-8*) CPL Biblios.

Bibliography of Social Surveys. Allen Eaton & Shelby H. Harrison. LC 75-17218. (Social Problems & Social Policy Ser.). 1976. reprint ed. 42.95 (*0-405-07489-1*) Ayer.

Bibliography of Soil Taxonomy, 1960-1979. Ed. by G. D. Bailey. 194p. (Orig.). 1987. pap. text ed. 27.00 (*0-85198-588-2*) CAB Intl.

Bibliography of Songsters Printed in America Before 1821. Irving Lowens. LC 75-5021. 1976. 25.00 (*0-912296-05-4*, U Pr of Va) Am Antiquarian.

Bibliography of Sources in Christianity & the Arts. Daven M. Kari. LC 94-9769. (Studies in Art & Religious Interpretation: Vol. 16). 780p. 1995. 139.95 (*0-7734-9094-9*) E Mellen.

Bibliography of Sources on Yugoslavia. Rusko Matulic. LC 80-53861. 260p. 1981. per. 18.00 (*0-918660-13-0*) Ragusan Pr.

Bibliography of South Asia. David N. Nelson. LC 94-613. (Area Bibliographies Ser.: No. 4). 484p. 1994. text ed. 52.50 (*0-8108-2854-5*) Scarecrow.

Bibliography of South Dakota Government. Loren M. Carlson. 1951. 5.00 (*1-55614-024-X*) U of SD Gov Res Bur.

Bibliography of South Dakota Government & Politics. Alan L. Clem & George M. Platt. 1965. 5.00 (*1-55614-023-1*) U of SD Gov Res Bur.

Bibliography of Soy Fiber - Okara (Soymilk Pulp), Soy Bran (Ground Hulls), & Soy Isolate Fiber: 468 References from 1716 to 1989, Partially Annotated. Ed. by Akiko Aoyagi. (Bibliographies of Soya Ser.). 105p. (Orig.). 1989. spiral bd., pap. 53.00 (*0-933332-64-5*) Soyfoods Center.

Bibliography of Soy Flour & Cereal-Soy Blends: 3,085 References from 3rd Century B.C. to 1990, Extensively Annotated. Ed. by Akiko Aoyagi. (Bibliographies of Soya Ser.). 427p. (Orig.). 1990. spiral bd., pap. 213.00 (*0-933332-66-1*) Soyfoods Center.

Bibliography of Soy Ice Cream, Yogurt, & Cheese: 1,071 References from 1910 to 1989. Ed. by Akiko Aoyagi. (Bibliographies of Soya Ser.). 209p. (Orig.). 1989. spiral bd. 105.00 (*0-933332-53-X*) Soyfoods Center.

Bibliography of Soy Protein Isolates, Concentrates, & Textured Soy Protein Products: 2,528 References from 1883 to 1989. Ed. by Akiko Aoyagi. (Bibliographies of Soya Ser.). 328p. (Orig.). 1989. spiral bd. 164.00 (*0-933332-63-7*) Soyfoods Center.

Bibliography of Soy Sauce, Shoyu, & Tamari, from A. D. 535 to 1988: 2,150 Plus References from A. D. 535 to 1988. Ed. by Akiko Aoyagi. (Bibliographies of Soya Ser.). 204p. (Orig.). 1989. spiral bd., pap. 132.00 (*0-933332-45-9*) Soyfoods Center.

Bibliography of Soy Sprouts: 655 References from 3rd Century A.D. to 1991. Ed. by Akiko Aoyagi. 185p. (Orig.). 1991. spiral bd. 92.00 (*0-933332-76-9*) Soyfoods Center.

Bibliography of Soya in Africa: 736 References from 1881 to 1989. Ed. by Akiko Aoyagi. (Bibliographies of Soya Ser.). 125p. (Orig.). 1989. spiral bd. 62.00 (*0-933332-59-9*) Soyfoods Center.

Bibliography of Soya in Latin America: 1,520 References from 1880 to 1989. Ed. by Akiko Aoyagi. (Bibliographies of Soya Ser.). 215p. (Orig.). 1989. spiral bd. 108.00 (*0-933332-62-9*) Soyfoods Center.

Bibliography of Soya in the Indian Subcontinent (South Asia) 1,118 References from 1679 to 1989. Ed. by Akiko Aoyagi. (Bibliographies of Soya Ser.). 180p. (Orig.). 1989. spiral bd. 90.00 (*0-933332-61-0*) Soyfoods Center.

Bibliography of Soya Nutrition, Biochemistry, & Medicinal Uses: 5,456 References from 200 B.C. to 1991, Extensively Annotated. Ed. by Akiko Aoyagi. 800p. (Orig.). 1991. spiral bd., pap. 399.00 (*0-933332-75-0*) Soyfoods Center.

Bibliography of Soybean Crushing, Soy Oil, & Soybean Meal: 4,183 References from A.D. 980 to 1990, Extensively Annotated. Ed. by Akiko Aoyagi. (Bibliographies of Soya Ser.). 647p. (Orig.). 1990. spiral bd., pap. 324.00 (*0-933332-74-2*) Soyfoods Center.

Bibliography of Soybean Cultural Practices, Harvesting, & Storage: 2,108 References from 120 B. C. to 1990. Ed. by Akiko Aoyagi. (Bibliographies of Soya Ser.). 286p. (Orig.). 1990. spiral bd., pap. 148.00 (*0-933332-68-8*) Soyfoods Center.

Bibliography of Soybean Varietal Development, Breeding, Genetics, & Biotechnology: 1,601 References from 1804 to 1990. Ed. by Akiko Aoyagi. (Bibliographies of Soya Ser.). 256p. (Orig.). 1990. spiral bd., pap. 134.00 (*0-933332-69-6*) Soyfoods Center.

Bibliography of Soymilk & Soymilk Products: 2,612 References from A. D. 1500 to 1989. Ed. by Akiko Aoyagi. (Bibliographies of Soybeans & Soyfoods Ser.). 323p. (Orig.). 1989. pap. text ed., spiral bd. 162.00 (*0-933332-49-1*) Soyfoods Center.

Bibliography of Sporting Books. John C. Phillips. 639p. 1991. 75.00 (*1-882860-00-4*) J Cummins Bksell.

Bibliography of Stained Glass. David Evans. 214p. 1982. 100.00 (*0-85991-087-3*) Boydell & Brewer.

Bibliography of State Land Resources Planning, Nineteen Seventy to Nineteen Seventy-Five: Indexed by State-Topic-Year-Agency, Nos. 848-850. David Hess. 1975. 12.50 (*0-686-20365-8*) CPL Biblios.

Bibliography of State Land Resources Planning, Nineteen Sixty to Nineteen Seventy-Four: Indexed by Year, Topic, State & Agency, Nos. 769-771. Ed. by David Hess. 1975. 12.50 (*0-686-20347-X*) CPL Biblios.

Bibliography of State of Ohio, Vols. I & II. Peter G. Thomson. 490p. 1993. reprint ed. lib. bdg. 49.50 (*0-8328-2836-X*) Higginson Bk Co.

Bibliography of Statistical Bibliographies. H. O. Lancaster. 1968. 18.00 (*0-934454-12-4*) Lubrecht & Cramer.

Bibliography of Statistical Literature, Set. Maurice Kendall & Alison G. Doig. 1981. reprint ed. lib. bdg. 82.95 (*0-405-13881-4*) Ayer.

Bibliography of Statistical Literature, Vol. I: 1950 to 1958. Maurice Kendall & Alison G. Doig. 1981. reprint ed. Vol. I, 1950 To 1958. write for info. (*0-318-50792-7*) Ayer.

Bibliography of Statistical Literature, Vol. II: 1940 to 1949. Maurice Kendall & Alison G. Doig. 1981. reprint ed. Vol. II, 1940 To 1949. write for info. (*0-318-50793-5*) Ayer.

Bibliography of Statistical Literature, Vol. III: Pre-1940. Maurice Kendall & Alison G. Doig. 1981. reprint ed. Vol. III, Pre-1940. write for info. (*0-318-50794-3*) Ayer.

Bibliography of Steel Columns. ASCE Committee on Compression Members Staff. 214p. 1990. pap. text ed. 20.00 (*0-87262-780-2*) Am Soc Civil Eng.

An Asterisk (*) at the beginning of an entry indicates that the title is appearing in BIP for the first time.

Bibliography of Studies & Translations of Modern Chinese Literature 1918-1942. Donald A. Gibbs et al. (East Asian Monographs: No. 61). 400p. 1975. 26.00 (*0-674-07111-5*) HUP.

Bibliography of Studies in Metaphysical Poetry, Nineteen Thirty-Nine to Nineteen Sixty. Ed. by Lloyd E. Berry. 112p. 1964. 25.00 (*0-299-03120-9*) U of Wis Pr.

Bibliography of Studies on Hindi Language & Linguistics. 2nd rev. ed. Narindar K. Aggarwal. 1986. 36.00 (*0-317-47418-9*, Pub. by Indian Doc Serv II) S Asia.

Bibliography of Stylistics & Related Criticism, 1967-1983. James R. Bennett. LC 85-25867. 405p. 1986. 37.50 (*0-87352-142-0*); pap. text ed. 19.75 (*0-87352-143-9*) Modern Lang.

Bibliography of Sun Yat-sen in China's Republican Revolution, 1885-1925. Ed. by Sidney H. Chang & Leonard H. Gordon. 374p. (Orig.). (C). 1990. lib. bdg. 63.00 (*0-8191-7961-2*) U Pr of Amer.

Bibliography of Swift Studies, 1945-1965. James J. Stathis. LC 67-17563. 122p. reprint ed. pap. 34.80 (*0-8357-3262-2*, 2039483) Bks Demand.

***Bibliography of Syrian Archaeological Sites to 1980.** Howard C. Bybee & Conrad L'Heureux. LC 94-26074. 248p. 1995. text ed. 89.95 (*0-7734-9040-X*) E Mellen.

Bibliography of Targum Literature, Vol. 1. B. Grossfeld. 1972. 49.50 (*0-685-02910-7*) Ktav.

Bibliography of Targum Literature, Vol. III. Bernard Grossfeld. xx, 92p. 1990. text ed. 39.95 (*0-87203-132-2*) Hermon.

Bibliography of Taxonomic Literature 1753-1821. D. H. Pfister et al. (Mycologia Memoirs Ser.: No. 17). 162p. 1991. pap. text ed. 55.00 (*3-443-76007-4*, Pub. by Cramer-Borntraeger GW) Lubrecht & Cramer.

Bibliography of Telecommunication Socio-Economic Development. Heather Hudson. 234p. 1988. text ed. 29.00 (*0-89006-288-9*) Artech Hse.

Bibliography of Tennyson. Richard Shepherd. LC 73-116802. (Studies in Tennyson: No. 27). 1970. reprint ed. lib. bdg. 39.95 (*0-8383-1044-3*) M S G Haskell Hse.

Bibliography of Texas Government & Politics. Arnold Fleischmann et al. (Policy Research Institute Ser.: No. 2). 106p. 1985. 10.00 (*0-89940-151-1*) LBJ Sch Pub Aff.

Bibliography of Texas, Seventeen Ninety-Five to Eighteen Forty-Five. 2nd rev. ed. Thomas Streeter. Ed. by Archibald Hanna. 584p. 1983. 290.00 (*0-89235-060-1*) Res Pubns CT.

***Bibliography of the Algonquian Languages.** James C. Pilling. (Bureau of American Ethnology Bulletins Ser.). 614p. 1995. lib. bdg. 149.00 (*0-7812-4013-1*) Rprt Serv.

Bibliography of the Algonquian Languages, 2 pts. James C. Pilling. 1988. reprint ed. lib. bdg. 75.00 (*0-7812-0312-0*) Rprt Serv.

Bibliography of the Amarna Period: The Reigns of Akhenaten Smenkhkare, Tutankhamun & Ay. Geoffrey T. Martin. (Studies in Egyptology). 120p. (C). 1991. text ed. 55.00 (*0-7103-0413-7*, A5621, Pub. by Kegan Paul Intl UK) Routledge Chapman & Hall.

Bibliography of the American Theatre, Excluding New York City. Carl J. Stratman. LC 65-3359. 413p. reprint ed. pap. 117.80 (*0-8357-7200-4*, 2002956) Bks Demand.

Bibliography of the Ashendene Press, Eighteen Ninety Five to Nineteen Thirty-Five. St. John Hornby. (Illus.). 224p. 1976. 150.00 (*0-915346-11-7*) A Wofsy Fine Arts.

***Bibliography of the Athapascan Languages.** James C. Pilling. (Bureau of American Ethnology Bulletins Ser.). 125p. 1995. lib. bdg. 79.00 (*0-7812-4014-X*) Rprt Serv.

Bibliography of the Bacon-Shakespeare Controversy. William H. Wyman. LC 71-178379. reprint ed. 32.50 (*0-404-07065-5*) AMS Pr.

Bibliography of the Black Sparrow Press 1966-1978. Bradford Morrow & Seamus Cooney. LC 80-24229. (Illus.). 302p. 1981. 40.00 (*0-87685-465-X*) Black Sparrow.

Bibliography of the Blackfoot. Hugh A. Dempsey & Lindsay Moir. LC 89-6444. (Native American Bibliography Ser.: No. 13). 255p. 1989. 27.50 (*0-8108-2211-3*) Scarecrow.

Bibliography of the British Coal Industry. John Benson. Ed. by Robert Neville & Charles Thompson. 1982. 120.00 (*0-19-920120-X*) OUP.

Bibliography of the Catawba. Thomas J. Blumer. (Native American Bibliography Ser.). 575p. 1987. 59.50 (*0-8108-1986-4*) Scarecrow.

Bibliography of the Chickasaw. Anne K. Hoyt. LC 87-4871. (Native American Bibliography Ser.: No. 11). 230p. 1987. 25.00 (*0-8108-1995-3*) Scarecrow.

***Bibliography of the Chinookan Languages, Including the Chinook Jargon.** James C. Pilling. (Bureau of American Ethnology Bulletins Ser.). 81p. 1995. lib. bdg. 79.00 (*0-7812-4015-8*) Rprt Serv.

Bibliography of the Collective Biography of Spanish America. Josefina Del Toro. 1976. lib. bdg. 59.95 (*0-87968-741-X*) Gordon Pr.

Bibliography of the Communist International 1919-1979, Vol. 1. Ed. by Vilem Kahan. LC 90-2678. 400p. (ENG, FRE, GER, ITA, POR, RUS & SPA.). 1990. 100.00 (*90-04-09320-6*) E J Brill.

Bibliography of the Computer in Environmental Design, 3 Vols., Set. 2nd ed. Ed. by Kaiman Lee. LC 73-158197. 650p. 1973. 110.00 (*0-915250-03-9*) Environ Design.

Bibliography of the County Histories of Alabama. Ed. by Robert D. Ward & William W. Rogers. 45p. 1991. lib. bdg. 12.00 (*0-942301-19-6*) Birm Pub Lib.

Bibliography of the Dance Collection of Doris Niles & Serge Leslie: A-Z, Pt. 4. Serge Leslie. 283p. 1981. 59.95 (*0-903102-56-0*, Pub. by Dance Bks UK) Princeton Bk Co.

Bibliography of the English Colonial Treaties with the American Indians. Henry F. De Puy. LC 78-164820. reprint ed. 27.50 (*0-404-07123-6*) AMS Pr.

Bibliography of the English Colonial Treaties with the American Indians. Henry F. De Puy. 1988. reprint ed. lib. bdg. 59.00 (*0-7812-0049-0*) Rprt Serv.

Bibliography of the English Colonial Treaties with the American Indians. Henry F. De Puy. LC 78-108471. 1917. reprint ed. 23.00 (*0-403-00425-X*) Scholarly.

***Bibliography of the Eskimo Languages.** James C. Pilling. (Bureau of American Ethnology Bulletins Ser.). 161p. 1995. lib. bdg. 79.00 (*0-7812-4001-8*) Rprt Serv.

Bibliography of the Federation of Riding for the Disabled International. Pref. by Barbara T. Engel. 95p. (Orig.). 1994. pap. text ed. 25.00 (*0-9633065-4-5*) B E Therapy.

Bibliography of the First Editions in Book Form of the Writings of Henry Wadsworth Longfellow. Jacob C. Chamberlain. LC 72-3116. (American Literature Ser.: No. 49). 1972. reprint ed. lib. bdg. 49.95 (*0-8383-1513-5*) M S G Haskell Hse.

Bibliography of the Foulis Press. 2nd ed. Philip Gaskell. 484p. 1986. reprint ed. 36.00 (*0-906795-13-3*) Oak Knoll.

Bibliography of the Fowler Architectural Collection of the Johns Hopkins University. Laurence H. Fowler & Elizabeth Baer. (Illus.). 429p. 1991. 150.00 (*1-55660-128-X*) A Wofsy Fine Arts.

***Bibliography of the Frederick Douglass Library at Cedar Hall.** William L. Petrie & Douglas E. Stover. (Illus.). 496p. (Orig.). 1995. pap. 30.00 (*1-887188-00-2*) Silesia Cos.

Bibliography of the French in India. Henry Scholberg & Emmanuel Divien. 216p. (C). 1975. lib. bdg. 12.50 (*0-88253-738-5*) Ind-US Inc.

Bibliography of the Gehenna Press, 1942-1975. 2nd ed. Stephen Brook. 1976. 40.00 (*0-686-18219-7*) J P Dwyer.

Bibliography of the Giant Clams. Ed. by J. L. Munro & W. J. Nash. (Bibliographies Ser.: No. 5). 26p. 1986. pap. 4.50 (*971-10-2222-2*, Pub. by ICLARM PH) Intl Spec Bk.

Bibliography of the Golden Cockerel Press, Nineteen Twenty-One to Nineteen Forty-Nine. LC 75-14604. 1975. boxed 150.00 (*0-915346-46-X*) A Wofsy Fine Arts.

Bibliography of the Grabhorn Press, Nineteen Fifteen to Nineteen Fifty-Six. David Magee. LC 75-14603. 1975. 150.00 (*0-915346-04-4*) A Wofsy Fine Arts.

Bibliography of the Grand Canyon & the Lower Colorado River, from 1540. E. Spamer. LC 90-82533. 360p. 1990. 25.00 (*0-938216-37-6*) GCNHA.

Bibliography of the Helminth Parasites of New Zealand. A. S. Baker. 79p. (Orig.). 1973. pap. text ed. 19.00 (*0-85198-265-4*) CAB Intl.

Bibliography of the History & Organisation of Horse Racing & Thoroughbred Breeding in Great Britain & Ireland. Ed. by Eileen P. Loder. 352p. 1990. 110.00 (*0-85131-297-7*, Pub. by J A Allen & Co UK) St Mut.

***Bibliography of the History of British Metal Mining.** R. Burt & P. Waite. 189p. 1988. 75.00x (*0-85989-319-7*, Pub. by Northern Mine Res UK) St Mut.

Bibliography of the History of California, 3 vols. Robert E. Cowan. 1992. reprint ed. lib. bdg. 225.00 (*0-7812-5019-6*) Rprt Serv.

Bibliography of the History of Medicine. 1992. lib. bdg. 88.00 (*0-8490-5256-4*) Gordon Pr.

Bibliography of the History of Medicine, No. 25: 1985-1989. National Institutes of Health, Health & Human Services Dept. Staff. 1464p. 1990. text ed. 25.00 (*0-16-026803-6*) USGPO.

Bibliography of the History of Medicine of the United States & Canada, 1939-1960. Genevieve Miller. 1979. 37.95 (*0-405-10616-5*) Ayer.

Bibliography of the History of Music Theory. 2nd ed. David R. Williams. (C). 1971. pap. 19.00 (*0-918194-08-3*) Accura.

Bibliography of the History of Printing in the Library of Congress, Vol. 1. Pref. by Horace Hart. 466p. 1987. 139.00 (*0-9622165-1-8*); ring bd. write for info. (*0-9622165-0-X*) H Hart Pub.

Bibliography of the History of Printing in the Library of Congress, Vol. 2. Pref. by Horace Hart & Philip A. Harriman. 1990. write for info. (*0-9622165-2-6*) H Hart Pub.

Bibliography of the Icelandic Sagas & Minor Tales. Halldor Hermannsson. LC 08-19528. (Islandica Ser.: Vol. 1). 1908. 20.00 (*0-527-00331-X*) Periodicals Srv.

***Bibliography of the International Conferences on Sino-Tibetan Languages & Linguistics I-XXV.** Randy J. LaPolla & John B. Lowe. Ed. by James A. Matisoff. LC 94-72182. (STEDT Monograph Ser.: 1A). 308p. (Orig.). (C). 1994. pap. text ed. 28.00 (*0-944613-22-5*) UC Berkeley Ctrs SE Asia.

Bibliography of the International Court of Justice, No. 41. (ENG & FRE.). pap. 5.00 (*0-685-13037-1*, ICJ/565) UN.

Bibliography of the International Court of Justice, No. 42. 1992. 5.00 (*0-685-52691-7*, ICJ/574) UN.

Bibliography of the International Court of Justice: 1989, No. 43. 360p. 1992. 5.00 (*0-685-52692-5*, ICJ/583) UN.

Bibliography of the Ionosphere: An Annotated Survey Through 1960. Laurence A. Manning. xvi, 613p. 1962. 69.50 (*0-8047-0125-3*) Stanford U Pr.

***Bibliography of the Iroquoian Languages.** James C. Pilling. (Bureau of American Ethnology Bulletins Ser.). 208p. 1995. lib. bdg. 89.00 (*0-7812-4006-9*) Rprt Serv.

Bibliography of the Kalenjin Peoples of East Africa. Robert E. Daniels et al. LC 87-31643. (Bibliographies in African Studies: No. 1). (Orig.). 1987. pap. 15.00 (*0-942615-03-4*) U Wis African Stud.

Bibliography of the Kelmscott Press. William S. Peterson. (Soho Bibliographies Ser.). (Illus.). 1984. 74.00 (*0-19-818199-X*) OUP.

Bibliography of the King's Book or Eikon Basilike. Susan Howe. 64p. 1989. 13.00 (*0-945926-13-8*) Paradigm RI.

Bibliography of the King's Book or Eikon Basilike. deluxe ed. Susan Howe. 64p. 1989. 30.00 (*0-945926-14-6*) Paradigm RI.

Bibliography of the Languages of Native California: Including Closely Related Languages of Adjacent Areas. William Bright. LC 82-3331. (Native American Bibliography Ser.: No. 3). 234p. 1982. 20.00 (*0-8108-1547-8*) Scarecrow.

Bibliography of the Laws & Resolves of the Massachusetts Bay: 1642-1780. Comp. by John D. Cushing. LC 83-82991. 372p. 1984. 60.00 (*0-89453-383-5*, 33835G) Scholarly Res Inc.

Bibliography of the Little Golden Books. Comp. by Dolores B. Jones. LC 86-27090. (Bibliographies & Indexes in American Literature Ser.: No. 7). 193p. 1987. text ed. 49.95 (*0-313-25025-1*, JBL/, Greenwood Pr) Greenwood.

Bibliography of the Major French Artist Books, 1867-1957: Les Peintres et Livre, 1867-1957. rev. ed. Nicolas Rauch. (Illus.). 228p. (FRE.). 1991. 100.00 (*1-55660-127-1*) A Wofsy Fine Arts.

Bibliography of the Manuscripts of Charlotte Bronte. Ed. by Christine Alexander. 205p. 1982. text ed. 59.95 (*0-313-27665-X*) Greenwood.

Bibliography of the Manuscripts of Patrick Branwell Bronte. Ed. by Victor A. Neufeldt. LC 93-8646. 184p. 1993. 52.00 (*0-8153-1563-5*) Garland.

Bibliography of the Musical Works Published by John Walsh During the Years 1695-1720. William C. Smith. 215p. 1993. reprint ed. lib. bdg. 79.00 (*0-7812-9701-X*) Rprt Serv.

***Bibliography of the Muskhogean Languages.** James C. Pilling. (Bureau of American Ethnology Bulletins Ser.). 114p. 1995. lib. bdg. 79.00 (*0-7812-4009-3*) Rprt Serv.

Bibliography of the Nature & Role of the Holy Spirit in Twentieth-Century Writings. Watson E. Mills. LC 93-22748. 372p. 1993. text ed. 99.95 (*0-7734-2366-4*, Mellen Biblical Pr) E Mellen.

Bibliography of the Navaho Indians. Clyde Kluckhohn & Katharine Spencer. LC 79-171546. reprint ed. 20.00 (*0-404-07134-1*) AMS Pr.

Bibliography of the Neutrino. B. Kuchowicz. 446p. 1967. text ed. 459.00 (*0-677-11490-7*) Gordon & Breach.

Bibliography of the Official Publications of Louisana, 1803-1934. Comp. by L. B. Foote. (Historical Records Survey Monographs: No. 19). 1972. reprint ed. 40.00 (*0-527-01916-X*) Periodicals Srv.

Bibliography of the Oil & Gas Industry 1980-1989. Ed. by Edward B. Deakin & James J. Cappell. 256p. 1990. pap. 25.00 (*0-926969-01-3*) UNTIPA.

Bibliography of the Osage. Terry P. Wilson. LC 85-2087. (Native American Bibliography Ser.: No. 6). 172p. 1985. 20.00 (*0-8108-1805-1*) Scarecrow.

Bibliography of the Periodical Works of Charles Dickens. T Hatton & A. H. Cleaver. LC 72-1271. (Studies in Dickens: No. 52). 1972. reprint ed. lib. bdg. 75.00 (*0-8383-1435-X*) M S G Haskell Hse.

Bibliography of the Philosophy of Science; Nineteen Forty-Five to Nineteen Eighty-One. Comp. by Richard J. Blackwell. LC 83-5671. xvii, 585p. 1983. text ed. 105.00 (*0-313-23124-9*, BLB/, Greenwood Pr) Greenwood.

Bibliography of the Philosophy of Technology. Carl Mitcham & Robert Mackey. LC 74-168204. 288p. reprint ed. pap. 82.10 (*0-8357-7201-2*, 2007277) Bks Demand.

Bibliography of the Prairie Provinces to Nineteen Fifty Three: With Biographical Index. 2nd ed. Comp. by Bruce Peel. LC 72-97930. 1973. 85.00 (*0-8020-1972-2*) U of Toronto Pr.

Bibliography of the Printed Works of C. W. Von Gluck, 1714-1787. 2nd ed. Cecil Hopkinson. (Illus.). 100p. 1967. lib. bdg. 50.00 (*0-8450-7001-0*) Broude.

Bibliography of the Published Works of Charles M. Russell. Karl Yost & Frederic G. Renner. LC 68-11567. 331p. reprint ed. pap. 94.40 (*0-8357-7202-0*, 2024937) Bks Demand.

Bibliography of the Romance & Related Forms in Spanish America. Merle E. Simmons. LC 72-6210. 396p. 1972. reprint ed. text ed. 38.50 (*0-8371-6478-8*, SIBR, Greenwood Pr) Greenwood.

Bibliography of the "Rubaiyat" of Omar Khayyam. Ambrose G. Potter. xvi, 314p. reprint ed. write for info. (*0-318-71553-8*, Pub. by Georg Olms GW) Lubrecht & Cramer.

***Bibliography of the Salishan Languages.** James C. Pilling. (Bureau of American Ethnology Bulletins Ser.). 86p. 1995. lib. bdg. 79.00 (*0-7812-4016-6*) Rprt Serv.

Bibliography of the Samaritans. 2nd ed. Alan D. Crown. LC 92-42799. (American Theological Library Association Monograph: No. 32). (Illus.). 338p. 1993. 39.50 (*0-8108-2646-1*) Scarecrow.

Bibliography of the Sanskrit Drama with an Introductory Sketch of Dramatic Literature of India. Montgomery Schuyler. LC 74-181074. (Columbia University. Indo-Iranian Ser.: No. 3). reprint ed. 11.00 (*0-404-50473-6*) AMS Pr.

Bibliography of the Siouan Language. J. C. Pilling. 1977. lib. bdg. 59.95 (*0-8490-1501-4*) Gordon Pr.

***Bibliography of the Siouan Language.** James C. Pilling. (Bureau of American Ethnology Bulletins Ser.). 87p. 1995. lib. bdg. 79.00 (*0-7812-4005-0*) Rprt Serv.

Bibliography of the Sioux. Jack W. Marken & Herbert T. Hoover. LC 80-20106. (Native American Bibliography Ser.: No. 1). 388p. 1980. 27.50 (*0-8108-1356-4*) Scarecrow.

Bibliography of the Soviet Sciences Nineteen Sixty-Five to Nineteen Seventy-Five, 2 vols., Set. William S. Heiliger. LC 76-51039. 1977. 65.00 (*0-87875-111-4*) Whitston Pub.

Bibliography of the Soviet Union, Its Predecessors & Successors. Bradley L. Schaffner. LC 94-1673. (Area Bibliographies Ser.: No. 5). 1995. 72.50 (*0-8108-2860-X*) Scarecrow.

Bibliography of the Soybean Plant: Nomenclature, Physiology, Morphology, Botany, Taxonomy, & Wild Soybeans, with References from 1100 B. C. to 1991. Comp. by William Shurtleff & Akiko Aoyagi. (Bibliographies of Soya Ser.). 352p. 1992. spiral bd. 141.00 (*0-933332-77-7*) Soyfoods Center.

Bibliography of the Soyfoods Industry & Market: 1984 to January, 1989. Ed. by Akiko Aoyagi. (Soyfoods Market Studies). 66p. (Orig.). 1989. spiral bd. 95.00 (*0-933332-56-4*) Soyfoods Center.

Bibliography of the Soymilk Industry & Market: Worldwide & Country-by-Country Analysis, 1984 to January, 1989. Ed. by Akiko Aoyagi. (Soyfoods Market Studies). 84p. (Orig.). 1989. spiral bd. 95.00 (*0-933332-55-6*) Soyfoods Center.

Bibliography of the State of Maine. Ed. by Bangor Public Library Editors. 1970. lib. bdg. 110.00 (*0-8161-0636-3*, Hall Library) G K Hall.

Bibliography of the State of Maine from the Earliest Period to 1891. Joseph Williamson. LC 85-60621. 1985. reprint ed. Vol. I, 760 pg. Not sold separately (*0-89725-058-3*); reprint ed. Vol. II, 677 pg. Not sold separately (*0-89725-059-1*) Picton Pr.

Bibliography of the State of Maine from the Earliest Period to 1891, Set. Joseph Williamson. LC 85-60621. 1985. reprint ed. 65.00 (*0-89725-074-5*) Picton Pr.

Bibliography of the State of Ohio, 2 vols., 1. Peter G. Thomson. LC 63-21499. 548p. 1971. reprint ed. 18.95 (*0-405-03683-3*) Ayer.

Bibliography of the State of Ohio, 2 vols., 2. Peter G. Thomson. LC 63-21499. 548p. 1971. reprint ed. 18.95 (*0-405-03686-8*) Ayer.

Bibliography of the State of Ohio, 2 vols., Set. Peter G. Thomson. LC 63-21499. 548p. reprint ed. 30.95 (*0-405-03687-6*) Ayer.

Bibliography of the Summer Institute of Linguistics. Comp. by Alan C. Wares. LC 92-63212. 700p. 1992. 15.00 (*0-88312-824-1*); pap. 10.00 (*0-88312-821-7*); fiche 44.00 (*1-55671-995-7*) Summer Instit Ling.

Bibliography of the Tablet Collections of the University Museum. Pamela Gerardi. (Occasional Publications of the Babylonian Fund: No. 8). xxi, 277p. 1984. 30.00 (*0-934718-67-9*) U PA Mus Pubns.

Bibliography of the Thoreau Society Bulletin Bibliographies, 1941-1969: A Cumulation & Index. Ed. by Walter Harding & Jean C. Advena. LC 77-150335. 1971. 12.50 (*0-87875-008-8*) Whitston Pub.

Bibliography of the Typophile Chap Books 1935-1992. John F. Rathe. Ed. by Abe Lerner. (Typophile Chap Bks.: No. 60). 94p. 1992. 27.50 (*0-945074-02-6*) Dawsons.

Bibliography of the U. S. Navy & the Conflict in Southeast Asia, 1950-1975. 2nd ed. Ed. by Edward J. Marolda & James Lesher. 100p. (Orig.). (C). 1994. pap. text ed. 35.00 (*0-7881-0268-0*) Diane Pub.

Bibliography of the Village Press. Melbert B. Cary, Jr. LC 81-52218. 221p. 1981. reprint ed. 35.00 (*0-938768-05-0*) Oak Knoll.

Bibliography of the Virginia Indians, No. 2. Ed. by Lynn E. Kauffman et al. 92p. 1976. pap. 11.00 (*1-884626-00-9*) Archeolog Soc.

***Bibliography of the Wakashan Languages.** James C. Pilling. (Bureau of American Ethnology Bulletins Ser.). 70p. 1995. lib. bdg. 79.00 (*0-7812-4019-0*) Rprt Serv.

Bibliography of the White Mountains. rev. ed. Allen H. Bent. Ed. by Jack Hanrahan. LC 79-179457. (Bibliographies of New Hampshire History Ser.). 1972. reprint ed. pap. 15.00 (*0-912274-11-5*) Picton Pr.

Bibliography of the White Rabbit Press. Alastair M. Johnston. LC 85-16944. (Illus.). 1985. 30.00 (*0-918395-02-X*) Poltroon Pr.

Bibliography of the Work of Carl Van Vechten. Comp. by Bruce Kellner. LC 79-8409. (Illus.). 258p. 1980. text ed. 59.95 (*0-313-20767-4*, KBV/, Greenwood Pr) Greenwood.

Bibliography of the Works of Aleister Crowley. G. J. Yorke. (Orig.). 1993. pap. 6.95 (*1-55818-262-4*) Holmes Pub.

Bibliography of the Works of Alfred Thayer Mahan. Ed. by Lynn C. Hattendorf. LC 86-23520. (Historical Monograph Ser.: No. 7). (Illus.). 116p. (C). 1986. reprint ed. pap. 5.00 (*0-9637973-5-2*) Naval War Coll.

Bibliography of the Works of Dante Gabriel Rossetti. William M. Rossetti. LC 71-130242. reprint ed. 24.50 (*0-404-05439-0*) AMS Pr.

Bibliography of the Works of Eugene O'Neill with Collected Poems by O'Neill. Ed. by Ralph Sanborn & Barrett H. Clark. LC 65-16249. (Illus.). 1972. reprint ed. 19.95 (*0-405-08911-2*) Ayer.

Bibliography of the Works of Giacomo Puccini, 1858-1924. Cecil Hopkinson. (Illus.). 78p. 1968. lib. bdg. 50.00 (*0-8450-7002-9*) Broude.

Bibliography of the Works of Giuseppe Verdi, 1813-1901 Vol. I: Vocal & Instrumental Works. Cecil Hopkinson. (Illus.). 1973. lib. bdg. 60.00 (*0-8450-7003-7*) Broude.

Bibliography of the Works of Giuseppe Verdi, 1813-1901 Vol. II: Operatic Works. Cecil Hopkinson. (Illus.). 144p. 1978. lib. bdg. 85.00 (*0-8450-7004-5*) Broude.

Bibliography of the Works of Gregorio Leti. Nati Krivatsky. LC 81-85664. (Illus.). 123p. 1982. 35.00 (*0-938768-06-9*) Oak Knoll Pr.

Bibliography of the Works of Jean Piaget in the Social Sciences. Comp. by Judith A. McLaughlin. LC 87-26136. 156p. (C). 1988. lib. bdg. 39.00 (*0-8191-6730-4*) U Pr of Amer.

B

An Asterisk (*) at the beginning of an entry indicates that the title is appearing in BIP for the first time.

739

Bibliography of the Works of John Bunyan. Frank M. Harrison. 1977. lib. bdg. 59.95 (*0-8490-1502-2*) Gordon Pr.

Bibliography of the Works of Larry Eigner. Andrea Wyatt. 1970. 4.50 (*0-685-04666-4*) Oyez.

Bibliography of the Works of Neil M. Gunn. C. J. Stokoe. (Illus.). 256p. 1987. pap. text ed. 17.75 (*0-08-035079-8*, Pub. by Aberdeen U Pr) Macmillan.

Bibliography of the Works of Peter Martyr Vermigli. Ed. by John P. Donnelly. (Sixteenth Century Essays & Studies). (Illus.). 160p. 1990. 50.00 (*0-940474-14-X*) Sixteenth Cent.

Bibliography of the Works of Robinson Jeffers. S. S. Alberts. LC 66-21849. 1966. 45.00 (*0-685-83031-4*) SPD-Small Pr Dist.

Bibliography of the Works of Rudyard Kipling. E. W. Martindell. LC 72-3118. (English Literature Ser.: No. 33). 1972. reprint ed. lib. bdg. 75.00 (*0-8383-1514-3*) M S G Haskell Hse.

Bibliography of the Works of Samuel Daniel, 1585-1623 see Proof-Reading by English Authors of the Sixteenth & Seventeenth Centuries

Bibliography of the Works of William Morris. Temple Scott. 1972. 75.00 (*0-87968-742-8*) Gordon Pr.

Bibliography of the Writings & Criticisms of Edwin Arlington Robinson. Lillian Lippincott. LC 74-1423. (American Literature Ser.: No. 49). 1974. lib. bdg. 49.95 (*0-8383-2049-X*) M S G Haskell Hse.

Bibliography of the Writings of A. Edward Newton. G. H. Sargent. 1972. 59.95 (*0-87968-743-6*) Gordon Pr.

Bibliography of the Writings of Albert Pike. Ed. by Ray B. Harris. 109p. 1994. pap. 17.95 (*1-56459-448-3*) Kessinger Pub.

Bibliography of the Writings of Charles Dickens. James Cook. 1972. 59.95 (*0-87968-744-4*) Gordon Pr.

***Bibliography of the Writings of Dr. William Harvey 1578-1657.** 3rd rev. ed. Geoffrey Keynes. (Illus.). 136p. 1989. 125.00 (*0-906795-14-1*) Norman SF.

Bibliography of the Writings of Ernest Hemingway. Louis Cohn. LC 73-2635. (American Literature Ser.: No. 49). 1973. reprint ed. lib. bdg. 75.00 (*0-8383-1694-8*) M S G Haskell Hse.

Bibliography of the Writings of Harvey Cushing. 3rd ed. Ed. by Aans. 142p. 1993. write for info. (*1-879284-26-X*) Am Assn Neuro.

Bibliography of the Writings of Henry E. Sigerist. Genevieve Miller. LC 66-19764. 123p. reprint ed. pap. 35.10 (*0-8357-7205-5*, 2023831) Bks Demand.

Bibliography of the Writings of Irving Louis Horowitz. Irving L. Horowitz. 93p. 1984. pap. 9.95 (*0-88738-039-5*) Transaction Pubs.

Bibliography of the Writings of James Branch Cabell. G. Y Holt. LC 72-757. (Bibliography Ser.: No. 59). 1972. reprint ed. lib. bdg. 42.95 (*0-8383-1424-4*) M S G Haskell Hse.

Bibliography of the Writings of Jeremy Taylor to 1700: With a Section of Tayloriana. Ed. by Robert Gathorne-Hardy & William P. Williams. LC 71-149932. 159p. 1971. 25.00 (*0-87580-023-8*) N Ill U Pr.

Bibliography of the Writings of John Cowper Powys. Dante Thomas. 25.00 (*0-911858-28-8*) Appel.

Bibliography of the Writings of Jonathan Swift. 2nd ed. Herman Teerink. Ed. by Arthur H. Scouten. LC 62-11270. 488p. reprint ed. pap. 139.10 (*0-8357-7206-3*, 2051018) Bks Demand.

Bibliography of the Writings of Roscoe Pound. Franklyn C. Setaro. 1942. 25.00 (*0-678-08043-7*) Kelley.

Bibliography of the Writings of Roscoe Pound. Franklyn C. Setaro. vi, 193p. 1942. 5.50 (*0-8377-2601-8*) Rothman.

Bibliography of the Writings of Roscoe Pound. Franklyn C. Setaro. (Harvard Series of Legal Bibliographies: Vol. 3). vi, 193p. 1980. reprint ed. lib. bdg. 42.00 (*0-89941-134-7*, 301420) W S Hein.

Bibliography of the Writings of W. H. Hudson. G. F. Wilson. LC 72-3094. (English Literature Ser.: No. 33). 1972. reprint ed. lib. bdg. 55.95 (*0-8383-1510-0*) M S G Haskell Hse.

Bibliography of the Writings of William Somerset Maugham. F. T. Bason. LC 74-6376. (Bibliography Ser.: No. 59). 1974. lib. bdg. 75.00 (*0-8383-1880-0*) M S G Haskell Hse.

Bibliography of the Writings of Wyndham Lewis. Bradford Morrow & Bernard Lafourcade. LC 78-12751. (Illus.). 350p. 1978. 40.00 (*0-87685-419-6*) Black Sparrow.

Bibliography of the Writings on Georgia History, Nineteen Hundred to Nineteen Seventy. Arthur R. Rowland & James E. Dorsey. LC 77-21733. 1978. 15.00 (*0-87152-254-3*) Reprint.

Bibliography of Theatre History in Canada: The Beginnings to 1984. John Ball & Richard Plant. 400p. (C). 1993. text ed. 85.00 (*1-55022-120-5*, Pub. by ECW Press CN) Genl Dist Srvs.

Bibliography of Theatre Technology: Acoustics & Sound, Lighting, Properties, & Scenery. John T. Howard, Jr. LC 81-7204. xii, 345p. 1982. text ed. 59.95 (*0-313-22839-6*, HTT/, Greenwood Pr) Greenwood.

Bibliography of Theses & Dissertations in Recreation & Parks, 1979. Betty Van der Smissen. 164p. reprint ed. pap. 46.80 (*0-7837-1538-2*, 2041821) Bks Demand.

***Bibliography of Theses & Dissertations on Ethnic Textiles & Dress.** Catherine A. Cerny et al. (ITAA Special Publication: No. 6). 60p. (C). 1993. pap. text ed. 20.00 (*1-885715-02-1*) Intl Textile.

Bibliography of Theses & Dissertations on Ohio Floristics & Vegetation in Ohio Colleges & Universities. Marvin L. Roberts & Ronald L. Stuckey. (Informative Circular Ser.: No. 7). 1974. 2.00 (*0-86727-074-8*) Ohio Bio Survey.

Bibliography of Thomas Heywood see Index to Rawlinson's Collections (Circa 1700-1750) for a New Edition of "Anthenae Oxonienses"

Bibliography of Tofu & Tofu Products: 3,939 References from A. D. 950 to 1989. Ed. by Akiko Aoyagi. (Bibliographies of Soya Ser.). 468p. (Orig.). 1989. pap. text ed., spiral bd. 234.00 (*0-933332-48-3*) Soyfoods Center.

Bibliography of Tofutti & Other Soy Ice Creams: Non-Dairy Frozen Dessert Industry & Market, 1985 to January 1989. Ed. by Akiko Aoyagi. (Soyfoods Market Studies). 66p. (Orig.). 1989. spiral bd. 95.00 (*0-933332-54-8*) Soyfoods Center.

Bibliography of Tourism & Travel: Research Studies, Reports & Articles, 9 vols., Set. 1980. 60.00 (*0-318-61875-3*) Travel & Tour Res.

Bibliography of Tourism & Travel Research Studies, Reports, & Articles, 9 vols., Set. Karen Dicke & C. R. Goeldner. 1980. 60.00 (*0-89478-052-2*) U CO Busn Res Div.

Bibliography of Trouchus (Trochus Niloticus L.) W. J. Nash. (Bibliographies Ser.: No. 7). 1987. pap. 3.00 (*971-10-2232-X*, Pub. by ICLARM PH) Intl Spec Bk.

Bibliography of Twentieth Century Art Publications. Hans Bolliger. (Illus.). 608p. (GER.). 1991. 150.00 (*1-55660-079-8*) A Wofsy Fine Arts.

Bibliography of United States Government Bibliographies: 1974-1976. Ed. by Roberta A. Scull. LC 75-4281. 1979. 29.50 (*0-87650-111-0*) Pierian.

Bibliography of United States Government Bibliographies: 1974-1976, Set. Ed. by Roberta A. Scull. LC 75-4281. 1979. 50.00 (*0-685-04041-0*) Pierian.

Bibliography of United States Government Bibliographies 1968-1973. Ed. by Roberta A. Scull. LC 75-4281. 1974. 24.50 (*0-87650-056-4*) Pierian.

Bibliography of United States-Latin American Relations since 1810: A Selected List of Eleven Thousand Published References. suppl. ed. Ed. by David F. Trask et al. LC 67-14421. 219p. Supp., 219p. pap. 62.50 (*0-8357-3809-4*, 2036536) Bks Demand.

Bibliography of United States-Latin American Relations since 1810: A Selected List of Eleven Thousand Published References. Ed. by David F. Trask et al. LC 67-14421. 473p. reprint ed. Text, 473p. pap. 134.90 (*0-8357-3808-6*, 2036536) Bks Demand.

Bibliography of Urban History, No. 897. Allen M. Wakstein. 1975. 5.00 (*0-686-20370-4*) CPL Biblios.

Bibliography of Vermont; or, a List of Books & Pamphlets Relating in Any Way to the State with Biographical & Other Notes. M. D. Gilman. 349p. 1992. reprint ed. lib. bdg. 45.00 (*0-685-54709-4*) Higginson Bk Co.

Bibliography of Vietnamese Literature in the Wason Collection at Cornell University. Marion W. Ross. LC 74-173511. (Cornell University, Southeast Asia Program, Data Paper Ser.: No. 90). 196p. reprint ed. pap. 55.90 (*0-8357-3679-2*, 2036403) Bks Demand.

Bibliography of Virginia Woolf. 3rd ed. Ed. by B. J. Kirkpatrick. (Soho Bibliographies Ser.). (Illus.). 1981. 98.00 (*0-19-818185-X*) OUP.

Bibliography of Vocational Education: An Annotated Guide. Ed. by Francesco Cordasco. LC 76-5961. (Studies in Education: No. 4). 47.50 (*0-404-10125-9*) AMS Pr.

Bibliography of Washington State Folklore & Folklife. Ed. by Robert E. Walls. (Illus.). 296p. 1987. 35.00 (*0-295-96514-2*) U of Wash Pr.

Bibliography of Welsh Americana. Henry Blackwell. (Sidewinder Studies in History & Sociology: No. 5). 92p. Date not set. lib. bdg. write for info. (*0-89370-828-3*); pap. write for info. (*0-89370-928-X*) Borgo Pr.

Bibliography of Whitley Stokes Works on the Celtic Language & Literature. R. I. Best. 1987. pap. text ed. 17.50 (*0-89979-041-0*) British Am Bks.

Bibliography of William Dean Howells. Ed. by William M. Gibson & George Arms. LC 71-137708. (New York Public Library Publications in Reprint). 1971. reprint ed. 20.95 (*0-405-01743-X*) Ayer.

Bibliography of William Hazlitt. 2nd rev. ed. Geoffrey Keynes. (Illus.). 152p. 1981. 20.00 (*0-906795-01-X*) Oak Knoll.

Bibliography of Women & Literature, 2 Vols., Set. Ed. by Florence Boos & Lynn F. Miller. LC 81-6989. 808p. 1989. 145.00 (*0-8419-0693-9*) Holmes & Meier.

Bibliography of Women Writers from the Caribbean. Brenda Berrian. LC 86-51311. 250p. (Orig.). 1989. 25.00 (*0-89410-600-7*); pap. 15.00 (*0-89410-601-5*) Three Continents.

Bibliography of Word Formation in the Germanic Languages. Richard K. Seymour. LC 68-18780. 174p. reprint ed. pap. 49.60 (*0-8357-7207-1*, 2023446) Bks Demand.

Bibliography of Works About Sir Christopher Wren see American Association of Architectural Bibliographers' Papers

Bibliography of Works in English on Playing Cards & Gaming see Bibliographies of Works on Playing Cards & Gaming

Bibliography of Works of Richard Price. D. O. Thomas et al. 280p. 1993. 94.95 (*0-85967-916-0*, Pub. by Scolar Pr UK) Ashgate Pub Co.

***Bibliography of Writings by & about Women in Photography, 1850-1990.** 2nd ed. Peter E. Palmquist. 332p. 1995. reprint ed. lib. bdg. 57.00x (*0-8095-5956-0*) Borgo Pr.

Bibliography of Writings for the History of the English Language. 2nd ed. Ed. by Jacek Fisiak. 216p. (C). 1988. text ed. 106.95 (*0-89925-057-2*) Mouton.

Bibliography of Writings of George Meredith & Meredithiana, 2 vols., Set. Maurice B. Forman. LC 78-122982. (Studies in George Meredith: No. 21). 1970. reprint ed. lib. bdg. 150.00 (*0-8383-1114-8*) M S G Haskell Hse.

***Bibliography of Writings on British History 1914-1989.** Keith Robbins. 1200p. 1995. 125.00 (*0-19-822496-6*) OUP.

Bibliography of Writings on Judaism, 2 vols., 1. David B. Griffiths. LC 88-30700. (Jewish Studies: Vol. 2). 810p. 1989. lib. bdg. 139.95 (*0-88946-254-2*) E Mellen.

Bibliography of Writings on Judaism, 2 vols., 2. David B. Griffiths. LC 88-30700. (Jewish Studies: Vol. 2). 810p. 1989. lib. bdg. 129.95 (*0-88946-257-7*) E Mellen.

Bibliography of Yaws. 106p. (ENG, FRE & RUS.). 1963. pap. 3.60 (*92-4-052003-1*) World Health.

Bibliography of Yuba: 161 References from 1587 to 1989. Ed. by Akiko Aoyagi. (Bibliographies of Soya Ser.). 56p. (Orig.). 1989. spiral bd., pap. 45.00 (*0-933332-60-2*) Soyfoods Center.

Bibliography Old & New. Herman Liebert. LC 72-619564. (Bibliographical Monograph: No. 6). (Illus.). 1974. 10.00 (*0-87959-050-5*) U of Tex H Ransom Ctr.

Bibliography on a Human Theory of Organization, No. 1293. Guy B. Adams. 1977. 5.50 (*0-686-19694-5*) CPL Biblios.

Bibliography on Abstract Data Types. B. Kutzler & F. Lichtenberger. (Informatik-Fachberichte Ser.: Vol. 68). 194p. 1983. pap. 27.00 (*0-387-12312-1*) Spr-Verlag.

Bibliography on Animal Rights & Related Matters. Charles R. Magel. LC 80-5636. 622p. (C). 1981. lib. bdg. 75.00 (*0-8191-1488-X*) U Pr of Amer.

Bibliography on Antisemitism: The Library of the Zentrum fur Antisemitismusforschung at the Technical University of Berlin, 4 vols., Set. Ed. by Herbert A. Strauss. 1407p. 1992. 565.00 (*3-598-10868-0*) U Pubns Amer.

Bibliography on Autism. Nancy M. Palvino. (Bibliographies Ser.: No. 4). 9p. (C). 1992. 3.50 (*1-883215-03-X*) Ramdil.

Bibliography on Bilharziasis, Nineteen Forty-Nine to Nineteen Fifty-Eight. 1960. 2.80 (*92-4-052002-3*) World Health.

Bibliography on California's Congressional Delegation: 1955 to the Present. Comp. by Richard C. Burnweit. 256p. 1992. pap. text ed. 30.00 (*1-883638-15-1*) Rose Inst.

Bibliography on Chaos. Ed. by S. Y. Zhang. 300p. (C). 1991. text ed. 86.00 (*981-02-0580-5*); pap. text ed. 40.00 (*981-02-0581-3*) World Scientific Pub.

Bibliography on Computational Molecular Biology & Genetics. Sarah Barron et al. 115p. (Orig.). (C). 1992. pap. text ed. 40.00 (*0-941375-91-9*) Diane Pub.

Bibliography on Copper Smelting Nineteen-Forty to Nineteen Seventy-Three. Subhash C. Malhotra. LC 73-87447. 300p. 1973. 31.45 (*0-686-05581-0*) Malhotra.

Bibliography on Deafness. rev. ed. Ed. by George W. Fellendorf. LC 77-86323. 1977. pap. 4.95 (*0-88200-111-6*, L9214) Alexander Graham.

Bibliography on Education in Development & Social Change in Sub-Saharan Africa. Mark A. Grey. LC 88-12774. (Studies in African Education & Development: Vol. 1). 192p. 1988. lib. bdg. 79.95 (*0-88946-381-6*) E Mellen.

Bibliography on Educational Broadcasting. Isabella M. Cooper. LC 76-161184. (History of Broadcasting: Radio to Television Ser.). 1977. reprint ed. 51.95 (*0-405-03587-X*) Ayer.

Bibliography on German Unification: Economic & Social Developments in Eastern Germany, November 1989-November 1992. Ed. by Frauke Siefkes & Library of the Kiel Institute of World Economics in the Federal Republic of Germany Staff. 365p. 1992. lib. bdg. 96.00 (*3-598-11147-9*) K G Saur.

Bibliography on Holocaust Literature. Abraham J. Edelheit & Hershel Edelheit. 564p. (C). 1992. text ed. 85.00 (*0-8133-1412-7*) Westview.

Bibliography on Holocaust Literature: Supplement. Abraham J. Edelheit & Hershel Edelheit. 684p. 1990. text ed. 111.00 (*0-8133-0896-8*) Westview.

Bibliography on Human Relations Training & Related Subjects. Comp. by Fred Massarik. 1985. pap. 8.00 (*0-9610392-3-X*) NTL Inst.

Bibliography on India in 2000 A. D. Nirmal Ruprail. (C). 1991. 28.00 (*0-8364-2739-4*, Pub. by Abhinav II) S Asia.

Bibliography on Indo-Pacific Red Tides. J. L. Maclean & R. M. Temprosa. 1990. pap. text ed. 5.00 (*971-10-2259-1*, Pub. by ICLARM PH) Intl Spec Bk.

Bibliography on International Peacekeeping. Gunnar Fermann. LC 92-34737. (C). 1992. lib. bdg. 112.00 (*0-7923-2011-5*) Kluwer Ac.

Bibliography on Israel & Zionism. Ed. by Yona Alexander & Mordecai Chertoff. 1980. write for info. (*0-318-53298-0*) Herzl Pr.

Bibliography on Kenya. John B. Webster et al. (Foreign & Comparative Studies Program, Eastern Africa Ser.: No. 3). 461p. 1967. pap. 10.00 (*0-686-70995-0*) Syracuse U Foreign Comp.

Bibliography on Land-Locked States. Martin I. Glassner. LC 80-51737. 60p. 1980. lib. bdg. 43.00 (*90-286-0290-9*) Kluwer Ac.

Bibliography on Land-Locked States. 3rd enl. rev. ed. Ed. by Martin I. Glassner. 1991. lib. bdg. 97.00 (*0-7923-1320-8*) Kluwer Ac.

***Bibliography on Land-Locked States.** 4th enl. rev. ed. Ed. by Martin I. Glassner. LC 94-44456. 280p. (C). 1995. lib. bdg. 125.00 (*0-7923-3300-4*, Pub. by M Nijhoff) Kluwer Ac.

Bibliography on Liberia: Part One, Books. Svend E. Holsoe. No. 1. 123p. 1971. write for info. (*0-318-65079-7*) Arden Assocs.

Bibliography on Liberia: Part Three. Ed. by Svend E. Holsoe. (Liberian Research Working Papers: No. 5). 1976. 11.00 (*0-686-17779-7*) Arden Assocs.

Bibliography on Liberia: Part Two. Svend E. Holsoe. (Liberian Studies Research Working Papers: No. 3). 1971. 6.00 (*0-686-11768-9*) Arden Assocs.

Bibliography on Liquid Exclusion Chromatography (Gel Permeation Chromatography) - AMD 40. suppl. ed. 1974. First supplement (1972-75), AMD 40-S1. pap. 9.50 (*0-8031-0293-3*, PCN 10-040010-3); Second supplement (1976-78), AMD 40-S2. pap. 14.00 (*0-8031-0294-1*, PCN 10-040020-3) ASTM.

Bibliography on Nonassociative Algebras. Ed. by M. L. Tomber et al. 545p. (C). 1984. reprint ed. pap. 40.00 (*0-911767-17-7*) Hadronic Pr Inc.

Bibliography on Orgone Biophysics. Ed. & Intro. by James DeMeo. 57p. (C). 1986. pap. text ed. 10.00 (*0-9621855-1-5*) Natural Energy.

***Bibliography on Ozone, Its Biological Effects & Technical Applications.** Harald Rosenthal & J. Scott Wilson. 249p. (Orig.). (C). 1993. pap. text ed. 95.00x (*0-7881-0110-2*) Diane Pub.

Bibliography on Peace Research & Peaceful International Relations: The Contributions of Psychology 1900-1991. Ed. by Marianne Muller-Brettel. 384p. 1993. lib. bdg. 85.00 (*3-598-11072-3*) K G Saur.

Bibliography on Plato's Laws, Nineteen Twenty to Nineteen Seventy: With Additional Citations Through May, 1975. Trevor J. Saunders. LC 75-13281. (History of Ideas in Ancient Greece Ser.). 1979. reprint ed. 12.95 (*0-405-07324-0*) Ayer.

Bibliography on Portraiture: Selected Writings on Portraiture As an Art Form & As Documentation. Comp. by Irene Heppner. (Library Reference Ser.). 850p. 1989. lib. bdg. 215.00 (*0-8161-0481-6*) G K Hall.

Bibliography on Postsecondary Accreditation. Ed. by M. T. Neal et al. 107p. 1984. 9.50 (*0-318-17661-0*) Coun Postsecondary Accredit.

Bibliography on Pre-stressed Concrete. 2nd ed. American Concrete Institute Staff. (American Concrete Institute Bibliography Ser.: No. 1). 106p. reprint ed. pap. 30.30 (*0-8357-3596-6*, 2004254) Bks Demand.

Bibliography on Publishing & Book Development in the Third World, 1980-1993. Philip G. Altbach & Hyaeweol Choi. LC 93-34124. (Bellagio Studies in Publishing: No. 3). 152p. 1993. 39.50 (*1-56750-084-6*); pap. 19.95 (*1-56750-085-4*) Ablex Pub.

Bibliography on Rare Earth Elements: Including Scandium & Yttrium. K. E. Mironov & L. A. Chernikova. 440p. 1970. text ed. 106.50 (*0-685-13629-9*, Pub. by Keter Pub IS) Coronet Bks.

Bibliography on Reinvestment Policy. Robert Stumberg. 33p. 1990. 5.00 (*0-685-56597-1*) CPA Washington.

Bibliography on Representation & Redistricting. Comp. by Leroy C. Hardy. 426p. 1992. pap. text ed. 75.00 (*1-883638-01-1*) Rose Inst.

Bibliography on Scientific Fraud. A. C. Higgins. LC 94-71496. 176p. (Orig.). Date not set. pap. text ed. 44.95 (*1-885343-00-0*) Exams Unltd.

Bibliography on Size Exclusion Chromatography (Gel Permeation Chromatography) - AMD 40-S3. Ed. by Plastics Committee D-20. LC 85-6242. (Atomic & Molecular Data Series AMD-S3). 298p. 1985. pap. text ed. 29.00 (*0-8031-0439-1*, PCN10-040030-39) ASTM.

Bibliography on South American Economic Affairs: Articles in Nineteenth Century Periodicals. Tom B. Jones et al. LC 55-7033. 162p. reprint ed. pap. 46.20 (*0-8357-3597-4*, 2055885) Bks Demand.

Bibliography on State Bar Admission Practices & Procedures & Effects Upon Lawyer Competence & Delivery of Legal Services. National Center for State Courts Staff. 52p. 1980. 3.12 (*0-685-16748-8*, FR-004) Natl Ctr St Courts.

Bibliography on Taxation in Developing Countries. Richard M. Bird. LC 68-20366. 198p. (Orig.). 1968. pap. 5.00 (*0-915506-08-4*) Harvard Law Intl Tax.

Bibliography on Taxation of Foreign Operations & Foreigners. Elisabeth A. Owens. LC 68-23792. 112p. (Orig.). 1968. pap. 5.00 (*0-915506-09-2*) Harvard Law Intl Tax.

Bibliography on Taxation of Foreign Operations & Foreigners, 1968-1975. Elisabeth A. Owens & Gretchen A. Hovemeyer. LC 76-14456. 122p. (Orig.). 1976. pap. 7.50 (*0-915506-21-1*) Harvard Law Intl Tax.

Bibliography on Taxation of Foreign Operations & Foreigners, 1976-1982. Elisabeth A. Owens & Gretchen A. Hovemeyer. LC 83-18402. 206p. (Orig.). 1983. pap. text ed. 12.50 (*0-915506-27-0*) Harvard Law Intl Tax.

Bibliography on Technology & Social Change in China & Japan. Roberta Abraham. (Reports on Technology & Social Change Ser.). 262p. 1974. 12.00 (*0-945271-21-2*) ISU-TSCP.

Bibliography on Temples of the Ancient Near East & Mediterranean World: Arranged by Subject & by Author. Donald W. Parry & Stephen D. Ricks. Ed. by John W. Welch. LC 91-516. (Ancient Near Eastern Texts & Studies: Vol. 9). 324p. 1991. lib. bdg. 99.95 (*0-7734-9775-7*) E Mellen.

Bibliography on the Assessment Center Method & Education Administration. Frederick C. Wendel. 124p. (Orig.). (C). 1988. pap. text ed. 11.25 (*0-922971-06-4*, RD-1403) Univ Council Educ Admin.

Bibliography on the Botany of the Eastern Himalayas. K. Thothathri & A. R. Das. (Botanical Survey of India Ser.). 72p. 1984. pap. text ed. 12.50 (*0-945345-57-7*, Pub. by Mahendra Pal Singh II) Lubrecht & Cramer.

Bibliography on the Communist Problem in the United States. LC 71-169651. (Civil Liberties in American History Ser.). 474p. 1971. reprint ed. lib. bdg. 65.00 (*0-306-70234-7*) Da Capo.

Bibliography on the Constitutions of Nigeria: A Sourcebook on the Constitutional Law. Oluremi Jegede. (Collection of Bibliographic & Research Resources). 124p. 1988. 50.00 (*0-379-20917-9*) Oceana.

An Asterisk (*) at the beginning of an entry indicates that the title is appearing in BIP for the first time.

Bibliography on the Epidemiology of Cancer: Bibliography on the Epidemiology of Cancer: Nineteen Forty-Six to Nineteen Sixty. 168p. (ENG, FRE, RUS & SPA.). 1963. pap. 4.80 (*92-4-052000-7*) World Health.

Bibliography on the Fatigue of Materials, Components & Structures, Vol. 2: 1951-1960. Incl. 1978. (*0-318-57468-3*); 1978. 208.00 (*0-08-021713-3*, Pub. by Pergamon Repr UK) Franklin.

Bibliography on the Fatigue of Materials, Components & Structures, Vol. 3: 1961-1965. J. Y. Mann. 510p. 1983. 205.00 (*0-08-025449-7*, Pub. by Pergamon Repr UK) Franklin.

Bibliography on the Fatigue of Materials, Components & Structures, Vol. 4: 1966-1969. J. Y. Mann. 509p. 1990. 216.00 (*0-08-040507-X*, Pub. by PPL UK) Franklin.

Bibliography on the Germans from Russia: Material Found in the New York Public Library, 1970. Marie M. Olson. 29p. 1976. 7.00 (*0-914222-21-X*) Am Hist Soc Ger.

Bibliography on the Law of the Sea 1968-1988: Two Decades on Law-Making State Practice & Doctrine. 483p. 1991. 25.00 (*92-1-022068-4*, 91.V.7) UN.

Bibliography on Tides Sixteen Sixty-Five to Nineteen Thirty-Nine. No. 14. 220p. 1955. (*0-318-61388-3*) Intl Assoc Phys Sci Ocean.

Bibliography on Women in Yemen. Joke Buringa. 160p. (C). 1992. pap. text ed. 10.00 (*1-882557-00-X*) Am Inst Yemeni.

Bibliography Publications: All Subjects Cumulative Index for Health Occupations, Vol. 1. American Health Research Institute Staff. 180p. 1994. 51.50 (*0-7883-0202-7*); pap. 45.50 (*0-7883-0203-5*) ABBE Pubs Assn.

Bibliography Publications: All Subjects Cumulative Index for Health Occupations, Vol. 2. American Health Research Institute Staff. 180p. 1994. 51.50 (*0-7883-0204-3*); pap. 45.50 (*0-7883-0205-1*) ABBE Pubs Assn.

Bibliography Supplement 1. E. Spamer. LC 93-70396. 156p. 1993. 10.00 (*0-938216-47-3*) GCNHA.

Bibliography to the Classical Tradition in English Literature. Hanne Carlsen. 164p. (Orig.). 1985. pap. text ed. 36.00x (*87-88648-06-0*) Coronet Bks.

Bibliography Without Footnotes. 2nd ed. Herbert H. Hoffman. LC 78-100270. 93p. 1978. pap. 4.00 (*0-89537-013-1*) Headway Pubns.

Bibliogrpahie de l'Histoire de Belgique. Henri Pirenne. viii, 440p. 1979. reprint ed. lib. bdg. 63.70 (*3-487-06722-6*, Pub. by Georg Olms GW) Lubrecht & Cramer.

Bibliogrpahy on Forecasting & Planning. Kwok K. Kwong. Ed. by Chaman L. Jain et al. LC 94-75680. 328p. (Orig.). 1995. pap. text ed. 56.95 (*0-932126-16-2*) Graceway.

Biblioholism: The Literary Addiction. Tom Raabe. LC 91-7260. (Illus.). 193p. (Orig.). 1991. pap. 8.95 (*1-55591-080-7*) Fulcrum Pub.

Bibliohrafiia ukrains'koi presy, 1816-1916. Varfolmii A. Ihnatiieako. LC 74-220297. (Bibliohrafiia I Bibliotekonznavstvo Ser.). (Illus.). 285p. (UKR.). 1968. 35.00 (*0-918884-13-6*, R6956.R9137) Slavia Lib.

BiblioMania, Vol. 1. Ed. by Richard Spiegel & Barbara Fisher. (Illus.). 36p. (Orig.). (J). (gr. 2-6). 1991. pap. 3.00 (*0-934830-48-7*) Ten Penny.

BiblioMania, Vol. 2. Richard Spiegel. Ed. by Barbara Fisher. (Illus.). 52p. (Orig.). (YA). (gr. 7-12). 1991. pap. 3.00 (*0-934830-49-5*) Ten Penny.

***Bibliomania: May 6, 1995.** Ed. by Barbara Fisher & Richard Spiegel. (Illus.). 48p. (Orig.). (YA). (gr. 7-12). 1995. pap. 3.00 (*0-934830-60-6*) Ten Penny.

Bibliomania in the Middle Ages. F. Somner Merryweather. 1977. lib. bdg. 59.95 (*0-8490-1503-0*) Gordon Pr.

Bibliomania in the Middle Ages. rev. ed. F. Somner Merryweather. Ed. by H. B. Copinger. LC 72-83748. 1972. reprint ed. 24.95 (*0-405-08787-X*, Pub. by Blom Pubns UK) Ayer.

Bibliomania Three, Vol. 1. Ed. by Barbara Fisher & Richard Spiegel. 47p. (Orig.). (J). (gr. k-6). 1993. pap. 3.00 (*0-934830-54-1*) Ten Penny.

Bibliomania Three, Vol. 2. Ed. by Barbara Fisher & Richard Spiegel. 47p. (Orig.). (YA). (gr. 7-12). 1993. pap. 3.00 (*0-934830-55-X*) Ten Penny.

***Bibliomania V - May 13, 1995.** Ed. by Barbara Fisher & Richard Spiegel. (Illus.). 48p. (Orig.). (J). (gr. 1-6). 1995. pap. 3.00 (*0-934830-61-4*) Ten Penny.

Bibliometrics: An Annotated Bibliography, 1970-1990. Mark K. Sellen. (Professional Librarian Ser.). 200p. 1993. text ed. 38.50 (*0-8161-1954-6*, Hall Reference) Macmillan.

Bibliopegia, Vol. 5. John Hannett. Ed. by Sidney F. Huttner. (History of Bookbinding & Design Ser.). (Illus.). 504p. 1990. 100.00 (*0-8240-4018-X*) Garland.

Bibliophile Dictionary: A Biographical Record of the Great Authors. International Bibliophile Society Staff. 1972. 75.00 (*0-87968-745-2*) Gordon Pr.

Bibliophile of the Future: His Complaints About the Twentieth Century. Jacques Barzun. 1976. 3.00 (*0-89073-048-2*) Boston Public Lib.

Bibliophiles Philadelphia Style: An Exhibit of Sixty Rare Books Once Owned by Notable Philadelphians. (Illus.). 23p. (Orig.). 1982. pap. 2.00 (*0-914076-56-6*) Lib Co Phila.

Bibliortecas Antiquas y Nuevas, 3 vols. Felix De Latassa y Ortin. lxvi, 1720p. reprint ed. write for info. (*0-318-71624-0*, Pub. by Georg Olms GW) Lubrecht & Cramer.

Bibliorum Codex Sinaiticus Petropolitanus, 4 vols. Ed. by C. Tischendorf. xcvi, 715p. 1969. reprint ed. write for info. (*0-318-70719-5*, Pub. by Georg Olms GW) Lubrecht & Cramer.

Bibliorum Codex Sinaiticus Petropolitanus, 4 vols., Vol. I. Ed. by C. Tischendorf. xcvi, 715p. 1969. reprint ed. write for info. (*0-318-70720-9*, Pub. by Georg Olms GW) Lubrecht & Cramer.

Bibliorum Codex Sinaiticus Petropolitanus, 4 vols., Vol. II. Ed. by C. Tischendorf. xcvi, 715p. 1969. reprint ed. write for info. (*0-318-70721-7*, Pub. by Georg Olms GW) Lubrecht & Cramer.

Bibliorum Codex Sinaiticus Petropolitanus, 4 vols., Vol. III. Ed. by C. Tischendorf. xcvi, 715p. 1969. reprint ed. write for info. (*0-318-70722-5*, Pub. by Georg Olms GW) Lubrecht & Cramer.

Bibliorum Codex Sinaiticus Petropolitanus, 4 vols., Vol. IV. Ed. by C. Tischendorf. xcvi, 715p. 1969. reprint ed. write for info. (*0-318-70723-3*, Pub. by Georg Olms GW) Lubrecht & Cramer.

Bibliorum Sacrorum Latinae Versiones Antiquae, 3 vols., Set. Pierre Sabatier. cxxxii, 3134p. Date not set. write for info. (*0-318-71219-9*, Pub. by Georg Olms GW) Lubrecht & Cramer.

Bibliotaph & Other People. Leon H. Vincent. LC 72-8578. (Essay Index Reprint Ser.). 1977. reprint ed. 21.95 (*0-8369-7335-6*) Ayer.

Biblioteca Andina, Pt. One: The Chroniclers, or, the Writers of the Sixteenth & Seventeenth Centuries Who Treated of the Pre-Hispanic History & Culture of the Andean Countries. Philip A. Means. (Connecticut Academy of Arts & Sciences Ser., Trans.: Vol. 29). 1928. pap. 100.00 (*0-685-22806-1*) Elliots Bks.

Biblioteca Basica de Rotary. David H. Bailey & Louise Gottlieb. Ed. by Willmon L. White & Mark Perlberg. (Illus.). 506p. (SPA.). 1982. 16.75 (*0-915062-15-1*) Rotary Intl.

Biblioteca Curiosa, 3 vols. in 1. Edmund Goldsmid. xxxvi, 373p. 1976. reprint ed. write for info. (*3-487-05814-6*, Pub. by Georg Olms GW) Lubrecht & Cramer.

Biblioteca Empresarial Deusto: Deusto Library of Business, 40 vols., Set. Ediciones Deusto Staff. (SPA.). 1,495.00 (*0-8288-8256-8*) Fr & Eur.

Biblioteca Entomologica, 2 vols. in 1. Hermann A. Hagen. xii, 1078p. 1960. reprint ed. write for info. (*0-318-71788-3*, Pub. by Georg Olms GW) Lubrecht & Cramer.

Biblioteca Espanola, 2 vols., Set. Jose Rodriguez De Castro. (Textos y Estudios Clasicos De las Literaturas Hispanicas Ser.). 1417p. 1977. reprint ed. write for info. (*3-487-06272-0*, Pub. by Georg Olms GW) Lubrecht & Cramer.

Biblioteca Espanola-Portugeza-Judaica. rev. ed. Meyer Kayserling. 1971. 45.00 (*0-87068-146-X*) Ktav.

Biblioteca Familiar. deluxe ed. (SPA.). 995.00 (*0-7859-0861-7*, S37347) Fr & Eur.

Biblioteca Topographica Britannica, 10 Vols. John Nichols & Richard Gough. LC 70-138264. reprint ed. 1,750.00 (*0-404-04740-8*) AMS Pr.

Bibliotecas Antiguas y Nuevas, 3 vols. Felix D. Latassa y Ortin. reprint ed. write for info. (*0-318-71836-7*, Pub. by Georg Olms GW) Lubrecht & Cramer.

Biblioteka Ruskoi Khuzoxhestvennoi Publitsistiki. Peterburga Fitzioloģiia. 304p. 1984. 39.00 (*0-317-40698-1*, Pub. by Collets UK) St Mut.

Bibliotesauri: Or, Jewels from the Shelves of the Library Company of Philadelphia. Ed. by Edwin Wolf, II. (Illus.). 68p. (Orig.). 1966. pap. 5.00 (*0-914076-65-5*) Lib Co Phila.

Bibliotheca Americana: Eighteen Fifty-Two to Eighteen Sixty-One, 3 vols. in 1, Vols. 2, 3 & 4. O. A. Roorbach. 30.00 (*0-8446-1389-4*) Peter Smith.

Bibliotheca Americana, Books to 1674, 3 Vols, Set. 3rd ed. Brown University, John Carter Brown Library Staff. 1972. reprint ed. 150.00 (*0-527-46200-4*) Periodicals Srv.

***Bibliotheca Amploiana: Ihre Bedeutung Im Spannungsfeld Von Aristotelismus, Nominalismus und Humanismus.** Ed. by Andreas Speer. (Miscellanea Mediaevalia: Bd. 23). 533p. (GER.). (C). 1995. lib. bdg. 238.50 (*3-11-014098-5*) De Gruyter.

Bibliotheca Anatomica, 2 vols., Set. Albrecht V. Haller. 1969. reprint ed. write for info. (*0-318-71791-3*, Pub. by Georg Olms GW) Lubrecht & Cramer.

Bibliotheca Astrologica: A Catalog of Astrological Publications of the 15th Through the 19th Centuries. F. Leigh Gardner. Ed. by William W. Westcott. 184p. 1993. pap. 16.95 (*1-56459-300-2*) Kessinger Pub.

Bibliotheca Austroasiatica. Arun Ghosh. (C). 1988. 16.00 (*0-8364-2372-0*, Pub. by Firma KLM) S Asia.

Bibliotheca Bibliothecarum Manuscriptorum Nova, 2 vols., Set. Bernard De Montfaucon. cclviii, 1669p. 1982. reprint ed. write for info. (*3-487-07162-2*, Pub. by Georg Olms GW) Lubrecht & Cramer.

Bibliotheca Biographica Lutherana. Ernest G. Vogel. x, 145p. 1967. reprint ed. write for info. (*0-318-71873-1*, Pub. by Georg Olms GW) Lubrecht & Cramer.

Bibliotheca Botanica. Carl Linnaeus. 1968. 12.00 (*0-934454-13-2*) Lubrecht & Cramer.

Bibliotheca Botanica, 2 vols., Set. Albrecht V. Haller. 1969. reprint ed. write for info. (*0-318-71792-1*, Pub. by Georg Olms GW) Lubrecht & Cramer.

Bibliotheca Chemica. Friedrich Roth-Scholtz. 238p. 1971. reprint ed. write for info. (*3-487-04117-0*, Pub. by Georg Olms GW) Lubrecht & Cramer.

Bibliotheca Chemica, Vols. 1 & 2. John Ferguson. 1085p. 1992. reprint ed. pap. 75.00 (*1-56459-001-1*) Kessinger Pub.

Bibliotheca Chemica: A Catalogue of Alchemical & Pharmaceutical Books in the Collection of the Late James Young of Kelly & Durris, 2 vols., Set. John Ferguson. 1974. reprint ed. write for info. (*3-487-05340-3*, Pub. by Georg Olms GW) Lubrecht & Cramer.

Bibliotheca Chemica Curiosa, 2 vols., Set. J. Jacob Manget. Date not set. write for info. (*0-318-71843-X*, Pub. by Georg Olms GW) Lubrecht & Cramer.

Bibliotheca Chemico-Mathematica: Catalogue of Works in Many Tongues on Exact & Applied Science with a Subject-Index, Vols. 1 & 2. Comp. by H. Zeitlinger & H. C. Sotheran. 1952. 420.00 (*0-8115-3813-3*) Periodicals Srv.

Bibliotheca Chimica, Sue Catalogus Librorum Philosophicorum Hermeticorum, in Quo 4000 Circiter Authorum Chimicorum, ... Usque Annum 1653 Continentur. Petrus Borellius. 254p. 1969. reprint ed. write for info. (*0-318-71746-8*, Pub. by Georg Olms GW) Lubrecht & Cramer.

Bibliotheca Chirurgica, 2 vols., Set. Albrech V. Haller. 1971. reprint ed. write for info. (*0-318-71793-X*, Pub. by Georg Olms GW) Lubrecht & Cramer.

Bibliotheca Crowleyana: The Collection of J. F. C. Fuller. J. F. Fuller. 1989. pap. 5.95 (*1-55818-153-9*, Sure Fire) Holmes Pub.

Bibliotheca Curiosa: A Treatise of Magic Incantations (1700) Christianus Pazig. Ed. by Edmund Goldsmid. 54p. 1994. pap. 12.95 (*1-56459-437-8*) Kessinger Pub.

Bibliotheca De Re Metallica: The Herbert Clark Hoover Collection of Mining & Metallurgy. Ed. by David Kuhner et al. LC 80-82055. (Illus.). 219p. 1980. 125.00 (*0-937368-00-8*) Lib Claremont Coll.

Bibliotheca Ecclesiastica Continens Graecorum Theologorum Opera. Andronicus Demetrakopulos. xliv, 415p. 1965. reprint ed. write for info. (*0-318-70907-4*, Pub. by Georg Olms GW) Lubrecht & Cramer.

Bibliotheca Ecclesiastica Continens Graecorum Theologorum Opera. Ed. by Andronicus Demetrakopulos. xliv, 415p. 1965. reprint ed. write for info. (*0-318-71763-8*, Pub. by Georg Olms GW) Lubrecht & Cramer.

Bibliotheca Entomologica, 2 vols. in 1. H. A. Hagen. 1960. 140.00 (*3-7682-0035-3*) Lubrecht & Cramer.

Bibliotheca Epidemiographica. Heinrich Haeser. xv, 230p. 1971. reprint ed. write for info. (*3-487-04919-8*, Pub. by Georg Olms GW) Lubrecht & Cramer.

Bibliotheca Familiarum Nobilium, 2 vols., Set. O. Gundlach. reprint ed. write for info. (*0-318-71909-6*, Pub. by Georg Olms GW) Lubrecht & Cramer.

Bibliotheca Faustiana. Karl D. Engel. xii, 764p. 1970. reprint ed. write for info. (*0-318-71769-7*, Pub. by Georg Olms GW) Lubrecht & Cramer.

Bibliotheca Graeca, 12 vols. Johann A. Fabricius. ccxii, 991p. 1970. reprint ed. write for info. (*0-318-70746-2*, Pub. by Georg Olms GW) Lubrecht & Cramer.

Bibliotheca Graeca, 12 vols., Set. Johann A. Fabricius. 1970. reprint ed. write for info. (*0-318-71778-6*, Pub. by Georg Olms GW) Lubrecht & Cramer.

Bibliotheca Graeca et Latina Suppletoria, Bd. I: Damascii Vitae Isidori Reliquiae. Ed. by Clemens Zintzen et al. xiv, 376p. 1967. write for info. (*0-318-70724-1*, Pub. by Georg Olms GW) Lubrecht & Cramer.

Bibliotheca Graeca et Latina Suppletoria, Bd. II: Physica Plinii Bambergensis. Ed. by Alf Onnerfors et al. 174p. 1976. write for info. (*0-318-70725-X*, Pub. by Georg Olms GW) Lubrecht & Cramer.

***Bibliotheca Grammaticorum: Antiquity; L'Antiquite Circa 2000 Ante Christum - Circa 200 Ante Christum.** Florent A. Tremblay. LC 95-7455. Vol. 1. 700p. 1995. text ed. 129.95 (*0-7734-8965-7*) E Mellen.

***Bibliotheca Grammaticorum: Antiquity; L'Antiquite Circa 2000 Ante Christum - Circa 200 Ante Christum, Bk. 1.** Florent A. Tremblay. LC 95-7455. Vol. 1. 700p. 1995. text ed. 129.95 (*0-7734-8967-3*) E Mellen.

***Bibliotheca Grammaticorum Vol. IV: The Middle Ages - Le Moyen Age Circa 6th to End of 15th Century, Bk. 1.** Florent A. Tremblay. LC 95-7455. 700p. 1996. text ed. 129.95 (*0-7734-8937-1*) E Mellen.

***Bibliotheca Grammaticorum Vol. IV: The Middle Ages - Le Moyen Age Circa 6th to End of 15th Century, Bk. 2.** Florent A. Tremblay. LC 95-7455. 700p. 1996. text ed. 129.95 (*0-7734-8939-8*) E Mellen.

Bibliotheca Hamiltoniana. Paul L. Ford. LC 74-168120. reprint ed. 29.50 (*0-404-02513-7*) AMS Pr.

Bibliotheca Hebraica Post-Mendelssohniana. Ed. by William Zeithlin & Steven Katz. LC 79-7154. (Jewish Philosophy, Mysticism & History of Ideas Ser.). 1980. reprint ed. lib. bdg. 49.95 (*0-405-12291-8*) Ayer.

Bibliotheca Hebraica Post-Mendelssohniana. William Zeitlin. vii, 548p. 1983. reprint ed. write for info. (*3-487-07351-X*, Pub. by Georg Olms GW) Lubrecht & Cramer.

Bibliotheca Historico-Naturalis. Wilhelm Engelmann. ix, 746p. 1960. reprint ed. write for info. (*0-318-71770-0*, Pub. by Georg Olms GW) Lubrecht & Cramer.

Bibliotheca Indosinica, 5 pts. in 2, Set. Henri Cordier. vii, 3030p. 1972. reprint ed. write for info. (*3-487-04196-0*, Pub. by Georg Olms GW) Lubrecht & Cramer.

Bibliotheca Japonica. Henri Cordier. xii, 762p. 1992. reprint ed. write for info. (*3-487-02193-5*, Pub. by Georg Olms GW) Lubrecht & Cramer.

Bibliotheca Judaica, 3 pts. in 2, Set. Julius Furst. 1960. reprint ed. write for info. (*0-318-71782-4*, Pub. by Georg Olms GW) Lubrecht & Cramer.

Bibliotheca Lexicologiae Medii Aevi: Bibliography of Mediaeval Latin Lexicology, 10 vols., Set. Florent Tremblay. LC 87-26515. 1989. lib. bdg. write for info. (*0-88946-208-9*) E Mellen.

Bibliotheca Librorum Germanicorum Classica. Georg Draud. viii, 791p. reprint ed. write for info. (*0-318-71767-0*, Pub. by Georg Olms GW) Lubrecht & Cramer.

Bibliotheca Librorum Rariorum Universalis. Johann J. Bauer. 2543p. 1982. reprint ed. write for info. (*3-487-07122-3*, Pub. by Georg Olms GW) Lubrecht & Cramer.

Bibliotheca Livoniae Historica. Eduard Winkelmann. xviii, 608p. 1969. reprint ed. write for info. (*0-318-71879-0*, Pub. by Georg Olms GW) Lubrecht & Cramer.

Bibliotheca Magica et Pneumatica. Johann G. Grasse. iv, 175p. 1986. reprint ed. write for info. (*3-487-04770-5*, Pub. by Georg Olms GW) Lubrecht & Cramer.

Bibliotheca Magica et Pneumatica, Oder Wissenschaftlich Geordnete Bibliographie, des Zauber, Wunder, Geister & Sonstigen Aberglaubens, Etc. G. T. Graesse. 175p. (GER & LAT.). 1986. reprint ed. lib. bdg. 40.95 (*0-685-64746-3*, Pub. by Georg Olms GW) Lubrecht & Cramer.

Bibliotheca Masonica. F. Leigh Gardner. reprint ed. pap. 6.95 (*1-55818-123-7*) Holmes Pub.

Bibliotheca Mechanico-Technologica. Wilhelm Engelmann. vii, 683p. 1970. reprint ed. write for info. (*0-318-71771-9*, Pub. by Georg Olms GW) Lubrecht & Cramer.

Bibliotheca Medicinae Practicae, 4 vols., Set. Albrecht V. Haller. 1987. reprint ed. write for info. (*3-487-07334-X*, Pub. by Georg Olms GW) Lubrecht & Cramer.

Bibliotheca Medico-Chirurgica et Anatomico-Physiologica, 2 vols. in 1. Wilhelm Engelmann. viii, 1084p. 1965. reprint ed. write for info. (*0-318-71772-7*, Pub. by Georg Olms GW) Lubrecht & Cramer.

Bibliotheca Medico-Historia. Johann L. Choulant. 279p. reprint ed. lib. bdg. 57.20 (*3-487-00014-8*, Pub. by Georg Olms GW) Lubrecht & Cramer.

Bibliotheca Mejicana. Puttick & Simpson. LC 71-168027. reprint ed. 40.00 (*0-404-02388-6*) AMS Pr.

Bibliotheca Musico-Liturgica. Walter H. Frere. xi, 353p. 1967. reprint ed. write for info. (*0-318-71781-6*, Pub. by Georg Olms GW) Lubrecht & Cramer.

Bibliotheca Musico-Liturgica, 2 vols., Set. Walter H. Frere. (Illus.). xi, 353p. 1967. reprint ed. write for info. (*0-318-71260-1*, Pub. by Georg Olms GW) Lubrecht & Cramer.

Bibliotheca Musico-Liturgica: A Descriptive Handlist of the Musical & Latin-Liturgical Mss. of the Middle Ages, 2 vols. Walter H. Frere. 1967. reprint ed. 122.20 (*0-685-66465-1*, 05101599, Pub. by Georg Olms GW) Lubrecht & Cramer.

Bibliotheca Oeconomica. Wilhelm Engelmann. iv, 438p. reprint ed. write for info. (*0-318-71773-5*, Pub. by Georg Olms GW) Lubrecht & Cramer.

Bibliotheca Orientalis Clementino-Vaticana, 3 vols., Set. Giuseppe S. Assemani. mxxxiv, 2002p. 1975. reprint ed. write for info. (*3-487-05500-7*, Pub. by Georg Olms GW) Lubrecht & Cramer.

Bibliotheca Orientalis Clementino-Vaticana, 3 vols., Vol. I. Giuseppe S. Assemani. mxxxiv, 2002p. 1975. reprint ed. write for info. (*0-318-71481-7*, Pub. by Georg Olms GW) Lubrecht & Cramer.

Bibliotheca Orientalis Clementino-Vaticana, 3 vols., Vol. II. Giuseppe S. Assemani. mxxxiv, 2002p. 1975. reprint ed. write for info. (*0-318-71482-5*, Pub. by Georg Olms GW) Lubrecht & Cramer.

Bibliotheca Orientalis Clementino-Vaticana, 3 vols., Vol. III. Giuseppe S. Assemani. mxxxiv, 2002p. 1975. reprint ed. write for info. (*0-318-71483-3*, Pub. by Georg Olms GW) Lubrecht & Cramer.

Bibliotheca Patrum Latinorum Britannica, 3 vols. in 1. Ed. by Heinrich Schenkl. 989p. 1969. write for info. (*0-318-70726-8*, Pub. by Georg Olms GW) Lubrecht & Cramer.

Bibliotheca Patrum Latinorum Hispaniensis, 4 vols., Set. Ed. by Gustav Loewes & Wilhelm Von Hartel. (Sitzungsberichte der Pilosophisch-Historischen Classe der Kaiserlichen Akademie der Wissenschaften Ser.: Vols. 111-113 & 169). 6385p. 1973. reprint ed. write for info. (*3-487-04428-5*, Pub. by Georg Olms GW) Lubrecht & Cramer.

Bibliotheca Patrum Latinorum Italica, 2 vols. in 1. Ed. by August Reifferscheid. 1033p. 1976. reprint ed. write for info. (*3-487-05966-5*, Pub. by Georg Olms GW) Lubrecht & Cramer.

Bibliotheca Piscatoria. A Catalogue of Books on Angling, the Fisheries & Fish-Culture by...1883. Thomas Westwood & Thomas Satchell. 260p. 1991. 75.00 (*1-882860-08-X*); 400.00 (*1-882860-09-8*) J Cummins Bksell.

Bibliotheca Politica: or, an Inquiry into the Ancient Constitution of the English Government. James Tyrrell. Ed. by Gerald M. Straka. LC 72-83174. (English Studies Ser.). 1972. reprint ed. lib. bdg. 59.00 (*0-8420-1430-6*) Scholarly Res Inc.

Bibliotheca Rabbinica, eine Sammlung Alter Midraschim. 3278p. (GER.). 1993. reprint ed. write for info. (*0-318-70550-8*, Pub. by Georg Olms GW) Lubrecht & Cramer.

Bibliotheca Realis Iuridica, 6 vols., Set. Martin Lipenius. 1967. reprint ed. write for info. (*0-318-71838-3*, Pub. by Georg Olms GW) Lubrecht & Cramer.

Bibliotheca Realis Philosophica, 2 vols., Set. Martin Lipenius. 1967. reprint ed. write for info. (*0-318-71839-1*, Pub. by Georg Olms GW) Lubrecht & Cramer.

Bibliotheca Realis Theologica, 2 vols., Set. Martin Lipenius. 1973. reprint ed. write for info. (*3-487-04594-X*, Pub. by Georg Olms GW) Lubrecht & Cramer.

***Bibliotheca Rosenthaliana: Treasures of Jewish Booklore: Marketing the 200th Anniversary of the Birth of Leeser Rosenthal, 1794-1994.** A. K. Offenberg et al. 130p. 1994. 39.50 (*90-5356-088-2*) IBD Ltd.

Bibliotheca Rosicruciana: A Catalogue Raisonne of Works on the Occult Sciences. F. Leigh Gardner. 101p. 1992. reprint ed. pap. 9.95 (*1-56459-014-3*) Kessinger Pub.

Bibliotheca Rosicruciana, Vol. 1: A Catalogue Raisonne of Works on the Occult Sciences. F. Leigh Gardner. 1992. pap. 22.95 (*1-55818-193-8*) Holmes Pub.

Bibliotheca Scholastica Instructissima: Or a Treasure of Ancient Adagies. Thomas Draxe. LC 76-57378. (English Experience Ser.: No. 796). 1977. reprint ed. lib. bdg. 24.00 (*90-221-0796-5*) Walter J Johnson.

Bibliotheca Scriptorum Classicorum et Graecorum et Latinorum, 2 vols. Rudolf Klussmann. 2115p. 1976. reprint ed. Bd. I: Scriptores Graeci. write for info. (*0-318-70772-1*, Pub. by Georg Olms GW); reprint ed. Bd. II: Scriptores Latini. write for info. (*0-318-70773-X*, Pub. by Georg Olms GW) Lubrecht & Cramer.

Bibliotheca Scriptorum Classicorum et Graecorum et Latinorum, 2 vols., Set. Rudolf Klussmann. 2115p. 1976. reprint ed. write for info. (*3-487-06253-4*, Pub. by Georg Olms GW) Lubrecht & Cramer.

Bibliotheca Sinica, 5 vols. in 3, Set. Henri Cordier. 1971. reprint ed. write for info. (*0-318-71760-3*, Pub. by Georg Olms GW) Lubrecht & Cramer.

Bibliotheca Susanna: A Used Book Sales Record. 3rd ed. Ed. by M. McGill. 322p. 1993. 49.95 (*0-9623826-0-4*) Chinook OR.

Bibliotheca Washingtoniana. W. S. Baker. 1973. 59.95 (*0-87968-746-0*) Gordon Pr.

Bibliothecae Bodleianae Codicum Manuscriptorum Catalogi Partis Secundae Volumen Secundum, Arabicos Complectens, 2 vols in 1. A. Nicoll & E. B. Pusey. (Illus.). viii, 535p. reprint ed. write for info. (*0-318-71539-2*, Pub. by Georg Olms GW) Lubrecht & Cramer.

Bibliothecae Bodleianae Codicum Manuscriptorum Orientalium, 2 vols. Johannes Uri. (Illus.). 1099p. reprint ed. write for info. (*0-318-71571-6*, Pub. by Georg Olms GW) Lubrecht & Cramer.

Bibliothek der Schonen Wissenschaften und der Freyen Kunste, 12 vols. in 6, Set. Ed. by Christoph F. Nicolai et al. 1979. reprint ed. write for info. (*3-487-06659-9*, Pub. by Georg Olms GW) Lubrecht & Cramer.

Bibliothek der Symbole und Glaubensregeln der Alten Kirche. August Hahn & Georg L. Hahn. xvi, 412p. 1962. reprint ed. write for info. (*0-318-70754-3*, Pub. by Georg Olms GW); reprint ed. write for info. (*0-318-71789-1*, Pub. by Georg Olms GW) Lubrecht & Cramer.

Bibliothekarische Klassifikationstheorie. Brian Buchanan. Tr. by Ute Reimer-Bohner. 150p. (GER.). 1989. lib. bdg. 28.00 (*3-598-10788-9*) K G Saur.

***Bibliothekarisches Grundwissen.** Rupert Hacker. 406p. (GER.). 1992. pap. text ed. 17.00 (*3-598-11078-2*) K G Saur.

Bibliothekswesen der Volksrepublik China. Claudia Lux. (Bibliothekspraxis Ser.: No. 26). (Illus.). 119p. (GER.). 1986. lib. bdg. 19.00 (*3-598-21127-9*) K G Saur.

Bibliothekswesen in den U. S. A. Eine Einfuhrung. Elisabeth Simon et al. 155p. (GER.). 1988. lib. bdg. 19.00 (*3-598-10667-X*) K G Saur.

Bibliothekswesen in England: Eine Einfuhrung. Elisabeth Simon. 74p. (GER.). 1985. lib. bdg. 10.00 (*3-598-10567-3*) K G Saur.

Bibliothekswesen in Italien. Gunther Nather. 96p. (GER.). 1991. pap. text ed. 22.00 (*3-598-10759-5*) K G Saur.

Bibliotheque Choisie des Livres de Droit. M. Camus. viii, 376p. 1976. reprint ed. write for info. (*3-487-05992-4*, Pub. by Georg Olms GW) Lubrecht & Cramer.

Bibliotheque de Base du Rotary. David H. Bailey & Louise Gottlieb. Ed. by Willmon L. White & Mark Perlberg. (Illus.). 506p. (FRE.). 1982. 16.75 (*0-915062-10-0*) Rotary Intl.

Bibliotheque des croisades, 4 vols., Set. Joseph F. Michaud. LC 76-29846. (FRE.). reprint ed. 325.00 (*0-404-15450-6*) AMS Pr.

Bibliotheque Du Conservatoire National De Musique et De Declamation. Jean B. Weckerlin. xxxi, 512p. 1973. reprint ed. write for info. (*3-487-04701-2*, Pub. by Georg Olms GW) Lubrecht & Cramer.

Bibliotheque Musicale Du Theatre De l'Opera, 2 vols., Set. Theodore D. De Lajarte. 724p. 1969. reprint ed. write for info. (*0-318-71361-6*, Pub. by Georg Olms GW) Lubrecht & Cramer.

Bibliotherapy: A Clinical Approach for Helping Children. Ed. by John T. Pardeck & Jean A. Pardeck. LC 92-49528. (Special Aspects of Education Ser.: Vol. 16). 1993. pap. text ed. 24.00 (*3-7186-5347-8*) Gordon & Breach.

Bibliotherapy: A Guide to Using Books in Clinical Practice. John T. Pardeck. Ed. by Jean A. Pardeck. LC 92-49235. 168p. 1992. pap. text ed. 59.95 (*0-7734-1954-3*) E Mellen.

Bibliotherapy & Its Widening Applications. Eleanor F. Brown. LC 74-28187. 414p. 1975. 35.00 (*0-8108-0782-3*) Scarecrow.

Bibliotherapy in Rehabilitation, Educational & Mental Health Settings. Joseph S. Zaccaria et al. 1978. pap. text ed. 8.80 (*0-87563-149-5*) Stipes.

Bibliotherapy Sourcebook. Ed. by Rhea J. Rubin. LC 78-939. (Neal-Schuman Professional Book Ser.). 416p. 1978. lib. bdg. 39.50 (*0-912700-04-1*) Oryx Pr.

Bibliotics. Persifor Frazer. LC 70-156017. (Illus.). reprint ed. 43.50 (*0-404-09117-2*) AMS Pr.

Bibliotics, or the Study of Documents: Determinations of the Individual Character of Handwriting & Detection of Fraud & Forgery. Percifor Frazer. 1977. lib. bdg. 59.95 (*0-8490-1504-9*) Gordon Pr.

Bibliotoons: A Mischievous Meander Through the Stacks & Beyond. Gary Handman. LC 89-13620. 112p. 1990. pap. 16.95x (*0-89950-481-7*) McFarland & Co.

***Bibliotraphie Linguistique de l'Annee 1992-Linguistic Bibliography for the Year 1992.** Ed. by Mark Janse. (LIBI - Yearbook Ser.). 1344p. (C). 1995. lib. bdg. 460.00 (*0-7923-3139-7*) Kluwer Ac.

Biblisch-Talmudische Medizin: Beitraege zur Geschichte der Heilkunde und der Kultur Ueberhaupt. Julius Preuss. viii, 736p. 1990. reprint ed. 160.00 (*3-8055-4976-8*) S Karger.

Biblische Lehren. Von S. Speck & H. M. Riggle. 343p. 1982. pap. 4.00 (*0-686-36267-5*) Faith Pub Hse.

Biblische Rosenkranz (German) Christianica Staff. (Illus.). (GER.). 1988. 7.95 (*0-911346-10-4*) Christianica.

Biblischen Erzahlungen Im Qoran. Heinrich Speyer. xiii, 509p. 1988. reprint ed. write for info. (*3-487-00085-7*, Pub. by Georg Olms GW) Lubrecht & Cramer.

***Biblisches und Emblematisches Woerterbuch.** Friedrich Oetinger. 930p. (GER.). 1994. 650.00 (*0-7859-8267-1*, 3110049031) Fr & Eur.

Biblisches und Emblematisches Worterbuch. Friedrich C. Oetinger. 880p. (GER.). 1988. reprint ed. write for info. (*3-487-02345-8*, Pub. by Georg Olms GW) Lubrecht & Cramer.

***Biblisches Woerterbuch.** 4th ed. Grunzweig. 413p. (GER.). 1992. 39.95 (*0-614-00354-7*, 3417240816) Fr & Eur.

Biblographic Guide to Psychology, 1991. Research Libraries of the New York Public Library Staff & Library of Congress Staff. (Bibliographic Guides Ser.). 154p. 1992. text ed. 185.00 (*0-8161-7168-8*) G K Hall.

Biblohrafiia Ukrains'koi Presy, 1816-1916. Varfolomii Adrianovych Ihnatiienko. LC 74-220297. (Bibliohrafiia I Bibliotekoznavstvo Ser.). (UKR.). 1968. pap. 30.00 (*0-685-89029-5*) Slavia Lib.

Biblyografye Fun Artiklen Vegn Khurbn un Gvure. Josef Gar. Incl. Vol. 1. 306p. 1966. 10.00 (*0-914512-22-6*); Vol. 2. 338p. 1969. 10.00 (*0-914512-31-5*); write for info. (*0-318-59438-2*) Yivo Inst.

Bibs & Boots. Alison Lester. (Illus.). 16p. (J). (ps-00). 1989. 3.50 (*0-670-81988-3*) Viking Child Bks.

Bicameral Politics: Conference Committees in Congress. Lawrence D. Longley. LC 88-27766. 400p. (C). 1989. 20.00 (*0-300-04544-1*) Yale U Pr.

BICC PLC & Sterling Greengate Cable Company Ltd. Monopolies & Mergers Ccommission Report. 69p. 1990. pap. 18.00 (*0-10-111312-9*, HM9213) UNIPUB.

Bicentenary History of the Linnean Society of London. Ed. by Andrew T. Gage & William T. Stearn. 242p. 1988. text ed. 72.00 (*0-12-273150-6*) Acad Pr.

Bicentennial Blues: Two Hundred Years of the American Presidency. Enoch Dillon. 64p. (Orig.). 1988. pap. 6.95 (*0-936784-57-1*, Fithian Pr) J Daniel.

Bicentennial Census: New Directions for Methodology in 1990. Ed. by Constance F. Citro & Michael L. Cohen. LC 85-51816. (Illus.). 420p. reprint ed. pap. 119.70 (*0-7837-2595-7*, 2042758) Bks Demand.

Bicentennial Concordance: Indexes to the Constitution of the United States of America. Ed. by Albert P. Blaustein. LC 92-9674. xiv, 202p. 1992. 45.00 (*0-8377-0361-1*) Rothman.

Bicentennial Conference on the Constitution: A Report to the Academy. Ed. by Marvin E. Wolfgang & Richard D. Lambert. LC 76-5778. (Annals Ser.: No. 426). 1976. 27.00 (*0-87761-227-7*); pap. 18.00 (*0-87761-228-5*) Am Acad Pol Soc Sci.

Bicentennial Festschrift for Jacob Rader Marcus. Bertram Korn. 50.00 (*0-87068-457-4*) Ktav.

Bicentennial Gleanings from "South of the Mountains" 1976. pap. 1.00 (*0-911183-13-2*) Rockland County Hist.

Bicentennial Guide to Greater Cincinnati: A Portrait of Two Hundred Years, 2 vols., Set. deluxe ed. Geoffrey J. Giglierano et al. (Illus.). 1988. boxed 39.95 (*0-685-44557-7*) Cinc Hist Soc.

Bicentennial History of Georgetown University, Vol. 1: From Academy to University 1789-1889. Robert E. Curran. LC 92-47499. (Illus.). 463p. 1993. 25.00 (*0-87840-485-6*) Georgetown U Pr.

Bicentennial History of Sullivan Maine, 1789-1989. limited ed. Sullivan-Sorrento Historical Society Staff. Ed. by Josephine Cooper. (Illus.). 400p. 1989. 26.25 (*0-9623511-0-5*) Sullivan-Sorrento.

***Bicentennial History of Union Presbyterian Church: Robinson Township, Pennsylvania, Pittsburgh Presbytery, 1794-1994.** Bicentennial Book Committee. (Illus.). 128p. 1993. 19.95 (*1-881576-15-9*) Providence Hse.

Bicentennial Images. Robert Baxter. 1976. per. 14.95 (*0-913384-19-4*) Rail-Europe-Baxter.

Bicentennial Mini Puppet Theatre. Beverly A. Scott, Jr. 1976. pap. 1.50 (*0-686-15355-3*) B A Scott.

Bicentennial Minutes: New York's Role in the Ratification of the Constitution. limited ed. Ed. by Dominic R. Massaro et al. (Illus.). 64p. reprint ed. boxed 30.00 (*0-318-35285-0*) NYS Bar.

Bicentennial Monograph on Hearing Impairment. Ed. by Robert Frisina. LC 76-16454. 1976. pap. 3.95 (*0-88200-100-0*, L9338) Alexander Graham.

Bicentennial of American Independence on Foreign Stamps. 66p. 1979. 6.00 (*0-318-13296-6*) Am Topical Assn.

Bicentennial of John James Audubon. Alton A. Lindsey et al. LC 84-47791. (Illus.). 192p. 1985. 25.00 (*0-253-10650-8*) Ind U Pr.

Bicentennial of Materials: National SAMPE Technical Conference, 8th, Sea-Tac Motor Inn, Seattle, Washington, October 12-14, 1976. National SAMPE Technical Conference Staff. LC 76-381464. (National SAMPE Technical Conference Ser.: No. 8). 518p. reprint ed. pap. 147.70 (*0-7837-1288-X*, 2041429) Bks Demand.

Bicentennial Space Symposium. Ed. by W. C. Schneider. (Advances in the Astronautical Sciences Ser.: Vol. 35). 1977. lib. bdg. 25.00 (*0-87703-090-1*, Pub. by Am Astro Soc) Univelt Inc.

Bicentennial Two Dollar Bill Cancellations, 2 vols., Set. Andrew J. Vero. Incl. Vol. I. Those Incredible B2FDC-B2J4C's! 3rd ed. 1978. pap. 4.35 (*0-686-25771-5*); Vol. II. Grading Guide for Bicentennial Two Dollar Bill Cancellations. 2nd ed. 1979. pap. 3.49 (*0-686-26083-X*); (Illus.). Set pap. 6.95 (*0-939368-02-1*) B-TwoC.

Bicentennials. Mark Dunster. 1977. pap. 4.00 (*0-89642-003-5*) Linden Pubs.

Bichareh Esfandiyar. Ali-Akbar Saidi-Sirjani. LC 92-70480. (Illus.). 304p. (Orig.). (PER.). 1992. 60.00 (*0-936347-24-4*) Iran Bks.

Bichitra Naatik: A Part of Sikh Scriptures. Ujagar S. Bawa. (Books on Sikhism Ser.). 172p. (YA). (gr. 8-12). 1991. pap. 10.00 (*0-942245-06-7*) Wash Sikh Ctr.

Bichon Frise. Martin Weil. (Illus.). 128p. 1981. 11.95 (*0-86622-448-3*, KW-140) TFH Pubns.

Bichon Frise Champions, 1973-1986. Camino E. E. & B. Co. Staff. (Illus.). 113p. 1988. pap. 36.95 (*0-940808-71-4*) Camino E E & Bk.

Bicicletas Son para el Verano. Fernando Fernan-Gomez. (Nueva Austral Ser.: Vol. 109). (SPA.). 1991. pap. text ed. 24.95x (*84-239-1909-9*) Elliots Bks.

Bicicross. Norman S. Barrett. LC 90-70885. (Picture Library). (Illus.). 32p. (SPA.). (J). (gr. k-4). 1990. lib. bdg. 12.60 (*0-531-07904-X*) Watts.

Bicknell's Victorian Buildings. Bicknell, A. J., & Co. Staff. LC 79-52830. (Illus.). 1980. pap. 7.95 (*0-486-23904-7*) Dover.

BiCMOS - CMOS Systems Design. James E. Buchanan. 336p. 1991. text ed. 50.00 (*0-07-008712-1*) McGraw.

***BiCMOS Advanced Logic Handbook.** 200p. (Orig.). 1995. pap. 125.00 (*0-7605-1820-3*) Rector Pr.

BiCMOS Bus Interface Logic Data Book. Texas Instruments Engineering Staff. 200p. 1989. 9.95 (*0-685-62486-2*, SCBD001A) Tex Instr Inc.

BiCMOS Integrated Circuit Design: With Analog, Digital & Smart Power Applications. Ed. by M. I. Elmasry. LC 94-2478. 528p. 1994. 79.95 (*0-7803-0430-6*, PC03467) Inst Electrical.

BICMOS Technology & Applications. Ed. by Anthony R. Alvarez. (C). 1989. lib. bdg. 79.00 (*0-7923-9033-4*) Kluwer Ac.

BICMOS Technology & Applications. 2nd ed. Ed. by A. R. Alvarez. LC 93-14295. (International Series in Engineering & Computer Science, VLSI, Computer Architecture, & Digital Screen Processing). 424p. (C). 1993. lib. bdg. 95.00 (*0-7923-9384-8*) Kluwer Ac.

Bicmos Technology & Design. (Electrical Engineering Ser.). 1990. text ed. write for info. (*0-442-00271-8*) Van Nos Reinhold.

BiComos Asics. Trontelj. 1996. text ed. 39.95 (*0-07-707777-6*) McGraw.

Bicultural & Trilingual Education: The Foyer Model in Brussels, No. 54. Michael Byram & Leman. 250p. 1990. 89.00 (*1-85359-044-4*, Pub. by Multilingual Matters UK); pap. 36.00 (*1-85359-043-6*) Taylor & Francis.

Bicultural-Bilingual Education for Latino Students. Vinicio H. Reyes. Ed. by Francesco Cordasco. LC 77-90553. (Bilingual-Bicultural Education in the U. S. Ser.). 1978. lib. bdg. 36.95 (*0-405-11092-8*) Ayer.

Bicultural Heritage: Themes for the Exploration of Mexican & Mexican-American Culture in Books for Children & Adolescents. Isabel Schon. LC 78-4332. 164p. 1978. 20.00 (*0-8108-1128-6*) Scarecrow.

Biculturalism of French-Canadian Music, 1534-1759: Indian-French. Lucie Therrien. 51p. 1991. spiral bd. 20.00 (*1-883365-01-5*) French Am Mus.

Biculturalism of Quebec Music, 1759-1850: French-English. Lucie Therrien. 41p. 1991. spiral bd. 17.00 (*1-883365-02-3*) French Am Mus.

Bicycle. Phillip DiLavore. 58p. 1975. 15.00 (*0-318-41558-5*, PT2) Am Assn Physics.

Bicycle. Phillip DiLavore. 26p. 1976. teacher ed 5.00 (*0-318-41559-3*, PT2A) Am Assn Physics.

Bicycle: Le Biciclette. Fermo Galbiati & Nino Ciravegna. LC 93-47375. (Bella Cosa Ser.). (Illus.). 144p. 1994. pap. 12.95 (*0-8118-0750-9*) Chronicle Bks.

Bicycle: The Image & the Dream. Ed. by Nick Sanders. (Illus.). 176p. 1992. pap. 18.95 (*1-873558-00-7*, Pub. by A&C Black UK) Talman.

Bicycle: Vehicle for a Small Planet. Marcia D. Lowe. (Orig.). (C). 1989. pap. write for info. (*0-916468-91-7*) Worldwatch Inst.

Bicycle Accident Reconstruction: A Guide for the Attorney & Forensic Engineer. 3rd ed. James M. Green. (Illus.). 280p. 1993. 49.00 (*0-88450-091-8*) Lawyers & Judges.

Bicycle & City Traffic: Principle & Practice. Hugh McClintock. LC 92-20664. 224p. 1992. text ed. 51.95 (*0-470-21928-9*) Halsted Pr.

***Bicycle & City Traffic: Principles & Practices.** Ed. by Hugh McClintock. 1993. text ed. 59.95 (*0-471-94720-2*) Wiley.

Bicycle As a Factor in Genito Urinary Diseases, Prostratis, Prostatorrhea, or Prostatic Catarrh. H. H. Kane. 24p. 1983. pap. 10.00 (*0-87556-575-1*) Saifer.

Bicycle Bear. Michaela Muntean. LC 93-15458. (Parents Magazine Read Aloud Original Ser.). (Illus.). (J). 1994. lib. bdg. 14.60 (*0-8368-0963-7*) Gareth Stevens Inc.

Bicycle Bear. Michaela Muntean. LC 83-3980. (Illus.). 48p. (J). (ps-3). 1983. 5.95 (*0-8193-1103-0*); lib. bdg. 5.95 (*0-8193-1104-9*) Parents.

Bicycle Bear Rides Again. Michaela Muntean. LC 93-15470. (Parents Magazine Read Aloud Original Ser.). (Illus.). (J). 1995. 14.60 (*0-8368-0964-5*) Gareth Stevens Inc.

Bicycle Bear Rides Again. Michaela Muntean. LC 89-27823. (Illus.). 48p. (J). (ps-3). 1989. 5.95 (*0-8193-1193-6*) Parents.

Bicycle Bibliography Nineteen Fifty to Nineteen Seventy-Two, Pt. 1. David J. Luebbers. (Bicycle Bibliographies Ser.: No. 5). (Illus.). 96p. 1977. pap. 5.00 (*0-9607406-5-1*) D Luebbers.

Bicycle Bibliography Nineteen Seventy-Six. David J. Luebbers. (Bicycle Bibliographies Ser.: No. 4). (Illus.). 106p. 1977. pap. 5.00 (*0-9607406-4-3*) D Luebbers.

***Bicycle Book.** Gail Gibbons. LC 95-5911. (Illus.). 32p. (J). 1995. lib. bdg. 15.95 (*0-8234-1199-0*) Holiday.

Bicycle Book: A Complete Maintenance Guide. Geoff Apps. 1993. 9.99 (*0-517-08743-X*) Random Hse Value.

Bicycle Commuting Book: Using the Bicycle for Utility & Transportation. Rob Van der Plas. LC 89-61364. (Illus.). 128p. (Orig.). 1989. pap. 7.95 (*0-933201-19-2*) Bicycle Books.

Bicycle Commuting Book: Using the Bike for Utility & Transportation. Rob Van der Plas. LC 89-61364. (Illus.). 128p. (Orig.). 1989. pap. 7.95 (*0-933201-29-X*) Bicycle Books.

Bicycle Dealers, 1995. American Business Directories Staff. 1995. spiral bd., pap. 580.00 (*1-56105-593-X*) Am Busn Direct.

***Bicycle Expeditions.** Paul Vickers. (C). 1989. 21.00x (*0-907649-45-9*, Pub. by Expedit Advisory Centre UK) St Mut.

Bicycle Fitness Book: Riding Your Bike for Health & Fitness. rev. ed. Rob Van der Plas. LC 89-61366. (Illus.). 144p. (Orig.). 1990. pap. 7.95 (*0-933201-23-0*) Bicycle Books.

Bicycle for Rosaura. Daniel Barbot. (Illus.). 24p. (J). (ps-3). 1991. 9.95 (*0-916291-34-0*) Kane-Miller Bk.

***Bicycle for Rosaura.** Daniel Barbot. (Illus.). 24p. (J). (ps-3). Date not set. pap. 5.95 (*0-916291-51-0*) Kane-Miller Bk.

Bicycle Frames. Joe Kossack. LC 74-16790. (Illus.). 48p. 1978. pap. 2.50 (*0-89037-062-1*) Anderson World.

Bicycle Gearing: A Practical Guide: Everything You Will Ever Need to Know to Use & Choose the Best Gearing Strategies for Pleasure & Performance Cycling. Dick Marr. LC 89-2986. (Illus.). 136p. (Orig.). 1989. pap. 8.95 (*0-89886-184-5*) Mountaineers.

Bicycle Hills: How One Halloween Almost Got out of Hand. John Bibee. LC 89-15316. (Spirit Flyer Ser.). (Illus.). 204p. (Orig.). (J). (gr. 7-8). 1989. pap. 6.99 (*0-8308-1203-2*, 1203) InterVarsity.

Bicycle Man. Allen Say. (Illus.). 48p. (J). (gr. k-3). 1982. 14.95 (*0-395-32254-5*); 11.95 (*0-685-05704-6*) HM.

Bicycle Man. Allen Say. (Illus.). (J). (ps-1). 1989. pap. 5.95 (*0-395-50652-2*, Sandpiper) HM.

Bicycle Manual. Whiter. 1972. 9.95 (*0-87505-131-6*) Borden.

***Bicycle Market.** 129p. (Orig.). 1995. pap. 1,295.00 (*0-7605-2065-8*) Rector Pr.

Bicycle Mechanics: In Workshop & Competition. 2nd ed. Steve Snowling & Ken Evans. LC 89-12191. (Illus.). 160p. 1990. 19.95 (*0-88011-384-7*, PSNO0384) Human Kinetics.

Bicycle Mystery. Gertrude C. Warner. LC 79-126428. (Boxcar Children Mysteries Ser.: No. 15). (Illus.). 128p. (J). (gr. 2-7). 1971. lib. bdg. 10.95 (*0-8075-0708-3*); pap. 3.50 (*0-8075-0709-1*) A Whitman.

Bicycle Race. Donald Crews. LC 84-27912. (Illus.). 24p. (J). (ps-1). 1985. 16.00 (*0-688-05171-5*); lib. bdg. 15.93 (*0-688-05172-3*) Greenwillow.

Bicycle Racing. Nancy J. Nielsen. LC 87-30489. (Super-Charged Ser.). (Illus.). 48p. (J). (gr. 5-6). 1988. text ed. 11.95 (*0-89686-361-1*, Crstwood Hse) Silver Burdett Pr.

Bicycle Racing Guide: Technique & Training for Bicycle Racers & Triathletes. rev. ed. Rob Van der Plas. LC 85-73276. (Illus.). 256p. (Orig.). 1988. pap. 9.95 (*0-933201-13-3*) Bicycle Books.

Bicycle Repair Book: Maintenance & Repair of the Modern Bicycle. 2nd exp. rev. ed. Robert Van der Plas. LC 93-83823. (Illus.). 192p. (Orig.). 1993. pap. 9.95 (*0-933201-55-9*) Bicycle Books.

Bicycle Repair Step-by-Step: The Full-Color Manual of Bicycle Repair. Robert Van der Plas. 1994. pap. 14.95 (*0-933201-58-3*) Bicycle Books.

Bicycle Resource Guide 1981. David J. Luebbers. (Bicycle Bibliographies Ser.: No. 8). (Illus.). 136p. (Orig.). 1981. pap. 5.00 (*0-9607406-0-0*) D Luebbers.

Bicycle Retailers Guide to Getting Rich in the Recession: Companion Manual to Principles of Bicycle Retailing. Randy W. Kirk. LC 89-84111. (Illus.). 110p. 1989. pap. 19.95 (*0-924272-02-3*) Info Net Pub.

Bicycle Rider. Mary Scioscia. LC 82-47702. (Trophy Picture Bk.). (Illus.). 48p. (J). (gr. 2-6). 1993. pap. 4.95 (*0-06-443295-5*, Trophy) HarpC Child Bks.

Bicycle Rides: Inland Empire. Don Brundige & Sharron Brundige. (Illus.). 154p. (Orig.). 1993. pap. 8.95 (*0-9619151-4-5*) BD Enterprises.

Bicycle Rides: Los Angeles County. Don Brundige & Sharron Brundige. LC 88-72328. (Illus.). 218p. (Orig.). 1991. pap. 10.95 (*0-9619151-3-7*) BD Enterprises.

Bicycle Rides: Orange County. Don Brundige & Sharron Brundige. LC 88-71407. (Illus.). 162p. (Orig.). 1993. pap. 9.95 (*0-9619151-2-9*) BD Enterprises.

Bicycle Rides: San Diego & Imperial Counties. Don Brundige & Sharron Brundige. LC 90-93234. (Illus.). 218p. (Orig.). 1992. pap. 11.95 (*0-9619151-5-3*) BD Enterprises.

Bicycle Rides: San Fernando Valley & Ventura County. Donald G. Brundige & Sharron L. Brundige. LC 88-70353. (Illus.). (Orig.). 1988. pap. 7.95 (*0-9619151-1-0*) BD Enterprises.

***Bicycle Rides: Santa Barbara & Ventura Counties.** Don Brundige & Sharron Brundige. LC 94-94025. (Illus.). 280p. (Orig.). 1994. pap. 10.95 (*0-9619151-6-1*) BD Enterprises.

An Asterisk (*) at the beginning of an entry indicates that the title is appearing in BIP for the first time.

B

An Asterisk (*) at the beginning of an entry indicates that the title is appearing in BIP for the first time.

743

Bifidobacteria & Their Use. J. Kurmann & J. Rasic. (Experientia Supplementa Ser.: Vol. 39). 304p. 1983. text ed. 150.00 (0-8176-1214-9) Birkhauser.

Bifocals Without Tears. Les Swift. (C). 1989. 40.00 (0-89771-745-7, Pub. by Assn Brit Dispen Opticians UK) St Mut.

Bifunctional Compounds. Robert S. Ward. LC 93-33958. (Oxford Chemistry Primers Ser.: Vol. 17). (Illus.). 96p. (C). 1994. text ed. 29.95 (0-19-855809-0); pap. text ed. 9.95 (0-19-855808-2) OUP.

Bifurcated Politics: Evolution & Reform in the National Party Convention. Byron E. Shafer. LC 87-33493. 416p. 1988. 37.50x (0-674-07256-1) HUP.

Bifurcation: Analysis, Algorithms, Applications. Ed. by T. Kupper et al. (International Series of Numerical Mathematics: No. 79). 368p. 1987. 85.00 (0-8176-1798-1) Birkhauser.

Bifurcation Analysis. Ed. by Michiel Hazewinkel et al. 1984. lib. bdg. 90.00 (90-277-1446-0) Kluwer Ac.

Bifurcation & Chaos: Analysis, Algorithms, Applications. Ed. by T. Kupper et al. (International Series of Numerical Mathematics: Vol. 97). 392p. 1991. 108.50 (0-8176-2593-3) Spr-Verlag.

***Bifurcation & Chaos: Theory & Applications.** Ed. by J. Awrejcewicz. LC 94-39751. (Nonlinear Dynamics Ser.). 1994. 84.00 (3-540-58531-1) Spr-Verlag.

Bifurcation & Chaos in Coupled Oscillators. J. Awrejcewicz. 256p. (C). 1991. text ed. 61.00 (981-02-0579-1) World Scientific Pub.

Bifurcation & Chaos in Simple Dynamical Systems. Ed. by J. Awrejcewicz. 136p. (C). 1989. text ed. 33.00 (981-02-0038-2) World Scientific Pub.

Bifurcation & Stability of Dissipative Systems. Ed. by Q. S. Nguyen. (CISM International Centre for Mechanical Sciences Ser.: Vol. 327). (Illus.). v, 291p. 1993. pap. 65.00 (0-387-82437-5) Spr-Verlag.

Bifurcation & Symmetry: Cross Influence Between Mathematics & Applications. Ed. by E. Allgower et al. LC 92-11639. (International Series of Numerical Mathematics: Vols. 104). 336p. 1992. pap. 99.50 (0-8176-2739-1, Pub. by Birkhauser Vlg SZ) Birkhauser.

Bifurcation in Rotating Bodies. P. J. Rabier & J. Tinsley Oden. Ed. by P. G. Ciarlet & J. L. Lions. (Recherches en Mathematiques Appliquees Ser.: Vol. 11). vii, 150p. 1990. pap. 35.00 (0-387-51551-8) Spr-Verlag.

Bifurcation of Extremals in Optimal Control. J. Kogan. (Lecture Notes in Mathematics Ser.: Vol. 1216). viii, 106p. 1986. pap. 18.00 (0-387-16818-4) Spr-Verlag.

Bifurcation Phenomena & Chaos in Thermal Convection. Ed. by H. H. Bau et al. (HTD Series, Vol. 214: AMD: Vol. 138). 120p. 1992. 37.50 (0-7918-1055-0, G00699) ASME.

Bifurcation Theory & Applications: Lectures Given at the Second Session of the Centro Internationale Mathematico Estivo Held at Montecatini, Italy, June 24-July 2, 1983. Centro Internationale Mathematico Estivo Staff. Ed. by L. Salvadori. (Lecture Notes in Mathematics Ser.: Vol. 1057). vii, 223p. 1984. pap. 27.00 (0-387-12931-6) Spr-Verlag.

Bifurcation Theory & Applications in Scientific Disciplines, Vol. 316. Otto E. Rossler. Ed. by Okan Gurel. (Annals Ser.). 708p. (Orig.). 1979. pap. 87.00 (0-89766-000-5) NY Acad Sci.

***Bifurcation Theory & Methods of Dynamical Systems.** D. J. Luo et al. (Advanced Series in Dynamical Systems). 400p. 1995. text ed. 86.00 (981-02-2094-4) World Scientific Pub.

Bifurcation Theory for Fredholm Operators. Jorge Ize. LC 76-25186. (Memoirs of the American Mathematical Society Ser.: No. 7/174). 128p. 1976. pap. 22.00 (0-8218-2174-1, MEMO 7/174) Am Math.

Bifurcations & Periodic Orbits of Vector Fields: Proceedings of the NATO Advanced Study Institute & Semiaaire de Mathematique Superieures, Montreal, Canada, July 13-24, 1992. Ed. by Dana Schlomiuk. LC 93-5095. (NATO Advanced Study Institutes Series C, Mathematical & Physical Sciences: Vol. 408). 492p. (C). 1993. lib. bdg. 180.00 (0-7923-2392-0) Kluwer Ac.

Bifurcations of Planar Vector Fields: Nilpotent Singularities & Abelian Integrals. F. Dumortier et al. Ed. by A. Dold et al. (Lecture Notes in Mathematics Ser.: Vol. 1480). (Illus.). viii, 226p. 1991. pap. 32.00 (0-387-54521-2) Spr-Verlag.

Bifurcations of Planar Vector Fields: Proceedings of a Meeting Held in Luminy, France, September 18-22, 1989. Ed. by J. P. Francoise & R. Roussarie. (Lecture Notes in Mathematics Ser.: Vol. 1455). vi, 396p. 1991. pap. 54.00 (0-387-53509-8) Spr-Verlag.

Big: Bulkbuilding Instructional Guide. Ellington Darden. (Illus.). 224p. (Orig.). 1990. pap. 16.00 (0-399-51630-1, Perigree Bks) Berkley Pub.

Big Abel & the Little Manhattan. Cornelius Mathews. 1972. reprint ed. 24.50 (0-8422-8093-6) Irvington.

***Big Action Bible Skits.** Christine Yount. Ed. by Mike Nappa. LC 95-1374. (Illus.). 40p. 1995. pap. 19.99 (1-55945-258-7) Group Pub.

Big Activities for Little Hands: Science. Veronica Terrill. (Illus.). 64p. (J). (ps-k). 1994. 8.95 (0-86653-826-7, GA1518) Good Apple.

Big Addition Book. Becky Daniel & Charlie Daniel. 64p. (J). (gr. k-3). 1979. 8.95 (0-916456-44-7, GA118) Good Apple.

Big Aiiieeeee! An Anthology of Chinese-American & Japanese-American Literature. Ed. by Jeffrey P. Chan et al. (Illus.). 650p. (Orig.). 1991. pap. 15.00 (0-452-01076-4, Mer) NAL-Dutton.

Big Al. Andrew Clements. (Illus.). (J). 1991. pap. 3.95 (0-590-44455-7, Blue Ribbon Bks) Scholastic Inc.

Big Al. Andrew Clements. LC 88-15129. (Illus.). 28p. (J). (ps up). 1991. pap. 14.95 (0-88708-075-8, Picture Book Studio) S&S Childrens.

Big Al. 2nd ed. Andrew Clements. LC 88-15129. (Pixies Ser.). (Illus.). 32p. (J). (gr. k up). 1991. reprint ed. pap. 4.95 (0-88708-154-1, Picture Book Studio) S&S Childrens.

Big Al & My Side of the Story: Two One-Act Plays. Bryan Goluboff. 1992. 4.75 (0-8222-1324-9) Dramatists Play.

Big Alfie & Annie Rose Storybook. Shirley Hughes. LC 88-11149. (Illus.). 64p. (J). (ps-1). 1989. 15.00 (0-688-07672-6); lib. bdg. 14.88 (0-688-07673-4) Lothrop.

Big Alfie Out of Doors Storybook. Shirley Hughes. LC 91-28635. (Illus.). 64p. (J). (ps up). 1992. 17.00 (0-688-11428-8) Lothrop.

Big Alma: San Francisco's Alma Spreckels. Bernice Scharlach. (Illus.). 352p. 1990. 24.95 (0-942087-05-4) Scottwall Assocs.

***Big American Southwest Activity Book.** Walter D. Yoder. (Illus.). 80p. (Orig.). (J). (gr. 8-12). 1994. pap. 10.95 (0-86534-216-4) Sunstone Pr.

Big & Bright: A History of the McDonald Observatory. David S. Evans & J. Derral Mulholland. LC 86-7044. (History of Science Ser.: No. 4). (Illus.). 224p. 1986. 19.95 (0-292-70759-2); pap. 9.95 (0-292-70762-2) U of Tex Pr.

Big & Easy Art. Rick Chacon. (Illus.). 32p. (J). (ps-1). 1986. student ed 5.95 (1-55734-074-9) Tchr Create Mat.

Big & Easy Art for Fall. Dianna J. Sullivan. (Illus.). 48p. (J). (ps-2). 1987. student ed 6.95 (1-55734-082-X) Tchr Create Mat.

Big & Easy Art for Spring & Summer. Dianna J. Sullivan. (Illus.). 64p. (J). (ps-2). 1987. student ed 7.95 (1-55734-084-6) Tchr Create Mat.

Big & Easy Art for Winter. Dianna J. Sullivan. (Illus.). 48p. (J). (ps-2). 1987. student ed 6.95 (1-55734-083-8) Tchr Create Mat.

Big & Easy Community Helpers. Dianna J. Sullivan. (Illus.). 48p. (J). (ps-2). 1988. student ed 5.95 (1-55734-106-0) Tchr Create Mat.

Big & Easy Health. Dianna J. Sullivan. (Illus.). 48p. (J). (ps-2). 1988. student ed 6.95 (1-55734-104-4) Tchr Create Mat.

Big & Easy Science. Dianna J. Sullivan. (Illus.). 48p. (J). (ps-2). 1988. student ed 6.95 (1-55734-105-2) Tchr Create Mat.

Big & Hairy. Brian Daly. Ed. by Ruth Ashby. 144p. (Orig.). (J). 1994. pap. 3.50 (0-671-87111-0, Minstrel Bks) PB.

Big & Little. William J. Smith. LC 91-66057. (Illus.). 32p. (J). (gr. 5 up). 1992. 15.95 (1-56397-023-6, Wordsong) Boyds Mills Pr.

***Big & Little Animal Book.** David Taylor. LC 95-8332. (Animal Opposites Ser.). (Illus.). (J). 1995. write for info. (0-8172-3950-2) Raintree Steck-V.

Big & Little, Same & Different. Walt Disney Productions Staff. (Walt Disney's Fun-to-Learn Library Ser.: Vol. 4). (Illus.). 44p. (J). (gr. 1-6). reprint ed. 2.99 (0-9619525-5-5) Advance Pubs.

***Big & Little Sweaters.** Kagan. 1994. pap. 9.99 (0-517-12643-5) Random.

***Big Animals.** (Information Square Ser.). (J). Date not set. 3.95 (0-614-02680-6) Ladybird Bks.

Big Annie: An American Tall Tale. Sandra Robbins. (See-More's Stories Ser.). (Illus.). 32p. (Orig.). (J). (ps-4). 1993. pap. 4.95 (1-882601-09-2); audio, pap. 9.98 (1-882601-03-3) See-Mores Wrkshop.

***Big Annie of Calumet.** Jerry Stanley. Date not set. write for info. (0-517-70097-2); lib. bdg. write for info. (0-517-70098-0) Random.

Big Anthony & the Magic Ring. Tomie De Paola. LC 78-23631. (Illus.). 32p. (J). (gr. k up). 1979. 14.95 (0-15-207124-5); pap. 4.95 (0-15-611907-2) HarBrace.

Big Apple: Deco Dances of the Twenties, Charleston, Black Bottom, Shag, Suzy Q, Truckin. 1986. lib. bdg. 79.95 (0-8490-3440-X) Gordon Pr.

Big Apple: Deco Dances of the Twenties, Charleston, Black Bottom, Shag, Suzy Q, Truckin. (Ballroom Dance Ser.). 1985. lib. bdg. 69.00 (0-87700-743-8) Revisionist Pr.

Big Apple Almanac. Patrick M. Reynolds. (Illus.). 112p. (Orig.). 1989. pap. 14.95 (0-932514-19-7) Red Rose Studio.

Big Apple Almanac, No. 2. Patrick M. Reynolds. (Illus.). 112p. (Orig.). 1991. pap. 14.95 (0-932514-24-3) Red Rose Studio.

Big Apple Almanac, No. 3. Patrick M. Reynolds. (Illus.). 112p. (Orig.). 1994. pap. 14.95 (0-932514-29-4) Red Rose Studio.

Big Apple Baby. Helen R. Freedman. (Illus.). 240p. 1988. pap. 9.95 (0-318-21768-6) Laurel-Howard.

***Big Apple Baseball: A Pictorial History, from the Boroughs to the Ballparks.** Harvey Frommer. 1995. 30.00 (0-87833-880-2) Taylor Pub.

Big Apple Guide. 1992. 9.95 (0-942361-53-9) MasterMedia Ltd.

Big Apple Street Smarts. Ed. by Robert S. Persky. 128p. 1992. pap. 14.95 (0-913069-33-7) Consultant Pr.

Big Arms in Six Weeks. Ellington Darden. (Illus.). 128p. 1988. pap. 12.95 (0-399-51432-5, Perigree Bks) Berkley Pub.

***Big as Life: Stories about Men.** Rand R. Cooper. LC 94-48922. 1995. 21.95 (0-385-31422-1, Dial) Doubleday.

Big As Texas: The A to Z Tour of Texas Cities & Places. Linda Michael. Ed. by Karen Lowdermilk. LC 87-36793. (Illus.). 64p. (J). (gr. k-3). 1988. pap. 6.95 (0-937460-34-6) Hendrick-Long.

***Big Babies.** Michael Kinsley. LC 95-14364. 1995. write for info. (0-688-12452-6) Morrow.

Big Baby. Anthony Browne. LC 93-20210. (Illus.). (J). (gr. 1-3). 1994. 13.00 (0-679-84737-5) Knopf Bks Yng Read.

Big Bad Bruce. Bill Peet. LC 76-62502. (Illus.). (J). (gr. k-3). 1977. 14.95 (0-395-25150-8) HM.

Big Bad Bruce. Bill Peet. LC 76-62502. (Illus.). (J). (gr. k-3). 1982. pap. 5.95 (0-395-32922-1) HM.

Big Bad Bruce. Bill Peet. (Book & Cassette Favorites Ser.). (J). (gr. 3 up). 1987. Incl. cass. pap. 8.95 (0-395-45741-6) HM.

Big Bad Bruce Literature Mini-Unit. Janet Lovelady. (Illus.). 32p. (J). (gr. 2-4). 1989. student ed 4.95 (1-56096-001-9) Mari.

Big Bad Love. Larry Brown. 230p. 1990. 17.95 (0-945575-46-7) Algonquin Bks.

Big Bad Love. Larry Brown. LC 91-50044. (Vintage Contemporaries Ser.). 240p. 1991. pap. 11.00 (0-679-73491-0, Vin) Random.

Big Bad Wolf: Level 2. Robert Lado. (Reading Playhouse Ser.). (Illus.). 24p. (J). (ps). 1985. pap. 3.95 (1-879580-53-5); 1.95 (1-879580-52-7) Lado Intl Pr.

Big Bad Wolf in Texas. Russ Huebel. (Illus.). 48p. (Orig.). (J). 1983. pap. 6.25 (0-9611604-2-X) C Del Grullo.

Big Ball of String. 2nd ed. Marion Holland. LC 92-16355. (Beginner Bks.). (Illus.). 72p. (J). (gr. 1-2). 1993. 6.95 (0-394-80005-2); lib. bdg. 7.99 (0-394-90005-7) Random Bks Yng Read.

Big Balloon Race. Eleanor Coerr. LC 91-13606. (I Can Read Bk.). (Illus.). 64p. (J). (gr. k-3). 1981. 13.00 (0-06-021352-3); lib. bdg. 12.89 (0-06-021353-1) HarpC Child Bks.

Big Balloon Race. Eleanor Coerr. LC 91-13607. (Trophy I Can Read Bk.). (Illus.). 64p. (J). (gr. k-3). 1984. pap. 3.50 (0-06-444053-2, Trophy) HarpC Child Bks.

***Big Balloon Race.** Duncan Searl. Ed. by J. Friedland & R. Kessler. (Novel-Ties Ser.). (J). (gr. 1-3). 1994. student ed, pap. text ed. 15.95 (1-56982-053-8) Lrn Links.

Big Band Almanac. rev. ed. Leo Walker. (Quality Paperbacks Ser.). (Illus.). 476p. 1989. reprint ed. pap. 16.95 (0-306-80345-3) Da Capo.

Big Band Combos: Duets-Solos. 1990. 9.95 (0-685-32233-5, 7649) Hansen Ed Mus.

Big Band Era. Jim Morse. Ed. by Kirsten Skogen. (Illus.). 120p. (Orig.). 1992. 5.95 (1-881550-00-1) Hiawatha Pubs.

Big Band Primer. Edward B. Soph. 86p. (C). 1992. 9.18 (1-56870-012-1) RonJon Pub.

Big Band Singers' Songbook. G. Simon. Date not set. pap. 17.00 (0-06-096937-7) HarpC.

Big Bands. 4th ed. George T. Simon. (Illus.). 640p. 1981. pap. 23.00 (0-02-872430-5) Schirmer Bks.

Big Bands Go to War. Chris Way. (Illus.). 288p. 1992. 34.95 (1-85158-457-9, Pub. by Mnstream UK) Trafalgar.

Big Bang: Improvised PETN & Mercury Fulminate. John Galt. (Illus.). 32p. 1987. pap. 8.00 (0-87364-437-9) Paladin Pr.

Big Bang: The Creation & Evolution of the Universe. rev. ed. Joseph Silk. LC 88-16497. (Illus.). 487p. (C). 1995. pap. text ed. write for info. (0-7167-1812-X) W H Freeman.

Big Bang: The Creation & Evolution of the Universe. 2nd rev. ed. Joseph Silk. LC 88-16497. (Illus.). 487p. (C). 1995. text ed. write for info. (0-7167-1997-5) W H Freeman.

Big Bang & Acceleration: Models for the Postcommunist Economic Transformation. Valdas Samonis & Csilla Hunyadi. LC 93-22071. (Illus.). 64p. 1993. pap. 24.95 (1-56072-097-2) Nova Sci Pubs.

Big Bang & George Lemaitre. Ed. by A. Berger. 1984. lib. bdg. 127.50 (90-277-1848-2) Kluwer Ac.

***Big Bang & Other Explosions in Nuclear & Particle Astrophysics.** David N. Schramm. 450p. 1995. text ed. 99.00 (981-02-2024-3); pap. text ed. 48.00 (981-02-2025-1) World Scientific Pub.

Big Bang? Baloney! Joe E. Pierce. LC 91-74062. 137p. (Orig.). 1991. pap. 8.50 (0-913244-27-9) Hapi Pr.

Big-Bang Cannons: The Carbide Cannon, a Unique American Toy. Raymond V. Brandes. LC 93-83909. 160p. 1993. pap. 19.95 (0-9636127-7-8) Ray-Vin Pub.

Big Bang Never Happened. Eric Lerner. 1992. 14.00 (0-679-74049-X, Vin) Random.

Big Bang Never Happened: A Startling Refutation of the Dominant Theory of the Origin of the Universe. Eric Lerner. 480p. 1991. 21.45 (0-8129-1853-3, Times Bks) Random.

Big Bang Theory - or Rotating Universe? Cosmatom Staff. (C). 1992. pap. 35.00 (1-874686-06-8, Pub. by Cosmatom UK) St Mut.

Big Bang Theory - or Rotating Universe? Ian McCrimmon. (C). 1992. text ed. 25.00 (0-9514698-7-8, Pub. by Cosmatom UK) St Mut.

Big Bank. G. Galletly & R. Ritchie. 1990. pap. 21.00 (0-7463-0549-4, Pub. by Northcote UK) St Mut.

Big Bank Take Little Bank. Paul Beatty. LC 90-62908. (New Cafe Poets Ser.). 74p. (Orig.). 1990. pap. 9.95 (0-9627842-7-3) Nuyorican Poets.

Big Bankroll: The Life & Times of Arnold Rothstein. Leo Katcher. (Illus.). 389p. 1994. reprint ed. pap. 14.95 (0-306-80565-0) Da Capo.

Big Base Hit. Dean Hughes. LC 89-37875. (Angel Park All-Stars Ser.). (Illus.). 96p. (Orig.). (J). (gr. 2-6). 1990. lib. bdg. 9.99 (0-679-90427-1) Knopf Bks Yng Read.

***Big Basics Book of Microsoft Office.** Alpha Development Group Staff. (Illus.). 600p. (Orig.). 1995. pap. 19.99 (1-56761-623-2) Alpha Bks IN.

***Big Basics Book of PCs.** Alpha Development Group Staff. (Illus.). 600p. (Orig.). 1995. pap. 19.99 (1-56761-624-0) Alpha Bks IN.

***Big Basics Book of Windows 3.1.** Alpha Development Group Staff. (Illus.). 600p. (Orig.). 1995. pap. 19.99 (1-56761-625-9) Alpha Bks IN.

***Big Bazoohley.** Peter Carey. LC 95-15282. (Illus.). (J). 1995. 14.95 (0-8050-3855-8) H Holt & Co.

***Big Bazoohley.** Peter Carey. (Storybridge Ser.). 96p. (J). 1995. pap. 9.95 (0-7022-2832-X, Pub. by Univ Queensland Pr AT) Intl Spec Bk.

Big Bead Mesa: An Archaeological Study of Navaho Acculturation, 1745-1812. Dorothy L. Keur. LC 76-43760. (Memoirs of the Society for American Archaeology Ser.: No. 1). reprint ed. 12.50 (0-404-15613-4) AMS Pr.

Big Bear: The End of Freedom. Hugh A. Dempsey. LC 84-13105. (Illus.). 227p. 1984. pap. 8.95 (0-8032-6566-2) U of Nebr Pr.

***Big Bear & the Picnic.** (J). 3.99 (0-517-13999-5) Random Hse Value.

***Big Bear Has a Birthday.** (J). 3.99 (0-517-13996-0) Random Hse Value.

Big Bear of Arkansas, & Other Sketches. Ed. by William T. Porter. LC 75-144673. reprint ed. 29.50 (0-404-05079-4) AMS Pr.

Big Bears. Melvin Berger. Ed. by Lisa Trumbauer. (Early Science Big Bks.). (Illus.). 16p. (J). (ps-2). 1994. pap. text ed. 14.95 (1-56784-015-9) Newbridge Comms.

***Big Bears: Mini Books.** Melvin Berger. Ed. by Lisa Trumbauer. (Early Science Big Bks.). 16p. (J). (ps-2). Date not set. pap. text ed. 2.95 (1-56784-042-6) Newbridge Comms.

***Big Bear's Book.** Christina Bjork. Tr. by Joan Sandin. (Illus.). 80p. (J). 1994. 17.95 (91-92962-91-2); 17.95 (91-29-62912-8) FS&G.

***Big Bear's Treasury: A Children's Anthology, Vol. 4.** (Illus.). (J). 1995. 19.95 (1-56402-495-4) Candlewick Pr.

Big Bear's Treasury Vol. 1: A Children's Anthology. LC 91-71859. (Illus.). 96p. (J). (ps up). 1992. 19.95 (1-56402-002-9) Candlewick Pr.

Big Bear's Treasury Vol. 2: A Children's Anthology. LC 91-71859. (Illus.). 96p. (J). (ps up). 1992. 19.95 (1-56402-113-0) Candlewick Pr.

Big Bear's Treasury Vol. 3: A Children's Anthology. Candlewick Press Staff. LC 91-71859. (Illus.). 96p. (J). (ps up). 1994. 19.95 (1-56402-309-5) Candlewick Pr.

Big Bear's Treasury, the Green Collection: A Family Anthology. LC 91-71859. (J). (ps up). 1994. pap. 12.99 (1-56402-363-X) Candlewick Pr.

Big Beast Book: Dinosaurs & How They Got That Way. Jerry Booth. LC 87-36206. (Brown Paper School Bks.). (Illus.). (J). (gr. 3-7). 1988. pap. 10.95 (0-316-10266-0) Little.

Big Beat Heat. John A. Jackson. (Illus.). 400p. 1991. text ed. 24.95 (0-02-871155-6) Schirmer Bks.

Big Beat Heat: Alan Freed & the Early Years of Rock & Roll. John A. Jackson. 1995. pap. 15.00 (0-02-871156-4) Macmillan.

***Big Bedtime Book of Stories & Prayers.** Debbie T. O'Neal. 64p. 1995. 9.95 (0-687-00126-9) Abingdon.

Big Ben Hood. Emanuel Fried. 320p. (Orig.). 1987. pap. 9.95 (0-9603888-5-0) Labor Arts.

Big Bend: A Homesteader's Story. J. O. Langford & Fred Gipson. (Illus.). 191p. 1974. reprint ed. pap. 8.95 (0-292-70734-7) U of Tex Pr.

Big Bend: Three Steps to the Sky. Frank Deckert. Ed. by John R. Pearson. (Illus.). 40p. (Orig.). 1981. pap. 3.95 (0-912001-03-8) Big Bend.

Big Bend Adventure Guide. Doug Rudig. Ed. by John R. Pearson & Frank J. Deckert. (Illus.). 32p. (Orig.). (J). (gr. k-6). 1983. pap. 2.00 (0-912001-10-0) Big Bend.

Big Bend Ambush. Erle Adkins. 224p. 1991. pap. 3.50 (0-8217-3421-0) Zebra.

Big Bend Country. Ross A. Maxwell. Ed. by John R. Pearson. (Illus.). 88p. 1986. 14.95 (0-912001-13-5); pap. 9.95 (0-912001-12-7) Big Bend.

Big Bend Country: Song Voices of the Southwest. Zelma H. Wright, Jr. (Illus.). (Orig.). 1975. pap. 3.00 (0-917016-32-7, M S Wright) Z H Wright.

Big Bend National Park, TX. rev. ed. by Trails Illustrated Staff. (Illus.). 1994. Folded topographical map. 8.99 (0-925873-77-2) Trails Illustrated.

Big Bend of the Rio Grande, a Guide to the Rocks, Landscape, Geologic History, & Settlers of the Area of Big Bend National Park. 5th ed. R. A. Maxwell. (Guidebook Ser.: GB 7). (Illus.). 138p. 1990. reprint ed. 5.00 (0-686-29315-0) Bur Econ Geology.

Big Bend on the Rio Grande: Biography of a National Park. John R. Jameson. (American University Studies: History: Ser. IX, Vol. 18). 172p. (C). 1987. text ed. 32.00 (0-8204-0300-8) P Lang Pubs.

Big Betrayal, Vol. 2. Jack T. Chick. (Illus.). 64p. (Orig.). 1981. pap. 2.95 (0-937958-08-5) Chick Pubns.

Big Bible Banners & Room Decorations. Sally Boscalijon. (Teacher Helper Ser.). (Illus.). 96p. 1992. 10.95 (0-86653-635-3, SS2808, Shining Star Pubns) Good Apple.

Big Bible Story Coloring Book. Corbin Hillam. (Illustrated Bible Ser.). (Illus.). 240p. (J). (ps-3). 1992. 8.95 (0-86653-700-7, SS2830, Shining Star Pubns) Good Apple.

Big Big Big Boat, & Other Bible Stories about Obedience. Christine H. Tanvald. LC 93-9234. (Read Aloud, Read Alone Ser.). (Illus.). (J). 1993. 7.99 (0-7814-0926-8, Chariot Bks) Chariot Family.

Big Big Book of Mother Goose: Favorite Rhymes Selected from the Original Volland Edition. Frederick Richardson. 1987. 4.99 (0-517-64628-5) Random Hse Value.

Big Big Book of Peter Rabbit & His Friends. Beatrix Potter. LC 87-15671. 1988. 5.99 (0-517-64374-X) Random Hse Value.

Big Big Book Series, 7 bks. Bob Reese et al. (Illus.). (J). (gr. k-6). 1987. pap. 140.00 (0-89868-244-4) ARO Pub.

***Big, Big Carrot.** Ret. by Jean Warren. (Cut & Tell Cutouts Ser.). (Illus.). 8p. (J). Date not set. 8.85 (0-614-07349-9) Totline Bks.

Big Big Sea. Martin Waddell. LC 93-33228. (Illus.). 32p. (J). 1994. 15.95 (1-56402-066-5) Candlewick Pr.

***Big Bike Race.** Lucy J. Bledsoe. LC 95-7165. (Illus.). 64p. (J). 1995. pap. 13.95 (0-8234-1206-7) Holiday.

An Asterisk (*) at the beginning of an entry indicates that the title is appearing in BIP for the first time.

Big Bill Blues: William Broonzy's Story. William Broonzy. LC 92-18376. (Illus.). 176p. 1992. reprint ed. pap. 10.95 (*0-306-80490-5*) Da Capo.

Big Bill Haywood. Melvyn Dubofsky. LC 87-17355. 150p. 1987. text ed. 24.95 (*0-312-01272-1*) St Martin.

Big Bill Haywood & the Radical Union Movement. Joseph R. Conlin. LC 79-80015. 264p. reprint ed. pap. 75.30 (*0-8357-3598-2*, 2030116) Bks Demand.

***Big Bird at Bat.** Albee. (J). 1995. 4.99 (*0-679-87090-3*) Random.

***Big Bird Brings Spring to Sesame Street.** Little Golden Books Staff. (J). Date not set. pap. 1.59 (*0-307-02019-3*, Golden Pr) Western Pub.

Big Bird Flies Alone. Felice Haus. LC 88-62523. (Sesame Street Mini-Storybooks Ser.). (Illus.). 32p. (Orig.). (J). (ps-3). 1989. pap. 1.50 (*0-394-83932-3*) Random Bks Yng Read.

Big Bird in China. Jon Stone. (Illus.). (J). (gr. 4-8). 1983. lib. bdg. 7.99 (*0-394-95645-1*) Random Bks Yng Read.

***Big Bird in the Bush: Stories & Sketches.** Earle Birney. 96p. 1995. lib. bdg. 27.00 (*0-8095-4907-7*) Borgo Pr.

Big Bird Is Yellow: A Sesame Street Book of Colors. Photos by John E. Barrett. LC 89-63996. (Board Bks.). (Illus.). 14p. (J). (ps). 1990. bds. 3.95 (*0-679-80752-7*) Random Bks Yng Read.

Big Bird Says...A Game to Read & Play. Sharon Lerner. LC 85-1959. 1985. 3.50 (*0-394-87499-4*) Random Bks Yng Read.

Big Bird Visits Granny Bird. Gail Herman. LC 90-60822. (Sesame Street Mini-Storybooks Ser.). (Illus.). 32p. (Orig.). (J). (ps-3). 1991. pap. 1.50 (*0-679-81050-1*) Random Bks Yng Read.

Big Bird Visits the Dodos. Illus. by Joe Mathieu. LC 84-43051. (Pictureback Ser.). 32p. (J). (ps-3). 1985. lib. bdg. 5.99 (*0-394-97373-9*) Random Bks Yng Read.

Big Birds. Denise Casey. LC 92-17275. (Illus.). 48p. (J). (gr. 1-5). 1993. 14.99 (*0-525-65121-7*, Cobblehill Bks) Dutton Child Bks.

Big Bird's Animal Game. Illus. by Tom Cooke. (Golden Sturdy Shape Bks.). 14p. (J). (ps). 1993. bds. 3.95 (*0-307-12395-2*, 12395, Golden Pr) Western Pub.

Big Bird's Bedtime Story. Rick Wetzel & Maggie Swanson. LC 87-4764. (Pictureback Ser.). (Illus.). 32p. (J). (ps-1). 1987. pap. 2.50 (*0-394-89126-0*) Random Bks Yng Read.

Big Bird's Big Bike. Anna Ross. LC 92-60305. (Sesame Street Chunky Shape Bks.). (Illus.). 22p. (J). (ps). 1993. 3.25 (*0-679-83271-8*) Random Bks Yng Read.

Big Bird's Big Book. Joe Mathieu. (Illus.). 12p. (J). (ps-1). 1987. 29.95 (*0-394-89128-7*) Random Bks Yng Read.

Big Bird's Color Game. (Golden Sturdy Shape Bks.). (Illus.). 14p. (J). (ps). 1980. write for info. (*0-307-12254-9*, Golden Bks) Western Pub.

Big Bird's Copycat Day: A Step 1 Book. Sharon Lerner. LC 84-6869. (Step into Reading Bks.). (Illus.). 32p. (J). (ps-2). 1984. lib. bdg. 7.99 (*0-394-96912-X*); pap. 3.50 (*0-394-86912-5*) Random Bks Yng Read.

Big Bird's Farm. Sesame Street Staff. LC 81-50537. (Board Bks.). (Illus.). 14p. (J). (ps). 1981. bds. 3.95 (*0-394-84812-8*) Random Bks Yng Read.

Big Bird's Mother Goose. Photos by John E. Barrett & View-Master International. LC 83-63404. (Chunky Bks.). (Illus.). 28p. (J). (ps). 1984. bds. 3.25 (*0-394-86745-9*) Random Bks Yng Read.

Big Bird's New Nest & Other Good-Night Stories. Justine Korman. (Big Golden Book Ser.). (Illus.). (J). (ps-1). 1989. write for info. (*0-307-12060-0*, 12060) Western Pub.

Big Bird's Red Book. (J). 1987. pap. 1.00 (*0-307-01029-5*) Western Pub.

Big Bird's Rhyming Book. Sesame Street Staff. LC 78-68790. (Sesame Street Pop-up Ser.: No. 13). (Illus.). (J). (ps-3). 1979. 8.99 (*0-394-84140-9*) Random Bks Yng Read.

Big Bird's Shape Book see Sesame Street Little Library

Big Bird's Yellow Book: Oral Development Language Kit. Zion. 1984. audio 17.50 (*0-19-434172-0*); 4.50 (*0-19-434157-7*); 23.95 (*0-19-434192-5*) OUP.

Big Bird's Yellow Book: Oral Development Language Kit. Zion. 1984. teacher ed 15.95 (*0-19-434156-9*); pap. text ed. 7.50 (*0-19-434155-0*) OUP.

Big Bird's Yellow Book: Oral Development Language Kit. Zion. 1985. 165.95 (*0-19-434179-8*) OUP.

***Big Bite: Barbecue.** Meg Jansz. (Illus.). 80p. 1995. 7.98 (*0-8317-0758-5*) Smithmark.

***Big Bite: Burgers.** Meg Jansz. LC 94-26752. 80p. 1994. 9.98 (*0-8317-0715-1*) Smithmark.

***Big Bite: Pizzas.** Meg Jansz. LC 94-26753. 80p. 1994. 9.98 (*0-8317-0716-X*) Smithmark.

***Big Bite: Salads.** Meg Jansz. (Illus.). 80p. 1995. 7.98 (*0-8317-0759-3*) Smithmark.

Big Black Bear. Wong H. Yee. LC 92-40862. (Illus.). (J). 1993. 14.95 (*0-395-66359-8*) HM.

***Big Black Buzzard & Little Rabbit.** Myldred Lawson. Tr. by Thomas Rowden. (Illus.). 32p. (Orig.). (J). (ps-5). 1994. per., pap. text ed. 5.95 (*0-9642481-1-5*) NE Texas Pub.

***Big-Block Chevy Performance.** Dave Emanuel. 176p. (Orig.). 1995. pap. 15.00 (*1-55788-216-9*, HP Books) Berkley Pub.

Big Block of Chocolate. Redhead. (J). 1989. pap. 19.95 (*0-590-50157-7*) Scholastic Inc.

Big Blow...Union Pacific's Super Turbines. Harold Keekley. LC 75-27729. (Great Railroading Ser.). (Illus.). 1977. pap. 7.95 (*0-916160-02-5*) G R Cockle.

Big Blue: A Trail Guide. Elizabeth Johnston. LC 87-72051. 83p. 1987. 6.00 (*0-915746-36-0*) Potomac Appalach.

Big Blue BASIC: Programming the IBM PC & Compatibles. 2nd ed. Peter Rob. 591p. (C). 1988. pap. 41.95 (*0-534-08706-X*) Boyd & Fraser.

***Big Blue Bottom Line: The Story Behind the Turnaround at IBM.** Mills. Date not set. text ed. 27.95 (*0-471-11622-X*) Wiley.

Big Blue Box of Books: Five Picture-Book Favorites. Incl. My First Picture Dictionary. 1978. (*0-318-55415-1*); Grover's Hide & Seek. 1978. (*0-318-55416-X*); Mother Goose. 1978. (*0-318-55417-8*); Berenstain Bears' New Baby. 1978. (*0-318-55418-6*); Richard Scarry's Find Your ABC's. 1978. (*0-318-55419-4*); (Picturebacks Ser.). (J). (ps-2). 1978. Set. Set boxed 9.75 (*0-394-83971-4*) Random Bks Yng Read.

Big Blue Soldier. large type ed. Grace L. Hill. LC 92-19030. (Nightingale Ser.). 136p. 1992. pap. 14.95 (*0-8161-5600-X*, Nightingale) Hall.

Big Blue Soldier. Grace L. Hill. 1976. reprint ed. lib. bdg. 18.95 (*0-89190-002-0*, Rivercity Pr) Amereon Ltd.

Big Blue Train: Poems. Paul Zimmer. 80p. 1993. 18.00 (*1-55728-296-X*); pap. 12.00 (*1-55728-297-8*) U of Ark Pr.

Big Blues: The Unmaking of IBM. Paul Carroll. 1994. pap. 14.00 (*0-517-88221-3*, Crown) Crown Pub Group.

Big Blues: The Unmaking of IBM. Paul Carroll. 1993. 24.00 (*0-517-59197-9*) Random Hse Value.

***Big Boasting Battle.** Wilhelm. 1995. pap. 3.95 (*0-590-22211-2*) Scholastic Inc.

Big Boats, Little Boats. Jack C. Harris. (Golden Little Look-Look Book Ser.). (Illus.). 24p. (J). (ps). 1990. pap. write for info. (*0-307-11667-0*, Golden Bks) Western Pub.

Big Bombers. Robert F. Dorr & Jim Benson. (Illus.). 128p. 1989. pap. 4.98 (*0-87938-374-7*) Motorbooks Intl.

Big Boobs Is. George Woodward. (Illus.). (Orig.). 1979. pap. 2.95 (*0-8431-0473-2*) Putnam Pub Group.

Big Book - Tape Set. (Cuento Mas Ser.). (Illus.). 143p. (ENG & SPA.). (J). 1989. teacher ed, audio 199.00 (*0-917837-26-6*) Hampton-Brown.

Big Book - Tape Set. (Rimas y Risas Red Ser.). (Illus.). (ENG & SPA.). (J). (gr. k-3). 1990. Set incls. 4 big bks. 16p. ea., 2 cass. tapes & tchr's. ed. pap. text ed. 192.00 (*0-917837-61-4*) Hampton-Brown.

Big Book Favorite Crochet Patterns. Mary C. Waldrep. 1990. pap. 5.95 (*0-486-26359-2*) Dover.

Big Book for Our Planet. Ed. by Ann Durell et al. LC 92-33433. 144p. (J). (gr. k-12). 1993. 17.99 (*0-525-45119-6*, DCB) Dutton Child Bks.

Big Book for Peace. Ed. by Ann Durell & Marilyn Sachs. LC 89-37595. (Illus.). 128p. (YA). (gr. 7-12). 1990. 17.50 (*0-525-44605-2*, DCB) Dutton Child Bks.

***Big Book of Adventure Travel.** 2nd ed. James C. Simmons. LC 94-46924. 1995. 17.95 (*1-56261-219-0*) John Muir.

Big Book of Airbrush. Jose M. Parramon & Miquel Ferron. (Illus.). 144p. 1990. pap. 24.95 (*0-8230-0164-4*, Watsn-Guptill) Watsn-Guptill.

Big Book of America. Illus. by David Atkinson. LC 93-85538. (Courage Children's Classics Ser.). 56p. (J). (gr. 3 up). 1994. 9.98 (*1-56138-390-2*) Courage Bks.

Big Book of America. Illus. by David Atkinson. 56p. (J). 1994. 9.98 (*0-685-71553-1*) Running Pr.

Big Book of Animal Masks. Angela Holroyd. (Illus.). 32p. (J). (gr. k-4). 1990. pap. 8.95 (*0-671-72580-7*, Litl Simon S&S) S&S Childrens.

Big Book of Animal Patterns. Marilynn Barr. (Illus.). 64p. (J). (ps-2). 1994. teacher ed, pap. 12.95 (*1-878279-67-X*, MM 1988) Evan-Moor Corp.

Big Book of Art Centers. Joy Evans. (Illus.). 64p. (J). (gr. 1-4). 1992. pap. 11.95 (*1-55799-221-5*, EMC307) Evan-Moor Corp.

Big Book of Baby Names & Announcements. Sandra B. Bailey. 1991. pap. 8.00 (*0-399-51710-3*, Body Pr-Perigree) Berkley Pub.

***Big Book of Beautiful Babies.** David Ellwand. (Illus.). 32p. (J). (ps). 1995. 14.99 (*0-525-45499-3*, DCB) Dutton Child Bks.

Big Book of Bible Crafts & Projects. Joy MacKenzie. (Illus.). 212p. (Orig.). (J). (ps-4). 1981. pap. 15.99 (*0-310-70151-1*, 14019P) Zondervan.

Big Book of Bible Games & Puzzles. Joy MacKenzie et al. 192p. (J). (gr. 1-6). 1982. reprint ed. pap. 15.99 (*0-310-70271-2*, 14029P) Zondervan.

Big Book of Blues: A Biographical Encyclopedia. Robert Santelli. LC 93-4127. (Illus.). 448p. (Orig.). 1994. pap. 15.95 (*0-14-015939-8*, Penguin Bks) Viking Penguin.

Big Book of Boat Canvas: A Complete Guide to Fabric Work on Boats. Karen Lipe. (Illus.). 256p. 1991. pap. 18.95 (*0-915160-34-X*, 60210P) Intl Marine.

Big Book of Boat Canvas: A Complete Guide to Fabric Work on Boats. Karen Lipe. 1991. pap. 19.95 (*0-07-038000-7*) McGraw.

Big Book of Boat Canvas: A Complete Guide to Fabric Work on Boats. Karen Lipe. 1991. pap. 19.95 (*0-915160-35-8*) Seven Seas.

***Big Book of Books & Activities: An Illustrated Guide for Teacher, Parents, & Anyone Who Works With Kids!** Dinah Zike. (Illus.). 131p. 1992. pap. 19.95 (*1-882796-07-1*, CCC 100) Dinah-Might Act.

***Big Book of Books & Activities Religious Supplement: New Testament Religious Supplement for Christian Schools, Sunday Schools, Bible Schools, & Home Schools.** Dinah Zike. (Illus.). 70p. 1993. pap. 12.95 (*1-882796-00-4*, CCC 94) Dinah-Might Act.

***Big Book of Books & Activities Religious Supplement: Old Testament Religious Supplement for Christian & Jewish Schools, Sunday Schools, Bible Schools, & Home Schools.** Dinah Zike. (Illus.). 71p. 1993. pap. text ed. 12.95 (*1-882796-04-7*, CCC 93) Dinah-Might Act.

Big Book of Borders & Frames. Carol B. Grafton. LC 94-13896. (Dover Pictorial Archive Ser.). 1994. write for info. (*0-486-28243-0*) Dover.

***Big Book of Bowling.** Howard Stallings. (Illus.). 96p. 1995. pap. 17.95 (*0-87905-662-2*) Gibbs Smith Pub.

Big Book of Boxes. Taro Gomi. (Illus.). 12p. (J). (ps up). 1991. pap. 14.95 (*0-8118-0067-9*) Chronicle Bks.

Big Book of Boxes (cutouts) (J). (gr. 2-6). 1992. 10.00 (*1-56021-140-7*) W J Fantasy.

***Big Book of Brewing.** Dave Line. (Illus.). 254p. (Orig.). pap. 12.95 (*0-9619072-9-0*) G W Kent.

***Big Book of Broadway.** (Piano-Vocal-Guitar Ser.). 316p. 1994. 19.95 (*0-7935-3154-3*) H Leonard.

***Big Book of Busts.** John Watson & Eric Schiller. (Competitive Chess Ser.). (Illus.). 240p. 1994. pap. 19.95 (*1-886040-16-8*) Hypermodern Pr.

Big Book of Buttons. Elizabeth Hughes & Marion Lester. 818p. 1991. 125.00 (*0-9629046-0-0*) New Leaf Pubs.

***Big Book of Camaro Data 1967-1973.** John Hooper. (Illus.). 160p. 1995. pap. 21.95 (*0-87938-973-7*) Motorbooks Intl.

Big Book of Cartooning, Bk. I. Vic Lockman. (Illus.). 104p. (Orig.). 1990. spiral bd., pap. 12.00 (*0-936175-08-7*) V Lockman.

Big Book of Cartooning, Bk. II: Animals. Vic Lockman. (Illus.). 48p. 1991. spiral bd. 8.00 (*0-936175-15-X*) V Lockman.

Big Book of Cartooning Drawing for Girls. Vic Lockman. (Illus.). 70p. 1993. spiral bd. 10.00 (*0-936175-26-5*) V Lockman.

Big Book of Ceramics: A Guide to the History, Materials, Equipment & Techniques of Hand-building, Throwing, Molding, Kiln-Firing, & Glazing Pottery & other Ceramic Objects. Joaquim Chavarria. LC 94-11057. (Illus.). 192p. 1994. pap. 32.50 (*0-8230-0508-9*) Watsn-Guptill.

Big Book of Children's Songs. 128p. 1988. pap. 10.95 (*0-88188-942-3*, 00359261) H Leonard.

Big Book of Children's Songs. (Big-Note Piano Ser.). 144p. 1990. pap. 12.95 (*0-7935-0042-7*, HL00290255) H Leonard.

Big Book of Christmas Plays. Ed. by Sylvia E. Kamerman. LC 88-15691. (J). (gr. 4-12). 1988. 18.95 (*0-8238-0288-4*) Plays.

Big Book of Christmas Songs. (Piano-Vocal-Guitar Ser.). 272p. (Orig.). 1991. pap. 19.95 (*0-7935-0783-9*, 00311520) H Leonard.

***Big Book of Combinations.** Eric Schiller. (Competitive Chess Ser.), 208p. 1994. pap. 17.95 (*1-886040-14-1*) Hypermodern Pr.

Big Book of Comedies. Ed. by Sylvia E. Kamerman. (YA). 1989. 18.95 (*0-8238-0289-2*) Plays.

***Big Book of Conspiracies.** D. Moench. Ed. by Taggart. (Illus.). 224p. 1995. pap. 12.95 (*1-56389-186-7*, Paradox) DC Comics.

***Big Book of Country Music: A Biographical Encyclopedia.** Richard Carlin. LC 94-39275. 1995. 16.95 (*0-14-023509-4*, Penguin Bks) Viking Penguin.

***Big Book of Death.** B. Carlton. Ed. by A. Helfer. (Illus.). 224p. 1995. pap. 12.95 (*1-56389-166-2*, Paradox) DC Comics.

Big Book of Decorative Painting: How to Paint if You Don't Know How -- & How to Improve If You Do. Jackie Shaw. LC 93-38486. (Illus.). 336p. 1994. 35.00 (*0-8230-0265-9*, Watsn-Guptill) Watsn-Guptill.

Big Book of Dinosaurs. 1989. 14.99 (*0-517-67601-X*) Random Hse Value.

Big Book of Dinosaurs. Angela Wilkes. LC 94-4675. (Illus.). 32p. (J). (ps). 1994. 12.95 (*1-56458-718-5*) Dorling Kindersley.

Big Book of Disney Songs for Electronic Keyboards. (Illus.). 112p. (Orig.). (J). 1987. pap. 16.95 (*0-88188-915-6*, 00243065) H Leonard.

Big Book of Dramatized Classics: 25 Adaptations of Favorite Novels, Stories, & Plays for Stage & Round-the-Table Reading. Ed. by Sylvia E. Kamerman. LC 93-3387. 400p. (J). (gr. 1-8). 1993. 18.95 (*0-8238-0299-X*) Plays.

Big Book of Drawing. Jose M. Parramon. (Illus.). 192p. 1993. pap. 27.50 (*0-8230-0492-9*, Watsn-Guptill) Watsn-Guptill.

Big Book of Folder Games for the Primary Classroom. Elaine Commins. LC 88-9104. 256p. (Orig.). 1989. pap. 17.95 (*0-89334-113-4*) Humanics Ltd.

Big Book of Folder Games for the Primary Classroom. Elaine Commins. LC 88-9104. (Illus.). 256p. (Orig.). 1989. lib. bdg. 27.95 (*0-89334-181-9*, 181-9) Humanics Ltd.

Big Book of Folktale Plays. Ed. by Sylvia E. Kamerman. 336p. (J). (gr. 3-7). 1991. 18.95 (*0-8238-0294-9*) Plays.

***Big Book of Freaks.** Gahan Wilson. Ed. by Taggart. (Illus.). 224p. 1995. pap. 12.95 (*1-56389-218-9*, Paradox) DC Comics.

Big Book of Fun: Creative Learning Activities for Home & School. Carolyn B. Haas. LC 87-20325. (Illus.). 288p. (Orig.). (J). (ps-7). 1987. reprint ed. pap. 9.95 (*1-55652-020-4*) Chicago Review.

Big Book of Gardening Skills. Garden Way Publishing Editors. Ed. by Andrea Chesman. LC 92-53949. (Illus.). 352p. 1993. 29.95 (*0-88266-796-3*, Garden Way Pub); pap. 18.95 (*0-88266-795-5*, Garden Way Pub) Storey Comm Inc.

Big Book of Geography Rhymes & Chants. Robert DeWeese. (Illus.). 32p. 1994. pap. text ed. 11.95 (*1-55799-268-1*) Evan-Moor Corp.

Big Book of Gifts to Make. Kate Yeates. Date not set. pap. 15.99 (*0-517-10342-7*) Random Hse Value.

Big Book of Graphic Design & Devices. Kiyoshi Takshashi. 1990. pap. 6.95 (*0-486-26261-8*) Dover.

Big Book of Harley-Davidson. rev. ed. Tom Bolfert. (Illus.). 300p. 1991. pap. text ed. 39.95 (*0-9624113-1-0*) Harley-Davidson.

Big Book of Hearts. Running Press Staff. (Visions of Love in Word & Image Ser.). (Illus.). 112p. 1994. 4.95 (*1-56138-416-X*) Running Pr.

Big Book of Hell. Matt Groening. Date not set. pap. 8.99 (*0-517-11260-4*) Random Hse Value.

Big Book of Holiday Plays. Ed. by Sylvia E. Kamerman. LC 90-7615. 335p. (J). 1990. 18.95 (*0-8238-0291-4*) Plays.

Big Book of Home Learning, Vols. 1-4. Mary Pride. LC 89-81254. 1991. pap. 82.50 (*0-89107-567-4*) Crossway Bks.

Big Book of How Things Work. (Illus.). 160p. (J). 1993. 14.98 (*1-56173-091-2*) Pubns Intl Ltd.

Big Book of Jazz. 288p. 1992. pap. 19.95 (*0-7935-1247-6*, 00311557) H Leonard.

Big Book of Jewish Humor. William Novak & Moshe Waldoks. LC 81-47234. (Illus.). 320p. 1981. pap. 17.00 (*0-06-090917-X*, CN 917, PL) HarpC.

Big Book of Kites. Jim Rowlands. (Illus.). 132p. 1988. pap. 14.95 (*0-312-02047-3*) St Martin.

***Big Book of Large-Cast Plays: Twenty-Seven One-Act Plays for Young Actors.** Ed. by Sylvia E. Kamerman. 350p. (J). 1994. text ed. 18.95 (*0-8238-0302-3*) Plays.

Big Book of Latin American Songs. 272p. 1992. pap. 19.95 (*0-7935-1383-9*, 00311562) H Leonard.

Big Book of Library Grant Money: Profiles of 1,471 Private & Corporate Foundations & Direct Corporate Givers Receptive to Library Grant Proposals. Taft Group Staff. LC 94-1383. 1300p. 1994. pap. 140.00 (*0-8389-0636-2*) ALA.

***Big Book of Life's Instructions.** Ed. by Sheree Bykofsky & Paul Fargis. LC 95-8648. 1995. pap. 19.95 (*0-06-273371-0*, Harper Ref) HarpC.

***Big Book of Little Criminals.** Ed. by Taggart. (Illus.). 224p. 1995. pap. 12.95 (*1-56389-217-0*, Paradox) DC Comics.

Big Book of Love & Wedding Songs. 256p. 1992. pap. 19.95 (*0-7935-1440-1*, 00311567) H Leonard.

Big Book of Magic Tricks. unabridged ed. Karl Fulves. LC 94-16495. (Illus.). 208p. 1994. pap. text ed. 9.95 (*0-486-28228-7*) Dover.

Big Book of Math Rhymes & Chants. Robert DeWeese & Jo E. Moore. (Illus.). 32p. (J). (gr. k-3). 1994. teacher ed, pap. 11.95 (*1-55799-267-3*, EMC 383) Evan-Moor Corp.

Big Book of Mazes & Labyrinths. Walter Shepherd. LC 72-97817. 112p. (Orig.). 1973. pap. 3.95 (*0-486-22951-3*) Dover.

Big Book of Monster Masks. Angela Holroyd. (Illus.). 32p. (J). (gr. k-4). 1990. pap. 8.95 (*0-671-72579-3*, Litl Simon S&S) S&S Childrens.

Big Book of Movie & TV Themes. Hal Leonard Publishing Staff. 352p. 1993. pap. 19.95 (*0-7935-1627-7*, 00311582) H Leonard.

Big Book of Mr. Small. Lois Lenski. (Illus.). (J). (ps-3). 1980. pap. 9.95 (*0-8098-6026-0*) McKay.

Big Book of Nursery Rhymes see Mother Goose's Nursery Rhymes

Big Book of Oil Painting. Jose M. Parramon. (Illus.). 192p. 1990. pap. 27.50 (*0-8230-0498-8*, Watsn-Guptill) Watsn-Guptill.

Big Book of Painting Nature in Oil. S. Allyn Schaeffer. (Illus.). 400p. 1991. pap. 29.95 (*0-8230-0503-8*, Watsn-Guptill) Watsn-Guptill.

Big Book of Painting Nature in Pastel. S. Allyn Schaeffer. (Illus.). 192p. (Orig.). 1993. pap. 29.95 (*0-8230-0504-6*, Watsn-Guptill) Watsn-Guptill.

Big Book of Painting Nature in Watercolor. Ferdinand Petrie. (Illus.). 400p. 1990. pap. 29.95 (*0-8230-0499-6*, Watsn-Guptill) Watsn-Guptill.

Big Book of Pencil Pastimes: The Best Word Games, Quizzes & Brain Ticklers. James F. Minter. 1991. pap. 6.95 (*0-88486-039-6*) Arrowood Pr.

Big Book of Photocopier Humor: A Treasury of High-Tech Grafitti, Left-Brain Witticisms, & Generic Humor. Wayne B. Norris. LC 84-90667. (Illus.). 256p. (Orig.). 1984. reprint ed. pap. 8.96 (*0-685-10088-X*) Norris Assocs Pr.

Big Book of Playground Rhymes & Chants. Ed. by Robert DeWeese. (Illus.). 32p. 1994. pap. text ed. 11.95 (*1-55799-266-5*) Evan-Moor Corp.

***Big Book of Projects: Fast & Easy Projects for Everyone From Kindergarten Through College.** Dinah Zike. Ed. by Jan Dorough. (Illus.). 144p. 1995. pap. 19.95 (*1-882796-03-9*) Dinah-Might Act.

Big Book of Puzzlers: Picture Puzzles, Brainteasers, Games, Mazes, & More. Karen C. Anderson. LC 91-73805. (Illus.). 176p. (J). (gr. 2-7). 1992. pap. 9.95 (*1-56282-067-2*) Disney Pr.

Big Book of Questions & Answers. Consumer Guide Editors. (Illus.). 192p. 14.98 (*1-56173-411-X*) Pubns Intl Ltd.

***Big Book of Real Estate Ads: 1001 Ads That Sell.** William H. Pivar & Bradley A. Pivar. 320p. 1995. pap. 29.95 (*0-7931-1430-6*, 1926-1101, Real Estate Ed) Dearborn Finan.

***Big Book of Relaxation: Simple Skills & Practices for a Calmer Life.** Shakti Gawain. 1994. pap. 14.95 (*1-55961-282-7*) Relaxtn Co.

Big Book of Riddles. Running Press Staff. (Miniature Editions Ser.). (Illus.). 128p. 1994. 4.95 (*1-56138-421-6*) Running Pr.

Big Book of Rock. 320p. 1992. pap. 19.95 (*0-7935-1434-7*, 00311566) H Leonard.

Big Book of Science Charts: Dinosaurs. Patricia L. Miriani & Karen J. Goldfluss. (Illus.). 26p. (Orig.). 1992. student ed 14.95 (*1-55734-571-6*) Tchr Create Mat.

Big Book of Science Charts: My Body. Breck Nichols. (Illus.). 26p. (Orig.). 1992. student ed 14.95 (*1-55734-570-8*) Tchr Create Mat.

Big Book of Science Rhymes & Chants. Jo E. Moore & Leslie Tryon. (Illus.). 64p. (J). (gr. k-2). 1991. pap. 11.95 (*1-55799-211-8*, EMC306) Evan-Moor Corp.

B

An Asterisk (*) at the beginning of an entry indicates that the title is appearing in BIP for the first time. 745

Big Book of Science Stories. Jo E. Moore & Leslie Tryon. (Illus.). 64p. (J). (gr. k-2). 1991. pap. 11.95 (1-55799-210-X) Evan-Moor Corp.

Big Book of Science Stories, Vol. 2. Jo E. Moore. (Illus.). 64p. 1994. pap. text ed. 11.95 (1-55799-265-7) Evan-Moor Corp.

Big Book of Secret Hiding Places. Jack Luger. (Illus.). 136p. (Orig.). 1987. pap. 14.95 (0-915179-66-0, 10048) Loompanics.

***Big Book of Small Household Repairs: Your Goof-Proof Guide to Fixing Over Two-Hundred Annoying Breakdowns.** Charlie Wing. (Illus.). 352p. 1995. 27.95 (0-87596-649-7) Rodale Pr Inc.

Big Book of Small Needlework Gifts. Annette Feldman. 159p. 1980. 27.50 (0-87559-210-4) Shalom.

Big Book of Software for the Atari ST. Bill Skurski & Michael Wilder. 200p. 1989. 16.95 (0-685-29926-0) B Skurski Enter.

***Big Book of Space.** William Edmonds. LC 94-28252. (Illus.). 48p. (J). (gr. 2-7). 1995. 15.95 (0-89577-648-0) RD Assn.

Big Book of Staff Paper. 512p. 1993. pap. 8.95 (0-7935-1688-9, 00210045) H Leonard.

Big Book of Stuffed Toy & Doll Making: Instructions & Full-Size Patterns for 45 Playthings. Margaret Hutchings. (Illus.). 256p. (J). (gr. 7 up). 1983. reprint ed. pap. 8.95 (0-486-24266-8) Dover.

Big Book of Things That Go. LC 94-643. (Illus.). 32p. (J). (ps). 1994. 12.95 (1-56458-462-3) Dorling Kindersley.

***Big Book of Things to Make & Play With: Games, Toys, Puppets.** Comp. by Highlights Editors Staff. LC 94-79103. 80p. (J). (gr. 1-5). 1995. 7.95 (1-56397-473-8) Boyds Mills Pr.

Big Book of Time. William Edmonds. LC 93-35709. (Illus.). 48p. (J). (gr. 2-7). 1994. 15.95 (0-89577-579-4) RD Assn.

Big Book of TV Guide Crosswords, No. 2. TV Guide Editors. 1993. pap. 8.95 (0-06-096969-5, PL) HarpC.

Big Book of "TV Guide" Crosswords: Test Your TV IQ with More Than 250 Great Puzzles from "TV Guide!", No. 1. TV Guide Editors. 288p. (Orig.). 1993. pap. 9.95 (0-06-096968-7, PL) HarpC.

Big Book of U. S. Presidents: A Young Person's Guide to American History. Victoria Sherrow. (Illus.). 56p. (J). 1994. 9.98 (1-56138-427-5) Running Pr.

***Big Book of Urban Legends.** Robert Fleming & R. Boyd, Jr. Ed. by B. Taggart. 224p. 1994. pap. 12.95 (1-56389-165-4, Paradox) DC Comics.

Big Book of Watercolor. Jose M. Parramon. (Illus.). 192p. 1984. 32.50 (0-8230-0496-1, Watsn-Guptill) Watsn-Guptill.

***Big Book of Weirdos.** Carl Posey. Ed. by B. C. Taggart. (Illus.). 224p. 1995. pap. 12.95 (1-56389-180-8, Paradox) DC Comics.

Big Book of Whittling & Woodcarving. E. J. Tangerman. 1990. pap. 12.95 (0-486-26171-9) Dover.

Big Book of Words: Primary Dictionary. William A. Kottmeyer & Audrey Claus. (Basic Goals in Spelling Ser.). 288p. 1988. text ed. 15.96 (0-07-034682-8) McGraw.

***Big Book of Words for Curious Kids.** Tr. by Vicky Holifield. LC 95-13123. (Illus.). (J). 1995. write for info. (1-56145-111-8) Peachtree Pubs.

Big Book on Small Groups. Jeffrey Arnold. LC 91-37115. 300p. (Orig.). 1992. pap. 10.99 (0-8308-1377-2, 1377) InterVarsity.

Big Book Package, 4 vols., Set. K. Beal. (Multicultural Sing-Along Big Book Program Ser.). (Illus.). 16p. (J). (gr. 1-3). 1990. pap. text ed. 80.25 (0-201-52205-5) Addison-Wesley.

Big Book Set: Level 2. (Wonders! Ser.). (Illus.). (Orig.). 1992. pap. 232.00 (1-56334-221-9); ring bd. 232.00 (1-56334-208-1) Hampton-Brown.

Big Book Study Guide. Joe McQuany. 145p. 1986. pap. text ed. 8.95 (1-883094-00-3) Kelly Fnd.

Big-Bore Rifle: The Book of Fine Magazine & Double Rifles, .375 - .700 Calibers. Michael McIntosh. LC 89-81948. (Illus.). 240p. 1990. 39.00 (0-924357-09-6) Countrysport Pr.

Big-Bore Rifle: The Book of Fine Magazine & Double Rifles, .375 - .700 Calibers. deluxe limited ed. Michael McIntosh. LC 89-81948. (Illus.). 240p. 1990. 95.00 (0-924357-12-6) Countrysport Pr.

Big Bore Rifles & Cartridges. 1990. 26.00 (1-879356-00-7) Wolfe Pub Co.

Big Boss Charger. Helen Kienlen & Lois Sandercock. (Illus.). 16p. (J). (gr. k-4). 1989. pap. text ed. 4.00 (0-9626864-1-7) Holistic Learning.

Big Bosses. Charles W. Van Devander. LC 73-19182. (Politics & People Ser.). 318p. 1974. reprint ed. 23.95 (0-405-05903-5) Ayer.

Big Bounce. Intro. by Elmore Leonard. LC 88-38210. 208p. 1989. reprint ed. 25.00 (0-922890-00-5); reprint ed. 18.95 (0-922890-05-6) Armchair Detective.

Big Bow Mystery. E. F. Bielier. 17.95 (0-8488-0063-X, Amereon Hse) Amereon Ltd.

Big Bow Mystery. Israel Zangwill. 160p. 1986. pap. 2.95 (0-88184-238-9) Carroll & Graf.

Big Bow Mystery. Israel Zangwill. 16.95 (0-8488-0856-8) Amereon Ltd.

Big Box. T. McTaggart. (C). 1989. pap. 60.00 (0-907526-27-6, Alloway Pub) St Mut.

Big Boy. Tololwa M. Mollel. (Illus.). (J). 1995. write for info. (0-318-72305-0, Clarion Bks) HM.

***Big Boy.** Tolowa M. Mollel. (J). (ps-3). 1994. 14.95 (0-395-67403-4, Clarion Bks) HM.

Big Boy: The Story of a Dog. Albert Pennington. 320p. 1971. 3.00 (0-685-04706-7); pap. 1.00 (0-685-04707-5) Pennington.

Big Boys (& Girls) Do Cry. Lester Dotson. (Illus.). 123p. (Orig.). 1990. pap. text ed. 8.95 (0-9626664-0-8) Halt Counseling.

Big Boys, Little Lies. Ed. by John Patrick. LC 92-82591. 448p. (Orig.). 1994. pap. 14.95 (1-877978-65-5) Woldt.

Big Brand. large type ed. Elmer Kelton. (Nightingale Series Large Print Bks.). 311p. (Orig.). 1992. pap. 14.95 (0-8161-5321-3, Nightingale) Hall.

Big Brave Brother Ben. Kara May. LC 91-530234. (Illus.). (J). (ps-3). 1992. 14.00 (0-688-11234-X); lib. bdg. 13.93 (0-688-11235-8) Lothrop.

Big Breakup, No. 5. Michael J. Pellowski. LC 91-73839. (Riverdale High Ser.). (Illus.). 128p. (YA). (gr. 4-8). 1992. pap. 2.99 (1-56282-147-4) Hyprn Child.

Big Broccoli Book. Georgia Downard. 1992. pap. 10.00 (0-679-74382-0) Random.

Big Brother. Mary Rogers. (Cityscapes Ser.). 19p. (J). (gr. k). 1992. pap. text ed. 23.00 (1-56843-010-8); pap. text ed. 4.50 (1-56843-060-4) BGR Pub.

Big Brother. Gilbert M. Woten. 1992. pap. 5.95 (1-55673-456-5, 7911) CSS OH.

Big Brother: The Soviet Union & Soviet Europe. Helene C. D'Encausse. Tr. by George Holoch. LC 86-31885. 380p. (C). 1987. 39.50 (0-8419-1042-1); pap. 24.50 (0-8419-1043-X) Holmes & Meier.

***Big Brother, Big Sister, Big Deal.** Dianne Dannhauss. Ed. by Debbie Bowen. (Professional Mom Ser.). (Illus.). 24p. (J). (gr. 1-4). Date not set. lib. bdg. 11.95 (1-56763-151-7); pap. text ed. 5.95 (1-56763-152-5) Ozark Pub.

Big Brother, Bunny. Pamela Kennedy. (CottonTale Book Ser.). (Illus.). 1992. bds. 4.99 (1-56179-087-7) Focus Family.

Big Brother Game. Scott French. 1976. 14.00 (0-8184-0240-7); pap. 14.95 (0-8184-0241-5) Carol Pub Group.

Big Brother Is Watching. Elaine Landau. (J). 1992. 14.95 (0-8027-8160-8); lib. bdg. 15.85 (0-8027-8161-6) Walker & Co.

Big Brother Mike. Dan Yaccarino. LC 92-72017. (Illus.). 32p. (J). (ps-2). 1993. 13.95 (1-56282-329-9); lib. bdg. 13.89 (1-56282-330-2) Hyprn Child.

Big Brown Box. David Drew. LC 92-30673. (Voyages Ser.). (Illus.). (J). 1993. 2.50 (0-383-03619-4) SRA Schl Grp.

Big Brush Watercolour. Ron Ranson. (Illus.). 128p. 1993. 24.95 (0-7153-9301-4, Pub. by D & C Pub UK) Sterling.

Big Bubble. Pratt. 220p. 1995. pap. write for info. (0-912451-34-3) Florida Classics.

Big Bucks: Selling Your Photography. Cliff Hollenbeck. LC 90-81632. 352p. (Orig.). 1990. pap. 19.95 (0-9626865-0-6) Hot Shot Prodns.

Big Bucks by Selling Your Property. Wade B. Cook & Paul D. Cook. (Orig.). pap. 24.95 (0-910019-09-6) United Support.

***Big Bucks Selling Your Photography.** rev. ed. Cliff Hollenbeck. (Illus.). 340p. 1995. pap. 15.95 (0-936262-39-7) Amherst Media.

Big Bug Big Book Package, 6 bks., 6 Bks., Set. Ed. by Janet L. Bolinske. (Illus.). 24p. (J). (gr. k-1). 1987. spiral bd. 80.00 (0-88335-760-7) Milliken Pub Co.

Big Bug Book of Counting. Patricia McKissack & Fredrick McKissack. LC 87-61655. (Big Bug Bks.). (Illus.). 24p. (Orig.). (J). (gr. k-1). 1987. pap. text ed. 4.95 (0-88335-772-0); spiral bd. 14.95 (0-88335-762-3) Milliken Pub Co.

Big Bug Book of Exercise. Roberta L. Duyff. Ed. by Patricia McKissack & Fredrick McKissack. LC 87-61656. (Big Bug Bks.). (Illus.). 24p. (Orig.). (J). (gr. k-1). 1987. pap. text ed. 4.95 (0-88335-771-2); spiral bd. 14.95 (0-88335-761-5) Milliken Pub Co.

Big Bug Book of Opposites. Patricia McKissack & Fredrick Mckissack. LC 87-61654. (Big Bug Bks.). (Illus.). 24p. (Orig.). (J). (gr. k-1). 1987. pap. text ed. 4.95 (0-88335-773-9); spiral bd. 14.95 (0-88335-763-1) Milliken Pub Co.

Big Bug Book of Places to Go. Patricia McKissack & Fredrick McKissack. LC 87-61652. (Big Bug Bks.). (Illus.). 24p. (Orig.). (J). (gr. k-1). 1987. pap. text ed. 4.95 (0-88335-775-5); spiral bd. 14.95 (0-88335-765-8) Milliken Pub Co.

Big Bug Book of the Alphabet. Patricia McKissack & Fredrick McKissack. LC 87-61653. (Big Bug Bks.). (Illus.). 24p. (Orig.). (J). (gr. k-1). 1987. pap. text ed. 4.95 (0-88335-774-7); spiral bd. 14.95 (0-88335-764-X) Milliken Pub Co.

Big Bug Book of Things to Do. Patricia McKissack & Fredrick McKissack. LC 87-61651. (Big Bug Bks.). (Illus.). 24p. (Orig.). (J). (gr. k-1). 1987. pap. text ed. 4.95 (0-88335-776-3); spiral bd. 14.95 (0-88335-766-6) Milliken Pub Co.

Big Bug Softcover Package, 6 Bks., Set. Ed. by Janet L. Bolinske. (Big Bug Bks.). (Illus.). 24p. (Orig.). (J). (gr. k-1). 1989. pap. 27.00 (0-88335-539-6) Milliken Pub Co.

***Big Bugattis Types 46 & 50.** Barrie Price. (Illus.). 128p. 1995. 59.95 (1-874105-43-X, Pub. by Veloce Pub UK) Motorbooks Intl.

***Big Bugs.** (Information Square Ser.). (J). Date not set. 3.95 (0-7214-9634-2) Ladybird Bks.

Big Bugs. Yolla Bolly Press Staff. LC 93-27516. (Gulliver Green Book Ser.). (Illus.). (J). 1994. pap. 14.95 (0-15-200693-1, Gulliver Bks) HarBrace.

Big Buildings of the Ancient World. Joanne Jessop. LC 93-36704. (X-Ray Picture Bks.). (Illus.). 48p. (J). (gr. 5-8). 1994. lib. bdg. 14.98 (0-531-14286-8); pap. 8.95 (0-531-15709-1) Watts.

Big Buildings of the Modern World. Joanne Jessop. LC 93-40315. (X Ray Picture Book Ser.). (J). 1994. lib. bdg. 14.98 (0-531-14307-4) Watts.

***Big Buildings of the Modern World.** Joanne Jessop. (X-Ray Picture Book Ser.). (Illus.). 48p. 1994. pap. 8.95 (0-531-15716-4) Watts.

Big Bull Falls, Postcard Views of Wausau Wisconsin. John Janke & Jane Janke. (Illus.). 68p. 1986. 14.95 (0-9617780-0-8) Birch Lake Pr.

Big Bulletin Boards: A Cooperative Approach. Karen R. Bigler. (Illus.). 96p. (Orig.). (J). (gr. k-5). 1990. pap. 8.95 (0-673-46240-4) GdYrBks.

Big Bunny & the Easter Egg. Steven Kroll. (Illus.). 32p. (J). (gr. k-3). 1988. pap. 3.95 (0-590-41660-X) Scholastic Inc.

Big Bunny & the Easter Eggs. Steven Kroll. LC 81-11613. (Illus.). 32p. (J). (ps-3). 1982. lib. bdg. 15.95 (0-8234-0436-6) Holiday.

Big Bunny & the Easter Eggs. Steven Kroll. (Illus.). (J). 1992. pap. 2.95 (0-685-54832-5) Scholastic Inc.

Big Bunny & the Magic Show. Steven Kroll. LC 85-14147. (Illus.). 32p. (J). (ps-3). 1986. lib. bdg. 15.95 (0-8234-0589-3) Holiday.

Big Bunny & the Magic Show. Steven Kroll. (Illus.). 32p. (J). (ps-2). 1987. reprint ed. pap. 3.95 (0-590-44633-9) Scholastic Inc.

Big Business. Leon Stein & Gene Brown. (Great Contemporary Issues Ser.). 1979. 27.95 (0-405-11196-7) Ayer.

Big Business: A New Era. David E. Lilienthal. LC 73-2517. (Big Business; Economic Power in a Free Society Ser.). 1973. reprint ed. 19.95 (0-405-05097-6) Ayer.

Big Business: Economic Power in a Free Society, 51 bks., Set. Ed. by Leon Stein et al. 1973. 1,231.50 (0-405-05070-4) Ayer.

Big Business & Industrial Conflict in Nineteenth-Century France: A Social History of the Parisian Gas Company. Lenard R. Berlanstein. LC 90-47352. (Illus.). 352p. 1991. 45.00 (0-520-07234-0) U CA Pr.

Big Business & Radio. Gleason L. Archer, Jr. LC 76-161133. (History of Broadcasting: Radio to Television Ser.). 1976. reprint ed. 40.95 (0-405-03558-6) Ayer.

Big Business & the American University. Bettina Aptheker. 1966. pap. 0.40 (0-87898-009-1) New Outlook.

Big Business & the Policy of Competition. Corwin D. Edwards. LC 79-26189. 180p. 1980. reprint ed. text ed. 35.00 (0-313-22256-8, EDBB, Greenwood Pr) Greenwood.

Big Business & the State: Changing Relations in Western Europe. Ed. by Raymond Vernon. LC 73-91784. 506p. 1974. 40.00 (0-674-07275-8) HUP.

Big Business, Efficiency & Fascism. Kemper Simpson. LC 78-63717. (Studies in Fascism: Ideology & Practice). (Illus.). 216p. reprint ed. 45.00 (0-404-16529-X) AMS Pr.

Big Business in China: Sino-Foreign Rivalry in the Cigarette Industry, 1890-1930. Sherman Cochran. LC 79-23907. (Studies in Business History: No. 33). (Illus.). 342p. 1980. 22.50 (0-674-07262-6) HUP.

***Big Business in Mining & Petroleum.** Ed. by Christopher Schmitz. (International Library of Critical Writings in Business History: Vol. 10). 704p. 1995. 136.95 (1-85898-048-8, Pub. by Gower UK) Ashgate Pub Co.

Big Business in the Third Reich. Arthur Schweitzer. LC 63-62857. 751p. reprint ed. pap. 180.00 (0-8357-3599-0, 2056057) Bks Demand.

Big Busy Building. Chuck Reasoner. (Illus.). 10p. (J). (ps up). 1994. bds. 12.95 (0-8431-3659-6) Price Stern.

***Big Butterfly Book.** Susanne S. Whayne. LC 95-2960. (Illus.). 24p. (J). (gr. k-2). 1995. pap. text ed. 2.95 (0-8167-3697-9, Whistlstop) Troll Assocs.

Big Byte. Peter J. Ognibene. 320p. (Orig.). 1984. pap. 2.95 (0-345-31418-2) Ballantine.

Big Camp Secret. Francine Pascal. (Sweet Valley Twins Ser.: No. 3). 1989. 3.50 (0-553-15707-8) Bantam.

***Big Carrot Book.** Georgia Downard. LC 95-14768. 1995. 11.00 (0-679-43824-6) Random.

Big Carrot Vegetarian Cookbook: From the Kitchen of Big Carrot Natural Food Mart. Lukin. (NFS Canada). Date not set. pap. 14.95 (0-929005-05-8, Pub. by Second Story Pr CN) InBook.

Big Cat Discover Library, 6 bks., Set. Lynn Stone. (Illus.). (J). (gr. k-5). 1989. lib. bdg. 71.64 (0-86592-500-3) Rourke Corp.

Big Catalogue: How to Get Information about Almost Anything for Little or Nothing. 1991. lib. bdg. 79.95 (0-8490-4237-2) Gordon Pr.

***Big Catch: A Practical Introduction.** Robertson. (C). 1995. pap. text ed. 17.95 (0-8133-2522-6) Westview.

***Big Cats.** Bobbie Kalman & Tammy Everts. LC 94-5312. (Crabapple Ser.). (Illus.). 32p. (J). (ps-3). 1994. lib. bdg. 14.95 (0-86505-610-2); pap. 5.95 (0-86505-710-9) Crabtree Pub Co.

Big Cats. Markus Kappeler. (Animal Families Ser.). (Illus.). 32p. (J). (gr. 4-6). 1991. lib. bdg. 18.60 (0-8368-0685-9) Gareth Stevens Inc.

Big Cats. Susan Lumpkin. LC 92-26838. (Great Creatures of the World Ser.). (Illus.). 72p. (YA). (gr. 6-9). 1993. 17.95 (0-8160-2847-8) Facts on File.

Big Cats. Joyce Milton. LC 94-7361. (All Aboard Reading Ser.). (Illus.). (J). 1994. write for info. (0-448-40565-2, G&D) Putnam Pub Group.

***Big Cats.** Joyce Milton. LC 94-7361. (All Aboard Reading Ser.). (Illus.). (J). 1994. pap. write for info. (0-448-40564-4, G&D) Putnam Pub Group.

Big Cats. Seymour Simon. LC 90-36374. (Illus.). 40p. (J). (gr. k-3). 1991. 17.00 (0-06-021646-8); lib. bdg. 16.89 (0-06-021647-6) HarpC Child Bks.

Big Cats. Seymour Simon. LC 90-36374. (Trophy Nonfiction Bk.). (Illus.). 40p. (J). (gr. k-3). 1994. pap. 5.95 (0-06-446119-X, Trophy) HarpC Child Bks.

Big Cats. John B. Wexo. (Zoobooks Ser.). 24p. (J). 1989. lib. bdg. 14.95 (0-88682-264-5) Creative Ed.

Big Cats. Wildlife Education, Ltd. Staff. (Zoobooks Ser.). (Illus.). 20p. (Orig.). (YA). (gr. 5 up). 1981. pap. 2.75 (0-937934-04-6) Wildlife Educ.

Big Cats: A Postcard Book. (Postcard Book Ser.). (Illus.). 64p. (Orig.). 1989. pap. 7.95 (0-89471-773-1) Running Pr.

Big Cats & Other Animals: Their Beauty, Dignity & Survival. Joseph R. Spies. Ed. by Kathy Leth. (Illus.). 240p. 1988. 29.95 (0-8119-0737-6) LIFETIME.

Big Cats, Little Cats. American Society for the Prevention of Cruelty to Animals Staff. (Illus.). 48p. (Orig.). (J). (gr. k-4). 1991. 4.95 (1-879326-09-4) Living Planet Pr.

Big Chair for Little Bear. Claire Schumacher. LC 89-10968. (Pictureback Ser.). (Illus.). 32p. (Orig.). (J). (ps-1). 1990. pap. 2.25 (0-679-80500-1) Random Bks Yng Read.

Big Change: America Transforms Itself: 1900-1950. Frederick L. Allen. LC 92-11261. 322p. (C). 1992. pap. 21.95 (1-56000-639-0) Transaction Pubs.

Big Change: America Transforms Itself, 1900-1950. Frederick L. Allen. LC 82-18395. xii, 308p. 1983. reprint ed. text ed. 35.00 (0-313-23791-3, ALBC, Greenwood Pr) Greenwood.

Big Change: America Transforms Itself, 1900-1950. Frederick L. Allen. LC 86-45061. 288p. 1988. reprint ed. pap. text ed. 14.00 (0-06-132082-X, TB 2082, Torch) HarpC.

Big Changes in the U. S. S. R. Leafing Through Soviet Journal Kommunist. Collets Staff. 310p. (C). 1988. 50.00 (0-685-31683-1, Pub. by Collets UK) Pro-Am Music.

Big Cheese. Trevor Romain. (Illus.). 32p. (Orig.). (J). (ps-3). 1992. pap. 5.25 (1-880092-00-X) Bright Bks TX.

***Big Cheese Pop-up Surprise Book.** Speirs. (J). 1995. 3.50 (0-307-14407-0, Golden Pr) Western Pub.

***Big Chocolate Cookbook.** Gertrude Parke. 1994. pap. 8.98 (0-88365-609-4) Galahad Bks.

***Big Christmas Coloring & Activity, Bk. C.** (Illus.). 160p. (Orig.). (J). (gr. k-2). 1994. pap. 4.95 (1-56144-512-6, Honey Bear Bks) Modern Pub NYC.

***Big Christmas Coloring & Activity, Bk. D.** (Illus.). 160p. (Orig.). (J). (gr. k-2). 1994. pap. 4.95 (1-56144-513-4, Honey Bear Bks) Modern Pub NYC.

***Big Christmas Coloring & Activity, Bk. A.** (Illus.). 160p. (Orig.). (J). (gr. k-2). 1994. pap. 4.95 (1-56144-510-X, Honey Bear Bks) Modern Pub NYC.

***Big Christmas Coloring & Activity, Bk. B.** (Illus.). 160p. (Orig.). (J). (gr. k-2). 1994. pap. 4.95 (1-56144-511-8, Honey Bear Bks) Modern Pub NYC.

Big City ABC. Allen Moak. (Illus.). 32p. (J). (ps up). 1989. text ed. 14.95 (0-88776-161-5, U of Toronto Pr); pap. 6.95 (0-88776-238-7, U of Toronto Pr) Tundra Bks.

Big City Boss in Depression & War: Mayor Edward J. Kelly of Chicago. Roger Biles. LC 83-19391. 219p. 1984. 22.50 (0-87580-098-X) N Ill U Pr.

Big City Fish. David Wilk. Ed. by James B. Van Treese. 480p. 1993. pap. 12.95 (1-56901-031-5) NW Pub.

Big City Mayors: The Crisis in Urban Politics. Ed. by Leonard I. Ruchelman. LC 80-15673. xi, 371p. 1981. reprint ed. text ed. 69.50 (0-313-22605-9, RUBC, Greenwood Pr) Greenwood.

Big-City Police. Robert M. Fogelson. LC 77-5096. (Urban Institute Study Ser.). 390p. 1977. reprint ed. pap. 111.20 (0-7837-1696-6, 2057225) Bks Demand.

Big City Politics Governance, & Fiscal Constraints. Ed. by George E. Peterson. (Urban Opportunity Ser.). 325p. (Orig.). (C). 1994. lib. bdg. 55.00 (0-87766-572-9); pap. text ed. 26.50 (0-87766-573-7) Urban Inst.

Big City Politics in Transition. H. V. Savitch & John C. Thomas. (Urban Affairs Annual Reviews Ser.: Vol. 38). (Illus.). 320p. 1991. text ed. 54.00 (0-8039-4030-0); pap. text ed. 24.00 (0-8039-4031-9) Sage.

Big City Port. Betsy Maestro & Ellen DelVecchio. 32p. (J). (gr. k-3). 1984. pap. 4.95 (0-590-41577-8) Scholastic Inc.

Big City Port. Betsy Maestro & Ellen DelVecchio. LC 85-4339. (Illus.). 32p. (J). (gr. k-3). 1984. text ed. 14.95 (0-02-762110-3, Four Winds Pr) S&S Childrens.

Big City Primer: Reading New York at the End of the Twentieth Century. John Yau. LC 91-20931. (Illus.). 132p. 1991. pap. 25.00 (0-943221-13-7) Timken Pubs.

Big City Stories by Modern American Writers. Tom Cahill & Sue Cahill. 1976. 26.95 (0-8488-0440-6) Amereon Ltd.

Big Clock. Kenneth Fearing. 1976. 22.95 (0-8488-1000-7) Amereon Ltd.

Big Clock: or No Way Out. large type ed. Kenneth Fearing. (Nightingale Ser.). 279p. 1991. pap. 13.95 (0-8161-5138-5, Nightingale) Hall.

Big Clown, Small Clown. Jennifer Daniel. (Circus Train Ser.). (Illus.). 12p. (J). (ps). Date not set. 2.95 (1-56828-061-0) Red Jacket Pr.

***Big Comprehension of Little Words.** Jean G. DeGaetano. 84p. 1991. pap. text ed. 22.00 (1-886143-11-0) Grt Ideas Tching.

Big Concrete Lorry: A Tale of Trotter Street. Shirley Hughes. LC 89-8051. (Illus.). 32p. (J). (ps-1). 1990. 13.95 (0-688-08534-2) Lothrop.

Big Creatures from the Past: A Pop-up Book. Claire Watson. (Illus.). 14p. (J). (gr. k-4). 1990. 14.95 (0-399-22159-X, Putnam) Putnam Pub Group.

Big Creek Album: Yesterday & Today. Elsie Bush. LC 82-173212. (Illus.). 132p. 1982. 9.95 (0-9609440-0-1) D & E Bush.

Big Cry Quandary. C. A. Malkasian. 1991. text ed. write for info. (0-9631541-0-9) W Dewey.

Big Cypress National Preserve. 2nd ed. Michael J. Duever et al. LC 86-60782. (National Audubon Society Research Report: No. 8). (Illus.). 455p. 1986. reprint ed. pap. 30.00 (0-930698-22-3) Natl Audubon.

Big Cypress Swamp & the Ten Thousand Islands: Eastern America's Last Great Wilderness. Jeff Ripple. LC 92-6025. (Illus.). 137p. 1992. 24.95 (0-87249-842-5) U of SC Pr.

B

An Asterisk (*) at the beginning of an entry indicates that the title is appearing in BIP for the first time.

An Asterisk (*) at the beginning of an entry indicates that the title is appearing in BIP for the first time.

747

Big Healey's: Collector's Guide. Graham Robson. (Collector's Guide Ser.). (Illus.). 1982. 27.95 (0-900549-55-6, Pub. by Motor Racing UK) Motorbooks Intl.

Big Heart. Margaret McDowell & Maxine Trottier. (Illus.). 32p. (J). (ps-2). 1991. pap. 29.50 (1-55037-186-X, Pub. by Annick CN) Firefly Bks Ltd.

Big Heart. rev. ed. Mulk R. Anand. 231p. 1980. reprint ed. 19.95 (0-86578-086-2); reprint ed. pap. 3.95 (0-86578-144-3) Ind-US Inc.

***Big Heart: Proceedings of the International School of Medical Sciences, Ettore Majorana Centre for Scientific Culture 1990, Italy.** LC 93-46071. (Ettore Majorana International Life Sciences Ser.: Vol. 14). 214p. 1994. text ed. 50.00 (3-7186-5510-1) Gordon & Breach.

Big Heat. Colin McArthur. (BFI Film Classics Ser.). 1993. pap. 9.95 (0-85170-342-9, Pub. by British Film Inst UK) Ind U Pr.

Big Hello. Janet Schulman. LC 75-33672. (Greenwillow Read-Alone Bks.). (Illus.). (J). (gr. 1-4). 1976. 13.95 (0-688-80036-X) Greenwillow.

Big Hello. braille ed. Janet Schulman. 8p. (J). 1992. vinyl bd. 0.64 (1-56956-194-X, BR8409) W A T Braille.

Big Hello. Janet Schulman. LC 75-33672. (Illus.). 56p. (J). (ps up). reprint ed. pap. 3.95 (0-688-08405-2, Mulberry) Morrow.

***Big Help.** Anna G. Hines. LC 94-3632. 1995. 13.95 (0-395-68702-0, Clarion Bks) HM.

Big Hit. James H. Readus. (Orig.). 1975. pap. 2.25 (0-87067-218-5, BH218) Holloway.

Big Hole Journal: Notes & Excerpts. Mary P. Berthold. 1973. 5.25 (0-8187-0022-X) Harlo Press.

Big Hollow: A Mountaintop History. Elwood Hitchcock. (Illus.). 140p. (Orig.). 1993. pap. 14.95 (0-9628523-7-6) Blk Dome Pr.

Big Honey Hunt. Stan Berenstain & Janice Berenstain. LC 62-15115. (Illus.). 64p. (J). (gr. 1-2). 1962. 7.99 (0-394-80028-1) Beginner.

Big Horn Gunfighter. Robert Kamman. 240p. 1987. pap. 2.50 (0-8217-1975-0) Zebra.

Big Horn Hellriders. Robert Kammen. 1991. pap. 3.50 (0-8217-3449-0) Zebra.

Big Horn Legacy. W. Michael Gear. 400p. 1988. pap. 3.95 (1-55817-135-5, Pinnacle NY) Windsor NY.

Big Horn Massacre. Jess McCreede. 1991. mass mkt. 3.99 (1-55817-569-5, Pinnacle NY) Windsor NY.

Big Horn Range see Field Book

Big House. (Key Words Readers Ser.: B Series, No. 641-8b). (Illus.). (J). (ps-5). 3.50 (0-7214-0544-4) Ladybird Bks.

Big House. Charles N. Aronson. LC 74-81876. (Illus.). 288p. (C). 1974. 20.00 (0-915736-04-7) C N Aronson.

Big House. Tom Tolnay. 188p. 1992. 19.95 (0-8027-3218-6) Walker & Co.

Big House. Mildred Wasson. LC 26-13914. 298p. 1980. reprint ed. pap. 4.95 (0-89101-043-2) U Maine Pr.

Big House: How American Prisons Work. Tony Lesce. LC 91-62781. 192p. (Orig.). 1991. pap. 19.95 (1-55950-075-1, 40071) Loompanics.

Big House, a Little Girl & a Few Things That Made Them Laugh. Cindy Bee. (Illus.). 20p. (Orig.). (J). (ps-5). 1990. pap. 2.75 (0-9616308-1-7) Hearthstn Inn.

Big House, Little House, Back House, Barn: The Connected Farm Buildings of New England. Thomas C. Hubka. LC 84-40303. (Illus.). 240p. 1984. pap. 24.95 (0-87451-356-1) U Pr of New Eng.

Big I & Little i: A Collection of Poems. James S. Benedict. (Illus.). 222p. (Orig.). 1992. 15.00 (0-9633524-0-7); pap. 10.00 (0-9633524-1-5) JB Press.

Big Idea. C. H. Douglas. 1973. 59.95 (0-87968-747-9) Gordon Pr.

Big Idea. C. H. Douglas. 76p. 1986. pap. 4.00 (0-88636-000-5, Pub. by Veritas Pubng AT) Noontide.

Big Ideas. Pride in America Company Staff. LC 78-58760. 96p. 1978. 3.00 (0-9614917-0-1) Pride in Am.

Big Ideas: Explanations, True Stories, Love, Nutrition, Advice, & More. Lynda Barry. LC 92-53412. 128p. 1993. pap. 9.00 (0-06-096902-4, PL) HarpC.

Big Ideas for Little People Book. Ted Marsters & Bridget Marsters. (Illus.). (Orig.). 1981. pap. 4.00 (0-939562-00-6) Parker Pr.

Big Ideas for Small Service Businesses: How to Successfully Advertise, Publicize, & Maximize Your Business or Professional Practice. Marilyn Ross & Tom Ross. 289p. 1994. pap. 15.95 (0-918880-16-5) Comm Creat.

***Big Ideas in Geography: Mini Page Resource Book.** Betty Debnam. (Illus.). 32p. (J). 1994. pap. 4.95 (0-8362-4318-8) Andrews & McMeel.

Big Illusion. Mel Wood. Ed. by John E. Wood. (Illus.). 73p. 1981. 20.00 (0-9604644-0-9) Sheephead Bks.

Big Instruction Book of Small Business: (Alabama Edition) Carole Marsh. (Carole Marsh Alabama Bks.). (Illus.). 1994. lib. bdg. 39.95 (0-7933-2324-X); pap. 29.95 (0-7933-2779-2) Gallopade Pub Group.

Big Instruction Book of Small Business: (Alaska Edition) Carole Marsh. (Carole Marsh Alaska Bks.). (Illus.). 1994. lib. bdg. 39.95 (0-7933-2325-8); pap. 29.95 (0-7933-2780-6) Gallopade Pub Group.

Big Instruction Book of Small Business: (Arizona Edition) Carole Marsh. (Carole Marsh Arizona Bks.). (Illus.). 1994. lib. bdg. 39.95 (0-7933-2342-8); pap. 29.95 (0-7933-2781-4) Gallopade Pub Group.

Big Instruction Book of Small Business: (California Edition) Carole Marsh. (Carole Marsh California Bks.). (Illus.). 1994. lib. bdg. 39.95 (0-7933-2360-6); pap. 29.95 (0-7933-2782-2) Gallopade Pub Group.

Big Instruction Book of Small Business: (Colorado Edition) Carole Marsh. (Carole Marsh Colorado Bks.). (Illus.). 1994. lib. bdg. 39.95 (0-7933-2369-X); pap. 29.95 (0-7933-2783-0) Gallopade Pub Group.

Big Instruction Book of Small Business: (Connecticut Edition) Carole Marsh. (Carole Marsh Connecticut Bks.). (Illus.). 1994. lib. bdg. 39.95 (0-7933-2378-9); pap. 29.95 (0-7933-2784-9) Gallopade Pub Group.

Big Instruction Book of Small Business: (Delaware Edition) Carole Marsh. (Carole Marsh Delaware Bks.). (Illus.). 1994. lib. bdg. 39.95 (0-7933-2387-8); pap. 29.95 (0-7933-2785-7) Gallopade Pub Group.

Big Instruction Book of Small Business: (Florida Edition) Carole Marsh. (Carole Marsh Florida Bks.). (Illus.). 1994. lib. bdg. 39.95 (0-7933-2405-X); pap. 29.95 (0-7933-2787-3) Gallopade Pub Group.

Big Instruction Book of Small Business: (Georgia Edition) Carole Marsh. (Carole Marsh Georgia Bks.). (Illus.). 1994. lib. bdg. 39.95 (0-7933-2414-9); pap. 29.95 (0-7933-2788-1) Gallopade Pub Group.

Big Instruction Book of Small Business: (Hawaii Edition) Carole Marsh. (Carole Marsh Hawaii Bks.). (Illus.). 1994. lib. bdg. 39.95 (0-7933-2423-8); pap. 29.95 (0-7933-2789-X) Gallopade Pub Group.

Big Instruction Book of Small Business: (Idaho Edition) Carole Marsh. (Carole Marsh Idaho Bks.). (Illus.). 1994. lib. bdg. 39.95 (0-7933-2432-7); pap. 29.95 (0-7933-2790-3) Gallopade Pub Group.

Big Instruction Book of Small Business: (Illinois Edition) Carole Marsh. (Carole Marsh Illinois Bks.). (Illus.). 1994. lib. bdg. 39.95 (0-7933-2441-6); pap. 29.95 (0-7933-2791-1) Gallopade Pub Group.

Big Instruction Book of Small Business: (Indiana Edition) Carole Marsh. (Carole Marsh Indiana Bks.). (Illus.). 1994. lib. bdg. 39.95 (0-7933-2450-5); pap. 29.95 (0-7933-2792-X) Gallopade Pub Group.

Big Instruction Book of Small Business: (Iowa Edition) Carole Marsh. (Carole Marsh Iowa Bks.). (Illus.). 1994. lib. bdg. 39.95 (0-7933-2459-9); pap. 29.95 (0-7933-2793-8) Gallopade Pub Group.

Big Instruction Book of Small Business: (Kansas Edition) Carole Marsh. (Carole Marsh Kansas Bks.). (Illus.). 1994. lib. bdg. 39.95 (0-7933-2468-8); pap. 29.95 (0-7933-2794-6) Gallopade Pub Group.

Big Instruction Book of Small Business: (Kentucky Edition) Carole Marsh. (Carole Marsh Kentucky Bks.). (Illus.). 1994. lib. bdg. 39.95 (0-7933-2477-7); pap. 29.95 (0-7933-2795-4) Gallopade Pub Group.

Big Instruction Book of Small Business: (Louisiana Edition) Carole Marsh. (Carole Marsh Louisiana Bks.). (Illus.). 1994. lib. bdg. 39.95 (0-685-72456-5); pap. 29.95 (0-7933-2796-2) Gallopade Pub Group.

Big Instruction Book of Small Business: (Maine Edition) Carole Marsh. (Carole Marsh Maine Bks.). (Illus.). 1994. lib. bdg. 39.95 (0-7933-2495-5); pap. 29.95 (0-7933-2797-0) Gallopade Pub Group.

Big Instruction Book of Small Business: (Maryland Edition) Carole Marsh. (Carole Marsh Maryland Bks.). (Illus.). 1994. lib. bdg. 39.95 (0-7933-2504-8); pap. 29.95 (0-7933-2798-9) Gallopade Pub Group.

Big Instruction Book of Small Business: (Massachusetts Edition) Carole Marsh. (Carole Marsh Massachusetts Bks.). (Illus.). 1994. lib. bdg. 39.95 (0-7933-2513-7); pap. 29.95 (0-7933-2799-7) Gallopade Pub Group.

Big Instruction Book of Small Business: (Michigan Edition) Carole Marsh. (Carole Marsh Michigan Bks.). (Illus.). 1994. lib. bdg. 39.95 (0-7933-2522-6); pap. 29.95 (0-7933-2800-4) Gallopade Pub Group.

Big Instruction Book of Small Business: (Minnesota Edition) Carole Marsh. (Carole Marsh Minnesota Bks.). (Illus.). 1994. lib. bdg. 39.95 (0-7933-2531-5); pap. 29.95 (0-7933-2801-2) Gallopade Pub Group.

Big Instruction Book of Small Business: (Mississippi Edition) Carole Marsh. (Carole Marsh Mississippi Bks.). (Illus.). 1994. lib. bdg. 39.95 (0-7933-2540-4); pap. 29.95 (0-7933-2802-0) Gallopade Pub Group.

Big Instruction Book of Small Business: (Missouri Edition) Carole Marsh. (Carole Marsh Missouri Bks.). (Illus.). 1994. lib. bdg. 39.95 (0-7933-2549-8); pap. 29.95 (0-7933-2803-9) Gallopade Pub Group.

Big Instruction Book of Small Business: (Montana Edition) Carole Marsh. (Carole Marsh Montana Bks.). (Illus.). 1994. lib. bdg. 39.95 (0-7933-2558-7); pap. 29.95 (0-7933-2804-7) Gallopade Pub Group.

Big Instruction Book of Small Business: (Nebraska Edition) Carole Marsh. (Carole Marsh Nebraska Bks.). (Illus.). 1994. lib. bdg. 39.95 (0-7933-2567-6); pap. 29.95 (0-7933-2805-5) Gallopade Pub Group.

Big Instruction Book of Small Business: (Nevada Edition) Carole Marsh. (Carole Marsh Nevade Bks.). (Illus.). 1994. lib. bdg. 29.95 (0-7933-2576-5); ring bd. 29.95 (0-7933-2806-3) Gallopade Pub Group.

Big Instruction Book of Small Business: (New Hampshire Edition) Carole Marsh. (Carole Marsh New Hampshire Bks.). (Illus.). 1994. lib. bdg. 39.95 (0-7933-2585-4); pap. 29.95 (0-7933-2807-1) Gallopade Pub Group.

Big Instruction Book of Small Business: (New Jersey Edition) Carole Marsh. (Carole Marsh New Jersey Bks.). (Illus.). 1994. lib. bdg. 39.95 (0-7933-2594-3); pap. 29.95 (0-7933-2808-X) Gallopade Pub Group.

Big Instruction Book of Small Business: (New Mexico Edition) Carole Marsh. (Carole Marsh New Mexico Bks.). (Illus.). 1994. lib. bdg. 39.95 (0-685-72457-3); pap. 29.95 (0-7933-2809-8) Gallopade Pub Group.

Big Instruction Book of Small Business: (New York Edition) Carole Marsh. (Carole Marsh New York Bks.). (Illus.). 1994. lib. bdg. 39.95 (0-7933-2612-5); pap. 29.95 (0-7933-2810-1) Gallopade Pub Group.

Big Instruction Book of Small Business: (North Carolina Edition) Carole Marsh. (Carole Marsh North Carolina Bks.). (Illus.). 1994. lib. bdg. 39.95 (0-7933-2621-4); pap. 29.95 (0-7933-2811-X) Gallopade Pub Group.

Big Instruction Book of Small Business: (North Dakota Edition) Carole Marsh. (Carole Marsh North Dakota Bks.). (Illus.). 1994. lib. bdg. 39.95 (0-7933-2630-3); pap. 29.95 (0-7933-2812-8) Gallopade Pub Group.

Big Instruction Book of Small Business: (Ohio Edition) Carole Marsh. (Carole Marsh Ohio Bks.). (Illus.). 1994. lib. bdg. 39.95 (0-7933-2639-7); pap. 29.95 (0-7933-2813-6) Gallopade Pub Group.

Big Instruction Book of Small Business: (Oklahoma Edition) Carole Marsh. (Carole Marsh Oklahoma Bks.). (Illus.). 1994. lib. bdg. 39.95 (0-7933-2648-6); pap. 29.95 (0-7933-2814-4) Gallopade Pub Group.

Big Instruction Book of Small Business: (Oregon Edition) Carole Marsh. (Carole Marsh Oregon Bks.). (Illus.). 1994. lib. bdg. 39.95 (0-7933-2657-5); pap. 29.95 (0-7933-2815-2) Gallopade Pub Group.

Big Instruction Book of Small Business: (Pennsylvania Edition) Carole Marsh. (Carole Marsh Pennsylvaniza Bks.). (Illus.). 1994. lib. bdg. 39.95 (0-7933-2666-4); pap. 29.95 (0-7933-2816-0) Gallopade Pub Group.

Big Instruction Book of Small Business: (Rhode Island Edition) Carole Marsh. (Carole Marsh Rhode Island Bks.). (Illus.). 1994. lib. bdg. 39.95 (0-7933-2675-3); pap. 29.95 (0-7933-2817-9) Gallopade Pub Group.

Big Instruction Book of Small Business: (South Carolina Edition) Carole Marsh. (Carole Marsh South Carolina Bks.). (Illus.). 1994. lib. bdg. 39.95 (0-7933-2684-2); pap. 29.95 (0-7933-2818-7) Gallopade Pub Group.

Big Instruction Book of Small Business: (South Dakota Edition) Carole Marsh. (Carole Marsh South Dakota Bks.). (Illus.). 1994. lib. bdg. 39.95 (0-7933-2693-1); pap. 29.95 (0-7933-2819-5) Gallopade Pub Group.

Big Instruction Book of Small Business: (Tennessee Edition) Carole Marsh. (Carole Marsh Tennessee Bks.). (Illus.). 1994. lib. bdg. 39.95 (0-7933-2702-4); pap. 29.95 (0-7933-2820-9) Gallopade Pub Group.

Big Instruction Book of Small Business: (Texas Edition) Carole Marsh. (Carole Marsh Texas Bks.). (Illus.). 1994. lib. bdg. 39.95 (0-7933-2711-3); pap. 29.95 (0-7933-2821-7) Gallopade Pub Group.

Big Instruction Book of Small Business: (Utah Edition) Carole Marsh. (Carole Marsh Utah Bks.). (Illus.). 1994. lib. bdg. 39.95 (0-7933-2720-2); pap. 29.95 (0-7933-2822-5) Gallopade Pub Group.

Big Instruction Book of Small Business: (Vermont Edition) Carole Marsh. (Carole Marsh Vermont Bks.). (Illus.). 1994. lib. bdg. 39.95 (0-7933-2729-6); pap. 29.95 (0-7933-2823-3) Gallopade Pub Group.

Big Instruction Book of Small Business: (Virginia Edition) Carole Marsh. (Carole Marsh Virginia Bks.). (Illus.). 1994. lib. bdg. 39.95 (0-7933-2738-5); pap. 29.95 (0-7933-2824-1) Gallopade Pub Group.

Big Instruction Book of Small Business: (Washington D. C. Edition) Carole Marsh. (Washington, D.C. Bks.). (Illus.). 1994. lib. bdg. 39.95 (0-7933-2396-7); pap. 29.95 (0-7933-2786-5) Gallopade Pub Group.

Big Instruction Book of Small Business: (Washington Edition) Carole Marsh. (Carole Marsh Washington Bks.). (Illus.). 1994. lib. bdg. 39.95 (0-7933-2747-4); pap. 29.95 (0-7933-2825-X) Gallopade Pub Group.

Big Instruction Book of Small Business: (West Virginia Edition) Carole Marsh. (Carole Marsh West Virginia Bks.). (Illus.). 1994. lib. bdg. 39.95 (0-7933-2756-3); pap. 29.95 (0-7933-2826-8) Gallopade Pub Group.

Big Instruction Book of Small Business: (Wisconsin Edition) Carole Marsh. (Carole Marsh Wisconsin Bks.). (Illus.). 1994. lib. bdg. 39.95 (0-7933-2765-2); pap. 29.95 (0-7933-2827-6) Gallopade Pub Group.

Big Instruction Book of Small Business: (Wyoming Edition) Carole Marsh. (Carole Marsh Wyoming Bks.). (Illus.). 1994. lib. bdg. 39.95 (0-7933-2774-1); pap. 29.95 (0-7933-2828-4) Gallopade Pub Group.

Big Island. Jeff Raines. 224p. 1989. pap. 3.95 (0-380-70552-4) Avon.

***Big Island Calendar.** Peter W. Cannon. (Illus.). 24p. (Orig.). 1995. pap. 5.95 (1-886229-02-3) Hawaiian Resources.

***Big Island History Makers.** LaRue W. Piercy. 48p. 1994. pap. 3.95 (1-56647-063-3) Mutual Pub HI.

***Big Island of Hawaii Handbook.** rev. ed. J. D. Bisignani. (Illus.). 350p. Date not set. pap. 13.95 (0-614-04504-5) Island Heritage.

Big Island of Hawaii Handbook. 2nd ed. J. D. Bisignani. (Illus.). 350p. 1994. pap. 13.95 (1-56691-006-4) Moon Pubns CA.

Big Issues in the Passage to Adulthood. Richard A. Hawley. 1988. 17.95 (0-8027-1033-6) Walker & Co.

***Big Jaguars 3 1/2 Litre-420G.** Graham Robson. 192p. 1995. 34.95 (1-85223-922-0, Pub. by Crowood UK) Motorbooks Intl.

Big Jake. Dave Sargent & Pat Sargent. (Animal Pride Ser.). (Illus.). 48p. (Orig.). (J). (gr. k-8). 1993. text ed. 11.95 (1-56763-030-8); pap. text ed. 5.95 (1-56763-031-6) Ozark Pub.

Big Joe's Trailer Truck. Joseph Mathieu. LC 74-2538. (Pictureback Ser.). (Illus.). 32p. (Orig.). (J). (ps-1). 1993. pap. 2.25 (0-394-82925-5) Random Bks Yng Read.

Big Kids: A Parents' Guide to Weight Control for Children. Gregory Archer. 176p. (Orig.). 1989. 24.95 (0-934986-68-1); pap. text ed. 11.95 (0-934986-67-3) New Harbinger.

Big Kill. large type ed. Mickey Spillane. LC 92-23380. 1993. 21.95 (0-7927-1424-5, Curley Lrg Print); pap. 19. 95 (0-7927-1423-7, Curley Lrg Print) Chivers N Amer.

Big Kiss. O'Neil De Noux. 1991. mass mkt. 4.50 (0-8217-3531-4) Zebra.

Big Kiss-Off. large type ed. Day Keene. 1990. pap. 12.95 (0-7089-6903-8, Linford) Ulverscroft.

Big Knife. Clifford Odets. 1963. pap. 4.75 (0-8222-0115-1) Dramatists Play.

Big Knockover. Dashiell Hammett. Ed. by Lillian Hellman. (Vintage Crime Ser.). 1989. pap. 12.00 (0-679-72259-9, Vin) Random.

Big League. Charles E. Van Loan. LC 75-152961. (Short Story Index Reprint Ser.). 1977. reprint ed. 19.95 (0-8369-3876-3) Ayer.

Big League Baseball Puzzlers. Dom Forker. LC 90-24038. (Illus.). 128p. 1991. 13.95 (0-8069-7336-6) Sterling.

Big League Baseball Puzzlers. Dom Forker. LC 90-24038. 128p. 1992. pap. 4.95 (0-8069-7337-4) Sterling.

Big League Break. Mark Freeman. (Rookies Ser.: No. 3). 144p. (J). (gr. 4 up). 1989. pap. 4.99 (0-345-35904-6) Ballantine.

Big League Business Thinking: The Heavy Hitter's Guide to Top Managerial Performance. Paul C. Miller & Tom Gorman. LC 94-6310. 1994. write for info. (0-13-289042-9) P-H.

Big League Play. Mark Freeman. (Rookies Ser.: No. 4). (J). 1989. 3.99 (0-345-35905-4) Ballantine.

Big Leagues: Professional Baseball, Football, & Basketball in National Memory. Stephen Fox. LC 94-6155. 1994. 24.00 (0-688-09300-0) Morrow.

Big Learning for Little Learners: Easy Guide for Teaching Early Childhood Activities. Sally Stauros & Ruth Bell. 1987. pap. 29.95 (0-933212-30-5) Partner Pr.

***Big-Leg Music.** David K. Kirby. LC 94-42449. 100p. (Orig.). 1995. pap. 12.95 (0-914061-48-8) Orchises Pr.

Big Lie: A True Story. Isabella Leitner & Irving Leitner. (J). 1992. 13.95 (0-590-45569-9, 025, Scholastic Hardcover) Scholastic Inc.

***Big Lie: A True Story.** Isabella Leitner. (J). (gr. 4-7). 1994. pap. 2.95 (0-590-45570-2) Scholastic Inc.

Big Life. Susan Johnson. 320p. 1993. 22.95 (0-571-16957-0) Faber & Faber.

Big Life. Susan Johnson. 320p. 1994. reprint ed. pap. 10.95 (0-571-17156-7) Faber & Faber.

Big Lifters. Dean Ing. 256p. 1994. mass mkt. 3.99 (0-8125-1614-1) Tor Bks.

Big Like Me. Anna G. Hines. LC 88-18772. (Illus.). 32p. (J). (ps up). 1989. 16.00 (0-688-08354-4); lib. bdg. 15.93 (0-688-08355-2) Greenwillow.

Big Little GTO Book. Albert Drake. (Illus.). 185p. 1983. pap. 17.95 (0-87938-112-4) Motorbooks Intl.

Big Lonely. Sam Brown. 203p. 1993. 19.95 (0-8027-1234-7) Walker & Co.

Big Lonely. large type ed. Sam Brown. LC 93-13779. 1993. 17.95 (1-56054-779-0) Thorndike Pr.

Big Long Animal Song. 2nd ed. Mike Artell. (Let Me Read Ser.). 8p. (J). (ps-2). 1994. text ed. 2.95 (0-673-36190-X) GdYrBks.

Big Love. Florence Aadland. 192p. 1986. 3.95 (0-446-30159-0) Warner Bks.

***Big Luke, Little Luke.** Dawn Stewardson. (Superromance Ser.). 1995. mass mkt. 3.75 (0-373-70653-7, 1-70653-0) Harlequin Bks.

Big Mac Secrets. Ken Maki. 1992. pap. 39.95 (0-88022-992-6) Que.

Big Machines. Angela Royston. LC 93-16019. (Illus.). (J). (gr. 3 up). 1994. 12.95 (0-316-76070-6) Little.

Big Mama. Lois J. Harris. (Illus.). 16p. (J). 1994. 5.95 (0-8059-3483-9) Dorrance.

Big Mama Stories. Shay Youngblood. LC 89-1315. 112p. (Orig.). 1989. lib. bdg. 18.95 (0-932379-58-3); pap. 8.95 (0-932379-57-5) Firebrand Bks.

Big Man. Ed McBain. 176p. 1991. mass mkt. 4.50 (0-380-71123-0) Avon.

Big Mary. Mark Medoff. 1989. pap. 4.75 (0-8222-0117-8) Dramatists Play.

***Big Mary's Year O Fun '96.** Mary A. Moore. 370p. (Orig.). 1995. pap. text ed. 9.95 (1-56383-042-6, 9230) G & R Pub.

Big Max. Kin Platt. LC 91-14742. (I Can Read Bk.). (Illus.). 64p. (J). (gr. k-3). 1965. lib. bdg. 12.89 (0-06-024751-7) HarpC Child Bks.

Big Max. Kin Platt. LC 91-14743. (Trophy I Can Read Bk.). (Illus.). (J). (gr. k-3). 1978. pap. 3.50 (0-06-444006-0, Trophy) HarpC Child Bks.

***Big, Mean Pig & Other Stories.** Sarah-Catherine Carroll. 1994. 7.95 (0-533-11031-9) Vantage.

***Big Meeting.** Dee P. Woodtor. LC 95-15299. (Illus.). (J). 1995. write for info. (0-689-31933-9, Atheneum Bks Young) S&S Childrens.

Big Meeting, Big Results. Tom McMahon. 1994. 19.95 (0-8442-3192-4, NTC Busn Bks) NTC Pub Grp.

Big Men: NBA Matchups. (J). (gr. 4-7). 1993. pap. 2.95 (0-307-20302-6, Golden Pr) Western Pub.

***Big Men & Small Boys: Power, Ideology & the Burden of History in Rawlings' Ghana, 1982-1994.** Paul Nugent. LC 95-12503. 1995. write for info. (0-7201-2309-7, Mansell Pub) Cassell.

Big Men, Big Country: A Collection of American Tall Tales. Paul R. Walker. LC 91-45128. (J). (gr. 4-7). 1993. 16.95 (0-15-207136-9) HarBrace.

Big Midget Murders. Craig Rice. 365p. pap. 6.95 (1-55882-112-0) Intl Polygonics.

Big Mile Race. Leonard Kessler. LC 82-9274. (Greenwillow Read-Alone Bks.). (Illus.). 48p. (J). (gr. 1-3). 1983. 9.00 (0-688-01420-8) Greenwillow.

Big Mini Book. Johannes Hubner. (Illus.). 128p. 1992. 29. 95 (1-870979-21-4, Pub. by Bay View Bks UK) Motorbooks Intl.

Big Mirror. Mohammed Mrabet. Tr. by Paul Bowles. 80p. 1990. pap. 10.95 (0-7206-0730-2, Pub. by P Owen Ltd UK) Dufour.

Big Mistake. Elizabeth L. Clarke. LC 94-60126. (J). (gr. k-3). 1994. pap. 5.95 (1-55523-673-1) Winston-Derek.

An Asterisk (*) at the beginning of an entry indicates that the title is appearing in BIP for the first time.

An Asterisk (*) at the beginning of an entry indicates that the title is appearing in BIP for the first time.

Big Sleep: A Film Adaptation Directed by Howard Hawks. Raymond Chandler. Ed. by George Garrett et al. LC 71-135273. (Film Scripts Ser.). 1989. reprint ed. pap. 19.95 (*0-89197-677-9*) Irvington.

***Big Sleep & Farewell My Lovely.** Chandler. 1995. 16.50 (*0-679-60140-6*) Random.

Big Small Church Book. David R. Ray. LC 92-30774. 256p. (Orig.). 1992. pap. 14.95 (*0-8298-0936-8*) Pilgrim OH.

Big Smith Snatch. Jane L. Curry. LC 89-8036. 224p. (J). (gr. 4-7). 1989. text ed. 14.95 (*0-689-50478-0*, McElderry) S&S Childrens.

Big Smoke. Peter Brimblecombe. 1987. 42.50 (*0-416-90080-1*, Routledge NY) Routledge Chapman & Hall.

Big Sneeze. Ruth Brown. LC 84-23385. (Illus.). 32p. (J). (ps-1). 1985. 16.00 (*0-688-04665-7*); lib. bdg. 15.93 (*0-688-04666-5*) Lothrop.

Big Snow. Elmer Hader & Berta Hader. LC 48-10240. (Illus.). 48p. (J). (gr. 1-3). 1967. text ed. 14.95 (*0-02-737910-8*, Mac Bks Young Read) S&S Childrens.

Big Snow. Elmer Hader & Berta Hader. LC 48-10240. (Illus.). 48p. (J). (gr. 1-3). 1972. pap. 4.95 (*0-02-043300-X*, Mac Bks Young Read) S&S Childrens.

Big Snow. 2nd ed. Berta Hader & Elmer Hader. LC 92-46365. (Illus.). 48p. (J). (gr. k-4). 1993. reprint ed. pap. 4.95 (*0-689-71757-1*, Aladdin Paperbacks) S&S Childrens.

Big Snowy. Jim Slater. LC 80-53066. (A. Mazing Monsters Ser.). (Illus.). (J). (ps-3). 1981. pap. 1.25 (*0-394-84736-9*) Random Bks Yng Read.

Big Something. Ron Padgett. 64p. 1990. per. 7.50 (*0-935724-38-9*) Figures.

Big South Fork Country. Photos by Howard Baker & John Netherton. LC 93-28260. (Illus.). 120p. (YA). (gr. 9 up). 1993. 29.95 (*1-55853-258-7*) Rutledge Hill Pr.

***Big South Fork NRA, TN - KY.** Ed. by Trails Illustrated Staff. 1995. 8.99 (*1-56695-012-0*) Trails Illustrated.

***Big Spirits, Little Bodies: Parenting Your Way to Wholeness.** Linda C. Aronson. Ed. by Ken Skidmore. 242p. 1995. pap. 14.95 (*0-87604-337-6*, 396) ARE Pr.

Big Splash: A Scientific Discovery That Revolutionizes the Way We View the Origin of Life, the Water We Drink, The Death of Dinosaurs, the Creation of the Oceans, the Nature of the Cosmos, & the Very Future of the Earth Itself. Louis A. Frank. 1990. 21.95 (*1-55972-033-6*, Birch Ln Pr) Carol Pub Group.

Big Splash in a Small Pond: Finding a Great Job in a Small, High-Growth Company. R. Linda Resnick & Kerry Pechter. LC 93-5708. 1994. 11.00 (*0-671-79807-3*, Fireside) S&S Trade.

Big Spread Cookbook: Cooking for Groups. Beth Tartan. 200p. 1985. 7.95 (*0-317-17400-2*) TarPar.

Big Squeeze. Jim Cirni. LC 90-19851. 224p. 1991. 18.95 (*0-939149-46-X*) Soho Press.

Big Squeeze: Balancing the Needs of Aging Parents, Dependent Children & You. Barbara Shapiro et al. LC 91-18195. 240p. (Orig.). 1991. 12.95 (*0-938179-29-2*) Mills Sanderson.

Big Squeeze: Balancing the Needs of Aging Parents, Dependent Children & You. Barbara A. Shapiro. 1995. mass mkt. 5.99 (*0-345-38145-9*) Ballantine.

Big Stakes of Detente. Gus Hall. 48p. 1974. pap. 0.50 (*0-87898-112-8*) New Outlook.

***Big Star Fallin' Mama: Five Women in Black Music.** Hettie Jones. (Illus.). 144p. (YA). 1995. 14.99 (*0-670-85621-5*, Viking) Viking Penguin.

Big Steal: The Screenplay. David Porter. 1991. pap. 12.95 (*0-7022-2372-7*, Pub. by Univ Queensland Pr AT) Intl Spec Bk.

Big Steel: Black Politics & Corporate Power in Gary, Indiana. Edward Greer. LC 79-13178. 287p. 1981. 16.50 (*0-85345-490-6*); pap. 6.50 (*0-85345-562-7*) Monthly Rev.

***Big Stink: And Five Other Mysteries.** Richie Chevat. (Ghostwriter Ser.). (J). (gr. 4-7). 1995. pap. 3.50 (*0-553-48221-1*) Bantam.

Big Stony. Howard T. Walden, II. (Fifty Greatest Bks.). (Illus.). 401p. (YA). (gr. 10 up). 1993. reprint ed. 40.00 (*1-56416-045-9*) Derrydale Pr.

Big Storm. Bruce Hiscock. LC 92-13973. (Illus.). 32p. (J). (gr. 1-5). 1993. text ed. 14.95 (*0-689-31770-0*, Atheneum Bks Young) S&S Childrens.

Big Storm. Rhea Tregebov. LC 92-55040. (Illus.). 32p. (J). (ps-3). 1993. 13.95 (*1-56282-461-9*); lib. bdg. 13.89 (*1-56282-462-7*) Hyprn Child.

Big Storm Knocked It Over. Laurie Colwin. LC 92-56219. 1994. pap. 12.00 (*0-06-092546-9*, PL) HarpC.

Big Storm Knocked It Over. large type ed. Laurie Colwin. LC 93-44178. 1994. 21.95 (*0-7862-0155-X*) Thorndike Pr.

Big Story. large type ed. Morris West. 1970. 21.95 (*0-7089-0204-9*) Ulverscroft.

Big Story: American Press & Television Reported & Interpreted the Crisis of Tet 1968 in Vietnam & Washington. Peter Braestrup. LC 82-11041. 632p. 1983. text ed. 45.00 (*0-300-02953-5*) Yale U Pr.

Big Story: How the American Press & Television Reported & Interpreted the Crisis of Tet 1968 in Vietnam & Washington. abr. ed. Peter Braestrup. 632p. 1994. pap. 16.95 (*0-89141-531-9*) Presidio Pr.

Big Strike. Mike Quin. LC 79-14101. 1991. reprint ed. pap. 7.50 (*0-7178-0504-2*) Intl Pubs Co.

Big Strike at Spindletop. Bonnie Bader. (Stories of the States Ser.). 80p. (J). (gr. 4-6). 1995. lib. bdg. 12.95 (*1-881889-60-2*) Silver Moon.

Big Strikes: Queensland 1889-1965. Ed. by D. J. Murphy. LC 82-23881. (Illus.). 303p. 1983. pap. 18.95 (*0-7022-1721-2*) Intl Spec Bk.

Big Structures, Large Processes, Huge Comparisons. Charles Tilly. LC 84-60264. (Russell Sage Foundation 75th Anniversary Ser.). 176p. 1989. pap. 9.95 (*0-87154-880-1*) Russell Sage.

Big Subtraction Book. Becky Daniel & Charlie Daniel. 64p. (J). (gr. k-3). 1979. 8.95 (*0-916456-43-9*, GA117) Good Apple.

Big Sugar: Seasons in the Cane Fields of Florida. Alec Wilkinson. LC 90-50164. 272p. 1990. pap. 9.95 (*0-679-73187-3*, Vin) Random.

Big Sundae. Randy Horton. Ed. by Liz Parker. (Take Ten Bks.). (Illus.). 49p. (Orig.). (YA). (gr. 6-12). 1993. pap. text ed. 2.95 (*1-56254-094-7*) Saddleback Pubns.

Big Sur. Frank Gagliano. 1971. pap. 2.75 (*0-8222-0118-6*) Dramatists Play.

Big Sur. Jack Kerouac. 320p. (FRE.). 1979. pap. 11.95 (*0-7859-2415-9*, 2070370941) Fr & Eur.

Big Sur. Jack Kerouac. 256p. 1992. pap. 10.95 (*0-14-016812-5*, Penguin Bks) Viking Penguin.

Big Sur. Donald Pike & David Muench. LC 78-51408. (Illus.). 48p. 1979. pap. 6.95 (*0-916122-67-0*) KC Pubns.

Big Sur & the Central Coast. David Muench & Jeff Whitmore. (Illus.). 96p. 1988. 19.95 (*1-55652-045-X*) Chicago Review.

Big Sur & the Monterey Peninsula: A Picture Book to Remember Her By. 1992. 3.99 (*0-517-34172-7*) Random Hse Value.

Big Sur & the Oranges of Hieronymus Bosch. Henry Miller. LC 57-5542. 1964. pap. 12.95 (*0-8112-0107-4*, NDP161) New Directions.

***Big Surprise!** Pam Jarrell. (HighReach Learning Big Bks.). 8p. (J). (ps-k). 1994. pap. text ed. 10.95 (*1-57332-007-2*) HighReach Lrning.

Big Surprise. Ski Michaels. LC 85-14017. (Illus.). 48p. (J). (gr. 1-3). 1986. lib. bdg. 10.59 (*0-8167-0576-3*); pap. text ed. 3.50 (*0-8167-0577-1*) Troll Assocs.

Big Sweep. Stephen Callis. 1994. pap. 9.95 (*1-879395-10-X*) CA Classics Bks.

***Big Switch: Creating Jobs, Saving Money, & Protecting the Environment in the 21st Century.** Gavin Gilchrist. (Illus.). 196p. 1995. pap. 16.95 (*1-86373-750-2*, Pub. by Allen Unwin AT) Paul & Co Pubs.

Big-Tailed Birds: Story of the 319th Bomb Group in WW II. Victor C. Tannehill. (Illus.). 80p. 1990. pap. 17.95 (*0-9605900-5-6*) Boomerang.

Big Ten. Peggy A. Griffin. 1986. student ed write for info. (*1-884056-00-8*) Scribes Pubns.

Big Ten Basketball. Peter Bjarkman. LC 95-45142. (Illus.). 192p. 1994. pap. 12.95 (*1-57028-003-7*) Masters Pr IN.

Big Thicket: An Ecological Reevaluation. 2nd rev. ed. A. Y. Gunter. LC 93-2305. (Philosophy & the Environment Ser.: No. 2). (Illus.). 250p. 1993. reprint ed. pap. 16.95 (*0-929398-52-1*) UNTX Pr.

Big Thicket Legacy. Ed. by Campbell Loughmiller & Lynn Loughmiller. LC 76-46329. (Illus.). 253p. 1977. pap. 14.95 (*0-292-70733-9*) U of Tex Pr.

***Big Thicket Legacy.** fac. ed. Ed. by Campbell Loughmiller & Lynn Loughmiller. LC 76-46329. (Illus.). 254p. 1994. pap. 72.40 (*0-7837-7641-1*, 2047394) Bks Demand.

Big Thicket National Preserve. Laurence E. Parent. Ed. by T. J. Priehs & Ronald J. Foreman. LC 92-62154. 16p. (Orig.). 1993. pap. 2.95 (*1-877856-21-5*) SW Pks Mnmts.

Big Thoughts for Little People. Kenneth N. Taylor. (J). (ps-3). 1983. 10.99 (*0-8423-0164-X*) Tyndale.

Big Three. Peter May. 1994. 22.00 (*0-671-79955-X*) S&S Trade.

***Big Three: Solids, Liquids & Gases.** J. M. Patten. LC 94-47599. (Let's Wonder About Science Ser.). (J). 1995. write for info. (*1-55916-126-4*) Rourke Bk Co.

Big Thunder Magic. Craig K. Strete. LC 89-34613. (Illus.). 32p. (J). (ps up). 1990. 12.95 (*0-688-08853-8*); lib. bdg. 12.88 (*0-688-08854-6*) Greenwillow.

Big Time. Phil Berger. 1990. 16.95 (*0-87833-696-6*) Dryad Pr.

Big Time. Fritz Leiber. 1976. reprint ed. lib. bdg. 18.95 (*0-88411-931-9*, Aeonian Pr) Amereon Ltd.

Big Time. Fritz Leiber. 1990. reprint ed. lib. bdg. 16.95 (*0-89968-537-4*) Buccaneer Bks.

Big Time. Fritz Leiber. (Collier Nucleus Science Fiction Ser.). 192p. 1991. reprint ed. mass mkt., pap. 4.95 (*0-02-069841-0*, Collier S&S) S&S Trade.

Big Time. Marcel Montecino. Ed. by Julie Rubenstein. 544p. 1991. reprint ed. mass mkt. 5.99 (*0-671-70971-2*, Pocket Star Bks) PB.

Big Time: How Success Really Works in 14 Top Business Careers. Glenn Kaplan. LC 82-8311. 384p. 1990. pap. 4.95 (*0-312-92052-0*) Congdon & Weed.

Big Time & After School Special. Keith Reddin. 61p. (Orig.). 1987. pap. 4.95 (*0-88145-063-4*) Broadway Play.

Big-Time Football at Harvard, 1905: The Diary of Coach Bill Reid. Ed. by Ronald A. Smith. LC 93-10247. (Illus.). 376p. (C). 1994. 27.50 (*0-252-02047-2*) U of Ill Pr.

Big-Time Golf. LeRoy Neiman. (Illus.). 176p. 1992. 45.00 (*0-8109-3666-6*) Abrams.

Big Time Tommy Sloane. Reardon. 1988. pap. 3.95 (*0-317-67578-8*) St Martin.

Big Time Tommy Sloane. James Reardon. LC 86-31957. 320p. 1987. 18.95 (*0-88191-043-0*) Freundlich.

Big Times in a Small Town - The Martha's Vineyard Tapes. Cheryl Wheeler et al. Ed. by Milton Okun. 1994. pap. 19.95 (*0-89524-799-2*) Cherry Lane.

Big Top Boss: John Ringling North & the Circus. David L. Hammarstrom. (Illus.). 384p. (C). 1992. 29.95 (*0-252-01901-6*) U of Ill Pr.

Big Top Boss: John Ringling North & the Circus. David L. Hammarstrom. 1994. pap. 16.95 (*0-252-06405-4*) U of Ill Pr.

Big-Top Circus. Neil Johnson. LC 93-40274. (J). 1995. 14.99 (*0-8037-1602-8*); lib. bdg. 14.89 (*0-8037-1603-6*) Dial Bks Young.

Big Top Circus Days. Larry G. Freeman. LC 64-7599. (Illus.). 132p. 1974. 20.00 (*0-87282-053-X*, 87282) Am Life Foun.

***Big Town.** Doug J. Swanson. 1994. pap. 4.50 (*0-06-109213-4*, Harp PBks) HarpC.

Big Town: A Novel of Suspense. Doug J. Swanson. LC 93-29503. 224p. 1994. 18.00 (*0-06-017749-7*, HarpT) HarpC.

Big Town, Little Town: Nudes for the Urban Environment. Frank H. Wallis. LC 94-92088. (Illus.). 34p. (Orig.). 1994. pap. 11.95 (*0-9638332-8-6*) Source Pub CT.

Big Town Trees: From an Original Article which Appeared in Ranger Rick Magazine, Copyright National Wildlife Federation. Illus. by Cathy Beylon. LC 92-34778. (Adventures of Ranger Rick Ser.). 20p. (J). (gr. k-3). 1993. 6.95 (*0-924483-83-0*); audio 9.95 (*0-924483-84-9*); audio 35.95 (*0-924483-87-3*); audio 21.95 (*0-924483-89-X*) Soundprints.

Big Towns, Big Talk. Patricia Smith. LC 92-53829. 128p. 1992. pap. 9.95 (*0-944072-24-0*) Zoland Bks.

Big Trail. Max Brand. 1976. reprint ed. lib. bdg. 20.95 (*0-88411-513-5*, Aeonian Pr) Amereon Ltd.

Big Tree. Bruce Hiscock. LC 89-18286. (Illus.). 32p. (J). (gr. 1-5). 1991. text ed. 14.95 (*0-689-31598-8*, Atheneum Bks Young) S&S Childrens.

Big Tree. Bruce Hiscock. LC 93-25564. (Illus.). 32p. (J). (gr. 1-5). 1994. reprint ed. pap. 4.95 (*0-689-71803-9*, Aladdin Paperbacks) S&S Childrens.

Big Trees & Lokies. David James. (Illus.). 1989. 7.95 (*0-935693-10-6*) Mason Cty Hist.

Big Trouble: Six Ten-Minute Plays from Actors Theatre of Louisville. Michael B. Dixon & Valerie Smith. (Illus.). 80p. (Orig.). 1990. pap. 5.00 (*0-88680-324-1*) I E Clark.

Big Trouble for Roxie. Hilda Stahl. LC 91-38945. (Best Friends Ser.: No. 2). 160p. (J). (gr. 4-7). 1992. pap. 3.99 (*0-89107-658-1*) Crossway Bks.

Big Trouble for Tricky Rabbit! Illus. & Ret. by Gretchen W. Mayo. LC 93-29749. (Native American Trickster Tales Ser.). 48p. (J). (gr. 2-3). 1994. 12.95 (*0-8027-8275-2*); lib. bdg. 13.85 (*0-8027-8276-0*) Walker & Co.

***Big Trucks.** (Information Square Ser.). (J). Date not set. 3.95 (*0-7214-9633-4*) Ladybird Bks.

***Big Twin High-Performance Guide.** D. William Denish. (Illus.). 238p. 1994. per. 24.95 (*0-9640115-0-6*) Crystal Publns.

Big V: A History of the Vitagraph Company. Anthony Slide & Alan Gevinson. LC 87-12731. (Illus.). 356p. 1987. 35.00 (*0-8108-2030-7*) Scarecrow.

Big Walks: Challenging Mountain Walk & Scrambles in the British Isles. Ken Wilson & Richard Gilbert. (Illus.). 256p. 1980. 55.00 (*0-906371-60-0*, Pub. by H & S UK) Trafalgar.

***Big Walls.** John Long & John Middendorf. (How to Rock Climb Ser.). (Illus.). 160p. 1994. pap. 11.95 (*0-934641-63-3*) Chockstone Pr.

Big Walls. Reinhold Messner. (Illus.). 1978. 35.00 (*0-19-520062-4*) OUP.

Big Wander. Will Hobbs. LC 92-825. 192p. (J). (gr. 5-9). 1992. text ed. 14.95 (*0-689-31767-0*, Atheneum Bks Young) S&S Childrens.

Big Wander. Will Hobbs. 192p. (J). (gr. 5). 1994. reprint ed. pap. 3.99 (*0-380-72140-6*, Camelot) Avon.

***Big Water.** John Engels. LC 94-30963. 112p. 1995. 22.95 (*1-55821-357-0*); pap. 14.95 (*1-55821-358-9*) Lyons & Burford.

Big Water: Flight to Okeechobee. Eugene Arnold. LC 92-61845. (Illus.). 201p. (YA). (gr. 12). 1993. pap. 12.95 (*0-9628828-2-8*) Prospector Pr.

Big Water: West To the Everglades, Vol. II: A Novel of 19th Century Florida. Eugene Arnold. Ed. by Denton R. Moore. LC 92-61845. (Illus.). 264p. (Orig.). 1994. pap. 9.95 (*0-9628828-4-4*) Prospector Pr.

Big Wave. Pearl S. Buck. LC 48-244. (Illus.). 80p. (J). (gr. 2-6). 1973. lib. bdg. 14.89 (*0-381-99923-8*, Crowell Jr Bks) HarpC Child Bks.

Big Wave. Pearl S. Buck. LC 85-45402. (Trophy Bk.). (Illus.). 80p. (J). (gr. 3-6). 1986. pap. 3.95 (*0-06-440171-5*, Trophy) HarpC Child Bks.

Big Wave: A Study Guide. Joyce Friedland & Rikki Kessler. (Novel-Ties Ser.). (J). (gr. 4-6). 1982. student ed, teacher ed 15.95 (*0-88122-000-0*) Lrn Links.

Big Way. William Peil. 1983. 2.00 (*0-89536-952-4*, 7503) CSS OH.

Big Wedding on a Small Budget Planner & Organizer. Diane Warner. 128p. 1992. pap. 12.95 (*0-89879-530-3*) Writers Digest.

Big Week: The Classic Story of the Crucial Air Battle of WWII. Glenn Infield. (Brassey's WWII Commemorative Ser.). 144p. 1993. 16.95 (*0-02-881068-6*) Brasseys Inc.

Big Weenies. H. Kavet. 96p. 1993. 5.95 (*0-88032-432-5*) Ivory Tower Pub.

Big Wheel. Marilyn Singer. LC 93-31912. 160p. (J). (gr. 5-9). 1993. 14.95 (*1-56282-583-6*); lib. bdg. 14.89 (*1-56282-584-4*) Hyprn Child.

Big Wheel: Rock & Roll & Roadside Attractions. Bruce Thomas. 192p. (Orig.). 1991. 10.95 (*0-571-12944-7*) Faber & Faber.

***Big Wheels, Little Wheels: Little Peek-in Books.** 1995. 2.99 (*0-88705-782-9*) Joshua Morris.

Big White Lie: The CIA & the Cocaine-Crack Epidemic. Michael Levine. 1993. 22.95 (*1-56025-064-X*) Thunders Mouth.

Big White Lie: The Deep Cover Operation That Exposed the CIA Sabotage of the Drug War. Michael Levine & Laura Kavanau-Levine. 448p. 1994. pap. 13.95 (*1-56025-084-4*) Thunders Mouth.

Big Win. Paul Ader. 180p. 1984. 30.00 (*0-946270-04-X*, Pub. by Pentland Pr UK) St Mut.

***Big Wind.** rev. ed. Beatrice Coogan. 686p. 1995. pap. 12.95 (*1-57098-031-4*) R Rinehart.

Big Windows. Peadar O'Donnell. (Classic Irish Fiction Ser.). 212p. 1984. 15.95 (*0-8159-5117-5*) Devin.

Big Windows. Peadar O'Donnell. 211p. 1988. pap. 7.95 (*0-86278-090-X*, Pub. by OBrien Pr IE) Dufour.

Big Winds, Glass Mornings, Shadows Cast by Stars: Poems: 1972-1980. 3rd ed. Morton Marcus. 80p. 1988. reprint ed. pap. 5.95 (*0-9621321-1-X*) Brown Bear.

Big-Wing Paper Gliders. Michael Johnson. (Illus.). 96p. (Orig.). 1992. pap. 19.95 (*0-312-06731-3*) St Martin.

Big Witness (Living in Wishes) Terry Allen. Terry Allen & Dave Hickey. (Illus.). 56p. 1989. pap. 9.00 (*0-930495-05-5*) San Fran Art Inst.

Big Wolves. Wilbur Sanders. 252p. 1991. 18.95 (*1-56131-005-0*) New Amsterdam Bks.

Big Woods: The Hunting Stories. William Faulkner. 1994. pap. 9.00 (*0-679-75252-8*, Vin) Random.

Big World of Love, Vol. I. Dennis L. Askew. (Orig.). 1993. pap. 5.99 (*0-9640773-0-2*, TXU 559-748) Estlin Staples.

Big World of Love, Vol. II. Dennis L. Askew. (Illus.). (Orig.). Date not set. pap. 5.99 (*0-9640773-1-0*) Estlin Staples.

Big World, Small Screen: The Role of Television in American Society. Aletha C. Huston et al. LC 91-13520. (Child, Youth, & Family Services Ser.). (Illus.). viii, 196p. 1992. pap. 12.00 (*0-8032-7263-4*) U of Nebr Pr.

Big World, Small World. Jeanne Titherington. LC 84-4140. (Illus.). 24p. (J). (ps-1). 1985. 11.75 (*0-688-04022-5*); lib. bdg. 11.88 (*0-688-04023-3*) Greenwillow.

Big Yellow School Bus. Bernard Wiseman. LC 91-58787. (Disney's First Readers Ser.). (Illus.). 48p. (J). (gr. k-3). 1992. 9.95 (*1-56282-048-6*); lib. bdg. 9.89 (*1-56282-226-8*) Disney Pr.

Bigallo: The Oratory & Residence of the Compagnia del Bigallo e della Misericordia in Florence. Howard Saalman. LC 69-18285. (College Art Association Monograph Ser.: Vol. 19). (Illus.). 120p. 1985. reprint ed. 35.00 (*0-271-00405-3*) Pa St U Pr.

***Bigbang.** James Drey. 28p. (Orig.). 1995. pap. 3.95 (*0-9641986-7-3*) Poetry Harbor.

***Bigby's Curse.** Carl Sargent. (Endless Quest Ser.). 192p. (Orig.). 1995. pap. 3.95 (*0-7869-0178-0*) TSR Inc.

Bigelow Families in 1850, Extracted from the 1850 U. S. Census. Bigelow Society, Inc. Staff. Ed. by Patricia Bigelow. 165p. (Orig.). 1986. pap. 18.95 (*0-9616682-0-2*) Bigelow Soc.

Bigelow Family Genealogy: The First Six Generations in America, Vol. 1. Bigelow Society, Inc. Staff. Ed. by Patricia Bigelow. LC 86-72956. (Family Genealogy Ser.). 385p. (Orig.). 1987. 55.00 (*0-9616682-1-0*) Bigelow Soc.

Bigelow Papers. James Russell Lowell. LC 71-107179. 1970. reprint ed. 15.00 (*0-403-00235-4*) Scholarly.

***Bigfoot.** Julie S. Bach. LC 94-11570. (Exploring the Unknown Ser.). (J). 1995. 17.95 (*1-56006-160-X*) Lucent Bks.

Bigfoot. Mary B. Christian. LC 87-9024. (Mystery of...Ser.). (Illus.). 48p. (J). (gr. 5-6). 1987. text ed. 12.95 (*0-89686-341-7*, Crstwood Hse) Silver Burdett Pr.

Bigfoot. Richard Hoyt. 1995. pap. 4.99 (*0-8125-1948-5*) Tor Bks.

Bigfoot: Man, Monster, or Myth? Carrie Carmichael. LC 77-21317. (Great Unsolved Mysteries Ser.). (Illus.). 48p. (J). (gr. 4 up). 1977. lib. bdg. 21.36 (*0-8172-1052-0*) Raintree Steck-V.

Bigfoot: Opposing Viewpoints. Norma Gaffron. LC 88-24376. (Great Mysteries Ser.). (Illus.). 112p. (J). (gr. 5-8). 1989. lib. bdg. 16.95 (*0-89908-058-8*) Greenhaven.

Bigfoot & other Legendary Creatures. P. Walker. (J). 1992. 15.95 (*0-15-207147-4*, HB Juv Bks) HarBrace.

Bigfoot & the Wilderness Artist of the Adirondacks. George Junghanns. (Illus.). 100p. (Orig.). 1994. pap. 4.75 (*1-881946-05-3*) Gauntlet Bks.

Bigger. Patricia Calvert. LC 93-14415. 144p. (J). (gr. 4-6). 1994. text ed. 14.95 (*0-684-19685-9*, C Scribner Sons Young) S&S Childrens.

Bigger & Blacker. Octavus R. Cohen. LC 78-106268. (Short Story Index Reprint Ser.). 1977. 27.95 (*0-8369-3305-2*) Ayer.

Bigger Bang: Growth of a Financial Revolution. G. Webb. (Waterlow Publications). 72p. 1987. pap. 14.00 (*0-08-033100-9*, Pergamon Pr) Elsevier.

Bigger Muscles in Forty-Two Days. Ellington Darden. (Illus.). 224p. (Orig.). 1992. pap. 16.00 (*0-399-51706-5*, Perigree Bks) Berkley Pub.

Bigger Profits for the Smaller Firm. E. G. Wood. 184p. 1972. 25.00 (*0-8464-0193-2*) Beekman Pubs.

Bigger Secrets: More Than One Hundred Twenty-Five Things They Prayed You'd Never Find Out. William Poundstone. 320p. 1989. pap. 10.95 (*0-395-53008-3*) HM.

Bigger, Stronger, Faster. Greg Shepard. (Illus.). 1977. pap. 12.95 (*0-89036-102-9*) Hawkes Pub Inc.

Bigger Than Biggest. Frank Smulders. (Count Me in Bks.). (Illus.). 24p. (Orig.). (J). (ps-1). 1994. pap. 4.95 (*1-55037-360-9*, Pub. by Annick CN) Firefly Bks Ltd.

Bigger Than Life: A Biography of Francis X. Shields. William X. Shields. LC 85-39389. 204p. 1986. 17.95 (*0-88191-028-7*) Freundlich.

Bigger Than Life: A Place Where Hearts Run Free. Jack W. Conaway, Jr. LC 93-71259. (Illus.). 132p. (Orig.). 1993. pap. 6.95 (*0-9636627-0-8*) Crosspt Pub.

Bigger Than Life: The Creator of Doc Savage. Marilyn Cannaday. LC 89-85739. (Illus.). 200p. (C). 1990. 34.95 (*0-87972-471-4*); pap. 17.95 (*0-87972-472-2*) Bowling Green Univ.

An Asterisk (*) at the beginning of an entry indicates that the title is appearing in BIP for the first time.

750

An Asterisk (*) at the beginning of an entry indicates that the title is appearing in BIP for the first time.

B

Bilateral Investment Treaties. UN Centre on Transnational Corporations Staff. (C). 1988. lib. bdg. 73.50 (1-85333-106-6, Pub. by Graham & Trotman UK) Kluwer Ac.

Bilateral, Regional & Multilateral Agreements...Co-operation...Nuclear Safety. (Legal Ser.: No. 15). 543p. 1990. pap. 105.00 (92-0-076090-2, STI/PUB/850) UNIPUB.

Bilateral Relations in an Uncertain World Context: Canada-U.S. Relations in 1978. Canadian-American Committee. LC 78-71435. (Canadian-American Committee Ser.). 112p. 1978. 4.00 (0-88806-044-0) Natl Planning.

Bilaterial Bergman Shift. G. Adams. LC 86-17404. (Memoirs of the American Mathematical Society Ser.: Vol. 63/355). 75p. 1986. pap. text ed. 17.00 (0-8218-2417-1, MEMO 63/355) Am Math.

Bilayer Lipid Membranes (BLM) Theory & Practice. H. Ti Tien. LC 72-95843. (Illus.). 669p. reprint ed. pap. 180.00 (0-7837-0707-X, 2041039) Bks Demand.

Bilbao Looking Glass. Charlotte MacLeod. 208p. 1984. pap. 3.50 (0-380-67454-8) Avon.

Bilbliography of Writings on Varieties of English, 1965-1983. Wolfgang Viereck et al. (Varieties of English Around the World General Ser.: No. G3). iv, 319p. (Orig.). 1984. pap. 59.00x (90-272-4861-3) Benjamins North Am.

Bilbo's Last Song. J. R. R. Tolkien. (Illus.). 32p. (J). 1990. 14.95 (0-395-53810-6) HM.

Bilbury Chronicles. Chilton Designs Publishers Staff. (C). 1992. 45.00 (0-9503527-5-6, Pub. by Chilton Designs UK) St Mut.

Bilbury Grange. Chilton Designs Publishers Staff. (C). 1992. pap. 45.00 (0-9503527-7-2, Pub. by Chilton Designs UK) St Mut.

Bild der Antike in der Deutschen Romantik. Helene M. Kastinger Riley. (German Language & Literature Monographs: No. 10). xiv, 288p. (GER.). 1981. 62.00x (90-272-4003-5) Benjamins North Am.

Bild und Lied: Archaologische Beitrage Zur Geschichte der Griechischen Heldensage. Carl Robert. LC 75-10653. (Ancient Religion & Mythology Ser.). (Illus.). (GER.). 1976. reprint ed. 18.95 (0-405-07277-5) Ayer.

Bildarchiv Preussischer Kulturversitz, Berlin, Pt. 1, 1933-1939, 2 vols. Ed. by Roland Klemig & Sybil Milton. LC 89-16915. (Archives of the Holocaust Ser.: Vol. 1). 712p. 1990. reprint ed. 410.00 (0-8240-5483-0) Garland.

Bildbeschreibungen: Picture Descriptions in German. Harris Winitz. Tr. by Josef Rohrer. (Intermediate Ser.). (Illus.). (YA). (gr. 7 up). 1988. Incl. 2 cassettes. pap. 32.00 (0-939990-59-8) Intl Linguistics.

Bildbeschreibungen: Picture Descriptions in German, 2 bks. Walter Zeller. (Basic Ser.). 130p. (YA). (gr. 7 up). 1988. Bk. I incl. 2 cassettes. 32.00 (0-939990-57-1); Bk. II incl. 2 cassettes. 32.00 (0-939990-58-X) Intl Linguistics.

Bilder Och Berattelser Om Smnadsredskap. Barbara D. Gullers. Tr. by Gertrud Grenander-Nyberg. (Illus.). 118p. (SWE.). 1992. 50.00 (0-941250-03-2) Gullers Pict.

Bilder und Gedanke: Poems. Russell W. Gilbert. LC 74-26228. (Pennsylvania German Folklore Ser.: Vol. 9). 1975. 12.50 (0-911122-31-1) Penn German Soc.

***Bilder zum Conversations Lexicon: Selections Heck's Pictorial Archive of Military Science, Geography & History.** J. G. Heck. LC 94-25894. (Illus.). 1994. write for info. (0-486-28290-2) Dover.

Bilderbergers. (Finance & Banking Ser.). 1992. lib. bdg. 69.95 (0-8490-5265-3) Gordon Pr.

Bilderbergers Conspiracy: Myth or Reality. 1992. lib. bdg. 189.95 (0-8490-9905-6) Gordon Pr.

Bildermann, Vol. 1. 1972. 35.00 (0-8115-0034-9) Periodicals Srv.

Bildgebende Systeme in der Urologie. Ed. by H. Melchior. (Beitraege zur Urologie Ser.: Vol. 4). (Illus.). xiv, 386p. (GER.). 1986. 173.75 (3-8055-4335-2) S Karger.

Bildhaften Vergleiche in Den Fragmenten der Stoiker von Zenon Bis Panaitios. Karl-Hermann Rolke. (Spudasmata Ser.: Bd. 32). vii, 531p. (GER.). 1975. write for info. (3-487-05595-3, Pub. by Georg Olms GW) Lubrecht & Cramer.

***Bildhauer Arno Breker.** Volker G. Probst. (Illus.). 168p. (Orig.). 1978. pap. 15.00 (0-914301-25-X, Pub. by Marco GW) West-Art.

***Bildhauer Kurt Arentz.** Joe F. Bodenstein. (Illus.). 144p. 1984. text ed. 30.00 (0-914301-29-2, Pub. by Marco GW) West-Art.

***Bildkatalog der Skulpteren des Vatikanischen Museums: Band I: Museo Chiaramonti, 3 pts.** B. Andreade et al. Ed. by P. Liverani & M. Mathea-Foertsch. 1106p. (GER.). (C). 1994. lib. bdg. 646.15 (3-11-013899-9) De Gruyter.

Bildkunst Des Tacitus. Uwe Rademacher. (Spudasmata Ser.: Bd. 29). xi, 298p. (GER.). 1975. write for info. (3-487-05754-9, Pub. by Georg Olms GW) Lubrecht & Cramer.

Bildliche Ausdrucksweise in den Tragodien des Euripides. Ewald Kurtz. (Heuremata Studien Zu Literatur, Sprachenn & Kultur der Antike: Vol. 8). vi, 669p. (Orig.). (GER.). 1985. pap. 74.00 (90-6032-228-2, Pub. by B R Gruener NE) Benjamins North Am.

Bildung & Verbildung in the Prose Fiction Works of Otto Julius Bierbaum. Roy L. Ackermann. (European University Studies: German Language & Literature: Ser. 1, Vol. 101). 95p. 1974. pap. 24.80 (3-261-01424-5) P Lang Pubs.

Bildung, Kultur, Existenz, 2 pts. Ed. by Richard Schwarz. Incl. Menschliche Existenz und Moderne Welt: Ein Internationales Symposion Zum Selbstverstaendnis des heutigen Menschen, Teil 1. xvi, 810p. (C). 1967. 150.00 (3-11-000486-0); Menschliche Existenz und Moderne Welt: Teil 2. x, 885p. (C). 1967. 215.00 (3-11-000487-9); (GER.). (C). write for info. (0-318-51615-2) De Gruyter.

Bildwoerterbuch der Kunst. 2nd ed. H. Leutzeler. 404p. (GER.). 1962. 45.00 (3-427-85012-9, M-7310) Fr & Eur.

***Bildwoerterbuch German-English-French, Vol. 29 Grosses Lexikon.** Meyers Staff. 937p. (ENG, FRE & GER.). 1981. 275.00 (0-7859-6917-9) Fr & Eur.

Bildworterbuch. (Duden Ser.: Vol. 3). (Illus.). 672p. 1993. 29.95 (3-411-04034-3, Pub. by Bibliogr Inst Brockhaus GW) Langenscheidt.

Bile Acids: Chemistry, Physiology & Metabolism. Ed. by P. P. Nair & David Kritchevsky. Incl. Chemistry. LC 71-138520. 384p. 1971. 65.00 (0-306-37131-6); Physiology & Metabolism. LC 71-138520. 330p. 1973. 65.00 (0-306-37132-4); Vol. 3. Pathophysiology. LC 71-138520. 242p. 1976. 55.00 (0-306-37133-2); LC 71-138520. write for info. (0-318-55308-2, Plenum Pr) Plenum.

Bile Acids & Atherosclerosis. Ed. by Scott M. Grundy. (Atherosclerosis Reviews Ser.: Vol. 15). (Illus.). 200p. 1986. text ed. 101.00 (0-88167-243-2) Raven.

Bile Acids & Cholesterol in Health & Disease. Ed. by G. Paumgartner et al. 350p. 1983. lib. bdg. 143.00 (0-85200-729-9) Kluwer Ac.

Bile Acids & the Hepatobiliary System - From Basic Science to Clinical Practice: Proceedings of the 68th Falk Symposium Held in Basel, Switzerland, October 12-14, 1992. Falk Symposium Staff. Ed. by G. Paumgartner et al. LC 93-19224. 1993. Casebound. lib. bdg. 100.00 (0-7923-8829-1) Kluwer Ac.

Bile Acids & the Liver. Ed. by G. Paumgartner et al. (Falk Ser.: No. 45). (C). 1987. lib. bdg. 150.50 (0-85200-675-6) Kluwer Ac.

Bile Acids As Therapeutic Agents from Basic Science to Clinical Practice. Ed. by G. Paumgartner et al. (Falk Symposia Ser.). (C). 1991. lib. bdg. 161.50 (0-7923-8954-9) Kluwer Ac.

Bile Acids: Chemistry, Physiology, & Metabolism, Vol. 4: Methods & Applications. Ed. by K. D. Setchell et al. LC 71-138520. (Illus.). 604p. 1987. 135.00 (0-306-42622-6, Plenum Pr) Plenum.

Bile Acids in Health & Disease. Ed. by T. C. Northfield. (C). 1988. lib. bdg. 104.00 (0-7462-0076-5) Kluwer Ac.

Bile Pigments & Jaundice: Molecular, Metabolic & Medical Aspects. Ostrow. (Liver: Normal Function & Disease Ser.: Vol. 4). 744p. 1986. 215.00 (0-8247-7428-0) Dekker.

Biles-Herzog Genealogy. Frances H. Biles. LC 84-81998. 88p. 1984. 22.50 (0-943480-58-2) Friis-Pioneer Pr.

Bilhana's Vikramankadevacarita: And Its Neo-Expounders. 2nd ed. Murari L. Nagar. (Illus.). 339p. (Orig.). 1992. pap. 55.00 (0-943913-23-3) Intl Lib Ctr.

Bilharzia: A History of Imperial Tropical Medicine. John Farley. (Cambridge History of Medicine Ser.). (Illus.). 350p. (C). 1991. 69.95 (0-521-40086-4) Cambridge U Pr.

Bilharziasis & Malaria. (Bulletin of WHO Ser.: Vol. 35, No. 3). 178p. 1966. pap. 3.60 (0-686-09213-9) World Health.

Biliary Atresia: The Japanese Experience. Daniel M. Hays & Ken Kimura. LC 79-24677. (Commonwealth Fund Publications). (Illus.). 232p. 1980. 32.00 (0-674-07325-8) HUP.

Biliary Excretion of Drugs & Other Chemicals. Claus-Peter Siegers & J. B. Watkins. (Progress in Pharmacology & Clinical Pharmacology Ser.: Vol. 8, No. 4). (Illus.). 240p. (Orig.). 1992. pap. text ed. 165.00 (1-56081-320-2, Pub. by Gustav Fischer Verlag) VCH Pubs.

Biliary Lithotripsy. Ferruci. 336p. 1988. 105.00 (0-8151-3202-6, Yr Bk Med Pubs) Mosby Yr Bk.

Biliary Lithotripsy, Vol. 2. Burhenne. 256p. 1989. 105.00 (0-8151-1375-7, Yr Bk Med Pubs) Mosby Yr Bk.

Biliary Tract. Gerald S. Dowdy, Jr. LC 73-78536. (Illus.). 330p. reprint ed. pap. 94.10 (0-8357-9396-6, 2014541) Bks Demand.

Biliary Tract Surgery Tactics & Techniques. Jacob Glassman. 1989. text ed. 90.00 (0-07-105343-3) McGraw.

Bilindex: A Bilingual Spanish-English Subject Heading List. 533p. (ENG & SPA.). 1986. 65.00 (0-685-45620-X) Floricanto Pr.

Bilindex: A Bilingual Spanish-English Subject Heading List: Spanish Equivalents to Library of Congress Subject Headings. California Spanish Language Data Base Staff. LC 83-25285. 1983. 95.95 (0-915745-00-3) Floricanto Pr.

Bilindex: Supplement I, 1985-86. Ed. by Roberto Cabello-Arpandona. 334p. 1988. pap. text ed. 55.00 (0-915745-02-X) Floricanto Pr.

Bilindex: Supplement II, 1987-1990. Ed. by Roberto Cabello-Argandona. 365p. 1990. pap. text ed. 75.00 (0-915745-22-4) Floricanto Pr.

Bilinear Transformation Method: Monograph. Yoshimasa Matsuno. (Mathematics in Science & Engineering Ser.). 1984. text ed. 91.00 (0-12-480480-2) Acad Pr.

Bilingual ABC: Spanish & English. Elizabeth Reid. (Illus.). 64p. (ENG & SPA.). (J). (gr. k-3). 1995. pap. text ed. 2.50 (0-9627080-6-2) In One EAR.

Bilingual & ESL Classrooms: Teaching in Multicultural Contexts. Carlos Ovando & Virginia Collier. 1985. text ed. 25.95 (0-07-047951-8) McGraw.

Bilingual & Multicultural Education: Canadian Perspectives. Ed. by Stan Shapson & Vincent D'Oyley. 170p. 1984. 69.00 (0-905028-36-8, Pub. by Multilingual Matters UK); pap. 24.95 (0-905028-35-X, Pub. by Multilingual Matters UK) Taylor & Francis.

Bilingual Aphasia Test, Nineteen Ninety-One. M. Paradis. Single language stimulus book. 34.50 (1-56321-087-8) LEA S&AM.

Bilingual Background & Its Relation to Certain Aspects of Character & Responsibility of Elementary School Children. Herman C. Axelrod. Ed. by Francesco Cordasco. LC 77-90406. (Bilingual-Bicultural Education in the U. S. Ser.). 1979. lib. bdg. 23.95 (0-405-11075-8) Ayer.

Bilingual-Bicultural Child & the Question of Intelligence: An Original Anthology. Ed. by Francesco Cordasco. LC 77-90568. (Bilingual-Bicultural Education in the U. S. Ser.). 1978. lib. bdg. 47.95 (0-405-11107-X) Ayer.

Bilingual-Bicultural Education: A Privilege or a Right? Illinois State Advisory Committee, the United States Commission on Civil Rights Staff. Ed. by Francesco Cordasco. LC 77-90410. (Bilingual-Bicultural Education in the U. S. Ser.). 1978. reprint ed. lib. bdg. 19.95 (0-405-11079-0) Ayer.

Bilingual Bicultural Education for the Spanish Speaking in the U. S., A Bibliography. H. Trueba. 1977. pap. 6.80 (0-87563-130-4) Stipes.

Bilingual-Bicultural Education in the U. S. Series, 37 bks., Set. Ed. by Francesco Cordasco. (Illus.). 1978. lib. bdg. 1,090.00 (0-405-11071-5) Ayer.

***Bilingual Blues.** Gustavo P. Firmat. LC 94-32331. (Orig.). 1994. pap. 11.00 (0-927534-47-9) Biling Rev-Pr.

Bilingual Brain: Neuropsychological & Neurolinguistic Aspects of Bilingualism. Martin L. Albert & Loraine K. Obler. LC 78-51243. (Perspectives in Neurolinguistics & Psycholinguistics Ser.). 1978. text ed. 53.00 (0-12-048750-0) Acad Pr.

Bilingual Children: A Resource Document. Muriel Saville-Troike. (Papers in Applied Linguistics: Bilingual Education Ser.: No. 2). 155p. reprint ed. pap. 44.20 (0-8357-3355-6, 2039591) Bks Demand.

Bilingual Children: From Birth to Teens. George Saunders. 1988. 59.00 (1-85359-010-X, Pub. by Multilingual Matters UK); pap. 19.50 (1-85359-009-6, Pub. by Multilingual Matters UK) Taylor & Francis.

Bilingual Commercial, Accounting & Legal Dictionary: Diccionario Bilingue, Comercial Contable y Legal. A. Daniel Hughes. 268p. (ENG & SPA.). 1982. 29.95 (0-8288-0127-4, S14503) Fr & Eur.

Bilingual Common Branches (One to Six) (Spanish), Elementary School. Jack Rudman. (Teachers License Examination Ser.: T-68). 1994. pap. 23.95 (0-8373-8068-5) Nat Learn.

Bilingual Concepts: Learning Center. Irene Handberg. (Bilingual Education Ser.). 176p. 1992. teacher ed write for info. (1-56831-711-5) Lrning Connect.

Bilingual Concepts: Learning Center, Set. Irene Handberg. (Bilingual Education Ser.). 176p. 1992. write for info. (1-56831-700-X) Lrning Connect.

Bilingual Conversation. J. C. Auer. LC 85-7404. (Pragmatics & Beyond Ser.: Vol. V-8). ix, 116p. (Orig.). 1984. pap. 46.00x (0-915027-49-6) Benjamins North Am.

Bilingual Cooking: La Cocina Bilingue. Ed. & Tr. by Elizabeth Reid. (Illus.). 224p. (Orig.). (ENG & SPA.). 1992. pap. 12.95 (0-9627080-3-8) In One EAR.

***Bilingual Court Glossaries - Glosarios Judiciales Bilingues No. 1: Crimes - Delitos.** Cuauhtemoc Gallegos. 48p. (Orig.). 1993. pap. 10.00 (1-886347-00-X) Merl Pubns.

***Bilingual Court Glossaries - Glosarios Judiciales Bilingues No. 2: Criminal Procedure.** Cuauhtemoc Gallegos. 52p. (Orig.). 1994. pap. 12.00 (1-886347-01-8) Merl Pubns.

Bilingual Courtroom: Court Interpreters in the Judicial Process. Susan Berk-Seligson. (Language & Legal Discourse Ser.). (Illus.). 320p. 1990. lib. bdg. 50.00 (0-226-04371-1); pap. text ed. 19.95 (0-226-04373-8) U Ch Pr.

Bilingual-Crosscultural Teacher Aides: A Resource Guide. California Department of Education Staff. 48p. 1984. pap. 3.50 (0-8011-0216-2) Calif Education.

Bilingual Dictionaries for Indigenous Languages. Doris A. Bartholomew & Louise C. Schoenhals. 370p. 1983. fiche 16.00 (0-88312-390-8) Summer Instit Ling.

***Bilingual Dictionary, French-English, English-French.** 1992. write for info. (0-7859-7848-8, 2-253-00660-2) Fr & Eur.

Bilingual Dictionary of Computer Graphics. Ferid Jemaa. 268p. (ENG & FRE.). 1992. 95.00 (0-8288-9193-1, 2212008104) Fr & Eur.

Bilingual-Dictionary of Criminal Justice Terms. Gould Editorial Staff. 250p. (ENG & SPA.). 1991. ring bd., pap. 19.95 (0-87526-379-8) Gould.

Bilingual Dictionary of Dental Terms - Diccionario Bilingue de Terminos Odontologicos. Marcos Freiberg. LC 89-24537. 111p. (ENG & SPA.). 1990. 18.00 (0-910383-22-7) Ism Pr.

Bilingual Dictionary of International Telecommunications, Vol. 1: Antenna Theory. Marcel Nouvel. 128p. (ENG & FRE.). 1983. 49.95 (0-8288-9448-5) Fr & Eur.

Bilingual Dictionary of International Telecommunications, Vol. 2: Transmission Equipment. Andy Lauriston. 506p. (ENG & FRE.). 1985. 225.00 (0-8288-9449-3) Fr & Eur.

Bilingual Dictionary of International Telecommunications, Vol. 3: Switching Equipment. Andy Lauriston. 544p. (ENG & FRE.). 1988. 225.00 (0-8288-9450-7) Fr & Eur.

Bilingual Dictionary of International Telecommunications, Vol. 4: Telecommunications Services. Andy Lauriston. 547p. (ENG & FRE.). 225.00 (0-8288-9451-5) Fr & Eur.

Bilingual Dictionary of School Terminology: English-Spanish. rev. ed. Barbara Thuro. LC 85-70097. 110p. (Orig.). (J). (ps-12). 1985. pap. 14.95 (0-932825-00-1) Ammie Enter.

Bilingual Education. National Advisory Council on Bilingual Education. Ed. by Francesco Cordasco. LC 77-90411. (Bilingual-Bicultural Education in the U. S. Ser.). 1978. reprint ed. lib. bdg. 19.95 (0-405-11080-4) Ayer.

Bilingual Education: A Sourcebook. Alba N. Ambert & Sarah E. Melendez. LC 86-23125. 356p. reprint ed. pap. 101.50 (0-7837-2178-1, 2042516) Bks Demand.

Bilingual Education: An Experience in Peruvian Amazonia. Ed. by Mildred L. Larson & Patricia M. Davis. LC 81-51059. 417p. 1981. pap. 12.00 (0-88312-918-3); fiche 20.00 (0-88312-596-X) Summer Instit Ling.

Bilingual Education: An Experience in Peruvian Amazonia. Mildred L. Larson & Patricia M. Davis. LC 81-51059. 435p. reprint ed. pap. 124.00 (0-8357-3358-0, 2039595) Bks Demand.

Bilingual Education: Evaluation, Assessment & Methodology. Carl Dodson. x, 183p. 1985. 35.00 (0-7083-0888-0, Pub. by U of Wales UK) Bks Intl VA.

Bilingual Education: Focusschrift in Honor of Joshua A. Fishman on the Occasion of his 65th Birthday, Vol. 1. Ed. by Ofelia Garcia. LC 91-16166. x, 344p. 1991. 94.00x (1-55619-116-2) Benjamins North Am.

Bilingual Education: History, Politics, Theory & Practice. James Crawford. Ed. by Patricia Crane et al. LC 89-60152. 204p. (Orig.). (C). 1989. pap. text ed. 20.98 (0-89075-556-6) Bilingual Ed Serv.

Bilingual Education: Issues & Strategies. Ed. by Amado M. Padilla et al. (Focus Editions Ser.: Vol. 112). (Illus.). 272p. (C). 1990. 46.00 (0-8039-3638-9, D1478); pap. 23.95 (0-8039-3639-7, D1478) Corwin Pr.

Bilingual Education: Policy, Practice, & Research. Ed. by M. Beatriz Arias & Ursula Casanova. (National Society for the Study of Education Publication Ser.: No. 92, Pt. 2). 262p. (C). 1993. 24.95 (0-226-60160-9) U Ch Pr.

Bilingual Education & Bilingual Special Education: A Guide for Administrators. Ed. by Sandra H. Fradd & William J. Tikunoff. LC 87-3851. 335p. (C). 1987. pap. text ed. 31.00 (0-89079-356-5, 1662) PRO-ED.

Bilingual Education & English As a Second Language: A Research Handbook 1988-1990. Alba N. Ambert. LC 91-2418. 398p. 1991. 40.00 (0-8240-5410-5); pap. 18.95 (0-8153-0466-8) Garland.

Bilingual Education & FLES: Keeping the Child in Focus. American Association of Teachers of French. Ed. by John F. Kunkle. (Reports of the FLES & Bilingual Education Section). v, 71p. (Orig.). 1975. pap. 10.00 (0-87352-168-4) Modern Lang.

Bilingual Education & Language Maintenance: A Southern Peruvian Quechua Case. N. Hornberger. (Topics in Sociolinguistics Ser.). xvi, 278p. 1988. pap. 34.95 (90-6765-357-8) Mouton.

Bilingual Education & Nationalism with Special Reference to South Africa. A. J. Aucamp. Ed. by Francesco Cordasco. LC 77-90405. (Bilingual-Bicultural Education in the U. S. Ser.). 1978. reprint ed. lib. bdg. 26.95 (0-405-11074-X) Ayer.

Bilingual Education for American Indians. U. S. Bureau of Indian Affairs Staff. Ed. by Francesco Cordasco. LC 77-90552. (Bilingual-Bicultural Education in the U. S. Ser.). 1978. reprint ed. lib. bdg. 24.95 (0-405-11091-X) Ayer.

Bilingual Education for Hispanic Students in the United States. Ed. by Joshua A. Fishman & Gary D. Keller. LC 80-27776. (Bilingual Education Ser.). (Orig.). (C). 1981. pap. 25.95 (0-8077-2603-6) Tchrs Coll.

Bilingual Education for Latinos. Ed. by Leonard Valverde. LC 78-70710. 120p. 1978. pap. text ed. 6.75 (0-87120-092-9, 611-78142) Assn Supervision.

Bilingual Education Handbook: Designing Instruction for LEP Students. California Department of Education Staff. (Illus.). 78p. 1990. pap. 6.00 (0-8011-0890-X) Calif Education.

Bilingual Education, Health, & Manpower Programs. U. S. Senate Committee on Labor & Public Welfare. Ed. by Francesco Cordasco. LC 77-90563. (Bilingual-Bicultural Education in the U. S. Ser.). 1978. reprint ed. lib. bdg. 21.95 (0-405-11101-0) Ayer.

Bilingual Education in New York City. Ed. by Francesco Cordasco. LC 77-92284. (Bilingual-Bicultural Education in the U. S. Ser.). 1978. lib. bdg. 36.95 (0-405-11081-2) Ayer.

Bilingual Education Programs, Hearings. U. S. House of Representative Committee on Education & Labor, General Subcommittee on Education. Ed. by Francesco Cordasco. LC 77-90565. (Bilingual-Bicultural Education in the U. S. Ser.). 1978. reprint ed. lib. bdg. 56.95 (0-405-11104-5) Ayer.

Bilingual Education, Vols. 1-5: Current Perspectives, 5 vols., Vol. 1: Social Science. Center for Applied Linguistics Staff. LC 77-80381. 153p. reprint ed. pap. 41.40 (0-8357-3383-1, 2039643) Bks Demand.

Bilingual Education, Vols. 1-5: Current Perspectives, 5 vols., Vol. 2: Linguistics. Center for Applied Linguistics Staff. LC 77-80381. 199p. reprint ed. pap. 56.80 (0-8357-3384-X) Bks Demand.

Bilingual Education, Vols. 1-5: Current Perspectives, 5 vols., Vol. 3: Law. Center for Applied Linguistics Staff. LC 77-80381. 89p. reprint ed. pap. 25.40 (0-8357-3385-8) Bks Demand.

Bilingual Education, Vols. 1-5: Current Perspectives, 5 vols., Vol. 4: Education. Center for Applied Linguistics Staff. LC 77-80381. 161p. reprint ed. pap. 45.90 (0-8357-3386-6) Bks Demand.

Bilingual Education, Vols. 1-5: Current Perspectives, 5 vols., Vol. 5: Synthesis. Center for Applied Linguistics Staff. LC 77-80381. 152p. reprint ed. pap. 43.40 (0-8357-3387-4) Bks Demand.

Bilingual Educations. U. S. Senate Committee on Labor & Public Welfare. Ed. by Francesco Cordasco. LC 77-18316. (Bilingual-Bicultural Education in the U. S. Ser.). 1978. reprint ed. lib. bdg. 64.95 (0-405-11103-7) Ayer.

Bilingual English-French, French-English Computers Dictionary: Dictionnaire Bilingue d'Informatique Anglais-Francais-Anglais. Alain Wiard & Ilya Virgatchik. 256p. (ENG & FRE.). 1985. pap. 19.95 (0-8288-1350-7, F28700) Fr & Eur.

An Asterisk (*) at the beginning of an entry indicates that the title is appearing in BIP for the first time.

Bilingual Fables & Folk Tales. Incl. Perez y Martina. Dorothy S. Bishop et al. 1988. pap. 4.95 (*0-8442-7167-5*); Pajaro Cu: The Cu Bird. Dorothy S. Bishop et al. 1988. pap. 4.95 (*0-685-73622-9*, 7163-5); Manchos del Sapo: How the Toad Lost Its Spots. Dorothy S. Bishop et al. 1988. pap. 4.95 (*0-685-73623-7*, 7171-5); Chiquita y Pepita: The City Mouse & the Country Mouse. Dorothy S. Bishop et al. 1988. pap. 4.95 (*0-8442-7446-1*); Tina la Tortuga y Carlos el Conejo: The Tortoise & the Hare. Dorothy S. Bishop et al. 1988. pap. 4.95 (*0-8442-7444-5*); Leonardo el Leon y Ramon el Raton: The Lion & The Mouse. Dorothy S. Bishop et al. 1988. pap. 4.95 (*0-8442-7445-3*); Poniendo el Cascabel el Gato: Belling the Cat. Dorothy S. Bishop et al. 1988. pap. 4.95 (*0-8442-7282-5*); Muchacho Que Grito el Lobo!: The Boy Who Cried Wolf. Dorothy S. Bishop et al. 1988. pap. 4.95 (*0-685-73624-5*, 7295-5); Lechera y Su Cubeta: The Milkmaid & Her Pail. Dorothy S. Bishop et al. 1991. pap. 4.95 (*0-8442-7250-7*); Illus.). 72p. (ENG & SPA.). (J). (gr. 4 up). 1988. Set pap. write for info. (*0-318-57683-X*, Natl Textbk) NTC Pub Grp.

Bilingual Family: A Handbook for Parents. Edith Harding & Philip F. Riley. 169p. 1986. pap. 15.95 (*0-521-31194-2*) Cambridge U Pr.

***Bilingual First Language Acquisition: French & German Grammatical Development.** Ed. by Jurgen M. Meisel. LC 94-23215. (Language Acquisition & Language Disorders (LALD) Ser.: No. 7). 250p. 1994. lib. bdg. 70.00x (*1-55619-242-8*) Benjamins North Am.

***Bilingual First Language Acquisition: French & German Grammatical Development.** Ed. by Jurgen M. Meisel. LC 94-23215. (Language Acquisition & Language Disorders (LALD) Ser.: No. 7). 1994. pap. 29.95x (*1-55619-243-6*) Benjamins North Am.

Bilingual French-Japanese, Japanese-French Dictionary: Dictionnaire Pair Francais-Japonais-Francais. Tuneki Shigenobu & T. Kigoshi. 638p. (FRE & JPN.). 1984. 65.00 (*0-8288-1015-X*, M9999) Fr & Eur.

Bilingual Glossary of Business Terms. M. Lapidus. 213p. (ENG & SPA.). 1982. pap. 14.95 (*0-8288-0133-9*, S 19416) Fr & Eur.

Bilingual Grammar of English-Spanish Syntax: A Manual with Exercises. Sam Hill & William Bradford. 368p. (Orig.). (C). 1991. pap. text ed. 38.00 (*0-8191-8187-0*) U Pr of Amer.

Bilingual Guide to Business & Professional Correspondence: Spanish-English, English-Spanish. J. Harvard. 1970. text ed. 102.00 (*0-08-015793-9*, Pub. by Pergamon Repr UK) Franklin.

Bilingual Guide to Business & Professional Correspondence, English-German, German-English. J. Harvard. 1973. text ed. 89.00 (*0-08-017654-2*, Pub. by Pergamon Repr UK) Franklin.

***Bilingual Handbook for Public Safety Professionals with Cassette.** (SPA.). 1995. audio 23.95 (*0-87526-427-1*) Gould.

Bilingual Homilies for Feast Days & Other Occasions. Frederick J. Murphy. LC 91-40302. 96p. (Orig.). 1992. pap. 4.95 (*0-8189-0622-7*) Alba.

Bilingual Introduction to Personal Computers Bk. 1: Hardware. German Calderon. LC 95-75139. (Illus.). 192p. (ENG & SPA.). 1995. pap. 14.95 (*0-9645037-1-9*) BilinguaTec. "DEFINITELY, the best way to learn about computers while I practice my foreign language skills."--Marcela Nicol, President of the Gulf Coast LATIN Chamber of Commerce. "VERY INTERESTING, I can see a huge need for this book."--Louis H. Sanchez, Director of region VI, United States Hispanic Chamber of Commerce. "I want to buy a copy of your book because I always wanted to learn computers & Spanish." Two weeks later... "I want another copy of your book to give away to a friend of mine."--Wilbur Woodruff, retired teacher. "Well German, you have a different concept here, we'll see what we can do."--Ron Smith, President of BookWorld Services, Inc., my distributor in the US. This book explains & describes all the different electronic components & equipment currently available for personal computers. Concise definitions guide the reader through the vast world of computer peripherals. ALL LEFT PAGES OF THE BOOK ARE IN ENGLISH & A FAITHFUL TRANSLATION TO SPANISH APPEARS ON THE RIGHT PAGES. Designed very carefully so there is no need to use a dictionary. Order from either BilinguaTec, 1410 Commerce Blvd., Suite D, Sarasota, FL 34243, (813) 351-8886 or from BookWorld (800) 444-2524.** ***Publisher Provided Annotation.

Bilingual Language, Speech, & Hearing Dictionary. Larry J. Mattes. 96p. (Orig.). 1985. pap. text ed. 9.00 (*0-930951-01-8*) Acad Comm.

Bilingual Learners & Mainstream Curriculum: Integrated Approaches to Learning & the Teaching & Learning of English As a Second Language. Josie Levine. 225p. 1990. 75.00 (*1-85000-494-3*, Falmer Pr); pap. 35.00 (*1-85000-495-1*, Falmer Pr) Taylor & Francis.

Bilingual Lexicon. Ed. by Robert Schreuder & Bert Weltens. LC 93-13893. (Studies in Bilingualism: No. 6). viii, 307p. (Orig.). 1993. 70.00x (*1-55619-536-2*); pap. 29.95 (*1-55619-538-9*) Benjamins North Am.

Bilingual Mathematics: Grade 3. Bearl Brooks. (Math Ser.). 24p. 1977. student ed 5.00 (*0-8209-0136-9*, BLM-2) ESP.

Bilingual Mathematics: Grade 4. Bearl Brooks. (Math Ser.). 24p. 1977. student ed 5.00 (*0-8209-0137-7*, BLM-3) ESP.

Bilingual Multicultural: Learning Center. Irene Handberg. (Multicultural Education Ser.). 128p. 1992. teacher ed write for info. (*1-56831-511-2*) Lrning Connect.

Bilingual Multicultural: Learning Center, Set. Irene Handberg. (Multicultural Education Ser.). 128p. 1992. write for info. (*1-56831-500-7*) Lrning Connect.

Bilingual-Multicultural Education in Canada: Interpretation & Bibliography. David H. Kelly. LC 86-2325. (Special Studies in Comparative Education: No. 15). 59p. 1986. pap. text ed. 10.00 (*0-937033-06-5*) SUNY GSE Pubns.

Bilingual Performance in Reading & Writing. Ed. by Alister H. Cumming. LC 94-9591. (Best of Language Learning Ser.: Vol. 1). 1994. 29.95 (*1-55619-714-4*) Benjamins North Am.

Bilingual Poet. Aurelio Valls. 64p. (Orig.). 1987. pap. 7.50 (*0-9614304-1-9*) Ariel Bks.

Bilingual Poet. deluxe limited ed. Aurelio Valls. 64p. (Orig.). 1987. pap. 20.00 (*0-9614304-2-7*) Ariel Bks.

Bilingual Puzzle Book: Rompecabezas Para Personas Bilingues. Sherman J. Marcus. 143p. (Orig.). 1986. pap. 4.95 (*0-9610444-2-X*) Cambita Bks.

Bilingual Reading: Level One. Bearl Brooks. (Reading Ser.). 24p. 1979. student ed 5.00 (*0-8209-0196-2*, BLR-1) ESP.

Bilingual Reading: Level Two. Bearl Brooks. (Reading Ser.). 24p. 1981. student ed 5.00 (*0-8209-0197-0*, BLR-2) ESP.

Bilingual Recipes: Recetas Bilingues. Ed. & Tr. by Elizabeth Reid. (Illus.). 64p. (Orig.). (ENG & SPA.). 1992. pap. 2.95 (*0-9627080-4-6*) In One EAR.

***Bilingual Rite of Baptism.** M. A. C. C. Team Staff. 47p. (SPA.). 1991. write for info. (*0-614-04879-6*) Mex Am Cult.

Bilingual School. Ernest G. Malherbe. Ed. by Francesco Cordasco. LC 77-90547. (Bilingual-Bicultural Education in the U. S. Ser.). 1978. reprint ed. lib. bdg. 19.95 (*0-405-11086-3*) Ayer.

Bilingual Schooling & the Miami Experience. Von N. Beebe & William F. Mackey. (Illus.). 223p. (C). 1991. 19.95 (*0-935501-20-7*, CP332) U Miami N-S Ctr.

Bilingual Selections from Sophocles' Antigone: An Introduction to the Text for the Greekless Reader. Joan V. O'Brien. LC 76-50116. 136p. 1977. 6.95 (*0-8093-0826-6*) S Ill U Pr.

Bilingual Singer: A Study in Albanian & Serbocroatian Oral Epic Tradition. John Kolsti. Ed. by Albert B. Lord. LC 90-42672. (Folklore & Oral Tradition Ser.). 410p. 1990. lib. bdg. 82.00 (*0-8240-2872-4*) Garland.

***Bilingual Songs & Fingerplays for the Mitt: Cantemos Chiquitos.** Georgette Baker. (Illus.). 12p. (Orig.). (J). (gr. k-6). Date not set. pap. text ed. 29.95 (*0-9623930-3-7*) Talented.

Bilingual Special Education Dictionary: A Resource for Special Educators & Parents. Richard A. Figueroa & Nadeen T. Ruiz. Ed. by Rogelio Diaz-Guerrero. 290p. (Orig.). 1983. pap. text ed. 16.50 (*0-318-02998-7*) Natl His Univ.

Bilingual Special Education Dictionary: A Resource for Special Educators & Parents. 2nd ed. Richard A. Figueroa et al. Ed. by Rogelio Diaz-Guerrero. (Illus.). 245p. (Orig.). (C). 1990. pap. text ed. 19.50 (*0-943803-07-1*) Natl His Univ.

Bilingual Special Education Interface. 2nd ed. Leonard M. Baca. 400p. (C). 1990. text ed. write for info. (*0-675-20833-5*, Merrill Pub Co) Macmillan.

Bilingual Special Education Resource Guide. Ed. by James L. Thomas & Carol H. Thomas. LC 82-8149. 208p. 1982. lib. bdg. 39.50 (*0-89774-008-4*) Oryx Pr.

***Bilingual Speech-Language Pathology.** Ed. by Hortencia Kayser. (Culture, Rehabilitation, & Education Ser.). (Illus.). 256p. (Orig.). (C). 1995. pap. text ed. 39.95 (*1-56593-205-6*, 0528) Singular Publishing.

Bilingual Teacher in School & Community Relations. Jack Rudman. (Teachers License Examination Ser.: T-66). 1994. pap. 23.95 (*0-8373-8066-9*) Nat Learn.

Bilingual Teacher (Junior & Senior High School) Jack Rudman. (Teachers License Examination Ser.: T-70). 1994. pap. 23.95 (*0-8373-8070-7*) Nat Learn.

Bilingual Two Language Battery of Tests. Adolph Caso. (ENG, FRE, ITA, SPA & VIE.). 1983. teacher ed, pap. 15.00 (*0-8283-1857-3*) Branden Pub Co.

Bilingual Vocabulary for the Medical Profession. R. Escandon. 248p. (ENG & SPA.). 1982. pap. 17.95 (*0-8288-0577-6*, S 40307) Fr & Eur.

Bilingual Vocational Education. Joan Friedenberg & Curtis Bradley. 53p. 1984. 5.75 (*0-318-17781-1*, IN269) Ctr Educ Trng Employ.

Bilingual Women: Anthropological Approaches to Second Language Use. Ed. by Shirley Ardener & Pauline Burton. 224p. 1994. 49.95 (*0-85496-737-0*); pap. 15.95 (*0-85496-864-4*) Berg Pubs.

Bilingualism. Suzanne Romaine. (Language in Society Ser.). (Illus.). 384p. 1989. pap. text ed. 19.95 (*0-631-15226-1*) Blackwell Pubs.

Bilingualism. 2nd ed. Suzanne Romaine. LC 94-9462. (Language in Society Ser.: Vol. 13). 416p. 1994. pap. 24.95 (*0-631-19539-4*) Blackwell Pubs.

Bilingualism: Basic Principles. 2nd ed. Hugo B. Beardsmore. 205p. 1986. 49.00 (*0-905028-69-4*, MM1, Pub. by Multilingual Matters UK); pap. 19.00 (*0-905028-63-5*, Pub. by Multilingual Matters UK) Taylor & Francis.

Bilingualism: Social & Psychological Implications. Ed. by Peter A. Hornby. 1977. text ed. 64.00 (*0-12-356350-X*) Acad Pr.

Bilingualism Across the Lifespan: Aspects of Acquisition, Maturity & Loss. Ed. by Kenneth Hyltenstam & Loraine K. Obler. (Illus.). 300p. (C). 1989. pap. 24.95 (*0-521-35998-8*) Cambridge U Pr.

Bilingualism Among American Slovaks: Analysis of Loans see Use of the Dictionary of American English & the Dictionary of Americanisms

Bilingualism & Bilinguality. Josiane F. Hamers & Michel Blanc. (Illus.). 400p. 1989. 79.95 (*0-521-33279-6*); pap. 24.95 (*0-521-33797-6*) Cambridge U Pr.

Bilingualism & Language Contact. Georgetown University Round Table Meeting on Linguistics & Language Studies Staff. Ed. by James E. Alatis. LC 58-31607. 390p. reprint ed. pap. 111.20 (*0-7837-6354-9*, 2046066) Bks Demand.

Bilingualism & Learning Disabilities: Policy & Practice for Teachers & Administrators. Ed. by Ann C. Willig & Hinda F. Greenberg. LC 85-28677. 214p. 1986. pap. text ed. 18.95 (*0-934598-92-4*) Am Lib Pub Co.

Bilingualism & Mathematics Learning. P. C. Clarkson. 60p. (C). 1991. pap. 51.00x (*0-7300-1292-1*, ECT403, Pub. by Deakin Univ AT) St Mut.

Bilingualism & Mental Development. Seth Arsenian. LC 75-176525. (Columbia University. Teachers College. Contributions to Education Ser.: No. 712). reprint ed. 37.50 (*0-404-55712-0*) AMS Pr.

Bilingualism & National Development. Ed. by Gary M. Jones & A. Conrad Ozog. LC 93-14134. 1993. 59.00 (*1-85359-208-0*, Pub. by Multilingual Matters UK) Taylor & Francis.

Bilingualism & Special Education: Issues in Assessment & Pedagogy. Jim Cummins. LC 90-22601. 306p. (C). 1984. pap. text ed. 29.00 (*0-89079-363-8*, 1639) PRO-ED.

Bilingualism & Special Education: Issues in Assessment & Pedagogy. Jim Cummins. 306p. 1984. write for info. (*0-905028-14-7*, MM6, Pub. by Multilingual Matters UK); pap. write for info. (*0-905028-13-9*, Pub. by Multilingual Matters UK) Taylor & Francis.

Bilingualism & Testing: A Special Case of Bias. Guadalupe Valdes & Richard Figueroa. LC 94-9902. (Second Language Learning Ser.). 264p. 1994. 47.50 (*0-89391-774-5*); pap. 22.50 (*0-89391-775-3*) Ablex Pub.

Bilingualism & the Bilingual Child: Challenges & Problems (an Original Anthology) Ed. by Francesco Cordasco. LC 77-90569. (Bilingual-Bicultural Education in the U. S. Ser.). 1978. lib. bdg. 51.95 (*0-405-11108-8*) Ayer.

Bilingualism & the Individual. Ed. by A. Holmen et al. (Copenhagen Studies in Bilingualism: Vol. 4). 240p. 1989. 42.00 (*0-685-21952-6*, Pub. by Multilingual Matters UK) Taylor & Francis.

Bilingualism As It Relates to Intelligence Test Scores & School Achievement among Culturally Deprived Spanish-American Children. Robert R. Galvan. Ed. by Francesco Cordasco. LC 77-92301. (Bilingual-Bicultural Education in the U. S. Ser.). 1978. lib. bdg. 18.95 (*0-405-11083-9*) Ayer.

***Bilingualism in Education.** Inger Ahlgren & Kenneth Hytenstam. 312p. 1994. 39.95 (*3-927731-54-4*, Pub. by Signum-Verlag GW) Gallaudet Univ Pr.

Bilingualism in Education. United Kingdom, Department of Education & Science, National Commission for U. N. E. S. C. O. Ed. by Francesco Cordasco. LC 77-17708. (Bilingual-Bicultural Education in the U. S. Ser.). 1978. reprint ed. lib. bdg. 26.95 (*0-405-11099-5*) Ayer.

Bilingualism in Northern England see Word List from Olney, Illinois

Bilingualism in Society & School. Ed. by J. N. Jorgensen et al. (Copenhagen Studies in Bilingualism: Vol. 5). 270p. 1989. 59.00 (*1-85359-016-9*, MM43, Pub. by Multilingual Matters UK) Taylor & Francis.

Bilingualism in the Americas: A Bibliography & Research Guide. Einar Haugen. (Publications of the American Dialect Society: No. 26). 159p. 1956. pap. 15.95 (*0-8173-0626-9*) U of Ala Pr.

Bilingualism in the Bicentennial & Beyond. Ed. by Gary D. Keller et al. LC 76-45292. 1976. lib. bdg. 15.00 (*0-916950-15-8*) Biling Rev-Pr.

Bilingualism in the History of Jewish Literature. Shmuel Niger. Tr. by Joshua A. Fogel. LC 89-24789. 140p. (C). 1990. lib. bdg. 33.00 (*0-8191-7382-7*) U Pr of Amer.

Bilingualism in the Primary School: A Handbook for Teachers. Ed. by Richard W. Mills & Jean Mills. LC 92-32058. 144p. 1993. 59.95 (*0-415-08860-7*, B0407); pap. write for info. (*0-415-08861-5*) Routledge.

Bilingualism in the United States: Conflict & Controversy. Judith Harlan. LC 91-18518. (Impact Bks.). (Illus.). 128p. (YA). (gr. 9-12). 1991. lib. bdg. 14.42 (*0-531-13001-0*) Watts.

Bilingualism, Multiculturalism, & Second Language Learning: The McGill Conference in Honour of Wallace E. Lambert. A. G. Reynolds. 288p. (C). 1991. text ed. 49.95 (*0-8058-0694-6*) L Erlbaum Assocs.

Bilingualism or Not: The Education of Minorities. Tove Skutnabb-Kangas. 378p. 1984. 79.00 (*0-905028-18-X*, Pub. by Multilingual Matters UK); pap. 29.95 (*0-905028-17-1*, Pub. by Multilingual Matters UK) Taylor & Francis.

Bilingualism Through Schooling: Cross-Cultural Education for Minority & Majority Students. Arnulfo G. Ramirez. LC 83-24246. 275p. 1985. 64.50 (*0-87395-891-8*); pap. 21.95 (*0-87395-892-6*) State U NY Pr.

Bilirubin, 2 vols. Ed. by Karel P. Heirwegh. Incl. Vol. I. Chemistry. 168p. 1982. 119.00 (*0-8493-6155-9*, QP671); Vol. II. Metabolism. 240p. 1982. 110.00 (*0-8493-6156-7*, QP671); 1982. write for info. (*0-318-56977-9*, CRC Reprint) Franklin.

Bilirubin Metabolism in the Newborn. Ed. by Daniel Bergsma et al. (International Congress Ser.: No. 380). 1976. 79.50 (*0-444-15216-4*, Excerpta Medica) Elsevier.

Biliteracy: Theory & Practice. David Spener. 1993. pap. write for info. (*0-13-094285-5*) P-H.

Bill. Chap Reaver. (J). 1994. 14.95 (*0-385-31175-3*) Delacorte.

***Bill: How the Adventures of Clinton's National Service Bill Reveal What Is Corrupt, Comic, Cynical, & Noble about Washington.** Steven Waldman. 320p. 1995. 22.95 (*0-670-85300-3*, Viking) Viking Penguin.

Bill & Al's Excellent Adventure. Jim Becker & Andy Mayer. (Illus.). 32p. (Orig.). 1993. pap. 9.99 (*0-312-10427-8*) St Martin.

Bill & Bev Beatty's Wild Plant Cookbook. Bill Beatty & Bev Beatty. (Illus.). 174p. 1987. 16.95 (*0-87961-158-8*); pap. 8.95 (*0-87961-159-6*) Naturegraph.

Bill & Hillary: Working Together in the White House. Keith E. Greenberg. (Partners Ser.). (Illus.). 48p. (J). (gr. 2-5). 1994. lib. bdg. 12.95 (*1-56711-067-3*); pap. 6.95 (*1-56711-069-X*) Blackbirch.

***Bill & Hillary Joke Book.** Laura Crenshaw. (Illus.). 64p. (Orig.). 1995. pap. 5.95 (*0-9632280-1-3*) Peroxide Pr.

***Bill & Hillary's Twelve-Step Recovery Guide: How to Recover from Anything.** Glenn Eichler. 144p. (Orig.). 1995. pap. 10.00 (*1-57297-030-8*, Berkley Trade) Berkley Pub.

Bill & Pete. Tomie De Paola. LC 78-5330. (Illus.). (J). (gr. k-2). 1978. 14.95 (*0-399-20646-9*, Putnam) Putnam Pub Group.

Bill & Pete. Tomie De Paola. (J). (ps-1). 1992. pap. 5.95 (*0-399-22402-5*, Sandcastle Bks) Putnam Pub Group.

Bill & Pete Go Down the Nile. Tomie De Paola. (Illus.). 32p. (J). (ps-1). 1987. 14.95 (*0-399-21395-3*, Putnam) Putnam Pub Group.

Bill & Pete Go down the Nile. Tomie De Paola. (Illus.). 32p. (J). (ps-3). 1990. pap. 5.95 (*0-399-22003-8*, Sandcastle Bks) Putnam Pub Group.

Bill & the Burning Bush. Bruce Porter. (Illus.). 40p. (Orig.). (J). (gr. 1 up). 1987. pap. 3.95 (*0-939925-12-5*) R C Law & Co.

Bill & the Ghost of Grimley Grange. Anthony Stones. 32p. 1988. 9.95 (*0-86327-194-4*, Pub. by Wolfhound Pr IE) Dufour.

Bill & the Maze at Grimley Grange. Anthony Stones. (Illus.). 32p. (Orig.). (J). (gr. k-2). 1990. 10.95 (*0-86327-249-5*, Pub. by Wolfhound Pr IE) Dufour.

Bill Anthony's Greatest Hits: Drawings 1963-1987. William Anthiny. LC 87-80709. (Illus.). 84p. 1988. 20.00 (*0-912330-62-7*) Jargon Soc.

Bill Anthony's Greatest Hits: Drawings 1963-1987. limited ed. William Anthiny. LC 87-80709. (Illus.). 84p. 1988. 100.00 (*0-912330-63-5*) Jargon Soc.

Bill Arp. James C. Austin. LC 68-24308. (Twayne's United States Authors Ser.). 1969. lib. bdg. 8.95 (*0-89197-678-7*); pap. text ed. 4.95 (*0-8290-0081-X*) Irvington.

Bill Arp, So Called: A Side Show of the Southern Side of the War. Charles H. Smith. (Illus.). reprint ed. lib. bdg. 16.00 (*0-8398-1866-1*) Irvington.

Bill Arp, So Called: Side Show of the Southern Side of the War. Bill Arp, pseud. LC 72-158277. (Illus.). reprint ed. 39.50 (*0-404-00213-7*) AMS Pr.

Bill Arp's Peace Papers. Bill Arp, pseud. LC 79-158276. (Illus.). reprint ed. 39.50 (*0-404-00405-9*) AMS Pr.

Bill Austin's Freshwater Fishing Digest. William Austin. (Illus.). 224p. 1983. pap. 9.95 (*0-911007-02-4*) Prairie Hse.

Bill Bailey, Vol. 1. large type ed. Catherine Cookson. (General Ser.). 387p. 1990. 20.95 (*0-8161-4485-0*, Large Print Bks) Hall.

Bill Bailey Came Home: As a Farm Boy, As a Stowaway at the Age of Nine, a Trapper at the Age of Fifteen & a Hobo at the Age of Sixteen. William A. Bailey. Ed. by Austin Fife & Alta Fife. LC 73-79904. (Illus.). 195p. reprint ed. pap. 55.60 (*0-8357-6039-1*, 2034601) Bks Demand.

Bill Bailey's Daughter, Vol. 3. large type ed. Catherine Cookson. (General Ser.). 321p. 1990. 20.95 (*0-8161-4768-X*, Large Print Bks) Hall.

Bill Bernbach's Book: A History of the Advertising that Changed the History of Advertising. Bob Levenson. LC 86-4013. (Illus.). 240p. 1987. 50.00 (*0-394-54920-1*, Villard Bks) Random.

Bill Berry: From Life & Memory. Mary Goodwin. (Illus.). 23p. (Orig.). 1989. pap. 10.00 (*0-931163-05-6*) U Alaska Museum.

Bill Bissett & His Works. Karl Jirgens. 91p. (C). 1992. pap. text ed. 9.95 (*1-55022-068-3*, Pub. by ECW Press CN) Genl Dist Srvs.

Bill Bowerman & Phil Knight: Building the Nike Empire. Keith E. Greenberg. Ed. by Bruce Glassman. LC 94-12747. (Partners Ser.). (Illus.). 48p. (J). (gr. 2-5). 1994. lib. bdg. 12.95 (*1-56711-085-1*) Blackbirch.

Bill Brandt: Photographs 1926-1983. Ed. by Ian Jeffrey. LC 93-60536. (Illus.). 192p. 1994. pap. 24.95 (*0-500-27726-5*) Thames Hudson.

Bill Brandt: Selected Texts & Bibliography. Ed. by Nigel Warburton. LC 93-33541. (World Photographers Ser.: No. 5). (Illus.). 180p. 1994. text ed. 85.00 (*0-8161-0616-9*) G K Hall.

Bill Bresnan Speaks on Mutual Fund in Words of One Syllable. Bill Bresnan. (Illus.). 224p. 1988. pap. 20.50 (*0-13-078270-X*, Busn) P-H.

B

An Asterisk (*) at the beginning of an entry indicates that the title is appearing in BIP for the first time.

753

Bill Bresnan Speaks on Tax Planning under the New Tax Law...in Words of One Syllable. Bill Bresnan. (Illus.). 224p. 1987. 20.50 (*0-13-076472-8*) P-H.

Bill Bresnan Speaks on the Stock Market. Bill Bresnan. (Illus.). 224p. 1988. 16.95 (*0-13-077314-X*) P-H.

***Bill Carlisle, Lone Bandit.** William Carlisle. (American Autobiography Ser.). 220p. 1995. reprint ed. lib. bdg. 79.00 (*0-7812-8473-2*) Rprt Serv.

Bill Clinton. Elaine Landau. LC 92-39174. (Illus.). (J). (gr. 5-8). 1993. lib. bdg. 13.23 (*0-531-11143-1*); pap. 5.95 (*0-531-15670-2*) Watts.

Bill Clinton. Victoria Sherrow. LC 93-1747. (Taking Sides Ser.). (Illus.). 72p. (J). (gr. 4-6). 1993. text ed. 13.95 (*0-87518-620-3*, Dillon Silver Burdett) Silver Burdett Pr.

Bill Clinton: As They Know Him. David Gallen. 1994. 21.95 (*0-9636477-2-5*) Gallen Pub Fnd.

Bill Clinton: Eyes on the Future. Leslie Kitchen. (Illus.). 96p. 1994. pap. 14.50 (*0-917882-39-3*); boxed 17.50 (*0-917882-38-5*) MD Hist Pr.

***Bill Clinton: Forty-Second President of the United States.** Carol Greene. LC 94-36410. (Rookie Biographies Ser.). (Illus.). 48p. (J). (gr. k-3). 1995. lib. bdg. 12.90 (*0-516-04267-X*) Childrens.

Bill Clinton: Friend or Foe? 2nd ed. Ann Wilson. Ed. by Sue Cooley. (Illus.). 243p. Date not set. pap. 11.95 (*0-9640180-0-4*) J W Pubng.

Bill Clinton: Our Forty-Second President. Robert Cwiklik. (Gateway Biographies Ser.). (Illus.). 48p. (J). (gr. 2-4). 1993. lib. bdg. 12.90 (*1-56294-387-1*) Millbrook Pr.

Bill Clinton: Our Forty-Second President. Robert Cwiklik. (Gateway Biographies Ser.). (Illus.). 48p. (J). (gr. 2-4). 1993. pap. 4.95 (*1-56294-764-8*) Millbrook Pr.

Bill Clinton: President from Arkansas. Gene L. Martin & Aaron Boyd. (Illus.). 104p. (YA). (gr. 7-12). 1993. lib. bdg. 17.95 (*0-936389-31-1*) Tudor Pubs.

Bill Clinton: The Inside Story. Robert E. Levin. (Illus.). 320p. 1992. 5.50 (*1-56171-177-2*, S P I Bks) Sure Sellers.

Bill Clinton: The 42nd President of the United States. Bob Italia. LC 93-24849. (All the President's Men & Women Ser.). (J). 1993. lib. bdg. 13.99 (*1-56239-249-2*) Abdo & Dghtrs.

Bill Clinton: United States President. Michael D. Cole. LC 93-37411. (People to Know Ser.). (Illus.). 112p. (J). (gr. 6 up). 1994. lib. bdg. 17.95 (*0-89490-437-X*) Enslow Pubs.

Bill Clinton on Stump, State, & Stage: The Rhetorical Road to the White House. Ed. by Stephen A. Smith. 384p. (Orig.). 1994. 34.00 (*1-55728-365-6*); pap. 20.00 (*1-55728-372-9*) U of Ark Pr.

Bill Clinton Story: Winning the Presidency. John Hohenberg. 260p. 1994. 24.95 (*0-8156-0284-7*) Syracuse U Pr.

***Bill Clinton You're No John F. Kennedy.** David L. Lantz. (Illus.). 151p. (Orig.). Date not set. pap. text ed. 9.95 (*0-9639611-0-1*) Joshua Hse.

Bill Clinton's Agenda for America: Will It Make You Rich or Poor. Peter Navarro. write for info. (*0-9635289-0-4*) Williams OR.

Bill Clinton's Pre-Presidential Career: An Annotated Bibliography. Allan Metz. LC 94-3017. (Bibliographies & Indexes in American History Ser.: Vol. 27). 248p. 1994. text ed. 59.95 (*0-313-29285-X*, Greenwood Pr) Greenwood.

Bill Cook's Strategic Planning for America's Schools. 2nd ed. William J. Cook, Jr. 222p. 1990. pap. 19.95 (*0-87652-132-4*, 021-00295) Am Assn Sch Admin.

Bill Cosby. Solomon Herbert & George Hill. (Black Americans of Achievement Ser.). (Illus.). 104p. (YA). (gr. 5 up). 1992. lib. bdg. 17.95 (*0-7910-1121-6*) Chelsea Hse.

***Bill Cosby: Actor & Comedian.** Michael A. Schuman. LC 95-9811. (People to Know Ser.). (Illus.). 128p. (YA). (gr. 6 up). 1995. lib. bdg. 17.95 (*0-89490-548-1*) Enslow Pubs.

Bill Cosby: America's Most Famous Father. Jim Haskins. 128p. (J). (gr. 7-9). 1988. 13.95 (*0-8027-6785-0*); lib. bdg. 14.85 (*0-8027-6786-9*) Walker & Co.

Bill Cosby: Entertainer. George Hill. (J). (gr. 4-7). 1992. pap. 7.95 (*0-7910-1146-1*) Chelsea Hse.

Bill Cosby: Family Funny Man. Larry Kettelkamp. LC 86-23809. 128p. (J). (gr. 3 up). 1987. lib. bdg. 12.98 (*0-671-62382-6*, Julian Messner); pap. 3.95 (*0-671-64029-1*, Julian Messner) Silver Burdett Pr.

Bill Cosby: Family Man. Bruce W. Conord. (Junior Black Americans of Achievement Ser.). (Illus.). 80p. (J). (gr. 3-6). 1993. lib. bdg. 14.95 (*0-7910-1761-3*) Chelsea Hse.

***Bill Cosby: Family Man.** Bruce W. Conord. (Junior Black Americans of Achievement Ser.). (Illus.). 80p. (J). (gr. 3-6). 1993. pap. 4.95 (*0-7910-2107-6*) Chelsea Hse.

Bill Cosby: In Words & Pictures. Robert Johnson. (Illus.). 1986. pap. 12.95 (*0-87485-084-3*) Johnson Chi.

Bill Cosby: Making America Laugh & Learn. Harold Woods & Geraldine Woods. LC 82-23497. (Taking Part Ser.). (Illus.). 48p. (J). (gr. 3 up). 1989. text ed. 13.95 (*0-87518-240-2*, Dillon Silver Burdett) Silver Burdett Pr.

Bill Cosby: Superstar. Patricia S. Martin. (Reaching Your Goal Bks.). (Illus.). 24p. (J). (gr. 1-4). 1987. 10.95 (*0-685-67569-6*); lib. bdg. 14.60 (*0-86592-169-5*) Rourke Corp.

Bill Cosby: The Changing Black Image. Robert Rosenberg. (YA). 1992. pap. 5.92 (*0-395-63615-9*) HM.

Bill Cosby: The Changing Black Image. Robert Rosenberg. (New Directions Ser.). (Illus.). 96p. (YA). (gr. 7 up). 1991. lib. bdg. 15.40 (*1-878841-17-3*); pap. 5.95 (*1-56294-828-8*) Millbrook Pr.

Bill Cosby, Entertainer. Marianne Ruuth. Ed. by Raymond F. Locke. (Black American Ser.). (Illus.). 1993. pap. 3.95 (*0-87067-596-6*, Melrose Sq) Holloway.

***Bill Culbert.** 84p. 1995. pap. 20.00 (*2-908257-16-5*, Pub. by F R A C FR) Dist Art Pubs.

Bill Doolin: Outlaw O. T. Bailey C. Hanes. LC 68-15673. (Western Frontier Library: Vol. 41). (Illus.). 256p. 1994. pap. 12.95 (*0-8061-1652-8*) U of Okla Pr.

Bill Douglas: A Lanternist's Account. Ed. by Eddie Dick et al. (Illus.). 240p. (C). 1993. 49.95 (*0-85170-347-X*, Pub. by British Film Inst UK); pap. 19.95 (*0-85170-348-8*, Pub. by British Film Inst UK) Ind U Pr.

Bill Elliott: Fastest Man Alive. Al Thomy. 208p. 1988. pap. 12.95 (*0-934601-38-0*) Peachtree Pubs.

Bill Emrich: Photographs of Men. Bill Emrich. (Illus.). 64p. 1993. 34.95 (*3-924163-00-6*, Pub. by Janssen GW) InBook.

Bill Frank's Delaware. Bill Frank. 320p. (Orig.). 1987. pap. 9.95 (*0-912608-53-6*) Mid Atlantic.

Bill Freeland. Robert Murdock. (Illus.). 52p. (Orig.). 1989. pap. 15.00 (*0-944751-02-4*) Maxwells Busn.

Bill Gaines. Steven Otfinoski. LC 93-16177. (Made in America Ser.). (J). 1993. write for info. (*0-86592-080-X*) Rourke Enter.

***Bill Garner's Cartoons.** Bill Garner. (Illus.). 160p. 1995. pap. text ed. 8.95 (*1-56554-127-8*) Pelican.

Bill Graham Presents. Bill Graham & Greenfield. 1993. pap. 12.95 (*0-385-31141-9*, Delta) Dell.

***Bill Graham Presents & the Family Dog: Dry Bones Research Database, Numbered Posters, Tickets & Memorabilia.** Ed. by Jimmie R. Rankin. 100p. (Orig.). 1996. pap. 25.00 (*1-883938-20-1*) Dry Bones Pr.

Bill Greene's One Hundred & One New Loopholes. Bill Greene. 112p. 1982. pap. 3.95 (*0-936602-32-5*) J C Print.

Bill Griffeth's Ten Steps to Financial Prosperity: CNBC's Award Winning Anchor Shows You How to Achieve Financial Independence. Bill Griffeth. 1994. 21.95 (*1-55738-575-0*) Probus Pub Co.

***Bill Griffeth's 10 Steps to Financial Prosperity.** Bill Griffeth. 1996. pap. write for info. (*0-446-67176-2*) Warner Bks.

Bill Guest Anthology of Fiddle Tunes. Bill Guest. 1993. 8.95 (*1-56222-143-4*, 94039); audio 9.98 (*1-56222-619-3*, 94039) Mel Bay.

Bill Gunston's Plane Speaking. Bill Gunston. (Illus.). 192p. 1991. 29.95 (*1-85260-166-3*) Motorbooks Intl.

Bill Hall & the Killer Chicken. Ed. by Bill Hall. (Illus.). 102p. 1981. pap. 4.95 (*0-9607506-0-6*) News Rev Pub.

Bill Hall's Land & Lakes Cookbook. Channel Four, Nashville Staff. LC 93-73580. 1993. write for info. (*0-87197-391-X*) Favorite Recipes.

Bill Hall's Son of Killer Chicken. Bill Hall. (Illus.). (Orig.). 1983. pap. 4.95 (*0-9607506-2-2*) News Rev Pub.

Bill Henry: An Approved History of the Olympic Games. 504p. 1984. pap. 6.00 (*0-317-56276-2*) S CA Committee.

Bill Hogg's Most Excellent Guide to Praying. Bill Hogg. (Orig.). 1993. pap. 12.95 (*0-86065-885-6*, Kingsway Pubns Ltd UK) Trans-Atl Phila.

Bill Horan's Modelling Masterclass. Bill Horan. (Illus.). 128p. 1994. 24.95 (*1-872004-09-1*, Pub. by Windrow & Green UK) Motorbooks Intl.

Bill Hutson: Paintings 1978-1987. Studio Museum in Harlem Staff. Ed. by Kellie Jones. (Illus.). 24p. (Orig.). 1987. pap. text ed. write for info. (*0-942949-01-3*) Studio Mus Harlem.

Bill James Historical Baseball Abstract. Bill James & Mary A. Wirth. LC 87-40570. (Illus.). 619p. 1985. 29.95 (*0-394-53713-0*, Villard Bks); pap. 15.95 (*0-394-75805-6*, Villard Bks) Random.

Bill James Player Ratings Book, 1993. Bill James. 320p. (Orig.). 1993. pap. 10.00 (*0-02-041563-X*, Collier S&S) S&S Trade.

Bill James Player Ratings Book, 1994. 192p. 1994. pap. 12.00 (*0-02-041564-8*, Collier S&S) S&S Trade.

Bill James Player Ratings Book, 1994. Bill James. 320p. 1994. 12.00 (*0-02-041465-X*, Collier S&S) S&S Trade.

***Bill James Player Ratings, 1995.** Bill James. 1995. pap. 12.95 (*0-684-80089-6*, Fireside) S&S Trade.

Bill James Presents STATS Major League Handbook 1992. STATS, Inc. Staff & Bill James. Ed. by John Dewan. 344p. (Orig.). (C). 1991. per. 17.95 (*0-9625581-3-3*) Sports Team Analysis.

Bill James Presents STATS Major League Handbook, 1993. Bill James. 1992. write for info. (*0-9625581-6-8*) Sports Team Analysis.

Bill James Presents STATS Minor League Handbook, 1993. STATS, Inc. Staff et al. 340p. 1992. 17.95 (*0-9625581-7-6*) Sports Team Analysis.

Bill James Presents Stats 1992 Minor League Handbook. STATS, Inc. Staff et al. 336p. (Orig.). (C). 1991. per. 17.95 (*0-9625581-5-X*) Sports Team Analysis.

Bill James Presents the Great American Baseball Stat Book. Project Scoresheet Staff & Bill James. LC 87-40610. 600p. 1988. pap. 14.95 (*0-394-75925-7*, Villard Bks) Random.

Bill Jensen. Eliza E. Rathbone. LC 87-27312. (Illus.). 45p. 1987. pap. 15.00 (*0-943044-10-3*) Phillips Coll.

***Bill Knapke - a Railroad Legend: Sketches from the Life of an Oldtime Boomer.** Dick Murdock. Ed. by Ruth Rockefeller & Joyce Gibbs. LC 95-6797. (Illus.). 144p. (Orig.). (YA). (gr. 8-10). 1996. pap. 12.95 (*0-932916-18-X*) May-Murdock.

Bill Koch on Cross Country Skiing. Bill Koch. (Illus.). 192p. 1993. pap. 14.00 (*0-02-028755-0*, Collier S&S) S&S Trade.

Bill Mack. Anna McDonnel. (Illus.). 166p. (C). 1989. write for info. (*0-318-65799-6*) Maresa Editions.

Bill Martin Junior Connection. Will C. Howell. 1991. 10.99 (*0-86653-991-3*) Fearon Teach Aids.

Bill Martin Junior Library. (J). 1993. 149.00 (*0-8050-3073-5*) H Holt & Co.

Bill Mason's Non-Nonsense Guide to Fly Fishing Idaho. Bill Mason. Ed. by David Banks et al. (Illus.). 64p. (Orig.). 1994. pap. text ed. 14.95 (*0-9637256-1-0*) D Mktg Comm.

Bill Mauldin's Army: Bill Mauldin's Greatest World War II Cartoons. Bill Mauldin. (Illus.). 384p. 1983. reprint ed. 30.00 (*0-89141-180-1*); reprint ed. pap. 14.95 (*0-89141-159-3*) Presidio Pr.

Bill Mazer's Amazin' Baseball Book. Bill Mazer. 1990. 19.95 (*0-8217-2947-0*) Zebra.

Bill Mazer's Amazin' Baseball Book. Bill Mazer. 416p. 1991. pap. 8.95 (*0-8217-3361-3*) Zebra.

Bill McDonald's Poems of Life. William A. McDonald. 1991. 12.95 (*0-533-09162-4*) Vantage.

Bill Monroe's Grande Ole Opry USM Song Folio No. 1. Bill Monroe. pap. 8.95 (*0-686-09065-9*, Peer-Southern) CPP Belwin.

Bill Neal's Southern Cooking. enl. rev. ed. Bill Neal. LC 88-37258. xv, 204p. 1989. 24.95 (*0-8078-1859-3*); pap. 13.95 (*0-8078-4255-9*) U of NC Pr.

Bill Nunn's Column Book: Essays on the Unbought Graces of Life Everyday. Bill Nunn. 12.95 (*0-915637-00-6*) Westphalia Pr.

Bill Nye. David B. Kesterson. LC 76-45132. (Western Writers Ser.: No. 22). 48p. 1976. pap. 3.95 (*0-88430-021-8*) Boise St U W Writ Ser.

Bill Nye: His Own Life Story. Edgar W. Nye. (BCL1-PS American Literature Ser.). 412p. 1992. reprint ed. lib. bdg. 99.00 (*0-7812-6815-X*) Rprt Serv.

Bill Nye: His Own Life Story. Edgar W. Nye & Frank W. Nye. LC 70-145216. (Illus.). 1971. reprint ed. 24.00 (*0-403-01133-7*) Scholarly.

Bill Nye & Boomerang. Edgar W. Nye. LC 70-166823. 1971. reprint ed. 29.00 (*0-403-01449-2*) Scholarly.

Bill Nye, His Own Life Story. Bill Nye. LC 78-124246. (Select Bibliographies Reprint Ser.). 1977. reprint ed. 24.95 (*0-8369-5434-3*) Ayer.

Bill Nye the Science Guy's Big Blast of Science. Bill Nye. (Illus.). 176p. (YA). 1993. pap. 12.45 (*0-201-60864-2*) Addison-Wesley.

Bill Nye's History of the United States. Edgar W. Nye. LC 75-96891. (Illus.). 1970. reprint ed. lib. bdg. 22.00 (*0-8398-1352-X*) Irvington.

Bill of Rights. LC 86-5096. (Milestone Documents in the National Archives Ser.). (Illus.). 28p. 1986. pap. 3.50 (*0-911333-42-8*, 200102) National Archives & Recs.

Bill of Rights. Warren Colman. LC 86-33437. (New True Bks.). (Illus.). 48p. (J). (gr. k-4). 1987. lib. bdg. 13.50 (*0-516-01232-0*); pap. 5.50 (*0-516-41232-9*) Childrens.

Bill of Rights. R. Conrad Stein. LC 91-41541. (Cornerstones of Freedom Ser.). (Illus.). 32p. (J). (gr. 3-6). 1992. lib. bdg. 12.30 (*0-516-04853-8*) Childrens.

Bill of Rights. R. Conrad Stein. LC 91-41541. (Cornerstones of Freedom Ser.). (Illus.). 32p. (J). (gr. 3-6). 1992. pap. 3.95 (*0-516-44853-6*) Childrens.

Bill of Rights. Hugo L. Black. (Reprint Series in Political Science). (C). 1993. reprint ed. pap. text ed. 1.90 (*0-8290-2615-0*, P-26) Irvington.

***Bill of Rights: A Bicentennial Assessment.** Ed. by Gary C. Bryner & A. D. Sorensen. LC 94-1729. 280p. 1994. 39.50 (*0-7914-2225-9*) State U NY Pr.

Bill of Rights: A Lively Heritage. Ed. by Jon Kukla. x, 178p. 1987. 25.00 (*0-88490-141-6*) VA State Lib.

***Bill of Rights: A User's Guide.** 248p. Date not set. 12.95 (*0-614-04361-1*) Close Up.

Bill of Rights: A User's Guide. Linda Monk. (Illus.). 248p. (Orig.). 1991. pap. text ed. 12.95 (*0-932765-38-6*, 996-920) Close Up.

Bill of Rights: A User's Guide. suppl. ed. Linda Monk. Ed. by David Zack. (Illus.). 248p. (Orig.). 1991. teacher ed 9.95 (*0-685-57437-7*) Close Up.

Bill of Rights: Bicentennial Reflections. Ed. by Yeager Hudson & Creighton Peden. LC 93-9179. 436p. 1993. text ed. 109.95 (*0-7734-9264-X*) E Mellen.

Bill of Rights: Opposing Viewpoints. Ed. by William Dudley. LC 93-4575. (American History Ser.). 1994. lib. bdg. 19.95 (*1-56510-088-3*); pap. 11.55 (*1-56510-087-5*) Greenhaven.

Bill of Rights: Original Meaning & Current Understanding. Eugene W. Hickok, Jr. 487p. 1991. text ed. 40.00 (*0-8139-1297-0*); pap. text ed. 18.95 (*0-8139-1336-5*) U Pr of Va.

Bill of Rights: Our Written Legacy. Joseph A. Melusky & Whitman H. Ridgway. 268p. (C). 1993. text ed. 26.50 (*0-89464-533-1*); pap. 18.50 (*0-89464-827-6*) Krieger.

Bill of Rights & Landmark Cases. Edmund Lindop. LC 89-8960. (Illus.). 144p. (J). (gr. 7-9). 1989. lib. bdg. 14.98 (*0-531-10790-6*) Watts.

***Bill of Rights & Limited Government.** (Becoming Informed Citizens Ser.: Vol. II). 204p. (YA). (gr. 8-12). 1995. spiral bd. 19.50 (*0-941690-61-X*) Regina Bks.

***Bill of Rights & Roman Law: A Comparative Study.** Joseph Plescia. 300p. (Orig.). 1995. 69.95 (*1-57292-005-X*); pap. 49.95 (*1-57292-004-1*) Austin & Winfield.

Bill of Rights & the Japanese American World War II Experience. Ed. by Rosalyn Tonai et al. 89p. 1992. teacher ed 6.50 (*1-881506-00-2*) Natl Japnse Am HS.

Bill of Rights & the Politics of Interpretation. Robert S. Peck. Ed. by Lippert. 371p. (C). 1992. text ed. 26.75 (*0-314-90881-1*) West Pub.

Bill of Rights & the States. Ed. by Paul L. Murphy. (Bill of Rights & American Legal History Ser.). 540p. 1990. reprint ed. 69.00 (*0-8240-5866-6*) Garland.

Bill of Rights & the States: The Colonial & Revolutionary Origins of American Liberties. Ed. by Patrick T. Conley & John P. Kaminski. (Illus.). 568p. 1992. 39.95 (*0-945612-26-5*); pap. 24.95 (*0-945612-29-X*) Madison Hse.

Bill of Rights & What It Means Today. Edward Dumbauld. LC 78-12307. (Illus.). xv, 242p. 1979. reprint ed. text ed. 59.75 (*0-313-21215-5*, DUBR, Greenwood Pr) Greenwood.

***Bill of Rights Cancelled.** Bill Uselton. 30p. (Orig.). 1992. pap. 2.50 (*1-879366-33-9*) Hearthstone OK.

Bill of Rights Debate. Robert Blackburn. (Citizenship & the Law Ser.). 224p. 1994. text ed. 70.00 (*0-7201-2123-X*, Mansell Pub) Cassell.

Bill of Rights for Future Generations. Jacques-Yves Cousteau. 33p. (Orig.). (gr. 8-12). 1980. pap. 1.50 (*0-913098-29-9*) Myrin Institute.

Bill of Rights in Modern America: After 200 Years. Ed. by David J. Bodenhamer & James W. Ely, Jr. LC 92-15815. (C). 1993. 29.95 (*0-253-31223-X*); pap. 12.95 (*0-253-20767-3*, MB 767) Ind U Pr.

Bill of Rights in the Welfare State. Ed. by Geoffrey R. Stone et al. LC 92-9397. 608p. (C). 1992. lib. bdg. 55.00 (*0-226-77531-3*); pap. text ed. 19.95 (*0-226-77532-1*) U Ch Pr.

Bill of Rites, a Bill of Wrongs, a Bill of Goods. Wright Morris. LC 80-389. x, 177p. 1980. reprint ed. 17.95 (*0-8032-3065-6*); reprint ed. pap. 5.95 (*0-8032-8107-2*) U of Nebr Pr.

***Bill Payer by Homefile: Monthly Bill Organizer.** J. Michael Martin & Mary E. Martin. Ed. by Mary E. Martin. (Financial Advantage Ser.). (Illus.). 96p. (Orig.). 1995. pap. 19.95 (*0-9628718-5-0*) Fin Advantage.

Bill Peet: An Autobiography. Bill Peet. (Illus.). (J). (gr. 3 up). 1989. 17.95 (*0-395-50932-7*) HM.

Bill Peet: An Autobiography. Bill Peet. (J). (gr. 4-7). 1994. pap. 9.95 (*0-395-68982-1*) HM.

Bill Pickett, Bulldogger: The Biography of a Black Cowboy. Bailey C. Hanes. LC 76-54937. (Illus.). 232p. 1989. pap. 13.95 (*0-8061-2203-X*) U of Okla Pr.

Bill Red Coyote Is a Nut. Hap Gilliland. (Beginning Reading for All Ages Ser.). 1981. 4.95 (*0-89992-101-9*) Coun India Ed.

***Bill Reid: Beyond the Essential Form.** Karen Duffek. (Illus.). 64p. 1986. pap. 14.95 (*0-7748-0263-4*) U of Wash Pr.

Bill Rodgers & Priscilla Welch on Masters Running & Racing. Bill Rodgers et al. LC 91-11263. (Illus.). 192p. 1991. 16.95 (*0-87857-972-9*, 12-751-0) Rodale Pr Inc.

Bill Russell. Miles Shapiro. (Black Americans of Achievement Ser.). (Illus.). 112p. (YA). (gr. 5 up). 1991. lib. bdg. 17.95 (*0-7910-1136-4*) Chelsea Hse.

Bill Russell's American Music. Mike Hazeldine. LC 93-73571. (Illus.). 200p. (Orig.). 1993. pap. 39.95 (*0-9638890-0-1*, Jazzology Pr) GHB Jazz Fnd.

Bill S: Shakespeare for Kids. Carole Marsh. (Quantum Leap Ser.). (Illus.). (J). (gr. 4-12). 1994. lib. bdg. 24.95 (*1-55609-156-7*); pap. 14.95 (*0-935326-10-3*) Gallopade Pub Group.

***Bill Saiff's Rod & Reel: Recipes for Hookin' & Cookin'** WNPE-WNPI TV Public Television Staff. 1994. pap. 12.95 (*0-87197-264-6*) Favorite Recipes.

Bill Severn's Amazing Magic. Bill Severn. LC 92-6210. (Illus.). 192p. 1992. pap. 12.95 (*0-8117-2530-8*) Stackpole.

Bill Severn's Best Magic: 50 Top Tricks to Entertain & Amaze Your Friends on All Occasions. Bill Severn. LC 89-11569. (Illus.). 224p. (Orig.). 1990. pap. 12.95 (*0-8117-2229-5*) Stackpole.

***Bill Severn's Complete Book of Magic.** Severn. 1995. 10.98 (*0-88365-898-4*) Galahad Bks.

***Bill Severn's Magic Comedy.** Bill Severn. LC 94-19787. 1995. write for info. (*0-8117-2529-4*) Stackpole.

Bill Severn's Magic in Four Acts. Bill Severn. LC 93-45672. (Illus.). 224p. 1994. pap. 12.95 (*0-8117-2536-7*) Stackpole.

Bill Severn's Magic in Mind: Mystifying Mental Tricks. Bill Severn. LC 92-20478. (Illus.). 160p. 1993. reprint ed. pap. 12.95 (*0-8117-2531-6*) Stackpole.

Bill Severn's Magic Money: Tricks with Coins & Bills. Bill Severn. LC 92-22101. (Illus.). 160p. 1993. pap. 12.95 (*0-8117-2532-4*) Stackpole.

Bill Severn's Magic with Rope, Ribbon, & String. Bill Severn. LC 93-17893. Orig. Title: Magic with Rope, Ribbon, & String. (Illus.). 224p. (J). 1994. pap. 12.95 (*0-8117-2533-2*) Stackpole.

***Bill Severn's Magic Workshop.** Bill Severn. (Illus.). 192p. 1995. pap. 12.95 (*0-8117-2528-6*) Stackpole.

Bill Shepherd Paintings. Jerry Schefcik. LC 86-62856. 20p. 1986. pap. 7.50 (*0-935037-13-6*) G Peters Gallery.

Bill Shields Is Dead. Bill Shields. 100p. (Orig.). 1994. pap. 10.00 (*1-885466-01-3*) Smoke The Soul.

Bill Shields of Youngwood, PA Is God. Bill Shields. 80p. (Orig.). 1992. pap. 8.00 (*1-885466-07-2*) Smoke The Soul.

Bill Sienkiewicz Sketchbook, Vol. 1. Bill Sienkiewicz. Ed. by Gary Groth. (Illus.). 160p. 1990. 39.95 (*1-56097-041-3*); pap. 19.95 (*1-56097-040-5*) Fantagraph Bks.

Bill Steinbock's Pocket MDL Programmer's Guide. Bill Steinbock. 256p. 1991. pap. 24.95 (*0-934605-32-7*, OnWord Pr) High Mtn.

Bill Sublette: Mountain Men. John E. Sunder. LC 59-7492. (Illus.). 1959. reprint ed. pap. 13.95 (*0-8061-1111-9*) U of Okla Pr.

Bill, the Galactic Hero. Harry Harrison. 192p. 1979. mass mkt. 4.50 (*0-380-00395-3*) Avon.

Bill the Galactic Hero: On the Planet of Tasteless Pleasure, No. 3. Harry Harrison & David Bischoff. 240p. (Orig.). 1991. pap. 3.95 (*0-380-75664-1*) Avon.

Bill, the Galactic Hero: On the Planet of Ten Thousand Bars, No. 5. Harry Harrison & David Bischoff. 208p. (Orig.). 1991. mass mkt. 3.99 (*0-380-75666-8*) Avon.

Bill, the Galactic Hero: On the Planet of Zombie Vampires, No. 4. Harry Harrison & Jack C. Haldeman, II. (Illus.). 240p. 1991. pap. 3.95 (*0-380-75665-X*) Avon.

Bill, the Galactic Hero: The Final Incoherent Adventure, No. 6. Harry Harrison & David Harris. 240p. (Orig.). 1992. mass mkt. 4.50 (*0-380-75667-6*, AvoNova) Avon.

Bill, the Galactic Hero: The Planet of the Robot Slaves, No. 1. Harry Harrison. 256p. (Orig.). 1989. mass mkt. 4.50 (*0-380-75661-7*) Avon.

An Asterisk (*) at the beginning of an entry indicates that the title is appearing in BIP for the first time.

An Asterisk (*) at the beginning of an entry indicates that the title is appearing in BIP for the first time.

Billy Bluefish: A Tale of Big Blues. Suzanne Tate. LC 88-92517. (Suzanne Tate's Nature Ser.: No. 2). (Illus.). 28p. (Orig.). (J). (gr. k-4). 1988. pap. 3.95 (0-9616344-4-8) Nags Head Art.

Billy Bob Walker Got Married. Lisa G. Brown. 1993. mass mkt. 4.50 (0-06-108071-3, Harp PBks) HarpC.

Billy Bowlegs War, 1856-58: Final Stand of the Seminoles Against the Whites. James W. Covington. LC 82-80100. (Illus.). 94p. 1981. 12.95 (0-913122-06-8) Mickler Hse.

Billy Bray: The King's Son. F. W. Bourne. pap. 3.99 (0-88019-004-3) Schmul Pub Co.

Billy Brazil: A Novella. Emilio DeGrazia. 1992. pap. 9.95 (0-89823-130-2) New Rivers Pr.

Billy Budd. Robert Chapman & Louis O. Coxe. (Mermaid Dramabook Ser.). 90p. 1962. pap. 7.95 (0-8090-1204-9) Hill & Wang.

Billy Budd. Herman Melville. Bd. with The Encantadas (Airmont Classics Ser.). (J). (gr. 9 up). 1966. Set pap. 1.75 (0-8049-0116-3, CL-116) Airmont.

Billy Budd. Guy Williams. LC 91-50833. 60p. (Orig.). (YA). 1992. pap. 5.00 (0-88734-415-1) Players Pr.

Billy Budd: And Other Stories. Herman Melville. 416p. 1993. pap. 4.95 (0-460-87205-2, Everyman's Classic Lib) C E Tuttle.

Billy Budd & Other Stories. Herman Melville. (Classics Ser.). 416p. 1986. mass mkt. 6.95 (0-14-039053-7, Penguin Classics) Viking Penguin.

Billy Budd & Other Tales. Herman Melville. 336p. 1961. pap. 2.50 (0-451-52237-0, Sig Classics) NAL-Dutton.

Billy Budd & Typee (Melville) Laskin. (Book Notes Ser.). (C). 1984. pap. 2.50 (0-8120-3404-X) Barron.

Billy Budd & Typee Notes. O. B. Emerson. (Orig.). 1991. pap. 3.75 (0-8220-0238-8) Cliffs.

Billy Budd, KGB. Jerome Charyn. (Illus.). 128p. (Orig.). 1991. pap. 17.95 (0-87416-111-8) Catalan Communs.

Billy Budd Readalong. Herman Melville. (Illustrated Classics Collection 5). 64p. 1994. audio, pap. 13.50 (1-56103-617-X) Lake Pub Co.

Billy Budd, Sailor. Herman Melville. Ed. by Harrision Hayford & Merton M. Sealts, Jr. LC 62-17135. (Orig.). 1962. pap. 7.95 (0-226-32132-0, P99) U Ch Pr.

Billy Budd, Sailor & Other Stories. Herman Melville. (Bantam Classics Ser.). 288p. (gr. 7-12). 1982. 3.95 (0-553-21274-5) Bantam.

Billy Budd, Sailor, & Other Stories. Herman Melville. Ed. by Harold Beaver. Incl. Cock-a-Doddle-Doo. 1968. (0-318-55012-1); Encantada. 1968. (0-318-55013-X); Bell Tower. 1968. (0-318-55014-8); Benito Cereno. 1968. (0-318-55015-6); John Marr. 1968. (0-318-55016-4); Daniel Orme. 1968. (0-318-55017-2); (English Library). 466p. 1968. Set pap. 2.50 (0-14-043029-6) Viking Penguin.

Billy-Club Puppets see Five Plays: Comedies & Tragicomedies

Billy Goat Escapes. (Little Fish Books about Bible Animals). (J). 1991. 0.79 (0-8307-1058-2, 5608605) Regal.

Billy Goat Show. Joan Kaghan. 32p. (J). 1993. 14.00 (0-374-30711-3) FS&G.

***Billy Goes to Town.** Matthew V. Smith. (Illus.). 17p. (J). (gr. k-4). 1995. pap. 10.95 (1-895583-72-1) MAYA Pubs.

***Billy Goose Bombs Bullies.** S. Bernadine Riske. (Illus.). 20p. (Orig.). (J). (gr. 2 up). Date not set. pap. 7.95 (1-885981-09-0, Brisk Pubns) Brisk Pubng.

Billy Graham. Nathan Asseng. (Today's Heroes Ser.). 112p. (J). (gr. 3-7). 1993. 4.99 (0-310-39841-X) Zondervan.

Billy Graham: The Pastor's Dilemma. Erroll Hulse. pap. 3.99 (0-87377-045-5) GAM Pubns.

Billy Graham Christian Worker's Handbook. Billy Graham. 240p. 1982. pap. 7.95 (0-89066-042-5); spiral bd. 8.95 (0-89066-140-5) World Wide Pubs.

Billy Groat. Carol V. Munger. LC 87-71679. (Illus.). 23p. (Orig.). (J). 1990. pap. 4.00 (0-916383-45-8) Aegina Pr.

Billy Hughes: Full Version. Charles Knox. Ed. by Arnold Bell et al. (C). 1989. 50.00 (1-85098-155-8, Pub. by Jordanhill College UK) St Mut.

Billy Hughes Topic Outline. Ed. by Arnold Bell et al. (C). 1989. 45.00 (1-85098-076-4, Pub. by Jordanhill College UK) St Mut.

Billy Ireland. Lucy S. Caswell & George A. Loomis, Jr. LC 81-119198. (Illus.). 235p. (Orig.). 1980. pap. 20.00 (0-88215-051-0) Friends Ohio St U Lib.

Billy Irish. Thomas Babe. 1982. pap. 4.75 (0-8222-0120-8) Dramatists Play.

Billy Is Nice. Alex Holland. (Illus.). 12p. (J). (gr. k-3). 1994. pap. 12.95 (1-56606-023-0) Bradley Mann.

Billy Jean. Matthew V. Smith. (Illus.). 14p. (J). (gr. k-3). 1993. pap. 9.95 (1-895583-57-8) MAYA Pubs.

Billy Joel - Ballads. 88p. (Orig.). 1993. pap. 14.95 (0-7935-2326-5, 00308181) H Leonard.

Billy Joel - River of Dreams. Intro. by Billy Joel. (Piano-Vocal-Guitar Ser.). (Illus.). 72p. (Orig.). 1993. pap. 14.95 (0-7935-2733-3, HL00308201) H Leonard.

Billy Joel Complete, Vols. 1 & 2. 1993. Boxed set. boxed 55.90 (0-7935-1980-2, 00308169) H Leonard.

Billy Joel Greatest Hits, Set. 135p. 1991. 14.95 (0-7935-0370-1, HL00356299) H Leonard.

Billy Joel, Vol. One: Complete. Leonard Hal. 1991. pap. 27.95 (0-7935-2070-3, HL00356297) H Leonard.

Billy Joel, Vol. Two: Complete. Leonard Hal. 1991. pap. 27.95 (0-7935-1524-6, HL00356298) H Leonard.

Billy Killdeere. Baldwin. Tr. by Ingram. 250p. 1995. pap. 8.95 (1-56901-275-X) NW Pub.

Billy King's Tombstone: The Private Life of an Arizona Boom Town. Charles L. Sonnichsen. LC 72-86559. (Southwest Chronicle Ser.). (Illus.). 270p. reprint ed. pap. 77.00 (0-8357-3176-6, 2039441) Bks Demand.

***Billy Lazroe & the King of the Sea: A Northwest Legend.** Eric A. Kimmel. LC 95-11715. (Illus.). (J). 1996. write for info. (0-15-200108-5, Browndeer Pr) HarBrace.

Billy Lump's Adventure. Alvin Westcott. LC 68-56817. (Illus.). 32p. (J). (gr. 2-4). 1968. lib. bdg. 9.95 (0-87783-002-9) Oddo.

Billy Mink. Thornton W. Burgess. (J). 18.95 (0-8488-0397-3) Amereon Ltd.

Billy Mink. Thornton Burgess. 91p. (J). 1981. reprint ed. lib. bdg. 17.95 (0-89966-352-4) Buccaneer Bks.

Billy Mink. Thornton Burgess. 178p. (J). 1981. reprint ed. lib. bdg. 17.95 (0-89967-026-1) Harmony Raine.

Billy Moon. H. B. Gilmour. LC 93-12117. Date not set. 17.95 (0-932279-44-9) World Citizens.

Billy Morrow Jackson: Interpretations of Time & Light. Howard E. Wooden. (Visions of Illinois Ser.). (Illus.). 160p. 1990. 19.95 (0-252-01735-8) U of Ill Pr.

Billy 'n' Bear Go to a Birthday Party see Billy 'n' Bear Series

Billy 'n' Bear Go to Church see Billy 'n' Bear Series

Billy 'n' Bear Go to Sunday School see Billy 'n' Bear Series

Billy 'n' Bear Go to the Doctor see Billy 'n' Bear Series

Billy 'n' Bear Go to the Grocery Store see Billy 'n' Bear Series

Billy 'n' Bear Series. Robin Gunn. Incl. Billy 'n' Bear Go to Sunday School. 1985. pap. 3.95 (0-570-08900-X, 56-1546); Billy 'n' Bear Go to Church. 1985. pap. 3.95 (0-570-08901-8, 56-1547); Billy 'n' Bear Go to the Grocery Store. 1985. pap. 3.95 (0-570-08902-6, 56-1548); Billy 'n' Bear Go to a Birthday Party. 1985. pap. 3.95 (0-570-08903-4, 56-1549); Billy 'n' Bear Go to the Doctor. 1985. pap. 3.95 (0-570-08904-2, 56-1550); Billy 'n' Bear Visit Grandma & Grandpa. 1985. pap. 3.95 (0-570-08905-0, 56-1551); (Illus.). 24p. (Orig.). (J). (gr. 2-5). 1985. Set pap. write for info. (0-317-20512-9) Concordia.

Billy 'n' Bear Visit Grandma & Grandpa see Billy 'n' Bear Series

Billy Name: Stills from the Warhol Films. Ed. by Debra Miller. (Illus.). 128p. 1994. pap. 29.95 (3-7913-1367-3, Pub. by Prestel) TeNeues.

Billy Phelan's Greatest Game. William P. Kennedy. 1983. pap. 10.95 (0-14-006340-4, Penguin Bks) Viking Penguin.

Billy Pridemore. Charles Moore. Ed. by James B. Van Treese. 124p. (Orig.). 1993. pap. 7.95 (1-880416-45-X) NW Pub.

Billy Ray Cyrus: A Photographic Scrapbook. Rick Baumgartner. (Illus.). 168p. 1993. pap. 21.95 (0-9628866-9-6) Blue Acorn Pr.

Billy Rose Sculpture Garden. Photos by Leonardo Bezzola. (Illus.). 116p. 1982. pap. 14.95 (0-295-96479-0) U of Wash Pr.

Billy Sheehan - The Talas Years. pap. 14.95 (0-89524-518-3) Cherry Lane.

Billy Sunday. William T. Ellis. (Golden Oldies Ser.). 1959. pap. 4.99 (0-8024-0042-6) Moody.

Billy Sunday: Baseball Preacher. Fern N. Stocker. (Preteen Biography Ser.). (Orig.). (J). (gr. 2-7). 1985. pap. text ed. 4.50 (0-8024-0442-1) Moody.

Billy Sunday: Homerun to Heaven. Robert A. Allen. Ed. by Louise Rock. (Sower Ser.). (Illus.). (J). (gr. 3-7). 1985. pap. 6.95 (0-88062-125-7) Mott Media.

Billy Sunday & Other Poems. Carl Sandburg. Ed. by Willene Hendrick. LC 93-4863. 1993. 19.95 (0-15-162130-6); pap. 9.95 (0-15-662144-4) HarBrace.

Billy Sunday & the Redemption of Urban America. Lyle W. Dorsett. Ed. by Mark Noll & Nathan Hatch. (Library of Religious Biography). 224p. (Orig.). 1991. pap. 12.99 (0-8028-0151-X) Eerdmans.

Billy the Bean. Maria E. Buria. (Illus.). 36p. (Orig.). (J). (ps-00). 1989. pap. 5.95 (1-878926-04-7) Colorful Lrngs.

Billy the Brave. Anne-Marie Chapouton. Tr. by Anthea Bell. LC 85-63307. (Illus.). 32p. (J). (gr. k-2). 1986. 8.95 (1-55858-070-0) North-South Bks NYC.

Billy the Great. Rosa Guy. (J). (ps-3). 1994. mass mkt. 4.99 (0-440-40920-9) Dell.

Billy the Kid. Carl R. Green & William R. Sanford. LC 91-18124. (Outlaws & Lawmen of the Wild West Ser.). (Illus.). 48p. (J). (gr. 4-10). 1992. lib. bdg. 14.95 (0-89490-364-0) Enslow Pubs.

***Billy the Kid: "Killed" in New Mexico--DIED in Texas.** Jannay Valdez & Bob Hefner. (Illus.). 240p. (Orig.). (YA). 1995. pap. 9.95 (1-886709-00-9) Outlaw Publ.

Billy the Kid: A Handbook. Jon Tuska. LC 85-20969. xvi, 237p. 1986. reprint ed. pap. 9.95 (0-8032-9406-9, Bison Books) U of Nebr Pr.

Billy the Kid: A Short & Violent Life. Robert M. Utley. LC 89-30022. (Illus.). xii, 328p. 1989. reprint ed. pap. 12.00 (0-8032-9558-8, Bison Books) U of Nebr Pr.

Billy the Kid: An Anthology of Tough Verse. B. Baldwin. (C). 1987. pap. 11.95 (0-09-067881-8, Pub. by S Thornes UK) Dufour.

Billy the Kid: His Life & Legend. Jon Tuska. LC 93-40176. 320p. 1994. text ed. 49.95 (0-313-28589-6, Greenwood Pr) Greenwood.

Billy the Kid: The Good Side of a Bad Man. rev. ed. Lee Priestley & Marquita Peterson. LC 93-61580. (Illus.). 72p. 1993. pap. 7.95 (1-881325-10-5) Yucca Tree Pr.

Billy the Kid: The Illustrated Life & Times. Bob B. Bell. (Old West Ser.). (Illus.). 120p. 1992. pap. 24.95 (0-9639549-0-3) Honkytonk Sue.

Billy the Kid: The Legend of El Chivato. Elizabeth Fackler. 480p. 1995. 24.95 (0-312-85559-1) Forge NYC.

***Billy the Kid: The Story - The Trial.** Randy Russell. LC 94-74143. (Illus.). (Orig.). 1995. pap. 15.95 (0-9644476-3-0) Crystal Pr NM.

***Billy the Kid & Me Were the Same.** William Tunstill. 105p. Date not set. write for info. (1-886709-07-6) Outlaw Publ.

Billy the Squid (Piano-Vocal) Tom Chapin. Ed. by Milton Okun. (Illus.). 96p. (Orig.). 1993. pap. text ed. 14.95 (0-89524-804-2) Cherry Lane.

Billy Watson's Croker Sack, Set. Franklin Burroughs. 160p. 1992. pap. 9.95 (0-395-61900-9) HM.

Billy Watson's Croker Sack. Franklin Burroughs. 1991. 18.95 (0-393-02893-3) Norton.

Billy Whiskers: Autobiography of a Goat. Frances T. Montgomery. (Illus.). 159p. (J). (gr. 2 up). 1985. reprint ed. pap. 4.50 (0-486-22345-0) Dover.

Billy Wilder in Hollywood. Maurice Zolotow. LC 87-4206. (Illus.). 396p. 1988. reprint ed. pap. 17.95 (0-87910-070-2) Limelight Edns.

Billy Yank. Bellerophon Books Staff. (J). (gr. 4-7). 1992. pap. 3.95 (0-88388-155-1) Bellerophon Bks.

Billy's Beetle. Mick Inkpen. (J). (ps-3). 1992. 13.95 (0-15-200427-0, HB Juv Bks) HarBrace.

***Billy's Brother.** Martin. Date not set. pap. 8.95 (0-85449-109-0, Pub. by Gay Mens Pr UK) InBook.

Billy's Button. William Accorsi. LC 91-37742. (Illus.). 24p. (J). (ps-3). 1992. 14.00 (0-688-10686-2); lib. bdg. 13.93 (0-688-10687-0) Greenwillow.

Bilma. B. Wongar. LC 84-5103. (Illus.). 71p. 1984. 18.95 (0-8142-0370-1) Ohio St U Pr.

Bilog 3: Item Analysis & Test Scoring with Binary Logistic Models. 2nd ed. Robert Mislevy & R. Darrell Bock. 1990. ring bd. 30.00 (0-89498-026-2) Sci Ware.

Bilouist & Other American Tales & Pieces. Charles B. Brown. (Works of Charles Brockden Brown). 1989. reprint ed. lib. bdg. 79.00 (0-7812-2077-7) Rprt Serv.

Biloxi Blues. Neil Simon. LC 85-24173. 96p. 1986. 11.95 (0-394-55139-7) Random.

Biloxi's Ethnic Cultures: Images of Change & Tradition. D. C. Young & Stephen Young. LC 89-61147. (Illus.). 24p. 1989. pap. 15.00 (0-938896-57-1) Mississippi Archives.

Biltmore Estate: Frederick Law Olmsted's Landscape Masterpiece. Pamela L. Messer. Ed. by Kathryn L. Hall. LC 93-60162. (Illus.). 336p. (Orig.). 1993. pap. 24.95 (1-56664-022-9) WorldComm.

Biltmore Estate: The Most Distinct Private Place. John M. Bryan. LC 94-14245. 160p. 1994. 45.00 (0-8478-1811-X) Rizzoli Intl.

***Biltmore Estate Specialities of the House.** Oxmoor Staff. 1994. 22.95 (0-8487-1246-3) Oxmoor Hse.

Biltmore Forest. Gifford Pinchot. LC 70-125757. (American Environmental Studies). 1974. reprint ed. 16.95 (0-405-02683-8) Ayer.

Biltmore House Classroom Gamebook. Carole Marsh. (Carole Marsh Bks.). (Illus.). (Orig.). (J). (gr. 1-12). 1994. lib. bdg. 24.95 (0-935326-83-9) Gallopade Pub Group.

Biltmore Oswald. Thorne Smith. 16.95 (0-8488-1173-9) Amereon Ltd.

Bily Brothers: Wood Carvers & Clock Makers. Duane Hutchinson. LC 93-11205. (Illus.). 160p. (Orig.). 1993. pap. 9.95 (0-934988-30-7) Foun Bks.

Bim le Petit Ane. Jacques Prevert & Albert Lamorisse. (Illus.). 48p. (FRE.). 1976. pap. 10.95 (0-7859-1445-5, 2211040659) Fr & Eur.

BIMAIN 2: Multiple-Group IRT Analysis & Test Maintenance for Binary Items. Michele F. Zimowski et al. 1994. 30.00 (0-89498-034-3) Sci Ware.

Bimal in Bog, 2 vols., Set. Baldev K. Vaid. 1972. 28.00 (0-88253-818-7); pap. text ed. 9.60 (0-88253-819-5) Ind-US Inc.

***Bimal Roy: A Man of Silence.** Rinki Bhattacharya. (C). 1994. 28.00 (81-7223-154-7, Pub. by Indus Pub II) S Asia.

***Bimbamana of Gautamiyasastra: As Hexard by Sariputra.** Ed. by E. W. Marasinghe. (C). 1994. 14.00 (81-7030-417-2, Pub. by Sri Satguru Pubns II) S Asia.

Bimbashi Baruk of Egypt. Sax Rohmer. 1970. 8.50 (0-685-26777-6) Bookfinger.

Bimbo Dirt. Elmslie & Tisa. (Illus.). 1990. pap. 18.00 (0-915990-24-5) Z Pr.

Bimbo the Bumble Bee & Rose the Rose Bud. A. C. Doyle. 20p. (J). (gr. 4-7). 1982. 3.50 (0-939476-74-6, Biblio Pr) Prosperity & Profits.

Bimbos of the Death Sun. Sharyn Mccrumb. LC 86-1267. 1987. pap. 3.95 (0-88038-455-7) TSR Inc.

Bimetallic Catalysts Discoveries, Concepts, & Applications. John H. Sinfelt. LC 83-6738. 176p. 1983. 34.95 (0-471-88321-2) Wiley.

Bimetallic Trade Tokens of the United States. David E. Schenkman. LC 89-92521. (Illus.). 163p. 1990. text ed. 40.00 (0-942596-02-1) Jade Hse Pubns.

Bimmi Finds a Cat. Elisabeth J. Stewart. LC 94-12780. (J). 1995. write for info. (0-395-64652-9, Clarion Bks) HM.

Bimwili & the Zimwi. Verna Aardema. LC 85-4449. (Illus.). 32p. (J). (ps-3). 1985. 14.99 (0-8037-0212-4); lib. bdg. 12.89 (0-8037-0213-2) Dial Bks Young.

Bimwili & the Zimwi. Verna Aardema. LC 85-4449. (Pied Piper Paperback Ser.). (Illus.). 32p. (J). (ps-3). 1988. pap. 4.95 (0-8037-0553-0) Dial Bks Young.

BIN Number Directory of All VISA & MasterCard Issuing Banks. 8th ed. Larry Schwartz & Pearl Sax. 505p. 1993. 1,175.00 (0-914801-04-X) Nat Assn Credit.

Binah: Studies in Jewish History, Vol. I. Ed. by Joseph Dan. LC 88-5813. (Studies in Jewish History, Culture, & Thought). 205p. 1989. text ed. 65.00 (0-275-93036-X, C3036, Praeger Pubs) Greenwood.

Binah: Studies in Jewish History, Vol. I. Ed. by Joseph Dan. LC 88-5813. (Studies in Jewish History, Culture, & Thought). 205p. 1989. pap. text ed. 25.95 (0-275-93035-1, B3035, Praeger Pubs) Greenwood.

Binah: Studies in Jewish Thought, Vol. II, Vol. 2. Ed. by Joseph Dan. LC 88-5813. (Studies in Jewish History, Culture, & Thought). 262p. 1989. text ed. 65.00 (0-275-93038-6, C3038, Praeger Pubs); pap. text ed., ring bd. 59.95 (0-275-93037-8, B3037, Praeger Pubs) Greenwood.

Binaries As Tracers of Stellar Formation. Ed. by Antoine Duquennoy & Michael Mayor. (Illus.). 302p. (C). 1993. 59.95 (0-521-43358-4) Cambridge U Pr.

Binary Alloy Phase Diagrams, 3 vols., Set. 2nd ed. Ed. by P. R. Subramanian & L. Kacprzak. (Illus.). 3589p. (C). 1990. text ed. 1,275.00 (0-87170-403-X) ASM.

Binary & Multiple Stars As Tracers of Stellar Evolution. Zdenek Kopal & Jurgen Rahe. 1982. lib. bdg. 145.50 (90-277-1436-3) Kluwer Ac.

Binary & Multiple Systems of Stars. A. H. Batten. LC 72-88026. 288p. (C). 1973. 120.00 (0-08-016986-4, Pub. by Pergamon Repr UK) Franklin.

Binary Functions & Their Applications. H. Stormer. Ed. by Martin J. Beckmann & W. Krelle. (Lecture Notes in Economics & Mathematical Systems Ser.: Vol. 348). (Illus.). viii, 151p. 1990. pap. 31.00 (0-387-52812-1) Spr-Verlag.

Binary Logic Diagrams for Process Operations. 1981. reprint ed. pap. 25.00 (0-87664-331-4, S5.2) Instru Soc.

***Binary Polynomial & Nonlinear Digital Filters.** S. Agaian et al. LC 95-5438. (Monographs & Textbooks in Pure & Applied Mathematics: Vol. 191). 1995. pap. write for info. (0-8247-9642-X) Dekker.

Binary Quadratic Forms. D. A. Buell. 255p. 1989. 42.00 (0-387-97037-1, 2985) Spr-Verlag.

Binary Stars: A Pictorial Atlas. Dirk Terrell et al. 396p. (C). 1992. 57.50 (0-89464-041-0); pap. 42.50 (0-89464-698-2) Krieger.

Binary Systems. H. Stephen & T. Stephen. LC 79-40319. (Solubilities of Inorganic & Organic Compounds Ser.: Vol. 1, Pt. 1). 1963. 396.00 (0-08-009923-8, Pub. by Pergamon Repr UK) Franklin.

Binary Systems. H. Stephen & T. Stephen. LC 79-40319. (Solubilities of Inorganic & Organic Compounds Ser.: Vol. 1, Pt. 2). 1963. 403.00 (0-08-009924-6, Pub. by Pergamon Repr UK) Franklin.

Binary Time Series. Kedem. (Lecture Notes in Pure & Applied Mathematics Ser.: Vol. 52). 160p. 1980. 99.75 (0-8247-6920-1) Dekker.

BiNational: American Art of the Late 80's. David Ross. (Illus.). 1988. 19.95 (0-87846-301-1) ICA Inc.

Bind Us Together: Supplemental Activities for the Christian Initiation of Adults into the Catholic Church. Gerard Weber & Robert Miller. LC 92-75790. (Illus.). 154p. (Orig.). 1993. pap. 12.95 (0-87946-082-2, 129) ACTA Pubns.

Binder Characterization & Evaluation, Vol. 1. Peterson et al. 152p. (Orig.). (C). 1994. pap. text ed. 15.00 (0-309-05809-0, SHRP-A-367) SHRP.

Binder Characterization & Evaluation, Vol. 2: Chemistry. J. F. Branthaver et al. 479p. (Orig.). (C). 1993. pap. text ed. 15.00 (0-309-05620-9, SHRP-A-368) SHRP.

Binder Characterization & Evaluation, Vol. 3: Physical Characterization. David A. Anderson et al. 475p. (Orig.). (C). 1994. pap. text ed. 20.00 (0-309-05767-1, SHRP-A-369) SHRP.

Binder Characterization & Evaluation, Vol. 4: Test Methods. Petersen et al. 193p. (Orig.). (C). 1994. pap. text ed. 15.00 (0-309-05806-6, SHRP-A-370) SHRP.

Binder Insolubilization: How to Achieve It. 61p. 1988. pap. 19.00 (0-89852-455-5, 0101R155) TAPPI.

***Binder Twine & Rabbit Stew: Fireside Stories of Our Country Past.** Joan Kent. 160p. 1995. 29.95 (0-7126-5776-2, Pub. by Century UK) Trafalgar.

Bindery Worker. Jack Rudman. (Career Examination Ser.: C-84). 1994. pap. 23.95 (0-8373-0084-3) Nat Learn.

Binding & Filtering. Ed. by Frank Heny. 336p. 1982. 37.50 (0-262-08117-2) MIT Pr.

Binding & Finishing. Ralph Lyman. Ed. by Pamela Groff. LC 92-85317. (Illus.). 200p. 1993. text ed. 55.00 (0-88362-163-0) Graphic Arts Tech Found.

Binding & Linkage: Functional Chemistry of Biological Macromolecules. Jeffrey Wyman & Stanley Gill. (Illus.). 336p. (C). 1990. text ed. 54.00 (0-935702-56-3) Univ Sci Bks.

***Binding (Aqedah) & Its Transformations in Judaism & Islam: The Lambs of God.** Mishael Caspi & Sascha B. Cohen. LC 94-30514. 1995. write for info. (0-7734-2389-3, Mellen Biblical Pr) E Mellen.

Binding Constants: The Measurement of Molecular Complex Stability. Kenneth A. Connors. 411p. 1987. text ed. 145.00 (0-471-83083-6, Wiley-Interscience) Wiley.

Binding Contract. large type ed. Alison A. York. 254p. 1994. 17.95 (0-7505-0604-0, Pub. by Magna Print Bks) Ulverscroft.

Binding Cultures: Black Women Writers in Africa & the Diaspora. Gay Wilentz. LC 91-27069. (Blacks in the Diaspora Ser.). 176p. 1992. text ed. 29.95 (0-253-36585-6); pap. text ed. 10.95 (0-253-20714-2, MB-714) Ind U Pr.

Binding of Books. Herbert P. Horne. LC 68-25314. (Reference Ser.: No. 44). 1969. reprint ed. lib. bdg. 75.00 (0-8383-0957-7) M S G Haskell Hse.

Binding of Isaac & Messiah: Law, Martyrdom, & Deliverance in Early Rabbinic Religiosity. Aharon E. Agus. LC 87-24496. (SUNY Series in Judaica: Hermeneutics, Mysticism, & Religion). 368p. 1988. 74.50 (0-88706-735-2); pap. 24.95 (0-88706-736-0) State U NY Pr.

Binding of Proteus: Proceedings of the Colloquium on Myth in Literature, Bucknell & Susquehanna Universities, Mar. 21-22, 1974. Colloquium on Myth in Literature Staff et al. Ed. by Marjorie W. McCune et al. LC 76-49774. (Illus.). 352p. 1978. 28.50 (0-8387-1708-X) Bucknell U Pr.

Binding Passions: Tales of Magic, Marriage, & Power at the End of the Renaissance. Guido Ruggiero. LC 92-24005. 296p. 1993. 55.00 (0-19-507930-2); pap. 18.95 (0-19-508320-2) OUP.

An Asterisk (*) at the beginning of an entry indicates that the title is appearing in BIP for the first time.

Binge. Charles Ferry. LC 92-93408. 94p. (Orig.). (YA). (gr. 7 up). 1992. pap. 8.95 (0-9632799-0-4) DaisyHill Pr. DISNEY Educational Productions: "An incredible book that would make an equally incredible movie to motivate teenagers to stop & think BEFORE driving under the influence." AN ALA BEST BOOK FOR YOUNG ADULTS. VOYA: "A vitally important book...an incredibly powerful, mesmerizing, tragic, read-in-one-sitting little book with an authenticity & understanding rare in adolescent literature...It pulls no punches, offers no pat endings, just describes a kid mired in his own alcoholic denial...an absolutely superb book, highly readable, & relentlessly constructed to make its point without being a tract...We have needed a book like this for a very long time." Recommended by The National Council of Teachers of English & The New York Public Library. To order: DaisyHill Press, P.O. Box 1681, Rochester, MI 48308. Publisher Provided Annotation.

B

An Asterisk (*) at the beginning of an entry indicates that the title is appearing in BIP for the first time.

757

Bioactive Spin Labels. Ed. by R. J. Zhdanov. (Illus.). 650p. 1992. 233.00 (*0-387-53811-9*) Spr-Verlag.

Bioactive Volatile Compounds from Plants. Ed. by Roy Teranishi et al. LC 93-18309. (Symposium Ser.: Vol. 525). (Illus.). 309p. 1993. 79.95 (*0-8412-2639-3*) Am Chemical.

Bioadhesive Drug Delivery Systems. Ed. by Vincent M. Lenaerts & Robert Gurny. 272p. 1989. 191.00 (*0-8493-5367-X*, RS201) CRC Pr.

Bioaerosals: Handbook of Samplers & Sampling. Cox. 1995. write for info. (*0-87371-615-9*) Lewis Pubs.

Bioaffinity Chromatography. Jaroslava Turkova. LC 93-11627. (Journal of Chromatography Library: Vol. 55). 1993. write for info. (*0-444-89030-0*) Elsevier.

Bioanalysis of Drugs & Metabolites: Especially Anti-Inflammatory & Cardiovascular. Ed. by E. Reid et al. LC 88-22412. (Methodological Surveys in Biochemistry & Analysis Ser.: Vol. 18). (Illus.). 430p. 1988. 110.00 (*0-306-42996-9*, Plenum Pr) Plenum.

***Bioanalytic Production of Amino Acids & Derivatives.** Ed. by J. David Rozzell & Fritz Wagner. 1993. text ed. 79.95 (*0-471-03717-6*) Wiley.

Bioanalytical Applications of Enzymes. Clarence H. Suelter & Larry J. Kricka. (Methods of Biochemical Analysis Ser.: No. 2180). 280p. 1992. text ed. 114.95 (*0-471-55880-X*) Wiley.

Bioanalytical Instrumentation. Ed. by Clarence H. Suelter. (Methods of Biochemical Analysis Ser.: Vol. 37). 1993. text ed. 110.95 (*0-471-58260-3*) Wiley.

Bioassay of Pesticides in the Laboratory. L. Banki. 490p. 1978. 175.00 (*0-569-08448-2*, Pub. by Collets UK) Pro-Am Music.

***Bioassay of Pesticides in the Laboratory: Research & Quality Control.** L. Banki. 490p. (C). 1978. 90.00x (*963-05-1306-4*, Pub. by Akad Kiado HU) St Mut.

Bioastronautics: Proceedings of the Nineteenth International Astronautical Congress, New York, 1968. M. Lunc & P. Contensou. LC 58-23647. (International Astronautical Congress Ser.: Vol. 4). 1970. 128.00 (*0-08-006932-0*, Pub. by Pergamon Repr UK) Franklin.

Bioastronomy: The Next Steps. Ed. by George Marx. (C). 1988. lib. bdg. 157.50 (*90-277-2714-7*) Kluwer Ac.

Bioastronomy - The Search for Extraterrestrial Life: The Exploration Broadens, Proceedings of the Third International Symposium on Bioastronomy Held at Val Cenis, Savoie, France, 18-23 June 1990. Ed. by Jean Heidmann & M. J. Klein. (Lecture Notes in Physics Ser.: Vol. 390). xvii, 413p. 1991. 70.00 (*0-387-54752-5*) Spr-Verlag.

Bioavailability: Physical, Chemical, & Biological Interactions. Ed. by Jerry L. Hamelink. LC 93-49061. (SETAC Special Publications Ser.). 1994. write for info. (*1-56670-086-8*) Lewis Pubs.

Bioavailability of Drugs: Proceedings. Conference on Bioavailability of Drugs, Washington, D.C., Nov. 1971. Ed. by B. B. Brodie & W. M. Heller. (Pharmacology Journal: Vol. 8, Nos. 1-3). (Illus.). 1972. 52.00 (*3-8055-1456-5*) S Karger.

Bioavailability of Drugs - Principles & Problems: Proceedings of the WHO Scientific Group, Geneva, 1973. WHO Staff. (Technical Report Ser.: No. 536). 1974. pap. 1.60 (*92-4-120536-9*) World Health.

***Bioavailability of Nutrients for Animals: Amino Acids, Minerals, Vitamins.** Ed. by Clarence B. Ammerman et al. (Illus.). 432p. 1995. text ed. 64.95 (*0-12-056250-2*) Acad Pr.

Biobalance: Using Acid-Alkaline Nutrition to Solve the Food-Mood-Health Puzzle. rev. ed. Rudolph A. Wiley. LC 88-13740. (Illus.). 201p. 1990. pap. 12.95 (*0-943685-05-2*, RC630.W55) Life Sci Pr.

Biobehavioral Bases of Coronary Heart Disease. Ed. by T. M. Dembroski et al. (Biobehavioral Medicine Ser.: Vol. 2). (Illus.). xviii, 482p. 1983. 127.25 (*3-8055-3629-1*) S Karger.

Biobehavioral Control of AIDS. Ed. by David G. Ostrow. (Illus.). 250p. (C). 1987. text ed. 29.50 (*0-8290-2354-2*) Irvington.

Biobehavioral Measures of Dyslexia. Ed. by David Gray & James Kavanagh. LC 85-52392. 328p. 1985. text ed. 33.00 (*0-912752-10-6*) York Pr.

Biobibliography of Native American Writers 1772-1924: A Supplement. Daniel F. Littlefield, Jr. & James W. Parins. LC 85-2045. (Native American Bibliography Ser.: No. 5). 350p. 1985. 29.50 (*0-8108-1802-7*) Scarecrow.

Bioburst: The Impact of Modern Biology on the Affairs of Man. Richard N. Re. LC 86-7422. (Illus.). xvi, 254p. 1986. text ed. 29.95 (*0-8071-1289-5*) La State U Pr.

***BioBusiness Handbook: How to Organize & Operate a Biotechnology Business.** Michael G. Pappas. LC 93-1612. (Including the Most Promising Applications for the 1990s Ser.). (Illus.). 480p. 1994. ring bd. 189.50 (*0-89603-218-3*) Humana.

BioBusiness Search Guide. 288p. 1990. ring bd. 60.00 (*0-916246-23-X*) BIOSIS.

BioBusiness Search Guide - 1994 Edition. 278p. 1994. 70.00 (*0-916246-28-0*) BIOSIS.

Biocatalysis. D. Abramowicz. 1990. text ed. 105.00 (*0-442-23848-7*) Chapman & Hall.

Biocatalysis & Biomimetics. Ed. by James D. Burrington & Douglas S. Clark. LC 89-307. (ACS Symposium Ser.: No. 392). (Illus.). xi, 172p. 1989. 39.95 (*0-8412-1611-8*) Am Chemical.

Biocatalysis at Extreme Temperatures: Enzyme Systems near & above 100 Degrees C. Ed. by Michael W. Adams & Robert M. Kelly. LC 92-16399. (Symposium Ser.: Vol. 498). (Illus.). 206p. 1992. 54.95 (*0-8412-2458-7*) Am Chemical.

Biocatalysis in Agricultural Biotechnology. Ed. by John R. Whitaker & Philip E. Sonnet. LC 89-65. (ACS Symposium Ser.: No. 389). (Illus.). 394p. 1989. 84.95 (*0-8412-1571-5*) Am Chemical.

Biocatalysis in Non-Conventional Media: Proceedings of an International Symposium, Noordwijkerhout, 26-29 April 1992. Ed. by J. Tramper et al. LC 92-28341. (Progress in Biotechnology Ser.: Vol. 8). 1992. write for info. (*0-444-89046-7*) Elsevier.

Biocatalysis in Organic Media. Ed. by C. Laane et al. 438p. 1987. 146.25 (*0-444-42785-6*) Elsevier.

Biocatalyst Design for Stability & Specificity. Ed. by Michael E. Himmel & George Georgiou. LC 92-38473. (ACS Symposium Ser.: No. 516). (Illus.). 352p. 1992. 89.95 (*0-8412-2518-4*) Am Chemical.

Biocatalysts for Industry. Ed. by J. S. Dordick. LC 91-9029. (Topics in Applied Chemistry Ser.). (Illus.). 350p. 1991. 85.00 (*0-306-43652-3*, Plenum Pr) Plenum.

Biocatalysts in Organic Syntheses: Proceedings of an International Symposium Organized under Auspices of the Working Party on Immobilized Biocatalysis of the European Federation of Biotechnology, Noordwijkerhout, The Netherlands, 14-17 April, 1985. Ed. by J. Tramper et al. (Studies in Organic Chemistry: No. 22). 260p. 1985. 115.50 (*0-444-42541-1*) Elsevier.

Biocatalysts in Organic Synthesis. Jan Halgas. LC 92-11638. (Studies in Organic Chemistry: Vol. 46). 1992. write for info. (*0-444-98698-7*) Elsevier.

***Bioceramics, Vol. 6.** Ducheyne & Christiansen. 1995. 110.00 (*0-08-042143-1*, Pergamon Pr) Elsevier.

Bioceramics: Material Characteristics versus In Vivo Behavior. Ed. by Paul Ducheyne & Jack Lemons. (Annals Ser.: Vol. 523). 298p. 1988. 75.00 (*0-89766-437-X*) NY Acad Sci.

***Bioceramics: Materials & Applications.** Ed. by Gary Fischman et al. (Ceramic Transactions Ser.: Vol. 48). 1995. 83.00 (*0-944904-82-3*, 1CBB00A) Am Ceramic.

Bioceramics: Materials, Properties, Applications. A. Ravaglioli & A. Krajewski. 416p. 1991. 125.00 (*0-412-34960-4*, A6082) Chapman & Hall.

***Bioceramics Vol. 7.** Ed. by O. H. Andersson et al. 480p. 1995. 145.00 (*0-08-042144-X*, Pergamon Pr) Elsevier.

Bioceramics of Calciumphosphate. Klaas De Groot. 152p. 1983. 102.95 (*0-8493-6456-6*, RK655, CRC Reprint) Franklin.

Biochemic Handbook. J. B. Chapman & Edward L. Perry. Orig. Title: Biochemic Theory & Practice. 1976. pap. 1.50 (*0-89378-051-0*) Formur Intl.

Biochemic System of Medicine. 26th ed. George W. Carey. 535p. 1965. spiral bd. 22.00 (*0-7873-0144-2*) Mokelumne.

Biochemic Theory & Practice see Biochemic Handbook

Biochemical Actions of Hormones, Vols. 1-7. Incl. Vol. 2. LC 70-107567. 1972. 73.00 (*0-12-452802-3*); LC 70-107567. write for info. (*0-318-50233-X*) Acad Pr.

Biochemical Actions of Progesterone & Progestins, Vol. 286. Ed. by Erlio Gurpide. (Annals Ser.). 449p. 1977. 43.00 (*0-89072-032-0*) NY Acad Sci.

Biochemical Adaptation. Peter W. Hochachka & George N. Somero. LC 83-43076. (Illus.). 480p. 1984. pap. 27.95 (*0-691-08344-4*) Princeton U Pr.

Biochemical Adaptation. Peter W. Hochachka & George N. Somero. LC 83-43076. 558p. reprint ed. pap. 159.10 (*0-8357-3300-9*, 2039523) Bks Demand.

Biochemical Adaptation in Parasites. C. Bryant & Carol Behm. 250p. 1989. 79.95 (*0-412-32530-6*) Chapman & Hall.

Biochemical Adaptation in Parasites. C. Bryant & Carol Behm. 250p. 1988. text ed. 79.95 (*0-318-32871-2*, Pub. by Croom Helm UK) Routledge Chapman & Hall.

Biochemical & Biophysical Perspectives in Marine Biology, Vol. 4. Ed. by D. C. Malins & J. R. Sargent. 1979. text ed. 178.00 (*0-12-466604-3*) Acad Pr.

***Biochemical & Cellular Mechanisms of Stress Tolerance in Plants.** Ed. by Joe H. Cherry. LC 94-21155. (NATO ASI Ser, Series H, Cell Biology: Vol. 86). 1994. 259.00 (*0-387-58215-0*) Spr-Verlag.

***Biochemical & Clinical Aspects of Pteridines Vol. 4: Cancer - Immunology - Metabolic Diseases. Proceedings, Fourth Winter Workshop on Pteridines, February 23-March 2, 1985, St. Christoph, Arlberg, Austria.** Ed. by H. Wachter et al. (Illus.). xxi, 686p. 1985. 315.40 (*3-11-010182-3*) De Gruyter.

***Biochemical & Clinical Aspects of Pteridines Vol. 5: Cancer - Immunology - Metabolic Diseases.** Ed. by W. Pfleiderer et al. 408p. (C). 1987. lib. bdg. 176.95 (*3-11-011251-5*) De Gruyter.

Biochemical & Clinical Aspects of Pteridines, Vol. 2: Cancer, Immunology, Metabolic Diseases: Proceedings, Second Winter Workshop on Pterdines, March 6-9, 1983, St. Christoph, Arlberg, Austria. Ed. by H. C. Curtius et al. LC 83-24079. xv, 435p. 1984. 173.10 (*3-11-009813-X*) De Gruyter.

Biochemical & Clinical Aspects of Pteridines, Vol. 4: Cancer - Immunology - Metabolic Diseases. Proceedings, Fourth Winter Workshop on Pteridines, February 23-March 2, 1985, St. Christoph, Arlberg, Austria. Ed. by H. Wachter et al. (Illus.). xxi, 686p. 1985. 315.40 (*0-89925-083-1*) De Gruyter.

Biochemical & Clinical Aspects of Pteridines, Vol. 5: Cancer - Immunology - Metabolic Diseases. Ed. by W. Pfleiderer et al. 408p. (C). 1987. lib. bdg. 176.95 (*0-89925-334-2*) De Gruyter.

Biochemical & Immunologic Diagnosis of Cancer. Ed. by A. M. Neville. (Journal: Tumor Biology: Vol. 8, No. 2-3, 1987). (Illus.). 124p. 1987. pap. 65.75 (*3-8055-4665-3*) S Karger.

Biochemical & Medical Aspects of Tryptophan Metabolism. Ed. by Osamu Hayaishi et al. (Developments in Biochemistry Ser.: Vol. 16). 1981. 92.50 (*0-444-80297-5*) Elsevier.

Biochemical & Molecular Aspects of Selected Cancers, Vol. 1. Ed. by Thomas G. Pretlow, II & Theresa P. Pretlow. (Illus.). 444p. 1991. text ed. 121.00 (*0-12-564498-1*) Acad Pr.

Biochemical & Molecular Aspects of Selected Cancers, Vol. 2. Ed. by Thomas G. Pretlow, II & Theresa P. Pretlow. (Illus.). 542p. 1994. text ed. 120.00 (*0-12-564499-X*) Acad Pr.

Biochemical & Morphological Aspects of Ageing. Ed. by Werner E. Muller & Johannes W. Rohen. (Research in Molecular Biology Ser.: No. 10). (Illus.). 226p. (Orig.). 1981. pap. text ed. 67.50 (*3-515-03457-9*) Coronet Bks.

Biochemical & Neuro-Physio Correlation Centrally Act Drug: Proceedings of Second International Pharmacological Meeting, Prague, August 1963, Vol. 2. E. Trabucchi & Rodolfo Paoletti. LC 64-15320. 1964. 127.00 (*0-08-010804-0*, Pub. by Pergamon Repr UK) Franklin.

Biochemical & Pharmacological Aspects of Depression. Ed. by M. B. Youdim & Keith F. Tipton. (Topics in Neurochemistry & Neuropharmacology Ser.: Vol. 3). 250p. 1988. 90.00 (*0-85066-375-X*) Taylor & Francis.

Biochemical & Pharmacological Mechanisms Underlying Behavior. P. B. Bradley & R. W. Brimblecombe. (Progress in Brain Research Ser.: Vol. 36). 1972. 63.75 (*0-444-40992-0*) Elsevier.

Biochemical & Pharmacological Roles of Adenosylmethionine & the Central Nervous System: Proceedings of an International Round Table on Adenosylmethionine & the Central Nervous System, Naples, Italy, May 1978. Ed. by V Zappia et al. (Illus.). 1979. 81.00 (*0-08-024929-9*, Pub. by Pergamon Repr UK) Franklin.

Biochemical & Physiological Aspects of Ethylene Production in Lower & Higher Plants. Ed. by H. Clijsters et al. (Advances in Agricultural Biotechnology Ser.). (C). 1989. lib. bdg. 112.50 (*0-7923-0201-X*) Kluwer Ac.

Biochemical & Structural Dynamics of the Cell Nucleus. Ed. by Eugenia Wang et al. (Illus.). 269p. 1990. text ed. 68.00 (*0-12-734575-2*) Acad Pr.

Biochemical Applications of Raman & Resonance Raman Spectroscopies. P. R. Carey. (Molecular Biology Ser.). 1982. text ed. 95.00 (*0-12-159650-8*) Acad Pr.

Biochemical Approach to Nutrition. R. A. Freedland & S. Briggs. 1977. pap. 13.95 (*0-412-13040-8*, NO.6113) Chapman & Hall.

Biochemical Approaches to Cancer. E. Reid. LC 65-24229. 1965. 88.00 (*0-08-011493-8*, Pub. by Pergamon Repr UK) Franklin.

Biochemical Aspects of Copper: Copper Proteins, Ceruloplasmin, & Copper Protein Binding. Charles A. Owen, Jr. LC 81-18988. (Copper in Biology & Medicine Ser.). 205p. 1982. 28.00 (*0-8155-0891-3*) Noyes.

Biochemical Aspects of Crop Improvement. Ed. by Khanna. 1990. 236.00 (*0-8493-5418-8*, SB123) CRC Pr.

Biochemical Aspects of Insect Development. P. S. Chen. (Monographs in Developmental Biology: Vol. 3). (Illus.). 1971. 57.75 (*3-8055-1265-1*) S Karger.

Biochemical Aspects of New Protein Food. Ed. by J. Adler-Nissen & B. O. Eggum. LC 77-30603. (Federation of European Biochemical Societies Ser.). 228p. 1978. 100.00 (*0-08-022625-6*, Pub. by Pergamon Repr UK) Franklin.

Biochemical Aspects of Physical Exercise. Ed. by G. Benzi et al. 504p. 1987. 159.00 (*0-444-80800-0*) Elsevier.

Biochemical Aspects of Plant & Animal Coevolution. Ed. by Jeffrey B. Harborne. (Phytochemical Society of Europe Symposia Ser.). 1978. text ed. 191.00 (*0-12-324672-5*) Acad Pr.

Biochemical Aspects of Plant Disease Resistance: Preformed Inhibitory Substance 'Prohibitions', Pt. 1. A. Mahadevan. (International Bioscience Monographs: No. 11). (Illus.). xiv, 400p. 1989. reprint ed. 59.00 (*0-88065-225-X*, Pub. by Today & Tomorrows P & P II) Scholarly Pubns.

Biochemical Aspects of Plant Diseases Resistance Vol. 2: Post Infectional Defence Mechanisms. A. Mahadevan. (Illus.). 800p. 1991. 95.00 (*1-55528-231-8*, Pub. by Today & Tomorrows P & P II) Scholarly Pubns.

Biochemical Aspects of Renal Function: Journal: Renal Physiology & Biochemistry, Vol. 12, Nos. 5 & 6, 1989. Ed. by W. Guder. (Illus.). iv, 124p. 1989. pap. 94.50 (*3-8055-5119-3*) S Karger.

Biochemical Aspects of Renal Function: Proceedings of a Symposium Held in Honour of Professor Sir Hans Krebs FRS, at Merton College, Oxford, 16-19 September 1979. Ed. by D. B. Ross & W. G. Guder. (Illus.). 340p. 1980. pap. 67.00 (*0-08-025517-5*, Pergamon Pr) Elsevier.

Biochemical Bases of the Development of Physiological Functions. Ed. by Olga Greengard. (Enzyme Ser.: Vol. 15, Nos. 1-6). (Illus.). 386p. 1974. pap. 77.00 (*3-8055-1713-0*) S Karger.

Biochemical Basis of Chemical Carcinogenesis. Ed. by Helmut Greim et al. (Workshop-Conference HOECHST Ser.: Vol. 13). 326p. 1984. text ed. 119.50 (*0-89004-961-0*) Raven.

Biochemical Basis of Functional Neuroteratology. Ed. by G. J. Boer et al. (Progress in Brain Research Ser.). 560p. 1988. 217.50 (*0-444-80970-8*) Elsevier.

Biochemical Basis of Inherited Human Disease. Shintaro Okada et al. 1973. 29.50 (*0-8422-7087-6*) Irvington.

Biochemical Basis of Neuropharmacology. 6th ed. Jack R. Cooper et al. (Illus.). 464p. 1991. pap. 26.95 (*0-19-507118-2*) OUP.

Biochemical Basis of Pediatric Disease. Ed. by Steven J. Soldin et al. 564p. 1992. 85.00 (*0-915274-60-4*) Am Assn Clinical Chem.

***Biochemical Basis of Pediatric Disease.** 2nd ed. Ed. by Steven J. Soldin et al. LC 95-15260. 1995. write for info. (*0-915274-78-7*) Am Assn Clinical Chem.

Biochemical Basis of Plant Breeding, Vol. II. Ed. by Carlos A. Neyra. 192p. 1986. 144.00 (*0-8493-5742-X*, SB123, CRC Reprint) Franklin.

Biochemical Basis of Pulmonary Function. Ed. by Ronald G. Crystal. LC 75-25165. (Lung Biology in Health & Disease Ser.: Vol. 2). 556p. reprint ed. pap. 158.50 (*0-8357-7215-2*, 2027073) Bks Demand.

***Biochemical Basis of Suicide.** David Lester. (Illus.). 150p. 1988. pap. 24.95 (*0-398-06229-3*) C C Thomas.

Biochemical Basis of Suicide. David Lester. (Illus.). 150p. (C). 1988. text ed. 37.95x (*0-398-05443-6*) C C Thomas.

Biochemical Basis Plant Breeding: Carbon Metabolism, Vol. I. Carlos A. Neyra. 176p. 1985. 144.00 (*0-8493-5741-1*, SB123, CRC Reprint) Franklin.

Biochemical Calculations: How to Solve Mathematical Problems in General Biochemistry. 2nd ed. Irwin H. Segel. LC 75-23140. 441p. (C). 1976. Net. pap. text ed. write for info. (*0-471-77421-9*) Wiley.

Biochemical Clinical Pharmacology: Proceedings of the 7th International Congress of Pharmacology, Paris 1978. J. Tillement & J. Boissier. LC 78-41030. (Advances in Pharmacology & Therapeutics Ser.: Vol. 7). 1979. 140.00 (*0-08-023197-7*, Pub. by Pergamon Repr UK) Franklin.

Biochemical Development of the Fetus & Neonate. Ed. by C. T. Jones. 908p. 1983. 333.00 (*0-444-80422-6*) Elsevier.

Biochemical Engineering. Ed. by W. R. Vieth et al. (Annals Ser.: Vol. 326). (Orig.). 1979. pap. 57.00 (*0-89766-019-6*) NY Acad Sci.

Biochemical Engineering, No. 3, Vol. 413. Ed. by K. Venkatasubramanian et al. 112.00 (*0-89766-220-2*); pap. 112.00 (*0-89766-221-0*) NY Acad Sci.

Biochemical Engineering: A Challenge for Interdisciplinary Cooperation. Ed. by H. Chmiel et al. 515p. (Orig.). 1988. pap. text ed. 85.00 (*0-89574-259-4*, Pub. by Gustav Fischer Verlag) VCH Pubs.

Biochemical Engineering: Proceedings of 2nd International Symposium on Biochemical Engineering, Stuttgart. Ed. by Matthias Reuss et al. (Illus.). 472p. (Orig.). 1991. pap. text ed. 80.00 (*1-56081-319-9*, Pub. by Gustav Fischer Verlag) VCH Pubs.

Biochemical Engineering & Biotechnology Handbook. 2nd ed. B. Atkinson & F. Mavituna. 1285p. 1991. 265.00 (*1-56159-012-6*, Stockton Pr) Groves Dictionaries.

Biochemical Engineering for Two Thousand One: Proceedings of Asia-Pacific Biochemical Engineering Conference 1992. Ed. by S. Furusaki et al. (Illus.). 870p. 1992. 159.00 (*0-387-70091-9*) Spr-Verlag.

Biochemical Engineering Fundamentals. 2nd ed. James Bailey & David F. Ollis. (Chemical Engineering Ser.). 1008p. 1986. text ed. write for info. (*0-07-003212-2*) McGraw.

Biochemical Engineering II: Proceedings of the Biochemical Engineering Conference, 2nd, Henniken, New Hampshire, July 13-18, 1980. Biochemical Engineering Conference Staff. Ed. by A. Constantinides et al. (Annals Ser.: Vol. 369). 384p. 1981. 75.00 (*0-89766-127-3*); pap. 75.00 (*0-89766-128-1*) NY Acad Sci.

Biochemical Engineering IV. Ed. by Henry C. Lim & K. Venkatqsubramanian. (Annals Ser.: Vol. 469). 112.00 (*0-89766-333-0*); pap. 112.00 (*0-89766-334-9*) NY Acad Sci.

Biochemical Engineering V. Ed. by William A. Weigand. (Annals Ser.: Vol. 506). (Illus.). 690p. 1987. 172.00 (*0-89766-408-6*) NY Acad Sci.

Biochemical Engineering VII. Ed. by Henrik Pedersen et al. LC 92-23487. (Annals Ser.: Vol. 665). 1992. write for info. (*0-89766-735-2*); pap. write for info. (*0-89766-736-0*) NY Acad Sci.

***Biochemical Engineering VIII.** Ed. by Robert M. Kelly et al. LC 94-41383. (Annals Ser.: Vol. 745). 1994. write for info. (*0-89766-913-4*); pap. write for info. (*0-89766-914-2*) NY Acad Sci.

Biochemical Evolution & the Origin of Life. Ed. by E. Schoffeniels. 1971. 37.00 (*0-444-10081-4*) Elsevier.

Biochemical Evolution in the Slimy Salamanders of the Plethodon Glutinosus Complex in the Eastern United States. Ed. by Richard Highton et al. (Illinois Biological Monographs: No. 57). (Illus.). 160p. 1989. pap. 18.95 (*0-252-06007-5*) U of Ill Pr.

Biochemical Factors Concerned in the Functional Activity of the Nervous System. Ed. by D. Richter. LC 75-80290. 1969. pap. 103.00 (*0-08-013311-8*, Pub. by Pergamon Repr UK) Franklin.

Biochemical Factors in Alcoholism. R. Maickel. LC 66-27641. 1967. 115.00 (*0-08-012045-8*, Pub. by Pergamon Repr UK) Franklin.

***Biochemical Fluorescence Vol. 2: Concepts.** Ed. by Raymond F. Chen & Harold Edelhoch. LC 74-31689. 603p. 1976. reprint ed. pap. 171.90 (*0-7837-8325-6*, 2049112) Bks Demand.

Biochemical Genetics: A Laboratory Manual. Emmanuel Shapira et al. (Illus.). 160p. 1989. Ringbound flexicover. ring bd. 29.95 (*0-19-505135-1*) OUP.

Biochemical Genetics of Man. 2nd ed. Ed. by D. J. Brock & Oliver Mayo. 1979. text ed. 227.00 (*0-12-134760-5*) Acad Pr.

Biochemical Identification of Meat Species: Proceedings of a Seminar in the CEC Programme of Coordination of Livestock Productivity Management, Brussels, Belgium, 27-28 November, 1984. Ed. by R. L. Patterson. 224p. 1986. 57.75 (*0-85334-408-6*, Pub. by Elsevier Applied Sci UK) Elsevier.

Biochemical Insect Control: Its Impact on Economy, Environment, & Natural Selection. Mohammed S. Quraishi. LC 76-29701. 288p. reprint ed. pap. 82.10 (*0-8357-7216-0*, 2056304) Bks Demand.

An Asterisk (*) at the beginning of an entry indicates that the title is appearing in BIP for the first time.

Biochemical Interactions at the Endothelium. A. Cryer. 1983. 161.00 (*0-444-80478-1*, I-007-83) Elsevier.

Biochemical Journal: Reviews 1991. Ed. by W. H. Evans. 240p. 1992. 25.00 (*1-85578-020-8*, Pub. by Portland Pr Ltd UK) Ashgate Pub Co.

Biochemical Journal: Reviews 1992. Ed. by W. H. Evans. 228p. 1993. 31.50 (*1-85578-040-2*, Pub. by Portland Pr Ltd UK) Ashgate Pub Co.

Biochemical Journal Reviews 1989. Ed. by P. J. England. 1990. 25.00 (*1-85578-000-3*, Pub. by Portland Pr Ltd UK) Ashgate Pub Co.

Biochemical Journal Reviews 1990. Ed. by P. J. England & W. H. Evans. 1991. 20.00 (*1-85578-006-2*, Pub. by Portland Pr Ltd UK) Ashgate Pub Co.

Biochemical Lesions & Lethal Synthesis. Reiner Peters & P. Alexander. LC 63-11698. (International Series of Monographs on Pure & Applied Mathematics: Vol. 18). 1963. 141.00 (*0-08-013779-2*, Pub. by Pergamon Repr UK) Franklin.

Biochemical Markers for Cancer. Ed. by T. Ming Chu. LC 81-19601. (Clinical & Biochemical Analysis Ser.: No. 11). (Illus.). 391p. reprint ed. pap. 111.50 (*0-7837-0653-7*, 2040992) Bks Demand.

Biochemical Markers in the Population Genetics of Forest Trees: Proceedings of the Joint Meeting of the Working Parties S2.04-01 Population Genetics & Ecological Genetics & S2.04-05 Biochemical Genetics of the International Union of Forest Research Organizations (IUFRO), Porano, Italy, October 1988. Ed. by S. Fineschi et al. (Illus.). vi, 251p. 1991. pap. 55.00 (*90-5103-055-X*, Pub. by SPB Acad Pub NE) Koeltz Sci Bks.

Biochemical Measurement & Control. G. K. McMillan. LC 87-2954. 150p. 1987. text ed. 50.00 (*0-87664-942-8*, 1942-8) Instru Soc.

Biochemical Mechanisms Involved in Plant Growth Regulation. Ed. by C. J. Smith et al. LC 93-32094. (Proceedings of the Phytochemical Society of Europe Ser.: No. 36). (Illus.). 288p. 1994. 83.00 (*0-19-857764-8*, Clarendon Pr) OUP.

Biochemical Messengers: Hormones, Neurotransmitters & Growth Factors. D. Grahame Hardie. 250p. 1990. 65.00 (*0-412-30340-X*, A4999); pap. 19.95 (*0-412-30350-7*, A5003) Chapman & Hall.

Biochemical Methodology for the Assessment of Carotenes. Kenneth L. Simpson et al. (Illus.). 47p. (Orig.). 1987. pap. 9.00 (*0-944398-01-4*) ILSI.

Biochemical Methodology for the Assessment of Vitamin A Status. International Nutritional Anemia Consulative Group Staff et al. Ed. by C. O. Chichester et al. (Illus.). 92p. 1982. 18.00 (*0-935368-27-2*) ILSI.

Biochemical Methods for Monitoring Risk Pregnancies. Ed. by P. J. Keller. (Contributions to Gynecology & Obstetrics Ser.: Vol. 2). 1976. 65.75 (*3-8055-2386-6*) S Karger.

Biochemical Monitoring of the Fetus. Ed. by Molly S. Chatterjee. LC 93-1477. 1993. 29.95 (*0-387-97892-5*) Spr-Verlag.

***Biochemical Oscillations & Cellular Rhythms: The Molecular Bases of Periodic & Chaotic Behavior.** Albert Goldbeter. (Illus.). 450p. (C). 1992. write for info. (*0-521-40307-3*) Cambridge U Pr.

Biochemical Pharmacology of Blood & Blood-Forming Organs. Ed. by J. W. Fisher et al. (Handbook of Experimental Pharmacology Ser.: Vol. 101). (Illus.). 576p. 1992. 342.00 (*0-387-52844-X*) Spr-Verlag.

Biochemical Pharmacology of Obesity. Ed. by P. B. Curtis-Prior. 472p. 1984. 212.00 (*0-444-80353-X*, I-076-84) Elsevier.

***Biochemical Plant Pathology.** fac. ed. Ed. by J. A. Callow. LC 82-19963. 496p. 1983. reprint ed. pap. 141.40 (*0-7837-8265-9*, 2049046) Bks Demand.

Biochemical Principles of the Use of Xylitol in Medicine & Nutrition with Special Consideration of Dental Aspects. K. K. Makinen. (Experientia Supplementa Ser.: No. 30). (Illus.). 160p. 1980. 40.95 (*0-8176-0961-X*) Birkhauser.

Biochemical Protozoology As a Basis for Drug Design. Ed. by Graham H. Coombs. 500p. 1991. 180.00 (*0-7484-0000-1*, Pub. by Tay Francis Ltd UK); pap. 69.00 (*0-7484-0001-X*, Pub. by Tay Francis Ltd UK) Taylor & Francis.

Biochemical Regulation of Blood Pressure. Ed. by Richard L. Soffer. LC 80-39522. 464p. 1981. 83.50 (*0-471-05600-6*) Wiley.

Biochemical Research Techniques: A Practical Introduction. J. M. Wrigglesworth. LC 82-21963. 239p. 1983. text ed. 126.95 (*0-471-10323-3*, Wiley-Interscience) Wiley.

Biochemical Responses Induced by Herbicides. Ed. by Donald E. Moreland et al. LC 81-20645. (ACS Symposium Ser.: No. 181). 274p. 1982. 43.95 (*0-8412-0699-6*) Am Chemical.

Biochemical Structure Determination by NMR. Ed. by Aksel A. Bothner-By et al. LC 81-22055. (Illus.). 246p. reprint ed. pap. 70.20 (*0-7837-4738-1*, 2044546) Bks Demand.

Biochemical Techniques: Theory & Practice. John F. Robyt & Bernard J. White. LC 86-26874. (Illus.). 407p. (C). 1990. reprint ed. text ed. 32.95x (*0-88133-556-8*) Waveland Pr.

***Biochemical Techniques for Filamentous Fungi.** R. R. Paterson & P. D. Bridge. (IMI Technical Handbooks Ser.: No. 1). 125p. 1994. pap. 30.00x (*0-85198-899-7*) CAB Intl.

Biochemical Thermodynamics. Ed. by M. N. Jones. (Studies in Modern Thermodynamics: Vol. 1). 390p. 1979. 120.50 (*0-444-41761-3*) Elsevier.

Biochemical Thermodynamics. Ed. by M. N. Jones. (Studies in Modern Thermodynamics: Vol. 8). 404p. 1988. 143.75 (*0-444-42943-3*) Elsevier.

Biochemical Toxicology. Ed. by Keith Snell & B. Mullock. (Practical Approach Ser.). 304p. 1987. pap. 39.00 (*0-947946-52-7*, IRL Pr) OUP.

Biochemical Toxicology of Environmental Agents. A. De Bruin. 154p. 1976. 383.00 (*0-444-41455-X*) Elsevier.

Biochemical Values in Clinical Medicine. 7th ed. R. D. Eastham. (Illus.). 482p. 1985. 32.95 (*0-7236-0820-2*) Buttrwrth-Heinemann.

Biochemist. Jack Rudman. (Career Examination Ser.: C-85). 1994. pap. 27.95 (*0-8373-0085-1*) Nat Learn.

Biochemist Trainee. Jack Rudman. (Career Examination Ser.: C-1171). 1994. pap. 23.95 (*0-8373-1171-3*) Nat Learn.

Biochemistry. Abeles et al. 864p. (C). 1992. boxed 65.00 (*0-86720-212-2*) Jones & Bartlett.

Biochemistry. Ed. by T. Briggs & A. M. Chandler. (Oklahoma Notes Ser.). 250p. (C). 1991. pap. 15.95 (*0-387-96341-3*) Spr-Verlag.

Biochemistry. Mary K. Campbell. 688p. (C). 1991. text ed. 64.00 (*0-03-052213-7*) SCP.

***Biochemistry.** (Blond's Medical Guides Ser.). (Illus.). 264p. (Orig.). (C). 1994. pap. text ed. 19.99 (*0-945819-49-8*) Sulzburger & Graham Pub.

Biochemistry. Alex F. Huang. (Licensing Examination Review Pop-up Book Series for Advanced Medical Study). 96p. (C). 1993. pap. text ed. 35.95 (*1-884142-03-6*) AFH Softech.

Biochemistry. Lyman. (Applied Science Review Ser.). 1993. 11.95 (*0-87434-572-3*) Springhouse Pub.

Biochemistry. Mathews & Kensal E. Van Holde. Ed. by Diane Bowen. 1100p. (C). 1990. text ed. 70.95 (*0-8053-5015-2*); trans. 215.25 (*0-8053-5016-0*); sl. 17.25 (*0-8053-5017-9*) Benjamin-Cummings.

***Biochemistry.** Robert Roskoski, Jr. LC 95-1002. (Illus.). 528p. 1995. pap. text ed. write for info. (*0-7216-5174-7*) Saunders.

Biochemistry. William M. Southerland. (Foundations of Medicine Ser.). (Illus.). 634p. 1989. pap. text ed. 29.95 (*0-443-08570-6*) Churchill.

Biochemistry. Keshav Trehan. (C). 1987. pap. 10.00 (*0-85226-907-2*, Pub. by Wiley Eastern II) S Asia.

***Biochemistry.** Voet. 1990. write for info. (*0-471-52147-7*) Wiley.

Biochemistry. Donald Voet & Judith G. Voet. 1216p. 1990. Net. trans. write for info. (*0-471-50242-1*) Wiley.

Biochemistry. Donald Voet & Judith G. Voet. 1216p. 1990. Net. text ed. write for info. (*0-471-61769-5*); Net. text ed. write for info. (*0-471-54010-2*) Wiley.

Biochemistry. 2nd ed. T. Briggs. Ed. by A. M. Chandler. (Oklahoma Notes Ser.). (Illus.). 224p. 1992. 16.95 (*0-387-97781-3*) Spr-Verlag.

Biochemistry. 2nd ed. Marks. (Board Review Ser.). 1994. 19.95 (*0-685-75161-9*) Williams & Wilkins.

Biochemistry. 2nd ed. Dawn B. Marks. (Board Review Ser.). (Illus.). 330p. 1994. 19.95 (*0-683-05597-6*) Williams & Wilkins.

***Biochemistry.** 2nd ed. Donald Voet & Judith Voet. 1995. text ed. write for info. (*0-471-58651-X*) Wiley.

Biochemistry. 3rd ed. Frank B. Armstrong. (Illus.). 704p. (C). 1989. text ed. 49.95 (*0-19-505356-7*) OUP.

***Biochemistry.** 3rd ed. Ed. by Thomas Briggs & Albert M. Chandler. LC 95-14197. (Oklahoma Notes Ser.). 1995. write for info. (*0-387-94398-6*) Spr-Verlag.

Biochemistry. 3rd ed. Victor Davidson & Donald Sittman. LC 93-20237. (National Medical Series for Independent Study). (Illus.). 500p. 1994. pap. 25.00 (*0-683-06205-0*) Williams & Wilkins.

Biochemistry. 3rd ed. Marks. (National Medical Ser.). 1993. 25.00 (*0-685-75166-X*) Williams & Wilkins.

Biochemistry. 3rd ed. Lubert Stryer. (Illus.). 1104p. (C). 1988. Companion text. write for info. (*0-318-62757-4*) W H Freeman.

Biochemistry. 3rd ed. Geoffrey Zubay et al. 1120p. (C). 1993. text ed. 81.92 (*0-697-14267-1*) Wm C Brown Pubs.

Biochemistry. 3rd ed. Geoffrey Zubay et al. 1120p. (C). 1993. Solutions guide. teacher ed write for info. (*0-697-14789-4*) Wm C Brown Pubs.

***Biochemistry.** 4th ed. Lubert Stryker. LC 94-22832. (Illus.). (C). 1995. text ed. write for info. (*0-7167-2009-4*) W H Freeman.

Biochemistry, 1. 3rd ed. Geoffrey Zubay et al. 1120p. (C). 1992. text ed. write for info. (*0-697-14878-5*) Wm C Brown Pubs.

Biochemistry, 2. 3rd ed. Geoffrey Zubay et al. 1120p. (C). 1992. text ed. write for info. (*0-697-14879-3*) Wm C Brown Pubs.

Biochemistry, 3. 3rd ed. Geoffrey Zubay et al. 1120p. (C). 1992. text ed. write for info. (*0-697-14880-7*) Wm C Brown Pubs.

Biochemistry, Set. Donald Voet & Judith G. Voet. 1216p. 1991. Net. text ed. write for info. (*0-471-56927-5*) Wiley.

Biochemistry: A Case-Oriented Approach. 5th ed. Montgomery et al. (Illus.). 896p. 1990. pap. text ed. 44.95 (*0-8016-3549-7*); International ed. pap. text ed. 20.95 (*0-8016-5495-5*) Mosby Yr Bk.

Biochemistry: A Manual for Universities. D. K. Knorre & S. D. Mysina. (Illus.). 459p. (C). 1994. lib. bdg. 74.00 (*1-56072-165-0*) Nova Sci Pubs.

Biochemistry: A Problems Approach. 2nd ed. W. B. Wood et al. (C). 1981. pap. text ed. 27.95 (*0-8053-9840-6*) Benjamin-Cummings.

Biochemistry: A Review with Questions. 3rd ed. Paul J. Friedman. 1987. 23.50 (*0-316-29374-1*) Little.

Biochemistry: A Review with Questions & Explanations. Paul J. Friedman. LC 94-14756. 1994. pap. 27.95 (*0-316-29428-4*) Little.

***Biochemistry: Examination & Board Review.** Balcauage. (C). 1995. pap. text ed. 28.95 (*0-8385-0661-5*) Appleton & Lange.

***Biochemistry: PreTest Self-Assessment & Review.** 8th ed. Francis J. Chlapowski. LC 95-1129. (PreTest Basic Science Ser.). (Illus.). 224p. 1995. pap. 16.95 (*0-07-052089-5*) Hlth Prof Div.

Biochemistry: PSAAR. 7th ed. Francis J. Chlapowski. (Basic Sciences PreTest Ser.). (Illus.). 224p. 1993. pap. text ed. 16.95 (*0-07-052001-1*) Hlth Prof Div.

Biochemistry: Review for New National Boards. Ajit Kumar & Kurt E. Johnson. LC 92-76134. 211p. 1993. pap. text ed. 25.00 (*0-9632873-1-1*) J & S Pub VA.

Biochemistry: The Molecular Basis of Cell Structure & Function. 2nd ed. Albert L. Lehninger. LC 75-11082. 1975. text ed. 69.95x (*0-87901-047-9*) Worth.

Biochemistry & Biology of Plasma Lipoproteins. Scanu & Spector. (Biochemistry of Disease Ser.: Vol. 11). 536p. 1986. 165.00 (*0-8247-7529-5*) Dekker.

Biochemistry & Cell Biology of Artemia. Ed. by Thomas H. MacRae et al. 272p. 1988. 156.00 (*0-8493-4897-8*, QL444, CRC Reprint) Franklin.

Biochemistry & Genetic Regulation of Commercially Important Antibiotics. Ed. by L. P. Vining. LC 83-2492. (Biotechnology Ser.: No. 2). (Illus.). 370p. (C). 1983. text ed. write for info. (*0-201-10984-0*) Addison-Wesley.

Biochemistry & Genetics of Cellulose Degradation. Ed. by Jean-Paul Aubert et al. (Fems Symposia Ser.). 428p. 1988. text ed. 94.00 (*0-12-067575-7*) Acad Pr.

Biochemistry & Metabolism of Plant Lipids: Proceedings of the International Symposium on the Biochemistry & Metabolism of Plant Lipids, Fifth, Groningen, the Netherlands, June 7-10, 1982. Ed. by J. F. Wintermans & P. J. Kuiper. (Developments in Plant Biology Ser.: Vol. 8). 600p. 1982. 142.00 (*0-444-80457-9*) Elsevier.

Biochemistry & Molecular Biology of "Anaerobic" Protozoa. Ed. by D. Lloyd et al. xii, 290p. 1989. pap. text ed. 95.00 (*3-7186-4943-8*) Gordon & Breach.

Biochemistry & Molecular Biology of Fishes, Vol. 1: Phylogenetic & Biochemical Perspectives. Peter W. Hochachka & T. P. Mommsen. 1991. 146.25 (*0-444-89124-2*) Elsevier.

Biochemistry & Molecular Biology of Plant-Pathogen Interactions. Ed. by C. J. Smith. (Proceedings of the Phytochemical Society of Europe Ser.: No. 32). (Illus.). 312p. 1991. 85.00 (*0-19-857734-6*) OUP.

Biochemistry & Molecular Genetics of Cancer Metastasis. Ed. by Karoly Lapis et al. (Developments in Oncology Ser.). 1986. lib. bdg. 85.00 (*0-89838-785-X*) Kluwer Ac.

Biochemistry & Oral Biology. 2nd ed. A. S. Cole & J. E. Eastoe. (Illus.). 555p. 1988. 80.00 (*0-7236-0834-2*, Pub. by John Wright UK) Buttrwrth-Heinemann.

Biochemistry & Pathology of Basement Membranes: Proceedings of the Colloquium, Paris, October 14-15, 1977. International Colloquium, Paris Staff. Ed. by L. Robert. (Frontiers of Matrix Biology Ser.: Vol. 7). (Illus.). 1979. 125.75 (*3-8055-2894-9*) S Karger.

Biochemistry & Pharmacology of Free Fatty Acids. Ed. by W. L. Holmes & W. M. Bortz. (Progress in Biochemical Pharmacology Ser.: Vol. 6). 1971. 77.75 (*3-8055-1211-2*) S Karger.

Biochemistry & Pharmacology of Platelets. Ciba Foundation Staff. (Ciba Foundation Symposium: New Ser.: No. 35). 360p. reprint ed. pap. 102.60 (*0-8357-7217-9*, 2022163) Bks Demand.

Biochemistry & Physiology of Bifidobacteria. Anatoly Bezkorovainy & Robin Miller-Catchpole. 192p. 1989. 242.00 (*0-8493-4753-X*, QR82) CRC Pr.

Biochemistry & Physiology of Gibberellins, 2 vols., 1. Alan Crozier. LC 83-13862. 576p. 1983. text ed. 110.00 (*0-275-90963-8*, C09631, Praeger Pubs) Greenwood.

Biochemistry & Physiology of Gibberellins, 2 vols., Vol. 2. Alan Crozier. LC 83-13862. 576p. 1983. text ed. 105.00 (*0-275-90964-6*, C09642, Praeger Pubs) Greenwood.

Biochemistry & Physiology of Herbicide Action. Carl Fedtke. (Illus.). 250p. 1982. 124.00 (*0-387-11231-6*) Spr-Verlag.

Biochemistry & Physiology of Plant Hormones. 2nd ed. T. C. Moore. (Illus.). xv, 330p. 1989. 69.00 (*0-387-96984-5*, 2731) Spr-Verlag.

Biochemistry & Physiology of Plant Immunity. B. Rubin & Y. Artsikhovskaya. LC 93-10063. 1963. 156.00 (*0-08-010190-9*, Pub. by Pergamon Repr UK) Franklin.

Biochemistry & Physiology of Polyamines in Plants. Robert D. Slocum & Hector E. Flores. 264p. 1991. 205.00 (*0-8493-6865-0*, OK898) CRC Pr.

Biochemistry & Physiology of Substance Abuse, 2 vols., I. Ed. by Ronald Watson. 272p. 1990. 190.00 (*0-8493-4461-1*, RC564) CRC Pr.

Biochemistry & Physiology of Substance Abuse, 2 vols., II. Ed. by Ronald Watson. 272p. 1990. 205.00 (*0-8493-4462-X*) CRC Pr.

Biochemistry & Physiology of Substance Abuse, Vol. III. Ed. by Ronald Watson. 1991. 191.00 (*0-8493-4463-8*, RC564) CRC Pr.

Biochemistry & Physiology of the Lemon & Other Citrus Fruits. Walton B. Sinclair. LC 83-72137. (Illus.). 962p. (Orig.). 1984. 75.00 (*0-931876-64-8*, 3306) ANR Pubns CA.

Biochemistry & Physiology of the Neutrophil. Steven W. Edwards. LC 93-31732. (Illus.). 300p. (C). 1994. 54.95 (*0-521-41698-1*) Cambridge U Pr.

Biochemistry & Physiology of the Skin, 2 vols., Set. 2nd ed. Ed. by Lowell A. Goldsmith. (Illus.). 1376p. 1991. 250.00 (*0-19-505612-4*) OUP.

Biochemistry & Physiology of Thiamin Diphosphate Enzymes: Proceedings of the International Meeting on the Function of Thiamin Diphosphate Enzymes. Ed. by H. Bisswanger & J. Ullrich. (Illus.). 453p. 1991. lib. bdg. 170.00 (*1-56081-142-0*) VCH Pubs.

Biochemistry & Uses of Pesticides: Structure, Metabolism, Mode of Action & Uses in Crop Protection. Kenneth A. Hassall. 536p. 1990. lib. bdg. 95.00 (*0-89573-976-3*) VCH Pubs.

Biochemistry, Cell & Molecular Biology. (Graduate Record Examination Ser.: GRE-22). 39.95 (*0-8373-5272-X*, GRE-22); 23.95 (*0-8373-5222-3*, GRE-22) Nat Learn.

Biochemistry Collections. Ed. by Bernard S. Schlessinger. LC 81-13408. (Special Collections Ser.: Vol. 1, No. 2). 147p. 1982. 49.95 (*0-917724-48-8*) Haworth Pr.

Biochemistry Explained. Bob Villanti. 1985. student ed 9.00 (*0-943008-79-4*, 125); audio 239.00 (*0-943008-80-8*) Bergwall.

Biochemistry for Medical Sciences. Isidore Danishefsky. 1980. text ed. 34.00 (*0-316-17198-0*) Little.

Biochemistry for the Medical Sciences. Eric A. Newsholme & Anthony R. Leech. 952p. 1984. pap. text ed. 89.95 (*0-471-90058-3*) Wiley.

Biochemistry for the Medical Sciences: An Integrated Case Approach. S. J. Higgins et al. LC 93-2354. 1994. pap. text ed. 32.95 (*0-470-22148-8*) Wiley.

Biochemistry for the Medical Sciences: An Integrated Case Approach. S. J. Higgins et al. LC 93-2354. 1994. write for info. (*0-582-10129-8*) Longman.

Biochemistry Illustrated. 2nd ed. Peter N. Campbell & Anthony D. Smith. (Illus.). 288p. 1988. pap. text ed. 37.00 (*0-443-03454-0*) Churchill.

Biochemistry Illustrated: An Illustrated Summary of the Subject for Medical & Other Students of Biochemistry. 3rd ed. Peter N. Campbell & Anthony D. Smith. LC 93-3365. (Illus.). 336p. 1994. pap. 32.95 (*0-443-04573-9*) Churchill.

Biochemistry in Clinical Practice. Ed. by David L. Williams & Vincent Marks. 720p. 1985. 89.50 (*0-444-00969-8*); pap. 52.00 (*0-444-00964-7*) Elsevier.

Biochemistry in Clinical Practice. 2nd ed. David Williams & Vincent Marks. (Scientific Foundations of Clinical Biochemistry Ser.). (Illus.). 896p. 1995. 190.00 (*0-7506-0167-1*) Buttrwrth-Heinemann.

Biochemistry Labfax. Ed. by J. A. Chambers & David Rickwood. (Labfax Ser.). (Illus.). 357p. 1993. pap. 49.95 (*0-12-167340-5*) Acad Pr.

Biochemistry Laboratory Manual. 3rd ed. Frank M. Strong & Gilbert H. Koch. 320p. (C). 1981. spiral bd. write for info. (*0-697-04705-9*) Wm C Brown Pubs.

Biochemistry, Molecular Biology, & Physiology of Phospholipase A2 & Its Regulatory Factors. Ed. by A. B. Mukherjee. (Advances in Experimental Medicine & Biology Ser.: Vol. 279). (Illus.). 270p. 1990. 85.00 (*0-306-43699-X*, Plenum Pr) Plenum.

Biochemistry of Antivirals: Mechanism of Action & Pharmacology. Rudolf K. Zahn. Ed. by Werner E. Nuller. (Research in Molecular Biology Ser.: No. 9). (Illus.). 87p. (Orig.). 1978. pap. text ed. 34.00 (*3-515-02878-1*) Coronet Bks.

Biochemistry of Arachidonic Acid Metabolism. Ed. by William E. Lands. LC 85-4853. (Prostaglandins, Leukotrienes, & Cancer Ser.). 1985. lib. bdg. 118.00 (*0-89838-717-5*) Kluwer Ac.

Biochemistry of Archaea (Archaebacteria) Ed. by M. Kates et al. LC 93-33456. (New Comprehensive Biochemistry Ser.: No. 26). 1993. write for info. (*0-444-81713-1*) Elsevier.

Biochemistry of Bacterial Cytochromes. T. Yamanaka. (Illus.). xiii, 251p. 1992. 100.00 (*0-387-55499-8*) Spr-Verlag.

***Biochemistry of Cell Membranes.** Ed. by S. Papa & J. M. Tager. LC 95-10623. (Molecular & Cell Biology Updates Ser.). 1995. pap. write for info. (*0-8176-5056-3*) Birkhauser.

Biochemistry of Cell Walls & Membranes in Fungi. Ed. by P. J. Kuhn et al. (Illus.). 312p. 1989. 98.00 (*0-387-50437-0*, 3019) Spr-Verlag.

Biochemistry of Cellular Regulation Vol. I: Gene Expression. Michael J. Clemens. 1980. 132.00 (*0-8493-5454-4*, QH450, CRC Reprint) Franklin.

Biochemistry of Cellular Regulation Vol. II: Clinical & Science Aspects. 1980. 143.00 (*0-8493-5455-2*, QP171, CRC Reprint) Franklin.

Biochemistry of Cellular Regulation Vol. III: Development & Differentiation. Margaret E. Buckingham. 272p. 1981. 144.00 (*0-8493-5456-0*, QH607, CRC Reprint) Franklin.

Biochemistry of Cellular Regulation Vol. IV: The Cell Surface. Ed. by Peter Knox. 336p. 1981. 143.00 (*0-8493-5457-9*, QH607, CRC Reprint) Franklin.

Biochemistry of Characterized Neurons. Ed. by Neville N. Osborne. LC 76-55379. 1978. 139.00 (*0-08-021503-3*, Pub. by Pergamon Repr UK) Franklin.

Biochemistry of Chemical Carcinogenesis. R. C. Garner & J. Hradec. LC 89-23090. (Illus.). 276p. 1989. pap. 85.00 (*0-306-43381-8*, Plenum Pr) Plenum.

Biochemistry of Cholesterol. G. F. Gibbons et al. 370p. 1982. 169.75 (*0-444-80348-3*) Elsevier.

Biochemistry of Copper. M. C. Linder. (Biochemistry of the Elements Ser.: Vol. 10). (Illus.). 430p. 1991. 95.00 (*0-306-43658-2*, Plenum Pr) Plenum.

***Biochemistry of Dementia: Based on a Workshop on Biochemistry of the Dementias, Held at University of Southampton, March, 1979.** fac. ed. Workshop on Biochemistry of the Dementias Staff. Ed. by P. J. Roberts. LC 79-42895. (Illus.). 286p. Date not set. pap. 81.60 (*0-7837-7364-1*, 2047173) Bks Demand.

Biochemistry of Development. Jean Brachet & P. Alexander. LC 59-14176. (International Series of Monographs on Pure & Applied Mathematics: Vol. 2). 1960. 134.00 (*0-08-009227-6*, Pub. by Pergamon Repr UK) Franklin.

B

An Asterisk (*) at the beginning of an entry indicates that the title is appearing in BIP for the first time.

759

Biochemistry of Dioxygen. Lloyd L. Ingraham & Damon Meyer. LC 85-12055. (Biochemistry of the Elements Ser.: Vol. 4). 300p. 1985. 89.50 (*0-306-41948-3*, Plenum Pr) Plenum.

Biochemistry of Energy Utilization in Plants. D. T. Dennis. (Tertiary Level Biology Ser.). (Illus.). 200p. 1987. text ed. 55.00 (*0-412-00981-1*, 9438, Chap & Hall NY); pap. text ed. 29.50 (*0-412-00991-9*, 9439, Chap & Hall NY) Chapman & Hall.

Biochemistry of Exercise, VII. Ed. by Albert W. Taylor. LC 89-24627. (International Series on Sport Sciences: Vol. 21). (Illus.). 432p. 1990. text ed. 65.00x (*0-87322-260-1*, BTAY0260) Human Kinetics.

Biochemistry of Exercise & Metabolic Adaptation. Wayne C. Miller. 152p. (C). 1992. pap. text ed. write for info. (*0-697-16707-0*) Brown & Benchmark.

Biochemistry of Exercise V. Ed. by Howard G. Knuttgen et al. LC 82-84696. (International Series on Sport Sciences: Vol. 13). 960p. (C). 1983. text ed. 72.00x (*0-931250-41-2*, BKNU0041) Human Kinetics.

Biochemistry of Exercise VI: Metabolic Regulation & Its Practical Significance. Ed. by Bengt Saltin. LC 86-7192. (International Series on Sport Sciences: Vol. 16). 592p. 1986. text ed. 65.00x (*0-87322-052-8*, BSAL0052) Human Kinetics.

Biochemistry of Foods. 2nd ed. N. A. Eskin. 557p. 1990. text ed. 69.00 (*0-12-242351-8*) Acad Pr.

Biochemistry of Foreign Compounds. D. V. Parke. 1968. 120.00 (*0-08-012202-7*, Pub. by Pergamon Repr UK) Franklin.

Biochemistry of Fruit Ripening. Ed. by G. Seymour et al. LC 92-38655. 454p. 1993. 99.95 (*0-412-40830-9*) Chapman & Hall.

Biochemistry of Gene Expression in Higher Organisms: Proceedings. Ed. by J. K. Pollak & J. W. Lee. LC 72-97960. 656p. 1973. lib. bdg. 145.50 (*90-277-0289-6*) Kluwer Ac.

Biochemistry of Grain & Breadmaking. Ed. by V. I. Kretovich. 272p. 1965. pap. 67.00 (*0-7065-0359-7*, Pub. by Keter Pub IS) Coronet Bks.

Biochemistry of Halogenated Organic Compounds. K. L. Kirk. LC 91-10708. (Biochemistry of the Elements Ser.: Vol. 9B). (Illus.). 360p. 1991. 85.00 (*0-306-43657-4*, Plenum Pr) Plenum.

Biochemistry of Human Nutrition: A Desk Reference. Eva M. Hamilton & Sareen S. Gropper. (Illus.). 324p. (Orig.). (C). 1987. pap. text ed. 41.00 (*0-314-29520-8*) West Pub.

Biochemistry of Hypertension. Ed. by J. Rosenthal et al. (Journal: Clinical Physiology & Biochemistry: Vol. 6, No. 3-4, 1988). (Illus.). 124p. 1988. pap. 53.75 (*3-8055-4849-4*) S Karger.

Biochemistry of Inflammation. Ed. by J. T. Wicher & S. W. Evansa. (Immunology & Medicine Ser.). (C). 1992. lib. bdg. 132.50 (*0-7923-8985-9*) Kluwer Ac.

Biochemistry of Inorganic Compounds of Sulphur. A. B. Roy & P. A. Trudinger. LC 78-79056. 414p. reprint ed. pap. 118.00 (*0-8357-7218-7*, 2025595) Bks Demand.

Biochemistry of Inorganic Polyphosphates. I. S. Kulaev. LC 78-31627. 255p. 1980. text ed. 195.00 (*0-471-27574-3*, Wiley-Interscience) Wiley.

Biochemistry of Inorganic Polyphosphates. Igor S. Kulaev. Tr. by R. F. Brookes. LC 78-31627. (Illus.). 269p. reprint ed. pap. 76.70 (*0-8357-7219-5*, 2030474) Bks Demand.

Biochemistry of Insects. Ed. by Morris Rockstein. LC 77-1121. 1978. text ed. 118.00 (*0-12-591640-X*) Acad Pr.

Biochemistry of Ionizing Radiation. Thomas L. Walden, Jr. & Nushin K. Farzaneh. 256p. 1990. 105.00 (*0-88167-679-9*, 2145) Raven.

Biochemistry of Kidney Functions. Ed. by F. Morel. (INSERM Symposia Ser.: Vol. 21). 462p. 1982. 134.00 (*0-444-80417-X*) Elsevier.

Biochemistry of Lactation. Ed. by T. B. Mepham. 500p. 1983. 169.75 (*0-444-80489-7*) Elsevier.

Biochemistry of Macrophages: Symposium on Biochemistry of Macrophages Held at the CIBA Foundation, 16-18 April 1985. CIBA Foundation Staff. (Ciba Foundation Symposium: New Ser.: No. 118). (Illus.). 266p. reprint ed. pap. 75.90 (*0-8357-4562-7*, 2037464) Bks Demand.

Biochemistry of Membrane Transport. I. C. West. (Outline Studies in Biology). 96p. 1983. pap. 12.95 (*0-412-24190-0*, NO. 6063) Chapman & Hall.

Biochemistry of Mental Disorders: New Vistas. Ed. by Earl Usdin & Arnold J. Mandell. LC 76-52655. (Modern Pharmacology-Toxicology Ser.: No. 13). (Illus.). 302p. reprint ed. pap. 86.10 (*0-7837-0813-0*, 2041128) Bks Demand.

Biochemistry of Mental Disorders: Proceedings of the WHO Scientific Group, Geneva, 1968. WHO Staff. (Technical Report Ser.: No. 427). 1969. pap. 2.00 (*92-4-120427-3*) World Health.

Biochemistry of Methylotrophs. Christopher Anthony. 1982. text ed. 138.00 (*0-12-058820-X*) Acad Pr.

Biochemistry of Microbial Degradation. Ed. by Colin Ratledge. LC 93-10260. 584p. (C). 1994. lib. bdg. 265.00 (*0-7923-2273-8*) Kluwer Ac.

Biochemistry of Migraine. Ed. by M. J. Eadie & J. H. Tyrer. 1985. lib. bdg. 112.50 (*0-85200-731-0*) Kluwer Ac.

***Biochemistry of Milk Products.** Ed. by A. T. Andrews & J. Varley. (Special Publication Ser.: No. 150). 190p. 1994. 79.95 (*0-85186-702-2*, R6702) CRC Pr.

Biochemistry of Neuroectodermal Tumors. Ed. by G. Melino et al. (Clinical Chemistry & Enzymology Communications Ser.). 180p. 1990. pap. text ed. 182.00 (*3-7186-5019-3*) Gordon & Breach.

Biochemistry of Nickel. R. Hausinger. (Biochemistry of the Elements Ser.: Vol. 12). 1994. 79.50 (*0-306-44541-7*, Plenum Pr) Plenum.

Biochemistry of Nonheme Iron. Anatoly Bezkorovainy. LC 80-16477. (Biochemistry of the Elements Ser.: Vol. 1). 456p. 1981. 120.00 (*0-306-40501-6*, Plenum Pr) Plenum.

Biochemistry of Normal & Abnormal Epidermal Differentiation. Ed. by I. A. Bernstein & M. Seiji. (Current Problems in Dermatology Ser.: Vol. 10). (Illus.). x, 442p. 1981. pap. 109.00 (*3-8055-1915-X*) S Karger.

Biochemistry of Parasites: Proceedings of Satellite Conference of the 13th Annual Meeting of the Federation of European Biochemical Societies (FEBS), Jerusalem, August 1980. Ed. by Gerald M. Slutzky. (Illus.). 236p. 1981. 103.00 (*0-08-026381-X*, Pub. by Pergamon Repr UK) Franklin.

Biochemistry of Peptide Antibiotics: Recent Advances in the Biotechnology of B-Lactams & Microbial Peptides. Ed. by Horst Kleinkauf & Hans Von Dohren. (Illus.). xiv, 522p. (C). 1990. lib. bdg. 238.50 (*3-11-011928-5*); lib. bdg. 200.00 (*0-89925-551-5*) De Gruyter.

Biochemistry of Photosynthesis. 3rd ed. R. P. Gregory. 257p. 1989. text ed. 99.95 (*0-471-91899-7*) Wiley.

Biochemistry of Plant Phenolics. C. F. Van Sumere. Ed. by Peter J. Lea. (Annual Proceedings of the Phytochemical Society of Europe: Vol. 25). (Illus.). 352p. 1986. 47.50 (*0-19-854170-8*) OUP.

Biochemistry of Plants: A Comprehensive Treatise, Vol. 10. Ed. by Paul K. Stumpf et al. 429p. 1987. text ed. 134.00 (*0-12-675410-1*) Acad Pr.

Biochemistry of Plants: A Comprehensive Treatise, Lipids: Structure & Function, Vol. 9. Ed. by Paul K. Stumpf et al. 336p. 1987. text ed. 134.00 (*0-12-675409-8*) Acad Pr.

Biochemistry of Plants: A Comprehensive Treatise, Photosynthesis, Vol. 8. Ed. by Paul K. Stumpf & M. D. Hatch. 1981. text ed. 134.00 (*0-12-675408-X*) Acad Pr.

Biochemistry of Plants: A Comprehensive Treatise, Secondary Plant Products, Vol. 7. Ed. by Paul K. Stumpf & E. E. Conn. LC 80-13168. 1981. text ed. 134.00 (*0-12-675407-1*) Acad Pr.

Biochemistry of Plants: A Comprehensive Treatise, Vol. 6: Proteins & Nucleic Acids. Ed. by Paul K. Stumpf et al. 1981. text ed. 134.00 (*0-12-675406-3*) Acad Pr.

Biochemistry of Plants Vol. 11: A Comprehensive Treatise, Biochemistry of Metabolism. Ed. by Paul K. Stumpf et al. 388p. 1987. text ed. 134.00 (*0-12-675411-X*) Acad Pr.

Biochemistry of Plants Vol. 12: A Comprehensive Treatise, Physiology of Metabolism. Ed. by Paul K. Stumpf et al. 357p. 1987. text ed. 134.00 (*0-12-675412-8*) Acad Pr.

Biochemistry of Plants Vol. 13: A Comprehensive Treatise, Methodology. Ed. by Paul K. Stumpf et al. 294p. 1987. text ed. 108.00 (*0-12-675413-6*) Acad Pr.

Biochemistry of Plants Vol. 15: A Comprehensive Treatise. Ed. by Abraham Marcus et al. (Molecular Biology Ser.). 1100p. 1989. text ed. 213.00 (*0-12-675415-2*) Acad Pr.

Biochemistry of Plants Vol. 16: A Comprehensive Treatise, Intermediary Nitrogen Metabolism. Ed. by B. J. Miflin et al. 402p. 1990. text ed. 160.00 (*0-12-675416-0*) Acad Pr.

Biochemistry of Plants, Carbohydrates Vol. 14: A Comprehensive Treatise. Ed. by Jack Preiss et al. 529p. 1988. text ed. 163.00 (*0-12-675414-4*) Acad Pr.

***Biochemistry of Psychiatric Disturbances.** fac. ed. Ed. by Gerald Curzon. LC 80-40498. (Illus.). 156p. Date not set. pap. 44.50 (*0-7837-7361-7*, 2047170) Bks Demand.

Biochemistry of Pulmonary Emphysema. Ed. by C. Grassi et al. LC 92-2315. (Current Topics in Rehabilitation Ser.). 1992. 52.00 (*0-387-19775-3*) Spr-Verlag.

Biochemistry of Redox Reactions. Ed. by Bernard Testa. (Illus.). 512p. 1994. text ed. 115.00 (*0-12-685391-6*) Acad Pr.

Biochemistry of S-Methyl-L-Cysteine & Its Principal Derivatives. G. A. Maw. (Sulfur Report Ser.). 31p. (Orig.). 1982. pap. text ed. 65.00 (*3-7186-0112-5*) Gordon & Breach.

Biochemistry of Schuessler. Sydney B. Flower. 87p. 1970. spiral bd. 4.40 (*0-7873-0327-5*) Mokelumne.

Biochemistry of Selenium. Raymond J. Shamberger. (Biochemistry of the Elements Ser.: Vol. 2). 346p. 1983. 95.00 (*0-306-41090-7*, Plenum Pr) Plenum.

Biochemistry of Silage. 2nd ed. P. McDonald et al. (Illus.). 340p. (C). 1991. text ed. 110.00 (*0-948617-22-5*, Pub. by Chalcombe Pubns UK) Scholium Intl.

Biochemistry of Smooth Muscle, Vol. I. Ed. by Newman L. Stephens. 208p. 1983. 144.00 (*0-8493-6575-9*, QP321, CRC Reprint) Franklin.

Biochemistry of Smooth Muscle, Vol. II. Ed. by Newman L. Stephens. 304p. 1983. 168.00 (*0-8493-6576-7*, QP321, CRC Reprint) Franklin.

Biochemistry of Smooth Muscle, Vol. III. Ed. by Newman L. Stephens. 208p. 1983. 124.95 (*0-8493-6577-5*, CRC Reprint) Franklin.

Biochemistry of Storage Carbohydrates in Green Plants. P. M. Dey & R. A. Dixon. LC 84-16778. 1985. text ed. 139.00 (*0-12-214680-8*) Acad Pr.

Biochemistry of Sulfur. Ryan J. Huxtable. (Biochemistry of the Elements Ser.: Vol. 6). 460p. 1986. 110.00 (*0-306-42348-0*, Plenum Pr) Plenum.

Biochemistry of the Brain. Sudhir Kumar. (Illus.). 1980. 258.00 (*0-08-021345-6*, Pub. by Pergamon Repr UK) Franklin.

Biochemistry of the Brain During the Process of Dying & Resuscitation. Mariya S. Gaevskaya. LC 64-17205. 106p. reprint ed. pap. 30.30 (*0-8357-7220-9*, 2020665) Bks Demand.

Biochemistry of the Carotenoids, Vol. I. 2nd ed. T. W. Goodwin. (Plants Ser.). 377p. 1980. 79.95 (*0-412-21690-6*, NO. 6412) Chapman & Hall.

Biochemistry of the Developing Brain, 2 vols., Vol. 1. Williamina A. Himwich. LC 72-90961. (Illus.). 414p. reprint ed. pap. 111.80 (*0-7837-0877-7*, 2041185) Bks Demand.

Biochemistry of the Developing Brain, 2 vols., Vol. 2. Williamina A. Himwich. LC 72-90961. (Illus.). 335p. reprint ed. pap. 95.50 (*0-7837-0878-5*) Bks Demand.

Biochemistry of the Elemental Halogens & Inorganic Halides. K. L. Kirk. LC 90-25111. (Biochemistry of the Elements Ser.: Vol. 9A). (Illus.). 290p. 1991. 85.00 (*0-306-43653-1*, Plenum Pr) Plenum.

Biochemistry of the Essential Ultratrace Elements. Ed. by Earl Frieden. LC 84-17973. (Biochemistry of the Elements Ser.: Vol. 3). 444p. 1984. 105.00 (*0-306-41682-4*, Plenum Pr) Plenum.

Biochemistry of the Eye. Ed. by Robert E. Anderson. (Illus.). 267p. 1983. 27.50 (*0-317-94078-3*) Am Acad Ophthal.

Biochemistry of the Eye. E. R. Berman. LC 90-14353. (Perspectives in Vision Research Ser.). (Illus.). 490p. 1991. 95.00 (*0-306-43633-7*, Plenum Pr) Plenum.

Biochemistry of the Eye. David R. Whikehart. (Illus.). 272p. 1994. pap. 39.95 (*0-7506-9074-7*) Buttrwrth-Heinemann.

Biochemistry of the Human Body. Peter G. Markow. 80p. (C). 1994. 11.54 (*1-56870-030-X*) RonJon Pub.

Biochemistry of the Lanthanides. C. H. Evans. LC 89-8703. (Biochemistry of the Elements Ser.: Vol. 8). (Illus.). 460p. 1990. 95.00 (*0-306-43176-9*, Plenum Pr) Plenum.

Biochemistry of the Mevalonic Acid Pathway to Terpenoids. Ed. by G. H. Towers & H. A. Stafford. LC 90-7265. (Recent Advances in Phytochemistry Ser.: Vol. 24). (Illus.). 352p. 1990. 89.50 (*0-306-43604-3*, Plenum Pr) Plenum.

Biochemistry of the Nucleic Acids. 11th ed. R. L. Adams et al. (Illus.). 544p. (C). 1992. text ed. 79.95 (*0-412-46030-0*, A5278); pap. 39.95 (*0-412-39940-7*, A5282) Chapman & Hall.

Biochemistry of the Poliomyelitis Viruses. E. Kovacs. 1964. 117.00 (*0-08-010111-9*, Pub. by Pergamon Repr UK) Franklin.

Biochemistry of the Reproductive Years: Proceedings of the Seventh Arnold O. Beckman Conference in Clinical Chemistry. Paige E. Besch et al. LC 84-9171. 343p. 1985. 20.00 (*0-915274-24-8*) Am Assn Clinical Chem.

Biochemistry of the Tissues. 2nd ed. Peter Banks et al. LC 75-26739. 509p. reprint ed. pap. 145.10 (*0-8357-7221-7*, 2052241) Bks Demand.

Biochemistry of Trace Metal. Adriano. 1992. 79.95 (*0-87371-523-3*, TD196) Lewis Pubs.

Biochemistry of Virus-Infected Plants. R. S. Fraser. LC 86-24794. (Botanical Research Studies). 259p. 1987. text ed. 145.00 (*0-471-91299-9*) Wiley.

Biochemistry of Viruses. Ed. by Hilton B. Levy. LC 75-90149. (Illus.). 671p. reprint ed. pap. 180.00 (*0-7837-0951-X*, 2041256) Bks Demand.

Biochemistry of Vitamin A. Ed. by Jagannath Ganguly. 1989. 191.00 (*0-8493-6890-1*, QP772) CRC Pr.

***Biochemistry of Vitamin B6 & PQQ.** Ed. by G. Marino et al. (Advances in Life Science Ser.). 384p. 1994. 85.00 (*0-8176-5067-9*) Birkhauser.

***Biochemistry of Vitamin B6 & PQQ.** Ed. by G. Marino et al. (Advances in Life Sciences Ser.). 1994. write for info. (*3-7643-5067-9*) Birkhauser.

Biochemistry of Zinc. Ed. by A. S. Prasad. (Biochemistry of the Elements Ser.: Vol. 11). (Illus.). 328p. (C). 1994. 79.50 (*0-306-44399-6*, Plenum Pr) Plenum.

Biochemistry of 2',5' - Oligadenylates. Wu. 1992. write for info. (*0-8493-4819-6*, CRC Reprint) Franklin.

Biochemistry, Pathology & Genetics of Pulmonary Emphysema: Proceedings of a Meeting on Emphysema Held at Porto Conte, Sassari (Sardinia), April 27-30, 1980. Ed. by J. Bignon & G. L. Scarpa. (Illus.). 430p. 1981. 184.00 (*0-08-027379-3*, Pub. by Pergamon Repr UK) Franklin.

***Biochemistry Primer for Exercise Science.** Michael E. Houston. LC 94-41211. (Illus.). 144p. (Orig.). (C). 1995. pap. text ed. write for info. (*0-87322-577-5*, BHOU0577) Human Kinetics.

Biochemistry Through Questions: Self-Assessment & Review. Philip W. Kuchel & Gregory B. Ralston. (Illus.). 208p. 1993. pap. text ed. 22.50 (*0-07-470019-7*) Hlth Prof Div.

Biochemistry, Ultrastructure & Physiology of Cerebral Anoxia, Hypoxia & Ischaemia. Ed. by M. M. Cohen et al. (Monographs in Neural Sciences: Vol. 1). (Illus.). 1973. 39.25 (*3-8055-1420-4*) S Karger.

Biochimestry of Food Proteins. Ed. by B. J. Hudson. LC 92-3541. 419p. 1992. 110.00 (*1-85166-768-7*) Elsevier.

Biochimica et Biophysica Acta: The Story of a Biochemical Journal. E. C. Slater. 136p. 1987. 44.00 (*0-444-80769-1*) Elsevier.

Biochromy: Natural Coloration of Living Things. Denis L. Fox. LC 78-57309. (Illus.). 1979. 55.00 (*0-520-03699-9*) U CA Pr.

Biochronological Correlations. J. Guex. (Illus.). xiv, 252p. 1991. pap. 70.00 (*0-387-53937-9*) Spr-Verlag.

Biocircuits: Amazing New Tools for Energy Health. Leslie Patten & Terry Patten. Ed. by Gregory Armstrong & Suzanne Lipsett. LC 88-81720. (Illus.). 240p. 1988. pap. 10.95 (*0-915811-13-8*) H J Kramer Inc.

Bioclimatology & the Adaptation of Livestock. H. D. Johnson. (World Animal Science Ser.: Vol. 2, No. 5). 1987. 133.50 (*0-444-42690-6*) Elsevier.

Biocompatability of Dental Materials Vol. I: Characteristics of Dental Tissues & Their Response to Dental Materials. Ed. by D. F. Williams & D. C. Smith. (CRC Uniscience Series on Biocompatibility). 240p. 1982. 123.95 (*0-8493-6617-8*, RK652, CRC Reprint) Franklin.

Biocompatability of Dental Materials Vol. II: Biocompatability of Preventive Dental Materials & Bonding Agents. Ed. by D. F. Williams & D. C. Smith. 296p. 1982. 146.00 (*0-8493-6618-6*, RK652, CRC Reprint) Franklin.

Biocompatability of Dental Materials Vol. III: Biocompatability of Dental Restorative Materials. Ed. by D. F. Williams & D. C. Smith. 312p. 1982. 166.00 (*0-8493-6619-4*, RK652, CRC Reprint) Franklin.

Biocompatability of Dental Materials Vol. IV: Biocompatability of Proshtodonic Materials. Williams & Smith. 288p. 1982. 146.00 (*0-8493-6620-8*, RK652, CRC Reprint) Franklin.

Biocompatibility in Hemodialysis. Ed. by C. A. Baldamus et al. (Contributions to Nephrology Ser.: Vol. 36). (Illus.). viii, 140p. 1983. pap. 77.00 (*3-8055-3601-1*) S Karger.

Biocompatibility: Interactions of Biological & Implantable Materials, Vol. I: Polymers. Frederik Silver & Charles Doillon. 306p. 1989. lib. bdg. 55.00 (*0-89573-317-X*) VCH Pubs.

Biocompatibility of Clinical Implant Materials, 2 vols., Vol. I. D. F. Williams. 288p. 1981. 146.00 (*0-8493-6625-9*, R857, CRC Reprint) Franklin.

Biocompatibility of Clinical Implant Materials, 2 vols., Vol. II. D. F. Williams. 288p. 1981. 149.95 (*0-8493-6626-7*, R857, CRC Reprint) Franklin.

Biocompatibility of Co-Cr-Ni Alloys. Ed. by H. F. Hildebrand & M. Champy. (NATO ASI Series A, Life Sciences: Vol. 158). (Illus.). 390p. 1989. 95.00 (*0-306-43095-9*, Plenum Pr) Plenum.

Biocompatibility of Orthopedic Implants, Vol. 1. David F. Williams. 328p. 1982. 159.95 (*0-8493-6613-5*, RD755, CRC Reprint) Franklin.

Biocompatibility of Orthopedic Implants, Vol. II. Ed. by David F. Williams. 264p. 1982. 139.95 (*0-8493-6614-3*, RD755, CRC Reprint) Franklin.

Biocompatibility of Tissue Analogs, Vol. I. Ed. by David F. Williams. LC 84-14974. 176p. 1985. 119.95 (*0-8493-6634-8*, R857, CRC Reprint) Franklin.

Biocompatibility of Tissue Analogs, Vol. II. Ed. by David F. Williams. LC 84-14974. 208p. 1985. 124.95 (*0-8493-6635-6*, CRC Reprint) Franklin.

Biocompatibility Testing of Disposable Medical Devices (Seminar Notes - April 1993) ring bd. 50.00 (*1-56676-045-3*) Technomic.

Biocompatible Materials for the Human Body, No. GB-072R. Business Communications Co., Inc. Staff. 104p. 1990. 1,950.00 (*0-89336-625-0*) BCC.

Biocompatible Polyurethanes: Medical & Pharmaceutical Applications (Seminar Notes - Oct. 1991) ring bd. 75.00 (*0-87762-904-8*) Technomic.

Biocompatible Surfaces: Design, Characterization & Applications (Seminar Notes - Oct. 1991) ring bd. 125.00 (*0-87762-914-5*) Technomic.

Biocomputers: The Next Generation from Japan. T. Kaminuma & G. Matsumoto. (Illus.). 288p. 1991. pap. 51.95 (*0-442-31156-7*) Chapman & Hall.

Biocomputing: Informatics & Genome Projects. Ed. by Douglas W. Smith. (Illus.). 336p. 1993. text ed. 49.95 (*0-12-653035-1*) Acad Pr.

***Bioconjugate Techniques.** Greg T. Hermanson. (Illus.). 721p. 1995. boxed write for info. (*0-12-342335-X*) Acad Pr.

Biocontrol of Arthropods Affecting Livestock & Poultry. Ed. by Donald A. Rutz & Richard S. Patterson. (Studies in Insect Biology). 316p. (C). 1990. pap. text ed. 66.00 (*0-8133-7850-8*) Westview.

Biocontrol of Medical & Veterinary Pests. Marshall Laird. LC 81-12083. 256p. 1981. text ed. 69.50 (*0-275-91346-5*, C1346, Praeger Pubs) Greenwood.

Biocontrol of Plant Diseases. Ed. by K. G. Mukerji & K. L. Garg. 1988. write for info. (*0-318-62925-9*, SB732) CRC Pr.

Biocontrol of Plant Diseases, Vol. I. Ed. by K. G. Mukerji & K. L. Garg. 224p. 1988. 204.00 (*0-8493-4595-2*, SB732) CRC Pr.

Biocontrol of Plant Diseases, Vol. II. Ed. by K. G. Mukerji & K. L. Garg. 224p. 1988. 121.00 (*0-8493-4596-0*, SB732, CRC Reprint) Franklin.

Bioconversion of Cereal Products. Ed. by B. Godon & Armand Boudreau. Tr. by Deirdre Ni Eidhin. LC 93-26665. (ENG.). 1993. write for info. (*1-56081-600-7*) VCH Pubs.

Bioconversion of Forest & Agricultural Plant Residues. J. N. Saddler. (Biotechnology in Agriculture Ser.). 335p. 1993. text ed. 109.25 (*0-85198-798-2*) CAB Intl.

Bioconversion of Waste Materials to Industrial Products. A. M. Martin. 1991. 153.00 (*1-85166-571-4*) Elsevier.

Biocultural Aspects of Disease. Ed. by Henry R. Rothschild. LC 81-12714. 1981. text ed. 148.00 (*0-12-598720-X*) Acad Pr.

Biocultural Basis of Health: Expanding Views of Medical Anthropology. Lorna G. Moore et al. (Illus.). 278p. (C). 1987. reprint ed. pap. text ed. 14.95 (*0-88133-255-0*) Waveland Pr.

***Biocultural Dimensions of Chronic Pain: Implications for Treatment of Multi-Ethnic Populations.** Maryann S. Bates. (SUNY Series in Medical Anthropology). 192p. 1995. text ed. 49.50x (*0-7914-2735-8*) State U NY Pr.

***Biocultural Dimensions of Chronic Pain: Implications for Treatment of Multi-Ethnic Populations.** Maryann S. Bates. (SUNY Series in Medical Anthropology). 192p. (C). 1995. pap. 16.95x (*0-7914-2736-6*) State U NY Pr.

Biodata: Biographical Indicators of Business Performance. Barrie Gunter et al. 176p. 1993. 59.95 (*0-415-08229-3*, B0176) Routledge.

Biodata Handbook: Theory, Research, & Use of Biographical Information for Selection & Performance Prediction. LC 90-2294. 672p. 1994. 69.95 (*0-89106-063-4*) Consulting Psychol.

Biodata: Potentials & Challenges in Public Sector Employee Selection see IPMA Assessment Council Monograph Series

B

An Asterisk (*) at the beginning of an entry indicates that the title is appearing in BIP for the first time.

B

An Asterisk (*) at the beginning of an entry indicates that the title is appearing in BIP for the first time.

761

Bioethics & the Fetus: Medical, Moral, & Legal Issues. Ed. by James M. Humber & Robert F. Almeder. LC 84-640015. (Biomedical Ethics Reviews, 1991 Ser.). 200p. 1991. 39.50 (*0-89603-220-5*) Humana.

***Bioethics & the Future of Medicine: Toward a Christian Agenda.** Ed. by Nigel M. De S Cameron et al. 301p. (Orig.). 1995. pap. 18.99 (*0-8028-4081-7*) Eerdmans.

Bioethics & the Law: Medical, Socio-Legal, & Philosophical Directions for a Brave New World. George P. Smith, II. LC 93-16036. 352p. (Orig.). (C). 1993. lib. bdg. 56.00 (*0-8191-9177-9*); pap. text ed. 29.50 (*0-8191-9178-7*) U Pr of Amer.

Bioethics & the New Medical Technology. Margot C. Mabie. LC 92-22642. 176p. (YA). (gr. 7 up). 1993. text ed. 14.95 (*0-689-31637-2*, Atheneum Bks Young) S&S Childrens.

Bioethics Committees: The Health Care Provider's Guide. Bowen Hosford. 350p. 1985. 80.00 (*0-87189-253-7*) Aspen Pub.

Bioethics in a Liberal Society. Max Charlesworth. LC 93-18160. 176p. (C). 1993. 39.95 (*0-521-44503-5*); pap. 12.95 (*0-521-44952-9*) Cambridge U Pr.

Bioethics Today: A New Ethical Vision. James W. Walters et al. LC 87-83558. 116p. (Orig.). 1988. pap. 6.95 (*0-685-23293-X*) La Sierra U Pr.

Bioethics Yearbook Vol. 1: Theological Developments in Bioethics, 1988-1990. Ed. by B. Andrew Lustig. 232p. (C). 1991. lib. bdg. 119.50 (*0-7923-1280-5*) Kluwer Ac.

Bioethics Yearbook Vol. 2: Regional Developments in Bioethics: 1989-1991. Ed. by B. Andrew Lustig. 448p. (C). 1992. lib. bdg. 175.00 (*0-7923-1893-5*) Kluwer Ac.

***Bioextraction & Biodeterioration of Metals.** Ed. by Christine C. Gaylarde & Hector A. Videla. (Biology of World Resources Ser.). (Illus.). 250p. (C). 1995. 99.95 (*0-521-41757-0*) Cambridge U Pr.

B

Biofeedback. Wilfred Hume. LC 80-15617. (Biofeedback Research Review Ser.: Vol. III). 83p. 1981. 29.95 (*0-87705-969-1*) Human Sci Pr.

***Biofeedback: A Practitioner's Guide.** 2nd ed. Mark S. Schwartz. 1995. lib. bdg. 60.00 (*0-89862-806-7*) Guilford Pr.

***Biofeedback: A Practitioner's Guide.** 2nd ed. Mark S. Schwartz. 1995. pap. text ed. 35.00 (*0-89862-821-0*) Guilford Pubns.

Biofeedback: A Source Guide. 1991. lib. bdg. 75.00 (*0-8490-4871-0*) Gordon Pr.

Biofeedback: An Introduction & Guide. David G. Danskin & Mark A. Crow. LC 80-84020. 116p. (Orig.). (C). 1981. pap. text ed. 16.95 (*0-87484-530-0*) Mayfield Pub.

Biofeedback: Basic Problems in Clinical Applications. E. Richter-Heinrich & Norman E. Miller. 141p. 1983. 51.50 (*0-444-86345-1*, I-122-82, North Holland) Elsevier.

Biofeedback: Methods & Procedures in Clinical Practice. George D. Fuller. (Orig.). 1977. pap. 18.00 (*0-686-25138-5*) Biofeed Pr.

Biofeedback: Principles & Practice for Clinicians. 3rd ed. John V. Basmajian. (Illus.). 396p. 1989. 56.00 (*0-683-00357-7*) Williams & Wilkins.

Biofeedback: Report. American Psychiatric Association, Task Force on Biofeedback Staff. LC 80-66989. (American Psychiatric Association Task Force Report Ser.: No. 19). 125p. reprint ed. pap. 35.70 (*0-8357-7801-0*, 2036170) Bks Demand.

Biofeedback: Studies in Clinical Efficacy. Ed. by John P. Hatch et al. LC 86-30358. 384p. 1987. 55.00 (*0-306-42347-2*, Plenum Pr) Plenum.

Biofeedback & Behavioral Strategies in Pain Treatment. Alfred J. Nigl. LC 84-14083. 368p. 1984. text ed. 42.50 (*0-89335-203-9*) PMA Pub Corp.

Biofeedback & Self-Regulation. Ed. by Niels Birbaumer & H. D. Kimmel. LC 79-19203. 480p. reprint ed. pap. 136.80 (*0-8357-2583-9*, 2040288) Bks Demand.

Biofeedback & Sports Science. Ed. by Jack H. Sandweiss & Steven L. Wolf. LC 85-12423. 220p. 1985. 39.50 (*0-306-41995-5*, Plenum Pr) Plenum.

Biofeedback & the Modification of Behavior. Aubrey J. Yates. LC 79-400. (Illus.). 524p. 1980. 60.00 (*0-306-40226-2*, Plenum Pr) Plenum.

Biofeedback, Behavior Therapy, & Hypnosis: Potentiating the Verbal Control of Behavior for Clinicians. Ed. by Ian Wickramasekara. LC 76-18294. 607p. 1976. 49.95 (*0-88229-193-9*) Nelson-Hall.

Biofeedback Frontiers: Self-Regulation of Stress Reactivity. Lilian Rosenbaum. LC 86-82030. (Stress in Modern Society Ser.: No. 15). 1988. 32.50 (*0-404-63266-1*) AMS Pr.

Biofeedback Guide. D. Heisel. 282p. 1977. text ed. 49.00 (*0-677-00020-0*) Gordon & Breach.

Biofeedback in Neuromuscular Re-Education: History, Uses, Procedures. Susanne Owen et al. LC 27-954. (Illus.). 1975. pap. 5.50 (*0-685-64751-X*) Biofeedback Research.

Biofeedback Primer. Edward B. Blanchard & Leonard H. Epstein. LC 76-74321. (Illus.). 218p. (C). 1978. pap. text ed. 10.50 (*0-394-34759-5*) Random.

Biofeedback Without Machines: A Strategy for Living. George E. Soroka. 171p. (Orig.). 1995. 9.95 (*1-881374-20-3*) Flash Blasters.

Biofertilizers. L. L. Somani & S. C. Bhandari. Ed. by K. K. Vyas & S. N. Saxena. 361p. (C). 1990. 150.00 (*81-85046-89-1*, Scientific) St Mut.

Biofertilizers: Potentialities & Problems. Ed. by S. P. Sen & P. Palit. (C). 1988. 44.00 (*81-85109-86-9*, Pub. by Naya Prokash IA) S Asia.

Biofertilizers in Agriculture. N. S. Subba. 200p. (C). 1982. text ed. 45.00 (*90-6191-405-1*, Pub. by A A Balkema NE) Ashgate Pub Co.

Biofertilizers in Agriculture & Forestry. N. S. Subbarao. 260p. (C). 1993. text ed. 50.00 (*1-881570-29-0*) Intl Sci Pub.

Biofertilizers in Agriculture & Forestry. N. S. Rao. (C). 1993. reprint ed. 32.00 (*81-204-0791-1*, Pub. by Oxford IBH II) S Asia.

Biofields: The New Physics of Health. Glen Swartwout. 102p. (Orig.). (C). 1992. pap. 21.95 (*0-9630503-1-1*) Aerai Pub.

***Biofilm Reactors.** Rogalla & Harremoes. (Water Science & Technology). 548p. 1994. pap. 270.00 (*0-08-042544-5*, Pergamon Pr) Elsevier.

Biofilms: Formation & Consequences. William G. Characklis & Kevin Marshall. (Environmental & Applied Microbiology Ser.). 1990. text ed. 149.95 (*0-471-82663-4*) Wiley.

***Biofilms: Methods for Enzymatic Release of Microorganisms.** Jean Brisou. LC 95-14237. 240p. 1995. 99.95 (*0-8493-4791-2*, 4791) CRC Pr.

Biofilms - Science & Technology. Ed. by L. F. Melo et al. LC 92-34848. (NATO Advanced Study Institutes Series E, Applied Sciences: Vol. 223). 1992. lib. bdg. 262.00 (*0-7923-2022-0*) Kluwer Ac.

Bioflavonoids. Jeffrey Bland. Ed. by Earl Mindell & Richard Passwater. (Good Health Guide Ser.). 32p. 1984. pap. 2.50 (*0-87983-330-0*) Keats.

Bioflavour '87, Analysis - Biochemistry - Biotechnology: Proceedings of the International Conference Wurzburg, Federal Republic of Germany, September 29-30, 1987. Ed. by Peter Schreier. 584p. (C). 1988. lib. bdg. 244.65 (*0-89925-290-7*) De Gruyter.

***Bioflavour '87, Analysis - Biochemistry - Biotechnology: Proceedings of the International Conference Wurzburg, Federal Republic of Germany, September 29-30, 1987.** Ed. by Peter Schreier. 584p. (C). 1988. lib. bdg. 244.65 (*3-11-011204-3*) De Gruyter.

***Biofluid & Tissue Analysis for Drugs, Including Hypolipidaemics.** Ed. by Eric Reid et al. 434p. 1994. 180.00 (*0-85186-644-1*, R6644) CRC Pr.

Biofluid Mechanics. J. Mazumdar. 200p. 1992. text ed. 43.00 (*981-02-0927-4*) World Scientific Pub.

Biofluid Mechanics: Blood Flow in Large Vessels: Proceeding of the Second International Symposium, June 25-18, 1989. Ed. by D. W. Liepsch. (Illus.). 500p. 1991. pap. 96.00 (*0-387-52730-3*) Spr-Verlag.

Biofouling & Biocorrosion in Industrial Water Systems. Gill G. Geesey. 1993. 79.95 (*0-87371-928-X*, TD353) Lewis Pubs.

Biofouling & Biocorrosion in Industrial Water Systems: Proceedings of the International Workshop on Industrial Biofouling & Biocorrosion, Stuttgart, September 13-14, 1990. Ed. by H. C. Flemming & G. G. Geesey. (Illus.). 228p. 1991. 77.00 (*0-387-53887-9*) Spr-Verlag.

Biofouling Control Procedures: Technology & Ecological Effects. Ed. by Loren D. Jensen. LC 77-2120. (Pollution Engineering & Technology Ser.: No. 5). 127p. reprint ed. pap. 36.20 (*0-7837-0123-3*, 2040402) Bks Demand.

***Biofuels.** OECD Staff. 80p. (Orig.). 1994. pap. 28.00x (*92-64-14233-9*) OECD.

Biofuels, Air Pollution, & Health: A Global Review. K. R. Smith. (Modern Perspectives in Energy Ser.). (Illus.). 476p. 1987. 95.00 (*0-306-42519-X*, Plenum Pr) Plenum.

Biofuels Bibliography: January 1986-August 1992. 60p. (Orig.). (C). 1993. pap. text ed. 30.00 (*1-56806-928-6*) Diane Pub.

Biofuture: Confronting the Genetic Era. Burke K. Zimmerman. (Illus.). 318p. 1984. 19.95 (*0-306-41315-9*, Plenum Pr) Plenum.

Biogas End-Use in the European Community. M. Constant et al. 346p. 1989. 88.25 (*1-85166-339-8*) Elsevier.

Biogas Plants: Design & Details of Simple Biogas Plants. 2nd ed. Ludwig Sasse. (GATE Ser.). (Illus.). 85p. 1988. pap. 14.00 (*3-528-02004-0*, Pub. by Vieweg & Sohn GW) Ballen Bkslr.

Biogas Plants in Animal Husbandry: A Practical Guide. Uli Werner et al. Ed. by Deutsches Zentrum fur Entwicklungs-technologien-GATE. (GATE Ser.). (Illus.). 153p. 1989. pap. 21.00 (*3-528-02048-2*, Pub. by Vieweg & Sohn GW) Ballen Bkslr.

Biogas Plants in Europe: A Practical Handbook. Ed. by M. Demuynck et al. (Solar Energy in the European Community Ser.: No. E, Vol. 6). 1984. lib. bdg. 111.50 (*90-277-1780-X*) Kluwer Ac.

Biogas Systems in India. Robert J. Lichtman. 130p. 1990. 19.25 (*0-86619-167-4*) Vols Tech Asst.

Biogas Technology, Transfer & Diffusion. Ed. by M. M. El-Halwagi. (Elsevier Applied Science Ser.). 736p. 1986. 124.25 (*1-85166-000-3*) Elsevier.

Biogas Utilization Handbook. James L. Walsh et al. (Illus.). 133p. (C). 1988. 15.00 (*0-9624647-4-0*) GA Tech Rsch Inst.

Biogeneration of Aromas. Ed. by Thomas H. Parliment & Rodney Croteau. LC 86-3534. (ACS Symposium Ser.: No. 317). (Illus.). ix, 399p. 1986. 82.95 (*0-8412-0987-1*) Am Chemical.

Biogenesis & Function of Plant Lipids: Proceedings of the Paris Meeting, June 1980. P. Mazliak. (Developments in Plant Biology Ser.: Vol. 6). 1980. 106.75 (*0-444-80273-8*) Elsevier.

Biogenesis & Turnover of Membrane Macromolecules. Ed. by John S. Cook. LC 75-25111. (Society of General Physiologists Ser.: No. 31). (Illus.). 304p. reprint ed. pap. 86.70 (*0-7837-7090-1*, 2046915) Bks Demand.

Biogenesis of Natural Compounds. 2nd rev. ed. P. Bernfeld. LC 62-21549. 1967. 494.00 (*0-08-011962-X*, Pub. by Pergamon Repr UK) Franklin.

Biogenetic Structuralism. Charles D. Laughlin, Jr. & Eugene G. D'Aquili. LC 74-13245. (Illus.). 211p. 1974. text ed. 37.00 (*0-231-03817-8*) Col U Pr.

Biogenetics of Neurohormonal Peptides. Ed. by Rolf Hakanson & Jan Thorell. 1985. text ed. 108.00 (*0-12-317450-3*) Acad Pr.

Biogenic Amines & Physiological Membranes in Drug Therapy, 2 pts., Pt. A. Ed. by John H. Biel & Leo G. Abood. LC 77-180643. (Medicinal Research Ser.: No. 5). 174p. reprint ed. pap. 47.00 (*0-7837-0738-X*, 2041061) Bks Demand.

Biogenic Amines & Physiological Membranes in Drug Therapy, 2 pts., Pt. B. Ed. by John H. Biel & Leo G. Abood. LC 77-180643. (Medicinal Research Ser.: No. 5). 376p. reprint ed. pap. 107.20 (*0-7837-0739-8*) Bks Demand.

Biogenic Amines in Development. S. Parvez & H. Parvez. 1980. 128.25 (*0-444-80215-0*) Elsevier.

Biogenic Meditation: Biogenic Self-Analysis, Creative Microcosmos. Edmond B. Szekely. (Illus.). 40p. 1978. pap. 3.50 (*0-89564-051-1*) IBS Intl.

Biogenic Monamines & Their Metabolites in the Urine, Plasma & Cerebrospinal Fluid of Normal, Psychiatric, & Neurological Subjects. Bruce A. Davis. 464p. 1990. 252.00 (*0-8493-4611-8*, RC455, CRC Reprint) Franklin.

Biogenic Reducing: The Wonder Week. Edmond B. Szekely. (Illus.). 56p. 1977. pap. 4.50 (*0-89564-055-4*) IBS Intl.

Biogenic Revolution. Edmond B. Szekely. (Illus.). 226p. (Orig.). 1985. pap. 9.50 (*0-89564-021-X*) IBS Intl.

Biogenic Structures: Their Use in Interpreting Depositional Environments. Ed. by H. Allen Curran. (Special Publications Ser.: No. 35). 364p. 1985. 49.00 (*0-918985-15-3*) SEPM.

Biogenic Sulfur in the Environment. Ed. by Eric S. Saltzman & William J. Cooper. LC 89-6566. (ACS Symposium Ser.: No. 393). (Illus.). xi, 584p. 1989. 99.95 (*0-8412-1612-6*) Am Chemical.

Biogeochemical Cycling of Mineral-Forming Elements. Ed. by P. A. Trudinger & D. J. Swaine. LC 79-21297. (Studies in Environmental Science: Vol. 3). 616p. 1979. 166.75 (*0-444-41745-1*) Elsevier.

Biogeochemical Cycling of Sulfur & Nitrogen in the Remote Atmosphere. Ed. by James N. Galloway et al. 1985. lib. bdg. 80.50 (*90-277-2130-0*) Kluwer Ac.

Biogeochemical Exploration for Mineral Deposits. A. L. Kovalevsky. Ed. by R. R. Brooks. Tr. by M. E. Rosenberg. 234p. 1987. lib. bdg. 144.00 (*90-6764-099-9*, Pub. by VSP NE) Coronet Bks.

***Biogeochemical Monitoring in Small Catchments: Refereed Papers for BIOGEOMON, the Symposium of Ecosystem Behaviour: Evaluation of Integrated Monitoring in Small Catchments Held in Prague, Czech Republic, September 18-20, 1993.** BIOGEOMON, the Symposium on Ecosystem Behaviour: Evaluation of Integrated Monitoring in Small Catchments Staff. Ed. by Jiri Cerny et al. LC 95-14. 432p. (C). 1995. lib. bdg. 259.00 (*0-7923-3383-7*) Kluwer Ac.

Biogeochemical Processes at the Land-Sea Boundary. Ed. by P. Lasserre & J. M. Martin. (Oceanography Ser.: No. 43). 224p. 1986. 79.50 (*0-444-42675-2*) Elsevier.

Biogeochemistry: An Analysis of Global Change. William H. Schlesinger. (Illus.). 443p. (C). 1991. text ed. 85.00 (*0-12-625156-8*); pap. text ed. 42.50 (*0-12-625157-6*) Acad Pr.

Biogeochemistry of a Forested Ecosystem. Gene E. Likens et al. LC 76-50113. 1991. pap. 28.00 (*0-387-90225-2*) Spr-Verlag.

***Biogeochemistry of a Forested Ecosystem.** 2nd ed. G. E. Likens & F. H. Bormann. LC 94-41866. (Illus.). 168p. 1995. 49.95 (*0-387-94502-4*) Spr-Verlag.

***Biogeochemistry of a Forested Ecosystem.** 2nd ed. Gene E. Likens & F. Herbert Bormann. LC 94-41866. (Illus.). 168p. 1995. 29.95 (*0-387-94351-X*) Spr-Verlag.

Biogeochemistry of a Subalpine Ecosystem: Loch Vale Watershed. Ed. by J. Baron. (Ecological Studies: Vol. 90). (Illus.). 240p. 1991. 98.00 (*0-387-97605-1*) Spr-Verlag.

Biogeochemistry of Amino Acids. P. E. Hare et al. LC 79-25824. 576p. 1980. 98.50 (*0-471-05493-3*) Krieger.

Biogeochemistry of Blue, Snow, & Ross' Geese. Harold C. Hanson & Robert L. Jones. LC 76-46617. (Illus.). 298p. 1976. 15.00 (*0-8093-0751-0*) S Ill U Pr.

***Biogeochemistry of Global Change: Radiatively Active Trace Gases.** R. S. Oremland. LC 93-19052. 879p. 1993. 99.50 (*0-412-04141-3*) Routledge.

Biogeochemistry of Global Change: Radiatively Active Trace Gases. Ed. by Ronald S. Oremland. LC 93-19052. 1993. write for info. (*0-04-120304-6*) Routledge Chapman & Hall.

Biogeochemistry of Lead in the Environment, Vol I, Pts. A & B: Topics in Environmental Health, Set. Jerome O. Nriagu. 1991. 177.25 (*0-685-50936-2*) Elsevier.

Biogeochemistry of Major World Rivers. Ed. by Egon T. Degens et al. (Scientific Committee on Problems of the Environment Ser.: No. 42). 356p. 1991. text ed. 229.95 (*0-471-92676-0*) Wiley.

Biogeochemistry of Mercury in the Environment. Jerome O. Nriagu. (Topics in Environmental Health Ser.: Vol. 3). 696p. 1980. 217.50 (*0-444-80110-3*) Elsevier.

Biogeochemistry of Small Catchments: A Tool for Environmental Research. Ed. by Bedrich Moldan & Jiri Cerny. LC 93-5685. 465p. 1994. text ed. 125.00 (*0-471-93723-1*) Wiley.

***Biogeodynamic of Pollutants in Soils & Sediments: Risk Assessment of Delayed & Non-Linear Responses.** Ed. by W. Salomons & W. M. Stigliani. LC 95-13009. (Environmental Science Ser.). 1995. write for info. (*0-387-58732-2*); write for info. (*3-540-58732-2*) Spr-Verlag.

Biogeografia de America Latina. 2nd ed. Organization of American States General Secretariat, Dept. of Echnological & Scientific Affairs Staff. (Serie de Biologia: No. 13). (Illus.). 122p. (SPA.). (C). 1980. pap. 3.50 (*0-8270-1233-0*) OAS.

Biogeographic Analysis of the Herpetofauna of Northwestern Nuclear Central America. Jerry D. Johnson. (Contributions in Biology & Geology Ser.: No. 76). 80p. 1989. 10.00 (*0-89326-160-2*) Milwaukee Pub Mus.

Biogeographical Analysis of the Chihuahuan Desert Through Its Herpetofauna. David J. Morafka. (Biogeographica Ser.: No. 9). (Illus.). 1977. lib. bdg. 103.00 (*90-6193-210-6*) Kluwer Ac.

Biogeographical Evolution of the Malay Archipelago. T. C. Whitmore. (Oxford Monographs on Biogeography: No. 4). (Illus.). 160p. 1987. 65.00 (*0-19-854185-6*) OUP.

Biogeographical Processes. (Processes in Physical Geography Ser.: No. 5). 136p. 1982. pap. text ed. 9.95 (*0-04-574016-X*) Routledge Chapman & Hall.

Biogeography. James H. Brown & Arthur C. Gibson. LC 82-14124. (Illus.). 656p. 1983. 44.95 (*0-8016-0824-4*) Mosby Yr Bk.

Biogeography. R. L. Jones. (C). 1980. text ed. 95.00 (*0-7175-0872-2*, Pub. by S Thornes Pubs UK) St Mut.

Biogeography. Gareth Nelson & Norman Platnick. Ed. by John J. Head. LC 83-70604. (Carolina Biology Readers Ser.: No. 119). (Illus.). 16p. (C). (gr. 10 up). 1986. pap. 2.75 (*0-89278-319-2*, 45-9719) Carolina Biological.

Biogeography. 2nd ed. James H. Brown & Arthur C. Gibson. (Illus.). 656p. (C). 1991. text ed. 44.95 (*0-8016-0672-1*) Mosby Yr Bk.

Biogeography. E. C. Pielou. LC 92-7291. 366p. (C). 1992. reprint ed. lib. bdg. 49.95 (*0-89464-739-3*) Krieger.

Biogeography: A Study of Plants in the Ecosphere. 3rd ed. Joy Tivy. 452p. 1993. pap. text ed. 46.95 (*0-470-22078-3*) Halsted Pr.

Biogeography: An Ecological & Evolutionary Approach. 5th ed. C. B. Cox & P. D. Moore. (Illus.). 320p. 1993. pap. text ed. 34.95 (*0-632-02967-6*) Blackwell Sci.

Biogeography: An Ecological Perspective. Pierre M. Dansereau. LC 57-6819. 408p. reprint ed. pap. 116.30 (*0-8357-7224-1*, 2056305) Bks Demand.

Biogeography: Recent Advances & Future Directions. Ed. by J. A. Taylor. LC 84-12428. 432p. (C). 1984. 65.00 (*0-389-20507-9*, BNB-08065) B&N Imports.

Biogeography & Adaptation: Patterns of Marine Life. Geerat J. Vermeij. LC 78-3722. (Illus.). 352p. 1978. 37.50 (*0-674-07375-4*) HUP.

Biogeography & Adaptation: Patterns of Marine Life. Geerat J. Vermeij. LC 78-3722. (Illus.). 352p. 1980. pap. 14.50 (*0-674-07376-2*) HUP.

Biogeography & Ecology of Forest Bird Communities. Ed. by A. Keast. (Illus.). vi, 410p. 1990. 135.00 (*90-5103-047-9*, Pub. by SPB Acad Pub NE) Koeltz Sci Bks.

Biogeography & Ecology of New Guinea, 2 vols. J. L. Gressitt. 1981. lib. bdg. 421.00 (*90-6193-094-4*) Kluwer Ac.

Biogeography & Ecology of Southern Africa, 2 vols., Set. Ed. by M. J. Werger. (Monographiae Biologicae: No. 31). 1978. lib. bdg. 373.50 (*90-6193-083-9*) Kluwer Ac.

Biogeography & Ecology of the Island of Newfoundland. R. South. 1983. lib. bdg. 281.50 (*90-6193-101-0*) Kluwer Ac.

Biogeography & Ecology of the Rain Forests of Eastern Africa. Ed. by Jon C. Lovett & Samuel K. Wasser. (Illus.). 390p. (C). 1993. 120.00 (*0-521-43083-6*) Cambridge U Pr.

Biogeography & Ecology of Turkmenistan. Ed. by Victor Fet & Khabibulla Atamuradov. LC 94-6952. (Monographiae Biologicae: Vol. 72). 1994. lib. bdg. 270.00 (*0-7923-2738-1*) Kluwer Ac.

Biogeography & Plate Tectonics. J. C. Briggs. (Developments in Palaeontology & Stratigraphy Ser.: Vol. 10). 1987. 79.50 (*0-444-42743-0*) Elsevier.

Biogeography & Quaternary History in Tropical America. Ed. by T. C. Whitmore & G. T. Prance. (Oxford Monographs in Biogeography: No. 3). (Illus.). 226p. 1987. 95.00 (*0-19-854546-0*) OUP.

Biogeography & Raxonomy of Honeybees. F. Ruttner. (Illus.). 290p. 1987. 149.00 (*0-387-17781-7*) Spr-Verlag.

Biogeography & Systematics of Poitea (Leguminosae) Matt Lavin. Ed. by Christiane Anderson. (Systematic Botany Monographs: Vol. 37). (Illus.). 87p. 1993. pap. 11.00 (*0-912861-37-1*) Am Soc Plant.

***Biogeography of Fire in the San Bernardino Mountains of California: A Historical Study.** Richard A. Minnich. LC 88-9997. (University of California Publications in Entomology: No. 28). 170p. 1988. pap. 48.50 (*0-7837-7494-X*, 2049216) Bks Demand.

Biogeography of Mediterranean Invasions. Ed. by R. H. Groves & F. Di Castri. (Illus.). 600p. (C). 1991. 125.00 (*0-521-36040-4*) Cambridge U Pr.

Biogeography of the British Isles: An Introduction. Peter Vincent. (Illus.). 368p. 1990. 92.00 (*0-415-03470-1*, A3961) Routledge.

Biogeography of the Herpetofauna of the Pine-Oak Woodlands of the Sierra Madre Occidental of Mexico. James McCranie & Larry Wilson. (Contributions in Biology & Geology Ser.: No. 72). 30p. 1987. pap. text ed. 5.95 (*0-89326-153-X*) Milwaukee Pub Mus.

Biogeography of the Island Region of Western Lake Erie. Ed. by Jerry F. Downhower. (Illus.). 368p. 1988. 85.00 (*0-8142-0448-1*) Ohio St U Pr.

Biogeography of the Island Region of Western Lake Erie: A Laboratory for Experiments in Ecology & Evolution. Jerry F. Downhower. Ed. by Veda M. Cafazzo. LC 85-61221. (Informative Circular Ser.: No. 15). (Illus.). 15p. 1985. pap. text ed. 2.00 (*0-86727-101-9*) Ohio Bio Survey.

***Biogeography of the Reptiles of South Asia.** Indraneil Das. (Illus.). (C). 1995. write for info. (*0-89464-935-3*) Krieger.

An Asterisk (*) at the beginning of an entry indicates that the title is appearing in BIP for the first time.

B

An Asterisk (*) at the beginning of an entry indicates that the title is appearing in BIP for the first time.

Biographical Dictionary of English Women Writers, 1958-1720. Maureen Bell et al. (Monograph Ser.). 208p. (C). 1990. text ed. 32.50 (*0-8161-1806-X*, Hall Reference) Macmillan.

***Biographical Dictionary of European Labor Leaders.** A. Thomas Lane. LC 94-24945. 1204p. 1995. text ed. 225.00 (*0-313-26456-2*, Greenwood Pr) Greenwood.

Biographical Dictionary of Fiddlers Including Performers on the Violin, Cello & Double Bass. A. Mason Clarke. LC 79-166225. 360p. 1895. reprint ed. 39.00 (*0-403-01352-6*) Scholarly.

Biographical Dictionary of Fiddlers Including Performers on the Violin, Cello & Double D. A. Mason Clarke. 1988. reprint ed. lib. bdg. 59.00 (*0-7812-0677-4*) Rprt Serv.

Biographical Dictionary of Film. David Thomson. 1994. pap. 25.00 (*0-679-75564-0*) Knopf.

***Biographical Dictionary of Film.** 3rd ed. David Thomson. 1994. 40.00 (*0-394-58165-2*) Random.

Biographical Dictionary of Founders of Modern Nations. Neil Hamilton. 300p. 1995. lib. bdg. 60.00 (*0-87436-750-6*) ABC-CLIO.

Biographical Dictionary of French Political Leaders since 1870. Ed. by David Bell et al. 448p. 1990. 50.00 (*0-13-084690-2*) P-H.

Biographical Dictionary of Geography. Robert P. Larkin & Gary L. Peters. LC 92-18364. 384p. 1993. text ed. 69.50 (*0-313-27622-6*, LBG, Greenwood Pr) Greenwood.

***Biographical Dictionary of Gerontologists.** W. Andrew Achenbaum & Daniel M. Albert. LC 95-8002. 416p. 1995. text ed. 85.00 (*0-313-29274-4*, Greenwood Pr) Greenwood.

Biographical Dictionary of Gifted Education. Monaco. 1988. pap. 15.00 (*0-89824-183-9*) Trillium Pr.

Biographical Dictionary of Hispanic Literature in the United States: The Literature of Puerto Ricans, Puerto Rican Americans, Cuban Americans, & Other Hispanic Writers. Ed. by Nicolas Kanellos. LC 88-37288. 374p. 1989. text ed. 55.00 (*0-313-24465-0*, KBI/) Greenwood.

Biographical Dictionary of Indians of the Americas, 2 vols., Set. Illus. by Marion E. Gridley. (American Indian Dictionary Ser.). 570p. 1984. lib. bdg. 145.00 (*0-317-17420-7*) Am Indian Pubs.

***Biographical Dictionary of Indians of the Americas, 2 vols., Set.** Illus. by Marion E. Gridley. (American Indian Dictionary Ser.). 570p. 1984. lib. bdg. 145.00 (*0-937862-29-0*) Am Indian Pubs.

Biographical Dictionary of Internationalists. Ed. by Warren F. Kuehl. LC 82-15416. xvi, 934p. 1983. text ed. 135.00 (*0-313-22129-4*, KBD/, Greenwood Pr) Greenwood.

Biographical Dictionary of Latin American & Caribbean Political Leaders. Ed. by Robert J. Alexander. LC 87-17899. 519p. 1988. text ed. 105.00 (*0-313-24353-0*, ADL/, Greenwood Pr) Greenwood.

Biographical Dictionary of Latin American Historians & Historiography. Jack R. Thomas. LC 83-8558. xiv, 420p. 1984. text ed. 59.95 (*0-313-23004-8*, TLA/, Greenwood Pr) Greenwood.

Biographical Dictionary of Life Peers. W. D. Rubinstein. 400p. 1991. text ed. 75.00 (*0-312-01911-4*) St Martin.

Biographical Dictionary of Marxism. Ed. by Robert A. Gorman. LC 84-29016. 398p. 1986. text ed. 69.50 (*0-313-24851-6*, GMX/, Greenwood Pr) Greenwood.

Biographical Dictionary of Mathematicians, 4 vols., Set. Ed. by Charles Scribner's Sons Staff. 2200p. 1991. text ed. 225.00 (*0-684-19282-9*, Scribners) S&S Trade.

Biographical Dictionary of Medicine. Elmer Bendiner & Jessica Bendiner. 304p. 1990. 40.00 (*0-8160-1864-2*) Facts on File.

***Biographical Dictionary of Military Leaders.** Wallach. 1994. 55.00 (*0-13-017310-X*) P-H.

Biographical Dictionary of Modern European Radicals & Socialists: 1780-1815, Vol. I. Ed. by David Nicholls & Peter Marsh. LC 87-36961. 360p. 1988. text ed. 55.00 (*0-312-01968-8*) St Martin.

Biographical Dictionary of Modern Peace Leaders. Ed. by Harold Josephson et al. LC 84-26514. xxix, 1133p. 1985. text ed. 145.00 (*0-313-22565-6*, JPL/, Greenwood Pr) Greenwood.

Biographical Dictionary of Modern Rationalists. Joseph McCabe. 1977. lib. bdg. 75.95 (*0-8490-1506-5*) Gordon Pr.

Biographical Dictionary of Musicians. James D. Brown. No. 157. vii, 637p. 1970. reprint ed. write for info. (*0-318-71889-8*, Pub. by Georg Olms GW) Lubrecht & Cramer.

Biographical Dictionary of Musicians. Rupert Hughes. 1988. reprint ed. lib. bdg. 59.00 (*0-7812-0553-0*) Rprt Serv.

Biographical Dictionary of Musicians. Rupert Hughes. Ed. by Deems Taylor & Russell Kerr. LC 73-166237. 481p. 1972. reprint ed. 69.00 (*0-403-01364-X*) Scholarly.

Biographical Dictionary of Musicians, with a Bibliography of English Writings on Music. James D. Brown. (Anglistica & Americana Ser.: No. 157). 644p. 1970. reprint ed. 115.70 (*0-685-25149-7*, 05102577, Pub. by Georg Olms GW) Lubrecht & Cramer.

Biographical Dictionary of Neo-Marxism. Robert A. Gorman. LC 84-27968. x, 463p. 1985. text ed. 89.50 (*0-313-23513-9*, GBD/, Greenwood Pr) Greenwood.

Biographical Dictionary of New Zealand Composers. J. M. Thomson. (Illus.). 168p. (Orig.). 1990. pap. 30.00 (*0-86473-095-0*, Pub. by Victoria Univ Pr NZ) Lubrecht & Cramer.

Biographical Dictionary of North American Classicists. Ward W. Briggs. LC 94-4785. 880p. 1994. text ed. 115.00 (*0-313-24560-6*, Greenwood Pr) Greenwood.

Biographical Dictionary of Old English Music. Jeffrey Pulver. LC 69-16666. (Music Ser.). 538p. 1973. reprint ed. lib. bdg. 59.50 (*0-306-71103-6*) Da Capo.

Biographical Dictionary of Old English Music. Jeffrey Pulver. 537p. 1990. reprint ed. lib. bdg. 99.00 (*0-7812-9008-2*) Rprt Serv.

Biographical Dictionary of Philadelphia Architects & Master Builders: 1760-1930. Sandra L. Tatman & Roger W. Moss. 1984. lib. bdg. 110.00 (*0-8161-0437-9*, Hall Reference) Macmillan.

Biographical Dictionary of Psychology. Leonard Zusne. LC 83-18326. xxi, 563p. 1984. text ed. 115.00 (*0-313-24027-2*, ZDP/, Greenwood Pr) Greenwood.

Biographical Dictionary of Republican China, 4 vols. Ed. by Howard L. Boorman & Richard C. Howard. Incl. Vol. 1. Ai-Ch'u. LC 67-12006. 1967. text ed. 83.50 (*0-231-08955-4*); Vol. 3. Mao-Wu. LC 67-12006. 1970. text ed. 84.00 (*0-231-08957-0*); Vol. 4. Yang-Bibliography. LC 67-12006. 1971. text ed. 84.00 (*0-231-08958-9*); LC 67-12006. write for info. (*0-318-51404-4*) Col U Pr.

Biographical Dictionary of Republican China: A Personal Name Index, Vol. 5. Ed. by Howard L. Boorman & Janet Krompart. 1979. text ed. 84.00 (*0-231-04558-1*) Col U Pr.

Biographical Dictionary of Russian-Soviet Composers. Ed. by Allan Ho & Dmitry Feofanov. LC 88-34810. 764p. 1989. text ed. 105.00 (*0-313-24485-5*, FDR/, Greenwood Pr) Greenwood.

Biographical Dictionary of Scenographers: 500 B. C. to 1900 A. D. Robin T. Lacy. LC 90-14004. 784p. 1990. text ed. 99.50 (*0-313-27429-0*, LBD/, Greenwood Pr) Greenwood.

Biographical Dictionary of Science Fiction & Fantasy Artists. Robert Weinberg. LC 87-17651. 352p. 1988. text ed. 65.00 (*0-313-24349-2*, WFA/, Greenwood Pr) Greenwood.

***Biographical Dictionary of Scientists.** 2nd ed. Ed. by Roy Porter. (Illus.). 960p. 1994. text ed. 85.00 (*0-19-521083-2*) OUP.

Biographical Dictionary of Scrimshaw Artists in the Kendall Whaling Museum. Stuart M. Frank. (Museum Monograph Ser.). (Illus.). 34p. 1990. pap. text ed. 6.50 (*0-937854-28-X*) Kendall Whaling.

Biographical Dictionary of Social Welfare in America. Ed. by Walter I. Trattner. LC 85-9831. 911p. 1986. text ed. 145.00 (*0-313-23001-3*, TDW/, Greenwood Pr) Greenwood.

Biographical Dictionary of Soviet Dissidents. S. P. De Boer et al. 1982. lib. bdg. 355.00 (*90-247-2538-0*) Kluwer Ac.

Biographical Dictionary of the American Left. Ed. by Bernard K. Johnpoll & Harvey E. Klehr. LC 85-27252. 506p. 1986. text ed. 105.00 (*0-313-24200-3*, JDA/, Greenwood Pr) Greenwood.

Biographical Dictionary of the Board of Governors of the Federal Reserve. Ed. by Bernard S. Katz. LC 91-11329. 408p. 1991. text ed. 99.50 (*0-313-26658-1*, KBG/, Greenwood Pr) Greenwood.

Biographical Dictionary of the British Colonial Service, 1940-1966. Anthony Kirk-Greene. 420p. 1991. lib. bdg. 165.00 (*0-905450-96-5*, Pub. by H Zell Pubs UK) Bowker-Saur.

Biographical Dictionary of the Byzantine Empire. Donald M. Nicol. (Illus.). 156p. 39.95 (*1-85264-048-0*, Pub. by Seaby UK) Trafalgar.

Biographical Dictionary of the Comintern. rev. ed. Branko Lazitch & Milorad M. Drachkovitch. (Publication Ser.: No. 340). 550p. (C). 1986. text ed. 44.95 (*0-8179-8401-1*) Hoover Inst Pr.

Biographical Dictionary of the Common Law. Ed. by A. W. Simpson. 1984. 84.00 (*0-406-51657-X*, U.K.) Butterworth Legal Pubs.

Biographical Dictionary of the Confederacy. Jon L. Wakelyn. Ed. by Frank E. Vandiver. LC 72-13870. 601p. 1977. text ed. 85.00 (*0-8371-6124-X*, WCL, Greenwood Pr) Greenwood.

Biographical Dictionary of the Extreme Right since 1890. Philip Rees. 428p. 1991. 75.00 (*0-13-089301-3*) S&S Trade.

Biographical Dictionary of the Former Soviet Union. 2nd ed. Jeanne Vronskaya & Vladimir Chuguev. 661p. 1992. lib. bdg. 275.00 (*0-86291-621-6*) Bowker-Saur.

***Biographical Dictionary of the History of Technology.** Ed. by Ian McNeil & Lance Day. 800p. 1995. 125.00 (*0-415-06042-7*, B0378) Routledge.

Biographical Dictionary of the Middle East: 1900 to the Present. Yaacov Shimoni. 296p. 1992. lib. bdg. 40.00 (*0-8160-2458-8*) Facts on File.

Biographical Dictionary of the Saints: With a General Introduction on Hagiology. F. G. Holweck. LC 89-63016. xxix, 1053p. 1990. reprint ed. lib. bdg. 82.00 (*1-55888-846-2*) Omnigraphics Inc.

Biographical Dictionary of the Soviet Union: 1917-1992. 2nd ed. Jeanne Vronskaya & Vladimir Chuguev. 704p. 1992. lib. bdg. 275.00 (*0-685-39254-6*, Pub. by H Zell Pubs UK) Bowker-Saur.

***Biographical Dictionary of the Union.** Ed. by John T. Hubbell & James W. Geary. LC 94-46934. 696p. 1995. text ed. 99.50 (*0-313-20920-0*, Greenwood Pr) Greenwood.

Biographical Dictionary of the Virgin Islands: Selected Living & Deceased Persons, Vol. 1. Robert V. Vaughn. 151p. (Orig.). 1993. pap. text ed. 16.95 (*0-9627257-4-9*) Aye Aye Pr.

Biographical Dictionary of the Virgin Islands: Selected Living & Deceased Persons, Vol. 2. Robert V. Vaughn. (Orig.). 1995. pap. 16.95 (*0-9627257-7-3*) Aye Aye Pr.

Biographical Dictionary of the Youngs (Born 1600-1870) From Essex & Old Norfolk Counties, Massachusetts Bay Colony, Which Once Contained Parts of Present-Day Rockingham Co., NH. Louise R. Young. 413p. (Orig.). 1994. pap. text ed. 30.00 (*1-55613-949-7*) Heritage Bk.

Biographical Dictionary of World War I. Holger H. Herwig & Neil M. Heyman. LC 81-4242. (Illus.). xiv, 424p. 1982. text ed. 85.00 (*0-313-21356-9*, HBD/, Greenwood Pr) Greenwood.

Biographical Directory of American Colonial & Revolutionary Governors, 1607-1789. Ed. by John W. Raimo. LC 80-13279. 536p. 1980. text ed. 125.00 (*0-313-28133-5*, RAK/, Greenwood Pr) Greenwood.

Biographical Directory of American Territorial Governors. Thomas A. McMullin & David Walker. LC 84-9095. 350p. 1984. text ed. 79.50 (*0-313-28101-7*, MTN/, Greenwood Pr) Greenwood.

***Biographical Directory of Decision Makers in Russia & Successor States.** 704p. 1994. 152.00 (*0-582-20999-4*, Pub. by Longman UK) Longman.

Biographical Directory of Librarians in the Field of Slavic & East European Studies. Ed. by Peter A. Goy & Lawrence H. Miller. LC 67-28101. 97p. reprint ed. pap. 27.70 (*0-8357-7225-X*, 2001783) Bks Demand.

Biographical Directory of National Librarians. F. L. Carroll & P. Schwartz. 152p. 1989. text ed. 80.00 (*0-7201-1875-1*, Mansell Pub) Cassell.

***Biographical Directory of Native American Painters.** Ed. by Patrick D. Lester. LC 95-69012. 704p. 1995. 49.95 (*0-8061-9936-9*) U of Okla Pr.

***Biographical Directory of Native American Painters.** limited ed. Ed. by Patrick D. Lester. LC 95-69012. 704p. 1995. 245.00 (*0-9640706-3-4*) U of Okla Pr.

Biographical Directory of One Hundred Leading Soviet Officials. Alexander Rahr. 211p. (C). 1991. text ed. 51.50 (*0-8133-8015-4*) Westview.

Biographical Directory of the Eighth Air Force, 1942-1945: Command & Staff Officers. Russell A. Strong. 190p. 1985. pap. 26.00 (*0-89126-142-7*) MA-AH Pub.

Biographical Directory of the Executive Branch, 1774-1989. Ed. by Robert Sobel. LC 89-25779. 600p. 1990. text ed. 95.00 (*0-313-26593-3*, SBM/, Greenwood Pr) Greenwood.

Biographical Directory of the Governors of the United States, 1789-1978. Ed. by Robert Sobel. LC 77-10435. 1816p. 1988. text ed. 375.00 (*0-313-28093-2*, SXZ/, Greenwood Pr) Greenwood.

Biographical Directory of the Governors of the United States, 1978-1983. Ed. by John W. Raimo. LC 84-20717. 400p. 1985. text ed. 75.00 (*0-313-28098-3*, RBM/, Greenwood Pr) Greenwood.

Biographical Directory of the Governors of the United States, 1988-1993. Marie M. Mullaney. LC 93-37875. 425p. 1994. text ed. 75.00 (*0-313-28312-5*, Greenwood Pr) Greenwood.

Biographical Directory of the South Carolina House of Representatives, 4 vols., Vol. I: 1692-1973. Ed. by Walter Edgar & N. Louise Bailey. LC 73-13630. xiv, 842p. 1977. Vol. I, 1692-1973. 29.95 (*0-87249-304-0*) U of SC Pr.

Biographical Directory of the South Carolina House of Representatives, 4 vols., Vol. II: 1692-1775. Ed. by Walter Edgar & N. Louise Bailey. LC 73-13630. xiv, 842p. 1977. Vol. II, 1692-1775. 29.95 (*0-87249-350-4*) U of SC Pr.

Biographical Directory of the South Carolina House of Representatives, 4 vols., Vol. III: 1775-1790. Ed. by Walter Edgar & N. Louise Bailey. LC 73-13630. xiv, 842p. 1977. Vol. III, 1775-1790. 29.95 (*0-87249-406-3*) U of SC Pr.

Biographical Directory of the South Carolina House of Representatives, 4 vols., Vol. IV: 1791-1815. Ed. by Walter Edgar & N. Louise Bailey. LC 73-13630. xiv, 842p. 1977. Vol. IV, 1791-1815. 29.95 (*0-87249-439-X*) U of SC Pr.

Biographical Directory of the South Carolina House of Representatives, 1816-1828, Vol. V. Ed. by Alex Moore & Carolyn Quickmire. 384p. 1992. write for info. (*1-880067-07-2*) SC Dept of Arch & Hist.

Biographical Directory of the Tennessee General Assembly, 1901-1931. Ilene J. Cornwell. Vol. III. 1300p. 1988. write for info. (*0-318-61810-9*) TN Hist Comm.

Biographical Directory of the United States Congress, 1774-1989. 2115p. 1988. boxed 82.00 (*0-16-006384-1*, S/N 052-071-006) USGPO.

Biographical Directory of the United States Congress, 1774-1989, 4 vols., Set. 1992. lib. bdg. 1,995.75 (*0-8490-5255-6*) Gordon Pr.

Biographical Directory 1988. rev. ed. Ed. by American Political Science Association Staff. 607p. (C). 1988. pap. text ed. 20.00 (*0-915654-81-4*) Am Political.

Biographical Directory 1989. American Psychiatric Association Staff. LC 85-645241. 1956p. 1989. text ed. 137.50 (*0-89042-186-2*, 2185); pap. text ed. 93.50 (*0-89042-185-4*) Am Psychiatric.

Biographical Encyclopedia of Kentucky: Of the Dead & Living Men of the Ninteenth Century. Armstrong, J. M. Company Staff. 1978. reprint ed. 42.50 (*0-89308-193-0*) Southern Hist Pr.

Biographical Encyclopedia of Scientists. 2nd ed. Ed. by J. Daintith et al. 1100p. 1994. 190.00 (*0-7503-0287-9*) IOP Pub.

Biographical Encyclopedia of Scientists. 2nd ed. John Daintith. LC 93-48736. 1994. write for info. (*0-7503-0286-0*) IOP Pub.

Biographical Encyclopedia of the Negro Leagues. James Riley. (Illus.). 1280p. 1994. 39.50 (*0-7867-0065-3*) Carroll & Graf.

Biographical Essays. Lytton Strachey. LC 49-11684. 295p. 1969. reprint ed. pap. 6.95 (*0-15-612616-8*, Harvest Bks) HarBrace.

Biographical Essays on Twentieth-Century Percussionists. Geary Larrick. LC 92-18731. 336p. 1992. lib. bdg. 99.95 (*0-7734-9559-2*) E Mellen.

Biographical Essays, 1790-1890. Edward Boyle. LC 68-54331. (Essay Index Reprint Ser.). 1977. 20.95 (*0-8369-0237-8*) Ayer.

Biographical Gazetteer of Texas, 6 vols., Set. William Ming & Virginia Ming. (Orig.). 1988. pap. 117.00 (*0-317-93433-3*) W M Morrison.

Biographical Gazetteer of Texas, 6 vols., Vol. 1: A-B. William Ming & Virginia Ming. (Orig.). 1988. Vol. 1, A-B. pap. 19.50 (*0-685-74070-6*) W M Morrison.

Biographical Gazetteer of Texas, 6 vols., Vol. 2: C-F. William Ming & Virginia Ming. (Orig.). 1988. Vol. 2, C-F. pap. 19.50 (*0-685-74071-4*) W M Morrison.

Biographical Gazetteer of Texas, 6 vols., Vol. 3: G-J. William Ming & Virginia Ming. (Orig.). 1988. Vol. 3, G-J. pap. 19.50 (*0-685-74072-2*) W M Morrison.

Biographical Gazetteer of Texas, 6 vols., Vol. 4: K-M. William Ming & Virginia Ming. (Orig.). 1988. Vol. 4, K-M. pap. 19.50 (*0-685-74073-0*) W M Morrison.

Biographical Gazetteer of Texas, 6 vols., Vol. 5: N-Smiley. William Ming & Virginia Ming. (Orig.). 1988. Vol. 5, N-Smiley. pap. 19.50 (*0-685-74074-9*) W M Morrison.

Biographical Gazetteer of Texas, 6 vols., Vol. 6: Smith-Z. William Ming & Virginia Ming. (Orig.). 1988. Vol. 6, Smith-Z. pap. 19.50 (*0-685-74075-7*) W M Morrison.

Biographical Guide to the Divina Commedia of Dante. F. A. Locock. 1972. 59.95 (*0-87968-750-9*) Gordon Pr.

Biographical Guide to the Divinna Commedia. Frances Locock. LC 74-6466. (Studies in Dante: No. 9). 1974. lib. bdg. 49.95 (*0-8383-1986-6*) M S G Haskell Hse.

Biographical Handbook of Education: Five Hundred Contributions to the Field. Ann K. Nauman. 238p. 1985. pap. text ed. 16.95 (*0-8290-0722-9*) Irvington.

Biographical History of Baseball. David Dewey & Nicholas Acocella. 308p. 1995. 21.00 (*0-7867-0138-2*) Carroll & Graf.

Biographical History of Greene County, Pennsylvania. Samuel P. Bates. 338p. 1993. reprint ed. pap. 28.50 (*0-685-65700-0*, 390) Clearfield Co.

Biographical History of Lancaster County (Pennsylvania) Being a History of Eminent Men of the County. Alexander Harris. 638p. 1992. reprint ed. pap. 45.00 (*0-685-66229-2*, 2570) Clearfield Co.

Biographical History of Sir William Blackstone. D. Douglas. 489p. 1971. reprint ed. 35.00 (*0-8377-2025-7*) Rothman.

Biographical History of the French Revolution. J. Mills Whitham. LC 68-24860. (Essay Index Reprint Ser.). 1977. reprint ed. 22.95 (*0-8369-0989-5*) Ayer.

Biographical History of Tippecanoe, White, Jasper, Newton, Benton & Pulaski Counties, Indiana, 2 vols., Set. (Illus.). 1074p. 1992. reprint ed. lib. bdg. 99.50 (*0-8328-2563-8*) Higginson Bk Co.

Biographical History of Unarius, Vol. 1. Ruth Norman. (Illus.). 1985. 17.95 (*0-932642-57-8*) Unarius Acad Sci.

Biographical History of Unarius, Vol. 2. Ruth Norman. (Illus.). 1985. 17.95 (*0-932642-58-6*) Unarius Acad Sci.

Biographical Index of American Artists. Ralph C. Smith. 1973. 69.95 (*0-87968-751-7*) Gordon Pr.

Biographical Index to American Science: The Seventeenth Century to 1920. Comp. by Clark A. Elliott. LC 90-31735. (Bibliographies & Indexes in American History Ser.: No. 16). 336p. 1990. text ed. 75.00 (*0-313-26566-6*, EBI, Greenwood Pr) Greenwood.

Biographical Index to California & Western Artists. Edward L. Korb. LC 83-80368. 172p. 1983. 35.00 (*0-685-08462-0*) DeRu's Fine Art.

Biographical Index to California & Western Artists. Edward L. Korb. LC 83-80368. 172p. 1983. 35.00 (*0-685-09123-6*) Old Master Gallery Pr.

Biographical Index to Children's & Young Adult Authors & Illustrators: 1993 Edition. David V. Loertscher. 400p. 1993. ring bd. 55.00 (*0-931510-47-3*) Hi Willow.

Biographical Index to the History of England. S. Y. McMasters. 1973. 59.95 (*0-87968-752-5*) Gordon Pr.

Biographical Memoir of Adam Smith. Dugald Stewart. LC 66-15560. 1966. reprint ed. 45.00 (*0-678-00141-3*) Kelley.

Biographical Memoir of Daniel Boone. Timothy Flint. Ed. by James K. Folsom. (Masterworks of Literature Ser.). 1967. 16.95 (*0-8084-0061-4*); pap. 11.95x (*0-8084-0062-2*) NCUP.

Biographical Memoirs. Dugald Stewart. LC 78-72784. reprint ed. 48.50 (*0-404-17684-4*) AMS Pr.

Biographical Memoirs, Vol. 44. National Academy of Sciences Staff. xii, 370p. 1974. 29.50 (*0-309-02238-X*) Natl Acad Pr.

Biographical Memoirs, Vol. 45. National Academy of Sciences Staff. vii, 465p. 1974. 29.50 (*0-309-02239-8*) Natl Acad Pr.

Biographical Memoirs, Vol. 46. National Academy of Sciences Staff. 435p. 1975. 29.50 (*0-309-02240-1*) Natl Acad Pr.

Biographical Memoirs, Vol. 47. National Academy of Sciences Staff. 551p. 1975. 29.50 (*0-309-02245-2*) Natl Acad Pr.

Biographical Memoirs, Vol. 48. (Biographical Memoirs Ser.). 399p. 1976. 29.50 (*0-309-02349-1*) Natl Acad Pr.

Biographical Memoirs, Vol. 50. National Academy of Sciences Staff. 416p. 1979. text ed. 29.50 (*0-309-02549-4*) Natl Acad Pr.

Biographical Memoirs, Vol. 51. National Academy of Sciences Staff. 418p. 1980. text ed. 29.50 (*0-309-02888-4*) Natl Acad Pr.

Biographical Memoirs, Vol. 53. National Academy of Sciences Staff. 400p. 1982. text ed. 29.50 (*0-309-03287-3*) Natl Acad Pr.

Biographical Memoirs, Vol. 54. National Academy of Sciences Staff. 448p. 1983. text ed. 29.50 (*0-309-03391-8*) Natl Acad Pr.

764

An Asterisk (*) at the beginning of an entry indicates that the title is appearing in BIP for the first time.

TITLE INDEX

BIOGRAPHY AS THEOLOGY: HOW LIFE STORIES

Biographical Memoirs, Vol. 55. National Academy of Sciences Staff. LC 05-26629. 636p. reprint ed. pap. 180.00 (*0-7837-2594-9*, 2042757) Bks Demand.

Biographical Memoirs, Vol. 56. National Academy of Sciences Staff. 640p. 1987. text ed. 29.50 (*0-309-03693-3*) Natl Acad Pr.

Biographical Memoirs, Vol. 57. National Academy of Sciences. (Illus.). 560p. 1987. text ed. 29.50 (*0-309-03729-8*) Natl Acad Pr.

Biographical Memoirs, Vol. 58. National Academy of Sciences Staff. 556p. 1989. text ed. 29.50 (*0-309-03938-X*) Natl Acad Pr.

Biographical Memoirs, Vol. 59. National Academy of Sciences Staff. 500p. (C). 1990. text ed. 29.50 (*0-309-04198-8*) Natl Acad Pr.

Biographical Memoirs, Vol. 61. National Research Council, Office of the Home Secretary Staff. 512p. (C). 1992. text ed. 59.00 (*0-309-04746-3*) Natl Acad Pr.

Biographical Memoirs, Vol. 64. National Research Council, Office of the Home Secretary Staff. 500p. 1994. 59.00 (*0-309-04978-4*) Natl Acad Pr.

Biographical Memoirs, Vol. 65. National Academy of Sciences, Office of the Home Secretary Staff. 500p. 1994. 59.00 (*0-309-05037-5*) Natl Acad Pr.

Biographical Memoirs: Of Eminent Novelists, & Other Distinguished Persons. Walter D. Scott. LC 72-377. (Essay Index Reprint Ser.). 1977. reprint ed. 58.95 (*0-8369-2822-9*) Ayer.

Biographical Memoirs of Extraordinary Painters. William Beckford. Ed. by Robert J. Gemmett. LC 69-19434. (Illus.). 112p. 1975. 24.50 (*0-8386-7367-8*) Fairleigh Dickinson.

Biographical Memoirs of Extraordinary Painters (1780) William Beckford. Ed. by Philip Ward. (Language & Literature Ser.: Vol. 6). 1977. pap. 25.00 (*0-900891-13-0*) Oleander Pr.

Biographical Memoirs of Saint John Bosco, 14 vols., Set. Incl. Vol. I. G. B. Lemoyne et al. Tr. by Diego Borgatello. LC 65-3104. 415p. 1965. lib. bdg. 29.95 (*0-89944-001-0*); Vol. II. G. B. Lemoyne et al. Tr. by Diego Borgatello. LC 65-3104. 479p. 1966. lib. bdg. 29.95 (*0-89944-002-9*); Vol. III. G. B. Lemoyne et al. Tr. by Diego Borgatello. LC 65-3104. 502p. 1966. lib. bdg. 29.95 (*0-89944-003-7*); Vol. IV. G. B. Lemoyne et al. Tr. by Diego Borgatello. LC 65-3104. 697p. 1967. lib. bdg. 34.95 (*0-89944-004-5*); Vol. V. G. B. Lemoyne et al. Tr. by Diego Borgatello. LC 65-3104. 674p. 1969. lib. bdg. 34.95 (*0-89944-005-3*); Vol. VI. G. B. Lemoyne et al. Tr. by Diego Borgatello. LC 65-3104. 697p. 1971. lib. bdg. 34.95 (*0-89944-006-1*); Vol. VII. G. B. Lemoyne et al. Tr. by Diego Borgatello. LC 65-3104. 541p. 1972. lib. bdg. 34.95 (*0-89944-007-X*); Vol. VIII. G. B. Lemoyne et al. Tr. by Diego Borgatello. LC 65-3104. 468p. 1973. lib. bdg. 34.95 (*0-89944-008-8*); Vol. IX. G. B. Lemoyne et al. Tr. by Diego Borgatello. LC 65-3104. 503p. 1975. lib. bdg. 29.95 (*0-89944-009-6*); Vol. X. G. B. Lemoyne et al. Tr. by Diego Borgatello. LC 65-3104. 620p. 1977. lib. bdg. 29.95 (*0-89944-010-X*); Vol. XI. G. B. Lemoyne et al. Tr. by Diego Borgatello. LC 65-3104. 525p. 1964. lib. bdg. 34.95 (*0-89944-011-8*); Vol. XII. G. B. Lemoyne et al. Tr. by Diego Borgatello. LC 65-3104. 503p. 1980. lib. bdg. 29.95 (*0-89944-012-6*); Vol. XIII. G. B. Lemoyne et al. Tr. by Diego Borgatello. LC 65-3104. 725p. 1983. lib. bdg. 39.95 (*0-89944-013-4*); LC 65-3104. Orig. Title: Memorie Biografiche di Don Giovanni Bosco. 1898. Set lib. bdg. write for info. (*0-89944-000-2*) Don Bosco Multimedia.

Biographical Memoirs of Saint John Bosco, Vol. XIV (1879-80) Eugenio Ceria. Ed. by Diego Borgatello. LC 65-3104. 649p. 1985. 34.95 (*0-89944-014-2*) Don Bosco Multimedia.

Biographical Memoirs of Saint John Bosco, Vol. XV (1881-1882), Vol. XV. Eugenio Ceria. Ed. by Diego Borgatello. 1989. 34.95 (*0-89944-015-0*) Don Bosco Multimedia.

Biographical Memoirs of St. Clair County, Michigan. (Illus.). 695p. 1993. reprint ed. lib. bdg. 72.00 (*0-8328-3079-8*) Higginson Bk Co.

Biographical Memoirs, Vol. 60: 1991. National Academy of Sciences Staff. LC 05-26629. 429p. reprint ed. pap. 122.30 (*0-7837-3573-1*, 2043432) Bks Demand.

Biographical Notes Upon Botanists, 3 Vols, Set. Comp. by New York Botanical Garden Library Staff. 1974. lib. bdg. 370.00 (*0-8161-0695-9*, Hall Library) G K Hall.

Biographical Notice of Nicolo Paganini. Francois J. Fetis. LC 74-24081. (Illus.). reprint ed. 32.50 (*0-404-12909-9*) AMS Pr.

Biographical Process: Studies in the History & Psychology of Religion. Ed. by Frank E. Reynolds & Donald Capps. (Religion & Reason, Method & Theory in the Study & Interpretation of Religion Ser.: No. 11). 1976. text ed. 75.40 (*90-279-7522-1*) Mouton.

Biographical Questionnaires of One Hundred & Fifty Prominent Tennesseans. Ed. by Colleen M. Elliott & John T. Moore. 400p. 1982. 20.00 (*0-89308-222-8*) Southern Hist Pr.

***Biographical Record of Boone County, Iowa.** (Illus.). 664p. 1993. lib. bdg. 67.50 (*0-8328-3533-1*) Higginson Bk Co.

***Biographical Record of Whiteside County.** (Illus.). 522p. 1995. reprint ed. lib. bdg. 52.50 (*0-8328-4596-5*) Higginson Bk Co.

Biographical Rectory of the Council of Economic Advisers. Ed. by Robert Sobel & Bernard S. Katz. LC 86-14984. 320p. 1988. text ed. 65.00 (*0-313-22554-0*, SEA/, Greenwood Pr) Greenwood.

Biographical Register of Members, Virginia State Convention of 1861: First Session. William H. Gaines, Jr. LC 74-628577. 87p. 1969. pap. 7.95 (*0-88490-059-2*) VA State Lib.

Biographical Register of the University of Oxford to AD 1500 Vol. 2: F to O. A. B. Emden. 774p. 1989. 140.00 (*0-19-951563-8*) OUP.

Biographical Register of the University of Oxford to AD 1500 Vol. 3: P to Z. A. B. Emden. 874p. 1989. 175.00 (*0-19-951564-6*) OUP.

Biographical Register of the University of Oxford to AD 1500, Vol. 1: A to E. A. B. Emden. 722p. 1989. 140.00 (*0-19-951562-X*) OUP.

Biographical Review of the Leading Citizens of Hampshire County, Massachusetts. (Illus.). 580p. 1993. reprint ed. lib. bdg. 59.50 (*0-8328-3080-1*) Higginson Bk Co.

***Biographical Roster of the Immortal 600: Foreign Language Translation from What Language.** Mauriel P. Joslyn. 232p. (Orig.). (C). 1995. pap. 25.00 (*0-942597-98-2*) White Mane Pub.

Biographical Sketch & Essays. I. M. Sechenov. LC 73-3028. (Classics in Psychology Ser.). 1977. reprint ed. 19.95 (*0-405-05161-1*) Ayer.

Biographical Sketch of C. H. Spurgeon. Ken Connolly. 1990. pap. 2.50 (*1-56186-418-8*) Pilgrim Pubns.

Biographical Sketch of G. Campbell Morgan. Silas Chan. (CHI.). 1984. pap. write for info. (*0-941598-21-7*) Living Spring Pubns.

Biographical Sketch of the Life of the Late Captain Michael Cresap with Notes & Appendix. John J. Jacob. LC 73-146404. (First American Frontier Ser.). 1971. reprint ed. 25.95 (*0-405-02863-6*) Ayer.

Biographical Sketches. Nassau W. Senior. LC 72-452. (Essay Index Reprint Ser.). 1977. reprint ed. 31.95 (*0-8369-2824-5*) Ayer.

Biographical Sketches & Records of the Ezra Olin Family. G. S. Nye. 441p. 1989. reprint ed. lib. bdg. 78.50 (*0-8328-0920-9*); reprint ed. pap. 68.50 (*0-8328-0921-7*) Higginson Bk Co.

Biographical Sketches of Gen. Pat Cleburne & T.C. Hindman. Charles E. Nash. (Illus.). 1977. 17.50 (*0-89029-039-3*) Morningside Bkshop.

Biographical Sketches of Joseph Smith, the Prophet & His Progenitors for Many Generations. Lucy M. Smith. LC 73-83439. (Religion in America, Ser. 1). 1971. reprint ed. 18.95 (*0-405-00264-5*) Ayer.

Biographical Sketches of Loyalists of the American Revolution. Gregory Palmer. LC 83-12137. 1200p. 1984. text ed. 395.00 (*0-313-28102-5*, PBL/, Greenwood Pr) Greenwood.

***Biographical Sketches of Loyalists of the American Revolution, 2 vols., Set.** Lorenzo Sabine. 1208p. 1994. pap. 80.00 (*0-614-00879-4*, 5070) Clearfield Co.

Biographical Sketches of Prominent Negro Men & Women of Kentucky. William D. Johnson. (Illus.). 1977. 16.95 (*0-8369-9225-3*, 9079) Ayer.

Biographical Sketches of Richard Ellis, the First Settler of Ashfield, Mass. & His Descendants. E. R. Ellis. (Illus.). 483p. 1989. reprint ed. lib. bdg. 71.50 (*0-8328-0514-9*); reprint ed. pap. 61.50 (*0-8328-0515-7*) Higginson Bk Co.

Biographical Sketches of the Bench & Bar of South Carolina, 2 vols., Set. John B. O'Neall. Incl. Vol. 1. LC 75-1159. 470p. 1975. 22.50 (*0-87152-198-9*); Vol. 2. LC 75-1159. 620p. 1975. 22.50 (*0-87152-199-7*); LC 75-1159. 1975. reprint ed. 45.00 (*0-87152-300-0*) Reprint.

***Biographical Sketches of the Prophet Joseph Smith & His Progenitors.** Lucy M. Smith. 297p. (C). 1994. 24.95 (*0-910523-17-7*) Grandin Bk Co.

Biographical Sketches of Those Who Attended Harvard College in the Classes 1690-1771. Clifford K. Shipton. Incl. Vol. 4. 1975. (*0-934909-39-3*); Vol. 5. 1975. (*0-934909-40-7*); Vol. 6. 1975. (*0-934909-41-5*); Vol. 7. 1975. (*0-934909-42-3*); Vol. 8. 1975. (*0-934909-43-1*); Vol. 9. 1975. (*0-934909-44-X*); Vol. 10. 1975. (*0-934909-45-8*); Vol. 11. 1975. (*0-934909-46-6*); Vol. 12. 1975. (*0-934909-47-4*); Vol. 13. 1975. (*0-934909-48-2*); Vol. 14. 1975. (*0-934909-49-0*); Vol. 15. 1975. (*0-934909-50-4*); Vol. 16. 1975. (*0-934909-51-2*); Vol. 17. 1975. (*0-934909-52-0*); (Sibley's Harvard Graduates Ser.: Vols. 4-17). (Illus.). 650p. 1975. 40.00 (*0-685-03315-5*) Mass Hist Soc.

Biographical Sources in the Sciences: A Source Guide. 1991. lib. bdg. 250.00 (*0-8490-4857-5*) Gordon Pr.

Biographical Studies. Walter Bagehot. Ed. by Richard H. Hutton. LC 75-111469. (BCL Ser.: No. I). reprint ed. 21.50 (*0-404-00445-8*) AMS Pr.

Biographical Studies in Modern Indian Education. Henry V. Hampton. LC 78-136647. (Biography Index Reprint Ser.). 1977. 23.95 (*0-8369-8042-5*) Ayer.

Biographical Truth: The Representation of Historical Persons in Tudor-Stuart Writing. Judith H. Anderson. LC 83-14520. 243p. 1984. 35.00x (*0-300-03085-1*) Yale U Pr.

Biographical Works of Gregory of Nyssa. Ed. by Andreas Spira. LC 84-81655. (Patristic Monograph: No. 12). viii, 274p. pap. 12.00 (*0-915646-11-0*) N Amer Patristic Soc.

Biographie, Briefe und Schriften. Georg F. Handel. 219p. 1977. reprint ed. write for info. (*3-487-06331-X*, Pub. by Georg Olms GW) Lubrecht & Cramer.

Biographie d'Empedocle. Joseph Bidez. (Recueil de Travaux Publies par la Faculte de Philosophie et Lettres de l'Universite de Gande Ser.: No. 12). xii, 176p. 1973. reprint ed. lib. bdg. 25.87 (*3-487-04664-4*, Pub. by Georg Olms GW) Lubrecht & Cramer.

Biographie Friedrich Hebbels, 2 Vols, Set. Emil Kuh. reprint ed. 135.00 (*0-404-03784-4*) AMS Pr.

Biographie Legendaire D'Achille. Monique Roussel. x, 505p. (FRE.). 1991. pap. 79.00 (*90-256-0993-7*, Pub. by A M Hakkert SP) Benjamins North Am.

Biographie Luxembourgeoise, 3 vols., Set. Auguste Neyen. lii, 1463p. 1973. reprint ed. write for info. (*3-487-04295-9*, Pub. by Georg Olms GW) Lubrecht & Cramer.

Biographie Medicale par Ordre Cronologique, 2 Vols., Set. A. L. Bayle & A. J. Thillaye. 1510p. reprint ed. lib. bdg. 147.50 (*90-6078-015-9*, Pub. by B M Israel NE) Coronet Bks.

Biographie von Ludwig van Beethoven, 2 pts. in 1. Anton Schindler. xxv, 645p. 1970. reprint ed. write for info. (*0-318-71946-0*, Pub. by Georg Olms GW) Lubrecht & Cramer.

Biographie W. A. Mozarts. Georg N. Nissen. (Olms Paperbacks Ser.: Vol. 37). 1991. write for info. (*3-487-06076-0*, Pub. by Georg Olms GW); pap. write for info. (*3-487-04548-6*, Pub. by Georg Olms GW) Lubrecht & Cramer.

Biographies for Birdwatchers: The Lives of Those Commemorated in Western Palearctic Bird Names. Barbara Mearns & Richard Mearns. (Books about Birds). 490p. 1988. text ed. 39.95 (*0-12-487422-3*) Acad Pr.

Biographies Literature Set, 6 stories. L. Johnson. (Graphic Learning Literature Program Ser.). (Illus.). (ENG & SPA.). 1992. 225.00 (*0-87746-310-7*) Graphic Learning.

***Biographies of Alaska-Yukon Pioneers 1850-1950.** Ed Ferrell. 355p. (Orig.). 1994. pap. text ed. 24.00 (*0-7884-0087-8*) Heritage Bk.

Biographies of American Women: An Annotated Bibliography. Patricia E. Sweeney. 290p. 1990. lib. bdg. 75.00 (*0-87436-070-6*) ABC-CLIO.

Biographies of British Women. Patricia E. Sweeney. 300p. 1993. lib. bdg. 75.00 (*0-87436-628-3*) ABC-CLIO.

Biographies of Child Development: The Mental Growth Careers of Eight-Four Infants & Children. Arnold L. Gesell et al. LC 74-21409. (Classics in Child Development Ser.). (Illus.). 350p. 1978. reprint ed. 34.95 (*0-405-06461-6*) Ayer.

Biographies of Creative Artists: An Annotated Bibliography. Susan M. Stievater. LC 91-8008. 222p. 1991. 28.00 (*0-8240-4948-9*, H1185) Garland.

Biographies of Distinguished Scientific Men. Francois Arago. Tr. by W. H. Smyth et al. LC 72-39662. (Essay Index Reprint Ser.). 1977. reprint ed. 58.95 (*0-8369-2737-0*) Ayer.

***Biographies of Franklin, Jefferson, Washington, Crawford, & Gasconade Counties, MO.** Goodspeed Publishing Co. Staff. (Illus.). 478p. 1995. reprint ed. pap. text ed. 30.00 (*0-7884-0187-4*) Heritage Bk.

Biographies of Gender & Hermaphroditism in Paired Comparisons: Clinical Supplement to the Handbook of Sexology. J. Money. 388p. 1991. 262.00 (*0-444-81403-5*); pap. 60.00 (*0-444-89129-3*) Elsevier.

Biographies of Judges of Louisiana. J. C. Fruge. 1971. text ed. 12.50 (*0-685-42088-4*) Claitors.

Biographies of Rasik Saints. rev. ed. Swami P. Saraswati. (Illus.). 160p. reprint ed. pap. 10.00 (*1-881921-00-X*) Intl Soc Divine Love.

Biographies of Scientists for Sci-Tech Libraries: Adding Faces. Ed. by Tony Stankus. LC 91-31241. (Science & Technology Libraries). (Illus.). 232p. 1991. lib. bdg. 39.95 (*1-56024-214-0*) Haworth Pr.

Biographies of Shakespeare, Pope, Goethe, & Schiller. Thomas De Quincey. LC 75-164822. (Illus.). reprint ed. 42.50 (*0-404-02079-8*) AMS Pr.

Biographies of the Dalai Lamas. Ya Hanzhang. Tr. by Wang Wenjiong. (Illus.). 442p. 1991. 20.15 (*7-119-01267-3*, 11E-2534S) Cypress Co.

***Biographies of Western Photographers: A Reference Tool for Historians & Collectors.** Carl Mautz et al. (Illus.). 500p. 1995. 85.00 (*0-9621940-7-7*) C Mautz Pubng.

***Biographies of Western Photographers: A Reference Tool for Historians & Collectors.** Carl Mautz et al. (Illus.). 500p. 1995. pap. 50.00 (*0-9621940-8-5*) C Mautz Pubng.

Biographies of Words & the Home of the Aryas. Friedrich M. Muller. (C). 1987. reprint ed. 22.00 (*81-206-0299-4*, Pub. by Asian Educ Servs II) S Asia.

Biographisch-bibliographisches Handbuch der Lichenologie. Nach dem Tode des Verfassers ed. by O. Klement. V. Grumann. 1979. lib. bdg. 150.00 (*3-7682-0907-5*) Lubrecht & Cramer.

Biographisch-Literarisches Lexikon der Katholischen Deutschen Dichter, Volks- und Jugendschriftsteller Im 19 Jahrhundert, 2 vols., Set. Joseph Kehrein. 1983. fiche write for info. (*0-318-71921-5*, Pub. by Georg Olms GW) Lubrecht & Cramer.

Biographisch-Litterarisches Lexikon Fur die Haupt- und Residenzstadt Konigsberg und Ostpreuben. Julius N. Weisfert. iv, 259p. 1975. reprint ed. write for info. (*3-487-05657-7*, Pub. by Georg Olms GW) Lubrecht & Cramer.

***Biographisches Handbuch der deutschsprachigen wirtschaftswissenschaftlichen Emigration nach 1933, 2.** 1995. write for info. (*3-598-11284-X*) K G Saur.

***Biographisches Handbuch der SB2, 2.** 1996. write for info. (*3-598-11130-4*) K G Saur.

***Biographisches Handbuch der SB2: Bd 1: A-L, 1.** 1995. write for info. (*3-598-11176-2*) K G Saur.

***Biographisches Handbuch der SB2: Bd 2: M-Z, 2.** 1995. write for info. (*3-598-11177-0*) K G Saur.

Biographisches Lexikon der Hervorragenden: Aertze Aller Zeiten und Voelker Sambucus-Zypen, 6 vols., Set. 3rd ed. A. Hirsch. (GER.). 1962. 215.00 (*0-8288-6802-6*, M-7048) Fr & Eur.

Biographisches Lexikon der Hervorragenden Aerzte der Letzten Feunfzig Jahre, 1880-1930: Aaser-Komoto, 2 vols., Set. 3rd ed. J. Fischer. (GER.). 1962. 495.00 (*0-8288-6801-8*, M-7311) Fr & Eur.

***Biographisches Lexikon der Psychoanalyse.** Elke Muhleitner. 400p. (GER.). 1992. 125.00 (*0-7859-8542-5*, 3892955573) Fr & Eur.

Biographisches Lexikon Fur das Gebiet Zwischen Inn und Salzach. Max Furst. 1983. fiche write for info. (*0-318-71903-7*, Pub. by Georg Olms GW) Lubrecht & Cramer.

Biographisches Lexikon hervorragender Aerzte des 19, Jahrhunderts mit Einer historischen Einleitung. J. L. Pagel. (Illus.). xxxii, 998p. 1989. reprint ed. 233.75 (*3-8055-4817-6*) S Karger.

Biographisches Woerterbuch zur Deutschen Geschichte: Biographical Dictionary of German History, 3 vols., Set. Karl Bosl. (GER.). 1973. 595.00 (*0-8288-6232-X*, M7312) Fr & Eur.

***Biography.** Garrett Christopher. Ed. by J. Friedland & R. Kessler. (Novel-Ties Ser.). (J). (gr. 4-7). 1987. student ed, pap. text ed. 15.95 (*0-88122-866-4*) Lrn Links.

***Biography.** Parke. 1995. text ed. 22.95 (*0-8057-0965-7*) Macmillan.

Biography. Henry A. Peirce. 25p. 1983. pap. 2.00 (*0-87770-160-1*) Ye Galleon.

***Biography.** Carl Rollyson. (Magill Bibliographies Ser.). 215p. 1992. 40.00 (*0-8108-2803-0*) Scarecrow.

Biography see Popeiana

***Biography & Aging: Explorations in Adult Development.** Ed. by James E. Birren et al. (Illus.). 344p. 1995. write for info. (*0-8261-8980-6*) Springer Pub.

Biography & Bibliography of Shakespeare. Henry G. Bohn. LC 74-38033. reprint ed. 49.50 (*0-404-00920-4*) AMS Pr.

Biography & Books. LC 85-600291. 75p. 1986. 5.95 (*0-8444-0520-5*) Lib Congress.

Biography & Family Record of Lorenzo Snow. Eliza R. Smith. 1975. reprint ed. 15.00 (*0-914740-15-6*) Western Epics.

Biography & Genealogy Master Index, 8 vols., Set. 2nd ed. Ed. by Miranda C. Herbert & Barbara McNeil. (Biographical Index Ser.: No. 1). 5860p. 1981. 975.00 (*0-8103-1094-5*) Gale.

Biography & Genealogy Master Index, 1981-1982, 3 Vols. 81th rev. ed. Ed. by Miranda C. Herbert & Barbara McNeil. 2064p. 1982. 305.00 (*0-8103-1095-3*) Gale.

Biography & Genealogy Master Index, 1981-85, 5 vols., Set. Ed. by Barbara McNeil. 4423p. 1985. 925.00 (*0-8103-1506-8*) Gale.

Biography & Genealogy Master Index 1983, 2 Vols., Set. Ed. by Miranda C. Herbert & Barbara McNeil. (Biographical Index Ser.: No. 1). 1592p. 1983. 305.00 (*0-8103-1509-2*) Gale.

Biography & Genealogy Master Index 1984. Ed. by Barbara McNeil. 936p. 1984. 305.00 (*0-8103-1508-4*) Gale.

Biography & Genealogy Master Index 1985. Ed. by Barbara McNeil. 664p. 1985. 305.00 (*0-8103-1507-6*) Gale.

Biography & Genealogy Master Index, 1986. Ed. by Barbara McNeil. 650p. 1986. 305.00 (*0-8103-1511-4*) Gale.

Biography & Genealogy Master Index, 1986-1990: Cumulation of Supplements, 3 vols., Set. Ed. by Barbara McNeil. 3600p. 1990. 925.00 (*0-8103-4803-9*) Gale.

Biography & Genealogy Master Index, 1987. Ed. by Barbara McNeil. 823p. 1986. 305.00 (*0-8103-1513-0*) Gale.

Biography & Genealogy Master Index, 1988. Ed. by Barbara McNeil. 1080p. 1987. 305.00 (*0-8103-1514-9*) Gale.

Biography & Genealogy Master Index, 1989. Ed. by Barbara McNeil. 1988. 305.00 (*0-8103-2794-5*) Gale.

Biography & Genealogy Master Index, 1990. Barbara McNeil. 1100p. 1989. 305.00 (*0-8103-4800-4*) Gale.

Biography & Genealogy Master Index, 1991. Ed. by Barbara McNeil. 1200p. 1990. 305.00 (*0-8103-4801-2*) Gale.

Biography & Genealogy Master Index, 1992. Barbara McNeil. 1991. 305.00 (*0-8103-4802-0*) Gale.

Biography & Genealogy Master Index, 1993. Barbara McNeil. 1992. 305.00 (*0-8103-7605-9*) Gale.

Biography & Genealogy Master Index, 1994. Barbara McNeil. 1993. 305.00 (*0-8103-8021-8*) Gale.

Biography & Genealogy Master Index 91-95 Cumulation, 3 Vols. 1994. 925.00 (*0-8103-5516-7*) Gale.

Biography & Genealogy Master Index 91-95 Cumulation, Vol. 1. 95th ed. 1994. write for info. (*0-8103-8343-8*) Gale.

Biography & Genealogy Master Index 91-95 Cumulation, Vol. 2. 95th ed. 1994. write for info. (*0-8103-8344-6*) Gale.

Biography & Genealogy Master Index 91-95 Cumulation, Vol. 3. 95th ed. 1994. write for info. (*0-8103-8345-4*) Gale.

***Biography & Source Studies, 2 vols., Set.** Ed. by Frederick R. Karl. 1995. 99.00 (*0-404-63410-9*) AMS Pr.

***Biography & Source Studies, Vol. 1.** Ed. by Frederick R. Karl. 1994. 49.50 (*0-404-63411-7*) AMS Pr.

***Biography & Source Studies, Vol. 2.** Ed. by Frederick R. Karl. 1995. 49.50 (*0-404-63412-5*) AMS Pr.

Biography & the Human Heart. Gamaliel Bradford. LC 68-58772. (Essay Index Reprint Ser.). 1977. 21.95 (*0-8369-1023-0*) Ayer.

Biography & Truth. Stanley Weintraub. LC 67-28300. (Composition & Rhetoric Ser.). 1967. pap. 2.50 (*0-672-60901-0*, CR15, Bobbs) Macmillan.

Biography As High Adventure: Life-Writers Speak on Their Art. Ed. by Stephen B. Oates. LC 85-20847. 160p. (Orig.). 1986. lib. bdg. 22.50 (*0-87023-513-3*); pap. 11.95 (*0-87023-514-1*) U of Mass Pr.

Biography as History. Stephen B. Oates. LC 90-63742. (Charles Edmondson Historical Lectures). 37p. (Orig.). 1991. pap. text ed. 4.50 (*0-918954-54-1*) Baylor Univ Pr.

Biography As Theology: How Life Stories Can Remake Today's Theology. rev. ed. James W. McClendon, Jr. LC 90-49778. 224p. (C). 1990. pap. 13.95 (*0-334-02482-X*) TPI PA.

An Asterisk (*) at the beginning of an entry indicates that the title is appearing in BIP for the first time.

B

***Biography Authors Handbook.** 200p. (C). 1995. 135.00 (0-7605-1620-0) Rector Pr.

Biography East & West. Ed. by Carol Ramelb. (Literary Studies: East & West: No. 3). 256p. (Orig.). 1990. pap. text ed. 18.00 (0-8248-1284-0) UH Pr.

Biography, Elizabeth Swift Brengle. Eileen Douglas. 1990. reprint ed. 5.95 (0-86544-060-3) Salv Army Suppl South.

***Biography for Beginners.** Ed. by Laurie L. Harris. (J). 1995. lib. bdg. 40.00x (0-7808-0091-5) Omnigraphics Inc.

***Biography for Beginners: Sketches for Early Readers.** Ed. by Laurie L. Harris. (J). 1995. lib. bdg. 40.00x (0-7808-0064-8) Omnigraphics Inc.

***Biography for Beginners: Sketches for Early Readers.** Ed. by Laurie L. Harris. (J). 1995. lib. bdg. 40.00x (0-7808-0065-6) Omnigraphics Inc.

***Biography Handbook.** 300p. (C). 1995. 155.00 (0-7605-1619-7) Rector Pr.

Biography, Identity & Schooling: Episodes in Educational Research. Ivor F. Goodson & Rob Walker. 232p. 1990. pap. 31.00 (1-85000-802-7, Falmer Pr) Taylor & Francis.

Biography in Late Antiquity: A Quest for the Holy Man. Patricia Cox. LC 82-4946. (Transformation of the Classical Heritage Ser.: Vol. V). 208p. 1983. 45.00 (0-520-04612-9) U CA Pr.

Biography in Waldorf Education. Willi Aeppli. Tr. by Angelika V. Ritscher. 1987. pap. 3.50 (0-88010-165-2) Anthroposophic.

Biography Index: 1946-994. LC 47-6532. 190.00 (0-685-73471-4) Wilson.

***Biography Monograph Ser. A Glossary of Terms in Biography, Autobiography, & Related Forms.** 2nd ed. Donald J. Winslow. LC 94-40735. (Biography Monograph Ser.). 112p. (C). 1995. pap. text ed. 13.00x (0-8248-1713-3) UH Pr.

Biography of a Baby. Milicent W. Shinn. 256p. 1985. pap. 8.61 (0-201-16466-3) Addison-Wesley.

Biography of a Baby. Milicent W. Shinn. LC 74-21427. (Classics in Child Development Ser.). 256p. 1975. reprint ed. 24.95 (0-405-06476-4) Ayer.

Biography of a Business, 1792-1942: Insurance Company of North America. Marquis James. LC 75-43409. (Companies & Men: Business Enterprises in America Ser.). (Illus.). 1976. reprint ed. 46.95 (0-405-08079-4) Ayer.

Biography of a Century & Other Poems. Leon L. Lerner. 80p. 1976. pap. 8.95 (0-9607964-1-X) Galaxy Pr MD.

Biography of a Grizzly. Ernest T. Seton. (Illus.). 167p. (YA). 1994. pap. 12.95 (1-885529-02-3) Stevens Pub.

Biography of a Grizzly. Ernest T. Seton. LC 87-10887. (Illus.). 167p. 1987. reprint ed. pap. 9.95 (0-8032-9184-1, Bison Books) U of Nebr Pr.

Biography of a Legal Dispute. Franklin. 1968. pap. text ed. 11.50 (0-88277-408-5) Foundation Pr.

***Biography of a Man-Beast.** Raymond Way. 1995. 13.95 (0-8062-5133-6) Carlton.

Biography of a Progressive: Franklin K. Lane, 1864-1920. Keith W. Olson. LC 78-57766. (Contributions in American History Ser.: No. 78). 233p. 1979. text ed. 59. 95 (0-313-20613-9, OBP/, Greenwood Pr) Greenwood.

Biography of a River: The Mississippi. Edith McCall. (Illus.). (YA). (gr. 7 up). 1990. 16.95 (0-8027-6914-4); lib. bdg. 17.85 (0-8027-6915-2) Walker & Co.

Biography of a River Town: Memphis--Its Heroic Age. 2nd deluxe limited ed. Gerald M. Capers, Jr. (Illus.). 318p. 1980. reprint ed. 27.95 (0-937130-10-9) Burke's Bk Store.

Biography of a River Town: Memphis--Its Heroic Age. 2nd ed. Gerald M. Capers, Jr. (Illus.). 318p. 1980. reprint ed. 17.95 (0-937130-09-5) Burke's Bk Store.

Biography of a Runaway Slave. Miguel Barnet. Tr. by W. Nick Hill. 224p. 1994. reprint ed. pap. 11.95 (1-880684-18-7) Curbstone.

Biography of a Small Town. Elvin Hatch. LC 79-313. 1979. text ed. 50.00 (0-231-04694-4) Col U Pr.

Biography of a Tree. James P. Jackson. LC 77-2818. (Illus.). 1979. 12.50 (0-8246-0216-1) Jonathan David.

Biography of a Yogi. Swami Satyeswarananda Giri. (Illus.). 206p. (Orig.). 1985. pap. write for info. (0-318-65288-9) Sanskrit Classics.

Biography of Ahjan Man. Ruth-Inge Heinze. (Asian Folklore & Social Life Monographs: No. 89). 12.00 (0-89986-296-9) Oriental Bk Store.

Biography of Alice B. Toklas. Linda Simon. LC 91-16848. (Illus.). xvi, 427p. 1991. reprint ed. pap. 12.95 (0-8032-9203-1, Bison Books) U of Nebr Pr.

Biography of an Archangel: The Accomplishments of Uriel. Ruth Norman. (Illus.). 365p. 1989. 24.95 (0-935097-19-8) Unarius Acad Sci.

Biography of an Idea. Ruth N. Anshen. 240p. (Orig.). 1987. reprint ed. pap. 9.95 (0-918825-57-1) Moyer Bell.

Biography of an Idea: John Maynard Keynes & the General Theory of Employment, Interest & Money. David Felix. LC 93-39855. 300p. (C). 1994. 34.95 (1-56000-149-6) Transaction Pubs.

Biography of an Institution: The Civil Service Commission of Canada, 1908-1967. J. E. Hodgetts et al. (Canadian Public Administration Ser.). 540p. 1972. pap. 15.95 (0-7735-0159-2, Pub. by McGill CN) U of Toronto Pr.

Biography of an Institution: The Civil Service Commission of Canada, 1908-1967. J. E. Hodgetts. LC 72-87185. (Canadian Public Administration Ser.). 544p. reprint ed. pap. 155.10 (0-7837-6913-X, 2046743) Bks Demand.

Biography of an Island: General C. C. Pinckney's Sea Island Plantation. Merrill G. Christophersen. Ed. by John E. Westburg. LC 76-18611. (Illus.). 1976. pap. 10.00 (0-87423-020-9) Westburg.

Biography of Arthur Diosy, Founder of the Japan Society: Home to Japan. John Adlard. LC 91-4247. (Japanese Studies: Vol. 2). 188p. 1991. lib. bdg. 79.95 (0-7734-9758-7) E Mellen.

Biography of Britain's First Professional Mycologist, Mordecai Cubitt Cooke: Victorian Naturalist, Mycologist, Teacher & Eccentric. Mary P. English. (Illus.). xviii, 349p. 1987. lib. bdg. 45.00 (0-948737-02-6) Lubrecht & Cramer.

Biography of Bruce Lee. Robert Clouse. (Illus.). 200p. (Orig.). 1988. pap. 12.95 (0-86568-133-3, 144) Unique Pubns.

Biography of Calvin. Ed. by Richard C. Gamble. LC 92-31346. (Articles on Calvin & Calvinism Ser.: Vol. 1). 184p. 1992. 37.00 (0-8153-1042-0) Garland.

Biography of Cancer. O. Cameron Gruner. 22p. 1961. spiral bd. 2.75 (0-7873-0361-5) Mokelumne.

Biography of Cesar Moro: Signatary of the Surrealist Manifesto. Andre Coyne. 1990. write for info. (0-318-67003-8) Extramares Edit.

Biography of Christopher Merkley: Written by Himself. Christopher Merkley. LC 70-38363. (Select Bibliographies Reprint Ser.). 1977. reprint ed. 16.95 (0-8369-6780-1) Ayer.

Biography of Edgard Varese. Fernand Quellette. (Illus.). xiv, 270p. 1981. reprint ed. lib. bdg. 27.50 (0-306-76103-3) Da Capo.

Biography of Eld. Barton Warren Stone, Written by Himself: With Additions & Reflections. Barton W. Stone. LC 79-38463. (Religion in America, Ser. 2). 476p. 1972. reprint ed. 29.95 (0-405-04089-X) Ayer.

Biography of Fr. Alexander Menn: A Modern Saint of Russia. Y. Montand. Tr. by Steven Bigham. 150p. 1995. write for info. (1-879038-12-9) Oakwood Pubns.

Biography of Frances Slocum, the Lost Sister of Wyoming: A Complete Narrative of Her Captivity & Wanderings Among the Indians. John F. Meginness. LC 74-3963. (Women in America Ser.). 260p. 1977. reprint ed. 23.95 (0-405-06112-9) Ayer.

Biography of Francis Schlatter, the Healer. Harry B. Magill. 198p. 1968. reprint ed. spiral bd. 4.95 (0-7873-0580-4) Mokelumne.

Biography of Francis Schlatter, the Healer: Life, Works & Wanderings - 5000 Healings a Day. H. B. Magill. 1991. lib. bdg. 75.95 (0-8490-4130-9) Gordon Pr.

Biography of George F. Kennan: The Education of a Realist. Michael Polley. LC 89-27727. (Studies in Twentieth Century American History: Vol. 4). 256p. 1990. lib. bdg. 89.95 (0-88946-693-9) E Mellen.

Biography of Gerald R. Ford. L. David LeRoy. 1974. 4.75 (0-87948-036-X) Beatty.

Biography of Gerry Adams. Colm Keena. 175p. (Orig.). 1990. pap. 14.95 (0-85342-906-5, Pub. by Mercier Pr IE) Dufour.

Biography of Gospel Song & Hymn Writers. Jacob H. Hall. LC 70-144626. reprint ed. 49.50 (0-404-07226-7) AMS Pr.

Biography of Henry Green. Jeremy Treglow. Date not set. write for info. (0-679-43303-1) Random.

Biography of Henry Stimson. Godfrey Hodgson. 1988. write for info. (0-670-81226-9) Viking Penguin.

Biography of Herman Melville. Robertson-Lorant Laurie. 1995. 35.00 (0-517-59314-9) Crown Pub Group.

Biography of Homicide. Poulos. 1976. pap. text ed. 19.25 (0-88277-421-2) Foundation Pr.

Biography of Hutton see System of the Earth, 1785

Biography of James G. Blaine. Mary A. Dodge. (Notable American Authors Ser.). 1992. reprint ed. lib. bdg. 75.00 (0-7812-2663-5) Rprt Serv.

Biography of James Parker, Colonial Printer: 1715-1770. Alan Dyer. LC 80-52545. 441p. 1982. 32.50 (0-87875-202-1) Whitston Pub.

Biography of John Buchan & His Sister Anna: The Personal Background of Their Literary Work. Martin Green. LC 90-5569. (Studies in British Literature: Vol. 8). 232p. 1990. lib. bdg. 89.95 (0-88946-945-8) E Mellen.

Biography of Me. Diane Kostic. (Illus.). 160p. (J). (gr. 5-9). 1992. student ed 12.95 (0-86653-687-6, 1421) Good Apple.

Biography of Mildmay Fane, Second Earl of Westmorland (1601-1666) The Unknown Cavalier. Gerald W. Morton. LC 90-24436. (Studies in British History: Vol. 22). (Illus.). 168p. 1991. lib. bdg. 79.95 (0-88946-261-5) E Mellen.

Biography of Ottmar Mergenthaler. Ed. by Carl Schlesinger. (Illus.). 144p. 1993. reprint ed. pap. 12.95 (0-938768-40-9) Oak Knoll.

Biography of Ottmar Mergenthaler & History of the Linotype, Its Invention & Development see Biography of Ottmar Mergenthaler Inventor of the Linotype

Biography of Ottmar Mergenthaler Inventor of the Linotype. Carl Schlesinger. LC 88-92646. (History of the Book Ser.: Vol. 4). Orig. Title: Biography of Ottmar Mergenthaler & History of the Linotype, Its Invention & Development. 144p. 1988. reprint ed. 35.00 (0-938768-12-3) Oak Knoll.

Biography of Percy & Marion MacKaye. Arvia MacKaye Ege. (Illus.). 730p. 1991. write for info. (0-318-66785-1) Kennebec River.

***Biography of Philosophy.** Julian Marias. Tr. by Harold C. Raley. LC 83-6939. 269p. 1984. pap. 76.70 (0-7837-8393-0, 2059204) Bks Demand.

Biography of Rev. David Smith. David Smith. LC 77-168520. (Black Heritage Library Collection). 1977. reprint ed. 19.95 (0-8369-8872-8) Ayer.

Biography of Richard Cromwell, 1626-1712, the Second Protector. John A. Butler. LC 93-44167. (Studies in British History: Vol. 33). (Illus.). 260p. 1994. text ed. 89. 95 (0-7734-9417-0) E Mellen.

Biography of Rombauer Becker. Anne Mendelson. Date not set. 17.95 (0-8050-2904-4) H Holt & Co.

Biography of San Francisco State University. Arthur Chandler. (Illus.). 120p. 1986. 29.95 (0-938530-34-8); pap. 19.95 (0-938530-33-X) Lexikos.

Biography of Satan. 4th ed. Kersey Graves. 153p. 1971. spiral bd. 8.25 (0-7873-0353-4) Mokelumne.

Biography of Satan: A Historical Exposition of the Devil & His Fiery Dominions. Kersey Graves. 1991. lib. bdg. 79.00 (0-8490-4132-5) Gordon Pr.

***Biography of Satan: Exposing the Origins of the Devil.** 5th ed. Kersey Graves. 158p. 1995. reprint ed. pap. 13. 95 (1-885395-11-6) Book Tree.

Biography of Satan: Or A Historical Exposition of the Devil & His Fiery Dominions. Kersey Graves. 160p. 1993. pap. 17.95 (1-56459-329-0) Kessinger Pub.

Biography of Siegfried Sassoon. John Keegan. 1987. write for info. (0-670-81340-0) Viking Penguin.

Biography of Sir Charles Hartley, Civil Engineer (1825-1915) The Father of the Danube, 2 vols., Set. C. W. Hartley. LC 88-37971. (Studies in British History: Vol. 9). 800p. 1989. lib. bdg. 129.95 (0-88946-461-8) E Mellen.

Biography of the Brothers Davenport. Thomas L. Nichols. LC 75-36912. (Occult Ser.). 1976. reprint ed. 29.95 (0-405-07969-9) Ayer.

Biography of the English Language. C. M. Millward. 432p. (C). 1989. text ed. 31.25 (0-03-059431-6) HB Coll Pubs.

Biography of the Gods. Albert E. Haydon. LC 74-37848. (Essay Index Reprint Ser.). 1977. reprint ed. 21.95 (0-8369-2595-5) Ayer.

Biography of the Reverend Robert Finley. Isaac V. Brown. LC 73-82178. (Anti-Slavery Crusade in America Ser.). 1979. reprint ed. 24.95 (0-405-00617-9) Ayer.

***Biography of the Tennessee Walking Horses.** 2nd rev. ed. Ben A. Green. Ed. by Allanna L. Jackson. (Illus.). 280p. Date not set. reprint ed. 35.00 (0-9639644-2-9) Four Craftsmen.

Biography of Thomas Wolfe. Neal F. Austin. (Illus.). 1968. 25.00 (0-911796-00-2) Beacham.

Biography of Wilmer McLean, May 3, 1814 - June 5, 1882. Frank P. Cauble. (Illus.). 114p. 1987. 12.95 (0-930919-39-4) H E Howard.

Biography, Songs, & Musical Compositions of Stephen C. Foster. Stephen C. Foster. LC 74-24086. reprint ed. 49. 50 (0-404-12915-3) AMS Pr.

***Biography Today.** Ed. by Laurie L. Harris. (Artists Ser.: Vol. 1). 200p. (YA). Date not set. lib. bdg. 30.00x (0-7808-0067-2) Omnigraphics Inc.

***Biography Today.** Ed. by Laurie L. Harris. (Scientists & Inventors Ser.: Vol. 1). 200p. (J). (gr. 3-12). 1995. lib. bdg. 30.00x (0-7808-0068-0) Omnigraphics Inc.

***Biography Today.** Ed. by Laurie L. Harris. (Sports Ser.: Vol. 1). (J). (gr. 3-12). 1995. lib. bdg. 30.00 (0-7808-0069-9) Omnigraphics Inc.

Biography Today: Profiles of People of Interest to Young Readers, 1992. annuals Ed. by Laurie L. Harris. 498p. (J). 1993. lib. bdg. 47.00 (1-55888-139-5) Omnigraphics Inc.

Biography Today: Profiles of People of Interest to Young Readers, 1992. annuals Laurie L. Harris. (Illus.). 450p. 1993. lib. bdg. 47.00 (1-55888-345-2) Omnigraphics Inc.

Biography Today Authors Ser. Ed. by Laurie L. Harris. 200p. 1995. lib. bdg. 30.00 (0-7808-0014-1) Omnigraphics Inc.

Biography Today 1994 Annual Cumulation: Profiles of People of Interest to Young Readers. Laurie L. Harris. (J). 1994. lib. bdg. 47.00x (0-7808-0022-2) Omnigraphics Inc.

***Biohazard - Urban Discipline.** 109p. Date not set. pap. 19. 95 (0-89524-879-4, 02501247) Cherry Lane.

Biohazard Testing, No. C-126. Business Communications Co., Inc. Staff. 335p. 1990. 2,850.00 (0-89336-787-7) BCC.

Biohazards in Biological Research: Proceedings of a Conference Held at the Asilomer Conference Center, Pacific Grove, CA, January 22-24, 1973. Conference on Biohazards in Cancer Research Staff et al. Ed. by A. Hellman. LC 73-84153. 379p. reprint ed. pap. 108.10 (0-7837-2083-1, 2042357) Bks Demand.

Biohazards Management Handbook. Liberman & Gordon. (Occupational Safety & Health Ser.: Vol. 17). 737p. 1989. 170.00 (0-8247-7897-9) Dekker.

***Biohazards Management Handbook.** 2nd expanded rev. ed. Daniel F. Liberman. LC 94-1164. (Occupational Safety & Health Ser.: Vol. 26). 1995. write for info. (0-8247-8995-4) Dekker.

Biohazards of Drinking Water Treatment. Ed. by Richard A. Larson. (Illus.). 294p. 1988. 79.95 (0-87371-110-6, TD433) Lewis Pubs.

Biohazards Reference Manual. American Industrial Hygiene Association Biohazards Committee. 160p. 1985. 35.00 (0-932627-19-6) Am Indus Hygiene.

Biohistory: The Interplay Between Human Society & the Biosphere. Ed. by Stephen Boyden. (Man & the Biosphere Ser.: Vol. 8). (Illus.). 250p. (C). 1992. 68.00 (1-85070-371-X) Prthnon Pub.

Biohistory: The Interplay Between Human Society & the Biosphere. H. Regier et al. (Man & the Biosphere Ser.). 350p. 1992. 98.00 (92-3-102747-6, U6720) UNIPUB.

Biohydrometallurgy. Giovanni Rossi. 620p. 1990. text ed. 90.00 (0-07-053931-6) McGraw.

Bioimaging & Two-Dimensional Spectroscopy. Ed. by L. Smith. 1990. 53.00 (0-8194-0246-X, VOL. 1205) SPIE.

Bioindicators & Environmental Management. Ed. by D. W. Jeffrey & B. Madden. (Illus.). 458p. 1991. text ed. 83.00 (0-12-382590-3) Acad Pr.

Bioindustrial Ecosystems. Ed. by D. J. Cole & George C. Brander. (Ecosystems of the World Ser.: No. 21). 295p. 1986. 107.75 (0-444-42421-0) Elsevier.

Bioinformatics: Information Transduction & Processing Systems from Cell to Whole Body: Proc. of the Internat. Symp., Takamatsu, Kagawa, Japan, 12-16 March, 1989. Ed. by O. Hatase & J. H. Wang. 444p. 1989. 131.00 (0-444-81130-3) Elsevier.

Bioinformatics, Supercomputing & Complex Genome Analysis: International Conference. H. A. Lim et al. 400p. 1993. text ed. 118.00 (981-02-1157-0) World Scientific Pub.

Bioinorganic Catalysis. Jan Reedijk. 496p. 1993. 195.00 (0-8247-9004-9) Dekker.

Bioinorganic Chemistry. (Structure & Bonding Ser.: Vol. 70). (Illus.). 190p. 1989. 115.00 (0-387-50130-4) Spr-Verlag.

Bioinorganic Chemistry. (Structure & Bonding Ser.: Vol. 72). (Illus.). 210p. 1990. 96.00 (0-387-51574-7, 3441) Spr-Verlag.

***Bioinorganic Chemistry.** Contrib by I. Bertini et al. LC 95-12983. (Structure & Bonding Ser.: Vol. 83). 1995. write for info. (0-387-59105-2); write for info. (3-540-59105-2) Spr-Verlag.

Bioinorganic Chemistry. Ivano Bertini et al. LC 91-67870. (Illus.). 822p. (C). 1993. text ed. 58.00 (0-935702-57-1) Univ Sci Bks.

***Bioinorganic Chemistry: An Inorganic Perspective of Life: Proceedings of the NATO Advanced Study Institute on Bioinorganic Chemistry: An Inorganic Perspective of Life, Rhodes Island, Greece, June 5-17, 1994.** Ed. by Dimitris P. Kessissoglou. LC 95-31. (NATO ASI, Series C, Mathematical & Physical Sciences: No. 459). 1995. lib. bdg. 198.00 (0-7923-3380-2) Kluwer Ac.

Bioinorganic Chemistry: Inorganic Elements in the Chemistry of Life - an Introduction & Guide. Wolfgang Kaim & Brigitte Schwederski. LC 94-6718. (Inorganic Chemistry Ser.). 1994. text ed. 89.95 (0-471-94368-1); pap. text ed. 39.95 (0-471-94369-X) Wiley.

Bioinorganic Chemistry of Copper. Kenneth D. Karlin & Zoltan Tyeklar. LC 93-12323. 1993. write for info. (0-412-03631-2) Chapman & Hall.

Bioinorganic Chemistry of Nickel. Ed. by Jack R. Lancaster, Jr. LC 88-140028. 337p. 1988. lib. bdg. 115. 00 (0-89573-338-2) VCH Pubs.

Bioinstrumentation: Research, Development & Applications. Ed. by Donald L. Wise. 1563p. 1990. text ed. 170.00 (0-409-90234-9) Buttrwrth-Heinemann.

Bioinstrumentation & Biosensors. Ed. by Donald L. Wise. 824p. 1991. 195.00 (0-8247-8337-9) Dekker.

Biokinesiology Workbook. Wayne W. Topping. (Illus.). 105p. 1986. reprint ed. student ed 13.95 (0-935299-01-7) Topping Inst.

BIOkinetic: Wendy Jacob, Gary Justis, Michael Paha, John Pakosta, John Ploof, Thomas Skomski. Contrib by Peter F. Spooner. (Illus.). 24p. 1989. 7.00 (0-945558-06-6) ISU Univ Galls.

Biokinetics of Flying & Swimming. Akira Azuma. LC 92-590. 1993. 198.00 (0-387-70106-0) Spr-Verlag.

Biolab: A Laboratory Manual for Biology & Ecology. Stephen Wilson. 176p. (C). 1991. spiral bd. 18.95 (0-8403-6876-3) Kendall-Hunt.

Biolab Book. Lundy Pentz. LC 82-49066. (Illus.). 144p. reprint ed. pap. 41.10 (0-8357-6040-5, 2034145) Bks Demand.

BioLab Book: Laboratory Studies in Life. 2nd ed. Robert Elgart. (Illus.). 195p. (C). 1995. pap. text ed. 22.95 (0-9609098-3-4) Biomat Pub Co.

***BioLab I: A Laboratory Notebook for General Biology.** Joel G. Zachry. 80p. Date not set. pap. text ed. 8.75 (1-882194-07-1) TN Valley Pub.

Biolaminated Deposits. G. Gerdes & W. E. Krumbein. (Lecture Notes in Earth Sciences Ser.: Vol. 9). ix, 183p. 1987. pap. 28.00 (0-387-17937-2) Spr-Verlag.

BioLaw, 2 vols. 415.00 (0-318-36509-X) U Pubns Amer.

Bioelectroanalysis No. 2: Second Symposium Held at Matrafured, Hungary 11-15 October, 1992. Ed. by E. Pungor. (Illus.). 450p. 1993. 75.00 (963-05-6529-3, Pub. by A K HU) Intl Spec Bk.

***Biolexicon: A Guide to the Language of Biology.** Charles Blinderman. (Illus.). 380p. 1990. pap. 25.95 (0-398-06023-1) C C Thomas.

Biolexicon: A Guide to the Language of Biology. Charles Blinderman. (Illus.). 380p. (C). 1990. text ed. 45.95x (0-398-05671-4) C C Thomas.

Biolog. Howard. 1992. 800.00 (0-87371-786-4, T) Lewis Pubs.

Biologia: Estudio de la Vida Texto Programado. Rafael A. Torres-Ortiz. (Illus.). 466p. (SPA.). (YA). (gr. 10-12). 1985. reprint ed. teacher ed 9.95 (0-939081-01-6); reprint ed. pap. 23.50 (0-939081-00-8); reprint ed. pap. text ed. 18.75 (0-685-17446-8); reprint ed. 10.95 (0-939081-02-4) Edit Roche.

***Biologia Animal: Manual de Laboratorio.** Angel Berrios. 195p. (C). 1994. 24.95 (1-881375-19-6) Libreria Univ.

Biologia Animal: Manual de Laboratorio. 2nd ed. Yesmin A. De Figueroa & Angel Berrios. 142p. (C). 1985. 19.95 (1-881375-06-4) Libreria Univ.

Biologia Centrali-Americana: Reptilia & Batrachia. Gunther. LC 87-60187. 1987. write for info. (0-916984-17-6) SSAR.

Biologia Moderna: Serie de Modulos Para Laboratorio Primer Semestre. 2nd rev. ed. Hilda Rivera de Hernandez. 265p. (C). 1991. 19.95 (1-881375-07-2) Libreria Univ.

Biologia Moderna: Serie de Modulos Para Laboratorio Segundo Semestre. Hilda Rivera de Hernandez. 291p. (C). 1991. 19.95 (1-881375-08-0) Libreria Univ.

Biologia y Origenes: Biology & Origins. Willen Ouweneel. (SPA.). 4.95 (84-7645-002-8, 223063, Pub. by Edit Clie SP) TSELF.

Biologic: Designing with Nature to Protect the Environment. rev. ed. David Wann. LC 94-2328. (Illus.). 288p. 1994. pap. 14.95 (1-55566-122-X) Johnson Bks.

Biologic Applications of Radiotracers. Ed. by Howard J. Glenn. 224p. 1982. 132.00 (0-8493-6009-9, QH324, CRC Reprint) Franklin.

An Asterisk (*) at the beginning of an entry indicates that the title is appearing in BIP for the first time.

Biologic Basis of Orthodontics. Anthony A. Gianelly & Henry M. Goldman. LC 70-123421. 431p. reprint ed. pap. 122.90 (*0-8357-7226-8*, 2056511) Bks Demand.

Biologic Basis of Pigmentation: Proceedings of the International Pigment Cell Conference, 10th, Cambridge, Mass., October, 1977. International Pigment Cell Conference Staff. Ed. by S. N. Klaus. (Pigment Cell Ser.: Vol. 4). (Illus.). 1979. 127.25 (*3-8055-2972-4*) S Karger.

Biologic Effect of Ultraviolet Radiation Emphasis on Skin: 1st International Conference on Skin & Cancer, Hospital Temple University Health Science. Frederick Urbach. LC 68-14721. 1969. 291.00 (*0-08-012042-3*, Pub. by Pergamon Repr UK) Franklin.

Biologic Effects of Light: Proceedings of a Symposium, Atlanta, Georgia, U. S. A., October 13-15, 1991. Ed. by Michael F. Holick & Albert M. Kligman. LC 92-22295. (Illus.). xiv, 466p. (C). 1992. 269.25 (*3-11-013473-X*) De Gruyter.

Biologic Effects of Light, 1993: Proceedings of a Symposium - Basel, Switzerland, June 3-5, 1993. Ed. by Ernst Jung & Michael Holick. LC 94-4068. 647p. (C). 1994. lib. bdg. 367.70 (*3-11-014096-9*) De Gruyter.

Biologic Effects of Light 1993: Proceedings of a Symposium, Basel, Switzerland 1993. Ed. by Ernst G. Jung & Michael F. Holick. LC 94-4068. 1994. 318.70 (*0-318-72595-9*) De Gruyter.

Biologic Effects of NonIonizing Radiation. Ed. by Paul E. Tyler. (Annals Ser.: Vol. 247). 1975. 64.75 (*0-89072-761-9*) NY Acad Sci.

Biologic Evolution. Fox. (C). 1995. pap. text ed. write for info. (*0-7167-1870-7*) W H Freeman.

Biologic Ionization Applied to Farming & Soil Management: Principles & Techniques. A. F. Beddoe. 210p. 1992. pap. text ed. 100.00 (*1-881201-06-6*); spiral bd. 100.00 (*1-881201-00-7*) S & J Unltd.

Biologic Ionization As Applied to Human Nutrition: Principles & Technique. A. F. Beddoe. 310p. 1992. pap. text ed. 100.00 (*1-881201-05-8*); spiral bd. 100.00 (*1-881201-01-5*) S & J Unltd.

Biologic Markers in Immunotoxicology. 224p. (C). 1992. pap. text ed. 37.95 (*0-309-04389-1*) Natl Acad Pr.

Biologic Markers in Reproductive Toxicology. 420p. 1989. 42.95 (*0-309-03930-4*) Natl Acad Pr.

Biologic Markers in Reproductive Toxicology. National Research Council Staff. 420p. 1989. pap. 32.95 (*0-309-03979-7*) Natl Acad Pr.

***Biologic Markers in Urinary Toxicology.** National Research Council Staff. 210p. (Orig.). (C). 1995. pap. text ed. 27.00 (*0-309-05228-9*) Natl Acad Pr.

Biologic Markers of Air-Pollution Stress & Damage in Forests. National Research Council (U. S.), Committee on Biologic Markers of Air-Pollution Damage in Trees Staff. LC 89-62584. 377p. reprint ed. pap. 107.50 (*0-7837-0345-7*, 2040664) Bks Demand.

Biologic Markers of Pulmonary Toxicology. National Research Council Staff. 196p. 1989. 34.95 (*0-309-03992-4*); pap. 24.95 (*0-309-03990-8*) Natl Acad Pr.

Biologic Response Styles: Clinical Implications. Ed. by Howard Klar & Larry J. Siever. LC 85-13403. (Clinical Insights Ser.). 107p. reprint ed. pap. 30.50 (*0-8357-7832-0*, 2036206) Bks Demand.

Biologic Rhythms in Clinical & Laboratory Medicine. Ed. by Yvan Touitou & E. Haus. (Illus.). 730p. 1992. 198.00 (*0-387-54461-5*) Spr-Verlag.

Biologic Rhythms in Clinical Laboratory & Medicine. Ed. by Y. Touitou & E. Haus. xviii, 730p. 1994. 94.00 (*0-387-57592-8*) Spr-Verlag.

Biologic Role of Dehydropiandrosterone (DHEA) Ed. by M. Y. Kalimi & W. Regelson. (Illus.). viii, 450p. (C). 1990. lib. bdg. 261.55 (*3-11-012243-X*) De Gruyter.

Biologic System Evaluation with Ultrasound. J. F. Greenleaf & C. M. Sehgal. (Illus.). ix, 127p. 1992. 65.00 (*0-387-97851-8*) Spr-Verlag.

***Biologic Therapy of Cancer.** 2nd ed. Ed. by Vincent T. DeVita, Jr. et al. LC 94-40512. 1994. write for info. (*0-397-51416-6*) Lippincott.

Biologic Therapy of Cancer: Principles & Practice. Vincent T. DeVita, Jr. et al. (Illus.). 800p. 1991. text ed. 135.00 (*0-397-51027-6*) Lippincott.

Biological - Biomedical Applications of Liquid Chromatography. Liquid Chromatography Symposium Staff. Ed. by Gerald L. Hawk et al. LC 78-26628. (Chromatographic Science Ser.: No. 10). (Illus.). 756p. reprint ed. pap. 180.00 (*0-7837-0794-0*, 2041108) Bks Demand.

Biological - Biomedical Applications of Liquid Chromatography, No. II. Liquid Chromatography Symposium Staff. Ed. by Gerald L. Hawk et al. LC 79-18918. (Chromatographic Science Ser.: No. 12). (Illus.). 520p. reprint ed. pap. 148.20 (*0-7837-0798-3*, 2041112) Bks Demand.

Biological - Biomedical Applications of Liquid Chromatography, No. III. Ed. by Gerald L. Hawk et al. LC 81-17416. (Chromatographic Science Ser.: No. 18). (Illus.). 440p. reprint ed. pap. 125.40 (*0-7837-0903-X*, 2041208) Bks Demand.

Biological - Biomedical Applications of Liquid Chromatography, No. IV. Ed. by Gerald L. Hawk et al. LC 82-2546. (Chromatographic Science Ser.: No. 20). (Illus.). 389p. reprint ed. pap. 110.90 (*0-7837-0668-5*, 2041003) Bks Demand.

Biological Actions & Medical Applications of Dimethyl Sulfoxide. 1983. 80.00 (*0-89766-215-6*, VOL. 411); pap. 80.00 (*0-89766-216-4*) NY Acad Sci.

Biological Actions of Dimethyl Sulfoxide, Vol. 243. 508p. 1975. pap. 27.00 (*0-89766-155-9*) NY Acad Sci.

Biological Activities for the Elementary Classroom: A Process Approach. Ernest L. Kern. Ed. by Robert E. Cook. (KSAM Activity Guide Ser.: Vol. 1). (Illus.). 294p. (gr. k-6). 1990. teacher ed 11.95 (*0-934426-24-4*) NAPSAC Reprods.

Biological Activities of Alpha-Fetoprotein, I. Ed. by Gerald J. Mizejewski & Herbert I. Jacobson. 256p. 1989. 155.00 (*0-8493-5637-7*, QP552, CRC Reprint) Franklin.

Biological Activities of Alpha-Fetoprotein, II. Ed. by Gerald J. Mizejewski & Herbert I. Jacobson. 256p. 1989. 174.00 (*0-8493-5638-5*, CRC Reprint) Franklin.

Biological Activities of Alpha-Fetoprotein, Set. Ed. by Gerald J. Mizejewski & Herbert I. Jacobson. 256p. 1989. 110.00 (*0-8493-5636-9*, QP552) CRC Pr.

Biological Activities of Complement: Proceedings of the International Symposium of the Canadian Society for Immunology, 5th, Guleph, 1970. Canadian Society for Immunology Staff. Ed. by D. G. Ingram. (Illus.). 1972. 67.25 (*3-8055-1310-0*) S Karger.

Biological Activities of Polymers. Ed. by Charles E. Carraher, Jr. & Charles G. Gebelein. LC 82-3988. (ACS Symposium Ser.: No. 186). 293p. 1982. 43.95 (*0-8412-0719-4*) Am Chemical.

Biological Aging Measurement: Clinical Applications. 2nd ed. Ward Dean. Ed. by Hans U. Weber. (Illus.). 472p. 1988. per., pap. text ed. 59.95 (*0-937777-00-5*) Ctr Bio-Gerontology.

Biological Aging Measurement: Clinical Applications. 2nd rev. ed. Ward Dean. Ed. by Hans U. Weber et al. LC 85-63822. (Illus.). 472p. 1988. text ed. 95.00 (*0-937777-01-3*) Ctr Bio-Gerontology.

Biological Aide. Jack Rudman. (Career Examination Ser.: C-86). 1994. pap. 23.95 (*0-8373-0086-X*) Nat Learn.

Biological & Agricultural Index, Vols. 1964-89. LC 17-8906. Date not set. 250.00 (*0-685-22239-X*) Wilson.

Biological & Agricultural Index, Vols. 1989-1994. Date not set. write for info. (*0-318-56450-5*) Wilson.

Biological & Behavioral Determinants of Language Development. Ed. by Norman Krasnegor et al. 544p. (C). 1991. text ed. 99.95 (*0-8058-0635-0*); pap. 39.95 (*0-8058-0993-7*) L Erlbaum Assocs.

Biological & Behavioral Technologies & the Law. Michael H. Shapiro & Stephen Morse. LC 81-19986. 396p. 1982. text ed. 65.00 (*0-275-90900-X*, C0900, Praeger Pubs) Greenwood.

Biological & Biomechanical Performance of Biomaterials. Ed. by P. Christel et al. 550p. 1986. 172.00 (*0-444-42666-3*) Elsevier.

Biological & Chemical Methods of Plant Protection. Ed. by I. S. Popushoi. Tr. by V. Kothekar. (Illus.). 64p. 1987. text ed. 55.00 (*90-6191-492-2*, Pub. by A A Balkema NE) Ashgate Pub Co.

Biological & Clinical Aspects of Phagocyte Function: (International Congress, Pavia, Italy, Sept. 1986) C. Mauri. Ed. by S. Roath & M. Corn. (Hematology Reviews & Communications Ser.: Vol. 1). vii, 182p. 1986. pap. text ed. 145.00 (*3-7186-0354-3*) Gordon & Breach.

Biological & Clinical Aspects of Reproduction. Ed. by F. J. Ebling & I. W. Henderson. (International Congress Ser.: No. 394). 1976. 107.75 (*90-219-0324-5*, Excerpta Medica) Elsevier.

Biological & Clinical Concepts see Current Trends in Histocompatability

Biological & Cultural Anthropology at Emory University. Ed. by Robert A. Paul. (Cultural Anthropology Ser.: Vol. 2, No. 1). 1987. 7.50 (*0-317-66356-9*) Am Anthro Assn.

***Biological & Cultural Evolution.** Mary Midgley. 23p. 1984. pap. 4.00 (*0-904674-08-8*, Pub. by Octagon Pr UK) ISHK Bk Service.

Biological & Cultural Tests for Control of Plant Diseases, Vol. 7. Ed. by David Wysong. 137p. 1992. pap. 25.00 (*0-685-62272-X*, SB731) Am Phytopathol Soc.

Biological & Cultural Tests for Control of Plant Diseases, Vol. 8. Ed. by David Wysong. 146p. 1993. pap. 28.00 (*0-685-70979-5*) Am Phytopathol Soc.

Biological & Cultural Tests for Control of Plant Diseases, Vol. 9. Ed. by David Wysong. 1994. pap. 28.00 (*0-685-74806-5*) Am Phytopathol Soc.

***Biological & Cultural Tests for Control of Plant Diseases, Vol. 10.** Ed. by Craig H. Canaday. 150p. 1995. pap. 28.00 (*0-614-06938-6*) Am Phytopathol Soc.

Biological & Environmental Aspects of Chromium. S. Langard. (Topics in Environmental Health Ser.). 1983. 142.00 (*0-444-80441-2*, I-008-83) Elsevier.

***Biological & Environmental Chemistry of Chromium.** Sidney A. Katz & Harry Salem. LC 94-5417. 1994. write for info. (*1-56081-629-5*) VCH Pubs.

Biological & Environmental Effects of Arsenic. Ed. by B. A. Fowler. (Topics in Environmental Health Ser.: Vol. 6). 288p. 1984. 126.75 (*0-444-80513-3*, I-379-83) Elsevier.

Biological & Environmental Reference Materials for Trace Elements, Nuclides & Organic Microcontaminants: A Survey. E. Cortes Toro et al. 114p. (Orig.). (C). 1994. pap. text ed. 50.00 (*0-7881-0303-2*) Diane Pub.

Biological & Health Sciences: Report of the Project 2061 Phase I Biological & Health Science Panel. Mary Clark. LC 89-76. 34p. 1989. pap. 7.50 (*0-87168-343-1*, 89-02S) AAAS.

Biological & Inorganic Copper Chemistry, Vol. I. Ed. by K. D. Karlin & J. Zubieta. (Illus.). 273p. 1986. lib. bdg. 95.00 (*0-940030-11-X*) Adenine Pr.

Biological & Inorganic Copper Chemistry, Vol. II. Ed. by K. Karlin & J. Zubieta. 288p. 1986. lib. bdg. 95.00 (*0-940030-15-2*) Adenine Pr.

Biological & Inorganic Factors in the Destruction of Limestone Coasts. J. Schneider. (Contributions to Sedimentology Ser.: No. 6). (Illus.). 112p. 1976. pap. text ed. 42.00 (*3-510-57006-5*) Lubrecht & Cramer.

Biological & Medical Electronics. Ralph W. Stacy. LC 59-14465. 320p. reprint ed. pap. 91.20 (*0-8357-7227-6*, 2055293) Bks Demand.

***Biological & Molecular Aspects of Mast Cell & Basophil Differentiation & Function.** Ed. by Stephen J. Galli et al. LC 95-2737. 1995. write for info. (*0-7817-0314-X*) Raven.

Biological & Neurobehavioral Studies of Borderline Personality Disorder. Ed. by Kenneth R. Silk. LC 93-44846. (Progress in Psychiatry Ser.: Vol. 45). 1994. boxed 34.00 (*0-88048-480-2*) Am Psychiatric.

Biological & Physical Aspects of Dredging, Kings Bay, Georgia. Ed. by Stephen V. Cofer-Shabica & Orville T. Magoon. LC 91-4237. (Coastlines of the World Ser.). 159p. 1991. pap. text ed. 22.00 (*0-87262-839-6*) Am Soc Civil Eng.

Biological & Physical Basis of Psychosomatic Disease: Based on Papers Presented at a Conference on Psychological Load & Stress in the Work Environment, Bergen, Norway, 1980. Ed. by H. Ursin & R. Murison. (Illus.). 304p. 1983. 127.00 (*0-08-029774-9*, Pub. by Pergamon Repr UK) Franklin.

Biological & Psychological Aspects of Orofacial Pain. Sessle et al. Ed. by Christian S. Stohler & David S. Carlson. (Craniofacial Growth Ser.: Vol. 29). (Illus.). 195p. 1994. 49.00 (*0-929921-25-9*) UM CHGD.

Biological & Psychological Factors in Cardiovascular Disease. Ed. by T. F. Schmidt et al. (Illus.). 650p. 1986. 71.00 (*0-387-16577-0*) Spr-Verlag.

Biological & Social Factors in Psycholinguistics. Ed. by John Morton. LC 70-137819. (Illus.). 215p. reprint ed. 61.30 (*0-8357-9666-3*, 2014924) Bks Demand.

Biological & Synthetic Polymer Networks: Proceedings of the 8th Polymer Network Group Meeting Held in Elsinore, Denmark, 31 August to 5 September 1986. Ed. by O. Kramer. 540p. 1988. 158.50 (*1-85166-166-2*) Elsevier.

Biological Anomalies No. I: Humans I. William R. Corliss. (Catalog of Biological Anomalies Ser.). (Illus.). 304p. 1992. 19.95 (*0-915554-26-7*) Sourcebook.

Biological Anomalies No. II: Humans II. William R. Corliss. LC 91-68541. (Catalog of Biological Anomalies Ser.). (Illus.). 297p. (C). 1993. 19.95 (*0-915554-27-5*) Sourcebook.

***Biological Anomalies No. III: Humans III.** William R. Corliss. (Catalog of Biological Anomalies Ser.). (Illus.). 212p. 1984. 19.95 (*0-915554-29-1*) Sourcebook.

***Biological Anthropology: The State of the Science.** Ed. by Noel T. Boaz & Linda D. Wolfe. 264p. (Orig.). 1995. pap. text ed. 39.95x (*0-614-04085-X*) Intl Inst Human Evol.

Biological Anthropology & Aging: Perspectives on Human Variation over the Span. Ed. by Dougalas E. Crews & Ralph M. Garruto. 472p. 1994. 75.00 (*0-19-506829-7*) OUP.

Biological Applications of Anti-Idiotypes, 2 vols., Vol. I. Constantin A. Bona. 224p. 1988. 120.00 (*0-8493-6941-X*, QR186, CRC Reprint) Franklin.

Biological Applications of Anti-Idiotypes, 2 vols., Vol. II. Constantin A. Bona. 224p. 1988. 114.00 (*0-8493-6942-8*, QR186, CRC Reprint) Franklin.

Biological Applications of Flouresence. Schwartz. 1991. write for info. (*0-8493-0163-7*, CRC Reprint) Franklin.

Biological Applications of Photochemical Switches. Ed. by Harry Morrison. 316p. 1993. text ed. 84.95 (*0-471-57293-4*) Wiley.

***Biological Applications of Tracer Elements.** Cold Spring Harbor Symposia on Quantitative Biology Staff. LC 34-8174. (Cold Spring Harbor Symposia on Quantitative Biology Ser.: Vol. 13). (Illus.). 240p. 1949. pap. 68.40 (*0-7837-8971-8*, 2049752) Bks Demand.

Biological Approaches & Evolutionary Trends in Plants. Ed. by Shoichi Kawano. (Illus.). 417p. 1990. text ed. 77.00 (*0-12-402960-4*) Acad Pr.

Biological Approaches to Cancer Treatment: Biomodulation. Malcolm S. Mitchell. (Illus.). 608p. 1992. text ed. 95.00 (*0-07-105397-2*) Hlth Prof Div.

***Biological Approaches to Illicit Drug Demand Reduction.** 1995. lib. bdg. 253.99 (*0-8490-6838-X*) Gordon Pr.

Biological Approaches to Rational Drug Design. Ed. by David B. Weiner & William V. Williams. LC 94-11157. (Pharmacology & Toxicology Ser.). 1994. write for info. (*0-8493-9422-8*) CRC Pr.

Biological Approaches to the Controlled Delivery of Drugs. Ed. by R. L. Juliano. (Annals Ser.: Vol. 507). (Illus.). 364p. 1987. 91.00 (*0-89766-409-4*) NY Acad Sci.

Biological Approaches to the Study of Human Intelligence. Philip Veron. 352p. (C). 1993. text ed. 72.95 (*0-89391-798-2*) Ablex Pub.

Biological Aspects of Affective Disorders. Ed. by Roger Horton & Cornelius Katona. (Neuroscience Perspectives Ser.). (Illus.). 359p. 1991. text ed. 69.95 (*0-12-356510-3*) Acad Pr.

Biological Aspects of Alcohol Consumption. O. Forsander & K. Eriksson. (Finnish Foundation for Alcohol Studies: Vol. 20). 1972. pap. 6.50 (*951-9192-09-3*) Rutgers Ctr Alcohol.

Biological Aspects of Alcoholism. rev. ed. Boris Tabakoff & Paula L. Hoffman. LC 94-19261. (WHO Expert Series on Biological Psychiatry: Vol. 4). (Illus.). 360p. 1995. text ed. 39.00 (*0-88937-130-X*) Hogrefe & Huber Pubs.

Biological Aspects of Alzheimer's Disease. Ed. by Robert Katzman. LC 82-19713. (Banbury Report Ser.: No. 15). 495p. 1983. 55.00 (*0-87969-213-8*) Cold Spring Harbor.

Biological Aspects of Brain Tumors: Proceedings of the 8th Nikko Brain Tumor Conference Karatsu (Saga) 1990. Ed. by K. Tabuchi. (Illus.). 512p. 1991. 173.00 (*0-387-70078-1*) Spr-Verlag.

Biological Aspects of Cancer & Aging: Studies in Pure Line Mice. L. Strong & P. Alexander. LC 68-18533. (International Series of Monographs on Pure & Applied Mathematics: Vol. 31). 1968. 104.00 (*0-08-012645-6*, Pub. by Pergamon Repr UK) Franklin.

Biological Aspects of Copper: Occurrence, Assay & Interrelationships. Charles A. Owen, Jr. LC 82-7931. (Copper in Biology & Medicine Ser.). 156p. 1983. 28.00 (*0-8155-0918-9*) Noyes.

Biological Aspects of Human Migration. Ed. by C. G. Mascie-Taylor & G. Lasker. (Cambridge Studies in Biological Anthropology: No. 3). (Illus.). 250p. 1988. 74.95 (*0-521-33109-9*) Cambridge U Pr.

Biological Aspects of Human Sexuality. rev. ed. Herant A. Katchadourian. (Illus.). 256p. (C). 1990. text ed. 24.00 (*0-03-032852-7*); pap. text ed. 13.25 (*0-03-032788-1*) HB Coll Pubs.

Biological Aspects of Mental Disorder. Solomon H. Snyder. 1981. pap. 12.95 (*0-19-502888-0*) OUP.

***Biological Aspects of Metals & Metal-Related Diseases.** Ed. by Bibudhendra Sarkar. LC 81-40759. (Illus.). Date not set. reprint ed. pap. 94.10 (*0-7837-9551-3*, 2060300) Bks Demand.

Biological Aspects of Rare Plant Conservation: Proceedings of an International Conference Held at King's College, Cambridge, England, 14-19 July, 1980. Ed. by Hugh Synge. LC 80-42067. (Illus.). 586p. reprint ed. pap. 167.10 (*0-8357-7228-4*, 2030469) Bks Demand.

B

Biological Aspects of Schizophrenia & Addiction. Ed. by Gwynneth Hemmings. LC 81-16040. 293p. reprint ed. pap. 83.60 (*0-8357-7229-2*, 2031937) Bks Demand.

Biological Assessment & Treatment of Posttraumatic Stress Disorder. Ed. by Earl Giller. LC 89-17972. (Progress in Psychiatry Ser.). 250p. 1990. text ed. 30.00 (*0-88048-189-7*) Am Psychiatric.

Biological Assessment Criteria. Wayne S. Davis. 1995. write for info. (*0-87371-894-1*) Lewis Pubs.

***Biological Assessment of the Alto Madidi Region & Adjacent Areas of Northwest Bolivia, May 18 - June 15, 1990.** Ed. by Theodore A. Parker, 3rd & Brent Bailey. LC 91-78133. 108p. 1991. pap. 7.00 (*1-881173-05-4*) Conser Intl.

***Biological Assessment of the Columbia River Forest Reserve, Toledo District, Belize.** Theodore A. Parker, 3rd et al. LC 93-71145. 81p. 1993. pap. 7.00 (*1-881173-03-8*) Conser Intl.

Biological Asymmetry & Handedness. CIBA Foundation Symposium Staff & CIBA Foundation Staff. (CIBA Foundation Symposia Ser.: No. 162). 327p. 1991. text ed. 89.00 (*0-471-92961-1*) Wiley.

Biological Balance & Thermal Modification see Towards a Plan of Actions for Mankind

Biological Barriers in Behavioral Medicine. Ed. by W. Linden. LC 87-36137. (Behavioral Psychophysiology Ser.). (Illus.). 348p. 1988. 60.00 (*0-306-42651-X*, Plenum Pr) Plenum.

Biological Barriers to Protein Delivery. Ed. by K. L. Audus & T. L. Raub. (Pharmaceutical Biotechnology Ser.: Vol. 4). (Illus.). 522p. (C). 1993. 85.00 (*0-306-44368-6*, Plenum Pr) Plenum.

Biological Based Risk Assessment. Cox. 1995. write for info. (*0-87371-540-3*) Lewis Pubs.

Biological Bases of Brain Function & Disease. Alan Frazer et al. Ed. by Perry Molinoff & Andrew Winokur. LC 93-16859. 464p. 1994. 69.00 (*0-7817-0089-2*); pap. 39.00 (*0-7817-0085-X*) Raven.

Biological Bases of Drug Tolerance & Dependence. Ed. by Judith Pratt. (Neuroscience Perspectives Ser.). (Illus.). 301p. 1992. text ed. 69.95 (*0-12-564250-4*) Acad Pr.

Biological Bases of Human Social Behavior. Robert A. Hinde. (Illus.). 416p. (C). 1974. text ed. 39.95 (*0-07-028932-8*) McGraw.

Biological Basis & Therapy of Neuroses. Ed. by Ashoka J. Prasad. 208p. 1988. 119.00 (*0-8493-4899-4*, RC530, CRC Reprint) Franklin.

Biological Basis for Cancer Diagnosis, Vol. 4. Ed. by A. Canonico. (Illus.). 1979. 137.00 (*0-08-024387-8*, Pub. by Pergamon Repr UK) Franklin.

Biological Basis for Risk Assessment of Dioxins & Related Compounds. Ed. by Michael A. Gallo et al. (Banbury Report Ser.: No. 35). (Illus.). 400p. (C). 1991. text ed. 95.00 (*0-87969-235-9*) Cold Spring Harbor.

Biological Basis for the Propagation of Woody Plants by Cuttings. D. A. Komissarov. 256p. 1968. text ed. 74.00 (*0-7065-0667-7*, Pub. by Keter Pub IS) Coronet Bks.

Biological Basis of Clinical Effect of Bleomycin. Ed. by A. Caputo. (Progress in Biochemical Pharmacology Ser.: Vol. 11). (Illus.). 200p. 1976. 101.75 (*3-8055-2338-6*) S Karger.

Biological Basis of Detoxification. Ed. by John Caldwell & William B. Jakoby. LC 82-18933. (Biochemical Pharmacology & Toxicology Ser.). 1983. text ed. 127.00 (*0-12-155060-5*) Acad Pr.

Biological Basis of Early Human Reproductive Failure: Applications to Medically-Assisted Conception. Ed. by Jonathan Van Blerkom. (Illus.). 464p. 1994. 85.00 (*0-19-506036-9*) OUP.

Biological Basis of Facial Plastic Surgery. Arlen D. Meyers. (American Academy of Facial Plastic & Reconstructive Surgery Monograph). (Illus.). 216p. 1993. text ed. 59.00 (*0-86577-443-9*) Thieme Med Pubs.

Biological Basis of Immunodeficiency. Ed. by Erwin W. Gelfand & Hans-Michael Dosch. 334p. 1980. text ed. 94.50 (*0-89004-361-2*) Raven.

Biological Basis of Mental Activity. John I. Hubbard. 224p. (C). 1975. pap. write for info. (*0-201-03086-1*) Addison-Wesley.

Biological Basis of Oncologic Thermotherapy. C. Streffer et al. (Clinical Thermology Ser.: Vol. 1). 160p. 1990. 96.00 (*0-387-51432-5*, 3612) Spr-Verlag.

An Asterisk (*) at the beginning of an entry indicates that the title is appearing in BIP for the first time. 767

Biological Basis of Personality. H. J. Eysenck. (Illus.). 420p. 1977. 66.95x (*0-398-00538-9*) C C Thomas.
***Biological Basis of Personality.** H. J. Eysenck. (Illus.). 420p. 1977. pap. 34.95 (*0-398-06111-4*) C C Thomas.
Biological Basis of Psychiatric Treatment. Ed. by S. Gershon & R. Pohl. (Progress in Basic & Clinical Pharmacology Ser.: Vol. 3). (Illus.). x, 328p. 1990. 227.25 (*3-8055-5007-3*) S Karger.
Biological Basis of Radiotherapy. G. G. Steel et al. 1983. 90.25 (*0-444-80511-7*) Elsevier.
Biological Basis of Radiotherapy. Ed. by G. G. Steel et al. 336p. 1989. 184.75 (*0-444-81099-4*); pap. 106.25 (*0-444-81187-7*) Elsevier.
Biological Basis of Schizophrenic Disorders. Ed. by T. Nakazawa. (Taniguchi Symposia on Brain Sciences Ser.: Vol. 14). (Illus.). x, 248p. 1991. 134.50 (*3-8055-5503-2*) S Karger.
Biological Basis of Substance Abuse. Ed. by Stanley G. Korenman & Jack D. Barchas. LC 92-49780. (Illus.). 536p. 1993. 75.00 (*0-19-507154-9*) OUP.
Biological Basis of the Human Chondrodysplasias. Ed. by W. A. Horton. (Journal: Pathology & Immunopathology Research: Vol. 7, No. 1-2, 1988). (Illus.). 148p. 1988. pap. 76.00 (*3-8055-4855-9*) S Karger.
Biological Carcinogenesis. Ed. by Marvin A. Rich & Philip Furmanski. LC 82-4996. (Illus.). 320p. reprint ed. pap. 91.20 (*0-7837-0886-6*, 2041192) Bks Demand.
Biological Century: Friday Evening Talks at the Marine Biological Laboratory. Robert Barlow et al. (Illus.). 303p. 1993. text ed. 45.00 (*0-674-07403-3*) HUP.
Biological Chemistry of Iron. H. B. Dunford et al. 1982. lib. bdg. 136.50 (*90-277-1444-4*) Kluwer Ac.
***Biological Chemistry of Magnesium.** James A. Cowan. LC 94-26741. 1995. write for info. (*1-56081-627-9*) VCH Pubs.
Biological Chemistry of Marine Copepods. Ed. by E. D. Corner & S. C. O'Hara. (Illus.). 270p. 1986. 73.00 (*0-19-854714-5*) OUP.
Biological Chemistry of Organelle Formation: Proceedings. Ed. by T. Buecher et al. (Colloquium Mosbach Ser.: Vol. 31). (Illus.). 254p. 1981. 55.00 (*0-387-10458-5*) Spr-Verlag.
Biological Chemistry of the Elements: The Inorganic Chemistry of Life. J. J. Frausto da Silva & R. J. Williams. (Illus.). 582p. 1991. 75.00 (*0-19-855598-9*) OUP.
Biological Chemistry of the Elements: The Inorganic Chemistry of Life. J. J. Frausto da Silva & R. J. Williams. (Illus.). 582p. (C). 1994. reprint ed. pap. text ed. 42.50 (*0-19-855802-3*) OUP.
Biological, Clinical & Cultural Perspectives of Anxiety, Vol. 1. Ed. by M. Roth, Jr. et al. (Handbook of Anxiety Ser.: Vol. 1). 400p. 1988. 201.25 (*0-444-90475-1*) Elsevier.
***Biological Clocks.** Cold Spring Harbor Symposia on Quantitative Biology Staff. LC 34-8174. (Cold Spring Harbor Symposia on Quantitative Biology Ser.: Vol. 25). (Illus.). 538p. 1960. pap. 153.40 (*0-7837-8978-5*, 2049759) Bks Demand.
Biological Clocks & Environmental Time. Ed. by Serge Daan & Eberhard Gwinner. 197p. 1989. lib. bdg. 40.00 (*0-89862-585-8*) Guilford Pr.
Biological Coherence & Response to External Stimuli. H. F. Frohlich. (Illus.). 340p. 1988. 161.00 (*0-387-18739-1*) Spr-Verlag.
Biological Components of Human Reproduction; Studies of Their Variations in Population Groups: Proceedings of the WHO Scientific Group, Geneva, 1968. WHO Staff. (Technical Report Ser.: No. 435). 1969. pap. 2.00 (*92-4-120435-4*) World Health.
Biological Components of Substance Abuse & Addiction: Background Paper. 1994. lib. bdg. 250.00 (*0-8490-8607-8*) Gordon Pr.
Biological Compounds see Comprehensive Organic Chemistry
Biological Consequences of Oxidative Stress: Implications for Carcinogenesis & Cardiovascular Disease. Ed. by Lawrence Spatz & Arthur D. Bloom. (The Conte Institute Ser.: No. 1). (Illus.). 208p. 1992. 39.95 (*0-19-507296-0*) OUP.
Biological Conservation. Ian F. Spellerberg & Steven R. Hardes. (Biology in Focus Ser.). (Illus.). 128p. 1992. pap. 17.00 (*0-521-39786-3*) Cambridge U Pr.
Biological Contaminants in Indoor Environments. Ed. by Philip R. Morey et al. LC 90-21115. (Special Technical Publication Ser.: STP 1071). (Illus.). 260p. 1990. text ed. 49.00 (*0-8031-1290-4*, 04-010710-17) ASTM.
Biological Contributions to Crime Causation. Ed. by Terrie E. Moffitt & Sarnoff A. Mednick. 1988. lib. bdg. 125.50 (*90-247-3655-2*) Kluwer Ac.
***Biological Control: Benefits & Risks.** Ed. by Heikki M.T. Hokkanen & James M. Lynch. (Plant & Microbiotechnology Research Ser.: 4). (Illus.). 480p. (C). 1995. write for info. (*0-521-47353-5*) Cambridge U Pr.
Biological Control: Pacific Prospects Supplement 1. D. F. Waterhouse & K. R. Norris. 125p. (C). 1989. text ed. 215.00 (*0-949511-98-6*, Pub. by ACIAR) St Mut.
Biological Control by Natural Enemies. 2nd ed. Paul DeBach & David Rosen. (Illus.). 448p. (C). 1991. 54.95 (*0-521-39191-1*) Cambridge U Pr.
Biological Control in Crop Production. Ed. by George C. Papavizas. LC 81-65017. (Beltsville Symposia in Agricultural Research Ser.: No. 5). 474p. 1982. text ed. 64.50 (*0-86598-037-3*) Rowman.
***Biological Control in the Western United States.** Ed. by James Nechols. (Illus.). 376p. 1995. pap. 25.00 (*1-879906-21-X*, 3361) ANR Pubns CA.
Biological Control of Insects: A Source Guide. 1991. lib. bdg. 76.00 (*0-8490-4852-4*) Gordon Pr.
Biological Control of Locusts & Grasshoppers. Ed. by C. Prior & C. J. Lomer. 394p. 1992. pap. 64.50 (*0-85198-779-6*) CAB Intl.
Biological Control of Microbial Plant Pathogens. R. Campbell. (Illus.). (C). 1989. 69.95 (*0-521-34088-8*) Cambridge U Pr.
Biological Control of Microbial Plant Pathogens. R. Campbell. (Illus.). (C). 1989. pap. 22.95 (*0-521-34900-1*) Cambridge U Pr.
Biological Control of Mosquitoes. Ed. by Harold C. Chapman. (Illus.). (Orig.). 1985. pap. 10.00 (*0-9606210-2-4*) Am Mosquito.
Biological Control of Pests by Mites: Proceedings of a Conference. Marjorie A. Hoy et al. LC 83-72136. (Illus.). 186p. (Orig.). 1983. pap. 12.50 (*0-931876-63-X*, 3304) ANR Pubns CA.
Biological Control of Photosynthesis. Ed. by R. Marcelle et al. (Advances in Agricultural Biotechnology Ser.). 1986. lib. bdg. 95.50 (*90-247-3287-5*) Kluwer Ac.
Biological Control of Plant Diseases: Progress & Challenges for the Future. Ed. by E. C. Tjamos et al. (NATO ASI Series A, Life Sciences: Vol. 230). (Illus.). 476p. (C). 1992. 115.00 (*0-306-44230-2*, Plenum Pr) Plenum.
Biological Control of Plant Parasitic Nematodes. G. R. Stirling. 282p. 1991. 76.50 (*0-85198-703-6*) CAB Intl.
Biological Control of Plant Pathogens. Kenneth F. Baker & R. James Cook. LC 73-18420. (Biology of Plant Pathogens Books Ser.). 451p. reprint ed. pap. 128.60 (*0-8357-7230-6*, 2055548) Bks Demand.
Biological Control of Postharvest Diseases: Theory & Practice. Ed. by Charles L. Wilson & Michael E. Wisniewski. LC 93-33268. 1994. 149.95 (*0-8493-4567-7*, SB608) CRC Pr.
Biological Control of Salvinia Molesta in Sri Lanka: An Assessment of Costs & Benefits. J. A. Doeleman. (C). 1989. text ed. 60.00 (*0-949511-97-8*, Pub. by ACIAR) St Mut.
***Biological Control of Social Forest & Plantation Crops Insects.** Ed. by T. N. Ananthakrishnan. 270p. 1995. text ed. 72.00 (*1-886106-13-4*) Science Pubs.
Biological Control of Soil-Borne Plant Pathogens. Ed. by D. Hornby. 496p. (Orig.). 1990. text ed. 104.50 (*0-85198-637-4*) CAB Intl.
Biological Control of Water Pollution. Ed. by Joachim T. Tourbier & Robert W. Pierson, Jr. LC 76-8593. (Illus.). 350p. reprint ed. pap. 99.80 (*0-8357-7231-4*, 2056736) Bks Demand.
Biological Control of Weeds: A World Catalogue of Agents & Their Target Weeds. 3rd ed. Ed. by M. H. Julien. 194p. 1992. pap. 35.00 (*0-85198-766-4*) CAB Intl.
***Biological Control of Weeds & Plant Diseases: Advances in Applied Allelopathy.** Elroy L. Rice. LC 94-23242. (Illus.). 439p. 1995. 55.00x (*0-8061-2698-1*) U of Okla Pr.
Biological Control on the Phylloplane. Ed. by C. E. Windels & S. E. Lindow. LC 85-71121. 169p. 1985. pap. 26.00x (*0-89054-067-5*) Am Phytopathol Soc.
Biological Control Programme Against Insects & Weeds in Canada 1969-1980. Ed. by J. S. Kelleher & M. A. Hulme. 410p. (Orig.). 1984. pap. text ed. 69.50 (*0-85198-536-X*) CAB Intl.
***Biological Control with Egg Parasitoids.** Ed. by E. Wajnberg & S. A. Hassan. 280p. 1994. 81.00x (*0-85198-896-2*) CAB Intl.
Biological Data Analysis: A Practical Approach. Ed. by John C. Fry. LC 92-27977. (Practical Approach Ser.: No. 115). (Illus.). 448p. 1993. 50.00 (*0-19-963340-1*) OUP.
Biological Data Analysis: A Practical Approach. Ed. by John C. Fry. LC 92-27977. (Practical Approach Ser.: No. 115). (Illus.). 448p. 1993. pap. 48.00 (*0-19-963339-8*) OUP.
Biological Data in Water Pollution Assessment: Quantitative & Statistical Analyses - STP 652. Ed. by K. L. Dickson & J. Cairns. 193p. 1978. 17.50 (*0-8031-0803-6*, 04-652000-16) ASTM.
Biological Degradation & Bioremediation of Toxic Chemicals. G. Rasul Chaudhry. LC 93-25453. (Illus.). 500p. 1995. 69.95 (*0-931146-27-5*, Dioscorides) Timber.
Biological Delay Systems: Linear Stability Theory. N. MacDonald. (Cambridge Studies in Mathematical Biology). (Illus.). 200p. 1989. 74.95 (*0-521-34084-5*) Cambridge U Pr.
Biological Determinants of Reinforcement Vol. 7: Quantitative Analyses of Behavior. Ed. by Michael L. Commons et al. 312p. 1988. 69.95 (*0-89859-551-7*) L Erlbaum Assocs.
Biological Determinants of Sexual Behaviour. Ed. by John B. Hutchison. LC 76-57753. 840p. reprint ed. pap. 180.00 (*0-8357-7232-2*, 2030416) Bks Demand.
Biological Differences & Social Equality: Implications for Social Policy. Ed. by Masako N. Darrough & Robert H. Blank. LC 82-11914. (Illus.). 272p. 1983. text ed. 55.00 (*0-313-23022-6*, DAS/, Greenwood Pr) Greenwood.
Biological Disposition of Morphine & Its Surrogates. Ed. by E. L. Way & T. K. Adler. (WHO Bulletin Reprint Ser.). 1962. pap. 2.00 (*92-4-056004-1*) World Health.
Biological Diversification in the Tropics: Proceedings of the Fifth International Symposium of the Association for Tropical Biology, Held at Macuto Beach, Caracas, Venezuela, February 8-13, 1979. Ed. by Ghillean T. Prance. LC 81-367. 730p. reprint ed. pap. 180.00 (*0-7837-0419-4*, 2040742) Bks Demand.
***Biological Diversity: Problems & Challenges.** Ed. by S. K. Majumdar et al. LC 93-87463. (Illus.). x, 461p. (C). 1994. 45.00 (*0-945809-09-3*) Penn Science.
Biological Diversity: Saving All the Pieces. George D. Davis. (Twenty Twenty Vision: Fulfilling the Promise of the Adirondack Park Ser: Vol. 1). (Illus.). 64p. (Orig.). 1988. pap. 10.00 (*0-9621202-0-0*) Adirondack Council.
Biological Diversity: The Coexistence of Species on Changing Landscapes. Michael A. Huston. (Illus.). 600p. (C). 1994. 100.00 (*0-521-36093-5*); pap. 34.95 (*0-521-36930-4*) Cambridge U Pr.
Biological Diversity Conservation & the Law. 292p. (C). 1993. pap. text ed. 30.00 (*2-8317-0192-9*, Pub. by IUCN SZ) Island Pr.
Biological Diversity in Forest Ecosystems. (Resource Policy Ser.). 52p. (Orig.). 1991. pap. 9.00 (*0-939970-45-7*) Soc Am Foresters.
Biological Diversity of Mexico: Origins & Distributions. Ed. by T. P. Ramamoorthy et al. (Illus.). 856p. 1993. 79.95 (*0-19-506674-X*) OUP.
Biological Effects & Exposure Criteria for Radiofrequency Electromagnetic Fields. National Council on Radiation Protection & Measurements Editors. LC 86-2451. (Report Ser.: No. 86). 400p. 1986. pap. text ed. 40.00 (*0-913392-80-4*) NCRP Pubns.
Biological Effects & Health Implications of Radiofrequency Radiation. Sol M. Michaelson & James C. Lin. 688p. 1987. 135.00 (*0-306-41580-1*, Plenum Pr) Plenum.
Biological Effects & Medical Applications of Electromagnetic Energy. Om P. Gandhi. 544p. 1990. text ed. 130.00 (*0-13-082728-2*) P-H.
Biological Effects & Physics of Solar & Galactic Cosmic Radiation: Part A. Ed. by Charles E. Swenberg et al. LC 93-8450. (NATO ASI Series A, Life Sciences: Vol. 243A). 1993. 95.00 (*0-306-44417-8*, Plenum Pr) Plenum.
Biological Effects & Physics of Solar & Galactic Cosmic Radiation: Part B. Ed. by Charles E. Swenberg et al. LC 93-8449. (NATO ASI Series A, Life Sciences: Vol. 243B). 938p. 1993. 155.00 (*0-306-44418-6*, Plenum Pr) Plenum.
Biological Effects of Asbestos: Proceedings of a Working Conference Held 2-6 October 1972. International Agency for Research on Cancer Staff. LC 74-193499. (IARC Scientific Publications: No. 8). (Illus.). 368p. reprint ed. pap. 104.90 (*0-8357-6447-8*, 2035818) Bks Demand.
Biological Effects of Asbestos: Proceedings of the International Agency for Research on Cancer Working Conference, Lyon, France, October 2-6, 1972. International Agency for Research on Cancer Staff. Ed. by P. Bogovski et al. (IARC Scientific Pub.: No. 8). 1973. 32.00 (*0-686-16778-3*) World Health.
Biological Effects of Cholesterol Oxides. 1991. 119.95 (*0-685-54332-3*, CRC Reprint) Franklin.
Biological Effects of Cholesterol Oxides. Peng Shi-Kaung & Robert J. Morin. (Illus.). 224p. 1991. 156.00 (*0-8493-6776-X*, QP752) CRC Pr.
Biological Effects of Deuterium. J. Thomson & P. Alexander. LC 63-19255. (International Series of Monographs on Pure & Applied Mathematics: Vol. 19). 1963. 65.00 (*0-08-010225-5*, Pub. by Pergamon Repr UK) Franklin.
Biological Effects of Electric & Magnetic Fields, Vol. 1: Sources & Mechanisms. Ed. by David O. Carpenter & Sinerik Ayrapetyan. (Illus.). 369p. 1994. text ed. 99.00 (*0-12-160261-3*) Acad Pr.
Biological Effects of Electric & Magnetic Fields, Vol. 2: Clinical Applications & Therapeutic Effects. Ed. by David O. Carpenter & Sinerik Ayrapetyan. (Illus.). 357p. 1994. text ed. 99.00 (*0-12-160262-1*) Acad Pr.
Biological Effects of Electropollution: Brain Tumors & Experimental Models. Ed. by Sisir K. Dutta & Richard M. Millis. LC 86-82834. (Illus.). x, 245p. (C). 1986. text ed. 48.00 (*0-9617314-1-9*) Info Ventures Inc.
Biological Effects of External X & Gamma Radiation, Part 2. AEC Technical Information Center Staff. Ed. by Raymond E. Zirkle. (National Nuclear Energy Ser.: Vol. 22C). 487p. 1956. pap. 52.00 (*0-87079-146-X*, TID-5220); fiche 9.00 (*0-87079-147-8*, TID-5220) DOE.
Biological Effects of Extremely Low Frequency Electromagnetic Fields: Proceedings. Ed. by R. D. Phillips & M. F. Gillis. LC 79-607778. (DOE Symposium Ser.). 593p. 1979. pap. 22.50 (*0-87079-118-4*, CONF-781016); fiche 9.00 (*0-87079-148-6*, CONF-781016) DOE.
Biological Effects of Glutamic Acid & Its Derivatives. Victor A. Najjar. 1982. lib. bdg. 183.00 (*90-6193-841-4*) Kluwer Ac.
Biological Effects of Heavy Metals, II. Ed. by E. C. Foulkes. 447p. 1990. 167.00 (*0-8493-4242-2*, RA1231) CRC Pr.
Biological Effects of Heavy Metals, Vols. I-II. Ed. by E. C. Foulkes. 447p. 1990. 179.00 (*0-8493-4241-4*, RA1231) CRC Pr.
Biological Effects of Low Level Exposures: Dose-Response Relationships. Ed. by Edward J. Calabrese. LC 93-50076. 320p. 1994. 75.00 (*1-56670-093-0*, L1093) Lewis Pubs.
Biological Effects of Low Level Exposures to Chemicals. Calabnese. 1992. 64.95 (*0-87371-665-5*, RA1199) Lewis Pubs.
Biological Effects of Magnetic Fields. Ed. by Madeline F. Barnothy. Incl. Vol. 1. LC 64-13146. 336p. 1964. 59.50 (*0-306-37601-6*); Vol. 2. LC 64-13146. 328p. 1969. 59.50 (*0-306-37602-4*); LC 64-13146. write for info. (*0-318-55309-0*, Plenum Pr) Plenum.
Biological Effects of Mineral Fibres: Effects Biologiques des Fibres Minerales: Proceedings of a Symposium Organized by IARC, l'Institut National De la Sante et De la Recherche Medicale (National Institute of Health & Medical Research), & the MRC Pneumoconiosis Unit, Penarth, U. K. Held at the International Agency for Research on Cancer, Lyon, France, 25-27 September 1979, Vol. 1. International Agency for Research on Cancer Staff. Ed. by J. C. Wagner. LC 81-169877. (IARC Scientific Publications: No. 30). 539p. reprint ed. pap. 145.60 (*0-7837-4001-8*, 2043832) Bks Demand.
Biological Effects of Mineral Fibres: Effects Biologiques des Fibres Minerales: Proceedings of a Symposium Organized by IARC, l'Institut National De la Sante et De la Recherche Medicale (National Institute of Health & Medical Research), & the MRC Pneumoconiosis Unit, Penarth, U. K. Held at the International Agency for Research on Cancer, Lyon, France, 25-27 September 1979, Vol. 2. International Agency for Research on Cancer Staff. Ed. by J. C. Wagner. LC 81-169877. (IARC Scientific Publications: No. 30). 489p. reprint ed. pap. 139.40 (*0-7837-4002-6*) Bks Demand.
Biological Effects of Non-Ionizing Radiations: Cellular Properties & Interactions. Herman P. Schwan. LC 86-33279. (Taylor Lecture Ser.: No. 10). 50p. 1987. pap. text ed. 20.00 (*0-913392-85-5*) NCRP Pubns.
Biological Effects of Nonionizing Radiation. Ed. by Karl H. Illinger. LC 81-2652. (ACS Symposium Ser.: No. 157). 342p. 1981. 43.95 (*0-8412-0634-1*) Am Chemical.
Biological Effects of Organolead Compounds. Ed. by Philippe Grandjean. 288p. 1984. 180.00 (*0-8493-5309-2*, RA1231) CRC Pr.
Biological Effects of Physical Activity. Ed. by R. Sanders Williams & Andrew G. Wallace. LC 89-1757. (HKP Sport Science Monograph Ser.). 192p. 1989. pap. text ed. 23.00x (*0-87322-218-0*, BWIL0218) Human Kinetics.
Biological Effects of Power Frequency Electric & Magnetic Fields. LC 89-600708. (Illus.). 109p. 1989. pap. 4.75 (*0-16-005560-1*, S/N 052-003-011) USGPO.
Biological Effects of Power Line Fields: Scientific Advisory Panel's Final Report. (Illus.). 169p. (Orig.). (C). 1994. pap. text ed. 55.00 (*0-7881-0571-X*) Diane Pub.
Biological Effects of Radiation. 2nd ed. Daniel S. Grosch & Larry E. Hopwood. LC 79-51677. 1979. text ed. 92.00 (*0-12-304150-3*) Acad Pr.
Biological Effects of Static Magnetic Fields. Nancy J. Simon. LC 92-70942. (Illus.). 300p. 1992. pap. 50.00 (*1-881160-04-1*) Intl Cryogenic.
Biological Effects of Transmission Line Fields. Edwin L. Carstensen. LC 86-42117. 400p. 1987. 69.50 (*0-444-01018-1*) P-H.
Biological Effects of Ultrasound. Ed. by Wesley L. Nyborg & Marvin C. Ziskin. (Clinics in Diagnostic Ultrasound Ser.: Vol. 16). (Illus.). 191p. 1985. text ed. 36.00 (*0-443-08314-2*) Churchill.
Biological Effects of Ultrasound: Mechanisms & Clinical Implications. LC 84-61833. (Report Ser.: No. 74). 1983. 30.00 (*0-913392-64-2*) NCRP Pubns.
Biological Effects of Ultraviolet Radiation. Walter Harm. LC 77-88677. (IUPAB Biophysics Ser.: No. 1). (Illus.). 1980. pap. 24.95 (*0-521-29362-6*) Cambridge U Pr.
Biological Effects of UVA Radiation. Frederick Urbach. Ed. by Richard W. Gange. LC 85-16877. 346p. 1985. text ed. 95.00 (*0-275-92047-X*, C2047, Praeger Pubs) Greenwood.
Biological Effects of 224 Ra. W. A. Muller & H. G. Ebert. 1978. lib. bdg. 84.00 (*90-247-2081-8*) Kluwer Ac.
Biological Efficiency in Agriculture. C. R. Spedding et al. 1981. text ed. 117.00 (*0-12-656560-0*) Acad Pr.
Biological Electron Microscopy: Theory, Techniques, & Troubleshooting. Michael J. Dykstra. (Illus.). 335p. (C). 1992. 49.50 (*0-306-44277-9*, Plenum Pr) Plenum.
Biological Environmental Impact Studies: Theory & Methods. Diana V. Ward. LC 78-10595. 1978. text ed. 44.00 (*0-12-735350-X*) Acad Pr.
Biological Evaluation of Medical Devices. AAMI Staff. (Illus.). 106p. (Orig.). 1994. pap. 150.00 (*1-57020-011-4*, BIO11) Assn Adv Med Instrn.
Biological Explorations: A Human Approach. 2nd rev. ed. Stanley E. Gunstream. LC 93-25338. (Illus.). 384p. (C). 1993. pap. write for info. (*0-02-348525-6*) Macmillan.
***Biological Exposure Values for Occupational Toxicants & Carcinogens: Critical Data Evaluation for BAT & EKA Values.** Ed. by D. Henschler & G. Lehnert. LC 94-41515. 1994. write for info. (*3-527-27032-9*) VCH Pubs.
***Biological Factors in Learning.** Ed. by Michael D. Zeiler & Peter Harzem. LC 82-23900. (Advances in Analysis of Behavior Ser.: No. 3). 420p. 1983. pap. 119.70 (*0-7837-8493-7*, 2049300) Bks Demand.
Biological Feedback. Ed. by Thomas. 1990. 190.00 (*0-8493-6766-2*, QH508) CRC Pr.
Biological Foundations of Behavior. Leger. (C). 1991. text ed. 54.50 (*0-06-043894-0*) HarpCollege.
Biological Foundations of Behavior. Frederick Toates. LC 86-5158. (Guides to Psychology Ser.). 160p. 1986. 29.00 (*0-335-15333-X*, Open Univ Pr) Taylor & Francis.
Biological Foundations of Gestures: Motor & Semiotic Aspects. J. L. Nespoulous et al. 336p. (C). 1986. text ed. 69.95 (*0-89859-645-9*) L Erlbaum Assocs.
Biological Foundations of Human Sexuality. William H. Masters et al. (C). 1993. 20.50 (*0-06-501517-7*) HarpCollege.
Biological Foundations of Linguistic Communication: Towards a Biocybernetics of Language. Thomas Ballmer. (Pragmatics & Beyond Ser.: Vol. III, No. 7). x, 161p. (Orig.). 1983. pap. 52.00 (*90-272-2520-6*) Benjamins North Am.
***Biological Foundations of Psychiatry Vol. 1.** fac. ed. Ed. by Robert G. Grenell & Sabit Gabay. LC 74-15664. (Illus.). 613p. Date not set. pap. 174.80 (*0-7837-7151-7*, 2047145) Bks Demand.
Biological Function of Gangliosides: Proceedings of Novel Symposium 93. Ed. by Lars Svennerholm et al. LC 93-30538. (Progress in Brain Research Ser.: Vol. 101). 1994. 231.25 (*0-444-81658-5*) Elsevier.
Biological Functions of Proteases & Inhibitors. Ed. by N. Katunuma et al. (Illus.). xii, 274p. 1994. 198.50 (*3-8055-5954-2*) S Karger.
Biological Functions of Proteinases. Ed. by H. Holzer & J. Tschesche. (Colloquium Mosbach Ser.: Vol. 30). (Illus.). 1979. 59.00 (*0-387-09683-5*) Spr-Verlag.

An Asterisk (*) at the beginning of an entry indicates that the title is appearing in BIP for the first time.

An Asterisk (*) at the beginning of an entry indicates that the title is appearing in BIP for the first time.

Biological Polyelectrolytes. Arthur Veis. LC 72-107758. (Biological Macromolecules Ser.: No. 3). (Illus.). 303p. reprint ed. pap. 86.40 (*0-7837-0884-X*, 2041190) Bks Demand.

Biological Principles with Human Applications. 3rd ed. Gideon Nelson. 435p. 1989. Net. pap. text ed. write for info. (*0-471-61775-X*); Net. student ed 22.95 (*0-471-61867-5*) Wiley.

Biological Process Design for Wastewater Treatment. Larry D. Benefield & Clifford W. Randall. (C). 1985. reprint ed. text ed. 35.00 (*0-935005-02-1*); reprint ed. 4.95 (*0-935005-03-X*) Lincoln-Rembrandt.

Biological Processes. Ed. by Harry M. Freeman & P. R. Sferra. LC 90-70257. (Innovative Hazardous Waste Treatment Technology Ser.: Vol. 3). 210p. 1990. 49.00 (*0-87762-618-9*) Technomic.

Biological Processes & Soil Fertility. Ed. by J. Tinsley & J. F. Darbyshire. LC 83-22002. (Developments in Plant & Soil Sciences Ser.). 1984. lib. bdg. 152.50 (*90-247-2902-5*) Kluwer Ac.

Biological Processes & Wastes in the Ocean. Judith M. Capuzzo & Dana R. Kester. Ed. by Iver. W. Duedall et al. LC 84-29733. (Oceanic Processes in Marine Pollution Ser.: Vol. 1). 280p. (C). 1986. lib. bdg. 59.50 (*0-89874-810-0*) Krieger.

Biological Product Freeze-Drying & Formulation. Ed. by J. C. May & F. Brown. (Developments in Biological Standardization Ser.: Vol. 74). (Illus.). x, 382p. 1992. pap. 224.00 (*3-8055-5466-4*) S Karger.

Biological Products & Actions: Index of Modern Information. Katie L. Holt. LC 88-48003. 150p. 1990. 49.50 (*1-55914-166-2*); pap. 39.50 (*1-55914-167-0*) ABBE Pubs Assn.

Biological Properties of Peptidoglycan: Proceedings of the International Workshop, 2nd, Munich, Federal Republic of Germany, May 20-21, 1985. Ed. by P. H. Seidl & K. H. Schleifer. xiv, 436p. 1986. lib. bdg. 203.85 (*0-89925-262-1*) De Gruyter.

***Biological Properties of Peptidoglycan: Proceedings of the International Workshop, 2nd, Munich, Federal Republic of Germany, May 20-21, 1985.** Ed. by P. H. Seidl & K. H. Schleifer. xiv, 436p. 1986. lib. bdg. 203.85 (*3-11-010737-6*) De Gruyter.

Biological Protection with Prostaglandins, Vol. I. Ed. by Max M. Cohen. 288p. 1985. 155.00 (*0-8493-5962-7*, QP801, CRC Reprint) Franklin.

Biological Protection with Prostaglandins, Vol. II. Max M. Cohen. 272p. 1986. 155.00 (*0-8493-5963-5*, QP801, CRC Reprint) Franklin.

***Biological Psychiatry.** Robert J. Hedaya. 192p. (C). 1995. 25.00 (*0-393-70191-3*) Norton.

Biological Psychiatry. Michael R. Trimble. 1988. text ed. 128.95 (*0-471-91622-6*) Wiley.

Biological Psychiatry, Nineteen Eighty-One. Carlo Perris et al. (Developments in Psychiatry Ser.: Vol. 5). 1982. 300.50 (*0-444-80404-8*) Elsevier.

Biological Psychiatry Today: Proceedings of the World Conference, 2nd, Spain, 1978, Set. Ed. by J. Obiols et al. (Developments in Psychiatry Ser.: Vol. 2). 1979. 218.00 (*0-444-80117-0*, North Holland) Elsevier.

Biological, Psychological, & Environmental Factors in Delinquency & Mental Disorder: An Interdisciplinary Bibliography. Ed. by Deborah W. Denno & Ruth M. Schwarz. LC 85-5620. (Bibliographies & Indexes in Sociology Ser.: No. 4). xv, 222p. 1985. text ed. 55.00 (*0-313-24939-3*, DBP/) Greenwood.

Biological Psychology. Daniel P. Kimble. LC 87-17633. (Illus.). 480p. (C). 1988. text ed. 43.25 (*0-03-069636-4*) HB Coll Pubs.

Biological Psychology. 2nd ed. Daniel P. Kimble. LC 91-32911. (Illus.). 482p. (C). 1992. text ed. 48.00 (*0-03-040487-8*) HB Coll Pubs.

Biological Psychology. 4th ed. James W. Kalat. 704p. (C). 1991. text ed. 57.95 (*0-534-16254-1*) Brooks-Cole.

Biological Psychology. 4th ed. James W. Kalat. 704p. (C). 1992. student ed, pap. 18.95 (*0-534-16255-X*) Brooks-Cole.

***Biological Psychology.** 5th ed. James W. Kalat. LC 94-27415. 688p. 1995. text ed. 58.95 (*0-534-21108-9*) Brooks-Cole.

Biological Psychology: A Cybernetic Science. F. J. McGuigan. LC 93-35572. 1993. text ed. write for info. (*0-13-146655-0*) P-H.

Biological Psychology: An Evolutionary Perspective. Eugene H. Galluscio. (Illus.). 900p. (C). 1990. text ed. write for info. (*0-02-340472-8*) Macmillan.

Biological-Psychosocial Interactions in Early Adolescence: A Life-Span Perspective. Ed. by Richard M. Lerner & Terryl Foch. (Child Psychology Ser.). 408p. 1987. text ed. 69.95 (*0-89859-787-0*) L Erlbaum Assocs.

Biological Radiation Effects. J. C. Kiefer. (Illus.). 456p. 1990. 89.00 (*0-387-51089-3*, 2883) Spr-Verlag.

Biological Reactions within the Extracorporeal Blood Circuit During Hemodialysis. Ed. by K. M. Koch & E. Streicher. (Contributions to Nephrology Ser.: Vol. 59). (Illus.). viii, 168p. 1988. 115.25 (*3-8055-4578-9*) S Karger.

Biological Reactive Intermediates III: Mechanisms of Action in Animal Model & Human Disease. Ed. by James J. Kocsis et al. LC 86-4973. (Advances in Experimental Medicine & Biology Ser.: Vol. 197). 1076p. 1986. 175.00 (*0-306-42264-6*, Plenum Pr) Plenum.

Biological Reactive Intermediates IV: Molecular & Cellular Effects & Their Impact on Human Health. Ed. by Charlotte M. Witmer et al. LC 90-14326. (Advances in Experimental Medicine & Biology Ser.: Vol. 283). (Illus.). 880p. 1991. 175.00 (*0-306-43737-6*, Plenum Pr) Plenum.

Biological Recording of Changes in British Wildlife. Ed. by P. T. Harding. 86p. 1992. pap. 45.00 (*0-11-701560-1*, HM15601, Pub. by HMSO UK) UNIPUB.

Biological Regulation & Development Vol. 3A: Hormone Action. Ed. by Robert F. Goldberger et al. LC 82-9841. 360p. 1982. 85.00 (*0-306-40925-9*, Plenum Pr) Plenum.

Biological Regulation & Development Vol. 3B: Hormone Action. Ed. by Robert F. Goldberger & Keith Yamamoto. LC 82-9841. 326p. 1984. 85.00 (*0-306-41442-2*, Plenum Pr) Plenum.

Biological Regulation of the Chondrocyte. Adolphe. 1992. 184.00 (*0-8493-6733-6*, QP88) CRC Pr.

Biological Relationships Between Africa & South America. Ed. by Peter Goldblatt. LC 93-18210. (Illus.). 648p. (C). 1993. 85.00 (*0-300-05375-4*) Yale U Pr.

Biological Research in Schizophrenia: Proceedings of the WHO Scientific Group, Geneva, 1969. WHO Staff. (Technical Report Ser.: No. 450). pap. 2.00 (*92-4-120450-8*) World Health.

Biological Response Modifiers: A Self-Instruction Manual for Health Professionals. Kimberly A. Rumsey & Paula T. Rieger. LC 92-81530. 134p. 1992. 29.95 (*0-944496-30-X*) Precept Pr.

Biological Response Modifiers: New Approaches to Disease Intervention. Ed. by Paul F. Torrence. 1985. text ed. 105.00 (*0-12-695770-3*); pap. text ed. 70.00 (*0-12-695771-1*) Acad Pr.

Biological Response Modifiers & Cancer Research. Chiao. (Immunology Ser.: Vol. 40). 464p. 1988. 175.00 (*0-8247-7860-X*) Dekker.

Biological Response Modifiers for Ophthalmic Tissue Repair. Ed. by Gary R. Grotendorst et al. (Advances in Applied Biotechnology Ser.: Vol. 8). (Illus.). 256p. (C). 1990. 55.00 (*0-943255-06-6*) Portfolio Pub.

Biological Responses in Cancer: Progress Toward Potential Applications, Vol. 1. Ed. by Enrico Mihich. LC 82-18041. 322p. 1982. 85.00 (*0-306-41146-6*, Plenum Pr) Plenum.

Biological Responses in Cancer: Progress Toward Potential Applications, Vol. 2. Ed. by Enrico Mihich. LC 82-18041. 258p. 1984. 79.50 (*0-306-41583-6*, Plenum Pr) Plenum.

Biological Responses in Cancer: Progress Toward Potential Applications, Vol. 3: Immunomodulation by Anticancer Drugs. Ed. by Enrico Mihich & Yoshio Sakurai. LC 84-18041. 230p. 1985. 79.50 (*0-306-41879-7*, Plenum Pr) Plenum.

Biological Responses in Cancer: Progress Toward Potential Applications, Vol. 4. Ed. by Enrico Mihich. LC 82-18041. 270p. 1985. 79.50 (*0-306-42044-9*, Plenum Pr) Plenum.

Biological Responses to Ultraviolet A Radiation: 2nd International Symposium. Ed. by Frederick Urback. (American Society for Photobiology Symposium Ser.). 433p. 1992. 80.00 (*0-9632105-0-5*); pap. 65.00 (*0-9632105-1-3*) Valdenmar.

Biological Rhythms. Ed. by Jurgen Aschoff. LC 80-21037. (Handbook of Behavioral Neurobiology Ser.: Vol. 4). 582p. 1981. 115.00 (*0-306-40585-7*, Plenum Pr) Plenum.

***Biological Rhythms: Implications for the Worker - New Developments in Neuroscience.** (Illus.). 249p. (Orig.). (C). 1994. pap. text ed. 55.00x (*0-7881-0738-0*) Diane Pub.

Biological Rhythms: Sleep & Shift Work. Ed. by L. C. Johnson et al. (Advances in Sleep Research Ser.: Vol. 7). 640p. 1981. text ed. 65.00 (*0-88331-115-1*) Luce.

Biological Rhythms & Behavior. J. Mendlewicz & Herman M. Van Praag. (Advances in Biological Psychiatry Ser.: Vol. 11). (Illus.). iv, 150p. 1983. pap. 79.25 (*3-8055-3672-0*) S Karger.

Biological Rhythms & Clocks of Intertidal Animals. John D. Palmer. (Illus.). 224p. 1995. 65.00 (*0-19-509435-2*) OUP.

Biological Rhythms & Living Clocks. 2nd ed. J. D. Palmer. Ed. by J. J. Head. LC 84-70786. (Carolina Biology Readers Ser.: No. 92). (Illus.). 16p. (J). (gr. 10 up). 1984. pap. 2.75 (*0-89278-192-0*, 45-9692) Carolina Biological.

Biological Rhythms & Mental Disorders. Ed. by David J. Kupfer et al. LC 88-24598. 357p. 1988. lib. bdg. 50.00 (*0-89862-746-X*) Guilford Pr.

Biological Rhythms & Shift Work. 1992. lib. bdg. 95.00 (*0-8490-8850-X*) Gordon Pr.

Biological Rhythms in Human & Animal Physiology. Gay G. Luce. Orig. Title: Biological Rhythms in Psychiatry & Medicine. 1971. reprint ed. pap. text ed. 6.95 (*0-486-22586-0*) Dover.

Biological Rhythms in Psychiatry & Medicine see Biological Rhythms in Human & Animal Physiology

Biological Rhythms, Mood Disorders, Light Therapy & the Pineal Gland. Mohammad Shafii & Sharon Shafii. LC 89-18447. (Progress in Psychiatry Ser.). 250p. 1990. text ed. 28.00 (*0-88048-169-2*) Am Psychiatric.

Biological Rhythms, Sleep & Performance. Ed. by Wilse B. Webb. LC 81-14754. (Wiley Series on Studies in Human Performance). (Illus.). 295p. reprint ed. pap. 84.10 (*0-8357-7234-9*, 2033054) Bks Demand.

Biological Risk Factors for Psychosocial Disorders. Ed. by Michael Rutter & Paul Casaer. (European Network on Longitudinal Studies on Individual Development). 384p. (C). 1991. 74.95 (*0-521-40103-8*) Cambridge U Pr.

Biological Risks of Medical Irradiations: Proceedings of the AAPM Spring Symposium Held at the University of Texas Health Science Center, San Antonio, Texas, March 26-28, 1980. Ed. by Gary D. Fullerton et al. (American Association of Physicists in Medicine Symposium Ser.: No. 5). 340p. 1980. 42.00 (*0-88318-278-5*) Am Inst Physics.

Biological Role of Plant Lipids. Ed. by P. A. Biacs. LC 88-43522. (Illus.). 644p. 1990. 135.00 (*0-306-43181-5*, Plenum Pr) Plenum.

***Biological Role of Plant Lipids: Proceedings of the 8th International Symposium on the Biological Role of Plant Lipids Held at Budapest, Hungary, July 25-28, 1988.** Pater A. Blacs. Ed. by Katalin Gruiz & Tibor Kremmer. 625p. (C). 1989. 150.00x (*963-05-5375-9*, Pub. by Akad Kiado HU) St Mut.

Biological Role of Porphyrins & Related Structures. Ed. by Alan D. Adler. (Annals Ser.: Vol. 244). 694p. 1975. 60.00 (*0-89072-758-9*) NY Acad Sci.

Biological Roles of Copper. Ciba Foundation Staff. LC 80-23396. (Ciba Foundation Symposium: New Ser.: 79). 351p. reprint ed. pap. 100.10 (*0-8357-7235-7*, 2022198) Bks Demand.

Biological Roots of Human Nature: Forging Links Between Evolution & Behavior. Timothy H. Goldsmith. (Illus.). 176p. 1991. 24.95 (*0-19-506288-4*) OUP.

Biological Roots of Human Nature: Forging Links Between Evolution & Behavior. Timothy H. Goldsmith. (Illus.). 176p. 1994. reprint ed. pap. 14.95 (*0-19-509393-3*) OUP.

Biological Science. William T. Keeton & James L. Gould. 1200p. (C). 1987. trans. 40.00 (*0-393-95392-0*); disk write for info. (*0-318-59751-9*) Norton.

Biological Science. William T. Keeton et al. LC 92-19326. (C). 1993. student ed, pap. text ed. 15.95 (*0-393-96226-1*) Norton.

Biological Science. William T. Keeton et al. LC 92-19326. (C). 1993. pap. text ed. write for info. (*0-393-96227-X*) Norton.

Biological Science, 1. William T. Keeton et al. LC 92-19326. (C). 1992. pap. text ed. 36.95 (*0-393-96224-5*) Norton.

Biological Science, 1. 5th ed. William T. Keeton et al. LC 92-19326. (C). 1992. text ed. 67.95 (*0-393-96223-7*) Norton.

Biological Science, 2. William T. Keeton et al. LC 92-19326. (C). 1992. pap. text ed. 36.95 (*0-393-96225-3*) Norton.

Biological Science: Interaction of Experiments & Ideas (BSCS Second Course) 3rd ed. Biological Sciences Curriculum Study Staff. (gr. 10-12). 1977. teacher ed 15.96 (*0-13-076919-3*); text ed. 30.64 (*0-13-076562-7*) P-H.

Biological Science: Red Patterns & Processes, Teacher's Edition. 3rd ed. BSCS Staff. 816p. 1992. ring bd. 38.90 (*0-8403-5864-4*) Kendall-Hunt.

Biological Sciences. Jack Rudman. (Graduate Record Area Examination Ser.: GRE-41). 1994. pap. 23.95 (*0-8373-5241-X*) Nat Learn.

Biological Shielding of Maritime Reactors. D. L. Broder et al. 362p. 1970. text ed. 90.50 (*0-7065-1006-2*, Pub. by Keter Pub IS) Coronet Bks.

Biological Signal Transduction. Ed. by E. M. Ross & K. W. A. Wirtz. (NATO ASI Series H: Cell Biology: Vol. 52). xi, 540p. 1991. 198.00 (*0-387-51773-1*) Spr-Verlag.

Biological Significance of Superantigens. Ed. by B. Fleischer. (Chemical Immunology Ser.: Vol. 55). (Illus.). x, 200p. 1992. 157.00 (*3-8055-5587-3*) S Karger.

***Biological Standard of Living on Three Continents: Further Explorations in Anthropometric History.** Ed. by John Komlos. LC 94-42328. 1995. text ed. 54.95 (*0-8133-2055-0*) Westview.

Biological Substances: International Standards & Reference Preparations. 1975. pap. 2.80 (*92-4-154049-4*) World Health.

Biological Substances: International Standards & Reference Reagents, 1986. 94p. 1987. pap. 9.00 (*92-4-154213-6*) World Health.

Biological Substrates of Alzheimer's Disease. Arnold B. Scheibel & Adam F. Wechsler. (UCLA Forum in Medical Sciences Ser.: No. 27). 1986. text ed. 71.00 (*0-12-623130-3*) Acad Pr.

Biological Survey for the Nation. National Research Council, Commission on Life Sciences Staff. 224p. (Orig.). (C). 1993. pap. text ed. 26.00 (*0-309-04984-9*) Natl Acad Pr.

Biological Survey Reports, 12 vols., Set. Bureau of Biological Survey Staff. 1993. reprint ed. lib. bdg. 900.00 (*0-7812-5140-0*) Rprt Serv.

Biological Systematics: The State of the Art. A. Minelli. LC 93-3578. 1993. write for info. (*0-412-36440-9*) Chapman & Hall.

Biological Systems: Papers from Science, 1988-1989. Ed. by Barbara R. Jasny & Daniel E. Koshland, Jr. LC 89-18005. (AAAS Publication Ser.: No. 89-16S). (Illus.). 282p. (Orig.). reprint ed. pap. 80.40 (*0-7837-6735-8*, 2046363) Bks Demand.

Biological Themes in Modern Science Fiction. Helen N. Parker. LC 84-8768. (Studies in Speculative Fiction: No. 6). 115p. reprint ed. pap. 32.80 (*0-8357-1577-9*, 2070516) Bks Demand.

Biological Transmutations. C. L. Kervran. (Illus.). 180p. 1980. text ed. 20.00 (*0-8464-1069-9*) Beekman Pubs.

Biological Transmutations: A New Science Practiced by Physicians, Chemists, Nutritionists, & Biologists. (Alternative Medicine Ser.). 1991. lib. bdg. 79.95 (*0-8490-4308-5*) Gordon Pr.

Biological Transmutations: The Movement of Life Stems from Change. C. Louis Kervran. 163p. 1989. 18.50 (*0-916508-47-1*) Happiness Pr.

Biological Transport of Radiotracers, I. L. Colombetti. 447p. 1982. pap. 156.00 (*0-8493-6017-X*, QP519, CRC Reprint) Franklin.

Biological Treatment of Food Processing Wastewater Design & Operations Manual. Scientific Publishers Staff. (C). 1988. 250.00 (*0-685-54215-7*, Scientific) St Mut.

Biological Treatment of Waste Water. 2nd ed. Michael Winkler. 500p. 1995. text ed. 109.95 (*0-13-084187-0*) P-H.

Biological Treatments in Psychiatry. Malcolm H. Lader & Reginald Herrington. (Illus.). 416p. 1990. 80.00 (*0-19-261644-7*); pap. 37.50 (*0-19-261939-X*) OUP.

***Biological Variation in Health & Illness: Race, Age, & Sex Differences.** 2nd ed. Theresa Overfield. LC 94-42293. 240p. 1995. 139.95 (*0-8493-4577-4*, 4577) CRC Pr.

Biological Vulnerability to Drug Abuse. 1993. lib. bdg. 261.95 (*0-8490-8910-7*) Gordon Pr.

Biological Vulnerability to Drug Abuse: Genetics in the Etiology of Drug Abuse. 1991. lib. bdg. 79.00 (*0-8490-4344-1*) Gordon Pr.

Biological Warfare in the Twenty-First Century. Malcolm Dando. 226p. 1994. 40.00 (*1-85753-064-0*, Pub. by Brasseys UK) Brasseys Inc.

Biological Waste Treatment. W. Wesley Eckenfelder & D. O'Connor. LC 61-10913. 1961. 124.00 (*0-08-009547-X*, Pub. by Pergamon Repr UK) Franklin.

Biological Wastewater Treatment: Theory & Applications. Grady & Lim. LC 80-20171. (Pollution Engineering & Technology Ser.: Vol. 12). 984p. 1980. 225.00 (*0-8247-1000-2*) Dekker.

Biological Wastewater Treatment Systems: Theory & Operation. N. J. Horan. 1990. text ed. 69.95 (*0-471-92258-7*) Wiley.

Biological Weapons: Weapons of the Future? Ed. by Brad Roberts. LC 92-47356. (Significant Issues Ser.: Vol. 15, No. 1). 1993. pap. 15.00 (*0-89206-210-X*) CSI Studies.

Biological Woman: The Convenient Myth. Ruth Hubbard et al. 376p. 1982. 24.95 (*0-87073-702-3*); pap. 16.95 (*0-87073-703-1*) Schenkman Bks Inc.

Biologically Active Amines Found in Man: Their Biochemistry, Pharmacology, Pathophysiological Importance. F. Franzen & K. Eysell. LC 75-78590. 1969. 103.00 (*0-08-013877-2*, Pub. by Pergamon Repr UK) Franklin.

Biologically Active Atrial Peptides. Ed. by Barry M. Brenner & John H. Laragh. (American Society of Hypertension Symposium Ser.: Vol. 1). (Illus.). 654p. 1987. text ed. 121.50 (*0-88167-306-4*) Raven.

Biologically Active Ether Lipids. Ed. by P. Braquet et al. (Progress in Biochemical Pharmacology Ser.: Vol. 22). (Illus.). vi, 198p. 1988. 132.00 (*3-8055-4669-6*) S Karger.

Biologically Active Natural Products: Potential Use in Agriculture. Ed. by Horace G. Cutler. LC 88-7859. (Symposium Ser.: No. 380). (Illus.). xi, 496p. 1988. 89.95 (*0-8412-1556-1*) Am Chemical.

Biologically Active Peptides: Design, Synthesis & Utilization. Ed. by William V. Williams & David B. Weiner. LC 92-56712. (Biomedical Applications of Biotechnology Ser.: Vol. 1). 350p. 1992. 85.00 (*0-87762-935-8*) Technomic.

Biologically Active Phytochemicals & Their Activities Database. Duke. 1992. 205.00 (*0-8493-3671-6*, TK) CRC Pr.

Biologically Active Substances: Exploration & Exploitation. Ed. by D. A. Hems. LC 76-58496. (Illus.). 337p. reprint ed. pap. 96.10 (*0-8357-7236-5*, 2030463) Bks Demand.

Biologically-Based Methods for Cancer Risk Assessment. Ed. by C. C. Travis. (NATO ASI Series A, Life Sciences: Vol. 159). (Illus.). 340p. 1989. 95.00 (*0-306-43117-3*, Plenum Pr) Plenum.

Biologically Closed Electric Circuits: Clinical, Experimental & Theoretical Evidence for an Additional Circulatory System. Bjorn E. Nordenstrom. (Illus.). 374p. 1983. 247.50x (*91-970432-0-6*, Pub. by Almqv & Wiksell SW) Coronet Bks.

Biologically Induced Corrosion. Ed. by S. C. Dexter. LC 86-60402. (NACE Reference Bks.: No. 8). (Illus.). 357p. 1986. 10.00 (*0-915567-20-2*) NACE Intl.

Biologically Inspired Physics. Ed. by L. Peliti. (NATO ASI Series B, Physics: Vol. 263). (Illus.). 396p. 1991. 120.00 (*0-306-44000-8*, Plenum Pr) Plenum.

Biologically Inspired Robots: Serpentile Locomotors & Manipulators. Shigeo Hirose. Tr. by Peter Cave & Charles Goulden. LC 92-34986. 1993. 59.95 (*0-19-856261-6*) OUP.

Biologicals from Recombinant Micro-organisms & Animal Cells: Production & Recovery: Proceedings of the 34th Oholo Conference, Eilat, Israel 1990. Ed. by M. D. White et al. 569p. 1991. text ed. 210.00 (*0-89573-967-4*) VCH Pubs.

***Biologics Development: A Regulatory Overview.** Ed. by Mark Mathieu. 310p. 1993. 135.00 (*1-882615-00-X*) Parexel Intl.

Biologie see Lesestoff Nach Wahl

Biologie der Hemipteren. H. Weber. (Illus.). 1968. 70.00 (*90-6123-179-5*) Lubrecht & Cramer.

Biologie der Suesswasserinsekten. C. Wesenberg-Lund. viii, 682p. 1981. reprint ed. 177.00 (*3-87429-189-8*) Koeltz Sci Bks.

Biologie der Suesswasserinsekten. C. Wesenberg-Lund. (Illus.). 682p. 1980. reprint ed. lib. bdg. 120.00 (*3-7682-1281-5*) Lubrecht & Cramer.

Biologie der Suesswassertiere. C. Wesenberg-Lund. xi, 817p. 1939. reprint ed. 177.00 (*3-87429-203-7*) Koeltz Sci Bks.

Biologie der Suesswassertiere: Wirbellose Tiere. C. Wesenberg-Lund. (Illus.). 1967. 140.00 (*3-7682-0426-X*) Lubrecht & Cramer.

Biologie des Menschen. 4th ed. J. Wunderli. (Illus.). xiv, 194p. 1982. pap. 19.25 (*3-8055-2613-X*) S Karger.

Biologising of Childhood: Developmental Psychology & the Darwinian Myth. John R. Morss. 320p. 1990. 59.95 (*0-86377-129-7*) L Erlbaum Assocs.

Biologist. Jack Rudman. (Career Examination Ser.: C-2013). 1994. pap. 27.95 (*0-8373-2013-5*) Nat Learn.

Biologist's Advanced Mathematics. David R. Causton. (Illus.). 288p. (C). 1987. pap. 37.95 (*0-04-574037-2*) Routledge Chapman & Hall.

Biologists & Their World Series, 55 bks, Set. Ed. by Keir B. Sterling. (Illus.). 1978. lib. bdg. 3,356.50 (*0-405-10641-6*) Ayer.

An Asterisk (*) at the beginning of an entry indicates that the title is appearing in BIP for the first time.

***Biologist's Guide to Principles & Techniques of Practical Biochemistry.** Keith Wilson & Kenneth H. Goulding. 396p. 1992. 75.00 (*81-85618-12-7*, Pub. by Print Hse II) St Mut.

Biologos & Biopsychosocial Synthesis: The SAMA Foundation Lectures, Calabar, West Africa, 1982. Stacey B. Day. LC 84-82409. 130p. 1985. 35.00 (*0-934314-75-6*) Intl Found Biosocial Dev.

Biology. James M. Barrett et al. (Illus.). 1056p. 1985. text ed. write for info. (*0-13-076597-X*) P-H.

***Biology.** Ruth Bernstein & Stephen Bernstein. 720p. (C). 1995. boxed write for info. (*0-697-04456-4*) Wm C Brown Pubs.

***Biology.** Ruth Bernstein & Stephen Bernstein. 720p. (C). 1995. student ed write for info. (*0-697-10149-5*) Wm C Brown Pubs.

***Biology.** Ruth Bernstein & Stephen Bernstein. 720p. (C). 1995. pap. write for info. (*0-697-15105-0*) Wm C Brown Pubs.

Biology. Eva M. Bushman. 205p. (Orig.). (C). 1980. pap. text ed. 9.55 (*0-89420-110-7*, 238040); audio 242.20 (*0-89420-203-0*, 238000) Natl Book.

Biology. Neil A. Campbell. 1987. text ed. 52.75 (*0-8053-1840-2*) Benjamin-Cummings.

Biology. Neil A. Campbell. Ed. by Robin Williams. (C). 1990. teacher ed 11.95 (*0-8053-1801-1*); teacher ed 11.95 (*0-8053-1803-8*) Benjamin-Cummings.

Biology. Neil A. Campbell. LC 92-45736. (Series in the Life Sciences). (C). 1993. Lab manual. teacher ed, spiral bd. 33.50 (*0-8053-1830-5*) Benjamin-Cummings.

Biology. J. Chisholm. (Introductions Ser.). (Illus.). 48p. (J). (gr. 3-6). 1984. pap. 6.95 (*0-86020-707-2*) EDC.

***Biology.** Sylvia Mader. (C). 1995. student ed write for info. (*0-697-28182-5*) Wm C Brown Pubs.

Biology. Minkoff. (Barron's E Z 101 Study Keys Ser.). 144p. 1991. pap. 5.95 (*0-8120-4569-6*) Barron.

Biology. Mix et al. (C). 1992. text ed. 69.00 (*0-673-39869-2*) HarpCollege.

Biology. Mix et al. (C). 1992. student ed 23.00 (*0-673-52139-7*) HarpCollege.

Biology. Mix et al. (C). 1992. student ed 30.50 (*0-673-52227-X*) HarpCollege.

Biology. Jack Rudman. (College Proficiency Examination Ser.: CPEP-5). 1994. pap. 23.95 (*0-8373-5405-6*) Nat Learn.

Biology. Jack Rudman. (Graduate Record Examination Ser.: GRE-1). 1994. pap. 23.95 (*0-8373-5201-0*) Nat Learn.

Biology. Jack Rudman. (Undergraduate Program Field Test Ser.: UPFT-2). 1994. pap. 23.95 (*0-8373-6002-1*) Nat Learn.

Biology. Claude A. Villee et al. LC 57-7051. (Illus.). 1224p. (C). 1985. text ed. 53.25 (*0-685-02363-X*) SCP.

Biology. N. K. Wessells. 1988. text ed. write for info. (*0-07-554560-8*) McGraw.

Biology. Norman Wessels & Janet L. Hopson. 1200p. (C). 1988. 12.95 (*0-685-17435-2*); text ed. 49.95 (*0-685-17434-4*); student ed 14.90 (*0-07-554561-6*) Random.

Biology. Zwolski. (Science Review Ser.). 1992. 11.95 (*0-87434-453-0*); 19.75 (*0-87434-459-X*) Springhouse Pub.

Biology. 2nd ed. Neil A. Campbell. Ed. by Robin Williams. (C). 1990. text ed. 59.95 (*0-8053-1800-3*); student ed, teacher ed 46.25 (*0-8053-1805-4*); trans. 322.75 (*0-8053-1804-6*) Benjamin-Cummings.

Biology. 2nd ed. Wayne H. Garnsey. (Science Ser.). (Illus.). 352p. 1992. pap. text ed. 4.13 (*0-685-59638-9*) N & N Pub Co.

Biology. 2nd ed. Leland G. Johnson. 1152p. (C). 1987. write for info. (*0-697-04998-1*) Wm C Brown Pubs.

Biology. 2nd ed. Peter Raven & George Johnson. 1260p. (C). 1993. student ed write for info. (*0-697-23506-8*) Wm C Brown Pubs.

Biology. 2nd ed. Donald D. Ritchie & Robert Carola. LC 82-11318. (Biology Ser.). (Illus.). 672p. (C). 1983. teacher ed write for info. (*0-201-06357-3*); text ed. write for info. (*0-201-06356-5*); student ed write for info. (*0-201-06358-1*); sl. write for info. (*0-201-06393-X*); write for info. (*0-201-06359-X*) Addison-Wesley.

Biology. 2nd ed. Claude A. Villee et al. 1400p. (C). 1989. text ed. write for info. (*0-03-029562-9*) SCP.

Biology. 3rd ed. Karen Arms & Pamela S. Camp. 1176p. (C). 1987. text ed. 64.00 (*0-03-003644-5*); teacher ed, pap. text ed. 28.50 (*0-03-003647-X*); student ed, pap. text ed. 20.50 (*0-03-003648-8*); pap. text ed. 36.25 (*0-03-003652-6*) SCP.

Biology. 3rd ed. Neil A. Campbell. LC 92-45736. (Series in the Life Sciences). (C). 1993. text ed. 66.75 (*0-8053-1880-1*); Study guide. student ed, pap. text ed. 20.50 (*0-8053-1881-X*) Benjamin-Cummings.

Biology. 3rd ed. Sylvia Mader. 880p. (C). 1990. student ed write for info. (*0-697-11247-0*) Wm C Brown Pubs.

Biology. 3rd ed. Sylvia Mader. 880p. (C). 1990. text ed. write for info. (*0-697-05638-4*) Wm C Brown Pubs.

Biology. 3rd ed. Sylvia Mader. 880p. (C). 1990. text ed write for info. (*0-697-05640-6*) Wm C Brown Pubs.

Biology. 3rd ed. Peter Raven & George Johnson. 1260p. (C). 1993. write for info. (*0-697-23498-3*); text ed. write for info. (*0-697-23494-0*) Wm C Brown Pubs.

***Biology.** 3rd ed. John Snyder & C. Leland Rodgers. (College Review Ser.). 1995. student ed 11.95 (*0-8120-1862-1*) Barron.

Biology. 4th ed. John W. Kimball. LC 77-74322. (Life Sciences Ser.). 1978. write for info. (*0-201-03692-4*); student ed write for info. (*0-201-03764-5*); text ed. write for info. (*0-201-03761-0*) Addison-Wesley.

Biology, 6 pts. 4th ed. Sylvia Mader. 896p. (C). 1992. pap. write for info. (*0-697-15096-8*) Wm C Brown Pubs.

Biology, 6 pts. 4th ed. Sylvia Mader. 896p. (C). 1992. student ed write for info. (*0-697-12384-7*); student ed, disk write for info. (*0-697-12386-3*) Wm C Brown Pubs.

Biology. 4th ed. Raven & Johnson. 1994. write for info. (*0-8016-6908-1*) Mosby Yr Bk.

Biology. 5th ed. Helena Curtis et al. (gr. 12 up). 1989. 65.95 (*0-87901-394-X*) Worth.

Biology. 5th ed. Helena Curtis et al. (YA). (gr. 12 up). 1989. Study Guide by Fox. student ed 12.95x (*0-87901-395-8*) Worth.

Biology. 5th ed. John W. Kimball. LC 82-11636. (Biology Ser.). (Illus.). 1040p. (C). 1983. teacher ed write for info. (*0-201-10247-1*); text ed. 54.95 (*0-201-10245-5*); Student guide. student ed, pap. text ed. 16.25 (*0-201-10246-3*); write for info. (*0-201-10265-X*) Addison-Wesley.

***Biology.** 5th ed. Sylvia Mader. 896p. (C). 1995. pap. write for info. (*0-697-21819-8*) Wm C Brown Pubs.

Biology. 6th ed. Bennett et al. 128p. 1991. pap. text ed. 9.95 (*0-88725-164-1*) Hunter Textbks.

Biology. 8th ed. Claude A. Villee et al. LC 57-7051. (Illus.). 1224p. (C). 1985. pap. text ed. 29.75 (*0-03-063174-2*) SCP.

Biology, No. 3. Peter H. Raven & Johnson. 1344p. 1991. 56.95 (*0-8016-6372-5*) Mosby Yr Bk.

Biology, 6 pts., Pt. I: The Cell. 4th ed. Sylvia Mader. 896p. (C). 1992. text ed. write for info. (*0-697-15098-4*) Wm C Brown Pubs.

Biology, 6 pts., Pt. II: Genetic Basics of Life. 4th ed. Sylvia Mader. 896p. (C). 1992. text ed. write for info. (*0-697-15099-2*) Wm C Brown Pubs.

Biology, 6 pts., Pt. III: Evolution & Diversity. 4th ed. Sylvia Mader. 896p. (C). 1992. text ed. write for info. (*0-697-15100-X*) Wm C Brown Pubs.

Biology, 6 pts., Pt. IV: Plant Structure & Function. 4th ed. Sylvia Mader. 896p. (C). 1992. text ed. write for info. (*0-697-15101-8*) Wm C Brown Pubs.

Biology, 6 pts., Pt. V: Biology of Animal Structure & Function. 4th ed. Sylvia Mader. 896p. (C). 1992. text ed. write for info. (*0-697-15102-6*) Wm C Brown Pubs.

Biology, 6 pts., Pt. VI: Biology of Behavior & Ecology. 4th ed. Sylvia Mader. 896p. (C). 1992. text ed. write for info. (*0-697-15103-4*) Wm C Brown Pubs.

Biology: A Critical Thinking Approach. Robert D. Allen. 320p. (C). 1995. pap. text ed. write for info. (*0-697-14749-5*) Wm C Brown Pubs.

***Biology: A Critical Thinking Approach.** Robert D. Allen. 184p. (C). 1995. teacher ed, pap. text ed. write for info. (*0-697-28134-5*) Wm C Brown Pubs.

***Biology: A Critical Thinking Approach.** Robert D. Allen. 80p. (C). 1995. student ed, pap. text ed. write for info. (*0-697-27526-4*) Wm C Brown Pubs.

Biology: A Human Endeavor. Vernon L. Avila. 270p. (C). 1992. student ed 15.00 (*1-880161-02-8*); text ed. 50.00 (*1-880161-00-1*) Bookmark Pubs.

Biology: A Human Endeavor. David J. Cotter. 216p. (C). 1992. write for info. (*1-880161-01-X*) Bookmark Pubs.

Biology: A Journey into Life. 2nd ed. Karen Arms. 1991. text ed. 56.00 (*0-03-076511-0*); pap. text ed. 56.00 (*0-03-033363-6*) SCP.

Biology: A Personalized Approach. Kelly et al. 688p. 1989. boxed 33.90 (*0-8403-4332-9*) Kendall-Hunt.

Biology: A Personalized Approach - Teacher's Guide. Kelly et al. 384p. 1989. 45.90 (*0-8403-4333-7*) Kendall-Hunt.

Biology: A Personalized Approach Logbook. Kelly et al. 272p. 1989. pap. text ed. 7.90 (*0-8403-5195-X*) Kendall-Hunt.

Biology: A Self-Teaching Guide. Steven D. Garber. 374p. 1989. pap. text ed. 17.95 (*0-471-62581-7*) Wiley.

***Biology: An Exploration of Life.** Carol H. Fadden & William T. Keeton. LC 93-1530. (Illus.). (C). 1995. teacher ed, pap. text ed. write for info. (*0-393-95720-9*) Norton.

***Biology: An Exploration of Life.** William T. Keeton & Carol H. McFadden. (Illus.). (C). 1995. text ed. 75.95 (*0-393-96693-3*) Norton.

***Biology: An Exploration of Life.** Carol H. McFadden & William T. Keeton. (Illus.). (C). 1995. text ed. 75.95 (*0-393-96692-5*); student ed, pap. text ed. 19.95 (*0-393-95718-7*); student ed, pap. text ed. write for info. (*0-393-95947-3*) Norton.

Biology: An Exploration of Life. 4th ed. Carol H. McFadden & William T. Keeton. LC 93-1530. (Illus.). 700p. (C). 1995. text ed. 63.95 (*0-393-95716-0*) Norton.

Biology: An Introduction. K. Johnson et al. 1984. teacher ed 7.50 (*0-8053-7889-8*); text ed. 44.25 (*0-8053-7887-1*); student ed 16.25 (*0-8053-7888-X*); trans. 161.50 (*0-8053-7891-X*) Benjamin-Cummings.

Biology: An Introduction to Plants & Animals. Vernon Grosvenor. 472p. (C). 1994. per., pap. text ed. 44.76 (*0-8403-9433-0*) Kendall-Hunt.

Biology! Bringing Science to Life. John N. Postlethwait et al. 1991. text ed. write for info. (*0-07-050631-0*); Study guide. student ed, pap. text ed. write for info. (*0-07-050638-8*) McGraw.

Biology: Cell Structure & Function. 2nd ed. Mark Taylor. 208p. 1991. spiral bd. 25.95 (*0-8403-7044-X*) Kendall-Hunt.

Biology: Concepts & Applications. 2nd ed. Cecie Starr. 645p. (C). 1994. text ed. 53.95 (*0-534-17616-X*); pap. 47.95 (*0-534-17635-6*) Intl Thomson.

Biology: Concepts & Connections. Neil A. Campbell et al. LC 93-30071. (C). 1994. text ed. 58.25 (*0-8053-0920-9*); Study guide. student ed, pap. text ed. 20.50 (*0-8053-0921-7*) Benjamin-Cummings.

Biology: Concepts & Connections. Neil A. Campbell et al. LC 93-30071. (C). 1995. Lab manual. teacher ed, spiral bd. 37.75 (*0-8053-0922-5*) Benjamin-Cummings.

***Biology: Continuity & Diversity of Life.** Eldon Enger et al. 512p. (C). 1995. pap. write for info. (*0-697-27862-X*) Wm C Brown Pubs.

Biology: Discovering Life, 4 vols. Joseph S. Levine & Kenneth R. Miller. LC 90-82264. 898p. (C). 1990. text ed. 37.50 (*0-669-12008-1*); Study guide. student ed 13.50 (*0-669-12009-X*); Study guide for Core Concepts vol. student ed write for info. (*0-669-28947-7*); Instr.'s guide. teacher ed 2.00 (*0-669-12014-6*); Transparencies/slides. trans. write for info. (*0-669-27697-9*) Heath.

***Biology: Discovering Life.** 2nd ed. Joseph Levine & Kenneth R. Miller. 988p. 1994. text ed. write for info. (*0-669-33494-4*) Heath.

Biology: Discovering Life, 4 vols., Vol. I: Core Concepts. Joseph S. Levine & Kenneth R. Miller. LC 90-82264. 419p. (C). 1990. Vol. I, Core Concepts, 419 p. pap. text ed. write for info. (*0-669-28840-3*) Heath.

Biology: Discovering Life, 4 vols., Vol. II: Diversity. Joseph S. Levine & Kenneth R. Miller. LC 90-82264. 97p. (C). 1990. Vol. II, Diversity, 97 p. pap. text ed. write for info. (*0-669-28841-1*) Heath.

Biology: Discovering Life, 4 vols., Vol. III: Plant Systems. Joseph S. Levine & Kenneth R. Miller. LC 90-82264. 71p. (C). 1990. Vol. III, Plant Systems, 71 p. pap. text ed. write for info. (*0-669-28842-X*) Heath.

Biology: Discovering Life, 4 vols., Vol. IV: Animal Systems. Joseph S. Levine & Kenneth R. Miller. LC 90-82264. 308p. (C). 1990. Vol. IV, Animal Systems, 308 p. pap. text ed. write for info. (*0-669-28843-8*) Heath.

Biology: Exploring Life. Gil D. Brum. 1989. Net. write for info. (*0-471-61903-5*); Net. student ed, text ed. write for info. (*0-471-51540-X*); Net. text ed. write for info. (*0-471-51766-6*); Net. student ed write for info. (*0-471-61902-7*) Wiley.

Biology: Exploring Life. Gil D. Brum & Larry K. McKane. 1993. pap. text ed. write for info. (*0-471-59806-2*) Wiley.

Biology: Exploring Life. 2nd ed. Gil D. Brum & Larry K. McKane. LC 93-23383. 1083p. 1993. Net. text ed. write for info. (*0-471-54408-6*) Wiley.

***Biology: Exploring Life, Incl. Student Study Guide.** 2nd ed. Gil Brum et al. 1994. text ed. write for info. (*0-471-10958-4*) Wiley.

***Biology: Exploring Life, Set, Units 1-2 & 4-6.** 2nd ed. Gil Brum et al. 1994. pap. text ed. write for info. (*0-471-11025-6*) Wiley.

***Biology: Exploring Life, Set; Units 1, 3, & 6.** 2nd ed. Gil Brum et al. 1994. text ed. write for info. (*0-471-11076-0*) Wiley.

***Biology: Exploring Life, Set, Units 1 & 4-6.** 2nd ed. Gil Brum et al. 1994. pap. text ed. write for info. (*0-471-10657-7*) Wiley.

***Biology: Exploring Life, Set; Vols. 1, 4, & 6.** 2nd ed. Gil Brum et al. 1994. text ed. write for info. (*0-471-11232-1*) Wiley.

***Biology: Exploring Life, Set, Vols. 1 & 4-5.** 2nd ed. Gil Brum et al. 1994. text ed. write for info. (*0-471-11140-6*) Wiley.

***Biology: Exploring Life, Vols. 1 & 6.** 2nd ed. Gil Brum et al. 1994. text ed. write for info. (*0-471-11192-9*) Wiley.

Biology: Human Perspectives Preliminary Edition. Charles K. Levy. 256p. 1993. spiral bd. 34.95 (*0-8403-8945-0*) Kendall-Hunt.

Biology: In a Flash. Elizabeth Burchard. (Exambusters Ser.). 480p. (J). (gr. 7-12). 1994. pap. 9.95 (*1-881374-00-9*) Flash Blasters.

***Biology: Investigating Life on Earth.** 2nd ed. Vernon L. Avila. LC 94-39326. (Bookmark Series in Biology). 1995. write for info. (*0-86720-942-9*) Jones & Bartlett.

Biology: Its Principles & Implications. 3rd ed. Garrett Hardin & Carl Bajema. (Illus.). 790p. 1978. teacher ed write for info. (*0-318-56350-9*) W H Freeman.

Biology: Lab & Field Theory & Techniques with Exercises. James L. Koevenig. 224p. (C). 1993. pap. text ed., spiral bd. 19.95 (*0-8403-9159-5*) Kendall-Hunt.

Biology: Laboratory Manual. Ritch. 608p. 1989. spiral bd. 27.50 (*0-8403-5394-4*) Kendall-Hunt.

Biology: Life on Earth. 3rd ed. Gerald Audesirk & Teresa Audesirk. (Illus.). 1136p. (C). 1992. text ed. write for info. (*0-02-304811-5*) Macmillan.

Biology: Life on Earth. 3rd ed. Gerald Audesirk & Teresa Audesirk. (Illus.). 1136p. (C). 1993. student ed, pap. write for info. (*0-02-304831-X*) Macmillan.

Biology: Life on Earth - Laboratory Manual. 3rd ed. Don M. Fritsch. (Illus.). 384p. (C). 1993. pap. write for info. (*0-02-339825-6*) Macmillan.

Biology: Principles & Perspectives. 2nd ed. John E. Silva. 448p. (C). 1994. per., pap. text ed. 52.96 (*0-8403-9031-9*) Kendall-Hunt.

***Biology: Realm of Life.** 3rd ed. Gibart. (C). 1995. student ed, text ed. write for info. (*0-673-46699-X*) HarpCollege.

***Biology: Realm of Life, Vol. 1.** Wallace & Ferl. (C). 1995. text ed. write for info. (*0-673-99805-3*) HarpCollege.

***Biology: Realm of Life, Vol. 2.** 3rd ed. Wallace & Ferl. (C). 1995. text ed. write for info. (*0-673-99806-1*) HarpCollege.

***Biology: Realm of Life, Vol. 3.** 3rd ed. Wallace & Ferl. (C). 1995. text ed. write for info. (*0-673-99807-X*) HarpCollege.

Biology: Special Edition. 2nd ed. Raven & Johnson. 1264p. 1991. 51.95 (*0-8016-6371-7*) Mosby Yr Bk.

Biology: Study Guide. John P. Harley & Sweeney. (C). 1986. pap. text ed. write for info. (*0-13-076605-4*) P-H.

Biology: Study Guide. 2nd ed. Martha Taylor. Ed. by Robin Williams. (C). 1990. pap. text ed. 18.25 (*0-8053-1802-X*) Benjamin-Cummings.

Biology: The Essential Principles. Thomas Graham. 768p. 1991. per. 39.95 (*0-8403-6654-X*) Kendall-Hunt.

Biology: The Foundations. 2nd ed. Stephen L. Wolfe. 585p. (C). 1983. text ed. 47.95 (*0-534-01169-1*) Intl Thomson.

***Biology: The Realm of Life.** 3rd ed. Robert A. Wallace & Robert J. Ferl. LC 94-32575. Orig. Title: Biosphere: The Realm of Life. (C). 1992. 66.50 (*0-673-46624-8*) HarpCollege.

Biology: The Science of Life. 3rd ed. Wallace et al. (C). 1990. text ed. 78.50 (*0-673-38044-0*) HarpCollege.

***Biology: The Study of Life.** John C. Williams. 282p. (C). 1994. pap. text ed. 49.95 (*1-885827-00-8*) NatureGraphics.

***Biology: The Study of Living Organisms: A Complete Course with 900 Questions & Answers.** George H. Fried. LC 94-44786. (Schaum's Outline Ser.). 1995. pap. text ed. 14.95 (*0-07-022402-1*) McGraw.

Biology: The Unity & Diversity of Life. 6th ed. Cecie Starr & Ralph Taggart. 921p. (C). 1992. text ed. 58.95 (*0-534-16566-4*) Intl Thomson.

***Biology: The Unity & Diversity of Life.** 7th ed. Cecie Starr & Ralph Taggart. LC 94-44432. 1995. text ed. 58.95 (*0-534-21060-0*) Intl Thomson.

Biology: The Web of Life, Vol. I. Daniel D. Chiras. Ed. by Westby. 350p. (C). 1993. pap. text ed. 24.00 (*0-314-01344-X*) West Pub.

Biology: The Web of Life, Vol. II. Daniel D. Chiras. Ed. by Westby. 425p. (C). 1993. pap. text ed. 24.00 (*0-314-01345-8*) West Pub.

Biology: The Web of Life, Vol. III. Daniel D. Chiras. Ed. by Westby. 375p. (C). 1993. pap. text ed. 24.00 (*0-314-01346-6*) West Pub.

Biology: The World of Life. 5th ed. Robert A. Wallace. (C). 1990. text ed. 39.00 (*0-673-38320-2*) HarpCollege.

Biology: World of Life. Wallace. (C). 1992. 22.00 (*0-673-46626-4*) HarpCollege.

Biology: World of Life. 6th ed. Wallace. (C). 1991. text ed. 69.00 (*0-673-46480-6*) HarpCollege.

***Biology Chaps. 1-17: Exploring Life, Cell Biology & Genetics, Vol. 1.** 2nd ed. Gil Brum et al. 1994. pap. text ed. write for info. (*0-471-01827-9*) Wiley.

***Biology Chaps. 18-21: Exploring Life, Form & Function of Plant Life, Vol. 2.** 2nd ed. Gil Brum et al. 1993. pap. text ed. write for info. (*0-471-01831-7*) Wiley.

***Biology Chaps. 22-32: Exploring Life, Form & Function of Animal Life, Vol. 3.** 2nd ed. Gil Brum et al. 1993. pap. text ed. write for info. (*0-471-01830-9*) Wiley.

***Biology Chaps. 33-35: Exploring Life, Evolution, Vol. 4.** 2nd ed. Gil Brum et al. 1993. pap. text ed. write for info. (*0-471-01829-5*) Wiley.

***Biology Chaps. 36-39: Exploring Life, Diversity & Classification, Vol. 5.** 2nd ed. Gil Brum et al. 1993. pap. text ed. write for info. (*0-471-01828-7*) Wiley.

***Biology Chaps. 40-44: Exploring Life, Ecology & Animal Behavior, Vol. 6.** 2nd ed. Gil Brum et al. 1993. pap. text ed. write for info. (*0-471-01832-5*) Wiley.

Biology No. 3: Lab Manual. Vodopich & Moore. 558p. 1992. spiral bd. 22.95 (*0-8016-6602-3*) Mosby Yr Bk.

Biology No. 3: Raven Text Plus Vodopich Lab Manual. Raven & Vodopich. 1992. 67.95 (*0-8016-7267-8*) Mosby Yr Bk.

Biology No. 3: Study Guide. Burke & Taylor. 480p. 1992. pap. 16.95 (*0-8016-6601-5*) Mosby Yr Bk.

Biology & Activities of Yeasts. Ed. by Frederick A. Skinner et al. LC 80-41362. (Society for Applied Bacteriology Symposium Ser.: No. 9). 1981. text ed. 115.00 (*0-12-648080-X*) Acad Pr.

Biology & Biochemistry. Ed. by P. Shubik. (Physiopathology of Cancer Ser.: Vol. 1). (Illus.). 412p. 1974. 39.25 (*3-8055-1545-6*) S Karger.

Biology & Biochemistry of Nitrogen Fixation. Ed. by M. J. Dilworth & A. R. Glenn. (Studies in Plant Science: No. 1). 438p. 1991. 120.00 (*0-444-88960-4*) Elsevier.

Biology & Biochemistry of Normal & Cancer Cell Growth. L. Castagnetta & I. Nenci. 288p. 1988. text ed. 160.00 (*3-7186-4816-4*) Gordon & Breach.

Biology & Biomechanics of the Traumatized Synovial Joint: The Knee As a Model. Ed. by Gerald A. Finerman. 608p. 1992. 105.00 (*0-89203-070-4*) Amer Acad Ortho Surg.

Biology & Chemistry of Polyamines. Sarah M. Goldemberg & Israel D. Algranati. Ed. by Karen M. Williams. (ICSU Symposium Ser.: Vol. 12). (Illus.). 264p. 1990. pap. 60.00 (*0-19-963147-6*, IRL Pr) OUP.

Biology & Chemistry of the Carbonic Anhydrases. Intro. by Richard E. Tashian & David Hewett-Emmett. LC 84-1190. (Annals Ser.: Vol. 429). 640p. 1984. lib. bdg. 140.00 (*0-89766-252-0*); pap. 140.00 (*0-89766-253-9*) NY Acad Sci.

Biology & Chemistry of the Umbelliferae. Ed. by Vernon H. Heywood. (Botanical Journal of the Linnean Society: Vol. 64, Suppl. 1). 1972. text ed. 198.00 (*0-12-346940-6*) Acad Pr.

Biology & Clinical Applications of Interleukin-2. Ed. by R. C. Rees. (Illus.). 200p. 1991. 55.00 (*0-19-963137-9*, IRL Pr) OUP.

Biology & Cognitive Development: The Case of Face Recognition. Mark H. Johnson & John Morton. (Cognitive Development Ser.). 160p. (C). 1991. pap. text ed. 17.95 (*0-631-17454-0*) Blackwell Pubs.

Biology & Computation: A Physicist's Choice. H. Gutfreund & G. Toulouse. (Lecture Notes in Physics Ser.). 868p. 1994. text ed. 162.00 (*981-02-1405-7*); pap. text ed. 99.00 (*981-02-1406-5*) World Scientific Pub.

Biology & Control of Weeds in Sugar Cane. S. Y. Peng. (Developments in Crop Science Ser.: Vol. 4). 250p. 1984. 107.75 (*0-444-42133-5*) Elsevier.

Biology & Cultivation of Edible Mushrooms. Ed. by S. T. Chang & W. A. Hayes. LC 77-6591. 1978. text ed. 151.00 (*0-12-168050-9*) Acad Pr.

Biology & Culture of Mussels of the Genus Perna. J. M. Vakily. 1989. pap. 5.50 (*971-10-2270-2*, Pub. by ICLARM PH) Intl Spec Bk.

Biology & Culture of Tropical Oysters. C. L. Angell. (ICLARM Studies & Reviews: No. 13). (Illus.). 42p. (Orig.). (C). 1986. pap. 6.00 (*971-10-2224-9*, Pub. by ICLARM PH) Intl Spec Bk.

Biology & Disease Transmission see Flies & Disease

B

An Asterisk (*) at the beginning of an entry indicates that the title is appearing in BIP for the first time.

Biology & Diseases of Dermal Pigmentation. Thomas B. Fitzpatrick et al. 376p. 1981. 112.50 (*0-86008-292-X*, Pub. by U of Tokyo JA) Col U Pr.

Biology & Diseases of the Ferret. Ed. by James G. Fox. LC 87-26096. (Illus.). (C). 1988. text ed. 49.50 (*0-8121-1139-7*) Williams & Wilkins.

Biology & Ecology of Benthic Marine Algae with Special Reference to Hypnea (Rhodophyta, Gigartinales: A Review of the Literature. K. E Mshigeni. (Bibliotheca Phycologica Ser.: No. 37). 1978. pap. 26.80 (*3-7682-1166-5*) Lubrecht & Cramer.

***Biology & Ecology of Fishes.** James S. Diana. (Illus.). 425p. (Orig.). (C). 1994. pap. text ed. 45.00 (*1-884125-24-7*) Cooper Pubng.

Biology & Emotion. Neil McNaughton. (Problems in the Behavioral Sciences Ser.). (Illus.). 175p. (C). 1989. pap. 21.95 (*0-521-31938-2*) Cambridge U Pr.

Biology & Evolution of Australian Lizards. Allan Greer. 264p. (C). 1990. text ed. 125.00 (*0-949342-21-1*, Pub. by Surrey Beatty & Sons AT) St Mut.

Biology & Evolution of Fossil Plants. Thomas N. Taylor & Edith L. Taylor. 976p. 1993. text ed. 100.00 (*0-13-651589-4*) P-H.

Biology & Evolution of Language. Philip Lieberman. LC 83-22582. (Illus.). 392p. 1984. 40.28 (*0-674-07412-2*) HUP.

Biology & Evolution of Language. Philip Lieberman. 392p. 1987. pap. 16.95 (*0-674-07413-0*) HUP.

Biology & Exploitation of the Minke Whale. Joseph Horwood. 240p. 1989. text ed. 180.00 (*0-8493-6069-2*, QL737) CRC Pr.

Biology & Feminism: A Dynamic Interaction. Sue V. Rosser. (Feminist Impact on the Arts & Sciences Ser.). 200p. 1992. pap. 14.95 (*0-8057-9755-6*, Twayne) Macmillan.

Biology & Feminism: A Dynamic Interaction. Sue V. Rosser. (Feminist Impact on the Arts & Sciences Ser.). 200p. 1993. text ed. 26.95 (*0-8057-9770-X*, Twayne) Macmillan.

Biology & General Science. Jack Rudman. (National Teachers Examination Ser.: NT-3). 1994. pap. 23.95 (*0-8373-8413-3*) Nat Learn.

Biology & General Science Sr. H. S. Jack Rudman. (Teachers License Examination Ser.: T-4). 1994. pap. 23.95 (*0-8373-8004-9*) Nat Learn.

Biology & Geology of Coral Reefs, 4 vols. Ed. by O. A. Jones & R. Endean. Incl. Biology Pt. 2. 1976. 95.50 (*0-12-389603-7*); write for info. (*0-318-50235-6*) Acad Pr.

Biology & Human Concerns. 3rd ed. E. Peter Volpe. 704p. 1983. student ed write for info. (*0-697-04747-4*) Wm C Brown Pubs.

Biology & Human Concerns. 3rd ed. E. Peter Volpe. 704p. (C). 1983. write for info. (*0-697-04746-6*) Wm C Brown Pubs.

Biology & Human Progress. 5th ed. C. Tanzer. 1977. student ed 9.92 (*0-13-076620-8*); teacher ed 11.40 (*0-13-076638-0*); text ed. 28.52 (*0-13-076612-7*) P-H.

Biology & Management of Australasian Carnivorous Marsupials. Ed. by Miles Roberts et al. (Illus.). 158p. 1993. pap. text ed. 20.00 (*0-9638408-1-9*) C & RC Nat Zool.

Biology & Management of Lobsters: Vol. 1, Physiology & Behavior. Ed. by J. Stanley Cobb & Bruce F. Phillips. LC 79-6803. 1980. text ed. 128.00 (*0-12-177401-5*) Acad Pr.

Biology & Management of Lobsters: Vol. 2, Ecology & Management. Ed. by J. Stanley Cobb & Bruce F. Phillips. LC 79-6803. 1980. text ed. 106.00 (*0-12-177402-3*) Acad Pr.

Biology & Management of Lung Cancer. Ed. by F. Anthony Greco. 1983. lib. bdg. 97.00 (*0-89838-554-7*) Kluwer Ac.

Biology & Management of Red Alder. Ed. by Dean S. DeBell & Robert F. Tarrant. LC 93-42131. (Illus.). 272p. 1994. text ed. 22.95 (*0-87071-382-5*) Oreg St U Pr.

Biology & Management of Rice Insects. E. A. Heinrichs. 779p. 1995. text ed. 89.95 (*0-470-21814-2*) Halsted Pr.

Biology & Management of the Cervidae. Christen Wemmer. LC 86-600124. (National Zoological Park Symposia for the Public Ser.). (Illus.). 578p. (C). 1987. 47.00 (*0-87474-980-8*); pap. 29.95 (*0-87474-981-6*) Smithsonian.

Biology & Management of the Soybean Cyst Nematode. Ed. by Robert D. Riggs & J. Allen Wrather. LC 92-70943. (Illus.). 186p. (Orig.). 1992. pap. 26.00 (*0-89054-125-6*) Am Phytopathol Soc.

Biology & Medicine into the 21st Century. Ed. by M. A. Hardy & R. K. Kinne. (Issues in Biomedicine, Monographs in Interdisciplinary: Vol. 15). (Illus.). viii, 200p. 1991. 180.00 (*3-8055-5392-7*) S Karger.

Biology & Medicine of Rabbits & Rodents. John E. Harkness & Joseph E. Wagner. LC 88-13330. (Illus.). 230p. 1989. pap. text ed. 28.50 (*0-8121-1176-1*) Williams & Wilkins.

Biology & Medicine of Signal Transduction. Yasutomi Nishizuka et al. (Advances in Second Messenger & Phosphoprotein Research Ser.: Vol. 24). 784p. 1990. 109.50 (*0-88167-670-5*) Raven.

Biology & Molecular Genetics of Lung Cancer. Adi F. Gazdar & David P. Carbone. LC 94-2335. (Medical Intelligence Unit Ser.). 152p. 1994. 89.95 (*1-57059-008-7*) R G Landes.

Biology & Neurophysiology of the Conditioned Reflex & Its Role in Adaptive Behavior. Peter K. Anokhin. Tr. by Samuel A. Corson. LC 73-744. 592p. (C). 1977. 240.00 (*0-08-017160-5*, Pub. by Pergamon Repr UK) Franklin.

Biology & Paleobiology of Ostracoda: Symposium, 1972, No. 282. (Bulletin of American Paleontology Ser.). (Illus.). 1975. pap. 25.00 (*0-87710-294-5*) Paleo Res.

Biology & Pathology of Astrocyte-Neuron Interactions. Ed. by S. Fedoroff et al. (Altschul Symposia Ser.: Vol. 2). 478p. (C). 1993. 125.00 (*0-306-44565-4*, Plenum Pr) Plenum.

Biology & Pathology of Elastic Tissues. Ed. by A. M. Robert & L. Robert. (Frontiers of Matrix Biology Ser.: Vol. 8). (Illus.). viii, 232p. 1980. 99.25 (*3-8055-3078-1*) S Karger.

Biology & Pathology of Platelet-Vessel Wall Interactions. Ed. by Georges Jolles et al. 350p. 1987. text ed. 108.00 (*0-12-388178-1*) Acad Pr.

Biology & Physiology of Amphibians: Physiology of Amphibians (Proceedings) Held at Karlsruhe, FRG, Aug, 31-Sept. 3, 1988. Ed. by Wilfried Hanke. (Progress in Zoology Ser.: Vol. 38). 413p. 1990. 140.00 (*0-685-48101-8*); lib. bdg. 165.00 (*0-89574-314-0*) G F Verlag.

Biology & Physiology of the Osteoclast. Rifkin. 1992. 173.00 (*0-8493-5437-4*, QP88) CRC Pr.

Biology & Politics: Recent Explorations. Ed. by A. Somit. (Publications of the International Social Science Council: No. 19). (Orig.). 1976. pap. text ed. 49.25 (*3-10-800138-8*) Mouton.

Biology & Prevention of Aerodigestive Tract Cancers. Ed. by Guy R. Newell & Waun K. Hong. LC 92-21811. (Advances in Experimental Medicine & Biology Ser.: Vol. 320). 1992. 65.00 (*0-306-44244-2*, Plenum Pr) Plenum.

***Biology & Sexual Orientation.** William Byne. 1997. write for info. (*0-88163-203-1*) Analytic Pr.

Biology & Social Behavior. Allan Mazur & Leon S. Robertson. LC 72-169236. 1974. 19.95 (*0-02-920450-X*) Free Pr.

Biology & Social Thought 1850-1914. Peter J. Bowler. Ed. by J. L. Heilbron. LC 92-64057. (Berkeley Papers in History of Science: No. 15). 120p. (Orig.). 1993. pap. text ed. 18.00 (*0-918102-19-7*) U Cal Hist Sci Tech.

***Biology & Technology of Intelligent Autonomous Agents.** L. Steels. (NATO ASI F Computer & Systems Sciences Ser.: Vol. 144). 518p. 1995. 135.00 (*3-540-59052-8*) Spr-Verlag.

Biology & Technology of the Cultivated Mushroom. Ed. by Peter B. Flegg et al. LC 83-3169. (Illus.). 359p. reprint ed. pap. 102.40 (*0-8357-6303-X*, 2035576) Bks Demand.

Biology & the Future of Man: Papers by Nathan Hershey & Merril Eisenbud. Ed. by Charles Angoff. LC 77-92564. (Leverton Lecture Ser.: No. 6). 52p. 1978. 14.50 (*0-8386-2222-4*) Fairleigh Dickinson.

Biology & the Mechanics of the Wave-Swept Environment. Mark W. Denny. (Illus.). 400p. 1988. text ed. 85.00 (*0-691-08486-6*); pap. text ed. 29.95 (*0-691-08487-4*) Princeton U Pr.

Biology & the Social Crisis. John K. Brierley. LC 71-120071. (Illus.). 260p. 1975. 28.50 (*0-8386-7719-3*) Fairleigh Dickinson.

Biology & Therapy of Acute Leukemia. Lawrence H. Baker et al. (Developments in Oncology Ser.). 1985. lib. bdg. 80.00 (*0-89838-728-0*) Kluwer Ac.

Biology & Treatment of Colorectal Cancer Metastasis. Ed. by Anthony J. Mastromarino. (Developments in Oncology Ser.). 1986. lib. bdg. 80.50 (*0-89838-786-8*) Kluwer Ac.

Biology & Treatment of Dementia in the Elderly. Ed. by Charles A. Shamoian. LC 84-6226. (Clinical Insights Ser.). 120p. reprint ed. pap. 34.20 (*0-8357-7811-8*, 2036183) Bks Demand.

Biology & Utilization of Shrubs. Ed. by Cyrus M. McKell. 850p. 1988. text ed. 202.00 (*0-12-484810-9*) Acad Pr.

Biology & Utilization of the Cucurbitaceae. Ed. by David M. Bates et al. LC 89-42885. (Comstock Book Ser.). (Illus.). 520p. 1989. 72.50 (*0-8014-1670-1*) Cornell U Pr.

Biology & Violence: From Birth to Adulthood. Deborah W. Denno. (Illus.). 192p. (C). 1990. 49.95 (*0-521-36219-9*) Cambridge U Pr.

Biology As Destiny: Scientific Fact or Social Bias? Ed. by SFP Sociobiology Study Group Staff. (Illus.). 52p. 1984. pap. 4.00 (*0-317-06088-0*) Sci People.

Biology as Ideology: The Doctrine of DNA. Richard C. Lewontin. LC 92-54487. 112p. 1993. pap. 10.00 (*0-06-097519-9*, PL) HarpC.

***Biology As Society, Society As Biology: Metaphors.** Sabine Maasen. Ed. by Everett Mendelsohn et al. LC 94-36251. (Sociology of the Sciences (Yearbook) Ser.). 364p. (C). 1995. lib. bdg. 160.00 (*0-7923-3174-5*) Kluwer Ac.

Biology Builder for Standardized Tests. Research & Education Association Staff. 512p. 1994. pap. text ed. 12.95 (*0-87891-940-6*) Res & Educ.

Biology Building Blocks. Marie-Francoise Chevallier-Le Guyader. (Focus on Science Ser.). 80p. 1989. pap. 4.95 (*0-8120-4212-3*) Barron.

Biology, Chemistry, & Pathology of Collagen. Ed. by Raul Fleischmajer et al. (Annals Ser.: Vol. 460). 537p. 1986. text ed. 124.00 (*0-89766-315-2*); pap. text ed. 124.00 (*0-89766-316-0*) NY Acad Sci.

Biology Coloring Book. Robert D. Griffin. (Illus.). 256p. (Orig.). 1986. pap. 15.00 (*0-06-460307-5*, Harper Ref) HarpC.

Biology Concepts: Illustrated Lecture Outline. Robert C. Gray. (Illus.). 154p. (Orig.). (C). 1982. pap. text ed. 7.50 (*0-9606666-1-3*) Greenfield Pubns.

Biology Concepts: The Laboratory Manual. Erdie Morris & Kimberly J. Weldon. (Illus.). 80p. (C). 1992. 16.00 (*1-880948-01-X*) Bold Ent.

Biology, Crime & Ethics: A Study of Biological Explanations for Criminal Behavior. Frank Marsh & Janet Katz. (C). 1985. pap. 19.95 (*0-87084-477-6*) Anderson Pub Co.

Biology Crossword Puzzle Book. Carol Crowder. 192p. (C). 1993. pap. text ed., spiral bd. 14.95 (*0-8403-8639-7*) Kendall-Hunt.

Biology Data & Resource Book. J. Hawes et al. (C). 1985. pap. 30.00 (*0-7175-1291-6*, Pub. by S Thornes UK) Dufour.

Biology Diagrams, 2 bks. D. P. Bennett. (Illus.). (C). 1988. write for info. (*0-318-65625-6*); 75.00 (*0-7157-2601-3*); 75.00 (*0-7157-2610-2*) St Mut.

Biology Dictionary. 2nd ed. Rita B. St. Pierre. LC 92-35770. (J). 1992. write for info. (*0-89420-291-X*) Natl Book.

Biology Dictionary: Five Thousand Terms for Beginning or First-Year Biology Students. Rita B. St. Pierre. Ed. by Mark Salser. 470p. (Orig.). 1985. pap. 16.95 (*0-89420-234-0*, 238100) Natl Book.

Biology Discovery Activities Kit: Lessons, Labs & Worksheets for Secondary Students. Mary L. Bellamy. 336p. 1990. pap. 29.95 (*0-87628-186-2*) P-H.

Biology, Epidemiology & Management of Pyrodinium Red Tides. Ed. by G. M. Hallegraeff & J. L. MacLean. 1989. pap. 40.00 (*971-10-2264-8*, Pub. by ICLARM PH) Intl Spec Bk.

Biology, Ethics, & Animals. Rosemary Rodd. 280p. 1992. reprint ed. pap. 18.95 (*0-19-824052-X*) OUP.

Biology Ethics & the Origin of Life. Holmes Rolston, III. (Philosophy Ser.). 300p. (C). 1994. pap. text ed. 26.25 (*0-86720-875-9*) Jones & Bartlett.

Biology Experience. Kenneth J. Curry. (Illus.). 300p. (C). 1991. pap. text ed. 26.95 (*0-89892-097-3*) Contemp Pub Co of Raleigh.

***Biology Experience: Laboratory Manual.** abr. ed. Dearing/NVCC Staff. 152p. (C). 1994. pap. text ed., spiral bd. 15.25 (*0-8403-9643-0*) Kendall-Hunt.

Biology Experience: Laboratory Manual. 7th ed. Stuart J. Dearing et al. 336p. (C). 1994. pap. text ed., spiral bd. 20.25 (*0-8403-5421-5*) Kendall-Hunt.

Biology Experiments for Children. Ethel Hanauer. LC 68-9305. (Illus.). 96p. (J). (gr. 5 up). 1969. pap. 2.95 (*0-486-22032-X*) Dover.

***Biology: Exploring Life: With Moral Matters, Set.** 2nd ed. Gil Brum & Arthur Caplan. 1994. text ed. write for info. (*0-471-12127-4*) Wiley.

Biology Flipper. Maurice Becker. (Illus.). 49p. (YA). (gr. 7 up). 1988. reprint ed. 6.25 (*1-878383-05-1*) C Lee Pubns.

Biology for Elementary Teachers. Simpson & Coulter. 272p. (C). 1991. pap. text ed. 25.95 (*0-8403-6806-2*) Kendall-Hunt.

Biology for Every Kid: One Hundred & One Easy Experiments That Really Work. Janice P. Vancleave. (J). 1990. pap. text ed. 10.95 (*0-471-50381-9*) Wiley.

Biology for Living. Bruce Wallace & George M. Simmons, Jr. LC 86-10292. (Illus.). 464p. (C). 1986. text ed. 34.95 (*0-8018-3221-7*) Johns Hopkins.

Biology for Science Majors. Hufford & Lipscomb. 240p. 1988. spiral bd. 23.50 (*0-8403-5107-0*) Kendall-Hunt.

Biology-Functional, Systematic & Environmental. G. B. Thomas & M. F. Thomas. (C). 1978. text ed. 80.00 (*0-7175-0759-9*, Pub. by S Thornes Pubs UK) St Mut.

***Biology Fundamentals.** Gil Brum et al. 1995. pap. text ed. write for info. (*0-471-59401-6*) Wiley.

Biology Illustrated. Gerald G. Farr. (Illus.). 234p. 1979. pap. text ed. 29.95 (*0-89641-054-4*) American Pr.

Biology in Human Affairs. Ed. by Edward M. East. LC 72-313. (Essay Index Reprint Ser.). 1977. reprint ed. 25.95 (*0-8369-2790-7*) Ayer.

Biology in Profile: An Introduction to the Many Branches of Biology. Ed. by P. N. Campbell. (Illus.). 148p. 1981. text ed. 40.00 (*0-08-026846-3*, Pub. by Pergamon Repr UK) Franklin.

Biology in Secondary Schools & the Training of Biology Teachers. Charles W. Finley. LC 77-176772. (Columbia University. Teachers College. Contributions to Education Ser.: No. 199). reprint ed. 37.50 (*0-404-55199-8*) AMS Pr.

***Biology in the Health Sciences: Index of Modern Authors & Subjects with Guide for Rapid Research.** rev. ed. 143p. 1995. pap. 39.50 (*0-7883-0665-0*) ABBE Pubs Assn.

***Biology in the Health Sciences: Index of Modern Authors & Subjects with Guide for Rapid Research.** rev. ed. J. H. Vickery. 143p. 1995. 44.50 (*0-7883-0664-2*) ABBE Pubs Assn.

Biology in the Laboratory. Doris Helms. 1985. pap. 24.95 (*0-87901-323-0*) Worth.

Biology in the Laboratory. Hughes. (Life Science Ser.). 1995. spiral bd., pap. 20.00 (*0-86720-196-7*) Jones & Bartlett.

Biology in the Laboratory. 2nd ed. Helms. 1994. pap. 29.95 (*0-87901-687-6*) Worth.

Biology in the Nineteenth Century. W. Coleman. LC 77-83989. (Cambridge History of Science Ser.). (Illus.). 1978. pap. 15.95 (*0-521-29293-X*) Cambridge U Pr.

Biology Lab Book. Michael B. Clark & Michael R. Riddle. 274p. (C). 1993. 18.50 (*1-885380-50-X*) Suspended Animat.

Biology Lab Manual, No. 101. Mark R. Fregeau. 71p. (C). 1993. 3.97 (*1-56870-054-7*) RonJon Pub.

Biology Laboratory. 3rd ed. Stetler. 236p. 1992. spiral bd. 23.95 (*0-88725-186-2*) Hunter Textbks.

***Biology Laboratory: An Inquiry.** Frank Romano et al. 256p. (C). 1994. pap. text ed., ring bd. 41.95 (*0-8403-8456-4*) Kendall-Hunt.

Biology Laboratory Experiences. Robert C. Gray. (Illus.). 160p. (Orig.). (C). 1983. 7.50 (*0-9606666-2-1*) Greenfield Pubns.

***Biology Laboratory Manual.** Fred Adams et al. 176p. (C). 1994. pap. text ed., spiral bd. 13.56 (*0-8403-9630-9*) Kendall-Hunt.

***Biology Laboratory Manual.** Warren D. Dolphin. 496p. (C). 1995. spiral bd. write for info. (*0-697-15903-5*) Wm C Brown Pubs.

Biology Laboratory Manual. Kim Wilson. 108p. 1991. spiral bd. 16.95 (*0-8403-7023-7*) Kendall-Hunt.

Biology Laboratory Manual. 2nd ed. Charlie J. Salter. 142p. 1984. pap. 14.95 (*0-88725-027-0*) Hunter Textbks.

Biology Laboratory Manual. 2nd ed. TCJCD (Pirkey) Staff. 320p. 1991. spiral bd. 24.95 (*0-8403-6815-1*) Kendall-Hunt.

Biology Laboratory Manual. 3rd ed. Marjorie Sharp. 212p. (C). 1984. 20.95 (*0-88725-009-2*) Hunter Textbks.

Biology Laboratory Manual. 7th ed. A. M. Winchester. 288p. (C). 1987. spiral bd. write for info. (*0-697-04929-9*) Wm C Brown Pubs.

Biology Laboratory Manual for Majors. Judith A. Parks. 184p. 1992. spiral bd. 16.95 (*0-8403-8072-0*) Kendall-Hunt.

Biology, Medicine & Society: 1840 to 1940. Ed. by Charles Webster. LC 80-41752. (Past & Present Publications). 344p. 1981. 79.95 (*0-521-23770-X*) Cambridge U Pr.

Biology of Acinetobacter: Taxonomy, Clinical Importance, Molecular Biology, Physiology, Industrial Relevance. Ed. by K. J. Towner et al. (FEMS Symposium Ser.: No. 57). (Illus.). 444p. 1991. 115.00 (*0-306-43902-6*, Plenum Pr) Plenum.

Biology of Adolescent Behavior & Development. Ed. by Gerald R. Adams et al. (Advances in Adolescent Development Ser.: Vol. 1). 384p. (C). 1989. text ed. 52.00 (*0-8039-3403-3*); pap. text ed. 24.00 (*0-8039-3404-1*) Sage.

Biology of Adventitious Root Formation. Ed. by Tim D. Davis & B. E. Haissig. LC 93-46186. (Basic Life Sciences Ser.: Vol. 62). (Illus.). 343p. 1994. 89.50 (*0-306-44627-8*, Plenum Pr) Plenum.

Biology of Aging. John W. Brookbank. 256p. (C). 1990. text ed. 43.50 (*0-06-041019-1*) HarpCollege.

Biology of Aging. James L. Christiansen & Grzybowski. 344p. 1992. pap. 26.95 (*0-8016-6363-6*) Mosby Yr Bk.

Biology of Aging. Morris Rockstein & Marvin Sussman. 203p. (C). 1979. pap. 18.95 (*0-534-00687-6*) Intl Thomson.

Biology of Aging. Ed. by Richard L. Sprott et al. LC 93-31559. 144p. 1993. 24.95 (*0-8261-8370-0*) Springer Pub.

Biology of Aging. Ed. by R. Zwilling & C. Balduini. (Reihe der Villa Vigoni Ser.: Vol. 1). (Illus.). 192p. 1992. pap. 69.00 (*0-387-54488-7*) Spr-Verlag.

Biology of Aging: Observation & Principles. Robert Arking. 368p. (C). 1990. text ed. write for info. (*0-13-084583-5*) P-H.

Biology of Agoraphobia. Ed. by James C. Ballenger. LC 84-6157. (Clinical Insights Ser.). 125p. reprint ed. pap. 35.70 (*0-8357-7823-1*, 2036196) Bks Demand.

Biology of AIDS. 2nd ed. Hung Fan et al. 208p. (Orig.). 1991. pap. 28.75 (*0-86720-178-9*) Jones & Bartlett.

Biology of AIDS. 3rd ed. Hung Fan et al. (Life Science Ser.). 190p. (C). 1994. pap. text ed. 26.25 (*0-86720-346-3*) Jones & Bartlett.

Biology of Alcoholism, 5 vols. Ed. by Benjamin Kissin & Henri Begleiter. Incl. Vol. 1. Biochemistry. LC 74-131883. 658p. 1971. 110.00 (*0-306-37111-1*); Vol. 5. Treatment & Rehabilitation of the Chronic Alcoholic. LC 74-131883. 656p. 1977. 110.00 (*0-306-37115-4*); LC 74-131883. (Illus.). write for info. (*0-318-55310-4*, Plenum Pr) Plenum.

Biology of Alcoholism Vol. 6: Pathogenesis of Alcoholism: Psychosocial Factors. Ed. by Benjamin Kissin & Henri Begleiter. LC 82-19029. 734p. 1983. 120.00 (*0-306-41052-4*, Plenum Pr) Plenum.

Biology of Alcoholism Vol. 6: Pathogenesis of Alcoholism: Psychosocial Factors, Vol. 6 & 7. Ed. by Benjamin Kissin & Henri Begleiter. LC 82-19029. 734p. 1983. Vols. 6 & 7. 175.00 (*0-685-18632-6*, Plenum Pr) Plenum.

Biology of Alcoholism Vol. 7: Pathogenesis of Alcoholism: Biological Factors. Ed. by Henri Begleiter & Benjamin Kissin. LC 82-22284. 666p. 1983. 120.00 (*0-306-41053-2*, Plenum Pr) Plenum.

Biology of Alcoholism Vol. 7: Pathogenesis of Alcoholism: Biological Factors, Vols. 6 & 7. Ed. by Henri Begleiter & Benjamin Kissin. LC 82-22284. 666p. 1983. 175.00 (*0-685-06438-7*, Plenum Pr) Plenum.

Biology of Algae & Diverse Other Verses. Ralph A. Lewin. 1987. pap. 9.95 (*0-940168-11-1*) Boxwood.

Biology of Alligators & Crocodiles: Index of New Information & Research Bible. Alex D. Ruppert. 150p. 1994. 44.50 (*0-7883-0112-8*); pap. text ed. 39.50 (*0-7883-0113-6*) ABBE Pubs Assn.

***Biology of Alpha B2-Macroglobulin, Its Receptor, & Related Proteins.** Ed. by Wolfgang Borth. LC 94-30081. (Annals of the New York Academy of Sciences Ser.: Vol. 737). 1994. write for info. (*0-89766-886-3*) NY Acad Sci.

Biology of Amphibians. William E. Duellman & Linda Trueb. LC 93-24401. 694p. (C). 1994. pap. text ed. 39.95 (*0-8018-4780-X*) Johns Hopkins.

Biology of Anaerobic Bacteria: Proceedings of the International Seminar, Lillie, France, June 17-18, 1986. Ed. by H. C. Dubourguier et al. (Progress in Biotechnology Ser.: No. 2). 270p. 1987. 97.50 (*0-444-42726-0*) Elsevier.

Biology of Anaerobic Microorganisms. Ed. by Alexander J. Zehnder. LC 87-28036. (Environmental & Applied Microbiology Ser.). 872p. 1988. text ed. 184.95 (*0-471-88226-7*) Wiley.

***Biology of & Novel Therapeutic Approaches for Epithelial Cancers of the Aerodigestive Tract.** 1995. lib. bdg. 252.99 (*0-8490-6721-9*) Gordon Pr.

Biology of Animal Behavior. 2nd ed. James W. Grier & Burk. (Illus.). 890p. 1991. 47.95 (*0-8016-2699-4*) Mosby Yr Bk.

Biology of Animal Behavior. 2nd ed. James W. Grier & Ted Burk. 800p. (C). 1993. text ed. write for info. (*0-697-23492-4*) Wm C Brown Pubs.

B

An Asterisk (*) at the beginning of an entry indicates that the title is appearing in BIP for the first time.

An Asterisk (*) at the beginning of an entry indicates that the title is appearing in BIP for the first time.

Biology of Major Psychosis. Ed. by D. Freedman. 1975. 31.00 (0-7204-7560-0) Elsevier.

Biology of Malaria Parasites. (Technical Report Ser.: No. 743). 229p. 1987. pap. 19.20 (92-4-120743-4) World Health.

Biology of Mallomonas: Morphology, Taxonomy & Ecology. Peter A. Siver. (Developments in Hydrobiology Ser.). (C). 1991. lib. bdg. 161.50 (0-7923-1166-3) Kluwer Ac.

Biology of Mammalian Germ-Cell Mutagenesis. Ed. by James W. Allen et al. (Banbury Report Ser.: No. 34). (Illus.). 350p. 1990. 95.00 (0-87969-234-0) Cold Spring Harbor.

Biology of Man in History Vol. 1: Selections from the Annales: Economies Societes, Civilisations. Ed. by Robert Forster & Orest Ranum. LC 74-24382. 1975. text ed. 32.50x (0-8018-1690-4) Johns Hopkins.

Biology of Mao Zedong. Philip Short. 1996. 35.00 (0-8050-3115-4) H Holt & Co.

Biology of Marine Plants. Matthew H. Dring. (Illus.). 208p. 1982. pap. 27.95 (0-521-42765-7) Cambridge U Pr.

Biology of Meiofauna. Ed. by C. Heip. (Developments in Hydrobiology Ser.). 1984. lib. bdg. 94.00 (90-6193-513-X) Kluwer Ac.

Biology of Memory Symposia Medica Hoechst Twenty-Three. Larry R. Squire. 1991. pap. text ed. 217.00 (0-471-56101-0) Wiley.

Biology of Menopause: The Causes & Consequences of Ovarian Ageing. R. C. Gosden. LC 84-14516. (Monograph Ser.). 1985. text ed. 99.00 (0-12-291850-9) Acad Pr.

***Biology of Mental Disorders.** Research & Education Staff. 192p. 1994. pap. text ed. 14.95 (0-87891-960-0) Res & Educ.

Biology of Methylotrophs. Israel Goldberg & J. Stefan Rokem. (Biotechnology Ser.). (Illus.). 382p. 1991. text ed. 36.00 (0-7506-9188-3) Buttrwrth-Heinemann.

Biology of Microorganisms. 6th ed. Thomas D. Brock & Michael T. Madigan. 880p. 1990. text ed. 67.00 (0-13-083817-9) P-H.

Biology of Microorganisms. 7th rev. ed. Thomas D. Brock et al. LC 93-8549. 1993. reprint ed. text ed. 77.00 (0-13-042169-3) P-H.

Biology of Millipedes. Stephen P. Hopkin & Helen J. Read. (Illus.). 248p. 1992. 70.00 (0-19-857699-4) OUP.

Biology of Moral Systems. Richard D. Alexander. (Foundations of Human Behavior Ser.). 323p. (C). 1987. lib. bdg. 48.95 (0-202-01173-9); pap. text ed. 24.95 (0-202-01174-7) Aldine de Gruyter.

Biology of Mosquitoes, Vol. 1: Development, Nutrition & Reproduction. A. N. Clements. (Illus.). 540p. (C). 1992. 89.95 (0-412-40180-0, A6946) Chapman & Hall.

Biology of Music Making - 1984 Conference: Proceedings. Ed. by Frank Wilson. 316p. (Orig.). 1988. pap. 14.95 (0-918812-51-8, ST 009) MMB Music.

Biology of Mutualism: Ecology & Evolution. Ed. by Douglas H. Boucher. (Illus.). 400p. 1988. pap. 25.95 (0-19-505392-3) OUP.

Biology of Nectaries. Ed. by Barbara Bentley & Thomas S. Elias. LC 82-4200. (Illus.). 336p. 1983. text ed. 56.00 (0-231-04446-1) Col U Pr.

Biology of Negative Strand Viruses. Ed. by B. W. Mahy & D. Kolakofsky. 436p. 1987. 177.00 (0-444-80833-7) Elsevier.

Biology of Nematocysts. Ed. by David A. Hessinger & Howard M. Lenhoff. 500p. 1988. text ed. 125.00 (0-12-345320-8) Acad Pr.

Biology of Neuropeptide Y & Related Peptides. Ed. by William F. Colmers & Claes Wahlestedt. LC 92-28742. (Contemporary Neuroscience Ser.). (Illus.). 576p. 1993. 99.50 (0-89603-241-8) Humana.

Biology of New World Microtus. Ed. by Robert H. Tamarin. (American Society of Mammalogists Special Publication Ser.: No. 8). 893p. 1985. 55.00 (0-943612-07-1) Am Soc Mammalogists.

Biology of Nicotine: Current Research Issues. Ed. by Patrick M. Lippiello et al. 240p. 1992. 89.50 (0-88167-860-0) Raven.

Biology of Nicotine Dependence. CIBA Foundation Symposium Staff. (CIBA Foundation Symposia Ser.: No. 152). 264p. 1990. text ed. 89.95 (0-471-92688-4) Wiley.

Biology of Nitric Oxide Pt. 1: Physiological & Clinical Aspects. Ed. by S. Moncada et al. (Proceedings Ser.: Vol. 1). 420p. 1992. 160.00 (1-85578-012-7, Pub. by Portland Pr Ltd UK) Ashgate Pub Co.

Biology of Nitric Oxide Pt. 2: Enzymology, Biochemistry, & Immunology. Ed. by S. Moncada et al. (Proceedings Ser.: Vol. 1). 230p. 1993. 110.00 (1-85578-013-5, Pub. by Portland Pr Ltd UK) Ashgate Pub Co.

Biology of Nitrogen Fixing Organisms. Janet I. Sprent. (Illus.). 1979. text ed. write for info. (0-07-084087-3) McGraw.

Biology of Non-Specific DNA Protein Interaction. Ed. by Revzin. 1990. 179.00 (0-8493-6177-X, QP624) CRC Pr.

***Biology of Normal Human Growth: Transactions of the First Karolinska Institute Nobel Conference.** fac. ed. Karolinska Institute Nobel Conference Staff. Ed. by Martin Ritzen et al. LC 80-5837. (Illus.). 349p. Date not set. pap. 99.50 (0-7837-7160-6, 2047137) Bks Demand.

Biology of Normal Proliferating Cells in Vitro Relevance for in vivo Aging. A. Macieira-Coelho. (Interdisciplinary Topics in Gerontology Ser.: Vol. 23). (Illus.). vi, 218p. 1987. 136.00 (3-8055-4660-2) S Karger.

Biology of Nutrition, Set. Ed. by R. N. Fiennes. Incl. Pt. 1. Evolution & Nature of Living Systems. 1972. (0-318-55140-3); Pt. 2. Organizations & Nutritional Methods of Life Forms. 1972. (0-318-55141-1); 688p. 1972. 285.00 (0-08-016470-6, Pub. by Pergamon Repr UK) Franklin.

Biology of Occlusal Development: Proceedings of a Sponsored Symposium Honoring Professor Robert E. Moyers, Held March 4 & 5, 1977, in Ann Arbor, Michigan. Symposium on Craniofacial Growth Staff. Ed. by James A. McNamara, Jr. (Craniofacial Growth Monograph Ser.: No. 7). (Illus.). 341p. reprint ed. pap. 97.20 (0-8357-8666-8, 2052309) Bks Demand.

Biology of Organisms, Pt. 2. 5th ed. Helena Curtis & N. Sue Barnes. 1989. pap. 24.95 (0-87901-436-9) Worth.

Biology of Oxygen. Peter Nicholls. Ed. by J. J. Head. LC 81-67981. (Carolina Biology Readers Ser.: No. 100). (Illus.). 16p. (gr. 10 up). 1982. pap. 2.75 (0-89278-300-1, 45-9700) Carolina Biological.

Biology of Paramecium. 2nd ed. Ralph Wichterman. LC 85-19317. 620p. 1986. 120.00 (0-306-42027-9, Plenum Pr) Plenum.

Biology of Parasitic Flowering Plants. Job Kuijt. LC 68-9722. (Illus.). 1969. 75.00 (0-520-01490-1) U CA Pr.

Biology of Parasitism. Paul T. Englund. (MBL Lectures in Biology). 544p. 1988. pap. text ed. 59.95 (0-471-56247-5) Wiley.

Biology of Parasitism: A Molecular & Immunological Approach. Ed. by Paul T. Englund & Alan Sher. 544p. 1988. text ed. 159.95 (0-471-50264-2) Wiley.

Biology of Particles in Aquatic Systems. Ed. by R. S. Wotton. 320p. 1990. 219.00 (0-8493-5450-1, QH) CRC Pr.

Biology of Peromyscus (Rodentia) Ed. by John A. King. (ASM Special Publication Ser.: No. 2). (Illus.). xiii, 593p. 1968. 25.00 (0-943612-01-2) Am Soc Mammalogists.

Biology of Phagocytes in Health & Disease: Proceedings of the International Congress on the Biological & Clinical Aspects of Phagocyte Function, 7-10 September, 1986, Pavia, Italy. Ed. by C. Mauri et al. 651p. 1988. 120.00 (0-08-036133-1, Pergamon Pr) Elsevier.

Biology of Plants. 5th ed. Peter H. Raven et al. 791p. 1992. text ed. 62.95x (0-87901-532-2); Laboratory Topics in Botany by Every & Eichhorn. pap. 25.95x (0-87901-521-7) Worth.

Biology of Plants: Laboratory Exercises. 6th ed. Henry L. Dean & Robert W. Schuhmacher. 304p. (C). 1987. spiral bd. write for info. (0-697-00644-1) Wm C Brown Pubs.

Biology of Platelet-Derived Growth Factor. Ed. by B. Westermark & C. Sorg. (Cytokines Ser.: Vol. 5). (Illus.). viii, 168p. 1992. 196.00 (3-8055-5635-7) S Karger.

Biology of Polar Bryophytes & Lichens. R. E. Longton. (Studies in Polar Research). (Illus.). 280p. 1988. 120.00 (0-521-25015-3) Cambridge U Pr.

Biology of Population Growth. Raymond Pearl. Ed. by Frank N. Egerton, 3rd. LC 77-74245. (History of Ecology Ser.). 1978. reprint ed. lib. bdg. 24.95 (0-405-10414-6) Ayer.

Biology of Populations, Pt. 3. 5th ed. Helena Curtis & N. Sue Barnes. 1989. pap. 24.95 (0-87901-437-7) Worth.

Biology of Poxviruses. S. Dales & Beatriz G. Pogo. (Virology Monographs: Vol. 18). (Illus.). 140p. 1981. 51.90 (0-387-81643-7) Spr-Verlag.

Biology of Proteoglycans. Ed. by Thomas N. Wight & Robert P. Mecham. (Biology of Extracellular Matrix Ser.). 356p. 1987. text ed. 114.00 (0-12-750650-0) Acad Pr.

Biology of Pseudoscorpions. Peter Weygoldt. LC 70-82300. (Harvard Bks. in Biology: No. 6). (Illus.). 159p. reprint ed. pap. 45.40 (0-7837-1737-7, 2057267) Bks Demand.

Biology of Race. rev. ed. James C. King. LC 81-1345. (Illus.). 220p. 1981. 40.00 (0-520-04223-9); pap. 12.00 (0-520-04224-7) U CA Pr.

***Biology of Radiation Carcinogenesis.** fac. ed. Ed. by John M. Yuhas et al. LC 74-14486. (Illus.). 371p. Date not set. pap. 105.80 (0-7837-7221-1, 2047077) Bks Demand.

Biology of Radiodine: Proceedings of Hanford Symposium Bio Radioactive, Richland, July 17-19. L. Bustad. 1964. 151.00 (0-08-010815-6, Pub. by Pergamon Repr UK) Franklin.

Biology of Religion. Antonio T. De Nicolas. 29p. 1990. pap. 3.50 (0-914910-96-5) Buddhist Bks.

Biology of Rice. Ed. by S. Tsunoda & N. Takahashi. (Developments in Crop Science Ser.: Vol. 7). 300p. 1984. 97.50 (0-444-99615-X, I-142-84) Elsevier.

Biology of Rickettsial Diseases, 2 vols., Vol. I. David H. Walker. 160p. 1988. text ed. 94.00 (0-8493-4382-8, RC114, CRC Reprint) Franklin.

Biology of Rickettsial Diseases, 2 vols., Vol. II. David H. Walker. 176p. 1988. text ed. 103.00 (0-8493-4383-6, RC114, CRC Reprint) Franklin.

Biology of Salmonella. Ed. by Felipe Cabello. LC 93-4806. (NATO ASI Series A, Life Sciences: Vol. 245). 470p. 1993. 115.00 (0-306-44492-5, Plenum Pr) Plenum.

Biology of Schistosomes: From Genes to Latrines. Ed. by David Rollinson & Andrew J. Simpson. 472p. 1988. text ed. 117.00 (0-12-593692-3) Acad Pr.

***Biology of Schizophrenia: Proceedings of the 7th International Symposium of the Tokyo Institute of Psychiatry, Tokyo, Japan, October 19-20, 1992.** Ed. by T. Moroji. LC 94-3420. (Developments in Psychiatry Ser.). 1994. write for info. (0-444-81772-7) Elsevier.

***Biology of Schizophrenia & Affective Disease.** Ed. by Stanley J. Watson. 464p. 1995. boxed 58.50 (0-88048-746-1, 8746) Am Psychiatric.

Biology of Scorpions. Ed. by Gary A. Polis. LC 84-40330. (Illus.). 614p. 1990. 89.50 (0-8047-1249-2) Stanford U Pr.

Biology of Seagrasses: A Treatise of Seagrasses with Special Reference to the Australian Region. Ed. by A. W. Larkum et al. (Aquatic Plant Studies: No. 2). 885p. 1989. 174.50 (0-444-87403-8) Elsevier.

Biology of Seaweeds. Ed. by Christopher S. Lobban & Michael J. Wynne. LC 81-69858. (Botanical Monographs: Vol. 17). (Illus.). 784p. 1982. 100.00 (0-520-04585-8) U CA Pr.

***Biology of Seed Plants.** Dennis Homan et al. 256p. (C). 1995. pap. text ed., ring bd. 24.95 (0-7872-0965-1) Kendall-Hunt.

Biology of Senescence. 3rd ed. A. Comfort. 414p. 1979. 45.25 (0-444-00266-9) Elsevier.

Biology of Serotonergic Transmission. Ed. by Neville N. Osborne. LC 81-14671. (Illus.). 536p. reprint ed. pap. 152.80 (0-8357-7242-X, 2029646) Bks Demand.

Biology of Sexually Transmitted Diseases. Gerald J. Stine. 384p. (C). 1991. pap. write for info. (0-697-11897-5) Wm C Brown Pubs.

Biology of Sleep Substances. Shojiro Inoue. 224p. 1989. 156.00 (0-8493-4822-6, QP425) CRC Pr.

Biology of Spermatozoa: Proceedings of the Inserm Symposium at Nouzilly, Nov. 4-7, 1973. Inserm-International Symposium Staff. Ed. by E. S. Hafez & C. G. Thibault. (Illus.). vii, 256p. 1975. 88.00 (3-8055-2104-9) S Karger.

Biology of Spiders. Rainer F. Foelix. 316p. 1987. pap. 18.95 (0-674-07432-7) HUP.

Biology of Stress in Farm Animals: An Integrative Approach. Ed. by P. R. Wiepkema & P. W. Van Adrichem. (Current Topics in Veterinary Medicine & Animal Science Ser.). (C). 1987. lib. bdg. 95.00 (0-89838-895-3) Kluwer Ac.

Biology of Suicide: Journal of Suicide & Life-Treatening Behaviors, Vol. 16, No. 2. Ed. by Ronald W. Maris. LC 86-14207. 216p. 1986. lib. bdg. 35.00 (0-89862-578-5) Guilford Pr.

Biology of Surfactant. Brian A. Hills. (Illus.). ix, 408p. 1988. 105.00 (0-521-30728-7) Cambridge U Pr.

Biology of Survival in Human & Animal Life: Index of New Information with Authors & Subjects. Howard A. Schultz. 180p. 1993. 49.50 (1-55914-886-1); pap. 39.50 (1-55914-887-X) ABBE Pubs Assn.

Biology of Suspension Feeding. C. K. Jorgensen & G. A. Kerkut. LC 64-7812. (International Series of Monographs on Pure & Applied Mathematics: Vol. 27). 1966. 156.00 (0-08-011068-1, Pub. by Pergamon Repr UK) Franklin.

Biology of Symbiosis. D. C. Smith & A. E. Douglas. 320p. (C). 1992. pap. 39.95 (0-521-42783-5) Cambridge U Pr.

Biology of Symbiotic Fungi. Roderic C. Cooke. LC 76-56175. (Illus.). 294p. reprint ed. pap. 83.80 (0-8357-7244-6, 2030496) Bks Demand.

Biology of Taurine: Methods & Mechanisms. Ed. by Ryan J. Huxtable et al. LC 87-20335. (Advances in Experimental Medicine & Biology Ser.: Vol. 217). (Illus.). 418p. 1987. 95.00 (0-306-42665-X, Plenum Pr) Plenum.

Biology of Terrestrial Isopods. Ed. by S. L. Sutton & D. M. Holdich. (Symposia of the Zoological Society of London Ser.: No. 53). (Illus.). 1985. 85.00 (0-19-854001-9) OUP.

Biology of the Algae. Philip Sze. 264p. (C). 1986. pap. write for info. (0-697-00741-3) Wm C Brown Pubs.

Biology of the Algae. 2nd ed. Philip Sze. 272p. (C). 1992. pap. text ed. write for info. (0-697-01373-1) Wm C Brown Pubs.

Biology of the Antarctic Seas, Vol. XIX. Ed. by L. S. Kornicker. (Antarctic Research Ser.: Vol. 47). 113p. 1988. 33.00 (0-87590-171-9) Am Geophysical.

***Biology of the Antarctic Seas Eight, 3 Papers, Papers 2 & 3: Nonasellote Isopod Crustaceans from.** Ed. by D. L. Pawson & L. S. Kornicker. (Antarctic Research Ser.). 50p. 1978. write for info. (0-87590-142-5) Am Geophysical.

Biology of the Antarctic Seas Eight, 3 papers, Set 28-3. Ed. by D. L. Pawson & L. S. Kornicker. (Antarctic Research Ser.: Vol. 28). 70p. 1978. Minibk. Set. 20.00 (0-685-55231-4) Am Geophysical.

Biology of the Antarctic Seas Eight: Morphology & Distribution of Species in the Genus Pogonophryne (Pices, Harpagiferidae), 3 Papers, Paper 1: Morphology & Distribution of Species in t. Ed. by D. L. Pawson & L. S. Kornicker. (Antarctic Research Ser.: Vol. 28). 20p. 1978. write for info. (0-87590-137-9) Am Geophysical.

Biology of the Antarctic Seas Eleven, 3 papers, Set 34-3. Ed. by L. Kornicker. (Antarctic Research Ser.: Vol. 34). 335p. 1983. Minibk. Set. 34.50 (0-685-55235-7); Paper 1: Antarctic & Subantarctic Scleractinia, 74p. write for info. (0-87590-180-8); Paper 2: Calanoid Copepods of the Genus Scaphocalanus from Antarctic & Subantarctic Waters, 52p. write for info. (0-87590-183-2); Paper 3: Antarctic Chaetognatha: United States Antarctic Research Program Eltanin Cruises 8-28, Pt. write for info. (0-87590-187-5) Am Geophysical.

Biology of the Antarctic Seas Fifteen. Ed. by Louis S. Kornicker. (Geophysical Monograph Ser.: Vol. 40). 288p. 1984. 35.00 (0-87590-192-1) Am Geophysical.

Biology of the Antarctic Seas Five, Paper 3: Bathypelagic Isopid Crustacea from the Antarctic & Southern Seas. Ed. by D. L. Pawson. (Antarctic Research Ser.: Vol. 23). 59p. 1977. write for info. (0-87590-127-1) Am Geophysical.

Biology of the Antarctic Seas 4. Ed. by George A. Llano & I. Eugene Wallen. LC 64-60030. (Antarctic Research Ser.: Vol. 17). (Illus.). 362p. 1971. 39.00 (0-87590-117-4) Am Geophysical.

Biology of the Antarctic Seas Fourteen, 5 papers, Set 39-5. Ed. by L. Kornicker. (Antarctic Research Ser.: Vol. 39). 364p. 1983. Minibk. Set. 26.00 (0-685-55236-5); Paper 1: Some Antarctic & Sub-Antarctic Sea Anemones (Coelenterata: Ptychodactiaria & Actiniaria), 6. write for info. (0-87590-188-3); Paper 2: Antarctic Chaetognatha: United States Antarctic Research Program Eltanin Cruises 10-23, 25,. write for info. (0-87590-189-1); Papers 3-5: Polychaetes of the Family Spionidae from South America, & Adjacent Seas & Islands; Antar. write for info. (0-87590-190-5) Am Geophysical.

Biology of the Antarctic Seas Nine, 5 papers, Set 31-5. Ed. by L. Kornicker. (Antarctic Research Ser.: Vol. 31). 158p. 1981. Minibk. Set. 39.00 (0-685-55233-0); Paper 1: Osteology of the Ross Seal Ommatophoca Rossi Gray, 1844, 24p. write for info. (0-87590-150-6); Paper 2: Calanoid Copepods of the Genus Scolecithricella from Antarctic & Subantarctic Waters, 1980,. write for info. (0-87590-151-4); Papers 3-5: Osteology & Relationships of the Fishes of the Antarctic Family Harpagiferidae (Pisces,. write for info. (0-87590-153-0) Am Geophysical.

Biology of the Antarctic Seas Seven, 4 papers, Set 27-4. Ed. by D. L. Pawson. (Antarctic Research Ser.: Vol. 27). 302p. 1978. Minibk. Set. 62.00 (0-685-55230-6); Paper 1: Systematics & Morphology of the Antarctic Cranchild Squid Galiteuthis Glacialis (Chun), 40p. write for info. (0-87590-133-6); Paper 2: Systematics & Ecology of Ciliated Protozoa from King George Island, South Shetland Islands,. write for info. (0-87590-134-4); Paper 3: More Planktonic Isopod Crustaceans from Subantarctic & Antarctic Seas, 34p. write for info. (0-87590-135-2); Paper 4: Calanoid Copepods (Aetideidae, Euchaetidae) from Anatarctic & Subantarctic Waters, 200p. write for info. (0-87590-136-0) Am Geophysical.

Biology of the Antarctic Seas Seventeen. Louis S. Koricker. (Antarctic Research Ser.: Vol. 44). 96p. 22.50 (0-87590-169-7) Am Geophysical.

Biology of the Antarctic Seas Six, Set. Ed. by D. L. Pawson. (Antarctic Research Ser.: Vol. 26). 51.00 (0-87590-144-1) Am Geophysical.

Biology of the Antarctic Seas Six, Paper Four: Polychaeta from the Weddell Sea Quadrant, Antarctica. Ed. by D. L. Pawson. (Antarctic Research Ser.: Vol. 26). 60p. 1978. write for info. (0-87590-132-8) Am Geophysical.

Biology of the Antarctic Seas Sixteen, Papers 1-2: 1985. Ed. by Louis S. Kornicker. (Geophysical Monograph Ser.: Vol. 41). 60p. Papers 1-2, 1985, 60p. 14.75 (0-87590-193-X) Am Geophysical.

Biology of the Antarctic Seas Sixteen, Papers 3 & 4. Ed. by L. Kornicker. (Antarctic Research Ser.: Vol. 41). 148p. 1986. 26.00 (0-87590-198-0) Am Geophysical.

Biology of the Antarctic Seas Ten, 5 papers, Set 32-5. Ed. by L. Kornicker. (Antarctic Research Ser.: Vol. 32). 165p. 1982. Minibk. Set. 21.00 (0-685-55234-9); Paper 1: A Representative of the Genus Dendrogaster (Cirripedia: Ascothoracica) Parasitic in an Anta. write for info. (0-87590-176-X); Papers 2 & 3: Species of Protallocoxoidea & Stenentrioidea (Isopoda, Asellota) from the Antarctic &. write for info. (0-87590-178-6); Paper 4: Some Antarctic Deep-Sea Tunicates in the Smithsonian Collections, 36p. write for info. (0-87590-177-8); Paper 5: A Faunistic Study of the Planktonic Ostracods (Myodocopa, Halocyprididae) Collected on Elev. write for info. (0-87590-179-4) Am Geophysical.

***Biology of the Antarctic Seas Thirteen.** Ed. by S. Cairns. (Antarctic Research Ser.: Vol. 63). 99p. 1994. 33.00 (0-87590-844-6, AR0638446) Am Geophysical.

Biology of the Antarctic Seas Thirteen. Ed. by Louis S. Kornicker. (Geophysical Monograph Ser.: Vol. 38). 262p. 1983. 40.00 (0-87590-186-7) Am Geophysical.

Biology of the Antarctic Seas Three. Ed. by George A. Llano & Waldo L. Schmitt. LC 64-60030. (Antarctic Research Ser.: Vol. 11). (Illus.). 261p. 1967. 17.00 (0-87590-111-5) Am Geophysical.

Biology of the Antarctic Seas Twelve. Ed. by D. Pawson. (Antarctic Research Ser.: Vol. 35). (Illus.). 110p. 1982. 20.00 (0-87590-181-6) Am Geophysical.

Biology of the Antarctic Seas Twenty-One. Ed. by L. S. Kornicker. (Antarctic Research Ser.: Vol. 52). 236p. 1990. 47.00 (0-685-53519-3, AR052761X) Am Geophysical.

Biology of the Antarctic Seas 22. Ed. by Stephen Cairns. (Antarctic Research Ser.: Vol. 58). 1993. 38.00 (0-87590-826-8) Am Geophysical.

Biology of the Antarctic Seas 2. Ed. by George A. Llano. LC 64-60030. (Antarctic Research Ser.: Vol. 5). (Illus.). 280p. 1965. 15.00 (0-87590-105-0) Am Geophysical.

Biology of the Antarctic Seas XVII. Louis S. Kornicker. (Antarctic Research Ser.: Vol. 45). 192p. 34.00 (0-87590-170-0) Am Geophysical.

Biology of the Autistic Syndromes. 2nd ed. Christopher Gillberg & Mary Coleman. (Clinics in Developmental Medicine Ser.: No. 126). 300p. (C). 1993. 64.95 (0-521-43228-6) Cambridge U Pr.

Biology of the Blastocyst. Ed. by Richard J. Blandau. LC 70-128713. 574p. reprint ed. pap. 163.60 (0-8357-3595-8, 2019955) Bks Demand.

Biology of the Brain: From Neurons to Networks. Ed. by Rodolfo R. Llinas. (Illus.). 192p. (C). 1995. text ed. 13.95 (0-7167-2037-X) W H Freeman.

Biology of the Cell Cycle. J. M. Mitchinson. LC 72-160100. (Illus.). 1972. 55.00 (0-521-08251-X) Cambridge U Pr.

Biology of the Cell Surface. Ernest Just. LC 88-14164. (Genes Cells & Organisms Ser.). (Illus.). 408p. 1988. 20.00 (0-8240-1380-8) Garland.

Biology of the Cervix. Ed. by Richard J. Blandau & Kamran Moghissi. LC 72-91429. 463p. reprint ed. pap. 132.00 (0-8357-7245-4, 2019956) Bks Demand.

***Biology of the Chemokine RANTES.** Alan M. Krensky. LC 95-7283. (Molecular Biology Intelligence Unit Ser.). 126p. 1995. 69.00 (1-57059-253-5) R G Landes.

Biology of the Chemotactic Response. Ed. by J. P. Armitage & J. M. Lackie. (Society for General Microbiology Symposium Ser.: No. 46). 400p. (C). 1991. 125.00 (0-521-40313-8) Cambridge U Pr.

Biology of the Crustacea: Itegument, Pigments, & Hormonal Process, Vol. 9. Ed. by Dorothy E. Bliss & Linda H. Mantel. 1985. text ed. 125.00 (0-12-106409-3) Acad Pr.

An Asterisk (*) at the beginning of an entry indicates that the title is appearing in BIP for the first time.

Biology of the Crustacea Vol. 6: Economic Aspects: Pathobiology, Culture & Fisheries. Ed. by Dorothy E. Bliss & J. Provenzano. LC 82-4058. 1983. text ed. 125.00 (0-12-106406-9) Acad Pr.

Biology of the Epidermis: Molecular & Functional Aspects: Proceedings of the Fifth Japan-United States Symposium on the Biology of the Epidermis, Niseko, Hokkaido, 21-25 July 1991. Ed. by Akira Ohkawara & Joseph McGuire. LC 92-22112. 1992. write for info. (0-444-89232-X) Elsevier.

Biology of the Eucestoda, Vol. 1. Peter Pappas. Ed. by Christopher Arme. 1984. text ed. 139.00 (0-12-062101-0) Acad Pr.

Biology of the Eucestoda, Vol. 2. Ed. by Christopher Arme & Peter Pappas. 1984. text ed. 139.00 (0-12-062102-9) Acad Pr.

Biology of the Germ Line: In Animals & Man. Ed. by H. Mohri et al. (Illus.). x, 304p. 1993. 157.00 (3-8055-5773-6) S Karger.

Biology of the Grapevine. Michael G. Mullins et al. (Biology of Horticultural Crops Ser.). (Illus.). 250p. (C). 1992. 69.95 (0-521-30507-1) Cambridge U Pr.

Biology of the Guinea Pig. Ed. by J. Wagner & P. Manning. 317p. 1979. write for info. (0-318-59895-7) ACLAM.

Biology of the Guinea Pig. Ed. by Joseph E. Wagner & Patrick J. Manning. 1976. text ed. 151.00 (0-12-730050-3) Acad Pr.

Biology of the Honey Bee. Mark L. Winston. LC 86-31940. (Illus.). 288p. 1987. 42.50 (0-674-07408-4) HUP.

Biology of the Honey Bee. Mark L. Winston. (Illus.). 296p. 1991. pap. 18.95x (0-674-07409-2, WINBIX) HUP.

Biology of the Integument: Invertebrates, Vol. 1. Ed. by K. S. Richards. (Illus.). 800p. 1984. 299.00 (0-387-13062-4) Spr-Verlag.

Biology of the Integument: Vertebrates. Ed. by J. Bereiter-Hahn et al. (Biology of the Integument Ser.: Vol. 2). (Illus.). 870p. 1986. 299.00 (0-387-13244-9) Spr-Verlag.

Biology of the Interferon System 1983: Proceedings of the Second International TNO Meeting on the Biology of the Interferon System, Held in Rotterdam, the Netherlands, 18-22 April, 1983. Ed. by Edward De Maeyer & H. Schellekens. 564p. 1983. 144.75 (0-444-80531-1, I-335-83) Elsevier.

Biology of the Interferon System, 1984: Proceedings of the 1984 TNO-ISIR Meeting on the Biology of the Interferon System, Held in Heidelberg, FRG, 21-25 October, 1984. Ed. by H. Kirchner & H. Schellekens. 654p. 1985. 184.00 (0-444-80661-X) Elsevier.

Biology of the Interferon System 1985. Ed. by W. E. Stewart & H. Schellenkens. 520p. 1986. 159.50 (0-444-80786-1, Excerpta Medica) Elsevier.

Biology of the Interferon System 1986. Ed. by K. Cantell & H. Schellekens. 1987. lib. bdg. 184.00 (90-247-3468-1) Kluwer Ac.

Biology of the Intervertebral Disc, Vol. I. Ed. by Peter Ghosh. 256p. 1988. 204.00 (0-8493-6711-5, RD771) CRC Pr.

Biology of the Intervertebral Disc, Vol. II. Ed. by Peter Ghosh. 224p. 1988. 191.00 (0-8493-6712-3, RD771) CRC Pr.

Biology of the Invertebrates. 2nd ed. Jan A. Pechenik. 592p. (C). 1991. pap. write for info. (0-697-14203-5) Wm C Brown Pubs.

Biology of the Kinetoplastida, Vol. 2. Ed. by W. H. Lumsden & D. A. Evans. 1979. text ed. 248.00 (0-12-460202-9) Acad Pr.

Biology of the Koala. Ed. by A. K. Lee et al. 346p. (C). 1991. text ed. 125.00 (0-949324-34-5, Pub. by Surrey Beatty & Sons AT) St Mut.

Biology of the Laboratory Rabbit. 2nd ed. Ed. by Patrick J. Manning et al. (American College of Laboratory Animal Medicine Ser.). (Illus.). 483p. 1994. text ed. 120.00 (0-12-469235-4) Acad Pr.

Biology of the Land Crabs. Ed. by Warren W. Burggren & Brian R. McMahon. (Illus.). 350p. 1988. 94.95 (0-521-30690-6) Cambridge U Pr.

***Biology of the Lobstor; Homarus Americanus.** Ed. by Jan R. Factor. (Illus.). 368p. 1995. text ed. write for info. (0-12-247570-4) Acad Pr.

***Biology of the Major Psychoses: A Comparative Analysis.** fac. ed. Ed. by Daniel X. Freedman. LC 75-14571. (Association for Research in Nervous & Mental Disease Research Publications: No. 54). (Illus.). 384p. Date not set. pap. 109.50 (0-7837-7297-1, 2047009) Bks Demand.

Biology of the Mollusca. 2nd ed. R. D. Purchon & G. Kerkut. LC 76-10804. (International Series of Monographs on Pure & Applied Mathematics: No. 57). 1977. 236.00 (0-08-021028-7, Pub. by Pergamon Repr UK) Franklin.

Biology of the Muscidae of the World. Peter Skidmore. LC 84-3871. (Entomalogica Ser.). 1985. lib. bdg. 242.00 (90-6193-139-8) Kluwer Ac.

Biology of the Mycobacteria, Vol. 1. Ed. by Colin Ratledge & John L. Stanford. 1982. text ed. 189.00 (0-12-582301-0) Acad Pr.

Biology of the Mycobacteria Vol. 2: Immunological & Environmental Aspects. Ed. by Colin Ratledge & John L. Stanford. 1983. text ed. 189.00 (0-12-582302-9) Acad Pr.

Biology of the Mycobacteria Vol. 3: Clinical Aspects of Mycobacterial Disease. Ed. by Colin Ratledge et al. 621p. 1989. text ed. 187.00 (0-12-582303-7) Acad Pr.

Biology of the Naked Mole-Rat. Ed. by Paul W. Sherman et al. (Monographs in Behavior & Ecology). (Illus.). 529p. 1991. text ed. 75.00 (0-691-08585-4); pap. text ed. 27.95 (0-691-02448-0) Princeton U Pr.

Biology of the Ocular Microcirculation: Proceedings of the Symposium on Ocular Microcirculation, Lake Louise, Alberta, U. S. A. 19-21 September 1991. Ed. by Robert N. Weinreb et al. LC 92-17967. 1992. write for info. (0-444-89729-1, Excerpta Medica) Elsevier.

Biology of the Ovary. Ed. by P. M. Motta & E. S. Hafez. (Developments in Obstetrics & Gynecology Ser.: No. 2). 345p. 1980. lib. bdg. 154.50 (90-247-2316-7) Kluwer Ac.

Biology of the Pneumococcus see Pneumonia

Biology of the Red Algae. Ed. by Kathleen M. Cole & Robert G. Sheath. (Illus.). 750p. (C). 1990. 130.00 (0-521-34301-1) Cambridge U Pr.

Biology of the Rhodophyta. Peter S. Dixon. (University Reviews of Botany Ser.: No. 4). (Illus.). 285p. 1977. reprint ed. pap. text ed. 50.00 (3-87429-124-3) Koeltz Sci Bks.

Biology of the Salivary Gland. Dobrosielski-Ve. 1992. 177.95 (0-8493-8847-3, QP191) CRC Pr.

***Biology of the Sialic Acids.** Ed. by Abraham Rosenberg. 375p. 1995. 95.00 (0-306-44974-9) Plenum.

Biology of the Southern Ocean. George A. Knox. LC 93-28273. (Studies in Polar Research). (Illus.). 488p. (C). 1995. 130.00 (0-521-32211-1) Cambridge U Pr.

Biology of the Species Porphyromanes Gingi. Shah. 1993. 189.95 (0-8493-6648-8, QR201) CRC Pr.

Biology of the Sperm Cell. B. Bacetti & B. Afzelius. (Monographs in Developmental Biology: Vol. 10). (Illus.). 250p. 1976. 101.75 (3-8055-2204-5) S Karger.

Biology of the Timber Rattlesnake. Brown. 1993. write for info. (0-916984-29-X) SSAR.

Biology of the Uterus. 2nd rev. ed. Ed. by R. M. Wynn & W. Jollie. (Illus.). 608p. 1989. 120.00 (0-306-43057-6, Plenum Med Bk) Plenum.

Biology of Ticks, Vol. 1. Daniel E. Sonenshine. (Illus.). 472p. 1992. 95.00 (0-19-505910-7) OUP.

Biology of Ticks, Vol. 2. Daniel E. Sonenshine. (Illus.). 488p. 1993. 95.00 (0-19-508431-4) OUP.

Biology of Tooth Movement. Ed. by Louis A. Norton & Charles J. Burstone. 1988. 234.00 (0-8493-4733-5, QP88) CRC Pr.

Biology of Trophoblast. Ed. by Y. W. Loke & A. Whyte. 706p. 1983. 224.75 (0-444-80477-3, I-333-83) Elsevier.

Biology of Trypansoma & Leishmania: Parasites of Man & Domestic Animals. D. H. Molyneux et al. 274p. 1983. 71.00 (0-8002-3078-7) Taylor & Francis.

Biology of Tumor Malignancy. G. V. Sherbet. LC 81-69599. 1982. text ed. 97.00 (0-12-639880-1) Acad Pr.

Biology of Turbellaria. Ed. by Ernest R. Schockaert & Ian R. Ball. 316p. 1981. lib. bdg. 149.50 (90-6193-757-4) Kluwer Ac.

***Biology of Turbellaria & Some Related Flatworms: Proceedings of the Seventh International Symposium on the Biology of the Turbellaria, Held at Abo/Turku, Finland, 17-22 June 1993.** International Symposium on the Biology of the Turbellaria Staff. Ed. by Lester R. Cannon. LC 95-14932. (Developments in Hydrobiology Ser.: Vol. 108). 1995. write for info. (0-7923-3506-6) Kluwer Ac.

Biology of Twinning in Man. M. G. Bulmer. LC 71-498413. 215p. reprint ed. pap. 61.30 (0-8357-7246-2, 2051313) Bks Demand.

Biology of Two Species of Lake Erie Mayflies. N. Wilson Britt. (Bulletin New Ser.: Vol. 1, No. 5). 1962. 4.00 (0-86727-047-0) Ohio Bio Survey.

Biology of Vascular Disease. Ed. by Goran Holm & Magnus Bjorkholm. (Acta Medica Scandinavica Symposium Ser.: No. 3). (Illus.). 171p. 1987. 108.00x (91-22-00866-7, Pub. by Almqv & Wiksell SW) Coronet Bks.

Biology of Vines. Ed. by F. E. Putz & Harold A. Mooney. (Illus.). 448p. (C). 1992. 125.00 (0-521-39250-0) Cambridge U Pr.

Biology of Viruses. Voyles. 320p. 1993. 46.95 (0-8016-6391-1) Mosby Yr Bk.

Biology of Vitronectins & Their Receptors: Proceedings of the First International Vitronectin Workshop. Ed. by Klaus T. Preissner et al. LC 93-33787. (International Congress Ser.: Vol. 1042). 1993. 203.25 (0-444-81680-1, Excerpta Medica) Elsevier.

Biology of Whiptail Lizards: Genus Cnemidophorus. Ed. by John W. Wright & Laurie J. Vitt. (Illus.). 417p. 1993. 29.00 (1-883090-01-6) OK Museum.

Biology of Women. 2nd ed. Ethel Sloane. 656p. 1985. pap. text ed. 34.95 (0-8273-4366-3) Delmar.

Biology of Women. 3rd ed. Ethel Sloane. LC 92-48339. 760p. 1993. pap. text ed. 34.95 (0-8273-4938-6) Delmar.

Biology of Wool & Hair. Ed. by G. E. Rogers et al. (Illus.). 500p. 1988. text ed. 105.00 (0-412-32120-3) Chapman & Hall.

Biology One Hundred Twenty-One L: Principles of Biology. TVI Staff. 176p. (C). 1992. pap. text ed. 15.95 (0-8403-7869-6) Kendall-Hunt.

Biology One Hundred Twenty-Two Lab Manual. Lyly R. Berger. 160p. (C). 1992. pap. text ed. 7.95 (0-8403-7653-7) Kendall-Hunt.

Biology or Oblivion. Brian Hocking. (Illus.). 118p. 1965. pap. 6.95 (0-87073-801-1) Schenkman Bks Inc.

Biology-Particles in Aquatic Systems. Wotton. 1994. 79.95 (0-87371-905-0, QH541) Lewis Pubs.

Biology Problem Solver. rev. ed. Research & Education Association Staff. LC 78-63610. (Illus.). 1088p. 1994. pap. text ed. 23.95 (0-87891-514-1) Res & Educ.

Biology Projects for Young Scientists. Salvatore Tocci. (J). 1989. pap. 6.95 (0-531-15127-1) Watts.

Biology, Pt. 2 see Biology & Geology of Coral Reefs

Biology, Purpose & Ethics. Conrad H. Waddington. LC 78-154538. (Heinz Werner Lecture Ser.: No. 5). 1971. 9.00 (0-685-01114-3) Clark U Pr.

Biology Quick Review. David N. Knowlton. (Cliffs Quick Reviews Ser.). (Illus.). 179p. (Orig.). 1993. pap. text ed. 6.95 (0-8220-5305-5) Cliffs.

***Biology Quick Review.** David N. Knowlton. (Orig.). 1994. pap. 6.95 (0-614-07036-8) Cliffs.

Biology Quizzes & Puzzles Spiritmasters. S. Curtis. (C). 1985. text ed. 190.00 (0-7175-1372-6, Pub. by S Thornes Pubs UK) St Mut.

Biology, Rearing, & Care of Young Primates. James A. Kirkwood & Katherine Stathatos. (Illus.). 168p. 1992. 75.00 (0-19-854733-1) OUP.

Biology Research Activities. Barbara Newman. Ed. by Eugene Kutscher. (Illus.). 1988. teacher ed write for info. (0-318-64016-3); student ed write for info. (0-318-64017-1) Alpha Pub MD.

Biology Reviews, Vol. 1. Ed. by V. P. Skulachev. (Soviet Scientific Reviews Ser.: Section D). 486p. 1980. text ed. 342.00 (3-7186-0020-X) Gordon & Breach.

Biology Reviews, Vol. 2. Ed. by V. P. Skulachev. (Soviet Scientific Reviews Ser.: Section D). 400p. 1981. text ed. 342.00 (3-7186-0058-7) Gordon & Breach.

Biology Reviews, Vol. 3. Ed. by V. P. Skulachev. (Soviet Scientific Reviews Ser.: Section D). 452p. 1982. text ed. 342.00 (3-7186-0111-7) Gordon & Breach.

Biology, Structure & Systematics of the Cycadales: Proceedings of the Symposium CYCAD 87, Beaulieu-sur-Mer, France, April 17-22, 1987. Ed. by Dennis Wm. Stevenson. LC 89-13570. (Memoirs Ser.: No. 57). (Illus.). 210p. 1990. pap. text ed. 49.50 (0-89327-350-3) NY Botanical.

Biology Teacher's Handbook. 3rd ed. Biological Sciences Curriculum Study Staff. LC 77-27548. 585p. (C). 1978. text ed. write for info. (0-02-310170-9) Macmillan.

Biology Teacher's Instant Vocabulary Kit: With Ready-to-Use Crosswords & Wordsearches for Grades 7-12. Michael Roa & Donnell Tonkelenberg. 212p. 1990. 24.95 (0-87628-189-7) P-H.

Biology Teacher's Instant Vocabulary Kit with Ready to Use Crossword Puzzles & Word Searches. Michael Roa & Donnell Tinkelenberg. 368p. 1990. pap. text ed. 29.95 (0-13-083841-1) P-H.

Biology Teacher's Survival Guide. Michael Fleming. 288p. 1993. spiral bd. 29.95 (0-87628-181-1) Ctr Appl Res.

Biology Teaching Methods. Doris Falk. LC 79-19132. 302p. 1980. reprint ed. lib. bdg. 25.50 (0-89874-038-X) Krieger.

Biology the Easy Way. 2nd ed. Gabrielle I. Edwards. (Easy Way Ser.). 336p. 1990. pap. 9.95 (0-8120-4286-7) Barron.

Biology: The Science of Life: Lab Manual. 3rd ed. Tietgen & Sanders. (C). 1990. write for info. (0-318-68470-5) HarpCollege.

Biology: The Science of Life: Study Guide. 3rd ed. Wallace et al. (C). 1991. 24.50 (0-673-38045-9) HarpCollege.

Biology, the Web of Life. Daniel D. Chiras. Ed. by Westby. LC 92-34101. (Illus.). 1005p. (C). 1993. text ed. 61.00 (0-314-01251-6); pap. text ed. 54.25 (0-314-01343-1) West Pub.

Biology Through the Eyes of Faith. Richard T. Wright. LC 88-45686. (Christian College Coalition Ser.). 220p. 1989. pap. text ed. 12.00 (0-06-069695-8) Harper SF.

Biology Today. Gottfried. 1992. pap. 45.95 (0-8016-7288-0) Mosby Yr Bk.

Biology Today. Sandra S. Gottfried et al. LC 92-30357. 800p. 1992. 48.95 (0-8016-7464-6) Mosby Yr Bk.

Biology Today & Tomorrow. Jack A. Ward & Howard R. Hetzel. (Illus.). 557p. 1984. teacher ed, pap. text ed. 11.25 (0-314-79148-5); student ed, pap. text ed. 20.50 (0-314-71135-X); student ed, teacher ed 30.50 (0-314-79150-7); student ed, teacher ed 13.95 (0-685-07871-X) West Pub.

Biology Today & Tomorrow. 2nd ed. Jack A. Ward & Howard R. Hetzel. (Illus.). 557p. 1984. text ed. 53.75 (0-314-69684-9) West Pub.

Biology Today Text & Lab Manual. Gottfried. 1993. 60.95 (0-8016-7517-0); pap. 58.95 (0-8016-7516-2) Mosby Yr Bk.

Biology Today Text & Study Guide. Gottfried. 1993. 57.95 (0-8016-7519-7); pap. 52.95 (0-8016-7518-9) Mosby Yr Bk.

Biology, Toxicology & Carcinogenesis of Respiratory Epithelium. David G. Thomassen & Paul Nettesheim. 1989. 79.00 (0-89116-941-5) Hemisp Pub.

Biology Two: Laboratory Manual. Vodopich & Moore. (Illus.). 320p. 1989. 17.95 (0-8016-5289-8); teacher ed write for info. (0-318-65135-1) Mosby Yr Bk.

Biology Two Hundred Fourteen Lab Manual. University of Toledo, Biology Dept. Staff. (C). 1993. student ed 10.00 (1-881592-25-1) Hayden-McNeil.

Biology Two Hundred Sixteen Lab Manual. University of Toledo, Biology Dept. Staff. 1993. student ed 10.00 (1-881592-26-X) Hayden-McNeil.

Biology Two Hundred Twelve Lab Manual. University of Toledo, Biology Dept. Staff. (C). 1993. 10.00 (1-881592-24-3) Hayden-McNeil.

Biology with Student Study Art Notebook. 6th ed. John W. Kimball. LC 93-70167. 800p. (C). 1993. text ed. write for info. (0-697-14257-4) Wm C Brown Pubs.

Biology with Student Study Art Notebook. 6th ed. John W. Kimball. LC 93-70167. 752p. (C). 1993. pap. text ed. 43.50 (0-697-20284-4) Wm C Brown Pubs.

Biology with Student Study Art Notebook. 6th ed. John W. Kimball. 800p. 1994. Art study notebook. ring bd. write for info. (0-697-22360-4) Wm C Brown Pubs.

Biology with Student Study Art Notebook. 6th ed. John W. Kimball. LC 93-70167. 800p. (C). 1994. Study guide. student ed write for info. (0-697-14259-0) Wm C Brown Pubs.

Biology Write Now. T. Taigen. 1992. pap. text ed. write for info. (0-07-003143-6) McGraw.

***Biology 101 & 102 Lab Manual.** Wayne Seifert. 111p. (C). 1994. 11.66 (1-56870-157-8) RonJon Pub.

Biology 105 Lab Manual. Joseph Griswold & Aaron Wasserman. 256p. (C). 1994. pap. text ed., spiral bd. 28.95 (0-8403-9214-1) Kendall-Hunt.

Biology 106: Laboratory Manual for Ecology, Evolution & Behavior. Bretton W. Kent & Irwin N. Forseth. 208p. 1991. spiral bd. 15.95 (0-8403-6809-7) Kendall-Hunt.

Biology 110 Lab Manual. 2nd rev. ed. George Labanick. (Illus.). 110p. (C). 1990. 11.00 (1-878045-03-2) Whittier Pubns.

Biology 1110 Laboratory Manual. Marc J. Pline. 128p. (C). 1993. pap. text ed., spiral bd. 15.95 (0-8403-8990-6) Kendall-Hunt.

Biology 1112 Laboratory Manual. Marc J. Pline. 96p. (C). 1993. pap. text ed., spiral bd. 12.95 (0-8403-8787-3) Kendall-Hunt.

Biology 120: Human Anatomy & Physiology - Lecture & Laboratory Manual. L. Jack Pierce. 352p. 1992. spiral bd. 21.95 (0-8403-7514-X) Kendall-Hunt.

Biology 121 Lab Manual. University of New Mexico Ligon Staff. 160p. (C). 1992. spiral bd. 7.95 (0-8403-7841-6) Kendall-Hunt.

***Biology 121L.** TVI Staff. 176p. (C). 1994. pap. text ed., spiral bd. 14.36 (0-7872-0325-4) Kendall-Hunt.

Biology 124L: Biology for Health Sciences. TVI (Albuquerque) Staff. 176p. (C). 1994. pap. text ed., spiral bd. 16.95 (0-8403-9348-2) Kendall-Hunt.

***Biology 131 Lab Manual.** Spencer Bowers. 96p. (C). 1995. pap. text ed. 16.95 (0-7872-0805-1) Kendall-Hunt.

***Biology 141 Instructor Notes.** Gregg Orloff. (Illus.). 113p. (C). 1995. 6.00 (1-886855-02-1) Tavenner Pub.

***Biology 143 Laboratory Exercises.** Ed. by Gregg Orloff. (Illus.). 100p. (C). 1995. 5.50 (1-886855-00-5) Tavenner Pub.

***Biology 190 Lab Manual.** James Botsford. 176p. (C). 1994. pap. text ed., spiral bd. 11.96 (0-7872-0105-7) Kendall-Hunt.

Biology 2A Syllabus. Gary Ogden. 72p. 1993. spiral bd. 10.95 (0-8403-8385-1) Kendall-Hunt.

Biology 331 Laboratory Manual. USAF (Biology) Staff. 84p. (C). 1993. pap. text ed., spiral bd. 11.35 (0-8403-8833-0) Kendall-Hunt.

BiolRes on Industrial Yeast, 3 vol., Set. Stewart. 1987. 261.00 (0-8493-4900-1, QR151) CRC Pr.

Bioluminescence Analysis. Sven E. Brolin & K. G. Wettermark. 151p. 1992. text ed. 95.00 (0-89573-995-X) VCH Pubs.

Bioluminescence & Chemiluminescence: Current Status. Ed. by Philip E. Stanley & Larry J. Kricka. 570p. 1991. text ed. 275.00 (0-471-92993-X) Wiley.

***Bioluminescence & Chemiluminescence: Fundamentals of Applied Aspects.** Ed. by Campbell et al. Date not set. text ed. write for info. (0-471-95548-5) Wiley.

Bioluminescence & Chemiluminescence; New Perspectives: Proceedings of the IV International Bioluminescence & Chemiluminescence Symposium, Freiburg, September, 1986, Vol. 198. Ed. by J. Scholmerich et al. LC 87-2136. 620p. 1987. text ed. 287.95 (0-471-91470-3) Wiley.

Bioluminescence & Chemiluminescence-Status Report: Proceedings of the 7th International Syposium on Bioluminescence & Chemiluminescence, Banff, March 1993. Ed. by A. Szalay et al. LC 93-29413. 1993. text ed. 160.00 (0-471-94164-6) Wiley.

Bioluminescence & Chemiluminesence Instruments & Applications, 2 vols., Vol. I. Ed. by Knox Van Dyke. 256p. 1985. 174.00 (0-8493-5863-9, QP517) CRC Pr.

Bioluminescence & Chemiluminesence Instruments & Applications, 2 vols., Vol. II. Ed. by Knox Van Dyke. 208p. 1985. 204.00 (0-8493-5864-7, QP517) CRC Pr.

Bioluminescence in Progress. Ed. by F. H. Johnson & Y. Haneda. 1966. 99.50 (0-691-07917-X) Princeton U Pr.

BIOM-pc: A Package of Statistical Programs. F. James Rohlf. 70p. (C). 1981. pap. 60.00 (0-925031-01-1) Exeter NY.

Biomac Sig Directory. American Crystallographic Association Staff. pap. 5.00 (0-317-43255-9) Polycrystal Bk Serv.

Biomachanics Workbook to Accompnay Software. Cheryl W. Maglischo. 137p. (C). 1991. pap. write for info. (0-697-14842-4) Brown & Benchmark.

BioMagnetic Handbook. William H. Philpott & Sharon Taplin. 97p. 1989. 17.95 (0-9636964-0-8) Enviro-Tech.

Biomagnetic Stimulation. Ed. by S. Ueno. (Illus.). 132p. (C). 1994. 65.00 (0-306-44707-X) Plenum.

Biomagnetism. Douglas Baker. (C). 1987. 75.00 (0-317-90360-8, Pub. by Claregate Coll UK) St Mut.

Biomagnetism. Romuald S. Wadas. 224p. 1991. text ed. write for info. (0-13-084666-X) P-H.

Biomagnetism: An Interdisciplinary Approach. Ed. by Samuel J. Williamson et al. LC 83-8087. (NATO ASI Series A, Life Sciences: Vol. 66). 726p. 1983. 125.00 (0-306-41369-8, Plenum Pr) Plenum.

Biomagnetism: Clinical Aspects: Proceedings of the 8th International Conference on Biomagnetism, Munster, 19-24 August, 1991. Ed. by Manfried Hoke et al. LC 92-48227. (International Congress Ser.: No. 988). 1992. write for info. (0-444-89268-0, Excerpta Medica) Elsevier.

Biomanagement of Wastewater & Wastes. Paul N. Cheremisinoff. LC 93-41767. 1993. text ed. 68.00 (0-13-501230-9) P-H Gen Ref & Trav.

Biomarker Guide: Interpreting Molecular Fossils in Petroleum & Ancient Sediments. Kenneth E. Peters & J. Michael Moldowan. 352p. 1992. text ed. 75.00 (0-13-086752-7) P-H.

Biomarkers: Biochemical, Physiological, & Histological Markers of Anthropogenic Stress. Robert J. Huggett et al. 500p. 1992. 85.00 (0-87371-505-5, Q) Lewis Pubs.

Biomarkers: The Ten Keys to Prolonging Vitality. William Evans et al. (Illus.). 304p. 1992. pap. 12.00 (0-671-77898-6, Fireside) S&S Trade.

***Biomarkers & Occupational Health: Progress & Perspectives.** Ed. by Mortimer L. Mendelsohn et al. 335p. (Orig.). (C). 1995. text ed. 54.95 (0-309-05187-8) Natl Acad Pr.

An Asterisk (*) at the beginning of an entry indicates that the title is appearing in BIP for the first time.

Biomarkers & Risk Assessment: Concept & Principles. WHO Staff. 92p. 1993. pap. 16.20 (*92-4-157155-1*) World Health.

BioMarkers of Environmental Contamination. Ed. by John F. McCarthy & Lee R. Shugart. (Illus.). 487p. 1990. 79.95 (*0-87371-284-6*, QH541) Lewis Pubs.

Biomarkers of Human Exposure of Pesticides: Developed from a Symposium Sponsored by the Division of Argochemicals at the 204th National Meeting of the American Chemical Society, Washington, DC, August 23-28, 1992. Ed. by Mahmoud A. Saleh et al. LC 93-36410. (ACS Symposium Ser.: No. 542). 326p. 1993. 79.95 (*0-8412-2738-1*) Am Chemical.

***Biomarkets: Forecasts & Analyses of 40 Opportunities.** 160p. 1995. spiral bd., vinyl bd. 1,700.00 (*1-56217-018-X*) Tech Insights.

Biomass: Applications, Technology & Production, Vol. 5. Cherimisinoff et al. (Energy, Power & Environment Ser.: Vol. 5). 232p. 1980. 125.00 (*0-8247-6933-3*) Dekker.

Biomass: Recent Economic Studies. Ed. by J. C. Sourie & L. Killen. 188p. 1986. 57.75 (*1-85166-028-3*, Pub. by Elsevier Applied Sci UK) Elsevier.

Biomass: Regenerable Energy. Ed. by D. O. Hall & R. P. Overend. (World Energy Options Ser.). 504p. 1987. text ed. 345.00 (*0-471-90919-X*) Wiley.

Biomass Conversion Processes for Energy & Fuels. Ed. by Samir S. Sofer & Oskar R. Zaborsky. LC 81-15721. 436p. 1981. 89.50 (*0-306-40663-2*, Plenum Pr) Plenum.

Biomass Conversion Technology, Principles & Practice: Symposium on Biomass Conversion Technology 1984. Ed. by M. Moo-Young et al. (Illus.). 224p. 1987. 97.00 (*0-08-033174-2*, Pergamon Pr) Elsevier.

Biomass Energies: Resources, Links, Constraints. Vaclav Smil. LC 83-9611. (Modern Perspectives in Energy Ser.). 474p. 1983. 105.00 (*0-306-41312-4*, Plenum Pr) Plenum.

Biomass Energy & Coal in Africa. Ed. by David A. Hall & Mao Yushi. LC 94-2290. (African Energy Policy Research Ser.). (Illus.). 192p. (C). 1994. text ed. 55.00 (*1-85649-235-4*, Pub. by Zed Books UK) Humanities.

Biomass Energy Development. Ed. by Wayne H. Smith. LC 85-31172. 682p. 1986. 115.00 (*0-306-42221-2*, Plenum Pr) Plenum.

Biomass Energy Directory (1993) 88p. (Orig.). (C). 1994. pap. text ed. 35.00 (*0-7881-0616-3*) Diane Pub.

Biomass for Energy & Chemicals in Europe: Industry & Agriculture (C50) D. O. Hall & J. Morton. 58p. (C). 1987. 100.00 (*0-685-33093-1*, Pub. by Interntl Solar Energy Soc UK) St Mut.

Biomass for Energy & Industry: E. C. Conference, 4th. G. Grassi et al. 1987. 189.00 (*1-85166-164-6*) Elsevier.

Biomass for Energy & Industry: Proceedings of the Seventh International E. C. Conference Held in Florence, Italy, 5-9 October 1992. Ed. by D. O. Hall et al. 1312p. (Orig.). 1994. 120.00 (*3-920328-09-4*, Pub. by Ponte Pr GW) Bks Intl VA.

Biomass for Energy & Industry: 5th E. C. Conference: Proceedings of the International Conference, Lisbon, Portugal, 9-13 October, 1989, 2 vols. Ed. by G. Grassi et al. 1888p. 1990. Vol. 1: Policy, Environment, Production & Harvesting. write for info. (*0-318-67334-7*); Vol. 2: Conversion & Utilization of Biomass. write for info. (*0-318-67335-5*) Elsevier.

Biomass for Energy & Industry: 5th E. C. Conference: Proceedings of the International Conference, Lisbon, Portugal, 9-13 October, 1989, 2 vols., Set. Ed. by G. Grassi et al. 1888p. 1990. 351.00 (*1-85166-494-7*) Elsevier.

Biomass for Energy in the Developing Countries: Current Role, Potential, Problems, Prospects. D. Hall & G. Barnard. LC 82-322. 1982. 110.00 (*0-08-029313-1*, Pub. by Pergamon Repr UK) Franklin.

Biomass Forestry in Europe: A Strategy for the Future. Ed. by F. C. Hummel et al. 600p. 1988. 128.00 (*1-85166-255-3*) Elsevier.

Biomass Handbook. Ed. by Osamu Kitani & Carl W. Hall. 1000p. 1989. text ed. 419.00 (*2-88124-269-3*) Gordon & Breach.

Biomass-Hydrocarbons-Hydrogen see Alternative Energy Sources V: Energy Research

Biomass Industry Profile Directory. (Illus.). 77p. (Orig.). (C). 1993. pap. text ed. 40.00 (*1-56806-798-4*) Diane Pub.

Biomass Production by Fast-Growing Trees. Ed. by J. S. Pereira & J. J. Landsberg. (C). 1989. lib. bdg. 115.50 (*0-7923-0208-7*) Kluwer Ac.

Biomass Pyrolysis Liquids Upgrading & Utilization. Ed. by A. V. Bridgwater & G. Grassi. 374p. 1991. 144.00 (*1-85166-565-X*) Elsevier.

***Biomass Regenerable Energy.** fac. ed. Ed. by David O. Hall & R. P. Overend. LC 86-15685. (World Energy Options Ser.). (Illus.). 514p. 1994. pap. 146.50 (*0-7837-7661-6*, 2047414) Bks Demand.

Biomass Stoves: Engineering, Design, Development, & Dissemination. Sam Baldwin. Ed. by Margaret Crouch. 287p. 1987. 35.75 (*0-86619-274-3*) Vols Tech Asst.

Biomaterial-Tissue Interfaces: Proceedings of the Ninth European Conference on Biomaterials, Chester, U. K., September 9-11, 1991. Ed. by P. J. Doherty et al. LC 92-49135. (Advances in Biomaterials Ser.: Vol. 10). 1992. write for info. (*0-444-89065-3*) Elsevier.

Biomaterials. D. Byrom. 365p. 1992. 100.00 (*1-56159-037-1*, Stockton Pr) Groves Dictionaries.

Biomaterials: An Interfacial Approach. Larry L. Hench & E. C. Ethridge. (Biophysics & Bioengineering Ser.). 335p. 1982. text ed. 92.00 (*0-12-340280-8*) Acad Pr.

Biomaterials: An Introduction. 2nd ed. J. B. Park & R. S. Lakes. (Illus.). 395p. (C). 1992. 55.00 (*0-306-43992-1*, Plenum Pr) Plenum.

Biomaterials: Hard Tissue Repair & Replacement. Ed. by D. Muster et al. LC 92-22652. 1992. write for info. (*0-444-88350-9*, North Holland) Elsevier.

Biomaterials: Interfacial Phenomena & Applications. Ed. by Stuart L. Cooper & Nicholas A. Peppas. LC 82-6763. (ACS Advances in Chemistry Ser.: No. 199). 539p. 1982. lib. bdg. 76.95 (*0-8412-0631-7*) Am Chemical.

Biomaterials & Biomechanics, 1983: Proceedings of the 4th European Conference on Biomaterials, Leuven, Belgium, Aug. 31-Sept. 2, 1983. Ed. by P. G. Ducheyne et al. (Advances in Biomaterials Ser.: No. 5). 500p. 1984. 151.50 (*0-444-42352-4*) Elsevier.

Biomaterials & Clinical Applications: Proceedings of the Sixth European Conference on Biomaterials, Bologna, Italy, Sept. 14-17, 1986. Ed. by A. Pizzoferrato et al. (Advances in Biomaterials Ser.: Vol. 7). 808p. 1987. 187.25 (*0-444-42883-6*) Elsevier.

Biomaterials Degradation: Fundamental Aspects & Related Clinical Phenomena. Ed. by M. A. Barbosa. (European Materials Research Society Monographs: No. 1). 436p. 1991. 131.50 (*0-444-88867-5*, North Holland) Elsevier.

Biomaterials for Drug & Cell Delivery, Vol. 331: Materials Research Society Symposium Proceedings. Ed. by A. G. Mikos et al. 1994. text ed. 78.00 (*1-55899-230-8*) Materials Res.

Biomaterials for the Nineteen Nineties: Polyurethanes, Silicones, & Ion Beam Modification Techniques (Seminar Notes) Oct. 29-31, 1990, Basel, Switzerland. Michael Szycher et al. 620p. 1990. ring bd. 125.00 (*0-87762-760-6*) Technomic.

Biomaterials in Otology. Ed. by J. J. Grote. 324p. 1983. lib. bdg. 131.50 (*0-89838-610-1*) Kluwer Ac.

Biomaterials' Mechanical Properties. Ed. by Helen E. Kambic & A. Toshimitsu Yokobori, Jr. LC 93-48490. (STP Ser.: Vol. 1173). (Illus.). 310p. 1994. 89.00 (*0-8031-1894-5*, 04-011730-54) ASTM.

Biomaterials, Medical Devices & Tissue Engineering: An Integrated Approach. F. H. Silver. (Illus.). 304p. 1993. text ed. 89.95 (*0-412-41260-8*) Chapman & Hall.

***Biomaterials, Organic & Intelligent Materials: Proceedings of the Symposia of the 3rd IUMRS International Conference on Advanced Materials, Sunshine City, Ikebukuro, Tokyo, Japan, August 31-September 4, 1993.** International Union of Materials Research Societies Staff & IUMRS International Conference of Advanced Materials Staff. Ed. by Hideki Aoki. (Transactions of the Materials Research Society of Japan: Vol. 15 A). 1994. write for info. (*0-444-81992-4*) Elsevier.

Biomaterials Science & Engineering. J. B. Park. LC 84-16016. 474p. 1984. 55.00 (*0-306-41689-1*, Plenum Pr) Plenum.

Biomaterials, 1980. World Biomaterials Congress (1st: 1980: Baden, Austria) Staff. Ed. by George D. Winter et al. LC 81-15923. (Advances in Biomaterials Ser.: Vol. 3). (Illus.). 855p. reprint ed. pap. 180.00 (*0-8357-7247-0*, 2030450) Bks Demand.

Biomathematical Problems in Optimization of Cancer Radiotherapy. Leonid G. Hanin et al. 160p. 1993. 79.95 (*0-8493-8648-9*, RC271) CRC Pr.

Biomathematics & Cell Kinetics. Ed. by M. Rotenberg. (Developments in Cell Biology Ser.: Vol. 8). 424p. 1981. 97.50 (*0-444-80371-8*) Elsevier.

Biomathematics & Its Applications in Plant Cultivation. I. Ban. 204p. 1988. 95.00 (*0-444-98970-6*) Elsevier.

Biomathematics & Related Computational Problems. Ed. by Luigi M. Ricciardi. (C). 1988. lib. bdg. 212.00 (*90-277-2726-0*) Kluwer Ac.

Biomathematics in Nineteen Eighty. Ed. by L. Ricciardi & A. Scott. (Mathematics Studies: Vol. 58). 298p. 1982. 77.00 (*0-444-86355-9*, North Holland) Elsevier.

Biomathematics of Malaria. Norman T. Bailey. (Charles Griffin Series- Mathematics in Medicine). (Illus.). 224p. 1987. 37.50 (*0-19-520565-0*) OUP.

Biomechanical Analysis of the Musculoskeletal Structure for Medicine & Sports. Ali Seireg & R. Arvikar. 700p. 1989. 105.00 (*0-89116-423-5*) Hemisp Pub.

Biomechanical & Human Factors Symposium: Proceedings of the Biomechanical & Human Factors Conference, 2nd, Washington, D. C., 1967. Biomechanical & Human Factors Conference Staff. Ed. by Howard Gage. LC 67-21480. (Illus.). 184p. reprint ed. pap. 52.50 (*0-8357-7248-9*, 2016814) Bks Demand.

Biomechanical & Morphological Analysis of Human Hand Joints. J. Koebke. (Advances in Anatomy, Embryology & Cell Biology Ser.: Vol. 80). (Illus.). 105p. 1983. pap. 38.00 (*0-387-12438-1*) Spr-Verlag.

***Biomechanical Basis of Human Movement.** Joe Hamill & Kathleen Knutzen. LC 94-22325. 1995. write for info. (*0-683-03863-X*) Williams & Wilkins.

Biomechanical Basis of Orthotic Management. Ed. by P. Bowker et al. LC 93-7836. (Illus.). 290p. 1993. 99.00 (*0-7506-1380-7*) Buttrwrth-Heinemann.

Biomechanical Cardiac Assist: Cardiomyoplasty & Muscle-Powered Devices. Ed. by Ray Chu-Jeng Chiu. (Illus.). 275p. 1986. 42.50 (*0-87993-289-9*) Futura Pub.

Biomechanical Measurement in Orthopaedic Practice. Ed. by Whittle & Harris. 1985. 59.95 (*0-19-857610-2*) OUP.

Biomechanical Mechanisms & Regulations of Intercellular Communication. Ed. by Harry A. Milman & Eugene Elmore. LC 87-61833. (Advances in Modern Environmental Toxicology Ser.). (Illus.). 325p. 1987. 65.00 (*0-911131-15-9*) Princeton Sci Pubs.

Biomechanical Transport Processes. Ed. by F. Mesera et al. LC 90-4246. (NATO ASI Series A, Life Sciences: Vol. 193). (Illus.). 410p. 1990. 110.00 (*0-306-43676-0*, Plenum Pr) Plenum.

Biomechanics. 98p. 1984. 9.00 (*0-685-72906-0*, P-40) Am Phys Therapy Assn.

Biomechanics. Yuan-Cheng Fung. (Illus.). 584p. 1990. 69.50 (*0-387-97124-6*) Spr-Verlag.

Biomechanics. Ed. by Jaroslav Valenta. LC 92-10085. (Clinical Aspects of Biomedicine Ser.: Vol. 2). 1993. write for info. (*0-444-98764-9*) Elsevier.

Biomechanics: A Qualitative Approach for Studying Human Movement. 3rd ed. Ellen Kreighbaum & Katharine Barthels. 901p. (C). 1990. write for info. (*0-02-366310-3*) Macmillan.

Biomechanics: An Approach to Vertebrate Biology. Carl Gans. LC 80-18705. 272p. (C). 1980. pap. text ed. 13.95x (*0-472-08016-4*) U of Mich Pr.

Biomechanics: Basic & Applied Research. Ed. by C. Bermann et al. (Developments in Biomechanics Ser.). (C). 1987. lib. bdg. 276.00 (*0-89838-961-5*) Kluwer Ac.

Biomechanics: Current Interdisciplinary Research. Ed. by S. M. Perren & E. Schneider. (Developments in Biomechanics Ser.). 1985. lib. bdg. 239.00 (*0-89838-755-8*) Kluwer Ac.

Biomechanics: Mechanical Properties of Living Tissues. Yuan-Cheng Fung. (Illus.). 400p. 1990. 49.50 (*0-387-90472-7*) Spr-Verlag.

Biomechanics: Mechanical Properties of Living Tissues. 2nd ed. Yuan-Cheng Fung. LC 92-33749. 1993. 49.50 (*0-387-97947-6*) Spr-Verlag.

Biomechanics: Principles & Applications. R. Huiskes. 1982. lib. bdg. 140.00 (*90-247-3047-3*) Kluwer Ac.

Biomechanics: Problem Solving for Functional Activity. Roberts. (Illus.). 194p. 1991. 25.95 (*0-8016-4047-4*) Mosby Yr Bk.

Biomechanics - Materials: A Practical Approach. Ed. by Julian F. Vincent. LC 92-9681. (Practical Approach Ser.). (Illus.). 240p. (C). 1992. 88.00 (*0-19-963223-5*, IRL Pr) OUP.

Biomechanics - Materials: A Practical Approach. Ed. by Julian F. Vincent. LC 92-9681. (Practical Approach Ser.: No. 105). (Illus.). 272p. (C). 1992. pap. 48.00 (*0-19-963222-7*, IRL Pr) OUP.

Biomechanics & Cells. Ed. by Fiona Lyall & A. J. El Haj. LC 93-42046. (Society for Experimental Biology Seminar Ser.: No. 54). (Illus.). 400p. (C). 1994. 74.95 (*0-521-45454-9*) Cambridge U Pr.

Biomechanics & Exercise Physiology. Arthur T. Johnson. 1991. text ed. 114.95 (*0-471-85398-4*) Wiley.

Biomechanics & Medical Aspects of Lower Limb Injuries. 1986. 35.00 (*0-89883-749-9*, P186) Soc Auto Engineers.

Biomechanics & Medicine in Swimming. Ed. by T. Reilly et al. 400p. 1991. 89.95 (*0-419-15600-3*, A6115, E & FN Spon) Routledge Chapman & Hall.

Biomechanics & Motor Control of Human Movement. 2nd ed. David A. Winter. 296p. 1990. text ed. 69.95 (*0-471-50908-6*) Wiley.

Biomechanics & Osteosynthesis of Condylar Neck Fractures of the Mandible. Christian Krenkel. LC 93-30260. 1994. text ed. 98.00 (*0-86715-264-8*) Quint Pub Co.

Biomechanics & Related Bio-Engineering Topics: Proceedings of Symposium, Glasgow, September 1964. R. Kenedi. LC 65-18422. 1965. 209.00 (*0-08-010934-9*, Pub. by Pergamon Repr UK) Franklin.

Biomechanics in Clinical Dentistry. Caputo & Standlee. (Illus.). 224p. 1987. text ed. 78.00 (*0-86715-178-1*) Quint Pub Co.

Biomechanics in Evolution. Ed. by J. M. Rayner & R. J. Wootton. (Society for Experimental Biology Seminar Ser.: Vol. 36). 288p. 1992. 74.95 (*0-521-34421-2*) Cambridge U Pr.

Biomechanics in Orthodontics. Marcotte. 200p. 1990. 52.00 (*1-55664-168-0*) Mosby Yr Bk.

Biomechanics in Orthopedia Trauma: One Fracture & Fixation. Allen F. Tencer & Kenneth D. Johnsion. LC 94-586. 320p. 1994. 79.95 (*0-397-51462-X*) Lippincott.

Biomechanics in Orthopedics. Ed. by S. Niwa et al. LC 92-49957. 1993. write for info. (*4-431-70108-7*); write for info. (*3-540-70108-7*); 165.00 (*0-387-70108-7*) Spr-Verlag.

Biomechanics IX, 2 vols., Set. Ed. by David A. Winter et al. LC 82-84703. (International Series on Biomechanics). 1985. text ed. 120.00x (*0-931250-52-8*, BWIN0052) Human Kinetics.

Biomechanics IX-A. Ed. by David A. Winter et al. LC 82-84703. (International Series on Biomechanics). 608p. 1985. text ed. 67.00x (*0-931250-53-6*, BWIN0053) Human Kinetics.

Biomechanics IX-B. Ed. by David A. Winter et al. LC 82-84703. (International Series on Biomechanics). 576p. 1985. text ed. 67.00x (*0-931250-54-4*, BWIN0054) Human Kinetics.

Biomechanics Manual for Coaches & Physical Educators. Alan J. Stockholm. LC 85-1269. 150p. 1985. pap. 12.00 (*0-935496-04-1*) AC Pubns.

Biomechanics of Active Movement & Division of Cells: Proceedings of the NATO ASI on Biomechanics of Active Movement & Division of Cells, Held in Istanbul, Turkey, Sept. 19-29, 1993. Ed. by Nuri Akkas. LC 94-15684. (NATO ASI, Series H, Cell Biology: Voll 84). 1994. 239.00 (*0-387-57951-6*) Spr-Verlag.

Biomechanics of Cell Division. Ed. by Nuri Akkas. LC 87-12349. (NATO ASI Series A, Life Sciences: Vol. 132). 382p. 1987. 105.00 (*0-306-42592-0*, Plenum Pr) Plenum.

Biomechanics of Diarthrodial Joints, 2 vols., Vol. I. Ed. by V. C. Mow et al. (Illus.). xix, 450p. 1990. 69.50 (*0-387-97378-8*) Spr-Verlag.

Biomechanics of Diarthrodial Joints, 2 vols., Vol. II. Ed. by V. C. Mow et al. (Illus.). xx, 464p. 1990. 69.50 (*0-387-97379-6*) Spr-Verlag.

Biomechanics of Distance Running. Ed. by Peter R. Cavanagh. LC 89-29302. (Illus.). 376p. 1990. text ed. 44.00x (*0-87322-268-7*, BCAV0268) Human Kinetics.

Biomechanics of Engineering. A. Morecki. (CISM International Centre for Mechanical Sciences Ser.: No. 291). (Illus.). vi, 186p. 1987. pap. 35.00 (*0-387-81974-6*) Spr-Verlag.

Biomechanics of Feeding in Vertebrates. Ed. by R. Gilles et al. (Advances in Comparative & Environmental Physiology Ser.: Vol. 18). (Illus.). 376p. 1994. 185.00 (*0-387-54847-5*) Spr-Verlag.

***Biomechanics of Human Gait: An Electronic Bibliography.** Ed. by Christopher L. Vaughan et al. (Illus.). 24p. 1992. 5.25 hd 49.00x (*0-87322-374-8*, BVAU0374) Human Kinetics.

***Biomechanics of Human Gait: An Electronic Bibliography.** 3rd ed. Ed. by Christopher L. Vaughan et al. (Illus.). 24p. 1992. 3.5 hd 49.00x (*0-87322-373-X*, BVAU0373) Human Kinetics.

Biomechanics of Human Movement. 2nd ed. Marlene J. Adrian & John M. Cooper. 592p. (C). 1995. boxed write for info. (*0-697-16242-7*) Brown & Benchmark.

***Biomechanics of Impact Injury & Injury Tolerances of the Abdomen, Lumbar Spine & Pelvic Complex.** Ed. by Stanley H. Backaitis. 60p. Date not set. pap. 119.00 (*1-56091-592-7*, PT47) Soc Auto Engineers.

Biomechanics of Impact Injury & Injury Tolerances of the Head-Neck Complex. Ed. by Stan Backaitis. 69p. 1993. 149.00 (*1-56091-363-0*, PT-43) Soc Auto Engineers.

Biomechanics of Impact Injury & Injury Tolerances of the Thorax-Shoulder Complex. Ed. by Stan Backaitis. (Progress in Technology Ser.). 1306p. 1994. 119.00 (*1-56091-501-3*, PT-45) Soc Auto Engineers.

Biomechanics of Medical Devices. D. Ghista. LC 80-15480. (Biomedical Engineering & Instrumentation Ser.: Vol. 7). 704p. 1981. 215.00 (*0-8247-6848-5*) Dekker.

Biomechanics of Motion. Ed. by A. Morecki. (CISM Courses & Lectures Ser.: Vol. 263). (Illus.). 217p. 1981. pap. 43.00 (*0-387-81611-9*) Spr-Verlag.

Biomechanics of Normal & Pathological Human Articulating Joints. Ed. by Necip Berme et al. (NATO Advanced Science Institutes Series C: Mathematical & Physical Sciences). 1985. lib. bdg. 121.50 (*90-247-3164-X*) Kluwer Ac.

Biomechanics of Running Shoes. Ed. by Benno M. Nigg. LC 85-2460. 192p. 1986. text ed. 40.00x (*0-87322-002-1*, BNIG0002) Human Kinetics.

Biomechanics of Spine Stabilization: Principles & Clinical Practice. Edward C. Benzel. 278p. 1995. text ed. 85.00 (*0-07-005091-0*) Hlth Prof Div.

Biomechanics of Sport. Ed. by Christopher L. Vaughan. 368p. 1988. 138.00 (*0-8493-6820-0*, RC1235) CRC Pr.

Biomechanics of Sport: A Research Approach. Doris I. Miller & Richard C. Nelson. LC 73-3173. (Health Education, Physical Education, & Recreation Ser.). 273p. reprint ed. pap. 77.90 (*0-8357-7249-7*, 2056571) Bks Demand.

Biomechanics of Sports Techniques. 4th ed. James G. Hay. LC 92-27506. 592p. (C). 1993. text ed. 32.00 (*0-13-084534-5*) P-H.

Biomechanics of the Foot & Ankle. Ed. by Robert Donatelli. LC 89-25675. (Contemporary Perspectives in Rehabilitation Ser.). (Illus.). 284p. (C). 1990. text ed. 38.00 (*0-8036-2696-7*) Davis Co.

***Biomechanics of the Foot & Ankle.** 2nd ed. Robert Donatelli. (Contemporary Perspectives in Rehabilitation Ser.). (Illus.). 420p. (C). 1995. 43.00 (*0-8036-0031-3*) Davis Co.

Biomechanics of the Hand. Ed. by Y. S. Chao et al. 204p. (C). 1989. text ed. 70.00 (*9971-5-0103-1*); pap. text ed. 30.00 (*9971-5-0104-X*) World Scientific Pub.

Biomechanics of the Hip. P. G. Maquet. (Illus.). 320p. 1984. 199.00 (*0-387-13257-0*) Spr-Verlag.

Biomechanics of the Knee. 2nd ed. P. G. Maquet. (Illus.). 330p. 1983. 184.00 (*0-387-12489-6*) Spr-Verlag.

Biomechanics of the Locomotor Apparatus. F. Pauwels. (Illus.). 520p. 1980. 248.00 (*0-387-09131-9*) Spr-Verlag.

Biomechanics of the Musculo-Skeletal System. B. M. Nigg & W. Herzog. LC 94-1827. 1994. text ed. 59.95 (*0-471-94444-0*) Wiley.

Biomechanics of the Spine: Clinical & Surgical Perspective. Ed. by Vijay K. Goel & James N. Weinstein. 288p. 1989. 144.00 (*0-8493-6649-6*, RD768) CRC Pr.

Biomechanics of the Wrist Joint. Ed. by K. N. An et al. (Illus.). 192p. 1991. 59.50 (*0-387-97674-4*) Spr-Verlag.

***Biomechanics Research at the Olympic Games: 1984-1994.** 544p. 1994. pap. text ed. write for info. (*0-87322-845-6*, JIJSBBRO) Human Kinetics.

Biomechanics: Structures & Systems: A Practical Approach. A. A. Biewener. (Practical Approach Ser.: No.). (Illus.). 312p. 1992. pap. 52.00 (*0-19-963267-7*) OUP.

Biomechanics: Structures & Systems: A Practical Approach. A. A. Biewener. (Practical Approach Ser.: No. 94). (Illus.). 312p. 1992. 96.00 (*0-19-963268-5*) OUP.

Biomechanics Symposium, 1977: Presented at the 1977 Joint Applied Mechanics, Fluids Engineering, & Bioengineering Conference, Yale University, New Haven, CT, June 15-17, 1977, (Sponsored by the Applied Mechanics Division, ASME, the Bioengineering Division, ASME, the Fluids Engineering Division, ASME. Biomechanics Symposium (1977, Yale University). Ed. by Richard Skalak & Albert B. Schultz. LC 77-151677. (AMD Ser.: Vol. 23). 244p. reprint ed. pap. 69.60 (*0-8357-7250-0*, 2056162) Bks Demand.

Biomechanics Symposium, 1979: Presented at the Joint ASME-CSME Applied Mechanics, Fluids Engineering, & Bioengineering Conference, Niagara. American Society of Mechanical Engineers Staff. Ed. by William C. Van Buskirk. LC 79-113524. (AMD Ser.: Vol. 32). (Illus.). 243p. reprint ed. pap. 69.30 (*0-8357-2858-7*, 2039093) Bks Demand.

Biomechanics Symposium, 1983, Vol. 1. 7th ed. Ed. by S. Wod & R. E. Mates. (AMD Ser.: Vol. 56). 246p. 1983. pap. text ed. 40.00 (*0-317-02553-8*, G00228) ASME.

Biomechanics VIII, 2 Vols. Ed. by Hideji Matsui & Kando Kobayashi. (International Series on Biomechanics). 1983. text ed. 120.00x (*0-931250-42-0*, BMAT0042) Human Kinetics.

An Asterisk (*) at the beginning of an entry indicates that the title is appearing in BIP for the first time.

B

***Biomembranes: Structural & Functional Aspects.** Ed. by Meir Shinitzky. 383p. 1994. 135.00 (*1-56081-772-0*) VCH Pubs.

Biomembranes: Structure, Biogenesis & Transport Proceedings of Biomembrane Symposium. Ed. by C. Rajamanickam & Lester Packer. (Current Trends in Life Sciences Ser.: Vol. XIII). (Illus.). 358p. 1987. 95.00 (*1-55528-142-7*, Messers Today & Tomorrow) Scholarly Pubns.

***Biomembranes Vol. 3: Signal Transduction Across Membranes.** Ed. by Meir Shinitzky. 325p. 1995. 135.00 (*3-527-30023-6*) VCH Pubs.

Biomembranes see Methods in Enzymology

Biomembranes & Cell Function, Vol. 414. Ed. by Fred A. Kummerow et al. 40.00 (*0-89766-222-9*); pap. 40.00 (*0-89766-223-7*) NY Acad Sci.

Biomembranes Vol. 11: Pathological Membranes. Ed. by Alois Nowotny. LC 82-22343. 494p. 1983. 110.00 (*0-306-41065-6*, Plenum Pr) Plenum.

Biomembranes, Vol. 12: Membrane Fluidity. Ed. by Morris Kates & Lionel A. Manson. LC 84-4877. 714p. 1984. 135.00 (*0-306-41548-8*, Plenum Pr) Plenum.

Biometeorological Aspects of Plants, Trees & Animals in Human Life see Progress in Human Biometeorology, Vol. 1: The Effect of Weather & Climate on Man & His Living Environment, Period 1963 to 1970-75

Biometeorology: Proceedings of the Second International Bioclimatological Congress, Society of Medicine, September, 1960. S. Tromp. LC 61-11154. 1962. 291.00 (*0-08-009683-2*, Pub. by Pergamon Repr UK) Franklin.

Biometric Industry Directory, 1990. 5th ed. Benjamin L. Miller. (Illus.). 90p. 1990. pap. 65.00 (*1-878413-00-7*) Warfel & Miller.

Biometrical Techniques in Breeding & Genetics. R. K. Singh & B. D. Chaudhury. 350p. 1977. 10.00 (*0-88065-193-8*, Messers Today & Tomorrow) Scholarly Pubns.

Biometrika Tables for Statisticians, Vol. 1. 3rd ed. Ed. by E. S. Pearson & H. O. Hartley. 270p. 1976. lib. bdg. 75.00 (*0-904653-10-2*) Lubrecht & Cramer.

Biometrika Tables for Statisticians: Reprint with Corrections, Vol. 2. Ed. by E. S. Pearson & H. O. Hartley. 385p. 1976. reprint ed. lib. bdg. 75.00 (*0-904653-11-0*) Lubrecht & Cramer.

***Biometrisches Woerterbuch.** 3rd ed. Deutsch Staff. 965p. (CZE, ENG, FRE, GER, HUN, ITA, POL & RUS.). 1988. write for info. (*0-614-00671-6*, 3817110529) Fr & Eur.

Biometry. 3rd ed. Sokal. LC 94-11120. (C). 1995. text ed. write for info. (*0-7167-2411-1*) W H Freeman.

Biometry - Clinical Trials & Related Topics: Proceedings of the ISI Satellite Meeting Held in Osaka, Japan, 21st Sept., 1987. Ed. by T. Okuno. (International Congress Ser.: No. 787). 132p. 1988. 72.00 (*0-444-81009-9*, Excerpta Medica) Elsevier.

Biomimetic & Bioorganic Chemistry II. Ed. by Fritz Vogtle & Eicke R. Weber. (Topics in Current Chemistry Ser.: Vol. 132). (Illus.). 190p. 1986. 77.00 (*0-387-16023-X*) Spr-Verlag.

Biomimetic & Bioorganic Chemistry III. Ed. by F. Vogtle & E. Weber. (Topics in Current Chemistry Ser.: Vol. 136). (Illus.). 185p. 1986. 76.00 (*0-387-16724-2*) Spr-Verlag.

Biomimetic Chemistry. Ed. by David Dolphin et al. LC 80-22864. (ACS Advances in Chemistry Ser.: No. 191). 437p. 1980. 65.95 (*0-8412-0514-0*) Am Chemical.

Biomimetic Chemistry. Ed. by Z. I. Yoshida & N. Ise. (Studies in Organic Chemistry: Vol. 13). 304p. 1983. 100.00 (*0-444-99660-5*) Elsevier.

Biomimetic Polymers. Ed. by G. G. Gebelein. (Illus.). 290p. 1990. 85.00 (*0-306-43708-2*, Plenum Pr) Plenum.

***Biomimetics: Design & Processing of Materials.** I. Aksay & M. Sarikaya. (Polymers & Complex Materials Ser.). 352p. (C). 1995. text ed. 65.00 (*1-56396-196-2*, AIP Pr) Am Inst Physics.

Biomineralization: Cell Biology & Mineral Deposition. Kenneth Simkiss & Karl M. Wilbur. 337p. 1989. text ed. 97.00 (*0-12-643830-7*) Acad Pr.

Biomineralization: Chemical & Biochemical Perspectives. Ed. by S. Mann et al. LC 89-14840. 541p. 1989. lib. bdg. 220.00 (*0-89573-672-1*) VCH Pubs.

Biomineralization & Biological Metal Accumulation. P. Westbroek & E. W. De Jong. 1983. lib. bdg. 69.50 (*0-686-39596-4*) Kluwer Ac.

Biomineralization in Lower Plants & Animals. Ed. by Barry S. Leadbeater & Robvert Riding. (Illus.). 400p. 1986. 80.00 (*0-19-857702-8*) OUP.

Biominerals. Ed. by Driessens. 1990. 240.00 (*0-8493-5280-0*, QP88) CRC Pr.

Biomirror. Todd Siler. (Illus.). 60p. (Orig.). 1983. pap. 6.00 (*0-914661-01-9*) Feldman Fine Arts.

Biomolecular Data: A Resource in Transition. Ed. by Rita Colwell. (Illus.). 382p. 1989. 64.00 (*0-19-854247-X*) OUP.

Biomolecular Engineering in the European Community. Ed. by E. Magnien. 1986. lib. bdg. 294.50 (*90-247-3400-2*) Kluwer Ac.

Biomolecular Materials. Ed. by S. T. Case et al. (Materials Research Society Symposium Proceedings Ser.: Vol. 292). 1993. text ed. 69.00 (*1-55899-187-5*) Materials Res.

Biomolecular Materials by Design, Vol. 330: Materials Research Society Symposium Proceedings. Ed. by H. Bayley et al. 1994. text ed. 78.00 (*1-55899-229-4*) Materials Res.

***Biomolecular NMR Spectroscopy.** Jeremy N. Evans. 416p. (C). 1995. text ed. 85.00 (*0-19-854767-6*); pap. text ed. 42.00 (*0-19-854766-8*) OUP.

Biomolecular Spectroscopy, Vol. 20. R. J. Clark & R. E. Hester. LC 92-27822. (Advances in Spectroscopy Ser.: Vol. 20). 400p. 1993. text ed. 345.00 (*0-471-93806-8*) Wiley.

Biomolecular Spectroscopy: 1989 Los Angeles Symposium - OE-LASE '89 (January 1989) Ed. by R. R. Birge & H. H. Mantsch. (Proceedings Ser.: Vol. 1057). 186p. 1989. 42.00 (*0-8194-0092-0*) SPIE.

Biomolecular Spectroscopy Pt. B, Vol. 2. Ed. by Robin J. Clark & Ronald E. Hester. (Advances in Spectroscopy Ser.: Vol. 21). 400p. 1993. text ed. 247.00 (*0-471-93832-7*) Wiley.

Biomolecular Spectroscopy Two, Vol. 1432. R. R. Birge & L. A. Nafie. 1991. 42.00 (*0-8194-0522-1*) SPIE.

Biomolecular Stereodynamics, Vol. IV. Ed. by R. H. Sarma & M. H. Sarma. (Illus.). 324p. 1986. lib. bdg. 100.00 (*0-940030-18-7*) Adenine Pr.

Biomolecular Stereodynamics III. Ed. by R. H. Sarma & M. H. Sarma. (Illus.). 380p. (C). 1986. lib. bdg. 100.00 (*0-940030-14-4*) Adenine Pr.

Biomolecular Structure, Conformation, Function & Evolution, 2 vols. R. Srinivasan. Incl. Vol. 1. Diffraction & Related Studies. 1981. (*0-318-55142-X*); Vol. 2. Physico-Chemical & Theoretical Studies. 1981. (*0-318-55143-8*); 1981. Set. 535.00 (*0-08-023187-X*, Pub. by Pergamon Repr UK) Franklin.

Biomolecules: Electronic Aspects. Ed. by C. Nagata et al. (Studies in Physical & Theoretical Chemistry: No. 36). 300p. 1985. 110.25 (*0-444-99551-X*) Elsevier.

Biomolecules in Organic Solvents. Gomez. 1992. 179.00 (*0-8493-4823-4*, TP248) CRC Pr.

Biomonitoring Air Pollutants with Plants. W. J. Manning & W. A. Feder. (Pollution Monitoring Ser.: No. 2). (Illus.). 142p. 1980. 41.50 (*0-85334-916-9*, Pub. by Elsevier Applied Sci UK) Elsevier.

Biomonitoring & Toxicity Reduction Evaluations 1994. Jones. 1995. write for info. (*0-87371-338-9*) Lewis Pubs.

Biomonitoring for Control of Toxicity in Effluent Discharges to the Marine Environment. (Illus.). 58p. (Orig.). (C). 1992. pap. text ed. 40.00 (*1-56806-121-8*) Diane Pub.

Biomonitoring of Coastal Waters & Estuaries. Ed. by Kees J. M. Kramer. LC 94-10065. 1994. write for info. (*0-8493-4895-1*) CRC Pr.

Biomonitoring of Trace Aquatic Contaminants. David J. Phillips & Philip S. Rainbow. LC 92-18802. 1992. write for info. (*1-85166-884-5*) Elsevier.

Biomusicology: Neurophysiological, Neuropsychological, & Evolutionary Perspectives on the Origins & Purposes of Music. Nils L. Wallin. LC 91-11808. (Illus.). 1992. lib. bdg. 38.00 (*0-945193-20-3*) Pendragon NY.

Bion & Group Psychotherapy. Ed. by Malcolm Pines. (International Library of Group Psychotherapy & Group Process). 336p. 1985. 49.95 (*0-7100-9949-5*, 99495, RKP) Routledge.

Bion & Group Psychotherapy. Ed. by Malcolm Pines. (International Library of Group Psychotherapy & Group Process). 416p. 1991. pap. 19.95 (*0-415-07181-X*, A6940, Tavistock) Routledge.

Biona Report Five - Bat Flight. Ed. by W. Nachtigall. 1987. pap. text ed. 40.00 (*0-89574-239-X*) VCH Pubs.

Bioneers. Ausubel. Date not set. pap. 16.00 (*0-06-251018-5*, PL) HarpC.

Bionic Bunny Show. Marc Brown. (Reading Rainbow Ser.). (Illus.). 32p. (J). (ps-3). 1984. 14.95 (*0-316-11120-1*, Joy St Bks) Little.

Bionic Bunny Show. Marc Brown. (Reading Rainbow Ser.). (Illus.). 32p. (J). (ps-3). 1985. mass mkt. 5.95 (*0-316-10992-4*, Joy St Bks) Little.

Bionomics: Economy As Ecosystem. Michael Rothschild. 448p. 1992. pap. 17.95 (*0-8050-1979-0*, Owl) H Holt & Co.

Bioorganic Chemistry. (Advanced Texts in Chemistry Ser.). (Illus.). xv, 651p. 1988. 65.00 (*0-387-96795-8*) Spr-Verlag.

Bioorganic Chemistry, 2 vols. Ed. by E. E. Van Tamelen. Incl. Vol. 1. Enzyme Action. 1977. 73.50 (*0-12-714301-7*); Vol. 2. 1978. 77.00 (*0-12-714302-5*); write for info. (*0-318-50237-2*) Acad Pr.

Bioorganic Chemistry: A Chemical Approach to Enzyme Action. H. Dugas & C. Penney. (Advanced Texts in Chemistry Ser.). (Illus.). 508p. 1981. 42.00 (*0-387-90491-3*) Spr-Verlag.

***Bioorganic Chemistry: A Chemical Approach to Enzyme Action.** 3rd ed. Hermann Dugas. LC 95-8361. 1995. 49.95 (*0-387-94494-X*) Spr-Verlag.

Bioorganic Chemistry Frontiers, Vol. 1. Ed. by H. Dugas. (Illus.). 224p. 1990. 83.00 (*0-387-51931-9*) Spr-Verlag.

Bioorganic Chemistry Frontiers, Vol. 2. Ed. by H. Dugas. (Illus.). 240p. 1991. 96.00 (*0-387-53365-6*) Spr-Verlag.

Bioorganic Chemistry Frontiers, Vol. 3. Ed. by H. Dugas & F. P. Schmidtchen. (Illus.). 280p. 1993. 122.00 (*0-387-56518-3*) Spr-Verlag.

Bioorganic Chemistry in Healthcare & Technology. Ed. by U. K. Pandit & F. C. Alderweireldt. (NATO ASI Series A, Life Sciences: Vol. 207). (Illus.). 326p. 1991. 95.00 (*0-306-44007-5*, Plenum Pr) Plenum.

Bioorganic Chemistry of Enzymatic Catalysis. Myron L. Bender et al. LC 83-19857. 312p. 1984. text ed. 89.95 (*0-471-05991-9*, Wiley-Interscience) Wiley.

Bioorganic Chemistry of Enzymatic Catalysis: An Homage to Myron L. Bender. Valerian D'Sousa. 208p. 1991. 156.00 (*0-8493-6823-5*, QP601) CRC Pr.

Bioorganic Marine Chemistry, Vol. 1. (Illus.). 210p. 1987. 91.00 (*0-387-17884-8*) Spr-Verlag.

Bioorganic Marine Chemistry, Vol. 3. Ed. by Paul J. Scheuer. (Illus.). viii, 175p. 1989. 104.00 (*0-387-50870-8*, 3271) Spr-Verlag.

Bioorganic Marine Chemistry, Vol. 4. Ed. by Paul J. Scheuer. (Illus.). 176p. 1991. 95.00 (*0-387-53522-5*) Spr-Verlag.

Biopathology of the Liver: An Ultrastructural Approach. Ed. by P. M. Motta. (C). 1988. lib. bdg. 168.00 (*0-7462-0049-8*) Kluwer Ac.

Biopesticides & Alternative Agriculture. Business Communications Co., Inc. Staff. 125p. 1990. 1,850.00 (*0-89336-741-9*, C-082B) BCC.

BioPharm Conference Proceedings '92: Key Issues & New Developments in Biopharmaceuticals. LC 91-648748. (Illus.). 313p. 1992. pap. text ed. 45.00 (*0-943330-29-7*) Advanstar Commns.

BioPharm Conference Proceedings '93. Ed. by Anne Montgomery. 133p. 1993. pap. text ed. 45.00 (*0-943330-39-4*) Advanstar Commns.

***BioPharm Conference Proceedings '95.** 300p. 1995. pap. 105.00 (*0-943330-54-8*) Advanstar Commns.

BioPharm Conference 1991 Proceedings. 135p. (Orig.). 1991. pap. text ed. 45.00 (*0-943330-28-9*) Advanstar Commns.

Biopharmaceutical Sequential Statistical Applications. Ed. by Peace. (Statistics: Vol. 128). 376p. 1992. 125.00 (*0-8247-8628-9*) Dekker.

Biopharmaceuticals of Occular Drug Delivery. 1992. 95.00 (*0-8493-7296-8*, RE994) CRC Pr.

Biopharmaceutics & Clinical Pharmacokinetics. 4th ed. Milo Gibaldi. LC 90-5614. (Illus.). 406p. 1991. text ed. 47.95 (*0-8121-1346-2*) Williams & Wilkins.

Biopharmaceutics & Clinical Pharmacokinetics: An Introduction. 4th rev. ed. Notari. 440p. 1987. 49.75 (*0-8247-7523-6*) Dekker.

Biopharmaceutics & Drug Interactions. 3rd ed. Donald E. Cadwallader. (Illus.). 162p. 1983. pap. 38.50 (*0-89004-704-9*) Raven.

Biopharmaceutics & Relevant Pharmacokinetics. John G. Wagner. LC 75-160736. (Illus.). 375p. (C). 1971. 46.00 (*0-914768-18-2*) Drug Intell Pubns.

Biophilia. Edward O. Wilson. LC 84-9052. 176p. 1984. 23.00 (*0-674-07441-6*) HUP.

Biophilia. Edward O. Wilson. 176p. 1986. pap. text ed. 9.95 (*0-674-07442-4*) HUP.

Biophilia Hypothesis. Ed. by Stephen R. Kellert & Edward O. Wilson. LC 93-2021. 1993. 29.95 (*1-55963-148-1*) Island Pr.

***Biophilia Hypothesis.** Ed. by Stephen R. Kellert & Edward O. Wilson. LC 93-2021. 450p. (C). 1995. reprint ed. pap. text ed. 17.95 (*1-55963-147-3*) Island Pr.

Biophilosophy. Bernhard Rensch. 1971. text ed. 55.00 (*0-231-03299-4*) Col U Pr.

Biophilosophy. Bernhard Rensch. Tr. by Cecilia Sym. LC 72-132692. 1971. 52.50 (*0-685-01146-1*) Col U Pr.

Biophosphates & Their Analogues - Synthesis, Structure, Metabolism & Activity: Proceedings of the 2nd International Symposium on Phosphorous Chemistry Directed Towards Biology, Lodtz, Poland, 8-12 September, 1986. Ed. by K. S. Bruzik & W. J. Stec. (Bioactive Molecules Ser.: No. 3). 598p. 1987. 187.25 (*0-444-42766-X*) Elsevier.

Biophosphonates & Tumor-Osteolysis. Ed. by K. W. Brunner et al. (Recent Results in Cancer Research Ser.: Vol. 116). (Illus.). 95p. 1989. 43.00 (*0-387-50560-1*) Spr-Verlag.

Biophysical & Biochemical Aspects of Fluorescence Spectroscopy. Ed. by T. G. Dewey. (Illus.). 310p. 1990. 79.50 (*0-306-43627-2*, Plenum Pr) Plenum.

Biophysical Applications of Crystallographic Techniques. Ed. by Warner Love & Eaton Lattman. (Transactions of the American Crystallographic Association Ser.: Vol. 9). 140p. 1973. pap. 25.00 (*0-686-60380-X*) Polycrystal Bk Serv.

Biophysical Approach to Complex Biological Phenomena. Ed. by E. I. Volkov. (Proceedings of the Lebedev Physics Institute Ser.: Vol. 194). (Illus.). 189p. (C). 1992. pap. text ed. 110.00 (*1-56072-047-6*) Nova Sci Pubs.

Biophysical Approach to Excitable Systems: A Volume in Honor of Kenneth S. Cole on His 80th Birthday. Ed. by William J. Adelman, Jr. & David E. Goldman. LC 81-15759. 270p. 1981. 65.00 (*0-306-40784-1*, Plenum Pr) Plenum.

Biophysical Aspects. Ed. by J. F. Liebman & A. Geenberg. (Molecular Structure & Energetics Ser.: Vol. 4). 407p. 1987. lib. bdg. 95.00 (*0-89573-336-6*) VCH Pubs.

Biophysical Aspects of Cerebral Circulation. Ed. by Yu E. Moskalenko. LC 78-41243. (Illus.). 174p. 1980. 74.00 (*0-08-022672-8*, Pub. by Pergamon Repr UK) Franklin.

Biophysical Aspects of Radiation Quality. Incl. (Illus.). 560p. 1971. pap. 85.00 (*92-0-010271-9*, ISP286, IAEA); write for info. (*0-318-62071-5*) UNIPUB.

Biophysical Basis of Excitability. Hugo G. Ferreira & M. W. Marshall. 512p. 1985. 120.00 (*0-521-30151-3*) Cambridge U Pr.

Biophysical Chemistry. Ed. by P. R. Bergethon & E. R. Simons. xiv, 340p. 1989. 65.00 (*0-387-97053-3*, 3010) Spr-Verlag.

Biophysical Chemistry Metal Ions DNA: Interactions. P. K. Banerjee. (International Bioscience Monographs: No. 8). 1979. 10.00 (*0-88065-022-2*, Messers Today & Tomorrow) Scholarly Pubns.

Biophysical Chemistry of Membrane Functions. K. Kotyk et al. LC 87-13325. 377p. 1988. text ed. 123.95 (*0-471-91657-9*) Wiley.

Biophysical Chemistry, Part I: The Conformation of Biological Macromolecules. Charles R. Cantor & Paul R. Schimmel. LC 79-22043. (Illus.). 365p. (C). 1995. text ed. write for info. (*0-7167-1042-0*); pap. text ed. write for info. (*0-7167-1188-5*) W H Freeman.

Biophysical Chemistry, Part II: Techniques for the Study of Biological Structure & Function. Charles R. Cantor & Paul R. Schimmel. LC 79-24854. (Illus.). 554p. (C). 1995. pap. text ed. write for info. (*0-7167-1190-7*) W H Freeman.

Biophysical Chemistry, Part III: The Behavior of Biological Macromolecules. Charles R. Cantor & Paul R. Schimmel. LC 79-27860. (Illus.). 597p. (C). 1995. pap. text ed. write for info. (*0-7167-1192-3*) W H Freeman.

Biophysical Control of Microfibril Orientation in Plant Cell Walls. J. D. Boyd. (Forestry Sciences Ser.). 1985. lib. bdg. 97.50 (*90-247-3101-1*) Kluwer Ac.

Biophysical Ecology. D. Oates. (Advanced Texts in Life Sciences Ser.). (Illus.). 1980. 84.00 (*0-387-90414-X*) Spr-Verlag.

Biophysical Electron Microscopy: Basic Concepts & Modern Techniques. Ed. by Peter W. Hawkes & Ugo Valdre. 517p. 1991. text ed. 154.00 (*0-12-333355-5*) Acad Pr.

Biophysical Lab Manual. LeRoy Scott et al. 1976. spiral bd. 32.00 (*0-88252-057-1*) Paladin Hse.

Biophysical Labeling Methods in Molecular Biology. Gertz I. Likhtenshtein. LC 92-19487. (Illus.). 256p. (C). 1993. 54.95 (*0-521-43132-8*) Cambridge U Pr.

Biophysical Modelling of Radiation Effects: Proceedings of the Workshop on Biophysical Modelling of Radiation Effects, Padua, Italy, 2-5 September 1991. Ed. by K. H. Chadwick et al. (Illus.). 368p. 1992. 118.00 (*0-7503-0187-2*) IOP Pub.

Biophysical Models in Radiation Oncology. Ed. by Lionel Cohen. 192p. 1982. 132.00 (*0-8493-6055-2*, RC271, CRC Reprint) Franklin.

Biophysical Plant Physiology & Ecology. Park S. Nobel. LC 82-20974. (Illus.). 608p. (C). 1995. text ed. write for info. (*0-7167-1447-7*) W H Freeman.

Biophysical Properties of Articular Cartilage. Mow. 1995. write for info. (*0-318-70404-8*) CRC Pr.

Biophysical Research for Asian Agroforestry. M. Avery. (C). 1992. text ed. 18.00 (*81-204-0569-2*, Pub. by Oxford IBH II) S Asia.

Biophysical Research for Asian Agroforestry. Ed. by M. E. Avery et al. 292p. (Orig.). (C). 1991. text ed. 14.00x (*0-933595-32-8*) Winrock Intl.

Biophysical Thermodynamics of Intracellular Processes: Molecular Machines of the Living Cell. Lev A. Blumenfeld & Alexander N. Tikhonov. LC 93-35826. (Illus.). 200p. 1994. 69.00 (*0-387-94179-7*) Spr-Verlag.

Biophysics. Ed. by W. Hoppe et al. (Illus.). 980p. 1983. 188.00 (*0-387-12083-1*) Spr-Verlag.

Biophysics. M. V. Volkenstein. 640p. 1983. 85.00 (*0-317-46581-3*, Pub. by Collets UK) Pro-Am Music.

Biophysics: An Introduction. Ed. by Christiaan Sybesma. (C). 1989. lib. bdg. 134.00 (*0-7923-0029-7*); pap. text ed. 60.00 (*0-7923-0030-0*) Kluwer Ac.

Biophysics & Cancer. Claudio Nicolini. LC 86-4926. 480p. 1986. 125.00 (*0-306-42122-4*, Plenum Pr) Plenum.

Biophysics & Physiology of Carbon Dioxide. Ed. by C. Bauer et al. (Proceedings in Life Sciences Ser.). (Illus.). 480p. 1980. 65.00 (*0-387-09892-5*) Spr-Verlag.

Biophysics for Physicists. R. H. Austin & S. Chan. 400p. (C). 1995. text ed. 78.00 (*981-02-0500-7*); pap. text ed. 37.00 (*981-02-0501-5*) World Scientific Pub.

Biophysics of Gap Junction Channels. Ed. by Peracchia. 1990. 229.00 (*0-8493-6337-3*, QP603, CRC Reprint) Franklin.

Biophysics of Hair Cell S. H Duifhuis & S. Van Netten. 432p. 1993. text ed. 121.00 (*981-02-1522-3*) World Scientific Pub.

Biophysics of Organ Cryopreservation. Ed. by D. E. Pegg & A. M. Karow, Jr. LC 87-36059. (NATO ASI Series A, Life Sciences: Vol. 147). (Illus.). 496p. 1988. 135.00 (*0-306-42812-1*, Plenum Pr) Plenum.

Biophysics of Photoreceptors & Photomovements in Microorganisms. Ed. by Francesco Lenci et al. (NATO ASI Series A, Life Sciences: Vol. 211). (Illus.). 364p. 1991. 115.00 (*0-306-44022-9*, Plenum Pr) Plenum.

Biophysics of the Cell Surface. Ed. by R. Glaser et al. (Biophysics Ser.: Vol. 5). (Illus.). 376p. 1990. 128.00 (*0-387-50801-5*) Spr-Verlag.

Biophysics of the Pancreatic B-Cell. Ed. by Illani Atwater et al. LC 87-7713. (Advances in Experimental Medicine & Biology Ser.: Vol. 211). 506p. 1987. 125.00 (*0-306-42555-6*, Plenum Pr) Plenum.

Biophysics of the Skeletal Muscle Extracellular Potentials. Alexander Gydikov. (C). 1992. lib. bdg. 126.00 (*0-7923-1468-9*) Kluwer Ac.

Biophysics of Water: Proceedings of a Working Conference, Held at Girton College, Cambridge, June 29-July 3, 1981. Ed. by Felix Franks & Sheila F. Mathias. LC 82-2839. (Illus.). 426p. reprint ed. pap. 121.50 (*0-8357-3096-4*, 2039353) Bks Demand.

Biophysics Progression: Some Physical, Mathematical & Logical Aspects, Vol. 37, No. 1. A. Noble. LC 50-11295. (Illus.). 48p. 1981. pap. 28.00 (*0-08-027133-2*, Pergamon Pr) Elsevier.

Biopoesis. Ed. by Harvey Bialy. 350p. 1974. pap. 5.00 (*0-913028-25-8*) North Atlantic.

Biopolitics. Ferenc Feher & Agnes Heller. (Public Policy & Social Welfare Ser.). 104p. 1994. pap. 28.95 (*1-85628-890-0*, Pub. by Avebury Pub UK) Ashgate Pub Co.

***Biopolitics: An Ecofeminist Reader on Biotechnology.** Ed. by Vandana Shiva & Ingunn Moser. (C). 1995. text ed. 59.95 (*1-85649-335-0*, Pub. by Zed Books UK); pap. 25.00 (*1-85649-336-9*, Pub. by Zed Books UK) Humanities.

Biopolitics & Gender. Ed. by Meredith W. Watts. LC 83-18597. (Women & Politics Ser.: Vol. 3, Nos. 2 & 3). 210p. 1984. text ed. 39.95 (*0-86656-250-8*) Haworth Pr.

Biopolymeric Controlled Release Systems, Vol. I. Ed. by Donald L. Wise. 240p. 1984. 143.00 (*0-8493-5403-X*, RS201) CRC Pr.

Biopolymeric Controlled Release Systems, Vol. II. Ed. by Donald L. Wise. 256p. 1985. 168.00 (*0-8493-5404-8*, RS201, CRC Reprint) Franklin.

Biopolymers, Vol. 28. No. 1. Ed. by Ettore Benedetti et al. 1989. pap. text ed. 69.95 (*0-471-50943-4*) Wiley.

778

An Asterisk (*) at the beginning of an entry indicates that the title is appearing in BIP for the first time.

Biopolymers: Making Materials Nature's Way. (Illus.). 95p. (Orig.). (C). 1994. pap. text ed. 60.00 (*0-7881-0445-4*) Diane Pub.

Biopolymers: Making Materials Nature's Way. (Orig.). 1994. lib. bdg. 250.00 (*0-8490-8414-8*) Gordon Pr.

Biopolymers I. Ed. by E. Doelker et al. (Advances in Polymer Science Ser.: Vol. 107). (Illus.). 292p. 1993. 159.00 (*0-387-56148-X*) Spr-Verlag.

***Biopolymers II.** Ed. by N. A. Peppas & R. S. Langer. (Advances in Polymer Science Ser.: Vol.122). (Illus.). 379p. 1995. 171.00 (*3-540-58788-8*) Spr-Verlag.

***Biopolymers-Natural Polymers: The Technology Is Ready, the Markets Are Waiting, a Host of Opportunities Can Now Be Exploited.** 140p. 1994. spiral bd. 1,770.00 (*1-56217-008-2*) Tech Insights.

Biopolymers: Non-Exclusion HPLC, Vol. 79. (Advances in Polymer Science Ser.). (Illus.). 250p. 1986. 102.00 (*0-387-16422-7*) Spr-Verlag.

Biopotency: Your Guide to Problem-Free Sexual Fulfillment. Richard Berger & Deborah Berger. 272p. 1990. mass mkt. 4.95 (*0-380-70816-7*) Avon.

Biopotentials of Cerebral Hemispheres in Brain Tumors. Natal'ia P. Bekhtereva. Tr. by Basil Haigh & Percival Bailey. LC 61-17724. (International Behavioral Sciences Ser.). 191p. reprint ed. pap. 54.50 (*0-8357-7254-3*, 2020644) Bks Demand.

Bioprocess Engineering. Ajit K. Ghose. 1990. boxed write for info. (*0-318-68282-6*) P-H.

Bioprocess Engineering: Basic Concepts. Michael L. Shuler & Fikret Kargi. 448p. 1991. text ed. 71.00 (*0-13-478215-1*) P-H.

Bioprocess Engineering: Kinetics, Mass Transport, Reactors & Gene Expression. Wolf R. Vieth. LC 93-44655. 388p. 1994. text ed. 69.95 (*0-471-03534-3*, Wiley-Interscience) Wiley.

Bioprocess Engineering: Systems, Equipment & Facilities. Kim L. Nelson. Ed. by Bjorn K. Lyderson et al. LC 93-44639. 1994. text ed. 89.95 (*0-471-03544-0*, Wiley-Interscience) Wiley.

***Bioprocess Engineering Principles.** Pauline M. Doran. (Illus.). 464p. 1995. text ed. 130.00 (*0-12-220855-2*); pap. text ed. 39.95 (*0-12-220856-0*) Acad Pr.

Bioprocess Engineering Symposium. Ed. by B. K. Henon & S. Ostrove. (BED Ser.: Vol. 23). 116p. 1992. 36.00 (*0-7918-1118-2*, G00762) ASME.

Bioprocess Engineering 1993. Ed. by B. Henon. LC 89-46291. 87p. Date not set. pap. 35.00 (*0-7918-1255-3*) ASME.

***Bioprocess Monitoring & Control.** Ed. by Marie N. Pons. 1993. text ed. 74.95 (*0-471-03714-1*) Wiley.

Bioprocess Parameter Control. Ed. by A. Agrawal. (Advances in Biochemical Engineering-Biochemistry Ser.: Vol. 30). (Illus.). 210p. 1984. 81.00 (*0-387-13539-1*) Spr-Verlag.

Bioprocess Production of Flavor Ingredients. Alan Gabelman. LC 93-46797. 1994. text ed. 69.95 (*0-471-03821-0*, Wiley-Interscience) Wiley.

Bioprocess Technology: Modelling & Transport Phenomena. Biotol Board Staff. (Illus.). 335p. 1992. pap. 32.95 (*0-7506-1507-9*) Buttrwrth-Heinemann.

Bioprocess Technology - Kinetics & Reactors. A. Moser. (Illus.). 455p. 1988. 189.00 (*0-387-96603-X*) Spr-Verlag.

Bioprocesses & Engineering. (Advances in Biochemical Engineering-Biotechnology Ser.: Vol. 40). (Illus.). 188p. 1989. 109.00 (*0-387-51446-5*, 3297) Spr-Verlag.

Bioprocesses Including Animal Cell Culture. (Advances in Biochemical Engineering-Biotechnology Ser.: Vol. 37). (Illus.). 180p. 1988. 96.00 (*0-387-19004-X*) Spr-Verlag.

Bioprocessing. Richard K. Miller & Terri C. Walker. LC 88-80910. (Survey on Technology & Markets Ser.: No. 26). 50p. 1989. pap. text ed. 200.00 (*1-55865-025-3*) Future Tech Surveys.

Bioprocessing. Owen P. Ward. Ed. by Marjorie Spencer. (Illus.). 192p. 1991. text ed. 57.95 (*0-442-31439-6*) Chapman & Hall.

Bioprocessing & Biotreatment of Coal. Ed. by Donald L. Wise. 760p. 1990. 199.00 (*0-8247-8305-0*) Dekker.

Bioprocessing for Environmental Benefits, Hydro-, Hydrous-, & Thermal Pyrolsis, Processing & Product Selectivity of Synthetic Fuels, Upgrading Strategies, General Papers & Mass Transfer in Coal Conversion Processes, Developments in Clean Coal Technology: Preprints of Papers Presented at the 204th ACS National Meeting, Washington, DC, August 23-28, 1992. American Chemical Society, Division of Fuel Chemistry Staff. (Preprints of Papers: Vol. 37, No. 4). 499p. reprint ed. pap. 142.30 (*0-7837-3204-X*, 2043198) Bks Demand.

Bioprocessing Safety: Worker & Community Safety & Health Considerations. Ed. by Warren C. Hyer, Jr. LC 89-18140. (Special Technical Publication Ser.: No. 1051). (Illus.). 175p. 1990. text ed. 39.00 (*0-8031-1264-5*, 04-010510-43) ASTM.

Bioproducts & Bioprocesses. Ed. by A. Fiechter et al. (Illus.). 385p. 1989. 141.00 (*0-387-50461-3*) Spr-Verlag.

Bioproducts & Bioprocesses 2: Third Conference to Promote Japan-U.S. Joint Projects & Cooperation in Biotechnology, Honolulu, Hawaii, January 6-10, 1991. Ed. by Toshiomi Yoshida & Robert D. Tanner. LC 93-3246. 1993. write for info. (*0-387-56508-6*) Spr-Verlag.

Biopsie und Operationspraeparat. U. E. Bonk. (Illus.). viii, 134p. 1983. pap. 17.75 (*3-8055-3702-6*) S Karger.

Biopsy Diagnosis of Liver Disease. Dale C. Snover. (Illus.). 320p. 1992. 82.00 (*0-683-07815-1*) Williams & Wilkins.

Biopsy Diagnosis of the Digestive Tract, 2 vols., Set. 2nd ed. Heidrun Rotterdam et al. (Biopsy Interpretation Ser.). 872p. 1993. 168.00 (*0-88167-968-2*) Raven.

Biopsy Interpretation of Lymph Nodes. Steven H. Swerdlow. (Biopsy Interpretation Ser.). 416p. 1992. 92.50 (*0-88167-840-6*) Raven.

Biopsy Interpretation of the Lung. Ed. by Yukio Shimosato & Roberta R. Miller. LC 94-954. (Biopsy Interpretation Ser.). 416p. 1994. 85.00 (*0-7817-0168-6*) Raven.

Biopsy Notes. N. T. Late. 14p. (Orig.). 1994. pap. write for info. (*0-9641448-7-5*) N Late Pub.

Biopsy of Bone in Internal Medicine: An Atlas & Sourcebook. R. Bartl & B. Frisch. LC 93-20357. (Current Histopathology Ser.: Vol. 21). 240p. (C). 1993. lib. bdg. 167.50 (*0-7923-8802-X*) Kluwer Ac.

Biopsy Pathology of Bone & Bone Marrow. B. Frisch et al. (Biopsy Pathology Ser.). (Illus.). 250p. 1985. text ed. 66.50 (*0-88167-162-2*) Raven.

Biopsy Pathology of Muscle. 2nd ed. Michael Swash & Martin S. Schwartz. LC 91-70213. (Illus.). 247p. 1991. lib. bdg. 87.00 (*0-89089-449-3*) Carolina Acad Pr.

Biopsy Pathology of the Bronchi. Elizabeth M. McDowell & Theodore F. Beals. (Illus.). 410p. 1987. text ed. 98.95 (*0-03-012119-1*) Saunders.

Biopsy Pathology of the Endometrium. C. H. Buckley & H. Fox. (Biopsy Pathology Ser.). 300p. 1989. 78.50 (*0-88167-600-4*) Raven.

Biopsy Pathology of the Skin. N. Kirkham. (Illus.). 408p. 1992. 99.95 (*0-442-31545-7*) Chapman & Hall.

Biopsy Pathology of the Thyroid & Parathyroid. Otto Ljungberg. LC 92-49004. (Biopsy Pathology Ser.). 1992. write for info. (*0-412-34890-X*) Chapman & Hall.

Biopsy Techniques in Pulmonary Disorders. Ko Pen Wang. 197p. 1989. 96.50 (*0-88167-518-0*) Raven.

Biopsychology. John P. Pinel. 608p. 1989. teacher ed write for info. (*0-318-66398-8*, H20530); text ed. 50.00 (*0-205-12052-0*, H20522); student ed 20.00 (*0-685-29845-0*, H20555); write for info. (*0-318-66399-6*, H22445); write for info. (*0-318-66400-3*, H20548) Allyn.

Biopsychology. 2nd ed. John P. Pinel. LC 92-49418. 1992. text ed. 38.25 (*0-205-13897-7*) Allyn.

Biopsychology of Mood & Arousal. Robert E. Thayer. (Illus.). 256p. 1989. 35.00 (*0-19-505162-9*) OUP.

Biopsychology of Mood & Arousal. Robert E. Thayer. (Illus.). 256p. 1990. reprint ed. pap. 19.95 (*0-19-506827-0*) OUP.

Biopsychosocial Aspects of Bereavement: Progress in Psychiatry. Ed. by Sidney Zisook. LC 86-28865. (Progress in Psychiatry Ser.). 192p. 1987. text ed. 21.50 (*0-88048-135-8*, 48-135-8) Am Psychiatric.

Biopsychosocial Health. Stacey B. Day et al. LC 80-85218. 225p. (C). 1980. pap. 15.00 (*0-934314-02-0*) Intl Found Biosocial Dev.

Biopsychosocial Imperative: Understanding the Biologos & General Systems Theory Approach to Biocommunications As the Psychospiritual Anatomy of Good Health. Stacey B. Day. LC 81-84483. 60p. 1981. 25.00 (*0-934314-06-3*) Intl Found Biosocial Dev.

Bioptics: Optics in Biomedicine & Environmental Sciences (Mar 1991, Porto, Portugal) O. D. Soares. 1992. write for info. (*0-8194-0652-X*, 1524) SPIE.

Bioquimica. 2nd ed. Robert C. Bohinski. 1987. pap. 41.75 (*0-201-64017-1*) Addison-Wesley.

Bioraphical Studies. Walter Bagehot. Ed. by Richard H. Hutton. LC 70-144862. vii, 368p. 1972. reprint ed. 12.00 (*0-403-00850-6*) Scholarly.

***Biorational Pest Control Agents: Formulation & Delivery.** American Chemical Society, Division of Agricultural & Food Chemistry Staff. Ed. by Franklin R. Hall & John W. Barry. LC 95-13986. (ACS Symposium Ser.: No. 595). (Illus.). 320p. 1995. 84.95 (*0-8412-3226-1*) Am Chemical.

Bioreaction Engineering: Reactions Involving Microorganisms & Cells, Vol. 1. Karl Schugerl. 1987. text ed. 286.00 (*0-471-91309-X*) Wiley.

Bioreaction Engineering Vol. 2: Characteristic Features of Bioreactors, Vol. 2. Karl Schugerl. 393p. 1991. text ed. 380.00 (*0-471-92593-4*) Wiley.

Bioreaction Engineering Principles. J. Nielsen & J. Villadsen. (Illus.). 440p. 1994. 79.50 (*0-306-44688-X*, Plenum Pr) Plenum.

Bioreactor Design & Product Yield. Biotol Board Staff. 275p. 1992. pap. 32.95 (*0-7506-1509-5*) Buttrwrth-Heinemann.

Bioreactor Design Fundamentals. Norton G. McDuffie. 137p. 1991. text ed. 42.95 (*0-7506-9107-7*) Buttrwrth-Heinemann.

Bioreactor Immobilized Enzymes & Cells: Fundamentals & Applications. Ed. by M. Moo-Young. 328p. 1988. 77.50 (*1-85166-160-3*) Elsevier.

***Bioreactor System Design.** Juan A. Asenjo & J. C. Merchuk. LC 94-35424. (Bioprocess Technology Ser.: Vol. 21). 1994. 195.00 (*0-8247-9002-2*) Dekker.

Bioreactors & Biotransformations. Ed. by G. W. Moody & P. B. Baker. 406p. 1987. 83.00 (*1-85166-162-X*, Pub. by Elsevier Applied Sci UK) Elsevier.

Bioreactors in Biotechnology: A Practical Approach. A. H. Scragg. 300p. 1991. text ed. 110.00 (*0-13-085143-4*) P-H.

Bioreclamation of Chlorinated Compounds. Battelle. 1994. 79.95 (*0-87371-983-2*) Lewis Pubs.

Bioreclamation of Hydrocarbons. Battelle. 1993. 69.95 (*0-87371-984-0*) Lewis Pubs.

Bioreductive Activation of Quinoid Compounds: Chemical, Biochemical & Toxicological Aspects. Ed. by H. Sies et al. (Free Radical Research Communications Ser.). 214p. 1990. pap. text ed. 197.00 (*3-7186-5028-2*) Gordon & Breach.

Bioregulators: Chemistry & Uses. Robert L. Ory & Falk R. Rittig. LC 84-10987. (ACS Symposium Ser.: No. 257). 296p. 1984. 49.95 (*0-8412-0853-0*) Am Chemical.

Bioregulators for Crop Protection & Pest Control. Ed. by Paul A. Hedin. LC 94-14287. (ACS Symposium Ser.: Vol. 557). 1994. 59.95 (*0-8412-2918-X*) Am Chemical.

Bioremedial Treatment Technology. Kaufman. 1995. write for info. (*0-87371-355-9*) Lewis Pubs.

Bioremediation. Katherine H. Baker. 1994. text ed. 55.00 (*0-07-003360-9*) McGraw.

***Bioremediation.** Richard K. Miller & Marcia E. Rupnow. (Survey on Technology & Markets Ser.: No. 226). 50p. 1994. pap. text ed. 200.00 (*1-55865-257-4*) Future Tech Surveys.

Bioremediation: Field Experience. Ed. by Paul E. Flathman et al. 544p. 1993. 79.95 (*0-87371-740-6*, TD192) Lewis Pubs.

Bioremediation: Nature's Cleanup Tool. Michael Sims. Ed. by Tricia Clark & Charles W. Ward. (Illus.). 29p. (Orig.). (C). 1993. pap. text ed. 17.95 (*1-56806-551-5*) Diane Pub.

Bioremediation -- The Use of Genetically Engineered or Adapted Microorganisms in the Treatment of Hazardous Waste. 1988. 55.00 (*0-944989-89-6*, 0100188P) Hazardous Mat Control.

Bioremediation - Hazardous Waste Treatment by Genetically Engineered or Adapted Organisms, 1988. 145p. 1988. pap. 35.00 (*0-685-50439-5*, 0100188) Hazardous Mat Control.

Bioremediation - Hazardous Waste Treatment by Genetically Engineered or Adapted Organisms, 1988. 145p. 1988. pap. 20.00 (*0-944989-90-X*, 010088) Hazardous Mat Control.

***Bioremediation Desk Manual for the Environmental Professional Bioremediation.** Pollution Engineering Staff. 97p. 1994. 24.95 (*0-934165-33-5*) Gulf Pub.

Bioremediation Engineering: Design & Applications. John T. Cookson, Jr. 1994. text ed. 79.95 (*0-07-012614-3*) McGraw.

Bioremediation Fundamentals & Effective Applications: Proceedings of the 3rd Annual Symposium, Gulf Coast Hazardous Substance Research Center, Lamar University, Beaumont, Texas, February 21-22, 1991. 253p. 1991. 35.00 (*0-685-60860-3*, 200091) Hazardous Mat Control.

***Bioremediation of Ground Water & Geological Material: A Review of In-situ Technologies.** Robert S. Kerr. 156p. (Orig.). 1994. pap. text ed. 75.00 (*0-86587-404-2*) Gov Insts.

***Bioremediation of Hazardous Waste.** U. S. Environmental Protection Agency, Office of Wetlands, Oceans, & Watersheds Staff. (EPA Research Ser.). 188p. (Orig.). 1994. pap. text ed. 55.00 (*0-86587-388-7*) Gov Insts.

***Bioremediation of Hazardous Wastes: Proceedings of the Fifth Annual Symposium.** (Illus.). 119p. (C). 1994. reprint ed. pap. text ed. 40.00x (*0-7881-1463-8*) Diane Pub.

Bioremediation of Hazardous Wastes, Wastewater, & Municipal Waste. 248p. 1993. 2,650.00 (*0-89336-952-7*, C-110R) BCC.

***Bioremediation of Pollutants in Soil & Water.** Ed. by Brian S. Shepart. LC 95-15010. (STP Ser.: Vol. 1235). 1995. write for info. (*0-8031-1891-0*) ASTM.

***Bioremediation of Pollutants in Soil & Water, STP 1235.** Ed. by Brian S. Schepart. (Special Technical Publication Ser.). (Illus.). 260p. 1995. text ed. 89.00 (*0-614-06764-2*, 04-012350-48) ASTM.

***Bioremediation Through Rhizosphere Technology.** Ed. by Todd A. Anderson & Joel R. Coats. LC 94-5331. (ACS Symposium Ser.: No. 563). (Illus.). 216p. 1994. 59.95 (*0-8412-2942-2*) Am Chemical.

Bioresonance & Multiresonance Therapy (BRT) New, Forward-Looking Forms of Therapy with Ultrafine Body Energies & Environmental Signals. Ed. by Hans Brugemann. Tr. by Robert E. Williams. (Illus.). 277p. 1993. text ed. 49.95 (*2-8043-4010-4*, Pub. by Edits Haug Intl) Medicina Bio.

Bioresources Ecology. T. N. Ananthakrishnan. 172p. (C). 1982. text ed. 70.00 (*90-6191-402-7*, Pub. by A A Balkema NE) Ashgate Pub Co.

Bioresources Ecology. Anantha Krishnan. (C). 1987. 15.00 (*0-317-66874-9*, Pub. by Oxford IBH II) S Asia.

Biorganic Photochemistry, Vol. 1: Photochemistry & the Nucleic Acids. Harry Morrison. 437p. 1990. text ed. 94.95 (*0-471-62987-1*) Wiley.

Biorheology: Abstracts of the Second International Congress, No. 2. Ed. by A. Copley. 1975. pap. 29.00 (*0-08-019962-3*, Pergamon Pr) Elsevier.

Biorheology: Proceedings of the Second International Congress. Ed. by A. Copley. 1975. pap. 47.00 (*0-08-019963-1*, Pergamon Pr) Elsevier.

Biorhythm: A Personal Science, 1991-1993. Bernard Gittelson. 1991. mass mkt. 4.99 (*0-446-36207-7*) Warner Bks.

Biorhythm: A Personal Science, 1994-1996. Bernard Gittelson. 432p. (Orig.). 1993. mass mkt. 5.50 (*0-446-60031-8*) Warner Bks.

Biorhythm for Life. Howard M. Thomson. LC 76-29578. (Illus.). 84p. (Orig.). 1976. pap. 9.95 (*0-9601070-1-0*) Evergreen MA.

***Biorhythms & Epilepsy.** Ed. by A. Martins Da Silva et al. LC 85-11860. (Illus.). Date not set. reprint ed. pap. 72.40 (*0-7837-9570-X*, 2060319) Bks Demand.

Biorhythms & Stress in the Physiopathology of Reproduction. Ed. by Paolo Pancheri & Lucio Zichella. (Series in Health Psychology & Behavioral Medicine). 580p. 1988. 110.00 (*0-89116-567-3*) Hemisp Pub.

Biorhythms, Biological Clocks & Periodicity: Index of New Information with Authors & Subjects. Preston G. Parke. 180p. 1993. 49.50 (*1-55914-900-0*); pap. 39.50 (*1-55914-901-9*) ABBE Pubs Assn.

Biorhythms in Your Life. Daniel Cohen. 1981. pap. 2.50 (*0-449-14168-3*, GM) Fawcett.

***Biorhythms of Natal Moon: Mysteries of Pancha Pakshi.** Ed. by U. S. Pulippani. (C). 1994. 16.00 (*0-8364-2900-1*, Pub. by Ranjan Pubs II) S Asia.

Biorthogonality & Its Applications to Numerical Analysis. Ed. by Brezinski. (Pure & Applied Mathematics Ser.: Vol. 156). 184p. 1991. 99.75 (*0-8247-8616-5*) Dekker.

Bios: Student Study Guide. 2nd ed. Perry Haalman. 192p. 1993. spiral bd. 18.95 (*0-8403-8805-5*) Kendall-Hunt.

Biosafety in Microbiological & Biomedical Laboratories. 3rd ed. Ed. by Jonathan Y. Richmond & Robert W. McKinney. 177p. (Orig.). (C). 1994. pap. text ed. 45.00 (*0-7881-0548-5*) Diane Pub.

Biosafety in Microbiological & Biomedical Laboratories: Working with Infectious Agents in Laboratory Settings. 1992. lib. bdg. 250.00 (*0-8490-5539-3*) Gordon Pr.

Biosafety in the Laboratory: Prudent Practices for Handling & Disposal of Infectious Materials. 244p. 1989. 39.95 (*0-309-03975-4*) Natl Acad Pr.

***Biosafety Results of Field Tests of Genetically Modified Plants & Microorganisms: Proceedings of an International Symposium, Kiawah Island Conference, Sponsored by ARI, November 27-30, 1990.** Ed. by D. R. MacKenzie & Suzanne C. Henry. 303p. Date not set. pap. 25.00 (*0-614-04327-1*) Agri Research Inst.

***Bioscan: The Worldwide Biotech Industry Reporting Service, Vol. 9, Suppl. 4.** Ed. by Arthur H. Stickney & Janet Woolum. 1995. pap. 975.00 (*0-614-07010-4*, 2264) Oryx Pr.

***Bioscan: The Worldwide Biotech Industry Reporting Service, Vol. 10, Suppl. 4.** Ed. by Arthur H. Stickney & Janet Woolum. 1995. pap. 975.00 (*0-614-07011-2*, 2412) Oryx Pr.

Bioscience: An Outline Approach. rev. ed. Anthony V. DeFina. (Illus.). 268p. 1992. reprint ed. teacher ed 20.00 (*0-916209-05-9*); reprint ed. student ed. pap. 15.00 (*0-916209-03-2*) Owlet Pubns.

Bioscience - Society: Report of the Schering Workshop, Berlin 1990, November 25-30. D. J. Roy et al. 408p. 1991. text ed. 137.95 (*0-471-93152-7*, Wiley-Liss) Wiley.

Bioscience at the Physical Science Frontier. Ed. by C. Nicolini. 270p. 1988. 115.00 (*0-89603-131-4*) Humana.

***Bioscience Directory: 1995 San Diego County Edition.** Ed. & Frwd. by Bruce E. Ahern. (Version 5.0 Ser.). 1995. spiral bd. 44.95 (*1-885062-00-1*) Tech Directory.

Bioscience II: An Advanced Biology Course Manual. rev. ed. Anthony V. DeFina. (Illus.). 396p. 1993. teacher ed 27.50 (*0-916209-10-5*); student ed 25.00 (*0-916209-11-3*) Owlet Pubns.

Biosciences: Information Sources & Services. Y. R. Alston & James Combs. 407p. 1993. 99.00 (*1-56159-065-7*, Stockton Pr) Groves Dictionaries.

Bioscientific Terminology. Donald M. Ayers. LC 74-163010. 325p. (C). 1972. pap. 11.95 (*0-8165-0305-2*) U of Ariz Pr.

Biosemiotics: The Semiotic Web 1991. Ed. by Thomas A. Sebeok & Jean Umiker-Sebeok. (Approaches to Semiotics Ser.: Vol. 106). xii, 498p. (C). 1992. lib. bdg. 252.35 (*3-11-012947-7*) Mouton.

Biosensor Design & Application. Ed. by Paul R. Mathewson & John W. Finley. LC 92-31003. (ACS Symposium Ser.: No. 511). (Illus.). 230p. 1992. 54.95 (*0-8412-2494-3*) Am Chemical.

Biosensor Principles & Applications. Ed. by Blum & Coulet. (Bioprocess Technology Ser.: No. 15). 376p. 1991. 145.00 (*0-8247-8546-0*) Dekker.

Biosensor Technology: Fundamentals & Applications. Buck et al. 408p. 1990. 140.00 (*0-8247-8414-6*) Dekker.

Biosensors. Ed. by M. Akhtar et al. (Illus.). 190p. 1987. text ed. 86.00 (*0-85403-324-6*) Scholium Intl.

Biosensors. Elizabeth Hall. 368p. 1990. text ed. 84.00 (*0-13-084526-4*) P-H.

Biosensors. Minh C. Tran. LC 93-12538. (Sensor Physics & Technology Ser.: Vol. 1). 1993. write for info. (*0-412-48190-1*) Chapman & Hall.

Biosensors: A Practical Approach. Ed. by A. E. Cass. (Practical Approach Ser.). (Illus.). 288p. 1990. 79.00 (*0-19-963046-1*, IRL Pr) OUP.

Biosensors: A Practical Approach. Ed. by A. E. Cass. (Practical Approach Ser.: No. 107). (Illus.). 288p. 1990. pap. 44.00 (*0-19-963047-X*, IRL Pr) OUP.

Biosensors: A Survey on Technology & Markets, No. 16. Richard K. Miller & Terri C. Walker. LC 88-80900. (Survey on Technology & Markets Ser.: No. 16). 50p. 1989. pap. text ed. 200.00 (*1-55865-015-6*) Future Tech Surveys.

Biosensors: Applications in Medicine, Environmental Protection & Process Control. Ed. by R. D. Schmid & F. Scheller. (Society for Biotechnology Research Ser.: Vol. 13). 428p. 1989. pap. text ed. 115.00 (*0-89573-955-0*) VCH Pubs.

Biosensors: Fundamentals, Technologies & Applications. Ed. by F. Scheller & R. D. Schmid. (GBF Monographs: Vol. 17). 548p. 1993. pap. 110.00 (*1-56081-220-6*) VCH Pubs.

Biosensors: Material Research Society International Symposium Proceedings-IMAM, No. 14. Ed. by I. Karube. 246p. 1989. text ed. 65.00 (*1-55899-043-7*) Materials Res.

Biosensors: May 31-June 1, 1988, Sunshine City, Ikebukuro, Tokyo, Japan. MRS International Meeting on Advanced Materials, First, Tokyo, Japan Staff. LC 90-174424. (Proceedings of the MRS International Meeting on Advanced Materials Ser.: No. 14). (Illus.). 268p. reprint ed. pap. 76.40 (*0-7837-1931-0*, 2042146) Bks Demand.

Biosensors: Microelectrochemical Devices. M. Lambrechts & W. Sansen. (Illus.). 320p. 1992. 112.00 (*0-7503-0112-0*) IOP Pub.

Biosensors: Theory & Applications. Donald Buerk. LC 92-61490. 220p. 1993. text ed. 85.00 (*0-87762-975-7*) Technomic.

Biosensors & Chemical Biosensors, No. C-053U. 1994. 2,850.00 (*1-56965-012-8*) BCC.

Biosensors & Chemical Sensors. Business Communications Co., Inc. Staff. 205p. 1989. pap. 2,650.00 (*0-89336-484-3*, C-053R) BCC.

B

An Asterisk (*) at the beginning of an entry indicates that the title is appearing in BIP for the first time.

Biosensors & Chemical Sensors: Optimizing Performance Through Polymeric Materials. Ed. by Peter G. Edelman & Joseph Wang. LC 92-6330. (ACS Symposium Ser.: No. 487). (Illus.). 340p. 1992. 79.95 (*0-8412-2218-5*) Am Chemical.

***Biosensors & Technical Medicine: Index of Modern Authors & Subjects with Guide for Rapid Research.** rev. ed. Peter B. Zeiderhof. LC 94-32971. 171p. 1994. text ed. 44.50 (*0-7883-0442-9*); pap. 39.50 (*0-7883-0443-7*) ABBE Pubs Assn.

Biosensors International Workshop 1987. Ed. by R. D. Schmid et al. LC 87-29557. (Society for Biotechnology Research Monograph Ser.: Vol. 10). 346p. 1987. pap. text ed. 120.00 (*0-89573-683-7*) VCH Pubs.

Biosensors with Fiberoptics. Ed. by Lemuel B. Wingard, Jr. LC 91-6350. (Contemporary Instrumentation & Analysis Ser.). (Illus.). 384p. 1991. 99.50 (*0-89603-190-X*) Humana.

***Bioseparation Processes in Food.** Rizvi Singh. (IFT Basic Symposium Ser.). 543p. 1995. write for info. (*0-8247-9608-X*) Dekker.

Bioseparations: Downstream Processing for Biotechnology. Paul A. Belter et al. 368p. 1988. text ed. 79.95 (*0-471-84737-2*) Wiley.

Biosignal Transduction Mechanisms. Ed. by M. Kasai et al. 230p. 1989. 77.00 (*0-387-50708-6*) Spr-Verlag.

BIOSIS Previews Search Guide, 2 vols., Set. enl. rev. ed. 792p. 1991. ring bd. 95.00 (*0-916246-24-8*) BIOSIS.

***BIOSIS Search Guide.** rev. ed. 550p. 1995. 115.00 (*0-916246-30-2*) BIOSIS.

Biosocial Aspects of Social Class. Ed. by C. G. Mascie-Taylor. (Biosocial Society Ser.: No. 2). (Illus.). 160p. 1990. 45.00 (*0-19-857724-9*) OUP.

Biosocial Background see Man in Adaptation

Biosocial Basis of Mental Retardation. Ed. by Sonia F. Osler & Robert E. Cooke. LC 65-17078. 168p. reprint ed. pap. 47.90 (*0-8357-7255-1*, 2020731) Bks Demand.

Biosocial Construction of Femininity: Mothers & Daughters in Nineteenth Century America. Nancy M. Theriot. LC 87-29545. (Contributions in Women's Studies: No. 93). 184p. 1988. text ed. 45.00 (*0-313-25483-4*, TBL/, Greenwood Pr) Greenwood.

Biosocial Interrelations in Population Adaptation. Ed. by Elizabeth S. Watts et al. (World Anthropology Ser.). (Illus.). xii, 412p. 1975. 51.55 (*90-279-7719-4*) Mouton.

Biosocial Nature of Man. Ashley Montagu. LC 72-11331. 123p. 1973. reprint ed. text ed. 45.00 (*0-8371-6658-6*, MOBN, Greenwood Pr) Greenwood.

Biosocial Perspectives on the Family. Ed. by Erik E. Filsinger. LC 87-26613. (Sage Focus Editions Ser.: No. 96). 208p. reprint ed. pap. 59.30 (*0-7837-6586-X*, 2046151) Bks Demand.

Biosocial Psychopathology: Epidemiologic Perspectives. Donald I. Templer et al. LC 93-25832. 344p. 1993. text ed. 46.95 (*0-8261-8290-9*) Springer Pub.

Biosorption of Heavy Metals. Ed. by Volesky. 1990. 240.00 (*0-8493-4917-6*, QR92) CRC Pr.

Biospeology, the Biology of Cavernicolous Animals. A. Vandel. 1965. 218.00 (*0-08-010242-5*, Pub. by Pergamon Repr UK) Franklin.

Biosphere. I. Bradbury. 213p. (C). 1991. 500.00 (*81-7089-154-X*, Pub. by Intl Bk Distr II) St Mut.

Biosphere. Ian Bradbury. 224p. 1992. text ed. 72.95 (*1-85293-037-3*, Pub. by Pinter Pubs Ltd UK); pap. text ed. 30.95 (*1-85293-038-1*, Pub. by Pinter Pubs Ltd UK) CRC Pr.

***Biosphere.** Ian K. Bradbury. LC 09-24076. 1994. text ed. 79.95 (*0-471-94489-0*); pap. text ed. 34.95 (*0-471-94491-2*) Wiley.

Biosphere: The Realm of Life. 2nd ed. Robert A. Wallace et al. (C). 1987. text ed. 74.50 (*0-673-16717-8*) HarpCollege.

Biosphere II Thousand: Protecting Our Global Environment Casebook. Donald G. Kaufman & Cecilia Franz. (C). 1993. Case studies. 24.50 (*0-06-500771-9*) HarpCollege.

Biosphere Politics: A New Consciousness for a New Century. Jeremy Rifkin. 1991. 20.00 (*0-517-57746-1*, Crown) Crown Pub Group.

Biosphere-Problems & Solutions: Proceedings of Miami International Symposium on Biosphere, September 23-24, 1984. Ed. by T. Nejat Veziroglu. (Studies in Environmental Science: Vol. 25). 1985. 207.75 (*0-444-42424-5*) Elsevier.

Biosphere: The Realm of Life see Biology: The Realm of Life

***Biosphere 2000.** Donald Kaufman & Cecilia Franz. 608p. (C). 1995. boxed 59.00 (*0-7872-0460-9*) Kendall-Hunt.

Biosphere 2000: Protecting Our Global Environment. Donald G. Kaufman & Cecilia Franz. LC 92-19689. (C). 1992. 70.00 (*0-06-043576-3*) HarpCollege.

Biosphere 2000: Protecting Our Global Environment. Donald G. Kaufman & Cecilia Franz. (C). 1993. student ed 23.00 (*0-06-043577-1*) HarpCollege.

Biospheres: Metamorphosis of Planet Earth. Dorion Sagan. 208p. 1990. text ed. 19.95 (*0-07-054426-3*) McGraw.

Biospherians, the New Pioneers. Stephen Dubin. (From Earth to Space Ser.). 40p. (J). (gr. 2 up). 1994. pap. 7.95 (*1-882428-05-6*) Biosphere Pr.

Biostatistical Microcomputing in Pascal. Jerome H. Klotz & R. Daniel Meyer. LC 84-27546. (Probability & Statistics Ser.). (Illus.). 176p. (C). 1985. 38.50 (*0-8476-7357-X*) Rowman.

Biostatistician. Jack Rudman. (Career Examination Ser.: C-1135). 1994. pap. 29.95 (*0-8373-1135-7*) Nat Learn.

Biostatistics. Brian K. Williams. LC 93-3336. 1993. Acid-free paper. write for info. (*0-412-46220-6*) Chapman & Hall.

Biostatistics: A Foundation for Analysis in the Health Sciences. 5th ed. Wayne W. Daniel. (Series in Probability & Mathematics). 740p. 1991. Net. text ed. write for info. (*0-471-52514-6*) Wiley.

***Biostatistics: A Foundation for Analysis in the Health Sciences.** 6th ed. Wayne W. Daniel. LC 94-26060. 1994. text ed. write for info. (*0-471-58852-0*) Wiley.

Biostatistics: A Methodology for the Health Sciences. Gerald Van Belle & Lloyd Fisher. LC 92-24336. (Analysis of Linear Models: Regression & Analysis of Variance Ser.). 832p. 1993. text ed. 79.95 (*0-471-58465-7*) Wiley.

Biostatistics: Experimental Design & Statistical Inference. James F. Zolman. LC 92-22605. (Illus.). 368p. 1993. 45.00 (*0-19-507810-1*) OUP.

BioStatistics: Statistics in Biomedical Public Health & Environmental Sciences. Ed. by Pranab K. Sen. 1985. 115.50 (*0-444-87694-4*) Elsevier.

Biostatistics: The Bare Essentials. Geoffrey R. Norman & David L. Streiner. LC 92-48446. 1993. write for info. (*0-8016-2186-0*) Mosby Yr Bk.

Biostatistics: The Bare Essentials. Geoffrey R. Norman & David L. Streiner. 260p. 1994. pap. 32.95 (*1-55664-369-1*) Mosby Yr Bk.

Biostatistics & Epidemiology: A Primer for Health Professionals. 2nd ed. S. Wassertheil-Smoller. (Illus.). 119p. 1992. pap. 28.00 (*0-387-97312-5*) Spr-Verlag.

***Biostatistics & Epidemology: A Primer for Health Professionals.** 2nd ed. Sylvia Wassertheil-Smoller. LC 94-44484. 1995. write for info. (*0-387-94388-9*) Spr-Verlag.

Biostatistics for Epidemiologists. Anders Ahlbom. 1993. 45.00 (*0-87371-912-3*, RA652) Lewis Pubs.

***Biostatistics for the Medical Boards.** Anthony N. Glaser. (Illus.). 128p. (Orig.). (YA). (gr. 10 up). 1994. pap. 14.95 (*0-941406-47-4*) Betz Pub Co Inc.

Biostatistics in Clinical Medicine. 3rd ed. Joseph A. Ingelfinger et al. LC 93-13482. (Illus.). 418p. 1994. 35.00 (*0-07-105415-4*) Hlth Prof Div.

Biostatistics in Medicine. Edmond A. Murphy. LC 81-48191. (Illus.). 560p. (C). 1982. text ed. 60.00x (*0-8018-2727-2*) Johns Hopkins.

Biostatistics in Pharmacology. Ed. by A. L. Delaunois. LC 78-40220. (International Encyclopedia of Pharmacology & Therapeutics Ser.: Section 7, Vol. 3). (Illus.). 1979. 116.00 (*0-08-021514-9*, Pub. by Pergamon Repr UK) Franklin.

Biostatistics in Pharmacology. Ed. by A. L. Delaunois. LC 78-40220. (International Encyclopedia of Pharmacology & Therapeutics Ser.). 1979. 574.00 (*0-08-023168-3*, Pub. by Pergamon Repr UK) Franklin.

Biostatistics in Pharmacology, Set. Ed. by A. L. Delaunois. 1128p. (C). 1973. 458.00 (*0-08-016556-7*, Pub. by Pergamon Repr UK) Franklin.

Biostats: A Primer for Health Care Professionals. 2nd ed. Dennis B. Gillings & Chester W. Douglass. LC 85-14927. (Illus.). 293p. (Orig.). (YA). 1985. 23.00 (*0-932137-02-4*) Cavco Pubns.

Biostats: Data Analysis for Dental Health Care Professionals. 4th ed. Jane A. Weintraub et al. (Illus.). 297p. (Orig.). (C). 1985. 23.00 (*0-932137-01-6*) Cavco Pubns.

Biostereometric Technology & Applications, Vol. 1380. R. E. Herron. 1991. 53.00 (*0-8194-0447-0*) SPIE.

Biostereometrics, '88: Fifth International Meeting (November 1988, Basel, Switzerland) Ed. by J. U. Baumann & R. E. Herron. (Proceedings Ser.: Vol. 1030). 398p. 1989. 64.00 (*0-8194-0065-3*) SPIE.

Biostratigraphic Studies of the Niagaran Inter-Reef Formations of Northeastern Illinois. Heinz A. Lowenstam. (Scientific Papers: Vol. IV). (Illus.). 146p. 1948. 3.00 (*0-89792-093-7*); pap. 2.00 (*0-89792-005-8*) Ill St Museum.

Biostratigraphic Zoning Trilobites of the Upper Cambrian & Lower Ordovician of the Northwestern Siberian Platform. A. V. Rozova. Tr. by R. Chakravarthy. 279p. (ENG.). (C). 1984. text ed. 95.00 (*90-6191-434-5*, Pub. by A A Balkema NE) Ashgate Pub Co.

Biostratigraphy of Jamaica. Ed. by R. M. Wright. (Memoir Ser.: No. 182). 1994. 118.75 (*0-8137-1182-7*) Geol Soc.

Biosurfactants: Production, Properties, Applications. Kosaric. 496p. 1993. 190.00 (*0-8247-8811-7*) Dekker.

Biosurfactants & Bioengineering. Kosaric. (Surfactant Science Ser.: Vol. 25). 344p. 1987. 160.00 (*0-8247-7679-8*) Dekker.

***Biosyntheses.** Georges N. Cohen. LC 94-30699. 1994. write for info. (*0-412-99551-4*) Chapman & Hall.

Biosynthesis. Ed. by C. A. Smith & E. J. Wood. (Molecular & Cell Biochemistry Ser.: No. 5). (Illus.). 176p. 1991. pap. 25.00 (*0-412-40760-4*, A6151) Chapman & Hall.

Biosynthesis, Vols. 1-5. Incl. Vol. 2. 1972 Literature. LC 76-6662. 1973. 38.00 (*0-85186-513-5*); Vol. 3. 1973 Literature. LC 76-6662. 1975. 38.00 (*0-85186-523-2*); Vol. 4. 1974 Literature. LC 76-6662. 1976. 43.00 (*0-85186-533-X*); Vol. 5. 1975-76 Literature. LC 72-83455. 1977. 57.00 (*0-85186-543-7*); LC 72-83455. write for info. (*0-318-50463-4*, Pub. by Royal Soc Chem UK) Am Chemical.

Biosynthesis & Biodegradation of Cellulose. Ed. by Haigler & Weimer. 704p. 1991. 225.00 (*0-8247-8387-5*) Dekker.

Biosynthesis & Biodegradation of Wood Components. Ed. by Takayoshi Higuchi. LC 84-12298. 1985. text ed. 198.00 (*0-12-347880-4*) Acad Pr.

Biosynthesis & Function of Plant Lipids. Ed. by William W. Thomson et al. 281p. 1983. pap. 14.00 (*0-943088-01-1*) Am Soc of Plan.

Biosynthesis & Manipulation of Plant Products. Ed. by Donald Grierson. (Plant & Microbial Biotechnology Ser.). 1992. 159.95 (*0-7514-0060-2*, A6872, Pub. by Blackie Acad & Prof UK) Routledge Chapman & Hall.

Biosynthesis & the Integration of Cellular Metabolism: Biotol Board. (Illus.). 1992. pap. 32.95 (*0-7506-1506-0*) Buttrwrth-Heinemann.

Biosynthesis, Metabolism & Mode of Action of Inverterbrate Hormones. Ed. by J. Hoffmann & M. Porchet. (Proceedings in Life Sciences Ser.). (Illus.). 570p. 1984. 126.00 (*0-387-13667-3*) Spr-Verlag.

Biosynthesis of Anematic Isoprenoids. M. F. Grundon. 1978. pap. 15.50 (*0-08-020469-4*, Pergamon Pr) Elsevier.

Biosynthesis of Branched Chain Amino Acids: Proceedings of the Workshop on the Biosynthesis of Branched Chain Amino Acids, Beer-Sheva, Israel, November, 1988. Ed. by Z. Barak et al. LC 90-11983. 527p. 1990. lib. bdg. 140.00 (*0-89573-961-5*) VCH Pubs.

Biosynthesis of Ergot Alkaloids & Related Compounds. Ed. by Heinz C. Floss. 1976. pap. 15.50 (*0-08-021232-8*, Pergamon Pr) Elsevier.

Biosynthesis of Heme & Chlorophylis. Harry Dailey. 608p. 1990. text ed. 94.00 (*0-07-015088-5*) McGraw.

Biosynthesis of Isoprenoid Compounds, Vol. 1. John W. Porter. Ed. by Sandra L. Spurgeon. LC 80-28511. 574p. reprint ed. pap. 163.60 (*0-8357-7256-X*, 2056302) Bks Demand.

Biosynthesis of Proteins. H. Chantrenne & P. Alexander. LC 61-14246. (International Series of Monographs on Pure & Applied Mathematics: Vol. 14). 1961. 100.00 (*0-08-009344-2*, Pub. by Pergamon Repr UK) Franklin.

Biosynthesis of Secondary Metabolites. 2nd ed. R. B. Herbert. (Illus.). 224p. 1989. 69.95 (*0-412-27540-6*); pap. 29.50 (*0-412-27720-4*) Chapman & Hall.

Biosynthesis of the Major Crop Products: The Biochemistry, Cell Physiology & Molecular Biology Involved in the Synthesis by Crop Plants of Sucrose, Fructan, Starch, Cellulose, Oil, Rubber & Proteins. Philip John. 150p. 1993. text ed. 84.95 (*0-471-93585-9*); pap. text ed. 37.95 (*0-471-93816-5*) Wiley.

***Biosynthesis of the Tetrapyrrole Pigments, No. 180.** CIBA Foundation Symposia Staff. (Ciba Foundation Symposia Ser.). 1994. text ed. 76.00 (*0-471-93947-1*) Wiley.

Biosynthesis, Transport & Functions of Glycoconjugates. Ed. by F. Wieland & W. Reutter. LC 93-47463. (Baden Ser.: Vol. 44). (Illus.). 201p. 1994. 133.00 (*0-387-57581-2*) Spr-Verlag.

Biosynthetic Products for Cancer Chemotherapy. G. R. Pettit et al. 400p. 1989. 148.75 (*0-444-88049-6*) Elsevier.

Biosystematic Monograph of the Genus Cucumis (Cucurbitaceae) Botanical Identification of Cucumbers & Melons. Joseph H. Kirkbride, Jr. LC 92-82126. (Illus.). 159p. (C). 1993. 47.50 (*0-9635752-0-1*) Pkway Pubs.

Biosystematic Studies of Ceylonese Wasps, Pt. 19. Karl V. Krombein. LC 82-600154. (Smithsonian Contributions to Zoology Ser.: No. 515). (Illus.). 45p. 1991. reprint ed. pap. 25.00 (*0-7837-1177-8*, 2041705) Bks Demand.

Biosystematic Studies of Ceylonese Wasps: A Revision of Gastrosericus Spinola (Hymenoptera: Sphecoidea: Larridae, Part 16. Karl V. Krombein & Wojciech J. Pulawski. LC 85-600250. (Smithsonian Contributions to Zoology Ser.: No. 436). 24p. 1986. reprint ed. pap. 25.00 (*0-8357-7257-8*, 2027314) Bks Demand.

Biosystematic Studies of Ceylonese Wasps, XIV: A Revision of Carinostigmus Tsuneki (Hymenoptera, Sphecoidea, Pemphredonidae. Karl V. Krombein. LC 84-600058. (Smithsonian Contributions to Zoology Ser.: No. 396). 41p. 1984. reprint ed. pap. 25.00 (*0-8357-7258-6*, 2024352) Bks Demand.

Biosystematic Study of the European Stratiomyidae (Diptera) R. Rozkosny. 1982. lib. bdg. 172.50 (*90-6193-132-0*) Kluwer Ac.

Biosystematic Study of the Genus Brodiaea (Amaryllidaceae) Theodore F. Niehaus. LC 77-170326. (University of California Publications in Social Welfare: No. 60). (Illus.). 73p. reprint ed. pap. 25.00 (*0-8357-7259-4*, 2030678) Bks Demand.

Biosystematics, Genetics, & Physiological Ecology of the Erythranthe Section of Mimulus. William M. Hiesey et al. LC 40-14859. (Experimental Studies on the Nature of Species: Vol. 5). (Illus.). 219p. 1971. 12.00 (*0-87279-639-6*, 628) Carnegie Inst.

Biosystematics in the Nordic Flora. Ed. by Bengt Jonsell & Lena Jonsell. (Symbolae Botanicae Upsalienses Ser.: Vol. XXVII). (Illus.). 256p. (Orig.). 1987. pap. 45.50x (*91-554-1941-0*, Pub. by Uppsala Univ Acta Univ Uppsaliensis SW) Coronet Bks.

Biosystematics of American Crows. David W. Johnston. LC 61-11576. (Illus.). 127p. 1961. 25.00 (*0-295-73724-7*) U of Wash Pr.

Biosystematics of Haematophagous Insects. Ed. by M. W. Service. (Systematics Association Special Volume Ser.: Vol. 37). (Illus.). 376p. 1988. 112.00 (*0-19-857709-5*) OUP.

Biosystematics of Social Insects. Ed. by P. E. Howse & Jean-Luc Clement. (Systematics Association Special Ser.: Vol. 19). 1981. text ed. 148.00 (*0-12-357180-4*) Acad Pr.

Biosystematics of the Nymphomyiidae (Insecta: Diptera) Life History, Morphology, & Phylogenetic Relationships. Gregory W. Courtney. LC 93-40217. (Smithsonian Contributions to Zoology Ser.: No. 550). (Illus.). 45p. reprint ed. pap. 25.00 (*0-7837-6893-1*, 2046723) Bks Demand.

Biosystematics of the Yellow-Faced Pocket Gopher, Cratogeomys Castanops (Rodentia: Geomyidae) in the United States. Ed. by Robert R. Hollander. (C). 1990. pap. 14.00 (*0-89672-229-5*) Tex Tech Univ Pr.

Biosystematische Studien an Lophozia Subgen. Schistochilopsis (Hepaticae) Irene Bisang. (Bryophytorum Bibliotheca Ser.: Vol. 43). (Illus.). 225p. 1991. pap. text ed. 69.60 (*3-443-62015-9*, Pub. by Cramer-Borntraeger GW) Lubrecht & Cramer.

Biosystematische Untersuchungen an den Porlingsgattungen Phellinus Quel und Inonotus Karst. Michael Fischer. (Bibliotheca Mycologica Ser.: Vol. 107). (Illus.). 134p. (GER.). (C). 1987. pap. text ed. 42.00 (*3-443-59008-X*) Lubrecht & Cramer.

Biotape Aquarium. Rainer Stawikowski. Tr. by T. F. H. Publications, Inc. Staff. (Illus.). 208p. 1993. text ed. 14.95 (*0-86622-519-6*, TT026) TFH Pubns.

Biotaxonomische Untersuchungen an Einigen Hefen der Gattung Saccharomyces. I. Neumann. 1972. 24.00 (*3-7682-5440-2*) Lubrecht & Cramer.

Biotec Two: Biosensors & Environmental Biotechnology, Vol. 2. Ed. by C. P. Hollenberg & H. Sahm. c, 149p. 1988. pap. text ed. 60.00 (*0-89574-264-0*, Pub. by Gustav Fischer Verlag) VCH Pubs.

Biotech Business: Financial Outlook & Analysis. (Special Report Series on Biotechnology: No. 3). 134p. 1989. 95.00 (*1-55871-156-2*, BSP-154) BNA.

Biotech Business Handbook: How to Organize & Operate a Biotechnology Business. Michael G. Pappas. (Including the Most Promising Applications for the 1990s Ser.). (Illus.). 480p. 1994. ring bd. 189.50 (*0-89603-320-1*) Humana.

Biotech Research Reagents Markets. (Theta Market Report: No. 240). (Illus.). 108p. 1991. 295.00 (*0-317-04304-8*) Theta Corp.

***Biotech Resource Manual.** Jack Chirikjian. (Life Science Ser.). 200p. Date not set. pap. 30.00 (*0-86720-895-3*) Jones & Bartlett.

***Biotech Resource Manual, Vol. 2.** Jack Chirikjian. (Life Science Ser.). 200p. Date not set. pap. 30.00 (*0-86720-896-1*) Jones & Bartlett.

Biotech Risk Assess: Issues & Methods for Environmental Introductions. Ed. by J. Fiksel & Vincent T. Covello. (Illus.). 160p. 1986. 82.00 (*0-08-034213-2*) Franklin.

Biotechnical Engineering: Equipment & Processes. James R. Critser, Jr. (Ser. 14-81). 1982. pap. 210.00 (*0-914428-92-6*) Lexington Data.

Biotechnical Engineering: Equipment & Processes. James R. Critser, Jr. (Ser. 14-82). 267p. 1983. pap. 210.00 (*0-88178-011-1*) Lexington Data.

Biotechnical Engineering: Equipment & Processes. James R. Critser, Jr. (Ser. 14-83). 318p. 1984. pap. 210.00 (*0-88178-012-X*) Lexington Data.

Biotechnical Engineering: Equipment & Processes. James R. Critser, Jr. (Ser. 14-84). 293p. 1985. pap. 210.00 (*0-88178-023-5*) Lexington Data.

Biotechnical Engineering: Equipment & Processes. James R. Critser, Jr. (Ser. 14-85). 321p. 1986. pap. 210.00 (*0-88178-032-4*) Lexington Data.

Biotechnical Engineering: Equipment & Processes. James R. Critser, Jr. (Ser. 14-86). 380p. 1987. pap. 210.00 (*0-88178-042-1*) Lexington Data.

Biotechnical Engineering: Equipment & Processes. James R. Critser, Jr. (Ser. 14-87). 1988. pap. 210.00 (*0-88178-060-X*) Lexington Data.

Biotechnical Engineering: Equipment & Processes, No. 14-88. James R. Critser, Jr. (Illus.). (C). 1989. pap. 210.00 (*0-88178-067-7*) Lexington Data.

Biotechnical Engineering: Equipment & Processes, No. 14-89. James R. Critser, Jr. (Illus.). (C). 1990. pap. 225.00 (*0-88178-072-3*) Lexington Data.

Biotechnical Engineering: Equipment & Processes, No. 14-91. James R. Critser, Jr. (C). 1992. pap. 225.00 (*0-88178-081-2*) Lexington Data.

Biotechnical Engineering: Equipment & Processes, No. 14-92. James R. Critser, Jr. (Illus.). (C). 1993. pap. 225.00 (*0-88178-085-5*) Lexington Data.

Biotechnical Engineering: Equipment & Processes, No. 14-90. James R. Critser, Jr. (Illus.). (Orig.). (C). 1991. pap. 225.00 (*0-88178-078-2*) Lexington Data.

***Biotechnical Engineering: Indexes & Summaries of U. S. Patents.** James R. Critser, Jr. (Fourteen-Ninety Three MPS Ser.). (Illus.). (C). 1994. pap. 160.00x (*0-88178-091-X*) Lexington Data.

***Biotechnical Engineering: Indexes & Summaries of U. S. Patents.** James R. Critser, Jr. (Fourteen-Ninety Four MPS Ser.). (Illus.). (C). 1995. pap. 160.00x (*0-88178-092-8*) Lexington Data.

***Biotechnical Engineering: Indexes & Summaries of U. S. Patents.** James R. Critser, Jr. (Fourteen-Ninety Two MPS Ser.). (Illus.). (C). 1994. pap. 160.00x (*0-88178-090-1*) Lexington Data.

Biotechnical Slope Protection & Erosion Control. Donald H. Gray & Andrew T. Leiser. LC 89-31979. 288p. (C). 1989. reprint ed. 49.50 (*0-89464-259-6*) Krieger.

Biotechnics - Wastewater. Ed. by A. Fiechter. (Advances in Biochemical Engineering-Biotechnology Ser.: Vol. 51). (Illus.). 150p. 1994. 109.00 (*0-387-57319-4*) Spr-Verlag.

Biotechnics & Society: The Rise of Industrial Genetics. Sheldon Krimsky. LC 90-23214. 280p. 1991. text ed. 55.00 (*0-275-93859-X*, C3859, Praeger Pubs); pap. text ed. 18.95 (*0-275-93860-3*, B3860, Praeger Pubs) Greenwood.

Biotechniques for Air Pollution Abatement & Odour Control Policies: Proceedings of an International Symposium, Maastricht, the Netherlands, 28-29 October 1991. J. Van Ham. Ed. by A. J. Dragt. LC 92-13147. (Studies in Environmental Science: No. 51). 1992. write for info. (*0-444-89263-X*) Elsevier.

Biotechnological Advances in Processing Municipal Wastes for Fuels & Chemicals. A. A. Antonopoulos. LC 86-31144. (Illus.). 488p. 1987. 45.00 (*0-8155-1122-1*) Noyes.

Biotechnological Applications of Lipid Microstructures. Ed. by B. P. Gaber et al. (Advances in Experimental Medicine & Biology Ser.: Vol. 238). (Illus.). 394p. 1988. 115.00 (*0-306-43014-2*, Plenum Pr) Plenum.

Biotechnological Applications of Plant Cultures. Shargool. 1994. write for info. (*0-8493-8262-9*) CRC Pr.

An Asterisk (*) at the beginning of an entry indicates that the title is appearing in BIP for the first time.

B

An Asterisk (*) at the beginning of an entry indicates that the title is appearing in BIP for the first time.

781

Biotechnology Guide U. S. A. Companies, Data & Analysis. 2nd ed. M. Dibner. 652p. 1991. 199.00 (1-56159-015-0, Stockton Pr) Groves Dictionaries.

*__Biotechnology Guide U. S. A. Companies, Data & Analysis.__ 3rd ed. Mark D. Dibner. 692p. 1995. pap. text ed. 249.00 (1-886041-02-4) Inst Biotech Info.

Biotechnology in a Global Economy. (Illus.). 283p. (Orig.). (C). 1992. pap. text ed. 50.00x (0-941375-60-9) Diane Pub.

Biotechnology in Agricultural Chemistry. Ed. by Homer M. LeBaron et al. LC 87-1803. (Symposium Ser.: No. 334). (Illus.). xxii, 354p. 1987. 71.95 (0-8412-1019-5) Am Chemical.

Biotechnology in Agriculture. Business Communications Co., Inc. Staff. 192p. 1985. pap. 1,750.00 (0-89336-440-1, GA-051R) BCC.

Biotechnology in Agriculture. S. Natesh et al. 1987. 47.50 (81-204-0241-3, Pub. by Oxford IBH II) S Asia.

Biotechnology in Agriculture: Diseases & Other Environmental Considerations Bibliography. 276p. (Orig.). (C). 1993. pap. text ed. 60.00 (1-56806-930-8) Diane Pub.

Biotechnology in Agriculture: Proceedings of the First Asia-Pacific Conference on Agricultural Biotechnology, Beijing, China, 20-24 August, 1992. Ed. by Chongbiao You. (Current Plant Science & Biotechnology in Agriculture Ser.). 532p. (C). 1993. lib. bdg. 192.00 (0-7923-2168-5) Kluwer Ac.

Biotechnology in Animal Agriculture. Richard K. Miller & Terri C. Walker. LC 88-80913. (Survey on Technology & Markets Ser.: No. 25). 50p. 1989. pap. text ed. 200.00 (1-55865-024-5) Future Tech Surveys.

Biotechnology in Blood Transfusion. Ed. by C. T. Sibinga. (Developments in Hematology & Immunology Ser.). (C). 1988. lib. bdg. 67.00 (0-89838-404-4) Kluwer Ac.

Biotechnology in China. National Academy of Sciences, Office of International Affairs Staff. 116p. 1989. 15.00 (0-309-03988-6) Natl Acad Pr.

Biotechnology in Clinical Medicine. Ed. by Alberto Albertini et al. 384p. 1987. text ed. 116.50 (0-88167-375-7) Raven.

Biotechnology in Developing Countries. P. A. Van Hemert. 168p. (Orig.). 1983. pap. text ed. 23.50 (90-6275-138-5, Pub. by Delft U Pr NE) Coronet Bks.

Biotechnology in Diagnostics: Proceedings of the International Symposium on the Impact of Biotechnology on Diagnostics Held in Rome, Italy, April 16-18, 1985, No. 21. Ed. by Hilary Koprowski et al. 326p. 1985. 96.50 (0-444-80703-9) Elsevier.

Biotechnology in Europe & Latin America: Prospects for Co-Operation. Ed. by Bernardo Sorj et al. (C). 1989. lib. bdg. 91.50 (0-7923-0278-8) Kluwer Ac.

Biotechnology in Food Processing. Ed. by Susan K. Harlander & Theodore P. Labuza. LC 86-5242. (Illus.). 323p. 1986. 48.00 (0-8155-1073-X) Noyes.

Biotechnology in Future Society. 2nd ed. Ed. by Edward Yoxen & Vittorio Di Martino. 147p. 1989. text ed. 55.95 (1-85521-016-9, Pub. by Dartmth Pub UK) Ashgate Pub Co.

Biotechnology in Growth Regulation. R. B. Heap et al. (Illus.). 304p. 1989. text ed. 52.95 (0-407-01473-X) Buttrwrth-Heinemann.

Biotechnology in International Argricultural Research. International Rice Research Institute Staff. (Illus.). 444p. 1985. pap. 16.95 (0-8138-0103-6) Iowa St U Pr.

Biotechnology in Japan. Malcolm Brock. 144p. 1989. 55.00 (0-415-03495-7, A3695) Routledge.

Biotechnology in Japan - a Comprehensive Guide. R. D. Schmid. (Illus.). 800p. 1991. 309.00 (0-387-53554-3) Spr-Verlag.

Biotechnology in Plant Agriculture. Richard K. Miller & Terri C. Walker. LC 88-80908. (Survey on Technology & Markets Ser.: No. 24). 50p. 1989. pap. text ed. 200.00 (1-55865-023-7) Future Tech Surveys.

Biotechnology in Plant Breeding. 187p. 1989. 2,650.00 (0-89336-686-2, C-106) BCC.

Biotechnology in Plant Science: Relevance to Agriculture in the Eighties. Milton Zaitlin et al. 1986. text ed. 114.00 (0-12-775310-9) Acad Pr.

Biotechnology in Pulp & Paper Manufacture. T. Kent Kirk & Hou-Min Chang. 696p. 1990. text ed. 84.95 (0-409-90192-X) Buttrwrth-Heinemann.

Biotechnology in Renal Replacement Therapy. Ed. by V. Bonomini et al. (Contributions to Nephrology Ser.: Vol. 70). (Illus.). xiv, 346p. 1989. 166.00 (3-8055-4893-1) S Karger.

Biotechnology in Schools: A Handbook for Teachers. Jenny Henderson & Stephen Knutton. 160p. 1990. 95.00 (0-335-09369-8, Open Univ Pr); pap. 34.00 (0-335-09368-X, Open Univ Pr) Taylor & Francis.

Biotechnology in Tall Fescue Improvement. Ed. by Michael J. Kasperbauer. 176p. 1990. 179.00 (0-8493-4891-9, SB201) CRC Pr.

Biotechnology in the Bay Area: The Job Hunters Guide to 100 Plus Leading Companies. rev. ed. Ed. by Emily A. Rosenberg. 90p. (Orig.). 1990. pap. 65.00 (0-9624687-4-6) Venture Info.

Biotechnology in the San Francisco Bay Area. 213p. 1988. 6.00 (0-317-05641-7, P88002PLN) Assn Bay Area.

Biotechnology in the School Curriculum. C. Gayford. (C). 1989. text ed. 125.00 (0-09-173080-5, Pub. by S Thornes Pubs UK) St Mut.

Biotechnology in the U. S. Pharmaceutical Industry. 3rd ed. North Carolina Biotechnology Center Institute for Biotechnology Information Staff. 479p. 1993. pap. 595. 00 (0-945597-20-7) NC Biotech Ctr.

*__Biotechnology in the U. S. Pharmaceutical Industry 1995: A Special Report.__ 4th ed. Institute for Biotechnology Information Staff. 525p. 1995. pap. text ed. 695.00 (1-886041-01-6) Inst Biotech Info.

Biotechnology in the 1990s: Taking Stock. 385p. 1991. 2, 850.00 (0-89336-886-5, C143) BCC.

Biotechnology in Western Europe. 1990. lib. bdg. 79.95 (0-8490-4041-8) Gordon Pr.

Biotechnology Information '86. Ed. by R. Wakeford. 268p. 1987. pap. 64.00 (1-85221-009-5, IRL Pr) OUP.

Biotechnology Instrumentation & Software: Pharmaceutical Growth Expands Supplier Markets. Market Intelligence Staff. 293p. 1993. 1,895.00 (1-56753-468-6) Frost & Sullivan.

Biotechnology Instrumentation Market. (Market Research Reports: No. 344). 266p. 1993. 795.00 (0-317-05451-1) Theta Corp.

Biotechnology Japan. Mark D. Dibner. 336p. 1989. text ed. 180.00 (0-07-016762-1) McGraw.

Biotechnology Law for the 1990s: Analysis & Perspective. LC 90-1306. (Special Report Series on Biotechnology: No. 4). 1989. 95.00 (1-55871-153-8, BSP 155) BNA.

Biotechnology Marketplace. Ed. by Lewis B. Sckolnick. 450p. (Orig.). (C). 1994. pap. 995.00 (1-57205-315-1) Rector Pr.

Biotechnology Methods. (Advances in Biochemical Engineering-Biotechnology Ser.: Vol. 35). (Illus.). 190p. 1987. 96.00 (0-387-17627-6) Spr-Verlag.

Biotechnology of Algae: A Bibliography. Virginia Stone et al. 60p. (Orig.). (C). 1994. pap. text ed. 40.00 (0-7881-0587-6) Diane Pub.

Biotechnology of Amino Acid Production. Ed. by K. Aida et al. (Progress in Industrial Microbiology Ser.: No. 24). 350p. 1986. 123.00 (0-444-99502-1) Elsevier.

Biotechnology of Amylodextrin Oligosaccharides. Ed. by Robert B. Friedman. LC 91-13893. (ACS Symposium Ser.: No. 458). (Illus.). 352p. 1991. 84.95 (0-8412-1993-1) Am Chemical.

Biotechnology of Antibiotics & Other Bioactive Microbial Metabolites. G. Lancini & R. Lorenzetti. (Illus.). 195p. (C). 1994. 59.50 (0-306-44603-0, Plenum Pr) Plenum.

Biotechnology of Blood. Jack Goldstein. (Biotechnology Ser.). (Illus.). 477p. 1991. text ed. 46.00 (0-7506-9120-4) Buttrwrth-Heinemann.

Biotechnology of Cotton. Ed. by J. M. Stewart. (International Cotton Advisory Committee Review Articles on Cotton Production Research Ser.: No. 3). 50p. (Orig.). 1991. pap. 33.25 (0-85198-714-1) CAB Intl.

Biotechnology of Dyslipoproteinemias: Applications in Diagnosis & Control. Claude Lenfant et al. (Atherosclerosis Reviews Ser.: Vol. 20). 352p. 1990. 104. 50 (0-88167-616-0) Raven.

Biotechnology of Endophytic Fungi of Grasses. Ed. by Charles W. Bacon & James F. White, Jr. 224p. 1994. 169.95 (0-8493-6276-8, 6276) CRC Pr.

Biotechnology of Filamentous Fungi: Technology & Products. David B. Finkelstein & Christopher Ball. (Biotechnology Ser.). 535p. 1992. text ed. 46.00 (0-7506-9115-8) Buttrwrth-Heinemann.

Biotechnology of Food Crops: Rice Biotechnology & Genetic Engineering. Paul Christou. LC 94-60643. 210p. 1994. pap. text ed. 65.00 (1-56676-150-6) Technomic.

Biotechnology of Fungi for Improving Plant Growth. Ed. by J. M. Whipps & R. D. Lumsden. (British Mycological Society Symposium Ser.: No. 16). 300p. (C). 1990. 94.95 (0-521-38236-X) Cambridge U Pr.

Biotechnology of Insulin Therapy. J. C. Pickup. (Frontiers in Pharmacology & Therapeutics Ser.). (Illus.). 186p. 1991. 115.00 (0-632-03038-0) Blackwell Sci.

Biotechnology of Malting & Brewing. James S. Hough. LC 84-14313. (Cambridge Studies in Biotechnology: No. 1). (Illus.). 168p. 1985. 59.95 (0-521-25672-0) Cambridge U Pr.

Biotechnology of Malting & Brewing. James S. Hough. LC 84-14313. (Cambridge Studies in Biotechnology: No. 1). (Illus.). 182p. (C). 1991. pap. 24.95 (0-521-39553-4) Cambridge U Pr.

Biotechnology of Marine Polysaccharides. Ed. by Rita Colwell et al. LC 84-25221. (Illus.). 550p. 1985. 121.00 (0-89116-433-2) Hemisp Pub.

Biotechnology of Microbial Exopolysaccharides. Ed. by Ian W. Sutherland. (Studies in Biotechnology: No. 9). 180p. (C). 1990. 74.95 (0-521-36350-0) Cambridge U Pr.

Biotechnology of Perennial Fruit Crops. Ed. by F. Hammerschlag & R. Litz. (Biotechnology in Agriculture Ser.: No. 8). 575p. 1992. text ed. 142.50 (0-85198-708-7) CAB Intl.

Biotechnology of Plant Fats & Oils. Ed. by James B. Rattray. 184p. (C). 1991. 70.00 (0-935315-33-0) AOCS Pr.

Biotechnology of Plant-Microbe Interactions. James P. Nakas & Charles Hagedorn. 336p. 1990. text ed. 65.00 (0-07-045867-7) McGraw.

Biotechnology of Plants & Microorganisms. Ed. by O. J. Crocomo et al. LC 86-23890. 488p. 1987. 89.50 (0-8142-0375-2) Ohio St U Pr.

Biotechnology of Plasma Proteins: Haemostasis, Thrombosis & Iron Proteins. Ed. by Alberto Albertini et al. (Current Studies in Hematology & Blood Transfusion: No. 58). (Illus.). x, 216p. 1991. 168.00 (3-8055-5250-5) S Karger.

Biotechnology of Secondary Products of Plant Cells. Rudolf Endress. LC 93-28522. 1994. 136.00 (0-387-56947-2) Spr-Verlag.

Biotechnology of Vitamins, Pigments & Growth Factors. Ed. by E. J. Vandamme. (Applied Biotechnology Ser.). 444p. 1989. 122.50 (1-85166-325-8) Elsevier.

Biotechnology Patents: A Business Manager's Legal Guide. LC 89-17384. (Special Report Series on Biotechnology: No. 1). 1989. 95.00 (1-55871-133-3, BSP 143) BNA.

Biotechnology: Plant Nutrition: A Bibliography, January 1988-April 1993. Janet Saunders & Robert Warmbrodt. 92p. (Orig.). (C). 1994. pap. text ed. 40.00 (0-7881-0733-X) Diane Pub.

Biotechnology R & D in the European Communities, EUR 14089. Ed. by B. Nieuwenhuis. 96p. 1992. pap. 9.00 (92-826-3743-3, CD-NA-14089-EN-C, Pub. by Europ Com) UNIPUB.

Biotechnology R & D Trends: Science Policy for Development. Ed. by George T. Tzotzos. LC 93-45346. (Annals Ser.: Vol. 700). 1993. write for info. (0-89766-819-7); pap. 70.00 (0-89766-820-0) NY Acad Sci.

Biotechnology Research & Applications: Papers Presented at the Internat. Conf. "Canbiocon 1988" Held at the Palais de Congres, Montreal, Quebec, Canada, 12-14 April 1988. Ed. by J. Gavora et al. 324p. 1989. 66.75 (1-85166-270-7) Elsevier.

Biotechnology Research Directory: 4000 Faculty Profiles. LC 91-27536. 662p. 1991. 125.00 (1-55871-226-7, RDBF) BNA.

Biotechnology Revolution. Ed. by Martin Fransman et al. LC 94-6313. (Illus.). 432p. 1994. pap. 29.95 (0-631-19596-3) Blackwell Pubs.

Biotechnology Revolution: An International Perspective. Alan M. Russell. LC 87-35590. 278p. 1988. text ed. 49. 95 (0-312-01876-2) St Martin.

Biotechnology, Selection Experiments, Parameter Estimation, Design of Breeding Programs, Management of Genetic Resources, Vol. XII. Ed. by G. E. Dickerson & R. K. Johnson. (Proceedings of 3rd World Congress on Genetics Applied to Livestock Production Ser.). 1986. lib. bdg. write for info. (0-9616828-3-3) U Nebr IANR.

Biotechnology Sourcebook. Fairmont Press Staff et al. 372p. 1988. pap. text ed. 95.00 (0-13-079815-0) P-H.

Biotechnology Sourcebook. Shawn L. Linam & M. Todd Jarvis. LC 88-45788. 372p. 1989. pap. text ed. 95.00 (0-88173-073-4) Fairmont Pr.

*__Biotechnology Sources: North & South America.__ Ed. by Barbara Rapp. 144p. 1994. pap. 32.50 (0-938734-87-3) Learned Info.

Biotechnology: Teacher's Guide: A Guide for Saskatchewan Teachers. (Illus.). 80p. (Orig.). (C). 1993. pap. text ed. 45.00 (0-7881-0023-8) Diane Pub.

Biotechnology, Vol. 4: Measuring, Modeling & Control. 2nd ed. Ed. by H. J. Rehm & G. Reed. 658p. 1991. lib. bdg. 365.00 (1-56081-154-4) VCH Pubs.

Biotelemetry International Symposium, 2nd, Davos, May 1974. Biotelemetry International Symposium Staff. Ed. by P. A. Neukomm et al. 1975. 51.25 (3-8055-2103-0) S Karger.

Biotelemetry X. Ed. by Charles J. Amlaner, Jr. LC 88-34782. 755p. 1989. 40.00 (1-55728-082-7) U of Ark Pr.

Biotherapy: A Comprehensive Overview. Paula Rieger. (Nursing Ser.). 500p. 1994. pap. 49.95 (0-86720-707-8) Jones & Bartlett.

Biotherm. limited ed. Frank O'Hara. (Illus.). 1990. 2,750.00 (0-685-56696-X) Arion Pr.

Biothermal-Fluid Sciences. Ed. by Wen-Jei Yang. (Principles & Applications Ser.). (Illus.). 425p. 1989. 136.00 (0-89116-869-9); pap. text ed. 65.00 (0-89116-974-1) Hemisp Pub.

*__Biothermodynamics: The Study of Biochemical Processes at Equilibrium.__ John T. Edsall & H. Gutfreund. LC 82-15971. (Monographs in Molecular Biophysics & Biochemistry). 262p. 1983. pap. 74.70 (0-7837-8490-2, 2049297) Bks Demand.

*__Biothiols in Health & Disease.__ Ed. by Packer & Cadenas. (Antioxidants in Health & Disease Ser.). 721p. 1995. write for info. (0-8247-9654-3) Dekker.

Biotic Communities: Southwestern United States & Northwestern Mexico. Ed. by David E. Brown. LC 94-20777. (Illus.). 344p. 1994. reprint ed. pap. 24.95 (0-87480-459-0) U of Utah Pr.

Biotic Diversity & Germplasm Preservation, Global Imperatives. Ed. by Lloyd Knutson & Allan K. Stoner. (Beltsville Symposia in Agricultural Research Ser.). (C). 1989. lib. bdg. 175.50 (0-7923-0178-1) Kluwer Ac.

Biotic Diversity of Southern Africa: Concepts & Conservation. Ed. by B. J. Huntley. (Illus.). 400p. 1990. 35.00 (0-19-570549-1) OUP.

*__Biotic Feedbacks in the Global Climatic System: Will the Warming Feed the Warming?__ George M. Woodwell & Fred T. MacKenzie. (Illus.). 432p. 1995. text ed. 65.00 (0-19-508640-6) OUP.

Biotic Interactions & Global Change. Ed. by Peter Kareiva et al. LC 92-19162. (Illus.). 480p. 1993. text ed. 68.00x (0-87893-429-4); pap. text ed. 35.95x (0-87893-430-8) Sinauer Assocs.

Biotic Interactions & Soil-Borne Diseases, No. 23: Developments in Agricultural & Managed-Forest Ecology. Ed. by A. B. Beemster et al. 424p. 1991. 120. 00 (0-444-88728-8) Elsevier.

Biotic Interactions in Recent & Fossil Benthic Communities. Ed. by Michael J. Tevesz & Peter L. McCall. LC 83-13953. (Topics in Geobiology Ser.: Vol. 3). 856p. 1983. 145.00 (0-306-41292-6, Plenum Pr) Plenum.

Biotic Message: Evolution Versus Message Theory. Walter J. ReMine. LC 93-92637. 538p. (C). 1993. text ed. 44.95 (0-9637999-0-8) St Paul Sci.

Biotin. Ed. by Hemmige N. Bhagavan. (Annals Ser.: Vol. 447). 441p. 1985. text ed. 100.00 (0-89766-288-1); pap. text ed. 100.00 (0-89766-289-X) NY Acad Sci.

*__Biotransformation: Microbial Degradation of Health-Risk Compounds.__ Ed. by Ved P. Singh. LC 95-11660. (Progress in Industrial Microbiology Ser.: Vol. 32). 1995. write for info. (0-444-81977-0) Elsevier.

Biotransformation of Organic Nitrogen Compounds. Ed. by A. K. Cho & B. Lindeke. (Progress in Basic & Clinical Pharmacology Ser.: Vol. 1). (Illus.). x, 218p. 1988. 158. 50 (3-8055-4650-5) S Karger.

Biotransformations, Vol. 5. 1993. 225.00 (0-85186-147-4, Pub. by Royal Soc Chem UK) CRC Pr.

Biotransformations: A Survey of the Biotransformation of Drugs & Chemicals in Animals, Vol. 1. Ed. by David R. Hawkins. 512p. 1989. 188.95 (0-85186-157-1, Q, Pub. by Royal Soc Chem UK) CRC Pr.

*__Biotransformations Vol. 6: A Survey of the Biotransformations of Drugs & Chemicals in Animals.__ Ed. by David R. Hawkins. 411p. 1994. 235.00 (0-85186-127-X, R6127) CRC Pr.

Biotransformations in Organic Chemistry. K. Faber. LC 92-27806. (Illus.). ix, 319p. 1992. 86.00 (0-387-55762-8) Spr-Verlag.

*__Biotransformations in Organic Chemistry.__ 2nd rev. ed. K. Faber. 366p. 1995. pap. 39.50 (3-540-58503-6) Spr-Verlag.

*__Biotransformations in Organic Chemistry.__ 2nd rev. ed. Kurt Faber. LC 94-45683. 366p. 1995. pap. text ed. 39. 50 (0-387-58503-6) Spr-Verlag.

Biotransformations in Preparative Organic Chemistry: The Use of Isolated Enzymes & Whole Cell Systems in Synthesis. G. H. Davies et al. (Best Synthetic Methods Ser.). 300p. 1989. text ed. 104.00 (0-12-206230-2) Acad Pr.

Biotreatment: The Use of Microorganisms in the Treatment of Hazardous Materials & Hazardous Wastes. 150p. 1989. pap. 35.00 (0-685-50425-5, 0100189) Hazardous Mat Control.

Biotreatment of Agricultural Wastewater. Ed. by Mark E. Huntley. 176p. 1989. 144.00 (0-8493-6378-0, TD755) CRC Pr.

Biotreatment of Hazardous Wastes. Sachchidananda Bhattacharya. (Industrial Health & Safety Ser.). 1992. pap. write for info. (0-442-00940-2) Van Nos Reinhold.

Biotreatment of Industrial & Hazardous Waste. Morris A. Levin. 1993. text ed. 60.00 (0-07-037554-2) McGraw.

Biotreatment Systems, 3 vols., Vol. I. Ed. by Donald L. Wise. (Illus.). 336p. 1988. 110.00 (0-8493-4848-X, TD755, CRC Reprint) Franklin.

Biotreatment Systems, 3 vols., Vol. II. Ed. by Donald L. Wise. (Illus.). 256p. 1988. 148.00 (0-8493-4849-8, TD755, CRC Reprint) Franklin.

Biotreatment Systems, 3 vols., Vol. III. Ed. by Donald L. Wise. (Illus.). 224p. 1988. 129.00 (0-8493-4850-1, TD755, CRC Reprint) Franklin.

*__Biotutorial: A Modular Program for Introductory Biology.__ 5th ed. Edward Samuels. 270p. 1994. pap. text ed. 34. 00 (0-89787-132-4) Gorsuch Scarisbrick.

Biowarning System in the Brain. Ed. by Hiroshi Tagaki et al. 364p. 1989. 97.50 (0-86008-431-0, Pub. by U of Tokyo JA) Col U Pr.

Bio1000, World Biotechnology Company Directory 1987-88. Ed. by Thomas Mysiewicz. (BioEngineering News World Biotechnology Company Directory Ser.). 221p. 1987. pap. write for info. (0-936451-01-7) D Mysiewicz.

Bio1000, 1988-1989. Ed. by Thomas Mysiewicz. LC 78-12345. 304p. 1988. pap. write for info. (0-936451-02-5, 987A) D Mysiewicz.

Bio1000 1991-1992: World Biotechnology Company Directory. Intro. by Thomas Mysiewicz. LC 78-12345. 255p. 1991. pap. write for info. (0-936451-06-8, 987A) D Mysiewicz.

Biped Locomotion. M. Vukobratovic et al. (Communications & Control Engineering Ser.: No. 7). (Illus.). 365p. 1990. 102.00 (0-387-17456-7, 3758) Spr-Verlag.

Bipersonal Field. Robert J. Langs. LC 75-42530. 480p. 1976. 40.00 (0-87668-246-8) Aronson.

Biplane. Richard Bach. 1990. mass mkt. 4.99 (0-440-20657-X) Dell.

Biplane. Richard Bach. (Illus.). 176p. 1983. text ed. 17.95 (0-02-504670-5) Macmillan.

*__Bipolar & Bipolar-MOS Integration.__ Ed. by P. A. H. Hart. LC 94-34771. 1994. write for info. (0-444-81510-4, North Holland) Elsevier.

Bipolar & MOS Analog Integrated Circuit Design. Alan B. Grebene. 894p. 1984. text ed. 119.00 (0-471-08529-4, Wiley-Interscience) Wiley.

Bipolar Junction Transistor. Gerold W. Neudeck. LC 81-14977. (Modular Series on Solid State Devices: No. 3). (Illus.). 85p. 1983. pap. write for info. (0-201-05322-5) Addison-Wesley.

Bipolar Junction Transistor. 2nd ed. Gerold W. Neudeck. (Modular Series on Solid State Devices: Vol. III). (Illus.). 128p. (C). 1989. pap. text ed. 20.50 (0-201-12297-9) Addison-Wesley.

Bipolar Semiconductor Devices. David J. Roulston. 1990. text ed. write for info. (0-07-054120-5) McGraw.

Bipolar Theory of Living Processes: How to Treat Chronic Fatigue, Exhaustion & Death from an Electrical Energy Standpoint. G. W. Crile. 1991. lib. bdg. 88.95 (0-8490-4933-4) Gordon Pr.

*__Bippity Boppity Beads: Beaded Earring Projects for Everyone.__ Janice S. Ackerman. Ed. by Denise E Knight & Monte Smith. (Illus.). 64p. (Orig.). (YA). 1995. pap. 8.95 (0-943604-47-8) Eagles View.

Biproducts. (Advances in Biochemical Engineering-Biotechnology Ser.: Vol. 33). (Illus.). 180p. 1986. 86.00 (0-387-16380-8) Spr-Verlag.

Bipyridinium Herbicides. L. A. Summers. LC 79-41550. 1980. text ed. 168.00 (0-12-676450-6) Acad Pr.

Birational Theory of Degenerations. Ed. by Robert Friedman & David Morrison. (Progress in Mathematics Ser.: Vol. 29). 386p. (C). 1982. text ed. 49.50 (0-8176-3111-9) Birkhauser.

Bircas Kohanim: The Priestly Blessing. Avie Gold. (ArtScroll Mesorah Ser.). 96p. 1986. 13.95 (0-89906-183-4); pap. 10.95 (0-89906-184-2) Mesorah Pubns.

Birch: Bright Tree of Life & Legend. John L. Peyton. LC 94-8264. (Illus.). 74p. (Orig.). 1994. 9.95 (0-939923-42-4) M & W Pub Co.

B

An Asterisk (*) at the beginning of an entry indicates that the title is appearing in BIP for the first time.

Birch Bark Books of Henry Abbott: Sporting Adventures & Nature Observations in the Adirondacks in the Early 1900s. Henry Abbott. LC 80-11071. (Illus.). 1980. reprint ed. 22.50 (*0-916346-40-4*) Harbor Hill Bks.

***Birch Fever.** Martin Pyx. (Orig.). 1994. pap. 5.95 (*1-56201-055-7*) Blue Moon Bks.

Birch Lane Press Presents American Fiction: Best Unpublished Short Stories by Emerging Authors. 1991. pap. 14.95 (*1-55972-074-3*, Birch Ln Pr) Carol Pub Group.

Birch Lane Press Presents American Fiction: Best Unpublished Short Stories By Emerging Authors. Michael White. 1990. pap. 12.95 (*1-55972-029-8*, Birch Ln Pr) Carol Pub Group.

Birch Lane Press Presents American Fiction: The Best Unpublished Short Stories by Emerging Writers, No. 3. Ed. by Michael C. White & Alan Davis. 336p. 1992. pap. 14.95 (*1-55972-121-9*, Birch Ln Pr) Carol Pub Group.

Birchard Music Series: A Comprehensive Book of Music & Activities for the First Grade, Bk. 1. Summy-Birchard Co. Staff. 191p. reprint ed. pap. 54.50 (*0-8357-7262-4*, 2005329) Bks Demand.

Birchard Music Series: A Comprehensive Book of Music & Activities for the First Grade, Bk. 2. Summy-Birchard Co. Staff. 210p. reprint ed. pap. 59.90 (*0-8357-7263-2*, 2005340) Bks Demand.

Birchard Music Series: A Comprehensive Book of Music & Activities for the First Grade, Bk. 3. Summy-Birchard Co. Staff. 212p. reprint ed. pap. 60.50 (*0-8357-7264-0*, 2005341) Bks Demand.

Birchard Music Series: A Comprehensive Book of Music & Activities for the First Grade, Bk. 4. Summy-Birchard Co. Staff. 259p. reprint ed. pap. 73.90 (*0-8357-7265-9*, 2005342) Bks Demand.

Birchard Music Series: A Comprehensive Book of Music & Activities for the First Grade, Bk. 5. Summy-Birchard Co. Staff. 323p. reprint ed. pap. 92.10 (*0-8357-7266-7*, 2005343) Bks Demand.

Birchard Music Series: A Comprehensive Book of Music & Activities for the First Grade, Bk. 6. Summy-Birchard Co. Staff. 384p. reprint ed. pap. 109.50 (*0-8357-7267-5*, 2005344) Bks Demand.

Birchard Music Series: An Extensive Collection of Songs & Music Activities for the General Music Class, Bk. 7. Summy-Birchard Co. Staff. 256p. reprint ed. pap. 73.00 (*0-8357-7268-3*, 2005345) Bks Demand.

Birchard Music Series: An Extensive Collection of Songs & Music Activities for the General Music Class, Bk. 8. Summy-Birchard Co. Staff. 288p. reprint ed. pap. 82.10 (*0-8357-7269-1*, 2005346) Bks Demand.

Birchbark Belles. Ed. by Larry B. Massie. (Illus.). 310p. (Orig.). 1993. 18.95 (*0-9626408-8-3*); pap. 10.95 (*0-9626408-7-5*) Priscilla Pr.

Birchbark Canoe: The Story of an Apprenticeship with the Indians. David Gidmark. (Illus.). 160p. (Orig.). 1989. pap. 14.95 (*0-919431-44-5*) Prairie Hse.

Bircher-Benner Children's Diet Book. M. Bircher-Benner. LC 76-58766. 64p. 1977. pap. 2.50 (*0-87983-141-3*) Keats.

Birches. Robert Frost. LC 87-46359. (Illus.). 32p. (J). (gr. 2-4). 1988. 13.95 (*0-8050-0570-6*, Bks Young Read) H Holt & Co.

Birches. Robert Frost. LC 87-46359. (Illus.). 32p. (J). (gr. 2-4). 1990. pap. 5.95 (*0-8050-1316-4*) H Holt & Co.

Bird. David Burnie. LC 87-26441. (Eyewitness Bks.). (Illus.). 64p. (J). (gr. 5 up). 1988. 16.00 (*0-394-89619-X*); lib. bdg. 16.99 (*0-394-99619-4*) Knopf Bks Yng Read.

Bird. Moira Butterfield. (Nature Chains Ser.). (Illus.). 24p. (J). (ps-1). 1992. pap. 3.95 (*0-671-75892-6*, Litl Simon S&S) S&S Childrens.

Bird. Western Promotional Books Staff. 1993. 2.49 (*0-307-13251-X*) Western Pub.

Bird: Master of Flight. Colin Harrison & Howard Loxton. LC 92-44566. (Illus.). 288p. 1993. 50.00 (*0-8120-6325-2*) Barron.

Bird: The Christmastide Battle. S. L. Marshall. (Vietnam War Ser.: No. 4). (Illus.). 216p. 1983. reprint ed. 22.95 (*0-89839-072-9*) Battery Pr.

Bird: The Legend of Charlie Parker. Ed. by Robert G. Reisner. LC 74-30084. (Roots of Jazz Ser.). (Illus.). 256p. 1975. reprint ed. lib. bdg. 29.50 (*0-306-70677-6*); reprint ed. pap. 12.95 (*0-306-80069-1*) Da Capo.

Bird: The Making of an American Sports Legend. Lee D. Levine. 1989. mass mkt. 5.50 (*0-425-11781-2*) Berkley Pub.

Bird - Parasite Interactions: Ecology, Evolution & Behavior. Ed. by J. E. Loye & M. Zuk. (Oxford Ornithology Ser.: No. 2). (Illus.). 424p. 1991. 69.95 (*0-19-857738-9*) OUP.

Bird Alphabet Book. Jerry Pallotta. (Jerry Pallotta's Alphabet Bks.). (Illus.). 32p. (J). (ps-3). 1989. 14.95 (*0-88106-457-2*); pap. 6.95 (*0-88106-451-3*) Charlesbridge Pub.

***Bird Alphabet Book.** Jerry Pallotta. (Jerry Pallotta's Alphabet Bks.). (Illus.). 32p. (J). (ps-3). 1989. lib. bdg. 15.88 (*0-88106-677-X*) Charlesbridge Pub.

Bird Anatomy, No. 2: Avian Structure & Function. Noble S. Proctor & Patrick J. Lynch. mac hd 75.00 (*0-300-05403-3*) Yale U Pr.

Bird & Bough. John Burroughs. (Works of John Burroughs). 1989. reprint ed. lib. bdg. 79.00 (*0-7812-2193-5*) Rprt Serv.

Bird & I. Fazil Husnu Daglarca. Ed. by Stanley H. Barkan. Tr. by Talat Sait Halman. (Cross-Cultural Review Chapbook Ser.: No. 4: Turkish Poetry 1). 16p. (ENG & TUR.). 1980. 15.00 (*0-89304-846-1*, CCC129); pap. 5.00 (*0-89304-803-8*); audio 10.00 (*0-89304-828-3*) Cross-Cultrl NY.

Bird & Nature Photography. Laurie Campbell. (Illus.). 160p. 1990. 29.95 (*0-7153-9470-3*, Pub. by D & C Pub UK) Sterling.

Bird & the Bell, with Other Poems. Christopher P. Cranch. LC 72-4960. (Romantic Tradition in American Literature Ser.). 344p. 1978. reprint ed. 28.95 (*0-405-04632-4*) Ayer.

Bird Artist. Howard Norman. 1994. 20.00 (*0-374-11330-0*) FS&G.

***Bird Artist.** large type ed. Howard Norman. LC 95-3156. (Large Print Book Ser.). 1995. pap. 19.95 (*1-56895-094-2*) Wheeler Pub.

***Bird Artist: A Novel.** Howard Norman. 320p. 1995. pap. 13.00 (*0-312-13027-9*) St Martin.

Bird Artist in Scotland. Donald Watson. (Illus.). 160p. 1989. 34.95 (*0-85493-167-8*, Pub. by V Gollancz UK) Trafalgar.

Bird Atlas. Barbara Taylor. LC 93-18225. (Illus.). 64p. (J). (gr. 4 up). 1993. 19.95 (*1-56458-327-9*) Dorling Kindersley.

***Bird Atlas of Botswana.** Huw Penry. (Illus.). 320p. Date not set. 55.75 (*0-86980-894-X*, Pub. by Univ Natal Pr SA); pap. 45.15 (*0-86980-895-8*, Pub. by Univ Natal Pr SA) Intl Spec Bk.

Bird Banding. Elliott McClure. (Illus.). 340p. (Orig.). 1984. pap. 15.00 (*0-910286-65-5*) Boxwood.

Bird Behavior. Robert Burton. Ed. by Charles Elliott & Bruce Campbell. LC 84-48677. (Illus.). 224p. 1985. 18. 95 (*0-394-53957-5*) Knopf.

Bird Biographies of W. H. Hudson. W. H. Hudson. LC 88-34095. 210p. (Orig.). (C). 1988. reprint ed. lib. bdg. 27. 00x (*0-8095-4000-2*) Borgo Pr.

Bird Blow Flies (Protocalliphora) in North America: (Diptera: Calliphoridae), with Notes on the Palearctic Species. Curtis W. Sabrosky et al. LC 89-30488. 336p. 1990. pap. 17.95 (*0-87474-865-8*) Smithsonian.

Bird Book & the Bird Feeder. Neil Dawe & Karen Dawe. LC 88-40225. (J). (gr. k-7). 1988. pap. 10.95 (*0-89480-614-9*, 1614) Workman Pub.

Bird Books & Bird Art: An Outline of the Literary History & Iconography of Descriptive Ornithology, Based Principally on the Collection in the University Library at Copenhagen. Jean Anker. LC 73-17795. (Natural Sciences in America Ser.). (Illus.). 326p. 1974. reprint ed. 25.95 (*0-405-05705-9*) Ayer.

Bird Books & Bird Arts: An Outline of the Literary History & Iconography of Descriptive Ornithology. Jean Anker. (Illus.). 251p. 1990. reprint ed. lib. bdg. 55. 00 (*0-685-48747-4*) Lubrecht & Cramer.

Bird Boy. Sidney Berger. (Illus.). 36p. (Orig.). (J). (gr. 2 up). 1988. pap. 4.00 (*0-88680-295-4*) I E Clark.

***Bird Brains: The Intelligence of Crows, Ravens, Magpies & Jays.** Candace Savage. LC 95-1169. (Illus.). 144p. 1995. 25.00 (*0-87156-379-7*) Sierra.

Bird Buddies. Meredith Corporation, Better Homes & Gardens Staff. (Max the Dragon Project Book Ser.). (Illus.). 32p. (J). (ps-12). 1991. reprint ed. lib. bdg. 10.95 (*1-878363-31-X*) Forest Hse.

Bird Business. 121p. 1981. reprint ed. 5.00 (*0-318-14370-4*, GR3042) Humane Soc.

Bird by Bird: Instructions on Writing & Life. Anne Lamott. LC 94-5448. 1994. 21.00 (*0-679-43520-4*) Pantheon.

***Bird by Bird: Some Instructions on Writing & Life.** Anne Lamott. LC 95-10225. 1995. write for info. (*0-385-48001-6*, Anchor NY) Doubleday.

Bird Call on Hood Canal: A Sharing of Bird Sightings along This Inland Saltwater Shoreline. Evelyn S. Walseth. LC 92-75667. (Illus.). 58p. (Orig.). 1993. pap. 5.95 (*0-9635361-1-7*) Burton Bks.

Bird Care Book. 2nd rev. ed. Sheldon L. Gerstenfeld. 1989. pap. 13.46 (*0-201-09559-9*) Addison-Wesley.

Bird Carving Basics: Bills & Beaks. Curtis J. Badger. LC 90-9491. (Illus.). 96p. (Orig.). 1991. pap. 12.95 (*0-8117-2340-2*) Stackpole.

Bird Carving Basics: Eyes. Curtis J. Badger. LC 90-9491. (Illus.). 96p. (Orig.). 1990. pap. 12.95 (*0-8117-2334-8*) Stackpole.

Bird Carving Basics: Feet. Curtis J. Badger. LC 90-9491. (Illus.). 96p. (Orig.). 1990. pap. 12.95 (*0-8117-2338-0*) Stackpole.

Bird Carving Basics: Habitat. Curtis J. Badger. LC 90-9491. (Illus.). 96p. 1992. pap. 12.95 (*0-8117-3053-0*) Stackpole.

Bird Carving Basics: Heads. Curtis J. Badger. LC 90-9491. (Illus.). 96p. (Orig.). 1991. pap. 12.95 (*0-8117-2339-9*) Stackpole.

Bird Carving Basics: How to Compete. Curtis J. Badger. (Illus.). 96p. 1994. pap. 17.95 (*0-8117-3056-5*) Stackpole.

Bird Carving Basics: Painting. Curtis J. Badger. LC 90-9491. (Illus.). 96p. 1991. pap. 17.95 (*0-8117-3051-4*) Stackpole.

Bird Carving Basics: Songbird Painting. Curtis J. Badger. (Illus.). 96p. (Orig.). 1993. pap. 17.95 (*0-8117-3055-7*) Stackpole.

Bird Carving Basics: Special Painting Techniques. Curtis J. Badger. LC 90-9491. (Illus.). 96p. 1992. pap. 17.95 (*0-8117-3052-2*) Stackpole.

Bird Carving Basics: Texturing. Curtis J. Badger. LC 90-9491. (Illus.). 112p. 1991. pap. 12.95 (*0-8117-3050-6*) Stackpole.

Bird Carving Basics: Tools. Curtis J. Badger. (Illus.). 96p. (Orig.). 1993. pap. 12.95 (*0-8117-3054-9*) Stackpole.

Bird CCP Review Course. Floyd Bird. 280p. 1989. Book & cassette. 265.00 (*0-9616174-1-1*) Bird Prof Pubns.

Bird CDP Review Course. Floyd Bird. 300p. 1989. audio 250.00 (*0-9616174-0-3*) Bird Prof Pubns.

Bird Census Techniques. Colin J. Bibby et al. (Illus.). 257p. 1992. text ed. 42.00 (*0-12-095830-9*) Acad Pr.

Bird Chain. Pauline Cartwright. LC 93-20805. (J). 1994. 4.25 (*0-383-03736-0*) SRA Schl Grp.

Bird Conservation, No. 1. Ed. by Stanley A. Temple. LC 83-50082. 192p. 1983. 17.50 (*0-299-08980-0*); pap. 12.95 (*0-299-08984-3*) U of Wis Pr.

Bird Conservation, No. 3. Ed. by Jerome A. Jackson. LC 84-641048. 156p. 1989. text ed. 17.50 (*0-299-11120-2*); pap. text ed. 12.95 (*0-299-11124-5*) U of Wis Pr.

Bird Conservation, Vol. 2. Ed. by Stanley A. Temple. LC 84-641048. (Illus.). 156p. 1986. 17.50 (*0-299-10220-3*); pap. text ed. 12.95 (*0-299-10224-6*) U of Wis Pr.

Bird Conservation & Farming Policy in the European Community. Ed. by Deborah Pain & James Dixon. (Illus.). 400p. 1996. boxed write for info. (*0-12-544280-7*) Acad Pr.

Bird Day Afternoon. Matsuo Allard. 32p. 1978. pap. 3.50 (*0-913719-06-4*) High-Coo Pr.

Bird Decoy: An American Art Form. A Catalog of Carvings Exhibited at the Sheldon Memorial Art Gallery, Lincoln Nebraska. Ed. by Paul A. Johnsgard. LC 76-2072. (Illus.). xii, 191p. 1976. 25.00 (*0-8032-0887-1*) U of Nebr Pr.

Bird Designs Stained Glass Pattern Book. Carolyn Relei. (Illus.). 64p. 1989. pap. 4.95 (*0-486-25947-1*) Dover.

Bird Discovery Library, 6 bks., Set. Lynn Stone. (Illus.). 144p. (J). (gr. k-5). 1989. lib. bdg. 71.64 (*0-86592-320-5*) Rourke Corp.

Bird Disease by Stroud. Robert Stroud. 17.95 (*0-86622-731-8*, AP-926) TFH Pubns.

Bird Diseases: 'An Introduction to the Study of Birds in Health & Disease' L. Arnall & I. F. Keymer. (Illus.). 1975. 39.95 (*0-87666-950-X*, H-964) TFH Pubns.

Bird Dogs & Upland Game Birds. Jack Stuart. LC 83-14247. (Other Dog Bks.). (Illus.). 1983. 24.95 (*0-87714-107-X*); pap. 14.95 (*0-685-73690-3*) Denlingers.

Bird Dogs Can't Fly. Mary J. Auch. LC 93-2746. (Illus.). (J). (ps-3). 1993. lib. bdg. 15.95 (*0-8234-1050-1*) Holiday.

***Bird-Eating Spider.** James E. Gerholdt. LC 95-12366. (J). 1995. write for info. (*1-56239-507-6*) Abdo & Dghtrs.

Bird Eating Spiders. L. Martin. (Spider Discovery Library). (Illus.). 24p. (J). (gr. k-5). 1988. lib. bdg. 11.94 (*0-86592-966-1*) Rourke Corp.

Bird Egg Feather Nest. Maryjo Koch. 96p. 1994. 30.00 (*0-00-255456-9*) Collins SF.

Bird Embryology. V. V. Rol'nik. 386p. 1970. text ed. 102. 50 (*0-7065-1014-3*, Pub. by Keter Pub IS) Coronet Bks.

Bird Etchings: The Illustrators & Their Books, 1655-1855. Christine E. Jackson. LC 84-27438. (Illus.). 288p. (C). 1985. 58.95 (*0-8014-1695-7*); pap. 19.95 (*0-8014-9684-5*) Cornell U Pr.

Bird-Eyes. Madelyn Arnold. LC 88-4439. 201p. 1988. pap. 8.95 (*0-931188-62-8*) Seal Pr Feminist.

Bird Facts. A. Ganeri. (Facts & Lists Ser.). (Illus.). 48p. (J). (gr. 3-7). 1991. lib. bdg. 12.96 (*0-88110-530-9*, Usborne); pap. 5.95 (*0-7460-0619-5*, Usborne) EDC.

Bird Family History. Booth, Maycock & Poulson Staff. 171p. 1994. reprint ed. lib. bdg. 36.50 (*0-8328-4116-1*); reprint ed. pap. 26.50 (*0-8328-4117-X*) Higginson Bk Co.

Bird Feeder Banquet. Michael Martchenko. (Illus.). 24p. (Orig.). (J). (gr. k-3). 1990. 14.95 (*1-55037-147-9*, Pub. by Annick CN); pap. 4.95 (*1-55037-146-0*, Pub. by Annick CN) Firefly Bks Ltd.

Bird Feeder Book: An Easy Guide to Attracting, Identifying, & Understanding Your Feeder Birds. Donald W. Stokes. (Illus.). 128p. 1987. pap. 11.95 (*0-316-81733-3*) Little.

Bird Feeder Book: How to Build Unique Bird Feeders from the Purely Practical to the Simply Outrageous. Thom Boswell. LC 92-40584. (Illus.). 144p. 1993. 19.95 (*0-8069-0295-7*) Sterling.

***Bird Feeder Book: How to Build Unique Bird Feeders from the Purely Practical to the Simply Outrageous.** Thom Boswell. (Illus.). 144p. 1995. pap. 14.95 (*0-8069-0296-5*) Sterling.

Bird Feeder Book & Kit. (Illus.). 1995. 40.00 (*0-8069-0460-7*) Sterling.

Bird Finder: A Guide to Common Birds of Eastern North America. Roger J. Lederer. (Illus.). 60p. 1990. pap. 2.50 (*0-912550-18-X*, T) Nature Study.

Bird Finder's Three-Year Notebook. 4th rev. ed. Paul S. Eriksson. (Illus.). 384p. 1989. spiral bd. 15.95 (*0-8397-1031-3*) Eriksson.

***Bird Finding Guide to Alaska.** Letheby. (Illus.). 152p. (Orig.). 1994. pap. 14.95 (*0-9637765-9-2*) Cinclus Pubns.

***Bird Finding Guide to Denali National Park.** K. Kertell & A. Seegert. (Illus.). 32p. 1995. pap. 3.00 (*0-9602876-7-1*) Alaska Natural.

Bird-Finding Guide to Ontario. enl. rev. ed. Clive E. Goodwin. (Illus.). 384p. 1995. pap. 24.95 (*0-8020-6904-5*) U of Toronto Pr.

Bird-Finding Guide to Ontario. Clive E. Goodwin. (Illus.). 256p. 1982. reprint ed. pap. 16.95 (*0-8020-6494-9*) U of Toronto Pr.

Bird Fisherman. Nicole Schneegans. (I Love to Read Collection). (Illus.). (J). (gr. 3-8). 1992. lib. bdg. 12.79 (*0-89565-896-8*) Childs World.

Bird Flew By: And Other Topics from the File. Katherine N. Eckhart. (Illus.). 128p. (Orig.). 1993. pap. text ed. 19. 95 (*1-879243-08-3*) Writers Helpers.

Bird Habitats in Britain. R. J. Fuller. (Illus.). 352p. 1990. text ed. 39.95 (*0-85661-031-3*, 784631, Pub. by Poyser UK) Acad Pr.

Bird Habitats in Britain. R. J. Fuller. (Illus.). 352p. 1990. 31.50 (*0-685-47236-1*, 784629, Pub. by Poyser UK) Acad Pr.

Bird House Book & Kit: How to Build Fanciful Bird Houses & Feeders, from the Purely Practical to the Absolutely Outrageous. Bruce Woods & David Schoonmaker. (Illus.). 144p. 1991. 19.95 (*0-8069-8324-8*) Sterling.

Bird House Book & Kit: How to Build Fanciful Bird Houses & Feeders, from the Purely Practical to the Absolutely Outrageous. Bruce Woods & David Schoonmaker. (Illus.). 144p. 1995. 40.00 (*0-8069-5902-9*) Sterling.

Bird House Man. Walter P. Eaton. LC 72-6078. (Short Story Index Reprint Ser.). (Illus.). 1977. reprint ed. 22. 95 (*0-8369-4215-9*) Ayer.

Bird Houses see Homes for Wildlife

Bird Hunter. James Nichols & C. M. Nichols. 192p. 1984. pap. 2.25 (*0-8439-2081-5*) Dorchester Pub Co.

Bird Hunter. large type ed. Nichols. 1991. 17.95 (*0-7451-8044-2*, AH092, Atlantic Lrg Print); pap. 15.95 (*0-7927-0508-4*, AS0128, Atlantic Lrg Print) Chivers N Amer.

Bird Hunter's Handbook. Bob Gooch. LC 88-82701. (Illus.). 264p. (Orig.). 1988. pap. 9.95 (*0-937866-16-4*) Atlantic Pub Co.

Bird Hunting Know-How see Bird Hunting Tactics

Bird Hunting Tactics. rev. ed. David M. Duffey. Orig. Title: Bird Hunting Know-How. (Illus.). 168p. 1989. 19. 50 (*0-932558-52-6*) Willow Creek Pr.

B

Bird Impressions: A Personal View of Birds. Darren Rees. (Illus.). 128p. 1994. 42.95 (*1-85310-286-5*) Voyageur Pr.

***Bird in a Cage.** Lee Martin. LC 95-14723. 1995. 20.95 (*0-312-13028-7*) St Martin.

Bird in Her Hair. Phillip Bonosky. Ed. by Adelaide Bean. LC 87-3432. (Illus.). 180p. (Orig.). 1987. pap. 5.95 (*0-7178-0661-8*) Intl Pubs Co.

Bird in the Bush. Kenneth Rexroth. LC 75-111860. (Essay Index Reprint Ser.). 1977. 21.95 (*0-8369-1623-9*) Ayer.

Bird in the Bush: A Naturalist's Guide to Watching Birds. Don A. Hall. LC 86-50859. (Illus.). 160p. (Orig.). 1986. pap. 7.95 (*0-9619886-0-6*) Words & Pictures Unltd.

Bird in the Hand. Ann Cleeves. 1987. mass mkt. 4.99 (*0-449-13349-4*, GM) Fawcett.

Bird in the Hand. Mann. 1994. 22.00 (*0-671-88995-8*); pap. 12.00 (*0-671-88994-X*) P-H Gen Ref & Trav.

Bird in the Hand. Mann. 1994. pap. 12.00 (*0-671-89779-9*) P-H Gen Ref & Trav.

Bird in the Hand. Nigel Snell. (Illus.). 32p. (J). (ps-1). 1992. 13.95 (*0-237-60295-4*, Pub. by Evans Bros Ltd UK) Trafalgar.

Bird in the House: Stories. Margaret Laurence. (Phoenix Fiction Ser.). 208p. (C). 1993. pap. 9.95 (*0-226-46934-4*) U Ch Pr.

Bird in the House: The Story of Wing Haven Garden. Mary N. Kratt. LC 90-72015. (Illus.). 80p. (Orig.). 1991. pap. 9.50 (*0-9628692-0-1*) Wing Haven.

Bird in the Tree. Elizabeth Goudge. 339p. 1976. lib. bdg. 25.95 (*0-89966-099-1*) Buccaneer Bks.

Bird in the Tree. Elizabeth Goudge. 1976. 22.95 (*0-8488-1337-5*) Amereon Ltd.

Bird in the Tree. Elizabeth Goudge. 288p. 1992. pap. 10.99 (*0-89283-758-6*) Servant.

Bird in the Waterfall. J. Dennis. Date not set. 22.50 (*0-06-017094-8*, HarpT) HarpC.

Bird, Kansas. Tony Parker. 1989. 19.95 (*0-394-57794-9*) Knopf.

Bird, Kansas. Tony Parker. 352p. 1990. pap. 8.95 (*0-380-71137-0*) Avon.

***Bird Language.** Diana Rivera. LC 93-30723. 114p. 1994. 10.00 (*0-927534-41-X*) Biling Rev-Pr.

Bird Life. (Golden Guide Ser.). (Illus.). (YA). 1991. write for info. (*0-307-24079-7*, Golden Pr) Western Pub.

Bird Life. Ian Wallace et al. (Mysteries & Marvels Ser.). (Illus.). 32p. (J). (gr. 4-7). 1985. lib. bdg. 13.96 (*0-88110-172-9*); pap. 5.95 (*0-86020-841-9*) EDC.

Bird Life in Hawaii. Andrew J. Berger. LC 83-81140. (Illus.). 72p. 1983. pap. 7.95 (*0-89610-090-1*) Island Heritage.

Bird Life in Hawaii. 2nd ed. Andrew J. Berger. (Illus.). 72p. 1993. pap. 6.95 (*0-89610-282-3*, 24525-000) Island Heritage.

Bird Life in Wington: Practical Parables for Young People. John C. Reid. (Illus.). 142p. (J). (gr. 1-4). 1990. reprint ed. pap. 7.99 (*0-8028-4062-0*) Eerdmans.

Bird Life of Coasts & Estuaries. Peter N. Ferns. (Bird Life Ser.: No. 2). (Illus.). 350p. (C). 1993. 54.95 (*0-521-34569-3*) Cambridge U Pr.

Bird Life of Mountain & Upland. Derek A. Ratcliffe. (Bird Life Ser.). (Illus.). 280p. (C). 1991. 44.95 (*0-521-33123-4*) Cambridge U Pr.

***Bird Life of North Carolina's Shining Rock Wilderness.** Marcus B. Simpson, Jr. Ed. by Eloise F. Potter. (Occasional Papers of the North Carolina Biological Survey). (Illus.). 32p. (Orig.). 1994. pap. text ed. 5.00 (*0-917134-20-6*) NC Natl Sci.

***Bird Life of Woodland & Forest.** Robert J. Fuller. (Bird Life Ser.: No. 3). (Illus.). 250p. (C). 1995. 64.95 (*0-521-33118-8*) Cambridge U Pr.

Bird-Lover in the West. Olive T. Miller. LC 76-125753. (American Environmental Studies). 1971. reprint ed. 19. 95 (*0-405-02679-X*) Ayer.

Bird Lovers. Jens Bjorneboe. Tr. by Fred Wasser. (Sun & Moon Classics Ser.: No. 43). 96p. (Orig.). 1994. pap. 9.95 (*1-55713-146-5*) Sun & Moon CA.

Bird-Lovers Anthology. Comp. by Clinton Scollard & Jessie B. Rittenhouse. LC 72-11919. (Granger Index Reprint Ser.). 1977. reprint ed. 23.95 (*0-8369-6407-1*) Ayer.

Bird-Lovers' Anthology. Clinton Scollard. (Granger Index Reprint Ser.). 320p. 1982. reprint ed. lib. bdg. 18.00 (*0-8290-0813-6*) Irvington.

Bird Lover's Life List & Journal. Boston Museum of Fine Arts Staff & Norman Boucher. (Illus.). 240p. 1992. 24. 95 (*0-8212-1993-6*) Bulfinch Pr.

An Asterisk (*) at the beginning of an entry indicates that the title is appearing in BIP for the first time.

Bird Lover's Life List & Journal. Norman Boucher & Museum of Fine Arts, Boston Staff. (Illus.). 240p. 1994. 14.95 (*0-8212-2138-8*) Little.

Bird Magic. Blake Johnson. (Illus.). 128p. 1985. lib. bdg. 12.95 (*0-9615685-1-8*) Blke.

Bird Mazes. Patricia Wynne. (Little Activity Bks.). (J). 1994. pap. 1.00 (*0-486-28112-4*) Dover.

Bird Mazes: Educational Activity-Coloring Book. Peter M. Spizzirri. Ed. by Linda Spizzirri. (Illus.). 32p. (J). (gr. k-5). 1984. pap. 1.00 (*0-86545-060-9*) Spizzirri.

Bird Meets Fish. Florita Chipangu. (Illus.). 36p. (J). 1993. pap. 2.50 (*1-878181-07-6*) Discovery Comics.

Bird Migration. Thomas Alerstam. Tr. & Pref. by David A. Christie. (Illus.). 428p. (C). 1993. pap. 37.95 (*0-521-44822-0*) Cambridge U Pr.

Bird Migration. Roma Gans. (J). Date not set. 13.95 (*0-06-020224-6*, HarpT); lib. bdg. 13.89 (*0-06-020225-4*, HarpT) HarpC.

Bird Migration. Liz Oram & R. Robin Baker. LC 91-12120. (Migrations Ser.). (Illus.). 48p. (J). (gr. 4-8). 1992. lib. bdg. 22.80 (*0-8114-2925-3*) Raintree Steck-V.

Bird Migration. Donald R. Griffin. LC 74-76321. (Illus.). 192p. 1974. reprint ed. pap. 4.95 (*0-486-20529-0*) Dover.

Bird Migration: A General Survey. Peter Gerthold. Tr. by Hans-Gunther Baueer & Tricia Tomlinson. LC 93-33020. (Ornithology Ser.: No. 3). (Illus.). 256p. (C). 1994. 52.50 (*0-19-854692-0*); pap. 26.50 (*0-19-854691-2*) OUP.

Bird Migration: An Illustrated Account. Robert Burton. (Illus.). 160p. 1992. lib. bdg. 29.95 (*0-8160-2781-1*) Facts on File.

Bird Migration: Physiology & Ecophysiology. Ed. by Eberhard Gwinner. (Illus.). 440p. 1990. 122.00 (*0-387-50855-4*) Spr-Verlag.

Bird Migration in Africa, Vol. I. Kai Curry-Lindahl. LC 80-40245. 1982. text ed. 92.00 (*0-12-200101-X*) Acad Pr.

Bird Migrations: Ecological & Physiological Factors. B. E. Bykhovski. 304p. 1973. text ed. 73.50 (*0-7065-1347-9*, Pub. by Keter Pub IS) Coronet Bks.

Bird Migrations: Ecological & Physiological Factors. Ed. by B. E. Bykohovskii. LC 73-12279. 298p. 1979. 39.50 (*0-470-12890-9*) Krieger.

Bird Navigation. 2nd ed. Geoffrey V. Matthews. LC 68-23181. (Cambridge Monographs in Experimental Biology: Vol. 3). 207p. reprint ed. pap. 59.00 (*0-8357-7270-5*, 2027236) Bks Demand.

Bird Navigation: The Solution of a Mystery? R. Robin Baker. 256p. (C). 1984. 37.50 (*0-8419-0946-6*); pap. 24.50 (*0-8419-0947-4*) Holmes & Meier.

Bird Nests. Photos by Gerry Ellis. LC 92-44031. (Illus.). 1993. 17.95 (*0-00-255110-1*) Collins SF.

***Bird of Barjag.** Elsebeth Rowe. 1995. 10.95 (*0-8062-5240-5*) Carlton.

Bird of Endless Time. James Laughlin. LC 88-63226. 128p. (Orig.). 1989. 15.00 (*1-55659-020-2*); pap. 9.00 (*1-55659-021-0*) Copper Canyon.

Bird of Happiness. large type ed. Sally Stewart. 593p. 1993. 21.95 (*0-7505-0450-1*, Pub. by Magna Print Bks) Ulverscroft.

Bird of Jove. David Bruce. LC 93-21439. (Louise Lindsey Merrick Natural Environment Ser.: No. 17). (Illus.). 288p. 1994. reprint ed. pap. 13.95 (*0-89096-604-4*) Tex A&M Univ Pr.

Bird of Light. John Hay. 160p. 1993. pap. 8.95 (*0-393-31001-9*) Norton.

Bird of Nothing & Other Poems: Prospero Saiz. Prospero Saiz. (Illus.). 167p. (Orig.). 1993. pap. 20.00 (*0-941160-11-4*) Ghost Pony Pr.

***Bird of Nothing & Other Poems: Prospero Saiz.** deluxe limited ed. Prospero Saiz. (Illus.). 167p. (Orig.). 1993. pap. 35.00 (*0-614-04767-6*) Ghost Pony Pr.

Bird of Paradise. Vicki Covington. 256p. 1991. mass mkt. 4.95 (*0-8041-0798-X*) Ivy Books.

Bird of Paradise. Elizabeth Daniels. 448p. (Orig.). 1991. pap. 4.50 (*0-8439-3185-X*) Dorchester Pub Co.

Bird of Paradise. Barney Vincelette. (Illus.). 200p. 1985. lib. bdg. 7.00 (*0-9614096-0-6*) Excelsior Pub.

Bird of Paradise. large type ed. Vicki Covington. (General Ser.). 322p. 1991. lib. bdg. 19.95 (*0-8161-5118-0*, Large Print Bks) Hall.

Bird of Paradise & Other Sabbath Stories. Steven M. Rosman. (Illus.). (Orig.). 1994. pap. 8.95 (*0-8074-0529-9*, 123725) UAHC.

***Bird of Paradox: Unpublished Writings of Wilson Duff.** E. N. Anderson. 1995. pap. 24.95 (*0-88839-360-1*) Hancock House.

Bird of Passage. Nicola Thorne. 1993. mass mkt. 4.99 (*0-06-100584-3*, Harp PBks) HarpC.

Bird of Passage. large type ed. Nicola Thorne. 1992. 19.95 (*0-7927-1257-9*, E0037, Eagle Lrg Print) Chivers N Amer.

Bird of Passage. large type ed. Nicola Thorne. 1992. pap. 17.95 (*0-7927-1256-0*, Paragon Lrg Print) Chivers N Amer.

Bird of Passage: Recollections of a Physicist. Rudolf Peierls. 350p. 1988. reprint ed. pap. text ed. 14.95 (*0-691-02416-2*) Princeton U Pr.

Bird of Passage: The Story of My Life. Otto Lang. Ed. by Marnie H. Pavelich. (Illus.). 416p. 1994. 40.00 (*1-56044-294-8*); pap. 24.00 (*1-56044-281-6*) Falcon Pr MT.

Bird of Peace Is Born in Petersburg. J. Wayne Beachy. (Illus.). (Orig.). (J). (gr. 5). 1981. pap. 2.50 (*0-9608084-0-X*) B Hawkins Studio.

Bird of Prey. Mary Hoffman. LC 86-17832. (Animals in the Wild Ser.). (Illus.). 24p. (J). (gr. k-5). 1987. lib. bdg. 9.95 (*0-8172-2701-6*); pap. 3.95 (*0-8114-6872-0*) Raintree Steck-V.

***Bird of Time.** Melvin Hall. (American Autobiography Ser.). 307p. 1995. reprint ed. lib. bdg. 89.00 (*0-7812-8544-5*) Rprt Serv.

Bird of Utica: Life, Thought & Art of Sylvia H. Bliss, 1870-1963. Forest K. Davis. LC 86-20558. 1986. 15.00 (*0-912362-05-7*) Adamant Pr.

Bird on Basketball: How-to Strategies from the Great Celtics Champion. 3rd rev. ed. Larry Bird & John Bischoff. (Illus.). 128p. 1988. pap. 12.50 (*0-201-14209-0*) Addison-Wesley.

Bird Paintings of C. G. Finch-Davies. C. G. Finch-Davies. 310p. 1986. boxed 160.00 (*0-87556-263-9*) Saifer.

Bird Paintings of C. G. Finch-Davies. Alan Kemp. (Illus.). 1989. 160.00 (*0-87556-736-3*) Saifer.

Bird Paintings of CG Finch Davies. Alan Kemp. 312p. (C). 1989. 600.00 (*1-85368-065-6*, Pub. by New Holland Pubs UK) St Mut.

Bird Path: Collected Longer Poems. Kenneth White. 240p. 1992. 29.95 (*1-85158-245-2*, Pub. by Mnstream UK) Trafalgar.

Bird Poems. Ed. by Miriam Irwin. (Illus.). 32p. 1984. 18.00 (*0-88014-067-4*) Mosaic Pr OH.

Bird Population Studies: Relevance to Conservation & Management. Ed. by Christopher M. Perrins et al. (Ornithology Ser.: No. 1). (Illus.). 704p. 1993. pap. 37.50 (*0-19-854082-5*) OUP.

Bird Populations of Aspen Forests in Western North America. J. A. Douglas Flack. 97p. 1976. 7.50 (*0-943610-19-2*) Am Ornithologists.

Bird Respiration, 2 vols., Set. Ed. by Seller. 1987. 220.00 (*0-8493-4690-8*, QL698) CRC Pr.

***Bird Song: Biological Themes & Variations.** C. K. Catchpole & P. J.B. Slater. (Illus.). 250p. (C). 1995. 32.95 (*0-521-41799-6*) Cambridge U Pr.

Bird Sounds & Their Meaning. Rosemary Jellis. LC 83-73212. (Illus.). 256p. 1984. pap. 18.95 (*0-8014-9276-9*) Cornell U Pr.

Bird Stencil Designs. Robert G. Bush. (Pictorial Archive Ser.). (Illus.). 64p. (Orig.). 1991. pap. 4.95 (*0-486-26704-0*) Dover.

Bird Stickers. Nina Barbaresi. (Illus.). (J). (gr. k-3). 1991. pap. 1.00 (*0-486-26813-6*) Dover.

Bird Student: An Autobiography. George M. Sutton. (Corrie Herring Hooks Ser.: No. 4). (Illus.). 232p. 1980. 22.95 (*0-292-70727-4*) U of Tex Pr.

Bird Study. Boy Scouts of America. (Illus.). 64p. (J). (gr. 6-12). 1984. pap. 1.85 (*0-8395-3282-2*, 33282) BSA.

Bird Table Book: How to Attract Wild Birds to Your Garden. Tony Soper. (Illus.). 192p. 1994. 19.95 (*0-7153-0053-9*, Pub. by D & C Pub UK) Sterling.

Bird Talk. Caroline Dorman. 1969. 6.95 (*0-87511-024-X*) Claitors.

***Bird Talk.** Keeshig-Tobias. Date not set. per. 6.95 (*0-920813-89-5*, Pub. by Sister Vision CN) InBook.

Bird That Never Flew. John Steele. (Illus.). 320p. 1992. 34.95 (*1-85619-124-9*, Sinclair-Stevenson) Trafalgar.

Bird, the Beast & the Fishes Tail. A. W. Spacey. (C). 1989. 40.00 (*1-85022-017-4*, Pub. by Dyllansow Truran UK) St Mut.

Bird, the Frog, & the Light: A Fable. Avi. LC 93-4886. (Illus.). 32p. (J). (ps-2). 1994. 15.95 (*0-531-06808-0*); lib. bdg. 15.99 (*0-531-08658-5*) Orchard Bks Watts.

Bird Trapping & Bird Banding: A Handbook for Trapping Methods All over the World. Hans Bub. Tr. by Frances Hamerstrom & Karin Wuertz-Schaefer. LC 90-34188. (Illus.). 448p. 1991. 72.50 (*0-8014-2525-5*) Cornell U Pr.

***Bird Trapping & Bird Banding: A Handbook for Trapping Methods All over the World.** Hans Bub. Tr. by Frances Hamerstrom & Karin Wuertz-Schaefer. (Illus.). 448p. 1995. pap. 29.95 (*0-8014-8312-3*) Cornell U Pr.

Bird Turd Peppers & Other Delights. Burley Packwood. (Illus.). 313p. (Orig.). 1993. pap. 7.95 (*0-9624358-1-3*) Quantum Pr AZ.

Bird Walk Through the Bible. Virginia C. Holmgren. 224p. 1988. reprint ed. pap. 4.95 (*0-486-25566-2*) Dover.

Bird Watch. Jane Yolen. (Illus.). 48p. (J). 1990. 15.95 (*0-399-21612-X*, Philomel Bks) Putnam Pub Group.

Bird Watch: An Integrated Activity Unit. Bev McKay. (Illus.). 32p. 1993. pap. text ed. 4.95 (*0-86530-226-X*) Incentive Pubns.

Bird Watchers. May Taylor. 148p. 1984. 35.00 (*0-7212-0607-7*, Pub. by Regency Press) St Mut.

Bird Watcher's Adventures in Tropical America. Alexander F. Skutch. LC 77-3478. (Corrie Herring Hooks Ser.: No. 3). (Illus.). 343p. 1977. reprint ed. 22.50 (*0-292-70722-3*); reprint ed. pap. 14.95 (*0-292-70766-5*) U of Tex Pr.

Bird Watcher's Book of Lists-Western Region. Lester Short. 1987. pap. 7.95 (*0-394-75198-1*) Knopf.

Bird Watcher's Guide to Japan. Mark Brazil. LC 87-81675. (Illus.). 220p. 1988. pap. 13.95 (*0-87011-849-8*) Kodansha.

Bird Watcher's Guide to Mexico. Margaret L. Wheeler. (Illus.). 96p. 1967. pap. 5.50 (*0-912434-07-4*) Ocelot Pr.

Bird Watcher's Journal. Nancy S. Taylor. 25p. 1990. 4.50 (*0-937745-13-8*) Traditions Pr.

Bird Watching for Everyone. Hockley Clarke. 128p. 1980. 29.00 (*0-905418-30-1*, Pub. by Gresham Bks UK) St Mut.

***Bird Watching for Kids.** (Outdoor Kids Ser.). (Illus.). 96p. (J). (gr. k-5). 1995. pap. write for info. (*1-55971-457-3*) NorthWord.

Bird Who Cleans the World: And Other Mayan Fables. Victor Montejo. Tr. by Wallace Kaufman. LC 90-52757. (Illus.). 128p. (Orig.). (J). 1991. 22.95 (*0-915306-93-X*); pap. 13.95 (*1-880684-03-9*) Curbstone.

Bird Who Steals Everything Shining. Dieter Weslowski. pap. write for info. (*0-938621-01-7*) MSS-New Myths.

***Bird with a Broken Wing.** L. J. Bellarts. LC 95-76647. (Illus.). 144p. 1995. pap. 12.95 (*0-8323-0514-6*) Binford Mort.

Bird with the Word Talks about Self-Control. Claudia Rees. (Illus.). (Orig.). (J). (gr. 1-3). 1987. pap. 0.98 (*0-89274-451-0*) Harrison Hse.

***Bird Without Feathers.** Mike Derzack et al. 320p. 1994. 19.95 (*1-56901-590-2*) NW Pub.

Bird Woman. Gene S. Porter. 27.95 (*0-8488-1527-0*) Amereon Ltd.

Bird Woman: Sacajawea, Guide of Lewis & Clark. J. W. Schultz. 1977. lib. bdg. 59.95 (*0-8490-1507-3*) Gordon Pr.

Bird World. Struan Reid. (Young Readers' Nature Library). (Illus.). 64p. (J). (gr. 4-6). 1991. lib. bdg. 15.40 (*1-56294-009-0*) Millbrook Pr.

Bird Year: A Book for Birders with Special Reference to the Monterey Bay Area. John Davis & Alan Baldridge. 1987. reprint ed. pap. 9.95 (*0-910286-62-0*) Boxwood.

Bird You Care For. Felicia Ames. (J). 1970. pap. 1.75 (*0-451-07527-7*, E7527, Sig) NAL-Dutton.

***Birddog Tape.** Barry Norman. 1995. 19.95 (*0-312-11753-1*) St Martin.

Birder's Dozen. Brendan Galvin. LC 84-72325. 36p. (Orig.). 1984. pap. 3.50 (*0-9604740-6-4*) Ampersand RI.

Birder's Guide to Alabama & Mississippi. Ray Vaughan. 200p. 1994. 14.95 (*0-88415-055-0*) Gulf Pub.

***Birder's Guide to Arkansas.** Mel White. Ed. by Paul J. Baicich. LC 95-75099. (ABA Birdfinding Guide Ser.). (Illus.). 272p. (Orig.). 1995. spiral bd., pap. 16.95 (*1-878788-09-4*, 117) Amer Birding Assn.

Birder's Guide to Bed & Breakfasts: United States & Canada. Peggy Van Hulsteyn. (Illus.). 288p. 1993. pap. 15.95 (*1-56261-106-2*) John Muir.

***Birder's Guide to Bed & Breakfasts: United States & Canada.** 2nd ed. Peggy Van Hulsteyn. LC 95-2943. 1995. pap. write for info. (*1-56261-225-5*) John Muir.

***Birder's Guide to Churchill.** 3rd rev. ed. Bonnie Chartier. Ed. by Paul J. Baicich. LC 93-74273. (Lane Birdfinding Guide Ser.). (Illus.). 132p. (Orig.). 1994. spiral bd., pap. 14.95 (*1-878788-07-8*) Amer Birding Assn.

Birder's Guide to Coastal North Carolina. John O. Fussell, III. LC 93-32475. (Illus.). 560p. (C). 1994. 29.95 (*0-8078-2146-2*); pap. 16.95 (*0-8078-4453-5*) U of NC Pr.

***Birder's Guide to Eastern Massachusetts.** Bird Observer Staff & Barry W. Van Dusen. Ed. by Paul J. Baicich. LC 94-71892. (ABA Birdfinding Guide Ser.). (Illus.). 292p. (Orig.). 1994. pap. text ed., spiral bd. 16.95 (*1-878788-08-6*, 266) Amer Birding Assn.

Birder's Guide to France. Tr. by Tony Williams. 270p. 1992. 16.95 (*0-88415-054-2*) Gulf Pub.

Birder's Guide to Japan. Jane W. Robinson. (Illus.). 358p. 1988. reprint ed. 15.95 (*0-934797-02-1*) Cornell U Pr.

Birder's Guide to Minnesota: A County-by-County Guide to over 800 Birding Areas with Annotated List of Minnesota Birds. 3rd rev. ed. Kim R. Eckert. 256p. 1994. pap. 17.95 (*0-9641437-0-4*) Williams MN.

Birder's Guide to Montana. Terry McEneaney. LC 92-55084. (Falcon Guidebook Ser.). (Illus.). 316p. (Orig.). 1993. pap. 14.95 (*1-56044-189-5*) Falcon Pr MT.

***Birder's Guide to North American Hotspots.** Jerry A. Cooper. Ed. by Paul J. Baicich. (ABA Birdfinding Guides Ser.). (Illus.). 300p. (Orig.). 1995. pap. 16.95 (*1-878788-10-8*, 333) Amer Birding Assn.

Birder's Guide to Northern California. Lolo Westrich. 322p. 1990. pap. 16.95 (*0-87201-063-5*) Gulf Pub.

Birder's Guide to Oregon. Joseph E. Evanich, Jr. (Illus.). 288p. (Orig.). 1990. pap. 12.95 (*0-931686-09-1*) Audubon Soc Portland.

***Birder's Guide to Pennsylvania.** Paula Ford & Stan Kotala. LC 94-34830. 304p. 1995. 17.95 (*0-88415-073-9*) Gulf Pub.

***Birder's Guide to Southeastern Arizona.** 4th rev. ed. Richard C. Taylor. Ed. by Paul J. Baicich. LC 95-75101. (ABA-Lane Birdfinding Guide Ser.). (Illus.). 256p. 1995. spiral bd., pap. 16.95 (*1-878788-06-X*, 102) Amer Birding Assn.

Birder's Guide to Southern California. 3rd ed. Harold R. Holt. Ed. by Paul J. Baicich. LC 90-84063. (ABA-Lane Birdfinding Guide Ser.). (Illus.). 238p. (Orig.). 1990. pap. 14.95 (*1-878788-00-0*) Amer Birding Assn.

Birder's Guide to Texas. 2nd ed. Edward A. Kutac. (Illus.). 282p. 1989. pap. 13.95 (*0-88415-550-1*) Gulf Pub.

Birder's Guide to the Atlin Valley. Richard S. Lee. (Illus.). 120p. (Orig.). 1989. pap. text ed. 14.95 (*0-317-93502-X*) Moose Mtn Pubns.

***Birder's Guide to the Cincinnati Tristate.** 2nd expanded ed. Robert Folzenlogen. (Orig.). 1995. 12.95 (*0-9620685-8-6*) Willow Pr OH.

Birder's Guide to the Coast of Maine. Elizabeth C. Pierson & Jan Erik Pierson. LC 81-67953. (Illus.). 224p. 1981. pap. 9.95 (*0-89272-118-9*, PIC471) Down East.

***Birder's Guide to the Kenai Peninsula, Alaska.** George C. West. (Illus.). 154p. (Orig.). 1994. pap. 14.95 (*0-9619026-2-0*) Homer Soc.

Birder's Guide to the Rio Grande Valley of Texas. rev. ed. Harold R. Holt & Paul J. Baicich. LC 91-73556. (ABA-Lane Birdfinding Guide Ser.). (Illus.). 189p. (Orig.). 1992. pap. 16.95 (*1-878788-01-9*) Amer Birding Assn.

Birder's Guide to the Texas Coast. rev. ed. Harold R. Holt. Ed. by Paul J. Baicich. LC 93-70809. (ABA-Lane Birdfinding Guide Ser.). (Illus.). 224p. 1993. pap. 14.95 (*1-878788-03-5*) Amer Birding Assn.

Birder's Guide to Trinidad & Tobago. William L. Murphy. (Illus.). v, 124p. (Orig.). 1986. pap. 12.95 (*0-941475-01-8*) Peregrine Enter.

***Birder's Guide to Washington.** Diann MacRae. LC 95-1573. (Illus.). 332p. 1995. 17.95 (*0-88415-126-3*) Gulf Pub.

Birder's Guide to Wyoming. Oliver K. Scott. Ed. by Paul J. Baicich. LC 92-74478. (ABA-Lane Birdfinding Guide Ser.). (Illus.). 246p. (Orig.). 1992. pap. 14.95 (*1-878788-02-7*) Amer Birding Assn.

Birder's Handbook: A Field Guide to the Natural History of North American Birds. Paul R. Ehrlich et al. (Illus.). 752p. 1988. pap. 17.00 (*0-671-65989-8*, Fireside) S&S Trade.

Birder's Journal. Mel Baughman. (Illus.). 416p. 1993. pap. 14.95 (*0-8117-2514-6*) Stackpole.

Birder's Journal: And Illustrated Lifelist. George W. Reiger. Ed. by Mel M. Baughman. (Illus.). 1989. 30.00 (*0-9623149-0-0*) Baughman Co.

Birder's Life List & Diary. Cornell Laboratory of Ornithology Staff. Ed. by Steven C. Sibley. 214p. (Orig.). 1986. spiral bd. 8.25 (*0-938027-00-X*) Crows Nest Bird.

Birder's List of Birds of the World. Ernest P. Edwards. (Illus.). x, 78p. 1990. pap. 5.90 (*0-911882-13-8*) E P Edwards.

Birder's Sourcebook. Sheila Buff. 160p. 1994. pap. 13.95 (*1-55821-278-7*) Lyons & Burford.

Birdfeeder's Handbook. Sheila Buff. (Illus.). 160p. 1991. pap. 10.95 (*1-55821-123-3*) Lyons & Burford.

***Birdfinding in Forty National Forests & Grasslands.** American Birding Association Staff & USDA Forest Service Staff. Ed. by William J. Boyle, Jr. & Roland H. Wauer. LC 94-7047. (Illus.). 192p. (Orig.). 1994. pap. 12.95 (*1-878788-29-9*) Amer Birding Assn.

Birdhouses, Feeders You Can Make. Hi Sibley. 1991. pap. 11.00 (*0-87006-843-1*) Goodheart.

Birdhousing. Peri Wolfman & Charles Gold. LC 92-1607. 1993. 22.50 (*0-517-58827-7*, C P Pubs) Crown Pub Group.

***Birdies: How to Tell a Duck Hooker from a Deep-Rough Thrasher.** Roy Benjamin. (Illus.). 96p. (Orig.). 1992. pap. write for info. (*0-9633960-0-5*) Golfing Birds Ent.

Birdies: How to Tell a Duck Hooker from a Deep-Rough Thrasher. Roy Benjamin. LC 92-35932. (Illus.). 94p. (Orig.). 1993. pap. 12.00 (*0-02-016589-7*, Collier S&S) S&S Trade.

***Birdies in the Boardroom: Golfing Your Way Up the Corporate Ladder.** Joey West. (Illus.). 145p. (Orig.). 1995. pap. 6.95 (*0-929957-09-1*, Push-Pull Pr) JSA Pubns.

Birdies in the Oven: Aces in the Kitchen. Trish Leverett. (Illus.). 228p. (Orig.). 1986. pap. 10.00 (*0-317-58354-9*) Miss Annie's Pubns.

***Birdie's Lighthouse.** Deborah Hopkinson. LC 94-24097. (Illus.). (J). 1996. 16.00 (*0-679-86998-0*); lib. bdg. 16.99 (*0-679-96998-5*) Knopf.

***Birding.** John Forshaw. Ed. by Terence Lindsey. LC 95-8608. (Nature Company Guide Ser.). (Illus.). 288p. 1995. write for info. (*0-7835-4752-8*) Time-Life.

Birding Around the World. Aileen R. Lotz. (Science Editions Ser.). 1988. pap. text ed. 10.95 (*0-471-62092-0*) Wiley.

***Birding Around the World: A Guide to Observing Birds Everywhere You Travel.** Aileen R. Lotz. 1987. pap. 10.95 (*0-396-09024-9*) WC Stone PMA.

***Birding Basics.** Sandy Cortright. LC 94-27655. (Illus.). 160p. (J). 1995. 19.95 (*0-8069-1262-6*) Sterling.

***Birding by Ear: Eastern & Central North America.** Richard K. Walton & Robert W. Lawson. 64p. 1994. 35.00 (*0-395-71258-0*) HM.

***Birding by Ear: Western North America.** Robert W. Lawson & Richard K. Walton. 1994. 35.00 (*0-395-71257-2*) HM.

Birding by Ear: Western: Guide to Bird-Song Identification, 2 Vols. Richard K. Walton & Robert W. Lawson. (Peterson Field Guide Ser.). (Illus.). 64p. 1990. pap. 35.00 (*0-395-52811-9*) HM.

Birding Crane River: Nebraska's Platte. Gary R. Lingle. 124p. 1994. spiral bd. 11.95 (*0-9641219-0-5*) Harrier Pubng.

Birding for Beginners. Sheila Buff. (Illus.). 192p. 1993. pap. 14.95 (*1-55821-209-4*) Lyons & Burford.

Birding for the Amateur Naturalist. Laura O'biso Socha. LC 88-36348. (Illus.). 192p. 1989. reprint ed. pap. 8.95 (*0-87106-615-7*) Globe Pequot.

Birding in Ohio. 2nd ed. Tom Thomson. LC 94-2448. (Illus.). Date not set. 29.95 (*0-253-35995-3*); pap. 13.95 (*0-253-20874-2*) Ind U Pr.

Birding in Ohio. Tom Thomson. LC 82-49012. (Illus.). 266p. reprint ed. pap. 77.00 (*0-8357-3941-4*, 2057036) Bks Demand.

Birding in Seattle & King County. Eugene S. Hunn. LC 82-61828. (Trailside Ser.). (Illus.). 1982. pap. 7.95 (*0-914516-05-1*) Seattle Audubon Soc.

Birding in the Cayuga Lake Basin. Cornell Laboratory of Ornithology Staff. Ed. by Mildred C. Comar et al. (Illus.). 108p. (Orig.). 1974. pap. 8.25 (*0-938027-04-2*) Crows Nest Bird.

Birding in the San Juan Islands. Mark Lewis. LC 87-23997. (Illus.). 224p. (Orig.). 1987. pap. 10.95 (*0-89886-133-0*) Mountaineers.

Birding Sites Around Perth. Ron Van Delft. 1988. pap. 9.95 (*0-85564-259-9*, Pub. by Univ of West Aust Pr AT) Intl Spec Bk.

Birding the Delaware Valley Region: A Comprehensive Guide to Birdwatching in Southeastern Pennsylvania, Central & Southern New Jersey, & Northcentral Delaware. John J. Harding & Justin J. Harding. LC 80-10279. 233p. 1980. pap. 14.95 (*0-87722-182-0*) Temple U Pr.

***Birding the Front Range: A Guide to Seasonal Highlights.** Robert Folzenlogen. LC 95-60112. (Illus.). 159p. 1995. 12.95 (*0-9620685-7-8*) Willow Pr OH.

Birding with a Purpose: Of Raptors, Gaboons, & Other Creatures. Frances Hamerstrom. LC 83-12684. (Illus.). 138p. 1984. reprint ed. pap. 10.95 (*0-8138-0229-6*) Iowa St U Pr.

Birdkeeper's Guide to Breeding Birds. David Alderton. (Illus.). 118p. 10.95 (*3-923880-72-3*, 16083) Tetra Pr.

An Asterisk (*) at the beginning of an entry indicates that the title is appearing in BIP for the first time.

An Asterisk (*) at the beginning of an entry indicates that the title is appearing in BIP for the first time.

785

Birds in Art Exhibition Catalogue: 1989. Intro. by Kathy K. Foley. LC 89-13088. (Illus.). 132p. (Orig.). 1989. pap. 10.00 (0-945529-02-3) Le Yawkey.

Birds in Art Exhibition Catalogue, 1990. Intro. by Kathy K. Foley. (Illus.). 132p. (Orig.). 1990. pap. 10.00 (0-945529-04-X) Le Yawkey.

Birds in Art, Nineteen Ninety-One. Intro. by Kathy K. Foley. (Birds in Art Exhibition Catalogue Ser.). (Illus.). 132p. 1991. pap. 12.50 (0-945529-06-6) Le Yawkey.

Birds in Brazil: A Natural History. Helmut Sick. Tr. by William Belton. LC 92-19971. (Illus.). 932p. (C). 1993. text ed. 125.00 (0-691-08569-2) Princeton U Pr.

Birds in Europe: Their Conservation Status. G. Tucker et al. (Birdlife Conservation Ser.). (Illus.). 625p. 1994. pap. 40.00 (1-56098-527-5) Smithsonian.

Birds in Ireland. Clive D. Hutchinson. 212p. 1990. text ed. 39.95 (0-85661-052-6, 784652, Pub. by Poyser UK) Acad Pr.

Birds in Jeopardy: The Imperiled & Extinct Birds of the United States & Canada: Including Hawaii & Puerto Rico. Paul R. Ehrlich et al. LC 91-29555. (Illus.). 272p. 1992. 45.00 (0-8047-1967-5); pap. 17.95 (0-8047-1981-0) Stanford U Pr.

Birds in Kansas, Vol. I. Max C. Thompson & Charles Ely. (Public Education Ser.: No. 11). (Illus.). 404p. 1989. 25.00 (0-89338-028-8); pap. 14.95 (0-89338-027-X) U of KS Mus Nat Hist.

Birds in Kansas, Vol. II. Max C. Thompson & Charles Ely. (Public Education Ser.: No. 12). 320p. 1992. 25.00 (0-89338-039-3); pap. 14.95 (0-89338-040-7) U of KS Mus Nat Hist.

Birds in Langfoot's Belfry. Paul Zech. Tr. by Elena B. Odio. (GERM Ser.). xvii, 105p. 1994. 35.00 (1-57113-007-1) Camden Hse.

Birds in Literature. Leonard Lutwack. LC 93-30647. 304p. (C). 1994. lib. bdg. 29.95 (0-8130-1254-6) U Press Fla.

Birds in Literature. Nancy Polette. (Illus.). 48p. (J). (gr. k-3). 1990. pap. 5.95 (0-913839-86-8) Bk Lures.

Birds in London. William H. Hudson. reprint ed. 64.50 (0-404-03397-0) AMS Pr.

Birds in Minnesota. Robert B. Janssen. LC 87-5860. (Illus.). 367p. 1987. text ed. 44.95 (0-8166-1568-3); pap. 14.95 (0-8166-1569-1) U of Minn Pr.

***Birds in Origami.** John Montroll. LC 94-40618. 1994. pap. write for info. (0-486-28341-0) Dover.

***Birds in Paradise.** Intro. by Bridget Barnes. (Illus.). 14p. 1995. pap. 5.00 (0-614-07332-4) Sesnon Art Gall.

Birds in Scotland. Valerie M. Thom. (Illus.). 392p. 1990. text ed. 39.95 (0-85661-040-2, 784640, Pub. by Poyser UK) Acad Pr.

Birds in Town & Village. William H. Hudson. reprint ed. 64.50 (0-404-03409-8) AMS Pr.

Birds in Your Backyard. Virginia S. Eifert. (Popular Science Ser.: Vol. II). (Illus.). 224p. 1986. pap. 5.00 (0-89792-031-7) Ill St Museum.

Bird's Nest. Shirley Jackson. 20.95 (0-317-27727-8, Amereon Hse) Amereon Ltd.

Bird's Nest. Shirley Jackson. 284p. 1993. 21.95 (1-56723-064-4) Yestermorrow.

Birds' Nest. Barrie Watts. (Stopwatch Ser.). (Illus.). 25p. (J). (gr. k-4). 1991. pap. 3.95 (0-382-24015-4) Silver Burdett Pr.

Birds' Nest. Barrie Watts. (Stopwatch Ser.). (Illus.). 25p. (J). (gr. k-4). 1991. 6.95 (0-382-09443-3); lib. bdg. 9.95 (0-382-09439-5) Silver Pr.

Bird's Nest Fungi. H. J. Brodie. LC 75-18476. 1975. pap. 12.95 (0-8020-6766-2) U of Toronto Pr.

Bird's Nest Fungi. Harold J. Brodie. LC 75-19476. (Illus.). 216p. reprint ed. pap. 61.60 (0-8357-3774-8, 2036504) Bks Demand.

Bird's Nest Soup. Manna Greeley. 144p. (C). 1987. pap. 9.95 (0-946211-47-7, Pub. by Attic IE) InBook.

Birds Nests. Eileen Curran. LC 84-8658. (Illus.). 32p. (J). (gr. k-2). 1985. lib. bdg. 11.59 (0-8167-0341-8); pap. text ed. 2.95 (0-8167-0342-6) Troll Assocs.

***Birds, Nests, & Eggs.** Mel Boring. (Take-Along Guide Ser.). (Illus.). 48p. (J). (gr. 3-7). 1996. write for info. (1-55971-480-8) NorthWord.

Birds New to Britain & Ireland. Ed. by J. T. Sharrock. (Illus.). 456p. 1990. text ed. 34.95 (0-85661-033-X, 784633, Pub. by Poyser UK) Acad Pr.

Birds of a Feather. Philipp P. Fehl. (Illus.). 132p. (Orig.). pap. 19.95 (0-252-06241-8) U of Ill Pr.

Birds of a Feather. Susan Murray. 192p. 1994. 17.95 (0-8034-9057-7, Avalon Bks) Bouregy.

Birds of a Feather. A. R. Plumb. (Further Adventures of Aladdin Ser.: No. 2). (Illus.). 64p. (Orig.). (J). (gr. k-3). 1994. 3.50 (0-7868-4017-X) Disney Pr.

Birds of a Feather. large type ed. Victor Canning. 304p. 1986. 21.95 (0-7089-1428-4) Ulverscroft.

Birds of a Feather: And Other Aesop's Fables. Tom Paxton. LC 92-2909. (Illus.). 40p. (J). (ps up). 1993. 15.00 (0-688-10400-2); lib. bdg. 14.93 (0-688-10401-0) Morrow Jr Bks.

Birds of a Maryland Farm: Local Study of Economic Ornithology. Sylvester D. Judd. Ed. by Frank N. Egerton, 3rd. LC 77-74233. (History of Ecology Ser.). (Illus.). 1978. reprint ed. lib. bdg. 17.95 (0-405-10402-2) Ayer.

Birds of Acadia National Park. Mary J. Perkins. (Illus.). 8p. 1990. 2.99 (0-934745-23-4) Acadia Pub Co.

Birds of Africa. Ed. by L. B. Brown et al. LC 81-69594. 1982. text ed. 201.00 (0-12-137301-0) Acad Pr.

Birds of Africa. deluxe ed. Ed. by L. B. Brown et al. LC 81-69594. 1982. ring bd. 460.00 (0-685-06092-6) Acad Pr.

Birds of Africa, Vol. 2. Ed. by Emil K. Urban et al. 596p. 1986. text ed. 201.00 (0-12-137302-9) Acad Pr.

Birds of Africa, Vol. 3. Ed. by C. Hilary Fry et al. 611p. 1988. text ed. 201.00 (0-12-137303-7) Acad Pr.

Birds of Africa Vol. 4: Broadbills to Chats. Ed. by Stuart Keith et al. 609p. 1992. text ed. 199.00 (0-12-137304-5) Acad Pr.

Birds of Alberta. David Hancock. (Illus.). 72p. 1989. pap. 5.95 (0-88839-222-2) Hancock House.

***Birds of Algonquin Legend.** Nichols. 1995. (0-472-10611-2) U of Mich Pr.

Birds of America. Audubon Society Staff. (Illus.). 29.95 (0-02-504440-0) Macmillan.

***Birds of America.** Mary McCarthy. 1994. lib. bdg. 24.95x (1-56849-426-2) Buccaneer Bks.

Birds of America. Mary McCarthy. 1992. pap. 10.95 (0-15-612630-3) HarBrace.

Birds of America, 5 vols., Set. John J. Audubon. (Illus.). reprint ed. write for info. (0-8446-1567-6) Peter Smith.

Birds of America, 5 vols., Vols. 1, 5, 6, 7. John J. Audubon. (Illus.). reprint ed. 10.50 (0-318-55248-5) Peter Smith.

Birds of America - Selections see Treasury of Audubon Birds in Full Color: Two Hundred Twenty-Four Plates from The Birds of America

Birds of an Indian Garden. T. Fletcher. 201p. 1984. 200.00 (81-7089-065-9, Pub. by Intl Bk Distr II) St Mut.

Birds of Ancient Egypt, Vol. 1: Natural History of Egypt. Houlihan. 1986. 95.00 (0-85668-521-6, Pub. by Aris & Phillips UK); pap. 59.95 (0-85668-283-7, Pub. by Aris & Phillips UK) David Brown.

***Birds of Another Feather...My Musical Colleagues.** Rivka Golani. 80p. 1995. lib. bdg. 25.00 (0-8095-4911-5) Borgo Pr.

***Birds of Antartica.** Lynn M. Stone. LC 95-5985. (Antarctica Ser.). (J). 1995. write for info. (1-55916-141-8) Rourke Bk Co.

Birds of Arizona. Allan R. Phillips et al. LC 64-17265. (Illus.). 292p. reprint ed. pap. 83.30 (0-7837-1910-8, 2042114) Bks Demand.

Birds of Australia: A Book of Identification. Ken Simpson & Nicolas Day. LC 84-8812. (Illus.). 352p. 1985. 45.00 (0-88072-076-X) Hollowbrook.

Birds of B. C. David Hancock. (Illus.). 72p. 1989. pap. 7.95 (0-88839-221-4) Hancock House.

Birds of Bahrain. Tom Nightingale & Mike Hill. 288p. (C). 1990. 150.00 (0-907151-79-5, Pub. by IMMEL Pubng UK) St Mut.

Birds of Baja California. Sanford R. Wilbur. 1987. 50.00 (0-520-05820-8) U CA Pr.

Birds of Britain & Europe. Peterson & Guy Mountfort. 1987. 22.95 (0-685-43762-0) Viking Penguin.

Birds of Burma. B. E. Smythies. 589p. 1984. 410.00 (81-7089-068-3, Pub. by Intl Bk Distr II) St Mut.

Birds of Burma. B. E. Smythies. 589p. (C). 1984. reprint ed. 750.00 (0-685-21820-1, Pub. by Intl Bk Distr II) St Mut.

Birds of Calcutta. F. Finn. 166p. (C). 1978. text ed. 45.00 (0-89771-606-X, Pub. by Intl Bk Distr II) St Mut.

Birds of Calcutta. F. Finn. 166p. 1978. reprint ed. 95.00 (0-685-21743-4, Pub. by Intl Bk Distr II) St Mut.

Birds of California. J. K. Anderson. (J). (gr. 1-9). 1992. pap. 3.95 (0-88388-101-2) Bellerophon Bks.

Birds of California. William L. Dawson. 1992. reprint ed. lib. bdg. 75.00 (0-7812-5023-4) Rprt Serv.

Birds of Cambridgeshire. P. M. Bircham. (Illus.). (C). 1989. 44.95 (0-521-32863-2) Cambridge U Pr.

Birds of Canada. rev. ed. W. Earl Godfrey. 1986. 39.95 (0-226-56289-1, 56289-1) U Ch Pr.

Birds of Cattaraugus County, New York. Stephen W. Eaton. LC 82-134257. (Bulletin Ser.: Vol. 29). (Illus.). 91p. (Orig.). (C). 1981. pap. 3.95 (0-944032-37-0) Buffalo SNS.

Birds of Chile: A Field Guide. Braulio Araya & Sharon Chester. (Illus.). 400p. (C). 1993. pap. 24.95 (0-9638511-0-1) Wander Albatross.

Birds of China. Rodolphe M. De Schauensee. Ed. by Eleanor D. Brown. LC 83-10314. (Illus.). 602p. 1984. pap. 37.00 (0-87474-363-X, DEBCP) Smithsonian.

Birds of Colonial Williamsburg: A Historical Portfolio. Alan Feduccia. LC 89-7220. (Illus.). 162p. 1989. 24.95 (0-87935-113-6) Colonial Williamsburg.

Birds of Darjeeling & India. L. J. Mackintosh. 226p. 1986. reprint ed. 175.00 (81-7089-047-0, Pub. by Intl Bk Distr II) St Mut.

Birds of Darjeling & India. J. J. Mackintosh. 226p. 1986. 135.00 (81-7089-147-7, Pub. by Intl Bk Distr II) St Mut.

***Birds of East Africa.** Date not set. 22.00 (0-00-219179-2, HarpT) HarpC.

Birds of East Central Idaho. Hadley B. Roberts. (Illus.). 128p. (Orig.). (C). 1993. pap. text ed. 9.95 (0-9634903-0-3) H B Roberts.

Birds of Egypt. Ed. by Steven M. Goodman & Peter L. Meininger. (Illus.). 574p. 1989. 125.00 (0-19-857644-7) OUP.

Birds of Erie County Pennsylvania. Jean Stull et al. LC 84-73239. (Illus.). 175p. 1985. pap. 9.95 (0-910042-47-0) Allegheny.

Birds of Eucalypt Forests & Woodlands. Ed. by A. Keast et al. 400p. (C). 1985. text ed. 150.00 (0-949324-06-X, Pub. by Surrey Beatty & Sons AT) St Mut.

***Birds of Europe.** Ed. by Expert-Center for Taxonomic Identification (ETI) Staff. 1995. cd-rom 99.00 (3-540-14189-8); cd-rom 99.00 (3-540-14190-1) Spr-Verlag.

Birds of Europe: With North Africa & the Middle East. Lars Jonsson. Tr. by David Christie. LC 92-41334. (C). 1993. 45.00 (0-691-03326-9) Princeton U Pr.

***Birds of Florida.** 2nd rev. ed. Frances W. Hall. (Illus.). 1994. pap. 3.95 (0-8200-0907-5) Great Outdoors.

Birds of Gibraltar. Ed. by J. E. Cortes et al. (C). 1988. pap. text ed. 50.00 (0-948466-00-6, Pub. by Gibraltar Bks UK) St Mut.

Birds of Grand Teton: And the Surrounding Area. Bert Raynes. Ed. by Debbie Broadus. (Illus.). 90p. (Orig.). reprint ed. pap. 7.95 (0-931895-00-6) Grand Teton NHA.

Birds of Heaven, & Other Stories. Vladimir G. Korolenko. Tr. by Clarence A. Manning. LC 79-167458. (Short Story Index Reprint Ser.). 1977. reprint ed. 19.95 (0-8369-3984-0) Ayer.

***Birds of Hoboken.** William Wenthe. LC 94-42458. 64p. (Orig.). 1995. pap. 12.95 (0-914061-49-6) Orchises Pr.

Birds of Houston. B. C. Robison & John L. Tveten. LC 90-53175. (Illus.). 144p. 1990. 22.50 (0-89263-303-4); pap. 12.95 (0-89263-304-2) Rice Univ.

Birds of Illinois. H. David Bohlen. LC 89-45203. (Illus.). 240p. 1989. 49.95 (0-253-31560-3) Ind U Pr.

Birds of India: A Guide to Indian Ornithology, 2 vols., Set. H. A. Barnes. 449p. 1981. text ed. 87.50 (0-685-14044-X) Coronet Bks.

Birds of Indiana. Russell E. Mumford & Charles E. Keller. LC 83-49454. (Illus.). 400p. 1984. 59.95 (0-253-10736-9) Ind U Pr.

Birds of Indianapolis: A Guide to the Region. Charles E. Keller & Timothy C. Keller. LC 92-46532. 145p. (C). 1993. 25.00 (0-253-33119-6); pap. 12.95 (0-253-28534-8) Ind U Pr.

Birds of Ireland. Gordon D'Arcy. (Appletree Pocket Guide Ser.). (Illus.). 72p. (Orig.). 1986. pap. 7.95 (0-86281-162-7, Pub. by Appletree Pr IE) Irish Bks Media.

Birds of Israel. Hadoram Shirihai. (Illus.). 800p. 1995. text ed. write for info. (0-12-640255-8) Acad Pr.

Birds of Jamaica: A Photographic Field Guide. Audrey Downer et al. (Illus.). 128p. (C). 1990. 20.50 (0-521-38309-9) Cambridge U Pr.

Birds of Japan. Mark A. Brazil. LC 90-62321. (Illus.). 480p. (C). 1991. text ed. 55.00 (1-56098-030-3) Smithsonian.

Birds of Java & Bali. Derek Holmes. (Images of Asia Ser.). (Illus.). 144p. 1989. 19.95 (0-19-588927-4) OUP.

Birds of John Burroughs: A Great Naturalist's Meditations & Essays on Bird Watching. John Burroughs. (Illus.). 240p. 1989. pap. 9.95 (0-87951-312-8) Overlook Pr.

Birds of John Burroughs: A Great Naturalist's Meditations & Essays on Bird Watching. John Burroughs. LC 87-42888. (Illus.). 240p. 1988. reprint ed. 18.95 (0-87951-301-2) Overlook Pr.

Birds of Kent, 2 vols., Set. James M. Harrison. (Illus.). 1953. 100.00 (0-8464-0199-1) Beekman Pubs.

Birds of Kentucky. Robert M. Mengel. Ed. by American Ornithologists' Union Staff. 581p. 1965. 15.00 (0-943610-03-6) Am Ornithologists.

Birds of Kentucky. Burt L. Monroe, Jr. LC 93-44364. (C). 1994. 49.95 (0-253-33892-1) Ind U Pr.

Birds of Konza: The Avian Ecology of the Tallgrass Prairie. John L. Zimmerman. LC 92-42414. (Illus.). 176p. 1993. 19.95 (0-7006-0597-5) U Pr of KS.

Birds of La Plata. William H. Hudson. reprint ed. 64.50 (0-404-03411-X) AMS Pr.

Birds of Land Between the Lakes. Photos by Fred J. Alsop, III. LC 91-76141. (Miscellaneous Publication Ser.: No. 5). (Illus.). 234p. 1991. 7.00 (1-880617-00-5) APSU Ctr Fld Bio.

Birds of Lesotho. Kurt Bonde. (Illus.). 108p. 1993. pap. text ed. 29.95 (0-86980-881-8, Pub. by A K HU) Intl Spec Bk.

Birds of Malheur National Wildlife Refuge, Oregon. Carroll D. Littlefield. LC 89-77930. (Illus.). 304p. 1990. text ed. 29.95 (0-87071-360-4); pap. 18.95 (0-87071-361-2) Oreg St U Pr.

Birds of Manhattan. Dan Witz. 36p. 1983. pap. 9.95 (0-912499-00-1) Skinny Bks.

Birds of Massachusetts. Richard R. Veit & Wayne R. Petersen. LC 93-2931. (Natural History of New England Ser.). 1993. 39.95 (0-932691-11-0) MA Audubon Soc.

Birds of Michigan. James Granlund et al. LC 94-8521. (Illus.). 1994. 59.95 (0-253-30122-X) Ind U Pr.

Birds of Missouri: Their Distribution & Abundance. Mark B. Robbins & David A. Easterla. (Illus.). 416p. (C). 1991. text ed. 59.95 (0-8262-0791-X) U of Mo Pr.

Birds of Nevada. J. R. Alcorn. LC 88-80743. (Illus.). 450p. 1988. 55.00 (0-9620221-0-1) Fairview West Pub.

Birds of New Guinea. Bruce Beehler et al. LC 85-42673. (Illus.). 370p. 1986. 85.00 (0-691-08385-1); pap. 39.50 (0-691-02394-8) Princeton U Pr.

***Birds of New Jersey.** Charles Leck. 1975. pap. 9.95 (0-8135-0838-X) Rutgers U Pr.

Birds of New York, 2 vols. E. H. Eaton. 1993. reprint ed. lib. bdg. 150.00 (0-7812-5143-5) Rprt Serv.

Birds of New York State: Including the 1976 Supplement. John Bull. LC 85-17415. (Illus.). 720p. (C). 1986. reprint ed. 52.50 (0-8014-1897-6); reprint ed. pap. 24.95 (0-8014-9314-5) Cornell U Pr.

Birds of North America. (Spotter's Guides Ser.). (Illus.). 64p. (J). (gr. 7 up). 1992. pap. 4.95 (0-7460-1145-8, Usborne) EDC.

Birds of North America. David Hancock. (Illus.). 56p. 1989. pap. 4.95 (0-88839-219-2) Hancock House.

Birds of North America. rev. ed. Chandler S. Robbins et al. (Golden Field Guide Ser.). (Illus.). 360p. 1983. write for info. (0-307-37002-X); pap. 11.95 (0-307-33656-5) Western Pub.

Birds of North America: Eastern Region. John Bull et al. (Quick Reference Field Guide Ser.). (Illus.). 160p. 1985. pap. 13.95 (0-02-079660-9, Collier S&S) S&S Trade.

Birds of North America: The Descriptions of Species Based Chiefly on the Collections in the Museum of the Smithsonian Institution, 2 vols. in one. Spencer F. Baird et al. LC 73-17799. (Natural Sciences in America Ser.). (Illus.). 1974. 80.95 (0-405-05715-6) Ayer.

Birds of North America, Western Region: The Quick Identification Guide for All Birdwatchers. John Bull & Edith Bull. (Illus.). 160p. 1989. pap. 12.95 (0-02-062580-4, Collier S&S) S&S Trade.

Birds of North Central Texas. Warren M. Pulich. LC 87-9143. (W. L. Moody, Jr. Natural History Ser.: No. 9). (Illus.). 472p. 1988. 45.00 (0-89096-319-3); pap. 16.95 (0-89096-322-3) Tex A&M Univ Pr.

***Birds of Northeast Oregon.** 2nd rev. ed. Joseph E. Evanich, Jr. 1992. pap. 5.00 (1-877693-20-0) Oregon Field.

Birds of Nova Scotia. Robie Tufts. (Illus.). 478p. 1991. pap. 19.95 (0-920852-66-1, Pub. by Nimbus Publishing Ltd CN) Chelsea Green Pub.

Birds of Ohio. Bruce G. Peterjohn. LC 89-45202. (Illus.). 256p. 1989. 49.95 (0-253-34183-3) Ind U Pr.

Birds of Ohio, 2 vols., Set. William L. Dawson. 1993. reprint ed. lib. bdg. 150.00 (0-7812-5355-1) Rprt Serv.

Birds of Oman. Michael Gallagher & Martin Woodcock. (Illus.). 138p. 1981. 75.00 (0-685-01041-4, Pub. by Quartet UK) Charles River Bks.

Birds of Omen in Shetland. Jessie M. Saxby & W A. Clouston. Bd. with And Notes on the Folklore of the Raven & Owl. LC 76-43950. LC 76-43950. (Viking Society for Northern Research Ser.: Vol. 1). 40p. reprint ed. 32.50 (0-404-60021-2) AMS Pr.

***Birds of Oregon: Status & Distribution.** Jeff Gilligan et al. 360p. 1994. lib. bdg. 35.00 (0-9637765-5-X); pap. 24.95 (0-9637765-1-7) Cinclus Pubns.

Birds of Orkney. Cuthbert Booth & Reynolds Booth. (C). 1986. 80.00 (0-907618-07-3, Pub. by Orkney Pr UK) St Mut.

Birds of Pakistan Vol. 1: Regional Studies & Non-Passeriformes. Tom J. Roberts. (Illus.). 666p. 1991. 85.00 (0-19-577404-3, 8452) OUP.

Birds of Pakistan Vol. 2. Tom J. Roberts. (Illus.). 682p. 1992. 85.00 (0-19-577405-1) OUP.

Birds of Paradise. Susan Murray. 192p. 1994. 17.95 (0-8034-9065-8, Avalon Bks) Bouregy.

Birds of Paradise. Paul Scott. 280p. 1986. pap. 4.50 (0-88184-232-X) Carroll & Graf.

Birds of Passage. Maria Illo. 96p. (Orig.). (C). 1994. per., pap. 8.00 (0-9613159-2-X) Emerald Forest.

Birds of Passage: Five Englishwomen in Search of America. Richard Mullen. LC 94-14200. 1994. text ed. 45.00 (0-312-12228-4) St Martin.

Birds of Passage: Migrant Labor & Industrial Societies. Michael J. Piore. LC 78-12067. 239p. reprint ed. pap. 68.20 (0-8357-7272-1, 2024518) Bks Demand.

Birds of Pompeii. John Ciardi. LC 84-28077. 80p. 1985. pap. 8.95 (0-938626-45-0) U of Ark Pr.

Birds of Prey. (Zoobooks Ser.). (J). 1991. lib. bdg. 14.95 (0-88682-332-3) Creative Ed.

Birds of Prey. (American Nature Guide Ser.). 1992. 9.98 (0-8317-6950-5) Smithmark.

Birds of Prey. Jill Bailey & Tony Seddon. (Nature Watch Ser.). (Illus.). 64p. (J). (gr. 5 up). 1988. 15.95 (0-8160-1655-0) Facts on File.

Birds of Prey. Norman S. Barrett. LC 90-46306. (Picture Library). (Illus.). 32p. (J). (gr. k-4). 1991. lib. bdg. 12.53 (0-531-14151-9) Watts.

Birds of Prey. Steven W. Carothers & Dorothy House. (Plateau Ser.). 48p. 1992. pap. 6.95 (0-89734-110-4) Mus Northern Ariz.

Birds of Prey. David Drake. 352p. 1984. 14.95 (0-671-55909-5); pap. 7.95 (0-671-55912-5) Baen Bks.

Birds of Prey. David Drake. 352p. 1991. pap. 3.95 (0-8125-1356-8) Tor Bks.

Birds of Prey. John P. Mackenzie. LC 86-62790. (Birds of the World Ser.). (Illus.). 144p. 1986. 24.95 (1-55971-019-5) NorthWord.

Birds of Prey. Ed. by Ian Newton & Penny Olsen. (Illus.). 240p. 1990. 40.00 (0-8160-2182-1) Facts on File.

Birds of Prey. Glenda P. Olsen. LC 93-2670. (Naturebooks Ser.). (J). (gr. 2-6). 1993. lib. bdg. 22.79 (1-56766-059-2) Childs World.

***Birds of Prey.** Malcolm Penny. (Remarkable World Ser.). (Illus.). 48p. (J). (gr. 4 up). 1996. 15.95 (1-56847-414-8) Thomson Lrning.

Birds of Prey. Philip Perry. 1990. 19.99 (0-517-03167-1) Random Hse Value.

Birds of Prey. Floyd Scholz. LC 93-12426. (Illus.). 352p. 1993. 59.95 (0-8117-0242-1) Stackpole.

Birds of Prey. Lynn M. Stone. LC 82-17909. (New True Bks.). (Illus.). 48p. (J). (gr. k-4). 1983. lib. bdg. 12.90 (0-516-01676-8); pap. 4.95 (0-516-41676-6) Childrens.

Birds of Prey. Wildlife Education, Ltd. Staff. (Zoobooks Ser.). (Illus.). 20p. (Orig.). (YA). (gr. 5 up). 1980. pap. 2.75 (0-937934-01-1) Wildlife Educ.

Birds of Prey: Aircraft, Nose Art & Mission Markings of Operation Desert Shield - Desert Storm. David F. Brown. LC 92-62609. (Illus.). 160p. (Orig.). 1993. pap. 29.95 (0-88740-472-3) Schiffer.

Birds of Prey: Blue Ribbon Techniques. William Veasey. LC 84-51190. (Illus.). 303p. 1986. 47.50 (0-88740-052-3) Schiffer.

Birds of Prey: Hunters of the Sky. Alan Richards. (Illus.). 144p. 1992. 16.98 (1-56138-176-4) Courage Bks.

Birds of Prey: Natural History & Conservation of North American Raptors. Noel Snyder & Helen Snyder. (Illus.). 224p. 1991. 39.95 (0-89658-131-4) Voyageur Pr.

***Birds of Prey in Florida.** 2nd ed. Ray Ovington. 1995. pap. 3.95 (0-8200-0908-3) Great Outdoors.

Birds of Rottnest Island. D. Saunders & Perry De Rebeira. 102p. 1993. 90.00 (0-9593247-3-9, Pub. by Surrey Beatty & Sons AT) St Mut.

Birds of S. E. Asia. Ben King et al. 1975. pap. 24.95 (0-685-43764-7) Viking Penguin.

Birds of San Diego County. Philip Unitt. Ed. by Amadeo Rea. LC 84-71043. (Illus.). 316p. 1984. 20.00 (0-918969-01-8); pap. 14.00 (0-918969-02-6) San Diego Soc Nat Hist.

Birds of Singapore. Clive Briffett. LC 92-41708. (Images of Asia Ser.). (Illus.). 146p. 1994. 29.95 (0-19-588606-2) OUP.

786

An Asterisk (*) at the beginning of an entry indicates that the title is appearing in BIP for the first time.

Birds of Sorrow: Notes from a River Junction in Northern New Mexico. Tom Ireland. LC 91-65949. (Illus.). 232p. 1991. pap. 12.95 (*0-939010-19-4*) Zephyr Pr.

Birds of South America: The Suboscine Passerines, Vol. 2. Robert S. Ridgley. (Illus.). 940p. (C). 1994. 85.00 (*0-292-77063-4*) U of Tex Pr.

Birds of South America, Vol. I: The Oscine Passerines. Robert S. Ridgely & Guy Tudor. (Illus.). 562p. 1989. 70.00 (*0-292-70756-8*); 12.50 (*0-292-70777-0*) U of Tex Pr.

Birds of South Dakota. rev. ed. South Dakota Ornithologists' Union Staff. (Illus.). 450p. 1991. 29.95 (*0-9628650-0-1*) SD Ornith Union.

Birds of Southeastern Michigan & Southwestern Ontario. Alice H. Kelley. LC 78-54302. (Bulletin Ser.: No. 57). 99p. 1978. pap. 4.50 (*0-87737-034-6*) Cranbrook.

Birds of Southern California's Deep Canyon. Wesley W. Weathers. LC 82-13382. (Illus.). 267p. 1983. 45.00 (*0-520-04754-0*) U CA Pr.

Birds of Sumatra & Kalimantan. Derek Holmes. (Images of Asia Ser.). (Illus.). 122p. 1991. 24.95 (*0-19-588971-1*) OUP.

***Birds of Summer: An Ojibwa Tale.** Illus. & Ret. by Kristina Rodanas. LC 95-7103. (J). 1996. write for info. (*0-316-75333-5*) Little.

Birds of Sydney. Ern Hoskin. 310p. (C). 1991. text ed. 85.00 (*0-949324-40-X*, Pub. by Surrey Beatty & Sons AT) St Mut.

Birds of Texas. John L. Tveten. (Illus.). 384p. 1993. text ed. 39.95 (*0-940672-62-6*); pap. 24.95 (*0-940672-63-4*) Shearer Pub.

Birds of Texas: A Field Guide. John H. Rappole & Gene W. Blacklock. LC 93-8448. (W. L. Moody, Jr. Natural History Ser.: Vol. 14). (Illus.). 372p. 1994. 39.95 (*0-89096-544-7*); pap. 14.95 (*0-89096-545-5*) Tex A&M Univ Pr.

Birds of the Adirondacks. A. Bessette et al. 240p. 1993. pap. 16.95 (*0-932052-94-0*) North Country.

Birds of the Antarctic & Sub-Antarctic. George E. Watson. LC 75-34547. (Antarctic Research Ser.: Vol. 24). (Illus.). 350p. 1975. 18.00 (*0-87590-124-7*) Am Geophysical.

Birds of the Athenian Agora. Robert D. Lamberton & Susan I. Rotroff. (Excavations of the Athenian Agora Picture Bks.: No. 22). (Illus.). 32p. 1985. pap. 3.00 (*0-87661-627-9*) Am Sch Athens.

Birds of the Bible. Gene S. Porter. 50.95 (*0-8488-0884-3*) Amereon Ltd.

Birds of the Bible. Henry Harbaugh. (Notable American Authors Ser.). 1992. reprint ed. lib. bdg. 75.00 (*0-7812-3009-8*) Rprt Serv.

Birds of the Bible. Gene S. Porter. 1986. reprint ed. lib. bdg. 35.95 (*0-89966-529-2*) Buccaneer Bks.

Birds of the Blue Ridge Mountains: A Guide for the Blue Ridge Parkway, Great Smoky Mountains, Shenandoah National Park, & Neighboring Areas. Marcus B. Simpson, Jr. LC 91-24620. (Illus.). xviii, 354p. (C). 1992. 29.95 (*0-8078-2018-0*); pap. 14.95 (*0-8078-4363-6*) U of NC Pr.

Birds of the Carolinas. Eloise F. Potter et al. LC 79-14201. (Illus.). viii, 408p. 1986. reprint ed. pap. 17.95 (*0-8078-4155-2*) U of NC Pr.

Birds of the Cayman Islands. Patricia Bradley. (Illus.). 246p. 1985. 25.00 (*0-903826-76-3*) World FL.

Birds of the Central Rockies. Jan Wassink. (Illus.). 187p. 1991. pap. 14.00 (*0-87842-235-8*) Mountain Pr.

Birds of the Chesapeake Bay. John W. Taylor. (Illus.). 96p. 1992. 36.95 (*0-8018-4380-4*) Johns Hopkins.

Birds of the Chukchi Peninsula & Wrangel Island, Vol. 2. L. A. Portenko. 1989. 39.50 (*81-205-0088-1*, Pub. by Oxford IBH II) S Asia.

Birds of the Coachella Valley: A Checklist. Theo Glenn. 5p. (Orig.). 1983. 1.50 (*0-937794-08-2*) Nature Trails.

Birds of the Colorado Valley: A Repository of Scientific & Popular Information Concerning North American Ornithology, Vol. 11. Elliott Coues. LC 73-17814. (Natural Sciences in America Ser.). 820p. 1974. reprint ed. 59.95 (*0-405-05730-X*) Ayer.

Birds of the Department of Lima, Peru. Maria Koepcke. Tr. by Erma J. Fisk. LC 83-12582. (Illus.). 1983. reprint ed. 16.95 (*0-915180-11-1*) Harrowood Bks.

Birds of the Grand Canyon Region: An Annotated Checklist. 2nd ed. Bryan Brown et al. LC 84-80860. 53p. 1985. pap. 15.00 (*0-938216-22-8*) GCNHA.

Birds of the Great Basin: A Natural History. Fred A. Ryser, Jr. LC 84-25763. (Max C. Fleischmann Series in Great Basin Natural History). (Illus.). 642p. (Orig.). 1985. pap. 39.95 (*0-87417-080-X*) U of Nev Pr.

Birds of the Great Plains: Breeding Species & Their Distribution. Paul A. Johnsgard. LC 79-1419. (Illus.). xlviii, 539p. 1979. 35.00 (*0-8032-2550-4*) U of Nebr Pr.

Birds of the Indian Hills. D. Dewar. 1986. 150.00 (*0-685-54029-4*, Pub. by Intl Bk Distr II) St Mut.

Birds of the Indian Hills. Ed. by D. Dewar. 264p. (C). 1987. text ed. 150.00 (*0-89771-594-2*, Pub. by Intl Bk Distr II) St Mut.

Birds of the Indiana Dunes. Kenneth J. Brock. LC 85-45312. (Illus.). 190p. 1986. 25.00 (*0-253-31201-9*); pap. 7.95 (*0-253-20369-4*, MB 369) Ind U Pr.

Birds of the Labrador Peninsula. W. E. Clyde Todd. LC 80-66715. (Illus.). 1980. 75.00 (*0-931130-06-9*) Harrell Bks.

Birds of the Lake Tahoe Region. Robert T. Orr & James Moffitt. (Illus.). 150p. 1971. 8.00 (*0-940228-08-4*) Calif Acad Sci.

Birds of the Ligonier Valley. Robert C. Leberman. (Special Publication CMNH Ser.: No. 3). (Illus.). 77p. (Orig.). 1976. pap. 6.00 (*0-911239-07-3*) Carnegie Mus.

Birds of the Limberlost. Gene S. Porter. 35.95 (*0-8488-1526-2*) Amereon Ltd.

Birds of the Lower Colorado River Valley. Kenneth V. Rosenberg et al. LC 90-11120. (Illus.). 416p. 1990. 45.00 (*0-8165-1174-8*) U of Ariz Pr.

***Birds of the Mayas: Field Guide to Birds of the Maya World.** Anne LaBastille. (Illus.). Date not set. 12.00 (*0-614-04833-8*) W Wind Pubns.

Birds of the Mayas: Field Guide to Birds of the Maya World. Anne Labastille. (Illus.). 120p. 1994. pap. 12.00 (*0-9632846-5-7*) W Wind Pubns.

Birds of the Middle East & North Africa. P. A. Hollom et al. LC 87-72278. (Illus.). 280p. 1988. 32.50 (*0-931130-15-8*) Harrell Bks.

Birds of the Night. Jean De Sart. LC 93-31749. (Illus.). (J). 1994. 14.95 (*0-88106-671-0*); lib. bdg. 15.88 (*0-88106-691-5*) Charlesbridge Pub.

***Birds of the Night Sky - Stars of the Field: Poems.** Pamela Gross. LC 95-13857. 1995. pap. write for info. (*0-8203-1776-4*) U of Ga Pr.

Birds of the North Gulf Coast-Prince William Sound Region, Alaska. M. E. Isleib & Brina Kessel. (Illus.). 160p. 1989. pap. 7.95 (*0-912006-39-0*) U of Alaska Pr.

Birds of the Northeast. Winston Williams. 128p. 15.95 (*0-911977-08-2*) World FL.

Birds of the Northern Rockies. rev. ed. Tom J. Ulrich. LC 84-2048. (Illus.). 159p. 1988. reprint ed. pap. 12.00 (*0-87842-169-6*) Mountain Pr.

Birds of the Northwest: A Handbook of the Ornithology of the Region Drained by the Missouri River & Its Tributaries. Elliott Coues. LC 73-17815. (Natural Sciences in America Ser.). 808p. 1974. reprint ed. 58.95 (*0-405-05731-8*) Ayer.

Birds of the Outer Hebrides. Peter Cunningham. 246p. (C). 1986. 60.00 (*0-906664-19-5*, Pub. by Mercat Pr Bks UK) St Mut.

Birds of the Pacific Northwest Mountains: The Cascade Range, the Olympic Mountains, the Insular Range, & the Coast Mountains. Jan L. Wassink. Ed. by Kathleen Ort. (Illus.). 192p. 1995. per., pap. 14.00 (*0-87842-308-7*) Mountain Pr.

Birds of the Pacific Slope: Biography by Lois Chambers Stone, 2 vols., Set. limited ed. Andrew J. Grayson. Ed. by Glenn Todd. (Illus.). 1986. 4,500.00 (*0-910457-10-7*) Arion Pr.

Birds of the Republic of Panama, 3 pts. Alexander Wetmore. Incl. Tinamidae (Tinamous) to Rynchopidae (Skimmers) LC 66-61061. (Illus.). 484p. 1965. 32.50 (*0-87474-063-0*, WEBP); Columbidae (Pigeons) to Picidae (Woodpeckers) LC 66-61061. (Illus.). 606p. 1965. 32.50 (*0-87474-064-9*, WEB2); Passeriformes: Dendrocolaptidae (Woodcreepers) to Oxyruncidae (Sharpbills) LC 66-61061. 632p. 1965. 32.50 (*0-87474-122-X*, WEBS); LC 66-61061. (Illus.). 1968. write for info. (*0-318-55737-1*) Smithsonian.

Birds of the Republic of Panama: Part 4. Passeriformes: Hirundinidae (Swallows) to Fringillidae (Finches) Alexander Wetmore et al. LC 66-61061. (Illus.). 670p. 1984. 37.50 (*0-87474-956-5*, WEB4) Smithsonian.

Birds of the Rocky Mountains. Paul A. Johnsgard. LC 91-42200. (Illus.). xii, 524p. 1992. reprint ed. pap. 19.95 (*0-8032-7574-9*, Bison Books) U of Nebr Pr.

Birds of the Seaward Peninsula, Alaska: Their Biogeography, Seasonality & Natural History. Brina Kessel. LC 89-5030. (Illus.). 330p. 1989. 34.95 (*0-912006-29-3*) U of Alaska Pr.

Birds of the Smokies. Fred J. Alsop, III. Ed. by Steve Kemp. (Natural History Handbooks Ser.). (Illus.). 168p. (Orig.). 1991. pap. 9.95 (*0-937207-05-5*) GSMNH.

***Birds of the South: Permanent & Winter Birds.** Charlotte H. Green. LC 94-37761. (Chapel Hill Bks. Ser.). (Illus.). 340p. 1995. pap. 16.95 (*0-8078-4516-7*) U of NC Pr.

Birds of the Southwestern Desert. Gusse T. Smith. LC 56-2505. (Illus.). 68p. 1989. pap. 6.95 (*0-935182-20-9*) Gem Guides Bk.

Birds of the Strait of Gibraltar. Clive Finlayson. (Poyser Popular Bird Bks.). (Illus.). 534p. 1991. text ed. 49.95 (*0-85661-066-6*, 784666) Acad Pr.

Birds of the Texas Coastal Bend: Abundance & Distribution. John H. Rappole & Gene W. Blacklock. LC 84-40567. (W. L. Moody, Jr. Natural History Ser.: No. 7). (Illus.). 184p. 1985. 19.50 (*0-89096-221-9*) Tex A&M Univ Pr.

Birds of the Wadden Sea: Final Report of the Section "Birds" of the Wadden Sea Working Group. Ed. by C. J. Smit & W. J. Wolff. 308p. (C). 1981. pap. text ed. 70.00 (*90-6191-056-0*, Pub. by A A Balkema NE) Ashgate Pub Co.

Birds of the Western Palearctic Volume I: Ostrich to Ducks. Ed. by Stanley Cramp et al. (Illus.). 1978. 150.00 (*0-19-857358-8*) OUP.

Birds of the Western Palearctic Volume V: Tyrant Flycatchers to Thrushes, Vol. V: Tyrant Flycatchers to Thrushes. Ed. by Stanley Cramp. (Illus.). 1080p. 1988. 150.00 (*0-19-857508-4*) OUP.

Birds of the Western Palearctic Volume VII: Old World Flycatchers to Shrikes. Ed. by Stanley Cramp & Christopher M. Perrins. (Illus.). 610p. 1993. 150.00 (*0-19-857510-6*) OUP.

Birds of the Western Palearctic Volume VIII: Crows to Finches. Ed. by Stanley Cramp & C. M. Perrins. (Illus.). 912p. 1994. 150.00 (*0-19-854679-3*) OUP.

Birds of the World. Colin Harrison & Alan Greensmith. LC 93-7065. (Eyewitness Handbks.). (Illus.). 416p. 1993. 29.95 (*1-56458-296-5*); Flexibinding. 19.95 (*1-56458-295-7*) Dorling Kindersley.

Birds of the World: Over Four Hundred of John Gould's Classic Bird Illustrations. Maureen Lambourne. LC 92-50130. (Illus.). 304p. 1992. 75.00 (*0-8478-1566-8*) Rizzoli Intl.

Birds of the World: With Latin, English & Chinese Names. Science Press Staff. 470p. (CHI, ENG & LAT.). 1989. lib. bdg. 49.95 (*0-7859-3663-7*, 7030013891) Fr & Eur.

Birds of Tikal: An Annotated Checklist for Tikal National Park & Peten, Guatemala. Randell A. Beavers. LC 92-2919. (W. L. Moody, Jr. Natural History Ser.: No. 12). (Illus.). 168p. 1992. 29.50 (*0-89096-525-0*); pap. 12.95 (*0-89096-518-8*) Tex A&M Univ Pr.

Birds of Tropical America. Alexander F. Skutch. LC 82-8597. (Corrie Herring Hooks Ser.: No. 5). (Illus.). 317p. 1983. 29.95 (*0-292-74634-2*) U of Tex Pr.

Birds of Tropical America: A Watcher's Introduction to Behavior, Breeding & Diversity. Steven L. Hilty. (Curious Naturalist Ser.). (Illus.). 304p. 1994. pap. 12.95 (*1-881527-56-5*) Chapters Pub.

Birds of Washtenaw County, Michigan. Michael A. Kielb et al. LC 92-46398. (Illus.). 262p. 1993. pap. text ed. 14.95 (*0-472-06535-1*) U of Mich Pr.

Birds of Water, Sea & Shore. Sandra D. Romashko. LC 77-81169. (Illus.). 64p. 1990. pap. 4.95 (*0-89317-016-X*) Windward Pub.

***Birds of West Africa.** Date not set. 22.00 (*0-00-219204-7*, HarpT) HarpC.

Birds of Western Pennsylvania & Adjacent Regions. Robert C. Leberman. (Special Publication CMNH Ser.: No. 13). 52p. 1988. pap. 6.00 (*0-911239-29-4*) Carnegie Mus.

Birds of Winter. Kit Harrison & George H. Harrison. (Illus.). 208p. 1990. 19.95 (*0-394-58196-2*) Random.

Birds of Yosemite & the East Slope. rev. ed. David Gaines. (Illus.). 360p. 1992. 12.00 (*0-932347-05-3*) Artemisia Pr.

Birds on a Wire. Roger A. Faber. (Illus.). (J). (ps-1). Date not set. pap. write for info. (*1-880122-06-5*) White Stone.

Birds on Lowland Farms. Peter Lack. 149p. 1992. pap. 35.00 (*0-11-242922-X*, HM2922X, Pub. by HMSO UK) UNIPUB.

Birds on the Horizon: Wingshooting Adventures Around the World. Stuart Williams. LC 92-74035. (Illus.). 288p. 1992. 49.00 (*0-924357-28-2*, 11200-A) Countrysport Pr.

Birds on the Horizon: Wingshooting Adventures Around the World. deluxe limited ed. Stuart Williams. LC 92-74035. (Illus.). 288p. 1992. 95.00 (*0-924357-29-0*, 11200-B) Countrysport Pr.

Birds on the Move: A Guide to New England's Avian Invaders. Neal Clark. LC 88-15216. (Illus.). 196p. (Orig.). 1988. pap. 8.95 (*0-945980-04-3*) Nrth Country Pr.

Birds on the Trees. Nina Bawden. (Modern Classic Ser.). 196p. 1993. pap. 10.95 (*1-85381-373-7*, Pub. by Virago Pr UK) Trafalgar.

***Birds on the Trees.** large type ed. Nina Bawden. LC 94-48848. 1995. write for info. (*0-7862-0412-5*) Thorndike Pr.

Birds or Massachusetts & Other New England States, Pts. 1, 2 & 3. Edward H. Forbush. Ed. by Keir B. Sterling. LC 77-81083. (Biologists & Their World Ser.). (Illus.). 1978. reprint ed. lib. bdg. 171.95 (*0-405-10659-9*) Ayer.

Birds over Troubled Forests. Russell Greenberg & Susan Lumpkin. (Illus.). 32p. (Orig.). (YA). 1991. pap. 5.00 (*1-881230-00-7*) Smiths Migratory.

Birds Pack. 32p. (J). (gr. k-2). 1993. pap. 8.95 (*1-882563-00-X*) Lamont Bks.

Birds Punch-Out Stencils. Ellen Sandbeck. (Illus.). (J). (gr. k-3). 1991. pap. 3.95 (*0-486-26801-2*) Dover.

Birds, Roots, Weeds, & the Good Ground. John F. Avanzini. (Illus.). 32p. 1980. pap. 3.00 (*0-941117-06-5*) HIS Publish.

Birds Sticker Jigsaw Book. (Illus.). (J). (gr. 3-6). 1992. pap. 3.95 (*1-56680-511-2*) Mad Hatter Pub.

Birds, the Bees & the Real Story: A Guide for Teens. Kay R. Todd & Nancy Abbey-Harris. 122p. 1980. 10.95 (*0-941816-00-1*) ETR Assocs.

Birds Throughout the World. Franz Robiller. 262p. 1980. 60.00 (*0-905418-39-5*, Pub. by Gresham Bks UK) St Mut.

Birds to Watch: The World List of Threatened Birds, No. 2. N. J. Collar et al. (Birdlife Conservation Ser.). 320p. 1994. pap. 25.00 (*1-56098-528-3*) Smithsonian.

Birds Tomorrow: Their Management & Enjoyment. Norval Barger. (Illus.). 350p. 1989. 20.95 (*0-87961-192-8*); pap. 12.95 (*0-87961-193-6*) Naturegraph.

Birds We Know. Margaret Friskey. LC 81-7745. (New True Bks.). (Illus.). 48p. (J). (gr. k-4). 1981. lib. bdg. 12.90 (*0-516-01609-1*); pap. 4.95 (*0-516-41609-X*) Childrens.

Birds Who Flew Beyond Time. Anne Baring. LC 93-5616. (Illus.). 40p. 1994. 15.00 (*1-56957-907-5*) Barefoot Bks.

Birds with Human Souls: A Guide to Bird Symbolism. Beryl Rowland. LC 77-4230. 232p. reprint ed. pap. 66.20 (*0-7837-3025-X*, 2042915) Bks Demand.

Birds Without a Nest: A Story of Indian Life in Peru. Clorinda Matto de Turner. 1977. lib. bdg. 59.95 (*0-8490-1508-1*) Gordon Pr.

Birds Worth Watching. George M. Sutton. LC 86-1314. (Illus.). 224p. (C). 1992. pap. 12.95 (*0-8061-2401-6*) U of Okla Pr.

Birdscaping Your Garden: A Practical Guide to Backyard Birds & the Plants That Attract Them. George Adams. LC 93-43391. 1994. 29.95 (*0-87596-635-7*) Rodale Pr Inc.

Birdsong: Fifty-Three Short Poems by Rumi. Jelaluddin Rumi. Tr. & Intro. by Coleman Barks. 64p. (Orig.). 1993. pap. 9.00 (*0-9618916-7-X*) Maypop.

Birdsong Ascending. Sam Harrison. 1992. 21.95 (*0-15-100060-3*) HarBrace.

Birdsong Lullaby. Diane Stanley. LC 85-5654. (Illus.). 32p. (J). (ps-2). 1985. 12.95 (*0-688-05804-3*) Morrow Jr Bks.

Birdsongs in Literature. Joseph W. Krutch. (Illus.). 1967. write for info. (*0-395-07559-9*) HM.

Birdstone Summer. Mavis Scott. (J). (ps-3). 1993. pap. 6.95 (*1-86373-231-4*, Pub. by Allen & Unwin Aust Pty AT) IPG Chicago.

Birdwashing Song: The Willow Tree Loon. Jacqueline B. Martin. LC 94-11787. (J). 1995. text ed. 15.95 (*0-02-762442-0*) Macmillan.

Birdwatch. Bates Littlehales. (Illus.). 136p. 1990. 34.95 (*0-912347-58-9*) Fulcrum Pub.

Birdwatcher's Bible. rev. ed. George Laycock. LC 93-32541. 1994. pap. 12.00 (*0-385-46835-0*) Doubleday.

Birdwatcher's Book of Lists-Eastern Region. Lester Short. 1987. pap. 7.95 (*0-394-75197-3*) Knopf.

Birdwatcher's Cookbook. Erma J. Fisk. (Illus.). 1987. 15.95 (*0-393-02502-0*) Norton.

Birdwatcher's Dictionary. Peter Weaver. (Illus.). 156p. 1990. text ed. 24.95 (*0-85661-028-3*, 784628, Pub. by Poyser UK) Acad Pr.

Birdwatchers Guide to the Sydney Region. Peter Roberts. (Illus.). 204p. (Orig.). 1994. pap. 15.95 (*0-86417-565-5*, Pub. by Kangaroo Pr AT) Seven Hills Bk.

Birdwatcher's Handbook: A Field Guide to the Natural History of the Birds of Britain & Europe: Including 515 Species That Regularly Breed in Europe & Adjacent Parts of the Middle East & North Africa. Paul R. Ehrlich et al. LC 93-41606. (Illus.). 580p. 1994. 22.00 (*0-19-858407-5*) OUP.

Birdwatching with American Women: A Selection of Nature Writings. Comp. by Deborah Strom. 1989. pap. 8.95 (*0-393-30598-8*) Norton.

Birdwise: Forty Fun Feats for Finding Out about Our Feathered Friends. Pamela M. Hickman. 1989. pap. 9.57 (*0-201-51757-4*) Addison-Wesley.

Birdy. William Wharton. 1992. 12.00 (*0-679-73412-0*, Vin) Random.

B

Birdy & the Ghosties. Jill Paton Walsh. 1989. 10.95 (*0-374-30716-4*) FS&G.

Birdy & the Ghosties. Jill Paton Walsh. 1991. pap. 4.95 (*0-374-40675-8*) FS&G.

Birger Sandzen: An Illustrated Biography. Emory K. Lindquist. LC 92-23467. (Illus.). 200p. 1993. 29.95 (*0-7006-0575-4*) U Pr of KS.

Birgit Nilsson: My Memoirs in Pictures. Birgit Nilsson. Tr. by Thomas Teal. (Quality Paperbacks Ser.). (Illus.). 127p. 1982. reprint ed. pap. 14.95 (*0-306-80180-9*) Da Capo.

Birgitta of Sweden: Life & Selected Writings. Marguerite T. Harris. (Classics of Western Spirituality Ser.). 1990. 22.95 (*0-8091-0434-2*); pap. 15.95 (*0-8091-3139-0*) Paulist Pr.

***Birjia: Society & Culture.** Samira Dasgupta. (C). 1994. text ed. 28.00 (*81-7102-018-6*, Pub. by Firma KLM) S Asia.

Birka V--Filigree & Granulation Work of the Viking Period: An Analysis of Materials from Bjorko. W. Duczko. (Illus.). 118p. 1985. lib. bdg. 33.50 (*91-7402-162-1*) Coronet Bks.

Birkat HaMazon Manual. pap. write for info. (*0-686-96116-1*) United Syn Bk.

Birkenau, The Camp of Death. Marco Nahon. Ed. by Steven Bowman. Tr. by Jacqueline H. Bowers. LC 89-4661. (Judaic Studies). (Illus.). 176p. 1989. 24.95 (*0-8173-0449-5*) U of Ala Pr.

Birkett Diary: Voyage & Visit to America, 1784-1785. Joseph Birkett. Ed. by C. W. Tazewell. LC 90-84741. 86p. (Orig.). 1990. pap. 12.00 (*1-878515-53-5*) W S Dawson.

Birkhoff Interpolation. George G. Lorentz et al. (Encyclopedia of Mathematics & Its Applications Ser.: No. 19). 1984. 64.95 (*0-521-30239-0*) Cambridge U Pr.

Birmingham. Gordon E. Cherry. (World Cities Ser.). 256p. 1994. text ed. 49.95 (*0-470-21994-7*) Halsted Pr.

Birmingham: A Study in Geography, History, & Planning. Gordon E. Cherry. LC 93-46899. (Belhaven World Cities Ser.). 254p. 1994. text ed. 49.95 (*0-471-94900-0*) Wiley.

Birmingham: Magic City Renaissance. Joe O'Donnell & Ruth B. Reuse. Ed. by James E. Turner & Mary S. Hughes. LC 92-73285. 1992. text ed. 45.00 (*0-9630029-3-7*) Community Comm.

***Birmingham: The Valley & the Hil.** Leah R. Atkins. 21.95 (*0-89781-031-7*) Preferred Mktg.

Birmingham & the Midland Hardware District. Ed. by S. Timmins. 720p. 1967. 35.00 (*0-7146-1147-6*, Pub. by F Cass Pubs UK) Intl Spec Bk.

Birmingham & West Bloomfield Cemeteries, Oakland County, Michigan. Intro. by Joan Pate. 182p. (Orig.). 1990. pap. 11.00 (*1-879766-15-9*) OCG Society.

Birmingham at War in Photographs, Vol. 1. (C). 1987. 50.00 (*0-317-89838-8*, Pub. by Birmingham Midland Soc UK) St Mut.

Birmingham at War in Photographs, Vol. 2. (C). 1987. 50.00 (*0-317-89839-6*, Pub. by Birmingham Midland Soc UK) St Mut.

***Birmingham Dine-a-Mate Book.** 272p. 1994. pap. 30.00 (*1-57393-003-2*) Dine-A-Mate.

Birmingham Dining Guide. Ed. by James R. Lunsford et al. (Illus.). 80p. 1991. pap. 3.95 (*0-9624032-1-0*) Best Times Inc.

Birmingham District: An Industrial History & Guide. Marjorie L. White. LC 81-70145. (Illus.). 324p. (Orig.). 1981. 20.00 (*0-943994-01-2*); pap. 14.95 (*0-943994-00-4*) Birmingham Hist Soc.

***Birmingham Gun.** Steve Smith & Laurie Morrow. (Illus.). 1998. 49.00 (*1-885106-20-3*) Wild Adven Pr.

Birmingham Heritage Hike Guide. 32p. (J). (gr. 4 up). 1979. pap. 2.00 (*0-943994-09-8*) Birmingham Hist Soc.

Birmingham, JFK & the Civil Rights Act of 1963: Implications for Elite Theory. John W. Cotman. (American University Studies: Political Science: Ser. X, Vol. 17). 211p. (C). 1989. text ed. 32.60 (*0-8204-0806-9*) P Lang Pubs.

Birmingham, Municipal Court Project Supporting Study. National Center for State Courts Staff. 250p. 1979. write for info. (*0-318-61194-5*, NRCO-074) Natl Ctr St Courts.

Birmingham River. Roy Fisher. 64p. 1994. pap. 10.95 (*0-19-282342-6*) OUP.

An Asterisk (*) at the beginning of an entry indicates that the title is appearing in BIP for the first time. 787

Birmingham's Best. Ed. by Michael C. Randle. (Illus.). 125p. (Orig.). 1989. pap. 4.95 (*1-878225-01-4*) First Pub Inc.

Birmingham's Commercial Real Estate - Review & Forecast. Ed. by Mike Randle & Mitzi McWhorter. (Illus.). 1989. pap. 2.95 (*0-685-29149-9*) First Pub Inc.

Birmingham's Health Care - Review & Forecast. Ed. by Mike Randle & Colleen White. (Illus.). 1989. pap. 2.95 (*0-685-29150-2*) First Pub Inc.

Birmingham's Rabbi: Morris Newfield & Alabama, 1895-1940. Mark Cowett. LC 85-20897. (Judaic Studies). 240p. 1986. 26.50 (*0-8173-0284-0*) U of Ala Pr.

***Birnbaum Bahamas - 96.** 208p. Date not set. 12.00 (*0-06-278217-7*, Harper Ref) HarpC.

***Birnbaum's Berlin, 1995.** Alexandra M. Birnbaum. (Birnbaum Travel Guides Ser.). 224p. 1994. pap. 12.00 (*0-06-278183-9*, Harper Ref) HarpC.

Birnbaum's Bermuda, 1995. Alexandra M. Birnbaum. 176p. 1994. pap. 12.00 (*0-06-278168-5*) HarpC.

***Birnbaum's Boston, 1995.** Alexandra M. Birnbaum. (Birbaum Travel Guides Ser.). 208p. 1994. pap. 12.00 (*0-06-278184-7*, Harper Ref) HarpC.

***Birnbaum's Canada 1995.** Alexandra M. Birnbaum. 1994. pap. 18.00 (*0-06-278185-5*, HarpT) HarpC.

***Birnbaum's Cancun, Cozumel & Isla Mujeres, 1996.** Alexandra M. Birnbaum. 196p. Date not set. 12.00 (*0-06-278215-0*, Harper Ref) HarpC.

***Birnbaum's Caribbean.** Alexandra M. Birnbaum. 864p. Date not set. 18.00 (*0-06-278214-2*, Harper Ref) HarpC.

***Birnbaum's Chicago, 1995.** Alexandra M. Birnbaum. 1994. pap. 12.00 (*0-06-278186-3*, HarpT) HarpC.

***Birnbaum's Country Inns North America 1995.** Ed. by Alexandra M. Birnbaum. (Birnbaum Travel Guide Ser.). (Illus.). 448p. 1995. pap. 12.00 (*0-06-278203-7*, Harper Ref) HarpC.

Birnbaum's Disneyland: The Official Guide 1994. Ed. by Steve Birnbaum. (Birnbaum Travel Guides Ser.). (Illus.). 160p. 1993. pap. 9.95 (*1-56282-804-5*) Hyperion.

Birnbaum's Disneyland: The Official Guide 1995. Birnbaum Travel Guides Staff. (Illus.). 160p. 1994. pap. 10.95 (*0-7868-8038-4*) Hyperion.

***Birnbaum's Disneyland: The Official Guide 1996.** (Birnbaum Travel Guides Ser.). (Illus.). 160p. 1995. pap. 10.95 (*0-7868-8110-0*) Hyperion.

Birnbaum's Disneyland 1993. Steve Birnbaum. (Illus.). 160p. 1992. pap. 9.95 (*1-56282-945-9*) Hyperion.

Birnbaum's Eastern Europe, 1994. Alexandra M. Birnbaum. (Birnbaum Travel Guides Ser.). (Illus.). 1994. pap. 18.00 (*0-06-278124-3*, Harper Ref) HarpC.

***Birnbaum's Eastern Europe 1995.** Ed. by Alexandra M. Birnbaum. (Birnbaum Travel Guide Ser.). (Illus.). 624p. 1995. pap. 18.00 (*0-06-278187-1*, Harper Ref) HarpC.

***Birnbaum's Europe for Business Travelers 1995.** Ed. by Alexandra M. Birnbaum. (Birnbaum Travel Guide Ser.). (Illus.). 912p. 1995. pap. 16.00 (*0-06-278189-8*, Harper Ref) HarpC.

Birnbaum's Europe, 1994. Alexandra M. Birnbaum. (Birnbaum Travel Guide Ser.). (Illus.). 1994. pap. 19.00 (*0-06-278125-1*, Harper Ref) HarpC.

***Birnbaum's Europe 1995.** Ed. by Alexandra M. Birnbaum. (Birnbaum Travel Guide Ser.). (Illus.). 2160p. 1995. pap. 20.00 (*0-06-278188-X*, Harper Ref) HarpC.

Birnbaum's France 1994. Ed. by Alexandra M. Birnbaum. (Birnbaum Travel Guides Ser.). (Illus.). 896p. 1993. pap. 18.00 (*0-06-278104-9*, Harper Ref) HarpC.

***Birnbaum's France, 1995.** Alexandra M. Birnbaums. 1995. pap. 18.00 (*0-06-278190-1*, HarpT) HarpC.

***Birnbaum's Germany, 1995.** Ed. by Alexandra M. Birnbaum. (Birnbaum's Travel Guides Ser.). (Illus.). 496p. (Orig.). 1994. pap. 18.00 (*0-06-278191-X*, Harper Ref) HarpC.

Birnbaum's Great Britain, 1994. Alexandra M. Birnbaum. (Birnbaum Travel Guides Ser.). (Illus.). 1994. pap. 18.00 (*0-06-278128-6*, Harper Ref) HarpC.

***Birnbaum's Great Britain, 1995.** Alexandra M. Birnbaum. 1995. pap. 18.00 (*0-06-278192-8*, HarpT) HarpC.

Birnbaum's Guide to Caribbean, Bermuda & the Bahamas, 1990. 1990. 13.95 (*0-317-99659-2*) HM.

***Birnbaum's Ireland, 1995.** Ed. by Alexandra M. Birnbaum. (Birnbaum's Travel Guides Ser.). (Illus.). 576p. (Orig.). 1994. pap. 18.00 (*0-06-278193-6*, Harper Ref) HarpC.

Birnbaum's Italy, 1987. Steve Birnbaum. 1987. pap. 12.95 (*0-317-56466-8*) HM.

***Birnbaum's Italy, 1995.** Alexandra M. Birnbaum. 1995. pap. 18.00 (*0-06-278194-4*, HarpT) HarpC.

***Birnbaum's London, 1995.** Alexandra M. Birnbaum. 1994. pap. 12.00 (*0-06-278195-2*, HarpT) HarpC.

***Birnbaum's Los Angeles, 1995.** Alexandra M. Birnbaum. 1994. pap. 12.50 (*0-06-278178-2*, HarpT) HarpC.

***Birnbaum's Miami and Ft. Lauderdale 96.** Date not set. pap. 12.00 (*0-06-278212-6*) HarpC.

***Birnbaum's Montreal & Quebec City.** Alexandra M. Birnbaum. 1994. pap. 12.00 (*0-06-278179-0*, HarpT) HarpC.

***Birnbaum's New Orleans, 1995.** Alexandra M. Birnbaum. 1994. pap. 12.50 (*0-06-278180-4*, HarpT) HarpC.

***Birnbaum's New York, 1995.** Alexandra M. Birnbaum. 1994. pap. 12.00 (*0-06-278181-2*, HarpT) HarpC.

Birnbaum's Paris, 1994. Ed. by Alexandra M. Birnbaum. (Birnbaum Travel Guides Ser.). (Illus.). 240p. 1993. pap. 12.00 (*0-06-278144-8*, Harper Ref) HarpC.

***Birnbaum's Paris, 1995.** Alexandra M. Birnbaum. 1995. pap. 12.00 (*0-06-278182-0*, HarpT) HarpC.

***Birnbaum's Portugal 1995.** Alexandra M. Birnbaum. 1994. pap. 18.00 (*0-06-278177-4*, HarpT) HarpC.

***Birnbaum's Rome, 1995.** Alexandra M. Birnbaum. 1995. pap. 12.00 (*0-06-278170-7*, HarpT) HarpC.

***Birnbaum's San Francisco, 1995.** Alexandra M. Birnbaum. 1994. pap. 12.00 (*0-06-278171-5*, HarpT) HarpC.

***Birnbaum's Santa Fe & Taos, 1995.** Alexandra M. Birnbaum. 1994. pap. 12.00 (*0-06-278172-3*, HarpT) HarpC.

***Birnbaum's South America, 1995.** Alexandra M. Birnbaum. (Birnbaum's Travel Guides Ser.). (Illus.). 976p. (Orig.). 1994. pap. 20.00 (*0-06-278162-6*, Harper Ref) HarpC.

***Birnbaum's Spain, 1995.** Ed. by Alexandra M. Birnbaum. (Birnbaum's Travel Guides Ser.). (Illus.). 640p. (Orig.). 1994. pap. 18.00 (*0-06-278173-1*, Harper Ref) HarpC.

Birnbaum's U. S. A. for Business Travelers, 1986. Steve Birnbaum. 1985. pap. 7.95 (*0-685-11176-8*) HM.

Birnbaum's United States 1994. Ed. by Alexandra M. Birnbaum. (Birnbaum Travel Guides Ser.). (Illus.). 1408p. 1994. pap. 19.00 (*0-06-278114-6*, Harper Ref) HarpC.

***Birnbaum's United States, 1995.** Alexandra M. Birnbaum. 1995. pap. 19.00 (*0-06-278174-X*, HarpT) HarpC.

***Birnbaum's United States 96.** rev. ed. 1995. pap. 19.00 (*0-06-278241-X*) HarpC.

Birnbaum's Walt Disney World: The Official Guide 1994. Ed. by Steve Birnbaum. (Birnbaum Travel Guides Ser.). (Illus.). 256p. 1993. pap. 11.95 (*1-56282-803-7*) Hyperion.

Birnbaum's Walt Disney World: The Official Guide 1995. Birnbaum Travel Guides Staff. (Illus.). 256p. 1994. pap. 12.95 (*0-7868-8040-6*) Hyperion.

***Birnbaum's Walt Disney World: The Official Guide 1996.** (Birnbaum Travel Guides Ser.). (Illus.). 256p. 1995. pap. 12.95 (*0-7868-8111-9*) Hyperion.

Birnbaum's Walt Disney World for Kids by Kids. rev. ed. Birnbaum Travel Guides Staff. (Illus.). 160p. 1994. pap. 9.95 (*0-7868-8041-4*) Hyperion.

Birnbaum's Walt Disney World for Kids by Kids, 1994. Ed. by Steve Birnbaum. (Birnbaum Travel Guides Ser.). (Illus.). 128p. (J). 1993. pap. 9.95 (*1-56282-750-2*) Hyperion.

***Birnbaum's Walt Disney World for Kids by Kids 1996.** (Birnbaum Travel Guides Ser.). (Illus.). 160p. (J). 1995. pap. 9.95 (*0-7868-8112-7*) Hyperion.

***Birnbaum's Walt Disney World Without Kids: The Official Guide for Fun-Loving Adults.** (Birnbaum Travel Guides Ser.). (Illus.). 224p. 1995. pap. 10.95 (*0-7868-8121-6*) Hyperion.

Birnbaum's Walt Disney World 1993. Steve Birnbaum. (Illus.). 256p. 1992. pap. 11.95 (*1-56282-946-7*) Hyperion.

Birnbaum's Washington, D. C., 1994. Alexandra M. Birnbaum. (Birnbaum Travel Guides Ser.). (Illus.). 1994. pap. 12.00 (*0-06-278156-1*, Harper Ref) HarpC.

***Birnbaum's Washington D. C., 1995.** Alexandra M. Birnbaum. 1994. pap. 12.00 (*0-06-278176-6*, HarpT) HarpC.

BIRPS Atlas: Deep Seismic Reflection Profiles Around the British Isles. Ed. by Simon L. Klemperer & Richard Hobbs. (Illus.). 128p. (C). 1992. 150.00 (*0-521-41828-3*) Cambridge U Pr.

Birsay Bay Project, Vol. 1: Excavations 1976-1982. Christopher D. Morris. (Illus.). 334p. 1993. text ed. 66.00 (*0-905096-08-8*) A Sutton Pub.

Birth. Gene Edwards. (Orig.). 1991. 7.99 (*0-8423-0158-5*) Tyndale.

Birth. James Tucker. (Stone Ser.: No. 1). 1981. pap. 2.95 (*0-8217-0760-4*) Zebra.

Birth: A Guide for Prayer. Jacqueline Bergan & S. Marie Schwan. (Take & Receive Ser.). (Illus.). 154p. (Orig.). 1985. pap. 6.95 (*0-88489-170-4*) St Marys.

Birth after Cesarean: The Medical Facts. Bruce L. Flamm. 224p. 1992. pap. 11.00 (*0-671-79218-0*, Fireside) S&S Trade.

Birth & Childhood among the Arabs. Hilma N. Granqvist. LC 72-9643. reprint ed. 45.00 (*0-404-57447-5*) AMS Pr.

Birth, & Copulation, & Death. Harry Morris. LC 79-94804. 68p. reprint ed. pap. 25.00 (*0-7837-5079-X*, 2044777) Bks Demand.

Birth & Death & Cybernation: Cybernetics of the Sacred. Paul Ryan. 190p. 1973. text ed. 62.00 (*0-677-04320-1*) Gordon & Breach.

Birth & Death of Companies: An Historical Perspective. Philippe Jobert & Michael Moss. (Illus.). 242p. 1990. 65.00 (*1-85070-332-9*) Prthnon Pub.

Birth & Death of Meaning. 2nd ed. Ernest Becker. LC 62-15359. 228p. 1971. 14.95 (*0-02-902170-7*); pap. 12.95 (*0-02-902190-1*) Free Pr.

Birth & Death Processes & Markov Chains. Z. K. Wang & Z. Q. Yang. ix, 361p. 1993. 109.00 (*0-387-10820-3*) Spr-Verlag.

Birth & Development of the Geoogical Sciences. Frank D. Adams. 1990. pap. 10.95 (*0-486-26372-X*) Dover.

Birth & Early Years of the Bell Telephone System, 1876-1880. Rosario J. Tosiello. Ed. by Stuart Bruchey & Vincent P. Carosso. LC 78-18979. (Dissertations in Broadcasting Ser.). 1979. lib. bdg. 40.95 (*0-405-11481-8*) Ayer.

Birth & Evolution of Massive Stars & Stellar Groups. Ed. by Wilfried Boland & Hugo Van Woerden. 1985. lib. bdg. 121.50 (*90-277-2135-1*) Kluwer Ac.

Birth & Fertility Rates by Education: 1980 & 1985 PHS 91-1927. (Vital & Health Statistics, Series 21: Data on Natality, Marriage, & Divorce: No. 49). 46p. 2.50 (*0-685-61588-X*, 017-022-01123-9) Natl Ctr Health Stats.

***Birth & Fertility Rates for States, United States, 1990.** Sally C. Clarke & Stephanie J. Ventura. Ed. by National Center for Health Statistics (U.S.) Staff. LC 94-24746. (Vital & Health Statistics Ser. 21, Data on Natality, Marriage, & Divorce: Vol. 52). 1994. write for info. (*0-8406-0502-1*) Natl Ctr Health Stats.

Birth & Fortune: The Impact of Numbers on Personal Welfare. 2nd rev. ed. Richard A. Easterlin. 240p. 1987. pap. text ed. 12.95 (*0-226-18032-8*) U Ch Pr.

Birth & Growth. (How Our Bodies Work Ser.). (Illus.). 48p. (J). (gr. 5-8). 1988. lib. bdg. 12.95 (*0-382-09708-4*) Silver Burdett Pr.

Birth & Growth. Anita Ganeri. (First Starts Ser.). (Illus.). 32p. (J). (gr. 2-4). 1994. lib. bdg. 19.97 (*0-8114-5519-X*) Raintree Steck-V.

Birth & Growth of Industrial England: 1714-1867 see Harbrace History of England

Birth & Infancy of Stars: Proceedings of the Les Houches Summer School, Session XLI, 8 August-2 September 1983, Vol. 41. Ed. by R. Lucas et al. 846p. 1985. 233.50 (*0-444-86917-4*, North Holland) Elsevier.

Birth & Ministry of Jesus. (J). (ps-3). 1992. pap. 4.99 (*0-529-07194-0*) World Bible.

Birth & Rebirth see Rites & Symbols of Initiation: The Mysteries of Birth & Rebirth

Birth & Rebirth of Pictorial Space. 3rd ed. John White. LC 87-1592. (Illus.). 384p. 1987. pap. 18.50 (*0-674-07475-0*) HUP.

Birth & Relationships: How Your Birth Affects Your Relationships. Sondra Ray & Bob Mandel. LC 86-28404. 172p. 1987. pap. 8.95 (*0-89087-486-7*) Celestial Arts.

Birth & the Dialogue of Love. Marilyn A. Moran. LC 81-81200. (Illus.). 233p. (Orig.). (C). 1981. pap. 24.95 (*0-940128-01-2*) New Nativity.

Birth & Youth of Jesus, by Mary, Mother of Jesus. Daniel G. Samuels. 1966. 5.00 (*0-686-12714-5*) Found Ch Divine Truth.

Birth As an American Rite of Passage. Robbee E. Davis-Floyd. (C). 1993. pap. 14.00 (*0-520-08431-4*) U CA Pr.

Birth As an American Rite of Passage. Robbie Davis-Floyd. 1992. 35.00 (*0-520-07439-4*) U CA Pr.

Birth at Dawn. Driss Chraibi. Tr. by Ann Woollcombe. LC 86-51006. Orig. Title: Le Noussance de l'Aube. 144p. 1990. 22.00 (*0-89410-576-0*); pap. 11.00 (*0-89410-577-9*) Three Continents.

Birth Atlas. 6th rev. ed. Maternity Center Association Staff. (Illus.). 19p. 1993. reprint ed. 53.00 (*0-912758-00-7*) Maternity Ctr.

Birth Bond: Reunions Between Birthparents & Adoptees, What Happens After. . . Judith S. Gediman & Linda P. Brown. Ed. by Joan S. Dunphy. LC 89-43405. 285p. 1991. pap. 13.95 (*0-88282-072-9*) New Horizon NJ.

Birth Book: Everything You Need to Know to Have a Safe & Satisfying Birth. William M. Sears & Martha Sears. LC 93-5748. 1994. 12.95 (*0-316-77907-5*) Little.

Birth by Fire: A Guide to Hawaii's Volcanoes. Bob Krauss. (Illus.). 92p. (Orig.). 1992. pap. 11.95 (*0-89610-228-9*) Island Heritage.

Birth Center: An Approach to the Birth Experience. Salee Berman & Victor Berman. write for info. (*0-318-59682-2*) S&S Trade.

Birth Control. Maududi Abu-Ala. pap. 5.50 (*0-935782-52-4*) Kazi Pubns.

Birth Control. Malcolm Potts. Ed. by J. J. Head. LC 84-45839. (Carolina Biology Readers Ser.: No. 178). (Illus.). 16p. (gr. 10 up). 1987. pap. 2.75 (*0-89278-104-1*, 45-9778) Carolina Biological.

Birth Control: Why Are They Lying to Women? J. Espinosa. 1980. 5.00 (*0-533-03922-3*, 001) Human Life Intl.

Birth Control & Christian Discipleship. John F. Kippley. 36p. (Orig.). 1993. 2.00 (*0-926412-10-8*) Couple to Couple.

Birth Control & Controlling Birth: Women-Centered Perspectives. Betty Hoskins & Michael Gross. Ed. by Helen B. Holmes. LC 80-82173. (Contemporary Issues in Biomedicine, Ethics, & Society Ser.). 352p. 1980. 39.95 (*0-89603-022-9*); pap. 19.95 (*0-89603-023-7*) Humana.

Birth Control & Family Planning in Nineteenth Century America. LC 73-20645. (Sex, Marriage & Society Ser.). (Illus.). 349p. 1977. reprint ed. 31.95 (*0-405-05795-4*) Ayer.

Birth Control & Morality in Nineteenth Century America. Incl. Fruits of Philosophy. Charles Knowlton. LC 78-169362. 1972. (*0-318-50795-1*); Moral Physiology. Robert D. Owen. LC 78-169362. 1972. (*0-318-50796-X*); LC 78-169362. (Family in America Ser.). 150p. 1974. 17.95 (*0-405-03883-6*) Ayer.

Birth Control & the Population Question in England, 1877-1930. Richard A. Soloway. LC 81-14791. xx, 418p. 1982. 39.95 (*0-8078-1504-7*) U of NC Pr.

Birth Control & You. Elizabeth K. White et al. (Illus.). 40p. 1994. pap. 3.60 (*0-317-59872-4*) Budlong.

Birth Control Book. Philip A. Belcastro. 144p. (C). 1986. pap. 26.25 (*0-86720-068-5*) Jones & Bartlett.

Birth Control by Injection: The Story of Depo-Provera. Thomas J. Vecchio. 1993. pap. 9.95 (*0-533-10695-8*) Vantage.

Birth Control in Germany 1871-1933. James Woycke. (Wellcome Institute Series in the History of Medicine). 176p. (C). 1988. lib. bdg. 59.95 (*0-415-00373-3*, A1728) Routledge.

Birth Control in Practice. Marie E. Kopp. LC 72-169390. (Family in America Ser.). 294p. 1974. reprint ed. 19.95 (*0-405-03867-4*) Ayer.

Birth Control Laws. M. W. Dennett. LC 70-119053. (Civil Liberties in American History Ser.). 1970. 35.00 (*0-306-71942-8*) Da Capo.

Birth Control Movement & American Society: From Private Vice to Public Virtue, with a New Preface on the Relationship Between Historical Scholarship & Feminist Issues. James Reed. LC 83-60459. 482p. reprint ed. pap. 137.40 (*0-7837-1420-3*, 2041775) Bks Demand.

Birth Control Politics in the United States, 1916-1945. Carole R. McCann. 256p. 1994. 29.95 (*0-8014-2490-9*) Cornell U Pr.

Birth Control Review, 24 vols. in 9, Set. Margaret Sanger. LC 69-11320. 1970. reprint ed. lib. bdg. 650.00 (*0-686-85844-1*) Da Capo.

Birth Control Technologies: Prospects by the Year 2000. Michael J. Harper. LC 82-15940. 281p. 1983. text ed. 27.50 (*0-292-70739-8*); pap. 10.95 (*0-292-70757-6*) U of Tex Pr.

Birth Control Vaccines. Ed. by Gursaran P. Talwar & Raj Raghupathy. (Medical Intelligence Unit Ser.). 165p. 1995. 79.00 (*1-57059-126-1*) R G Landes.

Birth Customs. Lucy Rushton. LC 92-42174. (Comparing Religions Ser.). (Illus.). 32p. (J). (gr. 4-8). 1993. 13.95 (*1-56847-030-4*) Thomson Lrning.

Birth Day. Benson. 1994. pap. 10.95 (*1-56924-952-0*) Marlowe & Co.

***Birth Day: Baby Animals Come into the World.** Midas Dekkers. LC 94-35394. (Illus.). 96p. (J). (gr. 1 up). 1995. text ed. 17.95 (*0-7167-6581-0*, Sci Am Yng Rdrs) W H Freeman.

***Birth Days: A Nurse-Midwife's Account.** Frances Wirvin. 160p. (Orig.). 1994. pap. 17.95 (*1-55059-079-0*) Temeron Bks.

Birth, Death, & Motherhood in Classical Greece. Nancy Demand. LC 93-39828. 1994. text ed. 39.95 (*0-8018-4762-1*) Johns Hopkins.

Birth Defects. (Encyclopedia of Health - Medical Disorders & Their Treatment Ser.). (Illus.). 112p. 1993. lib. bdg. 18.95 (*0-7910-0058-3*) Chelsea Hse.

Birth Defects Compendium. 2nd ed. Ed. by Daniel Bergsma. 1979. text ed. 189.95 (*0-471-83298-7*) Wiley.

Birth Defects Encyclopedia, 2 vols., Set. M. Buyse. 1991. 250.00 (*0-86542-228-1*) Blackwell Sci.

Birth Environments: Emerging Trends & Implications for Design. Alice Lerman. (Publications in Architecture & Urban Planning: No. R91-3). (Illus.). 110p. (C). 1991. 15.00 (*0-938744-76-3*) U of Wis Ctr Arch-Urban.

***Birth Expectations of U. S. Women: 1973 to 1988.** Linda S. Peterson. 9940. write for info. (*0-8406-0501-3*) Natl Ctr Health Stats.

Birth in Four Cultures: A Crosscultural Ivestigation of Childbirth in Yucatan, Holland, Sweden, & the United States. 4th rev. ed. Brigette Jordan. (Illus.). 235p. (C). 1993. pap. text ed. 10.50 (*0-88133-717-X*) Waveland Pr.

Birth Index for Buda Jewry: Covering the Years 1820-49 for Neolog Jews in Buda (Budapest), Hungary. Richard Panchyk. 56p. (Orig.). 1993. pap. text ed. 3.75 (*0-9622473-6-7*) No Ink.

Birth Injuries: Medical Subject Analysis with Research Bibliography. Michele Y. Kobayashi. LC 84-45647. 150p. 1987. 44.50 (*0-88164-236-3*); pap. 39.50 (*0-88164-237-1*) ABBE Pubs Assn.

Birth, Interaction & Attachment. Ed. by Marshall H. Klaus & Martha O. Robertson. (Pediatric Round Table Ser.: No. 6). 144p. 1982. 10.00 (*0-931562-03-1*) J & J Consumer Prods.

Birth Is More Than Once: The Inner World of Adopted Korean Children. H. Sook Wilkinson. LC 85-62489. 73p. (Orig.). 1985. pap. 7.95 (*0-9615674-0-6*) Sunrise Vent.

Birth Lottery: Prenatal Diagnosis & Selective Abortion. Judith A. Boss. LC 92-49738. (Values & Ethics Ser.: Vol. 5). 272p. 1993. 23.95 (*0-8294-0740-5*) Loyola Univ Pr.

Birth-Mark: Unsettling the Wilderness in American Literary History. Susan Howe. LC 92-56905. (Illus.). 208p. (C). 1993. text ed. 40.00 (*0-8195-5256-9*, Wesleyan Univ Pr); pap. 16.95 (*0-8195-6263-7*, Wesleyan Univ Pr) U Pr of New Eng.

Birth Marks. Sarah Dunant. LC 92-14735. 1992. 17.00 (*0-385-42318-7*) Doubleday.

Birth Marks. Dennis Guernsey & Lucy Guernsey. 1991. 12.99 (*0-8499-0904-X*) Word Inc.

Birth, Marriage, & Death Register, Church Records & Epitaphs of Lancaster, Massachusetts, 1643-1850. Henry S. Nourse. 508p. (Orig.). 1993. reprint ed. pap. text ed. 31.00 (*1-55613-801-6*) Heritage Bk.

Birth Mother: America's First Legal Surrogate Mother Tells the Story of Her Change of Heart. Elizabeth Kane. LC 87-23810. 320p. 1988. 17.95 (*0-15-112811-1*) HarBrace.

Birth Mother Search: Some Day I'll Find Her. E. B. Schumacher. Ed. by Frances B. Goodman. (Life Management Ser.). 120p. 1993. pap. 9.95 (*0-89896-379-6*) Larksdale.

Birth of a Book. Jess Carr. LC 74-84706. 151p. 1974. 6.95 (*0-89227-010-1*) Commonwealth Pr.

Birth of a Breed: The History of Polled Herefords - America's First Beef Breed. Orville K. Sweet. Ed. by Doris Morris. LC 75-18757. (Illus.). 386p. (C). 1975. 12.95 (*0-913504-25-4*) Lowell Pr.

Birth of a Century: Early Color Photographs of America. Jim Hughes. (Illus.). 224p. 1994. 40.00 (*1-85043-646-0*, Pub. by I B Tauris UK) St Martin.

***Birth of a Constitution.** Ed. by Bertus De Villiers. 444p. 1994. pap. 50.00 (*0-7021-3216-0*, Pub. by Juta SA) W W Gaunt.

Birth of a Cooperative: Hoedads Inc., A Worker Owned Forest Labor Coop. Hal Hartzell, Jr. LC 87-2656. (Illus.). 352p. (Orig.). 1987. pap. 12.95 (*0-938493-09-4*) Hulogosi Inc.

Birth of a Dilemma: The Conquest & Settlement of Rhodesia. Philip P. Mason. LC 82-9162. (Illus.). xii, 367p. 1982. reprint ed. text ed. 65.00 (*0-313-23547-3*, MABI, Greenwood Pr) Greenwood.

Birth of a Father. Martin H. Greenberg. 256p. 1986. mass mkt. 4.95 (*0-380-70156-1*) Avon.

Birth of a Foal. Hans-Heinrich Isenbart. LC 85-17406. (Nature Watch Bks.). (Illus.). 48p. (J). (gr. 2-5). 1986. lib. bdg. 19.95 (*0-87614-239-0*, Carolrhoda) Lerner Group.

B

An Asterisk (*) at the beginning of an entry indicates that the title is appearing in BIP for the first time.

B

An Asterisk (*) at the beginning of an entry indicates that the title is appearing in BIP for the first time.

Birth of the Nation: A Portrait of the American People on the Eve of Independence. Arthur M. Schlesinger, Jr. 228p. 1988. pap. 9.95 (*0-317-64564-1*) HM.

Birth of the Nation: The First Federal Congress, 1789-1791. Charlene B. Bickford & Kenneth R. Bowling. LC 89-14541. (Illus.). 128p. 1989. reprint ed. pap. 12.95 (*0-945612-14-1*) Madison Hse.

Birth of the National Park Service: The Founding Years, 1913-1933. Horace M. Albright. LC 85-19743. (Institute of the American West Bks.: Vol. 2). (Illus.). 340p. 1985. 19.95 (*0-935704-32-9*); pap. 10.95 (*0-935704-33-7*) Howe Brothers.

Birth of the New Testament: The Origin & Development of the First Christian Generation. Raymond F. Collins. 324p. 1993. 29.95 (*0-8245-1276-6*) Crossroad NY.

Birth of the Oil Industry. Paul H. Giddens. LC 72-2839. (Use & Abuse of America's Natural Resources Ser.). (Illus.). 292p. 1978. reprint ed. 25.95 (*0-405-04507-7*) Ayer.

Birth of the Other. Rosine Lefort. Tr. by Marc Du Ry et al. LC 93-40386. 344p. (C). 1994. 49.95 (*0-252-01900-8*); pap. 18.95 (*0-252-06393-7*) U of Ill Pr.

Birth of the Palestinian Refugee Problem, 1947-1949. Benny Morris. (Cambridge Middle East Library: No. 15). 416p. 1989. pap. 21.95 (*0-521-33889-1*) Cambridge U Pr.

***Birth of the People's Republic of Antarctica: A Novel.** John C. Batchelor. 416p. 1995. pap. 14.00 (*0-8050-3786-1*, Owl) H Holt & Co.

Birth of the Republic, 1763-89. Edmund S. Morgan. LC 92-8871. (Chicago History of American Civilization Ser.). 224p. (C). 1992. pap. text ed. 9.95 (*0-226-53757-9*) U Ch Pr.

Birth of the Republic, 1763-89. 3rd ed. Edmund S. Morgan. LC 92-8871. (Chicago History of American Civilization Ser.). 224p. (C). 1992. lib. bdg. 29.95 (*0-226-53756-0*) U Ch Pr.

Birth of the Senses. Boris Cyrulnik. 1992. pap. text ed. 11.95 (*0-07-015044-3*) McGraw.

Birth of the Sun: Selected Poems 1935-1985. Pablo A. Cuadra. Tr. by Steven F. White. (Illus.). 171p. 1988. 25.00 (*0-87775-204-4*); pap. 14.95 (*0-87775-205-2*) Unicorn Pr.

Birth of the Synoptic Gospels. Jean Carmignac. Tr. by Michael J. Wrenn. 1986. 5.95 (*0-8199-0887-8*, Frncscn Herld) Franciscan Pr.

Birth of the Talkies: From Edison to Jolsen. Harry M. Geduld. LC 74-11887. 350p. reprint ed. pap. 99.80 (*0-8357-7273-X*, 2056228) Bks Demand.

Birth of the Theotokos. Monks of New Skete Staff The. Tr. by Laurence Mancuso. (Liturgical Music Series I: Great Feasts: Vol. 3). 25p. 1986. pap. text ed. 10.00 (*0-935129-04-9*) Monks of New Skete.

Birth of the Universe: The Big Bang & After. Trinh X. Thuan. Tr. by I. Mark Paris. (Discoveries Ser.). (Illus.). 160p. 1993. pap. 12.95 (*0-8109-2815-9*) Abrams.

Birth of Tragedy. Friedrich Nietzsche. 1974. 300.00 (*0-87968-172-1*) Gordon Pr.

Birth of Tragedy. Friedrich Nietzsche. Tr. by Shaun Whiteside. 160p. 1994. pap. 8.95 (*0-14-043339-2*, Penguin Classics) Viking Penguin.

Birth of Tragedy. Friedrich Nietzsche. Tr. by Walter Kaufmann. Bd. with Case of Wagner. 1967. Set pap. 9.00 (*0-394-70369-3*, Vin) Random.

***Birth of Tragedy.** unabridged ed. Friedrich Nietzsche. (Thrift Editions Ser.). 96p. 1995. pap. text ed. 1.00 (*0-486-28515-4*) Dover.

Birth of Tragedy: A Commentary. David Lenson. (Twayne's Masterwork Studies). 152p. 1987. text ed. 21.95 (*0-8057-7968-X*, Twayne); pap. 12.95 (*0-8057-8008-4*, Twayne) Macmillan.

Birth of Tragedy & the Genealogy of Morals. Friedrich Nietzsche. Tr. by Francis Golffing. Incl. Genealogy of Morals. LC 56-7535. 1956. (*0-318-51722-1*); LC 56-7535. 1956. Set mass mkt. 8.95 (*0-385-09210-5*, A81, Anchor NY) Doubleday.

Birth of Vietnam. Keith W. Taylor. (Illus.). 418p. 1991. pap. 16.00 (*0-520-07417-3*) U CA Pr.

Birth of Western Canada: A History of the Riel Rebellions. 2nd ed. George F. Stanley. LC 61-1393. 508p. reprint ed. pap. 144.80 (*0-8357-7274-8*, 2023672) Bks Demand.

Birth of Western Canada: A History of the Riel Rebellions. 2nd ed. George F. Stanley. (Reprints in Canadian History Ser.). 500p. 1992. pap. 24.95 (*0-8020-6931-2*) U of Toronto Pr.

Birth or Abortion: Private Struggles in a Political World. K. Maloy & M. Patterson. (Illus.). 420p. (C). 1992. 26.95 (*0-306-44327-9*, Plenum Pr) Plenum.

Birth Order & Life Roles. Lucille K. Forer. 184p. 1969. 25.95x (*0-398-00596-6*) C C Thomas.

Birth Order & You: How Your Sex & Position in the Family Affects Your Personality & Relationships. Ron Richardson & Lois A. Richardson. (Psychology Ser.). 280p. (Orig.). 1990. pap. text ed. 7.95 (*0-88908-876-4*) Self-Counsel Pr.

Birth-Order Blues. Joan Drescher. (Illus.). 32p. (J). (ps-3). 1993. 13.99 (*0-670-83621-4*) Viking Child Bks.

Birth Order Book. Kevin Leman. 192p. 1985. pap. 4.99 (*0-8007-8596-7*) Revell.

Birth Order Book. Kevin Leman. 1992. mass mkt. 9.95 (*0-440-50471-6*, Dell Trade Pbks) Dell.

Birth Order Challenge: Expanding Your Horizons. Clifford E. Isaacson. LC 90-45409. (Illus.). 183p. (Orig.). 1991. 19.95 (*0-945156-01-4*); pap. 11.95 (*0-945156-02-2*) Upper Des Moines Counsel.

***Birth (Out of) Control: The Failure of Government Family Planning Programs.** Jacqueline R. Kasun. 19p. 1994. pap. 2.00 (*1-55922-034-1*) Human Life Intl.

Birth over Thirty. Sheila Kitzinger. (Nonfiction Ser.). 160p. 1985. mass mkt. 6.95 (*0-14-007610-7*, Penguin Bks) Viking Penguin.

***Birth Over Thirty-Five.** Sheila Kitzinger. LC 94-21963. (Illus.). 192p. 1995. pap. text ed. 9.95 (*0-14-024141-8*, Penguin Bks) Viking Penguin.

Birth Pangs of New Man. J. W. Kaiser. Tr. by R. Van Vlissingen. 80p. 1989. pap. 15.00 (*0-943185-03-3*) JWK Pubns.

Birth Partner: Everything You Need to Know to Help a Woman Through Childbirth. Penny Simkin. (Illus.). 256p. 1989. pap. 10.95 (*1-55832-010-5*) Harvard Common Pr.

Birth Partner's Handbook: How to Help a Woman Through Childbirth. Penny Simkin. LC 87-31537. 1989. pap. 5.95 (*0-671-66403-4*) S&S Trade.

Birth Pattern Psychology: Personality Assessment Through the Birth Chart. Tamise Van Pelt. Ed. by Marah Ren. LC 83-63066. (Illus.). 272p. (Orig.). 1984. pap. 14.95 (*0-914918-33-8*, Whitford Pr) Schiffer.

Birth Plan Guide. Jeanne Raycher. (Illus.). (Orig.). (C). 1988. pap. 9.95 (*0-944252-00-1*) CC Services.

Birth Power: The Case for Surrogacy. Carmel Shalev. 224p. (C). 1989. 30.00 (*0-300-04216-7*) Yale U Pr.

Birth Power: The Case for Surrogacy. Carmel Shalev. 210p. (C). 1991. reprint ed. pap. text ed. 13.00 (*0-300-05118-2*) Yale U Pr.

Birth Prevention Quizzes to a Street Preacher. Charles Carty & Leslie Rumble. (Radio Replies Quizzes to a Street Preacher Ser.). 32p. 1976. reprint ed. pap. 1.00 (*0-89555-110-1*) TAN Bks Pubs.

Birth Psychology. Ed. by Leslie Feher. (Illus.). 183p. (Orig.). 1984. pap. 29.50 (*0-9612182-0-7*) Assn Birth Psych.

Birth Rates of the White Population in the United States, 1800-1860: An Economic Study. Yasukichi Yasuba. LC 78-64236. (Johns Hopkins University. Studies in the Social Sciences. Thirtieth Ser. 1912: 2). reprint ed. 19.50 (*0-404-61341-1*) AMS Pr.

***Birth Reborn.** rev. ed. Michel Odent. (Illus.). 123p. 1994. pap. 17.95 (*0-9642036-9-3*) Birth Works.

Birth Records Before 1900, Mason Co., Illinois. 60p. (Orig.). 1988. pap. text ed. 6.00 (*1-877869-11-2*) Mason Cnty Hist Proj.

Birth Records Counselling: A Practical Guide. Ed. by P. Hodgkins. (C). 1989. 39.00 (*0-903534-97-5*, Pub. by Brit Ag for Adopt & Fost UK) St Mut.

Birth Rights: Can We Win the Freedom to Make Our Own Choices? Ed. by Sandy Smith. (Southern Exposure Ser.). (Illus.). 64p. (Orig.). 1990. pap. 5.00 (*0-943810-45-0*) Southern Exposure.

Birth Risks. Ed. by J. David Baum. LC 92-48554. (Nestle Nutrition Workshop Ser.: Vol. 31). 256p. 1993. 68.50 (*0-7817-0073-6*) Raven.

Birth Sores - Bands. Louis Hammer. LC 80-52553. 93p. (Orig.). 1980. pap. 4.95 (*0-937584-00-2*) Sachem Pr.

Birth Statistics, England & Wales, 1986. (Office of Population Censuses & Surveys Reference Series AB: No. 15). 107p. (Orig.). 1988. pap. 25.00 (*0-11-691216-2*, HM1807, Pub. by HMSO UK) UNIPUB.

Birth Statistics, 1989. (Office of Population Censuses & Surveys Reference Series AB: No. 18). 107p. 1991. pap. 25.00 (*0-11-691336-3*, HM6733) UNIPUB.

Birth Statistics 1990. (Office of Population Censuses & Surveys Reference Series AB). 107p. 1992. pap. 30.00 (*0-11-691382-7*, HM13827, Pub. by HMSO UK) UNIPUB.

Birth Statistics 1991. (Office of Population Censuses & Surveys Reference Series AB: No. 20). 82p. 1993. pap. 19.00 (*0-11-691528-5*, HM15285, Pub. by HMSO UK) UNIPUB.

Birth Stories: Mystery, Power, & Creation. Jane Dwinell. LC 92-3348. 200p. 1992. pap. text ed. 12.95 (*0-89789-304-2*, G304, Bergin & Garvey) Greenwood.

Birth Stories: Mystery, Power, & Creation. Jane Dwinell. LC 92-3348. 200p. 1992. text ed. 45.00 (*0-89789-296-8*, H296, Bergin & Garvey) Greenwood.

Birth Stories of the Ten Bodhisattvas. Dasabodhisattappattikatha. Tr. by Ven H. Saddhatissa. (C). 1975. 33.00 (*0-86013-089-4*, Pub. by Pali Text) Wisdom MA.

Birth, Suffering, & Death: Catholic Perspectives at the Edges of Life. Ed. by Kevin W. Wildes. (Philosophy & Medicine Ser.). 248p. (C). 1992. lib. bdg. 94.00 (*0-7923-1547-2*) Kluwer Ac.

Birth, Suffering, & Death: Catholic Perspectives at the Edges of Life. Ed. by Kevin W. Wildes. (Catholic Theology Ser.). 248p. (C). 1994. pap. text ed. 39.00 (*0-7923-2545-1*) Kluwer Ac.

Birth That We Call Death. Dunn & Eyre. 7.95 (*0-88494-297-X*) Bookcraft Inc.

***Birth That We Call Death.** Paul H. Dunn & Richard M. Eyre. 1994. pap. 1.95 (*0-88494-943-5*) Bookcraft Inc.

Birth-Through Children's Eyes. Sandra Van Dam Anderson & Penny Simkin. LC 81-82791. (Illus.). 150p. (Orig.). 1981. pap. 12.95 (*0-937604-05-4*) Pennypress.

Birth to Five: Early Childhood Special Education. Frank G. Bowe. LC 94-11494. (Illus.). 600p. 1995. 43.95 (*0-8273-6471-7*) Delmar.

Birth to Five Case Studies. Ed. by Roberta Weiner. 96p. (Orig.). 1987. 29.00 (*0-937925-34-9*, BTFC) Capitol VA.

Birth to Maturity. Jerome Kagan & Howard Moss. LC 62-19148. (C). 1983. text ed. 45.00x (*0-300-02998-5*, Y-460) Yale U Pr.

Birth to Old Age: Health & Disease in Transition. Open University Health & Disease Course Team Staff. (Health & Disease Ser.). 204p. 1985. pap. 32.00 (*0-335-15054-3*, Open Univ Pr) Taylor & Francis.

***Birth to Old Age: Health in Transition.** Ed. by Basiro Davey. LC 94-27569. (Health & Disease Ser.: Bk. 5). 224p. (Orig.). 1995. pap. text ed. 24.95x (*0-335-19207-6*, Open Univ Pr) Taylor & Francis.

Birth to Presence. Jean-Luc Nancy. Tr. by Brian Holmes et al. LC 92-30596. 440p. 1993. 47.50 (*0-8047-2060-6*) Stanford U Pr.

Birth to Presence. Jean-Luc Nancy. 440p. (C). 1993. pap. 15.95 (*0-8047-2189-0*) Stanford U Pr.

Birth Traditions & Modern Obstetrics. Priya. 1992. pap. 10.95 (*1-85230-321-2*) Element MA.

Birth Weight & Economic Growth: Women's Living Standards in the Industrializing West. W. Peter Ward. LC 93-3046. (Illus.). 248p. 1993. 38.00 (*0-226-87322-6*) U Ch Pr.

Birth Without Violence. Frederick Leboyer. 1975. 18.95 (*0-394-49581-0*) Knopf.

***Birth Without Violence.** Frederick Leboyer. 1995. pap. 12.95 (*1-85230-632-7*) Element MA.

***Birth Without Violence: The Book that Revolutionized the Way We Bring Our Children into the World.** Frederick Leboyer. LC 95-13382. (Illus.). 128p. 1995. 14.95 (*0-89281-545-0*, Heal Arts VT) Inner Tradit.

Birthday. Richardson. (Can You Find Ser.: No. 2). (J). 1994. 2.95 (*0-671-89312-2*, Litl Simon S&S) S&S Childrens.

Birthday. John Steptoe. LC 72-182782. (Illus.). 32p. (J). (ps-2). 1991. 14.95 (*0-8050-1849-2*, Bks Young Read) H Holt & Co.

Birthday. Dorothea Tanning. LC 86-81277. (Illus.). 185p. 1987. 19.95 (*0-932499-15-5*); pap. 10.95 (*0-932499-16-3*) Lapis Pr.

Birthday. Margaret Yorke. 192p. 1991. reprint ed. 19.00 (*0-7278-4165-3*) Severn Hse.

Birthday: Voices from the Heart. 15p. 1984. 2.50 (*0-934383-13-8*) Pride Prods.

Birthday ABC. Eric Metaxes. LC 93-46896. (J). 1995. 15.00 (*0-671-88306-2*, S&S Bks Young Read) S&S Childrens.

Birthday Astrologer. Great Quotations Staff. (Illus.). 168p. (Orig.). 1994. pap. 5.95 (*1-56245-086-7*) Great Quotations.

Birthday Basket for Tia. Pat Mora. LC 91-15753. (Illus.). 32p. (J). (ps-1). 1992. text ed. 13.95 (*0-02-767400-2*, Mac Bks Young Read) S&S Childrens.

Birthday Basket for Tia. Pat Mora. (One World Friends & Neighbors Ser.). (Illus.). (J). (gr. k-4). 1993. 13.95 (*0-685-64816-8*); audio 11.00 (*1-882869-78-8*) Varsity Read Servs.

Birthday Bear. (Teddy Bear Tales Ser.: No. S897-3). (J). 1989. boxed 3.95 (*0-7214-5226-4*) Ladybird Bks.

Birthday Bear. Paul Stickland. (Illus.). 14p. (J). (ps). 1994. 4.99 (*0-525-45147-1*) Dutton Child Bks.

Birthday Bears. Ruth G. Bragg. LC 90-7385. (Illus.). 28p. (J). (gr. k up). 1991. pap. 14.95 (*0-88708-139-8*, Picture Book Studio) S&S Childrens.

Birthday Bike for Brimhall. Judy Delton. LC 83-21025. (On My Own Bks.). (Illus.). 56p. (J). (gr. k-3). 1985. 15.95 (*0-87614-256-0*, Carolrhoda) Lerner Group.

Birthday Bird. Orfeo Funesti. 104p. 1972. 11.95 (*0-912282-03-7*) Pulse-Finger.

Birthday Blessings. William J. Freburger. (Greeting Book Line Ser.). 32p. (Orig.). 1985. pap. 1.95 (*0-89622-242-X*) Twenty-Third.

Birthday Blizzard. Bonnie Pryor. LC 92-1713. (Illus.). 32p. (J). (gr. k up). 1993. 15.00 (*0-688-09423-6*); lib. bdg. 14.93 (*0-688-09424-4*) Morrow Jr Bks.

Birthday Book. (Ariel Bks.). (Illus.). 80p. 1992. 4.95 (*0-8362-3012-4*) Andrews & McMeel.

***Birthday Book.** (Janet Bolton Ser.). (Illus.). 112p. 1995. 9.95 (*0-8069-3970-2*) Sterling.

Birthday Book. Linda C. Franklin. (Old Fashioned Keepbook Ser.). (Illus.). 128p. 1980. 12.00 (*0-934504-06-7*) Michel Pub Co.

Birthday Book. Jane Newdick. (Illus.). 160p. 1995. 9.98 (*0-8317-0689-9*) Smithmark.

Birthday Book. William Shakespeare. Ed. by Levi Fox. (Shakespeare Collection). 160p. 1993. 4.95 (*0-85306-091-6*, Pub. by Jarrold Pub UK); 5.95 (*0-85306-092-4*, Pub. by Jarrold Pub UK) Seven Hills Bk.

Birthday Book: A Birthdate & Birthplace Index to Biographies of American Children's Authors. Mary H. Munroe & Judith Banja. 500p. (Orig.). (C). 1991. text ed. 49.95 (*1-55570-051-9*) Neal-Schuman.

Birthday Book: Stickers to Stick & Cards to Create for Every Month of the Year. Debi Perna. (Illus.). 36p. (J). (ps up). 1992. 6.95 (*0-920775-57-8*, Pub. by Greey dePencier CN) Firefly Bks Ltd.

Birthday Book of Peter Rabbit. Beatrix Potter. (Illus.). 256p. (J). (ps up). 1983. 5.99 (*0-517-40303-X*) Random Hse Value.

Birthday Book (The Metropolitan Museum of Art) (Illus.). 160p. 1978. 14.95 (*0-8109-7498-3*) Abrams.

Birthday Boy: Reading Level 3. (Sundown Fiction Collection). 1993. 3.75 (*0-88336-211-2*); audio 13.50 (*0-88336-223-6*); audio 10.50 (*0-88336-777-7*) New Readers.

Birthday Boys. Beryl Bainbridge. 192p. 1994. 18.95 (*0-7867-0071-8*) Carroll & Graf.

***Birthday Boys.** Beryl Bainbridge. 192p. 1995. pap. 9.95 (*0-7867-0207-9*) Carroll & Graf.

***Birthday Boys.** large type ed. Beryl Bainbridge. LC 94-22433. 251p. 1995. pap. 17.95 (*0-7862-0310-2*) Thorndike Pr.

Birthday Buddies. Laura Damon. LC 87-10866. (Illus.). 32p. (J). (gr. k-2). 1988. lib. bdg. 11.59 (*0-8167-1091-0*); pap. text ed. 2.95 (*0-8167-1092-9*) Troll Assocs.

Birthday Burglar & a Very Wicked Headmistress. Margaret Mahy. LC 92-46599. (Illus.). 144p. (J). (gr. 5 up). 1993. pap. 4.95 (*0-688-12470-4*, Pub. by Beech Tree Bks) Morrow.

Birthday Cake: A Lift-the-Flap Pop-up Book. Ron Van der Meer. LC 91-62464. (Illus.). 14p. (J). (ps-1). 1993. 8.99 (*0-679-82849-4*) Random Bks Yng Read.

Birthday Cake Book. Sylvia Thompson. LC 92-15076. (Illus.). 1993. 12.95 (*0-8118-0227-2*) Chronicle Bks.

Birthday Cake Candles, Counting. Monica Weiss. LC 91-16033. (Frimble Family First Learning Adventures Ser.). (Illus.). 24p. (J). (gr. k-2). 1992. lib. bdg. 10.59 (*0-8167-2496-2*); pap. text ed. 2.95 (*0-8167-2497-0*) Troll Assocs.

Birthday Cakes. Sylvia Coward & Shelley Birnie. (C). 1989. 35.00 (*1-85368-042-7*, Pub. by New Holland Pubs UK) St Mut.

***Birthday Cakes: Exciting Designs with Full Step-by-Step Instructions.** Sylvia Coward & Shelley Birnie. (Illus.). 80p. 1995. pap. 14.95 (*1-85368-292-6*, Pub. by New Holland Pubs UK) Sterling.

Birthday Cakes for Kids. (Favorite All Time Recipes Ser.). (Illus.). 96p. 1993. spiral bd. 3.50 (*0-7853-0319-7*, 2100900) Pubns Intl Ltd.

Birthday Car. Margaret Hillert. (Illus.). (J). (ps-00). 1966. lib. bdg. 8.99 (*0-8136-5031-3*, TK2278); pap. 4.79 (*0-8136-5531-5*, TK2279) Modern Curr.

Birthday Cat. Leslie A. Ivory. LC 93-129. (Illus.). 32p. (J). (ps-3). 1993. 15.00 (*0-8037-1622-2*) Dial Bks Young.

Birthday Celebrations. Ariel Books Staff. 1994. 4.95 (*0-8362-3051-5*) Andrews & McMeel.

Birthday Chickens. Shirley Kurtz. (Illus.). 32p. (J). (gr. 4-7). 1994. pap. 6.95 (*1-56148-110-6*) Good Bks PA.

Birthday (Den Rosdenia) Alexsandr Ostrovsky. (Childrens Ser.). (Illus.). 16p. (Orig.). (RUS.). (J). 1982. pap. 14.95 (*0-934393-17-6*) Rector Pr.

Birthday Directory of Famous & Infamous People. Dennis Crossland. LC 93-91102. 184p. 1994. pap. 16.95 (*0-9639928-3-X*) CAVA Pr.

Birthday Doll. Ed. by Miriam Irwin. (Illus.). 48p. 1979. 24.00 (*0-88014-012-7*) Mosaic Pr OH.

Birthday for Blue. Kerry R. Lydon. Ed. by Abby Levine. LC 88-21697. (Illus.). 32p. (J). (gr. k-3). 1989. 13.95 (*0-8075-0774-1*) A Whitman.

Birthday for Frances. Russell Hoban. LC 68-24321. (Trophy Picture Bk.). (Illus.). (J). (ps-2). 1976. pap. 4.95 (*0-06-443007-3*, Trophy) HarpC Child Bks.

Birthday for Frances. Russell Hoban. LC 68-24321. (Illus.). 32p. (J). (gr. k-3). 1968. 15.00 (*0-06-022338-3*) HarpC Child Bks.

Birthday for Frances. Russell Hoban. LC 68-24321. (Illus.). 32p. (J). (gr. k-3). 1968. lib. bdg. 14.89 (*0-06-022339-1*) HarpC Child Bks.

Birthday Friend. Marla Martin. (Jewel Bks.). 1993. pap. 2.15 (*0-317-05266-7*) Rod & Staff.

Birthday Fun. Judith H. Corwin. (Holiday Library). (Illus.). 64p. (J). (gr. 3 up). 1985. lib. bdg. 10.98 (*0-671-55519-7*, Julian Messner); lib. bdg. 5.95 (*0-671-60126-1*, Julian Messner); lib. bdg. 7.71 (*0-685-47048-2*, Julian Messner); pap. 3.71 (*0-685-47049-0*, Julian Messner) Silver Burdett Pr.

***Birthday Fun: Great Things to Make & Do.** Ronne Randall. (Illus.). 32p. (J). (gr. 2-6). 1995. pap. 4.95 (*1-85697-548-7*, Kingfisher LKC) LKC.

***Birthday Galore Birthday Book.** Michele Breckenridge et al. (J). (gr. 1-3). 1995. write for info. (*0-939979-01-2*) Discovery Toys.

Birthday Gift for Mommi. Gilbert V. Beers. (Muffin Family Ser.). (Illus.). 32p. (Orig.). (J). 1994. pap. 2.99 (*1-56476-313-7*, Victor Books) SP Pubns.

Birthday Gift That Beeped. Jim Laster. Ed. by George Knight. LC 83-176266. (Illus.). 56p. (J). (gr. k-4). 1983. 10.95 (*0-9612780-0-5*) J Laster Pub Co.

Birthday Girls: I'm Not Telling. Jean Thesman. 128p. (Orig.). (J). (gr. 4-8). 1992. pap. 2.99 (*0-380-76523-3*, Camelot) Avon.

Birthday Girls: Mirror, Mirror. Jean Thesman. 128p. (Orig.). (J). (gr. 4-8). 1992. pap. 2.99 (*0-380-76271-4*, Camelot) Avon.

Birthday Girls: Who Am I, Anyway? Jean Thesman. 128p. (Orig.). (J). (gr. 4-8). 1992. pap. 2.99 (*0-380-76524-1*, Camelot) Avon.

Birthday in a Bathtub. Marcia Leonard. Ed. by Bonnie Brook. (What Next Ser.). (Illus.). 24p. (J). (ps-1). 1989. 4.95 (*0-671-68592-9*); lib. bdg. 6.95 (*0-671-68588-0*) Silver Pr.

***Birthday Jingo.** Gary Grimm & Phoebe Wear. 32p. (J). 1993. 10.00 (*1-56490-007-X*) G Grimm Assocs.

Birthday Letter to Lynn: Mandy Learns to Make a Cake. Helen S. Allen. (Mandy Monkey "Read to Me" Book Ser.). 16p. (J). (ps). 1992. pap. text ed. 5.00 (*1-881907-04-X*) Two Bytes Pub.

Birthday Magic. James W. Baker. LC 88-2717. (Holiday Magic Ser.). (Illus.). 48p. (J). (gr. 2-5). 1988. lib. bdg. 11.95 (*0-8225-2226-8*, Lerner Publctns); pap. 3.95 (*0-8225-9536-2*, Lerner Publctns) Lerner Group.

Birthday Moon. Lois Duncan. (J). (gr. 3-5). 1991. pap. 4.50 (*0-14-050876-7*, Puffin) Puffin Bks.

Birthday Mystery. Bill Graham. 18p. (J). (ps). 1991. 10.95 (*1-879680-05-X*) About You.

Birthday Mystery: Adventure Mystery for Kids. Patricia Lakin. (Puzzling Pen Pal Mysteries Ser.). (Illus.). 13p. (J). (gr. 3-6). 1991. 14.00 (*0-922242-21-6*) Lombard Mktg.

Birthday Numerology. Dusty Bunker et al. LC 82-60411. 240p. (Orig.). 1982. pap. 13.95 (*0-914918-39-7*, Whitford Pr) Schiffer.

Birthday of a King. Bob Hartman. (Illus.). 24p. (J). (ps-2). 1993. 7.99 (*1-56476-043-X*, Victor Books) SP Pubns.

Birthday of a New World: The Future of International Governance. Harlan Cleveland. 260p. (Orig.). (C). 1992. lib. bdg. 57.00 (*0-8191-8879-4*, Aspen Inst for Humanistic Studies); pap. text ed. 24.00 (*0-8191-8880-8*, Aspen Inst for Humanistic Studies) U Pr of Amer.

Birthday of the Infanta. Janet Lewis. 22p. 1981. 25.00 (*0-936576-03-0*) Symposium Pr.

790

An Asterisk (*) at the beginning of an entry indicates that the title is appearing in BIP for the first time.

B

An Asterisk (*) at the beginning of an entry indicates that the title is appearing in BIP for the first time.

791

Bishop Healy: Beloved Outcaste. Albert S. Foley. LC 79-94130. (American Negro: His History & Literature, Ser. No. 3). 1970. reprint ed. 19.95 (*0-405-01925-4*) Ayer.

Bishop Henry McNeal Turner & African-American Religion in the South. Stephen W. Angell. LC 91-21032. (Illus.). 352p. (C). 1992. text ed. 36.00x (*0-87049-734-0*) U of Tenn Pr.

Bishop Hill Colony. Michael A. Mikkelsen. LC 78-63808. (Johns Hopkins University. Studies in the Social Sciences. Thirtieth Ser. 1912: 1). reprint ed. 11.50 (*0-404-61071-4*) AMS Pr.

Bishop Hill Colony: A Religious, Communistic Settlement in Henry County, Illinois. M. A. Mikkelsen. LC 72-187466. (American Utopian Adventure Ser.). 167p. 1973. reprint ed. lib. bdg. 29.50 (*0-87991-014-3*) Porcupine Pr.

Bishop in Check. Adam Hall. 1991. mass mkt. 3.95 (*0-06-100133-3*, Harp PBks) HarpC.

Bishop in Honan: Mission & Museum in the Life of William C. White. Lewis C. Walmsley. LC 74-82288. 278p. reprint ed. pap. 79.30 (*0-8357-7277-2*, 2023678) Bks Demand.

Bishop Joseph Hall & Protestant Meditation in Seventeenth-Century England: A Study, with Texts of the Art of Divine Meditation (1606) & Occasional Meditations (1633) Frank L. Huntley. (Medieval & Renaissance Texts & Studies: Vol. 1). (Illus.). 232p. 1981. 18.00 (*0-86698-000-8*); pap. 9.00 (*0-86698-005-9*) MRTS.

Bishop Murder Case. S. S. Van Dine. reprint ed. lib. bdg. 22.95 (*0-89190-512-X*, Rivercity Pr) Amereon Ltd.

Bishop Museum & the Changing World of Hawaii. Nelson Foster. (Special Publication Ser.: No. 95). (Illus.). 96p. 1993. pap. 24.95 (*0-930897-77-3*) Bishop Mus.

Bishop Museum Bulletins in Botany: The Ethnobotany of Tonga: The Plants, Their Tongan Names, & Their Uses. W. A. Whistler. LC 91-73202. (Bishop Museum Bulletin in Botany Ser.: No. 2). (Illus.). 155p. (Orig.). 1991. 49.95 (*0-930897-57-9*) Bishop Mus.

Bishop Museum Bulletins in Entomology: World Catalog of Genus-Group Names of Bee Flies (Diptera: Bombyliidae) Neal L. Evenhuis. LC 91-72826. (Bishop Museum Bulletin in Entomology Ser.: No. 5). 105p. (Orig.). 1991. pap. 24.95 (*0-930897-56-0*) Bishop Mus.

Bishop of Cottontown: A Story of the Southern Cotton Mills. John T. Moore. LC 72-4610. (Black Heritage Library Collection). (Illus.). 1977. reprint ed. 35.95 (*0-8369-9113-3*) Ayer.

Bishop of the Land War: Dr. Patrick Duggan, Bishop of Clonfert, 1813-1896. Veritas Publications Staff. 1989. pap. 15.00 (*0-86217-284-5*, Pub. by Veritas IE) St Mut.

Bishop Paul Jones: Witness for Peace. 2nd ed. John H. Melish. 56p. 1992. pap. 2.95 (*0-88028-128-6*, 1159) Forward Movement.

Bishop Percy's Folio Manuscript Ballads & Romances, 3 vols. Bishop Percy et al. Ed. by John W. Hales. 1968. reprint ed. 210.00 (*1-55888-936-1*) Omnigraphics Inc.

Bishop Pike: Ham, Heretic, or Hero. Frederick M. Morris. LC 67-28381. 32p. reprint ed. pap. 25.00 (*0-8357-7278-0*, 2012934) Bks Demand.

Bishop Reginald Pecock & the Lancastrian Church: Securing the Foundations of Cultural Authority. Charles W. Brockwell, Jr. LC 85-26017. (Texts & Studies in Religion: Vol. 25). 280p. 1985. lib. bdg. 89.95 (*0-88946-813-3*) E Mellen.

Bishop Samuel Gerber: A Brief Look at the Lives & Times of His Ancestors, Family, & Descendants. Ruth G. King. (Illus.). 344p. 1991. write for info. (*0-9631085-0-6*) R C Roth.

Bishop Speaks His Mind. Earl G. Hunt. LC 87-1794. 160p. 1987. 14.95 (*0-687-03565-1*) Abingdon.

Bishop Stirling of the Falklands. Frederick Macdonald. 1976. lib. bdg. 59.95 (*0-8490-1509-X*) Gordon Pr.

Bishop Stock's "Narrative" of the Year of the French: 1798. Joseph Stock. Ed. by Grattan Freyer. LC 82-71112. (Illus.). 118p. 1982. 15.95 (*0-906462-07-X*, Pub. by Irish Humanities IE); pap. 7.95 (*0-906462-08-8*, Pub. by Irish Humanities IE) Dufour.

Bishop V. Knight Endings, Rook V. Minor Pierce Endings, Vol. 2. Y. Averbakh. Tr. by Kenneth P. Neat. (Illus.). 320p. 1985. 39.90 (*0-08-026902-8*, Pergamon Pr) Elsevier.

Bishop Westcott & the Platonic Tradition. David Newsome. LC 78-409427. (Bishop Westcott Memorial Lecture Ser.: Vol. 1968). 39p. reprint ed. pap. 25.00 (*0-8357-7279-9*, 2051381) Bks Demand.

Bishop Whipple's Southern Diary. Bishop Whipple. Ed. by Lester B. Shippee. LC 68-13637. (American Scene Ser.). (Illus.). 1968. lib. bdg. 29.50 (*0-306-70987-2*) Da Capo.

Bishop William Henry Benade: Founder & Reformer. Richard R. Gladish. (Illus.). 615p. 1983. 15.00 (*0-910557-07-1*) Acad New Church.

Bishophill, York: A Pictorial Appraisal by the Late George Pace, Friba. William Sessions Ltd., Staff. (C). 1988. 30.00 (*0-900657-22-7*, Pub. by W Sessions UK) St Mut.

Bishops: The Eternal Crusade. Loren Miller. (Primal Order Ser.). 128p. 1994. pap. 12.95 (*1-880992-19-1*) Wizards Coast.

Bishops & Brookes: The Anglican Mission & the Brooke Raj in Sarawak 1848-1941. Graham Saunders. (South-East Asian Historical Monographs). 320p. 1992. 49.95 (*0-19-588566-X*) OUP.

Bishops & Their Priests in the United States. Robert F. Trisco. LC 88-2442. (Heritage of American Catholicism Ser.). 200p. 1988. 155.00 (*0-8240-4083-X*) Garland.

Bishop's Bounty Cookbook. St. Mary's Parent's Group, Inc. LC 87-70591. (Illus.). 320p. 1987. 14.95 (*0-9618271-0-6*) St Marys Parents Group.

Bishop's Boys: A Life of Wilbur & Orville Wright. Tom D. Crouch. 1990. pap. 16.95 (*0-393-30695-X*) Norton.

Bishops by Ballot: An Eighteenth-Century Ecclesiastical Revolution. Frederick V. Mills, Sr. 1978. 22.95 (*0-19-502411-7*) OUP.

Bishops' Committee on the Liturgy Newsletter, 1976-1980. NCCB, Bishops' Committee on the Liturgy Staff. 271p. 1981. 5.95 (*1-55586-803-7*) US Catholic.

Bishops Extraordinary. Karl Pruter. LC 86-2284. 58p. 1985. reprint ed. lib. bdg. 20.00x (*0-89370-544-6*); reprint ed. pap. 10.00x (*0-912134-04-6*) Borgo Pr.

Bishop's Heir. Katherine Kurtz. (Histories of King Kelson Ser.: Bk. 1). 1987. pap. text ed. 4.99 (*0-345-34761-7*, Del Rey) Ballantine.

Bishop's Jaegers. Thorne Smith. 22.95 (*0-89190-434-4*, Am Repr) Amereon Ltd.

Bishop's Landing. Richard Forsythe. 368p. 1983. pap. 3.50 (*0-8439-2053-X*) Dorchester Pub Co.

Bishops on Birth Control: A Chronicle of Obstruction. Denise Shannon & Maggie Hume. (Powerful Conceptions Ser.). (Illus.). 20p. 1991. pap. 5.00 (*0-915365-19-7*) Cath Free Choice.

Bishop's Pawn, No. 4. Ritchie Perry. 192p. 1981. pap. 2.25 (*0-345-28971-4*) Ballantine.

Bishop's Progress: A Historical Ethnography of Catholic Missionary Experience on the Sepik Frontier. Mary T. Huber. LC 87-23562. (Ethnographic Inquiry Ser.). (Illus.). 272p. (C). 1988. 34.50 (*0-87474-544-6*) Smithsonian.

Bishop's Revenge: A Bishop Regan & Davey Goldman Myster. William F. Love. LC 92-54462. 1993. 20.00 (*1-55611-351-X*) D I Fine.

***Bishop's Tale.** Margaret Frazer. 208p. (Orig.). 1994. pap. text ed. 4.50 (*0-425-14492-5*, Prime Crime) Berkley Pub.

Bishops' Transcripts & Marriage. (C). 1987. 30.00 (*0-317-89803-5*, Pub. by Birmingham Midland Soc UK) St Mut.

Bishop's Transcripts of the Registers of the Parish of Elmdon, Warwicks, 1742-1846. (C). 1987. 35.00 (*0-317-89847-7*, Pub. by Birmingham Midland Soc UK) St Mut.

Bishop's University, 1843-1970. Christopher Nicholl. (Illus.). 360p. 1994. 39.95 (*0-7735-1176-8*, Pub. by McGill CN) U of Toronto Pr.

Bishops' Wars: Charles I's Campaigns Against Scotland, 1638-1640. Mark C. Fissel. (Studies in Early Modern British History). (Illus.). 350p. (C). 1994. pap. 27.95 (*0-521-46686-5*) Cambridge U Pr.

Bishopthrope Palace: History of the Residence of the Archbishops of York. Eric Gee. (C). 1988. 55.00 (*0-900657-84-7*, Pub. by W Sessions UK); 30.00 (*0-900657-77-4*, Pub. by W Sessions UK) St Mut.

Bisi & the Golden Disc. Carol Olu Easmon. LC 89-77347. (Illus.). 32p. (J). 1990. 13.95 (*0-940793-56-3*, Crocodile Bks) Interlink Pub.

Bismaleimide Resins. J. A. Harvey. (Chemical Engineering Ser.). Date not set. text ed. write for info. (*0-442-00855-4*) Chapman & Hall.

Bismarck. Bruce Waller. (Historical Association Studies). 96p. 1985. pap. 9.95 (*0-631-13962-1*) Blackwell Pubs.

Bismarck. Martin Booth et al. Ed. by Martin Yapp et al. (World History Ser.). (Illus.). 32p. (YA). (gr. 6-11). 1980. reprint ed. pap. text ed. 4.35 (*0-89908-023-5*) Greenhaven.

Bismarck: Some Secret Pages of His History. Moritz Busch. LC 70-144925. (Illus.). 1971. reprint ed. 49.00 (*0-403-00815-8*) Scholarly.

Bismarck: Some Secret Pages of His History, 2 vols. in 1, Vol. 1. Moritz Busch. 1988. reprint ed. lib. bdg. 99.00 (*0-7812-0455-0*) Rprt Serv.

Bismarck: The Man & the Statesman. Alan J. Taylor. 1967. pap. 9.00 (*0-394-70387-1*, Vin) Random.

Bismarck: 1815-1871, I. Lothar Gall. Tr. by J. A. Underwood. 1990. pap. 19.95 (*0-04-445778-2*) Routledge Chapman & Hall.

Bismarck: 1815-1871, Vol. 1. Lothar Gall. Tr. by J. A. Underwood. 1990. pap. 21.95 (*0-04-445779-0*) Routledge Chapman & Hall.

Bismarck - Mandan: The Cities & the People. Jeff Olson & Tammy Swift. (Illus.). 112p. (Orig.). 1995. pap. 14.95 (*1-56037-069-6*) Am Wrld Geog.

Bismarck & His Times. George O. Kent. LC 78-2547. 192p. 1978. pap. 15.95 (*0-8093-0859-2*) S Ill U Pr.

Bismarck & Mitteleuropa. Bascom B. Hayes. LC 92-55062. 1994. write for info. (*0-8386-3512-1*) Fairleigh Dickinson.

Bismarck & State Socialism: An Exposition of the Social & Economic Legislation of Germany since 1804. William H. Dawson. LC 79-106366. 1970. reprint ed. 8.00 (*0-403-00192-7*) Scholarly.

Bismarck & the Foundation of the German Empire. James Headlam-Morley. LC 73-14447. (Heroes of the Nations Ser.). reprint ed. 30.00 (*0-404-58265-6*) AMS Pr.

***Bismarck & the German Empire, 1871-1918.** Lynn Abrams. LC 94-22013. (Lancaster Pamphlets Ser.). 86p. 1994. pap. 9.95 (*0-415-07781-8*, B2249) Routledge.

Bismarck, Andrassy, & Their Successors. Gyula Andrassy. 1977. 20.95 (*0-8369-7101-9*, 7935) Ayer.

Bismarck Episode. Russell Grenfell. (Illus.). 11.25 (*0-8446-4024-7*) Peter Smith.

Bismarck in the Franco-German War, 1870-1871. Moritz Busch. 711p. 1987. reprint ed. lib. bdg. 49.50 (*0-86527-010-4*) Fertig.

Bismarck, Some Secret Pages of His History, 2 vols., Set. Moritz Busch. LC 76-112347. (BCL Ser. I). reprint ed. 155.00 (*0-404-01242-6*) AMS Pr.

Bismarck's Rival: A Political Biography of General & Admiral Albrecht von Stosch. Frederic B. M. Hollyday. LC 60-7077. (Duke Historical Publications). 328p. reprint ed. pap. 93.50 (*0-8357-7280-2*, 2026204) Bks Demand.

Bismark & the Development of Germany, Set. Otto Pflanze. (Illus.). 1531p. (C). 1990. 140.00 (*0-691-05673-0*) Princeton U Pr.

Bismark & the Development of Germany, Vol. 1: The Period of Unification, 1815-1871. Otto Pflanze. (Illus.). 1531p. (C). 1990. Vol. 1; The Period of Unification, 1815-1871. text ed. 55.00 (*0-691-05587-4*) Princeton U Pr.

Bismark & the Development of Germany, Vol. 2: The Period of Consolidation, 1871-1880. Otto Pflanze. (Illus.). 1531p. (C). 1990. Vol. 2; The Period of Consolidation, 1871-1880. text ed. 55.00 (*0-691-05588-2*) Princeton U Pr.

Bismark & the Development of Germany, Vol. 3: The Period of Fortification, 1880-1898. Otto Pflanze. (Illus.). 1531p. (C). 1990. Vol. 3; The Period of Fortification, 1880-1898. text ed. 55.00 (*0-691-05589-0*) Princeton U Pr.

Bismuth & Thallium Cuprate Superconductors: A Special Issue of the Journal Phase Transitions. Ed. by C. N. Rao. 96p. 1989. pap. text ed. 165.00 (*0-677-25930-1*) Gordon & Breach.

Bison. Carl R. Green & William R. Sanford. LC 85-6624. (Wildlife Habits & Habitats Ser.). (Illus.). 48p. (J). (gr. 5). 1985. text ed. 12.95 (*0-89686-275-5*, Crstwood Hse) Silver Burdett Pr.

Bison: Distant Thunder. Douglas Gruenau. LC 94-60217. (Illus.). 104p. 1995. 29.95 (*1-883489-07-5*) Takarajima.

Bison: Symbol of the American West. Michael S. Sample. LC 86-82740. (Illus.). 80p. (Orig.). 1987. pap. 9.95 (*0-937959-06-5*) Falcon Pr MT.

BISON: The YACC - Compatible Parser Generator. Charles Donnelly & Richard Stallman. 100p. (C). 1992. pap. 15.00 (*1-882114-30-2*) Free Software.

Bison & the Great Plains. Dave Taylor. (Animals & Their Ecosystems Ser.). (Illus.). 32p. (J). (gr. 3-4). 1990. lib. bdg. 15.95 (*0-86505-366-9*); pap. 7.95 (*0-86505-396-0*) Crabtree Pub Co.

Bison for Kids. Todd Wilkinson. (Wildlife for Kids Ser.). (Illus.). 48p. (J). (gr. k-8). 1994. pap. 6.95 (*1-55971-431-X*) NorthWord.

Bison in Art: A Graphic Chronicle of the American Bison. Larry Barsness & Barbara Tyler. LC 76-52543. (Illus.). 142p. 1977. pap. 14.50 (*0-87358-158-X*) Amon Carter.

***Bisonte Americano.** Ruth Berman. (Illus.). 48p. (SPA.). (J). (gr. 3-6). 1994. 19.95 (*0-87614-976-X*, Carolrhoda) Lerner Group.

Bispecific Antibodies. Michael W. Fanger. (Molecular Biology Intelligence Unit Ser.). 152p. 1995. 59.00 (*1-57059-166-0*) R G Landes.

Bispham: Memoranda Concerning the Family of Bispham in Great Britain & the U. S. W. Bispham. 348p. (YA). 1992. reprint ed. lib. bdg. 67.00 (*0-8328-2635-9*); reprint ed. pap. 57.00 (*0-8328-2636-7*) Higginson Bk Co.

***Bisphosphonates & Metastatic Bone Disease.** Ed. by R. D. Rubens. (Illus.). 86p. 1994. pap. text ed. 25.00 (*1-85070-643-3*) Prthnon Pub.

Biss: Selected Works by Earl Biss. Earl Biss. Ed. by Gail S. Abbo. (Illus.). 72p. (Orig.). 1988. pap. 19.95 (*0-317-91306-9*) V L Abbo.

Bistability & Nonlinearities in Laser Diodes. Hitoshi Kawaguchi. LC 94-7669. 379p. 1994. 88.00 (*0-89006-671-X*) Artech Hse.

***Bistatic Radar.** rev. ed. Nicholas J. Willis. (Illus.). 329p. (C). 1995. 55.00 (*0-9645923-0-4*) Technol Serv Corp.

Bistro Cooking. Patricia Wells. LC 89-40376. (Illus.). 320p. (Orig.). 1989. 22.95 (*0-89480-622-X*, 1622); pap. 12.95 (*0-89480-623-8*, 1623) Workman Pub.

Bit. Ed. by Vivian Carmona-Agosto. Tr. by Fernando Albornoz. (Rotary Drilling Ser.: Unit I, Lesson 2). (Illus.). 55p. (Orig.). (SPA.). 1981. pap. text ed. 14.00 (*0-88698-030-5*, 2.10232) PETEX.

Bit. 4th ed. Intro. by Kathy Bork. (Rotary Drilling Ser.: Unit I). (Illus.). 65p. 1994. pap. text ed. 15.00 (*0-88698-167-0*, 2.10240) PETEX.

Bit: Canadian Metric Edition. 3rd ed. Ed. by Jodie Leecraft. (Rotary Drilling Ser.: Unit I, Lesson 2). (Illus.). 55p. 1980. pap. text ed. 14.00 (*0-88698-018-6*, 2.10231) PETEX.

Bit Bookie of Verse. Daniel M. Henderson. (Notable American Authors Ser.). 1992. reprint ed. lib. bdg. 75.00 (*0-7812-3082-9*) Rprt Serv.

Bit by Bit. Steve Sanfield. LC 94-8752. 1995. 15.95 (*0-399-22736-9*, Philomel Bks) Putnam Pub Group.

Bit-Mapped Graphics. Steve Rimmer. 1990. 38.95 (*0-07-155670-2*); pap. text ed. 26.95 (*0-07-155681-8*) McGraw.

Bit-Mapped Graphics. Steve Rimmer. 1992. pap. 26.95 (*0-07-052998-1*) McGraw.

Bit-Mapped Graphics. Steve Rimmer. (Illus.). 512p. 1990. pap. 26.95 (*0-8306-3558-0*, 3558, Windcrest) TAB Bks.

Bit-Mapped Graphics. Steve Rimmer. 1991. 5.25 hd 24.95 (*0-8306-6750-4*); 3.5 hd 24.95 (*0-8306-6751-2*) TAB Bks.

Bit-Mapped Graphics. 2nd ed. Steve Rimmer. 1992. 38.95 (*0-07-052997-3*) McGraw.

Bit-Mapped Graphics. 2nd ed. Steve Rimmer. (Illus.). 496p. 1992. 38.95 (*0-8306-4209-9*, 4266, Windcrest); pap. 26.95 (*0-8306-4208-0*, 4266, Windcrest) TAB Bks.

Bit Mapped Graphics: For the Commodore C-64 & C-128, Vol. III. James L. Farvour. (Commodore Information Ser.). (Illus.). 96p. 1985. pap. 9.95 (*0-932679-04-8*) Blue Cat.

Bit Microprocessors, 16-32. Wunnava Subbarao. 480p. (C). 1990. write for info. (*0-675-21119-0*, Merrill Pub Co) Macmillan.

Bit of a Blue: The Life & Work of Frances Fuller Victor. Jim Martin. LC 91-90607. (Illus.). 320p. (Orig.). 1992. pap. 14.95 (*0-9632066-0-5*) Deep Well Pub.

Bit of a Flutter: Popular Gambling in England, c. 1820-1961. Mark Clapson. (International Studies in the History of Sport). 240p. 1992. text ed. 59.95 (*0-7190-3436-1*, Pub. by Manchester Univ Pr UK) St Martin.

Bit of Applesoft BASIC. Thomas A. Dwyer & Margot A. Critchfield. (Illus.). 240p. 1985. pap. 12.95 (*0-201-11161-6*) Addison-Wesley.

Bit of LOGO Magic: Adventures for Intermediate Programmers. Donna Bearden. 1984. Apple Version. pap. 13.95 (*0-8359-0495-4*, Reston); TI Version. pap. text ed. 12.95 (*0-8359-0494-6*, Reston) P-H.

Bit of Seventh Cavalry History with Warts. Carroll. 1976. pap. 12.95 (*0-8488-1600-5*, J M C & Co) Amereon Ltd.

Bit of the Blarney. John Ocallachan. 1992. pap. 6.95 (*1-882255-00-3*) Hot To Trot.

Bit on the Side. Jan Harvard. (MRP Ser.). (Illus.). 208p. 1992. 34.95 (*0-947981-66-7*) Motorbooks Intl.

Bit Parts in Shakespeare's Plays. M. M. Mahood. 266p. (C). 1993. 64.95 (*0-521-41612-4*) Cambridge U Pr.

***Bit Players: How the Creators of New Information Technology Will Change Our Lives Forever, But There Still Won't Be Anything to Watch on TV.** Robert X. Cringely. 336p. 1996. 24.95 (*0-7868-6080-4*) Hyperion.

Bitburg & Beyond. Ilya Levkov. 1987. 29.95 (*0-933503-94-6*) Sure Sellers.

Bitburg in Moral & Political Perspective. Ed. by Geoffrey Hartman. LC 85-45960. 304p. 1986. 29.95 (*0-253-34430-1*); pap. 9.95 (*0-253-20383-X*, MB-383) Ind U Pr.

Bitch. Jackie Collins. 256p. 1990. mass mkt. 5.99 (*0-671-73785-6*) PB.

Bitch. rev. ed. J. Jason Grant. (Orig.). 1985. pap. 2.95 (*0-87067-354-8*, BH354) Holloway.

Bitch: The Autobiography of Lady Lawford. Mary S. Lawford & Beauregard B. Galon. (Illus.). 178p. 17.95 (*0-8283-1995-2*) Branden Pub Co.

Bitch Goddess Success. LC 68-15189. 105p. 1968. 20.00 (*0-87130-000-1*); pap. 12.50 (*0-87130-001-X*) Eakins.

Bitch of Buchenwald. Julius Balbin. Ed. by Stanley H. Barkan. Tr. by Charlz Rizzuto. (Review Holocaust Chapbook Ser.: No. 1, CCC180). 48p. 1986. 15.00 (*0-89304-300-1*); pap. 5.00 (*0-89304-301-X*) Cross-Cultrl NY.

Bitches, Bastards & Lovers. Kurt Meyer. LC 81-83570. 1983. 9.95 (*0-87212-157-7*) Libra.

Bitches Ride Alone. Laura Chester. LC 91-31699. 204p. (Orig.). 1991. 25.00 (*0-87685-848-5*); pap. 12.00 (*0-87685-847-7*) Black Sparrow.

Bitches Ride Alone, signed ed. deluxe ed. Laura Chester. LC 91-31699. 204p. (Orig.). 1991. 35.00 (*0-87685-849-3*) Black Sparrow.

Bitchin Mac Programs. Owen Linzmayer. LC 93-87703. 135p. 1994. pap. 19.99 (*0-7821-1507-1*) Sybex.

Bitchu Province Sword Groups. Kizu. 1990. pap. 4.95 (*0-910704-06-6*) Hawley.

Bite Makes Right. B. B. Calhoun. (Dinosaur Detective Ser.: No. 3). (Illus.). 128p. (J). (gr. 3-7). 1995. text ed. 12.95 (*0-7167-6542-X*, Sci Am Yng Rdrs); pap. text ed. 3.95 (*0-7167-6550-0*, Sci Am Yng Rdrs) W H Freeman.

Bite of Black History: A Collective of Narrative & Short Poems of Afro-American History for Juveniles & Young Adults. Beatrice Garrett. LC 91-74117. 72p. (YA). (gr. 6 up). 1991. 14.95 (*0-9629887-1-5*); pap. 9.95 (*0-9629887-0-7*) Bosck Pub Hse.

A BITE OF BLACK HISTORY: A COLLECTION OF NARRATIVE & SHORT POEMS OF AFRO-AMERICAN HISTORY FOR JUVENILES & YOUNG ADULTS... This new book of poetry embraces such poems as BLACK CARGO, SLAVERY, FREEDOM DAY & FORTY ACRES & A MULE. Running the gamut with electrifying rhythmic gyrating explosions of imagery leaving you breathless. These vivid dramatic poems also manage to paint eloquent portraits of famous black pioneers of freedom with such giants as Mary McLeod Bethune, Marcus Garvey, Malcolm X & Martin Luther King, Jr. A BITE OF BLACK HISTORY enables the reader to witness this historic part of our history that embraced this "peculiar institution" known as slavery. Beatrice Garrett has truly found her niche in this moving but delicate tough subject... Hardcover: $14.95 ISBN 0-9629887-1-5, Paperback, $9.95 ISBN 0-9629887-0-7, Library purchase orders welcome... Discounts available. Bosck Publishing House, (213) 758-2782, P. O. Box 2311, Los Angeles, CA 90051-0311. ***Publisher Provided Annotation.***

Bite of Seattle Cookbook, 8 vols., 1. Ed. by Judith Deak & Gretchen Flickinger. 210p. write for info. (*0-939449-00-5*) Ink Plus.

Bite of Seattle Cookbook, 8 vols., 2. Ed. by Judith Deak & Gretchen Flickinger. 210p. write for info. (*0-939449-01-3*) Ink Plus.

792

An Asterisk (*) at the beginning of an entry indicates that the title is appearing in BIP for the first time.

Bite of Seattle Cookbook, 8 vols., 3. Ed. by Judith Deak & Gretchen Flickinger. 210p. write for info. (0-939449-02-1) Ink Plus.

Bite of Seattle Cookbook, 8 vols., 4. Ed. by Judith Deak & Gretchen Flickinger. 210p. write for info. (0-939449-03-X) Ink Plus.

Bite of Seattle Cookbook, 8 vols., 5. Ed. by Judith Deak & Gretchen Flickinger. 210p. write for info. (0-939449-04-8) Ink Plus.

Bite of Seattle Cookbook, 8 vols., 6. Ed. by Judith Deak & Gretchen Flickinger. 210p. write for info. (0-939449-05-6) Ink Plus.

Bite of Seattle Cookbook, 8 vols., 7. Ed. by Judith Deak & Gretchen Flickinger. 210p. write for info. (0-939449-06-4) Ink Plus.

Bite of Seattle Cookbook, 8 vols., 8. Ed. by Judith Deak & Gretchen Flickinger. 210p. write for info. (0-939449-07-2) Ink Plus.

Bite of the Gold Bug: A Story of the Alaskan Gold Rush. Barthe DeClements. (Illus.). 64p. (J). (gr. 2-6). 1994. pap. 3.99 (0-14-036081-6) Puffin Bks.

Bite of the Night. Howard Barker. 224p. (Orig.). 1989. pap. 9.95 (0-7145-4124-9) Riverrun NY.

Bite off the Living Dead. J. R. Black. (Shadow Zone Ser.). 132p. (Orig.). (J). (gr. 3-7). 1994. pap. 3.99 (0-679-86853-4, Bullseye Bks) Random Bks Yng Read.

***Bite-Taking for the Edentulous Jaw.** Toshio Hosoi. (Illus.). 55p. 1994. per. 30.00 (1-56386-024-4) Ishiyaku Euro.

Bite the Hand & Mooncastle. Ara Watson. 1985. pap. 4.75 (0-8222-0122-4) Dramatists Play.

Bite the Wall! Victor J. Ross. LC 84-10316. 408p. 1986. 19.95 (0-88280-108-2) ETC Pubns.

Bites & Stings: The World of Venomous Animals. John Nichol. 160p. 1989. 19.95 (0-8160-2233-X) Facts on File.

Bites from Boulder Cookbook. S. Creevy & A. Hakanson. (Illus.). 160p. (Orig.). 1987. pap. write for info. (0-9619649-0-1) Hakanson-Creevy.

Biting at the Grave: The Irish Hunger Strikes & the Politics of Despair. Padraig O'Malley. LC 89-43076. 344p. 1991. pap. 14.00 (0-8070-0209-7) Beacon Pr.

Biting off the Bracelet: A Study of Children in Hospitals. 2nd ed. Ann H. Beuf. LC 88-15329. 164p. (C). 1988. pap. text ed. 17.95x (0-8122-1278-9) U of Pa Pr.

Biting Silence. Arturo Von Vacano. 208p. 1987. mass mkt. 6.95 (0-380-75060-0) Avon.

Biting Sun. Thalia Kitrilakis. Ed. by Rena Rosenwasser. (Illus.). 48p. 1983. 5.00 (0-932716-17-2) Kelsey St Pr.

Biting the Bullet: Some Personal Reflections on Religious Education. Ed. by Chris Arthur. 194p. (C). 1990. pap. text ed. 40.00 (0-7152-0635-4) St Mut.

Biting the Bullet: Some Personal Reflections on Religious Education. Christ Arthur. 194p. (C). 1992. pap. 59.00 (0-685-60691-0, Pub. by St Andrew UK) St Mut.

Biting the Hand That Feeds Them: Organizing Women on Welfare at the Grass Roots Level. Jacqueline Pope. LC 88-27505. (Illus.). 170p. 1989. text ed. 47.95 (0-275-92922-1, C2922, Praeger Pubs) Greenwood.

Biting the Wall. J. M. Johnston. 240p. 1992. 15.95 (0-9629880-8-1) ACME Pr.

Biting the Wax. Peter McDonald. LC 89-82484. 64p. 1990. pap. 11.95 (1-85224-077-6, Pub. by Bloodaxe Bks UK) Dufour.

Bitmapped Graphics Programming in C Plus Plus. Marv Luse. LC 92-38363. 1993. pap. 37.95 (0-201-63209-8) Addison-Wesley.

BITNET for VMS Users. Michael Moore & Ronald Sawey. (Networking & Data Communications Ser.). (Illus.). 161p. 1992. pap. 25.95 (1-55558-094-7, EY-L464E-DP, Digital DEC) Buttrwrth-Heinemann.

Bits - Their History, Use & Misuse. Louis Taylor. 1981. pap. 10.00 (0-87980-231-6) Wilshire.

Bits & Bitting Manual: Getting the Horse to Understand Man, the Bit, the Rein, & the Leg. William G. Langdon, Jr. LC 93-206482. (Illus.). 113p. 1989. spiral bd. 29.95 (1-883714-03-6) Langdon Ent.

Bits & Pieces. Merline Lovelace. 224p. (Orig.). 1993. pap. 2.95 (1-56597-041-1, Kismet) Meteor Pub.

***Bits & Pieces: Forms, Leases, Applications, & Addenda for Landlords.** Roberta Mendel. (Real Estate Venture Ser.). (Orig.). Date not set. pap. 19.95 (0-936424-13-3) Pin Prick.

Bits & Pieces: Imaginative Uses for Children's Learning. Ed. by Sylvia Sunderlin. (Illus.). 1976. reprint ed. pap. text ed. 6.25 (0-87173-014-6) ACEI.

***Bits & Pieces: Maryland's Eastern Shore Counties, Talbot & Kent.** Baden. LC 92-62221. 1993. pap. text ed. 7.95 (0-9624619-5-4) Travel Tape.

Bits & Pieces: Textile Traditions. Ed. by Jeannette Lasansky. LC 90-27530. (Distributed for the Oral Traditions Project Ser.). (Illus.). 120p. (Orig.). (C). 1991. pap. 24.95 (0-8122-1362-9) U of Pa Pr.

Bits & Pieces: Two Plays. Corinne Jacker. 1975. pap. 4.75 (0-8222-0123-2) Dramatists Play.

***Bits & Pieces of a Lifetime: Stories of God's Work in a Layman's Life.** O. B. Spencer. 200p. 1993. pap. 9.95 (1-881576-08-6) Providence Hse.

Bits & Pieces of Eighty Years. Louise H. McBroom. 1993. 12.95 (0-533-10381-9) Vantage.

***Bits & Pieces of History along the 285 Corridor.** Harold Warren. (Illus.). 56p. (Orig.). 1994. pap. 5.95 (0-9644346-1-X) KR Syst.

Bits & Pieces of Ranchin' Life. Nina Waldie & Howard Waldie. (Illus.). 132p. (Orig.). 1990. pap. 14.23 (0-9626574-0-9) Waltronics.

***Bits, Bridles & Saddles.** Doris Culshaw. (Illus.). 176p. 1995. 35.00 (0-7134-7134-4, Pub. by Batsford UK) Trafalgar.

***Bits, Bytes & Big Brother: Federal Information Control in the Technological Age.** Shannon E. Martin. LC 94-32929. (Praeger Series in Political Communication). 184p. 1995. text ed. 52.95 (0-275-94900-1, Praeger Pubs) Greenwood.

Bits 'n Pieces Quilt. Anne Dease. (Illus.). 36p. 1994. 9.95 (0-922705-48-8) Quilt Day.

Bits of Background in One-Act Plays. Emma B. Brunner. LC 77-94334. (One-Act Plays in Reprint Ser.). 1978. reprint ed. 17.50 (0-8486-2034-8) Roth Pub Inc.

Bits of Experience. Larnders Roy. 109p. 1992. pap. 5.99 (0-9634432-0-8) Croy & Assocs.

Bits of Honey: Essays for Samson H. Levey. Ed. by Stanley F. Chyet & David H. Ellenson. LC 93-21881. (USF Studies in the History of Judaism: No. 74). 335p. 1993. 79.95 (1-55540-850-8, 240074) Scholars Pr GA.

Bits of Solace, Guidance & Consolation. Gladys E. Deck. 97p. 1984. 7.50 (0-913382-30-2, 101-30) Prow Bks-Franciscan.

Bits of Talk about Home Matters. Helen H. Jackson. (Notable American Authors Ser.). 1992. reprint ed. lib. bdg. 75.00 (0-7812-3347-X) Rprt Serv.

Bits of Travel. Helen H. Jackson. (Notable American Authors Ser.). 1992. reprint ed. lib. bdg. 75.00 (0-7812-3346-1) Rprt Serv.

Bits of Travel at Home. Helen H. Jackson. (Notable American Authors Ser.). 1992. reprint ed. lib. bdg. 75.00 (0-7812-3353-4) Rprt Serv.

Bits, Patterns & Reining: Teaching Horses to Rein. William G. Langdon, Jr. LC 93-206517. 157p. 1990. spiral bd. 29.95 (1-883714-04-4) Langdon Ent.

Bitten by Britain: Enjoying England. I. Travel. LC 78-58515. (Illus.). 96p. 1978. pap. 3.25 (0-915010-22-4) Sutter House.

Bitten by Devils. Lester Sumrall. 66p. (Orig.). 1987. pap. text ed. 1.95 (0-937580-98-8) LeSEA Pub Co.

Bitter Air of Exile: Russian Writers in the West, 1922-1972. rev. ed. Ed. by Simon Karlinsky & Alfred Appel, Jr. LC 74-84147. 450p. 1976. reprint ed. pap. 12.00 (0-520-02895-3) U CA Pr.

Bitter Almonds: Recollections & Recipes from a Sicilian Girlhood. Maria Grammatico & Mary T. Simeti. LC 94-6944. (Illus.). 1994. 20.00 (0-688-12449-6) Morrow.

Bitter Almonds: The True Story of Mothers, Daughters & the Seattle Cyanide Murders. Gregg Olsen. 552p. (Orig.). 1993. mass mkt. 6.99 (0-446-36359-6) Warner Bks.

Bitter Angel. Amy Gerstler. LC 89-16083. 112p. 1990. pap. 12.95 (0-86547-408-7, North Pt Pr) FS&G.

Bitter Bananas. Isaac Olaleve. LC 93-73306. (Illus.). 32p. (J). (ps-3). 1994. 14.95 (1-56397-039-2) Boyds Mills Pr.

Bitter Be Thy Bread. Gabriel Plesea. LC 89-92290. 307p. (Orig.). 1989. pap. 7.00 (0-9624498-0-6) G Plesea.

Bitter Berry: The Life of Byron Herbert Reece. Bettie Sellers. (Georgia Humanities Council Publications). (Illus.). 72p. 1992. pap. 9.95 (0-8203-1522-2) U of Ga Pr.

Bitter Betrayal. Penny Jordan. (Presents Ser.: No. 1369). 1991. pap. 2.75 (0-373-11369-2) Harlequin Bks.

Bitter Bierce: A Mystery of American Letters. Clinton H. Gratton. (BCL1-PS American Literature Ser.). 291p. 1992. reprint ed. lib. bdg. 79.00 (0-7812-6676-9) Rprt Serv.

Bitter, Bitter Tears: Nineteenth-Century Diarists & Twentieth-Century Brief Theories. Paul C. Rosenblatt. LC 83-3485. 214p. reprint ed. pap. 61.00 (0-7837-2924-3, 2057530) Bks Demand.

Bitter Blood. Jerry Bledsoe. 576p. 1989. pap. 4.95 (0-451-40149-2, Onyx) NAL-Dutton.

Bitter Blood. Ed. by Scott Siegel. (Warhunter Ser.: No. 4). (Orig.). 1981. pap. 2.25 (0-89083-905-0) Zebra.

Bitter Blood: A True Story of Southern Family Pride, Madness, & Multiple Murder. Jerry Bledsoe. 576p. 1989. pap. 5.99 (0-451-40210-3, Onyx) NAL-Dutton.

Bitter Bread. Albert Leberge. Tr. by Conrad Dion. LC 78-305999. (French Writers of Canada Ser.). 128p. reprint ed. pap. 36.50 (0-8357-7281-0, 2026119) Bks Demand.

Bitter Bread: The Famine in Norrbotten, 1867-1868. Marie C. Nelson. (Studia Historica Upsaliensia: No. 153). 192p. (Orig.). 1988. pap. 43.50x (91-554-2264-0, Pub. by Uppsala Univ Acta Univ Upsaliensis SW) Coronet Bks.

***Bitter Business.** Gini Hartzmark. Date not set. 21.00 (0-449-90989-1) Fawcett.

Bitter Canaan: The Story of the Negro Republic. Charles S. Johnson. 329p. (C). 1992. pap. 21.95 (1-56000-630-7) Transaction Pubs.

Bitter Carnival: Ressentiment & the Abject Hero. Michael A. Berstein. 264p. 1992. text ed. 32.50 (0-691-06939-5) Princeton U Pr.

Bitter Choices: Blue Collar Women In & Out of Work. Ellen I. Rosen. LC 87-5867. (Women in Culture & Society Ser.). (Illus.). 232p. (C). 1987. 25.95 (0-226-72644-4) U Ch Pr.

Bitter Choices: Blue Collar Women In & Out of Work. Ellen I. Rosen. LC 87-5867. (Women in Culture & Society Ser.). (Illus.). 232p. (C). 1990. pap. text ed. 12.95 (0-226-72645-2) U Ch Pr.

Bitter Communion Alters of Hemlock. Gyeorgos C. Hatonn. Tr. by Dharma. 198p. (Orig.). (C). 1991. pap. 10.00 (0-922356-37-8) Amer West Pubs.

***Bitter Conflict.** Kel Gleeson. 300p. Date not set. pap. 9.95 (0-7610-0242-1) NW Pub.

Bitter Conquest. Blackstock. 19.95 (0-88411-068-0) Amereon Ltd.

Bitter Conquest. Charity Blackstock. 18.95 (0-685-10844-9, Aeonian Pr) Amereon Ltd.

Bitter Dreams. Dolores Hughes. 480p. 1987. reprint ed. pap. 3.95 (0-8439-2458-6) Dorchester Pub Co.

Bitter Ends: The Selected Stories of Robert Bloch, Vol. 2. Robert Bloch. 1990. 12.95 (0-8065-1201-6, Citadel Pr) Carol Pub Group.

Bitter Fame: A Life of Sylvia Plath. Anne Stevenson. 192p. 1990. pap. 10.95 (0-395-53846-7, P Davison Bk) HM.

***Bitter Feast: Amerindians & Europeans in the American Northeast, 1600-64.** Denys Delage. 414p. 1993. pap. 29.95 (0-7748-0451-3) U of Wash Pr.

Bitter Finish. Linda Barnes. 208p. 1985. mass mkt. 4.95 (0-449-20690-4, Crest) Fawcett.

***Bitter Finish.** Linda Barnes. 1995. pap. 4.99 (0-440-21606-0) Dell.

Bitter Fruit: Black Politics & the Chicago Machine, 1931-1991. William J. Grimshaw. LC 92-4489. (Illus.). 264p. 1992. 24.95 (0-226-30893-6) U Ch Pr.

***Bitter Fruit: Black Politics & the Chicago Machine, 1931-1991.** William J. Grimshaw. 248p. 1995. pap. text ed. 12.95 (0-226-30894-4) U Ch Pr.

Bitter Fruit: The Untold Story of the American Coup in Guatemala. Stephen Kinzer & Stephen E. Schlesinger. LC 80-1728. (Illus.). 336p. 1983. pap. 11.95 (0-385-18354-2, Anchor NY) Doubleday.

Bitter Fruit: Women's Experiences of Unplanned Pregnancy, Abortion, & Adoption. Rita Townsend & Ann Perkins. LC 91-36208. (Illus.). 304p. (Orig.). 1992. 21.95 (0-89793-107-6); pap. 12.95 (0-89793-090-8) Hunter Hse.

Bitter Gold Hearts. Glen Cook. 256p. 1990. reprint ed. pap. 3.95 (0-451-45072-8, ROC) NAL-Dutton.

Bitter Grain: Huey Newton & the Black Panther Party. Michael Newton. (Orig.). 1991. pap. 3.95 (0-87067-751-9) Holloway.

Bitter Grass. large type ed. T. V. Olsen. LC 93-30322. 1994. 18.95 (0-7927-1871-2, Roundup Lrg Print Westerns); pap. 16.95 (0-7927-1870-4, Roundup Lrg Print Westerns) Chivers N Amer.

Bitter Grounds: Roots of Revolt in El Salvador. rev. ed. Liisa North. LC 85-17632. 144p. (C). 1985. pap. 8.95 (0-88208-193-4) L Hill Bks.

Bitter Harvest. John Montague. 128p. 1989. text ed. 22.50 (0-684-19032-X, Scribners) S&S Trade.

Bitter Harvest: A History of California Farmworkers, 1870-1941. Cletus E. Daniel. 348p. 1982. pap. 15.00 (0-520-04722-2) U CA Pr.

Bitter Harvest: A Modern History of Palestine. rev. ed. Sami Hadawi. LC 91-7951. (Illus.). 384p. 1991. pap. 14.95 (0-940793-76-8, Olive Branch Pr) Interlink Pub.

Bitter Harvest: A Modern History of Palestine. 4th rev. ed. Sami Hadawi. LC 91-7951. (Illus.). 384p. 1991. 29.95 (0-940793-81-4, Olive Branch Pr) Interlink Pub.

Bitter Harvest: A Personal Story of PBB Contamination. Frederic Halbert & Sandra Halbert. LC 78-23531. 159p. reprint ed. 45.40 (0-8357-9123-8, 2012732) Bks Demand.

Bitter Harvest: Palestine Between 1914-1979. Sami Hadawi. LC 79-16750. 1979. 35.00 (0-88206-025-2) Caravan Bks.

Bitter Harvest: The Odyssey of a Teacher. Constance Melaro. 1965. 12.95 (0-8392-1148-1) Astor-Honor.

Bitter Healing: German Women Writers from 1700 to 1830 - An Anthology. Ed. by Jeannine Blackwell & Susanne Zantop. LC 89-24953. (European Women Writers Ser.). (Illus.). viii, 539p. 1990. 45.00x (0-8032-1207-0); pap. 18.00 (0-8032-9909-5) U of Nebr Pr.

Bitter Herbs. Natasha Cooper. LC 93-32546. 1994. 22.00 (0-517-59023-9, Crown) Crown Pub Group.

Bitter Homecoming. Robyn Donald. (Presents Ser.: No. 1263). 1990. pap. 2.50 (0-373-11263-7) Harlequin Bks.

***Bitter Honey.** large type ed. Helen Brooks. (Harlequin Romance Ser.). 1994. 18.95 (0-263-13819-4) Thorndike Pr.

Bitter Legacy. Jean Davidson. 368p. (Orig.). 1993. pap. 4.50 (0-8439-3308-9) Dorchester Pub Co.

Bitter Legacy: Ideology & Politics in the Arab World. Paul Salem. (Contemporary Issues in the Middle East Ser.). 260p. 1994. text ed. 45.00x (0-8156-2628-2); pap. text ed. 17.95 (0-8156-2629-0) Syracuse U Pr.

Bitter Legacy: Polish-American Relations in the Wake of World War II. Richard C. Lukas. LC 82-1972. (Illus.). 200p. 1982. 22.00 (0-8131-1460-8) U Pr of Ky.

Bitter Lemons. Lawrence Durrell. 1976. 20.95 (0-8488-0480-5) Amereon Ltd.

***Bitter Lemons.** Lawrence Durrell. 256p. 1995. pap. 10.95 (1-56924-839-7) Marlowe & Co.

Bitter Medicine. Sara Paretsky. 272p. 1988. mass mkt. 5.95 (0-345-34722-6) Ballantine.

Bitter Medicine: Healing the Ills of America's Health-Care System. Jeanne Kassler. LC 93-43774. 1994. 21.95 (1-55972-223-1, Birch Ln Pr) Carol Pub Group.

Bitter Melon: Inside America's Last Rural Chinese Town. 2nd ed. James Motlow. Ed. by Jeff Gillenkirk. (Illus.). 144p. 1993. pap. 19.95 (0-930588-58-4) Heyday Bks.

Bitter Melon: Inside America's Last Rural Chinese Town. Jeff Gillenkirk & James Motlow. (Illus.). 144p. (C). 1993. reprint ed. lib. bdg. 47.00x (0-8095-4978-6) Borgo Pr.

Bitter Milk: Women & Teaching. Madeleine R. Grumet. LC 87-22679. 248p. (Orig.). (C). 1988. pap. 16.95x (0-87023-613-X) U of Mass Pr.

Bitter Money: Cultural Economy & Some African Meanings of Forbidden Commodities. Ed. by Parker Shipton. 1989. write for info. (0-913167-29-0) Am Anthro Assn.

Bitter Music: Collected Journals, Essays, Introductions & Librettos. Harry Partch. Ed. by Thomas McGeary. (Music in American Life Ser.). (Illus.). 520p. 1991. 44.95 (0-252-01660-2) U of Ill Pr.

Bitter Night. large type ed. Wayne D. Overholser. LC 93-5485. 1993. pap. 17.95 (0-7927-1786-4, Curley Lrg Print) Chivers N Amer.

Bitter Night, Sweet Dawn. Janet Q. Bedley. LC 92-10229. 1992. pap. 7.99 (0-7814-0942-X, LifeJourney) Chariot Family.

***Bitter Peace.** Michael Peterson. LC 94-37559. 1995. write for info. (0-671-72695-1) PB.

Bitter Pill: Tough Choices in America's Health Policy. Richard Sorian. LC 88-12830. 256p. 1988. pap. text ed. 29.95 (0-07-059736-7) Hlth Prof Div.

Bitter Pills: Medicines & the Third World Poor. Dianna Melrose. 277p. (C). 1982. pap. text ed. 40.00 (0-85598-065-6, Pub. by Oxfam Pubns UK) St Mut.

Bitter Rivals. Created by Francine Pascal. (Sweet Valley High Ser.: No. 29). 160p. (Orig.). 1986. 3.25 (0-553-27590-9) Bantam.

Bitter Roses: An Inside Look at the Washington Huskies' Turbulent Year. Sam Farmer. LC 93-84960. (Illus.). 357p. 1993. 19.95 (0-915611-80-5) Sagamore Pub.

Bitter Sage. Frank Gruber. Bd. with Bushwhackers. (Signet Pound Double Western Ser.). 1984. Set pap. 3.50 (0-451-12920-2, Sig) NAL-Dutton.

Bitter Sage. large type ed. Frank Gruber. 1991. pap. 13.95 (0-7089-6963-1) Ulverscroft.

Bitter Sea: The Human Cost of Minamata Disease. Akio Mishima. 248p. 1992. pap. 10.95 (4-333-01479-4, Pub. by Kosei Pub Co JA) C E Tuttle.

Bitter Seed: A Fictional History of Shaniko, Oregon. Arthur L. Fine. Ed. by Paul M. Clemens. (Illus.). 180p. (Orig.). 1986. pap. 7.95 (0-931892-06-6) B Dolphin Pub.

Bitter Strength: A History of the Chinese in the United States, 1850-1870. Gunther P. Barth. LC 64-21785. 319p. 1964. reprint ed. pap. 91.00 (0-7837-1669-9, 2057201) Bks Demand.

Bitter Sweet. LaVyrle Spencer. 496p. 1991. pap. text ed. 6.50 (0-515-10521-X) Jove Pubns.

Bitter Sweet: Governance of India in Transition. B. Sivaraman. (C). 1991. 54.00 (81-7024-403-X, Pub. by Ashish II) S Asia.

***Bitter-Sweet Harvests for Global Supermarkets: Sustainability & Equity in Latin America's Agroexport Boom.** Lori A. Thrupp et al. LC 95-14320. 1995. write for info. (1-56973-029-6) World Resources Inst.

Bitter Sweet of Ambrosia. Ginia L. Hurtado. 352p. 1995. pap. 6.95 (0-8059-3548-7) Dorrance.

***Bitter Teaching & Learning in College: Using Scholarship to Improve Practice.** Ed. by Robert J. Menges & Maryellen Wermer. (Higher & Adult Education Ser.). 1995. 32.95 (0-7879-0133-4) Jossey-Bass.

***Bitter Thistle, Sweet Rose.** Ruth Glover. 206p. 1994. pap. 8.95 (0-8341-1528-X) Beacon Hill.

***Bitter Thorns.** Chris A. Wolfe. (From the Muse Ser.). (Illus.). 210p. (Orig.). 1994. pap. 10.95 (1-886383-12-X) Pride OH.

Bitter Trumpet. large type ed. Fred Grove. LC 90-26276. 403p. 1991. reprint ed. lib. bdg. 16.95 (1-56054-107-5) Thorndike Pr.

Bitter Truth: The Avant-Garde Art & the Great War. Richard Cork. (Illus.). 256p. 1994. 55.00 (0-300-05704-0) Yale U Pr.

Bitter Water. large type ed. Thomas Thompson. (Nightingale Ser.). 235p. 1992. pap. 14.95 (0-8161-5405-8, Nightingale) Hall.

Bitter Winds. Joe E. Pierce. LC 77-71932. 184p. 1977. 6.95 (0-913244-12-0) Hapi Pr.

Bitter Winds: A Memoir of My Years in China's Gulag. Harry Wu & Carolyn Wakeman. LC 93-15799. 304p. 1993. text ed. 22.95 (0-471-55645-9) Wiley.

***Bitter Winds: A Memoir of My Years in China's Gulag.** Harry Wu & Carolyn Wakeman. 1995. pap. text ed. 14.95 (0-471-11425-1) Wiley.

Bitter Winds of Love. Barbara Cartland. 1976. 18.95 (0-89190-899-4, Am Repr) Amereon Ltd.

Bitter Woods. John S. Eisenhower. (Battery Classics Ser.). 506p. 1987. reprint ed. 29.95 (0-89839-106-7) Battery Pr.

***Bitter Woods: The Battle of the Bulge.** John S. Eisenhower. (Illus.). 550p. 1995. reprint ed. pap. 17.95 (0-306-80652-5) Da Capo.

Bitter Wounds: German Victims of the Great War 1914-1939. Robert W. Whalen. LC 83-45938. (Illus.). 288p. 1984. 34.95 (0-8014-1653-1) Cornell U Pr.

Bitter Years: MacArthur & Sutherland. Paul P. Rogers. LC 90-36984. 376p. 1990. text ed. 69.50 (0-275-92919-1, C2919, Praeger Pubs) Greenwood.

***Bitterbrush. Angela K. Black. Ed. by Jody Reid. 285p. (Orig.). 1994. pap. 9.95 (0-9642571-0-6) ABCDE Pubng. Elizabeth Harrison was young, pretty, & had everything going for her...until her battered body turned up near a stand of bitterbrush in Emigration Canyon. For Dectective Hal Lund, solving this case is more than just part of the job. It may be his last chance to set the record straight. Young, savvy attorney Jenifer Sullivan finds herself thrown from a simple divorce case into the middle of a homicide as she defends Craig Harrison in the murder of his wife. Fortunately, she's practiced law long engouth to know how to distance herself from her clients, whoever they are...or has she? The majestic Wasatch Mountains looming over Salt Lake City form the backdrop for a spine-tingling story of passion & deception. No one could guess that Elizabeth Harrison would die, victim of a gruesome crime, a crime that would entangle the lives of a twisted murderer & those bent on stopping him before another body will be found...Angela Black creates a**

B

An Asterisk (*) at the beginning of an entry indicates that the title is appearing in BIP for the first time. 793

masterful tale of suspense as she intertwines the lives of a beautiful defense attorney & her client with Salt Lake City's finest in the classic mystery BITTERBRUSH. For ordering information contact: ABCDE Publishing, P.O. Box 374, Spanish Fork, UT 84660-0374, 801-798-8832.
Publisher Provided Annotation.

Bitterest Age. Raymond Kennedy. LC 93-30337. 224p. 1994. 22.95 (*0-395-68629-6*) Ticknor & Fields.
Bitterleaf. Candace Camp. 1992. mass mkt. 4.50 (*0-06-104145-9*, Harp PBks) HarpC.
Bitterness. Robert S. McGee & Pat Springle. 56p. 1991. pap. 2.99 (*0-945276-38-9*) Rapha Pub.
Bitterness in Foods & Beverages. Ed. by R. Rouself. (Developments in Food Science Ser.: No. 25). 356p. 1990. 133.50 (*0-444-88175-1*) Elsevier.
Bitterness of Job: A Philosophical Reading. John T. Wilcox. LC 89-35811. 256p. (C). 1993. pap. text ed. 16. 95x (*0-472-08247-7*) U of Mich Pr.
Bitterness Road: The Mojave, 1604 to 1860. Lorraine M. Sherer. Ed. by Sylvia B. Vane & Lowell J. Bean. LC 94-6467. (Anthropological Paper Ser.: No. 41). 126p. (Orig.). 1994. pap. 13.95 (*0-87919-128-7*) Ballena Pr.
Bitterroot. Richard S. Wheeler. 1991. mass mkt. 4.50 (*0-8125-1305-3*) Tor Bks.
Bitterroot Landing. Sheri Reynolds. LC 94-4915. 1994. write for info. (*0-399-13994-X*, Putnam) Putnam Pub Group.
Bitterroot Landing. Sheri Reynolds. 240p. 1995. 19.95 (*0-685-73076-X*) Putnam Pub Group.
Bitterroot Marathon. John Russell & Mort Arkava. LC 87-50939. (Illus.). 472p. 1987. boxed 10.95 (*0-9611596-7-7*) Wilderness Adventure Bks.
***Bitterroot Montana State Flower.** Jerry DeSanto. (Illus.). 120p. Date not set. pap. 13.00 (*0-9637889-0-6*) Falcon Pr MT.
Bitterroot to Beartooth: Hiking Southwest Montana. Ruth Rudner. LC 84-22218. (Totebook Ser.). (Illus.). 288p. (Orig.). 1985. pap. 10.95 (*0-87156-834-9*) Sierra.
Bittersweet. Ed. by Rebecca S. Bell & C. Sherman Severin. (Collection of National Poetry Ser.: No. 8). (Illus.). 225p. (Orig.). 1985. pap. 9.95 (*0-317-39877-6*) CSS Pubns.
Bittersweet. Ave Jeanne. 1983. 2.00 (*0-932593-01-1*) Black Bear.
Bittersweet. Gay Lewis. LC 84-62706. 207p. 1985. pap. 4.95 (*0-88270-583-0*) Bridge Pub.
***Bittersweet.** Leslie Li. 512p. 1994. pap. 12.95 (*0-8048-3036-3*) C E Tuttle.
Bittersweet. Laura L. Schnap. 1994. 8.95 (*0-533-10633-8*) Vantage.
Bittersweet. Sylvie Sommerfield. 1991. 19.95 (*0-7278-4282-X*) Severn Hse.
Bittersweet. Sylvie F. Sommerfield. 352p. 1991. mass mkt. 4.99 (*0-446-35534-8*) Warner Bks.
***Bittersweet.** Mary Summer Rain. 288p. (Orig.). 1995. pap. 12.95 (*1-57174-032-5*) Hampton Roads Pub Co.
Bittersweet: Poems. Richard Mack, Jr. LC 94-6754. Date not set. 10.95 (*0-944957-45-5*) Rivercross Pub.
Bittersweet: The Recovery of an Adult Child of an Alcoholic. Mary Ann Haske. 183p. (Orig.). 1987. pap. 7.95 (*0-9619475-0-0*) M A Haske.
***Bittersweet: The Story of the Heath Candy Company.** Richard J. Heath & Ray Elliott. 415p. 1994. 22.95 (*0-9641423-1-7*) Tales Pr.
Bittersweet Aspartame: A Diet Delusion. Barbara A. Mullarkey. 88p. (Orig.). 1992. pap. 11.00 (*0-944366-00-7*) Hlth Watch Bk.
Bittersweet Aspartame, a Diet Delusion. 2nd ed. Barbara A. Mullarkey. (Illus.). 86p. 1993. pap. 11.00 (*0-944366-01-5*) Hlth Watch Bk.
Bittersweet Beginnings. Hedy Fleishmann & Devorah E. Fleishmann. LC 92-70696. 140p. (YA). 1992. write for info. (*1-56062-125-7*); pap. write for info. (*1-56062-126-5*) CIS Comm.
Bittersweet Bondage. Sonya Y. Pelton. 1984. pap. 3.75 (*0-8217-1368-X*) Zebra.
Bittersweet Century: Speculations on Modern Science & American Democracy. Paul N. Goldstene. Ed. by Victor Jones. LC 88-39765. (Publications in Political Science). 252p. (Orig.). (C). 1989. 27.95 (*0-88316-560-0*); pap. text ed. 12.95 (*0-88316-559-7*) Chandler & Sharp.
Bittersweet Country. Elaine Long. 1993. mass mkt. 4.99 (*0-312-92916-1*) St Martin.
Bittersweet Country. Ed. & Intro. by Ellen G. Massey. LC 86-40091. (Illus.). 464p. (Orig.). 1986. reprint ed. pap. 14.95 (*0-8061-2018-5*) U of Okla Pr.
Bittersweet Earth. Ellen G. Massey. LC 84-20991. (Illus.). 422p. 1985. 26.95 (*0-8061-1927-6*) U of Okla Pr.
Bittersweet Earth. Ellen G. Massey. LC 84-20991. (C). 1993. pap. 14.95 (*0-8061-2528-4*) U of Okla Pr.
Bittersweet Ecstasy. Janelle Taylor. 512p. 1992. mass mkt. 4.99 (*0-8217-3502-0*) Zebra.
Bittersweet Encounter: The Afro-American & the American Jew. Robert G. Weisbord & Arthur Stein. LC 72-127828. (Contributions in Afro-American & African Studies: No. 5). 242p. 1970. text ed. 29.95 (*0-8371-5093-0*, WBS&, Negro U Pr) Greenwood.
Bittersweet Honeymoon. large type ed. Majorie Lewty. (Classic Romance Ser.). 1992. 18.95 (*0-263-13343-5*, Pub. by Mills & Boon Ltd UK) Chivers N Amer.
Bittersweet Legacy. Jenna Ryan. (Intrigue Ser.). 1993. pap. 2.89 (*0-373-22221-1*, 1-22221-5) Harlequin Bks.
Bittersweet Legacy: The Black & White "Better Classes" in Charlotte, 1850-1910. Janette T. Greenwood. LC 93-32060. (Fred W. Morrison Series in Southern Studies). xvi, 334p. 1994. 45.00 (*0-8078-2133-0*) U of NC Pr.
***Bittersweet Memories.** Ed. by Celia H. Feldman. (Illus.). 58p. (Orig.). 1995. pap. text ed. write for info. (*0-9639999-0-7*) Jay St Pubs.
Bittersweet Notes from a Therapist. Dorothy Wagner. (Illus.). 240p. (Orig.). 1988. pap. 9.95 (*0-9621652-0-4*) Wagner Pub.
Bittersweet Pieces: A Collection of Dutch Short Stories. Ed. by Gerrit Bussink. 112p. 1991. pap. 12.00 (*0-920717-48-9*) SPD-Small Pr Dist.
Bittersweet Promises. Trana M. Simmons. 400p. (Orig.). 1994. pap. 4.99 (*0-505-51934-8*, Love Spell) Dorchester Pub Co.
Bittersweet Revenge. large type ed. Rosemary Hammond. 1991. reprint ed. lib. bdg. 18.95 (*0-263-12554-8*, Pub. by Mills & Boon UK) Thorndike Pr.
***Bittersweet Summer.** Rosalie Braend. 150p. 1995. pap. 7.95 (*1-56901-719-0*) NW Pub.
Bittersweet Temptation. John Donovan. (Orig.). 1979. pap. 2.50 (*0-89083-445-8*) Zebra.
***Bittersweet Time.** Jean S. Ducey. LC 94-41585. 115p. (J). (gr. 4-7). 1995. 12.99 (*0-8028-5096-0*) Eerdmans.
Bittersweet Trail. Bernice M. Chappel. LC 84-80978. (Illus.). 470p. 1990. pap. 9.95 (*0-923568-14-X*) Wilderness Adventure Bks.
Bittersweet Trail: An American Saga of the 1800's. Bernice M. Chappel. LC 84-80978. (Illus.). 480p. 1985. 12.95 (*0-9606400-1-0*); pap. 9.95 (*0-9606400-2-9*) Great Lakes Bks.
Bittersweet Years Smiling Through Tears (1920-1941) Homer R. Ankrum. LC 93-79072. (Illus.). 414p. 1993. 23.50 (*0-89279-082-2*) Graphic Pub.
Bittersweet Yesterdays. Kate Proctor. (Presents Ser.). 1994. mass mkt. 2.99 (*0-373-11710-8*, 1-11710-0) Harlequin Bks.
Bittersweet Yesterdays. large type ed. Kate Proctor. (Romance Ser.). 1993. 17.95 (*0-263-13425-3*, Pub. by Mills & Boon Ltd UK) Chivers N Amer.
Bittersweet...Hellogoodbye: A Resource in Planning Farewell Rituals When a Baby Dies. Ed. by Jane M. Lamb. (Illus.). 220p. (Orig.). 1989. pap. 15.00 (*0-918533-68-6*) Prairie Lark.
Bitting. Elwyn H. Edwards. 100p. (C). 1990. 28.00 (*0-85131-527-5*, Pub. by J A Allen & Co UK) St Mut.
Bittinger, Bittner, Biddinger, & Bidinger Families: And Their Kin of Garrett County, Maryland. Wayne Bittinger. 836p. 1986. 30.00 (*0-317-69991-1*) W Bittinger.
Bittle 'en Ting' Gullah Cooking with Maum Chrish. Virginia M. Geraty. LC 91-26004. (Illus.). 78p. 1992. 15. 95 (*0-87844-110-7*); pap. 9.95 (*0-87844-107-7*) Sandlapper Pub Co.
Bittner, Genealogical Record & History of the Bittner-Werley Families: Descendants of Michael Bittner & Sebastian Werley, 1753-1930. J. W. Bittner. (Illus.). 239p. 1992. reprint ed. lib. bdg. 38.00 (*0-8328-2637-5*); reprint ed. pap. 28.00 (*0-8328-2638-3*) Higginson Bk Co.
Bitty Business Book: Everyday Success Strategies for the Office. Maureen LaJoy. 84p. (Orig.). 1989. pap. 9.95 (*0-9623686-1-X*) Castalia MN.
Bitty Goes to School. Elizabeth Greenaway. (Pictureback Shapes Ser.). (Illus.). 24p. (Orig.). (J). (ps-2). 1994. pap. 2.50 (*0-679-86182-3*) Random Bks Yng Read.
Bitty's Halloween Surprise. Ruth Brook. LC 86-30730. (Illus.). 32p. (J). (gr. k-3). 1988. lib. bdg. 11.89 (*0-8167-0916-5*); pap. text ed. 2.95 (*0-8167-0917-3*) Troll Assocs.
Bitumens in Ore Deposits. J. Parnell et al. LC 92-36492. (Society for Geology Applied to Mineral Deposits Special Publication Ser.: No. 9). 1993. 179.00 (*0-387-55621-4*) Spr-Verlag.
Bituminous Coal in Texas. T. J. Evans. (Handbook Ser.: HB 4). (Illus.). 65p. 1982. reprint ed. 3.50 (*0-686-29325-8*) Bur Econ Geology.
Bituminous Coal Mining Vocabulary of the Eastern United States. Dennis R. Preston. (Publications of the American Dialect Society: No. 59). (Illus.). 128p. (Orig.). 1973. pap. 8.50 (*0-8173-0659-5*) U of Ala Pr.
Bituminous Materials, 3 vols., Set. Ed. by Arnold J. Hoiberg. Incl. Vol. 1. General Aspects. LC 79-4525. 446p. 1979. reprint ed. 45.00 (*0-88275-961-2*); Vol. 2. Asphalts. LC 79-4525. 716p. 1979. reprint ed. (*0-88275-962-0*); Vol. 3. Coal Tars & Pitches. LC 79-4525. 604p. 1979. reprint ed. (*0-88275-963-9*); LC 79-4525. 1766p. 1979. Set lib. bdg. 160.00 (*0-89874-020-7*) Krieger.
Bitwa O Warszawe. Stanislaw Strzetelski. 144p. 1945. 3.00 (*0-940962-02-0*) Polish Inst Art & Sci.
Bivad (David) For Parents of Learning Disabled Children. Anne Sheppard. 24p. (Orig.). 1983. pap. 1.75 (*0-8298-0650-4*) Pilgrim OH.
Bivalve: Proceedings of a Memorial Symposium in Honour of Sir Charles Maurice Yonge. Brian Morton. 364p. (C). 1990. pap. text ed. 144.00 (*962-209-254-3*, Pub. by Hong Kong U Pr HK) St Mut.
Bivalve Filter Feeders: In Estuarine & Coastal Ecosystem Processes. Ed. by Richard F. Dame. (NATO ASI Series G: Ecological Sciences: Vol. 33). (Illus.). vi, 580p. 1993. write for info. (*3-540-56952-9*) Spr-Verlag.
Bivalve Filter Feeders in Estuarine & Coastal Ecosystem Processes. Ed. by Richard F. Dame. LC 93-28010. (NATO ASI Series G: Ecological Sciences: Series G, Vol. 33). 1993. 240.00 (*0-387-56952-9*) Spr-Verlag.
Bivariate Discrete Distributions. Ed. by Kocherlakota. 384p. 1992. 140.00 (*0-8247-8702-1*) Dekker.
Bivectors & Waves in Mechanics & Optics. Philippe Boulanger & Michael A. Hayes. LC 93-17173. (Applied Mathematics & Mathematical Computation Ser.: Vol. 4). 1993. write for info. (*0-412-46460-8*) Chapman & Hall.
Biweekly Payment Handbook for Accelerated Mortgage Paybacks. Financial Publishing Co. Staff. 264p. 1988. pap. 15.00 (*0-87600-598-9*) Finan Pub.
Bixby: A Genealogy of the Descendants of Joseph Bixby, 1621-1701, of Ipswich & Boxford, Mass. W. G. Bixby. (Illus.). 707p. 1990. reprint ed. lib. bdg. 109.00 (*0-8328-1440-7*); reprint ed. pap. 99.00 (*0-8328-1441-5*) Higginson Bk Co.
Bixel Family History: Descendants of Abraham Bixel & Magdalena Schumacher, 1843-1984. Betty A. Miller & Oscar R. Miller. (Illus.). 94p. 1984. pap. 7.50 (*0-317-17479-7*) O R Miller.
Biz Jets: Technology & Market Structure in the Corporate Jet Aircraft Industry. Almarin Phillips et al. LC 93-42692. (Economics of Science, Technology & Innovation Ser.). 288p. (C). 1994. lib. bdg. 94.50 (*0-7923-2660-1*) Kluwer Ac.
Biz Kids Guide to Success: Money-Making Ideas for Young Entrepreneurs. Terri Thompson. (Illus.). 96p. (J). (gr. 3 up). 1992. pap. 4.95 (*0-8120-4831-8*) Barron.
Biz-Op: How to Get Rich with "Business Opportunity: Frauds & Scams. Bruce Easley. LC 94-75058. (Illus.). 167p. (Orig.). (C). 1994. pap. 14.95 (*1-55950-109-X*, 64155) Loompanics.
Biz Talk-1: American Business Slang & Jargon. David Burke. Ed. by Robert Graul. (Illus.). 260p. (Orig.). 1994. pap. 14.95 (*1-879440-17-2*) Optima CA.
Bizagolaa: An Apache Girl. Jan Mike & Cathie Lowmiller. (Illus.). 32p. (Orig.). (J). (gr. k-6). 1995. 3.95 (*0-918080-46-0*, 20976) Treas Chest Bks.
Bizantinishke Forschungen: Dedicated to Father Dr. Joseph Gill. Ed. by John Haldon & John Koumoulides. (Perspectives in Byzantine History & Culture Ser.: Vol. 10). (Illus.). xii, 307p. 1985. pap. 76.00 (*90-256-0916-3*, Pub. by A M Hakkert NE) Benjamins North Am.
Bizarre & Beautiful Ears. Santa Fe Writers Group. (Bizarre & Beautiful Ser.). (Illus.). 48p. (J). (gr. 3 up). 1993. 14. 95 (*1-56261-122-4*) John Muir.
***Bizarre & Beautiful Ears.** Santa Fe Writers Group. (Bizarre & Beautiful Ser.). (Illus.). 48p. (J). 1994. pap. 9.95 (*1-56261-184-4*) John Muir.
Bizarre & Beautiful Eyes. Santa Fe Writers Group. (Bizarre & Beautiful Ser.). (Illus.). 48p. (J). (gr. 3 up). 1993. 14. 95 (*1-56261-121-6*) John Muir.
***Bizarre & Beautiful Eyes.** Santa Fe Writers Group. (Bizarre & Beautiful Ser.). (Illus.). 48p. (J). 1994. pap. 9.95 (*1-56261-183-6*) John Muir.
Bizarre & Beautiful Feelers. Santa Fe Writers Group. LC 93-2034. (Bizarre & Beautiful Ser.). (Illus.). 48p. (J). 1993. text ed. 14.95 (*1-56261-125-9*) John Muir.
***Bizarre & Beautiful Feelers.** Santa Fe Writers Group. (Bizarre & Beautiful Ser.). (Illus.). 48p. (J). 1994. pap. 9.95 (*1-56261-187-9*) John Muir.
Bizarre & Beautiful Noses. Santa Fe Writers Group. (Bizarre & Beautiful Ser.). (Illus.). 48p. (J). (gr. 3 up). 1993. 14.95 (*1-56261-124-0*) John Muir.
***Bizarre & Beautiful Noses.** Santa Fe Writers Group. (Bizarre & Beautiful Ser.). (Illus.). 48p. (J). 1994. pap. 9.95 (*1-56261-186-0*) John Muir.
***Bizarre & Beautiful Tongues.** Santa Fe Writers Group. (Bizarre & Beautiful Ser.). (Illus.). 48p. (J). 1994. pap. 9.95 (*1-56261-185-2*) John Muir.
Bizarre & Beautiful Tongues. Santa Fe Writer's Group Staff. (Bizarre & Beautiful Ser.). (Illus.). 48p. (J). (gr. 4-7). 1993. text ed. 14.95 (*1-56261-123-2*) John Muir.
Bizarre & Ornamental Alphabets. Carol B. Grafton. (Illus.). 128p. (Orig.). 1981. pap. 5.95 (*0-486-24105-X*) Dover.
Bizarre Behaviours. Herschel Prins. (Tavistock Bk.). 128p. 1990. 57.00 (*0-415-01835-8*, A4677); pap. 17.95 (*0-415-01836-6*, A4681) Routledge.
Bizarre! Bizarre! Roald Dahl. (FRE.). 1973. pap. 11.95 (*0-7859-1747-0*, 2070363953) Fr & Eur.
Bizarre Brain Benders. Rolf Heimann. (Illus.). 32p. (J). (gr. 4-7). 1993. pap. 3.95 (*0-8167-3035-0*) Troll Assocs.
Bizarre Bugs. Kaye Quinn. (Science Crossword Puzzles Ser.). 48p. (Orig.). (J). 1990. pap. 2.95 (*0-8431-2811-9*) Price Stern.
***Bizarre Bugs.** Doug Wechsler. LC 94-27432. (Illus.). (J). (gr. 1-8). 1995. 14.99 (*0-525-65181-0*, Cobblehill Bks) Dutton Child Bks.
Bizarre Comix, Vol. 11. (Illus.). 1980. pap. 8.00 (*0-914646-30-3*) Belier Pr.
Bizarre Comix, Vol. 12. (Illus.). 1980. pap. 8.00 (*0-914646-31-1*) Belier Pr.
Bizarre Comix, Vol. 19. (Illus.). 1984. pap. 8.00 (*0-914646-42-7*) Belier Pr.
Bizarre Comix, Vol. 20. (Illus.). 1984. pap. 8.00 (*0-914646-43-5*) Belier Pr.
Bizarre Comix, Vol. 24. (Illus.). 1986. pap. 8.00 (*0-914646-47-8*) Belier Pr.
Bizarre Crime. Brad Steiger. 288p. (Orig.). 1992. pap. 4.99 (*0-451-17219-1*, Sig) NAL-Dutton.
Bizarre Detective. Bill Blackbeard. Ed. by Dave Schreiner. (Illus.). 36p. 1993. ring bd. 10.95 (*0-87816-183-X*) Kitchen Sink.
Bizarre Dreams. Ed. by Stanislaus Tal & Caro Soles. (Orig.). 1994. pap. text ed. 4.95 (*1-56333-187-X*) Masquerade.
Bizarre Hockey Tournament. Jerry Jenkins. (Dallas O'Neil & the Baker Street Sports Club Ser.). (Orig.). (YA). (gr. 7-12). 1986. pap. text ed. 4.99 (*0-8024-8236-8*) Moody.
***Bizarre Insects.** Margaret J. Anderson. LC 94-23725. (Weird & Wacky Science Ser.). (J). 1996. lib. bdg. write for info. (*0-89490-613-5*) Enslow Pubs.
***Bizarre Leisure Book: From the Alan Whicker Appreciation Society to Zen Archery - a Fun, A-Z Guide to 150 Offbeat Leisure Pursuits.** Stephen Jarvis. 290p. 1995. pap. 12.95 (*0-86051-878-7*, Robson-Parkwest) Parkwest Pubns.
Bizarre Murderers. Rose G. Mandelsberg. 1991. mass mkt. 4.95 (*1-55817-486-9*, Pinnacle NY) Windsor NY.
Bizarre Phenomena. Reader's Digest Editors. LC 92-31739. (Quest for the Unknown Ser.). (Illus.). 144p. 1992. 16.98 (*0-89577-464-X*) RD Assn.
Bizarre Sex & Other Crimes of Passion. Ed. by Stanislaus Tal. 1994. pap. 12.95 (*1-56333-213-2*) Masquerade.
***Bizarre Tales of the Cape Fear Country.** John E. Hair. LC 94-61603. 96p. (Orig.). 1994. per., pap. 9.95 (*1-884570-17-8*) Research Triangle.
Bizarre Will. Robert Pinget. Tr. by Barbara Wright. 150p. 1989. 10.95 (*0-87376-065-4*) Red Dust.
Bizarro. Dan Piraro. (Illus.). 104p. (Orig.). 1986. pap. 5.95 (*0-87701-402-7*) Chronicle Bks.
***Bizarro, No. 9.** Dan Piraro. (Illus.). 112p. (Orig.). 1995. pap. 6.95 (*0-8362-0430-1*) Andrews & McMeel.
***Bizarro Facts & Radical Earthlings: Outrageous Trivia & Incredible Information.** Tracy S. Burroughs. 160p. (Orig.). (YA). 1995. pap. 3.99 (*0-451-17950-1*, Sig) NAL-Dutton.
***Bizcomps 1994 Release Database.** ValuSource Staff. (Valusource Accounting Software Products Ser.). 1995. pap. text ed. 195.00 (*0-471-11893-1*) Wiley.
Bizen Schools of Swordsmiths. Kizu. 1991. pap. 5.95 (*0-910704-34-1*) Hawley.
Bizet: Music Book Index. Winton Dean. 262p. 1993. reprint ed. lib. bdg. 79.00 (*0-7812-9587-4*) Rprt Serv.
Bizet & His World. Mina Curtiss. LC 76-55412. 477p. 1977. reprint ed. text ed. 75.00 (*0-8371-9427-X*, CUBI, Greenwood Pr) Greenwood.
Bizet's Carmen. Georges Bizet. (Music Ser.). 96p. (Orig.). 1984. pap. 2.95 (*0-486-24556-X*) Dover.
Bizzare Comix, Vol. 21. (Illus.). 1985. pap. 8.00 (*0-914646-44-3*) Belier Pr.
Bizzy Bones & the Lost Quilt. Jacqueline B. Martin. LC 87-13577. (Illus.). (J). (ps-3). 1988. 16.00 (*0-688-07407-3*); lib. bdg. 12.88 (*0-688-07408-1*) Lothrop.
Bizzy Bubbles: Santa's Littlest Elf. Jeri Jurie. LC 77-82535. (Illus.). (J). (gr. k-6). 1977. 10.95 (*0-686-01311-5*); pap. 6.95 (*0-686-01312-3*) Al Fresco.
***BJ & Scooter.** Mary A. Dudko & Margie Larsen. (Illus.). 24p. (Orig.). (J). (ps-3). 1995. pap. 2.50 (*1-57064-043-2*) Barney Pub.
BJ Bernard Grows up. Marion Duckworth. (Little Deer Bks.). (Illus.). 28p. (J). (ps-00). 1993. 5.49 (*0-7847-0065-6*, 24-03845) Standard Pub.
***BJ Makes Music.** Mary A. Dudko. LC 94-79378. (Illus.). 22p. (J). (ps-k). 1995. bds. 3.95 (*1-57064-038-6*) Barney Pub.
Bjenok na Megilu Visokopreosvjashchennago Mitropolita Vladimira. 94p. reprint ed. pap. 4.00 (*0-317-29222-6*) Holy Trinity.
BJO Nordfeldt. Lois Sherman & Marlou J. Quintana. 46p. 1981. pap. 15.00 (*0-935037-04-7*) G Peters Gallery.
***Bjorklund Legacy: Bjorklund's Daughter.** Betty L. Halliwell. LC 94-92334. 544p. 1995. 19.95 (*1-886087-06-7*); pap. 11.95 (*1-886087-07-5*) Pribiloff Pr.
***Bjorklund Legacy: Philanth at 25.** Betty L. Halliwell. LC 94-92333. 864p. 1995. 24.95 (*1-886087-02-4*); pap. 14.95 (*1-886087-03-2*) Pribiloff Pr.
***Bjorklund Legacy: The Farber-Bjorklund Presidency Ended Strangely.** Betty L. Halliwell. LC 94-92335. 896p. 1995. 27.50 (*1-886087-08-3*); pap. 17.50 (*1-886087-09-1*) Pribiloff Pr.
***Bjorklund Legacy: The Seduction of the Chief of Staff.** Betty L. Halliwell. LC 94-92336. 384p. 1996. 12.50 (*1-886087-04-0*); pap. 4.95 (*1-886087-05-9*) Pribiloff Pr.
B.J.'s Billion Dollar Bet. Julie A. Peters. LC 93-36132. (J). 1994. 12.95 (*0-316-70254-4*) Little.
BJ's Fun Week. Mary A. Dudko & Margie Larsen. LC 94-72001. (Illus.). 20p. (J). (ps-k). 1994. bds. 3.95 (*1-57064-015-7*) Barney Pub.
BJ's Silly Story. Stephen White. LC 94-71998. (Lift & Peek Ser.). (Illus.). 16p. (J). (ps-k). 1994. bds. 4.95 (*1-57064-018-1*) Barney Pub.
Bk. 1: Counting My Money see Using Money Series
Bk. 1: Operations on Integers see Key to Algebra Series
Bk. 1: Percent Concepts see Key to Percents Series
Bk. 10: Square Roots & Quadratic Equations see Key to Algebra Series
Bk. 2: Making My Money Count see Using Money Series
Bk. 2: Percents & Fractions see Key to Percents Series
Bk. 2: Variables, Terms, & Expressions see Key to Algebra Series
Bk. 3: Buying Power see Using Money Series
Bk. 3: Equations see Key to Algebra Series
Bk. 3: Percents & Decimals see Key to Percents Series
Bk. 4: Polynomials see Key to Algebra Series
Bk. 5: Rational Numbers see Key to Algebra Series
Bk. 6 see Warsaw Requiem
Bk. 6: Multiplying & Dividing Rational Expressions see Key to Algebra Series
Bk. 7: Adding & Subtracting Rational Expressions see Key to Algebra Series
Bk. 8: Graphs see Key to Algebra Series
Bk. 9: Systems of Equations see Key to Algebra Series
BKSTS Dictionary of Image Technology. 3rd rev. ed. BKSTS Staff. LC 94-2192. 168p. 1994. 29.95 (*0-240-51364-9*, Focal) Buttrwrth-Heinemann.
BL Lac Objects. Ed. by L. Maraschi et al. (Lecture Notes in Physics Ser.: Vol. 334). xii, 500p. 1989. 73.00 (*0-387-51389-2*, 3453) Spr-Verlag.
***Bl Lexikon der Wein.** Karl-Dieter Gussek. 400p. (GER.). 1990. 45.00 (*0-7859-8295-7*, 3323003217) Fr & Eur.

An Asterisk (*) at the beginning of an entry indicates that the title is appearing in BIP for the first time.

Blab!, No. 4. Ed. by Monte Beauchamp. (Illus.). 128p. (Orig.). 1989. pap. 7.95 (*0-87816-063-9*) Kitchen Sink.

Blab!, No. 5. Ed. by Monte Beauchamp. (Illus.). 128p. (Orig.). 1990. pap. 7.95 (*0-87816-088-4*) Kitchen Sink.

Blab, No. 6. Ed. by Monte Beauchamp. (Illus.). 128p. (Orig.). 1991. pap. 7.95 (*0-87816-131-7*) Kitchen Sink.

Blab, No. 7. Ed. by Monte Beauchamp. (Illus.). 144p. (Orig.). 1992. pap. 8.95 (*0-87816-194-5*) Kitchen Sink.

***Blabber Mouth.** Morris Gleitzman. LC 94-33929. 1995. pap. 5.00 (*0-15-200370-3*) HarBrace.

***Blabber Mouth.** Morris Gleitzman. LC 94-33929. (J). 1995. 11.00 (*0-15-200369-X*) HarBrace.

Blabbermouths. Gerda B. Mantinband. LC 91-3006. (J). (ps-3). 1992. 14.00 (*0-688-10602-1*); lib. bdg. 13.93 (*0-688-10604-8*) Greenwillow.

Blabla de los Gemelos. Francois Pratte. (Coleccion Rosa Ser.). (Illus.). 60p. (SPA.). (J). (gr. 5 up). 1994. pap. 5.95 (*958-07-0068-0*) Firefly Bks Ltd.

Black. Benjamin F. Gardner. LC 74-178472. (Black Heritage Library Collection). 1977. reprint ed. 15.95 (*0-8369-8921-X*) Ayer.

Black: One Man's Mind One Black Man's Mind. Curtis L. Crisler et al. Ed. by Rhonda White & Marcia Tapp-Sanders. (C). Date not set. pap. text ed. 5.95 (*1-883517-12-5*) Alef Bet Comns.

Black - White Writing: Essays on South African Literature. Ed. by Pauline Fletcher. LC 92-58217. (Bucknell Review Ser.: Vol. 37, No. 1). 160p. 1993. 22.00 (*0-8387-5262-4*) Bucknell U Pr.

Black, a Mexican, & a Jew. abr. ed. Robert M. Freedman. 316p. 1995. pap. 7.95 (*1-56901-364-0*) NW Pub.

Black Abolitionist Papers, Vol. I: The British Isles, 1830-1865. Ed. by C. Peter Ripley et al. LC 84-13131. (Illus.). xxx, 609p. 1985. 50.00 (*0-8078-1625-6*) U of NC Pr.

Black Abolitionist Papers, Vol. II: Canada, 1830-1865. Ed. by C. Peter Ripley et al. LC 84-13131. (Illus.). xviii, 560p. 1987. 50.00 (*0-8078-1698-1*) U of NC Pr.

Black Abolitionist Papers, Vol. III: The United States, 1830-1846. Ed. by C. Peter Ripley et al. LC 84-13131. (Illus.). xxx, 522p. (C). 1991. 50.00 (*0-8078-1926-3*) U of NC Pr.

Black Abolitionist Papers, Vol. IV: The United States, 1847-1858. Ed. by C. Peter Ripley. LC 84-13131. (Illus.). xxxvi, 444p. (C). 1991. 50.00 (*0-8078-1974-3*) U of NC Pr.

Black Abolitionist Papers, Vol. V: The United States, 1859-1865. Ed. by C. Peter Ripley. LC 84-13131. (Illus.). xxviii, 436p. (C). 1992. 50.00 (*0-8078-2007-5*) U of NC Pr.

Black Abolitionists. Benjamin Quarles. (Quality Paperbacks Ser.). 310p. 1991. reprint ed. pap. 13.95 (*0-306-80425-5*) Da Capo.

Black Academic Libraries & Research Collections: An Historical Survey. Jessie C. Smith. LC 77-71857. (Contributions in Afro-American & African Studies: No. 34). 303p. 1977. text ed. 59.95 (*0-8371-9546-2*, SBA/, Greenwood Pr) Greenwood.

Black Access: A Bibliography of Afro-American Bibliographies. Comp. by Richard Newman. LC 83-8537. xxviii, 249p. 1984. text ed. 49.95 (*0-313-23282-2*, NEB/, Greenwood Pr) Greenwood.

***Black Achievers (1880-1920)** Ebraska D. Ceasor. Ed. by Dolores Laney & Dorothy Rambo. (Black History Bks.: No. III). (Illus.). (Orig.). (J). (gr. 4-8). 1995. pap. 12.95 (*0-913678-28-7*) New Day Pr.

Black Action Films: Plots, Critiques, Cast & Credits for 235 Theatrical & Made-for-TV Releases. James R. Parish & George H. Hill. LC 89-42871. 399p. 1989. lib. bdg. 49.95x (*0-89950-456-6*) McFarland & Co.

Black Actor's Book of Original Scenes & Monologues. Gus Edwards et al. Ed. by Tanya Kersey-Henley. LC 93-81080. 72p. (Orig.). 1995. pap. 9.95 (*0-9627515-9-6*) Love Child.

Black Adolescence: Current Issues & Annotated Bibliography. Consortium for Research on Black Adolescence Staff & Patricia Bell-Scott. 168p. 1990. text ed. 35.00 (*0-8161-9080-1*, Hall Reference) Macmillan.

Black Adolescent Parent. Ed. & Intro. by Stanley F. Battle. LC 87-332. (Child & Youth Services Ser.: Vol. 9, No. 1). 142p. 1987. text ed. 29.95 (*0-86656-554-X*) Haworth Pr.

Black Adolescents. Ed. by Reginald L. Jones. 454p. 1989. text ed. 36.95 (*0-943539-01-3*); pap. text ed. 25.95 (*0-943539-02-1*) Cobb & Henry Pubs.

Black Adolescents & Juvenile Justice: Background Report to the 1990 Arizona Black Town Hall. M. A. Bortner et al. 122p. (C). 1990. pap. write for info. (*1-879286-00-9*) AZ Bd Regents.

Black Adonis. Linn B Porter. LC 72-2028. (Black Heritage Library Collection). 1977. reprint ed. 30.95 (*0-8369-9060-9*) Ayer.

Black Adult Development & Aging. Ed. by Reginald L. Jones. 448p. 1989. text ed. 36.95 (*0-943539-03-X*); pap. text ed. 25.95 (*0-943539-04-8*) Cobb & Henry Pubs.

Black Advancement in the South African Economy. Ed. by Roy Smollan. LC 86-6500. 276p. 1987. text ed. 39.95 (*0-312-08253-3*) St Martin.

Black Aesthetic Criticism: An Annotated Bibliography. Reginald Martin. (Bibliographies of Modern Critics & Critical Schools Ser.: Vol. 16). 250p. 37.00 (*0-8240-6890-4*, H1290) Garland.

Black Africa: A Comparative Handbook. 2nd ed. Donald G. Morrison et al. LC 89-2879. (Illus.). 768p. 1989. disk 249.50 (*0-8290-2477-8*); text ed. 169.50 (*0-8290-2466-2*) Irvington.

Black Africa: A Comparative Handbook. 2nd ed. Donald G. Morrison et al. LC 89-2879. 716p. 1989. 169.50 (*0-88702-042-9*) Washington Inst Pr.

Black Africa: The Economic & Cultural Basis for a Federated State. rev. ed. Cheikh A. Diop. LC 87-17704. 128p. 1987. pap. 9.95 (*1-55652-061-1*) L Hill Bks.

Black Africa Cookbook. Monica Bayley. (Illus.). 1977. reprint ed. pap. 2.50 (*0-915696-04-5*) Determined Prods.

Black Africa, Nineteen Forty-Five to Nineteen Eighty: Economic Decolonization & Arrested Development. D. K. Fieldhouse. 272p. (C). 1986. pap. text ed. 22.95 (*0-04-325018-1*) Routledge Chapman & Hall.

Black African Cinema. N. Frank Ukadike. LC 92-29076. 1993. 50.00 (*0-520-07747-4*); pap. 17.00 (*0-520-07748-2*) U CA Pr.

Black African Literature in English: A Guide to Information Sources. Ed. by Bernth Lindfors. LC 73-16983. (American Literature, English Literature, & World Literatures in English Information Guide Ser.: Vol. 23). 512p. 1978. 68.00 (*0-8103-1206-9*) Gale.

Black African Literature in English: 1977-1981. Ed. by Bernth Linfors. LC 86-1021. 412p. 1986. 45.00 (*0-8419-0962-8*, Africana) Holmes & Meier.

Black African Literature in English: 1982-1986. Ed. by Bernth Linfors. Date not set. write for info. (*0-8419-1241-6*, Africana) Holmes & Meier.

Black African Literature in English, 1982-86. Bernth Lindfors. 550p. 1989. lib. bdg. 85.00 (*0-905450-75-2*, Pub. by H Zell Pubs UK) Bowker-Saur.

***Black African Literature in English, 1987-1991.** Bernth Lindfors. (Bibliographical Research in African Literature Ser.: No. 3). 472p. 1995. 125.00 (*1-873836-16-3*, Pub. by H Zell Pubs UK) Bowker-Saur.

Black Aged: Understanding Diversity & Service Needs. Ed. by Zev Harel et al. (Focus Editions Ser.: Vol. 120). (Illus.). 264p. (C). 1990. text ed. 49.95 (*0-8039-3836-5*); pap. text ed. 24.95 (*0-8039-3837-3*) Sage.

Black Aged in the United States: A Selectively Annotated Bibliography. Comp. by Lenwood G. Davis. LC 88-32359. (Bibliographies & Indexes in Afro-American & African Studies: No. 23). 291p. 1989. text ed. 69.50 (*0-313-25931-3*, DVB/, Greenwood Pr) Greenwood.

***Black Album.** Hanif Kureishi. 1995. 22.00 (*0-684-81342-4*, Scribners) S&S Trade.

Black Alcohol Abuse & Alcoholism: A Bibliography. Thomas D. Watts & Roosevelt Wright, Jr. LC 85-28245. 210p. 1986. text ed. 65.00 (*0-275-92083-6*, C2083, Praeger Pubs) Greenwood.

Black Alice. Thomas M. Disch & John T. Sladek. 186p. 1989. pap. 3.95 (*0-88184-506-X*) Carroll & Graf.

Black Amber. Phyllis A. Whitney. 1991. mass mkt. 4.99 (*0-06-100264-X*, Harp PBks) HarpC.

Black America. Scott Nearing. LC 69-17730. (Illus.). 275p. 1986. pap. 10.00 (*0-685-16626-0*) Schocken.

Black America: A Study of the Ex-Slave - His Late Master. William L. Clowes. LC 78-109322. 240p. 1970. reprint ed. text ed. 38.50 (*0-8371-3588-5*, CBA&, Negro U Pr) Greenwood.

Black America: Special Edition with National Holiday Epilogue. Roger A. Hammer. (Illus.). 28p. 1987. pap. 4.95 (*0-932991-01-7*) Place in the Woods.

Black American African American: Vietnam Through the Gulf War. Mullen. 1991. 17.35 (*0-536-58069-3*) Ginn Pr.

Black American Cinema: Aesthetics & Spectatorship. Ed. by Manthia Diawara. LC 92-32907. (AFI Film Readers Ser.). 1992. 45.00 (*0-415-90396-3*, A5299, Routledge NY); pap. 14.95 (*0-415-90397-1*, A5303, Routledge NY) Routledge.

Black American Colleges & Universities: Profiles of Two-Year, Four-Year, & Professional Schools. Ed. by Levirn Hill. LC 94-3898. 800p. (C). 1994. 55.00 (*0-8103-9166-X*) Gale.

Black American Cookbook, 1. Willa Mitchell. 400p. lib. bdg. 5.95 (*0-9603014-0-2*) Evang Assn.

Black American Cookbook, 2. Willa Mitchell. 400p. lib. bdg. 6.95 (*0-9603014-1-0*) Evang Assn.

Black American Culture & Scholarship: Contemporary Issues. Ed. by Bernice J. Reagon. (Illus.). 184p. (Orig.). (C). 1985. pap. text ed. 3.00 (*0-929847-00-8*) Natl Mus Am.

Black American Culture & Society: An Annotated Bibliography. Ed. by S. T. Rustavo. (Illus.). 167p. 1994. 67.00 (*1-56072-172-3*) Nova Sci Pubs.

Black American Elderly: Research on Physical & Psychosocial Health. Ed. by James S. Jackson. LC 88-4922. 400p. 1988. 43.95 (*0-8261-5810-2*) Springer Pub.

Black American Families, 11965 to 1984: A Classified, Selectively Annotated Bibliography. Ed. by Walter R. Allen et al. LC 86-14959. (Bibliographies & Indexes in Afro-American & African Studies: No. 16). 514p. 1986. text ed. 59.95 (*0-313-25613-6*, ALB/) Greenwood.

Black American Fiction: A Bibliography. Carol Fairbanks & Eugene A. Engeldinger. LC 78-1351. 359p. 1978. 29.50 (*0-8108-1120-0*) Scarecrow.

Black American Health: An Annotated Bibliography. Comp. by Mitchell F. Rice & Woodrow Jones, Jr. LC 86-25745. (Bibliographies & Indexes in Afro-American & African Studies: No. 17). 133p. 1987. text ed. 49.95 (*0-313-24887-7*, RBH/, Greenwood Pr) Greenwood.

Black American History: Rap & Rhyme. Poet's Workshop Staff. 8p. (YA). (gr. 6-12). 1989. pap. text ed. 2.50 (*0-913597-53-8*) Prosperity & Profits.

Black American History Word Search Puzzles: The Black Contribution to the World of America, Vol. 1. Ersie L. Nelson. 64p. 1993. write for info. (*0-9635801-0-8*) Ersie Nelson.

Black American in Books for Children: Readings in Racism. 2nd ed. Ed. by Donnarae MacCann & Gloria Woodard. LC 85-10893. (Illus.). 310p. 1985. 29.50 (*0-8108-1826-4*) Scarecrow.

Black American Inventors: A Rhyme. Story Time Staff. 10p. (Orig.). 1993. pap. text ed. 4.00 (*1-56820-095-1*) Story Time.

Black American Literature: A Critical History. Roger Whitlow. (Quality Paperback Ser.: No. 278). 288p. 1974. reprint ed. pap. 9.95 (*0-8226-0278-4*) Littlefield.

Black American Literature & Humanism. Ed. by R. Baxter Miller. LC 80-5179. 128p. 1981. 14.00 (*0-8131-1436-5*) U Pr of Ky.

Black American Music: Past & Present. 2nd ed. Hildred Roach. LC 82-25860. 390p. (C). 1992. 52.50 (*0-89464-580-3*); pap. 42.50 (*0-89464-766-0*) Krieger.

Black American Music: Past & Present. 2nd ed. Hildred Roach. LC 82-25860. 390p. 1994. pap. 42.50 (*0-89464-865-9*) Krieger.

Black American Poetry since Nineteen Forty-Four: A Preliminary Checklist. Frank Deodene & William French. 41p. 1971. pap. 7.00 (*0-911860-07-X*) Chatham Bkseller.

Black American Poets & Dramatists: Before the Harlem Renaissance. Ed. by Harold Bloom. LC 93-8433. (Writers of English: Lives & Works). (Illus.). 1994. 24.95 (*0-7910-2205-6*, Am Art Analog); pap. write for info. (*0-7910-2230-7*, Am Art Analog) Chelsea Hse.

Black American Poets & Dramatists of the Harlem Renaissance. Intro. by Harold Bloom. LC 94-5881. (Writers of English Ser.). Date not set. write for info. (*0-7910-2207-2*); pap. write for info. (*0-7910-2232-3*) Chelsea Hse.

Black American Poets Between Worlds, 1940-1960. Ed. by R. Baxter Miller. LC 85-22644. (Tennessee Studies in Literature: Vol. 30). 206p. (C). 1986. text ed. 25.00x (*0-87049-499-6*); pap. 14.00x (*0-87049-590-9*) U of Tenn Pr.

Black American Politics: From the Washington Marches to Jesse Jackson. rev. ed. Manning Marable. (Haymarket Ser.). 384p. 1985. text ed. 32.95 (*0-86091-108-X*, Pub. by Verso UK); pap. text ed. 12.95 (*0-86091-816-5*, Pub. by Verso UK) Routledge Chapman & Hall.

Black American Politics: From the Washington Marches to Jesse Jackson. 2nd ed. Manning Marable. 416p. 1993. 64.95 (*0-86091-205-1*, A1915, Pub. by Verso UK) Routledge Chapman & Hall.

Black American Politics: From the Washington Marches to Jesse Jackson, Vol. 1. 2nd ed. Manning Marable. 416p. 1992. pap. 18.95 (*0-86091-923-4*, A1919, Pub. by Verso UK) Routledge Chapman & Hall.

Black American Prose Theory: Studies in Black American Literature, Vol. I. Joe Wexlmann & Chester Fontenot. 230p. 1983. 15.00 (*0-913283-00-2*) Penkevill.

Black American Prose Writers Before the Harlem Renaissance. Intro. by Harold Bloom. LC 93-13022. (Writers of English: Lives & Works). (Illus.). 1994. 24.95 (*0-7910-2202-1*, Am Art Analog); pap. 12.95 (*0-7910-2227-7*, Am Art Analog) Chelsea Hse.

Black American Prose Writers of the Harlem Renaissance. Intro. by Harold Bloom. LC 93-17979. (Writers of English: Lives & Works). (Illus.). 1994. 24.95 (*0-7910-2203-X*, Am Art Analog); pap. write for info. (*0-7910-2228-5*, Am Art Analog) Chelsea Hse.

Black American Scholars: A Study of Their Beginnings. Horace M. Bond. LC 72-78234. 210p. 1972. 8.95 (*0-913642-01-0*); pap. 3.95 (*0-913642-04-5*) Balamp Pub.

Black American Short Stories. rev. ed. Ed. by John H. Clarke. LC 92-16249. (American Century Ser.). 1993. 10.95 (*0-374-52354-1*) Hill & Wang.

Black American Short Story in the Twentieth Century: A Collection of Critical Essays. Ed. by Peter Bruck. viii, 209p. 1977. pap. 26.00 (*90-6032-085-9*, Pub. by B R Gruener NE) Benjamins North Am.

Black American Street Life: South Philadelphia, 1969-1971. Dan Rose. LC 87-17830. (Conduct & Communication Ser.). (Illus.). 288p. (C). 1987. text ed. 46.95 (*0-8122-8071-7*); pap. text ed. 17.95x (*0-8122-1245-2*) U of Pa Pr.

***Black American Witness: Reports from the Front by Earl Caldwell.** Earl Caldwell. Ed. by Kenneth Walker & Lurma Rackley. 279p. 1994. write for info. (*1-886446-10-5*) Lion Hse Pub.

***Black American Women.** Craig Werner. (Magill Bibliographies Ser.). 286p. 1989. 40.00 (*0-8108-2787-5*) Scarecrow.

Black American Women, No. 3. H. K. Ross. (Illus.). 160p. (YA). (gr. 6-12). 1990. lib. bdg. 14.95 (*0-87460-365-X*) Lion Bks.

Black-American Women African Men: Myths Misconceptions & Misunderstandings. Jean Otumokala et al. Ed. by Geneieve Ettah. 197p. (Orig.). 1994. pap. 19.95 (*0-9629214-4-0*) Intl Spectrum.

Black American Women Fiction Writers. Intro. by Harold Bloom. LC 94-5887. (Writers of English Ser.). Date not set. write for info. (*0-7910-2208-0*); pap. write for info. (*0-7910-2233-1*) Chelsea Hse.

Black American Women in Literature: A Bibliography, 1976 Through 1987. Ronda Glikin. LC 88-43488. 263p. 1989. lib. bdg. 38.50x (*0-89950-372-1*) McFarland & Co.

Black American Women in Olympic Track & Field: A Complete Illustrated Reference. Michael D. Davis. LC 91-50946. 188p. 1992. lib. bdg. 27.50x (*0-89950-692-5*) McFarland & Co.

Black American Women Poets & Dramatists. Ed. by Harold Bloom. LC 94-4337. (Writers of English Ser.). 1995. write for info. (*0-7910-2209-9*); pap. write for info. (*0-7910-2234-X*) Chelsea Hse.

Black American Women Writers: A Quilt of Many Colors. Eva Birch. 304p. 1994. pap. text ed. 26.95 (*0-13-302340-0*) P-H.

Black American Writers Past & Present: A Biographical & Bibliographical Dictionary, 2 vols., Set. Theressa G. Rush et al. LC 74-28400. 865p. 1975. 72.50 (*0-8108-0785-8*) Scarecrow.

Black American Writing from the Nadir: The Evolution of a Literary Tradition, 1877-1915. Dickson D. Bruce, Jr. LC 88-22039. (Illus.). 272p. (C). 1989. pap. text ed. 11.95 (*0-8071-1806-0*) La State U Pr.

Black Americans. 4th ed. Alphonso Pinkney. 256p. 1992. pap. text ed. write for info. (*0-13-034240-8*) P-H.

Black Americans: A History in Their Own Words. rev. ed. Milton Meltzer. LC 83-46160. (Illus.). 320p. (YA). (gr. 7 up). 1984. lib. bdg. 15.89 (*0-690-04418-6*, Crowell Jr Bks) HarpC Child Bks.

Black Americans: A History in Their Own Words, 1619-1983. rev. ed. Milton Meltzer. LC 83-46160. (Trophy Nonfiction Bk.). (Illus.). 320p. (YA). (gr. 7 up). 1987. pap. 9.95 (*0-06-446055-X*, Trophy) HarpC Child Bks.

***Black Americans: A Statistical Sourcebook, 1995.** rev. ed. Ed. & Intro. by Louise L. Hornor. 350p. 1995. lib. bdg. 50.00 (*0-929960-18-1*) Info Pubns.

Black Americans: A Study Guide & Source Book. Lynn P. Dunn. LC 74-31621. 1975. pap. 9.95 (*0-88247-306-9*) R & E Pubs.

Black Americans: Images in Conflict. Ed. by Phyllis M. Banks & Virginia M. Burke. LC 72-121891. (Composition & Rhetoric Ser.). (Orig.). (C). 1970. pap. write for info. (*0-672-61177-5*, CR4, Bobbs) Macmillan.

Black Americans: Issues & Concerns. Ed. by N. N. Rachveli. (Illus.). 221p. 1994. lib. bdg. 59.00 (*1-56072-173-1*) Nova Sci Pubs.

B

Black Americans: The FBI Files. Kenneth O'Reilly. Ed. by David Gallen. 512p. 1994. 24.95 (*0-7867-0010-6*); pap. 14.95 (*0-7867-0027-0*) Carroll & Graf.

Black Americans see How & Where to Research Your Ethnic-American Cultural Heritage

Black Americans & Public Policy: Perspectives of the National Urban League. National Urban League Staff. LC 88-61131. 98p. (Orig.). (C). 1988. pap. text ed. 14.95 (*0-685-33317-5*) Natl Urban.

Black Americans & the Middle East Conflict. Henry Winston. 1970. pap. 0.25 (*0-87898-058-X*) New Outlook.

Black Americans & the Missionary Movement in Africa. Ed. by Sylvia M. Jacobs. LC 81-13230. (Contributions in Afro-American & African Studies: No. 66). (Illus.). xii, 255p. 1982. text ed. 55.00 (*0-313-23280-6*, JAA/, Greenwood Pr) Greenwood.

Black Americans & the Shaping of U. S. Foreign Policy: Proceedings of a JCPS Roundtable. JCPS Office of Research Staff. 56p. 1981. pap. 12.25 (*0-941410-18-8*) Jt Ctr Pol Studies.

Black Americans in Autobiography: An Annotated Bibliography of Autobiographies & Autobiographical Books Written since the Civil War. expanded rev. ed. Russell Brignano. LC 83-20505. xi, 193p. (C). 1984. text ed. 31.95 (*0-8223-0559-3*) Duke.

Black Americans in Autobiography: An Annotated Bibliography of Autobiographies & Autobiographical Books Written since the Civil War. Russell Brignano. LC 73-92535. 126p. reprint ed. pap. 36.00 (*0-8357-7282-9*, 2023373) Bks Demand.

Black Americans in Cleveland. Russell H. Davis. (Illus.). (YA). 1990. pap. 10.00 (*0-87498-075-5*) Assoc Pubs DC.

***Black Americans in Congress.** 1995. lib. bdg. 250.00 (*0-8490-6514-3*) Gordon Pr.

Black Americans in Congress. Mark Salser. 207p. 1991. pap. text ed. 14.95 (*0-89420-273-1*, 297150) Natl Book.

Black Americans in Congress: 1870-1989. 1991. lib. bdg. 69.00 (*0-8490-4575-4*) Gordon Pr.

Black Americans in Congress, Eighteen Seventy to Nineteen Eighty-Nine. Bruce A. Ragsdale & Joel D. Treese. LC 89-600409. (Illus.). 1990. per., pap. 12.00 (*0-16-018476-2*, S/N 052-071-008); boxed 16.00 (*0-16-018477-0*, S/N 052-071-00892-6) USGPO.

***Black Americans in Defense of Our Nation.** 1995. lib. bdg. 250.00 (*0-8490-6515-1*) Gordon Pr.

Black Americans in the Roosevelt Era: Liberalism & Race. John B. Kirby. LC 79-10315. (Twentieth-Century America Ser.). 272p. 1980. pap. 16.00x (*0-87049-349-3*) U of Tenn Pr.

Black Americans Information Directory. 3rd ed. Furtaw. 1993. 79.00 (*0-8103-8082-X*) Gale.

Black Americans of Achievement, 104 vols., Set. (Illus.). 1994. write for info. (*0-7910-2577-2*, Am Art Analog) Chelsea Hse.

Black Americans of Achievement Series, 50 vols., Set. Intro. by Coretta Scott King. (Illus.). 8400p. 1987. lib. bdg. 897.50 (*1-55546-568-4*) Chelsea Hse.

Black Americans of Achievement Series, 25 vols., Set. Intro. by Coretta Scott King. (Illus.). (J). 1991. lib. bdg. 448.75 (*0-7910-1112-7*) Chelsea Hse.

Black Americans on Postage Stamps. Garland McLaughlin. (Illus.). 1982. 20.00 (*0-933184-39-5*); pap. 10.00 (*0-933184-44-1*) Flame Intl.

Black Americans' Views of Racial Inequality: The Dream Deferred. Lee Sigelman & Susan Welch. (Illus.). 232p. (C). 1991. 29.95 (*0-521-40015-5*) Cambridge U Pr.

Black Americans' Views of Racial Inequality: The Dream Deferred. Lee Sigelman & Susan Welch. (Illus.). 232p. (C). 1994. pap. 15.95 (*0-521-45767-X*) Cambridge U Pr.

Black & African Theologies: Siblings or Distant Cousins? Josiah U. Young. LC 85-32090. (Bishop Henry McNeal Turner Studies in North American Black Religion: No. 2). 160p. (Orig.). reprint ed. pap. 45.60 (*0-8357-8557-2*, 2034903) Bks Demand.

Black & Beautiful. Marius Fortie. LC 78-168515. (Black Heritage Library Collection). 1977. reprint ed. 30.95 (*0-8369-8867-1*) Ayer.

Black & Beautiful: A Self-Discovery Coloring Book. Wallace Y. McNair. (Illus.). 26p. (Orig.). (J). (gr. 2 up). 1992. pap. 10.00 (*0-9627600-3-X*) Wstrn Images.

Black & Blue. Octavus R. Cohen. LC 71-106269. (Short Story Index Reprint Ser.). 1977. 28.95 (*0-8369-3306-0*) Ayer.

An Asterisk (*) at the beginning of an entry indicates that the title is appearing in BIP for the first time. 795

Black & Blue. Barry Singer. 444p. 1992. text ed. 28.00 (0-02-872395-3) Schirmer Bks.

Black & Blue: Policing in South Africa. John D. Brewer. (Illus.). 400p. 1994. 59.00 (0-19-827382-7) OUP.

Black & Blue: Profiles of Blacks in IBM. Charles Thomas. 181p. (C). 1995. 17.95 (0-942683-15-3) Aaron Pr.

Black & Blue Magic. Zilpha K. Snyder. LC 94-791. (Illus.). (J). 1994. pap. 3.95 (0-689-71848-9, Aladdin Paperbacks) S&S Childrens.

***Black & Blues.** Kamau Brathwaite. 96p. 1995. reprint ed. pap. 9.95 (0-8112-1313-7, NDP815) New Directions.

Black & Catholic: The Challenge & Gift of Black Folk: Contributions of African American Experience & World View to Catholic Theology. Ed. by James T. Phelps. (Studies in Theology). (Orig.). 1995. pap. write for info. (0-87462-629-3) Marquette.

Black & Catholic in Savannah, Georgia. Gary W. McDonogh. LC 93-15389. (Illus.). 360p. (Orig.). (C). 1993. 42.95x (0-87049-810-X); pap. 18.95 (0-87049-811-8) U of Tenn Pr.

Black & Deadly. Charlie A. Harris. (Orig.). 1977. pap. 2.95 (0-87067-550-8, BH550-8) Holloway.

Black & Deaf in America. Ernest Hairston & Linwood Smith. 1983. pap. 5.95 (0-932666-18-3) T J Pubs.

Black & Ethnic Leaderships in Britain: The Cultural Dimensions of Political Action. Ed. by Pnina Werbner & Muhammad Anwar. 304p. (C). 1991. text ed. 65.00 (0-415-04166-X, A5131) Routledge.

Black & Other Minority Participation in the All Voluntary Navy & Marine Corps. Herbert R. Northrup. LC 78-72037. (Pennsylvania University, Wharton School of Finance & Commerce, Industrial Research Unit Study Ser.: No. 57). 265p. reprint ed. pap. 75.60 (0-8357-7283-7, 2011212) Bks Demand.

Black & Red: The Historical Meeting of Africans & Native Americans. David McCord & William Cleveland. (Illus.). (Orig.). 1989. pap. 16.95 (0-685-26486-6) Dreamkeeper Pr.

Black & Red: W. E. B. Du Bois & the Afro-American Response to the Cold War, 1944-1963. Gerald Horne. LC 85-26127. 457p. 1985. 59.50 (0-88706-087-0); pap. 19.95 (0-88706-088-9) State U NY Pr.

Black & Reformed: Apartheid, Liberation, & the Calvinist Tradition. Allan A. Boesak. LC 84-7212. 192p. (Orig.). 1984. pap. 14.95 (0-88344-148-9) Orbis Bks.

Black & Single: Meeting & Choosing a Partner Who's Right for You. Larry E. Davis. LC 93-21565. 214p. (Orig.). 1993. pap. 12.95 (1-879360-29-2) Noble Pr.

***Black & Tan Bombshell: The Field Gordon Setter.** Suzanne Sorby & Norman B. Sorby. (Illus.). 365p. 1987. text ed. 32.50 (0-9618884-0-7) Springset Gordon.

Black & Tan Coonhounds. Anna K. Nicholas. 1990. 11.95 (0-86622-774-1, KW-190) TFH Pubns.

Black & White. Robyn Green & Bronwen Scarffe. LC 92-21393. (Illus.). (J). (gr. 4 up). 1993. 2.50 (0-383-03555-4) SRA Schl Grp.

Black & White. David Macaulay. (Illus.). 32p. (J). 1990. 14.95 (0-395-52151-3) HM.

Black & White. Carol Stetser. LC 76-46884. (Illus.). 1977. pap. 19.95 (0-917960-01-7) Padma.

Black & White. Ed. by J. C. Byars, Jr. LC 75-173602. (Black Heritage Library Collection). 1977. reprint ed. 19.95 (0-8369-8914-7) Ayer.

Black & White: Cultural Interaction in the Antebellum South. Ed. by Ted Ownby. LC 92-45586. (Chancellor's Symposium on Southern History Ser.). 264p. 1993. text ed. 42.00 (0-87805-620-3); pap. text ed. 18.95 (0-87805-621-1) U Pr of Miss.

Black & White: Land, Labor & Politics in the South. T. Thomas Fortune. 310p. Date not set. reprint ed. 35.00 (0-933121-70-9) Black Classic.

Black & White: Land, Labor & Politics in the South. Timothy T. Fortune. LC 68-28995. (American Negro: His History & Literature, Ser. No. 1). 1968. reprint ed. 16.95 (0-405-01814-2) Ayer.

Black & White: Reflections of a White Southern Sociologist. Lewis M. Killian. LC 93-79475. 239p. 1994. text ed. 34.95 (1-882289-12-9) Gen Hall.

Black & White & Said All Over-Riddles: Riddles. Catherine H. Ainsworth. LC 72-5461. (Clyde Press Folklore Bks.). 36p. (J). (ps-12). 1976. 5.00 (0-933190-02-6) Clyde Pr.

Black & White Are Colors: Paintings of the 1950's-1970's. David S. Rubin & David W. Steadman. LC 78-68735. (Illus.). 59p. 1979. 3.50 (0-915478-13-7) Galleries Coll.

Black & White Britain: The Third P. S. I. Survey. Colin Brown. xvii, 420p. (Orig.). 1985. 74.50 (0-566-05150-8) Ashgate Pub Co.

Black & White Cats. Ed. by J. C. Suares. 96p. 1992. 14.95 (0-00-255056-3) Collins SF.

Black & White Copy Preparation. William Levy. LC 80-730006. 1979. student ed 6.00 (0-8064-0059-5, 311); audio 199.00 (0-8064-0060-9) Bergwall.

Black & White Darkroom Techniques (KW-15) Hubert C. Birnbaum. LC 81-67033. (Kodak Workshop Ser.). (Illus.). 96p. (Orig.). 1992. pap. 11.95 (0-87985-274-7) Saunders Photo.

Black & White Families: A Study in Complementarity. Charles V. Willie. LC 85-80416. 308p. 1985. lib. bdg. 36.95 (0-930390-64-4); pap. text ed. 17.95 (0-930390-63-6) Gen Hall.

Black & White Home Developing & Printing. Herb Taylor et al. LC 81-71226. (Modern Photo Guides Ser.). (Illus.). 120p. (Orig.). 1982. pap. 7.95 (0-385-18164-7) Avalon Comm.

Black & White Identity Formation. 2nd ed. Stuart T. Hauser & E. Kasendorf. LC 82-16221. 252p. 1983. pap. 12.50 (0-89874-055-X) Krieger.

Black & White in American Culture: An Anthology from "The Massachusetts Review" Ed. by Jules Chametzky & Sidney Kaplan. LC 74-76045. (Illus.). 496p. 1969. 37.50 (0-87023-046-8) U of Mass Pr.

Black & White in Colour: Black People in British Television since 1936. Ed. by Jim Pines. (Illus.). 256p. 1992. 55.00 (0-85170-329-1, Pub. by British Film Inst UK); pap. 22.95 (0-85170-328-3, Pub. by British Film Inst UK) Ind U Pr.

Black & White in East Africa: The Fabric of a New Civilization. Richard C. Thurnwald. (B. E. Ser.: No. 175). 1935. 42.00 (0-8115-3085-X) Periodicals Srv.

Black & White in School: Trust, Tension, or Tolerance? Janet W. Schofield. 272p. 1989. reprint ed. pap. text ed. 18.95 (0-8077-2982-5) Tchrs Coll.

Black & White in Southern Zambia: The Tonga Plateau Economy & British Imperialism, 1890-1939. Kenneth P. Vickery. LC 85-27264. (Contributions in Comparative Colonial Studies: No. 21). (Illus.). 261p. 1986. text ed. 55.00 (0-313-25106-1, VBW/) Greenwood.

***Black & White in the Nineties.** Sharone L. Teamer. 40p. 1995. pap. 7.00 (0-8059-3691-2) Dorrance.

Black & White Keys. Hugh Hood. 298p. (C). 1982. 17.95 (0-920802-35-4, Pub. by ECW Press CN); pap. 8.95 (0-920802-37-0, Pub. by ECW Press CN) Genl Dist Srvs.

Black & White Keys. Hugh Hood. 298p. 1985. pap. 4.95 (0-7736-7101-3, Pub. by Stoddart Pubng CN) Genl Dist Srvs.

***Black & White Magic.** Anna Riva. 64p. (Orig.). 1994. pap. 4.50 (0-943832-22-5) Intl Imports.

Black & White New York. Bill Harris. (Illus.). 80p. 1994. 14.95 (1-56566-061-7) Thomasson-Grant.

Black & White of Finance. Debra Buhay. (Black & White Philosophy Ser.). 30p. (YA). (gr. 12). 1990. pap. 2.00 (1-878056-02-6) D Hockenberry.

Black & White of It. Ann A. Shockley. 144p. 1987. reprint ed. pap. 7.95 (0-930044-96-7) Naiad Pr.

Black & White of Marriage. Debra Buhay. (Black & White Philosophy Ser.). 30p. (YA). (gr. 12). 1990. pap. 2.00 (1-878056-04-2) D Hockenberry.

Black & White of Politics. Debra Buhay. (Black & White Philosophy Ser.). 30p. (YA). (gr. 12). 1990. pap. 2.00 (1-878056-03-4) D Hockenberry.

Black & White of Success. Debra Buhay. (Black & White Philosophy Ser.). 30p. (YA). (gr. 12). 1990. pap. 2.00 (1-878056-01-8) D Hockenberry.

Black & White of Writing. Debra Buhay. (Black & White Philosophy Ser.). 30p. (YA). (gr. 12). 1990. pap. 2.00 (0-685-37411-4) D Hockenberry.

Black & White Photography. Glenn M. Rand & David R. Litschel. Ed. by Jucha. LC 93-14290. 300p. (C). 1994. pap. text ed. 28.25 (0-314-02460-3) West Pub.

Black & White Photography: A Basic Manual. rev. ed. Henry Horenstein. (Illus.). 256p. 1983. reprint ed. pap. 19.95 (0-316-37314-1) Little.

Black-and-White Printing: A Practical Guide to Effective Darkroom Techniques. George Schaub. (Illus.). 144p. 1991. 29.95 (0-8174-3604-9, Amphoto); pap. 22.50 (0-8174-3605-7, Amphoto) Watsn-Guptill.

Black & White Rabbit's ABC. Alan Baker. LC 93-29760. (Little Rabbit Bks.: Vol. 3). (Illus.). 24p. (J). (ps). 1994. 7.95 (1-85697-951-2, Kingfisher LKC) LKC.

Black & White Racial Identity: Theory, Research, & Practice. Ed. by Janet E. Helms. LC 89-17030. (Contributions in Afro-American & African Studies: No. 129). 256p. 1990. text ed. 49.95 (0-313-26352-3, HBT/, Greenwood Pr) Greenwood.

Black & White Racial Identity: Theory, Research, & Practice. Ed. by Janet E. Helms. LC 93-11989. 256p. 1993. pap. text ed. 17.95 (0-275-94612-6, B4612, Praeger Pubs) Greenwood.

Black & White Sat Down Together: Reminiscences of an NAACP Founder. Mary W. Ovington. Ed. by Ralph E. Luker. 200p. 1995. 19.95 (1-55861-099-5) Feminist Pr.

Black & White Since Nineteen Sixty: Prints from the Reba & Dave Williams Collection. Reba Williams & Dave Williams. (Illus.). 32p. (Orig.). (C). 1989. pap. text ed. 5.00 (0-9621077-2-7) City Gallery Cntmprry Art.

Black & White Skin Diseases. C. Archer. 1994. write for info. (0-632-02529-8) Blackwell Sci.

Black & White Solution: Bar Code & the IBM PC. Russ Adams & Joyce Lane. 172p. (Orig.). 1987. pap. 19.95 (0-911261-01-X) Helmers Pub.

***Black & White Strangers: Race & American Literary Realism.** Kenneth W. Warren. 168p. 1995. pap. text ed. 10.95 (0-226-87385-4) U Ch Pr.

Black & White Styles in Conflict. Thomas Kochman. LC 81-3405. vi, 178p. 1981. lib. bdg. 24.00 (0-226-44954-8) U Ch Pr.

Black & White Styles in Conflict. Thomas Kochman. LC 81-3405. vi, 178p. 1983. pap. 8.95 (0-226-44955-6) U Ch Pr.

Black & White Styles of Youth Ministry: Two Congregations in America. William R. Myers. LC 90-43961. 240p. (Orig.). 1990. pap. 12.95 (0-8298-0868-X) Pilgrim OH.

Black & White Tangled Threads. Zara Wright. LC 73-18566. reprint ed. 45.00 (0-404-11378-8) AMS Pr.

Black & White Tangled Threads: Band, Kenneth. Zara Wright & Maggie Sale. LC 94-21459. 1995. text ed. 25.00 (0-8161-1626-1) G K Hall.

Black & White Urban-to-Suburban Outmigrants Vol. O4: A Comparative Analysis 1975-1980. Dennis E. Gale et al. 1986. 2.50 (0-317-01832-9) GWU CWAS.

***Black & White Washington.** Bill Harris. (Illus.). 80p. 1995. 14.95 (1-56566-070-6) Thomasson-Grant.

Black & White Women of the Old South: The Peculiar Sisterhood in American Literature. Minrose C. Gwin. LC 85-3238. 248p. 1985. text ed. 28.00x (0-87049-469-4) U of Tenn Pr.

Black Angel. Cordia Byers. (Orig.). 1993. mass mkt. 4.99 (0-449-14783-5, GM) Fawcett.

Black Angel. Michael Cristofer. 1984. pap. 4.75 (0-8222-0124-0) Dramatists Play.

Black Angel Delivers a Message. La Verne Dinckney. Ed. by Zulma Gonzalez-Parker. (Illus.). (Orig.). 1989. pap. write for info. (0-318-65768-6) Heartfelt Pr.

Black Anger. Wulf Sachs. LC 68-23323. 324p. 1968. reprint ed. text ed. 59.75 (0-8371-0244-8, SABA, Greenwood Pr) Greenwood.

Black Anglo-Saxons. Nathan Hare. 1992. pap. 12.95 (0-88378-130-1) Third World.

Black Anima. N. J. Loftis. (New Writers Ser.). 1973. 4.95 (0-87140-562-8) Liveright.

Black Anti-Semitism Controversy: Protestant Views & Perspectives. Hubert G. Locke. LC 93-50999. 144p. 1994. text ed. 29.50 (0-945636-51-2) Susquehanna U Pr.

Black Apathy (Poetry) Jessie Ivey. 29p. pap. 3.00 (0-9600864-3-9) Ivey Pubns.

Black Apollo of Science: The Life of Ernest Everett Just. Kenneth R. Manning. (Illus.). 416p. 1983. 35.00 (0-19-503299-3) OUP.

Black Apollo of Science: The Life of Ernest Everett Just. Kenneth R. Manning. (Illus.). 416p. 1985. pap. 12.95 (0-19-503498-8) OUP.

***Black Apple.** Eric H. Edwards. 20p. 1994. pap. 5.00 (1-885141-02-5) Harlequin Ink.

Black April. Julia Peterkin. 22.95 (0-89190-527-8, Am Repr) Amereon Ltd.

Black Armed Forces Officers, 1736-1971: A Documented Pictorial History. Jesse J. Johnson. LC 75-178014. (Illus.). 170p. 10.00 (0-915044-10-2) Carver Pub.

Black Arrow. Robert Louis Stevenson. (Airmont Classics Ser.). (J). (gr. 6 up). 1964. pap. 2.95 (0-8049-0020-5, CL-20) Airmont.

Black Arrow. Robert Louis Stevenson. 19.95 (0-8488-1182-8) Amereon Ltd.

Black Arrow. Robert Louis Stevenson. pap. 2.95 (0-89375-781-0) Troll Assocs.

Black Arrow: A Tale of the Two Roses. Robert Louis Stevenson. LC 87-9669. (Scribners Illustrated Classics Ser.). (Illus.). 336p. (J). 1987. text ed. 24.95 (0-684-18877-5, C Scribner Sons Young) S&S Childrens.

Black Arrow: A Tale of the Two Roses. deluxe ed. Robert Louis Stevenson. LC 87-9669. (Scribners Illustrated Classics Ser.). (Illus.). 336p. 1987. 75.00 (0-684-18897-X, C Scribner Sons Young) S&S Childrens.

Black Art: Ancestral Legacy: The African Impulse in African-American Art. Alvia J. Wardlaw et al. Ed. by Robert V. Rozelle. (Illus.). 304p. (Orig.). 1989. 45.00 (0-8109-3104-4); pap. 24.95 (0-936227-04-4) Dallas Mus.

Black Art in Houston: The Texas Southern University Experience. John Biggers et al. LC 77-99276. (Illus.). 122p. 1978. 20.00 (0-89096-046-1) Tex A&M Univ Pr.

Black Art of Cooking. Carl Loeb. 127p. 1993. reprint ed. spiral bd. 5.50 (0-7873-0568-5) Mokelumne.

Black Art of Cooking: How Cooked Food Produces Disease, an Introduction to the Unfired Diet. C. Loeb. 1991. lib. bdg. 79.95 (0-8490-4547-9) Gordon Pr.

***Black Art of Visual Basic Game Programming.** Tegliaferri. 512p. Date not set. cd-rom, pap. 34.95 (1-57169-005-0) Waite Group Pr.

***Black Art of Windows Game Programming.** Eric R. Lyons. 600p. Date not set. cd-rom, pap. 34.95 (1-878739-95-6) Waite Group Pr.

***Black Art of 3D Game Programming: Writing Your Own High-Speed 3D Polygon Video Games in C.** Andre Lamothe. 1000p. 1995. cd-rom, pap. 49.95 (1-57169-004-2) Waite Group Pr.

Black Artist in America: An Index to Reproductions. Comp. by Dennis Thomison. LC 91-33050. 456p. 1991. 47.50 (0-8108-2503-1) Scarecrow.

Black Artists in America. (Shorewood Art Programs for Education Ser.). 20p. 1974. 107.00 (0-88185-011-X); teacher ed 131.75 (0-88185-062-4); 130.00 (0-685-10056-1) Shorewood Fine Art.

Black Artists in the United States: An Annotated Bibliography of Books, Articles, & Dissertations on Black Artists, 1779-1979. Lenwood G. Davis & Janet L. Sims. LC 79-8576. 160p. 1980. text ed. 45.00 (0-313-22082-4, DBA/) Greenwood.

Black Artists on Art, 2 vols, 1. rev. ed. Samella S. Lewis & Ruth Waddy. LC 76-97788. 1971. pap. 15.00 (0-941248-04-6) Hancraft.

Black Artists on Art, 2 vols, 2. rev. ed. Samella S. Lewis & Ruth Waddy. LC 76-97788. 1971. 20.00 (0-941248-02-X); pap. 15.00 (0-941248-05-4) Hancraft.

Black Artists on Art, 2 vols, Set. rev. ed. Samella S. Lewis & Ruth Waddy. LC 76-97788. 1971. 40.00 (0-941248-00-3); pap. 30.00 (0-941248-03-8) Hancraft.

Black Artists on Art, 2 vols, Vol. 1. rev. ed. Samella S. Lewis & Ruth Waddy. LC 76-97788. 1971. 20.00 (0-941248-01-1) Hancraft.

Black Arts. Richard Cavendish. 1968. pap. 11.00 (0-399-50035-9, Perigree Bks) Berkley Pub.

Black Arts Annual: 1988-89. Ed. by Donald Bogle. LC 10-427104. (Illus.). 266p. 1990. 59.95 (0-8240-4943-8, 1206) Garland.

Black Arts Annual, 1989-90. Ed. by Donald Bogle. LC 10-427104. 180p. 1992. 59.95 (0-8240-6099-7, H1411) Garland.

Black As He Is Painted. Ngaio Marsh. 1976. reprint ed. lib. bdg. 21.95 (0-88411-472-4, Aeonian Pr) Amereon Ltd.

Black As He's Painted. Ngaio Marsh. (Mystery Ser.). 224p. 1984. pap. 3.99 (0-515-07627-9) Jove Pubns.

Black As He's Painted. Ngaio Marsh. 1994. reprint ed. lib. bdg. 27.95 (1-56849-307-X) Buccaneer Bks.

Black As He's Painted see Ngaio Marsh

Black As You Wanna Be: A Collection of Fun, Thought-Provoking Questions for the 1990-2000's. Deborah A. Williams. LC 91-67334. 180p. (Orig.). 1991. pap. 7.95 (0-963151-3-8) Syan Bks.

Black Athena Vol. II: The Archaeological & Documentary Evidence. Martin Bernal. (Illus.). 750p. (C). 1991. text ed. 65.00 (0-685-48854-3); pap. 17.95 (0-685-48855-1) Rutgers U Pr.

***Black Athena Revisited.** Ed. by Mary R. Lefkowitz & Guy M. Rogers. LC 95-8903. 1996. write for info. (0-8078-2246-9); pap. write for info. (0-8078-4555-8) U of NC Pr.

Black Athena, Vol. I: The Afroasiatic Roots of Classical Civilization: The Fabrication of Ancient Greece, 1785-1985. Martin Bernal. 575p. 1987. lib. bdg. 60.00 (0-8135-1276-X); pap. text ed. 16.95 (0-8135-1277-8) Rutgers U Pr.

Black Athlete: His Story in American History. Jack Orr. (J). (gr. 6 up). 1969. lib. bdg. 14.95 (0-87460-104-5) Lion Bks.

Black Athletes in the United States: A Bibliography of Books, Articles, Autobiographies & Biographies on Black Professional Athletes in the United States, 1880 to 1981. Comp. by Lenwood G. Davis & Belinda S. Daniels. LC 81-6334. 288p. 1981. text ed. 65.00 (0-313-22976-7, DBL/) Greenwood.

Black Atlantic: Modernity & Double-Consciousness. Paul Gilroy. 275p. 1993. text ed. 24.95 (0-674-07605-2) HUP.

***Black Atlantic: Modernity & Double-Consciousness.** Paul Gilroy. 275p. 1995. pap. 14.95 (0-674-07606-0, GILBLX) HUP.

***Black Atlantic Writers of the Eighteenth Century: Living the New Exodus in England & the Americas.** Ed. by Adam Potkay & Sandra Burr. LC 94-36117. 1995. text ed. 39.95 (0-312-12133-4) St Martin.

***Black Atlantic Writers of the Eighteenth Century: Living the New Exodus in England & the Americas.** Ed. by Adam Potkay & Sandra Burr. 288p. 1995. text ed. 16.95 (0-312-12518-6) St Martin.

***Black August.** Timothy Williams. 256p. 1995. pap. 8.95 (0-575-05602-9, Pub. by V Gollancz UK) Trafalgar.

Black Authors & Illustrators of Children's Books: A Biographical Dictionary. 2nd ed. Barbara Rollock. LC 91-37402. (Illus.). 252p. 1992. 35.00 (0-8240-7078-X, H01316) Garland.

Black Authors & Published Writers Directory, 1994. Ed. by Grace Adams. (Illus.). 320p. (Orig.). 1994. pap. 24.95 (1-877807-50-8) Grace Pub MI.

Black Authors Books in Print, 1994-95. Ed. by Grace Adams. (Illus.). (Orig.). 1996. pap. 24.95 (1-877807-60-5) Grace Pub MI.

Black Awakening in Capitalist America. Robert L. Allen. LC 90-80153. 305p. (C). 1990. 29.95 (0-86543-172-8); pap. 9.95 (0-86543-157-4) Africa World.

Black Back-Ups. Kate Rushin. LC 92-46886. 96p. (Orig.). 1993. lib. bdg. 18.95 (1-56341-026-5); pap. 8.95 (1-56341-025-7) Firebrand Bks.

Black Bahamian: His Indomitable Quest for Metaphysical, Ontological, & Political Balance. Lowell Moree. 1990. 10.95 (0-533-08544-6) Vantage.

Black Bait. rev. ed. Leo Guild. 224p. (Orig.). 1985. pap. 3.95 (0-87067-393-9) Holloway.

Black Balloon. Date not set. 5.95 (1-56222-049-7, 94512); audio 10.98 (1-56222-346-1, 94512C); cd-rom 15.98 (0-685-75039-6, 94512CD) Mel Bay.

Black Ballots: Voting Rights in the South 1944-1969. Steven F. Lawson. LC 76-18886. (Contemporary American History Ser.). 474p. 1976. pap. text ed. 23.50 (0-231-08352-1) Col U Pr.

Black Baltimore: A New Theory of Community. Harold A. McDougall. LC 92-32548. 288p. 1993. 39.95 (1-56639-037-0); pap. 18.95 (1-56639-193-8) Temple U Pr.

Black Baltimore, Eighteen Twenty to Eighteen Seventy. Ralph Clayton. (Illus.). vii, 199p. (Orig.). 1987. pap. 12.00 (1-55613-080-5) Heritage Bk.

Black Baptist Secondary Schools in Virginia, 1887-1957: A Study in Black History. Lester F. Russell. LC 80-22414. 218p. 1981. 22.50 (0-8108-1373-4) Scarecrow.

Black Baptists & African Missions: The Origins of a Movement, 1880-1915. Sandy D. Martin. LC 89-39041. 180p. (C). 1990. 24.95 (0-86554-353-4, MUP/H287) Mercer Univ Pr.

Black Barque. Thornton J. Hains. LC 70-37304. (Black Heritage Library Collection). (Illus.). 1977. reprint ed. 26.95 (0-8369-8941-4) Ayer.

***Black Barr, Boulevardier Bandit: The Saga of California's Most Mysterious Stagecoach Robber & the Men Who Sought to Capture Him.** George Hoeper. LC 94-61458. (Illus.). 176p. 1995. pap. 9.95 (1-884995-05-5) Word Dancer.

Black Bart Says Draw. Bill Amend. 128p. (Orig.). 1991. pap. 8.95 (0-8362-1869-8) Andrews & McMeel.

Black Basalt. Diana Edwards. (Illus.). 370p. 1994. 89.50 (1-85149-161-9) Antique Collect.

Black Baseball Journal, Vol. 1, No. 1. Ed. by James A. Riley. (Illus.). 64p. (Orig.). (YA). 1990. pap. 6.95 (0-9614023-5-0) TK Pubs.

Black Bass & the Fly Rod. Charles F. Waterman. LC 92-28802. (Illus.). 256p. 1993. 19.95 (0-8117-1630-9) Stackpole.

Black Bass Biology & Management. Ed. by Richard H. Stroud & Henry Clepper. 1975. 25.00 (0-686-21850-7); pap. 20.00 (0-686-21851-5) Sport Fishing.

Black Bear. Mark E. Ahlstrom. LC 85-22872. (Wildlife Habits & Habitats Ser.). (Illus.). 48p. (J). (gr. 5). 1985. text ed. 12.95 (0-89686-276-3, Crstwood Hse) Silver Burdett Pr.

An Asterisk (*) at the beginning of an entry indicates that the title is appearing in BIP for the first time.

An Asterisk (*) at the beginning of an entry indicates that the title is appearing in BIP for the first time.

797

B

Black Cat Inn. Brandy O'Shea. LC 91-67920. (Illus.). (J). Date not set. pap. 8.00 (*1-56002-180-2*, Univ Edtns) Aegina Pr.

Black Cat Made Me Buy It! Alice L. Muncaster & Ellen Y. Sawyer. (Illus.). 96p. 1988. pap. 12.95 (*0-517-56891-8*, Crown) Crown Pub Group.

Black Cat Named Smokey: On Vacation. Robyn Dean. LC 92-93502. (Illus.). 64p. (Orig.). (J). (gr. k-3). 1992. pap. 7.95 (*0-9633466-0-1*) Zyxalon Pr.

Black Cat Raiders of WWII. Richard C. Knott. 1984. pap. 3.25 (*0-8217-1381-7*) Zebra.

Black Cat Squadron: Night Bombing in World War I. Humphrey Wynn. LC 89-61563. 250p. 1990. 27.50 (*0-87474-992-1*) Smithsonian.

***Black Cats & Blue Birds.** Francis R. McNulty. 220p. 1995. pap. 8.95 (*1-56901-825-1*) NW Pub.

Black Cats & Outside Loops: Aerobatic Ace. Walt Bohrer. LC 89-92104. (Illus.). 221p. (Orig.). 1990. 29.95 (*0-929734-03-3*) Plere Pubs.

Black Cats, Hoot Owls, & Water Witches: Beliefs, Superstitions, & Sayings from Texas. Ed. by Kenneth W. Davis & Everett A. Gillis. LC 89-27779. 112p. (Orig.). 1989. pap. 8.95 (*0-929398-06-8*) UNTX Pr.

Black Cauldron. (Classics Ser.). 96p. (J). 1990. 6.98 (*1-57082-035-X*) Mouse Works.

Black Cauldron. (Penguin-Disney Ser.). (J). 1990. 6.98 (*0-8317-5795-7*) Viking Child Bks.

Black Cauldron. Lloyd Alexander. 192p. (J). (gr. k-6). 1980. mass mkt. 3.99 (*0-440-40649-8*, YB) Dell.

Black Cauldron. Lloyd Alexander. LC 65-13868. 224p. (J). (gr. 4-6). 1965. 16.95 (*0-8050-0992-2*, Bks Young Read) H Holt & Co.

Black Cauldron. William Heinesen. Tr. by W. Glyn Jones. (Dedalus European Fiction Classics Ser.). 304p. 1992. pap. 14.95 (*0-7818-0000-5*, Pub. by Dedalus Bks UK) Hippocrene Bks.

Black Cauldron. Walt Disney Staff. (J). (ps-3). 1993. 6.98 (*0-453-03154-4*) Viking Child Bks.

Black Celebrations. Aisha Nanji. Ed. by Taji Nanji & Joyce Mills. 62p. (Orig.). 1987. pap. 6.00 (*0-929003-00-4*) Prgrssv Pubs.

Black Characters in the Brazilian Novel. Giorgio Marotti. Tr. by Maria O. Marotti & Harry Lawton. (Afro-American Culture & Society Monograph Ser.: Vol. 6). (Illus.). 448p. 1987. 50.95 (*0-934934-24-X*); pap. 19.95 (*0-934934-25-8*) UCLA CAAS.

Black Charlestonians: A Social History, 1822-1885. Bernard E. Powers, Jr. LC 94-7861. (Illus.). 384p. 1994. 36.00 (*1-55728-364-8*) U of Ark Pr.

Black Cherry Blues. James L. Burke. 336p. 1990. reprint ed. mass mkt. 5.50 (*0-380-71204-0*) Avon.

Black Cheyenne. Charles R. Goodman. 1993. pap. 3.95 (*0-87067-854-X*, Melrose Sq) Holloway.

Black Chicago: The Making of a Negro Ghetto, 1890-1920. Allan H. Spear. LC 67-21381. 1969. reprint ed. pap. text ed. 12.95 (*0-226-76857-0*, P332) U Ch Pr.

Black Child Development in America, 1927-1977: An Annotated Bibliography. Comp. by Hector F. Myers et al. LC 78-20028. 470p. 1979. text ed. 49.95 (*0-313-20719-4*, FBC/, Greenwood Pr) Greenwood.

Black Child, White Child: The Development of Racial Attitudes. Judith D. Porter. (Illus.). 278p. 1971. pap. 12.95 (*0-674-07611-7*) HUP.

Black Children. Harriette McAdoo & John L. McAdoo. (Focus Editions Ser.: Vol. 72). 1985. 49.95 (*0-8039-2461-5*); pap. 24.95 (*0-8039-2462-3*) Sage.

Black Children: Their Roots, Culture, & Learning Styles. rev. ed. Janice E. Hale-Benson. LC 86-45459. (Illus.). 240p. 1986. reprint ed. pap. text ed. 13.95x (*0-8018-3383-3*) Johns Hopkins.

Black Children & American Institutions: An Ecological Review & Resource Guide. Valora Washington & Velma LaPoint. LC 88-16490. (Source Books on Education). 464p. 1988. lib. bdg. 73.00 (*0-8240-8517-5*, SS382) Garland.

Black Children & Poverty: A Developmental Perspective. Ed. by Diana T. Slaughter. LC 85-644581. (New Directions for Child Development Ser.: No. CP 42). 1988. 17.95 (*1-55542-885-1*) Jossey-Bass.

Black Children in the Public Care System. Ravinder Barn. (Illus.). 160p. 1993. pap. 29.95 (*0-7134-7136-0*, Pub. by Batsford UK) Trafalgar.

Black Christ. Kelly B. Douglas. LC 93-35821. (Bishop Henry McNeal Turner Studies: Vol. 9). 140p. (Orig.). 1994. pap. 12.95 (*0-88344-939-0*) Orbis Bks.

Black Christian Nationalism: New Directions for the Black Church. Albert B. Cleage, Jr. 350p. 1987. reprint ed. 14.95 (*0-941205-00-2*); reprint ed. pap. 10.00 (*0-941205-01-0*) Luxor Pubs PAOCC.

Black Christians & the Church in South Africa (Bishop Zwane of Swaziland) CIIR Staff. 1979. 20.00 (*0-904393-43-7*) Cath Inst Inter.

Black Christians & White Missionaries. Richard Gray. 144p. (C). 1991. text ed. 23.00x (*0-300-04910-2*) Yale U Pr.

Black Christians: The Untold Lutheran Story. Jeff Johnson. (Scholarship Today Ser.). 336p. (Orig.). 1991. pap. 14.95 (*0-570-04558-4*, 12-3162) Concordia.

Black Church & the Harold Washington Story: The Man, the Message, the Movement. Ed. by Henry J. Young. LC 88-40117. (Illus.). (Orig.). (C). 1988. pap. 19.95 (*1-55605-045-3*) Wyndhall Pr.

Black Church in the African American Experience. C. Eric Lincoln & Lawrence Mamiya. LC 90-34050. 472p. (C). 1990. pap. text ed. 21.95 (*0-8223-1073-2*) Duke.

Black Church Life-Styles. Emmanuel L. McCall. LC 86-17591. 1986. pap. 5.99 (*0-8054-5665-1*) Broadman.

Black Church Since Frazier see Negro Church in America

Black Churches of Brooklyn. Clarence Taylor. LC 94-5546. (Columbia History of Urban Life Ser.). 297p. 1994. 27.50 (*0-231-09980-0*) Col U Pr.

***Black Churches Reaching College Students.** John H. Corbitt. LC 95-3511. 1995. write for info. (*0-910683-30-1*) Townsnd-Pr.

Black Cinema Aesthetics: Issues in Independent Black Filmmaking. Gladstone Yearwood et al. (Papers on Afro-American, African & Caribbean Studies). (Illus.). 120p. (Orig.). 1983. pap. 5.00 (*0-911393-03-X*) Ctr Afro Stud Ohio.

Black Cinema Treasures: Lost & Found. G. William Jones. LC 91-10882. (Illus.). 258p. 1991. 29.95 (*0-929398-26-2*) UNTX Pr.

Black Cipher. Payne Harrison. LC 94-9849. 1994. 22.00 (*0-517-58753-X*) Crown Pub Group.

Black City Stage. Jack Sheperd. LC 68-59115. (Orig.). 1968. pap. 3.00 (*0-87574-162-2*) Pendle Hill.

***Black Civil Rights Champions.** Kimberly H. Taylor. LC 94-45652. (Profiles Ser.). (J). 1995. 14.95 (*1-881508-22-6*) Oliver Pr MN.

Black Civilization: A Social Study of an Australian Tribe. rev. ed. W. Lloyd Warner. (Illus.). 13.25 (*0-8446-0954-4*) Peter Smith.

Black Cliffs. Gunnar Gunnarsson. Tr. by Cecil Wood. (Nordic Translation Ser.). 260p. 1967. 8.00x (*0-299-04471-8*) U of Wis Pr.

Black Cloth: A Collection of African Folk Tales. Bernard B. Dadie. Tr. by Karen C. Hatch. LC 86-25043. 176p. 1987. pap. 12.95 (*0-87023-557-5*) U of Mass Pr.

Black Cloud. Fred Hoyle. 1993. reprint ed. lib. bdg. 18.95 (*0-89968-344-4*, Lghtyr Pr) Buccaneer Bks.

Black Cloud, White Cloud. limited ed. Ellen Douglas. LC 89-5524. (Author & Artist Ser.). (Illus.). 260p. 1989. reprint ed. 60.00 (*0-87805-397-2*) U Pr of Miss.

Black Cloud, White Cloud. Ellen Douglas. LC 89-5524. (Author & Artist Ser.). (Illus.). 260p. 1989. reprint ed. 25.00 (*0-87805-393-X*) U Pr of Miss.

Black Coal Miners in America: Race, Class, & Community Conflict, 1780-1980. Ronald L. Lewis. LC 87-2086. (Illus.). 256p. 1987. 28.00 (*0-8131-1610-4*) U Pr of Ky.

Black Cocktail. Jonathan Carroll. (Illus.). 80p. 1991. 13.95 (*0-312-06304-0*) St Martin.

Black Coffee Blues. Rollins. 142p. (Orig.). 1992. reprint ed. pap. 11.00 (*1-880985-05-5*) Two Thirteen Sixty-one.

Black Coffin. large type ed. Bill Reno. 304p. 1989. pap. 12.95 (*0-8161-4778-7*, Large Print Bks) Hall.

Black Collectibles: Mammy & Her Friends. rev. ed. Jackie Young. LC 88-62979. (Illus.). 128p. 1991. reprint ed. pap. 14.95 (*0-88740-365-4*) Schiffer.

Black College Career Guide. Joan Carroll. 140p. (YA). (gr. 9-12). 1992. pap. 6.95 (*1-881223-00-0*) Zulema Ent.

Black College Football, 1892-1992: One Hundred Years of History, Education, & Pride. Michael Hurd. LC 93-20988. 1993. 29.50 (*0-89865-882-9*) Donning Co.

Black Colleges & Public Policy. Ed. by Andrew Billingsley & Julia Elam. (NAFEO Conference Ser.). 100p. 1987. pap. 10.95 (*0-695-60050-8*) Follett Pr.

Black Colleges & Universities: Challenges for the Future. Ed. by Antoine M. Garibaldi. LC 83-22943. 320p. 1984. text ed. 59.95 (*0-275-91163-2*, C1163, Praeger Pubs) Greenwood.

Black Colleges & Universities: Charcoals to Diamonds. Ed. by Injay. 100p. 1992. pap. 15.95 (*1-881954-25-0*) Sssh Ent.

Black Colossus. Robert E. Howard. (Illus.). 1979. 20.00 (*0-937986-03-8*) D M Grant.

***Black Columbiad: Defining Moments in African American Literature & Culture.** Ed. by Maria Diedrich & Werner Sollors. LC 94-19727. (Harvard English Studies: 19). (Illus.). 416p. 1995. text ed. 39.95 (*0-674-07617-6*, SOLBLA) HUP.

***Black Columbiad: Defining Moments in African American Literature & Culture.** Werner Sollors. Ed. by Maria Diedrich. LC 94-19727. (Harvard English Studies: 19). (Illus.). 416p. 1995. pap. text ed. 16.95 (*0-674-07618-4*, SOLBLX) HUP.

Black Communication in White Society. Roy Cogdell & Sybil Wilson. LC 79-93302. 160p. 1980. 15.00 (*0-86548-004-4*) R & E Pubs.

Black Communications: Breaking Down the Barriers. Evelyn B. Dandy. 186p. 1992. pap. 10.95 (*0-913543-23-3*) African Am Imag.

Black Community. 3rd ed. Blackwell. (C). 1991. pap. text ed. 30.00 (*0-06-040737-9*) HarpCollege.

***Black Community Crusade & Covenant for Protecting Children.** Black Community Crusade for Children Staff. 1995. pap. write for info. (*1-881985-09-1*) Childrens Defense.

Black Company. Glen Cook. 1992. mass mkt. 4.99 (*0-8125-2139-0*) Tor Bks.

Black Computer Survival Guide. Eno Essien. (Illus.). 84p. (Orig.). (C). 1992. pap. text ed. 8.75 (*0-9632302-0-4*) Blackk Inkk.

***Black Conductors.** D. Antoinette Handy. LC 94-34560. (Illus.). 570p. 1995. 69.50 (*0-8108-2930-4*) Scarecrow.

Black Confederates & Afro-Yankees in Civil War Virginia. Ervin L. Jordan, Jr. LC 94-16923. (Nation Divided Ser.). 1995. text ed. 67.50 (*0-8139-1544-9*); pap. text ed. 18.95 (*0-8139-1545-7*) U Pr of Va.

Black Connection. Randolph Harris. (Orig.). 1974. pap. 2.50 (*0-87067-271-1*, BH077) Holloway.

Black Consciousness, Identity, & Achievement: A Study of Students in Historical Black Colleges. Patricia Gurin & Edgar Epps. LC 75-5847. 559p. reprint ed. pap. 159.40 (*0-8357-7285-3*, 2019891) Bks Demand.

Black Consciousness in South Africa: The Dialectics of Ideological Resistance to White Supremacy. Robert Fatton, Jr. LC 85-2855. (African Politics & Society Ser.). 189p. 1986. 64.50 (*0-88706-127-3*); pap. 21.95 (*0-88706-129-X*) State U NY Pr.

Black Consumer Profiles: Food Purchasing in the Inner City. Marcus Alexis et al. LC 80-622236. 97p. reprint ed. pap. 27.70 (*0-8357-7286-1*, 2056358) Bks Demand.

Black Cop. Joe Nazel. 1993. pap. 3.95 (*0-87067-761-6*) Holloway.

Black Cops. James N. Reaves. Ed. by William Wartman. (Illus.). 216p. 1991. 21.95 (*0-9627161-4-6*) QLP Phila PA.

Black Corps: A Collector's Guide to the History & Regalia of the SS. Robin Lumsden. (Illus.). 176p. (Orig.). 1992. pap. 19.95 (*0-7818-0112-5*) Hippocrene Bks.

Black Corps: The Structure & Power Struggles of the Nazi SS. Robert L. Koehl. LC 81-69824. (Illus.). 474p. 1983. 29.50 (*0-299-09190-2*) U of Wis Pr.

Black Corps d'Elite: An Egyptian Sudanese Conscript Battalion with the French Army in Mexico, 1863-1867, & Its Survivors in Subsequent African History. Richard Hill & Peter Hogg. 1995. 29.95 (*0-87013-339-X*) Mich St U Pr.

Black Country at War in Photographs. (C). 1987. 50.00 (*0-317-89842-6*, Pub. by Birmingham Midland Soc UK) St Mut.

Black Country Christmas. Ed. by Robin Pearson. (Christmas Ser.). (Illus.). 160p. 1992. pap. 15.00 (*0-7509-0071-7*) A Sutton Pub.

Black Country Elites: The Exercise of Authority in an Industrialized Area. Richard H. Trainor. (Oxford Historical Monographs). (Illus.). 464p. 1994. 75.00 (*0-19-820355-1*) OUP.

Black Cowboy. Harry Knill. (J). (gr. 1-9). 1993. pap. 2.50 (*0-88388-176-4*) Bellerophon Bks.

Black Cowboy: The Life & Legend of George McJunkin. 3rd ed. Franklin Folsom. (Illus.). 162p. (YA). 1992. pap. 7.95 (*1-879373-14-9*) R Rinehart.

Black Cowboys. Paul W. Stewart & Wallace Y. Ponce. Ed. by Linda C. Phillips. (Illus.). 248p. 1986. 29.95 (*0-938657-00-3*) Phillips Pub.

Black Crane, No. 1: An Anthology of Korean Literature. Ed. by David R. McCann. (Cornell East Asia Ser.: No. 14). 153p. 1977. 9.00 (*0-939657-14-7*) Cornell East Asia Pgm.

Black Creators, Vol. I. Corliss V. Grimes. (Illus.). 32p. (J). (gr. 1-3). 1994. 16.95 (*0-86543-288-0*); pap. 8.95 (*0-86543-289-9*) Africa World.

Black Critics & Kings: The Hermeneutics of Power in Yoruba Society. Andrew Apter. (Illus.). 312p. 1992. lib. bdg. 39.95 (*0-226-02342-7*); pap. text ed. 17.95 (*0-226-02343-5*) U Ch Pr.

Black Crook & Other 19th Century American Plays see Nineteenth-Century American Plays

***Black Cross.** Greg Iles. 480p. 1995. 19.95 (*0-525-93829-X*, Dutton) NAL-Dutton.

***Black Cross.** large type ed. Greg Iles. 1995. pap. 22.95 (*1-56895-225-2*) Wheeler Pub.

Black Crow. Francis H. Wise. Ed. & Illus. by Joyce M. Wise. (Learn to Read Ser.: No.11). 21p. (J). (gr. k-1). 1983. pap. 1.50 (*0-915766-62-0*) Wise Pub.

Black Crow, Black Crow. Ginger F. Guy. LC 89-34619. (Illus.). 24p. (J). (ps up). 1991. 13.95 (*0-688-08956-9*); lib. bdg. 13.88 (*0-688-08957-7*) Greenwillow.

***Black Crowes: America.** Ed. by Aaron Stang. 132p. (Orig.). (YA). 1995. pap. text ed. 22.95 (*0-89724-565-2*) Warner Brothers.

Black Crowes- Shake Your Money Maker (Guitar-Vocal) Black Crowes. Ed. by Mark Phillips. (Illus.). 80p. (Orig.). 1991. pap. 17.95 (*0-89524-655-4*); pap. 14.95 (*0-89524-630-9*) Cherry Lane.

***Black Crows.** Date not set. pap. 16.00 (*0-7119-3214-X*) Omnibus NY.

Black Crusoe. Alfred Seguin. LC 73-38022. (Black Heritage Library Collection). (Illus.). 1977. reprint ed. 29.95 (*0-8369-8995-3*) Ayer.

Black Cubena's Thoughts. Carlos G. Wilson. Tr. by Elba D. Birmingham-Pokorny & Rosangela Vieira- King. LC 90-86133. (Coleccion Ebano y Canela Ser.). 53p. (Orig.). (SPA.). 1991. pap. 6.95 (*0-89729-593-5*) Ediciones.

Black Culture & Black Consciousness: Afro-American Folk Thought from Slavery to Freedom. Lawrence W. Levine. LC 76-9223. 1978. reprint ed. pap. 13.95 (*0-19-502374-9*) OUP.

***Black Culture & Social Inequality in Colombia.** Peter Wade. 24p. 1989. pap. 7.00 (*0-904674-16-9*, Pub. by Octagon Pr UK) ISHK Bk Service.

Black Culture & the Harlem Renaissance. Cary D. Wintz. LC 88-42620. 277p. 1989. pap. 10.95 (*0-89263-271-2*) Rice Univ.

Black Culture & the Harlem Renaissance. Cary D. Wintz. LC 88-42620. 278p. 1992. text ed. 27.50 (*0-89263-267-4*) Rice Univ.

Black Dahlia. James Ellroy. 384p. 1988. mass mkt. 5.99 (*0-445-40525-2*, Mysterious Paperbk) Warner Bks.

Black Daisies for the Bride. Tony Harrison. 64p. (Orig.). 1994. pap. 10.95 (*0-571-17129-X*) Faber & Faber.

Black Dance. Lynne Emery. 392p. 1991. pap. 19.95 (*0-916622-63-0*) Princeton Bk Co.

Black Dance. Edward Thorpe. LC 89-8785. (Illus.). 192p. 1990. 35.00 (*0-87951-379-9*) Overlook Pr.

Black Dance. Edward Thorpe. (Illus.). 192p. 1994. reprint ed. pap. 19.95 (*0-87951-563-5*) Overlook Pr.

Black Dance in America: A History Through Its People. James S. Haskins. LC 89-35529. (Trophy Nonfiction Bk.). (Illus.). 240p. (YA). (gr. 7 up). 1992. pap. 6.95 (*0-06-446121-1*, Trophy) HarpC Child Bks.

Black Dance in the United States: From 1619 to Today. 2nd rev. ed. Lynne F. Emery. LC 88-61031. (Dance Ser.). 1980. lib. bdg. 42.95 (*0-88143-074-9*) Ayer.

Black Dawn Bright Day. Sun Bear. (Illus.). 246p. 1990. pap. 9.95 (*0-943404-18-5*) Bear Tribe.

Black Dawn, Bright Day: Indian Prophecies for the Millenium That Reveal the Fate of the Earth. Sun Bear & Wabun Wind. 256p. (Orig.). 1992. pap. 11.00 (*0-671-75900-0*, Fireside) S&S Trade.

Black Death. Timothy L. Biel. LC 89-112269. (World Disasters Ser.). (Illus.). 64p. (J). (gr. 5-8). 1989. lib. bdg. 14.95 (*1-56006-001-8*) Lucent Bks.

***Black Death.** E. R. Chamberlin. (Jackdaws Ser.). (Illus.). 1991. 24.95 (*1-56696-043-6*) Golden Owl NY.

Black Death. Basil Copper. (Illus.). 380p. (C). 1991. 32.00 (*1-878252-04-6*) Fedogan & Bremer.

Black Death. J. F. Hecker. Tr. by B. G. Babington. 78p. 1972. pap. 2.50 (*0-87291-038-5*) Coronado Pr.

Black Death. Tr. by Rosemary Horrox. LC 93-50558. (Medieval Sources Ser.). 1994. text ed. 69.95 (*0-7190-3497-3*, Pub. by Manchester Univ Pr UK) St Martin.

Black Death. R. Karl Largent. 368p. (Orig.). 1988. pap. 3.95 (*0-8439-2591-4*) Dorchester Pub Co.

***Black Death.** R. Karl Largent. 368p. 1995. mass mkt., pap. text ed. 4.99 (*0-8439-3797-1*) Dorchester Pub Co.

***Black Death.** Tom McGowen. LC 95-2122. (First Bks.). (J). 1995. lib. bdg. 13.93 (*0-531-20199-6*) Watts.

Black Death. Derek Turner. Ed. by Marjorie Reeves. (Then & There Ser.). (Illus.). 96p. (YA). (gr. 7-12). 1978. pap. text ed. 10.02 (*0-582-31097-0*, 78068) Longman.

Black Death. limited ed. Basil Copper. (Illus.). 380p. (C). 1991. 60.00 (*1-878252-05-4*) Fedogan & Bremer.

***Black Death.** E. R. Chamberlin. (Jackdaws Ser.). (Illus.). 1995. reprint ed. student ed 32.95 (*0-614-03232-6*) Golden Owl NY.

Black Death. Philip Ziegler. 1971. reprint ed. pap. text ed. 14.00 (*0-06-131550-8*, TB1550, Torch) HarpC.

Black Death. Philip Ziegler. (Illus.). 258p. 1991. reprint ed. 36.00 (*0-86299-838-7*) A Sutton Pub.

Black Death: A Turning Point in History? Ed. by William M. Bowsky. LC 77-21196. (European Problem Studies). 134p. 1978. reprint ed. pap. 9.50 (*0-88275-636-2*) Krieger.

Black Death: Mini-Play & Activities. Lawrence Stevens. (World History Ser.). (YA). (gr. 7 up). 1981. 6.50 (*0-89550-342-5*) Stevens & Shea.

Black Death: Natural & Human Disaster in Medieval Europe. Robert S. Gottfried. LC 82-48745. 240p. (C). 1985. 24.95 (*0-02-912630-4*); pap. 14.95 (*0-02-912370-4*) Free Pr.

Black Death: The Impact of the Fourteenth-Century Plague. Ed. by Daniel Williman. LC 82-12435. (Medieval & Renaissance Texts & Studies: Vol. 13). (Illus.). 160p. 1982. 25.00 (*0-86698-050-4*) MRTS.

Black Death & Men of Learning. Anna M. Campbell. LC 31-29792. reprint ed. 37.50 (*0-404-01368-6*) AMS Pr.

Black Death & Pastoral Leadership: The Diocese of Hereford in the Fourteenth Century. William J. Dohar. (Middle Ages Ser.). 192p. (C). 1995. text ed. 32.95 (*0-8122-3262-3*) U of Pa Pr.

Black Death in the Middle East. Michael W. Dols. LC 76-3254. 408p. reprint ed. pap. 116.30 (*0-8357-3301-7*, 2039524) Bks Demand.

Black Death of Thirteen Forty-Eight & Thirteen Forty-Nine. 2nd ed. Francis A. Gasquet. LC 75-23713. reprint ed. 47.50 (*0-404-13264-2*) AMS Pr.

Black Debacle - From a Thundering Voice to a Confused Whimper: (Recollections & Observations on the United Mine Workers & Collective Bargaining in the Coal Industry) Melvin Triolo. 320p. 1991. 19.95 (*0-9628040-0-2*) McClain.

Black Destiny. Stanley J. Goodwin. 89p. 1983. pap. 2.40 (*0-686-28004-0*) Northland Pubns WA.

Black Detroit & the Rise of the UAW. August Meier & Elliott Rudwick. (Illus.). 1981. pap. 9.95 (*0-19-502895-3*) OUP.

Black Diamond. Karen Blomain. 28p. 1987. pap. 3.50 (*0-9613465-7-4*) Great Elm.

Black Diamond. Jennie Gallant. 224p. (Orig.). 1981. pap. 2.25 (*0-449-24424-5*, Crest) Fawcett.

Black Diamond. large type ed. Jennie Gallant. 432p. (Orig.). 1984. 15.95 (*0-7089-1127-7*) Ulverscroft.

Black Diamond. 2nd rev. ed. Karen Blomain. Ed. by Roy Zarucchi & Carolyn Page. (Chapbook Ser.). (Illus.). 32p. 1990. pap. 5.00 (*1-879205-00-9*) Nightshade Pr.

Black Diamond: Mining the Memories. Diane Olson & Cory Olson. LC 88-83375. (Illus.). 236p. 1988. pap. 12.95 (*0-939116-19-7*) Frontier OR.

Black Diamond: The Story of the Negro Baseball Leagues. Patricia C. McKissack & Fredrick McKissack, Jr. LC 93-22691. (Illus.). 192p. (J). (gr. 3-9). 1994. 13.95 (*0-590-45809-4*) Scholastic Inc.

Black Diamonds. John B. Holway. 250p. 1989. 32.50 (*0-88736-334-2*) Mecklermedia.

Black Diamonds: Life in the Negro Leagues from the Men Who Lived It. John B. Holway. (Illus.). 200p. 1991. pap. 14.95 (*0-9625132-3-7*) Cyberbooks.

***Black Diamonds: The Wisdom of Booker T. Washington.** Ed. by Frank Hill. 150p. 1995. 9.95 (*1-55874-343-X*, 343X) Health Comm.

Black Diamonds; or Humor, Satire & Sentiment... William H. Levison. LC 75-91083. (American Humorists Ser.). reprint ed. lib. bdg. 29.50 (*0-8398-1156-X*) Irvington.

Black Diaspora. Howard University Staff. 1990. 24.00 (*0-536-57714-5*) Ginn Pr.

Black Diaspora: Colonization of Colored People. Edward L. Jones. LC 89-217080. 160p. (Orig.). 1988. pap. text ed. 16.95 (*0-9602458-5-5*) Ed-Lynne Jones.

***Black Diaspora: Five Centuries of the Black Experience Outside Africa.** Ronald Segal. 416p. Date not set. 25.00 (*0-374-11396-3*) FS&G.

Black Diva (Selected Poems: 1982-1986) Jean-Paul Daoust. 48p. 1991. pap. 8.00 (*0-920717-54-3*) SPD-Small Pr Dist.

Black Dixie: Afro-Texan History & Culture in Houston. Ed. by Howard Beeth & Cary D. Wintz. (Centennial Series of the Association of Former Students). 312p. 1992. 47.50 (*0-89096-494-7*) Tex A&M Univ Pr.

B

An Asterisk (*) at the beginning of an entry indicates that the title is appearing in BIP for the first time.

An Asterisk (*) at the beginning of an entry indicates that the title is appearing in BIP for the first time.

Black Family & the Black Woman: A Bibliography. Ed. by Phyllis R. Klotman & Wilmer H. Baatz. LC 77-81865. (Individual Publications Ser.). 1978. lib. bdg. 18.95 (*0-405-10523-1*) Ayer.

Black Family Dinner Quilt Cookbook. Dorothy Height. 1994. pap. 12.00 (*0-671-79630-5*, Fireside) S&S Trade.

Black Family in a Changing Black Community. Richard A. Davis. LC 92-27491. (Library of Sociology: Vol. 26). 144p. 1993. 22.00 (*0-8153-0878-7*, H838) Garland.

Black Family in Slavery & Freedom, 1750-1925. Herbert G. Gutman. 1977. pap. 20.00 (*0-394-72451-8*) Random.

Black Family in the United States: A Revised, Updated, Selectively Annotated Bibliography. Comp. by Lenwood G. Davis. LC 86-9926. (Bibliographies & Indexes in Afro-American & African Studies: No. 14). 244p. 1986. text ed. 75.00 (*0-313-25237-8*, DFR/, Greenwood Pr) Greenwood.

Black Family in the United States: A Selected Bibliography of Annotated Books, Articles, & Dissertations on Black Families in America. Lenwood G. Davis. LC 77-89109. 1978. lib. bdg. 35.00 (*0-8371-9851-8*, DBF/, Greenwood Pr) Greenwood.

Black Family in Urban Areas in the U. S., 1965-1974: A Bibliography of Published Works on the Black Family in Urban Areas in the U. S., Nos. 808-809. 2nd ed. Ed. by Lenwood G. Davis. 1975. 8.50 (*0-686-20354-2*) CPL Biblios.

Black Family Reunion Cookbook: Recipes & Food Memories from the National Council of Negro Women, Inc. National Council of Negro Women Staff. LC 92-41128. (Illus.). 224p. 1993. pap. 12.00 (*0-671-79629-1*, Fireside) S&S Trade.

Black Family Social Support Networks: Key to Educational Attainment for Adolescent Mothers. Diane Tait. 23p. (Orig.). 1995. pap. 2.95 (*0-9646450-0-9*) DeeMar Commun. BLACK FAMILY SOCIAL SUPPORT NETWORKS...was chosen by peer review for presentation at the Hartman National Biennial Conference on Children & Their Families, New London, CT, June 1995. It covers the controversial topic of adolescent mothers. One-half million adolescents give birth each year in America. Adolescent mothers earn only one-half the income over their lifetimes as adolescents who postpone pregnancy because of early termination of their education. Black adolescents give birth at a higher rate than white adolescents. Diane Tait theorizes that the black family social support network is an untapped resource which enables adolescent mothers to continue their education, & thereby, reduces their risk of living a life of poverty. Published by DeeMar Communications, Box 46330, Raleigh, NC 27620. E-mail DEEMAR@aol.com.** ***Publisher Provided Annotation.

Black Family Violence: Current Research & Theory. Ed. by Robert L. Hampton. 256p. 1991. pap. 35.00 (*0-669-21858-8*) Free Pr.

***Black Fatherhood: A Guide to Male Parenting.** rev. ed. Earl O. Hutchinson. LC 92-71110. 147p. 1995. pap. 10.95 (*1-881032-09-4*) Middle Passage.

Black Fatherhood II: Black Women Talk about Their Men. Earl O. Hutchinson. 184p. (Orig.). 1994. pap. 11.95 (*1-881032-10-8*) Middle Passage.

Black Feeling, Black Talk, Black Judgement. Nikki Giovanni. LC 70-119846. 1971. pap. 7.45 (*0-688-25294-X*, Quill) Morrow.

Black Female Domestics During the Depression in New York City, 1930-1940. Brenda C. Gray. LC 92-44921. (Studies in African American History & Culture). 216p. 1993. 51.00 (*0-8153-1013-7*) Garland.

Black Female Playwrights: An Anthology of Plays Before 1950. Ed. by Kathy A. Perkins. LC 88-46040. (Blacks in the Diaspora Ser.). (Illus.). 298p. (Orig.). 1989. 35.00 (*0-253-34358-5*); pap. 14.95 (*0-253-20623-5*, MB-623) Ind U Pr.

Black Females in the United States: A Bibliography from 1967 to 1987. Ed. by Christine C. Hall et al. (Bibliographies in Psychology Ser.: No. 3). 198p. 1989. pap. 25.00 (*1-55798-048-9*) Am Psychol.

Black Feminist Criticism: Perspectives on Black Women Writers. Barbara Christian. LC 84-22805. (Athene Ser.). 350p. 1985. text ed. 50.00 (*0-08-031956-4*, Pergamon Pr); pap. text ed. 19.95 (*0-08-031955-6*, Pergamon Pr) Elsevier.

Black Feminist Criticism: Perspectives on Black Women Writers. Barbara Christian. (Athene Ser.). 276p. (C). pap. text ed. 19.95 (*0-8077-6253-9*) Tchrs Coll.

Black Feminist Thought: Knowledge, Consciousness, & the Politics of Empowerment. Patricia H. Collins. (Perspectives on Gender Ser.: No. 2). 288p. (C). 1990. text ed. 49.95 (*0-04-445137-7*); pap. text ed. 16.95 (*0-415-90597-4*) Routledge Chapman & Hall.

Black Fiction. Roger Rosenblatt. LC 74-81387. 272p. 1974. 29.00 (*0-674-07620-6*) HUP.

Black Fiction. Roger Rosenblatt. LC 74-81387. 272p. 1976. pap. 11.50 (*0-674-07622-2*) HUP.

Black Fighting Men: A Proud History. Catherine Reef. (African-American Soldiers Ser.). (Illus.). 80p. (J). (gr. 4-7). 1994. bds. 14.98 (*0-8050-3106-5*) TFC Bks NY.

Black Film As Genre. Thomas Cripps. LC 77-23630. 192p. reprint ed. pap. 54.80 (*0-8357-7288-8*, 2056029) Bks Demand.

Black Fire. Stuart Fox. 320p. 1994. mass mkt. 4.99 (*0-8125-1643-5*) Tor Bks.

***Black Fire: The Making of a Revolutionary.** Nelson Peery. 352p. 1995. pap. 11.95 (*1-56584-159-X*) New Press NY.

Black Fire: The Making of an American Revolutionary. Nelson Peery. 352p. 1994. 22.95 (*1-56584-158-1*) New Press NY.

Black Firsts. Jessie C. Smith. Ed. by Casper L. Jordon & Robert L. Johns. LC 93-44155. 475p. 1994. 39.95 (*0-8103-8902-9*) Gale.

Black Firsts: Two Thousand Years of Extraordinary Achievements. Jessie C. Smith. 1994. pap. 16.95 (*0-8103-9490-1*) Gale.

Black Flag: Guerrilla Warfare on the Western Border, 1861-1865. Thomas Goodrich. LC 94-20849. 1995. 24.95 (*0-253-32599-4*) Ind U Pr.

***Black Flag: True Tales of Twentieth-Century Piracy.** James Hepburn. (Illus.). 288p. 1995. pap. 11.95 (*0-7472-4439-1*, Pub. by Headline UK) Trafalgar.

Black Flame. Stanley G. Weinbaum. 1976. reprint ed. 19.95 (*0-88411-988-2*, Aeonian Pr) Amereon Ltd.

Black Flame: A Trilogy, 3 vols., Set. W. E. B. Du Bois. Incl. Bk. 1. Ordeal of Mansart. 1957. 19.00 (*0-527-25270-0*); Bk. 2. Mansart Builds a School. 1976. 22.00 (*0-527-25271-9*); Bk. 3. Worlds of Color. 1961. 21.00 (*0-527-25272-7*); 1976. 55.00 (*0-527-25286-7*) Kraus Intl.

Black Flames. Sam Witt. (Advanced Dungeons & Dragons, Second Edition; Al-Qadim Ser.). (Illus.). 1994. pap. 14.95 (*1-56076-580-1*) TSR Inc.

***Black Flamingo.** Kenneth Sherman. 80p. 1995. lib. bdg. 25.00 (*0-8095-4526-8*) Borgo Pr.

Black Flies: Ecology, Population Management & Annotated World List. Ed. by Ke Chung Kim & Richard W. Merritt. LC 85-43562. (Illus.). 540p. 1988. 65.00 (*0-271-00417-7*) Pa St U Pr.

***Black Florida.** Kevin McCarthy. (Illus.). 317p. (Orig.). 1995. pap. 16.95 (*0-7818-0291-1*) Hippocrene Bks.

Black Focus on Multicultural Education. Beryle Banfield. 87p. 1979. pap. 5.95 (*0-685-00778-2*) Blyden Pr.

Black Folk Art in America, 1930-1980. Jane Livingston & John Beardsley. LC 81-24072. (Illus.). 176p. 1989. reprint ed. lib. bdg. 45.00 (*0-87805-398-0*); reprint ed. pap. 29.95 (*0-87805-158-9*) U Pr of Miss.

Black Folk Here & There: An Essay in History & Anthropology, Vols. 1 & 2. St. Clair Drake. (Afro-American Culture & Society Monograph Ser.: Vols. 7 & 9). (Illus.). 757p. 1991. Boxed Set. boxed 58.95 (*0-934934-28-2*); Boxed Set. boxed 35.95 (*0-934934-29-0*) UCLA CAAS.

Black Folk Here & There, Vol. 1: An Essay in History & Anthropology. St. Clair Drake. (Afro-American Culture & Society Monograph Ser.: Vol. 7). (Illus.). 387p. 1987. 29.95 (*0-934934-20-7*); pap. 18.95 (*0-934934-21-5*) UCLA CAAS.

Black Folk Here & There, Vol. 2: An Essay in History & Anthropology. St. Clair Drake. (Afro-American Culture & Society Monograph Ser.: Vol. 9). (Illus.). 376p. 1991. 29.95 (*0-934934-30-4*); pap. 18.95 (*0-934934-31-2*) UCLA CAAS.

Black Folk Medicine: The Therapeutic Significance of Faith & Trust. Ed. by Wilbur H. Watson. 152p. 1984. 29.95x (*0-87855-494-7*) Transaction Pubs.

Black Folk Then & Now: An Essay in the History & Sociology of the Negro Race. W. E. B. Du Bois. LC 30-17726. 1975. reprint ed. 24.00 (*0-527-25275-1*) Kraus Intl.

Black Folks & Christian Liberty: Be Christian, Be Black, Be Culturally & Socially Free. 2nd ed. Walter A. McCray. (Black Light Fellowship Ser.). 210p. (Orig.). 1987. pap. 10.00 (*0-933176-08-2*) Black Light Fellow.

Black Folks' Guide to Making Big Money in America. George Trower-Subira. 184p. 1980. 11.00 (*0-9605304-0-1*) VSBE.

***Black Folks' Little Instruction Book.** Denise L. Stinson. 1995. pap. 6.95 (*0-385-47623-X*) Doubleday.

Black Folktales. Julius Lester. 1991. pap. 9.95 (*0-8021-3242-1*) Grove-Atltic.

***Black-Footed Ferret.** Alvin Silverstein et al. LC 94-44676. (Endangered in America Ser.). (Illus.). 64p. (J). (gr. 4-6). 1995. 15.40 (*1-56294-552-1*) Millbrook Pr.

Black Footprints. Zenobia M. Johnson. (Illus.). 32p. (Orig.). (J). (gr. 4-7). 1979. student ed 3.50 (*0-9617411-1-2*) Z M Johnson.

Black for Remembrance. Carlene Thompson. 336p. 1992. mass mkt. 4.99 (*0-380-71715-8*) Avon.

Black Forbidden Things: Cryptical Secrets from the Crypt of Cthulhu. Ed. by Robert M. Price. LC 93-201926. (Starmont Studies in Literary Criticism: No. 44). iv, 200p. 1992. lib. bdg. 31.00x (*1-55742-249-4*); pap. 21.00x (*1-55742-248-6*) Borgo Pr.

Black Foremothers: Three Lives. Feminist Press Staff. (Women's Lives-Women's Work Ser.). (Illus.). (gr. 10-12). 1979. text ed. 9.60 (*0-07-020433-0*) McGraw.

Black Foremothers: Three Lives. 2nd ed. Dorothy Sterling. LC 87-19746. (Women's Lives - Women's Work Ser.). (Illus.). 224p. 1988. pap. 11.95 (*0-935312-89-7*) Feminist Pr.

Black Forest. 2nd ed. (Visitor's Guides Ser.). (Illus.). 256p. 1994. pap. 14.95 (*0-86190-507-5*) Hunter NJ.

***Black Forest Clockmaker & the Cuckoo Clock: 1995 Edition.** 6th enl. rev. ed. 262p. 1991. per. 22.50 (*0-933396-30-9*, BFCM90) Antique Clocks.

Black Forest Clocks. Rick Ortenburger. LC 90-63797. (Illus.). 300p. 1991. 79.95 (*0-88740-300-X*) Schiffer.

Black Forest Village Stories. Berthold Auerbach. Tr. by Charles Goepp. LC 70-101791. (Short Story Index Reprint Ser.). 1979. 23.95 (*0-8369-3179-3*) Ayer.

Black Fortune. Eldred K. Means. LC 72-4739. (Black Heritage Library Collection). 1977. reprint ed. 27.95 (*0-8369-9110-9*) Ayer.

Black Forty-One: The West Point Class of 1941 & the American Triumph in World War Two. William Yenne. 400p. 1991. text ed. 24.95 (*0-471-54197-4*) Wiley.

Black Fox. Matt Braun. 1994. mass mkt. 4.99 (*0-312-95355-0*) St Martin.

***Black Fox: Aunt Carrie's War Against the Black Fox Nuclear Power Plant.** Carrie B. Dickerson. 312p. 1995. 24.95 (*1-57178-009-2*) Coun Oak Bks.

Black Frames: Critical Perspectives on Independent Black Cinema. Mbye Cham & Claire Andrade-Watkins. (Celebration of Black Cinema Ser.). (Illus.). 116p. (Orig.). 1988. pap. 9.95 (*0-262-53080-5*) MIT Pr.

Black Freedom - White Violence, 1865-1900. Intro. by Donald G. Nieman. LC 93-29265. (African American Life in the Post-Emancipation South Ser.: Vol. 7). 1994. 68.00 (*0-8153-1444-2*) Garland.

Black, French, & African: A Life of Leopold Sedar Senghor. Janet G. Vaillant. (Illus.). 388p. 1990. text ed. 32.50 (*0-674-07623-0*) HUP.

Black Frenchmen: The Political Integration of the French Antilles. Arvin Murch. 184p. 1971. 18.95 (*0-87073-034-7*) Schenkman Bks Inc.

Black Friar: Champion of the Poor. Arthur L. McLaughlin. LC 82-51216. 54p. 1983. 6.95 (*0-938232-21-5*) Winston-Derek.

Black Friday. David Goodis. LC 90-50249. (Vintage Crime - Black Lizard Ser.). 144p. 1990. pap. 7.95 (*0-679-73255-1*, Vin) Random.

Black Friday. David Goodis. LC 86-70425. 144p. 1987. reprint ed. pap. 3.95 (*0-88739-028-5*, Blk Lizard) Creat Arts Bk.

Black Friday Coming Down. David Hunter. 1992. mass mkt. 4.99 (*0-425-13135-1*) Berkley Pub.

***Black Frigate of Monterey.** Kristiana Gregory. LC 94-42299. (J). 1995. 14.95 (*0-590-48822-8*) Scholastic Inc.

Black from the Edge. Kevin Gilbert. 96p. Date not set. pap. 24.95 (*1-875657-22-3*, Pub. by Hyland Hse AT) Intl Spec Bk.

Black Frontiers. Schlissel. (J). Date not set. 14.00 (*0-671-73853-4*) S&S Trade.

Black Frontiersmen: Afro-Hispanic Culture of Ecuador & Colombia. Norman E. Whitten. 221p. (C). 1986. reprint ed. pap. text ed. 9.95 (*0-88133-199-6*) Waveland Pr.

***Black Furies Tribebook.** (Werewolf). Date not set. 10.00 (*1-56504-093-7*) White Wolf.

Black Fury. Joseph Nazel. (Orig.). 1976. pap. 2.95 (*0-87067-058-1*, BH058) Holloway.

Black Future? Jesus & Salvation in South Africa. Ronald Nicholson. LC 89-28280. 288p. (Orig.). (C). 1990. pap. text ed. 18.95 (*0-334-00120-X*) TPI PA.

Black Gangster. rev. ed. Donald Goines. 288p. (Orig.). 1983. pap. 3.50 (*0-87067-192-8*) Holloway.

Black Gauntlet: A Tale of Plantation Life in South Carolina. Henry R. Schoolcraft. LC 78-138345. (Black Heritage Library Collection). 1977. 28.95 (*0-8369-8737-3*) Ayer.

Black Genealogy. Charles L. Blockson. LC 90-82688. 233p. 1992. reprint ed. text ed. 24.95 (*0-933121-54-7*); reprint ed. pap. 14.95 (*0-933121-53-9*) Black Classic.

Black Genealogy: A Record Keeping Book. Lewis E. Brooks. 198p. 1992. Wkbk. student ed 19.95 (*0-9635328-0-4*) L E Brooks.

Black Genesis. L. Ron Hubbard. (Mission Earth Ser.: Vol. 2). 512p. 1994. pap. 5.99 (*0-88404-283-9*) Bridge Pubns Inc.

Black Georgetown Remembered: A History of Its Black Community from the Founding of the "Town of George" in 1751 to the Present Day. Kathleen M. Lesko et al. LC 91-29357. (Illus.). 210p. 1991. reprint ed. pap. 25.00 (*0-87840-526-7*) Georgetown U Pr.

Black Georgia in the Progressive Era, 1900-1920. John Dittmer. LC 77-24249. (Blacks in the New World Ser.). 251p. 1977. pap. 11.95 (*0-252-00813-8*) U of Ill Pr.

Black Georgia in the Progressive Era, 1900-1920. John Dittmer. LC 77-24249. (Blacks in the New World Ser.). 251p. reprint ed. pap. 71.60 (*0-8357-6042-1*, 2034430) Bks Demand.

Black Ghetto. Geraldine Davenport. 1991. 6.95 (*0-533-09263-9*) Vantage.

Black Girl. Vernita Y. Crenshaw. Ed. by Dr. Aqu. 290p. (Orig.). Date not set. pap. 19.95 (*0-9635763-0-5*) V Crenshaw.

Black Girl. J. E. Franklin. 1971. pap. 4.75 (*0-8222-0125-9*) Dramatists Play.

Black Girl from Genesis to Revelations. J. E. Franklin. LC 74-30386. 1977. 12.95 (*0-88258-019-1*) Howard U Pr.

Black Girl Lost. Donald Goines. (Orig.). 1973. pap. 3.50 (*0-87067-186-3*) Holloway.

***Black Girl Lost.** Donald Goines. 208p. (Orig.). 1994. 4.95 (*0-87067-952-X*) Holloway.

***Black Girl Talk.** Black. Date not set. per. 14.95 (*0-920813-03-8*, Pub. by Sister Vision CN) InBook.

Black Girl, White Girl. Patricia Moyes. LC 89-7440. 224p. 1990. pap. 4.95 (*0-8050-1149-8*, Owl) H Holt & Co.

Black Girl, White Girl. large type ed. Patricia Moyes. (General Ser.). 326p. 1991. lib. bdg. 19.95 (*0-8161-5011-7*, Large Print Bks) Hall.

Black Glass: A Sea Myth. Stuart Edelson. 400p. 1993. 19.95 (*0-931625-22-X*) DIMI Pr.

***Black Glass Buttons.** Edith M. Fuess. 312p. 1994. pap. 25.00 (*0-9629046-2-7*) New Leaf Pubs.

Black Globe. Vicente Segrelles. (Mercenary Ser.). 48p. 1994. pap. 9.95 (*1-56163-097-7*) NBM.

Black Glove. Geoffrey Miller. 254p. 1984. pap. 3.50 (*0-88184-080-7*) Carroll & Graf.

***Black Godfather.** Fletcher. 1984. mass mkt. 2.25 (*0-87067-244-4*) Holloway.

Black Godfather. rev. ed. Omar Fletcher. (Orig.). 1984. pap. 3.95 (*0-87067-382-3*, BH382) Holloway.

Black Gods-Orisa Studies in the New World. Gary Edwards & John Mason. (Illus.). 96p. (Orig.). 1985. reprint ed. pap. 8.00 (*1-881244-02-4*) Yoruba Theol Arch.

Black Gold. Anita R. Bunkley. LC 93-30611. 400p. 1994. 21.95 (*0-525-93752-8*, Dutton) NAL-Dutton.

***Black Gold.** Anita R. Bunkley. 448p. 1995. pap. 5.99 (*0-451-17973-0*, Sig) NAL-Dutton.

Black Gold. large type ed. Anita R. Bunkley. LC 94-4869. 592p. 1994. reprint ed. 22.95 (*0-8161-7434-2*) Hall.

Black Gold. 2nd ed. Marguerite Henry. LC 91-4907. (Illus.). 176p. (J). (gr. 3-7). 1992. pap. 3.95 (*0-689-71562-5*, Aladdin Paperbacks) S&S Childrens.

Black Gold, Red Death. David L. Lindsay. 256p. 1986. mass mkt. 5.99 (*0-449-13121-1*, GM) Fawcett.

***Black Gourmet Cookbook.** Mademoiselles Noires, Inc., Staff. (Illus.). 80p. (Orig.). Date not set. spiral bd. 15.95 (*0-9643335-0-3*) Mmlle Noires.

Black Grandparents As Parents. Lenora M. Poe. (Orig.). 1992. pap. text ed. 13.95 (*0-9633992-0-9*) L M Poe.

Black Gryphon. Mercedes Lackey & Larry Dixon. 464p. 1994. pap. 22.00 (*0-88677-577-9*) DAW Bks.

***Black Gryphon.** Mercedes Lackey & Larry Dixon. 464p. 1995. 5.99 (*0-88677-643-0*) DAW Bks.

Black Guard. Kevin Barrett. Ed. by S. Coleman Charlton. (Metal Express Ser.). (Illus.). 40p. (Orig.). (YA). (gr. 12). 1990. pap. 8.00 (*1-55806-115-0*, 7012) Iron Crown Ent Inc.

Black Gulf. Konstantin G. Paustovskii. Tr. by Eugenia Schimanskaya. LC 75-39008. (Soviet Literature in English Translation Ser.). 124p. 1977. reprint ed. 16.00 (*0-88355-411-9*) Hyperion Conn.

Black Hair Is... The Complete Hair Care Guide for Today's Black Woman. Marilyn Singleton. (Illus.). 56p. 1992. pap. 9.95 (*0-9632805-7-0*) Image Perfect. Secrets to beautiful, healthy hair lie within the pages of this book. This exciting, handy, mini-reference guide is chock-full of accessible hair care & styling information for the black woman. Advice is offered by hair care specialists, dermatologists, & clinical professors of dermatology. Never before has ONE book so thoroughly covered the black woman's hair care & styling needs, including: hair growth, grooming, hair loss, breakage, afros, press & curl, relaxers, curly perms, braids, weaves, wigs & more! Since its debut, this book has remained in the spotlight, with over FIFTY articles appearing in ethnic & general population publications. The editors of ESSENCE magazine declares it as the book that offers tips to keep the black woman's hair in TIP TOP SHAPE! MADEMOISELLE magazine's editors STRONGLY RECOMMEND it for ALL of its black readers. ALLURE magazine uses it as an authority for black hair care advice. CLASS magazine heralds BLACK HAIR IS... as the book that presents a WEALTH OF INFORMATION FOR THE BLACK WOMAN WHO WANTS TO BE IN TUNE WITH HER HAIR. BLACK HAIR CARE magazine, the premier magazine for hair care & styling ideas for black women, devoted a four page spread to BLACK HAIR IS... This book is truly loved. Please make sure that it is on your shelf for your customers to see & buy. BLACK HAIR IS...available from IMAGE PERFECT COMMUNICATIONS, INC., 1480-F Terrell Mill Rd., Ste. 289, Marietta, GA 30067, (404) 956-8104. Quantity discounts available. ***Publisher Provided Annotation.***

Black Hand: A Chapter in Ethnic Crime. Thomas M. Pitkin. 274p. 1977. pap. 10.00 (*0-8226-0333-0*) Junius-Vaughn.

Black Hands of Beijing: Lives of Defiance in China's Democracy Movement. George Black & Robin Munro. (Robert L. Bernstein Book). (Illus.). 384p. 1993. text ed. 24.95 (*0-471-57977-7*) Wiley.

Black Harris. Jerome Peltier. 158p. 1986. 15.95 (*0-87770-388-4*) Ye Galleon.

***Black Hawk.** Gary Hanzak & Juanita Mucha. 200p. Date not set. pap. 8.95 (*0-7610-0304-5*) NW Pub.

Black Hawk: An Autobiography. Black Hawk. Ed. by Donald Jackson. LC 55-11217. (Prairie State Bks.). (Illus.). 178p. 1964. reprint ed. pap. 9.95 (*0-252-72325-2*) U of Ill Pr.

800

An Asterisk (*) at the beginning of an entry indicates that the title is appearing in BIP for the first time.

Black Hawk & Jim Thorp: Super Heroes; Sauk Indian Stories for Children. Betty Greison et al. (J). (gr. 5-12). 1983. pap. 4.95 (*0-89992-085-3*) Coun India Ed.

Black Hawk & the Warrior's Path. Roger Nichols. Ed. by Alan M. Kraut & Jon L. Wakelyn. (American Biographical History Ser.). 190p. 1992. pap. text ed. write for info. (*0-88295-884-4*) Harlan Davidson.

Black Hawk, Frontier Warrior. Joanne Oppenheim. LC 78-18049. (Illus.). 48p. (J). (gr. 4-6). 1979. lib. bdg. 10.59 (*0-89375-157-X*); pap. 3.50 (*0-89375-147-2*) Troll Assocs.

Black Hawk, Sac Rebel. Nancy Vonvillain. LC 93-19330. (North American Indians of Achievement Ser.). (J). 1993. write for info. (*0-7910-1711-7*); pap. write for info. (*0-7910-1997-7*) Chelsea Hse.

Black Hawk War. Frank E. Stevens. (Illus.). 440p. 1993. reprint ed. pap. text ed. 22.00 (*1-55613-859-8*) Heritage Bk.

Black Hawk War, Why? Lloyd H. Efflandt. (Illus.). 25p. (YA). 1987. reprint ed. pap. 2.00 (*0-9617938-0-5*, 5M) Rock Isl Arsenal Hist Soc.

Black Hawk War, 1831-1832: Vol. 2, Letters & Papers. Pt. 1, April 30, 1831-June 23, 1832. Ed. by Ellen M. Whitney. LC 70-634702. (Illinois Historical Collections: Vol. 36). 1973. 25.00 (*0-912154-22-5*) Ill St Hist Lib.

Black Hawk War, 1831-1832: Volume I, Illinois Volunteers. Ed. by Ellen M. Whitney. LC 70-634702. (Illinois Historical Collections: Vol. 35). 682p. 1970. 20.00 (*0-912154-20-9*) Ill St Hist Lib.

Black Hawk War, 1831-1832: Volume 2, Letters & Papers, Pt. 2, June 24, 1832-October 14, 1834. Ed. by Ellen M. Whitney. LC 70-634702. (Illinois Historical Collections: Vol. 37). (Illus.). 697p. 1975. 27.50 (*0-912154-23-3*) Ill St Hist Lib.

Black Hawk War, 1831-1832, Vol. 2: Letters & Papers, Part 3 Appendices & Index. Comp. by Ellen M. Whitney. LC 70-634702. (Illinois Historical Collections: Vol. 38). 1978. 14.00 (*0-912154-24-1*) Ill St Hist Lib.

Black Health Library Guide to Diabetes. Walter L. Henry et al. Ed. by Linda Villarosa. LC 93-7152. (Black Health Library). 176p. 1993. 22.50 (*0-8050-2285-6*); pap. 8.95 (*0-8050-2286-4*) H Holt & Co.

Black Health Library Guide to Heart Disease. Paul Jones & Angela Mitchell. Ed. by Linda Villarosa. 176p. (Orig.). 1993. pap. 8.95 (*0-8050-2268-6*, Owl) H Holt & Co.

Black Health Library Guide to Obesity. Kirth Johnson. Ed. by Linda Villarosa. LC 93-7151. (Black Health Library). 176p. 1993. 22.50 (*0-8050-2287-2*); pap. 8.95 (*0-8050-2288-0*) H Holt & Co.

Black Health Library Guide to Stroke. Lafayette Singleton & Kirk Johnson. Ed. by Linda Villarosa. LC 92-37377. 192p. (Orig.). 1993. pap. 8.95 (*0-8050-2290-2*, Owl) H Holt & Co.

Black Heart. Eric Van Lustbader. 1986. mass mkt. 5.95 (*0-449-21151-7*, Crest) Fawcett.

Black Heart: A Voyage into Central Africa. large type ed. Paul Hyland. 464p. 1992. 23.95 (*0-7089-8625-0*, Charnwood) Ulverscroft.

Black Hearts & Slow Dancing. Earl W. Emerson. 272p. 1989. mass mkt. 5.95 (*0-14-011732-6*, Penguin Bks) Viking Penguin.

Black Heart's Truth: The Early Career of W. D. Howells. John W. Crowley. LC 84-20908. xv, 192p. 1985. 29.95 (*0-8078-1632-9*) U of NC Pr.

***Black Helicopters over America: Strikeforce for the New World Order.** Jim Keith. LC 94-23888. (Illus.). 160p. (Orig.). 1994. pap. 12.95 (*1-881532-05-4*) IllumiNet Pr.

Black Hen: or The Underground Inhabitants. Antony Pogorelsky. LC 92-28599. (Illus.). 32p. (J). (gr. 2-5). 1994. 14.99 (*0-525-65133-0*, Cobblehill Bks) Dutton Child Bks.

Black Heralds. Cesar Vallejo. Ed. by Yvette E. Miller. Tr. by Kathleen Ross & Richard Schaaf. LC 89-13959. 174p. (ENG & SPA.). 1990. pap. 12.95 (*0-935480-43-9*) Lat Am Lit Rev Pr.

Black Heritage Recipes to Treasure. Willa Mitchell. LC 77-94215. (Black American Cookbook Ser.: Vol. 3). (Illus.). 200p. 1984. lib. bdg. 8.95 (*0-9603014-2-9*) Evang Assn.

***Black Heritage Sites: An African-American Odyssey & Finder's Guide.** Nancy C. Curtis. (Illus.). 575p. 1995. text ed. 45.00x (*0-8389-0643-5*) ALA.

Black Heritage Unveiled. 2nd ed. George S. Lewis. LC 86-62546. (Illus.). 200p. 1987. text ed. 15.95 (*0-937771-09-0*); lib. bdg. 14.95 (*0-937771-10-4*); pap. text ed. 10.95 (*0-937771-08-2*) Spencers Intl.

Black Hermit. Ngugi Wa Thiongo. (African Writers Ser.). (C). 1968. pap. 9.95 (*0-435-90051-X*) Heinemann.

Black Heroes: Seven Plays. Intro. by Errol Hill. 320p. (Orig.). 1989. pap. 12.95 (*1-55783-027-4*) Applause Theatre Bk Pubs.

Black Heroes & Heroines, Bk. 1. Ida R. Bellegarde. LC 79-51798. (C). 1979. 8.95 (*0-918340-08-X*) Bell Ent.

Black Heroes & Heroines, Bk. 2. Ida R. Bellegarde. LC 79-51798. 1981. 8.95 (*0-918340-10-1*) Bell Ent.

Black Heroes & Heroines, Bk. 3. Ida R. Bellegarde. LC 79-51798. 61p. (J). (gr. 5 up). 1983. 8.95 (*0-918340-11-X*) Bell Ent.

Black Heroes & Heroines, Bk. 4. Ida R. Bellegarde. LC 79-51798. 64p. (J). (gr. 5 up). 1984. 8.95 (*0-918340-13-6*) Bell Ent.

Black Heroes & Heroines, Bk. 6. Ethel Waters. 1991. 8.95 (*0-918340-15-2*) Bell Ent.

Black Heroes & Heroines, Bk 5: Benjamin Banneker's Great Achievements. Bellegarde. 64p. (J). (gr. 5 up). 1985. 8.95 (*0-918340-14-4*) Bell Ent.

Black Heroes of the American Revolution. Burke Davis. (J). (gr. 5 up). 1992. pap. 4.95 (*0-15-208561-0*, HB Juv Bks) HarBrace.

Black Heroes of the American Revolution. braille ed. Burke Davis. 98p. 1992. Braille. vinyl bd. 7.84 (*1-56956-337-3*, BR8881) W A T Braille.

***Black Heroes of the Martial Arts.** Ron Van Clief. LC 94-46817. 1995. 39.95 (*1-881316-87-4*); pap. 24.95 (*1-881316-78-5*) A&B Bks.

Black Heroes of the Wild West. Ruth Pelz. LC 89-63500. (Illus.). (gr. 4-12). 1989. 12.95 (*0-940880-25-3*); pap. 6.95 (*0-940880-26-1*) Open Hand.

Black Higher Education in Kentucky, 1879-1930: The History of Simmons University. Lawrence H. Williams. LC 86-23474. (Studies in American Religion: Vol. 24). 320p. 1986. lib. bdg. 99.95 (*0-88946-668-8*) E Mellen.

Black Higher Education in the United States: A Selected Bibliography on Negro Higher Education & Historically Black Colleges & Universities. Comp. by Frederick Chambers. LC 77-91100. 268p. 1978. text ed. 42.95 (*0-313-20037-8*, CBH/, Greenwood Pr) Greenwood.

Black Hills: Or, the Last Hunting Grounds of the Dakotahs. Annie D. Tallent. LC 75-126. (Mid-American Frontier Ser.). (Illus.). 1975. reprint ed. 68.95 (*0-405-06891-3*) Ayer.

Black Hills: Sacred Hills. Tom C. Eagle & Ron Zeilinger. (Illus.). 60p. (Orig.). 1987. pap. 3.50 (*1-877976-08-3*, 406-0006) Tipi Pr.

Black Hills - Badlands: The Web of the West. Mike Link. (Voyageur Wilderness Ser.). (Illus.). 120p. 1980. reprint ed. pap. 14.95 (*0-89658-017-2*) Voyageur Pr.

Black Hills - White Justice: The Sioux Nation vs. the United States, 1775 to the Present. Edward Lazarus. LC 90-56383. 1992. pap. 15.00 (*0-06-092207-9*, PL) HarpC.

Black Hills Ghost Towns. Watson Parker & Hugh K. Lambert. (Illus.). 215p. 1993. reprint ed. pap. 24.95 (*0-8040-0638-5*, Swallow) Swallow.

Black Hills Hay Camp: Images & Perspectives of Early Rapid City, South Dakota. Dave Strain & Chuck Nauman. Ed. by Norm Nelson. (Illus.). 217p. 1989. 35.00 (*0-912410-10-8*) Dakota West.

Black Hills Lady. W. H. O'Gara. Ed. by Jean O. Meyers. (Illus.). (Orig.). 1990. pap. 8.95 (*0-934904-12-X*) J & L Lee.

***Black Hills North, SD.** Ed. by Trails Illustrated Staff. 1995. 8.99 (*1-56695-021-X*) Trails Illustrated.

Black Hills; or, the Last Hunting Ground of the Dakotahs. deluxe limited ed. Annie D. Tallent. LC 74-76330. 594p. 1974. reprint ed. 50.00 (*0-685-50457-3*) Brevet Pr.

Black Hills or the Last Hunting Ground of the Dakotas. Annie D. Talent. (Illus.). 713p. 1994. reprint ed. lib. bdg. 72.50 (*0-8328-3923-X*) Higginson Bk Co.

Black Hills Restaurant Guide. 1994. pap. 6.95 (*0-9641490-0-1*) Black Hills.

Black Hills, Southeast, SD. (Illus.). 1995. 8.99 (*1-56695-011-2*) Trails Illustrated.

Black Hills Souvenir: A Pictorial & Historic Description of the Black Hills. John J. Sanford. (Illus.). 223p. 1994. reprint ed. lib. bdg. 29.50 (*0-8328-3924-8*) Higginson Bk Co.

Black Hills Trails: A History of the Struggles of the Pioneers... Jesse Brown & A. M. Willard. LC 75-83. (Mid-American Frontier Ser.). (Illus.). 1975. reprint ed. 48.95 (*0-405-06852-2*) Ayer.

Black History. Ed. by Patricia J. Rosof et al. LC 83-87. (Trends in History Ser.: Vol. 3, No. 1). 99p. 1983. text ed. 19.95 (*0-86656-135-8*) Haworth Pr.

Black History: A Guide to Civilian Records in the National Archives. Comp. by Debra L. Newman. LC 84-16597. (Illus.). 379p. 1984. pap. 15.00 (*0-911333-31-2*, 200030); boxed 25.00 (*0-911333-21-5*, 100030) National Archives & Recs.

Black History - A Different Approach. Eva M. Noles. 57p. (Orig.). 1989. pap. 9.95 (*0-9624731-1-1*) Noles Pub.

Black History & the Historical Profession, 1915-1980. August Meier & Elliott Rudwick. LC 85-16817. (Blacks in the New World Ser.). 400p. 1986. pap. 16.95 (*0-252-01274-7*) U of Ill Pr.

Black History Biographies. Delores Holt. LC 77-87843. (Illus.). 62p. 1978. pap. 8.00 (*0-913866-09-1*) US Games Syst.

Black History for Beginners. D. Dennis & W. Willmorth. 1990. pap. 21.00 (*0-685-67970-5*, Pub. by Northcote UK) St Mut.

Black History for Beginners. Denise Dennis & Susan Willmarth. (Illus.). 176p. 1984. 14.95 (*0-86316-069-7*); pap. 9.00 (*0-86316-068-9*) Writers & Readers.

Black History Heroes, Vol. I. P. Hilton Taylor. 110p. 1991. pap. 9.99 (*0-9638528-3-3*) Brainpower Pubng.

***Black History Month: How to Celebrate It at Home.** (Illus.). 30p. 1995. pap. 19.95 (*0-935483-21-7*) Praxis Madison.

Black History Month Activity & Enrichment Handbook. Just Us Books Editors. LC 90-60068. 24p. (J). (gr. 3-12). 1990. 8.95 (*0-940975-25-4*); pap. 6.50 (*0-940975-14-9*) Just Us Bks.

Black History Month Resource Book. Ed. by Mary E. Snodgrass. 250p. 1993. 34.95 (*0-8103-9151-1*, 101751) Gale.

Black History of Richmond: Concise & Condensed. Odell R. Byrd, Jr. Ed. by Trudy Bass. (Illus.). 100p. 1992. lib. bdg. 15.00 (*0-9621739-1-6*) Tambuzi Pubns.

Black History Quiz Book, Vol. 2. Melvett G. Chambers. LC 88-91979. (Illus.). 110p. 1988. pap. 8.95 (*0-9616522-7-6*) M G Chambers.

Black History Series 1, 6 bks, Set. Incl. Vol. 1. George Abraham Jefferson Thinks about Freedom. Martha Smith. 15p. (J). (gr. 2-3). 1988. (*0-913678-01-5*); Vol. 2. Terrible Tuesday. Edith Gaines. 13p. (J). (gr. 2-3). 1988. (*0-913678-02-3*); Vol. 3. Free; The Contraption; The First Freedom Ride. Edith Gaines & Martha Smith. 40p. (J). (gr. 3-4). 1988. (*0-913678-03-1*); Vol. 4. I Cannot Be a Traitor; the Cannon That Talked Back. Brenda Johnston & Mary Woodrich. 31p. (J). (gr. 4-5). 1988. (*0-913678-04-X*); Vol. 5. Adventures of Olaudah, the African Boy; Move Feet Move. Suzanne Hartman & Mary Shepard. 35p. (J). (gr. 5-6). 1988. (*0-913678-05-8*); Vol. 6. Disguise. Mary Shepard. 15p. (J). (gr. 5-6). 1988. (*0-913678-06-6*); (Illus.). (J). (gr. 2-6). 1988. Set pap. 8.00 (*0-913678-00-7*) New Day Pr.

Black History Trivia Quiz Book. Melvett G. Chambers & Emma F. Chambers. LC 85-91568. (Illus.). 80p. 1986. pap. 8.95 (*0-9616522-0-9*) M G Chambers.

Black History Trivia Quiz Book, 1990. rev. ed. Melvett G. Chambers. (Illus.). 120p. 1990. pap. 10.95 (*1-878807-12-9*) M G Chambers.

Black Hit Woman. Laurie Miles et al. 224p. (Orig.). 1983. pap. 2.25 (*0-87067-221-5*, BH221) Holloway.

Black Hole Affair. Jeffrey Klein. 1991. mass mkt. 4.95 (*0-8217-3470-9*) Zebra.

Black Hole of Calcutta. Noel Barber. (Dorset Press Reprints Ser.). (Illus.). 254p. 1990. 16.95 (*0-88029-421-3*) Dorset Pr.

Black Hole Physics: Proceedings of the NATO Advanced Study Institute (12th Course of the Ettore Majorana Centre for Scientific Culture), Erice, Italy, May 12-22, 1991. Ed. by Venzo De Sabbata. 436p. (C). 1992. lib. bdg. 147.00 (*0-7923-1679-7*) Kluwer Ac.

Black Hole Tariffs & Endogenous Policy Theory: Political Economy in General Equilibrium. Ed. by Stephen P. Magee et al. (Illus.). (C). 1989. 74.95 (*0-521-36247-4*); pap. 24.95 (*0-521-37700-5*) Cambridge U Pr.

Black Holes. Ed. by Steven Detweiler. 112p. 1982. 18.00 (*0-318-41403-1*, RB-35) Am Assn Physics.

Black Holes. Jean-Pierre Luminet. (Illus.). 300p. (C). 1992. 59.95 (*0-521-40029-5*); pap. 19.95 (*0-521-40906-3*) Cambridge U Pr.

Black Holes: An Annotated Bibliography, 1975-1983. Steven I. Danko. LC 85-14382. 1985. text ed. 27.50 (*0-8108-1836-1*) Scarecrow.

Black Holes: The Membrane Paradigm. Ed. by Kip S. Thorne et al. LC 86-50486. 416p. 1986. text ed. 50.00 (*0-300-03769-4*); pap. 19.00 (*0-300-03770-8*, Y-616) Yale U Pr.

***Black Holes & Baby Universes & Other Essays.** Stephen Hawking. 1994. pap. 12.95 (*0-553-37411-7*) Bantam.

Black Holes & Baby Universes & Other Essays. Stephen W. Hawking. LC 93-8269. 1993. 21.95 (*0-553-09523-4*) Bantam.

***Black Holes & Other Space Phenomena.** Philip Steele. LC 95-6106. (Young Observer Ser.). (J). 1995. write for info. (*1-85697-573-8*, Kingfisher LKC) LKC.

Black Holes & Tepee Rings: On Cosmic Mysteries & Spiritual Mythology. Robert M. Watkins. LC 93-90417. (Illus.). 272p. (Orig.). 1994. pap. 13.00 (*0-9637006-2-6*) Black Wolf.

***Black Holes & the Universe.** Igor Novikov. (Canto Bk.). (Illus.). 184p. (C). Date not set. pap. 8.95 (*0-521-55870-0*) Cambridge U Pr.

Black Holes & the Universe. Igor D. Novikov. Tr. by Vitaly I. Kisin. (Illus.). 200p. (C). 1990. pap. 19.95 (*0-521-36683-6*) Cambridge U Pr.

Black Holes & Time Warps: Einstein's Outrageous Legacy. Kip S. Thorne. LC 93-2014. 1994. 30.00 (*0-393-03505-0*) Norton.

***Black Holes & Time Warps: Einstein's Outrageous Legacy.** Kip S. Thorne. 1995. pap. 14.95 (*0-393-31276-3*, Norton Paperbks) Norton.

Black Holes, Gravitational Waves & Cosmology: Introduction to Current Research. Martin Rees et al. 436p. 1974. text ed. 190.00 (*0-677-04580-8*) Gordon & Breach.

Black Holes in Space-Time. Kitty Ferguson. LC 91-2111. (Venture Bks.). (Illus.). 128p. (J). (gr. 7-9). 1991. lib. bdg. 14.28 (*0-531-12524-6*) Watts.

Black Holes, White Dwarfs, & Neutron Stars: The Physics of Compact Objects. Stuart L. Shapiro & Saul A. Teukolsky. LC 82-20112. 645p. 1983. pap. text ed. 89.95 (*0-471-87316-0*, Wiley-Interscience) Wiley.

Black Holiness: A Guide to the Study of Black Participation in Wesleyan Perfectionist & Glossolalic Pentecostal Movements. Charles E. Jones. LC 86-21893. (American Theological Library Association Monograph: No. 18). 422p. 1987. 39.50 (*0-8108-1948-1*) Scarecrow.

Black Hollywood: From Nineteen Seventy to Today. Gary Null. LC 92-37551. 1993. pap. 16.95 (*0-8065-1216-4*) Carol Pub Group.

Black Hollywood: The Negro in Motion Pictures. Gary Null. 256p. 1984. pap. 15.95 (*0-8065-0908-2*, Citadel Pr) Carol Pub Group.

***Black Holocaust for Beginners.** S. E. Anderson. (Illus.). 192p. 1995. pap. 11.00 (*0-86316-178-2*) Writers & Readers.

Black Home Ownership: A Sociological Case Study of Metropolitan Jacksonville. William A. Stacey. LC 73-186201. (Special Studies in U. S. Economic, Social & Political Issues). 1972. 49.50 (*0-275-04810-1*) Irvington.

Black Homelands of South Africa: The Political & Economic Development of Bophuthatswana & Kwa-Zulu. Jeffrey Butler et al. LC 76-7755. (Perspectives on Southern Africa Ser.: No. 21). 1977. pap. 12.00 (*0-520-03716-2*) U CA Pr.

Black Hoods. Walter E. Adams. 144p. 1993. pap. 6.95 (*0-937408-88-3*) GMI Pubns Inc.

Black Hope Horror. Ben Williams et al. 288p. (Orig.). 1993. mass mkt. 5.50 (*0-425-13910-7*) Berkley Pub.

Black Hope Horror: The True Story of a Haunting. Ben Williams et al. (Illus.). 224p. 1991. 19.00 (*0-688-05176-6*) Morrow.

Black Hornet. James Sallis. 208p. 1994. 18.95 (*0-7867-0118-8*) Carroll & Graf.

***Black Horse Butte: A Dakota Homestead Community.** Elizabeth M. Johnson. 1995. write for info. (*0-9644024-0-8*) E M Johnson.

Black House. Patricia Highsmith. 1989. 19.95 (*0-89296-227-5*); pap. 9.95 (*0-89296-963-6*) Mysterious Pr.

Black Humor. Charles Johnson. (Illus.). 1970. pap. 3.95 (*0-87485-036-3*) Johnson Chi.

Black Humor: Critical Essays. Ed. by Alan R. Pratt. LC 92-7387. (Studies in Humor: Vol. 2). 408p. 1992. 60.00 (*0-8153-0619-9*, H1503) Garland.

Black Hundred: The Rise of the Extreme Right in Russia. Walter Laqueur. (Illus.). 336p. 1994. reprint ed. pap. 15.00 (*0-06-092534-5*, PL) HarpC.

***Black Hunter: Forms of Thought & Forms of Society in the Greek World.** Pierre Vidal-Naquet. LC 85-45870. 393p. 1986. pap. 112.10 (*0-7837-7454-0*, 2049176) Bks Demand.

Black Hymnody: A Hymnological History of the African-American Church. Jon M. Spencer. LC 91-31896. 256p. (Orig.). 1992. text ed. 31.00x (*0-87049-745-6*); pap. 18.95 (*0-87049-760-X*) U of Tenn Pr.

Black Ice. Lorene Cary. LC 90-52988. 238p. 1991. 24.00 (*0-394-57465-6*) Knopf.

Black Ice. Lorene Cary. 1992. pap. 10.00 (*0-679-73745-6*) McKay.

Black Ice. Michael Connelly. LC 92-33500. 1993. 19.95 (*0-316-15382-6*) Little.

Black Ice. Michael Connelly. 384p. 1994. mass mkt. 5.99 (*0-312-95281-3*) St Martin.

Black Ice. C. Dunne. (Critic's Choice Paperbacks Ser.). 1988. pap. 2.95 (*1-55547-277-X*, Univ Books) Carol Pub Group.

Black Ice. Pat Graversen. 256p. 1993. mass mkt. 4.50 (*0-8217-4093-8*) Zebra.

Black Ice. large type ed. Connelly. 1993. 17.95 (*0-7862-0041-3*) Thorndike Pr.

Black Ice. Albion W. Tourgee. LC 70-104581. reprint ed. lib. bdg. 18.00 (*0-8398-1962-5*) Irvington.

Black Ice: Modern Fiction, No. 2. Ed. by Dale Shank. 87p. (Orig.). 1985. pap. 5.00 (*0-918411-01-7*) Black I Press.

Black Ice: Modern Fiction Anthology, No. 3. Ed. by Dale Shank. 120p. (Orig.). 1987. pap. 6.00 (*0-918411-02-5*) Black I Press.

Black Ice: Modern Fiction Anthology, No. 4. Ed. by Dale Shank. 96p. (Orig.). 1988. pap. 6.00 (*0-918411-03-3*) Black I Press.

Black Ice: Modern Fiction, No. 1. Ed. by Dale Shank. 135p. (Orig.). 1984. pap. 4.00 (*0-918411-00-9*) Black I Press.

Black Ice Score. large type ed. Richard Stark. 1991. 12.95 (*0-7451-9820-1*, C0313, Atlantic Lrg Print); pap. 9.95 (*0-7927-0266-2*, Atlantic Lrg Print) Chivers N Amer.

Black Image in the New Deal: The Politics of FSA Photography. Nicholas Natanson. LC 91-14344. (Illus.). 320p. (C). 1992. text ed. 45.00x (*0-87049-723-5*); pap. 18.95 (*0-87049-724-3*) U of Tenn Pr.

Black Image in the White Mind: The Debate on Afro-American Character & Destiny, 1817-1914. George M. Fredrickson. LC 86-19022. 367p. 1987. pap. 16.95 (*0-8195-6188-6*, Wesleyan Univ Pr) U Pr of New Eng.

Black Image Makers. Edith M. Gaines et al. Ed. by Kenyette Adrine-Robinson. (Illus.). (Orig.). (J). (gr. 5-9). 1988. pap. 5.00 (*0-913678-17-1*) New Day Pr.

Black Images. Wilfred G. Cartey. LC 75-113096. (Columbia University, Center for Education in Asia, Publications). 200p. reprint ed. pap. 57.00 (*0-8357-7289-6*, 2025998) Bks Demand.

Black Images in Contemporary Children's Books: An Annotated Bibliography. Jeanette Lambert. 20p. (Orig.). 1991. pap. 5.50 (*0-9632736-0-4*) Edit Cetera.

Black Immigration & Ethnicity in the United States: An Annotated Bibliography. Center for Afro-American & African Studies Staff. Ed. by University of Michigan Staff. LC 84-12886. (Bibliographies & Indexes in Afro-American & African Studies: No. 2). xi, 170p. 1985. text ed. 55.00 (*0-313-24366-2*, SBI/) Greenwood.

Black in a White Paradise. rev. ed. Amos Brooke. (Orig.). 1985. pap. 2.50 (*0-87067-255-X*, BH255) Holloway.

***Black in Focus: A Guide to Aboriginality in Literature for Young People.** annot. ed. Ed. by Margaret Dunkle. 260p. 1994. pap. 25.00 (*1-875589-47-3*) D W Thorpe.

Black in Selma: The Uncommon Life of J. L. Chestnut, Jr. 1991. pap. 13.00 (*0-385-41938-4*, Anchor NY) Doubleday.

Black in Selma: The Uncommon Life of J. L. Chestnut, Jr. J. L. Chestnut, Jr. & Julia Cass. 1990. 22.95 (*0-374-11404-8*) FS&G.

Black Income in India. Suraj B. Gupta. LC 92-32148. (Illus.). 192p. (C). 1992. text ed. 29.95 (*0-8039-9453-2*) Sage.

Black Indian Genealogy Research. Angela Walton-Raji. 180p. (Orig.). 1993. pap. text ed. 18.50 (*1-55613-856-3*) Heritage Bk.

Black Indians: A Hidden Heritage. William Katz. LC 85-28770. (Illus.). 208p. (J). (gr. 5 up). 1986. text ed. 16.95 (*0-689-31196-6*, Atheneum Bks Young) S&S Childrens.

Black Infantry in the West, 1869-1891. Arlen L. Fowler. LC 78-105985. (Contributions in Afro-American & African Studies: No. 6). (Illus.). 167p. 1971. text ed. 27.50 (*0-8371-3313-0*, FON&, Negro U Pr) Greenwood.

Black Initiative & Governmental Responsibility. Committee on Policy for Racial Justice Staff. 22p. 1987. pap. 10.50 (*0-941410-61-7*) Jt Ctr Pol Studies.

B

An Asterisk (*) at the beginning of an entry indicates that the title is appearing in BIP for the first time. 801

Black Inner City As Frontier Outpost. David Ley. LC 74-82116. (Monograph Ser.: No. 7). 1974. pap. 10.00 (0-89291-086-0) Assn Am Geographers.

Black Innocence: The Immigrant. David Wilde. 165p. (Orig.). 1993. 21.95 (1-882204-00-X) Wilde Pub.

***Black Innovators in Technology: Inspiring a New Generation.** (Illus.). 52p. (Orig.). (C). 1994. pap. text ed. 30.00x (0-7881-0623-6) Diane Pub.

***Black Insider.** Dambudzo Marechera. Date not set. pap. 7.99 (0-85315-739-1, Pub. by Lawrence & Wishart UK) Humanities.

Black Intellectuals & the Dilemmas of Race & Class in Trinidad. Ivar Oxaal. LC 72-170653. 334p. 1982. pap. text ed. 22.95 (0-87073-417-2) Schenkman Bks Inc.

Black into White: Race & Nationality in Brazilian Thought. Thomas E. Skidmore. LC 92-28497. 334p. (C). 1993. pap. text ed. 16.95 (0-8223-1320-0) Duke.

Black Inventors, Vol. II. Corliss V. Grimes. (Illus.). 32p. (J). (gr. 1-3). 1994. 16.95 (0-86543-430-1); pap. 8.95 (0-86543-431-X) Africa World.

Black Inventors of America. McKinley Burt, Jr. 1969. pap. 11.95 (0-89420-095-X, 296959) Natl Book.

Black Iris. Jeane Harris. 256p. (Orig.). 1991. pap. 8.95 (0-941483-68-1) Naiad Pr.

Black Iris. Jean Joubert. Tr. by Denise Levertov. LC 88-70584. 120p. (Orig.). 1988. pap. 9.00 (1-55659-015-6) Copper Canyon.

Black Is Beautiful. T. Schuman. 1989. write for info. (0-935090-18-5) Almanac Pr.

Black Is Brown Is Tan. Arnold Adoff. LC 73-9855. (Illus.). 32p. (J). (ps-3). 1973. 15.00i (0-06-020083-9); lib. bdg. 14.89 (0-06-020084-7) HarpC Child Bks.

Black Is Brown Is Tan. Arnold Adoff. LC 73-9855. (Trophy Picture Bk.). (Illus.). 32p. (J). (ps-3). 1992. pap. 3.95 (0-06-443269-6, Trophy) HarpC Child Bks.

Black Is My Truelove's Hair. Elizabeth Madox Roberts. Ed. by Elizabeth Hardwick. LC 76-51675. (Rediscovered Fiction by American Women Ser.). 1977. reprint ed. lib. bdg. 33.95 (0-405-10053-1) Ayer.

Black Is OK! Andras Adorjan. (Illus.). 160p. 1989. pap. 12.95 (0-7134-5790-2, Trafalgar Sq Pub) Trafalgar.

Black Is the Color of My True Love's Heart. Ellis Peters. 208p. 1992. mass mkt. 4.99 (0-446-40072-6, Mysterious Paperbk) Warner Bks.

Black Is the Color of My TV Tube. Gil Noble. (Illus.). 1981. 12.00 (0-8184-0297-0) Carol Pub Group.

Black is the Color of My TV Tube. Gil Noble. 1991. pap. 9.95 (0-8184-0538-4) Carol Pub Group.

Black Is the Color of the Cosmos: Essays on Afro-American Literature & Culture, 1942-81. Charles T. Davis. Ed. by Henry L. Gates, Jr. 376p. 1989. pap. 16.95 (0-88258-166-X) Howard U Pr.

Black Island. Herge. (Illus.). 62p. (J). 19.95 (0-8288-5012-7) Fr & Eur.

Black Island. Herge. LC 74-21624. (Adventures of Tintin Ser.). (J). (gr. k up). 1975. mass mkt. 7.95 (0-316-35835-5, Joy St Bks) Little.

Black Islanders: A Personal Perspective of Bougainville, 1937-1991. Douglas Oliver. LC 91-57969. (Illus.). 348p. (C). 1992. pap. text ed. 19.95 (0-8248-1434-7) UH Pr.

Black Itinerants of the Gospel: The Narratives of John Jea & George White. Ed. by Graham R. Hodges. LC 92-39713. (Illus.). 208p. 1993. 29.95 (0-945612-32-X) Madison Hse.

Black Ivory: A History of British Slavery. James Walvin. LC 94-1281. 1994. 19.95 (0-88258-182-1) Howard U Pr.

***Black Jack: John A. Logan & Southern Illinois in the Civil War Era.** James P Jones. LC 94-42300. (Shawnee Classics Ser.). (C). 1995. pap. 12.95 (0-8093-2002-9) S Ill U Pr.

***Black Jack: John A. Logan & Southern Illinois in the Civil War Era.** James P. Jones. LC 94-42300. (Shawnee Classics Ser.). 360p. (C). 1995. reprint ed. 29.95 (0-8093-2001-0) S Ill U Pr.

Black Jack: The Life & Times of John J. Pershing, 2 vols. Frank E. Vandiver. LC 76-51729. (Illus.). 1246p. 1977. 47.50 (0-89096-024-0) Tex A&M Univ Pr.

Black Jack Brogan. Julie Kistler. (American Romance Ser.). 1993. mass mkt. 3.39 (0-373-16485-8, 1-16485-4) Harlequin Bks.

Black Jacobins. C. L. James. 1963. pap. 8.95 (0-394-70242-5) Random.

Black Jacobins: Toussaint L'Ouverture & the San Domingo Revolution. Cyril L. James. 1989. pap. 14.00 (0-679-72467-2, Vin) Random.

Black, Jacquard. 80p. 1990. 3.00 (0-9620519-9-3) Iris Bks.

Black Jamaica: A Study in Evolution. W. P. Livngstone. 1976. lib. bdg. 59.95 (0-8490-1512-X) Gordon Pr.

Black Jargon in White America. David Claerbaut. LC 72-77176. 89p. reprint ed. pap. 25.40 (0-8357-7290-X, 2012858) Bks Demand.

Black Jesus. Emery George. LC 74-84182. 64p. (C). 1974. 4.95 (0-914408-01-1); pap. 2.45 (0-914408-02-X) Kylix Pr.

Black-Jewish Relations in the United States, 1752-1984: A Selected Bibliography. Lenwood G. Davis. LC 84-4685. (Bibliographies & Indexes in Afro-American & African Studies: No. 1). xv, 130p. 1984. text ed. 49.95 (0-313-23329-2, DBB/) Greenwood.

Black Jews. 2nd ed. James H. Boykin. LC 81-90626. iv, 98p. 1982. reprint ed. pap. 3.25 (0-9603342-1-1) Boykin.

Black "Jography" The Paths of Our Black Pioneers. Carole Marsh. (Our Black Heritage Ser.). (J). (gr. 3-12). 1994. lib. bdg. 24.95 (1-55609-321-7); pap. 14.95 (1-55609-320-9); disk 29.95 (1-55609-322-5) Gallopade Pub Group.

Black John of Halfaday Creek. James B. Hendryx. 1976. reprint ed. lib. bdg. 22.95 (0-88411-831-2, Aeonian Pr) Amereon Ltd.

Black Journalists: The NABJ Story. Wayne Dawkins. LC 92-83827. 208p. (Orig.). 1993. pap. 12.95 (0-9635720-0-8) August Pr.

Black Journalists in Paradox: Historical Perspectives & Current Dilemmas. Clint C. Wilson, II. LC 90-25217. (Contributions in Afro-American & African Studies: No. 145). 208p. 1991. text ed. 45.00 (0-313-26690-5, WBN/, Greenwood Pr) Greenwood.

Black Journals of the United States. Walter C. Daniel. LC 81-13440. (Historical Guides to the World's Periodicals & Newspapers Ser.). x, 432p. 1982. text ed. 79.50 (0-313-20704-6, DBJ/, Greenwood Pr) Greenwood.

***Black Judges on Justice: Perspectives from the Bench.** Linn Washington. LC 94-27447. 288p. 1995. 22.95 (1-56584-104-2) New Press NY.

Black Jupiter. Mary-Katherine MacDougall. Ed. by Kate E. Gruver. (Illus.). 181p. (J). (gr. 5 up). 1983. 8.95 (0-940175-01-0) Now Comns.

Black Keys Only. Troy W. Parsons. Ed. by Wanda Ingram. (Illus.). 200p. 1993. 13.95 (0-9637109-0-7) Fayette Pub.

Black Knight. Jack B. Carmichael. (Trilogy of the Cousin Ser.). 89p. (Orig.). (YA). (gr. 12). 1991. pap. 9.95 (0-9626948-1-9) Dynamics MI.

Black Knight in Red Square. limited ed. Stuart M. Kaminsky. 224p. 1993. reprint ed. 75.00 (1-56287-036-X) Armchair Detective.

Black Knight in Red Square. Stuart M. Kaminsky. 224p. 1993. reprint ed. 19.95 (1-56287-034-3); reprint ed. 25.00 (1-56287-035-1) Armchair Detective.

Black Knights Tango. Georgi Orlov. Ed. by Michael J. Franett. (Illus.). 24p. (Orig.). 1991. pap. 5.95 (1-879479-03-6) ICE WA.

***Black-Korean Encounter: Toward Understanding & Alliance.** Ed. by Eui-Young Yu. LC 94-19786. 1994. write for info. (0-941690-60-1) Regina Bks.

***Black Labor - White Wealth: The Search for Economic Justice.** Claud Anderson. LC 93-72794. (Illus.). 250p. 1994. 19.95 (1-878647-11-3) Duncan & Duncan.

Black Labor & the American Legal System: Race, Work, & the Law. Herbert Hill. LC 85-40762. 480p. 1985. reprint ed. text ed. 27.50 (0-299-10590-3); reprint ed. pap. 14.50 (0-299-10594-6) U of Wis Pr.

Black Labor in America. Ed. by Milton Cantor. LC 74-111265. (Contributions in Afro-American & African Studies: No. 2). (Illus.). 170p. 1970. text ed. 49.95 (0-8371-4667-4, CLM&, Negro U Pr) Greenwood.

Black Labor in America, 1865-1983: A Selected Annotated Bibliography. Ed. by Thomas Weissinger. LC 86-349. (Bibliographies & Indexes in Afro-American & African Studies: No. 11). 131p. 1986. text ed. 42.95 (0-313-25267-X, WBL/) Greenwood.

Black Labor in Richmond, 1865-1890. Peter Rachleff. LC 88-29432. 264p. 1989. reprint ed. pap. 11.95 (0-252-06026-1) U of Ill Pr.

Black Labor on a White Canal: Panama, 1904-1981. Michael L. Conniff. LC 84-21970. (Latin American Ser.). (Illus.). 240p. 1985. 49.95 (0-8229-3509-0) U of Pittsburgh Pr.

Black Labor Unions in South Africa. 1990. lib. bdg. 79.95 (0-8490-4050-7) Gordon Pr.

Black Labor Unions in South Africa: Report of a Symposium. Ed. by Anthony G. Freeman & Diane B. Bendahame. LC 86-60599. (State Department Publications). 69p. (Orig.). 1987. pap. 4.50 (0-16-004442-1, S/N 044-000-02163-3) USGPO.

Black Lace & Linen. Susan Carroll. (Silhouette Desire Ser.). 1994. mass mkt. 2.99 (0-373-05840-3, 5-05840-9) Silhouette.

Black Lamb & Grey Falcon. Rebecca West. 1982. pap. 20.00 (0-14-006355-2, Penguin Bks) Viking Penguin.

Black Lamb & Grey Falcon: A Journey Through Yugoslavia. Rebecca West. 1200p. 1995. 20.00 (0-14-018847-9, Penguin Classics) Viking Penguin.

Black Land, Red River: A Pictorial History of Grayson County, Texas. Sherrie S. McLeRoy. LC 93-23092. 1993. write for info. (0-89865-868-3) Donning Co.

Black Laws: Nature of African Reality. LaRue E. Nedd. 126p. 1990. pap. write for info. (1-883762-00-6, 029916637) HomeBased Comm.

Black Laws in the Old Northwest: A Documentary History. Stephen Middleton. LC 91-47063. (Contributions in Afro-American & African Studies: No. 152). 464p. 1993. text ed. 55.00 (0-313-28016-9, MKL, Greenwood Pr) Greenwood.

Black Leaders: Texans for Their Times. Ed. by Alwyn Barr & Robert A. Calvert. (Illus.). x, 237p. 1990. pap. 9.95 (0-87611-056-1) Tex St Hist Assn.

Black Leaders of the Nineteenth Century. Leon Litwack & August Meier. (Blacks in the New World Ser.). (Illus.). 360p. 1991. pap. 11.95 (0-252-06213-2) U of Ill Pr.

Black Leaders of the Nineteenth Century. Ed. by Leon F. Litwack & August Meier. LC 87-19439. (Blacks in the New World Ser.). 360p. 1988. 29.95 (0-252-01506-1) U of Ill Pr.

Black Leaders of the Twentieth Century. Ed. by John Hope Franklin & August Meier. LC 81-11454. (Blacks in the New World Ser.). (Illus.). 390p. 1982. 29.95 (0-252-00870-7); pap. 11.95 (0-252-00939-8) U of Ill Pr.

Black Leadership in America: From Booker T. Washington to Jesse Jackson. 2nd ed. John White. (Studies in Modern History). 232p. (C). 1990. pap. text ed. 23.95 (0-582-06372-8, 78648) Longman.

Black Leather. David Schow. 1994. 29.95 (0-929480-34-1) Mark Ziesing.

Black Leather. limited ed. David Schow. 1994. 65.00 (0-929480-30-9) Mark Ziesing.

***Black Leather Required.** David Schow. 1994. 29.95 (0-929480-29-5) Mark Ziesing.

Black Legacy: America's Hidden Heritage. William D. Piersen. LC 92-41003. 280p. (C). 1993. pap. 15.95 (0-87023-859-0) U of Mass Pr.

Black Legend in England: The Development of Anti-Spanish Sentiment, 1558-1660. William S. Maltby. LC 78-161356. (Duke Historical Publications). 188p. reprint ed. pap. 53.60 (0-8357-7291-8, 2023764) Bks Demand.

Black Legends & Catholic Hispanic Culture: Liberation Theology & the History of the New World. Antonio Caponnetto. Tr. by Jose R. Lopez-Gaston & Rosa M. Lopez-Gaston. (Orig.). 1991. pap. 10.00 (0-9626257-3-6) CBCCU Amer.

***Black Liberation: A Comparative History of Black Ideologies in the United States & South Africa.** George M. Fredrickson. 448p. 1995. 30.00 (0-19-505749-X) OUP.

Black Liberation in Kentucky: Emancipation & Freedom, 1862-1884. Victor B. Howard. LC 82-40461. 230p. reprint ed. pap. 65.60 (0-7837-5815-4, 2045482) Bks Demand.

Black Liberation-Red Scare: Ben Davis & the Communist Party. Gerald Horne. LC 92-53778. 1994. write for info. (0-87413-472-2) U Delaware Pr.

Black Librarian in America Revisited. Intro. by E. J. Josey. LC 93-47270. 390p. 1994. 42.50 (0-8108-2830-8) Scarecrow.

Black Libraries, Museums, Halls of Fame, Colleges, Art Galleries, Etc: A How to Find or Locate Reference Workbook Bibliotheca Press Research Project. 62p. 1992. text ed. 19.95 (0-939476-90-8, Biblio Pr) Prosperity & Profits.

***Black Lies - White Lies: The Truth According to Tony Brown.** Tony Brown. LC 95-13315. 1995. write for info. (0-688-13270-7) Morrow.

Black Life in Corporate America: Swimming in the Mainstream. George Davis & Glegg Watson. LC 81-43064. 216p. 1985. pap. 10.95 (0-385-14702-3) Doubleday.

Black Life in Secondary Cities: A Comparative Analysis of the Black Communities of Camden & Elizabeth, N.J., 1860-1920. Spencer R. Crew. LC 93-2772. 232p. 1993. 61.00 (0-8153-1011-0) Garland.

Black Life Poetic Thinking: One-Hundred Original Works. R. S. Bunyon. 1992. 8.95 (0-533-10155-7) Vantage.

Black Light. Talbot Munday. 288p. 1991. 10.95 (0-89804-157-0) Ariel GA.

Black Light: The African American Hero. Paul C. Harrison. (Illus.). 196p. 1993. pap. 14.95 (1-56025-060-7) Thunders Mouth.

***Black Lightning.** John Saul. 400p. 1995. 23.00 (0-449-90864-X) Fawcett.

Black Lightning. Roger Mais. (Caribbean Writers Ser.). 159p. (Orig.). (C). 1983. reprint ed. pap. 8.95 (0-435-98584-1) Heinemann.

Black Like Kyra, White Like Me. Judith Vigna. Ed. by Kathleen Tucker. LC 92-1203. (Albert Whitman Concept Bks.). (Illus.). 32p. (J). (gr. 2-6). 1992. 13.95 (0-8075-0778-4) A Whitman.

Black Like Me. John H. Griffin. 160p. 1962. pap. 4.99 (0-451-16317-6, Sig) NAL-Dutton.

Black Like Me. John H. Griffin. 160p. (YA). (gr. 8). 1962. pap. 3.95 (0-451-15530-0, Sig) NAL-Dutton.

Black Like Me Notes. Margaret Mansfield. 1971. pap. 4.50 (0-8220-0245-0) Cliffs.

Black Lipstick: The Big Dipper Performance Jan. 14, 1990. Terry Trueman. (Illus.). 58p. (Orig.). 1991. pap. 4.95 (0-9629744-2-0) Siobhan Pr.

Black List. Paul J. Payack. (Illus.). 1977. 1.00 (0-686-19654-6) Chthon Pr.

***Black Literature & Literary.** Henry Gates. 1993. pap. 13.95 (0-415-90334-3) Routledge Chapman & Hall.

Black Literature & Literary Theory. Ed. by Henry L. Gates, Jr. 350p. 1984. pap. 15.95 (0-416-37240-6, NO. 4089) Routledge Chapman & Hall.

Black Literature Criticism, 3 vols., 1. 2nd ed. Draper. 1996. write for info. (0-8103-8575-9) Gale.

Black Literature Criticism, 3 vols., 2. 2nd ed. Draper. 1996. write for info. (0-8103-8576-7) Gale.

Black Literature Criticism, 3 vols., 3. 2nd ed. Draper. 1996. write for info. (0-8103-8577-5) Gale.

Black Literature Criticism, 3 vols., Set. 2nd ed. Draper. 1996. 275.00 (0-8103-8574-0, 101388) Gale.

Black Literature Criticism, Vol. 1. Draper. 1991. write for info. (0-8103-7930-9) Gale.

Black Literature Criticism, Vol. 2. Draper. 1991. write for info. (0-8103-7931-7) Gale.

Black Literature Criticism, Vol. 3. Draper. 1992. write for info. (0-8103-7932-5) Gale.

Black Literature Criticism: Excerpts from Criticism of the Most Significant Works of Black Authors over the Past 200 Years, 3 vols., Set. Ed. by James P. Draper. 706p. 1991. 275.00 (0-8103-7929-5) Gale.

Black Literature in America. Houston A. Baker, Jr. 1971. text ed. write for info. (0-07-003365-X) McGraw.

Black Literature Resources: Analysis & Organization. Doris H. Clack. LC 75-23582. (Books in Library & Information Science: No. 16). 217p. reprint ed. pap. 61.90 (0-8357-6043-X, 2034523) Bks Demand.

Black Literature, 1827-1940: Author - Title Index, Pt. 1. 1988. lib. bdg. 2,200.00 (0-89887-057-7) Chadwyck-Healey.

Black Lives, White Lives: Three Decades of Race Relations in America. Bob Blauner. 350p. (C). 1989. 38.00 (0-520-06261-2); pap. 14.00 (0-520-06950-1) U CA Pr.

Black Lizard Anthology of Crime Fiction. Ed. by Edward Gorman. LC 86-72053. 352p. (Orig.). 1987. pap. 8.95 (0-88739-039-0, Blk Lizard) Creat Arts Bk.

Black Lizard's Startling Encounter. Chip Hill. LC 91-16081. (Chronicles of Chuck Christian Ser.). (Illus.). (J). (gr. 4-9). 1991. 4.00 (0-915541-75-0) Star Bks Inc.

Black Local Stamp & 1862 Provisional of Local Stamp Type see Sweden: Skilling Banco Stamps, 1855-1858

Black Lodge. Robert Weinberg. Ed. by Sally Peters. 272p. (Orig.). 1991. mass mkt. 4.50 (0-671-70108-8) PB.

Black Lodge in White America: True Reformer Browne & His Economic Strategy. David M. Fahey. LC 93-48399. (C). 1994. 55.00 (1-882090-07-1) U Pr of Amer.

***Black London: Life Before Emancipation.** Gretchen H. Gerzina. (Illus.). 256p. (C). 1995. text ed. 29.95 (0-8135-2259-5) Rutgers U Pr.

Black Looks: Race & Representation. Bell Hooks. 1992. 30.00 (0-89608-434-5); pap. 14.00 (0-89608-433-7) South End Pr.

Black Lotus. Tony Reeder. 175p. (C). 1990. 39.00 (0-947333-17-7, Pub. by Pascoe Pub AT) St Mut.

Black Loyalists: The Search for a Promised Land in Nova Scotia & Sierra Leone 1783-1870. James W. Walker. (Reprints in Canadian History Ser.). 450p. 1992. reprint ed. pap. 19.95 (0-8020-7402-2) U of Toronto Pr.

Black Lung Claims Before the Department of Labor: A Manual of Substansive Law. 200p. 1987. 20.00 (0-317-02681-X, 42,880) NCLS Inc.

Black Lyon. Jude Deveraux. 288p. 1980. mass mkt. 5.99 (0-380-75911-X) Avon.

Black Lyon. Jude Deveraux. 1991. reprint ed. 18.95 (0-7278-4049-5) Severn Hse.

Black Mac Say. Frank S. Jenkins. (Illus.). 16p. (Orig.). 1982. pap. 2.00 (0-942048-01-6) Shockley Pr.

Black Macho & the Myth of the Superwoman. Michelle Wallace. 300p. 1990. pap. 15.95 (0-86091-518-2, A4980, Pub. by Verso UK) Routledge Chapman & Hall.

Black Madonna. Fred Gustafson. (Illus.). 143p. 1991. 27.50 (0-938434-49-7); pap. 15.95 (0-938434-48-9) Sigo Pr.

Black Madonna Within: Drawings, Dreams, Reflections. Tataya Mato. LC 94-5690. (Dreamcatchers Ser.: Vol. 1). 217p. 1994. 44.95 (0-8126-9248-9); pap. 16.95 (0-8126-9249-7) Open Court.

Black Madonnas: Feminism, Religion, & Politics in Italy. Lucia C. Birnbaum. 320p. 1993. text ed. 35.00 (1-55553-156-3) NE U Pr.

***Black Madonnas & Young Lions: A Rites of Passage for African American Adolescents.** rev. ed. Bernida Thompson. 125p. (YA). Date not set. pap. 18.95 (0-9632940-1-6) Roots Act.

Black Magic: A Pictorial History of the African-American in the Performing Arts. Langston Hughes & Milton Meltzer. (Quality Paperbacks Ser.). (Illus.). 384p. 1990. reprint ed. pap. 19.95 (0-306-80406-9) Da Capo.

Black Magic: Steve Jobs & the Next Big Thing. Randall E. Stross. Ed. by Lee Goerner. (Illus.). 352p. 1993. text ed. 24.00 (0-689-12135-0, Atheneum S&S) S&S Trade.

Black Magic & Stolen Timber. Yvonne M. Madden. Ed. by Christine W. Madden. 296p. 1993. text ed. 25.00 (0-9619080-0-9); pap. text ed. 20.00 (0-9619080-1-7) Vonnie Pub.

***Black Magic & Stolen Timber.** Yvonne M. Madden. Ed. by Christine W. Madden. 1995. digital audio 50.00 (0-9619080-2-5) Vonnie Pub.

Black Magistrates: A Study of Selection & Recruitment to the Bench. Michael King et al. 208p. (C). 1988. 21.00 (0-900137-24-X, Pub. by NCCL UK) St Mut.

Black Mail. Doris M. Disney. 1989. pap. 2.95 (0-8217-2662-5) Zebra.

Black Mail. large type ed. Neville Steed. (Mystery Ser.). 560p. 1992. 21.95 (0-7089-2685-1) Ulverscroft.

***Black Male: Representations of Masculinity in Contemporary American Art.** Thelma Golden. LC 94-23212. 1994. pap. write for info. (0-87427-093-6) Whitney Mus.

***Black Male: Representations of Masculinity in Contemporary American Art.** Thelma Golden. (Illus.). 224p. 1995. pap. 39.95 (0-8109-6816-9) Abrams.

Black Male - White Female. Ed. by Doris Y. Wilkinson. 190p. 1975. pap. 18.95 (0-87073-167-X) Schenkman Bks Inc.

Black Male Adolescents: Parenting & Education in Community Context. Benjamin P. Bowser. 352p. (Orig.). (C). Date not set. pap. text ed. 29.50 (0-8191-9115-9) U Pr of Amer.

Black Male Adolescents: Parenting & Education in Community Context. Ed. by Benjamin P. Bowser. 352p. (Orig.). (C). 1990. lib. bdg. 53.00 (0-8191-7975-2) U Pr of Amer.

Black Male Crisis. J. Carroll George. 100p. 1993. pap. text ed. 6.95 (1-881223-02-7) Zulema Ent.

Black Male Crisis Workbook: A Forum of Issues & Strategies for Action. J. Carroll George. 100p. 1993. pap. text ed. 7.95 (1-881223-04-3) Zulema Ent.

Black Male Deviance. Anthony J. Lemelle. LC 94-25040. 208p. 1994. text ed. 52.95 (0-275-95004-2, Praeger Pubs) Greenwood.

Black Male Entrepreneurs & Adult Development. James I. Herbert. LC 88-26046. 253p. 1989. text ed. 59.95 (0-275-93023-8, C3023, Praeger Pubs) Greenwood.

Black Male-Female Relationships: A Resource Book of Selected Materials. Delores Aldridge. 256p. 1989. pap. text ed. 29.95 (0-8403-5553-X) Kendall-Hunt.

Black Male in America: Perspectives on His Status in Contemporary Society. Ed. by Doris Y. Wilkinson & Ronald L. Taylor. LC 76-44310. 384p. (C). 1977. 36.95 (0-88229-227-7) Nelson-Hall.

***Black Male-White Male.** Fani-Kayode. Date not set. per. 25.00 (0-85449-080-9, Pub. by Gay Mens Pr UK) InBook.

Black Males: An African American View on Raising Young Men. Best, Inc. Staff. 160p. 1994. per. 16.95 (0-8403-9482-9) Kendall-Hunt.

Black Males & the Psychology of Love: A Visionary & Theoretical Look at a New Breed of Black Men for the 21st Century. Nathaniel Bracey. 39p. (Orig.). 1992. pap. 3.95 (1-56411-037-0) Untd Bros & Sis.

802

An Asterisk (*) at the beginning of an entry indicates that the title is appearing in BIP for the first time.

B

An Asterisk (*) at the beginning of an entry indicates that the title is appearing in BIP for the first time.

803

Black Noise: Rap Music & Black Culture in Contemporary America. Tricia Rose. LC 93-41386. (Music - Culture Ser.). (Illus.). 257p. (C). 1994. text ed. 35.00x (*0-8195-5271-2*, Wesleyan Univ Pr); pap. 14.95 (*0-8195-6275-0*, Wesleyan Univ Pr) U Pr of New Eng.

Black North in Nineteen One: A Social Study. W. E. B. Du Bois. LC 70-92229. (American Negro: His History & Literature, Ser. No. 3). 1970. reprint ed. 11.95 (*0-405-01921-1*) Ayer.

Black Novelist As White Racist: The Myth of Black Inferiority in the Novels of Oscar Micheaux. Joseph A. Young. LC 88-38305. (Contributions in Afro-American & African Studies: No. 123). 193p. 1989. text ed. 45.00 (*0-313-25749-3*, YNM/) Greenwood.

***Black O: How Racism & Arrogance Brought down an American Corporate Empire.** Steve Watkins. (Illus.). 256p. 1995. 20.00 (*1-56352-230-6*) Longstreet Pr Inc.

Black Obelisk. Erich M. Remarque. Tr. by Denver Lindley. LC 57-8840. 440p. 1957. 19.95 (*0-15-113181-3*) HarBrace.

Black Odyssey. Nathan I. Huggins. 1978. pap. 7.95 (*0-394-72687-1*) Random.

Black Odyssey: The Afro-American Ordeal in Slavery. Nathan I. Huggins. LC 89-40483. 1990. pap. 12.00 (*0-679-72814-7*, Vin) Random.

Black Odyssey: The Seafaring Traditions of Afro-Americans. James B. Farr. (Culture, Ethnicity & Nation Ser.: Vol. 1). 310p. (C). 1989. text ed. 53.95 (*0-8204-0803-4*) P Lang Pubs.

Black of Moonlit Sea: Poetry from the Mist. Abby L. Bogomolny. 60p. 1991. pap. 6.00 (*0-939821-02-8*) HerBooks.

Black Ohio & the Color Line, 1860-1915. David A. Gerber. LC 76-27285. 512p. reprint ed. pap. 146.00 (*0-8357-7294-2*, 2021155) Bks Demand.

Black Olympian Medalists. James A. Page. 190p. 1991. pap. 27.50 (*0-87287-618-7*) Libs Unl.

Black Olympic Guide to Los Angeles 1984. Alfred Williamson. 34p. (Orig.). (C). 1984. pap. 9.95 (*0-934033-01-3*) Williamson Ad Agcy.

***Black on Black Crime: Facing Facts - Challenging Fiction.** Ed. by P. Ray Kedia. 225p. (C). 1994. pap. text ed. 19.95 (*1-55605-246-4*) Wyndhall Pr.

***Black on Black Crime: Facing Facts - Challenging Fiction.** Ed. by P. Ray Kedia. 225p. (C). 1994. text ed. 29.95 (*1-55605-247-2*) Wyndhall Pr.

Black-on-Black Violence: The Psychodynamics of Black Self-Annihilation in Service of White Domination. Amos N. Wilson & Sababu N. Plata. 240p. (Orig.). (C). 1990. pap. 15.00 (*1-879164-00-0*) African World.

***Black on Steel.** Perata. 1996. 27.95 (*0-8057-4520-3*) Macmillan.

Black on White. Tana Hoban. LC 92-18897. (Illus.). 12p. (J). (ps up). 1993. bds. 4.95 (*0-688-11918-2*) Greenwillow.

Black One Hundred: A Ranking of the Most Influential African-Americans, Past & Present. Columbus Salley. (Illus.). 320p. 1992. 19.95 (*0-8065-1299-7*, Citadel Pr) Carol Pub Group.

Black One Hundred: A Ranking of the Most Influential African-Americans, Past & Present. Columbus Salley. LC 94-20041. 1994. 18.95 (*0-8065-1550-3*, Citadel Pr) Carol Pub Group.

***Black Opal.** Victoria Holt. 1994. mass mkt. 5.99 (*0-449-22271-3*, Crest) Fawcett.

Black Orator's Workbook. Edward L. Jones. 1982. pap. 16.00 (*0-9602458-4-7*) Ed-Lynne Jones.

Black Orchid. Neil Gaiman. Ed. by Karen Berger & Tom Peyer. (Illus.). 160p. 1991. pap. 19.95 (*0-930289-55-2*, Vertigo) DC Comics.

Black Orchids. Rex Stout. 1992. mass mkt. 4.99 (*0-553-25719-6*) Bantam.

Black Ordeal of Slave Trading & Slavery in the French West Indies, 1625-1715, 3 vols., 1. Clarence J. Munford. LC 91-22009. 300p. 1991. lib. bdg. 89.95 (*0-7734-9741-2*) E Mellen.

Black Ordeal of Slave Trading & Slavery in the French West Indies, 1625-1715, 3 vols., 2. Clarence J. Munford. LC 91-22009. 300p. 1991. lib. bdg. 89.95 (*0-7734-9431-6*) E Mellen.

Black Ordeal of Slave Trading & Slavery in the French West Indies, 1625-1715, 3 vols., 3. Clarence J. Munford. LC 91-22009. 300p. 1991. lib. bdg. 89.95 (*0-7734-9433-2*) E Mellen.

Black Organizations: A Directory & Community Events Planning Calendar. Doug McNair & Wallace Y. McNair. 96p. 1992. pap. 35.00 (*0-9627600-4-8*) Wstrn Images.

Black Organizations: Issues on Survival Techniques. Ed. by Lennox S. Yearwood. LC 79-5500. 286p. 1980. pap. 22.00 (*0-8191-0898-7*) U Pr of Amer.

Black Organized Crime in Harlem, 1920-1930. Rufus Schatzberg. LC 92-37543. (Studies in African-American History & Culture). 160p. 1993. 48.00 (*0-8153-1193-1*) Garland.

Black Orpheus. (Illus.). 1982. 6.95 (*0-88188-061-2*, 00309175) H Leonard.

Black Orpheus. Jean-Paul Sartre. 1976. pap. 12.95 (*0-7859-5398-1*) Fr & Eur.

Black Out. Jack Gregory. 1993. mass mkt. 4.99 (*0-312-95009-8*) St Martin.

***Black Out.** John Lawton. LC 95-1264. 1995. 22.95 (*0-670-85767-X*, Viking) Viking Penguin.

Black over White: Negro Political Leadership in South Carolina During Reconstruction. Thomas Holt. LC 77-7513. (Blacks in the New World Ser.). 276p. 1979. 29.95 (*0-252-00585-6*); pap. 11.95 (*0-252-00775-1*) U of Ill Pr.

Black Ox: A Study in the History of a Folk-Tale. Archer Taylor. Ed. by Richard M. Dorson. LC 80-798. (Folklore of the World Ser.). 1981. reprint ed. lib. bdg. 17.95 (*0-405-13338-3*) Ayer.

Black Oxen. Gertrude F. Atherton. (BCL1-PS American Literature Ser.). 346p. 1992. reprint ed. lib. bdg. 89.00 (*0-7812-6670-X*) Rprt Serv.

Black Pagoda. Robert Ebersole. LC 57-12929. (Illus.). 118p. reprint ed. pap. 33.70 (*0-7837-4918-X*, 2044583) Bks Demand.

Black Panther. Shelley S. Sateren. LC 89-28267. (Wildlife Ser.). (Illus.). 48p. (J). (gr. 5). 1990. text ed. 12.95 (*0-89686-519-3*, Crstwood Hse) Silver Burdett Pr.

Black Panther "Panther's Prey", No. 1. Don McGregor & Dwayne Turner. 48p. 1991. 3.95 (*0-87135-723-2*) Marvel Entmnt.

Black Panther "Panther's Prey", No. 2. Don McGregor & Dwayne Turner. 48p. 1991. 3.95 (*0-87135-724-0*) Marvel Entmnt.

Black Panther "Panther's Prey", No. 3. Don McGregor & Dwayne Turner. 48p. 1991. 3.95 (*0-87135-725-9*) Marvel Entmnt.

Black Panther "Panther's Prey", No. 4. Don McGregor & Dwayne Turner. 48p. 1991. 3.95 (*0-87135-726-7*) Marvel Entmnt.

***Black Panthers Speak.** Ed. by Philip S. Foner. (Illus.). 310p. 1995. reprint ed. pap. 13.95 (*0-306-80627-4*) Da Capo.

Black Paradise: The Rastafarian Movement. rev. ed. Peter B. Clarke & Bonnie F. Petry. LC 93-32884. (Black Political Studies: No. 5). 126p. 1994. pap. 15.00 (*0-8095-8005-5*) Borgo Pr.

Black Paradise: The Rastafarian Movement. rev. ed. Peter B. Clarke & Bonnie L. Petry. LC 93-32884. (Black Political Studies: No. 5). 126p. 1994. lib. bdg. 25.00x (*0-8095-8008-X*) Borgo Pr.

Black Parenting: Strategies for Training. Kirby T. Alvy. 260p. 1992. reprint ed. pap. 19.95 (*0-8290-2636-3*) Irvington.

Black Parent's Handbook to Educating Your Children: Outside of the Classroom. Baruti K. Kafele. LC 91-91992. (Illus.). 88p. (Orig.). 1991. pap. 5.95 (*0-9629369-0-1*) Baruti Pub.

Black Path of Fear. Cornell Woolrich. 17.95 (*0-88411-864-9*, Aeonian Pr) Amereon Ltd.

Black Patie: The Life & Times of Patrick Stewart, Earl of Orkney, Lord of Shetland. Peter D. Anderson. 250p. (C). 1989. 75.00 (*0-85976-355-2*, Pub. by J Donald) St Mut.

Black Pearl. Scott O'Dell. 96p. (gr. 7 up). 1977. mass mkt. 3.99 (*0-440-90803-5*, LFL) Dell.

Black Pearl. Scott O'Dell. LC 67-23311. (Illus.). 160p. (J). (gr. 7 up). 1967. 14.95 (*0-395-06961-0*) HM.

Black Pearl: A Literature Unit. Concetta D. Ryan. (Literature Units Ser.). (Illus.). 48p. (Orig.). (gr. 3-5). 1992. student ed 6.95 (*1-55734-410-8*) Tchr Create Mat.

Black Pearl: A Study Guide. Anita Tuchman. (Novel-Ties Ser.). (YA). (gr. 7-12). 1984. student ed, teacher ed 15.95 (*0-88122-106-6*) Lrn Links.

Black Pearls: Blues Queens of the 1920s. Daphne D. Harrison. (Illus.). 1988. 19.95 (*0-8135-1279-4*) Rutgers U Pr.

Black Pearls: Blues Queens of the 1920s. Daphne D. Harrison. (Illus.). 225p. 1990. pap. 13.95 (*0-8135-1280-8*) Rutgers U Pr.

Black Pearls: Daily Meditations, Affirmations, & Inspirations for African Americans. Eric V. Copage. LC 92-33186. 1993. 10.00 (*0-688-12291-4*) Morrow.

***Black Pearls for Parents: Meditations, Affirmations & Inspirations for African-American...** Eric V. Copage. LC 94-33073. 1995. pap. 10.00 (*0-688-13098-4*, Quill) Morrow.

***Black Pearls Journal.** Eric V. Copage. LC 94-3417. 1995. write for info. (*0-688-13967-1*) Morrow.

Black Pentecostalism: Southern Religion in an Urban World. Arthur E. Paris. LC 81-16169. 192p. 1982. lib. bdg. 25.00 (*0-87023-353-X*) U of Mass Pr.

***Black People in the British Empire.** Fryer. (C). 1988. pap. text ed. 17.00 (*0-7453-0342-0*) Westview.

Black People in the British Empire: An Introduction. Peter Fryer. 174p. (C). 1988. text ed. 55.50 (*0-7453-0268-8*, Pub. by Pluto Pr UK) Westview.

Black People in the Methodist Church: Whither Thou Goest? William B. McClain. 160p. (Orig.). 1985. pap. 8.95 (*0-687-03588-0*) Abingdon.

Black People Who Made the Old West. William L. Katz. LC 92-26779. (Illus.). 1992. 35.00 (*0-86543-363-1*); pap. 14.95 (*0-86543-364-X*) Africa World.

Black Pete - Outlaw. large type ed. John Dyson. (Linford Western Library). 272p. 1993. pap. 14.95 (*0-7089-7434-1*, Linford) Ulverscroft.

Black Phalanx: A History of the Negro Soldiers of the U. S. in the Wars of 1775-1812, 1861-1865. Joseph T. Wilson. LC 68-29023. (American Negro: His History & Literature, Ser. No. 1). (Illus.). 1974. reprint ed. 41.95 (*0-405-01845-2*) Ayer.

Black Phalanx: African American Soldiers in the War of Independence, the War of 1812, & the Civil War. Joseph T. Wilson. (Illus.). 534p. reprint ed. pap. 16.95 (*0-306-80550-2*) Da Capo.

Black Phoenix. George Bernau. 304p. 1994. 22.95 (*0-446-51610-4*) Warner Bks.

Black Phoenix. George Bernau. 304p. 1995. mass mkt. 5.99 (*0-446-60182-9*) Warner Bks.

Black Phoenix: A Volume of Values. Michael A. Williams. 135p. 1988. lib. bdg. write for info. (*1-878527-01-0*) Black Phoenix Pr.

Black Photographers, Illustrated Bio-Bibliography, 1940-1980. Deborah Willis-Thomas. LC 88-11200. (Illus.). 500p. 1989. 95.00 (*0-8240-8389-X*) Garland.

Black Physician's Story: Bringing Hope in Mississippi. Douglas L. Conner & John F. Marszalek. LC 85-9106. (Illus.). 197p. reprint ed. pap. 56.20 (*0-8357-4339-X*, 2037141) Bks Demand.

Black Picture Show. Bill Gunn. LC 75-27165. 1975. pap. 2.95 (*0-918408-03-2*) Reed & Cannon.

***Black Pig Bk. 1: In Red Ochre.** Denis Mahoney. 1994. pap. 7.00 (*0-614-04109-0*) Hozomeen Pr.

***Black Pioneers in a White Denomination.** 3rd ed. Mark D. Morrison-Reed & Andrew J. Young. LC 94-32438. 1994. 17.00 (*1-55896-250-6*) Unitarian Univ.

Black Pioneers of Science & Invention. Louis Haber. (J). (gr. 5 up). 1992. pap. 5.95 (*0-15-208566-1*, HB Juv Bks) HarBrace.

***Black Plays Three.** Yvonne Brewster. 256p. 1995. pap. 17.95 (*0-413-69130-6*, A0727) Heinemann.

Black Plumes. Margery Allingham. 276p. 1993. 19.95 (*0-89190-191-4*, Am Repr) Amereon Ltd.

***Black Plumes.** Margery Allingham. 1994. lib. bdg. 18.95x (*1-56849-458-0*) Buccaneer Bks.

***Black Plumes.** Margery Allingham. 192p. 1995. mass mkt. 3.95 (*0-7867-0290-7*) Carroll & Graf.

Black Plumes. Margery Allingham. 20.95 (*1-56723-002-4*) Yestermorrow.

Black Poets. Ed. by Dudley Randall. (Illus.). 384p. 1985. mass mkt. 5.95 (*0-553-27563-1*, Bantam Classics) Bantam.

Black Point. Jerome T. Burke. 325p. (Orig.). 1994. pap. text ed. 12.00 (*0-9639096-0-6*) HollyCourt Pr.

Black Police, White Society. Stephen H. Leinen. LC 83-23622. 250p. 1985. 45.00x (*0-8147-5008-7*); pap. 17.50x (*0-8147-5017-6*) NYU Pr.

Black Political Mobilization, Leadership, Power, & Mass Behavior. Minion K. Morrison. LC 86-30051. (Afro-American Studies). 303p. 1987. 64.50 (*0-88706-515-5*); pap. 21.95 (*0-88706-516-3*) State U NY Pr.

Black Political Participation: Patterns & Trends in Voting Representation. David Bositis & Milton Morris. 200p. (C). 1992. lib. bdg. 45.00 (*0-941410-97-8*); pap. text ed. 17.50 (*0-941410-98-6*) Jt Ctr Pol Studies.

Black Politicians & Reconstruction in Georgia: A Splendid Failure. Edmund L. Drago. LC 82-232. xii, 204p. (C). 1982. text ed. 30.00 (*0-8071-1021-3*) La State U Pr.

Black Politicians & Reconstruction in Georgia: A Splendid Failure. Edmund L. Drago. LC 91-47033. (Brown Thrasher Bks.). (Illus.). 232p. 1992. reprint ed. pap. 17.95 (*0-8203-1438-2*) U of Ga Pr.

Black Politics: A Study & Annotated Bibliography of the Mississippi Freedom Democratic Party. Ed. by Jennifer McDowell. LC 68-58320. 1971. pap. 6.95 (*0-930142-02-0*) Merlin Pr.

Black Politics & Black Political Behavior: A Linkage Analysis. Hanes Walton. LC 93-50062. 416p. 1994. text ed. 59.95 (*0-275-94832-3*, Praeger Pubs) Greenwood.

Black Politics & Black Political Behavior: A Linkage Analysis. Ed. by Hanes Walton. LC 93-50062. 416p. 1994. pap. text ed. 19.95 (*0-275-94988-5*, Praeger Pubs) Greenwood.

Black Politics in Britain. Ed. by Harry Goulbourne. (Illus.). 213p. 1990. text ed. 59.95 (*0-566-07148-7*, Pub. by Avebury Pub UK) Ashgate Pub Co.

Black Politics in Conservative America. Marcus D. Pohlmann. 271p. (Orig.). (C). 1990. pap. text ed. 27.50 (*0-582-28684-0*, 71697) Longman.

***Black Pope.** David L. Anderson. 360p. 1995. pap. 9.95 (*0-614-05128-2*) NW Pub.

Black Popular Culture: A Project by Michele Wallace. Michele Wallace et al. LC 89-650815. (Discussions in Contemporary Culture Ser.: No. 8). (Illus.). 84p. (Orig.). 1993. pap. 18.95 (*0-941920-23-2*) Bay Pr.

Black Popular Music in America: From the Spirituals, Minstrels, & Ragtime to Soul, Disco, & Hip-Hop. Arnold Shaw. 1986. text ed. 21.95 (*0-02-872310-4*) Schirmer Bks.

***Black Population in the United States.** 1995. lib. bdg. 250.00 (*0-8490-6516-X*) Gordon Pr.

Black Population in the United States: A Statistical Profile. (Illus.). 112p. (Orig.). (C). 1994. pap. text ed. 45.00 (*0-7881-0236-2*) Diane Pub.

Black Pottery of Coyotepec, Oaxaca, Mexico. Paul Van de Velde & Henrietta Van de Velde. 43p. 1939. pap. 5.00 (*0-916561-10-0*) Southwest Mus.

***Black Powder.** David Thompson. (Wilderness Ser.: Vol. 21). 176p. 1995. mass mkt. 3.99 (*0-8439-3820-X*) Dorchester Pub Co.

Black Powder Guide. 2nd ed. George C. Nonte, Jr. LC 79-82028. (Illus.). 256p. 1979. pap. 14.95 (*0-88317-069-8*) Stoeger Pub Co.

Black Powder Hobby Gunsmithing. Sam Fadala & Dale Storey. (Illus.). 256p. (Orig.). 1994. pap. 17.95 (*0-87349-153-X*) DBI.

Black-Powder Hunting Secrets. John Phillips. LC 93-79798. (Illus.). 160p. (Orig.). 1993. pap. text ed. 11.95 (*0-936513-38-1*) Larsens Outdoor.

Black Powder Justice. David Thompson. (Wilderness Ser.: No. 6). 176p. (Orig.). 1991. pap. 2.95 (*0-8439-3149-3*) Dorchester Pub Co.

Black Powder Notebook. Sam Fadala. 1993. 22.50 (*1-879356-36-8*) Wolfe Pub Co.

Black Powder Posse. Eric Allen. 224p. 1985. pap. 2.50 (*0-8217-1567-4*) Zebra.

***Black Power.** Richard Wright. 384p. 1995. pap. 12.00 (*0-06-092566-3*, PL) HarpC.

Black Power: A Record of Reactions in a Land of Pathos. Richard A. Wright. LC 73-13457. (Illus.). 358p. 1974. reprint ed. text ed. 59.75 (*0-8371-7136-9*, WRBP, Greenwood Pr) Greenwood.

Black Power: The Politics of Liberation in America. Stokely S. Carmichael & Charles V. Hamilton. 1967. pap. 6.95 (*0-394-70033-3*, V33, Vin) Random.

Black Power: The Politics of Liberation in America. Stokely S. Carmichael & Charles V. Hamilton. LC 92-60284. 1992. pap. 10.00 (*0-679-74313-8*, Vin) Random.

Black Power Gary Style: The Making of Mayor Richard Gordon Hatcher. Alex Poinsett. LC 72-128545. 1970. 6.95 (*0-87485-042-8*) Johnson Chi.

Black Power Ideologies: An Essay in African-American Political Thought. John T. McCartney. 256p. (C). 1992. 44.95 (*0-87722-914-7*); pap. 18.95 (*1-56639-145-8*) Temple U Pr.

Black Power Imperative: Racial Inequality & the Politics of Nonviolence. Theodore Cross. LC 84-80109. 907p. 1984. 19.95 (*0-916631-00-1*) Faulkner Bks.

Black Power Imperative: Racial Inequality & the Politics of Nonviolence. rev. ed. Theodore Cross. 950p. 1986. pap. 9.95 (*0-685-13558-6*) Faulkner Bks.

Black Power in Chicago: Harold Washington & the Crisis of the Black Middle Class: Mass Protest, Vol. 1. Abdul Alkalimat. (Black Power in Chicago Ser.). 150p. 1987. 15.95 (*0-940103-10-9*); pap. 5.95 (*0-940103-11-7*) Twenty First Bks.

Black Power in South Africa: The Evolution of an Ideology. Gail M. Gerhart. LC 75-13149. (Perspectives on Southern Africa Ser.: No. 19). 1978. pap. 16.00 (*0-520-03933-5*) U CA Pr.

Black Power in the Caribbean. W. F. Elkins. 1976. lib. bdg. 250.00 (*0-87700-234-7*) Revisionist Pr.

Black Power Revolt. Ed. by Floyd B. Barbour. LC 67-31432. (Extending Horizons Ser.). 288p. (C). 1968. 5.95 (*0-87558-038-6*) Porter Sargent.

Black Preacher to White America: The Collected Writings of Lemuel Haynes, 1774-1833. Ed. by Richard Newman. LC 89-48246. 291p. 1989. 75.00 (*0-926019-24-4*) Carlson Pub.

Black Preaching: The Recovery of a Powerful Art. Henry H. Mitchell. LC 90-38642. 1990. pap. 12.95 (*0-687-03614-3*) Abingdon.

Black Presence in the Bible & the Table of Nations (Genesis 10: 1-32), Vol. 2: With Emphasis on the Hamitic Genealogical Line from a Black Perspective. Walter A. McCray. LC 90-83436. (Illus.). 210p. (Orig.). (C). 1991. pap. 19.95 (*0-933176-13-9*) Black Light Fellow.

Black Presence in the Bible, Vol. 1: Discovering the Black & African Identity of Biblical Persons & Nations. Walter A. McCray. LC 90-80108. (Illus.). 208p. (Orig.). (C). 1991. pap. 19.95 (*0-933176-12-0*) Black Light Fellow.

Black Presence in the Era of the American Revolution. rev. ed. Sidney Kaplan & Emma N. Kaplan. LC 88-22111. (Illus.). 320p. 1989. pap. 17.95 (*0-87023-663-6*) U of Mass Pr.

Black Presidential Politics in America: A Strategic Approach. Ronald Walters. LC 86-30160. (Afro-American Studies). 255p. (C). 1987. 64.50 (*0-88706-546-5*); pap. 21.95 (*0-88706-547-3*) State U NY Pr.

Black Press & the Struggle for Civil Rights. Carl Senna. (African-American Experience Ser.). (Illus.). 176p. (YA). (gr. 7-12). 1993. lib. bdg. 14.98 (*0-531-11036-2*) Watts.

Black Press & the Struggle for Civil Rights. Carl Senna. (African-American Experience Ser.). (Illus.). (YA). (gr. 7-12). 1994. pap. 6.95 (*0-531-15693-1*) Watts.

Black Press in America: A Bibliography. Henry G. La Brie. 1974. pap. 3.50 (*0-89080-003-0*) Mercer Hse.

Black Press in Mississippi, 1865-1985. Julius E. Thompson. LC 92-28135. (Illus.). 240p. 1993. 34.95 (*0-8130-1174-4*) U Press Fla.

***Black Press in the Middle West, 1865-1985.** Ed. by Henry Lewis Suggs. LC 95-4668. (Contributions in Afro-American & African Studies: Vol. 177). 1996. text ed. write for info. (*0-313-25579-2*, Greenwood Pr) Greenwood.

Black Press in the South, Eighteen Sixty-Five to Nineteen Seventy-Nine. Ed. by Henry L. Suggs. LC 83-825. (Contributions in Afro-American & African Studies: No. 74). xi, 468p. 1983. text ed. 79.50 (*0-313-22244-4*, SBL/, Greenwood Pr) Greenwood.

Black Press, U. S. A. 2nd ed. Roland E. Wolseley. LC 89-31302. (Illus.). 478p. 1990. pap. text ed. 22.95 (*0-8138-0496-5*) Iowa St U Pr.

Black Press Views American Imperialism (1898-1900) George P. Marks. 1973. 24.95 (*0-405-01985-8*, 19466) Ayer.

Black Priest, White Church: Catholics & Racism. Lawrence E. Lucas & Bruce M. Wright. LC 88-71876. 280p. (C). 1989. 29.95 (*0-86543-108-6*); pap. 9.95 (*0-86543-109-4*) Africa World.

Black Prince. Iris Murdoch. 224p. 1983. pap. 12.95 (*0-14-003934-1*, Penguin Bks) Viking Penguin.

Black Prince. David Birt. (Resouces Units: Middle Ages, 1066-1484 Ser.). (Illus.). 24p. 1974. reprint ed. pap. text ed. 12.95 (*0-582-39382-5*) Longman.

Black Printmakers & the WPA. Leslie King-Hammond & Elisabeth Lorin. LC 89-80391. (Illus.). 35p. 1989. 10.00 (*0-685-70926-4*) Gal Assn NY.

***Black Progress Question: Explaining the African-American Predicament.** Stephen Burman. (Sage Series on Race & Ethnic Relations: Vol. 9). 240p. 1994. 49.95 (*0-8039-5060-8*); pap. 24.00 (*0-8039-5061-6*) Sage.

Black Property Owners in the South, 1790-1915. Loren Schweninger. (Blacks in the New World Ser.). (Illus.). 448p. 1990. 49.95 (*0-252-01678-5*) U of Ill Pr.

Black Prophets of Justice: Activist Clergy Before the Civil War. David E. Swift. LC 88-30327. (Illus.). xiii, 376p. 1989. text ed. 42.50 (*0-8071-1461-8*) La State U Pr.

Black Protagonist in the Cuban Novel. Pedro Barreda. Tr. by Page Bancroft. LC 78-19689. 192p. 1979. lib. bdg. 25.00 (*0-87023-262-2*) U of Mass Pr.

Black Protest. Ed. by Joann E. Grant. (Black History Titles Ser.). 1986. mass mkt. 4.95 (*0-449-30044-7*) Fawcett.

Black Protest: Issues & Tactics. Robert C. Dick. LC 72-794. 320p. 1974. text ed. 75.00 (*0-8371-6366-8*, DNAPB, Greenwood Pr) Greenwood.

B

An Asterisk (*) at the beginning of an entry indicates that the title is appearing in BIP for the first time.

An Asterisk (*) at the beginning of an entry indicates that the title is appearing in BIP for the first time.

805

B

Black Sisters, Speak Out. Thiam Awa. (C). 1986. pap. text ed. 18.95 (*0-7453-0050-2*) Westview.

Black Skimmer: The Social Dynamics of a Colonial Species. Joanna Burger & Michael Gochfeld. (Illus.). 416p. 1990. text ed. 47.50 (*0-231-07106-X*) Col U Pr.

Black Skin: Structure & Function. Ed. by William Montagna et al. LC 93-14784. 158p. 1993. text ed. 49.95 (*0-12-505260-X*) Acad Pr.

Black Skin, White Masks. Frantz Fanon. Tr. by Charles Markmann. 240p. 1989. pap. 10.95 (*0-8021-5084-5*) Grove-Atltic.

Black Sky. William H. Lovejoy. 1990. mass mkt. 4.50 (*0-8217-3236-6*) Zebra.

Black Slave Woman: Protagonist for Freedom. A. Faulkner Watts. pap. write for info. (*0-914110-10-1*) Blyden Pr.

Black Slaveowners: Free Black Slave Masters in South Carolina, 1790-1860. Larry Koger. LC 84-43203. 300p. 1985. lib. bdg. 32.50x (*0-89950-160-5*) McFarland & Co.

***Black Slaveowners: Free Black Slave Masters in South Carolina, 1790-1860.** Comp. by Larry Koger. LC 94-43848. 1995. pap. write for info. (*1-57003-037-5*) U of SC Pr.

Black Slavery in the Americas: An Interdisciplinary Bibliography, 1865-1980, 2 vols., 1. Comp. by John D. Smith. LC 82-11737. xxix, 2712p. 1982. text ed. 95.00 (*0-313-23675-5*, SMB/01) Greenwood.

Black Slavery in the Americas: An Interdisciplinary Bibliography, 1865-1980, 2 vols., Set. Comp. by John D. Smith. LC 82-11737. xxix, 2712p. 1982. text ed. 175.00 (*0-313-23118-4*, SMB/) Greenwood.

Black Slavery in the Americas: An Interdisciplinary Bibliography, 1865-1980, 2 vols., Vol. 2. Comp. by John D. Smith. LC 82-11737. xxix, 2712p. 1982. text ed. 95.00 (*0-313-23676-3*, SMB/02) Greenwood.

Black Slip. Terry Wolverton. 91p. (Orig.). 1992. pap. 7.95 (*1-878533-05-3*) Clothespin Fever Pr.

***Black-Smart.** Mba Mbulu. 1995. pap. 10.00 (*1-883885-09-4*) The People.

Black Smiles: Or, the Sunny Side of Sable Life. Franklin H. Bryant. LC 72-178469. (Black Heritage Library Collection). 1977. reprint ed. 15.95 (*0-8369-8917-1*) Ayer.

Black Snow. Liu Heng. Tr. by Howard Goldblatt. 256p. 1994. pap. 11.00 (*0-8021-3389-4*) Grove-Atltic.

Black Snow. Keith Reddin. 1993. 4.75 (*0-8222-1371-0*) Dramatists Play.

Black Snowball. Leydel J. Willis. LC 76-57069. 1977. 8.95 (*0-8187-0027-0*) Clodele.

Black Snowman. Phil Mendez. (Illus.). (J). (gr. 2-5). 1989. 14.95 (*0-590-40552-7*) Scholastic Inc.

Black Snowman. Phil Mendez. (Illus.). 48p. (J). 1991. pap. 4.95 (*0-590-44873-0*, Blue Ribbon Bks) Scholastic Inc.

Black Society. Geri Major. 1977. 25.00 (*0-87485-075-4*) Johnson Chi.

***Black Soldiers in Jim Crow Texas, 1899-1917.** Garna L. Christian. (Centennial Series of the Association of Former Students: No. 57). (Illus.). 256p. 1995. 35.00x (*0-89096-637-0*) Tex A&M Univ Pr.

Black Soldiers in the Colonial Militia: Documents from 1639 to 1780. Ed. by Edward Sandel. 100p. 1994. spiral bd. 22.50 (*0-9636425-1-0*) Tabor-Lucas.

Black Soul White Artifact: Fanon's Clinical Psychology & Social Theory. Jock McCulloch. LC 82-14605. 240p. 1983. 54.95 (*0-521-24700-4*) Cambridge U Pr.

Black South African Writing Today. Jane Watts. 272p. 1989. text ed. 45.00 (*0-312-02732-X*) St Martin.

Black Southern Voices: An Anthology of Fiction, Poetry, Nonfiction, Drama, & Critical Essays. Ed. by John O. Killens & Jerry W. Ward, Jr. 496p. (Orig.). 1992. pap. 15.00 (*0-452-01096-9*, Mer) NAL-Dutton.

Black Southerners & the Law, 1865-1900. Intro. by Donald G. Nieman. LC 93-29263. (African American Life in the Post-Emancipation South Ser.: Vol. 12). 488p. 1994. 73.00 (*0-8153-1449-3*) Garland.

Black Spider. Jeremias Gotthelf. Tr. by H. M. Waidson. (Orig.). 1980. pap. 9.95 (*0-7145-0126-3*) Riverrun NY.

***Black Spider over Tiegenhof.** James D. Yoder. 232p. (Orig.). 1995. pap. 10.95 (*0-8361-9012-2*) Herald Pr.

Black Spine. TSR, Inc. Staff. (Illus.). Date not set. 25.00 (*1-56076-824-X*) TSR Inc.

Black Spirits & White: A Book of Ghost Stories. Ralph A. Cram. LC 70-167445. (Short Story Index Reprint Ser.). 1977. reprint ed. 17.95 (*0-8369-3971-9*) Ayer.

Black Spiritual Movement: A Religious Response to Racism. Hans A. Baer. LC 83-14559. 232p. 1984. pap. 16.00 (*0-87049-515-1*) U of Tenn Pr.

Black Spring. Henry Miller. 244p. 1989. pap. 10.95 (*0-8021-3182-4*) Grove-Atltic.

Black Square & Compass: 200 Years of Prince Hall Freemasonry. rev. ed. Joseph A. Walkes, Jr. LC 79-112352. xvi, 176p. 1994. reprint ed. text ed. 16.95 (*0-88053-061-8*, M 324) Macoy Pub.

Black Squares on White Pieces. Alex Varenne. Ed. by Bernd Metz. Tr. by Elizabeth Bell. (Illus.). 49p. (Orig.). 1991. pap. 9.95 (*0-87416-132-0*) Catalan Communs.

Black Stallion. Walter Farley. LC 85-19927. (Illus.). (J). (gr. 3-7). 1944. lib. bdg. 13.99 (*0-394-90601-2*) Random Bks Yng Read.

Black Stallion see Walter Farley's Black Stallion Books

Black Stallion & Satan see Walter Farley's Black Stallion Books

Black Stallion Challenged. Walter Farley. LC 64-15094. (Illus.). (J). (gr. 5-9). 1980. pap. 3.95 (*0-394-84371-1*) Random Bks Yng Read.

Black Stallion Mystery see Walter Farley's Black Stallion Books

Black Stallion Returns see Walter Farley's Black Stallion Books

Black Stallion's Blood Bay Colt. Walter Farley. LC 50-9584. 288p. (J). (gr. 4-7). 1994. pap. 3.95 (*0-679-81347-0*) Random Bks Yng Read.

Black Stallion's Filly. Walter Farley. LC 52-7216. (Illus.). (J). (gr. 4-6). 1978. pap. 3.95 (*0-394-83916-1*) Random Bks Yng Read.

***Black Stallion's Ghost.** Farley. (J). 1995. 4.99 (*0-679-86950-6*) Random.

Black Stallion's Ghost. Walter Farley. (Illus.). (J). (gr. 5-9). 1978. pap. 3.95 (*0-394-83919-6*) Random Bks Yng Read.

***Black Stallion's Shadow.** Steven Farley. LC 94-41239. (Black Stallion Ser.). (J). 1995. 13.00 (*0-679-85004-X*) Random.

Black Star. Johnston McCulley. reprint ed. lib. bdg. 20.95 (*0-89190-995-8*, Rivercity Pr) Amereon Ltd.

Black Star, Bright Dawn. Scott O'Dell. 112p. 1989. mass mkt. 3.99 (*0-449-70340-1*, Juniper) Fawcett.

Black Star, Bright Dawn. Scott O'Dell. LC 87-35351. 144p. (J). (gr. 5-9). 1988. 14.95 (*0-395-47778-6*) HM.

Black Starlet. Bobbye B. Vance. (Orig.). 1983. pap. 2.25 (*0-87067-217-7*, BH217) Holloway.

Black Star's Campaign. Johnston McCulley. reprint ed. lib. bdg. 20.95 (*0-89190-996-6*, Rivercity Pr) Amereon Ltd.

Black Stars in Orbit: NASA's African-American Astronauts. Khephra Burns & William Miles. LC 93-44624. (J). 1995. 18.95 (*0-15-200432-7*) HarBrace.

***Black Stars in Orbit: NASA's African-American Astronauts.** Khephra Burns & William Miles. LC 93-44624. (J). (gr. 3 up). 1995. pap. 8.95 (*0-15-200276-6*) HarBrace.

Black Star's Return. Johnston McCulley. reprint ed. lib. bdg. 20.95 (*0-89190-997-4*, Rivercity Pr) Amereon Ltd.

Black State of the Arts: A Guide to Developing a Successful Career As a Black Performing Artist. Tanya Monique-Kersey & Bruce Hawkins. LC 90-91817. (Illus.). 352p. 1995. pap. 19.95 (*0-9627515-0-2*) Love Child.

Black Steel. Steve Perry. 1992. mass mkt. 4.99 (*0-441-06698-4*) Ace Bks.

Black Stone. Abdus Samad Sharfuddin. 24p. (Orig.). 1985. pap. 1.50 (*1-56744-235-8*) Kazi Pubns.

***Black Stork: Eugenics & the Death of "Defective" Babies in American Medicine & Motion Pictures.** Martin S. Pernick. (Illus.). 256p. 1995. 34.95 (*0-19-507731-8*) OUP.

Black Street. Wallace J. Robertson. 1972. 1.00 (*0-685-67932-2*) Windless Orchard.

Black Street Speech: Its History, Structure, & Survival. John Baugh. (Texas Linguistics Ser.). 160p. (C). 1983. pap. 9.95 (*0-292-70745-2*) U of Tex Pr.

Black Streets of Oakland. rev. ed. Kelly Eagle. (Orig.). 1985. pap. 3.50 (*0-87067-577-X*, BH577) Holloway.

Black Struggle for Public Schooling in Nineteenth-Century Illinois. Robert L. McCaul. LC 86-26004. 208p. 1987. text ed. 24.95 (*0-8093-1335-9*) S Ill U Pr.

Black Students: Psychosocial Issues & Academic Achievement. Ed. by Gordon L. Berry & Joy K. Asamen. (Focus Editions Ser.: Vol. 109). 320p. (C). 1989. 46.00 (*0-8039-3664-8*, D1478); pap. text ed. 23.95 (*0-8039-3665-6*, D1478) Corwin Pr.

Black Students & School Failure: Policies, Practices & Perscriptions. Jacqueline J. Irvine. LC 89-27162. (Contributions in Afro-American & African Studies: No. 131). 168p. 1990. text ed. 39.95 (*0-313-27215-8*, IBA/, Greenwood Pr) Greenwood.

Black Students & School Failure: Policies, Practices, & Prescriptions. Jacqueline J. Irvine. LC 91-3033. 176p. 1991. pap. text ed. 15.95 (*0-275-94094-2*, B4094, Praeger Pubs) Greenwood.

***Black Student's Guide to College Success.** Ruby D. Higgin. LC 94-27944. 392p. 1994. text ed. 39.95 (*0-313-29431-3*, Greenwood Pr); pap. text ed. 35.00 (*0-313-29432-1*, Greenwood Pr) Greenwood.

Black Student's Guide to Colleges: Profiles of 182 Colleges, Black & White. 3rd ed. Barry Beckham. 496p. 1995. pap. 16.95 (*0-931761-07-7*) Beckham House.

Black Student's Guide to Scholarships. Ed. by Ernestine Whiting. 147p. 1995. pap. 9.95 (*0-931761-27-1*) Beckham House.

Black Students in Higher Education: Conditions & Experiences in the 1970's. Ed. by Gail E. Thomas. LC 80-1702. (Contributions to the Study of Education Ser.: No. 1). (Illus.). xx, 405p. 1981. text ed. 89.50 (*0-313-22477-3*, TBS/, Greenwood Pr) Greenwood.

Black Students in Interracial Schools: A Guide for Students, Teachers, & Parents. rev. ed. Ed Smith. LC 94-11686. 126p. 1994. pap. 10.95 (*1-880774-07-0*) Garrett Pk.

Black Students on White Campuses: The Impacts of Increased Black Enrollments. Marvin W. Peterson et al. LC 78-60965. 384p. 1978. 18.00 (*0-87944-221-2*) Inst Soc Res.

Black Studies: A Select Catalog of National Archives Microfilm Publications. National Archives & Records Administration Staff. LC 83-15134. 97p. (Orig.). 1984. pap. text ed. 2.00 (*0-911333-08-8*, 200011) National Archives & Recs.

Black Studies: Pitfalls & Potential. William E. Sims. LC 77-18563. 1978. pap. text ed. 18.50 (*0-8191-0316-0*) U Pr of Amer.

Black Studies: Theory, Method, & Cultural Perspectives. Ed. by Talmadge Anderson. LC 90-42949. 227p. (Orig.). (C). 1990. pap. 15.00x (*0-87422-074-2*) Wash St U Pr.

Black Studies in the Community College. John Lombardi. LC 72-186575. (ERIC Clearinghouse for Junior Colleges, American Association of Junior Colleges, Monograph Ser.: No. 13). 74p. reprint ed. pap. 25.00 (*0-8357-7298-5*, 2020551) Bks Demand.

Black Studies, Rap, & the Academy. Houston A. Baker, Jr. LC 92-42997. (Black Literature & Culture Ser.). (Illus.). 112p. (C). 1993. 16.95 (*0-226-03520-4*) U Ch Pr.

***Black Studies, Rap & the Academy.** Houston A. Baker, Jr. (Illus.). xii, 110p. 1995. pap. 9.95 (*0-226-03521-2*) U Ch Pr.

Black Sun. Edward Abbey. 20.95 (*0-8488-0900-9*) Amereon Ltd.

Black Sun. Edward Abbey. 160p. 1982. mass mkt. 4.95 (*0-380-58503-0*) Avon.

Black Sun. Robert Leininger. 320p. (Orig.). 1991. mass mkt. 4.50 (*0-380-76012-6*) Avon.

Black Sun. rev. ed. Edward Abbey. LC 90-36308. 176p. 1990. reprint ed. pap. 9.95 (*0-88496-319-5*) Capra Pr.

Black Sun. Edward Abbey. 1991. reprint ed. lib. bdg. 21.95 (*1-56849-082-8*) Buccaneer Bks.

Black Sun: A Novel. Edward Abbey. LC 89-7106. 168p. 1990. reprint ed. lib. bdg. 27.00x (*0-8095-4064-9*) Borgo Pr.

Black Sun: Depression & Melancholia. Julia Kristeva. Tr. by Leon S. Roudiez. 300p. 1992. text ed. 31.00 (*0-231-06706-2*) Col U Pr.

Black Sun: The Brief Transit & Violent Eclipse of Harry Crosby. Geoffrey Wolff. 1985. 14.00 (*0-394-72472-0*, Vin) Random.

Black Sun: The Eyes of Four. Mark Holborn. (Illus.). 80p. 1986. 25.00 (*0-89381-185-8*) Aperture.

Black Sun Rising. C. S. Friedman. 496p. (Orig.). 1991. 18.95 (*0-88677-485-3*) DAW Bks.

Black Sun Rising. C. S. Friedman. 592p. (Orig.). 1992. mass mkt. 5.99 (*0-88677-527-2*) DAW Bks.

Black Sunday. Thomas Harris. 318p. 1991. reprint ed. lib. bdg. 24.95 (*0-89966-876-3*) Buccaneer Bks.

Black Sunday. Thomas Harris. 1990. reprint ed. mass mkt. 5.99 (*0-440-20614-6*) Dell.

***Black Sunday: Ploesti!** Michael Hill. (Illus.). 256p. 1993. 45.00 (*0-88740-519-3*) Schiffer.

Black Sunlight. Dambudzo Marechera. (African Writers Ser.). (Orig.). (C). 1981. pap. 9.95 (*0-435-90237-7*) Heinemann.

***Black Survival in White America: From Past History to the Next Century.** Jeanette Davis-Adeshote. Ed. by Gwendolynne A. Blakeley. LC 94-79897. 128p. (Orig.). (C). 1995. pap. 10.95 (*0-9638672-3-7*) Bryant & Dillon.

Black Swan. Farrukh Dhondy. LC 92-30425. 208p. (YA). (gr. 6 up). 1993. 14.95 (*0-395-66076-9*) HM.

Black Swan. Paula Z. Hogan. LC 78-27416. (Life Cycles Bks.). (Illus.). 32p. (J). (gr. 1-4). 1979. lib. bdg. 19.97 (*0-8172-1254-X*) Raintree Steck-V.

Black Swan. Paula Z. Hogan. LC 78-27416. (Life Cycles Clippers Ser.). (Illus.). 32p. (J). (gr. 1-4). 1984. audio, lib. bdg. 29.28 (*0-8172-2225-1*) Raintree Steck-V.

Black Swan. Thomas Mann. Tr. by Willard R. Trask. 155p. 1990. 22.00 (*0-520-07008-9*); pap. 12.00 (*0-520-07009-7*) U CA Pr.

Black Swan. large type ed. Catherine Dunn. 1990. 21.95 (*0-7089-2169-8*) Ulverscroft.

Black Swan. large type ed. Victoria Holt. 1992. pap. 16.95 (*0-7927-0670-6*, Paragon Lrg Print) Chivers N Amer.

Black Swan. Raphael Sabatini. 1976. reprint ed. lib. bdg. 22.95 (*0-89190-741-6*, Rivercity Pr) Amereon Ltd.

Black Swan & the Green See Saw. Blanche Greer. LC 75-261399. (Illus.). (J). (gr. 5 up). 1977. 4.50 (*0-930422-07-4*) Dennis-Landman.

***Black Swan, White Crow.** J. Patrick Lewis. (Illus.). 1995. 14.00 (*0-689-31899-5*, Atheneum Bks Young) S&S Childrens.

Black Swans: Stories. Eve Babitz. LC 92-42924. 1993. 22.00 (*0-679-40518-6*) Knopf.

Black Swans (a Russian Folktale) Tr. & Ret. by Eli Weinerman. (Illus.). 32p. (J). (gr. k-3). 1995. 15.95 (*0-945912-19-6*) Pippin Pr.

Black-Tailed Prairie Dog: Social Life of a Burrowing Mammal. John L. Hoogland. LC 94-13897. (Wildlife Behavior & Ecology Ser.). 1995. lib. bdg. 90.00 (*0-226-35117-3*); pap. text ed. 34.95 (*0-226-35118-1*) U Ch Pr.

***Black Talent Resource Guide: 1994 Edition.** Tanya Kersey-Henley. 176p. 1995. pap. 14.95 (*1-882613-03-1*) Love Child.

Black Talent Resource Guide, 1992. Ed. by Tanya-Monique Kersey & Bruce Hawkins. 170p. (Orig.). 1992. pap. 14.95 (*0-9627515-5-3*) Love Child.

Black Talent Resource Guide '94. Ed. by Tanya Kersey. 104p. (Orig.). 1994. pap. 14.95 (*1-882613-00-7*) Love Child.

Black Talk. Ben Sidran. LC 83-28567. (Roots of Jazz Ser.). xvii, 201p. 1981. reprint ed. lib. bdg. 27.50 (*0-306-76056-8*) Da Capo.

Black Talk. Ben Sidran. LC 82-23652. (Quality Paperbacks Ser.). 244p. 1983. reprint ed. pap. 9.95 (*0-306-80184-1*) Da Capo.

Black Talk: Words & Phrases from the Hood to the Amen Corner. Geneva Smitherman. 1994. 17.95 (*0-395-67410-7*); pap. 10.95 (*0-395-69992-4*) HM.

Black Teacher & the Dramatic Arts: A Dialogue, Bibliography & Anthology. William R. Reardon & Thomas D. Pawley. LC 73-90789. 487p. 1970. text ed. 65.00 (*0-8371-1850-6*, RET&, Negro U Pr) Greenwood.

Black Tears. Gerd Darner. 1993. 17.95 (*0-533-10478-5*) Vantage.

Black Teenage Mothers: Pregnancy & Child Rearing from Their Perspective. Constance W. Williams. 208p. 1990. 24.95 (*0-669-24313-2*) Heath.

Black Tennesseans, Nineteen Hundred to Nineteen Thirty. Lester C. Lamon. LC 76-49583. (Twentieth-Century America Ser.). 338p. reprint ed. pap. 96.40 (*0-8357-7299-3*, 2025561) Bks Demand.

Black Tents. Fazullah Rouhani. (Middle Eastern Ser.: No. 19). Orig. Title: Chadur-ha-ye Siah. (Illus.). 350p. (Orig.). 1986. pap. 17.00 (*0-936665-06-8*) Jahan Bk Co.

Black Texas Women: One Hundred Fifty Years of Trial & Triumph. Ruthe Winegarten. LC 94-7418. (Illus.). 448p. (C). 1995. text ed. 60.00x (*0-292-79087-2*); pap. 24.95 (*0-292-79089-9*) U of Tex Pr.

Black Theater, Dance, & Ritual in South Africa. Peter F. Larlham. Ed. by Oscar Brockett. LC 85-8758. (Theater & Dramatic Studies: No. 29). 172p. reprint ed. 54.50 (*0-8357-1658-9*, 2070473) Bks Demand.

Black Theater in America. James S. Haskins. LC 81-43874. (Illus.). 160p. (YA). (gr. 7 up). 1991. lib. bdg. 14.89 (*0-690-04129-2*, Crowell Jr Bks) HarpC Child Bks.

Black Theater, U. S. A. Forty-Five Plays by Black Americans, 1847-1974. Ed. by James V. Hatch & Ted Shine. LC 75-169234. 1974. 39.95 (*0-02-914160-5*) Free Pr.

Black Theatre: Premise & Presentation. rev. ed. Carlton W. Molette & Barbara J. Molette. LC 86-50584. 266p. (C). 1992. pap. text ed. 19.95 (*0-932269-94-X*) Wyndhall Pr.

Black Theatre: Premise & Presentation. 2nd rev. ed. Carlton W. Molette & Barbara J. Molette. LC 86-50584. 266p. (C). 1992. text ed. 29.95 (*1-55605-212-X*) Wyndhall Pr.

Black Theatre & Performance: A Pan-African Bibliography. Comp. by John Gray. LC 89-25836. (Bibliographies & Indexes in Afro-American & African Studies: No. 25). 448p. 1990. text ed. 55.00 (*0-313-26875-4*, GBT/, Greenwood Pr) Greenwood.

Black Theatre in the Nineteen Sixties & Seventies: A Historical-Critical Analysis of the Movement. Mance Williams. LC 84-22506. (Contributions in Afro-American & African Studies: No. 87). (Illus.). i, 188p. 1985. text ed. 55.00 (*0-313-23835-9*, WBT/) Greenwood.

Black Theology, 2 vols., Set. 2nd ed. James H. Cone & Gayraud S. Wilmore. 1993. boxed 34.95 (*0-88344-868-8*) Orbis Bks.

Black Theology: A Critical Assessment & Annotated Bibliography. Comp. by James H. Evans, Jr. LC 87-142. (Bibliographies & Indexes in Religious Studies: No. 10). 217p. 1987. text ed. 49.95 (*0-313-24822-2*, EBT/, Greenwood Pr) Greenwood.

Black Theology: A Documentary History, 1966-1979. Ed. by Gayraud S. Wilmore & James H. Cone. LC 79-12747. 669p. reprint ed. pap. 180.00 (*0-8357-8817-2*, 2033468) Bks Demand.

Black Theology: A Documentary History, 1966-1979, Vol. 1. 2nd abr. rev. ed. James H. Cone & Gayraud S. Wilmore. LC 92-44927. 400p. 1993. pap. 18.95 (*0-88344-853-X*) Orbis Bks.

Black Theology: Removing the Veil. Kenneth L. Johnson. 112p. (C). 1989. lib. bdg. 8.00 (*0-9622324-0-8*) Fertil Soil Pub.

Black Theology Vol. 2: A Documentary History, 1980-1992. James H. Cone & Gayraud S. Wilmore. LC 79-12747. 400p. (Orig.). 1993. pap. 18.95 (*0-88344-773-8*) Orbis Bks.

Black Theology & Black Power. James H. Cone. LC 70-76462. (Orig.). 1969. pap. 5.95 (*0-8164-2003-3*, SP59) Harper SF.

***Black Theology & Black Power.** James H. Cone. (Orig.). 1989. pap. text ed. 11.00 (*0-06-254864-6*, HarpT) HarpC.

Black Theology II: Essays on the Formation & Outreach of Contemporary Black Theology. Ed. by Calvin E. Bruce & William R. Jones. LC 75-39113. 285p. 1978. 35.00 (*0-8387-1893-0*) Bucknell U Pr.

Black Theology in Dialogue. J. Deotis Roberts. LC 86-15665. 132p. (Orig.). 1987. pap. 13.99 (*0-664-24022-4*, Westminster) Westminster John Knox.

Black Theology of Liberation: Twentieth Anniversary with Critical Responses. James H. Cone. LC 90-43041. 1990. pap. 14.95 (*0-88344-685-5*) Orbis Bks.

Black Theology Today: Liberation & Contextualization. James D. Roberts. LC 83-17246. (Toronto Studies in Theology: Vol. 12). 218p. 1984. lib. bdg. 99.95 (*0-88946-755-2*) E Mellen.

Black Thorn, White Rose. Ed. by Ellen Datlow & Terri Windling. 1994. 22.00 (*0-688-13713-X*, AvoNova) Avon.

Black Thorne's Rose. Susan King. 384p. (Orig.). 1994. pap. 4.99 (*0-451-40544-7*, Topaz) NAL-Dutton.

Black Thoroughbred the Only Success Formula for Colored People. Frederick L. Davison, II. 320p. (Orig.). 1991. pap. 13.95 (*0-9628544-0-9*) Blk Thoroughbred.

***Black Thoroughbred the Only Success Formula to Make Colored People the New Leaders of the World.** Frederick L. Davison, II. 680p. (Orig.). 1995. 30.00 (*0-9628544-1-7*) Blk Thoroughbred.

Black Throne. Roger Zelazny & Fred Saberhagen. (Orig.). 1990. mass mkt. 4.95 (*0-671-72013-9*) Baen Bks.

Black Thunder: An Anthology of African American Drama. Intro. by William B. Branch. 496p. 1992. pap. 5.99 (*0-451-62844-6*, Ment) NAL-Dutton.

Black Thunder: Gabriel's Revolt: Virginia, 1800. Arna Bontemps. LC 91-34123. 254p. 1992. pap. 14.00 (*0-8070-6337-1*) Beacon Pr.

Black Tickets. George Phillips. 1979. pap. 11.95 (*0-385-28088-2*, Delta) Dell.

***Black Tide: A Lewis Cole Mystery.** Brendan Dubios. LC 94-28920. 1995. 22.00 (*1-883402-58-1*) S&S Trade.

***Black Tides: The Alaska Oil Spill.** B. O'Donoghue. (Illus.). 40p. 1995. pap. 4.95 (*0-930931-05-X*) Alaska Natural.

Black-Tie Affair. Jane Bierce. (Lucky in Love Ser.). 288p. 1992. mass mkt. 3.99 (*0-8217-3834-8*) Zebra.

Black Tie Optional: The Ultimate Guide to Planning & Producing Successful Special Events. Harry A. Freedman & Karen F. Smith. LC 91-70500. 247p. 1993. text ed. 27.95 (*0-930807-17-0*, 600219) Fund Raising.

***Black Ties.** Danielle V. Laguerre. Date not set. pap. 15.00 (*0-9646413-0-5*) Tenaj Pub Hse.

An Asterisk (*) at the beginning of an entry indicates that the title is appearing in BIP for the first time.

B

***Black Women in the Academy: The Secrets to Success & Achievement.** Sheila T. Gregory. 186p. (C). 1995. lib. bdg. 32.50 (0-8191-9890-0) U Pr of Amer.

Black Women in the Cities, Eighteen Seventy-Two to Nineteen Seventy-Five: A Bibliography of Published Works on the Life & Achievements of Black Women in Cities in the U. S., Nos. 751-752. 2nd ed. Lenwood G. Davis. 1975. 7.50 (0-686-20343-7) CPL Biblios.

Black Women in the Fiction of James Baldwin. Trudier Harris. LC 84-27022. 240p. 1985. pap. 18.00 (0-87049-534-8) U of Tenn Pr.

***Black Women in the Middle West Project: A Comprehensive Resource Guide, Illinois & Indiana.** Darlene C. Hine et al. 238p. 1986. pap. 5.00 (1-885323-47-6) IN Hist Bureau.

Black Women in the Workplace: Impacts of Structural Change in the Economy. Bette Woody. LC 91-28745. (Contributions in Women's Studies: No. 126). 224p. 1992. text ed. 55.00 (0-313-25591-1, WBK/, Greenwood Pr) Greenwood.

Black Women in White: Racial Conflict & Cooperation in the Nursing Profession, 1890-1950. Darlene C. Hine. LC 88-46023. (Blacks in the Diaspora Ser.). (Illus.). 288p. 1989. 35.00 (0-253-32773-3); pap. 12.95 (0-253-20529-8, MB-529) Ind U Pr.

B

Black Women in White America: A Documentary History. Ed. by Gerda Lerner. LC 72-8643. 672p. 1988. pap. 12.00 (0-394-71880-1, Vin) Random.

Black Women in White America: A Documentary History. Gerda Lerner. 1992. pap. 15.00 (0-679-74314-6, Vin) Random.

Black Women Models of Houston, Texas. Sheryl H. Clayton. LC 86-61778. 1986. 20.00 (0-9607958-9-8); pap. 16.00 (0-9607958-8-X) Essai Seay Pubns.

Black Women Novelists: The Development of a Tradition, 1892-1976. Barbara Christian. LC 79-8953. (Contributions in Afro-American & African Studies: No. 52). xiv, 275p. 1980. text ed. 55.00 (0-313-20750-X, CBW/) Greenwood.

Black Women Novelists: The Development of a Tradition, 1892-1976. Barbara Christian. LC 79-8953. (Contributions in Afro-American & African Studies: No. 52). xiv, 275p. 1985. pap. text ed. 12.95 (0-313-25057-X, CWBPB) Greenwood.

Black Women Novelists & the Nationalist Aesthetic. Madhu Dubey. LC 93-14343. 1994. 29.95 (0-253-31841-6); pap. 12.95 (0-253-20855-6) Ind U Pr.

***Black Women of the Old West.** William L. Katz. LC 95-9969. (Illus.). (J). 1995. write for info. (0-689-31944-4, Atheneum S&S) S&S Trade.

Black Women Role Models of Greater St. Louis. Ed. by Sheryl H. Clayton. LC 81-71873. 381p. (Orig.). (J). (gr. 6 up). 1982. 14.95 (0-9607958-0-4) Essai Seay Pubns.

Black Women Role Models of Waco, Texas. Sheryl H. Clayton. LC 86-61779. 1986. 16.95 (0-9607958-6-3); pap. 12.95 (0-9607958-7-1) Essai Seay Pubns.

Black Women Writers, 1950-1980: A Critical Evaluation. Ed. by Mari Evans. LC 81-43914. 576p. 1984. pap. 14.95 (0-385-17125-0, Anchor NY) Doubleday.

Black Women, Writing, & Identity: Migrations of the Subject. Carole B. Davies. LC 93-44335. 240p. 1994. 55.00x (0-415-10086-0, B3141, Routledge NY); pap. 16.95 (0-415-10087-9, B3145, Routledge NY) Routledge.

Black Women Writing Autobiography: A Tradition Within a Tradition. Joanne M. Braxton. 240p. (C). 1989. 29.95 (0-87722-639-3) Temple U Pr.

Black Women Writing Autobiography: A Tradition Within a Tradition. Joanne M. Braxton. (Illus.). 240p. 1991. pap. 18.95 (0-87722-803-5) Temple U Pr.

Black Women's Blues: A Literary Anthology: 1934-Present. Rita Dandridge. (G. K. Hall Reference Ser.). 300p. 1992. text ed. 40.00 (0-8161-9084-4, Hall Reference) Macmillan.

Black Women's Health Book: Speaking for Ourselves. 2nd ed. Ed. by Evelyn C. White. LC 93-28901. 396p. (Orig.). 1993. pap. 16.95 (1-878067-40-0) Seal Pr Feminist.

Black Women's History: Theory & Practice, 2 vols., Set. Pref. by Darlene C. Hine. LC 90-1395. (Black Women in United States History Ser.: Vols. 9-10). 740p. 1990. 175.00 (0-926019-16-3) Carlson Pub.

Black Women's Psychology. G. Grant. Date not set. pap. 12.00 (0-06-092475-6) HarpC.

Black Women's Writing. Gina Wisker. 1993. pap. 16.95 (0-312-10582-7) St Martin.

Black Words, White Page: Aboriginal Literature 1929-88. Adam Shoemaker. 256p. (Orig.). (C). 1989. pap. text ed. 29.95 (0-7022-2149-X, Pub. by Univ Queensland Pr AT) Intl Spec Bk.

Black Worker in the Deep South. Hosea Hudson. LC 72-82078. 140p. 1991. pap. 4.95 (0-7178-0683-9) Intl Pubs Co.

Black Workers & the Class Struggle. Roscoe Proctor. 40p. 1972. pap. 0.45 (0-87898-078-4) New Outlook.

Black Workers & the New Unions. Horace R. Cayton & George S. Mitchell. 18.95 (0-405-18493-X) Ayer.

Black Workers in an Industrial Suburb: The Struggle Against Discrimination. Bruce Williams. 238p. 1987. text ed. 40.00 (0-8135-1191-7) Rutgers U Pr.

Black Workers Selections: A Documentary History from Colonial Times to the Present. Ed. by Philip S. Foner & Ronald L. Lewis. LC 88-29591. 440p. (C). 1988. 39.95 (0-87722-592-3); pap. text ed. 16.95 (0-87722-554-0) Temple U Pr.

Black Worker's Struggles in Detroit's Auto Industry 1935-1975. Kuniko Fujita. LC 79-93300. 125p. 1980. 12.00 (0-86548-010-9) R & E Pubs.

Black Writers: A Selection of Sketches from Contemporary Authors. Ed. by Linda Metzger. 600p. 1988. 89.00 (0-8103-2772-4) Gale.

Black Writers - Black Baseball: An Anthology of Articles from Black Sportswriters Who Covered the Negro Leagues. Jim Reisler. 183p. 1994. lib. bdg. 21.95 (0-7864-0002-1) McFarland & Co.

***Black Writers & Latin America.** 1995. 29.95 (0-614-06546-1, JABW) Howard U Pr.

Black Writers in Britain: An Anthology. Ed. by Paul Edwards & David Dabydeen. 256p. 1992. 45.00 (0-7486-0267-4, Pub. by Edinburgh U Pr UK) Col U Pr.

Black Writers in Britain: 1760-1890. Ed. by Paul Edwards & David Dabydeen. (Early Black Writers Ser.). 256p. 1993. pap. 25.00 (0-7486-0343-3, Pub. by Edinburgh U Pr UK) Col U Pr.

Black Writers in Britain 1760-1890. Ed. by Paul Edwards & David Dabydeen. 239p. 1993. pap. 25.00 (0-7486-0327-1, Pub. by Edinburgh U Pr UK) Col U Pr.

Black Writers in French: An Interpretive History. Lilyan Kesteloot. 1990. pap. 19.95 (0-88258-066-3) Howard U Pr.

Black Writers in Latin America. Richard L. Jackson. LC 78-21431. 238p. reprint ed. pap. 67.90 (0-8357-7301-9, 2029320) Bks Demand.

Black Writers in New England. Edward Clark. (Illus.). 76p. (Orig.). (C). 1985. pap. 10.00 (0-934441-01-4) Boston Afro Am.

Black Writers of America: A Comprehensive Anthology. Richard Barksdale & Keneth Kinnamon. 980p. (C). 1972. pap. write for info. (0-02-306080-8) Macmillan.

Black Writers of the Thirties. James O. Young. LC 72-96402. 271p. reprint ed. pap. 77.30 (0-8357-7302-7, 2051672) Bks Demand.

Black Writers Redefine the Struggle: A Tribute to James Baldwin. Ed. by Jules Chametzky. LC 88-29585. 92p. 1989. pap. 9.95 (0-87023-677-6) U of Mass Pr.

Black Writers, White Audience: A Critical Approach to African Literature. Phanuel A. Egejuru. LC 77-94306. (Exposition-University Book Ser.). 255p. reprint ed. pap. 72.70 (0-8357-7303-5, 2055581) Bks Demand.

Black Writers 2: Sketches from Contemporary Authors. 2nd ed. Ed. by Sharon Malinowski. 1993. 89.00 (0-8103-7788-8) Gale.

Black Yankees: The Development of an Afro-American Subculture in Eighteenth-Century New England. William D. Piersen. LC 87-13862. 256p. (Orig.). (C). 1988. pap. 16.95x (0-87023-587-7) U of Mass Pr.

***Black Young Adult Test (Christian Version) How Mature Are You?** Walter A. McCray. LC 94-96612. 48p. (Orig.). (YA). (gr. 11 up). 1995. pap. 2.99 (0-933176-15-5) Black Light Fellow.

***Black Young Adult Test (General Version) How Mature Are You?** Walter A. McCray. LC 94-96611. 48p. (Orig.). 1995. pap. 2.99 (0-933176-16-3) Black Light Fellow.

Black Young Adults - How to Reach Them, What to Teach Them: Strengthening the Black Church & Community by Educating Black Young Adults. 2nd ed. Walter A. McCray. LC 92-72415. 144p. (gr. 12 up). 1992. reprint ed. pap. 8.95 (0-933176-09-0) Black Light Fellow.

Black Youth Employment Crisis. Ed. by Richard R. Freeman & Harry J. Holzer. LC 85-20989. 480p. 1986. lib. bdg. 55.00 (0-226-26164-6) U Ch Pr.

Black Youth in Crisis: Facing the Future. Ed. by David Everatt & Elinor Sisulu. 104p. (C). 1993. pap. text ed. 12.95 (0-86975-429-7, Pub. by Ravan Pr ZA) Ohio U Pr.

Black Youth, Racism & the State: The Politics of Ideology & Policy. John Solomos. (Comparative Ethnic & Race Relations Ser.). (Illus.). 270p. 1988. 64.95 (0-521-36019-6) Cambridge U Pr.

Black Youth, Racism & the State: The Politics of Ideology & Policy. John Solomos. (Comparative Ethnic & Race Relations Ser.). (Illus.). 272p. (C). 1992. pap. 32.95 (0-521-42381-3) Cambridge U Pr.

***Black Youths, Delinquency, & Juvenile Justice.** Janice Joseph. LC 95-7987. 1995. text ed. write for info. (0-275-94909-5, Praeger Pubs) Greenwood.

Black Zeus. Edward L. Jones. 1972. pap. 6.50 (0-9602458-1-2) Ed-Lynne Jones.

Blackball. J. Sangster. Date not set. pap. write for info. (0-8050-0929-9) H Holt & Co.

Blackball Stars: Negro League Pioneers. John B. Holway. 416p. 1992. pap. 11.95 (0-88184-764-X) Carroll & Graf.

Blackball Stars: Negro League Pioneers. John B. Holway. (Baseball & American Society Ser.: No. 1). 400p. 1988. lib. bdg. 37.50 (0-88736-094-7) Mecklermedia.

Blackbeard & Other Pirates of the Atlantic Coast. Nancy Roberts. LC 93-698. 1993. 9.95 (0-89587-098-3) Blair.

Blackbeard the Pirate. Victor G. Ambrus. (Illus.). 32p. (J). (gr. 2 up). 1990. reprint ed. pap. 5.95 (0-19-272220-4) OUP.

Blackbeard the Pirate: A Reappraisal of His Life & Times. Robert E. Lee. LC 74-75752. 264p. 1984. pap. 8.95 (0-89587-032-0) Blair.

***Blackbeard the Pirate & Other Stories of the Pine Barrens.** Larona Homer. (Illus.). 96p. (J). (gr. 3-5). 1987. pap. 8.95 (0-912608-26-9) Mid Atlantic.

Blackbeard the Pirate's Missing Head Mystery Spook Kit. Carole Marsh. (S. P. A. R. K. Ser.). (Illus.). (J). (ps-6). 1994. lib. bdg. 24.95 (0-935326-19-7) Gallopade Pub Group.

Blackbeard's Cup & Stories of the Outer Banks. Charles H. Whedbee. LC 89-32193. 175p. 1988. 9.95 (0-89587-070-3) Blair.

Blackbelt in Blackjack. Arnold Snyder. 124p. 1983. pap. 12.95 (0-910575-02-9) R G Enterprises.

Blackberries. Nancy Deisroth. Ed. & Illus. by Carolyn Page. 36p. (Orig.). 1991. pap. 6.50 (1-879205-26-2) Nightshade Pr.

Blackberries & Dust. Nancy L. Nielsen. 20p. (Orig.). 1984. pap. 4.00 (0-914473-01-8) Stone Man Pr.

***Blackberries in the Dark.** Garrett Christopher. Ed. by J. Friedland & R. Kessler. (Novel-Ties Ser.). (J). (gr. 1-3). 1995. student ed, pap. text ed. 15.95 (1-56982-262-X) Lrn Links.

Blackberries in the Dark. Mavis Jukes. LC 85-4259. (Illus.). 48p. (J). (gr. 2-6). 1993. 15.00 (0-394-87599-0) Knopf Bks Yng Read.

Blackberries in the Dark. Mavis Jukes. (Illus.). 64p. (J). (gr. 2-6). 1994. pap. 3.50 (0-679-86570-5, Bullseye Bks) Random Bks Yng Read.

Blackberry Delights! A Blackberry Connoisseur's Specialty Cookbook. 2nd rev. ed. Lynda L. Harter. Ed. by Christene Brewster. LC 89-91375. (Illus.). 110p. 1989. pap. 8.95 (0-9622788-0-7) Ideas Unique.

Blackberry Delights! A Blackberry Connoisseurs Specialty Cookbook. Lynda L. Harter. Ed. by Christene Brewster. (Illus.). 110p. (Orig.). 1989. reprint ed. 8.95 (0-9622788-1-5) Ideas Unique.

Blackberry Delights! The Blackberry Connoisseurs Speciality Cookbook. Lynda Harter. (Illus.). 110p. (Orig.). 1989. pap. 8.95 (0-317-94014-7) Ideas Unique.

Blackberry Hollow. Paul Peabody. LC 92-8968. (Illus.). 160p. (J). (gr. 3-7). 1993. 15.95 (0-399-22500-5, Philomel Bks) Putnam Pub Group.

Blackberry Ink. Eve Merriam. LC 84-16633. (Illus.). 40p. (J). (ps-2). 1985. 15.00 (0-688-04150-7); lib. bdg. 13.93 (0-688-04151-5) Morrow Jr Bks.

Blackberry Ink. Eve Merriam. Ed. by Amy Cohn. LC 84-16633. (Illus.). 40p. (J). (ps up). 1994. reprint ed. pap. 4.95 (0-688-13080-1, Mulberry) Morrow.

Blackberry Juice from Blues Bones. David P. Bickham. (Orig.). 1988. pap. 4.00 (0-938535-80-3) Salt-Works Pr.

Blackberry Organ. David C. Wilson. LC 91-67985. 48p. (J). (gr. 3-7). 1992. pap. write for info. (0-9632765-6-5) Spirit Light.

***Blackberry Ramble.** Thatcher Hurd. LC 88-14188. (Illus.). 32p. (J). 1995. pap. 4.95 (0-06-443384-6, Trophy) HarpC Child Bks.

Blackberry Season: A Time to Mourn, a Time to Heal. H. H. Price. Ed. by Lura J. Geiger. LC 92-44882. 176p. (Orig.). 1993. pap. 14.95 (0-931055-93-8) LuraMedia.

Blackberry Vines & Winter Fruit for Orchestra. Marga Richter. (Illus.). 1978. pap. 15.00 (0-8258-0063-3, 0-5073) Fischer Inc NY.

Blackberry Wilderness. Sylvia Berkman. LC 79-116939. (Short Story Index Reprint Ser.). 1977. 20.95 (0-8369-3441-5) Ayer.

***Blackberry Winter.** Margaret Mead. 24.75 (0-614-03203-2) Peter Smith.

***Blackberry Winter.** Jack Stanley. 523p. 1995. pap. 12.95 (1-56901-783-2) NW Pub.

***Blackberry Winter: My Earlier Years.** Margaret Mead & Nancy Lutkehaus. Ed. by Philip Turner. (Globe Trade Paperback Ser.). (Illus.). 320p. 1995. pap. 14.00 (1-56836-069-X, Kodansha Globe) Kodansha.

Blackbird. Cartano. 1987. 18.95 (0-02-529270-6) Macmillan.

Blackbird. Larry Duplechan. (Stonewall Inn Editions Ser.). 192p. 1987. pap. 7.95 (0-312-00998-4) St Martin.

Blackbird. Jack Merek. 368p. 1992. mass mkt. 5.99 (0-446-36192-5) Warner Bks.

Blackbird. David W. Snow. 1989. pap. 30.00 (0-85263-854-X, Pub. by Shire UK) St Mut.

Blackbird: A Book of Poems on the World & Work of Franz Kafka. Emery George. LC 93-7116. (Illus.). 88p. 1993. pap. 12.95 (0-7734-0031-1) E Mellen.

Blackbird: The Life & Times of Paul McCartney. Geoffrey Giuliano. LC 92-53562. (Illus.). 400p. 1992. pap. 12.00 (0-452-26858-3, Plume) NAL-Dutton.

Blackbird Bye Bye. April Bernard. 1989. 16.95 (0-318-41456-2); pap. 9.95 (0-679-72195-9, Vin) Random.

***Blackbirds & Butterflies.** Bili M. Shelburne. 370p. 1995. pap. 9.95 (0-7610-0145-X) NW Pub.

Blackbirds of Mulhouse. Eric Maisel. LC 83-60319. 287p. (Orig.). 1984. pap. 7.95 (0-910997-01-2) Maya Pr.

Blackbirds of the Americas. Gordon H. Orians. LC 85-40352. (Illus.). 164p. 1985. 35.00 (0-295-96253-4) U of Wash Pr.

***Blackbird's Tale.** large type ed. Erma Blair. LC 94-34970. 876p. 1995. 22.95 (0-7838-1156-X, Large Print Bks) Hall.

Blackboard Architectures & Applications. Ed. by V. Jagannathan et al. (Perspectives in Artificial Intelligence Ser.). 560p. 1989. text ed. 68.00 (0-12-379940-6) Acad Pr.

Blackboard Bear. Martha Alexander. (Pied Piper Bks.). (Illus.). (J). (ps-2). 1988. pap. 3.50 (0-8037-0629-4) Dial Bks Young.

Blackboard Bear. Martha Alexander. (J). (ps-3). 1993. pap. 4.99 (0-14-054609-X) Dial Bks Young.

Blackboard Blackmail. Suzanne Clark. 242p. (Orig.). 1988. pap. 10.95 (1-877818-00-3) Footstool Pubns.

***Blackboard Jungle.** Evan Hunter. 1994. lib. bdg. 24.95x (1-56849-399-1) Buccaneer Bks.

Blackboard Systems. Ian D. Craig. Ed. by Masoud Yazdani. (Tutorial Monographs in Artificial Intelligence). 240p. (C). 1994. text ed. 49.50 (0-89391-594-7); pap. text ed. 24.50 (1-56750-029-3) Ablex Pub.

Blackboard Systems. Robert Engelmore & Anthony Morgan. (Illus.). 608p. (C). 1988. text ed. 43.25 (0-201-17431-6) Addison-Wesley.

Blackboard Unions: The AFT & the NEA, 1900-1980. Marjorie Murphy. LC 89-46175. (Illus.). 304p. 1991. 35.00 (0-8014-2365-1) Cornell U Pr.

Blackboard Unions: The AFT & the NEA, 1900-1980. Marjorie Murphy. LC 89-46175. (Illus.). 304p. 1992. pap. 14.95 (0-8014-8076-0) Cornell U Pr.

***Blackburn: A Novel.** Bradley Denton. 304p. 1995. pap. 12.00 (0-312-13029-5) St Martin.

Blackburn Affair. Dorothy W. Riley. 25p. (YA). (gr. 4-12). 1986. pap. write for info. (1-880234-04-1) Winbush Pub.

Blackburn Aircraft Since 1909. A. J. Jackson. LC 88-62582. (Putnam Aviation Ser.). (Illus.). 576p. 1989. 44.95 (0-87021-024-6) Naval Inst Pr.

Blackburn College 1837-1987: An Anecdotal & Analytical History of the Private College. Glenn L. McConagha. (Illus.). 533p. (C). 1988. 20.00 (0-9621555-0-0) Blackburn Univ.

Blackburne's Chess Games. Joseph H. Blackburne. Ed. by P. Anderson Graham. (Illus.). 1979. reprint ed. pap. 7.95 (0-486-23857-1) Dover.

Blackburn's Introduction to Clinical Radiation Therapy Physics. Ed. by Benjamin Blackburn. (Illus.). 220p. (Orig.). (C). 1989. text ed. 48.00 (0-944838-06-5) Med Physics Pub.

Blackcap & the Garden Warbler. Ernest Garcia. 1989. pap. 25.00 (0-7478-0025-1, Pub. by Shire UK) St Mut.

Blackchannel: A Cold War Novel. Richard N. Perle. 1992. 20.50 (0-394-56552-5) Random.

Blackcoated Worker: A Study in Class Consciousness. 2nd ed. David Lockwood. 272p. 1989. 64.00 (0-19-827840-3) OUP.

Blackcoats among the Delaware: David Zeisberger on the Ohio Frontier. Earl P. Olmstead. LC 90-47576. (Illus.). 296p. 1991. 29.00 (0-87338-422-9); pap. 17.50 (0-87338-434-2) Kent St U Pr.

***Blackening Song.** Aimee Thurlo & David Thurlo. 384p. 1995. 22.95 (0-312-85652-0) Forge NYC.

Blacker Than a Thousand Midnights. Susan Straight. LC 93-30432. 400p. 1994. 21.95 (0-7868-6003-0) Hyperion.

***Blacker Than a Thousand Midnights.** Susan Straight. LC 94-23924. 1995. 11.00 (0-385-47434-2) Doubleday.

Blacker the Berry. Wallace Thurman. reprint ed. 17.00 (0-404-00217-X) AMS Pr.

Blacker the Berry. Wallace Thurman. LC 69-18594. (American Negro: His History & Literature, Ser. No. 2). 1978. reprint ed. 24.95 (0-405-01897-5) Ayer.

Blacker the Berry. Wallace Thurman. Ed. by Charles R. Larson. (African-American Library). (Illus.). 256p. (J). (gr. 11 up). 1970. reprint ed. pap. 7.00 (0-02-054750-1, Collier Bks Young) S&S Childrens.

Blackeyes. Dennis Potter. (Orig.). 1988. pap. 6.95 (0-679-72047-2, Vin) Random.

Blackface. N. George. 1994. 22.00 (0-06-017120-0, HarpT) HarpC.

Blackface Minstrelsy & the American Working Class. Eric Lott. LC 92-41071. (Race & American Culture Ser.). 1993. 35.00 (0-19-507832-2) OUP.

Blackface to Blacklist: Al Jolson, Larry Parks, & "The Jolson Story" Doug McCelland. LC 86-29797. (Illus.). 298p. 1987. 29.50 (0-8108-1965-1) Scarecrow.

***Blackfeet.** Theresa J. Lacey. Ed. by Frank W. Porter, 3rd. LC 94-38594. (Indians of North America Ser.). (Illus.). 144p. (YA). (gr. 5 up). 1995. 18.95 (0-7910-1681-1); pap. 7.95 (0-7910-2491-1) Chelsea Hse.

Blackfeet: Raiders on the Northwestern Plains. John C. Ewers. LC 58-7778. (Civilization of the American Indian Ser.: No. 49). (Illus.). 377p. 1983. reprint ed. pap. 15.95 (0-8061-1836-9) U of Okla Pr.

Blackfeet & Buffalo: Memories of Life Among the Indians. James W. Schultz. Ed. by Keith C. Seele. LC 62-10762. 384p. 1981. pap. 13.95 (0-8061-1700-1) U of Okla Pr.

Blackfeet: Artists of the Northern Plains: The Scriver Collection of Blackfeet Indian Artifacts & Related Objects 1894-1990. Bob Scriver. LC 90-31476. (Illus.). 320p. 1992. 60.00 (0-932845-38-X) Lowell Pr.

Blackfeet Crafts. John C. Ewers. LC 86-70332. (Illus.). 68p. 1986. reprint ed. pap. 5.95 (0-936984-09-0) Schneider Pubs.

Blackfeet Indian Stories. George B. Grinnell. LC 92-40295. 1993. reprint ed. 10.95 (1-55709-201-X) Applewood.

Blackfeet Indians. W. Reiss & F. B. Linderman. 1977. lib. bdg. 75.95 (0-8490-1513-8) Gordon Pr.

Blackfeet Tales of Glacier National Park. J. W. Schultz. 1977. lib. bdg. 69.95 (0-8490-1514-6) Gordon Pr.

Blackfeet Tales of Glacier National Park. James W. Schultz. 144p. 1992. 7.95 (0-915463-52-0, Jameson Bks) Green Hill.

Blackflies: The Future for Biological Methods in Integrated Control. Ed. by Marshall Laird. LC 81-66373. 1982. text ed. 157.00 (0-12-434060-1) Acad Pr.

Blackflies (Simuliidae) I. A. Rubtsov. LC 89-71184. (Fauna of the U. S. S. R. Diptera Ser.: Vol. 6, Pt. 6). (Illus.). xxviii, 1042p. 1990. 171.50 (90-04-08871-7) E J Brill.

Blackfoot Craftworker's Book. Adolf Hungrywolf & Beverly Hungrywolf. LC 91-18003. (Illus.). 80p. 1991. pap. 11.95 (0-913990-80-9) Book Pub Co.

Blackfoot Dictionary of Stems, Roots & Affixes. D. G. Frantz & N. J. Russell. 492p. 1989. 70.00 (0-8020-2691-5) U of Toronto Pr.

***Blackfoot Dictionary of Stems, Roots & Affixes.** Donald G. Frantz & Norma J. Russell. (C). 1995. pap. 24.95 (0-8020-7136-8) U of Toronto Pr.

***Blackfoot Dictionary of Stems, Roots & Affixes.** 2nd ed. Donald G. Frantz & Norma J. Russell. 492p. (C). 1995. 65.00 (0-8020-0767-8) U of Toronto Pr.

Blackfoot-English Vocabulary. Christianus C. Uhlenbeck & R. H. Van Gulik. LC 76-44086. (Verhardelingen der Koninklijke Akademie Van Wetenschappen Te Amsterdam. Afdeeling Letterkunde. Nieuwe Reeks Ser.: 33, No. 2). (BLA & ENG.). reprint ed. 72.00 (0-404-15795-5) AMS Pr.

Blackfoot Getaways. Suzanne M. Vernon. 200p. (Orig.). 1992. pap. 8.95 (0-9620902-5-5) Vernon Print & Pub.

Blackfoot Grammar. Donald G. Frantz. 200p. 1991. 45.00 (0-8020-5964-3) U of Toronto Pr.

***Blackfoot Indians.** (Junior Library of American Indians). (Illus.). 80p. (J). (gr. 3-7). Date not set. lib. bdg. 14.95 (0-7910-1659-5) Chelsea Hse.

An Asterisk (*) at the beginning of an entry indicates that the title is appearing in BIP for the first time.

B

An Asterisk (*) at the beginning of an entry indicates that the title is appearing in BIP for the first time.

809

Blacks in the Pacific Northwest, 1788-1974: A Biography of Published Works & Unpublished Source Materials on the Life & Contributions of Black People on the Pacific Northwest, Nos. 767-768. 2nd ed. 1975. 9.00 (0-686-20346-1) CPL Biblios.

Blacks in the Republican Party? Jackson R. Champion. LC 75-29732. (Illus.). 1976. 7.50 (0-917230-03-5) LenChamps Pubs.

Blacks in the State of Ohio, 1800-1976: A Preliminary Survey, Nos. 1208-1209. Lenwood G. Davis. 1977. 8.50 (0-686-19690-2) CPL Biblios.

Blacks in the West. W. Sherman Savage. LC 75-44657. (Contributions in Afro-American & African Studies: No. 23). 288p. (Orig.). 1976. text ed. 55.00 (0-8371-8775-3, SBW/, Greenwood Pr) Greenwood.

Blacks in the West. W. Sherman Savage. LC 75-44657. (Contributions in Afro-American & African Studies: No. 23). xvi, 230p. (Orig.). 1977. pap. text ed. 6.95 (0-313-20161-7, SBWPB, Greenwood Pr) Greenwood.

Blacks in the White Establishment? A Study of Race & Class in America. Richar L. Zweigenhaft & G. William Domhoff. 208p. (C). 1991. text ed. 29.50 (0-300-04788-6) Yale U Pr.

Blacks in the White Establishment? A Study of Race & Class in America. Richard L. Zweigenhaft & G. William Domhoff. 208p. (C). 1992. reprint ed. pap. 12.00 (0-300-05433-5) Yale U Pr.

***Blacks in Topeka, Kansas, 1865-1915: A Social History.** Thomas C. Cox. LC 81-14310. 248p. 1982. pap. 70.70 (0-7837-8527-5, 2049336) Bks Demand.

Blacks in Undergraduate Science & Engineering Education. (Illus.). 109p. (Orig.). (C). 1993. pap. text ed. 35.00 (0-7881-0152-8) Diane Pub.

Blacks, Latinos & Asians in Urban America: Status & Prospects for Politics & Activism. Ed. by James Jennings. LC 94-8340. 192p. 1994. text ed. 49.95 (0-275-94746-7, Praeger Pubs); pap. text ed. 14.95 (0-275-94934-6, Praeger Pubs) Greenwood.

Black's Law Dictionary. 6th abr. ed. Henry C. Black et al. Ed. by M. J. Connolly et al. 1119p. 1992. reprint ed. pap. text ed. 19.50 (0-314-88536-6) West Pub.

Black's Law Dictionary. 6th ed. Henry C. Black et al. 1618p. 1990. reprint ed. text ed. 49.50 (0-314-77165-4) West Pub.

Black's Law Dictionary. 6th ed. Henry C. Black et al. 1657p. 1993. reprint ed. text ed. 29.50 (0-314-76271-X) West Pub.

Black's Medical Dictionary. Ed. by Gordon Macpherson. 656p. (C). 1992. text ed. 95.00 (0-389-20989-9) B&N Imports.

Black's Medical Dictionary. 36th ed. Ed. by C. W. Havard. (Illus.). (C). 1990. lib. bdg. 85.00 (0-389-20901-5) B&N Imports.

Blacks on John Brown. Ed. by Benjamin Quarles. LC 72-188132. (Illus.). 180p. reprint ed. pap. 51.30 (0-8357-7306-X, 2020221) Bks Demand.

Blacks on Television: A Selectively Annotated Bibliography. George H. Hill & Sylvia S. Hill. LC 84-23639. 237p. 1985. 25.00 (0-8108-1774-8) Scarecrow.

Blacks on White Campuses: Whites on Black Campuses. Ed. by Andrew Billingsley & Ada Elam. (NAFEO Conference Ser.). 178p. 1987. pap. text ed. 18.95 (0-695-60052-4) Follett Pr.

Blacks, Science, & American Education. Ed. by Willie Pearson, Jr. & Kenneth Bechtel. 1989. 35.00 (0-8135-1397-9) Rutgers U Pr.

Black's Texas Evidence Manual, 2 vols., Set. Thomas Black. LC 85-393. 1990. 165.00 (0-8321-0024-2) Bancroft Whitney Co.

Black's Veterinary Dictionary. 17th ed. Geoffrey West. 672p. (C). 1992. text ed. 99.00 (0-389-20994-5) B&N Imports.

***Black's Veterinary Dictionary.** 18th ed. Ed. by Geoffrey West. 624p. 1994. lib. bdg. 99.00 (0-7136-3946-6) B&N Imports.

Blacks Who Died for Jesus. Mark Hyman. LC 83-62818. (Illus.). 107p. (C). 1988. reprint ed. pap. 9.95 (1-55523-136-5) Winston-Derek.

Blacks Who Stole Themselves: Advertisements for Runaways in the Pennsylvania Gazette, 1728-1790. Billy G. Smith & Richard Wojtowicz. LC 88-32636. (Illus.). 222p. (C). 1989. text ed. 35.95 (0-8122-8145-4) U of Pa Pr.

***Black's Wing & Clay.** annuals Ed. by Jim Black. (Illus.). 410p. 1995. pap. 9.95 (1-57028-059-2) Masters Pr IN.

Blacksmith. Jack Rudman. (Career Examination Ser.: C-107). 1994. pap. 27.95 (0-8373-0107-6) Nat Learn.

Blacksmith: Ironworker & Farrier. Aldren A. Watson. 1990. pap. 14.95 (0-393-30683-6) Norton.

Blacksmith & the Fairies & Other Scottish Folk-Tales. Comp. by Elizabeth Howden. 128p. 1990. pap. 10.95 (0-86315-067-5, 1314, Pub. by Floris Books UK) Anthroposophic.

Blacksmith & the Farmer: Rural Manufacturing in Sub-Saharan Africa. David Poston. 160p. (Orig.). 1994. pap. 28.50 (1-85339-127-1, Pub. by Intermed Tech UK) Women Ink.

Blacksmith Guide to Ruger Flattops & Super Blackhawks. H. W. Ross. (Illus.). 96p. 1982. reprint ed. pap. 12.50 (0-941540-08-1) Blacksmith Corp.

Blacksmith Shop & Iron Forging. 1983. reprint ed. pap. 6.50 (0-917914-07-4) Lindsay Pubns.

Blacksmithing Instructors' Guide: Sixteen Lesson Plans with Teaching Advice. David Harries. 70p. (Orig.). 1994. pap. 28.50 (0-317-06160-7, Pub. by Intermed Tech UK) Women Ink.

Blacksmithing Made Easy. International Correspondence Schools Staff. (Illus.). 110p. 1991. reprint ed. 20.00 (1-877767-30-1); reprint ed. pap. 10.00 (1-877767-24-7) Univ Publng Hse.

Blacksmiths & Farriers Tools at Shelburne Museum. H. R. Smith. LC 82-3269. (Illus.). 72p. (Orig.). 1966. pap. 9.50 (0-939384-07-8) Shelburne.

Blacksmith's Daughter. large type ed. Joanna Dessau. (General Ser.). 320p. 1993. 21.95 (0-7089-2908-7) Ulverscroft.

Blacksmith's Helper. Jack Rudman. (Career Examination Ser.: C-108). 1994. pap. 23.95 (0-8373-0108-4) Nat Learn.

Blackstick Papers. Anne I. Ritchie. LC 71-76911. (Essay Index Reprint Ser.). 1977. 21.95 (0-8369-0027-8) Ayer.

Blackstone Book of Magic & Illusion. Harry Blackstone, Jr. et al. LC 84-29486. (Illus.). 248p. (J). (gr. 7 up). 1985. 22.95 (0-937858-45-5) Newmarket.

Blackstone Book of Magic & Illusion. rev. ed. Harry Blackstone, Jr. et al. (Illus.). 248p. 1993. 35.00 (1-55704-182-2); pap. 16.95 (1-55704-177-6) Newmarket.

Blackstone Franks Guide to Living in Spain. Blackstone Franks. 208p. (Orig.). 1989. pap. 22.95 (0-8464-1393-0) Beekman Pubs.

Blackstone Valley: A Sketch of Its River, Its Canal & Its People. Patrick T. Conley. 19p. 1983. pap. 2.75 (0-917012-41-0) RI Pubns Soc.

***Blackstone's Commentaries, 4 vols., Set.** W. Blackstone. 1915. 37.95 (0-87511-493-8) Claitors.

Blackstone's Commentaries on the Laws of England, 4 vols., Set. William Blackstone. LC 91-73627. 1993. reprint ed. 295.00 (0-89941-775-2, 307250) W S Hein.

Blackstone's Criminal Practice. P. Murphy. (C). 1991. text ed. 350.00 (1-85431-200-6, Pub. by Blackstone Pr UK) W W Gaunt.

***Blackstone's Criminal Practice.** P. Murphy. 1995. 169.00 (1-85431-402-5, Pub. by Blackstone Pr UK) W W Gaunt.

Blackstone's Criminal Practice. Ed. by Peter Murphy. 2550p. 1993. 194.00 (1-85431-255-3, Pub. by Blackstone Pr UK) W W Gaunt.

Blackstone's Criminal Practice. 4th ed. Ed. by Peter Murphy. 2446p. 1994. 194.00 (1-85431-325-8) W W Gaunt.

Blackstone's EC Legislation. 4th ed. Nigel Foster. 493p. 1993. pap. 28.00 (1-85431-283-9, Pub. by Blackstone Pr UK) W W Gaunt.

***Blackstone's EC Legislation: 1994-95.** 5th ed. Nigel Foster. 494p. pap. 28.00 (1-85431-344-4, Pub. by Blackstone Pr UK) W W Gaunt.

Blackstone's EEC Legislation. 3rd ed. Nigel Foster. 1992. pap. 32.00 (1-85431-240-5, Pub. by Blackstone Pr UK) W W Gaunt.

Blackstone's Guide to Australian Legal Books, 1986-1990. 604p. 1993. 185.00 (1-875114-21-1, Blckstone AT) W W Gaunt.

Blackstone's Guide to the Criminal Justice Act 1991. Ed. by M. Wasik & R. Taylor. 292p. (C). 1991. pap. 31.00 (1-85431-149-2, Pub. by Blackstone Pr UK) W W Gaunt.

Blackstone's Guide to the Criminal Justice Act 1991. 2nd ed. Martin Wasik & Richard D. Taylor. 351p. 1994. pap. 40.00 (1-85431-304-5, Pub. by Blackstone Pr UK) W W Gaunt.

***Blackstone's Guide to the Criminal Justice & Public Order Act 1994.** Martin Wasik & Richard Taylor. 349p. 1995. pap. 44.00 (1-85431-401-7, Pub. by Blackstone Pr UK) W W Gaunt.

Blackstone's Guide to the Food Safety Act 1990. Geraint Howells et al. 132p. (C). 1990. text ed. 25.00 (1-85431-108-5, Pub. by Blackstone Pr UK) W W Gaunt.

Blackstone's Guide to the Human Fertilisation & Embryology Act 1990: Abortion & Embryo Research, the New Law. Ed. by Derek Morgan & Robert G. Lee. 276p. (C). 1991. text ed. 33.00 (1-85431-105-0, Pub. by Blackstone Pr UK) W W Gaunt.

Blackstone's Guide to the Road Traffic Act 1991. Ed. by S. Cooper. vii, 190p. (C). 1991. pap. 33.00 (1-85431-120-4, Pub. by Blackstone Pr UK) W W Gaunt.

***Blackstone's Guide to the Trade Marks Act 1994.** Ruth Annand & Helen Norman. 1994. text ed. 44.00 (1-85431-384-3, Pub. by Blackstone Pr UK) W W Gaunt.

***Blackstone's International Human Rights Documents.** P. R. Ghandhi. 354p. 1995. pap. 30.00 (1-85431-409-2, Pub. by Blackstone Pr UK) W W Gaunt.

Blackstone's International Law Documents. Ed. by Malcolm Evans. 353p. (C). 1991. text ed. 34.00 (1-85431-148-4, Pub. by Blackstone Pr UK) W W Gaunt.

Blackstone's Modern Card Tricks. Harry Blackstone. 1974. pap. 7.00 (0-87980-282-0) Wilshire.

Blackstone's Secrets of Magic. Harry Blackstone. 1980. pap. 7.00 (0-87980-260-X) Wilshire.

***Blackstone's Statues on Intellectual Property.** 2nd ed. Andrew Christie & Stephen Gare. 388p. 1995. pap. 34.00 (1-85431-386-X, Pub. by Blackstone Pr UK) W W Gaunt.

Blackstone's Statutes on Commercial Law. 2nd ed. Francis Rose. 1992. pap. 34.00 (1-85431-247-2, Pub. by Blackstone Pr UK) W W Gaunt.

***Blackstone's Statutes on Contract, Tort & Restitution: 1994-95.** 5th ed. F. D. Rose. 309p. 1994. pap. 22.00 (1-85431-385-1, Pub. by Blackstone Pr UK) W W Gaunt.

Blackstone's Statutes on Criminal Law. 2nd ed. Peter Glazebrook. 1991. pap. 26.00 (0-685-65116-9, Pub. by Blackstone Pr UK) W W Gaunt.

***Blackstone's Statutes on Criminal Law 1994-95.** 4th ed. P. R. Glazebrook. 249p. Date not set. text ed. 22.00 (1-85431-381-9, Pub. by Blackstone Pr UK) W W Gaunt.

Blackstone's Statutes on Employment Law. Richard Kidner. 1991. pap. 26.00 (1-85431-021-6, Pub. by Blackstone Pr UK) W W Gaunt.

Blackstone's Statutes on English Legal System. Ed. by David Howarth & Stephen Wilson. (C). 1989. text ed. 26.00 (1-85431-038-0, Pub. by Blackstone Pr UK) W W Gaunt.

Blackstone's Statutes on Evidence. Ed. by Phil Huxley & Michael O'Connell. (C). 1991. text ed. 21.00 (1-85431-027-5, Pub. by Blackstone Pr UK) W W Gaunt.

Blackstone's Statutes on Evidence. 2nd ed. Phil Huxley & Michael O'Connell. 260p. 1993. pap. 22.00 (1-85431-256-1, Pub. by Blackstone Pr UK) W W Gaunt.

Blackstone's Statutes on Family Law. 2nd ed. Mika Oldham. pap. 32.00 (1-85431-220-0, Pub. by Blackstone Pr UK) W W Gaunt.

***Blackstone's Statutes on Family Law, Vol. 1.** 3rd ed. Mika Oldham. 385p. 1994. pap. text ed. 28.00 (1-85431-346-0, Blckstone AT) W W Gaunt.

Blackstone's Statutes on Landlord & Tenant. Stuart Bridge. (C). 1991. text ed. 33.00 (1-85431-118-2, Pub. by Blackstone Pr UK) W W Gaunt.

Blackstone's Statutes on Medical Law. Ed. by Michael Jones & Anne Morris. (C). 1992. 40.00 (1-85431-142-5, Pub. by Blackstone Pr UK) W W Gaunt.

Blackstone's Statutes on Planning Law. Victor Moore & David Hughes. 444p. (C). 1995. pap. 30.00 (1-85431-125-5, Pub. by Blackstone Pr UK) W W Gaunt.

Blackstone's Statutes on Property Law. Meryl Thomas. 1989. pap. 26.00 (1-85431-039-9, Pub. by Blackstone Pr UK) W W Gaunt.

***Blackstone's Statutes on Property Law: 1994-95 Edition.** Meryl Thomas. 367p. 1994. pap. 28.00 (1-85431-267-7, Pub. by Blackstone Pr UK) W W Gaunt.

Blackstone's Statutes on Public Law. 3rd ed. Ed. by Peter Wallington & Bob Lee. 1992. text ed. 30.00 (1-85431-221-9, Pub. by Blackstone Pr UK) W W Gaunt.

***Blackstone's Statutes on Public Law: 1994-1995 Edition.** 4th ed. Peter Wallington & Robert G. Lee. 393p. Date not set. text ed. 28.00 (1-85431-345-2, Pub. by Blackstone Pr UK) W W Gaunt.

Blackstone's Tricks Anyone Can Do. Harry Blackstone. 240p. (C). 1983. pap. 7.95 (0-8065-0862-0, Citadel Pr) Carol Pub Group.

Blacktail Deer Hunting Adventures: A Refreshingly Candid Account Valuable for Hunters Everywhere. Wesley Murphey. LC 94-76671. (Illus.). 176p. 1995. pap. 12.95 (0-9641320-4-4) Lost Creek.

***Blackthorn.** Gillian Allnutt. 64p. 1994. pap. 14.95 (1-85224-270-1, Pub. by Bloodaxe Bks UK) Dufour.

***Blackthorn.** Larry Clutter. 1995. 19.95 (0-8062-5172-7) Carlton.

Blackthorn. large type ed. Arlene J. Fitzgerald. (Large Print Ser.). 400p. 1994. 20.95 (0-7089-3005-0) Ulverscroft.

Blackthorn Lore & the Art of Making Walking Sticks. J. M. Douglas. 96p. 1984. 40.00 (0-907526-16-0, Alloway Pub) St Mut.

***Blackthorne's Woman.** Victoria Leigh. (Loveswept Ser.: No. 712). 1994. pap. 3.50 (0-553-44446-8, Loveswept) Bantam.

Blacktop Champion of Ickey Honey & Other Stories. Robert T. Sorrells. LC 88-14311. 239p. (Orig.). 1988. 18.95 (1-55728-045-2); pap. 9.95 (1-55728-046-0) U of Ark Pr.

Blackwalls & Other Stories. Liu Xinwu. Ed. by Don J. Cohn. xiii, 200p. 1992. reprint ed. pap. 9.50 (962-7255-06-8, Pub. by Renditions Papbk HK) SPD-Small Pr Dist.

Blackwater: Historical Studies in Race, Class Consciousness & Revolution. Manning Marable. 1992. pap. 14.95 (0-87081-274-2) Univ Pr Colo.

***Blackwater Anthology: Verse & Prose of a Mainly Gothic Kind.** Ed. by Cynthia Hendershot & Antony Oldknow. 214p. (Orig.). (C). 1993. pap. text ed. 20.00 (1-881604-06-3) Scopcraeft.

***Blackwater Anthology 2.** Ed. by Cynthia Hendershot & Antony Oldknow. 223p. (C). 1994. pap. text ed. 17.00 (1-881604-08-X) Scopcraeft.

***Blackwater Anthology 3.** Ed. by Cynthia Hendershot et al. 223p. (C). 1994. pap. text ed. 20.00 (1-881604-13-6) Scopcraeft.

Blackwater Country. 3rd ed. J. Lawrence Smith. 1984. reprint ed. pap. 5.00 (0-87012-083-2) McClain.

***Blackwater Spirits.** Miriam G. Monfredo. 1995. 21.95 (0-312-11754-X, Pub. by Thomas Dunne Bks) St Martin.

Blackwater Swamp. Bill Wallace. LC 93-28439. 208p. (J). 1994. 15.95 (0-8234-1120-6) Holiday.

***Blackwater Swamp.** Bill Wallace. Ed. by Pat MacDonald. 160p. (YA). 1995. pap. 3.50 (0-671-51156-4, Minstrel Bks) PB.

Blackways of Kent. Hylan Lewis. 1955. pap. 13.95x (0-8084-0064-9) NCUP.

Blackways of Kent. Hylan Lewis. 1955. 20.00 (0-8078-0676-5) U of NC Pr.

Blackweall Frigates. Basil Lubbock. (C). 1987. 114.00 (0-85174-108-8, Pub. by Brwn Son Ferg) St Mut.

Blackwell Biographical Dictionary of British Political Life in the Twentieth Century. Ed. by Keith Robbins. 360p. 1990. 83.95 (0-631-15768-9) Blackwell Pubs.

***Blackwell Book of Education.** Michael Farrell et al. LC 94-27461. 1995. 59.95 (0-631-19279-4); pap. 24.95 (0-631-19281-6) Blackwell Pubs.

Blackwell Companion to Jewish Culture: From the Eighteenth Century to the Present. Ed. by Glenda Abramson et al. (Illus.). 512p. 1989. 79.95 (0-631-15111-7) Blackwell Pubs.

***Blackwell Companion to Philosophy.** Ed. by Nicholas Bunnin & E. P. Tsui-James. LC 95-6545. 600p. (C). 1995. write for info. (0-631-18788-X) Blackwell Pubs.

***Blackwell Companion to Philosophy.** Ed. by Nicholas Bunnin & E. P. Tsui-James. LC 95-6545. 600p. (C). 1995. pap. write for info. (0-631-18789-8) Blackwell Pubs.

Blackwell Companion to the Enlightenment. Ed. by John Yolton. 608p. 1992. 74.95 (0-631-15403-5) Blackwell Pubs.

***Blackwell Companion to the Enlightenment.** Ed. by John Yolton. 608p. 1992. pap. write for info. (0-631-19688-9) Blackwell Pubs.

Blackwell Dictionary of Cognitive Psychology. Ed. by Michael W. Eysenck. (C). 1991. text ed. 69.95 (0-631-15682-8) Blackwell Pubs.

Blackwell Dictionary of Cognitive Psychology. Ed. by Michael W. Eysenck. (Illus.). 416p. (C). 1994. pap. 29.95 (0-631-19257-3) Blackwell Pubs.

***Blackwell Dictionary of Evangelical Biography 1730-1860.** Intro. by Donald M. Lewis. 1200p. 1995. lib. bdg. 150.00 (0-631-17384-6) Blackwell Pubs.

Blackwell Dictionary of Historians. Ed. by John Cannon. 600p. 1988. 94.95 (0-631-14708-X) Blackwell Pubs.

Blackwell Dictionary of Judaica. Ed. by Dan Cohn-Sherbok. 624p. 1992. pap. 24.95 (0-631-18728-6) Blackwell Pubs.

***Blackwell Dictionary of Neuropsychology.** Ed. by J. Graham Beaumont et al. (Illus.). 704p. 1996. write for info. (0-631-17896-1, Pub. by NCC Blackwell UK) Blackwell Pubs.

***Blackwell Dictionary of Sociology: A User's Guide to Sociological Language.** Allan Johnson. 352p. Date not set. write for info. (1-55786-116-1); pap. write for info. (1-55786-117-X) Blackwell Pubs.

Blackwell Dictionary of Twentieth-Century Social Thought. Ed. by William Outhwaite & Tom Bottomore. LC 92-20837. 1993. 59.95 (0-631-15262-8) Blackwell Pubs.

Blackwell Dictionary of Twentieth-Century Social Thought. Ed. by William Outhwaite & Tom Bottomore. 880p. (C). 1994. pap. text ed. 27.95 (0-631-19575-0) Blackwell Pubs.

Blackwell Encyclopedia of Industrial Archaeology. Ed. by Barry Trinder. (Illus.). 600p. 1993. 150.00 (0-631-14216-9) Blackwell Pubs.

Blackwell Encyclopedia of Modern Christian Thought. Intro. by Alister McGrath. 700p. 1993. 94.95 (0-631-16896-6) Blackwell Pubs.

Blackwell Encyclopedia of Political Science. Vernon Bogdanor. 1992. pap. 24.95 (0-631-18304-3) Blackwell Pubs.

***Blackwell Encyclopedia of Political Thought.** Ed. by David Miller. 1991. pap. 27.95 (0-631-17944-5) Blackwell Pubs.

Blackwell Encyclopedia of Social Psychology. Ed. by Antony S. Manstead & Miles Hewstone. (Illus.). (C). 1994. text ed. 125.00 (0-631-18146-6) Blackwell Pubs.

Blackwell Encyclopedia of the American Revolution. Ed. by Jack P. Greene & J. R. Pole. (Illus.). 1991. 54.95 (1-55786-244-3) Blackwell Pubs.

Blackwell Encyclopedia of the American Revolution. Ed. by Jack P. Greene & J. R. Pole. (Illus.). xvi, 850p. 1994. pap. text ed. 26.95 (1-55786-547-7) Blackwell Pubs.

Blackwell Encyclopedia of the Russian Revolution. H. Shukman. 418p. (C). 1988. 350.00 (0-685-31472-3, Pub. by Collets UK) Pro-Am Music.

Blackwell Encyclopedia of the Russian Revolution. Ed. by Harold Shukman. LC 94-11241. (Illus.). 300p. (C). 1994. pap. text ed. 24.95 (0-631-19525-4) Blackwell Pubs.

***Blackwell Encyclopedia of Writing Systems.** Florian Coulmas. (Illus.). 640p. Date not set. text ed. 65.00 (0-631-19446-0) Blackwell Pubs.

***Blackwell Encyclopedic Dictionary of Organizational Behavior.** Ed. by Nigel Nicholson. (Encyclopedia of Management Ser.). 550p. 1995. write for info. (0-631-18781-2) Blackwell Pubs.

Blackwell Genealogy, Bk. 1 Genealogy Only: Ancestors, Descendants & Connections of Moore Carter & Sarah Alexander (Foote) Blackwell. E. M. Blackwell. (Illus.). 126p. 1993. reprint ed. lib. bdg. 33.00 (0-8328-3268-5); reprint ed. pap. 23.00 (0-8328-3269-3) Higginson Bk Co.

Blackwell Guide to Blues Records. Paul Oliver. 1991. pap. 15.95 (0-631-18301-9) Blackwell Pubs.

Blackwell Guide to Contemporary Composers on Disc. Brian Morton. (Blackwell Guides Ser.). 352p. 1995. 24.95 (0-631-18881-9) Blackwell Pubs.

Blackwell Guide to Musical Theatre. Kurt Ganzl. 1990. 34.95 (0-631-16517-7) Blackwell Pubs.

Blackwell Guide to Recorded Country Music. Bob Allen. (Blackwell Studies). 496p. 1994. 24.95 (0-631-19106-2) Blackwell Pubs.

Blackwell Guide to Recorded Jazz. Barry Kernfeld. 1991. 29.95 (0-631-17164-9) Blackwell Pubs.

Blackwell Guide to Recorded Jazz. Barry Kernfeld. 1992. pap. 15.95 (0-631-18531-3) Blackwell Pubs.

***Blackwell Guide to Recorded Jazz.** 2nd ed. Ed. & Pref. by Barry Kernfeld. (Music Guides Ser.). 450p. 1995. pap. write for info. (0-631-19552-1) Blackwell Pubs.

Blackwell Guide to Soul Recordings. Ed. by Robert Pruter. LC 93-12312. (Reference Bks.). 496p. 1993. 24.95 (0-631-18595-X) Blackwell Pubs.

Blackwell History of Music in Britain: Sixteenth Century. Ed. by Roger Bray. (History of Music in Britain Ser.). (Illus.). 400p. (C). 1995. 100.00 (0-631-17924-0) Blackwell Pubs.

Blackwell History of Music in Britain Vol. 4: The Eighteenth Century. Ed. by H. Diack Johnstone & Roger Fiske. 500p. 1989. 125.00 (0-631-16519-3) Blackwell Pubs.

810

An Asterisk (*) at the beginning of an entry indicates that the title is appearing in BIP for the first time.

B

An Asterisk (*) at the beginning of an entry indicates that the title is appearing in BIP for the first time.

Blanche Ames: Artist & Activist. Bonnie L. Crane. (Illus.). 40p. (Orig.). 1982. pap. 4.95 (*0-934358-10-9*) Fuller Mus Art.

Blanche among the Talented Tenth. Barbara Neely. 240p. 1994. 19.95 (*0-312-11248-3*) St Martin.

***Blanche among the Talented Tenth.** Barbara Neely. 240p. 1995. 5.95 (*0-14-025036-0*, Penguin Bks) Viking Penguin.

Blanche Knott's Book of Etiquette. Blanche Knott. 1987. pap. 3.50 (*0-312-90590-4*) St Martin.

Blanche Knott's Treasury of Tastelessness. Blanche Knott. 192p. 1994. 12.95 (*0-312-11343-9*) St Martin.

Blanche Knott's Truly Tasteless Joke-a-Date Book 1990. Blanche Knott. 1990. pap. 3.50 (*0-312-92226-4*) St Martin.

Blanche Lazzell. John Clarkson. LC 89-61664. (Provincetown Classics in History, Literature, & Art Ser.: Vol. 2). (Illus.). 44p. 1988. reprint ed. pap. 7.00 (*0-945135-01-7*) Cape Cod Pilgrim.

***Blanche-Neige - Snow White.** Adapt. by Sarah Harris. (Comes to Life Bks.). 16p. (ENG & FRE.). (J). (ps-2). 1995. write for info. (*1-57234-037-1*) YES Ent.

Blanche of Brandywine. George Lippard. LC 77-76926. (American Fiction Reprint Ser.). 1977. 18.95 (*0-8369-7005-5*) Ayer.

Blanche on the Lam. Barbara Neely. 192p. 1993. mass mkt. 5.95 (*0-14-017439-7*, Penguin Bks) Viking Penguin.

***Blanchot Reader.** Ed. by Michael Holland. 288p. (C). Date not set. write for info. (*0-631-19083-X*) Blackwell Pubs.

***Blanchot Reader.** Ed. by Michael Holland. 288p. (C). 1995. pap. write for info. (*0-631-19084-8*) Blackwell Pubs.

Blanco County, Texas. Blanco County News Staff. (Illus.). 835p. 1987. 62.50 (*0-88107-102-1*) Curtis Media.

Blanco en Negro. Tana Hoban. LC 93-42643. Orig. Title: White on Black. (Illus.). (SPA.). (J). (ps up). 1994. bds. 4.95 (*0-688-13653-2*) Greenwillow.

Blanco White: Self-Banished Spaniard. Martin Murphy. LC 88-26139. 152p. (C). 1989. text ed. 37.00 (*0-300-04458-5*) Yale U Pr.

Blancs: The Collected Last Plays. Lorraine Hansberry. 1994. pap. 11.00 (*0-679-75532-2*, Vin) Random.

Bland Ambition. Steve W. Tally. LC 92-16198. 1992. pap. 10.95 (*0-15-613140-4*, Harvest Bks) HarBrace.

Bland Beginning. Julian Symons. 1987. pap. 3.95 (*0-88184-337-7*) Carroll & Graf.

Blandings Castle. P. G. Wodehouse. 255p. (C). 1988. pap. 4.95 (*0-88029-274-1*) Marboro Bks.

Blandy's Urology. 2nd ed. J. Blandy et al. (Illus.). 672p. 1994. 175.00 (*0-632-03679-6*, Pub. by Blckwell Sci Pubns UK) Blackwell Sci.

Blank. (Blank Bks.). 32p. (J). 1986. 2.95 (*0-88682-116-9*, 95167-098) Creative Ed.

Blank Books Series, 8 bks., Set. Philly Murtha. (Illus.). (J). 1986. 2.55 (*0-88682-117-7*, 31196-098) Creative Ed.

Blank Canvas: Inviting the Muse. Anna H. Audette. LC 93-9524. (Illus.). 120p. (Orig.). 1993. pap. 8.00 (*0-87773-938-2*) Shambhala Pubns.

Blank Check: The Pentagon's Black Budget. Tim Weiner. 288p. 1990. 21.95 (*0-446-51452-7*) Warner Bks.

Blank Darkness: Africanist Discourse in French. Christopher L. Miller. LC 85-1157. (Illus.). xii, 268p. 1986. pap. text ed. 13.95 (*0-226-52622-4*) U Ch Pr.

Blank Darkness: Africanist Discourse in French. Christopher L. Miller. LC 85-1157. (Illus.). xii, 268p. 1986. lib. bdg. 30.00 (*0-226-52621-6*) U Ch Pr.

Blank Tapes, Boots & Salads. Stephanie H. Piro. 64p. 1992. pap. 4.95 (*1-880053-01-2*) Pge One Pubs.

Blank Verse. J. A. Symonds. 1972. 59.95 (*0-87968-754-1*) Gordon Pr.

Blank Verse & Chronology in Milton. Ants Oras. LC 66-63667. (University of Florida Humanities Monographs: No. 20). (Illus.). 86p. reprint ed. pap. 25.00 (*0-7837-4921-X*, 2044586) Bks Demand.

Blank Wall & the Innocent Mrs. Duff, 2 vols. in 1. Elizabeth S. Holding. 432p. 1991. reprint ed. pap. 10.00 (*0-89733-366-7*) Academy Chi Pubs.

Blanket. Margot Apple. (Illus.). 32p. (J). (ps-3). 1990. 13.95 (*0-395-51522-X*) HM.

Blanket. 2nd ed. John Burningham. LC 93-24288. (Illus.). 24p. (J). (ps up). 1994. 6.95 (*1-56402-337-0*) Candlewick Pr.

***Blanket Brigade: The Soldiers Story of the 16th Maine, Vol. II.** Cyndi Dalton. 300p. 1995. pap. 13.95 (*0-9642029-2-1*) Union Pubng.

Blanket Burgler. Sandra G. Garrett & Philip C. Williams. LC 93-31883. (Screech Owl Mysteries Ser.). (J). 1994. write for info. (*0-86625-503-6*) Rourke Pubns.

Blanket-Land. Tony Hickey. 112p. 1990. pap. 6.95 (*1-85371-043-1*, Pub. by Poolbeg Pr IE) Dufour.

Blanket Makers, Sixteen Sixty-Nine to Nineteen Sixty-Nine: A History of Charles Early & Marriott Whitney Ltd. Alfred Plummer & Richard E. Early. LC 69-17112. (Illus.). 205p. 1969. 24.95 (*0-678-06508-X*) Kelley.

Blanket Mounting on the Offset Press. 12p. 1988. teacher ed 3.00 (*0-88362-103-7*, 0640); text ed. 16.00 (*0-88362-102-9*, 0641) Graphic Arts Tech Found.

***Blankets: A Grief Journey. Jane L. Wipf. LC 93-94143. (Illus.). 36p. (Orig.). 1993. pap. 14.95 (*0-9638512-0-9*) Spiritseeker. How can we ever survive the death of a child? BLANKETS is a story of love, of hope & of courage written by a grieving mother to her son. So deeply grieved over her 7 year-old son's death from a rare infection, author Jane Wipf composes a heartbreaking letter to her son, telling him all of the things she wants him to know. "God is a blanket all around you, in your heart, in your soul...He comforts you wherever you are. Even when you are dying..." "Then, one night I held you in my arms without a blanket. But a larger & grander blanket of wings surrounded us. Jesus held you & our family as you took your last breaths. He wrapped His everlasting arms about us & took you home to heaven." This book proves invaluable to people who are experiencing grief, schools, hospitals, hospices. Elisabeth Kubler-Ross says of the book, "BLANKETS is a beautiful book to help people if they have lost a child. It is highly recommendable, touching, moving & when you read it you feel you are being wrapped in the love of God." This is a tough book, dealing with tough material, but one that is so badly needed in these times of increasing awarenesses. Soft cover, 35 pages. "I love you, little guy! Mommy." Order from Spiritseeker Publishing, Inc., Box 2441, Fargo, ND 58108.**

Publisher Provided Annotation.

Blankets & Moccasins: Plenty Coups & His People, the Crows. Glendolin D. Wagner & William A. Allen. LC 86-19316. (Illus.). 304p. 1987. pap. 8.95 (*0-8032-9713-0*) U of Nebr Pr.

Blanksmanship. John M. Bennett. 21p. (Orig.). 1994. pap. 5.00 (*0-935350-47-0*); audio, pap. 10.00 (*0-935350-49-7*); audio 6.00 (*0-935350-48-9*) Luna Bisonte.

Blankwaffen des Dritten Reichs, 1993-94. Bernd Stephan. (Illus.). 122p. (ENG & GER.). 1994. pap. 17.50 (*3-9801358-5-3*) Johnson Ref Bks.

Blannerhassett Papers, Embodying the Private Journal of Harman Blannerhassett. William H. Safford. LC 75-146418. (First American Frontier Ser.). (Illus.). 1971. reprint ed. 48.95 (*0-405-02882-2*) Ayer.

Blanquerna. Ramon Lull. (Dedalus European Classics Ser.). 550p. 1987. pap. 14.95 (*0-87052-376-7*, Pub. by Dedalus Bks UK) Hippocrene Bks.

Blanquerna: A Thirteenth Century Romance Translated from the Catalan. Tr. by E. Allison Peers. 1977. lib. bdg. 59.95 (*0-8490-1515-4*) Gordon Pr.

Blas Hernandez y La Revolucion De 1933: La Campana En los Campos de Cuba. Angel A. Laurencio. LC 93-73414. (Coleccion Cuba y Sus Jueces Ser.). (Illus.). 183p. (Orig.). (SPA.). 1994. pap. 19.95 (*0-89729-706-7*) Ediciones.

Blas Meala: Gaelic Folksongs with Translation. Brian O'Rourke. (Illus.). 128p. 1985. 25.00 (*0-7165-2358-2*, Pub. by Irish Acad Pr IE) Intl Spec Bk.

Blaschke Products: Bounded Analytic Functions. Peter Colwell. 152p. 1985. text ed. 34.50x (*0-472-10065-3*) U of Mich Pr.

Blaschke's Rolling Theorem in RN. J. Brooks & J. Strantzen. LC 89-7017. (MEMO Ser.: Vol. 80/405). 101p. 1989. pap. 20.00 (*0-8218-2466-X*, MEMO 80/405) Am Math.

Blasket Island Guide. Ray Stagles. 64p. 1990. pap. 8.95 (*0-86278-197-3*, Pub. by OBrien Pr IE) Dufour.

Blasket Islands: Next Parish America. Joan Stagles & Ray Stagles. 144p. 1980. pap. 16.95 (*0-86278-071-3*, Pub. by OBrien Pr IE) Dufour.

***Blaskets: People & Literature.** rev. ed. Muiris MacConghail. (Illus.). 176p. 1995. pap. 16.95 (*1-57098-033-0*) R Rinehart.

Blason d'un Corps. Rene Etiemble. 256p. (FRE.). 1975. pap. 10.95 (*0-7859-2350-0*, 2070366235) Fr & Eur.

Blason Populaire De la France: Blason Populaire from France. Gaidoz Henri & Paul Sebillot. Ed. by Richard M. Dorson. LC 77-70595. (International Folklore Ser.). (Illus.). 1977. reprint ed. lib. bdg. 33.95 (*0-405-10093-0*) Ayer.

Blasphemer & Reformer: A Study of James Leslie Mitchell-Lewis Grassic Gibbon. Ed. by W. K. Malcolm. 224p. 1984. text ed. 27.90 (*0-08-030373-0*, Pergamon Pr) Elsevier.

Blasphemous Rumors: Is Satanic Ritual Abuse Fact or Fantasy?--an Investigation. Andrew Boyd. 320p. 1992. 9.99 (*0-00-627597-4*) Harper SF.

Blasphemy. David Lawton. LC 93-19145. 228p. (Orig.). (C). 1993. text ed. 39.95 (*0-8122-3219-4*); pap. 16.95 (*0-8122-1503-6*) U of Pa Pr.

Blasphemy: A Radical Critique of Our Technological Culture. Ivan Illich. 1993. pap. 6.95 (*1-882206-02-9*) Argonaut Pr.

Blasphemy: An Anglo-American History of Free Expression. Leonard W. Levy. LC 92-36345. 1993. 35.00 (*0-679-40236-5*) Knopf.

Blasphemy: Ancient & Modern. Nicholas Walter. 96p. (Orig.). 1990. pap. 10.00 (*0-301-90001-9*) Left Bank.

***Blasphemy: Verbal Offense Against the Sacred, from Moses to Salman Rushdie.** Leonard W. Levy. LC 94-31365. 688p. 1995. pap. 18.95 (*0-8078-4515-9*) U of NC Pr.

Blasphemy in Massachusetts: Freedom of Conscience & the Abner Kneeland Case. Leonard W. Levy. LC 70-16634. 592p. 1973. lib. bdg. 65.00 (*0-306-70221-5*) Da Capo.

Blassiah. Dexter G. Harrison. LC 91-67915. 165p. (Orig.). 1993. pap. 12.00 (*1-56002-182-9*, Univ Edtns) Aegina Pr.

***Blassingame Families, Vol. 1.** LC 73-92924. Date not set. 28.85 (*0-8418-4594-8*) Blassingame Family.

Blassingame Families, Vol. 2. W. Doak Blassingame. (Illus.). 555p. 1988. 47.82 (*0-9620041-2-X*) Blassingame Family.

Blast & Ballistic Loading of Structures. P. D. Smith & J. G. Hetherington. LC 94-10813. (Illus.). 384p. 1994. 84.95 (*0-7506-2024-2*) Buttrwrth-Heinemann.

Blast & Counterblast: Contemporary Writings on the Scottish Reformation. Ed. by I. B. Cowan. 76p. 1986. 20.00 (*0-85411-008-9*, Pub. by Saltire Soc) St Mut.

Blast Cleaning & Allied Processes, 2 vols., Set. H. J. Plaster. 826p. (C). 1989. 370.00 (*0-901994-03-0*, Pub. by Fuel Metallurgical Jrnl UK) St Mut.

***Blast from the Past.** B. Eric Rhoads. (Illus.). 300p. 1995. 75.00 (*1-886745-06-4*) Streamline Pr.

Blast from the Past: The Amazing Ernie Bowen. Phil Snow. (Illus.). 200p. (Orig.). 1987. pap. 4.95 (*0-9619079-0-8*) P Snow.

Blast Furnace: Theory & Practice, 2 Vols, Vol. 2. Ed. by J. H. Strassburger. 1062p. 1969. Set. text ed. 529.00 (*0-677-10420-0*) Gordon & Breach.

Blast Furnace Phenomena & Modelling. Comp. by Iron & Steel Instute of Japan. 632p. 1987. 158.50 (*1-85166-057-7*, Pub. by Elsevier Applied Sci UK) Elsevier.

Blast Furnace Technology, Science & Practice: Proceedings. Ed. by Julian Szekely. LC 77-190096. 413p. reprint ed. pap. 117.80 (*0-8357-7312-4*, 2055021) Bks Demand.

Blast Furnace, Vol. 1: Theory & Practice. J. H. Strassburger. lxxii, 534p. 1969. text ed. 369.00 (*0-677-13720-6*) Gordon & Breach.

Blast Furnace, Vol. 2: Theory & Practice, Vol. 2. J. H. Strassburger. lxxii, 506p. 1969. text ed. 329.00 (*0-677-13730-3*) Gordon & Breach.

Blast Off! Poems about Space. Illus. by Melissa Sweet. LC 93-24536. (I Can Read Book Ser.). 48p. (J). (gr. k-3). 1995. 14.00 (*0-06-024260-4*) HarpC Child Bks.

Blast Off! Poems about Space. Illus. by Melissa Sweet. LC 93-24536. (J). (gr. k-6). 1995. lib. bdg. 13.89 (*0-06-024261-2*) HarpC Child Bks.

Blast Off! see Guided Research Discovery Units: Six Project Books

Blast Off! A Space Counting Book. Norma Cole. LC 93-28794. (Illus.). 32p. (J). (ps-4). 1994. 14.95 (*0-88106-499-8*); lib. bdg. 15.88 (*0-88106-493-9*); pap. 6.95 (*0-88106-498-X*) Charlesbridge Pub.

Blast off to Earth! A Look at Geography. Loreen Leedy. LC 92-2567. (Illus.). 32p. (J). (ps-3). 1992. lib. bdg. 14.95 (*0-8234-0973-2*) Holiday.

Blast off with Book Reports. Debbie Robertson. 64p. (J). (gr. 3-8). 1985. student ed 7.95 (*0-86653-327-3*, GA 682) Good Apple.

Blast One. Wyndham Lewis. (Illus.). 167p. (C). 1992. reprint ed. pap. 15.00 (*0-87685-521-4*) Black Sparrow.

Blast Three. Wyndham Lewis. Ed. by Seamus Cooney et al. (Illus.). 300p. (Orig.). 1984. pap. 20.00 (*0-87685-591-5*) Black Sparrow.

Blast Two. Wyndham Lewis. (Illus.). 111p. 1993. reprint ed. pap. 15.00 (*0-87685-523-0*) Black Sparrow.

Blast Vibration Analysis. G. A. Bollinger. LC 79-22421. (Illus.). 149p. 1980. reprint ed. pap. 8.95 (*0-8093-0951-3*) S Ill U Pr.

***Blast Vibration Monitoring & Control.** Charles H. Dowding. (Illus.). 297p. (C). 1995. pap. text ed. 55.00 (*0-9644313-0-0*) C H Dowding.

Blast with the Past: Puzzling History Mysteries. Christin Wilsdon. (Ghostwriter Ser.). (J). (gr. 4-7). 1994. pap. 1.99 (*0-553-37285-8*) Bantam.

Blasted Allegories: An Anthology of Artists' Writings. Ed. by Brian Wallis. 320p. 1987. 21.95 (*0-262-23128-X*) New Mus Contemp Art.

Blasted Allegories: An Anthology of Writings by Contemporary Artists. Ed. by Brian Wallis. (Illus.). 448p. 1989. reprint ed. pap. 23.00x (*0-262-73086-3*) MIT Pr.

Blasted Beloved Breckenridge. Mark Fiester. (Illus.). 1994. reprint ed. 34.95 (*0-9640927-3-5*) Webers Bks.

Blaster: The Blaster Al Ackerman Omnibus. Blaster A. Ackerman. Ed. by Simeon Stylites et al. (Illus.). 304p. (Orig.). 1994. pap. 12.95 (*0-945209-09-6*) Popular Reality.

***Blaster Fun!** Bradygames Staff. (Illus.). 128p. (Orig.). 1995. pap. 9.99 (*1-56686-297-3*) Brady Compu Bks.

Blaster Mastery. Allen L. Wyatt, Sr. 496p. 1993. disk 34.95 (*0-672-30352-3*) Sams.

Blastin' Out of Abilene. Elliot Richmaw. 1988. 3.00 (*0-685-25017-2*) Windless Orchard.

Blasting & Bombardiering. Wyndham Lewis. 350p. (Orig.). 1982. pap. 11.95 (*0-7145-0130-1*) Riverrun NY.

Blasting & Bombardiering. 2nd rev. ed. Wyndham Lewis. LC 67-17112. (Illus.). 359p. (Orig.). reprint ed. pap. 102.40 (*0-8357-7313-2*, 2029954) Bks Demand.

Blasting Cap Explosives. 1991. lib. bdg. 69.95 (*0-8490-4718-8*) Gordon Pr.

Blasting Cap Tin Catalog. Andy Martin. LC 91-90085. (Illus.). 80p. (Orig.). 1991. pap. 8.00 (*0-9628762-0-8*) Old Adit.

Blasting in Ground Excavations & Mines. B. Singh et al. 186p. (C). 1993. text ed. 65.00 (*90-6191-956-8*, Pub. by A A Balkema NE) Ashgate Pub Co.

***Blasting Technology for Mining & Civil Engineers.** Gour C. Sen. 1995. pap. 29.95 (*0-86840-294-X*, Pub. by New South Wales Univ Pr AT) Intl Spec Bk.

Blasting the Historical Blackout. Harry E. Barnes. 1971. 250.00 (*0-87700-027-1*) Revisionist Pr.

Blasting the Lid Off of Buddhism. John R. Terry. 200p. 1993. pap. 7.50 (*0-933704-99-2*) Dawn Pr.

Blastocyst-Endometrium Relationships. Ed. by F. Leroy. (Progress in Reproductive Biology & Medicine Ser.: Vol. 7). (Illus.). 338p. 1980. 158.50 (*3-8055-0988-X*) S Karger.

Blastocyst Implantation. Ed. by Koji Yoshinaga. (Illus.). 248p. (C). 1989. text ed. 50.00 (*0-944903-04-5*) Adams Pub Group.

Blastogenesis: Normal & Abnormal. John M. Opitz. 424p. 1993. text ed. 185.95 (*0-471-59789-9*, Wiley-Liss) Wiley.

Blastomycosis. Ed. by Y. Al-Doory & A. F. DiSalvo. (Current Topics in Infectious Disease Ser.). (Illus.). 256p. 1991. 65.00 (*0-306-43958-1*, Plenum Med Bk) Plenum.

Blasts & Benedictions: Articles & Stories. Sean O'Casey. Ed. by Ronald Ayling. LC 75-8487. 314p. 1976. reprint ed. text ed. 45.00 (*0-8371-8158-5*, OCBB, Greenwood Pr) Greenwood.

BLAT Manual. Ernest T. Newland. 1971. pap. 7.50 (*0-252-00886-3*) U of Ill Pr.

Blatant Artifice: An Annual Anthology of Short Fiction Visiting Writers, 1984-85. Ed. by Edmund Cardoni. 142p. (Orig.). 1987. pap. 5.95 (*0-936739-03-7*) Hallwalls Inc.

Blatant Artifice 2-3: An Anthology of Short Fiction by Visiting Writers, 1985-1987. Anderson et al. Tr. by Helen Lane et al. (Illus.). 168p. (Orig.). 1988. pap. 10.00 (*0-936739-16-9*) Hallwalls Inc.

Blatant Millions: Clayton Williams' Buying Texas. Arthur F. Ide. LC 90-6078. (Illus.). 110p. (Orig.). (C). 1990. pap. 5.00 (*0-934659-10-9*) Liberal Pr.

***Blatant Opportunist Vol. I: Selected Reprints from Midnight Engineering.** Don Lancaster. (Illus.). 144p. (Orig.). 1994. pap. 24.50 (*1-882193-21-0*) Synergetics Pr.

Blatant Raw Foodist Propaganda: or, Consider Your True Nature, or Sell Your Stove to the Junkman & Feel Great! Joe Alexander. LC 90-84154. (Illus.). 160p. (Orig.). 1990. pap. 12.95 (*0-931892-14-7*) B Dolphin Pub.

Blatchford: Memorial II: A Genealogy Record of the Family of Rev. Samuel Blatchford. E. Blatchford. (Illus.). 123p. 1990. reprint ed. lib. bdg. 31.00 (*0-8328-1578-0*); reprint ed. pap. 21.00 (*0-8328-1579-9*) Higginson Bk Co.

Blathwayt Atlas: Vol. II, Commentary. Ed. by Jeannette D. Black. LC 73-7118. 255p. 1975. text ed. 40.00 (*0-87057-139-7*) U Pr of New Eng.

Blatnoi. Mikhail Dyomin. LC 80-54025. 364p. (Orig.). (RUS.). 1981. pap. 18.50 (*0-89830-027-4*) Russica Pubs.

Blattodea, Mantodea, Isoptera, Grylloblaatodea, Plasmatodea, Dermaptera & Embioptera. Michael White. (Animal Cytogenetics Ser.: Vol. 3: Insecta 2). (Illus.). 75p. 1976. pap. text ed. 36.00 (*3-443-26005-5*, Pub. by Gebrueder Borntraeger GW) Lubrecht & Cramer.

Blattstellung und Sprossentwicklung bei Bluetenpflanzen unter Besonderer Beruecksichtigung der Nelkengewaechse. Rolf Rutishauser. (Dissertationes Botanicae Ser.: Vol. 62). (Illus.). 200p. (GER.). 1981. pap. text ed. 27.50 (*3-7682-1304-8*) Lubrecht & Cramer.

Blaue Engel. Ed. by Hart Wegner. 214p. (GER.). (C). 1982. pap. text ed. 15.50 (*0-15-517350-2*) HB Coll Pubs.

Blaue Lotos. Herge. (Illus.). 62p. (GER.). (J). pap. 19.95 (*0-8288-5013-5*) Fr & Eur.

Blaue Reiter Almanac. Tr. by Wassily Kandinsky & Franz Marc. (Quality Paperbacks Ser.). (Illus.). 296p. 1989. reprint ed. pap. 13.95 (*0-306-80346-1*) Da Capo.

Blaustein's Pathology of the Female Genital Tract. 3rd ed. Ed. by Robert J. Kurman. LC 93-23252. (Illus.). 1000p. 1993. 165.00 (*0-387-96452-5*) Spr-Verlag.

Blaustein's Pathology of the Female Genital Tract. 4th ed. Ed. by Robert J. Kurman. (Illus.). 1240p. 1994. 155.00 (*0-387-94166-5*) Spr-Verlag.

***Blauvelt Family Genealogy: A Comprehensive Compilation of the Descendants of Gerrit Hendricksen (Blauvelt), 1620-1687, Who Came to America in 1638.** Louis L. Blauvelt. (Illus.). 1064p. 1995. reprint ed. lib. bdg. 145.00 (*0-8328-4446-2*); reprint ed. pap. 135.00 (*0-8328-4447-0*) Higginson Bk Co.

Blavatsky & the Secret Doctrine. Max Heindel. 133p. 1967. reprint ed. spiral bd. 8.25 (*0-7873-0405-0*) Mokelumne.

Blayde R. I. P. large type ed. John Wainwright. 528p. 1984. 22.95 (*0-7089-1121-8*) Ulverscroft.

Blaze. Susan Johnson. 1992. pap. 5.50 (*0-553-29957-3*) Bantam.

Blaze Allen. Lillian B. Ross. 281p. 1986. pap. 9.95 (*0-88496-241-5*) Coast Pub.

Blaze & the Forest Fire: Billy & Blaze Spread the Alarm. 2nd ed. C. W. Anderson. LC 91-26586. (Illus.). 56p. (J). (gr. k-3). 1992. reprint ed. pap. 3.95 (*0-689-71605-2*, Aladdin Paperbacks) S&S Childrens.

Blaze & the Lost Quarry: Billy & Blaze Find the Way. C. W. Anderson. LC 93-10721. (Illus.). 48p. (J). (gr. k-3). 1994. reprint ed. pap. 3.95 (*0-689-71775-X*, Aladdin Paperbacks) S&S Childrens.

Blaze & the Mountain Lion: Billy & Blaze to the Rescue. C. W. Anderson. LC 92-27148. (Illus.). 48p. (J). (gr. k-3). 1993. reprint ed. pap. 3.95 (*0-689-71711-3*, Aladdin Paperbacks) S&S Childrens.

Blaze & Thunderbolt: Billy & Blaze Head West. C. W. Anderson. LC 92-27153. (Illus.). 48p. (J). (gr. k-3). 1993. reprint ed. pap. 3.95 (*0-689-71712-1*, Aladdin Paperbacks) S&S Childrens.

Blaze in the Darkening Gloom: The Life of Rav Meir Shapiro. Yehoshva Baumol. Tr. by Charles Wengrov. 1994. 19.95 (*0-87306-675-8*) Feldheim.

Blaze of Autumn. Roe Richmond. 1980. pap. 1.95 (*0-8439-0841-6*) Dorchester Pub Co.

Blaze of Embers. Andre P. De Mandiargues. Tr. by April Fitzlyon. 128p. (Orig.). 1996. pap. 11.95 (*0-7145-0132-8*) Riverrun NY.

An Asterisk (*) at the beginning of an entry indicates that the title is appearing in BIP for the first time.

B

An Asterisk (*) at the beginning of an entry indicates that the title is appearing in BIP for the first time.

813

***Blessed Eucharist: Our Greatest Treasure.** Michael Muller. LC 93-61595. 297p. 1994. pap. 9.00 (*0-89555-507-7*) TAN Bks Pubs.

Blessed Eucharist: Our Greatest Treasure. Michael Muller. LC 79-112490. 1973. reprint ed. pap. 13.00 (*0-89555-040-7*) TAN Bks Pubs.

Blessed Events & the Bottom Line: Financing Maternity Care in the United States. Alan Guttmacher Institute Staff. Ed. by Richard Lincoln. LC 87-72461. (Illus.). 64p. (Orig.). 1987. pap. 12.00 (*0-939253-06-2*) Guttmacher Inst.

Blessed Everyday with Miracles, Prosperity & Success: A Poetry Book. Data Notes Staff. 22p. 1986. pap. text ed. 3.00 (*0-911569-92-8*) Prosperity & Profits.

Blessed Grieving: Reflections on Life's Losses. Joan Guntzelman. Ed. by Carl Koch. (Illus.). 125p. (Orig.). 1994. pap. 6.95 (*0-88489-304-9*) St Marys.

Blessed Hope. George E. Ladd. 1956. pap. 9.99 (*0-8028-1111-6*) Eerdmans.

Blessed Hope. Robert Whitelaw. pap. 1.49 (*0-87377-096-X*) GAM Pubns.

Blessed Is He Who Considers the Poor. Gloria Dalessandro. Ed. by Phyllis MacKall. 1989. text ed. write for info. (*0-318-64884-9*) G Dalessandro.

Blessed Is the Spot. Baha'u'llah. LC 58-8815. (Illus.). (J). (gr. k-2). 1958. 14.50 (*0-87743-014-4*, 352-040) Bahai.

Blessed Isle: Hal B. Fullerton & His Image of Long Island, 1897-1927. Charles L. Sachs. LC 90-27112. (Illus.). 104p. 1991. pap. 19.95 (*1-55787-078-0*) Hrt of the Lakes.

Blessed John, the Wonderworker. rev. ed. Abbot Herman. Ed. by St. Herman of Alaska Brotherhood Staff. LC 86-90658. (Illus.). 480p. 1987. pap. 15.00 (*0-938635-01-8*) St Herman AK.

Blessed Kateri Takakwitha: Mohawk Maiden. Daughters of St Paul. LC 80-20403. 1980. 3.75 (*0-8198-1100-9*); pap. 2.25 (*0-8198-1101-7*) Pauline Bks.

Blessed Kateri Tekakwitha. Mary F. Windeatt. (Catholic Story Coloring Book Ser.). (Illus.). 32p. (J). (gr. 1-5). 1989. reprint ed. student ed 3.00 (*0-89555-378-3*) TAN Bks Pubs.

Blessed Life. Ed. by Grace Y. Song et al. LC 83-26389. 664p. (Orig.). 1984. pap. 4.95 (*0-916075-00-1*) Intl Life Mess.

***Blessed Marie of New France: The Story of the First Missionary Sisters in Canada.** Ed. by Mary F. Windeatt. LC 93-61383. Orig. Title: Mere Marie of New France. (Illus.). 190p. (J). (gr. 5-8). 1994. pap. 7.00 (*0-89555-432-1*) TAN Bks Pubs.

Blessed McGill. Edwin Shrake. LC 86-30078. (Contemporary Fiction Ser.). 240p. 1987. reprint ed. pap. 9.95 (*0-87719-077-1*, Lone Star Bks) Gulf Pub.

***Blessed Mother.** 7.99 (*0-517-12441-6*) Random Hse Value.

Blessed Ordinary: Wounds & Healing. Gwenana. Ed. by Jonnie Taylor-Leidt. LC 87-80379. (Illus.). 101p. (Orig.). 1987. per., pap. text ed. 6.95 (*0-931721-03-2*) La Jolla Poets.

Blessed Paisius Velichkovsky, Vol. 1: The Man Behind the Philokalia. 2nd ed. Schema-monk Plato n. Ed. by St. Herman of Alaska Brotherhood Staff. Tr. by Seraphim Rose. LC 76-12010. (Illus.). 300p. 1994. pap. 17.00 (*0-938635-13-1*) St Herman AK.

Blessed Rage for Order: Deconstruction, Evolution, & Chaos. Alexander J. Argyros. (Illus.). 364p. (C). 1991. text ed. 42.50 (*0-472-10221-4*) U of Mich Pr.

***Blessed Rage for Order: The New Pluralism in Theology.** David Tracy. xviii, 272p. 1995. pap. 15.95x (*0-226-81129-8*) U Ch Pr.

Blessed Revolution: English Politics & the Coming of War, 1621-1624. Thomas Cogswell. (Cambridge Studies in Early Modern British History). (Illus.). 348p. (C). 1989. 69.95 (*0-521-36078-1*) Cambridge U Pr.

Blessed Sacrament. Frederick W. Faber. LC 78-66302. 1978. reprint ed. pap. 16.50 (*0-89555-077-6*) TAN Bks Pubs.

Blessed Simon Fidati of Cascia. Pietro Bellini & John E. Rotelle. Tr. by Audrey Fellowes. LC 88-70284. (Augustinian Ser.: Vol. 13). (Illus.). 112p. 1988. pap. 5.95 (*0-941491-18-8*) Augustinian Pr.

Blessed Thomas Belson: His Life & Times 1563-1589. Christine Kelly. LC 87-73289. (Illus.). 160p. 1988. 18.95 (*0-86140-282-0*, Pub. by Colin Smythe Ltd UK) Dufour.

Blessed Timothy Giaccardo. Eugenio Fornasari. LC 91-26364. 230p. (Orig.). 1992. pap. 12.95 (*0-8189-0627-8*) Alba.

Blessed to Be a Blessing. James K. Wagner. LC 80-52615. 144p. (Orig.). 1980. pap. 8.95 (*0-8358-0410-0*) Upper Room Bks.

Blessed Town: Oxford, Georgia, at the Turn of the Century. Polly S. Buck. (American Places of the Heart Ser.: No. II). 179p. 1986. 14.95 (*0-912697-38-5*) Algonquin Bks.

Blessed Trinity. Isabella A. Gregory. 1985. pap. 5.95 (*0-86140-228-6*, Pub. by Colin Smythe Ltd UK) Dufour.

Blessed Virgin Mary. Muzaffer O. Al-Jerrahi. Ed. by Louis Rogers. Tr. by Muhtar Holland. 81p. (Orig.). 1992. pap. 9.95 (*1-879708-04-3*) Pir Pubns.

Blessed Virgin Mary: Excerpt from the Glories of Mary. Alphonse Liguori. LC 82-50587. 96p. 1974. reprint ed. pap. 4.50 (*0-89555-177-2*) TAN Bks Pubs.

Blessed Virgin Mary: Her Life & Mission. Corinne Heline. (Illus.). 152p. 1986. pap. text ed. 10.95 (*0-933963-12-2*) New Age Bible.

Blessed Virgin Mary As Mediatrix in the Latin & Old French Legend Prior to the Fourteenth Century. M. Vincentine Gripkey. LC 72-94166. (Catholic University of America. Studies in Romance Languages & Literatures: No. 17). 1969. reprint ed. 37.50 (*0-404-50317-9*) AMS Pr.

Blessed Virgin Mary in Early Christian Latin Poetry. A. B. Heyden. 1972. 59.95 (*0-87968-755-X*) Gordon Pr.

Blessed Virgin Mary in Medieval Drama of England. Joannes Vriend. 1972. 69.95 (*0-87968-756-8*) Gordon Pr.

Blessed Women of Islam. M. S. Siddiqui. 18.50 (*0-935782-53-2*) Kazi Pubns.

Blessed Yoke. Emil N. Grunfeld. 304p. (Orig.). 1982. pap. 5.95 (*0-686-42885-4*) Makor Pub.

Blessing. Debbi Bedford. (Historical Ser.). 1993. mass mkt. 3.99 (*0-373-28787-9*, 1-28787-9) Harlequin Bks.

Blessing. Christopher J. Corkery. LC 84-42879. (Contemporary Poets Ser.). 64p. 1985. text ed. 21.95 (*0-691-06631-0*); pap. 9.95 (*0-691-01418-3*) Princeton U Pr.

Blessing. Nancy Mitford. 222p. 1989. pap. 4.95 (*0-88184-498-5*) Carroll & Graf.

Blessing. William Zaranka. (Illus.). 42p. 1986. pap. 7.00 (*0-933573-07-3*) Wayland Pr.

Blessing. limited ed. William Zaranka. (Illus.). 42p. 1986. 15.00 (*0-933573-06-5*) Wayland Pr.

Blessing & Curse in Syro-Palestinian Inscriptions of the Iron Age. Timothy G. Crawford. LC 91-19608. (American University Studies: Theology & Religion: Ser. VII). 259p. (C). 1992. text ed. 46.95 (*0-8204-1662-2*) P Lang Pubs.

Blessing Cards. Kathy Tyler & Joy Drake. 1p. 1990. 14.00 (*0-88079-374-0*) US Games Syst.

Blessing Cup: Forty Simple Rites for Family Prayer - Celebrations. rev. ed. Rock Travnikar. 64p. 1994. 3.95 (*0-86716-190-6*) St Anthony Mess Pr.

Blessing Discussion Guide. John Trent & Gary Smalley. 108p. 1988. 6.00 (*0-89109-275-7*) NavPress.

Blessing: Giving the Gift of Power. Myron C. Madden. LC 88-2599. (Orig.). 1988. pap. 10.99 (*0-8054-5056-4*) Broadman.

***Blessing in Disguise.** LC 94-13073. 1995. 14.95 (*0-385-32103-1*) Delacorte.

Blessing in Disguise. Eileen Goudge. 608p. 1994. 22.95 (*0-670-84961-8*, Viking) Viking Penguin.

***Blessing in Disguise.** Eileen Goudge. 496p. 1995. mass mkt. 6.99 (*0-451-18404-1*, Sig) NAL-Dutton.

Blessing in Disguise. large type ed. Marie Ferrarella. (Silhouette Special Edition Ser.). 1994. 17.95 (*0-373-58857-7*, Silhouette Lrg Print) Chivers N Amer.

Blessing in Disguise. large type ed. Eileen Goudge. LC 94-17130. (Basic Ser.). 736p. 1994. 23.95 (*0-7862-0238-6*) Thorndike Pr.

Blessing in Disguise. large type ed. Eileen Goudge. LC 94-17130. (Basic Ser.). 736p. 1995. pap. 18.95 (*0-7862-0239-4*) Thorndike Pr.

Blessing Is. Lily Cavell. (Illus.). 24p. (J). 1993. spiral bd. 8.95 (*1-885038-03-8*); audio 4.00 (*1-885038-06-2*) Uriel Press.

Blessing of Animals. Millicent Vetterlein. 24p. (J). (gr. k-2). 1992. pap. 7.95 (*0-963547-0-5*) St George ME.

Blessing of Business. E. W. Howe. (Collected Works of E. W. Howe). 1988. reprint ed. lib. bdg. 79.00 (*0-7812-1296-0*) Rprt Serv.

Blessing of Business see Collected Works of E. W. Howe

Blessing of Ikons. Mother Thekla. 1988. pap. 1.95 (*0-937032-60-3*) Light&Life Pub Co MN.

Blessing of Not Getting, No. 23. pap. 0.15 (*0-87377-148-6*) GAM Pubns.

***Blessing of Safe Travel.** Jeanne Foster. (QRL Poetry Book Ser.: Vol. XXI). 20.00 (*0-614-06378-7*); pap. 15.00 (*0-614-06379-5*) Quarterly Rev.

Blessing of the Fleet. Irv Broughton. LC 77-8971. (Lost Roads Poetry Ser.: No. 6). 1978. 6.00 (*0-918786-10-X*); pap. 3.00 (*0-918786-11-8*) Lost Roads.

Blessing or Curse: You Can Choose. Derek Prince. LC 90-38671. 1990. pap. 8.99 (*0-8007-9166-5*) Chosen Bks.

Blessing over Ashes. Howard Schwartz. 48p. (Orig.). 1975. pap. 5.00 (*0-686-10818-3*) Tree Bks.

Blessing Power of the Buddhas. Norma Levine. 1993. pap. 15.95 (*1-85230-305-0*) Element MA.

Blessing Way. Tony Hillerman. LC 89-18623. 224p. 1990. reprint ed. 18.95 (*0-922890-09-9*); reprint ed. Collector edition. 25.00 (*0-922890-10-2*) Armchair Detective.

Blessing Way. Tony Hillerman. LC 73-96009. 320p. 1990. reprint ed. mass mkt. 5.99 (*0-06-100001-9*) HarpC.

Blessing Way: A Joe Leaphorn Mystery. large type ed. Tony Hillerman. LC 92-17118. (General Ser.). 304p. 1992. text ed. 20.95 (*0-8161-5430-9*); pap. 16.95 (*0-8161-5431-7*) G K Hall.

Blessing Your Enemies, Forgiving Your Friends: A Scriptural Journey into Personal Peace. Kristen J. Ingram. 128p. 1993. pap. text ed. 5.95 (*0-89243-523-2*) Liguori Pubns.

***Blessings.** Debbie Friedman. Ed. by Randee Friedman & Velvel Pasternak. 46p. 1990. 13.95 (*0-9626286-0-3*) Sounds Write.

***Blessings.** Melanie H. Greenberg. (Illus.). (J). (ps-3). 1995. 15.95 (*0-8276-0540-4*) JPS Phila.

Blessings. Chris Thornton. 100p. 1992. pap. 7.50 (*1-56770-255-4*) S Scheewe Pubns.

Blessings. large type ed. Belva Plain. LC 93-45469. 1994. pap. 17.95 (*0-8161-5793-6*, Large Print Bks) Hall.

Blessings. Belva Plain. 1990. reprint ed. mass mkt. 6.99 (*0-440-20652-9*) Dell.

Blessings: A Reappraisal of Their Nature, Purpose, & Celebration. Thomas G. Simons. LC 80-54275. 168p. 1981. pap. 10.95 (*0-89390-026-5*) Resource Pubns.

Blessings: Reflections on the Beatitudes. John M. Talbot. 128p. (Orig.). 1991. pap. 8.95 (*0-8245-1077-1*) Crossroad NY.

Blessings: Reflections on the Beatitudes. Ed. by John M. Talbot. (Orig.). (C). 1990. 35.00 (*0-85439-377-3*, Pub. by St Paul Pubns UK) St Mut.

***Blessings: Transforming My Vietnam Experience.** Donald J. Yost. 178p. (Orig.). 1995. pap. 12.95 (*1-55612-804-5*) Sheed & Ward MO.

Blessings & Bible Stories: For the Family Table. Judith Ransom. Ed. by Ellen Rolfes. 96p. 1992. spiral bd. 5.95 (*1-879958-20-1*) Tradery Hse.

Blessings & Curses. Christopher Stasheff & Bill Fawcett. (Crafters Ser.: Vol. 2). 288p. (Orig.). 1992. pap. 4.50 (*0-441-12131-4*) Ace Bks.

***Blessings & Cursings of the Lord Jehovah God.** 53p. 1988. pap. 10.00 (*1-57277-006-6*) Truth Center.

***Blessings & Prayers.** Illus. by Judy Jarrett. 48p. (J). 1995. 15.95 (*1-56854-062-0*, BLESS) Liturgy Tr Pubns.

***Blessings & Prayers.** Illus. by Judy Jarrett. 48p. (J). 1995. pap. 8.95 (*1-56854-105-8*) Liturgy Tr Pubns.

Blessings & Sorrows. large type ed. Christine Thomas. 649p. 1993. 21.95 (*0-7505-0507-9*, Pub. by Magna Print Bks) Ulverscroft.

Blessings by Your Bedside. rev. ed. John M. Drescher. (Visitation Pamphlet Ser.). 1988. 1.95 (*0-8361-3476-1*) Herald Pr.

***Blessings for God's People: A Book of Blessings for all Occasions.** rev. ed. Thomas G. Simons. LC 95-76732. 128p. 1995. pap. 8.95 (*0-87793-592-0*) Ave Maria.

Blessings for Your Birthday. Fiona Macmath. LC 91-71041. 24p. 1992. 4.50 (*0-8066-2565-1*, 9-2565) Augsburg Fortress.

Blessings for Your Graduation. Fiona Macmath. LC 91-71040. 24p. 1992. 4.50 (*0-8066-2566-X*, 9-2566) Augsburg Fortress.

Blessings for Your Marriage. Fiona Macmath. LC 91-71038. 24p. 1992. 4.50 (*0-8066-2568-6*, 9-2568) Augsburg Fortress.

Blessings for Your New Baby. Fiona Macmath. LC 91-71039. 24p. 1992. 4.50 (*0-8066-2567-8*, 9-2567) Augsburg Fortress.

Blessings from the Cross: Expositional Highlights from the Book of Romans. Dan Bond. 140p. 1989. write for info. (*0-318-64925-X*) Word Transfer.

Blessings from the Kitchen. Church of Jesus Christ of Latter Day Saints, Santa Barbara Third Ward Relief Society Staff. 1972. 6.00 (*0-686-17209-4*) Sandollar Pr.

Blessings in Disguise. David Clewell. 96p. 1991. pap. 12.50 (*0-14-058672-5*, Penguin Bks) Viking Penguin.

Blessings in Disguise. Alec Guinness. 256p. 1986. 17.95 (*0-394-55237-7*) Knopf.

Blessings in Disguise. Alec Guinness. 272p. 1987. pap. 9.95 (*0-446-38426-7*) Warner Bks.

Blessings in Disguise. Lydia E. Ringwald. 36p. (Orig.). 1989. pap. 8.00 (*0-685-29073-5*) Creative Realities.

Blessings in Disguise, or, the Morality of Evil. Jean Starobinski. Tr. by Arthur Goldhammer. LC 92-17519. 243p. 1993. 45.00x (*0-674-07647-8*) HUP.

Blessings of Abraham Coloring Book. Susan Tate. (Petal Pals Ser.). (Illus.). 12p. (Orig.). (J). (gr. k-3). 1993. pap. 0.39 (*1-884395-06-6*) Clear Blue Sky.

Blessings of Babel: Bilingualism & Language Planning - Problems & Pleasures. Einar Haugen. LC 87-7882. (Contributions to the Sociology of Language Ser.: No. 46). (Illus.). 188p. (C). 1987. lib. bdg. 42.95 (*0-89925-226-5*) Mouton.

Blessings of Diligence. Al Houghton. 32p. (Orig.). 1981. pap. 1.50 (*0-940252-00-7*) A H Ministries.

Blessings of Illness. Basilea Schlink. 1973. pap. 2.50 (*0-551-00446-0*, Pub. by Marshall Morgan & Scott UK) Evang Sisterhood Mary.

Blessings of Imperfection: Reflections on the Mystery of Everyday Life. G. Peter Fleck. LC 87-47538. 224p. 1988. pap. 14.00 (*0-8070-1605-5*, BP814) Beacon Pr.

Blessings of Jesus. Joy Dueland. (Illus.). 1979. 8.95 (*0-931942-01-2*) Phunn Pubs.

Blessings of Liberty: An Enduring Constitution in a Changing World. Ed. by Jack David & Robert B. McKay. LC 88-26554. 400p. 1989. 24.95 (*0-394-56993-8*) Random.

Blessings of Liberty: Bicentennial Lectures at the National Archives. 176p. 1986. pap. 4.95 (*0-89707-265-0*, 468-0005) Amer Bar Assn.

Blessings of Liberty: Safeguarding Civil Rights. William C. Lowe. LC 92-9756. (Human Rights Ser.). (YA). 1992. 22.60 (*0-86593-173-9*); 16.95 (*0-685-59325-8*) Rourke Corp.

Blessings of Liberty: The Constitution & the Practice of Law. Frwd. by Paul A. Wolkin. (Illus.). 276p. 1988. text ed. 88.00 (*0-8318-0605-2*, B605) Am Law Inst.

Blessings of Light. John Roger. 1981. pap. 5.00 (*0-914829-02-5*, 949-1) Mandeville LA.

Blessings of Obedience. Andrew Murray. Orig. Title: School of Obedience; Believer's Secret of Obedience. 107p. 1984. pap. text ed. 3.99 (*0-88368-155-2*) Whitaker Hse.

***Blessings of the Blood.** Amerston. 1936. per. 14.95 (*0-88878-299-3*, Pub. by Beach Holme CN) InBook.

Blessings of the Heart. Jane M. Choate. 192p. 1994. 17.95 (*0-8034-9061-5*, Avalon Bks) Bouregy.

Blessings Out of Buffetings: Studies in Second Corinthians. Alan Redpath. (Alan Redpath Library). 240p. 1993. reprint ed. pap. 11.99 (*0-8007-5488-3*) Revell.

Blessings That Flow from Windows of Heaven: The Tithe Goes to God! The Blessings Come to You! Marvin L. Smith. LC 93-72123. 52p. (Orig.). 1993. pap. 4.00 (*1-882581-03-2*) Campbell Rd Pr.

Blessings That Make Us Be. Susan Muto. (C). 1988. 39.00 (*0-85439-219-X*, Pub. by St Paul Pubns UK) St Mut.

Blessings That Make Us Be: A Formative Approach to Living the Beatitudes. Susan A. Muto. LC 82-13102. 137p. 1991. reprint ed. pap. 7.95 (*0-932506-88-7*) St Bedes Pubns.

Blessings That Make Us Be: Living the Beatitudes. Susan Muto. LC 82-13102. 176p. 1982. 8.95 (*0-8245-0516-6*) Crossroad NY.

Blessingway. Leland C. Wyman. LC 66-28786. (Illus.). 660p. 1970. 50.00 (*0-8165-0178-5*) U of Ariz Pr.

***Blessingway. With Three Versions of the Myth Recorded & Translated from the Navajo.** Leland C. Wyman. Tr. by Berard Haile. LC 66-28786. (Illus.). 688p. 1970. pap. 180.00 (*0-7837-8021-4*, 2047777) Bks Demand.

Blest Be the Quilts: That Bind...Our Hearts in Christian Love. Dorothy Bond. (Illus.). 52p. 1992. pap. 12.00 (*0-9606086-1-3*) D Bond.

Bletzacker's OBBC Study Guide. 2nd ed. Richard W. Bletzacker et al. 310p. 1990. 74.00 (*0-8322-0264-9*) Banks-Baldwin.

Bleu du Ciel. Georges Bataille. (Imaginaire Ser.). (FRE.). 1991. pap. 12.95 (*2-07-072328-3*) Schoenhof.

Bleubite. Alphonse Boudard. (FRE.). 1976. pap. 10.95 (*0-7859-1829-9*, 2070367991) Fr & Eur.

Blew & the Death of the Mag. Wendy Lichtman. (Illus.). 74p. (J). (gr. 3-9). 1975. 5.00 (*0-913512-53-2*) Freestone Pub Co.

Blex. Mark Dunster. 16p. (Orig.). 1994. pap. 4.00 (*0-89642-243-7*) Linden Pubs.

***Bley's Barn.** John D. Brown. reprint ed. pap. 25.00 (*0-7837-9163-1*, 2049864) Bks Demand.

Blick of Tzurik. Chana Faiga Brander. (Illus.). 126p. (Orig.). (J). (gr. 4). 1990. pap. text ed. 9.50 (*0-9629684-0-4*) K K Aharon.

Blickensderfer: History of the Blickensderfer Family in America. Jacob Blickensderfer. 56p. 1994. reprint ed. pap. 11.00 (*0-8328-4185-4*) Higginson Bk Co.

Blickiling Homilies, Pts. I-III. Ed. by R. Morris. (EETS, OS Ser.: Vols. 58 & 63, 73). 1874. 45.00 (*0-8115-3354-9*) Periodicals Srv.

Blickling Hall. National Trust Staff & John Maddison. (Illus.). 96p. 1988. pap. 9.95 (*0-7078-0086-2*, Pub. by Natl Trust UK) Trafalgar.

Blickling Homilies see Early English Manuscripts in Facsimile

Blickling Spirituality & the Old English Vernacular Homily. Jane E. Jeffrey. LC 88-39955. (Studies in Medieval Literature: Vol. 1). 197p. 1989. lib. bdg. 79.95 (*0-88946-315-8*) E Mellen.

Blickpunkt Deutschland. 2nd ed. Jack R. Moeller. (C). 1982. teacher ed, pap. 13.88 (*0-395-32894-2*) HM.

Blickpunkt Deutschland. 2nd ed. Jack R. Moeller. (C). 1982. text ed. 44.12 (*0-395-32689-3*); student ed, pap. 12.76 (*0-395-32691-5*); audio 132.16 (*0-395-32692-3*) HM.

Blickwechsel. Jacqueline Vansant et al. (C). 1990. pap. 27.16 (*0-395-50231-4*) HM.

Bligh: A Chronicle of Mutiny Aboard His Majesty's Ship The Bounty. Sam McKinney. 1989. 22.95 (*0-318-41504-6*) TAB Bks.

Bligh: A True Account of Mutiny Aboard His Majesty's Ship The Bounty. Sam McKinney. (Illus.). 208p. 1992. pap. 12.95 (*0-87742-355-5*, 60132) Intl Marine.

Bligh: A True Account of the Mutiny Aboard His Majesty's Ship Bounty. Sam McKinney. 1992. pap. 12.95 (*0-07-045186-9*) McGraw.

Bligh: History's Most Famous Mutiny. Sam McKinney. 1989. text ed. 22.95 (*0-07-157331-3*) McGraw.

Blight. D. H. Melhem. LC 94-13017. (Illus.). 160p. 1995. 21.95 (*0-7145-4274-1*) Riverrun NY.

Blighted Harvest: The World Bank & African Agriculture in the 1980s. Peter Gibbon et al. LC 93-3606. 175p. 1993. 39.95 (*0-86543-387-9*); pap. 14.95 (*0-86543-388-7*) Africa World.

Blimey, Limey! Wha'd He Say? Shirley Herd. LC 83-14020. 96p. (Orig.). 1983. pap. text ed. 5.95 (*0-930006-02-X*) S Deal Assoc.

Blimps. Roxie Munro. LC 88-18138. (Illus.). 32p. (J). (gr. 2-7). 1988. 12.95 (*0-525-44441-6*, DCB) Dutton Child Bks.

Blimps. Roxie Munro. (Illus.). 32p. (J). (gr. 2-5). 1994. pap. 4.99 (*0-14-055292-8*, Puff Unicorn) Puffin Bks.

Blimps & U-Boats: U. S. Navy Airships in the Battle of the Atlantic. J. Gordon Vaeth. LC 91-37161. (Illus.). 205p. 1992. 39.95 (*1-55750-876-3*) Naval Inst Pr.

Blind. Jack Rudman. (Teachers License Examination Ser.: T-5). 1994. pap. 23.95 (*0-8373-8005-7*) Nat Learn.

Blind Alleys in Social Psychology: A Search for Ways Out. A. Eskola et al. (Advances in Psychology Ser.: Vol. 48). 324p. 1988. 92.50 (*0-444-70360-8*, North Holland) Elsevier.

Blind & Partially Sighted Adults in Britain. I. W. Bruce et al. (Illus.). 352p. 1991. pap. 45.00 (*0-11-701479-6*, HM6497) UNIPUB.

Blind & Partially Sighted Children in Britain, Vol. 2: The RNIB Survey. 292p. 1992. pap. 45.00 (*0-11-701626-8*, HM16268, Pub. by HMSO UK) UNIPUB.

Blind Archer. John G. Betancourt. 240p. 1988. pap. 2.95 (*0-380-75146-1*) Avon.

Blind Argus: A Novel. Gesualdo Bufalino. Tr. by Patrick Creagh. 175p. (Orig.). 1993. pap. 14.00 (*0-00-271048-X*, Pub. by HarpC UK) HarpC.

Blind Bargain. Philip J. Riley. LC 88-90745. (Ackerman Archives Ser.: Vol. 2). (Illus.). 208p. 1988. 24.95 (*1-882127-00-5*) Magicimage Filmbooks.

Blind Bargain. Philip J. Riley. (Ackerman Archives Ser.). (Illus.). 1991. 24.95 (*0-929127-00-5*) Magicimage Filmbooks.

Blind Bargain. deluxe limited ed. Philip J. Riley. (Ackerman Archives Ser.). (Illus.). 1991. boxed 49.00 (*0-685-50114-0*) Magicimage Filmbooks.

Blind Beasts: Chaucer's Animal World. Beryl Rowland. LC 77-104839. (Illus.). 206p. reprint ed. pap. 58.80 (*0-7837-0569-7*, 2040913) Bks Demand.

Blind Beggar of Bednal Green. John Day & Henry Chettle. (Tudor Facsimile Texts. Old English Plays Ser.: No. 143). reprint ed. 49.50 (*0-404-53443-0*) AMS Pr.

Blind Bess, Buddy, & ME. Ruby C. Tolliver. Ed. by Karen Welch. (Illus.). 104p. (J). (gr. 4 up). 1990. lib. bdg. 12.95 (*0-937460-63-X*) Hendrick-Long.

Blind Bow-Boy. Carl Van Vechten. LC 77-78305. 272p. reprint ed. 39.50 (*0-404-15125-6*) AMS Pr.
Blind Brag. large type ed. John Wainwright. 1991. 21.95 (*0-7089-2398-4*) Ulverscroft.
Blind Came Out of Darkness. Alexis Satchell. Ed. by Roswitha Petretschek. LC 84-51969. (Illus.). 69p. (Orig.). 1984. pap. 7.25 (*0-931841-00-3*) Satchells Pub.
Blind Children in Family & Community. Marietta B. Spencer. LC 60-11834. 152p. reprint ed. pap. 43.40 (*0-8357-7319-1*, 2056203) Bks Demand.
Blind Colt. Illus. & Adapt. by Glen Rounds. LC 89-1779. 84p. (J). (gr. 3-6). 1989. reprint ed. 15.95 (*0-8234-0010-7*); reprint ed. pap. 5.95 (*0-8234-0758-6*) Holiday.
Blind Corners: Adventures on Seven Continents. Geoff Tabin. LC 93-28138. (Illus.). 224p. 1993. 24.99 (*0-934802-03-3*) ICS Bks.
***Blind Courage.** Bill Irwin & David McCasland. (Illus.). 224p. (Orig.). 1995. pap. 12.95 (*1-56796-092-8*); audio 14.95 (*1-56796-093-6*) WRS Group.
Blind Courage: A Two Thousand-Mile Journey of Faith. Bill Irwin & David McCasland. LC 92-60012. (Illus.). 208p. 1992. 19.95 (*0-941539-86-5*) WRS Group.
Blind Date. Horton Foote. 1986. pap. 2.75 (*0-8222-0126-7*) Dramatists Play.
Blind Date. Bruce Richards. (Freddy Krueger's Tales of Terror Ser.: No. 1). 164p. (YA). 1994. mass mkt. 3.99 (*0-8125-5168-0*) Tor Bks.
Blind Date. Brad Sachs. 64p. 1992. pap. 6.95 (*0-932616-43-7*) New Poets Chestnut Hills.
Blind Date. R. L. Stine. (Orig.). (YA). 1986. pap. 3.95 (*0-590-43125-0*, Point) Scholastic Inc.
Blind Date Book of Romance. 64p. (C). 1990. 30.00 (*1-85283-272-X*, Pub. by Boxtree Ltd UK) St Mut.
Blind Date Survival Guide: A Practical & Funny (Well, Practically Funny) Step-by-Step Guide to Meeting the Person of Your Dreams. Jeff Nagel. (Illus.). 128p. (Orig.). 1988. pap. 5.95 (*0-923032-00-2*) Blockbuster Pubns Inc.
Blind Deconvolution. Simon Haykin. 350p. 1993. text ed. 73.00 (*0-13-087362-4*) P-H.
Blind Devotion of the People: Popular Religion & the English Reformation. Robert Whiting. (Cambridge Studies in Early Modern British History). (Illus.). 320p. (C). 1989. 64.95 (*0-521-35606-7*) Cambridge U Pr.
Blind Devotion of the People: Popular Religion & the English Reformation. Robert Whiting. (Cambridge Studies in Early Modern British History). (Illus.). 320p. (C). 1991. pap. 22.95 (*0-521-42439-9*) Cambridge U Pr.
Blind Eagle. (Stony Man Ser.). 1994. mass mkt. 4.99 (*0-373-61896-4*, 1-61896-6) Harlequin Bks.
Blind Eye of History: A Study of the Origins of the Present Police Era (With Intro. Added) Charles Reith. LC 74-26636. (Criminology, Law Enforcement, & Social Problems Ser.: No. 203). (C). 1975. reprint ed. 25.00 (*0-87585-203-3*) Patterson Smith.
Blind Eye to Murder: Britain, America & the Purging of Nazi Germany - A Pledge Betrayed. Tom Bower. (Illus.). 544p. 1983. pap. 11.00 (*0-586-08422-3*, Pub. by Granada UK) Academy Chi Pubs.
Blind Faith. Joe McGinnis. 1990. pap. 5.99 (*0-451-16806-2*, Sig) NAL-Dutton.
***Blind Faith: Confronting Contemporary Religion.** Chester Dolan. 350p. (C). 1995. 27.95 (*0-87975-931-3*) Prometheus Bks.
Blind Faith - William Moon: 1818-1894. Edna Stroud. (C). 1988. 40.00 (*1-85072-116-5*, Pub. by W Sessions UK) St Mut.
Blind Field. George Szirtes. LC 93-48951. (Oxford Poets Ser.). 64p. 1994. pap. 10.95 (*0-19-282387-6*) OUP.
***Blind Fortune.** Marti Jones. 368p. (Orig.). 1995. mass mkt., pap. 4.99 (*0-8439-3866-8*) Dorchester Pub Co.
Blind Fury. Anna Flowers. (Illus.). 352p. 1993. mass mkt. 4.99 (*1-55817-719-1*, Pinnacle NY) Windsor NY.
Blind Geometer. deluxe limited ed. Kim S. Robinson. (Illus.). 96p. (Orig.). 1986. boxed 95.00 (*0-941826-13-9*) Cheap St.
Blind Guards of Easter Island. Miriam W. Meyer. LC 77-14528. (Great Unsolved Mysteries Ser.). (Illus.). 48p. (J). (gr. 4 up). 1983. reprint ed. lib. bdg. 21.36 (*0-8172-1048-2*) Raintree Steck-V.
***Blind Hog: Memoirs of a Wall Street Maverick.** Bill Hackett. 1995. 15.95 (*0-8062-5049-6*) Carlton.
Blind Hunger. David Darke. 256p. 1993. mass mkt. 4.50 (*1-55817-714-0*, Pinnacle NY) Windsor NY.
Blind in One Ear: The Avenger Returns. Patrick Macnee. LC 89-32147. 304p. 1992. pap. 9.95 (*0-916515-85-0*) Mercury Hse Inc.
Blind in School & Society: A Psychological Study. Thomas D. Cutsforth. 288p. 1951. pap. 21.95 (*0-89128-011-1*) Am Foun Blind.
Blind in Society & Blindness, a New Seeing of the World. Jacques Lusseyran. Tr. by Dorothea Winkler. 32p. (gr. 7-12). 1978. pap. 1.50 (*0-913098-11-6*) Myrin Institute.
Blind Injustice. Bill Sardi. 100p. (Orig.). 1993. pap. 11.95 (*0-9637874-0-3*) Eye Commns.
Blind Intersection: Policy & the Automobile Industry. Clifford M. Winston. LC 87-806. 108p. 1987. 26.95 (*0-8157-9466-5*); pap. 9.95 (*0-8157-9465-7*) Brookings.
Blind Journey. Bruce Lancaster. 1976. reprint ed. lib. bdg. 22.95 (*0-88411-685-9*, Aeonian Pr) Amereon Ltd.
Blind Jump: The Story of Shaike Dan. Amos Ettinger. LC 90-55654. (Illus.). 392p. 1992. 24.50 (*0-8453-4834-5*, Cornwall Bks) Assoc Univ Prs.
Blind Justice. William Bernhardt. (Southwest Mysteries Ser.). 1992. mass mkt. 5.99 (*0-345-37483-5*) Ballantine.
Blind Justice. Ray Gibson. 1992. mass mkt. 4.99 (*0-312-92866-1*) St Martin.
Blind Justice. J. R. Roberts. (Gunsmith Ser.: No. 147). 192p. (Orig.). 1994. pap. 3.99 (*0-515-11340-9*) Jove Pubns.
Blind Justice: A Sir John Fielding Mystery. Bruce Alexander. LC 94-15059. 224p. 1994. 19.95 (*0-399-13978-8*) Putnam Pub Group.
Blind Leading the Blind. Jan M. Sherrill. Ed. by Clarinda H. Lott. (New Poets Ser.: Vol. 6). (Illus.). 50p. 1978. pap. 3.95 (*0-932616-04-6*) New Poets Chestnut Hills.
Blind Learning Aptitude Test. Ernest T. Newland. 1971. 50.00 (*0-252-00881-2*) U of Ill Pr.
Blind Lion. Paula G. Allen. LC 74-10806. (Orig.). 1974. pap. 2.00 (*0-914476-31-9*) Thorp Springs.
Blind Love. Wilkie Collins. 312p. 1986. reprint ed. pap. 8.95 (*0-486-25189-6*) Dover.
Blind Luck. Mandy Sayer. 140p. Date not set. pap. 16.95 (*0-7022-2560-6*, Pub. by Univ Queensland Pr AT) Intl Spec Bk.
Blind Man & the Cripple - Orchard Village: Folklore: English - Cambodian Version. Wonder Kids Publications Group Staff. Ed. by Emily Ching et al. Tr. by Wonder Kids Publications Staff. (Chinese Children's Stories Ser.). (Illus.). 28p. (J). (gr. 3-6). 1992. reprint ed. 12.95 (*1-56162-128-5*) Wonder Kids.
Blind Man & the Cripple - Orchard Village: Folklore: English - Spanish Version. Wonder Kids Publications Group Staff. Ed. by Emily Ching et al. Tr. by Wonder Kids Publications Staff. (Chinese Children's Stories Ser.). (Illus.). 28p. (J). (gr. 3-6). 1992. reprint ed. 12.95 (*1-56162-126-9*) Wonder Kids.
Blind Man & the Cripple - Orchard Village: Folklore: English - Vietnamese Version. Wonder Kids Publications Group Staff. Ed. by Emily Ching et al. Tr. by Wonder Kids Publications Staff. (Chinese Children's Stories Ser.). (Illus.). 28p. (J). (gr. 3-6). 1992. reprint ed. 12.95 (*1-56162-127-7*) Wonder Kids.
Blind Man on a Freeway: The Community College Administrator. William Moore. LC 72-168858. (Jossey-Bass Higher Education Ser.). 201p. reprint ed. pap. 57.30 (*0-8357-7320-5*, 2025664) Bks Demand.
Blind Man with a Pistol. Chester Himes. (Vintage Crime Ser.). 191p. 1989. pap. 9.00 (*0-394-75998-2*, Vin) Random.
Blind Man's Bluff. Phil Weidman. 40p. (Orig.). 1980. pap. 4.00 (*0-935390-05-7*) Wormwood Bks & Mag.
Blind Man's Dog. Slightly Off-Center Writers Group, Ltd. Staff. (Illus.). 60p. (J). (gr. 3-6). 1994. pap. 6.95 (*1-56721-048-1*) Twnty-Fifth Cent Pr.
Blind Man's Meal. Bryan Aspden. 72p. 1988. pap. 13.95 (*0-907476-99-6*, Pub. by Poetry Wales Pr UK) Dufour.
Blind Man's Peep Show. Julia Vinograd. (Illus.). 60p. (Orig.). 1990. pap. 4.95 (*0-929730-29-1*) Zeitgeist Pr.
***Blind Melon.** (Authentic Guitar-Tab Ser.). 140p. (Orig.). 1994. pap. 26.95 (*0-89724-149-5*) Warner Brothers.
***Blind Melon.** 96p. (Orig.). 1994. pap. 19.95 (*0-89724-145-2*) Warner Brothers.
***Blind Men & Elephants: Perspectives on Humor.** Arthur A. Berger. 200p. (C). 1994. 32.95 (*1-56000-185-2*) Transaction Pubs.
Blind Men & the Elephant, Level 3. Karen Backstein. (Hello Reader! Ser.). (J). 1992. 2.95 (*0-590-45813-2*) Scholastic Inc.
***Blind Men of Hindoostan.** K. Sundarji. (C). 1993. 24.00x (*81-85944-58-X*, Pub. by UBS Pubs Dist II) S Asia.
***Blind Mirror.** Christopher Pike. 1995. 21.95 (*0-312-85895-7*) Tor Bks.
Blind Musician. V. G. Korolenko. 1973. 34.95 (*0-87968-757-6*) Gordon Pr.
Blind Musician. Vladimir G. Korolenko. LC 69-13961. 187p. 1970. reprint ed. text ed. 49.75 (*0-8371-4093-5*, KOBM, Greenwood Pr) Greenwood.
Blind Needle. Trevor Hoyle. 260p. 1994. pap. 15.95 (*0-7145-4252-0*) Riverrun NY.
Blind on the Temple. John M. Bennett. 10p. (Orig.). 1993. pap. 2.50 (*0-935350-46-2*) Luna Bisonte.
Blind Owl. Sadegh Hedayat. Tr. by D. P. Costello. 144p. 1989. pap. 8.95 (*0-8021-3180-8*) Grove-Atltic.
Blind Paltu. Michael Uris. Ed. by James B. Van Treese. 520p. 1994. pap. 9.95 (*1-56901-070-6*) NW Pub.
Blind Panels of English Binders. James B. Oldham. (History of Bookbinding & Design Ser.). (Illus.). 144p. 1990. reprint ed. 80.00 (*0-8240-4048-1*) Garland.
Blind Passion. large type ed. Anne Mather. 282p. 1991. reprint ed. lib. bdg. 18.95 (*0-263-12694-3*, Pub. by Mills & Boon UK) Thorndike Pr.
Blind People: The Private & Public Life of Sightless Israelis. Shlomo Deshen. LC 91-20397. (SUNY Series, The Body in Culture, History, & Religion). 197p. 1992. 59.50 (*0-7914-1035-8*); pap. 19.95 (*0-7914-1036-6*) State U NY Pr.
***Blind Pig: A Detective Sergeant Mulheisen Novel.** Jon A. Jackson. 1995. pap. 4.99 (*0-440-21714-8*) Dell.
Blind Raftery: Seven Nights of a Wake. Peg E. Mayo. 166p. 1991. pap. 14.95 (*1-880797-00-3*) RiverVoice Pr.
***Blind Rage.** Gary C. King. 352p. (Orig.). 1995. mass mkt. 5.99 (*0-451-40532-3*, Onyx) NAL-Dutton.
Blind Realism: An Essay on Human Knowledge & Natural Science. Robert F. Almeder. 288p. (C). 1991. text ed. 52.00 (*0-8476-7709-5*) Rowman.
Blind Reflections: Gender in Elias Canetti's "Die Blendung" Kristie A. Foell. (Studies in Austrian Literature, Culture, & Thought. Translation Ser.). 241p. 1994. 33.50 (*0-929497-79-1*) Ariadne CA.
Blind Side. George G. Gilman. (Edge Ser.: No. 44). 192p. (Orig.). 1992. pap. 3.50 (*1-55817-628-4*, Pinnacle NY) Windsor NY.
Blind Side. Patricia Wentworth. 21.95 (*0-8488-0662-X*) Amereon Ltd.
Blind Side. Patricia Wentworth. 224p. 1991. mass mkt. 4.50 (*0-446-35689-1*) Warner Bks.
Blind Side of Eden: The Sexes in Perspective. Carol Lee. 224p. 1991. pap. 13.95 (*0-7475-0572-1*, Pub. by Bloomsbury Pub Ltd UK) Trafalgar.
Blind Spot in the Mind. Manly P. Hall. pap. 4.00 (*0-89314-306-5*) Philos Res.
Blind Spots & Spider Webs. Bradley B. Williams. 92p. (Orig.). 1993. pap. 5.95 (*0-9620486-2-3*) B B Williams.
***Blind Squirrel & Other Arizona Animal Stories.** Jack Grenard et al. (Illus.). (Orig.). 1995. pap. text ed. 14.95 (*0-9631487-1-0*) Carefree Comm.
Blind Trust. Linda Grant. 1991. mass mkt. 4.99 (*0-8041-0791-2*) Ivy Books.
Blind Trust. John J. Nance. Ed. by Howard Cady. LC 86-22502. (Illus.). 416p. 1987. pap. 15.00 (*0-688-06967-3*, Quill) Morrow.
Blind Trust. large type ed. Susannah Bamford. LC 90-45201. 456p. 1990. reprint ed. lib. bdg. 18.95 (*1-56054-066-4*) Thorndike Pr.
Blind Victorian: Henry Fawcett & British Liberalism. Ed. by Lawrence Goldman. (Illus.). 192p. (C). 1989. 54.95 (*0-521-35032-8*) Cambridge U Pr.
Blind Voices. Tom Reamy. LC 78-3817. 254p. 1978. 25.00 (*0-399-12240-0*) Ultramarine Pub.
Blind Watchmaker: Why the Evidence of Evolution Reveals a Universe Without Design. Richard Dawkins. (Illus.). 1987. pap. 10.95 (*0-393-30448-5*) Norton.
Blind Welfare in South Asia. Usha Bhalerao. 1992. 20.00 (*81-207-1286-2*, Pub. by Sterling Pubs II) Apt Bks.
Blind Women's Emancipation Movement: A World Perspective. Usha Bhalerao. 128p. 1986. text ed. 15.95 (*81-207-0118-6*, Pub. by Sterling Pubs II) Apt Bks.
Blinde Sehen: Die Eschatologie im Traditionsgeschichtlichen Prozess des Johannesevaneliums. Alois Stimpfle. (Beiheft zur Zeitschrift fuer die Neuetestamentliche Wissenschaft Ser.: No. 57). x, 324p. (GER.). (C). 1989. lib. bdg. 86.15 (*3-11-012017-8*) De Gruyter.
Blinded by the Light: New Theories about the Sun & the Search for Dark Matter. John Gribbin. (Illus.). 288p. 1991. 20.00 (*0-517-57827-1*, Harmony) Crown Pub Group.
Blinded Eye: Five Hundred Years of Christopher Columbus. Ziauddin Sardar et al. (Illus.). 92p. (Orig.). 1994. pap. 9.50 (*0-945257-52-X*) Apex Pr.
Blinded Veterans of the Vietnam Era. Robert L. Robinson. LC 74-191191. 39p. reprint ed. pap. 25.00 (*0-8357-7321-3*, 2027342) Bks Demand.
***Blindfold.** Kevin J. Anderson. (Orig.). 1995. mass mkt. 5.99 (*0-446-60247-7*, Aspect) Warner Bks.
Blindfold. Siri Hustvedt. 208p. 1992. 20.00 (*0-671-75953-1*) S&S Trade.
Blindfold. Siri Hustvedt. LC 92-45868. 220p. 1993. pap. 8.95 (*0-393-31013-2*) Norton.
Blindfold. Patricia Wentworth. 1976. reprint ed. lib. bdg. 22.95 (*0-88411-732-4*, Aeonian Pr) Amereon Ltd.
Blindfold Horse: Memories of a Persian Childhood. Shusha Guppy. LC 88-47883. 1993. pap. 12.00 (*0-8070-7043-2*) Beacon Pr.
Blinding Insights & Blind Alleys. Glenn Pickering. LC 88-62110. 128p. 1989. pap. 6.95 (*1-55523-185-3*) Winston-Derek.
Blinding Torch: Modern British Fiction & the Discourse of Civilization. Brian W. Shaffer. LC 92-36623. 224p. (C). 1993. lib. bdg. 27.50 (*0-87023-831-0*) U of Mass Pr.
Blindman's Bluff. large type ed. Margaret Carr. (Linford Mystery Library). 272p. 1987. pap. 11.95 (*0-7089-6360-9*, Linford) Ulverscroft.
Blindman's Daughter. Ed. by Edward B. Adams. (Korean Folk Story for Children Ser.: Bk. 1). (Illus.). 32p. (J). (gr. 3). 1981. 10.95 (*0-8048-1472-4*, Pub. by Seoul Intl Tourist KO) C E Tuttle.
Blindness. Elaine Landau. (Understanding Illness Ser.). (Illus.). 64p. (J). (gr. 5-8). 1994. lib. bdg. 15.98 (*0-8050-2992-3*) TFC Bks NY.
Blindness: Medical Subject Analysis with Bibliography. Edward G. Amaura. LC 87-47621. 160p. 1987. 44.50 (*0-88164-544-3*); pap. 39.50 (*0-88164-545-1*) ABBE Pubs Assn.
Blindness & Autobiography: Al-Ayyam of Taha Husayn. Fedwa Malti-Douglas. 248p. 1988. text ed. 37.50 (*0-691-06733-3*) Princeton U Pr.
Blindness & Children: An Individual Differences Approach. David H. Warren. LC 93-42678. (Illus.). 400p. (C). 1994. 59.95 (*0-521-45109-4*); pap. 22.95 (*0-521-45719-X*) Cambridge U Pr.
Blindness & Early Childhood Development. rev. ed. David Warren. LC 84-16796. 384p. 1984. pap. 29.95 (*0-89128-123-1*) Am Foun Blind.
Blindness & Insight: Essays in the Rhetoric of Contemporary Criticism. rev. ed. Paul De Man. (Theory & History of Literature Ser.: Vol. 7). 339p. (C). 1983. pap. text ed. 15.95 (*0-8166-1135-1*) U of Minn Pr.
Blindness & the Electrical Activity of the Brain: Electroencephalographic Studies of the Effects of Sensory Impairment. Liubov A. Novikova. Ed. by Z. S. Jastzembska. Tr. by B. Sznycer & L. Zielinski. LC 75-155920. (American Foundation for the Blind Research Ser.: No. 23). 359p. reprint ed. pap. 102.40 (*0-7837-0129-2*, 2040413) Bks Demand.
Blindness & Visual Handicap: The Facts. John H. Dobree & Eric Boulter. (Facts Ser.). (Illus.). 1982. 13.95 (*0-19-261328-6*) OUP.
Blindness in a Culture of Light: Especially the Case of Oedipus at Colonus of Sophocles. Eleftheria A. Bernidake-Aldous. LC 89-12752. (American University Studies: Classical Languages & Literature: Ser. XVII, Vol. 8). 243p. 1990. text ed. 40.50 (*0-8204-1024-1*) P Lang Pubs.
Blindness in Children. Miriam Norris & Patricia J. Spaulding. LC 57-6983. 195p. reprint ed. pap. 55.60 (*0-8357-7322-1*, 2020139) Bks Demand.
Blindside: Why Japan Is Still on Track to Overtake the U. S. by the Year 2000. Eamonn Fingleton. LC 94-44958. 384p. 1995. 27.50 (*0-395-63316-8*) HM.
Blindside Blitz. David Halecroft. (J). (gr. 4-7). 1991. pap. 3.99 (*0-14-034906-5*, Puffin) Puffin Bks.
Blindsided. Jack Myers. 96p. 1993. pap. 12.95 (*0-87923-956-5*) Godine.
Blindsided. Dick Richmond-Donahue & Leigh Richmond-Donahue. 172p. (Orig.). 1993. pap. 10.95 (*0-943975-03-4*) Interdimens Sci.
Blindsight. Robin Cook. 352p. 1993. mass mkt. 6.99 (*0-425-13619-1*) Berkley Pub.
Blindsight. large type ed. Robin Cook. LC 92-18297. (General Ser.). 544p. 1992. lib. bdg. 23.95 (*0-8161-5518-6*) G K Hall.
Blindsight. large type ed. Robin Cook. LC 92-18297. (General Ser.). 544p. 1993. pap. 16.95 (*0-8161-5519-4*) G K Hall.
Blindsight: A Case Study & Implications. L. Weiskrantz. (Oxford Psychology Ser.: No. 12). (Illus.). 200p. 1986. 32.50 (*0-19-852129-4*) OUP.
Blindsighted: One Man's Journey from Sight to Insight. Marty Klein. 182p. (Orig.). 1993. pap. 9.95 (*0-9638669-4-X*) Baba Doofus.
Blink. Tom Philbin. 1994. pap. 4.50 (*0-515-11397-2*) Jove Pubns.
Blink of an Eye. Ruth Jespersen. 448p. 1989. write for info. (*0-945009-03-8*) Mother Ashes Pr.
Blink of an Eye: The Invisibility Theme in Modern Fantastic Literature. Frank D. McSherry, Jr. (I. O. Evans Studies in the Philosophy & Criticism of Literature: No. 12). 128p. Date not set. lib. bdg. write for info. (*0-89370-311-7*); pap. write for info. (*0-89370-411-3*) Borgo Pr.
Blinkers & Buzzers: Building & Experimenting with Electricity & Magnetism. Bernie Zubrowski. LC 90-44519. (Illus.). 112p. (J). (gr. 3 up). 1991. pap. 4.95 (*0-688-09965-3*, Pub. by Beech Tree Bks) Morrow Jr Bks.
Blinky & the Blends. Elizabeth Gregory. (Illus.). (J). 1981. 6.95 (*0-933184-11-5*); pap. 4.95 (*0-933184-12-3*) Flame Intl.
Blinky Bill. Dorothy Wall. (Illus.). 356p. (J). (ps-7). 1993. 7.00 (*0-207-16732-X*) HarperColl Wrld.
***Blip in the Continuum.** Robin Williams. (Illus.). 96p. 1995. disk, pap. 19.95 (*1-56609-188-8*) Peachpit Pr.
Blish Family Genealogy, 1637-1905. J. K. Blish. (Illus.). 366p. 1990. reprint ed. lib. bdg. 68.50 (*0-8328-1442-3*); reprint ed. pap. 58.50 (*0-8328-1443-1*) Higginson Bk Co.
Bliss. Claudia Crawford. 432p. (Orig.). 1994. pap. 5.50 (*0-451-17937-4*, Sig) NAL-Dutton.
***Bliss.** Judy Cuevas. 384p. (Orig.). 1995. pap. text ed. 5.99 (*0-515-11587-8*) Jove Pubns.
BLISS: The Berkeley Interactive Statistical System. D. Mark Abrahams & Fran Rizzardi. (Orig.). (C). 1988. pap. text ed. 26.95 (*0-393-95586-9*) Norton.
Bliss, & Other Short Stories. Katherine Mansfield. 1977. 23.95 (*0-8369-4240-X*, 6051) Ayer.
***Bliss Bibliographic Classification: Class A-AL: Philosophy & Logic.** 2nd rev. ed. Ed. by Jack Mills & Vanda Broughton. 56p. 1992. text ed. 65.00 (*1-85739-025-3*) Bowker-Saur.
Bliss Bibliographic Classification: Class AM-AW, Mathematics, Probability & Statistics. 145p. 1993. lib. bdg. 60.00 (*1-85739-072-5*) Bowker-Saur.
Bliss Bibliographic Classification: Class GR-GZ: Applied Biology & Agriculture. 2nd ed. Ed. by Jack Mills & Vanda Broughton. 1992. write for info. (*0-408-70835-2*) Bowker-Saur.
Bliss Bibliographic Classification: Class H: Anthropology, Human Biology & Life Sciences. 2nd ed. Ed. by Jack Mills & Vanda Broughton. 326p. 1981. text ed. 67.00 (*0-408-70828-X*) Bowker-Saur.
Bliss Bibliographic Classification: Class I: Psychology & Psychiatry. Ed. by Jack Mills & Vanda Broughton. 62p. 1978. text ed. 35.00 (*0-408-70841-7*) Bowker-Saur.
Bliss Bibliographic Classification: Class K: Society. 2nd ed. Ed. by Jack Mills & Vanda Broughton. 167p. 1984. text ed. 61.00 (*0-408-70830-1*) Bowker-Saur.
Bliss Bibliographic Classification: Class P: Religion, the Occult, Morals & Ethics. 2nd ed. Ed. by Jack Mills & Vanda Broughton. 43p. 1977. text ed. 31.00 (*0-408-70832-8*) Bowker-Saur.
Bliss Bibliographic Classification: Class T: Economics, Management of Economic Enterprises. 2nd ed. Ed. by Jack Mills & Vanda Broughton. 36p. 1977. text ed. 95.00 (*0-408-70834-4*) Bowker-Saur.
Bliss Bibliographic Classification: Class W: Fine Arts & Music. 2nd ed. Ed. by Jack Mills & Vanda Broughton. 1995. write for info. (*0-408-70838-7*) Bowker-Saur.
Bliss Bibliographic Classification: Class X-Z: Language & Literature. 2nd ed. Ed. by Jack Mills & Vanda Broughton. 1995. write for info. (*0-408-70839-5*) Bowker-Saur.
Bliss Bibliographic Classification: Introduction & Auxiliary Schedules. 2nd ed. Ed. by Jack Mills & Vanda Broughton. 268p. 1992. 75.00 (*0-408-70865-4*) Bowker-Saur.
Bliss Bibliographic Classification Class J, 1990: Education. 2nd rev. ed. Douglas Foskett & Joy Foskett. 84p. 1990. lib. bdg. 65.00 (*0-86291-278-4*) Bowker-Saur.
***Bliss Bibliographic Classification Class R: Politics & Public Administration.** J. J. Mills et al. (Bliss Bibliographic Classification). 155p. 1995. 55.00 (*1-85739-077-6*) Bowker-Saur.
***Bliss Bibliographic Classification Class S: Law.** J. J. Mills et al. (Bliss Bibliographic Classification Ser.). 225p. 1995. 60.00 (*1-85739-067-9*) Bowker-Saur.
***Bliss Bibliographic Classification: Social Welfare and Criminology.** 2nd ed. Ed. by Jack Mills & Vanda Broughton. 200p. 1994. 50.00 (*1-85739-121-7*) Bowker-Saur.
Bliss Carman. Odell Shepard. 1972. 59.95 (*0-87968-758-4*) Gordon Pr.

B

An Asterisk (*) at the beginning of an entry indicates that the title is appearing in BIP for the first time. 815

Bliss Carman: A Reappraisal. Ed. & Intro. by Gerald Lynch. 208p. 1990. pap. 21.00 (*0-7766-0286-1*, Pub. by Univ Ottawa Pr CN) Paul & Co Pubs.

Bliss Carman & His Works. Terry Whalen. 58p. (C). 1983. pap. text ed. 9.95 (*0-920763-45-6*, Pub. by ECW Press CN) Genl Dist Srvs.

Bliss Carman & the Literary Currents & Influences of His Time. J. Cappon. 1972. 59.95 (*0-87968-759-2*) Gordon Pr.

Bliss Case. Michael A. Rockland. LC 89-36392. 176p. (Orig.). (C). 1989. pap. 9.95 (*0-918273-55-2*) Coffee Hse.

Bliss on Music: Selected Writings of Arthur Bliss, 1920-1975. Arthur Bliss. Ed. by Gregory Roscow. (Illus.). 304p. 1991. 45.00 (*0-19-816222-7*, 12065) OUP.

Bliss, Peacemaker: The Life & Letters of General Tasker Howard Bliss. Frederick Palmer. LC 70-130562. (Select Bibliographies Reprint Ser.). 1977. reprint ed. 28.95 (*0-8369-5535-8*) Ayer.

Blissed Out: The Apocalypse of Rock. Simon Reynolds & Bill Albert. LC 90-60291. 192p. (Orig.). 1990. pap. 15.95 (*1-85242-199-1*) Serpents Tail.

Blister D Whistle. Date not set. 7.50 (*0-685-75006-X*, 95196WW) Mel Bay.

Blisters & Bliss. 2nd rev. ed. David Foster & Wayne Aitken. (Illus.). 112p. 1991. pap. 9.95 (*0-938567-27-6*) Cloudcap.

Blithe Images. Nora Roberts. (NR Flowers Ser.: No. 38). 1993. mass mkt. 3.59 (*0-373-51038-1*, 1-51038-7) Silhouette.

Blithe Spirit see Three Plays

Blithedale Romance. Nathaniel Hawthorne. Ed. by Malcom Bradbury. 250p. 1993. pap. 4.95 (*0-460-87403-9*, Everyman's Classic Lib) C E Tuttle.

Blithedale Romance. Nathaniel Hawthorne. 1981. pap. 3.95 (*0-452-00990-1*, Mer) NAL-Dutton.

Blithedale Romance. Nathaniel Hawthorne. 1981. pap. 3.50 (*0-451-52027-0*, Sig Classics) NAL-Dutton.

Blithedale Romance. Nathaniel Hawthorne. Ed. by Tony Tanner & John Dugdale. (World's Classics Ser.). 320p. 1991. pap. 5.95 (*0-19-282598-4*) OUP.

Blithedale Romance. Nathaniel Hawthorne. (American Library). 256p. 1983. mass mkt. 6.95 (*0-14-039028-6*, Penguin Classics) Viking Penguin.

Blithedale Romance. Nathaniel Hawthorne. Ed. by Seymour L. Gross & Rosalie Murphy. (Critical Editions Ser.). (C). 1977. pap. text ed. 10.95 (*0-393-09150-3*) Norton.

Blithedale Romance. Nathaniel Hawthorne. (Notable American Authors Ser.). 1992. reprint ed. lib. bdg. 75.00 (*0-7812-3040-3*) Rprt Serv.

Blithedale Romance see Novels

Blithedale Romance & Fanshawe. Nathaniel Hawthorne. Ed. by William Charvat et al. (Centenary Edition of the Works of Nathaniel Hawthorne: Vol. 3). (Illus.). 559p. 1965. 55.00 (*0-8142-0061-3*) Ohio St U Pr.

Blitz! braille ed. Molly Lefebure. 728p. 1992. vinyl bd. 58. 24 (*1-56956-197-4*, BR8325) W A T Braille.

Blitz: Northern Ireland & the Second World War. Brian Barton. LC 89-81778. 339p. 1990. pap. 27.00 (*0-85640-426-8*, Pub. by Blackstaff Pr IE) Dufour.

Blitz Call: A System for Fear Free Prospecting & Making Cold Calls. Bill Truax & Sue Truax. Ed. by Ellen Schutter. LC 93-94068. 110p. (Orig.). 1993. pap. 12.95 (*1-883826-00-4*); audio 20.00 (*1-883826-01-2*); 69.95 (*1-883826-02-0*) Trufield Pub.

Blitz Call Prospecting Kit: Includes the Blitz Call Book, Unabridged Book on Audio Tape, & Comprehensive Self-Instruction Manual. Bill Truax & Sue Truax. 1993. 89.95 (*1-883826-03-9*) Trufield Pub.

Blitz Cartooning Kit. Bruce Blitz. (Illus.). 56p. 1991. 14.95 (*1-56138-011-3*) Running Pr.

Blitz over Britain. John Duncan & Edwin Webb. 192p. (C). 1991. 100.00 (*0-946771-89-8*, Pub. by Spellmount UK) St Mut.

Blitz over Britain. Spellmount Ltd. Publishers Staff. (C). 1986. 125.00 (*0-685-60260-5*, Pub. by Spellmount UK) St Mut.

Blitzcat. Robert Westall. 240p. (YA). (gr. 7 up). 1990. pap. 3.25 (*0-590-42771-7*) Scholastic Inc.

***Blitzen!** Julian Wiles. 1994. write for info. (*0-87129-451-6*, B79) Dramatic Pub.

Blitzkreig Era & the German General Staff, 1865-1941. Larry H. Addington. LC 75-163955. (Illus.). 302p. reprint ed. 86.10 (*0-8357-9528-4*, 2050453) Bks Demand.

Blitzkrieg. Wallace B. Black & Jean F. Blashfield. LC 90-46580. (World War II 50th Anniversary Ser.). (Illus.). 48p. (J). (gr. 5-6). 1991. text ed. 4.95 (*0-89686-552-5*, Crstwood Hse) Silver Burdett Pr.

Blitzkrieg. Len Deighton. 1982. pap. 12.95 (*0-345-29426-2*, Ballantine Trade) Ballantine.

***Blitzkrieg.** Len Deighton. 1994. pap. 6.99 (*0-06-100803-6*, Harp PBks) HarpC.

Blitzkrieg & Books: British & European Libraries As Casualties of World War II. Hilda U. Stubbings. LC 92-64467. (Illus.). xiii, 471p. (C). 1993. lib. bdg. 62.50 (*1-880622-02-5*) Rubena Pr.

Bliven, Five Families of Charlestown, R. I. Bliven, Crandall, Macomber, Money & Taylor, with Appendix. Earl P. Crandall. 285p. 1993. lib. bdg. 39.00 (*0-8328-3216-2*); pap. 29.00 (*0-8328-3217-0*) Higginson Bk Co.

Blix. Frank Norris. LC 74-95150. reprint ed. 37.50 (*0-404-04787-4*) AMS Pr.

Blix. Frank Norris. (BCL1-PS American Literature Ser.). 339p. 1992. reprint ed. lib. bdg. 89.00 (*0-7812-6807-9*) Rprt Serv.

Blizzard. Christopher Lampton. (Disaster! Ser.). (Illus.). 64p. (J). (gr. 4-6). 1991. lib. bdg. 13.90 (*1-56294-029-5*); pap. 5.95 (*1-56294-775-3*) Millbrook Pr.

Blizzard. Michael Norton. 368p. (Orig.). 1988. pap. 3.95 (*0-8439-2706-2*) Dorchester Pub Co.

Blizzard. Jim O'Connor. (Survive! Ser.). (Illus.). 160p. (J). (gr. 3-7). 1994. pap. 3.50 (*0-448-40435-4*, G&D) Putnam Pub Group.

Blizzard: A Disaster Book. Christopher Lampton. (J). (gr. 4-7). 1992. pap. 5.92 (*0-395-63641-8*) HM.

Blizzard! The Great Storm of Eighty-Eight. Judd Caplovich. Ed. by Wayne W. Westbrook. LC 87-51196. (Illus.). 242p. 1987. 24.95 (*0-9619282-0-4*) Vero Pub.

***Blizzard Bk. 3: Journeys of the Stranger.** Al Lacy. 1995. pap. 9.99 (*0-88070-702-X*) Questar Pubs.

Blizzard Blows. large type ed. Ed. by Kenneth Jernigan. (Kernel Book Ser.: No. 7). (Illus.). 84p. (Orig.). 1994. pap. 3.00 (*0-9624122-9-5*) Natl Fed Blind.

Blizzard of Eighteen Ninety-Six. E. J. Bird. (Tall Tales Ser.). (Illus.). 72p. (J). (gr. 2-6). 1990. lib. bdg. 14.95 (*0-87614-651-5*, Carolrhoda) Lerner Group.

***Blizzard Pass.** T. V. Olsen. 1995. 15.95 (*0-7451-4630-9*) Chivers N Amer.

Blizzard Pass. T. V. Olsen. 160p. 1982. pap. 2.95 (*0-449-12360-X*, GM) Fawcett.

Blizzard Pass. large type ed. T. V. Olsen. (Linford Western Library). 1991. pap. 13.95 (*0-7089-7040-0*, Linford) Ulverscroft.

Blizzard Voices. Ted Kooser. LC 84-12510. (Illus.). 1986. 125.00 (*0-931460-17-4*); pap. 8.95 (*0-931460-20-4*) Bieler.

Blizzard, 1949. Roy V. Alleman. Ed. by Betty Burnett. (Illus.). 194p. (Orig.). 1991. pap. 9.95 (*0-935284-88-5*) Patrice Pr.

***Blizzards.** Arlene Erlbach. LC 94-36339. (New True Bks.). 48p. (J). (gr. k-4). 1995. lib. bdg. 13.50 (*0-516-01073-5*) Childrens.

Blizzards. Steven Otfinoski. (When Disaster Strikes Ser.). (Illus.). 64p. (J). (gr. 5-8). 1994. lib. bdg. 15.98 (*0-8050-3093-X*) TFC Bks NY.

Blizzard's Book of Woodworking. Richard Blizzard. (Illus.). 208p. 1993. 22.95 (*1-55870-273-3*) Betterway Bks.

Bloat in Large Dogs. Siegfried Zahn. (Illus.). 24p. 1983. pap. 3.00 (*0-912183-00-4*) Univelt Inc.

Blob. Ian Thorne. LC 81-19633. (Monsters Ser.). (Illus.). 48p. (J). (gr. 4-8). 1982. text ed. 11.95 (*0-89686-212-7*, Crstwood Hse) Silver Burdett Pr.

Blob That Ate Oaxaca & Other Travel Tales. Carlos A. Amantea. LC 91-19828. 457p. 1992. pap. 12.95 (*0-685-59078-X*); write for info. (*0-917320-32-8*) Mho & Mho.

Bloc of One: The Political Career of Hiram W. Johnson. Richard C. Lower. LC 93-6975. (C). 1993. 45.00 (*0-8047-2081-9*) Stanford U Pr.

Bloc That Failed: Soviet-East European Relations in Transition. Charles Gati. LC 89-36971. 242p. 1990. 29. 95 (*0-253-32531-5*); pap. 12.95 (*0-253-20561-1*, MB-561) Ind U Pr.

Blocade: The Queensland Loans Affair, 1920-1924. Tom Cochrane. 250p. (Orig.). 1989. pap. 29.95 (*0-7022-2104-X*, Pub. by Univ Queensland Pr AT) Intl Spec Bk.

Block: Getting out of Your Own Way. Abigail Lipson & David N. Perkins. 1990. 18.95 (*0-8184-0516-3*) Carol Pub Group.

***Block: Poems.** Langston Hughes. LC 95-12336. (J). 1995. write for info. (*0-670-86501-X*, Viking) Viking Penguin.

Block Adventures: Build Creativity & Concepts Through Block Play. Karen Stephens. Ed. by Martha A. Hayes. (Illus.). 48p. 1991. pap. 6.95 (*1-878727-10-9*) First Teacher.

Block & Graft Copolymerization, Vol. 1. R. J. Ceresa. LC 72-5713. 389p. reprint ed. pap. 110.90 (*0-8357-7323-X*, 2024001) Bks Demand.

Block & Graft Copolymerization, Vol. 2. Ed. by R. J. Ceresa. LC 72-5713. 420p. reprint ed. pap. 119.70 (*0-8357-7324-8*, 2024808) Bks Demand.

Block Book. rev. ed. Ed. by Elisabeth S. Hirsch. LC 84-60160. (Illus.). 216p. 1984. pap. 7.00 (*0-912674-86-5*, NAEYC 132) Natl Assn Child Ed.

***Block Building for Children: Making Buildings of the World with the Ultimate Construction Toy.** Lester Walker & Witold Rybczynski. (Illus.). 167p. (J). 1995. 22.95 (*0-87951-609-7*) Overlook Pr.

Block City. Robert Louis Stevenson. LC 87-33397. (Illus.). 32p. (J). (ps-2). 1988. 12.95 (*0-525-44399-1*, DCB) Dutton Child Bks.

Block City. Robert Louis Stevenson. (Illus.). 32p. (J). (ps-2). 1992. pap. 4.99 (*0-14-054551-4*, Puff Unicorn) Puffin Bks.

Block Clustering Approach to the Definition of Site Classes & an Examination of the Relationship Between Data Recording Strategies & Intrasite Spatial Analysis. Jeffrey H. Altschul & Martin R. Rose. (Statistical Research Technical Ser.: Nos. 3 & 4). (Illus.). 160p. 1985. spiral bd. 12.50 (*1-879442-02-7*) Stats Res.

Block Copolymers. D. C. Allport. 1991. 160.00 (*0-85334-557-0*) Elsevier.

Block Copolymers: Science & Technology. Ed. by D. Meier. (MMI Press Symposium Ser.: Vol. 3). 210p. 1983. text ed. 174.00 (*3-7186-0144-3*) Gordon & Breach.

Block Grants: Set-Asides & Cost Ceilings since 1982. 64p. (Orig.). (C). 1992. pap. text ed. 29.95 (*1-56806-039-4*) Diane Pub.

Block Housing. Pere J. Ravetllat. (Illus.). 192p. 1992. 59.95 (*84-252-1567-6*) Rizzoli Intl.

Block Island. Daniel Berrigan. 100p. (Orig.). 1984. 20.00 (*0-87775-175-7*); pap. 9.95 (*0-87775-176-5*) Unicorn Pr.

Block Island. John C. Pine. 18p. (Orig.). 1982. pap. 2.50 (*0-943430-01-1*) Moveable Feast Pr.

***Block Island Geology: History Processes & Field Excursions.** Les Sirkin. (Illus.). 203p. 1994. pap. text ed. 15.00 (*0-910258-20-1*) Book & Tackle.

Block Level Planning. Girish Misra et al. 1987. 35.00 (*0-317-89538-9*, Pub. by Rawat II) S Asia.

Block Method for Solving the Laplace Equation & for Constructing Conformal Mappings. E. A. Volkov. LC 94-9091. 1994. write for info. (*0-8493-9406-6*) CRC Pr.

Block Printing. Susie O'Reilly. LC 92-43263. (Arts & Crafts Ser.). 32p. (J). (gr. 4-6). 1993. 14.95 (*1-56847-065-7*) Thomson Lrning.

Block Printing. Susie O'Reilly. (Arts & Crafts Ser.). (Illus.). 32p. (J). (gr. 4-6). 1995. reprint ed. pap. 5.95 (*1-56847-301-X*) Thomson Lrning.

Block Pulse Functions & Their Applications in Control Systems. Z. Jiang & W. Schoufelberger. Ed. by M. Thoma & A. Wyner. LC 92-9164. (Lecture Notes in Control & Information Sciences Ser.: Vol. 179). (Illus.). x, 237p. 1992. pap. 50.00 (*0-387-55369-X*) Spr-Verlag.

Block Salt & Candles: A Rhondda Childhood. Mary D. Parnell. (Illus.). 192p. 1991. 27.50 (*1-85411-056-X*, Pub. by Seren Bks UK) Dufour.

Block Salt & Candles: A Rhondda Childhood. Mary D. Parnell. (Illus.). 200p. 1994. pap. 16.95 (*1-85411-103-5*, Pub. by Seren Bks UK) Dufour.

***Block Scheduling: A Catalyst for Change in High Schools.** Robert L. Canady & Michael D. Rettig. (Illus.). 275p. 1995. 39.95x (*1-883001-14-5*) Eye On Educ.

Block Survey of Writing Readiness. Donna Connell. 1990. 19.00 (*0-88047-225-1*, D9008) DOK Pubs.

Block System Modelling by Discontinuous Deformation Analysis. Gen-Hua Shi. LC 90-81262. (Topics in Engineering Ser.: Vol. 11). 228p. 1992. 89.00 (*0-945824-38-6*) Computational Mech MA.

Blockade. (Civil War Ser.). (Illus.). 176p. 1983. 19.93 (*0-8094-4708-8*); lib. bdg. 25.93 (*0-8094-4709-6*) Time-Life.

Blockade. rev. ed. Aron Nimzowitsch. Tr. by Joseph Platz. (Illus.). 65p. (Orig.). 1983. pap. 5.00 (*0-931462-07-X*) Chess Ent Inc.

Blockade! A Guide to Non-Violent Intervention. Richard K. Taylor. LC 76-30600. 191p. reprint ed. pap. 54.50 (*0-8357-8818-0*, 2033469) Bks Demand.

Blockade & the Cruisers. James R. Soley. (Illus.). 266p. 1990. reprint ed. 25.00 (*0-916107-81-7*) Broadfoot.

Blockade Diary. Elena I. Kochina. Tr. by Samuel C. Ramer. 1990. 17.95 (*0-87501-065-2*) Ardis Pubs.

Blockade Law: Research Design & Sources. Michael N. Schmitt. LC 91-24109. (Legal Research Guides Ser.: Vol. 12). vi, 63p. 1991. lib. bdg. 32.50 (*0-89941-774-4*, 307220) W S Hein.

Blockaded Family. Parthenia A. Hague. LC 78-157371. (Black Heritage Library Collection). 1977. 24.95 (*0-8369-8809-4*) Ayer.

***Blockaded Family: Life in Southern Alabama During the Civil War.** Parthenia A. Hague. LC 94-40032. 192p. 1995. pap. 12.95 (*1-55709-247-8*) Applewood.

Blockaded Family: Life in Southern Alabama during the Civil War. Parthenia A. Hague. LC 91-26605. xxviii, 176p. 1991. reprint ed. pap. 7.95 (*0-8032-7254-5*, Bison Books) U of Nebr Pr.

Blockaders, Refugees, & Contrabands: Civil War on Florida's Gulf Coast, 1861-1865. George E. Buker. LC 92-46425. 256p. (C). 1993. 29.95 (*0-8173-0682-X*) U of Ala Pr.

Blockbuster Complex: Conglomerates, Show Business, & Book Publishing. Thomas Whiteside. LC 81-7453. 217p. reprint ed. pap. 61.90 (*0-8357-6878-3*, 2056883) Bks Demand.

Blockbuster Quilts. Margaret J. Miller. Ed. by Liz McGehee & Shellie Tucker. LC 90-15476. (Illus.). 168p. 1991. pap. 12.95 (*0-943574-75-7*) That Patchwork.

***Blockbuster Video Guide to Movies & Videos 1995.** 1994. pap. 7.99 (*0-440-21766-0*) Dell.

Blockbusting in Baltimore: The Edmondson Village Story. W. Edward Orser. LC 94-8631. (Illus.). 256p. 1994. lib. bdg. 39.95x (*0-8131-1870-0*) U Pr of Ky.

Blocked Heart. Edwin Brock. LC 75-6528. 64p. 1976. 7.25 (*0-8112-0577-0*); pap. 2.45 (*0-8112-0578-9*, NDP399) New Directions.

Blocking & Unblocking Plays in Bridge. Terence Reese & Roger Trezel. (Master Bridge Ser.). (Illus.). 128p. 1991. pap. 9.95 (*0-575-02749-5*, Pub. by V Gollancz UK) Trafalgar.

Blocking Board: How to Make & Use the Sewing Tool You'll Never Want to Be Without. Shirley M. McKeown. 52p. 1991. pap. text ed. 11.95 (*0-9629970-0-5*) S M McKeown.

Blocking for Machine Knitters. Pat Hampton. (Illus.). 67p. 1982. pap. 7.75 (*0-9614397-1-8*) P K Hampton.

Blocking, Unblocking, & Safety Plays in Bridge. Terence Reese & Roger Trezel. LC 92-35310. 128p. 1993. pap. 8.95 (*0-395-65669-9*) HM.

Blocks. Jay Allan. (My New Book Ser.). (Illus.). (J). (ps). 1993. pap. 5.95 (*0-9631798-1-0*) Silver Seahorse.

Blocks & Drilling Line. Ed. by Jodie Leecraft. Tr. by Fernando Albornoz. (Rotary Drilling Ser.: Unit I, Lesson 5). (Illus.). 67p. (Orig.). (SPA.). 1982. pap. text ed. 14.00 (*0-88698-033-X*, 2.10522) PETEX.

Blocks & Drilling Line. 3rd ed. Intro. by Kathy Bork. (Rotary Drilling Ser.: Unit I). (Illus.). 65p. 1994. pap. text ed. 14.00 (*0-88698-170-0*, 2.10530) PETEX.

Blocks & Drilling Line: Canadian Metric Edition. 2nd ed. Ed. by Jodie Leecraft. (Rotary Drilling Ser.: Unit I, Lesson 5). (Illus.). 50p. 1980. pap. text ed. 14.00 (*0-88698-021-6*, 2.10521) PETEX.

Blocks, Bears & Building Math Skills. Jeanne James & Patricia Biggar. 1991. 12.95 (*0-88076-148-2*) Kaplan Pr.

Blocks of Tame Representation Type & Related Algebras. K. Erdmann. Ed. by A. Dold et al. (Lecture Notes in Mathematics Ser.: Vol. 1428). xv, 312p. 1990. pap. 45.20 (*0-387-52709-5*) Spr-Verlag.

Blodeuwedd. Tony Conran. LC 88-70904. 72p. (Orig.). 1988. pap. 11.95 (*0-907476-78-3*, Pub. by Poetry Wales Pr UK) Dufour.

Blodgett: Asahel Blodgett of Hudson & Dorchester, N. H. I. D. Blodgett. (Illus.). 144p. 1990. reprint ed. lib. bdg. 33.00 (*0-8328-1580-2*); reprint ed. pap. 23.00 (*0-8328-1581-0*) Higginson Bk Co.

***Blodin the Beast.** Michael Morpurgo. (Illus.). 32p. 1995. 15.95 (*1-55591-211-7*) Fulcrum Pub.

Bloedel Reserve: Gardens in the Forest. Lawrence Kreisman. LC 88-71534. (Illus.). 112p. (Orig.). 1988. 24. 95 (*0-9621076-0-3*); pap. 14.95 (*0-9621076-1-1*) Bloedel Reserve.

Blomfield Letters Covering the Period 1799 to 1845. rev. ed. Eve Buscombe. (Illus.). 70.00 (*0-646-08235-3*, Pub. by Eureka Res AT); pap. 25.00 (*0-646-08236-1*, Pub. by Eureka Res AT) Eureka Resch.

Blond Barbarians & Noble Savages. L. Sprague De Camp. LC 85-28944. (Essays on Fantastic Literature Ser.: No. 2). 49p. 1986. reprint ed. lib. bdg. 17.00x (*0-89370-545-4*) Borgo Pr.

Blond Ghost. David Corn. 1994. 27.50 (*0-671-69525-8*) S&S Trade.

Blond Knight of Germany. Raymond F. Toliver & Trevor J. Constable. 1986. pap. text ed. 19.95 (*0-07-157012-8*) McGraw.

Blond Knight of Germany. Raymond F. Toliver. (Illus.). 384p. pap. 17.95 (*0-8306-8189-2*, 24189, TAB-Aero) TAB Bks.

Blond Knight of Germany. Raymond F. Toliver & Trevor J. Constable. Ed. by Ernest J. Gentle. (Illus.). 318p. 1985. 21.95 (*0-8168-4188-8*, 24189, TAB-Aero); pap. 16.95 (*0-8168-4189-6*, TAB-Aero) TAB Bks.

Blonde & Brunette. Jedediah V. Huntington. (Notable American Authors Ser.). 1992. reprint ed. lib. bdg. 75.00 (*0-7812-3293-7*) Rprt Serv.

Blonde Chicana Bride's Mexican Cookbook. Helen C. Duran. (Wild & Woolly West Ser.: No. 40). (Illus.). (Orig.). 1980. pap. 3.50 (*0-910584-96-6*) Filter.

Blonde Jokes. E. C. Stangland. 1991. pap. 2.95 (*1-880104-01-6*) Norse Pr.

Blondes in Venetian Paintings, the Nine-Banded Armadillo & Other Essays in Biochemistry. Konrad Bloch. LC 94-16906. 1995. 30.00 (*0-300-05881-0*) Yale U Pr.

Blondie: Another Masterpiece! Dean Young & Stan Drake. 128p. (Orig.). 1991. mass mkt. 6.00 (*0-380-76599-3*) Avon.

Blondie & Dagwood, America's Favorite Family. Dean Young. 1990. pap. 6.95 (*1-55698-222-4*, Pioneer Bks) Movie Pubs Servs.

Blond's Administrative Law. rev. ed. Neil Blond et al. (Blond's Law Guides Ser.). (Illus.). 280p. (C). 1993. pap. 14.99 (*0-945819-52-8*) Sulzburger & Graham Pub.

Blond's Civil Procedure. rev. ed. Neil Blond et al. (Blond's Law Guides Ser.). (Illus.). 352p. (Orig.). (C). 1992. pap. 14.99 (*0-945819-35-8*); disk 27.99 (*0-945819-37-4*) Sulzburger & Graham Pub.

***Blond's Civil Procedure.** rev. ed. Neil C. Blond et al. (Blond's Law Guides Ser.). (Illus.). 330p. (C). 1995. pap. text ed. 14.99 (*0-945819-85-4*) Sulzburger & Graham Pub.

Blond's Civil Procedure for Yeazel. Neil Blond et al. (Blond's Law Guides Ser.). (Illus.). 196p. (Orig.). (C). 1993. pap. 14.99 (*0-945819-45-5*) Sulzburger & Graham Pub.

Blond's Constitutional Law. 3rd ed. Neil Blond et al. (Blond's Law Guides Ser.). (Illus.). 440p. (Orig.). (C). 1993. pap. 14.99 (*0-945819-44-7*) Sulzburger & Graham Pub.

Blond's Contracts. rev. ed. Neil C. Blond et al. (Blond's Law Guides Ser.). (Illus.). 462p. (Orig.). (C). 1992. pap. 14.99 (*0-945819-28-5*); disk 27.99 (*0-945819-29-3*) Sulzburger & Graham Pub.

***Blond's Contracts.** rev. ed. Neil C. Blond et al. (Blond's Law Guides Ser.). (Illus.). 433p. (Orig.). (C). 1995. pap. text ed. 14.99 (*0-945819-84-6*) Sulzburger & Graham Pub.

Blond's Contracts Essay Questions: Essay Questions. Daniel Desario et al. (Blond's Essay Ser.). 160p. (Orig.). 1992. pap. 19.99 (*0-945819-22-6*) Sulzburger & Graham Pub.

Blond's Contracts for Farnsworth. Neil C. Blond et al. (Blond's Law Guides Ser.). (Illus.). 208p. (Orig.). (C). 1992. pap. 14.99 (*0-945819-27-7*) Sulzburger & Graham Pub.

Blond's Corporate Tax. Neil C. Blond et al. (Blond's Law Guides Ser.). 284p. (C). 1991. pap. 14.99 (*0-945819-13-7*) Sulzburger & Graham Pub.

Blond's Corporations. Neil C. Blond et al. (Blond's Law Guides Ser.). 372p. (C). 1991. pap. 14.99 (*0-945819-14-5*) Sulzburger & Graham Pub.

***Blond's Corporations.** rev. ed. Neil C. Blond et al. (Blond's Law Guides Ser.). (Illus.). 349p. (C). 1995. pap. text ed. 14.99 (*0-945819-82-X*) Sulzburger & Graham Pub.

***Blond's Criminal Law.** rev. ed. Neil C. Blond et al. (Blond's Law Guides Ser.). (Illus.). 349p. (Orig.). (C). 1995. pap. text ed. 14.99 (*0-945819-83-8*) Sulzburger & Graham Pub.

Blond's Criminal Law. 3rd ed. Neil C. Blond. (Blond's Law Guides Ser.). (Illus.). 340p. (Orig.). (C). 1994. pap. 14.99 (*0-945819-55-2*) Sulzburger & Graham Pub.

Blond's Criminal Procedure. 3rd ed. Neil C. Blond. (Blond's Law Guides Ser.). (Illus.). 295p. (Orig.). (C). 1994. pap. 14.99 (*0-945819-53-6*) Sulzburger & Graham Pub.

Blond's Essays Questions for Torts. Daniel Desario et al. (Blond's Essay Ser.). 160p. (Orig.). (C). 1992. pap. 19.99 (*0-945819-21-8*) Sulzburger & Graham Pub.

Blond's Evidence. 3rd ed. Neil C. Blond. (Blond's Law Guides Ser.). 456p. (Orig.). (C). Date not set. pap. 14.99 (*0-945819-56-0*) Sulzburger & Graham Pub.

An Asterisk (*) at the beginning of an entry indicates that the title is appearing in BIP for the first time.

Blond's Family Law. Neil C. Blond et al. (Blond's Law Guides Ser.). 346p. (C). 1991. pap. 14.99 (*0-945819-16-1*) Sulzburger & Graham Pub.

***Blond's Family Law.** rev. ed. Neil Blond et al. (Blond's Law Guides Ser.). (Illus.). 355p. (C). 1994. pap. text ed. 14.99 (*0-945819-67-6*) Sulzburger & Graham Pub.

Blond's Federal Income Taxation. rev. ed. Neil C. Blond & David Minars. (Blond's Accounting Ser.). (Illus.). 283p. (C). 1994. text ed. 36.99 (*0-945819-54-4*) Sulzburger & Graham Pub.

Blond's Income Tax (Personal) rev. ed. Neil Blond et al. (Blond's Law Guides Ser.). (Illus.). 296p. (C). 1993. pap. 14.99 (*0-945819-51-X*) Sulzburger & Graham Pub.

Blond's International Law. Neil C. Blond et al. (Blond's Law Guides Ser.). 312p. (C). 1991. pap. 14.99 (*0-945819-12-9*) Sulzburger & Graham Pub.

Blond's Multistate. 4th ed. Neil C. Blond et al. (Blond's Law Guides Ser.). 508p. (C). 1992. pap. 29.99 (*0-945819-17-X*) Sulzburger & Graham Pub.

Blond's Professional Responsibility. Brett Harris. (Blond's Multiple Choice Questions Ser.). 200p. (Orig.). (C). 1992. pap. 19.99 (*0-945819-34-X*) Sulzburger & Graham Pub.

Blond's Property. rev. ed. Neil Blond et al. (Blond's Law Guides Ser.). (Illus.). 336p. (Orig.). (C). 1992. pap. 14.99 (*0-945819-31-5*) Sulzburger & Graham Pub.

Blond's Property for Dukeminier. Neil Blond et al. (Blond's Law Guides Ser.). (Illus.). 192p. (Orig.). (C). 1992. pap. 14.99 (*0-945819-30-7*) Sulzburger & Graham Pub.

Blond's Torts. rev. ed. Neil Blond et al. (Blond's Law Guides Ser.). (Illus.). 272p. (Orig.). (C). 1992. pap. 14.99 (*0-945819-24-2*) Sulzburger & Graham Pub.

Blond's Torts for Henderson. Neil Blond et al. (Blond's Law Guides Ser.). (Illus.). 186p. (Orig.). (C). 1993. pap. 14.99 (*0-945819-47-1*) Sulzburger & Graham Pub.

Blond's Torts for Prosser. Neil Blond et al. (Blond's Law Guides Ser.). (Illus.). 256p. (Orig.). (C). 1992. pap. 13.99 (*0-945819-25-0*); disk 27.99 (*0-945819-26-9*) Sulzburger & Graham Pub.

***Blond's Torts (Wade Edition)** rev. ed. Neil C. Blond et al. (Blond's Law Guides Ser.). 235p. (C). 1994. pap. text ed. 14.99 (*0-945819-66-8*) Sulzburger & Graham Pub.

Blood. Harwant S. Bains. (Methuen New Theatrescripts Ser.). 47p. (Orig.). (C). 1989. pap. 11.95 (*0-413-19520-1*, A0365, Pub. by Methuen UK) Heinemann.

Blood. Ron Dee. Ed. by Dana Isaacson. 320p. (Orig.). 1993. mass mkt. 4.99 (*0-671-79242-3*) PB.

Blood. Janice Galloway. LC 91-50135. 192p. 1991. 19.00 (*0-679-40594-1*) Random.

Blood. Benny Hinn. 180p. 1993. 14.99 (*0-88419-346-2*, Creation Hse) Strang Comms Co.

Blood. Dennis W. Ross. LC 87-70225. (Carolina Biology Readers Ser.: No. 184). (Illus.). 16p. (Orig.). (YA). (gr. 10 up). 1988. pap. text ed. 2.75 (*0-89278-184-X*, 45-9784) Carolina Biological.

***Blood: A Southern Novel.** Michael Moorcock. LC 95-15749. 1995. write for info. (*0-688-14362-8*) Morrow.

Blood: A Tale. J. M. DeMatteis & Williams. (Illus.). 192p. 1989. pap. 17.95 (*0-87135-492-6*) Marvel Entmnt.

Blood: Atlas & Sourcebook of Hematology. Carola T. Kapff & James H. Jandl. 1981. 79.50 (*0-316-48276-5*) Little.

Blood: Atlas & Sourcebook of Hematology. 2nd ed. Carola T. Kapff. 1991. 120.00 (*0-316-48274-9*) Little.

***Blood: Hemostasis, Transfusion, & Alternatives in the Perioperative Period.** Carol L. Lake & Roger A. Moore. 496p. 1995. 125.00 (*0-7817-0267-4*) Raven.

Blood: Pathophysiology. Jandl. 1990. 49.95 (*0-86542-122-6*) Blackwell Sci.

Blood: Principles & Practice of Hematology. Handin et al. (C). 1994. text ed. 195.00 (*0-397-50944-8*) Lippincott.

Blood: Rheology, Hemolysis, Gas & Surface Interactions. Ed. by D. N. Ghista et al. (Advances in Cardiovascular Physics Ser.: Vol. 3). (Illus.). 1979. 78.50 (*3-8055-2852-3*) S Karger.

Blood: Textbook of Hematology. James H. Jandl. (Illus.). 1246p. 1987. 150.00 (*0-316-45729-9*, Little Med Div) Little.

Blood about the Heart. Sarah Menefee. LC 91-58997. 80p. (Orig.). 1992. pap. 10.95 (*0-915306-53-0*) Curbstone.

Blood Alcohol Testing in the Clinical Laboratory. (Proposed Guideline Ser.: Vol. 8). 1988. 40.00 (*1-56238-094-X*, TOM6-P) Natl Comm Clin Lab Stds.

Blood Alone. Elaine Bergstrom. 336p. 1994. pap. text ed. 4.99 (*0-441-00088-6*) Ace Bks.

Blood & Ashes. Gyerogos C. Hatonn. 245p. (Orig.). (C). 1990. pap. 10.00 (*0-922356-25-4*) Amer West Pubs.

Blood & Banquets: A Berlin Diary. Bella Fromm. 1990. 21.95 (*1-55972-055-7*, Birch Ln Pr) Carol Pub Group.

Blood & Belief: Family Survival & Confessional Identity among the Provincial Huguenot Nobility. Raymond A. Mentzer, Jr. LC 93-25955. 288p. 1994. 32.95 (*1-55753-041-6*) Purdue U Pr.

Blood & Belonging: Journeys Into the New Nationalism. Michael Ignatieff. LC 93-30954. 1994. reprint ed. 21.00 (*0-374-11440-4*) FS&G.

***Blood & Belongings.** Michael Ignatieff. 288p. Date not set. 11.00 (*0-374-52448-3*) FS&G.

Blood & Bone: The Call of Kinship in Somali Society. I. M. Lewis. LC 93-47165. 286p. 1994. 45.95 (*0-932415-92-X*); pap. 16.95 (*0-932415-93-8*) Red Sea Pr.

Blood & Bones. Clifton Snider. 80p. 1987. 14.95 (*0-930090-32-2*); pap. 6.95 (*0-930090-33-0*) Applezaba.

Blood & Family. Thomas Kinsella. (Oxford Poets Ser.). 96p. 1989. pap. 9.95 (*0-19-282182-2*) OUP.

Blood & Feathers: Selected Poems of Jacques Prevert. Jacques Prevert. Tr. by Harriet Zinnes. 144p. 1993. reprint ed. pap. 11.95 (*1-55921-056-7*) Moyer Bell.

Blood & Flesh: Black American & African Identifications. Josephine M. Moikobu. LC 80-1706. (Contributions in Afro-American & African Studies: No. 59). (Illus.). xii, 226p. 1981. text ed. 49.95 (*0-313-22549-4*, MBF/, Greenwood Pr) Greenwood.

Blood & Guts. Linda Allison. (Brown Paper School Bks.). (Illus.). (J). (gr. 5-12). 1976. pap. 11.95 (*0-316-03443-6*) Little.

Blood & Guts Dingbats Book. Carole Marsh. (Carole Marsh Dingbats Book Ser.). (Illus.). (YA). (gr. 3-12). 1994. lib. bdg. 24.95 (*0-7933-5398-X*); pap. 14.95 (*0-7933-5399-8*); disk 29.95 (*0-7933-5400-5*) Gallopade Pub Group.

Blood & Guts in High School. Kathy Acker. 176p. 1989. pap. 10.95 (*0-8021-3193-X*) Grove-Atltic.

Blood & Honor. George Anastasia. 448p. 1993. mass mkt. 4.99 (*0-8217-4254-X*) Zebra.

Blood & Honor. Simon R. Green. 336p. (Orig.). 1993. pap. 4.99 (*0-451-45242-9*, ROC) NAL-Dutton.

Blood & Honor: Inside the Scarfo Mob - The Story of the Most Violent Mafia Family. George Anastasia. (Illus.). 336p. 1991. 22.00 (*0-688-09260-8*) Morrow.

***Blood & Iron: Story & Storytelling in Homer's Odyssey.** S. Douglas Olson. LC 94-45655. (Mnemosyne, Bibliotheca Classica Batava Ser.: Vol. 145). 1995. write for info. (*90-04-10251-5*) E J Brill.

Blood & Its Third Anatomical Element. A. Bechamp. 1991. lib. bdg. 250.00 (*0-87700-927-9*) Revisionist Pr.

Blood & Its Third Anatomical Element. Bechamp. reprint ed. 22.50 (*0-685-71643-0*) Mokelumne.

Blood & Judgement. Michael Gilbert. 200p. 1994. 16.50 (*0-7451-8629-7*, Black Dagger) Chivers N Amer.

Blood & Judgment. large type ed. Jonathan Havard. 512p. 1986. 23.95 (*0-7089-8331-6*, Charnwood) Ulverscroft.

Blood & Knavery: A Collection of English Renaissance Pamphlets & Ballads of Crime & Sin. Joseph H. Marshburn & Alan R. Velie. LC 72-3523. (Illus.). 215p. 1973. 25.00 (*0-8386-1010-2*) Fairleigh Dickinson.

Blood & Lust. Paul Lockborn et al. Ed. by Sam Shirley. (Pendragon Roleplaying Game System Ser.). (Illus.). 128p. (Orig.). (J). (gr. 7 up). 1991. pap. 18.95 (*0-933635-84-2*, 2711) Chaosium.

Blood & Milk Poems. Ruth Whitman. 1963. 7.95 (*0-8079-0016-8*) October.

Blood & Oil in the Orient. Bey Essad. Tr. by Elsa Talmey. LC 72-1046. reprint ed. 12.50 (*0-404-00796-1*) AMS Pr.

Blood & Pity: A True Story of Deceit & Murder. M. E. Cooper. LC 94-70390. (Illus.). 216p. (Orig.). 1994. pap. 11.95 (*0-918751-37-3*, 24) J O Flores.

Blood & Plasma: Artificial & Substitutes: Index of Modern Authors & Subjects with Guide for Rapid Research. Science & Life Consultants Association Staff. LC 90-56298. 160p. 1991. 44.50 (*1-55914-360-6*); pap. 39.50 (*1-55914-361-4*) ABBE Pubs Assn.

Blood & Power: Organized Crime in Twentieth-Century America. Stephen Fox. (Illus.). 512p. 1990. pap. 10.95 (*0-14-013438-7*, Penguin Bks) Viking Penguin.

Blood & Rage: The Japanese Red Army. William R. Farrell. 256p. 1990. text ed. 24.95 (*0-669-19756-4*) Free Pr.

Blood & Roses. Sharon Bainbridge. 288p. (Orig.). 1994. pap. 4.99 (*1-55773-985-4*) Diamond.

***Blood & Sacrifice: The Civil War Journal of a Confederate Soldier.** William P. Chambers. Ed. & Intro. by Richard A. Baumgartner. (Illus.). 288p. 1994. 21.95 (*1-885033-01-X*) Blue Acorn Pr.

Blood & Sand Tango Including the Famous "Veloz & Yolanda" Parallel Pattern. (Ballroom Dance Ser.). 1985. lib. bdg. 250.00 (*0-87700-733-0*) Revisionist Pr.

Blood & Sand Tango Including the Famous Veloz & Yolanda Parallel Pattern. (Ballroom Dance Ser.). 1986. lib. bdg. 79.95 (*0-8490-3437-X*) Gordon Pr.

***Blood & Soil.** John Haberstroh. (Illus.). 120p. 1995. pap. 12.00 (*0-8059-3642-4*) Dorrance.

Blood & Thunder. M. W. Disher. LC 73-21683. (English Literature Ser.: No. 33). 1974. lib. bdg. 75.00 (*0-8383-1761-8*) M S G Haskell Hse.

***Blood & Thunder: A Nathan Heller Novel.** Max A. Collins. LC 94-45895. 1995. 21.95 (*0-525-93759-5*, Dutton) NAL-Dutton.

Blood-&-Thunder Adventure on Hurricane Peak. Margaret Mahy. LC 89-8098. (Illus.). 144p. (J). (gr. 4-7). 1989. text ed. 13.95 (*0-689-50488-8*, McElderry) S&S Childrens.

***Blood & Treasure: Confederate Empire in the Southwest.** Donald S. Frazier. LC 94-39221. (Military History Ser.: No. 41). (Illus.). 336p. 1995. 29.95 (*0-89096-639-7*) Tex A&M Univ Pr.

Blood & War. Created by Gordon R. Dickson. (Harriers Ser.: Bk. 2). 256p. 1993. mass mkt. 4.99 (*0-671-72181-X*) Baen Bks.

Blood & Water. Eilis NiDhuibhne. 148p. (C). 1991. pap. 9.95 (*0-946211-54-X*, Pub. by Attic IE) InBook.

***Blood & Water: The Death & Resurrection of Jesus in John 18-21.** John P. Heil. LC 95-10479. (Catholic Biblical Quarterly Monographs: Vol. 27). 1995. write for info. (*0-915170-26-4*) Catholic Bibl Assn.

Blood & White Apples. Stella V. Radulescu. LC 93-29557. 64p. 1993. pap. 12.95 (*0-7734-2769-4*, Mellen Poetry Pr) E Mellen.

Blood & Wine: The Unauthorized Story of the Gallo Wine Empire & the Family Scandal That Threatened to Destroy It. Ellen Hawkes. 1993. 25.00 (*0-671-64986-8*) S&S Trade.

Blood Assassins. Jerry Ahern. (Survivalist Ser.: No. 24). 384p. 1992. pap. 3.50 (*0-8217-3909-3*) Zebra.

***Blood at Fort Bridger.** Legg. 1995. mass mkt. 4.99 (*0-312-95447-6*) St Martin.

Blood at Sand Creek: The Massacre Revisited. Bob Scott. LC 94-15664. (Illus.). 235p. 1994. pap. 8.95 (*0-87004-361-7*) Caxton.

Blood at the Root. Aisha Eshe. Ed. by Yoly Zentella. 71p. (Orig.). 1990. pap. 6.95 (*0-943557-01-1*) Esoterica Pr.

Blood at the Root. 2nd ed. Aisha Eshe. Ed. by Yoly Zentella. 71p. (Orig.). 1990. pap. 8.50 (*0-943557-03-8*) Esoterica Pr.

***Blood Autumn: A Taggart Roper Mystery.** William Saunders. LC 94-45768. 1995. 21.00 (*0-312-11755-8*) St Martin.

Blood Bank GMPS. Ed. by Thomas G. Crouthamel. LC 92-81865. (Handi-Regs Ser.: No. 9206). 112p. (Orig.). 1992. pap. 21.95 (*0-940701-26-X*) Keystone Pr.

Blood Banking, Vol. 1. Ed. by Tibor J. Greenwalt et al. LC 76-27688. (Clinical Lab Science Ser.: Pt. D). 616p. 1977. 89.00 (*0-8493-7011-6*, RB37, CRC Reprint) Franklin.

Blood Banking, Vol. 2. Ed. by Tibor J. Greenwalt & Edwin A. Steane. (Clinical Lab Science Ser.: Pt. D). 400p. 1981. 89.00 (*0-8493-7012-4*, RB37, CRC Reprint) Franklin.

Blood Banking, Vol. 3. Ed. by Tibor J. Greenwalt & Edwin A. Steane. (Clinical Lab Science Ser.: Pt. D). 336p. 1981. 89.00 (*0-8493-7013-2*, RB37, CRC Reprint) Franklin.

Blood Banking Markets. (Market Research Reports: No. 320). (Illus.). 148p. 1992. 795.00 (*0-317-05031-1*) Theta Corp.

Blood Bath. Linda Stahl Borlik. 448p. 1987. pap. 3.95 (*0-8217-2040-6*) Zebra.

Blood Beast. Don D'Ammassa. 448p. 1988. pap. 3.95 (*1-55817-096-0*, Pinnacle NY) Windsor NY.

Blood, Blood Products, & AIDS. Ed. by R. Madhok et al. LC 87-21530. (Contemporary Medicine & Public Health Ser.). 244p. 1988. text ed. 55.00x (*0-8018-3608-5*) Johns Hopkins.

Blood, Blood Products, & HIV. 2nd ed. R. Madhok et al. 256p. 1993. 69.00 (*0-412-40400-1*) Chapman & Hall.

Blood-Boiling Black Blues. Odimumba Kwamdela, pseud. LC 83-82046. 50p. 1983. pap. 3.50 (*0-941266-03-6*) Kibo Bks.

Blood Bond. William W. Johnstone. 1989. pap. 2.95 (*0-8217-2724-9*) Zebra.

Blood Bond: Death in Snake Creek, No. 8. William W. Johnstone. 224p. 1994. mass mkt. 3.99 (*0-8217-4784-3*) Zebra.

Blood Bond: Devil Creek Crossfire. William W. Johnstone. 288p. 1992. pap. 3.50 (*0-8217-3799-6*) Zebra.

Blood Bond: Gunshot Crossing, No. 3. William W. Johnstone. 1991. pap. 3.95 (*0-8217-3473-3*) Zebra.

Blood Bond: Gunsmoke & Gold. William W. Johnstone. 1992. pap. 3.50 (*0-8217-3664-7*) Zebra.

Blood Book: All about Blood & Blood Tests. B. Birkner & G. Hoffmann. Ed. by John Ultmann. 212p. 1992. pap. 11.95 (*0-88179-084-2*) Hartley & Marks.

Blood Bound Brotherhood of Gun. William W. Johnstone. 1990. pap. 3.95 (*0-8217-3044-4*) Zebra.

***Blood Bounty.** Jake McMasters. (White Apache Ser.: No. 7). 176p. (Orig.). 1995. mass mkt., pap. text ed. 3.99 (*0-8439-3790-4*) Dorchester Pub Co.

Blood Bounty. Dan Raburn. 1985. pap. 2.50 (*0-8217-1580-1*) Zebra.

Blood Bounty. Jon Sharpe. (Canyon O'Grady Ser.: No. 18). 176p. (Orig.). 1992. pap. 3.50 (*0-451-17198-5*, Sig) NAL-Dutton.

Blood-Brain Barrier: Cellular & Molecular Biology. Ed. by William M. Pardridge. LC 92-48543. 496p. 1993. 95.00 (*0-7817-0015-9*) Raven.

Blood-Brain Barrier Amino Acids. M. B. Segal & B. V. Zlokovic. (C). 1989. lib. bdg. 96.50 (*0-7462-0122-2*) Kluwer Ac.

Blood-Brain Barrier in Physiology & Medicine. Stanley I. Rapoport. LC 75-26280. 328p. 1976. 80.00 (*0-89004-079-6*) Raven.

Blood, Bread & Poetry. Adrienne Rich. 1994. pap. 9.95 (*0-393-31162-7*) Norton.

Blood, Bread & Poetry: Selected Prose 1979-1985. Adrienne Rich. 1986. 15.95 (*0-393-02376-1*) Norton.

Blood, Bread, & Roses: How Menstruation Created the World. Judy Grahn. LC 93-7701. 384p. 1993. 22.00 (*0-8070-7504-3*) Beacon Pr.

***Blood, Bread, & Roses: How Menstruation Created the World.** Judy Grahn. 352p. 1994. pap. 14.00 (*0-8070-7505-1*) Beacon Pr.

Blood Brook. Ted Levin. 208p. 1992. 24.95 (*0-930031-56-3*) Chelsea Green Pub.

Blood Brook: A Naturalist's Home Ground. Ted Levin. 1992. pap. 14.95 (*0-930031-60-1*) Chelsea Green Pub.

Blood Brother. Elliott Arnold. LC 78-26788. x, 454p. 1979. reprint ed. pap. 13.95 (*0-8032-5901-8*) U of Nebr Pr.

Blood Brotherhood. Robert Barnard. 196p. 1983. mass mkt. 5.95 (*0-14-006552-0*, Penguin Bks) Viking Penguin.

Blood Brothers. Elias Chacour & David Hazard. LC 84-9510. 224p. 1988. pap. 8.99 (*0-8007-9096-0*) Chosen Bks.

Blood Brothers. Patrick DeVine. 1987. 17.95 (*0-911349-01-4*) English Fact.

Blood Brothers. Brian Lumley. 576p. 1993. mass mkt. 5.99 (*0-8125-2061-0*) Tor Bks.

Blood Brothers. Wiley Russell. 1989. pap. 22.00 (*0-7487-0182-6*) Dufour.

Blood Brothers. Willy Russell. (Illus.). 68p. 1993. pap. 17.95 (*0-7119-2221-7*) Music Sales.

Blood Brothers. Ron Soble. 1994. pap. 4.99 (*0-451-40547-1*, Onyx) NAL-Dutton.

Blood Brothers. T. Lucien Wright. 1992. mass mkt. 4.50 (*1-55817-580-6*, Pinnacle NY) Windsor NY.

Blood Brothers: A Short History of the Civil War. Frank E. Vandiver. LC 92-10985. (Military History Ser.: No. 26). (Illus.). 224p. 1992. 24.50 (*0-89096-523-4*); pap. 10.95 (*0-89096-524-2*) Tex A&M Univ Pr.

Blood Brothers: B-Movie Monsters & Adventures. Ed. by John B. Monroe. (Call of Cthulhu Roleplaying Game System Ser.). (Illus.). 128p. (Orig.). (YA). (gr. 12 up). 1990. pap. 18.95 (*0-933635-69-9*, 2329) Chaosium.

Blood Brothers: Ryan, Chris, & Hemophilia. rev. ed. Nancy Shaw. LC 90-9509. (Orig.). 1990. pap. 4.00 (*0-915541-60-2*) Star Bks Inc.

Blood Brothers: Siblings As Writers. Norman Kiell. LC 83-12677. xv, 434p. 1982. text ed. 55.00 (*0-8236-0545-0*) Intl Univs Pr.

Blood Brothers 2. Geoff Gillan et al. Ed. by Lynn Willis. (Call of Cthulhu Roleplaying Game System Ser.). (Illus.). 128p. (Orig.). 1992. pap. text ed. 18.95 (*0-933635-91-5*, 2340) Chaosium.

Blood Bullets. Ed Newsom. (Brannigan Ser.: No. 3). (Orig.). 1982. pap. 2.25 (*0-89083-920-4*) Zebra.

***Blood Cell Biochemistry, Vol. 6.** Ed. by J. P. Cartron & P. Rouger. (Illus.). 486p. (C). 1995. 110.00 (*0-306-44853-X*, Plenum Pr) Plenum.

Blood Cell Biochemistry Vol. 1: Erythroid Cells. Ed. by James R. Harris. (Illus.). 529p. 1990. 110.00 (*0-306-43462-8*, Plenum Pr) Plenum.

Blood Cell Biochemistry Vol. 4: Basophil & Mast Cell Degranulation & Recovery. A. M. Dvorak. (Illus.). 420p. 1991. 95.00 (*0-306-43752-X*, Plenum Pr) Plenum.

Blood Cell Biochemistry Vol. 5: Macrophages & Related Cells. Ed. by M. A. Horton. (Illus.). 440p. (C). 1993. 89.50 (*0-306-44362-7*, Plenum Pr) Plenum.

Blood Cell Growth Factors: Their Present & Future Use in Hematology & Oncology. Ed. by Martin J. Murphy, Jr. 225p. (C). 1991. pap. text ed. 89.00 (*1-880854-00-7*) AlphaMed Pr.

Blood Cell Morphology, 6 vols. Lynn Maedel & Sandra Sommer. 1993. sl. 100.00 (*0-89189-329-6*) Am Soc Clinical.

Blood Cell Morphology, 6 vols., Set. Lynn Maedel & Sandra Sommer. 1993. sl. 540.00 (*0-685-74782-4*) Am Soc Clinical.

Blood Cells & Arteries in Hypertension & Atherosclerosis. Philippe Meyer & Pierre Marche. (Atherosclerosis Reviews Ser.: Vol. 19). 300p. 1989. 163.50 (*0-88167-475-3*) Raven.

Blood Cells & Vessel Walls: Functional Interactions. Ciba Foundation Staff. LC 79-26528. (Ciba Foundation Symposium: New Ser.: 71). 369p. reprint ed. pap. 105.20 (*0-8357-7325-6*, 2022190) Bks Demand.

Blood Cells As a Tissue: Proceedings of a Conference Held at the Lankenau Hospital, Oct. 30-31, 1969. Ed. by William L. Holmes. LC 78-136210. 383p. reprint ed. pap. 109.20 (*0-8357-7326-4*, 2019395) Bks Demand.

Blood Cells in Nuclear Medicine, Pt. I. Ed. by M. R. Hardeman et al. LC 84-8100. (Developments in Nuclear Medicine Ser.). 1984. lib. bdg. 167.00 (*0-89838-653-5*) Kluwer Ac.

Blood Cells in Nuclear Medicine, Pt. II. Ed. by M. R. Hardeman et al. LC 84-8100. (Developments in Nuclear Medicine Ser.). 1984. lib. bdg. 167.00 (*0-89838-654-3*) Kluwer Ac.

Blood Cells in Nuclear Medicine, Set. Ed. by M. R. Hardeman et al. LC 84-8100. (Developments in Nuclear Medicine Ser.). 1987. lib. bdg. 208.00 (*0-89838-660-8*) Kluwer Ac.

***Blood Chemistry & Clinical Nutrition.** Jack Tips. 123p. 1995. 44.95 (*0-929167-07-4*) Apple-a-Day.

Blood Cinema: The Reconstruction of National Identity in Spain. Marsha Kinder. LC 92-31697. 1993. 45.00 (*0-520-08153-6*); pap. 17.00 (*0-520-08157-9*) U CA Pr.

Blood Circulation in the Brain. B. N. Klosovskii. 320p. 1963. text ed. 88.00 (*0-7065-0269-8*, Pub. by Keter Pub IS) Coronet Bks.

Blood, Class, & Nostalgia: Anglo-American Ironies. Christopher Hitchens. 398p. 1990. 22.95 (*0-374-11443-9*) FS&G.

Blood Club: Featuring Big Baby. Charles Burns. (Illus.). 36p. 1993. pap. 5.95 (*0-87816-179-1*) Kitchen Sink.

Blood Club: Featuring Big Baby. deluxe limited ed. Charles Burns. (Illus.). 36p. 1993. 19.95 (*0-87816-178-3*) Kitchen Sink.

Blood, Coagulants & Anticoagulants to Cardiovascular Agents see Encyclopedia of Chemical Technology

Blood Coagulation. Ed. by R. F. Zwaal & H. Coenraad Hemker. (New Comprehensive Biochemistry Ser.: No. 13). 321p. 1987. 111.00 (*0-444-80794-2*) Elsevier.

Blood Coagulation & Hemostasis: A Practical Guide. 4th ed. Ed. by Jean M. Thomson. (Illus.). 300p. 1991. text ed. 99.00 (*0-443-04383-3*) Churchill.

Blood Coin. Whittington. 1994. mass mkt. 4.50 (*0-06-100768-4*, Harp PBks) HarpC.

Blood Collection: Special Procedures. Susan Phelan. 1991. vhs 135.00 (*0-89189-309-1*, D47-9-055-VH) Am Soc Clinical.

***Blood Collection: The Difficult Draw.** Deanna Klosinski. 1992. vhs 135.00 (*0-89189-350-4*) Am Soc Clinical.

Blood Collection: The Pediatric Patient. Susan Phelan. (NLM Ser.: No. WB382). 1990. vhs 135.00 (*0-89189-302-4*, 47-9-052-VH) Am Soc Clinical.

Blood Collection: The Routine Venipuncture. Deanna Klosinski et al. 1989. vhs 135.00 (*0-89189-291-5*, 47-9-051VH) Am Soc Clinical.

Blood Collection on Filter Paper for Neonatal Screening Programs: Approved Standard, Vol. 9. National Committee for Clinical Laboratory Standards. 1988. 40.00 (*1-56238-074-5*, LA4-A) Natl Comm Clin Lab Stds.

Blood Compatibility, 2 vols., Set. Ed. by Williams. 1987. 220.00 (*0-8493-6608-9*, R857, CRC Reprint) Franklin.

Blood Compatibility, Vol. 1. D. Williams. LC 86-34337. 1987. reprint ed. 127.00 (*0-8493-6604-6*, CRC Reprint) Franklin.

Blood Compatibility, Vol. 2. D. Williams. LC 86-34337. 1987. reprint ed. 93.00 (*0-8493-6605-4*, CRC Reprint) Franklin.

Blood Compatible Materials & Devices. Ed. by Chandra P. Sharma & Michael Szycher. LC 90-71281. 300p. 1990. 65.00 (*0-87762-733-9*) Technomic.

B

An Asterisk (*) at the beginning of an entry indicates that the title is appearing in BIP for the first time. 817

Blood Compatible Materials & Their Testing. Ed. by Steen Dawids & A. Bantjes. (Developments in Hematology & Immunology Ser.). 1986. lib. bdg. 170.00 (0-89838-813-9) Kluwer Ac.
Blood Confessions. Albert DiBartolomeo. 304p. 1992. pap. 4.50 (0-451-17270-1, Sig) NAL-Dutton.
Blood Conservation in Anesthesia & Surgery. Salem. 300p. Date not set. pap. 35.00 (0-8016-4310-4) Mosby Yr Bk.
***Blood Conservation with Aprotinin.** Ed. & Intro. by Roque Pifarre. LC 95-6759. (Illus.). 407p. 1995. text ed. 55.00 (1-56053-151-7) Hanley & Belfus.
Blood Conspiracy: How to Avoid Getting AIDS & Hepatitis in a Transfusion. Joleen Ottosen. Ed. by Marilyn Ross. LC 92-71818. 326p. 1993. 24.95 (0-9632963-3-7) Aspen Leaf Pr.
***Blood Countess: A Novel.** Andrei Codrescu. 1995. 23.00 (0-684-80244-9) S&S Trade.
Blood Countess, Erzebet of Hungary (1560-1614) Robert Peters. LC 86-17570. (Illus.). 120p. 1987. 16.00 (0-916156-80-X); pap. 8.00 (0-916156-81-8) Cherry Valley.
Blood Country. Ivan Ruff. 1989. 18.95 (0-8027-1066-2) Walker & Co.
***Blood Covenant.** Ronald E. Griego, Sr. Date not set. pap. 5.95 (1-886045-14-3) Covenant Marriages.
Blood Covenant. Theo Wolmarans. 175p. (Orig.). 1984. pap. text ed. 9.95 (0-914307-26-6) R Tilton Ministries.
Blood Covenant. H. Clay Trumbull. 404p. 1975. reprint ed. pap. 10.95 (0-89228-029-8) Impact Christian.
Blood Dance. James W. Brown. 1993. 22.95 (0-15-113214-3) HarBrace.
***Blood Debt.** (Stony Man Ser.). 1995. pap. 4.99 (0-373-61899-9, 1-61899-0) Harlequin Bks.
Blood-Dimmed Tide: The Battle of the Bulge by the Men Who Fought It. Gerald Astor. LC 91-58657. (Illus.). 560p. 1992. 28.00 (1-55611-281-5) D I Fine.
Blood-Dimmed Tide: The Battle of the Bulge by the Men Who Fought It. Gerald Astor. 1994. mass mkt. 5.99 (0-440-21574-9) Dell.
Blood Diseases of Infancy & Childhood. 6th ed. Miller. (Illus.). 992p. 1989. 99.00 (0-8016-3914-X) Mosby Yr Bk.
***Blood Diseases of Infancy & Childhood: In the Tradition of C. H. Smith.** 7th ed. Ed. by Denis R. Miller et al. LC 94-30133. 1994. write for info. (0-8151-6137-9) Mosby Yr Bk.
Blood Disorders. Anne E. Belcher. LC 93-7369. (Clinical Nursing Ser.). 288p. 1993. 29.95 (0-8016-7801-3) Mosby Yr Bk.
Blood Disorders in Pregnancy. Ed. by Russell K. Laros. LC 85-24012. 257p. reprint ed. pap. 73.30 (0-7837-2724-0, 2043104) Bks Demand.
Blood Disputes among Bedoin & Rural Arabs in Israel. Joseph Ginat. LC 86-14609. (Illus.). 192p. 1987. 49.95 (0-8229-3820-0) U of Pittsburgh Pr.
Blood Donor Collection Practices. Ed. by Christina Kasprisin & Barbara Laird-Fryer. (Illus.). (C). 1993. text ed. 40.00 (1-56395-021-9) Am Assn Blood.
Blood Dreams. Jack MacLane. 352p. 1989. pap. 3.95 (0-8217-2680-3) Zebra.
Blood-Drenched Altars. Francis C. Kelley. 1976. lib. bdg. 59.95 (0-87968-760-6) Gordon Pr.
Blood-Drenched Altars: A Catholic Commentary on the History of Mexico. Francis C. Kelley. LC 87-71867. 502p. 1987. reprint ed. pap. 18.00 (0-89555-319-8) TAN Bks Pubs.
Blood Echoes. Thomas H. Cook. (Illus.). 352p. 1993. pap. 4.99 (0-451-40349-5, Onyx) NAL-Dutton.
Blood Evidence. Craig Lewis. 288p. 1992. mass mkt. 5.50 (0-425-13212-9) Berkley Pub.
Blood Evidence. Craig A. Lewis. 1990. 17.95 (0-87483-116-4) August Hse.
Blood Feast. Herschell G. Lewis. 43p. 1991. pap. 4.95 (0-944735-82-7) Malibu Graphics.
Blood Feast. 2nd ed. Herschell G. Lewis. (Illus.). 160p. 1988. reprint ed. pap. 9.95 (0-938782-07-X) Fantaco.
Blood Feud. Sam Siciliano. 320p. 1993. mass mkt. 4.50 (1-55817-705-1, Pinnacle NY) Windsor NY.
Blood Feud & Other Stories. Yusuf Sharouni. Tr. by Denys Johnson-Davies. 143p. 1992. pap. 9.95 (977-424-268-8, Pub. by Am Univ Cairo Pr UA) Col U Pr.
Blood Feuds. Jerry Pournelle. (War World Ser.: No. 4). 1993. mass mkt. 5.99 (0-671-72150-X) Baen Bks.
Blood Fever. Bruce Forester. 1990. pap. 3.95 (0-8217-2964-0) Zebra.
Blood Filtration & Blood Cell Deformability. Ed. by John A. Dormandy. 1985. pap. text ed. 52.50 (0-89838-714-0) Kluwer Ac.
Blood Flow: Theory & Practice. D. E. Taylor & A. L. Stevens. (Biology Engineering Society Ser.). 1983. text ed. 115.00 (0-12-683880-1) Acad Pr.
Blood Flow in Artificial Organs & Cardiovascular Prostheses. Ed. by J. C. Barbenel et al. (Oxford Medical Engineering Ser.: No. 8). (Illus.). 282p. 1989. 75.00 (0-19-857647-1) OUP.
Blood Flow in Large Arteries: Applications to Atherogenesis & Clinical Medicine. Ed. by Dieter W. Liepsch. (Monographs on Atherosclerosis: Vol. 15). (Illus.). viii, 288p. 1989. 216.00 (3-8055-4983-0) S Karger.
Blood Flow in the Brain. Ed. by W. J. Angerson et al. (Oxford Medical Engineering Ser.: No. 7). (Illus.). 152p. 1989. 49.95 (0-19-857646-3) OUP.
Blood Flow in the Heart & Large Vessels. Ed. by M. Sugawara et al. (Illus.). xiv, 226p. 1989. 210.00 (0-387-70032-3, 1524) Spr-Verlag.
Blood Flow Measurement in Man. Robert T. Mathie. 250p. 1982. 44.50 (0-7194-0078-3) Raven.
Blood Flower. Denise Newman. 8p. 1993. 15.00 (0-9632085-3-5) Em Pr.
Blood for the Ghosts: Classical Influences in the Nineteenth & Twentieth Centuries. Hugh Lloyd-Jones. LC 82-49061. 312p. 1983. text ed. 45.00x (0-8018-3017-6) Johns Hopkins.
Blood Forge. Kathryn M. Griffith. 368p. (Orig.). 1989. pap. 3.95 (0-8439-2722-4) Dorchester Pub Co.
Blood from the Mummy's Tomb. Ret. by Derek Allen. (Fleshcreepers Ser.). 160p. (J). (gr. 6 up). 1988. pap. 2.95 (0-8120-4074-0) Barron.
Blood Fury. David Thompson. (Wilderness Ser.: No. 4). 176p. 1993. pap. 3.50 (0-8439-3512-X) Dorchester Pub Co.
Blood Games: A True Account of Family Murder. Jerry Bledsoe. 448p. 1992. pap. 5.99 (0-451-40344-4, Onyx) NAL-Dutton.
Blood Gas Preanalytical Considerations: Specimen Collection, Calibration, & Controls - Tentative Guideline, Vol. 9. National Committee for Clinical Laboratory Standards. 1989. 40.00 (1-56238-015-X, C27-T) Natl Comm Clin Lab Stds.
Blood Gases: Hemoglobin, Base Excess & Maldistribution; Nomograms for Normal & Abnormal Bloods, Effects of Maldistribution. Albert J. Olszowka et al. LC 72-12923. 179p. reprint ed. pap. 51.10 (0-8357-7327-2, 2055439) Bks Demand.
Blood Gases & Acid-Base Physiology. 2nd ed. Norman L. Jones. (Illus.). 225p. 1987. text ed. 45.00 (0-86577-254-1) Thieme Med Pubs.
Blood, Gold, & the Superstition Mountains. Mitchell Waite. LC 91-68228. (Illus.). 160p. (Orig.). 1991. pap. text ed. 9.95 (1-881260-00-3) Southwest Pubns.
Blood, Gold, & the Superstition Mountains: The Return. Mitchell Waite. LC 92-60037. (Illus.). 160p. (Orig.). 1992. pap. text ed. 9.95 (1-881260-04-6) Southwest Pubns.
Blood Group Antigens & Antibodies. Marjory Stroup & Margaret Treacy. (Illus.). 255p. (Orig.). 1982. pap. text ed. 35.00 (0-910771-00-6) Ortho Diag.
Blood Group Antigens-Related Glycoepitopes. G. V. Glinsky. (Medical Intelligence Unit Ser.). 114p. 1992. text ed. 89.95 (1-879702-44-4) R G Landes.
Blood Group Serology. 6th ed. Kathleen E. Boorman et al. (Illus.). 448p. 1987. text ed. 95.00 (0-443-02636-X) Churchill.
Blood Group Systems: ABH & Lewis. Ed. by Margaret E. Wallace & Frances Gibbs. LC 86-22259. 1986. text ed. 24.00 (0-915355-25-6) Am Assn Blood.
Blood Group Systems: Duffy, Kidd & Lutheran. Steven R. Pierce & Colin Macpherson. LC 88-19267. 1988. 25.00 (0-915355-55-8) Am Assn Blood.
Blood Group Systems: Kell. Ed. by Barbara Laird-Fryer. LC 90-949. (C). 1990. text ed. 35.00 (0-915355-80-9) Am Assn Blood.
Blood Group Systems: MN & Gerbich. Phyllis Unger & Barbara Laird-Fryer. LC 89-17694. (Illus.). (C). 1989. text ed. 25.00 (0-915355-65-5) Am Assn Blood.
Blood Group Systems: Rh. Ed. by Virginia Vengelen-Tyler & Steven R. Pierce. LC 87-14518. 1987. text ed. 16.00 (0-915355-41-8) Am Assn Blood.
Blood Group Topics. Barbara E. Dodd. (Current Topics in Immunology Ser.: Vol. 3). (Illus.). 1978. pap. 21.25 (0-8151-2710-3, Yr Bk Med Pubs) Mosby Yr Bk.
Blood Groups. Laurence Snyder. LC 72-97619. (Basic Concepts in Anthropology Ser.). 39p. (C). reprint ed. 25.00 (0-8357-9046-0, 2013325) Bks Demand.
Blood Groups: Ch-Rg, Kn-McC-Yk, Cromer. Ed. by JoAnn M. Moulds & Barbara Laird-Fryer. LC 92-49706. 1992. 43.00 (1-56395-009-X) Am Assn Blood.
Blood Groups: P, I, Sda & Pr. JoAnn M. Moulds & Laura L. Woods. LC 91-4870. (Illus.). (C). 1991. text ed. 40.00 (1-56395-002-2) Am Assn Blood.
Blood Groups & Other Red Cell Surface Markers in Health & Disease. Ed. by Charles Salmon. LC 82-13096. (Illus.). 150p. 1982. 47.50 (0-89352-193-0, Yr Bk Med Pubs) Mosby Yr Bk.
***Blood Guilt.** David Rice. 247p. 1995. pap. 12.95 (0-85640-531-0) Dufour.
Blood Heat. (New Doctor Who Adventures Ser.). 1993. pap. 5.95 (0-426-20399-2, Dr Who) Carol Pub Group.
Blood Heat. Steve Pieczenik. 352p. 1988. 17.95 (0-15-113216-X) HarBrace.
Blood, Hook & Eye. Dara Wier. LC 76-30772. (University of Texas Press Poetry Ser.: No. 2). 80p. 1977. pap. 4.95 (0-292-70721-5) U of Tex Pr.
Blood-Hound. large type ed. Andrew Puckett. (Dales Mystery Ser.). 317p. 1993. pap. 16.95 (1-85389-410-9, Dales) Ulverscroft.
Blood Hunter. Sidney Williams. 1990. pap. 3.95 (1-55817-437-0, Pinnacle NY) Windsor NY.
Blood in Contact with Natural & Artificial Surfaces. Ed. by Edward F. Leonard et al. (Annals Ser.: Vol. 516). 688p. 1987. 172.00 (0-89766-427-2) NY Acad Sci.
Blood in My Eye. George L. Jackson. LC 90-81539. 200p. 1990. reprint ed. pap. 11.95 (0-933121-23-7) Black Classic.
Blood in the Ashes. William W. Johnstone. 1985. pap. 3.50 (0-8217-1537-2) Zebra.
Blood in the Desert's Eyes. Syl Cheney-Coker. (African Writers Ser.). (Illus.). 85p. (Orig.). (C). 1990. pap. 7.95 (0-435-90574-0, 90574) Heinemann.
Blood in the Face: The Ku Klux Klan, Aryan Nations, Nazi Skinheads, & the Rise of a New White Culture. James Ridgeway. (Illus.). 208p. 1991. pap. 19.95 (1-56025-003-8) Thunders Mouth.
Blood in the Sky. Dan Brennan. 1977. pap. 1.50 (0-8439-0464-X) Dorchester Pub Co.
Blood in the Snow. John Legg. 304p. 1993. pap. 3.50 (0-8217-4136-5) Zebra.
Blood in the Streets: Investment Profits in a World Gone Mad. James D. Davidson & William Rees-Mogg. 1988. mass mkt. 6.99 (0-446-35316-7) Warner Bks.
***Blood in Zion.** Saul Zadka. 256p. 1995. 29.95 (1-85753-136-1) Macmillan.
Blood Industry, No. C-071N. 2,750.00 (1-56965-017-9) BCC.
Blood Industry (Update) Business Communications Co., Inc. Staff. 135p. 1991. 2,250.00 (0-89336-763-X, C-071R) BCC.
Blood into Ink: South Asian & Middle Eastern Women Write War. Miriam Cooke. (C). 1994. pap. text ed. 19.95 (0-8133-8662-4) Westview.
Blood into Ink: South Asian & Middle Eastern Women Write War. Ed. by Roshni Rustomji-Kerns. LC 94-1770. 1994. text ed. 59.95 (0-8133-8661-6) Westview.
***Blood Is Not Enough.** Ellen Datlow. 230p. 1994. pap. text ed. 4.99 (0-441-00109-2) Ace Bks.
Blood Is Their Argument: Warfare among the Mae Enga Tribesmen of the New Guinea Highlands. Mervyn Meggitt. Ed. by Robert B. Edgerton & L. L. Langness. LC 76-28116. (Illus.). 223p. (C). 1977. pap. text ed. 14.95 (0-87484-394-4) Mayfield Pub.
Blood Is Thicker. Ann C. Fallon. 256p. (Orig.). 1990. pap. 3.95 (0-671-70623-3) PB.
***Blood Is Thicker Than Beaujolais: A Wine Taster's Mystery.** Tony Aspler. 224p. 1994. 19.95 (1-895629-39-X, Pub. by Warwick Pub CN) Firefly Bks Ltd.
Blood Justice. Jory Sherman. (Gunn Ser.: No. 4). 256p. (Orig.). 1980. pap. 1.95 (0-89083-670-1) Zebra.
Blood Justice. Gordon D. Shirreffs. Bd. with Valiant Bugles. 1985. Set pap. 3.50 (0-451-13339-0, Sig) NAL-Dutton.
Blood Justice: The Lynching of Mack Charles Parker. Howard Smead. (Illus.). 264p. 1988. pap. 10.95 (0-19-505429-6) OUP.
Blood Kin. Elizabeth Fackler. LC 91-31908. (Novel of the West Ser.). 208p. 1992. 16.95 (0-87131-667-6) M Evans.
Blood Kin. Elizabeth Fackler. 352p. 1993. mass mkt. 3.99 (0-8125-3338-0) Tor Bks.
Blood Kin. large type ed. Marjorie Dorner. 608p. 1994. 23.95 (0-7089-3108-1) Ulverscroft.
Blood Kin: A Novel. Majorie Dorner. 1992. 20.00 (0-688-09531-3) Morrow.
Blood Kiss. Dennis Etchison. (Illus.). 224p. lib. bdg. 22.50 (0-910489-18-1) Scream Pr.
***Blood Kiss: Vampire Erotica.** Ed. & Intro. by Cecilia Tan. 152p. (Orig.). 1994. pap. 9.95 (1-885865-00-7) Circlet Pr.
Blood Knife. Jack Slade. (Sundance Ser.). 224p. 1984. pap. 2.50 (0-8439-2138-2) Dorchester Pub Co.
Blood Knot. Bruce Algozin. (Orig.). 1982. pap. 2.95 (0-8217-1073-7) Zebra.
Blood Knot. David Hayes. 1991. mass mkt. 4.95 (0-312-92519-0) St Martin.
Blood Knot. large type ed. Sam Llewellyn. 497p. (Orig.). 1993. 21.95 (0-7505-0403-X, Pub. by Magna Print Bks) Ulverscroft.
Blood Knot. Sam Llewellyn. Ed. by Jane Chelius. 336p. (Orig.). 1993. reprint ed. mass mkt. 4.99 (0-671-86951-5) PB.
Blood Knot & Other Plays. Athol Fugard. LC 90-29029. 240p. 1991. 22.95 (1-55936-019-4); pap. 10.95 (1-55936-020-8) Theatre Comm.
***Blood Labyrinth.** Peter F. Wilson. LC 90-55250. 616p. (Orig.). 1994. pap. 6.95 (1-56002-059-8) Aegina Pr.
Blood Lactate Response to Exercise. Arthur Weltman. LC 94-15638. (Current Issues in Exercise Science Ser.). 128p. 1994. pap. text ed. 20.00x (0-87322-769-7, BWEL0769) Human Kinetics.
Blood Lake. Frank McConnell. 256p. 1987. 16.95 (0-8027-5673-5) Walker & Co.
Blood Libel Legend: A Casebook in Anti-Semitic Folklore. Ed. by Alan Dundes. LC 91-12592. (Illus.). 396p. (Orig.). (C). 1991. lib. bdg. 42.50 (0-299-13110-6); pap. 17.50 (0-299-13114-9) U of Wis Pr.
Blood Lies. Patricia Wallace. 320p. 1991. mass mkt. 4.50 (0-8217-3394-X) Zebra.
Blood Line: Stories of Fathers & Sons. David Quammen. LC 87-81374. (Short Fiction Ser.). 178p. (Orig.). 1988. pap. 8.00 (1-55597-100-8) Graywolf.
Blood Lines. Walter Griffin. 1973. 1.00 (0-685-67930-6) Windless Orchard.
Blood Lines. 2nd ed. Nash Buckingham. (Nash Buckingham Collection Ser.). (Illus.). 227p. 1986. reprint ed. 20.00 (1-56416-051-3) Derrydale Pr.
Blood Lines. 2nd ed. Nash Buckingham. (Fifty Greatest Bks.). (Illus.). 227p. 1991. reprint ed. 35.00 (1-56416-004-1) Derrydale Pr.
Blood Lines, Bk. 3. Tanya Huff. 272p. (Orig.). 1993. mass mkt. 4.99 (0-88677-530-2) DAW Bks.
Blood Lord: Poems. deluxe ed. Hugh Seidman. Ed. by Michael Andre. LC 73-10546. (Zerox Editions Ser.). 113p. (C). 1990. reprint ed. lib. bdg. 24.95 (0-934450-18-8) Unmuzzled Ox.
Blood Lord: Poems. Hugh Seidman. Ed. by Michael Andre. LC 73-10546. (ZeroX Editions Ser.). 113p. (C). 1990. reprint ed. pap. 9.95 (0-934450-17-X) Unmuzzled Ox.
Blood Lust: Portrait of a Serial Sex Killer. Gary C. King. (Illus.). 352p. (Orig.). 1992. pap. 5.99 (0-451-40352-5, Sig) NAL-Dutton.
Blood Magic: The Anthropology of Menstruation. Ed. by Thomas Buckley & Alma Gottlieb. 1988. 55.00 (0-520-06085-7); pap. 15.00 (0-520-06350-3) U CA Pr.
***Blood, Medicine & the Jehovah's Witnesses: A Century of a Cult in Chaos.** Steve Devore & Steve Lagoon. 1995. 9.95 (1-883858-56-9) Witness CA.
Blood-Membrane Internation in Extracorporal Circuits. Ed. by L. W. Henderson & D. Chenoweth. (Journal: Blood Purification: Vol. 5, No. 2-3, 1987). (Illus.). 96p. 1987. 55.25 (3-8055-4580-0) S Karger.
Blood Memory. Martha Graham. Ed. by Jane Rosenman. 288p. 1992. reprint ed. pap. 12.00 (0-671-78217-7, WSP) PB.
Blood Meridian. Cormac McCarthy. 1994. 21.50 (0-8446-6793-5) Peter Smith.
Blood Meridian. Cormac McCarthy. 1992. pap. 11.00 (0-679-72875-9, Vin) Random.
Blood Mist. Robert James. 368p. (Orig.). 1987. pap. 3.95 (0-8439-2523-X) Dorchester Pub Co.
Blood Money. Franklin W. Dixon. (Hardy Boys Casefiles Ser.: No. 32). 160p. (Orig.). (YA). 1991. pap. 3.50 (0-671-74665-0, Archway) PB.
Blood Money. Aaron Fletcher. (Bounty Hunter Ser.: No. 2). 176p. 1981. pap. 1.95 (0-8439-1018-6) Dorchester Pub Co.
Blood Money. Clifford Linedecker. (Illus.). 384p. 1993. mass mkt. 4.99 (1-55817-773-6, Pinnacle NY) Windsor NY.
Blood Money: Getting Rich Off a Woman's Right to Choose. Carol Everett. 210p. 1992. pap. 8.99 (0-88070-548-5, Multnomah Bks) Questar Pubs.
Blood Moon. Mason Burgess. 352p. (Orig.). 1986. pap. 3.75 (0-8439-2425-X) Dorchester Pub Co.
Blood Moon: Featuring Psychological Profile Investigator Robert Payne. Ed Gorman. 274p. 1994. 20.95 (0-312-10943-1) St Martin.
***Blood Muse: Timeless Tales of Vampires in the Arts.** Ed. by Esther M. Friesner & Martin H. Greenberg. 272p. 1995. 21.95 (1-55611-470-2) D I Fine.
Blood Music. Jessi P. Hunter. 1993. 20.00 (0-679-41824-5) Random.
Blood Music. Jessie P. Hunter. 1994. mass mkt. 5.99 (0-8041-1084-0) Ivy Books.
Blood Oath. David Morrell. 240p. 1983. mass mkt. 4.95 (0-449-20391-3) Fawcett.
Blood Oath. Robert Todaro. (Orig.). 1992. mass mkt. 4.99 (0-06-100399-9, Harp PBks) HarpC.
***Blood Oath Vol. 1.** David Morrell. 1994. pap. 5.99 (0-312-95345-3) St Martin.
Blood of a Dragon. Lawrence Watt-Evans. 1991. mass mkt. 4.99 (0-345-36410-4, Del Rey) Ballantine.
Blood of Abraham: Insights into the Middle East. Jimmy Carter. 1993. reprint ed. pap. 15.00 (1-55728-293-5) U of Ark Pr.
Blood of Amber. Roger Zelazny. (Chronicles of Amber Ser.: Bk. 7). 224p. 1995. reprint ed. mass mkt. 4.99 (0-380-89636-2, AvoNova) Avon.
Blood of an Aries: A Zodiac Mystery. Linda Mather. 208p. 1994. 18.95 (0-312-10429-4) St Martin.
Blood of an Englishman. large type ed. James McClure. 498p. 1982. 15.95 (0-7089-0744-X) Ulverscroft.
Blood of Apache Mesa. Patrick E. Andrews. 1988. pap. 2.95 (0-8217-2538-6) Zebra.
Blood of Brothers. Stephen Kinzer. 1992. 14.00 (0-385-42258-X, Anchor NY) Doubleday.
Blood of Eagles. Dean Ing. 288p. 1988. pap. 3.95 (0-8125-4106-5) Tor Bks.
Blood of God. Malcolm Webber. 272p. (Orig.). Date not set. pap. 9.95 (0-9626908-4-8) Pioneer Kimmell.
Blood of Heroes. Andrew Keith. (BattleTech Ser.). 288p. (Orig.). 1993. pap. 4.99 (0-451-45259-3, ROC) NAL-Dutton.
***Blood of Innocents.** Reel et al. 432p. 1995. pap. 4.99 (0-7860-0177-1) Windsor NY.
Blood of Jesus. William Reid. 1969. pap. 3.00 (0-914053-02-7) Liberty Bell Pr.
Blood of Kings: Dynasty & Ritual in Maya Art. Linda Schele & Mary Miller. LC 86-80193. (Illus.). 348p. 1992. 50.00 (0-8076-1159-X); pap. 29.95 (0-8076-1278-2) Braziller.
Blood of My Blood. Richard Gambino. 396p. 1991. reprint ed. lib. bdg. 27.95 (0-89966-784-8) Buccaneer Bks.
Blood of Our Fathers. Sonny Girard. 1992. mass mkt. 5.99 (0-671-72741-9) PB.
Blood of Our Silence. Kelwyn Sole. 123p. 1988. pap. text ed. 16.95 (0-86975-338-X, Pub. by Ravan Pr ZA) Ohio U Pr.
Blood of Peace: And Other Poems. Tanure Ojaide. (African Writers Ser.). 128p. (Orig.). 1991. pap. 8.95 (0-435-91193-7) Heinemann.
Blood of Prophets. Edgar L. Masters. 1972. 59.95 (0-87968-761-4) Gordon Pr.
Blood of the Albatross. Ridley Pearson. 1993. mass mkt. 5.99 (0-312-95183-3) St Martin.
Blood of the Boar. large type ed. Margaret Abbey. LC 93-13142. 1993. 17.95 (1-56054-617-4) Thorndike Pr.
Blood of the Breed. large type ed. T. V. Olsen. 1985. 15.95 (0-7089-1262-1) Ulverscroft.
Blood of the Colyn Muir. Paul E. Zimmer & Jon DeCles. 256p. (Orig.). 1988. pap. 3.50 (0-380-75368-5) Avon.
Blood of the Conquerors. Harvey Fergusson. Ed. by Carlos E. Cortes. LC 76-1232. (Chicano Heritage Ser.). 1977. reprint ed. lib. bdg. 18.95 (0-405-09500-7) Ayer.
Blood of the Cross. Andrew Murray. 1992. pap. 5.50 (0-87508-374-9) Chr Lit.
Blood of the Cross. Andrew Murray. 144p. 1981. reprint ed. pap. 4.50 (0-88368-103-X) Whitaker Hse.
Blood of the Eagle. Fred Dickey. 1985. pap. 3.50 (0-8217-1607-7) Zebra.
Blood of the Innocent: Victims of the Contras' War in Nicaragua. Teofilo Cabestrero. Tr. by Robert R. Barr. LC 85-13658. 112p. (Orig.). reprint ed. pap. 32.00 (0-8357-8541-6, 2034850) Bks Demand.
Blood of the Lamb. Thomas F. Monteleone. 448p. 1993. mass mkt. 5.99 (0-8125-2222-2) Tor Bks.
Blood of the Land: Government & Corporate War Against Indigenous America. 2nd ed. Rex Weyler. (Illus.). 308p. 1992. lib. bdg. 39.95 (0-86571-240-9); pap. 16.95 (0-86571-241-7) New Soc Pubs.
***Blood of the Lion.** John McRae. 240p. 1994. 16.98 (0-88290-509-0, 1981) Horizon Utah.

An Asterisk (*) at the beginning of an entry indicates that the title is appearing in BIP for the first time.

Blood of the Martyrs. Naomi Mitchison. Ed. by James S. Bell, Jr. (Christian Epics Ser.). 325p. 1994. pap. 9.99 (*0-8024-7107-2*) Moody.

Blood of the Monster: The Character of Coyote in Nez Perce Myths. Deward E. Walker, Jr. LC 94-76343. (Illus.). 192p. 1994. 27.50 (*1-881019-09-8*) High Plns WY.

***Blood of the Monster: The Character of the Coyote in Nez Perce Myths.** Deward E. Walker, Jr. (Illus.). 192p. Date not set. 27.50 (*1-881019-10-1*) High Plns WY.

Blood of the Mountain Man. William W. Johnstone. 256p. 1992. pap. 3.50 (*0-8217-3931-X*) Zebra.

Blood of the North. James B. Hendryx. 1976. reprint ed. lib. bdg. 21.95 (*0-88411-832-0*, Aeonian Pr) Amereon Ltd.

Blood of the Poet: Selected Poems. William Everson. Ed. by Albert Gelpi. LC 93-71566. 304p. (Orig.). 1993. pap. 14.95 (*0-913089-42-7*) Broken Moon.

Blood of the Poet see Two Screenplays: The Blood of a Poet: The Testament of Orpheus

Blood of the Walsungs: Selected Poems. Otto Orban. 94p. 1994. pap. 13.95 (*1-85224-203-5*, Pub. by Bloodaxe Bks UK) Dufour.

Blood of the Wolf. Jeffrey Goddin. 368p. (Orig.). 1987. pap. 3.95 (*0-8439-2558-2*) Dorchester Pub Co.

Blood of Their Blood: An Anthology of Polish-American Poetry. Victor Contoski. 1981. pap. 4.95 (*0-89823-020-9*) New Rivers Pr.

Blood on Frisco Bay. Jay Flynn. 1976. pap. 1.25 (*0-8439-0360-0*, LB36OZK) Dorchester Pub Co.

***Blood on the Arrows.** Jake McMasters. (Cheyenne Giant Edition Ser.). 368p. (Orig.). 1995. mass mkt. 4.99 (*0-8439-3839-0*) Dorchester Pub Co.

Blood on the Border: Criminal Behavior & Illegal Immigration along the Southern U. S. Border. Venson C. Davis. 1993. 15.95 (*0-533-10016-X*) Vantage.

Blood on the Dining-Room Floor: A Murder Mystery. 2nd ed. Gertrude Stein. Ed. & Aft. by John H. Gill. LC 82-70118. (Saturday Night Special Ser.). 100p. (Orig.). 1982. 12.95 (*0-916870-50-2*, Blk Lizard) Creat Arts Bk.

Blood on the Dining-Room Floor: A Murder Mystery. 2nd ed. Gertrude Stein. LC 82-70118. (Saturday Night Special Ser.). (Illus.). 64p. (Orig.). (C). 1994. pap. 8.95 (*0-916870-47-2*, Blk Lizard) Creat Arts Bk.

***Blood on the Doorposts: Receiving Blessings Through Victorians Prayer.** William Schnoebelen & Sharon Schnoebelen. (Orig.). (C). 1994. pap. 11.50 (*0-937958-43-3*) Chick Pubns.

Blood on the Forge. William Attaway. LC 92-31051. 1993. mass mkt. 9.00 (*0-385-42542-2*, Anchor NY) Doubleday.

Blood on the Forge. William Attaway. (Voices of Resistance Ser.). 320p. 1987. reprint ed. pap. 11.00 (*0-85345-722-0*) Monthly Rev.

Blood on the Half Shell. Al Qualman. LC 82-73152. (Illus.). 168p. 1982. pap. 6.95 (*0-8323-0411-5*) Binford Mort.

Blood on the Happy Highway. large type ed. Sheila Radley. 1985. 16.95 (*0-7089-1316-4*) Ulverscroft.

Blood on the Land. large type ed. Frank Bonham. LC 94-11945. 339p. 1994. 17.95 (*0-8161-7400-8*) Hall.

Blood on the Lotus. Lawrence C. Vetter. 1990. mass mkt. 4.95 (*0-8041-0614-2*) Ivy Books.

Blood on the Moon. James Ellroy. 272p. 1985. mass mkt. 4.99 (*0-380-69851-X*) Avon.

Blood on the Moon. large type ed. Luke Short. LC 93-7858. Orig. Title: Gunman's Chance. 334p. 1993. 17.95 (*1-56054-225-X*) Thorndike Pr.

Blood on the Moon: A Novel of Old Florida. Steve Glassman. 324p. (Orig.). 1990. pap. 9.95 (*0-934040-16-8*) Pathway Bk Serv.

Blood on the Moon: Valentine McGillycuddy & the Sioux. Julia B. McGillycuddy. LC 90-35176. (Illus.). xx, 291p. 1990. reprint ed. pap. 10.95 (*0-8032-8170-6*, Bison Books) U of Nebr Pr.

***Blood on the Painted Mountain: Zulu Victory & Defeat, Hlobane & Kambula, 1879.** Ron Lock. (Illus.). 208p. 1995. 35.00 (*1-85367-201-7*, Pub. by Greenhill Bks UK) Stackpole.

Blood on the Plains. Judd Cole. (Cheyenne Ser.: No. 5). 176p. (Orig.). 1993. pap. 3.50 (*0-8439-3441-7*) Dorchester Pub Co.

Blood on the Prairie. John Benteen. (Sundance Ser.: No. 18). 1978. pap. 1.50 (*0-8439-0577-8*) Dorchester Pub Co.

Blood on the Rails. Ned Stone. (Breed Ser.: No. 3). 176p. (Orig.). 1990. pap. 2.95 (*0-8439-2930-8*) Dorchester Pub Co.

Blood on the Range. Owen G. Irons. 1980. pap. 1.95 (*0-89083-686-8*) Zebra.

Blood on the Range. large type ed. Paul E. Lehman. 1991. pap. 15.95 (*1-55504-818-8*, 98, Curley Lrg Print) Chivers N Amer.

Blood on the Republican. Jeff O'Donnell. LC 91-29076. (Novel of the West Ser.). 192p. 1992. 16.95 (*0-87131-665-X*) M Evans.

Blood on the Risers: An Airborne Soldier's Thirty-Five Months in Vietnam. John Leppelman. (Orig.). 1991. mass mkt. 4.95 (*0-8041-0562-6*) Ivy Books.

***Blood on the Sea: American Destroyers Lost in WWII.** Robert S. Parkin. (Illus.). 304p. 1995. 24.95 (*1-885119-17-8*) Sarpedon.

Blood on the Shamrock: An American Bishop Ponders Northern Ireland, 1968-1989. Mark J. Hurley. (American University Studies: History: Ser. IX, Vol. 91). 384p. (C). 1990. text ed. 39.95 (*0-8204-1262-7*) P Lang Pubs.

Blood on the Shores: Soviet Naval Commandos in World War II. Viktor Leonov & James Gebhardt. LC 93-27869. 224p. 1993. 26.95 (*1-55750-506-3*) Naval Inst Pr.

***Blood on the Shores: Soviet SEALs in World War II.** Viktor Leonov. Tr. by James F. Gebhardt. (Orig.). 1994. mass mkt. 5.99 (*0-8041-0732-7*) Ivy Books.

Blood on the Stage: A Checklist of Cornerstone Crime, Mystery, & Detection Plays. Anno. & Comp. by Amnon Kabatchnik. (Illus.). Date not set. lib. bdg. write for info. (*1-55742-105-6*); pap. write for info. (*1-55742-104-8*) Borgo Pr.

Blood on the Street. Annette Meyers. 1993. mass mkt. 4.99 (*0-553-29731-7*) Bantam.

Blood on the Streets. Larry Edwards. 1991. pap. 13.95 (*0-87949-309-7*) Ashley Bks.

Blood on the Strip - Hijacking Manhattan. Chet Cunningham. (Double Penetrator Ser.). 368p. 1990. pap. 4.50 (*0-8439-3019-5*) Dorchester Pub Co.

***Blood on the Sun.** Chad Merriman. 1994. 15.95 (*0-7451-4615-5*, Gunsmoke) Chivers N Amer.

Blood on the Thistle: A Casebook of Twentieth-Century Scottish Murder. Douglas Skelton. (Illus.). 224p. 1993. pap. 15.95 (*1-85158-468-4*, Pub. by Mnstream UK) Trafalgar.

Blood on the Turf. large type ed. Glenis Wilson. 432p. 1993. 21.95 (*0-7089-2997-4*) Ulverscroft.

Blood on the Unicorn. abr. ed. Mitchel Maxine. 370p. 1995. pap. 9.95 (*1-56901-452-3*) NW Pub.

Blood on the Walls: Memoirs of an Anti-Royalist from Miner's Row to Royal Palace. Willie Hamilton. (Illus.). 218p. 1994. 39.95 (*0-7475-1116-0*, Pub. by Bloomsbury Pub Ltd UK) Trafalgar.

Blood on the Wind. large type ed. Helga Moray. 400p. 1985. 15.95 (*0-7089-1270-2*) Ulverscroft.

Blood on the Wind River Mountains. James A. Janke. 1993. 13.95 (*0-8034-9028-3*) Bouregy.

Blood on Their Banner: Nationalist Struggles in the South Pacific. David Robie. LC 89-28954. (Illus.). 304p. (C). 1989. text ed. 49.95 (*0-86232-864-0*, Pub. by Zed Books UK); pap. 17.50 (*0-86232-865-9*, Pub. by Zed Books UK) Humanities.

***Blood on Whose Hand? The Killing of Women & Children in Domestic Homicides.** Women's Coalition Against Family Violence Staff. 155p. 1994. pap. 14.00 (*0-646-17924-1*) W W Gaunt.

***Blood or Justice.** 216p. (YA). 1993. pap. 15.00 (*0-9634738-0-8*) Instep Pub.

Blood Orange. large type ed. Sam Llewellyn. 1990. 21.95 (*0-7089-2174-4*) Ulverscroft.

Blood Oranges. John Hawkes. LC 74-152516. 1972. pap. 9.95 (*0-8112-0061-2*, NDP338) New Directions.

Blood Orchid. Charles Bowden. Date not set. 23.00 (*0-679-43336-8*) Random.

Blood Pact. Debra Franklin. (Scream Ser.: No. 1). 224p. 1993. pap. 3.50 (*0-8217-4355-4*) Zebra.

Blood Pact. Tanya Huff. 336p. 1993. mass mkt. 4.99 (*0-88677-582-5*) DAW Bks.

Blood Plasma: The Promise & the Politics. Thomas Drees. LC 82-11617. (Illus.). 1983. 29.95 (*0-87949-225-2*) Ashley Bks.

Blood Platelet Function & Medicinal Chemistry. Ed. by A. Lasslo. 336p. 1984. 71.25 (*0-444-00790-3*) Elsevier.

Blood Platelets in Man & Animals, 2 vols., Set. B. Maupin. 1969. 427.00 (*0-08-006405-1*, Pub. by Pergamon Repr UK) Franklin.

Blood Prairie. Jon Sharpe. (Trailsman Ser.: No. 125). 176p. (Orig.). 1992. pap. 3.50 (*0-451-17238-8*, Sig) NAL-Dutton.

Blood Pressure. Sandra M. Gilbert. 1989. pap. 7.95 (*0-393-30624-0*) Norton.

Blood Pressure. Andrew R. Nara et al. Ed. by Mary J. Pramik-Holdaway. (Biophysical Measurement Ser.). 109p. (Orig.). (C). 1989. 28.00 (*0-9627449-0-5*) SpaceLabs.

Blood Pressure: Questions You Have--Answers You Need. Charles B. Inlander. LC 93-2000. 1993. reprint ed. 4.99 (*0-517-08902-5*) Wings Bks.

Blood Pressure: Questions You Have, Answers You Need. Ed Weiner. 1992. pap. 5.95 (*0-9627334-3-1*) Peoples Med Soc.

Blood Pressure & Drug Effects: Medical Analysis Index with Reference Bibliography. Dancilla Horaibe. LC 85-47867. 150p. 1987. 44.50 (*0-88164-408-0*); pap. 39.50 (*0-88164-409-9*) ABBE Pubs Assn.

Blood Pressure & Heart Rate Variability: Computer Analysis, Methodology & Clinical Applications. Ed. by M. Di Rienzo et al. LC 91-59040. (Studies in Health Technology & Informatics: Vol. 4). 293p. 1992. 110.00 (*90-5199-077-4*, Pub. by IOS Pr NE) IOS Press.

Blood Pressure Control: A Matter of Choices. Nancy R. Hull et al. Ed. by Faye Hoffman. LC 88-9829. (Illus.). 48p. (Orig.). 1993. pap. text ed. 3.75 (*0-939838-24-9*) Pritchett & Hull.

Blood Pressure Control Programs in Industrial Settings. John C. Erfurt & Andrea Foote. 83p. 1979. pap. 7.00 (*0-87736-334-X*) U of Mich Inst Labor.

Blood Pressure Equipment Market. (Market Research Reports: No. 212). 179p. 1992. 795.00 (*0-317-05453-8*) Theta Corp.

Blood Pressure Measurements. W. Meyer-Sabellek et al. 340p. 1990. 80.00 (*0-387-91332-7*, 1915) Spr-Verlag.

***Blood Pressure Transducers: BP22-1994.** rev. ed. AAMI Staff. (ANSI-AAMI American National Standard Ser.). (Illus.). 14p. Date not set. pap. 59.00 (*1-57020-023-8*) Assn Adv Med Instrn.

Blood Pressure Transducers - General. 12p. 1986. 49.00 (*0-910275-63-7*, BP22-113) Assn Adv Med Instrn.

Blood Pressure Transducers - Interchangeability & Performance of Resistive Bridge Type. 12p. 1986. 49.00 (*0-910275-64-5*, BP23-113) Assn Adv Med Instrn.

Blood Price. Tanya Huff. (Orig.). 1991. mass mkt. 4.99 (*0-88677-471-3*) DAW Bks.

Blood Processing Systems. James R. Critser, Jr. (Ser. 10 BPS-86). 1987. pap. 58.00 (*0-88178-046-4*) Lexington Data.

Blood Purification in Perspective: New Insights & Future Trends. Ed. by N. K. Man et al. 65.00 (*0-936022-28-0*) ICAOT Pr.

Blood Rain. James E. Morrison. 350p. 1994. pap. 9.95 (*1-56901-309-8*) NW Pub.

Blood Ransom. Jim Austin. (Fury Ser.: Bk. 2). 176p. (Orig.). 1992. pap. 3.99 (*0-425-13485-7*) Berkley Pub.

Blood Red Angel. Adrian Cole. 384p. (Orig.). 1993. mass mkt. 4.99 (*0-380-76889-5*, AvoNova) Avon.

***Blood Red Blues.** Julia Vinograd. (Illus.). 56p. 1995. pap. text ed. 4.95 (*0-929730-50-X*) Zeitgeist Pr.

Blood Red Roses. Katherine Deauxville. 320p. (Orig.). 1991. mass mkt. 4.99 (*0-312-92571-9*) St Martin.

Blood Red Sky. Anton Emmerton. 1985. pap. 3.50 (*0-8217-1586-0*) Zebra.

Blood Red, Snow White. Diane Henry & Nicholas Horrock. Ed. by Sally Peters. 352p. 1993. mass mkt. 5.50 (*0-671-79551-1*) PB.

***Blood Red Sunset.** Ma Bo. Tr. by Howard Goldblatt. 384p. 1995. 24.95 (*0-670-84181-1*, Viking) Viking Penguin.

Blood Relations. Eilis Dillon. 1995. pap. 14.95 (*0-285-63131-4*, Pub. by Souvenir UK) Atrium Pubs.

Blood Relations. Eilis Dillon. 1979. pap. 2.25 (*0-449-24043-6*, Crest) Fawcett.

Blood Relations. Bernard Feld. 224p. 1988. pap. 3.95 (*0-380-70339-4*) Avon.

Blood Relations. Otto Hoff. 1981. 23.00 (*0-7223-1343-8*, Pub. by A H S Ltd UK) St Mut.

***Blood Relations.** Carlos Montemayor. Tr. by Dale Carter & Alfonso Gonzalez. LC 95-1265. (Contemporary Latin-American Classics in English Translation Ser.). 111p. 1995. 17.95 (*0-917635-16-7*) Plover Pr.

Blood Relations: Blood Groups & Anthropology. A. E. Mourant. (Illus.). 1985. pap. 15.95 (*0-19-857631-5*) OUP.

Blood Relations: Menstruation & the Origins of Culture. Chris Knight. (Illus.). 448p. 1991. 45.00 (*0-300-04911-0*) Yale U Pr.

Blood Relative. Carolyn Hougan. 1994. mass mkt. 5.99 (*0-449-22053-2*, Crest) Fawcett.

Blood Relative. Crocker Stephenson. 226p. 1993. 20.00 (*0-929387-91-0*) Bonus Books.

Blood Relative. George Vandeman. (Outreach Ser.). 48p. 1986. pap. 0.49 (*0-8163-0681-8*) Pacific Pr Pub Assn.

Blood Relative: A Jacob Lomax Mystery. Michael Allegretto. 224p. 1992. text ed. 20.00 (*0-684-19409-0*, Scribners) S&S Trade.

Blood Relatives: The Family in Contemporary Photography. Tom Hamberger. (Illus.). 16p. (Orig.). 1991. pap. 4.95 (*0-944110-10-X*) Milwauk Art Mus.

***Blood Reunion.** Harrell. (Vampire Twins Ser.: No. 4). (J). 1995. mass mkt. 3.99 (*0-06-106283-9*, Harp PBks) HarpC.

Blood Revenge: The Enactment & Management of Conflict in Montenegro & Other Tribal Societies. Christopher Boehm. LC 86-24904. (Ethnohistory Ser.). (Illus.). 282p. (C). 1986. pap. text ed. 19.95 (*0-8122-1241-X*) U of Pa Pr.

***Blood Revenge, War & Victory Feasts among the Jibaro Indians of Eastern Ecuador.** Ed. by Rafael Karsten. (Bureau of American Ethnology Bulletins Ser.). 94p. 1995. lib. bdg. 79.00 (*0-7812-4079-4*) Rprt Serv.

Blood Rich: When Oil Billions, High Fashion, & Royal Intimacies Are Not Enough. Jane Wolfe. 1993. 22.95 (*0-316-95092-0*) Little.

Blood Ride. Paul Hofrichter. (Roadblaster Ser.: No. 3). 192p. (Orig.). 1988. pap. 3.95 (*0-8439-2616-3*) Dorchester Pub Co.

Blood Rites. Eliane Bergstrom. 336p. 1994. reprint ed. pap. text ed. 4.99 (*0-441-00074-6*) Ace Bks.

Blood River. Aneb Kgositsile. (YA). (gr. 12 up). 1983. pap. 5.00 (*0-685-18304-1*) Broadside Pr.

Blood River. Tom Willard. (Strike Fighters Ser.: No. 7). (Orig.). 1991. mass mkt. 3.99 (*0-06-100263-1*, Harp PBks) HarpC.

Blood River. large type ed. Bob Langley. 1991. 21.95 (*0-7089-2431-X*) Ulverscroft.

Blood River: Lassiter. large type ed. Jack Slade. (Linford Western Library). 1991. pap. 13.95 (*0-7089-6968-2*, Linford) Ulverscroft.

***Blood River: The War for the Northwest Territory.** Roarke. 1995. mass mkt. 4.99 (*0-312-95420-4*) St Martin.

Blood River Down. Lionel Fenn. 320p. (Orig.). 1986. pap. 2.95 (*0-8125-3785-8*) Tor Bks.

Blood River Gold. Swain Adams. 224p. (Orig.). 1985. reprint ed. pap. 2.25 (*0-8439-2306-7*) Dorchester Pub Co.

***Blood Road: The Mystery of Shen Dingyi in Revolutionary China.** R. Keith Schoppa. LC 94-22072. 1995. 40.00 (*0-520-20015-2*) U CA Pr.

Blood Root. Alma Villanueva. (Illus.). 1982. lib. bdg. 35.00 (*0-916908-19-4*); pap. 9.95 (*0-916908-06-2*) Place Herons.

Blood Roots. Richie T. Cusick. Ed. by Claire Zion. 352p. (Orig.). 1992. mass mkt. 4.99 (*0-671-73497-0*) PB.

Blood Rose. William Heffernan. 432p. 1992. pap. 5.99 (*0-451-17163-2*, Sig) NAL-Dutton.

Blood Royal. large type ed. Dornford Yates. (Mainstream Ser.). 288p. 1987. reprint ed. 7.97 (*1-85089-163-X*, Pub. by ISIS UK) Transaction Pubs.

***Blood Royal of Britain: Being a Roll of the Living Descendants of Edward IV & Henry VII, Kings of England, & James III, King of Scotland.** Marquis of Ruvigny & Raineval. (Illus.). 632p. 1994. 45.00 (*0-614-03827-8*, 5046) Genealog Pub.

***Blood Royal of Britain & the Plantagenet Roll of the Blood Royal, Set.** Marquis of Ruvigny & Raineval. 1994. 235.00 (*0-614-03832-4*, 5051) Genealog Pub.

Blood Rules. John Trehaile. 1993. mass mkt. 5.99 (*0-06-109087-5*, Harp PBks) HarpC.

Blood Rush. Patricia Springer. 352p. 1994. pap. 4.99 (*0-7860-0002-3*, Pinnacle NY) Windsor NY.

Blood Sabbath. Leigh Clark. 320p. 1991. pap. 3.95 (*0-8217-3371-0*) Zebra.

Blood Sacrifice: A Mystery of the Yucatan. Gary Alexander. LC 92-37070. 1993. 17.00 (*0-385-46895-4*) Doubleday.

Blood Sacrifice Complex. Edwin M. Loeb. LC 24-4020. (American Anthropological Association Memoirs Ser.: No. 30). 1924. pap. 15.00 (*0-527-00529-0*) Periodicals Srv.

Blood Safety: Current Challenges. Ed. by Sandra T. Nance. LC 92-49346. 1992. 49.00 (*1-56395-015-4*) Am Assn Blood.

***Blood Saga.** Will Camp. 1994. pap. 3.99 (*0-06-100800-1*, Harp PBks) HarpC.

Blood! Said the Cat, No. 2. Louise M. Foley. 192p. (Orig.). 1992. pap. 3.50 (*0-425-12655-2*) Berkley Pub.

Blood Saving in Open Heart Surgery. Ed. by D. E. Birnbaum & H. E. Hoffmeister. 1991. pap. text ed. 37.00 (*0-471-56083-9*) Wiley.

Blood Season: Tyson & the World of Boxing. Phil Berger. 1990. mass mkt. 4.95 (*0-06-100073-6*, Harp PBks) HarpC.

Blood Secrets. Dale Ludwig. 304p. 1993. mass mkt. 4.50 (*1-55817-695-0*, Pinnacle NY) Windsor NY.

Blood Secrets: The True Story of Demon Worship & Ceremonial Murder. Isaiah Oke & Joe Wright. 1991. pap. 4.95 (*0-425-12852-0*) Berkley Pub.

Blood Secrets: The True Story of Demon Worship & Ceremonial Murder. Isaiah Oke & Joe Wright. 235p. 1989. text ed. 23.95 (*0-87975-568-7*) Prometheus Bks.

Blood Separation & Plasma Fractionation. James R. Harris. 510p. 1991. text ed. 179.95 (*0-471-56875-9*) Wiley.

Blood Shot. Sara Paretsky. 1989. mass mkt. 5.99 (*0-440-20420-8*) Dell.

Blood Shot. large type ed. Sara Paretsky. (General Ser.). 1989. 20.95 (*0-8161-4775-2*, Large Print Bks) Hall.

Blood Simple. Joel Coen & Ethan Coen. (Original Screenplay Ser.). (Illus.). 112p. 1989. pap. 9.95 (*0-312-02168-2*) St Martin.

Blood Sisters. Ken Englade. 1994. mass mkt. 4.99 (*0-312-95203-1*) St Martin.

Blood Sisters. Judith H. Wall. 384p. 1994. 4.99 (*0-451-40414-9*, Onyx) NAL-Dutton.

Blood Sisters: An Examination of Conscience. Valerie Miner. 224p. 1982. pap. 6.95 (*0-312-08462-5*) St Martin.

Blood Sisters: The French Revolution in Women's Memory. Marilyn Yalom. LC 92-54518. (Illus.). 288p. 1993. 25.00 (*0-465-09263-2*) Basic.

Blood Song. Hank Searls. 352p. 1985. pap. 3.95 (*0-345-30663-5*) Ballantine.

Blood Speaks. rev. ed. Larry Huggins. LC 93-70311. 95p. 1993. pap. 5.95 (*0-88270-661-6*) Bridge Pub.

Blood Sport. Dick Francis. 1988. mass mkt. 5.95 (*0-449-21262-9*) Fawcett.

Blood Sport. large type ed. Dick Francis. 1991. text ed. 21.95 (*0-8161-5226-8*, Large Print Bks); pap. 15.95 (*0-8161-5227-6*, Large Print Bks) Hall.

Blood Sport. limited ed. Dick Francis. 320p. 1993. 75.00 (*1-56287-042-4*) Armchair Detective.

Blood Sport. Dick Francis. 320p. 1993. reprint ed. 19.95 (*1-56287-040-8*); reprint ed. 25.00 (*1-56287-041-6*) Armchair Detective.

Blood Sport. Dick Francis. 1994. reprint ed. lib. bdg. 32.95 (*1-56849-282-0*) Buccaneer Bks.

Blood Sport: A Social History of Spanish Bullfighting. Timothy Mitchell. LC 91-7231. (Illus.). 288p. (C). 1991. text ed. 28.95x (*0-8122-3129-5*); pap. text ed. 14.95x (*0-8122-1346-7*) U of Pa Pr.

***Blood Stain Evidence at Crime Scenes.** Stuart H. James. 550p. 1995. write for info. (*0-8493-8108-8*, 8108) CRC Pr.

Blood Stem Cell Transplants. Ed. by Robert P. Gale et al. (Illus.). 200p. (C). 1994. 64.95 (*0-521-44210-9*) Cambridge U Pr.

Blood Stone. Michael Allegretto. 272p. 1990. reprint ed. pap. 3.50 (*0-380-71119-2*) Avon.

***Blood Stories.** Martha Ramsey. (CSU Poetry Ser.: No. XLIX). 75p. (Orig.). 1996. pap. 10.00 (*1-880834-44-8*) Cleveland St Univ Poetry Ctr.

Blood Storm. Kyle Maning. 288p. (Orig.). 1990. pap. 3.50 (*0-8439-2815-8*) Dorchester Pub Co.

Blood Strike. (Super Bolan Ser.). 1994. mass mkt. 4.99 (*0-373-61439-X*, 1-61439-5) Harlequin Bks.

Blood Substitutes. Chang & Geyer. 736p. 1989. 150.00 (*0-8247-8027-2*) Dekker.

Blood Substitutes: Preparation Physiology & Medical Applications. Ed. by K. C. Lowe. LC 88-8358. (Ellis Horwood Series in Biomedicine). 187p. 1988. lib. bdg. 140.00 (*0-89573-578-4*) VCH Pubs.

***Blood Substitutes: Psysiological Basis of Efficacy.** Ed. by Robert M. Winslow et al. LC 95-2118. (Illus.). 205p. 1995. text ed. 49.50 (*0-8176-3804-0*) Birkhauser.

Blood Substitutes & Oxygen Carriers. Thomas M. Chang. 896p. 1992. 190.00 (*0-8247-8810-9*) Dekker.

Blood Substitutes & Therapeutic Uses: Index of New Information with Authors, Subjects & Bibliography. Arthur T. Treadwell. 180p. 1993. 49.50 (*1-55914-762-8*); pap. 39.50 (*1-55914-763-6*) ABBE Pubs Assn.

Blood Sugar. De Filippi. 1993. mass mkt. 4.50 (*0-06-109106-5*, Harp PBks) HarpC.

***Blood Supply: Risks, Perceptions & Prospects for the Future.** Ed. by Sandra T. Nance. (Illus.). (C). 1994. text ed. 50.00 (*1-56395-033-2*) Am Assn Blood.

B

An Asterisk (*) at the beginning of an entry indicates that the title is appearing in BIP for the first time. 819

Blood Surface Interactions: Biological Principles Underlying Haemocompatibility with Artificial Materials. Ed. by J. P. Cazenave et al. 266p. 1987. 115.00 (0-444-80764-0) Elsevier.

Blood, Sweat, & Mahjong: Family & Enterprise in an Overseas Chinese Community. Ellen Oxfeld. LC 92-56779. (Anthropology of Contemporary Issues Ser.). (Illus.). 320p. 1993. 42.50 (0-8014-2593-X); pap. 16.95 (0-8014-9908-9) Cornell U Pr.

Blood Sweat & Stanley Poole. William Goldman & James Goldman. 1962. pap. 4.75 (0-8222-0127-5) Dramatists Play.

Blood, Sweat, & Tears. Lady Coleman. 106p. (Orig.). 1991. pap. 12.13 (0-685-48293-6) Dayspring Pr.

Blood Sympathy. Reginald Hill. 224p. 1994. 19.95 (0-312-11249-1, Pub. by Thomas Dunne Bks) St Martin.

Blood Tattoo. Ebi Gabor. LC 87-24840. (Woman in History Ser.: Vol. 85). (Illus.). ix, 206p. (Orig.). 1987. pap. 12.00 (0-930383-11-7) Monument Pr.

Blood, Tears & Folly. Len Deighton. 1994. pap. 15.00 (0-06-092557-4) HarpC.

Blood, Tears, & Folly: An Objective Look at World War II. Len Deighton. LC 92-56241. (Illus.). 416p. 1993. 30.00 (0-06-017000-X, HarpT) HarpC.

Blood Technology. James R. Critser, Jr. (Ser. 10BT-79). 101p. 1980. pap. 90.00 (0-914428-75-6) Lexington Data.

Blood Technology. James R. Critser, Jr. (Ser. 10BT-80). 1981. pap. 100.00 (0-914428-84-5) Lexington Data.

Blood Technology. James R. Critser, Jr. (Ser. 10BT-81). 1982. pap. 100.00 (0-914428-90-X) Lexington Data.

Blood Technology. James R. Critser, Jr. (Ser.10BT-82). 1983. pap. 100.00 (0-88178-004-9) Lexington Data.

Blood Technology. James R. Critser, Jr. (Ser. 10BT-83). 176p. 1984. pap. 100.00 (0-88178-015-4) Lexington Data.

Blood Technology. James R. Critser, Jr. (Ser. 10BT-84). 227p. 1985. pap. 100.00 (0-88178-052-9) Lexington Data.

Blood Technology. James R. Critser, Jr. (Ser. 10BT-85). 138p. 1986. pap. 100.00 (0-88178-034-0) Lexington Data.

Blood Tells. Stephen Robertson. (Decoy Ser.: No. 3). 1990. pap. 3.95 (1-55817-325-0, Pinnacle NY) Windsor NY.

*Blood Test. Jonathan Kellerman. LC 85-20020. 1995. mass mkt. 5.99 (0-553-56963-5) Bantam.

Blood Test. Jonathan Kellerman. LC 85-20020. 352p. 1987. pap. 5.99 (0-451-15929-2, Sig) NAL-Dutton.

Blood That Keeps Singing - La Sangre Que Sigue Cantando. Clemente S. Velez. Tr. by Martin Espada & Camilo Perez-Bustillo. LC 91-55409. 128p. (Orig.). 1991. pap. 9.95 (0-915306-78-6) Curbstone.

Blood Thirst. L. A. Freed. 1989. pap. 3.95 (1-55817-158-4, Pinnacle NY) Windsor NY.

Blood Thirsty Savages. Adrian C. Louis. 109p. 1994. 18.95 (1-56809-010-2); pap. 12.50 (1-56809-011-0) Time Being Bks.

Blood Ties. Warren Murphy & Richard Sapir. (Destroyer Ser.: No. 69). 1987. pap. 3.95 (0-451-14879-7, Sig) NAL-Dutton.

Blood Ties. Laurel Pace. (Intrigue Ser.). 1993. mass mkt. 2.99 (0-373-22247-5, 1-22247-0) Harlequin Bks.

Blood Ties. Stephen Robertson. (Decoy Ser.: No. 2). 1989. pap. 3.95 (1-55817-279-3, Pinnacle NY) Windsor NY.

Blood Ties. large type ed. Isobel Lambot. 1989. 17.95 (0-7089-2092-6) Ulverscroft.

Blood Ties. large type ed. A. J. Quinnell. (Adventure Suspense Ser.). 416p. 1985. 23.95 (0-7089-8286-7, Charnwood) Ulverscroft.

Blood Ties: Life & Violence in Rural Mexico. James B. Greenberg. LC 88-29538. 282p. 1993. reprint ed. pap. text ed. 14.95 (0-8165-1379-1) U of Ariz Pr.

Blood to Remember: American Poets on the Holocaust. Charles Fishman. 450p. 1991. pap. 16.95 (0-89672-215-5) Tex Tech Univ Pr.

Blood Trail. Frederic Bean. 224p. 1993. pap. 3.50 (0-8217-4369-4) Zebra.

Blood Trail. Tanya Huff. 304p. (Orig.). 1992. mass mkt. 4.50 (0-88677-502-7) DAW Bks.

Blood Trail South. Walt Denver. 1987. pap. 2.25 (0-8217-1349-3) Zebra.

Blood Trail to Kansas. Robert Lake. 1991. pap. 3.50 (0-8217-3541-1) Zebra.

Blood Trance: A Maddy & Alex Phillips Mystery of Hypnotic Detection. R. D. Zimmerman. LC 92-37921. 1993. 20.00 (0-688-12139-X) Morrow.

Blood Trance: A Novel of Hypnotic Detection. R. D. Zimmerman. 1994. mass mkt. 4.99 (0-440-21518-8) Dell.

Blood Transfusion. 9th ed. P. L. Mollison. (Illus.). 1056p. 1992. 135.00 (0-632-02584-0) Blackwell Sci.

Blood Transfusion: A Guide to the Formation & Operation of a Transfusion Service. Ed. by C. C. Bowley et al. 132p. 1971. pap. 5.60 (92-4-154013-3, 196) World Health.

Blood Transfusion & Problems of Bleeding. C. T. Sibinga & P. C. Das. 1982. lib. bdg. 84.00 (90-247-3058-9) Kluwer Ac.

Blood Transfusion ID Card & Book: For Safer Blood at the Time of AIDS, Hepatitis, VDs, etc. Antun Murkovic. 120p. (Orig.). (ENG & JPN.). 1989. pap. write for info. (0-929602-00-5) Mura Pub Co.

Blood Transfusion Micro-Filters. 12p. 1989. 49.00 (0-910275-93-9, BF7-113) Assn Adv Med Instrn.

*Blood Transfusion Services for the Developing World. Ed. by J. Leikola & M. Contreras. (Journal Ser.: Vol. 67, Supplement 5, 1994). (Illus.). iv, 66p. 1994. pap. 28.00 (3-8055-6094-X) S Karger.

Blood Transfusion Therapy: A Physician's Handbook. Ed. by Patricia T. Pisciotto. (Illus.). (C). 1993. pap. text ed. 7.00 (1-56395-027-8) Am Assn Blood.

Blood Transfusion Therapy: A Problem Oriented Approach. J. A. Napier. 430p. 1987. text ed. 130.00 (0-471-91283-2, A R Liss) Wiley.

Blood Transfusions: A History & Evaluation of the Religions, Biblical & Medical Objections. Jerry Bergman. 220p. (Orig.). (C). 1994. pap. 9.95 (1-883858-27-5) Witness CA.

Blood Transfusions & Infectious Diseases. E. G. Rondanelli. (Infectious Diseases Color Atlas Monographs: No. 2). 322p. 1989. text ed. 45.00 (1-57235-029-6) Piccin NY.

*Blood Treachery. Jake McMasters. (White Apache Ser.: No. 6). 176p. (Orig.). 1995. mass mkt. 3.99 (0-8439-3739-4) Dorchester Pub Co.

Blood Trillium. Julian May. 1993. mass mkt. 5.99 (0-553-56198-7) Bantam.

Blood Truce. David Thompson. (Wilderness Ser.: No. 16). 176p. (Orig.). 1993. pap. 3.50 (0-8439-3525-1) Dorchester Pub Co.

Blood Type: The New John Marshall Tanner Mystery. Stephen Greenleaf. 304p. 1992. 20.00 (0-688-11268-4) Morrow.

Blood Use in Cardiac Surgery. Ed. by N. Friedel et al. 320p. 1991. 87.00 (0-387-91372-6) Spr-Verlag.

Blood Vengeance. Created by Jerry Pournelle. 1994. mass mkt. 5.99 (0-671-72201-8) Baen Bks.

Blood Vengeance. large type ed. Martin Carroll. (Linford Mystery Library). 240p. 1988. pap. 11.95 (0-7089-6613-6, Linford) Ulverscroft.

Blood Vessel Changes in Hypertension, I. Ed. by Lee. 1989. 132.00 (0-8493-4883-8, RC685) CRC Pr.

Blood Vessel Changes in Hypertension, II. Ed. by Lee. 1989. 132.00 (0-8493-4884-6, RC685) CRC Pr.

Blood Vessel Wall & Thrombosis, 2 vols., Vol. I: Hemostasis. Ed. by Raymond Machovich. 320p. 1988. Vol. I, Hemostasis, 320 pogs. 191.00 (0-8493-5626-1, RC694) CRC Pr.

Blood Vessel Wall & Thrombosis, 2 vols., Vol. II: Thrombotic Processes in Atherogenesis. Ed. by Raymond Machovich. 280p. 1988. Vol. II, Thrombotic Processes in Atherogenesis, 280 pgs. 180.00 (0-8493-5627-X, RC694) CRC Pr.

Blood Vessel Wall Interactions in Thrombogenesis. Ed. by A. Nordoy. (Haemostasis Journal: Vol. 8, Nos. 3-5). 1979. pap. 62.50 (3-8055-0117-X) S Karger.

Blood Vessels. Walter J. Cliff. LC 74-31789. (Biological Structure & Function Ser.: No. 6). 224p. reprint ed. pap. 63.90 (0-8357-7328-0, 2029215) Bks Demand.

Blood Vessels & Circulation: Proceedings of the Brown University Symposium on Biology of Skin, 1960. W. Montagna & R. Ellis. LC 60-10839. (Advances in Biology of Skin Ser.: Vol. 2). 1961. 69.00 (0-08-009345-0, Pub. by Pergamon Repr UK) Franklin.

Blood Viscosity in Heart Disease & Cancer: Proceedings. Ed. by Leopold Dintenfass et al. (Illus.). 192p. 1981. 82.00 (0-08-024954-X, Pub. by Pergamon Repr UK) Franklin.

Blood Wager. Walt Denver. 1989. pap. 2.95 (0-8217-2798-2) Zebra.

*Blood War: The Blood Covenant & Spiritual Warfare. Randy Hix. 144p. (Orig.). (C). 1994. pap. text ed. 6.95 (1-879993-20-1) Embassy Pub.

Blood Warriors. Jory Sherman. 1984. pap. 2.25 (0-8217-1317-5) Zebra.

*Blood Water & Stone. Walter Orr. LC 95-60834. 159p. 1996. pap. 8.95 (1-55523-748-7) Winston-Derek.

Blood Wedding see Three Tragedies

Blood Wedding; Yerma. Federico G. Lorca. Tr. by Langston Hughes & W. S. Merwin. LC 93-51498. (TCG Translations Ser.: Vol. 5). 160p. 1994. 24.95 (1-55936-079-8); pap. 12.95 (1-55936-080-1) Theatre Comm.

Blood Wedding, Yerma, & The House of Bernard Alba: Garcia Lorca's Tragic Trilogy. Dennis A. Klein. (Twayne's Masterworks Ser.: No. 69). 152p. 1991. text ed. 21.95 (0-8057-8351-2, Twayne); pap. 12.95 (0-8057-8144-7, Twayne) Macmillan.

Blood Weddings: The Knanaya Christian of Kerala. Richard M. Swiderski. (C). 1988. 18.00 (0-8364-2454-9, Pub. by New Era Pubns) S Asia.

Blood Whispers: L. A. Writers on AIDS. Ed. by Terry Wolverton. LC 91-90365. 100p. 1991. pap. 7.95 (0-9629528-0-X) Silverton Bks.

Blood Whispers, Vol. 2: L.A. Writers on AIDS. Ed. by Terry Wolverton. LC 91-90365. 128p. (Orig.). 1994. pap. 9.95 (0-9629528-1-8) Silverton Bks.

Blood Will Have Blood. Linda Barnes. 192p. 1986. mass mkt. 5.99 (0-449-20901-6, Crest) Fawcett.

Blood Will Out. large type ed. Margaret Carr. (Linford Mystery Library). 295p. 1988. pap. 11.95 (0-7089-6564-4, Linford) Ulverscroft.

Blood Will Tell. Gary Cartwright. Ed. by Rebecca Todd. 488p. 1995. mass mkt. 5.99 (0-671-88330-5) PB.

Blood Will Tell. Benjamin R. Davenport. LC 78-38645. (Black Heritage Library Collection). (Illus.). 1977. reprint ed. 25.95 (0-8369-9003-X) Ayer.

Blood Will Tell: A True Story of Deadly Lust. Joseph Bosco. LC 93-17770. 1993. 23.00 (0-688-10889-X) Morrow.

Blood Wings. Stephen Gresham. 1990. pap. 3.95 (0-8217-2891-1) Zebra.

Blood Witness for Unity & Peace: The Life of Max Joseph Metzger. Leonard Swidler. 1986. pap. 6.95 (0-87193-077-3) Dimension Bks.

Blood Wolf. John Peel. (Shockers Ser.). (Illus.). 144p. (J). (gr. 3-7). 1993. pap. 2.95 (0-448-40527-X, G&D) Putnam Pub Group.

Blood, Women & Territory: An Analysis of Clan Feuds of Dongria Konds. P. K. Nayak. (Sociological Publications in Honour of Dr. K. Ishwaran: No. 2). xviii, 238p. 1990. text ed. 32.50 (81-85047-43-X, Pub. by Reliance Pub Hse II) Apt Bks.

Blood Work. Ron Padgett. 104p. 1993. pap. 12.00 (0-917453-26-3) Bamberger.

*Blood Work. Ron Padgett. 104p. 1994. lib. bdg. 31.00 (0-8095-6512-9) Borgo Pr.

Blood Work. Fay Zachary. 288p. (Orig.). 1994. mass mkt. 4.99 (0-425-14047-4) Berkley Pub.

*Bloodbath. Jake McMasters. (White Apache Ser.: No. 5). 176p. (Orig.). 1994. mass mkt. 3.99 (0-8439-3689-4) Dorchester Pub Co.

Bloodborne Pathogens: Four Color Edition. National Safety Council Staff. LC 93-26138. 1993. pap. 13.75 (0-86720-818-X) Jones & Bartlett.

*Bloodborne Pathogens: How to Write an Exposure Control Plan. 40p. 1994. ring bd. 79.99 (0-88711-255-2) Am Trucking Assns.

Bloodborne Pathogens - Academic. National Safety Council Staff. LC 92-49476. 80p. 1992. teacher ed 15.00 (0-86720-772-8); teacher ed 395.00 (0-86720-798-1); pap. text ed. 12.50 (0-86720-771-X); vhs 195.00 (0-86720-775-2); sl. 195.00 (0-86720-773-6) Jones & Bartlett.

Bloodborne Pathogens in the Workplace: Guidelines for Small Businesses. Erskine S. Walther. LC 94-77292. 89p. 1994. write for info. (1-885327-03-X) Walther Cnslt.

Bloodborne Pathogens (Smithkline) National Safety Council Staff. 1993. pap. 12.50 (0-86720-793-0) Jones & Bartlett.

Bloodbrothers. Richard Price. 288p. 1993. pap. 9.00 (0-380-77476-3) Avon.

*Bloodchoice. Janice Harrell. (Vampire Twins Ser.: No. 3). (YA). 1994. pap. 3.99 (0-06-106243-X, HarpT) HarpC.

Bloodeagle. large type ed. Roy Lewis. LC 93-43541. 1994. 22.95 (0-7927-1928-X, Curley Lrg Print); pap. 20.95 (0-7927-1927-1, Curley Lrg Print) Chivers N Amer.

Bloodeagle: An Arnold Landon Mystery. Roy Lewis. 224p. 1993. 19.95 (0-312-10431-6) St Martin.

Blooded on Arachne. Michael Bishop. LC 81-10830. (Illus.). 352p. 1982. 13.95 (0-87054-093-9) Arkham.

Bloodfang. Michael D. Weaver. (Bloodfang Trilogy Ser.). 224p. (Orig.). 1989. pap. 3.50 (0-380-75584-X) Avon.

Bloodfire. John Lutz. (Fred Carver Mystery Ser.). 224p. 1992. reprint ed. mass mkt. 3.99 (0-380-71446-9) Avon.

Bloodfire: Poems. Fred Chappell. LC 78-13578. 56p. 1978. text ed. 13.95 (0-8071-0451-5); pap. 6.95 (0-8071-0452-3) La State U Pr.

Bloodhound Champions: 1952-1986. Camino E. E. & B. Co. Staff. (Illus.). 210p. 1988. pap. 36.95 (0-940808-46-3) Camino E E & Bk.

Bloodhounds. Hylda Owen. (Illus.). 160p. 1989. 11.95 (0-86622-675-3, KW-166) TFH Pubns.

Bloodhype, No. 4. Alan D. Foster. 1988. mass mkt. 4.99 (0-345-33285-7) Ballantine.

Bloodied Ivy. large type ed. Robert Goldsborough. 1988. reprint ed. lib. bdg. 7.95 (0-89621-191-6) Thorndike Pr.

Bloodiest Day. (Civil War Ser.). (Illus.). 176p. 1984. 19.93 (0-8094-4740-1); lib. bdg. 25.93 (0-8094-4741-X) Time-Life.

Blooding. Joseph Wambaugh. 1989. mass mkt. 6.50 (0-553-28281-6) Bantam.

Blooding of the Guns. large type ed. Alexander Fullerton. 512p. 1987. 16.95 (0-7089-1726-7) Ulverscroft.

Bloodland. William W. Johnstone. 352p. 1986. pap. 3.95 (0-8217-1926-2) Zebra.

*Bloodless. Andy Murphy. LC 94-72730. 1995. write for info. (0-944435-33-5) Glenbridge Pub.

Bloodless Revolution: England, Sixteen Eighty-Eight. Stuart E. Prall. LC 79-175415. 368p. 1985. reprint ed. pap. 13.95 (0-299-10294-7) U of Wis Pr.

Bloodless Surgery. (Alternative Medicine Ser.). 1991. lib. bdg. 79.95 (0-8490-4296-8) Gordon Pr.

Bloodless Surgery: Technique with Treatment. Paul Wendel. 110p. 1974. reprint ed. spiral bd. 22.00 (0-7873-0953-2) Mokelumne.

Bloodletter. Warren N. Beath. 352p. 1994. 21.95 (0-312-85731-4) Tor Bks.

Bloodletter. K. W. Jeter. (Star Trek: Deep Space Nine Ser.: No. 3). 288p. (Orig.). 1993. mass mkt. 5.50 (0-671-87275-3) PB.

Bloodletter. abr. ed. George Guthridge. 190p. 1995. pap. 7.95 (1-56901-483-3) NW Pub.

Bloodletters & Badmen: A Narrative Encyclopedia of American Criminals from the Pilgrims to the Present. Jay R. Nash. LC 72-95977. (Illus.). 640p. 1992. 16.95 (0-87131-113-5); pap. 17.95 (0-87131-200-X) M Evans.

*Bloodletters & Badmen: A Narrative Encyclopedia of American Criminals from the Pilgrims to the Present. expanded rev. ed. Jay R. Nash. LC 94-49585. 1995. pap. 19.95 (0-87131-777-X) M Evans.

*Bloodletting. Julie Noterman. 80p. (Orig.). 1995. pap. 9.95 (0-9645666-0-5) Eco Cult Perspect.

Bloodletting: A Mind at Midlife. Lois Silverstein. (Illus.). 88p. (Orig.). 1991. pap. 12.95 (0-9603440-2-0) Red Shoes Pr.

Bloodletting in Appalachia. 8th ed. Howard B. Lee. (Illus.). 224p. 1988. reprint ed. pap. 8.00 (0-87012-041-7) McClain.

*Bloodline. Gerry Boyle. LC 94-24035. 1995. write for info. (0-399-14030-1, Putnam) Putnam Pub Group.

*Bloodline. Rex Burns. 1995. 19.95 (0-8027-3256-9) Walker & Co.

*Bloodline. Sidney Sheldon. (Sheldon Continuity Ser.). 320p. 1994. 12.95 (1-56865-094-9, GuildAmerica) Dbldy Bk Music.

Bloodline. Sidney Sheldon. 464p. 1988. mass mkt. 6.99 (0-446-35744-8) Warner Bks.

Bloodline. Sidney Sheldon. LC 77-21175. 1978. 23.00 (0-688-03196-X) Morrow.

*Bloodline Poems. Del Corey. (Illus.). 70p. (Orig.). 1994. pap. 50.00x (1-56439-043-8) Ridgeway.

*Bloodlines. James Axler. 1995. pap. 4.99 (0-373-62529-4, Wrldwide Lib) Harlequin Bks.

Bloodlines. Susan Conant. 1994. mass mkt. 4.99 (0-553-29886-0) Bantam.

Bloodlines. L. C. Phillips. LC 79-153403. 91p. 1971. 16.95 (0-912282-02-9) Pulse-Finger.

Bloodlines. Mark Weaver & John Jenkins. 343p. (Orig.). 1993. pap. 10.99 (0-89283-825-6, Vine Bks) Servant.

*Bloodlines. J. N. Williamson. LC 94-34545. 1994. 17.95 (0-681-00693-5) Longmeadow Pr.

Bloodlines: Odyssey of a Native Daughter. Janet C. Hale. LC 92-56816. 192p. 1993. 18.00 (0-679-41527-0) Random.

Bloodlines: Odyssey of A Native Daughter. Janet C. Hale. LC 94-3999. 224p. 1994. reprint ed. pap. 11.00 (0-06-097612-8, PL) HarpC.

Bloodmaster. Mary L. Quijano. 1989. pap. 3.95 (1-55817-251-3, Pinnacle NY) Windsor NY.

Bloodname: Legend of the Jade Phoenix, Vol. 2. Robert Thurston. (BattleTech Ser.). 272p. (Orig.). 1991. pap. 4.50 (0-451-45117-1, ROC) NAL-Dutton.

Bloodrock. Richard Ferrie. 400p. (Orig.). 1987. pap. 3.95 (0-8439-2433-0) Dorchester Pub Co.

Bloodrock Valley War. large type ed. Ray Hogan. 128p. 1992. reprint ed. lib. bdg. 15.95 (1-56054-573-9) Thorndike Pr.

Bloodroot. Russ Banks. Date not set. 22.00 (0-06-016860-9, HarpT) HarpC.

Bloodrun. large type ed. William S. Brady. Bd. with Whiplash. 1984. 12.50 (0-685-29743-8) Ulverscroft.

Bloodrush. Hugh Zachary. 1981. pap. 1.95 (0-8439-0857-2) Dorchester Pub Co.

Bloods: An Oral History of the Vietnam War by Black Veterans. Wallace Terry. 320p. 1985. mass mkt. 5.95 (0-345-31197-3) Ballantine.

*Bloodshed & Three Novellas. Cynthia Ozick. (Library of Modern Jewish Literature). 192p. 1995. pap. 14.95 (0-8156-0352-5) Syracuse U Pr.

Bloodshed in the Caucasus: Escalation of the Armed Conflict in Nagorno Karabakh. Ed. by Human Rights Watch Staff. 92p. (Orig.). 1992. pap. 7.00 (1-56432-081-2) Hum Rts Watch.

Bloodshed in the Caucasus: Violations of Humanitarian Law & Human Rights in the Georgia-South Ossetia Conflict. Ed. by Human Rights Watch Staff. 66p. (Orig.). 1992. pap. 7.00 (1-56432-058-8) Hum Rts Watch.

Bloodsong. Jill Neimark. LC 94-15060. 288p. 1994. pap. 9.95 (0-452-27296-3, Plume) NAL-Dutton.

Bloodsong. Jill Neimark. LC 93-261. 1993. 20.00 (0-679-42005-3) Random.

Bloodstained Bokhara. William C. Gault. (Black Dagger Crime Ser.). 200p. 1989. reprint ed. text ed. 16.50 (0-86220-756-8, Black Dagger) Chivers N Amer.

Bloodstains. Giuliana Morandini. Tr. by Blossom S. Kirschenbaum. 1987. pap. 8.95 (0-89823-094-2) New Rivers Pr.

Bloodstock Breeding. Charles Leicester. 536p. 1990. 100.00 (0-85131-349-3, Pub. by J A Allen & Co UK) St Mut.

Bloodstock Breeding: Theory & Practice. Charles Leicester. (Illus.). 1983. 40.00 (0-87556-148-9) Saifer.

*Bloodstone. large type ed. Evelyn Anthony. LC 95-14158. 655p. 1995. 24.95 (0-7862-0458-3) Thorndike Pr.

Bloodstone Inheritance. Serita D. Stevens. 384p. 1992. mass mkt. 3.99 (0-8217-3969-7) Zebra.

*Bloodstones. Evelyn Anthony. 288p. 1995. 23.00 (0-06-017221-5) HarpC.

*Bloodstones. large type ed. Evelyn Anthony. LC 95-14158. 1995. write for info. (0-614-05434-6) Thorndike Pr.

Bloodstoppers & Bearwalkers: Folk Traditions of the Upper Peninsula. Richard M. Dorson. LC 52-5394. (Illus.). 311p. 1952. pap. 14.50 (0-674-07665-6) HUP.

Bloodstorm: Five Books of Poems & Docupoems - Towards Liberation. Kiarri T. Cheatwood. LC 85-82524. 160p. 1986. per., pap. 10.50 (0-916418-62-6) Lotus.

*Bloodstream. P. M. Carlson. Ed. by Jane Chelius. 336p. 1995. 20.00 (0-671-76977-4) PB.

Bloodstream Infections: Laboratory Detection & Clinical Considerations. Calvin L. Strand & Jonas S. Shulman. LC 87-31884. (Illus.). 292p. 1988. text ed. 45.00 (0-89189-262-1, 45-7-014-00) Am Soc Clinical.

Bloodstream Seren Poets, No. 1: Seren Poets. Ed. by Ceri Meyrick. 100p. 1989. pap. 13.95 (1-85411-014-4, Pub. by Poetry Wales Pr UK) Dufour.

*Bloodsuckers. Ron Knapp. LC 94-23726. (Weird & Wacky Science Ser.). (J). 1996. lib. bdg. write for info. (0-89490-614-3) Enslow Pubs.

Bloodsuckers: Vampires at the Movies. Scott Nance. 1992. pap. 14.95 (1-55698-317-4) Movie Pubs Servs.

*Bloodsucking Friends: A Love Story. Christopher Moore. LC 95-7463. 1995. 23.50 (0-684-81097-2) S&S Trade.

Bloodsucking Witchcraft: An Epistemological Study of Anthropomorphic Supernaturalism in Rural Tlaxcala. Hugo G. Nutini & John M. Roberts. LC 92-34513. 475p. 1993. 40.00 (0-8165-1197-7) U of Ariz Pr.

Bloodtaking & Peacemaking: Feud, Law, & Society in Saga Iceland. William I. Miller. LC 89-77971. (Illus.). 416p. 1990. 29.95 (0-226-52679-8) U Ch Pr.

Bloodthirst. J. M. Dillard. Ed. by Dave Stern. (Star Trek Ser.: No. 37). 1990. mass mkt. 5.50 (0-671-70876-7) PB.

Bloodties. Gloria Murphy. LC 86-46383. 252p. 1987. 17.95 (1-55611-036-7) D I Fine.

Bloodties: Nature, Culture & the Hunt. Ted Kerasote. Ed. by Philip Turner. (Illus.). 277p. 1994. pap. 13.00 (1-56836-027-4) Kodansha.

Bloodties: Nature, Culture & the Hunt. Ted Kerasote. LC 92-56824. 320p. 1993. 22.00 (0-394-57609-8) Random.

An Asterisk (*) at the beginning of an entry indicates that the title is appearing in BIP for the first time.

Bloomsday: A City in Motion. Don Kardong & Phil Schofield. (Illus.). 100p. 1989. 19.95 (*0-923910-02-6*); pap. 15.95 (*0-923910-03-4*) Cowles Pub Co.

Blooper Man: The Rip Sewell Story. Elson Smith. (Illus.). 106p. (Orig.). 1981. pap. 6.95 (*0-939332-00-0*) J Pohl Assocs.

Blossom. Dale Butler. LC 92-34265. (Voyages Ser.). (Illus.). (J). 1993. 14.00 (*0-383-03620-8*) SRA Schl Grp.

Blossom. Andrew Vachss. 320p. 1991. mass mkt. 5.95 (*0-8041-0751-3*) Ivy Books.

Blossom. Rosemary Wallner. LC 92-14779. (TV's Hottest Teens Ser.). (J). 1992. lib. bdg. 12.94 (*1-56239-141-0*) Abdo & Dghtrs.

Blossom & the Fruit. Mabel Collins. 332p. 1974. reprint ed. spiral bd. 9.90 (*0-7873-1136-7*) Mokelumne.

Blossom Bird Falls in Love. Sherry Paul. (See How I Read Ser.). (Illus.). 32p. (Orig.). (J). (ps-2). 1981. pap. 14.10 (*0-685-01192-5*); pap. 16.20 (*0-685-01193-3*) CPI Pub.

Blossom Bird Finds a Family. Sherry Paul. (See How I Read Ser.). (Illus.). 32p. (Orig.). (J). (ps-2). 1981. 16.20 (*0-685-01194-1*) CPI Pub.

Blossom Bird Finds a Family, Set. Sherry Paul. (See How I Read Ser.). (Illus.). 32p. (Orig.). (J). (ps-2). 1981. pap. 14.10 (*0-686-31343-7*) CPI Pub.

Blossom Bird Goes South. Sherry Paul. (See How I Read Ser.). (Illus.). 32p. (Orig.). (J). (ps-2). 1981. 16.20 (*0-685-01195-X*) CPI Pub.

Blossom Bird Goes South, Set. Sherry Paul. (See How I Read Ser.). (Illus.). 32p. (Orig.). (J). (ps-2). 1981. pap. 14.10 (*0-675-01080-2*) CPI Pub.

Blossom Comes Home. James Herriot. (Illus.). (J). 1988. 13.00 (*0-312-02169-0*) St Martin.

Blossom Comes Home. James Herriot. (Illus.). 32p. (J). (gr. 1-8). 1993. pap. 6.95 (*0-312-09131-1*) St Martin.

Blossom Culp & the Sleep of Death. Richard Peck. (J). (gr. k-6). 1994. reprint ed. mass mkt. 3.99 (*0-440-40676-5*, YB) Dell.

Blossom of Bone: Reclaiming the Connections Between Homoeroticism & the Sacred. Randy P. Conner. LC 92-56126. 352p. 1993. pap. 18.00 (*0-06-250257-3*) Harper SF.

Blossom on the Bough: A Book of Trees. Illus. & Text by Anne O. Dowden. LC 93-22726. 80p. (J). (gr. 3 up). 1994. 16.95 (*0-395-68375-0*); pap. 9.95 (*0-395-68943-0*) Ticknor & Flds Bks Yng Read.

Blossom Promise. Betsy C. Byars. (Illus.). 160p. (J). (gr. k-6). 1989. reprint ed. pap. 3.50 (*0-440-40137-2*, YB) Dell.

Blossom, Stalk & Vine. Judy Odom. Ed. by Phyllis Tickle. 96p. 1990. pap. 8.95 (*0-918518-89-X*) Iris Pr.

Blossoming Love. Hilda Stahl. (Prairie Ser.: Bk. 1). 224p. (Orig.). 1991. pap. 6.99 (*0-934998-42-6*) Bethel Pub.

Blossoming Romance. large type ed. Moira Morton. (Linford Romance Library). 256p. 1989. pap. 11.95 (*0-7089-6693-4*, Linford) Ulverscroft.

Blossoming Thorn: Georg Trakl's Poetry of Atonement. Erasmo Leiva-Merikakis. LC 85-43246. 192p. 1987. 36.50 (*0-8387-5102-4*) Bucknell U Pr.

Blossoming Trends. Daphne W. Ntiri. (C). 1994. pap. 7.00 (*0-911557-06-7*) Bedford Publishers.

***Blossoms.** Mary Balogh et al. 352p. (Orig.). 1995. mass mkt., pap. 4.99 (*0-451-18249-9*) NAL-Dutton.

Blossoms & Blizzards. Ed. by Winter et al. (Illus.). 110p. 1986. 9.95 (*0-9617240-3-X*); pap. 5.95 (*0-9617240-1-3*) Pegasus Prose.

Blossoms & Bones: On the Life & Work of Georgia O'Keeffe. Christopher Buckley. LC 88-20691. (Illus.). 52p. (Orig.). 1988. pap. 9.95 (*0-8265-1232-1*) Vanderbilt U Pr.

Blossoms & Branches: A Gathering of Rogue Valley Orchard Memories. Kay Atwood. (Illus.). 231p. 1980. pap. 10.95 (*0-685-24086-X*) K Atwood.

Blossoms & the Green Phantom. Betsy C. Byars. (Illus.). 160p. (J). (gr. 4-6). 1987. pap. 14.95 (*0-385-29533-2*) Delacorte.

Blossoms & the Green Phantom. Betsy C. Byars. (Illus.). 160p. (J). (gr. k-6). 1988. reprint ed. pap. 3.50 (*0-440-40069-4*) Dell.

Blossom's Family Album. Devra Speregen. (J). (gr. 4-7). 1993. pap. 4.95 (*0-590-47234-8*) Scholastic Inc.

Blossoms from the Desert. Frank Nance. 94p. (Orig.). 1981. pap. 5.00 (*0-9615739-0-2*) F Nance.

Blossoms from the East: The China Cantos of Ezra Pound. John Nolde. LC 82-61491. (Ezra Pound Scholarship Ser.). 490p. 1983. 35.00 (*0-915032-05-8*); pap. 15.95 (*0-915032-06-6*) Natl Poet Foun.

Blossoms Meet the Vulture Lady. Betsy C. Byars. (J). (gr. k-6). 1987. pap. 2.75 (*0-440-40677-3*, YB) Dell.

Blossoms Meet the Vulture Lady. large type ed. Betsy Byars. (J). (gr. 1-8). 1990. 16.95 (*0-7451-0824-5*, Galaxy Child Lrg Print) Chivers N Amer.

Blossoms of Friendship: Celebrate the Joy of Friendship with This Gift of Verse & Watercolors. Helen S. Rice. LC 91-41049. 1992. 13.99 (*0-8007-1664-7*) Revell.

Blossoms of Kamakura. Hiroshi Harada. (Illus.). 100p. 1994. 46.95 (*4-7661-0759-4*, Pub. by Graphic Sha JA) Bks Nippan.

***Blossoms of the Prairie: The History of the Danish Lutheran Churches in Nebraska.** Jean M. Matteson & Edith M. Matteson. 247p. 1988. 30.95 (*0-9620787-0-0*) Blossoms Prairie.

***Blossomtime Festival Southwest Michigan: A Pictorial History 1906-1996.** Glenn Zerler & Kathryn Zerler. 1995. text ed. 25.00 (*0-9645873-0-0*) Bloomtime.

Blot the Spot: Tried & True Ways. Mary C. Martin. Ed. by Janet Hubbard-Brown. 175p. 1992. write for info. (*0-9611712-1-9*) Concepts Pub.

Blot upon the Brain: Studies in History & Psychology. William W. Ireland. LC 72-3424. (Essay Index Reprint Ser.). 1977. reprint ed. 23.95 (*0-8369-2909-8*) Ayer.

Blotting Book. Edward F. Benson. LC 75-32734. (Literature of Mystery & Detection Ser.). 1976. reprint ed. 23.95 (*0-405-07864-1*) Ayer.

Bloudy Tenent, Washed, & Made White in the Bloud of the Lambe. John Cotton. LC 78-141105. (Research Library of Colonial Americana). 1972. reprint ed. 33.95 (*0-405-03319-2*) Ayer.

Blount Collection of American Art. LC 93-20408. (Illus.). 52p. (J). (ps-12). 1993. pap. 18.00 (*0-89280-031-3*) Montgomery Mus.

Blount County, Tennessee Chancery Court Records, Bk. 0 & Bk. 1: 1852-1865. Albert W. Dockter, Jr. 172p. (Orig.). 1992. pap. 17.50 (*1-55613-589-0*) Heritage Bk.

Blount County, Tennessee, Deeds, 1819-1833. Jane K. Thomas. 283p. (Orig.). 1993. pap. text ed. 24.00 (*1-55613-768-0*) Heritage Bk.

Blount County, Tennessee, Marriages, 1795-1865. Will E. Parham. iv, 422p. 1982. 25.00 (*0-89308-240-6*, TN 52) Southern Hist Pr.

***Blount County, TN: Chancery Court Records 1866-1869 Including Divorce Proceedings 1860-1937 & Monroe County, TN Chancery Court Records 1832-1852 Mentioning Blount County.** Albert W. Dockter, Jr. 267p. (Orig.). 1994. pap. text ed. 24.00 (*0-7884-0024-X*) Heritage Bk.

Blount's Anvil. Don Hendrie, Jr. LC 79-93196. 180p. (Orig.). 1979. 11.00 (*0-89924-025-9*); pap. 7.50 (*0-89924-024-0*) Lynx Hse.

Blouse Pattern Pizazz. Shirley Adams. (Illus.). 1982. vhs 29.25 (*1-884389-11-2*) Sewing Connection.

Blouse Pattern Pizazz. rev. ed. Shirley Adams. Ed. by Rebecca Adams. (Illus.). 64p. 1982. student ed 14.95 (*1-884389-09-0*, BPPB01) Sewing Connection.

Blow. Bruce Porter. 1994. mass mkt. 5.99 (*0-06-109164-2*) HarpC.

Blow: How a Small Town Boy Made 100 Million Dollars with the Medellin Cartel & Lost it All. Bruce Porter. 1993. 20.00 (*0-06-179300-0*, HarpT) HarpC.

***Blow Anthology: 8 Anthems.** John Blow. Ed. by Deborah S. King. 64p. 1995. pap. 19.95 (*0-19-353058-9*) OUP.

Blow Away Seaweeds. May Davenport. LC 89-92456. 265p. (YA). (gr. 7-12). 1994. 29.95 (*0-943864-60-7*) Davenport.

Blow Away Soon. Betsy James. LC 93-27135. (Illus.). (J). 1995. 14.95 (*0-399-22648-6*, Putnam) Putnam Pub Group.

Blow Away the Black Clouds. Florence Littauer. LC 79-50380. 1986. pap. 7.99 (*0-89081-285-3*) Harvest Hse.

Blow Away the Black Clouds: A Woman's Answer to Depression. large type ed. Florence Littauer. 1988. pap. 14.95 (*0-8027-2606-2*) Walker & Co.

Blow for Batten's Crossing. Hazel B. Girard & Marvin E. Girard. (Illus.). 191p. 1979. 10.50 (*0-934884-00-5*); pap. 6.95 (*0-686-77587-2*) Glendon Pub.

Blow for the Landing: A Hundred Years of Steam Navigation on the Waters of the West. Fritz Timmen. LC 73-150815. (Illus.). 255p. reprint ed. pap. 72.70 (*0-8357-7556-9*, 2052320) Bks Demand.

Blow Me a Kiss, Miss Lilly. Nancy W. Carlstrom. LC 89-34505. (Illus.). 32p. (J). (ps-3). 1990. lib. bdg. 14.89 (*0-06-021013-3*) HarpC Child Bks.

Blow Molded Plastic Containers - Update, No. P-029X. Business Communications Co., Inc. Staff. 164p. 1990. 1,950.00 (*0-89336-781-8*) BCC.

Blow Molding Growth in Today's Environment: 8th Annual High Performance Blow Molding Conference, Wyndham Hotel, Itasca, IL, September 22-23, 1992. Society of Plastics Engineers Staff. 216p. reprint ed. pap. 61.60 (*0-7837-4494-3*, 2044271) Bks Demand.

Blow Molding Handbook. Donald V. Rosato & Dominick V. Rosato. 1010p. (C). 1989. text ed. 184.50 (*1-56990-089-2*) Hanser-Gardner.

Blow My Blues Away. George Mitchell. LC 82-7266. (Roots of Jazz Ser.). (Illus.). xiii, 208p. 1983. reprint ed. lib. bdg. 29.50 (*0-306-76173-4*) Da Capo.

Blow the Candle Out: "Unprintable" Ozark Folksongs & Folklore, Vol. II: Folk Rhymes & Other Lore. Vance Randolph. LC 91-17685. 392p. 1992. 45.00 (*1-55728-237-4*) U of Ark Pr.

Blow the Silver Trumpets. Larry D. Powell. 1991. pap. 8.50 (*1-55673-314-3*, 9135) CSS OH.

Blow the Trumpet in Zion. Richard Booker. 216p. (Orig.). 1992. pap. 8.99 (*1-56043-009-5*) Destiny Image.

Blow up & Other Stories. Julio Cortazar. LC 84-22792. 1985. pap. 13.00 (*0-394-72881-5*) Pantheon.

***Blow-Up in Quasilinear Parabolic Equations.** A. A. Samarskii et al. Tr. by Michael Grinfeld. (de Gruyter Expositions in Mathematics Ser.: No. 19). xxi, 535p. (C). 1995. lib. bdg. 198.95 (*3-11-012754-7*) De Gruyter.

Blow Your Little Tin Whistle: A Biography of Richard Clarke Sommerville. Peggy A. Pittas. LC 92-11142. 258p. (Orig.). (C). 1992. lib. bdg. 39.50 (*0-8191-8744-5*); pap. text ed. 24.50 (*0-8191-8745-3*) U Pr of Amer.

Blow Your Own Horn: How to Market Yourself & Your Career. Jeffrey P. Davidson. 1988. 10.95 (*0-671-66385-2*) S&S Trade.

Blowdown. Center for Occupational Research & Development Staff. (EUTEC Power Plant Operator Curriculum Ser.). (Illus.). 26p. (C). 1985. pap. text ed. write for info. (*1-55502-216-2*) CORD Commns.

Blower & Exhaust Systems, Dust, Stock & Vapor Removal or Conveying. (Eighty-Ninety Ser.). 1994. pap. 16.75 (*0-685-58176-4*, 91-94) Natl Fire Prot.

Blowflies (Diptera, Calliphoridae) of Fennoscandia & Denmark. Knut Rognes. LC 90-40545. (Fauna Entomologica Scandinavica Ser.: No. 24). (Illus.). 272p. 1990. 80.00 (*90-04-09304-4*) E J Brill.

Blowguns: The Breath of Death. Michael P. Janich. (Illus.). 88p. 1993. pap. 14.00 (*0-87364-707-6*) Paladin Pr.

Blowing Bubbles with the Enemy. Alison Jackson. LC 93-2888. 120p. (J). (gr. 3-7). 1993. 13.99 (*0-525-45056-4*, DCB) Dutton Child Bks.

Blowing Her Own Trumpet: European Ladies' Orchestras & Other Women Musicians in Sweden, 1870-1950. Margaret Myers. (Goteborg Univ. Dept. of Musicology Ser.: No. 30). 411p. (Orig.). 1993. pap. 93.00x (*91-85974-22-6*, Pub. by Almqv & Wiksell SW) Coronet Bks.

Blowing in the Wind. Bernice M. Chappel. LC 89-40634. 338p. (Orig.). 1990. pap. 11.95 (*0-923568-06-9*) Wilderness Adventure Bks.

Blowing Kisses to the Sharks. Jane L. Perel. 1978. pap. 4.50 (*0-914278-20-7*) Copper Beech.

Blowing Mouth: The Jazz Poems. Ray Bremser. LC 78-7956. 1978. pap. 5.00x (*0-916156-34-6*) Cherry Valley.

Blowing Our Horns Before Midnight. Dan Seiters & Steve Falcone. (Illus.). 42p. (Orig.). 1988. pap. 5.00 (*0-685-54974-7*) Years Pr.

***Blowing Reeds.** Wally Swist. 28p. (Orig.). 1995. 7.50 (*0-944048-06-4*) Timberline Missouri.

Blowing the Bridge: Essays on Hemingway & "For Whom the Bell Tolls" Ed. by Rena Sanderson. LC 92-3307. (Contributions in American Studies: No. 101). 216p. 1992. text ed. 49.95 (*0-313-28451-2*, SQE/, Greenwood Pr) Greenwood.

Blowing the Whistle: The Organizational & Legal Implications for Companies & Their Employees. Marcia P. Miceli & Janet P. Near. 224p. 1992. text ed. 27.95 (*0-669-19599-5*) Free Pr.

Blowing the Whistle on Intercollegiate Sports. J. Robert Evans. LC 74-78842. 168p. 1974. 26.95 (*0-911012-94-X*) Nelson-Hall.

Blowing up Hitler: A Life of Johann Georg Elser, Would-Be Assassin. Gerald Williams. LC 86-13430. (Illus.). 11p. (Orig.). 1986. pap. 5.95 (*0-9602574-6-2*) M E Coughlin.

Blowing Weather. John McIntyre. 1993. reprint ed. lib. bdg. 89.00 (*0-7812-5487-6*) Rprt Serv.

Blowing Your Nose. Donita Ingenthron et al. (Project MORE Daily Living Skills Ser.). (Illus.). 32p. 1979. reprint ed. pap. text ed. 5.95 (*0-685-67487-8*) PRO-ED.

Blowing Your Nose, Set. Donita Ingenthron et al. (Project MORE Daily Living Skills Ser.). (Illus.). 32p. 1979. reprint ed. pap. text ed. 149.00 (*0-685-05746-1*) PRO-ED.

Blown Away. Kirk Mitchell. 1994. mass mkt. 4.99 (*0-380-77844-0*) Avon.

***Blown Away.** Herb Payson. 256p. 1995. pap. 14.95 (*0-924486-95-3*) Sheridan.

Blown Away. Ronald Sukenick. (New American Fiction Ser.: No. 7). 177p. 1986. 16.95 (*0-940650-63-0*); pap. 10.95 (*0-940650-64-9*) Sun & Moon CA.

Blown Away: The Rolling Stones & the Death of the Sixties. A. E. Hotchner. (Illus.). 349p. 1990. 21.95 (*0-685-47237-X*) S&S Trade.

Blown in by the Draft: Camp Yarns Collected at One of the Great National Army Cantonments by an Amateur War Correspondent. Frazier Hunt, Jr. LC 79-37273. (Short Story Index Reprint Ser.). (Illus.). 1977. reprint ed. 24.95 (*0-8369-4084-9*) Ayer.

***Blown Sideways Through Life.** Claudia Shear. LC 94-43859. 1995. 17.95 (*0-385-31312-8*, Dial) Doubleday.

Blown to Hell. large type ed. P. A. Bechko. LC 93-11955. 1994. 19.95 (*0-7927-1812-7*, Curley Lrg Print); pap. 17.95 (*0-7927-1813-5*, Curley Lrg Print) Chivers N Amer.

***Blowout.** Jeffrey Layton. 400p. (Orig.). 1995. mass mkt. 4.99 (*0-380-78066-6*) Avon.

Blowout Prevention. 2nd ed. W. C. Goins & Riley Sheffield. LC 70-101145. (Practical Drilling Technology Ser.: Vol. 1). 336p. 1983. 47.00 (*0-87201-073-2*) Gulf Pub.

Blowout Prevention. 2nd rev. ed. Curtis Kruse. (Rotary Drilling Ser.: Unit III, Lesson 3). (Illus.). 99p. (SPA.). 1975. pap. text ed. 14.00 (*0-88698-130-1*, 2.30322) PETEX.

Blowout Prevention. 3rd rev. ed. (Rotary Drilling Ser.: Unit III, Lesson 3). (Illus.). 99p. (Orig.). 1980. pap. text ed. 14.00 (*0-88698-051-8*, 2.30330) PETEX.

Blowout Prevention: Theory & Applications. Mills. 193p. 1988. text ed. 59.00 (*0-13-080193-3*) P-H.

Blowout Prevention: Theory & Applications. Peter G. Mills. LC 84-4507. (Illus.). 193p. 1984. 40.00 (*0-934634-78-5*) Intl Human Res.

***Blowout Prevention & Well Control.** (French Oil & Gas Industry Association Publications). (Illus.). 184p. (C). 1990. pap. text ed. 56.00 (*2-7108-0397-6*) Technip.

Blows of Circumstance. Ann Turnbull & Joseph Wase. LC 89-5821. (Illus.). 298p. 1989. 19.95 (*0-942597-11-7*) White Mane Pub.

***Blowup for Nonlinear Hyperbolic Equations.** Serge Alinhac. LC 95-2743. (Progress in Nonlinear Differential Equations & Their Applications Ser.: Vol. 17). 113p. 1995. 42.50 (*0-8176-3810-5*) Birkhauser.

***Blowup for Nonlinear Hyperbolic Equations.** Serge Alinhac. LC 95-2743. (Progress in Nonlinear Differential Equations & Their Applications Ser.: Vol. 17). 1995. write for info. (*3-7643-3810-5*) Birkhauser.

BLR Encyclopedia of Performance Appraisal. Business & Legal Reports Staff. 1985. ring bd. 129.95 (*1-55645-536-4*) Busn Legal Reports.

BLR Encyclopedia of Personnel Forms: Employment & Termination, Vol. 1. Stephen D. Bruce. 1986. ring bd. 99.95 (*1-55645-548-8*) Busn Legal Reports.

BLR Encyclopedia of Prewritten Job Descriptions. Stephen D. Bruce. 1986. ring bd. 199.95 (*1-55645-550-X*) Busn Legal Reports.

BLR Encyclopedia of Prewritten Personnel Letters. Louise Pitone. 436p. 1988. 99.95 (*1-55645-527-5*) Busn Legal Reports.

BLR Encyclopedia of Safety & Health Training, 2 vols., Set. Ed. by John F. Brady. 778p. 1988. 199.95 (*1-55645-591-7*) Busn Legal Reports.

BLR Handbook of Practical Time Management. Barbara Stretton. 1986. pap. 24.95 (*1-55645-516-X*) Busn Legal Reports.

BLR Handbook of Training Techniques. David A. Gallup & Katherine V. Beauchemin. Ed. by Stephen D. Bruce. 251p. 1987. ring bd. 89.95 (*1-55645-503-8*) Busn Legal Reports.

***BLT.** Catherine Dunphy. (Degrassi Book Ser.). (YA). 1995. pap. 4.95 (*1-55028-372-3*); bds. 16.95 (*1-55028-374-X*) Formac Dist Ltd.

***Blubb & the Chocolate Treasure.** Mel Gilden. Ed. by Ruth Ashby. 144p. (Orig.). (J). 1995. pap. 3.50 (*0-671-88805-6*) PB.

Blubber. Judy Blume. 160p. (J). (gr. 3-6). 1976. pap. 3.50 (*0-440-40707-9*, YB) Dell.

Blubber. Judy Blume. 160p. (gr. 4-7). 1978. mass mkt. 3.99 (*0-440-90707-1*, LFL) Dell.

Blubber. Judy Blume. LC 73-94116. 160p. (J). (gr. 4-6). 1982. text ed. 14.95 (*0-02-711010-9*, Bradbury S&S) S&S Childrens.

Blubber see Judy Blume

Bluberry God: The Education of a Finnish American. Reino Hannula. LC 80-54183. 1990. 12.95 (*0-9605044-2-7*); pap. 7.50 (*0-685-06774-2*) Quality Hill.

Blucher & the Uprising of Prussia Against Napoleon: 1806-15. Ernest F. Henderson. LC 73-14448. (Heroes of the Nations Ser.). (Illus.). reprint ed. 57.50 (*0-404-58266-4*) AMS Pr.

Blue. Denise Ohio. LC 93-29091. 192p. 1993. pap. 12.00 (*0-929701-30-5*) McPherson & Co.

Blue. Gabrielle Woolfitt. (J). (gr. k-3). 1992. 17.50 (*0-87614-704-X*, Carolrhoda) Lerner Group.

Blue: Text of a Film. Derek Jarman. LC 94-5555. 1994. 14.95 (*0-87951-560-0*) Overlook Pr.

Blue see Spectrum of English

Blue - Yellow - Red: A Color Anagram. (Illus.). 76p. 1991. 30.00 (*3-906700-41-0*, Pub. by Lars Muller SZ) Dist Art Pubs.

Blue Adept. Piers Anthony. 336p. 1987. mass mkt. 5.95 (*0-345-35245-9*, Del Rey) Ballantine.

Blue Afternoon. William Boyd. 1995. pap. 23.00 (*0-679-43295-7*) Random.

***Blue Air.** Kate Harper. Date not set. pap. 7.95 (*0-9633481-3-2*) Blue Beginnings.

Blue & Beautiful: Planet Earth, Our Home. 48p. (J). (gr. 1 up). 1990. 9.95 (*92-1-100441-1*, 90.I.15); 5.95 (*0-685-39198-1*, 90.I.19) UN.

Blue & Brown Books. Ludwig Wittgenstein. 1942. pap. text ed. 13.00 (*0-06-131211-8*, TB1211, Torch) HarpC.

***Blue & Brown Books: Preliminary Studies for the "Philosophical Investigations"** Ludwig Wittgenstein. 192p. 1994. lib. bdg. 31.00 (*0-8095-9151-0*) Borgo Pr.

Blue & Buff: Portrait of an English Hunt. John Minoprio. (Illus.). 144p. 1992. 55.00 (*1-85310-264-4*, Pub. by Airlife Pub Ltd UK) Voyageur Pr.

Blue & Distant Hills. Judith Saxton. 528p. 1994. 25.95 (*0-312-10944-X*) St Martin.

***Blue & Gray Magazine's History & Tour Guide of the Antietam Battlefield.** Stephen W. Sears et al. LC 95-76686. (Illus.). 1995. pap. 9.95 (*0-9626034-5-7*) Generals Bks.

Blue & Gray Roses of Intrigue. Rebecca D. Larson. (Illus.). 72p. (C). 1993. pap. text ed. 5.95 (*0-939631-46-6*) Thomas Publications.

Blue & Some Other Dogs. John Graves. (Illus.). 29p. 1981. 20.00 (*0-88426-058-5*) Encino Pr.

Blue & the Gray. Ed. by Claudius M. Capps. LC 70-75710. (Granger Index Reprint Ser.). 1977. 19.95 (*0-8369-6005-X*) Ayer.

Blue & the Gray, 2 vols., Set. Ed. by Henry S. Commager. (Illus.). 1296p. 1982. 12.98 (*0-517-38379-9*) Random Hse Value.

Blue & the Gray: Oneida County Stoneware. Christopher Bensch. (Illus.). 80p. (Orig.). 1987. pap. 7.00 (*0-915895-05-6*) Munson Williams.

***Blue & the Gray Vol. I.** Henry S. Commager. 1995. pap. 13.95 (*0-452-01144-2*, Plume) NAL-Dutton.

Blue & the Gray with National Geographic Guide to the "Civil War National Battlefield Park" Thomas B. Allen. Ed. by Leah Bendavid-Val & Mary A. Harrell. (Illus.). 320p. 1992. 41.95 (*0-87044-877-3*) Natl Geog.

Blue & the Gray with National Geographic Guide to the "Civil War National Battlefield Park" Thomas B. Allen. Ed. by Leah Bendavid-Val & Mary Ann Harrell. LC 92-13567. (Illus.). 320p. 1992. 29.95 (*0-87044-876-5*) Natl Geog.

Blue & the Grey. Henry S. Commager. 1991. 14.99 (*0-517-06015-9*, Crown) Random Hse Value.

Blue & the Grey: The Story of the Civil War As Told by Participants. Ed. by Henry S. Commager. LC 94-18223. 1994. 13.95 (*0-452-01145-0*, Mer) NAL-Dutton.

Blue & the Yellow Stars of David: The Zionist Leadership in Palestine & the Holocaust, 1939-1945. Dina Porat. (Illus.). 334p. 1990. 36.00 (*0-674-07708-3*) HUP.

Blue & White China: Origins Western Influences. Ed. by John Esten. (Illus.). 160p. 1987. 40.00 (*0-316-28349-5*) Little.

Blue & White Stoneware. Kathryn McNerney. (Illus.). 160p. 1991. pap. 9.95 (*0-89145-179-X*) Collector Bks.

***Blue & White Transfer-Printed Pottery.** Robert Copeland. (C). 1989. pap. 25.00x (*0-85263-620-2*, Pub. by Shire UK) St Mut.

Blue & Yellow Don't Make Green: Or-How to Mix the Color You Really Want-Every Time. rev. ed. Michael Wilcox. (Illus.). 128p. 1994. 27.95 (*0-89134-622-8*) North Light Bks.

Blue Angel. Josef Von Sternberg. (Illus.). 111p. (Orig.). 1989. pap. 8.95 (*0-571-12563-8*) Faber & Faber.

An Asterisk (*) at the beginning of an entry indicates that the title is appearing in BIP for the first time.

An Asterisk (*) at the beginning of an entry indicates that the title is appearing in BIP for the first time.

823

B

Blue Corn & Chocolate. Elizabeth Rozin. 1992. 25.00 (*0-394-58308-6*) Knopf.

Blue Corn & Square Tomatoes: Unusual Facts about Common Garden Vegetables. Rebecca Rupp. Ed. by Deborah Burns. LC 87-45009. (Illus.). 232p. (Orig.). 1987. pap. 12.95 (*0-88266-505-7*, Garden Way Pub) Storey Comm Inc.

Blue Corn Cookbook. Celine-Marie Pascale. (Border Bks.). 103p. (Orig.). 1990. pap. 7.95 (*0-685-66859-2*) Out West Pub.

Blue Corn Cookbook. Celine-Marie Pascale. (Chile Pepper Cookbook Ser.). (Illus.). 125p. (Orig.). 1992. pap. 7.95 (*0-9623865-1-0*) Out West Pub.

Blue Crab, a Fable. R. F. Waite. (Illus.). 32p. 1992. 9.95 (*0-933858-30-2*) Kennebec River.

Blue Creek, by Cracky. Garry Baun. 118p. (Orig.). 1990. pap. 9.95 (*0-940151-18-9*) Statesman Exam.

Blue Cross: What Went Wrong? Sylvia A. Law. LC 76-11427. 1976. 40.00 (*0-300-02053-8*) Yale U Pr.

***Blue Cross & Blue Shield: Experiences of Weak Plans & the Role of Effective State Oversight.** (Illus.). 64p. (Orig.). (C). 1994. pap. text ed. 50.00x (*0-7881-1149-3*) Diane Pub.

Blue Dahlia: A Screenplay. Raymond Chandler. 1976. 19.95 (*0-8488-0960-2*) Amereon Ltd.

***Blue Darter: And Other Sports Stories.** Highlights Staff. LC 94-72487. (Illus.). 96p. (J). (gr. 2-5). 1995. 2.95 (*1-56397-446-0*, Wordsong) Boyds Mills Pr.

Blue Day on Main Street. Jose L. Navarro. LC 73-88742. 1973. pap. 4.00 (*0-88412-063-5*) TQS Pubns.

Blue Deep. Layne Heath. 416p. 1994. mass mkt. 5.99 (*0-380-71398-5*) Avon.

Blue Deep. Layne Heath. LC 92-27418. 384p. 1993. 20.00 (*0-688-10313-8*) Morrow.

Blue Demons: Great DePaul Teams & Traditions. Tim Stephens. (Illus.). 220p. 1991. 24.95 (*0-929387-56-2*) Bonus Books.

Blue Denim Blues. Anne W. Smith. 128p. (YA). (gr. 6 up). 1988. pap. 2.75 (*0-380-70379-3*, Flare) Avon.

Blue Desert. Charles Bowden. LC 86-11413. 179p. 1986. pap. 10.95 (*0-8165-1081-4*) U of Ariz Pr.

Blue Devil "Battle Mountain" Regiment in Italy: A History of the 350th Infantry Regiment 1944-1945. John E. Wallace. (Combat Arms Ser.: No. 7). (Illus.). 266p. 1981. reprint ed. 22.95 (*0-89839-052-4*) Battery Pr.

Blue Devils in Italy: A History of the 88th Infantry Division in World War II. John P. Delaney. (Divisional Ser.). (Illus.). 359p. 1988. reprint ed. 29.95 (*0-89839-107-5*) Battery Pr.

Blue Diamond. Joan Smith. 1987. pap. 2.50 (*0-449-21326-9*) Fawcett.

Blue Diesels & Black Diamonds. John Henderson. (Illus.). 84p. 1991. pap. 29.95 (*0-9629037-5-2*) H & M Prods.

Blue Dog. George Rodrigue & Lawrence S. Freundlich. LC 93-39794. (Illus.). 96p. 1994. 39.95 (*0-670-85538-3*, Viking Studio) Studio Bks.

***Blue Dog.** limited ed. George Rodrigue & Lawrence S. Freundlich. (Illus.). 96p. 1995. 50.00 (*0-670-86621-0*, Viking Studio) Studio Bks.

Blue Dolphin. Robert Barnes. Ed. by Nancy Carleton. LC 94-1514. 192p. 1994. pap. 9.95 (*0-915811-55-3*) H J Kramer Inc.

Blue Donkey Fables. Suniti Namjoshi. 1990. pap. 7.95 (*0-7043-4115-8*, Pub. by Womens Pr UK) Interlink Pub.

Blue Dragon White Tiger: A Tet Story. Tran Van Dinh. Ed. by Ann Levison. 334p. 1984. 14.95 (*0-914075-00-4*) TriAm Pr.

Blue Dragon White Tiger: Taoist Rites of Passage. Michael Saso. (Illus.). 232p. (Orig.). (C). 1990. pap. text ed. 16.00 (*0-8248-1361-8*, Taoist Ctr) UH Pr.

***Blue Dreams: Korean Americans & the Los Angeles Riots.** Nancy Abelmann & John Lie. (Illus.). 288p. 1995. text ed. 29.95 (*0-674-07704-0*, ABEBLU) HUP.

Blue Dress Girl. large type ed. E. V. Thompson. (Charnwood Ser.). 592p. 1994. 26.95 (*0-7089-8746-X*, Charnwood) Ulverscroft.

Blue Dynamite. John Millett. 100p. 1986. pap. 5.00 (*0-318-23493-9*) Samisdat.

***Blue Earth County, Minnesota.** Julie Schrader. (Illus.). 976p. 1990. 65.00 (*0-88107-165-X*) Curtis Media.

Blue Eden. Luke Salisbury. LC 94-66401. 160p. (Orig.). 1994. pap. 14.50 (*1-882986-15-6*) The Smith.

Blue Eden. Luke Salisbury. LC 94-66401. 160p. (Orig.). 1995. 21.95 (*1-882986-16-4*) The Smith.

Blue Elephant. Kate Noble. (Zoo Stories Ser.). (Illus.). 32p. (J). (ps-4). 1995. 14.95 (*0-9631798-3-7*) Silver Seahorse.

***Blue Equinox.** Aleister Crowley. 1994. text ed. 45.00 (*1-55818-312-4*, First Impress) Holmes Pub.

Blue Equinox, Vol. III, No. 1. Aleister Crowley. 456p. 1992. reprint ed. pap. 45.00 (*1-872736-13-0*, Pub. by Mandrake Pr UK) Holmes Pub.

***Blue Estuaries.** Louise Bogan. 136p. Date not set. 11.00 (*0-374-52461-0*) FS&G.

Blue Estuaries: Poems, 1923-1968. Louise Bogan. LC 76-46175. (American Poetry Ser.: Vol. 11). 1977. reprint ed. pap. 8.50 (*0-88001-192-0*) Ecco Pr.

Blue Eye of a Pond. Darby Mitchell. (Illus.). 10p. (J). (ps-5). 1991. 8.00 (*0-9631809-0-8*) Castle MI.

Blue Eye Shadow Should Absolutely Be Illegal. 3rd ed. Paula Begoun. Ed. by Sheree Bykofsky. Orig. Title: Blue Eyeshadow Should be Illegal. 256p. 1992. pap. 10.95 (*1-877988-04-9*) Beginning Pr.

Blue-Eyed Beast. Neal N. Jackson. (Illus.). 125p. (Orig.). 1993. pap. 10.00 (*1-56411-068-0*) Untd Bros & Sis.

Blue-Eyed Boy. Arthur Madson. Ed. by Carol Spelius. (Orig.). pap. 6.95 (*0-941363-13-9*) Lake Shore Pub.

Blue-Eyed Boy. large type ed. Clare Curzon. 416p. 1992. 21.95 (*0-7089-2585-5*) Ulverscroft.

Blue-Eyed Child of Fortune: The Civil War Letters of Colonel Robert Gould Shaw. Ed. by Russell Duncan. xxxii, 448p. 1994. pap. 12.50 (*0-380-72168-6*) Avon.

Blue-Eyed Child of Fortune: The Civil War Letters of Colonel Robert Gould Shaw. Ed. by Russell Duncan. LC 91-46644. (Illus.). 448p. 1992. 29.95 (*0-8203-1459-5*) U of Ga Pr.

Blue-Eyed Chippewa: A Tragic Indian Story. 2nd ed. Wilma M. Weatherwax. (Illus.). 150p. (J). 1987. 10.00 (*0-9614640-6-2*); pap. 7.50 (*0-9614640-7-0*) Broadblade Pr.

Blue-Eyed Daisy. Cynthia Rylant. LC 84-21554. 112p. (J). (gr. 5-7). 1985. text ed. 13.95 (*0-02-777960-2*, Bradbury S&S) S&S Childrens.

Blue-Eyed Enemy: Japan Against the West in Java & Luzon, 1942-1945. Theodore Friend. (Illus.). 330p. 1988. text ed. 55.00 (*0-691-05524-6*) Princeton U Pr.

Blue-Eyed Grass. limited ed. Judy Sutcliffe. (Illus.). 1984. 25.00 (*0-943164-06-0*) Geronima.

Blue Eyed Iroquois. Edith A. Haugh. 128p. 1983. pap. 6.95 (*0-932052-30-4*) North Country.

Blue-Eyed Ninja Warrior. Beverley Ashwill. LC 90-83313. (Illus.). 43p. (J). (gr. 3-9). 1990. pap. 5.98 (*0-941381-05-6*) BJO Enterprises.

***Blue-Eyed Son.** Chris Lynch. LC 94-18728. (J). 1995. lib. bdg. 13.89 (*0-06-025397-5*) HarpC.

Blue Eyes. Jerome Charyn. 240p. 1993. mass mkt. 5.99 (*0-446-40077-7*, Mysterious Paperbk) Warner Bks.

Blue Eyes & Gray. Emmuska Orczy. 1976. lib. bdg. 14.75 (*0-685-03051-2*, Lghtyr Pr) Buccaneer Bks.

Blue Eyes Gazing at Japan. R. T. Joyce. 180p. 1982. pap. 4.95 (*0-933704-34-8*) Dawn Pr.

Blue Eyeshadow Should Be Illegal see Blue Eye Shadow Should Absolutely Be Illegal

Blue Faience Hippopotamus. Joan Grant. LC 91-17133. (Illus.). 32p. (Orig.). (YA). (gr. 7-9). 1991. reprint ed. 11.95 (*0-671-74977-3*, Green Tiger S&S) S&S Childrens.

Blue Fairy Book. Ed. by Andrew Lang. LC 34-28315. (Airmont Classics Ser.). (Illus.). (J). (gr. 4 up). 1969. pap. 2.95 (*0-8049-0196-1*, CL-196) Airmont.

Blue Fairy Book. Ed. by Andrew Lang. LC 34-28315. (Illus.). 390p. (J). (gr. 1-6). 1965. pap. 6.95 (*0-486-21437-0*) Dover.

Blue Fairy Book. Andrew Lang. 25.95 (*0-89190-089-6*, Am Repr) Amereon Ltd.

Blue Fairy Book. Ed. by Andrew Lang. (Illus.). (J). 1994. 8.98 (*1-56731-059-1*, MJF Bks) Fine Comms.

Blue Fairy Book. Andrew Lang. (J). 19.25 (*0-8446-5495-7*) Peter Smith.

Blue Feather & Other Stories. Zane Grey. 1993. mass mkt. 3.99 (*0-06-100581-9*, Harp PBks) HarpC.

Blue Feather's Vision, the Dawn of Colonial America. James E. Knight. LC 81-23082. (Illus.). 32p. (J). (gr. 5-9). 1982. lib. bdg. 11.59 (*0-89375-722-5*); pap. text ed. 2.95 (*0-89375-723-3*) Troll Assocs.

Blue Fire. 1990. pap. 4.50 (*0-8216-5074-2*, Univ Books) Carol Pub Group.

Blue Fire. Phyllis A. Whitney. 1991. mass mkt. 4.99 (*0-06-100205-4*, Harp PBks) HarpC.

Blue Fire: A Season Inside the St. Louis Blues. Dave Simons. LC 92-82551. (Illus.). 424p. 1992. 22.95 (*0-915611-55-4*) Sagamore Pub.

Blue Fire: Selected Writings by James Hillman. James Hillman. LC 89-45043. 336p. 1991. reprint ed. pap. 13.00 (*0-06-092101-3*, PL) HarpC.

Blue Flame: The Love Letters of Kahlil Gibran to May Ziadah. Ed. by Bushrui & Kuzbari. 1983. 25.00 (*0-86685-387-1*) Intl Bk Ctr.

***Blue Flame: Woody Herman's Life in Music.** Robert C. Kriebel. LC 95-6045. (Illus.). 250p. (Orig.). 1995. pap. 16.95 (*1-55753-073-4*) Purdue U Pr.

***Blue Flame Lingers.** Jim Blair. 40p. (Orig.). 1994. pap. 7.00 (*0-9645871-1-4*) Jim Blair.

Blue Flower. Henry Van Dyke. LC 70-110221. (Short Story Index Reprint Ser.). 1977. 23.95 (*0-8369-3373-7*) Ayer.

Blue Flowers. Raymond Queneau. Tr. by Barbara Wright. LC 84-25544. (Revived Modern Classics Ser.). 224p. 1985. reprint ed. pap. 8.95 (*0-8112-0945-8*, NDP595) New Directions.

Blue Food: A Case of National Indigestion. Tom Linster. (Illus.). 90p. (Orig.). 1992. pap. 8.95 (*1-881631-00-1*) Byfor Fnd.

Blue-Footed Booby: Bird of the Galapagos. Margret Bowman & Nicholas Millhouse. LC 85-27617. (Illus.). 32p. (J). (gr. 1-7). 1986. 11.95 (*0-8027-6628-5*); lib. bdg. 11.85 (*0-8027-6629-3*) Walker & Co.

Blue for Beware. Jessie Haas. LC 94-4572. (Illus.). 64p. (J). (gr. 2 up). 1995. 14.00 (*0-688-13678-8*) Greenwillow.

Blue for the Plough. Dara Wier. (Poetry Ser.). 80p. (Orig.). 1992. lib. bdg. 16.95 (*0-88748-136-1*); pap. 9.95 (*0-88748-137-X*) Carnegie-Mellon.

Blue-Fronted Amazon Parrots. Edward J. Mulawka. (Illus.). 128p. 1983. 16.95 (*0-87666-834-1*, PS-782) TFH Pubns.

Blue Galoshes in Spring: God's Wonderful World of Seasons. Glenda Palmer. LC 92-34716. (Almost on My Own Ser.). (Illus.). (J). 1993. pap. 4.99 (*0-7814-0710-9*, Chariot Bks) Chariot Family.

Blue Garden. Barbara Howes. LC 72-3697. (Wesleyan Poetry Program Ser.: Vol. 62). 70p. 1972. pap. 10.95 (*0-8195-1062-9*, Wesleyan Univ Pr) U Pr of New Eng.

Blue Garter Club: Ties That Bind Fourteen Christian Women for 40 Years. Carol W. Lee. Ed. by Renee Hermanson. LC 92-4563. (Illus.). 260p. (Orig.). 1992. pap. 11.95 (*1-880292-20-3*) LangMarc.

Blue Ghost: Lafcadio Hearn's Work. J. Temple. LC 74-16485. (American Literature Ser.: No. 49). 1974. lib. bdg. 75.00 (*0-8383-2027-9*) M S G Haskell Hse.

Blue Glass. Sandra Tyler. 1993. pap. 19.95 (*0-15-613226-5*) HarBrace.

Blue Glass. large type ed. Sandra Tyler. LC 92-19387. 312p. 1992. reprint ed. lib. bdg. 17.95 (*1-56054-494-5*) Thorndike Pr.

***Blue Goose Legend.** Shari L. Fiock. LC 95-92072. (Illus.). 50p. (J). 1995. student ed, pap. 8.50 (*0-9628801-5-9*) Coyote Pub.

Blue Grass. Tyler. 1992. 19.95 (*0-15-113225-9*) HarBrace.

Blue-Grass & Rhododendron: Out-Doors in Old Kentucky. John Fox, Jr. LC 93-19675. (Illus.). 324p. 1993. 25.00 (*0-8131-1842-5*); pap. 12.00 (*0-8131-0820-9*) U Pr of Ky.

Blue Grass Ballads & Other Verse. William L. Visscher. LC 77-83902. (Black Heritage Library Collection). 1977. 24.95 (*0-8369-8676-8*) Ayer.

Blue-Grass Region of Kentucky: And Other Kentucky Articles. James L. Allen. LC 74-39712. (Essay Index Reprint Ser.). 1977. reprint ed. 28.95 (*0-8369-2734-6*) Ayer.

Blue Grass Region of Kentucky & Other Kentucky Articles. James L. Allen. (Principle Works of James Lane Allen). 1989. reprint ed. lib. bdg. 79.00 (*0-7812-1727-X*) Rprt Serv.

Blue-Green Algae: Current Research, 4 vols., Vol. 1. M. Rodriguez-Lopez et al. 213p. 1974. text ed. 26.50 (*0-8422-7187-2*) Irvington.

Blue-Green Algae: Current Research, 4 vols., Vol. 2. R. V. Smith et al. 249p. 1974. text ed. 26.50 (*0-8422-7188-0*) Irvington.

Blue-Green Algae: Current Research, 4 vols., Vol. 3. C. N. Kenyon et al. 264p. 1974. text ed. 26.50 (*0-8422-7189-9*) Irvington.

Blue-Green Algae: Current Research, 4 vols., Vol. 4. John B. Hall et al. 192p. (C). 1974. text ed. 26.50 (*0-8422-7190-2*) Irvington.

Blue Grove. W. G. Archer. LC 72-7219. (Select Bibliographies Reprint Ser.). 1977. reprint ed. 24.95 (*0-8369-6920-0*) Ayer.

Blue Guide: Barcelona. Michael Jacobs. (Illus.). 192p. 1992. pap. 19.95 (*0-393-30887-1*) Norton.

***Blue Guide: Berlin & Eastern Germany.** Anne Massey. 1994. pap. 20.95 (*0-393-31197-X*, Norton Paperbks) Norton.

Blue Guide: Boston & Cambridge. 2nd ed. John Freely. LC 92-31581. 1994. pap. 19.95 (*0-393-30988-6*) Norton.

Blue Guide: Burgundy. Ian Ousby. (Illus.). 212p. 1992. pap. 19.95 (*0-393-30886-3*) Norton.

Blue Guide: China. Frances Wood. (Illus.). 560p. 1992. pap. 29.95 (*0-393-30888-X*) Norton.

Blue Guide: Corsica. 2nd ed. Roland Gant. (Illus.). 176p. 1992. pap. 16.95 (*0-393-30967-3*) Norton.

Blue Guide: Czechoslovakia. Michael Jacobs. (Illus.). 432p. 1992. pap. 24.95 (*0-393-30840-5*) Norton.

Blue Guide: Denmark. W. Glyn Jones & Kristen Gade. (Illus.). 352p. 1992. pap. 24.95 (*0-393-30839-1*) Norton.

Blue Guide: Holland. 5th ed. Charles Ford. (Illus.). 440p. 1993. pap. 21.95 (*0-393-30968-1*) Norton.

Blue Guide: Ireland. 6th ed. Ian Robertson. (Illus.). 404p. 1992. pap. 22.50 (*0-393-30841-3*) Norton.

Blue Guide: Istanbul. 3rd ed. John Freely. 1991. pap. 20.95 (*0-393-30728-X*) Norton.

Blue Guide: Morocco. 2nd ed. Jane Holliday. (Illus.). 232p. 1993. pap. 16.95 (*0-393-30966-5*) Norton.

Blue Guide: Paris & Versailles. 8th ed. Ian Robertson. (Illus.). 294p. 1992. pap. 19.95 (*0-393-30889-8*) Norton.

***Blue Guide: Rome & Environs.** 5th ed. Alta Macadam. 1995. pap. 21.95 (*0-393-31259-3*, Norton Paperbks) Norton.

Blue Guide: Switzerland. 5th ed. Ian Robertson. (Illus.). 384p. 1992. pap. 21.95 (*0-393-30890-1*) Norton.

***Blue Guide: Western Germany.** 2nd ed. James Bentley. 1995. pap. 21.95 (*0-393-31196-1*, Norton Paperbks) Norton.

Blue Guide: Albania. James Pettifer. 192p. 1994. pap. 17.95 (*0-393-31056-6*) Norton.

Blue Guide: Country House of England. Geoffrey Tyack & Stephen Brindle. 608p. 1994. pap. 23.00 (*0-393-31057-4*) Norton.

Blue Guide: Sicily. 4th ed. Alta Macadam. 306p. 1993. pap. 19.95 (*0-393-31054-X*) Norton.

Blue Guide: Spain. 6th ed. Ian Robertson. 508p. 1993. pap. 23.00 (*0-393-31053-1*) Norton.

Blue Guide to Adult Film: 1989 Edition. rev. ed. Kenneth Highfill. 478p. 1989. pap. 19.95 (*0-685-26972-8*) Blue Guide.

Blue Guide to Adult Films: 1989 Edition. rev. ed. Kenneth Highfill. 568p. 1989. ring bd. 39.95 (*0-685-26971-X*) Blue Guide.

***Blue Guide to Turkey.** 2nd rev. ed. Bernard McDonagh. (Blue Guide Ser.). (Illus.). 736p. 1995. pap. 27.50 (*0-393-31195-3*, Norton Paperbks) Norton.

***Blue Guide to Wales.** 8th ed. John Tomes. (Blue Guide Ser.). (Illus.). 320p. 1995. pap. 22.50 (*0-393-31267-4*, Norton Paperbks) Norton.

Blue Guides: Northern Italy. Alta Macadam. 1991. pap. 25.95 (*0-393-30727-1*) Norton.

Blue Guides: Southern Italy. 7th ed. Paul Blanchard. 1991. pap. 22.95 (*0-393-30726-3*) Norton.

Blue Guides Vol. 1: Churches & Chapels - Northern England. Stephen Humphrey. 1991. pap. 18.95 (*0-393-30724-7*) Norton.

Blue Guides Vol. 2: Churches & Chapels - Southern England. Stephen Humphrey. 1991. pap. 18.95 (*0-393-30725-5*) Norton.

Blue Guides Vol. 3: Cyprus. Ian Robertson. 1991. pap. 18.95 (*0-393-30730-1*) Norton.

Blue Guitar. Wallace Stevens. LC 77-85169. (Illus.). 52p. 1977. 30.00 (*0-902825-03-8*) Petersburg Pr.

Blue Guitar: Political Representation & Community. Nancy L. Schwartz. 200p. 1988. 24.95 (*0-226-74237-7*) U Ch Pr.

Blue Hammer. Ross MacDonald. 21.95 (*0-89190-095-0*, Am Repr) Amereon Ltd.

Blue Hat Green Hat. Sandra Boynton. (Boynton Board Bks.). 14p. (J). 1984. 3.95 (*0-671-49320-5*, Litl Simon S&S) S&S Childrens.

Blue Hat Red Coat. Clara Vulliamy. LC 93-22737. (Illus.). 14p. (J). (ps). 1994. 4.95 (*1-56402-353-2*) Candlewick Pr.

Blue Hawk. Peter Dickinson. (J). (gr. 5-9). 1991. 21.50 (*0-8446-6478-2*) Peter Smith.

Blue Hearts. Jim Lehrer. LC 92-37167. 224p. 1993. 20.00 (*0-679-42216-1*) Random.

Blue Hearts. large type ed. Jim Lehrer. LC 93-39162. 1994. pap. 18.95 (*0-7862-0112-6*) Thorndike Pr.

Blue Heaven. Joe Keenan. 320p. 1988. pap. 10.00 (*0-14-010764-9*, Penguin Bks) Viking Penguin.

Blue Heaven. Alfonso Paso. 1962. pap. 4.75 (*0-8222-0128-3*) Dramatists Play.

Blue Heaven. Lewis Warsh. 7.00 (*0-686-65480-3*); pap. 3.50 (*0-686-65481-1*) Kulchur Foun.

Blue Heaven Bends over All: A Novel of the Life of Sir Walter Scott. Jane Oliver. 384p. (Orig.). 1993. pap. 12.95 (*0-85640-450-0*, Pub. by Blackstaff Pr IE) Dufour.

***Blue Heaven, Black Night.** Shannon Drake. 544p. 1995. pap. 5.99 (*0-8217-5034-8*) Zebra.

Blue Helmets. 449p. 1990. 14.95 (*92-1-100444-6*, 90.I.18) UN.

Blue Helmets: A Review of United Nations Peace-keeping. 350p. 1986. 8.95 (*92-1-100275-3*, E.86.I.18) UN.

Blue Hen's Chick: An Autobiography. A. B. Guthrie, Jr. LC 92-37591. (Illus.). x, 279p. 1993. reprint ed. 35.00 (*0-8032-2149-5*); reprint ed. pap. 11.95 (*0-8032-7038-0*) U of Nebr Pr.

Blue Heron. Avi. 192p. (YA). 1993. pap. 3.99 (*0-380-72043-4*, Camelot) Avon.

Blue Heron. Avi. LC 91-4308. 192p. (J). (gr. 5-9). 1992. text ed. 14.95 (*0-02-707751-9*, Bradbury S&S) S&S Childrens.

Blue Heron's Sky. Kenneth MacLean. 1991. pap. 10.00 (*0-941179-28-1*) Latitudes Pr.

Blue Highways. William Least Heat Moon. 1986. mass mkt. 5.95 (*0-449-21109-6*) Fawcett.

Blue Highways: A Journey into America. William L. Heat-Moon. (Illus.). 432p. 1991. pap. 11.95 (*0-395-58568-6*) HM.

Blue Hill Meadows & the Much-Loved Dog. Cynthia Rylant. LC 93-40538. (Illus.). (J). 1994. write for info. (*0-15-253155-6*) HarBrace.

Blue Hill Meteorological Observatory: The First 100 Years, 1885-1985. John H. Conover. (Illus.). 528p. 1990. 60.00 (*0-933876-89-0*) Am Meteorological.

Blue Hills. Elizabeth Goudge. 288p. 1976. lib. bdg. 21.95 (*0-89966-100-9*) Buccaneer Bks.

Blue Hills. Cornelius Weygandt. 1993. reprint ed. lib. bdg. 89.00 (*0-7812-5856-1*) Rprt Serv.

Blue Hills of Maryland. Paula Strain. LC 92-61978. 300p. 1993. pap. 14.00 (*0-915746-45-X*) Potomac Appalach.

Blue Hills Robbery. Leola Kahrimanis. Ed. by M. Roberts. (Illus.). 128p. (J). (gr. 6-8). 1991. 10.95 (*0-89015-753-7*) Sunbelt Media.

Blue Hole. Laurel Trivelpiece. LC 87-71105. 72p. (Orig.). 1987. 15.95 (*0-914086-74-X*); pap. 9.95 (*0-914086-75-8*) Alicejamesbooks.

Blue Horizons. Faith Baldwin. 1976. reprint ed. lib. bdg. 21.95 (*0-88411-618-2*, Aeonian Pr) Amereon Ltd.

Blue Horizons: Faces & Places from a Bicycle Journey along the Blue Ridge Parkway. Jerry Bledsoe. LC 93-71245. (Illus.). 150p. (Orig.). 1993. pap. 11.95 (*1-878086-05-7*) Down Home NC.

Blue Horizons: Paradise Isles of the Pacific. Ed. by Donald J. Crump. (Special Publications Series 20: No. 3). (Illus.). 1985. 12.95 (*0-87044-544-8*) Natl Geog.

Blue Horse of Morning. Rose Flint. (Orig.). 1991. pap. 15.95 (*1-85411-053-5*) Dufour.

Blue Horse of Morning. Rose Flint. 76p. (Orig.). 1992. pap. 13.95 (*0-685-59674-5*, Pub. by Seren Bks UK) Dufour.

Blue Horses. Alyce Ingram. (Chapbook Ser.: No. 4). 60p. 1976. pap. 3.00 (*0-912824-12-3*) Vagabond Pr.

Blue Horses for Navajo Women. Nia Francisco. LC 87-80179. (Illus.). 80p. 1988. pap. 9.95 (*0-912678-72-0*, Greenfld Rev Pr) Greenfld Rev Lit.

***Blue Hour.** Elizabeth Evans. 1994. 17.95 (*1-56512-093-0*) Algonquin Bks.

***Blue Hour.** Elizabeth Evans. 364p. 1995. pap. write for info. (*1-56512-124-4*) Algonquin Bks.

Blue Hour. J. P. Smith. Ed. by James Linville. 224p. 1989. 17.95 (*0-945167-12-1*) British Amer Pub.

***Blue Hour: A Novel.** Elizabeth Evans. LC 94-19749. 350p. 1994. 17.95 (*1-56512-018-3*) Algonquin Bks.

Blue House. Cheng Naishan. 400p. (Orig.). 1989. pap. 7.95 (*0-8351-2065-1*) China Bks.

***Blue Ice in Motion: The Story of Alaska's Glaciers.** S. Wiley. (Illus.). 64p. 1995. pap. 6.95 (*0-930931-06-8*) Alaska Natural.

***Blue Ink Runs Out on a Partly Cloudy Day.** Alan Minskoff. 36p. (Orig.). 1994. pap. 12.00 (*0-931659-16-7*) Limberlost Pr.

***Blue Ink Runs Out on a Partly Cloudy Day.** deluxe limited ed. Alan Minskoff. 36p. (Orig.). 1994. 25.00 (*0-931659-17-5*) Limberlost Pr.

Blue Is the Hero. Bill Berkson. 1976. 7.50 (*0-685-79245-5*); pap. 4.00 (*0-685-79247-1*) L Pubns.

Blue Is the Hero. deluxe ed. Bill Berkson. 1976. 15.00 (*0-685-79246-3*) L Pubns.

Blue Island. Jean Raspail. Tr. by Jeremy Leggatt. LC 90-49381. 192p. 1991. 17.95 (*0-916515-99-0*) Mercury Hse Inc.

Blue Island. W. T. Stead et al. 157p. 1970. reprint ed. spiral bd. 6.60 (*0-7873-0815-3*) Mokelumne.

Blue Jackal. Rashmi Sharma. (Illus.). 32p. (J). (gr. 2 up). 1992. 14.95 (*1-878099-50-7*); pap. 6.95 (*1-878099-51-5*) Vidya Bks.

B

Blue Jacket: War Chief of Shawnees. Allan W. Eckert. LC 69-10656. 177p. (J). (gr. 7 up). 1983. reprint ed. pap. 6.95 (0-913428-36-1) Landfall Pr.

Blue Jade from the Morning Star: An Essay & a Cycle of Poems on Quetzalcoatl. William I. Thompson. LC 82-84052. 80p. (Orig.). 1983. pap. 6.95 (0-940262-03-7) Lindisfarne Pr.

Blue-Jay Yarn. limited ed. Mark Twain. (Illus.). 1981. Ltd. to 500 copies, signed, numbered, hand-sewn. pap. 12.50 (0-937686-16-6) Turtles Quill.

Blue Jays Companion: Thirty-Two Top Writers Expound on the History, Heroes, Heartbreaks & Triumphs of "Canada's Team" Ed. by David Fulk. LC 93-79894. (Illus.). 224p. (Orig.). 1994. pap. 9.95 (1-879092-20-4) Keystone Commns.

*Blue Jay's Dance: A Writer's Year with Baby. Louise Erdrich. 224p. 1995. 21.00 (0-06-017132-4) HarpC.

Blue Jean Gum. Teri Probasco. 35p. (J). (ps-4). Date not set. pap. 5.90 (0-932970-95-8) Prinit Pr.

Blue Kangaroo. Mary J. Flynn. (Illus.). 24p. (Orig.). (J). (ps-00). 1992. pap. text ed. 8.95 (1-880812-03-7) S Ink WA.

*Blue Kangaroo at the Zoo. Mary J. Flynn. (Illus.). 24p. (Orig.). (J). (ps-1). 1994. pap. 8.95 (1-880812-13-4) S Ink WA.

Blue Knight. Joseph Wambaugh. 1973. mass mkt. 5.99 (0-440-10607-9) Dell.

Blue Lady's Hands. John Champagne. 60p. 1988. 12.95 (0-8184-0478-7) Carol Pub Group.

Blue Lagoon: Anthology of Russian Poetry, 9 vols., 2A. Ed. by K. Kuzminsky & G. Kovalev. (Illus.). (RUS.). 1983. write for info. (0-89250-067-0) Orient Res Partners.

Blue Lagoon: Anthology of Russian Poetry, 9 vols., 4A. Ed. by K. Kuzminsky & G. Kovalev. (Illus.). (RUS.). 1983. write for info. (0-89250-343-2) Orient Res Partners.

Blue Lagoon: Anthology of Russian Poetry, 9 vols., 4B. Ed. by K. Kuzminsky & G. Kovalev. (Illus.). (RUS.). 1983. write for info. (0-89250-344-0) Orient Res Partners.

Blue Lagoon: Anthology of Russian Poetry, 9 vols., Set. Ed. by K. Kuzminsky & G. Kovalev. (Illus.). (RUS.). 1983. 421.00 (0-685-07027-1) Orient Res Partners.

Blue Lagoon: Anthology of Russian Poetry, 9 vols., Vols. 1, 2A, 2B, 3A, 3B, 4A, 4B, 5A, 5B. Ed. by K. Kuzminsky & G. Kovalev. (Illus.). (RUS.). 1983. 46.00 (0-685-73575-3) Orient Res Partners.

Blue Lagoon Omnibus. rev. ed. Henry D. Stakpoole. 211p. (C). 1981. reprint ed. 10.95 (0-9605338-0-X) Blue Lagoon.

Blue Lake. Pat Cummings. LC 92-24354. (Illus.). 64p. (J). (gr. 1-5). Date not set. 18.00 (0-06-021535-6); lib. bdg. 17.89 (0-06-021536-4) HarpC Child Bks.

Blue Laws: The History, Economics, & Politics of Sunday Closing Laws. David N. Laband & Deborah Heinbuch. LC 85-45930. 240p. 1987. text ed. 37.95 (0-669-12416-8) Free Pr.

Blue Laws, Brahmins, & Breakdown Lanes: An Alphabetic Guide to Boston & Bostonians. Karen C. Taylor. LC 89-11822. 160p. (Orig.). 1989. pap. 9.95 (0-87106-648-3) Globe Pequot.

Blue Layer. Kathie Atkinson. LC 93-28993. (J). 1994. 4.25 (0-383-03747-6) SRA Schl Grp.

*Blue Light in the Dash. Brend Brooks. 96p. (Orig.). 1995. pap. 9.95 (0-919591-99-X, Pub. by Polestar Bk Pubs CN) Orca Bk Pubs.

Blue Light Responses, 2 vols., Set. Ed. by Senger. 1987. 322.00 (0-8493-5238-X, QH515) CRC Pr.

Blue Lightning. Charles Stella. 1990. 19.95 (0-446-51545-0) Warner Bks.

Blue Lightning. large type ed. Richard Banks. (Linford Western Library). 336p. 1985. pap. 11.95 (0-7089-6181-9, Linford) Ulverscroft.

Blue Lights & River Songs. Tom Dent. LC 81-82659. 75p. (YA). (gr. 9-12). 1982. per., pap. 4.50 (0-916418-31-6) Lotus.

Blue Like the Heavens: New & Selected Poems. Gary Gildner. LC 83-19746. (Poetry Ser.). 160p. 1984. pap. 12.95 (0-8229-5358-7) U of Pittsburgh Pr.

Blue Limbo. Frank Lauria. 352p. (Orig.). 1991. pap. 3.95 (0-380-76164-5) Avon.

Blue Line. Farnham Blair & Constance Hunting. 33p. 1989. pap. 6.95 (0-685-45308-1) Puckerbrush.

Blue Lion, & Other Essays. Robert S. Lynd. LC 68-55848. (Essay Index Reprint Ser.). 1977. 19.95 (0-8369-0638-1) Ayer.

Blue Lodge. Edmond Ronayne. 18.95 (0-685-38430-6) Wehman.

Blue Lodge & Chapter. Edmond Ronayne. 1947. 17.00 (0-685-19465-5) Powner.

Blue Lodge Enlightenment. 13.00 (0-685-19466-3) Powner.

*Blue Lonesome. Bill Pronzini. LC 95-13049. 1995. write for info. (0-8027-3268-2) Walker & Co.

*Blue Lonesome: An Evan Horne Mystery. Bill Pronzini. LC 95-13048. 1995. write for info. (0-8027-3269-0) Walker & Co.

Blue Lotus. Herge. 64p. (Orig.). 1984. mass mkt. 7.95 (0-316-35856-8, Joy St Bks) Little.

Blue Lotus. Herge. (Adventures of Tintin Ser.). (Illus.). 64p. (Orig.). (J). 1992. 12.95 (0-316-35891-6, Joy St Bks) Little.

Blue Lotus. Herge. (Illus.). (ENG.). (J). 19.95 (0-8288-5480-7) Fr & Eur.

Blue MAC (2-3) Test Administration Booklet. Jean D. Maculaitis. 96p. (C). 1991. pap. text ed. write for info. (0-13-544073-4) P-H.

Blue Magic. P. K. Saha. 80p. 1975. 14.00 (0-88253-825-X); pap. 8.00 (0-88253-826-8) Ind-US Inc.

Blue Magic: The People, Power & Politics Behind the IBM Personal Computer. James Chposky & Ted Leonsis. LC 88-509. 240p. reprint ed. pap. 68.40 (0-7837-5343-8, 2045085) Bks Demand.

Blue Man. Keith Carter. LC 89-43350. (Illus.). 144p. 1990. 39.95 (0-89263-272-0) Rice Univ.

Blue Match the Rhyme Book. (Match the Rhyme Ser.). (J). (gr. 2-6). 1990. 4.95 (1-879332-01-9) XYZ Group.

Blue Meditation of the Clocks. Hailji, pseud. (Orig.). 1994. pap. text ed. write for info. (0-930502-11-6) Pine Pr.

Blue Mesa Review No. 6, No. 3. Ed. by Rudolfo A. Anaya. 282p. 1991. pap. 10.00 (0-8263-1315-9) U of NM Pr.

*Blue Mesa Review No. 6, No. 6. Ed. by Rudolfo Anaya. 235p. 1994. pap. 10.00 (1-885290-05-5) Blue Mesa Rev.

Blue Mirage. Joseph D. McNamara. LC 90-30025. 324p. 1990. 19.95 (0-688-09518-6) Morrow.

Blue Mold of Tobacco. Ed. by W. E. McKeen. LC 88-83539. (Illus.). 288p. 1989. 39.00 (0-89054-097-7) Am Phytopathol Soc.

Blue Monday. Harper Barnes. 210p. (Orig.). 1991. pap. 9.95 (0-935284-92-3) Patrice Pr.

Blue Monday - Vocal Score. 44p. (Orig.). 1993. pap. 30.00 (0-89724-121-5) Warner Brothers.

Blue Monkey for the Tomb. Hubert Witheford. 64p. (Orig.). 1994. pap. 9.95 (0-571-17012-9) Faber & Faber.

Blue Moon. Luanne Rice. 1994. mass mkt. 5.99 (0-553-56818-3) Bantam.

Blue Moon. Luanne Rice. LC 92-50732. 320p. 1993. 21.00 (0-670-84301-6, Viking) Viking Penguin.

Blue Moon. large type ed. Luanne Rice. LC 93-44120. 547p. 1994. lib. bdg. 21.95 (0-7862-0148-7) Thorndike Pr.

Blue Moon Bayou. Katherine Compton. 352p. (Orig.). 1992. mass mkt. 4.50 (0-380-76412-1) Avon.

Blue Moon over Kentucky: A Biography of Kentucky's Troubled Highlands. James Vaughn. LC 85-71378. (Illus.). 134p. (Orig.). 1985. pap. 5.95 (0-87571-037-9) Delapr Inc.

Blue Moon over Thurman Street. Ursula K. Le Guin & Roger Dorband. 1993. pap. 16.95 (0-939165-22-8) NewSage Press.

Blue Moon Rising. Simon Green. 480p. 1991. pap. 5.50 (0-451-45095-7, ROC) NAL-Dutton.

Blue Moon Ruby Tuesday. Elizabeth Marraffino. (Illus.). 60p. (Orig.). 1981. pap. 3.00 (0-936556-02-1) Contact Two.

Blue Moon Soup Spoon. Mimi Otey. (J). (ps-3). 1993. 15.00 (0-374-30851-9) FS&G.

Blue Moon 4: Red Herring Fiction-Writers' Workshop Plus National Contest Winners. 4th ed. Ed. by Elizabeth Klein. 151p. 1987. pap. 5.00 (0-932884-30-X) Red Herring.

*Blue Moose & Return of the Blue Moose. Daniel M. Pinkwater. 1995. 17.50 (0-8446-6831-1) Peter Smith.

Blue Moose, & Return of the Moose. Daniel M. Pinkwater. LC 93-22614. (Illus.). 112p. (Orig.). (J). (gr. 2-7). 1993. pap. 3.99 (0-679-84717-0, Bullseye Bks) Random Bks Yng Read.

Blue Mother. Christer Kihlman. Tr. by Joan Tate. LC 89-4850. (Modern Scandinavian Literature in Translation Ser.). vi, 308p. 1990. 29.95 (0-8032-2721-3); pap. 11.95 (0-8032-7769-5) U of Nebr Pr.

Blue Mountain. John Balaban. LC 81-7505. 88p. 1982. 17.50 (0-87775-143-9); pap. 9.95 (0-87775-144-7) Unicorn Pr.

Blue Mountain. George Weider. (Illus.). 160p. 35.00 (1-55046-009-9, Pub. by Boston Mills Pr CN) Genl Dist Srvs.

Blue Mountain. large type ed. Margaret Gaan. 464p. 1989. 17.95 (0-7089-2009-8) Ulverscroft.

Blue Mountain College Cookbook: Presidential Edition. Ed. by Blue Mountain College Alumnae Association Cookbook Committee Staff. (Illus.). 304p. (Orig.). 1989. 12.00 (0-9624097-0-7) Blue Mntn Coll.

Blue Mountain Magic. Garda Parker. 416p. 1994. mass mkt. 4.50 (0-8217-4603-0) Zebra.

Blue Movie Murder & I Love My Gun. Peter Zagare & Jesse Sublett. (Gryphon Double Novel Ser.: No. 6). 1993. per. 9.95 (0-936071-34-6) Gryphon Pubns.

Blue Mules. Curt Porter. LC 92-61996. 136p. (Orig.). 1994. pap. 8.95 (1-56002-211-6, Univ Edtns) Aegina Pr.

Blue Muse: The Poetry of Doris I. Warren. Doris I. Warren. LC 87-92026. 63p. (Orig.). (C). 1988. pap. 5.95 (0-9619657-0-3) Tick-Tock Pr.

*Blue Myth: Corruption & Mismanagement in America's Police Force. Eugene Maloney. 336p. 1994. pap. 5.99 (1-56171-334-1, S P I Bks) Sure Sellers.

Blue Nile. Alan Moorehead. 1976. 18.95 (0-8488-0766-9) Amereon Ltd.

Blue Northers to Sea Breezes: Texas Weather & Climate. Donald R. Haragan. (Illus.). 98p. (YA). (gr. 7 up). 1983. pap. 12.95 (0-937460-10-9) Hendrick-Long.

Blue Note: The Album Cover Art. Ed. by Graham Marsh. (Illus.). 128p. (Orig.). 1991. pap. 24.95 (0-8118-0036-9) Chronicle Bks.

Blue Note Label: A Discography. Ed. by Michel Ruppli. LC 88-162. (Discographies Ser.: No. 29). 532p. 1988. text ed. 95.00 (0-313-22018-2, RBN/, Greenwood Pr) Greenwood.

*Blue Note Years: The Jazz Photography of Francis Wolff. Michael Cuscuna et al. LC 95-7383. (Illus.). 204p. 1995. 65.00 (0-8478-1912-4) Rizzoli Intl.

*Blue Notebook: Reports on Canadian Culture. Doug Fetherling. 160p. 1995. lib. bdg. 27.00 (0-8095-4909-3) Borgo Pr.

*Blue Notes & Blessing Songs. Melvin E. Brown. 64p. Date not set. pap. 7.95 (1-56167-152-5) Am Literary Pr.

Blue Notes under a Green Felt Hat. David Ritz. 320p. 1989. 18.95 (1-55611-130-4) D I Fine.

Blue Number Counting Book. Ellen Gould. (Illus.). 13p. (J). (ps-2). pap. 6.00 (0-938017-01-2) Learn Tools.

Blue Octavo. John Blackburn. (Black Dagger Crime Ser.). 128p. 1990. reprint ed. text ed. 16.50 (0-86220-766-5, Black Dagger) Chivers N Amer.

Blue Octavo Notebooks. Franz Kafka. Ed. by Max Brod. Tr. by Ernst Kaiser & Eithne Wilkins. 107p. 1991. reprint ed. pap. 13.95 (1-878972-04-9) Exact Change.

Blue of Capricorn. Eugene Burdick. LC 61-14728. 322p. 1987. reprint ed. pap. 5.95 (0-935180-36-2) Mutual Pub HI.

Blue of Noon. Georges Bataille. Tr. by Harry Matthews. 155p. 1986. reprint ed. pap. 12.95 (0-7145-2850-1) M Boyars Pubs.

*Blue on Blue: A History of Friendly Fire. Geoffrey Regan. LC 94-23280. 256p. (Orig.). 1995. pap. 12.50 (0-380-77655-3) Avon.

Blue Orchids. Julia Fenton. 416p. (Orig.). 1992. mass mkt. 5.99 (0-515-10875-8) Jove Pubns.

Blue Orleans. O'Neil DeNoux. 1991. mass mkt. 4.50 (0-8217-3472-5) Zebra.

Blue Out of Season. Audrey Penn & C. S. Ewing. LC 84-13584. (Illus.). (J). (gr. 3-6). 1985. 10.95 (0-915556-14-6) Great Ocean.

*Blue over You. Hal. (Illus.). 184p. (Orig.). 1995. pap. text ed. 14.95 (0-7935-3623-5, HL00311682) H Leonard.

*Blue Pages: Resources for Teachers: from Invitations. Regie Routman et al. LC 94-31701. 200p. 1994. pap. text ed. 13.50 (0-435-08835-1) Heinemann.

Blue Pearl. T. J. MacGregor. LC 93-49700. 384p. 1994. 21.95 (0-7868-6061-8) Hyperion.

Blue Pencil Authoring System. Robert J. Bator & Mitsuru Yamada. 96p. (C). 1989. pap. 70.00 (0-13-080250-6) P-H.

Blue Perfume: A Collection of Poetry. Victoria-Ann Bonanni. (Illus.). 52p. (Orig.). 1993. pap. write for info. (0-9636942-9-4) VB Document.

Blue Perfume: A Collection of Poetry. braille ed. Victoria-Ann Bonanni. (Illus.). 52p. (Orig.). 1993. Braille ed. write for info. (0-9636942-7-8) VB Document.

Blue Peter: Sea Yarns. Morley Roberts. LC 71-178458. (Short Story Index Reprint Ser.). 1977. reprint ed. 20.95 (0-8369-4059-8) Ayer.

Blue Peter Action Book. Lewis Bronze & Peter Brown. (Illus.). 65p. (YA). 1994. 8.95 (0-563-36495-5, BBC-Parkwest) Parkwest Pubns.

Blue Peter Green Book. Lewis Bronze et al. (Illus.). 64p. (J). (gr. 7-9). 1992. 9.95 (0-563-20886-4, BBC-Parkwest) Parkwest Pubns.

Blue Planet. B. E. Hehner. (J). 1993. 17.95 (0-15-200423-8, Gulliver Bks) HarBrace.

Blue Planet. Rodolpho Neri. 1989. 10.95 (0-533-08166-1) Vantage.

Blue Planet: A Portrait of Earth. Lydia Dotto. (Illus.). 64p. 1991. pap. 19.95 (0-8109-2472-2) Abrams.

*Blue Planet: An Introduction to Earth System Science. Brian J. Skinner & Stephen C. Porter. LC 94-25686. 1994. text ed. write for info. (0-471-54021-8) Wiley.

*Blue Planet: An Introduction to Earth System Science, Texbook & Laboratory Manual. Skinner & Porter. 1994. pap. text ed. write for info. (0-471-12560-1) Wiley.

Blue Planet: Seas & Oceans. Diane C. De Beauregard. Tr. by Vicki Bogard. LC 89-8912. (Young Discovery Library). (Illus.). 38p. (J). (gr. k-5). 1989. 5.95 (0-944589-22-7, 022) Young Discovery Lib.

Blue Plaque Guide. Lord Montagu. (Illus.). 132p. (Orig.). (C). 1991. pap. text ed. 18.00 (1-85172-005-7, Pub. by Journeyman Pr UK) Westview.

Blue Plate Special. Tom Edwards. 75p. (Orig.). 1985. pap. 4.95 (0-88145-025-1) Broadway Play.

Blue Plate Special. Damon Runyon. 17.95 (0-89190-360-7, Am Repr) Amereon Ltd.

Blue Poetry Book. Andrew Lang. LC 77-80375. (Granger Index Reprint Ser.). 1977. 25.95 (0-8369-6080-7) Ayer.

Blue Politics: Pornography & the Law in the Age of Feminism. Dany Lacombe. 288p. (C). 1994. 50.00 (0-8020-2854-3); pap. 18.95 (0-8020-7352-2) U of Toronto Pr.

Blue Potatoes, Orange Tomatoes: How to Grow a Rainbow Garden. Rosalind Creasy. LC 92-38800. (Illus.). 48p. (J). (gr. 2-6). 1994. 15.95 (0-87156-576-5) Sierra.

Blue Rags. David Meltzer. 1974. 5.00 (0-685-48375-4); pap. 1.50 (0-685-48377-0) Oyez.

Blue Rags. deluxe ed. David Meltzer. 1974. 15.00 (0-685-48376-2) Oyez.

Blue Ranger. (Mighty Morphin Power Rangers Small Flip-Ups Ser.). (Illus.). 8p. (J). (gr. k-2). 1994. bds. write for info. (1-56144-478-2, Honey Bear Bks) Modern Pub NYC.

Blue Remembered Hills. large type ed. Ivy Preston. (Linford Romance Library). 304p. 1988. pap. 10.95 (0-7089-6594-6, Linford) Ulverscroft.

Blue Remembered Hills: A Recollection. Rosemary Sutcliff. (Illus.). 144p. (YA). 1992. pap. 8.95 (0-374-40714-2, Sunburst Bks) FS&G.

Blue Review May-July, 1913, Nos. 1-3. Ed. by J. M. Murry & K. Mansfield. (Illus.). 220p. 1968. 65.00 (0-7146-2103-X, BHA-02103, Pub. by F Cass Pubs UK) Intl Spec Bk.

*Blue Revolution: Case-Study of Women in the Inland Fisheries Sector. Frances Sinha et al. (C). 1994. 14.00x (81-241-0195-7) S Asia.

Blue Riband of the Heather. E. B. Carpenter. (Illus.). 144p. 1989. 27.95 (0-85236-197-1, Pub. by Farming Pr UK) Diamond Farm Bk.

Blue Ribbon. L. E. Blair. (Girl Talk Ser.: No. 25). 128p. (J). (gr. 3-7). 1992. pap. 2.95 (0-307-22025-7, 22025, Golden Pr) Western Pub.

Blue Ribbon: A Social & Pictorial History of the Minnesota State Fair. Karal A. Marling. LC 90-5738. (Illus.). 328p. 1990. 39.95 (0-87351-251-0); pap. 24.95 (0-87351-252-9) Minn Hist.

Blue Ribbon Barbeque. John Uldrich. (Illus.). 84p. (Orig.). 1989. 5.95 (0-9622794-0-4) Nystrom MN.

Blue Ribbon Burgers. John Uldrich. LC 91-62179. 160p. (Orig.). 1992. pap. 7.95 (0-9622794-2-0) Nystrom MN.

Blue Ribbon Commission on Inmate Management. (Illus.). 161p. (Orig.). (C). 1993. pap. text ed. 30.00 (1-56806-820-4) Diane Pub.

Blue Ribbon Commissions & Higher Education: Changing Academe from the Outside. Janet R. Johnson & Laurence R. Marcus. Ed. & Frwd. by Jonathan D. Fife. LC 86-71526. (ASHE-ERIC Higher Education Report Ser.: No. 2, 1986). 111p. (Orig.). 1986. pap. 10.00 (0-913317-29-2) GWU Schl E&HD.

Blue Ribbon Cookbook. Florence L. Middlebrooks. LC 79-15295. 1980. 22.95 (0-87949-160-4) Ashley Bks.

Blue Ribbon Cookies. Maria P. Robbins. 144p. 1988. 11.95 (0-312-01738-3); pap. 7.95 (0-312-01739-1) St Martin.

Blue-Ribbon Friends. Lyn Calder. LC 90-85433. (Minnie 'n Me Ser.). (Illus.). 32p. (J). (gr. k-3). 1991. 5.95 (1-56282-034-6) Disney Pr.

Blue Ribbon of the Air: The Gordon Bennett Races. Henry S. Villard. LC 87-4709. (Illus.). 224p. (C). 1987. 34.00 (0-87474-942-5) Smithsonian.

Blue-Ribbon Pies. Maria P. Robbins. (Illus.). 128p. 1987. pap. 7.95 (0-312-00569-5) St Martin.

Blue Ribbon Schools: Outstanding Practices in Geography Education & History Education. 1994. lib. bdg. 250.00 (0-8490-8583-7) Gordon Pr.

*Blue Ribbon Schools: Outstanding Practices in the Arts. Eve Bither. 60p. (Orig.). (C). 1995. pap. text ed. 25.00x (0-7881-1546-4) Diane Pub.

Blue-Ribbon Science Fair Projects. Maxine Iritz. 1991. text ed. 17.95 (0-07-157630-4); pap. text ed. 9.95 (0-07-157629-0) McGraw.

Blue Ribbon Science Fair Projects. Maxine H. Iritz. (Illus.). 160p. 1991. 16.95 (0-8306-7615-5, 3615); pap. 9.95 (0-8306-3615-3) TAB Bks.

Blue Ribbon Techniques: Burning & Texturing Methods. William Veasey. LC 84-51182. (Illus.). 64p. 1984. pap. 7.95 (0-88740-013-2) Schiffer.

Blue Ribbon Winner's Bakebook. Fredlyn Kruglak. (Illus.). 320p. (Orig.). (J). (gr. 6-12). 1980. pap. 7.95 (0-9606686-0-8) Bakebks & Cookbks.

Blue Rider: In the Lenbachhaus, Munich. Intro. by Armin Zweite. (Illus.). 288p. 1989. 65.00 (3-7913-0850-5, Pub. by Prestel) TeNeues.

Blue Rider: Postcard Book. (Illus.). 18p. 1993. pap. 8.95 (3-7913-1310-X, Pub. by Prestel) TeNeues.

Blue Ridge. William A. Bake. (Illus.). 112p. 1984. pap. 12.95 (0-8487-0631-5) Oxmoor Hse.

*Blue Ridge. Jon Harper. LC 94-23221. (Illus.). (J). 1995. 8.95 (0-9611872-7-1) Our Child Pr.

Blue Ridge Dinnerware. 3rd ed. Betty Newbound. 1989. pap. 14.95 (0-89145-391-1) Collector Bks.

Blue Ridge Parkway. Harley E. Jolley. LC 68-9777. (Illus.). 186p. 1969. 23.50x (0-87049-091-5); pap. 14.00 (0-87049-100-8) U of Tenn Pr.

Blue Ridge Parkway: Four Seasons of Splendor. Catherine D. Joseph. 56p. (Orig.). (J). (ps-12). 1987. pap. text ed. 5.25 (0-936672-74-9) Aerial Photo.

Blue Ridge Parkway: The Story Behind the Scenery. Margaret R. Rives. LC 82-82578. (Illus.). 48p. (Orig.). 1982. pap. 6.95 (0-916122-81-6) KC Pubns.

Blue Ridge Parkway: Virginia-North Carolina. 32p. (J). (ps-12). 2.95 (0-936672-07-2) Aerial Photo.

Blue Ridge Parkway Guide: Grandfather Mountain to Great Smoky Mountain National Park. William G. Lord. LC 92-28238. (Illus.). 1992. reprint ed. 5.95 (0-89732-119-7) Menasha Ridge.

Blue Ridge Parkway Guide: Rockfish Gap to Grandfather Mountain 0.0 - 291.9 miles. William G. Lord. LC 92-28237. (Illus.). 1992. reprint ed. 5.95 (0-89732-118-9) Menasha Ridge.

Blue Ridge Range: The Gentle Mountains. Ron Fisher. LC 92-32429. 1992. 12.95 (0-87044-865-X) Natl Geog.

Blue River. Ethan Canin. 224p. 1991. 19.95 (0-395-49854-6) HM.

Blue River. Ethan Canin. 240p. 1992. reprint ed. pap. 10.99 (0-446-39447-5) Warner Bks.

Blue Road. Kenneth White. 144p. 1992. 29.95 (1-85158-279-7, Pub. by Mnstream UK) Trafalgar.

*Blue Rodeo. Jo-Ann Mapson. 1995. pap. 12.00 (0-06-092635-X, PL) HarpC.

Blue Rodeo: A Novel. Jo-Ann Mapson. LC 93-46453. 352p. 1994. 22.00 (0-06-016944-3, HarpT) HarpC.

Blue Rodeo: A Novel. large type ed. Jo-Ann Mapson. LC 94-12999. 536p. 1994. 21.95 (0-7862-0280-7) Thorndike Pr.

Blue Room. Georges Simenon. Tr. by Eileen Ellenbogen. LC 78-7423. 141p. 1978. reprint ed. pap. 2.95 (0-15-613267-2, Harvest Bks) HarBrace.

Blue Room: Trauma & Testimony among Refugee Women, a Pscho-Social Exploration. Inger Agger. LC 88-706. 192p. (C). 1994. text ed. 55.00 (1-85649-239-7, Pub. by Zed Books UK); pap. 17.50 (1-85649-240-0, Pub. by Zed Books UK) Humanities.

*Blue Rose. Alison Tyler. (Orig.). 1995. pap. text ed. 5.95 (1-56333-335-X) Masquerade.

*Blue Rose-Year 2094. Audrey Matthewson. 300p. Date not set. pap. 9.95 (0-7610-0340-1) NW Pub.

Blue Ruin. G. L. Hill. 21.95 (0-89190-058-6, Am Repr) Amereon Ltd.

Blue Ruin. Grace L. Hill. (Grace Livingston Hill Ser.: No. 41). 1992. pap. 4.99 (0-8423-0349-9) Tyndale.

*Blue Sage. Anne Stuart. (Western Lovers Ser.). 1995. mass mkt. 3.99 (0-373-88502-4, 1-88502-9) Harlequin Bks.

Blue Sea. Robert Kalan. LC 78-18396. (Illus.). 24p. (J). (gr. k-3). 1979. 14.95 (0-688-80184-6); lib. bdg. 14.93 (0-688-84184-8) Greenwillow.

Blue Sea. Robert Kalan. LC 78-18396. (Illus.). 24p. (J). (ps up). 1992. pap. 3.95 (0-688-11509-8, Mulberry) Morrow.

Blue Sense: Psychic Detectives & Crime. Arthur Lyons & Marcello Truzzi. 1991. 19.95 (0-89296-426-X) Mysterious Pr.

Blue Shovel. Robert Hershon. 1979. pap. 6.00 (0-914610-14-7) Hanging Loose.

An Asterisk (*) at the beginning of an entry indicates that the title is appearing in BIP for the first time. 825

Blue Shutters. large type ed. Anne Durham. (Linford Romance Library). 352p. 1988. pap. 11.95 (*0-7089-6574-1*, Linford) Ulverscroft.

Blue Skidoo Crew. Professor Glugg. LC 92-75278. (Galactic Glue Glugg Stories Ser.). (Illus.). 32p. (Orig.). (J). (ps up). 1993. pap. 3.95 (*1-881905-03-9*) Glue Bks.

Blue Skies. Robert Fromberg. (Orig.). 1992. pap. 6.00 (*0-912449-18-7*) Floating Island.

Blue Skies: The Autobiography of a Canadian Spitfire Pilot in World War II. (Illus.). 262p. 1988. pap. 16.95 (*0-7737-5213-7*, Pub. by Stoddart Pubng CN) Genl Dist Srvs.

Blue Skies, French Fries. Judy Delton. (Pee Wee Scouts Ser.: No. 4). 80p. (Orig.). (J). (gr. k-6). 1988. pap. 3.25 (*0-440-40064-3*, YB) Dell.

Blue Skies, Green Days. Jillian De Muth. (Illus.). 48p. (J). (gr. 1-6). 1993. 16.95 (*1-86373-062-1*, Pub. by Allen & Unwin Aust Pty AT) IPG Chicago.

Blue Skies, Green Politics: The Clean Air Act Of 1990. Gary C. Bryner. LC 92-34505. 203p. 1992. 20.95 (*0-87187-668-X*) Congr Quarterly.

***Blue Skies, Green Politics: The Clean Air Act of 1990 & Its Implementation.** rev. ed. Gary Bryner. 250p. 1995. pap. 20.95 (*1-56802-134-8*) Congr Quarterly.

Blue Skin of the Sea. Graham Salisbury. (YA). 1994. mass mkt. 3.99 (*0-440-21905-1*) Dell.

Blue Skin of the Sea: A Novel in Stories. Graham Salisbury. (J). (gr. 4-7). 1992. 15.95 (*0-385-30596-6*) Doubleday.

Blue Skin of the Sea: A Novel in Stories. large type ed. Graham Salisbury. LC 92-41152. 327p. 1993. reprint ed. lib. bdg. 15.95 (*1-56054-623-9*) Thorndike Pr.

Blue Sky. Sam Stewart. 1985. pap. write for info. (*0-318-59384-X*) PB.

Blue Sky Green Sea: And Other Stories. Liu Sola Cliu. Tr. & Intro. by Martha Cheung. xxv, 145p. (Orig.). 1993. pap. 11.95 (*962-7255-12-2*, Pub. by Renditions Papbk HK) SPD-Small Pr Dist.

Blue Sky Law, 2 vols. Joseph C. Long. LC 85-11377. (Securities Law Ser.). 1985. ring bd. 250.00 (*0-87632-468-5*) Clark Boardman Callaghan.

Blue Sky Laws 1993. (Corporate Law & Practice Course Handbook, 1985-86 Ser.: Vol. 818). 514p. 1993. 70.00 (*0-685-69722-3*, B4-7042) PLI.

Blue Sky, Night Thunder: The Utes of Colorado. Jess McCreede. 416p. Date not set. 19.95 (*1-879915-08-1*) Affil Writers America.

Blue Sky Pocket Poems, Vol. 1. Fred Wood. (Illus.). 112p. (Orig.). 1991. pap. 4.95 (*0-9631050-1-9*) Safe Harbour.

Blue Sky Practice Handbook, 1992-93. Peter M. Fass & Derek A. Wittner. 1993. pap. 97.50 (*0-87632-879-6*) Clark Boardman Callaghan.

Blue Sky Regulation, 4 vols. Bender's Editorial Staff & Hugh L. Sowards. 1977. ring bd. write for info. (*0-8205-1142-0*) Bender.

***Blue Sky Sideways & Other Stories.** Alison Tyler. (Orig.). Date not set. mass mkt., pap. 5.95 (*1-56333-394-5*) Masquerade.

Blue Spaders - Vietnam: A Private's Account, 1-26th Inf., 1965-1966. Carl W. Bradfield. LC 92-72472. (Illus.). 284p. 1992. boxed 19.95 (*0-9632319-0-1*) ASDA Pub.

***Blue Spruce.** David Long. 1995. 22.00 (*0-684-80033-0*) S&S Trade.

Blue Spruce & the Year of the Haiku: Poems. Irving C. Hall. LC 90-27872. (Target Poetry Ser.). 74p. 1991. pap. 7.25 (*0-933532-78-4*) BkMk.

Blue Star. Robert Fierro. 256p. 1986. pap. 10.00 (*0-452-25819-7*, Plume) NAL-Dutton.

Blue Star. Fletcher Pratt. 1981. pap. 2.50 (*0-345-29852-7*, Del Rey) Ballantine.

Blue Star: The Story of Corabelle Fellows, Teacher at Dakota Missions, 1884-1888. Kunigunde Duncan. LC 89-39848. (Illus.). xx, 216p. 1989. pap. 8.95 (*0-87351-245-6*) Minn Hist.

Blue Star over Amritsar. Harminder Kaur. 1990. 30.00 (*0-685-35163-7*, Pub. by Ajanta II) S Asia.

***Blue Star Over Red Square.** Carmela Raiz. LC 94-39654. 1994. write for info. (*0-87306-616-2*); pap. text ed. write for info. (*0-87306-617-0*) Feldheim.

Blue Steel. George Hall & John Lopez. (Osprey Colour Library). (Illus.). 128p. 1992. pap. 15.95 (*1-85532-207-2*, Pub. by Ospreу Pubng Ltd UK) Motorbooks Intl.

***Blue Stragglers No. 53.** Ed. by Rex A. Saffer. 200p. 1993. 40.00 (*0-937707-72-4*) Astron Soc Pacific.

Blue Strawberry Cookbook: Cooking (Brilliantly) Without Recipes. James Haller. LC 76-23990. 1983. pap. 8.95 (*0-916782-05-0*) Harvard Common Pr.

Blue Suede Brogans: Scenes from the Secret Life of Scottish Rock Music. Jim Wilke. 192p. 1992. pap. 22.95 (*1-85158-372-6*, Pub. by Mnstream UK) Trafalgar.

Blue Suede Shoes. Steven Yount. Date not set. write for info. (*0-345-38302-8*) Ballantine.

Blue Swan Review: Guide to Women's Fashion Catalogs. Ed. by Randall Cornish & Kimberly Swan. (Illus.). 1990. 7.95 (*0-317-93388-4*) Blue Swan.

Blue Sword. Robin McKinley. mass mkt. 4.99 (*0-441-06880-4*) Ace Bks.

Blue Sword. Robin McKinley. LC 82-2895. 288p. (YA). (gr. 7 up). 1982. 16.00 (*0-688-00938-7*) Greenwillow.

Blue Sword: The Naval War College & the American Mission, 1919-1941. Michael Vlahos. LC 81-9654. (Historical Monograph Ser.: No. 4). 222p. (C). 1981. pap. 6.00 (*1-884733-01-8*) Naval War Coll.

***Blue Tale & Other Stories.** Marguerite Yourcenar. Tr. by Alberto Manguel. LC 95-14507. 1995. pap. 7.95 (*0-226-96531-7*) U Ch Pr.

***Blue Tale & Other Stories.** Marguerite Yourcenar. Tr. by Alberto Manguel. LC 95-14507. 144p. 1995. 15.00 (*0-226-96530-9*) U Ch Pr.

Blue Tango. 1993. pap. 5.95 (*1-56201-048-4*) Blue Moon Bks.

Blue Tango. 1992. pap. 4.95 (*1-56333-037-7*) Masquerade.

Blue Tango: Poems by Michael van Walleghen. Michael Van Walleghen. LC 88-17394. 104p. (Orig.). 1989. pap. 9.95 (*0-252-06044-X*) U of Ill Pr.

***Blue Tattoo.** Lyn Lifshin. 80p. 1995. pap. 9.95 (*1-880391-12-0*) Event Horizon.

Blue Taxis: Stories about Africa. Eileen Drew. LC 89-12595. (National Fiction Prize Ser.). 160p. (Orig.). 1989. pap. 9.95 (*0-915943-41-7*) Milkweed Ed.

Blue That Speaks of Heaven. Daniel Gallik. 40p. (Orig.). 1991. pap. 6.00 (*1-879533-06-5*) Poetic Page.

Blue Thunder. Richard Throssel. (Indian Culture Ser.). 32p. (J). (gr. 6-12). 1976. 1.75 (*0-89992-046-2*) Coun India Ed.

Blue Tights. Garcia R. Williams. 1989. pap. 3.50 (*0-553-28293-X*) Bantam.

Blue Tights. Rita Williams-Garcia. LC 87-17156. 160p. (YA). (gr. 7 up). 1988. 12.95 (*0-525-67234-6*, Lodestar Bks) Dutton Child Bks.

Blue Tit. Jim Flegg. 1989. pap. 25.00 (*0-85263-716-0*, Pub. by Shire UK) St Mut.

Blue Tongue. Steve Levine. LC 76-14297. (Illus.). 24p. 1976. pap. 3.00 (*0-915124-19-X*, Toothpaste) Coffee Hse.

Blue Tongue, African Horse Sickness & Related Orbiviruses: International Symposium on Bluetongue, African Horse Sickness, & Related Orbiviruses, Second Conference, Paris, France, 1991. 1042p. 1992. 125.00 (*0-8493-5169-3*, SF809) CRC Pr.

Blue Tortoise. Alan Roger. LC 90-9833. (Little Giants Ser.). (Illus.). 16p. (J). (ps-1). 1990. lib. bdg. 14.60 (*0-8368-0404-X*) Gareth Stevens Inc.

Blue Train. Richard Manton. 1993. pap. 5.95 (*1-56201-043-3*) Blue Moon Bks.

Blue Train: And Other Poems. Ron Ellis. LC 89-90564. 90p. (Orig.). 1990. pap. 10.00 (*0-9624746-0-6*) Woodhenge.

Blue Train to Athens: A Bad Trip to Egypt. Gui De Angulo. (Illus.). 295p. (Orig.). 1993. pap. 9.95 (*1-879042-03-7*) Stonegarden Pr.

Blue Trout & Black Truffles. Joseph Wechsberg. (Illus.). 288p. 1985. pap. 10.00 (*0-89733-134-6*) Academy Chi Pubs.

Blue Truth. Cherokee P. McDonald. 1992. mass mkt. 4.99 (*0-312-92773-8*) St Martin.

Blue Truth: Walking the Thin Blue Line - One Cop's Story of Life in the Streets. Cherokee P. McDonald. 1991. 18.95 (*1-55611-246-7*) D I Fine.

***Blue Umbrella.** Ruskin Bond. (Orig.). (J). 1993. 4.00 (*0-8364-2896-X*, Pub. by Rupa II) S Asia.

Blue Unicorn. Sidney A. Wilson. (Illus.). 88p. 1989. 9.95 (*0-9621548-0-6*) Coppage Pub Co.

Blue Valentine. 2nd ed. Gwen Schultz. 1979. reprint ed. 10.00 (*0-688-32176-3*) Reading Gems.

Blue Valleys. Robert Morgan. 192p. 1989. 15.95 (*0-934601-71-2*) Peachtree Pubs.

Blue Velvet. 192p. 1992. pap. 5.95 (*1-56201-031-X*, 82) Blue Moon Bks.

***Blue Vitriol.** Alexei Parshchikov. Ed. by Cydney Chadwick. Tr. by Michael Palmer et al. 64p. 1994. pap. text ed. 9.50 (*1-880713-02-0*) AVEC Bks.

Blue Warrior (above the Line of Duty) Otto Moravek. 1994. 17.50 (*0-8062-4995-1*) Carlton.

Blue Water. Michael D. Welch. LC 93-5085. (Illus.). 64p. (Orig.). 1993. per., pap. 7.50 (*1-878798-08-1*) Press Here.

Blue Water Women. Lorena Reed. (Illus.). 320p. 1993. write for info. (*0-933858-12-4*) Kennebec River.

Blue Waters, Black Depths. Caroline Gray. 1991. 19.95 (*0-7278-4144-0*) Severn Hse.

***Blue Whale.** Robert L. Buyer. (Carving Sea Life Ser.). (Illus.). 32p. 1996. pap. 12.95 (*0-8117-2467-0*) Stackpole.

Blue Whale. Melissa Kim. LC 93-79973. (Creature Club Ser.). (Illus.). 32p. (J). (gr. 1-5). 1993. lib. bdg. 12.00 (*0-8249-8628-8*, Ideals Child); pap. 5.95 (*0-8249-8614-8*, Ideals Child) Hambleton-Hill.

Blue Whales. S. Palmer. (Whale Discovery Library). (Illus.). 24p. (J). (gr. k-5). 1988. lib. bdg. 11.94 (*0-86592-480-5*) Rourke Corp.

***Blue Whales.** John F. Prevost. LC 95-9676. (J). 1995. lib. bdg. 9.95 (*1-56239-475-4*) Abdo & Dghtrs.

Blue Wildfire. Faye Ashley. 320p. 1983. pap. 3.25 (*0-8439-2018-1*) Dorchester Pub Co.

Blue Willow. Doris Gates. LC 40-32435. (Illus.). (J). (gr. 4-6). 1976. pap. 3.99 (*0-14-030924-1*, VS30, Puffin) Puffin Bks.

Blue Willow. Doris Gates. LC 40-32435. (Illus.). 176p. (J). (gr. 4-7). 1940. pap. 14.99 (*0-670-17557-9*) Viking Child Bks.

Blue Willow. Deborah Smith. 1993. mass mkt. 5.50 (*0-553-29690-6*) Bantam.

Blue Willow. 2nd ed. Mary F. Gaston. 1990. pap. 14.95 (*0-89145-396-2*) Collector Bks.

Blue Willowware Book & Appraisal Guide. Joshua D. Young. 48p. 4.95 (*0-935069-37-2*) White Oak Pr.

Blue Wine & Other Poems. Ed. by John Hollander. LC 78-20514. 1979. pap. 6.95 (*0-8018-2221-1*) Johns Hopkins.

Blue Wine & Other Poems. John Hollander. LC 78-20514. (Johns Hopkins: Poetry & Fiction Ser.). 80p. reprint ed. pap. 25.00 (*0-8357-7331-0*, 2025854) Bks Demand.

***Blue Wings: One Woman's Guided Flight Toward Healing.** Rose A. Higashi. (Illus.). 176p. 1995. 14.95 (*0-8091-0475-X*) Paulist Pr.

Blue Witch of Oz. Eric Shanower. (Oz Ser.). (Illus.). 72p. (Orig.). (J). 1993. pap. 9.95 (*1-878574-44-2*) Dark Horse Comics.

***Blue Woman.** Mary Flanagan. LC 94-36700. 320p. 1995. 21.00 (*0-393-03803-3*) Norton.

Blue Woman Dancing in the Nerve. Joan Colby. LC 79-22754. 1979. pap. 3.50 (*0-934184-02-X*) Alembic Pr.

Blue World. Robert R. McCammon. Ed. by Sally Peters. 464p. 1990. mass mkt. 5.99 (*0-671-69518-5*) PB.

Blueback. large type ed. Bill Knox. 1990. pap. 12.95 (*0-7089-6949-6*, Linford) Ulverscroft.

Bluebeard. Max Frisch. Tr. by Geoffrey Skelton. LC 82-21250. (Helen & Kurt Wolff Bk.). 144p. 1984. pap. 3.95 (*0-15-613198-6*, Harvest Bks) HarBrace.

Bluebeard. Kurt Vonnegut, Jr. 1988. mass mkt. 5.99 (*0-440-20196-9*) Dell.

Bluebeard Room. Carolyn Keene. (Nancy Drew Ser.: No. 77). (J). 1988. pap. 3.50 (*0-671-66857-9*, Minstrel Bks) PB.

Bluebeards: Adventure on Skull Island. Tony Bradman. (Arch Bks.). (Illus.). 64p. (J). (gr. 3-6). 1990. pap. 2.95 (*0-8120-4421-5*) Barron.

Bluebeards: Mystery at Musket Bay. Tony Bradman. (Arch Bks.). (Illus.). 64p. (J). (gr. 3-6). 1990. pap. 2.95 (*0-8120-4422-3*) Barron.

Bluebeards: Peril at the Pirate School. Tony Bradman. (Arch Bks.). (Illus.). 64p. (J). (gr. 2-5). 1990. pap. 2.95 (*0-8120-4502-5*) Barron.

Bluebeards: Revenge at Ryan's Reef. Tony Bradman. 52p. (J). (ps-3). 1992. pap. 3.50 (*0-8120-4903-9*) Barron.

Bluebeard's Egg & Other Stories. Margaret Atwood. 336p. 1987. mass mkt. 5.95 (*0-449-21417-6*, Crest) Fawcett.

Bluebell Blue. large type ed. Jan Webster. (Romance Ser.). 512p. 1992. 21.95 (*0-7089-2724-6*) Ulverscroft.

Bluebell Pool. Sue Sully. 320p. 1994. 22.95 (*0-312-11281-5*) St Martin.

Bluebell Wood. large type ed. Catherine Dunn. (Linford Romance Library). 1991. pap. 13.95 (*0-7089-7055-9*) Ulverscroft.

Bluebell Wood. large type ed. Elizabeth Shepherd. (Linford Romance Library). 1991. pap. 13.95 (*0-7089-6986-0*, Linford) Ulverscroft.

Bluebells & Acorns. Norma J. Burk. 1993. 8.75 (*0-8062-4792-4*) Carlton.

Bluebells Forever: A Story about Bessie. Kenneth L. Hardin. 192p. (Orig.). 1985. pap. 5.00 (*0-9619153-0-7*) K L Hardin.

Blueberries, Barnacles & Licorice Shoestrings. Carol L. Zimmerman. (Illus.). 28p. (Orig.). 1982. pap. 3.00 (*0-936014-12-1*) Dawn Valley.

Blueberries for Sal. Robert McCloskey. LC 48-4955. (Illus.). (J). (ps-1). 1976. pap. 4.99 (*0-14-050169-X*, Puffin) Puffin Bks.

Blueberries for Sal. Robert McCloskey. (Story Tapes Ser.). (Illus.). (J). (ps-3). 1989. pap. 6.95 (*0-14-095032-X*, Puffin) Puffin Bks.

Blueberries for Sal. Robert McCloskey. (Illus.). (J). 1993. audio, pap. 6.99 (*0-14-095110-5*, Puffin) Puffin Bks.

Blueberries for Sal. Robert McCloskey. LC 48-4955. (Illus.). 56p. (J). (ps-1). 1948. pap. 14.95 (*0-670-17591-9*) Viking Child Bks.

Blueberry. David D. Hume. LC 93-29842. (Illus.). 120p. 1994. 22.50 (*1-880158-02-7*) J N Townsend.

***Blueberry Afternoon.** Carolyn Sibr. 80p. 1996. pap. 7.95 (*0-7610-0513-7*) NW Pub.

Blueberry & the Victorian House. Andrea Skiff. Ed. by Elizabeth J. Peterson. (Illus.). 27p. (Orig.). (J). (gr. 2-5). 1987. pap. 3.95 (*0-938911-03-1*) Indiv Educ Syst.

Blueberry Bear. Rebecca Kaler. 14p. (J). (ps). 1993. 12.95 (*0-9634637-0-5*) Inquir Voices.

Blueberry Connection. Beatrice R. Buszek. 1991. pap. 12.95 (*0-920852-32-7*, Pub. by Nimbus Publishing Ltd CN) Chelsea Green Pub.

Blueberry Culture. Ed. by Paul Eck & Norman F. Childers. 1966. 27.50 (*0-317-03719-6*) Horticult Pubns.

Blueberry Culture. Ed. by Paul Eck & N. F. Childers. 1967. 50.00x (*0-8135-0535-6*) Rutgers U Pr.

Blueberry Lieutenant: The Iron Horse. Charlier & Moebius. 48p. 1991. 8.95 (*0-87135-740-2*) Marvel Entmnt.

Blueberry, Lt. Steelfingers. Charlier & Moebius. 48p. 1991. 8.95 (*0-87135-741-0*) Marvel Entmnt.

Blueberry Sampler. Jan Siegrist. (Illus.). 48p. (Orig.). 1988. pap. 3.95 (*0-933050-57-7*) New Eng Pr VT.

Blueberry Science. Paul Eck. 275p. (C). 1988. text ed. 50.00 (*0-8135-1283-2*) Rutgers U Pr.

Blueberry Summer. Elisabeth Ogilvie. reprint ed. lib. bdg. 18.95 (*0-88411-327-2*, Aeonian Pr) Amereon Ltd.

Blueberry Summer Cookbook. Vicki L. Duchesneau & Judy I. Casey. (Illus.). 100p. (Orig.). 1982. pap. 6.95 (*0-9608432-0-5*) Valley View.

***Blueberry Train.** Martin. 1995. 14.00 (*0-689-80304-4*) Macmillan.

Blueberry, Vol. 1: Chihuahua Pearl. Charlier & Moebius. 96p. 1989. 12.95 (*0-87135-569-8*) Marvel Entmnt.

Blueberry, Vol. 2: Ballad for a Coffin. Charlier & Moebius. 120p. 1989. 14.95 (*0-87135-570-1*) Marvel Entmnt.

Blueberry, Vol. 3: Angel Face. Charlier & Moebius. 96p. 1989. 12.95 (*0-87135-571-X*) Marvel Entmnt.

Blueberry, Vol. 4: The Ghost Tribe. Charlier & Moebius. 96p. 1990. 12.95 (*0-87135-580-9*) Marvel Entmnt.

Blueberry, Vol. 5: The End of the Trail. Charlier & Moebius. 96p. 1990. 12.95 (*0-87135-581-7*) Marvel Entmnt.

Blueberry's Secret. Jean-Michel Charlier. Tr. by Starwatcher Graphics Staff. (Young Blueberry Ser.). (Illus.). 56p. (Orig.). 1989. pap. 7.95 (*0-87416-068-5*, Comcat Comics) Catalan Communs.

Bluebird: How You Can Help Its Fight for Survival. Lawrence Zeleny. LC 74-22832. (Illus.). 192p. 1976. pap. 8.95 (*0-253-20212-4*, MB-212) Ind U Pr.

***Bluebird & the Sparrow.** Janette Oke. 240p. 1995. pap. 8.99 (*1-55661-612-0*); pap. 12.99 (*1-55661-613-9*) Bethany Hse.

Bluebird Book: The Complete Guide to Attracting Bluebirds. Donald W. Stokes. 1991. pap. 11.95 (*0-316-81745-7*) Little.

Bluebird Cafe. Carmel Bird. LC 90-13243. 192p. 1991. 19.95 (*0-8112-1156-8*); pap. 10.95 (*0-8112-1155-X*, NDP707) New Directions.

***Bluebird of Happiness.** Emerson Moore. (J). 1995. 8.95 (*0-8062-5221-9*) Carlton.

Bluebird Rescue: A Harrowsmith Country Life Nature Guide. rev. ed. Joan R. Heilman. LC 91-40618. (Illus.). 48p. (J). (gr. 10 up). 1992. reprint ed. lib. bdg. 16.95 (*0-944475-27-2*, Pub. by Camden Hse CN); reprint ed. pap. 6.95 (*0-944475-24-8*, Pub. by Camden Hse CN) Firefly Bks Ltd.

Bluebird Son of the Sun. Rob Wyant. LC 83-80375. 112p. 1983. pap. 5.00 (*0-88100-029-9*) Natl Writ Pr.

***Bluebird Trails: A Guide to Success.** Dorene H. Scriven. (Illus.). 253p. (Orig.). 1993. pap. text ed. write for info. (*0-9639661-0-3*) Bluebird Rec.

Bluebirds. David W. Frasure. 1978. pap. 4.95 (*0-932298-08-7*) Tri-State Pr Corp.

Bluebirds. Steve Grooms. 1991. pap. 16.95 (*1-55971-095-0*) NorthWord.

Bluebirds: Their Daily Lives & How to Attract & Raise Bluebirds. Tina Dew et al. LC 86-70315. (Illus.). 224p. 1986. 14.95 (*0-912542-06-3*); pap. 10.95 (*0-685-13982-4*) Nature Bks Pubs.

***Bluebirds & Their Survival.** Wayne H. Davis & Philippe Roca. (Illus.). 160p. 1995. pap. 15.95 (*0-8131-0846-2*) U Pr of Ky.

Bluebirds Forever. Connie Toops. LC 94-11710. 1994. 35.00 (*0-89658-249-3*) Voyageur Pr.

Bluebonnet at Dinosaur Valley State Park. Mary B. Casad. LC 90-7338. (Bluebonnet Ser.). (Illus.). 32p. (J). (gr. k-3). 1990. 13.95 (*0-88289-776-4*) Pelican.

Bluebonnet at Johnson Space Center. Mary B. Casad. LC 92-37416. (Illus.). 32p. 1993. 14.95 (*0-88289-963-5*) Pelican.

Bluebonnet at the Alamo. Mary B. Casad. (Illus.). 40p. (J). (gr. 4-7). 1984. 11.95 (*0-89015-445-7*) Sunbelt Media.

Bluebonnet at the State Fair. Mary B. Casad. (Bluebonnet Bks.: No. 3). (Illus.). 40p. (J). (gr. 2-4). 1985. 12.95 (*0-89015-530-5*) Sunbelt Media.

Bluebonnet Books: Activities for 1993. Anne M. Perry. 144p. (Orig.). 1993. pap. 16.95 (*0-944459-72-2*) ECS Lrn Systs.

Bluebonnet of the Hill Country. Mary B. Casad. (Illus.). (J). (gr. k-4). 1983. 11.95 (*0-89015-395-7*) Sunbelt Media.

***Bluebonnet Trail Cookbook.** Anita Allison et al. 1995. write for info. (*0-9647290-0-8*) Bluebonnet Trail Cookbk.

Bluebonnets. Nellie McCaslin. LC 93-5271. 20p. (J). 1993. pap. 4.00 (*0-88734-439-9*) Players Pr.

Bluebook of Cleaning, Reconstruction & Repair Costs: A Complete Reference & Cost Guide of Cleaning Repairs & Reconstruction. annuals Daniel E. Josipovich. (Illus.). 420p. Date not set. pap. 59.95 (*0-918767-00-8*) Insur Indus.

***Bluecoats: The U. S. Army in the West, 1848-1897.** John P. Langellier. LC 95-15138. (G. I. Ser.: Vol. 2). (Illus.). 80p. 1995. pap. 12.95 (*1-85367-221-1*, Pub. by Greenhill Bks UK) Stackpole.

***Bluefeather Fellini.** Max Evans. 1994. 5.99 (*0-553-56539-7*) Bantam.

Bluefeather Fellini. Max Evans. 304p. 1993. 19.95 (*0-87081-307-2*) Univ Pr Colo.

Bluefeather Fellini in the Sacred Realm. Max Evans. 368p. 1994. 19.95 (*0-87081-345-5*) Univ Pr Colo.

***Bluefish Cookbook.** 5th ed. Greta Jacobs & Jane Alexander. LC 79-51760. 144p. 1995. pap. 8.95 (*1-56440-726-8*) Globe Pequot.

Bluefishing. Henry Lyman. (Illus.). 160p. (Orig.). 1987. pap. 10.95 (*0-941130-58-4*) Lyons & Burford.

Bluegate Fields. Anne Perry. 288p. 1985. mass mkt. 5.99 (*0-449-45317-0*, Crest) Fawcett.

Bluegate Fields. Anne Perry. 1989. mass mkt. 5.99 (*0-449-20766-8*) Fawcett.

Bluegrass. Bob Artis. 1977. reprint ed. pap. 1.75 (*0-8439-0452-6*) Dorchester Pub Co.

Bluegrass: A History. Neil V. Rosenberg. LC 84-15747. (Music in American Life Ser.). (Illus.). 464p. 1985. 29.95 (*0-252-00265-2*) U of Ill Pr.

Bluegrass: A History. Neil V. Rosenberg. LC 93-3590. 464p. (C). 1993. pap. 18.95 (*0-252-06304-X*) U of Ill Pr.

***Bluegrass: An Informal Guide.** Richard D. Smith. (Informal Guide Ser.). (Illus.). 240p. (Orig.). 1995. pap. 12.95 (*1-55652-240-1*) A cappella Bks.

Bluegrass & Country Music for Harmonica. Phil Duncan. 1993. 6.95 (*0-87166-646-4*, 93990); audio 15.95 (*0-87166-651-0*, 93990); audio 9.98 (*0-87166-647-2*, 93990) Mel Bay.

Bluegrass Banjo. Peter Wernick. LC 73-92396. (Illus.). 1974. pap. 17.95 (*0-8256-0148-7*, 000148, Oak); lp (*0-318-54415-6*, Oak) Music Sales.

Bluegrass Banjo Method. Sonny Osborne. 1993. 4.95 (*0-87166-578-6*, 93243) Mel Bay.

***Bluegrass Banjo Simplified!!** Wayne Erbsen. 1985. pap. 12.95 (*1-883206-12-X*) Native Ground.

Bluegrass Banjo Style of Douglas Flint Dillard. Ed. by Ronny Schiff. 1980. 9.95 (*0-89898-020-8*) Almo Pubns.

Bluegrass Breakdown: The Making of the Old Southern Sound. Robert Cantwell. LC 83-4861. (Music in American Life Ser.). 328p. 1984. 24.95 (*0-252-01054-X*) U of Ill Pr.

Bluegrass Breakdown: The Making of the Old Southern Sound. Robert Cantwell. (Illus.). 334p. 1992. reprint ed. pap. 13.95 (*0-306-80495-6*) Da Capo.

Bluegrass Conspiracy. Sally Denton. 408p. 1991. reprint ed. mass mkt. 5.99 (*0-380-71441-8*) Avon.

Bluegrass Country. Lynn M. Stone. LC 93-23002. (Back Roads Ser.). (J). 1993. write for info. (*0-86593-306-5*) Rourke Corp.

Bluegrass, Country & Folk. Date not set. pap. 0.95 (*0-87166-538-7*, 93709) Mel Bay.

An Asterisk (*) at the beginning of an entry indicates that the title is appearing in BIP for the first time.

Bluegrass Fiddle. Gene Lowringer. LC 73-92395. (Illus.). 1974. pap. 12.95 (*0-8256-0150-9*, 000150, Oak) Music Sales.

Bluegrass Fiddle Styles. Stacy Phillips & Kenny Kosek. (Illus.). 112p. pap. 11.95 (*0-8256-0185-1*, OK63487, Oak) Music Sales.

Bluegrass Fiddler. Burton Isaac. 1993. 4.95 (*0-87166-784-3*, 93341) Mel Bay.

Bluegrass Guitar. Happy Traum. LC 74-77312. (Illus.). 1974. pap. 17.95 (*0-8256-0153-3*, 000153, Oak); lp (*0-318-54416-4*, Oak) Music Sales.

Bluegrass Harp Book for Diatonic Harmonica. J. Yates. 1990. 7.95 (*0-685-32199-1*, O494) Hansen Ed Mus.

Bluegrass Land & Life: Land Character, Plants, & Animals of the Inner Bluegrass Region of Kentucky. Mary E. Wharton & Roger W. Barbour. LC 90-36745. (Illus.). 304p. 1991. 40.00 (*0-8131-1688-0*) U Pr of Ky.

Bluegrass Mandolin. Jack Tottle. LC 74-77692. (Illus.). 120p. (Orig.). 1975. pap. 17.95 (*0-8256-0154-1*, Oak); lp (*0-318-54417-2*, Oak) Music Sales.

Bluegrass Picture Chords & How to Use Them. Happy Taum. (Picture Chords Library: EFS190). (Illus.). 32p. 1978. pap. 6.95 (*0-8256-2190-9*, AM21684) Music Sales.

Bluegrass Secrets: A Resource Guide for the Home & Garden. Jane S. Offutt. (Illus.). 192p. (Orig.). Date not set. pap. text ed. 12.95 (*1-883554-01-2*) City Secrets.

Bluegrass Songbook. Peter Wernick. (Illus.). 140p. 1976. pap. 14.95 (*0-8256-0164-9*, 000164, Oak) Music Sales.

Bluegrass Winners. Garden Club of Lexington, Inc. Staff. LC 85-60214. (Illus.). 368p. 1985. per. 16.50 (*0-9614442-0-7*) Starr-Toof.

Bluegreen Tree. Agnes Smith. LC 76-50105. (Illus.). 180p. (Orig.). (J). 1977. 9.00 (*0-87012-271-1*) Westwind Pr.

Bluejacket: A Biography. Fred J. Buenzle & A. Grove Day. LC 86-8528. (Classics of Naval Literature Ser.). 1986. reprint ed. 32.95 (*0-87021-190-0*) Naval Inst Pr.

***Bluejacket: From Guadalcanal to Tokyo.** John A. Hitchinson. (Illus.). 1995. 29.95 (*0-533-11182-X*) Vantage.

Bluejackets' Manual. 21th rev. ed. Rev. by Bill Bearden. (Illus.). 672p. 1990. 24.95 (*0-87021-259-1*) Naval Inst Pr.

Bluejay in the Desert. Marlene Shigekawa. LC 92-35424. (Illus.). 36p. (J). (gr. k-4). 1993. 12.95 (*1-879965-04-6*) Polychrome Pub.

Bluejay Shaman: An Alex Thorssen Mystery. Lise M. Webb. LC 93-32769. 240p. 1994. 19.95 (*0-8027-3179-1*) Walker & Co.

Blueprint: A Study of Diderot & the "Encyclopedie" Plates. Stephen Werner. LC 93-83303. (Illus.). 174p. 1993. lib. bdg. 34.95 (*0-917786-96-3*) Summa Pubns.

***Blueprint No. 3: Msrng. Sustaining Development.** David Pearce. 1993. 15.95 (*1-85383-183-2*, Pub. by Erthscan Pubns UK) Island Pr.

***Blueprint No. 4: Sustaining Earth.** David Pearce & Edward Barbier. 1995. 15.95 (*1-85383-184-0*, Pub. by Erthscan Pubns UK) Island Pr.

Blueprint for a Democratic Education. Jonathan Kozol. 224p. 1992. 17.00 (*0-517-59161-8*, Crown) Crown Pub Group.

Blueprint for a Green Planet. John Seymour & Herbert Girardet. 1987. 25.95 (*0-317-56562-1*) P-H.

***Blueprint for a Green School.** Jayni Chase. LC 94-36126. (Leadership Policy Research Ser.). (Illus.). 688p. 1995. 59.95x (*0-590-49830-4*) Scholastic Inc.

Blueprint for a Longitudinal Study of Adolescent Boys. Jerald G. Bachman et al. LC 72-610663. (Michigan University Survey Research Center Youth in Transition Ser.: Vol. 1). 285p. reprint ed. pap. 81.30 (*0-8357-7332-9*, 2005413) Bks Demand.

Blueprint for a New Japan: The Rethinking of a Nation. Ichiro Ozawa. Tr. by Louisa Rubinfein. 224p. 1994. 25.00 (*4-7700-1871-1*) Kodansha.

***Blueprint for a New Japan: The Rethinking of a Nation.** Ichiro Ozawa. Tr. by Louisa Rubenfein. 208p. Date not set. 10.00 (*4-7700-2034-1*) FS&G.

Blueprint for a Strike: A Fragmentary Capsule History of the Ironworkers & Other Unions at NASSCO; Excerpts from the photo-text installation, BLUEPRINT FOR A STRIKE, Good News at NASSCO, Labor Link TV 26A&B. Fred Lonidier. (Illus.). 32p. (Orig.). 1992. pap. 8.00 (*0-930495-16-0*) San Fran Art Inst.

Blueprint for a Terrorist. large type ed. Hardiman Scott. Orig. Title: Deadly Nature. 432p. 1987. 16.95 (*0-7089-1631-7*) Ulverscroft.

Blueprint for Action: Achieving Center-Based Change Through Staff Development. Paula J. Bloom et al. (Illus.). 300p. (Orig.). (C). 1991. pap. text ed. 28.95 (*0-9621894-2-1*) New Horzns Lake Forest.

Blueprint for Building Strong Faith. Kenneth Hagin, Jr. 1980. pap. 0.75 (*0-89276-704-9*) Hagin Ministries.

Blueprint for Community Emergency Management: Managing Emergency Operations. Lavalla et al. (Illus.). 600p. 35.00 (*0-913724-33-5*) Emerg Response Inst.

Blueprint for Developing Conversational Competence: A Planning-Instruction Model with Detailed Scenarios. Patrick Stone. LC 88-71410. 175p. (Orig.). (C). 1988. pap. text ed. 18.95 (*0-88200-164-7*) Alexander Graham.

Blueprint for Essay Writing & a Glossary of Usage. 2nd ed. Scheman & Groner. 1992. 17.00 (*0-536-58199-1*) Ginn Pr.

Blueprint for Fostering Infants, Children, & Youth in the 1990s. Comp. by National Commission of Family Foster Care Staff. 155p. 1991. pap. 14.95 (*0-87868-441-7*) Child Welfare.

Blueprint for Franchising a Business. Steven S. Raab & Gregory Matusky. LC 87-15932. 244p. 1987. text ed. 45.00 (*0-471-85617-7*) Wiley.

Blueprint for Fundraising. James C. O'Brien & Claire Drenowatz. (Illus.). 800p. 1991. student ed 295.00 (*0-9628823-0-5*) Money Magnet.

***Blueprint for Green Management: Creating Your Company's Own Environmental Action Plan.** Georg Winter. LC 94-32037. 1994. write for info. (*0-07-709015-2*) McGraw.

Blueprint for Health. Annabelle Lee-Warren. 1994. 18.95 (*0-8329-0509-7*) New Win Pub.

***Blueprint for Health.** Annabelle Lee-Warren & Jo Willard. LC 95-14339. 1995. pap. write for info. (*0-8329-0512-7*) New Win Pub.

Blueprint for Humanity: Paul Tillich's Theology of Culture. Raymond F. Bulman. 248p. 36.50 (*0-8387-5000-1*) Bucknell U Pr.

***Blueprint for Immortality.** Burr. 1995. pap. 12.50 (*0-85435-281-3*) Atrium Pubs.

Blueprint for Immortality. 5th ed. Harold S. Burr. 192p. pap. 18.95 (*0-8464-4205-1*) Beekman Pubs.

Blueprint for Judicial Reform. Ed. by Patrick B. McGuigan & Randall R. Rader. LC 81-70375. (Orig.). 1981. pap. text ed. 27.25 (*0-942522-08-7*) Free Congr Res.

Blueprint for Larceny. Peter Chester. (Black Dagger Crime Ser.). 176p. 1992. reprint ed. 16.50 (*0-86220-826-2*, Black Dagger) Chivers N Amer.

Blueprint for Life. Casey Treat. 1989. pap. 5.95 (*0-89274-492-8*) Harrison Hse.

Blueprint for Modern America: Non-Military Legislation of the First Civil War Congress. Leonard P. Curry. LC 68-10827. 312p. reprint ed. pap. 89.00 (*0-8357-3252-5*, 2039473) Bks Demand.

Blueprint for Our Future: Creating Jobs, Preserving the Environment. East End Economic & Environmental Task Force Staff. Ed. by Tom Twomey. LC 93-51076. (Illus.). 192p. 1994. pap. 14.95 (*1-55704-202-0*) Newmarket.

Blueprint for Plastics Recycling. (Illus.). 39p. (Orig.). (C). 1993. pap. text ed. 20.00 (*1-56806-426-8*) Diane Pub.

Blueprint for Progress. Al-Anon Family Group Headquarters, Inc. Staff. 60p. 1987. 2.50 (*0-910034-59-1*) Al-Anon.

Blueprint for Quality: How Training Can Turn Strategy into Real Improvement. Ted Cocheu. LC 94-16214. (Management Ser.). 1994. 29.95 (*0-7879-0021-4*) Jossey-Bass.

***Blueprint for Reading the Machine Trades.** 2nd ed. Wilfred B. Pouler. LC 94-25405. (Illus.). 416p. 1995. 24.95 (*0-8273-6651-5*) Delmar.

Blueprint for Restructuring America's Financial Institutions: Report of a Task Force. 48p. 1989. pap. 5.95 (*0-8157-5275-X*) Brookings.

Blueprint for Scandal: The Engineering Business in New Jersey. John Kolesar et al. 1973. 15.00 (*0-943136-02-4*) Ctr Analysis Public Issues.

Blueprint for Space: Science Fiction to Science Fact. Ed. by Frederick I. Ordway, III & Randy Lieberman. LC 91-3160. (Illus.). 320p. (C). 1992. text ed. 60.00 (*1-56098-072-9*); pap. text ed. 24.95 (*1-56098-073-7*) Smithsonian.

Blueprint for Success: An In-Depth Analysis of NCAA Division III Athletics & Why It Should Be the Model for Intercollegiate Reform. David F. Salter. LC 93-77935. 156p. 1993. pap. 14.95 (*0-9636680-0-5*) F Merrick Pub.

Blueprint for Success: The Complete Guide to Starting a Business after Fifty. Albert Myers. 1990. pap. 12.95 (*0-87877-166-2*) Newcastle Pub.

Blueprint for the Environment: A Plan for Federal Action & Advice to President Bush from America's Environmental Community. Ed. by T. Allan Comp. 352p. (Orig.). 1989. pap. 13.95 (*0-935704-50-7*, 89-80293) Howe Brothers.

Blueprint for the Future: Final Report of Trends & Issues for the 1990s. (Illus.). 52p. (Orig.). (C). 1993. pap. text ed. 20.00 (*1-56806-818-2*) Diane Pub.

***Blueprint for Writing.** Rachel F. Ballon. 240p. 1995. pap. 15.00 (*1-56565-216-9*) Lowell Hse.

Blueprint for Writing. 2nd ed. Thelma Goodman. 1990. pap. 24.20 (*0-536-57773-0*) Ginn Pr.

Blueprint for Writing: A Writer's Guide to Creativity, Craft & Career. Rachel F. Ballon. LC 93-45926. 204p. 1994. 21.95 (*1-56565-125-1*) Lowell Hse.

Blueprint Machine Operator. Jack Rudman. (Career Examination Ser.: C-1136). 1994. pap. 23.95 (*0-8373-1136-5*) Nat Learn.

Blueprint of His Dissent: Madness & Method in Tennyson's Poetry. Roger S. Platizky. LC 87-46433. 144p. 1989. 28.50 (*0-8387-5151-2*) Bucknell U Pr.

Blueprint of the Plant: A Laboratory Manual of Botany. 2nd ed. Winifred Trakimas et al. 178p. pap. text ed. write for info. (*0-8087-3614-0*) Burgess MN Intl.

Blueprint Reading. Richard Hunter. (Series 907). (Orig.). 1984. student ed, pap. 8.00 (*0-8064-0381-0*, 907); audio 359.00 (*0-8064-0382-9*) Bergwall.

Blueprint Reading & Sketching. 1991. lib. bdg. 250.00 (*0-8490-5044-8*) Gordon Pr.

Blueprint Reading & Sketching. (Illus.). 223p. 1990. per., pap. 12.00 (*0-16-002092-1*, S/N 008-047-003) USGPO.

Blueprint Reading & Sketching for Carpenters: Residential. Leo McDonnell & John Ball. LC 80-66027. (Blueprint Reading Ser.). (Illus.). 151p. (C). 1981. teacher ed 12.00 (*0-8273-1355-1*); pap. text ed. 22.50 (*0-8273-1354-3*) Delmar.

Blueprint Reading & Technical Sketching for Industry. Thomas P. Olivo & C. Thomas Olivo. LC 83-26174. 464p. (C). 1985. teacher ed 12.00 (*0-8273-2206-2*); pap. text ed. 33.95 (*0-8273-2205-4*) Delmar.

Blueprint Reading & Technical Sketching for Industry. 2nd ed. C. Thomas Olivo & Associates Staff & Thomas P. Olivo. 464p. 1992. pap. 33.95 (*0-8273-5077-5*) Delmar.

Blueprint Reading & Technical Sketching for Industry: Instructor's Guide. 2nd ed. Thomas P. Olivo. 1992. 12.00 (*0-8273-5078-3*) Delmar.

Blueprint Reading Basics. Warren Hammer. (Illus.). 256p. 1989. pap. 19.95 (*0-8311-1186-0*) Indus Pr.

***Blueprint Reading Basics.** 2nd ed. Warren Hammer. (Illus.). 300p. (C). 1995. pap. 24.95 (*0-8311-3062-8*) Indus Pr.

Blueprint Reading for Commercial Construction. Charles D. Willis. LC 77-87887. (C). 1979. pap. 23.95 (*0-8273-1654-2*) Delmar.

Blueprint Reading for Construction. Walter C. Brown. 244p. (Orig.). 1990. text ed. 31.60 (*0-87006-825-3*) Goodheart.

***Blueprint Reading for Heating, Ventilating & Air Conditioning.** Frank C. Miller & Wilma B. Miller. LC 95-1920. 1995. teacher ed, text ed. write for info. (*0-8273-6872-0*) Delmar.

Blueprint Reading for Machinists. 4th ed. David L. Taylor. LC 85-6890. 224p. (C). 1985. teacher ed 10.00 (*0-8273-1088-9*); pap. text ed. 22.95 (*0-8273-1087-0*) Delmar.

Blueprint Reading for Machinists - Intermediate. 4th ed. LC 75-138355. 125p. 1984. teacher ed 10.00 (*0-8273-1086-2*) Delmar.

Blueprint Reading for Machinists - Intermediate. 4th ed. LC 75-138355. 125p. 1984. 21.50 (*0-8273-1085-4*) Delmar.

Blueprint Reading for Machinists - Intermediate. 5th ed. David L. Taylor. 145p. 1992. teacher ed 10.00 (*0-8273-4733-2*); pap. text ed. 22.50 (*0-8273-4732-4*) Delmar.

Blueprint Reading for Plumbers: Residential & Commercial. rev. ed. Bartholomew D'Arcangelo et al. (Blueprint Reading Ser.). 1989. teacher ed 12.00 (*0-8273-3460-5*) Delmar.

Blueprint Reading for Plumbers: Residential & Commercial. 5th rev. ed. Bartholomew D'Arcangelo et al. (Blueprint Reading Ser.). 1989. pap. text ed. 23.95 (*0-8273-3459-1*) Delmar.

Blueprint Reading for the Building Trades. John E. Traister. LC 85-19455. 192p. 1985. reprint ed. pap. 11.25 (*0-934041-05-9*) Craftsman.

Blueprint Reading for the Construction Trades. Peter A. Mann. (C). 1984. text ed. write for info. (*0-318-57574-4*, Reston) P-H.

Blueprint Reading for the Construction Trades. 2nd ed. Herbert F. Bellis & Walter A. Schmidt. (Illus.). 1978. text ed. 35.95 (*0-07-004410-4*) McGraw.

Blueprint Reading for the Machine Trades. Thomas Vanderloop. (C). 1982. pap. text ed. 26.67 (*0-8359-0515-2*, Reston); write for info. (*0-8359-0516-0*, Reston) P-H.

***Blueprint Reading for the Machine Trades.** 3rd ed. Russ Schultz. LC 95-13273. 1995. pap. text ed. 36.00 (*0-13-287541-1*) P-H.

Blueprint Reading for Welders. 4th ed. A. E. Bennett & L. Siy. 1988. teacher ed 14.00 (*0-8273-2998-9*); text ed. 22.95 (*0-8273-2997-0*) Delmar.

Blueprint Reading for Welders. 5th ed. A. E. Bennett & Louis J. Siy. Ed. by Thomas J. Robin. LC 92-28911. 340p. 1993. pap. text ed. 22.95 (*0-8273-5579-3*) Delmar.

Blueprint Reading for Welders: Instructor's Guide. 5th ed. A. E. Bennett & Louis J. Sly. 152p. 1993. 16.00 (*0-8273-5580-7*) Delmar.

Blueprint Reading Made Easy. Stanley H. Aglow. Ed. by Joanna Turpin. LC 92-24333. (Illus.). 133p. (C). 1992. 27.95 (*0-912524-71-5*) Busn News.

Blueprint to Bluewater. Satyindra Singh. (C). 1992. 52.00 (*81-7062-148-8*, Pub. by Lancer II) S Asia.

Blueprint Your Destiny. Ron Kurz. 12p. (Orig.). (C). 1986. pap. 2.95 (*0-939829-01-0*) R Kurz.

Blueprinter. Jack Rudman. (Career Examination Ser.: C-1621). 1994. pap. 23.95 (*0-8373-1621-9*) Nat Learn.

Blueprinting. Lande. Date not set. pap. 49.95 (*0-06-251049-5*, PL) HarpC.

Blueprints: A Problem Notebook to Accompany Essentials of Managerial Finance. 10th ed. J. Fred Weston & Eugene F. Brigham. 248p. (C). 1993. teacher ed, pap. text ed. 8.00 (*0-03-092973-3*) Dryden Pr.

Blueprints: Solving the Mystery of Evolution. Maitland A. Edey. Ed. by Donald C. Johanson. (Illus.). 456p. 1989. 19.95 (*0-316-21076-5*) Little.

Blueprints: Solving the Mystery of Evolution. Maitland A. Edey & Donald C. Johanson. (Illus.). 432p. 1990. pap. 14.95 (*0-14-013265-1*, Penguin Bks) Viking Penguin.

Blueprints & Blood: The Stalinization of Soviet Architecture, 1917-1937. Hugh D. Hudson, Jr. LC 93-17638. (Illus.). 280p. 1994. text ed. 35.00 (*0-691-03349-8*) Princeton U Pr.

Blueprints Five-Seven Science: Teacher's Resource. R. Whiteford & J. Fitzsimmons. (C). 1990. 80.00 (*0-7487-0430-2*, Pub. by S Thornes Pubs UK); 130.00 (*0-7487-0431-0*, Pub. by S Thornes Pubs UK) St Mut.

Blueprints for a Black Federal Theatre, 1935-1939. Rena Fraden. LC 93-31189. (Studies in American Literature & Culture: No. 80). (Illus.). 272p. (C). 1994. 54.95 (*0-521-44359-8*) Cambridge U Pr.

Blueprints for America's Past. Ed. by Lisa C. Mullins. (Architectural Treasures of Early America Ser.). (Illus.). 224p. 1988. 19.95 (*0-918678-33-1*) Natl Hist Soc.

Blueprints for Basic Tax Reform. 2nd rev. ed. U. S. Treasury Tax Policy Staff & David F. Bradford. 194p. 1984. pap. text ed. 34.95 (*0-918255-00-7*) Tax Analysts.

Blueprints for Continuous Improvement: Lessons from the Baldrige Winners. Richard M. Hodgetts. LC 93-5166. (AMA Management Briefing Ser.). 1993. 12.50 (*0-8144-2352-3*) AMACOM.

Blueprints for Exchange Rate Management. Ed. by Marcus Miller et al. 329p. 1989. text ed. 80.00 (*0-12-497060-5*) Acad Pr.

Blueprints for Exchange Rate Management. Marcus Miller et al. (Illus.). 329p. 1991. pap. text ed. 44.00 (*0-12-497061-3*) Acad Pr.

Blueprints for Life. Ed. by Roberta Conian. LC 93-21603. (Journey Through the Mind & Body Ser.). (Illus.). 144p. 1993. 14.99 (*0-7835-1004-7*); lib. bdg. 16.99 (*0-7835-1005-5*) Time-Life.

Blueprints for Memory: Your Guide to Remembering Business Facts, Figures & Faces. William D. Hersey. 170p. 1991. 14.95 (*0-8144-7757-7*) AMACOM.

***Blueprints for Service Quality: The Federal Express Approach.** 2nd ed. American Management Association, AMA Membership, Publications Division Staff. LC 94-25323. (Management Briefing Ser.). 1994. write for info. (*0-8144-2356-6*) AMACOM.

Blueprints for Successful Teaching, Pt. One: Setting the Stage for Instruction. Tom Contine. 103p. 1994. teacher ed 25.00 (*1-878276-47-6*) Educ Systs Assocs Inc.

Blueprints for Successful Teaching, Pt. Two: Elements of Effective Instruction. Tom Contine. 96p. 1994. teacher ed 25.00 (*1-878276-48-4*) Educ Systs Assocs Inc.

Blueprints for Thinking: The Role of Planning in Cognitive Development. Ed. by Sarah L. Friedman et al. (Illus.). 512p. 1987. 89.95 (*0-521-25605-4*) Cambridge U Pr.

Blueprints for Thinking in the Cooperative Classroom. 2nd ed. James Bellanca & Robin Fogarty. (Illus.). 384p. (J). (gr. k-12). 1990. reprint ed. pap. text ed. 45.00 (*0-932935-30-3*) IRI-Skylght.

Blueprints for Worship: A User's Guide for United Methodist Congregations. Andy Langford. LC 92-41992. 96p. (Orig.). 1993. pap. 9.95 (*0-687-03312-8*) Abingdon.

***Blueprints on Fabric: Innovative Uses for Cyanotype.** Barbara Hewitt. 96p. (Orig.). 1995. pap. 12.95 (*0-934026-91-2*) Interweave.

Blueprints Seven-Eleven Science: Teacher's Resource. J. Fitzsimmons & R. Whiteford. (C). 1990. 100.00 (*0-685-39379-8*, Pub. by S Thornes Pubs UK); 130.00 (*0-685-39380-1*, Pub. by S Thornes Pubs UK) St Mut.

Blues. John R. Hersey. (Illus.). 1987. 16.95 (*0-394-55960-6*) Knopf.

Blues. Comp. by Jerry Silverman. (Traditional Black Music Ser.). (Illus.). 80p. (YA). (gr. 5 up). 1992. lib. bdg. 15.95 (*0-7910-1830-X*, Am Art Analog) Chelsea Hse.

Blues. John Hersey. LC 87-45942. 224p. 1988. reprint ed. pap. 10.00 (*0-394-75702-5*, Vin) Random.

Blues: A Bibliographic Guide. Mary L. Hart et al. LC 89-34943. (Music Research & Information Guides Ser.: Vol. 7). 656p. 1989. 76.00 (*0-8240-8506-X*, H703) Garland.

Blues: An Anthology. Ed. by W. C. Handy. (Roots of Jazz Ser.). 224p. 1985. reprint ed. lib. bdg. 37.50 (*0-306-76244-7*) Da Capo.

Blues: An Anthology. W. C. Handy. (Quality Paperbacks Ser.). (Illus.). 228p. 1990. reprint ed. pap. 14.95 (*0-306-80411-5*) Da Capo.

Blues: An Ensemble Play in One Act. Jerome McDonough. 28p. (Orig.). 1990. pap. 3.50 (*0-88680-323-3*) I E Clark.

Blues: The Story Always Untold. Sterling Plumpp. LC 88-71680. 140p. (Orig.). 1989. pap. 9.50 (*0-9614644-8-8*) Another Chicago Pr.

Blues Ain't Nothing but a Good Soul Feeling Bad: Daily Steps to Spiritual Growth. Sheldon B. Kopp. (Fireside - Parkside Meditation Book Ser.). 384p. 1992. pap. 9.00 (*0-671-76838-7*, Fireside) S&S Trade.

Blues & Ballads. Robert Allen. LC 75-302484. 103p. 1974. 3.95 (*0-87886-047-9*, Greenfld Rev Pr) Greenfld Rev Lit.

Blues & Evil. Jon M. Spencer. LC 92-33008. (Illus.). 208p. (Orig.). (C). 1993. lib. bdg. 31.00x (*0-87049-782-0*); pap. 18.95 (*0-87049-783-9*) U of Tenn Pr.

Blues & Rags. James Drew. (Illus.). 13p. 1989. 3.50 (*0-9625023-0-8*) Art Pr Intl.

Blues & Rock Harmonica. Glenn Weiser. 96p. 1990. audio, pap. text ed. 16.95 (*0-931759-41-2*) Centerstream Pub.

Blues & Rock Harmonica Made Easy! Everything You Need to Know. David Harp. 1993. pap. 4.95 (*0-918321-85-9*); pap. 9.95 (*0-918321-86-7*) Musical Idiot.

Blues & Roots Rue & Bluets: A Garland for the Southern Appalachians. 2nd rev. ed. Jonathan Williams. LC 84-21126. (Illus.). 112p. 1985. 31.95 (*0-8223-0614-X*); pap. 14.95 (*0-8223-0615-8*) Duke.

Blues & the Poetic Spirit. Paul Garon. LC 78-2025. (Roots of Jazz Ser.). (Illus.). 1978. reprint ed. lib. bdg. 25.00 (*0-306-77542-5*); reprint ed. pap. 7.95 (*0-306-80108-6*) Da Capo.

Blues Band Rhythm Guitar. Larry McCabe. 1993. 15.00 (*1-56222-566-9*, 94825); audio 9.98 (*1-56222-795-5*, 94825) Mel Bay.

Blue's Bastards: A True Story of Valor under Fire. Randy Herrod. LC 89-37363. 215p. 1989. 17.95 (*0-89526-549-4*) Regnery Pub.

Blues Before Dawn. Shane Harrison. 153p. (Orig.). 1992. pap. 10.95 (*1-85371-174-8*, Pub. by Poolbeg Pr IE) Dufour.

***Blues Blood: New & Selected Poems.** Robert E. Price. LC 94-72477. 83p. (Orig.). 1994. pap. 12.00 (*0-9642183-0-5*) CAC Press.

Blues Boogie & Barrelhouse Piano Workbook. Aaron Blumenfeld. 1993. pap. 19.95 (*0-943748-56-9*) Ekay Music.

Blues, Boogie & Rock Guitar. Date not set. 8.95 (*0-87166-968-4*, 93996) Mel Bay.

Blues, Boogie & Rock Guitar. Larry McCabe. 1993. 8.95 (*0-685-63953-3*, 93996); audio 9.98 (*1-56222-614-2*, 93996) Mel Bay.

Blues Classic Songbook. Date not set. 12.95 (*1-56222-419-0*, 94746) Mel Bay.

B

An Asterisk (*) at the beginning of an entry indicates that the title is appearing in BIP for the first time. 827

Blues Deluxe: A Tragicomic Love Story. Harvey Griffin. LC 93-81145. 240p. 1994. 15.00 (*1-56352-131-8*) Longstreet Pr Inc.

***Blues Detective: A Study of African American Detective Fiction.** Stephen Soitos. 1996. pap. 15.95 (*0-87023-996-1*) U of Mass Pr.

***Blues Detective: A Study of African American Detective Fiction.** Stephen Soitos. 256p. (C). 1996. text ed. 40.00 (*0-87023-995-3*) U of Mass Pr.

Blues et Gospels: Album Photographique. Marguerite Yourcenar. 192p. (FRE.). 1984. 125.00 (*0-7859-0550-2*, 207011077X) Fr & Eur.

Blues Fell This Morning: Meaning in the Blues. 2nd ed. Frwd. by Paul Oliver & Richard Wright. (Canto Bk.). (Illus.). 372p. (C). 1994. pap. 11.95 (*0-521-47738-7*) Cambridge U Pr.

Blues Fiddle. Julie L. Lieberman. (Illus.). 112p. pap. 14.95 (*0-8256-0308-0*, OK64162, Oak) Music Sales.

Blues Fiddling Classics. Date not set. 7.95 (*1-56222-996-6*, 95159); audio 9.98 (*0-7866-0051-9*, 95159C) Mel Bay.

Blues for a Black Cat & Other Stories. Boris Vian. Ed. & Tr. by Julia Older. LC 91-34866. (French Modernist Library). xxvi, 118p. 1992. 19.95 (*0-8032-4661-7*) U of Nebr Pr.

Blues for a Lost Childhood. Antonio Torres. Tr. by John Parker. LC 89-61872. (Readers International Ser.). 200p. (Orig.). 1989. 17.95 (*0-930523-67-9*); pap. 9.95 (*0-930523-68-7*) Readers Intl.

***Blues for Mister Charlie: A Play.** James Baldwin. LC 94-23842. 1995. pap. 10.00 (*0-679-76178-0*, Vin) Random.

Blues for Mr. Baldwin. William Mitchum. (Illus.). 134p. (Orig.). 1985. 9.95 (*0-9612120-2-0*); pap. 5.95 (*0-9612120-3-9*) Para-Bk-Pr.

***Blues for Port City.** David Lunde. 24p. (Orig.). 1995. pap. 5.00x (*0-932412-07-6*) Mayapple Pr.

Blues for Rita. 2nd ed. Lonnie Sherman. Ed. by Rick Lopez. (Kangaroo Court Ser.: No. 2). (Illus.). 12p. 1986. 2.00 (*0-940381-01-X*) Kangaroo Ct Pub.

Blues for the Berkeley Inn. Julia Vinograd. (Illus.). 60p. (Orig.). 1991. pap. 4.95 (*0-929730-33-X*) Zeitgeist Pr.

Blues for the Prince. Bart Spicer. (C). 1989. 35.00 (*0-948353-46-5*, Pub. by Oldcastle Bks UK) St Mut.

Blues for Tom McGrath. Dale Jacobson. (Orig.). 1992. pap. text ed. 2.50 (*1-882191-01-3*) Spirit Horse Pr.

Blues from the Delta. William Ferris. (Quality Paperbacks Ser.). (Illus.). 226p. 1988. pap. 11.95 (*0-306-80327-5*) Da Capo.

Blues from the Delta. Intro. by William Ferris & Billy Taylor. LC 83-18916. (Roots of Jazz Ser.). (Illus.). iii, 247p. 1984. reprint ed. lib. bdg. 27.50 (*0-306-76215-3*) Da Capo.

Blues Guitar: An Introduction to Acoustic Blues Guitar. Kenny Sultan. 76p. 1991. audio, pap. text ed. 15.95 (*0-931759-57-9*) Centerstream Pub.

Blues Guitar: The Men Who Made the Music. Jas Obrecht. 1991. pap. 19.95 (*0-7935-0074-5*, HL00183632) H Leonard.

Blues Guitar: The Men Who Made the Music. 2nd ed. Ed. by Jas Obrecht. (Illus.). 256p. 1993. pap. 19.95 (*0-87930-292-5*) Miller Freeman.

Blues Guitar Inside & Out. Richard Daniels. (Illus.). (Orig.). 1982. pap. 14.95 (*0-89524-148-X*) Cherry Lane.

Blues Guitar Songbook. Date not set. 12.95 (*0-7866-0035-7*, 95064) Mel Bay.

Blues Guitar Styles. William Bay. 1993. 3.95 (*0-87166-368-6*, 93291) Mel Bay.

Blues Hanon. Leo Alfassy. 1980. pap. 7.95 (*0-8256-2224-7*) Music Sales.

Blues Harmonica: A Crash Course & Overview. Tom Ball. (Illus.). 72p. (Orig.). 1993. pap. text ed. 16.95 (*0-931759-72-2*) Centerstream Pub.

Blues Harmonica Starter Kit. Date not set. 19.95 (*1-56222-460-3*, 94574BW) Mel Bay.

Blues Harp. Phil Duncan. 1993. 7.95 (*0-87166-890-4*, 93814); audio 9.98 (*1-56222-355-0*, 93814) Mel Bay.

Blues Harp. Tony Glover. (Illus.). (Orig.). 1973. pap. 11.95 (*0-8256-0018-9*, 000018, Oak) Music Sales.

Blues Harp Songbook. Tony Glover. (Illus.). audio, pap. 11.95 (*0-8256-0157-6*, Oak) Music Sales.

Blues, Ideology & Afro-American Literature: A Vernacular Theory. Houston A. Baker, Jr. LC 84-2655. (Illus.). 288p. 1987. pap. text ed. 12.95 (*0-226-03538-7*) U Ch Pr.

Blues If You Want. William Matthews. 72p. 1989. pap. 9.95 (*0-395-51756-7*) HM.

Blues in the Night. Elizabeth Jordan. 384p. 1987. pap. 3.95 (*0-449-13289-7*, GM) Fawcett.

Blues JamTrax. Ralph Agresta. (JamTrax Ser.). (Illus.). 1991. pap. 11.95 (*0-8256-2583-1*, AM75888) Music Sales.

Blues JamTrax for Keyboard. Ralph Agresta. (Illus.). 1993. pap. 11.95 (*0-8256-1354-X*) Music Sales.

Blues Journeys Home. Houston A. Baker. LC 85-80142. (Illus.). 59p. (Orig.). (YA). (gr. 7-12). 1985. per., pap. 5.00 (*0-916418-61-8*) Lotus.

Blues Lead Guitar Method. Steve Griffin. 1993. 3.95 (*0-87166-611-1*, 93390); audio 12.95 (*0-87166-625-1*, 93390); audio 9.98 (*0-87166-624-3*, 93390) Mel Bay.

***Blues Legends.** Charles K. Cowdery. LC 95-13142. (Illus.). 96p. 1995. cd-rom, 3.5 hd 19.95 (*0-87905-688-6*) Gibbs Smith Pub.

Blues Line: A Collection of Blues Lyrics from Leadbelly to Muddy Waters. Illus. by Jonathan Shahn. LC 92-46336. 1993. reprint ed. pap. 14.95 (*0-88001-328-1*) Ecco Pr.

Blues Lyric Poetry: An Anthology. Michael Taft. LC 82-48266. 487p. 1983. lib. bdg. 50.00 (*0-8240-9235-X*) Garland.

Blues Makers. Samuel Charters. (Quality Paperbacks Ser.). (Illus.). 416p. (Orig.). 1991. pap. 16.95 (*0-306-80438-7*) Da Capo.

Blues of a Lifetime: The Autobiography of Cornell Woolrich. Ed. by Mark Bassett. LC 91-73287. 152p. (C). 1991. lib. bdg. 39.95 (*0-87972-535-4*); pap. text ed. 15.95 (*0-87972-536-2*) Bowling Green Univ.

Blues of the Egyptian Kings. Jim Brodey. (Orig.). 1976. 4.00 (*0-929844-10-6*) Big Sky Bolinas.

Blues of the Sky: Interpreted from the Original Hebrew Book of Psalms. David Rosenberg. LC 76-991. 53p. 1976. 15.00 (*0-89366-241-0*) Ultramarine Pub.

Blues off the Record: Thirty Years of Blues Commentary. Paul Oliver. (Quality Paperbacks Ser.). (Illus.). 1988. reprint ed. pap. 13.95 (*0-306-80321-6*) Da Capo.

Blues on CD: The Essential Guide. Charles S. Murray. 432p. 1993. pap. 22.95 (*1-85626-084-4*) Trafalgar.

***Blues on the Run: Haiku, Senryu, Sketches.** Francine Porad. (Illus.). 28p. (Orig.). (C). 1988. pap. text ed. 5.00 (*0-9618009-3-3*) Vandina Pr.

Blues People: Negro Music in White America. Leroi Jones, pseud. 1971. pap. 10.00 (*0-688-18474-X*, Quill) Morrow.

Blues People: Negro Music in White America. Imamu A. Baraka. LC 80-15648. xii, 244p. 1980. reprint ed. text ed. 49.50 (*0-313-22519-2*, JOBP, Greenwood Pr) Greenwood.

Blues Piano Styles. Matt Dennis. 1993. 3.95 (*0-87166-819-X*, 93331) Mel Bay.

Blues Picture Chords & How to Use Them. Happy Taum. (Picture Chords Library: EFS186). (Illus.). 32p. 1978. pap. 6.95 (*0-8256-2186-0*, AM21676) Music Sales.

Blues Project. Jared Carter. (City Ser.). 32p. 1991. pap. 3.00 (*1-880649-27-6*) Writ Ctr Pr.

***Blues Records: 1943-1970, Vol. 2 (L-Z)** Comp. by Mike Leadbitter et al. 810p. 1995. 115.00 (*0-907872-25-5*) Big Nickel.

Blues Riffs for Guitar. Mark Michaels. (Illus.). 48p. 1978. pap. 9.95 (*0-8256-2203-4*, AM23532) Music Sales.

Blues Riffs for Guitar Two. Jesse Gress. (Illus.). 64p. 1989. pap. 12.95 (*0-8256-2542-4*, AM71283) Music Sales.

Blues-Rock Guitar Handbook. Mark Loneregan. 1993. 4.95 (*0-87166-405-4*, 94172); audio 13.95 (*0-87166-407-0*, 94172); audio 9.98 (*0-87166-406-2*, 94172) Mel Bay.

Blues Saraceno - Never Look Back: Guitar - Vocal. Ed. by John Chappell & Mark Phillips. (Illus.). 92p. (Orig.). 1990. pap. text ed. 16.95 (*0-89524-454-3*) Cherry Lane.

Blues Solos for Acoustic Guitar. Johnny Norris. (Illus.). 1993. pap. 15.95 (*0-7119-2789-8*) Music Sales.

Blues Who's Who. Sheldon Harris. LC 81-7873. (Quality Paperbacks Ser.). (Illus.). 775p. 1981. reprint ed. pap. 32.50 (*0-306-80155-8*) Da Capo.

Blueschild Baby. George Cain. 1994. pap. 10.00 (*0-88001-349-4*) Ecco Pr.

Blueschists & Eclogites. Ed. by B. W. Evans & E. H. Brown. (Memoir Ser.: No. 164). (Illus.). 432p. 1986. 20.00 (*0-8137-1164-9*) Geol Soc.

Blueshirts. 2nd ed. Maurice Manning. (Illus.). 276p. 1987. reprint ed. pap. 21.95 (*0-7171-1515-1*, Pub. by Gill & MacMill IE) Irish Bks Media.

Bluesman: A Novel. Andre Dubus, III. 276p. 1993. 22.95 (*0-571-19812-0*) Faber & Faber.

Bluesman: A Novel. Andre Dubus, III. 276p. 1994. pap. 12.95 (*0-571-19841-4*) Faber & Faber.

Bluesman: The Musical Heritage of Black Men & Women in the Americas. Julio Finn. LC 91-25984. (Illus.). 272p. 1992. 29.95 (*0-940793-98-9*); pap. 14.95 (*0-940793-91-1*) Interlink Pub.

Bluest Eye. Aft. by Toni Morrison. LC 94-14448. 1994. pap. 9.95 (*0-452-27305-6*, Plume) NAL-Dutton.

Bluest Eye: A Novel. Toni Morrison. LC 93-43124. 1993. 22.00 (*0-679-43373-2*) Knopf.

Bluestocking. David Delman. 320p. 1994. 22.95 (*0-312-10432-4*, Pub. by Thomas Dunne Bks) St Martin.

Bluestocking Bride. Elizabeth Thornton. 1990. pap. 2.95 (*0-8217-2904-7*) Zebra.

Bluestocking Circle: Women, Friendship, & the Life of the Mind in Eighteenth-Century England. Sylvia H. Myers. (Illus.). 360p. 1990. 69.00 (*0-19-811767-1*) OUP.

Bluestones & Salt Hay: An Anthology of New Jersey Poets. Ed. by Loel Lewis. LC 89-36067. 210p. (Orig.). 1990. text ed. 35.00 (*0-8135-1485-1*); pap. 11.95 (*0-8135-1486-X*) Rutgers U Pr.

Bluestown Mockingbird Mambo. Sandra M. Esteves. 64p. (Orig.). 1990. 7.00 (*1-55885-017-1*) Arte Publico.

Bluetenanalysen Neuer Orchideen, 4 pts. in 1. R. Schlecter & S. Mansfield. (Feddes Beiheft Ser.: Nos. 58, 59, 68 & 74). (Illus.). 35p. (GER.). 1979. reprint ed. text ed. 114.00 (*3-87429-051-4*) Koeltz Sci Bks.

Bluetentragende Spross-Systeme Einiger Chenopodiaceae. K. Urmi-Koenig. (Dissertationes Botanicae Ser.: No. 63). (Illus.). 240p. 1981. pap. text ed. 30.00 (*3-7682-1322-6*) Lubrecht & Cramer.

Bluetezeit der Deutsche Hanse: Hansische Geschichte von der Zweiten Haelfte des XIV bis zum Cetzten Viertel des XV Jahrhunderts, 2 vols., Set. E. Daenell. 1035p. (C). 1973. reprint ed. 280.75 (*3-11-004562-1*) De Gruyter.

Bluethendiagramme, 2 vols., Set. A. E. Eichler. (Illus.). xxviii, 922p. 1974. reprint ed. 148.00 (*3-87429-003-4*) Koeltz Sci Bks.

Bluetongue Virus see African Swine Fever Virus

Bluetongue Viruses. Ed. by P. Roy & B. M. Gorman. (Current Topics in Microbiology & Immunology Ser.: Vol. 162). (Illus.). 192p. 1990. 95.00 (*0-387-51922-X*) Spr-Verlag.

Bluett: Local Government Handbook: New South Wales. 11th ed. Eric B. Stuckey. viii, 256p. 1987. pap. 28.00 (*0-455-20740-2*, Pub. by Law Bk Co) W W Gaunt.

***Bluett Local Government Handbook (NSW)** 13th ed. Eric Stuckey. 411p. 1994. pap. 42.00 (*0-455-21265-1*, Pub. by Law Bk Co) W W Gaunt.

***Bluewater Fly Fishing.** Trey Combs. (Illus.). 256p. 1995. 60.00 (*1-55821-331-7*) Lyons & Burford.

***BlueWater Hunting & Freediving.** Terry Maas. LC 95-75143. 200p. 1995. 39.95 (*0-9644966-0-7*) BlueWtr Freedivers.

Bluewater Journal: The Voyage of the Sea Tiger. Loretta Krupinski. 32p. (J). 1995. 14.95 (*0-06-023436-9*) HarpC Child Bks.

Bluewater Journal: The Voyage of the Sea Tiger. Loretta Krupinski. (J). (gr. 1-4). 1995. lib. bdg. 14.89 (*0-06-023437-7*) HarpC Child Bks.

Bluewater Seamanship. S. W. Mort. (C). 1987. 42.00 (*0-85174-403-6*, Pub. by Brwn Son Ferg) St Mut.

***Bluff Beckons.** Mary R. Dees. Ed. by Lana Canon. 256p. (Orig.). 1995. pap. 11.95 (*0-9630600-3-1*) Marmor.

Bluff Body Aerodynamics & Its Application: Papers Presented at the International Colloquium, Kyoto, Japan, 17-20, Oct., 1988. Ed. by Masao Ito et al. 460p. 1990. 146.25 (*0-444-88381-9*) Elsevier.

Bluff-Body Wakes, Dynamics, & Instabilities: Proceedings of the International Union of Theoretical & Applied Mechanics Symposium, Gottingen, 1992. H. Eckelmann et al. LC 93-3704. (International Union of Theoretical & Applied Mechanics Symposia Ser.). 1993. 129.00 (*0-387-56594-9*) Spr-Verlag.

Bluff City Cooks. 3rd ed. Junior League of Greater Alton, Inc. Staff. (Illus.). 187p. reprint ed. 8.95 (*0-9615898-0-9*) Greater Alton Jr League.

Bluff View from the Twin Cities: Poems from the West Bank. Ron Weber. 64p. 1993. 14.95 (*0-937360-24-4*) Harbor Hse MI.

***Bluff Your Way in Baseball.** Jerry Bobrow. (Bluffers Ser.). 77p. (Orig.). 1995. pap. 3.95 (*1-57143-042-3*) RDR Bks.

Bluff Your Way in British Theatre. Fidelis Morgan. (Bluffers Ser.). 74p. (Orig.). 1993. pap. 3.95 (*1-57143-001-6*) RDR Bks.

***Bluff Your Way in Football.** Jerry Bobrow & Alan Gilreath. (Bluffers Ser.). 78p. (Orig.). 1995. pap. 3.95 (*1-57143-012-1*) RDR Bks.

Bluff Your Way in Gourmet Cooking. Joseph T. Straub. (Bluffers Ser.). 76p. (Orig.). 1993. pap. 3.95 (*1-57143-007-5*) RDR Bks.

***Bluff Your Way in Hollywood.** Virginia J. Nelson & Colin Clements. (Bluffers Ser.). 75p. (Orig.). 1993. pap. 3.95 (*1-57143-032-6*) RDR Bks.

***Bluff Your Way in Home Maintenance.** David L. Gale. (Bluffers Ser.). 78p. (Orig.). 1993. pap. 3.95 (*1-57143-027-X*) RDR Bks.

***Bluff Your Way in Japan.** Robert Ainsley. (Bluffers Ser.). 78p. (Orig.). 1993. pap. 3.95 (*1-57143-030-X*) RDR Bks.

Bluff Your Way in Management. Joseph T. Straub & John Courtis. (Bluffers Ser.). 75p. (Orig.). 1993. pap. 3.95 (*1-57143-003-2*) RDR Bks.

Bluff Your Way in Marketing. Joseph T. Straub et al. (Bluffers Ser.). 75p. (Orig.). 1993. pap. 3.95 (*1-57143-004-0*) RDR Bks.

Bluff Your Way in Math. Robert Ainsley. (Bluffers Ser.). 76p. (Orig.). 1993. pap. 3.95 (*1-57143-005-9*) RDR Bks.

Bluff Your Way in Music. Russell Robinson & Peter Gammond. (Bluffers Ser.). 77p. (Orig.). 1993. pap. 3.95 (*1-57143-006-7*) RDR Bks.

***Bluff Your Way in New York.** Ken Lawless & Nan Lawless. (Bluffers Ser.). 78p. (Orig.). 1993. pap. 3.95 (*1-57143-028-8*) RDR Bks.

***Bluff Your Way in Office Politics.** Joseph T. Straub. (Bluffers Ser.). 76p. (Orig.). 1993. pap. 3.95 (*1-57143-026-1*) RDR Bks.

***Bluff Your Way in Paris.** Jim Hankinson. (Buffers Ser.). 74p. (Orig.). 1993. pap. 3.95 (*1-57143-031-8*) RDR Bks.

Bluff Your Way in Philosophy. Jim Hankinson. (Bluffers Ser.). 74p. (Orig.). 1993. pap. 3.95 (*1-57143-008-3*) RDR Bks.

Bluff Your Way in Sex. Don Steel & Eve Steel. (Bluffers Ser.). 76p. (Orig.). 1993. pap. 3.95 (*1-57143-010-5*) RDR Bks.

***Bluff Your Way in the Deep South.** Mary E. Snodgrass. (Bluffers Ser.). 78p. (Orig.). 1993. pap. 3.95 (*1-57143-029-6*) RDR Bks.

Bluff Your Way in the Great Outdoors. Brock Fowler & Kate Fowler. (Bluffers Ser.). 77p. (Orig.). 1993. pap. 3.95 (*1-57143-002-4*) RDR Bks.

Bluff Your Way in the Occult. P. J. Owens & Alexander C. Rae. (Bluffers Ser.). 77p. (Orig.). 1993. pap. 3.95 (*1-57143-009-1*) RDR Bks.

Bluffers Guide to Bluffing. Mary E. Snodgrass & Peter Gammond. (Bluffers Ser.). 78p. (Orig.). 1993. pap. 3.95 (*1-57143-000-8*) RDR Bks.

Bluffer's Guide to Philosophy. T. V. Morris. LC 89-1414. 129p. 1989. pap. 6.95 (*0-912083-35-2*) Diamond Communications.

Blum & Blum. Andrew Dolcart & Susan Tunick. 1992. pap. 20.00 (*0-930829-19-0*) Lumen Inc.

Blume. (Meyers Kleine Kinderbibliothek Ser.). 1992. 13.25 (*3-411-08521-5*, Pub. by Bibliogr Inst Brockhaus GW) Langenscheidt.

Blumenfeld Gambit. J. Przewoznik & M. Pein. (PECH Pergamon Chess Ser.). 128p. 1991. write for info. (*0-08-037132-9*, 6201, Pub. by CHES UK); pap. 15.95 (*0-08-037133-7*, 6201, Pub. by CHES UK) Macmillan.

Blumhardt's Battle. 1970. reprint ed. pap. 2.50 (*0-913926-01-9*) T E Lowe.

Blumpoe Grumpoe Meets Arnold C, Vol. 1. Jean D. Okimoto. (J). (ps-3). 1990. 13.95 (*0-316-63811-0*, Joy St Bks) Little.

Blumroch l'Admirable ou le Dejeuner du Surhomme. Louis Pauwels. (FRE.). 1978. pap. 10.95 (*0-7859-4104-5*) Fr & Eur.

Blunder Book: Colossal Errors, Minor Mistakes, & Surprising Slip-ups That Have Changed the Course of History. M. Hirsh Goldberg. LC 84-4658. (Illus.). 272p. 1988. pap. 9.00 (*0-688-07757-9*, Quill) Morrow.

Blunder Years. Bill Myers & Robert West. LC 93-964. (Illus.). (J). 1993. 4.99 (*0-8423-4117-X*) Tyndale.

Blunderbuss. Rupendra G. Majumdar. (Writers Workshop Redbird Ser.). 1975. 8.00 (*0-88253-510-2*); pap. text ed. 4.80 (*0-88253-509-9*) Ind-US Inc.

Blundering to Glory: Napoleon's Military Campaigns. Owen Connelly. LC 87-9507. 250p. (C). 1987. 40.00 (*0-8420-2231-7*); pap. text ed. 14.95 (*0-8420-2375-5*) Scholarly Res Inc.

Blunders & Brilliancies. I. Mullen. 1989. pap. 9.95 (*0-08-037136-1*, Pergamon Pr) Elsevier.

Blunders in International Business. David A. Ricks. LC 92-33483. 192p. 1993. 16.95 (*1-55786-414-4*) Blackwell Pubs.

Blunt & Penetrating Trauma. Allan E. Fisch & Helen C. Redman. (Advanced Exercises in Diagnostic Radiology Ser.: Vol. 16). (Illus.). 256p. 1982. pap. text ed. 50.50 (*0-7216-3677-2*) Saunders.

Blunt Chest Trauma: General Principles of Management. Marvin M. Kirsh & Herbert Sloan. 1977. text ed. 30.00 (*0-316-49501-8*, Little Med Div) Little.

Blunt Darts. Jeremiah Healy. Ed. by Jane Chelius. 192p. 1991. reprint ed. mass mkt. 5.50 (*0-671-73742-2*) PB.

Blunt Instrument. Georgette Heyer. reprint ed. lib. bdg. 21.95 (*0-89190-640-1*, Rivercity Pr) Amereon Ltd.

Blunt Instrument. Georgette Heyer. 256p. 1987. reprint ed. pap. 4.50 (*0-425-09641-6*, Prime Crime) Berkley Pub.

Blunted Sword: The Erosion of Military Power in Modern World Politics. Evan Luard. 194p. (C). 1989. 25.00 (*0-941533-48-4*) New Amsterdam Bks.

Bluntschli Rituals of Craft Masonry As Worked in the Grand Lodge of the Sun Bayreuth, Germany. Tr. by Art DeHoyos. 1992. pap. 9.95 (*1-56459-269-3*) Kessinger Pub.

Blunty. Colin Smithson. (Illus.). 32p. (J). (ps-1). 1994. 15.95 (*1-85681-025-9*, Pub. by J MacRae UK) Trafalgar.

Blur. John M. Bennett & Byron Smith. (Illus.). vii, 20p. (Orig.). 1987. pap. 7.98 (*0-935350-17-9*) Luna Bisonte.

***Blur: An Illustrated Biography.** Linda Holomy. (Illus.). 66p. (Orig.). (C). 1995. pap. 11.95 (*0-7119-5044-X*, OP 47777, Pub. by Omnibus Press UK) Omnibus NY.

Blurred Boundaries. Bill Nichols. LC 94-2205. 1994. 29.95 (*0-253-34064-0*); pap. 12.95 (*0-253-20900-5*) Ind U Pr.

Blurred Boundaries: My Therapist, My Friend. Marina C. Miller. (Orig.). 1993. pap. 14.95 (*0-9636710-5-7*) Shades Of Gray.

Blurred Vision: Challenges in Credit Union Research & Modeling. George A. Overstreet, Jr. & Geoffrey M. Rubin. 45p. 1991. pap. 50.00 (*1-880572-00-1*) Filene Res.

***Blurred Visions: Philosophy, Science, & Ideology in a Troubled World.** Rory J. Conces. LC 94-36246. (New Directions in Philosophy: Vol. 2). 1995. write for info. (*0-8204-2468-4*) P Lang Pubs.

Blurring Boundaries: Socio-Spatial Consequences of Working at Home. Sherry Ahrentzen. (Publications in Architecture & Urban Planning: No. R87-4). (Illus.). vii, 221p. (C). 1987. 16.50 (*0-938744-53-4*) U of Wis Ctr Arch-Urban.

Blurring the Lines: Candidates & Journalists in American Elections. Ed. by Gary R. Orren. 320p. 1992. 24.95 (*0-02-923476-X*) Free Pr.

Blush. Colin Sargent. 36p. 1988. 7.95 (*0-913341-11-8*) Coyote Love.

Blush of Shame: A Few Considerations on Verbal Obscenity in the Theatre. Barrett H. Clark. 1932. pap. 2.50 (*0-910664-01-3*) Gotham.

***Blushing Detectives.** Ruta Lucas. (Illus.). (Orig.). Date not set. 9.95 (*0-916897-21-4*) Andrew Mtn Pr.

Blut - Adel - Leistung. Karl-Heinz Kirsch. (Illus.). civ, 172p. 1987. write for info. (*3-487-07381-1*, Pub. by Georg Olms GW) Lubrecht & Cramer.

Bluttransfusion. H. Reissigl & D. Schonitzer. (Illus.). x, 214p. 1986. 93.75 (*3-8055-4491-X*) S Karger.

BMA of America (1950-1986) John W. Duggar. 332p. 1988. 10.00 (*0-89114-166-9*) Baptist Pub Hse.

BMDP Data Entry User's Guide. 106p. (Orig.). (C). 1990. disk write for info. (*0-935386-23-8*) BMDP Stat.

BMDP EM-286 User's Guide. 51p. (C). 1990. write for info. (*0-935386-22-X*) BMDP Stat.

BMDP for X Windows User's Guide. 112p. (Orig.). (C). 1991. disk write for info. (*0-935386-25-4*) BMDP Stat.

BMDP PC-90 User's Guide. 102p. (C). 1990. write for info. (*0-935386-21-1*) BMDP Stat.

BMDP Statistical Software Manual: To Accompany the 7.0 Software Release, 3 vols., 1. rev. ed. Ed. by W. J. Dixon. LC 92-34074. (C). 1992. 33.00 (*0-520-08138-2*) U CA Pr.

BMDP Statistical Software Manual: To Accompany the 7.0 Software Release, 3 vols., 2. rev. ed. Ed. by W. J. Dixon. LC 92-34074. (C). 1992. 33.00 (*0-520-08139-0*) U CA Pr.

BMDP Statistical Software Manual: To Accompany the 7.0 Software Release, 3 vols., 3. rev. ed. Ed. by W. J. Dixon. LC 92-34074. (C). 1992. 20.00 (*0-520-08140-4*) U CA Pr.

BMDP Statistical Software Manual: To Accompany the 7.0 Software Release, 3 vols., Set. rev. ed. Ed. by W. J. Dixon. LC 92-34074. (C). 1992. 72.50 (*0-520-08141-2*) U CA Pr.

BMDP Student Version User's Guide. 80p. (Orig.). (C). 1992. disk write for info. (*0-935386-27-0*) BMDP Stat.

BMDP User's Digest: Quick Reference for the BMDP Programs: to Accompany BMDP Release 7. Des. by BMDP Statistical Software, Inc. Staff. LC 92-33041. 1992. 16.50 (*0-520-08142-0*) U CA Pr.

BMDP-386 Dynamic User's Guide. 128p. (Orig.). (C). 1992. disk write for info. (*0-935386-26-2*) BMDP Stat.

BMDP-386 User's Guide. 112p. (Orig.). (C). 1991. disk write for info. (*0-935386-24-6*) BMDP Stat.

BMI vs. Minicom, Inc. 5th ed. Donald H. Beskind & Anthony J. Bocchino. 142p. 1990. 10.00 (*1-55681-165-9*, FBA0165) Natl Inst Trial Ad.

An Asterisk (*) at the beginning of an entry indicates that the title is appearing in BIP for the first time.

An Asterisk (*) at the beginning of an entry indicates that the title is appearing in BIP for the first time.

829

B

Boas, Pythons & Other Friendly Snakes. John Coborn. 1992. 24.95 (*0-86622-603-6*) TFH Pubns.

Boastful Bullfrog. Keith Faulkner. (Illus.). 22p. (J). (gr. 1-3). 1991. 5.95 (*0-681-41051-5*) Longmeadow Pr.

Boat. Monique Felix. (Mouse Bks.). (Illus.). 32p. (J). (ps-12). 1993. 7.95 (*1-56846-080-5*) Creative Ed.

Boat. Illus. by Monique Felix. LC 92-44059. (Mouse Books Ser.). 1993. 10.95 (*0-88682-603-9*) Creative Ed.

Boat. Eric Kentley. LC 91-53136. (Eyewitness Bks.). (Illus.). 64p. (J). (gr. 5 up). 1992. 16.00 (*0-679-81678-X*); lib. bdg. 16.99 (*0-679-91678-4*) Knopf Bks Yng Read.

Boat & Canoe Camping in the Everglades Backcountry. Dennis Kalma. (Illus.). 64p. 1988. pap. 4.95 (*0-9613236-8-X*) Florida Flair Bks.

Boat & the Town. large type ed. Geoffrey Moorhouse. 448p. 1983. 15.95 (*0-7089-0949-3*) Ulverscroft.

Boat Book. Helene Gaillard de Neergaard. Ed. by Marcia Wiley. LC 94-60430. (Illus.). 384p. 1994. pap. 22.95 (*0-918752-17-5*) Wescott Cove.

Boat Book. Gail Gibbons. LC 82-15851. (Illus.). 32p. (J). (ps-3). 1983. lib. bdg. 15.95 (*0-8234-0478-1*); pap. 5.95 (*0-8234-0709-8*) Holiday.

***Boat Book's Nautical Terms & Abbreviations.** Helene Gaillet de Neergaard. (Illus.). 88p. 1994. 9.95 (*0-9642148-0-6*) Near Field Pr.

Boat Builders. Ed. by ICC Information Group Staff. 1987. 600.00 (*1-85319-033-0*, Pub. by ICC Info Group Ltd UK) St Mut.

***Boat Building Techniques Illustrated.** Richard Birmingham. (Illus.). 320p. Date not set. 40.00 (*0-7136-3642-4*) Sheridan.

Boat Building with Plywood. 3rd ed. Glen L. Witt. LC 89-80228. (Illus.). 312p. 1989. 25.95 (*0-939070-07-3*) Glen-L Marine.

Boat Buyer's Guide: Answers to Questions You Have about Boating but Don't Know Who to Ask. rev. ed. LeKemp, pseud. Orig. Title: A Boat Buyer's Handbook. (Illus.). 1991. reprint ed. pap. 7.00 (*0-9627438-2-8*) L E Kemppainen.

Boat Buyer's Handbook see Boat Buyer's Guide: Answers to Questions You Have about Boating but Don't Know Who to Ask

Boat Child: A Comedy. Melinda C. Porter. LC 93-79300. 75p. 1994. pap. 9.95 (*0-9637552-0-X*) Blake Pr.

Boat Contest: The Lion & the Mouse. Shari Lewis. Ed. by Blaine Marshall. (Lamb Chop's Fables Ser.). (Illus.). 32p. (J). (ps-3). 1993. 9.95 (*0-8094-7446-8*) Time-Life.

Boat Cosmetics Made Simple. Sheri Board. (Illus.). 128p. 1989. 9.95 (*0-930030-56-7*) Western Marine Ent.

Boat Cosmetics Made Simple: How to Improve & Maintain a Boat's Appearance. rev. ed. Sherri Board. Ed. by James A. Ayers. (Illus.). 176p. 1993. pap. 12.95 (*0-9634767-8-5*) Tug Pr CA.

***Boat Data Book.** 3rd ed. Ian Nicholson. LC 94-35443. (Illus.). 192p. 1995. 30.00 (*0-924486-78-3*) Sheridan.

Boat Dealers, 1995. American Business Directories Staff. 1995. spiral bd., pap. 810.00 (*1-56105-594-8*) Am Busn Direct.

Boat Diving: The Diver's Field Guide to Planning & Procedures for Diving from Boats. Liam Rooney & Jon Hardy. 27p. 1986. pap. text ed. 5.50 (*0-943717-30-2*) Concept Sys.

Boat Diving Manual. Gary R. Clark. (Specialty Diver Ser.). 80p. 1990. pap. text ed. 10.95 (*0-943717-97-3*) Concept Sys.

Boat Electrics. James Yates. (Helmsman Guide Ser.). (Illus.). 128p. 1993. pap. 19.95 (*1-85223-698-1*, Pub. by Crowood Pr UK) Trafalgar.

Boat Engines. 2nd ed. Dick Hewitt. 96p. (C). 1993. text ed. 59.00 (*0-906754-82-8*, Pub. by Fernhurst Bks UK) St Mut.

Boat Fishing. Mike Millman et al. (Illus.). 112p. 1992. pap. 24.95 (*1-85223-685-X*, Pub. by Crowood Pr UK) Trafalgar.

Boat Handling under Power. John Mellor. (Illus.). 190p. 1993. pap. 16.50 (*0-924486-43-0*) Sheridan.

Boat House. large type ed. Stephen Gallagher. (Mystery Ser.). 592p. 1993. 21.95 (*0-7089-2954-0*) Ulverscroft.

Boat Hull Service Manual. 1985. pap. 7.95 (*0-87288-020-6*, BHS-1) Intertec Pub.

Boat Joinery & Cabinetmaking Simplified. Fred P. Bingham. 1993. pap. text ed. 21.95 (*0-87742-354-7*) McGraw.

Boat Log & Record. (Illus.). 160p. 1993. pap. 14.95 (*0-943400-71-6*) Marlor Pr.

Boat Modeling the Easy Way: A Scratch Builder's Guide. Harold H. Payson. (Illus.). 192p. 1992. pap. 17.95 (*0-87742-320-2*, 60303) Intl Marine.

Boat Modeling the Easy Way: A Scratch Builder's Guide. Harold H. Payson. 1992. pap. 17.95 (*0-07-048962-9*) McGraw.

Boat Modeling with Dynamite Payson: A Step-by-Step Guide to Building Models of Small Craft. Harold H. Payson. (Illus.). 160p. 1989. pap. text ed. 18.95 (*0-87742-983-9*) Intl Marine.

Boat Modeling with Dynamite Payson: A Step-by-Step Guide to Building Models of Small Craft. Harold H. Payson. 1989. pap. text ed. 19.95 (*0-07-157371-2*) McGraw.

Boat Naming Made Simple. Sue Artof. (Orig.). 1993. pap. 10.95 (*0-9626888-2-7*) Ctr Pr CA.

***Boat Navigation for the Rest of Us: Finding Your Way by Eye & Electronics.** Bill Brogdon. 1995. pap. text ed. 17.95 (*0-07-008164-6*) McGraw.

Boat of a Million Years. Poul Anderson. 544p. 1993. mass mkt. 5.99 (*0-8125-3135-3*) Tor Bks.

Boat of Longing. O. E. Rolvaag. Tr. by Nora O. Solum. LC 84-29466. 304p. (C). 1985. reprint ed. pap. 9.95 (*0-87351-184-0*, Borealis Book) Minn Hist.

Boat of Longing, a Novel. Ole E. Rolvaag. Tr. by Nora O. Solum. LC 73-11844. 304p. 1974. reprint ed. text ed. 59.75 (*0-8371-7069-9*, ROBL, Greenwood Pr) Greenwood.

Boat of Quiet Hours. Jane Kenyon. LC 86-81787. 85p. 1986. pap. 8.95 (*0-915308-87-8*) Graywolf.

Boat of Stone. Maureen Earl. LC 92-9861. 254p. 1993. 22.00 (*1-877946-21-4*) Permanent Pr.

Boat of the Dream. Elizabeth McKim. (Illus.). 108p. (Orig.). 1988. pap. 9.95 (*0-944941-01-X*) Talking Stone Pr.

Boat Officer's Handbook. 2nd ed. David D. Winters. (Illus.). 176p. 1991. pap. 19.95 (*1-55750-900-X*) Naval Inst Pr.

Boat Owner's Guide to Coastwise Navigation. B. P. Lipscombe. (C). 1987. 40.00 (*0-685-45082-1*, Pub. by Brwn Son Ferg) St Mut.

Boat Owner's Maintenance Book. Geoffrey O'Connell. 164p. 1989. 17.95 (*0-87201-221-2*) Gulf Pub.

Boat Owner's Mechanical & Electrical Manual: How to Maintain, Repair & Improve Your Boat's Essential Systems. Nigel Calder. (Illus.). 400p. 1989. text ed. 39.95 (*0-87742-982-0*) Intl Marine.

Boat-Owner's Practical Dictionary. Denny Desoutter. (Practical Handbooks for the Yachtsman Ser.). (Illus.). 1978. 14.95 (*0-370-30041-6*) Transatl Arts.

Boat People: A Novel. Mary Gardner. 288p. 1995. 21.00 (*0-393-03738-X*) Norton.

Boat People & Vietnamese Refugees in the United States. rev. ed. Lady Borton. Ed. by Jerold M. Starr. (Lessons of the Vietnam War Ser.). (Illus.). 32p. (C). 1991. pap. text ed. 5.00 (*0-945919-11-5*) Ctr Social Studies.

Boat Repair Manual. George Buchanan. LC 92-33040. (Illus.). 312p. 1992. pap. 24.95 (*1-55992-070-X*, 2070, Pisces Bks) Gulf Pub.

Boat Ride. Bill Gillespie. (Illus.). 24p. (J). 1988. pap. 3.50 (*0-940859-05-X*) Snd Dollar Pub.

Boat Ride to Destiny. Robin Myers. LC 93-93512. 200p. (Orig.). 1994. pap. 7.95 (*1-56002-366-X*, Univ Edtns) Aegina Pr.

Boat Ropes: A Guide to the Use of Rope & Lines on Sailing Cruisers. Bill Finnis. (Illus.). 128p. 1994. pap. 19.95 (*1-85310-509-0*) Voyageur Pr.

Boat Sailing: A Primer for the Beginner. William F. Crosby. 1977. lib. bdg. 69.95 (*0-8490-1517-0*) Gordon Pr.

Boat That Wouldn't Float. Farley Mowat. (J). 1984. mass mkt. 3.99 (*0-553-27788-X*) Bantam.

Boat to Nowhere. Maureen C. Wartski. 160p. 1981. pap. 4.99 (*0-451-16285-4*, Sig) NAL-Dutton.

Boat Trailers & Tow Vehicles: A User's Guide. Steve Henkel. (Illus.). 160p. 1991. pap. 14.95 (*0-87742-290-7*, 60264P) Intl Marine.

Boat Trailers & Two Vehicles. Steve Henkel. 1991. User's Guide. pap. text ed. 14.95 (*0-07-028205-6*) McGraw.

Boat Trips on New England Rivers. Henry P. Fellows. 1977. lib. bdg. 59.95 (*0-8490-1518-9*) Gordon Pr.

Boat-U. S. Equipment Catalog. 300p. write for info. (*0-318-59918-X*) Boat Own Assn US.

Boat We Are in Together. Anne Valley-Fox. 32p. write for info. (*0-938631-28-4*) Pennywhistle Pr.

Boat Without an Oar. Galina Vahnina. Ed. by Lewis B. Sckolnick. (Poetry Ser.). 88p. (Orig.). 1992. pap. 8.95 (*0-934393-11-7*) Rector Pr.

Boat Work. L. G. Taylor. (C). 1987. 48.00 (*0-85174-398-6*, Pub. by Brwn Son Ferg) St Mut.

Boatbuilder's Manual. Charles Walbridge. LC 86-12739. (Illus.). 136p. 1982. pap. 9.95 (*0-89732-022-0*) Menasha Ridge.

Boatbuilders of Muskoka. A. H. Duke & W. M. Gray. (Illus.). 154p. reprint ed. pap. 29.95 (*1-55046-074-9*, Pub. by Boston Mills Pr CN) Genl Dist Srvs.

Boatbuilding: A Complete Handbook of Wooden Boat Construction. Howard I. Chapelle. 1994. 39.95 (*0-393-03554-9*) Norton.

Boatbuilding in Your Own Backyard. 2nd ed. S. S. Rabl. LC 57-11361. (Illus.). 239p. 1958. 29.95 (*0-87033-009-8*) Cornell Maritime.

Boatbuilding Manual. 3rd ed. Robert M. Steward. (Illus.). 288p. 1987. text ed. 29.95 (*0-87742-236-2*, 60160) Intl Marine.

Boatbuilding Manual. 4th ed. Robert Steward. 1994. text ed. 34.95 (*0-07-061376-1*) McGraw.

Boatbuilding Manual. 4th ed. Robert M. Steward. 1993. text ed. 34.95 (*0-87742-379-2*) Intl Marine.

Boatbuilding Notes: An Unforgettable Experience. Florencio O. Garcia. (Illus.). 76p. 1990. pap. 13.00 (*0-929928-05-9*) Fog Pubns.

Boatbuilding with Aluminium. Stephen F. Pollard. 1993. text ed. 29.95 (*0-07-050426-1*) McGraw.

Boatbuilding with Aluminum. Stephen F. Pollard. 1993. 29.95 (*0-87742-377-6*) Intl Marine.

***Boatbuilding with Baltek DuraKore.** David G. Brown. 1994. text ed. 29.95 (*0-07-008212-X*) McGraw.

Boatbuilding with Steel. rev. ed. Gilbert Klingel. (Illus.). 258p. 1990. text ed. 24.95 (*0-87742-287-7*) Intl Marine.

Boatbuilding with Steel. rev. ed. Gilbert Klingel & Thomas W. Colvin. 1991. 24.95 (*0-07-156318-0*) McGraw.

Boatbuilding with Steel (Including Boatbuilding with Aluminum) Gilbert Klingel & Thomas Colvin. LC 72-97402. 258p. 1973. 24.95 (*0-87742-029-7*) Intl Marine.

Boatbuilding Woods: A Directory of Suppliers. WoodenBoat Magazine Staff. 1987. pap. text ed. 9.50 (*0-937-155578-1*) McGraw.

Boaters & Broomsticks. Lionel Wyld. (Illus.). 128p. 1987. pap. 9.95 (*0-932052-45-2*) North Country.

Boaters Guide to Lake Powell. Michael R. Kelsey. (Illus.). 288p. (Orig.). 1991. pap. 12.95 (*0-9605824-9-5*) Kelsey Pub.

Boater's Guide to the Upper Florida Keys: Jewfish Creek to Long Key. John O'Reilly. LC 70-125659. (Illus.). 64p. 1970. spiral bd., pap. 7.95 (*0-87024-175-3*) U of Miami Pr.

Boater's Medical Companion. Robert S. Gould. LC 89-43018. (Illus.). 128p. (Orig.). 1990. pap. 6.95 (*0-87033-402-6*) Cornell Maritime.

Boater's Safety Handbook. Ed. by Robert Brown. (Illus.). 52p. (Orig.). 1982. pap. 3.50 (*0-89886-072-5*) Mountaineers.

Boater's Weather Guide. Margaret Williams. LC 90-55451. (Illus.). 160p. (Orig.). 1991. pap. 6.95 (*0-87033-417-4*) Cornell Maritime.

Boating Accident Investigation. Kirsten et al. 366p. (C). 1993. pap. text ed. 20.00 (*1-55989-463-6*) Underwrtrs Labs.

Boating & Waterways Regulations in New South Wales. Comp. by Gerard Carter. 141p. 1991. 45.00 (*1-875114-15-7*, Blckstone AT) W W Gaunt.

Boating Basics: A Small Craft Primer. LC 85-61207. (Illus.). 1995. teacher ed, pap. write for info. (*0-916682-44-7*); student ed, pap. 2.50 (*0-916682-43-9*) Outdoor Empire.

Boating Bible: The Essential Handbook for Every Sailor. Jim Murrant. (Illus.). 320p. 1991. 24.95 (*0-924486-13-9*) Sheridan.

Boating Book: A Practical Guide to Safe Pleasure Boating-Sail & Power. John Roberts. 1991. 39.95 (*0-393-03342-2*) Norton.

Boating Fiascos: Adventures in Yachting. Steve Perry & Lora Perry. 232p. 1989. pap. 12.95 (*0-685-29176-6*) Robinhood Pub Co.

Boating for Less: How to Save Money When Buying, Owning, & Selling Your Power or Sail Boat. Steve Henkel. 1991. pap. text ed. 19.95 (*0-07-028206-4*) McGraw.

Boating for Less: How to Save Money When Buying, Owning or Selling Your Power or Sail Boat. Steve Henkel. 320p. 1991. pap. 19.95 (*0-87742-315-6*, 0305) Intl Marine.

Boating for the Handicapped: Guidelines for the Physically Handicapped. Eugene Hedley. LC 79-91181. (Illus.). 124p. 1979. 5.65 (*0-686-38820-8*) Human Res Ctr.

***Boating Guide to Mexico: West Coast Edition (Guidebook)** John Rains & Patricia Miller. 304p. 1995. 39.95 (*0-9644783-1-5*) Pt Loma Pubng.

Boating Guide to Western Lake Erie. William Gordon & Mary Gordon. LC 94-65030. (Illus.). 120p. (Orig.). 1994. pap. 24.95 (*0-913285-03-X*) Photomaker Pubng.

***Boating in Glacier Bay.** K. Heacox. (Illus.). 30p. 1995. pap. 3.00 (*0-930931-01-7*) Alaska Natural.

***Boating in Spanish (Lexicon for Adventurers)** John Rains & Patricia Miller. 1995. 22.95 (*0-9638470-5-8*) Pt Loma Pubng.

Boating on the Ohio. William Vernon. Ed. by Lorraine DeGennaro & Alana Sherman. 24p. (Orig.). 1993. pap. 5.00 (*0-939689-17-0*) Alms Hse Pr.

Boating Watersports: The Ultimate Get Started Guide to Towing Fun. Waterski Magazine Staff. Ed. by Jo Robertson. LC 89-52016. (Illus.). 100p. (YA). 1990. pap. 15.95 (*0-944406-07-6*) World Pub FL.

Boating with Cap'n Bob & Matey: An Encyclopedia for Kids of All Ages. LC 88-62045. (Illus.). 32p. (J). (gr. 1-9). 1989. boxed 12.95 (*0-931595-03-7*) Seascape Enters.

Boatkeeper: The Boatowner's Manual to Maintenance, Repair, & Construction. Ed. by Bernard Gladstone & Tom Bottomley. LC 84-80492. (Illus.). 288p. 1984. 18.95 (*0-688-03565-5*, Hearst Marine Bks) Morrow.

Boatload of Madmen: Surrealism & the American Avant-Garde, 1920-1950. Dickran Tashjian. LC 94-60289. (Illus.). 336p. 1995. 29.95 (*0-500-23687-9*) Thames Hudson.

Boatman's Handbook. 2nd rev. ed. Tom Bottomley. LC 87-23647. (Illus.). 320p. (Orig.). 1988. 10.95 (*0-688-07754-4*, Hearst Marine Bks) Morrow.

Boatman's Manual. 4th enl. rev. ed. Carl D. Lane. (Illus.). 1979. 25.95 (*0-393-03190-X*) Norton.

Boatowner's Energy Planner: How to Make & Manage Electrical Energy on Board. Kevin Jeffrey & Nan Jeffrey. (Illus.). 220p. 1991. pap. 19.95 (*0-915160-63-3*, 60234P) Seven Seas.

Boatowner's Guide to Marine Electronics. 3rd ed. Gordon West. 1993. pap. 19.95 (*0-87742-342-3*) Intl Marine.

Boatowner's Guide to Marine Electronics. 3rd ed. Gordon West et al. 1993. pap. 19.95 (*0-07-069549-0*) McGraw.

Boatowner's Guide to Radar. Jack West. (Illus.). 135p. 1988. pap. text ed. 13.95 (*0-87742-978-2*) Intl Marine.

Boatowner's Illustrated Handbook of Wiring. Charlie Wing. LC 93-9425. (Illus.). 1993. 29.95 (*0-87742-383-0*) Intl Marine.

Boatowner's Illustrated Handbook of Wiring. Charlie Wing. 1993. text ed. 29.95 (*0-07-071092-9*) McGraw.

Boatowner's Legal & Financial Advisor. Larry Rogers. (Illus.). 256p. 1993. pap. text ed. 17.95 (*0-87742-341-5*, 60270) Intl Marine.

Boatowner's Legal & Financial Advisor. Larry Rogers. 1994. pap. text ed. 17.95 (*0-07-158007-7*) McGraw.

Boatowner's Mechanical & Electrical Manual: How to Maintain, Repair & Improve Your Boat's Essential Systems. Nigel Calder. 1989. text ed. 39.95 (*0-07-157287-2*) McGraw.

Boatride with Lillian Two-Blossom. Patricia Polacco. (Illus.). 32p. 1989. 14.95 (*0-399-21470-4*, Philomel Bks) Putnam Pub Group.

Boats. LC 91-58216. (What's Inside? Ser.). (Illus.). 24p. (J). (ps-3). 1992. 8.95 (*1-56458-006-7*) Dorling Kindersley.

Boats. Byron Barton. LC 85-47900. (Illus.). 32p. (J). (ps-00). 1986. 4.95 (*0-694-00059-0*, Crowell Jr Bks); lib. bdg. 14.89 (*0-690-04536-0*, Crowell Jr Bks) HarpC Child Bks.

Boats. Byron Barton. (Illus.). 28p. (J). (ps). 1994. 2.95 (*0-694-00600-9*, Festival) HarpC Child Bks.

Boats. Illus. by Christian Broutin. LC 92-41414. (J). 1993. 11.95 (*0-590-47131-7*) Scholastic Inc.

Boats. Ralph S. Coventry. (How to Draw & Paint Ser.). (Illus.). 32p. (Orig.). 1989. pap. 5.95 (*0-929261-62-3*, HT98) W Foster Pub.

***Boats.** Ian Graham. (How it Goes Ser.). 1995. write for info. (*0-8120-6487-9*); pap. write for info. (*0-8120-9151-5*) Barron.

***Boats.** Dilwyn Jones. (Egyptian Bookshelf Ser.). (Illus.). 100p. (Orig.). 1995. pap. 17.95 (*0-292-74039-5*) U of Tex Pr.

Boats. Anne Rockwell. (Illus.). 24p. (J). 1993. pap. 4.99 (*0-14-054988-9*, Puff Unicorn) Puffin Bks.

Boats. Philip Steele. LC 90-41177. (Pocket Facts Ser.). (Illus.). 32p. (J). (gr. 5-6). 1991. text ed. 11.95 (*0-89686-522-3*, Crstwood Hse) Silver Burdett Pr.

Boats: A Manual for Their Documentation. Willits Ansel et al. Ed. by Paul Lipke et al. (Illus.). 408p. (Orig.). (C). 1994. pap. text ed. 37.95 (*0-942063-17-1*) AASLH.

Boats Against the Current: American Culture Between Revolution & Modernity, 1820-1860. Lewis Perry. LC 92-11094. 352p. (C). 1993. 35.00 (*0-19-506091-1*) OUP.

***Boats & Boating in the Adirondacks.** Hallie E. Bond. LC 95-8603. (Illus.). 328p. 1995. 49.95 (*0-8156-0373-8*) Syracuse U Pr.

Boats & Ships. J. Cooper. (Traveling Machines Ser.). (J). 1991. 8.95 (*0-86592-492-9*) Rourke Enter.

Boats, Boats, Boats. J. Ruane. (My First Reader Ser.). (Illus.). 28p. (J). (ps-2). 1990. 10.50 (*0-516-05351-5*); pap. 3.95 (*0-516-45351-3*) Childrens.

Boat's Gonna Leave: A Study of Children Learning a Second Language from Conversations with Other Children. Anca M. Nemoianu. (Pragmatics & Beyond Ser.: Vol. 1, No. 1). vi, 116p. 1980. pap. 29.00x (*90-272-2507-9*) Benjamins North Am.

Boats in Watercolor. Duane R. Light. (How to Draw & Paint Ser.). (Illus.). 32p. (Orig.). 1989. pap. 5.95 (*0-929261-70-4*, HT210) W Foster Pub.

Boats of "Glen Carrig" William H. Hodgson. LC 75-28855. (Classics of Science Fiction Ser.). 312p. 1991. reprint ed. 31.00 (*0-88355-369-4*) Hyperion Conn.

Boats on the River. Marjorie Flack. (Illus.). 32p. (J). (ps-3). 1991. 14.95 (*0-670-83918-3*) Viking Child Bks.

***Boats (Pleasure) Market.** 152p. (Orig.). 1995. pap. 1,295.00 (*0-7605-2067-4*) Rector Pr.

Boats, Ships, Submarines, & Other Floating Machines. Ian Graham. LC 92-33588. (How Things Work Ser.). (Illus.). 40p. (Orig.). (J). (gr. 3-8). 1993. lib. bdg. 10.95 (*1-85697-868-0*, Kingfisher LKC); pap. 5.95 (*1-85697-867-2*, Kingfisher LKC) LKC.

Boats Unlimited. Harold Wilson. (Illus.). 280p. 29.95 (*0-317-05889-4*, Pub. by Boston Mills Pr CN) Genl Dist Srvs.

Boats with an Open Mind: Seventy-Five Uninhibited Designs & Concepts. Philip C. Bolger. LC 94-19978. 1994. pap. text ed. 34.95 (*0-07-006376-1*) Intl Marine.

Boatspeed. Rodney Pattisson. 64p. (C). 1990. text ed. 59.00 (*0-906754-25-9*, Pub. by Fernhurst Bks UK) St Mut.

Boatswain's Manual. rev. ed. Rev. by A. G. Miller. (C). 1987. 84.00 (*0-85174-475-3*, Pub. by Brwn Son Ferg) St Mut.

Boatwatch. Averitt. (Orig.). 1979. pap. 1.95 (*0-684-16159-1*, Scribners) S&S Trade.

Boatwatch: Armchair Shopping Three Hundred Forty Sailboats 29'-35' Ed. & Illus. by M. W. Averitt. 192p. 1994. pap. 24.00 (*0-9627152-3-9*); pap. 24.00 (*0-9627152-2-0*) Boatwatch.

Boatwatch: Master Guide to Sailboats of the World. Illus. by Max W. Averitt. 592p. (ENG, FRE & GER.). 1992. pap. 64.00 (*0-9627152-1-2*) Boatwatch.

Boatwatch: On-the-Water Guide to Pleasure Boat Identification. 2nd ed. Illus. by Max W. Averitt. 384p. 1990. pap. 22.00 (*0-9627152-0-4*) Boatwatch.

Boatwatcher's Guide to San Francisco Bay. Jerry George & Mollie Rights. (Illus.). 160p. 1994. Perfect bdg. per. 12.95 (*1-883867-03-7*) Curiosity Pr.

Boatwords. Denny Desoutter. (Illus.). 224p. 1994. pap. 19.95 (*1-85310-299-7*) Voyageur Pr.

Boatwrights Companion: Repairs Below the Waterline. Allen Taube. LC 85-18032. (Illus.). 170p. 1987. pap. text ed. 18.95 (*0-87742-198-6*) Intl Marine.

Boatwright's Companion: Repairs Below the Waterline. Allen Taube. 1987. pap. text ed. 18.95 (*0-07-155592-7*) McGraw.

Boatyards & Marinas: A Boatowner's Guide to Smart Shopping. Ralph Naranjo. (Illus.). 180p. 1988. pap. text ed. 17.95 (*0-87742-962-6*) Intl Marine.

Boatyards & Marinas: Boatowner's Guide to Smart Shopping. Ralph Naranjo. 1988. pap. text ed. 17.95 (*0-07-155638-9*) McGraw.

Boaz & Ruth. Van Ryn. 1988. pap. 5.00 (*0-937396-73-7*) Walterick Pubs.

Bob & Bob: Selected Works. Al Nodal & Peter Frank. (Illus.). 48p. 1986. 10.00 (*0-930209-03-6*) Otis Art.

Bob & Bob: The First Five Years. Linda F. Burnham. LC 80-67655. (Illus.). 100p. (Orig.). 1980. pap. 12.00 (*0-937122-00-9*) Astro Artz.

Bob & Jack: A Boy & His Yak. Jeff Moss. LC 92-17458. (Illus.). 64p. (J). (gr. 4 up). 1992. 15.00 (*0-553-08931-5*) Bantam.

Bob & Jerry's Regional Graphic Research, No. 1: Fishing Lakes & Ponds. Robert L. Voss & Gerald G. Fuller. LC 94-94138. 163p. 1994. pap. 21.95 (*0-9641260-0-1*) J B Ent.

Bob & Rod: A Portrait of a Marriage. Tom Bianchi. (Illus.). 96p. 1994. 60.00 (*0-312-11471-0*) St Martin.

Bob & the Guides. Mary Andrews. LC 77-163019. (Short Story Index Reprint Ser.). 1977. reprint ed. 23.95 (*0-8369-3933-6*) Ayer.

An Asterisk (*) at the beginning of an entry indicates that the title is appearing in BIP for the first time.

B

An Asterisk (*) at the beginning of an entry indicates that the title is appearing in BIP for the first time.

831

Bobby & the Brockles. Adele Faber & Elaine Mazlish. LC 93-42283. (Illus.). 64p. (Orig.). (J). 1994. pap. 15.00 (0-380-77067-9) Avon.
Bobby & the Brockles Go to School. Adele Faber & Elaine Mazlish. LC 93-42884. (Illus.). 64p. (Orig.). (J). 1994. pap. 15.00 (0-380-77068-7) Avon.
Bobby Bagley POW. Rod Gragg. 1978. pap. 3.95 (0-89728-022-9, 678434) Omega Pubns OR.
Bobby Baseball. Robert K. Smith. (Illus.). (J). (gr. 3-7). 1989. 13.95 (0-385-29807-2) Delacorte.
Bobby Baseball. Robert K. Smith. (J). (gr. 4-7). 1991. pap. 3.50 (0-440-40417-7); pap. 3.25 (0-440-80212-1) Dell.
Bobby Bear & the Band. Judy Saul. LC 85-61831. (Bobby Bear Ser.). (Illus.). 32p. (J). (ps-1). 1985. 6.95 (0-87783-203-X) Oddo.
Bobby Bear & the Bees. M. O. Helmrath & J. L. Bartlett. LC 68-56806. (Bobby Bear Ser.). (Illus.). 32p. (J). (ps-1). 1968. ring bd. 12.35 (0-87783-003-7); audio 7.94 (0-87783-177-7) Oddo.
Bobby Bear & the Blizzard. Oana. LC 80-82950. (Bobby Bear Ser.). (Illus.). 32p. (J). (ps-1). 1981. lib. bdg. 9.95 (0-87783-151-3) Oddo.
Bobby Bear & the Friendly Ghost. Marilue. LC 85-61830. (Bobby Bear Ser.). (Illus.). 32p. (J). (ps-1). 1985. 6.95 (0-87783-204-8) Oddo.
Bobby Bear & Uncle Sam's Riddle. Lee Mountain. (Bobby Bear Ser.). (Illus.). 32p. (J). (ps-1). 1988. lib. bdg. 11.45 (0-87783-221-8) Oddo.
Bobby Bear at the Circus. Marilue. LC 89-62708. (Bobby Bear Ser.). (Illus.). 32p. (J). (ps-2). 1990. lib. bdg. 12.95 (0-87783-252-8) Oddo.
Bobby Bear Finds Maple Sugar. M. O. Helmrath & J. L. Bartlett. LC 68-56805. (Bobby Bear Ser.). (Illus.). 32p. (J). (ps-1). 1968. ring bd. 12.35 (0-87783-005-3); audio 7.94 (0-87783-178-5) Oddo.
Bobby Bear Goes Fishing. M. O. Helmrath & J. L. Bartlett. LC 68-56807. (Bobby Bear Ser.). (Illus.). 32p. (J). (ps-1). 1968. ring bd. 12.35 (0-87783-006-1); audio 7.94 (0-87783-179-3) Oddo.
Bobby Bear Goes to the Beach. Oana. LC 80-82951. (Bobby Bear Ser.). (Illus.). 32p. (J). (ps-1). 1981. lib. bdg. 9.95 (0-87783-153-X) Oddo.
Bobby Bear in the Spring. M. O. Helmrath & J. L. Bartlett. LC 68-56810. (Bobby Bear Ser.). (Illus.). 32p. (J). (ps-1). 1968. ring bd. 12.35 (0-87783-007-X); audio 7.94 (0-87783-180-7) Oddo.
Bobby Bear Meets Cousin Boo. Marilue. LC 80-82952. (Bobby Bear Ser.). (Illus.). 32p. (J). (ps-1). 1981. lib. bdg. 9.95 (0-87783-155-6) Oddo.
Bobby Bear Series, 18 bks. M. O. Helmrath & J. L. Bartlett. (Illus.). (J). (ps-1). audio 63.52 (0-87783-181-5) Oddo.
Bobby Bear Series, 18 bks., Set. M. O. Helmrath & J. L. Bartlett. (Illus.). (J). (ps-1). lib. bdg. 189.60 (0-87783-163-7) Oddo.
Bobby Bear's Birthday. Rae Oetting. LC 87-62508. (Bobby Bear Ser.). (Illus.). 32p. (J). (ps-1). 1988. lib. bdg. 11.45 (0-87783-220-X) Oddo.
Bobby Bear's Christmas. Marilue. LC 77-83628. (Illus.). 32p. (J). (ps-1). 1978. lib. bdg. 9.95 (0-87783-142-4) Oddo.
Bobby Bear's Halloween. M. O. Helmrath & J. L. Bartlett. LC 68-56808. (Bobby Bear Ser.). (Illus.). 32p. (J). (ps-1). 1968. lib. bdg. 9.95 (0-87783-004-5); audio 7.94 (0-87783-183-1) Oddo.
Bobby Bear's Kite Contest. Marilue. LC 87-62507. (Bobby Bear Ser.). (Illus.). 32p. (J). (ps-1). 1988. lib. bdg. 11.45 (0-87783-219-6) Oddo.
Bobby Bear's Magic Show. Marilue. LC 89-62707. (Bobby Bear Ser.). (Illus.). 32p. (J). (ps-2). 1990. lib. bdg. 12.95 (0-87783-253-6) Oddo.
Bobby Bear's New Home. Marilue. LC 78-190265. (Bobby Bear Ser.). (Illus.). 32p. (J). (ps-1). 1973. lib. bdg. 9.95 (0-87783-054-1); audio 7.94 (0-87783-184-X) Oddo.
Bobby Bear's Red Raft. Marilue. LC 71-190266. (Bobby Bear Ser.). (Illus.). 32p. (J). (ps-1). 1973. lib. bdg. 9.95 (0-87783-055-X); audio 7.94 (0-87783-185-8) Oddo.
Bobby Bear's Rocket Ride. M. O. Helmrath & J. L. Bartlett. LC 68-56809. (Bobby Bear Ser.). (Illus.). 32p. (J). (ps-1). 1968. ring bd. 12.35 (0-87783-008-8); audio 7.94 (0-87783-186-6) Oddo.
Bobby Bear's Thanksgiving. Marilue. LC 77-83623. (Bobby Bear Ser.). (Illus.). 32p. (J). (ps-1). 1978. lib. bdg. 9.95 (0-87783-143-2) Oddo.
Bobby Bobcat. Dave Sargent & Pat Sargent. (Animal Pride Ser.). 64p. (J). (gr. 2-6). 1992. pap. write for info. (1-56763-012-X) Ozark Pub.
Bobby Bonilla. Ken Rappoport. LC 92-34583. (Illus.). 144p. (J). (gr. 5 up). 1993. 14.95 (0-8027-8255-8); lib. bdg. 15.85 (0-8027-8256-6) Walker & Co.
*__Bobby Bumblebee Learns to Fly.__ Debra Cogburn. LC 94-92457. (Illus.). 32p. (Orig.). (J). (ps-2). 1995. pap. write for info. (0-9644825-0-9) Cogburn Enter.
Bobby Deerfield. Erich M. Remarque. 1978. pap. 1.95 (0-449-23367-7, Crest) Fawcett.
Bobby Fischer: Complete Games of the American World Chess Champion. Lou Hays. 315p. 1992. pap. 19.95 (1-880673-89-4) Hays Pub.
Bobby Fischer: His Approach to Chess. Elie Agur. 1992. 25.00 (1-85744-001-3, Maxwell Macmillan) Macmillan.
Bobby Fischer: Profile of a Prodigy. rev. ed. Frank Brady. 435p. 1989. pap. 8.95 (0-486-25925-0) Dover.
Bobby Fischer Teaches Chess. Bobby Fischer et al. (Illus.). 352p. 1982. mass mkt. 6.99 (0-553-26315-3) Bantam.
Bobby Fischer's Outrageous Chess Moves. Bruce Pandolfini. 1993. pap. 10.00 (0-671-87432-2, Fireside) S&S Trade.
Bobby Flay's Bold American Food: More Than 200 Revolutionary Recipes. Bobby Flay & Joan Schwartz. (Illus.). 224p. 1994. 34.95 (0-446-51724-0) Warner Bks.
Bobby Goldsboro's A Cat Named Bob. Bobby Goldsboro. (Comes to Life Bks.). 16p. (J). (ps-2). 1993. write for info. (1-883366-33-X) YES Ent.
*__Bobby Goldsboro's De Jongen die een Kikker Werd.__ Bobby Goldsboro. Tr. by DigiPro Staff. (Comes to Life Bks.). 16p. (DUT.). (J). (ps-2). 1994. write for info. (1-883366-95-X) YES Ent.
*__Bobby Goldsboro's Le Petit Garcon Qui Voulait Devenir une Grenouille.__ Bobby Goldsboro. Tr. by DigiPro Staff. (Comes to Life Bks.). 16p. (FRE.). (J). (ps-2). 1994. write for info. (1-883366-70-4) YES Ent.
Bobby Goldsboro's The Boy Who Became a Frog. Bobby Goldsboro. (Comes to Life Bks.). 16p. (J). (ps-2). 1993. write for info. (1-883366-12-7) YES Ent.
*__Bobby Goldsboro's the Boy Who Became a Frog.__ Bobby Goldsboro. (Come to Life Bks.). 16p. (J). (ps-2). 1994. write for info. (1-883366-79-8) YES Ent.
Bobby Jim's Down Home Cookin'. Robert J. Fithian. 1992. spiral bd. 9.95 (0-9633605-0-7) Bobby Jim Ent.
*__Bobby Joe: In the Mind of a Monster.__ Bernie Ward. LC 94-42954. (Illus.). 432p. (Orig.). 1994. pap. 12.95 (1-56790-093-3) Cool Hand Comms.
Bobby Jones on Golf. Robert T. Jones. 1976. 19.95 (0-8488-1391-X) Amereon Ltd.
Bobby Jones on Golf. Robert T. Jones. 256p. 1991. lib. bdg. 20.95 (0-89966-773-2) Buccaneer Bks.
Bobby Jones on Golf: The Classic Instructional by Golf's Greatest Legend. Bobby Jones. 1992. pap. 15.00 (0-385-42419-1) Doubleday.
Bobby Rex's Greatest Hit. Marianne Gingher. 352p. 1987. pap. 3.95 (0-345-34823-0) Ballantine.
Bobby Sands & the Tragedy of Northern Ireland. John Feehan. 160p. 1985. 22.00 (0-932966-63-2); pap. 16.00 (0-932966-65-9) Permanent Pr.
Bobby Sands: Irish Rebel: A Self-Portrait in Poetry & Polemics Issued on the 10th Anniversary of His Death. Bobby Sands. Ed. by Robert West. LC 91-24306. (Illus.). 156p. 1991. pap. 49.95 (0-7734-9870-2) E Mellen.
*__Bobby Short, Saloon Singer.__ Bobby Short & Robert Mackintosh. LC 95-6978. 1995. 25.00 (0-517-59564-8, Panache) Crown Pub Group.
Bobby Thatcher Together with Phil Hardy: An Original Compilation. George Storm. Ed. by Bill Blackbeard. LC 76-53056. (Classic American Comic Strips Ser.). (Illus.). 1977. 18.50 (0-88355-667-7); pap. 10.00 (0-88355-666-9) Hyperion Conn.
Bobby, the Babe & Me. Earl C. Fabritz. (Illus.). 128p. 1994. 14.00 (0-9627653-3-3) Witness Prods.
Bobby the Mostly Silky. David McKelvey. LC 83-73327. (Illus.). 32p. (J). (gr. 1-3). 1984. lib. bdg. 10.95 (0-931722-28-4); pap. 3.95 (0-931722-27-6) Corona Pub.
Bobby's Girl. Rochelle Ratner. LC 86-20794. 116p. (Orig.). 1986. pap. 9.95 (0-918273-22-6) Coffee Hse.
*__Bobby's World: A Bird in the Hand.__ 1995. 7.98 (1-57036-196-7, Bedrock Press) Turner Pub GA.
*__Bobby's World: Are We There Yet?__ 1995. 3.98 (1-57036-192-4, Bedrock Press) Turner Pub GA.
*__Bobby's World: Bobby on the Job.__ 1995. 5.98 (1-57036-195-9, Bedrock Press) Turner Pub GA.
*__Bobby's World: Bobby, That's My Name.__ 1995. 3.98 (1-57036-191-6, Bedrock Press) Turner Pub GA.
*__Bobby's World: I'm Not a Baby.__ 1995. 6.98 (1-57036-194-0, Bedrock Press) Turner Pub GA.
*__Bobby's World: Sleepover Scare.__ 1995. 4.98 (1-57036-189-4, Bedrock Press) Turner Pub GA.
*__Bobby's World: Things That Go Bump.__ 1995. 6.98 (1-57036-193-2, Bedrock Press) Turner Pub GA.
*__Bobby's World: Tooth Or Dare.__ 1995. 4.98 (1-57036-190-8, Bedrock Press) Turner Pub GA.
Bobby's Zoo. Carolyn Lunn. LC 88-36865. (Rookie Reader Ser.). (Illus.). 32p. (J). (ps-2). 1989. lib. bdg. 10.35 (0-516-02089-7); pap. 2.95 (0-516-42089-5) Childrens.
Bobby's Zoo Big Book. Carolyn Lunn. (Rookie Readers Big Bks.). (Illus.). 32p. (J). (ps-2). 1991. lib. bdg. 22.95 (0-516-49501-1) Childrens.
Bobcat. Hope Ryden. (Illus.). 64p. (J). 1992. pap. 9.95 (1-55821-143-8) Lyons & Burford.
Bobcat Action Book. 16p. 1980. pap. 1.15 (0-8395-3901-0, 33901) BSA.
Bobcat & Her Babies. Curt Jansen et al. (Wildlife Adventure Ser.: Vol. 3). (Orig.). (J). (gr. k-4). pap. write for info. (0-9614904-3-8) Adventure Prods.
Bobcat Hydraulics Manual. LC 92-85560. 210p. 1992. pap. text ed. write for info. (1-882370-00-7) Melroe.
Bobcat Trapper's Guide. Mitchell S. Ricketts. (Illus.). 116p. (Orig.). 1987. pap. 10.95 (0-9617720-0-X) Elk River Pr.
Bobcat Year. Hope Ryden. (Illus.). 240p. 1990. reprint ed. pap. 14.95 (1-55821-055-5) Lyons & Burford.
Bobe Mayse: A Tale of Washington Square. Nancy Bogen. LC 92-63378. 1993. 21.95 (0-936726-03-2); pap. 13.95 (0-936726-04-0) Twickenham Pr.
Bobi Jones. John Emyr. 125p. 1991. pap. 7.00 (0-7083-1101-6, Pub. by U of Wales UK) Bks Intl VA.
Bobio: A Fairy Tale for All Ages. Barbara Brown-Cathers. (Illus.). 36p. (Orig.). (J). (gr. 5). 1994. pap. 7.95 (0-9640122-0-0) Pen & Pr Unltd.
*__Bobke: A Ride on the Wild Side of Cycling.__ Bob Roll. 175p. 1995. pap. 11.95 (1-884737-12-9) VeloPress.
*__Bobo & the Greedy Tito.__ Funmi Ogun. (Illus.). 16p. (Orig.). (J). 1994. pap. 14.95 (1-882188-09-8) Magnolia Mktg.
Bobo Baxter: An Original Compilation, First Collection of the Complete Daily Strip, Which Ran from 1927 to 1928. Rube Goldberg. Ed. by Bill Blackbeard. LC 76-53042. (Classic American Comic Strips Ser.). (Illus.). 1993. 35.00 (0-88355-639-1) Hyperion Conn.
Bob's Joint: A Poetry Collection. Ed. by Bob Balo. 1994. write for info. (1-884391-05-2) Bobs Joint.
Bob's Letters. Robert Fox. 1980. 5.95 (0-87881-086-2) Mojave Bks.
Bob's Your Uncle: A Dictionary of Slang for British Mystery Fans. Jann Turner-Lord. LC 92-3858. 64p. (Orig.). 1992. pap. 8.95 (1-56474-022-6) Fithian Pr.
Bobsledding: Down the Chute! Stephen Gregory. LC 75-23407. (Illus.). 32p. (J). (gr. 5-10). 1976. lib. bdg. 10.79 (0-89375-002-6); pap. 2.95 (0-89375-018-2) Troll Assocs.
Bobst & Beyond: A Guide to Graduate Research in New York City with a Directory of Research Library Collections & Archives. Ed. by Lise Dyckman & George A. Thompson. (Illus.). 104p. (C). 1994. pap. write for info. (0-9641374-0-2) NYU Ofc Advert.
Bobwhite Quail. LC 73-96025. 1992. 50.00 (0-8135-0603-4) GSJ Press.
Bobwhite Quail: Its Habits, Preservation & Increase. Herbert L. Stoddard. LC 81-914570. (Illus.). 590p. 1992. 100.00 (0-914570-14-5) L'Avant Studios.
Bobwhites in the Rio Grande Plain of Texas. Val W. Lehmann. LC 83-40495. (Illus.). 394p. 1985. 40.00 (0-89096-186-7) Tex A&M Univ Pr.
Boby Yath'hab Ilal Madrasa. Eric Hill. (Lift-the-Flap Ser.). (Illus.). 24p. (ARA.). (J). (ps-2). 1988. 10.95 (0-940793-03-2, Crocodile Bks) Interlink Pub.
Boca Grande: A Series of Historical Essays. Charles D. Gibson. LC 82-90197. (Illus.). 250p. (Orig.). 1982. pap. text ed. 12.95 (0-9608996-0-X) Ensign Pr.
Bocadillos Para el Alma: Tidbits for the Soul. Rodolfo Loyola. (SPA.). 4.00 (84-7228-306-2, 220113, Pub. by Edit Clie SP) TSELF.
Boccaccian Novella: The Creation & Waning of a Genre. Corradina Caporello-Szykman. Ed. by Aldo Scaglione. (Studies in Italian Culture: Literature in History: Vol. 2). 167p. 1990. 49.95 (0-8204-1134-5) P Lang Pubs.
Boccaccio. W. J. Fielding. 1972. 59.95 (0-87968-763-0) Gordon Pr.
Boccaccio: "Decameron" David Wallace. (Landmarks of World Literature Ser.). (Illus.). 128p. (C). 1991. 29.95 (0-521-38182-7); pap. 10.95 (0-521-38851-1) Cambridge U Pr.
Boccaccio, Beauveau & Chaucer: Sources for Troilus & Criseyde. Michael G. Hanly. 235p. 1991. 32.95 (0-937664-83-9) Pilgrim Bks OK.
*__Boccaccio in English: A Bibliography of Editions, Adaptations, & Criticism.__ F. S. Stych. LC 94-41268. (Bibliographies & Indexes in World Literature Ser.: Vol. 48). 280p. 1995. text ed. 79.50 (0-313-28967-0, Greenwood Pr) Greenwood.
Boccaccio's & Chaucer's Cressida. Laura D. Kellogg. LC 94-17920. (Studies in the Humanities: Vol. 16). 144p. (C). 1995. text ed. 42.95 (0-8204-2559-1) P Lang Pubs.
Boccaccio's Revenge. N. R. Cartier. 1977. pap. text ed. 37.50 (90-247-1961-5) Kluwer Ac.
Boccaccio's Two Venuses. Robert Hollander. LC 77-5144. 1977. text ed. 42.00 (0-231-04224-8) Col U Pr.
*__Boccerini's Minuet.__ Gerald Burns. (Lucky Heart Book Ser.). reprint ed. pap. 25.00 (0-7837-9099-6, 2049849) Bks Demand.
Bocci Affair. 1994. lib. bdg. 258.95 (0-8490-9034-2) Gordon Pr.
Boccioni. Ester Coen. (Illus.). 328p. 1988. 49.50 (0-87099-522-7, Abrams) Metro Mus Art.
Boche & Bolshevik. Nesta Webster. 82p. reprint ed. pap. 4.95 (0-945001-03-7) GSG & Assocs.
Bocheck in Poland. (J). (gr. 2-8). 1980. 9.95 (0-317-02772-7) Polanie.
Bochner Technique in Differential Geometry. H. H. Wu. Ed. by J. Dieudonne. (Mathematical Reports: Vol. 3, No. 2). xii, 252p. 1988. pap. text ed. 143.00 (3-7186-0383-7) Gordon & Breach.
Bock. Darryl Richman. (Classic Beer Style Ser.). (Illus.). 165p. (Orig.). 1994. pap. 11.95 (0-937381-39-X) Brewers Pubns.
Bockus Gastroenterology, 7 vols. J. Edward Berk et al. (Illus.). 4730p. 1985. 100.00 (0-685-42732-3) Saunders.
Bockus Gastroenterology, Set. 5th ed. Ed. by William S. Haubrich et al. LC 93-2763. 1994. text ed. 595.00 (0-7216-3687-X) Saunders.
Bocuse's Regional French Cooking. Paul Bocuse. 256p. 1991. 17.98 (2-08-013517-1, Pub. by Flammarion) Abbeville Pr.
*__Boda! A Zapotec Wedding.__ Nancy Van Laan. LC 94-39169. (Illus.). (ENG & SPA.). 1995. 15.95 (0-316-89626-8) Little.
Bodacious Borders. B. Armstrong. LC 92-81600. 68p. (J). 1992. 9.95 (0-88160-214-0, LW208) Learning Works.
*__Bodacious Kid.__ Stan Lynde. Ed. by Jael Prezeau. LC 95-68395. (Illus.). 352p. 1996. 29.00 (1-886370-10-9) Cttnwd Pub.
Bodas de Sangre. Federico Garcia Lorca & Fernando Lazaro Carreter. (Nueva Austral Ser.: Vol. 26). (SPA.). 1991. pap. text ed. 12.95 (84-239-1826-2) Elliots Bks.
Bodas de Sangre. Garcia Lorca. 172p. (SPA.). 1987. 11.95 (0-8288-7011-X) Fr & Eur.
*__Bodas de Sangre.__ 4th ed. Federico G. Lorca. 232p. 1989. pap. 11.95 (0-7859-5200-4) Fr & Eur.
Bodas de Sangre. 5th ed. Federico G. Lorca. 176p. (SPA.). 1989. pap. 8.95 (0-7859-4977-1) Fr & Eur.
Bode Sketchbook Diaries, Vol. 1. Vaughn Bode. Ed. by Gary Groth. (Illus.). 64p. 1990. 9.95 (1-56097-028-6) Fantagraph Bks.
Bode Sketchbook Diaries, Vol. 2. Vaughn Bode. (Illus.). 64p. 1990. pap. 9.95 (1-56097-044-8) Fantagraph Bks.
Bode Sketchbook Diaries, Vol. 3. Vaughn Bode. (Illus.). 72p. 1991. pap. 10.95 (1-56097-053-7) Fantagraph Bks.
Bodega of Palenque, Chiapas Mexico. Linda Schele & Peter Mathews. LC 79-63728. (Illus.). 173p. 1978. pap. 24.00 (0-88402-085-1) Dumbarton Oaks.
Bodega Sold Dreams. Miguel Pinero. LC 79-90765. (Illus.). (Orig.). 1979. pap. 5.00 (0-934770-05-0) Arte Publico.
Bodega Sold Dreams. 2nd ed. Miguel Pinero. LC 79-90765. (Illus.). 1986. pap. 5.00 (0-685-18634-2) Arte Publico.
Bodelian Shelley Manuscripts. Ed. by Michael O'Neill. LC 86-4746. (Bodleian Shelley Manuscripts Ser.). 548p. 1994. 195.00 (0-8153-1155-9) Garland.
Boden als Anlageobjekt und Produktionsfaktor. Wolfgang Eckart. (European University Studies: Economics & Management: Ser. 5, Vol. 385). 173p. (GER.). 1982. 30.75 (3-8204-7222-3) P Lang Pubs.
Boden's Beasts. Arthur Boden & John Woodside. (Illus.). (J). (gr. 1-5). 1964. 8.95 (0-8392-3045-1) Astor-Honor.
Bodhgaya Interviews. Dalai Lama. Ed. & Intro. by Jose Ignacio Cabezon. LC 88-6713. 104p. (Orig.). 1988. pap. 8.95 (0-937938-62-9) Snow Lion Pubns.
Bodhidharma, the Greatest Zen Master. Osho Rajneesh. Ed. by Ma D. Gitika & Ma D. Sarito. (Zen Ser.). (Illus.). 780p. 1988. 21.95 (3-89338-025-6, Pub. by Rebel Hse GW) Osho Chidvilas.
Bodhisattva. Subhoranjan Dasgupta. 8.00 (0-89253-465-6); 4.00 (0-89253-466-4) Ind-US Inc.
Bodhisattva of Compassion: The Mystical Tradition of Kuan Yin. John Blofeld. LC 87-28524. (Dragon Editions Ser.). (Illus.). 158p. 1988. pap. 15.00 (0-87773-126-8) Shambhala Pubns.
Bodhisattva Vow: The Essential Practices of Mahayana Buddhism. Geshe Kelsang Gyatso. 144p. 1995. 13.95 (0-948006-14-5, Pub. by Tharpa UK); pap. 9.95 (0-948006-19-6, Pub. by Tharpa UK) Atrium Pubns.
Bodhisattva Warriors: The Origin, Inner Philosophy, History & Symbolism of the Buddhist Martial Art Within India & China. Shifu N. Tomio. (Illus.). 560p. (Orig.). 1994. pap. 19.95 (0-87728-785-6) Weiser.
Bodhisattvas Everywhere. Tokuso Sakakibara et al. Ed. by Ruth Tabrah. Tr. by Toshikazu Arai. LC 83-26247. 120p. (Orig.). 1983. pap. 7.95 (0-938474-03-0) Buddhist Study.
Bodhisatyas - Keys to Awakening. Paul Pursley. 1995. 29.95 (0-8062-5107-7) Carlton.
Bodhran Makers. John B. Keane. LC 91-33771. 320p. 1992. reprint ed. 18.95 (0-941423-80-8) FWEW.
Bodhran Tutor Book. Date not set. 12.95 (0-685-75007-8, 95179WW) Mel Bay.
Bodiam Castle. National Trust Staff. (Illus.). 64p. 1991. pap. 9.95 (0-7078-0137-0, Pub. by Natl Trust UK) Trafalgar.
Bodian's Publishing Desk Reference: A Comprehensive Dictionary of Practices & Techniques for Book & Journal Marketing & Bookselling. Nat G. Bodian. 448p. 1988. 49.50 (0-89774-454-3) Oryx Pr.
Bodie. large type ed. Alan Irwin. (Linford Western Library). 240p. 1993. pap. 14.95 (0-7089-7372-8, Linford) Ulverscroft.
Bodie Beauties. Dirk Fletcher. (Spur Ser.: No. 26). 192p. (Orig.). 1988. pap. 2.95 (0-8439-2635-X) Dorchester Pub Co.
Bodie Beauties - Frisco Foxes. Dirk Fletcher. (Spur Double Edition Ser.). 368p. 1993. pap. 4.99 (0-8439-3486-7) Dorchester Pub Co.
Bodie Boomtown of California. Douglas McDonald & Goldtown. (Illus.). 48p. 1988. pap. 4.95 (0-913814-88-1) Nevada Pubns.
Bodie Eighteen Fifty-Nine to Nineteen Hundred. Wedertz. LC 72-96763. 1969. pap. 12.95 (0-912494-20-4) Chalfant Pr.
Bodie Five: Hangtown. large type ed. Neil Hunter. (Western Ser.). 256p. 1994. pap. 14.95 (0-7089-7582-8, Linford) Ulverscroft.
Bodie Four: The Killing Trail. large type ed. Neil Hunter. (Linford Western Library). 240p. 1994. pap. 14.95 (0-7089-7504-6, Linford) Ulverscroft.
Bodie, No. 1: Trackdown. large type ed. Neil Hunter. (Linford Western Library). 272p. 1993. pap. 14.95 (0-7089-7316-7, Linford) Ulverscroft.
Bodie, No. 2: Bloody Bounty. large type ed. Neil Hunter. (Linford Western Library). 256p. 1993. pap. 14.95 (0-7089-7375-2, Linford) Ulverscroft.
*__Bodie Six: The Day of the Savage.__ large type ed. Neil Hunter. (Western Ser.). 1994. pap. 14.95 (0-7089-7591-7, Linford) Ulverscroft.
Bodie Three: High Hell. large type ed. Neil Hunter. (Linford Western Library). 256p. 1994. pap. 14.95 (0-7089-7495-3, Linford) Ulverscroft.
Bodied Spaces: Phenomenology & Performance in Contemporary Drama. Stanton B. Garner, Jr. 272p. 1994. 37.50 (0-8014-3039-9); pap. 14.95 (0-8014-8218-6) Cornell U Pr.
Bodies. James Saunders. 1979. pap. 4.75 (0-8222-0129-1) Dramatists Play.
*__Bodies.__ Ed. by David Walker & Julia Horne. 160p. 1994. 39.95 (0-7855-0338-2, Pub. by Deakin Univ AT) St Mut.
Bodies & Machines. Mark Seltzer. (Illus.). 248p. (Orig.). 1992. write for info. (0-415-90021-2, A1559, Routledge NY); pap. write for info. (0-415-90022-0, A1563, Routledge NY) Routledge Chapman & Hall.
Bodies & Soul: Musical Memoirs. 2nd ed. Al Young. 160p. 1981. pap. 6.95 (0-916870-39-1) Creat Arts Bk.
*__Bodies & Souls.__ Robbin Henderson. Ed. by Robert Schildgen. (Illus.). 32p. (Orig.). 1994. 9.00 (0-942744-03-9) Berkeley Art.
Bodies & Souls. John Rechy. 386p. (Orig.). 1983. pap. 8.95 (0-88184-004-1); pap. 4.50 (0-88184-102-1) Carroll & Graf.
Bodies at Sea: Stories. Erin McGraw. (Illinois Short Fiction Ser.). 168p. 1989. 14.95 (0-252-01631-9) U of Ill Pr.
Bodies Electric. Colin Harrison. 400p. 1994. mass mkt. 5.99 (0-380-72310-7) Avon.
Bodies Electric. Colin Harrison. LC 93-46521. 1994. 25.95 (0-7927-1995-6, Contemp Lrg Print); pap. 24.95 (0-7927-1994-8, Contemp Lrg Print) Chivers N Amer.
Bodies Electric. Colin Harrison. 1993. 20.00 (0-517-58491-3, Crown) Crown Pub Group.

B

An Asterisk (*) at the beginning of an entry indicates that the title is appearing in BIP for the first time.

An Asterisk (*) at the beginning of an entry indicates that the title is appearing in BIP for the first time.

833

Body Build & Behavior in Young Children, Pt. 1. R. N. Walker. (SRCD M: Vol. 27, No. 3). 1962. pap. 15.00 (0-527-01594-6) Periodicals Srv.

Body-Centered Psychotherapy: The Hakomi Method. Ron Kurtz. (Illus.). 212p. (Orig.). 1990. pap. 15.95 (0-940795-03-5) LifeRhythm.

*__Body Cleansing & Detoxification.__ rev. ed. Linda Rector-Page. (Healthy Healing Library Ser.). 32p. 1993. 2.95 (1-884334-31-8) Hlthy Healing.

Body Code: The Meaning in Movement. Warren Lamb & Elizabeth Watson. LC 87-60416. (Illus.). 190p. 1995. reprint ed. pap. 12.95 (0-916622-50-9) Princeton Bk Co.

Body Compass: Poems. David Steingass. LC 76-78534. 70p. reprint ed. pap. 25.00 (0-8357-7333-7, 2020623) Bks Demand.

Body Composition - Research Techniques & Nutritional Assessment. Ed. by Werner Overbeck & Dieter Bohm. (Internationale Zeitschrift fuer Infusionstherapie, Klinische Ernahrung und Transfusionsmedizin Ser.: Supplement 3 zu Band 17, April 1990). 1990. 17.00 (3-8055-5228-9) S Karger.

Body Composition in Biological Anthropology. Roy J. Shepard. (Studies in Biological Anthropology: No. 6). (Illus.). 300p. (C). 1991. 79.95 (0-521-36267-9) Cambridge U Pr.

*__Body Composition Techniques in Health & Disease.__ Ed. by Peter S.W. Davies & T. J. Cole. (Society for the Study of Human Biology Symposium Ser.: 36). (Illus.). 225p. (C). 1995. 54.95 (0-521-46179-0) Cambridge U Pr.

Body Conditioning: A Thinking Person's Guide to Aerobic Fitness. Kenneth France. LC 84-19801. 184p. (Orig.). 1985. pap. 12.95 (0-89334-080-4) Humanics Ltd.

Body Count. Ted Meyer. 166p. 1982. 8.50 (0-682-49840-8) Mey-Hse Bks.

Body Count: A Father Koesler Mystery. William X. Kienzle. (Midwest Mysteries Ser.). 1993. reprint ed. mass mkt. 5.99 (0-345-37767-2) Ballantine.

Body Criticism: Imaging the Unseen in Enlightenment Art & Medicine. Barbara M. Stafford. (Illus.). 608p. 1991. 60.00x (0-262-19304-3) MIT Pr.

Body Criticism: Imaging the Unseen in Enlightenment Art & Medicine. Barbara M. Stafford. 504p. 1993. pap. 29. 95x (0-262-69165-5) MIT Pr.

*__Body Decoration.__ Jillian Powell. (Traditions Around the World Ser.). (Illus.). 48p. (J). (gr. 5-7). 1995. 16.95 (1-56847-276-5) Thomson Lrning.

*__Body Detectives.__ Rita G. Gelman. (J). (ps-3). 1994. pap. 3.95 (0-590-47019-1) Scholastic Inc.

Body Divine: The Symbol of the Body in the Works of Teilhard de Chardin & Ramanuja. Anne H. Overzee. (Studies in Religious Traditions: No. 2). 224p. (C). 1992. 64.95 (0-521-38516-4) Cambridge U Pr.

Body Dynamics: The Body Shape-Up Book for Women. Susan Koch. LC 82-83947. (Illus.). 160p. (Orig.). 1984. pap. 15.00x (0-88011-115-1, PKOC0115) Human Kinetics.

Body Dynamics No. 1: The Easy Way to Great Legs. Gloria West. (Critic's Choice Paperbacks Ser.). 1988. pap. 2.50 (1-55547-278-8, Univ Books) Carol Pub Group.

*__Body Ecology: For a Healthy & Beautiful Body.__ Roe Gallo. Ed. by Nancy Watkins. (Illus.). 134p. (Orig.). 1994. pap. 10.00 (0-9642253-0-1) Gallo Pubns.

Body Ecology Diet: Recovering Your Health & Rebuilding Your Immunity. Donna Gates. 247p. (Orig.). 1993. pap. 19.95 (0-9638458-8-8) Body Ecol Diet.

Body Electric: Electromagnetism & the Foundation of Life. Robert O. Becker & Gary Selden. Ed. by Maria D. Guarnaschelli. LC 86-25168. (Illus.). 448p. 1987. pap. 11.00 (0-688-06971-1, Quill) Morrow.

Body Elite Gourmet. Wendi H. Schwartz. 123p. (Orig.). 1993. pap. write for info. (0-9635503-0-6) Bodyworks Pubs.

Body Embarrassed: Drama & the Disciplines of Shame in Early Modern England. Gail K. Paster. LC 92-36855. (Illus.). 304p. 1993. 42.95 (0-8014-2776-2); pap. 14.95 (0-8014-8060-4) Cornell U Pr.

*__Body Emblazoned: Dissection & the Human Body in Renaissance Culture.__ Jonathan Sawday. LC 94-36943. (Illus.). 336p. 1995. 45.00 (0-415-04444-8, C0196) Routledge.

Body Energy. James S. Skinner. LC 80-24094. (Illus.). 160p. (Orig.). 1981. pap. 5.95 (0-89037-174-1) Anderson World.

Body Experience in Fantasy & Behavior. Seymour Fisher. LC 71-111878. (Century Psychology Ser.). (C). 1970. 36.50 (0-89197-046-0); pap. text ed. 12.95 (0-89197-683-3) Irvington.

*__Body Exposed: 150 Years of Nude Photography.__ 224p. 1995. 45.00 (3-905514-47-8) Dist Art Pubs.

Body Exposures. Barbara Ess et al. (Illus.). 64p. 1993. 22.50 (3-906700-54-2, Pub. by Lars Muller SZ) Dist Art Pubs.

Body Facts. A. Ganeri. (Facts & Lists Ser.). (Illus.). 48p. (J). (gr. 3-7). 1993. lib. bdg. 12.96 (0-88110-599-6); pap. 5.95 (0-7460-0948-8) EDC.

Body Fantasy. William C. Schutz & Evelyn Turner. 135p. (C). 1985. reprint ed. 15.95 (0-8290-1330-X); reprint ed. pap. text ed. 6.95 (0-8290-0994-9) Irvington.

*__Body Farm.__ Patricia Cornwell. 368p. (Orig.). 1995. pap. 6.99 (0-425-14762-2) Berkley Pub.

*__Body Farm.__ Patricia D. Cornwell. 352p. 1995. pap. text ed. 6.99 (0-425-14863-7, Prime Crime) Berkley Pub.

*__Body Farm.__ large type ed. Patricia D. Cornwell. LC 94-34500. 403p. 1994. 24.95 (0-7838-1122-5) Hall.

*__Body Farm.__ large type ed. Patricia D. Cornwell. LC 94-34500. 1995. pap. 18.95 (0-7838-1123-3) Hall.

Body Farm: A Novel. Patricia Cornwell. 352p. 1994. text ed. 20.00 (0-684-19597-6, Scribners) S&S Trade.

Body Fat: A Loser's Manual. Don McDaniel. (Illus.). 185p. (Orig.). 1992. pap. 12.95 (0-9624378-2-4) Life Fitness.

Body Flex - Body Magic. Anja Langer & Bill Reynolds. (Illus.). 368p. 1992. pap. 14.95 (0-8092-3930-2) Contemp Bks.

Body Fluid Homeostasis. Ed. by Barry M. Brenner & Jay H. Stein. (Contemporary Issues in Nephrology Ser.: Vol. 16). (Illus.). 454p. 1986. text ed. 73.00 (0-443-08530-7) Churchill.

Body Fluids: Laboratory Examination of Amniotic, Cerebrospinal, Seminal, Serous & Synovial Fluids. 3rd ed. Carl R. Kjeldsberg & Joseph A. Knight. LC 92-23968. (Illus.). 436p. 1993. 135.00 (0-89189-344-X) Am Soc Clinical.

*__Body Fluids: Laboratory Examination of Amniotic, Cerebrospinal, Seminal, Serous & Synovial Fluids, 200-35mm Slides.__ 3rd ed. Carl R. Kjeldsberg & Joseph A. Knight. 1993. sl. 250.00 (0-614-02698-9) Am Soc Clinical.

Body Fluids & Electrolytes: A Programmed Presentation. Norma J. Weldy. (Illus.). 224p. 1991. 19.95 (0-8016-5577-3) Mosby Yr Bk.

*__Body Fluids & Electrolytes: A Programmed Presentation.__ 7th ed. Norma J. Weldy. LC 95-10053. 1995. write for info. (0-8151-9197-9) Mosby Yr Bk.

*__Body Flute.__ limited ed. Cortney Davis. 24p. (Orig.). 1994. pap. 8.00 (0-938566-66-0) Adastra Pr.

Body for Christmas. Richard Reinsmith. (Bodyguard Ser.). 240p. 1984. pap. 2.50 (0-8439-2071-8) Dorchester Pub Co.

Body for McHugh. large type ed. Jay Flynn. (Linford Mystery Library). 320p. 1993. pap. 14.95 (0-7089-7350-7, Linford) Ulverscroft.

*__Body Game.__ (DK Family Library). (J). Date not set. write for info. (0-7894-0238-6, 5-70646) Dorling Kindersley.

Body Guard. large type ed. Rex Burns. LC 91-46908. 431p. 1992. reprint ed. lib. bdg. 17.95 (1-56054-356-6) Thorndike Pr.

Body Guard: Sixth Carol Ashton Mystery. Claire McNab. 224p. 1994. pap. 10.95 (1-56280-073-6) Naiad Pr.

Body Guards: The Cultural Politics of Gender Ambiguity. Ed. by Julia Epstein & Kristina Straub. (Illus.). 400p. 1991. 52.50 (0-415-90388-2, A5275, Routledge NY); pap. 16.95 (0-415-90389-0, A5279, Routledge NY) Routledge.

Body Has Its Reasons. Therese Bertherat & Carol Bernstein. 176p. 1989. pap. 9.95 (0-89281-298-2, Heal Arts VT) Inner Tradit.

Body, Heart, & Text in the "Pearl"-Poet. Kevin Marti. LC 91-29879. (Studies in Mediaeval Literature: Vol. 12). 220p. 1991. lib. bdg. 89.95 (0-7734-9764-1) E Mellen.

Body Heat: Adventure. Elise Title. (Temptation Ser.). 1994. mass mkt. 2.99 (0-373-25573-X, 1-25573-6) Harlequin Bks.

Body Hispanic: Gender & Sexuality in Spanish & Spanish American Literature. Paul J. Smith. 232p. 1990. 49.95 (0-19-815863-7) OUP.

Body Hispanic: Gender & Sexuality in Spanish & Spanish American Literature. Paul J. Smith. (Illus.). 230p. 1992. pap. 18.95 (0-19-815874-2) OUP.

Body Image & Perceptual Dysfunction in Adults. Julia M. Van Deusen. (Illus.). 267p. 1992. pap. text ed. 33.50 (0-7216-3172-X) Saunders.

Body Image & the Image of the Brain. Warren Gorman. LC 68-8293. (Illus.). 298p. 1969. 10.60 (0-87527-037-9) Green.

Body Image Disturbance. Thompson. (Practitioner Guidebook Ser.). (C). 1990. pap. 25.95 (0-205-14482-9, H4482, Longwood Div) Allyn.

Body Image Trap: Understanding & Rejecting the Body Image Myth. Marion Crook. (Psychology Ser.). 128p. (Orig.). 1992. pap. 8.95 (0-88908-975-2) Self-Counsel Pr.

Body Imaged: The Human Form & Visual Culture since the Renaissance. Ed. by Kathleen Adler & Marcia Pointon. (Illus.). 228p. (C). 1993. pap. 19.95 (0-521-44768-2) Cambridge U Pr.

Body Imaged: The Human Form & Visual Culture since the Renaissance. Ed. by Kathleen Adler & Marcia Pointon. (Illus.). 228p. (C). 1993. 69.95 (0-521-41536-5) Cambridge U Pr.

Body Images: Development, Deviance & Change. Ed. by Thomas F. Cash & Thomas Pruzinsky. LC 90-3405. 361p. 1990. lib. bdg. 39.95 (0-89862-438-X) Guilford Pr.

Body in Blackwater Bay. Paula Gosling. 304p. 1992. 17.95 (0-89296-459-6) Mysterious Pr.

Body in Blackwater Bay. Paula Gosling. 288p. 1993. mass mkt. 4.99 (0-446-40319-9, Mysterious Paperbk) Warner Bks.

Body in Blackwater Bay. large type ed. Paula Gosling. 470p. 1992. reprint ed. lib. bdg. 19.95 (1-56054-570-4) Thorndike Pr.

Body in Brief: Essentials for Health Care. 2nd ed. Rebecca Rayman. (Illus.). 400p. 1993. 26.95 (0-944132-76-6) Skidmore Roth Pub.

Body in Four Parts. Janet Kauffman. LC 92-34193. 144p. 1993. 18.00 (1-55597-179-2) Graywolf.

Body in Illness & Health: Themes & Images in Jane Austen. Anita G. Gorman. LC 92-36595. (American University Studies: English Language & Literature: Ser. IV, Vol. 154). 212p. 1993. 45.95 (0-8204-1996-6) P Lang Pubs.

Body in Medical Thought & Practice. Ed. by Drew Leder. (Philosophy & Medicine Ser.). 272p. (C). 1992. lib. bdg. 109.50 (0-7923-1657-6) Kluwer Ac.

Body in Pain: The Making & Unmaking of the World. Elaine Scarry. LC 85-15585. 385p. 1985. 30.00 (0-19-503601-8) OUP.

Body in Pain: The Making & Unmaking of the World. Elaine Scarry. LC 85-15585. 385p. 1987. pap. 13.95 (0-19-504996-9) OUP.

Body in Paradise. Richard Reinsmith. (Bodyguard Ser.). 240p. 1984. pap. 2.50 (0-8439-2106-4) Dorchester Pub Co.

*__Body in Pieces: The Fragment As a Metaphor of Modernity.__ Linda Nochlin. LC 94-61110. (Walter Neurath Memorial Lecture Ser.). (Illus.). 64p. 1995. 14. 95 (0-500-55027-1) Thames Hudson.

Body in Psychotherapy. Edward W. Smith. LC 84-43201. (Illus.). 199p. 1985. lib. bdg. 23.95x (0-89950-169-9) McFarland & Co.

Body in Recovery: Somatic Psychotherapy & the Self. John Conger. LC 93-37231. 277p. (Orig.). 1994. pap. 16. 95 (1-883319-06-4) Frog CA.

Body in Swift & Defoe. Carol H. Flynn. (Cambridge Studies in Eighteenth-Century English Literature & Thought: No. 5). 256p. (C). 1990. 59.95 (0-521-38268-8) Cambridge U Pr.

Body in the Basement. Katherine P. Hall. 272p. 1994. 20. 95 (0-312-11470-2, Pub. by Thomas Dunne Bks) St Martin.

*__Body in the Basement.__ Katherine H. Page. (Faith Fairchild Mystery Ser.). 304p. 1995. reprint ed. mass mkt. 4.99 (0-380-72339-5) Avon.

Body in the Belfry. Katherine H. Page. 256p. 1991. reprint ed. mass mkt. 4.99 (0-380-71328-4) Avon.

Body in the Bouillon. Katherine H. Page. 224p. 1992. mass mkt. 4.50 (0-380-71896-0) Avon.

Body in the Bouillon. Katherine H. Page. 224p. 1991. 17.95 (0-312-06309-1, Pub. by Thomas Dunne Bks) St Martin.

*__Body in the Cast.__ Katherine H. Page. 272p. 1994. mass mkt. 4.99 (0-380-72338-7) Avon.

Body in the Cast. Katherine H. Page. 224p. 1993. 19.95 (0-312-09755-7, Pub. by Thomas Dunne Bks) St Martin.

Body in the Cornflakes. K. K. Beck. (Northwest Mysteries Ser.). 1994. mass mkt. 4.99 (0-8041-1175-8) Ivy Books.

Body in the Cornflakes. K. K. Beck. 224p. 1992. 17.95 (0-312-08146-4, Pub. by Thomas Dunne Bks) St Martin.

Body in the Kelp. Katherine H. Page. 1990. 16.95 (0-312-05392-4) St Martin.

Body in the Kelp. Katherine H. Page. 1992. mass mkt. 4.99 (0-380-71329-2) Avon.

Body in the Library. large type ed. Agatha Christie. (Popular Author Ser.). 249p. 1988. lib. bdg. 16.95 (0-8161-4458-3) G K Hall.

Body in the Library: A Miss Marple Mystery. Agatha Christie. 1992. mass mkt. 4.99 (0-06-100364-6, Harp PBks) HarpC.

Body in the Mind: The Bodily Basis of Meaning, Imagination, & Reason. Mark Johnson. (Illus.). xxxviii, 234p. 1990. pap. text ed. 15.95 (0-226-40318-1) U Ch Pr.

Body in the Mirror: Shapes of History in Italian Cinema. Angela D. Vacche. (Illus.). 357p. 1992. text ed. 59.50 (0-691-05566-1); pap. text ed. 21.95 (0-691-00872-8) Princeton U Pr.

*__Body in the Red Velvet Robe.__ Dorothy Abel. 1995. 17.95 (0-8034-9108-5, 095131) Bouregy.

*__Body in the Transept: A Dorothy Martin Mystery.__ Jeanne Dams. 1995. 19.95 (0-8027-3275-5) Walker & Co.

Body in the Vestibule. Katherine H. Page. 224p. 1993. mass mkt. 4.99 (0-380-72079-5) Avon.

Body in the Vestibule. Katherine H. Page. 234p. 1992. 17. 95 (0-312-08148-0, Pub. by Thomas Dunne Bks) St Martin.

Body in the Volvo. K. K. Beck. 1987. 16.95 (0-8027-5685-9) Walker & Co.

Body in the Volvo. large type ed. K. K. Beck. LC 92-795. 260p. 1992. reprint ed. lib. bdg. 17.95 (1-56054-379-5) Thorndike Pr.

Body India. Elizabeth McKim. (Illus.). 56p. 1981. 12.95 (0-938756-04-4); pap. 6.95 (0-938756-03-6) Yellow Moon.

Body Invaders: Panic Sex in America. Ed. by Arthur Kroker & Marilouise Kroker. 256p. 1988. pap. 14.95 (0-312-01380-9) St Martin.

Body Is a Clear Place & Other Statements on Dance. Erick Hawkins. 224p. 1992. pap. 14.95 (0-87127-166-4) Princeton Bk Co.

*__Body Is Water: A Novel.__ Julie Schumacher. 272p. 1995. 21.00 (1-56947-042-1) Soho Press.

Body Know-How: A Practical Guide to the Use of the Alexander Technique in Everyday Life. Jonathan Drake. 1992. pap. 12.95 (0-7225-2394-7) Thorsons SF.

*__Body Knows: A Theopoetics of Death & Resurrection.__ Melanie A. May. 128p. 1995. 16.95 (0-8264-0849-4) Continuum.

Body Language. (Teach Yourself Ser.). 220p. 1993. pap. 7.95 (0-8442-3909-7) NTC Pub Grp.

Body Language. Jill Briscoe. 108p. 1987. pap. 6.99 (0-89693-319-9, Victor Books) SP Pubns.

Body Language. Julius Fast. 1994. 6.98 (1-56731-004-4, MJF Bks) Fine Comms.

Body Language. Julius Fast. LC 72-106592. (Illus.). 192p. 1970. 12.95 (0-87131-039-2) M Evans.

Body Language. Garrison. (Power Japanese Ser.). 1991. pap. 10.00 (4-7700-1955-6) Kodansha.

Body Language: Figurative Aspects of Recent Art. Roberta Smith. (Illus.). 116p. (Orig.). 1982. pap. 10.00 (0-938437-02-X) MIT List Visual Arts.

Body Language & Emotion of Cats. Myrna M. Milani. LC 87-5772. 288p. 1987. 18.95 (0-688-06786-7) Morrow.

Body Language & Emotion of Cats. Myrna M. Milani. 1993. pap. 12.00 (0-688-12840-8, Quill) Morrow.

Body Language & Emotion of Dogs. Myrna M. Milani. 1993. pap. 12.00 (0-688-12841-6, Quill) Morrow.

Body Language & Emotions of Dogs. Myrna M. Milani. LC 86-8449. 288p. 1986. 17.95 (0-688-06239-3) Morrow.

Body Language for Competent Teachers. Sean Neill & Chris Caswell. LC 92-24744. 1993. pap. 17.95 (0-415-06660-3, A9892, Routledge NY) Routledge.

Body Language in the Workplace. Julius Fast. 256p. 1994. pap. 10.95 (0-14-017815-5, Penguin Bks) Viking Penguin.

Body Language Sex Signals. H. R. Samiy. 64p. 1993. pap. 5.95 (1-871964-06-7, Pub. by Ideas Unltd UK) Atrium Pubs.

Body Lightning. Mel Clay. (Illus.). 67p. (Orig.). 1983. pap. text ed. 2.50 (1-879594-06-4) Androgyne Bks.

Body Love: The Amazing Career of Bernarr Macfadden. William R. Hunt. LC 89-51126. (Illus.). 223p. (C). 1989. lib. bdg. 35.95 (0-87972-463-3); pap. 18.95 (0-87972-464-1) Bowling Green Univ.

Body Magnetic. abr. ed. Buryl Payne. (Illus.). 120p. 1991. pap. text ed. 12.00 (0-9628569-9-1) Psycho Physics.

Body Management. Bosworth et al. (Body Awareness Resource Network Ser.). (YA). (gr. 7-12). Date not set. disk 120.00 (0-912899-58-1) Lrning Multi-Systs.

Body-Marking in Southwestern Asia. H. Field. (Harvard University Peabody Museum of Archaeology & Ethnology Papers: Vol. 45, No. 1). 1972. reprint ed. 29. 00 (0-527-01318-8) Periodicals Srv.

*__Body Mastery: The Journey to Discovering the Perfect Body.__ Kris Gebhardt. (Illus.). 224p. (Orig.). 1995. pap. 14.95 (1-57028-042-8) Masters Pr IN.

Body Matters: Essays on the Sociology of the Body. Ed. by Sue Scott & David Morgan. 200p. 1993. 90.00 (0-7507-0942-1, Falmer Pr); pap. 32.50 (0-7507-0943-X, Falmer Pr) Taylor & Francis.

Body Matters: Essays on the Sociology of the Body. Ed. by Sue Scott & David Morgan. 200p. 1993. 79.00 (1-85000-942-2, Falmer Pr); pap. 27.00 (1-85000-943-0, Falmer Pr) Taylor & Francis.

Body Matters for Women. Aine McCarthy. (Attic Handbooks Ser.). (Illus.). 128p. (Orig.). (C). 1989. pap. 7.95 (0-946211-86-8, Pub. by Attic IE) InBook.

*__Body Mechanics of Tai Chi Chuan.__ William C. Chen. 176p. Date not set. pap. 14.95 (0-9644084-0-6) W C C Chen.

Body, Memory & Architecture. Kent C. Bloomer & Charles W. Moore. LC 77-76304. (Illus.). 1977. pap. 17.00 (0-300-02142-9) Yale U Pr.

Body Message for Beauty Therapy. 2nd ed. 1989. 24.95 (0-7506-0523-5) Buttrwrth-Heinemann.

Body Mike: The Unsparing Expose by the Mafia Insider Who Turned on the Mob. Joseph Cantalupo & Thomas C. Renner. LC 89-40196. 352p. 1989. 18.95 (0-394-56371-9, Villard Bks) Random.

Body, Mind & Death. Ed. by Antony G. Flew. 320p. 1964. pap. 6.95 (0-02-084840-4, Collier S&S) S&S Trade.

Body, Mind & Health: A Biblical Approach to Wholeness. Monte Kline. 128p. 1992. pap. 8.95 (0-9632948-0-6) Total Living.

Body, Mind, & Method. Ed. by Donald F. Gustafson & Bangs L. Tapscott. (Synthese Library: No. 138). 1979. lib. bdg. 64.00 (90-277-1013-9) Kluwer Ac.

Body, Mind, & Spirit: A Dictionary of New Age Ideas, People, Places, & Terms. Eileen Campbell. (Alternative Health Ser.). 256p. 1994. pap. 14.95 (0-8048-3010-X) C E Tuttle.

Body, Mind, & Spirit: Daily Meditations. Ed. by Kristen Ison. LC 91-75300. (Meditation Ser.). 400p. (Orig.). 1990. pap. 7.95 (0-942421-29-9) Hazelden.

*__Body, Mind, & Spirit: Daily Meditations.__ Ed. by Kristen Ison. LC 91-75300. (Meditation Ser.). 400p. (Orig.). 1990. pap. 7.95 (1-56838-077-1) Hazelden.

Body, Mind & Spirit: To Harmony Through Meditation. Louis Hughes. LC 91-65004. 128p. (Orig.). 1991. pap. 7.95 (0-89622-484-8, C56) Twenty-Third.

Body, Mind, & Sport: The Body-Type Guide to Health, Fitness, & Longevity. John Douillard. LC 93-26446. 1994. 22.00 (0-517-59455-2, Harmony) Crown Pub Group.

*__Body, Mind, & Sport: The Mind-Body Guide to Lifelong Fitness & Your Personal Best.__ John Douillard. 1995. pap. 13.00 (0-517-88383-X, Crown) Crown Pub Group.

Body Mind Connection in Human Movement Analysis. Susan Loman & Rose Brandt. LC 92-70393. 235p. (C). 1992. pap. text ed. 12.00 (1-881245-00-4) Antioch New Eng.

Body-Mind Workbook. Debbie Shapiro. 1990. pap. 13.95 (1-85230-167-8) Element MA.

Body Movement: Coping with the Environment. I. Bartenieff & D. Lewis. 304p. 1980. text ed. 60.00 (0-677-05500-5) Gordon & Breach.

Body Movement: Perspectives in Research, 10 vols, Set. Ed. by Martha Davis. (Illus.). 1975. 84.00 (0-405-06197-8) Ayer.

Body, Movement, & Culture: Kinesthetic & Visual Symbolism in a Philippine Community. Sally A. Ness. LC 92-15310. (Contemporary Ethnography Ser.). (Illus.). 312p. (Orig.). (C). 1992. text ed. 41.95 (0-8122-3110-4); pap. text ed. 17.95 (0-8122-1383-1) U of Pa Pr.

Body Movement & Speech in Medical Interaction. Christian Heath. (Cambridge Studies in Emotion & Social Interaction). (Illus.). 272p. 1986. 54.95 (0-521-25335-7) Cambridge U Pr.

Body Moves (Poems) Tim Seibles. LC 88-70160. (Poets Ser.). 60p. 1988. pap. 6.95 (0-931722-68-3) Corona Pub.

Body of a Crime. Michael C. Eberhardt. LC 93-30902. 352p. 1994. 19.95 (0-525-93623-8, Dutton) NAL-Dutton.

*__Body of a Crime.__ Michael C. Eberhardt. 448p. 1995. pap. 5.99 (0-451-40569-2, Onyx) NAL-Dutton.

Body of a Person. Virgil C. Aldrich. LC 88-19017. 114p. (Orig.). (C). 1988. lib. bdg. 32.00 (0-8191-7105-0); pap. text ed. 15.00 (0-8191-7106-9) U Pr of Amer.

Body of Beatrice. Robert P. Harrison. LC 88-3944. 256p. 1988. text ed. 34.00x (0-8018-3680-8) Johns Hopkins.

Body of Christ. Gary Teja. 1992. 4.50 (1-55955-126-7) CITE MI.

Body of Christ: A Reality. Watchman Nee. Tr. by Stephen Kaung. 90p. 1978. pap. 3.50 (0-935008-13-6) Christian Fellow Pubs.

An Asterisk (*) at the beginning of an entry indicates that the title is appearing in BIP for the first time.

Body of Christ Is Overweight. Beryle E. Whitten. Ed. by Florence Biros & Stan Scott. (Mini Teaching Ser.). 72p. (Orig.). 1987. pap. 3.95 (*0-936369-09-4*) Son-Rise Pubns.

Body of Dancers. Candice L. Brown. LC 93-70996. 250p. 1993. 18.00 (*1-880909-07-3*) Baskerville.

Body of Divinity. Thomas Watson. 1978. pap. 14.95 (*0-85151-383-2*) Banner of Truth.

Body of Divinity. Thomas Watson. 316p. 1993. reprint ed. 21.95 (*0-85151-144-9*) Banner of Truth.

Body of Earth. John Fandel. LC 79-181993. pap. 8.50 (*0-87957-000-8*) Roth Pub.

Body of Evidence. Patricia D. Cornwell. (Kay Scarpetta Mystery Ser.). 416p. 1995. mass mkt. 6.50 (*0-380-71701-8*) Avon.

Body of Evidence. Arnston Harrison. 1993. mass mkt. 5.99 (*0-06-100675-0*, Harp PBks) HarpC.

Body of Evidence. large type ed. Patricia D. Cornwell. LC 93-27186. 1994. 22.95 (*0-8161-5866-5*) Hall.

Body of Evidence: A Kay Scarpetta Novel. Patricia D. Cornwell. 256p. 1991. text ed. 18.95 (*0-684-19240-3*, Scribners) S&S Trade.

Body of Frankenstein's Monster: Essays in Myth & Medicine. Cecil Helman. 208p. 1992. 19.95 (*0-393-03104-7*) Norton.

Body of God: An Ecological Theology. Sallie McFague. LC 93-6584. 208p. 1993. pap. 15.00 (*0-8006-2735-0*, 1-2735) Augsburg Fortress.

Body of Knowledge: A Novel. Carol Dawson. LC 94-13355. 1994. write for info. (*1-56512-054-X*) Algonquin Bks.

Body of Knowledge: An Introduction to Body - Mind Psychology. Robert Marrone. LC 89-28863. (Transpersonal & Humanistic Psychology Ser.). 160p. 1990. 49.50 (*0-7914-0387-4*); pap. 16.95 (*0-7914-0388-2*) State U NY Pr.

Body of Liberties. Peter Gurnis. (Poetry Chapbooks). 32p. (Orig.). 1987. pap. 4.00 (*0-930901-45-2*) Burning Deck.

Body of Life. Thomas Hanna. LC 79-3503. (Illus.). 1980. 15.95 (*0-394-42383-6*) Knopf.

Body of Life: Creating New Pathways for Sensory Awareness & Fluid Movement. Thomas Hanna. 224p. 1993. pap. 10.95 (*0-89281-481-0*, Heal Arts VT) Inner Tradit.

Body of Light: History & Practical Techniques for Awakening Your Subtle Body. John Mann & Lar Short. (Illus.). 192p. (Orig.). 1993. reprint ed. 12.95 (*0-8048-1992-0*) C E Tuttle.

Body of Light, Life & Immortality Keys to Translation. Muriel Isis. 306p. (Orig.). 1991. pap. 25.00 (*1-879380-06-4*) Lighted Way.

Body of Love. Tee Corinne. 1994. pap. 9.95 (*0-934411-52-2*, Banned Bks) Edward-William Austin.

Body of Myth: Mythology, Shamanic Trance, & the Sacred Geography of the Body. J. Nigro Sansonese. (Illus.). 256p. (Orig.). 1994. pap. 24.95 (*0-89281-409-8*) Inner Tradit.

Body of Opinion. Susannah Stacey. Ed. by Jane Chelius. 224p. 1991. reprint ed. pap. 4.99 (*0-671-73427-X*) PB.

Body of Power, Spirit of Resistance: The Culture & History of a South African People. Jean Comaroff. LC 84-24012. (Illus.). 304p. 1985. pap. text ed. 14.95 (*0-226-11423-6*) U Ch Pr.

Body of the Work. Ryki Zuckerman. Ed. by Joy Walsh. (Illus.). (Orig.). 1984. pap. 3.50 (*0-938838-11-3*) Textile Bridge.

Body of Truth. Paul Ferrini. (Illus.). (Orig.). 1990. pap. 7.50 (*1-879159-02-3*) Heartways Pr.

Body of Truth. David L. Lindsay. 1993. mass mkt. 6.50 (*0-553-28964-0*) Bantam.

Body of Water. Judith Freeman. Date not set. pap. write for info. (*0-679-75271-4*) Random.

Body of Water. Jenna Zark. 1994. pap. 4.75 (*0-8222-1390-7*) Dramatists Play.

Body on the Beach see Murder in Washington

Body Packaging. Julian Robinson. LC 88-6888. (Illus.). 192p. (C). 1988. 32.95 (*1-55599-027-4*) Elysium.

***Body Parts.** Michael Bates. (Bloodlust Ser.: No. 4). (YA). 1995. mass mkt. 3.99 (*0-553-56700-4*) Bantam.

***Body Parts.** William A. Fahey. (Illus.). 32p. (Orig.). (C). 1993. pap. text ed. 5.00 (*1-878173-34-0*) Birnham Wood.

Body Parts. William C. Knott. 1991. pap. 3.95 (*0-312-92422-4*) St Martin.

Body Poems. limited ed. John Lane. 20p. 1991. pap. 4.50 (*0-685-64796-X*) New Native Pr.

Body Politic. Tony Flynn. 60p. 1993. pap. 14.95 (*1-85224-129-2*, Pub. by Bloodaxe Bks UK) Dufour.

Body Politics. Maggie Jaffee. (Everybody Books Ser.). 38p. (Orig.). 1989. pap. 4.00 (*0-941720-75-6*) Slough Pr TX.

Body Politics: Disease, Desire, & the Family. Ed. by Michael Ryan & Avery Gordon. LC 93-7934. (Politics & Culture Ser.: Vol. 1). 280p. 1993. text ed. 63.00 (*0-8133-1840-8*) Westview.

Body Politics: Disease, Desire, & the Family. Ed. by Michael Ryan & Avery Gordon. LC 93-7934. (Politics & Culture Ser.: Vol. 1). 280p. (C). 1993. pap. text ed. 22.50 (*0-8133-1841-6*) Westview.

Body Politics: Five Practices of the Christian Community Before the Watching World. John H. Yoder. LC 92-71308. 88p. 1992. pap. 8.95 (*0-88177-118-X*, DR118) Discipleship Res.

Body Politics: Power, Sex, & Nonverbal Communication. Nancy M. Henley. (Patterns of Social Behavior Ser.). (Illus.). 1977. pap. 4.95 (*0-13-079632-8*) P-H.

Body-Politics: Women & the Discourses of Science. Ed. by Mary Jacobus et al. 256p. 1989. 39.50 (*0-415-90130-8*, A3268, Routledge NY); pap. 13.95 (*0-415-90131-6*, A3272, Routledge NY) Routledge.

Body Posture. R. Magnus. (C). 1988. 47.50 (*81-205-0061-X*, Pub. by Oxford IBH II) S Asia.

Body Power. Jenny Vaughan. 1990. 3.99 (*0-517-69906-0*) Random Hse Value.

***Body Power Vision.** Nicholas Mirzoeff. LC 95-6735. (Visual Cultures Ser.). 1995. write for info. (*0-415-09800-9*); pap. write for info. (*0-415-09801-7*) Routledge.

Body Prints. Rochelle Nameroff. LC 73-155607. 54p. 1972. 2.95 (*0-87886-022-3*, Greenfld Rev Pr) Greenfld Rev Lit.

Body Process: Working with the Body in Psychotherapy. James I. Kepner. (Social & Behavioral Science Ser.). 256p. 1993. 27.95 (*1-55542-586-0*) Jossey-Bass.

Body Purification. Brown Landone. 69p. 1994. reprint ed. spiral bd. 5.50 (*0-7873-1132-4*) Mokelumne.

Body Purification: How to Transform Your Body. Brown Landone. 1992. lib. bdg. 79.95 (*0-8490-5278-5*) Gordon Pr.

Body Reading: The Complete Guide. Sasha Fenton. 1990. pap. 9.95 (*0-85030-772-4*, Pub. by Aquarian Pr UK) Thorsons SF.

Body Reflexology: Healing at Your Fingertips. Mildred Carter. LC 83-2422. 234p. 1986. 21.95 (*0-13-079699-9*, Parker Publishing Co); 6.95 (*0-13-079681-6*, Parker Publishing Co) P-H.

Body Reflexology: Healing at Your Fingertips. 2nd rev. ed. Mildred Carter & Tammy Weber. LC 94-15863. 1994. reprint ed. text ed. 29.95 (*0-13-299728-2*, Parker Publishing Co); reprint ed. pap. text ed. 9.95 (*0-13-299736-3*, Parker Publishing Co) P-H.

Body Repair Inspector. Jack Rudman. (Career Examination Ser.: C-3281). 1994. pap. 23.95 (*0-8373-3281-8*) Nat Learn.

Body Reveals: How to Read Your Own Body. Ron Kurtz & Hector Prestera. LC 83-48420. (Illus.). 160p. 1984. pap. 12.00 (*0-06-250488-6*, CN 4084) Harper SF.

Body Ritual Among the Nacirema. Horace Miner. (Reprint Series in Social Sciences). (C). 1993. reprint ed. pap. text ed. 1.30 (*0-8290-4182-6*, S-185) Irvington.

Body Schema & Body Image. D. Tiemersma. 1989. 55.00 (*90-265-1055-1*, Pub. by Swets Pub Serv NE) Taylor & Francis.

Body Science. Anita Ganeri. LC 92-22722. (Science Questions & Answers Ser.). (Illus.). 48p. (J). (gr. 5 up). 1993. text ed. 13.95 (*0-87518-576-2*, Dillon Silver Burdett) Silver Burdett Pr.

Body Scissors. Jerome Doolittle. Ed. by Bill Grose. 240p. (Orig.). 1991. reprint ed. mass mkt. 5.50 (*0-671-70753-1*) PB.

Body Sculpturing by Lipoplasty. Yves-Gerard Illouz & Yves T. De Villers. (Illus.). 496p. 1989. text ed. 195.00 (*0-443-03833-3*) Churchill.

Body Self & Psychological Self: A Developmental & Clinical Integration of Disorders of the Self. David W. Krueger. LC 88-26256. 184p. 1989. 29.95 (*0-87630-543-5*) Brunner-Mazel.

***Body, Self, & Society: The View from Fiji.** Anne E. Becker. (Illus.). 224p. 1995. text ed. 34.95 (*0-8122-3180-5*); pap. text ed. 14.95 (*0-8122-1397-1*) U of Pa Pr.

Body Self & Soul: Sustaining Integration. Jack Rosenberg et al. LC 85-2293. (Illus.). 352p. 1985. lib. bdg. 28.95 (*0-89334-196-7*, 196-7) Humanics Ltd.

Body, Self & Soul: Sustaining Integration. 2nd ed. Jack L. Rosenberg et al. LC 85-2293. 352p. (Orig.). 1985. pap. 18.95 (*0-89334-082-0*) Humanics Ltd.

Body-Self Appreciation. rev. ed. Nathan Liskey & Justine Hill. Ed. by Jason Loam. LC 88-6487. 116p. 1987. pap. 8.95 (*1-55599-019-3*) Elysium.

Body, Self-Cultivation, & Ki-Energy. Yasuo Yuasa. Tr. by Shigenori Nagatomo & Monte S. Hull. LC 92-36569. (SUNY Series, The Body in Culture, History, & Religion). 229p. (C). 1993. 49.50 (*0-7914-1623-2*); pap. 16.95 (*0-7914-1624-0*) State U NY Pr.

Body-Self Image. rev. ed. Williams Hartman & Marilyn Fithian. Ed. by Jason Loam. LC 88-6456. 116p. 1987. pap. text ed. 8.95 (*1-55599-018-5*) Elysium.

Body, Sex & Pleasure: Reconstructing Christian Sexual Ethics. Christine E. Gudorf. LC 94-5008. 288p. 1994. 19.95 (*0-8298-1014-5*) Pilgrim OH.

***Body, Sex, & Pleasure: Reconstructing Christian Sexual Ethics.** Christine E. Gudorf. 288p. 1995. reprint ed. pap. 14.95 (*0-8298-1062-5*) Pilgrim OH.

Body Shaping: A Slim-Down, Shape-Up Guide to Conquering Your Body's Trouble Spots. Michael Yessis & Porter Shimer. (Illus.). 256p. 1994. 24.95 (*0-87596-194-0*); pap. 16.95 (*0-87596-222-X*) Rodale Pr Inc.

Body Shaping Diet: A Leading Woman's Health Specialist Reveals the Hormonal Secrets That Can Change Your Shape Forever. Sandra Cabot. (Illus.). 320p. 1995. 19.95 (*0-446-51872-7*) Warner Bks.

***Body-Shaping Diet: A Leading Woman's Health Specialist Reveals the Hormonal Secrets That Can Change Your Shape Forever.** Sandra Cabot. 320p. 1996. mass mkt. 6.50 (*0-446-60290-6*) Warner Bks.

Body-Shaping for the Over-Thirties. Ros Cruickshank. 160p. 1995. pap. 7.95 (*0-572-01532-1*, Pub. by Foulsham UK) Atrium Pubs.

Body Sharers: A Novel. Elisabeth Rose. LC 92-28944. (Fiction Ser.). 205p. (C). 1993. 17.95 (*0-8135-1934-9*) Rutgers U Pr.

Body Shop Book: Skin, Hair, & Body Care. Body Shop International Staff. LC 94-20765. 1994. 26.95 (*0-525-93950-4*, Dutton) NAL-Dutton.

Body Shop Hazardous Materials Program Employee Training Manual. Mike Rager. (Illus.). (Orig.). (C). 1989. pap. write for info. (*0-318-65935-2*) Amer Hazmat.

Body-Signal Secret: You Know Diets Don't Work, Here's What Does. Steven C. Strauss & Gail North. LC 90-9096. 272p. 1991. 19.95 (*0-87857-931-1*, 05-826-0) Rodale Pr Inc.

***Body Signals.** Bruce L. Lowell. LC 95-9673. 1995. 25.00 (*0-06-270111-8*, HarpT) HarpC.

Body Silent. Robert F. Murphy. 1990. pap. 9.95 (*0-393-30702-6*) Norton.

Body Size in Mammalian Paleobiology: Estimation & Biological Implications. Ed. by John D. Damuth & Bruce J. MacFadden. (Illus.). 345p. (C). 1990. 64.95 (*0-521-36099-4*) Cambridge U Pr.

***Body Smart System: The Complete Guide to Cleansing & Rejuvenation.** rev. ed. Helene Silver. (Illus.). 248p. 1995. pap. text ed. 19.95 (*1-884334-60-1*) Hlthy Healing.

Body Snatcher. Juan C. Onetti. Tr. by Alfred M. Adam. LC 91-58061. 1992. pap. 13.00 (*0-679-73887-8*, Vin) Random.

Body Snatcher. Robert Louis Stevenson. Ed. by Raymond Harris. (Classics Ser.). (Illus.). 48p. (Orig.). (gr. 6-12). 1982. teacher ed 5.00 (*0-89061-257-9*, 461); pap. text ed. 4.00 (*0-89061-256-0*, 459); audio 13.00 (*0-89061-258-7*, 460) Jamestown Pubs.

Body Snatchers. James M. Ball. (Reprints Ser.). (Illus.). 216p. 1990. reprint ed. 17.95 (*0-88029-397-7*) Dorset Pr.

Body Snatchers. Jack Finney. 1993. reprint ed. lib. bdg. 21.95x (*0-89968-428-9*, Lghtyr Pr) Buccaneer Bks.

Body Snatchers: Stiffs & Other Goulish Delights. Frederick Drimmer. (Illus.). 224p. 1992. pap. 12.95 (*0-8065-1285-7*, Citadel Pr) Carol Pub Group.

Body Snatching: The Robbing of Graves for the Education of Physicians in Early Nineteenth Century America. Suzanne M. Shultz. LC 90-53522. 144p. 1992. lib. bdg. 23.95x (*0-89950-587-2*) McFarland & Co.

Body Social. Anthony Synnott. LC 92-40461. 1993. write for info. (*0-415-06296-9*) Routledge.

***Body, Soul, & Bioethics.** Gilbert C. Meilaender. LC 95-17486. (C). 1996. text ed. 21.95 (*0-268-00698-9*) U of Notre Dame Pr.

Body, Soul & Blood: Recovering the Human in Medicine. William T. Sayers. LC 79-56194. 112p. 1980. pap. 7.95 (*0-935718-00-1*) Asclepiad.

Body Space Expressions: The Development of Rudolf Laban's Movement & Dance Concepts. Vera Maletic. (Approaches to Semiotics Ser.: No. 75). (Illus.). xvi, 268p. 1987. lib. bdg. 90.80 (*0-89925-141-2*) Mouton.

Body Speaks: Therapeutic Dialogues for Mind-Body Problems. James Griffith & Melissa E. Griffith. (Illus.). 336p. 1994. text ed. 35.00 (*0-465-00716-3*) Basic.

Body, Spirit & Democracy. Don Johnson. LC 93-49887. 228p. (Orig.). 1993. pap. 12.95 (*1-55643-166-X*) North Atlantic.

***Body Star Signs: Your Shape & Stars Say about You.** Bel Hislop & Jane Oakley. (Illus.). 544p. 1995. pap. 17.95 (*0-09-178391-7*, Vermillion) Trafalgar.

Body Structures & Functions. 7th ed. Elizabeth Fong. (Illus.). 356p. 1989. teacher ed 14.00 (*0-8273-3482-6*); text ed. 25.95 (*0-8273-3481-8*) Delmar.

Body Structures & Functions. 8th ed. Elizabeth Fong et al. LC 92-49599. 337p. 1993. pap. text ed. 28.95 (*0-8273-5115-1*); disk 49.95 (*0-8273-5903-9*) Delmar.

Body Structures & Functions: Instructor's Guide. Elizabeth Fong et al. 113p. 1993. 14.00 (*0-8273-5117-8*) Delmar.

Body, Subject, & Power in China. Ed. by Angela Zito & Tani E. Barlow. LC 93-15596. 1994. Alk. paper. pap. text ed. 16.95 (*0-226-98727-2*) U Ch Pr.

Body, Subject, & Power in China. Ed. by Angela Zito & Tani E. Barlow. LC 93-15596. 1994. Alk. paper. lib. bdg. 45.00 (*0-226-98726-4*) U Ch Pr.

Body Surface Electrocardiographic Mapping. Ed. by David M. Mirvis. (Developments in Cardiovascular Medicine Ser.). (C). 1988. lib. bdg. 100.00 (*0-89838-983-6*) Kluwer Ac.

Body Surface Mapping of Cardiac Fields: Proceedings of the Symposium, Burlington, Vermont, 1972. Body Surface Mapping of Cardiac Fields Symposium Staff. Ed. by E. Lepeschkin & S. Rush. (Advances in Cardiology Ser.: Vol. 10). (Illus.). 344p. 1974. 113.75 (*3-8055-1566-9*) S Karger.

Body Surrounded by Water. large type ed. Eric Wright. (Nightingale Series Large Print Bks.). 264p. 1992. pap. 14.95 (*0-8161-5319-1*, Nightingale) Hall.

Body Symbolism. Richard Rybickl. 200p. (Orig.). 1985. pap. 5.95 (*0-9614341-1-2*) Future Dream Pr.

Body Systems. Lorraine Conway. 64p. (J). (gr. 5 up). 1984. student ed 7.95 (*0-86653-153-X*, GA 552) Good Apple.

***Body Talk.** 15.99 (*0-517-14035-7*) Random Hse Value.

Body Talk. Nigel Nelson. LC 93-27780. (Nonverbal Communications Ser.). (Illus.). 32p. (J). (gr. k-2). 1993. 12.95 (*1-56847-099-1*) Thomson Lrning.

Body Techniques. Lafrentiere. 1984. 26.50 (*0-89352-205-8*) Mosby Yr Bk.

Body Temperature: Regulation, Drug Effects, & Therapeutic Implications. Ed. by Peter Lomax & Eduard Schonbaum. LC 79-879. (Modern Pharmacology-Toxicology Ser.: No. 16). (Illus.). 680p. reprint ed. pap. 180.00 (*0-7837-0809-2*, 2041124) Bks Demand.

Body, the Desire Body. Max Heindel. Ed. by Rosicrucian Fellowship Staff. 159p. (C). 1975. reprint ed. pap. text ed. 9.95 (*0-911274-03-0*) Rosicrucian.

Body, the Vital Body. Max Heindel. Ed. by Rosicrucian Fellowship Staff. 196p. (C). 1991. reprint ed. pap. text ed. 9.95 (*0-911274-16-2*) Rosicrucian.

Body Theology. James B. Nelson. 176p. (Orig.). 1992. pap. 12.99 (*0-664-25379-2*) Westminster John Knox.

***Body to Die for.** Frankel. 1995. mass mkt. 5.50 (*0-671-79520-1*) PB.

Body to Dye For. Grant Michaels. 1991. pap. 8.95 (*0-312-05825-X*) St Martin.

Body to Earth: Three Artists from Brazil (Cildo Meireles, Mario Cravo Neto, Tunga) Susan M. Anderson. LC 92-73010. (Illus.). 40p. (Orig.). (C). 1993. pap. 15.00 (*0-945192-10-X*) USC Fisher Gallery.

Body Traffic. Stephen Dobyns. 160p. 1991. pap. 12.50 (*0-14-058650-4*) Viking Penguin.

Body Traps: Breaking the Binds That Keep You from Feeling Good about Your Body. Judith Rodin. 1993. pap. 12.00 (*0-688-12836-X*, Quill) Morrow.

Body Traps: How to Unlock the Cage of Body Obsessions. Judith Rodin. 1992. 22.00 (*0-688-08843-0*) Morrow.

Body Treatments & Dietetics for the Beauty Therapist. Ann Gallant. (Illus.). 400p. (Orig.). 1978. pap. 42.50 (*0-85950-401-8*, Pub. by Stanley Thornes UK) Trans-Atl Phila.

Body Types: The Enneagram of Essence Types. 2nd ed. Joel Friedlander. 1993. 10.95 (*0-936385-25-1*) J Friedlander.

Body Velocity: Reproductions of Poems & Objects. Kay Divant. (Illus.). 88p. (Orig.). 1989. pap. 22.00 (*0-9625038-1-9*) Geanie.

***Body Voices: Using the Power of Breath, Sound & Movement to Heal & Create New Boundaries.** Carolyn J. Braddock. 1995. pap. 19.95 (*1-879290-05-7*) Atrium Pubs.

***Body Voices: Using the Power of Breath, Sound & Movement to Heal & Create New Boundaries.** Carolyn J. Braddock. 1994. 25.00 (*1-879290-04-9*) PageMill Pr.

***Body Waits for Sound.** Forrest Hamer. 80p. (Orig.). 1995. pap. 9.95 (*1-882295-06-4*) Alicejamesbooks.

Body Watch: Know Your Insides. Anna Sproule. (Discovering Science Ser.). (Illus.). 48p. (J). (gr. 1-4). 1987. 12.95 (*0-8160-1782-4*) Facts on File.

Body Weight Regulatory System: Normal & Disturbed Mechanisms. Ed. by Luigi A. Cioffi et al. 398p. 1981. text ed. 101.50 (*0-89004-659-X*) Raven.

Body Wore Brocade. Jame Melville. 1994. mass mkt. 4.99 (*0-449-22189-X*) Fawcett.

Body Wore Brocade. large type ed. James Melville. (Ulverscroft Ser.). 304p. 1994. 20.95 (*0-7089-3064-6*) Ulverscroft.

Body Wore Brocade: A Superintendent Otani Mystery. James Melville. 224p. 1992. text ed. 20.00 (*0-684-19413-9*, Scribners) S&S Trade.

Body Work: Objects of Desire in Modern Narrative. Peter Brooks. LC 92-34163. (Illus.). 341p. 1993. 52.50 (*0-674-07724-5*); pap. 21.50 (*0-674-07725-3*) HUP.

Body Works. Sandi Johnson. 100p. 1992. pap. text ed. 9.95 (*0-9632412-0-6*) S Johnson.

BodyArt: Holidays. Carol Hauswald & Alice Maskowski. (Illus.). 80p. (J). (ps-1). 1992. teacher ed, pap. 8.95 (*1-878279-41-6*, MM 1958) Monday Morning Bks.

BodyArt: Nature. Carol Hauswald & Alice Maskowski. (Illus.). 80p. (J). (ps-1). 1992. teacher ed, pap. 8.95 (*1-878279-40-8*) Monday Morning Bks.

Bodybuilder's Nutrition Book. Franco Columbu & Lydia Fragomeni. LC 85-13317. (Illus.). 192p. (Orig.). 1985. pap. 11.95 (*0-8092-5457-3*) Contemp Bks.

Bodybuilder's Training Diary. Edie Leen & Ed Bertling. 160p. 1983. spiral bd. 7.95 (*0-89037-258-6*) Anderson World.

Bodybuilding: A Scientific Approach. Frederick C. Hatfield. (Illus.). 160p. (Orig.). 1984. pap. 15.95 (*0-8092-5458-1*) Contemp Bks.

Bodybuilding: The Weider Approach. Joe Weider. (Illus.). 224p. 1981. pap. 14.95 (*0-8092-5908-7*) Contemp Bks.

Bodybuilding a Realistic Approach: How You Can Have a Great Body. Frank A. Melfa. LC 94-66492. (Illus.). 315p. (Orig.). 1995. pap. 15.95 (*0-9641640-5-1*) Power Writings.

Bodybuilding a Realistic Approach: How You Can Have a Great Body. Frank A. Melfa. LC 94-66492. (Illus.). 315p. (Orig.). 1995. text ed. 23.95 (*0-9641640-4-3*) Power Writings.

Bodybuilding Basics. Robert Kennedy. LC 90-28701. (Illus.). 128p. 1991. pap. 9.95 (*0-8069-7392-7*) Sterling.

Bodybuilding Basics. Robert Kennedy. (Illus.). 128p. (C). 1991. reprint ed. lib. bdg. 27.00x (*0-8095-7598-1*) Borgo Pr.

Bodybuilding for Beginners. Bill Reynolds. (Illus.). 144p. (Orig.). 1983. pap. 11.95 (*0-8092-5499-9*) Contemp Bks.

Bodybuilding Nutrition: Recipes, Health & Diet Tips for the Active Athlete. Mandy Tanny. LC 90-55817. 256p. 1991. pap. 14.00 (*0-06-096497-9*, PL) HarpC.

BodyBusiness. Ken Cooper. LC 78-25971. (Illus.). 214p. 1987. pap. 6.95 (*0-932801-01-3*, HF5386.C78) Total Comm.

Bodybusiness: The Sender's & Receiver's Guide to Nonverbal Communications. Ken Cooper. LC 78-25971. 224p. 1981. 5.95 (*0-8144-7545-0*) Total Comm.

Bodycheck. large type ed. Elizabeth Oldfield. 264p. 1993. 21.95 (*0-7505-0555-9*, Pub. by Magna Print Bks) Ulverscroft.

Bodyclock. Milo Keynes & Martin Hughes. 192p. 1989. 24.95 (*0-8160-2223-2*) Facts on File.

Bodycraft: Creating the Body You Want While Loving the Body You Have. L. Ilizabethe Zelandais. (Illus.). 224p. (Orig.). 1994. pap. 12.00 (*0-9640961-0-2*) Anti-Gravity.

BodyFueling: The Ground-Breaking Approach to Eating for Health, Energy, Fitness, & Fat Loss. Robyn Landis. 320p. 1994. 21.95 (*0-446-51767-4*) Warner Bks.

BodyFueling: The Ground-Breaking Approach to Eating for Health, Energy, Fitness, & Fat Loss. Robyn Landis. 368p. 1995. mass mkt. 5.99 (*0-446-60194-2*) Warner Bks.

***Bodyguard.** Assorted. 1995. mass mkt. 5.50 (*0-373-20117-6*) Harlequin Bks.

***Bodyguard.** William C. Dietz. 240p. (Orig.). 1994. pap. text ed. 5.50 (*0-441-00105-X*) Ace Bks.

Bodyguard. Lawrence Kasdan. 1992. pap. 3.99 (*0-451-17777-0*, Sig) NAL-Dutton.

Bodyguard: From the Pages of Australian Penthouse. David De Vries & Glenn Lumsden. (Illus.). 70p. 1991. pap. 9.95 (*0-944735-18-5*) Malibu Graphics.

B

An Asterisk (*) at the beginning of an entry indicates that the title is appearing in BIP for the first time. 835

Bodyguard of Lies. Anthony C. Brown. LC 90-22531. 960p. 1991. reprint ed. pap. 17.95 (*0-688-10281-6*, Quill) Morrow.

Bodying Forth: Aesthetic Liturgy. Patrick W. Collins. LC 92-28045. 208p. 1993. pap. 12.95 (*0-8091-3352-0*) Paulist Pr.

***Bodylink.** Martin Sulway. (Illus.). 96p. 1995. text ed. write for info. (*0-07-470002-2*) Hlth Prof Div.

***Bodylore.** Young. (C). 1995. pap. text ed. 18.00 (*0-87049-890-8*) U of Tenn Pr.

Bodylore. Ed. by Katharine Young. LC 93-15390. (Illus.). 264p. (C). 1993. text ed. 28.00 (*0-87049-799-5*) U of Tenn Pr.

Bodylove: Learning to Like Our Looks - & Ourselves. Rita Freedman. LC 88-45511. (Illus.). 272p. 1990. reprint ed. pap. 12.00 (*0-06-091647-8*, PL) HarpC.

Bodymind. rev. ed. Ken Dychtwald. 320p. 1986. pap. 10.95 (*0-87477-375-X*) J P Tarcher.

Bodymind Energetics: Toward a Dynamic Model of Health. Mark Seem & Joan Kaplan. 1989. pap. 16.95 (*0-89281-246-X*, Heal Arts VT) Inner Tradit.

Bodymind Experience in Japanese Buddhism: A Phenomenological Study of Kukai & Dogen. David E. Shaner. LC 84-26747. (SUNY Series in Buddhist Studies). 250p. 1985. 59.50 (*0-88706-061-7*); pap. 19.95 (*0-88706-062-5*) State U NY Pr.

Bodypower. Vernon Coleman. 128p. 1989. reprint ed. pap. 8.95 (*1-878290-00-2*) Intl Hlth MD.

Bodyrhythms: Biological Clocks & Peak Performance. Lynne Lamberg. LC 93-40320. 1994. 25.00 (*0-87795-991-9*) Morrow.

Body's Memory. Jean Stewart. 288p. 1993. pap. 10.95 (*0-312-09253-9*) St Martin.

Body's Rapture. Jules Romains. (Black & Gold Library). 1937. 7.95 (*0-87140-855-4*) Liveright.

Body's Recollection of Being: Phenomenological Psychology & the Deconstruction of Nihilism. David M. Levin. 384p. 1985. pap. 15.95 (*0-7102-0478-7*, 04787, RKP) Routledge.

***Bodyscapes.** Allan T. Teger. Ed. by Malcolm E. Reding. (Illus.). 72p. (Orig.). 1995. 24.95 (*0-9638703-7-8*) Shade Tree Pr.

Bodysculpting: The Weisbeck Way. Chuck Weisbeck & Susan Malone. (Illus.). 176p. (Orig.). 1993. pap. 14.95 (*0-89015-925-4*) Sunbelt Media.

BodySkills Manual. Judy K. Werder & Robert H. Bruininks. 1988. pap. text ed. 48.95 (*0-88671-185-1*, 4901) Am Guidance.

Bodysmasher. Jan Stacy. 1989. pap. 3.95 (*0-8217-2668-4*) Zebra.

Bodysmasher No. 2: Death Match. Jan Stacy. 1989. pap. 3.95 (*0-8217-2747-8*) Zebra.

Bodyspace: Anthropometry, Ergonomics & Design. Stephen Pheasant. 276p. 1986. pap. 44.00 (*0-85066-352-0*) Taylor & Francis.

Bodyssey. (Illus.). 12.95 (*0-685-70823-3*) Fantagor Pr.

Bodyssey. Simon Revelstroke & Richard Corben. (Illus.). 64p. 1993. reprint ed. pap. 12.95 (*0-9623841-8-6*) Fantagor Pr.

Bodystories. Andrea Olsen. 1991. pap. 19.95 (*0-88268-106-0*) Station Hill Pr.

***Bodytalk: The Meaning of Human Gestures.** Desmond Morris. LC 94-30719. 1995. pap. 14.00 (*0-517-88355-4*, Crown) Crown Pub Group.

Bodytalk: When Women Speak in Old French Literature. E. Jane Burns. (New Cultural Studies). 304p. (Orig.). (C). 1993. text ed. 36.95 (*0-8122-3183-X*); pap. text ed. 14.95 (*0-8122-1405-6*) U of Pa Pr.

Bodywise. Joseph Heller & William A. Henkin. LC 86-3757. (Illus.). 260p. 1991. pap. 13.95 (*0-914728-73-3*) Wingbow Pr.

Bodywise. Peter Rowan. 64p. 1993. pap. 9.00 (*0-11-701707-8*, HM17078, Pub. by HMSO UK) UNIPUB.

Bodywise Woman. Melpomene Institute for Women's Health Research Staff. LC 93-22710. (Illus.). 304p. 1990. pap. 13.95 (*0-87322-551-1*, PMEL0551) Human Kinetics.

***Bodywork.** Lynn Davis. 120p. 1995. 45.00 (*3-905514-37-0*) Dist Art Pubs.

***Bodywork: What Type of Massage to Get & How to Make the Most of It.** Thomas Claire. 1995. write for info. (*0-688-12581-6*) Morrow.

Bodywork Tantra: On Land & in Water. Harold Dull. (Illus.). 112p. (Orig.). 1987. pap. 10.95 (*0-944202-00-4*) Harbin Springs.

Boecius de Consolacione Philosophie. Anicius Boethius. Tr. by Geoffrey Chaucer. LC 74-80164. (English Experience Ser.: No. 644). 1974. reprint ed. 45.00 (*90-221-0644-6*) Walter J Johnson.

Boehlendorff: A Short Story & Seven Poems. Johannes Bobrowski. Tr. by Francis Golffing. 44p. 1989. 25.00 (*0-930126-26-2*) Typographeum.

Boehm Woodwinds: A Fact Book on Theobald Boehm & Woodsinds on His System. K. Ventzke & D. Hilkenbach. (Illus.). 80p. pap. text ed. 50.99 (*0-933224-37-0*) Bold Strummer Ltd.

***Boehme: An Appreciation.** Alexander Whyte. Date not set. pap. 6.95 (*1-55818-287-X*, Sure Fire) Holmes Pub.

Boehme: An Intellectual Biography of the Seventeenth-Century Philosopher & Mystic. Andrew Weeks. LC 90-37130. 280p. 1991. 59.50 (*0-7914-0596-6*); pap. 19.95 (*0-7914-0597-4*) State U NY Pr.

Boeing Aircraft since Nineteen Sixteen. 2nd ed. Peter M. Bowers. (Putnam Aviation Ser.). (Illus.). 560p. 1989. 49.95 (*0-87021-037-8*) Naval Inst Pr.

***Boeing B-52: A Documentary History.** Walter Boyne. (Illus.). 160p. 1994. 29.95 (*0-88740-600-9*) Schiffer.

Boeing B-52: A Documentary History. Walter Boyne. (Illus.). 160p. 1982. 29.95 (*0-87474-246-3*, BOBO) Smithsonian.

***Boeing Company: A Report on the Company's Environmental Policies & Practices.** (Illus.). 34p. (C). 1994. reprint ed. pap. text ed. 200.00x (*0-7881-0901-4*, Coun on Econ) Diane Pub.

BOEING in Peace & War. Eugene E. Bauer. (Illus.). 1991. 21.95 (*1-879242-06-0*); pap. 14.95 (*1-879242-04-4*) Taba Pub.

***Boeing Jetliners.** Robbie Shaw. (Osprey Color Library). (Illus.). 128p. 1995. pap. 15.95 (*1-85532-528-4*, Pub. by Osprey Pubng Ltd UK) Motorbooks Intl.

Boeing 247. Henry M. Holden. (Flying Classics Ser.). (Illus.). 160p. 1991. pap. 14.95 (*0-8306-3593-9*, 3593, TAB-Aero) TAB Bks.

Boeing 247: The First Modern Airliner. F. Robert Van der Linden. LC 90-2476. (Illus.). 268p. 1991. 24.95 (*0-295-97094-4*) U of Wash Pr.

Boeing 707. P. R. Smith. (Airline Markings Ser.: Vol. 3). 1993. 14.95 (*1-85310-087-0*, Pub. by Airlife Pub Ltd UK) Voyageur Pr.

Boeing 727. P. R. Smith. (Airline Markings Ser.: Vol. 6). 1993. 14.95 (*1-85310-341-1*, Pub. by Airlife Pub Ltd UK) Voyageur Pr.

Boeing 727: Flight Engineer Manual. C. St. John. 475p. 1988. pap. 29.95 (*0-942397-04-5*) Buckeye Aviat Bk.

Boeing 727: Flight Engineer Written Test Guide. C. St. John. 75p. 1988. pap. 12.95 (*0-942397-05-3*) Buckeye Aviat Bk.

Boeing 727 Scrapbook. Len Morgan & Terry Morgan. LC 78-72164. 1978. pap. 12.60 (*0-8168-8349-1*, TAB-Aero) TAB Bks.

Boeing 737. David H. Minton. (Aero Ser.: Vol. 37). (Illus.). 112p. (Orig.). 1989. pap. 10.95 (*0-8306-8618-5*, TAB-Aero) TAB Bks.

Boeing 737. P. R. Smith. (Airline Markings Ser.: Vol. 7). 1993. 14.95 (*1-85310-312-8*, Pub. by Airlife Pub Ltd UK) Voyageur Pr.

***Boeing 747.** Peter Gilchrist. (Modern Civil Aircraft Ser.: No. 4). (Illus.). 112p. 1994. pap. 16.95 (*0-7110-2050-7*, Pub. by Ian Allan Pub UK) Howell Pr VA.

Boeing 747. Robbie Shaw. (Color Library). (Illus.). 128p. 1994. pap. 15.95 (*1-85532-420-2*, Pub. by Osprey Pubng Ltd UK) Motorbooks Intl.

Boeing 747. P. R. Smith. (Airline Markings Ser.: Vol. 1). 1993. 14.95 (*1-85310-077-3*, Pub. by Airlife Pub Ltd UK) Voyageur Pr.

***Boeing 757-767 Simulator Checkride: The Line Pilot's Survival Guide.** Michael J. Ray. 250p. 1995. pap. write for info. (*1-885591-88-8*) Morris Pubng.

Boeings & Bullock-Carts Vol. 3: Law Politics & Society in India. Ed. by Yogendra Malik & Dhirendra Vajpeyi. (C). 1990. text ed. 34.00 (*81-7001-065-9*, Pub. by Chanakya II) S Asia.

Boeings & Bullock Carts Vol. 5: State & Society in India. Ed. by Jayant Lele & Rajendra Vora. 1990. 54.00 (*81-7001-067-5*, Pub. by Chanakya II) S Asia.

Boeings & Bullock Carts: Studies in Change & Continuity in Indian Civilization Vol. 2: Indian Civilization in It's Local, Regional & National Aspects. Ed. by Dhirendra Vajpeyi. 1990. 30.00 (*81-7001-064-0*, Pub. by Chanakya II) S Asia.

Boeings & Bullock Carts: Studies in Change & Continuity in Indian Civilization: Essays in Honour of K. Ishwaran Vol. 1: India Culture & Society. Ed. by Yogendra Malik. 1990. 42.00 (*81-7001-063-2*, Pub. by Chanakya II) S Asia.

Boeing's Ed Wells. Mary W. Geer. LC 92-29582. (Illus.). 176p. 1992. 19.95 (*0-295-97204-1*) U of Wash Pr.

Boen Ou la Possession des Biens. Jules Romains. 160p. (FRE.). 1959. pap. 10.95 (*0-7859-1311-4*, 2070255247) Fr & Eur.

Boeotia Antiqua I: Papers on Recent Work in Boiotian Archaeology & History. Ed. by John M. Fossey. (McGill University Monographs in Classical Archaeology & History: Vol. 7). xii, 207p. (Orig.). 1989. pap. 74.00 (*90-5063-009-X*, Pub. by Gieben NE) Benjamins North Am.

Boeotia Antiqua II: Papers on Recent Work in Boiotian Archaeology & Epigraphy. Ed. by John M. Fossey. (McGill University Monographs in Classical Archaeology & History: No. 11). (Illus.). x, 63p. 1992. pap. 44.00 (*90-5063-083-9*, Pub. by Gieben NE) Benjamins North Am.

***Boeotia Antiqua III: Papers in Boiotian History, Institutions & Epigraphy in Memory of Paul Roesch.** Ed. by John M. Fossey. (McGill University Monographs in Classical Archaeology & History: No. 14). (Illus.). xii, 110p. 1993. lib. bdg. 46.00x (*90-5063-226-2*, Pub. by Gieben NE) Benjamins North Am.

***Boeotia Antiqua IV: Proceedings of the 7th International Congress on Boiotian Antiquities.** Ed. by John M. Fossey. (McGill University Monographs in Classical Archaeology & History: No. 15). (Illus.). xiv, 184p. 1994. pap. 69.00x (*90-5063-276-9*, Pub. by Gieben NE) Benjamins North Am.

Boer Commando: An Afrikaner Journal of the Boer War. Deneys Reitz. 288p. 1993. reprint ed. pap. 12.95 (*0-9627613-3-8*) Sarpedon.

***Boer Conspiracy: A Tale of Winston Churchill & Sherlock Holmes.** John C. Woods. (Illus.). 92p. 1992. per., pap. 15.00 (*0-943879-07-8*) Intl Churchill Soc.

Boer Fight for Freedom. Michael Davitt. 1972. 59.95 (*0-87968-764-9*) Gordon Pr.

Boer Fight for Freedom. Michael Davitt. LC 72-5540. (Black Heritage Library Collection). 1977. reprint ed. 66.95 (*0-8369-9137-0*) Ayer.

Boer War. Thomas Pakenham. LC 79-4779. 1979. 29.95 (*0-394-42742-4*) Random.

Boer War. Thomas Pakenham. LC 93-26234. (Illus.). 1994. 40.00 (*0-679-43047-4*) Random.

Boer War. Thomas Pakenham. 784p. 1992. reprint ed. pap. 15.00 (*0-380-72001-9*) Avon.

Boer War: A History. Allen Dulles. 1974. 250.00 (*0-87968-184-5*) Gordon Pr.

Boer War: From the Times War Correspondents. Ed. by Raymond Sibbald. (War Correspondents Ser.). (Illus.). 1993. text ed. 40.00 (*0-7509-0042-3*) A Sutton Pub.

***Boer War Afrikaaners P. O. W. Roll.** Roberts Staff. (C). 1993. 295.00x (*1-873058-16-0*, Pub. by Roberts UK) St Mut.

Boer War & Military Reform. Ed. by Bela K. Kiraly & Albert Nofi. write for info. (*0-318-60326-8*) Brooklyn Coll Pr.

Boer War & Military Reforms. Jay Stone & Erwin A. Schmidl. LC 87-25327. (War & Society in East Central Europe Ser.: Vol. 28). 358p. (Orig.). (C). 1988. lib. bdg. 44.00 (*0-8191-6652-9*, Atlantic Rsch & Pubns Inc) U Pr of Amer.

Boer War in American Politics & Diplomacy. Richard B. Mulanax. 248p. (Orig.). (C). 1994. lib. bdg. 46.50 (*0-8191-9356-9*) U Pr of Amer.

Boer War in Postcards. Ian McDonald. (Illus.). 192p. 1991. 30.00 (*0-86299-737-2*) A Sutton Pub.

Boerenverdriet: Violence Between Peasants & Soldiers in Early Modern Netherlands Art. Jane S. Fishman. LC 81-19655. (Studies in the Fine Arts: Iconography: No. 5). (Illus.). 166p. reprint ed. pap. 47.40 (*0-8357-1275-3*, 2070183) Bks Demand.

Boethian Apocalypse: Studies in Middle English Vision Poetry. Michael D. Cherniss. 330p. 1986. 29.95 (*0-937664-71-5*) Pilgrim Bks OK.

Boethian Fictions: Narratives in the Medieval French Versions of the Consolatio Philosophiae. Richard A. Dwyer. LC 75-36477. (Medieval Academy Bks.: No. 83). 1976. 20.00 (*0-910956-57-X*) Medieval Acad.

Boethius: The Consolations of Music, Logic, Theology, & Philosophy. Henry Chadwick. 336p. 1990. reprint ed. pap. 26.00 (*0-19-826549-2*) OUP.

***Boethius: The Poems from on the Consolation of Philosophy.** Ed. & Tr. by Peter Glassgold. 235p. (Orig.). (ENG.). 1994. pap. 10.95 (*1-55713-109-0*) Sun & Moon CA.

Boethius & Aquinas. Ralph McInerny. LC 89-15705. 268p. 1990. 34.95 (*0-8132-0709-6*) Cath U Pr.

Boethius & Dialogue: Literary Method in "The Consolation of Philosophy" Seth Lerer. LC 85-42937. 280p. 1985. text ed. 42.50 (*0-691-06653-1*) Princeton U Pr.

***Boethius & Dialogue: Literary Method in the Consolation of Philosophy.** Seth Lerer. LC 85-42937. reprint ed. pap. 79.00 (*0-7837-9372-3*, 2060116) Bks Demand.

Boethius Consolatio Philosophiae. James J. O'Donnell. (Latin Commentaries Ser.). 273p. (Orig.). (C). 1984. pap. text ed. 10.00 (*0-929524-37-3*) Bryn Mawr Commentaries.

Boethius Is "De topicis Differentiis" De Topicis Differentiis. Boethius. Ed. & Tr. by Eleonore Stump. LC 77-17275. (Illus.). 264p. 1978. 43.50 (*0-8014-1067-3*) Cornell U Pr.

Boethius on Signification & Mind. John Magee. LC 89-37962. (Philosophia Antiqua Ser.: Vol. LII). xiv, 165p. (Orig.). 1989. pap. text ed. 51.50 (*90-04-09096-7*) E J Brill.

Boethius's "In Ciceronis Topica" An Annotated Translation of a Medieval Dialectical Text. Boethius. Ed. & Tr. by Eleonore Stump. LC 87-23161. (In Ciceronis Topica Ser.). 296p. 1988. 43.50 (*0-8014-2017-2*) Cornell U Pr.

Boeuf Clandestin. Marcel Ayme. 72p. (FRE.). 1991. pap. 10.95 (*0-7859-1671-7*, 2070310760) Fr & Eur.

BOF Steelmaking, 2 vols, 1. Iron & Steel Society of AIME Staff. Ed. by J. M. Gaines. LC 77-152003. reprint ed. pap. 160.00 (*0-8357-3607-5*, 2025691) Bks Demand.

BOF Steelmaking, 2 vols, 2. Iron & Steel Society of AIME Staff. Ed. by J. M. Gaines. LC 77-152003. 625p. reprint ed. pap. 178.20 (*0-8357-7334-5*) Bks Demand.

Boffin: A Personal Story of the Early Days of Radar & Radio Astronomy & Quantum Optics. R. Hanbury Brown. (Illus.). 192p. 1991. 35.00 (*0-7503-0130-9*) IOP Pub.

Bofors: The Selling of a Nation. Prashant Bhushan. 1990. 27.50 (*81-7094-066-4*, Pub. by Vision) S Asia.

Bog Man & the Archaeology of People. Don R. Brothwell. LC 87-8435. (Illus.). 136p. 1987. pap. text ed. 14.95 (*0-674-07732-6*) HUP.

Bog-Myrtle & Peat: Being Tales Chiefly of Galloway. Samuel R. Crockett. LC 72-5909. (Short Story Index Reprint Ser.). 1977. reprint ed. 28.95 (*0-8369-4206-X*) Ayer.

Bog Nash na Njbesi i na zjemli. Protopresbyter Michael Pomazansky. 140p. 1985. pap. 5.00 (*0-317-29087-8*) Holy Trinity.

Bog of Stars, & Other Stories & Sketches of Elizabethan Ireland. Standish O'Grady. LC 74-125234. (Short Story Index Reprint Ser.). 1977. 16.95 (*0-8369-3601-9*) Ayer.

Bogardus: Genealogical History of the Ancestors & Descendants of Gen. Robert Bogardus. M. Gray. (Illus.). 281p. 1991. reprint ed. lib. bdg. 55.00 (*0-685-48714-8*); reprint ed. pap. 45.00 (*0-8328-1892-5*) Higginson Bk Co.

***Bogart: In Search of My Father.** Stephen H. Bogart. (Illus.). 320p. 1995. 24.95 (*0-525-93987-3*, Dutton) NAL-Dutton.

Bogart: The Bogart Family: Tunis Gysbert Bogaert & His Descendents. J. A. Bogart. (Illus.). 280p. 1992. reprint ed. lib. bdg. 54.00 (*0-8328-2305-8*); reprint ed. pap. 44.00 (*0-8328-2306-6*) Higginson Bk Co.

Bogdanovich's Picture Shows. Thomas J. Harris. LC 90-48649. (Illus.). 346p. 1990. 42.50 (*0-8108-2365-9*) Scarecrow.

Bogert, Five Bogert Families: Descendants of Evert, Jan Laurencz, Cornelis, Guysbert, & Harmense Myndertse Bogert. Herbert S. Ackerman. 528p. 1993. reprint ed. lib. bdg. 88.00 (*0-8328-3568-4*); reprint ed. pap. 78.00 (*0-8328-3569-2*) Higginson Bk Co.

Bogert, More Bogert Families: Descendants of Cornelise Jansen, Gysbert Uyten, & Henry Bogert, with Other Bogert Families. Herbert S. Ackerman. 430p. 1993. reprint ed. lib. bdg. 76.00 (*0-8328-3566-8*); reprint ed. pap. 66.00 (*0-8328-3567-6*) Higginson Bk Co.

Bogert's Nutrition & Physical Fitness. 11th ed. George M. Briggs & Doris H. Calloway. 736p. (C). 1984. text ed. 40.75 (*0-03-058587-2*) HB Coll Pubs.

Bogey: The Films of Humphrey Bogart. McCarty. (Illus.). 1970. pap. 16.95 (*0-8065-0001-8*, Citadel Pr) Carol Pub Group.

Bogey Beasts. Sidney Sime & Josef Holbrooke. (Illus.). 1975. reprint ed. pap. 10.00 (*0-9603300-0-3*) Purple Mouth.

Bogey Dust. Hal Kaiser. Ed. by Pam Nolf. 224p. (Orig.). 1993. pap. 9.95 (*1-881964-24-8*) Colin Grp.

Bogey Man: A Month on the PGA Tour. George Plimpton. 320p. 1993. pap. 13.95 (*1-55821-241-8*) Lyons & Burford.

Bogeyman Caper. Susan Pearson. (Eagle-Eye Ernie Mysteries Ser.). (Illus.). 80p. (J). (gr. 1-3). 1990. pap. 11.95 (*0-671-70565-2*, S&S Bks Young Read); pap. 2.95 (*0-671-70569-5*, S&S Bks Young Read) S&S Childrens.

Boggart. Susan Cooper. LC 92-15527. 208p. (J). (gr. 4-7). 1993. text ed. 14.95 (*0-689-50576-0*, McElderry) S&S Childrens.

Boggart's Sandwich. Martin Riley. (Illus.). 95p. (J). (gr. 7-9). 1992. pap. 3.95 (*0-563-20871-6*, BBC-Parkwest) Parkwest Pubns.

Boggin, Blizzy, & Sleeter the Cheater. Michael P. Waite. LC 87-35510. (Building Christian Character Ser.). (Illus.). 32p. (J). (ps-2). 1988. 7.99 (*1-55513-618-4*, Chariot Bks) Chariot Family.

Bogglers: Twenty-Two Smart Games (2k to 16k) in Timex-Sinclair BASIC. G. Charlton et al. 224p. 1983. pap. text ed. 9.95 (*0-07-023959-2*, BYTE Bks) McGraw.

Bogie. Jean-Philippe & Lesueur. 1990. pap. 9.95 (*0-913035-78-5*) Eclipse Bks.

***Bogle on Mutual Funds: New Perspectives for the Intelligent Investor.** John C. Bogle. 1994. pap. 12.95 (*0-440-50682-4*) Dell.

Bogle on Mutual Funds: New Perspectives for the Intelligent Investor. John C. Bogle. LC 93-22697. 320p. 1993. text ed. 25.00 (*1-55623-860-6*) Irwin Prof Pubng.

Bogman. Walter Macken. 288p. 1994. reprint ed. pap. 11.95 (*0-86322-184-X*, Pub. by Brandon Bk Pubs IE) Irish Bks Media.

Bogner's Complete Professional Bartender's Guide. Bogner's Limited Staff & Jerry L. Bogner. LC 87-50919. (Illus.). 150p. 1987. 30.95 (*0-943323-02-9*); pap. 14.95 (*0-943323-03-7*) Bogners Limited.

Bogojavlenije Gospodnje. Ed. by Moscow Synod Staff. 194p. reprint ed. pap. 8.00 (*0-317-29167-X*) Holy Trinity.

Bogomils: A Study in Balkan Neo-Manichaeism. Dmitri Obolensky. LC 77-84712. reprint ed. 39.00 (*0-404-16118-9*) AMS Pr.

Bogosluzhebncje Penije Russkoj Pravoslavnoj Tserkvi: Suschnost' Sistema I Istoria: Liturgical Chant of the Russian Orthodox Church: Its Essence, Structure & History, Vol. 1. Johann v. Gardner. LC 77-77086. (Illus.). (Orig.). (RUS.). 1979. text ed. 30.00 (*0-88465-008-1*); pap. text ed. 25.00 (*0-686-50014-8*) Holy Trinity.

Bogosluzhebnoje Penije Russkoj Pravoslavnoj Tserkvi: Istorija, Vol. 2. Johann V. Gardner. LC 77-77086. (Illus.). 1981. text ed. 30.00 (*0-88465-010-3*); pap. text ed. 25.00 (*0-317-30384-8*) Holy Trinity.

Bogs of the Northeast. Charles W. Johnson. LC 84-40587. (Illus.). 285p. 1985. pap. 15.95 (*0-87451-331-6*) U Pr of New Eng.

Bogue's Fortune. Julian Symons. 1988. pap. 3.95 (*0-88184-423-3*) Carroll & Graf.

Bogus Buddha. large type ed. James Melville. (Keating's Choice Ser.). 249p. 1992. 21.95 (*1-85089-569-4*, Pub. by ISIS UK) Transaction Pubs.

Bohannon's Country. Joseph Hansen. 192p. 1994. mass mkt. 5.95 (*0-14-023355-5*, Penguin Bks) Viking Penguin.

Bohannon's New Mexico Environmental Law Handbook, 1990-93. Paul M. Bohannon. 420p. 1993. ring bd. 95.00 (*0-409-25533-5*) Michie Butterworth.

Bohannon's New Mexico Environmental Law Handbook, 1990-93. suppl. ed. Paul M. Bohannon. 420p. 1993. 45.00 (*0-250-42722-2*) Butterworth Legal Pubs.

Boheme. Giacomo Puccini. Ed. by Nicholas John. Tr. by P. Pinkerton & W. Grist. (English National Opera Guide Series: Bilingual Libretto, Articles: No. 14). (Illus.). 128p. (Orig.). 1983. pap. 9.95 (*0-7145-3938-4*) Riverrun NY.

Boheme Depuis la Montagne-Blanche, 2 vols., Set. Ernest Denis. 1981. reprint ed. lib. bdg. 59.00 (*0-686-71907-7*) Scholarly.

Boheme Depuis la Montagne-Blanche, 2 vols., Set. Ernest Denis. LC 70-144973. (FRE.). Date not set. reprint ed. 59.00 (*0-403-00941-3*) Scholarly.

Bohemia: Digging the Roots of Cool. Herbert Gold. 1994. pap. 12.00 (*0-671-88608-8*, Touchstone Bks) S&S Trade.

Bohemia: Where Art, Angst, Love, & Strong Coffee Meet. Herbert Gold. 288p. 1993. pap. 21.00 (*0-671-76781-X*) S&S Trade.

Bohemia in the Eighteenth Century. Robert J. Kerner. 1972. 59.95 (*0-87968-765-7*) Gordon Pr.

Bohemia in the Eighteenth Century. Robert J. Kerner. LC 79-94315. reprint ed. 42.50 (*0-404-01948-X*) AMS Pr.

Bohemian Airs & Other Kefs. Robert Anbian. LC 81-90581. (Literature Ser.: No. 1). (Illus.). 74p. (Orig.). 1982. pap. 6.00 (*0-941842-00-2*) Night Horn Books.

836

An Asterisk (*) at the beginning of an entry indicates that the title is appearing in BIP for the first time.

Bohemian Brigade. Louis M. Starr. LC 86-51252. (Illus.). 424p. 1987. reprint ed. text ed. 35.00 (0-299-11340-X); reprint ed. pap. text ed. 13.50 (0-299-11344-2) U of Wis Pr.

***Bohemian Connection.** Susan Dunlap. 1994. pap. 4.99 (0-440-21569-2) Dell.

Bohemian Flats. Writers' Program, Minnesota Staff. LC 73-3628. (American Guide Ser.). reprint ed. 21.50 (0-404-57929-9) AMS Pr.

Bohemian Glass, 1400-1989. Ed. by Sylva Petrova & Jean-Luc Olivie. (Illus.). 240p. 1990. 75.00 (0-8109-1241-4) Abrams.

Bohemian Heart. James Dalessandro. 256p. 1993. 19.95 (0-312-09756-5, Pub. by Thomas Dunne Bks) St Martin.

Bohemian Mobility Tales. Emil Vopata. (Illus.). 80p. (Orig.). (J). (gr. 3-12). 1994. pap. 9.95 (0-9638668-0-X) AV Mobility.

Bohemian Paris of Today. Cucuel Morrow. 1977. lib. bdg. 59.95 (0-8490-1520-0) Gordon Pr.

Bohemian Register: An Annotated Bibliography of the Best Literary Movement. Morgen Hickey. LC 90-21657. (Illus.). 271p. 1990. 32.50 (0-8108-2397-7) Scarecrow.

***Bohemian Rhapsody & the Best of Queen for Guitar.** 72p. (Orig.). 1994. pap. 12.95 (0-89724-172-X) Warner Brothers.

Bohemians: American Adventures from Bret Harte's Overland Monthly. Robert A. Bennett. 365p. 1987. pap. 10.95 (0-936546-11-5) Pioneer Pr Bks.

Bohemians & Critics: American Theatre Criticism in the Nineteenth Century. Tice L. Miller. LC 80-24430. x, 190p. 1981. 22.50 (0-8108-1377-7) Scarecrow.

Bohemia's Case for Independence. Edvard Benes. LC 73-135792. (Eastern Europe Collection Ser.). 1971. reprint ed. 12.95 (0-405-02734-6) Ayer.

Bohemond I: Prince of the Antioch. Ralph B. Yewdale. LC 80-19742. (Crusades & Military Orders Ser.: Second Series). reprint ed. 21.00 (0-404-17048-X) AMS Pr.

Bohikee Creek. Robert Unger. 100p. (Orig.). 1988. pap. 6.95 (0-9620754-0-X) Phillipsport Assocs.

Bohin Manor. Tadeusz Konwicki. Tr. by Richard Lourie. 240p. 1990. 18.95 (0-374-11523-0) FS&G.

Bohn's Antiquarian Library, 28 titles in 38 vols., Set. reprint ed. 1,198.50 (0-404-50000-5) AMS Pr.

***Bohr Maker.** Nataga. 1995. mass mkt. 4.99 (0-553-56925-2, Spectra) Bantam.

Bohumil Kubista. Mahulena Neslehova. 328p. 1984. 158.00 (0-317-61238-7, Pub. by Collets UK) Pro-Am Music.

***Bohuslav Martinu.** Jaroslav Mihule. (20th Century Composers Ser.). (Illus.). 240p. 1995. pap. 19.95 (0-7148-3171-9, Pub. by Phaidon Press UK) Chronicle Bks.

Boiardo's Orlando Innamorato: An Ethics of Desire. Jo A. Cavallo. LC 92-37288. (C). 1993. 34.50 (0-8386-3534-2) Assoc Univ Prs.

Boiarynia. Lesia Ukrainka. 56p. 1970. pap. 2.00 (0-686-70594-7) Slavia Lib.

Boies Penrose: Symbol of an Era. Robert D. Bowden. LC 75-175690. (Select Bibliographies Reprint Ser.). 1977. reprint ed. 23.95 (0-8369-6605-8) Ayer.

Boil My Heart for Me. H. Baxter Liebler. LC 94-17862. (Illus.). 230p. 1994. reprint ed. pap. 14.95 (0-87480-464-7) U of Utah Pr.

Boiled Grass & the Broth of Shoes: Reconstructing Literary Deconstruction. Richard W. Nason. LC 91-52758. 176p. 1991. lib. bdg. 31.50x (0-89950-643-7) McFarland & Co.

Boiler & Pressure Vessel Code Ser. (Boiler & Pressure Vessel Code Ser.: Sec X). 1980. 55.00 (0-686-70011-2, P00100); ring bd., pap. 65.00 (0-686-70012-0, V00100) ASME.

Boiler Auxiliaries. Center for Occupational Research & Development Staff. (EUTEC Power Plant Operator Curriculum Ser.). (Illus.). 25p. (C). 1987. pap. text ed. write for info. (1-55502-231-6) CORD Commns.

Boiler Control Systems. David Lindsley. 1991. text ed. 43.00 (0-07-707374-6) McGraw.

Boiler Efficiency Manual. Ron Anderson. (Illus.). 128p. (C). 1986. text ed. 29.67 (0-13-079724-3) P-H.

***Boiler Emissions Legislation for the United Kingdom.** 60p. (Orig.). 1995. pap. 125.00 (0-7605-1611-1) Rector Pr.

Boiler Inspector. Jack Rudman. (Career Examination Ser.: C-87). 1994. pap. 29.95 (0-8373-0087-8) Nat Learn.

Boiler Operation. Center for Occupational Research & Development Staff. (EUTEC Power Plant Operator Curriculum Ser.). (Illus.). 64p. (C). 1985. pap. text ed. write for info. (1-55502-250-2) CORD Commns.

***Boiler Operation Engineering: Questions & Answers.** P. Chattopadhyay. LC 95-5964. 1995. text ed. 65.00 (0-07-460296-9) McGraw.

Boiler Operations. Billy C. Langley. 417p. (C). 1988. text ed. 39.00 (0-15-505526-7) SCP.

Boiler Operator's Dictionary. L. E. LaRocque. LC 87-18417. 151p. 1988. pap. 12.95 (0-912524-41-3) Busn News.

***Boiler Operator's Exam: Preparation Guide.** Theodore Sauselein. Ed. by Joanna Turpin. (Illus.). 300p. 1995. write for info. (0-912524-86-3) Busn News.

Boiler Operator's Guide. 2nd ed. Harry M. Spring & Anthony L. Kohan. (Illus.). 480p. 1981. text ed. 64.95 (0-07-060511-4) McGraw.

Boiler Operator's Guide. 3rd ed. Anthony L. Kohan. 1991. text ed. 54.00 (0-07-035697-1) McGraw.

Boiler Operators Handbook. National Industrial Fuel Efficiency Service Ltd. Staff. Ed. by Graham & Trotman Ltd. Staff. 155p. 1981. pap. text ed. 23.50 (0-86010-251-3) G & T Inc.

Boiler Operators Handbook. 2nd ed. National Fuel Efficiency Service Ltd. Staff. (C). 1990. lib. bdg. 39.50 (1-85333-285-2) G & T Inc.

Boiler Operator's Workbook. R. D. Wilson. (Illus.). 282p. 1991. 26.96 (0-8269-4491-4) Am Technical.

Boiler Plant & Distribution System Optimization Manual. Fairmont Press Staff & Harry Taplin. 345p. 1991. pap. text ed. 90.67 (0-685-50514-6) P-H.

Boiler Plant & Distribution System Optimization Manual. Harry Taplin. (Illus.). 328p. 1991. pap. 68.00 (0-88173-142-0, 0276) Fairmont Pr.

Boiler Ratings & Efficiencies: I-B-R Cast Iron, Steel & Copper Boilers. Hydronics Institute Staff. (Illus.). 116p. 1986. 10.00 (0-318-14378-X) Hydronics Inst.

***Boiler Room.** Reuben Gonzalez. 1994. 5.00 (0-87129-478-8, B17) Dramatic Pub.

Boiler Room Helper. Jack Rudman. (Career Examination Ser.: C-1138). 1994. pap. 23.95 (0-8373-1138-1) Nat Learn.

Boilermaker. Jack Rudman. (Career Examination Ser.: C-109). 1994. pap. 29.95 (0-8373-0109-2) Nat Learn.

Boilermaker Music Makers: Al Stewart & the Purdue Musical Organizations. Joseph L. Bennett. LC 86-61175. 182p. 1986. 19.95 (0-931682-21-5) Purdue U Pubns.

***Boilerplate: Koreshians, Potential Rioters, & Bureaucratic Complicity in American Self-Destruction: Being a List of Eight Ways in Which the Dead at Waco Were a Lot Like the Rest of Us.** Daniel X. O'Neil. 32p. 1994. pap. 5.00 (0-9646137-1-9) Juggernaut.

Boilerplating America: The Hidden Newspaper. Eugene C. Harter. Ed. by Dorothy Harter. 246p. (C). 1991. lib. bdg. 48.00 (0-8191-8082-3); pap. text ed. 28.50 (0-8191-8083-1) U Pr of Amer.

Boilers. Center for Occupational Research & Development Staff. (EUTEC Power Plant Operator Curriculum Ser.). (Illus.). 34p. (C). 1987. pap. text ed. write for info. (1-55502-230-8) CORD Commns.

Boilers & Ancillary Plants see Modern Power Station Practice

Boilers, Evaporators & Condensers. Sadik Kakac. 835p. 1991. text ed. 165.00 (0-471-62170-6) Wiley.

Boilers Simplified. Lionel LaRocque. LC 87-685. 240p. 1987. 27.95 (0-912524-40-5) Busn News.

Boilin' & Bakin in Boogar Hollow. 2.00 (0-936672-55-2) Aerial Photo.

Boiling, Condensation, & Gas-Liquid Flow. P. B. Whalley. (Oxford Engineering Sciences Ser.: No. 21). (Illus.). 304p. 1987. 80.00 (0-19-856181-4) OUP.

Boiling Crisis & Critical Heat Flux. L. S. Tong. LC 72-600190. (AEC Critical Review Ser.). 91p. 1972. pap. 10.25 (0-87079-154-0, TID-25887); fiche 9.00 (0-87079-155-9, TID-25887) DOE.

Boiling Energy: Community Healing among the Kalahari Kung. Richard Katz. LC 81-13383. 368p. 1984. pap. 16.50 (0-674-07736-9) HUP.

Boiling Heat Transfer: Modern Developments & Advances. Ed. by R. T. Lahey. LC 92-24921. 1992. write for info. (0-444-89499-3) Elsevier.

Boiling Heat Transfer & Two-Phase Flow. L. S. Tong. LC 74-26607. 256p. 1975. reprint ed. 25.50 (0-88275-251-0) Krieger.

Boiling Liquid-Metal Heat Transfer. O. E. Dwyer. LC 75-11012. (Nuclear Science Technology Ser.). (Illus.). 1976. text ed. 44.00 (0-89448-000-6, 300008) Am Nuclear Soc.

Boiling Phenomena, Set. Van Stralen. 1979. 154.00 (0-89116-513-4) Hemisp Pub.

Boiling Point: Republicans, Democrats, & the Decline of Middle-Class Prosperity. Kevin P. Phillips. 336p. 1994. pap. 13.00 (0-06-097582-2, PL) HarpC.

***Boiling Pool.** Gary Brandner. 1995. lib. bdg. 20.00 (0-7278-4749-X) Severn Hse.

Boiling Rock. Remar Sutton. 288p. 1991. 19.95 (0-945167-40-7) British Amer Pub.

***Boiling Water: The World's Best Vegetarian Recipes from America's Premier Vegetarian Chef - Fast, Simple, Filling.** Michael O'Sullivan. 114p. 1995. pap. 10.95 (0-9636867-0-4) Leichman Assocs.

***Boing!** Play Bac Publisher Staff. Date not set. write for info. (0-679-87486-0) Random.

Boise: An Illustrated History. Merle Wells. (Illus.). 208p. 1982. 22.95 (0-89781-042-2) Preferred Mktg.

Boise: The City & the People. Clay Morgan & Steve Bly. (Illus.). 112p. (Orig.). 1993. 22.95 (1-56037-053-X) Am Wrld Geog.

***Boise Baseball: The First 125 Years.** Arthur A. Hart. 110p. 1994. pap. 14.95 (0-9631258-6-9) Historic Idaho.

Boise Belle. Dirk Fletcher. (Spur Ser.: No. 30). 176p. 1989. pap. 2.95 (0-8439-2820-4) Dorchester Pub Co.

***Boise Cascade: A Report on the Company's Environmental Policies & Practices.** (Illus.). 52p. (C). 1994. reprint ed. pap. text ed. 200.00x (0-7881-0952-9, Coun on Econ) Diane Pub.

Boise Parent Guide. Patricia Rowan & Dennis Stevenson. 100p. (Orig.). 1990. pap. write for info. (0-318-66749-5) Boise Parent Guide.

***Boiseans: At Home.** Arthur A. Hart. 86p. 1984. pap. 9.95 (0-9631258-8-5) Historic Idaho.

Boit: Chronicles of the Boit Family & Their Descendants. R. Boit. (Illus.). 260p. 1990. reprint ed. lib. bdg. 49.00 (0-8328-1582-9); reprint ed. pap. 39.00 (0-8328-1583-7) Higginson Bk Co.

Boite aux Lettres. Victor Hugo. (FRE.). 1966. 24.95 (0-7859-1172-3, 2082103021) Fr & Eur.

Boites de Peinture. Marcel Ayme. (Folio - Cadet Bleu Ser.: No. 199). (Illus.). 72p. (FRE.). (J). (gr. 1-5). 1990. pap. 9.95 (2-07-031199-6) Schoenhof.

Boites en Porcelaines des Manufactures Europeennes au XVIII Siecle. B. Beaucamp. 604p. (FRE.). 1991. 350.00 (0-8288-7305-4, 2859170499) Fr & Eur.

Bojeffries Saga. Alan Moore & Steve Parkhouse. Ed. by Garry Leach & Paul Jenkins. (Illus.). 80p. 1993. pap. 9.95 (1-879450-65-8) Tundra MA.

Bokaro Steel Plant. P. Desai. 1972. pap. 18.00 (0-444-10388-0, North Holland) Elsevier.

Bokaro Steel Plant: Some Economic Aspects. Surinder. (C). 1991. 26.50 (81-7154-540-8, Pub. by Popular Prakashan II) S Asia.

Boke of Iustices of Peas, the Charge with All the Processe of the Cessions. LC 76-57391. (English Experience Ser.: No. 808). 1977. reprint ed. lib. bdg. 25.00 (90-221-0808-2) Walter J Johnson.

Boke of Surveying, Here Begynneth a Ryght Frutefull Mater: And Has to Name the Boke of Surveying. John Fitzherbert. LC 74-80175. (English Experience Ser.: No. 657). (Illus.). 131p. 1974. reprint ed. 25.00 (90-221-0657-8) Walter J Johnson.

Bokken: Art of the Japanese Sword. Dave Lowry. Ed. by Mike Lee. LC 85-63391. (Weapons Ser.). 192p. 1985. pap. 11.95 (0-89750-104-7, 443) Ohara Pubns.

Bokotola. Millard Fuller. LC 77-1277. 1978. pap. 6.95 (0-8329-1179-8) New Win Pub.

***Bol (Ferdinand), a Catalogue Raisonne of the Graphic Work.** George C. Kenney. (Illus.). 300p. 1995. 150.00 (1-55660-247-2) A Wofsy Fine Arts.

Bold Angel. Kat Martin. 1994. mass mkt. 4.99 (0-312-95303-8) St Martin.

Bold As a Lamb: Pastor Samuel Lamb & the Underground Church of China. Ken Anderson. 192p. 1991. pap. 9.99 (0-310-53221-3) Zondervan.

Bold, Bad '60s. James E. Jackson. LC 91-40617. xi, 136p. (Orig.). 1992. pap. 7.50 (0-7178-0693-6) Intl Pubs Co.

Bold Blades Flashing. Lorinda Hagen. 320p. 1987. reprint ed. pap. 3.50 (0-8439-2481-0) Dorchester Pub Co.

Bold Breathless Nights. Penelope Neri. 1989. mass mkt. 4.50 (0-8217-2780-X) Zebra.

***Bold Carnivore: An Alphabet of Predators.** Consie Powell. (Illus.). 32p. (J). (gr. k-6). 1995. 14.95 (1-57098-023-3) R Rinehart.

Bold Challenge. Walter A. Dawes. (Illus.). 103p. (Orig.). 1980. pap. 5.95 (0-938792-14-8) New Capernaum.

Bold Conquest. Virginia Henley. 384p. 1983. mass mkt. 4.99 (0-380-84830-9, 84830) Avon.

Bold Destiny. Jane Feather. 400p. 1990. mass mkt. 4.99 (0-380-75808-3) Avon.

Bold Dragoon: The Life of J. E. B. Stuart. Emory M. Thomas. LC 87-45928. (Vintage Civil War Library). 368p. 1988. pap. 13.00 (0-394-75775-0, Vin) Random.

***Bold Experiment: A Documentary History of Australian Immigration since 945.** Ed. by John Lack & Jacqueline Templeton. (Illus.). 304p. 1995. pap. 39.95 (0-19-553548-0) OUP.

Bold Experiment: The Story of Educational Television in American Samoa. Wilbur L. Schramm et al. LC 79-67777. xviii, 244p. 1981. 35.00 (0-8047-1090-2) Stanford U Pr.

Bold Galilean: The Power of Rome Encounters Christ. Legette Blythe. 1993. pap. 9.99 (0-8024-7103-X) Moody.

***Bold Ideas: Creative Approaches to the Challenge of Youth Programming.** Sherril L. York & Debra J. Jordan. Ed. by Debra J. Jordan. 83p. (C). 1995. pap. text ed. 10.00 (1-881516-04-0) U of NI Inst Youth Lead.

Bold Impostor. Helen Tucker. 192p. (Orig.). 1991. pap. 3.99 (0-8439-3164-7) Dorchester Pub Co.

Bold Journey: West with Lewis & Clark. Charles Bohner. LC 84-19328. (Illus.). 171p. (J). (gr. 5 up). 1985. 13.95 (0-395-36691-7); pap. 5.95 (0-395-54978-7) HM.

Bold Land, Bold Love. Connie Mason. 480p. pap. 4.99 (0-8439-3327-5) Dorchester Pub Co.

***Bold Legend.** Gordon D. Shirreffs. 320p. 1995. mass mkt. 4.50 (0-8439-3726-2) Dorchester Pub Co.

Bold Love: The Courageous Practice of Life's Ultimate Influence. Dan B. Allender. LC 92-60188. 320p. 1992. pap. 12.00 (0-89109-703-1) NavPress.

Bold Love Discussion Guide. Dan B. Allender. 72p. 1992. pap. 5.00 (0-89109-681-7) NavPress.

Bold Men Win. Marilyn Hickey. 48p. (Orig.). pap. write for info. (1-56441-121-4) M Hickey Min.

Bold Montana Bride. Karen A. Bale. 448p. 1991. mass mkt. 4.50 (0-8217-3391-5) Zebra.

***Bold New World: The Essential Road Map to the Twenty-First Century.** William Knoke. Ed. by Philip Turner. 352p. 1996. 25.00 (1-56836-095-9) Kodansha.

***Bold Prayers from the Heart.** Jean Maalouf. (Illus.). 100p. (Orig.). 1995. text ed. 16.95 (1-55612-773-1); pap. 9.95 (1-55612-850-9) Sheed & Ward MO.

Bold Rebel Love. Christine Dorsey. 432p. 1991. mass mkt. 4.50 (0-8217-3337-0) Zebra.

***Bold Riders: Behind Australia's Corporate Collapses.** Trevor Sykes. (Illus.). 750p. 1995. 45.00 (1-86373-702-2, Pub. by Allen Unwin AT) Paul & Co Pubs.

***Bold Stroke for a Wife.** Susanna Centlivre. Ed. by Nancy Copeland. 192p. 1995. pap. 12.95 (1-55111-021-0) Broadview Pr.

Bold Stroke for a Wife. Susanna Centlivre. Ed. by Thalia Stathas. LC 67-12640. (Regents Restoration Drama Ser.: No. BB267). 138p. reprint ed. pap. 39.40 (0-8357-7335-3, 2031607) Bks Demand.

Bold Surrender. Judith E. French. 368p. 1988. pap. 3.95 (0-380-75243-3) Avon.

Bold Texas Embrace. Victoria Thompson. 1989. mass mkt. 4.50 (0-8217-2835-0) Zebra.

Bold Thing. Mark Daniel. LC 93-18605. 1994. 19.95 (0-316-17266-9) Little.

Bold Vegetarian. B. Kirchner. 1995. pap. 16.00 (0-06-095056-0) HarpC.

Bold Venture: A History of Walla Walla College. Terrie D. Aamodt. 320p. 1992. text ed. 39.95 (0-9631859-0-X) Walla Walla Coll.

Bold Women. Helen B. Woodward. LC 71-160928. (Biography Index Reprint Ser.). 1977. reprint ed. 23.95 (0-8369-8091-3) Ayer.

***Bolden & Tackle's Practice Nurse Handbook.** 3rd ed. Gillian Hampson. (Illus.). 288p. 1994. pap. (0-632-03692-3, Pub. by Blckwell Sci Pubns UK) Blackwell Sci.

Bolder Dash! The Hound with Cash. Mark Soifer. (Illus.). 24p. (Orig.). 1987. pap. 4.95 (0-942991-00-1) Spectrum PA.

Boldstrokes & Quiet Gestures: Twentieth Century Drawings & Watercolors from the Santa Barbara Museum of Art. Susan Larsen. 1992. 25.00 (1-882603-00-1) Mid Am Arts.

***Boldt Castle - Heart Island.** 4th ed. Roger S. Lucas. (Illus.). 60p. 1995. reprint ed. 9.00 (1-887287-00-0) Res Rev Pubns.

***Boldt's Boats.** 2nd rev. ed. Roger S. Lucas. 62p. 1995. 9.00 (1-887287-01-9) Res Rev Pubns.

Bolero. large type ed. Irene Ord. (Linford Romance Library). 288p. 1993. pap. 14.95 (0-7089-7320-5, Linford) Ulverscroft.

Bolero-Rumba. (Ballroom Dance Ser.). 1985. lib. bdg. 250.00 (0-87700-742-X) Revisionist Pr.

Bolero-Rumba. Earl Atkinson. (Ballroom Dance Ser.). 1986. lib. bdg. 250.00 (0-8490-3620-8) Gordon Pr.

Bolero-Rumba. Earl Atkinson. (Ballroom Dance Ser.). 1983. lib. bdg. 250.00 (0-87700-488-9) Revisionist Pr.

Bolero-Rumba. (Ballroom Dance Ser.). 1986. lib. bdg. 79.95 (0-8490-3439-6) Gordon Pr.

Boleros. Jay Wright. (Contemporary Poets Ser.). 94p. 1991. text ed. 24.95 (0-691-06890-9); pap. 9.95 (0-691-01504-X) Princeton U Pr.

Boleslaus the Bold & Bishop Stanislaus. Tadeusz Grudzinski. Tr. by Lech Petrowicz. (Panorama of Polish History Ser.: Vol. I). (Illus.). 255p. 1987. pap. 6.95 (83-223-1988-6, Pub. by Interpress PO) Hippocrene Bks.

Boleslaw Limanowski, (1835-1935) Kazimiera J. Cottam. (East European Monographs: No. 41). 365p. 1978. text ed. 59.00 (0-914710-34-6) East Eur Quarterly.

Boletes of North America: A Compendium. Ernest E. Both. 431p. 1993. pap. 10.00 (0-944032-54-0, Lubrecht & Cramer) Buffalo SNS.

Boleti of North Carolina. William C. Coker & Alma H. Beers. (Illus.). 10.00 (0-8446-5016-1) Peter Smith.

Boleti of North Carolina. William C. Coker & Alma Beers. (Illus.). 163p. 1974. reprint ed. pap. 6.95 (0-486-20377-8) Dover.

Boleti of Northeastern North America. W. H. Snell & E. A. Dick. (Illus.). 1970. 90.00 (3-7682-0681-5) Lubrecht & Cramer.

***Boletin.** Ed. by Blanca Vazquez. (Illus.). 240p. (Orig.). 1993. pap. write for info. (1-878483-53-6) Hunter Coll CEP.

Boletin de Arqueologia (FIAN), Ano 3, Nos. 1-3. 1988. 10.00 (0-685-75382-4, Pub. by Siglo del Hombre CK) UPLAAP.

Boletin de Arqueologia (FIAN), Ano 4, Nos. 1-3. 1989. 10.00 (0-685-75383-2, Pub. by Siglo del Hombre CK) UPLAAP.

Boletin Estadistico de la OEA. Ed. by OAS, General Secretariat, Department of Publications Staff. 207p. (C). 4.00 (0-686-68291-2) OAS.

Boletin Estadistico de la OEA: Enero-Junio 1980, Vol. 2, Nos. 1-2. Ed. by OAS General Secretariat. 221p. 1980. pap. text ed. 4.00 (0-686-69867-3) OAS.

Boletin Estadistico de la OEA: Vol. 2, No. 3 Julio-Septiembre 1980. OAS General Secretariat. 212p. (SPA.). (C). 1980. pap. write for info. (0-318-54727-9) OAS.

Boletin Museo del Oro, No. 25. 1989. 13.50 (0-685-75384-0, Pub. by Siglo del Hombre CK) UPLAAP.

***Boletin Museo del Oro, No. 30.** 1991. 13.50 (0-614-03098-6, Pub. by Siglo del Hombre CK) UPLAAP.

Boletin Museo del Oro, Nos. 26-29. 1990. 13.50 (0-318-72971-7, Pub. by Siglo del Hombre CK) UPLAAP.

***Boletin Museo del Oro No. 30.** 1991. 13.50 (0-614-02963-5, Pub. by Siglo del Hombre CK) UPLAAP.

Boletinaceae of Mexico & Central America One & Two. R. Singer et al. (Nova Hedwigia Beiheft Ser.: No. 98). (Illus.). 72p. 1990. pap. text ed. 52.50 (3-443-51020-5, Pub. by Cramer-Borntraeger GW) Lubrecht & Cramer.

Boletinae of Florida with Notes on Extralimital Species: 4 Parts in One Vol. R. Singer. (Bibliotheca Mycologica Ser.: No. 58). (Illus.). 1977. lib. bdg. 40.00 (3-7682-1145-2) Lubrecht & Cramer.

Boletineae of Mexico & Central America, Pt. 3. R. Singer et al. (Nova Hedwigia Beiheft Ser.: No. 102). (Illus.). 120p. 1991. pap. 56.00 (3-443-51024-8, Pub. by Gebrueder Borntraeger GW) Lubrecht & Cramer.

Bolingbroke & France. Rex A. Barrell. LC 88-19852. (Illus.). 152p. (C). 1988. lib. bdg. 38.00 (0-8191-7127-1) U Pr of Amer.

Bolingbroke & His Circle: The Politics of Nostalgia in the Age of Walpole. Isaac Kramnick. LC 92-4257. 336p. 1992. pap. 16.95 (0-8014-8001-9) Cornell U Pr.

Bolingbroke & His Times, 2 Vols. Walter Sichel. LC 68-25265. (English Biography Ser.: No. 31). 1969. reprint ed. lib. bdg. 99.95 (0-8383-0170-3) M S G Haskell Hse.

Bolingbroke & Others. limited ed. Parker Grindal. 128p. 1994. 85.00 (1-881119-24-6) Pyncheon Hse.

Bolingbroke's Political Writings: The Conservative Enlightenment. Ed. by Bernard Cottret. LC 94-17767. 1995. write for info. (0-312-12322-1) St Martin.

Bolivar. Salvador De Madariaga. LC 79-16763. (Illus.). 711p. 1979. reprint ed. text ed. 95.00 (0-313-22029-8, MABO, Greenwood Pr) Greenwood.

Bolivar ante Marx y Otros Ensayos. Pedro J. Rua. (Norte Ser.). 148p. 1978. pap. 5.95 (0-940238-05-5) Ediciones Huracan.

B

An Asterisk (*) at the beginning of an entry indicates that the title is appearing in BIP for the first time. 837

Bolivar Burial Complex of Southwestern Missouri, Vol. 45. W. R. Wood & S. L. Brock. (Missouri Archaeologist Ser.). 1984. 6.00 (*0-943414-62-8*) MO Arch Soc.

Bolivar! Gulf Coast Peninsula. A. Pat Daniels. (Illus.). 113p. (Orig.). 1985. pap. 8.95 (*0-9614885-0-6*) Peninsula Pr TX.

Bolivarian Nations. Lawrence A. Clayton. LC 84-5961. (World of Latin America Ser.). (Illus.). 102p. (C). 1984. pap. text ed. write for info. (*0-88273-603-5*) Forum Pr IL.

Bolivarian Presidents: Conversations & Correspondence with Presidents of Bolivia, Peru, & Ecuador. Robert J. Alexander. LC 93-11892. 296p. 1994. text ed. 59.95 (*0-275-94661-4*, Praeger Pubs) Greenwood.

Bolivia. Karen Jacobsen. LC 91-8889. (New True Bks.). 48p. (J). (gr. k-4). 1991. lib. bdg. 12.90 (*0-516-01122-7*); pap. 4.95 (*0-516-41122-5*) Childrens.

Bolivia. Marion Morrison. LC 88-10877. (Enchantment of the World Ser.). (Illus.). 128p. (J). (gr. 5-9). 1988. lib. bdg. 20.55 (*0-516-02705-0*) Childrens.

***Bolivia.** Robert Pateman. (Cultures of the World Ser.). 128p. (J). (gr. 3-5). 1995. lib. bdg. 21.95 (*0-7614-0178-4*) Marshall Cavendish.

Bolivia. Karen Schimmel. (Let's Visit Places & Peoples of the World Ser.). (Illus.). 112p. (YA). (gr. 5 up). 1991. 14.95 (*0-7910-1109-7*) Chelsea Hse.

B

Bolivia. Gertrude M. Yeager. (World Bibliographical Ser.). 228p. 1988. lib. bdg. 60.00 (*1-85109-066-5*) ABC-CLIO.

Bolivia. Rosa Q. Mesa. LC 73-180800. (Latin American Serial Documents Ser.: Vol. 6). 190p. reprint ed. pap. 54.20 (*0-8357-7336-1*, 2013552) Bks Demand.

Bolivia: A Travel Survival Kit. 2nd ed. Deanna Swaney & Robert Strauss. (Illus.). 408p. (Orig.). 1992. pap. 16.95 (*0-86442-160-5*) Lonely Planet.

***Bolivia: Commercial Law.** 300p. (Orig.). 1994. pap. 295.00 (*0-7605-1230-2*) Rector Pr.

Bolivia: Land Divided. Harold Osborne. 1976. lib. bdg. 69.95 (*0-8490-1521-9*) Gordon Pr.

Bolivia: Land, Location, & Politics since 1825. J. Valerie Fifer. LC 72-139713. (Cambridge Latin American Studies: 13). 327p. reprint ed. pap. 93.20 (*0-8357-7337-X*, 2024453) Bks Demand.

Bolivia: Land of Struggle. Waltraud Q. Morales. 202p. 1992. text ed. 46.00 (*0-8133-0197-1*) Westview.

Bolivia: Past, Present, & Future of Its Politics. Robert J. Alexander. Ed. by Robert Wesson. LC 81-22661. (Politics in Latin America Ser.). 184p. 1982. text ed. 49.95 (*0-275-90751-1*, C0751, Praeger Pubs) Greenwood.

Bolivia: The Evolution of a Multi-Ethnic Society. 2nd ed. Herbert S. Klein. (Latin American Histories Ser.). (Illus.). 368p. (C). 1992. text ed. 45.00 (*0-19-505734-1*); pap. text ed. 15.95 (*0-19-505735-X*) OUP.

Bolivia: The Uncompleted Revolution. James M. Malloy. LC 77-101486. (Pitt Latin American Ser.). 406p. reprint ed. 115.80 (*0-8357-9751-1*, 2015449) Bks Demand.

Bolivia: 1952-1986. Jeffrey Sachs & Juan A. Morales. 48p. 1988. pap. 5.00 (*1-55815-036-6*) ICS Pr.

Bolivia see American Nations Past & Present

Bolivia see Statements of the Laws of the OAS Member States in Matters Affecting Business

Bolivia, a Land Divided. Harold Osborne. LC 85-24763. 193p. 1986. reprint ed. text ed. 49.75 (*0-313-24982-2*, OSBO, Greenwood Pr) Greenwood.

Bolivia & Coca: A Study in Dependency. James Painter. LC 93-32723. (Studies on the Impact of the Illegal Drug Trade: Vol. 1). 194p. 1994. lib. bdg. 36.50 (*1-55587-490-8*) Lynne Rienner.

Bolivia Business Forecaster. Ed. by Lewis B. Sckolnick. 70p. (Orig.). (C). 1994. pap. 675.00 (*1-57205-366-6*) Rector Pr.

***Bolivia Business Intelligence Handbook.** (Illus.). 70p. (Orig.). 1994. pap. 295.00 (*0-7605-1070-9*) Rector Pr.

***Bolivia Business Risk Outlook.** 70p. (Orig.). 1994. pap. 495.00 (*0-7605-1383-X*) Rector Pr.

Bolivia Fertilizer Situation & Recommendations. M. T. Frederick & R. T. Smith. (Technical Bulletin Ser.: No. T-15). (Illus.). 83p. (Orig.). 1979. pap. 4.00 (*0-88090-014-8*) Intl Fertilizer.

Bolivia in Pictures. Ed. by Lerner Publications, Department of Geography Staff. (Visual Geography Ser.). (Illus.). 64p. (YA). (gr. 5 up). 1987. lib. bdg. 18.95 (*0-8225-1808-2*, Lerner Publctns) Lerner Group.

Bolivian Diary of Ernesto Che Guevara. Ernesto C. Guevara. Tr. by Michael Taber. LC 93-85736. (Illus.). 350p. (Orig.). (ENG.). 1994. lib. bdg. 55.00 (*0-87348-767-2*); pap. 19.95 (*0-87348-766-4*) Pathfinder NY.

Bolivian Indian Textiles: Traditional Designs & Costumes. Tamara E. Wasserman & Jonathan S. Hill. (Pictorial Archive Ser.). (Illus.). 64p. (Orig.). 1981. pap. 7.95 (*0-486-24118-1*) Dover.

Bolivian Quechua Reader & Grammar-Dictionary, 2 vols. in 1. Richley H. Crapo & Percy Aitken. (Illus.). 236p. 1986. ring bd. 15.00 (*0-89720-080-2*) Karoma.

Bolivian Tubular Edging & Crossed-Warp Techniques. Adele Cahlander. 1994. 9.50 (*0-932394-22-1*) Dos Tejedoras.

Bolivia's Answer to Poverty, Economic Crisis, & Adjustment: The Emergency Social Fund. Ed. by Steen Jorgensen et al. LC 92-8591. (Regional & Sectorial Studies). 134p. 1992. 8.95 (*0-8213-2056-4*, 12056) World Bank.

***Boljsevici Kolju Sami Sebe.** Ivo Omrcanin. 72p. (CRO.). 1995. pap. 7.00 (*0-614-06282-9*) Ivor Pr.

Boll Weevil & the Triple Play. Louis D. Rubin. 1979. 5.00 (*0-937684-00-7*) Tradd St Pr.

Boll Weevil Mass Rearing Technology. P. P. Sikorowski et al. LC 83-17041. (Illus.). 180p. 1984. text ed. 20.00 (*0-87805-199-6*) U Pr of Miss.

Bollingen: An Adventure in Collecting the Past. William McGuire. LC 82-47625. (Bollingen Ser.). (Illus.). 340p. (C). 1989. 47.50 (*0-691-09951-0*); pap. text ed. 15.95 (*0-691-01885-5*) Princeton U Pr.

Bollinger Connections. Orenia Bollinger. Ed. by Ruth M. Maples. (Illus.). 563p. 1985. 40.00 (*0-9614324-0-3*) C B Williams.

Bologna, Pt. 2. Ed. by Anne Schnoebelen. LC 86-755546. (Solo Motets from the Seventeenth Century Ser.: Vol. 7). 288p. 1988. 40.00 (*0-8240-0642-9*) Garland.

Bologna Pt. 1, Vol. 6: Maurice Cazzati, Op. 6 - Venice 1648; Mauricio Cazzati Op. 13 - Venice 1651; Mauricio Cazzati, Op. 25 - Bologna 1661. Ed. by Anne Schnoebelen. (Solo Motets from the Seventeenth Century Ser.). 350p. 1988. lib. bdg. 45.00 (*0-8240-0641-0*) Garland.

***Bologna Annual Nonfiction '95.** North South Books Staff. 1995. pap. 39.95 (*1-55858-439-0*) North-South Bks NYC.

Bologna Annual, 1994. (Illus.). 104p. 1994. 39.95 (*1-55858-265-7*) North-South Bks NYC.

***Bologna Annual '95.** North South Books Staff. 1995. pap. 39.95 (*1-55858-368-8*) North-South Bks NYC.

Bologna, Civico Museo Bibliografico Musicale MM DD-53: Florence, Biblioteca del Conservatorio di Musica Luigi Cherubini, MS D, No. 2358. Ed. by Alexander Silbiger. (Keyboard Music Horologivm Ser.). 275p. 1987. lib. bdg. 30.00 (*0-8240-8009-2*) Garland.

Bolognese & Emilian Schools. Michael Jaffe. (Illus.). 320p. (C). 1994. 90.00 (*0-7148-2935-8*, Pub. by Phaidon Press UK) Chronicle Bks.

***Bolognese & Emilian Schools.** Michael Jaffe. (Illus.). 320p. (C). 1994. 90.00 (*0-614-03779-4*, Pub. by Phaidon Press UK) Chronicle Bks.

Bolos, Bk. 1: Honor of the Regiment. Created by Keith Laumer. 320p. (Orig.). 1993. mass mkt. 4.99 (*0-671-72184-4*) Baen Bks.

***Bolos, Bk. 3.** Created by Keith Laumer. 1995. mass mkt. 5.99 (*0-671-87683-X*) Baen Bks.

Bolossy Kiralfy, Creator of Great Musical Spectacles: An Autobiography. Ed. by Barbara M. Barker. LC 88-1278. (Theater & Dramatic Studies: No. 50). (Illus.). 310p. reprint ed. pap. 91.20 (*0-8357-1862-X*, 2070781) Bks Demand.

Bolsec Controversy on Predestination, from 1551 to 1555: The Statements of Jerome Bolsec, & the Responses on John Calvin, Theodore Beza, & Other Reformed Theologians, Vol. 1: Theological Currents, the Setting & Mood, & the Trial Itself, 2 bks., Bk. 1: Introduction & Pts. 1 & 2. Philip C. Holtrop. LC 92-47037. 1993. text ed. 109.95 (*0-7734-9248-8*) E Mellen.

Bolsec Controversy on Predestination, from 1551 to 1555: The Statements of Jerome Bolsec, & the Responses on John Calvin, Theodore Beza, & Other Reformed Theologians, Vol. 1: Theological Currents, the Setting & Mood, & the Trial Itself, 2 bks., Bk. 2: Pts. 3-6; Bibliography & Indexes. Philip C. Holtrop. LC 92-47037. 1993. text ed. 129.95 (*0-7734-9250-X*) E Mellen.

Bolshevik Culture: Experiment & Order in the Russian Revolution. Ed. by Abbott Gleason et al. LC 84-48253. (Special Study of the Kennan Institute for Advanced Russian Studies, the Wilson Center: No. 5). 318p. reprint ed. pap. 90.70 (*0-7837-3707-6*, 2057885) Bks Demand.

Bolshevik Feminist: The Life of Aleksandra Kollontai. Barbara E. Clements. LC 78-3240. (Illus.). 370p. reprint ed. pap. 107.80 (*0-7837-1746-6*, 2057280) Bks Demand.

Bolshevik Festivals, 1917-1920. James Von Geldern. LC 92-9074. (Studies on the History of Society & Culture: Vol. 15). (C). 1993. 40.00 (*0-520-07690-7*) U CA Pr.

Bolshevik Party in Conflict: The Left Communist Opposition of 1918. Ronald I. Kowalski. LC 90-21259. (Series in Russian & East European Studies). 290p. (C). 1991. 49.95 (*0-8229-1161-2*) U of Pittsburgh Pr.

Bolshevik Poster. Stephen White. (C). 1988. text ed. 50.00 (*0-300-04339-2*) Yale U Pr.

Bolshevik Poster. V. White. (C). 1990. 120.00 (*0-685-34374-X*, Pub. by Collets) St Mut.

Bolshevik Poster. Stephen White. 159p. (C). 1990. reprint ed. pap. 22.00 (*0-300-04869-6*) Yale U Pr.

Bolshevik Revolution, 1917-1918: Documents & Materials. James Bunyan & Harold H. Fisher. xii, 735p. 1934. 75.00 (*0-8047-0344-2*) Stanford U Pr.

Bolshevik Revolution 1917-1923, 3 vols., 1. Edward H. Carr. 1985. reprint ed. pap. 12.95 (*0-393-30195-8*) Norton.

Bolshevik Revolution 1917-1923, 3 vols., 2. Edward H. Carr. 1985. reprint ed. pap. 13.95 (*0-393-30197-4*) Norton.

Bolshevik Revolution 1917-1923, 3 vols., 3. Edward H. Carr. 1985. reprint ed. pap. 14.95 (*0-393-30199-0*) Norton.

Bolshevik Salute: A Modernist Chinese Novel. Meng Wang. Tr. by Wendy Larson. LC 89-22525. 168p. 1990. 19.95 (*0-295-96856-7*) U of Wash Pr.

Bolshevik Visions: First Phase of the Cultural Revolution in Soviet Russia, Pt. 1: The Culture of a New Society: Ethics, Gender & the Family, Law & Problems of Tradition. 2nd rev. ed. Ed. by William G. Rosenberg. LC 90-10958. 250p. 1990. text ed. 44.50 (*0-472-09424-6*); pap. text ed. 16.95 (*0-472-06424-X*) U of Mich Pr.

Bolshevik Visions: First Phase of the Cultural Revolution in Soviet Russia, Pt. 2: Creating Soviet Cultural Forms: Art, Architecture, Music, Film & the New Tasks of Education. 2nd rev. ed. Ed. by William G. Rosenberg. LC 90-10958. 250p. 1990. text ed. 44.50 (*0-472-09425-4*); pap. text ed. 16.95 (*0-472-06425-8*) U of Mich Pr.

Bolsheviks. Adam B. Ulam. 624p. 1968. pap. 14.95 (*0-02-038100-X*, Collier S&S) S&S Trade.

Bolsheviks & British Jews: The Anglo-Jewish Community, Britain & the Russian Revolution. Sharman Kadish. 312p. 1992. text ed. 45.00 (*0-7146-3371-2*, Pub. by F Cass Pubs UK) Intl Spec Bk.

Bolsheviks & the National & Colonial Question, 1917-1928. Demetrio Boersner. LC 79-2894. 285p. 1995. reprint ed. 36.50 (*0-8305-0062-6*) Hyperion Conn.

Bolsheviks & the Red Army 1918-1921. Francesco Benvenuti. Tr. by Christopher Woodall. (Cambridge Russian, Soviet & Post-Soviet Studies: No. 61). 256p. 1988. 59.95 (*0-521-25771-9*) Cambridge U Pr.

Bolsheviks & the World War: The Origins of the Third International. Olga H. Gankin & Harold H. Fisher. xviii, 856p. 1940. 79.50 (*0-8047-0345-0*) Stanford U Pr.

Bolsheviks & War. Sam Marcy. 165p. 1985. 4.95 (*0-89567-080-1*) World View Forum.

Bolsheviks & Worker's Control. Maurice Brinton. 1975. pap. 2.50 (*0-934868-05-0*) Black & Red.

Bolsheviks in the Tsarist Duma. A. Badayev. 1973. 35.00 (*0-86527-013-9*) Fertig.

Bolshevism: An International Danger; Its Doctrine & Its Practice Through War & Revolution. Pavel N. Miliukov. LC 79-2915. 303p. 1981. reprint ed. 25.75 (*0-8305-0084-7*) Hyperion Conn.

Bolshevism: Practice & Theory. Bertrand Russell. LC 72-4296. (World Affairs Ser.: National & International Viewpoints). 192p. 1979. reprint ed. 19.95 (*0-405-04587-5*) Ayer.

Bolshevism: Theory & Practice. Waldemar Gurian. Tr. by E. I. Watkin. LC 70-104052. reprint ed. 45.00 (*0-404-02963-9*) AMS Pr.

Bolshevism & Anarchism. Rudolf Rocker. 1976. lib. bdg. 250.00 (*0-8490-1522-7*) Gordon Pr.

Bolshevism & the West: A Debate. Scott Nearing & Bertrand Russell. 1973. 250.00 (*0-87968-070-9*) Gordon Pr.

Bolshevism, Fascism & Capitalism. LC 71-128211. (Essay Index Reprint Ser.). 1977. 21.95 (*0-8369-1866-5*) Ayer.

Bolshevism in Art & Its Propagandists. Veritas. 1976. lib. bdg. 59.95 (*0-8490-1523-5*) Gordon Pr.

Bolshevism's Terrible Record: An Indictment. Maitre Aubert. 1976. lib. bdg. 59.95 (*0-8490-1524-3*) Gordon Pr.

Bolshoi Ballet. G. M. Zapevalova. 272p. 1981. 193.00 (*0-317-61240-9*, Pub. by Collets UK) Pro-Am Music.

Bolshoi Theatre: History, Opera, Ballet. A. Zolotov et al. 248p. (C). 1988. 300.00 (*0-569-54811-X*, Pub. by Collets) St Mut.

***Bolsillo para Corduroy.** Don Freeman. (Illus.). (SPA.). (J). (gr. k-3). 1992. audio 22.95 (*0-87499-294-X*); audio, pap. 14.95 (*0-87499-293-1*) Live Oak Media.

***Bolsillo para Corduroy.** Don Freeman. (Illus.). 32p. (SPA.). (J). 1995. pap. 3.99 (*0-14-055283-9*) Puffin Bks.

***Bolsillo para Corduroy, 4 bks., Set.** Don Freeman. (Illus.). (SPA.). (J). (gr. k-3). 1992. audio, pap. 29.95 (*0-87499-295-8*) Live Oak Media.

Bolt. Dick Francis. 320p. 1988. mass mkt. 5.95 (*0-449-21239-4*, Crest) Fawcett.

Bolt Action Rifles. rev. ed. Frank De Haas. LC 73-16310. (Illus.). 448p. (Orig.). 1984. pap. 19.95 (*0-910676-69-0*) DBI.

Bolt Action-Trigger Guard, 2 vols. in 1. Roy LeBeau. (Double Buckskin Ser.). 400p. 1989. pap. 3.95 (*0-8439-2872-7*) Dorchester Pub Co.

Bolt from the Blue: A True Story. Ernest Pintoff. Ed. by James B. Van Treese. 232p. 1992. 14.95 (*1-880416-54-9*) NW Pub.

Bolt from the Blue: Five Hundred Fiftieth Airborne Infantry Battalion, 1941-1945. Justin P. Buckeridge. (Airborne Ser.: No. 6). (Illus.). 1978. reprint ed. pap. 10.00 (*0-89839-006-0*) Battery Pr.

Bolt, No. 1: First Blood. Cort Martin. (Orig.). 1981. pap. 2.25 (*0-89083-767-8*) Zebra.

Bolt, No. 10: Bawdy House Showdown. Cort Martin. 1983. pap. 2.25 (*0-8217-1176-8*) Zebra.

Bolt, No. 14: Virginia City Virgin. Cort Martin. pap. 2.25 (*0-8217-1360-4*) Zebra.

Bolt, No. 15: Bordello Backshooter. Cort Martin. 192p. 1984. pap. 2.25 (*0-8217-1411-2*) Zebra.

Bolt, No. 2: Dead Man's Bounty. Cort Martin. 1981. pap. 2.25 (*0-89083-783-X*) Zebra.

Bolt, No. 20: Six-Guns & Silk. Cort Martin. 1986. pap. 2.25 (*0-8217-1866-5*) Zebra.

Bolt, No. 21: Deadly Withdrawal. Cort Martin. 208p. 1986. pap. 2.25 (*0-8217-1956-4*) Zebra.

Bolt, No. 22: Climax Mountain. Cort Martin. 192p. 1987. pap. 2.25 (*0-8217-2024-4*) Zebra.

Bolt, No. 25: Hot on the Warpath. Cort Martin. 224p. 1988. pap. 2.50 (*0-8217-2265-4*) Zebra.

Bolt, No. 26: Maverick Mistress. Cort Martin. 224p. 1988. pap. 2.50 (*0-8217-2387-1*) Zebra.

Bolt, No. 3: Showdown at Black Mesa. Cort Martin. (Orig.). 1981. pap. 2.25 (*0-89083-812-7*) Zebra.

Bolt, No. 4: The Guns of Taos. Cort Martin. (Orig.). 1981. pap. 2.25 (*0-89083-873-9*) Zebra.

Bolt, No. 5: Shootout at Santa Fe. Cort Martin. (Orig.). 1982. pap. 2.25 (*0-89083-943-3*) Zebra.

Bolt, No. 6: The Tombstone Honeypot. Cort Martin. 1982. pap. 2.25 (*0-8217-1009-5*) Zebra.

Bolt, No. 7: Rawhide Woman. Cort Martin. (Orig.). 1982. pap. 2.25 (*0-8217-1057-5*) Zebra.

Bolt, No. 8: Hard in the Saddle. Cort Martin. 1982. pap. 2.25 (*0-8217-1095-8*) Zebra.

Bolt, No. 9: Badman's Bordello. Cort Martin. 1983. pap. 2.25 (*0-8217-1127-X*) Zebra.

Bolt of White Cloth. Leon Rooke. 176p. 1985. pap. 8.50 (*0-88001-078-9*) Ecco Pr.

Bolton. Susanne Baille et al. (Illus.). 96p. text ed. 10.00 (*1-55046-036-6*, Pub. by Boston Mills Pr CN) Genl Dist Srvs.

Bolton & Wodehouse & Kern: The Men Who Made Musical Comedy. Lee Davis. (Illus.). 480p. 1993. 29.95 (*0-87008-131-4*) JAS Heineman.

Bolton & Wodehouse & Kern: The Men Who Made Musical Comedy. Lee Davis. (Illus.). 480p. 1995. 29.95 (*0-87008-145-4*) JAS Heineman.

Bolton Soldiers & Sailors in the American Revolution. Esther K. Whitcomb & Dorothy O. Mayo. viii, 90p. (Orig.). 1985. pap. 12.50 (*0-917890-56-6*) Heritage Bk.

Bolton Twenty Years On: The Small Firm in the 1990's. John Stanworth. 144p. 1991. 68.00 (*1-85396-178-7*, Pub. by P Chapman Pub UK) Taylor & Francis.

Bolton 20 Years On: The Small Firm in the 1990's. John Stanworth. 224p. 1993. pap. 37.50 (*1-85396-229-5*, Pub. by Paul Chapman UK) Taylor & Francis.

Bolton's American Armory. Charles K. Bolton. (Illus.). 246p. 1989. reprint ed. 18.95 (*0-685-60340-7*, 555) Clearfield Co.

Bolton's Handbook of Canine & Feline Electrocardiography. 2nd ed. N. Joel Edwards. (Illus.). 408p. 1987. pap. text ed. 52.50 (*0-7216-1847-2*) Saunders.

Boltons of Old & New England. Charles K. Bolton. (Illus.). 98p. 1988. reprint ed. lib. bdg. 29.50 (*0-8328-0274-3*); reprint ed. pap. 19.50 (*0-8328-0275-1*) Higginson Bk Co.

Bolts & Nuts of Electronics: Industry History, Conversion Factors, Glossary & Pictorial Index. 115p. 1988. 39.95 (*0-911703-21-7*) CDS Assocs.

Boltzmann Equation & Its Applications. C. Cercignani. (Applied Mathematical Sciences Ser.: Vol. 67). (Illus.). xiii, 455p. 1987. 55.00 (*0-387-96637-4*) Spr-Verlag.

Bolyai Appendix. Ed. by F. Kartezi. (Colloquia Mathematica Societatis Janos Bolyai Ser.). 1988. 102.75 (*0-444-86528-4*, North Holland) Elsevier.

Bolzano & the Foundations of Mathematical Analysis. V. Jarnik. 90p. 1981. pap. 85.00 (*0-317-52903-X*, Pub. by Collets UK) Pro-Am Music.

Bom-Crioulo: The Black Man & the Cabin Boy. Adolfo Caminha. Tr. by E. A. Lacey. 144p. 1982. 25.00 (*0-685-06170-1*); pap. 7.95 (*0-917342-88-7*) Gay Sunshine.

Bom Dia! One-Minute Dialogues in Portugese. Albert R. Lopes. (C). 1980. reprint ed. pap. text ed. 4.95 (*0-89197-520-9*) Irvington.

***Boma's Guide to Writing a Commercial Real Estate Lease.** rev. ed. Boma Staff. 140p. (C). 1994. pap. 140.00 (*0-943130-08-5*) Build Own & Man.

Bomb. Makoto Oda. Tr. by D. H. Whittaker. 192p. 1990. 18.95 (*0-87011-981-8*) Kodansha.

***Bomb.** Theodore Taylor. LC 95-10683. (J). 1995. write for info. (*0-15-200867-5*) HarBrace.

Bomb. R. D. Zimmerman. (BePuzzled Ser.). 4p. (J). 1987. 20.00 (*0-922242-01-1*) Lombard Mktg.

Bomb. Keith Eubank. (Anvil Ser.). 248p. (Orig.). 1992. reprint ed. pap. 13.50 (*0-89464-237-5*) Krieger.

Bomb: Interviews. Ed. by Betsy Sussler. (Illus.). 224p. (Orig.). 1992. pap. 10.95 (*0-87286-261-5*) City Lights.

Bomb & the General. Umberto Eco. Tr. by William Weaver. (Illus.). 40p. (J). (ps up). 1989. 12.95 (*0-15-209700-7*) HarBrace.

Bomb in Bengal: The Rise of Revolutionary Terrorism in India, 1900-1910. Peter Heehs. (Illus.). 354p. 1994. 23.00 (*0-19-563350-4*) OUP.

Bomb in the Brain: A Heroic Tale of Science, Surgery & Survival. Steven J. Fishman. 336p. 1990. pap. 8.95 (*0-380-70898-1*) Avon.

***Bomb Ship.** Peter Tonkin. 608p. 1995. pap. 11.95 (*0-7472-4031-0*, Pub. by Headline UK) Trafalgar.

***Bomb Squad Officer: Expert with Explosives.** Keith Greenberg. Ed. by Bruce Glassman. (Risky Business Ser.). (Illus.). 32p. (J). (gr. 2-5). 1995. lib. bdg. 12.95 (*1-56711-155-6*) Blackbirch.

Bomb Squads & SWAT Teams. Jean Dick. LC 88-15907. (At Risk Ser.). (Illus.). 48p. (J). (gr. 5-6). 1988. text ed. 11.95 (*0-89686-401-4*, Crstwood Hse) Silver Burdett Pr.

***Bomb the Suburbs.** 2nd ed. William U. Wimsatt. (Illus.). 112p. 1995. pap. 7.00 (*0-9643855-0-3*) Subway & Elevator.

Bomb Vessel. Richard Woodman. LC 85-26611. 215p. 1986. 15.95 (*0-8027-0886-2*) Walker & Co.

***Bomb Vessel: Shore Bombardment Ships of the Age of Sail.** Chris Ware. (Conway's Ship Type Ser.). (Illus.). 128p. 1995. 38.95 (*1-55750-071-1*) Naval Inst Pr.

Bomb Vessel Granado. Peter Goodwin. LC 89-62379. (Anatomy of the Ship Ser.). (Illus.). 128p. 1990. 36.95 (*0-87021-178-1*) Naval Inst Pr.

Bombard Story. Alain Bombard. 224p. 1986. pap. 14.95 (*0-246-13038-5*, Pub. by Granada UK) Sheridan.

Bombardier. John W. Corrington. 1970. 25.00 (*0-399-10096-2*) Ultramarine Pub.

***Bombardier Beetles & Fever Trees: A Close-up Look at Chemical Warfare & Signals in Animals & Plants.** William Agosta. 272p. 1995. write for info. (*0-201-62658-6*) Addison-Wesley.

Bombardiers. Po Bronson. LC 94-20610. 1995. 22.00 (*0-679-43541-7*) Random.

Bombarding the Heavenlies. Ora Holloway. 68p. (Orig.). 1993. pap. 10.95 (*0-9631620-1-2*) O J Holloway.

Bombast & Broadsides: The Lives of George Johnstone. Robin F. Fabel. LC 86-19348. 264p. 1987. 29.50 (*0-8173-0337-5*) U of Ala Pr.

Bombay. Rahul Singh. 104p. (C). 1992. 295.00 (*81-7002-042-5*, Pub. by Himalayan Bks II) St Mut.

Bombay: Gateway of India. Raghubir Singh. (Illus.). 108p. 1994. 40.00 (*0-89381-583-7*) Aperture.

***Bombay: Metaphor for Modern India.** Ed. by Sujata Patel & Alice Thorner. (Illus.). 320p. 1995. 24.00 (*0-19-563688-0*) OUP.

***Bombay: Mosaic of Arts & Letters.** Ed. by Sujata Patel & Alice Thorner. (Illus.). 256p. 1995. 24.00 (*0-19-563689-9*) OUP.

An Asterisk (*) at the beginning of an entry indicates that the title is appearing in BIP for the first time.

An Asterisk (*) at the beginning of an entry indicates that the title is appearing in BIP for the first time.

839

Bond of Beauty: Poems. Leslie Konnyu. 1959. pap. 3.25 (*0-911862-01-3*) Hungarian Rev.

***Bond of Hatred.** Lynne Graham. (Presents Ser.). 1995. mass mkt. 3.25 (*0-373-11758-2*, 1-11758-9) Harlequin Bks.

Bond of Interest. Wilbert H. Treloar. (Illus.). 30p. (Orig.). 1978. pap. 2.50 (*0-938746-07-3*) Marquette Cnty.

Bond of Iron: Master & Slave at Buffalo Forge. Charles B. Dew. LC 93-6261. 1994. 27.50 (*0-393-03616-2*) Norton.

***Bond of Iron: Master & Slave at Buffalo Forge.** Charles B. Dew. (Illus.). 448p. 1995. pap. 14.00 (*0-393-31359-X*, Norton Paperbks) Norton.

Bond of Love. 1978. 6.50 (*0-685-68269-2*, MB-464); audio 10.98 (*0-685-68270-6*, TA-229C) Lillenas.

***Bond of Love.** Rosemary Joyce. (Dream Girls Ser.: No. 4). 160p. (J). (gr. 4-7). 1994. pap. 4.50 (*1-56171-371-6*, S P I Bks) Sure Sellers.

Bond on File. Comp. by Philip Roberts. (Methuen Writer-Files Ser.). 96p. (C). 1985. pap. 9.95 (*0-413-54040-5*, A0034) Heinemann.

Bond Orientational Order in Condensed Matter Systems. Ed. by K. J. Strandburg. (Partially Ordered Systems Ser.). (Illus.). 352p. 1991. 89.00 (*0-387-97638-8*) Spr-Verlag.

Bond-Plays One. Edward Bond. (Methuen World Dramatists Ser.). 312p. 1983. pap. 9.95 (*0-413-45410-X*, A0035) Heinemann.

***Bond Record Handbook: Moody's.** 300p. (Orig.). 1995. pap. 595.00 (*0-7605-1811-4*) Rector Pr.

Bond Risk Analysis: A Guide to Duration & Convexity. Livingston G. Douglas. 1990. 34.95 (*0-13-221037-1*) NY Inst Finance.

Bond Salesmanship. William W. Townsend. LC 75-2673. (Wall Street & the Security Market Ser.). 1975. reprint ed. 41.95 (*0-405-07236-8*) Ayer.

Bond Street Burlesque. Raymond Paul. 1987. 16.95 (*0-393-02402-4*) Norton.

***Bond Survey: Moody's.** 400p. (Orig.). 1995. pap. 1,595.00 (*0-7605-1812-2*) Rector Pr.

Bond to Halogens & Halogenoids, Pt. 1. Alan G. MacDiarmid. (Organometallic Compounds of the Group IV Elements Ser.: Vol. 2). (Illus.). 392p. reprint ed. pap. 111.80 (*0-8357-7338-8*, 2055068) Bks Demand.

Bond Values Tables. Financial Publishing Co. Staff. 1248p. 1981. 65.00 (*0-87600-183-5*) Finan Pub.

Bond with the Beloved: The Mystical Relationship of the Lover & the Beloved. Llewellyn Vaughan-Lee. 160p. (Orig.). 1993. pap. 12.00 (*0-9634574-0-3*) Golden Sufi Ctr.

Bond with the Beloved: The Relationship of the Lover & Beloved on the Sufi Path. Llewellyn Vaughan-Lee. 160p. 1993. pap. 12.00 (*0-9634576-8-3*) Patch Pub.

Bond Yield Tables: Annual Coupon. Financial Publishing Co. Staff. 222p. 1971. pap. 15.00 (*0-87600-154-1*) Finan Pub.

Bond Yield Tables: Semi-annual Coupons. Financial Publishing Co. Staff. 222p. 1971. pap. 15.00 (*0-87600-254-8*) Finan Pub.

Bondage. Patti Davis. 1994. 23.00 (*0-671-86953-1*) S&S Trade.

***Bondage.** Patti Davis. Ed. by Julie Rubenstein. 320p. 1995. mass mkt. 5.99 (*0-671-86954-X*) PB.

Bondage. W. L. Garrison. LC 78-72959. 1978. 5.95 (*0-933012-01-2*) Coker Pub.

Bondage Breaker. Neil Anderson. LC 90-30479. (Orig.). 1990. pap. 8.99 (*0-89081-787-1*) Harvest Hse.

Bondage Breaker Audiobook. Neil Anderson. 1994. audio 14.99 (*1-56507-018-6*) Harvest Hse.

Bondage Breaker Study Guide. Neil Anderson. 1992. pap. 5.99 (*0-89081-996-3*) Harvest Hse.

Bondage Breaker Youth Edition. Neil Anderson & Dave Park. (J). 1993. pap. 7.99 (*1-56507-139-5*) Harvest Hse.

***Bondage Breaker Youth Edition Study Guide.** Neil T. Anderson & Dave Park. (Orig.). (YA). 1995. student ed, pap. 5.99 (*1-56507-293-6*) Harvest Hse.

Bondage of the Will. J. I. Packer. LC 58-8662. 1990. pap. 12.99 (*0-8007-5342-9*) Revell.

Bonded Ceramic Inlays. Jean-Francois Roulet & Stefan Herder. (Illus.). 103p. 1991. text ed. 62.00 (*0-86715-244-3*) Quint Pub Co.

Bonded Electrical Resistance Strain Gage. William M. Murray & William R. Miller. (Illus.). 432p. 1992. text ed. 75.00 (*0-19-507209-X*) OUP.

Bonded Histories: Genealogies of Labor Servitude in Colonial India. Gyan Prakash. (Cambridge South Asian Studies: No. 44). (Illus.). 272p. (C). 1990. 59.95 (*0-521-36278-4*) Cambridge U Pr.

Bonded in Christ's Love: Being a Member of the Church. Denise L. Carmody & John T. Carmody. 240p. (Orig.). (C). 1986. pap. 9.95 (*0-8091-2791-1*) Paulist Pr.

***Bonded Labour: Caste & Cultural Identity among Tamil Plantation Workers in Sri Lanka.** Oddvar Hollup. (C). 1995. 32.00x (*81-207-1480-6*, Pub. by Sterling Plns Pvt II) S Asia.

Bonded Labour & Social Justice. S. S. Prakash. 1990. 17.00 (*81-7100-197-1*, Pub. by Deep) S Asia.

Bonded Labour & Social Justice. S. S. Prakash. (C). 1990. 60.00 (*0-89771-316-8*) St Mut.

***Bonded Labourers: A Study of Rehabilitation & Organisational Dynamics.** R. R. Prasad & K. Suman Chandra. (C). 1994. text ed. 22.00 (*81-241-0211-2*, Pub. by Har-Anand Pubns II) S Asia.

Bonded Repair of Aircraft Structures. Ed. by A. A. Baker & R. Jones. (C). 1988. lib. bdg. 140.00 (*90-247-3606-4*) Kluwer Ac.

Bonded Warehouse Manual for Proprietors, Importers & Customs Officers. 1992. lib. bdg. 86.95 (*0-8490-5544-X*) Gordon Pr.

Bonded Warehouse Manual for Proprietors, Importers, Customs Officers. 135p. 1990. per., pap. 7.00 (*0-16-027485-0*, S/N 048-002-001) USGPO.

Bondi Blues. John Baxter. 1994. pap. 5.95 (*1-86373-453-8*, Pub. by Allen & Unwin Aust Pty AT) IPG Chicago.

Bonding. Stanley Keleman. 131p. (Orig.). 1986. pap. 9.00 (*0-934320-11-X*) Center Pr.

***Bonding: Building the Foundations of Secure Attachment & Independence.** Phyllis H. Klaus et al. 1995. 22.00 (*0-201-62673-X*) Addison-Wesley.

Bonding: Relationships in the Image of God. Donald Joy. 199p. 1987. write for info. (*0-8499-3076-6*) Word Inc.

Bonding & Structure: Structural Principles in Inorganic & Organic Chemistry. N. W. Alcock. (Ellis Horwood Series in Inorganic Chemistry). 292p. 1991. text ed. 37.50 (*0-13-465246-0*, 520101) P-H.

Bonding & Structure of Solids. Ed. by R. Haydock. (Royal Society Discussion Volumes Ser.). (C). 1991. 69.95 (*0-521-41316-8*) Cambridge U Pr.

Bonding Before Birth. John W. Harris. Ed. by Robert Brown. (Illus.). (Orig.). student ed, pap. 8.95 (*0-9618411-0-9*); audio 8.95 (*0-9618411-1-7*) Prsnl Grwth ID.

Bonding Before Birth: Journey into Familyhood. Leni Schwartz. 325p. 1991. 37.50 (*1-879041-05-7*); pap. 16.95 (*1-879041-04-9*) Sigo Pr.

Bonding Book. Leon Nelson. 1985. 49.95 (*0-87814-267-3*, D4238) PennWell Bks.

Bonding Energetics in Organometallic Compounds. Ed. by Tobin J. Marks. LC 90-36268. (ACS Symposium Ser.: No. 428). (Illus.). 292p. 1990. 64.95 (*0-8412-1791-2*) Am Chemical.

Bonding, Energy Levels & Bands in Inorganic Solids. J. A. Duffy. 249p. 1990. pap. text ed. 42.95 (*0-470-21567-4*) Wiley.

Bonding in Cementitious Composites. Ed. by S. Mindess & S. Shah. (Symposium Proceedings Ser.: Vol. 114). 1988. text ed. 42.00 (*0-931837-82-0*) Materials Res.

Bonding-The Universal Glue. Thomas Bowman. Ed. by T. E. Dennison. (Illus.). 45p. Date not set. 5.00 (*0-923231-20-X*) Mohican Pub.

Bonding Versus Pay-As-You-Go in the Financing of School Buildings. Don L. Essex. LC 70-176757. (Columbia University. Teachers College. Contributions to Education Ser.: No. 496). reprint ed. 37.50 (*0-404-55496-2*) AMS Pr.

Bondmen & Rebels: A Study of Master-Slave Relations in Antigua. David B. Gaspar. LC 92-37509. 352p. (Orig.). 1993. pap. text ed. 18.95 (*0-8223-1336-7*) Duke.

Bonds. 2nd ed. Jan Seale. Ed. by Dorey Schmidt. (Poetry Ser.: No. 1). (Illus.). 60p. (Orig.). 1981. pap. 6.95 (*0-938884-04-2*) Riversedge Pr.

Bonds & Bondage: Daughter-Father Relationships in the Father Memoirs of German-Speaking Women Writers of the 1970s. Gisela Moffit. LC 92-35430. (Studies in Modern German Literature: Vol. 53). 284p. 1993. 56.95 (*0-8204-2014-X*) P Lang Pubs.

Bonds & the Money Market Simplified. Martin Torosian. 1987. 37.00 (*0-9603592-5-7*) MTA Financial Servs.

Bond's Franchise Guide. 8th ed. Robert E. Bond. 558p. (Orig.). 1995. pap. 29.95 (*1-887137-00-9*) Source Bk Pubns. Truly required reading for any serious franchisee. BOND'S FRANCHISE GUIDE - 1995 EDITION, now in its 8th Edition (previously published as THE SOURCE BOOK OF FRANCHISE OPPORTUNITIES), is the definitive directory of North American franchising. Published by America's most respected authority on the franchise selection process, the GUIDE lists over 2,200 franchise opportunities, divided into 54 distinct business categories. A detailed profile is provided on 1,120 franchises. Supplemental data is provided on over 1,100 others. All data has been 100% verified & represents the most up-to-date & comprehensive information about a potential franchisee's options. The profiles, which are the result of an exhaustive 40-point questionnaire, cover company history, capital requirements (initial cash investment & total investment, on-going royalty & advertising fees, staffing levels, space needs, etc.), initial training & start-up assistance, franchisee selection criteria, specific areas of geographic expansion & much, much more. Since receiving his MBA from Stanford University, the author has spent much of the past 13 years focusing on the franchising industry. As an author, lecturer & consultant, Bond is generally regarded as one of the industry's most knowledgeable & articulate spokesman. Source Book Publications, P.O. Box 12488, Oakland, CA 94604. (510) 839-5471.** ***Publisher Provided Annotation.

Bonds of Community: The Lives of Farm Women in Nineteenth-Century New York. Nancy G. Osterud. LC 90-41814. (Illus.). 320p. 1991. 45.00 (*0-8014-2510-7*); pap. 14.95 (*0-8014-9798-1*) Cornell U Pr.

Bonds of Enterprise: John Murray Forbes & Western Development in America's Railway Age. John L. Larson. 1984. text ed. 30.00 (*0-07-103279-7*) McGraw.

Bonds of Iron: Forging Lasting Male Relationships. James Osterhaus. 1994. 16.99 (*0-8024-7129-3*) Moody.

Bonds of Love. Candace Camp. 1992. mass mkt. 4.50 (*0-06-104063-0*, Harp PBks) HarpC.

Bonds of Love: Psychoanalysis, Feminism, & the Problem Domination. Jessica Benjamin. 1988. pap. 16.00 (*0-394-75730-0*) Pantheon.

***Bonds of Matrimony Hsing - Shih Yin - Yuan Chuan Vol. 1: A Seventeenth - Century Chinese Novel.** Tr. by Eve A. Nyren. LC 94-37609. (Chinese Studies: Vol. 1). 312p. (CHI.). 1995. text ed. 99.95 (*0-7734-9033-7*) E Mellen.

Bonds of Silk: The Human Factor in the British Administration of the Sudan. Martin W. Daly & Francis M. Deng. LC 89-43113. (African Studies: No. 1). (C). 1990. text ed. 26.00 (*0-87013-279-2*) Mich St U Pr.

Bonds of Sisterhood: A History of the RLDS Women's Organization, 1842-1983. Madelon Brunson. 170p. 1985. pap. 12.00 (*0-8309-0401-8*) Herald Hse.

Bonds of Unity. Melanie May. LC 88-37682. (American Academy of Religion Academy Ser.). 196p. 1989. 23.95 (*1-55540-308-5*, 01 01 65); pap. 15.95 (*1-55540-309-3*) Scholars Pr GA.

Bonds of Womanhood: "Woman's Sphere" in New England, 1780-1835. Nancy F. Cott. LC 76-49728. 1978. pap. 13.00x (*0-300-02289-1*) Yale U Pr.

Bonds, Preferred Stocks & the Money Market. Jeffrey B. Little & Paul A. Samuelson. (Basic Investors Library). (Illus.). 48p. 1988. lib. bdg. 12.95 (*1-55546-625-7*) Chelsea Hse.

Bonds Without Bondage: Explorations in Transcultural Interactions. Ed. by Krishna Kumar. LC 78-31546. 308p. 1979. pap. text ed. 12.00 (*0-8248-0636-0*, Eastwest Ctr Pr) UH Pr.

Bone. Tom Bacchus. (Orig.). 1994. pap. text ed. 4.95 (*1-56333-177-2*) Masquerade.

Bone. Fae M. Ng. 208p. 1994. reprint ed. pap. 11.00 (*0-06-097592-X*, PL) HarpC.

Bone: A Novel. Fae M. Ng. 208p. 1993. 19.95 (*1-56282-944-0*) Hyperion.

***Bone: Differentiation & Morphogenesis of Bone, Vol. 9.** Ed. by Brian K. Hall. 208p. 1994. 99.95 (*0-8493-8994-1*, 8994) CRC Pr.

Bone: Fundamentals of the Physiology of Skeletal Tissue. 3rd rev. ed. Franklin C. McLean & Marshall R. Urist. LC 68-16703. 336p. reprint ed. pap. 95.80 (*0-8357-7339-6*, 2024121) Bks Demand.

***Bone: Mechanisms of Bone Development & Growth, Vol. 8.** Ed. by Brian K. Hall. 256p. 1994. 119.95 (*0-8493-8903-8*, 8903) CRC Pr.

***Bone Vol. 1: Out from Boneville.** Jeff Smith. 144p. 1995. 19.95 (*0-9636609-9-3*) Cartoon Bks.

Bone Vol. 1: The Osteoclast & Osteocyte. Ed. by Brian K. Hall. 500p. 1989. 65.00 (*0-936923-24-5*) Telford Pr.

Bone Vol. 2: The Osteoclast. Ed. by Brian K. Hall. 500p. 1989. 65.00 (*0-936923-25-3*) Telford Pr.

Bone: A Treatise: The Osteoclast, II. Brian K. Hall. 500p. 1992. 91.95 (*0-8493-8822-8*, QP88) CRC Pr.

Bone: A Treatise: The Osteoclast, III. Brian K. Hall. 500p. 1992. 86.95 (*0-8493-8823-6*, QP88) CRC Pr.

Bone: A Treatise: The Osteoclast, IV. Brian K. Hall. 500p. 1992. 86.95 (*0-8493-8824-4*, QP88) CRC Pr.

Bone: A Treatise: The Osteoclast, V. Brian K. Hall. 500p. 1992. 86.95 (*0-8493-8825-2*) CRC Pr.

Bone: A Treatise: The Osteoclast, VI. Brian K. Hall. 500p. 1992. 86.95 (*0-8493-8826-0*) CRC Pr.

Bone: A Treatise: The Osteoclast, Vol. VII, 1992. Brian K. Hall. 500p. 1992. 83.95 (*0-8493-8827-9*) CRC Pr.

Bone & Bone Seeking Radionuclides: Physiology, Dosimetry, & Effects. Ed. by V. Volf. (European Applied Research Reports Special Topics Ser.). 160p. 1981. text ed. 136.00 (*3-7186-0061-7*) Gordon & Breach.

Bone & Cartilage Allografts: Biology & Clinical Applications. Ed. by Gary E. Friedlaender & Victor M. Goldberg. LC 91-4559. 308p. 1991. 95.00 (*0-89203-047-X*) Amer Acad Ortho Surg.

Bone & Mineral Research, Vol. 7. W. A. Peck et al. 364p. 1991. 200.00 (*0-444-81371-3*) Elsevier.

Bone & Mineral Research, Vol. 8. Ed. by J. Heersche & J. Kanis. 324p. 1994. 262.75 (*0-444-89659-7*) Elsevier.

Bone & Mineral Research Annual, No. 6. Ed. by W. A. Peck. 350p. 1989. 143.75 (*0-444-81061-7*) Elsevier.

Bone & Mineral Research Annual, Vol. 5. Ed. by W. A. Peck. 470p. 1987. 97.75 (*0-317-61525-4*) Elsevier.

Bone & Mineral Research Annual Vol. 3: A Yearly Survey of Developments in the Field of Bone & Mineral Metabolism. Ed. by W. A. Peck. 400p. 1985. 95.00 (*0-444-90347-X*) Elsevier.

Bone & Renal Failure. Ed. by Marc E. De Broe & F. L. Van de Vyver. (Contributions to Nephrology Ser.: Vol. 64). (Illus.). vi, 182p. 1988. 117.75 (*3-8055-4738-2*) S Karger.

Bone & Tooth: Proceedings of First European Symposium, Oxford, April 1963. H. Blackwood. LC 63-21445. 1964. 187.00 (*0-08-010623-4*, Pub. by Pergamon Repr UK) Franklin.

Bone Appetit! Gourmet Cooking for Your Dog. Suzan Anson. (Illus.). (Orig.). 1989. pap. 11.95 (*0-942257-13-8*) New Chapter Pr.

Bone Biodynamics in Orthodontic & Orthopedic Treatment. Ed. by Steven A. Goldstein & David S. Carlson. LC 93-135645. (Craniofacial Growth Ser.: Vol. 27). (Illus.). 388p. 1992. 59.00 (*0-929921-23-2*) UM CHGD.

Bone-Biomaterial Interface. Ed. by J. E. Davies. 352p. 1991. 140.00 (*0-8020-5941-4*) U of Toronto Pr.

***Bone, Breath, & Gesture: Practices of Embodiment, Vol. I.** Ed. by Don H. Johnson. 200p. (Orig.). 1995. pap. 12.95 (*1-55643-201-1*) North Atlantic.

***Bone Breath & the Vandals.** Peg Kehret. Ed. by Pat MacDonald. (Frightmares Ser.). (Orig.). 1995. 14.00 (*0-671-89190-1*, Minstrel Bks) PB.

***Bone Breath & the Vandals.** Peg Kehret. Ed. by Pat MacDonald. (Frimble Family First Learning Adventures Ser.). 144p. (Orig.). (J). 1995. pap. 3.50 (*0-671-89189-8*, Minstrel Bks) PB.

***Bone Builders Cookbook.** Edita M. Kaye. 496p. (Orig.). 1995. pap. 19.95 (*0-9635150-1-2*) Fndtn Youth Grp.

Bone by Bone: Stories. Gary Krist. LC 93-4865. 1994. 19.95 (*0-15-182064-3*) HarBrace.

Bone-Chilling Tales of Fright: Stories to Make You Scream. 128p. (J). 1994. pap. 4.95 (*1-56565-167-7*) Lowell Hse Juvenile.

Bone Circulation & Vascularization in Normal & Pathological Conditions. Ed. by A. Schoutens et al. (NATO ASI Series A, Life Sciences: Vol. 247). 1993. 110.00 (*0-306-44523-9*, Plenum Pr) Plenum.

Bone Dance: New & Selected Poems, 1965-1993. Wendy Rose. LC 93-21117. (Sun Tracks Ser.: Vol. 27). 120p. (Orig.). (C). 1994. lib. bdg. 19.95 (*0-8165-1412-7*); pap. 10.95 (*0-8165-1428-3*) U of Ariz Pr.

***Bone Deep.** Darian North. LC 95-12413. 1995. write for info. (*0-525-93849-4*, Dutton) NAL-Dutton.

Bone Disease in Renal Failure. Ed. by H. H. Malluche. (Mineral & Electrolyte Metabolism Journal: Vol. 17, No. 4). (Illus.). 92p. 1992. pap. 54.50 (*3-8055-5506-7*) S Karger.

Bone Disease in the Elderly. Colin R. Paterson & W. J. MacLennan. LC 84-3716. (Wiley Series on Disease Management in the Elderly: No. 3). (Illus.). 224p. reprint ed. pap. 63.90 (*0-8357-3926-0*, 2036661) Bks Demand.

***Bone-Duster.** John Morgan. (QRL Poetry Book Ser.: Vol. XXI). 20.00 (*0-614-06380-9*); pap. 15.00 (*0-614-06381-7*) Quarterly Rev.

Bone Flames. Colleen J. McElroy. LC 86-32463. (Wesleyan Poetry Ser.). 80p. 1987. 22.50 (*0-8195-2148-5*, Wesleyan Univ Pr); pap. 10.95 (*0-8195-1149-8*, Wesleyan Univ Pr) U Pr of New Eng.

Bone Forest. Robert Holdstock. 256p. (Orig.). 1992. mass mkt. 4.50 (*0-380-76781-3*, AvoNova) Avon.

***Bone Formation & Repair.** Ed. by Carl T. Brighton et al. (Illus.). 542p. 1994. 105.00 (*0-89203-116-6*) Amer Acad Ortho Surg.

Bone from a Dry Sea. Peter Dickinson. LC 92-20491. (J). 1993. 16.00 (*0-385-30821-3*) Delacorte.

***Bone from a Dry Sea.** Peter Dickinson. (YA). (gr. 7 up). 1995. mass mkt. 3.99 (*0-440-21928-0*) Dell.

Bone from a Dry Sea. large type ed. Peter Dickinson. LC 93-43769. (J). 1994. pap. 15.95 (*0-7862-0154-1*) Thorndike Pr.

Bone Game: A Novel. Louis Owens. LC 94-13882. (American Indian Literature & Critical Studies: Vol. 10). 1994. 19.95 (*0-8061-2664-7*) U of Okla Pr.

Bone Garden. William Wood. 1994. mass mkt. 5.99 (*0-671-68638-0*) PB.

***Bone Gnawers Tribebook.** (Werewolf). Date not set. 10.00 (*1-56504-094-5*) White Wolf.

Bone Grafts & Bone Substitutes. Mutaz B. Habal & A. Harri Reddi. (Illus.). 485p. 1992. text ed. 121.00 (*0-7216-2809-5*) Saunders.

Bone Grafts & Derivatives. B. T. O'Connor et al. (Illus.). 456p. 1994. 135.00 (*0-7506-1369-6*) Buttrwrth-Heinemann.

***Bone Hill.** Gene McLaughlin. 290p. Date not set. pap. 8.95 (*0-7610-0258-8*) NW Pub.

Bone Histomorphometry. Erik F. Eriksen et al. LC 93-24476. 88p. 1994. 15.00 (*0-7817-0122-8*) Raven.

Bone Histomorphometry: Techniques & Interpretation. Ed. by Robert R. Recker. 312p. 1983. 168.00 (*0-8493-5373-4*, QM569, CRC Reprint) Franklin.

Bone Hunters: The Heroic Age of Paleontology in the American West. Url Lanham. Orig. Title: The Bone Hunters. (Illus.). 304p. 1991. reprint ed. pap. 10.95 (*0-486-26917-5*) Dover.

Bone Hunters see Bone Hunters: The Heroic Age of Paleontology in the American West

Bone Hunters in Patagonia. John B. Hatcher. LC 84-25527. 212p. 1985. reprint ed. 26.00 (*0-918024-36-6*); reprint ed. pap. 15.95 (*0-918024-37-4*) Ox Bow.

***Bone Idle.** Susannah Stacey. LC 94-48227. 1995. 21.00 (*0-671-73531-4*) PB.

Bone Implant Grafting. Ed. by John Older. LC 92-2327. xviii, 226p. 1992. write for info. (*3-540-19720-6*); 198.00 (*0-387-19720-6*) Spr-Verlag.

***Bone In the Throat.** Bourdain. 1995. 20.00 (*0-679-43552-2*, Villard Bks) Random.

Bone Is Pointed. Arthur Upfield. (Napoleon Bonoparte Mysteries Ser.). 21.95 (*0-89190-568-5*, Am Repr) Amereon Ltd.

Bone Is Pointed. 2nd large type ed. Arthur Upfield. 385p. 1993. 21.95 (*1-85695-335-1*, Pub. by ISIS UK) Transaction Pubs.

Bone Is Pointed: An Inspector Napoleon Bonaparte Mystery. Arthur W. Upfield. 288p. 1984. pap. 6.00 (*0-684-18247-5*, Scribners) S&S Trade.

Bone Ischaemia & Infarction in Sickle Cell Disease. Stanley P. Bohrer & Abass Alavi. LC 79-50182. (Illus.). 347p. (C). 1981. 44.50 (*0-87527-188-X*) Green.

Bone Marrow & Stem Cell Processing: A Manual of Current Techniques. Ellen Areman et al. LC 92-4730. (Illus.). 487p. (C). 1992. text ed. 145.00 (*0-8036-0266-9*) Davis Co.

Bone Marrow Biopsies Revisited. R. Bartl et al. (Illus.). xiv, 138p. 1984. 46.50 (*3-8055-3937-1*) S Karger.

An Asterisk (*) at the beginning of an entry indicates that the title is appearing in BIP for the first time.

B

An Asterisk (*) at the beginning of an entry indicates that the title is appearing in BIP for the first time.

841

Bonjour, Ca Va? An Introductory Course. 3rd ed. Myrna B. Rochester et al. 1991. pap. text ed. 11.84 (*0-07-557445-4*) McGraw.

Bonjour, Ca Va? An Introductory Course. 3rd ed. Myrna B. Rochester et al. 1991. write for info. (*0-07-557441-1*); Cahier D'Exercices. pap. text ed. write for info. (*0-07-557443-8*); audio 100.00 (*0-07-557459-4*) McGraw.

Bonjour, Ca Va? An Introductory Course. 3rd ed. Myrna B. Rochester et al. 1991. write for info. (*0-07-053401-2*); write for info. (*0-07-053402-0*) McGraw.

Bonjour, la Bonjour. rev. ed. Tr. by Tremblay & John Van Burek. (NFS Canada Ser.). 1999. pap. 9.95 (*0-88922-252-5*, Pub. by Talonbooks CN) InBook.

Bonjour, Mes Amis - Hello, My Friends. Irene Bowers & Linda Weller. (Illus.). 32p. (J). (ps-3). 1994. audio, pap. 16.95 (*0-8120-8150-1*) Barron.

Bonjour, Mr. McGrue. Le Rap. (Nursery Rhymes Ser.). 15p. (J). (gr. k-2). 1991. pap. text ed. 23.00 (*1-56843-040-X*); pap. text ed. 4.50 (*1-56843-087-6*) BGR Pub.

Bonjour, Mister Satie. Edward Lear & Tomie De Paola. (Illus.). (J). (ps-3). 1991. 15.95 (*0-399-21782-7*, Putnam) Putnam Pub Group.

Bonjour, Paris. Florence R. Goss. (Illus.). 80p. (Orig.). 1993. pap. 7.95 (*0-938711-19-9*) Tecolote Pubns.

Bonjour, Tigre! Barbara Huneke & Ilona Gay. 40p. (J). (gr. 1). 1984. pap. 10.00 (*1-884488-00-5*) Bonjour Tigre.

Bonjour, Tigre! 2nd ed. Barbara Huneke & Ilona Gay. 40p. (J). (gr. 1). 1985. pap. 12.00 (*1-884488-01-3*) Bonjour Tigre.

Bonjour, Tigre! 3rd ed. Barbara Huneke & Ilona Gay. 28p. (J). (gr. 1). 1993. pap. 12.00 (*1-884488-03-X*) Bonjour Tigre.

Bonjour Tristesse. Francoise Sagan. 153p. (FRE.). 1990. pap. 10.95 (*0-7859-1487-0*, 2266038230) Fr & Eur.

Bonk! Goes the Ball. Philippa J. Stevens. LC 89-48561. (Rookie Reader Ser.). (Illus.). 32p. (J). (ps-2). 1990. lib. bdg. 10.35 (*0-516-02061-7*); pap. 2.95 (*0-516-42061-5*) Childrens.

***Bonkers.** Golden Western Staff. (J). Date not set. pap. 1.59 (*0-307-08221-0*, Golden Pr) Western Pub.

Bonkers: Why Women Get Stressed Out & What They Can Do about It. Kevin Leman. pap. 3.99 (*0-8007-8612-2*) Revell.

Bonkie the Great Bank Blagger. Seamus O'Mulgreavey. 264p. (C). 1990. 39.00 (*1-86305-003-5*, Pub. by Pascoe Pub AT) St Mut.

Bonkly Dribblefink Fables. James Magorian. LC 87-70706. (Illus.). 16p. (J). (gr. 1-4). 1987. pap. 3.00 (*0-930674-24-3*) Black Oak.

Bonko. Robert W. Schnell. LC 77-99446. (Illus.). 28p. (J). (ps-3). 8.95 (*0-87592-008-X*) Scroll Pr.

Bonn & Moscow: A Partnership in Progress? Robbin Laird. (C). 1990. 65.00 (*0-907967-97-3*, Pub. by Inst Euro Def & Strat UK) St Mut.

***Bonn & the Bomb: German Politics & the Nuclear Option.** Matthias Kuntzel. (Transnational Institute Ser.). (C). 1995. pap. text ed. 22.95 (*0-7453-0909-7*, Pub. by Pluto Pr UK) Westview.

***Bonn & the Bomb: German Politics & the Nuclear Option.** Matthias Kuntzel, Jr. Tr. by R. Range Cloyd & Helke Heino. LC 94-40247. (Transnational Institute Ser.). (C). 1995. text ed. 69.95 (*0-7453-0910-0*, Pub. by Pluto Pr UK) Westview.

Bonn Workshop on Combinatorial Optimization. Ed. by Achim Bachem et al. (Mathematics Studies: Vol. 66). 312p. 1982. pap. 87.25 (*0-444-86366-4*, I-320-82, North Holland) Elsevier.

***Bonnard.** Julian Bell. (Color Library). (Illus.). 128p. (C). 1994. pap. 14.95 (*0-7148-3052-6*, Pub. by Phaidon Press UK) Chronicle Bks.

***Bonnard.** Julian Bell. (Color Library). (Illus.). 128p. (C). 1994. 19.99 (*0-7148-3205-7*, Pub. by Phaidon Press UK) Chronicle Bks.

Bonnard. Raymond Cogniat. (CAL Art Ser.). (Illus.). 1988. 18.00 (*0-517-09889-X*, Crown) Crown Pub Group.

Bonnard. Andre Ferminger. (Masters of Art Ser.). 1984. 22. 95 (*0-8109-0732-1*) Abrams.

Bonnard. Nicholas Watkins. 1994. 49.95 (*0-7148-2895-5*, Pub. by Phaidon Press UK) Chronicle Bks.

Bonnard: The Complete Graphic Work. Francis Bouvet. (Illus.). 352p. 1981. 125.00 (*0-915346-74-5*) A Wofsy Fine Arts.

Bonnard: The Magic Ring. Jean Bouret. (Rhythem & Color Two Ser.). 1970. 9.95 (*0-8288-9514-7*) Fr & Eur.

Bonnard - Matisse: Letters Between Friends, 1925-1946. Tr. by Richard Howard. LC 92-12144. 1992. pap. 19.95 (*0-8109-2533-8*) Abrams.

Bonnard at le Cannet. Michel Terrasse. LC 92-64152. (Illus.). 128p. 1993. reprint ed. pap. 24.95 (*0-500-27672-2*) Thames Hudson.

Bonnard, ou le Bonheur de Voir. Annette Vaillant. (Illus.). 230p. (FRE.). 1965. lib. bdg. 195.00 (*0-8288-3931-X*) Fr & Eur.

Bonne Chanson. Paul Verlaine. 256p. (FRE.). 1979. pap. 10. 95 (*0-7859-1625-3*, 2070321843) Fr & Eur.

Bonne Chanson Jadis et Naguere. Paul Verlaine. (Poesie Ser.). (Illus.). (FRE.). 9.95 (*2-07-032184-3*) Schoenhof.

Bonne Chanson, Jadis et Naguere, Parallelement. Paul Verlaine. (FRE.). 1979. pap. 10.95 (*0-8288-3826-7*, F104939) Fr & Eur.

Bonne Chanson, Romances sans Paroles, Sagasse. Paul Verlaine. (Illus.). 1964. pap. 10.95 (*0-7859-3076-0*) Fr & Eur.

Bonne Cuisine: Cooking New Orleans Style. All Saints Episcopal Churchwomen Staff. (Illus.). 337p. 1980. pap. 11.95 (*0-9606880-0-5*) ECS Inc.

Bonne Cuisine: Cooking New Orleans Style Lagniappe. All Saints Episcopal Churchwomen Staff. 28p. 1986. pap. 3.50 (*0-9606880-1-3*) ECS Inc.

Bonne et Heureuse Annee. Roch Carrier. LC 91-65366. (Illus.). 24p. (FRE.). (J). (gr. 3 up). 1991. 14.95 (*0-88776-268-9*) Tundra Bks.

***Bonne Nouvelle pour Vous.** Charles Brock. Tr. by Renaud Balzora. 28p. (Orig.). (FRE.). 1993. pap. 1.00 (*1-885504-06-3*) Church Gwth.

Bonne Pratique des Essais Cliniques des Medicaments. A. Spriet & Therese Dupin-Spriet. (Illus.). vi, 250p. 1990. 107.25 (*3-8055-5220-3*) S Karger.

Bonne Table. Ludwig Bemelmans. LC 89-45382. (Illus.). 1989. pap. 14.95 (*0-87923-808-9*) Godine.

Bonne Vie. Jim Davis. (Garfield Ser.). (FRE.). (J). 1988. 18. 95 (*0-8288-4581-6*) Fr & Eur.

Bonner. large type ed. Paul K. McAfee. (Linford Western Library). 256p. 1993. pap. 14.95 (*0-7089-7439-2*, Linford) Ulverscroft.

Bonnes. Jean Genet. (Folio Ser.: No. 1060). (FRE.). 1963. pap. 8.95 (*2-07-037060-7*) Schoenhof.

Bonnes. Jean Genet. (FRE.). 1978. pap. 10.95 (*0-8288-3645-0*, M5078) Fr & Eur.

Bonnes see Oeuvres Completes

Bonnet & Shawl: An Album. Philip Guedalla. LC 70-121475. (Essay Index Reprint Ser.). 1977. 20.95 (*0-8369-1753-7*) Ayer.

Bonnet House: Coastal Wilderness Refined. Jayne R. Workman. Ed. by Alice Smith et al. (Illus.). 28p. 1992. pap. write for info. (*0-9624757-3-4*) Bonnet Hse.

Bonnet House: The Life & Gift. Jayne Rice. (Illus.). 48p. (Orig.). 1990. pap. text ed. write for info. (*0-9624757-1-8*) Bonnet Hse.

Bonneville! Quest for the Land Speed Record. Jay Schleifer. LC 94-765. (Out to Win Ser.). (J). 1994. text ed. 14.95 (*0-89686-817-6*, Crstwood Hse) Silver Burdett Pr.

Bonneville Blue. Joan Chase. 1993. mass mkt. 4.99 (*0-345-37822-9*) Ballantine.

Bonneville Blue: Stories. Joan Chase. 226p. 1991. 19.95 (*0-374-11539-7*) FS&G.

Bonneville Dream. Lorena S. Fisher. LC 91-76002. (Illus.). 152p. (Orig.). 1991. pap. 10.00 (*0-8323-0490-5*) Binford Mort.

Bonney's Gynaecological Surgery. 9th ed. John M. Monaghan. (Illus.). 605p. 1987. text ed. 73.50 (*0-7020-1019-7*, Bailliere-Tindall) Saunders.

Bonney's Place. Leon Hale. (Illus.). 264p. 1981. reprint ed. pap. 8.95 (*0-940672-02-2*) Shearer Pub.

Bonnie. Bonnie Consolo. (Illus.). 149p. (Orig.). 1990. pap. 12.50 (*0-9641198-0-3*) B Consolo.

Bonnie: The Development History of the Triumph Bonneville. John Nelson. 165p. pap. 17.95 (*0-85429-257-8*, F257, Pub. by G T Foulis Ltd) Haynes Pubns.

***Bonnie: The Development of the Triumph Bonneville.** J. R. Nelson. (Illus.). 184p. 1995. pap. 24.95 (*0-85429-957-2*) Motorbooks Intl.

Bonnie & Clyde. Sue Hamilton. Ed. by John Hamilton. LC 89-84921. (America's Most Wanted Ser.). (Illus.). 32p. (J). (gr. 4). 1989. lib. bdg. 11.96 (*0-939179-62-8*) Abdo & Dghtrs.

***Bonnie & Clyde - Villains or Victims?** Jannay Valdez. (Illus.). 120p. (YA). Date not set. write for info. (*1-886709-09-2*) Outlaw Publ.

***Bonnie Blair.** Bob Italia. LC 94-23383. (Reaching for the Stars Ser.). (J). 1994. lib. bdg. 12.94 (*1-56239-341-3*) Abdo & Dghtrs.

***Bonnie Blair.** Richard Rambeck. (Sports Superstars Ser.). (Illus.). (J). (gr. 2-6). 1995. lib. bdg. 14.95 (*0-614-04748-X*) Childs World.

Bonnie Blair: Speediest Skater. Cathy Breitenbucher. LC 94-5744. (Achievers Ser.). (J). (gr. 4-9). 1994. 17.50 (*0-8225-2883-5*, Lerner Publctns); pap. 5.95 (*0-8225-9665-2*, Lerner Publctns) Lerner Group.

Bonnie Bunnie's Bicycle. Susan Tate. (Petal Pals Ser.). (Illus.). 40p. (J). (gr. k-3). 1993. pap. 3.99 (*1-884395-01-5*) Clear Blue Sky.

Bonnie Creek Site: A Late Mississippian Homestead in the Upper Galum Creek Valley, Perry County, Illinois. Mark J. Wagner. LC 86-72635. (Preservation Ser.: No. 3). (Illus.). 277p. (Orig.). 1986. pap. 15.00 (*0-913415-02-2*) Am Resources.

Bonnie Dundee. Rosemary Sutcliff. (J). (gr. 7 up). 21.00 (*0-8446-6363-8*) Peter Smith.

Bonnie Jean, a Collection of Papers & Poems Relating to the Wife of Robert Burns. John D. Ross. LC 71-144471. reprint ed. 20.00 (*0-404-08526-1*) AMS Pr.

Bonnie Little Birthday Book. (Little Remembrance Gift Editions Ser.). (J). (ps-3). 6.95 (*0-87741-005-4*) Makepeace Colony.

Bonnie McSmithers Is at It Again! Sueann Alderson. (Annick Press Ser.: Series 9). (Illus.). 24p. (Orig.). (J). (ps-2). 1990. pap. 0.99 (*1-55037-110-X*, Pub. by Annick CN) Firefly Bks Ltd.

Bonnie McSmithers You're Driving Me Dithers. Sueann Alderson. (Annick Press Ser.: Series 9). (Illus.). 24p. (Orig.). (J). (ps-2). 1990. pap. 0.99 (*1-55037-108-8*, Pub. by Annick CN) Firefly Bks Ltd.

Bonnie Prince Charlie. Moray McLaren. (Dorset Reprints Ser.). 224p. 1990. 19.95 (*0-88029-508-2*) Marboro Bks.

***Bonnie Raitt - Longing in Their Hearts (Piano-Vocal-Guitar)** Ed. by Milton Okun. 71p. (Orig.). (YA). Date not set. pap. 16.95 (*0-89524-844-1*, 02502139) Cherry Lane.

Bonnie Raitt - Luck of the Draw. Ed. by Milton Okun. pap. 14.95 (*0-89524-646-5*) Cherry Lane.

Bonnie Raitt - Nick of Time. Ed. by Milton Okun. pap. 14. 95 (*0-89524-440-3*) Cherry Lane.

Bonnie Scotland: Romantic Scotland in Pictures & Verse. (Illus.). 32p. 1993. pap. 3.95 (*0-7117-0223-3*) Seven Hills Bk.

Bonnie Scottish Cookbook. Kay S. Nelson. LC 89-7778. 144p. (Orig.). 1989. pap. 10.95 (*0-939009-25-0*) EPM Pubns.

Bonnie the Black Bear. Illus. by Bob Storms. (World of Animals Ser.). 24p. (Orig.). (J). (gr. k-3). 1994. pap. 4.95 (*0-89346-794-4*) Heian Intl.

Bonnier's Swedish Dictionary: Bonniers Svenska Ordbok. S. Malmstrom. 744p. (SWE.). 1986. 150.00 (*0-8288-2072-4*, F60694) Fr & Eur.

***Bonnie's Beach Towel.** Judy Mullican. (HighReach Learning Big Bks.). 8p. (J). (ps-k). 1994. pap. text ed. 10. 95 (*1-57332-008-0*) HighReach Lrning.

Bonnie's Household Budget Book. 2nd rev. ed. Bonnie R. McCullough. 64p. 1987. pap. 8.95 (*0-312-00992-5*) St Martin.

Bonnie's Household Budget Book: The Essential Guide for Getting Control of Your Money. 3rd rev. ed. Bonnie R. McCullough. LC 92-34393. 1992. pap. 8.95 (*0-312-08708-X*) St Martin.

Bonnie's Household Organizer: The Essential Guide for Getting Control of Your Home. rev. ed. Bonnie R. McCullough. (Illus.). 192p. 1983. pap. 6.95 (*0-312-08795-0*) St Martin.

Bonnie's Thirteenth Summer. Betty Haith. 52p. (J). 1992. pap. 4.95 (*1-882185-01-3*) Crnrstone Pub.

Bonnin & Morris of Philadelphia: The First American Porcelain Factory, 1770-1772. Graham Hood. LC 72-81327. (Institute of Early American History & Culture Ser.). (Illus.). xiii, 78p. 1972. 24.95 (*0-8078-1200-5*) U of NC Pr.

***Bonnin & Morris of Philadelphia: The First American Porcelain Factory, 1770-1772.** Graham Hood. LC 72-81327. (Institute Book on the Arts & Material Culture in Early America Ser.). (Illus.). reprint ed. pap. 35.70 (*0-7837-9019-8*, 2049771) Bks Demand.

Bonnot Gang: The Story of the French Illegalists. Richard Parry. (Illus.). 190p. (Orig.). (C). 1987. pap. 12.00 (*0-946061-04-1*) Left Bank.

Bonny Case of Murder: Dr. Jean Montrose Mystery. C. F. Roe. 256p. (Orig.). 1994. pap. 3.99 (*0-451-18067-4*) NAL-Dutton.

Bonny's Big Day. James Herriot. (Illus.). 32p. (J). (gr. k up). 1987. 13.00 (*0-312-01000-1*) St Martin.

Bonny's Big Day. James Herriot. (Illus.). 32p. (J). 1991. pap. 6.95 (*0-312-06571-X*) St Martin.

Bono & Nonno. Arthur A. Levine. LC 93-35931. (Illus.). (J). 1995. write for info. (*0-688-13233-2*, Tambourine Bks); lib. bdg. write for info. (*0-688-13234-0*, Tambourine Bks) Morrow.

Bono el Mono En la Escuela Vol. 6: Pasitos Spanish Language Development Books. Darlyne F. Schott. (Pasitos Hacia la Lectura Ser.). 25p. (J). (gr. k-1). 1990. pap. text ed. 11.00 (*1-56537-055-4*) D F Schott Educ.

Bono Goes to School Vol. 6: Pasitos English Language Development Books. Darlyne F. Schott. (Pasitos Hacia la Lectura Ser.). 25p. (J). (gr. k-1). 1990. pap. text ed. 11.00 (*1-56537-065-1*) D F Schott Educ.

Bono Homini Donum: Essays in Historical Linguistics in Memory of J. Alexander Kerns, 2 vols., Set. Ed. by Yoel L. Arbeitman & Allan R. Bomhard. (Current Issues in Linguistic Theory Ser.: No. 16). 1981. 194.00x (*90-272-3507-4*) Benjamins North Am.

Bono in His Own Words. Dave Thompson. (Illus.). 96p. pap. 12.95 (*0-7119-1646-2*, OP44957) Omnibus NY.

Bonsai. Ed. by Ogawa. (Postcard Book Ser.). (Illus.). 56p. 1994. pap. 9.00 (*4-7700-1805-3*) Kodansha.

Bonsai. Sunset Editors. 96p. 1994. 9.99 (*0-376-03045-3*) Sunset Menlo Pk.

Bonsai. Harry Tomlinson. LC 94-19143. (RD Home Handbooks Ser.). (Illus.). 216p. 1995. pap. 16.00 (*0-89577-647-2*) RD Assn.

Bonsai. rev. ed. Alan Roger. (Wisley Handbooks Ser.). (Illus.). 64p. (Orig.). 1990. pap. 5.95 (*0-304-32001-3*, Pub. by Cassell UK) Sterling.

Bonsai: Art & Technique. Jennifer Wilkinson. Ed. by John Patrick. (Lothian Australian Garden Ser.). (Illus.). 64p. (Orig.). 1995. pap. 9.95 (*0-85091-551-1*, Pub. by Lothian Pub AT) Seven Hills Bk.

Bonsai: Blow up Edition. Peter Chan. 1989. 19.98 (*1-55521-383-9*) Bk Sales Inc.

***Bonsai: From Native Trees & Shrubs.** Werner Busch. (Illus.). 144p. 1995. 24.95 (*0-7153-0336-8*, Pub. by D & C Pub UK) Sterling.

Bonsai: In Cooperation with the Brooklyn Botanic Garden. Susan M. Resnick. (Illus.). 144p. 1992. 35.00 (*0-316-45630-6*) Little.

Bonsai: Its Art, Science, History & Philosophy. Deborah Koreshoff. 272p. (C). 1990. 150.00 (*0-908175-75-2*, Pub. by Boolarong Pubns AT) St Mut.

Bonsai: Its Art, Science, History & Philosophy. Deborah R. Koreshoff. (Illus.). 287p. 1984. 49.95 (*0-917304-68-3*) Timber.

Bonsai: Step by Step to Growing Success. Dave Pike. (Illus.). 128p. 1990. pap. 16.95 (*1-85223-128-9*, Pub. by Crowood Pr UK) Trafalgar.

Bonsai: The Art of Growing & Keeping Miniature Trees. McGovern. 1987. 12.98 (*0-89009-946-4*) Bk Sales Inc.

Bonsai: The Complete Guide to Art & Technique. Paul Lesniewicz. (Illus.). 192p. 1984. 24.95 (*0-7137-1362-3*, Pub. by Blandford Pr UK) Sterling.

Bonsai Art of Kimura. Katsuhito Onishi. Ed. by W. John Palmer. Tr. by Margaret Cullen. (Illus.). 176p. (Orig.). 1992. pap. 24.95 (*0-9634423-0-9*) Stone Lantern.

Bonsai Basics: A Step-by-Step Guide to Growing, Training & General Care. Christian Pessey & Remy Samson. LC 92-38557. (Illus.). 120p. 1993. pap. 10.95 (*0-8069-0327-9*) Sterling.

Bonsai Book of Practical Facts Plus Addenda. 5th ed. Jerome Meyer. LC 90-38869. (Illus.). 128p. 1992. 17.95 (*0-945487-00-2*) Purchase Pub.

***Bonsai Complete Illustrated Guide.** Crespi. 1995. (*0-7858-0215-0*) Bk Sales Inc.

Bonsai Creation & Design Using Propagation Techniques. William N. Valavanis. (Encyclopedia of Classical Bonsai Art: Vol. 1). (Illus.). 1975. pap. 3.95 (*0-916352-03-X*) Symmes Syst.

Bonsai in Australia. Dorothy Koreshoff & Vita Koreshoff. (C). 1990. pap. 30.00 (*0-908175-63-9*, Pub. by Boolarong Pubns AT) St Mut.

Bonsai in the Tropics. Dorothy Koreshoff & Vita Koreshoff. (C). 1990. pap. 30.00 (*0-86439-055-6*, Pub. by Boolarong Pubns AT) St Mut.

Bonsai in Your Home: An Indoor Grower's Guide. Paul Lesniewicz. LC 94-17466. (Illus.). 208p. 1994. 27.95 (*0-8069-0780-0*) Sterling.

Bonsai Masterclass. Peter Chan. (Illus.). 160p. 1993. pap. 16.95 (*0-8069-6763-3*) Sterling.

Bonsai Society. Thomas I. Saxon. Ed. by Renais J. Hill. LC 91-58533. 303p. (Orig.). 1992. pap. 10.95 (*1-55666-076-6*) Pubs Grp Toluca.

Bonsai: Special Techniques. Ed. by Kan Yashiroda. (Plants & Gardens Ser.). (Illus.). 1989. per., pap. 6.95 (*0-945352-02-6*) Bklyn Botanic.

Bonsai Theory of Church Growth. Ken Hemphill. (Orig.). 1992. pap. 3.99 (*0-8054-6045-4*) Broadman.

Bonsai Ways. Beatriz Botero de Borrero & Martha O. Botero de Borrero. (Illus.). 308p. 1993. 35.00 (*958-33-0058-6*, Pub. by Borrero & Gomez CK) Stone Lantern.

Bonsai with American Trees. Masakuni Kawasumi. LC 75-10588. (Illus.). 131p. 1984. pap. 17.00 (*0-87011-619-3*) Kodansha.

Bonsai with Australian Native Plants. Dorothy Koreshoff & Vita Koreshoff. (C). 1990. pap. 33.00 (*0-908175-66-3*, Pub. by Boolarong Pubns AT) St Mut.

Bonsai Workshop. Herb L. Gustafson. LC 93-43460. 208p. 1994. 29.95 (*0-8069-0556-5*) Sterling.

***Bonsai Year Book.** Paul Goff & Harry Tomlinson. (Illus.). 96p. 1994. 12.95 (*0-9634423-1-7*) Stone Lantern.

Bonsall: Securitisation. Ed. by David Bonsall. 1990. 180.00 (*0-406-11722-5*) Butterworth Legal Pubs.

Bonstonofavitch! Thomas Carlisle. LC 74-78089. (Illus.). 176p. (Orig.). 1974. pap. 4.95 (*0-914580-00-0*) Angst World.

Bontecou Genealogy: A Records of the Descendants of Pierre Bontecou, Huguenot Refugee from France, in the Lines of His Sons. John E. Morris. (Illus.). 271p. 1994. reprint ed. lib. bdg. 53.00 (*0-8328-4256-7*); reprint ed. pap. 43.00 (*0-8328-4255-9*) Higginson Bk Co.

Bontshe the Silent. Isaac L. Peretz. Tr. by A. S. Rappoport. LC 77-178454. (Short Story Index Reprint Ser.). 1977. reprint ed. 18.95 (*0-8369-4055-5*) Ayer.

***Bonus Deal.** Crail. 1993. per. 12.95 (*1-55050-031-7*, Pub. by Coteau Bks CN) InBook.

***Bonus-Malus Systems in Automobile Insurance.** Ed. by Jean Lemaire. LC 94-41825. (Huebner International Series on Risk, Insurance & Economic Security: Vol. 19). 312p. (C). 1995. lib. bdg. 85.00 (*0-7923-9545-X*) Kluwer Ac.

Bonus March: An Episode of the Great Depression. Roger Daniels. LC 75-133497. (Illus.). 352p. 1971. text ed. 35. 00 (*0-8371-5174-0*, DBM/, Greenwood Pr) Greenwood.

Bonus Options in Health Insurance. Peter Zweifel & Otto Waser. LC 92-9931. (Developments in Health Economics & Public Policy Ser.: Vol. 2). 160p. (C). 1992. lib. bdg. 87.50 (*0-7923-1722-X*) Kluwer Ac.

Bonvesin da la Riva, Volgari Scelti: Select Poems. Stefani Ruggero. Tr. by Patrick S. Diehl. (American University Studies: Romance Languages & Literature: Ser. II, Vol. 58). 498p. 1988. text ed. 69.50 (*0-8204-0427-6*) P Lang Pubs.

Bony & Kelly Gang. Arthur Upfield. 19.95 (*0-89190-554-5*) Amereon Ltd.

Bony & the Black Virgin. Arthur Upfield. (Napoleon Bonaparte Mysteries Ser.). reprint ed. lib. bdg. 18.95 (*0-89190-553-7*, Rivercity Pr) Amereon Ltd.

Bony & the Kelly Gang. Arthur W. Upfield. 192p. 1988. pap. 4.95 (*0-02-025880-1*, Collier S&S) S&S Trade.

Bony & the Mouse. A. Upfield. (Bon Mystery Ser.). 20.95 (*0-89190-561-8*, Am Repr) Amereon Ltd.

Bony Buys a Woman. Arthur Upfield. (Napoleon Bonaparte Mysteries Ser.). reprint ed. lib. bdg. 19.95 (*0-89190-555-3*, Rivercity Pr) Amereon Ltd.

Bony-Legs. Joanna Cole. (Illus.). 48p. (J). (ps-2). 1986. pap. 2.95 (*0-590-40516-0*) Scholastic Inc.

Bony-Legs. Joanna Cole. LC 85-5070. (Illus.). 48p. (J). (ps-3). 1984. text ed. 13.95 (*0-02-722970-X*, Four Winds Pr) S&S Childrens.

Bony Skeleton's Cut-Out Fun Book. (Illus.). 24p. (Orig.). (J). (ps-00). 1991. pap. 3.95 (*0-8249-8347-5*, Ideals Child) Hambleton-Hill.

***Boo.** 1995. 3.99 (*0-88705-745-4*) Joshua Morris.

Boo. Pat Conroy. 1976. 19.95 (*0-8488-1274-3*) Amereon Ltd.

***Boo!** Kirsten Hall. LC 95-10110. (My First Reader Ser.). (Illus.). (J). 1995. write for info. (*0-516-05370-1*) Childrens.

Boo. Pat Conroy. (Orig.). 1983. reprint ed. 15.95 (*0-937036-02-1*) Old NY Bk Shop.

Boo. Pat Conroy. (Illus.). 176p. (Orig.). 1993. reprint ed. pap. 5.95 (*0-8197-6041-2*, Mckingbird) R Bemis Pub.

Boo! A Parable for Children over & under 21. Jim Ballard. LC 75-25393. (Mandala Series in Education). (Illus.). 1975. pap. 3.50 (*0-916250-08-3*) Irvington.

Boo Baby Boo! Clara Vulliamy. LC 93-22736. (Illus.). 14p. (J). (ps). 1994. 4.95 (*1-56402-388-5*) Candlewick Pr.

Boo Baby Girl Meets the Ghost of Mable's Gable. Jim May. LC 92-72702. (Illus.). 32p. (J). (ps-5). 1992. lib. bdg. 14.95 (*1-878925-03-2*) Brotherstone Pubs.

842

An Asterisk (*) at the beginning of an entry indicates that the title is appearing in BIP for the first time.

An Asterisk (*) at the beginning of an entry indicates that the title is appearing in BIP for the first time.

843

Book Industry Trends, 1993. Statistical Service Center Staff. (Illus.). 260p. (Orig.). 1993. pap. 425.00 (0-940016-42-7) Bk Indus Study.

Book Introducing the E-Meter. L. Ron Hubbard. 8.75 (0-686-30797-6) Church Scient NY.

Book IV-the Teacher. Rebecca Daniel. (Life of Jesus Ser.). 32p. (YA). (gr. 2-7). 1984. student ed 7.95 (0-86653-225-0, SS 827, Shining Star Pubns) Good Apple.

Book-Keeper & The American Counting Room, 4 vols., Set. Ed. by Richard P. Brief. (Foundations of Accounting Ser.: No. 25). 1922p. 1989. reprint ed. 100.00 (0-8240-6141-1) Garland.

Book-Keeping - A Guide for Beginners, Vol. 1. Ed. by Stanley Thornes. (C). 1986. 40.00 (0-85950-514-6, Pub. by S Thornes Pubs UK) St Mut.

Book-Keeping - A Guide for Beginners, Vol. 2. Ed. by Stanley Thornes. (C). 1988. 55.00 (0-85950-645-2, Pub. by S Thornes Pubs UK) St Mut.

Book-Keeping - A Guide for Beginners, Vol. 1: Worked Solutions. M. J. Maloney. (C). 1986. 40.00 (0-85950-654-1, Pub. by S Thornes Pubs UK) St Mut.

Book-Keeping - A Guide for Beginners, Vol. 2: Worked Solutions. Stanley Thornes. (C). 1988. 50.00 (0-85950-657-6, Pub. by S Thornes Pubs UK) St Mut.

*Book-Keeping & Accounting. Geoffrey Whitehead. 256p. 1991. pap. 36.00 (0-273-03516-9, Pub. by Pitman Pubng UK) St Mut.

Book-Keeping Moderniz'd: Or, Merchant-Accounts by Double Entry, According to the Italian Form. John Mair. Ed. by Richard P. Brief. LC 77-87276. (Development of Contemporary Accounting Thought Ser.). 1978. reprint ed. lib. bdg. 52.95 (0-405-10904-0) Ayer.

Book Loft. Patricia Bille & Suzanne M. Williamson. (C). 1986. pap. 19.16 (0-395-39046-X) HM.

*Book Lover in Texas. Evelyn Oppenheimer. 176p. 1995. 16.95 (0-929398-89-0) UNTX Pr.

Book-Lovers, Bibliomaniacs & Book Clubs. H. H. Harper. 1973. 59.95 (0-87968-766-5) Gordon Pr.

Book Lovers' Borrow Book. (Orig.). 1987. pap. 6.95 (0-913515-24-8, Starrhill) Elliott & Clark.

Book Lover's Guide to Boston & Cape Cod. Lane Phalen. (Book Lover's Buide Ser.). 256p. (Orig.). 1992. pap. 14.95 (1-880339-08-0) Brigadoon Bay.

Book Lover's Guide to Chicagoland. Lane Phalen. LC 91-74136. (Book Lover's Guide Ser.). (Illus.). 256p. (Orig.). 1991. pap. 14.95 (1-880339-06-4) Brigadoon Bay.

Book Lover's Guide to Florida: Authors, Books & Literary Sites. Ed. by Kevin M. McCarthy. LC 92-20483. (Illus.). 512p. 1992. 27.95 (1-56164-012-3); pap. 18.95 (1-56164-021-2) Pineapple Pr.

Book Lover's Guide to Washington, D. C. Lane Phalen. (Book Lover's Guide Ser.). 288p. (Orig.). 1993. pap. 14.95 (1-880339-09-9) Brigadoon Bay.

Book Lover's Journal. 1986. 15.38 (0-201-10354-0) Addison-Wesley.

Book Lovers Quotations. Ed. by Helen Exley. (Quotable Quotations Ser.). (Illus.). 60p. 1992. 6.99 (1-85015-268-3) Exley Giftbooks.

*Book Makers. Zev Chafets. LC 94-32159. 1995. 21.00 (0-679-41456-8) Random.

*Book Maker's Desire: Writings on the Art of the Book. Buzz Spector. (Illus.). 84p. (Orig.). 1995. pap. 11.95 (0-9635042-1-5) Umbrella Assocs.

*Book Market. 500p. (Orig.). 1994. pap. 1,395.00 (1-57205-928-1) Rector Pr.

Book Market: How to Write, Publish & Market Your Book. Aron Mathieu. LC 80-71059. 474p. 1981. 19.95 (0-939014-00-9) Andover Pr.

*Book Marketing: A New Approach. 5th ed. Dan Poynter. (Book Publishing Consultation with Dan Poynter Ser.). (Illus.). 70p. 1994. student ed, pap. 14.95 (0-568-60009-6) Para Pub.

Book Marketing Handbook: Tips & Techniques for the Sale & Promotion of Scientific, Technical, Professional, & Scholarly Books & Journals, Vol. I. Nat G. Bodian. 482p. 1980. 64.95 (0-8352-1286-6) Bowker.

Book Marketing Handbook: Tips & Techniques for the Sale & Promotion of Scientific, Technical, Professional, & Scholarly Books & Journals, Vol. II. Nat G. Bodian. 607p. 1983. 64.95 (0-8352-1685-3) Bowker.

Book Marketing Made Easier. 3rd ed. John Kremer. (Illus.). 384p. 1991. pap. 19.95 (0-912411-34-1) Open Horizons.

Book Marketing Opportunities: A Database. Marie Kiefer. 180p. 1991. disk 150.00 (0-912411-12-0) Open Horizons.

Book Nobody Knows. Bruce Barton. 306p. 1992. reprint ed. lib. bdg. 23.95 (0-89966-950-6) Buccaneer Bks.

Book Notes, 1958-1993. Richard Kostelanetz. LC 93-61167. 1200p. 1994. write for info. (0-87875-451-2) Whitston Pub.

Book Numbering. (National Information Standards Ser.). 1980. 10.00 (0-88738-981-3, Z39.21) Transaction Pubs.

Book Numbering: Z39.21-1988. rev. ed. (National Information Standards Ser.). 20p. 1989. lib. bdg. 30.00 (0-88738-951-1) Transaction Pubs.

Book-o-Cards: San Francisco from the Air. Date not set. pap. 6.95 (0-916290-43-3) Squarebooks.

Book-o-Cards: Spanning the Gate. Date not set. pap. 6.95 (0-916290-41-7) Squarebooks.

Book-o-Cards: The Golden Gate Bridge. 1995. pap. 7.95 (0-916290-40-9) Squarebooks.

Book-o-Cards: The Napa Valley. Date not set. pap. 6.95 (0-916290-44-1) Squarebooks.

Book of a Naturalist. William H. Hudson. reprint ed. 64.50 (0-404-03410-1) AMS Pr.

Book of Abigail & John: Selected Letters of the Adams Family, 1762-1784. Abigail Adams & John Adams. Ed. by L. H. Butterfield et al. LC 74-27938. (Illus.). 459p. 1976. 36.00 (0-674-07855-1) HUP.

Book of Abigail & John: Selected Letters of the Adams Family, 1762-1784. Abigail Adams & John Adams. Ed. by L. H. Butterfield et al. LC 74-27938. (Illus.). 459p. 1977. pap. text ed. 9.95 (0-674-07854-3) HUP.

Book of Abstract Algebra. 2nd ed. C. C. Pinter. 1990. text ed. write for info. (0-07-050138-6) McGraw.

Book of Acquisition see Code of Maimonides

*Book of Acts. (Cross Training Ser.: Vol. 4). 72p. (YA). (gr. 10-12). 1995. 29.95 (1-57405-032-X) CharismaLife Pub.

Book of Acts. rev. ed. (New International Commentary on the New Testament Ser.). 1988. 24.99 (0-8028-2505-2) Eerdmans.

Book of Acts: A Radiant Commentary on the New Testament. Stanley M. Horton. LC 80-65892. 304p. (Orig.). (YA). (gr. 12). 1981. 8.95 (0-88243-317-2, 02-0317) Gospel Pub.

Book of Acts: Free to Live. Stephen Gaukroger. Ed. by Ian Coffey. (Baker Bible Guides Ser.). (Illus.). 232p. 1994. reprint ed. pap. 9.99 (0-8010-3873-1) Baker Bk.

Book of Acts & Church Growth. F. J. May. 1990. 7.99 (0-87148-113-8) Pathway Pr.

*Book of Acts & Paul in Roman Custody. Brian Rapske. Ed. by Bruce W. Winter. LC 94-34745. (Book of Acts in Its First Century Setting: Vol. 3). 600p. 1994. text ed. 37.50 (0-8028-2435-8) Eerdmans.

Book of Acts in Its Ancient Literary Setting. Bruce W. Winter. 1993. 37.50 (0-8028-2433-1) Eerdmans.

Book of Acts in Its Graeco-Roman Setting. Ed. by David W. Gill & Conrad Gempf. (Book of Acts in Its First-Century Setting Ser.). 450p. 1994. 37.50 (0-8028-2434-X) Eerdmans.

*Book of Acts in Its Palestinian Setting. Ed. by Richard Bauckham. (Book of Acts in Its First-Century Setting Ser.: Vol. 4). 600p. 1995. 37.50 (0-8028-2436-6) Eerdmans.

Book of Acts in the Setting of Hellenistic History. Colin J. Hemer. Ed. by Conrad H. Gempf. xiv, 482p. 1989. 88.50 (3-16-145451-0, Pub. by J C B Mohr GW) Coronet Bks.

Book of Acts in the Setting of Hellenistic History. Colin J. Hemer. Ed. by Conrad H. Gempf. LC 90-45799. xiv, 482p. 1990. reprint ed. 45.00 (0-931464-58-7) Eisenbrauns.

Book of Acupuncture Points: Volume I of a Complete Course in Acupuncture. James Tin-Yau So. Ed. by Robert L. Felt. (Illus.). 320p. text ed. 35.00 (0-912111-02-X) Paradigm Publns.

Book of Adam to Moses. Lore Segal. LC 87-2581. (Illus.). 144p. (J). (gr. k up). 1987. lib. bdg. 14.99 (0-394-96757-7) Knopf Bks Yng Read.

Book of Adirondack Firsts. David Cross & Joan Potter. (Pinto Press Firsts Ser.: Vol. 1). (Illus.). 200p. (Orig.). 1992. pap. 11.95 (0-9632476-0-3) Pinto Pr.

Book of Adoration. Maimondies & Moses Hyamson. (Mishneh Torah Ser.). 330p. 1981. 17.95 (0-87306-086-5) Feldheim.

Book of Aerial Stereo Photographs. Harold R. Wanless. (Illus.). spiral bd. 10.00 (0-8331-1703-3) Hubbard Sci.

Book of African Divination: Interpreting the Forces of Destiny with Techniques from the Venda, Zulu, & Yoruba. Raymond Buckland & Kathleen Binger. (Illus.). 144p. (Orig.). 1992. boxed, pap. 24.95 (0-89281-364-4) Inner Tradit.

Book of African Names. Molefi K. Asante. LC 91-72493. 64p. 1991. 24.95 (0-86543-254-6); pap. 8.95 (0-86543-255-4) Africa World.

Book of African Names. Chief Osuntoki. LC 90-82690. 32p. 1991. reprint ed. pap. 5.95 (0-933121-24-5) Black Classic.

Book of African Sayings. Issy K. Tindimwebwa. (Illus.). 64p. (Orig.). 1982. write for info. (0-318-50442-1) Akili Bks of Amer.

*Book of African Women's Poetry. Ed. by Stella Chipasula & Frank Chipasula. (African Writers Ser.). 256p. 1995. pap. 10.95 (0-435-90680-1) Heinemann.

Book of Afternoon Tea. Lesley Mackley. 120p. 1992. pap. 12.00 (1-55788-046-8, HP Books) Berkley Pub.

Book of Agriculture. Maimondies & Isaac Klein. LC 49-9495. (Yale Judaica Ser.: No. 7). 1979. text ed. 70.00 (0-300-02223-9) Yale U Pr.

Book of Air Shows. Philip Handleman. LC 92-62187. (Illus.). 176p. 1993. 49.95 (0-88740-471-5) Schiffer.

*Book of All-American Wisdom: Common Sense & Uncommon Genius from 101 Great Americans. Criswell Freeman. (Wisdom Ser.). 154p. (Orig.). 1994. pap. 5.95 (0-9640955-2-1) Walnut Gr Pr.

Book of Alze. Tr. by A. E. Waite. 1985. reprint ed. pap. 2.95 (0-916411-99-0) Holmes Pub.

Book of America: Inside Fifty States Today. Neal R. Pierce & Jerry Hagstrom. 1983. 27.50 (0-393-01639-0) Norton.

Book of American Clocks. Pati Palmer. 19.95 (0-02-594590-4) Macmillan.

Book of American Diaries. Ed. by Randall M. Miller & Linda Patterson Miller. LC 94-17807. 512p. (Orig.). 1995. pap. 12.50 (0-380-76583-7) Avon.

Book of American Negro Poetry. rev. ed. Ed. by James Weldon Johnson. LC 67-99475. 320p. 1969. reprint ed. pap. 10.95 (0-15-613539-6, Harvest Bks) HarBrace.

Book of American Presidents. Esse V. Hathaway. LC 70-93345. (Essay Index Reprint Ser.). 1977. 26.95 (0-8369-1576-3) Ayer.

Book of American Trade Marks, Vol. 1. Ed. by David E. Carter. LC 72-76493. (Trade Marks Ser.). 1978. reprint ed. 17.50 (0-88108-110-8) Art Dir.

Book of American Trade Marks, Vol. 2. Ed. by David E. Carter. LC 72-76493. (Trade Marks Ser.). 1978. reprint ed. 18.50 (0-910158-28-2) Art Dir.

Book of American Trade Marks, Vol. 3. Ed. by David E. Carter. LC 72-76493. (Trade Marks Ser.). 1978. reprint ed. 18.50 (0-910158-29-0) Art Dir.

Book of American Trade Marks, Vol. 4. Ed. by David E. Carter. LC 72-76493. (Illus.). 232p. 1976. 18.50 (0-910158-30-4) Art Dir.

Book of American Trade Marks, Vol. 5. Ed. by David E. Carter. LC 72-76493. (Illus.). 1977. 18.50 (0-910158-31-2) Art Dir.

Book of American Trademarks, Vol. 6. Ed. by David E. Carter. LC 72-76493. (Illus.). 208p. 1991. reprint ed. pap. text ed. 17.50 (0-88108-098-5) Art Dir.

Book of American Trademarks, Vol. 9. Ed. by David E. Carter. LC 72-76493. (Illus.). 1984. 18.50 (0-88108-020-9) Art Dir.

Book of American Trademarks, Vol. 11. Ed. by David E. Carter. 1989. 24.75 (0-88108-068-3) Art Dir.

Book of American Trademarks, Vol. 6. Ed. by David E. Carter. LC 72-76493. (Illus.). 1979. 18.50 (0-910158-39-8) Art Dir.

Book of American Trademarks, Vol. 7. Annual of Trade Mark Design Staff. Ed. by David E. Carter. LC 72-76493. (Illus.). 1980. 18.50 (0-910158-61-4) Art Dir.

Book of American Trademarks, Vol. 8. Ed. by David E. Carter. LC 72-76493. (Illus.). 1983. 18.50 (0-910158-94-0) Art Dir.

Book of American Trademarks 10. Ed. by David E. Carter. 1987. 18.50 (0-88108-034-9) Art Dir.

Book of American Twentieth-Century Poetry. Idear Garris. 1992. 8.95 (0-533-08461-X) Vantage.

Book of American Verse. Ed. by A. C. Ward. LC 71-128159. (Granger Index Reprint Ser.). 1977. 26.95 (0-8369-6188-9) Ayer.

*Book of American Women. John Sanford. 220p. (C). 1995. pap. 12.95 (0-252-06522-0) U of Ill Pr.

Book of Americans. Stephen Vincent Benet & Rosemary Benet. LC 33-27433. 128p. (J). (gr. 4-6). 1987. pap. 5.95 (0-8050-0297-9, Bks Young Read) H Holt & Co.

*Book of Ammon. 2nd ed. Ammon Hennacy. 510p. (Orig.). (C). 1994. pap. 23.95 (1-879175-14-2) Fortkamp.

Book of Analysis. Tr. by Ven U. Thittila. (C). 1969. 56.00 (0-86013-030-4, Pub. by Pali Text) Wisdom MA.

Book of Angels. Sophy Burnham. 1992. 18.00 (0-345-38078-9, Ballantine Trade) Ballantine.

*Book of Angels. Sophy Burnham. 1995. pap. 6.99 (0-345-40057-7) Ballantine.

Book of Angels. Terrie Tomko. 1986. 4.95 (0-8198-1115-7) Pauline Bks.

Book of Angels: Reflection on Angels Past & Present & True Stories of How They Touch Our Lives. large type ed. Sophy Burnham. (Illus.). 256p. 1991. pap. 12.95 (0-8027-2661-5) Walker & Co.

Book of Angels: Reflections on Angels Past & Present & True Stories of How They Touch Our Lives. Sophy Burnham. (Illus.). 256p. 1990. pap. 12.00 (0-345-36157-1, Ballantine Trade) Ballantine.

Book of Angels: Reflections on Angels Past & Present & True Stories of How They Touch Our Lives. Sophy Burnham. 320p. 1994. pap. 10.00 (0-345-37355-3, Ballantine Trade) Ballantine.

*Book of Angelus Silesius. Frederick Franck. LC 85-70839. (Illus.). 145p. (Orig.). Date not set. reprint ed. pap. 16.00x (1-56907-007-5) Beacon Pt Pr.

Book of Answers. 1992. pap. 10.00 (0-671-76192-7, Fireside) S&S Trade.

Book of Answers: The New York Public Library Telephone Reference Service's Most Unusual & Entertaining Questions. Barbara Berliner et al. 228p. 1990. 21.45 (0-13-957432-8) P-H.

Book of Antipasti. Lyn Rutherford. (Book of Ser.). (Illus.). 120p. (Orig.). 1992. pap. 10.95 (1-55788-040-9) Price Stern.

Book of Appetizers. June Budgen. (Book of...Ser.). (Illus.). 128p. (Orig.). 1992. 12.00 (0-89586-482-7, HP Books) Berkley Pub.

Book of Apples. Joan Morgan & Alison Richards. (Illus.). 288p. 1994. 29.95 (0-09-177759-3, Pub. by Ebury Pr UK) Trafalgar.

*Book of Aran: The Aran Islands, County Galway. Ed. by John Waddell et al. (Illus.). 334p. 1994. pap. 31.95 (0-614-03383-7, Pub. by Tir Eolas IE) Irish Bks Media.

*Book of Aran: The Aran Islands, County Galway. Ed. by John Waddell et al. (Illus.). 334p. 1994. 49.95 (1-873821-04-2, Pub. by Tir Eolas IE) Irish Bks Media.

Book of Architecture. James Gibbs. LC 68-17153. (Illus.). 1972. reprint ed. 38.95 (0-405-08560-5, Pub. by Blom Pubns UK) Ayer.

Book of Architecture. Sebastiano Serlio. LC 68-56509. (Illus.). 1972. reprint ed. 74.95 (0-405-08951-1) Ayer.

Book of Art Deco Alphabets: A Treasury of Original Alphabets from the 1920's & 30's. Comp. by Frederick S. Copley. (Graphic Arts Archives Ser.). 128p. (Orig.). 1990. pap. 7.95 (0-8069-7338-2, Sterling-Main St) Sterling.

Book of Art Nouveau Alphabets & Ornaments. LC 90-39132. (Illus.). 128p. (Orig.). 1990. pap. 7.95 (0-8069-7427-3) Sterling.

Book of Artifacts. Dave Cook. (Illus.). 160p. 1993. 20.00 (1-56076-672-7) TSR Inc.

Book of Artifacts. Ed. by Mary Ezzell et al. (Illus.). 32p. 1982. pap. 8.50 (0-940918-17-X, STK 82-002) Dragon Tree.

Book of Arts & Crafts. Marguerite Ickis & Reba S. Esh. (Illus.). 275p. 1965. pap. 5.95 (0-486-21472-9) Dover.

Book of Asseverations see Code of Maimonides

*Book of Atrix Wolfe. Patricia A. McKillip. LC 94-33999. 256p. 1995. text ed. 24.50 (0-441-00211-0) Ace Bks.

Book of Authentic Indian Life Crafts. rev. ed. Oscar E. Norbeck. LC 74-81910. (Illus.). 260p. 1974. 10.95 (0-87874-012-0) Galloway.

*Book of Ayurveda: A Holistic Approach to Health & Longevity. Judith Morrison. 1995. pap. 15.00 (0-684-80017-9) S&S Trade.

*Book of Babel: Words & the Way We See Things. Nigel Lewis. LC 94-61461. 320p. (Orig.). 1995. pap. 19.95 (0-87745-496-5) U of Iowa Pr.

Book of Babies: A First Picture Book of All the Things That Babies Do. Photos by Jo Foord. LC 90-39490. (Illus.). 32p. (J). (ps). 1991. 10.95 (0-679-80955-4) Random Bks Yng Read.

Book of Baby Names: Classic & Contemporary Names for Your Baby. Jane Resnick. 1994. 5.98 (0-8317-0668-6) Smithmark.

Book of Bad Habits see Farnam Horse Library Series

Book of Bad Virtues. Tony Hendra. 1994. pap. 8.00 (0-671-51928-X) PB.

Book of Bahamian Verse. Ed. by Jack Culmer. 1977. lib. bdg. 59.95 (0-8490-1529-4) Gordon Pr.

Book of Balaam (Numbers 22: 2 - 24: 25) A Study in Methods of Criticism & the History of Biblical Literature & Religion. Alexander Rofe. (Jerusalem Biblical Studies: Vol. 1). 77p. (HEB.). 1979. pap. text ed. 6.50 (0-685-49416-0, Pub. by Simor Ltd IS) Eisenbrauns.

Book of Ballads. Ed. by Bon Gautier et al. Bd. with Fermilion: Or the Student of Badajoz: A Spasmodic Tragedy. 338p. 1986. Set lib. bdg. 20.00 (0-8240-8620-1) Garland.

Book of Ballads. Ed. by John R. Crossland. LC 72-168779. (Granger Index Reprint Ser.). 1977. reprint ed. 21.95 (0-8369-6299-0) Ayer.

Book of Ballymote. Ed. by Robert Atkinson. LC 78-72618. (Celtic Language & Literature Ser.: Goidelic & Brythonic). reprint ed. 130.00 (0-404-17535-X) AMS Pr.

Book of Baltimore Orioles Lists. David Pugh & Linda Geeson. (Illus.). 144p. (Orig.). 1993. pap. 9.95 (1-56167-120-7) Am Literary Pr.

Book of Bamboo. I-Hsiung Ju. LC 82-70338. (Illus.). (Orig.). pap. 5.00 (0-9611726-0-6) Art Farm Gal.

Book of Baruch: Also Called I Baruch (Greek & Hebrew) Bible, O. T. Apocrypha Staff. Ed. by Emanuel Tov. LC 75-30775. (Texts & Translations Ser.: No. 8). 59p. reprint ed. pap. 25.00 (0-7837-5458-2, 2045223) Bks Demand.

Book of Baseball Cards, 1993. (Illus.). 320p. 1993. 15.98 (0-7853-0127-5, 3513300) Pubns Intl Ltd.

Book of Baseball Cards, 1994. Consumer Guide Editors. 320p. (Orig.). 1994. pap. 9.99 (0-451-82274-9, Sig) NAL-Dutton.

Book of Baseball Lists. Steve LaMar. LC 92-51044. 508p. 1993. lib. bdg. 39.95 (0-89950-661-5) McFarland & Co.

Book of Bathroom Design. Barry Dean. 1985. 24.95 (0-685-43049-9) S&S Trade.

Book of Be Attitudes: A Treasury of Positive Behaviors & Sage Advice. 192p. (Orig.). 1992. pap. 5.95 (0-399-51787-1, Perigee Bks) Berkley Pub.

Book of Bead Tips: One Hundred One of the Best Bead Tips. Linda Benmour. Ed. by Alice Scherer & Milton Firestone. (Illus.). 132p. (Orig.). 1995. pap. 16.95 (1-883153-14-X) Artstone Pr.

Book of Beads. Janet Coles. 1990. 22.95 (0-671-70525-3) S&S Trade.

Book of Beasts. T. H. White. (Illus.). 1993. 34.00 (0-7509-0206-X) A Sutton Pub.

Book of Beasts. T. H. White. (Literature Ser.). 304p. 1984. reprint ed. pap. 6.95 (0-486-24609-4) Dover.

Book of Bebb. Frederick Buechner. LC 90-80330. 544p. 1990. reprint ed. pap. 16.95 (0-00-001210-6) Harper SF.

Book of Bees: And How to Keep Them. Sue Hubbell. 1988. 17.95 (0-394-55894-4) Random.

Book of Beginnings. (Enchanted World Ser.). (Illus.). 144p. 1986. 19.93 (0-8094-5265-0); lib. bdg. 25.93 (0-8094-5266-9) Time-Life.

Book of Beginnings, Pt. 2: Natural Genesis, 2 vols., Set. Gerald Massey. 535p. 1989. reprint ed. spiral bd. 82.50 (0-7873-1242-8) Mokelumne.

Book of Being Born Again into the World. Richard Grossinger. 248p. 1974. pap. 5.00 (0-913028-29-0) North Atlantic.

Book of Bere Regis. E. P. Pittfield. 1988. 60.00 (0-686-75650-9) Dorset Pr.

Book of Berkshire: Describing & Illustrating Its Hills & Homes. Clark W. Bryan. LC 93-85392. (Great American Guidebook Ser.). (Illus.). 304p. 1993. reprint ed. pap. 24.95 (1-884022-00-6) Past Perfect.

Book of Bestial Nonsense. Simon Drew. (Illus.). 48p. 1986. 12.50 (1-85149-042-6) Antique Collect.

Book of Beth. Kent Klich. (Illus.). 96p. 1989. 29.95 (0-89381-370-2) Aperture.

Book of Bible Activities. N. J. Bull. (C). 1983. text ed. 35.00 (0-7175-0422-0, Pub. by S Thornes Pubs UK) St Mut.

Book of Bible History. Charles Baker. 1980. lib. bdg. 59.95 (0-8490-3159-1) Gordon Pr.

Book of Bible Knowledge. (Ichthus Ser.). 1987. pap. 3.95 (0-687-03670-4) Abingdon.

Book of Bible Knowledge. Ed. by W. M. Clow. 407p. 1994. reprint ed. pap. 8.99 (0-529-10185-8) World Bible.

Book of Billy. 2nd ed. David Birman. LC 92-97191. 209p. 1993. pap. 11.95 (0-9635181-0-0) Plutonia Pr.

*Book of Birth Poetry. Charlotte Otten. LC 94-27156. 1995. pap. 10.95 (0-553-37449-4) Bantam.

Book of Black Heroes Vol. 2: Great Women in the Struggle. Toyomi Igus et al. LC 91-90098. 112p. (J). (gr. 4-8). 1991. lib. bdg. 17.95 (0-940975-27-0); pap. 10.95 (0-940975-26-2) Just Us Bks.

Book of Black Magic. A. E. Waite. 1993. pap. 10.95 (0-942272-35-8) Original Pubns.

Book of Black Magic. Arthur E. Waite. LC 72-77557. 326p. 1972. reprint ed. pap. 10.95 (0-87728-207-2) Weiser.

Book of Black Magic & of Pacts. Arthur E. Waite. reprint ed. write for info. (0-318-72633-5) Mokelumne.

An Asterisk (*) at the beginning of an entry indicates that the title is appearing in BIP for the first time.

Book of Colt Firearms. 2nd ed. R. L. Wilson. (Illus.). 624p. 1993. text ed. 149.95 (0-9625943-7-7) Blue Bk Pubns. THE BOOK OF COLT FIREARMS is a complete Colt book library in a single volume. This book is a comprehensive pictorial & verbal study of Sam Colt & his company from its inception in 1832 through 1973. This new second edition presents valuable, detailed & authoritative text (over 1.25 million words) for the avid Colt collector, investor, or any gun enthusiast. Included are thousands of chronological facts, heretofore unpublished, drawn from years of specialized research, such as serial number sequences by year for all percussion & cartridge Colt handguns & long arms. If you are looking for any information regarding Colt firearms between 1832-1973 (including some important new information through 1993), this is the publication that gets used consistently.

The pictorial phase of this publication is explicitly emphasized through the use of 67 color pages, illustrating over 420 guns as well as 1,258 black & white photos covering the complete range of Colt firearms. Lavishly illustrated & with a unique 9 X 12 inch page-size format, this book is a must for any Colt aficionado. Literally, this book is a one-stop shopping center for all Colt related information & related facts. Retail $149.95, plus $7.50 s/h. Available from Baker & Taylor, Ingram or directly from the publisher by calling toll free 1-800-877-4867, 612-854-5229 or FAX 612-853-1486. *Publisher Provided Annotation.*

An Asterisk (*) at the beginning of an entry indicates that the title is appearing in BIP for the first time.

845

one volume come handsomely bound in three beautiful bindings. All editions are black with gold stampings, gold gilded page edges, six colored ribbon markers with gold/black headbands, & presentation pages. The leather editions include all of the cloth features plus, gold fillet on inner cover & a two-piece gift box. The classical Anglican devotional practise of Morning & Evening Prayer (prayer & scripture reading) can be conveniently engaged using this one book alone. To Order Direct: Send Check or Money Order for appropriate edition (include $6.50 s & h for the first book; $1 for every additional book) to Preservation Press, P.O. Box 612, Swedesboro, NJ 08085-0612, 609- 467-8902; Credit Card Orders: 800-264-5422; FAX: 609-467-3183, Quantity Discounts Available.
Publisher Provided Annotation.

***Book of Common Prayer (1928 Edition) & Authorized King James Bible with the Apocrypha, bonded leather. 2448p. 1995. 85.00 (*1-886412-01-4*) Preserv Press.**
One of the unique features of the English 'Reformation' - i.e., of the history of the Church of England - is the fact that it coincides with a climax in the history of English prose. The King James Bible (which originally contained the Apocrypha), the Book of Common Prayer are lasting monuments to this conjunction. These two particular books are the twin towers of English language & spirituality. This edition of these two classics of the English language & spirituality bound in one volume come handsomely bound in three beautiful bindings. All editions are black with gold stampings, gold gilded page edges, six colored ribbon markers with gold/black headbands, & presentation pages. The leather editions include all of the cloth features plus, gold fillet on inner cover & a two-piece gift box. The classical Anglican devotional practise of Morning & Evening Prayer (prayer & scripture reading) can be conveniently engaged using this one book alone. To Order Direct: Send Check or Money Order for appropriate edition (include $6.50 s & h for the first book; $1 for every additional book) to Preservation Press, P.O. Box 612, Swedesboro, NJ 08085-0612, 609- 467-8902; Credit Card Orders: 800-264-5422; FAX: 609-467-3183, Quantity Discounts Available.
Publisher Provided Annotation.

***Book of Common Prayer (1928 Edition) & Authorized King James Bible with the Apocrypha, leather. 2448p. 1995. 95.00 (*1-886412-00-6*) Preserv Press.**
One of the unique features of the English 'Reformation' - i.e., of the history of the Church of England - is the fact that it coincides with a climax in the history of English prose. The King James Bible (which originally contained the Apocrypha), The Book of Common Prayer are lasting monuments to this conjunction. These two particular books are the twin towers of English language & spirituality. This edition of these two classics of the English language & spirituality bound in one volume come handsomely bound in three beautiful bindings. All editions are black with gold stampings, gold gilded page edges, six colored ribbon markers with gold/black headbands, & presentation pages. The leather editions include all of the cloth features plus, gold fillet on inner cover & a two-piece gift box. The classical Anglican devotional practise of Morning & Evening Prayer (prayer & scripture reading) can be conveniently engaged using this one book alone. To Order Direct: Send Check or Money Order for appropriate edition (include $6.50 s & h for the first book; $1 for every additional book) to Preservation Press, P.O. Box 612, Swedesboro, NJ 08085-0612, 609- 467-8902; Credit Card Orders: 800-264-5422; FAX: 609-467-3183, Quantity Discounts Available.
Publisher Provided Annotation.

Book of Common Worship. Presbyterian Church, Theology & Worship Ministry Unit Staff & Cumberland Presbyterian Church Staff. 1008p. 1993. text ed. 30.00 (*0-664-21991-8*) Westminster John Knox.

Book of Common Worship, Daily Prayer. deluxe ed. Ed. by Cumberland Presbyterian Church Staff. LC 93-4547. 512p. 1993. 20.00 (*0-664-22032-0*) Westminster John Knox.

Book of Common Worship, Pastoral Edition. deluxe ed. Presbyterian Church (U. S. A.), Theology & Worship Ministry Unit Staff & Cumberland Presbyterian Church Staff. LC 93-4538. 368p. 1993. 25.00 (*0-664-22033-9*) Westminster John Knox.

Book of Comparing. Selma Wassermann & Jack Wassermann. (Smart Start Ser.). (Illus.). 32p. (J). (gr. k-3). 1990. lib. bdg. 12.85 (*0-8027-6944-6*); pap. 4.95 (*0-8027-9451-3*) Walker & Co.

Book of Complaints. Richard Katrovas. LC 92-74528. (Poetry Ser.). 1993. pap. 9.95 (*0-88748-157-4*) Carnegie-Mellon.

Book of Concord: The Confessions of the Evangelical Lutheran Church. Ed. & Tr. by Theodore G. Tappert. LC 59-11369. 1959. 28.00 (*0-8006-0825-9*, 1-825, Fortress Pr) Augsburg Fortress.

Book of Confidence. 2nd ed. Thomas De Saint Laurent. 95p. 1989. pap. 3.95 (*1-877905-14-3*) Am Soc Defense TFP.

Book of Consolations. Isho-Yabah. Ed. by Phillip Scott-Moncreiff. LC 77-87669. (Luzac's Semitic Text & Translation Ser.: No. 16). reprint ed. 21.50 (*0-404-11350-8*) AMS Pr.

Book of Container Gardening. Malcolm Hillier. 1991. 27.50 (*0-671-72253-0*) S&S Trade.

Book of Contemporary Myth. Ed. by D. C. Bradburd. (Illus.). 64p. (Orig.). 1988. pap. 5.50 (*0-317-92280-7*) Caitlin Pr.

Book of Cookies. Pat Alburey. (Illus.). 120p. 1988. pap. 10.95 (*0-89586-670-6*) Price Stern.

Book of Cool. Ronny P. Kaye. LC 90-55240. 47p. 1992. pap. 6.00 (*1-56002-024-5*) Aegina Pr.

Book of Corkman Jokes. Des MacHale. 1990. pap. 4.95 (*0-85342-478-0*) Dufour.

Book of Corn. Betty Fussell. 1992. pap. 35.00 (*0-394-57805-8*) Knopf.

Book of Corn Cookery. Mary L. Wade. 1979. pap. 5.95 (*0-916638-05-7*) Meyerbooks.

Book of Costs. Ed. by Terrill A. Mast. (Cost Containment Learning Modules Ser.). 85p. (Orig.). 1985. pap. text ed. 12.50 (*0-931369-18-5*) Southern IL Univ Sch.

Book of Costume: Or Annals of Fashion (1846) by a Lady of Rank, Countess of Wilton. annot. ed. Ed. by R. L. Shep & Pieter Bach. LC 86-90527. (Illus.). 528p. 1986. 45.00 (*0-914046-04-7*) R L Shep.

Book of Counsel: The Popol Vuh of the Quiche Maya of Guatemala. Munro S. Edmonson. LC 72-197628. (Tulane University. Middle American Research Institute Publication Ser.: No. 35). 293p. reprint ed. pap. 83.60 (*0-7837-4064-6*, 2044014) Bks Demand.

Book of Count Lucanor & Patronio: A Translation of Don Juan Manuel's El Conde Lucanor. Juan Manuel et al. LC 76-24342. (Studies in Romance Languages: No. 16). 207p. reprint ed. pap. 59.00 (*0-7837-5812-X*, 2045479) Bks Demand.

Book of Country Herbal Crafts: A Step-by-Step Guide to Making over 100 Beautiful Wreaths, Garlands, Bouquets, & Much More. Dawn Cusick. LC 91-10334. (Illus.). 176p. 1991. 24.95 (*0-87857-938-9*, 11-252-0) Rodale Pr Inc.

***Book of Country Music Wisdom: Common Sense & Uncommon Genius from 101 Country Music Greats.** Criswell Freeman. (Wisdom Ser.). 153p. (Orig.). 1994. pap. 5.95 (*0-9640955-1-3*) Walnut Gr Pr.

Book of Country Things. Walter Needham. LC 75-22098. (Illus.). 176p. 1992. reprint ed. pap. 11.95 (*0-911469-09-5*) A C Hood.

Book of Courtly Love: The Passionate Code of the Troubadours. Andrea Hopkins. LC 94-2926. 128p. 1994. 16.00 (*0-06-251115-7*) Harper SF.

Book of Creation. Pierre-Marie Beaude. Tr. by Andrew Clements. LC 90-35418. (Illus.). 56p. (J). (gr. 5 up). 1991. pap. 16.95 (*0-88708-141-X*, Picture Book Studio) S&S Childrens.

Book of Crepes & Omelets. Mary Norwak. Ed. by Jan Thiesen. LC 87-17602. (Book of...Ser.). 120p. (Orig.). 1988. pap. 9.95 (*0-89586-669-2*, HP Books) Berkley Pub.

Book of Crests of Scottish-American Clans. Mike McLaren. (Illus.). 273p. (Orig.). 1991. pap. 20.00 (*1-55613-401-0*) Heritage Bk.

Book of Cross-Stitch. Gail Lawther. (Illus.). 128p. 1994. 22.50 (*0-8230-0517-8*, Watsn-Guptill) Watsn-Guptill.

***Book of Cruising: Cruising Around the World West to East, Vol. 2.** Ed. by Rosalind Miranda. (Illus.). 464p. (Orig.). 1993. pap. text ed. 29.95 (*1-880465-03-5*) Chiodi Advert.

***Book of Cruising: Introduction to Cruising, Vol. 1.** Ed. by Rosalind Miranda. (Illus.). 148p. (Orig.). 1991. pap. text ed. 12.95 (*1-880465-02-7*) Chiodi Advert.

Book of Cryptic Crosswords. Wayne R. Williams. 1994. mass mkt. 8.99 (*0-440-50543-7*) Dell.

Book of Cucumbers, Melons & Squash. National Gardening Association Staff. 1987. pap. 4.95 (*0-394-74988-X*, Villard Bks) Random.

Book of Cups. Garth Clark. (Illus.). 96p. 1990. 14.95 (*1-55859-068-4*) Abbeville Pr.

Book of Curries & Indian Foods. Linda Fraser. (Illus.). 120p. 1989. pap. 11.00 (*0-89586-820-2*) Price Stern.

Book of Curtesye: Caxton's Book of Curtesye. Ed. by F. J. Furnivall. (EETS, ES Ser.: No. 3). 1972. reprint ed. pap. 15.00 (*0-527-00218-6*) Periodicals Srv.

Book of Cuttings for Acting & Directing. Marshall Cassady. 1989. pap. 16.95 (*0-8442-5120-8*, Natl Textbk) NTC Pub Grp.

Book of Daily Prayer. Robert Webber. 544p. 1993. 29.99 (*0-8028-3753-0*); pap. 19.99 (*0-8028-0678-3*) Eerdmans.

Book of Daily Thoughts & Prayers. Swami Paramananda. 1977. 7.95 (*0-911564-32-2*) Vedanta Ctr.

Book of Dakmonies, Bk. V. IGOS Staff. (Illus.). 220p. 1994. 25.00 (*1-57179-034-9*) Intern Guild ASRS.

Book of Daniel. R. J. Clifford. pap. 1.95 (*0-317-46870-7*, Frncscn Herld) Franciscan Pr.

Book of Daniel. E. L. Doctorow. 320p. 1987. mass mkt. 4.50 (*0-449-21430-3*, Crest) Fawcett.

Book of Daniel. E. L. Doctorow. LC 83-42866. 303p. 1984. 8.95 (*0-394-60501-2*, Modern Lib) Random.

Book of Daniel. E. L. Doctorow. LC 91-50222. (Vintage International Ser.). 320p. 1991. pap. 11.00 (*0-679-73657-3*, Vin) Random.

Book of Daniel. Douglas J. Simpson. 1974. pap. 6.95 (*0-89265-023-0*) Randall Hse.

Book of Daniel: A New Translation with Introduction & Commentary. Louis F. Hartman & Alexander A. Di Lella. LC 77-82762. (Anchor Bible Ser.: Vol. 23). 1978. pap. 28.00 (*0-385-01322-1*, Anchor NY) Doubleday.

Book of Daniel Drew. Bouck White. 1980. pap. 6.95 (*0-8065-0745-4*, Citadel Pr) Carol Pub Group.

Book of Daniel Drew. Bouck White. LC 73-2539. (Big Business; Economic Power in a Free Society Ser.). 1973. reprint ed. 29.95 (*0-405-05118-2*) Ayer.

***Book of Daniel Unsealed.** Freddie Robinson. 1995. pap. 12.95 (*0-9640487-3-6*) Transfig Prod.

Book of Danish Verse. C. W. Stork. 1973. 69.75 (*0-87968-767-3*) Gordon Pr.

Book of Days. 96p. 1993. 14.95 (*1-880317-12-5*) Biblical Arch Soc.

***Book of Days.** Budget Staff. 1994. 19.98 (*0-88365-880-1*) Galahad Bks.

Book of Days: A Miscellany of Popular Antiquities, 2 vols. Intro. by Robert Chambers & Tristram P. Coffin. (Illus.). 1990. reprint ed. Vol. 1, 831p. write for info. (*0-318-65969-7*); reprint ed. Vol. 2, 840p. write for info. (*0-318-65970-0*) Omnigraphics Inc.

Book of Days: A Miscellany of Popular Antiquities, 2 vols., Set. Intro. by Robert Chambers & Tristram P. Coffin. LC 89-63013. (Illus.). 1990. reprint ed. lib. bdg. 140.00 (*1-55888-848-9*) Omnigraphics Inc.

Book of Days: An Encyclopedia of Information Sources on Historical Figures & Events, Keyed to Calendar Dates, Vol. 1. Ed. by C. Edward Wall. 808p. 1987. 98.00 (*0-87650-224-9*) Pierian.

Book of Days: Celebrating Art in Children's Literature. (Illus.). 65p. 1993. 14.95 (*0-8109-3184-2*) Abrams.

Book of Days: Plates from Le Bon Genre. Pierre De La Mesangere & J. Dustin Wees. (Illus.). 80p. 1986. pap. 10.00 (*1-55660-183-2*) A Wofsy Fine Arts.

Book of Days & Nights. Thomas McNight. (Illus.). 128p. 1993. 14.95 (*0-8212-2021-7*) Bulfinch Pr.

Book of Days, 1988: An Encyclopedia of Information Sources on Historical Figures & Events, Keyed to Calendar Dates, Vol. 2. Ed. by C. Edward Wall. 776p. 1988. 98.00 (*0-87650-248-6*) Pierian.

Book of Days Nineteen Ninety. Ed. by Alen MacWeeney. (Illus.). 120p. 1989. 9.95 (*0-945618-03-4*) Dorsoduro Pr.

Book of Death. Tenney Nathanson. 1975. pap. 5.00 (*0-87924-024-5*) Membrane Pr.

Book of DEC Systems & Architectures. Carl Malamud. (Illus.). 256p. 1989. text ed. 50.00 (*0-07-039822-4*) McGraw.

Book of Deciding. Selma Wassermann & Jack Wassermann. LC 89-78073. (Smart Start Ser.). (Illus.). (J). (gr. k-3). 1990. lib. bdg. 12.85 (*0-8027-6952-7*); pap. 4.95 (*0-8027-9456-4*) Walker & Co.

Book of Decorative Knots. Peter Owen. (Illus.). 144p. 1994. pap. 12.95 (*1-55821-304-X*) Lyons & Burford.

Book of Dede Korkut. Tr. by Geoffrey L. Lewis. 224p. 1974. pap. 8.95 (*0-14-044298-7*, Penguin Classics) Viking Penguin.

Book of Dede Korkut: A Turkish Epic. Ed. by Faruk Sumer et al. (Illus.). 240p. 1991. reprint ed. pap. 14.95 (*0-292-70787-8*) U of Tex Pr.

Book of Delight & Other Papers. Israel Abrahams. Ed. by Steven Katz. LC 79-7124. (Jewish Philosophy, Mysticism & History of Ideas Ser.). 1980. reprint ed. lib. bdg. 29.95 (*0-405-12238-1*) Ayer.

***Book of Democracy.** James D. Barber. LC 94-36188. 1995. pap. text ed. 24.00 (*0-13-340068-9*) P-H.

Book of Desire. Stanley J. Goodwin. 1982. pap. 2.40 (*0-686-10271-1*) Northland Pubns WA.

Book of Destiny. Herman B. Kramer. LC 75-13556. (Illus.). 1975. pap. 18.00 (*0-89555-046-6*) TAN Bks Pubs.

Book of Destiny. Arthur E. Waite. 290p. 1994. pap. 19.95 (*1-56459-435-1*) Kessinger Pub.

Book of Destiny & the Art of Reading Therein. Grand Orient. 277p. 1986. spiral bd. 19.25 (*0-7873-0647-9*) Mokelumne.

Book of Devotions. Comp. by Joseph Coppolino. 68p. (Orig.). 1986. pap. 1.75 (*0-8189-0502-6*) Alba.

Book of Dialogue. Edmond Jabes. Tr. by Rosmarie Waldrop. LC 86-23338. 88p. 1988. 25.00 (*0-8195-5147-3*, Wesleyan Univ Pr) U Pr of New Eng.

Book of Diaries. Ronald Blythe. 1989. 24.95 (*0-394-58017-6*) Pantheon.

Book of Dilemmas. Laszlo Balogh. 1992. 12.95 (*0-533-10068-2*) Vantage.

Book of Dinosaur Dice Games. Moira Butterfield. (J). (gr. 3 up). 1994. 5.95 (*0-681-45374-5*) Longmeadow Pr.

Book of Dinosaurs. C. Bloch. (Illus.). 64p. (Orig.). (J). (gr. k-6). 1993. pap. 3.95 (*1-879424-46-0*) Nickel Pr.

***Book of Dinosaurs.** RH Value Publishing Staff. 1995. pap. 8.99 (*0-517-12354-1*) Random.

Book of Dinosaurs: The Natural History Museum Guide. Tom Gardom & Angela Milner. (Illus.). 124p. 1993. pap. 14.95 (*1-55958-350-9*) Prima Pub.

Book of Direction to the Duties of the Heart: Hovot Ha-Levavot. Bahya I. Pakuda. Ed. & Tr. by Menahem Mansoor. Tr. by Shoshana Dannhauser et al. (Littman Library of Jewish Civilization). 480p. 1973. 19.50 (*0-19-710020-1*, Pub. by Littman Lib Jew UK) Bnai Brith Bk.

Book of Discipline, Pt. 1. Tr. by I. B. Horner. (C). 1966. Vol. 1. 39.00 (*0-86013-037-1*) Wisdom MA.

Book of Discipline, Pt. 2. Tr. by I. B. Horner. (C). 1966. Vol. 2. 43.50 (*0-86013-038-X*) Wisdom MA.

Book of Discipline, Pt. 3. Tr. by I. B. Horner. (C). 1966. Vol. 3. 43.50 (*0-86013-039-8*) Wisdom MA.

Book of Discipline, Pt. 4. Tr. by I. B. Horner. (C). 1966. Vol. 4. 43.50 (*0-86013-040-1*) Wisdom MA.

Book of Discipline, Pt. 5. Tr. by I. B. Horner. (C). 1966. Vol. 5. 43.50 (*0-86013-044-4*) Wisdom MA.

Book of Discipline, Pt. 6. Tr. by I. B. Horner. (C). 1966. Vol. 6. 43.50 (*0-86013-049-5*) Wisdom MA.

Book of Discipline, 6 vols., Set. Tr. by I. B. Horner. (C). 1966. 245.00 (*0-86013-254-4*) Wisdom MA.

Book of Disquiet. Fernando Pessoa. Tr. by Alfred MacAdam. LC 90-53484. 320p. 1991. 25.00 (*0-679-40234-9*) Pantheon.

Book of Disquiet. Fernando Pessoa. Ed. by Maria J. De Lancastre. Tr. by Margaret J. Costa. 320p. 1992. pap. 14.99 (*1-85242-204-1*) Serpents Tail.

Book of Distinguished American Women. 2nd ed. Vincent Wilson, Jr. (Illus.). 1992. pap. 5.50 (*0-910086-05-2*) Am Hist Res.

Book of Divine Magic. 2nd ed. Omraam M. Aivanhov. (Izvor Collection: No. 226). 208p. 1993. reprint ed. pap. 8.95 (*2-85566-442-X*, Pub. by Prosveta FR) Prosveta USA.

Book of Do-In: Exercise for Physical & Spiritual Development. Michio Kushi. (Illus.). 224p. (Orig.). 1995. pap. 19.00 (*0-87040-382-6*) Japan Pubns USA.

Book of Dogs: An Illustrated Guide & Photos of All Breeds. James G. Lawson. 1991. lib. bdg. 88.00 (*0-8490-5222-X*) Gordon Pr.

Book of Dogs: Breeds, Training & Show Points. Stanley West. 1991. lib. bdg. 88.95 (*0-8490-5236-X*) Gordon Pr.

***Book of Doors: An Alchemical Oracle from Ancient Egypt.** Athon Veggi & Alison Davidson. LC 94-30284. 256p. 1994. boxed, pap. 29.95 (*0-89281-512-4*, Destiny Bks) Inner Tradit.

Book of Do's. Bern Porter. (Illus.). 400p. (Orig.). 1982. pap. 19.95 (*0-937966-11-8*) Tilbury Hse.

Book of Dracula. Ed. by Leslie Shepard. 560p. 1991. reprint ed. 10.99 (*0-517-03758-0*) Random Hse Value.

***Book of Dragons.** Ed. & Illus. by Michael Hague. LC 94-42958. (J). 1995. 18.00 (*0-688-10879-2*) Morrow Jr Bks.

***Book of Dream Symbols.** Peter Bentley. 1995. text ed. 7.95 (*0-8118-0664-2*) Chronicle Bks.

Book of Dreams. Jack Kerouac. LC 60-14774. (Orig.). 1908. pap. 8.95 (*0-87286-027-2*) City Lights.

Book of Dreams. Craig Nova. LC 93-23343. 336p. 1994. 22.95 (*0-395-63650-7*) Ticknor & Fields.

Book of Dreams & Ghosts. Andrew Lang. LC 71-108815. reprint ed. 37.50 (*0-404-03848-4*) AMS Pr.

Book of Dressings & Marinades. Janice Murfitt. (Illus.). 120p. (Orig.). 1989. pap. 10.95 (*0-89586-819-9*) Price Stern.

Book of Druidry: History, Sites, & Wisdom. Ross Nichols. (Illus.). 1992. reprint ed. pap. 16.00 (*1-85538-167-2*, Pub. by Aquarian Pr UK) Thorsons SF.

Book of Duarte Barbosa, 2 vols. Duarte Barbosa. Tr. by Mansel L. Dames. (Hakluyt Society Works Ser.: No. 2, Vols. 44 & 49). 1921. 120.00 (*0-8115-0352-6*) Periodicals Srv.

Book of Dublinman Jokes. Y. M. Hughes. 1990. pap. 5.95 (*0-85342-488-8*) Dufour.

Book of Dulwich. Evan Davies. 1977. 40.00 (*0-86023-003-1*) St Mut.

***Book of Dumb Movie Blurbs.** Jeff Rovin. 96p. (Orig.). 1995. pap. 8.00 (*0-425-14616-2*, Berkley Trade) Berkley Pub.

Book of During. Clark Coolidge. 1991. per. 15.00 (*0-935724-43-5*) Figures.

Book of During. deluxe ed. Clark Coolidge. 1991. per. 25.00 (*0-935724-49-4*) Figures.

Book of Dust: The Beginning & the End of Time & Thereafter. Agnes Denes. LC 88-51541. (Illus.). 120p. 1989. 75.00 (*0-89822-057-2*) Visual Studies.

***Book of E-Meter Drills.** L. Ron Hubbard. 172p. 1988. spiral bd. 40.00 (*0-88404-310-X*) Bridge Pubns Inc.

Book of E-Meter Drills. L. Ron Hubbard. 8.75 (*0-686-30796-8*) Church Scient NY.

Book of Eagles. Helen R. Sattler. LC 88-38806. (Illus.). 64p. (J). (gr. 3 up). 1989. lib. bdg. 14.93 (*0-688-07022-1*) Lothrop.

Book of Early Whisperings. Walter Russell. (Illus.). 103p. 1977. reprint ed. text ed. 15.00 (*1-879605-17-1*) U Sci & Philos.

***Book of Earth.** Marjorie B. Kellogg. (Dragon Quartet Ser.). 320p. (Orig.). 1995. pap. 4.99 (*0-88677-574-4*) DAW Bks.

An Asterisk (*) at the beginning of an entry indicates that the title is appearing in BIP for the first time.

B

An Asterisk (*) at the beginning of an entry indicates that the title is appearing in BIP for the first time.

847

B

Book of Gradual Sayings, Vol. 2. Tr. by F. L. Woodward & E. M. Hare. (C). 1936. 33.00 (0-86013-015-0) Wisdom MA.

Book of Gradual Sayings, Vol. 3. Tr. by F. L. Woodward & E. M. Hare. (C). 1936. 36.50 (0-86013-016-9) Wisdom MA.

Book of Gradual Sayings, Vol. 4. Tr. by F. L. Woodward & E. M. Hare. (C). 1936. 36.50 (0-86013-017-7) Wisdom MA.

Book of Gradual Sayings, Vol. 5. Tr. by F. L. Woodward & E. M. Hare. (C). 1936. 33.00 (0-86013-018-5) Wisdom MA.

Book of Graphic Problem Solving: How to Get Visual Ideas When You Need Them. John Newcomb. 256p. 1984. pap. 39.95 (0-8352-1895-3) Bowker.

Book of Great American Documents. 3rd ed. Ed. by Vincent Wilson, Jr. (Illus.). 1993. pap. 5.50 (0-910086-00-1) Am Hist Res.

Book of Great Breakfasts & Brunches. Terence Janericco. LC 92-46781. 1993. text ed. 34.95 (0-442-01355-8) Van Nos Reinhold.

Book of Great Desserts. Terence Janericco. (Illus.). 304p. 1994. text ed. 34.95 (0-442-01356-6) Van Nos Reinhold.

Book of Great Hors D'oeuvers. Terence Janericco. 1990. text ed. 39.95 (0-442-00183-5) Van Nos Reinhold.

Book of Great Irish Lies. Myler Magrath. 1989. pap. 7.95 (0-946645-10-8) Dufour.

Book of Great Mysteries. Ed. by Colin Wilson & Christopher Evans. (Dorset Press Reprints Ser.). 512p. 1990. reprint ed. 24.95 (0-88029-517-1) Dorset Pr.

Book of Greek Cooking. Lesley Mackley. (Illus.). 120p. (Orig.). 1993. pap. 10.95 (1-55788-062-X, HP Books) Berkley Pub.

Book of Grilling & Barbecuing. Cecilia Norman. (Book of... Ser.). (Illus.). 120p. (Orig.). 1989. pap. 12.00 (0-89586-790-7, HP Books) Berkley Pub.

*Book of Griswold & Wagner. David Smith & Charles Wafford. LC 95-68661. (Illus.). 320p. (Orig.). 1995. pap. 29.95 (0-88740-836-2) Schiffer.

Book of Gross. Mimi Aderton & Douglas Liss. (Illus.). 96p. (Orig.). 1983. pap. 3.95 (0-8065-0838-8, Citadel Pr) Carol Pub Group.

Book of Guys. large type ed. Garrison Keillor. LC 94-1129. 1994. 24.95 (1-56895-065-9) Wheeler Pub.

Book of Guys. Garrison Keillor. (Illus.). 352p. 1994. reprint ed. pap. 11.95 (0-14-023372-5, Penguin Bks) Viking Penguin.

Book of Handwoven Coverlets. rev. ed. Eliza C. Hall. (Illus.). 88p. 1988. reprint ed. pap. 6.95 (0-486-25688-X) Dover.

Book of Hard Criticisms: Watching the America Show (versus) A Revisioning for an Alternative America in the Twenty-First Century. Glen B. Page. LC 90-85738. 368p. 1991. 22.00 (0-9628845-0-2) Canopus Pub.

Book of Health. Susan Stockton. (Illus.). 228p. (Orig.). 1990. pap. text ed. 12.95 (0-9628770-0-X) S S Swimmer.

Book of Health Secrets. Boardroom's Experts & Editors. LC 89-577. 420p. 1989. 50.00 (0-88723-011-3) Boardroom.

Book of Heath. Ed. by Susan B. Silvester. LC 85-12421. (Illus.). 207p. 1985. 22.00 (0-913993-02-6) Paideia MA.

Book of Heaven & the Earth: Stories from the Confucian Analects. Ed. by Kojin Shimomura. Tr. by Nobuyoshi Okumura. 191p. 1973. 18.00 (0-86008-085-4, Pub. by U of Tokyo JA) Col U Pr.

Book of Hebrew Letters. Mark Podwal. LC 92-20241. 64p. 1992. 22.50 (0-87668-317-0) Aronson.

Book of Herbs. Edmond B. Szekely. (Illus.). 48p. 1981. pap. 3.50 (0-89564-044-9) IBS Intl.

Book of Heroic Verse. Ed. by Arthur Burrell. LC 78-168775. (Granger Index Reprint Ser.). 1977. reprint ed. 23.95 (0-8369-6295-8) Ayer.

Book of Hertford. Cyril Heath. 1977. 40.00 (0-86023-005-8) St Mut.

Book of Highland Verse. Ed. by Dugald Mitchell. LC 79-144528. reprint ed. 52.50 (0-404-08673-X) AMS Pr.

*Book of Hindu Festivals & Ceremonies. Om L. Bahadur. (C). 1995. 8.50x (81-86112-23-5, Pub. by UBS Pubs Dist II) S Asia.

*Book of Hindu Imagery: The Gods & Their Symbols. Eva R. Jansen. 158p. (Orig.). 1994. 19.95 (90-74597-10-6) Binkey Kok NE.

Book of Hindu Imagery: The Gods & Their Symbols. Eva R. Jansen. (Illus.). 158p. (Orig.). 1993. pap. 12.95 (90-74597-07-6, Pub. by Binkey Kok NE) Weiser.

Book of Holiness see Code of Maimonides

Book of Home Plans. Homestyles Publishing & Marketing Staff. 230p. 1989. pap. 9.95 (0-945471-22-X) HomeStyles Pub & Mkt.

*Book of Hope: Testament of a Master Guide. Ati. Ed. by Bob Murray & Alicia Fortinberry. 256p. (Orig.). 1995. pap. 11.95 (1-885610-09-2) European Amer.

*Book of Horrors. Diane Hoh. (Nightmare Hall Ser.: No. 16). (YA). 1994. pap. 3.50 (0-590-48358-7) Scholastic Inc.

Book of Hot & Spicy Foods. Louise Steele. LC 87-11907. 120p. 1987. pap. 9.95 (0-89586-642-0) Price Stern.

*Book of Hours. T. Tolley. 1995. 10.00 (0-06-251132-7) Harper SF.

Book of Hours. Elizabeth Yates. 1976. 5.95 (0-8164-0901-3) Harper SF.

Book of Hours. large type ed. Elizabeth Yates. 128p. 1985. pap. 4.95 (0-8027-2484-1) Walker & Co.

Book of Hours: Illuminations by Simon Marmion. Comment & Intro. by James Thorpe. (Illus.). 48p. 1990. pap. 5.95 (0-87328-130-6) Huntington Lib.

Book of Hours & Constellations. Eugen Gomringer. Tr. by Jerome Rothenberg. LC 68-31588. 1968. 15.00 (0-89366-054-X); pap. 7.50 (0-89366-055-8) Ultramarine Pub.

Book of Hours of Emperor Maximilian the First. Ed. by Walter L. Strauss. LC 73-81346. 345p. 1974. 75.00 (0-913870-01-3) Abaris Bks.

Book of Hours of Jeanne de L'Avenier. Ann Erickson. Ed. by Edward Mycue. (Took Modern Poetry in English Ser.: No. 17). (Illus.). 28p. (Orig.). 1991. pap. 4.00 (1-879457-16-4) Norton Coker Pr.

Book of Houses: An Astrological Guide to the Harvest Cycle in Human Life. Robert Cole. LC 80-16931. 132p. 1980. pap. 8.95 (0-934558-04-3); pap. 6.95 (0-934558-01-9) Entwhistle Bks.

Book of Hrabal. Peter Esterhazy. Tr. by Judith Sollosy. LC 94-11544. 168p. 1994. reprint ed. 22.50 (0-8101-1192-6) Northwestern U Pr.

Book of Hugs. Dave Ross. LC 79-7896. (Illus.). 32p. (J). (gr. k up). 1991. reprint ed. pap. 3.95 (0-06-107418-7) HarpC Child Bks.

Book of Humor. Eva M. Tappan. 22.00 (0-8196-1363-0) Biblo.

Book of Humorous Verse. Comp. by Carolyn Wells. LC 73-116419. (Granger Index Reprint Ser.). 1977. 50.95 (0-8369-6162-5) Ayer.

Book of Hymns. Ed. by Ian Bradley. LC 88-31254. 476p. 1989. 24.95 (0-87951-346-2) Overlook Pr.

Book of Hymns. Ed. by Ian Bradley. 480p. 1992. reprint ed. pap. 15.95 (0-87951-460-4) Overlook Pr.

Book of Hymns. Samuel Johnson. (Notable American Authors Ser.). 1992. reprint ed. lib. bdg. 75.00 (0-7812-3496-4) Rprt Serv.

Book of Hypotheses. Selma Wassermann & Jack Wassermann. LC 89-78082. (Smart Start Ser.). (Illus.). 32p. (J). (gr. k-3). 1990. lib. bdg. 12.85 (0-8027-6946-2); pap. 4.95 (0-8027-9452-1) Walker & Co.

Book of Ian Watson. Ian Watson. LC 85-50240. 380p. 1985. 18.50 (0-9612970-3-4) Mark Ziesing.

Book of Ian Watson. deluxe ed. Ian Watson. LC 85-50240. 380p. 1985. 35.00 (0-9612970-4-2) Mark Ziesing.

Book of Ice Creams & Sorbets. Jacki Passmore. LC 86-81043. 128p. 1987. pap. 9.95 (0-89586-503-3) Price Stern.

Book of Images. Rainer M. Rilke. Tr. by Edward Snow. 288p. 1991. 25.00 (0-86547-468-0, North Pt Pr) FS&G.

Book of Images. Rainer M. Rilke. Tr. by Edward Snow. 1994. pap. 12.00 (0-86547-477-X, North Pt Pr) FS&G.

Book of Imagining. Selma Wassermann & Jack Wassermann. LC 89-77869. (Smart Start Ser.). (Illus.). 32p. (J). (gr. k-3). 1990. lib. bdg. 12.85 (0-8027-6948-9); pap. 4.95 (0-8027-9454-8) Walker & Co.

Book of Incense: Enjoying the Traditional Art of Japanese Scents. Kiyoko Morita. Ed. by Meagan Calogeras. LC 92-11064. (Illus.). 144p. 1992. 15.00 (4-7700-1557-7) Kodansha.

Book of Indian Birds. 11th ed. Salim Ali. (Illus.). 332p. 1988. 29.95 (0-19-562167-0) OUP.

Book of Indian Crafts & Costumes. Bernard S. Mason. LC 46-6959. 128p. reprint ed. pap. 36.50 (0-8357-7341-8, 2055164) Bks Demand.

Book of Indian Crafts & Indian Lore. J. H. Salomon. 1977. lib. bdg. 250.00 (0-8490-1531-6) Gordon Pr.

*Book of Indian Names. Ed. by Raja R. Mehrotra. (C). 1994. 22.00 (81-7167-149-7, Pub. by Rupa II) S Asia.

*Book of Indian Sweets. Satarupa Banerjee. (C). 1994. 34.00 (81-7167-150-0, Pub. by Rupa II) S Asia.

Book of Indiana, Vol. I. Ed. by R. W. Haldeman & E. Hodge. (First of Annual Ser.). (Illus.). 196p. (Orig.). 1988. pap. 7.95 (0-317-91347-6) PennUltimate Pubs.

Book of Infinite Love. Louise M. De La Touche. Tr. by E. Patrick O'Connell. LC 79-90488. 1979. reprint ed. pap. 4.50 (0-89555-129-2) TAN Bks Pubs.

Book of Ingenious & Diabolical Puzzles. Jerry Slocum & Jack Botermans. LC 94-8033. 1994. 20.00 (0-8129-2153-4, Times Bks) Random.

Book of Ingenious Devices. Banu (Sons of) Musa Bin Shakir Staff. Tr. by Donald R. Hill. 1978. lib. bdg. 145.50 (90-277-0833-9) Kluwer Ac.

Book of Inside Information. Ed. by Bottom Line Personal, Experts Staff. LC 86-30972. 500p. 1985. 50.00 (0-88723-015-6) Boardroom.

Book of Inspirational Verse. Mary A. Mitra. (C). 1989. 40.00 (0-7223-2360-3, Pub. by A H S Ltd UK) St Mut.

Book of Insults & Irreverent Quotations. D. C. Hook & L. Kahn. 1980. 14.95 (0-8246-0250-1) Jonathan David.

*Book of Intercessions. Carmelites of Indianapolis Staff. 32p. 1994. pap. 5.95 (1-886873-05-4) Carmelites IN.

Book of Interesting & Amusing Puns. 1991. lib. bdg. 74.95 (0-8490-4167-8) Gordon Pr.

Book of Intimate Grammar. David Grossman. Tr. by Betsy Rosenberg. LC 93-46460. 1994. 22.00 (0-374-11547-8) FS&G.

*Book of Intimate Grammar. David Grossman. 1995. pap. 13.00 (1-57322-515-0) Riverhead Bks.

Book of Intrusions. Desmond MacNamara. LC 93-36126. 214p. 1994. 19.95 (1-56478-041-4) Dalkey Arch.

Book of Irish American Blessings & Prayers. Andrew Greeley. 1991. pap. 13.95 (0-88347-269-4) Thomas More.

Book of Irish Americans. D. William Griffin. 1990. pap. 16.95 (0-8129-1264-0, Times Bks) Random.

Book of Irish Bull. Des MacHale. 118p. 1991. reprint ed. pap. 10.95 (0-85342-822-0, Pub. by Mercier Pr IE) Dufour.

Book of Irish Curses. Patrick C. Power. 1975. pap. 5.95 (0-87243-060-X) Templegate.

Book of "Irish Families" Great & Small. Michael O'Laughlin. 320p. 1992. 28.00 (0-940134-08-X) Irish Genealog.

Book of Irish Names. Ida Grehan et al. LC 89-32660. (Illus.). 128p. 1994. pap. 9.95 (0-8069-6944-X) Sterling.

Book of Irish Names: First, Family & Place Names. Ida Grehan et al. (Illus.). 128p. (C). 1990. reprint ed. lib. bdg. 27.00x (0-8095-7584-1) Borgo Pr.

Book of Irish Poetry. enl. rev. ed. Ed. by Alfred P. Graves. LC 77-39394. (Granger Index Reprint Ser.). 1977. reprint ed. 23.95 (0-8369-6345-8) Ayer.

Book of Irish Quotations. Ed. by Sean McMahon. 240p. 1985. 16.95 (0-87243-127-4) Templegate.

Book of Irish School Jokes. Catherine McCurdy. 1990. pap. 4.95 (0-85342-778-X) Dufour.

*Book of Irish Verse: Irish Poetry from the Sixth Century to the Present. John Montague. 1995. 9.98 (0-88365-881-X) Galahad Bks.

Book of Irish Wit & Humour. Daniel O'Keeffe. 120p. 1989. pap. 9.95 (0-85342-873-5, Pub. by Mercier Pr IE) Dufour.

Book of Isaiah. Illus. by Chaim Gross. LC 78-188581. 200p. 1992. reprint ed. 45.00 (0-8276-0417-3) JPS Phila.

Book of Isaiah, Vol. 1. Tr. by A. J. Rosenberg. 261p. (HEB.). 1982. 17.95 (0-910818-50-9) Judaica Pr.

Book of Isaiah, Vol. 2. Tr. by A. J. Rosenberg. 292p. (HEB.). 1983. 17.95 (0-910818-52-5) Judaica Pr.

Book of Isaiah: An Introductory Commentary. Ronald F. Youngblood. LC 92-42721. 192p. (Orig.). 1993. pap. 10.99 (0-8010-9894-7) Baker Bk.

Book of Isaiah: Sample Edition with Introduction. M. H. Goshen-Gottenstein. 104p. 1965. text ed. 20.00 (0-685-74237-7, Pub. by Magnes Press IS) Eisenbrauns.

Book of Isaiah, Chapters 1-39. John N. Oswalt. (New International Commentary on the Old Testament Ser.). 672p. 1986. 34.99 (0-8028-2368-8) Eerdmans.

Book of Italian Cooking. 1993. 12.99 (0-517-10322-2) Random Hse Value.

Book of J. Harold Bloom. Tr. by David Rosenberg. LC 91-50220. 352p. 1991. pap. 12.00 (0-679-73624-7, Vin) Random.

*Book of Jabbo: Revelations in Six Languages. Mondo J. Hart. (Illus.). 160p. (Orig.). Date not set. pap. text ed. 19.95 (1-885214-04-9) Azul Edits.

Book of Jack London, 2 vols. Charmian London. 1976. 60.95 (0-8488-0886-X) Amereon Ltd.

Book of Jack London, 2 vols. Charmian London. 1992. reprint ed. lib. bdg. 150.00 (0-7812-5061-7) Rprt Serv.

Book of Jamaica. Russell Banks. 320p. 1986. mass mkt. 5.95 (0-345-33074-9) Ballantine.

Book of James. J. J. Turner. 1976. pap. 6.95 (0-89137-548-1) Quality Pubns.

Book of Jargon. Miller. 1982. 16.95 (0-02-584960-3) Macmillan.

Book of Jasher. Albinus Alciun. 291p. 1966. reprint ed. spiral bd. 13.75 (0-7873-0000-4) Mokelumne.

Book of Jasher. Tr. by M. Noah. LC 87-72939. 272p. (C). 1988. reprint ed. pap. 9.00 (0-934666-25-3) Artisan Sales.

Book of Jasher: One of the Sacred Books of the Bible Long Lost or Undiscovered. Tr. by Flaccus A. Alcuinus. 90p. 1993. pap. 14.95 (1-56459-340-1) Kessinger Pub.

Book of Jeremiah. Joseph Breuer. 1988. 22.95 (0-317-68133-8) Feldheim.

Book of Jeremiah. John A. Thompson. LC 79-16510. (New International Commentary on the Old Testament Ser.). 1980. 34.99 (0-8028-2369-6) Eerdmans.

Book of Jeremiah, Vol. 1. Tr. by A. J. Rosenberg. (Books of the Prophet Ser.). 474p. (HEB.). 1985. 17.95 (0-910818-59-2) Judaica Pr.

Book of Jeremiah, Vol. II. Tr. by A. J. Rosenberg. (Books of the Prophet Ser.). 464p. (HEB.). 1985. 17.95 (0-910818-60-6) Judaica Pr.

*Book of Jesus the Christ. Donald W. Garner. 114p. (Orig.). 1995. pap. 12.95 (0-9618970-2-3) Sea Crow Prodn.

Book of Jewelry: Create Your Own Jewelry with Beads, Clay, Papier-mache, Fabric & Other Everyday Items. Joo Moody. LC 94-1812. 1994. 22.95 (0-671-89096-4) S&S Trade.

Book of Jewish Belief. Louis Jacobs. 250p. (Orig.). 1984. pap. text ed. 8.95 (0-87441-379-6) Behrman.

Book of Jewish Curiosities. David M. Hausdorff. LC 55-11366. 1979. pap. 8.95 (0-8197-0466-0) Bloch.

*Book of Jewish Customs. Harvey Lutske. 400p. 1995. pap. 24.95 (1-56821-608-4) Aronson.

Book of Jewish Customs. Harvey Lutske. LC 86-22362. 400p. 1987. reprint ed. 30.00 (0-87668-916-0) Aronson.

Book of Jewish Ethical Concepts. Abraham P. Bloch. 1984. 25.00 (0-88125-039-2) Ktav.

Book of Jewish Holidays. Ruth Kozodoy. Ed. by Seymour Rossel. (Illus.). 192p. (Orig.). (J). (gr. 4-5). 1981. 12.50 (0-87441-367-2); By Morris J. Sugarman. student ed 4.25 (0-87441-338-9); pap. text ed. 7.95 (0-87441-334-6) Behrman.

Book of Jewish Knowledge: 613 Basic Facts about Judaism. David E. Cahn-Lipman. LC 91-10760. 478p. 1994. reprint ed. pap. 24.95 (1-56821-182-1) Aronson.

Book of Jewish Practice. Louis Jacobs. (YA). (gr. 9 up). 8.95 (0-317-70168-1) Behrman.

Book of Jewish Women's Prayers: Translations from the Yiddish. Ed. & Tr. by Norman Tarnor. LC 94-28363. 248p. 1995. 30.00 (1-56821-298-4) Aronson.

Book of Jewish Women's Tales. Barbara Rush. LC 93-34959. 344p. 1994. 35.00 (1-56821-087-6) Aronson.

Book of Jim. Jim Woodring. 120p. 1993. pap. 14.95 (1-56097-106-1) Fantagraph Bks.

Book of Job. Intro. by Harold Bloom. (Modern Critical Interpretations Ser.). 152p. 1987. lib. bdg. 24.95 (0-87754-913-3) Chelsea Hse.

Book of Job. Orlin Corey. 1961. 10.00 (0-87602-000-7) Anchorage.

Book of Job. Wayne Jackson. 1983. pap. 6.95 (0-89137-541-4) Quality Pubns.

Book of Job. Tr. & Intro. by Stephen Mitchell. LC 92-52637. 1992. pap. 10.00 (0-06-096959-8, PL) HarpC.

Book of Job. Cyril Rodd. LC 90-33941. (Narrative Commentaries Ser.). 160p. (Orig.). (C). 1990. pap. 12.95 (0-334-02473-0) TPI PA.

Book of Job. Ethelbert W. Bullinger. LC 90-36536. 204p. 1990. reprint ed. pap. 8.99 (0-8254-2291-4) Kregel.

Book of Job. Jeanne Guyon. Tr. by M. W. Russell. 265p. 1993. reprint ed. pap. 10.95 (0-940232-23-5) Seedsowers.

Book of Job: Commentary, New Translation & Special Studies. Robert Gordis. LC 78-2305. (Moreshet Studies in Jewish History, Literature & Thought: No. 2). 1977. 59.50 (0-87334-003-5) Ktav.

Book of Job: The New International Commentary on the Old Testament. John Hartley. (New International Commentary on the Old Testament Ser.). 1988. 32.99 (0-8028-2528-1) Eerdmans.

Book of Job - Hebrew Text & Commentary with English Translation: Hebrew Text, English Translation & Commentary Digest. Tr. by A. J. Rosenberg. (Books of Prophets & Holy Writings Ser.). 249p. (HEB.). 1989. 17.95 (0-910818-80-0) Judaica Pr.

Book of Job, a Commentary. Norman C. Habel. LC 84-21580. (Old Testament Library). 586p. (C). 1985. 40.00 (0-664-21831-8, Westminster) Westminster John Knox.

Book of Job As Sceptical Literature. Katharine J. Dell. (Beiheft zur Zeitschrift fuer die Alttestamentliche Wissenschaft Ser.: Vol. 197). x, 259p. (GER.). (C). 1991. lib. bdg. 80.00 (3-11-012554-4) De Gruyter.

Book of Joe. Mark Kessinger. (Cleveland Poets Ser.: No. 46). 64p. (Orig.). 1990. pap. 6.00 (0-914946-74-9) Cleveland St Univ Poetry Ctr.

Book of Johnson Family Group Sheets. Ed. by Verna Ellis. 200p. (Orig.). 1987. pap. 9.00 (0-9619668-0-7) Surname Pubns.

Book of Jonah. Illus. by Sant Bani School Children. LC 84-50924. (J). (gr. 1-6). 1984. pap. 6.95 (0-89142-044-4) Sant Bani Ash.

*Book of Jook: Chinese Medicinal Porridges, a Healthy Alternative to the Typical Western Breakfast. Bob Flaws. 225p. (Orig.). Date not set. pap. 18.95 (0-936185-60-0) Blue Poppy.

Book of Joshua. Marten H. Woudstra. LC 80-23413. (New International Commentary on the Old Testament Ser.). 400p. 1981. 28.99 (0-8028-2356-4) Eerdmans.

Book of Joshua: An Historical Biography. Susanrachel Balber & Joshua Greenspan. (Illus.). 206p. 1989. write for info. (0-318-64308-1) Galen Pr.

Book of Joshua - Hebrew Text & Commentary with English Translation: Hebrew Text, English Translation & Commentary Digest. Tr. by A. J. Rosenberg. 357p. (HEB.). 1984. 17.95 (0-910818-08-8) Judaica Pr.

Book of Joshua in Greek According to the Critically Restored Text with an Apparatus Containing the Variants of the Principal Recensions & of the Individual Witnesses, Pt. 5: Joshua 19: 39 - 24: 33. Max L. Margolis. LC 91-21422. xxvi, 457p. 1992. pap. 35.00 (0-900268-66-2) Eisenbrauns.

Book of Journeyman, Essays from the New Freeman. Albert J. Nock. LC 67-23253. (Essay Index Reprint Ser.). 1977. 18.95 (0-8369-0744-2) Ayer.

*Book of Joy. Sherwood E. Wirt. LC 94-35095. 256p. Date not set. 17.95 (1-56977-590-7) McCracken Pr.

Book of Joyous Children. James W. Riley. LC 79-98085. (Granger Index Reprint Ser.). 1977. 20.95 (0-8369-6087-4) Ayer.

Book of Jubilees. Tr. by Schodde. LC 80-53467. 96p. 1980. reprint ed. pap. 5.00 (0-934666-07-5) Artisan Sales.

Book of Jubilees: The Little Genesis. Ed. by R. H. Charles. 1988. reprint ed. lib. bdg. 59.00 (0-7812-0101-2) Rprt Serv.

Book of Jubilees: The Little Genesis. Ed. by R. H. Charles. 1984. reprint ed. 59.00 (0-403-08996-4, Regency) Scholarly.

Book of Judas: A Poem. Brendan Kennelly. (Orig.). 1991. 55.00 (1-85224-170-5, Pub. by Bloodaxe Bks UK); pap. 22.00 (1-85224-171-3, Pub. by Bloodaxe Bks UK) Dufour.

Book of Judges. Abraham Shoshana. 308p. (HEB.). (C). 1988. 14.95 (1-881255-03-4) OFEQ Inst.

Book of Judges: Hebrew Text, English Translation & Commentary Digest. Tr. by A. J. Rosenberg. 400p. (HEB.). 1979. 17.95 (0-910818-17-7) Judaica Pr.

Book of Judges see Code of Maimonides

Book of Judging. Selma Wassermann & Jack Wassermann. (Smart Start Ser.). (Illus.). 32p. (J). (gr. k-3). 1990. lib. bdg. 12.85 (0-8027-6950-0); pap. 4.95 (0-8027-9455-6) Walker & Co.

*Book of Judith. Stuart Hood. 160p. 1995. 26.95 (1-85754-186-3) Paul & Co Pubs.

Book of Juniper. Tom Paulin & Noel Connor. 24p. 1981. pap. 6.95 (0-906427-16-9, Pub. by Bloodaxe Bks UK) Dufour.

Book of Jupiter. Marilyn Waram. 320p. (Orig.). 1993. pap. 12.95 (0-935127-28-3) ACS Pubns.

*Book of Kapros. 1988. 12.00 (0-917828-03-8) Personal Dev Ctr.

Book of Karma. Shelly Marshall. 246p. (Orig.). 1994. pap. 12.99 (1-880197-99-5) Gylantic Pub.

Book of Kells. Date not set. 1.00 (0-486-27715-1) Dover.

Book of Kells. (Illus.). 680p. 1991. write for info. (0-8109-4987-3) Abrams.

*Book of Kells. Ben Mackworth-Praed. 1995. 10.00 (0-06-251131-9) Harper SF.

Book of Kells. rev. ed. Bernard Meehan. LC 94-60268. (Illus.). 96p. 1994. pap. 19.95 (0-500-27790-7) Thames Hudson.

Book of Kells: A Selection of Pages Reproduced with Description. George O. Simms. (Illus.). 32p. 1986. pap. 5.95 (0-85105-298-3, Pub. by Colin Smythe Ltd UK) Dufour.

Book of Kells: Proceedings of a Conference at Trinity College, Dublin, 1994. Ed. by Felicity O'Mahony. LC 94-38638. (Illus.). 640p. 1994. 129.95 (0-85967-967-5, Pub. by Scolar Pr UK) Ashgate Pub Co.

848

An Asterisk (*) at the beginning of an entry indicates that the title is appearing in BIP for the first time.

An Asterisk (*) at the beginning of an entry indicates that the title is appearing in BIP for the first time.

849

B

Book of Mark: Jesus - The Servant of Jehovah Fourteenth Annual Spiritual Sword Lectureship. Ed. by Jim Laws. 457p. 1989. 20.00 (*0-9615751-5-8*) Getwell Church.

Book of Marriage Charts. Emylu L. Hughes. LC 85-73303. 262p. 1986. 18.95 (*0-86690-309-7*, H2351-014) Am Fed Astrologers.

Book of Martyrs. Cornelia A. Comer. LC 77-94711. (Short Story Index Reprint Ser.). 1977. 18.95 (*0-8369-3090-8*) Ayer.

***Book of Martyrs.** John Foxe. 245p. Date not set. pap. text ed. write for info. (*0-614-02757-8*) Christ Stewards.

Book of Mary: Prayers in Honor of the Blessed Virgin Mary. rev. ed. 40p. (Orig.). 1987. pap. 1.95 (*1-55586-155-5*) US Catholic.

Book of Masks. Remy De Gourmont. Tr. by J. Lewis. LC 67-26745. (Essay Index Reprint Ser.). 1977. 18.95 (*0-8369-0490-7*) Ayer.

Book of Masks. Hwang Sun-won. Ed. by J. Martin Holman. LC 88-63251. (Readers International Ser.). 200p. (Orig.). 1989. 17.95 (*0-930523-57-1*); pap. 9.95 (*0-930523-58-X*) Readers Intl.

Book of Masonry Stoves: Rediscovering an Old Way of Warming. David Lyle. LC 83-3897. (Illus.). 224p. (Orig.). 1994. pap. 24.95 (*0-931790-57-3*) Brick Hse Pub.

Book of Massage. Lucy Lidell. 192p. 1984. pap. 14.00 (*0-671-54139-0*, Fireside) S&S Trade.

***Book of Massage & Aromatherapy.** Nitya LaCroix. 1994. 14.99 (*0-517-10256-0*) Random Hse Value.

Book of Matthew. Garland Elkins & Thomas B. Warren. 781p. 1988. 25.00 (*0-9615751-4-X*) Getwell Church.

Book of Matthew: What Would You Do If Your Child Was Faced with a Serious Medical Problem? Betty J. Wylie. 1994. pap. 4.99 (*1-56171-285-X*, S P I Bks) Sure Sellers.

Book of Medicines. Linda Hogan. LC 93-7677. 90p. (Orig.). 1993. pap. 11.95 (*1-56689-010-1*) Coffee Hse.

Book of Medieval & Renaissance Alphabets. Comp. by Main Street Press Staff. LC 91-14736. 128p. 1991. pap. 7.95 (*0-8069-8278-0*, Sterling-Main St) Sterling.

Book of Meditation for Everyday in Year. J. Allan. 366p. 1976. 14.95 (*0-318-36382-8*) Asia Bk Corp.

***Book of Meditations: Readings from Phillips Exeter Academy, 1983-1994.** Ed. by Douglas G. Rogers et al. (Orig.). 1995. pap. write for info. (*0-939618-09-5*) Phillips Exeter.

Book of Megillos. Meir Zlotowitz. (ArtScroll Tanach Ser.). 160p. 1986. 14.95 (*0-89906-225-3*) Mesorah Pubns.

Book of Meissen. Robert Rontgen. LC 84-51186. (Illus.). 333p. 1984. 95.00 (*0-88740-014-0*) Schiffer.

Book of Memories: Kent State University, 1910-1992. Ed. by William H. Hildebrand et al. LC 93-109. (Illus.). 336p. 1993. lib. bdg. 49.00 (*0-87338-488-1*) Kent St U Pr.

Book of Memory: A Study of Memory in Medieval Culture. Mary J. Carruthers. (Studies in Medieval Literature: No. 10). (Illus.). 400p. (C). 1992. pap. 22.95 (*0-521-42973-0*) Cambridge U Pr.

Book of Mercy. Leonard Cohen. 114p. 1994. pap. 10.95 (*0-7710-2182-8*, Pub. by McClelland & Stewart CN) Firefly Bks Ltd.

Book of Merlin: Insights from the First Merlin Conference, London, June 1986. Ed. by R. J. Stewart. LC 89-7278. (Illus.). 192p. (C). 1989. reprint ed. lib. bdg. 37.00x (*0-8095-7501-9*) Borgo Pr.

Book of Merlyn. T. H. White. mass mkt. 4.99 (*0-441-07015-9*) Ace Bks.

Book of Merlyn: The Unpublished Conclusion to "The Once & Future King" T. H. White. (Illus.). 159p. (YA). (gr. 10). 1988. reprint ed. pap. 10.95 (*0-292-70769-X*) U of Tex Pr.

***Book of Metaphors, Vol. II.** Michael A. Gass & AEE Staff. 160p. 1995. 28.95 (*0-7872-0306-8*) Kendall-Hunt.

Book of Mexican Foods. Christine Barrett. (Book of Ser.). 120p. 1991. pap. text ed. 10.95 (*1-55788-032-8*) Price Stern.

Book of Middle Eastern Food. Claudia Roden. (Illus.). 1974. pap. 16.00 (*0-394-71948-4*) Knopf.

Book of Middle English. J. A. Burrow & Thorlac Turville-Petre. 368p. (C). 1991. text ed. 64.95 (*0-631-16097-3*); pap. text ed. 22.95 (*0-631-16726-9*) Blackwell Pubs.

***Book of Middle English.** J. A. Burrow & Thorlac Turvill-Petre. (Illus.). (C). 1996. pap. write for info. (*0-631-19353-7*) Blackwell Pubs.

***Book of Middle English.** 2nd ed. J. A. Burrow & Thorlac Turvill-Petre. (Illus.). 384p. (C). 1996. write for info. (*0-631-19352-9*) Blackwell Pubs.

***Book of Middoth.** Rubbeinu Yechiel. Tr. by Shraga Silverstein. 355p. 1994. 15.95 (*0-614-01889-7*) Moznaim.

Book of Military Blunders. Geoffrey Regan. 192p. 1991. lib. bdg. 45.00 (*0-87436-668-2*) ABC-CLIO.

Book of Minerals. Edmond B. Szekely. (Illus.). 40p. 1978. pap. 3.50 (*0-89564-046-5*) IBS Intl.

Book of Miniatures: Furniture & Accessories. Helen Ruthberg. LC 76-451. (Creative Crafts Ser.). 264p. 1977. 19.95 (*0-8019-6366-4*) Chilton.

Book of Mint. Jackie French. (Illus.). 48p. 1993. 9.00 (*0-207-17852-6*, Pub. by Angus & Robertson AT) HarpC.

Book of Minutes: Nineteen Hundred Six to Nineteen Seventeen. (Vol. 1). 304p. 1978. 7.95 (*0-87148-103-0*) Pathway Pr.

Book of Miracles: A Young Person's Guide to Jewish Spirituality. Lawrence Kushner. (Illus.). 96p. (Orig.). (J). (gr. 4-6). 1987. pap. text ed. 7.95 (*0-8074-0323-7*, 123926) UAHC.

Book of Mirdad: A Lighthouse & a Haven. Mikhail Naimy. 192p. 1994. pap. 11.00 (*0-14-019332-4*, Arkana) Viking Penguin.

Book of Miso. William Shurtleff & Akiko Aoyagi. 768p. 1981. mass mkt. 5.99 (*0-345-29107-7*) Ballantine.

Book of Miso. rev. ed. William Shurtleff & Akiko Aoyagi. LC 83-70114. (Illus.). 278p. 1983. 16.95 (*0-89815-098-1*); pap. 16.95 (*0-89815-097-3*) Ten Speed Pr.

Book of Monograms. D. M. Campana. (Illus.). 10.00 (*0-939608-06-5*) Campana Art.

Book of Monologues for Aspiring Actors. 1994. pap. 16.95 (*0-8442-5771-0*, Passport Bks) NTC Pub Grp.

Book of Moonlight. Richard Behm. LC 78-61837. 1978. pap. 5.00 (*0-931350-01-8*) Moonlight Pubns.

Book of Moons. Rosemary Edghill. 1995. 20.95 (*0-312-85605-9*) Forge NYC.

Book of Mordechai: A Study of the Jews of Libya. Mordechai Hakohen. Ed. & Tr. by Harvey E. Goldberg. (C). 1993. 90.00 (*1-85077-230-4*, Darf Pubs Ltd); pap. 75.00 (*1-85077-231-2*, Darf Pubs Ltd) St Mut.

Book of Mormon: Alma, the Testimony of the Word. Ed. by Monte S. Nyman & Charles D. Tate, Jr. 1992. 11.95 (*0-88494-841-2*) Bookcraft Inc.

Book of Mormon: First Nephi, the Doctrinal Foundation. Ed. by Nyman & Tate. (Symposium Ser.: Vol. 2). 10.95 (*0-88494-647-9*) Bookcraft Inc.

Book of Mormon: Helaman Through 3 Nephi 8, According to Thy Word. Ed. by Nyman & Tate. 1992. 11.95 (*0-88494-864-1*) Bookcraft Inc.

Book of Mormon: Jacob Through Words of Mormon, to Learn with Joy. Ed. by Nyman & Tate. (Symposium Ser.: Vol. 4). 11.95 (*0-88494-734-3*) Bookcraft Inc.

Book of Mormon: Mosiah, Salvation Only Through Christ. 1992. 11.95 (*0-88494-816-1*) Bookcraft Inc.

Book of Mormon: Second Nephi, the Doctrinal Structure. Ed. by Nyman & Tate. (Symposium Ser.: Vol. 3). 11.95 (*0-88494-699-1*) Bookcraft Inc.

Book of Mormon: The Keystone Scripture. Ed. by Paul R. Cheesman. (Symposium Ser.: Vol. 1). 10.95 (*0-88494-637-1*) Bookcraft Inc.

Book of Mormon: Three Nephi 9-30, This Is My Gospel. BYU Religious Studies Center Staff. Ed. by Monte S. Nyman & Charles D. Tate, Jr. 1993. 11.95 (*0-88494-913-3*) Bookcraft Inc.

Book of Mormon - Key to Conversion. Glenn L. Pearson. pap. 3.95 (*0-88494-105-1*) Bookcraft Inc.

Book of Mormon Activity Book: Creative Scripture Learning Experiences for Children 4-12. Sandy Halverson. (Illus.). 80p. (J). (gr. 3-8). 1982. pap. 5.98 (*0-88290-188-5*, 4521) Horizon Utah.

***Book of Mormon Circle a Word, Bk. 2.** Matt Canaday & Cindi Canaday. Ed. by Grace Griffin. 51p. (Orig.). (YA). Date not set. student ed, pap. 2.95 (*1-56998-000-4*) Gospel Puzzles.

Book of Mormon Critical Text: A Tool for Scholarly Reference, 3 vols., Set. 2nd rev. ed. F.A.R.M.S. Staff. LC 86-81479. 1331p. 1987. pap. 55.00 (*0-934893-07-1*) FARMS.

Book of Mormon Digest. John D. Hawkes. 240p. 1966. pap. 4.95 (*0-89036-010-3*) Hawkes Pub Inc.

Book of Mormon Puzzles & Pictures for Young Latter-Day Saints. Jean D. Crowther. LC 77-74495. (Books for LDS Children). (Illus.). 56p. (J). (gr. 3 up). 1977. pap. 5.98 (*0-88290-080-3*) Horizon Utah.

Book of Mormon Reflections. Jim Lovalvo. Ed. by James B. Van Treese. 395p. 1993. 14.95 (*1-880416-34-4*) NW Pub.

Book of Mormon Stories for Little Children. Marjorie Johnson. LC 76-3991. (Books for LDS Children). (Illus.). 96p. (Orig.). (J). (ps-7). 1976. pap. 7.98 (*0-88290-063-3*) Horizon Utah.

Book of Mormon Stories for Young LDS. Emma M. Petersen. (J). 9.95 (*0-88494-019-5*) Bookcraft Inc.

Book of Mormon Story & Coloring Book. Illus. by Valerie A. Chadwick. (Orig.). (J). (gr. 3-6). 1993. pap. 4.95 (*0-87579-702-4*) Deseret Bk.

Book of Mormon Summer. Joy S. Lundberg. (J). (gr. 5-8). 1991. 6.95 (*0-915029-00-6*) Cherished Bks.

Book of Moss: Poems by Benjamin Saltman. Benjamin Saltman. 64p. 1992. pap. 7.95 (*0-9633481-0-8*) Blue Beginnings.

Book of Murder. Ron Cowen. 1974. pap. 4.75 (*0-8222-0133-X*) Dramatists Play.

Book of Murder. Ed. by Sebastian Wolfe. 256p. 1992. pap. 12.95 (*0-8184-0564-3*, L Stuart) Carol Pub Group.

Book of Murder. Frederick I. Anderson. 288p. 1987. reprint ed. pap. 5.95 (*0-486-25630-8*) Dover.

Book of Musical Anecdotes: Hundreds of Classic & Little-Known Stories about the World's Greatest Composers & Performers. Norman Lebrecht. LC 85-16809. 480p. 1985. 24.95 (*0-02-918710-9*) Free Pr.

Book of Musical Artwork: An Interpretation of the Musical Theories of Heinrich Schenker. Felix-Eberhard Von Cube. Tr. by David Neumeyer et al. LC 87-4819. (Studies in the History & Interpretation of Music: Vol. 10). 396p. 1987. lib. bdg. 99.95 (*0-88946-436-7*) E Mellen.

Book of Musical Documents. Paul Nettl. LC 73-88991. 381p. 1969. text ed. 65.00 (*0-8371-2116-7*, NEMD, Greenwood Pr) Greenwood.

Book of Musical Knowledge. Arthur Elson. 609p. 1991. reprint ed. lib. bdg. 109.00 (*0-7812-9335-9*) Rprt Serv.

Book of Mysterious & Fateful Stories. Nathaniel Hawthorne. 1991. lib. bdg. 75.00 (*0-8490-4160-0*) Gordon Pr.

Book of Myths. Thomas Bulfinch & H. Sewell. LC 42-25450. (Illus.). 128p. (J). (gr. 5-9). 1969. text ed. 15.95 (*0-02-782280-X*, Mac Bks Young Read) S&S Childrens.

Book of Myths. Amy Cruse. LC 93-17341. (J). 1993. 9.99 (*0-517-09335-9*, Pub. by Gramercy) Random Hse Value.

Book of Name Signs: Naming in American Sign Language. Samuel J. Supalla. 112p. 1992. 12.95 (*0-915035-30-8*, 2228) Dawn Sign.

Book of Names: New & Selected Poems. Barton Sutter. (American Poets Continuum Ser.: Vol. 25). 1993. 25.00 (*0-918526-96-5*); pap. 12.50 (*0-918526-97-3*) BOA Edns.

Book of Names Especially Relating to the Early Palatines & the First Settlers in the Mohawk Valley. Lou D. MacWethy. (Illus.). 209p. 1985. 15.00 (*0-8063-0231-3*, 3620) Genealog Pub.

***Book of Narnians: The Lion, the Witch & the Others.** C. S. Lewis. LC 94-29069. (Illus.). 96p. (J). (gr. 3 up). 1995. 16.95 (*0-06-025009-7*) HarpC Child Bks.

***Book of Narnians: The Lion, the Witch & the Others.** C. S. Lewis. LC 94-29069. (Illus.). 96p. (YA). (gr. 3 up). 1995. lib. bdg. 16.89 (*0-06-025014-3*) HarpC Child Bks.

Book of Narratives. Ed. by Oscar J. Campbell & Richard A. Rice. LC 72-5901. (Short Story Index Reprint Ser.). 1977. reprint ed. 30.95 (*0-8369-4196-9*) Ayer.

Book of National Trust Recipes. Sarah Edington. (Illus.). 160p. 1988. 17.95 (*0-7078-0092-7*, Pub. by Natl Trust UK) Trafalgar.

Book of Nations see **World Book Desk Reference Set**

***Book of Natural Pain Relief.** Chaitow. 1995. mass mkt. 5.99 (*0-06-100886-9*, Harp PBks) HarpC.

Book of Naturalists: An Anthology of the Best Natural History. Ed. by William Beebe. (Illus.). 520p. 1988. 69.50 (*0-691-08466-1*); pap. text ed. 19.95 (*0-691-02408-1*) Princeton U Pr.

Book of Nature. Olaf Pedersen. (C). 1992. pap. 9.95 (*0-268-00690-3*) U of Notre Dame Pr.

Book of Nature: The History of Insects. Thomas Flloyd & John Swammerdam. Ed. by Keir B. Sterling. LC 77-83844. (Biologists & Their World Ser.). (Illus.). 1978. reprint ed. lib. bdg. 56.95 (*0-405-10742-0*) Ayer.

Book of Nature Photography. Heather Angel. 160p. 1982. 50.00 (*0-85223-227-6*, Pub. by Ebury Pr UK) Trafalgar.

Book of Navy Songs. Ed. by Trident Society. LC 27-5084. 159p. 1987. reprint ed. pap. 10.95 (*0-87021-106-4*) Naval Inst Pr.

Book of Needlepoint Stitches. Susan Higginson. 112p. (C). 1989. 65.00 (*0-685-36100-4*, Pub. by Textile Institue UK) St Mut.

Book of Needs. Ed. by St. Tikhon's Monastery Monk. 408p. 1987. 15.00 (*1-878997-15-7*) St Tikhons Pr.

Book of Negro Humor. Langston Hughes. 300p. 1990. reprint ed. lib. bdg. 25.95 (*0-89966-733-3*) Buccaneer Bks.

Book of Neptune. Marilyn Waram. 256p. (Orig.). 1989. pap. 14.95 (*0-917086-84-8*) ACS Pubns.

Book of New Testament Prayers. Ed. by William Lane. 95p. 1988. reprint ed. pap. 5.95 (*1-85390-046-X*, Pub. by Veritas Publns IE) Ignatius Pr.

Book of New Testament Word Studies. (Bible Reference Library). 215p. 1988. pap. 7.95 (*1-55748-031-1*) Barbour & Co.

Book of New York. R. Shackleton. 1977. lib. bdg. 59.95 (*0-8490-1532-4*) Gordon Pr.

Book of New York Firsts. Bradford Moscow. 1989. 9.95 (*0-685-46247-1*, Collier S&S) S&S Trade.

***Book of New York Firsts: Unusual, Arcane, & Fascinating Facts in the Life of New York City.** Henry Moscow. LC 94-39250. (Illus.). 133p. 1995. pap. 14.95 (*0-8156-0308-8*) Syracuse U Pr.

Book of Night. Charles Vess. Ed. by Jerry Prosser. (Illus.). 112p. 1991. pap. 12.95 (*1-878574-25-6*) Dark Horse Comics.

Book of Night. deluxe limited ed. Charles Vess. Ed. by Jerry Prosser. (Illus.). 112p. 1991. 49.95 (*1-56971-034-1*) Dark Horse Comics.

Book of Night: Legends of Shadow & Silence. Daniel Kemp. LC 90-84141. (Illus.). 80p. (Orig.). 1990. pap. 7.77 (*0-9627623-1-8*) Iraya Pubns.

Book of Nightmares. Galway Kinnell. 1973. pap. 11.95 (*0-395-12098-5*) HM.

Book of Nights. Sylvie Germain. Tr. by Christine Donougher. 288p. 1993. 22.95 (*0-87923-975-1*) Godine.

***Book of Nod.** White Wolf Staff. Date not set. per., pap. 8.95 (*1-56504-078-3*, 2251) White Wolf.

Book of Nonsense. Edward Lear. LC 92-53176. (Everyman's Library of Children's Classics). (Illus.). 240p. (J). 1992. 12.95 (*0-679-41798-2*, Evrymans Lib Childs) Knopf.

Book of Nonsense. Mervyn Peake. LC 75-4108. 1975. 10.95 (*0-7206-0412-5*) Dufour.

Book of Nonsense. Comp. by Ernest Rhys. LC 83-45786. reprint ed. 27.50 (*0-404-20215-2*, PN6110) AMS Pr.

Book of North American Birds. Reader's Digest Editors. LC 89-70261. (Illus.). 576p. 1990. 32.95 (*0-89577-351-1*, Random) RD Assn.

***Book of North American Owls.** Helen R. Sattler. (J). (gr. 4-7). 1995. 15.95 (*0-395-60524-5*, Clarion Bks) HM.

Book of Numbers. Timothy R. Ashley. (New International Commentary on the Old Testament Ser.). 745p. (Orig.). 1993. text ed. 34.99 (*0-8028-2354-8*) Eerdmans.

Book of Numbers. Ruth S. Fajfr. pap. 1.99 (*1-56632-027-5*) Revival Lit.

Book of Numbers. Gopi Gyan. Ed. by Morningland Publications, Inc. Staff. 620p. (Orig.). 1980. pap. 10.00 (*0-935146-13-X*) Morningland.

Book of Numerology: Taking a Count of Your Life. Hal A. Lingerman. (Illus.). 160p. (Orig.). 1994. pap. 9.95 (*0-87728-804-6*) Weiser.

Book of Nurbs, Vol 1. Les Pirgl. (Monographs in Visual Communication). 1994. 79.00 (*0-387-55069-0*) Spr-Verlag.

Book of Nursery Songs & Rhymes. S. Baring-Gould. (J). (ps-4). 1972. 59.95 (*0-87968-768-1*) Gordon Pr.

Book of Object Oriented Knowledge. Brian Henderson-Sellers. 270p. 1991. pap. text ed. 45.00 (*0-13-059445-8*) P-H.

Book of Odds: Winning the Lottery, Finding True Love, Losing Your Teeth & Other Chances in Day-to-Day Life. Michael D. Shook & Robert L. Shook. 240p. (Orig.). 1993. pap. 4.99 (*0-451-17748-7*, Sig) NAL-Dutton.

Book of Offerings see **Code of Maimonides**

***Book of Offices & Services: After the Usage of the Order of Saint Luke.** 3rd ed. Timothy J. Crouch. 86p. (Orig.). 1994. 12.95 (*1-878009-24-9*) Order St Luke Pubns.

Book of Ogham: The Celtic Tree Oracle. Edred Thorsson. LC 92-13330. (Illus.). 240p. 1992. pap. 12.95 (*0-87542-783-9*) Llewellyn Pubns.

Book of Old English Ballads. Comp. by Hamilton W. Mabie. LC 79-121929. (Granger Index Reprint Ser.). 1977. 19.95 (*0-8369-6170-6*) Ayer.

Book of Old English Love Songs. Comp. by Hamilton W. Mabie. LC 73-121930. (Granger Index Reprint Ser.). 1977. 19.95 (*0-8369-6171-4*) Ayer.

Book of Old Roses. Dorothy Stemler. 10.95 (*0-8283-1413-6*) Branden Pub Co.

Book of Old Ships: From Egyptian Galleys to Clipper Ships. unabridged ed. Henry B. Culver. LC 92-21987. (Pictorial Archive Ser.). (Illus.). 256p. 1992. reprint ed. pap. text ed. 6.95 (*0-486-27332-6*) Dover.

Book of Old Silver: English, American, Foreign. Seymour B. Wyler. (Illus.). 1937. 26.00 (*0-517-00089-X*, Crown) Crown Pub Group.

Book of One-Hundred Hands. George B. Bridgman. (Illus.). 1972. reprint ed. pap. 4.95 (*0-486-22709-X*) Dover.

Book of One Hundred Type Face Alphabets. Jacob I. Biegeleisen. LC 65-15691. 1974. 12.95 (*0-911380-03-5*) ST Pubns.

Book of One Thousand One Home Health Remedies. Laura N. Beverly et al. Ed. by Cal Beverly. 590p. 1993. text ed. 27.95 (*0-915099-47-0*) FC&A Pub.

Book of One Thousand Plays: A Comprehensive Guide to the Most Frequently Performed Plays. Ed. by Stephen Fletcher & Norman Jopling. LC 88-38121. 352p. reprint ed. pap. 100.40 (*0-7837-6693-9*, 2046310) Bks Demand.

Book of One Tree. Annette R. Schober. LC 91-45466. 64p. (Orig.). 1992. pap. 9.95 (*0-87358-539-9*, Entrada Bks) Northland AZ.

***Book of One's Own.** Thomas Mallon. 318p. 1995. reprint ed. pap. 14.00 (*1-886913-02-1*) Hungry Mind.

Book of One's Own: Developing Literacy Through Making Books. Paul Johnson. LC 91-28908. 119p. 1991. pap. text ed. 19.00 (*0-435-08708-8*, 08708) Heinemann.

Book of Opening the Mouth: The Egyptian Texts with English Translations, 2 vols. in 1. E. Wallis Budge. LC 72-80498. (Illus.). 1980. reprint ed. 36.95 (*0-405-08315-7*, Pub. by Blom Pubns UK) Ayer.

Book of Operas; Their Histories, Plots, & Music: Music Book Index, 2 vols. in 1. Henry E. Drehbiel. 1993. reprint ed. lib. bdg. 99.00 (*0-7812-9720-6*) Rprt Serv.

Book of Operas, Their Histories, Their Plots & Their Music. Henry E. Krehbiel. LC 80-2279. reprint ed. 42.50 (*0-404-18851-6*) AMS Pr.

Book of Orchid. I-Hsiung Ju. LC 89-85946. (Illus.). 140p. 1990. pap. 10.00 (*0-9611726-1-4*) Art Farm Gal.

Book of Orgasms. Nin Andrews. LC 94-70672. 64p. (Orig.). 1994. pap. 8.95 (*1-878580-69-8*) Asylum Arts.

Book of Ornamental Knots. John J. Hensel. LC 89-77912. (Illus.). 176p. 1990. pap. 19.95 (*0-87033-410-7*) Cornell Maritime.

Book of Other Days. Lisa M. Steinman. 1993. 19.95 (*0-934847-17-7*); pap. 9.95 (*0-934847-18-5*) Arrowood Bks.

Book of Our Heritage, 3 vols. Eliyahu Kitov. Tr. by Nathan Bulman. Orig. Title: Sefer HaToda'ah. 1978. pap. 43.95 (*0-87306-157-8*); boxed 53.95 (*0-87306-151-9*) Feldheim.

Book of Our House. David Ballantine & Sylvia Weinberg. LC 86-18231. (Illus.). 288p. 1987. 21.95 (*0-87951-267-9*) Overlook Pr.

Book of Ours. Pat Smith. 64p. 1991. pap. 8.00 (*1-880280-01-9*) St Lazaire.

Book of Outdoor Knots. Peter Owen. (Illus.). 144p. 1993. pap. 12.95 (*1-55821-225-6*) Lyons & Burford.

Book of Owls. Lewis W. Walker. LC 92-30801. (Illus.). 272p. 1993. reprint ed. pap. 19.95 (*0-292-70788-6*) U of Tex Pr.

Book of Pagan Rituals, Vol. 1. Ed. by Herman Slater. 160p. 1978. pap. 13.95 (*0-87728-348-6*) Weiser.

Book of Pain Relief: A Comprehensive Self-Help Guide to Easing & Treating Both Chronic & Short-Term Pain. Leon Chaitow. (Illus.). 1993. pap. 11.00 (*0-7225-2820-5*) Thorsons SF.

Book of Paper Cutting: A Complete Guide to All the Techniques with More than 100 Project Ideas. Chris Rich. LC 92-21536. 128p. 1994. pap. 12.95 (*0-8069-0286-8*) Sterling.

Book of Paper Quilling: Techniques & Projects for Paper Filigree. Malinda Johnson. LC 93-37240. 1994. 24.95 (*0-8069-0598-0*) Sterling.

***Book of Paper Quilling: Techniques & Projects for Paper Filigree.** Malinda Johnston. (Illus.). 144p. 1995. pap. 12.95 (*0-8069-0599-9*) Sterling.

Book of Papercutting: A Complete Guide to All the Techniques with More Than 100 Project Ideas. Chris Rich. LC 92-21536. (Illus.). 128p. (YA). (gr. 10-12). 1993. 24.95 (*0-8069-0285-X*) Sterling.

Book of Pasta. Leslie Mackley. LC 87-8721. 120p. 1987. pap. 10.95 (*0-89586-641-2*) Price Stern.

***Book of Pastoral Prayers: For Special Occasions & Sundays Throughout the Year.** Ralph B. Johnson. 1992. pap. 9.95 (*1-881576-06-X*) Providence Hse.

Book of Pates & Terrines. Friedrich W. Ehlert et al. LC 83-83312. (Illus.). 192p. 1994. 30.00 (*0-688-03896-4*) Hearst Bks.

An Asterisk (*) at the beginning of an entry indicates that the title is appearing in BIP for the first time.

An Asterisk (*) at the beginning of an entry indicates that the title is appearing in BIP for the first time.

851

B

***Book of Saints.** Michael Walsh. LC 94-61084. (Illus.). 160p. (Orig.). 1995. pap. 9.95 (0-89622-628-X) Twenty-Third.

Book of Saints: A Dictionary of Servants of God. Comp. by St. Augustine's Abbey Benedictine Monks. LC 89-33515. (Illus.). 622p. 1993. reprint ed. pap. 24.95 (0-8192-1611-9) Morehouse Pub.

Book of Saints: True Stories of How They Touch Our Lives. Anne Gordon. LC 93-39437. 1994. pap. 12.95 (0-553-37272-6) Bantam.

Book of Salads. Lorna Rhodes. (Book of...Ser.). (Illus.). 120p. (Orig.). 1989. pap. 11.00 (0-89586-791-5, HP Books) Berkley Pub.

Book of Samuel, Vol. 1. Tr. by A. J. Rosenberg. 512p. (HEB.). 1981. 17.95 (0-910818-07-X) Judaica Pr.

Book of Samuel, Vol. 2. Tr. by A. J. Rosenberg. 450p. (HEB.). 1982. 17.95 (0-910818-11-8) Judaica Pr.

Book of Sananda. Thedra. 240p. 1989. pap. 12.95 (0-941131-03-3) ASSK Pub.

Book of Sand. large type ed. Jorge L. Borges. 185p. 1991. 11.47 (1-85290-022-9, Pub. by ISIS UK) Transaction Pubs.

Book of Sandwiches. Julia Ransome. (Book of...Ser.). (Illus.). 120p. (Orig.). 1989. pap. 12.00 (0-89586-789-3, HP Books) Berkley Pub.

Book of Sauces. Gordon Grimsdale. Ed. by Dru A. Degu. (Book of...Ser.). 128p. (Orig.). 1986. pap. 9.95 (0-89586-504-1, HP Books) Berkley Pub.

Book of Scenes for Acting Practice. Marshall Cassady. 128p. 1985. pap. 16.95 (0-8442-5125-9, Natl Textbk) NTC Pub Grp.

Book of Scenes for Aspiring Actors. 1994. pap. 16.95 (0-8442-5769-9, Passport Bks) NTC Pub Grp.

Book of Science. J. Chisholm. (Introductions Ser.). (Illus.). 48p. (J). (gr. 3-6). 1984. pap. 14.95 (0-7460-0830-9) EDC.

Book of Scientific Anecdotes. Ed. by Adrian Berry. LC 92-44255. 239p. (C). 1993. reprint ed. 29.95 (0-87975-806-6); reprint ed. pap. 15.95 (0-87975-836-8) Prometheus Bks.

***Book of Scorpio: An Enchiridion, Vol. 2.** N. K. Oo. (Enchiridions Ser.: Vol. 2 of 12). 80p. 1995. 14.95 (1-56313-639-2) BrownTrout Pubs Inc.

Book of Scottish Poetry. George B. Douglas. LC 77-144506. reprint ed. 64.50 (0-404-08635-7) AMS Pr.

Book of Scoundrels. Charles Whibley. LC 70-174393. 1972. reprint ed. 18.95 (0-405-09066-8) Ayer.

***Book of SCSI: A Guide for Adventurers.** Peter M. Ridge. LC 94-44670. 450p. 1995. pap. 34.95 (1-886411-02-6) No Starch Pr.

Book of Seance: Reaching Out to the Next World. Tom Cowan. 176p. 1994. pap. 8.95 (0-8092-3733-4) Contemp Bks.

Book of Seasons see Libro de las Estaciones

Book of Secrets. Ed. by Marion Buhagiar. LC 86-31050. 420p. 1988. 50.00 (0-88723-003-2) Boardroom.

Book of Secrets of Albertus Magnus of the Virtues of Herbs, Stones & Certain Beasts; Also, a Book of the Marvels of the World. Albertus Magnus. Ed. by Michael R. Best. (Illus.). 1974. reprint ed. pap. 7.95 (0-19-519786-0) OUP.

Book of Seeing with One's Own Eyes. Sharon Doubiago. LC 87-81373. (Short Fiction Ser.). 212p. 1988. pap. 10.95 (1-55597-101-6) Graywolf.

***Book of Self & Other Drawings.** Gary Turchin. (Illus.). 64p. (Orig.). 1995. pap. 9.95 (0-9646099-7-5) Little Green Man.

Book of Ser Marco Polo: The Venetian Concerning the Kingdom & Marvels of the East, 2 vols., Set. 3rd ed. Henry Yule & Henri Cordier. 1497p. 1993. 115.00 (81-215-0602-6, Pub. by M Manoharial II) Coronet Bks.

***Book of Serenity.** 1994. 34.95 (0-940262-24-X) Lindisfarne Pr.

Book of Services. United Reformed Church in England & Wales, Doctrine & Worship Committee. 1980. 8.95 (0-7152-0446-7) Outlook.

Book of Sex Lists. Albert B. Gerber. 1981. 12.00 (0-8184-0320-9) Carol Pub Group.

Book of Shadowboxes: A Story of the ABC's. Laura L. Seeley. (Illus.). 64p. (J). (ps-3). 1990. 16.95 (0-934601-65-8) Peachtree Pubs.

Book of Shadowboxes: A Story of the ABC's. Laura L. Seeley. (Illus.). 64p. (J). (ps-3). 1993. reprint ed. pap. 8.95 (1-56145-072-3) Peachtree Pubs.

Book of Shadows. Hilary Llewellyn-Williams. 104p. (Orig.). 1990. pap. 17.95 (1-85411-041-1, Pub. by Seren Bks UK) Dufour.

Book of Shadows: Personal Use. Papa Jim, pseud. Ed. by Leticia M. Ayala. (Illus.). 60p. 1990. pap. 3.95 (1-878575-05-8) El Rey Pub.

Book of Shadows: Players Guide. Phil Brucato. (Mage). 250p. 1994. per., pap. 18.00 (1-56504-119-4, 4050) White Wolf.

Book of Shaker Furniture. John Kassay. LC 79-4017. (Illus.). 288p. 1980. 60.00 (0-87023-275-4) U of Mass Pr.

Book of Shakespeare Plays & Pageants. Orie L. Hatcher. (BCL1-PR English Literature Ser.). 339p. 1992. reprint ed. lib. bdg. 89.00 (0-7812-7284-X) Rprt Serv.

Book of Shapes. Eric Hill. (S.S. Happiness Crew Ser.). (J). (ps). 6.95 (0-317-13666-6) Determined Prods.

Book of Shares. Edmond Jabes. Tr. by Rosmarie Waldrop. LC 89-4928. (Religion & Postmodernism Ser.). 112p. 1989. 14.95 (0-226-38886-7) U Ch Pr.

Book of Sharks. Richard Ellis. 1989. pap. 35.00 (0-679-72210-6) Knopf.

Book of Shiatsu. Paul Lundberg. (Illus.). 128p. (Orig.). 1992. pap. 14.95 (0-671-74488-7, Fireside) S&S Trade.

Book of Shiatsu: A Guide to a Traditional Healing Art. Saul Goodman. (Illus.). 230p. (Orig.). 1990. pap. 12.95 (0-89529-454-0) Avery Pub.

Book of Short Stories. Louise Neaderland. (Illus.). 1986. 25.00 (0-942561-11-2) Bone Hollow.

Book of Short Stories. Ed. by Stuart P. Sherman. LC 74-169562. (Short Story Index Reprint Ser.). 1977. reprint ed. 24.95 (0-8369-4025-3) Ayer.

Book of Sibyls. Margherita Guidacci. Tr. by Ruth Feldman. LC 89-61083. 64p. (ENG & ITA.). 1989. pap. 7.95 (0-937672-26-2) Rowan Tree.

Book of Signs. Rudolf Koch. Tr. by Vyvyan Holland. 1930. pap. 3.95 (0-486-20162-7) Dover.

Book of Silk. Philippa Scott. LC 92-80127. (Illus.). 274p. 1993. 65.00 (0-500-23662-3) Thames Hudson.

Book of Silly Lists. Patrick M. Reynolds. LC 92-38660. (J). 1993. 1.25 (0-89375-354-8) Troll Assocs.

Book of Similes (Gi) 1992. 50.00 (0-7189-0219-X, Pub. by Aris & Phillips UK) David Brown.

Book of Sir Marco Polo, the Venetian, Concerning the Kingdoms & Marvels of the East, 3 vols., 1. 3rd ed. Marco Polo. Ed. & Tr. by Henry Yule. LC 74-5240. reprint ed. write for info. (0-404-11541-1) AMS Pr.

Book of Sir Marco Polo, the Venetian, Concerning the Kingdoms & Marvels of the East, 3 vols., 2. 3rd ed. Marco Polo. Ed. & Tr. by Henry Yule. LC 74-5240. reprint ed. write for info. (0-404-11542-X) AMS Pr.

Book of Sir Marco Polo, the Venetian, Concerning the Kingdoms & Marvels of the East, 3 vols., 3. 3rd ed. Marco Polo. Ed. & Tr. by Henry Yule. LC 74-5240. reprint ed. write for info. (0-404-11543-8) AMS Pr.

Book of Sir Marco Polo, the Venetian, Concerning the Kingdoms & Marvels of the East, 3 vols., Set. 3rd ed. Marco Polo. Ed. & Tr. by Henry Yule. LC 74-5240. reprint ed. write for info. (0-404-11540-3) AMS Pr.

Book of Sir Thomas More. Ed. by W. W. Greg. (Malone Society Ser.: No. 28). (Illus.). 148p. 1991. 49.95 (0-19-729016-7) OUP.

Book of Sixteen Thousand to Sixty Thousand Dollar Post Office Jobs: Where They Are, What They Pay, & How to Get Them. Veltisezar B. Bautista. LC 88-72061. 192p. 1989. pap. 14.95 (0-931613-04-3) Bkhaus.

Book of Sixty Hand-Lettered Alphabets. J. I. Biegeleisen. 1976. 10.95 (0-911380-40-X) ST Pubns.

Book of Slice. Katherine Dunn. (Illus.). (Orig.). 1989. pap. 4.95 (0-9624513-0-4) City Roses News.

Book of Slugs: A Guide to Slug Fun in the Garden & the Home. Jeff Moore & Geoff Carlton. (Illus.). 140p. 1982. pap. 4.95 (0-9606752-1-3) Sauvie Island.

Book of Smith. Elsdon C. Smith. (Illus.). 228p. 1984. reprint ed. 18.95 (0-8290-2355-0) Irvington.

Book of Snakes. John Burton. 1991. 14.99 (0-517-06093-0) Random Hse Value.

Book of Snedekers. Walter C. Snedeker. 320p. 1993. 39.95 (1-878853-19-8) Venture Pr FL.

Book of Soba. James Udesky. LC 87-82855. 160p. 1988. 14.95 (0-87011-860-9) Kodansha.

***Book of Soba.** James Udesky. 240p. Date not set. 9.95 (4-7700-1956-4) FS&G.

Book of Sodom. Paul Hallam. 1993. 24.95 (0-86091-476-3, B2487, Pub. by Verso UK) Routledge Chapman & Hall.

***Book of Sodom.** Paul Hallam. 240p. 1995. pap. 18.95 (1-85984-042-6, C0507, Pub. by Verso UK) Routledge Chapman & Hall.

Book of Soldiers: The Journey from War to Peace. Chuck Dean. (Illus.). 1991. pap. write for info. (0-9622413-2-6) Wine Pr Pub.

Book of Solo Games. Gyles Brandreth. 1991. 7.99 (0-517-05949-5) Random Hse Value.

Book of Solving Problems. Selma Wassermann & Jack Wassermann. (Smart Start Ser.). (Illus.). 32p. (J). (gr. k-3). 1990. lib. bdg. 12.85 (0-8027-6954-3); pap. 4.95 (0-8027-9457-2) Walker & Co.

Book of Songs. David B. Hopes. 105p. (Orig.). 1991. pap. 12.04 (0-685-48257-X) Dayspring Pr.

Book of Sonnets. Alan Rickard. pap. 7.00 (0-936128-17-8) De Young Pr.

Book of Sound Therapy: Heal Yourself with Music & Voice. Olivea Dewhurst-Maddock. LC 92-13804. 1993. pap. 14.00 (0-671-78639-3, Fireside) S&S Trade.

***Book of Southern Wisdom: Common Sense & Uncommon Genius from 101 Great Southerns.** Criswell Freeman. (Wisdom Ser.). 156p. (Orig.). 1994. pap. 5.95 (0-9640955-3-X) Walnut Gr Pr.

Book of Soybeans: Nature's Miracle Protein. Tokuji Watanade & Asako Kishi. LC 81-80832. (Illus.). 192p. 1984. pap. 13.95 (0-87040-513-6) Japan Pubns USA.

Book of Space Contacts. Timothy G. Beckley. (Illus.). 72p. 1981. pap. 9.95 (0-938294-05-9) Glob Comm-Inner Lght.

Book of Space Facts & Records. Stuart Atkinson. 1990. 8.99 (0-517-03051-9) Random Hse Value.

Book of Spanish Cooking. Hilaire Walden. (Illus.). 120p. (Orig.). 1993. pap. 10.95 (1-55788-063-8, HP Books) Berkley Pub.

***Book of Special Days.** Charles Apt. Date not set. 16.00 (0-614-01773-4) Gibson.

***Book of Spells: First Third.** Gerald Burns. LC 79-2568. (Lucky Heart Book Ser.). reprint ed. pap. 25.00 (0-7837-9098-8, 2049848) Bks Demand.

Book of Spiders & Scorpions. Rod Preston. 1991. 14.99 (0-517-06092-2) Random Hse Value.

Book of Spinechillers. E. Fischel & K. Dolby. (Spinechillers Ser.). (Illus.). 144p. (J). (gr. 4 up). 1994. pap. 9.95 (0-7460-0718-3, Usborne) EDC.

Book of Splendours. Eliphas Levi. 191p. (ENG.). 1973. 10.95 (0-87728-614-0) Weiser.

Book of Sports Trophies. Brian A. Wynne & Jerry C. Wynne. LC 82-71438. 192p. 1984. 25.00 (0-8453-4746-2, Cornwall Bks) Assoc Univ Prs.

Book of Squares: Leonardo Pisano "Fibonacci"--An Annotated Translation into English by L. E. Sigler. L. E. Sigler. 100p. 1987. text ed. 41.00 (0-12-643130-2) Acad Pr.

Book of Stillmeadow. Gladys Taber. reprint ed. lib. bdg. 21.95 (0-89190-593-6, Rivercity Pr) Amereon Ltd.

***Book of Stillmeadow.** Gladys Taber. (American Autobiography Ser.). 273p. 1995. reprint ed. lib. bdg. 79.00 (0-7812-8649-2) Rprt Serv.

Book of Stir-Fry Dishes. Elizabeth Wolf-Cohen. (Illus.). 120p. 1994. pap. 11.00 (1-55788-085-9, HP Books) Berkley Pub.

Book of Stone: Alchemy & Pyramids, Vol. I. 2nd ed. Joseph Davidovits. Tr. by Andrew C. James & Jacqueline James. (Illus.). 252p. 1984. reprint ed. pap. text ed. 11.95 (2-902933-09-6) Geopolymer Inst.

Book of Stones. L. Dean James. 320p. (Orig.). 1993. pap. 4.50 (1-56076-639-5) TSR Inc.

Book of Stories. Caleb Gattegno. (Illus.). 99p. 1964. pap. 2.00 (0-87825-060-3) Ed Solutions.

***Book of Storyteller Secrets & Changeling Screen.** Deirdre Brooks & Ian Lemke. (Changeling Ser.). 64p. 1995. per., pap. 18.00 (1-56504-702-8, 7001) White Wolf.

Book of Strangers: A Novel. Ian Dallas. LC 88-16114. 151p. 1988. 44.50 (0-88706-990-8); pap. 14.95 (0-88706-991-6) State U NY Pr.

Book of Stratagems: Tactics for Triumph & Survival. Ed. & Tr. by Myron B. Gubitz. 416p. 1993. pap. 14.00 (0-14-016954-7, Penguin Bks) Viking Penguin.

Book of Stress Survival: Identifying & Reducing the Stress in Your Life. Alix Kirsta. (Illus.). 192p. 1987. pap. 14.00 (0-671-63026-1, Fireside) S&S Trade.

Book of Stupid Questions. Tom Weller. 1988. 3.95 (0-446-38972-2) Warner Bks.

Book of Subtyl Histories & Fables of Esope. Aesopus. Bd. with Siege of Rhodes. LC 76-14086. LC 76-14086. 1975. reprint ed. 60.00 (0-8201-1154-6) Schol Facsimiles.

Book of Success. Richard Shea. LC 93-30087. 192p. (J). 1993. 12.95 (1-55853-254-4) Rutledge Hill Pr.

Book of Sufi Healing. Shaykh H. Chishti. 1991. pap. 16.95 (0-89281-324-5) Inner Tradit.

Book of Superchallenging Puzzles. Wayne R. Williams. 1993. mass mkt. 8.99 (0-440-50542-9) Dell.

Book of Superiority of Dogs over Many of Those Who Wear Clothes. Al-Marzuban. 35.00 (0-85668-090-7, Pub. by Aris & Phillips UK) David Brown.

***Book of Surrealist Games.** Mel Gooding & Alistair Brotchie. 1995. pap. 10.00 (1-57062-084-9) Shambhala Pubns.

Book of Survey Techniques. Joseph M. Viladas. LC 82-90995. 278p. 1982. spiral bd. 86.50 (0-911397-00-0) Havemeyer Bks.

Book of Sushi. Kinjiro Omae & Yuzuru Tachibana. LC 81-80658. 128p. 1988. pap. 15.00 (0-87011-866-8) Kodansha.

***Book of Sushi.** Kinjiro Omae & Yuzuru Tachibana. 180p. Date not set. 9.95 (4-7700-1954-8) FS&G.

***Book of Swamp & Bog: Tres, Shrubs & Wildflowers of the Eastern Freshwater Wetlands.** John Eastman. LC 94-33396. (Illus.). 1994. 16.95 (0-8117-2518-9) Stackpole.

Book of Sweets. Marina Schinz. LC 94-1545. 1994. write for info. (0-8109-3131-1) Abrams.

Book of Synonyms. 1991. lib. bdg. 300.00 (0-8490-4161-9) Gordon Pr.

Book of Synonyms. Oliver Stonor. 1966. pap. 3.95 (0-8065-0191-X, 237, Citadel Pr) Carol Pub Group.

Book of Tahkemoni. Judah Al-Harizi. Tr. by David Segal. (Littman Library of Jewish Civilization). 1996. lib. bdg. write for info. (0-19-710062-7, Pub. by Littman Lib Jew UK) Bnai Brith Bk.

Book of Takes. Paul Zelevansky. LC 76-1809. 1976. 18.00 (0-9605610-0-5) P Zelevansky.

Book of Tales, Being Myths of the North American Indians. Charles E. Wood. 1973. 59.95 (0-87968-770-3) Gordon Pr.

Book of Tales by A. B. C. Tr. by John E. Keller & L. Clark Keating. LC 91-32595. (Iberica Ser.: Vol. 3). 300p. (C). 1992. text ed. 50.95 (0-8204-1731-9) P Lang Pubs.

***Book of Talismans, Amulets & Zodiacal Gems.** William Thomas & Kate Pavitt. (Illus.). 292p. 1994. pap. 18.95 (1-56459-461-0) Kessinger Pub.

Book of Tap. Jerry Ames & Jim Siegelman. (Illus.). 224p. 1977. pap. 6.95 (0-679-50632-2) McKay.

Book of Tarot: Companion to the Morgan Greer Deck. Susan Gerulskis-Estes. (Illus.). 96p. 1981. pap. 9.95 (0-88079-277-9) US Games Syst.

***Book of Tarts: Form, Function & Flavor at the City Bakery.** Maury Rubin. LC 94-32734. 1995. write for info. (0-688-12254-X) Morrow.

Book of Tax Knowledge. Boardroom's Experts & Editors. LC 88-13935. 340p. 1989. 50.00 (0-88723-012-1) Boardroom.

Book of Tea. (Illus.). 140p. 1989. boxed 15.95 (0-87011-941-9) Kodansha.

***Book of Tea.** John P. Beilenson. (Die-Cuts Ser.). (Illus.). 80p. (Orig.). 1995. pap. 5.99 (0-88088-928-4) Peter Pauper.

Book of Tea. Okakura Kakuzo. LC 56-13134. (Illus.). 154p. 1956. bds. 14.95 (0-8048-0069-3) C E Tuttle.

Book of Tea. Kakuzo Okakura. Ed. by Everett F. Bleiler. 1906. pap. 2.95 (0-486-20070-1) Dover.

Book of Tea. Alain Stella et al. (Illus.). 256p. 1992. 50.00 (2-08-013533-3, Pub. by Flammarion) Abbeville Pr.

Book of Tea. Kakuzo Okakura. 144p. 1991. reprint ed. pap. 8.00 (4-7700-1542-9) Kodansha.

Book of Tea. Kakuzo Okakura. LC 92-50737. (Illus.). 200p. 1993. reprint ed. pap. 6.00 (0-87773-918-8, Sham Pocket Class) Shambhala Pubns.

Book of Tempeh: Professional Edition. William Shurtleff & Akiko Aoyagi. LC 78-20185. (Illus.). 248p. 1980. reprint ed. 16.95 (0-933332-05-X) Soyfoods Center.

Book of Temple Service see Code of Maimonides

Book of Ten. Harriet Zinnes. 7.50 (0-317-39747-8) Bellevue Pr.

Book of Ten. deluxe ed. Harriet Zinnes. 12.50 (0-317-39746-X) Bellevue Pr.

Book of Tens. Mark Podwal. LC 93-43871. (Illus.). 24p. (J). 1994. 15.00 (0-688-12994-3); lib. bdg. 14.93 (0-688-12995-1) Greenwillow.

Book of Texas. H. Y. Benedict. 1993. reprint ed. lib. bdg. 75.00 (0-7812-5865-0) Rprt Serv.

Book of Texas Bests. Kirk Dooley. LC 88-10185. 192p. 1988. pap. 8.95 (0-87833-584-6, F600M) Taylor Pub.

***Book of Texas Wisdom: Common Sense & Uncommon Genius from 101 Great Texans.** Criswell Freeman. (Wisdom Ser.). 160p. (Orig.). Date not set. pap. 5.95 (0-9640955-8-0) Walnut Gr Pr.

Book of Thai Cooking. Hilaire Walden. (Book of Ser.). (Illus.). 120p. (Orig.). 1992. pap. 12.00 (1-55788-038-7, HP Books) Berkley Pub.

Book of Thanks. Helen S. Rice. LC 93-3967. (Illus.). 96p. 1993. 13.99 (0-8007-1695-7) Revell.

***Book of Thanksgiving.** Paul Dickson. LC 95-7694. 1995. pap. write for info. (0-399-52163-1, Perigee Bks) Berkley Pub.

Book of the Akita. Joan M. Brearley. (Illus.). 272p. 1985. text ed. 34.95 (0-86622-053-4, H-1075) TFH Pubns.

***Book of the Akita.** Joan M. Brearley. 1985. 34.95 (0-86622-048-8) TFH Pubns.

Book of the American Indian. Hamlin Garland. (Collected Works of Hamlin Garland). 1988. reprint ed. lib. bdg. 79.00 (0-7812-1248-0) Rprt Serv.

Book of the American Indian see Collected Works of Hamlin Garland

Book of the American Indians. Howard E. Bovert & Marlene S. Baranzini. LC 93-3068. (USKids History Ser.). (Illus.). (J). (gr. 1-8). 1993. 19.95 (0-316-96921-4) Little.

Book of the American Indians. Howard E. Bovert & Marlene S. Baranzini. LC 93-3068. (USKids History Ser.). (Illus.). (J). (gr. 1-8). 1994. pap. 10.95 (0-316-22208-9) Little.

Book of the American Pit Bull Terrier. Richard F. Stratton. (Illus.). 352p. 1989. 29.95 (0-86622-719-9, H-1024) TFH Pubns.

Book of the American Revolution. Howard E. Bovert et al. LC 93-21769. (USKids History Ser.). (Illus.). (YA). (gr. 9-12). 1994. 19.95 (0-316-96922-2) Little.

Book of the Archpriest of Hita (Libro de buen amor) Juan Ruiz. Tr. by Mack Singleton. x, 182p. 1975. 7.50 (0-942260-06-6) Hispanic Seminary.

Book of the Artists. Henry Tuckerman. 639p. 1993. reprint ed. lib. bdg. 109.00 (0-7812-5290-3) Rprt Serv.

Book of the Banshee. Anne Fine. LC 91-23715. (YA). (gr. 7 up). 1992. 13.95 (0-316-28315-0) Little.

Book of the Banshee. Anne Fine. (J). (gr. 4-7). 1994. pap. 2.95 (0-590-46926-6) Scholastic Inc.

Book of the Basques. Rodney Gallop. LC 79-174355. (Illus.). 1972. reprint ed. 18.95 (0-405-08548-6, Pub. by Blom Pubns UK) Ayer.

Book of the Basques. Rodney Gallop. LC 76-137133. (Basque Ser.). (Illus.). xv, 318p. 1970. reprint ed. 24.95 (0-87417-029-X) U of Nev Pr.

Book of the Beast: The Secret Books of Paradys Two. Tanith Lee. 240p. 1991. 19.95 (0-87951-417-5) Overlook Pr.

Book of the Beginnings. Gerald Massey. (African Heritage Classical Research Studies). 654p. reprint ed. 75.00 (0-938818-58-9) ECA Assoc.

Book of the Beginnings, 2 vols., 1. Gerald Massey. reprint ed. write for info. (0-933121-63-6) Black Classic.

Book of the Beginnings, 2 vols., 2. Gerald Massey. reprint ed. write for info. (0-933121-64-4) Black Classic.

Book of the Beginnings, 2 vols., Set. G. Massey. 1991. lib. bdg. 119.95 (0-8490-4294-1) Gordon Pr.

Book of the Beginnings, 2 vols., Set. Gerald Massey. 1187p. 1987. spiral bd. 82.50 (0-7873-0585-5) Mokelumne.

Book of the Beginnings, 2 vols., Set. Gerald Massey. reprint ed. 75.00 (0-685-72903-6) Black Classic.

Book of the Beginnings: Egypt, Africa & the Cultural & Historic Heritage of the Black Race, African Origins of Mankind, 2 vols. Gerald Massey. 1991. lib. bdg. 199.75 (0-8490-5040-5) Gordon Pr.

Book of the Beginnings, Vols. 1-2: Containing an Attempt to Recover & Reconstitute the Lost Origins of the Myths & Mysteries, Types & Symbols, Religion & Language, with Egypt for the Mouthpiece & Africa as the Birthplace, Set. Gerald Massey. 1187p. 1992. pap. 57.00 (1-56459-149-2) Kessinger Pub.

Book of the Bench. rev. ed. Lesley Ward. (Illus.). 78p. 1985. reprint ed. boxed, lib. bdg. 45.00 (0-379-20795-8) Oceana.

Book of the Blockade. Ales Adamovich & Danill Granin. 496p. 1983. 65.50 (0-317-53845-4, Pub. by Collets UK) Pro-Am Music.

Book of the Body Politic. Christine De Pizan. Ed. & Tr. by Kate L. Forhan. LC 93-37130. (Cambridge Texts in the History of Political Thought Ser.). 160p. (C). 1994. 44.95 (0-521-41050-9) Cambridge U Pr.

Book of the Body Politic. Christine De Pizan. Ed. & Tr. by Kate L. Forhan. LC 93-37130. (Cambridge Texts in the History of Political Thought Ser.). 160p. (C). 1994. pap. 14.95 (0-521-42259-0) Cambridge U Pr.

Book of the Book. Idries Shah. 146p. 1976. 18.00 (0-900860-12-X, Pub. by Octagon Pr UK) ISHK Bk Service.

Book of the Books, Vol. 1. Osho Rajneesh. Ed. by Rajneesh Foundation International. LC 82-50462. (Buddha Ser.). 360p. (Orig.). 1982. pap. 9.95 (0-88050-513-3) Osho Chidvilas.

Book of the Books, Vol. 2. Osho Rajneesh. Ed. by Ma P. Asha. LC 82-50462. (Buddha Ser.). 352p. (Orig.). 1983. pap. 4.95 (0-88050-514-1) Osho Chidvilas.

An Asterisk (*) at the beginning of an entry indicates that the title is appearing in BIP for the first time.

An Asterisk (*) at the beginning of an entry indicates that the title is appearing in BIP for the first time.

853

Book of the Thousand Nights & One Night, 4 vols., Set. E. Powys Mathers. 1986. 37.50 (*0-7102-0869-3*, A5329, RKP) Routledge.
Book of the Three Dragons. Kenneth Morris. Ed. by R. Reginald & Douglas Melville. LC 77-84257. (Lost Race & Adult Fantasy Ser.). 1978. reprint ed. lib. bdg. 23.95 (*0-405-11001-4*) Ayer.
Book of the Toad: A Natural & Magical History of Toad-Human Relations. Robert M. DeGraaff. (Illus.). 192p. 1991. pap. 19.95 (*0-89281-261-3*) Inner Tradit.
Book of the Torah. Thomas W. Mann. LC 87-25079. 1988. pap. 15.99 (*0-8042-0085-8*, John Knox) Westminster John Knox.
Book of the True Life, Vol. I. abr. ed. Tr. by Emilio B. Villanueva. Orig. Title: Libro de la Vida Verdadera. (Illus.). 376p. (Orig.). (SPA.). 1983. text ed. 12.00 (*0-912753-00-5*); pap. 6.00 (*0-912753-01-3*) True Life Found.
Book of the Twenty-Two: The All American Caliber. Sam Fadala. (Illus.). 288p. (Orig.). 1989. pap. 16.95 (*0-88317-149-X*) Stoeger Pub Co.
***Book of the Twilight Graphic Novel.** Mark Ricketts. (Illus.). 144p. 1994. 13.95 (*0-941613-63-1*) Stabur Pr.
Book of the Unknown. Harold Woods & Geraldine Woods. LC 82-3683. (Illus.). 72p. (J). (gr. 4-7). 1982. lib. bdg. 5.99 (*0-394-95233-2*) Random Bks Yng Read.
Book of the Vision Quest. Steven Foster. 1989. pap. 10.00 (*0-671-76189-7*) P-H.
Book of the Vision Quest. 2nd ed. Steven Foster & Meredith Little. LC 80-22810. (Illus.). 160p. reprint ed. pap. 8.95 (*0-943404-04-5*) Bear Tribe.
Book of the West Highland White Terrier. Anna K. Nicholas. (Illus.). 224p. 1993. 29.95 (*0-86622-663-X*, TS187) TFH Pubns.
Book of the West Indies. A. Verrill. 1976. lib. bdg. 59.95 (*0-8490-1533-2*) Gordon Pr.
Book of the Wilders: The History from 1497 in England, the Emigration of Martha, a Widow, & Her Family to Massachusetts Bay 1638, Her Family to 1875 with a Genealogical Table. W. Wilder. (Illus.). 410p. 1989. reprint ed. lib. bdg. 60.00 (*0-8328-1268-4*); reprint ed. pap. 50.00 (*0-8328-1269-2*) Higginson Bk Co.
Book of the Words. Albert Pike. 180p. 1992. pap. 24.95 (*1-56459-161-1*) Kessinger Pub.
Book of the Wyrm. (Werewolf). per., pap. 15.00 (*1-56504-041-4*, 3200) White Wolf.
Book of the Year: Middle American Calendrical Systems. Ed. by Munro S. Edmonson. LC 88-5642. 240p. 1988. 40.00 (*0-87480-288-1*) U of Utah Pr.
Book of the Yorkshire Terrier. Joan M. Brearley. LC 84-148045. (Illus.). 352p. 1984. 34.95 (*0-87666-940-2*, H-1066) TFH Pubns.
Book of Thel: A Facsimile & a Critical Text. William Blake. Ed. by Nancy Bogen. LC 74-155857. 98p. reprint ed. pap. 28.00 (*0-8357-7343-4*, 2023011) Bks Demand.
Book of Theodicy: A Translation & Commentary on the Book of Job by Saadiah Ben Joseph Al-Fayyumi. Lenn E. Goodman. (C). 1988. text ed. 75.00 (*0-300-03743-0*) Yale U Pr.
Book of Think: Or How to Solve Problems Twice Your Size. Marilyn Burns. (Brown Paper School Bks.). (Illus.). (J). (gr. 5 up). 1976. pap. 10.95 (*0-316-11743-9*) Little.
Book of Thoth. Aleister Crowley. LC 79-16399. (Illus.). 287p. 1977. pap. 10.95 (*0-913866-12-1*) US Games Syst.
Book of Thoth. Aleister Crowley. LC 79-16399. (Illus.). 308p. 1974. reprint ed. pap. 12.95 (*0-87728-268-4*) Weiser.
Book of Thoughts. Richard A. French. 1994. 8.95 (*0-533-11001-7*) Vantage.
Book of Three. Lloyd Alexander. (Prydain Chronicles Ser.). 192p. (J). (gr. k-6). 1978. mass mkt. 3.99 (*0-440-40702-8*, YB) Dell.
Book of Three. Lloyd Alexander. LC 64-18250. 224p. (J). (gr. 4-6). 1964. 16.95 (*0-8050-0874-8*, Bks Young Read) H Holt & Co.
Book of Thyme. Jackie French. (Illus.). 48p. 1993. 9.00 (*0-207-17855-0*, Pub. by Angus & Robertson AT) HarpC.
Book of Time. William Whallon. LC 89-81155. (Illus.). 67p. 1990. 20.00 (*0-9624631-2-4*) Bennett & Kitchel.
Book of Tobit. Tr. by Frank Zimmermann. LC 58-11288. (Jewish Apocryphal Literature Ser.). xii, 190p. (C). 1958. text ed. 15.00 (*0-685-46286-2*, Ctr Judaic Studies) Eisenbrauns.
Book of Tofu. William Shurtleff & Akiko Aoyagi. 1987. mass mkt. 5.99 (*0-345-35181-9*) Ballantine.
Book of Tofu. rev. ed. William Shurtleff & Akiko Aoyagi. LC 83-70113. (Illus.). 336p. 1983. pap. 15.95 (*0-89815-095-7*) Ten Speed Pr.
Book of Tokens: Tarot Meditations. enl. rev. ed. Paul F. Case. (Illus.). 200p. 1974. reprint ed. 16.00 (*0-938002-00-7*) Builders of Adytum.
Book of Tomatoes. National Gardening Association Staff. 1987. pap. 4.95 (*0-394-75000-4*, Villard Bks) Random.
Book of Topiary. Charles H. Curtis & W. Gibson. LC 84-50509. (Illus.). 80p. 1986. reprint ed. pap. 8.95 (*0-8048-1491-0*) C E Tuttle.
Book of Torts see Code of Maimonides
Book of Total Happiness: Stop AIDS! For Preventions, & Others, Read. Gabriel B. Atsepoyi. 130p. 1993. 13.95 (*0-9636951-0-X*) Gabriel Pubng.
Book of Totally Useless Information. Donald A. Voorhees. LC 92-38786. 1993. 7.95 (*0-8065-1405-1*, Citadel Pr) Carol Pub Group.
***Book of Traces.** Ed. by Volker Deikert & Grzegorz Rozenberg. LC 94-39387. 568p. 1995. text ed. 112.00 (*981-02-2058-8*) World Scientific Pub.
Book of Trades in the Iconography of Social Typology. Hellmut Lehmann-Haupt. 1976. 3.00 (*0-89073-010-5*) Boston Public Lib.
Book of Trades of Jan Van Vliet. Harry Bober. LC 81-69221. (Illus.). 39p. 1981. 8.00 (*0-317-64496-3*) Early Am Indus.
Book of Trades, or Library of the Useful Arts see Early Nineteenth-Century Crafts & Trades
Book of Trades, or Library of the Useful Arts see Old-Time Crafts & Trades
Book of Trades (Standebuch) Jost Amman & Hans Sachs. Tr. by Stanley Appelbaum & Benjamin Rifkin. LC 72-75581. (Pictorial Archive Ser.). Orig. Title: Eygentliche Beschreibung Aller Stande Auff Erden. (Illus.). 1973. reprint ed. 6.95 (*0-486-22886-X*) Dover.
Book of Travellers' Tales. Comp. by Eric Newby. 576p. 1987. pap. 10.95 (*0-14-009567-5*, Penguin Bks) Viking Penguin.
Book of Treasured Poems. Ed. by William R. Bowlin. LC 72-3090. (Granger Index Reprint Ser.). 1977. reprint ed. 22.95 (*0-8369-8234-7*) Ayer.
Book of Trials. Travers Humphreys. LC 79-8065. reprint ed. 26.50 (*0-404-18376-X*) AMS Pr.
Book of Tributes: Early Sixteenth-Century Nahuatl Censuses from Morelos - Museo De Antropologia E Historia, Archivo Historico, Coleccion Antigua, Vol. 549. Ed. & Tr. by S. L. Cline. LC 92-35264. (Latin American Studies - Nahuatl Ser.: Vol. 81, No. 4). 1993. 18.95 (*0-87903-082-8*) UCLA Lat Am Ctr.
Book of Troilus & Criseyde. Geoffrey Chaucer. (BCL1-PR English Literature Ser.). 572p. 1992. reprint ed. lib. bdg. 99.00 (*0-7812-7169-X*) Rprt Serv.
Book of Troth. Edred Thorsson. LC 89-38817. (Teutonic Magick Ser.). (Illus.). 256p. (Orig.). 1989. pap. 9.95 (*0-87542-777-4*) Llewellyn Pubns.
Book of True Love: Bilingual Edition. Juan Ruiz. Ed. by Anthony N. Zahareas. Tr. & Intro. by Saralyn R. Daly. LC 77-12820. (C). 1978. 29.95 (*0-271-00523-8*) Pa St U Pr.
Book of True Lovers. Alice French. LC 78-94722. (Short Story Index Reprint Ser.). 1977. 20.95 (*0-8369-3101-7*) Ayer.
Book of Truly Tasteless Anatomy Jokes. Blanche Knott. 1990. mass mkt. 3.99 (*0-312-92062-8*) St Martin.
Book of Trustees, Purdue University, 1865-1989. Robert W. Topping. LC 89-36309. (Illus.). 200p. 1989. 20.00 (*0-931682-26-6*) Purdue U Pubns.
Book of Twelve Prophets, Vol. I. Tr. by A. J. Rosenberg. 268p. (HEB.). 1986. 17.95 (*0-910818-70-3*) Judaica Pr.
Book of Twelve Prophets, Vol. II. Tr. by A. J. Rosenberg. 213p. (HEB.). 1988. 17.95 (*0-910818-78-9*) Judaica Pr.
Book of Tziril: A Family Chronicle. Bess Waldman. (Illus.). 215p. 1988. 17.95 (*1-55774-016-X*) Modan-Adama Bks.
Book of U. S. Government Jobs: Where They Are, What's Available & How to Get One. 5th rev. ed. Dennis V. Damp. Ed. by Michelle Macie. LC 93-70449. (Illus.). 224p. 1994. pap. 15.95 (*0-943641-09-8*) Bookhaven Pr.
***Book of U. S. Government Jobs: Where They Are, What's Available & How to Get One.** 6th rev. ed. Dennis V. Damp. Ed. by Michelle Macie. LC 98-7817. (Illus.). 288p. 1995. pap. 17.95 (*0-943641-12-8*) Bookhaven Pr.
Book of U. S. Postal Exams: How to Score Ninety-Five to One Hundred Percent & Get a Twenty Thousand Dollars-a-Year Job. rev. ed. Veltisezar B. Bautista. LC 87-62025. 230p. 1988. pap. 12.95 (*0-931613-02-7*) Bkhaus.
Book of U. S. Postal Exams: How to Score 95-100 Percent & Get a Job! 3rd enl. rev. ed. Veltisezar B. Bautista. LC 90-81541. (Illus.). 272p. 1990. pap. 13.95 (*0-931613-05-1*) Bkhaus.
Book of Ulster Surnames. Robert Bell. LC 88-7452. 285p. 1988. pap. 14.95 (*0-85640-405-5*, Pub. by Blackstaff Pr IE) Dufour.
Book of Uncommon Faith. Kenneth G. Phifer. LC 90-71862. 144p. (Orig.). 1991. pap. 8.95 (*0-8358-0632-4*) Upper Room Bks.
Book of Uncommon Prayer. Kenneth G. Phifer. LC 82-50945. 128p. 1983. reprint ed. pap. 8.95 (*0-8358-0451-8*) Upper Room Bks.
Book of Understanding: One Who Prayed for One Who Wrote. Two Hermits. LC 94-24327. Date not set. 23.95 (*0-9627925-2-7*); pap. 15.95 (*0-9627925-3-5*) BenYamin Pr.
Book of Unlikely Saints. Margaret T. Monro. LC 77-107727. (Essay Index Reprint Ser.). 1977. 21.95 (*0-8369-1528-3*) Ayer.
Book of Urizen. William Blake. LC 66-27494. 1966. pap. 7.95 (*0-87024-065-X*) U of Miami Pr.
Book of Urizen. William Blake. (BCL1-PR English Literature Ser.). 25p. 1992. reprint ed. lib. bdg. 59.00 (*0-7812-7443-5*) Rprt Serv.
Book of U.S. Postal Exams: How to Score 95-100 Percent & Get a Job! 4th ed. Veltisezar B. Bautista. LC 94-72176. (Illus.). 320p. 1994. Study Guide. student ed. pap. 17.95 (*0-931613-10-8*) Bkhaus.
Book of Vampires. Dudley Wright. 1987. 17.95 (*0-88029-154-0*) Dorset Pr.
Book of Vampires. 2nd ed. Dudley Wright. LC 89-34173. 220p. 1989. reprint ed. lib. bdg. 40.00 (*1-55888-817-9*) Omnigraphics Inc.
Book of Vegetarian Cooking. Louise Pickford. 120p. 1993. pap. 12.00 (*1-55788-076-X*, HP Books) Berkley Pub.
Book of Verse. William Morris. 1980. 424.95 (*0-85967-606-4*, Pub. by Scolar Pr UK) Ashgate Pub Co.
Book of Verses. Edgar L. Masters. 1972. 59.95 (*0-87968-773-8*) Gordon Pr.
Book of Verses for Children. Comp. by Edward V. Lucas. LC 71-121927. (Granger Index Reprint Ser.). 1977. 20.95 (*0-8369-6168-4*) Ayer.
***Book of Vices: Collection of Classic Immoral Tales.** Ed. & Comment by Robert J. Hutchinson. LC 94-41450. 1995. 18.00 (*1-57322-006-X*) Riverhead Bks.
Book of Victorian Ghost Stories. large type ed. Virago. 1989. 23.95 (*0-7089-8525-4*, Charnwood) Ulverscroft.
Book of Video Lists. Tom Wiener. 640p. (Orig.). 1993. pap. 16.95 (*0-8362-8031-8*) Andrews & McMeel.
Book of Video Lists. 3rd ed. Tom Wiener. 608p. (Orig.). 1991. 24.95 (*0-685-47172-1*); pap. 12.95 (*0-8191-7825-X*) Madison Bks UPA.
***Book of Virtues: A Treasury of Great Stories.** Ed. & Comment by William J. Bennett. LC 94-41655. (J). 1995. 19.95 (*0-382-24924-0*) Silver Burdett Pr.
Book of Virtues: A Treasury of the World's Great Moral Stories. William J. Bennett. (Illus.). 672p. 1993. 30.00 (*0-671-68306-3*) S&S Trade.
***Book of Virtues: Gift Wrapped Edition.** William J. Bennett. 1994. 30.00 (*0-671-51158-0*) S&S Trade.
***Book of Virtues for Young People.** William J. Bennett. (Illus.). 384p. (YA). (gr. 5 up). 1995. lib. bdg. 14.95 (*0-382-24923-2*) Silver Burdett Pr.
Book of Visual Illusions. Martin Gardner. LC 92-38502. (Illus.). 64p. (Orig.). 1993. pap. text ed. 4.95 (*0-486-27380-6*) Dover.
Book of Vitamins. Edmond B. Szekely. (Illus.). 40p. 1978. pap. 3.50 (*0-89564-045-7*) IBS Intl.
Book of Warsaw Palaces. Tadeusz Jaroszewski. 174p. 1985. 135.00 (*0-317-61241-7*, Pub. by Collets UK) Pro-Am Music.
Book of Weather Clues. 3rd ed. Ed. by Diane Kaiser. LC 86-90363. (Illus.). 64p. (Orig.). 1986. pap. 6.95 (*0-913515-11-6*, Starrhill) Elliott & Clark.
Book of Webster's. J. N. Williamson. LC 92-46747. 384p. 1993. 17.95 (*0-681-41598-3*) Longmeadow Pr.
Book of Weird: Being a Most Desirable Lexicon of the Fantastical... Barbara N. Byfield. LC 94-6573. Orig. Title: Glass Harmonica. (Illus.). 1994. reprint ed. 10.00 (*0-385-06591-4*) Doubleday.
Book of Were-Wolves: Being an Account of a Terrible Superstition. Sabine Baring-Gould. LC 89-61544. 266p. 1989. reprint ed. lib. bdg. 44.00 (*1-55888-818-7*) Omnigraphics Inc.
***Book of Western Films.** Ed. by Ian Cameron & Douglas Pye. LC 94-25280. 320p. 1995. 29.95 (*0-8264-0818-4*) Continuum.
Book of Whales. Richard Ellis. LC 80-7640. (Illus.). 1985. pap. 35.00 (*0-394-73371-1*) Knopf.
Book of Wheat: An Economic History & Practical Manual of the Wheat Industry. Peter T. Dondlinger. LC 72-89073. (Rural America Ser.). 1973. reprint ed. 32.00 (*0-8420-1481-0*) Scholarly Res Inc.
Book of Where: Or How to Be Naturally Geographic. Neill Bell. (Brown Paper School Bks.). 140p. (J). (gr. 7 up). 1982. pap. 10.95 (*0-316-08831-5*) Little.
Book of Whole Grains. Marlene A. Bumgarner. 1990. mass mkt. 4.95 (*0-312-92411-9*) St Martin.
***Book of Whole Grains: The Grain-by-Grain Guide to Cooking, Growing, & Grinding Whole Cereals, Nuts, Peas & Beans.** Marlene A. Bumgarner. (Illus.). Date not set. pap. 9.95 (*0-614-04803-6*); mass mkt. 4.95 (*0-614-04804-4*) Chesbro.
Book of Whole Meals: A Seasonal Guide to Assembling Balanced Vegetarian Breakfasts, Lunches & Dinners. Annemarie Colbin. 240p. (Orig.). 1985. pap. 12.00 (*0-345-33274-1*, Ballantine Trade) Ballantine.
Book of Wine Antiques. R. Butler & G. Walkling. (Illus.). 280p. 1986. 59.50 (*1-85149-022-1*) Antique Collect.
Book of Wine Antiques. Robin Butler & Gillian Walking. (Illus.). 288p. 1994. pap. 39.50 (*1-85149-185-6*) Antique Collect.
Book of Wines. William Turner. LC 41-26942. 1980. reprint ed. 50.00 (*0-8201-1200-3*) Schol Facsimiles.
Book of Winter. Sue Owen. (Journal Award in Poetry). 60p. 1988. 18.95 (*0-8142-0474-0*); pap. 12.95 (*0-8142-0475-9*) Ohio St U Pr.
Book of Wisdom. 1995. pap. 6.00 (*0-385-47845-3*) Doubleday.
Book of Wisdom. Judith DeFrain. Ed. by Arielweehawk et al. (Illus.). 269p. (Orig.). (C). 1988. pap. text ed. 150.00 (*0-9619008-3-0*) Eye Cat.
Book of Wisdom. Tr. by Joseph Reider. LC 53-5114. xi, 233p. 1957. text ed. 15.00 (*0-685-46287-0*, Ctr Judaic Studies) Eisenbrauns.
Book of Wisdom, Vol. 2. Osho Rajneesh. Ed. by Swami Krishna Prabhu. LC 82-23142. (Atisha Ser.). 416p. (Orig.). 1984. pap. 5.95 (*0-88050-531-1*) Osho Chidvilas.
Book of Wisdom: Discourses on Atisha's Seven Points of Mind Training. Osho. Ed. by Swami K. Prabhu. (Atisha Ser.). 545p. 1993. 24.95 (*3-89338-117-1*, Pub. by Rebel Hse GW) Osho Chidvilas.
Book of Wisdom: Ishopanished. Swami Rama. LC 77-150818. 121p. 1972. pap. 7.95 (*0-89389-003-0*) Himalayan Pubs.
Book of Wisdom & Lies. Sulkhan-Saba Orbeliani. Tr. by Katherine Vivian. 1982. 22.00 (*0-317-03152-X*, Pub. by Octagon Pr UK) ISHK Bk Service.
***Book of Wisdom for Speakers.** Best, Inc. Staff & Alston. 64p. 1994. per., pap. text ed. 2.10 (*0-8403-9756-9*) Kendall-Hunt.
Book of Wisdom, Song of Songs. James Reese. LC 82-83726. (Old Testament Message Ser.: Vol. 20). 1983. pap. 8.95 (*0-8146-5254-9*) Liturgical Pr.
Book of Wishes & Complaints. Zina Rohan. 214p. 1992. 23.95 (*0-09-174778-3*, Pub. by Hutchinson UK) Trafalgar.
Book of Woman, Vol. 1. Lea Sovran. 240p. (Orig.). 1988. spiral bd. 4.50 (*0-929000-00-5*) Life Force Pr.
Book of Woman, Vol. 1. rev. ed. Lea Sovran. 240p. (Orig.). 1990. pap. 10.95 (*1-882000-01-3*) Life Force Pr.
Book of Women: The Code of Maimonides, Bk. 4. Moses Maimonides & Isaac Klein. LC 49-9495. (Judaica Ser.: No. 19). 592p. 1972. 60.00 (*0-300-01438-4*) Yale U Pr.
Book of Women: Three Hundred Notable Women History Passed By. Lynne Griffin & Kelly McCann. (Illus.). 204p. 1992. 10.95 (*1-55850-106-1*) Adams Pubng.
***Book of Women: Three Hundred Notable Women History Passed By.** Lynne Griffin & Kelly McCann. (Illus.). 192p. 1995. pap. 7.95 (*1-55850-516-4*) Adams Pubng.
Book of Women Poets from Antiquity to Now. rev. ed. Ed. by Aliki Barnstone & Willis Barnstone. LC 91-52701. 832p. 1992. reprint ed. pap. 20.00 (*0-8052-0997-2*) Schocken.
Book of Women's Firsts: Break-Through Achievements of Over 1000 American Women. Phyllis J. Read & Bernard Witlieb. LC 92-16872. 1992. 24.00 (*0-679-40975-0*, Random Ref); pap. 16.00 (*0-679-74280-8*, Random Ref) Random.
Book of Wonder. Edward J. Dunsany. LC 72-6079. (Short Story Index Reprint Ser.). 1977. reprint ed. 21.95 (*0-8369-4213-2*) Ayer.
Book of Wood Carving: Technique, Designs & Projects. Charles M. Sayers. 1978. pap. 4.95 (*0-486-23654-4*) Dover.
Book of Woodcraft. Ernest Seton. LC 87-72796. (Illus.). 600p. 1988. reprint ed. pap. 12.95 (*0-88739-060-9*) Creat Arts Bk.
Book of Woodcraft & Indian Lore. Ernest T. Seton. (Illus.). 590p. (YA). 1994. pap. 29.95 (*1-885529-11-2*) Stevens Pub.
Book of Wooden Boats. Photos by Benjamin Mendlowitz. LC 92-10533. (Illus.). 192p. 1992. 50.00 (*0-393-03417-8*) Norton.
Book of Words. Rudyard Kipling. LC 76-128266. (Essay Index Reprint Ser.). 1977. 19.95 (*0-8369-1884-3*) Ayer.
Book of Words: Talking Spiritual Life, Living Spiritual Talk. Lawrence Kushner. LC 93-29004. (Illus.). 152p. 1993. 21.95 (*1-879045-35-4*) Jewish Lights.
Book of Work Sheets for the I-Ching (Yi-Jing) H. David Lloyd. (Illus.). 65p. 1991. student ed 15.95 (*1-880107-14-7*) D Lloyd Eng.
Book of World City Rankings. John T. Marlin et al. LC 85-25298. 766p. (C). 1986. text ed. 49.95 (*0-02-920230-2*) Free Pr.
Book of World-Famous Libretti: The Musical Theater from 1598 to Today. rev. ed. James J. Fuld. LC 93-39884. 1994. pap. 36.00 (*0-945193-48-3*) Pendragon NY.
***Book of World-Famous Music: Classical, Popular & Folk.** 4th enl. rev. ed. James J. Fuld. LC 94-23374. (Illus.). 752p. 1995. pap. text ed. 18.95 (*0-486-28445-X*) Dover.
Book of World-Famous Music: Classical, Popular & Folk. James J. Fuld. LC 84-21232. (Music Bks.). 800p. 1985. reprint ed. pap. 15.95 (*0-486-24857-7*) Dover.
Book of World Religions. E. G. Parrinder. (C). 1965. text ed. 70.00 (*0-7175-0443-3*, Pub. by S Thornes Pubs UK) St Mut.
Book of World Rugby Quotations: Wit Wisdom & Wisecracks from the Rugby Union Game. Derek Douglas. 30p. 1992. pap. 17.95 (*1-85158-435-8*, Pub. by Mnstream UK) Trafalgar.
Book of Worship: United Church of Christ. United Church of Christ Office for Church Life & Leadership. 563p. 1986. ring bd. 28.00 (*0-940615-00-2*) UCCOCLL.
Book of Worship: United Church of Christ. deluxe ed. United Church of Christ Office for Church Life & Leadership. 563p. 1986. 28.00 (*0-940615-01-0*) UCCOCLL.
Book of Yeats's Poems. Hazard Adams. 304p. 1989. lib. bdg. 37.95 (*0-8130-0944-8*); pap. 19.95 (*0-8130-0951-0*) U Press Fla.
Book of Yechezkel. Ed. by Rabbi Dr. Joseph Breuer Foundation Staff. LC 93-25424. (ENG & HEB.). 1993. 22.95 (*0-87306-956-0*) Feldheim.
Book of You. Bernard Asbell & Karen Wynn. 336p. 1992. pap. 9.00 (*0-449-90717-1*, Columbine) Fawcett.
***Book of Your Own: Angel.** 1995. 8.95 (*0-446-91021-X*) Warner Bks.
***Book of Your Own: Clock.** 1995. 8.95 (*0-446-91019-8*) Warner Bks.
Book of Your Own: Keeping a Diary or Journal. Carla Stevens. LC 92-33818. (J). 1993. 14.95 (*0-89919-256-4*, Clarion Bks) HM.
Book of Your Own: Keeping a Diary or Journal. Carla Stevens. (J). (gr. 4-7). 1993. pap. 7.95 (*0-395-67887-0*, Clarion Bks) HM.
***Book of Your Own: Rose.** 1995. 8.95 (*0-446-91023-6*) Warner Bks.
***Book of Your Own: Typewriter.** 1995. 8.95 (*0-446-91024-4*) Warner Bks.
***Book of 1001 Home Health Remedies.** Frank Cawood & Associates Inc. Staff. 1993. pap. 9.95 (*0-915099-54-3*) FC&A Pub.
Book of 35mm Photography. Curtin & London Editors. (Illus.). 167p. 1983. pap. text ed. 19.95 (*0-240-51763-6*, Focal) Buttrwrth-Heinemann.
Book on Angling: Being a Complete Treatise on the Art of Angling with Explanatory Plates. Francis Francis. (Fly Fisherman's Gold Ser.: Vol. 3). (Illus.). 529p. 1993. reprint ed. 42.90 (*1-56416-115-3*) Derrydale Pr.
Book on C. 3rd ed. Al Kelley & Ira Pohl. (C). 1995. pap. text ed. 41.95 (*0-8053-1677-9*) Benjamin-Cummings.
Book on C. 3rd ed. B. A. Meekings et al. (Illus.). 194p. (C). 1993. pap. text ed. 35.00 (*0-333-56919-9*, Pub. by Macmill Educ UK) Scholium Intl.
Book on C: Programming in C. 2nd ed. Al Kelley. 554p. (C). 1990. pap. text ed. 41.95 (*0-8053-0060-0*); pap. text ed. 11.95 (*0-8053-0061-9*) Benjamin-Cummings.
Book on Cataracts. G. Brock Magruder & Walter R. Gilbert, Jr. Ed. by Curley & Pynn Public Relations Management, Inc. Staff. (Illus.). (Orig.). (C). 1988. pap. text ed. 4.95 (*0-317-93288-8*) G B Magruder.
Book on Chickens. Lowell Davis. LC 98-23115. (Illus.). 64p. 1992. 19.95 (*0-88289-888-4*); pap. 12.95 (*0-88289-890-6*) Pelican.
***Book on Congress: Process, Procedure, & Structure.** Martin Gold et al. 367p. 1992. 72.50 (*0-9634954-0-2*) Big Eagle.

An Asterisk (*) at the beginning of an entry indicates that the title is appearing in BIP for the first time.

An Asterisk (*) at the beginning of an entry indicates that the title is appearing in BIP for the first time.

855

Booke Containing Divers Sortes of Hands, As Well As the English & French Secretarie. John De Beau Chesne & John Baildon. LC 77-6875. (English Experience Ser.: No. 867). 1977. reprint ed. lib. bdg. 20.00 (*90-221-0867-8*) Walter J Johnson.

Booke Conteining...Experienced Medicines: The Fourth & Finall Booke of His Secretes. Piemontese Alessio. Tr. by R. Androse. LC 77-6846. (English Experience Ser.: No. 841). 1977. reprint ed. lib. bdg. 35.00 (*90-221-0841-4*) Walter J Johnson.

Booke of Certaine Canons, Concernynge Some Parte of the Discipline of the Churche of England. Church of England Staff. LC 70-26475. (English Experience Ser.: No. 312). 1971. reprint ed. 7.00 (*90-221-0312-9*) Walter J Johnson.

Booke of Christian Ethicks or Moral Philosophie. William Fulbecke. LC 74-28856. (English Experience Ser.: No. 737). 1975. reprint ed. 15.00 (*90-221-0737-X*) Walter J Johnson.

Booke of Fishing with Hooke & Line (Taken from the Treatise of Fishing with an Angle) Leonard Mascall. LC 72-6017. (English Experience Ser.: No. 542). 92p. 1973. reprint ed. 25.00 (*90-221-0542-3*) Walter J Johnson.

Booke of Honor & Armes & Honor Military & Civil, 2 vols. in 1. William Segar. LC 74-20543. 475p. 1975. reprint ed. 60.00 (*0-8201-1138-4*) Schol Facsimiles.

Booke of Sundry Draughtes Principally for Glasiers: Whereunto Is Annexed How to Anniel in Glas, 4 pts., Set. Walter Gedde. LC 78-26524. (English Experience Ser.: No. 316). (Illus.). 136p. 1971. reprint ed. 45.00 (*90-221-0316-1*) Walter J Johnson.

Booke of the Arte & Manner How to Plant & Graffe All Sortes of Trees. Leonard Mascall. LC 74-80200. (English Experience Ser.: No. 679). 90p. 1974. reprint ed. 25.00 (*90-221-0679-9*) Walter J Johnson.

Booke of the Pylgremage of the Sowle. Guillaume De Deguilleville. Ed. by Katherine I. Cust. Tr. by William Caxton. LC 78-180445. (Illus.). reprint ed. 21.50 (*0-404-56612-X*) AMS Pr.

Booked on the Morning Train: A Journey Through America. George F. Scheer, III. 384p. 1991. text ed. 19.95 (*0-945575-40-8*) Algonquin Bks.

Booked to Die. John H. Dunning. 336p. 1993. mass mkt. 4.99 (*0-380-71883-9*) Avon.

Booked to Die: A Mystery Introducing Cliff Janeway. John H. Dunning. 288p. 1992. text ed. 19.95 (*0-684-19383-3*, Scribners) S&S Trade.

***Bookee Presents Colors, Shapes & Sounds.** Ron Kidd. (Talking Book Adventures Ser.). (Illus.). 12p. (J). 1995. text ed. 19.95 (*0-9627001-1-8*) Futech Educ Prods.

***Bookee's Sounds Around.** Stephen McTaggart & Debra McTaggart. (Talking Book Adventures Ser.). (Illus.). 12p. (J). 1995. 19.95 (*0-9627001-0-X*) Futech Educ Prods.

Bookends. Michele Borba & Dan Ungaro. 128p. (J). (gr. 1-4). 1982. 11.95 (*0-86653-065-7*, GA 432) Good Apple.

Booker T. Washington. (Story Clippers Ser.). (Illus.). (J). (gr. 2-5). 1989. 29.28 (*0-8172-2959-0*) Raintree Steck-V.

***Booker T. Washington.** Bass. Date not set. 24.95 (*0-8057-3977-7*, Twayne) Macmillan.

Booker T. Washington. Jan Gleiter & Kathleen Thompson. LC 87-26325. (Stories Ser.). (Illus.). 32p. (Orig.). (J). (gr. 2-5). 1987. lib. bdg. 19.97 (*0-8172-2663-X*) Raintree Steck-V.

***Booker T. Washington.** Jan Gleiter & Kathleen Thompson. LC 94-41001. (First Biographies Ser.). (Orig.). (J). 1995. 19.97 (*0-8114-8454-8*) Raintree Steck-V.

***Booker T. Washington.** Shirley Graham. 1995. pap. 9.95 (*0-86543-473-5*) Africa World.

Booker T. Washington. Alan Schroeder. (Black Americans of Achievement Ser.). (Illus.). 144p. (YA). (gr. 5 up). 1992. 17.95 (*1-55546-616-8*) Chelsea Hse.

Booker T. Washington. Ed. by Emma L. Thornbrough. LC 69-15336. (Great Lives Observed Ser.). 1969. pap. 1.95 (*0-13-945303-2*, Spectrum Bks) P-H.

Booker T. Washington: Builder of a Civilization. Emmett J. Scott. (BCL1 - U. S. History Ser.). 331p. 1991. reprint ed. lib. bdg. 89.00 (*0-7812-6092-2*) Rprt Serv.

***Booker T. Washington: Education & Racial Spokesman.** (Junior Black Americans of Achievement Ser.). (Illus.). 80p. (J). (gr. 3-6). Date not set. lib. bdg. 14.95 (*0-7910-2388-5*) Chelsea Hse.

***Booker T. Washington: Educator.** Alan Schroeder. Ed. by Nathan I. Huggins. (Black Americans of Achievement Ser.). (Illus.). 144p. (YA). (gr. 5 up). 1992. pap. 7.95 (*0-7910-0252-7*) Chelsea Hse.

***Booker T. Washington: Educator & Leader.** Jack L. Roberts. LC 94-21484. (Gateway Civil Rights Ser.). (Illus.). 32p. (J). (gr. 2-4). 1995. 13.40 (*1-56294-487-8*) Millbrook Pr.

Booker T. Washington: Leader & Educator. Patricia McKissack & Fredrick McKissack. LC 92-5356. (Great African Americans Ser.). (Illus.). 32p. (J). (gr. 1-4). 1992. lib. bdg. 12.95 (*0-89490-314-4*) Enslow Pubs.

Booker T. Washington: Leader of His People. Alan Schroeder. (Discovery Biographies Ser.). (Illus.). 80p. (J). (gr. 2-6). 1991. reprint ed. lib. bdg. 12.95 (*0-7910-1427-4*) Chelsea Hse.

Booker T. Washington: Mini Play. (Black Americans Ser.). (J). (gr. 5 up). 1977. 6.50 (*0-89550-361-1*) Stevens & Shea.

Booker T. Washington: Story Pak. L. Johnson. (Graphic Learning Literature Program Series: Folk Tales). (Illus.). (ENG & SPA.). 1992. 39.00 (*0-87746-259-3*) Graphic Learning.

Booker T. Washington: The Master Mind of a Child of Slavery. Frederick E. Drinker. LC 77-100288. 320p. 1970. reprint ed. text ed. 35.00 (*0-8371-2939-7*, DRW&, Greenwood Pr) Greenwood.

Booker T. Washington Vol. 1: The Making of a Black Leader, 1856-1901. Louis R. Harlan. LC 72-77499. (Illus.). 1975. pap. 15.95 (*0-19-501915-6*) OUP.

Booker T. Washington Vol. 2: The Wizard of Tuskegee, 1901-1915. Louis R. Harlan. (Illus.). 562p. 1983. 39.95 (*0-19-503202-0*) OUP.

Booker T. Washington Vol. 2: The Wizard of Tuskegee, 1901-1915. Louis R. Harlan. (Illus.). 562p. 1986. pap. 16.95 (*0-19-504229-8*) OUP.

Booker T. Washington & His Critics. 2nd ed. Ed. by Hugh Hawkins. (Problems in American Civilization Ser.). 228p. (C). 1974. pap. text ed. 8.50 (*0-669-87049-8*) Heath.

Booker T. Washington & the Adult Education Movement. Virginia L. Denton. LC 92-27094. (Illus.). 280p. 1993. 34.95 (*0-8130-1182-5*) U Press Fla.

Booker T. Washington & the Negro's Place in American Life. Samuel R. Spencer, Jr. (Library of American Biography). (C). 1987. pap. text ed. 16.00 (*0-673-39352-6*) HarpCollege.

Booker T. Washington, Educator. James Neyland. Ed. by Raymond F. Locke. (Black American Ser.). (Illus.). 192p. (YA). 1993. pap. 3.95 (*0-87067-599-0*, Melrose Sq) Holloway.

Booker T. Washington in Perspective: Essays of Louis R. Harlan. Ed. by Raymond W. Smock. LC 88-17338. (Illus.). 244p. 1988. text ed. 30.00 (*0-87805-374-3*) U Pr of Miss.

Booker T. Washington Papers, 14 vols., Set. Booker T. Washington. Ed. by Louis R. Harlan et al. (Illus.). 1989. 495.00 (*0-252-01152-X*) U of Ill Pr.

Booker T. Washington Papers, Vol. 1: The Autobiographical Writings. Booker T. Washington. Ed. by Louis R. Harlan. LC 75-186345. (Illus.). 509p. 1972. 45.00 (*0-252-00242-3*) U of Ill Pr.

Booker T. Washington Papers, Vol. 10: 1909-1911. Booker T. Washington. Ed. by Geraldine McTigue & Nan E. Woodruff. LC 75-186345. 688p. 1981. 45.00 (*0-252-00800-6*) U of Ill Pr.

Booker T. Washington Papers, Vol. 11: 1911-1912. Booker T. Washington. Ed. by Geraldine McTigue. LC 75-186345. 648p. 1981. 45.00 (*0-252-00887-1*) U of Ill Pr.

Booker T. Washington Papers, Vol. 12: 1912-14. Booker T. Washington. Ed. by Louis R. Harlan & Raymond W. Smock. (Illus.). 544p. 1982. 45.00 (*0-252-00974-6*) U of Ill Pr.

Booker T. Washington Papers, Vol. 13: 1914-1915. Booker T. Washington. Ed. by Susan Valenza & Sadie M. Harlan. LC 75-186345. 592p. 1984. 45.00 (*0-252-01125-2*) U of Ill Pr.

Booker T. Washington Papers, Vol. 14: Cumulative Index. Booker T. Washington. Ed. by Louis R. Harlan & Raymond W. Smock. (Illus.). 328p. 1989. 45.00 (*0-252-01519-3*) U of Ill Pr.

Booker T. Washington Papers, Vol. 2: 1860-1889. Booker T. Washington. Ed. by Pete Daniel et al. LC 75-186345. (Illus.). 597p. 1972. 45.00 (*0-252-00243-1*) U of Ill Pr.

Booker T. Washington Papers, Vol. 3: 1889-1895. Booker T. Washington. Ed. by Stuart B. Kaufman & Raymond W. Smock. LC 75-186345. (Illus.). 648p. 1974. 45.00 (*0-252-00410-8*) U of Ill Pr.

Booker T. Washington Papers, Vol. 4: 1895-1898. Booker T. Washington. Ed. by Stuart B. Kaufman et al. LC 75-186345. (Illus.). 623p. 1975. 45.00 (*0-252-00529-5*) U of Ill Pr.

Booker T. Washington Papers, Vol. 5: 1899-1900. Booker T. Washington. Ed. by Barbara S. Kraft. LC 75-186345. 784p. 1976. 45.00 (*0-252-00627-5*) U of Ill Pr.

Booker T. Washington Papers, Vol. 6: 1901-1902. Booker T. Washington. Ed. by Barbara S. Kraft. LC 75-186345. (Illus.). 691p. 1977. 45.00 (*0-252-00650-X*) U of Ill Pr.

Booker T. Washington Papers, Vol. 7: 1903-1904. Booker T. Washington. Ed. by Barbara S. Kraft. LC 75-186345. (Illus.). 602p. 1977. 45.00 (*0-252-00666-6*) U of Ill Pr.

Booker T. Washington Papers, Vol. 8: 1904-1906. Booker T. Washington. Ed. by Geraldine McTigue. LC 75-186345. (Illus.). 828p. 1979. 45.00 (*0-252-00728-X*) U of Ill Pr.

Booker T. Washington Papers, Vol. 9: 1906-1908. Booker T. Washington. Ed. by Nan E. Woodruff. LC 75-186345. 779p. 1980. 45.00 (*0-252-00771-9*) U of Ill Pr.

Booker Tropical Soil Manual: A Handbook for Soil Survey & Agricultural Land Evaluation in the Tropics & Sub-Tropics. Ed. by J. R. Landon. 474p. 1991. pap. text ed. 67.95 (*0-470-21713-8*) Halsted Pr.

Booker T's Child: The Life & Times of Portia Marshall Washington Pitman. Roy L. Hill. 164p. 1993. pap. 15.00 (*0-89410-749-6*) Three Continents.

Booker's Bunch, Bk. 1. Jerry Mallett & Marian Bartch. 80p. (J). (gr. 3-4). 1988. lib. bdg. 9.74 (*0-8000-4735-4*, 036417) Perma-Bound.

Booker's Bunch, Bk. 2. Jerry Mallett & Marian Bartch. 88p. (J). (gr. 3-4). 1988. lib. bdg. 9.74 (*0-8000-4736-2*, 036418) Perma-Bound.

Bookfinder, Vol. 4. Sharon S. Dreyer. 1989. text ed. 89.95 (*0-913476-50-1*, 7581); pap. text ed. 44.95 (*0-913476-51-X*, 7582) Am Guidance.

Bookful of Bob Getz. Bob Getz. 240p. (Orig.). 1992. pap. 9.95 (*1-880652-11-0*) Wichita Eagle.

***Booking & Tour Management for the Performing Arts.** Rena Shagan. LC 95-76687. 256p. 1995. reprint ed. pap. 19.95 (*1-880559-36-6*) Allworth Pr.

Booking in the Heartland. Jack Matthews. LC 86-7150. 176p. 1986. 16.95 (*0-8018-3332-9*) Johns Hopkins.

***Booking Pleasures.** Jack Matthews. 150p. 1995. 24.95 (*0-8214-1129-2*) Ohio U Pr.

Bookkeeper. Jack Rudman. (Career Examination Ser.: C-89). 1994. pap. 23.95 (*0-8373-0089-4*) Nat Learn.

Bookkeeper - Account Clerk: Federal - State - Municipal. 6th ed. Hy Hammer. 240p. 1992. pap. 12.00 (*0-685-51949-X*, Arco Test) P-H Gen Ref & Trav.

Bookkeeper-Account Clerk. 6th ed. Ed. by Hy Hammer. LC 82-11427. 240p. (Orig.). 1985. pap. 12.00 (*0-668-05398-4*, 5398, Arco Test) P-H Gen Ref & Trav.

Bookkeeper for Horse Owners, 1995. Tony Winter & Sue E. Marder. (Illus.). 96p. 1992. pap. 17.95 (*0-914327-48-8*) Breakthrgh NY.

Bookkeeping & Accounts. 3rd ed. Frank Wood. 400p. (Orig.). 1992. pap. 37.50 (*0-273-03770-6*, Pub. by Pitman Pub Ltd UK) Trans-Atl Phila.

Bookkeeping & Accounts. 22th ed. Spicer & Pegler. 1993. pap. 38.00 (*0-406-02236-4*) Butterworth Legal Pubs.

Bookkeeping Buddy: The Fun & Easy Way to Track Your Money. C. Mitch Gallon. (Illus.). 155p. 1994. Binder. 29.95 (*0-9641298-9-2*) Benebook Pubng.

***Bookkeeping for a Small Business.** 5th ed. Diane Bellavance. (Illus.). 24p. (Orig.). 1994. pap. 3.95 (*0-9605276-5-6*) DBA Bks.

Bookkeeping for Builders. Michael C. Thomsett. 208p. 1989. pap. 19.75 (*0-934041-42-3*) Craftsman.

***Bookkeeping for Churches.** James Wills. 80p. 1995. ring bd. 39.95 (*0-7872-0812-4*) Kendall-Hunt.

Bookkeeping for Nonprofits. Public Management Institute Staff. LC 79-90010. 1979. ring bd. 49.00 (*0-916664-14-7*) Datarex Corp.

Bookkeeping for Small Organizations: A Handbook for Treasurers & Finance Committees. enl. ed. Kenneth Ives et al. 48p. 1990. pap. 4.00 (*0-89670-008-9*) Progresiv Pub.

Bookkeeping Machine Operator. Jack Rudman. (Career Examination Ser.: C-1139). 1994. pap. 23.95 (*0-8373-1139-X*) Nat Learn.

Bookkeeping Machine Supervisor. Jack Rudman. (Career Examination Ser.: C-1140). 1994. pap. 27.95 (*0-8373-1140-3*) Nat Learn.

Bookkeeping Made Simple. rev. ed. Louis W. Fields. 1990. pap. 12.00 (*0-385-23882-7*) Doubleday.

Bookkeeping on Your Home-Based PC. Linda Stern. 1993. 24.95 (*0-07-061231-5*); pap. 14.95 (*0-07-061232-3*) McGraw.

Bookkeeping On Your Home-Based PC. Lisa Stern. LC 93-15875. 1993. 24.95 (*0-8306-4305-2*, Windcrest); pap. 14.95 (*0-8306-4304-4*, Windcrest) TAB Bks.

Bookkeeping Operations Supervisor. Jack Rudman. (Career Examination Ser.: C-2801). 1994. pap. 29.95 (*0-8373-2801-2*) Nat Learn.

Bookkeeping the Easy Way. 2nd ed. Wallace Kravitz. (Easy Way Ser.). 288p. 1990. pap. 9.95 (*0-8120-4371-5*) Barron.

Booklet Making at Home: A Professional Guide to Writing & Selling Your Knowledge. J. F. Jones. LC 87-51716. 40p. (Orig.). 1988. pap. 10.00 (*0-9617813-1-9*) Drakestone Pub.

***Booklet of Meaningful Quotes.** Comp. by Paul Tice. 51p. (Orig.). 1994. pap. 4.95 (*1-885395-07-8*) Book Tree.

Booklinks: Writing Connections to Children's Literature. Arlene Brown. 96p. 1993. pap. text ed. 13.95 (*0-944459-61-7*) ECS Lrn Systs.

***Booklinks to the First American Colonies.** Doris V. Jackson. (ECS Activity Book for Social Studies). 32p. (Orig.). 1994. pap. 4.95 (*1-57022-008-5*) ECS Lrn Systs.

Booklist, 1990-1991. 1990. write for info. (*0-318-67998-1*) Womans Inst-Cont Jewish Ed.

Booklist's Guide to the Year's Best Books: Definitive Reviews of over 1000 Fiction & Nonfiction Titles in All Fields. 408p. 1992. 49.95 (*1-880141-07-8*); pap. 14.95 (*1-880141-08-6*) Triumph Bks.

Booklover & His Books. Harry L. Koopman. 1972. 34.95 (*0-87968-775-4*) Gordon Pr.

Booklover's Birthday Book. (Illus.). 184p. 1984. 14.95 (*0-8109-0741-0*) Abrams.

Booklover's Booklist. (Illus.). 96p. 1986. 9.95 (*0-8109-0742-9*) Abrams.

***Bookmakers.** Zev Chafets. 261p. 1995. 21.00 (*0-615-00676-0*) Random Hse Value.

Bookmaker's Daughter: A Memory Unbound. Shirley Abbott. 320p. 1992. pap. 10.95 (*0-395-62944-6*) Ticknor & Fields.

Bookmaking: The Illustrated Guide to Design, Production, Editing. enl. rev. ed. Ed. by Marshall Lee. LC 79-65014. 485p. 1980. 49.95 (*0-8352-1097-9*) Bowker.

Bookmaking & Kindred Amenities. Ed. by Earl S. Miers & Richard Ellis. LC 70-80392. (Essay Index Reprint Ser.). 1977. 20.95 (*0-8369-1045-1*) Ayer.

Bookman. Ed Baldwin. LC 90-82854. 172p. (Orig.). 1990. pap. 10.95 (*0-9627167-0-7*) Brasfield Bks.

***Bookman's Fantasy: How Science Fiction Became Respectable & Other Essays.** Fred Lerner. LC 94-73980. iv, 97p. (Orig.). 1995. pap. 11.95 (*0-915368-65-X*) New Eng SF Assoc.

Bookman's Glossary. 6th ed. Ed. by Jean Peters. 223p. 1983. 39.95 (*0-8352-1686-1*) Bowker.

Bookman's Guide to Americana. 9th ed. J. Norman Heard & Charles F. Hamsa. LC 86-6467. viii, 468p. 1986. 42.50 (*0-8108-1894-9*) Scarecrow.

Bookman's Guide to Americana. 10th ed. Lee Shiflett. LC 91-25404. 524p. 1991. 49.50 (*0-8108-2464-7*) Scarecrow.

***Bookman's Guide to Archaeology: A Compilation of over 7,000 Books Pertaining to the Scientific Study of Prehistoric & Historic People, Their Artifacts, Inscriptions, & Monuments with Prices & Annotations, Both Bibliographical & Descriptive.** Richard A. Hand. LC 94-345523. 1036p. 1994. 110.00 (*0-8108-2946-0*) Scarecrow.

Bookman's Guide to Hunting, Shooting, Angling & Related Subjects: A Compilation of Over 13,450 Catalog Entries with Prices & Annotations, Both Bibliographical & Descriptive. Richard A. Hand. LC 90-37559. 1194p. 1991. 115.00 (*0-8108-2333-0*) Scarecrow.

Bookman's Guide to the Indians of the Americas: A Compilation of over 10,000 Catalogue Entries with Prices & Annotations, Both Bibliographical & Descriptive. Richard A. Hand. LC 88-38642. 764p. 1989. 72.50 (*0-8108-2182-6*) Scarecrow.

Bookman's Holiday: The Private Satisfactions of an Incurable Collector. Vincent Starrett. LC 79-167423. (Essay Index Reprint Ser.). 1977. reprint ed. 20.95 (*0-8369-2475-4*) Ayer.

Bookman's Price Index, Vol. 26. Ed. by Daniel F. McGrath. 896p. 1984. 245.00 (*0-8103-0639-5*) Gale.

Bookman's Price Index, Vol. 27. Ed. by Daniel F. McGrath. 920p. 1984. 245.00 (*0-8103-0640-9*) Gale.

Bookman's Price Index, Vol. 28. Ed. by Daniel F. McGrath. 880p. 1984. 245.00 (*0-8103-0641-7*) Gale.

Bookman's Price Index, Vol. 29. Ed. by Daniel F. McGrath. 992p. 1985. 245.00 (*0-8103-0642-5*) Gale.

Bookman's Price Index, Vol. 30. Daniel F. McGrath. 944p. 1985. 245.00 (*0-8103-0643-3*) Gale.

Bookman's Price Index, Vol. 31. Ed. by Daniel F. McGrath. 1020p. 1985. 245.00 (*0-8103-0636-0*) Gale.

Bookman's Price Index, Vol. 32. 1986. 245.00 (*0-8103-0637-9*) Gale.

Bookman's Price Index, Vol. 33. Ed. by Daniel F. McGrath. 1000p. 1986. 245.00 (*0-8103-1804-0*) Gale.

Bookman's Price Index, Vol. 34. Ed. by Daniel F. McGrath. 1232p. 1987. 245.00 (*0-8103-1805-9*) Gale.

Bookman's Price Index, Vol. 35. Daniel F. McGrath. 1250p. 1987. 245.00 (*0-8103-1806-7*) Gale.

Bookman's Price Index, Vol. 37. Ed. by Daniel F. McGrath. 1000p. 1988. 245.00 (*0-8103-1808-3*) Gale.

Bookman's Price Index, Vol. 38. Daniel F. McGrath. 1989. 245.00 (*0-8103-1811-3*) Gale.

Bookman's Price Index, Vol. 40. Ed. by Daniel F. McGrath. 1000p. 1990. 245.00 (*0-8103-1813-X*) Gale.

Bookman's Price Index, Vol. 41. Ed. by Daniel F. McGrath. 1990. 245.00 (*0-8103-1814-8*) Gale.

Bookman's Price Index, Vol. 42. Daniel F. McGrath. 1991. 245.00 (*0-8103-1815-6*) Gale.

Bookman's Price Index, Vol. 43. Daniel F. McGrath. 1991. 245.00 (*0-8103-1816-4*) Gale.

Bookman's Price Index, Vol. 44. Daniel F. McGrath. 1992. 245.00 (*0-8103-7493-5*) Gale.

Bookman's Price Index, Vol. 45. Daniel F. McGrath. 1992. 245.00 (*0-8103-7494-3*) Gale.

Bookman's Price Index, Vol. 46. 1993. 245.00 (*0-8103-8215-6*) Gale.

Bookman's Price Index, Vol. 47. 1993. 245.00 (*0-8103-8216-4*) Gale.

Bookman's Price Index, Vol. 48. Daniel F. McGrath. 1994. 245.00 (*0-8103-5602-3*, 004148) Gale.

Bookman's Price Index, Vol. 49. Daniel F. McGrath. 1994. 245.00 (*0-8103-5603-1*, 004149) Gale.

***Bookman's Price Index, Vol. 50.** Anne F. McGrath. 930p. 1995. pap. 245.00 (*0-8103-9147-3*) Gale.

Bookman's Price Index: A Guide to the Values of Rare & Other Out-of-Print Books, 25 vols. Ed. by Daniel F. McGrath. Incl. Vol. 1. LC 64-8723. 2008p. 1964. 245.00 (*0-8103-0601-8*); Vol. 2. LC 64-8723. 1314p. 1967. 245.00 (*0-8103-0602-6*); Vol. 3. LC 64-8723. 1098p. 1968. 245.00 (*0-8103-0603-4*); Vol. 5. LC 64-8723. 1032p. 1971. 245.00 (*0-8103-0605-0*); Vol. 6. LC 64-8723. 706p. 1973. 245.00 (*0-8103-0606-9*); Vol. 7. LC 64-8723. 678p. 1973. 245.00 (*0-8103-0607-7*); Vol. 8. LC 64-8723. 676p. 1974. 245.00 (*0-8103-0608-5*); Vol. 9. LC 64-8723. 730p. 1974. 245.00 (*0-8103-0609-3*); Vol. 10. LC 64-8723. 750p. 1975. 245.00 (*0-8103-0635-2*); Vol. 11. LC 64-8723. 804p. 1976. 245.00 (*0-8103-0611-5*); Vol. 12. LC 64-8723. 808p. 1977. 245.00 (*0-8103-0612-3*); Vol. 13. LC 64-8723. 768p. 1978. 245.00 (*0-8103-0613-1*); Vol. 14. LC 64-8723. 768p. 1978. 245.00 (*0-8103-0614-X*); Vol. 15. LC 64-8723. 760p. 1979. 245.00 (*0-8103-0615-8*); Vol. 16. LC 64-8723. 736p. 1979. 245.00 (*0-8103-0616-6*); Vol. 17. LC 64-8723. 768p. 1979. 245.00 (*0-8103-0617-4*); Vol. 18. LC 64-8723. 792p. 1980. 245.00 (*0-8103-0618-2*); Vol. 19. LC 64-8723. 808p. 1980. 245.00 (*0-8103-0619-0*); Vol. 21. LC 64-8723. 792p. 1981. 245.00 (*0-8103-0621-2*); Vol. 22. LC 64-8723. 880p. 1981. 245.00 (*0-8103-0622-0*); Vol. 23. LC 64-8723. 792p. 1983. 245.00 (*0-8103-0623-9*); Vol. 24. LC 64-8723. 792p. 1983. 245.00 (*0-8103-0624-7*); Vol. 25. LC 64-8723. 776p. 1983. 245.00 (*0-8103-0638-7*); LC 64-8723. 218.00 (*0-318-52353-1*) Gale.

Bookman's Price Index: Modern First Edition, Vol. 1. Ed. by Daniel F. McGrath. 1000p. 1987. 216.00 (*0-8103-2535-7*, 004340-99584) Gale.

Bookman's Price Index: CUM Index, Vol. 537-46. Ed. by Anne McGrath. 1000p. 1993. 245.00 (*0-8103-9554-1*) Gale.

Bookman's Price Index, Vol. 36, Vol. 36. Ed. by Daniel F. McGrath. 1000p. 1988. 245.00 (*0-8103-1807-5*) Gale.

Bookman's Price Index, Vol. 39, Vol. 39. Daniel F. McGrath. 1000p. 1989. 245.00 (*0-8103-1812-1*) Gale.

Bookman's Progress: Selected Writings. Lawrence C. Powell. Ed. by William Targ & Ward Ritchie. 246p. 1968. 15.00 (*0-910740-25-9*) Holmes.

Bookman's Quintet, Five Catalogues about Books, Bibliography, Printing History, Booksellers, Libraries, Presses, Collectors. Leona Rostenberg et al. (Illus.). 283p. 1980. 25.00 (*0-938768-03-4*) Oak Knoll.

Bookman's Tale. Berry Fleming. LC 90-53321. 160p. 1991. 22.00 (*1-877946-02-8*) Permanent Pr.

***Bookman's Wake.** John Dunning. 1995. 21.00 (*0-684-80003-9*) S&S Trade.

Bookmarks for Cooks: Markers for Your Cookbooks. Starrhill Press Staff. (Orig.). 1991. pap. 6.95 (*0-913515-72-8*) Elliott & Clark.

Bookmen's Bedlam of Literary Oddities. Walter H. Blumenthal. LC 77-80383. (Essay Index Reprint Ser.). 1977. 26.95 (*0-8369-1022-2*) Ayer.

An Asterisk (*) at the beginning of an entry indicates that the title is appearing in BIP for the first time.

An Asterisk (*) at the beginning of an entry indicates that the title is appearing in BIP for the first time.

857

Books for Young Explorers, 4 vols, Set 2. Incl. Animals in Danger. Peggy D. Winston. 1978. (*0-318-54519-5*); Animals That Live in the Sea. Joan A. Straker. 1978. (*0-318-54520-9*); Explore a Spooky Swamp. Wendy W. Cortesi. 1978. (*0-318-54521-7*); Zoo Babies. Donna K. Grosvenor. 1978. (*0-318-54522-5*); Honeybees. (*0-318-54523-3*); How Animals Hide. (*0-318-54524-1*); Namu. (*0-318-54525-X*); Pandas. (*0-318-54526-8*); Spiders. (*0-318-54527-6*); Creepy Crawly Things. (*0-318-54528-4*); Three Little Indians. (*0-318-54529-2*); Cats. (*0-318-54530-6*); Creatures of the Night. (*0-318-54535-7*); Blue Whale. (*0-318-54536-5*); Let's Go to the Moon. (*0-318-54537-3*); What Happens in the Spring. (*0-318-54538-1*); Cowboys. (*0-318-54539-X*); Day in the Woods. (*0-318-54540-3*); Tricks Animals Play. (*0-318-54541-1*); Wild Ponies of Assateague Island. lib. bdg. (*0-318-54542-X*); Wild Cats. Peggy D. Winston. (*0-318-57224-9*); Amazing Animal Groups. (*0-318-57225-7*); Koalas & Kangaroos: Strange Animals of Australia. Toni Eugene. (*0-318-57226-5*); Life in Ponds & Streams. William H. Amos. (*0-318-57227-3*); Animals That Travel. Jennifer C. Urquhart. (*0-318-57228-1*); Puppies. Judith E. Rinard. (*0-318-57229-X*); Animals in Winter. Ronald M. Fisher. (*0-318-57230-3*); What Happens in the Autumn. Suzanne Venino. (*0-318-57231-1*); (J). (ps-3). 1973. Set lib. bdg. 16.95 (*0-87044-305-4*) Natl Geog.

Books for Young Explorers, 4 vols., Set 3. Incl. Animals in Danger. Peggy D. Winston. 1978. (*0-318-54519-5*); Animals That Live in the Sea. Joan A. Straker. 1978. (*0-318-54520-9*); Explore a Spooky Swamp. Wendy W. Cortesi. 1978. (*0-318-54521-7*); Zoo Babies. Donna K. Grosvenor. 1978. (*0-318-54522-5*); Honeybees. (*0-318-54523-3*); How Animals Hide. (*0-318-54524-1*); Namu. (*0-318-54525-X*); Pandas. (*0-318-54526-8*); Spiders. (*0-318-54527-6*); Creepy Crawly Things. (*0-318-54528-4*); Three Little Indians. (*0-318-54529-2*); Cats. (*0-318-54530-6*); Creatures of the Night. (*0-318-54535-7*); Blue Whale. (*0-318-54536-5*); Let's Go to the Moon. (*0-318-54537-3*); What Happens in the Spring. (*0-318-54538-1*); Cowboys. (*0-318-54539-X*); Day in the Woods. (*0-318-54540-3*); Tricks Animals Play. (*0-318-54541-1*); Wild Ponies of Assateague Island. lib. bdg. (*0-318-54542-X*); Wild Cats. Peggy D. Winston. (*0-318-57224-9*); Amazing Animal Groups. (*0-318-57225-7*); Koalas & Kangaroos: Strange Animals of Australia. Toni Eugene. (*0-318-57226-5*); Life in Ponds & Streams. William H. Amos. (*0-318-57227-3*); Animals That Travel. Jennifer C. Urquhart. (*0-318-57228-1*); Puppies. Judith E. Rinard. (*0-318-57229-X*); Animals in Winter. Ronald M. Fisher. (*0-318-57230-3*); What Happens in the Autumn. Suzanne Venino. (*0-318-57231-1*); (Illus.). (J). (ps-3). 1974. Set. 13.95 (*0-87044-157-4*); Incl. (*0-318-54519-5*); (*0-318-54520-9*); (*0-318-54521-7*); (*0-318-54522-5*); (*0-318-54523-3*); (*0-318-54524-1*); (*0-318-54525-X*); (*0-318-54526-8*); (*0-318-54527-6*); (*0-318-54528-4*); (*0-318-54529-2*); (*0-318-54530-6*); (*0-318-54535-7*); (*0-318-54536-5*); (*0-318-54537-3*); (*0-318-54538-1*); (*0-318-54539-X*); (*0-318-54540-3*); (*0-318-54541-1*); lib. bdg. (*0-318-54542-X*); (*0-318-57224-9*); (*0-318-57225-7*); (*0-318-57226-5*); (*0-318-57227-3*); (*0-318-57228-1*); (*0-318-57229-X*); (*0-318-57230-3*); (*0-318-57231-1*); Set lib. bdg. 16.95 (*0-87044-310-0*) Natl Geog.

Books for Young Explorers, 4 vols., Set 4. Incl. Animals in Danger. Peggy D. Winston. 1978. (*0-318-54519-5*); Animals That Live in the Sea. Joan A. Straker. 1978. (*0-318-54520-9*); Explore a Spooky Swamp. Wendy W. Cortesi. 1978. (*0-318-54521-7*); Zoo Babies. Donna K. Grosvenor. 1978. (*0-318-54522-5*); Honeybees. (*0-318-54523-3*); How Animals Hide. (*0-318-54524-1*); Namu. (*0-318-54525-X*); Pandas. (*0-318-54526-8*); Spiders. (*0-318-54527-6*); Creepy Crawly Things. (*0-318-54528-4*); Three Little Indians. (*0-318-54529-2*); Cats. (*0-318-54530-6*); Creatures of the Night. (*0-318-54535-7*); Blue Whale. (*0-318-54536-5*); Let's Go to the Moon. (*0-318-54537-3*); What Happens in the Spring. (*0-318-54538-1*); Cowboys. (*0-318-54539-X*); Day in the Woods. (*0-318-54540-3*); Tricks Animals Play. (*0-318-54541-1*); Wild Ponies of Assateague Island. lib. bdg. (*0-318-54542-X*); Wild Cats. Peggy D. Winston. (*0-318-57224-9*); Amazing Animal Groups. (*0-318-57225-7*); Koalas & Kangaroos: Strange Animals of Australia. Toni Eugene. (*0-318-57226-5*); Life in Ponds & Streams. William H. Amos. (*0-318-57227-3*); Animals That Travel. Jennifer C. Urquhart. (*0-318-57228-1*); Puppies. Judith E. Rinard. (*0-318-57229-X*); Animals in Winter. Ronald M. Fisher. (*0-318-57230-3*); What Happens in the Autumn. Suzanne Venino. (*0-318-57231-1*); (J). Set lib. bdg. 16.95 (*0-87044-175-2*) Natl Geog.

Books for Young Explorers, 4 vols., Set 5. Ed. by National Geographic Society. Incl. Camping Adventures. (*0-318-54531-4*); Wonders of the Desert World. (*0-318-54532-2*); Playful Dolphins. (*0-318-54533-0*); Animals That Build Their Homes. (*0-318-54534-9*); (J). 13.95 (*0-87044-200-7*); Incl. (*0-318-54531-4*); (*0-318-54532-2*); (*0-318-54533-0*); (*0-318-54534-9*); Set lib. bdg. 16.95 (*0-87044-205-8*) Natl Geog.

Books for Young Explorers, 4 vols., Set 6. Incl. Animals in Danger. Peggy D. Winston. 1978. (*0-318-54519-5*); Animals That Live in the Sea. Joan A. Straker. 1978. (*0-318-54520-9*); Explore a Spooky Swamp. Wendy W. Cortesi. 1978. (*0-318-54521-7*); Zoo Babies. Donna K. Grosvenor. 1978. (*0-318-54522-5*); Honeybees. (*0-318-54523-3*); How Animals Hide. (*0-318-54524-1*); Namu. (*0-318-54525-X*); Pandas. (*0-318-54526-8*); Spiders. (*0-318-54527-6*); Creepy Crawly Things. (*0-318-54528-4*); Three Little Indians. (*0-318-54529-2*); Cats. (*0-318-54530-6*); Creatures of the Night. (*0-318-54535-7*); Blue Whale. (*0-318-54536-5*); Let's Go to the Moon. (*0-318-54537-3*); What Happens in the Spring. (*0-318-54538-1*); Cowboys. (*0-318-54539-X*); Day in the Woods. (*0-318-54540-3*); Tricks Animals Play. (*0-318-54541-1*); Wild Ponies of Assateague Island. lib. bdg. (*0-318-54542-X*); Wild Cats. Peggy D. Winston. (*0-318-57224-9*); Amazing Animal Groups. (*0-318-57225-7*); Koalas & Kangaroos: Strange Animals of Australia. Toni Eugene. (*0-318-57226-5*); Life in Ponds & Streams. William H. Amos. (*0-318-57227-3*); Animals That Travel. Jennifer C. Urquhart. (*0-318-57228-1*); Puppies. Judith E. Rinard. (*0-318-57229-X*); Animals in Winter. Ronald M. Fisher. (*0-318-57230-3*); What Happens in the Autumn. Suzanne Venino. (*0-318-57231-1*); (J). 13.95 (*0-87044-245-7*); Incl. (*0-318-54519-5*); (*0-318-54520-9*); (*0-318-54521-7*); (*0-318-54522-5*); (*0-318-54523-3*); (*0-318-54524-1*); (*0-318-54525-X*); (*0-318-54526-8*); (*0-318-54527-6*); (*0-318-54528-4*); (*0-318-54529-2*); (*0-318-54530-6*); (*0-318-54535-7*); (*0-318-54536-5*); (*0-318-54537-3*); (*0-318-54538-1*); (*0-318-54539-X*); (*0-318-54540-3*); (*0-318-54541-1*); lib. bdg. (*0-318-54542-X*); (*0-318-57224-9*); (*0-318-57225-7*); (*0-318-57226-5*); (*0-318-57227-3*); (*0-318-57228-1*); (*0-318-57229-X*); (*0-318-57230-3*); (*0-318-57231-1*); Set lib. bdg. 16.95 (*0-87044-250-3*) Natl Geog.

Books for Young Explorers, 4 vols, Set 7. Incl. Animals in Danger. Peggy D. Winston. 1978. (*0-318-54519-5*); Animals That Live in the Sea. Joan A. Straker. 1978. (*0-318-54520-9*); Explore a Spooky Swamp. Wendy W. Cortesi. 1978. (*0-318-54521-7*); Zoo Babies. Donna K. Grosvenor. 1978. (*0-318-54522-5*); Honeybees. (*0-318-54523-3*); How Animals Hide. (*0-318-54524-1*); Namu. (*0-318-54525-X*); Pandas. (*0-318-54526-8*); Spiders. (*0-318-54527-6*); Creepy Crawly Things. (*0-318-54528-4*); Three Little Indians. (*0-318-54529-2*); Cats. (*0-318-54530-6*); Creatures of the Night. (*0-318-54535-7*); Blue Whale. (*0-318-54536-5*); Let's Go to the Moon. (*0-318-54537-3*); What Happens in the Spring. (*0-318-54538-1*); Cowboys. (*0-318-54539-X*); Day in the Woods. (*0-318-54540-3*); Tricks Animals Play. (*0-318-54541-1*); Wild Ponies of Assateague Island. lib. bdg. (*0-318-54542-X*); Wild Cats. Peggy D. Winston. (*0-318-57224-9*); Amazing Animal Groups. (*0-318-57225-7*); Koalas & Kangaroos: Strange Animals of Australia. Toni Eugene. (*0-318-57226-5*); Life in Ponds & Streams. William H. Amos. (*0-318-57227-3*); Animals That Travel. Jennifer C. Urquhart. (*0-318-57228-1*); Puppies. Judith E. Rinard. (*0-318-57229-X*); Animals in Winter. Ronald M. Fisher. (*0-318-57230-3*); What Happens in the Autumn. Suzanne Venino. (*0-318-57231-1*); (Illus.). (J). (gr. 4-8). 1978. 13.95 (*0-87044-265-1*); Incl. (*0-318-54519-5*); (*0-318-54520-9*); (*0-318-54521-7*); (*0-318-54522-5*); (*0-318-54523-3*); (*0-318-54524-1*); (*0-318-54525-X*); (*0-318-54526-8*); (*0-318-54527-6*); (*0-318-54528-4*); (*0-318-54529-2*); (*0-318-54530-6*); (*0-318-54535-7*); (*0-318-54536-5*); (*0-318-54537-3*); (*0-318-54538-1*); (*0-318-54539-X*); (*0-318-54540-3*); (*0-318-54541-1*); lib. bdg. (*0-318-54542-X*); (*0-318-57224-9*); (*0-318-57225-7*); (*0-318-57226-5*); (*0-318-57227-3*); (*0-318-57228-1*); (*0-318-57229-X*); (*0-318-57230-3*); (*0-318-57231-1*); Set lib. bdg. 16.95 (*0-87044-270-8*) Natl Geog.

Books for Young Explorers, 4 vols., Set 12. Incl. Helping Our Animal Friends. Judith E. Rinard. 1985. (*0-318-59788-8*); Creatures of the Woods. Toni Eugene. 1985. (*0-318-59789-6*); World Beneath Your Feet. Judith E. Rinard. 1985. (*0-318-59790-X*); Penguins & Polar Bears. Sandra L. Crow. 1985. (*0-318-59791-8*); Baby Bears & How They Grow. Jane H. Buxton. (*0-318-60376-4*); Saving Our Animal Friends. Susan McGrath. (*0-318-60377-2*); Animals That Live in Trees. Jane R. McCauley. (*0-318-60378-0*); Animals & Their Hiding Places. Jane R. McCauley. (*0-318-60379-9*); (Illus.). 1985. Set. 13.95 (*0-87044-563-4*); Incl. (*0-318-59788-8*); (*0-318-59789-6*); (*0-318-59790-X*); (*0-318-59791-8*); (*0-318-60376-4*); (*0-318-60377-2*); (*0-318-60378-0*); (*0-318-60379-9*); Set lib. bdg. 16.95 (*0-87044-568-5*) Natl Geog.

Books for Young Explorers, 4 vols., Set 15. Ed. by National Geographic Society Staff. (J). (gr. k-4). 1988. lib. bdg. 16.95 (*0-87044-742-4*) Natl Geog.

Books for Young Explorers, 4 vols., Set 18. Incl. Deer Growing Up in the Wild. Judith E. Rinard. 1991. 13.95 (*0-87044-843-9*); Towns Down Underground. Gene S. Stuart. 1991. 13.95 (*0-87044-846-3*); Pets You Love. Jennifer C. Urquhart. 1991. 13.95 (*0-87044-845-5*); Dinnertime for Animals. Jane R. McCauley. 1991. 13.95 (*0-87044-844-7*); 1991. write for info. (*0-318-69251-1*) Natl Geog.

Books for Young Explorers: Along a Rocky Shore; Animal Families; Lions & Tigers & Leopards: The Big Cats; Our Amazing Animal Friends, 4 bks., Set. Ed. by Donald J. Crump. (J). (gr. k-4). 1990. 13.95 (*0-87044-821-8*) Natl Geog.

Books for Young Gentlemen. rev. ed. Joan J. Grubbs et al. (Illus.). 50p. (J). (gr. 6-8). 1993. 25.00 (*1-56611-024-6*); pap. 25.00 (*1-56611-071-8*) Jonas.

Books for Young Ladies. rev. ed. Joan Abell. (Illus.). (YA). Date not set. 25.00 (*1-56611-028-9*); pap. 25.00 (*1-56611-072-6*) Jonas.

Books Forever. Manoj Das. (Nehru Library for Children). (Illus.). (J). (gr. 2-8). 1979. pap. 2.50 (*0-89744-175-3*) Auromere.

Books from Chapel Hill, 1922-1972: A Complete Catalog of the University of North Carolina Press. LC 72-78422. xliv, 244p. 1972. pap. 5.00 (*0-8078-1198-X*) U of NC Pr.

Books in Action: The Armed Services Editions. LC 84-600198. 78p. 1984. 6.95 (*0-8444-0466-7*) Lib Congress.

Books in American History: A Basic List for High Schools & Junior Colleges. 2nd ed. John E. Wiltz & Nancy C. Cridland. LC 80-8766. 125p. reprint ed. pap. 35.70 (*0-8357-7346-9*, 2056727) Bks Demand.

Books in Black or Red. Edmund L. Pearson. LC 77-93371. (Essay Index Reprint Ser.). 1977. 23.95 (*0-8369-1267-5*) Ayer.

Books in Brazil: A History of the Publishing Trade. L. Hallewell. LC 82-10826. 537p. 1982. 37.50 (*0-8108-1591-5*) Scarecrow.

Books in Cambridge Inventories: Book-Lists from Vice-Chancellor's Court Probate Inventories in the Tudor & Stuart Periods, 2 vols. E. S. Leedham-Green. 1987. Catalogue, Vol. II, 867pp. 165.00 (*0-521-30888-7*) Cambridge U Pr.

Books in Cambridge Inventories: Book-Lists from Vice-Chancellor's Court Probate Inventories in the Tudor & Stuart Periods, 2 vols., Vol. I: The Inventories. E. S. Leedham-Green. 682p. 1987. The Inventories, Vol. I, 682pp. 165.00 (*0-521-30873-9*) Cambridge U Pr.

Books in Chains. J. Blades. 1976. lib. bdg. 59.95 (*0-8490-1537-5*) Gordon Pr.

Books in General. Victor S. Pritchett. LC 70-110378. 258p. 1970. reprint ed. text ed. 38.50 (*0-8371-4582-1*, PRBG, Greenwood Pr) Greenwood.

Books in General, First Series. John C. Squire. LC 70-142699. (Essay Index Reprint Ser.). 1977. 20.95 (*0-8369-2136-4*) Ayer.

Books in General, Second Series. John C. Squire. LC 70-142700. (Essay Index Reprint Ser.). 1977. 20.95 (*0-8369-2137-2*) Ayer.

Books in General, Third Series. John C. Squire. LC 73-142701. (Essay Index Reprint Ser.). 1977. 15.95 (*0-8369-2138-0*) Ayer.

Books in Manuscript. Falconer Madan. LC 68-25315. (Reference Ser.: No. 44). (Illus.). (C). 1972. reprint ed. lib. bdg. 39.95 (*0-8383-0213-0*) M S G Haskell Hse.

Books in My Baggage: Adventures in Reading & Collecting. Lawrence C. Powell. LC 73-726. 255p. 1973. reprint ed. text ed. 65.00 (*0-8371-6784-1*, POBB, Greenwood Pr) Greenwood.

Books in My Life. Henry Miller. LC 71-88728. 1969. reprint ed. pap. 10.95 (*0-8112-0108-2*, NDP280) New Directions.

Books in Our Future: Perspectives & Proposals. Ed. by John Y. Cole. LC 87-600047. 399p. 1987. 16.00 (*0-8444-0554-X*, 030-000-00188-5) Lib Congress.

***Books in Print & Subject Guide to Books in Print on Microfiche 1994-95.** Ed. by Bowker, R. R., Staff. Date not set. write for info. (*0-8352-3685-4*) Bowker.

Books in Print on Microfiche 1994-95. Ed. by Bowker, R. R., Staff. 1994. fiche 775.00 (*0-8352-3523-8*) Bowker.

***Books in Print on Microfiche 1995-96.** Ed. by Bowker, R. R., Staff. 1995. fiche write for info. (*0-8352-3690-0*) Bowker.

Books in Print Supplement 1994-95, 3 Vols., 1. Ed. by Bowker, R. R., Staff. 3600p. 1995. write for info. (*0-8352-3510-6*) Bowker.

Books in Print Supplement 1994-95, 3 Vols., 2. Ed. by Bowker, R. R., Staff. 3600p. 1995. write for info. (*0-8352-3511-4*) Bowker.

Books in Print Supplement 1994-95, 3 Vols., 3. Ed. by Bowker, R. R., Staff. 3600p. 1995. write for info. (*0-8352-3512-2*) Bowker.

Books in Print Supplement 1994-95, 3 Vols., Set. Ed. by Bowker, R. R., Staff. 3600p. 1995. 245.00 (*0-8352-3509-2*) Bowker.

***Books In Print Supplement, 1995-96, Set.** Ed. by Bowker, R. R., Staff. 6000p. 1996. 249.95 (*0-8352-3661-7*) Bowker.

Books in Print 1993-94, 10 vols. 46th ed. Ed. by Bowker, R. R., Staff. Incl. 1993. Set. 425.00 (*0-8352-3354-5*); 1. 1993. (*0-8352-3355-3*); 2. 1993. (*0-8352-3356-1*); 3. 1993. (*0-8352-3357-X*); 4. 1993. (*0-8352-3358-8*); 5. 1993. (*0-8352-3359-6*); 6. 1993. (*0-8352-3360-X*); 7. 1993. (*0-8352-3361-8*); 8. 1993. (*0-8352-3362-6*); 9. 1993. (*0-8352-3363-4*); 10. 1993. (*0-8352-3364-2*); 1993. Set microfiche. 775.00 (*0-8352-3433-9*); 1993. Set microfiche of Books in Print & Subject Guide to Books in Print combo. 1,095.00 (*0-8352-3480-0*); 1993. write for info. (*0-318-72255-0*) Bowker.

Books in Print 1994-95, 10 vols. Ed. by Bowker, R. R., Staff. 13800p. 1994. Vol. 8. (0-8352-3506-8). write for info. (*0-318-72441-3*) Bowker.

Books in Print 1994-95, 10 vols., 1. Ed. by Bowker, R. R., Staff. 13800p. 1994. write for info. (*0-8352-3499-1*) Bowker.

Books in Print 1994-95, 10 vols., 2. Ed. by Bowker, R. R., Staff. 13800p. 1994. write for info. (*0-8352-3500-9*) Bowker.

Books in Print 1994-95, 10 vols., 3. Ed. by Bowker, R. R., Staff. 13800p. 1994. write for info. (*0-8352-3501-7*) Bowker.

Books in Print 1994-95, 10 vols., 4. Ed. by Bowker, R. R., Staff. 13800p. 1994. write for info. (*0-8352-3502-5*) Bowker.

Books in Print 1994-95, 10 vols., 5. Ed. by Bowker, R. R., Staff. 13800p. 1994. write for info. (*0-8352-3503-3*) Bowker.

Books in Print 1994-95, 10 vols., 6. Ed. by Bowker, R. R., Staff. 13800p. 1994. write for info. (*0-8352-3504-1*) Bowker.

Books in Print 1994-95, 10 vols., 7. Ed. by Bowker, R. R., Staff. 13800p. 1994. write for info. (*0-8352-3505-X*) Bowker.

Books in Print 1994-95, 10 vols., Set. Ed. by Bowker, R. R., Staff. 13800p. 1994. 450.00 (*0-8352-3498-3*) Bowker.

Books in Print 1995-96, 10 vols. Ed. by Bowker, R. R., Staff. 14750p. 1995. 475.00 (*0-8352-3644-7*) Bowker. "Untangles the bibliographic knots... present(ed) at reference desks & on interlibrary loan request forms."--WILSON LIBRARY BULLETIN. "BIP has continued to expand (now over 1 million titles) & enhance the variety of information & accessibility to it."--REFERENCE & RESEARCH BOOK NEWS. "With its million plus titles & long established database, BIP has little competition...there is simply no other work that can replace it."--AMERICAN REFERENCE BOOK ANNUAL. With over 1.5 million entries, BOOKS IN PRINT 1995-96 is the definitive information resource for books published & distributed in the United States. Only BOOKS IN PRINT has: * entries for over 1.3 million books of all kinds - adult, juvenile, popular, scholarly & reprints - with over 174,000 new titles. * some 590,000 price entry revisions, plus a separate O.P./O.S.I. Volume that lists nearly 170,000 titles declared out-of-print or out-of-stock indefinitely from July 1994 through July 1995. * a stand alone Publishers Index to more than 44,000 firms. * the most complete & current bibliographic & ordering information for every title - UPDATED BY THE PUBLISHERS THEMSELVES THROUGH BOWKERPOWER - from pages to price & publisher, to edition, binding & ISBN. * thousands of Publisher Provided Annotations that summarize the books themselves. To ensure high information quality, electronic transfer methods enable leading publishers to download bibliographic information from their own computers directly in the BOOKS IN PRINT database. Indexing bars at the edge of the page mark off each alphabetical section of the Author & Title guides & boldface symbols flag new titles. Books in Print is the one resource that keeps you abreast of all book changes.** ***Publisher Provided Annotation.

***Books in Print 1995-96, Vol. 1.** Ed. by Bowker, R. R., Staff. 1995. write for info. (*0-8352-3645-5*) Bowker.

***Books in Print 1995-96, Vol. 2.** Ed. by Bowker, R. R., Staff. 1995. write for info. (*0-8352-3646-3*) Bowker.

***Books in Print 1995-96, Vol. 3.** Ed. by Bowker, R. R., Staff. 1995. write for info. (*0-8352-3647-1*) Bowker.

***Books in Print 1995-96, Vol. 4.** Ed. by Bowker, R. R., Staff. 1995. write for info. (*0-8352-3648-X*) Bowker.

***Books in Print 1995-96, Vol. 5.** Ed. by Bowker, R. R., Staff. 1995. write for info. (*0-8352-3649-8*) Bowker.

***Books in Print 1995-96, Vol. 6.** Ed. by Bowker, R. R., Staff. 1995. write for info. (*0-8352-3650-1*) Bowker.

***Books in Print 1995-96, Vol. 7.** Ed. by Bowker, R. R., Staff. 1995. write for info. (*0-8352-3651-X*) Bowker.

***Books in Print 1995-96, Vol. 8.** Ed. by Bowker, R. R., Staff. 1995. write for info. (*0-8352-3652-8*) Bowker.

***Books in Print 1995-96, Vol. 9.** Ed. by Bowker, R. R., Staff. 1995. write for info. (*0-8352-3653-6*) Bowker.

***Books in Print 1995-96, Vol. 10.** Ed. by Bowker, R. R., Staff. 1995. write for info. (*0-8352-3654-4*) Bowker.

Books in Series, 1985-89, 2 vols., 1. 2549p. 1989. write for info. (*0-8352-2680-8*) Bowker.

Books in Series, 1985-89, 2 vols., 2. 2549p. 1989. write for info. (*0-8352-2681-6*) Bowker.

Books in Series, 1985-89, 2 vols., Set. 2459p. 1989. 199.95 (*0-8352-2679-4*) Bowker.

Books in Spanish for Children & Young Adults: An Annotated Guide. Isabel Schon. LC 83-3315. (Series II). Orig. Title: Libros Infantiles y Juveniles en Espanol: Una Guia Anotada. 172p. 1983. 22.50 (*0-8108-1620-2*) Scarecrow.

Books in Spanish for Children & Young Adults: An Annotated Guide. Isabel Schon. LC 85-2196. (Series III). Orig. Title: Libros Infantiles y Juveniles en Espanol: Una Guia Anotada. 220p. 1985. 22.50 (*0-8108-1807-8*) Scarecrow.

Books in Spanish for Children & Young Adults: An Annotated Guide, No. IV. Isabel Schon. LC 87-9785. Orig. Title: Libros Infantiles y Juveniles en Espanol: Una Guia Anotada. 313p. 1987. 29.50 (*0-8108-2004-8*) Scarecrow.

An Asterisk (*) at the beginning of an entry indicates that the title is appearing in BIP for the first time.

Books in Spanish for Children & Young Adults: An Annotated Guide, Series V. Isabel Schon. LC 89-10526. 180p. 1989. 20.00 (*0-8108-2238-5*) Scarecrow.

Books in Spanish for Children & Young Adults - Libros Infantiles y Juveniles en Espanol, Ser. No. VI: An Annotated Guide - Una Guia Anotada. Isabel Schon. LC 92-33302. 305p. 1993. 35.00 (*0-8108-2622-4*) Scarecrow.

Books in the Western World: A Cultural History. Karl Schottenloher. Tr. by William D. Boyd & Irmgard H. Wolfe. LC 88-42501. 551p. 1989. lib. bdg. 62.50x (*0-89950-344-6*) McFarland & Co.

Books in the 1990s: Proceedings of the 23rd Congress of the International Publishers Association. Ed. by Gordon Graham. 125p. 1989. pap. text ed. 54.00 (*0-86291-855-3*) Bowker-Saur.

Books in World History: A Guide for Teachers & Students. W. Warren Wagar. LC 73-75791. 192p. reprint ed. pap. 54.80 (*0-8357-7347-7*, 2015837) Bks Demand.

Books Kids Will Sit Still For: The Complete Read-Aloud Guide. 2nd rev. ed. Judy Freeman. 660p. 1990. 45.00 (*0-8352-3010-4*) Bowker.
"Liberally sprinkled with titles, chock full of ideas, & supplemented with high-quality bibliographies...librarians will find helpful & few children will be able to resist."--BOOKLIST. This vital guide culls the best & most exciting picture books, poetry, folklore, fiction, & nonfiction books for children from preschool through the sixth grade. Each entry provides a brief plot summary, extension activities, related titles, & subject designations, as well as bibliographic details. Author, Title, Illustrator, & Subject Indexes complete each volume. BOOKS KIDS WILL SIT STILL FOR contains over 2,100 recommended titles through 1989. MORE BOOKS KIDS WILL SIT STILL FOR brings these listings up-to-date with 2,000 new titles. *Publisher Provided Annotation.*

Books, Libraries & Electronics: Essays on the Future of Written Communication. Efrem Sigel et al. LC 82-15229. (Professional Librarian Ser.). 139p. 1982. text ed. 27.95 (*0-86729-024-2*, Hall Reference) Macmillan.

Books, Libraries, & Information in Slavic & East European Studies: Proceedings of the Second International Conference of Slavic Librarians & Information Specialists. Ed. by Marianna T. Choldin. LC 85-43530. (Russica Bibliography Ser.: No. 8). 540p. (Orig.). 1986. pap. 37.50 (*0-89830-107-6*) Russica Pubs.

Books, Manuscripts, & the History of Medicine: Essays on the Fiftieth Anniversary of the Osler Library. Ed. by Philip M. Teigen. 112p. 1982. 14.95 (*0-88202-199-0*, Sci Hist) Watson Pub Intl.

Books of American Negro Spirituals, 2 vols. in one. Ed. by James Weldon Johnson & J. R. Johnson. LC 77-23414. 1977. reprint ed. text ed. 14.95 (*0-306-80074-8*) Da Capo.

Books of Amos & Hosea. Harry Mowvley. 176p. pap. 14.95 (*0-7162-0475-4*, Epworth Pr) TPI PA.

Books of Assumption of Scottish Benefices, c.1562. James Kirk. (Records of Social & Economic History, New Series British Academy: No. XXI). (Illus.). 1000p. 1995. 98.00 (*0-19-726125-6*) OUP.

Books of Autolykos: On a Moving Sphere & on Risings & Settings. Tr. by Frans Bruin & Alexander Vonjidis. (Illus.). 83p. (C). 1971. text ed. 12.00 (*0-8156-6034-0*, Am U Beirut) Syracuse U Pr.

Books of Contemplation: Medieval Jewish Mystical Sources. Mark Verman. LC 90-44905. (SUNY Series in Judaica: Hermeneutics, Mysticism, & Religion). 270p. (C). 1992. 59.50 (*0-7914-0719-5*); pap. 21.95 (*0-7914-0720-9*) State U NY Pr.

***Books of Eros: Art & Letters from Yellow Silk.** Ed. by Lily Pond & Richard A. Russo. LC 94-33164. 1995. 22.00 (*0-517-79962-6*, Crown) Crown Pub Group.

Books of Ezra & Nehemiah. F. Charles Fensham. (New International Commentary on the Old Testament Ser.). 288p. 1983. 34.99 (*0-8028-2362-9*) Eerdmans.

Books of Faith & Power. John T. McNeill. LC 75-134112. (Essay Index Reprint Ser.). 1977. 20.95 (*0-8369-1996-3*) Ayer.

Books of Haggai & Malachi. Pieter A. Verhoef. Ed. by R. K. Harrison. (New International Commentary on the Old Testament Ser.). 384p. 1987. 27.99 (*0-8028-2376-9*) Eerdmans.

***Books of History.** James E. Smith. LC 95-3858. (Old Testament Survey Ser.). 1995. 24.99 (*0-89900-424-5*) College Pr Pub.

Books of Kiu-Te in the Tibetan Buddhist Tantras. David Reigle. LC 83-60416. (Secret Doctrine Reference Ser.). (Illus.). 80p. (Orig.). 1983. pap. 6.00 (*0-913510-49-1*) Wizards.

Books of Light. Ed. by Robert R. Leichtman & Carl Japikse. (Illus.). 160p. (Orig.). 1986. pap. 4.95 (*0-89804-155-4*) Ariel GA.

Books of Magic. Neil Gaiman. Ed. by Bob Kahan. 200p. 1993. pap. 19.95 (*1-56389-082-8*, Vertigo) DC Comics.

***Books of Magic: Bindings.** J. Rieber. Ed. by Bob Kahan. (Illus.). 112p. 1995. pap. 12.95 (*1-56389-187-5*, Vertigo) DC Comics.

Books of Miles, Westland & Bristol Aircraft: An Original Anthology, 3 vols. in 1. Ed. by James B. Gilbert. LC 79-7281. (Flight: Its First Seventy-Five Years Ser.). (Illus.). 1980. lib. bdg. 73.95 (*0-405-12190-3*) Ayer.

Books of Nahum, Habakkuk, & Zephaniah. O. Palmer Robertson. (New International Commentary on the Old Testament Ser.). 384p. (C). 1990. 29.99 (*0-8028-2374-2*) Eerdmans.

Books of Nature & Scripture: Recent Essays on Natural Philosophy, Theology, & Biblical Criticism in the Netherlands of Spinoza's Time & the British Isles of Newton's Time. Ed. by James E. Force & Richard H. Popkin. LC 93-29487. (Archives Internationales d'Histoire des Idees (International Archives of the History of Ideas) Ser.: Vol. 139). 232p. (C). 1994. lib. bdg. 87.00 (*0-7923-2467-6*) Kluwer Ac.

Books of Rachel. large type ed. Joel Gross. 1985. 13.95 (*0-7089-8265-4*, Charnwood) Ulverscroft.

Books of Songs: The Ancient Chinese Classic of Poetry. Tr. by Arthur Waley. 368p. 1987. pap. 11.95 (*0-8021-3021-6*) Grove-Atltic.

Books of the Bible. Jerold C. Potter. Ed. by Bowen & Bowen Type Setters Staff. 36p. (J). 1988. pap. text ed. 1.50 (*0-925306-00-2*) WOFPPM.

Books of the Bible. Philip G. Roets. 155p. (Orig.). (C). 1992. pap. text ed. 19.95 (*0-911943-34-X*) Leadership Pub.

Books of the Bible, 2 vols., Set. Bernard W. Anderson. 888p. 1989. text ed. 179.00 (*0-684-18487-7*, Scribners) S&S Trade.

Books of the Brave: Being an Account of Books & of Men in the Spanish Conquest & Settlement of the Sixteenth-Century New World. Irving A. Leonard. (C). 1992. 45.00 (*0-520-07990-6*); pap. 16.00 (*0-520-07816-0*) U CA Pr.

Books of the California Gold Rush: A Centennial Selection. Carl I. Wheat. 50p. 1991. reprint ed. pap. 17.50 (*0-926158-11-2*) W M Morrison.

Books of the Colorado River: A Selective Bibliography. Francis Farquhar. 50p. 1991. reprint ed. pap. 17.50 (*0-926158-10-4*) W M Morrison.

Books of the Dead. Stanislav Grof. LC 92-62130. (Art & Imagination Ser.). (Illus.). 96p. 1994. pap. 15.95 (*0-500-81041-9*) Thames Hudson.

Books of the Keepers. Ann Downer. LC 92-30131. 256p. (J). (gr. 7 up). 1993. text ed. 15.95 (*0-689-31519-8*, Atheneum Bks Young) S&S Childrens.

Books of the New Testament. Julianne Booth. (Arch Books Supplement Ser.). (J). (gr. k-4). 1981. pap. 1.89 (*0-570-06150-4*, 59-1305) Concordia.

Books of the Old Testament. Julianne Booth. (J). (ps-3). 1988. pap. 1.89 (*0-570-06151-2*) Concordia.

Books of the Times: The New York Times Daily Book Reviews, 1980. (Illus.). 1981. 20.95 (*0-405-14021-5*) Ayer.

Books of Visions. John B. Jones. (Notable American Authors Ser.). 1992. reprint ed. lib. bdg. 75.00 (*0-7812-3513-8*) Rprt Serv.

Books of WAD, a Bibliography of the Books Designed by W. A. Dwiggins. limited rev. ed. Dwight Agner. LC 76-58639. (Illus.). 1977. 25.00 (*0-915346-26-5*) A Wofsy Fine Arts.

Books on Asia from the Near East to the Far East: A Guide for the General Reader. Eleazar Birnbaum. LC 75-151361. 357p. reprint ed. pap. 101.80 (*0-8357-7348-5*, 2014133) Bks Demand.

Books on Israel, Vol. I. Ed. by Ian S. Lustick. LC 87-26763. 111p. (C). 1988. 49.50 (*0-88706-776-X*); pap. 16.95 (*0-88706-777-8*) State U NY Pr.

Books on Tape Catalog, 1987. Ed. by Books on Tape, Inc. Staff. 1988. 5.00 (*0-318-41107-5*) Books on Tape.

***Books on Tape, 1995 Edition: World's Largest Selection of Unabridged Audio Books. Susan Jin. Ed. & Intro. by Duvall Y. Hecht. (Illus.). 1995. write for info. (*0-913369-12-8*) Books on Tape. Books on Tape, Inc. produces the world's largest selection of unabridged audio books. The 1995 Edition of Books on Tape Catalog contains more than 3,000 current & classic full-length bestsellers on cassette. Over 250 are new since the 1994 Edition. (All Books on Tape titles remain in circulation.) Superb professional readers project intelligence, feeling & understanding. Cover titles are: The Chamber (John Grisham); Debt of Honor (Tom Clancy); Thunder Point (Jack Higgins); Inca Gold (Clive Cussler); The Fist of God (Frederick Forsythe); "J" is for Judgement (Sue Grafton); JFK: Reckless Youth (Nigel Hamilton); Big Blues, the Unmaking of IBM (Paul Carroll). Audio book selections are grouped in the following categories: Adventure, Travel & the Sea; Biography; Classics & Family; Fiction; History & War; Humor; Mystery & Intrigue; Non-Fiction; Science Fiction. The Books on Tape, Inc. 1995 Catalog also includes Language Programs, Audio Programs & Abridgements; Management & Business & Personal Achievement. Contents indexed by reader & by title & author. Books on Tape, Inc. releases forty to fifty new full-length readings every other month covering the spectrum of literary genres. Books on Tape cassette recordings available concurrently (or virtually so) with hard cover publication date. Special library packaging, discounts, plans & services. Absolute satisfaction guaranteed.** *Publisher Provided Annotation.*

Books on the Horse & Horsemanship, Riding, Hunting, Breeding, & Racing, 1400-1941. John B. Podeschi. (Illus.). 427p. 1981. 50.00 (*0-905005-53-8*) Yale Ctr Brit Art.

Books on the Move: A Read-about-It, Go-There Guide to America's Best Family Destinations. Susan M. Knorr & Margaret Knorr. Ed. by Pamela Espeland. LC 93-11524. (Illus.). 368p. (Orig.). 1993. pap. 13.95 (*0-915793-53-9*) Free Spirit Pub.

Books on the Shelf. Thomas J. Hardy. LC 76-107708. (Essay Index Reprint Ser.). 1977. 20.95 (*0-8369-1510-0*) Ayer.

Books on the Table. Edmund W. Gosse. LC 74-156653. (Essay Index Reprint Ser.). 1977. reprint ed. 24.95 (*0-8369-2365-0*) Ayer.

Books, Our Eternal Companions. Edmond B. Szekely. (Illus.). 48p. 1971. pap. 3.50 (*0-89564-064-3*) IBS Intl.

Books Out of Print, 1984-88, 3 vols., 1. Ed. by Bowker, R. R., Staff. 3500p. 1988. write for info. (*0-8352-2507-0*) Bowker.

Books Out of Print, 1984-88, 3 vols., 2. Ed. by Bowker, R. R., Staff. 3500p. 1988. write for info. (*0-8352-2508-9*) Bowker.

Books Out of Print, 1984-88, 3 vols., 3. Ed. by Bowker, R. R., Staff. 3500p. 1988. write for info. (*0-8352-2554-2*) Bowker.

Books Out of Print, 1984-88, 3 vols., Set. Ed. by Bowker, R. R., Staff. 3500p. 1988. 110.00 (*0-8352-2506-2*) Bowker.

Books Printed in England Before 1640: A Descriptive Catalogue of 964 Facsimile Editions Now Available for Immediate Delivery. (English Experience Ser.). 257p. 1986. pap. write for info. (*90-221-9995-9*) Walter J Johnson.

Books, Puppets & the Mentally Retarded Student. John Champlin & Connie Champlin. (Illus.). 162p. (Orig.). (J). 1981. pap. 15.95 (*0-938594-00-1*) Spec Lit Pr.

***Books, Readers, Reading.** Ed. by David Walker & Julia Horne. 142p. 1994. 39.95 (*0-7855-0336-6*, Pub. by Deakin Univ AT) St Mut.

Books, Scribes & Learning in the Frankish Kingdoms, 6th-9th Centuries. Rosamond McKitterick. LC 94-7578. (Collected Studies: No. CS 452). (Illus.). 352p. 1994. 89.95 (*0-86078-406-1*, Pub. by Variorum UK) Ashgate Pub Co.

Books Speaking to Books: A Contextual Approach to American Fiction. William T. Stafford. LC 80-25892. 175p. reprint ed. pap. 49.90 (*0-7837-2459-4*, 2042612) Bks Demand.

Books That Bring Life. Eugene W. Brice. 112p. 1983. pap. 7.95 (*0-937462-00-4*) Net Pr.

Books That Bring Life, Vol. I. rev. ed. Eugene Bruce. 1988. pap. 9.95 (*0-937462-11-X*) Net Pr.

Books That Bring Life, Vol. II. Eugene Brice. 1987. pap. 9.95 (*0-937462-05-5*) Net Pr.

Books That Build Character. William Kilpatrick. 1994. pap. 10.00 (*0-671-88423-9*, Touchstone Bks) S&S Trade.

Books That Changed Our Minds. Ed. by Malcolm Cowley & Bernard Smith. LC 72-128230. (Essay Index Reprint Ser.). 1977. 23.95 (*0-8369-1912-2*) Ayer.

Books That Changed the World. Robert B. Downs. 1956. pap. 5.99 (*0-451-62698-2*, Ment) NAL-Dutton.

Books That Changed the World. braille ed. Robert B. Downs. 865p. 1992. vinyl bd. 69.20 (*1-56956-045-5*, BR8730) W A T Braille.

Books That Heal: A Whole Language Approach. Carolyn Mohr et al. 283p. 1991. pap. 23.50 (*0-87287-829-5*) Teacher Ideas Pr.

Books That Made a Difference: What People Told Us. Gordon Sabine & Patricia Sabine. LC 82-24977. viii, 176p. 1983. pap. 21.50 (*0-208-02022-5*, Lib Prof Pubns) Shoe String.

Books That Moved the World. Horace Shipp. 1977. lib. bdg. 250.00 (*0-8490-1538-3*) Gordon Pr.

***Books That Shaped Successful People.** Kelly. 1995. pap. text ed. 12.95 (*0-925190-44-6*) Fairview Press.

Books to Begin On. Nancy Polette. (Illus.). 48p. (J). (ps-1). 1994. pap. 5.95 (*1-879287-28-5*) Bk Lures.

Books to Bytes: Knowledge & Information in the Postmodern Era. Anthony Smith. 184p. 1994. 49.95 (*0-85170-401-8*, Pub. by British Film Inst UK); pap. 19.95 (*0-85170-402-6*, Pub. by British Film Inst UK) Ind U Pr.

Books to Help Children Cope with Separation & Loss: An Annotated Bibliography. 4th ed. Masha K. Rudman et al. 514p. 1994. 49.00 (*0-8352-3412-6*) Bowker.
"...an indispensable tool for librarians, counselors, parents & teachers who may be required to help children facing a separation or loss."--EDUCATION LIBRARIES. "A thorough & thoughtfully prepared reference."--AMERICAN REFERENCE BOOKS ANNUAL. The new 4th edition of this unique selection guide provides librarians, teachers, counselors, & parents with the information needed to choose "real-life" situation books appropriate for children ages 3 to 16 who face difficult times. Here are some 750 fiction & nonfiction books, from folklore to poetry, focusing on separation & loss themes for young people. Topics new to this edition include Homelessness; Economic Loss/ Parents Out of Work; Apartheid. BOOKS TO HELP CHILDREN COPE WITH SEPARATION & LOSS, 4TH EDITION, profiles only the best books, selected "classics" & recommended titles from SCHOOL LIBRARY JOURNAL, BULLETIN OF THE CENTER FOR CHILDREN'S BOOKS, PUBLISHERS WEEKLY, KIRKUS, HORN BOOK, & other publications. Arranged by topic, each annotated entry provides a review of plot & theme, interest/age level, suggestions for use, & complete bibliographic information. This is the ideal reference guide for those who have the opportunity to help children through separation & loss, ranging from going away to camp to the death of a sibling. With approximately half the titles new to this volume, BOOKS TO HELP CHILDREN COPE WITH SEPARATION & LOSS, 4TH EDITION, profiles only the best books: selected "classics" & recommended titles from SCHOOL LIBRARY JOURNAL, BULLETIN OF THE CENTER FOR CHILDREN'S BOOKS, PUBLISHERS WEEKLY, KIRKUS, HORN BOOK, & other publications. Arranged by topic, each annotated entry provides a review of plot & theme, interest/age level, suggestions for use, & complete bibliographic information. This is the ideal reference guide for those who have the opportunity to help children through separation & loss ranging from going away to camp to the death of a sibling. *Publisher Provided Annotation.*

Books to Learn & Live by, 5 bks., Set. Mildred Pfrimmer. Incl. Bk. ABC's of Creation. 1977. (*0-318-55947-1*); Bk. 2. ABC's of the Flood. 1977. (*0-318-55948-X*); Bk. 3. Aardvark in the Art. 1977. (*0-318-55949-8*); Bk. 4. Elephant in Eden. 1977. (*0-318-55950-1*); Bk. 5. Tale of the Whale. 1977. (*0-318-55951-X*); (Little Talkers Ser.). (J). (gr. 3-9). 1977. 17.50 (*0-685-80546-8*) Triumph Pub.

Books Too Good to Miss. Faye Day & Annette Geistfeld. (Illus.). 53p. 1984. pap. 7.50 (*0-912773-04-9*) One Hund Twenty Creat.

Books vs. CD-ROM. COINT Reports Staff. LC 85-641403. (COINT Reports: Vol. 6, No. 6). 22p. (Orig.). 1986. pap. 3.50 (*0-939670-12-7*) Info Digest.

Books We Love Best: A Unique Guide to Children's Books. Intro. by Bay Area Kids & Marilyn Sachs. (Illus.). 128p. (Orig.). 1991. pap. 4.95 (*0-935701-01-X*) Foghorn Pr.

***Books West Southwest.** Lawrence C. Powell. 137p. 1994. pap. 12.95 (*0-614-05596-2*) Bks West SW.

***Books with Manuscript.** R. C. Alston. (Manuscript Studies). 616p. 1994. 120.00 (*0-7123-0329-4*, Pub. by Brit Library UK) U of Toronto Pr.

Books Without Bias: A Guide to Evaluating Children's Literature for Handicapism. 2nd ed. Beverly Slapin. (Illus.). 80p. 1990. pap. 10.00 (*1-878458-51-5*) Squeaky Wheels Pr.

Books You Can Count On: Linking Mathematics & Literature. Rachel Griffiths & Margaret Clyne. LC 91-6662. 112p. 1991. pap. text ed. 15.00 (*0-435-08322-8*, 08322) Heinemann.

Books You Read: Business Edition. Charles E. Jones. (Books You Read: Vol. 1). 1985. 14.95 (*0-937539-00-7*) Executive Bks.

Books You Read: Devotional Edition. Ed. by Charles E. Jones & D. James Kennedy. (Books You Read: Vol. 3). 279p. 1985. 14.95 (*0-937539-02-3*) Executive Bks.

Books You Read: Historical Edition. Ed. by Charles E. Jones. 282p. 1992. 14.95 (*0-937539-03-1*) Executive Bks.

Books You Read: Professional Edition. Charles E. Jones. (Books You Read: Vol. 2). 275p. 1985. 14.95 (*0-937539-01-5*) Executive Bks.

Bookseller As Rogue: John Almon & the Politics of Eighteenth-Century Publishing. Deborah D. Rogers. (American University Studies: English Language & Literature: Ser. IV, Vol. 28). 153p. 1986. text ed. 28.50 (*0-8204-0221-4*) P Lang Pubs.

Booksellers & Stationers in the UK. Euromonitor Staff. (C). 1987. 825.00 (*0-86338-260-6*, Pub. by Euromonitor Pubns UK) Gale.

B

Booksellers Cookbook. Annie Adams. 1989. pap. 14.95 (*0-9624839-0-7*) Cohn Thompson.

***Booksellers Make a Difference: Selected Proceedings of the 1994 Convention of the American Booksellers Association.** American Booksellers Association Staff. 72p. (Orig.). 1994. pap. 10.00 (*1-879556-13-8*) ABA.

Bookselling Business in England. Thomas Joy. 1974. 25.00 (*0-8464-0205-X*) Beekman Pubs.

Bookselling, Reviewing & Reading. Ed. by Peter Davison et al. LC 77-90621. (Literary Taste, Culture & Mass Communication Ser.: Vol. 12). 282p. 1978. lib. bdg. 90.00 (*0-85964-047-7*) Chadwyck-Healey.

Booksharing: One Hundred One Programs to Use with Preschoolers. Margaret R. MacDonald. LC 87-35777. (Illus.). 236p. 1988. lib. bdg. 32.50 (*0-208-02159-0*, Lib Prof Pubns) Shoe String.

Booksharing: One Hundred One Programs to Use with Preschoolers. Margaret R. Macdonald. LC 87-35777. (Illus.). 236p. 1991. pap. text ed. 19.50 (*0-208-02314-3*, Lib Prof Pubns) Shoe String.

Bookshelf: A Guide for Librarians & Systems Managers. Jennifer Rowley & Shelagh Fisher. 300p. 1992. 79.95 (*1-85742-008-X*, Pub. by Ashgate UK) Ashgate Pub Co.

Bookshelf Adventures! see Guided Research Discovery Units: Six Project Books

***Bookshelf Collection Fifth-Eighth Graders.** Yuriko Nichols. (Reading Skills Discovery Ser.). 144p. (J). 1994. 14.00 (*1-880892-56-1*) Fam Lrng Ctr.

***Bookshelf Collection Third-Fourth Grades.** Debbie Ward. (Reading Skills Discovery Ser.). 160p. (J). 1994. 14.00 (*1-880892-55-3*) Fam Lrng Ctr.

Bookshelf of Brander Matthews. Brander Matthews. LC 79-134610. reprint ed. 31.50 (*0-404-04268-6*) AMS Pr.

Bookshelves & Cabinets. LC 86-82776. (Illus.). 96p. 1987. 8.99 (*0-376-01086-X*) Sunset Menlo Pk.

Bookshelves & Cabinets. Ed. by Southern Living Staff. (Southern Living Home Improvement Ser.). 96p. 1992. pap. 8.99 (*0-376-09038-3*) Oxmoor Hse.

Bookstock Management in Public Libraries. Tony Houghton. LC 85-169908. (Illus.). 138p. reprint ed. pap. 39.40 (*0-7837-5293-8*, 2045047) Bks Demand.

***Bookstore & Others.** Lee Ranaldo. (Illus.). 90p. (Orig.). 1995. pap. 7.00 (*1-885175-06-X*) Hozomeen Pr.

Bookstore Cat. Cindy Wheeler. LC 89-42635. (Step into Reading Ser.). (J). 1994. 3.50 (*0-394-84109-3*); lib. bdg. 7.99 (*0-394-94109-8*) Random.

Bookstore Cat: A Step One Book. Cindy Wheeler. (Step into Reading Bks.). (Illus.). 32p. (Orig.). (J). (ps-1). 1992. pap. 3.50 (*0-679-84109-1*) Random Bks Yng Read.

Bookstore Cat: A Step One Book. Cindy Wheeler. (Step into Reading Bks.). (Illus.). 32p. (Orig.). (J). (ps-1). 1994. lib. bdg. 7.99 (*0-679-94109-6*) Random Bks Yng Read.

***Bookstore Mouse.** Peggy Christian. LC 95-8454. (Illus.). (J). 1995. write for info. (*0-15-200203-0*) HarBrace.

Booktalk! Five: Booktalks!, No. 5. Ed. by Joni R. Bodart. LC 92-14017. 282p. 1993. 32.00 (*0-8242-0836-6*) Wilson.

Booktalk! Four: Selections from the Booktalker. Ed. by Joni R. Bodart. LC 92-13556. 1992. 32.00 (*0-8242-0835-8*) Wilson.

Booktalk! Three. Joni Bodart-Talbot. 371p. 1988. 32.00 (*0-8242-0764-5*) Wilson.

Booktalk! Two: Booktalking for All Ages & Audiences. Joni Bodart. LC 85-14223. 408p. 1985. 32.00 (*0-8242-0716-5*) Wilson.

***Booktalking the Award Winners: 1992-1993.** Ed. by Joni R. Bodart. 1995. 32.00 (*0-8242-0866-8*) Wilson.

Bookwebs: A Brainstorm of Ideas for the Primary Classroom. Barbara LeCroy & Bonnie Holder. (Illus.). 175p. 1994. pap. 21.00 (*1-56308-109-1*) Teacher Ideas Pr.

Bookworks. P. Klawitter. (Creative Writing Ser.). 64p. (J). (gr. 4-8). 1993. 8.95 (*0-88160-212-4*, LW204) Learning Wks.

***Bookworks: Making Books by Hand.** Gwenyth Swain. LC 94-28120. (J). 1995. write for info. (*0-87614-858-5*, Carolrhoda) Lerner Group.

Bookworm. Teng C. Yung. Ed. by John DeFrancis. LC 73-189613. (PALI Language Texts, Chinese Ser.). (Illus.). 72p. (Orig.). (C). 1975. pap. text ed. 8.00 (*0-8248-0223-3*) UH Pr.

Bookworm Who Hatched. Verna Aardema. LC 93-12002. (Meet the Author Ser.). (Illus.). 32p. 1995. 13.95 (*1-878450-39-5*) R Owen Pubs.

Bookworm's Big Apple: A Guide to Manhattan's Booksellers. Susan P. Barile. LC 94-8968. (Illus.). 400p. 1994. 44.00 (*0-231-08494-3*); pap. 15.95 (*0-231-08495-1*) Col U Pr.

***Bookworm's Feast: A Potluck of Poems.** J. Patrick Lewis. LC 94-31897. 1996. lib. bdg. write for info. (*0-8037-1693-1*) Dial Bks Young.

***Bookworm's Feast: A Potluck of Poems.** J. Patrick Lewis. LC 94-31897. (J). 1996. write for info. (*0-8037-1692-3*) Dial Bks Young.

Boola's Secrets. (Illus.). 26p. (J). (ps-1). 1988. pap. 2.95 (*0-671-66867-6*, Litl Simon S&S) S&S Childrens.

***Boolean Algebra & Its Applications.** J. Eldon Whitesitt. LC 94-25266. x, 182p. 1995. pap. text ed. 8.95 (*0-486-68483-0*) Dover.

Boolean Algebra & Switching Circuits. Elliot Mendelson. (Schaum's Outline Ser.). 1970. pap. text ed. 11.95 (*0-07-041460-2*) McGraw.

Boolean Calculus of Differences. A. Thayse. (Lecture Notes in Computer Science Ser.: Vol. 101). 144p. 1981. pap. 20.00 (*0-387-10286-8*) Spr-Verlag.

Boolean Constructions in Universal Algebras. A G Pinus. LC 92-44823. (Mathematics & Its Applications Ser.: Vol. 242). 1993. lib. bdg. 149.00 (*0-7923-2117-0*) Kluwer Ac.

Boolean Function Complexity. Ed. by M. S. Paterson. (London Mathematical Society Lecture Note Ser.: No. 164). 300p. (C). 1992. pap. 42.95 (*0-521-40826-1*) Cambridge U Pr.

Boolean Functions. W. Schneeweiss. (Illus.). 310p. 1989. 89.50 (*0-387-18892-4*) Spr-Verlag.

Boolean Functions & Equations. S. Rudeanu. 1975. 51.50 (*0-444-10520-4*) Elsevier.

Boolean Reasoning. Frank M. Brown. (C). 1990. lib. bdg. 69.00 (*0-7923-9121-7*) Kluwer Ac.

Boolean Semantics for Natural Language. Edward L. Keenan & Leonard M. Faltz. LC 84-22349. 1984. lib. bdg. 122.50 (*90-277-1768-0*); pap. text ed. 24.50 (*0-318-03670-3*) Kluwer Ac.

Boolean-Valued Models & Independence Proofs in Set Theory. 2nd ed. John L. Bell. (Oxford Logic Guides Ser.). 1985. 24.95 (*0-19-853241-5*) OUP.

Boole's Logic & Probability: A Critical Exposition from the Standpoint of Contemporary Algebra, Logic & Probability Theory. 2nd enl. rev. ed. T. Hailperin. (Studies in Logic & the Foundations of Mathematics: No. 85). 426p. 1987. 102.75 (*0-444-87952-8*, North Holland) Elsevier.

Boom, Again: The First Computer Boom is Over. The Next One Has Already Begun! Ed Gustafson. 224p. 1994. 23.95 (*1-884343-00-7*) Abbot-Hill Pubng.

Boom & Bust: The Historical Cycles of Matamoros & Brownsville. Milo Kearney & Anthony Knopp. 322p. 1991. pap. 15.95 (*0-89015-815-0*) Sunbelt Media.

Boom & Bust Cycle. Tom Mooney. pap. 3.00 (*0-317-28512-2*) Mooney.

***Boom Baby! The Sudden, Surprising Rise of the Indiana Pacers.** Conrad Brunner. LC 94-68643. (Illus.). 248p. (Orig.). 1994. pap. 14.95 (*1-57028-036-3*) Masters Pr IN.

Boom Baby Moon. Sean Kelly. 1993. mass mkt. 7.99 (*0-440-50573-9*) Dell.

***Boom Boom Boom.** Hayward. (J). 3.99 (*0-679-86755-4*) Random.

Boom, Cash, & Balderdash: A Different Look at Fairbanks During Pipeline Construction. Jerry Fears. LC 77-87430. (Illus.). 1978. 8.95 (*0-918270-02-2*) That New Pub.

Boom Chicka Rock. Martin & Archambault. (J). Date not set. 14.00 (*0-671-88689-4*, S&S Bks Young Read) S&S Childrens.

Boom Cities & Towns U. S. A. A How to Find or Locate Workbook. Bibliotheca Press Staff. 50p. 1983. 15.95 (*0-939476-51-7*, Biblio Pr) Prosperity & Profits.

Boom, Crisis, & Adjustment: The Macroeconomic Experience of Developing Countries. Ian M. Little et al. (World Bank Publication Ser.). 472p. 1994. 42.95 (*0-19-520891-9*, 60891) OUP.

Boom, Crisis, & Adjustment: The Macroeconomic Experience of Developing Countries. Ian M. Little et al. 472p. 1993. 42.95 (*0-685-71263-X*, 60891) World Bank.

***Boom, Crisis & Adjustment - a Summary: The Macroeconomic Experiences of Developing Countries, 1970-1990.** Richard N. Cooper. LC 94-33974. (Directions in Development Ser.). 1994. write for info. (*0-8213-3051-9*) World Bank.

Boom in Retrospect: A Reconsideration. Yvette E. Miller. Ed. by Raymond L. Williams. 248p. 1987. pap. 20.00 (*0-318-42060-0*) Lat Am Lit Rev Pr.

Boom of the Eighties in Southern California. 5th ed. Glenn S. Dumke. (Illus.). 336p. 1991. reprint ed. 24.95 (*0-87328-003-2*) Huntington Lib.

Boomba Lives in Africa. Caroline Singer & Cyrus L. Baldridge. LC 72-4556. (Black Heritage Library Collection). 1977. reprint ed. 17.95 (*0-8369-9125-7*) Ayer.

Boomer. Charles D. Taylor. 1991. mass mkt. 5.50 (*0-671-74330-9*) PB.

Boomer: Railroad Memoirs. Linda Niemann. 252p. (C). 1992. reprint ed. pap. 12.95 (*0-939416-55-7*) Cleis Pr.

Boomer Bible. R. F. Laird. LC 91-50385. 880p. (Orig.). 1991. pap. 14.95 (*1-56305-075-7*, 3075) Workman Pub.

Boomer Sawbones. large type ed. Lloyd Madison. (Linford Western Library). 304p. 1986. pap. 11.95 (*0-7089-6279-3*, Linford) Ulverscroft.

Boomerang. Raymond Q. Armington & William D. Ellis. 348p. (Orig.). 1988. pap. 9.95 (*0-9621126-1-5*) Ward & Ward.

Boomerang. Raymond Q. Armington & William D. Ellis. 348p. (Orig.). 1989. 14.95 (*0-9621126-0-7*) Ward & Ward.

Boomerang: A One-Act Play for Grades 7-9. Royce Schuyler. Ed. by Ellen S. Kester. (Illus.). 50p. (Orig.). (YA). 1989. pap. text ed. 6.95 (*0-685-26284-7*) Pickwick Pubs.

Boomerang: Drama for Study & Performance. Royce Schuyler. Ed. by Ellen S. Kester. (Illus.). 100p. (Orig.). (YA). 1989. pap. text ed. 35.00 (*0-685-26285-5*) Pickwick Pubs.

Boomerang & Never Die. Barry Hannah. (Banner Bks.). 320p. 1994. pap. 16.95 (*0-87805-702-1*) U Pr of Miss.

Boomerang Clue. large type ed. Agatha Christie. (Popular Author Ser.). 375p. 1988. lib. bdg. 16.95 (*0-8161-4535-0*) G K Hall.

Boomerang Clue. large type ed. Agatha Christie. (Popular Author Ser.). 375p. 1989. pap. 9.95 (*0-8161-4536-9*) G K Hall.

Boomerang Poems. R. Franklin Pate. LC 90-46508. xiv, 54p. (Orig.). 1990. pap. 6.00 (*0-926487-07-8*) Rowan Mtn Pr.

Boomerangs: How to Make & Throw Them. Bernard S. Mason. (Illus.). (J). (gr. 5 up). 17.75 (*0-8446-5062-5*) Peter Smith.

Boomerangs: How to Make & Throw Them. Bernard S. Mason. LC 73-94346. (Illus.). 99p. 1974. reprint ed. pap. 3.50 (*0-486-23028-7*) Dover.

Boomer's Big Day. Constance W. McGeorge. LC 93-27273. (Illus.). (J). 1994. 12.95 (*0-8118-0526-3*) Chronicle Bks.

Boomer's Gold. Jack Walker. LC 77-16196. 1978. 10.00 (*0-914476-74-2*) Thorp Springs.

Boomer's Kids. Ruby C. Tolliver. (Illus.). 128p. (J). (gr. 4 up). 1992. 14.95 (*0-937460-69-9*) Hendrick-Long.

Boomers: The Ageless Generation: Sell Them If You Can! Phil Goodman. 160p. 1991. pap. 12.95 (*1-880846-00-4*) Blue Bk CA.

Boomer's War. Molly Moore. LC 92-31278. 352p. 1993. text ed. 22.50 (*0-684-19418-X*, Scribners) S&S Trade.

Boomfell. Douglas Hobbie. 448p. 1993. pap. 10.95 (*0-8050-2663-0*) H Holt & Co.

Booming of Acre Hill & Other Reminiscences of Urban & Suburban Life. John K. Bangs. LC 79-98558. (Short Story Index Reprint Ser.). (Illus.). 1977. 20.95 (*0-8369-3132-7*) Ayer.

Booms & Mushrooms: The Saga of Susanvile & the McDow Boys from 1910 to 1930. George McDow, Jr. (Illus.). 171p. 1988. pap. 12.95 (*0-938373-05-6*) Lahontan Images.

Booms & Recessions in a Noisy Economy. Robert E. Hall. 96p. (C). 1991. text ed. 23.00x (*0-300-04857-2*) Yale U Pr.

Boomtown, No. 4. Gilbert Morris. 1992. pap. 9.99 (*0-8423-7789-1*) Tyndale.

Boomtown Blues: Colorado Oil Shale, 1885-1985. (Illus.). 208p. 1989. 19.95 (*0-87081-178-9*) Univ Pr Colo.

Boomtown Bust. E. J. Hunter. (White Squaw Ser.: No. 2). 1983. pap. 2.50 (*0-8217-1286-1*) Zebra.

Boomtowns. R. Shapley. (Wild West in American History Ser.). (Illus.). 32p. (J). (gr. 3-8). 1990. 13.50 (*0-685-58647-2*); lib. bdg. 18.00 (*0-86625-370-X*) Rourke Corp.

Boon the Raccoon & Easel the Weasel: A Fable by Bobby L. Jackson. Bobby L. Jackson. LC 92-62211. (Illus.). 32p. (J). (ps-4). 1993. 9.95 (*0-9634932-0-5*); pap. 5.95 (*0-9634932-1-3*) Multicult Pubns.

***Boondocker Ballet.** Melvin H. Thomas. 224p. 1995. pap. 13.00 (*0-8059-3759-5*) Dorrance.

Boondocks. Dave Etter. (Crow King Editions Ser.). 64p. (Orig.). 1982. pap. 3.00 (*0-930600-15-0*) Uzzano Pr.

***Boondocks Lawman.** Dan Sanders. 260p. 1995. pap. 8.95 (*1-56901-856-1*) NW Pub.

Boondoggle: A Book of Lanyard & Lacing. Klutz Press Staff. (Illus.). 46p. 1994. ring bd. 11.95 (*1-878257-72-2*) Klutz Pr.

Boondoggle see Lanyard: Having Fun with Plastic Lace

***Boone: A Novel Based on the Life & Times of Daniel Boone.** Judd. 1995. mass mkt. (*0-553-57383-7*) Bantam.

Boone & Clinton Counties, Indiana. (Illus.). 905p. 1992. reprint ed. lib. bdg. 89.00 (*0-8328-2536-0*) Higginson Bk Co.

Boone & Crockett Club's Twentieth Big Game Awards. Ed. by W. H. Nesbitt & Jack Reneau. (Illus.). 480p. 1990. 34.95 (*0-940864-16-9*) Boone & Crockett.

Boone & Crockett Clubs Twenty-First Big Game Award, 1989-1991. William H. Nesbitt. 1992. 39.95 (*1-879356-19-8*) Wolfe Pub Co.

Boone & Crockett Club's Twenty-First Big-Game Awards, 1989-1991. Ed. by Gary Sitton & Jack Reneau. 500p. 1992. 39.95 (*0-940864-19-3*) Boone & Crockett.

***Boone & Crockett Club's Twenty-Second Big Game Awards, 1992-1994.** Ed. by Jack Reneau & Susan Reneau. (Illus.). 498p. 1995. 39.95 (*0-940864-22-3*) Boone & Crockett.

Boone & Crockett Club's 18th Big Game Awards. Ed. by W. H. Nesbitt. (Illus.). 306p. 1984. 24.95 (*0-940864-05-3*) Boone & Crockett.

Boone County: Top of Kentucky. Ed. by William Conrad. (Illus.). 64p. (Orig.). 1992. pap. 5.95 (*0-9624673-7-5*) Picture This Bks.

Boone County Kentucky: 1810-1840 Censuses. Rowena Lawson. iv, 68p. (Orig.). 1986. pap. 10.00 (*0-917890-79-5*) Heritage Bk.

Boone County Kentucky: 1850 Census. Rowena Lawson. iv, 93p. (Orig.). 1986. pap. 12.50 (*0-917890-80-9*) Heritage Bk.

Boone Family: A Genealogical History of the Descendants of George & Mary Boone Who Came to America in 1717. Hazel A. Spraker. LC 74-839. (Illus.). 707p. 1993. reprint ed. 40.00 (*0-8063-0612-2*) Genealog Pub.

Boone's Florida Historical Markers & Sites. Floyd E. Boone. LC 87-9708. (Illus.). 372p. 1988. pap. 29.95 (*0-935834-62-1*) Rainbow Books.

Boone's Lick Salt Works, 1805-33. Ed. by Robert T. Bray. (Missouri Archaeologist Ser.: Vol. 48). (Illus.). 89p. (Orig.). (C). 1990. pap. 8.00 (*0-943414-70-9*) MO Arch Soc.

Boone's Wilderness Road see Historic Highways of America

Boonesborough: Its Founding, Pioneer Struggles, Indian Experiences, Transylvania Days, & Revolutionary Annals. George W. Ranck. LC 70-146414. (First American Frontier Ser.). (Illus.). 1971. reprint ed. 30.95 (*0-405-02878-4*) Ayer.

Boonsville Bombers. Alison C. Herzig. (Illus.). 96p. (J). (gr. 3-7). 1993. pap. 3.99 (*0-14-034578-7*, Puffin) Puffin Bks.

Boonsville Bombers. Alison C. Herzig. (J). (gr. 4-7). 1991. 11.95 (*0-670-83595-1*) Viking Child Bks.

Boontling: An American Lingo. rev. ed. Charles C. Adams. (Illus.). 272p. (C). 1990. 24.95 (*0-939665-03-4*); pap. 12.95 (*0-939665-05-0*) Mountain Hse Pr.

Boonville & Beyond: An Upstate Sampler. William Crosten. 72p. 1989. 14.95 (*0-932052-82-7*) North Country.

Boop! Boop! I'm Better. Karen Hodgson. (Illus.). 12p. (J). 1993. pap. 1.25 (*1-56794-046-3*, C2316) Star Bible.

***Booran.** G. Megerssa. (Heritage Library of African Peoples Ser.). (Illus.). 64p. 1995. 15.95 (*0-8239-1769-X*) Rosen Group.

***Boorstyn on Copyright Law, 2 vols.** 2nd ed. Neil Boorstyn. LC 94-27684. (IP Ser.). 1994. ring bd. 225.00 (*0-87632-152-X*) Clark Boardman Callaghan.

Boost Your Brainpower. Ellen Michaud et al. 1994. 9.98 (*1-56731-026-5*, MJF Bks) Fine Comms.

Boost Your Brainpower: A Total Program to Sharpen Your Thinking & Age-Proof Your Mind. Prevention Magazine Editors et al. LC 91-3914. 480p. 1991. 26.95 (*0-87857-975-3*, 05-317-0) Rodale Pr Inc.

Boost Your Business in Any Economy. Bill Gibson. LC 92-23220. (Orig.). 1993. pap. 9.95 (*0-89815-516-9*) Ten Speed Pr.

Boost Your Credibility As a Leader. Jack Pyle. 24p. 1993. student ed 7.00 (*1-882843-02-9*) Perf Pub MI.

Boost Your I. Q. Harold Gale. (MENSA Ser.). 1994. pap. 7.98 (*0-7858-0130-8*) Bk Sales Inc.

***Boost Your Memory.** 190p. (Orig.). 1994. pap. 14.95 (*1-57327-014-8*, M Pr CA) Busn Concepts.

Boosted Dart Theory. Jerry Irvine. (Advanced Information Report Ser.: No. 5). 20p. 1984. 4.95 (*0-912468-03-3*, AIR-5) CA Rocketry.

Booster Boycott. Francine Pascal. (Sweet Valley Twins Ser.). (J). (gr. 4-7). 1991. pap. 3.25 (*0-553-15933-X*) Bantam.

Boosters & Businessmen: Popular Economic Thought & Urban Growth in the Antebellum Middle West. Carl Abbott. LC 80-1795. (Contributions in American Studies: No. 53). (Illus.). xii, 266p. 1981. text ed. 59.95 (*0-313-22562-1*, ABB/, Greenwood Pr) Greenwood.

***Boosting Businesses: Advisory Services.** 196p. (Orig.). 1995. pap. 67.00 (*92-64-14321-1*, Pub. by Econ & Coop Dev FR) OECD.

Boosting Employee Performance Through Better Motivation. 17.00 (*0-87102-038-6*, 55-1540) Natl Ret Merch.

Boosting Self-Esteem. Nancy Going. (Active Bible Curriculum Ser.). 48p. (Orig.). (J). (gr. 6-8). 1990. pap. 9.99 (*1-55945-100-9*) Group Pub.

Boosting the Adolescent Underachiever: How Parents Can Change a "C" Student into an "A" Student. Victor Cogen. (Illus.). 275p. (C). 1992. 24.95 (*0-306-44328-7*, Plenum Pr) Plenum.

Boosting the Underachiever: How Busy Parents Can Unlock Their Child's Potential. Victor Cogen. 1992. mass mkt. 4.99 (*0-425-13272-2*) Berkley Pub.

Boosting the Underachiever: How Busy Parents Can Unlock Their Child's Potential. Victor Cogen. LC 90-40668. (Illus.). 330p. 1990. 21.95 (*0-306-43569-1*, Plenum Pr) Plenum.

Boosting Your Brain Power: Stress, the Brain, Exercise & Nutrition. 1991. lib. bdg. 250.00 (*0-8490-4651-3*) Gordon Pr.

Boot. Daniel Da Cruz. 1987. mass mkt. 4.99 (*0-312-90060-0*) St Martin.

***Boot Camp: Basic Training for Your Dog.** Ted Sutton. (Life Line Ser.). (Illus.). 175p. (Orig.). 1994. pap. 16.95 (*1-55059-085-5*) Temeron Bks.

Boot Fitting from A to Z Workbook. Doug Killham. 52p. 1986. pap. text ed. 4.25 (*0-943717-31-0*) Concept Sys.

***Boot Street Band.** Steve Attridge. 128p. (J). (gr. 7-8). 1995. pap. 5.95 (*0-563-40329-2*) Parkwest Pubns.

Boot Weather. Judith Vigna. Ed. by Ann Fay. LC 88-20563. (Illus.). 32p. (J). (ps-2). 1989. 13.95 (*0-8075-0837-3*) A Whitman.

Booth Again! George Booth. (Illus.). 152p. (Orig.). 1989. pap. 7.95 (*0-8362-1843-4*) Andrews & McMeel.

Boothill Bounty. Jory Sherman. (Gunn Ser.: No. 9). (Orig.). 1981. pap. 2.25 (*0-686-79736-1*) Zebra.

Boothill Brand. Lee Floren. 192p. 1983. pap. 2.25 (*0-8439-2059-9*) Dorchester Pub Co.

***Boothill Brand.** large type ed. Wade Bronson. (Western Ser.). 1994. pap. 14.95 (*0-7089-7597-6*, Linford) Ulverscroft.

Boothill Brand. large type ed. Lee Floren. (Nightingale Ser.). 241p. 1990. pap. 14.95 (*0-8161-4968-2*) G K Hall.

Boothill Court. large type ed. Lew Smith. (Linford Western Library). 304p. 1993. pap. 14.95 (*0-7089-7312-4*, Linford) Ulverscroft.

Boothill Riders. large type ed. Lee Floren. 1990. pap. 12.95 (*0-7089-6940-2*, Linford) Ulverscroft.

Booths: An American Theatrical Dynasty. Lawrence Estavan. Ed. by Paul D. Seldis. (Clipper Studies in the Theatre). (Illus.). 128p. Date not set. lib. bdg. write for info. (*0-8095-0300-X*); pap. write for info. (*0-8095-1300-5*) Borgo Pr.

Booths in History: Their Roots & Lives, Encounters & Achievements. John N. Booth. LC 82-5421. (Illus.). 243p. 1982. pap. text ed. 16.95 (*0-943230-01-2*) Ridgeway Pr.

Booths of Ancient Israel's Autumn Festival. William R. Scott. (Dissertation Ser.: No. 4). 224p. 1995. pap. write for info. (*0-941037-32-0*) BIBAL Pr.

***Bootleg: The Secret History of the Other Recording Industry.** Clinton Heylin. (Illus.). 448p. 1995. 29.95 (*0-312-13031-7*) St Martin.

Bootlegger's Boy. Barry Switzer & Bud Shrake. 1991. mass mkt. 5.99 (*0-515-10683-6*) Jove Pubns.

Bootlegger's Daughter. Margaret Maron. 272p. 1992. 18.95 (*0-89296-445-6*) Mysterious Pr.

Bootlegger's Daughter. Margaret Maron. 272p. 1993. mass mkt. 5.50 (*0-446-40323-7*, Mysterious Paperbk) Warner Bks.

Bootlegger's Daughter. Claire Vermilya. 481p. (Orig.). 1988. pap. 10.95 (*0-9618979-0-2*) Camelot Self.

Bootlegger's Lady. Ed Sager & Mike Frye. (Illus.). 144p. (Orig.). 1984. pap. 9.95 (*0-88839-976-6*) Hancock House.

Bootnanny's Trip to Town. Carinda Swann. LC 62-63255. (Illus.). 44p. (J). (gr. 2-5). 1993. lib. bdg. 12.95 (*1-55523-589-1*); pap. 7.95 (*1-55523-657-X*) Winston-Derek.

An Asterisk (*) at the beginning of an entry indicates that the title is appearing in BIP for the first time.

B

An Asterisk (*) at the beginning of an entry indicates that the title is appearing in BIP for the first time.

861

B

Border Terrier. David Van Goron Kline & Patricia B. Hoffman. Ed. by Luana Luther. LC 91-73751. (Pure Breds Ser.). (Illus.). 318p. 1993. 26.95 (*0-944875-20-3*) Doral Pub.

***Border Terrier Champions, 1952-1994.** Camino Book Co. Staff & Jan Linzy. (Illus.). 180p. 1995. pap. 0.95 (*1-55893-041-8*) Camino E E & Bk.

Border That Joins: Mexican Migrants & U. S. Responsibility. Ed. by Peter G. Brown & Henry Shue. 1983. 54.50 (*0-317-05217-9*); pap. 32.25 (*0-317-05218-7*) IPPP.

Border That Joins: Mexican Migrants & U. S. Responsibility. Ed. by Peter G. Brown & Henry Shue. LC 82-7526. (Maryland Studies in Public Philosophy). 264p. 1983. text ed. 59.00 (*0-8476-7072-4*, R7072); pap. text ed. 35.50 (*0-8476-7206-9*, R7206) Rowman.

Border to Terrorism. P. Jay Burchett & M. Ann Evans. 295p. (Orig.). 1988. pap. 4.95 (*0-929013-03-4*) Newport Pub Hse.

Border Town Law. David Critser. 160p. 1994. 19.95 (*0-8027-1278-9*) Walker & Co.

Border Towns of the Navajo Nation. 2nd ed. Aaron Yava. (Illus.). 80p. 1975. pap. 5.95 (*0-914974-06-8*) Holmgangers.

Border Tradition. William Cullen Bryant. Ed. by Bernard A. Drew. 48p. 1988. pap. 6.50 (*0-941583-13-9*) Attic Rev Pr.

Border Trials: Ricardo Flores Magon & the Mexican Liberals. Thomas A. Langham. (Southwestern Studies: No. 65). 1981. pap. 10.00 (*0-87404-123-6*) Tex Western.

Border Trumpet. Ernest Haycox. 288p. 1992. pap. 3.50 (*1-55817-670-5*, Pinnacle NY) Windsor NY.

Border Trumpet. Ernest Haycox. 1976. 20.95 (*0-8488-1360-X*) Amereon Ltd.

Border Trumpet. Ernest Haycox. Bd. with Wild Bunch. 1984. Set pap. 3.50 (*0-451-13166-5*, Sig) NAL-Dutton.

Border Vengeance. J. L. Bouma. 1978. pap. 1.25 (*0-8439-0605-7*) Dorchester Pub Co.

Border Vengeance. large type ed. J. L. Bouma. (Linford Western Library). 320p. 1986. pap. 11.95 (*0-7089-6217-3*, Linford) Ulverscroft.

Border War. Jack Slade. (Gatling Ser.: No. 3). 176p. pap. 2.95 (*0-8439-2807-7*) Dorchester Pub Co.

Border Wares. Jacqueline Pearce. 160p. 1992. pap. 65.00 (*0-11-290494-7*, HM04947, Pub. by HMSO UK) UNIPUB.

Border Warfare of New York During the Revolution: The Annals of Tryon County. William W. Campbell. 406p. 1992. reprint ed. pap. 26.00 (*1-55613-612-9*) Heritage Bk.

Border Wars of New England. S. A. Drake. 305p. 1973. reprint ed. 22.50 (*0-87928-045-X*) Corner Hse.

Border Wars of Texas. James T. DeShields. LC 93-15163. (Illus.). 448p. 1993. 29.95 (*0-938349-98-8*) State House Pr.

Border Watch. (Greyhawk Accessory Ser.). 1993. pap. 6.95 (*1-56076-631-X*) TSR Inc.

Border Watch. Joseph Altsheler. 1976. lib. bdg. 25.95 (*0-89968-001-1*, Lghtyr Pr) Buccaneer Bks.

Border Watch. Joseph A. Altsheler. 24.95 (*0-685-71959-6*) Amereon Ltd.

Border Way. Hank Edward. (Judge Ser.: No. 9). 1993. mass mkt. 3.50 (*0-06-100489-8*, Harp PBks) HarpC.

Border Writing: The Multidimensional Text. Emily D. Hicks. (Theory & History of Literature Ser.: Vol. 80). 256p. (C). 1991. text ed. 39.95 (*0-8166-1982-4*); pap. text ed. 14.95 (*0-8166-1983-2*) U of Minn Pr.

Borderers. William Wordsworth. Ed. by Robert Osborn. LC 80-11212. (Cornell Wordsworth Ser.). 784p. 1981. 105. 00 (*0-8014-1283-8*) Cornell U Pr.

Borderers: Or, the Wept of Wish-Ton-Wish. James Fenimore Cooper. LC 74-162892. (Bentley's Standard Novels Ser.: No. 33). (Illus.). reprint ed. 15.50 (*0-404-54433-9*) AMS Pr.

***Bordering.** Luanne Armstrong. 176p. 1995. pap. 10.95 (*0-921881-35-5*, Pub. by Gynergy-Ragweed CN) InBook.

***Bordering on Fiction: Chantal Akerman's D'Est.** Kathy Halbreich et al. LC 94-43489. (Illus.). 1995. pap. 14.95 (*0-935640-44-4*) Walker Art Ctr.

Bordering on the Body: The Racial Matrix of Modern Fiction & Culture. Laura A. Doyle. (Race & American Culture Ser.). 320p. 1994. 39.95 (*0-19-508654-6*); pap. 18.95 (*0-19-508655-4*) OUP.

Bordering on Treason? The Trial & Conviction of Arif Durrani. Lawrence Lifschultz et al. 56p. 1991. 5.50 (*0-9630587-0-3*) Pamphleteers.

Borderland. S. K. Epperson. LC 91-55180. 288p. 1992. 19. 95 (*1-55611-317-X*) D I Fine.

Borderland. S. K. Epperson. 304p. 1993. pap. 4.50 (*0-8439-3435-2*) Dorchester Pub Co.

Borderland. Marjorie McKusick. 252p. (Orig.). 1993. pap. 9.99 (*1-56043-653-0*) Destiny Image.

Borderland: A Casebook of True Supernatural Stories. W. T. Stead. LC 69-16361. 358p. 1970. 5.95 (*0-8216-0058-3*, Univ Bks) Carol Pub Group.

Borderland: Origins of the American Suburb, 1820-1939. John R. Stilgoe. 367p. (C). 1990. reprint ed. pap. 20.00 (*0-300-04866-1*) Yale U Pr.

Borderland, a Historical & Geographical Study of Burgenland, Austria. Andrew F. Burghardt. LC 62-15992. 389p. reprint ed. pap. 110.90 (*0-8357-7350-7*, 2015356) Bks Demand.

Borderland in Retreat: From Spanish Louisiana to the Far Southwest. Abraham P. Nasatir. LC 75-21183. 187p. reprint ed. pap. 53.30 (*0-8357-7351-5*, 2031005) Bks Demand.

Borderland in the Civil War. Edward C. Smith. LC 70-95078. (Select Bibliographies Reprint Ser.). 1977. 37.95 (*0-8369-5078-X*) Ayer.

Borderland in the Civil War. Edward C. Smith. LC 72-111783. reprint ed. 34.50 (*0-404-00214-5*) AMS Pr.

Borderland in the Civil War. Edward C. Smith. (History - United States Ser.). 412p. 1992. reprint ed. lib. bdg. 99. 00 (*0-7812-6172-4*) Rprt Serv.

Borderland of Embryology & Pathology. Rupert A. Willis. (Illus.). 671p. reprint ed. pap. 180.00 (*0-8357-7352-3*, 2025725) Bks Demand.

Borderland of Society. Charles B. Davis. LC 79-140328. (Short Story Index Reprint Ser.). 1977. reprint ed. 18.95 (*0-8369-3720-1*) Ayer.

Borderlands. Peter Carter. 1990. 17.00 (*0-374-30895-0*) FS&G.

Borderlands. Peter Carter. (YA). 1993. pap. 4.95 (*0-374-40883-1*) FS&G.

Borderlands. James Magorian. LC 91-75480. 36p. (Orig.). 1992. pap. 6.00 (*0-930674-36-7*) Black Oak.

Borderlands. Thomas F. Monteleone. 1990. pap. 3.95 (*0-380-75924-1*) Avon.

Borderlands. Ed. by Chase Twichell. 231p. (Orig.). (C). 1993. pap. 8.95 (*0-933277-09-1*) Ploughshares.

Borderlands: Essays in Canadian-American Relations. A. Artibise. Ed. by Robert Lecker. 328p. (C). 1991. pap. text ed. 45.00 (*1-55022-133-7*, Pub. by ECW Press CN) Genl Dist Srvs.

Borderlands: Nation & Empire. Scott L. Malcomson. 250p. 1994. 22.95 (*0-571-19815-5*) Faber & Faber.

Borderlands - La Frontera: The New Mestiza. Gloria Anzaldua. LC 87-60780. 203p. (Orig.). 1987. pap. 10.95 (*1-879960-12-5*) Aunt Lute Bks.

Borderlands of Normal & Early Pathologic Findings in Skeletal Radiography. enl. rev. ed. A. Kohler et al. Ed. & Tr. by Peter Winter. LC 92-49475. (Illus.). 918p. 1993. write for info. (*0-86577-461-7*) Thieme Med Pubs.

Borderlands of Normal & Early Pathologic Findings in Skeletal Radiography. 4th enl. rev. ed. A. Kohler et al. Ed. & Tr. by Peter Winter. LC 92-49475. (Illus.). 918p. 1993. text ed. 199.00 (*3-13-784104-6*) Thieme Med Pubs.

***Borderlands Reflections: The Untied States & Canada.** Lauren McKinsey & Victor Konrad. (Borderlands Monograph Ser.: No. 1). 37p. (C). 1989. pap. text ed. 5.00 (*0-614-04705-6*) Canadian-Amer Ctr.

Borderlands Sourcebook: A Guide to the Literature on Northern Mexico & the American Southwest. Ed. by Ellwyn R. Stoddard et al. LC 82-40331. (Illus.). 462p. 1983. 75.00 (*0-8061-1718-4*) U of Okla Pr.

Borderlands Town in Transition: Laredo, 1755-1870. Gilberto M. Hinojosa. LC 83-45096. (Illus.). 168p. 1983. 24.50 (*0-89096-160-3*) Tex A&M Univ Pr.

Borderlands Two. Ed. by Thomas F. Monteleone. 304p. (Orig.). 1991. mass mkt. 4.99 (*0-380-76517-9*) Avon.

Borderlands 1. White Wolf Staff. 1994. pap. 4.99 (*1-56504-107-0*, 11804) White Wolf.

Borderlands 2. Tom Monteleone. 1994. pap. 4.99 (*1-56504-108-9*, 11802) White Wolf.

Borderlands 3. White Wolf Staff. 1994. pap. 4.99 (*1-56504-109-7*, 11803) White Wolf.

Borderlands 4. White Wolf Staff. 1994. pap. 4.99 (*1-56504-110-0*, 11805) White Wolf.

Borderless World: Power & Strategy in the Interlinked Economy. Kenichi Ohmae. LC 90-56432. 224p. 1991. reprint ed. pap. 12.00 (*0-06-097412-5*, PL) HarpC.

Borderline. W. J. Amos. (Orig.). 1988. pap. 2.95 (*0-87067-351-3*) Holloway.

Borderline. Janette T. Hospital. 288p. 1995. pap. 14.95 (*0-8050-3295-9*) H Holt & Co.

Borderline. Sigmund Stoler. LC 91-58257. 144p. 1992. 16. 95 (*0-8453-4838-8*, Cornwall Bks) Assoc Univ Prs.

BorderLine: A Bibliography of the United States-Mexico Borderlands. Ed. by Barbara G. Valk. LC 88-4565. 736p. 1988. Individuals & Mexican agencies & institutions. 65.00 (*0-87903-112-3*) UCLA Lat Am Ctr.

Borderline: A Psychological Study of Paranoia & Delusional Thinking. Peter Chadwick. LC 91-23890. (Illus.). 208p. 1992. 75.00 (*0-415-07151-8*, A6941) Routledge.

Borderline: Current Empirical Research. Thomas H. McGlashan. LC 85-6102. (Progress in Psychiatry Ser.). 128p. 1985. boxed, pap. 22.00 (*0-88048-068-8*, 8068) Am Psychiatric.

***Borderline Adolescents.** Martijn Meijer. 141p. 1995. pap. 26.50 (*90-5170-338-4*, Pub. by Thesis Pubs NE) IBD Ltd.

Borderline & Acting-Out Adolescents: A Developmental Approach. Intro. by Gary Nielsen. LC 81-20223. (Illus.). 256p. 1983. 35.95 (*0-89885-109-2*) Human Sci Pr.

Borderline & Narcissistic Patients in Therapy. Ed. by Nonna Slavinska-Holy. 568p. (C). 1988. 70.00x (*0-8236-0572-8*) Intl Univs Pr.

Borderline & Other Self Disorders. Donald B. Rinsley. LC 81-20538. 336p. 1982. 40.00 (*0-87668-447-9*) Aronson.

Borderline Conditions & Pathological Narcissism. Otto Kernberg. LC 84-45864. 384p. 1992. pap. 35.00x (*0-87668-177-1*) Aronson.

Borderline Conditions & Pathological Narcissism. Otto F. Kernberg. LC 84-45864. 384p. 1990. reprint ed. 40.00 (*0-87668-762-1*) Aronson.

Borderline Crime & the Hidden Economy. 1991. lib. bdg. 250.00 (*0-8490-4722-6*) Gordon Pr.

Borderline Culture: The Politics of Identity in Four Twentieth-Century Slavic Novels. Tomislav Z. Longinovic. LC 92-20696. 216p. 1993. 24.00 (*1-55728-262-5*) U of Ark Pr.

Borderline Disorders: Clinical Models & Techniques. Eda G. Goldstein. LC 90-3400. 262p. 1990. lib. bdg. 32.95 (*0-89862-442-8*) Guilford Pr.

Borderline Patient: Emerging Concepts in Diagnosis, Etiology, Psychodynamics, & Treatment, 1. Ed. by J. S. Grotstein et al. (Psychoanalytic Inquiry Book Ser.: Vols. 6 & 7). 1987. text ed. 45.00 (*0-88163-037-3*) Analytic Pr.

Borderline Patient: Emerging Concepts in Diagnosis, Etiology, Psychodynamics, & Treatment, 2. Ed. by J. S. Grotstein et al. (Psychoanalytic Inquiry Book Ser.: Vols. 6 & 7). 1987. text ed. 45.00 (*0-88163-055-1*) Analytic Pr.

Borderline Patient: Emerging Concepts in Diagnosis, Etiology, Psychodynamics, & Treatment, Set. Ed. by J. S. Grotstein et al. (Psychoanalytic Inquiry Book Ser.: Vols. 6 & 7). 1987. text ed. 70.00 (*0-88163-056-X*) Analytic Pr.

Borderline Patients: Psychoanalytic Perspectives. Sander M. Abend et al. Ed. by Bernard D. Fine et al. LC 83-12750. (Kris Study Group Monograph: No. 7). viii, 255p. 1983. 34.50 (*0-8236-0576-0*) Intl Univs Pr.

Borderline Patients, the Psychosomatic Focus, & the Therapeutic Process. Peter Giovacchini. LC 92-49191. 296p. 1993. 35.00 (*0-87668-295-6*) Aronson.

Borderline Personality: Vision & Healing. Nathan Schwartz-Salant. LC 88-25079. 256p. (Orig.). (C). 1989. 24.95 (*0-933029-30-6*); pap. 16.95 (*0-933029-31-4*) Chiron Pubns.

Borderline Personality Disorder. John G. Gunderson. LC 84-18411. 224p. 1984. 34.50 (*0-88048-020-3*, 48-020-3) Am Psychiatric.

Borderline Personality Disorder: A Multidimensional Approach. Joel Paris. 1994. boxed 29.95 (*0-88048-655-4*) Am Psychiatric.

Borderline Personality Disorder: Clinical & Empirical Perspectives. Ed. by John F. Clarkin et al. LC 91-28304. (Personality Disorders Ser.). 352p. 1991. lib. bdg. 37.95 (*0-89862-262-X*) Guilford Pr.

Borderline Personality Disorder: Etiology & Treatment. Ed. by Joel Paris. LC 92-7020. 400p. 1992. text ed. 46. 50 (*0-88048-408-X*) Am Psychiatric.

Borderline Personality Disorders: The Concept, the Syndrome, the Patient. Ed. by Peter Hartocollis. LC 77-6152. 535p. 1977. 65.00 (*0-8236-0575-2*) Intl Univs Pr.

Borderline Phenomena & the Rorschach Test. Ed. by Jay S. Kwawer et al. LC 80-15693. 505p. 1980. text ed. 65. 00 (*0-8236-0577-9*) Intl Univs Pr.

Borderline Psychopathology & Its Treatment. Gerald Adler. LC 84-24171. 272p. 1991. reprint ed. 35.00 (*0-87668-739-7*) Aronson.

***Borderline Psychopathology & Its Treatment.** Gerald Adler. LC 84-24171. 272p. 1994. reprint ed. pap. 27.50 (*1-56821-400-6*) Aronson.

Borderliners. Peter Hoeg. Tr. by Barbara Haveland. LC 94-18892. 1994. 24.00 (*0-374-11554-0*) FS&G.

***Borderliners.** large type ed. Peter Hoeg. LC 95-3694. (Large Print Book Ser.). 1995. 21.95 (*1-56895-202-3*) Wheeler Pub.

Borderlines. John Bishop. 1989. pap. 4.75 (*0-8222-0135-6*) Dramatists Play.

Borderlines. Archer Mayor. 320p. 1991. mass mkt. 4.50 (*0-380-71600-3*) Avon.

Borderlines. Archer Mayor. 320p. 1994. mass mkt. 5.50 (*0-446-40443-8*, Mysterious Paperbk) Warner Bks.

***Borderlines.** Scott Rollins. (Essential Poets Ser.: No. 66). 160p. 1995. 15.00 (*1-55071-009-5*) Guernica Editions.

Borderlines. large type ed. Archer Mayor. LC 91-2310. 398p. 1991. reprint ed. lib. bdg. 19.95 (*1-56054-162-8*) Thorndike Pr.

***Borderlines & Borderlands in English Canada: The Written Line.** Russell Brown. (Borderlands Monograph Ser.: No. 4). 13-70p. (C). 1990. pap. text ed. 5.00 (*0-614-04706-4*) Canadian-Amer Ctr.

Borderlords. Terry C. Johnston. 1986. mass mkt. 5.99 (*0-553-26224-6*) Bantam.

Borderlords. Terry C. Johnston. LC 85-14763. (Frontier Library). 500p. 1985. 19.95 (*0-915463-11-3*) Green Hill.

Borderman: Memoirs of Federico Jose Maria Ronstadt. Ed. by Edward F. Ronstadt. LC 93-3853. (Illus.). 181p. 1993. 19.95 (*0-8263-1462-7*) U of NM Pr.

Borders. Mary Crow. 1989. 16.00 (*0-918526-70-1*); pap. 10. 00 (*0-918526-71-X*) BOA Edns.

Borders. 2nd ed. Pat Mora. LC 85-73352. 88p. (Orig.). 1993. pap. 7.00 (*0-685-64977-6*) Arte Publico.

Borders, Vol. 1. Ed. by Leslie Cabarga & Casey Robbins. LC 91-70262. (Illus.). 64p. 1991. pap. text ed. 7.95 (*0-88108-083-7*) Art Dir.

Borders, Vol. 2. Ed. by Leslie Cabarga & Casey Robbins. LC 91-70262. (Illus.). 64p. 1991. pap. 7.95 (*0-88108-084-5*) Art Dir.

Borders, Vol. 3. Comp. by Leslie Cabarga. LC 91-70262. 64p. 1991. pap. text ed. 7.95 (*0-88108-085-3*) Art Dir.

Borders, Vol. 4. Comp. by Leslie Carbarga. LC 91-70262. 64p. 1991. pap. text ed. 7.95 (*0-88108-086-1*) Art Dir.

Borders: The National Trust Guide. Penelope Hobhouse. (Illus.). 112p. 1993. pap. 19.95 (*1-85145-854-9*, Pub. by Pavilion UK) Trafalgar.

***Borders Vol. 5.** Ed. by Leslie Cabarga. 64p. 1991. pap. text ed. 7.95 (*0-88108-087-X*) Art Dir.

***Borders & Berwick: An Illustrated Architectural Guide.** Charles A. Strang. (Illus.). 288p. (C). 1994. pap. 35.00x (*1-873190-10-7*, Pub. by Rutland Pr UK) St Mut.

Borders & Boxes, No. 1454. (Illus.). 48p. 1987. reprint ed. 5.95 (*1-878259-09-1*) Neibauer Pr.

Borders & Districts in Biblical Historiography. N. Na'aman. (Jerusalem Biblical Studies: Vol. 4). 275p. 1986. pap. text ed. 28.00 (*0-685-74281-4*, Pub. by Simor Ltd IS) Eisenbrauns.

Borders & Frames of the Art Nouveau Period. Ed. by Carol B. Grafton. (Pictorial Archive Ser.). 128p. 1984. pap. 5.95 (*0-486-24610-8*) Dover.

Borders & Scrolls: American Brush-Stroke Wall Painting, 1790-1820. Margaret Coffin. (Illus.). 80p. (Orig.). 1987. pap. 14.95 (*0-939072-08-4*) Albany Hist & Art.

Borders, Boundaries & Frameworks. Ed. by Mae Henderson. LC 93-42245. (Essays from the English Institute Ser.). 1994. 49.95 (*0-415-90929-5*, Routledge NY); pap. 15.95 (*0-415-90930-9*, Routledge NY) Routledge.

***Borders by Design: Creative Ways to Border Your Quilt.** Paulette Peters. Ed. by Janet White. (Joy of Quilting Ser.). (Illus.). 56p. (Orig.). 1994. pap. 9.95 (*1-56477-082-6*) That Patchwork.

Borders for Calligraphy. rev. ed. Margaret Shepherd. 144p. 1984. pap. 14.95 (*0-02-029560-X*, Collier S&S) S&S Trade.

Borders, Frames & Decorative Motifs from the 1862 Derriey Typographic Catalog. Charles Derriey. (Pictorial Archive Ser.). 128p. 1987. reprint ed. pap. 7.95 (*0-486-25322-8*) Dover.

Borders-Grenzen. Riki K. Nelson. 128p. (ENG & GER.). 1991. 9.50 (*0-9614462-4-2*) Ariadne CA.

Borders-Grenzen. Peter P. Wiplinger. Tr. by Herbert Kuhner. LC 77-18422. (Bilingual Poetry Ser.: No. 1). 72p. (GER.). 1977. 15.00 (*0-89304-022-3*, CCC112); pap. 7.50 (*0-89304-023-1*) Cross-Cultrl NY.

***Border's Guide to Arizona.** Bill McMillan. (Falcon Guide Ser.). (Illus.). 200p. 1995. pap. 14.95 (*1-56044-230-1*) Falcon Pr MT.

Borders Made Easy. Ed. by Karen Brewer. (Illus.). 48p. (Orig.). Date not set. pap. text ed. 6.49 (*0-7847-0146-6*, 14-03312) Standard Pub.

Borders of Culture, Margins of Identity: Seventh Annual Colloquium of the Interdisciplinary Nineteenth Century Studies Association, New Orleans, 1992. Ed. by Michele F. Levy et al. (Occasional Publications Ser.: No. 3). (Illus.). 95p. (Orig.). 1994. pap. 8.95 (*1-883275-01-6*) Xavier Rev.

Borders of Nightmare: The Fiction of John Richardson. Michael Hurley. (Illus.). 224p. 1992. 40.00 (*0-8020-5009-3*); pap. 16.95 (*0-8020-6940-1*) U of Toronto Pr.

Borders of Time: Life in a Nursing Home. Walter H. Crandall & Rob Crandall. (Illus.). 136p. 1990. pap. 29.95 (*0-8261-6890-6*) Springer Pub.

Bordertown. Terri Windling. 256p. 1996. mass mkt. 4.99 (*0-8125-2262-1*) Tor Bks.

Bordertown Blues. Allen Taylor. 1981. pap. 1.95 (*0-8439-0854-8*) Dorchester Pub Co.

Bordertowns. Marc Gaede. Ed. by Marnie Gaede. (Illus.). 112p. 1987. 27.95 (*0-9616019-2-2*) Chaco Pr.

Borderwork: Feminist Engagements with Comparative Literature. Ed. by Margaret R. Higonnet. LC 94-11246. (Reading Women Writing Ser.). 352p. 1994. 44.95 (*0-8014-2869-6*); pap. 16.95 (*0-8014-8107-4*) Cornell U Pr.

Bordetella Pertussis: Immunological & Other Biological Activities. John J. Munoz & R. K. Bergman. LC 76-26453. (Immunology Ser.: No. 4). (Illus.). 249p. reprint ed. pap. 71.00 (*0-7837-0815-7*, 2041130) Bks Demand.

Bordieu: Critical Perspectives. Ed. by Craig Calhoun et al. LC 93-12631. 296p. 1993. lib. bdg. 49.95 (*0-226-09092-2*); pap. text ed. 16.95 (*0-226-09093-0*) U Ch Pr.

Bordism of Diffeomorphisms & Related Topics. M. Kreck. (Lecture Notes in Mathematics Ser.: Vol. 1069). iii, 144p. 1984. pap. 28.10 (*0-387-13362-3*) Spr-Verlag.

Bords: Mathematiciens, Precurseurs, Encyclopedistes. Raymond Queneau. 144p. (FRE.). 1978. pap. 24.95 (*0-7859-1607-5*, 270565402X) Fr & Eur.

***Bore No More! (For Every Pastor, Teacher, Speaker) 70 Creative Ways to Involve Your Audience in Unforgettable Bible Teaching.** Mike Nappa & Amy Nappa. LC 94-24039. 1995. 12.99 (*1-55945-266-8*) Group Pub.

Boreal Forest Adaptations: The Northern Algonkians. Ed. by A. Theodore Steegman, Jr. LC 83-3984. 372p. 1983. 85.00 (*0-306-41238-1*, Plenum Pr) Plenum.

Boreal Forests & Global Change: Proceedings of the International Boreal Forest Research Association Alaska International Conference. Sinyan Shen. (Global Warming International Center Ser.). (Illus.). 200p. (C). 1993. pap. 85.00 (*0-9634567-4-1*) Supcon Intl.

Boreal Lower Cretaceous: The Proceedings of an International Symposium Organized by Queen Mary College, University of London, & the Institute of Geological Sciences, 17-30 September, 1972. International Symposium on the Boreal Lower Cretaceous Staff. Ed. by R. Casey & P. F. Rawson. LC 75-302015. (Geological Journal Special Issues Ser.: No. 5). 520p. reprint ed. pap. 148.20 (*0-8357-7353-1*, 2024275) Bks Demand.

Borealis, No. 1: An Isle Royale Potpourri. Ed. by David Harmon. 100p. (Orig.). 1992. pap. 7.95 (*0-935289-03-8*) Isle Royale Hist.

Bored & Busy: An Analysis of Formal & Informal Organization in the Automated Office. Phyllis L. Baker. LC 90-25698. (American University Studies: Anthropology & Science: Ser. XI, Vol. 52). 152p. (C). 1991. text ed. 35.95 (*0-8204-1362-3*) P Lang Pubs.

Bored Betty's Wish. Myrna Perkins. (Illus.). 32p. (Orig.). (J). (gr. 2-5). 1986. pap. 5.95 (*0-937729-02-7*) Markins Enter.

Bored Blue. Cynthia Jabar. 1991. 14.95 (*0-316-88884-2*) Little.

Bored Blue? Think What You Can Do. Cynthia Jabar. (J). (ps-3). 1991. 14.95 (*0-316-43458-2*) Little.

Bored, Nothing to Do. Peter Spier. LC 77-20726. (Illus.). 48p. (J). (gr. k-3). 1987. mass mkt. 5.95 (*0-385-24104-6*, Zephyr-BFYR) Doubleday.

Bored of the Rings: Fifty-First Anniversary Edition. Harvard Lampoon Staff. 176p. 1993. pap. 8.00 (*0-451-45261-5*, ROC) NAL-Dutton.

An Asterisk (*) at the beginning of an entry indicates that the title is appearing in BIP for the first time.

B

An Asterisk (*) at the beginning of an entry indicates that the title is appearing in BIP for the first time.

863

Born Different: The Amazing Stories of Some Very Special People. Frederick Drimmer. LC 87-33354. (Illus.). 192p. (J). (gr. 5-9). 1988. text ed. 15.95 (*0-689-31360-8*, Atheneum Bks Young) S&S Childrens.

Born Early: A Premature Baby's Story for Children. Lida Lafferty & Bo Flood. LC 94-92186. (Illus.). 40p. (Orig.). (J). (ps-4). 1995. pap. 8.95 (*0-9641413-0-2*) Songbird Pubng.

Born Fi' Dead: A Journey Through the Jamaican Posse Underworld. Laurie Gunst. LC 94-34554. 1995. 23.00 (*0-8050-3205-3*) H Holt & Co.

Born for Battle. 9th ed. R. Arthur Matthews. 1988. pap. 7.95 (*9971-972-36-0*) OMF Bks.

Born for Battle: Thirty-One Studies on Spiritual Warfare. R. Arthur Matthews. 190p. 1993. pap. 7.99 (*0-87788-090-5*, OMF Books) Shaw Pubs.

Born for Battle see Nascido para a Batalha

Born for Liberty: A History of Women in America. Sara M. Evans. 1990. pap. 16.95 (*0-02-903090-0*) Free Pr.

Born for Love: Reflections on Loving. Leo F. Buscaglia. 320p. 1994. reprint ed. pap. 10.00 (*0-449-90929-8*, Columbine) Fawcett.

Born for Love: Thoughts for Lovers. Leo F. Buscaglia. 1992. 18.50 (*0-679-41393-6*) Random.

Born for Love: Thoughts for Lovers. large type ed. Leo F. Buscaglia. 1992. 21.00 (*0-679-41381-2*) Random.

Born for Opposition: Eighteen Twenty-One see Byron's Letters & Journals

Born for the Muses: The Life & Masses of Jacob Obrecht. Rob C. Wegman. LC 93-39022. (Monographs on Music). (Illus.). 448p. (C). 1994. 45.00 (*0-19-816382-7*, Clarendon Pr) OUP.

***Born Free.** Joy Adamson. LC 74-5073. (Illus.). 1994. reprint ed. lib. bdg. 44.95x (*1-56849-551-X*) Buccaneer Bks.

Born Free: A Lioness of Two Worlds. Joy Adamson. LC 86-42972. 1987. 11.95 (*0-679-56141-2*); pap. 14.00 (*0-394-74635-X*) Pantheon.

***Born Free: How to Find Radical Freedom & Infectious Joy in an Authentic Faith.** Steve Brown. 1993. 16.99 (*0-8010-1069-1*) Baker Bk.

***Born Free: The Complete Guide to the Mighty Columbia River, by Land, & Water.** William H. Schweizer. (Illus.). 282p. 1994. 19.95 (*0-925244-03-1*) EOS Pub.

Born Free & Equal. limited rev. ed. Ansel Adams. Ed. by Emily Medvec. LC 84-21125. (Illus.). 44p. 1984. pap. 50.00 (*0-931547-00-8*, BFE, Photogram) Gnu Vue.

***Born Free Study Guide.** Steve Brown. 1994. pap. 9.99 (*0-8010-1095-0*) Baker Bk.

Born from Above: The Anthropology of the Gospel of John. Jeffrey A. Trumbower. (Hermen. Unt. Suchungen zur Theologie Ser.: No. 29). 170p. 1992. 87.50 (*3-16-145806-0*, Pub. by J C B Mohr GW) Coronet Bks.

***Born Giving Birth.** Ed. by Mary H. Schertz & Phyllis Martens. LC 91-75974. 88p. 1991. pap. 19.95 (*0-87303-148-2*) Faith & Life.

***Born Guilty.** Reginald Hill. 240p. 1995. 20.95 (*0-312-13032-5*, Pub. by Thomas Dunne Bks) St Martin.

Born Hooked: Poisoned in the Womb. rev. ed. Ed. by Gary E. McCuen. (Ideas in Conflict Ser.). (Illus.). 159p. 1994. lib. bdg. 12.95 (*0-86596-091-7*) G E M.

***Born Hutterite.** Samuel Hofer. (Illus.). 140p. Date not set. pap. 9.95 (*0-9693056-4-8*) Ex Machina.

***Born in a Stable.** Joshua Morris Packager Staff. Date not set. 4.99 (*0-679-87479-8*) Random.

***Born in a Stable.** Rhona Pipe. (Illus.). 1995. pap. 4.99 (*0-8010-4040-X*) Baker Bk.

***Born in a Trunk...Outside the Center Door Fancy.** Billy Choate. 266p. (Orig.). 1994. pap. write for info. (*1-885591-42-X*) Morris Pubng.

Born in Blood. John J. Robinson. LC 89-23703. 396p. 1990. 18.95 (*0-87131-602-1*) M Evans.

Born in Brooklyn. John Montague. 128p. 1991. pap. 10.00 (*1-877727-13-X*) White Pine.

Born in Exile. George Gissing. 544p. 1993. pap. 6.95 (*0-460-87241-9*, Everyman's Classic Lib) C E Tuttle.

Born in Exile: A Novel, 3 Vols. in 1. George Gissing. LC 68-54266. reprint ed. 37.50 (*0-404-02786-5*) AMS Pr.

***Born in Fire.** Nora Roberts. 416p. (Orig.). 1994. pap. text ed. 5.99 (*0-515-11469-3*) Jove Pubns.

***Born in Fire.** large type ed. Nora Roberts. LC 94-41311. 506p. 1995. 22.95 (*0-7862-0373-0*) Thorndike Pr.

***Born in Ice.** Nora Roberts. 384p. (Orig.). 1995. pap. text ed. 5.99 (*0-515-11675-0*) Jove Pubns.

Born in New Orleans: Notables of Two Centuries. Al Rose. (Illus.). 1983. 17.50 (*0-916620-68-9*) Portals Pr.

Born in Ohio & Living in Southwest Michigan in 1860. Ann Burton & Conrad Burton. (Illus.). 78p. (Orig.). 1986. pap. 9.50 (*0-937505-02-1*) Glyndwr Resc.

Born in Paradise. Armine von Tempski. LC 84-27345. 342p. (J). 1985. reprint ed. 27.50 (*0-918024-65-X*); reprint ed. pap. 14.95 (*0-918024-34-X*) Ox Bow.

Born in the Bleachers. Steven Moore. 96p. 1989. pap. 5.95 (*0-02-040631-2*, Collier S&S) S&S Trade.

***Born in the Country: A History of Rural America.** David B. Danbom. (Revisiting Rural America Ser.). (Illus.). 232p. 1994. text ed. 42.50x (*0-8018-5039-8*); pap. text ed. 14.95x (*0-8018-5040-1*) Johns Hopkins.

Born in the Delta: Reflections on the Making of a Southern White Sensibility. Margaret J. Bolsterli. LC 90-45245. (Illus.). 152p. 1991. 22.95 (*0-87049-690-5*) U of Tenn Pr.

Born in the Fire: Case Studies in Christian Ethics & Globalization. Enoch H. Oglesby. LC 90-43875. 192p. (Orig.). (C). 1990. pap. 14.95 (*0-8298-0849-3*) Pilgrim OH.

Born in the Gravy. Denys Cazet. LC 92-44523. (Illus.). 32p. (J). (ps-1). 1993. 14.95 (*0-531-05488-8*); lib. bdg. 14.99 (*0-531-08638-0*) Orchard Bks Watts.

Born in the Spring: A Collection of Spring Wildflowers. June C. Roberts. LC 75-36979. (Illus.). 160p. 1976. reprint ed. pap. 21.95 (*0-8214-0226-9*) Ohio U Pr.

Born in the U. S. A. The Myth of America in Popular Music from Colonial Times to the Present. Timothy E. Scheurer. LC 90-29114. (Studies in Popular Culture Ser.). 1991. 37.50 (*0-87805-496-0*); pap. 15.95 (*0-87805-497-9*) U Pr of Miss.

Born in the Year of Courage. Emily Crofford. (Adventures in Time Ser.). 184p. (J). (gr. 4-7). 1991. lib. bdg. 19.95 (*0-87614-679-5*, Carolrhoda) Lerner Group.

Born in the Year of the Pink Sink. Lenore B. Wang. (Italian-American Women's Poetry (Chapbooks) Ser.). 20p. (Orig.). 1993. pap. 3.00 (*1-883112-04-4*) Malafemmina.

Born in Tibet. Chogyam Trungpa. 1985. pap. 9.95 (*0-394-74219-2*) Random.

***Born in Tibet.** Chogyam Trungpa. (Illus.). 296p. 1995. pap. 15.00 (*1-57062-116-0*) Shambhala Pubns.

***Born Indian.** Kinsella. Date not set. per. 12.95 (*0-88750-381-0*, Pub. by Oberon Pr CN) Pocahontas Pr.

Born Innocent. Christine Rimmer. (Silhouette Special Edition Ser.). 1993. mass mkt. 3.50 (*0-373-09833-2*, 5-09833-0) Silhouette.

***Born Naked.** large type ed. Farley Mowat. LC 94-31743. 1994. pap. 19.95 (*1-56895-076-4*) Wheeler Pub.

Born Naked: The Early Adventures of the Author of "Never Cry Wolf" Farley Mowat. LC 93-23702. 1994. 21.95 (*0-395-68927-9*) HM.

***Born Naked: The Early Adventures of the Author of Never Cry Wolf.** Farley Mowat. 1995. pap. 10.95 (*0-395-73528-9*) HM.

Born Near the Earth's Surface: Sedimentary Rocks. Sally M. Walker. LC 90-42436. (Earth Processes Ser.). (Illus.). 64p. (J). (gr. 6 up). 1991. lib. bdg. 15.95 (*0-89490-293-8*) Enslow Pubs.

Born of a Dream: Fifty Haiku by Basho, Buson, Taigi, Issa, Shiki. Tr. & Intro. by Cid Corman. LC 88-81708. 72p. (Orig.). 1989. pap. text ed. 7.50 (*0-917788-37-0*) Gnomon Pr.

Born of a Dream: Fifty Haiku by Basho, Buson, Taigi, Issa, Shiki. deluxe limited ed. Tr. & Intro. by Cid Corman. LC 88-81708. 72p. (Orig.). 1989. 25.00 (*0-917788-36-2*) Gnomon Pr.

Born of a Glorious Thunder: Real Life Accounts of Foreign Christian Work. Kenneth Oosterhouse et al. Tr. by Helen Kortenhoeven. 304p. (Orig.). 1986. pap. 6.95 (*0-318-22002-4*) West Indies Pub.

Born of a Woman: A Bishop Rethinks the Virgin Birth & the Treatment of Women by a Male-Dominated Church. John S. Spong. LC 91-55087. 1994. pap. 10.00 (*0-06-067523-3*) Harper SF.

***Born of Elven Blood.** Kevin J. Anderson & John G. Betancourt. (Illus.). (YA). (gr. 7 up). 1995. 15.00 (*0-689-31815-4*, Atheneum Bks Young) S&S Childrens.

Born of Fire: The Volcanic Origins of Yellowstone National Park. William H. Cottrell. 64p. (Orig.). 1987. pap. 11. 95 (*0-911797-35-1*) R Rinehart.

Born of Fire: Volcanoes & Igneous Rocks. Robert I. Tilling. LC 89-25781. (Earth Processes Ser.). (Illus.). 64p. (J). (gr. 6 up). 1991. lib. bdg. 15.95 (*0-89490-151-6*) Enslow Pubs.

Born of Flame: A Rosicrucian Story. Margaret B. Peeke. 299p. 1971. reprint ed. spiral bd. 11.00 (*0-7873-1139-1*) Mokelumne.

Born of Heat & Pressure: Mountains & Metamorphic Rocks. Patricia L. Barnes-Svarney. LC 89-25856. (Earth Processes Ser.). (Illus.). 64p. (J). (gr. 6 up). 1991. lib. bdg. 15.95 (*0-89490-276-8*) Enslow Pubs.

Born of Love. Arleen Lorrance. (Illus.). 200p. (Orig.). 1981. pap. 14.95 (*0-916192-16-4*) L P Pubns.

***Born of Man.** Gray. Date not set. per. 9.95 (*0-85449-107-4*, Pub. by Gay Mens Pr UK) InBook.

Born of the Poor: The Latin American Church Since Medellin. Ed. by Edward L. Cleary. LC 89-40746. 200p. (C). 1990. text ed. 23.95 (*0-268-00683-0*) U of Notre Dame Pr.

Born of the Poor: The Latin American Church since Medellin. Ed. by Edward L. Cleary. LC 89-40746. (From the Helen Kellogg Institute for International Studies). (C). 1992. pap. text ed. 9.95 (*0-268-00685-7*) U of Notre Dame Pr.

Born of the Same Roots: Stories of Modern Chinese Women. Ed. by Vivian L. Hsu. LC 81-47009. 317p. reprint ed. pap. 90.40 (*0-7837-6101-5*, 2059147) Bks Demand.

***Born of the Spirit: Renewal Movements in the Life of the Church.** 2nd ed. Paul J. Cordes. 138p. 1995. 11.95 (*0-937779-30-X*) Greenlawn Pr.

Born of the Storm. Nikolai A. Ostrovskii. Tr. by Louise L. Hiler. LC 74-10089. (Soviet Literature in English Translation Ser.). 251p. 1975. reprint ed. 20.00 (*0-88355-175-6*) Hyperion Conn.

Born of the Sun. Gillian Cross. LC 84-3740. (Illus.). 240p. (YA). (gr. 7 up). 1984. 11.95 (*0-8234-0528-1*) Holiday.

Born of the Sun. Joan Wolf. 1991. reprint ed. pap. 5.50 (*0-451-40225-1*, Onyx) NAL-Dutton.

Born of the Sun: A Namibian Novel. Joseph Diescho. 200p. 1988. 14.95 (*0-377-00188-0*); pap. 6.95 (*0-377-00187-2*) Friendship Pr.

Born of Water & Spirit: Teachings in Mystic Christianity. Andrew Lohr. LC 90-82118. 256p. (Orig.). 1990. pap. 11.95 (*0-9626563-4-8*) Folsom Lee.

Born on Snowhoes. Evelyn B. Shore. 301p. 1994. 20.00 (*0-9636511-8-8*) Herit Pr CA.

Born on the Fourth of July. Ron Kovic. 224p. 1990. mass mkt. 5.50 (*0-671-73914-X*) PB.

***Born, One of Us.** Marion Fairman. 1995. pap. write for info. (*0-7880-0571-5*) CSS OH.

Born Only Once: The Miracle of Affirmation. Conrad W. Baars. 1984. pap. 5.00 (*0-8199-0671-9*, Frncscn Herld) Franciscan Pr.

Born Out of Season. Ralph L. Hooker. Ed. by William H. Scurlock. LC 81-84090. 110p. 1981. pap. 5.95 (*0-9605666-1-9*) Scurlock Pub.

Born Out of Wedlock. Gil Fox. (Illus.). 40p. (Orig.). 1992. pap. 4.99 (*1-882676-00-9*) CT Post.

Born Permeable. Eunice De Chazeau. Ed. by Joseph D. Adams. LC 91-67822. xii, 68p. (Orig.). 1992. pap. 5.00 (*1-880016-09-5*) Road Pubs.

Born Red: A Chronicle of the Cultural Revolution. Gao Yuan. LC 86-23058. 416p. (Orig.). 1987. 45.00 (*0-8047-1368-5*); pap. 12.95 (*0-8047-1369-3*) Stanford U Pr.

Born Remembering. Elise Boulding. LC 74-30805. 32p. (Orig.). 1975. pap. 3.00 (*0-87574-200-9*) Pendle Hill.

Born Secret: The H-Bomb, the "Progressive" Case & National Security. Alexander De Volpi et al. (Illus.). 320p. 1981. 42.00 (*0-08-025995-2*, Pergamon Pr) Elsevier.

Born Smart: The Story of Paul Smith. Helen E. Tyler. (Illus.). 192p. 1988. pap. 12.95 (*0-932052-65-7*) North Country.

Born Substance Exposed, Educationally Vulnerable. Lisbeth J. Vincent et al. (Exceptional Children at Risk Ser.). 30p. 1991. 8.90 (*0-86586-212-5*, P355) Coun Exc Child.

Born That Way: A True Story of Overcoming Same-Sex Attraction. Erin Eldridge. LC 93-48687. vii, 192p. 1994. 13.95 (*0-87579-835-7*) Deseret Bk.

***Born This Day: A Daily Celebration of Famous Beginnings.** Ed Morrow. (Illus.). 324p. 1995. pap. 10.95 (*0-8065-1648-8*, Citadel Pr) Carol Pub Group.

Born This Way. Don Zivney. 54p. 1993. pap. 4.95 (*1-883412-01-3*) Woodrose Pr.

***Born to Be.** Taylor Gordon. (Blacks in the American West Ser.). (Illus.). 288p. 1995. pap. 11.00 (*0-8032-7052-6*, Bison Books) U of Nebr Pr.

Born to Be a Loser: The Jimmy Donley Story. Johnnie Allan & Bernice L. Webb. LC 92-72741. 341p. (Orig.). 1992. pap. 18.95 (*0-9619335-2-6*) Jadfel Pub.

Born to Be a Soldier: The Military Career of William Wing Loring of St. Augustine, Florida. LC 71-143789. (Texas Christian University Monographs in History & Culture: No. 8). 128p. reprint ed. pap. 36.50 (*0-8357-7356-6*, 2010133) Bks Demand.

Born to Be Bad. Naomi Horton. (Silhouette Intimate Moments Ser.). 1994. mass mkt. 3.50 (*0-373-07543-X*, 5-07543-7) Silhouette.

Born to Be Invisible see Absent from School: The Story of a Truancy Centre

Born to Be Lucky: An Autobiography by Daniel P. Benford. Daniel P. Benford. LC 94-71594. (Illus.). 300p. 1994. 9.95 (*1-882183-34-7*) Computer Pr.

Born to Be Rich. Illus. by Reynold J. Anschuetz. 232p. (Orig.). 1988. pap. 11.95 (*0-9619358-1-2*) Confectionery World Inc.

Born to be Wild. Barry Bowe. 304p. (Orig.). 1994. mass mkt. 5.99 (*0-446-36434-7*) Warner Bks.

Born to Be Wild. Kris Cassidy. 224p. (Orig.). 1990. pap. 2.75 (*1-878702-11-4*, Kismet) Meteor Pub.

***Born to Be Wild.** Timothy Williams. Date not set. pap. 3.50 (*0-87406-636-0*) Willowisp Pr.

Born to Be Wild: Hollywood & the Sixties Generation. rev. ed. Seth Cagin & Philip Dray. 236p. 1994. reprint ed. pap. 14.95 (*0-89777-148-6*, Coyte) Sirs Inc.

***Born to Build: A Parent's Guide to Academic Alternatives.** Paul Ridilla. LC 94-21564. 1994. 16.95 (*0-912524-93-6*) Busn News.

Born to Code in C. Herbert Schildt. 1989. pap. text ed. 28. 95 (*0-07-881468-5*) Osborne-McGraw.

Born to Crime: The Genetic Causes of Criminal Behavior. Lawrence Taylor. LC 83-12937. (Contributions in Criminology & Penology Ser.: No. 2). x, 179p. 1984. text ed. 37.50 (*0-313-24172-4*, TAB/, Greenwood Pr) Greenwood.

Born to Die? Deciding the Fate of Critically Ill Newborns. Earl E. Shelp. 288p. 1986. 27.95 (*0-02-929110-0*) Free Pr.

Born to Die in Medellin. Alonso Salazar. (Latin America Bureau Ser.). (Illus.). 130p. (Orig.). (C). 1992. pap. text ed. 10.00 (*0-85345-854-5*, Pub. by Lat Am Bur UK) Monthly Rev.

Born to Exile. Phyllis Eisenstein. 1989. pap. 3.95 (*0-451-16280-3*, 017) NAL-Dutton.

Born to Fly: How to Discover & Encourage Your Child's Natural Gifts. Tom Black & Lynda R. Stephenson. LC 93-47962. 1994. pap. write for info. (*0-310-40282-4*) Zondervan.

Born to Fly: How to Discover & Encourage Your Child's Natural Gifts. Tom Black & Lynda R. Stephenson. 224p. 1994. pap. 12.99 (*0-310-40281-6*) Zondervan.

Born to Fly: How to Discover & Encourage Your Child's Natural Gifts. Tom Black & Lynda R. Stephenson. 224p. 1994. Spiral wkbk. spiral bd. 5.99 (*0-310-40283-2*, Pyranee) Zondervan.

Born to Fly: The Story of General Edwin Rawlings. Edwin Rawlings. LC 87-82697. (Illus.). 309p. (C). 1987. 16.95 (*0-9619320-0-7*) Great Way Pub.

Born to Heal. Ruth Montgomery. 1985. pap. 3.50 (*0-449-21111-8*) Fawcett.

***Born to Kill: True Story of America's Most Notorious Vietnamese Gang.** T. J. English. LC 94-21474. 1995. (*0-688-12238-8*) Morrow.

Born to Lose. Trevor Clark. 154p. (Orig.). 1989. pap. 12.00 (*1-55022-081-0*, Pub. by ECW Press CN) Genl Dist Srvs.

Born to New Life - Cyprian of Carthage. Ed. by Oliver Davies. Tr. by Tim Witherow. 128p. (Orig.). 1992. pap. 7.95 (*1-56548-006-6*) New City.

Born to Play: The Life & Career of Hazel Harrison. Jean E. Cazort & Constance T. Hobson. LC 82-12169. (Contributions to the Study of Music & Dance Ser.: No. 3). (Illus.). 200p. 1983. text ed. 49.95 (*0-313-23643-7*, CBO/, Greenwood Pr) Greenwood.

Born to Power: Heirs to America's Leading Companies. Jan Pottker. 1992. pap. 12.95 (*0-8120-1456-1*) Barron.

Born to Raise: What Makes a Great Fundraiser, What Makes a Fundraiser Great. Jerold Panas. LC 88-61232. 228p. 1988. 40.00 (*0-944496-02-4*) Precept Pr.

Born to Raze Hell. Tom Franks. 112p. (Orig.). (YA). 1989. pap. 5.95 (*1-877717-00-2*) Mercedes Ministries.

Born to Rebel: An Autobiography by Benjamin E. Mays. Benjamin E. Mays. LC 86-19308. (Brown Thrasher Bks.). (Illus.). 440p. 1986. reprint ed. pap. 14.95 (*0-8203-0881-1*) U of Ga Pr.

Born to Rebel: The Life of Harriet Boyd Hawes. Mary Allsebrook. (Illus.). 263p. 1992. 25.00 (*0-946897-40-9*) David Brown.

Born to Rule: Autobiography of a Life President. Tah Asongwed. 228p. (Orig.). (C). 1993. pap. 17.95 (*0-9636439-0-8*) Herit Pub MD.

Born to Run. Mercedes Lackey & Larry Dixon. 1992. mass mkt. 5.99 (*0-671-72110-0*) Baen Bks.

Born to Sail: On Other People's Boats. Jennifer P. Stuart. (Illus.). 112p. (Orig.). 1991. pap. 13.95 (*0-924486-11-2*) Sheridan.

Born to Shine. Susan E. Schaefer. (Illus.). 36p. (J). 1994. 14.95 (*0-9638908-4-0*) Blink Bks.

Born to Shop Great Britain. 3rd ed. Suzy Gershman. (Born to Shop Ser.). (Illus.). 304p. (Orig.). 1994. pap. 12.00 (*0-06-273199-8*, Harper Ref) HarpC.

Born to Shop Hong Kong. 5th ed. Suzy K. Gershman. (Illus.). 304p. 1993. pap. 12.00 (*0-06-273200-5*, Harper Ref) HarpC.

Born to Shop in Mexico. 2nd ed. Suzy Gershman. (Born to Shop Ser.). 1994. pap. 12.00 (*0-06-273258-7*) HarpC.

Born to Shop London. 6th ed. Suzy Gershman. (Born to Shop Ser.). (Illus.). 304p. (Orig.). 1994. pap. 12.00 (*0-06-273203-X*, Harper Ref) HarpC.

Born to Shop New York. 5th ed. Suzy Gershman. (Born to Shop Ser.). (Illus.). 304p. (Orig.). 1994. pap. 12.00 (*0-06-273198-X*, Harper Ref) HarpC.

Born to Sing. Elisabeth Howard & Howard Austin. (Illus.). 125p. 1985. pap. 9.95 (*0-934419-00-0*) Vocal Power.

Born to Sing: An Interpretation & World Survey of Bird Song. Charles Hartshorne. 320p. 1992. 35.00 (*0-253-32729-6*); pap. 12.95 (*0-253-20743-6*, MB-743) Ind U Pr.

Born to Sing: An Interpretation & World Survey of Bird Song. Charles Hartshorne. LC 72-75392. 320p. reprint ed. pap. 91.20 (*0-8357-7357-4*, 2056037) Bks Demand.

Born to Sing: Vocal Harmony. Elisabeth Howard & Howard Austin. (Born to Sing Ser.). (Illus.). 88p. (Orig.). 1989. audio 19.95 (*0-934419-10-8*); pap. text ed. 12.95 (*0-317-93013-3*) Vocal Power.

Born to Spend: How to Overcome Compulsive Spending. Gloria Arenson. 1991. pap. text ed. 9.95 (*0-07-001652-6*) McGraw.

Born to Spend: How to Overcome Compulsive Spending. Gloria Arenson. 196p. 1991. pap. 9.95 (*0-8306-2155-5*, 2303, TAB-Human Servs Inst) TAB Bks.

Born to Succeed. Mark Nevin. (Illus.). 145p. (Orig.). 1983. pap. 7.95 (*0-553-13843-X*) M Nevin.

***Born to Succeed.** Colin Turner. 1995. pap. 10.95 (*1-85230-486-3*) Element MA.

Born to Survive, 1936-1946. George G. Whitney. (Illus.). 200p. 1982. pap. 12.95 (*0-916224-72-4*) Banyan Bks.

Born to Talk: An Introduction to Speech & Language Development. Lloyd M. Hulit & Merle R. Howard. LC 92-20404. 400p. (C). 1993. write for info. (*0-675-22155-2*, Merrill Pub Co) Macmillan.

Born to the Purple. S. L. Florian. 288p. 1992. mass mkt. 3.99 (*0-8217-3854-2*) Zebra.

Born to Triumph. C. Paul Willis. 392p. (Orig.). 1992. pap. 9.99 (*1-56043-651-4*) Destiny Image.

Born to Trot. 2nd ed. Marguerite Henry. LC 92-24139. (Illus.). 224p. (J). (gr. 3-6). 1993. reprint ed. pap. 3.95 (*0-689-71692-3*, Aladdin Paperbacks) S&S Childrens.

Born to Trouble. large type ed. Nelson Nye. (Nightingale Ser.). 278p. 1991. pap. 14.95 (*0-8161-4831-7*, Nightingale) Hall.

***Born to Wander: The Autobiography of John Ball.** John Ball. Ed. & Intro. by Gary Burbridge. (Illus.). 160p. (YA). (gr. 8 up). 1994. 24.95 (*0-9617708-4-8*) GRMI Hist Comm.

Born to Win. Muriel James & Dorothy Jongeward. 352p. 1978. 5.99 (*0-451-16521-7*, Sig) NAL-Dutton.

Born to Win. Lewis Timberlake & Marietta Reed. 224p. 1986. pap. 8.99 (*0-8423-0338-3*) Tyndale.

Born to Win. 3rd ed. Muriel James. 1990. pap. 11.54 (*0-201-55016-4*) Addison-Wesley.

***Born to Win: A Poetic Biography of African-Americans.** John Z. Reid. LC 95-68267. 64p. (YA). (gr. 6-12). 1995. 17.95 (*1-887214-01-1*); pap. 12.95 (*1-887214-02-X*) Caribbean TX.

Born to Win: Breed to Succeed. Patricia V. Craige. Ed. by Luana Luther. (Illus.). 320p. 1995. 29.95 (*0-944875-40-8*) Doral Pub.

Born to Win: Transactional Analysis with Gestalt Experiments. Muriel James & Dorothy Jongeward. LC 70-161224. (Business Ser.). 1971. pap. 8.95 (*0-201-03319-4*) Addison-Wesley.

Born to Win: Transactional Analysis with Gestalt Experiments. 10th ed. Muriel James & Dorothy Jongeward. 1978. pap. 4.95 (*0-451-15650-1*, Sig) NAL-Dutton.

***Born to Work: Child Labour in India.** Neera Burra. (Illus.). 296p. 1995. 24.00 (*0-19-563628-7*) OUP.

Born Too Soon. Elizabeth Mehren. 416p. 1993. mass mkt. 4.50 (*1-55817-751-5*, Pinnacle NY) Windsor NY.

An Asterisk (*) at the beginning of an entry indicates that the title is appearing in BIP for the first time.

An Asterisk (*) at the beginning of an entry indicates that the title is appearing in BIP for the first time.

865

B

Bosch Technical Instruction: Components for Compressed-Air Brake Systems. Robert Bosch. Date not set. pap. 11.95 (*0-8376-0499-0*) Bentley.

Bosch Technical Instruction: Compressed-Air Brake Systems. Robert Bosch. Date not set. pap. 11.95 (*0-8376-0498-2*) Bentley.

Bosch Technical Instruction: Diesel Fuel-Injection--An Overview. Robert Bosch. Date not set. pap. 11.95 (*0-8376-0494-X*) Bentley.

Bosch Technical Instruction: Diesel Fuel-Injection Pumps Types PE-PF. Robert Bosch. Date not set. pap. 11.95 (*0-8376-0496-6*) Bentley.

Bosch Technical Instruction: Distributor Fuel-Injection Pump Type VE. Robert Bosch. Date not set. pap. 11.95 (*0-8376-0495-8*); 44.95 (*0-8376-0598-9*) Bentley.

Bosch Technical Instruction: Electronics & Microcomputers. Robert Bosch. Date not set. pap. 11.95 (*0-8376-0481-8*) Bentley.

Bosch Technical Instruction: Emission Control for Spark-Ignition Engines. Robert Bosch. Date not set. pap. 11.95 (*0-8376-0474-5*) Bentley.

Bosch Technical Instruction: Engine Electronics. Robert Bosch. Date not set. pap. 11.95 (*0-8376-0475-3*) Bentley.

Bosch Technical Instruction: Governors for In-Line Pumps. Robert Bosch. Date not set. pap. 11.95 (*0-8376-0497-4*) Bentley.

Bosch Technical Instruction: Graphical Symbols & Circuit Diagrams for Automotive Electrics. Robert Bosch. Date not set. pap. 11.95 (*0-8376-0493-1*) Bentley.

Bosch Technical Instruction: Interference Suppression. Robert Bosch. Date not set. pap. 11.95 (*0-8376-0476-1*) Bentley.

Bosch Technical Instruction: K-Jetronic Fuel-Injection System. Robert Bosch. Date not set. pap. 11.95 (*0-8376-0468-0*) Bentley.

Bosch Technical Instruction: KE-Jetronic Fuel-Injection System. Robert Bosch. Date not set. pap. 11.95 (*0-8376-0469-9*) Bentley.

Bosch Technical Instruction: L-Jetronic Fuel-Injection System. Robert Bosch. Date not set. pap. 11.95 (*0-8376-0470-2*) Bentley.

Bosch Technical Instruction: Mono-Jetronic. Robert Bosch. Date not set. pap. 11.95 (*0-8376-0492-3*) Bentley.

Bosch Technical Instruction: Motronic Combined Ignition & Fuel-Injection System. Robert Bosch. Date not set. pap. 11.95 (*0-8376-0471-0*) Bentley.

Bosch Technical Instruction: Spark Plugs. Robert Bosch. Date not set. pap. 11.95 (*0-8376-0478-8*) Bentley.

Bosch Technical Instruction: Starting Systems. Robert Bosch. Date not set. pap. 11.95 (*0-8376-0480-X*) Bentley.

Bosch Technical Instruction: Symbols for Compressed-Air Brake Systems. Robert Bosch. Date not set. pap. 11.95 (*0-8376-0597-0*) Bentley.

Bose Algebras: Complex & Real Wave Representations. T. T. Nielsen. (Lecture Notes in Mathematics Ser.: Vol. 1472). v, 132p. 1991. pap. 24.00 (*0-387-54041-5*) Spr-Verlag.

Bose & His Statistics. G. Venkataraman. (Vignettes in Physics Ser.). 1993. pap. 5.95 (*0-86311-313-3*, Pub. by Universities Pr II) Apt Bks.

Bose-Einstein Condensation. Ed. by A. Griffin et al. 540p. (C). 1995. 79.95 (*0-521-46473-0*) Cambridge U Pr.

Boshblobberbosh: Runcible Poems for Mr. Lear. J. Patrick Lewis. LC 93-43749. (J). 1995. write for info. (*0-8037-1390-8*); lib. bdg. write for info. (*0-8037-1391-6*) Dial Bks Young.

Bosillo Para Corduroy: A Pocket for Corduroy. Don Freeman. (Illus.). 32p. (ENG & SPA.). (J). (ps-3). 1992. 13.00 (*0-670-84483-7*) Viking Child Bks.

Bosler Cookbook of Hors D'Oeuvres & Other Savory Recipes. Ed. by Barbara Lillich et al. (Illus.). 1988. spiral bd., pap. 10.95 (*0-9620870-0-9*) Friends Bosler.

Bosley Crowther: Social Critic of the Film, 1974. Frank E. Beaver. LC 73-21589. (Dissertations on Film Ser.: Vol. 8). 202p. 1977. 15.95 (*0-405-04870-X*) Ayer.

Bosnia: A Short History. Noel Malcolm. (Illus.). 340p. 1994. 26.95 (*0-8147-5520-8*) NYU Pr.

***Bosnia: Can There Ever Be Peace?** David Flint. LC 95-11749. (Hot Off the Press Ser.). (J). 1995. write for info. (*0-8172-4176-0*) Raintree Steck-V.

Bosnia & Hercegovina: A Tradition Betrayed. Robert J. Donia & John V. A. Vine, Jr. LC 94-16223. 1994. 24.95 (*0-231-10160-0*) Col U Pr.

***Bosnia & Herzegovina.** David W. Felder. (Illus.). 52p. 1995. pap. text ed. 5.00 (*0-910959-85-4*, B&G 17A) Felder Bks.

Bosnia, Croatia, Macedonia, Serbia, Montenegro, Slovenia: Business Risk Overview. Ed. by Lewis B. Sckolnick. 125p. (Orig.). (C). 1994. pap. text ed. 495.00 (*1-57205-603-7*) Rector Pr.

***Bosnia Teenage Refugees.** (Illus.). 70p. (YA). 1995. lib. bdg. 45.00 (*0-7605-1523-9*) Rector Pr.

Bosnian Chronicle. Ivo Andric. Tr. by Joseph Hitreck. 442p. 1993. reprint ed. pap. 10.95 (*1-55970-236-2*) Arcade Pub Inc.

***Bosnian Muslims.** Francine Friedman. (C). 1995. pap. text ed. 19.95 (*0-8133-2096-8*) Westview.

***Bosnian Muslims.** Francine Friedman. 1995. text ed. 62.50 (*0-8133-2097-6*) Westview.

Bosnian People Charge Genocide: Proceedings at the International Court of Justice Concerning Bosnia v. Serbia on the Prevention & Punishment of the Crime of Genocide. Francis A. Boyle. LC 94-11826. 1994. pap. text ed. write for info. (*1-880831-09-0*) Aletheia Pr.

Bosom Buddies. Anthony. 1991. pap. 5.95 (*0-88032-410-4*) Ivory Tower Pub.

Bosoms & Neglect. John Guare. 1979. pap. 4.75 (*0-8222-0137-2*) Dramatists Play.

Bosonization. Michael Stone. 300p. 1994. text ed. 104.00 (*981-02-1847-8*); pap. text ed. 54.00 (*981-02-1848-6*) World Scientific Pub.

Bosons in Nuclei: Proceedings of Workshop held in Drexel, Jan. 28-29, 1983. Ed. by Da-Hsuan Feng & M. Vallieres. 320p. 1984. 60.00 (*9971-950-18-9*); pap. 30.00 (*9971-950-19-7*) World Scientific Pub.

Bosque. J. M. Parramon. (J). (ps-3). 1991. pap. 6.95 (*0-8120-4712-5*) Barron.

Bosque Animado. Wenceslao Fernandez Florez. Ed. by Jose C. Mainer. (Nueva Austral Ser.: Vol. 128). (SPA.). 1991. pap. text ed. 24.95x (*84-239-1928-5*) Elliots Bks.

Bosque County: Land & People. rev. ed. Ed. by Bosque County History Book Committee. (Illus.). 801p. 1986. reprint ed. 60.00 (*0-88107-052-1*) Curtis Media.

Bosque County, Texas: Land & People. Ed. by Bosque County History Book Committee. (Illus.). 800p. 1985. 55.00 (*0-88107-029-7*) Curtis Media.

Bosque Indomado...Donde Chilla el Obsceno Pajaro de la Noche. Josefina A. Pujals. LC 81-69533. 134p. (Orig.). (SPA.). 1982. pap. 15.95 (*0-89729-304-5*) Ediciones.

Bosque Redondo: A Study of Cultural Stress at the Navajo Reservation, 1863-1868. Lynn R. Bailey. (Illus.). 275p. 19.95 (*0-87026-043-X*) Westernlore.

***Bosque Seco de Guanica.** Angel L. Torres et al. (Illus.). (J). 1994. 12.95 (*0-8477-0207-3*) U of PR Pr.

Bosque Tropical: Rain Forest. Helen Cowcher. (YA). 1992. 15.00 (*0-374-30900-0*) FS&G.

Bosquejos Biblicos, Tomo III. Daniel Campderros. 96p. 1988. reprint ed. pap. 3.50 (*0-311-43033-3*) Casa Bautista.

Bosquejos Biblicos Tomo I: Antiguo Testamento. Daniel Campderros. 96p. 1990. reprint ed. pap. 3.50 (*0-311-43025-2*) Casa Bautista.

Bosquejos Biblicos Tomo II. Daniel Campderros. 96p. 1990. reprint ed. pap. 3.50 (*0-311-43026-0*) Casa Bautista.

Bosquejos de Doctrina Cristiana: Outlines of Christian Doctrine. H. C. Moule. (SPA.). 6.95 (*84-7228-901-X*, 220114, Pub. by Edit Clie SP) TSELF.

Bosquejos de Doctrina Fundamental. Ernesto Trenchard. 144p. (SPA.). 1972. pap. 4.50 (*0-8254-1725-2*) Kregel.

Bosquejos de Sermones: Sermon Outlines. Matthew Henry. (SPA.). 5.50 (*84-7645-298-5*, 223382, Pub. by Edit Clie SP) TSELF.

Bosquejos de Sermones de Avivamiento. Ed. by Charles R. Wood. 64p. (SPA.). 1990. pap. 2.50 (*0-8254-1880-1*) Kregel.

Bosquejos de Sermones Evangelisticos. Ed. by Charles R. Wood. 64p. (SPA.). 1990. pap. 2.50 (*0-8254-1881-X*) Kregel.

Bosquejos de Sermones para Bodas y Funerales. Comp. by Jose L. Martinez. Orig. Title: Sermon Outlines for Weddings & Funerals. 112p. (Orig.). (SPA.). 1990. pap. 3.75 (*0-311-43042-2*) Casa Bautista.

Bosquejos de Sermones Para Celebracion de Bautismo y Cena del Senor: Sermon Outlines on Baptism & The Lord's Supper. Comp. by Jose L. Martinez. 112p. (Orig.). (SPA.). 1988. pap. 3.95 (*0-311-43040-6*) Casa Bautista.

Bosquejos de Sermones Para Dias y Ocasiones Especiales. Ed. by Charles R. Wood. 64p. (SPA.). 1991. pap. 2.80 (*0-8254-1882-8*) Kregel.

Bosquejos de Sermones Para la Juventud. Ed. by Charles R. Wood. 64p. (SPA.). 1993. pap. 2.50 (*0-8254-1895-X*) Kregel.

Bosquejos de Sermones Para Servicios Funerales. Ed. by Charles R. Wood. 64p. (SPA.). 1991. pap. 2.50 (*0-8254-1883-6*) Kregel.

Bosquejos de Sermones Selectos. Ernesto Barocio. 144p. 1990. reprint ed. pap. 4.50 (*0-311-43039-2*) Casa Bautista.

***Bosquejos de Sermones Sobre el Consuelo y la Seguridad.** Charles R. Wood. 64p. (SPA.). 1994. pap. 2.50 (*0-8254-1892-5*) Kregel.

Bosquejos de Sermones Sobre el Nuevo Nacimiento. Ed. by Charles R. Wood. 64p. (SPA.). 1993. pap. 2.50 (*0-8254-1887-9*) Kregel.

Bosquejos de Sermones Sobre Grandes Temas de la Biblia. Ed. by Charles R. Wood. 64p. (SPA.). 1993. pap. 2.50 (*0-8254-1894-1*) Kregel.

Bosquejos de Sermones sobre Hombres de la Biblia. Ed. by Charles R. Wood. 64p. (SPA.). 1993. pap. 2.50 (*0-8254-1884-4*) Kregel.

Bosquejos de Sermones Sobre la Oracion. Charles R. Wood. Orig. Title: Sermon Outlines on Prayer. 64p. (SPA.). 1994. pap. 2.50 (*0-8254-1896-8*) Kregel.

***Bosquejos de Sermones Sobre la Pascua y la Resurreccion.** Charles R. Wood. 64p. (SPA.). 1994. pap. 2.50 (*0-8254-1897-6*) Kregel.

Bosquejos de Sermones Sobre los Nombres y el Caracter de Dios. Ed. by Charles R. Wood. 64p. (SPA.). 1993. pap. 2.50 (*0-8254-1886-0*) Kregel.

Bosquejos de Sermones Sobre Mujeres de la Biblia. Ed. by Charles R. Wood. 68p. (SPA.). 1991. pap. 2.50 (*0-8254-1885-2*) Kregel.

Bosquejos de Sermones Sobre Temas Doctrinales. Charles R. Wood. Orig. Title: Sermon Outlines on Great Doctrines of the Bible. 64p. (SPA.). 1994. pap. 2.50 (*0-8254-1893-3*) Kregel.

Bosquejos Para Evangelizar (Outlines to Evangelize) Kittim Silva. (SPA.). 1992. 3.99 (*1-56063-114-7*, 498410) Editorial Unilit.

Bosquejos Para Predicadores Vol. 11: Sermon Outlines for Preachers. 112p. (SPA.). 1992. pap. 6.50 (*84-7645-552-6*, 223629, Pub. by Edit Clie SP) TSELF.

Bosquejos Para Predicadores, Vol. Four: Sermon Outlines For Preachers. Samuel Vila & Lidia Vila. (SPA.). 6.50 (*84-7645-417-1*, 223521, Pub. by Edit Clie SP) TSELF.

Bosquejos Para Predicadores, Vol. One: Sermon Outlines For Preachers. Samuel Vila & Lidia Vila. (SPA.). 6.50 (*84-7228-993-1*, 223084, Pub. by Edit Clie SP) TSELF.

Bosquejos Para Predicadores, Vol. Seven: Sermon Outlines. Samuel Vila. (SPA.). 6.50 (*84-7645-502-X*, 223589, Pub. by Edit Clie SP) TSELF.

Bosquejos Para Predicadores, Vol. Six: Sermon Outlines on Prayer. (SPA.). 6.50 (*84-7645-495-3*, 223581, Pub. by Edit Clie SP) TSELF.

Bosquejos Para Predicadores, Vol. Three: Sermon Outlines For Preachers. Samuel Vila & Lidia Vila. (SPA.). 6.50 (*84-7645-238-1*, 223426, Pub. by Edit Clie SP) TSELF.

Bosquejos Para Predicadores, Vol. Two: Sermon Outlines For Preachers. Samuel Vila & Lidia Vila. (SPA.). 6.50 (*84-7645-069-9*, 223277, Pub. by Edit Clie SP) TSELF.

Bosquejos Para Predicadores, Vol. 1: Sermon Outlines. Kittim Silva. (SPA.). 10.50 (*84-7228-973-7*, 223032, Pub. by Edit Clie SP) TSELF.

Bosquejos Para Predicadores, Vol. 2: Sermon Outlines. Kittim Silva. (SPA.). 8.95 (*84-7228-974-5*, 223033, Pub. by Edit Clie SP) TSELF.

Bosquejos Para Predicadores, Vol. 3: Sermon Outlines For. Kittim Silva. (SPA.). 8.95 (*84-7645-290-X*, 223278, Pub. by Edit Clie SP) TSELF.

Bosquejos Para Predicadores, Vol. 5: Sermon Outlines for Funerals. (SPA.). 6.50 (*84-7645-492-9*, 223582, Pub. by Edit Clie SP) TSELF.

Bosquejos Para Reuniones Oracion: Sermon Outlines for Prayer. Enrique Lund. (SPA.). 6.95 (*84-7645-040-0*, 223110, Pub. by Edit Clie SP) TSELF.

Bosquejos Para Reuniones Senoras: Sermon Outlines for Women's. Laurel Slade. (SPA.). 5.95 (*84-7228-464-6*, 220115, Pub. by Edit Clie SP) TSELF.

Bosquejos Utiles para Laicos. Roy B. Lyon. (Illus.). 96p. (SPA.). 1990. reprint ed. pap. 3.50 (*0-311-42401-5*) Casa Bautista.

Boss. Alfred H. Lewis. LC 67-29272. (Americans in Fiction Ser.). reprint ed. lib. bdg. 19.00 (*0-8398-1157-8*); reprint ed. pap. text ed. 6.95 (*0-89197-684-1*) Irvington.

Boss: Bruce Springsteen. Sharon Starbooks. (Illus.). 96p. (Orig.). 1984. pap. 5.95 (*0-317-00914-1*, Sig) NAL-Dutton.

Boss: Charles J. Haughey in Government. Joe Joyce & Peter Murtagh. (Illus.). 400p. 1983. pap. 10.95 (*0-905169-69-7*, Pub. by Poolbeg Pr IE) Dufour.

Boss: J. Edgar Hoover & the Great American Inquisition. Athan G. Theoharis & John S. Cox. LC 87-18105. 1988. 27.95 (*0-87722-532-X*) Temple U Pr.

Boss: Richard J. Daley of Chicago. Mike Royko. 1988. pap. 10.95 (*0-452-26167-8*, Plume) NAL-Dutton.

Boss: The Bill Stroppe Story. Tom Madigan. (Illus.). 204p. 1984. pap. 13.95 (*0-933506-13-9*) Darwin Pubns.

***Boss & Co. Makers of Fine "Best" Guns Only.** Donald Dallas. (Illus.). 1995. 75.00 (*0-614-04259-3*) Safari Pr.

***Boss & Co. Makers of Fine "Best" Guns Only.** limited ed. D. Dallas. (Illus.). 336p. 1995. 75.00 (*1-57157-014-4*) Safari Pr.

Boss & I: A Modern Day Success Story. Alfred Haller. Ed. by Laura Edwards. 68p. (Orig.). 1986. pap. 8.95 (*0-936887-00-1*) Allgau Bks.

Boss Came to Dinner & Other Stories. Bhisham Sahni. Tr. by Jai Ratan et al. (Greenbird Ser.). 95p. 1975. 14.00 (*0-88253-264-2*); pap. 6.75 (*0-88253-720-2*) Ind-US Inc.

Boss Cat. Louise Kantenwein. (J). 1993. 7.95 (*0-533-10628-1*) Vantage.

Boss Cowman: The Recollections of Ed Lemmon, 1857-1946. Ed Lemmon. LC 69-10313. (Pioneer Heritage Ser.: No. 6). 341p. reprint ed. pap. 97.20 (*0-7837-6464-2*, 2046468) Bks Demand.

Boss Cox's Cincinnati: Urban Politics in the Progressive Era. Zane L. Miller & Richard C. Wade. LC 81-6346. (Urban Life in America Ser.). xii, 301p. 1981. reprint ed. text ed. 59.75 (*0-313-22760-8*, MIBC, Greenwood Pr) Greenwood.

Boss Dog. large type ed. M. F. Fisher. 142p. 1991. reprint ed. lib. bdg. 17.95 (*1-56054-196-2*) Thorndike Pr.

Boss Dog. M. F. Fisher. 128p. 1991. reprint ed. 16.95 (*0-86547-465-6*, North Pt Pr) FS&G.

Boss Dog: A Story of Provence. M. F. Fisher. 1992. pap. 10.00 (*0-679-73860-6*) Knopf.

Boss Dog: A Story of Provence. M. F. Fisher. LC 91-53117. 128p. 1992. reprint ed. pap. 10.00 (*0-685-49285-0*) Pantheon.

Boss for a Week. Libby Handy. 32p. (J). (gr. k-3). Big Book. 28.67 (*0-590-64641-9*) Scholastic Inc.

Boss Gardener: The Life & Times of John McLaren. Tom G. Aikman. (Illus.). 118p. (Orig.). 1988. pap. 9.95 (*0-917583-18-3*) Lexikos.

Boss Girl: A Christmas Story, & Other Sketches. James W. Riley. LC 76-160948. (Short Story Index Reprint Ser.). 1977. reprint ed. 20.95 (*0-8369-3927-1*) Ayer.

Boss Island: The Subcontracting Network & Micro-Entrepreneurship in Taiwan's Development. Gwo-shyong Shieh. LC 91-48191. (American University Studies: Anthropology & Science: Ser. XI, Vol. 60). 247p. (C). 1993. text ed. 26.95 (*0-8204-1839-0*) P Lang Pubs.

Boss Kettering. Stuart W. Leslie. LC 82-17906. (Illus.). 382p. 1986. pap. text ed. 17.00 (*0-231-05601-X*) Col U Pr.

Boss Lady. large type ed. Norma Newcomb. (Dales Ser.). 192p. 1994. pap. 16.95 (*1-85389-435-4*, Dales) Ulverscroft.

Boss of Bosses. large type ed. Joseph O'Brien & Andris Kurins. 607p. 1992. reprint ed. lib. bdg. 22.95 (*1-56054-284-5*) Thorndike Pr.

Boss of Bosses. large type ed. Joseph O'Brien & Andris Kurins. 607p. 1992. reprint ed. pap. 14.95 (*1-56054-945-9*) Thorndike Pr.

Boss of Bosses: The FBI & Paul Castellano. Joseph F. O'Brien. 1992. mass mkt. 5.99 (*0-440-21229-4*) Dell.

Boss of Brightland. large type ed. Miriam MacGregor. 304p. 1993. 21.95 (*0-7505-0554-0*, Pub. by Magna Print Bks) Ulverscroft.

Boss of Panamint. Leslie Ernenwein. 1993. 14.95 (*0-7451-4566-3*, Gunsmoke) Chivers N Amer.

Boss of the Lazy Y. large type ed. Charles A. Seltzer. 1974. 21.95 (*0-85456-281-8*) Ulverscroft.

Boss of the Pool. Robin Klein. 96p. (J). (gr. 3-7). 1992. pap. 3.99 (*0-14-036037-9*) Puffin Bks.

Boss Platt & His New York Machine: A Study of the Political Leadership of Thomas C. Platt, Theodore Roosevelt, & Others. Harold F. Gosnell. LC 75-95153. reprint ed. 49.50 (*0-404-02884-5*) AMS Pr.

Boss Platt & His New York Machine: A Study of the Political Leadership of Thomas C. Platt, Theodore Roosevelt, & Others. Harold F. Gosnell. (BCL1 - United States Local History Ser.). 370p. 1991. reprint ed. text ed. 89.00 (*0-7812-6275-5*) Rprt Serv.

Boss Platt & His New York Machine - A Study of the Political Leadership of Thomas C. Platt, Theodore Roosevelt, & Others. Harold F. Gosnell. LC 70-145047. (Illus.). 1971. reprint ed. 59.00 (*0-403-00991-X*) Scholarly.

Boss, Prof. Medard Festschrift zum 85 Geburtstag Gewidmet: Journal: Daseinsanalyse, Vol. 5, No. 4, 1988. Ed. by G. Condrau. 140p. 1988. pap. 21.75 (*3-8055-4912-1*) S Karger.

Boss Ruef's San Francisco: The Story of the Union Labor Party, Big Business, & the Graft Prosecution. Walton Bean. 1952. pap. 12.00 (*0-520-00094-3*) U CA Pr.

Boss Rule: Portraits in City Politics. John T. Salter. LC 73-19176. (Politics & People Ser.). 282p. 1974. reprint ed. 23.95 (*0-405-05897-7*) Ayer.

Boss Rule in the Gilded Age: Matt Quay of Pennsylvania. James A. Kehl. LC 80-5254. (Illus.). 320p. 1981. 49.95 (*0-8229-3426-4*) U of Pittsburgh Pr.

Boss Should Be a Woman: How Women Can Manage Their Way to the Top & Compromise Nothing; How to Succeed Because You Are a Woman. Jack B. McAllen. LC 93-28066. (Illus.). 208p. 1993. pap. 12.95 (*0-931892-56-2*) B Dolphin Pub.

Boss Should Be a Woman: How Women Can Manage Their Way to the Top & Compromise Nothing; How to Succeed Because You Are a Woman. John B. McAllen. 264p. 1992. pap. text ed. 38.95 (*0-9634510-4-9*) Castlerock Pub.

Boss Tweed: Story of a Grim Generation. Denis T. Lynch. LC 73-19157. (Politics & People Ser.). (Illus.). 448p. 1974. reprint ed. 34.95 (*0-405-05879-9*) Ayer.

Boss Tweed: The Story of a Grim Generation. Denis T. Lynch. (BCL1 - United States Local History Ser.). 433p. 1991. reprint ed. lib. bdg. 99.00 (*0-7812-6277-1*) Rprt Serv.

Boss Tweed's New York. Seymour J. Mandelbaum. 216p. 1990. pap. 8.95 (*0-929587-20-0*, Elephant Paperbacks) I R Dee.

Boss Tweed's New York. Seymour J. Mandelbaum. Ed. by Norman F. Cantor. LC 81-13368. (New Dimensions in History Ser.: Historical Cities). (Illus.). ix, 196p. 1982. reprint ed. text ed. 49.75 (*0-313-23259-8*, MATY, Greenwood Pr) Greenwood.

Boss 1976: Proceedings of an International Conference on the Behavior of Off-Shore Structures, Norwegian Institute of Technology, Trondheim, 2-5 August 1976. Ed. by J. Kuvas. LC 77-75338. 1977. pap. 404.00 (*0-08-021739-7*, Pub. by Pergamon Repr UK) Franklin.

Boss 429 Performance Mustang Style. Stephen B. Strange. LC 84-73250. (Illus.). 100p. 1985. pap. 24.95 (*0-931417-02-3*) Boss Perform.

Bossa Nova. Earl Atkinson. (Ballroom Dance Ser.). 1983. lib. bdg. 250.00 (*0-87700-487-0*) Revisionist Pr.

Bossa Nova: Ballroom Dance Ser. Earl Atkinson. 1986. lib. bdg. 250.00 (*0-8490-3621-6*) Gordon Pr.

Bosses. Jim Wall. 208p. 1986. text ed. 19.95 (*0-669-13475-9*) Free Pr.

Bosses. Jim Wall. 208p. 1988. pap. 19.95 (*0-669-18138-2*) Free Pr.

Bosses. rev. ed. John Haeger et al. LC 78-73266. 1979. pap. text ed. write for info. (*0-88273-103-3*) Forum Pr IL.

Bosses & Other Reptiles. Comp. by Rodd Zolkos. 112p. 1994. 8.95 (*0-8092-3617-6*) Contemp Bks.

Bosses from Hell: True Tales from the Trenches. Matthew Sartwell. LC 93-37204. 1994. 7.95 (*0-452-27048-0*, Plume) NAL-Dutton.

Bosses, Machines, & Urban Voters. rev. ed. John M. Allswang. LC 85-24042. 192p. 1986. reprint ed. pap. text ed. 12.95x (*0-8018-3312-4*) Johns Hopkins.

Bossier Parish History, 1843-1993: The First 150 Years. Clifton D. Cardin. 253p. 1993. 29.95 (*0-9637507-1-2*); pap. 19.95 (*0-9637507-0-4*) C D Cardin.

***Bossier Parish, Louisiana Marriage Records 1843-1900.** John C. Head. 137p. (Orig.). 1989. pap. text ed. 17.50 (*1-57088-005-0*) J&W Ent.

Bossmen: Bill Monroe & Muddy Waters. James Rooney. (Quality Paperbacks Ser.). (Illus.). 163p. 1991. reprint ed. pap. 11.95 (*0-306-80427-1*) Da Capo.

Boss's Encyclopedia. Boardroom's Experts & Editors Staff. LC 86-30961. 600p. 1987. 50.00 (*0-932648-75-4*) Boardroom.

Boss's Wife. S. L. Stebel. 252p. 1992. 19.95 (*0-8027-1198-7*) Walker & Co.

Bossuet. Gustave Lanson. Ed. by J. P. Mayer. LC 78-67363. (European Political Thought Ser.). (FRE.). 1979. reprint ed. lib. bdg. 40.95 (*0-405-11711-6*) Ayer.

Bossuet & Vieira. Mary C. Gotaas. LC 75-128929. (Catholic University in Romance Languages & Literatures Ser.: No. 46). reprint ed. 37.50 (*0-404-50346-2*) AMS Pr.

Bossy Gallito: A Traditional Cuban Folk Tale. Illus. by Lulu Delacre. LC 93-15541. 32p. (J). (ps-2). 1994. 14.95 (*0-590-46843-X*) Scholastic Inc.

An Asterisk (*) at the beginning of an entry indicates that the title is appearing in BIP for the first time.

An Asterisk (*) at the beginning of an entry indicates that the title is appearing in BIP for the first time.

867

Boston Studies in the Philosophy of Science, Vol. 1: Proceedings of the Colloquium for the Philosophy of Science, Boston, 1961-1962. Colloquium for the Philosophy of Science Staff. Ed. by Marx W. Wartofsky. (Synthese Library: No. 6). 212p. 1970. lib. bdg. 51.50 (*90-277-0021-4*) Kluwer Ac.

Boston Studies in the Philosophy of Science, Vol. 14: Proceedings of the Colloquium for the Philosophy of Science, Boston, 1969-1972. Colloquium for the Philosophy of Science Staff. Ed. by R. S. Cohen & Marx W. Wartofsky. LC 73-83558. (Synthese Library: No.60). 405p. 1974. lib. bdg. 103.00 (*90-277-0392-2*); pap. text ed. 58.00 (*90-277-0378-7*) Kluwer Ac.

Boston Studies in the Philosophy of Science, Vol. 15: Scientific, Historical & Political Essays in Honor of Dirk J. Struik. Ed. by R. S. Cohen et al. LC 73-83556. (Synthese Library: No. 61). 652p. 1974. lib. bdg. 154.50 (*90-277-0393-0*); pap. text ed. 103.00 (*90-277-0379-5*) Kluwer Ac.

Boston Studies in the Philosophy of Science, Vol. 10: Scientific Procedures. Ladislav Tondl. Tr. by David Short. LC 72-77880. (Synthese Library: No. 47). 268p. 1972. lib. bdg. 70.00 (*90-277-0147-4*) Kluwer Ac.

Boston Studies in the Philosophy of Science, Vol. 10: Scientific Procedures. Ladislav Tondl. Tr. by David Short. LC 72-77880. (Synthese Library: No. 47). 268p. 1972. pap. text ed. 41.50 (*90-277-0323-X*) Kluwer Ac.

Boston Studies in the Philosophy of Science, Vol. 16: Selected Papers on Language & the Brain. Ed. by N. Geschwind. LC 75-8602. (Synthese Library: No. 68). 549p. 1974. lib. bdg. 136.50 (*90-277-0262-4*); pap. text ed. 44.50 (*90-277-0263-2*) Kluwer Ac.

Boston Studies in the Philosophy of Science, Vol. 20: Proceedings of the Philosophy of Science Association, Biennial Meeting, 1972. Philosophy of Science Association Staff. Ed. by Kenneth F. Schaffner & R. S. Cohen. LC 72-624169. (Synthese Library: Vol. 64). 1974. lib. bdg. 112.50 (*90-277-0408-2*); pap. text ed. 64.00 (*90-277-0409-0*) Kluwer Ac.

Boston Studies in the Philosophy of Science, Vol. 22: The Concepts of Space & Time - Their Structure & Their Development. Ed. by M. Capek. LC 73-75761. (Synthese Library: No. 74). 564p. 1975. pap. text ed. 58.00 (*90-277-0375-2*) Kluwer Ac.

Boston Studies in the Philosophy of Science, Vol. 25: The Methods of Analysis, Its Geometrical Origin & Its General Significance. Jaakko Hintikka. LC 74-81938. (Synthese Library: No. 75). 144p. 1974. lib. bdg. 51.50 (*90-277-0532-1*); pap. text ed. 36.50 (*90-277-0543-7*) Kluwer Ac.

Boston Studies in the Philosophy of Science, Vol. 23: The Understanding of Nature. Essays in the Philosophy of Biology. Marjorie Grene. LC 74-76477. (Synthese Library: No. 66). 366p. 1974. lib. bdg. 89.00 (*90-277-0462-7*); pap. text ed. 51.50 (*90-277-0463-5*) Kluwer Ac.

Boston Studies in the Philosophy of Science, Vol. 27: Topics in the Philosophy of Biology. Ed. by Marjorie Grene & Everett I. Mendelsohn. LC 75-12875. (Synthese Library: No. 84). 425p. 1975. lib. bdg. 121.50 (*90-277-0595-X*); pap. text ed. 63.00 (*90-277-0596-8*) Kluwer Ac.

Boston Studies in the Philosophy of Science, Vol. 37: Epistemological Writings, a New Selection. Hermann Von Helmholtz. Ed. by R. S. Cohen & Yahuda Elkana. Tr. by Yahuda Elkana. (Synthese Library: No. 79). 215p. 1977. lib. bdg. 65.50 (*90-277-0290-X*); pap. text ed. 36.50 (*90-277-0582-8*) Kluwer Ac.

Boston Studies in the Philosophy of Science, Vol. 43: Language in Focus-Foundations, Methods & Systems. Ed. by A. Kasher. (Synthese Library: No. 89). 700p. 1975. lib. bdg. 149.50 (*90-277-0644-1*); pap. text ed. 69.50 (*90-277-0645-X*) Kluwer Ac.

Boston Studies in the Philosophy of Science, Vol 8: Proceedings of the Philosophy of Science Association, Biennial Meeting, 1970. Philosophy of Science Association Staff. Ed. by R. Creighton Buck & R. S. Cohen. LC 73-20858. (Synthese Library: No. 39). 615p. 1971. lib. bdg. 136.50 (*90-277-0187-3*); pap. text ed. 65.50 (*90-277-0309-4*) Kluwer Ac.

Boston Studies in the Philosophy of Science, Vol 9: Foundations of the Logical Theory of Scientific Knowledge (Complex Logic) A. A. Zinov'ev. Tr. by Thomas J. Blakeley. LC 74-135109. (Synthese Library: No. 46). 301p. 1973. lib. bdg. 80.00 (*90-277-0193-8*); pap. text ed. 47.00 (*90-277-0324-8*) Kluwer Ac.

Boston Symphony Orchestra: Eighteen Eighty-One to Nineteen Thirty-One. rev. ed. Mark A. Howe. Ed. by John N. Burk. LC 77-16532. (Music Reprint Ser.: 1978). (Illus.). 1978. reprint ed. lib. bdg. 35.00 (*0-306-77533-6*) Da Capo.

Boston Taxpayers in Eighteen Twenty-One. rev. ed. Intro. by Lewis B. Rohrbach. LC 88-90540. 256p. 1988. reprint ed. 25.00 (*0-929539-01-X*) Picton Pr.

Boston Tea Parties: Recipes from the Museum of Fine Arts, Boston. Ed. by Judith F. Chamberlin & Janet R. Sears. LC 87-61474. (Illus.). 164p. (Orig.). 1987. pap. 13.50 (*0-87846-281-3*) Mus Fine Arts Boston.

Boston Tea Party. Walter Olesky. LC 92-26247. (First Bks.). (Illus.). 64p. (J). (gr. 4-6). 1993. lib. bdg. 13.93 (*0-531-20147-3*) Watts.

Boston Tea Party. Benjamin W. Labaree. LC 79-5423. (Illus.). 360p. 1979. reprint ed. text ed. 37.50 (*0-930350-16-2*); reprint ed. pap. text ed. 15.95 (*0-930350-05-7*) NE U Pr.

Boston Tea Party, Rebellion in the Colonies. James E. Knight. LC 81-23077. (Illus.). 32p. (J). (gr. 5-9). 1982. lib. bdg. 11.59 (*0-89375-734-9*); pap. text ed. 2.95 (*0-89375-735-7*) Troll Assocs.

Boston Terrier. Arthur R. Huddleston. LC 85-27371. (Breed Bks.). (Illus.). 1985. 29.95 (*0-87714-096-0*) Denlingers.

***Boston Terrier: An American Original.** Beverly Staley & Michael Staley. (Illus.). 224p. 1995. 25.95 (*0-87605-056-9*) Howell Bk.

Boston Terrier Champions, 1952-1987. Camino E. E. & B. Co. Staff. (Illus.). 372p. 1988. pap. 36.95 (*0-940808-76-5*) Camino E E & Bk.

Boston Terriers. Susan Bulanda. (Barron's Pet Owner's Manuals Ser.). 64p. 1994. pap. 5.95 (*0-8120-1696-3*) Barron.

Boston Terriers. Ed. by TFH Publications Staff. (Illus.). 128p. 1991. 11.95 (*0-86622-336-3*, KW-105) TFH Pubns.

Boston Then & Now: Sixty-Five Boston Sites Photographed in the Past & Present. Peter Vanderwarker. LC 81-17385. (Illus.). 128p. 1982. pap. 8.95 (*0-486-24312-5*) Dover.

Boston Track Map, July 1986. (Illus.). 1986. 4.95 (*0-938315-31-5*) Boston St Rwy.

Boston Transcript: A History of Its First Hundred Years. Joseph E. Chamberlin. LC 76-103646. (Select Bibliographies Reprint Ser.). 1977. 29.95 (*0-8369-5146-8*) Ayer.

Boston under Military Rule 1768-1769. Ed. by Oliver M. Dickerson. LC 70-118029. (Era of the American Revolution Ser.). 1970. reprint ed. 22.50 (*0-306-71943-6*) Da Capo.

Boston Unitarianism, 1820-1850: A Study of the Life & Work of Nathaniel Langdon Frothingham. Octavius B. Frothingham. (Notable American Authors Ser.). 1992. reprint ed. lib. bdg. 75.00 (*0-7812-2910-3*) Rprt Serv.

***Boston Women & City School Politics, 1872-1905.** rev. ed. Polly W. Kaufman. LC 94-25388. (Illus.). 325p. 1994. 85.00 (*0-8153-1669-0*) Garland.

Boston 1775. Brendan Morrissey. (Campaign Ser.). (Illus.). 96p. 1994. pap. 14.95 (*1-85532-362-1*, 9531, Pub. by Osprey UK) Stackpole.

Boston 1990: The Sixth Triennial Exhibition. Contrib by Peter J. Baldaia. (Illus.). 6p. 1990. 2.00 (*0-934358-27-3*) Fuller Mus Art.

Boston, 1995: The Complete Guide Including Cambridge, Lexington, Concord & the North Shore. Fodor's Travel Staff. (Illus.). 1994. pap. 12.00 (*0-679-02699-1*) Fodors Travel.

Bostoner: Stories & Recollections from the Colorful Chassidic Court of the Bostoner Rebbe. Hanoch Teller. (Illus.). 208p. 1990. 13.95 (*0-87306-507-7*) Feldheim.

Bostonians. Henry James. 1976. 25.95 (*0-8488-0542-9*) Amereon Ltd.

Bostonians see Novels, Eighteen Eighty-One to Eighteen Eighty-Six

Bostonians & Bullion: The Journal of Robert Livermore. Robert Livermore. Ed. by Gene M. Gressley. LC 68-12703. (Illus.). 222p. reprint ed. pap. 63.30 (*0-8357-5608-4*, 2056848) Bks Demand.

Bostoniennes. Henry James. 704p. (FRE.). 1992. pap. 11.95 (*0-7859-2324-1*, 2070364798) Fr & Eur.

Boston's Commuter Rail - Second Section. Thomas J. Humphrey & Norton D. Clark. (Bulletin Ser.: No. 20). (Illus.). 62p. (Orig.). 1986. pap. 9.95 (*0-938315-02-1*) Boston St Rwy.

Boston's First Neighborhood: The North End. Paula J. Todisco. 1976. 3.00 (*0-89073-009-1*) Boston Public Lib.

Boston's Freedom Trail. Terry Dunnahoo. LC 94-470. (Places in American History Ser.). (J). 1994. text ed. 14.95 (*0-87518-623-8*, Dillon Silver Burdett) Silver Burdett Pr.

Boston's Freedom Trail: An Illustrated Reference to 27 Legendary Landmarks of Early American History. 3rd ed. Robert Booth. Ed. by Shirley B. Moskow. LC 94-17379. (Illus.). 96p. 1994. pap. 5.95 (*1-56440-489-7*) Globe Pequot.

***Boston's Immigrants: Fiftieth Anniversary Ed.** Oscar Handlin. (Belknap Press Ser.). 398p. 1991. pap. 15.95 (*0-674-07986-8*) HUP.

Boston's Lower Criminal Courts, 1814-1850. Theodore Ferdinand. LC 90-50595. 240p. 1992. 38.50 (*0-87413-422-6*) U Delaware Pr.

Boston's Most Eligible Bachelors, 1989. Norma Nathan. (Illus.). 200p. (Orig.). 1988. pap. 8.95 (*0-9621200-0-6*) N Nathan.

Boston's Museum of Science Inventor's Workshop. (Discovery Kit Ser.). (Illus.). 64p. (J). 1994. 17.95 (*0-685-72752-1*) Running Pr.

Boston's North Shore, 1823-1890 & Boston's Gold Coast, 1890-1929. Joseph E. Garland. 1981. boxed 40.00 (*0-316-30432-8*) Little.

Boston's Water Resource Development: Past, Present, & Future. Ed. by Jonathan A. French. LC 86-25933. 52p. 1986. pap. 11.00 (*0-87262-570-2*) Am Soc Civil Eng.

Boston's Wayward Children: Social Services for Homeless Children, 1830-1930. Peter C. Holloran. LC 87-46425. (Illus.). 336p. 1989. 49.50 (*0-8386-3297-1*) Fairleigh Dickinson.

Boston's Wayward Children: Social Services for Homeless Children 1830-1930. Peter C. Holloran. 330p. 1994. reprint ed. pap. text ed. 15.95 (*1-55553-211-X*) NE U Pr.

Boston's Workers: A Labor History. James R. Green & Hugh C. Donahue. (Illus.). 1978. 10.00 (*0-89073-056-3*) Boston Public Lib.

***Bosun! Sound Your Pipe!** O. M. Chickory. 340p. 1995. pap. 9.95 (*1-56901-862-6*) NW Pub.

Boswell: "The Life of Johnson" Greg Clingham. (Landmarks of World Literature Ser.). (Illus.). 160p. (C). 1992. 34.95 (*0-521-37304-2*) Cambridge U Pr.

***Boswell: Citizen of the World, Man of Letters.** Ed. by Irma S. Lustig. 288p. 1995. text ed. 37.50 (*0-8131-1910-3*) U Pr of Ky.

Boswell: The Applause of the Jury: 1782-1785: The Yale Editions of the Private Papers of James Boswell. James Boswell. 1981. write for info. (*0-318-66903-X*) McGraw.

Boswell: The Ominous Years: 1774-1776: The Yale Editions of the Private Papers of James Boswell. James Boswell. 1963. write for info. (*0-318-66900-5*) McGraw.

Boswell, Burns & the French Revolution. Thomas Crawford. (C). 1989. 39.00 (*0-85411-046-1*, Pub. by Saltire Soc) St Mut.

Boswell for the Defence, 1769-1774: The Yale Editions of the Private Papers of James Boswell. James Boswell. 1962. write for info. (*0-318-66898-X*) McGraw.

Boswell in Extremes: 1776-1778: The Yale Editions of the Private Papers of James Boswell. James Boswell. 1970. write for info. (*0-318-66901-3*) McGraw.

Boswell in Holland, Seventeen Sixty-Two to Seventeen Sixty-Four: The Yale Editions of the Private Papers of James Boswell. James Boswell. 1952. write for info. (*0-318-66859-9*) McGraw.

Boswell in Search of a Wife, 1766-1769: The Yale Editions of the Private Papers of James Boswell. James Boswell. 1956. write for info. (*0-318-66897-1*) McGraw.

Boswell, Laird of Auchinleck: 1778-1782: The Yale Editions of the Private Papers of James Boswell. James Boswell. 1977. write for info. (*0-318-66902-1*) McGraw.

Boswell of Bagdad. Edward V. Lucas. LC 79-107722. (Essay Index Reprint Ser.). 1977. 20.95 (*0-8369-1579-8*) Ayer.

Boswell on the Grand Tour: Germany & Switzerland, 1764-1953: The Yale Editions of the Private Papers of James Boswell. James Boswell. 1953. write for info. (*0-318-66895-5*) McGraw.

Boswell on the Grand Tour: Italy, Corsica & France, 1765-1766: The Yale Editions of the Private Papers of James Boswell. James Boswell. 1955. write for info. (*0-318-66896-3*) McGraw.

Boswell the Biographer. George Mallory. 1972. 59.95 (*0-87968-778-9*) Gordon Pr.

Boswellian Studies: A Bibliography. 3rd ed. Ed. by Anthony E. Brown. 128p. 1992. 42.50 (*0-7486-0303-4*, Pub. by Edinburgh U Pr UK) Col U Pr.

Boswell's Johnson: A Preface to the "Life" Richard B. Schwartz. LC 78-4509. 142p. 1978. 27.50 (*0-299-07630-X*) U of Wis Pr.

Boswell's Journal of a Tour to the Hebrides see Life of Johnson

Boswell's Journal of a Tour to the Hebrides with Samuel Johnson, LL.D., 1773: The Yales Editions of the Private Papers of James Boswell. James Boswell. 1962. write for info. (*0-318-66899-8*) McGraw.

Boswell's Life of Johnson. James Boswell. Ed. by Frank Brady. 1968. pap. 3.95 (*0-452-00752-6*, Mer) NAL-Dutton.

Boswell's Life of Johnson: An Edition of the Original Manuscript, Vol. I: 1709-1765. Ed. by Marshall Waingrow. 528p. 1994. 75.00 (*0-300-06060-2*) Yale U Pr.

Boswell's Life of Johnson: New Questions, New Answers. Ed. by John A. Vance. LC 84-16351. 288p. 1988. pap. 15.00 (*0-8203-1024-7*) U of Ga Pr.

Boswell's Literary Art: An Annotated Bibliography of Critical Studies, 1900-1985. Hamilton E. Cochrane. LC 91-30751. 172p. 1991. 22.00 (*0-8240-1516-9*, H969) Garland.

Boswell's London Journal, Seventeen Sixty-Two to Seventeen Sixty-Three: The Yale Editions of the Private Papers of James Boswell. James Boswell. 1950. write for info. (*0-318-66858-0*) McGraw.

Boswell's London Journal, 1762-1763. James Boswell. Ed. by Frederick A. Pottle. 408p. (Orig.). (C). 1992. pap. text ed. 16.00 (*0-300-05735-0*) Yale U Pr.

Bosworth, Pts. V & VI. M. B. Clarke. (Illus.). 464p. 1991. reprint ed. lib. bdg. 79.50 (*0-8328-2029-6*); reprint ed. pap. 69.50 (*0-8328-2030-X*) Higginson Bk Co.

Bosworth Genealogy: History of the Descendants of Edward Bosworth Who Arrived in America in 1634. M. B. Clarke. (Illus.). 122p. 1993. reprint ed. lib. bdg. 33.00 (*0-8328-3647-8*); reprint ed. pap. 23.00 (*0-8328-3648-6*) Higginson Bk Co.

Botanic Drugs: Their Materia Medica, Pharmacology & Therapeutics. Thomas S. Blair. 1976. lib. bdg. 250.00 (*0-8490-1539-1*) Gordon Pr.

Botanic Manuscript. J. Colden. Ed. by H. W. Rickett & E. C. Hall. (Illus.). 1963. 20.00 (*0-934454-15-9*) Lubrecht & Cramer.

Botanical Atlas. D. Malpine. 1989. 14.99 (*0-517-68132-3*) Random Hse Value.

Botanical Bibliographies: A Guide to Bibliographic Materials Applicable to Botany. Lloyd H. Swift. LC 70-106633. 853p. reprint ed. pap. 180.00 (*0-8357-7361-2*, 2003489) Bks Demand.

Botanical Compendium of Dosages & Products. Peggy S. Wolf. LC 92-60207. (Illus.). 105p. (C). 1992. 50.00 (*0-9632598-0-6*) NaturePartners.

Botanical Exploration of Southern Africa: An Illustrated History of Early Botanical Literature on the Cape Flora, Biographical Accounts of the Leadings Plant Collectors & Their Activities in Southern Africa from the Days of the East India Company until Modern Times. Mary Gunn & L. E. Codd. 416p. (C). 1981. text ed. 130.00 (*0-86961-129-1*, Pub. by A A Balkema NE) Ashgate Pub Co.

Botanical Exploration of the Trans-Mississippi West, 1790-1850. Susan D. McKelvey. LC 91-24466. (Northwest Reprints Ser.). 1200p. 1991. 99.95 (*0-87071-513-5*) Oreg St U Pr.

Botanical Gardens & the World Conservation Strategy. Ed. by David Bramwell & Ole Hamann. Tr. by Hugh Synge. 367p. 1988. text ed. 104.00 (*0-12-125462-3*) Acad Pr.

***Botanical Gardens at the Huntington.** (Illus.). 192p. 1995. 29.95 (*0-614-03555-4*) Huntington Lib.

Botanical Gardens of China. Yu Dejun. (Illus.). 319p. 1983. text ed. 75.00 (*0-945345-08-9*, Pub. by Sci Pr CH) Lubrecht & Cramer.

Botanical Illustration: Preparation for Publication. Noel H. Holmgren & Bobbi Angell. LC 86-2548. (Illus.). 74p. (Orig.). 1986. pap. 10.00 (*0-89327-272-8*) NY Botanical.

Botanical Illustration in Watercolor. Eleanor B. Wunderlich. (Illus.). 144p. 1991. 29.95 (*0-8230-0529-1*, Watsn-Guptill) Watsn-Guptill.

Botanical Influences on Illness: A Sourcebook of Clinical Research. Melvyn R. Werbach & Michael T. Murray. LC 94-60010. 350p. 1994. text ed. 39.95 (*0-9618550-4-5*) Third Line Pr.

***Botanical Latin: History, Grammar, Syntax, Terminology & Vocabulary.** 4th ed. William T. Stearn. (Illus.). 562p. 1995. 39.95 (*0-88192-321-4*) Timber.

***Botanical Medicine: A European Professional Perspective.** Yves Requena & Dan Kenner. 250p. 35.00 (*0-912111-48-8*) Paradigm Publns.

Botanical Microscopy, 1985. Ed. by Anthony W. Robards. (Illus.). 378p. 1986. 32.50 (*0-19-854587-8*) OUP.

Botanical Misceliary: Containing Figures & Description of Plants Recommended in Medicine & Domestic Economy, Vols. 1-3. B. Hooker. (C). 1988. 1,000.00 (*0-317-92322-6*, Scientific) St Mut.

Botanical Miscellany, Set. W. J. Hooker. (C). 1988. text ed. 1,000.00 (*0-685-44247-0*, Scientific) St Mut.

Botanical Monkeys. E. J. Corner. (C). 1989. text ed. 70.00 (*0-685-63528-7*, Pub. by Pentland Pr UK) St Mut.

Botanical Pesticides in Agriculture. Anand Prakash. 1995. write for info. (*0-87371-825-9*) Lewis Pubs.

Botanical Prints. 1989. pap. 0.99 (*0-517-68806-9*) Random Hse Value.

Botanical Systematics, Vol. 1. Ed. by Vernon H. Heywood. 1976. text ed. 185.00 (*0-12-346901-5*) Acad Pr.

Botanical Text Book. Asa Gray. (Notable American Authors Ser.). 1992. reprint ed. lib. bdg. 75.00 (*0-7812-2942-1*) Rprt Serv.

Botanical Touch: Decoration, Gardens, Parties. Cynthia Gibson. Ed. by Coco Myers. LC 92-36160. (Illus.). 288p. 1993. 40.00 (*0-670-84292-3*, Viking Studio) Studio Bks.

Botanical World. David K. Northington & J. R. Goodin. (Illus.). 720p. (C). 1984. 39.95 (*0-8016-1893-2*) Mosby Yr Bk.

Botanical World. 2nd ed. Northington et al. (Illus.). 608p. 1991. pap. 37.95 (*0-8016-5169-7*) Mosby Yr Bk.

Botanical World - Laboratory Manual. Davis. 160p. 1984. pap. 17.95 (*0-8016-1233-0*) Mosby Yr Bk.

Botanical Wreaths. Laura M. Reinstatler. Ed. by Kerry Hoffman. LC 94-17052. (Illus.). 120p. (Orig.). 1994. pap. 21.95 (*1-56477-056-7*) That Patchwork.

Botanique. Fernand Moreau. (Methodique Ser.). 1534p. (FRE.). 1965. pap. 125.00 (*0-7859-1589-3*, 207010396X) Fr & Eur.

Botanique see Oeuvres Completes, Tome IV: Emile Education, Morale, Botanique

Botanique see Oeuvres Completes

***Botanisches Woerterbuch Fur Gartner und Floristen.** 19th ed. Hans Jessen. 143p. (GER.). 1992. 39.95 (*0-7859-8474-7*, 3794401395) Fr & Eur.

***Botanist & Her Muleskinner: Pioneer Botanists in the Siskiyou Mountains.** Golda Kirkpatrick et al. 150p. 1994. pap. text ed. 7.95 (*0-9645137-0-6*) Leach Garden.

Botanist's Garden, 1992. John Raven. 224p. (C). 1989. 90.00 (*1-85183-034-0*, Silent Bks) St Mut.

Botanist's Visit to Oahu in 1831. Franz J. Meyen. Ed. by Mary Anne Pultz. Tr. by Astrid Jackson. LC 81-7353. (Illus.). 90p. 1981. pap. 6.95 (*0-916630-23-4*) Pr Pacifica.

Botanizers: Amateur Scientists in Nineteenth-Century America. Elizabeth B. Keeney. LC 92-5022. (Illus.). xiv, 206p. (C). 1992. 34.95 (*0-8078-2046-6*) U of NC Pr.

Botany. Boy Scouts of America. (Illus.). 64p. (J). (gr. 6-12). 1983. pap. 1.85 (*0-8395-3379-9*, 33379) BSA.

Botany. Randall c. Moore et al. 104p. (C). 1994. student ed write for info. (*0-697-24309-5*); boxed write for info. (*0-697-16957-X*) Wm C Brown Pubs.

Botany. Randall c. Moore et al. 208p. (C). 1995. student ed, spiral bd. write for info. (*0-697-03776-2*) Wm C Brown Pubs.

Botany. Pratt. (Applied Science Review Ser.). 1993. 11.95 (*0-87434-570-7*) Springhouse Pub.

Botany. Peter Ray et al. 784p. (C). 1983. text ed. 54.00 (*0-03-089942-7*) SCP.

Botany. Incl. Vascular Plants. Johannes Grontved. LC 76-21756. (*0-318-50534-7*); Mosses. August Hesselbo. LC 76-21756. (*0-318-50535-5*); Lichens. Bernt Lynge. LC 76-21756. (*0-318-50536-3*); LC 76-21756. (Thule Expedition, 5th, 1921-1924 Ser.: Vol. 2, Nos. 1-3). (Illus.). reprint ed. 40.00 (*0-404-58308-3*) AMS Pr.

Botany: A Functional Approach. 4th ed. Walter H. Muller. (C). 1979. write for info. (*0-02-384700-X*) Macmillan.

Botany: A Laboratory Manual. Denny Jackson & Gary Hannan. 192p. 1993. spiral bd. 10.95 (*0-8403-9012-2*) Kendall-Hunt.

Botany: An Introduction to Plant Biology. James D. Mauseth. 1138p. (C). 1991. text ed. 61.25 (*0-03-030222-6*) SCP.

Botany: An Introduction to Plant Biology. 6th ed. T. Elliot Weier et al. LC 81-10304. (C). 1982. Net. text ed. write for info. (*0-471-01561-X*) Wiley.

Botany: Forty-Nine More Science Air Projects. Robert L. Bonnet & G. Daniel Keen. (Science Fair Project Ser.). 1990. pap. text ed. 10.95 (*0-07-156666-X*) McGraw.

Botany: Forty-Nine More Science Fair Projects. Robert L. Bonnet & G. Daniel Keen. (Illus.). 170p. (J). (gr. 4-7). 1990. 16.95 (*0-8306-7416-0*, 3416); pap. 9.95 (*0-8306-3416-9*) TAB Bks.

An Asterisk (*) at the beginning of an entry indicates that the title is appearing in BIP for the first time.

Bottom Line Basics: Understand & Control Business Finances. Robert J. Low. Ed. by Linda Pinkham. (Successful Business Library). 325p. (Orig.). 1994. pap. 19.95 (*1-55571-330-0*); ring bd. 39.95 (*1-55571-329-7*) Oasis Pr OR.

Bottom-Line Bidding: A Small Business Guide to Lucrative California-State Contracts. Linda S. Brewer. LC 89-60527. 256p. 1989. pap. 45.00 (*0-9622514-0-2*) Columbia San Fran.

Bottom Line Business Writing. John S. Fielden & Ronald E. Dulek. LC 83-19192. 156p. 1986. 6.95 (*0-13-080283-2*, Busn) P-H.

Bottom Line Is in Your Mind: Financial Success Through Attitude Analysis. Theresa M. Danna. LC 93-74401. (Illus.). 360p. (Orig.). 1994. pap. 12.95 (*0-9631074-1-0*) T M Danna.

Bottom Line Is Money: A Comprehensive Guide to Songwriting & the Nashville Music Industry. Jennifer E. Pierce. Ed. by A. Miccinello. (Illus.). 323p. 1994. 29.95 (*0-933224-86-9*); pap. 19.95 (*0-933224-77-X*) Bold Strummer Ltd.

Bottom Line on God's Gift to You. Don R. Womack. 64p. 1991. pap. 6.95 (*0-9629376-0-6*) Amos Pubns.

Bottom-Line Perspective on Health Care Costs. Ed. by Wendy B. Gray & Susan Henricksen. (Report Ser.: No. 939). xii, 68p. (Orig.). 1990. pap. text ed. 80.00 (*0-8237-0385-1*) Conference Bd.

Bottom-Line Plant Management. Martin Smith. 1991. 59.95 (*0-13-087594-5*, Busn) P-H.

Bottom Line Reader: A Financial Handbook for Librarians. Ed. by Betty C. Sellen & Betty J. Turock. 175p. 1990. pap. text ed. 39.95 (*1-55570-057-8*) Neal-Schuman.

Bottom Line Results from Strategic Human Resource Planning. Ed. by R. J. Niehaus & K. F. Price. (Illus.). 313p. (C). 1991. 85.00 (*0-306-44187-X*, Plenum Pr) Plenum.

*__Bottom Line 20th Anniversary Songbook.__ Ed. by Milton Okun. (Illus.). 149p. (Orig.). (YA). Date not set. pap. 19.95 (*0-89524-852-2*, 02502038) Cherry Lane.

Bottom Liner Blues. K. C. Constantine. 256p. 1993. 18.95 (*0-89296-289-5*) Mysterious Pr.

Bottom Liner Blues. K. C. Constantine. 272p. 1994. mass mkt. 5.99 (*0-446-40372-5*, Mysterious Paperbk) Warner Bks.

Bottom Lines: The Golden Rules for Executive Success. Murray Fisher. (Life's Golden Rules Ser.). 160p. 1994. 5.99 (*1-881649-12-1*) Genl Pub Grp.

Bottom of the Boat. Bob Hartman & Mike McGuire. (What Was It Like Ser.). (Illus.). 32p. (J). 1994. 7.99 (*1-56476-298-X*, Victor Books); audio 11.99 (*7-900882-31-6*, Victor Books) SP Pubns.

Bottom of the Harbor. Joseph Mitchell. 1994. 12.50 (*0-679-60093-0*, Modern Lib) Random.

*__Bottom of the Main Sequence--& Beyond: Proceedings of the ESO Workshop Held in Garching, Germany, 10-12 August, 1994.__ ESO Workshop Staff. Ed. by Chris G. Tinney. LC 95-15642. (ESO Astrophysics Symposia Ser.). 1995. write for info. (*3-540-59171-0*) Spr-Verlag.

*__Bottom Soils, Sediment, & Pond Aquaculture.__ Claude E. Boyd. LC 94-44496. 1995. 74.95 (*0-412-06941-5*) Chapman & Hall.

Bottom Stories. Grover S. McLeod. 194p. 1971. 19.95 (*1-884150-00-4*) Manchester AL.

Bottom Translation: Shakespeare & Marlowe & the Carnival Tradition. Jan Kott. Tr. by Daniela Miedzyrzecka & Lillian Vallee. 165p. (Orig.). 1987. pap. 14.95 (*0-8101-0738-4*) Northwestern U Pr.

Bottom-up Democracy. Community Service Editors. 1954. pap. 1.50 (*0-910420-07-6*) Comm Serv OH.

Bottom-up Marketing. Al Ries & Jack Trout. 240p. 1989. text ed. 22.95 (*0-07-052733-4*); audio 9.95 (*0-07-052734-2*) McGraw.

Bottom-up Marketing. Al Ries & Jack Trout. 240p. 1990. pap. 11.95 (*0-452-26418-9*, Plume) NAL-Dutton.

Bottomfeeder: A Fishhk Story. Mark Spitzer. Ed. & Illus. by Artemis Smith. (On-Demand Collectors' Editions Ser.). 500p. 1995. per., pap. 100.00 (*1-878998-27-7*) Savant Garde.

*__Bottoming Book: How to Get Terrible Things Done to You By wonderful People.__ Dossie Easton & Catherine A. Liszt. (Illus.). 112p. (Orig.). Date not set. pap. text ed. 11.95 (*0-9639763-1-1*) Greenery Pr.

*__Bottomland.__ Harry Humes. LC 94-43871. 1995. write for info. (*1-55728-377-X*); pap. write for info. (*1-55728-380-X*) U of Ark Pr.

Bottomless Bag. Karl Rohnke. 384p. 1991. pap. 29.00 (*0-8403-6633-7*) Kendall-Hunt.

Bottomless Baggie. Karl Rohnke. 144p. 1991. pap. text ed. 16.50 (*0-8403-6813-5*) Kendall-Hunt.

Bottomless Well. Walter S. Terry. (Illus.). 278p. 1991. pap. 8.95 (*0-9628984-0-6*) Hometown Pr.

Bottomline Banking: A Strategic Vision. John B. McCoy et al. 1993. 32.50 (*1-55738-389-8*) Probus Pub Co.

Bottoms Up. George J. Nathan. LC 70-148843. (Select Bibliographies Reprint Ser.). 1977. 15.95 (*0-8369-5657-5*) Ayer.

Bottoms Up. Jeff Putnam. LC 92-75410. 320p. 1993. 20.00 (*0-9627509-4-8*) Baskerville.

Bottoms Up! Joyce L. Vedral. LC 92-28685. 304p. (Orig.). 1993. pap. 12.99 (*0-446-39421-1*) Warner Bks.

Bottoms Up! A Pathologist's Essays on Medicine & the Humanities. William B. Ober. 1988. pap. 8.95 (*0-685-44374-4*, PL) HarpC.

Bottoms Up! A Pathologist's Essays on Medicine & the Humanities. William B. Ober. LC 87-13125. (Illus.). 356p. 1987. 19.95 (*0-8093-1419-3*) S Ill U Pr.

Botulinum & Tetanus Neurotoxins - Neurotransmission & Biomedical Aspects: Proceedings of an International Conference on Botulinum, Tetanus Neurotoxins - Neurotransmission & Biomedical Aspects, Held May 11-13, 1992, in Madison, Wisconsin. Ed. by Bibhuti R. DasGupta. LC 93-3845. (Illus.). 680p. (C). 1993. 135.00 (*0-306-44412-7*, Plenum Pr) Plenum.

Botulinum Neurotoxin & Tetanus Toxin. Ed. by Lance L. Simpson. 850p. 1989. text ed. 146.00 (*0-12-644445-5*) Acad Pr.

Botulism: The Organism, Its Toxins, the Disease. 2nd ed. Louis D. Smith & Hiroshi Sugiyama. (Illus.). 184p. 1988. 48.95 (*0-398-05446-0*) C C Thomas.

Botvinnik on the Endgame. Mikhail Botvinnik. Tr. by Jim Marfia. 81p. (Orig.). 1985. pap. 6.00 (*0-931462-43-6*) Chess Ent Inc.

Bouche Creole, No. I. Leon E. Soniat, Jr. LC 80-23178. (Illus.). 256p. 1981. 15.95 (*0-88289-805-1*) Pelican.

Bouche Creole, No. II. Leon Soniat & June Soniat. LC 85-3371. 272p. 1985. spiral bd. 13.95 (*0-88289-364-5*) Pelican.

Boucher Family, Bowsher, Bauscher, Bausher, Bousher, Comprising a Genealogy of Branches of Strawn, Harpster, Tedrow, Cryfer, et al: Descendants of Daniel Boucher of Albany Township, Berks Co., PA, with Notes of Other Boucher Families. F. A. Burkhardt. (Illus.). 402p. 1992. reprint ed. lib. bdg. 72.00 (*0-8328-2643-X*); reprint ed. pap. 62.00 (*0-8328-2644-8*) Higginson Bk Co.

Boucher's Clinical Dental Terminology: A Glossary of Accepted Terms in All Disciplines of Dentistry. 4th ed. Ed. by Thomas J. Zwemer. LC 92-24903. 433p. 1993. 35.95 (*0-8016-6706-2*) Mosby Yr Bk.

Boucher's Prosthodontic Treatment for Edentulous Patients, No. 10. Zarb et al. (Illus.). 640p. 1990. 64.95 (*0-8016-3310-9*) Mosby Yr Bk.

Bouches Inutiles. Simone de Beauvoir. (FRE.). 1972. pap. 10.95 (*0-8288-9675-5*, 2070320359) Fr & Eur.

Bouclier Arverne. Rene De Goscinny. (FRE.). (J). (gr. 7-9). 1990. 19.95 (*0-8288-5120-4*, FC883) Fr & Eur.

Bouclier Arverne. Rene De Goscinny & A. Uderzo. (FRE.). 1992. 19.95 (*0-7859-0985-0*, 2205002686) Fr & Eur.

Boucs. Driss Chraibi. 181p. (FRE.). 1989. pap. 11.95 (*0-7859-2122-2*, 2070381609) Fr & Eur.

*__Boudica.__ Paol Keineg. Tr. by Keith Waldrop. (Serie d'Ecriture: No. 8). (Illus.). 64p. (Orig.). 1994. pap. 6.00 (*0-930901-94-0*) Burning Deck.

Boudin. Jean Selz. (CAL Art Ser.). (Illus.). 96p. 1986. 14.95 (*0-517-54710-4*, Crown) Crown Pub Group.

Boudoir. 1991. mass mkt. 4.95 (*1-878320-85-8*) Masquerade.

Boudoir Art: The Celebration of Life. Clifford P. Catania. LC 94-65629. (Illus.). 144p. 1994. 59.95 (*0-88740-615-7*) Schiffer.

Boudoir Desserts. Jacqueline Kimmen. 70p. (Orig.). 1989. pap. 5.95 (*0-9622648-6-5*) Beeline Co.

Boudoir Photography. Mario Venticinque. (Illus.). 144p. 1986. pap. 18.95 (*0-8174-3562-X*, Amphoto) Watsn-Guptill.

Boudoir Studio. Robert Wortham & Roxanne Becker-Wortham. (Illus.). 144p. 1990. pap. 18.95 (*0-8174-3566-2*, Amphoto) Watsn-Guptill.

*__Boudu Saved from Drowning.__ Richard Boston. (BFI Film Classics Ser.). 1994. pap. 9.95 (*0-85170-467-0*) Ind U Pr.

Bougainville & the Northern Solomons. John N. Rentz. (Elite Unit Ser.: No. 22). (Illus.). 166p. reprint ed. 32.50 (*0-89839-137-7*) Battery Pr.

Bougainville Breakout. (McLeane's Rangers Ser.: No. 1). (Orig.). 1983. pap. 2.50 (*0-8217-1207-1*) Zebra.

Bougainville, 1943-1945: The Forgotten Campaign. Harry A. Gailey. LC 90-28496. (Illus.). 256p. 1991. 27.00 (*0-8131-1748-8*) U Pr of Ky.

Bouger Gravity Anomalies of the San Fernando Valley, California. Charles E. Carbato. LC 65-63511. (University of California Publications in Social Welfare: Vol. 46, No. 1). 49p. reprint ed. pap. 25.00 (*0-8357-7363-9*, 2011792) Bks Demand.

Boughs of Innocence. large type ed. Frances Melvin. 356p. 1983. 15.95 (*0-7089-1005-X*) Ulverscroft.

Bought with a Price. Peggy Albrecht. LC 91-67257. 128p. (Orig.). 1991. pap. 6.95 (*0-9627974-5-6*) Tabby Hse Bks.

Boughton House: The English Versailles. Ed. by Tessa Murdoch. (Illus.). 304p. 1993. 150.00 (*0-571-16338-6*) Faber & Faber.

Boulainvilliers & the French Monarchy: Aristocratic Politics in Early Eighteenth-Century France. Harold Ellis. LC 87-47971. 288p. 1988. 42.50 (*0-8014-2130-6*) Cornell U Pr.

Boulanger see Nouvelles Pieces Grincantes

Boulanger Affair Reconsidered: Royalism, Boulangism, & the Origins of the Radical Right in France. William D. Irvine. 256p. 1988. 39.95 (*0-19-505334-6*) OUP.

Boulanger, la Boulangere et le Petit Mitron. Jean Anouilh. (FRE.). 1980. pap. 10.95 (*0-7859-3563-0*, F81830) Fr & Eur.

Boulangere et le Petit Mitron see Nouvelles Pieces Grincantes

*__Boulangerie.__ Paul Rimbali. LC 94-5372. 1995. 20.00 (*0-02-600865-3*) Macmillan.

Boulder: Evolution of a City. Silvia Pettem. (Illus.). 208p. 1994. 29.95 (*0-87081-350-1*) Univ Pr Colo.

Boulder - Longmont (Close up) Atlas - Street Guide. 1994. pap. 9.95 (*0-914449-16-8*) Pierson Graph.

Boulder Canyon Project, Historical & Economic Aspects. Paul L. Kleinsorge. LC 41-6850. 120p. reprint ed. pap. 30.00 (*0-8357-7364-7*, 2024689) Bks Demand.

*__Boulder Climbs North.__ 2nd ed. Richard Rossiter. (Illus.). 130p. 1995. pap. write for info. (*0-614-05455-9*) Chockstone Pr.

Boulder Climbs South. Richard Rossiter. (Illus.). 420p. (Orig.). 1990. pap. 25.00 (*0-934641-15-3*) Chockstone Pr.

Boulder County Nature Almanac. RuthCarol & Stephen R. Jones. LC 93-6251. (Illus.). 340p. 1993. pap. 19.95 (*0-87108-819-3*) Pruett.

Boulder Dam. Zane Grey. 1990. mass mkt. 3.99 (*0-06-100111-2*, Harp PBks) HarpC.

*__Boulder Hiking Trails: The Best of the Plains, Foothills, & Mountains.__ Ruth C. Cushman & Glenn Cushman. (Illus.). 224p. (Orig.). 1995. pap. 18.00 (*0-87108-836-3*) Pruett.

Boulder Lecture Notes in Theoretical Physics, 1963, Vol. 6. Ed. by Wesley E. Brittin et al. 526p. 1964. text ed. 380.00 (*0-677-13030-9*) Gordon & Breach.

Boulder Lecture Notes in Theoretical Physics, 1964: Vol. 7-A, Lorentz Group, Vol. 7. Ed. by Wesley E. Brittin et al. 394p. 1968. text ed. 309.00 (*0-677-13040-6*) Gordon & Breach.

Boulder Lecture Notes in Theoretical Physics, 1964: Vol. 7-B, Elementary Particles, Vol. 7. Ed. by Wesley E. Brittin et al. 480p. 1968. text ed. 380.00 (*0-677-13050-3*) Gordon & Breach.

Boulder Lecture Notes in Theoretical Physics, 1964: Vol. 7-C, Statistical Physics, Weak Interactions, Field Theory, Vol. 8. Ed. by Wesley E. Brittin et al. 496p. 1968. text ed. 380.00 (*0-677-13060-0*) Gordon & Breach.

Boulder Lecture Notes in Theoretical Physics, 1965: Vol. 8-A, Statistical Physics & Solid State Physics. Ed. by Wesley E. Brittin et al. 364p. 1966. 181.00 (*0-685-01946-2*) Gordon & Breach.

Boulder Lecture Notes in Theoretical Physics, 1965: Vol. 8-B, Fundamental Particles & High Energy Physics, Vol. 8. Ed. by Wesley E. Brittin et al. 436p. 1966. text ed. 342.00 (*0-677-13080-5*) Gordon & Breach.

Boulder Lecture Notes in Theoretical Physics, 1965: Vol. 8-C, Nuclear Structure Physics, Vol. 8. Ed. by Wesley E. Brittin et al. 688p. 1966. text ed. 484.00 (*0-677-13090-2*) Gordon & Breach.

Boulder Lecture Notes in Theoretical Physics, 1966: Vol. 9-A, Mathematical Methods of Theoretical Physics, Vol. 9. Ed. by Wesley E. Brittin et al. 410p. 1967. text ed. 295.00 (*0-677-11600-4*) Gordon & Breach.

Boulder Lecture Notes in Theoretical Physics, 1966: Vol. 9-B, High Energy & Particle Physics, Vol. 9. Ed. by Wesley E. Brittin et al. 448p. 1967. text ed. 342.00 (*0-677-11610-1*) Gordon & Breach.

Boulder Lecture Notes in Theoretical Physics, 1966: Vol. 9-C, Kinetic Theory, Vol. 9. Ed. by Wesley E. Brittin et al. 804p. (Orig.). 1967. text ed. 329.00 (*0-677-11620-9*) Gordon & Breach.

Boulder Lecture Notes in Theoretical Physics, 1967: Vol. 10-B, High Energy Physics & Fundamental Particles, Vol. 10. Ed. by Wesley E. Brittin & A. O. Barut. 722p. 1968. text ed. 276.00 (*0-677-12900-9*) Gordon & Breach.

Boulder Lecture Notes in Theoretical Physics, 1968: Vol. 11-A, Elementary Particle Physics, Vol. 11. Ed. by Wesley E. Brittin et al. 650p. 1969. Pt. 1, 650p. text ed. 426.00 (*0-677-13110-0*); Pt. 2, 380p. text ed. 310.00 (*0-677-13400-2*) Gordon & Breach.

Boulder Lecture Notes in Theoretical Physics, 1968: Vol. 11-B, Quantum Fluids & Nuclear Matter, Vol. 11. Ed. by Wesley E. Brittin et al. 444p. 1969. text ed. 342.00 (*0-677-13120-8*) Gordon & Breach.

Boulder Lecture Notes in Theoretical Physics, 1968: Vol. 11-C, Atomic Collision Processes, Vol. 11. Ed. by Wesley E. Brittin et al. 352p. 1969. text ed. 275.00 (*0-677-13130-5*) Gordon & Breach.

Boulder Lecture Notes in Theoretical Physics, 1968: Vol. 11-D, Mathematical Methods, Vol. 11. Ed. by Wesley E. Brittin et al. 664p. 1969. text ed. 392.00 (*0-677-13140-2*) Gordon & Breach.

Boulder Lecture Notes in Theoretical Physics, 1969: Vol. 12-A, Ferromagnetism & Quantum Optics, Vol. 12. Ed. by K. T. Mahanthappa & Wesley E. Brittin. 220p. 1971. text ed. 134.00 (*0-677-14550-0*) Gordon & Breach.

Boulder Lecture Notes in Theoretical Physics, 1969: Vol. 12-B High Energy Collisions of Elementary Particles, Vol. 12. Ed. by K. T. Mahanthappa & Wesley E. Brittin. 384p. 1971. text ed. 197.00 (*0-677-14560-8*) Gordon & Breach.

Boulder Lecture Notes in Theoretical Physics, 1969: Vol. 12-C, Mathematical Methods in Field Theory & Complex Analytic Varieties, Vol. 12. Ed. by K. T. Mahanthappa & Wesley E. Brittin. 296p. 1971. text ed. 190.00 (*0-677-14570-5*) Gordon & Breach.

Boulder Lectures in Theoretical Physics, 1967: Quantum Theory & Statistical Physics, Vol. 10-A, Vol. 10. Ed. by A. O. Barut & W. E. Brittin. x, 572p. 1968. text ed. 200.00 (*0-677-12890-8*) Gordon & Breach.

*__Boulder Sport Climbs.__ Richard Rossiter. (Illus.). 120p. (Orig.). Date not set. pap. 12.95 (*0-614-05454-0*) Chockstone Pr.

Boulder Weather Log. William G. Callahan. 225p. (C). 1986. pap. 16.00 (*0-945527-00-4*) Upslope Pr.

Boulder Weather Log. 9th ed. William G. Callahan. (Illus.). 225p. (C). 1988. pap. 16.00 (*0-945527-08-X*) Upslope Pr.

Boulderides: The Mountain Biking Guide to Boulder, Colorado. Dave Rich. (Fat Tire Guides Ser.). (Orig.). 1993. pap. 7.95 (*0-9634607-1-4*) Little Rose Pub.

*__Bouldering in America: A Historical Guide to the Forgotton Art of Climbing.__ John Sherman. 1994. 30.00 (*0-930410-57-2*) Amer Alpine Club.

*__Bouldering with John Bachar.__ John Bachar & Steven Boga. (Illus.). 96p. 1996. pap. 10.95 (*0-8117-2517-0*) Stackpole.

Boule de Suif. Guy De Maupassant. (Folio Ser.: No. 904). (FRE.). 1961. pap. 9.95 (*2-07-036904-8*, 650) Schoenhof.

Boule de Suif, & Other Stories: Collected Novels & Stories, Vol. 1. Guy De Maupassant. Tr. by Ernest A. Boyd. LC 76-157786. (Short Story Index Reprint Ser.). 1977. reprint ed. 18.95 (*0-8369-3898-4*) Ayer.

Boule de Suif et Autres Contes Normands. Guy De Maupassant. Ed. by Marie-Claire Bancquart. (Coll. Prestige). 10.95 (*0-8288-9610-0*, M2452) Fr & Eur.

Boule de Suif, Maupassant: Critical Monographs in English. Peggy Chaplin. 80p. 1993. pap. 32.00 (*0-85261-250-8*, Pub. by Univ of Glasgow UK) St Mut.

Boulestin's Round-the-Year Cookbook. X. Marcel Boulestin. 256p. 1975. reprint ed. pap. 4.95 (*0-486-23214-X*) Dover.

Boulevard, Chevron, & Combination Weaves: Based on Dr. William G. Bateman's Manuscript. Ed. by Virginia I. Harvey. LC 87-91236. (Guild Monographs: No. 38). (Illus.). 94p. 1988. pap. 16.95 (*0-916658-42-2*) Shuttle Craft.

Boulevard des Illusions. Pierre Boulle. 214p. (FRE.). 1981. 11.95 (*0-7859-1183-9*, 2266009680) Fr & Eur.

Boulevard Durand. Armand Salacrou. (FRE.). 1977. pap. 10.95 (*0-7859-2884-7*) Fr & Eur.

Boulevard Durand. Armand Salacrou. (Folio Ser.: No. 779). (FRE.). 1972. 8.95 (*2-07-036779-7*) Schoenhof.

Boulevard of Broken Dreams: The Life, Times, & Legend of James Dean. Paul Alexander. (Illus.). 320p. 1994. 22.95 (*0-670-84951-0*, Viking) Viking Penguin.

Boulevard of Heroes. Eduardo G. Aguilar. Ed. by Yvette E. Miller. Tr. by Jay Miskowiec. LC 93-1491. 192p. 1993. pap. 16.95 (*0-935480-62-5*) Lat Am Lit Rev Pr.

Boulevard Stories. Robert Wintringer. 150p. (Orig.). 1985. ring bd., pap. 65.00 (*0-942424-08-5*) W Anglia Pubns.

Boulevard Theater & Revolution in Eighteenth- Century Paris. Michele Root-Bernstein. LC 84-2545. (Theater & Dramatic Studies: No. 22). (Illus.). 340p. reprint ed. pap. 96.90 (*0-8357-1551-5*, 2070573) Bks Demand.

Boulevards de Ceintures. Patrick Modiano. (FRE.). 1978. pap. 10.95 (*0-7859-3390-5*) Fr & Eur.

Boulevards de Ceintures. Patrick Modiano. (Folio Ser.: No. 1033). (FRE.). pap. 8.95 (*2-07-037033-X*) Schoenhof.

Boulez & the Modern Concept. Peter F. Stacey. LC 86-30818. xii, 151p. 1987. 50.00x (*0-8032-4183-6*) U of Nebr Pr.

*__Boulez-Cage Correspondence.__ Ed. by Jean-Jacques Nattiez. 192p. 1995. pap. 14.95 (*0-521-48558-4*) Cambridge U Pr.

Boulton & Paul. Gordon Kinsey. 1994. 54.00 (*0-86138-085-1*, Pub. by T Dalton UK) St Mut.

Bounce Bounce Bounce. Kathy Henderson. LC 93-3556. (Illus.). 24p. (J). (ps up). 1994. 9.95 (*1-56402-311-7*) Candlewick Pr.

Bounce, Stretch & Spring. Julie Fitzpatrick. (Science Spirals Ser.). (Illus.). 30p. (J). (gr. 3-5). 1991. 13.95 (*0-237-60212-1*, Pub. by Evans Bros Ltd UK) Trafalgar.

Bounce the Rhine: The Battle for the Heart of Germany. Charles Whiting. 248p. 1992. mass mkt. 4.99 (*0-380-71576-7*) Avon.

Bounceback. Jeff Magee. 1992. pap. 12.95 (*0-932845-50-9*) Lowell Pr.

Bouncers. John Godber. 1991. pap. 4.75 (*0-8222-0138-0*) Dramatists Play.

Bouncer's Guide to Barroom Brawling: Dealing with the Sucker Puncher, Streetfighter, & Ambusher. Peyton Quinn. (Illus.). 64p. 1990. pap. 17.95 (*0-87364-586-3*) Paladin Pr.

*__Bouncing.__ Hughes. LC 92-53001. 1995. pap. text ed. 3.99 (*1-56402-554-3*) Candlewick Pr.

Bouncing. Shirley Hughes. LC 92-53001. (Illus.). 24p. (J). (ps up). 1993. 12.95 (*1-56402-128-9*) Candlewick Pr.

Bouncing & Bending Light. Barbara Taylor. LC 89-36213. (Science Starters Ser.). (J). (gr. 4-6). 1990. lib. bdg. 13.23 (*0-531-14014-8*) Watts.

*__Bouncing & Bending Light.__ Steve Tomecek. LC 94-37820. (Phantastic Physical Phenomena Ser.). (Illus.). 48p. (J). (gr. 3-7). 1995. text ed. 14.95 (*0-7167-6541-1*, Sci Am Yng Rdrs); pap. text ed. 9.95 (*0-7167-6591-8*, Sci Am Yng Rdrs) W H Freeman.

Bouncing Back. Geoffrey Norman. Ed. by Paul McCarthy. 256p. 1992. reprint ed. mass mkt. 4.99 (*0-671-74635-9*) PB.

Bouncing Back: Handling the Humor & Heartaches of Frustration. Brent D. Earles. (Life Enrichment Ser.). 165p. 1986. pap. 6.99 (*0-8010-3435-3*) Baker Bk.

Bouncing Back: How to Stay in the Game When Your Career Is on the Line. Andrew J. Dubrin. 1992. text ed. 24.95 (*0-07-017901-8*); pap. text ed. 14.95 (*0-07-017900-X*) McGraw.

*__Bouncing Back: How to Turn Business Crises into Success.__ Harvey Reese. 224p. 1994. 18.95 (*1-57101-014-9*) MasterMedia Ltd.

*__Bouncing Back: What to Do after Mistakes, Embarrassment, & Other Daily Disasters.__ (Custom Curriculum Ser.). (Illus.). (J). (gr. 6-9). Date not set. 10.95 (*0-7814-5166-3*, 23101) Cook.

Bouncing Back after Divorce. Carol A. Vercz. 1993. 4.00 (*0-318-11854-8*) SOCO Pubns.

Bouncing Dinosaur. Emma C. Clark. (Illus.). 32p. (J). (ps-3). 1990. 13.95 (*0-374-30912-4*) FS&G.

Bouncing Hills - Dialect Tales & Light Verse. Jack Clemo. (C). 1989. 35.00 (*0-907566-38-3*, Pub. by Dyllansow Truran UK) St Mut.

*__Bouncing-Quitely Lessons: Winnie the Pooh.__ Leslie McGuire. (Comes to Life Bks.). 16p. (J). (ps-2). 1995. write for info. (*1-57234-053-3*) YES Ent.

Bouncy Bunny's Birthday: A Family Story about Bravery. Cathy J. Brown & Debi Paterson. LC 86-61065. (Illus.). 32p. (Orig.). (J). (gr. 1-3). 1985. pap. 8.75 (*0-9614796-0-4*) C J Brown.

An Asterisk (*) at the beginning of an entry indicates that the title is appearing in BIP for the first time.

Bouncy Bunny's Birthday: A Family Story about Bravery. Cathy J. Brown & Debi Paterson. (Illus.). 32p. (Orig.). (J). (gr. 1-3). 1985. pap. 8.75 (*0-318-19386-8*) Offset Hse.

Bound & Conjugated Pesticide Residues. Ed. by Donald D. Kaufman et al. LC 76-13011. (ACS Symposium Ser.: No. 29). 396p. 1976. 43.95 (*0-8412-0334-2*) Am Chemical.

***Bound & Determined: Captivity, Culture-Crossing & the White Womanhood from Mary Rowlandson to Patty Hearst.** Christopher Castiglia. (Women in Culture & Society Ser.). (Illus.). 216p. 1996. 36.00x (*0-226-09652-1*); pap. 13.95x (*0-226-09654-8*) U Ch Pr.

Bound & Ready. Kim Knox. (Illus.). 30p. (Orig.). 1994. per. 20.00 (*1-882313-02-X*) Ice Hse Pr.

Bound by Blood. Charles r. Goodman. 1985. pap. 3.95 (*0-87067-396-3*, BH396) Holloway.

Bound by Blood & Name: A History & Genealogies of the Podoll Families in Prussia & America. Brian A. Podoll. (Illus.). 600p. 1989. 40.00 (*0-9621809-0-4*) B A Podoll.

Bound by Desire. Rosemary Rogers. 416p. 1988. mass mkt. 4.95 (*0-380-75451-7*) Avon.

***Bound by Diversity: Essays, Prose & Poetry from Members of the Lesbian, Gay, Bisexual, & Transgender Communities.** James T. Sears. (Empathy Ser.). 272p. (Orig.). 1994. 25.95 (*0-9642502-1-7*) Sebastian Pr.

***Bound by Diversity: Essays, Prose & Poetry from Members of the Lesbian, Gay, Bisexual, & Transgender Communities.** James T. Sears. (Empathy Ser.). (Illus.). 272p. (Orig.). (C). 1994. pap. 14.95 (*0-9642502-0-9*) Sebastian Pr.

Bound by Ecstasy. Kristal L. Scott. 384p. 1991. mass mkt. 4.25 (*0-8217-3353-2*) Zebra.

Bound by Henry Hoffman. 136p. 1991. 19.95 (*0-89754-075-1*); pap. 8.95 (*0-89754-074-3*) Dan River Pr.

Bound by Love. Erin Yorke. (Historical Ser.). 1993. mass mkt. 3.99 (*0-373-28776-3*, 1-28776-2) Harlequin Bks.

Bound by Our Constitution: Women, Workers & the Minimum Wage. Vivian Hart. LC 94-1052. 1994. 35.00 (*0-691-03480-X*) Princeton U Pr.

Bound by the Heart. Marsha Canham. 1991. 21.95 (*0-7278-4235-8*) Severn Hse.

Bound by the Sea: A Summer Diary. Jean G. Howard. LC 86-50255. (Illus.). 96p. (YA). (gr. 6-12). 1986. text ed. 15.00 (*0-930954-25-4*); pap. 10.00 (*0-930954-26-2*) Tidal Pr.

Bound Carbohydrates in Nature. Leonard Warren. (Lezioni Lincee Lectures). (Illus.). 126p. (C). 1994. 39.95 (*0-521-44231-1*); pap. 16.95 (*0-521-44743-7*) Cambridge U Pr.

Bound for America: The Transportation of British Convicts to the Colonies, 1718-1775. A. Roger Ekirch. (Illus.). 300p. 1990. reprint ed. pap. 19.95 (*0-19-820211-3*) OUP.

Bound for Glory. Woody Guthrie. LC 83-13424. 320p. 1983. pap. 12.95 (*0-452-26445-6*, Plume) NAL-Dutton.

Bound for Glory. Woody Guthrie. 21.75 (*0-8446-6178-3*) Peter Smith.

Bound for Good Health: A Collection of Age Pages. 128p. (Orig.). (C). 1993. pap. text ed. 35.00 (*0-7881-0060-2*) Diane Pub.

Bound for Idaho: The 1864 Trail Journal of Julius Merrill. Ed. by Irving R. Merrill. LC 87-38315. (Illus.). 160p. (Orig.). 1989. pap. 13.95 (*0-89301-124-X*) U of Idaho Pr.

Bound for Oregon. Jean Van Leeuwen. LC 93-26709. (J). 1994. 14.99 (*0-8037-1526-9*); lib. bdg. 14.89 (*0-8037-1527-7*) Dial Bks Young.

Bound for Success: Guiding Your Child Toward Higher Self-Esteem. Bert Simmons & Betty J. Simmons. 101p. (Orig.). 1993. pap. 9.95 (*0-939007-79-7*) Lee Canter & Assocs.

Bound for the Kingdom. Joseph Linn. 1992. 6.50 (*0-8341-9279-9*, MB-636); audio 15.98 (*0-685-71337-7*, TA-9139C); audio 85.00 (*0-685-71339-3*, MU-9139C); cd-rom 85.00 (*0-685-71340-7*, MU-9139T); 7.00 (*0-685-71338-5*, L-9139C) Lillenas.

Bound for the Promised Land. Joan C. Cobb. (Illus.). 567p. 1992. write for info. (*0-318-69597-9*) Anchor Pub Co.

Bound for the Promised Land. Elva J. Hoover. LC 89-80329. (Radiant Life Ser.). 158p. 1989. pap. 3.95 (*0-88243-861-1*, 02-0861) Gospel Pub.

Bound for the Promised Land. Richard Marius. LC 93-18163. (C). 1993. reprint ed. pap. 12.95 (*1-55853-226-9*) Rutledge Hill Pr.

***Bound for the Promised Land: The Great Migration & How It Changed America.** Michael L. Cooper. LC 95-2611. (J). 1995. 15.99 (*0-525-67476-4*, Lodestar Bks) Dutton Child Bks.

Bound for the Promised Land Teacher's Guide. Rosemary L. Ford. (Radiant Life Ser.). 48p. 1990. 4.50 (*0-88243-201-X*, 32-0201) Gospel Pub.

Bound Girl of Cobble Hill. Lois Lenski. 21.95 (*0-89190-632-0*, Am Repr) Amereon Ltd.

Bound Man, & Other Stories. Ilse Aichinger. Tr. by Eric Mosbacher. LC 72-144151. (Short Story Index Reprint Ser., Suppl. 1955-58). 1977. reprint ed. 12.95 (*0-8369-3766-X*) Ayer.

Bound Pesticide Residues. Khan. 1995. write for info. (*0-8493-5058-1*) CRC Pr.

Bound to Be Free. Richard B. McKenzie. (Publication Ser.: No. 255). 210p. 1982. 15.95 (*0-8179-7551-9*) Hoover Inst Pr.

Bound to Be Teachers. Ed. by India L. Broyles. 72p. (Orig.). 1992. pap. text ed. write for info. (*0-939561-12-3*) Univ South ME.

Bound to Change: Consolidating Democracy in East Central Europe. Ed. by Peter M. Volten. LC 92-26640. 1992. 23.85 (*0-913449-34-2*) Inst EW Stud.

Bound to Change: Consolidating Democracy in East Central Europe. Ed. by Peter M. Volten. LC 92-26640. 240p. 1993. 23.85 (*0-8133-8704-3*) Westview.

Bound to Differ: The Dynamics of Theological Discourses. Wesley A. Kort. 160p. 1992. 25.00 (*0-271-00859-8*) Pa St U Pr.

Bound to Earth. James A. Swan & Roberta Swan. 176p. (Orig.). 1994. pap. 10.00 (*0-380-76971-9*) Avon.

Bound to Empire: The United States & the Philippines. H. W. Brands. 400p. 1992. 30.00 (*0-19-507104-2*) OUP.

Bound to Fail: Britain's Membership in the Common Market. 1991. lib. bdg. 72.95 (*0-8490-4560-6*) Gordon Pr.

***Bound to Forgive: The Pilgrimage to Reconciliation of a Beirut Hostage.** Lawrence M. Jenco. LC 95-75315. (Illus.). 144p. (Orig.). 1995. pap. 9.95 (*0-87793-554-8*) Ave Maria.

Bound to Happen. Elswyth Thane. 1976. reprint ed. lib. bdg. 24.95 (*0-88411-964-5*, Aeonian Pr) Amereon Ltd.

Bound to Lead: The Changing Nature of American Power. Joseph S. Nye, Jr. 307p. 1991. pap. 15.00 (*0-465-00744-9*) Basic.

Bound to Please. 2nd ed. Junior League of Boise, Inc. Staff. (Illus.). 480p. 1983. reprint ed. ring bd. 14.95 (*0-9613743-0-6*) Jr League Boise.

Bound to Please: Selected Rare Books about Louisiana from the Historic New Orleans Collection. Ed. by Florence M. Jumonville. LC 82-83113. (Illus.). xii, 82p. 1982. pap. 16.00 (*0-917860-11-X*) Historic New Orleans.

Bound to Violence. Yambo Ouologuem. (African Writers Ser.). 182p. 1971. pap. 9.95 (*0-435-90099-4*) Heinemann.

Bound Volume of Consumer Reports, 1992. Consumer Reports Editors. 850p. 1992. 29.95 (*0-89043-589-8*) Consumer Reports.

Bound with Them in Chains: A Biographical History of the Antislavery Movement. Jane H. Pease & William H. Pease. LC 74-175612. (Contributions in American History Ser.: No. 18). 284p. 1972. text ed. 59.95 (*0-8371-6265-3*, PEB/, Greenwood Pr) Greenwood.

Boundaries. Anne Katherine. 1993. pap. 10.00 (*0-671-79193-1*, Fireside) S&S Trade.

Boundaries: Gaining Control of Your Life. Henry Cloud & John Townsend. 256p. 1992. 17.99 (*0-310-58590-2*) Zondervan.

Boundaries: National Autonomy & Its Limits. Ed. by Peter G. Brown & Henry Shue. 1981. 45.00 (*0-317-05219-5*); pap. 17.75 (*0-317-05220-9*) IPPP.

Boundaries: National Autonomy & Its Limits. Ed. by Peter G. Brown & Henry Shue. LC 81-5896. (Maryland Studies in Public Philosophy). 234p. 1981. 50.00 (*0-8476-7011-2*, R7011) Rowman.

Boundaries: The Making of France & Spain in the Pyrenees. Peter Sahlins. 1989. 42.50 (*0-520-06538-7*) U CA Pr.

Boundaries: The Making of France & Spain in the Pyrenees. Peter Sahlins. (Illus.). 372p. 1991. pap. 15.00 (*0-520-07415-7*) U CA Pr.

Boundaries & Identities: Muslims, Work & Status in Aligarh. E. A. Mann. (Illus.). 188p. (C). 1992. text ed. 28.50 (*0-8039-9422-2*) Sage.

Boundaries & Landmarks. A. C. Mulford. 1977. reprint ed. pap. 15.00 (*0-686-18920-5*, 611) CARBEN Survey.

Boundaries & Passages: Rule & Ritual in Yup'ik Eskimo Oral Tradition. Ann Fienup-Riordan. LC 93-23220. (Civilization of the American Indian Ser.: Vol. 212). (Illus.). 416p. 1994. 47.50 (*0-8061-2604-3*) U of Okla Pr.

Boundaries & Relationships: Knowing, Protecting & Enjoying the Self. Charles Whitfield. 280p. (Orig.). 1993. pap. 11.95 (*1-55874-259-X*, 259X) Health Comm.

Boundaries Between Promotion & Progression During Carcinogenesis. Ed. by O. Sudilovsky et al. (Basic Life Sciences Ser.: Vol. 57). (Illus.). 360p. 1991. 95.00 (*0-306-44031-8*, Plenum Pr) Plenum.

Boundaries Dimly Perceived: Law, Religion, Education, & the Common Good. Christopher F. Mooney. LC 89-40393. (C). 1990. text ed. 26.95 (*0-268-00682-2*) U of Notre Dame Pr.

***Boundaries in China.** Ed. by John Hay. (Illus.). 360p. (C). 1995. 45.00 (*0-948462-37-X*, Reaktion Bks UK); pap. 27.00 (*0-948462-38-8*, Reaktion Bks UK) U of Wash Pr.

Boundaries in Mind: A Study of Immediate Awareness Based on Psychotherapy. Charles E. Scott. LC 81-18366. (American Academy of Religion, Studies in Religion). (C). 1982. 22.95 (*0-89130-554-8*, 01-00-27) Scholars Pr GA.

***Boundaries in Question: New Directions in International Relations.** Ed. by John MacMillan & Andrew Linklater. LC 95-3441. 1995. write for info. (*1-85567-265-0*, Pub. by Pinter Pubs UK); pap. write for info. (*1-85567-266-9*, Pub. by Pinter Pubs UK) St Martin.

Boundaries in the Mind: A New Psychology of Personality. Ernest Hartmann. LC 91-70061. 288p. 1993. reprint ed. pap. 14.50 (*0-465-00740-6*) Basic.

Boundaries of Art. David Novitz. 296p. (C). 1992. 44.95 (*0-87722-928-7*) Temple U Pr.

Boundaries of Change in Community Work. Ed. by Paul Henderson et al. 1980. 35.00 (*0-317-05779-0*, Pub. by Natl Inst Soc Work) St Mut.

***Boundaries of Charity: Cistercian Culture & Ecclesiastical Reform, 1098-1180.** Martha G. Newman. LC 95-14016. (Figurae: Reading Medieval Culture Ser.). (Illus.). 466p. 1996. 55.00x (*0-8047-2512-8*) Stanford U Pr.

Boundaries of Citizenship: Race, Ethnicity, & Nationality in the Liberal State. Jeff Spinner. LC 93-46089. 1994. text ed. 39.95x (*0-8018-4812-1*) Johns Hopkins.

***Boundaries of Citizenship: Race, Ethnicity, & Nationality in the Liberal State.** Jeff Spinner. 272p. 1995. reprint ed. pap. text ed. 14.95x (*0-8018-5239-0*) Johns Hopkins.

Boundaries of Civilizations in Space & Time. Ed. by Matthew Melko & Leighton R. Scott. LC 87-10718. (Illus.). 480p. (Orig.). (C). 1987. pap. text ed. 37.00 (*0-8191-6493-3*) U Pr of Amer.

Boundaries of Economics. Ed. by Gordon C. Winston & Richard F. Teichgraeber. (Murphy Institute Studies in Political Economy: 1). 208p. 1988. 44.95 (*0-521-34450-6*) Cambridge U Pr.

Boundaries of Eros: Sex Crime & Sexuality in Renaissance Venice. Guido Ruggiero. (Studies in the History of Sexuality). (Illus.). 240p. 1989. reprint ed. pap. 14.95 (*0-19-505696-5*) OUP.

Boundaries of Flame. Olena Teliha. Ed. by Orysia Prokopiw. LC 77-20575. (Illus.). 1978. 6.65 (*0-914834-13-4*) Smoloskyp.

Boundaries of Free Speech: Deciding How Free Is Too Free. abr. ed. National Issues Forum Staff. 32p. 1991. 2.95 (*0-8403-6927-1*) Kendall-Hunt.

Boundaries of Free Speech: How Free Is Too Free? National Issues Forum Institute Staff. 32p. 1991. 2.95 (*0-8403-6924-7*) Kendall-Hunt.

Boundaries of Genre. Gary S. Morson. 219p. 1988. pap. 12.95 (*0-8101-0811-9*) Northwestern U Pr.

Boundaries of Genre: Dostoevsky's "Diary of a Writer" & the Traditions of Literary Utopia. Gary S. Morson. (Slavic Ser.: No. 4). 230p. 1981. 25.00 (*0-292-70732-0*) U of Tex Pr.

Boundaries of Home: Mapping for Local Empowerment. Ed. by Doug Aberley. (Illus.). 144p. 1993. 34.95 (*0-86571-271-9*); pap. 9.95 (*0-86571-272-7*) New Soc Pubs.

Boundaries of Humanity: Humans, Animals, Machines. Ed. by James J. Sheehan & Morton Sosna. (Illus.). 264p. 1991. 38.00 (*0-520-07153-0*); pap. 13.00 (*0-520-07207-3*) U CA Pr.

Boundaries of Liberty & Tolerance: The Struggle Against Kahanism in Israel. Raphael Cohen-Almagor. LC 93-33425. 352p. (C). 1994. lib. bdg. 34.95 (*0-8130-1258-9*) U Press Fla.

***Boundaries of Love.** Kristin Hungenberg. 1995. 17.95 (*0-8034-9104-2*, 095123) Bouregy.

Boundaries of Love: And Other Stories. Henry H. Roth. 1990. 17.95 (*0-945167-31-8*) British Amer Pub.

Boundaries of Modern Iran. Ed. by Keith McLachlan. LC 93-40359. (SOAS-GRC Geopolitics Ser.). 1994. text ed. 49.95 (*0-312-12062-1*) St Martin.

Boundaries of Moral Discourse. Mane Hajdin. LC 93-11148. (Values & Ethics Ser.: Vol. 8). 230p. 1993. 29.95 (*0-8294-0747-2*, Campion Bks) Loyola Univ Pr.

Boundaries of Natural Science. Rudolf Steiner. Tr. by Frederick Amrine & Konrad Oberhuber. LC 83-9943. 144p. 1987. pap. 9.95 (*0-88010-187-3*) Anthroposophic.

Boundaries of Our Habitations: Tradition & Theological Construction. Delwin Brown. LC 93-27411. (SUNY Series in Religious Studies). 215p. (C). 1994. 49.50x (*0-7914-1965-7*); pap. 16.95x (*0-7914-1966-5*) State U NY Pr.

Boundaries of the Accounting Universe: Accounting Rules of Selection. George H. Sorter. Ed. by Richard P. Brief. LC 77-87308. (Development of Contemporary Accounting Thought Ser.). 1978. lib. bdg. 19.95 (*0-405-10947-4*) Ayer.

Boundaries of the City: The Architecture of Western Urbanism. Alan Waterhouse. (Illus.). 384p. 1993. 75.00 (*0-8020-0538-1*) U of Toronto Pr.

Boundaries of the Latin American Republics: An Annotated List of Documents, 1493-1943. Alexander N. De Armond Marchant. (Latin America Ser.). 1979. lib. bdg. 59.95 (*0-8490-2876-0*) Gordon Pr.

Boundaries of the Louisiana Purchase: A Historical Study. Louis Houck. LC 72-146401. (First American Frontier Ser.). 1976. reprint ed. 22.95 (*0-405-02855-5*) Ayer.

Boundaries of the Self: Chinese Portraits, 1600-1900. Richard Vinograd. (Illus.). 451p. (C). 1992. 105.00 (*0-521-38548-2*) Cambridge U Pr.

Boundaries of the Self: Gender, Culture, Fiction. Roberta Rubenstein. LC 86-11252. 272p. 1987. 29.95 (*0-252-01355-7*) U of Ill Pr.

Boundaries of the Soul: The Practice of Jung's Psychology. June Singer. LC 94-9070. 1994. 12.95 (*0-385-47529-2*, Anchor NY) Doubleday.

***Boundaries of the Soul: The Practice of Jung's Psychology.** rev. ed. June Singer. LC 94-72961. 528p. 1995. 35.00 (*1-56821-435-9*) Aronson.

Boundaries of the Text: Epic Performances in South & Southeast Asia. Ed. by Joyce B. Flueckiger & Laurie J. Sears. LC 90-85739. (Michigan Papers on South & Southeast Asia: No. 35). x, 161p. 1990. 28.95 (*0-89148-062-5*); pap. 16.95 (*0-89148-063-3*) Ctr S&SE Asian.

Boundaries of the Universe. John S. Glasby. LC 76-162638. (Illus.). 296p. 1971. 29.95 (*0-674-08015-7*) HUP.

Boundaries of Twilight: Czecho-Slovak Writing from the New World. Ed. by C. J. Hribal. 1991. pap. 14.95 (*0-89823-121-3*) New Rivers Pr.

Boundaries Where You End & I Began: How to Recognize & Set Healthy Boundaries. Anne Katherine. 133p. 1991. reprint ed. pap. 9.95 (*1-56838-030-5*) Hazelden.

***Boundaries Workbook.** Henry Cloud & John Townsend. 1995. pap. 8.99 (*0-310-49481-8*) Zondervan.

Boundary & Eigenvalue Problems. Hans Sagan. 1989. pap. 8.95 (*0-486-66132-6*) Dover.

Boundary & Space: An Introduction to the Work of D. W. Winnicott. Madeleine Davis & David Wallbridge. LC 90-48118. 240p. 1991. pap. 21.95 (*0-87630-641-5*) Brunner-Mazel.

Boundary Behavior of Holomorphic Functions of Several Complex Variables. E. M. Stein. LC 71-183062. (Mathematical Notes Ser.: No. 11). 84p. 1972. pap. 16.95 (*0-691-08109-3*) Princeton U Pr.

Boundary Behaviour of Conformal Maps. C. Pommerenke. Ed. by M. Berger et al. LC 92-10365. (Grundlehren der Mathematischen Wissenschaften Ser.: Vol. 299). (Illus.). 312p. 1992. 69.00 (*0-387-54751-7*) Spr-Verlag.

***Boundary Breaking.** Kay Allen et al. 352p. (C). 1994. per., pap. text ed. 34.95 (*0-7872-0274-6*) Kendall-Hunt.

Boundary Control & Boundary Variation: IFIP WG 7.2 Conference, Sophia-Antipolis, 15-17 October 1990. Ed. by J. P. Zolesio. (Lecture Notes in Control & Information Sciences Ser.: Vol. 178). (Illus.). iii, 406p. 1992. pap. 96.00 (*0-387-55351-7*) Spr-Verlag.

Boundary Control & Legal Principles. 3rd ed. Curtis M. Brown et al. LC 86-9181. 409p. 1986. text ed. 69.95 (*0-471-08384-4*) Wiley.

Boundary Control & Variation. Ed. by Jean-Paul Zolesio. LC 94-18489. (Lecture Notes in Pure & Applied Mathematics: Vol. 163). 424p. 1994. pap. 160.00 (*0-8247-9274-2*) Dekker.

Boundary Crossing of Brownian Motion. H. R. Lerche. (Lecture Notes in Statistics Ser.: Vol. 40). 142p. 1986. pap. 29.00 (*0-387-96433-9*) Spr-Verlag.

Boundary Disputes & How to Resolve Them. A. Anstey. 72p. (C). 1990. pap. text ed. 65.00 (*0-85406-463-X*, Pub. by R-I-C-S Bks UK) St Mut.

Boundary Element Analysis in Computational Fracture Mechanics. T. A. Cruse. (C). 1988. lib. bdg. 90.00 (*90-247-3614-5*) Kluwer Ac.

Boundary Element Analysis in Engineering Continuum Mechanics. James H. Kane. LC 93-3139. 1993. text ed. 77.00 (*0-13-086927-9*) P-H.

Boundary Element Analysis of Nonhomogeneous Biharmonic Phenomena. C. V. Camp & G. S. Gipson. Ed. by Carlos A. Brebbia & S. A. Orszag. (Lecture Notes in Engineering Ser.: Vol. 74). (Illus.). xii, 246p. 1992. pap. 62.00 (*0-387-55020-8*) Spr-Verlag.

Boundary Element Analysis of Plates & Shells. Ed. by D. E. Beskos & S. N. Atluri. (Computational Mechanics Ser.). (Illus.). viii, 368p. 1991. 105.00 (*0-387-54464-X*) Spr-Verlag.

Boundary Element Applications in Fluid Mechanics. Ed. by H. Power. (Advances in Fluid Mechanics Ser.: Vol. 4). 376p. 1995. 157.00 (*1-56252-212-4*) Computational Mech MA.

Boundary Element Method. W. S. Hall. LC 93-33793. (Solid Mechanics & Its Applications Ser.). 240p. (C). 1993. lib. bdg. 119.00 (*0-7923-2580-X*) Kluwer Ac.

Boundary Element Method: Principles & Applications: Proceedings of the Third Japan-China Symposium on Boundary Element Methods, Hachiohji, Tokyo, Japan, 4-7 April, 1990. Ed. by Masataka Tanaka & Qinghua Du. (Illus.). 428p. 1990. pap. 40.00 (*0-08-040201-1*, Pergamon Pr) Elsevier.

Boundary Element Method Applied to Inelastic Problems. J. C. Telles. (Lecture Notes in Engineering Ser.: Vol. 1). 243p. 1984. pap. 34.00 (*0-387-12387-3*) Spr-Verlag.

Boundary Element Method Educational Package. Ed. by C. A. Brebbia. 1993. boxed 2,600.00 (*1-56252-179-9*) Computational Mech MA.

Boundary Element Method for Groundwater Flow. E. Bruch. Ed. by Carlos A. Brebbia & S. A. Orszag. (Lecture Notes in Engineering Ser.: Vol. 70). (Illus.). 120p. 1991. pap. 27.00 (*0-387-54407-0*) Spr-Verlag.

Boundary Element Method for Solving Improperly Posed Problems. Derek B. Ingham & Yong Yuan. LC 94-70412. 160p. 1994. 74.00 (*1-56252-215-9*) Computational Mech MA.

Boundary Element Method in Engineering. A. A. Becker. 320p. 1992. text ed. 33.50 (*0-07-707415-7*) McGraw.

Boundary Element Method XVI: Proceedings of the Sixteenth International Conference. Ed. by C. A. Brebbia. LC 74-70404. (BEM Ser.: Vol. 16). 602p. 1994. text ed. 231.00 (*1-56252-207-8*) Computational Mech MA.

Boundary Element Methods. Goong Chen & Jianxin Zhou. (Computational Mathematics & Applications Ser.). (Illus.). 646p. 1992. text ed. 99.00 (*0-12-170940-X*) Acad Pr.

Boundary Element Methods: Current Research in Japan & China - Proceeding of the Fifth Japan-China Symposium on Boundary Element Methods, Sapporo, Japan, 1-4 June, 1993. Ed. by Masataka Tanaka et al. LC 93-19753. 1993. write for info. (*0-444-89973-1*) Elsevier.

Boundary Element Methods: Fundamentals & Applications, Proceedings of the IABEM Symposium, Kyoto, Japan, October 14-17, 1991. Ed. by Shoshichi Kobayashi & N. Nishimura. LC 92-32708. 1993. 145.00 (*0-387-55976-0*) Spr-Verlag.

Boundary Element Methods in Acoustics. Ed. by R. D. Ciskowski & C. A. Brebbia. LC 91-70445. (Computational Engineering Ser.). 292p. 1991. 125.00 (*0-945824-87-4*) Computational Mech MA.

Boundary Element Methods in Creep & Fracture. S. Mukherjee. (Illus.). 224p. 1983. 56.00 (*0-85334-163-X*, I-430-82, Pub. by Elsevier Applied Sci UK) Elsevier.

Boundary Element Methods in Elastodynamics. G. D. Manolis & D. E. Beskos. 288p. 1988. text ed. 75.00 (*0-04-620019-3*) Routledge Chapman & Hall.

Boundary Element Methods in Engineering. 2nd ed. P. K. Banerjee. LC 93-13475. 1994. text ed. write for info. (*0-07-707769-5*) McGraw.

Boundary Element Methods in Heat Transfer. Ed. by L. C. Wrobel & C. A. Brebbia. LC 91-76553. (Computational Engineering Ser.). 306p. 1992. 135.00 (*0-945824-86-6*) Computational Mech MA.

Boundary Element Methods in Mechanics. D. E. Beskos. (Computational Methods in Mechanics Ser.: Vol. 3). 1987. 159.00 (*0-444-87990-0*) Elsevier.

An Asterisk (*) at the beginning of an entry indicates that the title is appearing in BIP for the first time. 871

Boundary Element Methods in Nonlinear Fluid Dynamics: Developments in Boundary Element Methods, No. 6. Ed. by P. K. Banerjee & L. Morino. 358p. 1990. 113.50 (1-85166-429-7) Elsevier.

Boundary Element Methods in Solid Mechanics. Steven L. Crouch & Anthony M. Starfield. 322p. (C). 1990. text ed. 49.95 (0-685-46015-0); pap. text ed. 34.95 (0-04-445913-0) Routledge Chapman & Hall.

Boundary Element Methods in Structural Analysis. Ed. by D. E. Beskos. LC 89-6565. 352p. 1989. pap. text ed. 31.00 (0-87262-694-6, 694) Am Soc Civil Eng.

Boundary Element Methods in Transport Phenomena. P. A. Ramachandran. LC 93-72570. 424p. 1993. 160.00 (1-56252-184-5) Computational Mech MA.

Boundary Element Methods in Transport Phenomena. P. A. Ramachandran. 400p. 1993. 160.00 (1-85861-026-5, Pub. by Elsevier Applied Sci UK) Elsevier.

Boundary Element Reference Book. M. Mackerle. LC 87-72284. 350p. 1987. 77.00 (0-931215-67-6) Computational Mech MA.

Boundary Element Reference Book. 2nd ed. M. H. Aliabadi et al. 750p. 1995. disk 248.00 (1-56252-216-7) Computational Mech MA.

Boundary Element Research. Ed. by C. A. Brebbia. (Progress in Engineering Ser.). 100p. 1984. pap. 46.00 (0-931215-02-1) Computational Mech MA.

Boundary Element Starter Pack for Acoustics. Ed. by R. Adey et al. 1994. disk 275.00 (1-56252-261-2) Computational Mech MA.

Boundary Element Starter Pack for Stress Analysis. Ed. by R. Adey et al. 1994. disk 275.00 (1-56252-260-4) Computational Mech MA.

Boundary Element Starter Pack Set. Ed. by R. Adey et al. 1994. disk 715.00 (1-56252-263-9) Computational Mech MA.

Boundary Element Starter Packs for Fracture Mechanics & Crack Growth. Ed. by R. Adey et al. 1994. disk 275.00 (1-56252-262-0) Computational Mech MA.

Boundary Element Techniques. C. A. Brebbia et al. 478p. 1984. 85.00 (1-56252-143-8) Computational Mech MA.

Boundary Element Techniques: Applications in Fluid Flow & Computational Aspects. Ed. by C. A. Brebbia & W. S. Venturini. LC 78-70506. (BETECH Ser.: Vol. 3). 260p. (C). 1987. 72.00 (0-931215-77-3) Computational Mech MA.

Boundary Element Techniques: Applications in Stress Analysis & Heat Transfer. Ed. by C. A. Brebbia & W. S. Venturini. LC 87-70777. (BETECH Ser.: Vol. 3). 240p. 1987. 72.00 (0-931215-76-5) Computational Mech MA.

Boundary Element Techniques--Applications in Engineering. Ed. by C. A. Brebbia & N. G. Zamani. LC 89-60747. (BETECH Ser.: Vol. 4). 452p. 1989. 109.00 (0-945824-08-4) Computational Mech MA.

Boundary Element Techniques in Computer-Aided Engineering. Ed. by Carlos A. Brebbia. LC 84-16710. 1984. lib. bdg. 136.50 (90-247-3065-1) Kluwer Ac.

Boundary Element Techniques in Geomechanics. Ed. by G. Manolis & T. Davies. LC 93-72574. (Computational Engineering Ser.). 548p. 1993. 224.00 (1-56252-183-7) Computational Mech MA.

Boundary Element Techniques in Geomechanics. G. D. Manolis. 1993. 224.00 (1-85861-024-9, Pub. by Elsevier Applied Sci UK) Elsevier.

Boundary Element Technology, Vol. 6. Carlos A. Brebbia. 1991. 110.50 (1-85166-668-0) Elsevier.

Boundary Element Technology IX: Proceedings of the Ninth International Conference. Ed. by C. A. Brebbia & A. J. Kassab. LC 94-70127. (BETECH Ser.: Vol. 9). 357p. 1994. 139.00 (1-56252-206-X) Computational Mech MA.

Boundary Element Technology VI. Ed. by C. A. Brebbia. LC 91-71739. (BETECH Ser.: Vol. 6). 432p. 1991. 130.00 (1-56252-067-9) Computational Mech MA.

Boundary Element Technology VII: Proceedings of the Seventh International Conference on Boundary Element Technology (Betech 92) Held in Albuquerque, New Mexico, June 3-5, 1992. Ed. by C. A. Brebbia & M. S. Ingber. LC 92-70437. (BETECH Ser.: Vol. 7). 964p. 1992. 375.00 (1-56252-097-0) Computational Mech MA.

Boundary Element Technology VIII. Ed. by H. Pina & C. A. Brebbia. LC 93-71016. (BETECH Ser.: Vol. 8). 383p. 1993. 135.00 (1-56252-173-X) Computational Mech MA.

Boundary Element Technology X: Proceedings of the 10th International Conference. Ed. by C. A. Brebbia & A. J. Kassab. (BETECH Ser.: Vol. 10). 400p. 1995. 145.00 (1-56252-241-8) Computational Mech MA.

***Boundary Element Technology XI.** (Betech Ser.: Vol. 11). 370p. 1996. text ed. 145.00 (1-85312-394-3) Computational Mech MA.

Boundary Elements: An Introductory Course. Carlos A. Brebbia & J. Dominguez. 1989. write for info. (0-07-007415-1) McGraw.

Boundary Elements: An Introductory Course. 2nd rev. ed. C. A. Brebbia & J. Dominguez. LC 91-77179. 314p. (C). 1992. 59.95 (1-56252-087-3) Computational Mech MA.

Boundary Elements: Proceedings of the International Conference, Bejing, China, 14-17 October 1986. Ed. by Du Qinghua. 750p. 1986. 302.00 (0-08-034357-0) Franklin.

Boundary Elements for Engineers: Theory & Applications. Jon Trevelyan. LC 93-74383. 228p. 1994. 69.00 (1-56252-203-5) Computational Mech MA.

Boundary Elements in Dynamics. J. Dominguez. LC 93-72572. (Computational Engineering Ser.). 724p. 1993. disk 272.00 (1-56252-182-9) Computational Mech MA.

Boundary Elements in Dynamics. J. Dominiguez. 724p. 1993. 272.00 (1-85861-021-4, Pub. by Elsevier Applied Sci UK) Elsevier.

Boundary Elements in Fluid Dynamics: Proceedings of the International Conference on Boundary Elements & Fluid Dynamics Held in Southampton, UK, April 1992. Ed. by C. A. Brebbia & P. W. Partridge. LC 91-77631. 272p. 1992. 130.00 (1-56252-093-8) Computational Mech MA.

Boundary Elements in Fluid Dynamics & Computer Modelling of Seas & Coastal Regions, 2 vols., Set. Ed. by C. A. Brebbia & P. W. Partridge. 806p. 1992. 334.00 (1-56252-121-7) Computational Mech MA.

Boundary Elements in Mechanical & Electrical Engineering. Ed. by C. A. Brebbia & Mrs. Chaudet-Miranda. LC 90-80853. (EUROBEM Ser.). 1990. 134.00 (0-945824-44-0) Computational Mech MA.

Boundary Elements in Mechanical & Electrical Engineering: European Boundary Element Method Symposium, 15-17 May 1990, Nice, France. Ed. by Carlos A. Brebbia & A. Chaudouet-Miranda. (Illus.). 580p. 1990. 167.00 (0-387-52645-5) Spr-Verlag.

Boundary Elements in Non Linear Fracture Mechanics. Vitor Leitao. LC 94-72219. (Topics in Engineering Ser.: No. 21). 288p. 1994. text ed. 119.00 (1-56252-259-0) Computational Mech MA.

Boundary Elements IX, 3 vols., Vol. 1: Mathematical & Computational Aspects. W. L. Wendland & C. A. Brebbia. LC 87-71518. (BEM Ser.: Vol. 9). 1987. Mathematical & Computational Aspects, 650 pgs. 132.00 (0-931215-60-9) Computational Mech MA.

Boundary Elements IX, 3 vols., Vol. 2: Stress Analysis Applications. W. L. Wendland & C. A. Brebbia. LC 87-71518. (BEM Ser.). 1987. Stress Analysis Applications, 650 pgs. 132.00 (0-931215-82-X) Computational Mech MA.

Boundary Elements IX, 3 vols., Vol. 3: Fluid Flow & Potential Applications. W. L. Wendland & C. A. Brebbia. LC 87-71518. (BEM Ser.). 1987. Fluid Flow & Potential Applications, 650 pgs. 132.00 (0-931215-83-8) Computational Mech MA.

Boundary Elements Techniques: Theory & Applications in Engineering. 2nd ed. C. A. Brebbia & L. C. Wrobel. 1000p. 1995. 195.00 (1-56252-226-4) Computational Mech MA.

Boundary Elements V. Ed. by C. A. Brebbia. (BEM Ser.: Vol. 5). 1046p. 1983. 137.00 (0-931215-46-3) Computational Mech MA.

Boundary Elements VI. Ed. by C. A. Brebbia. (BEM Ser.: Vol. 6). 480p. 1984. 87.00 (0-931215-47-1) Computational Mech MA.

Boundary Elements VII, 2 vols., Set. Ed. by C. A. Brebbia & G. Maier. (BEM Ser.: Vol. 7). 1319p. 1985. 168.00 (0-931215-05-6) Computational Mech MA.

Boundary Elements VIII, 2 vols., Set. Ed. by M. Tanaka & C. A. Brebbia. (BEM Ser.: Vol. 8). 917p. 1986. 199.00 (0-931215-32-3) Computational Mech MA.

Boundary Elements X, 4 vols., Set. Ed. by Carlos A. Brebbia. 1920p. 1988. 521.00 (0-387-50095-2) Spr-Verlag.

Boundary Elements X Vol. 1: Mathematical & Computational Aspects. Ed. by C. A. Brebbia. LC 88-71494. (BEM Ser.: Vol. 10). 653p. 1988. 128.00 (0-945824-00-9) Computational Mech MA.

Boundary Elements X Vol. 2: Heat Transfer, Fluid Flow & Electrical Applications. Ed. by C. A. Brebbia. LC 88-71494. (BEM Ser.: Vol. 10). 632p. 1988. 106.00 (0-945824-01-7) Computational Mech MA.

Boundary Elements X Vol. 3: Stress Analysis. Ed. by C. A. Brebbia. LC 88-71494. (BEM Ser.: Vol. 10). 704p. 1988. 132.00 (0-945824-02-5) Computational Mech MA.

Boundary Elements X Vol. 4: Geomechanics, Wave Propagation & Vibrations. Ed. by C. A. Brebbia. LC 88-71494. (BEM Ser.: Vol. 10). 484p. 1988. 92.00 (0-945824-03-3) Computational Mech MA.

Boundary Elements XII: Proceedings of the Twelfth International Conference on Boundary Elements in Engineering, Held at Hokkaido University, Sapporo, Japan During September 24-27, 1990, 2 vols., Set. Masataka Tanaka et al. 1188p. 1990. 290.00 (0-387-53209-9) Spr-Verlag.

Boundary Elements XII: Proceedings of the Twelfth International Conference on Boundary Elements in Engineering, Held at Hokkaido University, Sapporo, Japan During September 24-27, 1990, 2 vols., Vol. 1: Applications in Stress Analysis, Potential. Masataka Tanaka et al. 604p. 1990. 165.00 (0-387-53207-2) Spr-Verlag.

Boundary Elements XII: Proceedings of the Twelfth International Conference on Boundary Elements in Engineering, Held at Hokkaido University, Sapporo, Japan During September 24-27, 1990, 2 vols., Vol. 2: Applications in Fluid Mechanics & Field Pr. Masataka Tanaka et al. 584p. 1990. 165.00 (0-387-53208-0) Spr-Verlag.

Boundary Elements XII Vol. 1: Applications in Stress Analysis, Potential & Diffusion. Ed. by M. Tanaka et al. LC 90-84147. (BEM Ser.: Vol. 12). 1990. 165.00 (0-945824-76-9) Computational Mech MA.

Boundary Elements XIII: Boundary Element Methods in Engineering. Ed. by C. A. Brebbia & G. S. Gipson. LC 91-73255. 1054p. 1991. 325.00 (1-56252-072-5) Computational Mech MA.

Boundary Elements XIII: Proceedings of the Thirteenth International Conference on Boundary Element Methods, BEM 13, August 1991, Tulsa, OK. Ed. by Carlos A. Brebbia & G. S. Gipson. 1054p. 1991. 297.50 (1-85166-696-6) Elsevier.

Boundary Elements XIV: Proceedings of the Fourteenth International Conference on Boundary Element Methods in Engineering Held in Seville, Spain, November 3-6, 1992, 2 vols., Set. Ed. by C. A. Brebbia et al. LC 92-82810. (BEM Ser.: Vol. 14). 1444p. 1992. 585.00 (1-56252-136-5) Computational Mech MA.

Boundary Elements XIV Vol. 1: Field Problems & Applications. Ed. by C. A. Brebbia et al. LC 92-82810. (BEM Ser.: Vol. 14). 708p. 1992. 286.00 (1-56252-108-X) Computational Mech MA.

Boundary Elements XIV Vol. 2: Stress Analysis & Computational Aspects. Ed. by C. A. Brebbia et al. LC 92-82810. (BEM Ser.: Vol. 14). 736p. 1992. 299.00 (1-56252-135-7) Computational Mech MA.

Boundary Elements XV. Ed. by C. A. Brebbia & J. J. Rencis. 1356p. 1993. 440.00 (1-85166-844-6, Pub. by Elsevier Applied Sci UK) Elsevier.

Boundary Elements XV, 2 vols., Set. Ed. by J. J. Rencis & C. A. Brebbia. LC 93-71026. (BEM Ser.: Vol. 15). 1330p. 1993. 440.00 (1-56252-161-6) Computational Mech MA.

Boundary Elements XV Vol. 1: Fluid Flow & Computational Aspects. Ed. by J. J. Rencis & C. A. Brebbia. (BEM Ser.: Vol. 15). 706p. 1993. 229.00 (1-56252-197-7) Computational Mech MA.

Boundary Elements XV Vol. 2: Stress Analysis. Ed. by J. J. Rencis & C. A. Brebbia. LC 93-71026. (BEM Ser.: Vol. 15). 650p. 1993. 211.00 (1-56252-198-5) Computational Mech MA.

Boundary Elements XVII: Proceedings of the 17th International Conference. Ed. by C. A. Brebbia et al. (BEM Ser.: Vol. 17). 750p. 1995. 279.00 (1-56252-248-5) Computational Mech MA.

***Boundary Function Method for Singular Perturbation Problems.** Adelaida B. Vasileva et al. LC 94-42996. (Studies in Applied Mathematics: Vol. 14). 221p. 1995. pap. 58.50 (0-89871-333-1) Soc Indus-Appl Math.

Boundary Integral & Singularity Methods for Linearized Viscous Flow. C. Pozrikidis. (Texts in Applied Mathematics Ser.: No. 8). (Illus.). 250p. (C). 1992. 79.95 (0-521-40502-5); pap. 29.95 (0-521-40693-5) Cambridge U Pr.

Boundary Integral Approach to Static & Dynamic Contact Problems: Equality & Inequality Methods. H. Antes & P. D. Panagiotopoulos. LC 92-25605. (International Series of Numerical Mathematics: Vol. 108). xv, 307p. 1992. 116.00 (0-8176-2592-5, Pub. by Birkhauser Vlg SZ) Birkhauser.

Boundary Integral Equation Analysis of Singular, Potential & Biharmonic Problems. D. B. Ingham & M. A. Kelmanson. (Lecture Notes in Engineering Ser.: Vol. 7). (Illus.). iv, 173p. 1984. pap. 26.00 (0-387-13646-0) Spr-Verlag.

Boundary Integral Equation Method in Axisymmetric Stress Analysis Problems. A. A. Bakr. (Lecture Notes in Engineering Ser.: Vol. 14). 213p. 1986. pap. 31.00 (0-387-16030-2) Spr-Verlag.

Boundary Integral Equation Methods in Eigenvalue Problems of Elastodynamics & Thin Plates. M. Kitahara. (Studies in Applied Mechanics: Vol. 10). 1985. 100.00 (0-444-42447-4) Elsevier.

Boundary Integral Methods in Fluid Mechanics. Ed. by H. Power & L. C. Wrobel. LC 94-70411. (Computational Engineering Ser.). 344p. 1995. 99.00 (1-56252-176-4) Computational Mech MA.

Boundary Integral Methods: Theory & Applications: Proceedings of the IABEM Symposium Rome, Italy, October 15-19, 1990. Ed. by L. Morino & R. Piva. (Illus.). 544p. 1991. 105.00 (0-387-53773-2) Spr-Verlag.

Boundary-Interior Layer Interactions in Nonlinear Singular Perturbation Theory. F. A. Howes. LC 78-8693. 108p. 1982. reprint ed. pap. 21.00 (0-8218-2203-9, MEMO 15/203) Am Math.

***Boundary Law in North Carolina.** John E. Keen. 111p. (C). 1995. pap. text ed. 40.00 (1-56569-008-7) Land Survey.

Boundary Layer Analysis. Joseph C. Schetz. 512p. 1992. text ed. 77.00 (0-13-086885-X) P-H.

Boundary Layer & Flow Control: Its Principles & Application, 2 vols., Set. G. Lachmann. LC 60-9645. 1961. 552.00 (0-08-009346-9, Pub. by Pergamon Repr UK) Franklin.

***Boundary Layer & Free Shear Flows.** Ed. by J. F. Dononvan et al. LC 94-71358. (Fluid Engineering Division Conference Ser.: Vol. 184). 243p. 1994. pap. 45.00 (0-7918-1367-3) ASME.

Boundary Layer Climates. 2nd ed. T. R. Oke. (Illus.). 416p. 1988. lib. bdg. 99.00 (0-416-04422-0, A1481); pap. text ed. 35.00 (0-416-04432-8, A1485) Routledge Chapman & Hall.

Boundary-Layer Method in Diffraction Problems. V. M. Babic & N. Y. Kirpichnikova. (Electroyphysics Ser.: Vol. 3). (Illus.). 1980. 26.00 (0-387-09605-1) Spr-Verlag.

Boundary Layer Structure. Ed. by H. Kaplan & Nathan Dinar. 1984. lib. bdg. 162.50 (90-277-1877-6) Kluwer Ac.

Boundary Layer Studies & Applications: A Special Issue of Boundary-Layer Meteorology in Honor of Dr. Hans A. Panofsky (1917-1988) Ed. by R. E. Munn. (C). 1989. lib. bdg. 172.00 (0-7923-0277-X) Kluwer Ac.

Boundary Layer Theory. 7th ed. Hermann T. Schlichting. Tr. by Joseph Kestin. (Mechanical Engineering Ser.). (Illus.). 1979. text ed. write for info. (0-07-055334-3) McGraw.

Boundary Layers. A. D. Young. (Educ Ser.). 267p. 1989. 54.95 (0-930403-57-6) AIAA.

Boundary Layers in Homogeneous & Stratified Rotating Fluids: Notes on Lectures by Allan R. Robinson & Victor Barcilon. Jay S. Fein. LC 78-400. (Monograph Publishing on Demand: Imprint Ser.: No. 45). 142p. reprint ed. pap. 40.50 (0-8357-7366-3, 2016493) Bks Demand.

Boundary Lines. Nora Roberts. (NR Flowers Ser.: No. 47). 1994. mass mkt. 3.59 (0-373-51047-0, 1-51047-8) Silhouette.

Boundary Lubrication: An Appraisal of World Literature. Frederick F. Ling et al. LC 70-79165. 586p. reprint ed. pap. 167.10 (0-8357-7367-1, 2016847) Bks Demand.

Boundary of Blur. Nick Piombino. LC 92-63355. (Language Poetics Ser.: No. 6). 122p. (Orig.). 1993. pap. 13.95 (0-937804-50-9) Segue NYC.

Boundary Politics of Independent Africa. Saadia Touval. LC 72-79312. (Center for International Affairs Ser.). (Illus.). 346p. 1972. 34.00 (0-674-08025-4) HUP.

***Boundary Power: How I Treat You, How I Let You Treat Me, How I Treat Myself.** Mike S. O'Neil & Charles E. Newbold, Jr. 190p. (Orig.). 1995. pap. 19.95 (0-9633454-2-7) Sonlight Pub.

Boundary Problems for Differential Equations. Incl. Vol. 1. Proceedings. Steklov Institute of Mathematics Staff. Ed. by V. P. Mihailov. 178p. 1969. 67.00 (0-8218-1891-0, STEKLO-91); Vol. 2. Proceedings. Steklov Institute of Mathematics Staff. Ed. by V. P. Mihailov. 213p. 1970. 58.00 (0-8218-3003-1, STEKLO-103); Vol. 3. Proceedings. Ed. by V. P. Mihailov. 256p. 1975. 84.00 (0-8218-3026-0, STEKLO-103); (Proceedings of the Steklov Institute of Mathematics Ser.: No. STEKLO-126). write for info. (0-318-59450-1) Am Math.

Boundary Problems in Differential Equations: Proceedings of a Symposium Conducted by the Mathematics Research Center at the University of Wisconsin, Madison, April 20-22, 1959. Ed. by Rudolph E. Langer. LC 60-60003. (U. S. Army. Mathematics Research Center Publication Ser.: No. 2). 334p. reprint ed. pap. 95.20 (0-8357-7368-X, 2021137) Bks Demand.

Boundary-Scan Handbook. Kenneth P. Parker. LC 92-27976. 288p. (C). 1992. lib. bdg. 93.50 (0-7923-9270-1) Kluwer Ac.

Boundary Stabilization of Thin Plates. John E. Lagnese. (Studies in Applied Mathematics: No. 10). viii, 176p. 1989. pap. 38.75 (0-89871-237-8) Soc Indus-Appl Math.

Boundary Stelae of Akhenaten. William J. Murnane & Charles C. Van Siclen, III. LC 93-7007. (Studies in Egyptology). 1993. write for info. (0-7103-0464-1, Pub. by Kegan Paul Intl UK) Routledge Chapman & Hall.

Boundary Value & Initial Value Problems in Complex Analysis: Studies in Complex Analysis & Its Applications to Partial Differential Equations. W. Tutschke & R. Kuhnau. (Pitman Research Notes in Mathematics Ser.: No. 1). 292p. 1991. pap. text ed. 63.95 (0-470-21796-0) Halsted Pr.

Boundary Value Problems. F. Gakhov & I. N. Sneddon. LC 62-10263. (International Series of Monographs on Pure & Applied Mathematics: Vol. 85). 240.00 (0-08-010067-8, Pub. by Pergamon Repr UK) Franklin.

Boundary Value Problems. F. D. Gakhov. 1990. pap. 12.95 (0-486-66275-6) Dover.

Boundary Value Problems. Ladis D. Kovach. (Illus.). 400p. 1984. text ed. 49.56 (0-201-11728-2) Addison-Wesley.

Boundary Value Problems. 3rd ed. David L. Powers. 351p. (C). 1987. text ed. 60.00 (0-15-505535-6) SCP.

***Boundary Value Problems & Integral Equations in Nonsmooth Domains.** Ed. by Martin Costabel et al. LC 94-32078. (Lecture Notes in Pure & Applied Mathematics Ser.: Vol. 167). 1994. 135.00 (0-8247-9320-X) Dekker.

Boundary Value Problems & Orthogonal Expansions: Physical Problems from a Sobolev Viewpoint. C. R. MacCluer. LC 94-20004. 368p. 1994. 64.95 (0-7803-1071-3, PC04226) Inst Electrical.

Boundary Value Problems & Partial Differential Equations. Humi & Miller. (C). 1992. text ed. 63.95 (0-534-92880-3) PWS Pubs.

Boundary Value Problems for Analytic Functions. J. K. Lu. (Series in Pure Mathematics: No. 16). 450p. 1994. text ed. 74.00 (981-02-1020-5) World Scientific Pub.

Boundary Value Problems for Elliptic Pseudodifferential Equations. G. I. Eskin. Tr. by S F. Smith. LC 80-39789. (Translations of Mathematical Monographs-MMONO: No. 52). 375p. 1981. reprint ed. pap. 108.00 (0-8218-4503-9, MMONO-52) Am Math.

***Boundary Value Problems for Elliptic Pseudofifferential Equations.** fac. ed. Grigorii I. Eskin. LC 80-39789. (Translations of Mathematical Monographs: No. 52). 389p. 1994. pap. 110.90 (0-7837-7553-9, 2047306) Bks Demand.

***Boundary Value Problems for Elliptic Systems.** J. T. Wloka et al. (Illus.). 515p. (C). 1995. write for info. (0-521-43011-9) Cambridge U Pr.

Boundary Value Problems for Linear Evolution-Partial Differential Equations. Ed. by H. G. Garnir. (NATO Advanced Study Institutes Series C, Mathematical & Physical Sciences: No. 29). 1977. lib. bdg. 112.50 (90-277-0788-X) Kluwer Ac.

Boundary Value Problems for Operator Differential Equations. V. I. Gorbachuk & M. L. Gorbachuk. (C). 1991. lib. bdg. 164.00 (0-7923-0381-4) Kluwer Ac.

Boundary Value Problems for Partial Differential Equations & Applications in Electrodynamics. N. E. Tovmasyan. 350p. 1994. text ed. 74.00 (981-02-1351-4) World Scientific Pub.

Boundary Value Problems from Higher Order Differential Equations. Ravi P. Agarwal. 310p. 1986. text ed. 51.00 (9971-5-0108-2) World Scientific Pub.

Boundary Value Problems in Abstract Kinetic Theory. W. Greenberg et al. (Operator Theory Ser.: Vol. 23). 532p. 1987. 120.00 (0-8176-1765-5) Birkhauser.

Boundary Value Problems in Queueing Systems Analysis. J. W. Cohen & O. J. Boxma. (Mathematical Studies: Vol. 79). 1991. 68.75 (0-444-86567-5, I-010-83) Elsevier.

Boundary Value Problems of Applied Mathematics. John L. Troutman & Maurino Bautista. LC 93-40335. 1994. text ed. 67.95 (0-534-19116-9) PWS Pubs.

Boundary Value Problems of Finite Elasticity. T. Valent. (Tracts in Natural Philosophy Ser.: Vol. 31). 190p. 1987. 69.00 (0-387-96550-5) Spr-Verlag.

872

An Asterisk (*) at the beginning of an entry indicates that the title is appearing in BIP for the first time.

Boundary Value Problems of Heat Conduction. Ozisik. 1989. pap. 11.95 (*0-486-65990-9*) Dover.

Boundary Value Problems of Linear Partial Differential Equations for Engineers & Scientists. S. S. Shu. 288p. 1987. text ed. 79.00 (*9971-5-0417-0*); pap. text ed. 47.00 (*9971-5-0418-9*) World Scientific Pub.

Boundary Value Problems of Mathematical Physics. Incl. Vol. 10. Ed. by O. A. Ladyzhenskaja. 213p. 1981. 101.00 (*0-8218-3068-6*); Vol. 9. Ed. by O. A. Ladyzhenskaja. 179p. 1977. 59.00 (*0-8218-3027-9*); Vol. 3. Proceedings. Steklov Institute of Mathematics, Academy of Sciences, U. S. S. R. Staff. Ed. by O. A. Ladyzhenskaja. 184p. 1967. 58.00 (*0-8218-1883-X*, STEKLO-83); Vol. 4. Proceedings. Steklov Institute of Mathematics, Academy of Sciences, U. S. S. R. Staff. Ed. by O. A. Ladyzhenskaja. 339p. 1968. 96.00 (*0-8218-1892-9*, STEKLO-92); Vol. 5. Proceedings. Ed. by O. A. Ladyzhenskaja. 185p. 1979. 57.00 (*0-8218-3002-3*, STEKLO-102); Vol. 6. Proceedings. Steklov Institute of Mathematics, Academy of Sciences, U. S. S. R. Staff. Ed. by O. A. Ladyzhenskaja. 210p. 1972. 58.00 (*0-8218-3010-4*, STEKLO-110); Vol. 7. Proceedings. Steklov Institute of Mathematics. Ed. by O. A. Ladyzhenskaja. 245p. 1973. 84.00 (*0-8218-3016-3*, STEKLO-116); Vol. 8. Ed. by O. A. Ladyzhenskaja. 226p. 1992. 77.00 (*0-8218-3084-8*); (Proceedings of the Steklov Institute of Mathematics Ser.). Date not set. write for info. (*0-318-59451-X*, STEKLO-159) Am Math.

Boundary Value Problems of Mathematical Physics. Olga A. Ladyzhenskaya. Tr. by J. Lohwater. (Applied Mathematical Sciences Ser.: Vol. 49). 350p. 1985. 87.00 (*0-387-90989-3*) Spr-Verlag.

Boundary Value Problems of Mathematical Physics & Related Aspects of Function Theory. Ed. by O. A. Ladyzhenskaya. LC 69-12506. (Seminars in Mathematics Ser.: Vol. 14, Pt. 4). (Illus.). 163p. (RUS.). reprint ed. pap. 46.50 (*0-8357-7369-8*, 2020698) Bks Demand.

Boundary Value Problems of Mathematical Physics VIII: Proceedings. Steklov Institute of Mathematics, Academy of Sciences, U. S. S. R. Staff. Ed. by O. A. Ladyzenskaja. LC 67-6187. (Proceedings of the Steklov Institute of Mathematics Ser.: No. 125). 217p. 1975. 89.00 (*0-8218-3025-2*, STEKLO-125) Am Math.

Boundary Value Problems of Mathematical Physics XIII. O. Ladyzhenskaya. LC 67-6187. (STEKLO Ser.: Vol. 179). 266p. 1989. pap. 139.00 (*0-8218-3127-5*, STEKLO-179) Am Math.

Boundary Value Problems of Mathematical Physics, XIV. Ed. by O. A. Ladyzhenskaya. LC 67-6187. (Proceedings of the Steklov Institute of Mathematics Ser.: Vol. 188). 239p. 1991. reprint ed. 132.00 (*0-8218-3141-0*, STEKLO/188C) Am Math.

Boundary-Value Problems with Free Boundaries for Elliptic Systems of Equations. V. N. Monakhov. Tr. by H. H. McFaden. LC 83-2754. (Translations of Mathematical Monographs: Vol. 57). 522p. 1983. 149.00 (*0-8218-4510-1*, MMONO/57C) Am Math.

Boundary Walls: Caste & Women in a Tamil Community. Kamala Ganesh. (C). 1993. 28.00 (*81-7075-023-7*, Pub. by Hindustan IA) S Asia.

Boundary Waters. Barbara Field. 1993. 4.75 (*0-8222-1325-7*) Dramatists Play.

Boundary Waters. Jerry Stebbins & Greg Breining. (Illus.). 94p. 1992. pap. 10.99 (*0-931714-48-6*) Nodin Pr.

*__Boundary Waters: Canoe Camping with Style.__ Cliff Jacobson. (Illus.). 144p. 1995. 11.95 (*1-57034-007-2*) ICS Bks.

*__Boundary Waters: The Fight for the Boundary Waters Canoe Area.__ Kevin Proescholdt & Rip Rapson. (Illus.). 160p. (Orig.). 1995. 12.95 (*0-87839-100-2*) North Star.

Boundary Waters Canoe Area: Wilderness Values & Motorized Recreation. James N. Gladden. LC 89-26813. (Illus.). 166p. 1990. text ed. 21.95 (*0-8138-0151-6*) Iowa St U Pr.

Boundary Waters Canoe Area, Vol. 1: The Western Region. 5th ed. Robert Beymer. (Illus.). 173p. 1994. pap. 14.95 (*0-89997-165-2*) Wilderness Pr.

Boundary Waters Canoe Area, Vol. 2: The Eastern Region. 3rd ed. Robert Beymer. LC 85-40197. (Illus.). 160p. 1991. 14.95 (*0-89997-124-5*) Wilderness Pr.

Boundary Waters Fishing Guide. Michael J. Furtman. LC 84-70248. (Illus.). 176p. 1984. 16.95 (*0-916691-01-2*); pap. 8.95 (*0-916691-00-4*) Birch Portage.

Boundary Waters Fishing Guide. Mike Furtman. 160p. 1988. pap. 9.95 (*1-55971-073-X*) NorthWord.

*__Boundaryless Organization: Breaking the Chains of Organizational Structure.__ Ron Ashkenas et al. (Management Ser.). 1995. write for info. (*0-7879-0113-X*) Jossey-Bass.

Bounded & Almost Periodic Solutions of Nonlinear Operator Differential Equations. A. A. Pankov. (C). 1990. lib. bdg. 115.50 (*0-7923-0585-X*) Kluwer Ac.

*__Bounded Arithmetic, Propositional Logic, & Complexity Theory.__ Jan Krajicek. (Encyclopedia of Mathematics & Its Applications Ser.: No. 60). 350p. (C). Date not set. write for info. (*0-521-45205-8*) Cambridge U Pr.

Bounded Integral Operatores on L Two Spaces. P. R. Halmos & V. S. Sunder. (Ergebnisse der Mathematik und Ihrer Grenzgebiete Ser.: Vol. 96). 1978. 42.00 (*0-387-08894-6*) Spr-Verlag.

Bounded Rational Behavior in Experimental Games & Markets. Ed. by R. Tietz et al. (Lecture Notes in Economics & Mathematical Systems Ser.: Vol. 314). vi, 368p. 1988. pap. 47.90 (*0-387-50036-7*) Spr-Verlag.

Bounded Rationality in Macroeconomics. Thomas J. Sargent. (Arne Ryde Memorial Lectures). 200p. 1993. 29.95 (*0-19-828864-6*) OUP.

Bounded Rationality in Macroeconomics. Thomas J. Sargent. (Arne Ryde Memorial Lectures). 200p. 1994. pap. 16.95 (*0-19-828869-7*) OUP.

Boundedness Results for Operators with Singular Kernels on Distribution Spaces. R. Torres. (MEMO Ser.: Vol. 90/442). 172p. 1991. 19.00 (*0-8218-2505-4*, MEMO 90/442) Am Math.

Bounden Duty: The Memoirs of a German Officer 1932-45. Alexander Stahlberg. (Illus.). 410p. 1990. text ed. 24.95 (*0-08-036714-3*, Pub. by Brasseys UK) Brasseys Inc.

*__Bounder & a Cad.__ George Ashley. 230p. 1995. pap. 8.95 (*1-56901-865-0*) NW Pub.

Bounding Approach to VLSI Circuit Simulation. Charles Zukowski. 1986. lib. bdg. 65.50 (*0-89838-176-2*) Kluwer Ac.

Boundless. Alexandra Thorne. 432p. 1994. mass mkt. 4.99 (*0-7860-0059-7*) Windsor NY.

*__Boundless Energy.__ Deepak Chopra. 1995. 15.00 (*0-517-79974-X*, Harmony) Crown Pub Group.

Boundless Function. Arthur Gibson. LC 87-73051. (Illus.). 96p. (Orig.). 1988. pap. 14.95 (*1-85224-038-5*, Pub. by Bloodaxe Bks UK) Dufour.

*__Boundless Grace.__ Mary Hoffman. LC 94-31209. (Illus.). (J). 1995. 14.99 (*0-8037-1715-6*) Dial Bks Young.

Boundless Privilege. Oren Arnold. LC 74-81628. 192p. 1974. 10.95 (*0-89052-007-0*) Madrona Pr.

Boundless Resource: A Prospectus for an Education-Work Policy. National Manpower Institute Staff & Willard Wirtz. 205p. 1975. 10.00 (*0-915220-10-5*) Natl Inst Work.

*__Bounds of Freedom: About the Eastern & Western Approaches to Freedom.__ Oded Balaban & Anan Erev. (American University Series V: Vol. 165). 200p. (C). 1995. pap. text ed. 41.95 (*0-8204-2514-1*) P Lang Pubs.

Bounds of Interpretation: Linguistic Theory & Literary Text. Ellen Schauber & Ellen Spolsky. LC 85-26218. 232p. 1986. 32.50 (*0-8047-1300-6*) Stanford U Pr.

Bounds of Logic: A Generalized Viewpoint. Gila Sher. (Illus.). 160p. 1991. 30.00 (*0-262-19311-6*, Bradford Bks) MIT Pr.

Bounds of Possibility: The Legacy of Steve Biko & Black Consciousness. Ed. by Barney Pityana et al. 288p. (C). 1991. text ed. 49.95 (*1-85649-047-5*, Pub. by Zed Books UK); pap. 17.50 (*1-85649-048-3*, Pub. by Zed Books UK) Humanities.

Bounds of Race: Perspectives on Hegemony & Resistance. Ed. by Dominick LaCapra. LC 91-11896. 360p. 1991. 44.50 (*0-8014-2553-0*); pap. 16.95 (*0-8014-9789-2*) Cornell U Pr.

Bounds of Reason: Cervantes, Dostoevsky, Flaubert. Anthony J. Cascardi. LC 85-99994. 288p. 1986. text ed. 44.00 (*0-231-06212-5*) Col U Pr.

Bounds of Sense: An Essay on Kant's Critique of Pure Reason. P. F. Strawson. 296p. 1966. pap. 17.95 (*0-415-04030-2*, NO.2532) Routledge Chapman & Hall.

Bounds on Transfer Principles for Algebraically Closed & Complete Discretely Valued Fields. Scott S. Brown. LC 78-9121. (Memoirs of the American Mathematical Society Ser.: Vol. 204). 92p. 1978. 19.00 (*0-8218-2204-7*, MEMO/15/204C) Am Math.

Bounteous Koran: A Translation of Meaning & Commentary. M. M. Khatib. 850p. 1989. 65.00 (*0-333-34738-2*) St Martin.

Bountiful. Michael Waters. (Poetry Ser.). 72p. (Orig.). 1992. lib. bdg. 16.95 (*0-88748-139-6*); pap. 9.95 (*0-88748-140-X*) Carnegie-Mellon.

Bountiful Blooms: Preserving Flowers with Colour. Margaret Burch. (Illus.). 106p. 1994. 19.95 (*1-86351-101-6*, Pub. by S Milner AT) Sterling.

*__Bountiful Harvest.__ Ed. by Mary B. Jung. 99p. 1994. 9.98 (*0-89821-118-2*) Reiman Pubns.

Bountiful Island: A Study of Land Tenure on a Micronesian Atoll. David Damas. (Illus.). (C). 1994. text ed. 55.00 (*0-88920-239-7*, Pub. by Wilfrid Laurier CN) Humanities.

Bountiful Ohio: Good Food & Stories from Where the Heartland Begins. James Hope & Susan Failor. (Illus.). 224p. (Orig.). 1993. 21.95 (*0-911861-06-8*); pap. 14.95 (*0-911861-05-X*) Gabriels Horn.

*__Bountiful Temple: Cross-Stitch Leaflet.__ Jean D. Crowther. 8p. 1994. pap. 3.98 (*0-88290-496-5*, 2838) Horizon Utah.

Bountiful Year: Cooking Through the Seasons in Maine. Ed. by Roberta Bailey & Jean English. (Cookbook Ser.). (Illus.). 220p. 1990. spiral bd. 12.00 (*0-9621498-2-9*, Robin Hood) R Hood Little.

Bounty Beware. Owen G. Irons. (Orig.). 1982. pap. 2.50 (*0-8217-1028-1*) Zebra.

Bounty Hunter. Bob Burton. (Illus.). 136p. 1984. pap. 12.00 (*0-87364-296-1*) Paladin Pr.

Bounty Hunter. Aaron Fletcher. 160p. 1981. pap. 1.75 (*0-8439-1006-2*) Dorchester Pub Co.

Bounty Hunter. Donna Kauffman. (Loveswept Ser.: No. 707). 1994. pap. 3.50 (*0-553-44425-5*) Bantam.

Bounty Hunter. Rick Miller. LC 88-7168. (Early West Ser.). (Illus.). 256p. 1988. 21.95 (*0-932702-41-4*) Creative Texas.

Bounty Hunter. Vicki L. Thompson. 1994. mass mkt. 2.99 (*0-373-25616-7*, 1-25616-3) Harlequin Bks.

Bounty Hunters. Elmore Leonard. 1993. mass mkt. 3.99 (*0-440-21306-1*) Dell.

Bounty in Bondage: The Anglican Church in Southern Africa, Essays in Honour of Edward King, Dean of Cape Town. Ed. by Frank England & Torquil Paterson. 222p. (Orig.). 1989. pap. text ed. 17.95 (*0-86975-383-5*, Pub. by Ravan Pr ZA) Ohio U Pr.

Bounty Killer. John Benteen. (Sundance Ser.: No. 15). 144p. 1981. pap. 1.75 (*0-8439-1050-X*) Dorchester Pub Co.

Bounty Lands. William D. Ellis. LC 52-5196. (Trilogy Ser.: No. 1). 495p. 1981. reprint ed. pap. 5.95 (*0-913428-20-5*) Landfall Pr.

Bounty Lands of the American Revolution in Ohio. William T. Hutchinson. Ed. by Stuart Bruchey. LC 78-56675. (Management of Public Lands in the U. S. Ser.). (Illus.). 1979. lib. bdg. 31.95 (*0-405-11336-6*) Ayer.

Bounty of Texas. Ed. by Francis E. Abernethy. LC 90-12417. (Publications of the Texas Folklore Society: No. 49). (Illus.). 254p. 1990. 19.95 (*0-929398-14-9*) UNTX Pr.

Bounty of the Chesapeake: Fishing in Colonial Virginia. James Wharton. (Jamestown 350th Anniversary Historical Booklet Ser.: No. 13). (Illus.). 96p. reprint ed. pap. 27.40 (*0-8357-3734-9*, 2036460) Bks Demand.

Bounty of the Earth Cookbook. Sylvia G. Bashline. 280p. 1994. pap. 14.95 (*1-55821-302-3*) Lyons & Burford.

Bounty of the Wayside. Walter B. Wilder. LC 72-93386. (Essay Index Reprint Ser.). 1977. 21.95 (*0-8369-1637-9*) Ayer.

Bounty on the Brandywine. Barbara B. Matuszewki. (Illus.). 324p. 1988. 35.00 (*0-912608-56-0*); pap. 24.95 (*0-912608-63-3*) Mid Atlantic.

Bounty Trilogy. Charles Nordhoff & James N. Hall. 1985. pap. 19.95 (*0-316-61166-2*) Little.

Bouquet. Henri Calet. 320p. (FRE.). 1983. pap. 12.95 (*0-7859-1974-0*, 2070374645) Fr & Eur.

Bouquet. Shirl Henke. 384p. (Orig.). 1994. pap. 4.99 (*0-451-40516-1*, Onyx) NAL-Dutton.

Bouquet. Tasha Tudor. Ed. by Jenny Wren. LC 89-51275. (Illus.). (Orig.). 1990. pap. text ed. 6.95 (*0-9621753-4-X*) Jenny Wren Pr.

Bouquet. deluxe limited ed. Harry Burrus. LC 88-63413. (Illus.). 75p. 1990. 30.00 (*0-941749-03-7*); pap. 20.00 (*0-941749-05-3*) Black Tie Pr.

Bouquet. limited ed. Harry Burrus. LC 88-63413. (Illus.). 75p. 1990. Contains print by author. 45.00 (*0-941749-07-X*) Black Tie Pr.

Bouquet de Bourgogne: Seasonal Recipes from La Cote St. Jacques, Joigny. Michel Lorain & Jean-Michel Lorain. (Illus.). 96p. 1994. 16.95 (*1-85793-396-6*, Pub. by Pavilion UK) Trafalgar.

Bouquet de Bretagne: Seasonal Recipes from Le Bretagne, Questembert. Georges Paineau. (Illus.). 96p. 1993. 17.95 (*1-85145-788-7*, Pub. by Pavilion UK) Trafalgar.

Bouquet for Murder. Jan Meins. (Illus.). 106p. 1987. pap. 13.95 (*0-914546-74-0*) Rose Pub.

Bouquet for Our Lives & Deaths. Ed. by Paul Wade. LC 79-67040. 1980. write for info. (*0-933838-02-6*) Swampgas.

Bouquet from the Kitchen. Jane Resnick. (Illus.). 64p. 1991. 5.95 (*0-681-41124-4*) Longmeadow Pr.

*__Bouquet of Flowers: A Treasury of Blossoms.__ (Miniature Pop-up Bks.). (Illus.). 12p. 1995. 4.95 (*1-56138-574-3*) Running Pr.

Bouquet of Flowers: Sweet Thoughts, Recipes, & Gifts from the Garden, with "The Language of Flowers" Barbara M. Ohrbach. (Illus.). 1990. 9.95 (*0-517-57428-4*, C P Pubs) Crown Pub Group.

Bouquet of Good-Byes. Carole G. Page. (Kasey Carlone Ser.). (YA). 1992. pap. 4.99 (*0-8024-8180-9*) Moody.

Bouquet of Memories for Mother. Frank Carpenter. Ed. by Judi Williams. (Bouquet of Memories Ser.). (Illus.). 80p. 1988. 9.95 (*0-937769-06-1*) Mark Inc CA.

Bouquet of Memories for Mother. Frank Carpenter. 1990. pap. 5.95 (*0-937769-14-2*) Mark Inc CA.

Bouquet of Memories from the Heart. Frank Carpenter. Ed. by Judi Williams. (Bouquet Ser.). (Illus.). 88p. 1990. 9.95 (*0-937769-40-1*) Mark Inc CA.

Bouquet of Memories from the Heart. Mark Publishing Staff. 1991. 9.95 (*0-937769-15-0*) Mark Inc CA.

Bouquet of Memories Journal. Judi Williams. (Bouquet Ser.). (Illus.). 144p. 1990. 9.95 (*0-937769-17-7*) Mark Inc CA.

*__Bouquet of Night Flowers: Journey of a Soul Through Loss, Grief & Healing.__ Ellie Rezabek-Turner. (Illus.). 80p. (Orig.). 1995. pap. 12.00 (*0-9646595-3-0*) LinkaAges.

Bouquet of Roses. Pat Nation. LC 89-83522. (Illus.). 110p. 1989. lib. bdg. 12.95 (*0-944419-09-7*) Everett Cos Pub.

Bouquets, Brambles, & Buena Vista or "Down Home". Susan Turner. LC 76-7852. 1976. 5.95 (*0-87397-094-2*) Strode.

Bourbaki Gambit: A Novel by Carl Djerassi. Carl Djerassi. LC 93-44392. 240p. (C). 1994. 19.95 (*0-8203-1652-0*) U of Ga Pr.

*__Bourbon County, Kentucky Taxpayers, 1787-1799.__ T.L.C. Genealogy Staff. LC 92-64441. 173p. (Orig.). 1992. spiral bd., pap. 12.00 (*1-886633-06-1*) TLC Genealogy.

Bourbon Democracy in Alabama, 1874-1890. Allen J. Going. (Library of Alabama Classics). 280p. 1992. reprint ed. pap. 19.95 (*0-8173-0580-7*) U of Ala Pr.

Bourbon Democracy of the Middle West, 1865-1896. Horace S. Merrill. LC 53-8592. (Americana Library Ser.: No. 2). (Illus.). 1969. reprint ed. 20.00 (*0-295-97857-0*, AL2); reprint ed. pap. 10.00 (*0-295-95032-3*, ALP2) U of Wash Pr.

Bourbon Restoration. Guillaume De Bertier De Sauvigny. Tr. by Lynn M. Case. LC 67-17175. 514p. reprint ed. 146.50 (*0-8357-9746-5*, 2051109) Bks Demand.

Bourbon Spain: Seventeen Hundred to Eighteen Hundred Eight. John Lynch. (History of Spain Ser.). (Illus.). 400p. (C). 1989. text ed. 59.95 (*0-631-14576-1*) Blackwell Pubs.

Bourbon Spain: 1700-1808. John Lynch. 1994. pap. 21.95 (*0-631-19245-X*) Blackwell Pubs.

*__Bourdon Advanced Pick: Database & Operating System 2E.__ 2nd ed. Bourdon. (C). 1996. pap. text ed. 39.75 (*0-201-87696-5*) Addison-Wesley.

Bourdon Tubes & Bourdon Tube Gages: An Annotated Bibliography. Ed. by Geza Kardos. LC 77-93948. 44p. reprint ed. pap. 25.00 (*0-8357-8705-2*, 2033636) Bks Demand.

Boure (Boo-Ray) A Louisiana Card Game. Nickens. 1972. 4.95 (*0-685-37721-0*) Claitors.

Bourgeois & the Bibelot. Remy G. Saisselin. LC 84-4701. (Illus.). 240p. (C). 1984. 35.00x (*0-8135-1062-7*) Rutgers U Pr.

Bourgeois As Hero. Heinz Schlaffer. Tr. by James Lynn. 200p. (C). 1989. text ed. 51.00 (*0-389-20889-2*, N 8447) B&N Imports.

Bourgeois Blues: An American Memoir. Jake Lamar. LC 92-53557. 176p. 1992. pap. 9.00 (*0-452-26911-3*, Plume) NAL-Dutton.

*__Bourgeois de la Compagnie du Nord-Ouest, Recits de Voyages, Lettres et Rapports Inedits Relatifs au Nord-Ouest Canadien Avec une Esquisse Historique et des Annotations Series 1, Vol. 2: McDonald, John-Autobiographical Notes; Keith, George-Letters to Mr. Roderic McKenzie 1807-1817, Johnston, John-an Account of Lake Superior 1792-1807, Wilcooke, Samuel H.-Death of Mr. Benjamin Frobisher 1819, Duncan, Cameron-Nipigon Country 1804, Peter, Grant-Sauteaux Indians, 1804, McKenzie, James-Extracts from His Journal 1799-1800, Athabasca District, McKenzie, James-King's Posts & Journal of a.__ Ed. by L. R. Masson. 499p. 1960. 100.00x (*0-614-01804-8*) Elliots Bks.

B

Bourgeois Element in the Dramas of Thomas Heywood. F. Mowbray Velte. LC 65-21092. (Studies in Drama: No. 39). 1969. reprint ed. lib. bdg. 75.00 (*0-8383-0641-1*) M S G Haskell Hse.

Bourgeois Epoch: Marx & Engels on Britain, France, & Germany. Richard F. Hamilton. LC 91-50252. xiv, 294p. (C). 1991. 39.95 (*0-8078-1976-X*); pap. 14.95 (*0-8078-4325-3*) U of NC Pr.

Bourgeois Experience-Victoria to Freud: Education of the Senses, Vol. I. Peter Gay. (Illus.). 576p. 1984. 35.00 (*0-19-503352-3*) OUP.

Bourgeois Experience-Victoria to Freud: Education of the Senses, Vol. I. Peter Gay. (Illus.). 576p. 1985. pap. 13.95 (*0-19-503728-6*) OUP.

Bourgeois Experience-Victoria to Freud: The Tender Passion, Vol. II. Peter Gay. 1986. 35.00 (*0-19-503741-3*) OUP.

Bourgeois Experience-Victoria to Freud: The Tender Passion, Vol. II. Peter Gay. (Illus.). 512p. 1987. pap. 15.95 (*0-19-505183-1*) OUP.

Bourgeois Gentilhomme. Moliere. Ed. by Jean Thoraval. 64p. (FRE.). 1975. 7.95 (*0-7859-0050-0*, FC1413) Fr & Eur.

Bourgeois Gentilhomme. Adapt. by Pierre Spierckel. 80p. 1993. pap. 6.95 (*0-8442-1188-5*, Natl Textbk) NTC Pub Grp.

Bourgeois Gentilhomme. Les Femmes Savantes. Le Malade Imaginaire. Moliere. (Folio Ser.: No. 334). 448p. (FRE.). 1973. pap. 10.95 (*2-07-036334-1*) Schoenhof.

Bourgeois Gentilhomme. Les Femmes Savantes. Le Malade Imaginaire. Moliere. (FRE.). 1973. pap. 12.95 (*0-7859-2874-X*, 2070363341) Fr & Eur.

Bourgeois Mind, & Other Essays. Nicolas Berdyaev. LC 67-22072. (Essay Index Reprint Ser.). 1977. 22.95 (*0-8369-0198-3*) Ayer.

*__Bourgeois Politics in France 1945-1951.__ Richard Vinen. (Illus.). 304p. (C). 1995. 59.95 (*0-521-47451-5*) Cambridge U Pr.

Bourgeois Revolution. 3rd ed. George Plechanoff. Tr. by Henry Kuhn. 1968. pap. text ed. 0.50 (*0-935534-05-9*) NY Labor News.

Bourgeois Society in the Nineteenth-Century. Ed. by Jurgen Kocka & Alan Mitchell. Tr. by Gus Fagan. 448p. 1993. 74.00 (*0-85496-676-5*) Berg Pubs.

Bourgeois Society in 19th Century Europe. Ed. by Jurgen Kocka & Allan Mitchell. 480p. 1994. pap. 19.95 (*0-85496-414-2*) Berg Pubs.

Bourgeois Utopias: The Rise & Fall of Suburbia. Robert Fishman. LC 87-47508. (Illus.). 272p. 1989. pap. text ed. 13.00 (*0-465-00747-3*) Basic.

Bourgeoisie Inside Out: A History of Clothing in the Nineteenth Century. Tr. by Philippe Perrot & Richard Bienvenu. LC 93-40094. 1994. 29.95 (*0-691-03383-8*); 16.95 (*0-691-00081-6*) Princeton U Pr.

Bourgmestre de Fumes, Malempin, les Inconnus Dans la Masion. Georges Simenon. 1148p. (FRE.). 1992. 49.95 (*0-7859-0494-8*, 2258035279) Fr & Eur.

Bourgmestre de Furnes. Georges Simenon. (FRE.). 1977. pap. 10.95 (*0-7859-4077-4*) Fr & Eur.

Bourgmestre de Stilmonde. Maurice Maeterlinck. 216p. (FRE.). 1967. reprint ed. pap. 11.95 (*0-7859-0931-1*) Fr & Eur.

Bourgmont: Explorer of the Missouri, 1698-1725. Frank Norall. LC 88-4013. (Illus.). x, 192p. 1988. 22.50 (*0-8032-3316-7*) U of Nebr Pr.

Bourgogne Green Guide. 3rd ed. (FRE.). Date not set. pap. 18.00 (*2-06-700307-0*, 307) Michelin.

*__Bourgogne Green Guide French Edition.__ Michelin Staff. (FRE.). Date not set. pap. 17.95 (*0-7859-7222-6*, 2067003070) Fr & Eur.

Bourke Cockran: A Free Lance in American Politics. James McGurrin. LC 74-172219. (Right Wing Individualist Tradition in America Ser.). 1972. reprint ed. 28.95 (*0-405-00428-1*) Ayer.

Bourke Engine Documentary. 1990. 24.50 (*0-914119-13-3*) Tesla Bk Co.

Bourke's Diary: From Journals of First Lieutenant John Gregory Bourke, from June 27-September 15, during Indian War of Eighteen Seventy-Six. John G. Bourke et al. Ed. & Intro. by James Willert. (Illus.). 270p. 1986. 40.00 (*0-930798-09-0*); pap. text ed. 25.00 (*0-930798-10-4*) J Willert.

An Asterisk (*) at the beginning of an entry indicates that the title is appearing in BIP for the first time. 873

Bourlinguer. Blaise Cendrars. (FRE.). 1974. pap. 11.95 (*0-7859-1789-6*, 2070366022) Fr & Eur.

Bourne Identity. Robert Ludlum. 544p. (Orig.). 1984. mass mkt. 6.99 (*0-553-26011-1*) Bantam.

Bourne Identity. Robert Ludlum. 1987. pap. 16.99 (*0-553-45053-0*) Bantam.

Bourne Shell Quick Reference Guide. Anatole Olczak. 44p. (Orig.). 1991. pap. text ed. 9.95 (*0-935739-22-X*) A System Pubns.

Bourne Supremacy. Robert Ludlum. 656p. 1987. mass mkt. 6.99 (*0-553-26322-6*) Bantam.

Bourne Ultimatum. Robert Ludlum. 1990. 21.95 (*0-394-58408-2*) Random.

Bourne Ultimatum. Robert Ludlum. 1991. mass mkt. 6.99 (*0-553-28773-7*) Bantam.

Bourne Ultimatum. large type ed. Robert Ludlum. 1312p. 1990. 24.45 (*0-679-40043-5*) Random.

Bournemouth Coast Path. Leigh Hatts. 80p. 1987. 35.00 (*0-905392-49-3*) St Mut.

Bournemouth Then & Now: A Pictorial Past. Ed. by John Peters & Roger Guttridge. (C). 1989. 39.00 (*1-85455-024-1*, Pub. by Ensign Pubns & Print UK) St Mut.

Bournonville Ballet Technique: Fifty Enchainements. Vivi Flindt & Knud A. Jurgensen. (Illus.). 142p. (C). 1992. text ed. 49.95 (*1-85273-035-8*, Pub. by Dance Bks UK) Princeton Bk Co.

B

Bournonville Ballet Technique: Piano Scores. Knud A. Jurgensen. 44p. (C). 1992. pap. text ed. 29.95 (*1-85273-036-6*, Pub. by Dance Bks UK) Princeton Bk Co.

Bournonville Ballets: A Photographic Record 1844-1933. Knud A. Jurgensen. (Illus.). 200p. 1987. lib. bdg. 100.00 (*0-903102-98-6*, Pub. by Dance Bks UK) Princeton Bk Co.

Bournonville Heritage: A Choreographic Record, 1829-1875; Twenty-Four Unknown Dances in Labanotation. Knud A. Jurgensen & Ann H. Guest. (Illus.). 208p. 1990. 100.00 (*1-85273-025-0*, Pub. by Dance Bks UK) Princeton Bk Co.

Bournonville School, Pt. 4: Labanotation. Ed. by Kirsten Ralov. LC 78-9554. (Dance Program Ser.: Vol. 12). 137p. reprint ed. Pt. 4 - Labanotation. pap. 39.10 (*0-8357-7370-1*, 2027074) Bks Demand.

Bourrichon. 2nd ed. Mary Kennedy. 1976. pap. 3.95 (*0-910664-40-4*) Gotham.

Bourton on the Water. Tony Wray & David Stratford. (Illus.). 96p. 1994. pap. 14.00 (*0-7509-0577-8*) A Sutton Pub.

Boussingault. F. W. McCosh. 1984. lib. bdg. 119.00 (*90-277-1682-X*) Kluwer Ac.

Bout-Galeux. Jean-Pierre Chabrol. (FRE.). 1978. pap. 11.95 (*0-7859-1865-5*, 2070369927) Fr & Eur.

Bouteneff Family Chronicle. Michael C. Bouteneff. (Illus.). 300p. (Orig.). 1989. pap. write for info. (*0-318-65398-2*) M C Bouteneff.

Boutique Bean Pot: Exciting Bean Varieties in Superb New Recipes! Kathleen Mayes & Sandra Gottfried. LC 92-7572. (Illus.). 208p. (Orig.). 1992. pap. 12.95 (*0-88007-196-6*) Woodbridge Pr.

Boutique Bonanza: Crochet, Knit, Tat, Plastic Canvas & More. Workbasket Staff. 1994. pap. 9.95 (*0-86675-308-7*) KC Pub.

Bouton Boughton Family. J. Boughton. (Illus.). 684p. 1988. reprint ed. lib. bdg. 100.00 (*0-8328-0286-7*); reprint ed. pap. 90.00 (*0-8328-0287-5*) Higginson Bk Co.

Bouts de Bois de Dieu. Ousmane Sembene. (FRE.). 1988. pap. 10.95 (*0-7859-3220-8*, 2266023195) Fr & Eur.

***Bouts of Glory & Fields of Dreams: Great Stadiums & Ballparks of North America.** Steve Blickstein. (Illus.). 128p. 1995. 29.95 (*1-882933-05-2*) Cherbo Pub Grp.

Bouvard & Pecuchet. Gustave Flaubert. Tr. by Alban J. Krailsheimer. (Classics Ser.). 336p. 1976. mass mkt. 9.95 (*0-14-044320-7*, Penguin Classics) Viking Penguin.

Bouvard et Pecuchet. Gustave Flaubert. Ed. by Maynial. (FRE.). 1954. pap. 10.95 (*0-7859-0123-X*, M5433) Fr & Eur.

Bouvard et Pecuchet; Le Dictionnaire des Idees Recues; Le Sottisier, etc. Gustave Flaubert. (Folio Ser.: No. 1137). (FRE.). pap. 12.95 (*2-07-037137-9*) Schoenhof.

Bouvard et Pecuchet suivi de les Sottisier. Gustave Flaubert. 570p. (FRE.). 1979. pap. 12.95 (*0-7859-2423-X*, 2070371379) Fr & Eur.

Bouvier des Flanders: The Dogs of Flanders Fields. James Engel. LC 90-28418. (Illus.). 256p. 1991. 28.95 (*0-931866-53-7*) Alpine Pubns.

Bouvier des Flandres. Gerene C. Legget. (Illus.). 192p. 1989. lib. bdg. 11.95 (*0-86622-691-5*, KW-168) TFH Pubns.

Bouvier des Flandres. 2nd ed. Claire McLean. LC 80-66115. (Breed Bks.). (Illus.). 1981. 29.95 (*0-87714-077-4*) Denlingers.

Bouvier Records. Claire D. McLean. (Breed Bks.). (Illus.). 1991. pap. 24.95 (*0-87714-149-5*) Denlingers.

Bouviers: From Waterloo to the Kennedys & Beyond. John H. Davis. 1993. 24.95 (*0-915765-84-5*) Natl Pr Bks.

***Bouviers: From Waterloo to the Kennedys & Beyond.** John H. Davis. (Illus.). 440p. 1995. pap. text ed. 14.95 (*1-882605-19-5*) Natl Pr Bks.

Bouvier's Law Dictionary, 2 vols., Set. John Bouvier. 1991. lib. bdg. 475.95 (*0-8490-5111-8*) Gordon Pr.

Bouvier's Law Dictionary & Concise Encyclopedia, 2 Vols. in 3 bks. 8th ed. John Bouvier. 3532p. 1994. reprint ed. lib. bdg. 175.00 (*0-89941-335-8*, 303280) W S Hein.

Bouvier's Law Dictionary & Concise Encyclopedia: 1914 Version. unabridged ed. John Bouvier. Ed. by W. E. Baldwin. 1360p. 1992. reprint ed. 120.00 (*1-877767-62-X*) Univ Publng Hse.

***Bouwsma's Notes on Wittgenstein's Philosophy, 1965-1975.** O. K. Bouwsma. Ed. by J. L. Craft & Ronald Hustwit. LC 95-9292. (Studies in the History of Philosophy: Vol. 37). 460p. 1996. text ed. 109.95 (*0-7734-8885-5*) E Mellen.

Boverbindungen-Boron Compounds. Planck, Max, Society for the Advancement of Science, Gmelin Institute for Inorganic Chemistry Staff. (Gmelin Handbuch der Anorganischen Chemie Ser.: Vol. 22, Pt. 4). (Illus.). 360p. 1975. 458.00 (*0-387-93289-5*) Spr-Verlag.

Bovine & Equine Urogenital Surgery. Donald F. Walker & J. T. Vaughan. LC 79-10980. (Illus.). 287p. reprint ed. pap. 81.80 (*0-7837-1500-5*, 2057196) Bks Demand.

Bovine Economy in India. A. Vaidyanathan. (C). 1988. 17.50 (*81-204-0312-6*, Pub. by Oxford IBH II) S Asia.

Bovine Medicine, Diseases & Husbandry of Cattle. A. H. Andrews et al. (Illus.). 940p. 1991. 170.00 (*0-632-03039-9*) Blackwell Sci.

Bovine Practice. William E. Boden. 1991. pap. text ed. 41.95 (*0-7020-1556-3*) Saunders.

Bovine Radiology. Uri Bargai et al. (Venture Series in Veterinary Medicine). (Illus.). 206p. (C). 1989. pap. text ed. 44.95 (*0-8138-0185-0*) Iowa St U Pr.

Bovine Respiratory Disease: A Symposium. Ed. by Raymond W. Loan. LC 83-40491. (Illus.). 544p. 1984. 27.50 (*0-89096-187-5*) Tex A&M Univ Pr.

Bovine Somatotropin & Emerging Issues: An Assessment. M. C. Hallberg. 324p. (C). 1992. pap. text ed. 54.00 (*0-8133-0603-5*) Westview.

Bow: Its History, Manufacture & Use. Henry Saint-George. (Strad Library: No. III). (Illus.). 144p. 1969. reprint ed. lib. bdg. 30.00 (*0-8450-2582-1*) Broude.

Bow & Arrow: The Complete Guide to Equipment, Technique, & Competition. Larry Wise. LC 91-34325. (Illus.). 288p. 1992. pap. 15.95 (*0-8117-2411-5*) Stackpole.

Bow & the Lyre: The Poem. The Poetic Revelation. Poetry & History. Octavio Paz. Tr. by Ruth L. Simms. (Texas Pan American Ser.). 293p. (C). 1987. reprint ed. pap. 12.95 (*0-292-70764-9*) U of Tex Pr.

Bow Angle Tables. Comp. by J. M. Peters. (C). 1987. 40.00 (*0-85174-135-5*, Pub. by Brwn Son Ferg) St Mut.

***Bow Down.** Rich Moore & Ron Rogalski. 1991. 25.00 (*0-614-03115-X*) Lillenas.

Bow Down. Ron Rogalski & Rich Moore. 1991. 5.25 (*0-685-72879-X*, MB-630); audio 10.98 (*0-685-72880-3*, TA-9132C); audio 60.00 (*0-685-72882-X*, MU-9132C); audio 45.00 (*0-685-72884-6*, MU-9132R); cd-rom 60.00 (*0-685-72883-8*, MU-9132T); 6.00 (*0-685-72881-1*, L-9132C); 8.00 (*0-685-72885-4*, MU-926); 36.00 (*0-685-72886-2*, OR-9132); 5.00 (*0-685-72887-0*, MB-630A) Lillenas.

Bow down in Jerico. Byron H. Reece. LC 85-21335. 160p. 1985. reprint ed. 15.95 (*0-87797-102-1*) Cherokee.

Bow Hunting Basics: Fundamentals for Successful Hunting. Dixon Thayer, Sr. Ed. by Vic Spadaccini. (Illus.). 22p. (Orig.). 1985. pap. 2.95 (*0-911493-07-7*) Blue Sky.

Bow Instruments: Their Form & Construction. J. W. Giltay. LC 75-181164. 129p. 1923. reprint ed. 59.00 (*0-403-01566-9*) Scholarly.

Bow Instruments, Their Form & Construction. J. W. Giltay. 129p. 1990. reprint ed. lib. bdg. 59.00 (*0-7812-0394-5*) Rprt Serv.

Bow Jest. Paul Zetter. 212p. (C). 1989. text ed. 59.00 (*1-85821-007-0*, Pub. by Pentland Pr UK) St Mut.

Bow Porcelain. 2nd ed. Elizabeth Adams et al. (Faber Monographs on Pottery & Porcelain). (Illus.). 272p. 1991. 120.00 (*0-571-14467-5*) Faber & Faber.

Bow Shot, Or a Dream from Out the Scrubby Oaks. Adam N. Gladefly. 1991. 13.95 (*0-533-09573-5*) Vantage.

Bow vs. Gun. John Smythe & Humphrey Barwick. 1976. reprint ed. 15.00 (*0-85409-881-X*) Charles River Bks.

Bow Wow! Alabama Dogs in History, Mystery, Legend, Lore, Humor & More! Carole Marsh. (Carole Marsh Alabama Bks.). (Illus.). (J). (gr. 3-12). 1994. lib. bdg. 24.95 (*0-7933-3467-5*); pap. 14.95 (*0-7933-3468-3*); disk 29.95 (*0-7933-3469-1*) Gallopade Pub Group.

Bow Wow! Alaska Dogs in History, Mystery, Legend, Lore, Humor & More! Carole Marsh. (Carole Marsh Alaska Bks.). (Illus.). (J). (gr. 3-12). 1994. lib. bdg. 24.95 (*0-7933-3470-5*); pap. 14.95 (*0-7933-3471-3*); disk 29.95 (*0-7933-3472-1*) Gallopade Pub Group.

Bow Wow! Arizona Dogs in History, Mystery, Legend, Lore, Humor & More! Carole Marsh. (Carole Marsh Arizona Bks.). (Illus.). (J). (gr. 3-12). 1994. lib. bdg. 24.95 (*0-7933-3473-X*); pap. 14.95 (*0-7933-3474-8*); disk 29.95 (*0-7933-3475-6*) Gallopade Pub Group.

Bow Wow! Arkansas Dogs in History, Mystery, Legend, Lore, Humor & More! Carole Marsh. (Carole Marsh Arkansas Bks.). (Illus.). (J). (gr. 3-12). 1994. lib. bdg. 24.95 (*0-7933-3476-4*); pap. 14.95 (*0-7933-3477-2*); disk 29.95 (*0-7933-3478-0*) Gallopade Pub Group.

Bow Wow! California Dogs in History, Mystery, Legend, Lore, Humor & More! Carole Marsh. (Carole Marsh California Bks.). (Illus.). (J). (gr. 3-12). 1994. lib. bdg. 24.95 (*0-7933-3479-9*); pap. 14.95 (*0-7933-3480-2*); disk 29.95 (*0-7933-3481-0*) Gallopade Pub Group.

Bow Wow! Colorado Dogs in History, Mystery, Legend, Lore, Humor & More! Carole Marsh. (Carole Marsh Colorado Bks.). (Illus.). (J). (gr. 3-12). 1994. lib. bdg. 24.95 (*0-7933-3482-9*); pap. 14.95 (*0-7933-3483-7*); disk 29.95 (*0-7933-3484-5*) Gallopade Pub Group.

Bow Wow! Connecticut Dogs in History, Mystery, Legend, Lore, Humor & More! Carole Marsh. (Carole Marsh Connecticut Bks.). (Illus.). (J). (gr. 3-12). 1994. lib. bdg. 24.95 (*0-7933-3485-3*); pap. 14.95 (*0-7933-3486-1*); disk 29.95 (*0-7933-3487-X*) Gallopade Pub Group.

Bow Wow! Delaware Dogs in History, Mystery, Legend, Lore, Humor & More! Carole Marsh. (Carole Marsh Delaware Bks.). (Illus.). (J). (gr. 3-12). 1994. lib. bdg. 24.95 (*0-7933-3488-8*); pap. 14.95 (*0-7933-3489-6*); disk 29.95 (*0-7933-3490-X*) Gallopade Pub Group.

Bow Wow! Florida Dogs in History, Mystery, Legend, Lore, Humor & More! Carole Marsh. (Carole Marsh Florida Bks.). (Illus.). (J). (gr. 3-12). 1994. lib. bdg. 24.95 (*0-7933-3494-2*); pap. 14.95 (*0-7933-3495-0*); disk 29.95 (*0-7933-3496-9*) Gallopade Pub Group.

Bow Wow! Georgia Dogs in History, Mystery, Legend, Lore, Humor & More! Carole Marsh. (Carole Marsh Georgia Bks.). (Illus.). (J). (gr. 3-12). 1994. lib. bdg. 24.95 (*0-7933-3497-7*); pap. 14.95 (*0-7933-3498-5*); disk 29.95 (*0-7933-3499-3*) Gallopade Pub Group.

Bow Wow! Hawaii Dogs in History, Mystery, Legend, Lore, Humor & More! Carole Marsh. (Carole Marsh Hawaii Bks.). (Illus.). (J). (gr. 3-12). 1994. lib. bdg. 24.95 (*0-7933-3500-0*); pap. 14.95 (*0-7933-3501-9*); disk 29.95 (*0-7933-3502-7*) Gallopade Pub Group.

Bow Wow! Idaho Dogs in History, Mystery, Legend, Lore, Humor & More! Carole Marsh. (Carole Marsh Idaho Bks.). (Illus.). (J). (gr. 3-12). 1994. lib. bdg. 24.95 (*0-7933-3503-5*); pap. 14.95 (*0-7933-3504-3*); disk 29.95 (*0-7933-3505-1*) Gallopade Pub Group.

Bow Wow! Illinois Dogs in History, Mystery, Legend, Lore, Humor & More! Carole Marsh. (Carole Marsh Illinois Bks.). (Illus.). (J). (gr. 3-12). 1994. lib. bdg. 24.95 (*0-7933-3506-X*); pap. 14.95 (*0-7933-3507-8*); disk 29.95 (*0-7933-3508-6*) Gallopade Pub Group.

Bow Wow! Indiana Dogs in History, Mystery, Legend, Lore, Humor & More! Carole Marsh. (Carole Marsh Indiana Bks.). (Illus.). (J). (gr. 3-12). 1994. lib. bdg. 24.95 (*0-7933-3509-4*); pap. 14.95 (*0-7933-3510-8*); disk 29.95 (*0-7933-3511-6*) Gallopade Pub Group.

Bow Wow! Iowa Dogs in History, Mystery, Legend, Lore, Humor & More! Carole Marsh. (Carole Marsh Iowa Bks.). (Illus.). (J). (gr. 3-12). 1994. lib. bdg. 24.95 (*0-7933-3512-4*); pap. 14.95 (*0-7933-3513-2*); disk 29.95 (*0-7933-3514-0*) Gallopade Pub Group.

Bow Wow! Kansas Dogs in History, Mystery, Legend, Lore, Humor & More! Carole Marsh. (Carole Marsh Kansas Bks.). (Illus.). (J). (gr. 3-12). 1994. lib. bdg. 24.95 (*0-7933-3515-9*); pap. 14.95 (*0-7933-3516-7*); disk 29.95 (*0-7933-3517-5*) Gallopade Pub Group.

Bow Wow! Kentucky Dogs in History, Mystery, Legend, Lore, Humor & More! Carole Marsh. (Kentucky Bks.). (Illus.). (J). (gr. 3-12). 1994. lib. bdg. 24.95 (*0-7933-3518-3*); pap. 14.95 (*0-7933-3519-1*); disk 29.95 (*0-7933-3520-5*) Gallopade Pub Group.

Bow Wow! Louisiana Dogs in History, Mystery, Legend, Lore, Humor & More! Carole Marsh. (Carole Marsh Louisiana Bks.). (Illus.). (J). (gr. 3-12). 1994. lib. bdg. 24.95 (*0-7933-3521-3*); pap. 14.95 (*0-7933-3522-1*); disk 29.95 (*0-7933-3523-X*) Gallopade Pub Group.

Bow Wow! Maine Dogs in History, Mystery, Legend, Lore, Humor & More! Carole Marsh. (Carole Marsh Maine Bks.). (Illus.). (J). (gr. 3-12). 1994. lib. bdg. 24.95 (*0-7933-3524-8*); pap. 14.95 (*0-7933-3525-6*); disk 29.95 (*0-7933-3526-4*) Gallopade Pub Group.

Bow Wow! Maryland Dogs in History, Mystery, Legend, Lore, Humor & More! Carole Marsh. (Carole Marsh Maryland Bks.). (Illus.). (J). (gr. 3-12). 1994. lib. bdg. 24.95 (*0-7933-3527-2*); pap. 14.95 (*0-7933-3528-0*); disk 29.95 (*0-7933-3529-9*) Gallopade Pub Group.

Bow Wow! Massachusetts Dogs in History, Mystery, Legend, Lore, Humor & More! Carole Marsh. (Massachusetts Bks.). (Illus.). (J). (gr. 3-12). 1994. lib. bdg. 24.95 (*0-7933-3530-2*); pap. 14.95 (*0-7933-3531-0*); disk 29.95 (*0-7933-3532-9*) Gallopade Pub Group.

Bow Wow! Michigan Dogs in History, Mystery, Legend, Lore, Humor & More! Carole Marsh. (Carole Marsh Michigan Bks.). (Illus.). (J). (gr. 3-12). 1994. lib. bdg. 24.95 (*0-7933-3533-7*); pap. 14.95 (*0-7933-3534-5*); disk 29.95 (*0-7933-3535-3*) Gallopade Pub Group.

Bow Wow! Minnesota Dogs in History, Mystery, Legend, Lore, Humor & More! Carole Marsh. (Carole Marsh Minnesota Bks.). (Illus.). (J). (gr. 3-12). 1994. lib. bdg. 24.95 (*0-7933-3536-1*); pap. 14.95 (*0-7933-3537-X*); disk 29.95 (*0-7933-3538-8*) Gallopade Pub Group.

Bow Wow! Mississippi Dogs in History, Mystery, Legend, Lore, Humor & More! Carole Marsh. (Carole Marsh Mississippi Bks.). (Illus.). (J). (gr. 3-12). 1994. lib. bdg. 24.95 (*0-7933-3539-6*); pap. 14.95 (*0-7933-3540-X*); disk 29.95 (*0-7933-3541-8*) Gallopade Pub Group.

Bow Wow! Missouri Dogs in History, Mystery, Legend, Lore, Humor & More! Carole Marsh. (Carole Marsh Missouri Bks.). (Illus.). (J). (gr. 3-12). 1994. lib. bdg. 24.95 (*0-7933-3542-6*); pap. 14.95 (*0-7933-3543-4*); disk 29.95 (*0-7933-3544-2*) Gallopade Pub Group.

Bow Wow! Montana Dogs in History, Mystery, Legend, Lore, Humor & More! Carole Marsh. (Carole Marsh Montana Bks.). (Illus.). (J). (gr. 3-12). 1994. lib. bdg. 24.95 (*0-7933-3545-0*); pap. 14.95 (*0-7933-3546-9*); disk 29.95 (*0-7933-3547-7*) Gallopade Pub Group.

Bow Wow! Nebraska Dogs in History, Mystery, Legend, Lore, Humor & More! Carole Marsh. (Carole Marsh Nebraska Bks.). (Illus.). (J). (gr. 3-12). 1994. lib. bdg. 24.95 (*0-7933-3548-5*); pap. 14.95 (*0-7933-3549-3*); disk 29.95 (*0-7933-3550-7*) Gallopade Pub Group.

Bow Wow! Nevada Dogs in History, Mystery, Legend, Lore, Humor & More! Carole Marsh. (Carole Marsh Nevada Bks.). (Illus.). (J). (gr. 3-12). 1994. lib. bdg. 24.95 (*0-7933-3551-5*); pap. 14.95 (*0-7933-3552-3*); disk 29.95 (*0-7933-3553-1*) Gallopade Pub Group.

Bow Wow! New Hampshire Dogs in History, Mystery, Legend, Lore, Humor & More! Carole Marsh. (Carole Marsh New Hampshire Bks.). (Illus.). (J). (gr. 3-12). 1994. lib. bdg. 24.95 (*0-7933-3554-X*); pap. 14.95 (*0-7933-3555-8*); disk 29.95 (*0-7933-3556-6*) Gallopade Pub Group.

Bow Wow! New Jersey Dogs in History, Mystery, Legend, Lore, Humor & More! Carole Marsh. (Carole Marsh New Jersey Bks.). (Illus.). (J). (gr. 3-12). 1994. lib. bdg. 24.95 (*0-7933-3557-4*); pap. 14.95 (*0-7933-3558-2*); disk 29.95 (*0-7933-3559-0*) Gallopade Pub Group.

Bow Wow! New Mexico Dogs in History, Mystery, Legend, Lore, Humor & More! Carole Marsh. (Carole Marsh New Mexico Bks.). (Illus.). (J). (gr. 3-12). 1994. lib. bdg. 24.95 (*0-7933-3560-4*); pap. 14.95 (*0-7933-3561-2*); disk 29.95 (*0-7933-3562-0*) Gallopade Pub Group.

Bow Wow! New York Dogs in History, Mystery, Legend, Lore, Humor & More! Carole Marsh. (Carole Marsh New York Bks.). (Illus.). (J). (gr. 3-12). 1994. lib. bdg. 24.95 (*0-7933-3563-9*); pap. 14.95 (*0-7933-3564-7*); disk 29.95 (*0-7933-3565-5*) Gallopade Pub Group.

Bow Wow! North Carolina Dogs in History, Mystery, Legend, Lore, Humor & More! Carole Marsh. (Carole Marsh North Carolina Bks.). (Illus.). (J). (gr. 3-12). 1994. lib. bdg. 24.95 (*0-7933-3566-3*); pap. 14.95 (*0-7933-3567-1*); disk 29.95 (*0-7933-3568-X*) Gallopade Pub Group.

Bow Wow! North Dakota Dogs in History, Mystery, Legend, Lore, Humor & More! Carole Marsh. (Carole Marsh North Dakota Bks.). (Illus.). (J). (gr. 3-12). 1994. lib. bdg. 24.95 (*0-7933-3569-8*); pap. 14.95 (*0-7933-3570-1*); disk 29.95 (*0-7933-3571-X*) Gallopade Pub Group.

Bow Wow! Ohio Dogs in History, Mystery, Legend, Lore, Humor & More! Carole Marsh. (Carole Marsh Ohio Bks.). (Illus.). (J). (gr. 3-12). 1994. lib. bdg. 24.95 (*0-7933-3572-8*); pap. 14.95 (*0-7933-3573-6*); disk 29.95 (*0-7933-3574-4*) Gallopade Pub Group.

Bow Wow! Oklahoma Dogs in History, Mystery, Legend, Lore, Humor & More! Carole Marsh. (Carole Marsh Oklahoma Bks.). (Illus.). (J). (gr. 3-12). 1994. lib. bdg. 24.95 (*0-7933-3575-2*); pap. 14.95 (*0-7933-3576-0*); disk 29.95 (*0-7933-3577-9*) Gallopade Pub Group.

Bow Wow! Oregon Dogs in History, Mystery, Legend, Lore, Humor & More! Carole Marsh. (Oregon Bks.). (Illus.). (J). (gr. 3-12). 1994. lib. bdg. 24.95 (*0-7933-3578-7*); pap. 14.95 (*0-7933-3579-5*); disk 29.95 (*0-7933-3580-9*) Gallopade Pub Group.

Bow Wow! Pennsylvania Dogs in History, Mystery, Legend, Lore, Humor & More! Carole Marsh. (Pennsylvania Bks.). (Illus.). (J). (gr. 3-12). 1994. lib. bdg. 24.95 (*0-7933-3581-7*); pap. 14.95 (*0-7933-3582-5*); disk 29.95 (*0-7933-3583-3*) Gallopade Pub Group.

Bow Wow! Rhode Island Dogs in History, Mystery, Legend, Lore, Humor & More! Carole Marsh. (Rhode Island Bks.). (Illus.). (J). (gr. 3-12). 1994. lib. bdg. 24.95 (*0-7933-3584-1*); pap. 14.95 (*0-7933-3585-X*); disk 29.95 (*0-7933-3586-8*) Gallopade Pub Group.

Bow Wow! South Carolina Dogs in History, Mystery, Legend, Lore, Humor & More! Carole Marsh. (South Carolina Bks.). (Illus.). (J). (gr. 3-12). 1994. lib. bdg. 24.95 (*0-7933-3587-6*); pap. 14.95 (*0-7933-3588-4*); disk 29.95 (*0-7933-3589-2*) Gallopade Pub Group.

Bow Wow! South Dakota Dogs in History, Mystery, Legend, Lore, Humor & More! Carole Marsh. (South Dakota Bks.). (Illus.). (J). (gr. 3-12). 1994. lib. bdg. 24.95 (*0-7933-3590-6*); pap. 14.95 (*0-7933-3591-4*); disk 29.95 (*0-7933-3592-2*) Gallopade Pub Group.

Bow Wow! Tennessee Dogs in History, Mystery, Legend, Lore, Humor & More! Carole Marsh. (Tennessee Bks.). (Illus.). (J). (gr. 3-12). 1994. lib. bdg. 24.95 (*0-7933-3593-0*); pap. 14.95 (*0-7933-3594-9*); disk 29.95 (*0-7933-3595-7*) Gallopade Pub Group.

Bow Wow! Texas Dogs in History, Mystery, Legend, Lore, Humor & More! Carole Marsh. (Texas Bks.). (Illus.). (J). (gr. 3-12). 1994. lib. bdg. 24.95 (*0-7933-3596-5*); pap. 14.95 (*0-7933-3597-3*); disk 29.95 (*0-7933-3598-1*) Gallopade Pub Group.

Bow Wow! Utah Dogs in History, Mystery, Legend, Lore, Humor & More! Carole Marsh. (Utah Bks.). (Illus.). (J). (gr. 3-12). 1994. lib. bdg. 24.95 (*0-7933-3599-X*); pap. 14.95 (*0-7933-3600-7*); disk 29.95 (*0-7933-3601-5*) Gallopade Pub Group.

Bow Wow! Vermont Dogs in History, Mystery, Legend, Lore, Humor & More! Carole Marsh. (Vermont Bks.). (Illus.). (J). (gr. 3-12). 1994. lib. bdg. 24.95 (*0-7933-3602-3*); pap. 14.95 (*0-7933-3603-1*); disk 29.95 (*0-7933-3604-X*) Gallopade Pub Group.

Bow Wow! Virginia Dogs in History, Mystery, Legend, Lore, Humor & More! Carole Marsh. (Virginia Bks.). (Illus.). (J). (gr. 3-12). 1994. lib. bdg. 24.95 (*0-7933-3605-8*); pap. 14.95 (*0-7933-3606-6*); disk 29.95 (*0-7933-3607-4*) Gallopade Pub Group.

Bow Wow! Washington D. C. Dogs in History, Mystery, Legend, Lore, Humor & More! Carole Marsh. (Washington, D.C. Bks.). (Illus.). (J). (gr. 3-12). 1994. lib. bdg. 24.95 (*0-7933-3491-8*); pap. 14.95 (*0-7933-3492-6*); disk 29.95 (*0-7933-3493-4*) Gallopade Pub Group.

Bow Wow! Washington Dogs in History, Mystery, Legend, Lore, Humor & More! Carole Marsh. (Washington Bks.). (Illus.). (J). (gr. 3-12). 1994. lib. bdg. 24.95 (*0-7933-3608-2*); pap. 14.95 (*0-7933-3609-0*); disk 29.95 (*0-7933-3610-4*) Gallopade Pub Group.

Bow Wow! West Virginia Dogs in History, Mystery, Legend, Lore, Humor & More! Carole Marsh. (West Virginia Bks.). (Illus.). (J). (gr. 3-12). 1994. lib. bdg. 24.95 (*0-7933-3611-2*); pap. 14.95 (*0-7933-3612-0*); disk 29.95 (*0-7933-3613-9*) Gallopade Pub Group.

Bow Wow! Wisconsin Dogs in History, Mystery, Legend, Lore, Humor & More! Carole Marsh. (Wisconsin Bks.). (Illus.). (J). (gr. 3-12). 1994. lib. bdg. 24.95 (*0-7933-3614-7*); pap. 14.95 (*0-7933-3615-5*); disk 29.95 (*0-7933-3616-3*) Gallopade Pub Group.

An Asterisk (*) at the beginning of an entry indicates that the title is appearing in BIP for the first time.

Bow Wow! Wyoming Dogs in History, Mystery, Legend, Lore, Humor & More! Carole Marsh. (Wyoming Bks.). (Illus.). (J). (gr. 3-12). 1994. lib. bdg. 24.95 (*0-7933-3617-1*); pap. 14.95 (*0-7933-3618-X*); disk 29.95 (*0-7933-3619-8*) Gallopade Pub Group.
Bow Wow House U. S. A. Invitational - 1993. Susan Brown & Barbara Jedda. LC 93-90295. (Illus.). 28p. (Orig.). 1993. 7.95 (*0-9615072-0-9*) Dog Museum.
Bowater: A History. W. J. Reader. LC 81-7681. (Illus.). 312p. 1981. 89.95 (*0-521-24165-0*) Cambridge U Pr.
Bowditch for Yachtsmen: Piloting. Nathaniel Bowditch. 1980. pap. 9.95 (*0-679-50930-5*) McKay.
Bowdoin Book Set, 10 vols., Set. Ruth Bowdoin. Tr. by Ana Wier. (Metodo Bowdoin Ser.). (Illus.). (Orig.). (SPA.). 1989. pap. text ed. write for info. (*1-55997-058-8*) Websters Intl.
Bowdoin College Museum of Art: Handbook of the Collections. Ed. by Margaret R. Burke. LC 81-66892. (Illus.). (Orig.). 1981. pap. 10.00 (*0-916606-01-5*) Bowdoin Coll.
Bowdoin Method Manual. 2nd ed. Ruth Bowdoin. (Illus.). 110p. 1978. pap. text ed. write for info. (*1-55997-002-2*) Websters Intl.
Bowdrie. Louis L'Amour. 1983. 3.99 (*0-553-28106-2*) Bantam.
Bowdrie's Law. Louis L'Amour. LC 85-824. (Orig.). 1984. mass mkt. 3.99 (*0-553-24550-3*) Bantam.
Bowed Tendon Book. Tom Ivers. (Illus.). 1994. 24.95 (*0-929346-25-4*) R Meerdink Co Ltd.
Bowel & Bladder Retraining of the Elderly Client. 1988. 5.95 (*0-941353-01-X*, 7120) Briggs Corp.
Bowel Cancer: The Facts. John M. Northover & Joel D. Kettner. LC 92-12443. 1992. pap. 10.50 (*0-19-262207-2*) OUP.
Bowel Cancer: The Facts. John M. Northover & Joel D. Kettner. (Facts Ser.). (Illus.). 184p. 1993. 22.50 (*0-19-261788-5*) OUP.
Bowel Management: A Manual of Ideas & Techniques. Ed. by Raymond C. Cheever & Charles D. Elmer. 32p. 1975. pap. 3.50 (*0-915708-02-7*, #1420) Cheever Pub.
Bowel Obstruction: Differential Diagnosis & Clinical Management. John P. Welch. (Illus.). 711p. 1989. text ed. 132.50 (*0-7216-1963-0*) Saunders.
Bowels of the Earth. John Elder. (Illus.). 1978. pap. 9.95 (*0-19-854413-8*) OUP.
Bowen & Hardin. Chuck Parsons & Marjorie Parsons. LC 91-24946. (Illus.). 112p. 1991. 21.95 (*0-932702-91-0*) Creative Texas.
***Bowen Family Systems Theory: Clinical Applications.** Ed. by Peter Titleman. (Illus.). 356p. (C). 1995. text ed. write for info. (*0-89876-220-0*) Gardner Pr.
Bowen Family Theory & Its Uses. C. Margaret Hall. LC 79-51905. 320p. 1992. reprint ed. 40.00 (*0-87668-373-1*) Aronson.
Bowers on Employment Law. 4th ed. John Bowers. 1993. 64.00 (*1-85431-289-8*, Pub. by Blackstone Pr UK) W W Gaunt.
Bowes & Church's Food Values of Portions Commonly. 16th ed. Pennington. (Illus.). 328p. 1992. pap. text ed. 29.95 (*0-397-55087-1*) Lippincott.
Bowfin. Edwin P. Hoyt. 264p. 1984. pap. 3.50 (*0-380-69817-X*) Avon.
Bowhunter. Stephen Altman. 192p. 1988. 17.95 (*0-8027-4085-5*) Walker & Co.
Bowhunter's Digest. 3rd ed. Chuck Adams. LC 73-91589. (Illus.). 288p. (Orig.). 1990. pap. 16.95 (*0-87349-108-4*) DBI.
Bowhunter's Encyclopedia: Practical, Easy-to-Find Answers to Your Bowhunting Questions. Dwight Schuh. LC 87-6473. (Illus.). 576p. 1987. pap. 24.95 (*0-8117-2412-3*) Stackpole.
Bowhunting Alternative. Adrian Benke. Ed. by Patty Mullins. (Illus.). (Orig.). 1989. pap. 7.95 (*0-685-28351-8*) B Todd Pr.
***Bowhunting Big Game.** Dan Dietrich. LC 92-62494. (Hunter's Information Ser.). 250p. 1993. write for info. (*0-914697-53-6*) N Amer Outdoor Grp.
Bowhunting Fireside Tales. Dan Bertalan. LC 94-70353. 128p. 1994. pap. 6.95 (*0-9623955-3-6*) Envisage Unlimited.
Bowhunting for Whitetails: Your Best Methods for Taking North America's Favorite Deer. Dave Bowring. LC 84-16187. (Illus.). 304p. 1985. pap. 18.95 (*0-8117-3076-X*) Stackpole.
Bowhunting's Whitetail Masters: The Techniques, Secrets & Successes of the Most Skilled Whitetail Bowhunters in America. Dan Bertalan. LC 91-77435. (Illus.). 344p. 1992. 29.95 (*0-9623955-1-X*) Envisage Unlimited.
Bowie. Hopkins. 1985. 17.95 (*0-02-553730-X*) Macmillan.
Bowie: Changes. Stuart Hoggard & Chris Charlesworth. (Illus.). 84p. pap. 9.95 (*0-86001-772-9*, OP40880) Omnibus NY.
Bowie: Glass Idol. David Currie. (Illus.). 96p. pap. 17.95 (*0-7119-1182-7*, OP44411) Omnibus NY.
Bowie: The Pitt Report. Ken Pitt. (Illus.). 230p. 1985. pap. 12.95 (*0-7119-0619-X*, OP43256) Omnibus NY.
Bowie in His Own Words. Comp. by Miles. (Illus.). 128p. 1980. pap. 15.95 (*0-86001-645-5*, OP40567) Omnibus NY.
Bowie Knife. R. Thorp. 167p. 1993. 9.95 (*0-685-70213-8*) Phillips Pubns.
Bowie Knives of the Ben Palmer Collection. Phillips et al. 245p. 1992. 34.95 (*0-932572-24-3*) Phillips Pubns.
Bowies of Their Kindred: A Genealogical & Biographical History. W. W. Bowie. (Illus.). 523p. 1991. reprint ed. lib. bdg. 88.50 (*0-8328-1963-8*); reprint ed. pap. 78.50 (*0-8328-1964-6*) Higginson Bk Co.
Bowker Annual Library & Book Trade Almanac 1994. 39th ed. Ed. by Catherine Barr. LC 55-12434. 800p. 1994. 155.00 (*0-8352-3481-9*) Bowker.
***Bowker Annual of Library & Book Trade Almanac 1995.** Ed. by Catherine Barr. LC 55-12434. 800p. 1995. 159.95 (*0-8352-3613-7*) Bowker.
Bowker's Complete Video Directory 1994, 3 vols., 2. Ed. by Bowker, R. R., Staff. 3624p. 1994. write for info. (*0-8352-3393-6*) Bowker.
Bowker's Complete Video Directory 1994, 3 vols., 3. Ed. by Bowker, R. R., Staff. 3624p. 1994. write for info. (*0-8352-3394-4*) Bowker.
Bowker's Complete Video Directory 1994, 3 vols., Set. Ed. by Bowker, R. R., Staff. 3624p. 1994. 219.95 (*0-8352-3391-X*); 139.95 (*0-8352-3410-X*) Bowker.
Bowker's Complete Video Directory 1994, 3 vols., Vol. 1: Entertainment. Ed. by Bowker, R. R., Staff. 3624p. 1994. Vol. 1, Entertainment. 109.95 (*0-8352-3392-8*) Bowker.
Bowker's Complete Video Directory 1995, 1. Ed. by Bowker, R. R., Staff. 1776p. 1995. 114.95 (*0-8352-3587-4*) Bowker.
Bowker's Complete Video Directory 1995, 2. Ed. by Bowker, R. R., Staff. 1995. write for info. (*0-8352-3588-2*) Bowker.
Bowker's Complete Video Directory 1995, 3. Ed. by Bowker, R. R., Staff. 1995. write for info. (*0-8352-3589-0*) Bowker.

Bowker's Complete Video Directory 1995, Set. Ed. by Bowker, R. R., Staff. 3976p. 1995. 229.95 (*0-8352-3586-6*) Bowker. "...the award for the MOST comprehensive guide to video programs has to go to BOWKER'S COMPLETE VIDEO DIRECTORY..."--BOX OFFICE. "An impressive...resource noteworthy for its large number of listings, its up-to-date ordering, price information, & other special features..."--PUBLIC LIBRARIES. "...one of the largest directories of this type..."--BOOKLIST. "...the essential reference for gaining access to the entire video market today."--THE BIG REEL. "...a valuable tool..."--VIDEO BUSINESS. This comprehensive, three-volume reference gives you a wide-angle view of the full range of videos available to make selection & collection development easier. Covering over 107, 000 videos--thousands more than other references--this up-to-date hardbound director lists virtually every one of them in all formats: VHS, Beta, 3/4", U-matic, 8mm, & laser disc. No other source can match BOWKER'S COMPLETE VIDEO DIRECTORY 1995 for: * Practicality---BOWKER'S COMPLETE VIDEO DIRECTORY offers separate volumes (ENTERTAINMENT & EDUCATION/SPECIAL INTEREST) for ready focus on the types of videos you need for your collection. * Comprehensiveness-Bowker brings you thousands more available videos than any other source. * Value--BOWKER'S COMPLETE VIDEO DIRECTORY is significantly less expensive than the competition. * Diversity--Bowker gives you ordering information on more foreign, Spanish-language, children's, silent, & feature films than anyone else; includes full series & performance rights information, & notes international standards, such as PAL & SECAM, where applicable. * Selection Guidance--provides information on preview tapes where applicable. * Selection Guidance--provides information on preview tapes when available. * Access--BOWKER'S COMPLETE VIDEO DIRECTORY contains a variety of indexes for ease of research, including Title, Genre, Cast/ Director, & more. As a reference tool... as a selection guide...for complete ordering information & valuable acquisition assistance...depend on BOWKER'S COMPLETE VIDEO DIRECTORY 1995. ***Publisher Provided Annotation.***

Bowker's Complete Video Directory 1995, Set, Vols. 2 & 3. Ed. by Bowker, R. R., Staff. 2200p. 1995. 146.95 (*0-8352-3590-4*) Bowker.
Bowl Judgments. pap. 0.95 (*0-937408-11-5*) GMI Pubns Inc.
Bowl Like a Pro: Winning Techniques That Will Raise Your Average. David Ozio & Dan Herbst. LC 92-11488. (Illus.). 224p. 1992. pap. 11.95 (*0-8092-4039-4*) Contemp Bks.
Bowl-O-Rama: The Visual Arts of Bowling. H. Thomas Steele. LC 85-30799. (Illus.). 96p. 1986. 21.95 (*0-89659-607-9*) Abbeville Pr.
Bowl of Baal. Robert A. Bennet. 1976. 10.00 (*0-937986-06-2*) D M Grant.
Bowl of Cherries. Shena Mackay. 192p. 1992. 16.95 (*1-55921-070-2*) Moyer Bell.
Bowl of Cherries. Shena Mackay. 192p. 1994. pap. 9.95 (*1-55921-114-8*) Moyer Bell.
Bowl of Heaven. Evangeline Adams. 275p. 1994. pap. 18.00 (*0-89540-196-7*, SB-196, Sun Bks) Sun Pub.
Bowl of Mischief. Ellen K. McKenzie. LC 92-24246. 144p. (J). (gr. 4-7). 1992. 14.95 (*0-8050-2090-X*, Bks Young Read) H Holt & Co.
Bowl of Night. Robert B. Dick & William Smith. Ed. by James B. Van Treese. 326p. 1994. pap. 9.95 (*1-56901-110-9*) NW Pub.
Bowl of Red. Frank X. Tolbert. LC 93-35691. 200p. 1994. reprint ed. pap. 9.95 (*0-89096-598-6*) Tex A&M Univ Pr.
Bowl of Saki. Inayat Khan. LC 85-22332. 128p. 1985. reprint ed. lib. bdg. 23.00x (*0-89370-583-7*) Borgo Pr.
Bowl of Saki Commentary. Samuel L. Lewis & Hazrat I. Khan. Ed. by Moineddin Jablonski & Saadi Klotz. 180p. (Orig.). 1981. pap. 18.00 (*0-915424-08-8*) PeaceWks Intl Ctr Dances Univ Peace.
Bowl of Sorrow. B. M. Bennani. 1977. per. 3.00 (*0-912678-36-4*, Greenfld Rev Pr) Greenfld Rev Lit.
***Bowl of Soup, a Crust of Bread, & Thou.** Patricia B. Mitchell. 1995. pap. 4.00 (*0-925117-78-1*) Mitchells.
***Bowlby Families in England & America.** Raymond E. Bowlby. 534p. 1994. reprint ed. lib. bdg. 89.50 (*0-8328-4297-4*); reprint ed. pap. 79.50 (*0-8328-4298-2*) Higginson Bk Co.
***Bowler's Start-Up: A Beginner's Guide to Bowling.** Doug Warner. (Start-Up Sports Ser.: Vol. 5). (Illus.). 128p. (Orig.). 1995. pap. 9.95 (*1-884654-05-3*) Tracks Pubng.
Bowlers Team Record Book. Tech Data Publications Staff. 1980. pap. 2.00 (*0-937816-32-9*) Tech Data.
Bowles & Gintis Revisited: Correspondence & Contradiction in Educational Theory. Ed. by Mike Cole. 245p. 1988. 70.00 (*1-85000-173-1*, Falmer Pr); pap. 33.00 (*1-85000-174-X*, Falmer Pr) Taylor & Francis.
Bowles, Byron & the Pope Controversy. Jacob J. Van Rennes. LC 68-734. (Studies in Byron: No. 5). 1969. reprint ed. lib. bdg. 75.00 (*0-8383-0640-3*) M S G Haskell Hse.
Bowlfood: Lowfat Foods to Serve in a Bowl. Deborah Fisher. (Illus.). 80p. (Orig.). 1992. pap. 8.00 (*0-9630532-1-3*) F & D Graphics.
Bowling. Charles Edgington. 124p. 1993. pap. 10.95 (*0-945483-27-9*) E Bowers Pub.
Bowling. Joyce M. Harrison & Ron Maxey. (Sport for Life Ser.). (C). 1986. pap. text ed. 11.00 (*0-673-18324-6*) HarpCollege.
Bowling. Connie Johnson. LC 93-21103. (Lifetime Sport & Fitness Ser.). 1993. pap. 14.50 (*0-89787-625-3*) Gorsuch Scarisbrick.
Bowling. H. Kavet. 64p. 1993. 8.95 (*0-88032-354-X*) Ivory Tower Pub.
Bowling. Les Palmer. (Illus.). 54p. 1981. pap. text ed. 5.95x (*0-89641-063-3*) American Pr.
Bowling. 5th rev. ed. Richard T. Mackey. LC 92-12893. 97p. (C). 1993. pap. text ed. 12.95 (*1-55934-161-0*) Mayfield Pub.
Bowling. 7th ed. Joan L. Martin et al. 128p. 1994. pap. write for info. (*0-697-12646-3*) Brown & Benchmark.
Bowling: Knowledge Is the Key. 2nd ed. Fred Borden & Jay Elias. (Illus.). 138p. (Orig.). (C). 1986. pap. 19.95 (*0-9619177-0-9*) Bowling Concepts.
Bowling: Steps to Success. Robert H. Strickland. LC 88-37740. (Illus.). 200p. (Orig.). 1989. pap. text ed. 14.95x (*0-88011-355-3*, PSTR0355) Human Kinetics.
Bowling: Ten Keys to Success. Fred Borden & Jay Elias. (Illus.). 114p. (Orig.). 1991. pap. 19.95 (*0-9619177-1-7*) Bowling Concepts.
Bowling Basics. 2nd ed. Gerald P. Carlson & E. Harold Blackwell. 128p. 1993. per. 10.95 (*0-8403-8644-3*) Kendall-Hunt.
Bowling Centers, 1995. American Business Directories Staff. 1995. spiral bd., pap. 495.00 (*1-56105-595-6*) Am Busn Direct.
Bowling Everyone. Scott & Carpenter. 138p. (Orig.). (C). 1985. pap. 12.95 (*0-88725-035-1*) Hunter Textbks.
Bowling Green Murder. May Taylor. 148p. 1988. 19.00 (*0-7212-0648-4*, Pub. by Regency Press) St Mut.
Bowling Madness: Hey Pops, You Hustled Me. Steve Raymond. LC 88-83761. 278p. (Orig.). 1989. pap. 8.95 (*0-927707-16-0*) FL Bay Pubs.
Bowling Proprietor. Ed. by Steve Welch. 88p. write for info. (*0-318-60102-8*) Bowling Prop Assn.
***Bowling Song.** Raffi. write for info. (*0-517-59382-3*) Random Hse Value.
Bowling Strikes. Dawson Taylor. 128p. 1991. pap. 9.95 (*0-8092-3977-9*) Contemp Bks.
Bowling Tough: Three Simple Methods to Improve Your Performance under Pressure. Will Powers & Bob Strickland. 112p. 1993. pap. text ed. 9.95 (*0-9635919-0-8*) R H Strickland.
Bowling Two Hundred Plus: Winning Strategies to up Your Average & Improve Your Game. Mike Aulby et al. (Illus.). 144p. 1989. pap. 11.95 (*0-8092-4338-5*) Contemp Bks.
Bowling 300: Top Pros Share Secrets to Rolling the Perfect Game. Dan Herbst. 192p. (Orig.). 1993. pap. 9.95 (*0-8092-3823-3*) Contemp Bks.
Bowman: The Bowmans, a Pioneering Family in Virginia, Kentucky & the Northwest Territory. J. W. Wayland. (Illus.). 185p. 1992. reprint ed. lib. bdg. 41.50 (*0-8328-2458-5*); reprint ed. pap. 31.50 (*0-8328-2459-3*) Higginson Bk Co.
***Bowman, N. Dakota War Book.** Aileen Doyle. (Illus.). 84p. 1993. 34.95 (*0-88107-235-4*) Curtis Media.
Bowman's Glory, or, Archery Revived. William Wood. 1976. 7.50 (*0-85409-552-7*) Charles River Bks.
Bowman's Kid. large type ed. Gordon D. Shirreffs. (Linford Western Library). 272p. 1987. pap. 11.95 (*0-7089-6343-9*, Linford) Ulverscroft.
***Bowman's Kid; Renegade's Trail, 2 vols. in 1.** Gordon D. Shirreffs. (Manhunter Ser.). 336p. 1995. mass mkt., pap. 4.99 (*0-8439-3850-1*) Dorchester Pub Co.
***Bowman's Line.** Brian A. Laird. LC 95-2822. 224p. 1995. 20.95 (*0-312-13033-3*) St Martin.
Bowne: William Bowne of Yorkshire, England & His Descendants. M. K. Reading. (Illus.). 47p. 1994. reprint ed. pap. 10.00 (*0-8328-4199-4*) Higginson Bk Co.
***Bowne - William Bowne of Yorkshire, England & His Descendants.** M. K. Reading. (Illus.). 47p. 1994. reprint ed. lib. bdg. 20.00 (*0-8328-4515-9*); reprint ed. pap. 10. 00 (*0-8328-4516-7*) Higginson Bk Co.
Bows & Arrows of the Native Americans. Jim Hamm. (Illus.). 160p. 1992. pap. 14.95 (*1-55821-168-3*) Lyons & Burford.
Bows, Arrows & Quivers of Ancient Japan. Seyssel & Hawley. 1994. pap. 30.00 (*0-910704-91-0*) Hawley.
***Bows, Hearts & Borders.** Patti Kinzie. (Clip Art Ser.). 23p. 1993. pap. text ed. 5.95 (*1-886046-11-5*) Dovetail Pr.
Bowser Family History. A. B. Bowser. (Illus.). 310p. 1992. reprint ed. lib. bdg. 57.00 (*0-8328-2468-2*); reprint ed. pap. 47.00 (*0-8328-2469-0*) Higginson Bk Co.
Bowser the Hound. Thornton W. Burgess. (J). 19.95 (*0-8488-0391-4*) Amereon Ltd.
Bowstring Murders. Carr Dickson. 256p. 1989. pap. 3.50 (*0-8217-2687-0*) Zebra.
Bowyer Ledgers: The Printing Accounts of William Bowyer Father & Son with a Checklist of Bowyer Printing 1699-1777, a Commentary, Indexes, & Appendixes. Ed. by Keith Maslen & John Lancaster. (Illus.). lxxv, 616p. 1991. 190.00 (*0-914930-13-3*, 12229) Biblio Soc Am.
Bowyer's Bible, Vol. 1. Jim Hamm. (Illus.). 326p. 1993. 19. 95 (*1-55821-206-X*) Lyons & Burford.
Bowyer's Bible, Vol. 2. Jim Hamm. (Illus.). 350p. 1993. 22. 95 (*1-55821-207-8*) Lyons & Burford.
Bowyer's Bible, Vol. 3. Ed. by Jim Hamm. (Illus.). 366p. 1994. 24.95 (*1-55821-311-2*) Lyons & Burford.
Box. Peter Babe. 1989. pap. 4.95 (*0-88739-126-5*) Creat Arts Bk.
***Box: An Oral History of Television, 1929-1961.** Jeff Kisselhoff. LC 95-10720. 1995. write for info. (*0-670-86470-6*, Viking) Viking Penguin.
Box & Cox. Grace Chetwin. LC 88-35337. (Illus.). 32p. (J). (gr. k-3). 1990. text ed. 13.95 (*0-02-718314-9*, Bradbury S&S) S&S Childrens.
Box & Quotations from Chairman Mao Tse-Tung: Two Inter-Related Plays. Edward Albee. 1968. pap. 4.75 (*0-8222-0139-9*) Dramatists Play.
***Box & the Bone.** Snyder. (Castle Court Kids Ser.: No. 2). (J). 1995. pap. 3.50 (*0-440-40986-1*) Dell.
Box Butte County, Nebraska. Box Butte Centennial Committee Staff. (Illus.). 465p. 1988. 57.50 (*0-88107-107-2*) Curtis Media.
***Box City: An Interdisciplinary Experience in Community Planning.** Ginny Graves & Dean Graves. 114p. 1994. 26.95 (*0-9632033-1-2*) Ctr Under Built.
Box Closet. Meigs. (NFS Canada Ser.). Date not set. pap. 13.95 (*0-88922-253-3*, Pub. by Talonbooks CN) InBook.
Box Crafts: Over 50 Things to Make & Do with Boxes of Every Size. Imogene Forte. LC 86-82933. (Tabletop Learning Ser.). (Illus.). 80p. (J). (gr. k-6). 1987. pap. text ed. 3.95 (*0-86530-123-9*, IP 942) Incentive Pubns.
Box Engineering: A Subsystem Designer's Handbook. David W. Weisman. 1992. text ed. 49.95 (*0-07-069014-6*) McGraw.
Box Engineering: A Subsystem Designer's Handbook. David W. Weisman. 304p. 1991. 34.95 (*0-8306-2188-1*) TAB Bks.
***Box It or Bag It Mathematics, 2 vols., Set.** Donna Burk et al. (Illus.). (C). 1988. teacher ed 64.00 (*1-886131-11-2*, BBT) Math Lrning.
***Box It or Bag It Mathematics: Teachers Resource Guide - First-Second, Incl. blackline masters.** Donna Burk et al. LC 88-61046. (Illus.). 296p. (C). 1988. teacher ed 36. 00 (*1-886131-01-5*, BB12) Math Lrning.
***Box It or Bag It Mathematics: Teachers Resource Guide - Kindergarten, Incl. blackline masters.** Donna Burk et al. LC 87-63571. (Illus.). 232p. (C). 1988. teacher ed 30. 00 (*1-886131-00-7*, BBK) Math Lrning.
Box Man. Kobo Abe. Tr. by E. Dale Saunders. 192p. 1991. reprint ed. pap. 11.00 (*0-86547-461-3*, North Pt Pr) FS&G.
Box Nine. Jack O'Connell. LC 91-52863. 272p. 1992. 17.95 (*0-89296-472-3*) Mysterious Pr.
Box Nine. Jack O'Connell. 336p. 1993. mass mkt. 4.99 (*0-446-40100-5*, Mysterious Paperbk) Warner Bks.
Box of Broadsides: Poets & Writers at the United Nations. Ed. by Stanley H. Barkan & David Curzon. 1991. boxed 250.00 (*0-89304-954-9*) Cross-Cultrl NY.
Box of Broadsides' International Poets & Writers. Ed. by Stanley H. Barkan. 1991. boxed 250.00 (*0-89304-955-7*) Cross-Cultrl NY.
Box of Night Mirrors. Ed. by John Caddy. (Illus.). 120p. (Orig.). (J). 1980. pap. 5.00 (*0-927663-11-2*) COMPAS.
Box of Peppermints. Libby Stopple. Ed. by Dick Dromgoole. LC 75-20957. (Illus.). 96p. (J). (gr. 2-10). 1975. 12.95 (*0-913632-08-2*); pap. 7.95 (*0-913632-07-4*) All Things Pr.
Box of Rain: Lyrics: 1965-1993. rev. ed. Robert Hunter. 368p. 1993. pap. 15.00 (*0-14-013451-4*, Penguin Bks) Viking Penguin.
Box of Roses. Lee Sharkey. 1980. pap. text ed. 3.00 (*0-913006-24-6*) Puckerbrush.

An Asterisk (*) at the beginning of an entry indicates that the title is appearing in BIP for the first time.

Box of Stars: A Practical Guide to the Mythology of the Night Sky. Catherine Tennant. (Illus.). 48p. 1993. 24.95 (*0-8212-2038-1*) Bulfinch Pr.

Box Office Blockbusters: Fifty-Five Movie Songs & Themes. Ed. by Carol Cuellar. 164p. (Orig.). (YA). 1994. pap. text ed. 12.95 (*0-89898-779-2*); pap. text ed. 14.95 (*0-89898-778-4*) CPP Belwin.

Box-Office Buckaroos: The Cowboy Hero from the Wild West Show to the Silverscreen. Robert Heide & John Gilman. (Illus.). 224p. 1990. pap. 19.95 (*1-55859-070-6*) Abbeville Pr.

Box Office Champions, 4 vols., Pt. 1: The Directors. 1992. Part 1: The Directors. 95.00 (*1-882333-00-4*) P Kagan Assocs.

Box Office Champions, 4 vols., Pt. 2: The Producers. 1992. Part 2: The Producers. 95.00 (*1-882333-01-2*) P Kagan Assocs.

Box Office Champions, 4 vols., Pt. 3: The Actors. 1992. Part 3: The Actors. 95.00 (*1-882333-02-0*) P Kagan Assocs.

Box Office Champions, 4 vols., Pt. 4: The Writers. 1992. Part 4: The Writers. 95.00 (*1-882333-03-9*) P Kagan Assocs.

Box Office Champions, 4 vols., Set. 1992. 285.00 (*1-882333-04-7*) P Kagan Assocs.

Box Office Champs. Eddie D. Kay. 1990. 14.99 (*0-517-69212-0*) Random Hse Value.

Box Poems & Old Sheets. Willa Schneberg & Larkin Warren. LC 78-74231. 88p. 1979. pap. 9.95 (*0-914086-25-1*) Alicejamesbooks.

Box Socials. W. P. Kinsella. 240p. 1993. pap. 9.00 (*0-345-38253-6*, Ballantine Trade) Ballantine.

Box Splines: Applied Mathematical Sciences Ser. Carl De Boor et al. (Vol. 98). (Illus.). 200p. 1993. write for info. (*3-540-94101-0*) Spr-Verlag.

Box Splines: Applied Mathematical Sciences Ser. Carl De Boor et al. LC 93-5263. (Vol. 98). 1993. 34.00 (*0-387-94101-0*) Spr-Verlag.

Box, the Amoeba, & the Egg: The Flow to Self-Discovery. Michael C. Giammatteo. (Illus.). 1974. pap. 7.00 (*0-918428-07-6*) Sylvan Inst.

Box Turtle at Long Pond. William T. George. LC 88-18787. (Illus.). 24p. (J). (ps-1). 1989. 15.00 (*0-688-08184-3*); lib. bdg. 14.93 (*0-688-08185-1*) Greenwillow.

Boxborough: A New England Town & Its People. Lucie C. Hager. (Illus.). 1891p. 1989. reprint ed. lib. bdg. 28.00 (*0-8328-0808-3*, MA0018) Higginson Bk Co.

Boxcar. Joanne Barkan. (Come Aboard Bks.). (Illus.). 12p. (J). (ps-00). 1992. pap. 3.50 (*0-689-71573-0*, Aladdin Paperbacks) S&S Childrens.

Boxcar Brigade: Saga of a Steam Locomotive Engineer 1890's-1960's. Mary E. Ester. (Illus.). 309p. 1993. 25.00 (*0-9636498-0-9*) M E Ester.

***Boxcar Children.** Garrett Christopher. Ed. by J. Friedland & R. Kessler. (Novel-Ties Ser.). (J). (gr. 2-4). 1993. student ed, pap. text ed. 15.95 (*0-88122-879-6*) Lrn Links.

***Boxcar Children.** braille ed. Gertrude C. Warner. 104p. (J). 1994. text ed., vinyl bd. 8.32 (*1-56956-534-1*, BR9507) W A T Braille.

Boxcar Children. Gertrude C. Warner. LC 42-1418. (Boxcar Children Mysteries Ser.: No. 1). (J). (gr. 2-7). 1942. reprint ed. lib. bdg. 10.95 (*0-8075-0851-9*); reprint ed. pap. 3.50 (*0-8075-0852-7*) A Whitman.

Boxcar Children. Gertrude C. Warner. (Illus.). 158p. (J). 1992. reprint ed. lib. bdg. 14.95 (*0-89966-902-6*) Buccaneer Bks.

Boxcar Children, Set, Nos. 1-4. Gertrude C. Warner. LC 42-1418. (Boxcar Children Mysteries Ser.: No. 1). (J). (gr. 2-7). 1942. reprint ed. boxed, pap. 14.00 (*0-8075-0854-3*) A Whitman.

Boxcar Children, Set, Nos. 5-8. Gertrude C. Warner. LC 42-1418. (Boxcar Children Mysteries Ser.: No. 1). (J). (gr. 2-7). 1942. reprint ed. boxed, pap. 14.00 (*0-8075-0857-8*) A Whitman.

Boxcar Children Cookbook. Diane Blain. Ed. by Kathy Tucker. LC 91-15080. (Illus.). 96p. (J). (gr. 2-8). 1991. 13.95 (*0-8075-0859-4*); pap. 9.95 (*0-8075-0856-X*) A Whitman.

Boxcar of Peaches: Our Family. Bruce Gjovig. (Illus.). 60p. (Orig.). 1990. pap. 15.00 (*0-9626855-0-X*) Ctr Innov & Bus.

Boxcar Sammy. Shirley Weldon. 1995. 7.95 (*0-8062-5111-5*) Carlton.

Boxcars. David Young. (American Poetry Ser.). 84p. 1990. reprint ed. 6.95 (*0-912946-06-7*); reprint ed. pap. 2.95 (*0-912946-07-5*) Ecco Pr.

Boxed-Dictionary of Occupational Titles, Version 2. United States Dept. of Labor Staff. 1992. pap. 40.00 (*0-8442-4144-X*, VGM Career Bks) NTC Pub Grp.

Boxed In: The Culture of TV. Mark C. Miller. (Illus.). 349p. 1988. pap. 14.95 (*0-8101-0792-9*) Northwestern U Pr.

Boxed Nightmares. Kevin Siembieda & Kevin Long. Ed. by Alex Marciniszyn & Thomas Bartold. (Beyond the Supernatural Game Supplement Ser.). (Illus.). 80p. (Orig.). (YA). (gr. 8 up). 1990. pap. 11.95 (*0-916211-41-X*, 701) Palladium Bks.

Boxelder Bug Variations: A Meditation on an Idea in Language & Music. Bill Holm. LC 85-61616. (Lakes & Prairies Ser.). 104p. 1985. pap. 10.95 (*0-915943-43-3*) Milkweed Ed.

Boxer Blueprint. Daniel A. Buchwald & Jean M. Buchwald. 102p. 1992. 22.95 (*0-944242-10-3*) Doral Pub.

Boxer Champions, 1952-1988. Camino E. E. & B. Co. Staff. 175p. 1995. pap. 36.95 (*0-940808-91-9*) Camino E E & Bk.

Boxer Rebellion. Lynn Bodin. (Men-at-Arms Ser.: No. 95). (Illus.). 48p. pap. 11.95 (*0-85045-335-6*, 9031, Pub. by Osprey UK) Stackpole.

Boxer Rebellion. Joel Goldman. 288p. 1990. mass mkt. 4.95 (*0-380-70866-3*) Avon.

Boxer Rebellion. Paul H. Clements. LC 79-15870. (Columbia University. Studies in the Social Sciences: No. 160). reprint ed. 29.50 (*0-404-51160-0*) AMS Pr.

Boxer Rebellion & Other Tales. Joel Goldman, Jr. 1988. 17.95 (*1-55611-105-3*) D I Fine.

Boxers. Herta E. Kraupa-Tuskany. 1988. pap. 5.95 (*0-8120-4036-8*) Barron.

***Boxers.** Kurt Markus. 112p. 1995. 50.00 (*0-944092-36-5*) Twin Palms Pub.

Boxers. Beverly Pisano. (Illus.). 160p. 1981. 11.95 (*0-86622-160-3*, KW-041) TFH Pubns.

***Boxers.** limited ed. Kurt Markus. 112p. 1995. 150.00 (*0-944092-37-3*) Twin Palms Pub.

Boxer's Break. Mick Uranich. (Illus.). 64p. (Orig.). 1987. pap. text ed. 6.00 (*0-9622474-2-1*) Past Tents Pr.

***Boxer's Shorts: (More Than Just a Brief Attempt at Humor) - Round 2.** Robert W. Boxer. LC 94-92101. (Illus.). 144p. (Orig.). 1994. pap. 9.95 (*0-9620687-1-3*) Punchline Pr.

Boxer's Shorts (More Than Just a Brief Attempt at Humor) Robert W. Boxer. LC 88-90962. (Illus.). 144p. (Orig.). 1988. pap. 7.95 (*0-9620687-0-5*) Punchline Pr.

Boxers Today. Jo Royle. (Book of the Breed Ser.). (Illus.). 176p. 1994. 22.95 (*0-948955-08-2*, Pub. by Ringpr Bks UK) Seven Hills Bk.

Boxer's Workout. Peter DePasquale. LC 90-82757. (Illus.). 176p. 1990. reprint ed. pap. 14.95 (*0-9627050-0-4*) Fighting Fit.

Boxes. Rose Griffiths. (First Step Math Ser.). (Illus.). 32p. (J). (gr. 1 up). 1995. lib. bdg. 17.27 (*0-8368-1179-8*) Gareth Stevens Inc.

Boxes for the Protection of Books: Their Design & Construction. rev. ed. Illus. by Margaret Brown et al. LC 93-1994. 1994. write for info. (*0-8444-0797-6*) Lib Congress.

***Boxes, Squares, & Other Things.** Marion I. Walter. LC 71-111259. (Illus.). 88p. (J). (gr. 1-10). Date not set. reprint ed. pap. write for info. (*0-87353-410-7*) NCTM.

Boxing. Edwin L. Haislet. LC 82-81591. (Illus.). 124p. 1982. reprint ed. pap. 6.95 (*0-943736-00-5*) Ormsby.

Boxing - This Is It! Hank Kaplan & Enrique Encinosa. LC 84-1649. (Illus.). 256p. 1985. 19.95 (*0-88280-105-8*) ETC Pubns.

***Boxing & Medicine.** Robert C. Cantu. LC 94-33961. (Illus.). 224p. 1995. text ed. 35.00 (*0-87322-797-2*, BCAN0797) Human Kinetics.

Boxing Babylon: Behind the Shadowy World of the Prize Ring. Nigel Collins. 1990. 18.95 (*0-8065-1183-4*, Citadel Pr) Carol Pub Group.

Boxing Champion. Roch Carrier. LC 90-70133. (Illus.). 24p. (J). (gr. 3 up). 1991. 14.95 (*0-88776-249-2*) Tundra Bks.

Boxing Champion. Roch Carrier. (Illus.). 24p. (J). (gr. 3 up). 1993. pap. 6.95 (*0-88776-308-1*) Tundra Bks.

***Boxing Champion.** Roch Carrier. (J). (ps-3). 1993. pap. 6.95 (*0-88776-257-3*) Tundra Bks.

Boxing Legends. Greg Garber. LC 94-7837. 1994. write for info. (*1-56799-101-7*, Friedman-Fairfax) M Friedman Pub Grp Inc.

Boxing Skills for Fun and Fitness. Charles R. Schroeder. (Illus.). 117p. (YA). (gr. 8 up). 1973. 10.95 (*0-914338-01-3*) Regmar Pub.

Boxing's Strangest Fights: Incredible but True Encounters from over 250 Years of Boxing History. Graeme Kent. 248p. 1992. 24.95 (*0-86051-715-2*, Robson-Parkwest) Parkwest Pubns.

Boxtime Charterparty: An Industry Report. J. W. Richardson. 1990. pap. 160.00 (*1-85044-285-1*) Lloyds London Pr.

Boxwood & Ivory: Stanley Traditional Rules, 1855-1975. Philip E. Stanley. LC 84-50516. (Illus.). 188p. 1984. 20.00 (*0-9613291-0-6*) Stanley Pub Co.

***Boxwood Handbook: A Practical Guide to Knowing & Growing Boxwood.** Lynn R. Batdorf. (Illus.). 124p. (Orig.). 1995. pap. 15.00 (*1-886833-00-1*) Am Boxwood Soc.

Boy. Roald Dahl. 176p. 1988. pap. 9.00 (*0-14-008917-9*, Penguin Bks) Viking Penguin.

Boy: Tales of Childhood. Roald Dahl. LC 85-117335. (Illus.). 176p. (J). (gr. 3 up). 1984. 16.00 (*0-374-37374-4*) FS&G.

Boy: Tales of Childhood. Roald Dahl. (J). (gr. 4-6). 1986. pap. 4.99 (*0-14-031890-9*, Puffin) Puffin Bks.

Boy, a Ball, a Dream. Chris Roche. LC 92-72559. (Illus.). 1993. 21.95 (*0-8158-0488-1*) Chris Mass.

Boy, a Ball, & a Dream: The Marvin Wood Story. Kerry Marshall. (Illus.). 192p. (Orig.). 1991. 19.95 (*0-9630362-0-3*); pap. 10.45 (*0-9630362-1-1*) Scott IN.

***Boy, a Bike & Buster: Fishing & Hunting in Northern Michigans Good Old Days.** Gordie Charles. LC 94-61375. (Illus.). 160p. 1994. pap. 12.95 (*0-9642948-0-X*) Traverse Outdoor.

***Boy, a Chicken & the Lion of Judah: How Ari Became a Vegetarian.** Roberta Kalubofsky. LC 94-42519. 56p. (J). 1995. pap. 8.00 (*0-916288-39-0*) Micah Pubns.

Boy, a Dog, a Frog & a Friend. Marianna Mayer. 1993. pap. 3.99 (*0-14-054610-3*) Puffin Bks.

Boy, a Dog, a Frog & a Friend. Mercer Mayer. LC 70-134857. (J). (ps-2). 1971. reprint ed. 8.95 (*0-8037-0754-1*) Dial Bks Young.

Boy, a Dog, a Frog & a Friend. Mercer Mayer. LC 70-134857. (J). (ps-2). 1978. reprint ed. lib. bdg. 8.89 (*0-8037-0755-X*); reprint ed. pap. 2.95 (*0-8037-0804-1*) Dial Bks Young.

Boy, a Dog & a Frog. Mercer Mayer. LC 67-22254. (Pied Piper Bks.). (Illus.). (J). (ps-3). 1985. lib. bdg. 9.89 (*0-8037-0767-3*) Dial Bks Young.

Boy, a Dog & a Frog. Mercer Mayer. LC 67-22254. (Pied Piper Bks.). (Illus.). 32p. (J). (ps-2). 1985. reprint ed. pap. 3.50 (*0-8037-0769-X*) Dial Bks Young.

***Boy Across the River.** Kelby Tyler. 1995. 12.95 (*0-8062-5347-9*) Carlton.

***Boy & a Man: Short Stories of Interactions & Relationships.** Calvin White. 1995. 11.95 (*0-8062-5244-8*) Carlton.

Boy & His Baseball: The Dave Dravecky Story. Judy Gire. 32p. (J). 1992. 14.99 (*0-310-58630-5*) Zondervan.

Boy & His Piano. Julian Wiles & Laura Beck. 80p. (Orig.). 1991. 4.95 (*0-87129-027-8*, B66) Dramatic Pub.

Boy & the Book: A Story of Early Christian Ireland. Francis McCrickard. 104p. 1989. pap. 30.00 (*1-85390-018-4*, Pub. by Veritas IE) St Mut.

Boy & the Cloth of Dreams. Jenny Koralek. LC 93-23091. (Illus.). 32p. (J). (ps up). 1994. 14.95 (*1-56402-349-4*) Candlewick Pr.

Boy & the Dog. Siv Widerberg. Tr. by Richard E. Fisher. (Illus.). 28p. (J). (ps up). 1991. bds. 13.95 (*91-29-59926-1*, Pub. by R & S Bks) FS&G.

Boy & the Dolphin. John C. Fine. Ed. by Jane Weinberger. LC 90-70094. (Illus.). 34p. (J). (gr. 4-8). 1990. 12.95 (*0-932433-60-X*); pap. 9.95 (*0-932433-79-0*) Windswept Hse.

Boy & the Donkey. Carol Barnett. (J). (ps-3). 1990. 7.95 (*0-8442-9417-9*, Natl Textbk) NTC Pub Grp.

Boy & the Ghost. Robert D. San Souci. (Illus.). (J). (ps-3). 1989. pap. 13.95 (*0-671-67176-6*, S&S Bks Young Read) S&S Childrens.

Boy & the Ghost. Robert D. San Souci. LC 89-418. 40p. (J). (ps-3). 1992. pap. 5.95 (*0-671-79248-2*, S&S Bks Young Read) S&S Childrens.

Boy & the Giants. Fiona Moodie. (J). (ps-3). 1993. 15.00 (*0-374-30927-2*) FS&G.

Boy & the Goats. Margaret Hillert. (Illus.). (J). (ps-00). 1982. lib. bdg. 8.99 (*0-8136-5092-5*, TK2160); pap. 4.79 (*0-8136-5592-7*, TK2161) Modern Curr.

Boy & the Gunfighter. Spencer Knight. (Gunsmoke Western Ser.). 184p. 1990. text ed. 12.95 (*0-86220-924-2*, Gunsmoke) Chivers N Amer.

Boy & the Hat. Neal Starkman. LC 91-16798. 32p. (Orig.). (J). (gr. 4-6). 1991. pap. text ed. 9.00 (*0-935529-27-6*) Comprehen Health Educ.

Boy & the Horse. Frank Endersby. LC 90-46601. (Illus.). 16p. (J). (ps-2). 1976. 11.95 (*0-85953-098-1*, Pub. by Childs Play UK) Childs Play.

Boy & the Quilt. Shirley Kurtz. LC 91-74050. (Illus.). 32p. (J). (gr. 4-7). 1991. pap. 6.95 (*1-56148-009-6*) Good Bks PA.

Boy & the Samurai. Erik C. Haugaard. LC 90-47535. 256p. (J). (gr. 5-9). 1991. 14.95 (*0-395-56398-4*) HM.

Boy & the Whale: A Christmas Fairy Tale. Eric Metaxas. (Illus.). 48p. 1994. 14.95 (*1-884506-15-1*) Third Story.

Boy Apprenticed to an Enchanter. Padraic Colum. (Illus.). (J). (gr. 3-7). 1991. 20.00 (*0-8446-6482-0*) Peter Smith.

***Boy at Fort Mackinac: The Diary of Harold Dunbar Corbusier 1883-1884, 1892.** Ed. by Phil Porter. (Illus.). vi, 97p. (Orig.). 1994. pap. text ed. 7.00 (*0-911872-62-0*) Mackinac Island.

Boy at the Window. Owen Dodson. 212p. 1972. reprint ed. 15.00 (*0-911860-10-X*) Chatham Bkseller.

Boy Becomes a Man at Wounded Knee. Ted Wood & Wanbli Numpa Afraid of Hawk. 42p. (YA). 1992. 15.95 (*0-8027-8174-8*); lib. bdg. 16.85 (*0-8027-8175-6*) Walker & Co.

***Boy Becomes a Man at Wounded Knee.** Ted Wood & Wanbli N. Afraid. 48p. (J). (gr. 3-7). 1995. pap. 6.95 (*0-8027-7446-6*) Walker & Co.

Boy Behind the Counter. Kalindi Handler. 160p. (Orig.). (YA). (gr. 7 up). 1989. pap. 2.50 (*0-380-75646-3*, Flare) Avon.

Boy Called Hopeless. David Melton. LC 86-27557. (Illus.). 231p. (J). (gr. 4-8). 1986. reprint ed. lib. bdg. 13.95 (*0-933849-32-X*) Landmark Edns.

Boy Called Hopeless. David Melton. LC 86-27557. (Illus.). 232p. (J). (gr. 4 up). 1986. reprint ed. pap. 5.95 (*0-933849-07-9*) Landmark Edns.

Boy Called Mish Mash. Myrnie O'Callaghan. LC 91-92177. 100p. (Orig.). (J). (gr. 5-8). 1991. pap. 9.95 (*0-9630075-0-5*) Creole Connect.

Boy Called Slow. Joseph Bruchac. LC 93-21233. (Illus.). (J). 1994. write for info. (*0-399-22692-3*, Philomel Bks) Putnam Pub Group.

Boy, Can He Dance! Eileen Spinelli. LC 92-12929. (Illus.). 32p. (J). (ps-2). 1993. text ed. 14.95 (*0-02-786350-6*, Four Winds Pr) S&S Childrens.

Boy Captive in Canada. Mary P. Smith. 1990. reprint ed. 11.75 (*0-9612876-6-7*) Pocumtuck Valley Mem.

Boy Captive of Deerfield. Mary P. Smith. 1991. reprint ed. 10.75 (*0-9612876-5-9*) Pocumtuck Valley Mem.

Boy Captive of Old Deerfield. Mary P. Smith. (Illus.). (J). (gr. 5-6). reprint ed. lib. bdg. 20.95 (*0-89190-961-3*, Rivercity Pr) Amereon Ltd.

Boy Colonel of the Confederacy: The Life & Times of Henry King Burgwyn, Jr. Archie K. Davis. LC 84-26958. (Illus.). xiv, 406p. 1985. 32.50 (*0-8078-1647-7*) U of NC Pr.

Boy-Crazy Stacey. Ann M. Martin. (Baby-Sitters Club Ser.: No. 8). (Orig.). (J). (gr. 4-7). 1987. pap. 3.50 (*0-590-43509-4*) Scholastic Inc.

Boy David, etc. see Works of J. M. Barrie

***Boy Detective.** Sobol. (Encyclopedia Brown Ser.: No. 1). (J). 1995. mass mkt. 1.99 (*0-553-56751-9*) Dell.

Boy Friends & Boyfriends. Dianna Booher. LC 87-28777. (Orig.). (YA). (gr. 7 up). 1988. pap. 5.99 (*0-8007-5274-0*) Revell.

Boy from Abilene: The Story of Dwight D. Eisenhower. Diane Sherman. 16.95 (*0-89190-786-6*, Am Repr) Amereon Ltd.

Boy from Custer: The First Twenty Five Years. Arthur J. Pejsa. (Illus.). 164p. (Orig.). 1992. pap. 19.95 (*0-9612776-5-3*) Kenwood Pub.

Boy from Kahaluu. Thomas H. Ige. LC 89-19761. (Illus.). 192p. 1990. 25.00 (*0-8248-1291-3*) UH Pr.

Boy from over There. Tamar Bergman. (J). (gr. 4-7). 1992. pap. 4.95 (*0-395-64370-8*) HM.

Boy Full of Joy. Brian Van Horn & Chris Van Horn. (Illus.). (J). (ps-5). 1989. write for info. (*1-877765-01-5*) Lambgel Family.

Boy Gets Car. Henry G. Felsen. (Illus.). (J). (gr. 7-11). 1968. lib. bdg. 5.39 (*0-394-90976-3*) Random Bks Yng Read.

Boy Harlequin & Other Stories. Girard Kent. 208p. (Orig.). 1983. pap. 7.95 (*0-917342-29-1*) Gay Sunshine.

Boy Helps Jesus. Kenneth N. Taylor. (Bible Treasures Ser.). (J). (ps-3). 1994. 3.99 (*0-8423-1292-7*) Tyndale.

Boy, Howdy! Jack Boyd. LC 90-33521. (Cedar Gap Archives Ser.: Vol. 2). 1990. 12.95 (*0-89672-227-9*) Tex Tech Univ Pr.

Boy Hunters. Thomas M. Reid. LC 68-23725. (Americans in Fiction Ser.). reprint ed. lib. bdg. 17.00 (*0-8398-1750-9*); reprint ed. pap. text ed. 4.95 (*0-89197-685-X*) Irvington.

Boy I Knew. Laurence Hutton. (Notable American Authors Ser.). 1992. reprint ed. lib. bdg. 75.00 (*0-7812-3319-4*) Rprt Serv.

Boy I Never Knew. Patricia Sierra. 128p. (YA). (gr. 7 up). 1988. pap. 2.50 (*0-380-75208-5*, Flare) Avon.

Boy in Rural Mississippi. S. G. Thigpen. (Illus.). 1966. 5.00 (*0-685-20525-8*) Thigpen.

Boy in the Air. Don Bajema. Ed. by Rollins. 140p. (Orig.). 1990. pap. 8.00 (*1-880985-06-3*) Two Thirteen Sixty-one.

Boy in the Alamo. Margaret Cousins. LC 83-72585. (Illus.). 180p. (J). (gr. 5-7). 1983. reprint ed. pap. 5.95 (*0-931722-26-8*) Corona Pub.

Boy in the Bush. D. H. Lawrence. Ed. by Paul Eggert. (Cambridge Edition of the Works of D. H. Lawrence). 560p. (C). 1990. 94.95 (*0-521-30704-X*) Cambridge U Pr.

Boy in the Bush. D. H. Lawrence. 400p. 1992. 9.95 (*0-14-018446-5*, Penguin Classics) Viking Penguin.

Boy in the Doghouse. Betsy Duffey. LC 90-47751. (Illus.). 96p. (J). 1991. pap. 12.00 (*0-671-73618-3*, S&S Bks Young Read) S&S Childrens.

Boy in the Doghouse. Betsy Duffey. LC 90-47751. (Illus.). 96p. (J). (gr. 2-6). 1993. pap. 2.95 (*0-671-86698-2*, Half Moon Paper) S&S Childrens.

Boy in the Drawer. Robert Munsch. 32p. (J). (gr. k-3). 1982. lib. bdg. 14.95 (*0-920236-34-0*, Pub. by Annick CN); pap. 4.95 (*0-920236-36-7*, Pub. by Annick CN) Firefly Bks Ltd.

Boy in the Drawer. Robert Munsch. (Annikin Ser.: Series 5). (Illus.). 24p. (J). (ps-1). 1987. pap. 0.99 (*0-920303-50-1*, Pub. by Annick CN) Firefly Bks Ltd.

Boy in the Mirror. Keith Chatfield. 1990. pap. 1.95 (*0-907018-51-3*, Pub. by Tabb Hse Pubs UK) Seven Hills Bk.

Boy in the Moon. Ron Koertge. 176p. (J). 1992. mass mkt. 3.99 (*0-380-71474-4*, Flare) Avon.

Boy in the Peninsular War. Robert Blakeney. 400p. 40.00 (*1-85367-029-4*, 5450) Stackpole.

***Boy in the Stone.** Badger. 150p. (Orig.). 1995. pap. 4.99x (*0-9647120-0-8*) Badger Publng.

***Boy in the Well.** Daniel M. Epstein. 80p. (Orig.). 1995. pap. 13.95 (*0-87951-597-X*) Overlook Pr.

***Boy in the Welland Other Poems.** Daniel M. Epstein. 80p. (Orig.). 1995. 19.95 (*0-87951-587-2*) Overlook Pr.

Boy Inside the American Businessman: Corporate Darwinism in Twentieth-Century American Literature. Carl S. Horner. LC 92-16088. 1992. 37.50 (*0-8191-8749-6*); pap. 16.50 (*0-8191-8750-X*) U Pr of Amer.

Boy into Man: A Fathers' Guide to Initiation of Teenage Sons. Bernard Weiner. (Illus.). 70p. (Orig.). 1992. pap. 9.95 (*0-9632636-0-9*) Transform CA. Most initiations of teenage boys are carried out by institutions: Boy Scouts, synagogues, churches, etc. BOY INTO MAN shows how parents can create & carry out coming-of-age ceremonies for their sons of a more personal, meaningful kind. The rite of passage described (with text & photos included) is based on one the author & fellow dads carried out over a weekend in the Sierra foothills. The author, the San Francisco Chronicle's theater critic from 1974-1990, used theatrical techniques & rituals from a wide variety of cultures to create "a template of what modern day rites of passage can be...a particularly innovative coming-of-age ceremony," according to Gordon Clay, Director of the National Men's Resource Center. As it turns out, doing a ceremony like the one described in BOY INTO MAN initiates everyone: boys, fathers, mothers. Also included are chapters on the mothers' ritual, storytelling, the boys' experiences in the woods, & helpful hints for fathers who might want to try something similar. Distributed by Inland Book Company, Moving Books, New Leaf Distributing. (ISBN 0-9632636-0-9). Transformation

Press, 197 Bonview Street, Box R, San Francisco, CA 94110. *Publisher Provided Annotation.*

Boy Inventor. Thomas Bulfinch. (Works of Thomas Bulfinch). 1989. reprint ed. lib. bdg. 79.00 (*0-7812-2164-1*) Rprt Serv.

Boy Is Something Special. (Little Remembrance Gift Editions Ser.). 6.95 (*0-87741-001-1*) Makepeace Colony.

Boy-Is-This-Place-Big Biltmore House Spark Kit. Carole Marsh. (S. P. A. R. K. Ser.). (Illus.). (Orig.). (J). (gr. 3-12). 1994. lib. bdg. 24.95 (*0-935326-22-7*) Gallopade Pub Group.

Boy Jesus Goes A-Walking & Other Stories. Mary Richardson. (Illus.). 96p. 1988. pap. 2.95 (*0-8091-6575-9*) Paulist Pr.

Boy King. Greg Stafford. Ed. by Sam Shirley. (Pendragon Roleplaying Game System Ser.). (Illus.). 136p. (Orig.). 1991. pap. 18.95 (*0-933635-78-8*, 2708) Chaosium.

Boy Knight, 1. G. A. Henty. 1986. pap. 5.99 (*0-88019-184-8*) Schmul Pub Co.

Boy Knight, 2. G. A. Henty. 1986. pap. 5.99 (*0-88019-199-6*) Schmul Pub Co.

Boy Life on the Prairie. Hamlin Garland. LC 61-16185. 471p. reprint ed. pap. 134.30 (*0-7837-0083-0*, 2040345) Bks Demand.

Boy Life on the Prairie. Hamlin Garland. (Collected Works of Hamlin Garland). 1988. reprint ed. lib. bdg. 79.00 (*0-7812-1228-6*) Rprt Serv.

Boy Life on the Prairie see Collected Works of Hamlin Garland

Boy Looked at Johnny: The Obituary of Rock & Roll. Julie Burchill & Tony Parsons. (Illus.). 128p. (Orig.). 1987. reprint ed. pap. 9.95 (*0-571-12992-7*) Faber & Faber.

Boy Mechanic, Bk. 1. 470p. (J). (gr. 5 up). reprint ed. 29.95 (*0-917914-89-9*); reprint ed. pap. 17.95 (*0-917914-88-0*) Lindsay Pubns.

Boy Meets Family: Manuscript Edition. Allan Rieser. 1990. pap. 13.00 (*0-8222-0141-0*) Dramatists Play.

Boy Meets Girl. H. Eugene Netherton. 112p. (Orig.). 1975. pap. 2.00 (*0-686-31977-X*) Netherton.

Boy Meets Girl & Spring Song: Manuscript Edition. Bella Spewack. 1946. pap. 13.00 (*0-8222-0142-9*) Dramatists Play.

Boy Meets Horn. Rex Stewart. Ed. by Claire P. Gordon. 250p. 1990. 27.95 (*0-472-10213-3*) U of Mich Pr.

Boy Meets Horn. Rex Stewart. Ed. by Claire P. Gordon. (Michigan Music Ser.). (Illus.). 264p. 1993. pap. 15.95 (*0-472-08229-9*) U of Mich Pr.

Boy My Very Special Friend. Mimi Petroske. Ed. by Mary Caroland. (Illus.). 44p. (J). (gr. k-3). 1991. 5.95 (*1-55523-381-3*) Winston-Derek.

Boy Named Chong. Brian Marchant & Heather Marchant. 40p. (J). (gr. k-9). 1993. pap. 11.95 (*1-885298-00-5*); vhs 14.95 (*1-885298-01-3*) Project Chong.

Boy Named Ossie: A Jamaican Childhood. Earl McKenzie. (Caribbean Writers Ser.). (Illus.). 104p. (Orig.). (YA). 1991. pap. 8.95 (*0-435-98816-6*, 98816) Heinemann.

Boy Next Door. Betty Cavanna. (J). (gr. 4-7). 1992. pap. 2.50 (*0-8167-1270-0*) Troll Assocs.

***Boy Next Door.** Quin-Harkin. (Love Stories Ser.: No. 4). 1995. mass mkt. 3.50 (*0-553-56663-6*) Bantam.

***Boy Next Door.** Sinclair Smith. (YA). 1995. pap. 3.50 (*0-590-48677-2*) Scholastic Inc.

Boy No More. Paxton Davis. LC 92-16715. (Illus.). 252p. 1992. 17.95 (*0-89587-094-0*) Blair.

Boy Not Say Name. (Illus.). (J). (ps-2). 1991. lib. bdg. 8.99 (*0-8136-5041-0*); pap. 4.79 (*0-8136-5541-2*) Modern Curr.

Boy of Blossom Prairie, Who Became Vice-President. Maurine W. Liles. (J). 1993. 14.95 (*0-89015-913-0*) Sunbelt Media.

Boy of Kanawha. McCoy. 1984. pap. 3.50 (*0-941092-12-7*) Mtn St Pr.

Boy of la Mancha. Nelson A. Ossorio & Michele B. Salvadeo. (Spark of Life Ser.). (Illus.). 60p. (J). (gr. 4-6). 1994. pap. 6.95 (*1-56721-068-6*) Twnty-Fifth Cent Pr.

Boy of Nazareth. Erwin W. Cook. (J). 1994. pap. 4.95 (*0-533-10728-8*) Vantage.

Boy of the Bells. Carly Simon. (J). 1990. 14.95 (*0-385-41587-7*) Doubleday.

Boy of the Land, Man of the Lord. Elaine Cannon. pap. 5.95 (*0-88494-722-X*) Bookcraft Inc.

Boy of the Painted Cave. Justin Denzel. 160p. (J). (gr. 3-7). 1988. 14.95 (*0-399-21559-X*, Philomel Bks) Putnam Pub Group.

Boy of the Three-Year Nap. Illus. by Allen Say. LC 87-30674. 32p. (J). (ps-3). 1988. 16.95 (*0-395-44090-4*) HM.

Boy of the Three-Year Nap. Dianne Snyder. (J). (ps-3). 1993. pap. 4.95 (*0-395-66957-X*) HM.

Boy on a Black Horse. Nancy Springer. LC 92-27158. 176p. (J). (gr. 5-9). 1994. lib. bdg. 14.95 (*0-689-31840-5*, Atheneum Bks Young) S&S Childrens.

***Boy on a Black Horse.** Nancy Springer. (J). (gr. 4-7). 1995. pap. 3.95 (*0-8167-3633-2*) Troll Assocs.

Boy on Platform One see Memory Boy

Boy on the Back Wall. James Plunkett. 208p. 1987. pap. 8.95 (*0-905169-60-3*, Pub. by Poolbeg Pr IE) Dufour.

Boy on the Beach. Margaret Meacham. (Illus.). 144p. (Orig.). (J). (gr. 4-8). 1992. pap. 8.95 (*0-87033-441-7*, Tidewtr Pubs) Cornell Maritime.

***Boy on the Bicycle.** Thom Nickels. LC 92-82592. 384p. (Orig.). 1993. pap. 13.95 (*1-877978-59-0*, STARbks Pr) Woldt.

***Boy on the Bus.** Diana Loski. (Illus.). 30p. (Orig.). (J). (ps-5). 1994. pap. 6.99 (*1-885101-02-3*) Writers Pr Srv.

***Boy on the Bus, 35 bks., Large Class Set.** Diana Loski. (Illus.). (Orig.). (J). (gr. k-5). Date not set. pap. 244.65 (*1-885101-26-0*) Writers Pr Srv.

***Boy on the Bus, 10 bks., Resource Room Set.** Diana Loski. (Illus.). (Orig.). (J). (gr. k-5). Date not set. pap. 69.90 (*1-885101-24-4*) Writers Pr Srv.

***Boy on the Bus, 25 bks., Small Class Set.** Diana Loski. (Illus.). (Orig.). (J). (gr. k-5). Date not set. pap. 174.75 (*1-885101-25-2*) Writers Pr Srv.

Boy on the Cover. Phoebe Matthews. (YA). (gr. 7 up). 1988. pap. 2.75 (*0-380-75407-X*, Flare) Avon.

Boy on the Rooftop. Tamas Szabo. Tr. by David Hughes. 12.00 (*0-8446-0931-5*) Peter Smith.

Boy on the Step. Stanley Plumly. 1989. 17.95 (*0-88001-228-5*) Ecco Pr.

Boy on the Step. Stanley Plumly. 1991. pap. 9.95 (*0-88001-229-3*) Ecco Pr.

Boy or Girl? Elizabeth M. Whelan. LC 76-44667. (Illus.). 1977. 7.95 (*0-672-52276-4*, Bobbs) Macmillan.

Boy or Girl? Elizabeth M. Whelan. 1991. mass mkt. 5.50 (*0-671-73901-8*) PB.

Boy or Girl? rev. ed. Elizabeth M. Whelan. LC 76-44667. 155p. 1984. write for info. (*0-672-52811-8*) Macmillan.

Boy or Girl? Fifty Fun Ways to Find Out. Shelly Lavigne. (Illus.). (Orig.). 1992. mass mkt. 5.99 (*0-440-50459-7*, Dell Trade Pbks) Dell.

Boy Picked up by the Wind: Poems. Robert Gregory. LC 92-33758. 84p. 1992. 18.00 (*1-878325-07-8*); pap. 9.95 (*1-878325-06-X*) Bluestem Press.

***Boy Poems.** Rod Smith. 36p. 1995. pap. 4.00 (*1-886353-01-8*) B Downs Bks.

Boy Sandwich. Beryl Gilroy. (Caribbean Writers Ser.). 122p. (Orig.). (C). 1989. pap. 7.50 (*0-435-98810-7*, 98810) Heinemann.

Boy Sarah. large type ed. Grace Thompson. (Romance Ser.). 528p. 1992. 21.95 (*0-7089-2756-4*) Ulverscroft.

Boy Scout Collector's Bibliography. Comp. & Frwd. by Bill Sheldon. 254p. (Orig.). (J). (gr. 6-12). 1987. pap. 13.50 (*0-9616668-0-3*) B Sheldon.

Boy Scout Handbook. 10th ed. Robert C. Birkby. (Illus.). 672p. (YA). (gr. 6-12). 1992. 5.00 (*0-685-48068-2*, 33229) BSA.

Boy Scout Requirements. 136p. 1991. pap. 1.75 (*0-8395-3216-4*, 33217) BSA.

Boy Scout Roundtable Commissioner Training. Boy Scouts of America Staff. (Illus.). 48p. (Orig.). 1988. pap. 7.00 (*0-8395-4256-9*, 34256) BSA.

Boy Scout Roundtable Planning Guide. rev. ed. Boy Scouts of America Staff. (Illus.). 326p. 1988. pap. 9.65 (*0-8395-4253-4*, 7263A) BSA.

Boy Scout Songbook. Boy Scouts of America. 128p. (J). (gr. 6-12). 1970. pap. 1.55 (*0-8395-3224-5*, 33224) BSA.

Boy Scouts. Carolyn Soto. 1988. 7.98 (*0-671-08914-5*) S&S Trade.

Boy Scouts: An American Adventure. Robert W. Peterson. (Illus.). 256p. 1985. pap. 12.95 (*0-685-42998-9*) HM.

Boy Scouts Beyond the Seas: My World Tour. Robert Baden-Powell. (Illus.). 250p. 1992. pap. 17.95 (*0-9632054-4-7*) Stevens Pub.

Boy Scout's Hike Book. Edward Cave. 243p. (YA). (gr. 10). 1992. pap. 12.95 (*0-9632054-0-4*) Stevens Pub.

Boy Sex Offender & His Later Career. Lewis J. Doshay. LC 69-14921. (Criminology, Law Enforcement, & Social Problems Ser.: No. 59). 1969. reprint ed. 20.00 (*0-87585-059-6*) Patterson Smith.

Boy That I Used to Be. Todd Tessmer. 1991. 7.95 (*0-533-09355-4*) Vantage.

Boy, the Devil, & Divorce. Richard Frede. Ed. by Bill Grose. 400p. 1994. reprint ed. mass mkt. 5.99 (*0-671-77662-2*) PB.

Boy Through the Ages. Dorothy M. Stuart. LC 89-43349. (Illus.). 288p. 1990. reprint ed. lib. bdg. 38.00 (*1-55888-869-1*) Omnigraphics Inc.

Boy Toy. Derek Adams. (Orig.). 1995. pap. text ed. 4.95 (*1-56333-260-4*) Masquerade.

Boy Toy. Phyllis Johnson. (Illus.). 32p. (J). (gr. k-3). 1988. pap. 5.95 (*0-914996-26-6*) Lollipop Power.

Boy Trouble. Francine Pascal. (Sweet Valley Ser.: No. 61). (YA). 1990. 2.95 (*0-553-28317-0*) Bantam.

Boy Trouble. Suzanne Weyn. LC 90-11142. (Sitting Pretty Ser.). 128p. (J). (gr. 4-8). 1991. lib. bdg. 9.89 (*0-8167-2011-8*); pap. text ed. 2.95 (*0-8167-2012-6*) Troll Assocs.

Boy Trouble for Tess & Ali. Janet Quin-Harkin. (Friends Ser.: No. 3). (YA). 1991. mass mkt. 3.50 (*0-06-106065-8*, Harp PBks) HarpC.

Boy under the Bed. Philip Dacey. LC 80-8858. (Poetry & Fiction Ser.). 1981. text ed. 16.50 (*0-8018-2601-2*); pap. text ed. 7.95 (*0-8018-2602-0*) Johns Hopkins.

Boy Wants a Dinosaur. Hiawyn Oram. (J). (ps-3). 1991. bds. 13.95 (*0-374-30939-6*) FS&G.

Boy Wants a Dinosaur. Hiawyn Oram. (J). (ps-3). 1993. pap. 4.95 (*0-374-40889-0*) FS&G.

Boy Who Adopted Me. Don Weldon. 260p. (Orig.). 1994. pap. 9.95 (*0-89896-284-6*) Larksdale.

Boy Who Ate Dog Biscuits. Betsy Sachs. LC 89-3905. (Stepping Stone Bks.). (Illus.). 64p. (J). (gr. 2-4). 1989. pap. 2.99 (*0-394-84778-4*) Random Bks Yng Read.

Boy Who Came Back to Life see Arch Books Series 20

Boy Who Could Make His Mother Stop Yelling. Ilse Sondheimer. (Illus.). 32p. (J). (ps-6). 1982. lib. bdg. 9.95 (*0-943156-00-9*); pap. 2.95 (*0-943156-01-7*) Rainbow Pr NY.

Boy Who Could Not Fly. John J. Dennis. 64p. (J). (gr. 4-8). pap. 7.95 (*0-9629036-0-4*) Grow Up Hlthy.

Boy Who Couldn't. Daryl Knauer. Ed. by Diane Stortz. (Little Deer Bks.). (Illus.). 28p. (J). (ps). 1994. 5.49 (*0-7847-0199-7*, 24-03879) Standard Pub.

Boy Who Couldn't Stop Washing: The Experience & Treatment of Obesessive-Compulsive Disorder. Judith L. Rapoport. 272p. 1990. pap. 9.95 (*0-452-26365-4*, Plume) NAL-Dutton.

Boy Who Couldn't Stop Washing: The Experience & Treatment of Obsessive-Compulsive Disorder. Judith L. Rapoport. 304p. 1991. pap. 5.99 (*0-451-17202-7*, Sig) NAL-Dutton.

Boy Who Counted Stars. David Harrison. LC 92-61632. (Illus.). 32p. (J). (gr. 1-5). 1994. 14.95 (*1-56397-125-9*, Wordsong) Boyds Mills Pr.

Boy Who Cried Wolf. Carol Barnett. (J). (ps-3). 1990. 7.95 (*0-8442-9419-5*, Natl Textbk) NTC Pub Grp.

Boy Who Cried Wolf! Illus. by Gary Chalk. (J). (gr. 4 up). 1994. 10.95 (*0-553-09043-7*) Bantam.

Boy Who Cried Wolf. Ellen Schecter. (Bank Street Ready-to-Read Ser.: No. 49). (J). (ps-3). 1994. 3.99 (*0-553-37232-7*) Bantam.

Boy Who Cried Wolf: The First Book to Break Masonic Silence. Richard P. Thorn. 1994. 18.95 (*0-87131-760-5*) M Evans.

Boy Who Didn't Believe in Spring. Lucille Clifton. (Unicorn Paperbacks Ser.). (Illus.). (J). (gr. 3-4). 1973. 14.99 (*0-525-27145-7*, DCB); pap. 1.95 (*0-525-45038-6*, DCB) Dutton Child Bks.

Boy Who Didn't Believe in Spring. Lucille Clifton. LC 87-27145. (Unicorn Paperbacks Ser.). (Illus.). 32p. (J). (ps-3). 1988. pap. 4.95 (*0-525-44365-7*, 0383-120, DCB) Dutton Child Bks.

Boy Who Didn't Believe in Spring. Lucille Clifton. (J). (ps-3). 1992. pap. 4.99 (*0-14-054739-8*) Viking Child Bks.

Boy Who Drank Too Much. Shep Greene. 144p. (YA). (gr. 7 up). 1980. pap. 3.50 (*0-440-90493-5*, LFL) Dell.

Boy Who Dreamed of an Acorn. Leigh Casler. LC 92-44902. (Illus.). 32p. (J). (ps up). 1994. lib. bdg. 15.95 (*0-399-22547-1*, Philomel Bks) Putnam Pub Group.

Boy Who Drew Cats. David Johnson. (We All Have Tales Book & Cassette Ser.). (Illus.). 40p. (J). (gr. k up). 1991. pap. 14.95 (*0-88708-194-0*, Rabbit); audio 19.95 (*0-88708-195-9*, Rabbit) S&S Childrens.

Boy Who Drew Cats: A Japanese Folktale. Arthur A. Levine. LC 91-46232. (J). (ps-3). 1994. 16.00 (*0-8037-1172-7*); 15.89 (*0-8037-1173-5*) Dial Bks Young.

Boy Who Followed Ripley. Patricia Highsmith. 1993. pap. 10.00 (*0-679-74567-X*, Vin) Random.

Boy Who Gave His Lunch Away: John 6: 1-15. Concordia Staff. (J). 1993. pap. 1.99 (*0-570-06027-3*) Concordia.

Boy Who Held Back the Sea. Illus. by Thomas Locker. LC 86-32893. (J). 1987. 15.99 (*0-8037-0406-2*) Dial Bks Young.

Boy Who Held Back the Sea. Thomas Locker. (J). (ps-3). 1991. pap. 4.95 (*0-8037-1049-6*, Puff Pied Piper) Puffin Bks.

Boy Who Held Back the Sea. Thomas Locker. (J). 1993. pap. 4.99 (*0-14-054613-8*, Puff Pied Piper) Puffin Bks.

Boy Who Knew the Language of the Birds. Margaret K. Wetterer. (Fiction Ser.). (Illus.). 48p. (J). (gr. 2-5). 1991. lib. bdg. 17.50 (*0-87614-652-3*, Carolrhoda) Lerner Group.

Boy Who Lived with Seals. Rafe Martin. (Illus.). 32p. (J). (ps-3). 1993. lib. bdg. 14.95 (*0-399-22413-0*, Putnam) Putnam Pub Group.

Boy Who Lived with the Bears: And Other Iroquois Stories. Joseph Bruchac. LC 94-9829. (Illus.). 64p. (J). (gr. 2 up). 1995. lib. bdg. 15.89 (*0-06-021288-8*, HarpT) HarpC Child Bks.

Boy Who Lived with the Bears: And Other Iroquois Stories. Joseph Bruchac. LC 94-9829. (Illus.). 64p. (J). (gr. 2 up). 1995. 15.95 (*0-06-021287-X*, HarpT) HarpC Child Bks.

Boy Who Looked Different. Bezalie P. Bautista. (Illus.). 24p. (Orig.). (J). (gr. k-2). 1990. pap. 3.50 (*971-10-0406-2*, Pub. by New Day Pub PH) Cellar.

Boy Who Looked for Spring. Susan Fleischman. LC 90-36819. (J). (gr. 4-7). 1993. 15.95 (*0-15-210699-5*) HarBrace.

Boy Who Lost His Face. Louis Sachar. LC 88-22622. 192p. (J). (gr. 5-9). 1989. 11.95 (*0-394-82863-1*) Knopf Bks Yng Read.

Boy Who Loved Alligators. Barbara Kennedy. LC 93-15982. 144p. (J). (gr. 3-7). 1994. text ed. 14.95 (*0-689-31876-6*, Atheneum Bks Young) S&S Childrens.

Boy Who Loved Bears: A Pawnee Folktale. Illus. by Charles W. Chapman. LC 94-9067. (Adventures in Storytelling Ser.). 48p. (J). (ps-3). 1994. lib. bdg. 13.80 (*0-516-05142-3*) Childrens.

Boy Who Loved Bears: A Pawnee Folktale. Illus. by Charles W. Chapman. LC 94-9067. (Adventures in Storytelling Ser.). 48p. (J). (ps-3). 1994. pap. 5.95 (*0-516-45142-1*) Childrens.

***Boy Who Loved Dumplings.** Sandra S. Yamate. Ed. by Lisa Trumbauer. (Multicultural Big Bks.). (Illus.). 16p. (J). (ps-2). 1994. pap. text ed. 14.95 (*1-56784-500-2*) Newbridge Comms.

Boy Who Loved Mammoths. Martin Rafe. (Storytelling-Folklore Ser.). (Illus.). 64p. (Orig.). Date not set. pap. 10.95 (*0-938756-42-7*) Yellow Moon.

Boy Who Loved Morning. Shannon K. Jacobs. (J). (ps-3). 1993. 15.95 (*0-316-45556-3*) Little.

Boy Who Made Dragonfly: A Zuni Myth. Illus. by Janet Grado. LC 86-6996. 85p. (J). (gr. 5 up). 1986. reprint ed. pap. 8.95 (*0-8263-0910-0*) U of NM Pr.

Boy Who Owned the School. Gary Paulsen. (J). 1991. pap. 3.50 (*0-440-70694-7*) Dell.

Boy Who Owned the School. Gary Paulsen. LC 89-23048. 112p. (J). (gr. 6-9). 1990. 14.95 (*0-531-05865-4*); lib. bdg. 14.99 (*0-531-08465-5*) Orchard Bks Watts.

Boy Who Owned the School. Gary Paulsen. (J). (gr. 4-7). 1991. pap. 3.50 (*0-440-40524-6*, YB) Dell.

Boy Who Picked the Bullets Up. Charles Nelson. (Meadowland Ser.). 1988. pap. 7.95 (*0-317-68068-4*) Carol Pub Group.

Boy Who Picked the Bullets Up. Charles Nelson. 1988. pap. 9.95 (*0-8216-2002-9*, Univ Books) Carol Pub Group.

Boy Who Remembered Everything. Jennie Abbott. LC 87-14986. (Super Squad Ser.). (Illus.). 96p. (J). (gr. 5-8). 1988. lib. bdg. 9.89 (*0-8167-1183-6*); pap. text ed. 2.95 (*0-8167-1184-4*) Troll Assocs.

Boy Who Rode a Lion. James Ngumy. (Junior African Writers Ser.). (Illus.). (J). (gr. 4-5). 1992. pap. 2.95 (*0-7910-2907-7*) Chelsea Hse.

Boy Who Sailed with Columbus. Michael Foreman. (Illus.). 80p. (J). (gr. 1-4). 1992. 16.95 (*1-55970-178-1*) Arcade Pub Inc.

Boy Who Saved His Family. Alyce Bergey & Betty Wind. (Arch Bks.: Set 3). 1966. 1.99 (*0-570-06017-6*, 59-1126) Concordia.

Boy Who Saved the Town. Brenda Seabrooke. LC 89-52027. (Illus.). 30p. (J). (gr. 2-5). 1990. 7.95 (*0-87033-405-0*, Tidewtr Pubs) Cornell Maritime.

Boy Who Saw True. 248p. 1961. 11.95 (*0-685-06950-8*, Pub. by C W Daniel UK) Atrium Pubs.

Boy Who Saw True. 11th ed. Intro. by Cyril Scott. 248p. 1994. pap. 17.95 (*0-8464-4204-3*) Beekman Pubs.

Boy Who Set the Fire & Other Stories. Mohammed Mrabet. Tr. by Paul Bowles. 144p. 1989. reprint ed. pap. 8.95 (*0-87286-230-5*) City Lights.

Boy Who Shot down an Airship. large type ed. Michael Green. 275p. 1991. 10.97 (*1-85089-431-0*, Pub. by ISIS UK) Transaction Pubs.

Boy Who Spoke Colors. David Gifaldi. LC 92-11301. (Illus.). 32p. (J). (gr. 2-5). 1993. 14.95 (*0-395-65025-9*) HM.

Boy Who Stopped Time. Anthony Taber. LC 92-398. (Illus.). 32p. (J). (ps-3). 1993. text ed. 13.95 (*0-689-50460-8*, McElderry) S&S Childrens.

Boy Who Swallowed a Rainbow. Trevor Romain. (Illus.). 32p. (J). (ps-5). 1993. 13.95 (*1-880092-05-0*) Bright Bks TX.

Boy Who Swallowed Snakes. Laurence Yep et al. LC 93-21822. (Illus.). 32p. (J). (gr. 5 up). 1994. 14.95 (*0-590-46168-0*) Scholastic Inc.

Boy Who Talked to Whales. Webster Smalley. (Orig.). 1981. 5.00 (*0-87602-232-8*) Anchorage.

Boy Who Turned into a TV Set. Stephen Manes. (Illus.). 32p. (Orig.). (J). (gr. 2-5). 1983. pap. 2.50 (*0-380-62000-6*, Camelot) Avon.

Boy Who Wanted the Moon. Betsy Hernandez et al. (Land of Pleasant Dreams Ser.). (Illus.). 26p. (J). (ps up). 1986. Book & Cassette. 7.95 (*1-55578-100-4*); audio (*0-318-61947-4*) Worlds Wonder.

Boy Who Was Followed Home. Margaret Mahy. LC 75-2866. (Pied Piper Bks.). (Illus.). 32p. (J). (ps-3). 1986. 14.99 (*0-8037-0286-8*) Dial Bks Young.

Boy Who Was Followed Home. Margaret Mahy. (J). (ps-3). 1993. pap. 5.99 (*0-14-054614-6*) Dial Bks Young.

Boy Who Was Followed Home. Margaret Mahy. (Pied Piper Bks.). (Illus.). 32p. (J). (ps-3). 1983. pap. 4.95 (*0-8037-0903-X*) Dial Bks Young.

Boy Who Wasn't There. Hans Wilhelm. LC 92-29874. (J). 1993. 14.95 (*0-590-46635-6*) Scholastic Inc.

Boy Who Would Be a Helicopter. Vivian G. Paley. 163p. 1990. 26.50 (*0-674-08030-0*) HUP.

Boy Who Would Be a Helicopter. Vivian G. Paley. 163p. 1991. pap. text ed. 9.95 (*0-674-08031-9*) HUP.

Boy Who Wouldn't Eat Breakfast. Eugene Coco. (Storytime Bks.). (Illus.). 24p. (J). (ps-2). 1993. pap. text ed. 0.99 (*1-56293-349-3*) McClanahan Bk.

Boy Who Wouldn't Speak. Steve Berry. (Illus.). 32p. (J). 1992. lib. bdg. 14.95 (*1-55037-231-9*, Pub. by Annick CN); pap. 4.95 (*1-55037-230-0*, Pub. by Annick CN) Firefly Bks Ltd.

Boy Will Come to Nothing: Freud's Ego Ideal & Freud As Ego Ideal. Leonard Shengold. LC 92-49700. 208p. (C). 1993. text ed. 30.00 (*0-300-05684-2*) Yale U Pr.

Boy with a Paintbox: The Story of Paul Cezanne. Rosalind Hoover. LC 91-67762. 88p. (Orig.). (J). 1994. pap. 15.95 (*1-56002-135-7*, Univ Edtns) Aegina Pr.

Boy with a Problem: Johnny Learns to Share His Troubles. Joan Fassler. LC 78-147125. (Illus.). 32p. (J). (ps-3). 1971. 16.95 (*0-87705-054-6*) Human Sci Pr.

Boy with a Sling. Mary P. Warren & Mathews. LC 65-15143. (Arch Bks.: Set 2). 1965. pap. 1.99 (*0-570-06012-5*, 59-1116) Concordia.

Boy with a Toucan in His Heart. Christina Bell. 160p. (J). 1990. 39.00 (*0-85439-397-8*, Pub. by St Paul Pubns UK) St Mut.

Boy with Goldfish: A Heroic Fantasy Oratorio - Music Theatre Piece. Malia Elliott & Leon Siu. Ed. & Tr. by Harvey Hess. 20p. 1992. pap. 3.00 (*0-931909-09-0*) Malama Arts.

Boy with Green Hair. F. Andrew Leslie. 1961. pap. 4.75 (*0-8222-0144-5*) Dramatists Play.

Boy with the Dad That Always Said No! Gary Bryant. 32p. 1993. pap. 4.95 (*1-881442-04-7*) New Legends Pub.

Boy with the Helium Head. Phyllis R. Naylor. (J). (ps-3). 1992. 3.50 (*0-440-40644-7*, YB) Dell.

Boy with the Square Eyes. Juliet Snape. LC 87-1293. (J). (gr. 4-7). 1990. pap. 6.95 (*0-671-69445-6*, S&S Bks Young Read) S&S Childrens.

Boy with Wings. Adele DeLeeuw. LC 74-15860. (J). (gr. 1-6). 1971. 8.95 (*0-87874-001-5*) Galloway.

Boy Without a Flag: Tales of the South Bronx. Abraham Rodriguez, Jr. LC 91-45672. (Illus.). 120p. (Orig.). 1992. pap. 11.00 (*0-915943-74-3*) Milkweed Ed.

***Boychiks in the Hood: Travels in the Hasidic Underground.** Robert Eisenberg. LC 95-9838. 1995. 20.00 (*0-06-251222-6*); pap. 10.00 (*0-06-251223-4*) Harper SF.

Boycott: The Autobiography. large type ed. Geoffrey Boycott. (Illus.). 592p. 1988. 23.95 (*0-7089-8462-2*, Charnwood) Ulverscroft.

Boycott & Backlist: A History of Arab Economic Warfare Against Israel. Aaron J. Sarna. LC 86-1891. (Illus.). 286p. (C). 1986. 61.00 (0-8476-7489-4) Rowman.

Boycott in American Trade Unions. Leo Wolman. LC 77-156442. (American Labor Ser., No. 2). 1971. reprint ed. 15.95 (0-405-02950-0) Ayer.

Boycott of the Milner Mission: A Study in Egyptian Nationalism. John McIntyre, Jr. (American University Studies: History: Ser. IX, Vol. 9). 222p. 1985. text ed. 28.00 (0-8204-0162-5) P Lang Pubs.

Boyd Christenson Interviews. Boyd Christenson & Nancy E. Hanson. (Illus.). 224p. 1983. 15.95 (0-911007-00-8); pap. 9.95 (0-911007-01-6) Prairie Hse.

Boyd Coddington's How to Build Hot Rod Bodywork. Tim Remus. (Power Pro Ser.). (Illus.). 160p. 1993. pap. 17.95 (0-87938-798-X) Motorbooks Intl.

Boyd Coddington's How to Build Hot Rod Chassis. Tim Remus. (Illus.). 160p. 1992. pap. 17.95 (0-87938-626-6) Motorbooks Intl.

Boyd Coddington's How to Build Hot Rod Engines & Drivelines. Timothy Remus. LC 92-43458. (MBI Ser.). (Illus.). 160p. 1993. pap. 17.95 (0-87938-721-1) Motorbooks Intl.

Boyd Coddington's How to Paint Your Hot Rod. Timothy Remus. (Boyd Coddington How-to Ser.). (Illus.). 160p. 1994. pap. 17.95 (0-87938-942-7) Motorbooks Intl.

Boyd Cruise. Boyd Cruise. LC 76-24712. (Illus.). vi, 74p. 1976. 20.00 (0-917860-01-2) Historic New Orleans.

Boyd Norton's PhotoJournal. Boyd Norton. LC 90-30864. (Illus.). 128p. (Orig.). 1990. spiral bd., pap. 2.99 (0-89658-126-8) Voyageur Pr.

Boyd Three: Two Warring Souls. Evangeline G. Briley & William A. Boyd. 200p. (Orig.). (C). 1992. pap. 19.95 (1-881575-00-4) Prison News Ntwrk.

Boyd Webb: Works 1988-1990. Boyd Webb. (Illus.). 108p. 1992. pap. 30.00 (2-908257-03-3, Pub. by F R A C FR) Dist Art Pubs.

Boydell Shakespeare Prints. Ed. by John Boydell. LC 68-21362. (Illus.). 1972. reprint ed. 48.95 (0-405-08299-1, Pub. by Blom Pubns UK) Ayer.

Boyden: Here & There in the Family Tree. Albert Byden. (Illus.). 294p. 1991. reprint ed. lib. bdg. 56.00 (0-8328-2211-6); reprint ed. pap. 46.00 (0-8328-2212-4) Higginson Bk Co.

Boyd's Bible Dictionary. James P. Boyd. Orig. Title: Vest Pocket Bible Dictionary, Orig. pap. 4.99 (0-87981-087-4) Holman Bible Pub.

Boyd's Introduction to the Study of Disease. 11th ed. Huntingdon Sheldon. (Illus.). 606p. 1992. text ed. 43.95 (0-8121-1561-9) Williams & Wilkins.

***Boyd's Mark.** Patsy C. Cabiness. 128p. 1995. pap. 12.95 (1-881576-49-3) Providence Hse.

Boyds of Black River: A Family Chronicle. Walter D. Edmonds. 264p. 1988. pap. 12.95 (0-8156-2454-9) Syracuse U Pr.

Boyer: American Boyers. rev. ed. Charles C. Boyer. 663p. 1993. reprint ed. lib. bdg. 109.50 (0-8328-3270-7); reprint ed. pap. 99.50 (0-8328-3271-5) Higginson Bk Co.

Boyer Gonzales, the Painter: A Retrospective Exhibition, 1930 to Present. Intro. by Harvey West. LC 79-21551. (Index of Art in the Pacific Northwest Ser.: No. 13). (Illus.). 64p. (Orig.). 1979. pap. 5.00 (0-935558-05-5) Henry Art.

Boyertown Area Cookery or the Boyertown Housewife & Kitchen Efficiency Guide & Companion. 2nd ed. Boyertown Area Historical Society Staff. (Illus.). 204p. 1985. pap. text ed. 8.00 (0-9616068-0-0) Boyertown Hist.

Boyfriend. R. L. Stine. 176p. (YA). (gr. 7 up). 1990. pap. 3.50 (0-590-43279-6, Point) Scholastic Inc.

***Boyfriend Blues.** Lauren Phelps. (Sweet Dreams Ser.: No. 224). (YA). 1995. 3.50 (0-553-56678-4) Bantam.

Boyfriend Mix-up. Katherine Applegate. LC 93-72888. (Little Mermaid Novels Ser.: No. 10). (Illus.). 80p. (J). (gr. 1-4). 1994. pap. 3.50 (1-56282-642-5) Disney Pr.

Boyfriend War. Francine Pascal. (Sweet Valley High Ser.: No. 101). (YA). 1994. pap. 3.50 (0-553-29858-5) Bantam.

Boyfriends: Getting Them, Keeping Them, Living without Them. Joyce L. Vedral. 1990. mass mkt. 4.99 (0-345-36258-6) Ballantine.

Boyfriends Live Longer Than Husbands Because... Karen Ireland. Ed. by Mac Anderson. (Illus.). 78p. (Orig.). 1990. pap. 7.95 (0-931089-96-4) Great Quotations.

Boyhood Days of Guy Fawkes: Or, the Conspirators of Old London. Ed. by R. Reginald & Douglas Menville. LC 75-46257. (Supernatural & Occult Fiction Ser.). (Illus.). (YA). (gr. 7 up). 1976. reprint ed. lib. bdg. 20.95 (0-405-08116-2) Ayer.

Boyhood, Growing up Male: A Multicultural Anthology. Ed. by Franklin Abbott. 200p. 1993. pap. 12.95 (0-89594-581-9) Crossing Pr.

***Boyhood in the Dustbowl.** Robert A. Rutland. (Illus.). 144p. 1995. 22.50 (0-87081-416-8) Univ Pr Colo.

Boyhood of Christ. Lew Wallace. 1991. lib. bdg. 79.00 (0-8490-5131-2) Gordon Pr.

Boyhood of Christ. Lew Wallace. 101p. 1967. reprint ed. spiral bd. 3.30 (0-7873-0926-5) Mokelumne.

Boyhood to War: History & Anecdotes of the 442nd Regimental Combat Team. Dorothy Matsuo. (Illus.). 240p. 1992. boxed 35.00 (1-56647-019-6) Mutual Pub HI.

Boyishness in American Culture: The Charms & Dangers of Social Immaturity. David Kirby. LC 90-29117. 204p. 1991. lib. bdg. 89.95 (0-88946-793-5) E Mellen.

Boyle Genealogy: John Boyle of Virginia & Kentucky; Notes on Lines of Descent with Some Collateral References. John Boyle. (Illus.). 174p. 1993. reprint ed. lib. bdg. 37.50 (0-8328-3096-8); reprint ed. pap. 27.50 (0-8328-3097-6) Higginson Bk Co.

***Boyle's Law.** J. N. Spencer. Ed. by H. A. Neidig. (Modular Laboratory Program in Chemistry Ser.). 8p. (C). 1987. pap. text ed. 1.25x (0-87540-331-X) Chem Educ Res.

Boylston Street Fishweir, Vol. 4. E. Barghoorn et al. Ed. by F. Johnson. LC 50-4864. 1949. 10.00 (0-939312-05-0) Peabody Found.

Boymans van Beuningen Museum. Hanneke De Man. (Illus.). 128p. 1993. 29.95 (1-870248-95-3) Scala Books.

Boymans van Beuningen Museum. Hanneke De Man. (Illus.). 128p. 1993. 29.95 (0-685-74830-8, Pub. by P Wilson Pubs) Sothebys Pubns.

Boyne: A Valley of Kings. Henry Boylan. LC 89-50989. (Illus.). 168p. (Orig.). 1989. pap. 15.95 (0-685-29818-3, Pub. by OBrien Pr IE) Dufour.

Boyne Valley Book & Tape of Irish Legends. Brenda Maguire. 48p. 1987. pap. 14.95 (0-86278-140-X, Pub. by OBrien Pr IE) Dufour.

Boyne Water: A Tale, 3 vols. in 2, Set. John Banim & Michael Banim. LC 79-8229. reprint ed. 84.50 (0-404-61761-1) AMS Pr.

Boynton on Board: Barnyard Dance! Sandra Boynton. (Illus.). 24p. (J). (ps). 1993. bds. 6.95 (1-56305-442-6, 3442) Workman Pub.

Boynton on Board: Birthday Monsters! Sandra Boynton. (Illus.). 24p. (J). (ps). 1993. bds. 6.95 (1-56305-443-4, 3443) Workman Pub.

Boynton on Board: Oh My Oh My Oh Dinosaurs! Sandra Boynton. (Illus.). 24p. (J). (ps). 1993. bds. 6.95 (1-56305-441-8, 3441) Workman Pub.

Boynton on Board: One, Two, Three! Sandra Boynton. (Illus.). 24p. (J). (ps). 1993. bds. 6.95 (1-56305-444-2, 3444) Workman Pub.

Boynton: The Classic Prints: A Portfolio of Twelve Great Drawings & Three Pretty Good Ones. Sandra Boynton. (Illus.). (Orig.). 1990. pap. 9.95 (0-89480-811-7, 1811) Workman Pub.

Boys: A Schoolmaster's Journal. Ronald Bazarini. 1988. 12.95 (0-8027-1053-0) Walker & Co.

***Boys: For Kids & Grandparents.** William Bockus, Jr. LC 95-69380. (Illus.). 192p. (Orig.). (YA). (gr. 6-12). 1995. pap. 12.95 (0-9647151-0-4) Print Place.

Boys: One Hundred Years of Everett Firefighting History. Charles Z. Henderson. LC 92-11941. 1992. write for info. (0-89865-840-3) Donning Co.

Boys: The Cinematic World of Laurel & Hardy. Scott A. Nollen. LC 89-42742. 167p. 1989. lib. bdg. 28.50x (0-89950-383-7) McFarland & Co.

Boys: The Inside Story of the Dallas Cowboys' Season on the Edge. Skip Bayless. (Illus.). 320p. 1993. 23.00 (0-671-79359-4) S&S Trade.

Boys Against Girls. Phyllis R. Naylor. LC 93-37683. (Illus.). (J). 1994. 14.95 (0-385-32081-7) Delacorte.

Boys Against Girls. Created by Francine Pascal. 112p. (Orig.). 1988. pap. 2.50 (0-318-33018-0) Bantam.

Boys Against Girls. Francine Pascal. (Sweet Valley Twins Ser.). (Orig.). (J). 1988. 3.25 (0-553-15666-7) Bantam.

Boys & Girls. (Key Words Readers Ser.: B Series, No. 641-3b). (Illus.). (J). (ps-5). 3.50 (0-7214-0015-9) Ladybird Bks.

Boys & Girls, No. 3. (Key Words Readers Ser.: B Series, No. 641-3b). (Illus.). (J). (ps-5). Series No. S705. student ed 1.95 (0-317-04007-3) Ladybird Bks.

Boys & Girls: Superheroes in the Doll Corner. Vivian G. Paley. LC 84-93. xii, 116p. (C). 1986. pap. 8.95 (0-226-64492-8) U Ch Pr.

Boys & Girls: The Development of Gender Roles. Carole R. Beal. LC 93-6422. 1993. pap. text ed. write for info. (0-07-004533-X) McGraw.

Boys & Girls & Doctors & Dentists. Jeannette N. Hafford. 24p. (Orig.). (J). 1986. pap. 7.22 (0-9616549-0-2) Tinys Self Help Bks.

Boys & Girls at Play: The Development of Sex Roles. Evelyn G. Pitcher & Lynn H. Schultz. 220p. 1983. text ed. 49.95 (0-275-91059-8, C1059, Praeger Pubs) Greenwood.

Boys & Girls at Play: The Development of Sex Roles. Evelyn G. Pitcher & Lynn H. Schultz. LC 82-16579. 224p. 1985. pap. text ed. 14.95 (0-89789-055-8, Bergin & Garvey) Greenwood.

Boys & Girls Book about Divorce. Richard A. Gardner. LC 84-2815. (Illus.). 160p. (J). (gr. 7 up). 1992. reprint ed. 25.00 (0-87668-664-1) Aronson.

Boys & Girls Book about One-Parent Families. Richard A. Gardner. LC 78-18388. (Illus.). 122p. (J). (gr. k-8). 1983. reprint ed. pap. 4.99 (0-933812-16-7) Creative Therapeutics.

Boys & Girls Book about Stepfamilies. Richard A. Gardner. (Illus.). 180p. (J). (gr. 3-10). 1985. reprint ed. pap. 4.99 (0-933812-13-2) Creative Therapeutics.

Boys' & Girls' Book of Dealing with Feelings. Eric Dlugokinski. 31p. (J). (gr. k-6). 1988. pap. 10.95 (1-882801-02-4) Feelings Factory.

Boys & Girls Come Out to Play: A Collection of Irish Singing Games. Maurice Leyden. (Illus.). 112p. (Orig.). 1994. pap. 13.95 (0-86281-432-4, Pub. by Appletree Pr IE) Irish Bks Media.

Boys & Girls Cookbook. (Illus.). 64p. (J). 1988. pap. 3.95 (0-8249-3079-7) Ideals.

Boys & Girls of Divorce. Richard A. Gardner. (YA). 1985. pap. 4.99 (0-553-27619-0) Bantam.

***Boys & Girls Study Skills Bingo: A Program to Help Students in Grades Kindergarten Through Third Grade to Learn, Understand, & Apply Good Study Skills.** JoAnn Cooper. 16p. (J). (gr. k-3). 1991. 10.95 (1-884063-28-4) Mar Co Prods.

Boys & Sex. 3rd ed. Wardell B. Pomeroy. (YA). 1991. pap. 3.95 (0-440-20811-4) Dell.

Boys & Their Baby. Larry Wolff. (Stonewall Inn Editions Ser.). 1989. pap. 9.95 (0-312-02878-4) St Martin.

Boys Are Back: The Return of the Dallas Cowboys. Mike Fisher & Richie Whitt. (Illus.). 176p. 1993. 29.95 (1-56530-061-0) Summit TX.

Boys at Bar Twelve Ranch. Eugene Borer. 1993. 16.50 (0-8062-4636-7) Carlton.

***Boys at Work.** Gary Soto. LC 94-25652. (Illus.). (YA). (gr. 5 up). 1995. 14.95 (0-385-32048-5) Delacorte.

Boys Beginning. Mark Dunster. 17p. 1984. pap. 4.00 (0-89642-108-2) Linden Pubs.

Boys Behind Bars: True Homosexual Accounts of Prison Sex. Ed. by Robert N. Boyd. 192p. (Orig.). 1992. pap. 14.95 (0-943595-36-3) Leyland Pubns.

Boy's Best Friend. Joan Alden. LC 92-8061. (Illus.). 32p. (J). (ps-2). 1992. 12.95 (1-55583-203-2, Alyson Wonderland) Alyson Pubns.

Boys! Boys! Boys, Vol. 7: True Gay Encounters. 160p. (Orig.). 1988. pap. 10.00 (0-943595-21-5) Leyland Pubns.

Boys Clubs' Guide to Youth Football. Edward M. Torba. LC 83-80714. (Illus.). 208p. (Orig.). 1984. pap. 12.95 (0-88011-178-X, PTOR0178) Human Kinetics.

Boys Don't Cry: Boys & Sexism in Education. Sue Askew & Carol Ross. (Gender & Education Ser.). 112p. 1988. pap. 27.00 (0-335-10296-4, Open Univ Pr) Taylor & Francis.

Boys' First Book of Radio & Electronics. Alfred Morgan. 1993. reprint ed. lib. bdg. 21.95 (1-56849-181-6) Buccaneer Bks.

Boys from Brazil. Ira Levin. 1991. mass mkt. 5.95 (0-553-29004-5) Bantam.

Boys from Brazil. Ira Levin. 1976. 8.95 (0-394-40267-7) Random.

Boys from Grover Avenue. George Dove. LC 84-73512. 166p. 1985. 18.95 (0-87972-321-1); pap. 8.95 (0-87972-322-X) Bowling Green Univ.

***Boys from New Jersey: How the Mob Beat the Feds.** Robert Rudolph. 431p. 1995. pap. 16.95 (0-8135-2154-8) Rutgers U Pr.

Boys from St. Petri. Bjarne Reuter. 192p. (J). (gr. 6 up). 1994. 14.99 (0-525-45121-8, DCB) Dutton Child Bks.

Boys from Syracuse. (Illus.). 1981. 7.95 (0-88188-062-0, 00312045); pap. 35.00 (0-88188-006-X, 00312046) H Leonard.

Boys from the Blackstuff. Alan Bleasdale. 1990. pap. 15.95 (0-7487-0350-0) Dufour.

Boys from the Blackstuff: Studio Script. B. Bleasdale. (C). 1984. 50.00 (0-09-159681-5, Pub. by S Thornes Pubs UK) St Mut.

Boys Here - Girls There. Riki Levinson. LC 92-5321. (Illus.). (J). 1993. 13.00 (0-525-67374-1, Lodestar Bks) Dutton Child Bks.

Boys I Didn't Kiss. Kathleen R. Lawrence. 1990. 17.95 (0-945167-34-2) British Amer Pub.

Boys in Autumn. Bernard Sabath. 77p. 1975. 5.45 (0-87129-110-X, B60) Dramatic Pub.

Boys in Blue. Phil Andros. 145p. 1993. reprint ed. pap. 7.95 (1-55583-221-0) Alyson Pubns.

Boys in the Back Room: Notes on California Novelists. Edmund Wilson. (BCL1-PS American Literature Ser.). 72p. 1993. reprint ed. lib. bdg. 59.00 (0-7812-6595-9) Rprt Serv.

Boys in the Sky Blue Pants. Dorothy C. Cragen. (Illus.). 1975. 15.00 (0-914330-07-1) Linrose Pub.

Boys in White: Student Culture in Medical School. rev. ed. Ed. by Howard S. Becker et al. LC 76-26951. 456p. 1991. reprint ed. pap. text ed. 21.95 (0-87855-622-2) Transaction Pubs.

Boys Jones vs. Johnson: The Feud That Rocked America's Team. Skip Bayless. 1994. pap. 5.99 (0-671-51141-6) S&S Trade.

Boy's King Arthur. Sidney Lanier. LC 73-13451. (Illustrated Classics Ser.). (Illus.). 336p. (J). 1989. text ed. 24.95 (0-684-19111-3, C Scribner Sons Young) S&S Childrens.

Boy's King Arthur. deluxe ed. Sidney Lanier. LC 73-13451. (Illustrated Classics Ser.). (Illus.). 336p. (J). 1989. 75.00 (0-684-19118-0, C Scribner Sons Young) S&S Childrens.

Boys' Life. Howard Korder. 1988. pap. 4.75 (0-8222-0140-2) Dramatists Play.

Boy's Life. large type ed. Robert R. McCammon. 644p. 1992. reprint ed. lib. bdg. 21.95 (1-56054-326-4) Thorndike Pr.

Boy's Life. large type ed. Robert R. McCammon. 644p. 1992. reprint ed. pap. 14.95 (1-56054-938-6) Thorndike Pr.

Boy's Life. Robert R. McCammon. Ed. by Sally Peters. 592p. 1992. reprint ed. pap. 6.50 (0-671-74305-8) PB.

Boy's Life and Other Plays: The Middle Kingdom; Lip Service; Fun; Nobody. Howard Korder. 240p. 1989. pap. 14.95 (0-8021-3170-0) Grove-Atltic.

Boy's Life of Robert E. Lee. Stanley F. Horn. 1972. 59.95 (0-87968-779-7) Gordon Pr.

Boys' Life of Theodore Roosevelt. Herman Hagedorn. 1976. 25.95 (0-8488-0280-2) Amereon Ltd.

Boys Like Us. Peter McGehee. (Stonewall Inn Editions Ser.). 176p. 1992. pap. 8.95 (0-312-06913-8) St Martin.

Boys Next Door. Tom Griffin. 1988. pap. 4.75 (0-8222-0143-7) Dramatists Play.

Boys of Bensonhurst. Salvatore La Puma. LC 86-7100. (Flannery O'Connor Award for Short Fiction Ser.). 136p. 1987. 15.95 (0-8203-0891-9) U of Ga Pr.

Boys of Life. Paul Russell. 320p. 1992. pap. 10.00 (0-452-26837-0, Plume) NAL-Dutton.

Boys of Summer. Roger Kahn. LC 86-46074. (Illus.). 464p. 1987. pap. 13.00 (0-06-091416-5, PL 1416, PL) HarpC.

Boys of Summer. Roger Kahn. (Illus.). 458p. 1992. reprint ed. lib. bdg. 29.95 (0-89966-850-X) Buccaneer Bks.

Boys of Vaseline Alley. Ed. by Robert N. Boyd. (Orig.). 1994. pap. 14.95 (0-943595-47-9) Leyland Pubns.

Boys of Winter. Wilfrid Sheed. 1987. 17.95 (0-317-58854-0) Knopf.

Boys on the Bus: Riding with the Campaign Press Corps. Timothy Crouse. 1986. mass mkt. 5.99 (0-345-34015-9) Ballantine.

Boys on the Gold Coast. Marvin Ferguson. 247p. (J). (gr. 7-12). 1993. pap. 9.95 (1-882286-00-6) Parker Pub IL.

Boys on the Rock. John Fox. 160p. 1994. pap. 8.95 (0-312-10433-2, Stonewall Inn) St Martin.

Boys on Their Bony Mules. Poems. Miller Williams. LC 83-905. 58p. 1983. pap. 6.95 (0-8071-1088-4) La State U Pr.

Boy's Own Story. Edmund White. LC 83-8212. 224p. 1983. pap. 7.95 (0-452-26123-6, Plume); pap. 9.00 (0-452-26352-2) NAL-Dutton.

Boy's Own Story: With a New Introduction by the Author. Edmund White. 240p. 1994. pap. 10.95 (0-452-27300-5, Plume) NAL-Dutton.

Boys' Preparatory Schools: A Photographic Essay. Patrick Briston & Dennis Weidner. (Illus.). 136p. 1990. 19.95 (0-9624570-0-0) Apertures.

Boys' Puberty. Alain Chirinian. 1991. pap. 6.95 (0-8125-1125-5) Tor Bks.

Boys' Ranch. Joe Simon & Jack Kirby. 208p. 1992. 39.95 (0-87135-859-X) Marvel Entmnt.

***Boy's Service with the 76th Ohio.** Charles A. Willison. (Illus.). 200p. 1995. 22.95 (1-885033-13-3) Blue Acorn Pr.

Boys Start the War. Phyllis R. Naylor. LC 92-249. (J). (gr. 4-7). 1993. 14.95 (0-385-30814-0) Doubleday.

Boys Start the War - The Girls Get Even. Phyllis R. Naylor. (J). (gr. 4-7). 1994. mass mkt. 4.99 (0-440-40971-3) Dell.

***Boy's Tale.** Margaret Frazer. 240p. (Orig.). 1995. pap. text ed. 4.99 (0-425-14899-8) Berkley Pub.

Boys Themselves. Michael Ruhlman. 1995. 25.00 (0-8050-3370-X) H Holt & Co.

Boy's Town. Art Bosch. LC 87-72875. 200p. (Orig.). 1988. pap. 7.95 (1-55583-126-5) Alyson Pubns.

Boys Town. Robert P. Hupp. LC 91-46629. (Illus.). 262p. (Orig.). 1992. pap. 12.95 (0-8189-0641-3) Alba.

Boy's Town. William Dean Howells. (Notable American Authors Ser.). 1992. reprint ed. lib. bdg. 75.00 (0-7812-3244-9) Rprt Serv.

Boy's Town. William Dean Howells. LC 75-131748. 247p. 1980. reprint ed. 10.00 (0-403-00635-X) Scholarly.

Boys Town: A Photographic History. Ed. by Barbara A. Lonnborg. LC 92-18878. 144p. 1992. 29.95 (0-938510-37-1, 19-001); pap. 19.95 (0-938510-31-2, 19-002) Boys Town Pr.

Boy's War. Paxton Davis. LC 90-970. (Illus.). 269p. 1990. 17.95 (0-89587-079-7) Blair.

Boys War. David Michell. 1988. pap. 6.95 (9971-972-71-9) OMF Bks.

Boys' War: Confederate & Union Soldiers Talk about the Civil War. Jim Murphy. (Illus.). 128p. (J). (gr. 4-9). 1990. 15.95 (0-89919-893-7, Clarion Bks) HM.

Boys' War: Confederate & Union Soldiers Talk about the Civil War. Jim Murphy. (Illus.). 128p. (J). (gr. 4-7). 1993. pap. 7.95 (0-395-66412-8, Clarion Bks) HM.

Boys Who Became Prophets. Lynda Cory. LC 92-29812. (Illus.). vii, 80p. (J). 1992. pap. 8.95 (0-87579-664-8) Deseret Bk.

Boys Who Stole the Funeral: A Novel Sequence. Les Murray. 80p. 1992. 20.00 (0-374-11603-2) FS&G.

Boy's Will. Erik C. Haugaard. (J). (gr. 4-7). 1990. pap. 5.95 (0-395-54962-0) HM.

Boy's Will & North of Boston. Robert Frost. (Thrift Editions Ser.). 96p. reprint ed. pap. 1.00 (0-486-26866-7) Dover.

Boys Will Be. Bruce Brooks. 144p. (YA). (gr. 6 up). 1993. 14.95 (0-8050-2420-4, Bks Young Read) H Holt & Co.

***Boys Will Be.** Bruce Brooks. LC 94-3599. 144p. (J). (gr. 5-9). 1995. pap. 4.50 (0-7868-1026-2) Hyprn Child.

Boys Will Be Boys: Breaking the Link Between Masculinity & Violence. Myriam Miedzian. 1992. mass mkt. 10.00 (0-385-42254-7, Anchor NY) Doubleday.

Boys Will Be Boys, Vol. 9: True Gay Encounters. Ed. by Winston Leyland. 160p. (Orig.). 1990. pap. 10.95 (0-943595-26-6) Leyland Pubns.

Boys Will Be Girls: The Feminine Ethic & British Children's Fiction, 1857-1917. Claudia Nelson. LC 90-20004. (Illus.). 216p. (C). 1991. text ed. 35.00 (0-8135-1681-1) Rutgers U Pr.

Boys Will Be Men: Masculinity in Troubled Times. Richard A. Hawley. LC 93-6870. 208p. 1993. 19.95 (0-8397-1193-X) Eriksson.

Boys Will Be Men: Masculinity in Troubled Times. Richard A. Hawley. LC 93-6870. 208p. reprint ed. pap. 12.95 (0-8397-1194-8) Eriksson.

Boysie's First Birthday. Gillian Osband. (Boysie Bks.). (Illus.). 32p. (J). (ps-3). 1990. lib. bdg. 14.95 (0-87614-404-0, Carolrhoda) Lerner Group.

Boysie's Kitten. Gillian Osband. (Boysie Bks.). (Illus.). 32p. (J). (ps-3). 1990. lib. bdg. 14.95 (0-87614-403-2, Carolrhoda) Lerner Group.

***Boyz II Men Success Story: Defying the Odds.** Rita E. Henderson. Ed. by Lawrence Aynesmith. LC 94-48534. (Illus.). (Orig.). 1995. pap. 12.95 (0-9644587-5-6) Aynderson Pr.

***Bozambo's Revenge.** Bertene Juminer. Tr. by Alexandre B. Warren. (Sun Lit Ser.). Orig. Title: La Revanche de Bozambo. 117p. 1981. 10.00 (0-914478-10-9) Three Continents.

Bozeman Trail, Vol. I. Grace R. Hebard & E. A. Brininstool. LC 90-12364. (Illus.). viii, 369p. 1990. reprint ed. pap. 11.95 (0-8032-7249-9, Bison Books) U of Nebr Pr.

Bozeman Trail, Vol. II. Grace R. Hebard & E. A. Brininstool. LC 90-12364. (Illus.). xii, 281p. 1990. reprint ed. pap. 10.95 (0-8032-7250-2, Bison Books) U of Nebr Pr.

An Asterisk (*) at the beginning of an entry indicates that the title is appearing in BIP for the first time.

An Asterisk (*) at the beginning of an entry indicates that the title is appearing in BIP for the first time.

879

B

Bragg Vegetarian Gourmet Recipes. 9th rev. ed. Paul C. Bragg & Patricia Bragg. (Illus.). 1993. pap. 7.95 (*0-87790-046-9*) Hlth Sci.

Braggart Warrior see Merchant

Bragg's Hunch. J. Lynch. (Bragg Ser.: No. 1). 1982. pap. 2.25 (*0-449-14449-6*) Fawcett.

Brahaus. Samuele Mazza. LC 93-5515. 192p. (ITA.). 1994. pap. 16.95 (*0-8118-0593-X*) Chronicle Bks.

Brahma-Knowledge, Philosophy of Vedanta. L. D. Barnett. 1973. 59.95 (*0-87968-780-0*) Gordon Pr.

Brahma Net Sutra, Set. Tr. by Buddhist Text Translation Society. (Illus.). 312p. (Orig.). (C). 1981. 50.00 (*0-685-57672-8*) Buddhist Text.

Brahma Net Sutra, Vol. I. Tr. by Buddhist Text Translation Society. (Illus.). 312p. (Orig.). (C). 1981. pap. 10.00 (*0-917512-79-0*) Buddhist Text.

Brahma Net Sutra, Vol. II Commentary by Hui Seng, Elder Master. Tr. by Buddhist Text Translation Society. (Illus.). 210p. (Orig.). 1982. pap. 8.00 (*0-917512-88-X*) Buddhist Text.

Brahma Sutra: The Philosophy of Spiritual Life. Badarayana. Tr. by Sarvepalli Radhakrishnan. LC 68-21330. 606p. 1968. reprint ed. text ed. 85.00 (*0-8371-0291-X*, BABS, Greenwood Pr) Greenwood.

Brahma-Sutra Bhasya of Sankaracarya. Badarayana. Tr. by Swami Gambhirananda. 1965. Bilingual ed. 12.95 (*0-87481-066-3*, Pub. by Advaita Ashrama II) Vedanta Pr.

Brahma Sutras & Their Principal Commentaries, 3 vols., 1. Ed. by B. N. Sharma. 1986. 40.00 (*81-215-0033-8*, Pub. by Munshiram Manoharial II) S Asia.

Brahma Sutras & Their Principal Commentaries, 3 vols., 2. Ed. by B. N. Sharma. 1986. 42.50 (*81-215-0034-6*, Pub. by Munshiram Manoharial II) S Asia.

Brahma Sutras & Their Principal Commentaries, 3 vols., 3. Ed. by B. N. Sharma. 1986. 54.00 (*81-215-0035-4*, Pub. by Munshiram Manoharial II) S Asia.

Brahma Sutras (Sri Ramanuja) Badarayana. 1979. 5.95 (*0-87481-189-9*, Pub. by Advaita Ashrama II) Vedanta Pr.

Brahma-Sutras (Vedanta-Sutras) Badarayana. Tr. by Swami Vireswarananda. Bilingual ed. 5.95 (*0-87481-076-0*, Pub. by Advaita Ashrama II) Vedanta Pr.

Brahma-Vaivarta Puranam, 2 vols., Set. Puranas. LC 73-3817. reprint ed. 74.50 (*0-404-57824-1*) AMS Pr.

Brahmanada: Sound, Mantra & Power. Shri Dhyanyogi Madhusudandasji. (Illus.). 102p. (Orig.). 1979. pap. 7.00 (*1-883879-02-7*) Dhyanyoga Ctr.

Brahmanda Purana, Pt. I. Ed. & Tr. by G. V. Tagare. (Ancient Indian Tradition & Mythology Ser.: Vol. 22). 1983. 26.00 (*0-8364-2502-2*, Pub. by Motilal Banarsidass II) S Asia.

Brahmanda Purana, Pt. II. Ed. & Tr. by G. V. Tagare. (Ancient Indian Tradition & Mythology Ser.: Vol. 23). 1983. 26.00 (*0-8364-2503-0*, Pub. by Motilal Banarsidass II) S Asia.

Brahmanda Purana, Pt. III. Ed. & Tr. by G. V. Tagare. (Ancient Indian Tradition & Mythology Ser.: Vol. 24). 1991. 26.00 (*0-8364-2504-9*, Pub. by Motilal Banarsidass II) S Asia.

Brahmanda Purana, Pt. IV. Ed. & Tr. by G. V. Tagare. (Ancient Indian Tradition & Mythology Ser.: Vol. 25). 1984. 26.00 (*0-8364-2505-7*, Pub. by Motilal Banarsidass II) S Asia.

Brahmanical Gods in Burma: A Chapter of Indian Art & Iconography. Nihar-Ranjan Ray. LC 77-87020. reprint ed. 16.50 (*0-404-16852-3*) AMS Pr.

Brahmanical Religion in Ancient Orissa. Satyendra Patnaik. 1987. 42.00 (*0-317-61786-9*, Pub. by Ashish II) S Asia.

Brahmanism Jainism & Buddhism in Andhra Desa. P. Arundhati. (C). 1990. text ed. 84.00 (*81-85067-30-9*) S Asia.

Brahmans of India. J. Radha Krishna. (C). 1987. 31.00 (*81-85076-24-3*, Pub. by Chugh Pubns II) S Asia.

Brahmans, Theists & Muslims of India. John C. Oman. LC 76-179231. (Illus.). reprint ed. 49.50 (*0-404-54858-X*) AMS Pr.

Brahmin's Castles in the Air. Rashmi Sharma. LC 92-61764. (Illus.). 32p. (J). (gr. k up). 1994. 14.95 (*1-878099-56-6*) Vidya Bks.

Brahmo Samaj & the Shaping of the Modern Indian Mind. David Kopf. LC 78-70303. 1979. text ed. 65.00x (*0-691-03125-8*) Princeton U Pr.

Brahmopanisat-Sara Sangraha. Tr. by Vidyatilaka. LC 73-3809. (Sacred Books of the Hindus: No. 18, Pt. 1). (ENG & SAN.). reprint ed. 18.00 (*0-404-57818-7*) AMS Pr.

Brahms. Paul Holmes. (Illustrated Lives of the Great Composers Ser.). (Illus.). 168p. 1987. pap. 14.95 (*0-7119-0826-5*, OP43710) Omnibus NY.

Brahms. Malcolm MacDonald. 1990. text ed. 29.95 (*0-02-871393-1*) Schirmer Bks.

Brahms. Malcolm MacDonald. LC 90-8545. 490p. 1993. pap. 18.00 (*0-02-872851-3*) Schirmer Bks.

Brahms. Ann Rachlin. (Famous Children Ser.). (Illus.). 24p. (J). (gr. k-3). 1993. pap. 5.95 (*0-8120-1542-8*) Barron.

Brahms. Henry C. Colles. LC 74-24060. (Music of the Masters Ser.). reprint ed. 16.50 (*0-404-12883-1*) AMS Pr.

Brahms. John A. Fuller-Maitland. 263p. 1990. reprint ed. lib. bdg. 69.00 (*0-7812-9052-X*) Rprt Serv.

Brahms. William D. Murdoch. LC 74-24161. reprint ed. 37.50 (*0-404-13056-9*) AMS Pr.

Brahms. Walter Niemann. 492p. 1990. reprint ed. lib. bdg. 89.00 (*0-7812-9054-6*) Rprt Serv.

Brahms: His Life & Work. 3rd ed. Karl Geiringer. (Music Ser.). (Illus.). xvii, 383p. 1981. reprint ed. lib. bdg. 45.00 (*0-306-76093-2*); reprint ed. pap. 13.95 (*0-306-80223-6*) Da Capo.

Brahms: Music Book Index. Peter Latham. 230p. 1993. reprint ed. lib. bdg. 79.00 (*0-7812-9574-2*) Rprt Serv.

***Brahms: The Vocal Music.** A. Craig Bell. LC 94-43514. 1995. write for info. (*0-8386-3597-0*) Fairleigh Dickinson.

Brahms & His Four Symphonies. Julius Harrison. LC 76-127285. (Music Ser.). (Illus.). 1971. reprint ed. lib. bdg. 35.00 (*0-306-70033-6*) Da Capo.

Brahms & His World. Ed. by Walter Frisch. (Illus.). 160p. (C). 1990. pap. 16.95 (*0-691-02713-7*) Princeton U Pr.

Brahms & the Principle of Developing Variation. Walter Frisch. LC 82-13675. (California Studies in 19th Century Music: No. 2). 232p. (C). 1984. 50.00 (*0-520-04700-1*); pap. 16.00 (*0-520-06958-7*) U CA Pr.

Brahms Arrangements for Piano - Four Hands of His String Quartets. Johannes Brahms. (Music Scores to Play & Study Ser.). 160p. 1985. reprint ed. pap. 9.95 (*0-486-24835-6*) Dover.

Brahms, His Life & Work: Music Book Index. Karl Geiringer. 383p. 1993. reprint ed. lib. bdg. 89.00 (*0-7812-9589-0*) Rprt Serv.

***Brahms-Keller Correspondence.** Ed. by George S. Bozarth & Wiltrud Martin. LC 95-16158. 1996. write for info. (*0-8032-1238-0*) U of Nebr Pr.

Brahms' Lullaby. (Sing-a-Song Sound Bks.). (Illus.). 6p. (J). (gr. k-2). 1993. bds. 14.95 (*1-56144-348-4*, Honey Bear Bks) Modern Pub NYC.

Brahms Studies, Vol. 1. David Brodbeck. (Illus.). 258p. 1994. 40.00 (*0-8032-1243-7*) U of Nebr Pr.

Brahms Symphonies. Walter Frisch. (Monuments of Western Music Ser.). (Illus.). 1995. text ed. 35.00 (*0-02-870765-6*) Schirmer Bks.

Brahms, the Man & His Music. Ernest M. Lee. LC 74-24138. (Illus.). reprint ed. 37.50 (*0-404-13001-1*) AMS Pr.

Brahms 2: Biographical, Documentary & Analytical Studies. Ed. by Michael Musgrave. (Illus.). 240p. 1987. 69.95 (*0-521-32606-0*) Cambridge U Pr.

Brahms's Choral Compositions & His Library of Early Music. Virginia Hancock. LC 83-18322. (Studies in Musicology: No. 76). (Illus.). 237p. reprint ed. pap. 67.60 (*0-8357-1496-9*, 2070338) Bks Demand.

Brahms's Lieder. Max Friedlaender. LC 74-24087. reprint ed. 22.50 (*0-404-12916-1*) AMS Pr.

Brahui & Dravidian Comparative Grammar. Murray B. Emeneau. LC 62-63439. (University of California Publications in Social Welfare: Vol. 27). 103p. reprint ed. pap. 29.40 (*0-8357-7372-8*, 2011685) Bks Demand.

Brahui Language. M. S. Andronov. (Languages of Asia & Africa Ser.). 112p. 1980. 30.00 (*0-317-56599-0*, Pub. by Collets UK) Pro-Am Music.

Brahui Language: Introduction & Grammar. Denys Bray. 248p. 1986. 39.95 (*0-8288-8421-8*) Fr & Eur.

***Braid & Chevron Updated.** Camille Remme. (Illus.). 72p. (Orig.). Date not set. pap. 17.95 (*0-929950-09-7*) ME Pubns.

Braid Group, Knot Theory & Statistical Mechanics. Ed. by C. N. Yang & M. L. Ge. 336p. (C). 1989. text ed. 86.00 (*9971-5-0828-1*); pap. text ed. 48.00 (*9971-5-0833-8*) World Scientific Pub.

Braid Group, Knot Theory & Statistical Mechanics II. C. N. Yang & M. L. Ge. (Advanced Series in Mathematical Physics). 400p. 1994. text ed. 109.00 (*981-02-1524-X*) World Scientific Pub.

Braid of Feathers: American Indian Law & Contemporary Tribal Life. Frank Pommersheim. LC 94-4846. 1995. 30.00 (*0-520-08857-3*) U CA Pr.

Braid of Literature: Children's Worlds of Reading. Shelby A. Wolf & Shirley B. Heath. 264p. 1992. 29.95x (*0-674-08040-8*) HUP.

***Braid of Literature: Children's Worlds of Reading.** Shelby A. Wolf & Shirley B. Heath. 264p. 1995. pap. text ed. 15.95x (*0-674-08041-6*, WOLBRX) HUP.

***Braided Borders.** John F. Flynn. 1991. 13.95 (*0-9627889-1-0*) Flynn Quilt Frame.

Braided Card: Memoirs of a School Librarian. Mary Gaver. LC 87-12738. (Illus.). 253p. 1988. 25.00 (*0-8108-2032-3*) Scarecrow.

Braided Dream: Robert Penn Warren's Late Poetry. Randolph P. Runyon. LC 89-48187. 264p. 1990. text ed. 28.00 (*0-8131-1722-4*) U Pr of Ky.

Braided Lives. Marge Piercy. 1986. mass mkt. 4.95 (*0-449-44526-7*, Crest); mass mkt. 5.95 (*0-449-21300-5*, Crest) Fawcett.

Braided Lives. Marge Piercy. 1987. 15.50 (*0-685-18687-3*) Summit Bks.

Braided Lives. Marge Piercy. LC 81-16695. 441p. 1982. 25.00 (*0-671-43834-4*) Ultramarine Pub.

Braided Lives: An Anthology of Multicultural American Writing. Ed. by Minnesota Humanities Commission Staff. 288p. (YA). (gr. 9-12). 1991. pap. text ed. 13.00 (*0-9629298-0-8*) MN Humanities.

***Braided River.** Peggy Shumaker. 36p. 1993. pap. 20.00 (*1-884236-00-6*) Limner Pr.

***Braided River.** deluxe limited ed. Peggy Shumaker. 36p. 1993. 50.00 (*0-9630863-9-1*) Limner Pr.

Braided Rivers. Ed. by J. L. Best & C. S. Bristow. (Geological Society Special Publications: No. 75). (Illus.). 432p. (C). 1993. 108.00 (*0-903317-93-1*, Pub. by Geol Soc Pub Hse UK) AAPG.

***Braided Rug Book: Creating Your Own American Folk Art.** Norma Sturges. Ed. by Deborah Morganthal. LC 95-14990. (Illus.). 112p. 1995. 21.95 (*0-937274-91-7*) Lark Books.

Braided Streams: Esther & a Woman's Way of Growing. Marjory Z. Bankson. Ed. by Marcia Broucek. LC 85-50203. (Illus.). 184p. (Orig.). 1985. pap. 11.95 (*0-931055-05-9*) LuraMedia.

Braided Streams Leader's Guide. Pat Backman & Lura J. Geiger. 128p. (Orig.). 1986. spiral bd., pap. 15.95 (*0-931055-09-1*) LuraMedia.

***Braided Wire Jewelry.** Loretta Henry. (Illus.). 64p. (Orig.). 1995. pap. 12.95 (*0-88740-867-2*) Schiffer.

Braiding. Marva Patterson. (Illus.). 192p. 1991. pap. 22.95 (*0-87350-386-4*) Milady Pub.

Braiding & Knotting: Techniques & Projects. C. A. Belash. LC 74-75266. 1974. reprint ed. pap. 3.95 (*0-486-23059-7*) Dover.

Braiding Rawhide Horse Tack. Robert L. Woolery. LC 84-46107. (Illus.). 132p. (Orig.). 1985. pap. 7.95 (*0-87033-333-X*) Cornell Maritime.

Braidmaking. Barbara Pegg. (Illus.). 80p. 1991. pap. 14.95 (*0-7136-3198-8*, Pub. by A&C Black UK) Talman.

Braids. J. Birman & A. Libgober. LC 88-26283. (CONM Ser.: Vol. 78). 730p. 1988. pap. 72.00 (*0-8218-5088-1*, CONM-78) Am Math.

Braids. Consumer Guide Editors. 128p. (Orig.). 1994. pap. 6.99 (*0-451-82271-4*, Sig) NAL-Dutton.

***Braids: 250 Patterns from Japan, Peru & Beyond.** Rodrick Owen. 160p. 1995. 24.95 (*1-883010-06-3*) Interweave.

Braids & Bows: A Book of Instruction. Anne A. Johnson & Robin Stoneking. (Illus.). 80p. (J). 1992. spiral bd. 18.95 (*1-878257-17-X*) Klutz Pr.

Braids & Bows for Kids. (Illus.). 64p. 1993. spiral bd. 5.98 (*0-7853-0075-9*, 3616300) Pubns Intl Ltd.

***Braids & Bows for Kids.** (Arts-Crafts-Cooking-Drawing Books for Children Ser.). (Illus.). 64p. (J). 1995. lib. bdg. 16.95 (*1-56674-098-3*) Forest Hse.

Braids & Coverings: Selected Topics. V. L. Hansen. (London Mathematical Society Student Texts Ser.: No. 18). 191p. (C). 1990. 74.95 (*0-521-38479-6*); pap. 29.95 (*0-521-38757-4*) Cambridge U Pr.

Braids, Links & Mapping Class Groups. Joan S. Birman. LC 74-2961. (Annals of Mathematics Studies: No. 82). 300p. 1974. 47.50x (*0-691-08149-2*) Princeton U Pr.

Braille. Bob Perelman. LC 75-319972. 61p. 1975. 3.50 (*0-87886-057-6*, Greenfld Rev Pr) Greenfld Rev Lit.

***Braille Enthusiast's Dictionary.** Ed. by Alan J. Koenig & M. Cay Holbrook. 548p. 1994. pap. 55.00 (*0-9634229-5-2*) Scalars Pub.

Braille for a Storm of Loss: Poems. William Ruddy. 1978. 6.95 (*0-685-50207-4*); pap. 3.50 (*0-685-50208-2*) Oyez.

Braille in the United States: Its Production, Distribution, & Use. Louis H. Goldish. LC 76-356837. 121p. reprint ed. pap. 34.50 (*0-8357-7373-6*, 2027343) Bks Demand.

Braille Me. Jean P. Brody. 64p. (Orig.). 1984. pap. 5.95 (*0-941374-02-5*) Grapetree Prods.

Brain. (Symposia on Quantitative Biology Ser.: Vol. LV). (Illus.). 1067p. 1991. text ed. 200.00 (*0-87969-059-3*); pap. text ed. 85.00 (*0-87969-060-7*) Cold Spring Harbor.

Brain. Robin Cook. 4.95 (*0-685-47356-2*) NAL-Dutton.

Brain. Robin Cook. 320p. 1982. pap. 5.99 (*0-451-15797-4*, Sig) NAL-Dutton.

Brain. Robin Cook. 1993. pap. 3.99 (*0-451-17622-7*, Sig) NAL-Dutton.

Brain. Douglas Mathers. LC 90-42883. (Illus.). 32p. (J). (gr. 4-6). 1992. lib. bdg. 11.89 (*0-8167-2090-8*); pap. 3.95 (*0-8167-2091-6*) Troll Assocs.

Brain. Richard M. Restak. 1988. mass mkt. 5.99 (*0-446-35540-2*) Warner Bks.

Brain: A Neuroscience Primer. 2nd ed. Richard F. Thompson. LC 92-48460. (Series of Books in Psychology). (C). 1995. pap. text ed. 24.95 (*0-7167-2485-5*) W H Freeman.

Brain: Aids to the Examination of the Peripheral Nervous System. (Illus.). 68p. 1987. pap. text ed. 13.50 (*0-7020-1165-7*, Bailliere-Tindall) Saunders.

Brain: An Introduction to the Psychology of the Human Brain & Behavior. Christine Temple. (Illus.). 240p. 1994. pap. 11.00 (*0-14-013385-2*, Arkana) Viking Penguin.

Brain: An Overview, a Source Guide. 1991. lib. bdg. 250.00 (*0-8490-4863-X*) Gordon Pr.

Brain: Biochemistry & Inherited Metabolic Disease. Ed. by N. R. Belton et al. 128p. 1983. lib. bdg. 71.50 (*0-85200-484-2*) Kluwer Ac.

Brain: Fetal & Infant. Samuel R. Berenberg. 1978. lib. bdg. 103.00 (*90-247-2022-2*) Kluwer Ac.

Brain: What It Is, What It Does. Ruth D. Bruun & Bertel Bruun. LC 88-21182. (Illus.). 64p. (J). 1989. 12.95 (*0-688-08453-2*); lib. bdg. 12.88 (*0-688-08454-0*) Greenwillow.

Brain Activation. P. E. Roland. LC 92-49741. (Series in Neuroscience). 600p. 1993. text ed. 94.95 (*0-471-50867-5*, Wiley-Liss) Wiley.

Brain Aging: Molecular Neurobiology, the Aging Process & Neurodegenerative Disease. Ed. by H. Hendrie et al. LC 89-15337. (Neuronal Control of Bodily Function Ser.: Vol. 5). (Illus.). 320p. (C). 1990. text ed. 69.00 (*0-920887-49-X*) Hogrefe & Huber Pubs.

Brain Aging: Neuropathology & Neuropharmacology. Ed. by J. Cervos-Navarro & H. I. Sarkander. (Aging Ser.: Vol. 21). (Illus.). 454p. 1983. text ed. 148.50 (*0-89004-739-1*) Raven.

Brain Allergies. William H. Philpott & Dwight K. Kalita. (Orig.). 1987. pap. 14.95 (*0-87983-426-9*) Keats.

Brain & Bannister's Clinical Neurology. 7th ed. Ed. by Roger Bannister. (Illus.). 588p. 1992. pap. 46.95 (*0-19-261913-6*) OUP.

Brain & Behavior: Assessing Cortical Dysfunction Through ADL. Arnadottir. (Illus.). 352p. 1990. 39.95 (*0-8016-0334-X*) Mosby Yr Bk.

Brain & Behavior: Proceedings, 2 vols. Incl. Vol. 1. Brain & Behavior. First Conference, 1961. 1961. 10.00 (*0-934454-17-5*); Vol. 2. Internal Environment & Alimentary Behavior. Second Conference, 1962. 1963. 10.00 (*0-934454-18-3*); write for info. (*0-318-54133-5*) Lubrecht & Cramer.

Brain & Behavior in Child Psychiatry. Ed. by A. Rothenberger. 496p. 1990. 109.00 (*0-387-52064-3*) Spr-Verlag.

Brain & Behaviour: Proceedings of the 28th International Congress of Physiological Sciences, Budapest, 1980. Ed. by G. Adam et al. LC 80-42186. (Advances in Physiological Sciences Ser.: Vol. 17). (Illus.). 500p. 1981. 228.00 (*0-08-027338-6*, Pub. by Pergamon Repr UK) Franklin.

Brain & Behavioural Development: Interdisciplinary Perspectives on Structure & Function. Ed. by John W. T. Dickerson & Harry McGurk. (Illus.). 266p. 1982. 69.95 (*0-903384-27-2*) Trans-Atl Phila.

Brain & Belief: Faith in Light of Brain Research. James B. Ashbrook. LC 88-40340. (Illus.). 250p. (Orig.). (C). 1988. text ed. 34.95 (*1-55605-041-0*); pap. text ed. 24.95 (*1-55605-040-2*) Wyndhall Pr.

Brain & Blood Pressure Control. Ed. by K. Nakamura. (International Congress Ser.: No. 695). 464p. 1986. 139.00 (*0-444-80810-8*) Elsevier.

Brain & Female Reproductive Function. Ed. by A. R. Genazzani et al. (Illus.). 640p. 1988. 85.00 (*1-85070-182-2*) Prthnon Pub.

Brain & Information: Even-Related Potentials. Intro. by Rathe Karrer et al. (Annals Ser.: Vol. 425). 1984. lib. bdg. 169.00 (*0-89766-242-3*); pap. 169.00 (*0-89766-243-1*) NY Acad Sci.

Brain & Intelligence in Vertebrates. Euan MacPhail. (Illus.). 1982. pap. 19.95 (*0-19-854551-7*) OUP.

Brain & Its Mind. 2nd ed. H. Kuhlenbeck & J. Gerlach. (Human Brain & Its Universe Ser.: Vol. 2). (Illus.). viii, 374p. 1982. 185.75 (*3-8055-2403-X*) S Karger.

Brain & Its Role in the Phylogenetic Transformation of the Human Skull. Franz Weidenreich. LC 78-72707. reprint ed. 19.50 (*0-404-18278-X*) AMS Pr.

Brain & Language: Cerebral Hemispheres & Linguistic Structure in Mutual Light. Roman Jakobson & Kathy Santilli. (New York University Slavic Papers: Vol. IV). 1980. pap. 5.95 (*0-89357-068-0*) Slavica.

Brain & Memory: Modulation & Mediation of Neuroplasticity. J. L. McGaugh et al. (Illus.). 416p. 1995. 75.00 (*0-19-508294-X*) OUP.

Brain & Mind. Ed. by David A. Oakley. LC 84-29604. (Psychology in Progress Ser.). 320p. 1985. pap. 14.95 (*0-416-31630-1*, 9627) Routledge Chapman & Hall.

Brain & Nervous System. (How Our Bodies Work Ser.). (Illus.). 48p. (J). (gr. 5-8). 1988. lib. bdg. 12.95 (*0-382-09703-3*) Silver Burdett Pr.

Brain & Nervous System. Ed. by Charles B. Clayman. LC 91-12825. (American Medical Association Home Medical Library). (Illus.). 144p. 1991. 16.98 (*0-89577-396-1*) RD Assn.

Brain & Nervous System. rev. ed. Steve Parker. (Human Body Ser.). (J). (gr. 5-7). 1990. lib. bdg. 13.93 (*0-531-14026-1*) Watts.

Brain & Nervous System. rev. ed. Steve Parker. (Human Body Ser.). (Illus.). 48p. (J). (gr. 5-8). 1991. pap. 6.95 (*0-531-24600-0*) Watts.

Brain & Nervous System; Head & Neck; Genitourinary System. Victor A. Levin et al. (Illus.). 105p. (Orig.). 1994. pap. text ed. 49.95 (*1-85922-620-5*) Current Science.

***Brain & Oral Functions: Oral Motor Function & Dysfunction: Selected Papers from the Osaka International Oral Physiology Symposium on Brain & Oral Function, Osaka, 3-5 September 1994.** Ed. by Toshifumi Morimoto et al. LC 95-8197. (International Congress Ser.: No. 1079). 1995. write for info. (*0-444-81963-0*) Elsevier.

Brain & Perception: Holonomy & Structure in Figural Processing. Karl H. Pribram. (John M. MacEachran Lectures Ser.). 400p. 1991. 79.95 (*0-89859-995-4*) L Erlbaum Assocs.

Brain & Personality. Graham Powell. LC 79-87638. 122p. 1979. text ed. 45.00 (*0-275-90408-3*, C0408, Praeger Pubs) Greenwood.

Brain & Pituitary Peptides. Ed. by W. Wuttke et al. (Illus.). 248p. 1980. 78.50 (*3-8055-0165-X*) S Karger.

Brain & Pituitary Peptides II: Pulsatile Administration of Gn-Rh in Hypothalmic Failure-Basic & Clinical Aspects, Ferring Symposium on Brain & Pituitary Peptides, June 1982. H. Stock & L. Wildt. Ed. by G. Leyendecker et al. (Illus.). viii, 188p. 1984. 78.50 (*3-8055-3811-1*) S Karger.

Brain & Space. Ed. by Jacques Paillard. (Illus.). 520p. 1991. 90.00 (*0-19-854284-4*) OUP.

Brain & Spinal Cord Tumors: Hope Through Research. 1994. lib. bdg. 250.00 (*0-8490-8546-2*) Gordon Pr.

***Brain & Spinal Cord Tumors: Hope Through Research.** 1995. lib. bdg. 251.99 (*0-8490-6717-0*) Gordon Pr.

Brain & the Bible: Is Psychology Compatible with Christianity? Robert A. Moss. 108p. 1993. pap. 8.95 (*0-9638848-1-6*) R A Moss.

Brain & the Universe. Orlando N. Acosta. LC 89-63297. (Illus.). 188p. (Orig.). 1990. pap. 15.95 (*0-9625266-1-4*) Outer Space Pr.

Brain As a Computer. 2nd ed. F. H. George. 1961. 202.00 (*0-08-017022-6*, Pub. by Pergamon Repr UK) Franklin.

Brain As an Endocrine Organ. Ed. by M. P. Cohen & Piero P. Foa. (Endocrinology & Metabolism Ser.: Vol. 3). (Illus.). 225p. 1988. 119.00 (*0-387-96644-7*) Spr-Verlag.

Brain Asymmetry. Ed. by Richard J. Davidson & Kenneth Hugdahl. 650p. 1994. 75.00 (*0-262-04144-8*, Bradford Bks) MIT Pr.

Brain Atlas & Functional Systems. Josephine C. Moore. (Illus.). 58p. (Orig.). (C). 1993. 22.00 (*1-56900-000-X*) Am Occup Therapy.

Brain Atlas of the Adult Swordtail Fish, Xiphophorus Helleri, & of Certain Developmental Stages. Ralf H. Anken & Hinrich Rachmann. LC 93-41657. 1993. pap. 60.00 (*1-56081-391-1*) VCH Pubs.

An Asterisk (*) at the beginning of an entry indicates that the title is appearing in BIP for the first time.

***Brain Attack: Mapping Out Early Recovery from Stroke.** Mary M. Castiglione & Cynthia C. Johnson. Ed. by Anna Hollingsworth. (Illus.). 48p. (Orig.). 1995. pap. text ed. write for info. (*0-939838-40-0*) Pritchett & Hull.

Brain Bafflers. Robert Steinwachs. (Illus.). 128p. (YA). (gr. 10-12). 1993. pap. 4.95 (*0-8069-8787-1*) Sterling.

Brain, Behaviour & Drugs: Introduction to the Neurochemistry of Behaviour. David M. Warburton. LC 74-20789. (Illus.). 290p. reprint ed. pap. 82.70 (*0-8357-7374-4*, 2030516) Bks Demand.

Brain, Behaviour, & Iron in the Infant Diet. Ed. by J. Dobbing. 208p. 1990. 64.00 (*0-387-19605-6*) Spr-Verlag.

Brain Benders. Joan Wheeler & Sharon Carter. (Enrichment & Gifted Ser.). 48p. (J). (gr. 4-6). 1982. 5.95 (*0-88160-048-2*, LW 234) Learning Wks.

Brain-Bending Mazes. (Activity Bks.). (J). (gr. 2-5). 1987. pap. 1.79 (*0-671-64357-6*, Litl Simon S&S) S&S Childrens.

Brain, Biochemistry & Behavior: Proceedings of the Sixth Arnold O. Beckman Conference in Clinical Chemistry. Ed. by Robert L. Habig. LC 83-14057. 335p. 1984. 20.00 (*0-915274-22-1*) Am Assn Clinical Chem.

Brain Biochemistry & Brain Disorders. Philip E. Strange. (Illus.). 360p. 1993. pap. 35.00 (*0-19-854775-7*) OUP.

Brain Blood Flow in Neurology & Psychiatry. D. C. Costa & P. J. Ell. (Clinician's Guide to Nuclear Medicine Ser.). (Illus.). 190p. 1991. text ed. 45.00 (*0-443-04282-9*) Churchill.

***Brain Blood Supply.** G. I. Mchedlishvili et al. 320p. (C). 1977. 54.00x (*963-05-1130-4*, Pub. by Akad Kiado HU) St Mut.

Brain Book. Peter Russell. 1984. pap. 12.95 (*0-452-26723-4*, Plume) NAL-Dutton.

Brain Boosters: Foods & Drugs That Make You Smarter. Beverly Potter & J. Sebastian Orfali. 257p. (Orig.). 1993. pap. 12.95 (*0-914171-65-8*) Ronin Pub.

***Brain Boosters for Business Advantage: Ticklers, Grabbags, Blue Skies, & Other Bionic Ideas.** Arthur B. VanGundy. LC 94-31011. 352p. 1994. 24.95 (*0-89384-267-2*) Pfeiffer & Co.

Brain Browser. Floyd E. Bloom et al. 220p. 1989. text ed. 350.00 (*0-12-107250-9*) Acad Pr.

Brain Browser: A Spinnaker Plus Based HyperText Application for Microsoft Windows. Floyd F. Bloom & Warren G. Young. 224p. 1994. spiral bd. 375.00 (*0-12-107240-1*) Acad Pr.

Brain Builder. Charles Gonher. 64p. 1991. write for info. (*1-56491-038-5*) Imagine Pubs.

***Brain Builders: A Lifelong Guide to Sharper Thinking, Better Memory, & an Age-Proof Mind.** Richard Leviton. 1995. pap. text ed. 12.95 (*0-13-303603-0*) P-H.

***Brain Builders: A Lifelong Guide to Sharper Thinking, Better Memory, & an Age-Proof Mind.** Richard Leviton. 1995. text ed. 27.95 (*0-13-303611-1*) P-H.

***Brain Builders Book One: A Workbook for Ages 4-6.** June Bailey. 1995. pap. 3.95 (*1-56565-227-4*) Lowell Hse Juvenile.

***Brain Builders Book One: A Workbook for Ages 6-8.** June Bailey. (Illus.). 1995. pap. 3.95 (*1-56565-229-0*) Lowell Hse Juvenile.

Brain Builders...Not! Lisa Eisenberg. (J). (gr. 4-7). 1993. pap. 1.95 (*0-590-47295-X*) Scholastic Inc.

Brain Building in Just Twelve Weeks. Marilyn Vos Savant. 1991. pap. 10.95 (*0-553-35348-9*) Bantam.

Brain Busters. Philip J. Carter & Ken A. Russell. (Illus.). 368p. (YA). (gr. 10-12). 1992. pap. 8.95 (*0-7063-7097-X*, Pub. by Ward Lock UK) Sterling.

Brain-Busting Decode Puzzles. Morris Bureloff. Ed. by Mary Laycock. (Illus.). 64p. (J). (gr. 7-10). 1985. pap. 7.95 (*0-918932-86-6*) Activity Resources.

Brain Cell Cultures: A Tool in Neurobiology. Ed. by Nicole Baumann. (Journal: Developmental Neuroscience: Vol. 7, No. 5-6, 1985). (Illus.). vi, 150p. 1986. 41.00 (*3-8055-4356-5*) S Karger.

Brain Chemistry & the French Connection (1791-1841) Donald B. Tower. LC 94-11631. 336p. 1994. 69.00 (*0-7817-0216-X*) Raven.

Brain Child. J. B. Dibble. 352p. (Orig.). 1987. pap. 3.95 (*0-8439-2504-3*) Dorchester Pub Co.

Brain Child. Stephen R. George. 352p. 1989. pap. 3.95 (*0-8217-2578-5*) Zebra.

Brain Child. George Turner. 416p. 1992. mass mkt. 5.50 (*0-380-71804-9*, AvoNova) Avon.

Brain Cholinergic Systems. Ed. by Mircea Steriade & D. Biesold. (Illus.). 468p. 1991. 150.00 (*0-19-854266-6*) OUP.

Brain Circuits & Functions of the Mind. Ed. by Colwyn Trevarthen. (Illus.). (C). 1990. pap. 44.95 (*0-521-37874-5*) Cambridge U Pr.

Brain Circuits & Functions of the Mind. Ed. by Colwyn Trevarthen. (Illus.). (C). 1990. 84.95 (*0-521-26102-3*) Cambridge U Pr.

Brain Code & Paleolinguistic. Valerii Chalidze. 88p. (ENG & RUS.). 1986. pap. write for info. (*1-56541-170-6*) Chalidze.

Brain Code Mechanisms of Information Transfer & the Role of the Corpus Callosum. Norman D. Cook. 300p. 1986. 42.50 (*0-416-40840-0*, 9834) Routledge Chapman & Hall.

Brain, Cognition, & Education. Ed. by Sarah L. Friedman et al. 400p. 1986. text ed. 66.00 (*0-12-268330-7*) Acad Pr.

Brain Control of Responses to Trauma. Ed. by Nancy J. Rothwell & Frank Berkenbosch. (Illus.). 330p. (C). 1994. 79.95 (*0-521-41939-5*) Cambridge U Pr.

Brain Control of the Reproductive System. Ed. by Akira Yokoyama. 1992. 83.95 (*0-8493-7754-4*, QP251) CRC Pr.

***Brain Corticosteroid Receptors: Studies on the Mechanism, Function, & Neurotoxicity of Corticosteroid Action.** Ed. by E. Ronald de Kloet et al. (Annals of the New York Academy of Sciences Ser.: 746). 1994. write for info. (*0-89766-907-X*) NY Acad Sci.

***Brain Corticosteroid Receptors: Studies on the Mechanism, Function, & Neurotoxicity of Corticosteroid Action.** Philip W. Landfield. Ed. by E. Ronald de Kloet et al. (Annals of the New York Academy of Sciences: 746). 1994. pap. write for info. (*0-89766-908-8*) NY Acad Sci.

Brain, Culture, & the Human Spirit: Essays from an Emergent Evolutionary Perspective. Ed. by James B. Ashbrook. (Illus.). 222p. (Orig.). (C). 1992. lib. bdg. 49.50 (*0-8191-8853-0*); pap. text ed. 23.50 (*0-8191-8854-9*) U Pr of Amer.

Brain-Culture or Phrenometry: Auto-Suggestion & Cerebral Stimulation. R. Dimsdale Stocker. 66p. 1985. reprint ed. spiral bd. 7.15 (*0-7873-1171-5*) Mokelumne.

Brain Damage. Herbert Burkholz. 288p. 1992. text ed. 20.00 (*0-689-12009-5*, Atheneum S&S) S&S Trade.

***Brain Damage Vol. 1: Medico Legas Aspects.** 200p. Date not set. 68.50 (*1-875114-36-X*, Pub. by Blackstone Pr UK) W W Gaunt.

Brain Damage & Recovery: Research & Clinical Perspectives. Stanley Finger & Donald Stein. (Historical & Contemporary Issues Ser.). 352p. 1982. text ed. 72.00 (*0-12-256780-3*) Acad Pr.

Brain Damage, Behaviour, & the Mind. Moyra Williams. LC 78-16370. (Illus.). 201p. reprint ed. pap. 57.30 (*0-8357-4630-5*, 2037559) Bks Demand.

Brain Damage Claims: Coping with Neuropsychological Evidence, 2 vols. David Faust et al. LC 91-72274. 1000p. 1991. Vol. 1, The Scientific & Professional Literature. write for info. (*1-879689-01-4*); Vol. II, Practical Guidelines, Cross-examination & Case Illustrations. write for info. (*1-879689-02-2*) Law & Psych.

Brain Damage Claims: Coping with Neuropsychological Evidence, 2 vols., Set. David Faust et al. LC 91-72274. 1000p. 1991. 175.00 (*1-879689-00-6*) Law & Psych.

Brain Damage in the Preterm Infant. Nigel Paneth et al. (Clinics in Developmental Medicine Ser.: No. 131). (Illus.). 300p. (C). 1995. 69.95 (*0-521-68300-9*) Cambridge U Pr.

Brain Dead. Linda Brieno. 384p. 1988. pap. 3.95 (*0-8439-2645-7*) Dorchester Pub Co.

Brain Dead, Brain Absent, Brain Donors: Human Subjects or Human Objects? Peter McCullagh. LC 92-49197. 200p. 1993. text ed. 95.00 (*0-471-93736-3*) Wiley.

Brain Death. Douglas N. Walton. LC 80-80845. (Science & Society: Series in Science, Technology, & Human Values: Vol. 5). 102p. 1980. pap. 6.95 (*0-931682-12-6*) Purdue U Pubns.

Brain Death. Sandra Wilkinson. 1988. pap. 3.95 (*1-55817-106-1*, Pinnacle NY) Windsor NY.

Brain Death: Interrelated Medical & Social Issues, Vol. 315. Ed. by Julius Korein. (Annals Ser.). 454p. 1978. pap. 61.00 (*0-89072-073-8*) NY Acad Sci.

Brain Death Criterion of Human Death. D. L. Stickel. (Illus.). 73p. 1982. pap. 23.00 (*0-08-025814-X*, Pergamon Pr) Elsevier.

***Brain Development: Relationship to Dietary Lipid & Lipid Metabolism.** Ed. by J. Jumpsen & M. T. Clandinin. 1995. write for info. (*0-935315-65-9*) AOCS Pr.

Brain Development & Cognition: A Reader. Ed. by Mark H. Johnson. LC 92-17620. 752p. 1993. 64.95 (*0-631-18222-5*); pap. 26.95 (*0-631-18223-3*) Blackwell Pubs.

***Brain Development & Epilepsy.** Ed. by Philip A. Schwartzkroin et al. (Illus.). 304p. 1995. 59.95 (*0-19-507846-2*) OUP.

Brain Diseases & Disorders: Diagnostics & Treatment Products. 275p. 1991. 2,650.00 (*0-89336-830-X*, C-139) BCC.

Brain Displacements & Deformations. Samuil Mikha'ilovich Blinkov & N. A. Smirnov. Ed. by Donald B. Lindsley. Tr. by George T. Onischenko. LC 70-107532. 230p. reprint ed. pap. 65.60 (*0-8357-7375-2*, 2020705) Bks Demand.

Brain Dopaminergic Imaging with Positron Tomography. Ed. by J. C. Baron et al. (Developments in Nuclear Medicine Ser.). 208p. 1991. lib. bdg. 77.50 (*0-7923-1476-X*) Kluwer Ac.

Brain Drain. Warren Murphy. (Destroyer Ser.: No. 22). (Orig.). 1989. pap. 3.50 (*1-55817-247-5*, Pinnacle NY) Windsor NY.

Brain Drain, 2 bks. Ernest R. Ranucci & Wilma E. Rollins. 70p. (J). (gr. 6-12). 7.50 (*0-685-74212-1*); Bk. A, 1975. write for info. (*1-878669-10-9*, 4301); Bk. B, 1978. write for info. (*0-318-66932-3*, 4420) Crea Tea Assocs.

Brain Drain, 2 bks., Bks. A & B. Ernest R. Ranucci & Wilma E. Rollins. 70p. (J). (gr. 6-12). teacher ed write for info. (*1-878669-09-5*, 4301) Crea Tea Assocs.

Brain Drain: Emigration & Return. William A. Glaser. LC 77-30576. (UNITAR Studies). 1978. 149.00 (*0-08-022419-9*, Pub. by Pergamon Repr UK) Franklin.

Brain Drain & Foreign Students. G. Lakshmana Rao. LC 78-10903. (Illus.). 1979. text ed. 32.50 (*0-312-09437-X*) St Martin.

Brain Drain & How to Reverse It. S. K. Chopra. 1986. 20.00 (*0-8364-1878-6*, Pub. by Lancer II) S Asia.

Brain Drain & Income Taxation. Ed. by Jagdish N. Bhagwati. 1977. pap. text ed. 16.25 (*0-08-020600-X*, Pergamon Pr) Elsevier.

Brain Drains Puzzle Book. 1990. pap. 1.50 (*0-89375-457-9*) Troll Assocs.

Brain Dysfunction in Children: Etiology, Diagnosis & Management. Ed. by Perry Black. 320p. 1981. text ed. 83.50 (*0-89004-022-2*) Raven.

Brain Dysfunction in Infantile Febrile Convulsions. Mary A. Brazier & Flavio Coceani. LC 75-14564. (International Brain Research Organization Monograph Ser.: Vol. 2). 384p. 1976. 88.00 (*0-89004-068-0*) Raven.

Brain Dysfunction in Metabolic Disorders. Ed. by Fred Plum. 1974. 33.50 (*0-7204-7521-X*, North Holland) Elsevier.

***Brain Dysfunction in Metabolic Disorders.** fac. ed. Ed. by Fred Plum. LC 74-79190. (Association for Research in Nervous & Mental Disease Research Publications: No. 53). (Illus.). 336p. Date not set. pap. 95.80 (*0-7837-7296-3*, 2047010) Bks Demand.

Brain Edema, No. VIII. Ed. by H. J. Reulen et al. (Acta Neurochirurgica - Supplementum Ser.: No. 51). (Illus.). xiii, 416p. 1991. 162.00 (*0-387-82240-2*) Spr-Verlag.

***Brain Edema: A Pathogenetic Analysts.** G. I. Mchedlishvili et al. 365p. (C). 1986. 120.00x (*963-05-4378-8*, Pub. by Akad Kiado HU) St Mut.

Brain Edema: Pathogenesis, Imaging, & Therapy. Donlin M. Long. (Advances in Neurology Ser.: Vol. 52). 640p. 1990. 149.00 (*0-88167-625-X*) Raven.

Brain Edema IX: Proceedings of the Ninth International Symposium, Tokyo, May 16-19, 1993. Ed. by Umeo Ito et al. LC 94-5220. (Acta Neurochirugica - Supplementum Ser.: Vol. 60). 1994. 184.00 (*0-387-82532-0*) Spr-Verlag.

Brain-Endocrine Interaction I: Median Eminence-Structure & Function: Proceedings of the International Symposium, Munich, 1971. International Symposium on Brain-Endocrine Interaction Staff. Ed. by K. M. Knigge et al. (Illus.). xii, 368p. 1972. 96.00 (*3-8055-1257-0*) S Karger.

Brain Endocrine Interaction II: The Ventricular System in Neuroendocrine Mechanisms: Proceedings of the International Symposium, 2nd, Tokyo, October, 1974. International Symposium on Brain-Endocrine Interaction Staff. Ed. by K. M. Knigge & D. E. Scott. (Illus.). x, 406p. 1975. 113.75 (*3-8055-2176-6*) S Karger.

Brain Endocrinology. 2nd ed. Marcella Motta. Ed. by Luciano Martini. (Comprehensive Endocrinology, Revised Ser.). 496p. 1991. 160.50 (*0-88167-768-X*) Raven.

Brain Energy Metabolism. B. K. Siesjo. LC 77-2666. 619p. reprint ed. pap. 176.50 (*0-8357-7376-0*, 2030383) Bks Demand.

Brain Failure. Ed. by D. J. Bihari & J. W. Holaday. (Update in Intensive Care & Emergency Medicine Ser.: Vol. 9). (Illus.). 360p. 1989. pap. 97.00 (*0-387-51655-7*, 3512) Spr-Verlag.

Brain Fields & Learning Process see Studies in the Psychology of Art

Brain Fluids & Metabolism. Gary A. Rosenberg. (Illus.). 224p. 1990. 39.95 (*0-19-505324-9*) OUP.

Brain Food Diet for Children. Ralph E. Minear & William Proctor. LC 83-3798. 228p. 1984. write for info. (*0-672-52755-3*) Macmillan.

Brain Fuel: The Book That Improves Your Mind As Well As Your Body! 2nd ed. L. A. Peterson et al. (Illus.). 256p. 1990. reprint ed. pap. 12.95 (*1-878459-01-5*) Total Rsch Pub.

Brain Function. Paul August. (Encyclopedia of Psychoactive Drugs Ser.: No. 2). (Illus.). 128p. (YA). (gr. 5 up). 1988. lib. bdg. 19.95 (*1-55546-204-9*) Chelsea Hse.

Brain Function & Psychotropic Drugs. Heather Ashton. (Illus.). 440p. 1992. 98.00 (*0-19-262243-9*); pap. 56.50 (*0-19-262242-0*) OUP.

Brain Functions in Neuropeptides: A Current View. Ed. by J. P. Burbach & D. De Wied. (Illus.). 150p. (C). 1993. 49.00 (*1-85070-453-8*) Prthnon Pub.

Brain Game: Twenty-Seven Fun-to Take Aptitude Tests. Rita Aero & Elliot Weiner. LC 83-61196. 1983. pap. 12.95 (*0-688-01923-4*, Quill) Morrow.

Brain Growth. Ed. by H. J. Kretschmann. (Bibliotheca Anatomica Ser.: No. 28). (Illus.). viii, 140p. 1986. 112.00 (*3-8055-4226-7*) S Karger.

Brain Gut Interactions. Ed. by Tache. 1991. 219.00 (*0-8493-5368-8*, QP145) CRC Pr.

Brain Gut Peptides & Reproductive Peptides. Barnes. 1991. 98.95 (*0-8493-8848-1*, QP552) CRC Pr.

Brain Gym. Paul Dennison & Gail Dennison. (Illus.). 8.00 (*0-685-64783-8*, 3); teacher ed 16.95 (*0-685-64784-6*, 3A); 2.00 (*0-685-64785-4*, 9); 2.00 (*0-685-64786-2*, 10); 20.00 (*0-685-64787-0*, 12A) Edu-Kinesthetics.

***Brain Gym for Business: Instant Brain Boosters for on-the-Job Success.** Gail E. Dennison et al. (Illus.). 52p. (Orig.). 1994. pap. 10.00 (*0-942143-03-5*) Edu-Kinesthetics.

Brain Gym Surfer. Sandra Hinsley. (Illus.). (J). 6.00 (*0-685-64789-7*, 5) Edu-Kinesthetics.

***Brain Gym Teacher's Education.** Paul E. Dennison & Gail E. Dennison. (Illus.). 45p. (Orig.). 1994. pap. 16.95 (*0-942143-02-7*) Edu-Kinesthetics.

Brain Has a Mind of Its Own: Insights from a Practicing Neurologist. Richard M. Restak. 192p. 1991. 18.00 (*0-517-57483-7*, Harmony) Crown Pub Group.

Brain Has a Mind of Its Own: Insights from a Practicing Neurologist. Richard M. Restak. 1993. 12.00 (*0-517-88080-6*, Crown) Crown Pub Group.

Brain Imaging: An Introduction. John R. Bradshaw. (Illus.). 264p. 1989. pap. 80.00 (*0-7236-0596-3*) Buttrwrth-Heinemann.

Brain Imaging: Applications in Psychiatry. Ed. by Nancy C. Andreasen. LC 88-16775. 396p. 1989. 80.00 (*0-88048-229-X*, 8229) Am Psychiatric.

Brain Imaging & Brain Function. Ed. by Louis Sokoloff. (Association for Research in Nervous & Mental Disease Research Publications: Vol. 63). (Illus.). 308p. 1985. text ed. 105.00 (*0-88167-084-7*) Raven.

Brain Imaging in Affective Disorders. Ed. by Peter Hauser. LC 91-4537. (Progress in Psychiatry Ser.: No. 34). 176p. 1991. text ed. 35.00 (*0-88048-456-X*, 8456) Am Psychiatric.

Brain Imaging in Psychiatry. Ed. by John M. Morihisa. LC 84-6303. (Clinical Insights Ser.). 103p. reprint ed. pap. 29.40 (*0-8357-7812-6*, 2036184) Bks Demand.

***Brain Imaging of Nicotine & Tobacco Smoking.** E. F. Domino. LC 95-67172. 344p. 1995. 95.00x (*0-916182-10-X*) NPP Bks.

***Brain Immune Axis & Substance Abuse: Proceedings of the Second Annual Symposium Held in Palm Beach, Florida, June 16-18, 1994.** Ed. by Burt M. Sharp et al. (Advances in Experimental Medicine & Biology Ser.: Vol. 373). 240p. 1995. 79.50 (*0-306-45017-8*) Plenum.

Brain in Health & Disease Abstracts. IBRO Staff. (Neuroscience Ser.: No. 468). 1982. pap. 125.00 (*0-08-028896-0*, Pergamon Pr) Elsevier.

Brain in Human Aging. Gene D. Cohen. (Adulthood & Aging Ser.). 272p. (C). 1988. 31.95 (*0-8261-5830-7*) Springer Pub.

Brain in Pediatric AIDS. Ed. by P. B. Kozloski et al. (Illus.). xvi, 204p. 1990. 157.00 (*3-8055-5216-5*) S Karger.

Brain Injuries: Medical Subject Analysis & Research Guide with Bibliography. Peter B. Zeiderhof. LC 83-45530. 152p. 1985. 39.50 (*0-88164-120-0*); pap. 34.50 (*0-88164-121-9*) ABBE Pubs Assn.

B

Brain Injury: Cognitive & Pre-Vocational Approaches to Rehabilition. J. Kenig et al. Ed. by Philip A. Morse. LC 84-52527. (Illus.). 192p. (Orig.). 1986. 10.95 (*0-913292-42-7*) Tiresias Pr.

Brain Injury & Protection During Heart Surgery. Ed. by Mark Hilberman. (C). 1987. lib. bdg. 82.50 (*0-89838-952-6*) Kluwer Ac.

Brain Injury & Recovery. Ed. by Stanley Finger et al. (Illus.). 362p. 1988. 79.50 (*0-306-42756-7*, Plenum Pr) Plenum.

Brain Injury & the Family: An Aid for Better Understanding. Lesley A. Sitkin & Bruce E. Murdoch. (Illus.). (Orig.). (C). 1987. pap. text ed. 9.47 (*0-943723-00-0*) Simmons & Hall Pub.

***Brain Injury Glossary.** Ed. by Don Lehmkuhl. 45p. 1992. pap. 9.50 (*1-882855-06-X*) HDI Pubs.

Brain Injury Rehabilitation: A Neuro-Functional Approach. Jo Clark-Wilson & Gordon M. Giles. LC 92-21407. (Therapy in Practice Ser.: Vol. 33). 1992. 47.50 (*1-56593-052-5*) Singular Publishing.

Brain Injury Rehabilitation: Clinical Considerations. Ed. by M. Alan Finlayson & Scott H. Garner. LC 92-48433. (Rehabilitation Medicine Library). 332p. 1994. 79.00 (*0-683-03224-0*) Williams & Wilkins.

Brain Insults in Infants & Children: Pathophysiology & Management. Ed. by Hector E. James et al. 304p. 1985. text ed. 70.50 (*0-8089-1723-4*, Grune) Saunders.

Brain Iron: Neurochemical & Behavioral Aspects. Ed. by M. B. Youdim. (Topics in Neurochemistry & Neuropharmacology Ser.: Vol. 2). 250p. 1988. 95.00 (*0-85066-393-8*) Taylor & Francis.

Brain Ischemia: From Basic Science to Treatment. Ed. by Louis R. Caplan. LC 93-49746. 1995. 165.00 (*0-387-19850-4*) Spr-Verlag.

Brain Ischemia: Quantitative EEG & Imaging Techniques. Ed. by G. Pfurtscheller et al. (Progress in Brain Research Ser.: Vol. 62). 1985. 151.50 (*0-444-80582-6*) Elsevier.

Brain Lateralization in Children: Developmental Implications. Ed. by Dennis L. Molfese & Sidney J. Segalowitz. LC 88-11269. 612p. 1988. lib. bdg. 65.00 (*0-89862-719-2*) Guilford Pr.

***Brain Lord: Official Players Guide.** Tim Rooney. (Illus.). 96p. (Orig.). 1994. pap. 9.95 (*1-57280-016-X*) IFTW Bks.

Brain Machine: The Development of Neurophysiological Thought. Marc Jeannerod. Tr. by David Urion. LC 85-7597. (Illus.). 192p. 1985. 26.50 (*0-674-08047-5*) HUP.

Brain Maps: Structure of the Rat Brain. Larry W. Swanson. LC 92-32374. 1992. 243.75 (*0-444-81414-0*) Elsevier.

Brain Maturation & Cognitive Development: Comparative & Cross-Cultural Perspectives. Ed. by Kathleen R. Gibson & Anne C. Petersen. (Foundations of Human Behavior Ser.). (Illus.). 399p. 1991. lib. bdg. 69.95 (*0-202-01187-9*) Aldine de Gruyter.

Brain Mechanisms: Papers in Memory of Robert Thompson. Ed. by Francis M. Crinella & Jen Yu. LC 93-41801. (Annals Ser.: Vol. 702). 1993. write for info. (*0-89766-759-X*); pap. 60.00 (*0-89766-760-3*) NY Acad Sci.

***Brain Mechanisms & Abnormal Behavior: Chemistry.** Ed. by Herman M. Van Praag et al. LC 81-5489. (Handbook of Biological Psychiatry Ser.: Pt. 4). 981p. 1981. reprint ed. pap. 180.00 (*0-7837-8331-0*, 2049118) Bks Demand.

***Brain Mechanisms & Abnormal Behavior: Genetics & Neuroendocrinology.** Ed. by Herman M. Van Praag et al. LC 80-21053. (Handbook of Biological, Experimental & Clinical Psychiatry Ser.: Pt. 3). (Illus.). 405p. Date not set. pap. 115.50 (*0-7837-8343-4*, 2049132) Bks Demand.

***Brain Mechanisms & Abnormal Behavior: Psychophysiology.** fac. ed. Ed. by Herman M. Van Praag et al. LC 80-22738. (Handbook of Biological Psychiatry Ser.: Pt. 2). (Illus.). 503p. 1980. pap. 143.40 (*0-7837-8344-2*, 2049133) Bks Demand.

Brain Mechanisms & Spatial Vision. Ed. by David J. Ingle et al. 1984. lib. bdg. 148.00 (*90-247-3117-8*) Kluwer Ac.

***Brain Mechanisms, Attention-Deficit, & Related Mental Disorders: A Clinical & Theoretical Assessment of Attention-Deficit.** Jordan Joseph. 620p. 1992. pap. 48.95 (*0-398-06195-5*) C C Thomas.

An Asterisk (*) at the beginning of an entry indicates that the title is appearing in BIP for the first time.

Brain Mechanisms, Attention-Deficit, & Related Mental Disorders: A Clinical & Theoretical Assessment of Attention-Deficit. Jordan Joseph. 620p. (C). 1992. text ed. 91.95x (*0-398-05765-6*) C C Thomas.

Brain Mechanisms in Problem Solving & Intelligence: A Lesson Survey of the Rat Brain. Richard F. Thompson et al. (Critical Issues in Neuropsychology Ser.). (Illus.). 238p. 1990. 39.50 (*0-306-43420-2*, Plenum Pr) Plenum.

Brain Mechanisms of Behaviour in Lower Vertebrates. Ed. by Peter R. Laming. LC 80-41368. (Society for Experimental Biology Seminar Ser.: No. 9). 200p. 1981. 59.95 (*0-521-23702-5*); pap. 27.95 (*0-521-28168-7*) Cambridge U Pr.

Brain Mechanisms of Perception & Memory: From Neuron to Behavior. Ed. by Taketoshi Ono et al. LC 92-49789. (Illus.). 722p. 1993. 95.00 (*0-19-507770-9*) OUP.

Brain Messengers & the Pituitary. Engenio E. Muller & Giuseppe Nistico. 711p. 1989. text ed. 201.00 (*0-12-510310-7*) Acad Pr.

Brain Metabolic Diseases (Melas Syndrome) Index of New Information, Bibliography & Reference Research Bible. 180p. 1994. 49.50 (*0-7883-0122-5*); pap. 45.50 (*0-7883-0123-3*) ABBE Pubs Assn.

***Brain Metallothionein in Neurological Disorders.** Ed. by M. Ebadi. (Journal: Biological Signals: Vol. 3, No. 4, 1994). (Illus.). 40p. 1994. pap. 28.00 (*3-8055-6057-5*) S Karger.

Brain, Mind & Behavior. 2nd ed. Floyd E. Bloom & Arlyne Lazerson. LC 87-30598. (Illus.). 394p. (C). 1995. teacher ed 4.95 (*0-7167-1895-2*); pap. text ed. 39.95 (*0-7167-1863-4*); student ed 15.95 (*0-7167-1894-4*) W H Freeman.

Brain, Mind & Medicine: Charles Richet & the Origins of Physiological Psychology. Stewart Wolf. 302p. (C). 1992. 49.95 (*1-56000-063-5*) Transaction Pubs.

Brain-Mind & Parapsychology: Proceedings of the International Conference, Aug. 24-25, 1978. International Conference, Montreal Canada Staff. Ed. by Betty Shapin & Lisette Coly. LC 79-84820. 1979. 17.00 (*0-912328-31-2*) Parapsych Foun.

Brain, Mind, & the External Signs of Intelligence. Bernard Hollander. LC 78-72802. 1931. 32.50 (*0-404-60864-7*) AMS Pr.

Brain Ninety-Three: Proceedings of the 16th International Symposium on Cerebral Blood Flow & Metabolism. Kyuya Kogure & Takashi Yoshimoto. (Journal of Cerebral Blood Flow & Metabolism Ser.: Vol. 13, Suppl. 1, 1993). 916p. 1993. 108.50 (*0-7817-0101-5*) Raven.

Brain of an Army - the Command of the Sea - the Brain of a Navy. Spenser Wilkinson. (Modern Revivals in Military History Ser.). 400p. 1992. 69.95 (*0-7512-0081-6*, Pub. by Gregg Pub UK) Ashgate Pub Co.

Brain of Robert Frost: A Cognitive Approach to Literature. Norman N. Holland. 208p. 1988. 39.50 (*0-415-90023-9*, A2320, Routledge NY); pap. 13.95 (*0-415-90083-2*, A2564, Routledge NY) Routledge.

***Brain of the Firm.** 2nd ed. Stafford Beer. (Stafford Beer Classic Library). Date not set. pap. text ed. 29.95 (*0-471-94839-X*) Wiley.

Brain of the Firm. 2nd ed. Stafford Beer. LC 80-49979. 417p. 1981. text ed. 125.00 (*0-471-27687-1*, Wiley-Interscience) Wiley.

Brain of the Tiger Salamander. Charles J. Herrick. LC 48-5790. (Illus.). 417p. reprint ed. 118.90 (*0-8357-9643-4*, 2015757) Bks Demand.

Brain Oncology. Ed. by M. Chatel et al. (Developments in Oncology Ser.). (C). 1987. lib. bdg. 228.50 (*0-89838-954-2*) Kluwer Ac.

Brain Opioid Systems in Reproduction. Ed. by R. G. Dyer & R. J. Bicknell. (Illus.). 388p. 1989. 89.00 (*0-19-857694-3*) OUP.

Brain Organization & Memory: Cells, Systems, & Circuits. Ed. by James L. McGaugh et al. (Illus.). 432p. 1990. 75.00 (*0-19-505496-2*) OUP.

Brain Organization & Memory: Cells, Systems, & Circuits. Ed. by James L. McGaugh et al. (Illus.). 448p. 1992. pap. 39.95 (*0-19-507712-1*) OUP.

Brain Organization of Language & Cognitive Processes. Ed. by A. Ardila & P. Ostrosky-Solis. LC 89-16051. (Critical Issues in Neuropsychology Ser.). (Illus.). 285p. 1989. 45.00 (*0-306-43169-6*, Plenum Pr) Plenum.

Brain People & the New Humans: A History. Robert E. Brooks. LC 86-70386. 340p. 1986. pap. 9.95 (*0-936339-07-1*) Circa Pr Portland.

Brain Peptides & Catecholamines in Cardiovascular Regulation. Ed. by Joseph P. Buckley & Carlos M. Ferrario. (Illus.). 448p. 1987. text ed. 83.00 (*0-88167-262-9*) Raven.

Brain Phosphoproteins: Characterization & Function: Proceedings of a Workshop at the State University of Utrecht, Sept. 1981. W. H. Gispen. (Progress in Brain Research Ser.: Vol. 56). 454p. 1982. 180.50 (*0-444-80412-9*) Elsevier.

Brain-Pituitary-Adrenal Interrelationships: Proceedings of the International Symposium, Cincinnati, Ohio, June, 1973. International Symposium on Brain-Pituitary-Adrenal Interrelationships Staff. Ed. by H. Brodish & S. Redgate. 1972. 117.00 (*3-8055-1457-3*) S Karger.

***Brain Plasticity & Behavior.** Bryan Kolb. (John M. MacEachran Memorial Lectures Ser.). 208p. 1995. text ed. 45.00 (*0-8058-1520-1*) L Erlbaum Assocs.

Brain Power. Norman Sullivan. (Illus.). 128p. (YA). (gr. 10-12). 1993. pap. 4.95 (*0-7063-7130-5*, Pub. by Ward Lock UK) Sterling.

Brain Power: A Neurosurgeon's Complete Program to Maintain & Enhance Brain Fitness Throughout Your Life. Vernon H. Mark & Jeffrey P. Mark. 256p. 1991. pap. 11.95 (*0-395-55001-7*) HM.

Brain Power: How to Boost Your Mind with Special Foods, What Drugs & Dangers to Avoid & Brain Exercises to Improve Thinking & Protect Against Memory Loss. 1992. lib. bdg. 188.95 (*0-8490-5519-9*) Gordon Pr.

Brain Power: How to Unleash Your Extraordinary Range of Mental Skills. 1991. 79.95 (*0-924967-23-4*) Intl Ctr Creat Think.

Brain Power Through Picture Books: Help Children Develop with Books That Stimulate Specific Parts of Their Minds. Nancy J. Polette. LC 91-50976. (Illus.). 144p. 1992. pap. text ed. 18.95x (*0-89950-708-5*) McFarland & Co.

Brain Puzzler's Delight. E. R. Emmet. LC 93-8555. (Illus.). 96p. (YA). (gr. 10-12). 1993. pap. 4.95 (*0-8069-8816-9*) Sterling.

Brain Puzzles. Tyler. (Brain Benders Ser.). (J). (gr. 2-5). 1980. lib. bdg. 12.96 (*0-88110-051-X*, Usborne); pap. 4.95 (*0-86020-437-5*, Usborne) EDC.

Brain Quest: Grade 1. Chris W. Feder. (J). (gr. 1). 1992. pap. 9.95 (*1-56305-258-X*, 3258) Workman Pub.

Brain Quest: Grade 2. Chris W. Feder. (J). (gr. 2). 1992. pap. 9.95 (*1-56305-259-8*, 3259) Workman Pub.

Brain Quest: Grade 3. Chris W. Feder. (J). (gr. 3). 1992. pap. 9.95 (*1-56305-260-1*, 3260) Workman Pub.

Brain Quest: Grade 4. Chris W. Feder. (J). (gr. 4). 1992. pap. 9.95 (*1-56305-261-X*, 3261) Workman Pub.

***Brain Quest American History.** Feder. (J). (gr. 4-6). 1995. 9.95 (*1-56305-879-0*) Workman Pub.

***Brain Quest English.** Feder. (J). (gr. 4-6). 1995. 9.95 (*1-56305-882-0*) Workman Pub.

***Brain Quest for the Car.** Gold. (J). (gr. 2-7). 1995. (*0-7611-0016-4*) Workman Pub.

Brain Quest for Threes: Ages Three-Four. Chris W. Feder. (J). (ps-3). 1994. 10.95 (*1-56305-633-X*) Workman Pub.

Brain Quest, Grade 5. Chris W. Feder. (J). (gr. 5). 1992. pap. 9.95 (*1-56305-262-8*, 3262) Workman Pub.

Brain Quest, Grade 6. Chris W. Feder. (J). (gr. 6). 1992. pap. 9.95 (*1-56305-263-6*, 3263) Workman Pub.

Brain Quest, Grade 7. Chris W. Feder. (J). (gr. 7). 1992. pap. 9.95 (*1-56305-264-4*, 3264) Workman Pub.

Brain Quest (Kindergarten) Chris W. Feder. (J). (gr. k-1). 1993. pap. 10.95 (*1-56305-352-7*, 3352) Workman Pub.

***Brain Quest Math.** Feder. (J). (gr. 4-6). 1995. 9.95 (*1-56305-880-4*) Workman Pub.

Brain Quest (Preschool) Chris W. Feder. (J). (ps-3). 1993. pap. 10.95 (*1-56305-351-9*, 3351) Workman Pub.

***Brain Quest Science.** Feder. (J). (gr. 4-6). 1995. 9.95 (*1-56305-881-2*) Workman Pub.

Brain Research & Learning. Mary Claycomb. 27p. reprint ed. pap. 25.00 (*0-8357-7377-9*, 2024754) Bks Demand.

Brain Reward Systems & Abuse: Proceedings of the Seventh International Berzelius Symposium. Ed. by Jorgen Engel et al. (Illus.). 208p. 1987. text ed. 83.00 (*0-88167-263-7*) Raven.

Brain Scale of Dr. Brunler. Arthur M. Young. (Broadside Editions Ser.). 20p. 1985. reprint ed. pap. 2.95 (*0-931191-01-7*) Rob Briggs.

***Brain Sell.** Tony Buzan & Richard Israel. 280p. 1995. 54.95 (*0-566-07658-6*, Pub. by Gower UK) Ashgate Pub Co.

Brain Sell: A Thinking Person's Guide to Selling Like the Pros. John C. Kiley. 128p. 1992. 17.95 (*1-56565-010-7*) Lowell Hse.

Brain Sex. Anne Moir & David Jessel. 1992. pap. 12.95 (*0-385-31183-4*, Delta) Dell.

Brain Sex: The Real Difference Between Men & Women. Anne Moir. 1991. 17.95 (*0-8184-0543-0*) Carol Pub Group.

Brain Signal Transduction & Memory. Ed. by Masao Ito & Yasutomo Nishizuka. 297p. 1990. text ed. 92.00 (*0-12-375655-3*) Acad Pr.

Brain Simulator: Tutorial Software for Neural Circuit Design. Neural Network Laboratory Staff. (Illus.). 91p. (C). 1988. pap. 99.00 (*0-944365-05-1*) Abbot Foster.

Brain Slices. Ed. by Raymond Dingledine. LC 83-22957. 460p. 1984. 85.00 (*0-306-41437-6*, Plenum Pr) Plenum.

Brain Slices: Fundamentals, Applications & Implications. Ed. by A. Schurr et al. (Illus.). vi, 194p. 1987. 136.00 (*3-8055-4490-1*) S Karger.

***Brain Slices in Basic & Clinical Research.** Ed. by Avital Schurr & Benjamin M. Rigor. LC 94-31343. 1995. write for info. (*0-8493-4760-2*) CRC Pr.

Brain States. Tom Kenyon. LC 93-23667. (Illus.). 297p. (Orig.). 1994. pap. 11.95 (*1-880698-04-8*) US Pub FL.

Brain Stations: A Center Approach to Thinking Skills. Greta Rasmussen. (Illus.). 112p. (Orig.). 1989. teacher ed 11.95 (*0-936110-07-4*) Tin Man Pr.

Brain Stem Control of Spinal Mechanisms: Proceedings of the First Eric K. Fernstrom Symposium, Lund, Sweden, 10-13 November, 1981. Anders T. Bjorklund. Ed. by B. H. Sjolund. (Fernstrom Foundation Ser.: Vol. I). 519p. 1983. 184.00 (*0-444-80429-3*) Elsevier.

Brain-Stem Localization & Function. Ed. by Louis R. Caplan et al. LC 93-5073. 1993. 90.00 (*0-387-56608-2*) Spr-Verlag.

Brain Storms: Recovery from Traumatic Brain Injury. John Cassidy. 160p. (Orig.). 1992. pap. 8.95 (*0-929162-39-0*) PIA Pr.

Brain Stretchers-Book I. Carolyn Anderson & Jackie Haller. 1975. pap. 6.95 (*0-910974-87-X*) Crit Think Soft.

Brain Structure & Aging. E. A. Wright et al. 297p. 1974. text ed. 26.50 (*0-8422-7175-9*) Irvington.

Brain Styles Be Who You Really Are. David Cherry & Marlane Miller. (Orig.). 1992. pap. 22.95 (*0-9634406-0-8*); audio 18.95 (*0-9634406-1-6*) BrainStyles.

Brain Surgery: Complication Avoidance & Management, 2 vols., Set. Ed. by Michael L. Apuzzo. (Illus.). 2616p. 1993. text ed. 495.00 (*0-443-08709-1*) Churchill.

Brain Surgery: What to Know & Ask. Elaine B. LePage. Ed. by Anna Hollingsworth. (Illus.). 36p. (Orig.). 1994. pap. text ed. 4.65 (*0-939838-36-2*) Pritchett & Hull.

***Brain Surgery for Beginners & Other Major Operations for Minors.** Steve Parker & David West. (Illus.). 64p. (J). (gr. 4-12). 1995. lib. bdg. 15.90 (*1-56294-604-8*) Millbrook Pr.

Brain, Symbol & Experience: Toward a Neurophenomenology of Human Consciousness. Charles D. Laughlin, Jr. et al. LC 92-22627. 424p. (Orig.). (C). 1993. pap. 20.00 (*0-231-08139-1*, Mrngside) Col U Pr.

Brain Systems & Psychological Concepts. John Boddy. LC 77-21203. 477p. reprint ed. pap. 136.00 (*0-8357-7378-7*, 2031022) Bks Demand.

Brain Systems, Disorders & Psychotropic Drugs. Ed. by Heather Ashton. (Illus.). 556p. 1987. 85.00 (*0-19-261436-3*) OUP.

Brain Teasers. Carol Eichel. Ed. by Amy LasCola. (Illus.). 80p. (J). (gr. 3-5). 1993. student ed 8.95 (*1-55734-490-6*) Tchr Create Mat.

Brain Teasers. Carol Eichel. Ed. by Amy LasCola. (Illus.). 80p. (J). (gr. 5-8). 1993. student ed 8.95 (*1-55734-491-4*) Tchr Create Mat.

Brain Teasers. Stuart A. Kallen. LC 92-14774. (J). 1992. lib. bdg. 12.94 (*1-56239-130-5*) Abdo & Dghtrs.

Brain Teasers! Over One Hundred Eighty Activities & Worksheets That Make Kids Think. Susan S. Petreshene. LC 94-11905. (Illus.). 1994. pap. 27.95 (*0-87628-123-4*) Ctr Appl Res.

Brain Teasers & Puzzles for Kids. Troll. 32p. (J). (ps-3). 1991. pap. 1.95 (*0-8167-2247-1*) Troll Assocs.

Brain, the Soul, God. Judy Ball & John Danich. 174p. 1986. pap. 6.95 (*0-88144-064-7*) Christian Pub.

Brain Theory. Ed. by G. Shaw & G. Palm. (Advance Series on Neuroscience: Vol. 1). 800p. (C). 1988. reprint ed. text ed. 116.00 (*9971-5-0483-9*); reprint ed. pap. text ed. 55.00 (*9971-5-0484-7*) World Scientific Pub.

Brain Theory: Spatio-Temporal Aspects of Brain Function. Ed. by A. M. Aertsen. LC 93-15872. ix, 306p. 1993. 145.75 (*0-444-89839-5*) Elsevier.

***Brain Train.** Palmer. 1995. pap. (*0-419-19830-X*) Routledge Chapman & Hall.

Brain Train: Ready-to-Use Tapes & Activities to Develop Confidence & Competence in Children with Learning Difficulties. Janna Spark. 356p. 1993. 69.95 (*0-87628-192-7*) Ctr Appl Res.

Brain Train: Studying for Success. Richard Palmer & Chris Pope. 230p. 1984. pap. 12.95 (*0-419-13110-8*, NO. 9185, E & FN Spon) Routledge Chapman & Hall.

***Brain Tricks: Coping with Your Defective Brain.** David L. Weiner. LC 95-1694. 358p. 1995. pap. 12.95 (*0-87975-989-5*) Prometheus Bks.

Brain Tricks: How to Win the Ultimate Mind Game. David L. Weiner. 358p. (C). 1993. 19.95 (*0-87975-829-5*) Prometheus Bks.

Brain Tumor Biology. Ed. by M. L. Rosenblum & C. B. Wilson. (Progress in Experimental Tumor Research Ser.: Vol. 27). (Illus.). xvi, 260p. 1984. 125.75 (*3-8055-3698-4*) S Karger.

Brain Tumor Invasiveness. Ed. by Ronald H. Goldfarb. LC 94-8764. 90p. (C). 1994. lib. bdg. 125.00 (*0-7923-2791-8*) Kluwer Ac.

Brain Tumor Therapy. Ed. by M. L. Rosenblum & C. B. Wilson. (Progress in Experimental Tumor Research Ser.: Vol. 28). (Illus.). xvi, 288p. 1984. 125.75 (*3-8055-3699-2*) S Karger.

Brain Tumors: A Comprehensive Text. Ed. by Morantz & Walsh. 864p. 1993. 215.00 (*0-8247-8826-5*) Dekker.

Brain Tumors: Pathology & Biological Correlates. Davide Schiffer. LC 92-49398. 1993. write for info. (*3-540-55864-0*); 225.00 (*0-387-55864-0*) Spr-Verlag.

Brain Tumors - Biopathology & Therapy: Proceedings of the Brain Tumor Workshop - Verona 1 Held in Verona, Italy, 13-14 June 1985. Ed. by M. A. Gerosa et al. LC 86-785. (Advances in the Biosciences Ser.: No. 58). (Illus.). 254p. 1986. 115.00 (*0-08-032013-9*, Pergamon Pr) Elsevier.

Brain Tumors Completely. 3rd rev. ed. K. J. Zulch. (Illus.). 752p. 1986. 273.00 (*0-387-10933-1*) Spr-Verlag.

Brain Tumors in Children: Principles of Diagnosis & Treatment. 2nd ed. Michael E. Cohen & Patricia K. Duffner. LC 93-34357. (International Review of Child Neurology Ser.). 512p. 1994. 99.00 (*0-7817-0064-7*) Raven.

Brain Tumors in the Chemical Industry, Vol. 381. Ed. by Irving Selkoff & E. Cuyler Hammond. 363p. 1982. 75.00 (*0-89766-151-6*) NY Acad Sci.

Brain Twister. Randall Garrett & Laurence M. Janifer. 144p. 1992. pap. 3.95 (*0-88184-845-X*) Carroll & Graf.

***Brain Twisters.** 90p. (YA). 1995. pap. 9.95 (*1-882664-13-2*) Prufrock Pr.

Brain Twisters. Hayes. (Mind Benders Ser.). (Illus.). 32p. (J). (gr. 2-6). 1988. pap. 2.95 (*0-88625-149-4*) Durkin Hayes Pub.

Brain Twisters. Norman Sullivan. (Illus.). 128p. (YA). (gr. 10-12). 1992. pap. 4.95 (*0-7063-7086-4*, Pub. by Ward Lock UK) Sterling.

Brain User's Guide. Tony Buzan. pap. 8.95 (*0-525-48363-2*, Dutton) NAL-Dutton.

Brain Wave. Poul Anderson. 1993. reprint ed. lib. bdg. 18.95 (*0-89968-327-4*, Lghtyr Pr) Buccaneer Bks.

Brain Without Oxygen: Causes of Failure & Mechanisms for Survival. Peter L. Lutz & G oran E. Nilsson. LC 94-16812. (Neuroscience Intelligence Unit Ser.). 1994. 89.95 (*1-57059-187-3*) R G Landes.

Brain Without Oxygen-Causes of Failure: Mechanisms for Survival. Peter L. Lutz & Goran Nilsson. (Medical Intelligence Unit Ser.). 118p. 1994. 89.95 (*1-879702-96-7*, LN0296) R G Landes.

Brain Work & Mental Activity. Lassen. (ABS Ser.: No. 31). 550p. 1991. 89.50 (*87-16-10698-9*) Mosby Yr Bk.

Brain World. Mack Reynolds. 1978. pap. 1.75 (*0-8439-0595-6*) Dorchester Pub Co.

Brain 85, Vol. 5: Proceedings of the Twelfth International Symposium on Cerebral Blood Flow & Metabolism. Ed. by David H. Ingvar et al. 704p. 1985. pap. text ed. 110.50 (*0-88167-169-X*) Raven.

Brain 87, Vol. 7: Proceedings of the Thirteenth International Symposium on Cerebral Blood Flow & Metabolism. Ed. by Antoine Hakim & Albert Gjedde. 716p. 1987. pap. text ed. 87.50 (*0-88167-359-5*) Raven.

Brain, 91: Proceedings of the Fifteenth International Symposium on Cerebral Blood Flow & Metabolism, Vol. 11, Suppl. 2. Myron D. Ginsberg & Peritz Scheinberg. 942p. 1991. 108.50 (*0-88167-829-5*) Raven.

Brainbenders. J. Tyler. (Illus.). 96p. (J). 1993. pap. 10.95 (*0-7460-1629-8*, Usborne) EDC.

Brainchild. David Brown. LC 88-81440. 130p. (Orig.). 1988. pap. 9.95 (*0-941404-92-7*) New Falcon Pubns.

Brainchild. John Saul. 352p. (Orig.). 1985. mass mkt. 5.99 (*0-553-26552-0*) Bantam.

Braindance: New Discoveries about Human Brain Evolution. Dean Falk. LC 91-14628. 1994. pap. 12.95 (*0-8050-3186-3*) H Holt & Co.

Brained-Whitefish Area Fishing Guide: Where the Experts Fish & How. Sybil Smith. LC 85-80435. (Illus.). 192p. 1988. pap. 9.95 (*0-9615221-2-7*) Fins Pubns.

Brainedness, Handedness, & Mental Abilities: The Foundations of Neuropsychology, 40 titles in 44 vols. write for info. (*0-404-60850-7*) AMS Pr.

Brainercise Mental Exercise Program: Arithmetic, Vol. 1, Bk. 7. large type ed. Steven Callaghan. 25p. (J). (gr. k up). 1991. spiral bd. 5.00 (*0-925395-22-6*) SGC Biomedical.

Brainercise Mental Exercise Program: Arithmetic, Vol. 1, Bk. 8. large type ed. Steven Callaghan. 25p. (J). (gr. k up). 1991. spiral bd. 5.00 (*0-925395-23-4*) SGC Biomedical.

Brainercise Mental Exercise Program: Arithmetic, Vol. 1, Bk. 9. large type ed. Steven Callaghan. 25p. (J). (gr. k up). 1991. spiral bd. 5.00 (*0-925395-29-3*) SGC Biomedical.

Brainercise Mental Exercise Program: Arithmetic, Vol. 1, Bk. 10. large type ed. Steven Callaghan. 25p. (J). (gr. k up). 1991. spiral bd. 5.00 (*0-925395-30-7*) SGC Biomedical.

Brainercise Mental Exercise Program: Arithmetic, Vol. 2, Bk. 1. large type ed. Steven Callaghan. 25p. (J). (gr. k up). 1991. spiral bd. 5.00 (*0-925395-27-7*) SGC Biomedical.

Brainercise Mental Exercise Program: Arithmetic, Vol. 2, Bk. 2. large type ed. Steven Callaghan. 25p. (J). (gr. k up). 1991. spiral bd. 5.00 (*0-925395-31-5*) SGC Biomedical.

Brainercise Mental Exercise Program: Arithmetic, Vol. 2, Bk. 3. large type ed. Steven Callaghan. 25p. (J). (gr. k up). 1991. spiral bd. 5.00 (*0-925395-32-3*) SGC Biomedical.

Brainercise Mental Exercise Program: Arithmetic, Vol. 3, Bk. 1. large type ed. Steven Callaghan. 25p. (J). (gr. k up). 1991. spiral bd. 5.00 (*0-925395-28-5*) SGC Biomedical.

Brainercise Mental Exercise Program, Vol. 1, Bk. 3: Arithmetic. large type ed. Steven Callaghan. 25p. (YA). (gr. k-12). 1991. spiral bd. 5.00 (*0-925395-16-1*) SGC Biomedical.

Brainercise Mental Exercise Program, Vol. 1, Bk. 4: Arithmetic. large type ed. Steven Callaghan. 25p. (YA). (gr. k-12). 1991. spiral bd. 5.00 (*0-925395-17-X*) SGC Biomedical.

Brainerd: Ancestry of Thomas Chalmers Brainerd. Comp. by D. L. Jacobus. 351p. 1991. reprint ed. lib. bdg. 64.00 (*0-8328-2103-9*); reprint ed. pap. 54.00 (*0-8328-2104-7*) Higginson Bk Co.

Brainerd Area Fishing Map Guide. James F. Billig & Thomas C. Billig. 1994. pap. 14.95 (*1-885010-04-4*) Sptsmans Connect.

Brainfever. Ron Dee. 283p. (Orig.). 1989. 3.95 (*1-55817-262-9*, Pinnacle NY) Windsor NY.

Brainfire. Campbell Armstrong. 1990. mass mkt. 4.95 (*0-06-100086-8*, Harp PBks) HarpC.

***Brainlift.** Tricia Warden. (Illus.). 160p. (Orig.). 1994. pap. 10.00 (*1-880985-18-7*) Two Thirteen Sixty-one.

***Brainlord Totally Unauthorized Strategy Guide.** 1994. pap. 9.99 (*1-56686-209-4*) Brady Compu Bks.

***Brainmakers.** David Freedman. 1995. pap. 12.00 (*0-671-51055-X*, Touchstone Bks) S&S Trade.

Brainmakers: How Scientists Are Moving Beyond Computers to Create a Rival to the Human Brain. David Freedman. 1994. 22.00 (*0-671-76079-3*) S&S Trade.

Brainpower for the Cold War: The Sputnik Crisis & National Defense Education Act of 1958. Ed. by Barbara B. Clowse. LC 81-1477. (Contributions to the Study of Education Ser.: No. 3). x, 225p. 1981. text ed. 55.00 (*0-313-22813-2*, CCW) Greenwood.

Brainpuzzlers: Amazing Math Games & Puzzles. Dan Nevins. (J). (gr. 4-7). 1994. pap. 2.95 (*0-8167-3193-4*) Troll Assocs.

Brainrose. Nancy Kress. 320p. 1991. pap. 3.95 (*0-380-71015-3*) Avon.

Brains & Numbers: Elitism, Comtism, & Democracy in Mid-Victorian England. Christopher Kent. LC 77-21722. 226p. reprint ed. pap. 64.50 (*0-7837-0530-1*, 2040858) Bks Demand.

***Brains & Parker McGoohan: Ben Franklin Beware.** Megan Stine & H. William Stine. 78p. (J). (gr. 4-6). 1993. pap. 3.95 (*1-56801-063-X*) Sundance Pub.

An Asterisk (*) at the beginning of an entry indicates that the title is appearing in BIP for the first time.

B

An Asterisk (*) at the beginning of an entry indicates that the title is appearing in BIP for the first time.

Brande Roms: Ein Apokalyptisches Motiv in der Antiken Historiographie. Gerhard J. Baudy. (Spudasmata Ser.: Bd. 50). 75p. (GER.). 1991. write for info. (*3-487-09480-0*, Pub. by Georg Olms GW) Lubrecht & Cramer.

Branded. Rosalie Cates. LC 79-19211. 1981. 19.95 (*0-87949-147-7*) Ashley Bks.

Branded Eye: Bunuels un Chien Andalou. rev. ed. Jenaro Talens. Tr. by Giulia Colaizzi. LC 93-3662. 218p. 1993. text ed. 39.95 (*0-8166-2046-6*); pap. 14.95 (*0-8166-2047-4*) U of Minn Pr.

Branded Hand: Trial & Imprisonment of Jonathan Walker. Jonathan Walker. LC 75-82228. (Anti-Slavery Crusade in America Ser.). 1975. reprint ed. 14.95 (*0-405-00667-5*) Ayer.

***Branded Hearts.** Shannon Drake. 432p. (Orig.). 1995. mass mkt. 5.99 (*0-380-77170-5*) Avon.

***Branded to Thrill: The Delirious Cinema of Suzuki Seijun.** Ed. by Simon Field & Tony Rayns. 48p. 1995. pap. 9.95 (*0-905263-44-8*) Ind U Pr.

Branded West: An Anthology. Western Writers of America Staff. Ed. by Don Ward. LC 73-116967. (Short Story Index Reprint Ser.). 1977. 20.95 (*0-8369-3471-7*) Ayer.

Brandeis: A Host at Last. rev. ed. Abram L. Sachar. LC 91-50821. (Illus.). 360p. (C). 1995. text ed. 39.95 (*0-87451-581-5*) U Pr of New Eng.

***Brandeis: A Host at Last.** rev. ed. Abram L. Sachar. LC 91-50821. (Illus.). (C). 1995. pap. 19.95 (*0-87451-585-8*) U Pr of New Eng.

Brandeis: An Intimate Biography. Lewis J. Paper. reprint ed. pap. 9.95 (*0-8065-0966-X*, Citadel Pr) Carol Pub Group.

Brandeis: Beyond Progressivism. Phillipa Strum. LC 93-18649. (American Political Thought Ser.). 240p. 1995. 25.00x (*0-7006-0603-3*) U Pr of KS.

***Brandeis: Beyond Progressivism.** Phillipa Strum. LC 93-18649. (American Political Thought Ser.). 240p. 1995. pap. 17.95x (*0-7006-0687-4*) U Pr of KS.

Brandeis: The Personal History of an American Ideal. Alfred Lief. LC 72-169768. (Select Bibliographies Reprint Ser.). 1977. reprint ed. 35.95 (*0-8369-5988-4*) Ayer.

Brandeis & America. Ed. by Nelson L. Dawson. LC 89-30929. 176p. 1989. text ed. 20.00 (*0-8131-1690-2*) U Pr of Ky.

Brandeis of Boston. Allon Gal. LC 79-15501. 282p. 1980. 29.00 (*0-674-08043-2*) HUP.

Brandeis on Democracy. Ed. by Philippa Strum. (Illus.). 240p. 1995. 29.95 (*0-7006-0678-5*); pap. 17.95 (*0-7006-0679-3*) U Pr of KS.

Brandeis on Zionism. Louis D. Brandeis. LC 75-6425. (Rise of Jewish Nationalism & the Middle East Ser.). 156p. 1975. reprint ed. 18.00 (*0-88355-312-0*) Hyperion Conn.

Brandeis University Summer Institute in Theoretical Physics: 1963 Lectures, 2 vols. Ed. by K. W. Ford. Incl. Vol. 63. Strong & Electromagnetic Interactions. 352p. 1964. text ed. 275.00 (*0-677-10630-0*); Vol. 63. Astrophysics & Weak Interactions. 478p. 1964. text ed. 342.00 (*0-677-10640-8*); 1964. write for info. (*0-318-52696-4*) Gordon & Breach.

Brandeis University Summer Institute in Theoretical Physics: 1965 Lectures, 2 vols. Incl. Vol. 65. Axiomatic Field Theory. Ed. by M. Chretien & S. Deser. 526p. 1966. text ed. 444.00 (*0-677-10705-6*); Vol. 2. Particle Symmetries. Ed. by M. Chretien & S. Deser. 704p. 1966. pap. text ed. 484.00 (*0-677-10755-2*); Vol. 68. Ed. by M. Chretien et al. 310p. 1969. text ed. 207.00 (*0-677-13480-0*); Vol. 68. 396p. 1971. text ed. 342.00 (*0-677-13490-8*); 1966. write for info. (*0-318-52694-8*) Gordon & Breach.

Brandeis University Summer Institute in Theoretical Physics: 1965 Lectures, 2 vols. Incl. Vol. 65. Axiomatic Field Theory. Ed. by M. Chretien & S. Deser. 526p. 1966. text ed. 444.00 (*0-677-10705-6*); Vol. 2. Particle Symmetries. Ed. by M. Chretien & S. Deser. 704p. 1966. pap. text ed. 484.00 (*0-677-10755-2*); Vol. 68. Ed. by M. Chretien et al. 310p. 1969. text ed. 207.00 (*0-677-13480-0*); Vol. 68. 396p. 1971. text ed. 342.00 (*0-677-13490-8*); 1969. write for info. (*0-318-52695-6*) Gordon & Breach.

Brandeis University Summer Institute in Theoretical Physics: 1966 Lectures: Statistical Physics, Phase Transitions & Superfluidity, 2 vols. Ed. by M. Chretien. Incl. Vol. 66. 336p. 1968. text ed. 274.00 (*0-677-10820-6*); Vol. 66. 490p. 1968. text ed. 275.00 (*0-677-10830-3*); 1968. write for info. (*0-318-52693-X*) Gordon & Breach.

Brandeis University Summer Institute in Theoretical Physics: 1967 Lectures: Elementary Particle Physics & Scattering Theory, 2 vols, Vol. 67. Ed. by M. Chretien & S. S. Schweber. 474p. 1970. Vol. 1, 474p. text ed. 272.00 (*0-677-12840-1*); Vol. 2, 446p. text ed. 323.00 (*0-677-12850-9*) Gordon & Breach.

Brandeis University Summer Institute in Theoretical Physics: 1969 Lectures: Atomic Physics & Astrophysics, 2 vols, Vol. 69. Ed. by M. Chretien & E. Lipworth. 228p. 1971. Vol. 1, 228p. 1971. text ed. 216.00 (*0-677-14900-X*) Gordon & Breach.

Brandeis University Summer Institute in Theoretical Physics: 1969 Lectures: Atomic Physics & Astrophysics, 2 vols, Vol. 69. Ed. by M. Chretien & E. Lipworth. 350p. 1973. Vol. 2, 350p. 1973. text ed. 285.00 (*0-677-14910-7*) Gordon & Breach.

Brandeis University Summer Institute in Theoretical Physics 1967 Lectures: Elementary Particle Physics & Scattering Theory, Vol. 67. Ed. by M. Chretien & S. S. Schweber. xii, 462p. 1970. pap. text ed. 87.00 (*0-677-12845-2*) Gordon & Breach.

Branden Papers. Quentin Bell. 224p. 1986. pap. 5.95 (*0-15-614045-4*, Harvest Bks) HarBrace.

Brander Matthews, Theodore Roosevelt, & the Politics of American Literature, 1880-1920. Lawrence J. Oliver. LC 91-24627. 272p. (C). 1992. text ed. 31.00x (*0-87049-738-3*) U of Tenn Pr.

***Brandi.** H. D. Myers. LC 93-86270. 1994. pap. 12.95 (*1-885487-03-7*) Brownell & Carroll.

***Brandiad.** Phyllis Omni. 1994. 18.95 (*0-533-11040-8*) Vantage.

Branding: A Key Marketing Tool. Ed. by J. M. Murphy. 272p. 1987. text ed. 24.95 (*0-07-044055-7*) McGraw.

***Brandis & Broun on North Carolina Evidence, 2 vols., Set.** 4th ed. Kenneth S. Broun. 1993. 160.00 (*1-55834-135-8*) Michie Butterworth.

Brandis on North Carolina Evidence, with 1991 Cumulative Supplements, 2 vols. 3rd ed. Henry Brandis, Jr. 1988. 150.00 (*0-87473-358-8*) Michie Butterworth.

Brandmaps: The Competitive Marketing Strategy Game. 2nd ed. Randall G. Chapman. 144p. 1991. pap. text ed. 33.33 (*0-13-093691-X*) P-H.

Brandmaps: The Competitive Marketing Strategy Game. 3rd ed. Randall G. Chapman. LC 93-5869. 1993. pap. text ed. write for info. (*0-13-177502-2*) P-H.

Brandnames: Who Owns What. rev. ed. Diane W. Frankenstein. LC 80-23592. 463p. reprint ed. pap. 132.00 (*0-8357-4243-1*, 2037031) Bks Demand.

***Brando.** Robert Tanitch. (Illus.). 192p. 1995. pap. 16.95 (*0-289-80138-9*, Pub. by Studio Vista Bks UK) Sterling.

Brando: A Life in Our Times. Richard Schickel. 1993. mass mkt. 5.99 (*0-312-92863-7*) St Martin.

Brando: Songs My Mother Taught Me. large type ed. Marlon Brando. 1994. pap. 24.00 (*0-679-75692-2*) Random.

Brando: The Biography. Peter Manso. (Illus.). 1172p. 1994. 29.95 (*0-7868-6063-4*) Hyperion.

***Brando: The Biography.** Peter Manso. (Illus.). 1172p. 1995. pap. 15.95 (*0-7868-8128-3*) Hyperion.

Brandon Amino Acid & Peptide Reference Guide. Brandon Associates Editorial Staff. LC 92-75779. 336p. 1993. 280.00 (*0-927230-11-9*) Brandon Associates.

Brandon Buyer's Guide to Fine Chemicals & Intermediates from India. Brandon Associates Editorial Staff. 75p. (Orig.). 1992. pap. 170.00 (*0-927230-07-0*) Brandon Associates.

Brandon Guide to Custom Chemical Synthesis Services - North America. 2nd ed. Brandon Associates Editorial Staff. 295p. 1994. 225.00 (*0-927230-14-3*) Brandon Associates.

Brandon Guide to Custom Processing & Packaging Services. Brandon Associates Editorial Staff. LC 90-80452. 240p. (Orig.). 1990. pap. 150.00 (*0-927230-03-8*) Brandon Associates.

Brandon Guide to Pharmaceuticals & Pharmaceutical Manufacturers in India. Brandon Associates Editorial Staff. 60p. (Orig.). 1992. pap. 170.00 (*0-927230-09-7*) Brandon Associates.

Brandon Maintenance Log. Larry L. Brandon & Kathleen M. Brandon. 356p. (Orig.). 1982. ring bd. 49.95 (*0-934114-38-2*, BK-284) Marine Educ.

Brandon Papers. Quentin Bell. LC 85-8573. 224p. 1985. 15.95 (*0-685-10655-1*) HarBrace.

Brandon Papers. Quentin Bell. 1986. pap. 5.95 (*0-317-53636-2*) HarBrace.

Brandon Worldwide Monomer Reference Guide & Sourcebook. 3rd ed. Brandon Associates Editorial Staff. 330p. 1994. 250.00 (*0-927230-13-5*) Brandon Associates.

Brandons. Angela Thirkell. (Barsetshire Novels Ser.). 358p. 1987. reprint ed. pap. 4.95 (*0-88184-361-X*) Carroll & Graf.

Brandon's First Baseball Game. Illus. by Famous Robinson. LC 90-63290. (I Promise to Do My Best Ser.). 37p. (Orig.). (J). (ps-6). 1990. pap. text ed. 5.00 (*0-9627951-0-0*) JRBB Pubs.

Brandon's Guide to Theater in Asia. James R. Brandon. LC 75-37506. 178p. 1976. pap. 3.95 (*0-8248-0369-8*) UH Pr.

Brands: A Marketing Game. Randall G. Chapman. 96p. 1992. pap. text ed. 17.50 (*0-13-087404-3*) P-H.

***Brands: A Marketing Game.** 2nd ed. Randall G. Chapman. LC 95-5515. 1995. pap. text ed. write for info. (*0-13-371667-8*) P-H.

Brands & Their Companies, 2 vols. 13th ed. Susan L. Stetler. 1994. write for info. (*0-318-68504-3*) Gale.

***Brands & Their Companies, 2 vols.** 13th ed. Susan L. Stetler. 1994. write for info. (*0-318-68503-5*) Gale.

Brands & Their Companies, 2 Vols., Set. 13th ed. Susan L. Stetler. (Trade Names Dictionary Ser.). 1994. 440.00 (*0-8103-5574-4*, 009699) Gale.

Brands & Their Companies, Vol. 1, A-K. 12th ed. Susan L. Stetler. 1993. write for info. (*0-8103-5572-8*) Gale.

Brands & Their Companies, Vol. 2, L-Z. 12th ed. Susan L. Stetler. (Trade Names Dictionary Ser.). 1993. write for info. (*0-8103-5573-6*, 101363) Gale.

Brands & Their Companies Supplement. 13th ed. Susan L. Stetler. (New Trade Names Ser.). 1995. 295.00 (*0-8103-5578-7*, 009710) Gale.

Brandy. Mark Dunster. (Rin Ser.: Part 13). 1977. pap. 4.00 (*0-89642-000-0*) Linden Pubs.

***Brandy & Bullets.** Jessica Fletcher & Donald Bain. (Murder, She Wrote Ser.). 304p. (Orig.). 1995. mass mkt. 4.99 (*0-451-18491-2*, Sig) NAL-Dutton.

Brandy in the Snow. Frederic Will. 1972. pap. 2.50 (*0-912284-30-7*) New Rivers Pr.

Brandywine. 2nd ed. Henry S. Canby. (Illus.). 285p. 1977. 9.95 (*0-916838-06-4*) Schiffer.

***Brandywine: A Legacy of Tradition in Du Pont-Wyeth Country.** Photos by Anthony Edgeworth. LC 94-43914. (Illus.). 224p. 1995. 45.00 (*1-56566-080-3*) Thomasson-Grant.

Brandywine Valley: An Introduction to Its Cultural Treasures. James S. Wamsley. (Illus.). 224p. 1992. 60.00 (*0-8109-3628-3*) Abrams.

Branemark Implant System: Clinical & Laboratory Procedures. S. Lewis & J. Beumer. (Illus.). 250p. 1990. 95.00 (*0-912791-62-4*) Ishiyaku Euro.

Branemark Osseointegrated Implant. Ed. by Albrektsson & Zarb. (Illus.). 262p. 1989. text ed. 128.00 (*0-86715-208-7*) Quint Pub Co.

Branemark System of Oral Reconstruction: A Clinical Atlas. Richard Rasmussen. Ed. by Gregory Hacke. (Illus.). 305p. 1992. text ed. 75.00 (*1-56386-003-1*) Ishiyaku Euro.

Branford, Connecticut Various Cemetery Records. Glenn Griswold. 34p. 1994. pap. 7.00 (*1-878545-05-1*) ACETO Bookmen.

Branford Marsalis: Jazz Musician. Bob Bernotas. LC 93-47358. (People to Know Ser.). (Illus.). 112p. (J). (gr. 6 up). 1994. lib. bdg. 17.95 (*0-89490-495-7*) Enslow Pubs.

Brangwen - The Poet & the Dancer: A Story Based on Letters from Poet Laureate John Masefield. Comp. by John Gregory. (Illus.). 207p. 1989. 26.95 (*0-87975-571-7*) Prometheus Bks.

***Branigan's Break.** Leslie D. Guccione. (Desire Ser.). 1995. pap. 2.99 (*0-373-05902-7*, 1-05902-1) Silhouette.

Branioci Kosova. Milos Acin-Kosta. 165p. (SER.). 1973. pap. 10.00 (*0-931931-08-8*) Ravnogorski.

Branioci Kosova. 2nd enl. ed. Milos Acin-Kosta. (Illus.). 515p. (SER.). 1989. pap. 25.00 (*0-931931-30-4*) Ravnogorski.

Brann & the "Iconoclast" Charles Carver. (Illus.). 214p. 1987. reprint ed. pap. 9.95 (*0-292-70765-7*) U of Tex Pr.

Brann, the Iconoclast: Collected Writings, 2 vols, Set. William C. Brann. 1976. 500.00 (*0-87968-782-7*) Gordon Pr.

Brannan Plan: Farm Politics & Policy. Reo M. Christenson. LC 74-10728. 207p. 1974. reprint ed. text ed. 55.00 (*0-8371-7650-6*, CHBP, Greenwood Pr) Greenwood.

Brannigan. Ed Newsom. 208p. (Orig.). 1981. pap. 1.95 (*0-89083-713-9*) Zebra.

Brannigan, No. 4: The Peacekeeper. Ed Newsom. 1983. pap. 2.25 (*0-8217-1163-6*) Zebra.

Brannon's Southampton. John E. Mann & Derek Whatley. (C). 1989. 39.00 (*1-85455-042-X*, Pub. by Ensign Pubns & Print UK) St Mut.

Brann's "Scrap Book" William C. Brann. LC 71-104422. (C). 1986. reprint ed. lib. bdg. 12.50 (*0-8398-0171-8*); reprint ed. pap. text ed. 4.95 (*0-8290-1895-6*) Irvington.

Branson: Country Themes, Neon Dreams. Leland Payton & Crystal Payton. (Illus.). 144p. 1994. text ed. 29.95 (*0-9636666-3-0*) Anderson MO.

Branson: On Stage in the Ozarks. Ron Sylvester & Jeff Hampton. Ed. by June Ford. (Illus.). 155p. 1994. 34.95 (*1-56530-079-3*) Summit TX.

***Branson & Beyond.** Buckstaff. 1995. mass mkt. 4.99 (*0-312-95482-4*) St Martin.

Branson Backroads - Ozark Tales. Roy English. 1994. 10.95 (*0-8062-4846-7*) Carlton.

***Branson Backstage.** 128p. 1995. pap. write for info. (*0-9647000-1-8*) Elf Publng NJ.

Branson Cookin' Country. Susan St. Marie-Martin. (Illus.). 96p. (Orig.). 1993. pap. 9.95 (*1-878686-13-5*) Two Lane Pr.

Branson Getaway Guide. Frank Shipe et al. 144p. 1993. pap. 12.95 (*1-883723-00-0*) Action MO.

Branson Getaway Guide: Summer. Frank Shipe et al. (Illus.). 56p. (Orig.). 1993. pap. 3.95 (*1-883723-01-9*) Action MO.

Branson, Missouri, Scrapbook: A Guide to the New Capital of Country Music. Scott Faragher. LC 93-22841. (Illus.). 192p. 1993. pap. 14.95 (*0-8065-1440-X*, Citadel Pr) Carol Pub Group.

Branson Souvenir Book. Date not set. pap. text ed. write for info. (*1-56944-020-4*); pap. text ed. write for info. (*1-56944-030-1*) Terrell Missouri.

Brant Broughton in the Nineteenth Century. Bill Couth. (C). 1984. text ed. 40.00 (*0-685-22176-8*, Pub. by Univ Nottingham UK) St Mut.

Branta & the Golden Stone. Walter Wangerin. LC 92-34891. (Illus.). (J). 1993. pap. 16.00 (*0-671-79693-3*, S&S Bks Young Read) S&S Childrens.

Brantome et le Sens de l'Histoire. Grimaldi. 12.50 (*0-685-34182-8*) Fr & Eur.

Brantub the Dancing Bear. Margaret Norton. (Illus.). 32p. (J). (ps-2). 1992. 15.95 (*0-370-31409-3*, Pub. by Bodley Head UK) Trafalgar.

Brantwood Diary of John Ruskin: Together with Selected Related Letters & Sketches of Persons Mentioned. John Ruskin. Ed. by Helen G. Viljoen. LC 72-99844. 650p. reprint ed. pap. 180.00 (*0-8357-7382-5*, 2022049) Bks Demand.

Braque. Raymond Cogniat. (CAL Art Ser.). 1984. 14.95 (*0-517-03300-3*, Crown) Crown Pub Group.

Braquemond: The Graphic Work, 1849-1859. Jean-Paul Bouillon. 232p. (FRE.). 1987. 125.00 (*1-55660-151-4*) A Wofsy Fine Arts.

Braque's Graphic Work. Dora Vallier. (Illus.). 320p. 1988. 95.00 (*0-915346-88-5*) A Wofsy Fine Arts.

***Bras.** Hawthorne. 1995. 7.95 (*0-285-63086-5*, Pub. by Souvenir UK) Atrium Pubs.

Brasada - Blood Justice, 2 vols. in 1. Gordon D. Shirreffs. 336p. 1993. pap. 4.50 (*0-8439-3410-7*) Dorchester Pub Co.

Brasil! Lingua e Cultura. Thomas Lathrop & Eduardo Dias. (Illus.). 392p. (C). 1992. 14.95 (*0-942566-15-7*); text ed. 41.95 (*0-942566-08-4*) LinguaText.

Brasilianische Flechten: Die Gattung Pyxine, Vol. 1. Klaus Kalb. (Bibliotheca Lichenologica Ser.: Vol. 24). (Illus.). 106p. (GER.). 1987. pap. text ed. 36.75 (*3-443-58003-3*) Lubrecht & Cramer.

Brass. Dee Lillegard. LC 87-32990. (Introduction to Musical Instruments Ser.). (Illus.). 32p. (J). (ps-3). 1988. lib. bdg. 11.85 (*0-516-02218-0*) Childrens.

Brass. Elizabeth Sharma. LC 93-20398. (Live Music! Ser.). (Illus.). 32p. (J). (gr. 4-6). 1993. 14.95 (*1-56847-114-9*) Thomson Lrning.

Brass. Alyn Shipton. LC 93-2895. (Exploring Music Ser.). (Illus.). 32p. (J). (gr. 5-8). 1993. lib. bdg. 19.97 (*0-8114-2317-4*) Raintree Steck-V.

Brass Anthology. 1991. 53.00 (*0-686-15890-3*) Instrumental.

Brass Ass. Tey Emel. LC 85-18708. 1987. pap. 13.95 (*0-87949-260-0*) Ashley Bks.

***Brass Bands & New Orleans Jazz.** William J. Schafer. LC 76-58469. 144p. 1977. pap. 41.10 (*0-7837-8463-5*, 2049268) Bks Demand.

Brass Bands & Snake Oil Stands: Colorful Glimpses of America's Early Entertainment. Dennis Goodwin. LC 93-90384. 90p. (Orig.). 1993. pap. 7.95 (*0-936885-02-5*) Activity Factory.

Brass Bed & Other Stories. Pearl Cleage. 1991. pap. 8.00 (*0-88378-127-1*) Third World.

Brass Bibliography: Sources on the History, Literature, Pedagogy, Performance, & Acoustics of Brass Instruments. Mark J. Fasman. LC 89-45198. 464p. 1990. 39.95 (*0-253-32130-1*) Ind U Pr.

Brass Book: American, English & European, 15th Century Thru 1850. Nancy Peter & Herbert F. Schiffer. LC 78-63428. 1978. 60.00 (*0-916838-17-X*) Schiffer.

Brass Boy. large type ed. Jim Miller. (Linford Western Library). 1990. pap. 12.95 (*0-7089-6803-1*, Linford) Ulverscroft.

Brass Brigade. Will Cook. 1994. lib. bdg. 15.95 (*0-7451-4607-4*, Gunsmoke) Chivers N Amer.

***Brass Bullet.** large type ed. John Hunt. (Western Library). 288p. 1995. pap. 14.95 (*0-7089-7690-5*, Linford) Ulverscroft.

Brass Button Broadcasters: A Lighthearted Look at Fifty Years of Military Broadcasting. Trent Christman. 1992. 39.95 (*1-56311-086-5*) Turner Pub KY.

Brass Chalice: Short Stories & Information on Drug Abuse Prevention Among Youth. Richard E. Hardy & John G. Cull. (Illus.). 100p. (Orig.). (J). (gr. 5-10). 1994. pap. 6.95 (*1-884507-01-8*) Boyer-Caswell. A silver chalice, bright & shining, may not be what it seems to be. Young people find excitement turns & silver may be brass. The sleep-over seemed like such fun & a great way to get to know new friends, but Karen soon learned these new friends had different ideas about how to enjoy a sleep-over. Karen will never forget that Friday night & how she nearly lost her life. Adolescents & teens can so easily become involved with drugs - many times inadvertently. Drs. Hardy & Cull have written a book especially for adolescents - grades 5-10 that is very interesting & informative. An "all you wanted to know about drugs" glossary is a big help for parents as well as kids. Truthful, objective & non-sensational real-life episodes about boys & girls. Drs. Hardy & Cull have received national & international awards for their respective work in addiction problems & drug & alcohol abuse. THE BRASS CHALICE serves as a teaching aid to parents, educators & children. The stories are adaptable as plays, "raps" & other presentations for drug prevention programs. Comments from youthful readers are quite encouraging! To order contact: Boyer-Caswell Publishing CO., 823 E. Main St., 14th Fl., Richmond, VA 23219. 804-648-6624. FAX 804-648- 9221.** ***Publisher Provided Annotation.

Brass Check. Upton Sinclair. LC 74-125715. (American Journalists Ser.). 1971. reprint ed. 38.95 (*0-405-01696-4*) Ayer.

Brass Cross. Bruce Blackie. LC 89-11201. 280p. (Orig.). 1989. pap. 9.95 (*1-877674-00-1*) Hampshire Bks.

Brass Eagle. Margaret Duffy. 256p. 1991. pap. 3.95 (*0-449-21887-2*, Crest) Fawcett.

Brass Eagle. large type ed. Margaret Duffy. 1991. 21.95 (*0-7089-2347-X*) Ulverscroft.

Brass Ensemble. Paul Anderson & Lisa Bontrager. 1987. 14.00 (*0-318-37568-0*) Instrumental.

Brass Ensemble Method for Music Educators. Jay D. Zorn. 174p. (C). 1977. Spiralbound. pap. 24.95 (*0-534-00503-9*) Intl Thomson.

***Brass Ensemble Methods for Music Educators.** 2nd ed. Jay Zorn. LC 94-35619. (Illus.). 179p. 1995. pap. 26.95 (*0-534-22969-7*) Intl Thomson.

Brass Entrepreneur. Jim Schell. 224p. 1994. pap. 12.95 (*0-8050-3089-1*) H Holt & Co.

Brass Go-Between. Ross Thomas. 240p. 1993. mass mkt. 4.99 (*0-446-40175-7*, Mysterious Paperbk) Warner Bks.

B

An Asterisk (*) at the beginning of an entry indicates that the title is appearing in BIP for the first time.

Brave the Wild Sea. large type ed. Joan Garrison. (Romance Ser.). 208p. 1993. 21.95 (*0-7089-2955-9*) Ulverscroft.

Brave the Wild Trail. Milly Howard. (Light Line Ser.). (Illus.). 129p. (Orig.). (J). (gr. 4-6). 1987. pap. 5.95 (*0-89084-384-8*) Bob Jones Univ Pr.

Brave the Wild Wind. Johanna Lindsey. 352p. 1984. mass mkt. 5.99 (*0-380-89284-7*) Avon.

***Brave Winds: Native American Experiences.** Caryn Curtis. (Petite Major Ser.). 134p. 1995. pap. 4.95 (*1-884754-17-1*) Potpourri Pubns.

***Braveheart.** Wallace. (Illus.). (J). 1995. mass mkt. 5.99 (*0-671-52281-7*) PB.

Braver Men Walk Away. large type ed. Peter Gurney. 320p. 1994. 25.95 (*0-7089-8762-1*) Ulverscroft.

Braverman's Introduction to the Biochemistry of Foods. 2nd rev. ed. Z. Berk. 316p. 1976. 68.75 (*0-444-41450-9*) Elsevier.

***Braves: An Illustrated History of America's Team.** Bob Klapisch. 1995. 29.95 (*1-57036-170-3*) Turner Pub GA.

***Braves: An Illustrated History of America's Team.** Bob Klapisch & Pete Van Woeren. 1995. pap. 27.95 (*1-57036-207-6*) Turner Publishing Co.

***Braves Encyclopedias.** Gary Caruso. (Baseball Encyclopedias Ser.). (Illus.). (C). 1995. 59.95 (*1-56639-384-1*) Temple U Pr.

Braves First Fifteen Years in Atlanta. J. Hudson Couch. LC 84-81647. 436p. (Orig.). 1984. pap. 9.95 (*0-931083-00-1*) Other Alligator.

Braves Fun Book I. Sherry Cawley. 80p. (Orig.). (J). 1986. pap. 3.95 (*0-937511-00-5*) Fun Bk Enter.

Braves Gens Ne Courent Pas les Rues. Flannery O'Connor. (FRE.). 1981. pap. 10.95 (*0-7859-4144-4*) Fr & Eur.

Bravest Battle: The Twenty-Eight Days of the Warsaw Ghetto Uprising. Dan Kurzman. (Illus.). 400p. 1993. reprint ed. pap. 14.95 (*0-306-80533-2*) Da Capo.

Bravest Dog Ever. Natalie Staniford. Date not set. pap. 2.99 (*0-517-11112-8*) Random Hse Value.

Bravest Dog Ever: The True Story of Balto. Natalie Standiford. Tr. by Donald Cook. LC 89-3465. (Step into Reading Bks.). (Illus.). 47p. (Orig.). (J). (gr. 1-3). 1989. pap. 3.50 (*0-394-89695-5*) Random Bks Yng Read.

Bravest Flute. Grifalaconi Ann. (Illus.). 96p. 1994. 15.95 (*0-316-32878-2*) Little.

Bravest of Bears. John McClelland. (Illus.). 32p. (J). (ps-1). 1994. bds. 12.95 (*0-86264-389-9*, Pub. by Andersen Pr UK) Trafalgar.

***Bravest Thing.** Donna J. Napoli. LC 94-48347. (J). 1995. 14.99 (*0-525-45397-0*, DCB) Dutton Child Bks.

Bravi: Lyric Opera of Chicago. Ed. by Andrew Porter & John Von Rhein. LC 94-6516. 1994. 50.00 (*1-55859-771-9*) Abbeville Pr.

***Braving the Elements.** Harry B. Gray et al. LC 94-45685. (Illus.). 413p. (C). 1995. pap. text ed. 29.50 (*0-935702-34-2*) Univ Sci Bks.

Braving the New World, 1619-1784: From the Arrival of the Enslaved Africans to the End of the American Revolution. Don Nardo. LC 94-2963. (Milestones in Black American History Ser.). (YA). (gr. 7 up). 1994. write for info. (*0-7910-2259-5*); pap. write for info. (*0-7910-2685-X*) Chelsea Hse.

***Braving Those Angry Skies: An American Pilot in the Battle of Britain.** F. Mackay Drapnell. (Orig.). 1993. pap. write for info. (*0-9639242-0-6*) Delfin Press.

Bravo. James Fenimore Cooper. Ed. by Donald A. Ringe. (Masterworks of Literature Ser.). 1963. 21.95 (*0-8084-0065-7*); pap. 16.95 (*0-8084-0066-5*) NCUP.

Bravo. James Fenimore Cooper. (Works of James Fenimore Cooper Ser.). 1990. reprint ed. lib. bdg. 79.00 (*0-7812-2380-6*) Rprt Serv.

Bravo! Communication et Grammaire. 2nd ed. Judith A. Muyskens et al. LC 92-38753. 1993. student ed, pap. 28. 95 (*0-8384-4418-0*) Heinle & Heinle.

Bravo! Communication et Grammaire. 2nd ed. Judith A. Muyskens et al. LC 92-38753. 1993. pap. 30.95 (*0-8384-4422-9*) Heinle & Heinle.

Bravo! Communication et Grammaire. 2nd ed. Judith A. Muyskens et al. LC 92-38753. 1993. 34.95 (*0-8384-4427-X*) Heinle & Heinle.

Bravo: Libretto by Gaetano Rossi & Others, after James Fenimore Cooper & Anicet Bourgeois. Music by Saverio Mercadante. Saverio Mercadante. LC 89-753690. (Italian Opera 1810-1840 Ser.: Vol. 21). 368p. 1990. 124.00 (*0-8240-6570-0*) Garland.

***Bravo for the Bride.** Elizabeth Eyre. 192p. 1995. 21.95 (*0-312-11756-6*) St Martin.

Bravo, Minski. Arthur Yorinks. (Illus.). (J). (ps up). 1988. 15.00 (*0-374-30951-5*) FS&G.

Bravo of Venice, A Romance. Matthew G. Lewis. LC 74-131327. (Gothic Novels Ser.). 1974. reprint ed. 51.95 (*0-405-00807-4*) Ayer.

Bravo Romeo. Ralph Peters. Ed. by Paul McCarthy. 320p. 1990. mass mkt. 4.95 (*0-671-68166-4*) PB.

Bravo, San Pedro, Ole! Dickhaut E. Wolfe. 160p. 1985. 14. 95 (*0-936810-04-1*) R&E Miles.

Bravo, Tanya. Patricia L. Gauch. (Illus.). 40p. (J). (ps-3). 1992. lib. bdg. 14.95 (*0-399-22145-X*, Philomel Bks) Putnam Pub Group.

Bravo Twenty: The Bombing of the American West. Richard Misrach & Myriam W. Misrach. LC 90-34150. (Creating the North American Landscape Ser.). (Illus.). 160p. 1990. 49.95 (*0-8018-4064-3*); pap. 29.95 (*0-8018-4065-1*) Johns Hopkins.

Bravo Two Zero: The Harrowing True Story of a Special Forces Patrol Behind the Lines in Iraq. Andy Mcnab. 1994. mass mkt. 5.99 (*0-440-21880-2*) Dell.

***Bravo! Wedding Organizer.** 1993. 19.95 (*0-9624634-7-7*) Bravo Pubns.

***Bravos of the West.** John Myers. 480p. 1995. pap. 15.00 (*0-8032-8222-2*, Bison Books) U of Nebr Pr.

Brawl. Gerard Bessette. Tr. by Marc Lebel & Ronald Sutherland. LC 77-473823. (French Writers of Canada Ser.). 230p. reprint ed. pap. 65.60 (*0-8357-7384-1*, 2024931) Bks Demand.

Brawl Ridiculous: Swordfighting in Shakespeare's Plays. Charles Edelman. (Revels Plays Companion Library). 256p. 1992. 59.95 (*0-7190-3507-4*, Pub. by Manchester Univ Pr UK) St Martin.

Brawn Drain: Foreign Student Athletes in American Universities. John Bale. 248p. 1991. 29.95 (*0-252-01732-3*) U of Ill Pr.

Brawny Wycherley, First Master in English Modern Comedy. Willard Connely. (BCL1-PR English Literature Ser.). 352p. 1992. reprint ed. lib. bdg. 89.00 (*0-7812-7419-2*) Rprt Serv.

Braxton Bragg: General of the Confederacy. Don C. Seitz. LC 72-179537. (Select Bibliographies Reprint Ser.). 1977. reprint ed. 33.95 (*0-8369-6666-X*) Ayer.

Braxton Bragg & Confederate Defeat, Vol. I. Grady McWhiney. 1991. 22.50 (*0-8173-0545-9*) U of Ala Pr.

Braxton Bragg & Confederate Defeat, Vol. II. Judith L. Hallock. 320p. 1991. 29.95 (*0-8173-0543-2*) U of Ala Pr.

***Bray House.** Eilis Ni Dhuibhne. 256p. (Orig.). 1990. pap. 11.95 (*0-614-05161-4*, Pub. by Attic IE) InBook.

Bray House. Eilis Ni Dhuibhne. (Orig.). (C). 1989. 39.00 (*0-946211-96-5*, Pub. by Attic Pr IE) St Mut.

***Brazen.** Ghislaine Dunant. Tr. by Rosette Lamont. 1995. pap. 10.95 (*1-56201-065-4*) Blue Moon Bks.

Brazen Altar of the Roman Letter. Leon Tucker. pap. 1.99 (*1-56632-021-6*) Revival Lit.

Brazen Ecstasy. Janelle Taylor. (Orig.). 1991. mass mkt. 4.99 (*0-8217-3499-7*) Zebra.

Brazen Face of History: Studies in the Literary Consciousness in America. Lewis P. Simpson. LC 80-12940. xx, 260p. 1980. text ed. 37.50 (*0-8071-0752-2*) La State U Pr.

Brazen Gambit. Lynn Abbey. (Dark Sun, Chronicles of Athas Ser.). 320p. (Orig.). 1994. pap. 4.95 (*1-56076-872-X*) TSR Inc.

Brazen Head. John C. Powys. 348p. text ed. 26.95 (*0-912568-11-9*) Colgate U Pr.

Brazen Heart. Rosalyn Alsobrook. 432p. 1991. mass mkt. 4.50 (*0-8217-3412-1*) Zebra.

Brazen Horn. Denis Johnston. 1976. 52.50 (*0-85105-259-2*, Pub. by Colin Smythe Ltd UK) Dufour.

***Brazen Rule.** Steven Burgauer. 278p. 1995. pap. 8.95 (*0-7610-0088-7*) NW Pub.

***Brazen Serpent.** Eilean N. Chuilleanain. LC 94-61973. 50p. 1994. 13.95 (*0-916390-65-9*); pap. 7.95 (*0-916390-64-0*) Wake Forest.

Brazen Tower: Essays on Mythological Imagery in French Renaissance & Baroque, 1550-1670. John C. Lapp. (Stanford French & Italian Studies: No. 7). 198p. 1978. pap. 46.50 (*0-915838-35-4*) Anma Libri.

Brazen Virginia Bride. Millie Criswell. 1990. mass mkt. 4.25 (*0-8217-3251-X*) Zebra.

Brazen Virtue. Nora Roberts. 1988. 5.99 (*0-553-27283-7*) Bantam.

Brazen Whispers. Jane Feather. 384p. (Orig.). 1990. pap. 3.95 (*0-380-76167-X*) Avon.

***Brazil.** (American Geographical Society Around the World Program Ser.). 1994. lib. bdg. 17.95 (*0-614-04838-9*) Am Geographical.

***Brazil.** (American Geographical Society Around the World Program Ser.). 1994. pap. 9.95 (*0-614-04839-7*) Am Geographical.

Brazil. Moyra Ashford. LC 90-19250. (World in View Ser.). (Illus.). 96p. (YA). (gr. 6-12). 1991. lib. bdg. 24.26 (*0-8114-2436-7*) Raintree Steck-V.

Brazil. Donna Bailey & Anna Sproule. LC 90-30534. (Where We Live Ser.). (Illus.). 32p. (J). (gr. 1-4). 1990. lib. bdg. 19.97 (*0-8114-2560-6*) Raintree Steck-V.

Brazil. Evelyn Bender. (Let's Visit Places & Peoples of the World Ser.). (Illus.). 112p. (J). (gr. 5 up). 1990. 14.95 (*0-7910-1108-9*) Chelsea Hse.

Brazil. Wilbur Cross. LC 84-7602. (Enchantment of the World Ser.). (Illus.). 128p. (J). (gr. 5-9). 1984. lib. bdg. 21.53 (*0-516-02753-0*) Childrens.

***Brazil.** Zoe Dawson. LC 95-10301. (Postcards From Ser.). (J). 1995. write for info. (*0-8172-4013-6*) Raintree Steck-V.

Brazil. Pierre Denis. 1977. lib. bdg. 59.95 (*0-8490-1541-3*) Gordon Pr.

Brazil. Karen Jacobsen. LC 89-10042. (New True Bks.). 48p. (J). (gr. k-4). 1989. lib. bdg. 12.90 (*0-516-01171-5*); pap. 4.95 (*0-516-41171-3*) Childrens.

***Brazil.** David C. King. LC 94-37253. (Dropping on On Ser.). (J). 1995. write for info. (*1-55916-082-9*) Rourke Bk Co.

***Brazil.** Anna Lewington & Edward Parker. (Illus.). 48p. (J). (gr. 6-8). Date not set. 15.95 (*1-56847-339-7*) Thomson Lrning.

Brazil. Marion Morrison. LC 93-26100. (Country Fact Files Ser.). (J). 1993. lib. bdg. 22.80 (*0-8114-1842-1*) Raintree Steck-V.

Brazil. Marion Morrison. LC 88-18294. (People & Places Ser.). (Illus.). 48p. (J). (gr. 4-8). 1988. lib. bdg. 12.95 (*0-382-09516-2*) Silver Burdett Pr.

Brazil. Christopher Richard. LC 90-22471. (Cultures of the World Ser.: Group 2: Latin America). (Illus.). 128p. (YA). (gr. 5-9). 1991. lib. bdg. 21.95 (*1-85435-382-9*) Marshall Cavendish.

Brazil. John Updike. LC 93-28632. 1994. 23.00 (*0-679-43071-7*) Knopf.

Brazil. John Updike. 1995. mass mkt. 6.99 (*0-449-22313-2*) Fawcett.

Brazil. Rosa Q. Mesa. LC 68-57259. (Latin American Serial Documents Ser.: Vol. 2). 365p. reprint ed. pap. 104.10 (*0-8357-7385-X*, 2013544) Bks Demand.

***Brazil: A Cook's Tour.** Christopher Idone. LC 94-37317. (Illus.). (J). 1995. write for info. (*0-517-59555-9*, Clarkson Potter) Crown Bks Yng Read.

Brazil: A Mask Called Progress. Neil MacDonald. 96p. (C). 1991. pap. text ed. 24.00 (*0-85598-091-5*, Pub. by Oxfam Pubns UK) St Mut.

Brazil: A New Regional Power in the World Economy. Bertha K. Becker & Claudio A. Egler. (Geography of the World Economy Ser.). (Illus.). 212p. (C). 1992. 49.95 (*0-521-37008-6*); pap. 16.95 (*0-521-37905-9*) Cambridge U Pr.

Brazil: A Study of Economic Types. Joao F. Normano. LC 67-29551. 1935. 24.00 (*0-8196-0208-6*) Biblo.

Brazil: A Travel Survival Kit. 2nd ed. Andrew Draffen et al. (Illus.). 632p. 1992. pap. 17.95 (*0-86442-141-9*) Lonely Planet.

Brazil: An Awakening Giant. Mark Carpenter. LC 87-13417. (Discovering Our Heritage Ser.). (Illus.). 128p. (J). (gr. 5 up). 1988. text ed. 14.95 (*0-87518-366-2*, Dillon Silver Burdett) Silver Burdett Pr.

Brazil: Anthropological Perspectives. Ed. by Maxine L. Margolis & William E. Carter. LC 79-11843. (Illus.). 448p. 1979. text ed. 53.00 (*0-231-04714-2*) Col U Pr.

***Brazil: Business Financing Handbook.** (Illus.). 70p. (Orig.). 1994. pap. 295.00 (*0-7605-1182-9*) Rector Pr.

Brazil: Business Risk Overview. Ed. by Lewis B. Sckolnick. 125p. (Orig.). (C). 1994. pap. text ed. 495.00 (*1-57205-567-7*) Rector Pr.

Brazil: Chapters by Manoel Cardozo & Others. Ed. by Lawrence F. Hill. LC 82-15848. (United Nations Ser.). (Illus.). xxi, 394p. 1982. reprint ed. text ed. 75.00 (*0-313-23503-1*, HILB, Greenwood Pr) Greenwood.

***Brazil: Commercial Law.** 300p. (Orig.). 1994. pap. 295.00 (*0-7605-1232-9*) Rector Pr.

Brazil: Controlled Decompression. (Report on the Americas: Vol. XIII, No. 3). 52p. 2.50 (*0-317-34955-4*) NA Cong Lat Am.

Brazil: Country Reporter. Lewis B. Sckolnick. (Illus.). 60p. 1994. pap. 895.00 (*1-57205-174-4*) Rector Pr.

Brazil: Economic, Social & Political Challenges of the 1990s. Ed. by Maria D. Kinzo. 256p. 1993. text ed. 59. 50 (*1-85043-613-4*, Pub. by I B Tauris UK) St Martin.

Brazil: Emerging World Power. rev. ed. Jordan M. Young. 248p. (Orig.). (C). 1991. reprint ed. pap. 16.50 (*0-89464-563-3*) Krieger.

Brazil: Foreign Financing Reporter. Ed. by Lewis B. Sckolnick. (Illus.). 60p. (Orig.). 1994. pap. 225.00 (*1-57205-237-6*) Rector Pr.

Brazil: Mixture or Massacre? Essays in the Genocide of a Black People. rev. ed. Abdias do Nascimento. Tr. by Elisa L. Nascimento. xviii, 214p. (Orig.). 1989. reprint ed. pap. text ed. 12.95 (*0-912469-26-9*) Majority Pr.

***Brazil: New Risks & Opportunities.** 160p. (Orig.). 1994. pap. 495.00 (*0-7605-0420-2*) Rector Pr.

Brazil: Politics in a Patrimonial Society. Riordan Roett. 1978. 16.95 (*0-275-90312-5*, C0312, Praeger Pubs); pap. 16.95 (*0-275-91475-5*, B1475, Praeger Pubs) Greenwood.

Brazil: Politics in a Patrimonial Society. 4th ed. Riordan Roett. LC 92-13657. 256p. 1992. text ed. 59.95 (*0-275-94121-3*, C4121, Praeger Pubs); pap. text ed. 19. 95 (*0-275-94122-1*, B4122, Praeger Pubs) Greenwood.

Brazil: Responses to the Debt Crisis. James Dinsmoor. 155p. 1990. write for info. (*0-940602-30-X*) IADB.

Brazil: Stray Notes from Bahia. James Wetherell. 1977. lib. bdg. 59.95 (*0-8490-1547-2*) Gordon Pr.

Brazil: The Forging of a Nation, 1798-1852. Roderick J. Barman. LC 88-2299. 352p. 1988. 42.50 (*0-8047-1437-1*) Stanford U Pr.

Brazil: The Forging of a Nation, 1798-1852. Roderick J. Barman. 1994. pap. 16.95 (*0-8047-2330-3*) Stanford U Pr.

***Brazil: The Future of the Real 1994.** 60p. (Orig.). 1994. pap. 195.00 (*0-7605-0459-8*) Rector Pr.

Brazil: Today & Tomorrow. L. E. Elliott. 1976. lib. bdg. 59. 95 (*0-87968-784-3*) Gordon Pr.

Brazil: Trade, Licensing & Investing Rules & Regulations. Ed. by Lewis B. Sckolnick. (Illus.). 80p. (Orig.). (C). 1994. pap. 225.00 (*1-57205-055-1*) Rector Pr.

***Brazil: Travel Survival Kit.** 3rd ed. Andrew Draffen et al. (Illus.). 688p. 1995. pap. 17.95 (*0-86442-317-9*) Lonely Planet.

Brazil: War on Children. Gilberto Dimenstein. 88p. 1992. pap. 10.00 (*0-85345-838-3*, Pub. by Lat Am Bur UK) Monthly Rev.

Brazil: World Frontier. Benjamin H. Hunnicutt. (Brazil Ser.). 1979. lib. bdg. 69.95 (*0-8490-2878-7*) Gordon Pr.

Brazil see American Nations Past & Present

Brazil see Statements of the Laws of the OAS Member States in Matters Affecting Business

Brazil & Cuba - Blacks. Lewis B. Sckolnick. (Civil Rights Reporter Ser.). (Illus.). 60p. (Orig.). (C). 1994. pap. 45. 00 (*1-57205-111-6*) Rector Pr.

Brazil & Her People of Today. N. Winter. 1976. lib. bdg. 69.95 (*0-8490-1542-1*) Gordon Pr.

Brazil & Latin-American Nuclear Proliferation: An Optimistic View. George H. Quester. (CISA Working Paper Ser.: No. 17). 36p. (Orig.). Date not set. pap. 10. 00 (*0-86682-016-7*) Ctr Intl Relations.

Brazil & Peru: Social & Economic Effects of Petroleum Development. Norman Gall & Eleodoro M. Alba. (Illus.). x, 123p. (Orig.). 1987. pap. 14.00 (*92-2-105506-X*) Intl Labour Office.

Brazil & the Brazilians. G. Bruce. 1976. lib. bdg. 59.95 (*0-8490-1543-X*) Gordon Pr.

Brazil & the Brazilians. 7th enl. rev. ed. Daniel P. Kidder & James C. Fletcher. LC 71-171063. (Illus.). reprint ed. 72.50 (*0-404-03668-6*) AMS Pr.

Brazil & the Challenge of Economic Reform. Ed. by Werner Baer & Joseph S. Tulchin. LC 93-30786. (Special Studies). 160p. (C). 1993. pap. text ed. 13.95 (*0-943875-53-6*) W Wilson Ctr Pr.

Brazil & the Great Powers, 1930-1939: The Politics of Trade Rivalry. Stanley E. Hilton & Jose H. Rodrigues. LC 75-17747. (Latin American Monographs: No. 38). 326p. reprint ed. pap. 93.00 (*0-8357-7745-6*, 2036102) Bks Demand.

Brazil & the Ivory Coast: The Impact of International Lending, Investment & Aid. Ed. by Werner Baer et al. (Contemporary Studies in Economic & Financial Analysis: Vol. 58). 1987. 73.25 (*0-89232-819-3*) Jai Pr.

Brazil & the Quiet Intervention, 1964. Phyllis R. Parker. (Texas Pan American Ser.). 161p. 1979. text ed. 14.50 (*0-292-78507-0*) U of Tex Pr.

Brazil & the Soviet Challenge, 1917-1947. Stanley E. Hilton. 303p. (C). 1991. text ed. 37.50 (*0-292-70781-9*) U of Tex Pr.

Brazil & the Struggle for Rubber: A Study in Environmental History. Warren Dean. (Studies in Environment & History). (Illus.). 240p. 1987. 44.95 (*0-521-33477-2*) Cambridge U Pr.

Brazil & the United States. Abraham F. Lowenthal. LC 86-81679. (Headline Ser.: No. 279). 64p. (Orig.). (C). 1986. pap. 5.95 (*0-87124-109-9*) Foreign Policy.

Brazil & the World System. Ed. by Richard Graham. (Institute of Latin American Studies Critical Reflections on Latin America Ser.). 135p. 1991. text ed. 22.50 (*0-292-70785-1*) U of Tex Pr.

Brazil Business Forecaster. Ed. by Lewis B. Sckolnick. 70p. (Orig.). (C). 1994. pap. 675.00 (*1-57205-367-4*) Rector Pr.

***Brazil Business Intelligence Handbook.** (Illus.). 70p. (Orig.). 1994. pap. 295.00 (*0-7605-1071-7*) Rector Pr.

***Brazil Business Risk Outlook.** 70p. (Orig.). 1994. pap. 495.00 (*0-7605-1393-7*) Rector Pr.

***Brazil Commercial Law, 2 vols.** 300p. (C). 1994. pap. 595. 00 (*0-7605-0086-X*) Rector Pr.

Brazil Company Handbook, 1992. 6th ed. Ed. by IMF Editora Staff. 148p. (Orig.). 1992. pap. 29.95 (*1-878753-10-X*, Pub. by IMF Edit Ltda BL) Ref Press.

Brazil Company Handbook, 1993. 7th ed. Ed. by IMF Editora Staff. 171p. 1993. pap. 29.95 (*1-878753-41-X*) Ref Press.

***Brazil Company Handbook, 1994-95.** 8th ed. 200p. 1994. pap. 34.95 (*1-878753-73-8*) Ref Press.

***Brazil Company Handbook, 1995-1996.** 9th ed. 200p. 1995. pap. 34.95 (*1-57311-001-9*) Ref Press.

***Brazil Corporate Guidebook 1995.** (Illus.). 225p. (Orig.). 1994. pap. 145.00 (*0-7605-0619-1*) Rector Pr.

Brazil: Empire & First Republic, 1822-1930: A Selection of Chapters from Volumes III & IV of the Cambridge History of Latin America. Ed. by Leslie Bethell. (Illus.). 368p. (C). 1989. 69.95 (*0-521-36293-8*); pap. 18.95 (*0-521-36837-5*) Cambridge U Pr.

Brazil Gold Ninety-One - the Economics, Geology, Geochemistry & Genesis of Gold Deposits: Proceedings of the Symposium Brazil Gold '91, Belo Horizonte, Minas Gerais, Brazil, 13-17 May, 1991. Ed. by E. A. Ladeira. (Illus.). 844p. (C). 1991. text ed. 120.00 (*90-6191-195-8*, Pub. by A A Balkema NE) Ashgate Pub Co.

Brazil Highlights Pocket Guide. Berlitz Editors. (Pocket Guides Ser.). (Illus.). 128p. 1989. pap. 7.95 (*2-8315-1425-8*) Berlitz.

Brazil in Pictures. rev. ed. Nathan A. Haverstock. (Visual Geography Ser.). (Illus.). 64p. (YA). (gr. 5 up). 1987. lib. bdg. 18.95 (*0-8225-1802-3*, Lerner Publctns) Lerner Group.

Brazil in Reference Books, 1965-1989: An Annotated Bibliography. annot. ed. Ann Hartness. LC 90-28356. 361p. 1991. 39.50 (*0-8108-2400-0*) Scarecrow.

Brazil in the Making. J. Jobim. 1976. lib. bdg. 59.95 (*0-8490-1544-8*) Gordon Pr.

Brazil in the Seventies. Riordan Roett. LC 76-54880. (AEI Studies: No. 132). 126p. reprint ed. pap. 36.00 (*0-8357-4437-X*, 2037271) Bks Demand.

Brazil in Transition. Ed. by Robert Wesson & David Fleischer. LC 82-16645. (Politics in Latin America Ser.). 208p. 1983. text ed. 55.00 (*0-275-91102-0*, C1102, Praeger Pubs) Greenwood.

Brazil, Its Condition & Prospects. C. C. Andrews. 1976. lib. bdg. 59.95 (*0-87968-783-5*) Gordon Pr.

Brazil Looks Forward. Benjamin H. Hunnicutt. 1978. lib. bdg. 75.00 (*0-8490-1545-6*) Gordon Pr.

Brazil-Maru. Karen T. Yamashita. LC 92-17857. 248p. 1992. 19.95 (*1-56689-000-4*) Coffee Hse.

Brazil-Maru. Karen T. Yamashita. LC 92-17857. 248p. 1993. pap. 12.95 (*1-56689-016-0*) Coffee Hse.

Brazil on the March. M. Cooke. 1976. lib. bdg. 59.95 (*0-8490-1546-4*) Gordon Pr.

Brazil on the Move. Dos Passos. 1994. pap. 10.95 (*1-56924-958-X*) Marlowe & Co.

Brazil on Your Own. Arnold Greenberg. (Illus.). 480p. 1988. pap. 12.95 (*0-8442-9640-6*, Passport Bks) NTC Pub Grp.

Brazil on Your Own. 2nd rev. ed. 1993. 14.95 (*0-8442-9642-2*, Natl Textbk) NTC Pub Grp.

Brazil, Portrait of Half a Continent. Thomas L. Smith. LC 73-138183. (Illus.). 466p. (C). 1972. reprint ed. text ed. 75.00 (*0-8371-5640-8*, SMBR, Greenwood Pr) Greenwood.

Brazil, Portugal, & Other Portuguese-Speaking Lands: A List of Books Primarily in English. Francis M. Rogers & David T. Haberly. LC 68-7564. (Texts from the Romance Languages Ser.: No. 4). 75p. (C). 1968. pap. 1.95 (*0-674-08050-5*) HUP.

***Brazil Tax Law, 2 vols.** 300p. (C). 1994. pap. 595.00 (*0-7605-0085-1*) Rector Pr.

An Asterisk (*) at the beginning of an entry indicates that the title is appearing in BIP for the first time.

Brazil Traveler. Selden Rodman. LC 75-13350. (Illus.). 104p. 1975. pap. 9.95 (0-8159-5113-2) Devin.

Brazil, 1954-64: End of a Civilian Cycle. Ed. by Jordan M. Young. LC 73-184921. (Interim History Ser.). 205p. reprint ed. pap. 58.50 (0-8357-7386-8, 2022898) Bks Demand.

Brazilian. Henri Meilhac & Lucovic Halevy. Tr. by Norman R. Shapiro. (Tour De Farce Ser.: Vol. 3). 56p. (Orig.). 1987. pap. 6.95 (0-936839-59-7) Applause Theatre Bk Pubs.

Brazilian Amazon: Institutions & Publications. Carmen M. Muricy. (Bibliography & Reference Ser.: No. 28). vii, 50p. 1991. pap. 26.00 (0-685-53178-3) SALALM.

Brazilian Bombshell: The Biography of Carmen Miranda. Martha Gil-Montero. (Illus.). 352p. 1989. 18.95 (1-55611-128-2) D I Fine.

Brazilian Capital Goods Industry, Nineteen Twenty-Nine to Nineteen Sixty-Four. Nathaniel H. Leff. LC 68-21976. (Center for International Affairs Ser.). 198p. 1968. 22.00 (0-674-08090-4) HUP.

Brazilian Cinema. Randal Johnson & Robert Stam. LC 80-66323. (Illus.). 260p. 1982. 49.50 (0-8386-3078-2) Fairleigh Dickinson.

Brazilian Citrus Industry: Situation & Outlook, 1992-93. 22p. (Orig.). (C). 1992. pap. text ed. 24.00 (0-941375-69-2) Diane Pub.

Brazilian Communism, 1935-1945: Repression During World Upheaval. John W. Dulles. (Illus.). 311p. 1983. text ed. 25.00 (0-292-70741-X) U of Tex Pr.

Brazilian Defense Industry. Patrice Franko-Jones. 262p. (C). 1991. pap. text ed. 43.50 (0-8133-7771-4) Westview.

Brazilian Diamond in Contracts, Contraband & Capital. Harry Bernstein. LC 87-25336. (Illus.). 170p. (Orig.). 1988. lib. bdg. 41.50 (0-8191-6531-X, Atlantic Rsch & Pubns Inc); pap. text ed. 20.00 (0-8191-6532-8, Atlantic Rsch & Pubns Inc) U Pr of Amer.

Brazilian Economy: Growth & Development. 2nd ed. Werner Baer. 368p. 1983. 40.95 (0-275-90938-7, C0938, Praeger Pubs) Greenwood.

Brazilian Economy: Growth & Development. 4th ed. Werner Baer. LC 94-15878. 440p. 1995. text ed. 65.00 (0-275-94509-X, Praeger Pubs); pap. text ed. 22.95 (0-275-94510-3, Praeger Pubs) Greenwood.

Brazilian Economy: Structure & Performance. Ed. by Maria J. Willumsen & Roberto B. Macedo. (University of Miami North-South Center Ser.). 400p. (C). 1993. pap. text ed. 21.95 (1-56000-684-6) Transaction Pubs.

Brazilian Economy in the Eighties. Ed. by Jorge Salazar-Carrillo & Roberto Fendt. (Illus.). 200p. 1985. 68.00 (0-08-031953-X, Pub. by PPI UK) Elsevier.

Brazilian Empire: Myths & Histories. Emilia Viotti da Costa. LC 85-16456. (Illus.). xxvi, 288p. 1986. 29.00 (0-226-85667-4) U Ch Pr.

Brazilian Exchange: The Study of an Inconvertible Currency. J. P. Wileman. LC 76-75583. 267p. 1970. reprint ed. text ed. 59.75 (0-8371-1082-3, WIBE, Greenwood Pr) Greenwood.

Brazilian Fiction: Aspects & Evolution of the Contemporary Narrative. Robert E. DiAntonio. LC 88-19882. 239p. (Orig.). 1989. 20.00 (1-55728-056-8); pap. 12.00 (1-55728-057-6) U of Ark Pr.

Brazilian Folk Narrative Scholarship: A Critical Survey & Selective Annotated Bibliography. Mary MacGregor-Villarreal. LC 94-20707. (Folklore Library: Vol. 8). 264p. 1994. reprint ed. 40.00 (0-8153-1243-1, H1683) Garland.

Brazilian Happenings. Richard O'Connell. 1966. pap. 10.00 (0-685-62617-2) Atlantis Edns.

Brazilian Industrialists & Democratic Change. Leigh A. Payne. LC 93-974. 224p. (C). 1993. text ed. 32.50 (0-8018-4648-X) Johns Hopkins.

Brazilian Informatics & the United States: Defending Infant Industry vs. Opening Foreign Markets. Anne Dibble & John Odell. (Pew Case Studies in International Affairs). 50p. (C). 1992. pap. text ed. 2.50 (1-56927-128-3) Geo U Inst Dplmcy.

Brazilian Jazz Guitar Styles. Date not set. 8.95 (0-7866-0026-8, 95111); audio 9.98 (0-7866-0039-X, 95111C) Mel Bay.

Brazilian Lectures, I & II. Wilfred R. Bion. 220p. 1990. reprint ed. pap. 36.95 (0-946439-78-8, Pub. by Karnac Bks UK) Brunner-Mazel.

Brazilian Legislature & Political System: Contributions in Political Science, No. 298. Abdo Baaklini. LC 91-44633. 256p. 1992. text ed. 59.95 (0-313-28450-4, BZG/, Greenwood Pr) Greenwood.

Brazilian Literature. Isaac Goldberg. 1975. 250.00 (0-87968-197-7) Gordon Pr.

Brazilian Literature. Isaac Goldberg. LC 78-58257. (Essay Index in Reprint Ser.). 1978. 24.50 (0-8486-3019-X) Roth Pub Inc.

Brazilian Literature, Vol. 1. Claude L. Hulet. LC 74-16331. 419p. reprint ed. pap. 119.50 (0-7837-6327-1, 2046042) Bks Demand.

Brazilian Literature, Vol. 2. Claude L. Hulet. LC 74-16331. 319p. reprint ed. pap. 91.00 (0-7837-6328-X, 2046042) Bks Demand.

Brazilian Literature, Vol. 3. Claude L. Hulet. LC 74-16331. 397p. reprint ed. pap. 113.20 (0-7837-6329-8, 2046042) Bks Demand.

Brazilian Literature: A Research Bibliography. David W. Foster & Walter Rela. LC 90-31766. 448p. 1990. 56.00 (0-8240-3442-2, H1162) Garland.

Brazilian Literature: An Outline. Erico Verissimo. LC 78-88987. 184p. 1970. reprint ed. text ed. 49.75 (0-8371-2319-4, VEBL, Greenwood Pr) Greenwood.

Brazilian Literature: Special Issue. Ed. by Kenneth D. Jackson & Yvette E. Miller. 208p. 1986. pap. 16.00 (0-317-47010-8) Lat Am Lit Rev Pr.

Brazilian Medical Contributions. Leonidio Ribeiro. 1976. lib. bdg. 69.95 (0-8490-1548-0) Gordon Pr.

Brazilian Monarchy & the South American Republics, 1822-1831: Diplomacy & State Building. Ron Seckinger. LC 83-25588. xvi, 184p. 1984. text ed. 30.00 (0-8071-1156-2) La State U Pr.

***Brazilian Mosaic: Portraits of a Diverse People & Culture.** Ed. by G. Harvey Summ et al. (Latin American Silhouettes Ser.). 272p. 1995. 50.00 (0-8420-2491-3); pap. 16.95 (0-8420-2492-1) Scholarly Res Inc.

Brazilian Music for Acoustic Guitar. Carlos Barbosa-Lima. 1993. 7.95 (1-56222-558-8, 94840); audio 9.98 (1-56222-794-7, 94840) Mel Bay.

Brazilian Mystic. Robert B. Cunninghame-Graham. LC 70-146856. (Select Bibliographies Reprint Ser.). 1977. 21.95 (0-8369-5623-0) Ayer.

Brazilian Mystic: Life & Miracles of Antonio Conselheiro. R. B. Graham. 1976. lib. bdg. 59.95 (0-87968-786-X) Gordon Pr.

Brazilian Nights. Odie Hawkins. 192p. (Orig.). 1992. pap. 3.95 (0-87067-375-0) Holloway.

Brazilian Palms: Notes on Their Uses, & Vernacular Names & Added Illustrations, Contributions from The New York Botanical Garden, Vol. 17. C. U. Pinheiro & M. J. Balick. LC 87-12201. (Illus.). 61p. 1987. pap. 8.75 (0-89327-317-1) NY Botanical.

Brazilian Peasantry. Shepard Forman. LC 75-16156. 319p. 1978. text ed. 50.00 (0-231-03106-8) Col U Pr.

Brazilian Phrasebook. 2nd ed. Mark Balla. (Phrasebooks Ser.). (Illus.). 96p. (Orig.). 1993. pap. 5.95 (0-86442-176-1) Lonely Planet.

Brazilian Poems. Richard O'Connell. 1928. 35.00 (0-87556-226-4) Saifer.

Brazilian Poetry (1950-1980) Ed. by Emanuel Brasil & William J. Smith. LC 83-199745. 197p. reprint ed. pap. 56.20 (0-7837-0209-4, 2040517) Bks Demand.

Brazilian Product Guide. Ed. by C. DePaula. 350p. 1993. pap. 70.00 (0-915344-40-8) Todd Pubns.

Brazilian Psalm. Jorge De Lima. Tr. by Willis Wager. 1977. lib. bdg. 59.95 (0-8490-1549-9) Gordon Pr.

***Brazilian Puzzle: Culture on the Borderlands of the Western World.** Ed. by David J. Hess & Roberto Da Matta. LC 94-29469. 1995. write for info. (0-231-10114-7); write for info. (0-231-10115-5) Col U Pr.

Brazilian Quandary: A Twentieth Century Fund Paper. Marcillo M. Morcira. 87p. (Orig.). (C). 1986. pap. 7.00 (0-87078-171-5) TCFP-PPP.

Brazilian Serial Documents: A Selective & Annotated Guide. Mary Lombardi. LC 73-16533. (Indiana University Latin American Studies Program). 485p. reprint ed. pap. 138.30 (0-8357-7387-6, 2015828) Bks Demand.

Brazilian Short Stories. Monteiro Lobato. 1977. lib. bdg. 59.95 (0-8490-1550-2) Gordon Pr.

Brazilian Sound. Chris McGowan & Ricardo Pessanha. (Illus.). 208p. 1991. pap. 18.95 (0-8230-7673-3, Billboard Bks) Watsn-Guptill.

Brazilian Species of "Hyla" Bertha Lutz & Gualter Lutz. LC 70-39502. (Illus.). 286p. 1973. 25.00 (0-292-70704-5) U of Tex Pr.

Brazilian Stone Meteorites: With a Brief General Introduction on the Significance, Classification, Mineralogy, Bulk Composition & Recognition of Stone Meteorites. Celso B. Gomes & Klaus Keil. LC 80-5333. 168p. reprint ed. pap. 47.90 (0-8357-7388-4, 2029321) Bks Demand.

***Brazilian Studies.** Alan L. Bryan & Ruth Gruhn. 168p. 1993. pap. 30.00 (0-912933-10-0) Ctr Study First Am.

Brazilian Tales. Machado J. Deassis et al. Tr. by Isaac Goldberg. 1977. lib. bdg. 59.95 (0-8490-1551-0) Gordon Pr.

Brazilian Tales. Ed. by Isaac Goldberg. Bd. with Attendant's Confession, the Fortune Teller, & Life. Joaquim M. Assis.; Aunt Zeze's Tears. Carmen Dolores.; Pigeons. Coelho Netto. Set pap. 4.95 (0-8283-1426-8, Intl Pocket Lib) Branden Pub Co.

Brazilian Tenement. Aluizio Azevedo. Tr. by Harry W. Brown. 1977. lib. bdg. 59.95 (0-8490-1552-9) Gordon Pr.

Brazilian Theatre: a Child Prodigy Comes of Age: An Illustrated Overview of the First Four Centuries. Sun L. Yu. LC 91-85024. (Illus.). 128p. 1992. 19.95 (1-878756-87-7); pap. 10.95 (1-878756-88-5) YCP Pubns.

Brazilian Three-Dimensional Embroidery: Instructions & 60 Transfer Patterns. Rosie Montague. (Embroidery, Needlework Designs Ser.). (Illus.). 64p. (Orig.). 1983. pap. 3.95 (0-486-24384-2) Dover.

Brazilian Voter: Mass Politics in Democratic Transition, 1974-1986. Kurt Von Mettenheim. (Pitt Latin American Ser.). 240p. (C). 1995. 49.95 (0-8229-3838-3) U of Pittsburgh Pr.

Brazilian Women Speak: Contemporary Life Stories. Daphne Patai. 404p. (Orig.). (C). 1988. text ed. 45.00 (0-8135-1300-6); pap. 15.00 (0-8135-1301-4) Rutgers U Pr.

Brazilian Workers' ABC: Class Conflict & Alliances in Modern Sao Paulo. John D. French. LC 91-50936. (Illus.). 368p. (C). 1992. 49.95 (0-8078-2029-6); pap. 18.95 (0-8078-4368-7) U of NC Pr.

Brazilian World. Robert Hayes. LC 81-69333. (World of Latin America Ser.). 1982. pap. text ed. write for info. (0-88273-602-7) Forum Pr IL.

***Brazilians.** Joseph A. Page. 560p. 1995. 26.50 (0-201-40913-5) Addison-Wesley.

***Brazillian Perspectives of Sustainable Development of the Amazon Region.** Ed. by M. Clusener-Godt & I. Sachs. LC 94-24324. (Man & the Biosphere Ser.: Vol. 15). (Illus.). 320p. (C). 1995. text ed. 68.00 (1-85070-576-3) Prthnon Pub.

Brazil's Developing Northeast: A Study of Regional Planning & Foreign Aid. Stefan H. Robock. LC 79-26655. (Illus.). xv, 213p. 1980. reprint ed. text ed. 55.00 (0-313-22295-9, ROBD, Greenwood Pr) Greenwood.

Brazil's Foreign Policy. W. Perry. write for info. (0-275-90004-5, C0004, Praeger Pubs) Greenwood.

Brazil's National Alcohol Program: Technology & Development in an Authoritarian Regime. F. Joseph Demetrius. LC 89-16243. 194p. 1990. text ed. 49.95 (0-275-93183-8, C3183, Praeger Pubs) Greenwood.

Brazil's State-Owned Enterprises: A Case Study of the State As Entrepreneur. Thomas J. Trebat. LC 82-9564. (Cambridge Latin American Studies: No. 45). 288p. 1983. 74.95 (0-521-23716-5) Cambridge U Pr.

Brazing. 455p. 1987. 130.00 (0-87170-246-0) ASM.

Brazing Handbook (BRH) (Illus.). 493p. 1991. 72.00 (0-87171-359-4) Am Welding.

Brazing, Soldering & Braze Welding-Terms in 17 Languages see Terms for Welding & Allied-Processes in Different Languages (11W): WT

Brazos. Cameron Judd. 1994. 3.99 (0-553-56550-8) Bantam.

Brazos County Texas, Eighteen Seventy Census. Mary Collie-Cooper. 243p. (Orig.). 1987. spiral bd., pap. 10.00 (0-943553-04-0) Collie-Cooper Ent.

Brazos County Texas, Eighteen Sixty Census (Also 1842 Tax Roll & Surnames on 1850 Census) Mary Collie-Cooper & Allie Whitley. 59p. (Orig.). 1983. pap. 6.25 (0-943553-01-6) Collie-Cooper Ent.

***Brazos County Texas Marriage Records: Books G-1 & G-2 1887-1895.** (Orig.). 1994. per., pap. 15.00 (0-943553-07-5) Collie-Cooper Ent.

Brazos County Texas Marriage Records, 1878-1887, Bks. E & F. Texas Research Ramblers Staff. 140p. (Orig.). 1993. pap. 15.00 (0-943553-06-7) Collie-Cooper Ent.

Brazos Dreamer: The Story of Major Robert S. Neighbors. Gene Shelton. LC 93-16243. (Texas Legends Ser.: Bk. 5). 1993. 15.00 (0-385-42491-4) Doubleday.

Brazos Vacios: Como Vivir con el Aborto la Muerte Prenatala y la Muerte Infantil: Empty Arms: Coping with Miscarriage, Stillbirth & Infant Loss. Sherokee Ilse. 96p. (SPA.). 1992. reprint ed. pap. 7.50 (0-9609456-7-9) Wntergrn.

Brazzaville Beach. William Boyd. 336p. 1992. mass mkt. 4.99 (0-380-71385-3) Avon.

***Brazzaville Beach.** William Boyd. 320p. 1995. pap. 11.00 (0-380-78049-6) Avon.

Brea: The City of Oil, Oranges, & Opportunity. Esther R. Cramer. 384p. 1992. 29.95 (0-9632638-0-3); boxed 104.50 (0-9632638-1-1) City Brea.

***Brea: The City of Oil, Oranges & Opportunity.** 75th ed. Esther Cramer. (Illus.). Date not set. 32.27 (0-614-04562-2) City Brea.

Breach: Kilimanjaro & the Conquest of Self. Rob Taylor. 254p. 1991. pap. 12.95 (0-9630188-0-9) Wildeyes.

Breach & Adaptation of International Contracts: An Introduction to Lex Mercatoria. Ralph B. Lake et al. 240p. 1992. boxed 105.00 (0-88063-750-1) Michie Butterworth.

***Breach in the Watershed.** Douglas Niles. 448p. (Orig.). 1995. pap. 13.00 (0-441-00208-0) Ace Bks.

Breach of Contract. J. W. Carter. xlvi, 551p. 1984. 94.00 (0-455-20505-1, Pub. by Law Bk Co) W W Gaunt.

Breach of Employment Contracts & Wrongful Dismissal. John McMullen. Date not set. U.K. pap. write for info. (0-406-11841-8) Butterworth Legal Pubs.

Breach of Ethics. Haskell H. Bishop. 156p. 1994. pap. 7.95 (1-56901-295-4) NW Pub.

Breach of Fate. John P. Evans & John B. Mannion. (Orig.). 1980. pap. 2.25 (0-449-14325-2, GM) Fawcett.

Breach of Immunity. Molly Hite. 256p. 1994. pap. 8.95 (0-312-10434-0, Stonewall Inn) St Martin.

Breach of Impunity: The Trial for the Murder of Jesuits in El Salvador: Report of the Observer of the International Commission of Jurists. International Commission of Jurists Staff. LC 92-26144. (Illus.). vii, 81p. (C). 1992. pap. 12.95 (0-8232-1443-5) Fordham.

Breach of Promise: Its History & Social Considerations... Charles J. MacColla. ix, 93p. 1993. reprint ed. lib. bdg. 25.00 (0-8377-2445-7) Rothman.

Breach of Promise: Portraits of Poverty in North America. James A. Gittings. 136p. 1988. pap. 4.95 (0-377-00181-3) Friendship Pr.

Breach of the Peace. Michael G. Christie. 1990. U.K. pap. 29.00 (0-406-14430-3) Butterworth Legal Pubs.

Breach of Treaty. Shabtai Rosenne. 154p. (C). 1985. 50.00 (0-906496-36-5, Pub. by Grotius Pubns UK) St Mut.

***Breach of Trust.** Preston Pairo. LC 95-14712. 1995. write for info. (0-312-13034-1) St Martin.

***Breach of Trust: Sexual Exploitation by Health Care Professionals & Clergy.** John C. Gonsiorek. 456p. 1994. 59.95 (0-8039-5556-1) Sage.

***Breach of Trust: Sexual Exploitation by Health Care Professionals & Clergy.** John C. Gonsiorek. 1994. pap. 26.95 (0-8039-5557-X) Sage.

Breaches of Trust in Singapore & Malaysia. W. J. Ricquier & Stanley Y. Heong. 98p. 1984. pap. 40.00 (0-406-18115-2) Butterworth Legal Pubs.

***Breaching Fortress Europe.** Berger. 288p. 1994. per., pap. text ed. 19.95 (0-8403-9516-7) Kendall-Hunt.

Breaching the Wall: Of Separation Between Church & State, Excessive Entanglement & the IRS. pap. 4.00 (0-915598-39-6) Church of Scient Info.

Bread. Judith Baskerville. Ed. by Rebecca Stefoff. LC 91-18189. (Threads Ser.). (Illus.). 32p. (J). (gr. 3-5). 1991. lib. bdg. 15.93 (1-56074-001-9) Garrett Ed Corp.

Bread. Beth Hensperger. LC 87-29620. (Illus.). 160p. 1988. 29.95 (0-87701-472-8); pap. 18.95 (0-87701-443-4) Chronicle Bks.

Bread. Ed McBain. 176p. 1987. mass mkt. 4.50 (0-380-70368-8) Avon.

Bread. Sarah Morgan. (Illus.). 120p. 1975. 15.00 (0-88426-042-9) Encino Pr.

Bread. Dorothy Turner. (Foods We Eat Ser.). (Illus.). 32p. (J). (gr. 1-4). 1989. lib. bdg. 14.96 (0-87614-359-1, Carolrhoda) Lerner Group.

Bread: Social, Nutritional, & Agricultural Aspects of Wheaten Bread. Ed. by Arnold Spicer. (Illus.). 358p. 1975. 93.75 (0-85334-637-2, Pub. by Elsevier Applied Sci UK) Elsevier.

Bread Afresh, Wine Anew: Sermons by Disciples Women. Women Ministers in the Christian Church (Disciples of Christ) Staff. Ed. by Joan Campbell. 168p. (Orig.). 1991. pap. 13.99 (0-8272-0218-0) Chalice Pr.

Bread Alone: Bold Fresh Loaves from Your Own Hands. Daniel Leader & Judith Blahnik. LC 92-47236. 1993. 25.00 (0-688-09261-6) Morrow.

Bread & a Stone. Alvah Bessie. LC 83-7488. 352p. 1983. pap. 7.95 (0-88316-553-8) Chandler & Sharp.

Bread & Authority in Russia: 1914-1921. Lars T. Lih. 1990. 40.00 (0-520-06584-0) U CA Pr.

Bread & Breakfast. Linda K. Bristow. LC 92-30279. (One Hundred One Productions Ser.). 134p. (Orig.). 1993. reprint ed. pap. 10.95 (1-56426-551-X, One Hund One Prods) Cole Group.

Bread & Butter Bidding. Brian Senior. 1992. pap. 11.95 (1-85744-504-X, Maxwell Macmillan) Macmillan.

Bread & Butter Days: A Biographical Novel Based on the Life of Clem Flickinger. large type ed. LaVerne Stevens. LC 92-90223. (Illus.). 154p. (Orig.). 1992. per., pap. 10.00 (0-9630441-1-7) B&B Pr.

Bread & Circuses: A Study of Federal Theatre. Willson Whitman. LC 74-37919. (Select Bibliographies Reprint Ser.). 1977. reprint ed. 18.95 (0-8369-6756-9) Ayer.

Bread & Circuses: The Politician's Primer for Beginning Politicians, Party Bosses, Military Dictators, & Other Assorted Suckwhatcrats. Y. H. Servant. 115p. (Orig.). 1994. pap. 19.95 (0-9639848-0-2) LCC Press.

Bread & Circuses: Theories of Mass Culture As Social Decay. Patrick Brantlinger. LC 83-45134. 312p. (Orig.). (C). 1983. pap. 15.95 (0-8014-9338-2) Cornell U Pr.

Bread & Democracy in Germany. Alexander Gerschenkron. LC 88-43394. 238p. 1989. pap. 14.95 (0-8014-9586-5) Cornell U Pr.

Bread & Fire: A Novel. Charles R. Walker. LC 74-22823. reprint ed. 18.00 (0-404-58482-9) AMS Pr.

Bread & Flour Confectionery: The International Market. Euromonitor Staff. 110p. (C). 1988. 2,925.00 (0-685-30331-4, Pub. by Euromonitor Pubns UK) Gale.

Bread & Freedom: Understanding & Acting on Human Rights. Ron O'Grady. LC 81-470289. (Risk Book Ser.: No. 4). (Illus.). 87p. reprint ed. pap. 25.00 (0-7837-5996-7, 2045806) Bks Demand.

Bread & Honey. (Parents Magazine Press Read-Aloud Library). (Illus.). 42p. (J). (ps-3). 1992. lib. bdg. 13.26 (0-8368-0880-0); lib. bdg. 14.60 (0-685-61512-X) Gareth Stevens Inc.

Bread & Honey. Frank Asch. LC 81-16893. (Illus.). 48p. (J). (ps-3). 1982. 5.95 (0-8193-1077-8); lib. bdg. 5.95 (0-8193-1078-6) Parents.

Bread & Honey. Frank Asch. (Sunny Day Bks.). (Illus.). 48p. (J). (ps-2). 1992. pap. 2.95 (0-448-40319-6, G&D) Putnam Pub Group.

Bread & Hyacinths: The Rise & Fall of Utopian Los Angeles. (Illus.). 224p. (Orig.). 1992. pap. text ed. 12.95 (1-879395-21-5) CA Classics Bks.

Bread & Jam for Frances. Russell Hoban. LC 92-13622. (Illus.). 32p. (J). (ps-3). 1964. 15.00 (0-06-022359-6) HarpC Child Bks.

Bread & Jam for Frances. Russell Hoban. LC 92-13622. (Illus.). 32p. (J). (ps-3). 1965. lib. bdg. 14.89 (0-06-022360-X) HarpC Child Bks.

Bread & Jam for Frances. Russell Hoban. LC 92-13622. (Trophy Picture Bk.). (Illus.). 32p. (J). (ps-3). 1986. pap. 4.95 (0-06-443096-0, Trophy) HarpC Child Bks.

Bread & Jam for Frances: Big Book. Russell Hoban. LC 92-13622. (Trophy Picture Bk.). (Illus.). 32p. (J). (ps-3). 1993. pap. 19.95 (0-06-443336-6, Trophy) HarpC Child Bks.

Bread & Jam for Frances Literature Mini-Unit. Janet Lovelady. (Illus.). 32p. (J). (gr. 2-4). 1989. student ed 4.95 (1-56096-002-7) Mari.

Bread & Justice: State & Society in Petrograd, 1917-1922. Mary McAuley. (Illus.). 488p. 1991. 85.00 (0-19-821982-2) OUP.

Bread & Politics: Multilateral Negotiations at the FAO Governing Conference. David C. McGaffey & Pamela S. Chasek. LC 93-2865. (FPI Case Studies: No. 23). 1993. write for info. (0-941700-83-6) JH FPI SAIS.

Bread & Puppet Theatre, 2 vols., 1. Stefan Brecht. 784p. 1988. pap. text ed. 22.50 (0-413-59890-X, 9820) Routledge.

Bread & Puppet Theatre, 2 vols., 2. Stefan Brecht. 784p. 1988. pap. text ed. 22.50 (0-413-60510-8, 1092) Routledge.

Bread & Puppet Theatre, 2 vols., Set. Stefan Brecht. 784p. 1988. pap. text ed. 35.00 (0-416-01691-X, 1269) Routledge.

***Bread & Rice.** Doris Rubens. (American Autobiography Ser.). 235p. 1995. reprint ed. lib. bdg. 79.00 (0-7812-8633-6) Rprt Serv.

Bread & Roses: The Struggle of American Labor, 1865-1911. Milton Meltzer. LC 67-19485. 1977. pap. 3.95 (0-451-62396-7, Ment) NAL-Dutton.

Bread & Roses: The Struggle of American Labor, 1865-1915. Milton Meltzer. (Library of American History). (Illus.). 192p. (YA). 1990. 17.95 (0-8160-2371-9) Facts on File.

***Bread & Roses Vol. 2: Gardening Books from 1560 to 1960, Vol. 2.** Hoyles. (C). 1995. text ed. 43.95 (0-7453-0802-3, Pub. by Pluto Pr UK) Westview.

B

An Asterisk (*) at the beginning of an entry indicates that the title is appearing in BIP for the first time.

Bread & Roses from Stone. Jack Gaerity. (Shorey Lost Arts Ser.). 92p. pap. 4.95 (0-8466-0126-5, S126) Shorey.
Bread & Roses Too. Joseph R. Conlin. LC 79-95505. (Contributions in American History Ser.: No. 1). 165p. 1970. text ed. 49.95 (0-8371-2344-5, COB/, Greenwood Pr) Greenwood.
Bread & Scripture: Trailer Folks Favorite Recipe, Chapter & Verse. Annie RVer. (Illus.). 96p. 1985. pap. 8.50 (0-9613607-1-2) RVer Annie.
Bread & Spirit: Therapy with the New Poor--Diversity of Race, Culture & Values. Harry J. Aponte. 256p. 1994. 27.00 (0-393-70176-X) Norton.
Bread & Tears. Adele Brook. 1993. 12.95 (0-533-10506-4) Vantage.
Bread & the Ballot: The United States & India's Economic Development, 1947-1963. Dennis Merrill. LC 90-50012. (Illus.). xvi, 282p. (C). 1990. 45.00 (0-8078-1920-4) U of NC Pr.
Bread & the British Economy, 1770-1870. Christian Petersen. Ed. by Andrew Jenkins. 1995. 84.95 (1-85928-117-6, Pub. by Scolar Pr UK) Ashgate Pub Co.
Bread & the Liturgy: The Symbolism of Early Christian & Byzantine Bread Stamps. George Galavaris. LC 75-98120. 253p. reprint ed. pap. 72.20 (0-8357-7389-2, 2015361) Bks Demand.
Bread & the Wine, No. Sixteen. Denise Ahern. (Arch Bks.). (Illus.). (J). (gr. k-4). 1979. 1.99 (0-570-06127-X, 59-1245) Concordia.
Bread & Water. Eileen Myles. 208p. (Orig.). 1987. pap. 5.95 (0-937815-02-0) Hanuman Bks.
Bread & Water. rev. ed. Alison Knowles. (Illus.). 96p. (Orig.). 1995. pap. 18.00 (1-880516-07-1) Left Hand Bks.
Bread & Wine. Ignazio Salone. 1977. pap. 4.95 (0-451-52500-0, Sig Classics) NAL-Dutton.
Bread & Wine. Charles Watts. 40p. pap. 6.00 (0-685-56998-5) SPD-Small Pr Dist.
Bread & Wine. rev. ed. Ignazio Silone. Tr. by Harvey Fergusson, Jr. (Orig.). pap. 2.95 (0-451-51757-1, Sig Classics) NAL-Dutton.
Bread Around the World. Cynthia Rothman. (Interactive Photo Big Bks.). 16p. (J). (ps-2). 1994. pap. 14.95 (1-56784-301-8) Newbridge Comms.
Bread Baking. rev. ed. Lou S. Pappas. 176p. (Orig.). 1992. pap. 8.95 (1-55867-042-4, Nitty Gritty Ckbks) Bristol Pub Ent CA.
Bread Baking: Problems & Their Solutions. 2nd rev. ed. Ken Moore. 32p. 1992. 2.25 (0-9632986-0-7) Moores Pub.
Bread Bonanza. Kathy Bremer. (Orig.). 1986. pap. 9.50 (0-9615766-1-8, 200) Bremer Bks.
Bread Book. Gail Duff. LC 93-9232. (Illus.). 192p. 1993. text ed. 30.00 (0-02-533585-5) Macmillan.
Bread Book. Meredith Books Staff. 1994. 29.95 (0-696-02564-7) Meredith Bks.
Bread Book: A Baker's Almanac. Ellen F. Johnson. LC 94-4196. 1994. pap. 14.95 (0-88266-701-7, Garden Way Pub) Storey Comm Inc.
Bread Book: A Natural, Whole-Grain Seed-to-Loaf Approach to Real Bread. Thom Leonard. 128p. 1990. pap. 8.95 (0-936184-09-4) E W-Nat Hlth Bks.
Bread Book: More Than Two Hundred Recipes & Techniques for Baking & Shaping Perfect Breads, Sweet & Savory, Muffins, Rolls, Buns, Biscuits, & Pizzas. Betsy Oppenneer. (Illus.). 416p. 1994. 27.50 (0-06-016716-5, HarpT) HarpC.
Bread, Bread, Bread. Ann Morris. LC 82-26677. (Illus.). 32p. (J). (ps-2). 1989. 16.00 (0-688-06334-9); lib. bdg. 15.93 (0-688-06335-7) Lothrop.
Bread, Bread, Bread. Ann Morris. LC 92-25547. (Illus.). 32p. (J). (gr. k up). 1993. reprint ed. pap. 4.95 (0-688-12275-2, Mulberry) Morrow.
Bread, Bread, Bread: Big Book Edition. Ann Morris. 32p. (J). (gr. k up). 1993. pap. 18.95 (0-688-12939-0, Mulberry) Morrow.
***Bread, Bricks, & Belief: Communities in Charge of Their Future.** Mary Lean. LC 95-14670. (Kumarian Press Books for a World That Works). (Illus.). 192p. 1995. pap. 15.95 (1-56549-046-0) Kumarian Pr.
Bread Dough Creations. Susan Roach. (Illus.). 68p. 1994. pap. 7.95 (1-86351-102-4, Pub. by S Milner AT) Sterling.
***Bread for All Seasons: Distinctive Recipes for Year-Round Baking.** Beth Hensperger. LC 94-43508. (Illus.). 1995. 18.95 (0-8118-0582-4) Chronicle Bks.
Bread for Body & Soul. Jean M. Howard. (Illus.). 160p. 1987. pap. 8.95 (0-9619410-0-6) JMH Pubs-Distbrs.
Bread for the Banquet: Experiencing Life in the Spirit. Elaine M. Ward. LC 90-41011. (Kaleidoscope Ser.). 168p. (Orig.). 1990. teacher ed, pap. 9.95 (0-8298-0859-0); vhs 29.95 (0-8298-0860-4) Pilgrim OH.
Bread for the Eating. Kelly B. Kelly. 121p. (Orig.). 1982. pap. 4.95 (0-914544-39-X) Living Flame Pr.
Bread for the Journey: Resources for Worship Based on the New Ecumenical Lectionary. Ruth C. Duck. LC 81-5046. 96p. 1981. pap. 8.95 (0-8298-0423-4) Pilgrim OH.
Bread for the Journey: The Mission of Transformation & the Transformation of Mission. Anthony J. Gittins. LC 92-42152. (American Society of Missiology Ser.: No. 17). 250p. (Orig.). 1993. pap. 18.95 (0-88344-857-2) Orbis Bks.
Bread for the Living. Mary Lasswell. 1976. 18.95 (0-8488-1405-3) Amereon Ltd.
Bread for the Living. Mary Lasswell. 1981. reprint ed. lib. bdg. 19.95 (0-89966-438-5) Buccaneer Bks.
Bread for the World. rev. ed. Arthur Simon. LC 84-238017. 219p. 1985. pap. 5.95 (0-8091-2670-2) Paulist Pr.
Bread for the World. Arthur R. Simon. LC 75-16672. 189p. reprint ed. pap. 53.90 (0-8357-7390-6, 2025343) Bks Demand.
Bread from My Oven. Marjorie Parker. (Quiet Time Books for Women). 128p. 1972. pap. 3.99 (0-8024-0910-5) Moody.
Bread from Stones. Julius Hensel. LC 91-72031. 102p. 1991. pap. 10.00 (0-911311-30-0) Halcyon Hse.
Bread from Stones. Julius Hensel. 112p. 1991. pap. 7.95 (0-932298-85-0) Tri-State Pr Corp.
Bread from Stones: A New & Rational System of Land Fertilization & Physical Regeneration. Julius Hensel. 50p. 1994. reprint ed. spiral bd. 4.95 (0-7873-1006-9) Mokelumne.
Bread Givers: A Struggle Between a Father of the Old World & a Daughter of the New World. Anzia Yezierska. LC 74-25319. 320p. 1975. pap. 7.95 (0-89255-014-7) Persea Bks.
Bread, Hashish & Moon: Four Modern Arab Poets. (Keepsake Ser.: Vol. 9). 72p. 1982. 19.95 (0-87775-134-X); pap. 7.95 (0-87775-135-8) Unicorn Pr.
Bread in Half the Time: Use Your Microwave & Food Processor to Make Real Yeast Bread in 90 Minutes. Linda W. Eckhardt & Diana C. Butts. (Illus.). 352p. 1991. 25.00 (0-517-58154-X, Crown) Crown Pub Group.
Bread in the Wilderness. Merton. 1986. pap. 5.95 (0-8146-0406-4) Liturgical Pr.
Bread in Time: Breadbaking Without Angst. Stuart Silverstein. Ed. by Nancy Priest. (Illus.). 128p. (Orig.). 1990. pap. text ed. 10.00 (0-9621498-5-3, Robin Hood) R Hood Little.
Bread in Time: Breadbaking Without Angst. rev. ed. Stuart Silverstein. Ed. by Nancy Priest. (Illus.). 128p. (Orig.). reprint ed. spiral bd. 12.50 (0-9621498-9-6, Robin Hood) R Hood Little.
***Bread in Time & Bread on Earth, 2 bks., Set.** Stuart Silverstein. (Illus.). 265p. (Orig.). 1994. spiral bd. 29.50 (1-883957-02-8) R Hood Little.
Bread Is for Eating. David Gershator. (J). 1995. 14.95 (0-8050-3173-1) H Holt & Co.
Bread Loaf Anthology of Contemporary American Essays. Ed. by Robert Pack & Jay Parini. LC 88-40352. (Bread Loaf Anthology Ser.). 389p. 1989. 35.00 (0-87451-476-2); pap. 15.95 (0-87451-475-4) U Pr of New Eng.
Bread Loaf Anthology of Contemporary American Poetry. Ed. by Robert Pack et al. LC 85-40489. (Bread Loaf Anthology Ser.). 367p. 1985. pap. 17.95 (0-87451-350-2) U Pr of New Eng.
Bread Loaf Anthology of Contemporary American Short Stories. Ed. by Robert Pack & Jay Parini. LC 86-40387. (Bread Loaf Anthology Ser.). 341p. (C). 1987. 40.00 (0-87451-392-8); pap. 16.95 (0-87451-401-0) U Pr of New Eng.
Bread Machine Bakery Book: How to Bake Wonderful Homemade Breads with Your Bread Machines. Richard W. Langer. 1991. pap. 10.95 (0-316-51388-1) Little.
Bread Machine Baking: Perfect Every Time. Lora Brody & Millie Apter. LC 92-23021. 1993. 20.00 (0-688-11843-7) Morrow.
Bread Machine Baking for Better Health: Delicious Bread Recipes for Brimming Good Health. Maureen B. Keane & Daniella Chace. LC 93-35452. 1994. 12.95 (1-55958-419-X) Prima Pub.
Bread Machine Bounty: More Than 100 Recipes for Your Bread Machine. Better Homes & Gardens Staff. 144p. 1992. 14.95 (0-696-01992-2) Meredith Bks.
Bread Machine Cookbook. Melissa Clark. 208p. (Orig.). 1993. mass mkt. 4.99 (0-425-13733-3) Berkley Pub.
Bread Machine Cookbook. Donna R. German. 176p. (Orig.). 1991. pap. 8.95 (1-55867-025-4) Bristol Pub Ent CA.
Bread Machine Cookbook II. Donna R. German. (Nitty Gritty Cookbks.). 176p. (Orig.). 1991. pap. 8.95 (1-55867-037-8, Nitty Gritty Ckbks) Bristol Pub Ent CA.
Bread Machine Cookbook III. Donna R. German. 192p. (Orig.). 1992. pap. 8.95 (1-55867-048-3, Nitty Gritty Ckbks) Bristol Pub Ent CA.
Bread Machine Cookbook IV: Whole Grains & Natural Sugars. Donna R. German. 176p. (Orig.). 1992. pap. 8.95 (1-55867-049-1, Nitty Gritty Ckbks) Bristol Pub Ent CA.
Bread Machine Cookbook V: Favorite Recipes from 100 Kitchens. Donna R. German. (Illus.). 176p. (Orig.). 1994. pap. 8.95 (1-55867-093-9, Nitty Gritty Ckbks) Bristol Pub Ent CA.
***Bread Machine Cookbook VI: Hand-Shaped Breads from the Dough Cycle.** Donna R. German. (Illus.). 176p. (Orig.). 1995. pap. 8.95 (1-55867-121-8, Nitty Gritty Ckbks) Bristol Pub Ent CA.
Bread Machine Gourmet: Simple Recipes for Extraordinary Breads. Shea MacKenzie. LC 93-977. 320p. 1993. pap. 13.95 (0-89529-560-1) Avery Pub.
Bread Machine Magic. Linda Rehberg & Lois Conway. 160p. (Orig.). 1992. pap. 10.95 (0-312-06914-6) St Martin.
Bread Machine Magic Book of Helpful Hints: Dozens of Problem-Solving Hints & Troubleshooting Techniques for Getting the Most Out of Your Bread Machine. Linda Rehberg & Lois Conway. (Illus.). 224p. (Orig.). 1993. pap. 10.95 (0-312-09759-X) St Martin.
Bread Machine Sweets & Treats: Featuring Tea Breads, Coffee Cakes, & Festive Desserts for all Occasions. Richard W. Langer. LC 93-16014. (Illus.). 1993. pap. 10.95 (0-316-51391-1) Little.
***Bread Machine Wholegrain Cookbook.** Zoe Caywood. 1992. write for info. (0-614-06218-7) War Eagle Cks.
***Bread Market.** 200p. (Orig.). 1995. pap. 2,195.00 (0-7605-2207-3) Rector Pr.
***Bread Not Stone: The Challenge of Feminist Biblical Interpretation.** Elisabeth S. Fiorenza. LC 94-48473. 224p. 1995. pap. 14.00 (0-8070-1231-9) Beacon Pr.
Bread Not Stone: The Challenge of Feminist Biblical Interpretation. Elisabeth S. Fiorenza. LC 84-14669. 208p. 1986. reprint ed. pap. 14.00 (0-8070-1103-7, BP 717) Beacon Pr.
Bread of Affliction: The Food Supply in the U. S. S. R. During World War II. William Moskoff. (Cambridge Russian, Soviet & Post-Soviet Studies: No. 76). (Illus.). 576p. (C). 1990. 69.95 (0-521-37499-5) Cambridge U Pr.
Bread of Blessing, Cup of Hope. Michael E. Dixon. 144p. (Orig.). 1987. pap. 7.99 (0-8272-0450-7) Chalice Pr.
Bread of Dreams: Food & Fantasy in Early Modern Europe. Piero Camporesi. Tr. by David Gentilcore. LC 89-4689. 230p. 1989. 27.50 (0-226-09257-7) U Ch Pr.
Bread of Faith: Thematic Communion Services for the Sick & Homebound. rev. ed. George Knab. 68p. 1992. pap. 2.95 (0-9631517-1-1) Jeremiah Pr.
Bread of Life. Ken Finn. 410p. 1994. pap. 9.95 (1-882972-32-5); pap. 9.95 (1-882972-29-5) Queenship Pub.
Bread of Life. Ken Finn. 410p. 1995. pap. 9.95 (1-882972-31-7) Queenship Pub.
Bread of Life. Emma Smiley. 1972. pap. 2.50 (0-87516-157-X) DeVorss.
Bread of Life, Cycle C. Ken Finn. Tr. by Josefina Long. 410p. (SPA.). 1994. pap. 9.95 (1-882972-35-X) Queenship Pub.
Bread of Life, Cycle A. Ken Finn. Tr. by Josefina Long. 410p. 1995. pap. 9.95 (1-882972-33-3) Queenship Pub.
Bread of Life, Cycle B. Ken Finn. Tr. by Josefina Long. 410p. 1995. pap. 9.95 (1-882972-34-1) Queenship Pub.
***Bread of Life: Diaries & Memories of a Dakota Family, 1936-1945.** Marian K. Towne. LC 94-90344. (Illus.). viii, 459p. (Orig.). 1994. pap. 25.00 (0-9642666-0-1) M K Towne.
Bread of Life & Cup of Joy: Newer Ecumenical Perspectives on the Eucharist. Horton Davies. 1992. pap. 14.99 (0-8028-0252-4) Eerdmans.
Bread of Life Catholic Bible Study, Cycle B. Kenneth J. Finn & Marie A. Finn. LC 92-61784. (Orig.). 1993. pap. write for info. (0-9634553-1-1) St Dismas Guild.
Bread of Life Catholic Bible Study, Vol. A, Cycle A. Kenneth J. Finn & Marie A. Finn. LC 92-61784. 396p. (Orig.). 1992. pap. text ed. write for info. (0-9634553-0-3) St Dismas Guild.
Bread of Salt & Other Stories. N. V. Gonzalez. LC 92-43922. 224p. (C). 1993. 30.00 (0-295-97246-7); pap. 14.95 (0-295-97275-0) U of Wash Pr.
Bread of the Imagined. Ricardo Pau-Llosa. LC 91-11914. 88p. 1992. pap. 8.00 (0-927534-16-9) Biling Rev-Pr.
Bread of the Word. Carlo Martini. 1989. 4.25 (0-685-28776-9) Catholic Bk Pub.
Bread of Those Early Years. Heinrich Boll. Tr. by Leila Vennewitz. LC 94-10923. (European Classics Ser.). 133p. 1994. reprint ed. 35.00 (0-8101-1178-0); reprint ed. pap. 10.95 (0-8101-1163-2) Northwestern U Pr.
Bread of Tomorrow: Prayers for the Church Year. Ed. by Janet Morley. LC 92-5619. 192p. 1992. pap. 8.95 (0-88344-831-9) Orbis Bks.
Bread on Earth: Crafting the Primal Loaf. Stuart Silverstein. (Breadbaking Ser.). (Illus.). 130p. (Orig.). 1994. spiral bd. 12.50 (1-883957-01-X) R Hood Little.
Bread, Politics & Political Economy in the Reign of Louis XV, Set. S. L. Kaplan. (International Archives of the History of Ideas Ser.: No. 86). 1976. lib. bdg. 206.00 (90-247-1873-2) Kluwer Ac.
Bread Pudding: Fifty & More Delicious Ways to Make Bread Pudding. rev. ed. Alpha Pyramis Publishing Staff. (Illus.). 70p. 1992. 21.95 (0-913597-16-3) Prosperity & Profits.
Bread Pudding Encyclopedia: 1001 Plus Variations. Data Notes Staff. 150p. 1991. ring bd. 39.95 (0-911569-75-8) Prosperity & Profits.
Bread Pudding Recipe Greetings for the Fax Machine. Bibliotheca Press Staff. (Illus.). 56p. (Orig.). 1992. pap. text ed. 16.95 (0-939476-81-9, Biblio Pr) Prosperity & Profits.
Bread Sister of Sinking Creek. Robin Moore. LC 89-36400. (Trophy Bk.). 160p. (J). (gr. 4-7). 1992. pap. 3.95 (0-06-440357-2, Trophy) HarpC Child Bks.
Bread to Time: Toward an Autobiography. Philip Levine. LC 93-22599. 1994. 23.00 (0-679-42406-7) Knopf.
Bread upon the Water: Federal Aids to the Maritime Industries. Gerald R. Jantscher. LC 75-1067. (Brookings Institution Studies in the Regulations of Economic Activity). 176p. reprint ed. pap. 50.20 (0-8357-7391-4, 2025383) Bks Demand.
Bread upon the Waters. Marion D. Hanks. 1991. 12.95 (0-88494-808-0) Bookcraft Inc.
Bread upon the Waters. Derek Worlock. 144p. (C). 1990. 49.00 (0-85439-394-3, Pub. by St Paul Pubns UK) St Mut.
Bread upon the Waters. large type ed. Irwin Shaw. 658p. 1982. 23.95 (0-7089-8050-3, Charnwood) Ulverscroft.
Bread upon the Waters. Rose Pesotta. 464p. (Orig.). 1987. reprint ed. 39.00 (0-87546-126-3); reprint ed. pap. 15.95 (0-87546-127-1) ILR Pr.
***Bread upon the Waters.** Rose Pesotta. (American Autobiography Ser.). 435p. 1995. reprint ed. lib. bdg. 99.00 (0-7812-8616-6) Rprt Serv.
Bread, Wine & Money: The Windows of the Trades at Chartres Cathedral. Jane W. Williams. LC 92-11269. (Illus.). 248p. (C). 1993. lib. bdg. 55.00 (0-226-89912-8); pap. text ed. 22.50 (0-226-89913-6) U Ch Pr.
***Bread, Wine & Women: The Ordination Debate in the Church of England.** Sue Dowell & Jane Williams. 133p. 1995. pap. 13.95 (1-85381-730-9, Pub. by Virago Pr UK) Trafalgar.
Bread Winner. Arvella Whitmore. (J). (gr. 4-7). 1990. 14.95 (0-395-53705-3) HM.
Bread-Winners. John Hay. Ed. by Charles Vandersee. 1972. 17.95 (0-8084-0010-X); pap. 14.95 (0-8084-0011-8) NCUP.
Bread-Winners: A Social Study. John Hay. LC 67-29270. (Americans in Fiction Ser.). 319p. reprint ed. lib. bdg. 9.00 (0-8398-0773-2) Irvington.
Bread-Winners: A Social Study. John Hay. (BCL1-PS American Literature Ser.). 319p. 1992. reprint ed. lib. bdg. 89.00 (0-7812-6734-X) Rprt Serv.
Bread-Winners: A Social Study. John Hay. (Americans in Fiction Ser.). 319p. (C). 1986. reprint ed. pap. text ed. 5.95 (0-8290-2356-9) Irvington.
Bread Without Sugar: Poems. Gerald Stern. 96p. 1992. 18.95 (0-393-03094-6) Norton.
Bread Without Sugar: Poems. Gerald Stern. 128p. 1993. pap. 8.95 (0-393-31010-8) Norton.
Breadbox Philosophy. Gloria G. Broyles. 1992. pap. 9.95 (1-55673-492-1, 7942) CSS OH.
Breadfruit of Tahiti. G. P. Wilder. (BMB Ser.: No. 50). 1972. reprint ed. 25.00 (0-527-02156-3) Periodicals Srv.
Breadloaf School of English: The First Fifty Years. George K. Anderson. 1969. pap. 3.50 (0-910408-15-7) Coll Store.
Breadman's Healthy Bread Book: Use Your Bread Machine to Make More Than 100 Delicious, Healing Breads. George Burnett. 288p. 1992. 15.00 (0-688-12025-3) Morrow.
Breadman's Healthy Sandwich Book: Learn to Make More Than 65 Delicious, Low-Fat, High-Flavor Sandwiches. George Burnett. LC 93-21351. 1994. 15.00 (0-688-12968-4) Morrow.
***Breadown: Deadly Technological Disasters.** Neil Y. Schlager. 300p. 1995. pap. 15.95 (0-7876-0478-X) Visible Ink Pr.
Breads. Miriam Canter. 160p. 1989. spiral bd. 5.50 (0-941016-59-5) Penfield.
Breads. Sharon T. Herbst. LC 94-14296. 288p. 1994. pap. 13.00 (1-55788-192-8, HP Books) Berkley Pub.
Breads. Ed. by Amanda Murray. 100p. 1992. pap. 5.95 (1-882232-02-X) Kitchen Collect.
Breads. Louise Stoltzfus. LC 94-14904. (Best of Favorite Recipes from Quilters Ser.). (Illus.). 64p. 1994. 7.95 (1-56148-111-4) Good Bks PA.
Breads. Sunset Editors. 128p. 1994. 9.99 (0-376-02749-5) Sunset Menlo Pk.
Breads: From Amish & Mennonite Kitchens. Ed. by Phyllis P. Good & Rachel T. Pellman. (Pennsylvania Dutch Cookbooks Ser.). (Illus.). 32p. (Orig.). 1982. pap. 2.95 (0-934672-06-7) Good Bks PA.
Breads at the Academy. Cynthia Scheer. LC 92-43677. (California Culinary Academy Ser.). 128p. 1993. reprint ed. pap. 11.95 (1-56426-051-8, Calif Culinary Acad) Cole Group.
Bread's Biological Transmutations. rev. ed. L. C. Kervan. Ed. by Jacques De Langre. LC 78-56122. pap. 6.00 (0-916508-06-4) Happiness Pr.
***Breads, Cakes, Cookies, Sweets, & Special Food of a Midwest German Christmas.** Erin M. Renn. (Illus.). 76p. 1994. spiral bd. 10.95 (1-57216-018-7) Penfield.
Breads from the Amish & Mennonite Kitchen. Phyllis P. Good. 1991. pap. 2.95 (1-56148-036-3) Good Bks PA.
Breads of France. Bernard Clayton, Jr. 288p. 1985. pap. 18.00 (0-02-009470-1, Collier S&S) S&S Trade.
Breads of Many Lands. Florence Laffal. LC 73-94308. 1975. pap. 12.95 (0-913622-01-X) Gallery Pr.
Breadsticks & Blessing Places. Candy D. Boyd. LC 84-43021. 216p. (gr. 5-9). 1985. lib. bdg. 14.95 (0-02-709290-9, Mac Bks Young Read) S&S Childrens.
Breadth & Balance in the Primary Curriculum. Ed. by R. J. Campbell. 208p. 1993. 90.00 (0-7507-0179-X, Falmer Pr); pap. 32.50 (0-7507-0180-3, Falmer Pr) Taylor & Francis.
Breadth & Depth of Continuum Mechanics. Ed. by C. M. Dafermos et al. (Illus.). 790p. 1986. reprint ed. pap. 81.00 (0-387-16219-4) Spr-Verlag.
Breadth of Physics: Proceedings of the Peirels 80th Birthday Symposium, Oxford, United Kingdom. Ed. by R. Dalitz & R. Stinchcombe. 252p. (C). 1988. pap. 29.00 (9971-5-0520-7) World Scientific Pub.
***Breadth of the Problem: Continence Management in an Extended Care Setting.** Heather Gibb & Anne Riggs. (Research Paper Ser.: No. 3). 1992. pap. 21.00 (0-7300-1483-5, Pub. by Deakin Univ AT) St Mut.
Breadth of Vision: The Ritz Collection. Comp. by Sue Taylor. LC 92-33781. 1992. pap. 20.00 (0-944110-28-2) Milwauk Art Mus.
Breadtime Stories: A Cookbook for Bakers & Browsers. Susan J. Cheney. (Illus.). 280p. (Orig.). 1990. pap. 17.95 (0-89815-315-8) Ten Speed Pr.
Breadtime Story. Adela Turin & Margherita Saccaro. (Feminist Fables for Children Ser.). Orig. Title: Storia Di Panini. (Illus.). 32p. (J). (gr. 3-6). 1980. 6.95 (0-904613-61-5) Writers & Readers.
Breadwinners. John M. Hay. (Notable American Authors Ser.). 1992. reprint ed. lib. bdg. 75.00 (0-7812-3055-1) Rprt Serv.
Break: Habermas, Heidegger, & the Nazis: Protocol of the Sixty-First Colloquy, 5 November 1989. Hans Sluga. Ed. by Christopher Ocker. LC 92-28288. (Colloquy Ser.: Vol. 61). 1992. write for info. (0-89242-062-6) Ctr Hermeneutical.
***Break a Leg.** John O'Brien. 1983. 5.00 (0-87129-489-3) Dramatic Pub.
Break a Leg! Daily Inspiration for the Actor. Paul Boynton. Date not set. pap. 11.95 (1-880399-39-3) Smith & Kraus.
Break a Leg! Famous Curses & Superstitions. John Vornholt. LC 94-5119. (Avon Camelot Book Ser.). 96p. (Orig.). (J). 1994. pap. 3.50 (0-380-76858-5, Camelot) Avon.

An Asterisk (*) at the beginning of an entry indicates that the title is appearing in BIP for the first time.

An Asterisk (*) at the beginning of an entry indicates that the title is appearing in BIP for the first time.

889

B

B

Breaking Blue. Timothy Egan. 272p. 1993. mass mkt. 4.99 (*0-425-13815-1*) Berkley Pub.

Breaking Blue. large type ed. Timothy Egan. LC 92-23144. 473p. 1992. reprint ed. lib. bdg. 21.95 (*1-56054-514-3*) Thorndike Pr.

Breaking Boundaries. Russell Woods. LC 92-61368. 50p. 1993. 6.95 (*1-55523-560-3*) Winston-Derek.

Breaking Boundaries: Latina Writing & Critical Readings. Ed. by Asuncion Horno-Delgado et al. LC 88-17141. 288p. (Orig.). (C). 1989. pap. 16.95 (*0-87023-636-9*) U of Mass Pr.

Breaking Bounds: The Dance Photography of Lois Greenfield. William A. Ewing. (Illus.). 120p. 1992. 35.00 (*0-8118-0210-8*); pap. 22.95 (*0-8118-0232-9*) Chronicle Bks.

***Breaking Bounds: Whitman & American Cultural Studies.** Ed. by Betsy Erkkila & Jay Grossman. (Illus.). 256p. 1995. 35.00 (*0-19-509349-6*); pap. 17.95 (*0-19-509350-X*) OUP.

Breaking Bread. Joyce R. Kornblatt. 6.95 (*0-931848-86-5*) Dryad Pr.

Breaking Bread: Insurgent Black Intellectual Life. Bell Hooks & Cornel West. 174p. (Orig.). 1991. 25.00 (*0-89608-415-9*); pap. 14.00 (*0-89608-414-0*) South End Pr.

Breaking Bread: The Spiritual Significance of Food. Sara C. Juengst. 112p. (Orig.). 1992. pap. 8.99 (*0-664-25383-0*) Westminster John Knox.

Breaking Bread: The Table Talk of Jesus. M. Basil Pennington. LC 85-51008. 160p. 1986. 10.95 (*0-86683-489-3*) Harper SF.

Breaking Camp. Jill W. Boyer. LC 83-82772. (Illus.). 61p. (YA). (gr. 9-12). 1984. per. 6.00 (*0-916418-52-9*) Lotus.

Breaking Camp: Poems. Marge Piercy. LC 68-16007. (Wesleyan Poetry Program Ser.: Vol. 39). 74p. 1968. pap. 10.95 (*0-8195-1039-4*, Wesleyan Univ Pr) U Pr of New Eng.

***Breaking Chains: Hope for Adult Children of Recovering Slaves.** Anthony L. Sutton. 200p. 1994. pap. 19.95 (*0-9643587-4-3*) Southside Pride.

Breaking Chains: Social Movements & Collective Action. Ed. by Michael P. Smith. (Comparative Urban & Community Research Ser.: Vol. 3). 196p. (C). 1990. pap. text ed. 21.95x (*0-88738-860-4*) Transaction Pubs.

Breaking Controlling Powers. rev. ed. Roberts Liardon. 110p. 1991. pap. 4.95 (*1-879993-09-0*) Embassy Pub.

***Breaking Convention with Intercultural Romances: Personal Accounts.** Ed. by Dianne Dicks. 304p. 1995. pap. 12.95 (*0-89594-757-9*) Crossing Pr.

Breaking Crime's Vicious Cycle. Don Dennis. (Orig.). 1993. pap. 9.99 (*0-8054-5114-5*) Broadman.

Breaking Destructive Patterns: Multiple Strategies for Treating Partner Abuse. Janet A. Geller. 1992. text ed. 29.95 (*0-02-911605-8*) Free Pr.

Breaking down the Barricades: Reforming Export Controls to Increase U. S. Competitiveness. Irwin M. Pikus & David Earnest. LC 93-44715. (CSIS Panel Report). 82p. (Orig.). (C). (gr. 13). 1994. pap. 21.00 (*0-89206-261-4*) CSI Studies.

Breaking Down the Boundaries: Artists & Museums. Ed. by Tamara Moats. LC 89-24501. (Illus.). 32p. 1989. pap. 7.95 (*0-935558-24-1*) Henry Art.

Breaking Down the Wall: Between Americans & East Germans - Jews & Christians Through Dialogue. Ed. by Leonard Swidler. 182p. (Orig.). (C). 1987. pap. text ed. 19.50 (*0-8191-6177-2*) U Pr of Amer.

Breaking down the Wall of Science: The Liberating Experience of Facing the Painful truth. Alice Miller. 192p. 1993. pap. 10.00 (*0-452-01111-6*, Plume) NAL-Dutton.

Breaking down the Walls of New Jericho. Elkan V. Kemp. (Illus.). 185p. 1994. pap. text ed. write for info. (*1-878455-09-5*) Markas Pub.

Breaking down Walls: A Model for Reconciliation in an Age of Racial Strife. Raleigh Washington & Glen Kehrein. 256p. 1993. 14.99 (*0-8024-2642-5*) Moody.

Breaking Earth. Keith Laumer. 288p. 1988. pap. 3.50 (*0-8125-4387-4*) Tor Bks.

Breaking Even: Financial Management in Human Service Organizations. Roger A. Lohmann. LC 79-23692. 336p. 1981. pap. text ed. 24.95 (*0-87722-247-9*) Temple U Pr.

Breaking Financial Boundaries: Global Capital, National Deregulation, & Financial Services Firms. David M. Meerschwam. 320p. 1990. 35.00 (*0-87584-253-4*) Harvard Busn.

Breaking Financial Boundaries: Global Capital, National Deregulation & Financial Services Firms. David M. Meerschwan. 1991. text ed. 35.00 (*0-07-103305-X*) McGraw.

Breaking Frame: Technology & the Visual Arts in the Nineteenth Century. Julie Wosk. (Illus.). 275p. (C). 1994. reprint ed. pap. text ed. 16.95 (*0-8135-1925-X*) Rutgers U Pr.

Breaking Frame: Technology & the Visual Arts, 1820-1900. Julie Wosk. LC 92-1623. (Illus.). 275p. 1993. text ed. 40.00 (*0-8135-1924-1*) Rutgers U Pr.

Breaking Free. LouAnn Gaeddert. LC 93-22600. 144p. (J). (gr. 3-7). 1994. text ed. 14.95 (*0-689-31883-9*, Atheneum Bks Young) S&S Childrens.

Breaking Free. Ivar Lo-Johansson. Tr. by Rochelle Wright. LC 89-24971. (Modern Scandinavian Literature in Translation Ser.). viii, 478p. 1990. 45.00 (*0-8032-2891-0*) U of Nebr Pr.

Breaking Free. Pia Mellody. 1989. pap. 16.00 (*0-06-250590-4*, PL) HarpC.

***Breaking Free: A Memoir of Love & Rebellion.** Susan Eisenhower. LC 94-46563. 288p. 1995. 23.00 (*0-374-26246-2*) FS&G.

Breaking Free: A Self-Help Guide for Adults Who Were Sexually Abused As Children. Carolyn Ainscough & Kay Toon. LC 93-37229. 256p. 1993. pap. 12.95 (*1-55561-057-9*) Fisher Bks.

Breaking Free: An Anthology of Human Rights Poetry. Sel. by Robert Hull. (Illus.). 64p. (J). (gr. 7-10). 1994. 17.95 (*1-56847-196-3*) Thomson Lrning.

Breaking Free: Glasnost & the Soviet Press. Committee to Protect Journalists Staff. Ed. by Peter Tarr. 80p. 1991. pap. text ed. 10.00 (*0-944823-05-X*) Comm to Protect Jrnlists.

Breaking Free! Rescuing Families from the Clutches of Legalism. David R. Miller. LC 91-35648. 176p. 1992. pap. 9.99 (*0-8010-6288-8*) Baker Bk.

Breaking Free: Self-Reparenting for a New Life. Muriel James. 1981. pap. 11.49 (*0-201-04665-2*) Addison-Wesley.

Breaking Free: The Further Adventures of Tintin. J. Daniels. (Illus.). 175p. (Orig.). 1993. pap. 8.95 (*0-9514261-0-9*, Pub. by Attack Intl UK) AK Pr Dist.

Breaking Free from Compulsive Eating. Geneen Roth. 1986. pap. 4.50 (*0-451-16132-7*, Sig) NAL-Dutton.

Breaking Free from Compulsive Eating. Geneen Roth. LC 93-13034. 224p. 1993. reprint ed. pap. 10.95 (*0-452-27084-7*, Plume) NAL-Dutton.

Breaking Free from Corporate Bondage: Do What You Really Want to Do & Control Your Own Future. Michael Dainard. LC 92-45058. 200p. 1993. pap. 17.95 (*0-7931-0575-7*, 561406) Dearborn Finan.

Breaking Free from Domestic Violence. Jerry L. Brinegar. Ed. by Jane Noland. LC 92-11973. 176p. (Orig.). 1992. pap. 11.95 (*0-89638-263-X*) Hazelden.

Breaking Free from Domestic Violence. Jerry L. Brinegar. Ed. by Howard Pearson. 308p. (Orig.). 1990. pap. 14.95 (*1-877652-00-8*) Valet Pub.

Breaking Free from Partner Abuse: Voices of Battered Women Caught in the Cycle of Domestic Violence. enl. rev. ed. Mary Marecek. Orig. Title: Say "No!" to Violence. (Illus.). 96p. 1993. pap. 7.95 (*0-930934-74-1*) Morning Glory.

Breaking Free from the Bondage of Sin. Henry Brandt. 1994. pap. 7.99 (*1-56507-188-3*) Harvest Hse.

Breaking Free from Wedlock Deadlock: Popular Myths That Cause, Christian Truths That Cure. Paul A. Mickey. LC 88-72131. 192p. (Orig.). 1988. pap. 7.95 (*0-917851-16-1*) Bristol Hse.

Breaking Free of Addictive Family Relationships. Barry Weinhold. LC 91-65767. 230p. 1991. pap. 11.95 (*0-913299-83-9*) Stillpoint.

Breaking Free of Birth Order. Ari Kiev. 1993. mass mkt. 4.99 (*0-345-35069-3*) Ballantine.

Breaking Free of the Co-Dependency Trap. Barry K. Weinhold & Janae B. Weinhold. LC 88-62957. 245p. (Orig.). 1989. pap. 11.95 (*0-913299-49-9*) Stillpoint.

Breaking Free of the Shame Trap: How Women Get into it, How Women Get Out of It. Christine B. Evans. LC 93-14513. 320p. (Orig.). 1994. pap. 10.00 (*0-345-38703-1*, Ballantine Trade) Ballantine.

Breaking from Taylorism: Changing Forms of Work in the Automobile Industry. Ulrich Jurgens et al. LC 92-26693. (Illus.). 496p. (C). 1994. 69.95 (*0-521-40544-0*) Cambridge U Pr.

Breaking from the Line: The Songs of Fred Small. Fred Small. (Illus.). 100p. 1986. pap. 12.95 (*0-938756-13-3*) Yellow Moon.

Breaking Ground: Teachers Relate Reading & Writing in the Elementary School. Jane Hansen et al. xi, 211p. (Orig.). (C). 1985. pap. text ed. 19.50 (*0-435-08219-1*) Heinemann.

***Breaking Ground in Youth Ministry: A Manual for Developing a Parish Youth Ministry.** Robert McCarty. 64p. Date not set. write for info. (*0-89944-322-2*) Don Bosco Multimedia.

Breaking Hard Ground: Stories of the Minnesota Farm Advocates. Dianna Hunter. LC 90-82293. (Illus.). 202p. (Orig.). 1990. pap. 12.95 (*0-930100-42-5*) Holy Cow.

Breaking Hearts: The Two Sides of Unrequited Love. Roy F. Baumeister & Sara R. Wotman. LC 92-2418. 241p. 1992. lib. bdg. 30.00 (*0-89862-543-2*) Guilford Pr.

Breaking Hearts: The Two Sides of Unrequited Love. Roy F. Baumeister & Sara R. Wotman. LC 92-2418. (Emotions & Social Behavior). 1994. pap. text ed. 16.95 (*0-89862-154-2*, 2154) Guilford Pr.

Breaking Ice: An Anthology of Contemporary American Black Fiction. Ed. by Terry McMillan. 400p. 1990. pap. 14.95 (*0-14-011697-4*, Penguin Bks) Viking Penguin.

Breaking into Advertising: Making Your Portfolio Work for You. Ken Musto. (Illus.). 144p. 1988. pap. 19.95 (*0-442-26424-7*) Van Nos Reinhold.

Breaking into Broadcasting. Donn Pearlman. 224p. 1986. 17.95 (*0-933893-16-7*) Bonus Books.

Breaking Into Hollywood Before Hollywood Breaks You. Robert L. Tranchant, III & Rianna Tranchant. (Illus.). 412p. 1995. pap. text ed. 23.95 (*0-9645733-0-X*) Starmaker Prodns. BREAKING INTO HOLLYWOOD BEFORE HOLLYWOOD BREAKS YOU is a 412 page narrative & instructional book. The purpose of the book is to give the reader the knowledge of the acting, modeling, singing, dancing, & music industries. The book can give advice on overcoming challenges & obstacles & how to solve problems & by solving problems they can obtain their chosen career. Whether they pursue a career in Hollywood or their own hometown, the basics contained in the book are the same. Hollywood is synonymous with the Entertainment Industry. We write about Hollywood because that is where our experience happened. The workbook section of the book is to give the reader, through practical use of instruction from the book to train their minds to grasp the material faster & comprehend easier. We are preparing the reader by giving them a portion of the work that lies ahead & enough knowledge for them to make an intelligent decision, & to be able to decide for themselves if the profession they have chosen is what they really want to pursue. Portions of the proceeds from the sale of the Book will go to Covenant House, AMFAR, & the Jenny Jones Foundation. Ordering Information: Starmaker Productions, ISBN 0-9645733-0-X, 1-713-684- 4754 or 1-800-460-5944 Retail: $23.95 Dealer: atten. $16.75** ***Publisher Provided Annotation.

Breaking into Nests of Sick People: A Treatise on Exploitation. rev. ed. Kenneth Koym. (Illus.). 245p. 1988. spiral bd., pap. 15.95 (*0-925291-01-3*); teacher ed, pap. 18.95 (*0-925291-02-1*) Advocacy Servs Pr.

Breaking into Print: A Guide to Writing Books & Manuals. Jane Evanson & LuAnne Dowling. 128p. (C). 1993. per., pap. text ed. 16.95 (*0-8403-8513-7*) Kendall-Hunt.

***Breaking into Print: Before & After the Printing Press.** Stephen Krensky. LC 95-13839. (Illus.). (J). 1996. write for info. (*0-316-50376-2*) Little.

Breaking into Print; Being a Compilation of Papers Wherein Each of a Select Group of Authors Tells of the Difficulties of Authorship & How Such Trials Are Met. Elmer Alder. LC 68-55840. (Essay Index Reprint Ser.). 1977. reprint ed. 18.95 (*0-8369-0247-5*) Ayer.

Breaking into Prison. Michael Rickenbaker. 176p. (Orig.). 1993. pap. 7.95 (*1-882673-00-X*) Spirit & Truth.

Breaking into the Big Leagues. Al Goldis & Rick Wolff. LC 87-15320. (Illus.). 176p. 1988. pap. 12.95 (*0-88011-298-0*, PGOL0298) Human Kinetics.

Breaking into the Boardroom. Jinx Melia. 1989. mass mkt. 4.50 (*0-312-91649-3*) St Martin.

Breaking into the Catering Business: A Learning Annex Book. Kara Levine & Erika Temko. LC 94-20349. 1994. 8.95 (*0-8065-1586-4*, Citadel Pr) Carol Pub Group.

Breaking into the Current: Boatwomen of the Grand Canyon. Louise Teal. LC 93-35400. (Illus.). 200p. (Orig.). (C). 1994. lib. bdg. 25.95 (*0-8165-1413-5*); pap. 14.95 (*0-8165-1429-1*) U of Ariz Pr.

Breaking into the Movies. Charles R. Jones. 1976. lib. bdg. 59.95 (*0-8490-1553-7*) Gordon Pr.

Breaking into the Music Business. Alan H. Siegel. 1991. 22.95 (*0-671-74257-4*, Fireside); pap. 13.00 (*0-671-72907-1*) S&S Trade.

Breaking into Windows. Matthew Lake. 1993. disk, pap. 24.95 (*1-56276-144-7*) Ziff-Davis.

***Breaking into Windows: A Guide to Using Windows 95.** Bill Stott & Mark Brear. 300p. 1995. pap. 24.95 (*0-7506-2085-4*) Buttrwrth-Heinemann.

***Breaking Legs.** Tom Dulack. (Illus.). 128p. 1993. 5.99 (*1-56865-035-3*, GuildAmerica) Dblday Bk Music.

Breaking Legs. Tom Dulack. 1992. pap. 4.75 (*0-8222-0147-X*) Dramatists Play.

Breaking Loose. David Halecroft. (J). (gr. 4 up). 1990. pap. 2.95 (*0-14-034546-9*, Puffin) Puffin Bks.

Breaking New Ground. Gifford Pinchot. LC 87-82038. (Conservation Classics Ser.). (Illus.). 522p. 1987. reprint ed. pap. 19.95 (*0-933280-42-4*) Island Pr.

Breaking New Ground. Gifford Pinchot. LC 87-82038. (Conservation Classics Ser.). (Illus.). 522p. 1988. reprint ed. 35.00 (*0-933280-50-5*) Island Pr.

Breaking New Ground: American Women, 1800-1848. Michael Goldberg. (Young Oxford History of Women in the United States Ser.: Vol. 4). (Illus.). 144p. (J). 1994. lib. bdg. 20.00 (*0-19-508202-8*) OUP.

Breaking New Ground: Community-Based Development Organizations. Barbara Puls et al. (Capitols & Communities Ser.). 21p. 1991. pap. text ed. 15.00 (*1-55516-804-3*, 3908) Natl Conf State Legis.

Breaking New Ground: Developing Innovative AIDS Care Residences. Betsy Lieberman & Donald Chamberlain. LC 93-71111. 250p. 1993. pap. text ed. 39.95 (*0-9636595-0-2*) AIDS Hse WA.

Breaking New Ground: Developing Innovative AIDS Care Residences. Betsy Lieberman & Donald Chamberlain. 311p. 1993. pap. 39.95 (*0-9639595-0-6*) AIDS Hse WA.

Breaking New Ground: The History of the Autauga Quality Cotton Association. Autauga Quality Cotton Association Staff & Faye Gibbons. LC 93-17238. 1993. 30.00 (*1-881320-08-1*) Black Belt Pr.

***Breaking New Ground: Thinking & Leading in the Twenty-First Century.** Gamma Vision, Inc. Staff. 223p. 1994. ring bd. 165.00 (*1-884031-04-8*) Gamma Vision.

Breaking New Ground in U. S. Trade Policy. 153p. 1990. pap. 22.95 (*0-87186-090-2*) Comm Econ Dev.

Breaking Ninety: A History of the Country Club of Ithaca, 1900-1989. Julian C. Smith. (Illus.). 215p. (Orig.). 1990. pap. 15.00 (*0-9625479-0-5*) Country Club Ithaca.

Breaking Nuclear Ties: New Zealand's Nuclear-Free Course. Kevin P. Clements. 232p. (C). 1929. pap. text ed. 39.95 (*0-8133-1505-0*) Westview.

***Breaking of Curses.** Frank Hammond. 94p. (Orig.). 1993. pap. 4.95 (*0-89228-109-X*) Impact Christian.

Breaking of Glass Horses & Other Poems. Edward J. Rielly. 40p. 1988. pap. 4.50 (*0-9613465-9-0*) Great Elm.

Breaking of Northwall, No. 1. Paul O. Williams. 288p. 1984. pap. 5.99 (*0-345-32434-X*, Del Rey) Ballantine.

Breaking of Seals: The French Resistance in Slovakia. B. Chnoupek & K. Brusak. Tr. by R. Pynsent. LC 88-25578. 110p. 1988. text ed. 51.00 (*0-08-034869-6*, Pub. by Pergamon Repr UK) Franklin.

***Breaking of Style: Hopkins, Heaney, Graham.** Helen Vendler. (Richard Ellman Lectures in Modern Literature). 144p. (C). 1995. text ed. 29.95 (*0-674-08120-X*); pap. 14.00 (*0-674-08121-8*) HUP.

Breaking of the Day & Other Poems. Peter Davison. LC 75-21578. (Yale Series of Younger Poets: No. 60). reprint ed. 18.00 (*0-404-53860-6*) AMS Pr.

Breaking of the Seals. Francis Ashton. Ed. by Hank Stine. LC 82-2386. (Illus.). 360p. 1982. pap. 6.95 (*0-89865-200-6*, Starblaze) Donning Co.

Breaking of the Treaty by the United States: By Keeping Nuclear Weapons "In Transit" on the Island, & Using It for Military Attacks in the Caribbean. Louise Cripps. 178p. 1989. pap. 6.95 (*0-685-28344-5*) Borinquen Bks.

Breaking Old Patterns Weaving New Ties: Alliance Building. Margo Adair & Sharon Howell. (Orig.). 1990. pap. 4.50 (*1-882098-24-2*) Tools Change.

Breaking Open the Gospel of Luke. Gerard P. Weber & Robert Miller. 101p. 1990. 5.95 (*0-86716-138-8*) St Anthony Mess Pr.

Breaking Open the Gospel of Mark. Gerard P. Weber & Robert Miller. 1994. write for info. (*0-86716-192-2*) St Anthony Mess Pr.

Breaking Open the Word of God: Resources for Using the Lectionary for Catechesis in the RCIA (Cycle A) Ed. by Karen H. Hinman & Joseph P. Sinwell. 192p. (Orig.). 1987. pap. 12.95 (*0-8091-2894-2*) Paulist Pr.

Breaking Open the Word of God: Resources for Using the Lectionary for Catechesis in the RCIA (Cycle A) Karen M. Hinman & Joseph P. Sinwell. 208p. (Orig.). 1986. pap. 12.95 (*0-8091-2822-5*) Paulist Pr.

Breaking Open the Word of God: Resources for Using the Lectionary for Catechists in the RCIA (Cycle C) Ed. by Karen H. Powell & Joseph P. Sinwell. 192p. (Orig.). 1988. pap. 12.95 (*0-8091-2973-6*) Paulist Pr.

Breaking Out. Barthe DeClements. (J). (gr. 4-7). 1993. pap. 3.50 (*0-440-40802-4*) Dell.

Breaking Out Again: Feminist Ontology & Epistomology. rev. ed. Liz Stanley & Sue Wise. LC 92-28809. 256p. 1993. pap. 15.95 (*0-415-07271-9*, B0233, Routledge NY) Routledge.

Breaking Out Again: Feminist Ontology & Epistomology. 2nd rev. ed. Liz Stanley & Sue Wise. LC 92-28809. 256p. 1993. 49.95 (*0-415-07270-0*, B0229, Routledge NY) Routledge.

Breaking out of Beginner's Spanish. Joseph J. Keenan. LC 94-4316. 232p. (ENG & SPA.). (C). 1994. text ed. 27.50x (*0-292-74321-1*); pap. 10.95 (*0-292-74322-X*) U of Tex Pr.

Breaking Out of Nine to Five: How to Revise Your Job to Fit You. Maria Laqueur & Donna Dickinson. 256p. (Orig.). 1994. pap. 12.95 (*1-56079-351-1*) Petersons Guides.

***Breaking Point: A Guide to Preventing Occupational Overuse Syndrome.** Pluto Press Staff. LC 95-1684. (International Labour Series, 1351-4530). (C). 1995. pap. text ed. 9.95 (*0-7453-1022-2*) Westview.

Breaking Political Gridlock: California's Experiment in Public-Private Cooperation for Hazardous Waste Policy. Daniel A. Mazmanian et al. LC 88-15342. (Environmental Studies: No. 8). (Illus.). 104p. (Orig.). 1988. pap. 20.00 (*0-912102-86-1*) Cal Inst Public.

Breaking Ranks. Melissa Everett. (Illus.). 252p. (Orig.). 1988. 39.95 (*0-86571-134-8*); pap. 14.95 (*0-86571-135-6*) New Soc Pubs.

Breaking Rules: Alternatives for Language Teachers. John Fanselow. (Reference Books-Methodology Ser.). (Illus.). 500p. (C). 1987. pap. text ed. 39.90 (*0-582-79733-0*, 74989) Longman.

Breaking Silence: An Anthology of Contemporary Asian American Poets. Intro. by Joseph Bruchac. LC 83-80759. 300p. (Orig.). 1984. pap. 9.95 (*0-912678-59-3*, Greenfld Rev Pr) Greenfld Rev Lit.

***Breaking Silence: Coming-Out Letters.** Bohlin-Davis et al. 128p. 1995. pap. 12.00 (*0-9638295-5-6*) Xanthus Pr.

Breaking Silence Before the Lord. E. Lee Phillips. (Pulpit Library). 160p. 1986. pap. 5.99 (*0-8010-7093-7*) Baker Bk.

***Breaking Silences: Asian Americans Today.** Ronald Takaki. (The Asian American Experience Ser.). (Illus.). 128p. (YA). (gr. 5 up). 1995. 18.95 (*0-7910-2183-1*) Chelsea Hse.

Breaking Story: South African Press. Gordon S. Jackson. 308p. (C). 1993. text ed. 37.00 (*0-8133-8453-2*) Westview.

Breaking Strain. Paul Preuss. (Arthur C. Clarke's Venus Prime Ser.: Vol. 1). 272p. 1987. mass mkt. 4.99 (*0-380-75344-8*) Avon.

Breaking Strongholds: How Spiritual Warfare Can Reap a Harvest of Evangelism. Thomas B. White. 200p. (Orig.). 1993. pap. 8.99 (*0-89283-782-9*, Vine Bks) Servant.

***Breaking Strongholds in the African-American Family: Strategies for Spiritual Warfare.** Clarence Walker. 160p. 1995. pap. 9.99 (*0-310-20007-5*) Zondervan.

An Asterisk (*) at the beginning of an entry indicates that the title is appearing in BIP for the first time.

An Asterisk (*) at the beginning of an entry indicates that the title is appearing in BIP for the first time.

Breaking Traditions: The Fiction of Clemente Palma. Nancy M. Kason. LC 86-73238. 136p. 1988. 29.50 (0-8387-5124-5) Bucknell U Pr.

Breaking Trail in the Central Appalachians - A Narrative. David Bates. LC 87-72050. 194p. 12.50 (0-915746-35-2) Potomac Appalach.

***Breaking Up.** David W. Felder. 1995. pap. text ed. 5.00 (0-910959-84-6, B&G 16E) Felder Bks.

Breaking Up. Norma Klein. 176p. 1981. pap. 2.50 (0-380-55830-0, Flare) Avon.

Breaking Up: From Heartache to Happiness in 48 Pages. Yolanda Nave. LC 84-40680. (Illus.). 48p. (Orig.). 1984. pap. 3.95 (0-89480-839-7, 839) Workman Pub.

Breaking up Is Hard to Do. Bruce Hart & Carole Hart. LC 86-90994. 256p. (YA). (gr. 7 up). 1987. mass mkt. 3.99 (0-380-89970-1, Flare) Avon.

Breaking up Is Hard to Do: Stories by Women. Alta et al. Ed. by Amber C. Sumrall. 1994. pap. 14.95 (0-89594-654-8) Crossing Pr.

Breaking up? Moving On . . . Carlan M. Robinson. LC 89-92013. (Illus.). 54p. 1989. pap. 14.95 (0-9623896-0-9) Cable Pub.

Breaking up the Bank: Rethinking an Industry under Seige. Lowell L. Bryan. 200p. 1988. text ed. 50.00 (1-55623-144-X) Irwin Prof Pubng.

Breaking Vicious Circles. H. J. Wahler. Ed. by Deborah Batjer. LC 89-92750. (Illus.). 170p. (Orig.). 1991. pap. text ed. 9.95 (0-9625926-0-9) Sky Island Pr.

Breaking Violence in a Relationship: Co-Dependent. Janet A. Blue. LC 94-65724. (Orig.). 1994. pap. 7.98 (1-882786-28-9) New Dawn NY.

Breaking Wave. Nevil S. Norway. 22.95 (0-405-18913-3) Ayer.

Breaking Wave. Nevil Shute. 21.95 (0-88411-315-9, Aeonian Pr) Amereon Ltd.

Breaking Wave. Nevil Shute. 224p. 1984. pap. 3.50 (0-345-32173-1) Ballantine.

Breaking Waves: IUTAM Symposium, Sydney, Australia, 1991. Ed. by M. L. Banner & R. H. Grimshaw. LC 92-30806. 1992. 129.00 (0-387-55944-2) Spr-Verlag.

Breaking Which Brings Us Anew: Poems. Charles Taylor. 1978. 7.95 (0-913152-01-3) Folder Edns.

Breaking with Burr: Harman Blennerhassett's Journal, 1807. Ed. by Raymond E. Fitch. LC 86-23814. (Illus.). 230p. 1988. 34.95 (0-8214-0860-7) Ohio U Pr.

Breaking with Communism: The Intellectual Odyssey of Bertram D. Wolfe. Ed. by Robert Hessen. (Publication Series: Archival Documentaries: No. 388). 311p. 1990. 24.95 (0-8179-8881-5); pap. 18.95 (0-8179-8882-3) Hoover Inst Pr.

Breaking with Moscow. Arkady N. Shevchenko. 512p. 1985. mass mkt. 4.95 (0-345-30088-2) Ballantine.

Breaking with Tradition. Felice N. Schwartz & Jean Zimmerman. 352p. 1992. 22.95 (0-446-51600-7) Warner Bks.

Breaking with Tradition: Diversity, Conflict & Change in Contemporary American Families. Marcia E. Bedard. LC 91-75940. 228p. 1992. lib. bdg. 36.95 (0-930390-15-6); pap. text ed. 18.95 (0-930390-14-8) Gen Hall.

Breaking with Tradition: Women & Work, the New Facts of Life. Felice N. Schwartz. 416p. 1993. pap. 12.99 (0-446-39480-7) Warner Bks.

Breaking Writer's Block..Write Now. John Wolcott. 70p. 1983. pap. 6.95 (0-931435-01-3) Features NW.

Breaking Your Addiction Habit. Billie J. Sahley & Katherine M. Birkner. LC 90-60548. (Illus.). 125p. (Orig.). 1990. pap. text ed. 8.95 (0-9625914-0-8) Pain & Stress.

Breaking Your Barriers: Living Life Without Limitations. Keith Hershey. 59p. (Orig.). 1989. pap. 3.95 (0-940487-01-2) Jubilee CA.

Breaking Your Child's TV Addiction: A Guide for Parents. David P. Demers. LC 88-62927. (Orig.). 1989. pap. 9.95 (0-922993-00-9) Marquette Bks.

Breaking Your Horse's Bad Habits. W. Dayton Sumner. (Illus.). 1984. reprint ed. text ed. 17.95 (0-914327-07-0) Breakthrgh NY.

Breaking Your Horse's Bad Habits. W. Dayton Sumner. 1977. reprint ed. pap. 10.00 (0-87980-334-7) Wilshire.

Breaking Your Time Barrier: Becoming A Strategic Time Manager. Ross A. Webber. 368p. 1991. pap. text ed. write for info. (0-13-085374-7) P-H.

Breakout: Profiles in African Rhythm. Gary Stewart. LC 91-30279. (Illus.). 168p. 1992. pap. 12.95 (0-226-77406-6) U Ch Pr.

***Breakout: The Evolving Threat of Drug-Resistant Disease.** Marc Lappe. LC 95-12016. Orig. Title: Revolutionary Medicine. (Illus.). 272p. 1995. pap. 14.00 (0-87156-382-7) Sierra.

Breakpoint: Business Process Redesign. Robert A. King et al. (Illus.). 160p. 1992. 39.95 (0-944533-04-3) Coopers Total Qlty.

Breakpoint & Beyond: Mastering the Future - Today. Beth J. Georgeland. (Illus.). 288p. 1993. pap. 13.00 (0-88730-604-7) Harper Busn.

Breakpoints: How Managers Exploit Radical Business Change. Paul Strebel. LC 92-10438. 272p. 1992. 27.95 (0-87584-369-7) Harvard Busn.

Breakpoints: How Managers Exploit Radical Business Change. Paul Strebel. 1992. pap. text ed. 27.95 (0-07-103376-9) McGraw.

Breaks. Richard Price. (Contemporary American Fiction Ser.). 448p. 1984. pap. 11.00 (0-14-007037-0, Penguin Bks) Viking Penguin.

Breaks in Monetary Series. S. L. Topping & S. L. Bishop. (Bank of England. Discussion Papers. Technical Ser.: No. 23). 88p. reprint ed. pap. 25.10 (0-8357-7907-6, 2036335) Bks Demand.

Breaks of the Game. David Halberstam. 480p. 1983. mass mkt. 5.99 (0-345-29625-7) Ballantine.

Breakthrough. Daisy Aldan. 1971. lib. bdg. 9.95 (0-913152-02-1) Folder Edns.

Breakthrough. Jason Winters. 66p. 1986. pap. 6.00 (1-885026-01-3) Vinton Pubng.

Breakthrough: Emerging New Thinking. Ed. by Anatoly Gromyko & Martin Hellman. LC 87-23009. 1988. 19.95 (0-8027-1015-8); pap. 9.95 (0-8027-1026-3) Walker & Co.

Breakthrough: Insights of the Great Religious Discoverers. Clifford G. Hospital. LC 85-5135. 208p. (Orig.). reprint ed. pap. 59.30 (0-7837-5516-3, 2045286) Bks Demand.

Breakthrough: Meister Eckhart's Creation Spirituality. Meister Eckhart. LC 80-909. 600p. 1980. 15.95 (0-385-17034-3, Image Bks) Doubleday.

Breakthrough: Stories of Conversion. Andre Papineau. (Illus.). 152p. (C). 1988. pap. 7.95 (0-89390-128-8) Resource Pubns.

Breakthrough: Tactics, Technology, & the Search for Victory on the Western Front in World War I. Hubert C. Johnson. LC 93-41188. 322p. 1994. 24.95 (0-89141-505-X) Presidio Pr.

Breakthrough: The Emergence of the Ecumenical Tradition. Robert S. Bilheimer. LC 89-7705. 245p. (Orig.). reprint ed. pap. 69.90 (0-7837-3179-5, 2042783) Bks Demand.

***Breakthrough: The Next Step.** Whitley Strieber. 1995. 23.00 (0-06-017653-9) HarpC.

Breakthrough: Women in Archaeology. Barbara Williams. LC 80-7687. (Walker's Breakthrough Ser.). (Illus.). 174p. (J). 1981. 9.95 (0-8027-6406-1) Walker & Co.

Breakthrough: Women in Politics. Barbara Williams. (Breakthrough Ser.). (Illus.). 1979. 9.95 (0-8027-6366-9) Walker & Co.

Breakthrough Advertising: How to Write Ads That Shatter Traditions & Sales Records. Eugene Schwartz. LC 84-2797. 236p. 1984. reprint ed. 50.00 (0-932648-54-1) Boardroom.

Breakthrough Bird Taxidermy Manual. Sallie Dahmes. Ed. by Bob Williamson & Ken Edwards. (Illus.). 156p. (C). 1988. pap. text ed. 24.95 (0-925245-08-9) WASCO Manufact.

Breakthrough Bridge. C. Knutson. 24p. (Orig.). 1985. pap. 2.00 (0-938451-00-6) Selena Pr.

Breakthrough Business Management Manual. Bob Williamson. (Illus.). 100p. (C). 1986. pap. text ed. 14.95 (0-925245-00-3) WASCO Manufact.

Breakthrough Business Meetings: Shared Leadership in Action. Robert E. Levasseur. 1994. pap. 8.95 (1-55850-395-1) Adams Pubng.

Breakthrough Creativity! Developing Ideas That Make a Difference. Marlene Caroselli. LC 94-14081. 98p. 1994. pap. 14.95 (0-527-76244-X) Qual Resc.

Breakthrough Dreaming: How to Tap the Power of Your 24-Hour Mind. Gayle Delaney. 1991. pap. 14.50 (0-553-35281-4) Bantam.

Breakthrough Fictioneers. Ed. by Richard Kostelanetz. LC 72-75710. (C). 1978. reprint ed. 50.00 (0-932360-17-3); reprint ed. pap. 30.00 (0-932360-16-5) Archae Edns.

Breakthrough Fish Carving Manual. Mark Frazier. Ed. by Ken Edwards. (Illus.). 160p. (C). 1994. pap. text ed. 24.95 (0-925245-12-7) WASCO Manufact.

Breakthrough Fish Painting Encyclopedia. rev. ed. Jim Hall & Tom Sexton. Ed. by Bob Williamson & Ken Edwards. (Illus.). 156p. (C). 1987. reprint ed. pap. text ed. 24.95 (0-925245-01-1) WASCO Manufact.

Breakthrough Fish Taxidermy Manual. rev. ed. Tom Sexton et al. Ed. by Ken Edwards. (Illus.). 162p. (C). 1988. reprint ed. pap. text ed. 24.95 (0-925245-06-2) WASCO Manufact.

Breakthrough for Back Pain! William V. Zucker & Brian W. Nelson. (Illus.). 213p. (Orig.). 1992. pap. 15.00 (0-9634440-0-X) Lester St Pub.

Breakthrough from Colonialism: An Interdisciplinary Study of Statehood, 2 Vols., I. Grupo de Investigadores Puertorriquenos Staff. LC 83-1326. xxiv, 1532p. pap. 20.00 (0-8477-2489-1) U of PR Pr.

Breakthrough from Colonialism: An Interdisciplinary Study of Statehood, 2 Vols., II. Grupo de Investigadores Puertorriquenos Staff. LC 83-1326. xxiv, 1532p. pap. 20.00 (0-8477-2490-5) U of PR Pr.

Breakthrough from Colonialism: An Interdisciplinary Study of Statehood, 2 Vols., Set. Grupo de Investigadores Puertorriquenos Staff. LC 83-1326. xxiv, 1532p. pap. 40.00 (0-8477-2491-3) U of PR Pr.

Breakthrough Habitat & Exhibit Manual. Bob Williamson et al. Ed. & Illus. by Ken Edwards. 156p. (C). 1986. pap. text ed. 24.95 (0-925245-07-0) WASCO Manufact.

Breakthrough Illusion: Corporate America's Failure to Move from Innovation to Mass Production. Richard Florida & Martin Kenney. LC 90-80248. (Illus.). 272p. 1992. pap. 13.00 (0-465-00760-0) Basic.

Breakthrough in Burma: Memoirs of a Revolution, 1939-1946. LC 67-24504. 504p. reprint ed. pap. 143.70 (0-8357-7395-7, 2003688) Bks Demand.

Breakthrough in Making Computers Friendly: The Macintosh Computer. Arden Group Staff & James Martin. (Illus.). 320p. 1985. text ed. 44.00 (0-13-081589-6); pap. 26.95 (0-685-10930-5) P-H.

Breakthrough in Making Computers Friendly: The Macintosh Computer. James Martin. write for info. (0-318-59634-2) S&S Trade.

Breakthrough in Medicine: From Superstition to Empirical & Scientific Medicine. David Erlik. 204p. 1992. 19.95 (965-229-078-5, Pub. by Gefen Pub Hse IS) Gefen Bks.

Breakthrough (La Brecha in Translation) Mercedes Valdivieso. Ed. by Yvette E. Miller. Tr. by Graciela Daichman. LC 87-33909. 96p. 1987. pap. 12.00 (0-935480-33-1) Lat Am Lit Rev Pr.

***Breakthrough Leadership: Achieving Organizational Alignment Through Hoshin Planning.** Mara M. Melum & Casey Collett. LC 94-48029. 1995. write for info. (1-55648-133-0) AHPI.

Breakthrough Mammal Taxidermy Manual. Jim Hall & Brent Housekeeper. Ed. by Bob Williamson. (Illus.). 160p. (C). 1990. pap. text ed. 24.95 (0-925245-09-7) WASCO Manufact.

***Breakthrough Management: How to Convert Objectives into Results.** Giorgio Merli. 1995. text ed. 39.95 (0-471-95351-2) Wiley.

Breakthrough Manual. Paul McGuire. 320p. (Orig.). 1992. pap. 9.95 (0-88270-658-6) Bridge Pub.

Breakthrough on Skis. Lito Tejada-Flores. LC 86-40146. (Illus.). 224p. 1986. pap. 11.00 (0-394-74703-8, Vin) Random.

Breakthrough on Skis: How to Get Out of the Intermediate Rut. Lito Tejada-Flores. 1993. pap. 12.00 (0-679-75081-9) Random.

Breakthrough on the Color Front. rev. ed. Lee Nichols. LC 93-24153. 1993. 24.00 (0-89410-771-2); pap. 15.00 (0-89410-772-0) Three Continents.

Breakthrough Parenting: Unlock the Secrets to a Great Relationship with Your Children. A. Jayne Major. 192p. 1993. pap. 9.95 (0-925190-69-1) Fairview Press.

Breakthrough Partnering: Creating a Collective Enterprise Advantage. Patricia E. Moody. LC 93-60669. 256p. 1993. 75.00 (0-939246-39-2) Oliver Wight.

Breakthrough Performance: Managing for Speed & Flexibility. William R. Daniels. Ed. by PRC, Inc. Staff. 1994. pap. 19.95 (1-882939-01-8) ACT Pub.

Breakthrough Performance: Managing for Speed & Flexibility. William R. Daniels. Ed. by PRC, Inc. Staff. 1994. 29.95 (1-882939-00-X) ACT Pub.
This book is for the REAL MANAGERS at work - individual contributors - & their bosses who want to encourage them to be more pro-active. With flatter & flatter organizations demanding more speed & flexibility, EVERYONE MUST MANAGE THEMSELVES & THEIR PEERS. Personal & organizational survival is at stake. For over 21 years clients like Intel, Motorola, Levi Strauss & Co., Xilinx & Northwestern Mutual Life Insurance have relied on Bill Daniels' system to achieve & sustain ever-increasing levels of productivity. Highlights of BREAKTHROUGH PERFORMANCE include how to: work successfully with the formal & informal power structures, develop a personal performance plan that focuses on key results, keep goals aligned with others, get into Breakthrough Systems (clear expectations, informal feedback systems & resource control), create a learning-rich environment. It also addresses that most vital skill of coordination: how to create real teamwork at meetings. Daniels' profound understanding of how organizations really work is shared in a practical, inviting text that offers readers a way to increase their value to their organizations. An easy read with a powerful message, each chapter has worksheets & guidelines that invite readers to take immediate action, either alone or in teams, one step at a time. Absolutely indispensable for anyone concerned about staying vital at work. To order: American Consulting & Training, Inc., 655 Redwood Highway, #395, Mill Valley, CA 94941; 415-388-6651; 800-995-6651; Fax: 415-388-6672.
Publisher Provided Annotation.

Breakthrough Process Redesign: New Pathways to Building Customer Value. Charlene B. Adair. 240p. 1993. 24.95 (0-8144-5150-0) AMACOM.

Breakthrough Quality Improvement for Leaders who Want Results. Robert F. Wickman & Robert S. Doyle. LC 93-13578. 221p. 1993. 27.95 (0-87389-213-5) ASQC Qual Pr.

Breakthrough Rapid Reading. Peter Kump. 256p. 1979. pap. 5.95 (0-13-081554-3, Reward) P-H.

Breakthrough Reptile & Amphibian Taxidermy Manual. Ken Edwards. Ed. by Bob Williamson. (Illus.). 172p. (C). 1992. pap. text ed. 24.95 (0-925245-11-9) WASCO Manufact.

Breakthrough Strategy. Robert H. Schaffer. 1990. pap. 17.00 (0-88730-404-4) Harper Busn.

Breakthrough Tennis: A Revolutionary Approach to the Game. Rolf Clark. LC 91-3070. (Illus.). 155p. (Orig.). 1991. pap. 9.95 (0-918535-11-5) Farragut Pub.

Breakthrough Thinking. Gerald Nadler & Shozo Hibino. 1989. 22.95 (1-55958-004-6) Prima Pub.

Breakthrough Thinking. 2nd rev. ed. Gerald Nadler & Shozo Hibino. LC 93-23559. 1994. 24.95 (1-55958-421-1) Prima Pub.

Breakthrough Thinking in Total Quality Management. Glen D. Hoffherr & Gerald Nadler. LC 93-4328. 434p. Date not set. 29.95 (0-13-090820-7) P-H.

Breakthrough to Creativity. Shafica Karagulla. 1967. pap. 13.95 (0-87516-034-4) DeVorss.

Breakthrough to Higher Psychism. Torkom Saraydarian. LC 90-90140. 150p. 1990. pap. 10.95 (0-929874-15-3) TSG Pub Found.

Breakthrough to Literacy, 3 bks., Bk. 1. J. Motta & K. Riley. 1981. pap. write for info. (0-318-50127-9); teacher ed, pap. write for info. (0-318-50128-7) Addison-Wesley.

Breakthrough to Literacy, 3 bks., Bk. 2. J. Motta & K. Riley. 1981. teacher ed write for info. (0-318-50130-9); Bk.2. write for info. (0-318-50129-5) Addison-Wesley.

Breakthrough to Literacy, 3 bks., Bk. 3. J. Motta & K. Riley. 1981. write for info. (0-318-50131-7) Addison-Wesley.

Breakthrough to Math, Level 1: Basic Skills with Whole Numbers, Reading Level 3-5. 1993. Set, incl. all material for level 1. 33.00 (0-88336-801-3); student ed 3.75 (0-88336-808-0); teacher ed 4.25 (0-88336-807-2); 4.00 (0-88336-847-1); 0.50 (0-88336-816-1); 1.00 (0-88336-848-X); 0.75 (0-88336-849-8) New Readers.

Breakthrough to Math, Level 1: Basic Skills with Whole Numbers, Reading Level 3-5, Bk. 1: Understanding Numbers. 1993. 3.75 (0-88336-810-2) New Readers.

Breakthrough to Math, Level 1: Basic Skills with Whole Numbers, Reading Level 3-5, Bk. 2: Adding Whole Numbers. 1993. 3.75 (0-88336-811-0) New Readers.

Breakthrough to Math, Level 1: Basic Skills with Whole Numbers, Reading Level 3-5, Bk. 3: Subtracting Whole Numbers. 1993. 3.75 (0-88336-812-9) New Readers.

Breakthrough to Math, Level 1: Basic Skills with Whole Numbers, Reading Level 3-5, Bk. 4: Multiplying Whole Numbers. 1993. 3.75 (0-88336-813-7) New Readers.

Breakthrough to Math, Level 1: Basic Skills with Whole Numbers, Reading Level 3-5, Bk. 5: Dividing Whole Numbers. 1993. 3.75 (0-88336-814-5) New Readers.

Breakthrough to Math, Level 1: Basic Skills with Whole Numbers, Reading Level 3-5, Bk. 6: Word Problems with Whole Numbers. 1993. 3.75 (0-88336-815-3) New Readers.

Breakthrough to Math, Level 2: Fractions, Decimals & Percents, Reading Level 4. 1993. Set, incl. all material for level 2. 33.00 (0-88336-802-1); student ed 3.75 (0-88336-829-3); teacher ed 4.25 (0-88336-827-7); write for info. (0-318-70327-0); 0.50 (0-88336-826-9); write for info. (0-318-70325-4); write for info. (0-318-70326-2) New Readers.

Breakthrough to Math, Level 2: Fractions, Decimals & Percents, Reading Level 4, Bk. 1: Understanding & Comparing Fractions. 1993. 3.75 (0-88336-820-X) New Readers.

Breakthrough to Math, Level 2: Fractions, Decimals & Percents, Reading Level 4, Bk. 2: Adding & Subtracting Fractions. 1993. 3.75 (0-88336-821-8) New Readers.

Breakthrough to Math, Level 2: Fractions, Decimals & Percents, Reading Level 4, Bk. 3: Multiplying & Dividing Fractions. 1993. 3.75 (0-88336-822-6) New Readers.

Breakthrough to Math, Level 2: Fractions, Decimals & Percents, Reading Level 4, Bk. 4: Decimal Fractions. 1993. 3.75 (0-88336-823-4) New Readers.

Breakthrough to Math, Level 2: Fractions, Decimals & Percents, Reading Level 4, Bk. 5: Percents. 1993. 3.75 (0-88336-824-2) New Readers.

Breakthrough to Math, Level 2: Fractions, Decimals & Percents, Reading Level 4, Bk. 6: Word Problems with Fractions, Decimals & Pe. 1993. 3.75 (0-88336-825-0) New Readers.

Breakthrough to Math, Level 3: Algebra, Reading Level 5, 5 bks. 1993. Set, incl. all material for Level 3. 33.50 (0-88336-803-X); student ed 5.00 (0-88336-806-4); teacher ed 4.75 (0-88336-805-6); write for info. (0-318-70330-0); 0.50 (0-88336-836-6); write for info. (0-318-70328-9); write for info. (0-318-70329-7) New Readers.

Breakthrough to Math, Level 3: Algebra, Reading Level 5, 5 bks., Bk. 1: Signed Numbers. 1993. 4.25 (0-88336-830-7) New Readers.

Breakthrough to Math, Level 3: Algebra, Reading Level 5, 5 bks., Bk. 2: Solving Equations. 1993. 4.25 (0-88336-831-5) New Readers.

Breakthrough to Math, Level 3: Algebra, Reading Level 5, 5 bks., Bk. 3: Word Problems in Algebra. 1993. 4.25 (0-88336-832-3) New Readers.

Breakthrough to Math, Level 3: Algebra, Reading Level 5, 5 bks., Bk. 4: Exponents, Roots & Polynomials. 1993. 4.25 (0-88336-833-1) New Readers.

Breakthrough to Math, Level 3: Algebra, Reading Level 5, 5 bks., Bk. 5: Algebraic Graphs. 1993. 4.25 (0-88336-834-X) New Readers.

Breakthrough to Math, Level 4: Geometry, Reading Level 5. 1993. Set, incl. all material for level 4. 23.85 (0-88336-804-8); student ed 3.25 (0-88336-835-8); teacher ed 4.25 (0-88336-809-9); write for info. (0-318-70333-5); 0.50 (0-88336-846-3); write for info. (0-318-70331-9); write for info. (0-318-70332-7) New Readers.

Breakthrough to Math, Level 4: Geometry, Reading Level 5, Bk. 1: Lines & Angles. 1993. 4.25 (0-88336-840-4) New Readers.

Breakthrough to Math, Level 4: Geometry, Reading Level 5, Bk. 2: Triangles & Quadrangles. 1993. 4.25 (0-88336-841-2) New Readers.

Breakthrough to Math, Level 4: Geometry, Reading Level 5, Bk. 3: Circles & Volume. 1993. 4.25 (0-88336-842-0) New Readers.

Breakthrough to Shakespeare. Forbes J. Monaghan. LC 76-29144. 1979. 12.00 (0-916620-07-7) Portals Pr.

892
An Asterisk (*) at the beginning of an entry indicates that the title is appearing in BIP for the first time.

Breakthrough to the Big League: The Story of Jackie Robinson. Jackie Robinson & Alfred Duckett. LC 90-48588. (American Cavalcade Ser.). (Illus.). 160p. (J). (gr. 6-10). 1991. lib. bdg. 9.95 (*1-55905-094-2*) Marshall Cavendish.

Breakthrough Waterfowl & Bird Finishing Manual. Kelly Seibels. Ed. by Bob Williamson & Ken Edwards. (Illus.). 192p. (C). 1987. pap. text ed. 24.95 (*0-925245-02-X*) WASCO Manufact.

Breakthrough Whitetail Taxidermy Manual. rev. ed. Bob Williamson & Tom Sexton. Ed. by Ken Edwards. (Illus.). 112p. (C). 1987. reprint ed. pap. text ed. 19.95 (*0-925245-05-4*) WASCO Manufact.

Breakthroughs: A Chronology of Great Achievements in Science & Mathematics, 1200-1930. Claire L. Parkinson. (Reference Books - Science). (Illus.). 624p. 1985. text ed. 40.00 (*0-8161-8706-1*, Hall Reference) Macmillan.

Breakthroughs! How Leadership & Drive Created Commerical Innovations That Sweep the World. John M. Ketteringham & P. Ranganath Nayak. 400p. 1993. 22.95 (*0-89384-250-8*) Pfeiffer & Co.

Breakthroughs: Re-Creating the American City. Neal R. Peirce & Robert Guskind. LC 93-17189. 203p. (C). 1993. text ed. 24.95 (*0-88285-145-4*) Ctr Urban Pol Res.

***Breakthroughs & Integragation.** Rowan. 1992. 49.95 (*1-56593-579-9*, 0310) Singular Publishing.

Breakthroughs in Commodity Technical Analysis 1985. J. D. Hamon. 65.00 (*0-930233-01-8*) Windsor.

Breakthroughs in Family Therapy with Drug Abusing & Problem Youth. Jose Szapocznik & William Kurtines. 208p. 1989. 26.95 (*0-8261-6850-7*) Springer Pub.

***Breakthroughs in Natural Healing.** David G. Williams. 25p. 1992. pap. 9.95 (*0-944649-09-2*) Mtn Home Pub.

Breakthroughs in Statistics, 2 vols. Ed. by N. I. Johnson et al. Vols. I & II. (Illus.). 1991. write for info. (*0-318-68828-X*) Spr-Verlag.

Breakthroughs in Statistics, 2 vols., Vol. 1: Fundations & Basic Theory. Ed. by N. I. Johnson et al. (Series in Statistics: Perspectives in Statistics: Vols. I & II). (Illus.). 680p. 1991. Vol. I, Fundations & Basic Theory, 680p. 89.00 (*0-387-97566-7*) Spr-Verlag.

Breakthroughs in Statistics, 2 vols., Vol. II: Methodology & Distribution. Ed. by N. I. Johnson et al. (Series in Statistics: Perspectives in Statistics: Vols. I & II). (Illus.). 600p. 1991. Vol. II, Methodology & Distribution, 600p. 89.00 (*0-387-97572-1*) Spr-Verlag.

Breakthroughs in Statistics: Foundations & Basic Theory. Ed. by Samuel I. Kotz & Norman L. Johnson. LC 93-3854. (Series in Statistics: Perspectives in Statistics: Vol. 1). 1994. pap. 49.00 (*0-387-94037-5*) Spr-Verlag.

Breakthroughs in Statistics Vol. 2: Methodology & Distribution. Ed. by Samuel I. Kotz et al. (Series in Statistics). (Illus.). 624p. 1993. pap. 54.95 (*0-387-94039-1*) Spr-Verlag.

Breakthroughs in Union-Management Cooperation. Ed. by Joseph Loftus & Beatrice Walfish. LC 77-24837. 49p. 1977. pap. text ed. 7.00 (*0-89361-002-X*) Work in Amer.

Breakthroughs on Hunger: A Journalist's Encounter with Global Change. Richard M. Harley. 1990. 29.95 (*1-56098-001-X*); pap. 15.95 (*1-56098-026-5*) Smithsonian.

Breakthroughts in Health-Care Management: Employer & Union Initiatives. Victoria George & William E. Hembree. 213p. 1986. 22.50 (*0-08-032798-2*) Work in Amer.

Breakthru. Clifton Brusso. 1991. 16.95 (*0-533-08817-8*) Vantage.

Breaktime & the School: Understanding & Changing Playground Behaviour. Ed. by Peter Blatchford & Sonia Sharp. LC 93-25944. Date not set. write for info. (*0-415-10099-2*) Routledge.

Breakup: The Coming End of Canada & the Stakes for America. Lansing Lamont. LC 93-43809. 1994. 25.00 (*0-393-03634-0*) Norton.

Breakup of Communism: The Soviet Union & Eastern Europe. Ed. by Matthew A. Kraljic. LC 92-42466. (Reference Shelf Ser.: Vol. 65, No. 2). 1993. 15.00 (*0-8242-0840-4*) Wilson.

Breakup of the Soviet Union: Opposing Viewpoints. Ed. by William Barbour. LC 93-1809. (YA). 1994. lib. bdg. 19.95 (*1-56510-068-9*); pap. 11.55 (*1-56510-067-0*) Greenhaven.

Breakup of the Soviet Union: 1993. Close Up Foundation Staff. LC 92-29579. 40p. (YA). 1992. pap. text ed. 6.95 (*0-932765-41-6*, 1149-93) Close Up.

Breakup of Yugoslavia. Martyn Rody. (Conflicts Ser.). (Illus.). 48p. (J). (gr. 6 up). 1994. text ed. 13.95 (*0-02-792529-3*, New Dscvry Bks) Silver Burdett Pr.

Breakwall. High School Student Participants of Huron Shores Summer Writing Institute Staff. (Orig.). 1986. pap. 5.95 (*0-939345-00-5*) H S S W I.

Breakwall, Vol. III. High School Student Participants of Huron Shores Summer Writing Institute Staff. (Illus.). 200p. (Orig.). 1988. pap. 5.75 (*0-939345-02-1*) H S S W I.

Breakwall, Vol. IV. Huron Shores Summer Writing Institute Participants. (Illus.). 250p. (Orig.). 1989. pap. 6.95 (*0-939345-03-X*) H S S W I.

Breakwall, Vol. 5. Huron Shores Summer Writing Institute Participants. (Illus.). 192p. (Orig.). 1990. pap. 6.97 (*0-939345-04-8*) H S S W I.

Breakwall, Vol. VI. International Writing Workshop Staff. (Illus.). (Orig.). (ENG & GER.). 1994. pap. 6.95 (*0-939345-05-6*) H S S W I.

Breakwall '87, Vol. II. Student Participants of Huron Shores Summer Writing Institute. (Illus.). (Orig.). 1987. pap. 6.95 (*0-939345-01-3*) H S S W I.

Breakwater. Ed. by Alun Morgan. 190p. (C). 1989. pap. 35.00 (*0-9500789-8-0*, Pub. by D Brown & Sons Ltd UK) St Mut.

Breast. Philip Roth. LC 93-43498. 1994. pap. 9.00 (*0-679-74901-2*, Vin) Random.

Breast. Penny Stanway & Andrew Stanway. (Illus.). 250p. 1982. pap. 8.00 (*0-583-13464-5*, Pub. by Granada UK) Academy Chi Pubs.

Breast: A Comprehensive Textbook for the Management of Benign & Malignant Diseases. Bland & Copeland. (Illus.). 1154p. 1990. text ed. 179.00 (*0-7216-2234-8*) Saunders.

***Breast: Anthology.** Ed. by Susan Thames et al. LC 95-75463. 256p. 1995. pap. 14.00 (*0-9641292-8-0*) Global Cty Pr.

Breast: Therapeutic Modalities. Martin D. Abeloff. Ed. by Ross Donehower & John Kirkwood. (Current Opinion in Oncology, 1993 Ser.). (Illus.). 1147p. (Orig.). 1993. pap. text ed. 49.95 (*1-85922-014-2*) Current Science.

***Breast: Therapeutic Modalities.** Martin D. Abeloff. Ed. by Donald Trump & John M. Kirkwood. (Current Opinion in Oncology Ser.). (Illus.). 632p. (Orig.). 1994. pap. text ed. 49.95 (*1-85922-623-X*) Current Science.

Breast & Gynecologic Cancer Epidemiology. J. L. Kelsey & N. G. Hildreth. LC 82-9629. 1983. 95.00 (*0-8493-6385-3*, CRC Reprint) Franklin.

***Breast Awareness: Breast Lumps & Cancer.** S. Eva Singletary. (OB-GYN Ser.). 32p. 1994. pap. text ed. 3.95 (*1-885274-04-1*) HIN.

Breast Cancer. Heinz Bohmert et al. (Illus.). 535p. 1989. text ed. 135.00 (*0-86577-326-2*) Thieme Med Pubs.

Breast Cancer. Lesley Fallowfield & Andrew Clark. Ed. by Psychology Staff. (Experience of Illness Ser.). 160p. 1992. pap. 12.95 (*0-415-03841-3*, A7633) Routledge.

Breast Cancer. Ed. by I. Fentiman & J. Taylor-Papadimitriou. (Cancer Surveys Ser.: Vol. 18). (Illus.). 235p. (C). 1994. text ed. 69.00 (*0-87969-394-0*) Cold Spring Harbor.

Breast Cancer. Ed. by Barth Hoogstraten & Robert W. McDivitt. 304p. 1981. 156.00 (*0-8493-5731-4*, RC280, CRC Reprint) Franklin.

Breast Cancer. Ed. by B. J. Kennedy. (Current Clinical Oncology Ser.). 1989. text ed. 94.00 (*0-471-56230-0*) Wiley.

***Breast Cancer.** Elaine Landau. LC 95-3831. (Venture Bks.). (J). 1995. 14.77 (*0-531-11242-X*) Watts.

Breast Cancer. Ed. by Richard G. Margolese. LC 83-10059. (Contemporary Issues in Oncology Ser.: Vol. 1). (Illus.). 318p. reprint ed. pap. 90.70 (*0-7837-6240-2*, 2045954) Bks Demand.

Breast Cancer, Vol. 1. Ed. by Edwin W. Salzman. (NEJM Reprint Collection). (Illus.). 420p. 1990. text ed. 65.00 (*0-910133-24-7*); pap. 39.00 (*0-910133-18-2*) MA Med Soc.

***Breast Cancer: A Family Survival Guide.** Lucille M. Pederson & Janet M. Trigg. LC 94-37836. 304p. 1995. text ed. 59.95 (*0-89789-293-3*, Bergin & Garvey) Greenwood.

***Breast Cancer: A Family Survival Guide.** Lucille M. Pederson & Janet M. Trigg. LC 94-37836. 304p. 1995. pap. text ed. 19.95 (*0-89789-438-3*, Bergin & Garvey) Greenwood.

Breast Cancer: A Guide for Every Woman. Michael Baum et al. (Illus.). 160p. 1994. pap. 14.95 (*0-19-262436-9*) OUP.

Breast Cancer: A Patient Guide. Patricia J. Anderson. LC 92-81894. 199p. 1992. pap. 14.95 (*1-881915-00-X*) Creat Hlth Srvs.

Breast Cancer: A Practical Guide to Diagnosis, Vol. 1. Wende W. Logan-Young & Nancy Yanes-Hoffman. (Illus.). 500p. 1994. Vol. 2. 160.00 (*0-9640886-2-2*); Set. write for info. (*0-9640886-0-6*) Mount Hope Pub.

Breast Cancer: A Practical Guide to Diagnosis, Vol. 1. Wende W. Logan-Young & Nancy Yanes-Hoffman. (Illus.). 500p. 1994. 160.00 (*0-9640886-1-4*) Mount Hope Pub.

Breast Cancer: A Practical Guide to Diagnosis & Treatment. Ed. by Lewis Venet. 1979. text ed. 30.00 (*0-88331-116-X*) Luce.

***Breast Cancer: A Psychological Treatment Manual.** Sandra Haber. LC 94-35284. (Illus.). 160p. 1994. 27.95 (*0-8261-8790-0*) Springer Pub.

Breast Cancer: Advances in Research & Treatment, Vol. 4. Ed. by William L. McGuire. LC 79-646815. 246p. 1981. 75.00 (*0-306-40667-5*, Plenum Med Bk) Plenum.

Breast Cancer: An Annotated Guide to the Current Literature. Ed. by N. G. Arashvili. 165p. 1994. pap. text ed. 69.00 (*1-56072-112-X*) Nova Sci Pubs.

Breast Cancer: Controversies in Management. Ed. by Leslie Wise & Houston Johnson, Jr. LC 93-31411. (Illus.). 608p. 1994. 105.00 (*0-87993-562-6*) Futura Pub.

Breast Cancer: From Biology to Therapy. Ed. by F. Squartini et al. LC 93-40875. (Annals Ser.: Vol. 698). 1993. write for info. (*0-89766-803-0*); pap. write for info. (*0-89766-804-9*) NY Acad Sci.

Breast Cancer: Origins, Detection, & Treatment. Ed. by Marvin A. Rich et al. (Developments in Oncology Ser.). 1986. lib. bdg. 80.50 (*0-89838-792-2*) Kluwer Ac.

Breast Cancer: Progress in Biology, Clinical Management & Prevention. Ed. by Marvin A. Rich et al. (Developments in Oncology Ser.). (C). 1989. lib. bdg. 79.00 (*0-7923-0507-8*) Kluwer Ac.

Breast Cancer: Scientific & Clinical Progress. Ed. by Marvin A. Rich et al. (C). 1988. lib. bdg. 127.00 (*0-89838-387-0*) Kluwer Ac.

Breast Cancer: Setting Priorities for Effectiveness Research: Report of a Study by a Committee of the Institute of Medicine, Division of Health Care Services. Ed. by Kathleen N. Lohr. LC 89-64426. 72p. reprint ed. pap. 25.00 (*0-8357-2694-0*, 2040231) Bks Demand.

***Breast Cancer: Strategies for Husbands to Support Their Wives.** James K. Eckmann. LC 94-69145. (Illus.). 102p. (Orig.). 1995. pap. 9.95 (*0-9644135-0-7*) Nehemiah Pubng.

Breast Cancer: Textbook for General Practitioners. Ed. by Europe Against Cancer Staff & U. Veronesi. (EC Series for General Practitioners). (Illus.). xi, 67p. 1990. pap. text ed. 38.00 (*0-387-53102-5*) Spr-Verlag.

Breast Cancer: The Complete Guide. Yashar Hirshaut. 1993. pap. 12.95 (*0-553-37203-3*) Bantam.

Breast Cancer: The Psychological Effects of the Disease & Its Treatment. Karin Gyllenskold. Tr. by Patricia Crampton. 1982. 29.50 (*0-422-76820-0*, NO. 3623, Pub. by Tavistock UK) Routledge Chapman & Hall.

Breast Cancer: Trends in Research & Treatment. EORTC Breast Cancer Working Conference Staff. Ed. by Jean-Claude Heuson et al. LC 76-381463. (Monograph Series of the European Organization for Research on Treatment of Cancer: No. 2). (Illus.). 343p. reprint ed. pap. 97.80 (*0-7837-7092-8*, 2046917) Bks Demand.

***Breast Cancer: Twenty Women's Stories.** Ed. by Susan D. Moch. 1995. pap. write for info. (*0-88737-654-1*) Natl League Nurse.

***Breast Cancer: What Every Woman Should Know.** Baron F. Rita. LC 94-32852. 1995. 23.00 (*0-688-12069-5*) Hearst Bks.

Breast Cancer: What Every Woman Should Know. Paul Rodriguez. (Illus.). 138p. (Orig.). 1988. pap. text ed. 11.45 (*0-9622118-0-X*) Aurora KS.

Breast Cancer: What Your Doctor Won't Tell You about Prevention, Diagnosis, & Treatment. Steve Austin & Cathy Hitchcock. LC 93-49716. 1994. pap. write for info. (*1-55958-362-2*) Prima Pub.

***Breast Cancer & Breast Care.** Carolyn Faulder. (Ward Lock Family Health Guides Ser.). (Illus.). 80p. 1995. pap. 9.95 (*0-7063-7411-8*, Pub. by Ward Lock UK) Sterling.

Breast Cancer & Stress. Ed. by Cary L. Cooper. 219p. 1988. text ed. 129.95 (*0-471-91744-3*) Wiley.

***Breast Cancer & You: Bettering the Odds.** Martha L. Grigg. Ed. by Adolph Caso. (Illus.). 204p. (Orig.). 1995. pap. 14.95 (*0-8283-2010-1*) Branden Pub Co.

Breast Cancer: Biological & Clinical Progress: Proceedings of the Conference of the International Association for Breast Cancer Research, St. Vincent, Aosta Valley, Italy, May 26-29, 1991. Ed. by L. Dogliotti. (Developments in Oncology Ser.). 336p. (C). 1992. lib. bdg. 109.00 (*0-7923-1655-X*) Kluwer Ac.

Breast Cancer-Black Woman. Edwin T. Johnson. (Illus.). 167p. 1994. 19.75 (*0-9635435-0-4*) Mont Urgent CC.

Breast Cancer? Breast Health! The Wise Woman Way. Susun S. Weed. LC 94-71323. (Wise Woman Herbal Ser.: No. 4). (Illus.). 356p. (Orig.). 1995. pap. 14.95 (*0-9614620-7-8*) Ash Tree. BREAST CANCER? BREAST HEALTH! THE WISE WOMAN WAY is for every woman who loves her breasts & doesn't want to lose them. Covering all aspects of healthy breast care, as well as alternative & complementary medicines for women diagnosed with breast cancer, this book offers safe, simple, & successful ways to regain & maintain breast health. If estimates that 80 percent of all cancers are environmentally caused are correct, the sections on cancer-preventive foods, building powerful immunity & reducing your breast cancer risk through lifestyle choices could save more than 25,000 lives a year. (46,000 women die annually in the U.S. of breast cancer.) For women dealing with cancer, individual sections on complementary homeopathic, herbal, & home remedies insure that the side-effects of surgery, radiation, & chemotherapy are held to a minimum. Of special note is her chapter focusing on the uses of massage & easily available, non-toxic, infused herbal oils to keep breasts in full health & to melt away painful lumps. Praised by M.D.s, naturopaths, & ordinary citizens, Susun Weed's books are immensely popular with women of all ages. Her current best-seller MENOPAUSAL YEARS: THE WISE WOMAN WAY, is cherished by hundreds of thousands of menopausal women. WISE WOMAN HERBAL FOR THE CHILDBEARING YEAR, her first book, is a classic used by millions of midwives & mothers throughout the world (in addition to English, German & French editions are in print). Weed's latest offering, her fourth, is guaranteed to be a strong-selling title now & far into the future. Release date: late September. ***Publisher Provided Annotation.***

Breast Cancer Collaborative Management. Ed. by Jay K. Harness et al. (Illus.). 390p. 1988. 89.95 (*0-87371-106-8*, RC280) Lewis Pubs.

Breast Cancer Companion. Kathy LaTour. 512p. 1994. reprint ed. pap. 15.00 (*0-380-71996-7*) Avon.

Breast Cancer Companion: From Diagnosis, Through Treatment, to Recovery, Everything You Need to Know for Every Step along the Way. Kathy LaTour. LC 93-7473. 1993. 22.00 (*0-688-11931-X*) Morrow.

Breast Cancer: Current Literature for Nonmedical People: A Bibliography. Rama K. Rao. (Social Science Resource Guides Ser.: No. 8). 30p. (C). 1992. pap. text ed. 9.95 (*0-9628998-6-0*) Ramdil.

Breast Cancer Detection: Mammography & Other Methods in Breast Imaging. 2nd ed. Lawrence W. Bassett & Richard Gold. 256p. 1987. text ed. 84.00 (*0-8089-1842-7*, 790451, Grune) Saunders.

Breast Cancer, Diagnosis & Management. Ed. by Gianni Bonadonna. LC 83-6898. (Wiley Series on Cancer Investigation & Management: No. 1). 359p. reprint ed. pap. 102.40 (*0-8357-3468-4*, 2039730) Bks Demand.

Breast Cancer Handbook: Taking Control - Knowing the Options - Making Decisions. Joan Swirsky & Barbara Balaban. 144p. (Orig.). 1994. pap. 10.00 (*0-06-095045-5*, PL) HarpC.

Breast Cancer Immunodiagnosis & Immunotherapy. Ed. by R. L. Ceriani. (Illus.). 272p. 1989. 85.00 (*0-306-43338-9*, Plenum Pr) Plenum.

Breast Cancer in the Life Course: Women's Experiences. Ed. by Julianne Oktay & Carolyn Walter. (Social Work Ser.: Vol. 20). 232p. 1991. 28.95 (*0-8261-7110-9*) Springer Pub.

Breast Cancer-Its Impact on the Patient, Family, & Community: Proceedings of the San Francisco Cancer Symposium, 11th, San Francisco, California, November, 1975. San Francisco Cancer Symposium Staff. Ed. by J. M. Vaeth. (Frontiers of Radiation Therapy & Oncology Ser.: Vol. 11). (Illus.). 200p. 1976. 70.50 (*3-8055-2340-8*) S Karger.

B

Breast Cancer Journal: A Century of Petals. Juliet Wittman. LC 92-54765. 320p. 1993. 21.95 (*1-55591-136-6*) Fulcrum Pub.

Breast Cancer Journal: A Century of Petals. Juliet Wittman. 304p. 1994. pap. 14.95 (*1-55591-194-3*) Fulcrum Pub.

Breast Cancer? Let Me Check My Schedule! Donna Cedenberg et al. 250p. 1994. pap. 12.95 (*0-9641386-0-3*) Innovat Med.

***Breast Cancer Nursing.** S. Denton. (Illus.). 256p. 1995. pap. text ed. 57.50 (*1-56593-033-9*, 0281) Singular Publishing.

***Breast Cancer Prevention Report: With John R. Lees, M.D., Revealing Interview on Natural Progesterone vs. the Estrogen Replacement Risk.** Daniel A. Herman. (Illus.). 100p. 1995. pap. text ed. 29.00 (*0-9644403-0-X*) Advances.

Breast Cancer Screening. Joan Austoker & John Humphreys. (Practical Guides for General Practice Ser.: No. 6). (Illus.). 66p. 1988. pap. 9.95 (*0-19-261789-3*) OUP.

Breast Cancer Screening in Europe. Ed. by A. Gad & M. Rosselli Del Turco. LC 93-13231. (Monographs of the European School of Oncology). 1993. Alk. paper. 100.00 (*0-387-56577-9*) Spr-Verlag.

Breast Cancer Treatment. Fowble et al. (Illus.). 672p. 1991. 99.00 (*0-8016-6207-9*) Mosby Yr Bk.

***Breast Cancers - Chemically Induced: Index of New Information.** John C. Bartone, Sr. (Illus.). 160p. 1995. 44.50 (*0-7883-0698-7*); pap. 37.50 (*0-7883-0699-5*) ABBE Pubs Assn.

Breast Carcinoma: Risk & Detection. Cushman D. Haagensen et al. LC 80-53370. 542p. 1981. text ed. 121.00 (*0-7216-4438-4*) Saunders.

Breast Carcinoma: The Radiologist's Expanded Role. Wende W. Logan. LC 77-13047. 396p. reprint ed. 112.90 (*0-8357-9848-8*, 2015195) Bks Demand.

Breast Care. Fit Magazine Editors. (Fit Self-Improvement Ser.: No. 2). 96p. 1983. pap. 7.95 (*0-89037-259-4*) Anderson World.

Breast Care Options. Paul Kuehn. LC 86-61100. (Illus.). 178p. 1986. 17.95 (*0-938539-00-0*) Newmark Pub.

Breast Care Options for the 1990's. Paul Kuehn. LC 91-60345. 255p. 1991. 19.95 (*0-938539-04-3*) Newmark Pub.

Breast Conservation in the Treatment of Early Breast Cancer. Frederick L. Moffat. (Medical Intelligence Unit Ser.). 115p. 1994. 89.95 (*1-57059-087-7*, LN9087) R G Landes.

***Breast Conservation vs. Mastectomy: Patient Survival in Day-to-Day Medical Practice & in Randomized Studies.** (Illus.). 48p. (Orig.). (C). 1995. pap. text ed. 35.00x (*0-7881-1691-6*) Diane Pub.

Breast Disease. Ed. by H. J. Stewart et al. (British Medical Bulletin Ser.: Vol. 47, No. 2). (Illus.). 264p. 1991. text ed. 72.00 (*0-443-04492-9*) Churchill.

Breast Disease for Gynecologists. William H. Hindle. (Illus.). 296p. 1989. boxed 85.00 (*0-8385-0826-X*, A0826-6) Appleton & Lange.

Breast Disease for Radiographers. Caseldine. 1988. 50.00 (*0-7236-1067-3*, Pub. by John Wright UK) Buttrwrth-Heinemann.

Breast Disease in Women & Men. Pam Shuler. (Illus.). (Orig.). 1993. pap. text ed. 12.95 (*0-929240-54-5*) Essential Med Info Syst Inc.

Breast Disease (Second Series) Test Syllabus. Edward A. Sickles et al. LC 93-41764. (Professional Self-Evaluation & Continuing Education Program Ser.: Vol. 36). (Illus.). 470p. 1993. 200.00 (*1-55903-037-2*) Am Coll Radiology.

Breast Diseases. Jay R. Harris et al. LC 65-9244. (Illus.). 751p. 1987. text ed. 99.00 (*0-397-50760-7*, Lippincott Medical) Lippincott.

Breast Diseases. 2nd ed. Jay R. Harris et al. (Illus.). 954p. 1991. text ed. 160.00 (*0-397-51079-9*) Lippincott.

An Asterisk (*) at the beginning of an entry indicates that the title is appearing in BIP for the first time. 893

Breast Epithelial Antigens. Ed. by R. L. Ceriani. (Illus.). 230p. 1991. 75.00 (*0-306-44009-1*, Plenum Pr) Plenum.

Breast Feeding & Child Development. B. K. Mishra. viii, 178p. 1993. 20.00 (*81-7024-567-2*, Pub. by Ashish Pub Hse II) Nataraj Bks.

Breast-Feeding & Fertility. Ed. by Malcolm Potts et al. (Journal of Biological Science, Supplement Ser.: No. 9). 170p. 1985. pap. 25.00 (*0-907232-04-3*) Portland NC.

Breast Feeding & the Mother. (Ciba Foundation Symposium Ser.: No. 45). 1976. 18.50 (*0-685-10184-3*) Elsevier.

Breast-Feeding & the Mother. Ciba Foundation Staff. LC 76-44816. (Ciba Foundation Symposium: New Ser.: No. 45). 288p. reprint ed. pap. 82.10 (*0-8357-7396-5*, 2022173) Bks Demand.

Breast Feeding & the Working Women of India. Rajendra Pandey. 1990. 40.00 (*81-85076-92-8*, Pub. by Chugh Pubns II) S Asia.

***Breast Health: What You Need to Know.** Charles Simone. 354p. 1995. pap. 15.95 (*0-89529-660-8*) Avery Pub.

Breast Imaging. Daniel B. Kopans. LC 65-9251. (Illus.). 304p. 1989. text ed. 89.50 (*0-397-50761-5*, Lippincott Medical) Lippincott.

Breast Imaging: Diagnosis & Morphology of Breast Diseases. Robert L. Egan. (Illus.). 656p. 1988. text ed. 129.00 (*0-7216-2320-4*) Saunders.

Breast Implant Problem Reports. Heidi M. Garrett. Date not set. 795.00 (*1-56363-072-9*) Med Econ Data.

Breast Implants: Everything You Need to Know. Nancy Bruning. LC 92-16101. (Illus.). 128p. 1992. pap. 7.95 (*0-89793-119-X*) Hunter Hse.

***Breast Implants: Everything You Need to Know.** Nancy Bruning. 1995. 21.95 (*0-89793-176-9*) Hunter Hse.

***Breast Implants: Everything You Need to Know.** 2nd ed. Nancy Bruning. 1995. pap. 11.95 (*0-89793-175-0*) Hunter Hse.

Breast Implants: Everything You Need to Know. Nancy Bruning. 128p. 1992. reprint ed. lib. bdg. 23.00x (*0-8095-6332-0*) Borgo Pr.

Breast Implants: Making Safe Choices. Kathlyn Gay. LC 92-35095. (Illus.). 128p. (J). (gr. 6 up). 1993. text ed. 13.95 (*0-02-737955-8*, Mac Bks Young Read) S&S Childrens.

***Breast Milk - Nature's Perfect Formula.** Margaret B. Salmon. Date not set. 10.95 (*0-614-05038-3*) Techkits.

***Breast Milk, Nature's Perfect Formula: More Than 100 Answers to the Most Frequently Asked Questions About Breast Milk.** Margaret B. Salmon. 1994. write for info. (*0-615-00270-6*) Techkits.

Breast of the Earth: A Survey of the History, Culture & Literature of Africa South of the Sahara. Kofi Awoonor. 1983. reprint ed. 19.95 (*0-685-03583-2*); reprint ed. pap. text ed. 7.95 (*0-88357-103-X*) NOK Pubs.

Breast Pathology. Robert E. Fechner & Stacey E. Mills. LC 90-647. (Illus.). 182p. 1990. text ed. 135.00 (*0-89189-298-2*, 16-1-049-00) Am Soc Clinical.

Breast Reconstruction Following Mastectomy for Carcinoma. William M. Cocke, Jr. 1977. text ed. 27.50 (*0-316-14920-9*, Little Med Div) Little.

Breast Self-Examination. Albert R. Milan. LC 79-56529. (Illus.). 128p. 1980. pap. 3.50 (*0-89480-124-4*, 419) Workman Pub.

Breast Self Examination & You. P. G. Nama et al. 1995. pap. 6.00 (*0-318-37463-3*) Budlong.

Breast Ultrasound. Bassett. 1986. 85.00 (*0-316-08314-3*) Little.

Breast Ultrasound Update. Ed. by H. Madjar et al. (Illus.). x, 376p. 1995. 100.00 (*3-8055-5860-0*) S Karger.

***Breastfeeding: A Biocultural Perspective.** Patricia Stuart-Macadam & Katherine Dettwyler. (Foundations of Human Behavior Ser.). 432p. 1995. lib. bdg. 65.95 (*0-202-01191-7*); pap. 31.95 (*0-202-01192-5*) Aldine de Gruyter.

Breastfeeding: A Guide for the Medical Profession. Lawrence. 650p. 1994. 46.95 (*0-8016-6858-1*) Mosby Yr Bk.

Breastfeeding: A Guide for the Medical Profession. 3rd ed. Lawrence. (Illus.). 672p. 1989. 44.95 (*0-8016-2803-2*) Mosby Yr Bk.

Breastfeeding: A Problem-Solving Manual. 3rd ed. Stephen Saunders et al. 1991. pap. 14.95 (*0-929240-28-6*) Essential Med Info Syst Inc.

Breastfeeding: Something Special for Mother & Baby. rev. ed. Toni Berg. (Illus.). 26p. 1992. reprint ed. pap. 2.95 (*0-945886-10-1*) New Futures.

Breastfeeding: The Art of Mothering. rev. ed. Maurice Teitel et al. (Illus.). 48p. 1988. vhs 49.95 (*0-317-93069-9*); pap. 5.95 (*0-317-93070-2*); vhs 49.95 (*0-317-93071-0*) Alive Prodns.

Breastfeeding & Human Lactation. Jan Riordan & Kathleen G. Auerbach. (Nursing-Health Science Ser.). 600p. (C). 1993. boxed 82.50 (*0-86720-343-9*) Jones & Bartlett.

Breastfeeding & Human Lactation Student Study Guide. Jan Riordan. 168p. (C). 1993. pap. text ed. 14.95 (*0-86720-632-2*) Jones & Bartlett.

Breastfeeding & Natural Child Spacing: How Ecological Breastfeeding Spaces Babies. 2nd rev. ed. Sheila K. Kippley. (Illus.). 208p. 1989. reprint ed. pap. 8.95 (*0-9601036-8-6*) Couple to Couple.

***Breastfeeding & the Active Woman.** Lillian A. Pfluke. 160p. 1995. pap. 11.95 (*1-56796-087-1*) WRS Group.

Breastfeeding & the Working Mother: The Complete Guide for Today's Nursing Mother. Diana J. Mason & Diane Ingersoll. (Illus.). 256p. 1986. pap. 11.95 (*0-312-09527-9*) St Martin.

Breastfeeding Answer Book. Nancy Mohrbacher & Julie Stock. LC 91-62087. 455p. 1991. spiral bd. 34.95 (*0-912500-33-6*) La Leche.

During the last decade, the average length of hospital stay following birth has been cut almost in half as the health-care industry strives to keep costs down. As a result, women are often sent home to grapple through common breastfeeding challenges without the information & support they need. This book presents a broad spectrum of information & explores in-depth all types of breastfeeding questions along with a variety of possible approaches & solutions. It is a concise, practical & well-documented guide to not only what to do in virtually any breastfeeding circumstance, but why. Although originally written for lay breastfeeding counselors, the non-medical language & easy to use format make this book an effective resource for anyone interested in obtaining or providing reliable information about breastfeeding. To order contact La Leche League International, 1400 N. Meacham Road, Schaumburg, IL 60173. 708-519-7730. No. 480, $34.95. ***Publisher Provided Annotation.***

***Breastfeeding Care: Setting the Environment, Supporting the Process.** Ruth A. Lawrence et al. LC 94-29660. 1994. write for info. (*0-86525-058-8*) March of Dimes.

Breastfeeding for the Working Woman see Working Woman's Guide to Breastfeeding

Breastfeeding Handbook: A Practical Reference for Physicians, Nurses & Other Health Professionals. rev. ed. Johanna Goldfarb & Edith Tibbetts. LC 88-30998. (Illus.). 256p. 1989. pap. 20.95 (*0-89490-186-9*) Enslow Pubs.

***Breastfeeding Product Guide, 1994.** Kittie Frantz. LC 94-96329. (Illus.). 218p. 1994. 23.95 (*1-885748-14-0*) Geddes Prods.

Breastfeeding Promotion Through the Women, Infants & Children (WIC) Program. (Illus.). 122p. (Orig.). (C). 1994. pap. text ed. 35.00 (*0-7881-0568-X*) Diane Pub.

Breastfeeding Pure & Simple. Gwen Gotsch. LC 93-80164. (Illus.). 117p. 1994. pap. 8.95 (*0-912500-42-5*) La Leche.

Parents-to-be have so much to do & so much to read! But because breastfeeding is such a natural way to nourish & nurture a baby, many new parents expect it to go smoothly without having all the information they need. This brand new breastfeeding book published by La Leche League International provides new parents with a basic but thorough & up-to-date introduction to the early months of nursing their babies. Written by an accredited La Leche League Leader & mother of three children, BREASTFEEDING PURE & SIMPLE is based on the experience of thousands of mothers who have successfully breastfed their babies. This book will help parents discover how simple & satisfying breastfeeding can be. Also available in Spanish. To order contact La Leche League International, 1400 N. Meacham Road, Schaumburg, IL 60173. 708-519-7730. No. 251, $8.95. ***Publisher Provided Annotation.***

Breastfeeding Secrets & Solutions. Janis Graham. Ed. by Claire Zion. 256p. (Orig.). 1993. pap. 10.00 (*0-671-74963-3*) PB.

Breastfeeding Source Book: Where to Get What You Need to Breastfeed Successfully. Marilyn Grams. LC 88-6191. (Illus.). 220p. (Orig.). 1988. pap. 9.95 (*0-932707-17-3*) Achievement Pr.

Breastfeeding Success for Working Mothers. Marilyn Grams. LC 85-71326. (Illus.). 160p. 1985. pap. 15.00 (*0-932707-14-9*) Achievement Pr.

***Breastfeeding the Adopted Baby.** Debra Peterson. (Illus.). 141p. (Orig.). 1995. pap. 8.95 (*0-931722-43-8*) Corona Pub.

***Breastfeeding the Healthy Newborn: A Nursing Perspective.** Marie Biancuzzo & Margaret Comberford Freda. Ed. by Karla Damus. 1994. write for info. (*0-86525-064-2*) March of Dimes.

Breastfeeding Today: A Mother's Companion. 2nd ed. Candace Woessner et al. LC 91-15434. (Illus.). 256p. (Orig.). 1991. pap. 9.95 (*0-89529-469-9*) Avery Pub.

BreastFeeding Your Baby. Joyce Fischer. (Illus.). 33p. (Orig.). 1990. pap. 6.50 (*0-944782-02-7*) Glover Pr.

Breastfeeding Your Baby. Sheila Kitzinger. (Illus.). 1989. pap. 19.00 (*0-679-72433-8*) Knopf.

Breastfeeding Your Baby: A Guide for the Contemporary Family. Carl Jones & Ruth A. Lawrence. LC 92-26521. 224p. 1993. pap. 10.00 (*0-02-080401-6*, Collier S&S) S&S Trade.

Breastfeeding Your Baby: A Practical Guide for the New Mother. 3rd ed. Nursing Council of the Boston Association for Childbirth Education. LC 89-387. (Illus.). 128p. (Orig.). 1989. pap. 3.95 (*0-89529-387-0*) Avery Pub.

Breastfeeding Your Premature Baby. Gwen Gotsch. 24p. 1990. pap. 2.25 (*0-912500-38-7*) La Leche.

Breastplate of Faith & Love. John Preston. 241p. 1979. reprint ed. 35.95 (*0-85151-289-5*) Banner of Truth.

Breasts, Bottles, & Babies. Valerie Fildes. 400p. 1985. 30.00 (*0-85224-462-2*, Pub. by Edinburgh U Pr UK) Col U Pr.

Breasts, Bottles, & Babies: A History of Infant Feeding. Valerie Fildes. (Illus.). 490p. 1989. pap. 18.00 (*0-85224-610-2*, Pub. by Edinburgh U Pr UK) Col U Pr.

***Breath Alcohol Technician Training.** 1995. lib. bdg. 601.75 (*0-8490-6699-9*) Gordon Pr.

Breath & Spirit: Rebirthing As a Healing Technique. Gunnel Minett. 208p. 1994. pap. 15.00 (*1-85538-353-5*) Thorsons SF.

Breath Awareness: Breath Awareness for Public Schools, Medical Profession. Lernard D. Orr. (YA). (gr. 7 up). 1988. pap. 10.00 (*0-945793-02-2*) Inspir Univ.

Breath Connection: How to Reduce Psychosomatic & Stress-Related Disorders with Ease. Robert Fried. (Illus.). 290p. 1990. 23.50 (*0-306-43433-4*, Plenum Insight) Plenum.

***Breath Deeply.** White Wolf Staff. 1995. pap. 5.99 (*1-56504-881-4*, 11300) White Wolf.

***Breath, Eyes, Memories.** Edwidge Danticat. (Vintage Contemporaries). 1995. 11.00 (*0-679-75661-2*, Vin) Random.

Breath, Eyes, Memory. Edwidge Danticat. LC 93-39256. 230p. 1994. 20.00 (*1-56947-005-7*) Soho Press.

Breath, Mind, & Consciousness. Harish Johari. (Illus.). 96p. 1989. pap. 9.95 (*0-89281-252-4*, Destiny Bks) Inner Tradit.

Breath of Air & a Breath of Smoke. John S. Marr. LC 70-161362. (Illus.). 48p. (J). (gr. 3 up). 1970. 4.95 (*0-87131-038-4*) M Evans.

Breath of Blood & Milk: Dry Long So Poems. Amir Rashidd & L. V. Williams. LC 88-70764. 64p. (Orig.). 1989. pap. 10.95 (*0-943767-05-9*) Audacious Pr.

Breath of Clarity. Linda Pizzi. LC 90-82582. 55p. (Orig.). 1990. pap. write for info. (*0-9627073-0-9*) Clarion Word Servs.

***Breath of Fire Authorized Game Secrets Vol. 1.** Rusel Demaria. 1994. pap. 14.95 (*1-55958-613-3*) Prima Pub.

Breath of Fresh Air: A Practical Guide for Filtering Out Indoor Air Pollution Utilizing House Plants. LaRonna DeBraak. Ed. by Ben McDonald. (Illus.). 138p. (Orig.). 1991. pap. 12.95 (*0-9630603-0-9*) Mtn Meadow.

Breath of Fresh Air: Christian Education of Adults in the 21st Century. Richard L. Spindle. 112p. 1989. pap. 5.95 (*0-8341-1300-7*) Beacon Hill.

Breath of Fresh Air - A Flash of Light. H. Emery Ball. 1993. 10.95 (*0-533-10693-1*) Vantage.

Breath of God. Swami Chetanananda. Ed. by Linda Barnes. 310p. (Orig.). 1988. pap. 15.95 (*0-915801-05-1*) Rudra Pr.

Breath of God: An Approach to Prayer. Nancy Roth. LC 89-29785. 174p. 1990. pap. 9.95 (*0-936384-92-1*) Cowley Pubns.

Breath of God - Portrait of a Prelate: A Biography of Archbishop Iakovos. George Poulos. 177p. 1984. pap. 12.95 (*0-916586-98-7*) Holy Cross Orthodox.

Breath of Life. Faith Baldwin. 1976. reprint ed. lib. bdg. 21.95 (*0-88411-617-4*, Aeonian Pr) Amereon Ltd.

Breath of Life. John Burroughs. (Works of John Burroughs). 1989. reprint ed. lib. bdg. 79.00 (*0-7812-2198-6*) Rprt Serv.

Breath of Life: A Simple Way to Pray. Ron DelBene et al. LC 91-65724. 128p. 1992. pap. 8.95 (*0-8358-0647-2*) Upper Room Bks.

Breath of Life: Discovering Your Breath Prayer. Ron Delbene & Herb Montgomery. 108p. (Orig.). 1981. pap. 3.95 (*0-86683-639-X*) Harper SF.

Breath of Life: Feminism in the American Jewish Community. Sylvia B. Fishman. 300p. 1993. text ed. 24.95 (*0-02-910342-8*) Free Pr.

***Breath of Life: Feminism in the American Jewish Community.** Sylvia B. Fishman. (Brandeis Series in American Jewish History, Culture, & Life). 320p. 1995. pap. 17.95 (*0-87451-706-0*) U Pr of New Eng.

Breath of Life: Mastering the Breathing Techniques of Pranayama & Qi Gong. George Ellis. Ed. by Gina R. Gross. (Illus.). 192p. (Orig.). 1993. pap. 12.95 (*0-87877-183-2*) Newcastle Pub.

Breath of Life: The Life & Work of Dr. Samuel James Meltzer. Adolph Meltzer. 1993. 18.95 (*0-533-09572-7*) Vantage.

Breath of Life & the Flame Devine. Hilton Hotema. 63p. 1957. reprint ed. spiral bd. 6.60 (*0-7873-0421-2*) Mokelumne.

Breath of Life at Birth Is the Beginning of Spiritual Existence. Lasan L. Vulani. (Illus.). 108p. (Orig.). 1993. pap. write for info. (*0-913491-30-6*) SCP Third.

Breath of Life or Mal-Respiration. George Catlin. (Works of George Catlin Ser.). 1990. reprint ed. lib. bdg. 79.00 (*0-7812-2250-8*) Rprt Serv.

Breath of Life Series: A Simple Way to Pray. Ron Delbene. 1992. pap. 24.95 (*0-8358-0669-3*) Upper Room Bks.

Breath of Light: Platinum Print Photography. Tom Shillea. (Illus.). 80p. (Orig.). 1986. pap. 14.95 (*0-938766-05-8*) NJ State Mus.

Breath of Scandal. Sandra Brown. 464p. 1991. mass mkt. 6.50 (*0-446-35963-7*) Warner Bks.

***Breath of Scandal.** Jeanne Carmichael. 1995. pap. 4.50 (*0-449-22372-8*) Fawcett.

Breath of Scandal. large type ed. Sandra Brown. LC 93-4569. 667p. 1993. lib. bdg. 20.95 (*1-56054-783-9*); pap. 13.95 (*1-56054-784-7*) Thorndike Pr.

Breath of Suspension. Alexander Jablokov. LC 93-38607. (Illus.). viii, 320p. 1994. 20.95 (*0-87054-167-6*) Arkham.

Breath of the Crowd. Howard Barker. 32p. (Orig.). 1987. pap. 9.95 (*0-7145-4099-4*) Riverrun NY.

Breath of the Dragon: Homebuilt Flamethrowers. Ragnar Benson. (Illus.). 80p. 1990. 12.00 (*0-87364-565-0*) Paladin Pr.

Breath of the Invisible. John Redtail Freesoul. LC 86-40124. (Illus.). 226p. (Orig.). 1986. pap. 11.95 (*0-8356-0611-2*, Quest) Theos Pub Hse.

Breath of Youth. Brown Landone. 75p. 1966. reprint ed. spiral bd. 4.40 (*0-7873-1147-2*) Mokelumne.

Breath on the Mirror: Walking the World of Mayan Myths. Dennis Tedlock. LC 92-56418. 272p. 1993. reprint ed. 21.00 (*0-06-250900-4*) Harper SF.

Breath on the Mirror: Walking the World of Mayan Myths. Dennis Tedlock. LC 92-56418. 272p. 1994. reprint ed. pap. 12.00 (*0-06-250901-2*) Harper SF.

Breath Sounds Methodology. Noam Gavriely. 1995. write for info. (*0-8493-5500-1*) CRC Pr.

Breath Taken: The Landscape & Biography of Asbestos. Bill Ravanesi et al. (Illus.). 50p. 1991. pap. 20.00 (*1-879842-91-2*) Ctr Vis Arts.

Breath-Taking: Stopping the Plunder of Our Planet's Air. Edna A. Zeavin. Ed. by Diane Parker. LC 92-54170. 205p. (Orig.). 1992. pap. 12.95 (*0-88247-925-3*) R & E Pubs.

Breath Tests in Health, Science & Medicine: Subject Analysis with Reference Bibliography. Stella S. Yardley. LC 85-48087. 150p. 1987. 44.50 (*0-88164-446-3*); pap. 39.50 (*0-88164-447-1*) ABBE Pubs Assn.

Breathe! An Anti-Smoking Anthology. Ed. by Shel Horowitz. (Illus.). 62p. 1981. pap. 5.00 (*0-942292-08-1*) Warthog Pr.

Breathe Again Naturally. Bernard Jensen. 1983. pap. 4.95 (*0-932615-08-2*) B Jensen.

Breathe All Seasons. Mark Raney. (Illus.). 241p. 1977. 10.00 (*0-933272-00-6*) Hurricane Co.

***Breathe & Stretch Your Stress Away: With Yoga.** Ina Townsend. 141p. 1995. pap. 12.95 (*0-9646116-0-0*) Tonti Assocs.

Breathe Deeply & Avoid Colds. Emanuel Josephson. (Natural Health Ser.). 127p. (Orig.). 1957. pap. 25.00 (*0-686-29302-9*, Chedney) A-albionic Res.

Breathe Deeply & Avoid Colds. Emanuel M. Josephson. (Orig.). 1979. 250.00 (*0-685-96457-4*) Revisionist Pr.

Breathe Deeply, My Son. Henry Wermuth. (Library of Holocaust Testimonies Ser.). (Illus.). 232p. 1993. pap. text ed. 19.50 (*0-85303-246-7*, Pub. by Vallentine Mitchell UK) Intl Spec Bk.

Breathe Easy: Young People's Guide to Asthma. Jonathan H. Weiss. (Illus.). 64p. (J). 1994. pap. 9.95 (*0-945354-62-2*) Magination Pr.

Breathe Free: Nutritional & Herbal Care for Your Respiratory System. Daniel Gagnon & Amadea Morningstar. LC 90-24413. 180p. (Orig.). (YA). 1991. pap. 14.95 (*0-914955-07-1*) Lotus Light.

Breathe in, Breathe Out. Rose Rosberg. 56p. (Orig.). 1992. pap. 7.50 (*1-880286-09-2*) Singular Speech Pr.

Breathe on Me Butterflies. Betty Trott. LC 93-60232. (Illus.). 44p. (J). (gr. k-3). 1994. pap. 8.95 (*1-55523-603-0*) Winston-Derek.

Breathe! You Are Alive: Sutra on the Full Awareness of Breathing. 2nd ed. Thich Nhat Hanh. Tr. by Annabel Laity. LC 90-48425. 68p. 1990. pap. 6.00 (*0-938077-38-4*) Parallax Pr.

Breathers. James Reiss. LC 73-86610. (American Poetry Ser.: Vol. 4). 64p. 1974. pap. 2.95 (*0-912946-17-2*) Ecco Pr.

Breathing. Anita Ganeri. (First Starts Ser.). (Illus.). 32p. (J). (gr. 2-4). 1994. lib. bdg. 19.97 (*0-8114-5520-3*) Raintree Steck-V.

Breathing: And Your Health. Brian Ward. LC 90-31226. (Health Guides Ser.). (Illus.). 32p. (J). (gr. 5-8). 1991. lib. bdg. 13.93 (*0-531-14094-6*) Watts.

Breathing: Expanding Your Power & Energy. Michael Sky. LC 90-840. 160p. (Orig.). 1990. pap. 9.95 (*0-939680-82-3*) Bear & Co.

Breathing: The Respiratory System. Jenny Bryan. LC 92-36353. (Body Talk Ser.). (Illus.). 48p. (J). (gr. 5 up). 1993. text ed. 13.95 (*0-87518-563-0*, Dillon Silver Burdett) Silver Burdett Pr.

Breathing & Relaxation: In Theory & Practice. Margarita Mayer. Ed. by Vesta Callender & Winifred Clark. Tr. by Thomas Mayer. (Illus.). 45p. (Orig.). (C). 1988. pap. text ed. write for info. (*0-318-62904-6*) W Clark.

Breathing Apparatus Guide: Leader's Guide. Shirley Ayers. 60p. (Orig.). 1992. pap. write for info. (*0-945790-03-1*) Detrick Lawrence.

Breathing Cathedral: Feeling Our Way into a Living Cosmos. Martha Heyneman. LC 92-34363. (Illus.). 224p. 1993. 25.00 (*0-87156-687-7*) Sierra.

Breathing Deeply of God's New Life: Preparing Spiritually for the Sacraments of Initiation. Mark Boyer. 170p. 1993. 7.95 (*0-86716-163-9*) St Anthony Mess Pr.

Breathing Disorders: Your Complete Exercise Guide. Neil F. Gordon. LC 92-42116. (Illus.). 144p. 1993. pap. 11.95 (*0-87322-426-4*, PGOR0426) Human Kinetics.

Breathing Disorders of Sleep. Ed. by Norman H. Edelman & Teodoro Santiago. (Contemporary Issues in Pulmonary Disease Ser.: Vol. 5). (Illus.). 274p. 1986. text ed. 47.00 (*0-443-08398-3*) Churchill.

An Asterisk (*) at the beginning of an entry indicates that the title is appearing in BIP for the first time.

An Asterisk (*) at the beginning of an entry indicates that the title is appearing in BIP for the first time.

895

Breeding Oat Cultivars Suitable for Production in Developing Countries. (Illus.). 120p. (Orig.). (C). 1993. pap. text ed. 40.00 (*1-56806-772-0*) Diane Pub.

Breeding of Pest Resistant Trees. Ed. by H. D. Gerhold et al. 1966. 214.00 (*0-08-011764-3*, Pub. by Pergamon Repr UK) Franklin.

Breeding Oilseed Brassicas. Ed. by K. S. Labana et al. (Monographs on Theoretical & Applied Genetics: Vol. 19). 296p. 1993. 139.00 (*0-387-55854-3*) Spr-Verlag.

Breeding Plants for Less Favorable Environments. Ed. by M. N. Christiansen & Charles F. Lewis. LC 81-10346. 469p. reprint ed. pap. 133.70 (*0-7837-2367-9*, 2040053) Bks Demand.

Breeding Plants Resistant to Insects. Ed. by Fowden G. Maxwell & Peter R. Jennings. LC 79-13462. (Environmental Science & Technology Ser.). 700p. reprint ed. pap. 180.00 (*0-7837-2811-5*, 2057661) Bks Demand.

Breeding Primates: Proceedings of the International Symposium on Breeding Non-Human Primates for Laboratory Use, Berne, 1971. International Symposium on Breeding Non-Human Primates for Laboratory Use Staff. Ed. by W. I. Beveridge. (Illus.). 300p. 1972. 51.25 (*3-8055-1369-0*) S Karger.

Breeding Programs for Dairy & Beef Cattle, Water Buffalo, Sheep & Goats, Vol. IX. Ed. by G. E. Dickerson & R. K. Johnson. (Proceedings of 3rd World Congress on Genetics Applied to Livestock Production Ser.). 1986. lib. bdg. write for info. (*0-9616828-0-9*) U Nebr IANR.

Breeding Programs for Swine, Poultry & Fish, Vol. X. Ed. by G. E. Dickerson & R. K. Johnson. (Proceedings of 3rd World Congress on Genetics Applied to Livestock Production Ser.). (Orig.). 1986. lib. bdg. write for info. (*0-9616828-1-7*) U Nebr IANR.

Breeding Purebred Cats. enl. rev. ed. Anne S. Moore. 132p. (Orig.). 1987. pap. 12.95 (*0-318-41068-0*) Abraxas Pub WA.

Breeding Rottweilers. Victoria Robertson. (Illus.). 128p. 1993. 11.95 (*0-86622-816-0*, KW229) TFH Pubns.

Breeding the Competition Horse. 2nd ed. John Rose & Sarah Pillider. LC 93-27092. 1993. 24.00 (*0-632-03727-X*) Blackwell Sci.

Breeding the Flock: Modern Research & Reproduction in Sheep. D. R. Lindsay. 1988. pap. 33.00 (*0-909605-45-9*, Pub. by Inkata Pr AT) Intl Spec Bk.

Breeding Vegetable Crops. Mark J. Bassett. (Illus.). 1985. text ed. 109.95 (*0-87055-499-9*) AVI.

Breeding, Whelping & Natal Care of Dogs. Louis L. Vine. LC 77-1817. 1977. pap. 2.50 (*0-668-04160-9*, Arco Test) P-H Gen Ref & Trav.

Breefe Declaration of That Which Is Happened As Well Within As Without Oastend. LC 70-171781. (English Experience Ser.: No. 406). 8p. 1971. reprint ed. 11.50 (*90-221-0406-0*) Walter J Johnson.

Breeze for a Bargeman. A. W. Roberts. 144p. 1994. pap. 22.00 (*0-86138-007-X*, Pub. by T Dalton UK) St Mut.

Breeze off the Ocean - Morgan Wade's Woman, 2 vols. in 1. Amii Lorin. 384p. 1994. mass mkt., pap. text ed. 4.99 (*0-505-51977-1*) Dorchester Pub Co.

Breeze Swept Through. Luci Tapahonso. 51p. (Orig.). 1987. pap. 7.95 (*0-931122-45-7*) West End.

Breezers: A Lighthearted History of the Open Trolley Car in America. Stephen L. Meyers. Ed. by Marion Harris. LC 93-33978. (Illus.). 184p. 1993. text ed. 56.00 (*0-933449-20-8*) Transport Trails.

Breezing Through the Change: Managing Menopause Naturally. Ellen H. Brown & Lynne P. Walker. LC 93-26662. 197p. 1994. 14.95 (*1-883319-12-9*) Frog CA.

Breezy. Leda Blumberg. 96p. (J). (gr. 3-7). 1988. pap. 2.50 (*0-380-89942-6*, Camelot) Avon.

Breezy. Helen M. Stearns. (Illus.). 40p. (J). (gr. k-1). 1984. 8.95 (*0-9614281-1-2*, Cricketfld Pr) Picton Pr.

Brega Path. Dennis McKiernan. 1987. pap. 4.99 (*0-451-45241-0*, ROC) NAL-Dutton.

Brega Path. Dennis L. McKiernan. 272p. 1987. pap. 3.95 (*0-451-16645-0*, Sig) NAL-Dutton.

Bregy, PA Intestate, Wills & Estates Provisions of PEF Code. Karen A. Fahrner et al. LC 90-84168. 1993. ring bd. 89.50 (*0-317-04142-8*) Bisel Co.

Brehon Laws: A Legal Handbook. Laurence Ginnell. vii, 249p. 1993. reprint ed. lib. bdg. 35.00 (*0-8377-2213-6*) Rothman.

Brehons, Serjeants & Attornies: Studies in the History of the Irish Legal Profession. Ed. by Daire Hogan & W. N. Osborough. 240p. 1990. 39.50 (*0-7165-2466-X*, Pub. by Irish Acad Pr IE) Intl Spec Bk.

Breitkoph & Hartel in Paris (1833-1844) The Letters of Heinrich Probst. Tr. & Comment by Hans Lenneberg. LC 90-7036. (Musical Life in Nineteenth-Century France Ser.: No. 5). (Illus.). 200p. (GER.). 1990. lib. bdg. 47.00 (*0-918728-64-9*) Pendragon NY.

***Breitling Timepieces: 1884-Present.** Benno Richter. (Illus.). 176p. 1995. 49.98 (*0-88740-864-8*) Schiffer.

***Breland Families of the Southern States, 1755-1875.** 2nd ed. Charles G. Breland. Ed. by Hunter M Breland. LC 95-69436. 100p. 1995. 20.00 (*0-9647379-0-6*) Queenstown Pr.

Bremen Town Musicians. Eugene Evans. LC 90-10974. (Fairy Tale Classics Ser.). (Illus.). 48p. (J). (gr. 1-5). 1990. 5.95 (*0-88101-102-9*) Unicorn Pub.

Bremen Town Musicians. Jacob Grimm & Wilhelm K. Grimm. Tr. by Anthea Bell. LC 88-15179. (Illus.). 32p. (J). (ps up). 1991. pap. 13.95 (*0-88708-071-5*, Picture Book Studio) S&S Childrens.

Bremen Town Musicians. Jacob Grimm & Wilhelm K. Grimm. LC 78-18064. (Illus.). 32p. (J). (gr. k-3). 1979. lib. bdg. 9.79 (*0-89375-133-2*); pap. 2.50 (*0-89375-111-1*) Troll Assocs.

Bremen Town Musicians. Jacob Grimm & Wilhelm K. Grimm. (Children's Classics Ser.). (Illus.). (J). 1991. 6.95 (*0-8362-4925-9*) Andrews & McMeel.

Bremen Town Musicians. Jacob Grimm & Wilhelm K. Grimm. LC 91-815. (Illus.). 32p. (J). (ps-3). 1992. lib. bdg. 15.95 (*0-8234-0939-2*) Holiday.

Bremen-Town Musicians. Ruth B. Gross. (Illus.). 32p. (Orig.). (J). (ps-2). 1985. pap. 2.50 (*0-590-42364-9*) Scholastic Inc.

***Bremen Town Musicians.** Rabbit. Date not set. pap. 19.95 (*0-689-80236-6*) Macmillan.

Bremen Town Musicians. Hans Wilhelm. 32p. (J). 1992. 13.95 (*0-590-44795-5*, Scholastic Hardcover) Scholastic Inc.

Bremen-Town Musicians. Ilse Plume. LC 86-42990. (Trophy Picture Bk.). (Illus.). 32p. (J). (ps-3). 1987. reprint ed. pap. 5.95 (*0-06-443141-X*, Trophy) HarpC Child Bks.

Bremen-Town Musicians Literature Mini-Unit. Janet Lovelady. (Illus.). 32p. (J). (gr. 2-4). 1989. student ed 4.95 (*1-56096-004-3*) Mari.

Brementown Musicians. (Read Along With Me Ser.: No. II). (Illus.). 24p. (J). (ps-3). 1993. 2.25 (*1-56288-166-3*) Checkerboard.

Bremer's Graphic Work. Detlev Rosenbach. (Illus.). 230p. 1974. 120.00 (*0-915346-98-2*) A Wofsy Fine Arts.

Bremia Dobra: Russkii Pisatel' Kak Vlastitel' Dum. Efimov I. Markovich. LC 93-15793. 204p. (Orig.). (RUS.). 1993. pap. 14.00 (*1-55779-064-7*) Hermitage.

Bremner's Bulletins, a Wee Sample. Walter D. Bremner. (Illus.). 135p. (Orig.). 1993. pap. 12.95 (*0-931563-13-5*) Wishing Rm.

***Bremsstrahlung from Radio-nuclides: Practical Guidance for Radiation Protection.** Ed. by I. S. McLintock. (C). 1994. 120.00x (*0-948237-23-6*, Pub. by H&H Sci Cnslts UK) St Mut.

***Brenda & Edward.** Maryann Kovalski. 1995. pap. 1.95 (*1-55074-139-X*) IPG Chicago.

Brenda Starr: The Red-Headed Bombshell. Dale Messick. (Illus.). 104p. 1989. pap. 12.95 (*0-944735-30-4*) Malibu Graphics.

Brenda the Cow & the Little White Hen. Walter Swan. Ed. by Deloris Swan. (Illus.). 16p. (Orig.). (J). (gr. 2-3). 1989. pap. 1.50 (*0-927176-02-5*) Swan Enterp.

Brendan: A Novel. Frederick Buechner. LC 88-45128. 256p. 1988. pap. 11.00 (*0-06-061178-2*) Harper SF.

Brendan Behan: An Annotated Bibliography of Criticism. E. H. Mikhail. 117p. 1980. text ed. 44.00 (*0-06-494826-9*, N6595) B&N Imports.

Brendan Behan's 'The Scarperer' P. J. O'Connor. (Adaptations Ser.). 1978. 6.95 (*0-685-04179-4*); pap. 2.95 (*0-912262-56-7*) Proscenium.

Brendan the Navigator. Jean Fritz. LC 78-13247. (Illus.). (J). (gr. 2-5). 1979. 14.95 (*0-698-20473-5*, Coward) Putnam Pub Group.

Brendan the Navigator: Exploring the Ancient World. George O. Simms. LC 89-82004. (Illus.). 96p. (YA). (gr. 7-12). 1989. 13.95 (*0-86278-202-3*, Pub. by OBrien Pr IE) Dufour.

Brendan the Navigator: Exploring the Ancient World. George O. Simms. (Illus.). 86p. 1990. pap. 9.95 (*0-86278-241-4*, Pub. by OBrien Pr IE) Dufour.

Brendan's Leather Book. Brendan Smith. (Illus.). 168p. (Orig.). 1972. pap. 4.50 (*0-686-02406-0*) Outer Straubville.

Brengle Treasury: A Samuel Logran Brengle Treasury. Sallie Chesham. 1988. 12.95 (*0-86544-049-2*) Salv Army Suppl South.

Brenhinedd y Saesson: or The Kings of the Saxons. Thomas Jones. (History & Law Ser.: No. 25). 439p. 1971. 28.50 (*0-904730-87-5*, Pub. by U of Wales UK) Bks Intl VA.

Brennan vs. Rehnquist: The Battle for the Constitution. LC 94-7708. 1994. 27.50 (*0-679-42436-9*) Knopf.

Brennan's Book. Garrett Anderson. 1976. text ed. 25.00 (*0-8464-0207-6*) Beekman Pubs.

Brennan's New Orleans Cookbook. Hermann B. Deutsch. LC 60-53567. (Illus.). 244p. 1982. 17.95 (*0-88289-382-3*) Pelican.

Brennan's Point. Daniel Lynch. 526p. 1988. 18.95 (*0-945167-03-2*) British Amer Pub.

Brennan's War: Vietnam 1965-1969. Matthew Brennan. 304p. 1989. mass mkt. 5.99 (*0-671-70595-4*) PB.

***Brenner & Rector's the Kidney, 2 Vols., Set.** 5th rev. ed. Barry M. Brenner. LC 95-3459. (Illus.). 2592p. 1995. text ed. write for info. (*0-7216-5075-9*) Saunders.

Brenner Debate: Agrarian Class Structure & Economic Development in Pre-Industrial Europe. Ed. by T. H. Aston & C. H. Philpin. (Past & Present Publications). 347p. 1987. pap. 22.95 (*0-521-34933-8*) Cambridge U Pr.

Brenner Restaurant Index: A Computerized Guide to Choice Restaurants in the Greater Los Angeles Area. Jules Brenner. 290p. (Orig.). 1984. pap. 12.95 (*0-685-42809-5*) NewTEK Indust.

Brenner Restaurant Index: A Computerized Guide to Choice Restaurants in the Greater Los Angeles Area. Jules Brenner. (Illus.). 274p. (Orig.). 1992. pap. 12.95 (*0-930437-00-4*) NewTEK Indust.

Brenner Restaurant Index: A Computerized Guide to Choice Restaurants in the Greater Los Angeles Area. 2nd ed. Jules Brenner. (Illus.). 268p. (Orig.). 1991. pap. 12.95 (*0-685-48586-2*) NewTEK Indust.

Brent: Descendants of Col. Giles Brent, Capt. George Brent & Robert Brent, Immigrants to Maryland & Virginia. C. H. Brent. (Illus.). 195p. 1993. reprint ed. lib. bdg. 41.00 (*0-8328-3649-4*); reprint ed. pap. 31.00 (*0-8328-3650-8*) Higginson Bk Co.

Brent Housekeeper: Open Mouth Coyote Head Mount. Brent Housekeeper. Ed. by Bob Williamson. (Illus.). 16p. (C). 1986. pap. text ed. 6.95 (*0-925245-24-0*) WASCO Manufact.

Brentano & Intrinsic Value. Roderick M. Chisholm. (Modern European Philosophy Ser.). 130p. 1986. 44.95 (*0-521-26437-5*); pap. 16.95 (*0-521-26989-X*) Cambridge U Pr.

Brenton: Plays One. Howard Brenton. (Methuen World Dramatists Ser.). 390p. 1988. pap. 9.95 (*0-413-40430-7*, A0040, Pub. by Methuen UK) Heinemann.

Brenton: Plays Two. Howard Brenton. (Methuen World Dramatists Ser.). 399p. (Orig.). (C). 1990. pap. 12.95 (*0-413-61490-5*, A0412, Pub. by Methuen UK) Heinemann.

Brenton the Playwright. Richard Boon. (Modern Theatre Profiles Ser.). (Illus.). 355p. (Orig.). (C). 1991. pap. 19.95 (*0-413-18980-5*, A0553, Pub. by Methuen UK) Heinemann.

Brentwood. Grace L. Hill. 20.95 (*0-89190-059-4*, Am Repr) Amereon Ltd.

Brer Rabbit & Boss Lion. Brad Kessler. (American Heroes & Legends Ser.). (Illus.). 40p. (J). (gr. k up). 1993. audio 19.95 (*0-88708-274-2*, Rabbit); 14.95 (*0-88708-273-4*, Rabbit) S&S Childrens.

Brer Rabbit & His Tricks. Ennis Rees. LC 93-32674. (Illus.). 48p. (J). (ps-4). 1994. pap. 5.95 (*1-56282-577-1*) Hyprn Ppbks.

Brer Rabbit & His Tricks. Ennis Rees. (J). (ps-3). 1990. pap. 5.95 (*0-929077-10-5*) WaterMark Inc.

Brer Rabbit & His Tricks. Ennis Rees. LC 93-32674. (Illus.). 56p. (J). (gr. k-5). 1992. reprint ed. 12.95 (*1-56282-215-2*) Hyprn Child.

Brer Rabbit & the Peanut Patch. rev. ed. Susan Dickinson. (Quality Time Easy Readers Ser.). (Illus.). 32p. (J). (gr. k-2). 1990. reprint ed. lib. bdg. 10.95 (*1-878363-18-2*) Forest Hse.

Brer Rabbit & the Wonderful Tar Baby. Illus. by Henrik Drescher. LC 90-7166. 32p. (J). (gr. k up). 1991. pap. 14.95 (*0-88708-144-4*, Rabbit); audio, pap. 19.95 (*0-88708-145-2*, Rabbit) S&S Childrens.

Brer Rabbit & the Wonderful Tar Baby. Joel C. Harris. (Illus.). 64p. (J). 1992. reprint ed. Mini-bk. audio 9.95 (*0-88708-250-5*, Rabbit) S&S Childrens.

Br'er Rabbit Stories. Rene Cloke. (J). 1988. 2.98 (*0-671-06187-9*) S&S Trade.

***Brer Rabbit's Adventures.** Cloke. 1995. (*0-517-12087-9*) Random Hse Value.

Brer Tiger & the Big Wind. William J. Faulkner. LC 94-15408. (Illus.). 32p. (J). (gr. k up). 1995. 15.00 (*0-688-12985-4*); lib. bdg. 14.93 (*0-688-12986-2*) Morrow Jr Bks.

Brereton Diaries. Lewis Brereton. (Politics & Strategy of World War II Ser.). 1976. reprint ed. lib. bdg. 45.00 (*0-306-70766-7*) Da Capo.

***Brereton Diaries.** Lewis Brereton. (American Autobiography Ser.). 450p. 1995. reprint ed. lib. bdg. 99.00 (*0-7812-8464-3*) Rprt Serv.

Bresilien Sans Peine: Portuguese for French Speakers. Assimil Staff. (FRE & POR.). 1990. 28.95 (*0-8288-4384-8*, F48125); audio 125.00 (*0-8288-9032-3*, F48121) Fr & Eur.

Breslov Haggadah. Yehoshua Starret & Chaim Kramer. Ed. by Moshe Mykoff. 256p. 1989. text ed. 15.95 (*0-930213-35-1*); pap. text ed. 16.00 (*0-930213-36-X*) Breslov Res Inst.

Breslov Music Book, Vol. 1: Azamer Bishvachin. Benzion Solomon. 120p. 1992. spiral bd. 20.00 (*0-930213-59-9*) Breslov Res Inst.

Breslov Music Book, Vol. 2: Asadeir LiSudose. Benzion Solomon. 132p. 1992. spiral bd. 20.00 (*0-930213-60-2*) Breslov Res Inst.

Brest Fortress: A Guide. M. Kudryashov. (Illus.). 86p. (C). 1987. 35.00 (*0-685-32382-X*, Pub. by Collets) St Mut.

Brest, Minsk, Smolensk, Moscow. Collets Staff. (Illus.). 151p. (C). 1982. 40.00 (*0-685-37529-3*, Pub. by Collets) St Mut.

Bret Harte. Patrick Morrow. LC 72-619588. (Western Writers Ser.: No. 5). (Illus.). 51p. (Orig.). (C). 1972. pap. 3.95 (*0-88430-004-8*) Boise St U W Writ Ser.

Bret Harte. Henry W. Boynton. LC 70-133513. (Select Bibliographies Reprint Ser.). 1977. reprint ed. 12.95 (*0-8369-5545-5*) Ayer.

Bret Harte: Great American Short Stories I. Illus. by James Balkovek. LC 94-75015. (Classic Short Stories Ser.). 80p. 1994. pap. 4.50 (*1-56103-005-8*) Lake Pub Co.

Bret Harte, Argonaut & Exile. George R. Stewart. LC 76-6593. reprint ed. 30.00 (*0-404-15298-8*) AMS Pr.

Bret Harte, Argonaut & Exile. George R. Stewart. 1992. reprint ed. lib. bdg. 75.00 (*0-7812-5093-5*) Rprt Serv.

Bret Harte the Goldrush Storyteller. Bret Harte et al. (Illus.). 264p. 1986. pap. 9.95 (*0-932458-33-5*) Star Rover.

Bret "Hit Man" Hart. Edward R. Ricciuti. Ed. by Bruce Glassman. (Face to Face Ser.). 25p. (Orig.). (J). (gr. 5 up). Date not set. text ed. 12.95 (*1-56711-075-4*, Topdog) Blackbirch.

Bret "Hit Man" Hart. Edward R. Ricciuti. Ed. by Bruce Glassman. (Face to Face Ser.). 25p. (Orig.). (J). (gr. 5 up). 1994. pap. text ed. 6.95 (*1-56711-070-3*) Blackbirch.

Bret (Rin, Pt. 23) A Play. Mark Dunster. LC 77-356479. 1976. 4.00 (*0-89642-012-4*) Linden Pubs.

Bretagne Green Guide. 3rd ed. (FRE.). Date not set. pap. 18.00 (*2-06-003094-3*, 309) Michelin.

***Bretagne Green Guide French Edition.** Michelin Staff. (FRE.). pap. 17.95 (*0-7859-7223-4*, 2060030943) Fr & Eur.

Brete Harte. Gary Scharnhorst. (Twayne's United States Authors Ser.). 150p. 1992. text ed. 20.95 (*0-8057-7648-6*, Twayne) Macmillan.

***Brethen Beginnings: The Origin of the Church of the Brethren in Early Eighteenth-Century Europe.** Donald F. Durnbaugh. (Monograph Ser.). 1992. 25.00 (*0-614-06603-4*) Brethren Encyclopedia.

***Brethen of the Brule.** rev. ed. William B. Bauer. (Illus.). 200p. 1995. pap. 14.95 (*0-9640154-0-4*) Brother Bills.

***Bretherick's Handbook of Reactive Chemical Hazards.** Rev. by Peter Urben. (Illus.). 1994. cd-rom 450.00 (*0-7506-2140-0*) Buttrwrth-Heinemann.

***Bretherick's Handbook of Reactive Chemical Hazards.** Rev. by Peter Urben. (Illus.). 1994. disk 450.00 (*0-7506-2141-9*) Buttrwrth-Heinemann.

***Bretherick's Handbook of Reactive Chemical Hazards, 2 vols., Set.** 5th ed. Rev. by Peter Urben. (Illus.). 2100p. 1994. 225.00 (*0-7506-1557-5*) Buttrwrth-Heinemann.

Bretherick's Handbook of Reactive Chemistry. 1990. 200.00 (*0-7506-0706-8*) Buttrwrth-Heinemann.

Brethern, I Would Not Have You Ignorant. Henry E. Griffin, Jr. 64p. (Orig.). 1986. pap. 2.25 (*0-934942-63-3*, 2262) White Wing Pub.

Brethren. Leonard Leventon. 208p. 1994. pap. 7.95 (*1-56901-400-0*) NW Pub.

Brethren. Shawn Ryan. 336p. (Orig.). 1993. mass mkt. 4.99 (*0-671-79243-1*) PB.

Brethren. Bob Woodward & Scott Armstrong. 592p. 1981. mass mkt. 6.99 (*0-380-52183-0*) Avon.

Brethren. H. Rider Haggard. reprint ed. lib. bdg. 26.95 (*0-89190-713-0*, Aeonian Pr) Amereon Ltd.

Brethren: A Poem in Four Books. Elizabeth Smith. LC 91-27141. 1992. 50.00 (*0-8201-1459-6*) Schol Facsimiles.

Brethren Beginnings: The Origin of the Church of the Brethren in Early Eighteenth-Century Europe. (Monograph Ser.). 99p. (C). 1992. text ed. 25.00 (*0-936693-23-1*) Brethren Encyclopedia.

***Brethren Dress: A Testimony to Faith.** Esther F. Rupel. (Monograph Ser.: No. 5). (Illus.). 200p. 1994. 45.00 (*0-936693-50-9*) Brethren Encyclopedia.

Brethren Encyclopedia, 1. (Illus.). 2126p. 1983. reprint ed. write for info. (*0-936693-01-0*) Brethren Encyclopedia.

Brethren Encyclopedia, 2. (Illus.). 2126p. 1983. reprint ed. write for info. (*0-936693-02-9*) Brethren Encyclopedia.

Brethren Encyclopedia, 3. (Illus.). 2126p. 1983. reprint ed. 75.00 (*0-936693-03-7*) Brethren Encyclopedia.

Brethren Encyclopedia, Set. (Illus.). 2126p. 1983. reprint ed. 130.00 (*0-936693-00-2*) Brethren Encyclopedia.

Brethren Hymn Books & Hymnals 1720-1884. Donald R. Hinks. (Illus.). 205p. 1986. 19.50 (*0-943429-01-3*) Brethren Heritage Pr.

Brethren in Colonial America. Donald F. Durnbaugh. (Illus.). 659p. 1967. 15.95 (*0-87178-110-7*) Brethren.

Brethren in Industrial America. Roger E. Sappington. 512p. 1985. 24.95 (*0-87178-111-5*) Brethren.

Brethren in the New Nation. Roger Sappington. (Illus.). 1976. 15.95 (*0-87178-113-1*) Brethren.

***Brethren of the Net: American Entomology, 1840-1880.** Conner Sorenson. LC 94-5258. (History of Science & Technology Ser.). 1995. 59.95 (*0-8173-0755-9*) U of Ala Pr.

***Brethren Patriots Again: A Thirteen Session Study Guide Proposing Nonviolence As the Potential Power for the Continuing American Revolution.** fac. ed. Vernon Miller. (Heritage Learning Program Ser.). 64p. 1994. pap. 25.00 (*0-7837-7347-1*, 2047300) Bks Demand.

Brethren Social Policy, Nineteen Hundred Eight to Nineteen Fifty-Eight. Roger E. Sappington. LC 61-4081. 221p. reprint ed. pap. 63.00 (*0-8357-7399-X*, 2022416) Bks Demand.

***Brethren Society: The Cultural Transformation of a "Peculiar People"** Carl F. Bowman. LC 94-19329. (Illus.). 512p. 1994. text ed. 59.95x (*0-8018-4904-7*); pap. text ed. 18.95x (*0-8018-4905-5*) Johns Hopkins.

Breton Dictionary: Dictionnaire Breton. Jakez Helias. 816p. (BRE & FRE.). 1986. 125.00 (*0-8288-1115-6*, F89680) Fr & Eur.

Breton-French Dictionary of the Vannes Dialect: Dictionnaire Breton-Francais du Dialecte de Vannes. Emile Ernault. 320p. (BRE & FRE.). 1991. reprint ed. pap. 32.95 (*0-7859-4748-5*) Fr & Eur.

Breton Lays in Middle English. Ed. by Thomas C. Rumble. LC 65-11629. (Waynebooks Ser.: No. 25). (Illus.). 270p. 1965. reprint ed. pap. 15.95 (*0-8143-1265-9*) Wayne St U Pr.

Breton Sans Peine (One) Breton for French Speakers (1) Assimil Staff. (BRE & FRE.). 1990. 28.95 (*0-8288-4467-4*, M14495); audio 125.00 (*0-8288-9033-1*, M14795) Fr & Eur.

Breton Sans Peine (Two) Breton for French Speakers (2) Assimil Staff. (BRE & FRE.). 1990. 28.95 (*0-8288-4469-0*, M4624); audio 125.00 (*0-8288-9034-X*, M14796) Fr & Eur.

Bretons. Patrick Galliou & Michael Jones. (Peoples of Europe Ser.). (Illus.). 240p. 1991. 29.95 (*0-631-16406-5*) Blackwell Pubs.

Brett. Brett Hull & Kevin Allen. 242p. 1992. pap. 5.95 (*1-895565-14-6*) Firefly Bks Ltd.

Brett Ashley. Ed. by Harold Bloom. (Major Literary Characters Ser.). 216p. 1991. lib. bdg. 29.95 (*0-7910-0951-3*) Chelsea Hse.

Brett Genealogy. L. B. Goodenow. (Illus.). 545p. 1993. reprint ed. lib. bdg. 94.00 (*0-8328-3015-1*); reprint ed. pap. 84.00 (*0-8328-3016-X*) Higginson Bk Co.

Brett Hull. Carl R. Green & Roxanne Green. LC 93-23424. (J). 1994. text ed. 13.95 (*0-89686-837-0*, Mac Bks Young Read) S&S Childrens.

Brett Hull: Hockey's Top Gun. Margaret J. Goldstein. (Sports Achievers Ser.). (Illus.). 64p. (J). (gr. 4-7). 1992. lib. bdg. 13.50 (*0-8225-0544-4*, Lerner Publctns); pap. 3.95 (*0-8225-9599-0*, Lerner Publctns) Lerner Group.

Brett, My Pet. Patty Carratello. Ed. by Darlene Spivak. (Easy Rainbow Reader Ser.). (Illus.). 16p. (J). (gr. k-2). 1988. student ed 1.95 (*1-55734-387-X*) Tchr Create Mat.

Brett Randall, Gambler. large type ed. E. B. Mann. (Linford Western Library). 352p. 1988. pap. 11.95 (*0-7089-6527-X*, Linford) Ulverscroft.

An Asterisk (*) at the beginning of an entry indicates that the title is appearing in BIP for the first time.

Brett Weston: A Personal Selection. Dody Thompson. Ed. by David Featherstone. LC 86-91436. (Illus.). 70p. 1986. 75.00 (*0-9616515-0-4*) Photog West Graphics.

Brett Weston: Master Photographer. Beaumont Newhall et al. Ed. by Carol W. Christopher & David Featherstone. (Illus.). 180p. 1989. 95.00 (*0-9616515-3-9*) Photog West Graphics.

***Brett Whiteley: Art & Life.** Barry Pearce & Wendy Whiteley. LC 95-60188. (Illus.). 240p. 1995. 45.00 (*0-500-09252-4*) Thames Hudson.

Bretton Woods: Birth of a Monetary System. Armand Van Dormael. LC 77-10651. 332p. 1979. 39.50 (*0-8419-0326-3*) Holmes & Meier.

***Bretton Woods: Rethinking Bretton Woods.** 70p. (Orig.). 1995. pap. 45.00 (*0-7605-1660-X*) Rector Pr.

***Bretton Woods & Dumbarton Oaks: American Economic & Political Post-War Planning in the Summer of 1944.** Georg Schild. LC 94-34125. 254p. 1995. text ed. 45.00 (*0-312-12216-0*) St Martin.

***Bretton Woods Commission Report July 1994.** (Illus.). 325p. (Orig.). 1995. pap. 195.00 (*0-7605-1682-0*) Rector Pr.

Bretton Woods Debates: A Memoir. Raymond F. Mikesell. LC 94-8984. (Essays in International Finance Ser.: No. 192). 1994. 8.00 (*0-88165-099-4*) Princeton U Int Finan Econ.

***Bretton Woods-GATT System: Retrospect & Prospect after Fifty Years.** Ed. by Orin Kirshner. 400p. 1995. 62.50 (*1-56324-629-5*); pap. 24.95 (*1-56324-630-9*) M E Sharpe.

Bretton Woods Plot: The Twin Evils of the International Monetary Fund & the World Bank for Reconstruction & Development. A. N. Field. 1979. lib. bdg. 69.95 (*0-8490-2879-5*) Gordon Pr.

Breu Diccionari Ideologic Catala. Xavier Romeu. 270p. (CAT.). 1977. pap. 19.95 (*0-8288-5291-X*, S50236) Fr & Eur.

Breughel's Pig. Robert Peters. (Orig.). 1988. pap. 9.95 (*0-89807-139-9*) Illuminati.

Breuiary of Helthe, for All Maner of Syckenesses & Diseases, the Whiche May Be in Man, or Woman Deth Folowe, 2 pts., Set. Andrew Borde. LC 71-38106. (English Experience Ser.: No. 362). 356p. 1971. reprint ed. 50.00 (*90-221-0362-5*) Walter J Johnson.

***Breuss Cancer Cure: Advice for the Prevention & Natural Treatment of Cancer, Leukemia & Other Seemingly Incurable Diseases.** Rudolf Breuss. LC 95-910587. 112p. (Orig.). 1995. pap. 11.95 (*0-920470-56-4*) Alive Bks.

Brev fra F. A. Reissiger-Letters from F. A. Reissiger. Bjarne Kortsen & Friedrich A. Reissiger. LC 76-506867. (Illus.). li, 90p. (Orig.). (ENG, GER & NOR.). 1975. pap. 24.00 (*0-934082-13-8*) Theodore Front.

***Brevard County: A History to 1955.** Ruth M. Erikson. 1994. pap. text ed. 15.95 (*1-886104-00-X*) Fla Hist Soc.

Brevard County: From Cape of the Canes to Space Coast. Elaine M. Stone. 136p. 1988. 27.95 (*0-89781-277-8*, 5316) Preferred Mktg.

***Brevard County: On the Edge of Sea & Space.** Elaine M. Stone & L. A. Davis. Ed. by Mary S. Hughes & James E. Turner. (Illus.). 144p. 1995. 35.00 (*1-885352-17-4*) Community Comm.

Breve Antologia Bibliografica de Puerto Rico (1493-1990) Comp. by Jose N. Davila-Lanausse. LC 89-82741. (Illus.). 84p. (Orig.). (C). 1990. pap. text ed. 8.00 (*0-9622522-4-7*) Editorial Academica.

Breve Apologia de la Cultura Cristiana Occidental. Carlos F. Aballi. LC 90-82590. (Coleccion Cuba y Sus Jueces Ser.). 64p. (Orig.). (SPA.). 1990. pap. 7.95 (*0-89729-567-6*) Ediciones.

***Breve Diccionario de Autores Griegos y Latinos.** B. Kytzler. 300p. (SPA.). 1993. 125.00 (*84-249-1395-7*) Elliots Bks.

Breve Diccionario de Filosofia: Brief Dictionary of Philosophy. Muller. 464p. (SPA.). 1977. 29.95 (*0-8288-5292-8*, S50199) Fr & Eur.

Breve Diccionario del Argentino Exquisito. Adolfo Bioy Casares. 162p. (SPA.). 1978. 19.95 (*0-8288-4865-3*, S33074) Fr & Eur.

Breve Diccionario Espanol-Ruso: Ruso-Espanol de Terminos Cientificos & Tecnicos. deluxe ed. J. C. Orts et al. 438p. (RUS & SPA.). 1960. 35.00 (*0-8288-6832-8*, S-31835) Fr & Eur.

***Breve Diccionario Etimologico de la Lengua Castellana.** J. Corominas. 628p. (SPA.). 1993. 125.00 (*84-249-1332-9*) Elliots Bks.

Breve e Facile Maniera. Giovanni Conforto. (Monuments of Music Literature in Facsimile: Ser. II, Vol. 115). 1978. reprint ed. lib. bdg. 30.00 (*0-8450-2315-2*) Broude.

Breve Estudio Sobre el Pentateuco: Lectures on the Pentateuch. James G. Chastain. (SPA.). 5.50 (*84-7645-062-1*, 223120, Pub. by Edit Clie SP) TSELF.

Breve Historia de la Iglesia Cristiana, Revisada. Howard F. Vos. Orig. Title: An Introduction to Church History. 160p. (SPA.). 1988. pap. 5.99 (*0-8254-1824-0*) Kregel.

Breve Historia de los Bautistas Hasta 1900. Enrique C. Vedder. Tr. by Teofilo Barocio. 272p. 1985. reprint ed. 3.75 (*0-311-15039-X*) Casa Bautista.

Breve Historia Del Cristianismo: A Concise History of the Christian. G. H. Lacy. (SPA.). 5.50 (*84-7645-274-8*, 223325, Pub. by Edit Clie SP) TSELF.

***Breve Historia Feminista de la Literatura Espanola: En Lengua Castellana, Tomo I.** Myriam Diaz-Diocaretz & Iris M. Zavala. 143p. 1993. pap. 10.50 (*84-7658-403-2*) U of PR Pr.

Brevedad de la Inocencia: Aventuras y Desventuras de un Cubano en el Exilio. Pancho Vives. LC 93-70237. (Coleccion Caniqui Ser.). 199p. (Orig.). (SPA.). 1993. pap. 16.00 (*0-89729-670-2*) Ediciones.

***Brevet Brigadier Generals in Blue.** Roger D. Hunt & Jack R. Brown. (Illus.). 700p. 1991. 65.00 (*1-56013-002-4*) Olde Soldier Bks.

Brevet's Illinois Historical Markers & Sites. Ed. by Lina S. Plucker & Kaye L. Roerick. LC 75-253. (Historical Markers-Sites Ser.). (Illus.). 300p. (Orig.). 1976. pap. 9.95 (*0-88498-029-4*) Brevet Pr.

Brevet's North Dakota Historical Markers & Sites. Ed. by Kaye L. Roehrick. LC 74-79978. (Historical Markers-Sites Ser.). (Illus.). 176p. 1975. 12.95 (*0-88498-024-3*) Brevet Pr.

Breviaire Poetique. Paul Claudel. (FRE.). pap. 10.95 (*0-8288-9108-7*, F93930) Fr & Eur.

Breviarium Aberdonense, 2 Vols, Set. Ed. by William Blew. LC 73-39874. (Bannatyne Club, Edinburgh. Publications: No. 96). reprint ed. 170.00 (*0-404-52844-9*) AMS Pr.

Breviary of Torment. Thomas Cashet. Ed. by John Hanley. (Illus.). 109p. (Orig.). 1991. 28.95 (*1-879194-04-X*); pap. 13.95 (*1-879194-03-1*) GLB Pubs.

Breviloquium. St. Bonaventure. Tr. by Jose De Vinck. 326p. 1963. 15.00 (*0-8199-0528-3*, Frncscn Herld) Franciscan Pr.

Brevis Collectio Artis Musicae. Bonaventura Da Brescia. Ed. by Albert Seay. (Critical Texts Ser.: No. 11). (Illus.). vi, 93p. 1981. pap. text ed. 6.00 (*0-933894-01-5*) Colo Coll Music.

***Brevisima Historia de Fray Bartolome de las Casas, Obispo de Chiapas.** Andres D. Puello. (Cuadernos Panamericanos Ser.). 44p. 1994. spiral bd. 11.95 (*0-9631210-2-2*) DPA Intl.

Brevities. Martin Booth. 1974. pap. 6.00 (*0-685-40884-1*) Elizabeth Pr.

Brew Free or Diet Beer & Brewing Vol. 11: AHA. American Homebrewers Association Staff & National Conference on Quality Beer & Brewing Staff. (Illus.). 240p. (Orig.). 1991. pap. 21.95 (*0-937381-26-8*) Brewers Pubns.

Brew Vocabulari Catala-Castella-Angles de Comerc Exterior. 43p. (CAT, ENG & SPA.). 13.50 (*0-7859-0718-1*, S33058) Fr & Eur.

Brew Your Own Real Ale at Home. Roger Protz & Graham Wheeler. (Illus.). 187p. (Orig.). 1993. per., pap. 14.99 (*1-85249-113-2*, Pub. by Camra Bks UK) Info Devels.

Brewed in America: A History of Beer & Ale in the United States. Stanley W. Baron. LC 72-5030. (Technology & Society Ser.). (Illus.). 424p. 1979. reprint ed. 36.95 (*0-405-04683-9*) Ayer.

Brewed in the Pacific Northwest: A History of Beer Making in Oregon & Washington. Gary Meier & Gloria Meier. LC 91-23402. (Western Writers Ser.: No. 3). 216p. (Orig.). 1991. 25.95 (*0-940242-54-0*) Fjord Pr.

Brewer & Holden (ME) Families. 26p. 1986. reprint ed. pap. 4.00 (*0-935207-38-4*) Danbury Hse Bks.

Brewer Medical Diet for Normal & High-Risk Pregnancy: A Leading Obstetrician's Guide to Every Stage of Pregnancy. Gail S. Brewer & Thomas H. Brewer. 1983. 8.95 (*0-686-44924-X*, Fireside) S&S Trade.

Breweries of Wisconsin. Jerry Apps. LC 92-10591. (North Coast Bks.). (Illus.). 272p. (Orig.). 1992. 29.95 (*0-299-13370-2*); pap. 19.95 (*0-299-13374-5*) U of Wis Pr.

Brewers, Beerhalls, & Boycotts: A History of Liquor in South Africa. Paul La Hausse. (History Workshop Topic Ser.: No. 2). (Illus.). 67p. (C). 1988. pap. 9.95 (*0-86975-332-0*, Pub. by Ravan Pr ZA) Ohio U Pr.

***Brewer's Cinema: A Phrase & Fable Dictionary.** Frwd. by Richard Attenborough. 640p. 1995. 29.95 (*0-304-34235-1*, Pub. by Cassell UK) Sterling.

***Brewer's Companion.** rev. ed. Randy Mosher. (Illus.). 1995. pap. 19.95 (*0-9640410-1-4*) Alephenalia.

Brewer's Myth & Legend. Ed. by J. C. Cooper. 320p. 1993. 21.95 (*0-304-34084-7*, Pub. by Cassell UK) Sterling.

Brewer's Politics: A Phrase & Fable Dictionary. Nicholas Comfort. 693p. 1994. 24.95 (*0-304-34085-5*, Pub. by Cassell UK) Sterling.

***Brewer's Politics: A Phrase & Fable Dictionary.** rev. ed. Nicholas Comfort. 704p. 1995. 29.95 (*0-304-34659-4*, Pub. by Cassell UK) Sterling.

***Brewer's Quotations: A Phrase & Fable Dictionary.** Nigel Rees. 448p. 1995. 24.95 (*0-304-34397-8*, Pub. by Cassell UK) Sterling.

Brewer's Star. 2nd ed. Paula Weber. 720p. 1993. pap. 24.95 (*0-9635968-1-0*) Bavaria Bks.

Brewer's Theater: A Phrase & Fable Dictionary. LC 94-16436. 1994. 35.00 (*0-06-270043-X*) HarpC.

***Brewer's Twentieth-Century Music.** David Pickering. 480p. 1995. 24.95 (*0-304-32049-8*, Pub. by Cassell UK) Sterling.

Brewer's Yeast, Wheat Germ, Lecithin & Other High Power Foods. Beatrice T. Hunter. (Good Health Guide Ser.). 1982. pap. 2.50 (*0-87983-278-9*) Keats.

Brewery Adventures in the Big East: A Travel Guide to East Coast Craft Breweries. Jack Erickson. (Illus.). 200p. (Orig.). 1994. pap. 14.95 (*0-941397-06-8*) Redbrick Pr.

Brewery Adventures in the Wild West. Jack Erickson. (Illus.). 220p. (Orig.). 1991. pap. 14.95 (*0-941397-04-1*) Redbrick Pr.

***Brewery Adventures in the Wild West II: A Travel Guide to West Coast Craft Breweries.** rev. ed. Jack Erickson. (Illus.). 276p. (Orig.). 1995. pap. 16.95 (*0-941397-07-6*) Redbrick Pr.

Brewery Operations Vol. 3: Microbrewers Conference 1986 Transcripts. Ed. by Virginia Thomas. (Illus.). 1986. 25.95 (*0-937381-04-7*) Brewers Pubns.

Brewery Operations Vol. 6: Microbrewers Conference 1989 Transcripts. Ed. by Virginia Thomas. (Illus.). 257p. 1990. pap. 25.95 (*0-937381-16-0*) Brewers Pubns.

Brewery Operations Vol. 7: Microbrewers Conference 1990 Transcripts. Ed. by Virginia Thomas. (Illus.). 226p. (Orig.). 1991. pap. 25.95 (*0-937381-23-3*) Brewers Pubns.

Brewery Planner. Institute for Brewing Studies Staff. 192p. 1991. pap. 80.00 (*0-937381-25-X*) Brewers Pubns.

***Brewing.** Lewis. 1995. pap. (*0-412-26420-X*) Chapman & Hall.

Brewing: Twenty Milwaukee Poets. Ed. & Frwd. by Martin J. Rosenblum. LC 72-89435. 1972. 6.95 (*0-89018-008-3*); pap. 6.00 (*0-89018-007-5*) Pentagram.

Brewing & Bottling Dictionary: Fachwoerterbuch der Brauerei und Abfuellpraxis. 2nd ed. K. U. Heyse. 240p. (ENG & GER.). 1981. 45.00 (*0-8288-0030-8*, M15346) Fr & Eur.

***Brewing & Breweries.** Maurice Lovett. (C). 1989. pap. 25.00x (*0-85263-568-0*, Pub. by Shire UK) St Mut.

Brewing Beer Like Those You Buy. Dave Line. (Illus.). 158p. (Orig.). 1993. reprint ed. pap. 10.95 (*0-9619072-3-1*) G W Kent.

Brewing in Trinidad, Colorado: A Beer History from Statehood to the Last Draught. Michael C. Hennech. (Illus.). 104p. (Orig.). 1992. pap. 14.95 (*1-881301-02-8*) Ale Pub.

Brewing Industry in England 1700-1830. Peter Mathias. (Modern Revivals in Economic & Social History Ser.). 63p. 1993. 92.95 (*0-7512-0150-2*, Pub. by Gregg Revivals UK) Ashgate Pub Co.

***Brewing Industry Report.** (Orig.). 1995. pap. 395.00 (*0-7605-2164-6*) Rector Pr.

Brewing Lager Beer. Gregory Noonan. (Illus.). 314p. 1986. pap. 14.95 (*0-937381-01-2*) Brewers Pubns.

Brewing Mead. Robert Gayre & Charlie Papazian. (Illus.). 202p. 1986. pap. 11.95 (*0-937381-00-4*) Brewers Pubns.

Brewing Microbiology. Ed. by F. G. Priest & I. Campbell. 278p. 1987. 84.75 (*1-85166-062-3*, Pub. by Elsevier Applied Sci UK) Elsevier.

Brewing Quality Beers. 2nd ed. Byron Burch. 1993. pap. 5.95 (*0-9604284-2-9*) Joby Bks.

Brewing Science, Vol. 1. Ed. by J. R. Pollock. (Food Science & Technology Ser.). 1979. text ed. 223.00 (*0-12-561001-7*) Acad Pr.

Brewing Science, Vol. 3. Ed. by J. R. Pollock. (Food Science & Technology Ser.). 611p. 1987. text ed. 223.00 (*0-12-561003-3*) Acad Pr.

Brewing Storms. Ed. by Scott A. Grover. (Illus.). (Orig.). Date not set. 24.95 (*1-883621-00-3*); teacher ed 11.95 (*1-883621-03-8*); lib. bdg. 29.95 (*1-883621-01-1*); pap. 9.95 (*1-883621-02-X*) S A Grover.

Brewing the World's Great Beers: A Step-By-Step Guide. Dave Miller. Ed. by Ben Watson. LC 91-50605. 160p. 1992. 22.95 (*0-88266-776-9*); pap. 12.95 (*0-88266-775-0*) Storey Comm Inc.

Brewing under Adversity Brewery Operations Vol. 8: Microbrewers Conference 1991 Transcripts. Ed. by Virginia Thomas. (Illus.). 248p. (Orig.). 1992. pap. 25.95 (*0-937381-29-2*) Brewers Pubns.

***Brewmaster's Recipe Manual.** Steve Snyder. Ed. by Alfred Haunold et al. (Illus.). 310p. 1994. ring bd. write for info. (*1-885591-07-1*) Morris Pubng.

Brewsie & Willie. Lisabeth Blake. 1960. pap. 2.75 (*0-8222-0149-6*) Dramatists Play.

Brewster & Wheatstone on Vision. Ed. by Nicholas J. Wade. 1984. text ed. 92.00 (*0-12-729550-X*) Acad Pr.

Brewster by Name, T. Barlow Hill. Brewster. LC 62-63251. 254p. 1994. 10.95 (*1-55523-586-7*) Winston-Derek.

Brewster Genealogy, 1566-1907: A Record of the Descendants of William Brewster of the Mayflower, 2 vols. Emma C. Jones. (Illus.). 1493p. 1988. reprint ed. lib. bdg. 197.50 (*0-8328-0314-6*); reprint ed. pap. 187.50 (*0-8328-0315-4*) Higginson Bk Co.

Brewster's Courage. Deborah Kovacs. LC 91-21481. (Illus.). 112p. (J). (gr. 2-6). 1992. pap. 14.00 (*0-671-74016-4*, S&S Bks Young Read) S&S Childrens.

Brewster's Millions. George B. McCutcheon. 1976. lib. bdg. 19.95 (*0-89968-058-5*, Lghtyr Pr) Buccaneer Bks.

Breyfogle's Lost Gold. John M. Townley & Jamison Station Press Staff. (Desert Rat Guidebook Ser.: No. 5). (Illus.). 16p. 1985. 1.95 (*0-317-01478-1*) Jamison Stn.

Brezhnev Era. Stuart A. Kallen. Ed. by Rosemary Wallner. LC 92-13475. (Rise & Fall of the Soviet Union Ser.). (J). 1992. lib. bdg. 13.99 (*1-56239-104-6*) Abdo & Dghtrs.

Brezhnev Years, 1964-1981 see Resolutions & Decisions of the Communist Party of the Soviet Union: 1898-1964

***Brhad Devata, 2 pts.** Arthur A. Macdonell. (C). 1994. text ed. 44.00 (*81-208-1141-0*, Pub. by Motilal Banarsidass II) S Asia.

Brhad-Devata, Attributed to Saunaka: A Summary of the Deities & Myths of the RgVeda, Vols. 5-6. Arthur A. Macdonnel. (Harvard Oriental Ser.). (C). 1965. 27.50 (*0-8364-2357-7*, Pub. by Motilal Banarsidass II) S Asia.

Brhadaranyaka Upanisad. Tr. by P. Lal. (Saffronbird Ser.). 117p. (ENG.). (C). 1975. pap. text ed. 6.75 (*0-88253-828-4*) Ind-US Inc.

***Brhadaranyaka Upanisad.** Nitya C. Yati. (C). 1994. 29.50x (*81-246-0007-4*, Pub. by DK Pubs Dist II) S Asia.

Brhadaranyaka Upanishad. Tr. by Swami Madhavananda. 1965. Bilingual ed. pap. 7.95 (*0-87481-063-9*, Pub. by Advaita Ashrama II) Vedanta Pr.

Brhadaranyaka Upanishad. 2nd ed. Tr. by Swami Jagadiswarananda. 1951. Bilingual ed. pap. 5.95 (*0-87481-415-4*, Pub. by Ramakrishna Math II) Vedanta Pr.

Brhaddesi of Sri Matanga Muni, Vol. 1. Matanga Muni. Ed. by Prem L. Sharma & Kapila Vatsyayan. (Kalamulasasatra Series Eight: Vol. 1). (C). 1995. 28.50x (*81-208-1031-7*, Pub. by Motilal Banarsidass II) S Asia.

***Brhaddesi of Sri Matanga Muni, Vol. 2.** Matanga Muni. Ed. by Oren Kata & Prem L. Sharma. (C). 1995. 28.50x (*81-208-1032-5*, Pub. by Motilal Banarsidass II) S Asia.

Brhatsamhita. Varahamihira. Ed. & Tr. by M. Ramakrishna Bhatt. 1985. 45.00 (*0-317-61104-6*, Pub. by Motilal Banarsidass II) S Asia.

***BRI Film & Television Handbook 1995: Nick Thomas.** (Illus.). 1995. pap. 28.95 (*0-85170-492-1*) Ind U Pr.

Brian Aldiss. Michael R. Collings. Ed. by Roger C. Schlobin. LC 85-17224. (Starmont Reader's Guide Ser.: Vol. 28). (Illus.). iv, 115p. (Orig.). 1986. lib. bdg. 25.00x (*0-916732-99-1*); pap. 15.00x (*0-916732-74-6*) Borgo Pr.

Brian Boru: Emperor of the Irish. Morgan Llywelyn. 160p. (Orig.). (J). (gr. 4 up). 1990. pap. 8.95 (*0-86278-230-9*, Pub. by OBrien Pr IE) Dufour.

***Brian Boru: Emperor of the Irish.** Morgan Llywelyn. (Illus.). 160p. (Orig.). (YA). (gr. 6 up). 1995. 14.95 (*0-312-85623-7*) Tor Bks.

Brian Clarke, No. 82. Ed. by Kyoichi Tsuzuki. (Art Random Ser.). (Illus.). 48p. 1991. 32.95 (*4-7636-8518-X*, Pub. by Kyoto Shoin JA) Bks Nippan.

Brian Clarke: Art & Design Monograph. (Illus.). 120p. 1994. pap. 38.00 (*1-85490-343-8*, Academy Edits) St Martin.

Brian de Palma. Michael Bliss. LC 83-3306. (Filmmakers Ser.: No. 6). 176p. 1983. 20.00 (*0-8108-1621-0*) Scarecrow.

***Brian Eno: His Music & the Vertical Color of Sound.** Eric Tamm. 242p. 1995. reprint ed. pap. 14.95 (*0-306-80649-5*) Da Capo.

Brian Friel. D. E. Maxwell. LC 76-125299. (Irish Writers Ser.). 110p. 1975. pap. 1.95 (*0-8387-7666-3*) Bucknell U Pr.

Brian Friel. George O'Brien. (Twayne's English Authors Ser.: No. 470). 182p. 1989. text ed. 23.95 (*0-8057-6980-3*, Twayne) Macmillan.

***Brian Friel: A Reference Guide.** George O'Brien. LC 94-30903. (Reference Guide to Literature Ser.). 152p. 1995. text ed. 40.00 (*0-8161-7273-0*) G K Hall.

Brian Friel & Ireland's Drama. Richard Pine. 208p. 1990. 69.95 (*0-415-04753-6*, A4244); pap. 18.95 (*0-415-04754-4*, A4248) Routledge.

Brian Has a Winning Day. Paul M. Quintilone. (J). (gr. 3-5). 1988. pap. write for info. (*0-9616980-2-0*) Quintilone Ent.

Brian Lumley. Brian Lumley. 1990. Boxed set. 13.85 (*0-8125-2858-1*) Tor Bks.

Brian Moore. Jeanne Flood. (Irish Writers Ser.). 98p. 1975. 8.50 (*0-8387-7823-2*); pap. 1.95 (*0-8387-7972-7*) Bucknell U Pr.

Brian Moore: A Critical Study. Jo O'Donoghue. 280p. (C). 1991. text ed. 44.95 (*0-7735-0850-3*, Pub. by McGill CN) U of Toronto Pr.

***Brian Piccolo: A Short Season.** 25th ed. Jeannie Morris. (Illus.). 200p. 1995. pap. text ed. 12.95 (*1-56625-024-2*) Bonus Books.

Brian Robertson's Favorite Texas Tales. Brian Robertson. LC 92-17115. (Illus.). 112p. (J). (gr. 4-7). 1992. 12.95 (*0-89015-862-2*) Sunbelt Media.

Brian Rust's Guide to Discography. Brian Rust. LC 79-6827. (Discographies Ser.: No. 4). (Illus.). x, 133p. 1980. text ed. 42.95 (*0-313-22086-7*, RGD/, Greenwood Pr) Greenwood.

Brian Wall. Seattle Art Museum Staff. LC 82-60696. (Illus.). 28p. (Orig.). 1982. pap. 6.95 (*0-932216-09-9*) Seattle Art.

***Brian Wildsmith 1, 2, 3.** Brian Wildsmith. LC 95-13987. (Illus.). 32p. (J). (ps-k). 1995. pap. 5.95 (*1-56294-905-5*) Millbrook Pr.

***Brian Wildsmith's A B C.** Brian Wildsmith. LC 95-14686. (Illus.). 56p. (J). (ps-k). 1995. pap. 6.95 (*1-56294-906-3*) Millbrook Pr.

Brian Wilson Aldiss: A Man for All Seasons: A Working Bibliography. Phil Stephensen-Payne & Gordon Benson, Jr. (Galactic Central Bibliographies Ser.: No. 26). ix, 138p. (C). 1990. lib. bdg. 23.00x (*0-8095-4724-4*) Borgo Pr.

Brian Wolf's Fantasy Finishes. Brian Wolf. (Illus.). 64p. 1991. 19.00 (*0-938655-33-7*) Columba Pub.

Brian Wolf's "Sketchbook of Designs" Brian Wolf. LC 89-62453. (Illus.). 32p. (Orig.). 1991. pap. text ed. 15.00 (*0-938655-30-2*) Columba Pub.

***Brianna et le Roi.** Diana Palmer. (Azur Ser.). (FRE.). 1994. pap. 3.50 (*0-373-34436-8*, 1-34436-5) Harlequin Bks.

Brian's Footsteps. Carol Gorman. LC 93-38322. (I Witness Ser.). (Illus.). 96p. (Orig.). (J). (gr. 4-7). 1994. pap. 3.99 (*0-570-04629-7*) Concordia.

Brian's Song. William Blinn. (Illus.). 128p. (Orig.). (J). (gr. 6 up). 1983. mass mkt. 3.99 (*0-553-26618-7*) Bantam.

***Briant Stringham & His People: With Additional Ashby Ancestors.** Nathaniel G. Stringham & Briant S. Hinckley. 448p. 1994. 24.98 (*0-88290-513-9*, 2024) Horizon Utah.

Briar Rose. Susan Wiggs. 400p. 1987. pap. 3.95 (*0-380-75430-4*) Avon.

***Briar Rose.** Susan Wiggs. 1994. pap. 4.50 (*0-06-108181-7*, Harp PBks) HarpC.

Briar Rose. Jane Yolen. Ed. by Terri Windling. (Fairy Tales Ser.: No. 3). 224p. 1993. mass mkt. 4.99 (*0-8125-5862-6*) Tor Bks.

Briard. Diane McLeroth. LC 83-138458. (Illus.). 240p. 1982. 20.00 (*0-9639860-0-7*) Aubry Assocs.

Briards. Alice B. Clark. (Illus.). 192p. 1994. 11.95 (*0-86622-761-X*, KW213) TFH Pubns.

Briarpatch. Ross Thomas. 384p. 1985. mass mkt. 5.95 (*0-14-007990-4*, Penguin Bks) Viking Penguin.

Briarpatch. Ross Thomas. LC 85-5814. (Fiction Ser.). 384p. 1988. mass mkt. 5.95 (*0-14-010581-6*, Penguin Bks) Viking Penguin.

***Bribage Cartooniano.** Fabio Doctorovich et al. (Illus.). 52p. (Orig.). 1994. pap. 9.00 (*0-935350-42-X*) Luna Bisonte.

B

Bribery & Extortion in World Business. Neil H. Jacoby et al. LC 77-6942. (Studies of the Modern Corporation). 1977. 19.95 (*0-02-916000-6*) Free Pr.

Bribes. John T. Noonan, Jr. LC 87-13924. 839p. 1988. pap. 17.00 (*0-520-06154-3*) U CA Pr.

Brice Marden: Boston. Trevor Fairbrother et al. (Illus.). 40p. 1992. pap. 17.50 (*0-87846-346-1*) Mus Fine Arts Boston.

Brice Marden: New Paintings, Drawings, Etchings. Brice Marden. (Illus.). 48p. 1993. 25.00 (*1-880146-07-X*) M Marks Inc.

Brice Marden: Paintings & Drawings. Klaus Kertess. (Illus.). 252p. 1992. 95.00 (*0-8109-3627-5*) Abrams.

***Brice Marden: Paintings & Drawings.** (Illus.). 120p. Date not set. pap. 35.00 (*1-880146-11-8*) M Marks Inc.

Brice Marden: Prints 1961-1991. Jeremy Lewison. (Illus.). 176p. 1992. 60.00 (*1-85437-092-8*, Pub. by Tate Gallery UK); pap. 35.00 (*1-85437-091-X*, Pub. by Tate Gallery UK) U of Wash Pr.

Brice Marden - Cold Mountain: The Way to Cold Mountain. Brenda Richardson. LC 92-16791. 1992. 35.00 (*0-939594-30-7*); 25.00 (*0-940619-09-1*) Menil Found.

Brice Marden Recent Drawings & Etchings: With an Interview by Pat Steir. Told to Pat Steir. (Illus.). 58p. 1991. pap. 15.00 (*1-880146-01-0*) M Marks Inc.

Brice Marden Recent Drawings & Etchings: With an Interview by Pat Steir. deluxe limited ed. Told to Pat Steir. (Illus.). 58p. 1991. 100.00 (*1-880146-02-9*) M Marks Inc.

***Brice Marden Sketchbook.** Brice Marden. (Illus.). 108p. Date not set. pap. 29.95 (*1-881616-49-5*) Dist Art Pubs.

***Brick: A Novel.** William Thompson. 192p. (Orig.). 1995. pap. 10.95 (*1-56474-142-7*) Fithian Pr.

Brick & Block Masonry: Proceedins of the Eighth International Conference Held in Trinity College, Dublin, Ireland, 19-21 Sept. 1988. Ed. by J. W. De Courcy. 1844p. 1989. 288.00 (*1-85166-265-0*) Elsevier.

Brick & Reinforced Brick Structures. P. Dayaratnam. 108p. (C). 1987. 14.00 (*81-204-0249-9*, Pub. by Oxford IBH II) S Asia.

Brick & the Rose. Lewis J. Carlino. 1959. pap. 2.75 (*0-8222-0150-X*) Dramatists Play.

Brick & Tile Industry in Stark County, 1809-1976: A History. C. Harold McCollam. LC 76-17281. 351p. reprint ed. pap. 100.10 (*0-8357-7400-7*, 2024925) Bks Demand.

Brick Architecture in Ancient Egypt. Spencer. 1979. 79.95 (*0-85668-128-8*, Pub. by Aris & Phillips UK) David Brown.

Brick Building in Britain. R. W. Brunskill. (Illus.). 208p. 1992. 50.00 (*0-575-04457-8*, Pub. by V Gollancz UK) Trafalgar.

***Brick City.** Lillian Whitlow. 400p. (Orig.). 1995. pap. 12.95 (*0-7610-0043-7*) NW Pub.

Brick-Clay, Common & Face - Wholesale & Manufacturers, 1995. American Business Directories Staff. 1995. spiral bd., pap. 210.00 (*1-56105-596-4*) Am Busn Direct.

Brick, Concrete, Stonework. Monte Burch. Ed. by Gail Kummings. LC 81-66575. (Illus.). 144p. (Orig.). 1980. pap. 9.95 (*0-932944-30-2*) Creative Homeowner.

Brick for Offissa Pupp. James M. LeCuyer. (Orig.). 1989. pap. 8.00 (*0-912449-31-4*) Floating Island.

Brick House Burglars. Peni R. Griffin. LC 93-22914. 144p. (J). (gr. 4-7). 1994. text ed. 14.95 (*0-689-50579-5*, McElderry) S&S Childrens.

Brick Moon & Other Stories. Edward E. Hale. LC 73-121555. (Short Story Index Reprint Ser.). 1977. 24.95 (*0-8369-3512-8*) Ayer.

Brick Oven Baking with Planned Pottery Bakeware, Vol. 1. rev. ed. Planned Pottery Staff. (Illus.). 1988. pap. 6.00 (*0-9620282-0-7*) Planned Pottery.

***Brick Pavement: The Architects & Builders Companion. Peter J. Harrison. LC 94-96169. (Architects & Builders Companion Ser.). (Illus.). 180p. 1994. 25.00 (*0-9636205-1-7*) P J Harrison. BRICK PAVEMENT: THE ARCHITECTS & BUILDERS COMPANION is the second in a series of detailed Architectural pattern books devoted to the study of 18th & early 19th century American styling; eleven bountiful chapters demonstrating COURSES & BONDS, JOININGS, CORNER,S BOARDERS, WALKS, ENTRANCE PAVEMENTS & TERRACES. 131 beautiful illustrations fashioned after 18th century copper plates. Included are two illustrating 21 antique bricklayer's tools; "with instructions to the Workmen on the lay of Brick for Foot Paths & Wide Ways." This most complete work concludes with a DICTIONARIAL INDEX of 93 terms "explaining the useful Art of Bricklayers Work, with Critical Remarks & Observations." Hard bound in tobacco brown fabric, gold stamped cover boards & spine, fine marbleized end sheets & printed with a period text; makes this a beautiful source book for every serious architect, landscaper & builder as well as historians & home owners with discerning tastes. Order from: Peter Joel Harrison, 2021 Fawndale Dr., Raleigh, NC 27612. 919-676-0659.** *Publisher Provided Annotation.*

Brick People. 2nd ed. Alejandro Morales. LC 88-10409. 320p. 1992. pap. 9.50 (*0-934770-91-3*) Arte Publico.

Brick Road to Boom Town: The Story of Santa Rosa County's "Old Brick Road" Brian R. Rucker. (Illus.). 58p. (Orig.). 1993. pap. 5.50 (*1-882695-07-0*) Patagonia Pr.

Brick, Stone & Concrete. Time-Life Books Staff. 1994. pap. 12.99 (*0-376-01912-3*) Sunset Menlo Pk.

Brick Temples of Bengal: From the Archives of David McCutchion. Ed. by George Michell. LC 82-3872. (Illus.). 450p. 1983. 125.00 (*0-691-04010-9*) Princeton U Pr.

Bricker Amendment Controversy: A Test of Eisenhower's Political Leadership. Duane Tananbaum. LC 88-3614. 280p. 1988. 39.95 (*0-8014-2037-7*) Cornell U Pr.

***Bricker's International Directory, University-Based Executive Programs, 1995.** 1004p. 1994. 295.00 (*1-56079-478-X*) Petersons Guides.

Brickhouse Dreams: Young Benjamin E. Mays. Melvin De Gree. (Illus.). 140p. (Orig.). (J). (gr. 3-10). 1992. pap. 11.95 (*0-9632895-0-0*) Trail of Success.

Bricklayer. Jack Rudman. (Career Examination Ser.: C-110). 1994. pap. 23.95 (*0-8373-0110-6*) Nat Learn.

Bricklaying. W. G. Nash. (Illus.). 128p. (Orig.). 1991. pap. 24.00 (*0-7487-1292-5*, Pub. by Stanley Thornes UK) Trans-Atl Phila.

Bricklaying: A Homeowner's Illustrated Guide. Charles R. Self. 1992. 22.95 (*0-07-157820-X*); pap. 14.95 (*0-07-157819-6*) McGraw.

Bricklaying: A Homeowner's Illustrated Guide. Charles R. Self. 176p. 1992. 22.95 (*0-8306-3918-7*); pap. 14.95 (*0-8306-3917-9*) TAB Bks.

Bricklaying Simplified. rev. ed. Donald R. Brann. LC 77-140968. (Illus.). 1976. lib. bdg. 5.95 (*0-87733-068-9*) Easi-Bild.

Bricklaying Simplified. Donald R. Brann. LC 77-140968. 1979. reprint ed. pap. 7.95 (*0-87733-668-7*) Easi-Bild.

Bricklaying Skill & Practice. 3rd ed. Robert Putnam. LC 73-84363. (Illus.). 272p. reprint ed. pap. 77.60 (*0-8357-7401-5*, 2006412) Bks Demand.

Brickmaking in Nebraska. William F. Rapp. (Illus.). 88p. 1993. pap. 9.00 (*0-916170-28-4*) J-B Pub.

Bricks. Terry Cash. Ed. by Rebecca Stefoff. LC 90-40249. (Threads Ser.). (Illus.). 32p. (J). (gr. 3-5). 1990. lib. bdg. 15.93 (*0-944483-68-2*) Garrett Ed Corp.

Bricks. Graham Rickard. LC 93-6833. (Resources Ser.). (Illus.). 32p. (J). (gr. 3-6). 1993. 13.95 (*1-56847-046-0*) Thomson Lrning.

***Bricks: A New Book of Poems by Daniel X. O'Neil.** Daniel X. O'Neil. 53p. 1992. pap. 10.00 (*0-9646137-0-0*) Juggernaut.

Bricks & Anchors. Jon Longhi. 128p. (Orig.). 1991. pap. 8.95 (*0-916397-12-2*) Manic D Pr.

Bricks & Brackets: A Lowell Activity Book. Ed. by Lewis T. Karabatsos. 19p. (Orig.). (J). (gr. 1-6). 1981. pap. 0.95 (*0-942472-04-7*) Lowell Museum.

Bricks & Brickmaking. Martin Hammond. (Album Ser.). (Illus.). 32p. 1981. pap. text ed. 5.25 (*0-7478-0067-7*, Pub. by Shire Pubns UK) Lubrecht & Cramer.

Bricks & Brickmaking: A Handbook for Historical Archaeology. Karl Gurcke. LC 87-5875. 326p. 1987. pap. 13.95 (*0-89301-118-5*) U of Idaho Pr.

Bricks & Brownstone: The New York Row House, 1783-1929. Charles Lockwood. (Illus.). 288p. 1988. 39.95 (*0-89659-785-7*) Abbeville Pr.

Bricks & Mortar: What's Left in Old Princess Anne County & New Virginia Beach. Ed. by C. W. Tazewell. LC 93-71162. (Illus.). 136p. 1993. pap. 17.00 (*1-878515-99-3*) W S Dawson.

Bricks Without Straw. Albion W. Tourgee. LC 67-29282. (Americans in Fiction Ser.). reprint ed. lib. bdg. 34.00 (*0-8398-1963-3*) Irvington.

Brickwork. (C). 1989. 45.00 (*1-85368-058-3*, Pub. by New Holland Pubs UK) St Mut.

Brickwork, Vol. 1. W. G. Nash. 152p. (C). 1983. pap. 30.00x (*0-7487-0266-0*, Pub. by S Thornes Pubs UK) St Mut.

Brickwork, Vol. 2. rev. ed. W. G. Nash. 204p. (C). 1988. pap. 33.00x (*0-7487-0310-1*, Pub. by S Thornes Pubs UK) St Mut.

Brickwork: Architecture & Design. Andrew Plumridge & Wim Meulenkamp. LC 92-24191. (Illus.). 224p. 1993. 39.95 (*0-8109-3123-0*) Abrams.

***Brickwork 2.** W. G. Nash. 224p. (C). 1988. pap. 30.00x (*0-7487-0265-2*, Pub. by S Thornes Pubs UK) St Mut.

Brickyard Summer. Paul B. Janeczko. LC 89-42542. (Illus.). 64p. (J). (gr. 7 up). 1989. 14.95 (*0-531-05846-8*); lib. bdg. 14.99 (*0-531-08446-9*) Orchard Bks Watts.

Bricolage Ex Machina. Carl Watson. Ed. & Illus. by Virginia Hoge. 90p. (Orig.). 1992. pap. text ed. 7.00 (*1-878883-00-3*) Lost Modern Pr.

Bridal Bargains: Secrets to Throwing a Fantastic Wedding on a Realistic Budget. Alan S. Fields & Denise C. Fields. 256p. (Orig.). 1990. pap. 9.95 (*0-9626556-0-0*) Windsor Peak Pr.

Bridal Bargains: Secrets to Throwing a Fantastic Wedding on a Realistic Budget. 2nd ed. Denise Fields & Alan Fields. (Illus.). 288p. (Orig.). 1993. pap. 10.95 (*0-9626556-1-9*) Windsor Peak Pr.

***Bridal Bargains: Secrets to Throwing a Fantastic Wedding on a Realistic Budget.** 3rd rev. ed. Denise Fields & Alan Fields. (Illus.). 320p. 1995. pap. 11.95 (*0-9626556-7-8*) Windsor Peak Pr.

Bridal Blues. Cathie Linz. 1994. mass mkt. 2.99 (*0-373-05894-2*, 1-05894-0) Harlequin Bks.

Bridal Bouquet: Penhaligon's Scented Treasury of Verse & Prose. Ed. by Sheila Pickles. (Illus.). 112p. 1991. 25.00 (*0-517-58507-3*, Harmony) Crown Pub Group.

***Bridal Buying Book: 1994-95 Macomb County Edition.** 184p. 1994. pap. text ed. 9.95 (*1-887177-00-0*) Bridal Buying Bur.

***Bridal Buying Book: 1995 Oakland County Edition.** 196p. 1994. pap. text ed. 9.95 (*1-887177-01-9*) Bridal Buying Bur.

***Bridal Buying Book: 1995-96 Wayne County Edition.** 190p. 1995. pap. text ed. 9.95 (*1-887177-02-7*) Bridal Buying Bur.

Bridal Creations. Kathy Lamancusa. (Illus.). 28p. (Orig.). 1987. pap. 5.95 (*0-933491-18-2*) Hot off Pr.

***Bridal Directory: Dallas-Fort Worth.** 2nd ed. Robert H. Sage. 220p. 1995. pap. 9.95 (*0-9639579-1-0*) Crtive Ventures.

Bridal Directory: Dallas-Fort Worth, 1994. Robert H. Sage. 165p. 1993. pap. 9.95 (*0-9639579-0-2*) Crtive Ventures.

Bridal Fashions: Victorian Era. Comp. by Donna Felger. (Illus.). 168p. 1986. pap. 12.95 (*0-87588-281-1*) Hobby Hse.

***Bridal Feast - the Lord's Supper.** Keith Harris. 151p. 1995. pap. text ed. 8.00 (*0-9636534-1-5*) Omega Pub KY.

Bridal Flowers: Arrangements for a Perfect Wedding. Maria McBride-Mellinger & William Stites. (Illus.). 96p. 1992. 24.95 (*0-8212-1917-0*) Bulfinch Pr.

Bridal Guide: The Complete Guide to Planning Your Wedding. 5th ed. Pamela Thomas. LC 92-71369. (Illus.). 350p. 1994. pap. 13.95 (*0-9615882-2-5*) Bridal Guide.

Bridal March & Other Stories. Bjornstjerne Bjornson. Tr. by Rasmos B. Anderson. LC 74-98562. (Short Story Index Reprint Ser.). 1977. 19.95 (*0-8369-3136-X*) Ayer.

Bridal Path. Alaina Hawthorne. (Silhouette Romance Ser.). 1994. pap. 2.75 (*0-373-19029-8*, 1-19029-7) Harlequin Bks.

Bridal-Quest Romance in Medieval Iceland. Marianne E. Kalinke. LC 89-22277. (Islandica Ser.: No. 46). 240p. 1990. 31.50 (*0-8014-2356-2*) Cornell U Pr.

Bridal Registry Budget & Service Guide. Frank M. Keesling. 180p. 1993. pap. 16.95 (*0-9637920-0-8*) Bridal Registry.

Bridal Sense: How to Get Married Without Going Crazy or Broke. Melanie Sonsini-Goodrich. Ed. by John K. Goodrich. (Illus.). 170p. 1985. pap. 9.95 (*0-933359-00-4*) Bridal Sense.

Bridal Shops, 1995. American Business Directories Staff. 1995. spiral bd., pap. 645.00 (*1-56105-597-2*) Am Busn Direct.

***Bridal Shower.** Elizabeth August. (Romance Ser.). 1995. mass mkt. 2.99 (*0-373-19091-3*, 1-19091-7) Silhouette.

Bridal Shower Guidebook. Myra M. Ishee. 96p. (Orig.). 1985. pap. 7.95 (*0-939298-44-9*, 449) J M Prods.

***Bridal Shower Journal.** Bruce A. Moulton. (Illus.). 22p. 1995. 16.95 (*0-9633573-2-8*) Lakeland Color.

Bridal Shower Keepsake. Nancy S. Taylor. 25p. 1990. spiral bd. 4.50 (*0-937745-10-3*) Traditions Pr.

Bridal Showers: Fifty Great Ideas for a Perfect Shower. Sharon E. Dlugosch & Florence E. Nelson. (Illus.). 144p. 1987. pap. 9.00 (*0-399-51344-2*, Perigree Bks) Berkley Pub.

Bridal Style. Nancy Davis. 1994. 60.00 (*0-88363-094-X*) H L Levin.

Bride. Zabel Asadour. Tr. by Nishan Parlakian. 1987. 12.00 (*0-918680-37-9*) Bagehot Council.

***Bride.** Stella Cameron. 416p. (Orig.). 1995. mass mkt. 5.99 (*0-446-60175-6*) Warner Bks.

Bride. Julie Garwood. Ed. by Linda Marrow. (Orig.). 1991. mass mkt. 5.99 (*0-671-73779-1*) PB.

***Bride.** Wallace H. Heflin. 168p. 1994. pap. 6.95 (*1-884369-10-3*, Treasures Pub) McDougal Pubng.

Bride: Renewing Our Passion for the Church. Charles R. Swindoll. LC 94-536. Orig. Title: Rise & Shine. 224p. 1994. 17.99 (*0-310-42070-9*) Zondervan.

Bride see Uncollected Poems, 1604-1617

Bride & Bear. Margaret Savides. 1980. pap. 2.00 (*0-685-04196-4*) Quixote.

Bride & Groom Handbook. Ronald H. Issacs. Ed. by Ruby G. Strauss. 64p. (Orig.). 1989. pap. text ed. 4.50x (*0-87441-476-8*) Behrman.

***Bride & the Baby.** Phyllis Halldorson. 1995. pap. 3.75 (*0-373-23999-8*, 1-23999-5) Silhouette.

Bride & the Bachelors. Calvin Tomkins. (Illus.). 1976. pap. 11.00 (*0-14-004313-6*, Penguin Bks) Viking Penguin.

Bride Book. Deborah Wood. 192p. 1987. pap. 10.95 (*0-937533-02-5*) TEC Pubns.

Bride-Bush, or a Wedding Sermon. William Whately. LC 74-28893. (English Experience Ser.: No. 769). 1975. reprint ed. 20.00 (*90-221-0769-8*) Walter J Johnson.

Bride Came C. O. D. Barbara Bretton. (American Romance Ser.). 1993. mass mkt. 3.50 (*0-373-16505-6*, 1-16505-9) Harlequin Bks.

Bride Comes to Yellow Sky. Stephen Crane. (Creative's Classic Short Stories Ser.). (Illus.). 40p. (J). (gr. 6 up). 1982. lib. bdg. 13.95 (*0-87191-827-7*) Creative Ed.

Bride Comes to Yellow Sky. adapted ed. Stephen Crane. 1970. pap. 2.75 (*0-8222-0152-6*) Dramatists Play.

***Bride Did What?! Etiquette for the Wedding Impaired.** Martha A. Woodham. 1995. 14.00 (*1-56352-198-9*) Longstreet Pr Inc.

Bride Fire. Elizabeth Chadwick. 448p. (Orig.). 1992. pap. 4.50 (*0-8439-3294-5*) Dorchester Pub Co.

Bride for a Tiger. large type ed. Jo Germany. 304p. 1985. 21.95 (*0-7089-1337-7*) Ulverscroft.

***Bride for Adam.** Muriel Jensen. (Historical Ser.). 1995. pap. 3.99 (*0-373-28853-0*, 1-28853-9) Harlequin Bks.

Bride for Anna's Papa. Isabel R. Marvin. LC 93-41175. (Illus.). 152p. (J). 1994. pap. 6.95 (*0-915943-93-X*) Milkweed Ed.

Bride for Donnigan. Janette Oke. 224p. (Orig.). (YA). 1993. pap. 7.99 (*1-55661-327-X*) Bethany Hse.

Bride for Donnigan. large type ed. Janette Oke. 224p. (Orig.). (YA). 1993. pap. 9.99 (*1-55661-328-8*) Bethany Hse.

Bride for Donnigan. large type ed. Janette Oke. LC 93-48240. (Orig.). 1994. 20.95 (*0-8161-5958-0*, Large Print Bks) Hall.

Bride for Hunter. Pat Warren. 1994. mass mkt. 3.50 (*0-373-09893-6*, 5-09893-4) Harlequin Bks.

Bride for Ransom. Renee Roszel. (Romance Ser.). 1993. pap. 2.89 (*0-373-03251-X*, 1-03251-5) Harlequin Bks.

Bride for Ransom. large type ed. Renee Roszel. 266p. 1993. reprint ed. lib. bdg. 13.95 (*1-56054-686-7*) Thorndike Pr.

Bride for the Guillotine. large type ed. Jo Germany. (General Ser.). 448p. 1993. 21.95 (*0-7089-2805-6*) Ulverscroft.

***Bride for the Taking.** Sandra Marton. (Presents Ser.). 1995. mass mkt. 3.25 (*0-373-11751-5*, 1-11751-4) Harlequin Bks.

Bride Goes West. Nannie T. Alderson & Helena H. Smith. LC 42-12918. (Illus.). viii, 273p. 1969. reprint ed. pap. 8.95 (*0-8032-5001-0*, Bison Books) U of Nebr Pr.

Bride Guide: The Perfect Wedding Planner. rev. ed. Dinah B. Griffin & Marla S. Schwartz. LC 91-18348. (Illus.). 192p. 1991. spiral bd. 17.95 (*0-942637-39-9*, Dembner NY) Barricade Bks.

Bride in Flight. large type ed. Essie Summers. (General Ser.). 384p. 1993. 21.95 (*0-7089-2794-7*) Ulverscroft.

Bride in Pink: Reading Level 3. Judith A. Bosley. Ed. by Annie Billups. (Sundown Fiction Collection). (Illus.). 95p. 1993. pap. text ed. 3.75 (*0-88336-761-0*); audio, pap. text ed. 21.00 (*0-88336-224-4*); audio 18.50 (*0-88336-799-8*) New Readers.

Bride of a Stranger. large type ed. Jennifer Blake. (Large Print Books General Ser.). 274p. 1990. lib. bdg. 17.95 (*0-8161-5022-2*) G K Hall.

Bride of a Thousand Cedars. Bruce Lancaster. (Illus.). 344p. 1975. reprint ed. lib. bdg. 23.95 (*0-89190-883-8*, Rivercity Pr) Amereon Ltd.

Bride of Acacias: Selected Poems of Forugh Farrokhzad. Jascha Kessler & Amin Banani. 1982. 26.50 (*0-88206-050-3*) Mazda Pubs.

Bride of Ambrose & Other Stories. Castle Freeman. LC 86-31522. 211p. 1987. 14.95 (*0-939149-01-X*) Soho Press.

Bride of Chance. large type ed. Vanessa Blake. 304p. 1988. 15.95 (*0-7089-1892-1*) Ulverscroft.

Bride of Christ. Chrysostemos Stratman. 1950. pap. 1.00 (*0-317-30422-4*) Holy Trinity.

Bride of Dark & Stormy: Yet More of the Best (?) from the Bulwer-Lytton Contest. Comp. by Scott Rice. (Illus.). 144p. 1988. pap. 7.00 (*0-14-010304-X*, Penguin Bks) Viking Penguin.

Bride of Desire. Theresa Scott. 448p. (Orig.). 1994. reprint ed. pap. 4.99 (*0-8439-3610-X*) Dorchester Pub Co.

Bride of Diamonds. Emma Darcy. (Presents Ser.: No. 1367). 1991. pap. 2.75 (*0-373-11367-6*) Harlequin Bks.

Bride of Diamonds. large type ed. Emma Darcy. 1991. reprint ed. lib. bdg. 18.95 (*0-263-12561-0*, Pub. by Mills & Boon UK) Thorndike Pr.

Bride of Film Book Reference Guide. David McDaniel. (Illus.). 56p. (Orig.). 1991. pap. 8.00 (*0-88734-901-3*) Players Pr.

Bride of Frankenstein. Michael Egremont. 1976. 8.50 (*0-685-80028-8*) Bookfinger.

Bride of Frankenstein: The Original Shooting Script. Ed. by Philip J. Riley. LC 89-92189. (Universal Filmscript Series: Classic Horror Films: Vol. 2). (Illus.). 176p. (Orig.). 1989. pap. 19.95 (*1-882127-06-4*) Magicimage Filmbooks.

Bride of Frankenstein: The Original Shooting Script. limited ed. Ed. by Philip J. Riley. LC 89-92189. (Universal Filmscript Series: Classic Horror Films: Vol. 2). (Illus.). 176p. (Orig.). 1989. 60.00 (*0-685-44928-9*) Magicimage Filmbooks.

Bride of Fu Manchu. Sax Rohmer. 1976. reprint ed. lib. bdg. 19.95 (*0-89190-801-3*, Rivercity Pr) Amereon Ltd.

Bride of Hatfield Castle. Beverly C. Warren. 384p. 1992. mass mkt. 3.99 (*0-8217-3811-9*) Zebra.

Bride of Innisfallen & Other Stories. Eudora Welty. 18.95 (*0-89190-515-4*, Am Repr) Amereon Ltd.

Bride of Jesus Christ. M. Basilea Schlink. Tr. by Evangelical Sisters of Mary Staff. Orig. Title: Braut Jesu Christi. 64p. (Orig.). 1989. pap. text ed. 1.75 (*3-87209-638-9*) Evang Sisterhood Mary.

Bride of Lammermoor. Walter Scott. 392p. 1993. pap. 7.95 (*0-685-67368-5*, Everyman's Classic Lib) C E Tuttle.

Bride of Lammermoor. Sir Walter Scott. Ed. by Fiona Robertson. (World's Classics Ser.). 518p. 1991. pap. 8.95 (*0-19-281791-4*) OUP.

***Bride of Life.** Eeva Joenpelto. Tr. by Ritva Cederstrom. 370p. 1995. pap. 15.00 (*1-880474-09-3*) FATA.

Bride of Messina. Friedrich Schiller. Tr. & Intro. by Charles E. Passage. Bd. with William Tell. LC 62-17091.; Demetrius. LC 62-17091. LC 62-17091. xxxvii, 299p. 1962. 10.50 (*0-8044-2785-2*, F Ungar Bks); Bd. with; Set pap. 7.95 (*0-8044-6816-8*, F Ungar Bks) Continuum.

Bride of Mistletoe. James L. Allen. (Principle Works of James Lane Allen). 1989. reprint ed. lib. bdg. 79.00 (*0-7812-1736-9*) Rprt Serv.

Bride of My Heart. Rebecca Winters. (Romance Ser.). 1994. mass mkt. 2.99 (*0-373-03325-7*, 1-03325-7) Harlequin Bks.

Bride of Newgate. John Dickson Carr. 256p. (Orig.). 1994. pap. 4.95 (*0-7867-0102-1*) Carroll & Graf.

Bride of Pegasus: Studies in Magic, Mythology & Folklore. W. R. Dawson. 1972. lib. bdg. 79.95 (*0-87968-514-X*) Krishna Pr.

898

An Asterisk (*) at the beginning of an entry indicates that the title is appearing in BIP for the first time.

B

Bridge Basics: An Introduction to the Game. 2nd ed. Mary A. McVey. 120p. 1982. pap. 5.50 (*0-910475-01-6*) KET.

Bridge Bearings & Expansion Joints. David J. Lee. LC 93-32192. 1994. write for info. (*0-419-14570-2*, E & FN Spon) Routledge Chapman & Hall.

Bridge Between. large type ed. Mary Williams. 306p. 1994. pap. 16.95 (*1-85389-425-7*, Dales) Ulverscroft.

Bridge Between Acupuncture & Modern Bio-Energetic Medicine. Stuart J. Zoll. (Illus.). 184p. 1993. pap. text ed. 29.95 (*2-8043-4001-5*, Pub. by Edits Haug Intl) Medicina Bio.

Bridge Between Control Science & Technology, Vol. 1. Ed. by J. Gertler & L. Keviczky. (IFAC Proceedings Ser.). 1985. 248.00 (*0-08-031667-0*) Franklin.

Bridge Between Control Science & Technology, Vol. 2. Ed. by J. Gertler & L. Keviczky. (IFAC Proceedings Ser.). 1985. 200.00 (*0-08-031668-9*) Franklin.

Bridge Between Control Science & Technology, Vol. 3. Ed. by J. Gertler & L. Keviczky. (IFAC Proceedings Ser.). 1985. 248.00 (*0-08-031669-7*) Franklin.

Bridge Between Control Science & Technology, Vol. 4. Ed. by J. Gertler & L. Keviczky. (IFAC Proceedings Ser.). 1985. 288.00 (*0-08-031670-0*) Franklin.

Bridge Between Control Science & Technology, Vol. 5. Ed. by J. Gertler & L. Keviczky. (IFAC Proceedings Ser.). 1985. 272.00 (*0-08-031671-9*) Franklin.

B

Bridge Between Neurology & Psychiatry. Ed. by Edward H. Reynolds & Michael R. Trimble. (Illus.). 400p. 1989. pap. text ed. 82.00 (*0-443-03344-7*) Churchill.

Bridge Between the Testaments: Reappraisal of Judaism from the Exile to the Birth of Christianity. 3rd rev. ed. Ed. by Donald E. Gowan. LC 86-9327. (Pittsburgh Theological Monographs: No. 14). 1986. text ed. 32.95 (*0-915138-88-3*) Pickwick.

Bridge Between Two Worlds. Leia A. Greene. (Little Angel Books Ser.). (Illus.). 36p. (J). (gr. k-12). 1992. pap. text ed. 4.95 (*1-880737-08-6*) Crystal Jrns.

Bridge Between Two Worlds. Abby A. Judson. 217p. 1972. reprint ed. spiral bd. 6.60 (*0-7873-0484-0*) Mokelumne.

Bridge Between Universal Spirituality & the Physical Constitution of Man. 2nd ed. Rudolf Steiner. Tr. by Dorothy S. Osmond. 64p. (Orig.). 1979. pap. 5.95 (*0-910142-03-3*) Anthroposophic.

***Bridge Between Us.** Julie Shigekuni. LC 94-3668. 253p. 1995. 18.95 (*0-385-47678-7*, Anchor NY) Doubleday.

Bridge Bidding: The Golden Rules. Liz Brinig. (Illus.). 149p. 1992. pap. 15.95 (*1-85223-282-X*, Pub. by Crowood Pr UK) Trafalgar.

Bridge Bidding Made Easy. Edwin Kantar. 1980. pap. 10.00 (*0-87980-012-7*) Wilshire.

Bridge Book, Vol. 1. Frank Stewart. 1988. pap. 9.95 (*0-910791-33-3*) Devyn Pr.

Bridge Book, Vol. 2. Frank Stewart. 1988. pap. 9.95 (*0-910791-34-1*) Devyn Pr.

Bridge Book, Vol. 4. Frank Stewart. 1989. pap. 7.95 (*0-910791-56-2*) Devyn Pr.

Bridge Book Vol. 3: For Advanced Players. Frank Stewart & Randall Baron. 1989. pap. 7.95 (*0-910791-55-4*) Devyn Pr.

***Bridge Builder's Story.** Howard Fast. 216p. 1995. 19.95 (*1-56324-691-0*) M E Sharpe.

Bridge Built Halfway: A History of Memorial University College, 1925-1950. Malcolm MacLeod. 416p. (C). 1990. text ed. 44.95 (*0-7735-0761-2*, Pub. by McGill CN) U of Toronto Pr.

Bridge (Collective Work) 1979. write for info. (*0-938838-00-8*) Textile Bridge.

Bridge Conventions. Edwin Kantar. 1980. pap. 10.00 (*0-87980-013-5*) Wilshire.

***Bridge Conventions Complete, 1990 Edition.** Kearse. Date not set. 24.95 (*0-910791-76-7*, 0610) Devyn Pr.

Bridge Conventions, Defences & Countermeasures. Ron Klinger. (Illus.). 144p. 1993. 24.95 (*0-575-05564-2*, Pub. by V Gollancz UK) Trafalgar.

***Bridge Conventions for You.** Ron Klinger & Andrew Kambites. 128p. 1995. pap. 13.95 (*0-575-05815-3*, Pub. by V Gollancz UK) Trafalgar.

Bridge Dancers. Carol Saller. (Fiction Ser.). (Illus.). 40p. (J). (gr. 2-4). 1991. lib. bdg. 17.50 (*0-87614-653-1*, Carolrhoda) Lerner Group.

Bridge Dancers. Carol Saller. (Illus.). (J). (gr. 2-5). 1993. pap. 5.95 (*0-87614-579-9*, Carolrhoda) Lerner Group.

Bridge Deck Analysis. Anthony R. Cusens & R. P. Pama. LC 74-3726. (Illus.). 294p. reprint ed. pap. 83.80 (*0-8357-6707-8*, 2035338) Bks Demand.

Bridge Deck Behaviour. 2nd ed. E. C. Hambly. 336p. 1991. 84.95 (*0-419-17260-2*, E & FN Spon) Routledge Chapman & Hall.

Bridge Deck Joint-Sealing Systems: Evaluation & Performance Specification. (National Cooperative Highway Research Program Report Ser.: No. 204). 46p. 1979. 5.60 (*0-309-02910-4*) Transport Res Bd.

Bridge Deck Joints. (National Cooperative Highway Research Program Report Ser.: No. 141). 66p. 1989. 9.00 (*0-309-04551-7*) Transport Res Bd.

Bridge Design: Aesthetics & Developing Technologies. Ed. by Adele F. Bacow & Kenneth Kruckemeyer. LC 86-61840. 186p. 1986. 20.00 (*0-9617326-0-1*, BD01) Am Soc Civil Eng.

Bridge Design & Performance & Composite Materials. (Research Record Ser.: No. 1223). 124p. 1989. 18.50 (*0-309-04820-6*) Transport Res Bd.

Bridge Design & Testing. (Transportation Research Record Ser.: No. 1180). 100p. 1988. 15.50 (*0-309-04720-X*) Transport Res Bd.

Bridge Design for Economy & Durability: Concepts for New, Strengthened & Replacement Bridges. Brian Pritchard. (Illus.). 172p. 1992. 79.00 (*0-7277-1671-9*, Pub. by T Telford UK) Am Soc Civil Eng.

***Bridge Design Reviewer.** Frank Talania. (Illus.). 300p. 1995. pap. 36.75 (*0-929176-20-0*) Burdick & Landreth Co.

Bridge Designs to Reduce & Facilitate Maintenance & Repair. (National Cooperative Highway Research Program Report Ser.: No. 123). 65p. 1985. 8.40 (*0-309-04007-8*) Transport Res Bd.

***Bridge Director's Companion.** 2nd ed. Harris. Date not set. 14.95 (*0-910791-61-9*, 0580) Devyn Pr.

Bridge Drainage Systems. (National Cooperative Highway Research Program Report Ser.: No. 67). 44p. 1980. 5.60 (*0-309-03013-7*) Transport Res Bd.

Bridge Engineering: Design, Rehabilitation & Maintenance of Modern Highway Bridges. Demetrius E. Tonias. 1994. text ed. 79.00 (*0-07-065073-X*) McGraw.

Bridge Evaluation, Repair & Rehabilitation. Ed. by Andrzej S. Nowak. (C). 1990. lib. bdg. 201.50 (*0-7923-0999-5*) Kluwer Ac.

Bridge for Ambitious Players. Terence Reese. 144p. 1988. pap. 15.95 (*0-575-04176-5*, Pub. by V Gollancz UK) Trafalgar.

Bridge for Bright Beginners. Terence Reese. 144p. 1973. reprint ed. pap. 3.95 (*0-486-22942-4*) Dover.

Bridge for Everyone: A Step by Step Text & Workbook. Shelly De Satnick. 160p. 1982. pap. 9.95 (*0-380-81083-2*) Avon.

Bridge for Improvers. Derrek Stubbings & Howard Melbourne. 176p. 1990. pap. 15.95 (*1-85223-184-X*, Pub. by Crowood Pr UK) Trafalgar.

Bridge for the Awful-to-Average Player. Richard C. Jennings. 87p. (C). 1989. 31.00 (*0-7223-2230-5*, Pub. by A H S Ltd UK) St Mut.

Bridge for the Connoisseur. Hugh Kelsey. (Master Bridge Ser.). 144p. 1991. 22.95 (*0-575-04996-0*, Pub. by V Gollancz UK) Trafalgar.

Bridge for the Girls & Their Boys. Aneta R. Sheridan. (Illus.). 75p. (Orig.). 1985. pap. 3.95 (*0-9613949-0-0*) R S Pr.

***Bridge in the Jungle.** B. Travern. LC 94-25692. Orig. Title: Brucke in Dschungel. 228p. 1994. pap. 11.95 (*1-56663-063-0*, Elephant Paperbacks) I R Dee.

Bridge in the Menagerie. Victor Mollo. 152p. 1977. reprint ed. pap. 8.95 (*0-571-11439-3*) Faber & Faber.

Bridge in Time. Elisabeth McNeill. 448p. 1994. pap. 8.95 (*1-85797-406-9*) Trafalgar.

Bridge in Time: The Complete Eighteen Fifty Census of Frederick County, Maryland. Mary F. Hitselberger & John P. Dern. LC 78-71854. (Illus.). (C). 1978. 25.00 (*0-913186-07-4*) Monocacy.

Bridge Inspection & Rehabilitation: A Practical Guide. Parsons, Brinckerhoff, Quade & Douglas, Inc. Staff. 312p. 1992. text ed. 84.95 (*0-471-53262-2*) Wiley.

Bridge Inspection & Structural Analysis: Handbook of Bridge Inspection. Sung H. Park. LC 80-81421. (Illus.). 312p. (Orig.). 1980. pap. text ed. 20.00 (*0-9604440-0-9*) S H Park.

***Bridge Inspector's Training Manual, 2 vols.** 1994. lib. bdg. 629.95 (*0-8490-6421-X*) Gordon Pr.

Bridge Inspector's Training Manual. (Illus.). 247p. 1987. reprint ed. pap. 13.00 (*0-16-005050-2*, S/N 050-002-00106-0) USGPO.

Bridge Inspector's Training Manual, 2 vols., Set. 1994. lib. bdg. 625.95 (*0-8490-9062-8*) Gordon Pr.

Bridge into Light: Your Connection to Spiritual Guidance. Pam Cameron & Fred Cameron. Ed. by Sara Benjamin. LC 92-35243. 112p. (Orig.). 1994. pap. 11.95 (*1-880666-07-3*) Oughten Hse.

***Bridge Is a Contact Sport.** Wendell Abern. (Illus.). 64p. (Orig.). 1995. pap. 8.95 (*0-9645895-0-8*) W Abern.

Bridge Is a Partnership Game. 252p. 1989. 13.95 (*0-940257-04-1*) Granovetter Bks.

Bridge Literature. Nick Smith. 1993. pap. 15.95 (*1-85744-503-1*, Maxwell Macmillan) Macmillan.

Bridge Made Easy, Bk. 1. Caroline Sydnor. LC 78-104076. (Illus.). 165p. (Orig.). 1975. pap. 4.00 (*0-318-23806-3*) C Sydnor.

Bridge Made Easy, Bk. 2: For Intermediates. Caroline Sydnor. LC 78-104076. (Illus.). 206p. (Orig.). 1977. pap. 4.00 (*0-318-23769-5*) C Sydnor.

Bridge Made Easy, Bk. 3: How to Win More Tricks. Caroline Sydnor. Tr. by Gerard Falardeau. LC 78-104076. (Illus.). 266p. (Orig.). (FRE.). 1981. pap. 5.00 (*0-318-23807-1*) C Sydnor.

Bridge Maintenance, Corrosion, Joint Seals, & Polymar Mortar Materials. (Research Record Ser.: No. 1113). 70p. 1987. 10.50 (*0-309-04465-0*) Transport Res Bd.

Bridge Maintenance Inspection & Evaluation. Ed. by White et al. 368p. 1992. 135.00 (*0-8247-8609-2*) Dekker.

Bridge Maintenance Inspection & Evaluation. Kenneth R. White et al. LC 80-22577. (Civil Engineering Ser.: No. 3). (Illus.). 269p. reprint ed. pap. 76.70 (*0-8357-7402-3*, 2032991) Bks Demand.

Bridge Maintenance Supervisor. Jack Rudman. (Career Examination Ser.: C-2289). 1994. pap. 29.95 (*0-8373-2289-8*) Nat Learn.

Bridge Management. OECD Staff. (Road Transport Research Ser.). 126p. (Orig.). 1992. pap. 43.00 (*92-64-13617-7*) OECD.

Bridge Management: Inspection, Maintenance, Assessment & Repair: Papers Presented at the First International Conference Held at The University of Surrey, Guildford, UK, from 28-30 March 1990. Ed. by J. E. Harding et al. 810p. 1990. 216.00 (*1-85166-456-4*) Elsevier.

Bridge Management Systems. (National Cooperative Highway Research Program Report Ser.: No. 300). 74p. 1987. 10.40 (*0-309-04569-X*) Transport Res Bd.

Bridge Mechanic. Jack Rudman. (Career Examination Ser.: C-1141). 1994. pap. 23.95 (*0-8373-1141-1*) Nat Learn.

***Bridge Modification: Proceedings of the Conference Bridge Modification Organized by the Institution of Civil Engineers, London, March 23-24, 1994.** Ed. by B. Pritchard. 302p. 1994. 67.20 (*0-7277-2028-7*) Am Soc Civil Eng.

Bridge Mountain Experience. Charles D. Floro. (Illus.). 60p. (Orig.). 1991. pap. 8.00 (*1-879765-00-4*) Earth & Sky.

***Bridge My Way.** Zia Mahmood. 1994. pap. 12.95 (*0-9634715-2-X*) L Cohen NJ.

Bridge Needs, Design, & Performance. (Research Record Ser.: No. 1118). 98p. 1987. 13.00 (*0-309-04471-5*) Transport Res Bd.

Bridge Odds for Practical Players. Hugh Kelsey & Michael Glauert. 128p. 1994. pap. 14.95 (*0-575-05742-4*, Pub. by V Gollancz UK) Trafalgar.

Bridge of Ashes see Today We Choose Faces

Bridge of Beyond. Simone Schwarz-Bart. Tr. by Barbara Bray. (Caribbean Writers Ser.). xviii, 174p. (C). 1982. reprint ed. pap. 10.95 (*0-435-98770-4*) Heinemann.

Bridge of Birds. Barry Hughart. 288p. 1985. mass mkt. 5.99 (*0-345-32138-3*, Del Rey) Ballantine.

Bridge of Change: Poems 1974-1980. John Logan. (American Poets Continuum Ser.: No. 7). pap. 8.00 (*0-918526-35-3*) BOA Edns.

Bridge of Courage: Life Stories of the Guatemalan Companeros & Companeras. Jennifer Harbury. LC 93-19685. 1993. text ed. 29.95 (*1-56751-017-5*); pap. 14.95 (*1-56751-016-7*) Common Courage.

***Bridge of Courage: Life Stories of the Guatemalan Companeros & Companeras.** Jennifer Harbury. 1995. 29.95 (*1-56751-069-8*); pap. 14.95 (*1-56751-068-X*) Common Courage.

Bridge of Darkness: The Return of the Master Assassin. Shotaro Ikenami. Ed. by Eric Chaline. Tr. by Gavin Frew. LC 92-37069. 180p. 1993. 22.00 (*4-7700-1728-6*, Pub. by Kodansha Ltd JA) Kodansha.

***Bridge of Dreams.** Christina Skye. 400p. (Orig.). 1995. mass mkt. 5.99 (*0-380-77386-4*) Avon.

Bridge of Dreams: A Poetics of 'The Tale of Genji' Haruo Shirane. LC 86-30031. (Illus.). 312p. 1987. 45.00 (*0-8047-1345-6*); pap. 13.95 (*0-8047-1719-2*) Stanford U Pr.

Bridge of Dreams: The Story of Paramananda, a Modern Mystic. Sara A. Levinsky & David Steindl-Rast. LC 83-82698. (Illus.). 632p. (Orig.). 1984. pap. 12.95 (*0-940262-12-6*) Lindisfarne Pr.

Bridge of Feathers. Eamon Kelly. LC 89-82490. 128p. (J). (gr. 4-8). 1990. pap. 6.95 (*1-85371-054-7*, Pub. by Poolbeg Pr IE) Dufour.

Bridge of Light: Tools of Light for Spiritual Transformation. 2nd rev. ed. LaUna Huffines. LC 93-37300. (Awakened Life Ser.: Bk. 1). 216p. 1993. pap. 9.95 (*0-915811-50-2*) H J Kramer Inc.

Bridge of Light: Tools of Light for Spiritual Transformations. LaUna Huffines. 1989. pap. 9.95 (*0-671-67089-1*, Fireside) S&S Trade.

Bridge of Light: Yiddish Film Between Two Worlds. J. Hoberman. (Orig.). 1991. 40.00 (*0-8052-4107-8*) Pantheon.

***Bridge of Light: Yiddish Film Between Two Worlds.** J. Hoberman. (Illus.). 409p. (Orig.). (C). Date not set. reprint ed. pap. write for info. (*0-614-06504-6*) Temple U Pr.

***Bridge of Longing: The Lost Art of Yiddish Storytelling.** David G. Roskies. (Illus.). 400p. 1995. text ed. 37.50 (*0-674-08139-0*, ROSBRI) HUP.

Bridge of Magpies. large type ed. Geoffrey Jenkins. 432p. 1983. 21.95 (*0-7089-0976-0*) Ulverscroft.

***Bridge of No Return: Burnside's Bridge at Antietam, the Thermopylae of the Civil War.** Phillip T. Tucker. (Illus.). 325p. 1995. 29.95 (*0-9632137-7-6*) Sergeant Kirk.

Bridge of San Luis Rey. Thornton Wilder. LC 85-45925. 160p. 1986. pap. 9.00 (*0-06-091341-X*, PL1341, PL) HarpC.

Bridge of San Luis Rey. Thornton Wilder. 150p. 1991. reprint ed. lib. bdg. 23.00x (*0-8095-9065-4*) Borgo Pr.

Bridge of San Luis Rey. Thornton Wilder. 300p. 1991. reprint ed. lib. bdg. 22.95 (*0-89966-853-4*) Buccaneer Bks.

Bridge of Sand. large type ed. Frank Gruber. 480p. 1992. 21.95 (*0-7089-2588-X*) Ulverscroft.

Bridge of Sighs: Poems. Steve Orlen. LC 92-8418. (Miami University Press Poetry Ser.). 60p. (C). 1992. 15.95 (*1-881163-00-8*); pap. 9.95 (*1-881163-01-6*) Miami Univ Pr.

Bridge of Sorrow, Bridge of Hope. 2nd rev. ed. Riva Chirurg. Ed. by Rebecca Fromer. Orig. Title: Henai Hem Ba'im. (Illus.). 208p. 1994. pap. 13.95 (*0-943376-61-0*) Magnes Mus.

Bridge of the Gods, Mountains of Fire. Chuck Williams. (Illus.). 192p. 1982. 29.50 (*0-913890-43-X*) Mountaineers.

***Bridge of Triangles.** John Burke. Date not set. pap. 16.95 (*0-7022-2639-4*, Pub. by Univ Queensland Pr AT) Intl Spec Bk.

Bridge of Voices. Werner Reichhold. (Illus.). 190p. (Orig.). (ENG, FRE, GER & ITA.). 1990. pap. 14.00 (*0-944676-13-8*) AHA Bks.

Bridge of Years. May Sarton. 352p. 1985. reprint ed. pap. 4.95 (*0-393-30239-3*) Norton.

Bridge on the Drina. Ivo Andric. Tr. by Lovett F. Edwards. 1977. pap. 10.95 (*0-226-02045-2*, P746) U Ch Pr.

Bridge Operating Engineer. (Career Examination Ser.: C-3573). 1994. 29.95 (*0-8373-3573-6*) Nat Learn.

Bridge Operations Supervisor. Jack Rudman. (Career Examination Ser.: C-1142). 1994. pap. 29.95 (*0-8373-1142-X*) Nat Learn.

Bridge Operator. Jack Rudman. (Career Examination Ser.: C-92). 1994. pap. 23.95 (*0-8373-0092-4*) Nat Learn.

Bridge Operator-in-Charge. Jack Rudman. (Career Examination Ser.: C-91). 1994. pap. 29.95 (*0-8373-0091-6*) Nat Learn.

Bridge or Barrier? Turkey & the West after the Cold War. Ian O. Lesser. LC 92-17308. 1992. write for info. (*0-8330-1256-8*, R-4204-AF/A) Rand Corp.

Bridge over Jordan. 2nd rev. ed. Amelia B. Robinson. Ed. by Christina Huth & Marianna Wertz. LC 90-62730. (Illus.). 415p. (YA). (gr. 12 up). 1991. reprint ed. pap. 10.00 (*0-9621095-4-1*) Schiller Inst.

Bridge over the River Kwai. Pierre Boulle. 19.95 (*0-89190-571-5*, Am Repr) Amereon Ltd.

Bridge over Time. Brenda Hiatt. (Superromance Ser.). 1994. mass mkt. 3.50 (*0-373-70592-1*, 1-70592-0) Harlequin Bks.

Bridge over Troubled Waters. Rasputin, pseud. Ed. by Avonelle Kelsey. 207p. (Orig.). (GER.). 1994. pap. 9.95 (*0-9640610-0-7*) Cheval Intl.

Bridge over Troubled Waters: Ministry to Baby Boomers: A Generation Adrift. James Bell. LC 93-3925. (Illus.). 312p. (Orig.). 1993. pap. 16.99 (*1-56476-112-6*, Victor Books) SP Pubns.

Bridge Painter. Jack Rudman. (Career Examination Ser.: C-93). 1994. pap. 23.95 (*0-8373-0093-2*) Nat Learn.

***Bridge Party Hostess.** Molly Anderson. 1995. pap. 9.95 (*0-572-01923-8*) Atrium Pubs.

Bridge Passages. George Szirtes. 72p. 1991. pap. 10.95 (*0-19-282821-5*) OUP.

Bridge People: Daily Life in a Camp of the Homeless. Jackson Underwood. 336p. (C). 1993. pap. text ed. 27.50 (*0-8191-8962-6*) U Pr of Amer.

Bridge People: Daily Life in a Camp of the Homeless. Jackson Underwood. 336p. (C). 1993. lib. bdg. 47.50 (*0-8191-8961-8*) U Pr of Amer.

Bridge Play from A to Z. 4th ed. George S. Coffin. (Illus.). 1979. reprint ed. pap. 6.95 (*0-486-23891-1*) Dover.

Bridge Player's Companion. Larry Harris. (Illus.). 160p. (Orig.). 1991. pap. 11.95 (*0-9628297-0-6*) C & T Bridge.

Bridge Players Comprehensive Guide. Frank Stewart. 1990. pap. 12.95 (*0-671-72460-6*) S&S Trade.

***Bridge Player's Dictionary.** Baron. Date not set. 19.95 (*0-939460-50-5*, 4710) Devyn Pr.

***Bridge Player's Supper Book.** Nicola Cox. 96p. 1995. pap. 11.95 (*0-575-05945-1*, Pub. by V Gollancz UK) Trafalgar.

Bridge Procedures Guide. ICS Staff. (C). 1988. 150.00 (*0-948691-42-5*, Pub. by Witherby & Co UK) St Mut.

Bridge Quiz for Improving Players. Hugh Kelsey & Tim Bourke. (Illus.). 128p. 1993. 22.95 (*0-575-05536-7*, Pub. by V Gollancz UK) Trafalgar.

Bridge Rail Design: Factors, Trends, & Guidelines. (National Cooperative Highway Research Program Report Ser.: No. 149). 49p. 1974. 4.00 (*0-309-02209-6*) Transport Res Bd.

Bridge Rehabilitation & Replacement (Bridge Repair Practice) Sung H. Park. LC 82-90094. (Illus.). 818p. (C). 1984. text ed. 70.00 (*0-9604440-1-7*) S H Park.

Bridge Rehabilitation & Strengthening. OECD Staff. (Road Transport Research Ser.). 104p. 1983. pap. 15.00 (*92-64-12528-0*) OECD.

Bridge Repair Supervisor. Jack Rudman. (Career Examination Ser.: C-2288). 1994. pap. 29.95 (*0-8373-2288-X*) Nat Learn.

Bridge Research Nineteen Ninety. (Transportation Research Record Ser.: No. 1275). 96p. 1990. 16.00 (*0-309-05061-8*) Transport Res Bd.

Bridge Squeezes Complete; or, Winning End Play Strategy. Clyde E. Love. LC 68-25410. (Illus.). 1968. pap. 4.95 (*0-486-21968-2*) Dover.

Bridge Strategy at Trick One. 2nd ed. Fred L. Karpin. LC 75-30256. 288p. 1976. reprint ed. pap. 6.95 (*0-486-23296-4*) Dover.

***Bridge Street.** E. Tim, 4th. 1994. 12.95 (*0-533-11002-5*) Vantage.

Bridge Substructure & Foundation Design. Petros Xanthakos. 1995. text ed. 90.00 (*0-13-300617-4*) P-H.

Bridge Summary Complete. George Coffin. (Illus.). (Orig.). pap. 3.95 (*0-8283-1427-6*, 40, Intl Pocket Lib) Branden Pub Co.

Bridge Team Murders. Matthew Granovetter. 400p. (Orig.). 1993. 19.95 (*0-940257-14-9*); pap. 14.95 (*0-940257-13-0*) Granovetter Bks.

Bridge the Gap: A Guide to the Development of Acquisition Activities. Jami Ferrer & Patty W. De Poleo. (Illus.). 148p. 1983. text ed. 9.95 (*0-685-06851-X*); pap. 19.95 (*0-13-084823-9*) Alemany Pr.

Bridge Through Time. Laila Abou-Saif. LC 92-10885. 284p. 1993. reprint ed. pap. 12.95 (*1-55652-119-7*) L Hill Bks.

Bridge to Abstract Mathematics: Mathematical Proof & Structures. 2nd ed. Ronald P. Morash. 389p. 1991. text ed. write for info. (*0-07-043043-8*) McGraw.

Bridge to Another World. Myron E. Gruenwald. 36p. 1986. pap. 3.50 (*0-9601536-4-0*) M E Gruenwald.

Bridge to Buddhist-Christian Dialogue. Seiichi Yagi & Leonard Swidler. 144p. 1990. pap. 9.95 (*0-8091-3169-2*) Paulist Pr.

***Bridge to Carryover S-R-L.** Jean G. DeGaetano. 49p. 1986. pap. text ed. 21.00 (*1-886143-12-9*) Grt Ideas Tching.

Bridge to College Success. Robertson. 1991. pap. 22.95 (*0-8384-2907-6*); teacher ed, pap. 8.95 (*0-8384-2908-4*) Heinle & Heinle.

Bridge to College Success. Robertson. 1991. audio 25.00 (*0-8384-3007-4*) Heinle & Heinle.

Bridge to College Success. Robertson. 1991. vhs 10.00 (*0-8384-3006-6*) Heinle & Heinle.

Bridge to College Success, 2 vols., Set. Robertson. 1991. vhs 75.00 (*0-8384-3009-0*) Heinle & Heinle.

Bridge to Courage. Ann Gabhart. 160p. (Orig.). (J). (gr. 6). 1993. pap. 3.50 (*0-380-76051-7*, Flare) Avon.

***Bridge to Cutter Gap.** Catherine Marshall. LC 95-13127. (Christy Juvenile Fiction Ser.: Vol. 1). (J). 1995. pap. write for info. (0-8499-3686-1) Word Pub.

Bridge to Dialogue: The Story of Jewish-Christian Relations. John Rousmaniere. 1991. pap. 8.95 (0-8091-3284-2) Paulist Pr.

Bridge to Eternity. Advaita. 538p. 1987. pap. 12.95 (0-87481-230-5, Pub. by Advaita Ashrama II) Vedanta Pr.

Bridge to France. Edward N. Hurley. LC 74-75241. (United States in World War I Ser.). (Illus.). xiii, 338p. 1974. reprint ed. lib. bdg. 39.95 (0-89198-105-5) Ozer.

Bridge to Freedom. Isabel Marvin. 148p. (YA). (gr. 5-9). 1991. 14.95 (0-8276-0377-0) JPS Phila.

Bridge to Heaven. Ruth E. Norman. 1969. 17.95 (0-932642-10-1) Unarius Acad Sci.

Bridge to Infinity - Harmonic 371244. rev. ed. Bruce L. Cathie. LC 88-33299. (Illus.). 200p. (C). 1989. pap. 11.95 (0-922356-00-9) Amer West Pubs.

Bridge to Learning: Motor Skill Development. Seagraves. 270p. (Orig.). (C). 1986. pap. 19.95 (0-88725-056-4) Hunter Textbks.

Bridge to Life: Gospel of John. (King James Version Ser.). 64p. 1991. pap. (1-880349-54-X) Pocket Testament.

Bridge to Nothingness: Gnosis, Kabala, Existentialism, & the Transcendental Predicament of Man. Shlomo G. Shoham. LC 89-46418. 1993. write for info. (0-8386-3396-X) Fairleigh Dickinson.

Bridge to Nowhere. Megan McDonald. LC 92-50844. 160p. (YA). (gr. 6 up). 1993. 15.95 (0-531-05478-0); lib. bdg. 15.99 (0-531-08628-3) Orchard Bks Watts.

Bridge to Prayer: Teacher's Guide, Vols. 1 & 2. 1989. pap. 6.00 (0-8074-0433-0, 201903) UAHC.

Bridge to Prayer: The Jewish Worship Workbook, Vol. II. Nachama S. Moskowitz. (Amidah, Torah Service, & Concluding Prayers Ser.). (Illus.). 144p. (J). (gr. 6-7). 1989. pap. text ed. 6.00 (0-8074-0432-2, 123596) UAHC.

Bridge to Prayer: The Jewish Worship Workbook: God, Prayer, & the Shema, Vol. 1. Nachama S. Moskowitz. (J). (gr. 4-6). 1988. pap. text ed. 6.00 (0-8074-0417-9, 123594) UAHC.

Bridge to Reality: A Heart Centered Approach to a Course in Miracles & the Process of Inner Healing. Paul Ferrini. (Illus.). (Orig.). 1990. pap. 12.00 (1-879159-03-1) Heartways Pr.

Bridge to Recovery: An Introduction to 12-Step Programs. Robert L. DuPont & John P. McGovern. LC 93-26758. 160p. 1994. text ed. 22.50 (0-88048-669-4, 8669) Am Psychiatric.

***Bridge to School: Entering a New World.** Liz Waterland. 88p. (Orig.). (C). 1995. pap. text ed. 8.50 (1-57110-020-2) Stenhse Pubs.

Bridge to Terabithia. Katherine Paterson. LC 77-2221. (Illus.). (J). (gr. 5 up). 1977. 14.95 (0-690-01359-0, Crowell Jr Bks) HarpC Child Bks.

Bridge to Terabithia. braille ed. Katherine Paterson. 182p. (J). 1992. vinyl bd. 14.56 (1-56956-199-0, BR8631) W A T Braille.

Bridge to Terabithia. Katherine Paterson. LC 77-2221. (Illus.). 144p. (J). (gr. 5 up). 1987. reprint ed. lib. bdg. 14.89 (0-690-04635-9, Crowell Jr Bks) HarpC Child Bks.

Bridge to Terabithia. Katherine Paterson. LC 77-2221. (Trophy Bk.). (Illus.). 144p. (J). (gr. 5-9). 1987. reprint ed. pap. 3.95 (0-06-440184-7, Trophy) HarpC Child Bks.

Bridge to Terabithia: (Puente Hasta Terabithia) Katherine Paterson. (SPA.). (J). (gr. 1-6). 8.95 (84-204-3633-X) Santillana.

Bridge to Terabithia: A Literature Unit. John Carratello & Patty Carratello. (Illus.). 48p. (Orig.). (gr. 5-8). 1991. student ed, pap. 6.95 (1-55734-401-9) Tchr Create Mat.

Bridge to Terabithia: A Study Guide. Joyce Friedland & Rikki Kessler. (Novel-Ties Ser.). (J). (gr. 4-6). 1982. student ed, teacher ed 15.95 (0-88122-001-9) Lrn Links.

Bridge to Terabithia: L-I-T Guide. Charlotte Jaffe & Barbara Roberts. (L-I-T Guides: Literature in Teaching Ser.). (J). (gr. 4-8). Date not set. Grades 4-8. 8.95 (0-910857-85-7) Educ Impress.

Bridge to the Future: A Centennial Celebration of the Brooklyn Bridge. Intro. by Margaret Latimer et al. LC 84-11444. (Annals Ser.: Vol. 424). 355p. 1984. lib. bdg. 75.00 (0-89766-246-6); pap. 75.00 (0-89766-247-4) NY Acad Sci.

Bridge to the Other Side. 2nd ed. Vikee Vaughn. LC 89-45150. 201p. (Orig.). 1988. reprint ed. pap. 10.95 (0-944534-01-5) Diamond Stockton.

Bridge to the Sun. Gwen Terasaki. xvi, 260p. 1986. reprint ed. 17.95 (0-9613859-2-8) Wakestone Bks.

Bridge to Understanding: Listening, Speaking, Thinking, the Differences Between Men & Women. Lisa A. Obroslinski. 104p. 1992. pap. 12.95 (0-9633649-4-4) L A Obroslinski.

Bridge to Wholeness: A Feminine Alternative to the Hero Myth. Jean B. Raffa. Ed. by Marcia Broucek. LC 92-10643. (Illus.). 208p. (Orig.). 1992. pap. 14.95 (0-931055-88-1) LuraMedia.

***Bridge to Yesterday.** Mittman. 1995. mass mkt. 4.50 (0-06-108364-X, Harp PBks) HarpC.

Bridge Today One Thousand One Workbook. Frank Stewart. 260p. (Orig.). 1990. pap. 14.95 (0-940257-07-6) Granovetter Bks.

***Bridge Too Far: The Classic History of the Greatest Airborne Battle of World War II.** Cornelius Ryan. 1995. pap. 15.00 (0-684-80330-5, Touchstone Bks) S&S Trade.

***Bridge Welding Code (D1.5-95)** (Illus.). 220p. 1995. pap. 64.00 (0-87171-453-1) Am Welding.

Bridge with the Blue Team. Pietro Forquet. Ed. by Ron Klinger. 384p. 1987. pap. 24.95 (0-575-04005-X, Pub. by V Gollancz UK) Trafalgar.

Bridge with the Professional Touch. Terence Reese & Jeremy Flint. (Master Bridge Ser.). 128p. 1991. pap. 13.95 (0-575-04998-7, Pub. by V Gollancz UK) Trafalgar.

Bridge Without Error. Ron Klinger. (Master Bridge Ser.). (Illus.). 128p. 1981. pap. 13.95 (0-575-02946-3, Pub. by V Gollancz UK) Trafalgar.

Bridge Works: A History of Chicago Bridge & Iron. CBI Industries, Inc. Staff. Ed. by Graham Harper. LC 86-63855. 224p. 1987. 10.00 (0-916371-05-0) Mobium Pr.

Bridge World Magazine - Swiss Match Challenge: Learn How to Bid & Play Like a Winner, & Have Fun Too! Jeff Rubens. LC 92-74745. 240p. 1992. pap. 11.95 (0-685-63269-5) Lawrence & Leong Pub.

Bridged Free Radicals. Leonard Kaplan. LC 72-81777. 501p. reprint ed. pap. 142.80 (0-7837-0644-8, 2040985) Bks Demand.

Bridegroom's Body see Three Short Novels

Bridgehead. David Drake. (Orig.). 1990. pap. 3.95 (0-8125-1168-9) Tor Bks.

***Bridgeport Initiative: The Lessons of One Community's Pioneering Attempt to Move the Poor from Welfare to Work.** 72p. 1991. pap. 10.00 (0-614-07232-8) Jobs for Future.

Bridgeport Township Site: Archaeological Investigation at 20SA620, Saginaw County, Michigan. Ed. by John M. O'Shea & Michael Shott. LC 89-48109. (Anthropological Papers: No. 81). (Illus.). xii, 304p. (Orig.). 1990. pap. 15.00 (0-915703-19-X) U Mich Mus Anthro.

Bridger: A Secular Humanist Odyssey. Jack W. Kennedy. Ed. by Dan Scanlan. 335p. (Orig.). 1991. 21.00 (0-9626280-1-8); pap. 16.00 (0-9626280-4-2); disk 8.00 (0-9626280-3-4); mac hd 8.00 (0-9626280-2-6) Pyramid Workers Pr.

Bridger: The Story of Mountain Man. David Kherdian. LC 86-7558. 160p. (J). (gr. 7 up). 1987. 11.75 (0-688-06510-4) Greenwillow.

Bridger Pass Overland Trail. Louise Erb. 1989. 23.75 (0-9626193-1-0); pap. 13.85 (0-9626193-0-2) Erbgem.

Bridger's Guide, Basics: Bridging Vocational & Academic Skills. National Center for Research in Vocational Education Staff. 1987. 75.00 (0-317-03855-9, SP300A) Ctr Educ Trng Employ.

Bridges. Neil Ardley. Ed. by Rebecca Stefoff. LC 90-40247. (How We Build Ser.). (Illus.). 48p. (J). (gr. 4-7). 1990. lib. bdg. 17.26 (0-944483-74-7) Garrett Ed Corp.

Bridges. David J. Brown. LC 93-9747. (Illus.). 176p. 1993. text ed. 30.00 (0-02-517455-X) Macmillan.

Bridges. Norman Carlisle & Madelyn Carlisle. LC 82-17874. (New True Bks.). (Illus.). 48p. (J). (gr. k-4). 1983. lib. bdg. 13.50 (0-516-01677-6) Childrens.

Bridges. J. Cooper. (Man-Made Wonders Ser.). (J). 1991. 8.95 (0-86592-628-X) Rourke Enter.

Bridges. Andrew Dunn. LC 93-6832. (Structures Ser.). 32p. (J). (gr. 5-8). 1993. 13.95 (1-56847-028-2) Thomson Lrning.

Bridges. John Flattau. (Illus.). 80p. 1985. 15.00 (0-912810-50-5) Lustrum Pr.

Bridges. Joy Richardson. LC 93-30058. (Picture Science Ser.). (Illus.). 32p. (J). (gr. 2-4). 1994. lib. bdg. 12.25 (0-531-14289-2) Watts.

Bridges. Ken Robbins. (Illus.). (J). 1991. lib. bdg. 13.89 (0-8037-0930-7) Dial Bks Young.

***Bridges: A Self-Esteem Activity Book for Students in Grades 4-6.** J. V. McGuire et al. LC 94-30011. (Illus.). (J). (gr. 4-6). 1994. 29.95 (0-205-16504-4, Longwood Div) Allyn.

Bridges: Analysis & Design of Reinforced Concrete Bridge Structures. 116p. 1988. 79.75 (0-317-32073-4, 343R-88) ACI.

Bridges: From Sentence to Paragraph. Beth Snyder & Barbara Auerbach. 160p. (C). 1986. pap. text ed. 13.50 (0-15-505550-X) HB Coll Pubs.

Bridges: Literature Across Cultures. Comp. by Gilbert H. Muller & John A. Williams. LC 93-3954. 1993. pap. text ed. write for info. (0-07-044216-9) McGraw.

***Bridges: Metaphor for Psychic Processes.** Rosemary Gordon. LC 94-44022. (History of Ideas Ser.). 1995. pap. write for info. (1-56000-819-9) Transaction Pubs.

Bridges: Poets of Dutchess & Ulster Counties. Ed. by D. Appelbaum & S. Lewis. 132p. (Orig.). (C). 1989. pap. 9.95 (0-941669-01-7) Springtown Pr.

***Bridges: Promising Programs for the Education of Immigrant Children.** Laurie Olsen. 176p. 1989. pap. 17.00 (1-887039-01-5) Calif Tomorrow.

Bridges: The Genealogy of Samuel Willard Bridges (1874-1943) & Caroline Britton Bridges (1873-1958) R. E. Thomas. (Illus.). 129p. 1991. reprint ed. pap. 19.50 (0-8328-2105-5) Higginson Bk Co.

Bridges: Ways to Understand Written Discourse. Rosentene B. Purnell. 112p. 1988. per. 22.95 (0-8403-4724-3) Kendall-Hunt.

Bridges Across the South: Technical Cooperation among Developing Countries. Bhashkar P. Menon. (Policy Studies). 1980. text ed. 56.00 (0-08-024645-1, Pergamon Pr); pap. text ed. 18.00 (0-08-024646-X, Pergamon Pr) Elsevier.

Bridges & Boundaries: African Americans & American Jews. Irving Howe et al. 272p. 1992. 45.00 (0-8076-1279-0); pap. 24.95 (0-8076-1280-4) Braziller.

Bridges & Cupolas. rev. ed. Janet A. Strombeck & Richard H. Strombeck. (Illus.). 104p. (Orig.). 1984. pap. 8.95 (0-912355-02-6) Sun Designs.

Bridges & Transmission Line Structures. Ed. by Lambert Tall. 512p. 1987. 49.00 (0-87262-613-X) Am Soc Civil Eng.

Bridges & Tunnels. Chris Oxlafe. LC 93-41962. (Technology Craft Topics Ser.). (Illus.). (J). 1994. lib. bdg. 12.60 (0-531-14328-7) Watts.

Bridges at Toko-Ri. James A. Michener. 1953. 16.95 (0-394-41780-1) Random.

Bridges at Toko-Ri. James A. Michener. 1984. mass mkt. 5.95 (0-449-20651-3, Crest) Fawcett.

Bridges Between Psychology & Linguistics: A Swarthmore Festschrift for Lila Gleitman. Ed. by D. Napoli & J. Kegl. 312p. (C). 1991. text ed. 59.95 (0-8058-0783-7) L Erlbaum Assocs.

Bridges from School to Working Life for Handicapped Youth: The View from Australia. Trevor Parmenter. (Monograph Ser.: No. 33). 76p. 1986. pap. text ed. 2.00 (0-939986-47-7) World Rehab Fund.

Bridges Go from Here to There. Forrest Wilson. (Illus.). 88p. (YA). 1993. 16.95 (0-89133-206-5) Preservation Pr.

Bridge's House. Dawn Powell. 1990. pap. 8.95 (0-679-72685-3, Vin) Random.

Bridges Not Walls: A Book about Interpersonal Communication. 3rd ed. John Stewart. (Illus.). 368p. (C). 1982. pap. text ed. 10.00 (0-394-34986-5) Random.

Bridges Not Walls: A Book About Interpersonal Communication. 5th ed. John Stewart. 480p. (C). 1990. pap. text ed. write for info. (0-07-061537-3) McGraw.

***Bridges Not Walls: A Book about Interpersonal Communication.** 6th ed. Ed. by John Stewart. LC 94-33881. 1994. pap. text ed. 12.75 (0-07-061549-7) McGraw.

Bridges of Consciousness. Kathy Oddenino. 300p. (Orig.). 1989. pap. 14.95 (0-923081-01-1) Joy Pubns MD.

Bridges of Faith Across the Seas. William J. Harvey, III. Ed. by Dorothy J. Rose. 338p. 1989. 27.95 (0-685-28911-7) Neibauer Pr.

Bridges of Faith Across the Seas. William J. Harvey, III. Ed. by Dorothy Rose. 338p. (C). 1989. 27.95 (0-685-29061-1) W J Harvey.

Bridges of God: A Study in the Strategy of Missions. Donald A. McGavran. LC 55-3682. 194p. reprint ed. pap. 55.30 (0-7837-1951-5, 2042168) Bks Demand.

***Bridges of Love.** Lois Oakland. 1995. 16.95 (0-8062-5299-5) Carlton.

Bridges of Madison County. Robert J. Waller. 192p. 1992. 17.95 (0-446-51652-X) Warner Bks.

Bridges of Madison County. Robert J. Waller. 208p. 1994. mass mkt. 4.99 (0-446-36449-5, Warner Vision) Warner Bks.

Bridges of Madison County. large type ed. Robert J. Waller. 170p. 1992. reprint ed. lib. bdg. 18.95 (1-56054-489-9) Thorndike Pr.

***Bridges of Madison County: The Film.** Ken Regan et al. 128p. 1995. 22.95 (0-446-51997-9) Warner Bks.

***Bridges of Madison County Memory Book.** Photos by Clint Eastwood. 48p. 1995. 11.95 (0-446-51998-7) Warner Bks.

Bridges of Power: Women's Multicultural Alliances. Ed. by Lisa Albrecht & Rose M. Brewer. 256p. (Orig.). 1990. lib. bdg. 39.95 (0-86571-183-6); pap. 14.95 (0-86571-184-4) New Soc Pubs.

Bridges of Respect. rev. ed. Katherine Whitlock. 1989. pap. 7.50 (0-910082-14-6) Am Fr Serv Comm.

Bridges of Respect. rev. ed. Katherine Whitlock. Ed. by Rachel Kamel. 1989. reprint ed. pap. 7.50 (0-910082-39-1) Am Fr Serv Comm.

Bridges of Steel, Ladders of Gold: Biography of Joseph Tanenbroum. Hanoch Teller. 1990. 13.95 (0-87306-526-3) Feldheim.

Bridges of Summer. Brenda Seabrooke. LC 92-11642. 160p. (J). (gr. 5 up). 1992. 14.99 (0-525-65094-6, Cobblehill Bks) Dutton Child Bks.

Bridges of Summer. Brenda Seabrooke. 160p. (J). (gr. 5 up). 1994. pap. 3.99 (0-14-036933-3) Puffin Bks.

Bridges of the Bodymind. 2nd ed. Jeanne Achterberg & Frank Lawlis. (Illus.). xv, 375p. 1980. reprint ed. pap. text ed. 24.95 (0-918296-19-6) Inst Personality & Ability.

Bridges on Secondary Highways & Local Roads: Rehabilitation & Replacement. (National Cooperative Highway Research Program Report Ser.: No. 222). 132p. 1980. 9.20 (0-309-03025-0) Transport Res Bd.

***Bridges over Bondage.** Mark Hyman. Ed. by Violet B. Johnson. 1994. pap. write for info. (0-915515-05-9) Way Pub.

Bridges Site (11-Mr-11) A Late Prehistoric Settlement in the Central Kaskaskia Valley. Michael L. Hargrave et al. LC 83-72630. (Center for Archaeological Investigations Research Paper Ser.: No. 38). (Illus.). xxi, 398p. (Orig.). 1983. pap. 15.00 (0-88104-014-2) Center Archaeo.

Bridges to Accessibility. Project Adventure Staff. 144p. 1992. per. 12.00 (0-8403-7891-2) Kendall-Hunt.

Bridges to Algebra. John L. Tilley & Roosevelt Gentry. 784p. (C). 1993. per. 49.95 (0-8403-8907-8) Kendall-Hunt.

***Bridges to Beginnings.** Agnes N. Johnston. Ed. by Joseph D. Adams. 96p. 1995. pap. 10.95 (1-880016-22-2) Road Pubs.

Bridges to Change: How Kids Live on a South Carolina Sea Island. Kathleen Krull. LC 93-42392. (World of My Own Ser.). (J). 1995. 15.99 (0-525-67441-1, Lodestar Bks) Dutton Child Bks.

Bridges to English, 6 bks.

Bridges to English, Bk. 1. E. Woodford Protase et al. (Bridges to English). (Illus.). 1981. text ed. 6.67 (0-07-034481-7); Wkbk. student ed 4.60 (0-07-034483-3); Tchr's. ed. teacher ed 4.60 (0-07-034482-5); Cassettes. audio 115.00 (0-07-034484-1); Cue cards. 74.75 (0-07-034485-X); Tests. 40.25 (0-07-034486-8) McGraw.

Bridges to English, Bk. 2. E. Woodford Protase & Doris Kernan. Ed. by J. Rebrisz. (Bridges to English). (Illus.). 1981. text ed. 6.67 (0-07-034487-6); Wkbk. student ed 4.05 (0-07-034489-2); Tchr's. ed. teacher ed 2.88 (0-07-034488-4); Cue cards. 74.75 (0-07-034491-4); Tests. 40.25 (0-07-034492-2) McGraw.

Bridges to English, Bk. 3. E. Woodford Protase & Doris Kernan. Ed. by J. Rebrisz. (Bridges to English). (Illus.). 1981. text ed. 6.67 (0-07-034493-0); Wkbk. student ed 4.60 (0-07-034495-7); Tchr's. ed. teacher ed 2.88 (0-07-034494-9); Cassettes. audio 140.30 (0-07-034496-5); Cue cards. 74.75 (0-07-034497-3); Tests. 40.25 (0-07-034498-1) McGraw.

Bridges to English, Bk. 4. E. Woodford Protase & Doris Kernan. Ed. by J. Rebrisz. (Bridges to English). (Illus.). 1981. text ed. 6.67 (0-07-034499-X); Tests. 40.25 (0-07-034504-X) McGraw.

Bridges to English, Bk. 5. E. Woodford Protase & Doris Kernan. Ed. by J. Rebrisz. (Bridges to English). (Illus.). 1981. Wkbk. student ed 4.60 (0-07-034507-4); Tchr's. ed. teacher ed 2.88 (0-07-034506-6); Cassettes. audio 140.30 (0-07-034508-2); Cue cards. 74.75 (0-07-034509-0); Tests. 40.25 (0-07-034510-4) McGraw.

Bridges to English, Bk. 6. E. Woodford Protase & Doris Kernan. Ed. by J. Rebrisz. (Bridges to English). (Illus.). 1981. text ed. 6.67 (0-07-034511-2); Wkbk. student ed 4.60 (0-07-034513-9); Tchr's. ed. teacher ed 2.88 (0-07-034512-0); Cassettes. audio 123.65 (0-07-034514-7); Cue cards. 74.75 (0-07-034515-5); Tests. 40.25 (0-07-034516-3) McGraw.

Bridges to Fantasy. Ed. by George E. Slusser et al. LC 81-13548. (Alternatives Ser.). 245p. 1982. 19.95 (0-8093-1043-0) S Ill U Pr.

Bridges to Heaven: How Well-Known Seekers Define & Deepen Their Connection with God. Jonathan Robinson. LC 94-67620. 256p. (Orig.). 1994. pap. 14.95 (0-913299-98-7) Stillpoint.

Bridges to Infinity: Nanotechnology & the Promise of Space. James Bennett. 1993. disk, pap. 19.95 (0-672-30387-6) Sams.

Bridges to Intimacy. C. Jesse Carlock & Patricia Hagerty. 1991. 14.95 (1-55691-037-1) Learning Pubns.

Bridges to Knowledge: Foreign Students in Comparative Perspective. Ed. by Elinor Barber et al. LC 84-16374. 264p. 1985. pap. text ed. 13.95 (0-226-03709-6) U Ch Pr.

Bridges to Knowledge: Foreign Students in Comparative Perspective. Ed. by Elinor Barber et al. LC 84-16374. 264p. 1985. lib. bdg. 27.50 (0-226-03708-8) U Ch Pr.

Bridges to Literacy: Children, Families & Schools. Intro. by David K. Dickinson. (Illus.). 288p. 1994. text ed. 54.95 (1-55786-372-5); pap. text ed. 21.95 (1-55786-373-3) Blackwell Pubs.

Bridges to Literacy: Learning from Reading Recovery. Ed. by Diane E. DeFord et al. LC 91-6551. (Illus.). 234p. (Orig.). 1991. pap. text ed. 19.00 (0-435-08575-1) Heinemann.

Bridges to Opportunity. Fred L. Pincus & Elayne Archer. 56p. 1989. pap. 2.00 (0-685-59931-0) Acad Educ Dev.

Bridges to Retirement: Older Workers in a Changing Labor Market. Ed. by Peter B. Doeringer. LC 89-26789. 248p. 1990. 32.00 (0-87546-159-X); pap. 45.00 (0-87546-160-3) ILR Pr.

Bridges to Science Fiction. Ed. by George E. Slusser et al. LC 80-16622. (Alternatives Ser.). 176p. 1980. 15.95 (0-8093-0961-0) S Ill U Pr.

Bridges to Success & Fulfillment: Techniques to Discover & Release Your Potential. William W. Hewitt. LC 92-35727. (Self-Improvement Ser.). 212p. 1993. 7.95 (0-87542-323-X) Llewellyn Pubns.

Bridges to the Natural World: A Natural History Guide for Teachers of Grades Pre K-6. Patricia Kane et al. (Illus.). 258p. (Orig.). 1992. teacher ed write for info. (0-9624065-1-1) NJ Audubon Soc.

Bridges to the World: Henry Noble MacCracken & Vassar College. Elizabeth A. Daniels. LC 94-31965. (Illus.). 318p. (Orig.). 1994. pap. 18.50 (1-883551-02-1, College Ave Pr) Attic Studio.

Bridges to Tomorrow: The Best of ACLD, Vol. 2. Ed. by William M. Cruickshank & Archie A. Silver. 1981. pap. 17.95x (0-8156-2237-6) Syracuse U Pr.

Bridgestone One Hundred Best Places to Stay in Ireland. John McKenna & Sally McKenna. (Bridgestone Guides Ser.). (Illus.). 140p. (Orig.). 1993. pap. 9.95 (1-874076-06-5, Pub. by Estragon Pr Ltd IE) Irish Bks Media.

Bridgestone One Hundred Best Restaurants in Ireland 1993. 2nd ed. John McKenna & Sally McKenna. (Bridgestone Guides Ser.). (Illus.). 144p. 1993. pap. 9.95 (1-874076-05-7, Pub. by Estragon Pr Ltd IE) Irish Bks Media.

Bridget of Cat's Head Point. Donna Winters. Ed. by Lynda S. Jolls & Pamela Q. Chambers. (Great Lakes Romances Ser.). (Illus.). 200p. (Orig.). 1994. pap. 8.95 (0-923048-82-0) Bigwater Pub.

***Bridget Riley: Five Dialogues on Art.** Ed. by R. Kudielka Shone. (Illus.). 1995. 25.00 (0-302-00667-2) Scala Books.

Bridgewater: History & Guide. Robert Dunning. LC 92-34326. 1992. 16.00 (0-7509-0192-6) A Sutton Pub.

Bridgewater College: The First Hundred Years 1880-1980. Francis F. Wayland. LC 93-27776. (Illus.). 960p. 1993. 34.95 (1-55618-134-5) Brunswick Pub.

Bridgewater Manuscript of Thomas Middleton's A Game at Chess (1624) Thomas Middleton. Ed. by T. H. Howard-Hill. LC 94-18381. 148p. 1994. text ed. 69.95 (0-7734-9113-9) E Mellen.

***Bridging.** Robert S. Cortright. LC 94-94550. (Illus.). 116p. (Orig.). 1994. pap. 24.95 (0-9641963-0-1) Bridge Ink.

Bridging: A Teacher's Guide to Metaphorical Thinking. Sharon Pugh et al. (Illus.). 150p. (Orig.). 1992. pap. 11.95 (0-8141-0384-7) NCTE.

Bridging Alaska: From the Big Delta to the Kenai. Ralph Soberg. LC 91-75800. (Illus.). 128p. (Orig.). 1991. pap. 12.50 (0-9625429-2-X) Hardscratch Pr.

B

Bridging Both Worlds: The Communication Consultant in Corporate America. Rebecca L. Ray. LC 93-28996. 194p. (Orig.). (C). 1993. lib. bdg. 49.50 (*0-8191-9278-3*); pap. text ed. 27.50 (*0-8191-9279-1*) U Pr of Amer.
Bridging Cultural Barriers for Corporate Success: How to Manage the Multicultural Work Force. Sondra Thiederman. 224p. 1990. text ed. 36.95 (*0-669-21930-4*) Free Pr.
***Bridging Cultures: A Program Kit for Schools & Public Libraries.** Barbara Blake & Tom Kruger. LC 94-28100. 1994. write for info. (*1-55570-166-3*) Neal-Schuman.
Bridging dBASE & Clipper Five. N. Dunlop. 1992. pap. 41.95 (*0-442-23823-1*) Van Nos Reinhold.
Bridging Differences: Effective Intergroup Communication. William B. Gudykunst. LC 93-43669. (Interpersonal CommTexts Ser.: Vol. 3). 256p. (C). 1994. pap. text ed. 17.95 (*0-8039-6479-X*) Sage.
Bridging Differences: Effective Intergroup Communication. 2nd ed. William B. Gudykunst. LC 93-43669. (Interpersonal CommTexts Ser.: Vol. 3). 256p. (C). 1994. text ed. 39.95 (*0-8039-5646-0*) Sage.
Bridging Early Services for Children with Special Needs & Their Families: A Practical Guide for Transition Planning. Sharon Rosenkoetter et al. 300p. (C). 1993. pap. text ed. 22.00 (*1-55766-160-X*, 160X) P H Brookes.
***Bridging East & West: Japanese Ceramics from the Kozan Studio: Selections from the Perry Foundation.** Kathleen Emerson-Dell. (Illus.). 64p. (Orig.). 1994. pap. 17.50 (*0-911886-39-7*) Walters Art.
Bridging English. Joseph O. Milner & Lucy F. Milner. LC 92-33936. 512p. (C). 1993. pap. write for info. (*0-675-21412-2*, Merrill Pub Co) Macmillan.
Bridging Environmental Science & Technology with Public Policy Decision Making. (Illus.). 60p. (Orig.). (C). 1993. pap. text ed. 40.00 (*1-56806-753-4*) Diane Pub.
Bridging Faults & IDDQ Testing. Y. K. Malaiya & R. Rajsuman. LC 92-30950. 136p. 1992. pap. 35.00 (*0-8186-3215-1*, 3215) IEEE Comp Soc.
Bridging Gap: The Contemporary Relationship of Architecture & Engineering. Building Arts Forum Staff. 1991. pap. 34.95 (*0-442-00135-5*) Van Nos Reinhold.
Bridging Japanese - North American Differences. William B. Gudykunst & Tsukasa Nishida. LC 93-43671. (Communicating Effectively in Multicultural Contexts Ser.: Vol. 1). 148p. (C). 1994. text ed. 36.00 (*0-8039-4834-4*); pap. text ed. 16.95 (*0-8039-4835-2*) Sage.
Bridging Mind & Model: Papers in Applied Mathematics. Ed. by Peter J. Costa. LC 93-86932. 325p. 1994. 24.95 (*0-9624229-7-5*) St Thomas Tech.
Bridging of Faiths: Religion & Politics in a New England City. N. J. Demerath, III & Rhys H. Williams. 368p. 1992. text ed. 35.00 (*0-691-07413-5*) Princeton U Pr.
Bridging Paradigms: Positive Development in Adulthood & Cognitive Aging. Ed. by Jan D. Sinnott & John C. Cavanaugh. LC 90-49073. 288p. 1991. text ed. 55.00 (*0-275-93617-1*, C3617, Praeger Pubs) Greenwood.
Bridging School & University. Ed. by M. H. Cantrell et al. 250p. 1993. pap. text ed. 40.00 (*90-5383-152-5*, Pub. by VU Univ Pr NE) Paul & Co Pubs.
Bridging Science & Spirit: Common Elements in David Bohm's Physics, the Perennial Philosophy, & Seth. Norman Friedman. Ed. by Sara Jenkins. 326p. (Orig.). 1994. pap. 14.95 (*0-9636470-0-8*) Living Lake.
Bridging the Age Gap: Module IV: Leader's Guide. Catherine D. Fyock. 75p. 1993. teacher ed 75.00 (*0-7863-0160-0*) Irwin Prof Pubng.
Bridging the Age Gap, Module IV Participants Workbook. Catherine D. Fyock. 32p. 1993. pap. 10.00 (*1-55623-828-2*) Irwin Prof Pubng.
***Bridging The Age Gap (Package of 10)** Catherine D. Fyock. 32p. 1993. 80.00 (*0-7863-0174-0*) Irwin Prof Pubng.
Bridging the Americas: The Literature of Paule Marshall, Toni Morrison, & Gayl Jones. Stelamaris Coser. 240p. (C). 1994. text ed. 49.95 (*1-56639-266-7*); pap. text ed. 18.95 (*1-56639-267-5*) Temple U Pr.
Bridging the Atlantic. Ed. by Philip H. Gibbs. LC 78-128245. (Essay Index Reprint Ser.). 1977. 19.95 (*0-8369-1928-9*) Ayer.
Bridging the Bereavement Gap: A Comprehensive Manual for the Preparation & Programming of Hospice Bereavement Services. 2nd ed. Donna R. O'Toole. 291p. (C). 1988. reprint ed. pap. 49.00 (*0-685-44864-9*); reprint ed. ring bd. 49.00 (*1-878321-01-3*) Rainbow NC.
Bridging the Communication Gap with the Elderly: Practical Strategies for Caregivers. Barbara J. Cox & Lois L. Waller. LC 91-31599. 126p. (Orig.). 1991. 25.95 (*1-55648-080-6*, 130104) AHPI.
Bridging the Computer GAP 10-14. Ronald MacKay & James Allan. (C). 1989. 75.00 (*0-685-52506-6*, Pub. by Jordanhill College UK) St Mut.
Bridging the Continent: A Sourcebook on the American West. Ed. by Carter Smith. LC 91-31129. (American Albums from the Collections of the Library of Congress). (Illus.). 96p. (YA). (gr. 5-8). 1992. lib. bdg. 18.90 (*1-56294-130-5*) Millbrook Pr.
Bridging the Gap. John Harvey. 128p. (C). 1988. pap. text ed. 45.00 (*0-7152-0607-9*) St Mut.
Bridging the Gap. J. Peter Kichline. 139p. 1989. 9.95 (*0-940257-06-8*) Granovetter Bks.
Bridging the Gap: A Learner's Guide to Transferable Skills. rev. ed. Urban Whitaker & Paul Breen. (Illus.). 32p. (Orig.). (C). 1983. pap. 5.00 (*0-918997-00-3*) Learning Ctr.
Bridging the Gap: A National Directory of Services for Women & Girls with Disabilities. Ed. by Merle Froschl. (Orig.). 1990. pap. text ed. 15.00 (*0-931629-09-8*) Educ Equity Con.
Bridging the Gap: African Traditional Religion & Bible Translation. Ed. by Philip C. Stine & Ernst R. Wendland. (UBS Monograph Ser.: No. 4). x, 226p. 1990. reprint ed. pap. text ed. 7.00 (*0-8267-0454-9*, 104643) Untd Bible Soc.
Bridging the Gap: College Reading. 3rd ed. Brenda D. Smith. (C). 1988. pap. text ed. 20.00 (*0-673-38259-1*) HarpCollege.
Bridging the Gap: College Reading. 4th ed. Brenda D. Smith. LC 92-22263. (C). 1992. 22.50 (*0-673-46691-4*) HarpCollege.
Bridging the Gap: Empirical Research in Simultaneous Interpretation. Ed. by Sylvie Lambert & Barbara Moser-Mercer. LC 94-9728. (Benjamins Translation Library: Vol. 3). 1994. 69.00 (*1-55619-481-1*) Benjamins North Am.
Bridging the Gap: Evangelism, Development & Shalom. Bruce Bradshaw. (Innovations in Mission Ser.). 183p. 1994. pap. 11.95 (*0-912552-84-0*) MARC.
Bridging the Gap: Examining Polarity in America. Ed. by Nancy L. Herron & Diane Zabel. 350p. 1994. lib. bdg. 50.00 (*1-56308-114-8*) Libs Unl.
Bridging the Gap: Implementing School-to-Work Transition in Austin, Texas. Kenneth W. Tolo & Robert W. Glover. (Policy Research Project Report Ser.: No. 103). 175p. 1993. 12.00 (*0-89940-711-0*) LBJ Sch Pub Aff.
Bridging the Gap: Literary Theory in the Classroom. J. M. Davies. LC 94-17926. (Locust Hill Literary Studies: No. 17). 373p. (C). 1994. lib. bdg. 38.00 (*0-933951-60-4*) Locust Hill Pr.
***Bridging the Gap: Student to Professional Actor.** Susan G. Cohen. (Classroom to the Stage & Screen Ser.: No. 1). (Illus.). 36p. (YA). (gr. 11 up). 1994. pap. 6.95 (*0-9641831-0-2*) Stage Coach.
Bridging the Gap: Tapping Foreign Personnel for U. S. Economic Development. Comp. by AILA Staff. 160p. (Orig.). 1991. pap. text ed. write for info. (*1-878677-19-5*) Amer Immi Law Assn.
Bridging the Gap: Theory & Practice in Foreign Policy. Alexander L. George. LC 92-45232. 1993. 24.95 (*1-878379-23-2*); pap. 14.95 (*1-878379-22-4*) US Inst Peace.
Bridging the Gap... Between an Understanding of the Physics & the Engineering Applications: Proceedings of the Institute of Environmental Sciences 9th Annual Meeting, 1963. Institute of Environmental Sciences Staff. (Illus.). 670p. 1963. pap. text ed. 75.00 (*0-915414-03-1*) Inst Environ Sci.
Bridging the Gap Between Computer Technicians & Users. M. C. Dobelis. (Illus.). 1976. reprint ed. pap. 0.50 (*0-918230-05-5*) Barnstable.
Bridging the Gap Between Ethical Theory & Conduct. Zalman F. Ury. 1.50 (*0-914131-07-9*, B130) Torah Umesorah.
Bridging the Gap Between Learning English in the Classroom & Using English in Lecture Halls, 2 Vols., I. Wu Yi So. xxi, 260p. 1979. pap. 15.00 (*0-87013-225-3*) Mich St U Pr.
Bridging the Gap Between Learning English in the Classroom & Using English in Lecture Halls, 2 Vols., II. Wu Yi So. xxi, 260p. 1979. pap. 15.00 (*0-87013-226-1*) Mich St U Pr.
Bridging the Gap Between Nonprofit & For-Profit Board Members. David M. Loscell & Cary M. Jensen. (Nonprofit Governance Ser.: No. 13). 14p. (Orig.). (C). 1992. pap. text ed. 10.00 (*0-925299-20-0*) Natl Ctr Nonprofit.
Bridging the Gap Between Rich & Poor: American Economic Development Policy Toward the Arab East, 1942-1949. Nathan Godfried. LC 87-8471. (Contributions in Economics & Economic History Ser.: No. 75). 256p. 1987. text ed. 65.00 (*0-313-25648-9*, GBG/) Greenwood.
Bridging the Gap Between the Media Specialist & the Classroom Teacher. Jan G. Philpot. 80p. 1989. pap. text ed. 7.95 (*0-86530-071-2*, IP 166-6) Incentive Pubns.
Bridging the Gap Between Theory & Practice: Exploring Clinical Practice Guidelines. Ed. by Hospital Research & Educational Trust Staff. (Illus.). 194p. (Orig.). 1993. pap. 19.95 (*0-87258-652-9*, 169511) Am Hospital.
Bridging the Gap Between Theory & Practice: Exploring Continuous Quality Improvement. Ed. by Hospital Research & Educational Trust Staff. (Illus.). 130p. (Orig.). 1992. pap. 19.95 (*0-87258-587-5*, 169510) Am Hospital.
Bridging the Gap Between Theory & Practice: Exploring Outcomes Management. Ed. by Hospital Research & Educational Trust Staff. (Illus.). 122p. (Orig.). 1994. pap. 19.95 (*0-87258-664-2*, 169512) Am Hospital.
Bridging the Gap: Philosophy, Mathematics, & Physics: Lectures on the Foundations of Science. Ed. by Giovanna Corsi et al. LC 92-12617. (Boston Studies in the Philosophy of Science: Vol. 140). 1992. lib. bdg. 112.00 (*0-7923-1761-0*) Kluwer Ac.
Bridging the Gaps: Contextualization among Korean Churches in America. In-Gyeong K. Lundell. LC 94-20468. (Asian Thought & Culture: Vol. 18). 168p. (C). 1995. text ed. 38.95 (*0-8204-2541-9*) P Lang Pubs.
***Bridging the Gender Gap.** Louise Y. Eberhardt. 192p. (Orig.). 1995. pap. 24.95 (*1-57025-023-5*) Whole Person.
Bridging the Global Gap: A Handbook to Linking Citizens on the First & Third Worlds. Medea Benjamin & Andrea Freeman. Ed. by Sarah Miles. LC 89-10508. 338p. 1989. pap. 12.95 (*0-932020-73-9*) Seven Locks Pr.
Bridging the Golden Gate. Kathy Pelta. (American Landmarks Ser.). (Illus.). 96p. (J). (gr. 4-8). 1987. pap. 5.95 (*0-8225-9521-4*, Lerner Publctns) Lerner Group.
Bridging the Golden Gate. Kathy Pelta. (American Landmarks Ser.). (Illus.). 96p. (J). (gr. 4 up). 1987. lib. bdg. 15.95 (*0-8225-1707-8*, Lerner Publctns) Lerner Group.
Bridging the Gulf: India's Manpower Migrations to West Asia. V. Chandra Mowli. xiii, 106p. 1992. 18.95 (*81-207-1416-4*, Pub. by Sterling Pubs II) Apt Bks.
Bridging the Information Gap for Small & Medium Enterprises: Proceedings of the Seminar "Distributed Database Systems for Small & Medium Enterprises" Beijing, China, May 8-12, 1989. Ed. by K. Ganzhorn & S. Faustoferri. (Illus.). x, 235p. 1990. pap. 32.00 (*0-387-52706-0*) Spr-Verlag.
***Bridging the Internet Gap.** 2nd ed. James E. Potter. (C). 1994. pap. text ed. 17.50 (*0-9632069-9-0*) Bridge Lrn Systs.
***Bridging the Internet Gap.** 4th ed. James E. Potter. (C). 1995. student ed, pap. text ed. 12.00 (*1-885587-07-4*) Bridge Lrn Systs.
Bridging the Learning Gap: Selecting & Implementing an Integrated Learning System. 46p. (Orig.). 1991. pap. text ed., vhs 125.00 (*0-88364-159-3*) Natl Sch Boards.
Bridging the Narrows. Joe Gotchy. Ed. by Gladys C. Para. (Illus.). 130p. (Orig.). 1990. 23.95 (*0-9626048-1-X*); pap. 17.95 (*0-9626048-0-1*) Pen Hist Soc.
***Bridging the Nonproliferation Divide: The United States & India.** Ed. by Francine R. Frankel. LC 95-14734. 1995. write for info. (*0-8191-9943-5*); pap. write for info. (*0-8191-9944-3*) U Pr of Amer.
Bridging the Sacred & the Secular: Selected Writings. John C. Murray. Ed. by J. Leon Hooper. LC 94-9698. 1994. 55.00 (*0-87840-561-5*) Georgetown U Pr.
Bridging the Silence: Nonverbal Modalities in the Treatment of Adult Survivors of Childhood Sexual Abuse. Susan L. Simonds. 220p. (C). 1994. 27.00 (*0-393-70175-1*) Norton.
Bridging the Skills Gap: Women & Job in a High Tech World. Vikki Gregory & Christine Kaplan. 1983. 10.00 (*0-934966-05-2*) Wider Oppor Women.
Bridging the Strait: Taiwan, China, & the Prospects for Reunification. Hsin-Hsing Wu. LC 93-42311. (Studies on Contemporary Taiwan). 320p. 1994. 75.00 (*0-19-585765-8*) OUP.
Bridging Three Worlds: Hungarian-Jewish Americans, 1848-1914. Robert Perlman. LC 90-11224. 320p. (C). 1991. lib. bdg. 40.00 (*0-87023-468-4*) U of Mass Pr.
Bridging Two Worlds. Martha Barham. Ed. by Tom Greene. LC 84-194533. (Illus.). 246p. (Orig.). 1981. pap. 6.95 (*0-9609680-0-8*) MJB Bks.
Bridging Two Worlds: Social Work & the Elderly Living Alone. Ian Sinclair et al. 233p. 1988. text ed. 53.00 (*0-566-05715-8*, Pub. by Gower UK) Ashgate Pub Co.
Bridging Worlds Through General Semantics. Ed. by Mary Morain. LC 84-82325. 347p. 1984. 15.00 (*0-918970-34-2*) Intl Gen Semantics.
Bridgman's Complete Guide to Drawing from Life. George B. Bridgman. 352p. 1992. reprint ed. 14.99 (*0-517-25546-4*, Pub. by Wings Bks) Random Hse Value.
Bridgman's Life Drawing. George B. Bridgeman. 18.75 (*0-8446-0038-5*) Peter Smith.
Bridgman's Life Drawings. George B. Bridgman. (Illus.). 1971. reprint ed. pap. 4.95 (*0-486-22710-3*) Dover.
Bridie & Finn. Harry Cauley. LC 93-37081. 1994. 22.95 (*0-15-113910-5*) HarBrace.
Bridle: Index of United States Patents 1790-1950. Susan Green. (Illus.). 92p. (Orig.). pap. text ed. 20.00 (*1-880499-01-0*) S Green PA.
Bridle Path. Bonnie Bryant. (Saddle Club Ser.: No. 27). (J). (gr. 4-7). 1993. 3.50 (*0-553-48074-X*) Bantam.
***Bridled Ambition: Why Countries Constrain Their Nuclear Capabilities.** Mitchell Reiss. LC 95-2646. (Special Studies). 360p. 1995. text ed. 45.00 (*0-943875-72-2*); pap. 16.95 (*0-943875-71-4*) W Wilson Ctr Pr.
***Bridled Groom: A Dead Letter Mystery.** Borthwick. 1995. mass mkt. 4.99 (*0-312-95505-7*) St Martin.
Bridled Groom: A Mystery. J. S. Borthwick. 304p. 1994. 20.95 (*0-312-10435-9*) St Martin.
***Bridles & Bits of Cowboy Poetry.** David N. Nelson. (Illus.). 60p. (Orig.). 1994. pap. text ed. 8.00 (*1-886615-00-4*) D N Nelson.
Bridling of Desire: Views of Sex in the Later Middle Ages. Pierre J. Payer. LC 92-95553. 285p. 1993. 35.00 (*0-8020-2919-1*) U of Toronto Pr.
Bridling of Pegasus: Prose Papers on Poetry. Alfred Austin. LC 67-22053. (Essay Index Reprint Ser.). 1977. 20.95 (*0-8369-0164-9*) Ayer.
Bridlington Book. Bryan Waites. (C). 1989. text ed. 35.00 (*0-948929-09-X*) St Mut.
***Brids of the Western Palearctic Volume IX: Buntings & New World Warblers, 9 Vols.** Stanley Cramp & C. M. Perrins. 1990. 1,200.00 (*0-19-854843-5*) OUP.
Brief Abstract of Lower Norfolk County & Norfolk County Wills. Charles F. McIntosh. 223p. 1994. reprint ed. pap. 25.50 (*0-8328-4019-X*) Higginson Bk Co.
Brief Abstracts of Norfolk County Wills, 1710-1753. Charles F. McIntosh. 344p. 1982. reprint ed. pap. 30.00 (*0-89308-324-0*) Southern Hist Pr.
Brief Account of the Military Orders in Spain. Georgiana G. King. LC 76-29841. reprint ed. 33.00 (*0-404-15421-2*) AMS Pr.
Brief American Lives: Four Studies in Collective Biography. Donald C. Yelton. LC 77-29102. 249p. 1978. 22.50 (*0-8108-1114-6*) Scarecrow.
Brief American Pageant, 2 vols. 3rd ed. David M. Kennedy et al. 688p. (C). 1993. pap. text ed. write for info. (*0-669-28899-3*); Instr.'s resource guide. teacher ed write for info. (*0-669-28904-3*); Guidebook. write for info. (*0-669-28903-5*) Heath.
Brief American Pageant, 2 vols., Vol. I: To 1877. 3rd ed. David M. Kennedy et al. 384p. (C). 1993. pap. text ed. write for info. (*0-669-28900-0*) Heath.
Brief American Pageant, 2 vols., Vol. II: Since 1865. 3rd ed. David M. Kennedy et al. 400p. (C). 1993. pap. text ed. write for info. (*0-669-28901-9*) Heath.
Brief American Pageant: A History of the Republic, 2 vols. 2nd ed. David M. Kennedy et al. LC 88-81497. 592p. (C). 1989. disk 150.00 (*0-669-18147-1*); 150.00 (*0-669-18144-7*) Heath.
Brief American Pageant: A History of the Republic, 2 vols., Set. 2nd ed. David M. Kennedy et al. LC 88-81497. 592p. (C). 1989. pap. text ed. 22.00 (*0-669-17839-X*) Heath.
Brief American Pageant: A History of the Republic, 2 vols., Vol. I. 2nd ed. David M. Kennedy et al. LC 88-81497. 320p. (C). 1989. pap. text ed. 14.00 (*0-669-17840-3*) Heath.
Brief American Pageant: A History of the Republic, 2 vols., Vol. II. 2nd ed. David M. Kennedy et al. LC 88-81497. 336p. (C). 1989. pap. text ed. 14.00 (*0-669-17841-1*) Heath.
Brief Analysis of the Cultural Revolution. Liu Guokai. Ed. by Anita Chan. Tr. by John Hsu. LC 87-4541. 151p. (C). 1987. pap. 22.95 (*0-87332-435-8*) M E Sharpe.
Brief & Extended Casework. William J. Reid & Ann W. Shyne. LC 70-79192. 1969. text ed. 35.50 (*0-231-03219-6*) Col U Pr.
Brief & Incomplete History of the Archaeology of the Kansas City Vicinity, Vol. 42. Carl H. Chapman et al. (Missouri Archaeologist Ser.). (Illus.). 108p. (Orig.). 1981. pap. 5.00 (*0-943414-59-8*) MO Arch Soc.
Brief & Practical Guide to EC Law. 2nd ed. David Medhurst. LC 93-46402. 256p. 1994. pap. write for info. (*0-632-03432-7*, Pub. by Blckwell Sci Pubns UK) Blackwell Sci.
Brief Anthology of French Poetry. Ed. by Marija Petrovska. LC 84-48026. 191p. (C). 1985. text ed. 23.80 (*0-8204-0170-6*) P Lang Pubs.
Brief Assessment of the New Hampshire State Law Library: Technical Assistance Report. David Steelman et al. 57p. 1987. 4.00 (*0-685-18271-1*, NERO,T/A-536) Natl Ctr St Courts.
***Brief Bedford Reader.** 5th ed. X. J. Kennedy et al. 512p. 1994. pap. text ed. 12.00 (*0-312-08636-9*) St Martin.
***Brief Bible Outline.** Cleyburn L. McCauley. Ed. by Lucy Foley. (Illus.). 245p. (Orig.). 1995. pap. text ed. 15.95 (*0-910531-21-8*) Wolcotts.
Brief Bible Studies for Busy People. Frances L. Carroll. LC 85-3470. 144p. 1985. 13.95 (*0-13-081993-X*) P-H.
Brief Biographical Sketch of the Life of Major-General Grenville M. Dodge. J. T. Granger. Ed. by Stuart Bruchey. LC 80-1310. (Railroads Ser.). 1981. reprint ed. lib. bdg. 18.95 (*0-405-13778-8*) Ayer.
Brief Business Statistics. Watson & Billingley. 625p. (C). 1988. student ed 17.00 (*0-685-18750-0*, H14251); student ed 19.00 (*0-685-18751-9*, H14244); Instr's. manual avail. teacher ed write for info. (*0-318-62195-9*, H14236); 17.00 (*0-685-18749-7*, H14251); Test manual avail. write for info. (*0-318-62196-7*, H14228) Allyn.
***Brief Calculus: With Student Solutions & Discovering Calculus with Mathematics.** 5th ed. Howard Anton. 1994. pap. text ed. write for info. (*0-471-11024-8*) Wiley.
Brief Calculus & Its Applications. 6th ed. Larry J. Goldstein et al. 560p. 1993. text ed. write for info. (*0-13-087131-1*) P-H.
Brief Calculus for Business, Economics, & the Social & Life Sciences. 5th ed. Laurence D. Hoffman & Gerald L. Bradley. LC 92-17331. 1992. text ed. write for info. (*0-07-029361-9*) McGraw.
Brief Calculus for Management & the Life & Social Sciences. 2nd ed. Donald Stancl & Mildred Stancl. 512p. (C). 1990. text ed. 62.95 (*0-256-08250-2*) Irwin.
***Brief Calculus for Management & the Life & Social Sciences.** 2nd ed. Donald Stancl & Mildred Stancl. 86p. (C). 1990. student ed, text ed. 53.95 (*0-256-09279-6*) Irwin.
Brief Calculus with Application. 2nd ed. Roland E. Larson & Robert P. Hostetler. LC 86-82096. 640p. (C). 1987. text ed. 37.00 (*0-669-12060-X*); Student soln. guide. student ed 8.50 (*0-669-12061-8*); Matrices suppl. 2.50 (*0-669-13013-3*); Answer key. 2.00 (*0-669-12063-4*) Heath.
Brief Calculus with Applications. Raymond F. Coughlin & David Zitarelli. 496p. (C). 1990. text ed. 56.00 (*0-03-031597-2*) SCP.
Brief Calculus with Applications. Chris Vancil & Cliff Swauger. 472p. (C). 1990. text ed. 66.50 (*0-06-046766-5*) HarpCollege.
Brief Calculus with Applications. 3rd ed. Roland E. Larson et al. LC 89-81072. 812p. (C). 1991. text ed. 37.00 (*0-669-21767-0*); Study guide & workbook. student ed 12.00 (*0-669-24500-3*); Student solutions guide. student ed 8.50 (*0-669-21769-7*); Instr.'s guide. teacher ed 2.00 (*0-669-21768-9*); Transparencies. trans. write for info. (*0-669-27336-8*); Systems of equations, matrices & determinants. write for info. (*0-669-21770-0*); Complete solutions guide. write for info. (*0-669-27149-7*); Test item file. write for info. (*0-669-27150-0*) Heath.
***Brief Calculus with Applications.** 4th ed. Roland E. Larson et al. 736p. (C). 1995. text ed. write for info. (*0-669-35165-2*) Heath.
Brief Calculus with Applications. 5th ed. Laurence D. Hoffmann & Gerald L. Bradley. 1993. pap. text ed. write for info. (*0-07-029362-7*) McGraw.
Brief Calculus with Applications: Alternate Third Edition. Roland E. Larson et al. LC 89-81072. 648p. (C). 1990. text ed. 35.00 (*0-669-21763-8*); Student solutions guide. student ed 8.50 (*0-669-21764-6*); Study guide & workbook. student ed write for info. (*0-318-68032-7*); Instr.'s guide. teacher ed 2.00 (*0-669-21765-4*); Complete solutions guide. write for info. (*0-669-27147-0*); Test item file. write for info. (*0-669-27148-9*) Heath.
Brief Calculus with Applications: Student Solution Manual. 5th ed. Margaret L. Liall et al. (C). 1993. text ed. 23.00 (*0-673-46755-4*) HarpCollege.

An Asterisk (*) at the beginning of an entry indicates that the title is appearing in BIP for the first time.

Brief Calculus with Applications Alternate. 2nd ed. Roland E. Larson & Robert P. Hostetler. LC 86-82095. 512p. (C). 1990. text ed. 35.00 (*0-669-12186-X*); Student soln. guide. student ed 8.50 (*0-669-12187-8*); Answer key. 2.00 (*0-669-12188-6*) Heath.

Brief Candle. Charles B. Garrigus. LC 86-30067. 540p. 1987. 15.95 (*0-89407-084-3*); pap. 9.95 (*0-89407-078-9*) Strawberry Hill.

Brief Candles. Craig P. Standish. LC 91-84025. 64p. (Orig.). 1994. pap. 5.95 (*0-943512-23-9*) Linwood Pub.

Brief Career of Eliza Poe. Geddeth Smith. LC 86-46406. (Illus.). 176p. 1988. 26.50 (*0-8386-3317-X*) Fairleigh Dickinson.

Brief Catechism for Adults: A Complete Handbook on How to Be a Good Catholic. rev. ed. William J. Cogan. LC 93-60780. 176p. 1993. reprint ed. pap. 9.00 (*0-89555-492-5*) TAN Bks Pubs.

Brief Cherishing: A Napa Valley Harvest. Hildegarde Flanner. LC 85-16107. (Illus.). 102p. 1985. pap. 10.00 (*0-936784-03-2*) J Daniel.

Brief Chronicles. James Agate. LC 79-92223. 1972. reprint ed. lib. bdg. 24.95 (*0-405-08183-9*, Pub. by Blom Pubns UK) Ayer.

Brief Commentary on Luke & Acts, 2 bks., Set. John J. Kilgallen. 1988. pap. 19.95 (*0-8091-3009-2*) Paulist Pr.

Brief Commentary on the Acts of the Apostles. John J. Kilgallen. 240p. 1988. pap. 12.50 (*0-8091-2977-9*) Paulist Pr.

Brief Commentary on the Gospel of John. John J. Kilgallen. LC 92-16596. 276p. 1992. lib. bdg. 89.95 (*0-7734-2346-X*) E Mellen.

Brief Commentary on the Gospel of Luke. John J. Kilgallen. 240p. 1988. pap. 12.50 (*0-8091-2928-0*) Paulist Pr.

Brief Commentary on the Gospel of Mark. John J. Kilgallen. 1989. pap. 14.95 (*0-8091-3059-9*) Paulist Pr.

Brief Commentary on the Gospel of Matthew. John J. Kilgallen. LC 89-37928. (Mellen Biblical Press Ser.). 348p. 1992. lib. bdg. 99.95 (*0-7734-2350-8*) E Mellen.

Brief Conversion & Other Stories. Earl Lovelace. (Caribbean Writers Ser.). 141p. (Orig.). (C). 1988. pap. 7.50 (*0-435-98882-4*, 98882) Heinemann.

Brief Counseling with Suicidal Persons. William L. Getz et al. LC 80-8375. 288p. 1982. text ed. 29.95 (*0-669-04090-8*) Free Pr.

Brief Counselling: A Practical Guide for Beginning Practitioners. Wendy Dryden & Colin Feltham. LC 92-8610. 1992. pap. 27.00 (*0-335-09972-6*, Open Univ Pr) Taylor & Francis.

Brief Course in Arithmetic. Ann Farber et al. 213p. 1985. write for info. (*0-912675-10-1*) Ardsley.

Brief Course in Arithmetic. 2nd ed. Ann Farber et al. 213p. 1985. pap. text ed. 35.95x (*0-912675-08-X*) Ardsley.

Brief Course in Business Statistics. Willam Mendenhall & Robert J. Beaver. LC 94-17706. 654p. 1995. text ed. 37.95 (*0-534-25290-7*) Intl Thomson.

Brief Course in Mediumship. Khei. 79p. 1965. spiral bd. 3.30 (*0-7873-0491-3*) Mokelumne.

Brief Course in QBasic: With an Introduction to Visual Basic. 2nd ed. David I. Schneider. LC 94-4806. 384p. (C). 1994. pap. write for info. (*0-02-407741-0*) Dellen Pub.

Brief Course in QBASIC with an Introduction to Visual Basic. 2nd ed. David I. Schneider. Orig. Title: Microsoft QuickBASIC. 1994. pap. write for info. (*0-318-72287-9*) Dellen Pub.

Brief Course of Higher Mathematics. V. A. Kudryavtsev & P. Demidovich. 694p. 1984. 80.00 (*0-317-52904-8*, Pub. by Collets UK) Pro-Am Music.

***Brief Description of the Geostellar Shell Theory: and Related Material.** rev. ed. Peter D. Hays. 90p. (C). 1992. pap. text ed. 13.95 (*1-885554-00-1*) P D Hays.

Brief Dictionary of Biology & Environmental Sciences. Ed. by Karen Arms. (Illus.). 128p. (Orig.). (C). 1992. pap. text ed. 4.95 (*0-9629275-1-1*) Halfmoon Pub.

Brief Dictionary of Hinduism. Usha. 1990. pap. 4.95 (*0-87481-048-5*) Vedanta Pr.

Brief Dictionary of Hinduism. Ed. by Brahmacharini Usha. (Orig.). 1962. pap. 4.95 (*0-87481-017-5*) Vedanta Pr.

Brief Discourse of the Christian Life & Godly Death of Mistris Katherin Brettergh (1602) see Death's Advantage Little Regarded

Brief Disquisition of the Law of Nature, According to the Principles & Method Laid down in the Reverend Dr. Cumberland's (Now Lord Bishop of Peterborough's) Latin Treatise on That Subject. As also His Confutations of Mr. Hobbs's Principles Put into Another Method. 2nd ed. James Tyrrell. (Illus.). ixxii, 380p. 1987. reprint ed. lib. bdg. 45.00 (*0-8377-2630-1*) Rothman.

Brief Enchantment. large type ed. MacLeod. 1991. 17.95 (*0-7451-9993-3*, AH029, Atlantic Lrg Print); pap. 15.95 (*0-7927-0458-4*, AS065, Atlantic Lrg Print) Chivers N Amer.

Brief Encounter. Richard Dyer. (Illus.). 72p. 1994. pap. 9.95 (*0-85170-362-3*, Pub. by British Film Inst UK) Ind U Pr.

***Brief Encounter: (Sealed with a Kiss)** Catherine George. (Romance Ser.). 1995. pap. 2.99 (*0-373-03360-5*, 1-03360-4) Harlequin Bks.

***Brief Encounters: A Dictionary of Briefs & Phrases for Court Reporting.** Laurie Boucke. Ed. by Linda Carlson. 450p. (Orig.). (C). 1995. pap. 50.00 (*0-9625006-8-2*) White-Boucke.

Brief Encounters (Brief Psychotherapy) Karl K. Lewin. LC 78-96987. 288p. 1970. 10.00 (*0-87527-048-4*) Green.

Brief Encyclopedia of Homosexuality. Stephen Wright. LC 78-62675. 1978. pap. 9.50 (*0-9601904-0-6*) Stephen Wright.

Brief Encyclopedia of the Materials & Techniques of Manuscript Illumination in Europe Before 1650 A. D. Robert Trump. (Illus.). 66p. (Orig.). 1984. pap. 3.50 (*0-939329-01-8*) Potboiler Pr.

Brief English Handbook. 4th ed. Edward A. Dornan & Charles W. Dawe. LC 93-13924. (C). 1993. text ed. 16.75 (*0-673-52308-X*) HarpCollege.

Brief English Workbook. Edward A. Dornan & Charles W. Dawe. (C). 1987. pap. text ed. 24.00 (*0-673-39252-X*) HarpCollege.

Brief Enquiry into the True Nature & Character of Our Federal Government. A. P. Upshur. LC 71-169643. (American Constitutional & Legal History Ser). 128p. 1971. reprint ed. lib. bdg. 19.50 (*0-306-70363-7*) Da Capo.

***Brief Eternity.** Eduard H. Strauch. LC 94-90275. 136p. (Orig.). 1995. pap. 10.00 (*1-56002-481-X*, Univ Edtns) Aegina Pr.

Brief Examination of the Practice of the Times. Ralph Sandiford. LC 76-82212. (Anti-Slavery Crusade in America Ser.). 1970. reprint ed. 13.95 (*0-405-00658-6*) Ayer.

Brief Exposition of the Constitution of the United States: With an Appendix, Containing the Declaration of Independence, & the Articles of Confederation, & a Copious Index. James Bayard. 178p. reprint ed. 27.50 (*0-8377-1953-4*) Rothman.

Brief Exposition with Practical Observation upon the Whole Book of Canticles. John Cotton. LC 71-141106. (Research Library of Colonial Americana). 1972. reprint ed. 26.95 (*0-405-03320-6*) Ayer.

***Brief Field of View & Elderly Drivers: A Research Study.** A. Thompson Perry, 2nd. (Illus.). 109p. (Orig.). (C). 1995. pap. text ed. 40.00 (*0-7881-1615-0*) Diane Pub.

Brief for the Prosecution. C. H. Douglas. 1972. 59.95 (*0-87968-787-8*) Gordon Pr.

Brief for the Prosecution. C. H. Douglas. 92p. 1986. pap. 7.50 (*0-949667-80-3*, Pub. by Veritas Pubng AT) Noontide.

Brief for the Trial of Criminal Cases. 2nd enl. ed. Austin Abbott. xx, 814p. 1994. reprint ed. lib. bdg. 75.00 (*0-8377-1911-9*) Rothman.

Brief French Reference Grammar. Colbert. 1972. 23.95 (*0-442-21615-7*) Heinle & Heinle.

Brief Gaudy Hour: A Novel of Anne Boleyn. Margaret C. Barnes. 23.95 (*0-8488-0423-6*) Amereon Ltd.

Brief Genealogical History of Robert Starkweather of Roxbury & Ipswich, Massachusetts, Who Was the Original American Ancestor, & of His Descendants in Various Lines. C. L. Starkweather. (Illus.). 356p. 1989. reprint ed. lib. bdg. 66.00 (*0-8328-1114-9*); reprint ed. pap. 56.00 (*0-8328-1115-7*) Higginson Bk Co.

Brief Greek Syntax. L. Bevier. (College Classical Ser.). (gr. 11-12). 1981. 25.00 (*0-89241-127-9*); pap. 14.00 (*0-89241-343-3*) Caratzas.

Brief Guide to Basic Writing. Roger D. Cherry & Kay Halasek. LC 92-10022. (C). 1992. teacher ed, pap. 10.00 (*0-06-041384-0*) HarpCollege.

Brief Guide to Basic Writing. Roger D. Cherry. (C). 1992. 16.50 (*0-06-041339-5*) HarpCollege.

Brief Guide to Brief Therapy. Brian Cade & William H. O'Hanlon. 280p. (C). 1993. 22.95 (*0-393-70143-3*) Norton.

Brief Guide to Current Methods of Assessing Vitamin A Status. International Vitamin A Consultative Group Staff. (Illus.). 37p. 1993. pap. 3.50 (*0-944398-10-3*) ILSI.

Brief Guide to Music. 2nd ed. Stanley Sadie. 576p. (C). 1989. boxed write for info. (*0-318-65461-X*) P-H.

Brief Guide to Music. 3rd ed. Stanley Sadie. 432p. 1993. pap. text ed. 42.00 (*0-13-086851-5*) P-H.

Brief Guide to Scholarly Editing. Robin Higham et al. 62p. (Orig.). 1982. pap. text ed. 3.50 (*0-89745-037-X*) Sunflower U Pr.

Brief Guide to Sources of Scientific & Technical Information. 2nd ed. Saul Herner. LC 80-81087. (Illus.). xi, 160p. 1980. 15.00 (*0-87815-031-5*) Info Resources.

Brief Guide to the Theory of Relativity. 1977. pap. 0.75 (*0-686-23350-6*) Chthon Pr.

Brief Guide to VP Planner Plus (3 & half inch Disk) West Publishing Company Staff. 36p. (C). 1988. 3.5 hd (*0-318-63012-5*) West Pub.

Brief Handbook for Writers. 3rd ed. James F. Howell & W. Dean Memering. LC 92-28552. 416p. 1992. pap. text ed. write for info. (*0-13-087024-2*) P-H.

Brief Handbook of English. 3rd ed. Hulon Willis & Enno Klammer. 334p. (C). 1986. pap. text ed. 16.00 (*0-15-505565-8*) HB Coll Pubs.

Brief Historical Relation of State Affairs from September 1678 to April 1714, 6 vols., Set. Narcissus Luttrell. Ed. by Gerald M. Straka. LC 72-83165. (English Studies Ser.). 1972. reprint ed. lib. bdg. 324.00 (*0-8420-1423-3*) Scholarly Res Inc.

Brief Historie of the English Renaissance: The Life & Tymes of Elizabeth Tudor. rev. ed. Wayne Wright. (Illus.). 59p. 1989. reprint ed. pap. 5.95 (*0-685-33273-X*) Bay Press.

Brief History of Ahmeek, Michigan. (Copper Country Local History Ser.: Vol. 18). (Illus.). 104p. 1981. 2.50 (*0-942363-17-5*) C J Monette.

Brief History of American Culture. Robert Crunden. 370p. 1994. 22.95 (*1-55778-705-0*) Paragon Hse.

Brief History of Bishop Henry Funck & Other Funk Pioneers & a Complete Genealogical Family History, with Biographies of Their Descendants from the Earliest Available Records to the Present. A. J. Fretz. (Illus.). 874p. 1989. reprint ed. lib. bdg. 141.00 (*0-8328-0556-4*); reprint ed. pap. 131.00 (*0-8328-0557-2*) Higginson Bk Co.

Brief History of Bullet Moulds. Codman Parkerson. 1974. 1.75 (*0-913150-26-6*) Pioneer Pr.

Brief History of Camouflage. Thaisa Frank. LC 91-39923. 250p. 1993. reprint ed. 25.00 (*0-87685-857-4*); reprint ed. pap. 12.50 (*0-87685-856-6*) Black Sparrow.

Brief History of Camouflage, signed ed. Thaisa Frank. LC 91-39923. 250p. 1993. reprint ed. 35.00 (*0-87685-858-2*) Black Sparrow.

Brief History of Central America. Hector Perez-Brignoli. Tr. by Ricardo B. Sawrey & Susana S. De Sawrey. 1989. 45.00 (*0-520-06049-0*) U CA Pr.

Brief History of Central America. Hector Perez-Brignoll. 1989. pap. 13.00 (*0-520-06832-7*) U CA Pr.

Brief History of Chinese & Japanese Civilizations. 2nd ed. Conrad Schirokauer. 673p. (Orig.). (C). 1988. pap. text ed. 29.50 (*0-15-505569-0*) HB Coll Pubs.

Brief History of Chinese & Japanese Civilizations. 2nd ed. Conrad Schirokauer. 673p. (Orig.). (C). 1989. pap. text ed. write for info. (*0-318-69123-X*) HB Coll Pubs.

Brief History of Chinese Civilization. Conrad Schirokauer. 415p. (C). 1990. pap. text ed. 21.50 (*0-15-505568-2*) HB Coll Pubs.

Brief History of Chinese Fiction. Lu Hsun, pseud. Tr. by Hsien-yi Yang & Gladys Yang. LC 73-870. (China Studies: from Confucius to Mao Ser.). (Illus.). 462p. 1990. reprint ed. 42.00 (*0-88355-065-2*) Hyperion Conn.

Brief History of Christian Worship. James F. White. 224p. (Orig.). 1993. pap. 14.95 (*0-687-03414-0*) Abingdon.

Brief History of Education. 2nd rev. ed. Francesco Cordasco. (Quality Paperback Ser.: No. 67). 192p. 1976. pap. 8.95 (*0-8226-0067-6*) Littlefield.

Brief History of English Bible Translations. Laurence M. Vance. LC 93-93831. 127p. (Orig.). 1993. pap. 5.95 (*0-9628898-1-4*) Vance FL.

Brief History of Hawaii. George T. Armitage. 1973. pap. 2.50 (*0-930492-04-8*) Hawaiian Serv.

Brief History of Imbecility: Poetry & Prose of Takamura Kotaro. Kotaro Takamura. Tr. by Hiroaki Sato. LC 92-11916. 296p. (C). 1992. pap. text ed. 16.95 (*0-8248-1456-8*) UH Pr.

Brief History of Italian Literature. Vincent Luciani. (C). 1967. 12.95 (*0-913298-09-3*) S F Vanni.

Brief History of Japanese Civilization. Conrad Schirokauer. 352p. (C). 1993. pap. text ed. 22.75 (*0-15-500282-1*) HB Coll Pubs.

Brief History of John & Christian Fretz & a Complete Genealogical Family Register. A. J. Fretz. (Illus.). 609p. 1989. reprint ed. lib. bdg. 93.00 (*0-8328-0554-8*); reprint ed. pap. 83.00 (*0-8328-0555-6*) Higginson Bk Co.

Brief History of John Valentine Kratz, & a Complete Genealogical Family Register. A. J. Fretz. (Illus.). 315p. reprint ed. lib. bdg. 51.50 (*0-8328-0741-9*); reprint ed. pap. 41.50 (*0-8328-0742-7*) Higginson Bk Co.

Brief History of Lancaster County, Pennsylvania. Israel S. Clare. (Illus.). 317p. 1994. reprint ed. lib. bdg. 32.50 (*0-8328-4004-1*) Higginson Bk Co.

***Brief History of Logan County, with Reminiscences by Pioneers.** Comp. by Emma B. Conklin. (Illus.). 354p. 1995. reprint ed. lib. bdg. 45.00 (*0-8328-4679-1*) Higginson Bk Co.

Brief History of Male Nudes in America: Stories by Dianne Nelson. Dianne Nelson. LC 93-809. (Flannery O'Connor Award for Short Fiction Ser.). 136p. (C). 1993. 19.95 (*0-8203-1571-0*) U of Ga Pr.

Brief History of Medicine in the Spartanburg Region & of the Spartanburg County Medical Society 1700-1990: To Which Are Added Biographies of the Spartanburg Physicians. William C. Herbert, Jr. LC 92-49376. 1992. 25.00 (*0-87152-461-9*) Reprint.

Brief History of Methodism in Texas. Homer S. Thrall. 304p. 1977. reprint ed. 12.50 (*0-87921-042-7*) Attic Pr.

Brief History of Mongolia in the Autonomous Period: Mongolian Text with an Introduction & Index in English by John G. Hangin. L. Dindub. (Mongolia Society Special Papers: No. 6). spiral bd. 20.00 (*0-910980-26-8*) Mongolia.

Brief History of New Mexico. Myra E. Jenkins & Albert H. Schroeder. LC 74-21917. (Illus.). 95p. 1974. reprint ed. pap. 9.95 (*0-8263-0370-6*) U of NM Pr.

Brief History of Okinawa: Based on the Omoro Soshi. Mitsugu Sakihara. 246p. 1987. pap. text ed. 25.00 (*0-8248-1130-5*) UH Pr.

Brief History of Pacifism from Jesus to Tolstoy. Peter Brock. 80p. (C). 1992. pap. text ed. 9.95 (*0-9690997-1-1*) Syracuse U Pr.

Brief History of Panics & Their Periodical Occurrence in the United States. 3rd ed. Clement Juglar. Tr. & Intro. by DeCourcy W. Thom. LC 87-17069. (Reprints of Economic Classics Ser.). 189p. 1989. reprint ed. 29.50 (*0-678-00168-5*) Kelley.

Brief History of Panics in the United States. Clement Juglar. Tr. by DeCourcy W. Thom. LC 93-73937. 189p. (C). reprint ed. pap. text ed. 14.00 (*0-87034-113-8*) Fraser Pub Co.

Brief History of Political Thought & Statecraft. Henry Paolucci. 9.95 (*0-918680-08-5*) Bagehot Council.

***Brief History of Pollution.** Adam Markham. LC 94-22231. 1994. text ed. 39.95 (*0-312-12368-X*) St Martin.

***Brief History of Pollution.** Adam Markham. LC 94-22231. 1995. pap. write for info. (*0-312-12369-8*) St Martin.

Brief History of Prince William Sound, Alaska. Ed. by Jim Lethcoe & Nancy Lethcoe. (Illus.). 80p. (Orig.). 1992. pap. 8.95 (*0-9613146-5-6*) Prince W Sound.

Brief History of Psychology. 3rd ed. Michael Wetheimer. 176p. (C). 1987. pap. text ed. 20.00 (*0-03-009504-2*) HB Coll Pubs.

Brief History of Sports in America. Elliott Gorn. 1993. pap. 11.95 (*0-8090-1561-7*) Hill & Wang.

Brief History of Tantra Literature. S. C. Banerjee. 576p. (C). 1986. 42.00 (*81-85109-46-X*, Pub. by Naya Prokash IA) S Asia.

Brief History of Technology & the Arts. Linda Bellow. Ed. by Mike Heinz. (Illus.). 110p. 1994. 11.95 (*0-9625476-7-0*) Carnegie.

Brief History of the Caribbean: From the Arawak & the Carib to the Present. Jan Rogozinski. (Illus.). 256p. 1992. lib. bdg. 29.95 (*0-8160-2451-0*) Facts on File.

Brief History of the Caribbean: From the Arawak & the Carib to the Present. Jan Rogozinski. (Illus.). 336p. 1994. pap. 13.95 (*0-452-01134-5*, Mer) NAL-Dutton.

Brief History of the Church of God Reformation Movement. John W. Smith. 1976. pap. 3.95 (*0-87162-188-6*, D2350) Warner Pr.

Brief History of the Coeur d'Alene Indians 1806-1909. Jerome Peltier. 94p. 1987. pap. 6.95 (*0-87770-256-X*) Ye Galleon.

Brief History of the Episcopal Church. David L. Holmes. LC 93-31234. 1993. pap. 17.00 (*1-56338-060-9*) TPI PA.

Brief History of the Future: The United States in a Changing World Order. Allan E. Goodman. 156p. (C). 1993. text ed. 50.00 (*0-8133-1620-0*); pap. text ed. 15.95 (*0-8133-1621-9*) Westview.

Brief History of the Greek-American Community of St. George, Memphis, Tennessee 1962-1982. Speros Vryonis, Jr. LC 82-50980. (Byzantina Kai Metabyzantina Ser.: Vol. 3). 130p. 1982. 26.25 (*0-89003-126-6*); pap. 13.75 (*0-89003-127-4*) Undena Pubns.

Brief History of the Indian Peoples. William W. Hunter. 1977. 19.95 (*0-8369-7142-6*, 7975) Ayer.

Brief History of the Military Career of Carpenter's Battery. C. A. Fonderden. 88p. 1983. reprint ed. 15.00 (*0-942211-80-4*) Olde Soldier Bks.

Brief History of the Pentecostal Holiness Church. A. D. Beacham, Jr. 1983. pap. 5.95 (*0-911866-21-3*) LifeSprings Res.

Brief History of the Pentecostal Holiness Church: Teacher's Guide. David R. Hopkins. 1983. pap. 4.95 (*0-911866-22-1*) LifeSprings Res.

Brief History of the Presbyterians: With a New Chapter by George Laird Hunt. 4th ed. Lefferts A. Loetscher. LC 83-21652. 224p. 1984. pap. 6.99 (*0-664-24622-2*, Westminster) Westminster John Knox.

***Brief History of the Quapaw Tribe of Indians.** Vern E. Thompson. 44p. 1994. pap. 7.95 (*1-882355-06-7*) Mostly Bks Pub.

Brief History of the Thirtieth Georgia Regiment. A. P. Adamson. (Illus.). 161p. 1993. reprint ed. 20.00 (*1-881454-02-9*) Amer Hist Bks.

Brief History of the Western World. 5th ed. Thomas H. Greer. 608p. (C). 1987. pap. text ed. 30.75 (*0-15-505573-9*) HB Coll Pubs.

Brief History of the Western World. 6th ed. Thomas H. Greer & Gavin Lewis. 650p. (C). 1992. pap. text ed. 33.25 (*0-15-505552-6*) HB Coll Pubs.

Brief History of Time. Stephen W. Hawking. 1990. pap. 13.95 (*0-553-34614-8*) Bantam.

Brief History of Time: From the Big Bang to Black Holes. Stephen W. Hawking. 240p. 1988. 24.95 (*0-553-05340-X*) Bantam.

Brief History of University of S. W. Louisiana. Florent J. Hardy. 1974. 10.00 (*0-87511-056-8*) Claitors.

Brief History of Vernon Parish, Louisiana. John T. Cupit. 1963. 12.50 (*0-685-08150-8*) Claitors.

Brief History of Western Magick. Frater Zarathustra, pseud. Bd. with Modern Magickal Lodge. LC 86-50418. LC 86-50418. (Ritual Magick Ser.: Nos. 2 & 3). (Illus.). 100p. (Orig.). 1986. Set pap. 18.00 (*0-939856-56-5*) Tech Group.

***Brief History Pollution.** Adam Markham. 1993. 16.95 (*1-85383-213-8*, Pub. by Erthscan Pubns UK) Island Pr.

Brief History with Tombstone Inscriptions of Old Little River Church, Abbeville County, South Carolina. Pauline Young. 24p. 1981. pap. 5.00 (*0-685-12043-0*) Southern Hist Pr.

Brief Infinity: A Love Story in Haiku. Jayne M. Murdock. Ed. by Dick Murdock. LC 80-83998. (Illus.). 64p. (Orig.). 1981. pap. 4.00 (*0-932916-06-6*) May-Murdock.

Brief Introduction to BASIC: Microsoft - GWBASIC Version. Seth Hochwald et al. 140p. (C). 1991. pap. text ed. 9.96 (*1-880634-01-5*) Access Pubs.

Brief Introduction to DOS 3.3. Seth Hochwald et al. 92p. (C). 1992. pap. text ed. 4.96 (*1-880634-04-X*) Access Pubs.

Brief Introduction to DOS 5.0. Seth Hochwald et al. 108p. (C). 1992. pap. text ed. 11.96 (*1-880634-05-8*) Access Pubs.

Brief Introduction to General, Organic, & Biological Chemistry. M. Lynn James & James O. Schreck. 480p. (C). 1982. teacher ed 2.00 (*0-318-40026-X*); 16.00 (*0-318-40028-6*); text ed. 32.50 (*0-318-40025-1*); student ed 13.00 (*0-318-40027-8*) Heath.

Brief Introduction to Health Occupations. Shirley Badasch & Doreen Chesebro. LC 93-24610. 1993. 18.45 (*0-89303-170-4*) P-H.

Brief Introduction to Hinduism: Religion, Philosophy & Ways of Liberation. A. L. Herman. 181p. (C). 1991. text ed. 47.50 (*0-8133-8109-6*); pap. text ed. 16.95 (*0-8133-8110-X*) Westview.

Brief Introduction to Organic Chemistry. 2nd ed. Robert C. Atkins & Frank A. Carey. 142p. (C). 1990. text ed. write for info. (*0-07-009919-7*) McGraw.

Brief Introduction to QBasic - QuickBasic Version. 208p. 1993. 14.96 (*1-880634-03-1*) Access Pubs.

Brief Introduction to Speech. 2nd ed. Donovan J. Ochs et al. 240p. (C). 1983. pap. text ed. 18.75 (*0-15-505585-2*); pap. text ed. 2.00 (*0-15-505586-0*) HB Coll Pubs.

Brief Introduction to Technology Forecasting: Concepts & Exercises. 2nd ed. James R. Bright. 266p. reprint ed. pap. 75.90 (*0-8357-7403-1*, 2007106) Bks Demand.

An Asterisk (*) at the beginning of an entry indicates that the title is appearing in BIP for the first time.

903

Brief Introduction to the Evidence: Jesus As Christ & God. Wallace L. Bornong. LC 91-90120. 60p. (Orig.). 1991. pap. 5.00 (*0-9629121-3-1*) W Bornong.

Brief Introduction to the Genius of Nietzsche. Richard D. Chessick. LC 83-10305. 160p. (Orig.). (C). 1983. pap. text ed. 24.00 (*0-8191-3337-X*) U Pr of Amer.

Brief Introduction to the Study of Theology: With Reference to the Scientific Standpoint & the Catholic System. Johann S. Drey. Tr. by Michael J. Himes. LC 93-42343. (Studies in Theology: Vol. 1). 1994. 32.95 (*0-268-01171-0*) U of Notre Dame Pr.

Brief Lessons in High Technology. Ed. by James D. Meindl. (Portable Stanford Book Ser.). 249p. 1991. 12.95 (*0-916318-41-9*) Stanford Alumni Assn.

Brief Life. Juan C. Onetti. 1994. pap. 15.99 (*1-85242-301-3*) Serpents Tail.

Brief Life of Christ. L. Rumble. 54p. 1974. reprint ed. pap. 2.00 (*0-89555-096-2*) TAN Bks Pubs.

Brief Lives. Anita Brookner. 1991. 20.00 (*0-394-58548-8*) Random.

Brief Lives. Anita Brookner. 1992. pap. 11.00 (*0-679-73733-2*, Vin) Random.

Brief Making & the Use of Law Books. Ed. by Nathan Abbott. LC 88-81235. (Legal Bibliographic & Research Reprint Ser.: Vol. 10). viii, 472p. 1988. reprint ed. lib. bdg. 47.50 (*0-89941-650-0*, 305630) W S Hein.

Brief Memoir of James Wilson, 1799-1828. James Wilson. LC 83-50321. 165p. 1983. reprint ed. 18.50 (*0-913129-01-1*) La Tienda.

Brief Memories. Elizabeth Wentzel. 0.95 (*0-8488-0893-2*) Amereon Ltd.

Brief Memories of the Life of Joseph Marello, Bishop of Acqui & of the Congregation He Founded. John Baptist Cortona. LC 93-78556. (Illus.). 180p. (Orig.). 1993. pap. 8.95 (*1-883839-02-5*) Guard Redeemer.

Brief Moments for Solo Tuba. Barton Cummings. (Contemporary Instrumental Ser.: No. 3). i, 5p. 1989. 5.00 (*1-56571-020-7*) PRB Prods.

Brief Narrative of the Ravages of the British & Hessians at Princeton in 1776-1777. Ed. by Varnum L. Collins. LC 67-29024. (Eyewitness Accounts of the American Revolution Ser., No. 1). 1975. reprint ed. 16.95 (*0-405-01110-5*) Ayer.

Brief Notices of Hayti. John Candler. 1977. 16.95 (*0-8369-9219-9*, 9074) Ayer.

Brief of the Pequot War. John L. Mason. LC 71-152995. (Select Bibliographies Reprint Ser.). 1977. reprint ed. 11.95 (*0-8369-5747-4*) Ayer.

Brief on Tensor Analysis. J. G. Simmonds. (Undergraduate Texts in Mathematics Ser.). (Illus.). 192p. 1982. 33.00 (*0-387-90639-8*) Spr-Verlag.

Brief on Tensor Analysis. 2nd ed. J. G. Simmonds. (Undergraduate Texts in Mathematics Ser.). (Illus.). 120p. (C). 1993. reprint ed. 29.95 (*0-387-94088-X*) Spr-Verlag.

Brief Outline. Rough Notes Co. Staff. 1992. 25.00 (*0-942326-05-9*, 26199) Rough Notes.

Brief Outline of Theology As a Field of Study. Friedrich Schleiermacher. LC 88-29222. (Schleiermacher Studies & Translations: Vol. 1). 1990. 79.95 (*0-88946-359-X*) E Mellen.

Brief Outlines for Relaxation Training (& Meditative Relaxation) Russell E. Mason. (Brief Outlines SeR.: No. 1). 1973. pap. 15.00 (*0-89533-022-9*) F I Comm.

Brief Outlines for Substitution Training & Positive Goal Achievement. Russell E. Mason. (Brief Outlines SeR.: No. 3). 1973. pap. 15.00 (*0-89533-024-5*) F I Comm.

Brief Pastoral Counseling: Short-Term Approach & Strategies. Howard W. Stone. LC 93-28167. 1994. 12.00 (*0-8006-2720-2*, 1-2720) Augsburg Fortress.

Brief Period of Time & Two Eggs Scrambled Soft. Don Rifkin. 1989. pap. 4.75 (*0-8222-0151-8*) Dramatists Play.

Brief Points: An Almanac for Parents & Friends of U. S. Naval Academy Midshipmen. Ross MacKenzie. LC 93-12792. (Illus.). 217p. 1993. pap. 14.95 (*1-55750-565-9*) Naval Inst Pr.

Brief Psychotherapies: Changing Frames of Mind. Thomas H. Peake et al. 280p. (C). 1988. text ed. 36.00 (*0-8039-2829-7*) Sage.

***Brief Psychotherapy: An Integrative Approach in Clinical Practice.** Francis Macnab. 1993. pap. text ed. 42.95 (*0-471-94078-X*) Wiley.

Brief Reader on the Virtues of the Human Heart. Josef Pieper. Tr. by Lothar Krauth. LC 90-81767. 54p. 1991. pap. 5.95 (*0-89870-303-4*) Ignatius Pr.

Brief Reconnaissance of Itzan see Excavations at Seibal: Department of Peten, Guatemala

Brief Review for Confirmation. Daughters of St. Paul. 1973. pap. 0.95 (*0-8198-0250-6*) Pauline Bks.

Brief Review of Connecticut's Judicial Department Biennial Reports for the Years 1982-84 & 1984-86: A Technical Assistance Report. Shirley Conti & Samuel Conti. 49p. 1987. 3.00 (*0-685-19933-9*, NERO, T/A-544) Natl Ctr St Courts.

Brief Review of Selected Facilities Issues in Hudson County, New Jersey. Samuel Conti. 11p. 1985. 1.00 (*0-685-15349-5*, NERO, T/A-526) Natl Ctr St Courts.

Brief Review of the Settlement of Upper Canada. D. M'Leod. 300p. 1992. reprint ed. pap. 21.50 (*1-55613-727-3*) Heritage Bk.

Brief Separations. Christoph M. Heinicke & Ilse Westheimer. LC 65-25911. 355p. 1966. text ed. 45.00x (*0-8236-0600-7*) Intl Univs Pr.

Brief Sketch of the First Settlement of the County of Schoharie by the Germans. John Brown. 1981. reprint ed. pap. 5.00 (*0-910746-85-0*, BSO01) Hope Farm.

Brief Sketch of the History of Political Parties in Japan. Arthur H. Lay. Bd. with Political Ideas of Modern Japan: An Interpretation Studies in Japanese Law & Government. LC 78-78387. 461p. 1979. reprint ed. Set text ed. 65.00 (*0-313-26997-1*, U6997, Greenwood Pr) Greenwood.

Brief Sketch of the Organization & Services of the Fifty-Ninth Regiment of United States Colored Infantry. Robert Cowden. LC 74-168514. (Black Heritage Library Collection). 1977. reprint ed. 29.95 (*0-8369-8866-3*) Ayer.

Brief Sojourn: Seven Months as Ambassador to the United States. Karan Singh. (C). 1991. 15.00 (*81-7018-647-1*, Pub. by BR Pub II) S Asia.

Brief Songs of the Kisang. Tr. by Wolhee Choe & Constantine Contogenis. LC 93-71569. (International Ser.). 128p. (Orig.). 1995. pap. 12.95 (*0-913089-41-9*) Broken Moon.

Brief Spanish Reference Grammar. Colbert. 1972. 28.95 (*0-442-21616-5*) Heinle & Heinle.

Brief Sparrow. Barry Spacks. 60p. (Orig.). 1988. pap. 7.95 (*0-89807-253-0*) Illuminati.

Brief Statement of the Claims of the Colonies. Thomas Hutchinson. (Notable American Authors Ser.). 1992. reprint ed. lib. bdg. 75.00 (*0-7812-3296-1*) Rprt Serv.

Brief Strategic Intervention for School Behavior Problems. Ellen S. Amatea. LC 89-45572. (Social & Behavioral Science Education Ser.). 224p. 1989. 29.95x (*1-55542-174-1*) Jossey-Bass.

Brief Study Course in Homoeopathy. Elizabeth Wright-Hubbard. Ed. by Alain Naude. 1977. pap. 2.95 (*0-89378-071-5*) Formur Intl.

Brief Survey of Printing. S. Morison & H. A. Jackson. 1972. 59.95 (*0-87968-788-6*) Gordon Pr.

Brief Survey of Recent Caseflow Management Trends in State Courts of Last Resort: A Technical Assistance Report for the Supreme Court of Vermont. David Steelman. 61p. 1989. 3.50 (*0-685-34850-4*, NERO, T/A-556) Natl Ctr St Courts.

***Brief Tests of Collection Strength: A Methodology for all Types of Libraries.** Howard D. White. LC 95-2904. (Contributions in Librarianship & Information Science Ser.: Vol. 88). 1995. text ed. write for info. (*0-313-29753-3*, Greenwood Pr) Greenwood.

Brief Therapy: Myths, Methods, & Metaphors. Jeffrey K. Zeig. Ed. by Stephen G. Gilligan. LC 90-1498. 492p. 1990. 51.95 (*0-87630-577-X*) Brunner-Mazel.

Brief Therapy: Short-Term Psychodynamic Intervention. Gregory P. Bauer & Joseph C. Kobos. LC 87-1487. 320p. 1993. pap. 35.00x (*1-56821-102-3*) Aronson.

***Brief Therapy & Eating Disorders: A Practical Guide to Solution-Focused Work with Clients.** Barbara McFarland. LC 94-38947. (Social & Behavioral Sciences-Health Ser.). 288p. 1995. 29.95 (*0-7879-0053-2*) Jossey-Bass.

***Brief Therapy & Managed Care: Readings for Contemporary Practice.** Michael F. Hoyt. (Social & Behavioral Sciences-Health Ser.). 352p. 1995. 34.95 (*0-7879-0077-X*) Jossey-Bass.

Brief Therapy Approaches to Treating Anxiety & Depression. Ed. by Michael D. Yapko. LC 89-15746. 384p. 1989. 41.95 (*0-87630-508-7*) Brunner-Mazel.

Brief Therapy with Single-Parent Families. Anita Morawetz & Gillian Walker. LC 83-21367. 294p. 1984. 36.95 (*0-87630-350-5*) Brunner-Mazel.

Brief Treatise on Ratios That Pertain to Music & A Little Treatise on the Method of Dividing the Monochord. Prosdocimo de'Beldomandi. Ed. & Tr. by Jan Herlinger. LC 87-10818. (Greek & Latin Music Theory Ser.). x, 182p. 1987. 25.00 (*0-8032-3677-8*) U of Nebr Pr.

Brief Treatise on the Police of the City of New York. Charles Christian. LC 76-112548. (Rise of Urban America Ser.). 1976. reprint ed. 17.95 (*0-405-02442-8*) Ayer.

Brief U. S. Foreign Policy. Gerald Combs. (C). 1986. text ed. write for info. (*0-07-554643-4*) McGraw.

Brief View of Astronomy. Jay M. Pasachoff. 336p. (C). 1986. pap. text ed. 37.25 (*0-03-058422-1*) SCP.

Brief View of the Constitution of the United States. Peter S. Du Ponceau. LC 72-124893. (American Constitutional & Legal History Ser). 1974. reprint ed. lib. bdg. 18.50 (*0-306-71986-X*) Da Capo.

***Brief vs. Long Psychotherapy: When, Why, & How.** James P. Gustafson. LC 94-49234. 1995. 45.00 (*1-56821-470-7*) Aronson.

Brief Welcome Speeches. Amy Bolding. (Pocket Pulpit Library). 1979. pap. 5.99 (*0-8010-0856-5*) Baker Bk.

Brief Writing & Argumentation. 3rd ed. Mario Pittoni. (University Textbook Ser.). 217p. 1991. reprint ed. pap. text ed. 11.95 (*0-88277-415-8*) Foundation Pr.

Brief Writing & Oral Argument. 7th ed. Edward D. Re & Joseph R. Re. LC 87-22068. 384p. 1993. lib. bdg. 37.50 (*0-379-20425-8*) Oceana.

Brief Writing & Oral Argument. 7th ed. Edward D. Re & Joseph R. Re. LC 87-22068. 384p. 1993. pap. text ed. 24.95 (*0-379-21203-X*) Oceana.

BriefBook: Biotechnology & Genetic Diversity. Steven C. Witt. LC 88-606951. (Illus.). 145p. (Orig.). 1985. pap. 14.50 (*0-912005-03-3*) Ctr Sci Info.

BriefBook: Biotechnology, Microbes & the Environment. Steven C. Witt. (Illus.). 159p. (Orig.). 1990. pap. 17.50 (*0-912005-04-1*) Ctr Sci Info.

Briefcase. David G. Fowler. 1979. pap. 5.00 (*0-930324-15-3*) Wings Pr.

BriefCASE: The Collegiate Systems Development Tool. Galen B. Crow. 192p. (C). 1990. Lab manual & IBM 5.25 Diskette. pap. text ed. 33.95 (*0-538-80304-5*, DH83A8H81) S-W Pub.

Briefcase Poetry of Yankee Jones, Vol. 1. Glenn R. Jones. (Illus.). 64p. 1978. pap. write for info. (*0-935910-00-X*) Jones Intl.

Briefcase Poetry of Yankee Jones, Vol. II. Glenn R. Jones. (Illus.). 68p. 1981. 5.00 (*0-935910-01-8*) Jones Intl.

Briefcase Poetry of Yankee Jones III: The Big Arena. Glenn R. Jones. (Illus.). 98p. (Orig.). pap. 7.00 (*0-935910-02-6*) Jones Intl.

Briefcase to Diaper Bag: A Mother's Journey to Find Balance at Home. Katie K. Dorn. (Illus.). 112p. 1994. pap. text ed. 10.99 (*0-9640435-1-3*) Nantucket Pubng.

Briefe, 3 vols., Set. Johann H. Voss. Ed. by G. Hay. xxviii, 1311p. 1971. reprint ed. write for info. (*3-487-04059-X*, Pub. by Georg Olms GW) Lubrecht & Cramer.

Briefe an Gail, Band 1. Paul Twitchell. Tr. by Eckankar Studiengruppe Munchen. (Illus.). 204p. (Orig.). (GER.). 1981. pap. 8.00 (*0-914766-41-4*, 0554) Illum Way Pub.

Briefe an Hildegard Jone und Josef Humplik see Letters to Hildegard Jone & Josef Humplik

Briefe An Ihre Fruhere Hofmeisterin A. K. von Harling, Geb. v. Uffeln, und Deren Gemahl GeheimRath F. von Harling Zu Hannover. Elisabeth C. Von Orleans. xxxii, 234p. reprint ed. write for info. (*0-318-71459-0*, Pub. by Georg Olms GW) Lubrecht & Cramer.

Briefe an Roman Ingarden. Edmund Husserl. (Phaenomenologica Ser.: No. 25). 1968. pap. text ed. 37.50 (*90-247-0256-9*) Kluwer Ac.

Briefe & Familiar Epistle Shewing His Maiesties Title to All His Kingdomes. Robert Fletcher. LC 72-5991. (English Experience Ser.: No. 516). 14p. 1973. reprint ed. 20.00 (*90-221-0516-4*) Walter J Johnson.

Briefe & Moderate Answer to H. Burton. Peter Heylyn. LC 76-57389. (English Experience Ser.: No. 806). 1977. reprint ed. lib. bdg. 22.00 (*90-221-0806-6*) Walter J Johnson.

Briefe & True Report of the New Found Land of Virginia. Thomas Harriot. (Illus.). 91p. 1972. pap. 8.95 (*0-486-21092-8*) Dover.

Briefe & True Report of the New Found Land of Virginia. Thomas Hariot. LC 71-171785. (English Experience Ser.: No. 384). 48p. 1971. reprint ed. 20.00 (*90-221-0384-6*) Walter J Johnson.

Briefe Apologie Against M. Sutcliffe. Thomas Cartwright. LC 78-25890. (English Experience Ser.: No. 237). 28p. 1970. reprint ed. 20.00 (*90-221-0237-8*) Walter J Johnson.

Briefe Aus Den Jahren 1853-1896, 2 vols., Set. Clara Schumann & Johannes Brahms. Ed. by Berthold Litzmann. 1989. reprint ed. write for info. (*3-487-03228-7*, Pub. by Georg Olms GW) Lubrecht & Cramer.

Briefe Declaration for What Manner of Speciall Nusance Man May Have His Remedy by Assise. LC 76-38169. (English Experience Ser.: No. 446). 1972. reprint ed. 7.00 (*90-221-0446-X*) Walter J Johnson.

Briefe der Herzogin Elisabeth Charlotte von Orleans Aus Den Jahren 1676 bis 1722. Elisabeth C. Von Orleans. (Bibliothek Des Literarischen Vereins in Stuttgart Ser.: Nos. 88-107-122-132-144-157). 3345p. 1988. reprint ed. write for info. (*3-487-07909-7*, Pub. by Georg Olms GW) Lubrecht & Cramer.

Briefe Des Libanius. Otto Seeck. 496p. 1966. reprint ed. write for info. (*0-318-71027-7*, Pub. by Georg Olms GW) Lubrecht & Cramer.

Briefe Description of the Notorious Life of J. Lambe. John Lambe. LC 76-57394. (English Experience Ser.: No. 811). 1977. reprint ed. lib. bdg. 15.00 (*90-221-0811-2*) Walter J Johnson.

Briefe Description of the Whole Worlde. George Abbot. LC 78-25701. (English Experience Ser.: No. 213). 68p. 1970. reprint ed. 25.00 (*90-221-0213-0*) Walter J Johnson.

Briefe Description of Universal Mappes & Cardes. Thomas Blundeville. LC 79-38159. (English Experience Ser.: No. 438). 44p. 1972. reprint ed. 20.00 (*90-221-0438-9*) Walter J Johnson.

Briefe Discourse Concerning the Power of the Peeres & Commons of Parliament. John Selden. LC 74-25562. (English Experience Ser.: No. 344). 10p. 1971. reprint ed. 15.00 (*90-221-0344-7*) Walter J Johnson.

Briefe Discourse of a Disease Called the Suffocation of the Mother. Edward Jorden. LC 77-171768. (English Experience Ser.: No. 392). 58p. 1971. reprint ed. 25.00 (*90-221-0392-7*) Walter J Johnson.

Briefe Discourse of Royall Monarchie, Wherunto Is Added a Collection of Italian Proverbes, Etc. Charles Merbury. LC 70-38209. (English Experience Ser.: No. 474). 94p. 1972. reprint ed. 14.00 (*90-221-0474-5*) Walter J Johnson.

Briefe Discourse of the Spanish State, with a Dialogue Intituled Philobasilis. Edward Daunce. LC 72-6281. (English Experience Ser.: No. 73). 52p. 1968. reprint ed. 20.00 (*90-221-0073-1*) Walter J Johnson.

Briefe Discourse of the Troubles Begonne at Franckford. William Whittingham. LC 71-38228. (English Experience Ser.: No. 492). 210p. 1972. reprint ed. 45.00 (*90-221-0492-3*) Walter J Johnson.

Briefe Discourse of the True (but Neglected) Use of Charact'ring the Degrees... Thomas Ravenscroft. (Monuments of Music & Music Literature in Facsimile: Series II, Vol. 22). 1976. reprint ed. lib. bdg. 45.00 (*0-8450-2222-9*) Broude.

Briefe Discovery of the Idle Animadversions of Mark Ridley, Doctor of Phisicke. William Barlow. LC 71-38149. (English Experience Ser.: No. 429). 16p. 1972. reprint ed. 20.00 (*90-221-0429-X*) Walter J Johnson.

Briefe, Easie & Necessary Tables for the Valuation of Leases. Thomas Clay. LC 76-57373. (English Experience Ser.: No. 791). 1977. reprint ed. lib. bdg. 15.00 (*90-221-0791-4*) Walter J Johnson.

Briefe Introduction to Geography. William Pemble. LC 77-7420. (English Experience Ser.: No. 883). 1977. reprint ed. lib. bdg. 20.00 (*90-221-0883-X*) Walter J Johnson.

Briefe Relation of the Discovery & Plantation of New England. LC 74-28876. (English Experience Ser.: No. 754). 1975. reprint ed. 20.00 (*90-221-0754-X*) Walter J Johnson.

Briefe Relation of the Persecution Lately Made Against the Catholike Christians in Japonia, Taken Out of the Annuall Letters of the Societie of Jesus. Tr. by William Wright. LC 75-26238. (English Experience Ser.: No. 159). 1969. reprint ed. 35.00 (*90-221-0159-2*) Walter J Johnson.

Briefe Report of the Militaire Services Done in the Low Countries by the Erle of Leicester. Robert Dudley. LC 72-192. (English Experience Ser.: No. 201). 36p. 1969. reprint ed. 20.00 (*90-221-0201-7*) Walter J Johnson.

Briefe Treatise Concerning the Burnynge of Bucer & Phagius at Cambridge. Martin Bucer. LC 76-57362. (English Experience Ser.: No. 780). 1977. reprint ed. lib. bdg. 30.00 (*90-221-0780-9*) Walter J Johnson.

Briefe Treatise of Testaments & Last Wils, Newly Corrected & Augmented. Henry Swinburne. LC 79-84140. (English Experience Ser.: No. 957). 620p. 1979. reprint ed. lib. bdg. 58.00 (*90-221-0957-7*) Walter J Johnson.

Briefing & Arguing Federal Appeals: With an Appendix of Late Authorities Including References to the Supreme Court's 1967 Rules. Fredrick B. Wiener. LC 61-10553. 543p. reprint ed. pap. 154.80 (*0-8357-7404-X*, 2026789) Bks Demand.

***Briefing Book on Peacekeeping: The U. S. Role in United Nations Peace Operations.** 2nd ed. Victoria K. Holt. (Illus.). 1995. pap. write for info. (*0-9646407-0-8*) CLWEF.

Briefing for a Descent into Hell. Doris Lessing. 1981. pap. 9.00 (*0-394-74662-7*) Knopf.

Briefing for a Descent into Hell. Doris Lessing. LC 80-6142. 308p. 1981. pap. 3.95 (*0-685-04268-5*, V-662, Vin) Random.

Briefing on Computer Viruses. F. Cohen. (Orig.). (C). 1987. pap. 25.00 (*1-878109-04-9*) ASP PA.

***Briefing on International Timeshare Law.** Elizabeth A. Wolfe & Amy Drachman. (Industry Issues Ser.). 187p. 1993. 50.00 (*0-614-04629-7*) ARDA.

Briefing Papers Collection, 9 vols., Vols. 1-9: 1970-1991. Vol. 1-8, 1970-89. 165.00 (*0-318-72407-3*) Fed Pubns Inc.

Briefing-Seminar on Video: The Future of Sunday School & Church Growth. Elmer Towns. 46p. 1988. 99.95 (*0-941005-06-2*); student ed, pap. 1.95 (*0-941005-05-4*) Chrch Grwth VA.

Briefing Sessions on Collective Bargaining Workbook 1985. BNA Editorial Staff. 1985. 95.00 (*0-685-07284-3*) BNA.

Briefing Sessions on Employee Relations Workbook. 125p. 1988. 95.00 (*0-318-35133-1*) BNA.

Briefings. A. R. Ammons. LC 70-119696. 1971. 6.00 (*0-393-04326-6*) Norton.

Briefings' Best Tips: Tactics & Techniques to Help You & Your Employees Work Smarter & Succeed. 1988. 25.00 (*1-878604-12-0*) Comn Pubns & Resources.

Briefly Speaking: A Guide to Public Speaking in College & Career. 4th ed. Calvin M. Logue et al. 350p. (C). 1991. pap. text ed. 16.00 (*0-205-12913-7*) Allyn.

***Briefs.** Diana Stoneberg. 124p. 1993. pap. write for info. (*0-9642796-4-9*) Snapping Turtle.

Briefs of Leading Cases in Corrections. Rolando V. Del Carmen et al. LC 92-75505. 260p. (C). 1993. pap. text ed. write for info. (*0-87084-186-6*) Anderson Pub Co.

Briefs of One Hundred Leading Cases in Law Enforcement. Rolando V. Del Carmen & Jeffery T. Walker. LC 90-82312. 203p. (C). 1990. pap. text ed. 11.95 (*0-87084-090-8*); write for info. (*0-685-47717-7*) Anderson Pub Co.

Briefs of the American Revolution. Ed. by John P. Reid. (School of Law Series in Anglo-American Legal History: Linden Studies in American Constitutional History). 176p. 1981. 55.00x (*0-8147-7384-2*) NYU Pr.

***Briefs of 100 Leading Cases in Law Enforcement.** 2nd ed. Rolando V. del Carmen & Jeffery T. Walker. LC 94-79463. 263p. (C). 1994. pap. text ed. write for info. (*0-87084-096-7*) Anderson Pub Co.

Briefwechsel. Johann Reuchlin. 372p. (GER.). 1973. reprint ed. write for info. (*0-318-70505-2*, Pub. by Georg Olms GW) Lubrecht & Cramer.

Briefwechsel. Beatus Rhenanus. xxiv, 700p. (GER.). 1966. reprint ed. write for info. (*0-318-70506-0*, Pub. by Georg Olms GW) Lubrecht & Cramer.

Briefwechsel. Beatus Rhenanus. Ed. by A. Horawitz & K. Hartfelder. xxiv, 700p. 1966. reprint ed. write for info. (*0-318-71276-8*, Pub. by Georg Olms GW) Lubrecht & Cramer.

Briefwechsel, 10 vols., Set. Edmund Husserl. (C). 1994. lib. bdg. 1,500.00 (*0-7923-1925-7*) Kluwer Ac.

Briefwechsel: Kritische Gesamtausgabe, Section 1, Vol. 1. Friedrich Nietzsche. Ed. by Giorgio Colli & Mazzino Montinari. xiv, 452p. (C). 1975. 156.95x (*3-11-005911-8*) De Gruyter.

Briefwechsel: Kritische Gesamtausgabe, Section 1, Vols. 2 & 3. Friedrich Nietzsche. Incl. Vol. 2. September 1864 - April 1869. 1975. 56.00 (*3-11-006514-2*); Vol. 3. October 1864 - March 1869. 1975. 52.00 (*3-11-006558-4*); (C). 1975. write for info. (*0-318-51616-0*) De Gruyter.

Briefwechsel Des M. T. Cicero Von Seinem Prokonsulat in Cilicien Bis Zu Caesars Ermordung. Otto E. Schmidt. 535p. 1988. reprint ed. write for info. (*3-487-07902-X*, Pub. by Georg Olms GW) Lubrecht & Cramer.

904

An Asterisk (*) at the beginning of an entry indicates that the title is appearing in BIP for the first time.

An Asterisk (*) at the beginning of an entry indicates that the title is appearing in BIP for the first time.

905

Bright Words for Dark Days: Meditations for Women Who Get the Blues. Caroline A. Miller. LC 94-15934. 1994. pap. 8.95 (*0-553-37181-9*) Bantam.

Brighten the Corner. John C. Holm. 1946. pap. 4.75 (*0-8222-0155-0*) Dramatists Play.

Brighten the Corner Where You Are. Fred Chappell. 1989. 15.95 (*0-312-03297-8*) St Martin.

Brighten the Corner Where You Are. Fred Chappell. 1990. pap. 8.95 (*0-312-05057-7*) St Martin.

Brighten up at Breakfast: Helpful Tips for Heavenly Bodies. Marylou Adams. LC 81-51601. (Illus.). 120p. (J). (gr. 2-7). 1981. spiral bd. 7.95 (*0-9606248-0-5*) Starbright.

Brightening Day. Michael McLaverty. 278p. 1987. pap. 10.95 (*0-905169-87-5*, Pub. by Poolbeg Pr IE) Dufour.

***Brighter Child Software: Beginning Sounds.** Garrett Christopher. (Brighter Child Ser.). (Illus.). 32p. (J). (ps-6). 1994. disk 24.99 (*1-56189-295-5*) Amer Educ Pub.

***Brighter Child Software: Letters: Capital & Small.** Voldi Way. (Brighter Child Ser.). (Illus.). 32p. (J). (ps-k). 1994. disk 24.99 (*1-56189-294-7*) Amer Educ Pub.

***Brighter Child Software: Same & Different.** Voldi Way. (Brighter Child Ser.). (Illus.). 32p. (J). (ps-k). 1994. disk 24.99 (*1-56189-296-3*) Amer Educ Pub.

***Brighter Child Software: Sorting & Ordering.** Voldi Way. (Brighter Child Ser.). (Illus.). 32p. (J). (ps-k). 1995. disk 24.99 (*1-56189-299-8*) Amer Educ Pub.

***Brighter Child Software: Sound Patterns.** Garrett Christopher. (Brighter Child Ser.). (Illus.). 32p. (J). (ps-k). 1995. disk 24.99 (*1-56189-297-1*) Amer Educ Pub.

***Brighter Child Software: Thinking Skills.** Bonita R. Ferraro. (Brighter Child Ser.). (Illus.). 32p. (J). (ps-k). 1995. disk 24.99 (*1-56189-298-X*) Amer Educ Pub.

Brighter Coming Day: A Frances Ellen Watkins Harper Reader. Ed. by Frances S. Foster. LC 89-26041. 432p. 1990. pap. 14.95 (*1-55861-020-0*) Feminist Pr.

Brighter Future for Rural America? Strategies for Communities & States. DeWitt John et al. Ed. by Karen Glass et al. (Orig.). (C). 1988. pap. text ed. 12.95 (*1-55877-000-3*) Natl Governor.

Brighter Garden. Emily Dickinson. (Illus.). 63p. (YA). 1990. 17.95 (*0-399-21490-9*, Philomel Bks) Putnam Pub Group.

Brighter Leaves of Grass. Richard E. Petitti. (Self Realization Bks.: Bk. VI). (Illus.). 100p. 1986. pap. 10.00 (*0-938582-11-9*) Sensitive Man.

Brighter Side of Human Nature: Altruism & Empathy in Everyday Life. Alfie Kohn. LC 89-43102. 416p. 1992. pap. 13.00 (*0-465-00758-9*) Basic.

Brighter Than a Thousand Suns: A Personal History of the Atomic Scientists. Robert Jungk. Tr. by James Cleugh. LC 58-8581. Orig. Title: Heller Als Tausend Sonnen. 369p. 1970. reprint ed. pap. 7.95 (*0-15-614150-7*, Harvest Bks) HarBrace.

***Brighter Tomorrow.** Andrew Jergens. Ed. by M. L. Jones. 347p. (Orig.). 1994. pap. 9.95 (*1-882270-19-3*) Old Rugged Cross.

Brighter Tomorrows. LC 89-110892. (Moments in American History Ser.). (Illus.). 48p. (J). (gr. 4-10). 1990. lib. bdg. 19.97 (*0-8114-2674-2*) Raintree Steck-V.

Brightest Light. Colleen O. McKenna. (YA). 1992. 13.95 (*0-590-45347-5*, Scholastic Hardcover) Scholastic Inc.

***Brightest Light.** Colleen O. McKenna. (YA). 1994. pap. 3.50 (*0-590-45348-3*) Scholastic Inc.

Brightest Stars. Ed. by C. De Jager. (Geophysics & Astrophysics Monographs: No. 19). 472p. 1980. lib. bdg. 145.50 (*90-277-1109-7*); pap. 31.50 (*0-685-02823-2*) Kluwer Ac.

***Brightness Falls.** McInerney. 1994. 3.99 (*0-517-13614-7*) Random Hse Value.

Brightness Falls. Jay McInerney. 1992. pap. 22.50 (*0-679-40219-5*) McKay.

Brightness Falls. Jay McInerney. LC 92-50604. 1993. pap. 12.00 (*0-679-74532-7*, Vin) Random.

Brightness Falls from the Air. James Tiptree, Jr. 384p. 1993. pap. 9.95 (*0-312-85407-2*) Orb NYC.

Brightness of His Presence: Theological Dissertation. William F. Myers. LC 82-90351. 64p. 1982. 6.95 (*0-87948-049-1*) Beatty.

***Brighton.** (Pevensey Heritage Guides Ser.). (Illus.). 112p. 1994. pap. 9.95 (*0-907115-60-8*) Sterling.

Brighton. Pevensey Pr. Staff. (C). 1987. pap. text ed. 35.00 (*0-685-44251-9*, Pub. by Pevensey UK) St Mut.

Brighton Beach Memoirs. Neil Simon. (Illus.). 144p. 1986. pap. 4.99 (*0-451-16344-3*, Sig); pap. 3.95 (*0-451-14765-0*, Sig) NAL-Dutton.

***Brighton Beach Memoirs.** Neil Simon. (Illus.). 156p. 1995. pap. 8.95 (*0-452-27528-8*, Plume) NAL-Dutton.

Brighton Beach Memoirs: A Play. Neil Simon. 1984. 14.95 (*0-394-53739-4*) Random.

Brighton Burglar. Dawn A. Poore. 256p. 1993. mass mkt. 3.99 (*0-8217-4104-7*) Zebra.

Brighton on the Rocks Monetarism & the Local State. Queens Spark Rate Book Group Staff. 192p. 1988. 39.00 (*0-317-43589-2*, Bertrand Russell Soc) St Mut.

Brighton Past & Present. John Montgomery. 96p. 1987. 30.00 (*0-905392-70-1*) St Mut.

Brighton Road, The Sugar Road, 2 bks. in 1. Susan Carroll. 1994. mass mkt. 3.99 (*0-449-14924-2*, GM) Fawcett.

Brighton Rock. Graham Greene. LC 92-54296. 1993. 15.00 (*0-679-42034-7*, Everymans Lib) Knopf.

Brighton Rock. Graham Greene. (Twentieth-Century Classics Ser.). 1991. 9.95 (*0-14-018492-9*, Penguin Bks) Viking Penguin.

Brighton Rock. large type ed. Graham Greene. 416p. 1983. 23.95 (*0-7089-8133-X*, Charnwood) Ulverscroft.

***Brighton Run.** Lord Montague of Beaulieu. (C). 1989. pap. 25.00x (*0-7478-0099-5*, Pub. by Shire UK) St Mut.

Brighton Story. Geraldine Collins. LC 86-6829. (Illus.). 224p. 1986. reprint ed. 13.95 (*0-918517-08-7*) Chauncy Pr.

Brights of Suffolk, England. J. B. Bright. (Illus.). 365p. 1988. reprint ed. lib. bdg. 67.50 (*0-8328-0322-7*); reprint ed. pap. 57.50 (*0-8328-0323-5*) Higginson Bk Co.

Bright's Old English Grammar. 3rd ed. F. J. Cassidy & R. Ringler. LC 76-179921. (C). 1972. text ed. 34.00 (*0-03-084713-3*) HB Coll Pubs.

Brightsuit Macbear. L. Neil Smith. 224p. 1988. pap. 2.95 (*0-380-75324-3*) Avon.

Brightwork: The Art of Finishing Wood. Rebecca Wittman. (Illus.). 192p. 1990. text ed. 34.95 (*0-87742-984-7*) Intl Marine.

Brightwork: The Art of Finishing Wood. Rebecca Wittman. 1990. text ed. 34.95 (*0-07-157981-8*) McGraw.

Brighty: Of the Grand Canyon. Marguerite Henry. LC 53-7233. (Illus.). 224p. (J). (gr. 3-7). 1991. text ed. 13.95 (*0-02-743664-0*, Mac Bks Young Read) S&S Childrens.

Brighty: Of the Grand Canyon. 2nd ed. Marguerite Henry. LC 90-28636. (Illus.). 224p. (J). (gr. 3-7). 1991. reprint ed. pap. 3.95 (*0-689-71485-8*, Aladdin Paperbacks) S&S Childrens.

***Brigid Beware.** Kathleen Leverich. LC 94-28614. (Illus.). Date not set. lib. bdg. write for info. (*0-679-95429-5*) Random.

***Brigid Beware.** Kathleen Leverich. LC 94-28614. (Illus.). 1995. pap. 3.99 (*0-679-85429-0*) Random.

Brigid, Bewitched. Kathleen Leverich. LC 93-43221. (First Stepping Stone Bks.). (Illus.). 80p. (Orig.). (J). (gr. 1-4). 1994. pap. 2.99 (*0-679-85433-9*) Random Bks Yng Read.

Brigid, Bewitched. Kathleen Leverich. LC 93-43221. (First Stepping Stone Bks.). (Illus.). 80p. (Orig.). (J). (gr. 1-4). 1994. lib. bdg. 9.99 (*0-679-95433-3*) Random Bks Yng Read.

***Brigid the Bad.** Kathleen Leverich. LC 95-5305. (Illus.). 1995. lib. bdg. write for info. (*0-679-97340-0*) Random.

***Brigid the Bad.** Kathleen Leverich. LC 95-5305. (Illus.). (J). 1995. pap. 3.99 (*0-679-87340-6*) Random.

Brigitta. Adalbert Stifter. Tr. by Helen Watanabe-O'Kelly. 1990. 25.00 (*0-8023-1288-8*, Pub. by Angel Bks UK); pap. 14.95 (*0-8023-1289-6*, Pub. by Angel Bks UK) Dufour.

***Brigitta & Other Tales: Brigitta, Abdias, Limestone, the Forest Path.** Adalbert Stifter. Tr. & Intro. by Helen Watanabe-O'Kelly. 256p. 1995. 10.95 (*0-14-044630-3*, Penguin Classics) Viking Penguin.

Brigitte Bardot & the Lolita Syndrome. Simone De Beauvoir. LC 78-169346. (Arno Press Cinema Program Ser.). (Illus.). 100p. 1980. reprint ed. 11.95 (*0-405-03912-3*) Ayer.

Brihadaranyaka Upanisad. Tr. by Srisa Chandra Vasu. LC 73-3802. (Sacred Books of the Hindus: No. 14). reprint ed. 57.50 (*0-404-57814-4*) AMS Pr.

Brihajjatakam of Varaha Mihira. Tr. by Vijnanananda of Belur Math. LC 73-3800. (Sacred Books of the Hindus: No. 12). reprint ed. 42.50 (*0-404-57812-8*) AMS Pr.

Brihat Parasara Hora Sastra: Guide to Hindu Astrology, 2 vols., Set. S. Maharishi Parasara. Tr. by R. Santhanam. (C). 1989. 58.50 (*0-8364-2545-6*, Pub. by Ranjan Pubs II) S Asia.

Brihat Samhita of Varaha Mihira. 2nd ed. Tr. by N. C. Iyer. (Sri Garib Dass Oriental Ser.: No. 43). 456p. (C). 1987. text ed. 25.00 (*81-7030-094-0*) S Asia.

Briles Report on Women in Healthcare: Changing Conflict to Collaboration in a Toxic Workplace. Judith Briles. LC 94-12540. (Health-Management Ser.). 261p. 1994. ring bd. 25.00 (*1-55542-671-9*) Jossey-Bass.

Brill of Exitorn. Peggy Downing. LC 93-50904. (J). 1994. write for info. (*0-89084-736-3*) Bob Jones Univ Pr.

Brillant Bean: Sophisticated Recipes for the World's Healthiest Food. Sally Stone & Martin Stone. LC 87-47793. 288p. (Orig.). 1988. pap. 14.95 (*0-553-34483-8*) Bantam.

Brillat-Savarin: The Judge & His Stomach. Giles MacDonogh. LC 93-13879. 256p. 1993. 27.50 (*1-56663-028-2*) I R Dee.

Brillhart: A Pictorial History of the Brillharts of America. J. A. Brillhart. (Illus.). 268p. 1991. reprint ed. lib. bdg. 52.00 (*0-8328-1893-3*); reprint ed. pap. 42.00 (*0-8328-1894-1*) Higginson Bk Co.

Brilliance Breakthrough: How to Talk & Write So That People Will Never Forget You. Eugene M. Schwartz. 296p. 1994. 29.98 (*0-9638684-0-3*) Instant Lrning.

Brilliance in Glass: The Lost Wax Glass Sculpture of Frederick Carder. Paul Hollister. Ed. by Robyn G. Peterson. (Illus.). 32p. 1993. pap. 9.95 (*0-9622038-5-8*) Rockwell NY.

***Brilliance Uncommon Voices from Uncommon Women: Thoughts to Inspire & Celebrate Your Achievements.** Daniel Zadra. (Illus.). 120p. Date not set. 12.95 (*0-9640178-0-6*) Compendium Inc.

Brilliancies & Blunders in the European Bridge Championship. Terence Reese. 1992. text ed. 11.95 (*1-85744-500-7*, Maxwell Macmillan) Macmillan.

Brilliant Alliance. Elizabeth Jackson. (Regency Romance Ser.). 224p. (Orig.). 1993. pap. 3.99 (*0-451-17502-6*, Sig) NAL-Dutton.

Brilliant Book of Promotions, Sales Tools, & Special Events: Tested Ideas & Tricks of the Trade for Selling Advertising Space. Naomi K. Shapiro. 209p. (Orig.). 1987. pap. 105.00 (*0-945139-00-4*) Creative Brilliance.

Brilliant Bylines: A Biographical Anthology of Notable Newspaperwomen in America. Barbara Belford. LC 86-6817. (Illus.). 448p. 1986. text ed. 49.50 (*0-231-05496-3*) Col U Pr.

Brilliant Bylines: A Biographical Anthology of Notable Newspaperwomen in America. Barbara Belford. (Illus.). 385p. 1988. pap. text ed. 16.50 (*0-231-05497-1*, King's Crown Paperbacks) Col U Pr.

Brilliant Career of Winnie-the-Pooh. Ann Thwaite. (Illus.). 192p. (J). 1994. 25.00 (*0-525-45248-6*, DCB) Dutton Child Bks.

Brilliant Deception: Powerful Testimony Out of Occult Control. Chris Kline. LC 91-78271. 192p. 1992. pap. 5.95 (*0-88270-652-7*) Bridge Pub.

Brilliant Divorces. June F. Singer. LC 93-6721. 1993. 20.00 (*0-688-12001-6*) Morrow.

Brilliant Function of Pain. Milton Ward. LC 65-92058. (Illus.). 96p. (Orig.). 1977. pap. 9.95 (*0-939835-00-2*) Optimus Bks.

Brilliant Idiot: An Autobiography of a Dyslexic. Abraham Schmitt. LC 92-4593. 179p. 1992. 16.95 (*1-56148-058-4*) Good Bks PA.

Brilliant Idiot: An Autobiography of a Dyslexic. Abraham Schmitt. 183p. 1994. pap. 9.95 (*1-56148-108-4*) Good Bks PA.

Brilliant Madness. Patty Duke. 1993. mass mkt. 5.99 (*0-553-56072-7*) Bantam.

Brilliant Mismatch. Elizabeth Mansfield. 224p. 1991. pap. text ed. 4.50 (*0-515-10545-7*) Jove Pubns.

***Brilliant Origami: A Collection of Original Designs by David Brill.** David Brill. 232p. (Orig.). Date not set. 17.00 (*1-56836-896-8*) FS&G.

***Brilliant Origami: A Collection of Original Designs by David Brill.** David Brill. (Illus.). 232p. (Orig.). 1995. pap. 19.00 (*0-87040-896-8*) Japan Pubns USA.

Brilliant Passage...A Schooning Memoir. Philip Gerard. (Illus.). viii, 81p. 1989. pap. 13.95 (*0-913372-50-1*) Mystic Seaport.

Brilliant Stars. H. T. Rost. 182p. 1979. pap. 9.95 (*0-85398-083-7*) G Ronald Pub.

***Brilliant the Dinosaur.** Richard Stilgoe. (Illus.). 96p. (J). (gr. k-2). 1995. 19.95 (*1-85793-283-8*, Pub. by Pavilion UK) Trafalgar.

Brilliant Traces. Cindy L. Johnson. 1989. pap. 4.75 (*0-8222-0156-9*) Dramatists Play.

Brimhall Keyboard Chart. (Keyboard Theory Ser.). 1990. 1.50 (*0-685-32008-1*, G121) Hansen Ed Mus.

Brimhall Piano Method, Bk. 1. John Brimhall. (Piano Method Ser.). 40p. (Orig.). 1985. pap. text ed. 4.95 (*0-8494-2768-1*, T101) Hansen Ed Mus.

Brimhall Piano Method, Bk. 3. John Brimhall. (Piano Method Ser.). 40p. (Orig.). 1985. pap. text ed. 4.25 (*0-8494-2770-3*, T103) Hansen Ed Mus.

Brimhall Piano Method, Bk. 4. John Brimhall. (Piano Method Ser.). 40p. (Orig.). 1985. pap. text ed. 4.95 (*0-8494-2771-1*, T104) Hansen Ed Mus.

Brimhall Turns Detective. Judy Delton. LC 82-9582. (On My Own Bks.). (Illus.). 48p. (J). (gr. k-3). 1983. 15.95 (*0-87614-203-X*, Carolrhoda) Lerner Group.

Brimhall's "Complete 88" Reversible Keyboard: Beginning Skills Ser. 1990. 2.95 (*0-685-32031-6*, G123) Hansen Ed Mus.

Brimming Cup. Dorothy C. Fisher. 1993. reprint ed. lib. bdg. 89.00 (*0-7812-5363-2*) Rprt Serv.

Brimming over. Grace Sandness. (Illus.). 303p. (Orig.). 1979. pap. 5.95 (*0-931323-01-0*) Mini-World Pubns.

Brimstone. large type ed. Richard Masefield. 544p. 1988. 15.95 (*0-7089-1774-7*) Ulverscroft.

Brimstone, No. 2. Shirvanian. 128p. (Orig.). 1988. pap. 1.95 (*0-8125-6275-5*) Tor Bks.

Brinca de Alegria Hacia la Primavera con las Matematicas y Ciencias. R. Adair et al. 94p. (ENG & SPA.). (J). (gr. k-1). 1988. pap. text ed. 16.95 (*1-881431-21-5*) AIMS Educ Fnd.

Brinch Hansen on Pascal Compilers. Brinch Hansen. (Illus.). 256p. (C). 1985. text ed. 70.00 (*0-13-083098-4*) P-H.

Brindle Mule. Robert Leeper. LC 83-15521. 1983. 11.95 (*0-913239-09-7*); pap. 7.95 (*0-913239-08-9*) Appalach Consortium.

Brine & Evaporities: Depositional Environments of Precipitates in Hypersaline Brines. Peter Sonnenfeld. 1984. text ed. 158.00 (*0-12-654780-7*) Acad Pr.

Briner Family History: A Genealogy of George Michael Breiner & Anna Catharina Loy. Forrest D. Myers & Jerry A. Clouse. LC 82-63190. (Illus.). 704p. (Orig.). 1984. 18.00 (*0-9602156-2-X*) A E Myers.

Brines & Evaporites. Ed. by P. Sonnenfeld & J. P. Perthuisot. (Short Course Ser.: Vol. 3). 126p. 1989. 21.00 (*0-87590-707-5*) Am Geophysical.

Bring an Author to Your Library. Stephen Weiner. 47p. (Orig.). 1993. pap. text ed. 6.95 (*0-913853-29-1*, 32537, Alleyside) Highsmith Pr.

***Bring Back the Birds: What You Can Do to Save Threatened Species.** Russell Greenberg & Jamie Reaser. LC 94-43772. (Illus.). 288p. 1995. pap. 19.95 (*0-8117-2519-7*) Stackpole.

***Bring Back the Bluebirds Even on Your Hand.** Andrew M. Troyer. 36p. 1994. 6.95 (*0-9642548-1-6*) Carlisle Press.

Bring Back the Deer. Jeffrey Prusski. (Illus.). 32p. (J). (ps-3). 1988. 13.95 (*0-15-200418-1*, Gulliver Bks) HarBrace.

Bring Back the Night. James Gray. LC 93-72227. 346p. (Orig.). 1993. pap. 14.95 (*1-56883-013-0*) Colonial Pr AL.

Bring Down the Night, Bk. 1. John R. Sansevere & Carol Q. Sansevere. (Illus.). 64p. 1987. 6.95 (*0-671-91540-1*) S&S Trade.

Bring 'Em Back Alive. Danny Lehman. 176p. (Orig.). 1992. pap. 4.99 (*0-88368-199-4*) Whitaker Hse.

Bring 'em Back Alive. Ed. by Frank Buck & Edward Anthony. (Illus.). 300p. 1990. reprint ed. lib. bdg. 26.95 (*0-89966-731-7*) Buccaneer Bks.

Bring Forth the Mighty Men: On Violence & the Jewish Character. Howard Singer. 280p. (C). Date not set. reprint ed. pap. text ed. 28.25 (*0-8191-7762-8*) U Pr of Amer.

Bring Forth Your Light. Frederick W. Babbel. 8.95 (*0-88494-714-9*) Bookcraft Inc.

Bring Home the World: A Management Guide for Community Leaders of International Exchange Programs. Stephen H. Rhinesmith. 223p. 1986. pap. 9.95 (*0-8027-7289-7*) Walker & Co.

Bring in the Arts: Lessons in Dramatics, Art & Story Writing for Elementary & Middle School Classrooms. Pam Walker. 1993. pap. text ed. 17.50 (*0-685-62971-6*, 0811) Heinemann.

Bring in the Arts: Lessons in Dramatics, Art, & Story Writing for Elementary & Middle School Classrooms. Pam P. Walker. LC 92-44692. (Illus.). 207p. 1993. pap. text ed. 19.00 (*0-435-08611-1*, 0811) Heinemann.

***Bring Me a Memory.** Rose Blue. (Illus.). (Orig.). (J). (gr. 6-9). 1995. pap. 9.95 (*0-931625-28-9*) DIMI Pr.

Bring Me a Story. Sally Benforado. (Mujer Latina Ser.). 66p. 14.95 (*0-915745-11-9*); pap. 9.95 (*0-685-45618-8*) Floricanto Pr.

Bring Me a Story. rev. ed. Sally Benforado. (J). (gr. 6-10). 14.95 (*0-915745-08-9*) Floricanto Pr.

Bring Me a Unicorn: Diaries & Letters of Anne Morrow Lindbergh, 1922-1928. Anne M. Lindbergh. 1993. pap. 8.95 (*0-15-614164-7*) HarBrace.

Bring Me All of Your Dreams. Nancy Larrick. LC 79-26892. 128p. (YA). (gr. 10 up). 1988. pap. 6.95 (*0-87131-550-5*) M Evans.

***Bring Me Children.** D. Martin. 1994. pap. 4.99 (*0-517-13036-X*) Random.

Bring Me Children. David Martin. Ed. by Claire Zion. 352p. 1994. reprint ed. mass mkt. 5.99 (*0-671-88611-8*, Pocket Star Bks) PB.

Bring Me Duck. rev. ed. Suzanne Tate. LC 86-60040. (Illus.). 48p. (Orig.). 1986. pap. 4.95 (*0-9616344-0-5*) Nags Head Art.

Bring Me His Ears. Clarence E. Mulford. (Hopalong Cassidy Ser.). 1976. reprint ed. 24.95 (*0-88411-228-4*, Aeonian Pr) Amereon Ltd.

Bring Me His Scalp. John Benteen. (Sundance Ser.: No. 8). 160p. 1981. pap. 1.75 (*0-8439-1047-X*) Dorchester Pub Co.

Bring Me the Head of Prince Charming. Roger Zelazny. 1992. mass mkt. 5.50 (*0-553-29935-2*, Spectra) Bantam.

***Bring Me the Head of Willy the Mailboy: A Dilbert Collection.** Scott Adams. (Illus.). 128p. 1995. pap. 8.95 (*0-8362-1779-9*) Andrews & McMeel.

***Bring Me the Ocean: Nature As Teacher, Messenger, & Intermediary.** Rebecca A. Reynolds. LC 94-61765. (Illus.). 120p. 1995. 21.95 (*0-9641089-2-5*) VanderWyk & Burnham.

Bring Me What I Ask: A Hawaiian Story about Numbers. Stacey S. Kaopuiki. Ed. by Cindy R. Despins. LC 91-72019. (Peter Panini Keiki Reader Ser.). (Illus.). 32p. (J). (ps-3). 1991. 12.95 (*1-878498-03-7*) Hawaiian Isl Concepts.

Bring Me Your Love. Charles Bukowski. LC 83-5023. (Illus.). 14p. 1995. reprint ed. 14.00 (*0-87685-608-3*); reprint ed. pap. 4.50 (*0-87685-606-7*) Black Sparrow.

***Bring on the Clowns: An Assessment of the Origin of the Shih Tzu.** Clarence E. Mann. 1995. 18.95 (*0-533-11461-6*) Vantage.

Bring on the Night. Don Davis & Jay Davis. 416p. (Orig.). 1993. mass mkt. 4.99 (*0-8125-1189-1*) Tor Bks.

Bring Out the Best in Your Child. Patrick J. Jeske. LC 86-91503. 160p. (Orig.). 1987. pap. 7.95 (*0-88289-499-4*) Pelican.

Bring Out Your Dead: The Great Plague of Yellow Fever in Philadelphia in 1793. J. H. Powell. (Studies in Health, Illness, & Caregiving). 334p. (C). 1993. reprint ed. text ed. 31.95 (*0-8122-3210-0*); reprint ed. pap. text ed. 13.95 (*0-8122-1423-4*) U of Pa Pr.

Bring Out Your Dead: The Great Plague of Yellow Fever in Philadelphia in 1793. John H. Powell. LC 77-112567. (Rise of Urban America Ser.). (Illus.). 1976. reprint ed. 23.95 (*0-405-02471-1*) Ayer.

Bring Phonics to Life: Individual Book. Jean Binnie. Date not set. text ed. write for info. (*0-943343-72-0*) Lrn Wrap-Ups.

Bring the Monkey. Miles Franklin. LC 84-17360. 248p. 1988. pap. 11.95 (*0-7022-1809-X*) Intl Spec Bk.

Bring the Noise: A Guide to Rap Music & Hip-Hop Culture. Havelock Nelson & Michael Gonzales. (Illus.). 224p. 1991. 12.00 (*0-517-58305-4*, Harmony) Crown Pub Group.

Bring to the Boil & Simmer Gently: Secrets of Making Delicious, Simple Homemade Soup. Diane Martin. 1988. pap. 9.95 (*0-931485-10-X*) Scriptorium Pr.

Bring TQM on the QT to Your Organization: How to Implement Quality Management Without Shoving It Down Your Employees's Throats. Hedy Abromovitz & Les Abromovitz. 250p. (Orig.). 1993. pap. 12.00 (*0-945320-34-5*) SPC Pr.

Bring Warm Clothes: Letters & Photos from Minnesota's Past. Peg Meier. LC 81-11236. (Illus.). 340p. (Orig.). 1981. pap. 14.95 (*0-932272-06-1*) Neighbors Pub.

Bring Your Body Along: Supplement Manual Programs & Catalog. Rain O. Crow. 124p. (C). 1991. 15.00 (*0-942815-02-5*) MDRE.

Bring Your Own Restaurant Guide. Henry J. Nunez. (Orig.). 1992. pap. 9.95 (*0-9634741-0-3*) Phoenix Comns.

Bring Your Own Restaurant Guide. 2nd enl. rev. ed. Henry J. Nunez. (Orig.). 1993. pap. 9.95 (*0-9634741-1-1*) Phoenix Comns.

***Bringer of Songs.** Richard Roe. 54p. (Orig.). 1994. pap. 6.00 (*1-878660-13-6*) Fireweed WI.

Bringers of the Dawn: Teachings from the Pleiadians. Barbara Marciniak. Ed. by Tera L. Thomas. LC 92-12393. 260p. (Orig.). 1992. pap. 10.95 (*0-939680-98-X*) Bear & Co.

An Asterisk (*) at the beginning of an entry indicates that the title is appearing in BIP for the first time.

An Asterisk (*) at the beginning of an entry indicates that the title is appearing in BIP for the first time.

Bristol Glass. Cleo Witt. 112p. 1988. 39.00 (*0-685-10640-3*, Pub. by Redcliffe Pr Ltd) St Mut.

Bristol: Maritime City. Frank Shipsides & Robert Wall. 144p. 1985. 50.00 (*0-905459-37-7*, Current Dist) St Mut.

Bristol Murder see Heinemann Guided Readers

Bristol-Myers Squibb: World's Largest Pharmaceutical Sales Force in Action. Market Intelligence Staff. 210p. (Orig.). 1992. 995.00 (*1-56753-047-8*) Frost & Sullivan.

Bristol Registers of Servants Sent to Foreign Plantations, 1654-1686. Peter W. Coldham. 491p. 1988. 30.00 (*0-8063-1223-8*, 1096) Genealog Pub.

Bristol, Rhode Island's Early Settlers. Dorothy C. Saunders. 209p. (Orig.). 1992. pap. 19.00 (*1-55613-649-8*) Heritage Bk.

Bristol Riots of 1831 & Social Reform in Britain. Jeremy N. Caple. LC 90-22628. (Studies in British History: Vol. 21). 312p. 1991. lib. bdg. 99.95 (*0-88946-224-0*) E Mellen.

Bristol, Tennessee - Virginia: A History, 1852-1900. V. N. Phillips. (Illus.). 492p. 1992. 27.95 (*0-932807-63-1*) Overmountain Pr.

Bristol Wagon & Carriage Illustrated Catalog, 1900. Bristol Wagon & Carriage Works Co., Ltd. Staff. LC 94-13893. (Illus.). 160p. 1994. reprint ed. pap. 7.95 (*0-486-28123-X*) Dover.

Brit-Think, Ameri-Think. Jane Walmsley. (Illus.). 144p. 1987. pap. 10.95 (*0-14-009367-2*, Penguin Bks) Viking Penguin.

B

Britain. (Driving Tours Ser.). (Illus.). 120p. (Orig.). 1991. pap. 17.95 (*0-13-917618-7*, P-H Travel) P-H Gen Ref & Trav.

Britain. Barbara Fuller. LC 93-45745. (Cultures of the World Ser.). (J). 1994. write for info. (*1-85435-587-2*) Marshall Cavendish.

Britain. Katherine McCormick. (Language & Travel Guides Ser.). (Illus.). 266p. (Orig.). 1994. pap. 14.95 (*0-7818-0290-3*) Hippocrene Bks.

Britain. Richard Trench. (C). 1989. 30.00 (*1-85368-052-4*, Pub. by New Holland Pubs UK) St Mut.

***Britain: A Travel Survival Kit.** Richard Everist et al. (Illus.). 1052p. 1995. pap. 24.95 (*0-86442-236-9*) Lonely Planet.

Britain: An Official Handbook 1993. Central Office of Information Staff. 538p. 1993. 39.95 (*0-11-701702-7*, HM17027, Pub. by HMSO UK) UNIPUB.

Britain: An Official Handbook 1994. Central Office of Information Staff. 482p. 1994. 39.95 (*0-11-701759-0*, HM17590, Pub. by HMSO UK) UNIPUB.

Britain: Aspects of Political & Social Life. D. Siegmund-Schultze. 154p. (C). 1980. 40.00 (*0-685-31593-2*, Pub. by Collets UK) Pro-Am Music.

Britain: England Scotland & Wales. Henry Weisser. (Companion Guides Ser.). 250p. (Orig.). 1993. pap. 14.95 (*0-7818-0147-8*) Hippocrene Bks.

Britain: Policy & Practice in Continuing Education. Ed. by Peter Jarvis. LC 85-644750. (New Directions for Continuing Education Ser.: No. ACE 40). 1988. 16.95 (*1-55542-881-9*) Jossey-Bass.

Britain: Progress & Decline, Vol. 17. Ed. by William B. Gwyn et al. LC 81-165801. 154p. 1980. lib. bdg. 17.50 (*0-930598-18-0*) Tulane Stud Pol.

Britain: The Best Places. D. Yeadon. Date not set. 12.95 (*0-06-270044-8*) HarpC.

***Britain: The First Colour Photographs - Images of Wartime Britain.** Roger A. Freeman. (Illus.). 160p. 1995. 29.95 (*0-7137-2471-4*, Pub. by Blandford Pr UK) Sterling.

Britain Against Itself: The Political Contradictions of Collectivism. Samuel H. Beer. 256p. (C). 1982. pap. text ed. 6.95 (*0-393-95288-6*) Norton.

Britain & Africa: Aspects of Britain. 92p. 1993. pap. 10.00 (*0-11-701731-0*, HM17310, Pub. by HMSO UK) UNIPUB.

Britain & America: A Study of Economic Change 1850-1939. 2nd ed. Philip S. Bagwell & G. E. Mingay. 328p. 1987. pap. 17.95 (*0-7102-1297-6*, RKP) Routledge.

Britain & Canada. Ed. by Peter Lyon. (Studies in Commonwealth Politics & History: No. 4). 191p. 1976. 35.00 (*0-7146-3052-7*, Pub. by F Cass Pubs UK) Intl Spec Bk.

Britain & Canada in the 1990s: Proceedings of a U. K. - Canada Colloquim. Ed. by David K. Adams. 1992. 59.95 (*1-85521-274-9*, Pub. by Dartmth Pub UK) Ashgate Pub Co.

Britain & China: 1941-1947. Aron Shai. LC 82-23030. 176p. 1984. text ed. 29.95 (*0-312-09976-3*) St Martin.

Britain & Decolonisation: The Retreat from Empire in the Post-War World. John Darwin. Ed. by Geoffrey Warner. (Making of the Twentieth Century Ser.). 380p. 1988. text ed. 49.95 (*0-312-02464-9*) St Martin.

Britain & East Germany since 1918. Ed. by Adolf M. Birke et al. (Prince Albert Studies: Vol. 9). 151p. 1992. lib. bdg. 55.00 (*3-598-21409-X*) K G Saur.

Britain & European Cooperation since 1945. Sean Greenwood. (Historical Association Studies). 128p. (C). 1992. 34.95 (*0-631-18108-3*); pap. 12.95 (*0-631-17654-3*) Blackwell Pubs.

***Britain & European Integration since 1945.** (Making Contemporary Britain Ser.). 144p. 1991. pap. write for info. (*0-631-16895-8*) Blackwell Pubs.

Britain & European Resistance, Nineteen Forty to Nineteen Forty-Five: A Survey of the Special Operations Executive, with Documents. David Stafford. LC 79-19224. 1980. pap. 13.95 (*0-685-05051-3*) U of Toronto Pr.

Britain & European Unity, 1945-92. John W. Young. LC 93-17300. 217p. 1994. text ed. 39.95 (*0-312-09979-7*) St Martin.

Britain & Germany in Africa: Imperial Rivalry & Colonial Rule. Ed. by Prosser Gifford & Roger W. Louis. LC 67-24500. 847p. reprint ed. pap. 180.00 (*0-8357-7405-8*, 2006158) Bks Demand.

Britain & Her People. Anthony Kamm. 1990. 29.99 (*0-517-03380-1*) Random Hse Value.

Britain & Hong Kong. HMSO Staff. (Illus.). 88p. 1992. pap. 12.00 (*0-11-701697-7*, HM16977, Pub. by HMSO UK) UNIPUB.

Britain & India: Requiem for Empire. Maurice Zinkin & Taya Zinkin. LC 64-17884. (Britain in the World Today Ser.). 191p. reprint ed. pap. 54.50 (*0-8357-7406-6*, 2011510) Bks Demand.

Britain & Ireland. Leslie Gardiner. (Family Library of World Travel). (Illus.). 64p. 1985. pap. 4.95 (*0-933521-15-4*) AGT Pub.

***Britain & Ireland: Charming Small Hotels, 1995.** Chris Gill. (Charming Small Hotels Ser.). (Illus.). 224p. (Orig.). 1995. pap. 12.95 (*1-55650-672-4*) Hunter NJ.

***Britain & Ireland, 1995.** (Les Routiers Guides Ser.). (Illus.). 400p. (Orig.). 1995. pap. 18.95 (*1-85733-141-9*, Pub. by Kuperard UK) Seven Hills Bk.

Britain & Irish Separatism: From the Fenians to the Free State 1867-1922. Thomas E. Hachey. LC 84-1832. 343p. (C). 1984. pap. 8.95 (*0-8132-0597-2*) Cath U Pr.

Britain & Japan: Biographical Portraits. Ed. by Ian Nish. 264p. (C). 1994. text ed. 70.00 (*1-873410-27-1*, Pub. by Japan Library) Humanities.

Britain & Japan 1859-1991: Themes & Personalities. Ed. by Gordon Daniels. (Illus.). 320p. 1991. 69.50 (*0-415-05966-6*, A6843) Routledge.

Britain & Latin America: A Changing Relationship. Ed. by Victor Bulmer-Thomas. (Illus.). (C). 1989. 54.95 (*0-521-37205-4*) Cambridge U Pr.

Britain & Latin America in the Nineteenth & Twentieth Centuries. Rory Miller. LC 92-35634. (Studies in Modern History). 228p. (C). 1993. text ed. 52.50 (*0-582-21877-2*, 79639) Longman.

Britain & Latin America in the Nineteenth & Twentieth Centuries. Rory Miller. LC 92-35634. (Studies in Modern History). 228p. (C). 1994. pap. text ed. 27.50 (*0-582-49721-3*, 79638) Longman.

Britain & NATO's Northern Flank. Ed. by Geoffrey Till. 224p. 1988. text ed. 45.00 (*0-312-01543-7*) St Martin.

Britain & Palestine During the Second World War. Ronald W. Zweig. (Royal Historical Society Ser.: No. 43). 198p. 1986. 63.00 (*0-86193-200-5*) Boydell & Brewer.

***Britain & Poland, 1939-1943: The Betrayed Ally.** Anita J. Prazmowska. (Cambridge Russian, Soviet & Post-Soviet Studies: 97). 270p. (C). 1995. 64.95 (*0-521-40309-X*); pap. 29.95 (*0-521-48385-9*) Cambridge U Pr.

Britain & Regional Cooperation in South-East Asia, 1945-49. Tilman Remme. LC 94-9183. 224p. 1994. 69.95x (*0-415-09753-3*, B4002) Routledge.

Britain & Russia: Contacts & Comparisons, 1700-1800. Ed. by A. G. Cross. (Illus.). 1979. 32.00 (*0-89250-109-X*) Orient Res Partners.

Britain & Saudi Arabia 1925-1939: The Imperial Oasis. Clive Leatherdale. 414p. 1983. text ed. 42.00 (*0-7146-3220-1*, Pub. by F Cass Pubs UK) Intl Spec Bk.

Britain & Slavery in East Africa. Moses Nwulia. LC 75-25756. (Illus.). 230p. (Orig.). 1975. 17.00 (*0-914478-11-7*); pap. 9.00 (*0-914478-12-5*) Three Continents.

Britain & South Africa. Dennis Austin. LC 81-4550. (Illus.). viii, 191p. 1981. reprint ed. text ed. 52.50 (*0-313-22994-5*, AUBS, Greenwood Pr) Greenwood.

Britain & South-East Asia. Saul Rose. LC 62-18415. (Britain in the World Today Ser.: No. 2). 208p. reprint ed. pap. 59.30 (*0-8357-7407-4*, 2005249) Bks Demand.

Britain & Sweden: Current Issues in Local Government. Eric Reade. xii, 170p. (Orig.). 1989. pap. 53.25x (*91-540-9318-X*, Pub. by Almqv & Wiksell SW) Coronet Bks.

Britain & the Arab-Israeli Conflict, 1948-51. Ilan Pappe. LC 87-22509. 320p. 1988. text ed. 55.00 (*0-312-01573-9*) St Martin.

Britain & the Arab States: A Survey of Anglo-Arab Relations, 1920-1948. M. V. Seton-Williams. LC 79-2881. (Illus.). 330p. 1981. reprint ed. 29.00 (*0-8305-0049-9*) Hyperion Conn.

Britain & the Balkan Crisis Eighteen Seventy-Five to Eighteen Seventy-Eight. Walter G. Wirthwein. LC 35-8932. (Columbia University. Studies in the Social Sciences: No. 407). reprint ed. 28.00 (*0-404-51407-3*) AMS Pr.

Britain & the British People. Ernest Barker. LC 75-28660. (Illus.). 186p. 1978. reprint ed. text ed. 49.75 (*0-8371-8483-5*, BABB, Greenwood Pr) Greenwood.

Britain & the British Seas. Halford J. Mackinder. LC 68-25248. (British History Ser.: No. 30). 1969. reprint ed. lib. bdg. 49.95 (*0-8383-0212-2*) M S G Haskell Hse.

Britain & the British Seas. Hanford J. MacKinder. LC 69-13982. 377p. 1970. reprint ed. text ed. 65.00 (*0-8371-2754-8*, MABR, Greenwood Pr) Greenwood.

Britain & the Cinema in the Second World War. Phillip M. Taylor. LC 87-27017. 224p. 1988. text ed. 39.95 (*0-312-01605-0*) St Martin.

Britain & the Cold War: Nineteen Forty-Five As Geopolitical Transition. Peter J. Taylor. LC 90-7201. (Political Geography & International Relations Ser.). 156p. (C). 1990. lib. bdg. 30.00 (*0-89862-538-6*) Guilford Pr.

Britain & the Commonwealth Aspects of Britain. HMSO Staff. 100p. 1992. pap. 12.00 (*0-11-701675-6*, HM16756, Pub. by HMSO UK) UNIPUB.

Britain & the Congo in the Nineteenth Century. Roger Anstey. LC 81-20224. (Illus.). viii, 260p. 1982. reprint ed. text ed. 67.50 (*0-313-23366-7*, ANBC, Greenwood Pr) Greenwood.

Britain & the Conquest of Africa: The Age of Salisbury. G. N. Uzoigwe. 403p. 1978. text ed. 21.95 (*0-88357-055-6*); pap. 9.95 (*0-88357-056-4*) NOK Pubs.

Britain & the Crimea, 1855-56: Problems of War and Peace. J. B. Conacher. LC 87-13053. 304p. 1988. text ed. 49.95 (*0-312-01242-X*) St Martin.

Britain & the Dictators. R. W. Seton-Watson. 1968. reprint ed. 49.50 (*0-86527-015-5*) Fertig.

Britain & the Egyptian Nationalist Movement, 1936-1952. Hoda G. Nasser. 1994. 65.00 (*0-86372-177-X*, Pub. by Ithaca UK) Paul & Co Pubs.

Britain & the European Community. Michael Franklin & Wilke. (Chatham House Papers). 144p. 1991. pap. 14.95 (*0-87609-095-1*) Coun Foreign.

Britain & the European Community: The Politics of Semi-Detachment. Ed. by Stephen George. (Illus.). 232p. 1992. 56.00 (*0-19-827315-0*) OUP.

Britain & the Falklands War. Lawrence Freedman. (Making Contemporary Britain Ser.). 128p. 1988. pap. text ed. 18.95 (*0-631-16088-4*) Blackwell Pubs.

Britain & the First Cold War. Ed. by Anne Deighton. LC 89-24065. 256p. 1990. text ed. 55.00 (*0-312-04020-2*) St Martin.

Britain & the French Revolution, 1789-1815. Ed. by H. T. Dickinson. 304p. 1989. text ed. 45.00 (*0-312-02840-7*) St Martin.

Britain & the Great War: 1914-1918. John Bourne. (Illus.). 256p. 1989. 49.95 (*0-7131-6523-5*, Pub. by E Arnold UK); pap. 14.95 (*0-7131-6592-8*, Pub. by E Arnold UK) Routledge Chapman & Hall.

Britain & the Gulf Crisis. HMSO Staff. (Aspects of Britain Ser.). 85p. 1993. pap. 10.00 (*0-11-701734-5*, HM17345, Pub. by HMSO UK) UNIPUB.

Britain & the Information Society. David Butler. (British Computer Society Workshop Ser.: Vol. 3). 38p. reprint ed. pap. 25.00 (*0-8357-7408-2*, 2032676) Bks Demand.

Britain & the Making of Europe. Ian D. Davidson. LC 74-182185. 1972. text ed. 29.95 (*0-312-09800-6*) St Martin.

Britain & the Marshall Plan. Henry Pelling. LC 88-18160. 192p. 1988. text ed. 49.95 (*0-312-02427-4*) St Martin.

Britain & the Middle East: An Economic History 1945-87. Frank Brenchley. 405p. 1991. text ed. 59.50 (*1-870915-07-0*, Pub. by I B Tauris UK) St Martin.

Britain & the Middle East in the 1930s: Security Problems 1935-39. Ed. by Michael J. Cohen & Martin Kolinsky. LC 91-32524. 256p. 1992. text ed. 45.00 (*0-312-07211-2*) St Martin.

Britain & the Modern World. David Tester. (C). 1989. text ed. 35.00 (*0-902662-90-2*, Pub. by R K Pubns UK) St Mut.

Britain & the Multinationals. John M. Stopford & Louis Turner. LC 85-12352. (IRM Series in Multinationals). 1986. text ed. 72.50 (*0-471-90839-8*) Wiley.

Britain & the Onset of Modernization in Brazil, 1850-1914. Richard Graham. LC 68-21393. (Cambridge Latin American Studies: No. 4). 401p. reprint ed. pap. 114.30 (*0-8357-7409-0*, 2025583) Bks Demand.

Britain & the Sino-Japanese War, 1937-1939: A Study in the Dilemmas of British Decline. Bradford A. Lee. LC 77-190526. xiv, 320p. 1973. 42.50 (*0-8047-0799-5*) Stanford U Pr.

Britain & the Soviet Union, 1917-89. Curtis Keeble. LC 89-36456. 358p. 1990. text ed. 49.95 (*0-312-03616-7*) St Martin.

Britain & the Sterling Area: From Devaluation to Convertibility in the 1950s. Catherine R. Schenk. LC 93-41630. 176p. 1994. 65.00x (*0-415-09772-X*, B3914) Routledge.

Britain & the Threat to Stability in Europe, 1918-47. Ed. by Peter Catterall & C. J. Morris. 240p. 1994. 59.00 (*0-7185-1483-1*, Pub. by Leicester Univ Pr) St Martin.

Britain & the U. S. A. Herbert G. Nicholas. LC 63-10195. (Albert Shaw Lectures on Diplomatic History: 1961). 192p. reprint ed. pap. 54.80 (*0-8357-7410-4*, 2020728) Bks Demand.

Britain & the U. S. in the Caribbean. Mary M. Proudfoot. 1976. lib. bdg. 69.95 (*0-8490-1555-3*) Gordon Pr.

Britain & the United States in the Caribbean: A Comparative Study in Methods of Development. Mary M. Proudfoot & Margery F. Perham. LC 74-385. (Illus.). 434p. 1977. reprint ed. text ed. 35.00 (*0-8371-7382-5*, PRBR, Greenwood Pr) Greenwood.

Britain & the Vatican During the Second World War. Owen Chadwick. 350p. 1987. 69.95 (*0-521-32242-1*) Cambridge U Pr.

Britain & the Vatican During the Second World War. Owen Chadwick. 350p. 1988. pap. 19.95 (*0-521-36825-1*) Cambridge U Pr.

Britain & the War for the Union, Vol. 2. Brian Jenkins. 480p. 1980. 39.95 (*0-7735-0354-4*, Pub. by McGill CN) U of Toronto Pr.

Britain & the War for Yugoslavia, Nineteen Forty to Nineteen Forty-Three. Mark C. Wheeler. (East European Monographs: No. 64). 351p. 1980. text ed. 58.00 (*0-914710-57-5*) East Eur Quarterly.

Britain & the War of Words in Neutral Europe, 1939-45: The Art of the Possible. Robert Cole. LC 89-34297. 256p. 1990. text ed. 49.95 (*0-312-03538-1*) St Martin.

Britain & World Trade. A. Loveday. LC 76-37894. (Select Bibliographies Reprint Ser.). 1977. reprint ed. 19.95 (*0-8369-6731-3*) Ayer.

***Britain As a Learning Society.** Ed. by David Bradshaw. 224p. 1995. 75.00x (*0-7507-0394-6*, Falmer Pr); pap. 29.00x (*0-7507-0395-4*, Falmer Pr) Taylor & Francis.

Britain Ascendant: Studies in British & Franco-British Economic History. Francois Crouzet. 350p. (C). 1991. 84.95 (*0-521-34434-4*) Cambridge U Pr.

Britain at Its Best. 2nd ed. Robert S. Kane. 1990. pap. 12.95 (*0-8442-9581-7*, Passport Bks) NTC Pub Grp.

Britain at the Polls, 1979: A Study of the General Election. Ed. by Howard R. Penniman. LC 80-27536. (AEI Studies: No. 296). (Illus.). 368p. reprint ed. pap. 104.90 (*0-8357-4439-6*, 2037273) Bks Demand.

Britain at the Polls, 1983: A Study of the General Election. Ed. by Austin Ranney. LC 84-24646. (At the Polls Ser.). xiv, 227p. 1985. 37.00 (*0-8223-0619-0*); pap. 16.95 (*0-8223-0620-4*) Duke.

Britain at the Polls, 1983: A Study of the General Election. Ed. by Austin Ranney. LC 84-24646. (Illus.). 239p. reprint ed. pap. 68.20 (*0-8357-4438-8*, 2037272) Bks Demand.

Britain At the Polls, 1992. Anthony King et al. LC 92-33413. 264p. (C). 1993. 25.00 (*0-934540-96-9*); pap. 19.95x (*0-934540-95-0*) Chatham Hse Pubs.

Britain at War. T. S. Eliot et al. LC 70-169301. (Museum of Modern Art Publications in Reprint). (Illus.). 98p. 1972. reprint ed. 18.95 (*0-405-01560-7*) Ayer.

Britain Between the Wars, Nineteen Eighteen to Nineteen Forty. Charles Mowat. LC 55-5139. 704p. reprint ed. pap. 180.00 (*0-8357-7411-2*, 2024060) Bks Demand.

***Britain by Britrail, 1995-1996: How to Tour Britain by Train.** 15th ed. George Ferguson & LaVerne Ferguson. LC 87-640215. (Illus.). 320p. 1994. pap. 13.95 (*1-56440-502-8*) Globe Pequot.

***Britain Can Take It: The British Cinema in the Second World War.** Anthony Aldgate. 256p. 1994. pap. 19.50 (*0-7486-0508-8*, Pub. by Edinburgh U Pr UK) Col U Pr.

Britain, China, & the Antimissionary Riots, 1891-1900. Edmund S. Wehrle. LC 66-15064. 235p. reprint ed. pap. 67.00 (*0-8357-7412-0*, 2055925) Bks Demand.

***Britain Confronts the Stalin Revolution: Anglo-Soviet Relations & the Metro-Vickers' Crisis.** Gordon W. Morrell. 232p. (C). 1995. text ed. 35.00 (*0-88920-250-8*, Pub. by Wilfrid Laurier CN) Humanities.

Britain, Detente & Changing East-West Relations. Brian White. LC 91-44854. 192p. 1992. 69.95 (*0-415-07841-5*, A7518) Routledge.

Britain Discover Guide. Berlitz Editors. (Discover Guides Ser.). (Illus.). 352p. 1994. pap. 17.95 (*2-8315-0676-X*) Berlitz.

Britain, Europe & the World, 1850-1986: Illusions of Grandeur. 2nd ed. Bernard Porter. 184p. 1987. pap. text ed. 17.95 (*0-04-909040-2*) Routledge Chapman & Hall.

Britain Fascism & the Popular Front. Merson. (C). 1985. pap. 19.95 (*0-85315-642-5*, Pub. by Lawrence & Wishart UK) Humanities.

Britain First. Oswald Mosley. 1984. lib. bdg. 79.95 (*0-87700-612-1*) Revisionist Pr.

Britain, France, & the New African States: A Study in Post-Independence Relationships. Charles O. Chikeka. LC 89-13073. (Studies in African Economic & Social Development: Vol. 3). 256p. 1989. lib. bdg. 89.95 (*0-88946-516-9*) E Mellen.

Britain, France, Belgium, 1939-1940. rev. ed. Brian Bond. (Illus.). 136p. 1990. 35.00 (*0-08-037700-9*, Pub. by Brasseys UK) Brasseys Inc.

Britain, Franco Spain & the Cold War, 1945-1950. Qasim Ahmad. LC 92-1114. (Modern European History Ser.: No. 2). 336p. 1992. 78.00 (*0-8153-0737-3*) Garland.

Britain from Space: An Atlas of Landsat Images. R. K. Bullard & R. W. Dixon-Gough. (Illus.). 128p. 1984. 45.00 (*0-85066-277-X*) Taylor & Francis.

Britain from the Air. Jane Struthers. (Illus.). 192p. 1994. 34.95 (*0-09-177175-7*, Pub. by Ebury Pr UK) Trafalgar.

***Britain, Germany, & Western Nuclear Strategy.** Christopher Bluth. (Nuclear History Program Ser.). 336p. 1995. 65.00 (*0-19-828004-1*) OUP.

Britain, Germany, & 1992: The Limits of Deregulation. Stephen Woolcock et al. 128p. pap. 14.95 (*0-87609-102-8*) Coun Foreign.

Britain, Greece & the Politics of Sanctions: Ethiopia 1935-1936. James Barros. (Royal Historical Society Ser.: No. 33). 248p. 1982. 63.00 (*0-901050-86-5*) Boydell & Brewer.

Britain in Close-Up. David McDowall. LC 92-18031. 1993. write for info. (*0-582-06461-9*) Longman.

Britain in Crisis. John Hughes. 106p. 1986. 40.00 (*0-85124-317-7*, Bertrand Russell Soc); pap. 15.00 (*0-685-12446-0*, Bertrand Russell Soc) St Mut.

Britain in Decline: Economic Policy, Political Strategy & the British State. 3rd ed. Andrew Gamble. LC 90-8196. 288p. 1990. text ed. 45.00 (*0-312-04726-6*) St Martin.

Britain in Decline: Economic Policy, Political Strategy & the British State. 4th ed. Andrew Gamble. LC 94-16020. 1994. write for info. (*0-312-12239-X*) St Martin.

***Britain in Europe in 2010.** Jim Northcott. 200p. (C). 1995. pap. 19.95 (*0-85374-645-1*, Pub. by Pol Studies Inst UK) Brookings.

Britain in the Age of Walpole. Ed. by Jeremy Black. LC 84-15089. 280p. 1985. text ed. 35.00 (*0-312-09826-X*) St Martin.

Britain in the Depression: Society & Politics, 1929-1939. 2nd ed. John Stevenson & Chris Cook. LC 94-2956. (C). 1994. pap. text ed. 25.95 (*0-582-22941-3*, Pub. by Longman UK) Longman.

Britain in the Early Nineteenth Century. A. D. Harvey. LC 77-15016. 1978. text ed. 27.50 (*0-312-09747-6*) St Martin.

Britain in the Far East: A Survey from 1819 to the Present. Peter Lowe. LC 79-42619. 272p. reprint ed. pap. 77.60 (*0-8357-6044-8*, 2034486) Bks Demand.

Britain in the First Age of Party, 1689-1750: Essays Presented to Geoffrey Holmes. Ed. by Clyve Jones. 304p. 1987. text ed. 58.00 (*0-907628-89-3*) Hambledon Press.

Britain in the International Economy, 1870-1939. Ed. by S. N. Broadberry & N. F. Crafts. 424p. (C). 1992. 64.95 (*0-521-41859-3*) Cambridge U Pr.

An Asterisk (*) at the beginning of an entry indicates that the title is appearing in BIP for the first time.

B

An Asterisk (*) at the beginning of an entry indicates that the title is appearing in BIP for the first time.

909

British & American Manufacturing Productivity: A Comparison & Interpretation, Vol. 54. Marvin E. Frankel. LC 82-2868. (University of Illinois Bulletin: No. 49). 130p. 1982. reprint ed. text ed. 55.00 (*0-313-23487-6*, FRAB, Greenwood Pr) Greenwood.

British & American Plans for International Currency Stabilization. J. H. Riddle. (Occasional Papers: No. 16). 48p. 1943. reprint ed. 20.00 (*0-87014-331-X*); reprint ed. mic. film 20.00 (*0-685-61247-3*) Natl Bur Econ Res.

British & American Poets: Chaucer to the Present. Ed. by W. Jackson Bate & David Perkins. 1048p. (C). 1986. pap. text ed. 26.75 (*0-15-505588-7*) HB Coll Pubs.

British & American Short Stories. (Fiction Ser.). (YA). 1993. pap. text ed. 6.50 (*0-582-09681-2*, 79816) Longman.

British & American Sporting Authors: Their Writings & Biographies. A. Henry Higginson. (Illus.). xvii, 443p. 1990. reprint ed. lib. bdg. 65.00 (*1-55888-887-X*) Omnigraphics Inc.

British & American Systems of Government. Malcolm Walles. 256p. 1988. 53.00 (*0-389-20795-0*, N8353) B&N Imports.

British & American Tanks of World War II. Peter Chamberlain & Christopher Ellis. LC 69-13591. (Illus.). 1981. 15.00 (*0-668-01867-4*, Arco Test) P-H Gen Ref & Trav.

British & American Women's Trade Union Leagues, 1890-1925: A Case Study of Feminism & Class. Robin M. Jacoby. LC 94-19126. (Scholarship in Women's History Ser.: Vol. 7). 200p. 1995. 55.00 (*0-926019-68-6*) Carlson Pub.

British & Americans Philhellenes During the War of Greek Independence, 1821-1833. Douglas Dakin. xii, 247p. 1987. reprint ed. pap. 42.00 (*90-256-0947-3*, Pub. by A M Hakkert NE) Benjamins North Am.

British & Argentina in the Nineteenth Century. Henry S. Ferns. Ed. by Mira Wilkins. LC 76-29757. (European Business Ser.). 1977. reprint ed. lib. bdg. 44.95 (*0-405-09772-7*) Ayer.

British & French Writers of the First World War: Comparative Studies in Cultural History. Frank Field. (Illus.). 300p. (C). 1991. 54.95 (*0-521-39277-2*) Cambridge U Pr.

British & German Deserters, Dischargees, & Prisoners of War Who May Have Remained in Canada & the United States, 1774-1783. Clifford N. Smith. (British-American Genealogical Research Monograph Ser.: No. 9, Pt. 2). 36p. (Orig.). 1989. pap. text ed. 15.00 (*0-915162-35-0*) Westland Pubns.

British & German Deserters, Dischargees, & Prisoners of War Who May Have Remained in Canada & the United States, 1774-1783, Pt. I. Clifford N. Smith. (British-American Genealogical Research Monograph Ser.: No. 9, Pt. 1). 24p. (Orig.). 1988. pap. 15.00 (*0-915162-34-2*) Westland Pubns.

British & German East Africa: Their Economic & Commercial Relations. Heinrich Brode. Ed. by Mira Wilkins. LC 76-29766. (European Business Ser.). (Illus.). 1977. reprint ed. lib. bdg. 18.95 (*0-405-09780-8*) Ayer.

British & German Parliamentarism. Ed. by Adolf M. Birke & Kurt Kluxen. (Prince Albert Studies: Vol. 3). 192p. (ENG & GER.). 1985. lib. bdg. 37.00 (*3-598-21403-0*) K G Saur.

British & Indian Armies in the East Indies: 1685-1935. Alan Hartfield. 411p. (C). 1987. 175.00 (*0-902633-95-3*, Pub. by Picton UK) St Mut.

British & Indian Armies in the East Indies: 1685-1935. deluxe ed. Alan Hartfield. 411p. (C). 1987. 665.00 (*0-317-90382-9*, Pub. by Picton UK) St Mut.

British & Indian Armies in the East Indies (1685-1935) Picton Publishing (Chippenham) Ltd. Staff. (C). 1987. 125.00 (*0-685-39343-7*, Pub. by Picton UK) St Mut.

British & Indian Armies in the East Indies (1685-1935) deluxe ed. Picton Publishing (Chippenham) Ltd. Staff. (C). 1987. 475.00 (*0-685-39344-5*, Pub. by Picton UK) St Mut.

British & Irish Archaeology: A Select Bibliography. Comp. by Anthony C. King. 1994. write for info. (*0-318-72155-4*, Pub. by Manchester Univ Pr UK) St Martin.

British & Irish Library Resources: A Bibliographical Guide. R. B. Downs. 442p. 1982. text ed. 110.00 (*0-7201-1604-X*, Mansell Pub) Cassell.

British & Irish Women Dramatists since 1958: A Critical Handbook. Trevor R. Griffiths & Margaret Llewellyn-Jones. LC 92-29695. (Gender in Writing Ser.). 1993. 90.00 (*0-335-09603-4*, Open Univ Pr); pap. 32.50 (*0-335-09602-6*, Open Univ Pr) Taylor & Francis.

British & Soviet Politics: Legitimacy & Convergence. Jerome M. Gilison. LC 72-4017. 204p. reprint ed. pap. 58.20 (*0-8357-7416-3*, 2020528) Bks Demand.

British & Western Literature. 3rd ed. G. Robert Carlsen & Miriam Gilbert. (Themes & Writers Ser.). (Illus.). 1979. text ed. 33.36 (*0-07-009871-9*) McGraw.

British & Western Literature: A Thematic Approach. 4th ed. G. Robert Carlsen et al. 800p. 1985. text ed. 32.80 (*0-07-009821-2*) McGraw.

British Animated Films, 1895-1985: A Filmography. Denis Gifford. LC 87-42507. 367p. 1987. lib. bdg. 49.95x (*0-89950-241-5*) McFarland & Co.

British Antique Furniture. John Andrews. (Illus.). 392p. 1990. 69.50 (*1-85149-090-6*) Antique Collect.

***British Appeasement & the Origins of World War II.** R. J. Adams. (Problems in European Civilization Ser.). 176p. (C). 1994. pap. text ed. write for info. (*0-669-33502-9*) Heath.

British Architect. 2nd ed. Abraham Swan. LC 67-25995. (Architecture & Decorative Art Ser.). (Illus.). 1967. reprint ed. lib. bdg. 95.00 (*0-306-70961-9*) Da Capo.

British Architect in Industry, 1841-1940. Harold Brockman. LC 74-189063. 186p. reprint ed. pap. 53.10 (*0-8357-7417-1*, 2023261) Bks Demand.

British Architectural Books & Writers, 1556-1785. Eileen Harris. (Illus.). 528p. (C). 1990. 150.00 (*0-521-38551-2*) Cambridge U Pr.

British Architectural Drawings. Ed. by Fumio Shimizu. (Illus.). 228p. 1993. pap. 60.00 (*1-85490-193-1*, Academy Edits) St Martin.

British Armoured Cars. Simon Dunstan. (Orig.). 1990. pap. 22.00 (*1-85368-994-7*, Pub. by New Holland Pubs UK) St Mut.

British Army & Jewish Insurgency in Palestine, 1945-1947. David A. Charters. 280p. 1989. text ed. 49.95 (*0-312-02502-5*) St Martin.

British Army & Signals Intelligence During the First World War, Vol. 8. Ed. by John Ferris. (Publications of the Army Records Society). 240p. (C). 1992. text ed. 60.00 (*0-7509-0247-7*) A Sutton Pub.

British Army & the Theory of Armored Warfare 1918-1940. Robert H. Larson. LC 83-47509. (Illus.). 272p. 1984. 45.00 (*0-87413-219-3*) U Delaware Pr.

British Army at Mackinac, Eighteen Twelve to Eighteen Fifteen. Brian L. Dunnigan. Ed. by David A. Armour. LC 83-109767. (Reports in Mackinac History & Archaeology: No. 7). (Illus.). 56p. (Orig.). 1981. pap. 6.00 (*0-911872-40-X*) Mackinac Island.

British Army in North America. Robin May. (Men-at-Arms Ser.: No. 39). (Illus.). 48p. pap. 11.95 (*0-85045-195-7*, 9161, Pub. by Osprey UK) Stackpole.

British Army in the 1980s. Mike Chappell. (Elite Ser.: No. 14). (Illus.). 64p. pap. 12.95 (*0-85045-796-3*, 9413, Pub. by Osprey UK) Stackpole.

British Army in Ulster, 3 Vols., Set. David Barzilay. (Illus.). 1976. reprint ed. 74.95 (*0-8464-0209-2*) Beekman Pubs.

***British Army of the Rhine.** Carl Schultz. (Europa Militaria Ser.: No. 19). (Illus.). 64p. 1995. pap. 15.95 (*1-85915-031-4*, Pub. by Windrow & Green UK) Motorbooks Intl.

British Army on Campaign 1816-1902 Vol. 1: 1816-53. Michael Barthorp. (Men-at-Arms Ser.: No. 193). (Illus.). 48p. pap. 11.95 (*0-85045-793-9*, 9126, Pub. by Osprey UK) Stackpole.

British Army on Campaign 1816-1902 Vol. 2: The Crimea 1854-56. (Men-at-Arms Ser.: No. 196). (Illus.). 48p. pap. 11.95 (*0-85045-827-7*, 9129, Pub. by Osprey UK) Stackpole.

British Army on Campaign, 1816-1902 Vol. 4. Michael Barthorp. (Men-at-Arms Ser.: No. 201). (Illus.). 48p. pap. 11.95 (*0-85045-849-8*, 9134, Pub. by Osprey UK) Stackpole.

British Army on Campaign, 1816-1907 Vol. 3. Michael Barthorp. (Men-at-Arms Ser.: No. 198). (Illus.). 48p. pap. 11.95 (*0-85045-835-8*, 9131, Pub. by Osprey UK) Stackpole.

***British Army Pensioners Abroad: 1772-1899.** Norman K. Crowder. 351p. 1995. 35.00 (*0-8063-1460-5*) Genealog Pub.

British Army 1660-1704. John Tincey. (Men-at-Arms Ser.). (Illus.). 48p. 1994. pap. 11.95 (*1-85532-381-8*, 9238, Pub. by Osprey UK) Stackpole.

British Army 1914-18. Robert Marrion & Don Fosten. (Men-at-Arms Ser.: No. 81). (Illus.). 48p. pap. 11.95 (*0-85045-287-2*, 9021, Pub. by Osprey UK) Stackpole.

British Art. Frank Trapp et al. (Mead Art Museum Monographs: Vols. 6 & 7). (Illus.). 63p. (Orig.). 1986. pap. text ed. 5.00 (*0-914337-07-6*) Mead Art Mus.

British Art & Antiques Yearbook, 1992. Ed. by Ebury Press Staff. 772p. 1991. 220.00 (*0-686-78855-9*, Pub. by Ebury Pr UK) Trafalgar.

British Art in the Twentieth Century. Ed. by Susan Compton. (Art in the Twentieth Century Ser.: Vol. 2). (Illus.). 457p. 1987. 80.00 (*3-7913-0798-3*, Pub. by Prestel) TeNeues.

British Art Now: An American Perspective-1980 Exxon International Exhibition. Intro. by Diane Waldman & Thomas M. Messer. LC 79-89380. (Illus.). 1980. 8.50 (*0-89207-020-X*) S R Guggenheim.

British Art since Nineteen Hundred. Frances Spalding. LC 85-51119. (World of Art Ser.). (Illus.). 1986. pap. 14.95 (*0-500-20204-4*) Thames Hudson.

British Art, 1740-1820: Essays in Honor of Robert R. Wark. John Hayes et al. Ed. by Sutherland & Guilland. LC 92-28356. (Illus.). 172p. 1992. 60.00 (*0-87328-135-7*) Huntington Lib.

British Artists & War: The Face of Battle in Paintings & Prints 1700-1914. Peter Harrington. (Illus.). 369p. 1993. 80.00 (*1-85367-157-6*, 5405) Stackpole.

British Artists Authority List. Anne-Marie Logan. 1987. 20.00 (*0-685-54075-8*) Visual Resources Assn.

British Ascomycetes. 3rd enl. rev. ed. R. W. Dennis. (Illus.). 1981. 130.00 (*3-7682-0552-5*) Lubrecht & Cramer.

British Ascomycotina: Annotated Checklist. P. F. Cannon et al. 302p. (Orig.). 1985. pap. text ed. 117.00 (*0-85198-546-7*) CAB Intl.

British Atlantic Empire Before the American Revolution. Ed. by Peter Marshall & Glyn Williams. 130p. 1980. 35.00 (*0-7146-3158-2*, Pub. by F Cass Pubs UK) Intl Spec Bk.

British Atlas of Historic Towns Vol. III: The City of London from Prehistoric Times to c. 1520. Ed. by Mary D. Lobel. (Illus.). 144p. 1990. 160.00 (*0-19-822979-8*) OUP.

British Attitudes Towards India 1748-1858. George D. Bearce. LC 81-20244. viii, 315p. 1982. reprint ed. text ed. 65.00 (*0-313-23367-5*, BEBA, Greenwood Pr) Greenwood.

British Auden: A Study in His Poetic Theory & Practice. Raghavendra N. Singh. 1993. text ed. 35.00 (*81-7045-067-5*, Pub. by Associated Pub Hse II) Advent Bks Div.

British Audit Practice 1884-1900: A Case Law Perspective. Ed. by Roy A. Chandler & John Edwards. LC 93-39273. (New Works in Accounting History.). 232p. 1994. 57.00 (*0-8153-1720-4*) Garland.

British Authors Before Eighteen Hundred: A Biographical Dictionary. Ed. by Stanley J. Kunitz & Howard Haycraft. LC 52-6758. (Illus.). 584p. 1952. 64.00 (*0-8242-0006-3*) Wilson.

British Authors of the Nineteenth Century. Ed. by Stanley J. Kunitz & Howard Haycraft. (Illus.). 677p. 1936. 68.00 (*0-8242-0007-1*) Wilson.

British Autobiographies: An Annotated Bibliography of British Autobiographies Published or Written Before 1951. William Matthews. (California Library Reprint Edition). 390p. reprint ed. pap. 111.20 (*0-7837-4836-1*, 2044483) Bks Demand.

British Ballads from Maine. Phillips Barry et al. LC 81-5548. (Music Ser.). (Illus.). 535p. 1982. reprint ed. lib. bdg. 49.50 (*0-306-76135-1*) Da Capo.

British Baptists: An Original Anthology. H. Wheeler Robinson & Ernest A. Payne. Ed. by Edwin S. Gaustad. LC 79-52583. (Baptist Tradition Ser.). 1980. lib. bdg. 33.95 (*0-405-12450-3*) Ayer.

British Barbarians. Grant Allen. LC 74-15943. (Science Fiction Ser.). (Illus.). 226p. 1975. reprint ed. 19.95 (*0-405-06272-9*) Ayer.

British Basidomycetaceae: A Handbook to the Larger British Fungi. C. Rea. 1968. pap. 60.00 (*3-7682-0561-4*) Lubrecht & Cramer.

British Battalions on the Somme. Ray Westlake. (Illus.). 320p. 1994. 42.50 (*0-85052-374-5*, Pub. by L Cooper Bks UK) Trans-Atl Phila.

British Battle Insignia Vol. 1: 1914-18. Mike Chappell. (Men-at-Arms Ser.: No. 182). (Illus.). 48p. pap. 11.95 (*0-85045-727-0*, 9114, Pub. by Osprey UK) Stackpole.

British Battle Insignia Vol. 2: 1939-45. Mike Chappell. (Men-at-Arms Ser.: No. 187). (Illus.). 48p. pap. 11.95 (*0-85045-739-4*, 9119, Pub. by Osprey UK) Stackpole.

British Battledress 1937-61. Brian Jewell. (Men-at-Arms Ser.: No. 112). (Illus.). 48p. pap. 11.95 (*0-85045-387-9*, 9045, Pub. by Osprey UK) Stackpole.

British Battles & Medals. L. L. Gordon. 1989. 60.00 (*0-685-51512-5*) S J Durst.

British Battleships, Eighteen Eighty-Nine to Nineteen Hundred Four. Ray Burt. LC 88-71711. (Illus.). 320p. 1989. 47.95 (*0-87021-061-0*) Naval Inst Pr.

British Battleships Eighteen Ninety-Two to Nineteen Fifty-Seven. Randolph Pears. 1981. 40.00 (*0-906223-14-8*) St Mut.

British Battleships, Eighteen Sixty to Nineteen Fifty. Oscar Parkes. LC 90-61164. (Illus.). 701p. 1990. 59.95 (*1-55750-075-4*) Naval Inst Pr.

British Battleships of World War I. R. A. Burt. LC 86-60257. (Illus.). 320p. 1986. 49.50 (*0-87021-863-8*) Naval Inst Pr.

British Beers, Wines & Spirits Industry. 195p. 1992. 500.00 (*0-85938-166-8*) St Mut.

British Beginnings in Bengal. P. Thankappan Nair. (C). 1991. text ed. 54.00 (*81-85094-36-5*, Pub. by Punthi Pus II) S Asia.

British Bibliographer, 4 Vols, Set. Samuel E. Brydges. LC 03-25390. reprint ed. 306.00 (*0-404-01200-0*) AMS Pr.

British Biographical Index, 4 vols. Comp. by Laureen Baillie. 2045p. 1991. lib. bdg. 1,060.00 (*0-86291-390-X*) U Pubns Amer.

British Birds. William H. Hudson. reprint ed. 64.50 (*0-404-03396-2*) AMS Pr.

British Biscuit Tins, 1864-1939. M. J. Franklin. 1994. 150.00 (*0-904568-11-3*, Pub. by New Cavendish UK) Pincushion Pr.

British Block Grants & Central-Local Finance. Reynold E. Carlson. LC 78-64203. (Johns Hopkins University. Studies in the Social Sciences. Thirtieth Ser. 1912: 1). 224p. 1980. reprint ed. 37.50 (*0-404-61309-8*) AMS Pr.

British Bomber since 1914. Francis K. Mason. (Illus.). 416p. 1994. 42.95 (*1-55750-085-1*) Naval Inst Pr.

British Borough Charters, 1042-1216. Ed. by Adolphus Ballard. LC 80-2236. reprint ed. 49.50 (*0-404-18750-1*) AMS Pr.

British Brewing Industry, 1830-1980. T. R. Gourvish & R. G. Wilson. (Illus.). 634p. (C). 1994. 84.95 (*0-521-45232-5*) Cambridge U Pr.

British Broadcasting in Transition. Burton Paulu. LC 61-8399. 260p. reprint ed. pap. 74.10 (*0-8357-7418-X*, 2055896) Bks Demand.

British Broadside Ballads of the Sixteenth Century Vol. I: A Catalogue of the Extant Sheets & an Essay. Carole R. Livingston. LC 90-48731. 928p. 1991. 96.00 (*0-8240-7226-X*, 1390) Garland.

British Brutality in Ireland. Jack O'Brien. LC 89-50971. 178p. 1989. pap. 15.95 (*0-85342-879-4*, Pub. by Mercier Pr IE) Dufour.

British Building Industry: Four Studies in Response & Resistance to Change. Marian Bowley. LC 65-14856. 502p. reprint ed. pap. 143.10 (*0-8357-3608-3*, 2027276) Bks Demand.

British Bureaucracy in India: Status, Policy & the I. C. S. in Late Nineteenth Century. Bradford Spangenburg. LC 76-52213. 1977. 17.50 (*0-88386-768-0*) S Asia.

British Business & Ghanaian Independence. Josephine F. Milburn. LC 76-50681. 166p. reprint ed. pap. 47.40 (*0-8357-6741-8*, 2035396) Bks Demand.

***British Business History.** LC 94-41739. 1995. text ed. (*0-7190-4133-3*, Pub. by Manchester Univ Pr UK) St Martin.

***British Business History.** John F. Wilson. LC 94-41739. 1995. text ed. write for info. (*0-7190-4132-5*) St Martin.

British Business in Asia since 1860. Ed. by R. P. Davenport-Hines & Geoffrey Jones. (Illus.). 320p. (C). 1989. 69.95 (*0-521-33527-2*) Cambridge U Pr.

British Butchers & Bunglers of World War I. John Laffin. LC 92-18632. (Illus.). 224p. (YA). (gr. 9-12). 1992. pap. text ed. 16.00 (*0-7509-0179-9*) A Sutton Pub.

British By-Elections: The Volatile Electorate. Pippa Norris. (Illus.). 280p. 1990. 69.00 (*0-19-827330-4*) OUP.

British Cabinet Government. Simon James. 272p. 1992. 72.50 (*0-415-07605-6*, A6943) Routledge.

***British Cabinet Government.** Simon James. 272p. 1993. pap. 24.95x (*0-415-07606-4*, A6947) Routledge.

British Calendar Customs, England Vol. III: Fixed Festivals, June to December, Inclusive, Index to Vols. I & III. A. R. Wright. Ed. by T. East Lones. (Folk-Lore Society, London, Monographs: Vol. 106). 1972. reprint ed. pap. 25.00 (*0-8115-0540-5*) Periodicals Srv.

British Calendar Customs, Orkney & Shetland. Ed. by M. M. Banks. (Folk-Lore Society, London Monographs: Vol. 112). 1972. reprint ed. 35.00 (*0-8115-0543-X*) Periodicals Srv.

British Calendar Customs, Scotland Vol. I: Movable Festivals, Harvest, March Ridings & Wappynshaws, Wells, Fairs. Ed. by M. M. Banks. (Folk-Lore Society, London, Monographs: Vol. 100). 1972. reprint ed. pap. 25.00 (*0-8115-0537-5*) Periodicals Srv.

British Calendar Customs, Scotland Vol. II: Fixed Festivals, The Quarters, Hogmanay, January to March, Inclusive. Ed. by M. M. Banks. (Folk-Lore Society, London, Monographs: Vol. 104). 1972. reprint ed. pap. 25.00 (*0-8115-0539-1*) Periodicals Srv.

British Calendar Customs, Scotland Vol. III: Fixed Festivals, June to December, Inclusive, Christmas, the Yules (Index to Vols. II & III) M. M. Banks. (Folk-Lore Society, London Monographs: Vol. 108). 1972. reprint ed. 25.00 (*0-8115-0541-3*) Periodicals Srv.

British Capitalism at the Crossroads, 1919-1932: A Study in Politics, Economics & International Relations. Robert Boyce. 496p. 1988. 79.95 (*0-521-32535-8*) Cambridge U Pr.

British Car Factories from Eighteen Ninety-Six. Paul Collins & Michael Straton. (Illus.). 224p. 1993. 59.95 (*1-874105-04-9*, Pub. by Veloce Pub UK) Motorbooks Intl.

British Caribbean from the Decline of Colonialism to the End of Federation. Elisabeth Wallace. LC 76-48191. 282p. reprint ed. pap. 80.40 (*0-8357-8049-X*, 2033996) Bks Demand.

British Carrier Aviation: The Evolution of the Ships & Their Aircraft. Norman Friedman. LC 88-62038. (Illus.). 352p. 1989. 49.95 (*0-87021-054-8*) Naval Inst Pr.

British Cars at Le Mans. Dominique Pascal. (Illus.). 148p. 1991. 34.95 (*0-85429-872-X*, Pub. by G T Foulis Ltd) Haynes Pubns.

British Castles. Charles W. Oman. 1989. pap. 11.95 (*0-486-26086-0*) Dover.

British Catalogue of Music 1957-1985, 10 vols. 1988. Set; ea. vol. 400p. lib. bdg. 2,705.00 (*0-86291-395-0*) U Pubns Amer.

British Catholic Press & the Educational Controversy, 1847-1865. Mary G. Holland. Ed. by William H. McNeill & Peter Stansky. (Modern European History Ser.). 400p. 1987. lib. bdg. 15.00 (*0-8240-7817-9*) Garland.

British Cavalry Equipments 1800-1941. Mike Chappell. (Men-at-Arms Ser.: No. 138). (Illus.). 48p. pap. 11.95 (*0-85045-479-4*, 9070, Pub. by Osprey UK) Stackpole.

British Cavalryman 1792-1815. Philip Haythornthwaite. (Warrior Ser.). (Illus.). 64p. 1994. pap. 12.95 (*1-85532-364-8*, 9607, Pub. by Osprey UK) Stackpole.

British Ceramic Art, 1870-1940. John A. Bartlett. LC 92-82036. (Illus.). 240p. 1993. 69.95 (*0-88740-456-1*) Schiffer.

***British Charitable Gambling 1956-1994: Towards a National Lottery.** Andrew Douglas. 320p. (C). 1995. text ed. 80.00 (*0-485-11472-0*, Pub. by Athlone Pr UK) Humanities.

British Chess. Ed. by G. S. Botterill. (Chess Ser.). (Illus.). 300p. 1983. 105.00 (*0-08-024134-4*, Pergamon Pr) Elsevier.

British Children's Authors: Interviews at Home. Cornelia Jones & Olivia R. Way. LC 76-44494. 184p. reprint ed. pap. 52.50 (*0-8357-7419-8*, 2023943) Bks Demand.

British Cinema in Pictures: The British Film Collection. Patricia Warren. (Illus.). 264p. 1994. pap. 34.95 (*0-7134-7284-7*, Pub. by Batsford UK) Trafalgar.

British Cinema Now. Ed. by Martyn Auty & Nick Roddick. (Illus.). 168p. 1985. 35.00 (*0-85170-130-2*, Pub. by British Film Inst UK); pap. 14.95 (*0-85170-131-0*, Pub. by British Film Inst UK) Ind U Pr.

British Cinemas & Their Audiences. J. P. Mayer. Ed. by Garth S. Jowett. LC 77-11387. (Aspects of Film Ser.). (Illus.). 1978. lib. bdg. 20.95 (*0-405-11141-X*) Ayer.

British Civil Engineering Literature, 1640-1840: A Bibliography of Contemporary Printed Reports, Plans & Books. A. W. Skempton. 320p. 1987. text ed. 130.00 (*0-7201-1746-1*, Mansell Pub) Cassell.

British Civilization: An Introduction. John Oakland. 272p. 1989. pap. 12.95 (*0-415-00670-8*, A2673) Routledge.

British Civilization: An Introduction. 2nd ed. John Oakland. (Illus.). 240p. 1992. pap. 13.95 (*0-415-06475-9*, A6944) Routledge.

***British Civilization: An Introduction.** 3rd ed. John Oakland. (Illus.). 368p. 1995. pap. 16.95 (*0-415-12258-9*, C0608) Routledge.

***British Clocks Illustrated.** Brian Loomes. (Illus.). 272p. Date not set. 45.00 (*0-7090-4547-6*, Hale-Parkwest) Parkwest Pubns.

An Asterisk (*) at the beginning of an entry indicates that the title is appearing in BIP for the first time.

British Co-Operative Movement. Jack Bailey. LC 73-19302. (Illus.). 178p. 1974. reprint ed. text ed. 49.75 (*0-8371-7116-4*, BABC, Greenwood Pr) Greenwood.

British Co-operative Movement in a Socialist Society. George D. Cole. LC 76-22523. 168p. 1976. reprint ed. text ed. 59.75 (*0-8371-9002-9*, COBCM, Greenwood Pr) Greenwood.

British Coal-Mining Industry During the War: R. A. S. Redmayne. Robert A. Redmayne. (Economic & Social History of the World War Ser.). 1923. 125.00 (*0-686-37864-4*) Elliots Bks.

British Coal-Tar Industry. Walter M. Gardner. Ed. by I. Bernard Cohen. LC 80-2122. (Development of Science Ser.). (Illus.). 1981. lib. bdg. 44.95 (*0-405-13845-8*) Ayer.

British Coal Trade. H. Stanley Jevons. LC 68-58858. (Illus.). xiv, 876p. 1969. reprint ed. 65.00 (*0-678-05559-9*) Kelley.

British Colonial Policy. George L. Beer. 327p. 1993. reprint ed. lib. bdg. 89.00 (*0-7812-5167-2*) Rprt Serv.

British Colonial Policy in Burma: An Aspect of Colonialism in South East Asia, 1840-1885. Aparna Mukherjee. 1988. 50.00 (*0-8364-2290-2*, Pub. by Abhinav II) S Asia.

British Colonial Policy in Burma: An Aspect of Colonialism in South-East Asia, 1840-1885. Aparna Mukherjee. LC 88-61303. 557p. 1988. 34.00 (*0-913215-37-6*) Riverdale Co.

British Colonial Policy, 1754-1765. George L. Beer. 13.25 (*0-8446-1065-8*) Peter Smith.

British Colonial Rule & the Resistance of the Malay Peasantry, 1900-1957. Donald M. Nonini. (Monograph Ser. - Yale University Southeast Asia Studies: No. 38). 350p. 1992. 30.00 (*0-938692-48-8*); pap. 17.00 (*0-938692-47-X*) Yale U SE Asia.

***British Columbia.** Vivien Bowers. LC 94-25539. (J). 2995. write for info. (*0-8225-2755-3*, Lerner Publctns) Lerner Group.

British Columbia. Suzanne LeVert. (Let's Discover Canada Ser.). (Illus.). 64p. (YA). (gr. 3 up). 1991. lib. bdg. 16.95 (*0-7910-1033-3*) Chelsea Hse.

British Columbia. Isabel Nanton. (Discover Canada Ser.). (Illus.). 144p. (J). (gr. 4 up). 1993. lib. bdg. 20.55 (*0-516-06619-6*) Childrens.

British Columbia. Ed. by J. Lewis Robinson. LC 72-197301. (Studies in Canadian Geography Ser.). 149p. reprint ed. pap. 42.50 (*0-8357-7420-1*, 2026536) Bks Demand.

British Columbia: Land of Rich Diversity. Judith A. McDowell & Jim Lyon. (Canadian Enterprise Ser.). 144p. 1991. 32.95 (*0-89781-371-5*) Preferred Mktg.

British Columbia Bicycling Guide. Teri Lydiard. (Illus.). 76p. (Orig.). 1984. pap. 9.95 (*0-9691693-0-2*) Gordon Soules Bk.

***British Columbia Business Directory, 1995-96.** 1408p. 1995. 235.00 (*1-56105-804-1*) Am Busn Direct.

British Columbia Coast Names, 1592-1906: Their Origin & History. John T. Walbran. LC 91-16304. (Illus.). 604p. 1991. reprint ed. pap. 19.95 (*0-295-97142-8*) U of Wash Pr.

British Columbia Handbook. 3rd ed. Jane King. (Illus.). 400p. 1994. pap. 15.95 (*1-56691-014-5*) Moon Pubns CA.

British Columbia Reconsidered: Essays on Women. Ed. by Creese & Strong-Boag. (NFS Canada Ser.). Date not set. pap. 21.95 (*0-88974-038-0*, Pub. by Press Gang CN) InBook.

***British Columbia Wildlife Viewing Guide.** Bill Wareham. 99p. Date not set. pap. 8.95 (*1-55105-000-5*) Falcon Pr MT.

British Columbia's Coast: The Canadian Inside Passage. Ed. by Alaska Geographic Staff. LC 72-92087. (Alaska Geographic Ser.: Vol. 13, No. 3). (Illus.). 1972. pap. 17.95 (*0-88240-178-5*) Alaska Geog Soc.

British Commandos in Action. (Illus.). 1987. pap. 8.95 (*0-89747-192-X*, 3008) Squad Sig Pubns.

British Commemorative Medals & Values. Christopher Eimer. (Illus.). 256p. 1987. 75.00 (*0-900652-94-2*, Pub. by Seaby UK) Trafalgar.

British Commemoratives: Royalty, Politics, War & Sport. Lincoln Hallinan. (Illus.). 350p. 1994. 59.50 (*1-85149-129-5*) Antique Collect.

British Commercial Banking & Commonwealth Development: An International Survey. Alaine M. Low. 320p. 1988. lib. bdg. 42.00 (*0-415-01945-1*) Routledge.

British Commercial Computer Digest. 11th ed. Computer Consultants Ltd. Staff. 1970. 132.00 (*0-08-016279-7*, Pub. by Pergamon Repr UK) Franklin.

British Commonwealth at War. Ed. by William Y. Elliot & Hessel D. Hall. LC 70-134072. (Essay Index Reprint Ser.). 1977. reprint ed. 30.95 (*0-8369-2106-2*) Ayer.

British Commonwealth of Nations in a Changing World: Law, Politics & Prospects. Zelman Cowen. LC 65-12096. (Julius Rosenthal Memorial Lecture Ser: 1964). 127p. reprint ed. 36.20 (*0-8357-9448-2*, 2015292) Bks Demand.

British Commonwealth, United States, United Nations, 1994, Vol. 1. 1993. 32.00 (*0-89487-190-0*) Scott Pub Co.

British Communist Party & the Trade Unions, 1933-45. Nina Fishman. LC 94-5837. 1994. 74.95 (*1-85928-116-8*, Pub. by Scolar Pr UK) Ashgate Pub Co.

British Companies Acts & the Practice of Accountancy: 1844-1962. Leonard W. Hein. Ed. by Richard P. Brief. LC 77-87299. (Development of Contemporary Accounting Thought Ser.). 1978. lib. bdg. 37.95 (*0-405-10938-5*) Ayer.

British Company Legislation & Company Accounts, 1844-1976, 2 vols. J. R. Edwards. Ed. by Richard P. Brief. LC 80-1456. (Dimensions of Accounting Theory & Practice Ser.). 1980. lib. bdg. 75.95 (*0-405-13478-9*) Ayer.

British Computers & Industrial Innovation: Implications of the Parliamentary Select Committee. Eric Moonman. 1971. 22.00 (*0-8464-0210-6*) Beekman Pubs.

British Conquest & Dominion of India. Penderel Moon. LC 89-2003. 1248p. 1989. 89.95 (*0-253-33836-0*) Ind U Pr.

British Constitution. N. Middleton. (C). 1978. Incl. 3 filmstrips & cassette. audio, flmstrp 430.00 (*0-86158-641-7*, Pub. by S Thornes Pubs UK) St Mut.

British Constitution, Time for Reform? The Rise & Decline of the Doctrine of Fundamental Breach in the English Law of Contact. P. Elias & L. S. Sealy. (Cambridge-Tilburg Law Lectures: No. 4). 76p. pap. 12.00 (*90-6544-108-5*) Kluwer Ac.

British Constitutional Crisis, 1909-1911. Klaus W. Epstein. Ed. by William H. McNeill & Peter Stansky. (Modern European History Ser.). 575p. 1987. lib. bdg. 15.00 (*0-8240-7805-5*) Garland.

British Consulate in Jerusalem in Relation to the Jews of Palestine, 1838-1914, 2 vols, Set. Ed. & Intro. by Albert M. Hyamson. LC 70-180348. reprint ed. 60.00 (*0-404-56278-7*) AMS Pr.

British Consuls in the Confederacy. Hilledge L. Bonham. LC 11-31660. (Columbia University. Studies in the Social Sciences: No. 111). reprint ed. 32.50 (*0-404-51111-2*) AMS Pr.

***British Contemporary Art, 1910-1990.** Alan Bowness. (Illus.). 160p. 1992. 35.00 (*0-614-06569-0*, Herbert Pr UK) New Amsterdam Bks.

British Cookery: A Complete Guide to Culinary Practice in England, Scotland, Ireland & Wales. Ed. by Lizzie Boyd. LC 78-60775. (Illus.). 640p. 1979. 37.95 (*0-87951-087-0*) Overlook Pr.

British Coracles & Irish Curraghs. James Hornell. LC 77-87671. (Illus.). reprint ed. 23.50 (*0-404-16464-1*) AMS Pr.

British Corporation Finance, 1775-1850. George H. Evans, Jr. LC 78-64292. (Johns Hopkins University. Studies in the Social Sciences. Thirtieth Ser. 1912: 23). 216p. 1983. reprint ed. 24.50 (*0-404-61392-6*) AMS Pr.

British Counter-Culture, 1966-1973: A Study of the Underground Press. Elizabeth Nelson. 256p. 1989. text ed. 45.00 (*0-312-02766-4*) St Martin.

***British Counterinsurgency in the Post-Imperial Era.** Thomas R. Mockaitis. LC 94-29769. (War, Armed Forces, & Society Ser.). 1995. text ed. write for info. (*0-7190-3919-3*) St Martin.

British Counterinsurgency, Nineteen Nineteen to Nineteen Sixty. Thomas R. Mockaitis. LC 90-30357. 192p. 1990. text ed. 49.95 (*0-312-04618-9*) St Martin.

British Countermarks on Copper & Bronze Coins. Gavin J. Scott. 1977. 30.00 (*0-685-51515-X*) S J Durst.

British Crime Survey, 1988. 133p. 1989. pap. 25.00 (*0-11-340965-6*, HM9656, Pub. by HMSO UK) UNIPUB.

British Critical Tradition: A Re-Evaluation. Ed. by Gary Day. LC 91-29661. 208p. 1992. text ed. 39.95 (*0-312-07481-6*) St Martin.

British Criticisms of American Writers, 2 vols, Set. W. B. Cairns. 1972. 250.00 (*0-87968-790-8*) Gordon Pr.

British Criticisms of American Writing. William B. Cairns. 1988. reprint ed. lib. bdg. 75.00 (*0-7812-0169-1*) Rprt Serv.

British Crown & Indian States. Chamber of Princes Staff. (C). 1988. reprint ed. 32.50 (*81-212-0141-1*, Pub. by Gian Publng Hse II) S Asia.

British Cultural Studies. Graeme Turner. (Media & Popular Culture Ser.: No. 7). 240p. (C). 1990. text ed. 39.95 (*0-04-445424-4*); pap. text ed. 14.95 (*0-04-445425-2*) Routledge Chapman & Hall.

British Culture & Economic Decline. Ed. by Bruce Collins & Keith Robbins. LC 90-31501. (Debates in Modern History Ser.). 224p. 1990. text ed. 45.00 (*0-312-04750-9*) St Martin.

British Defence: A Blueprint for Reform. M. Chichester & J. A. Wilkinson. 224p. 1987. 38.00 (*0-08-034745-2*, Pergamon Pr) Elsevier.

British Defence Choices for the Twenty-First Century: A Centre for Defence Studies Book. Ed. by Michael Clark & Philip Sabin. 272p. 1993. 45.00 (*1-85753-088-8*, Pub. by Brasseys UK) Brasseys Inc.

British Defence Policy & Nuclear War. Emanuel J. De Kadt. 144p. 1964. 36.00 (*0-7146-1550-1*, Pub. by F Cass Pubs UK) Intl Spec Bk.

British Defence Policy in the Nineteen-Nineties: A Guide to the Defence Debate. Christopher Coker. 186p. 1987. 38.00 (*0-08-035811-X*, Pub. by Brasseys UK) Brasseys Inc.

British Defence Policy since 1945. Ritchie Ovendale. LC 94-12637. (Documents in Contemporary History Ser.). 1994. text ed. 49.95 (*0-7190-4014-0*, Pub. by Manchester Univ Pr UK); text ed. 24.95 (*0-7190-4015-9*, Pub. by Manchester Univ Pr UK) St Martin.

***British Defence Problem in the Middle East 1946-7.** H. Rahman. 220p. 1995. 75.00 (*0-86372-186-9*, Pub. by Ithaca UK) Paul & Co Pubs.

British Defense: Policy & Process. Arthur Cyr. (CISA Working Paper Ser.: No. 13). 35p. (Orig.). Date not set. pap. 10.00 (*0-86682-012-4*) Ctr Intl Relations.

British Defense Policy: Striking the Right Balance. John Baylis. 180p. 1989. text ed. 49.95 (*0-312-02788-5*) St Martin.

British Defense since 1945. Michael Dockrill. (Making Contemporary Britain Ser.). 128p. 1988. pap. text ed. 19.95 (*0-631-16055-8*) Blackwell Pubs.

British Delft at Williamsburg. John Austin. LC 93-21045. (Decorative Arts Ser.). (Illus.). 299p. 1994. 135.00 (*0-87935-126-8*, Pub. by J Horne UK) Antique Collect.

British Deportees to America Pt. 1: 1760-1763. Clifford N. Smith. (British-American Genealogical Research Monograph Ser.: No. 1). 97p. (Orig.). 1987. reprint ed. pap. 15.00 (*0-915162-25-3*) Westland Pubns.

British Deportees to America Pt. 6: 1772-1773. Clifford N. Smith. (British-American Genealogical Research Monograph Ser.: No. 6). (Orig.). 1987. pap. 15.00 (*0-915162-31-8*) Westland Pubns.

British Deportees to America Pt. 7: 1774-1775. Clifford N. Smith. (British-American Genealogical Research Monograph Ser.: No. 7). 37p. 1987. pap. 15.00 (*0-915162-32-6*) Westland Pubns.

British Deportees to America Pt. 8: Cumulative Index, 1760-1775. Clifford N. Smith. (British-American Genealogical Research Monograph Ser.: No. 8). 22p. (Orig.). 1987. pap. 15.00 (*0-915162-33-4*) Westland Pubns.

British Deportees to America, Pt. 2: 1764-1765. Clifford N. Smith. (British-American Genealogical Research Monograph Ser.: No. 2). 100p. (Orig.). 1979. 15.00 (*0-915162-26-1*) Westland Pubns.

British Deportees to America, Pt. 3: 1766-1767. Clifford N. Smith. (British-American Genealogical Research Monograph Ser.: No. 3). 73p. (Orig.). 1981. pap. 15.00 (*0-915162-27-X*) Westland Pubns.

British Deportees to America, Pt. 4: 1768-1769. Clifford N. Smith. (British-American Genealogical Research Monograph Ser.: No. 4). 1986. pap. 15.00 (*0-915162-29-6*) Westland Pubns.

British Deportees to America, Pt. 5: 1770-1771. Clifford N. Smith. (British-American Genealogical Research Monograph Ser.: No. 5). 1986. pap. 15.00 (*0-915162-30-X*) Westland Pubns.

British Design & Art Direction, 1993. Clibborn E. Booth. 1994. 75.00 (*0-8478-5754-9*) Rizzoli Intl.

British Desmidieae. J. Ralfs. (Illus.). 1962. 52.00 (*3-7682-0144-9*) Lubrecht & Cramer.

British Diaries: An Annotated Bibliography of British Diaries Written Between 1442-1942. William Matthews. 11.25 (*0-8446-1304-5*) Peter Smith.

British Diaries: An Annotated Bibliography of British Diaries Written Between 1442-1942. William Matthews. (California Library Reprint). 373p. reprint ed. pap. 106.40 (*0-7837-4838-8*, 2044485) Bks Demand.

British Diplomacy & Finance in China, 1895-1914. E. W. Edwards. LC 86-28567. (Illus.). 230p. 1987. 65.00 (*0-19-822916-X*) OUP.

British Diplomacy & Foreign Policy 1782-1865. John Clarke. 272p. 1988. text ed. 60.00 (*0-04-445040-0*) Routledge Chapman & Hall.

British Diplomacy & Swedish Politics, 1758-1773. Michael Roberts. LC 80-11499. (Nordic Ser.: No. 1). 553p. reprint ed. pap. 157.70 (*0-7837-2925-1*, 2057529) Bks Demand.

British Direct Investment in Canada, 1890-1914. D. G. Paterson. LC 76-22429. 159p. reprint ed. pap. 45.40 (*0-8357-7421-X*, 2056122) Bks Demand.

British Discovery of Buddhism. Philip C. Almond. 192p. 1988. 59.95 (*0-521-35503-6*) Cambridge U Pr.

British Discovery of Hinduism in the 18th Century. Ed. by Peter J. Marshall. LC 73-111132. (European Understanding of India Ser.). 320p. reprint ed. pap. 91.20 (*0-8357-7422-8*, 2024493) Bks Demand.

British Documents on Foreign Affairs: From the First to the Second World War. Ed. by Donald C. Watt et al. LC 85-29635. (Series C, 1919-1939: Vols. 1-25). 12500p. 1986. 2,945.00 (*0-89093-605-6*) U Pubns Amer.

British Documents on Foreign Affairs: Reports & Papers from the Foreign Office Confidential Print, 20 vols., Set: Vol. 1-20. Ed. by David Gillard. LC 84-5216. (Near & Middle East, 1856-1914 Ser.). 10000p. 1985. Set. 2,355.00 (*0-89093-602-1*) U Pubns Amer.

British Documents on Foreign Affairs: Reports & Papers from the Foreign Office Confidential Print-Russia, 1859-1914, Part I. Kenneth Bourne. LC 86-11053. (Series C: Vols. 1-15). 7500p. 1986. 1,765.00 (*0-89093-604-8*) U Pubns Amer.

British Documents on Foreign Affairs: Reports & Papers from the Foreign Office Confidential Print-Russia, 1859-1914, 6 Vols., Set. Ed. by Kenneth Bourne et al. LC 82-21722. 2285p. 1983. 705.00 (*0-89093-600-5*) U Pubns Amer.

British Documents on Foreign Affairs, Complete Collection, 425 vols., Set. 40,015.00 (*0-318-72496-0*) U Pubns Amer.

British Documents on Foreign Affairs Part 2: Reports & Papers from the Foreign Office Confidential Print, 15 vols., Set. Ed. by D. Cameron Watt. LC 83-21722. (Soviet Union Ser.). 7500p. 1984. 2,000.00 (*0-89093-601-3*) U Pubns Amer.

British Documents on Foreign Affairs, Pt. 2: Reports & Papers from the Foreign Office Confidential Print, 35 vols, Set. Ed. by Robin Bidwell. LC 85-11148. (Turkey, Iran, & the Middle East Ser.). 17500p. 1986. 4,120.00 (*0-89093-603-X*) U Pubns Amer.

***British Documents on Foreign Affairs, Reports & Papers from the Foreign Office Confidential Print Part I: From the Mid-Nineteenth Century to the First World War, Series G, Africa. 1848-1914, Set.** David Throup. LC 95-3017. 1995. 3,060.00 (*0-89093-616-1*) U Pubns Amer.

***British Documents on Foreign Affairs, Reports & Papers from the Foreign Office Confidential Print Part II: From the First to the Second World War.** Ed. by Peter Woodward et al. LC 94-8149. (Series G, Africa, 1914-1939). 1994. 3,530.00 (*0-89093-617-X*) U Pubns Amer.

British Documents on Foreign Affairs, Reports & Papers from the Foreign Office Confidential Print Part I: From the Mid-Nineteenth Century to the First World War, 35 vols. Ed. by David Stevenson. LC 86-33988. (Series F, Europe, 1848-1914). 1987. 4,120.00 (*0-89093-610-2*) U Pubns Amer.

British Dominions in North America, 2 vols., 1. Joseph Bouchette. LC 68-56073. reprint ed. write for info. (*0-404-00937-9*) AMS Pr.

British Dominions in North America, 2 vols., 2. Joseph Bouchette. LC 68-56073. reprint ed. write for info. (*0-404-00938-7*) AMS Pr.

British Dominions in North America, 2 vols., Set. Joseph Bouchette. LC 68-56073. reprint ed. 295.00 (*0-404-00936-0*) AMS Pr.

British Drama: A Handbook & Brief Chronicle. Alan S. Downer. (Illus.). 1950. 44.50 (*0-89197-047-9*); pap. text ed. 24.50 (*0-89197-048-7*) Irvington.

British Drama: Sixteen Sixty Through Nineteen Hundred. Ed. & Intro. by Harold Bloom. (Critical Cosmos Ser.). 1990. 64.95 (*0-87754-981-8*) Chelsea Hse.

British Drama Beginnings to Sixteen Hundred Sixty. Jennifer R. Goodman. (Twayne's History of British Drama Ser.). 264p. (C). 1990. text ed. 25.95 (*0-8057-8953-7*, Twayne) Macmillan.

British Drama, Eighteen Ninety to Nineteen Fifty. Richard Dietrich. (Critical History of British Drama Ser.). 330p. (C). 1989. text ed. 25.95 (*0-8057-8951-0*, Twayne) Macmillan.

B

British Drama in the Eighties: Texts & Contexts. Ed. by P. S. Petersen & K. H. Westarp. (Dolphin Ser.: No. 14). 218p. (Orig.). 1986. pap. 29.50 (*0-685-33598-4*, Pub. by Aarhus Univ Pr DK) Coronet Bks.

British Drama Since Shaw. Emil Roy. LC 72-188699. (Crosscurrents-Modern Critiques Ser.). 158p. 1972. 8.50 (*0-8093-0579-8*) S Ill U Pr.

***British Drama, 1660-1779: A Critical History.** Frances Kavenik. (Critical History of British Drama Ser.). 1995. lib. bdg. 26.95x (*0-8057-8297-4*, Twayne) Macmillan.

***British Drama, 1660-1779: A Critical History.** Frances M. Kavenik. LC 94-26538. (Critical History of British Drama). 1995. write for info. (*0-8057-4533-5*, Twayne) Macmillan.

British Drama, 1950 to Present. Susan Rusinko. (Critical History of British Drama Ser.). 285p. (C). 1989. text ed. 25.95 (*0-8057-8952-9*, Twayne) Macmillan.

British Dramatists: Since World War Two, 2 Vols., Vol. 13. Ed. by Stanley Weintraub. (Dictionary of Literary Biography Ser.: Vol. 13). 679p. 1983. Set. pap. 128.00 (*0-8103-0936-X*, 006389-M99348) Gale.

British Dramatists from Dryden to Sheridan. 2nd ed. Ed. by George H. Nettleton & Arthur E. Case. LC 75-2443. 975p. (C). 1975. pap. 30.00 (*0-8093-0743-X*) S Ill U Pr.

British Drawings & Watercolors. Ed. by Frederick Den Broeder. (Illus.). 72p. 1974. 1.00 (*0-918386-13-6*) W Benton Mus.

British Economic & Social History Bk. 1: 1700-1870. Stanley Thornes. (C). 1987. 70.00 (*0-85950-619-3*, Pub. by S Thornes Pubs UK) St Mut.

British Economic & Social History Bk. 2: 1850 to Present Day. P. Sauvain. (C). 1987. 70.00 (*0-85950-620-7*, Pub. by S Thornes Pubs UK) St Mut.

British Economic & Social History, 1700-1950. Richard Korzeniewicz. 261p. 1985. 59.00 (*0-7212-0711-1*, Pub. by Regency Press) St Mut.

British Economic Fluctuations: Seventeen Ninety to Nineteen Thirty-Nine. Ed. by Derek H. Aldcroft & Peter Fearon. LC 77-178900. 1972. text ed. 29.95 (*0-312-10045-0*) St Martin.

British Economic Growth During the Industrial Revolution. N. F. Crafts. (Illus.). 220p. 1986. 24.95 (*0-19-873067-5*) OUP.

British Economic Growth 1688-1959: Trends & Structure. Phyllis Deane & W. A. Cole. (Modern Revivals in Economic & Social History Ser.). 1993. 67.95 (*0-7512-0197-9*, Pub. by Gregg Revivals UK) Ashgate Pub Co.

British Economic Growth, 1856-1973. R. C. Matthews et al. LC 80-53222. (Studies of Economic Growth in Industrialized Countries). 736p. 1982. 79.50 (*0-8047-1110-0*) Stanford U Pr.

British Economic Interests in the Far East. Edward M. Gull. LC 75-30058. (International Research Series of the Institute of Pacific Relations). 280p. 1983. reprint ed. 39.50 (*0-404-59528-6*) AMS Pr.

British Economic Thought in the Seventeenth & Eighteenth Centuries, 8 vols., Set. (History of British Economic Thought Ser.). 4096p. 1992. Boxed set. boxed 920.50 (*0-415-08107-6*, B0110, Pub. by Thoemmes Pr UK) Routledge.

British Economists & the Empire, 1860-1914. John C. Wood. LC 83-3400. 320p. 1983. text ed. 39.95 (*0-312-10089-2*) St Martin.

British Economy. William Mennell. 1964. pap. 12.00 (*0-8464-0211-4*) Beekman Pubs.

British Economy. Roy F. Harrod. LC 77-14391. (Economics Handbook Ser.). (Illus.). 240p. 1978. reprint ed. text ed. 38.50 (*0-8371-9832-1*, HABE, Greenwood Pr) Greenwood.

***British Economy in Transition: From the Old to the New?** Ed. by Royce Turner. LC 94-46808. 1995. write for info. (*0-415-11114-5*); pap. write for info. (*0-415-11115-3*) Routledge.

British Economy of the Nineteenth Century: Essays. Walt W. Rostow. LC 81-13312. 240p. 1982. reprint ed. text ed. 59.75 (*0-313-23208-3*, ROBR, Greenwood Pr) Greenwood.

British Economy since 1945. Ed. by N. F. Crafts & Nicholas W. Woodward. (Illus.). 560p. 1991. 74.00 (*0-19-877274-2*, 12227); pap. 29.95 (*0-19-877273-4*) OUP.

An Asterisk (*) at the beginning of an entry indicates that the title is appearing in BIP for the first time. 911

***British Economy since 1945.** 2nd ed. Alec Cairncross. (Making Contemporary Britain Ser.). (Illus.). 368p. (C). 1995. pap. write for info. (0-631-19961-6) Blackwell Pubs.

British Economy Since 1945: Economic Policy & Performance 1945-90. Alec Cairncross. Ed. by Anthony Seldon. (ICBH Ser.). 320p. 1992. pap. 19.95 (0-631-18277-2) Blackwell Pubs.

British Edda. L. A. Waddell. 331p. reprint ed. 12.00 (0-913022-41-1) Angriff Pr.

British Edge. Victor Burgin et al. (Illus.). 70p. (Orig.). 1987. pap. write for info. (0-910663-46-7) ICA Inc.

British Educational Theory, 1750-1850, 11 vols., Set. (History of British Educational Thought Ser.). 1992. Boxed set. boxed 999.95 (0-415-07974-8, A7719, Pub. by Thoemmes Pr UK) Routledge.

British Election of 1992 & Why It Did Not Help George Bush. Gerald A. Dorfman. LC 93-3008. (Essays in Public Policy Ser.: No. 40). 1993. 5.00 (0-8179-3662-9) Hoover Inst Pr.

British Election Studies, 1950. James K. Pollock et al. 1951. 10.00 (0-911586-27-X) Wahr.

***British Elections & Parties Yearbook.** Ed. by D. Broughton et al. 304p. 1995. pap. 30.00 (0-7146-4150-2, Pub. by F Cass Pubs UK) Intl Spec Bk.

***British Elections & Parties Yearbook.** Ed. by D. Broughton et al. 304p. 1995. 60.00 (0-7146-4620-2, Pub. by F Cass Pubs UK) Intl Spec Bk.

British Elections & Parties Yearbook, 1991. Ed. by Ivor Crewe et al. 450p. (C). 1992. text ed. 49.50 (0-472-10393-8) U of Mich Pr.

British Elections & Parties Yearbook 1993. Ed. by Ivor Crewe et al. 450p. text ed. 49.50 (0-472-10530-2) U of Mich Pr.

British Electoral Facts, 1832-1987. F. W. Craig. 256p. 1989. text ed. 59.95 (0-900178-30-2, Pub. by Dartmth Pub UK) Ashgate Pub Co.

British Electorate, 1963-1987: A Compendium of Data from the British Election Studies. Ivor Crewe et al. (Illus.). 544p. (C). 1991. 160.00 (0-521-32197-2) Cambridge U Pr.

British Empire, 12 vols, Set. Incl. Vol. 1. Dominions & Dependencies of the British Empire. Ed. by Hugh Gunn. (Illus.). 20.00 (0-404-54301-4); Vol. 2. Story of the Empire. C. Lucas. Ed. by Hugh Gunn. 14.00 (0-404-54302-2); Vol. 3. Constitution, Administration & Laws of the Empire. A. B. Keith. Ed. by Hugh Gunn. 15.00 (0-404-54303-0); Vol. 4. Resources of the Empire & Their Development. E. Lewin. Ed. by Hugh Gunn. 15.00 (0-404-54304-9); Vol. 5. Health Problems of the Empire, Past, Present & Future. A. Balfour & H. H. Scott. Ed. by Hugh Gunn. 17.50 (0-404-54305-7); Vol. 6. Press & Communications of the Empire. J. S. Mills. Ed. by Hugh Gunn. 17.50 (0-404-54306-5); Vol. 7. Trade, Commerce...of the Empire. C. C. McLeod. Ed. by Hugh Gunn. 17.50 (0-404-54307-3); Vol. 8. Makers of the Empire. H. Gunn. Ed. by Hugh Gunn. 17.50 (0-404-54308-1); Vol. 9. Native Races of the Empire. G. Lagden. Ed. by Hugh Gunn. 17.50 (0-404-54309-X); Vol. 10. Universities & Educational Systems of the British Empire. Ed. by Hugh Gunn. 17.50 (0-404-54310-3); Vol. 11. Literature of the Empire; the Art of the Empire. E. Salaman & A. A. Longden. Ed. by Hugh Gunn. 17.50 (0-404-54311-1); Vol. 12. Migration Within the Empire. E. A. Belcher & J. A. Williamson. Ed. by Hugh Gunn. 17.50 (0-404-54312-X); reprint ed. 200.00 (0-404-54300-6) AMS Pr.

British Empire at Its Zenith. A. J. Christopher. 288p. 1988. lib. bdg. 75.00 (0-7099-3418-1, A1760) Routledge Chapman & Hall.

British Empire, Fifteen Fifty-Eight to Nineteen Eighty-Three. T. O. Lloyd. (Short Oxford History of the Modern World Ser.). (Illus.). 1984. pap. 19.95 (0-19-873025-X) OUP.

British Empire in the Middle East, 1945-1951: Arab Nationalism, the United States, & Postwar Imperialism. William R. Louis. (Illus.). 820p. 1986. pap. 35.00 (0-19-822960-7) OUP.

British Empire, Seventeen Eighty-Four to Nineteen Thirty-Nine. James T. Admas. (Dorset Classic Reprints Ser.). 408p. 1992. 24.95 (0-88029-706-9) Dorset Pr.

British Empiricism & American Pragmatism: New Directions & Neglected Arguments. Robert J. Roth. LC 93-3064. 205p. 1993. 30.00 (0-8232-1391-9); pap. 19.95 (0-8232-1392-7) Fordham.

British Empiricists: Locke, Berkeley, Hume. John Dunn et al. (Past Masters Ser.). 304p. 1992. pap. 12.95 (0-19-283068-6) OUP.

British Employment in the Eighties: The Spatial, Structural & Compositional Change of the Workforce. Martin Frost & Nigel Spence. (Progress in Planning Ser.). (Illus.). 96p. 1991. pap. 57.00 (0-08-041151-7, Pergamon Pr) Elsevier.

***British English, A to Zed.** Norman W. Schur. LC 86-16754. 492p. 1987. reprint ed. pap. 140.30 (0-7837-8136-9, 2047944) Bks Demand.

British English, A to Zed. Norman W. Schur. LC 91-55008. 496p. 1991. reprint ed. pap. 17.00 (0-06-272501-7, Harper Ref) HarpC.

British English for American Readers: A Dictionary of the Language, Customs, & Places of British Life & Literature. David Grote. LC 91-45575. 728p. 1992. text ed. 85.00 (0-313-27851-2, GBW, Greenwood Pr) Greenwood.

British-English Language Dictionary: For More Effective Communication Between Americans & Britons. 2nd ed. Norman Moss. (Illus.). 192p. 1991. 14.95 (0-8442-9115-3, Natl Textbk); pap. 8.95 (0-8442-9116-1, Natl Textbk) NTC Pub Grp.

British Enterprise in Brazil: The St. John d'el Rey Mining Company & the Morro Velho Gold Mine, 1830-1960. Marshall C. Eakin. LC 89-33441. (Illus.). 336p. 1990. lib. bdg. 50.50 (0-8223-0914-9) Duke.

British Enterprise in Nigeria. Arthur N. Cook. 330p. 1964. reprint ed. 40.00 (0-7146-1644-3, Pub. by F Cass Pubs UK) Intl Spec Bk.

British Entry to the European Community under the Heath Government of 1970-74. Christopher Lord. 194p. 1993. 59.95 (1-85521-336-2, Pub. by Dartmth Pub UK) Ashgate Pub Co.

British Essays in American History. Ed. by H. C. Allen & C. P. Hill. LC 82-20916. x, 350p. (C). 1983. reprint ed. text ed. 65.00 (0-313-23789-1, ALBE, Greenwood Pr) Greenwood.

British Establishments on the Columbia & the State of the Fur Trade. William H. Ashley. 60p. 1981. 12.95 (0-87770-255-1) Ye Galleon.

British Ethical Societies. Ian MacKillop. 224p. 1986. 69.95 (0-521-26672-6) Cambridge U Pr.

British Experience with River Pollution, 1865-1876. Lawrence E. Breeze. LC 93-22308. (American University Studies: History: Ser. IX, Vols. 139). 297p. (C). 1994. text ed. 53.95 (0-8204-2162-6) P Lang Pubs.

British Experimental Jets. Barrie Hygate. (Illus.). 224p. 1990. 59.95 (1-85486-010-0, Pub. by Argus Pubs UK) Motorbooks Intl.

British External Policy-Making in the 1990s. Michael Clarke. 339p. (C). 1992. 39.95 (0-8157-1454-8); pap. 18.95 (0-8157-1453-X) Brookings.

British Factory-Japanese Factory: The Origins of National Diversity in Employment Relations. Ronald P. Dore. LC 72-78948. 1973. pap. 15.00 (0-520-02495-8) U CA Pr.

British Falling Block Breechloading Rifles from 1865. Jonathan G. Kirton. Ed. by Charles R. Suydam & George Hoyem. LC 85-71782. (Illus.). 250p. 1985. 39.95 (0-9604982-3-0) Armory Pubns.

British Family Names. Henry Barber. 1972. 59.95 (0-87968-791-6) Gordon Pr.

British Family Names: Their Origin & Meaning. Henry Barber. 298p. 1990. reprint ed. 20.00 (0-685-60517-5, 315) Clearfield Co.

***British Farming: Changing Policies & Production Systems.** Eric Carter & Malcolm Stansfield. (Illus.). 144p. 1994. text ed. 29.95 (0-85236-278-1, Pub. by Farming Pr UK) Diamond Farm Bk.

British Federation of Master Printers - How It Began. Mary Sessions. (C). 1989. pap. 31.00 (0-900657-10-3, Pub. by W Sessions UK) St Mut.

British Female Poets: With Biographical & Critical Notices. George W. Bethune. LC 75-38734. (Essay Index Reprint Ser.). 1977. reprint ed. 30.95 (0-8369-2636-6) Ayer.

British Feminism in the Twentieth Century. Ed. by Harold L. Smith. LC 89-20249. 224p. (C). 1990. lib. bdg. 27.50 (0-87023-705-5) U of Mass Pr.

British Feminist Thought: A Reader. Terry Lovell. 256p. (C). 1990. pap. text ed. 19.95 (0-631-16915-6) Blackwell Pubs.

British Fertility Decline: Demographic Transition in the Crucible of the Industrial Revolution. Michael S. Teitelbaum. LC 84-2152. (Illus.). 244p. 1984. text ed. 52.50x (0-691-09405-5) Princeton U Pr.

***British Fertility Decline: Demographic Transition in the Crucible of the Industrial Revolution.** Michael S. Teitelbaum. LC 84-2152. (Illus.). Date not set. reprint ed. pap. 81.60 (0-7837-9458-4, 2060200) Bks Demand.

British Fiction, 1750-1770: A Chronological Check-List of Prose Fiction Printed in Britain & Ireland. James Raven. LC 87-6041. 360p. 1987. 50.00 (0-87413-324-6) U Delaware Pr.

British Fighter since Nineteen Twelve. Francis K. Mason. (Putnam Aviation Ser.). (Illus.). 448p. 1993. 49.95 (1-55750-082-7) Naval Inst Pr.

British Figurative Painters of the Eighties, Nos. 46 & 1. Ed. by Kyoichi Tsuzuki. (Art Random Ser.). (Illus.). 48p. 1990. 32.95 (4-7636-8509-0, Pub. by Kyoto Shoin JA) Bks Nippan.

British Figurative Painters of the Eighties, Nos. 47 & 2. Ed. by Kyoichi Tsuzuki. (Art Random Ser.). (Illus.). 48p. 1990. 32.95 (4-7636-8510-4, Pub. by Kyoto Shoin JA) Bks Nippan.

British Film Actors' Credits, 1895-1987. Scott Palmer. LC 87-31098. 935p. 1988. lib. bdg. 82.00x (0-89950-316-0) McFarland & Co.

British Film Catalogue, 1895-1985: A Reference Guide. Denis Gifford. LC 86-6281. 1052p. reprint ed. pap. 180.00 (0-8357-3496-X, 2039756) Bks Demand.

British Film Character Actors: Great Names & Memorable Moments. Terence Pettigrew. LC 82-3913. (Illus.). 208p. (C). 1982. text ed. 38.00 (0-389-20289-4, N7112) B&N Imports.

British Film Documentary Movement: 1926-1946. Paul Swann. (Cambridge Studies in Film). (Illus.). 228p. (C). 1989. 64.95 (0-521-33479-9) Cambridge U Pr.

British Film Institute Broadcasting Debate, 7 bklts., Set. 1990. pap. 57.50 (0-253-31193-4, Pub. by British Film Inst UK) Ind U Pr.

British Film Music. John Huntley. LC 72-169331. (Literature of Cinema Ser.). (Illus.). 272p. 1978. reprint ed. 20.95 (0-405-03897-6) Ayer.

British Finance, 1930-1940. Walter A. Morton. Ed. by Mira Wilkins. LC 78-3942. (International Finance Ser.). (Illus.). 1979. reprint ed. lib. bdg. 35.95 (0-405-11242-4) Ayer.

***British Financial Markets & Institutions.** 2nd ed. J. Piesse et al. LC 95-8631. 1995. pap. write for info. (0-13-647165-X) P-H.

British Fingerpicking Guitar. Comp. by Stefan Grossman. (Guitar Workshop Ser.). 1993. 9.95 (1-56222-066-7, 94507); audio 9.98 (1-56222-086-1, 94507) Mel Bay.

British Fire Engines. Roger Pennington. (Color Library). (Illus.). 128p. 1994. pap. 15.95 (1-85532-426-1, Pub. by Osprey Pubng Ltd UK) Motorbooks Intl.

British Folk Art. James Ayres. LC 76-57876. (Illus.). 144p. 1977. 37.95 (0-87951-060-9) Overlook Pr.

British Folk Scene: Musical Performance & Social Identity. Niall Mackinnon. LC 93-4036. (Popular Music in Britain Ser.). 224p. 1994. 90.00 (0-335-09774-X, Open Univ Pr); pap. 27.50 (0-335-09773-1, Open Univ Pr) Taylor & Francis.

British Folk Tales: A Selection. large type ed. Kevin Crossley-Holland. (YA). (gr. 1-8). 1993. 16.95 (0-7451-1911-5, Galaxy Child Lrg Print) Chivers N Amer.

British Folk Tales: New Versions. Ret. by Kevin Crossley-Holland. LC 87-9918. 384p. 1987. 22.95 (0-531-05733-X) Orchard Bks Watts.

British Folktales. Ed. by Katharine Briggs. (Reprints Ser.). 336p. 1989. 9.95 (0-88029-288-1) Dorset Pr.

British Followers of Theodor Herzl: English Zionist Leaders, 1896-1904. Virginia H. Hein. Ed. by William H. McNeill & Peter Stansky. (Modern European History Ser.). 325p. 1988. lib. bdg. 15.00 (0-8240-7815-2) Garland.

British Food Policy During the First World War. L. Margaret Barnett. 256p. (C). 1985. text ed. 49.95 (0-04-942189-1) Routledge Chapman & Hall.

British Foot Guards: A Bibliography. Silverthorne & W. D. Gaskin. 1960. pap. 5.00 (0-910746-27-3, BFG01) Hope Farm.

***British Footpath Handbook: Independent Walking Tours of England, Wales & Scotland.** 3rd rev. ed. Richard Hayward. (Illus.). 100p. 1995. pap. 8.95 (1-880848-11-2) Brit Footpaths.

***British Footpath Sampler: Twenty-Eight Day Walks & 12 "Easy" Long Distance Paths.** 2nd rev. ed. Richard Hayward. (Illus.). 50p. (Orig.). 1995. pap. 3.95 (1-880848-09-0) Brit Footpaths.

***British Footpaths Bibliography: Guide to Guidebooks.** 2nd rev. ed. Richard Hayward. 104p. 1995. pap. 8.95x (1-880848-10-4) Brit Footpaths.

British Forces in Zululand 1879. Ian Knight. (Elite Ser.: No. 32). (Illus.). 64p. pap. 12.95 (1-85532-109-2, 9432, Pub. by Osprey UK) Stackpole.

***British Foreign Direct Investment in the United States 1974-1994.** Francis M. Jeffries. 400p. (Orig.). 1995. pap. 250.00 (1-878974-18-1) Jeffries & Assocs.

British Foreign Office: Japan Correspondence, 1856 - 1905: Indexes & Guides to the Microfilm Collection. LC 75-7622. 1975. 20.00 (0-8420-2064-0) Scholarly Res Inc.

British Foreign Office: Russia Correspondence, 1906-1913 & 1919-1940: Indexes & Guides to the Microfilm Collection. LC 07-85235. 1977. 60.00 (0-8420-2127-2) Scholarly Res Inc.

British Foreign Office: Russia Correspondence, 1914 - 1918: Indexes & Guides to the Microfilm Collection. British Foreign Office Staff. LC 76-44647. 1976. 20.00 (0-8420-2107-8) Scholarly Res Inc.

British Foreign Policy: Tradition, Change, & Transformation. Ed. by Steve Smith et al. 240p. 1988. text ed. 21.95 (0-04-327080-8); pap. text ed. 18.95 (0-04-327081-6) Routledge Chapman & Hall.

British Foreign Policy & Its Critics, 1830-1950. Andrew Rothstein. 128p. 1969. 19.95 (0-8464-0212-2) Beekman Pubs.

British Foreign Policy & the Atlantic Area: The Techniques of Accommodation. Arthur Cyr. LC 79-4331. 172p. 1979. 35.00 (0-8419-0489-8) Holmes & Meier.

***British Foreign Policy During the Curzon Period, 1919-24.** G. H. Bennett. LC 95-14910. 1995. write for info. (0-312-12650-6) St Martin.

British Foreign Policy in an Age of Revolution, 1783-1793. Jeremy Black. (Illus.). 448p. (C). 1994. 89.95 (0-521-45001-2); pap. 34.95 (0-521-46684-9) Cambridge U Pr.

British Foreign Policy in the Age of the American Revolution. H. M. Scott. 392p. 1991. 89.00 (0-19-820195-8) OUP.

British Foreign Policy in the Twentieth Century. C. J. Bartlett. LC 88-34583. 180p. 1989. text ed. 45.00 (0-312-02844-X) St Martin.

British Foreign Policy, Nineteen Eighteen to Nineteen Forty-Five: A Guide to Research & Research Materials. rev. ed. Ed. by Sidney Aster. LC 90-46466. (European Diplomatic History Ser.). 391p. 1991. 50.00 (0-8420-2310-0) Scholarly Res Inc.

British Foreign Policy, Nineteen Forty-Five to Fifty-Six. Ed. by M. Dockrill & John W. Young. LC 88-31825. 280p. 1989. text ed. 49.95 (0-312-02847-4) St Martin.

British Foreign Policy, 1660-1672. Keith Feiling. 385p. 1968. reprint ed. 37.50 (0-7146-1473-4, Pub. by F Cass Pubs UK) Intl Spec Bk.

British Foreign Policy under Thatcher. Ed. by Peter Byrd. LC 88-26380. 192p. 1988. text ed. 49.95 (0-312-02526-2) St Martin.

British Foreign Secretaries & Foreign Policy: From Crimean War to First World War. Ed. by Keith M. Wilson. 224p. 1986. 49.95 (0-7099-3678-8, Pub. by Croom Helm UK) Routledge Chapman & Hall.

British Foreign Service & the American Civil War. Eugene H. Berwanger. LC 94-6468. 216p. 1994. lib. bdg. 28.00x (0-8131-1876-X) U Pr of Ky.

British Freshwater Fishes. Margaret Varley. 1978. 40.00 (0-685-63394-2) St Mut.

British Fungus Flora, Agarics & Boleti No. 3: Bolbiticeae: Agrocybe, Bolbitius, & Conocybe. D. M. Henderson et al. 138p. 1982. pap. text ed. 32.00 (0-11-491750-7) Lubrecht & Cramer.

British Fungus Flora, Agarics & Boleti No. 6: Pluteaceae: Pluteus & Volvariella. D. M. Henderson et al. 98p. 1986. pap. text ed. 32.00 (0-9504270-4-7) Lubrecht & Cramer.

British Fungus Flora, Agarics & Boleti Pt. 5: Strophariaceae & Coprinaceae p.p., Hypholoma, Melanotus, Psilocybe, Stropharia, Lacrymaria & Panaeolus. Roy Watling & Norma M. Gregory. Ed. by D. M. Henderson & P. D. Orton. (Illus.). 121p. 1989. pap. 32.00 (0-9504270-7-1, Pub. by Royal Botanic Garden UK) Lubrecht & Cramer.

British Further Education. A. J. Peters. 1967. 164.00 (0-08-011893-3, Pub. by Pergamon Repr UK) Franklin.

British Fusilier in Revolutionary Boston. Frederick MacKenzie. Ed. by Allen French. LC 79-102237. (Select Bibliographies Reprint Ser.). 1977. 21.95 (0-8369-5122-0) Ayer.

British Gallantry Awards. P. E. Abbott & J. M. A. Tamplin. 334p. 1982. 75.00 (0-902633-74-0, Pub. by Picton UK) St Mut.

British Game Shooting. Martin. (Illus.). 172p. 1988. 29.95 (1-57157-008-X) Safari Pr.

British General Election Manifestos 1959-1987. F. W. Craig. (Parliamentary Research Services Ser.). 516p. 1990. text ed. 89.95 (0-900178-34-5, Pub. by Dartmth Pub UK) Ashgate Pub Co.

British General Election of 1931. Andrew Thorpe. 344p. 1991. 72.00 (0-19-820218-0, 12192) OUP.

British General Election of 1945. R. B. McCallum & Alison Readman. 311p. 1964. 35.00 (0-7146-1566-8, Pub. by F Cass Pubs UK) Intl Spec Bk.

British General Election of 1950. H. G. Nicholas. (Illus.). 353p. 1968. reprint ed. 35.00 (0-7146-1568-4, Pub. by F Cass Pubs UK) Intl Spec Bk.

British General Election of 1983. David E. Butler & Dennis A. Kavanagh. LC 83-26990. 350p. 1984. text ed. 32.50 (0-312-10256-9) St Martin.

British General Election of 1987. David E. Butler & Dennis A. Kavanagh. LC 87-32314. 392p. 1988. text ed. 45.00 (0-312-01870-3) St Martin.

***British General Elections: Since 1945.** 2nd ed. David Butler. (Making Contemporary Britain Ser.). (Illus.). 132p. (C). 1995. per., pap. write for info. (0-631-19828-8) Blackwell Pubs.

British General Elections since 1945. David Butler. (Making Contemporary Britain Ser.). (Illus.). 128p. 1989. pap. text ed. 17.95 (0-631-16053-1) Blackwell Pubs.

British Genres: Cinema & Society, 1930-1960. Marcia Landy. (Illus.). 620p. 1991. text ed. 75.00 (0-691-03176-2); pap. text ed. 23.95 (0-685-48016-X) Princeton U Pr.

British Gentlemen in the Wild West: The Era of the Intensely English Cowboy. Lawrence M. Woods. 352p. 1989. text ed. 27.95 (0-02-935601-6) Free Pr.

British Geography, 1918-1945. Ed. by Robert W. Steel. 200p. 1987. 59.95 (0-521-24790-X) Cambridge U Pr.

British Glass, 1800-1914. Charles R. Hajdamach. (Illus.). 465p. 1992. 89.50 (1-85149-141-4) Antique Collect.

British Goblins. Wirt Sikes. (Illus.). 1976. 20.00 (0-685-52214-8) Charles River Bks.

British Government & Politics. 5th ed. R. M. Punnett. 572p. (C). 1990. reprint ed. pap. text ed. 19.95 (0-88133-560-6) Waveland Pr.

British Government & Politics. 6th ed. R. M. Punnett. (Illus.). 608p. (C). 1994. text ed. 57.95 (1-85521-497-0, Pub. by Dartmth Pub UK); pap. text ed. 21.95 (1-85521-508-X, Pub. by Dartmth Pub UK) Ashgate Pub Co.

British Government & the Constitution: Text, Cases & Materials. Collin Turpin. (Law in Context Ser.). xxviii, 476p. 1985. 45.00 (0-297-78651-2) Rothman.

British Government, the Triumph of Elitism: A Study of the British Political Tradition & Its Major Challenges. A. P. Tant. 200p. 1993. 59.95 (1-85521-209-9, Pub. by Dartmth Pub UK) Ashgate Pub Co.

British Grand Prix. Maurice Hamilton. (Illus.). 270p. 1991. 39.95 (1-85223-589-6, Pub. by Crowood UK) Motorbooks Intl.

British Guiana: Issued Under the Auspices of the Royal Institute of International Affairs. Raymond T. Smith. LC 80-10964. (Illus.). vi, 218p. 1980. reprint ed. text ed. 55.00 (0-313-22142-1, SMBG, Greenwood Pr) Greenwood.

British Harpsichord Music Vol. 1: Sources. John Harley. 350p. 1992. text ed. 75.00 (0-85967-876-8, Pub. by Scolar Pr UK) Ashgate Pub Co.

British Harpsichord Music Vol. 2: History. John Harley. 352p. 1994. 75.00 (0-85967-899-7, Pub. by Scolar Pr UK) Ashgate Pub Co.

***British High Politics & a Nationalist Ireland: Criminality, Land, & the Law Under Forster & Balfour.** Margaret O'Callaghan. 220p. 1994. 55.00 (0-312-12497-X) St Martin.

British Hispanism & the Challenge of Literary Theory. Jordan. (Re-Reading Hispanic Studies). 1990. pap. 17.50 (0-85668-515-1, Pub. by Aris & Phillips UK) David Brown.

British Historical Facts, 1688-1760. Christopher Cook & John Stevenson. LC 88-7047. 264p. 1988. text ed. 49.95 (0-312-02106-2) St Martin.

British Historical Medals, 1760-1837: The Accession of George III to the Death of William IV, Vol. I. Laurence Brown. 1987. 125.00 (0-318-22505-0) Numismatic Fine Arts.

British Historical Medals, 1760-1837: The Accession of George III to the Death of William IV, Vol. I. Laurence Brown. (Illus.). 469p. 1980. 125.00 (0-900652-56-X, Pub. by Seaby UK) Trafalgar.

An Asterisk (*) at the beginning of an entry indicates that the title is appearing in BIP for the first time.

B

An Asterisk (*) at the beginning of an entry indicates that the title is appearing in BIP for the first time.

British Literary Magazines: The Victorian & Edwardian Age, 1837-1913. Ed. by Alvin Sullivan. LC 82-21136. (Historical Guides to the World's Periodicals & Newspapers Ser.). xxvi, 560p. 1984. text ed. 95.00 (0-313-24335-2, SVI/, Greenwood Pr) Greenwood.

British Literary Manuscripts: Series I. Ed. by Verlyn Klinkenborg. 259p. 1981. pap. 13.95 (0-486-24124-6) Dover.

British Literary Manuscripts: Series II. Ed. by Verlyn Klinkenborg. 1981. pap. 13.95 (0-486-24125-4) Dover.

British Literature, 2 vols. 3rd ed. Hazelton Spencer et al. (C). 1974. write for info. (0-318-53236-0) Heath.

British Literature, 2 vols, 1. 3rd ed. Hazelton Spencer et al. (C). 1974. text ed. 26.00 (0-669-84129-3) Heath.

British Literature, 2 vols, 2. 3rd ed. Hazelton Spencer et al. (C). 1974. text ed. 26.00 (0-669-84137-4) Heath.

British Literature since Nineteen Forty-Five. George Watson. LC 90-43361. 150p. 1991. text ed. 45.00 (0-312-05339-8) St Martin.

British Locomotive Catalogue 1825-1923, Vol. 1. D. Baxter. 1977. 30.00 (0-685-87550-4) St Mut.

British Locomotives, 1894. C. J. Bowen Cooke. 396p. 1980. 65.00 (0-905418-72-7, Pub. by Gresham Bks UK) St Mut.

British Longcase Clocks. Derek Roberts. LC 89-64089. (Illus.). 400p. 1989. 95.00 (0-88740-230-5) Schiffer.

British Look at America During the Age of Samuel Johnson: With an Address by Herman W. Liebert. (Illus.). 55p. 1971. pap. 15.00 (0-916617-07-6) J C Brown.

British Malaya. Frank A. Swettenham. LC 74-179244. reprint ed. 39.50 (0-404-54870-9) AMS Pr.

British Male Body Measurements. Wira Tech. Group Staff. (C). 1980. 125.00 (0-900820-13-6, Pub. by British Textile Tech UK) St Mut.

British Maps of Colonial America. William P. Cumming. LC 73-84190. 126p. reprint ed. pap. 36.00 (0-8357-7425-2, 2024089) Bks Demand.

British Maps of the American Revolution. Peter J. Guthorn. LC 72-79889. (Revolutionary War Bicentennial Ser.). (Illus.). 1972. lib. bdg. 15.95 (0-912480-07-6) Freneau.

British Marxist Historians: An Introductory Analysis. Harvey J. Kaye. 224p. 1985. pap. 21.95 (0-7456-0016-6) Blackwell Pubs.

British Master Tax Guide, 1992-1993. 11th ed. 800p. 1992. pap. 44.00 (0-685-68067-3, 5383) Commerce.

British Masters of Medicine. Ed. by D'Arcy Power. LC 79-99721. (Essay Index Reprint Ser.). 1977. 26.95 (0-8369-1375-2) Ayer.

British Masters of the Albumen Print: A Selection of Mid-Nineteenth Century Victorian Photography. International Museum of Photography, George Eastman House Staff. LC 76-16546. 1976. fiche, lib. bdg. 35.00 (0-226-69171-3) U Ch Pr.

British Medieval Literature. Ed. & Intro. by Harold Bloom. (Critical Cosmos Ser.). 1990. 64.95 (0-87754-968-0) Chelsea Hse.

British Mercantile Houses in Buenos Aires, 1810-1880. Vera B. Reber. LC 78-15743. (Studies in Business History: No. 29). (Illus.). 217p. 1979. 29.00 (0-674-08245-1) HUP.

British Mercantile Interests in the Making of the Peace of Paris, 1763: Trade, War & Empire. Barry M. Gough. LC 92-14031. (Studies in British History: Vol. 30). 148p. 1992. lib. bdg. 69.95 (0-7734-9548-7) E Mellen.

British Merchant see Manufacturer

British Merchant, or, Commerce Preserved, 3 Vols, Set. Ed. by Charles King. LC 67-29508. (Reprints of Economic Classics Ser.). 1968. reprint ed. 150.00 (0-678-00356-4) Kelley.

British Military Administration of Occupied Territories in Africa During the Years of 1941-1947. Francis J. Rennell. 1970. reprint ed. text ed. 85.00 (0-8371-4319-5, REBM, Greenwood Pr) Greenwood.

British Military & Naval Forces in West African History 1807-1874. Paul M. Mbaeyi. LC 77-23627. (Library of African Affairs). (Illus.). 263p. 1978. 21.95 (0-88357-029-7) NOK Pubs.

British Military Band Uniforms, Vol. 1: Cavalry Regiments. Spellmount Ltd. Publishers Staff. (C). 1986. 59.00 (1-873376-05-7, Pub. by Spellmount UK) St Mut.

British Military Band Uniforms, Vol. 1: Cavalry Regiments, Vol. 2: The Household Regiments. Spellmount Ltd. Publishers Staff. (C). 1986. 65.00 (1-873376-06-5, Pub. by Spellmount UK) St Mut.

British Military Band Uniforms, Vol. 1: Cavalry Regiments, Vol. 3: English Infantry Regiments. Spellmount Ltd. Publishers Staff. (C). 1986. 65.00 (1-873376-07-3, Pub. by Spellmount UK) St Mut.

British Military Dilemma in Ireland: Occupation Politics, 1886-1914. Elizabeth Muenger. LC 91-11120. (Modern War Studies). 288p. 1991. 29.95 (0-7006-0487-1) U Pr of KS.

British Military Firearms, 1650-1850. Howard L. Blackmore. (Illus.). 144p. 1994. 50.00 (1-85367-172-X, 5406) Stackpole.

British Military Intelligence, 1870-1914: The Development of a Modern Intelligence Organization. Thomas G. Fergusson. LC 83-17094. 308p. 1984. text ed. 55.00 (0-313-27002-3, U7002, Greenwood Pr) Greenwood.

British Military Thought after World War II. Julian Lider. LC 83-20724. 200p. 1985. text ed. 74.95 (0-566-00638-3) Ashgate Pub Co.

British Milk Marketing & the Common Agricultural Policy: The Origins of Confusion & Crisis. Michael A. Hollingham & Richard W. Howarth. 220p. 1989. pap. text ed. 89.95 (0-566-05542-2, Pub. by Avebury Pub UK) Ashgate Pub Co.

***British Mining No. 33: The Yorkshire & Lancashire Lead Mines.** M. C. Gill. 68p. 1990. 65.00x (0-901450-32-4, Pub. by Northern Mine Res UK) St Mut.

***British Mining No. 35: The Gorinan Mines.** S. J. Hughes. 88p. 1990. 65.00x (0-901450-33-2, Pub. by Northern Mine Res UK) St Mut.

***British Mining No. 38: A History of the Manor & Lead Mines of Marrick.** L. O. Tyson. 72p. 1990. 65.00x (0-901450-35-9, Pub. by Northern Mine Res UK) St Mut.

***British Mining No. 44: Mining on Dartmoor & the Tamar Valley after 1913.** P. H. Richardson. 159p. 1990. 65.00x (0-901450-38-3, Pub. by Northern Mine Res UK) St Mut.

***British Mining No. 46: The Grassington Mines.** M. C. Gill. 160p. 1990. 65.00x (0-901450-39-1, Pub. by Northern Mine Res UK) St Mut.

***British Mining No. 47: The Mines of Alston Moor.** R. A. Fairbairn. 192p. 1990. 65.00x (0-901450-40-5, Pub. by Northern Mine Res UK) St Mut.

***British Mining No. 49: The Wharfedale Mines.** M. C. Gill. 122p. 1990. 65.00x (0-901450-41-3, Pub. by Northern Mine Res UK) St Mut.

British Modernist Fiction, 1920-1945. Ed. & Intro. by Harold Bloom. (Critical Cosmos Ser.). 426p. 1987. 59.95 (0-87754-987-7) Chelsea Hse.

British Monetary Policy & the Balance of Payments, 1951-1957. Peter B. Kenen. LC 60-11556. (Economic Studies: No. 116). 339p. 1960. 20.00 (0-674-08275-3) HUP.

British Monetary Policy, 1924-1931: The Norman Conquest of Four Dollars & Eighty-Six Cents. D. E. Moggridge. (Modern Revivals in Economic & Social History Ser.). 302p. 1992. 59.95 (0-7512-0092-1, Pub. by Gregg Revivals UK) Ashgate Pub Co.

***British Moralists & the Internal 'Ought' 1640-1740.** Stephen Darwall. 553p. (C). 1995. pap. 18.95 (0-521-45782-3) Cambridge U Pr.

***British Moralists & the Internal 'Ought' 1640-1740.** Stephen Darwall. 553p. (C). 1995. 59.95 (0-521-45167-1) Cambridge U Pr.

British Moralists, 1650-1800, 2 vols. Intro. by D. D. Raphael. 1991. reprint ed. Vol. I, Hobbes-Gay. write for info. (0-318-68108-0); reprint ed. Vol. II, Hume-Bentham. write for info. (0-318-68109-9); reprint ed. Vol. I, Hobbes-Gay. write for info. (0-318-68110-2); reprint ed. Vol. II, Hume-Bentham. write for info. (0-318-68111-0) Hackett Pub.

British Moralists, 1650-1800, 2 vols., Set. Intro. by D. D. Raphael. LC 90-85423. 1991. reprint ed. lib. bdg. 67.50 (0-87220-121-X); reprint ed. pap. text ed. 25.00 (0-87220-120-1) Hackett Pub.

***British Motor Industry.** James Foreman-Peck et al. LC 94-33151. (British Industries in the Twentieth Century Ser.). 1995. text ed. write for info. (0-7190-2612-1) St Martin.

***British Motor Sport Year 1995-96.** (Illus.). 192p. 1996. 49.95 (1-874557-61-6, Pub. by Hazelton UK) Motorbooks Intl.

British Motorcycles since Nineteen Fifty, Vol. 5, Pt. 1: The Company. Steve Wilson. (Illus.). 176p. 1991. 31.95 (1-85260-021-7) Haynes Pubns.

***British Multinational Banking 1830-1990.** Geoffrey Jones. (Illus.). 528p. 1995. reprint ed. pap. 28.00 (0-19-820602-X) OUP.

British Multinationals: Origins, Growth & Performance. Geoffrey Jones. 200p. 1986. text ed. 75.00 (0-566-00997-8) Ashgate Pub Co.

British Museum Book of Ancient Egypt. Ed. by Stephen Quirke & Jeffrey Spencer. LC 92-80823. (Illus.). 240p. 1992. pap. 19.95 (0-500-01550-3) Thames Hudson.

British Museum Book of Chinese Art. Ed. by Jessica Rawson. LC 92-61337. (Illus.). 396p. 1993. pap. 24.95 (0-500-27700-1) Thames Hudson.

British Museum Book of Flowers. Ann S. James et al. (Illus.). 190p. 1994. 24.95 (0-7141-1700-5) Parkwest Pubns.

British Museum Book of Greek & Roman Art. Lucilla Burn. LC 91-75165. (Illus.). 224p. 1992. pap. 24.95 (0-500-27657-9) Thames Hudson.

British Museum Book of the Rosetta Stone. Carol Andrews. (Dorset Reprints Ser.). (Illus.). 64p. 1991. 19.95 (0-88029-607-0) Marboro Bks.

British Museum Cookbook: Four Thousand Years of International Cuisine. Michelle Berriedale-Johnson. (Illus.). 160p. 1992. 16.95 (1-55859-367-5) Abbeville Pr.

British Museum Cotton Nero A. see Early English Manuscripts in Facsimile

***British Museum Egyptian Art Day Book.** 1992. 14.99 (1-85145-612-0, Pavilion Bks) Viking Penguin.

British Museum Expedition to Middle Egypt. Guy Brunton. LC 77-86429. reprint ed. 45.00 (0-404-16626-1) AMS Pr.

***British Museum III Vol. III: Japanese Art: The Great European Collections.** Kodansha Ltd. 208p. Date not set. 350.00 (4-06-253203-4) FS&G.

British Museum Is Falling Down. David Lodge. 192p. 1989. pap. 10.95 (0-14-012419-5, Penguin Bks) Viking Penguin.

British Museum Library: A Short History & Survey. Arundell J. Esdaile. LC 78-31145. (Library Association Ser.). 388p. 1979. reprint ed. text ed. 65.00 (0-313-20940-5, ESBM, Greenwood Pr) Greenwood.

British Museum, London see Oriental Ceramics: The World's Great Collections

British Museum (Natural History): Collections of Natural History Specimens & Drawings from the Endeavour Voyage of Captain Cook, 1768-1771, Pt. I: Botany: Australia. 183p. 1985. 99.00 (0-930466-92-6) Chadwyck-Healey.

British Museum (Natural History): Collections of Natural History Specimens & Drawings from the Endeavour Voyage of Captain Cook, 1768-1771, Pt. II: Botany: Brazil, Java, Madeira, New Zealand, Society Islands & Tierra del Fuego. 200p. 1987. 99.00 (0-930466-93-4) Chadwyck-Healey.

British Museum (Natural History): Collections of Natural History Specimens & Drawings from the Endeavour Voyage of Captain Cook, 1768-1771, Pt. III: Zoology. 172p. 1988. 99.00 (0-930466-98-5) Chadwyck-Healey.

British Music of Our Time: Music Book Index. Alfred L. Bacharach. 256p. 1993. reprint ed. lib. bdg. 79.00 (0-7812-9565-3) Rprt Serv.

British Music Publishers, Printers & Engravers. Frank Kidson. LC 67-23861. 1972. reprint ed. 18.95 (0-405-08701-2, Pub. by Blom Pubns UK) Ayer.

British Music Yearbook, 1980. 6th ed. Ed. by Arthur Jacobs. 637p. 1980. pap. 10.50 (0-8476-6255-1) Rowman.

British Musical Biography: A Dictionary of Musical Artists, Authors & Composers Born in Britain & Its Colonies. James D. Brown & Stephen S. Stratton. LC 76-139197. (Music Ser.). 1971. reprint ed. lib. bdg. 55.00 (0-306-70076-X) Da Capo.

British Musical Theatre, 2 Vols., Set. Kurt Ganzl. 2400p. 1987. 145.00 (0-19-520509-X) OUP.

British Mystery Writers, 1860-1919, Vol. 70. Ed. by Bernard Benstock & Thomas F. Staley. (Dictionary of Literary Biography Ser.: Vol. 70). 1988. 128.00 (0-8103-1748-6) Gale.

British Mystery Writers, 1920-1939, Vol. 77. Ed. by Bernard Benstock & Thomas F. Staley. (Dictionary of Literary Biography Ser.: Vol. 77). 414p. 1988. pap. 128.00 (0-8103-4555-2, 006545-M99348) Gale.

British Narrative Drawings & Watercolors 1660-1880: Twenty-Two Examples from the Huntington Collection. Shelley M. Bennett. LC 85-27262. (Illus.). 60p. 1985. pap. 3.00 (0-87328-089-X) Huntington Lib.

British Nationality: The Agin Guide to the New Law. Ann Dummett & Ian Martin. (C). 1988. 21.00 (0-946088-10-1, Pub. by NCCL UK) St Mut.

British Nationalization: Nineteen Forty-Five to Nineteen Seventy-Three. R. Kelf-Cohen. LC 73-86069. (C). 1974. text ed. 26.00 (0-312-10360-3) St Martin.

British Naval Administration in the Age of Walpole. Daniel A. Baugh. (Illus.). 1965. 77.50 (0-691-05107-0) Princeton U Pr.

British Naval Aircraft since Nineteen Twelve. 6th ed. Owen Thetford. LC 90-62896. (Putnam Aviation Ser.). (Illus.). 512p. 1991. 49.95 (1-55750-076-2) Naval Inst Pr.

British Naval Aviation: The Fleet Air Arm, 1917-1990. Ray Sturtivant. (Illus.). 224p. 1990. 29.95 (0-87021-026-2) Naval Inst Pr.

British Naval Documents 1204-1960. Ed. by John B. Hattendorf et al. (Publications of the Navy Records Society: Vol. 131). 1176p. 1993. 119.95 (0-85967-947-0, Pub. by Scolar Pr UK) Ashgate Pub Co.

British Naval History since Eighteen Fifteen: A Guide to Literature. Eugene L. Rasor. LC 90-3310. (Military History Bibliographies Ser.: Vol. 13). 864p. 1990. 90.00 (0-8240-7735-0, 1069) Garland.

British New Left. Lin Chun. 256p. 1993. 55.00 (0-7486-0422-7, Pub. by Edinburgh U Pr UK) Col U Pr.

British Newspapers & Periodicals, 1641-1700: A Short-Title Catalogue of Serials Printed in England, Scotland, Ireland & British America. Ed. by Carolyn Nelson & Matthew Seccombe. LC 86-33171. xx, 724p. 1988. 300.00 (0-87352-174-9) Modern Lang.

British Nineteenth Century Marine Painting. Denys Brook-Hart. (Illus.). 370p. 1976. 69.50 (0-902028-32-4) Antique Collect.

***British "Non-elite" MPs 1715-1820.** Ian R. Christie. 256p. 1995. 45.00 (0-19-820557-0) OUP.

British North Borneo: An Account of Its History, Resources & Native Tribes. Owen Rutter. LC 77-87001. reprint ed. 32.50 (0-404-16775-6) AMS Pr.

British Novel: Scott Through Hardy. Ian Watt. LC 72-96559. (Goldentree Bibliographies Series in Language & Literature). (C). 1973. pap. text ed. write for info. (0-88295-533-0) Harlan Davidson.

British Novel, Defoe to Austen: A Critical History. John A. Stevenson. (Twayne's Critical History of the Novel Ser.: No. 184). 184p. 1990. text ed. 20.95 (0-8057-7852-7, Twayne) Macmillan.

***British Novel 1945 to Present.** Higdon. 1995. 22.95 (0-8057-7859-4, Twayne) Macmillan.

British Novelists & Their Styles. David Masson. LC 72-10853. (Essay Index Reprint Ser.). 1977. reprint ed. 23.95 (0-8369-7230-9) Ayer.

British Novelists since Nineteen Hundred. Ed. by Jack I. Biles. LC 85-48000. (Georgia State Literary Studies: No. 1). 1987. 45.00 (0-404-63201-7) AMS Pr.

British Novelists since Nineteen Sixty, 2 Vols., Vol. 14. Ed. by Jay L. Halio. LC 82-2977. (Dictionary of Literary Biography Ser.: Vol. 14). (Illus.). 5514p. (C). 1983. 250.00 (0-8103-0927-0) Gale.

British Novelists, 1660-1800, 2 Vols., Vol. 39. 39th ed. Ed. by Martin C. Battestin. (Dictionary of Literary Biography Ser.: Vol. 39). 1577p. 1985. 250.00 (0-8103-1717-6) Gale.

British Novelists, 1890-1921: Traditionalists, Vol. 34. Ed. by Thomas F. Staley. (Dictionary of Literary Biography Ser.: Vol. 34). 392p. 1984. 128.00 (0-8103-1712-5) Gale.

British Novelists, 1890-1929: Modernists, Vol. 36. Ed. by Thomas F. Staley. LC 84-18723. (Dictionary of Literary Biography Ser.: Vol. 36). (Illus.). 408p. 1985. 128.00 (0-8103-1714-1) Gale.

British Novelists, 1930-1959, 2 vols., Set. Ed. by Bernard Oldsey. (Dictionary of Literary Biography Ser.: Vol. 15). 713p. 1983. pap. 238.00 (0-8103-1637-4, 006392-M99348) Gale.

British Novelists, 1930-1959, 2 Vols., Vol. 15. Ed. by Bernard Oldsey. (Dictionary of Literary Biography Ser.: Vol. 15). (Illus.). 376p. 1983. Set. 250.00 (0-8103-0938-6) Gale.

***British Nuclear Deterrent after the Cold War: After the Cold War.** Nicholas K. Witney. LC 94-44369. 143p. 1995. pap. text ed. 9.00 (0-8330-1619-9) Rand Corp.

British Nuclear Policymaking. Christopher J. Bowie & Alan Platt. LC 83-22953. 1984. 7.50 (0-8330-0534-0, R-3085-AF) Rand Corp.

***British Object Relations Theory & Therapy: An Introductory Reading Program.** David E. Scharff. LC 94-24240. 1995. text ed. 40.00 (1-56821-419-7) Aronson.

British Object Sculptors of the Eighties, Nos. 48 & 1. Ed. by Kyoichi Tsuzuki. (Art Random Ser.). (Illus.). 48p. 1990. 32.95 (4-7636-8511-2, Pub. by Kyoto Shoin JA) Bks Nippan.

British Object Sculptors of the Eighties, Nos. 49 & 2. Ed. by Kyoichi Tsuzuki. (Art Random Ser.). (Illus.). 48p. 1990. 32.95 (4-7636-8512-0, Pub. by Kyoto Shoin JA) Bks Nippan.

British Officers Serving in America, 1754-1774. Worthington C. Ford. 1972. 59.95 (0-87968-792-4) Gordon Pr.

British Official Publications. 2nd ed. J. E. Pemberton. LC 73-16231. 328p. 1973. 137.00 (0-08-017797-2, Pub. by Pergamon Repr UK) Franklin.

British Official Publications Not Published by HMSO Catalogue. 1987. 290.00 (0-85964-209-7) Chadwyck-Healey.

British Official Publications Not Published by HMSO Catalogue. 1988. 310.00 (0-85964-214-3) Chadwyck-Healey.

British Official Publications Not Published by HMSO Catalogue. 1989. 335.00 (0-85964-219-4) Chadwyck-Healey.

British Official Publications Not Published by HMSO Catalogue. 1990. 365.00 (0-85964-225-9) Chadwyck-Healey.

British Oil Policy, 1919-1939. B. S. McBeth. (Illus.). 190p. 1985. 35.00 (0-7146-3229-5, Pub. by F Cass Pubs UK) Intl Spec Bk.

British Opera in America: Children in the Wood, 1795 & Blue Beard, 1811. Ed. by Susan L. Porter. LC 93-49049. (Nineteenth-Century American Musical Theater Ser.). (Illus.). 314p. 1994. 70.00 (0-8153-1368-3) Garland.

British Opinions on the Protecting System see Journal of the Proceedings of the Friends of Domestic Industry: In General Convention Met at the City of New York, October 26, 1831

British Orders, Decorations, & Medals in the Robert B. Honeyman, Jr. Collection of Orders, Decorations, & Medals. (Illus.). 110p. 1979. 14.00 (0-938644-12-2); pap. 9.00 (0-938644-11-4) Nat Hist Mus.

British Overseas Investment: 1918-1931. John M. Atkin. Ed. by Stuart Bruchey. LC 77-81821. (Dissertations in European Economic History Ser.). (Illus.). 1978. lib. bdg. 41.95 (0-405-10774-9) Ayer.

British Overseas Investments, 1907-1948: An Original Anthology. Mira Wilkins. LC 76-29782. (European Business Ser.). 1977. reprint ed. lib. bdg. 34.95 (0-405-09783-2) Ayer.

British Paediatric Association Manual on Infections & Immunizations in Children. Ed. by Angus Nicoll & Peter Rudd. (Illus.). 376p. 1989. pap. 19.95 (0-19-261785-0) OUP.

British Paediatric Association Manual on Infections & Immunizations in Children. 2nd ed. Ed. by Peter Rudd & Angus Nicoll. (Illus.). 320p. 1991. pap. 27.50 (0-19-262118-1) OUP.

British Paint Industry. F. Armitage. LC 66-3062. 1967. 75.00 (0-08-012351-1, Pub. by Pergamon Repr UK) Franklin.

British Painting in the Philadelphia Museum of Art. Richard Dorment. LC 86-8105. (Illus.). 485p. 1986. 69.95 (0-8122-8035-0, PA Mus Art) U of Pa Pr.

British Painting in the Philadelphia Museum of Art: From the Seventeenth Through the Nineteenth Century. Richard Dorment. LC 86-8105. 468p. (Orig.). 1986. pap. 25.00 (0-87633-065-0) Phila Mus Art.

British Paintings in the National Gallery of Art. Ed. by John Hayes. (Collections of the National Gallery of Art Systematic Catalogue). (Illus.). 350p. (C). 1993. 90.00 (0-521-41066-5) Cambridge U Pr.

British Paper Industry, Fourteen Ninety-Five to Eighteen Sixty: A Study in Industrial Growth. Donald C. Coleman. LC 75-74. (Illus.). 367p. 1975. reprint ed. text ed. 65.00 (0-8371-8015-5, COBP, Greenwood Pr) Greenwood.

British Paramountcy: British-Baroda Relations, 1818-1848. Mani Kamerkar. 253p. 1980. 34.50 (0-940500-75-2, Pub. by Popular Prakashan II) Asia Bk Corp.

British Parliamentary Democracy. 3rd ed. Sydney D. Bailey. LC 77-18752. (Illus.). 248p. 1978. reprint ed. text ed. 59.75 (0-313-20195-1, BABR, Greenwood Pr) Greenwood.

British Parliamentary Papers: 19th Century, 1112 vols. Irish University Press Staff. write for info. (0-318-68510-8, Pub. by Irish Acad Pr IE) Intl Spec Bk.

British Parliamentary Papers Relating to India (1662-1947), 3 vols., I. Ed. by Adrian Sever. (C). 1992. write for info. (81-7018-618-8, Pub. by BR Pub II) S Asia.

British Parliamentary Papers Relating to India (1662-1947), 3 vols., II. Ed. by Adrian Sever. (C). 1992. write for info. (81-7018-619-6, Pub. by BR Pub II) S Asia.

An Asterisk (*) at the beginning of an entry indicates that the title is appearing in BIP for the first time.

An Asterisk (*) at the beginning of an entry indicates that the title is appearing in BIP for the first time.

British Ranchero in Old California: The Life & Times of Henry Dalton & the Rancho Azusa. 2nd ed. Sheldon Jackson. LC 77-79745. (Western Frontiersmen Ser.: Vol. XVII). (Illus.). 265p. 1987. 24.50 (*0-87062-122-X*) A H Clark.

British Readings in Financial Management. Ed. by Stewart Ivison et al. 416p. (C). 1986. 40.00 (*0-06-318361-7*, Pub. by P Chapman Pub UK) St Mut.

***British Realist Theatre: The New Wave in Its Context, 1956-1965.** Stephen Lacey. LC 94-44677. 1995. write for info. (*0-415-07782-6*); pap. write for info. (*0-415-12311-9*) Routledge.

British Rearmament in the Thirties: Politics & Profits. Robert P. Shay, Jr. LC 76-45911. 1977. 49.50x (*0-691-05248-4*) Princeton U Pr.

***British Rearmament in the Thirties: Politics & Profits.** Robert P. Shay. LC 76-45911. (Illus.). Date not set. reprint ed. pap. 94.40 (*0-7837-9443-6*, 2060185) Bks Demand.

British Reference Catalogue of Current Literature, 1874-1940. 1972. 350.00 (*0-87968-793-2*) Gordon Pr.

British Regime in Wisconsin & the Northwest. Louise T. Kellogg. LC 74-124927. (American Scene Ser.). (Illus.). 1971. reprint ed. lib. bdg. 45.00 (*0-306-71047-1*) Da Capo.

British Regional Geology: Bristol & Gloucester Region. 3rd ed. 188p. 1993. pap. 16.00 (*0-11-884482-2*, HM44822, Pub. by HMSO UK) UNIPUB.

British Regionalism, 1900-2000. Ed. by P. Garside & M. Hebbert. 200p. 1989. text ed. 80.00 (*0-7201-2013-6*, Mansell Pub) Cassell.

British Regulars in Montreal: An Imperial Garrison, 1832-1854. Elinor K. Senior. LC 81-178941. 302p. reprint ed. pap. 86.10 (*0-7837-1044-5*, 2041355) Bks Demand.

British Regulation of the Colonial Iron Industry. Arthur C. Bining. LC 68-55481. (Library of Early American Business & Industry: No. 60). 1973. reprint ed. 29.50 (*0-678-00924-4*) Kelley.

British Relations with the Hill Tribes of Assam Since Eighteen Fifty-Eight. Birendra C. Chakravorty. 1981. 12.50 (*0-8364-0705-9*, Pub. by Mukhopadhyaya II) S Asia.

***British Relations with the Malay Rulers from Decentralization to Malayan Independence, 1930-1957.** Simon C. Smith. (South-East Asian Historical Monographs). (Illus.). 184p. 1995. 38.00 (*967-65-3089-1*) OUP.

British Republic, 1649-1660. Ronald Hutton. LC 89-24156. 160p. 1990. text ed. 45.00 (*0-312-04065-2*) St Martin.

British Research & Development Aircraft. Ray Sturtivant. (Illus.). 216p. 1990. 39.95 (*0-85429-697-2*, Pub. by G T Foulis Ltd) Haynes Pubns.

British Robot Association Annual Conference, 6th, 1984. T. E. Brock. 1984. 64.00 (*0-444-86685-X*, I-506-83, North Holland) Elsevier.

British Robot Association Annual Conference, 7th: Proceedings of the Conference, Cambridge, U. K., May 14-16, 1984. Ed. by T. E. Brock. 300p. 1984. 74.50 (*0-444-87532-8*, North Holland) Elsevier.

British Romantic Art & the Second World War. Stuart Sillars. LC 91-17375. 273p. 1991. text ed. 55.00 (*0-312-06719-4*) St Martin.

British Romantic Novelists, 1789-1832, Vol. 116. Ed. by Bradford K. Mudge. LC 92-9153. (Dictionary of Literary Biography Ser.: Vol. 116). 1992. 128.00 (*0-8103-7593-1*) Gale.

British Romantic Painting. Raymond Lister. (Illus.). 176p. (C). 1989. 59.95 (*0-521-35604-0*) Cambridge U Pr.

British Romantic Painting. Raymond Lister. (Illus.). 176p. (C). 1990. pap. 27.95 (*0-521-35687-3*) Cambridge U Pr.

British Romantic Writers & the East: Anxieties of Empire. Nigel Leask. LC 92-11690. (Cambridge Studies in Romanticism: No. 12). (Illus.). 276p. (C). 1993. 59.95 (*0-521-41168-8*) Cambridge U Pr.

British Royal Bookplates: And Ex-Libris of Related Families. Brian N. Lee. 280p. 1991. text ed. 120.00 (*0-85967-883-0*, Pub. by Scolar Pr UK) Ashgate Pub Co.

British Royal Commemorative. Geoffrey Warren. 1994. 10.98 (*0-7858-0153-7*) Bk Sales Inc.

British Royalty Commemoratives. Douglas Flynn & Alan Bolton. LC 94-65430. (Illus.). 176p. (Orig.). 1994. pap. 19.95 (*0-88740-601-7*) Schiffer.

British Rule in Burma, Eighteen Twenty-Four to Nineteen Forty-Two. Godfrey E. Harvey. reprint ed. 22.50 (*0-404-54834-2*) AMS Pr.

British Rule in Malaya: The Malayan Civil Service & Its Predecessors, 1867-1942. Robert Heussler. LC 80-658. (Contributions in Comparative Colonial Studies: No. 6). (Illus.). xx, 356p. 1981. text ed. 79.50 (*0-313-22243-6*, HBM/, Greenwood Pr) Greenwood.

British Rust Fungi. Malcolm Wilson & D. M. Henderson. 402p. reprint ed. pap. 114.60 (*0-8357-7429-5*, 2024560) Bks Demand.

British Samplers: A Concise History. Jane Toller. 64p. (C). 1980. 30.00 (*0-85033-383-0*) St Mut.

British Science & Politics Since 1945. Thomas Wilkie. (Making Contemporary Britain Ser.). 176p. (C). 1991. text ed. 34.95 (*0-631-16851-6*) Blackwell Pubs.

British Science Fiction: A Chronology, 1478-1990. Nicholas Ruddick. LC 92-6409. (Bibliographies & Indexes in World Literature Ser.: No. 35). 320p. 1992. text ed. 65.00 (*0-313-28002-9*, RBF, Greenwood Pr) Greenwood.

British Science Fiction Paperbacks, 1949-1956: An Annotated Bibliography & Guide. Philip Harbottle & Stephen Holland. LC 87-752. (Borgo Literary Guide Ser.: No. 7). 232p. 1994. lib. bdg. 31.00x (*0-89370-821-6*); pap. 21.00x (*0-89370-921-2*) Borgo Pr.

British Scientists & the Manhattan Project: The Los Alamos Years. Ferenc M. Szasz. LC 91-19904. 208p. 1992. text ed. 45.00 (*0-312-06167-6*) St Martin.

***British Sculpture & the Company Raj: Church Monuments & Public Statuary in Madras, Calcutta, & Bombay to 1858.** Barbara Groseclose. LC 94-25643. (Illus.). 152p. (C). 1995. 47.50x (*0-87413-406-4*) U Delaware Pr.

British Seaman. Christopher Lloyd. LC 76-118123. (Illus.). 319p. 1975. 32.50 (*0-8386-7708-8*) Fairleigh Dickinson.

British Seas: An Introduction to the Oceanography & Resources of the North-West European Continental Shelf. Jack Hardisty. 208p. 1990. 75.00 (*0-415-03586-4*, A4708) Routledge.

***British Season.** Cook. 1995. pap. text ed. 24.95 (*0-316-12485-0*) Little.

British Security Policy: The Thatcher Years & the End of the Cold War. Ed. by Stuart Croft. 240p. 1991. 49.95 (*0-04-445820-7*, A8156); pap. 18.95 (*0-04-445819-3*, A8157) Routledge Chapman & Hall.

British Service Rifles & Carbines 1888-1900. Alan M. Petrillo. (Illus.). 72p. (Orig.). 1994. pap. 11.95 (*1-880677-05-9*) Excalibur NY.

British Settlers in Natal, Vol. 5. Shelagh O. Spencer. 1990. 39.95 (*0-86980-700-5*, Pub. by Univ Natal Pr SA) Intl Spec Bk.

British Shipbuilding Industry Eighteen Seventy to Nineteen Fourteen. Sidney Pollard & Paul Robertson. LC 78-12500. (Studies in Business History: No. 30). 336p. 1979. 34.50 (*0-674-08287-7*) HUP.

British Shipping. 2nd ed. R. H. Thornton. LC 60-269. (Illus.). 298p. reprint ed. pap. 85.00 (*0-8357-7430-9*, 2022477) Bks Demand.

British Shipping: Its History, Organization & Importance. Adam W. Kirkaldy. LC 69-13756. (Illus.). 1970. reprint ed. 57.50 (*0-678-05558-0*) Kelley.

British Ships & Shipping. Peter Duff. 1977. lib. bdg. 59.95 (*0-8490-1556-1*) Gordon Pr.

British Shotgun, Vol. I (1850-1870) I. M. Crudgington & D. J. Baker. (Illus.). 256p. 1991. 60.00 (*0-940143-56-9*) Safari Pr.

British Shotgun, Vol. II (1871-1890) I. M. Crudgington & D. J. Baker. (Illus.). 250p. 1989. 60.00 (*0-940143-47-X*) Safari Pr.

British Sieges: Peninsular War. Spellmount Ltd. Publishers Staff. (C). 1986. 125.00 (*0-685-60256-7*, Pub. by Spellmount UK) St Mut.

British Sieges of the Peninsular War, 1811-1813. Frederick Myatt. 200p. (C). 1991. 95.00 (*0-946771-59-6*, Pub. by Spellmount UK) St Mut.

British Silhouette Artists & Their Work: 1760-1860. Sue McKechnie. (Illus.). 798p. 1978. 85.00 (*0-85667-036-7*) Sothebys Pubns.

British Silver in the Huntington Collection. Robert R. Wark. LC 78-4315. (Illus.). 172p. 1978. text ed. 12.00 (*0-87328-073-3*) Huntington Lib.

British Skeleton Clocks. Derek Roberts. 272p. 1987. 79.50 (*1-85149-059-0*) Antique Collect.

British Slave Emancipation: The Sugar Colonies & the Great Experiment, 1830-1865. William A. Green. (Illus.). 464p. 1991. pap. 24.95 (*0-19-820278-4*) OUP.

British Slave Trade Suppression Policies 1821-1865: Impact & Implications. E. Phillip LeVeen. Ed. by Stuart Bruchey. LC 77-77179. (Dissertations in European Economic History Ser.). (Illus.). 1978. lib. bdg. 26.95 (*0-405-10792-7*) Ayer.

British Social Attitudes: Cumulative Sourcebook. Ed. by Roger Jowell et al. 500p. 1991. text ed. 95.00 (*0-566-05829-4*, Pub. by Gower UK) Ashgate Pub Co.

British Social Attitudes: The Eighth Report. Ed. by Roger Jowell et al. 384p. 1991. 59.95 (*1-85521-258-7*, Pub. by Dartmth Pub UK) Ashgate Pub Co.

***British Social Attitudes: The Eleventh Report.** Ed. by Roger Jowell et al. 250p. 1994. text ed. 62.95 (*1-85521-605-1*, Pub. by Dartmth Pub UK) Ashgate Pub Co.

British Social Attitudes: The Fifth Report. Roger Jowell et al. 274p. 1988. text ed. 59.95 (*0-566-05699-2*, Pub. by Gower UK) Ashgate Pub Co.

British Social Attitudes: The Seventh Report. Roger Jowell et al. 300p. 1990. text ed. 64.95 (*0-566-05840-5*, Pub. by Gower UK); pap. text ed. 37.95 (*0-566-05844-8*, Pub. by Gower UK) Ashgate Pub Co.

British Social Attitudes: The 1985 Report. Ed. by Roger Jowell & Sharon Witherspoon. 271p. 1985. text ed. 64.95 (*0-566-00738-X*) Ashgate Pub Co.

British Social Attitudes: The 1987 Report. Roger Jowell et al. 250p. 1987. text ed. 64.95 (*0-566-00740-1*, Pub. by Gower UK) Ashgate Pub Co.

British Social Attitudes: Special International Report: The 6th Report. Ed. by Roger Jowell et al. (Illus.). 224p. 1989. text ed. 63.95 (*0-566-05821-9*, Pub. by Gower UK) Ashgate Pub Co.

British Social Attitudes 1992 - 9th Report. Ed. by Roger Jowell et al. 384p. 1992. 59.95 (*1-85521-328-1*, Pub. by Dartmth Pub UK) Ashgate Pub Co.

British Social Policy & Female Infanticide in India. Lalita Panigrahi. 1972. 16.00 (*0-8364-2617-7*, Pub. by Munshiram Manoharial II) S Asia.

***British Social Policy since 1945.** Howard Glennerster. (Making Contemporary Britain Ser.). 352p. (C). Date not set. write for info. (*0-631-18961-0*); pap. write for info. (*0-631-18962-9*) Blackwell Pubs.

British Social Politics. Carlton Hayes. LC 72-37885. (Select Bibliographies Reprint Ser.). 1977. reprint ed. 35.95 (*0-8369-6722-4*) Ayer.

British Social Reform & German Precedents: The Case of Social Insurance 1880-1914. E. P. Hennock. (Illus.). 256p. 1987. 58.00 (*0-19-820127-3*) OUP.

***British Social Welfare: Past, Present & Future.** Ed. by David Gladstone. 320p. 1995. pap. 24.95x (*1-85728-198-5*, Pub. by UCL Pr UK) Taylor & Francis.

British Social Work in the Nineteenth Century. Agnes F. Young & E. T. Ashton. LC 83-22739. (International Library of Sociology & Social Reconstruction). vii, 264p. 1984. reprint ed. text ed. 41.50 (*0-313-24390-5*, YBSW, Greenwood Pr) Greenwood.

British Socialists: The Journey from Fantasy to Politics. Stanley Pierson. LC 78-25820. 415p. 1979. reprint ed. pap. 118.30 (*0-7837-1720-2*, 2057249) Bks Demand.

British Socialists & the Politics of Popular Culture, 1884-1914. Chris Waters. LC 89-62182. 260p. 1990. 37.50 (*0-8047-1758-3*) Stanford U Pr.

British Society since Nineteen Forty-Five. Arthur Marwick. (Social History of Britain Ser.). 300p. 1983. mass mkt. 6.95 (*0-14-021906-4*, Penguin Bks) Viking Penguin.

British Society Since Nineteen Forty-Five. Arthur Marwick. (Pelican Social History of Britain Ser.). 302p. 1984. 15.95 (*0-317-00889-7*) Allen Lane.

***British Soldiers Firearm, 1850-1864.** C. H. Roads. (Illus.). 336p. 1994. reprint ed. 53.00 (*1-884849-13-X*) R&R Bks.

***British Sources of the Economic, Political & Social History of the Mysore State 1799-1812 Vol. 1: Purnaiah's Administration.** Ed. by M. H. Gopal. (C). 1993. 21.00x (*81-7154-570-X*, Pub. by Popular Prakashan II) S Asia.

***British Sources of the Economic, Political & Social History of the Mysore State 1813-1832 Vol. 2: Raja's Administration.** Ed. by M. H. Gopal. (C). 1993. 21.00x (*81-7154-571-8*, Pub. by Popular Prakashan II) S Asia.

***British South Africa Company's Medal: The 1890 Mashonsland Medal.** Roberts Staff. (C). 1989. 95.00x (*1-873058-45-4*, Pub. by Roberts UK) St Mut.

***British South Africa Company's Medal: The 1893 Metabeleland Medal.** Roberts Staff. (C). 1989. 95.00x (*1-873058-50-0*, Pub. by Roberts UK) St Mut.

***British South Africa Company's Medal: The 1896 Rhodesia Medal.** Roberts Staff. (C). 1989. 95.00x (*1-873058-55-1*, Pub. by Roberts UK) St Mut.

***British South Africa Company's Medal: The 1897 Mashonsland Medal.** Roberts Staff. (C). 1989. 95.00x (*1-873058-60-8*, Pub. by Roberts UK) St Mut.

***British South Africa Company's Medal Complete Roll.** Roberts Staff. (C). 1989. 360.00x (*1-873058-40-3*, Pub. by Roberts UK) St Mut.

British Special Operations Explored: Yugoslavia in Turmoil, 1941-1943, & the British Response. M. Deroc. 320p. 1988. text ed. 47.00 (*0-88033-139-9*) East Eur Quarterly.

British Specialist Cars: Low Volume Production Cars & Kit Cars since World War II. Chris Rees. (Illus.). 208p. 1993. 39.95 (*1-872004-22-9*, Pub. by Windrow & Green UK) Motorbooks Intl.

British Sport: A Social History. Dennis Brailsford. LC 92-32237. (Illus.). 160p. 1992. lib. bdg. 49.50 (*0-389-21002-1*) B&N Imports.

British Sporting & Animal Drawings, 1500-1850. Judy Egerton & Dudley Snelgrove. (Illus.). 126p. 1978. 50.00 (*0-905005-52-X*) Yale Ctr Brit Art.

British Sporting & Animal Paintings, 1655-1867. Judy Egerton. (Illus.). 382p. 1978. 50.00 (*0-905005-51-1*) Yale Ctr Brit Art.

British Sporting & Animal Prints, 1658-1874. Dudley Snelgrove. (Illus.). 257p. 1981. 50.00 (*0-905005-54-6*) Yale Ctr Brit Art.

British Sporting Art in the Twentieth Century. Stella A. Walker. (Illus.). 248p. 1990. 55.00 (*0-948253-36-3*, Pub. by Sportmans Pr UK) Trafalgar.

British Sporting Paintings: The Paul Mellon Collection in the Virginia Museum of Fine Arts. Judy Egerton. Ed. by Anne B. Barriault. LC 85-22551. (Illus.). 104p. 1985. 40.00 (*0-917046-24-2*, U of Wash Pr); pap. 19.95 (*0-917046-23-4*, U of Wash Pr) Va Mus Arts.

British Sporting Rifle Cartridges: A Summary of Case Types, Headstamps, Bullets, & Charge Variations. Bill Fleming. LC 93-8680. 1993. write for info. (*0-939683-11-3*) Armory Pubns.

British Spy Novel. John Atkins. 288p. 1989. pap. 14.95 (*0-7145-4056-0*) Riverrun NY.

British State & the Ulster Crisis: From Wilson to Thatcher. Paul Bew & Henry Patterson. 154p. 1985. text ed. 24.95 (*0-86091-107-1*, A0857, Pub. by Verso UK); pap. text ed. 12.95 (*0-86091-815-7*, A0861, Pub. by Verso UK) Routledge Chapman & Hall.

British Statutes in American Law. Elizabeth G. Brown. LC 73-21605. (American Constitutional & Legal History Ser). 1974. reprint ed. lib. bdg. 42.50 (*0-306-70610-5*) Da Capo.

British Statutes in American Law, 1776-1836. Elizabeth G. Brown. LC 64-64845. (Michigan Legal Publications). xii, 377p. 1984. reprint ed. lib. bdg. 45.00 (*0-89941-321-8*, 303130) W S Hein.

British Steel: An Industry Between the State & the Private Sector. Heidrun Abromeit. LC 85-4205. 288p. 1986. text ed. 39.95 (*0-312-10541-X*) St Martin.

British Steel Act, 1988, Chapter 35. 1988. pap. 8.00 (*0-10-543588-0*, HM3989, Pub. by HMSO UK) UNIPUB.

British Steel Corporation: A Report on the Efficiency & Costs in Discharging Its Functions of the British Steel Corporation. (Reports of the Monopolies & Mergers Commission). (Illus.). 225p. 1988. pap. 30.00 (*0-10-104372-4*, HM3948, Pub. by HMSO UK) UNIPUB.

British Strategic Bombing Policy from World War I Through 1940: Politics, Attitudes, & the Formation of a Lasting Pattern. Harvey B. Tress. LC 87-28931. (Studies in British History: Vol. 12). 450p. 1989. 109.95 (*0-88946-464-2*) E Mellen.

***British Studies Sampler.** Ed. by Richard D. Fulton. ii, 193p. 1994. pap. 12.95 (*0-614-04710-2*) Vic Periodicals.

British Subjects. Fred D'Aguiar. 64p. 1994. pap. 12.95 (*1-85224-248-5*, Pub. by Bloodaxe Bks UK) Dufour.

British Subministers & Colonial America, 1763-1783. Franklin B. Wickwire. 1966. 37.50 (*0-691-04509-7*) Princeton U Pr.

***British Subministers & Colonial America, 1763-1783.** Franklin B. Wickwire. LC 66-10274. Date not set. reprint ed. pap. 68.40 (*0-7837-9484-3*, 2060226) Bks Demand.

British System of Government. Anthony H. Birth. LC 92-1632. 1992. write for info. (*0-415-09082-2*, Routledge NY) Routledge.

British System of Government. 9th ed. Anthony H. Birch. LC 93-17073. 256p. 1993. pap. 19.95 (*0-415-08937-9*, B2483) Routledge.

British Tanganyika: An Essay & Documents on District Administration. Robert Heussler. LC 78-142291. 168p. reprint ed. pap. 47.90 (*0-8357-7431-7*, 2023401) Bks Demand.

British Tar in Fact & Fiction. Charles N. Robinson. (Illus.). 1968. reprint ed. 43.00 (*1-55888-938-8*) Omnigraphics Inc.

British Tax Review, 1956-1992, Set. 2,432.00 (*0-8377-9028-X*) Rothman.

British Teapots & Tea Drinking. (Illus.). 320p. 1991. pap. 36.95 (*0-11-701509-1*, HM8005, Pub. by HMSO UK) UNIPUB.

British Technology & European Industrialization: The Norwegian Textile Industry in the Mid-Nineteenth Century. Kristine Bruland. (Illus.). 206p. (C). 1989. 54.95 (*0-521-35083-2*) Cambridge U Pr.

British Television: An Illustrated Guide. Comp. by Tise Vahimagi. (Illus.). 360p. 1995. 39.95 (*0-19-812267-5*) OUP.

British Television Drama in the 1980s. Intro. by George W. Brandt. LC 92-41630. (Illus.). 284p. (C). 1993. pap. 17.95 (*0-521-42723-1*) Cambridge U Pr.

British Territorial Units 1914-18. R. Westlake. (Men-at-Arms Ser.: No. 245). (Illus.). 48p. pap. 11.95 (*1-85532-168-8*, 9208, Pub. by Osprey UK) Stackpole.

British Tertiary Volcanic Province. C. H. Emeleus & M. C. Gyopari. (Geological Conservation Review Ser.: No. 4). 192p. 1992. 155.00 (*0-412-47980-X*, A9670) Chapman & Hall.

British Textiles from 1850 to 1900: The Victoria & Albert Museum Textile Collection. 1993. pap. 19.95 (*1-55859-653-4*) Abbeville Pr.

British Theatre. Elizabeth Inchbald. 1988. reprint ed. lib. bdg. 75.00 (*0-7812-0235-3*) Rprt Serv.

British Theatre, 25 vols., Set. Elizabeth S. Inchbald. (BCL1-PR English Literature Ser.). 1992. reprint ed. lib. bdg. 2,250.00 (*0-7812-7151-7*) Rprt Serv.

British Theatre: Its Repertory & Practice, 1100-1900 A. D. Ernest J. Burton. LC 77-22954. (Illus.). 271p. 1977. reprint ed. text ed. 59.75 (*0-8371-9739-2*, BUBT, Greenwood Pr) Greenwood.

British Theatre & Other Arts. Shirley S. Kenny. LC 82-48158. (Illus.). 312p. 1984. 44.50 (*0-918016-65-7*) Folger Bks.

British Theatre Design, 1978-1988. John Goodwin. (Illus.). 208p. 1989. text ed. 55.00 (*0-312-03724-4*) St Martin.

British Theatre in the Eighteen Nineties: Essays on Drama & the Stage. Ed. by Richard Foulkes. (Illus.). 188p. (C). 1992. 64.95 (*0-521-41478-4*) Cambridge U Pr.

British Theatre: or A Collection of Plays, 25 vols., Set. Ed. by Elizabeth Inchbald. (Anglistica & Americana Ser.: No. 84). 9316p. 1970. reprint ed. 1,287.00 (*0-317-05064-8*, 05102833, Pub. by Georg Olms GW) Lubrecht & Cramer.

British Theatre Yearbook, 1989. Ed. by David Lemmon. 360p. 1989. text ed. 39.95 (*0-312-03198-X*) St Martin.

British Theatre Yearbook, 1990. Ed. by David Lemmon. 384p. 1990. text ed. 45.00 (*0-312-04531-X*) St Martin.

British Thought & Thinkers: From John of Salisbury & Roger Bacon to John Stuart Mill & Herbert Spencer. George S. Morris. 1977. lib. bdg. 59.95 (*0-8490-1557-X*) Gordon Pr.

British Thought & Thinkers: Introductory Studies, Critical, Biographical & Philosophical. George S. Morris. LC 75-3286. reprint ed. 26.00 (*0-404-59274-0*) AMS Pr.

British Tokens & Their Values. M. Dickinson & P. F. Purvey. (Illus.). 1984. lib. bdg. 16.00 (*0-685-43016-2*, Pub. by Seaby UK) S J Durst.

British Town & Country Planning. Ed. by Eric Reade. 288p. 1987. 90.00 (*0-335-15509-X*, Open Univ Pr); pap. 34.00 (*0-335-15508-1*, Open Univ Pr) Taylor & Francis.

British Tractors for World Farming: An Illustrated History. Michael Williams. (Illus.). 112p. pap. 10.95 (*0-7137-1407-7*, Pub. by Blndford Pr UK) Diamond Farm Bk.

***British Trade & the Opening of China, 1800-42.** Michael Greenberg. LC 79-12206. reprint ed. pap. 71.30 (*0-7837-9608-0*, 2060365) Bks Demand.

British Trade Cycles & American Bank Credit: Some Aspects of Economic Fluctuations in the United States, 1815-1840. Burke A. Parsons. Ed. by Stuart Bruchey. LC 76-39839. (Nineteen Seventy-Seven Dissertations Ser.). (Illus.). 1977. lib. bdg. 37.95 (*0-405-09919-3*) Ayer.

British Trade Fluctuations, 1868-1896: Dissertations in European Economic History II. Walt W. Rostow. Ed. by Stuart Bruchey. LC 80-2828. (Illus.). 1981. lib. bdg. 49.00 (*0-686-73124-7*) Ayer.

British Trade Unionism. Allen Hunt. 1975. pap. 25.00 (*0-8464-0216-5*) Beekman Pubs.

British Trade Unionism Against the Trades Union Congress. Gerald A. Dorfman. LC 82-83300. (Publication Ser.: No. 281). vii, 165p. 1983. 9.98 (*0-8179-7811-9*) Hoover Inst Pr.

916

An Asterisk (*) at the beginning of an entry indicates that the title is appearing in BIP for the first time.

British Trade Unionism, 1770-1990: A Reader in History. Keith Laybourn. (C). 1991. pap. text ed. 15.00 (*0-86299-784-4*) A Sutton Pub.

British Trade Unions & the Problem of Change. Will Paynter. LC 75-123196. 172p. reprint ed. pap. 49.10 (*0-8357-7432-5*, 2023835) Bks Demand.

British Trade Unions Today. C. Jenkins & J. E. Mortimer. 1965. 62.00 (*0-08-011169-6*, Pub. by Pergamon Repr UK) Franklin.

British Trademarks of the 1920s & 1930s. John Mendenhall. (Illus.). 130p. 1989. pap. 14.95 (*0-87701-577-5*) Chronicle Bks.

***British Tradition of Federalism.** Michael Burgess. LC 95-2304. 240p. 1995. 39.50 (*0-8386-3618-7*) Fairleigh Dickinson.

British Trans-Atlantic Slave Trade, Sixteen Fifty to Seventeen Seventy-Five. Richard N. Bean. LC 75-2575. (Dissertations in American Economic History Ser.). (Illus.). 1978. 28.95 (*0-405-07256-2*) Ayer.

British Transport Industry & the European Community. P. Mackie et al. (Institute for Transport Studies: Vol. 3). 120p. 1987. text ed. 54.95 (*0-566-05368-3*, Pub. by Avebury Pub UK) Ashgate Pub Co.

British Traveller in America, 1836-1860. Max Berger. LC 78-39433. (Columbia University. Studies in the Social Sciences: No. 502). reprint ed. 20.00 (*0-404-51502-9*) AMS Pr.

British Travellers in Holland During the Stuart Period: Edward Browne & John Locke as Tourists in the United Provinces. C. D. Van Strien. (Studies in Intellectual History, Vol. 42; Publications of the Sir Thomas Browne Institute, New Ser.: No. 13). 444p. 1992. 111.50 (*90-04-09482-2*) E J Brill.

British Unemployment, 1919-1939: A Study in Public Policy. W. R. Garside. (Illus.). 416p. (C). 1990. 79.95 (*0-521-36443-4*) Cambridge U Pr.

British Union-Catalogue of Early Music Printed Before the Year 1801: A Record of the Holdings of over One Hundred Libraries Throughout the British Isles, 2 vols., 1. Ed. by Edith B. Schnapper. LC 58-526. reprint ed. pap. 150.80 (*0-8357-7433-3*, 2025753) Bks Demand.

British Union-Catalogue of Early Music Printed Before the Year 1801: A Record of the Holdings of over One Hundred Libraries Throughout the British Isles, 2 vols., 2. Ed. by Edith B. Schnapper. LC 58-526. 595p. reprint ed. pap. 169.60 (*0-8357-7434-1*) Bks Demand.

British Unitarians Against American Slavery, 1833-1865. Charles D. Stange. LC 82-48436. 256p. 1984. 35.00 (*0-8386-3168-1*) Fairleigh Dickinson.

British United Provident Association Ltd & HCA United Kingdom Ltd. Monopolies & Mergers Commission Staff. (Monopolies & Mergers Commission Report Ser.). 92p. 1990. pap. 17.50 (*0-10-109962-2*, HM9622) UNIPUB.

British Universities & the State. Robert O. Berdahl. Ed. by Walter P. Metzger. LC 76-55198. (Academic Profession Ser.). 1977. reprint ed. lib. bdg. 21.95 (*0-405-10029-9*) Ayer.

British Universities of Teacher's Education. J. B. Thomas. 1990. 65.00 (*1-85000-706-3*, Falmer Pr); pap. 31.00 (*1-85000-707-1*, Falmer Pr) Taylor & Francis.

British Urban Policy & the Urban Development Corporations. Ed. by Rob Imrie & Huw Thomas. LC 93-25817. 1993. 34.00 (*1-85396-207-4*, Pub. by Paul Chapman UK) Taylor & Francis.

***British Victory in Egypt 1801: The End of Napoleon's Conquest.** Piers Mackesey. LC 94-26059. (Illus.). 304p. 1995. 79.95x (*0-415-04064-7*, B2238) Routledge.

***British Virgin Islands: Commercial Law.** 300p. (Orig.). 1994. pap. 295.00 (*0-7605-1233-7*) Rector Pr.

British Virgin Islands: Consolidated Index & Statutes & Subsidiary Legislation. Ed. by C. J. Hammett. (West Indian Legislation Indexing Project Ser.). vi, 74p. (Orig.). 1991. pap. text ed. 25.00 (*0-317-60536-4*, Pub. by UWI Fac Law BB) W W Gaunt.

British Virgin Islands Business Law. Commercial & Financial Trust Company Limited. 257p. 1980. 50.00 (*0-89499-011-X*) Bks Business.

British Virgin Islands Business Law. Commercial & Financial Trust Company Staff. LC 82-176238. 259p. reprint ed. pap. 73.90 (*0-7837-2412-8*, 2040097) Bks Demand.

***British Virgin Islands Commercial Law.** 150p. (C). 1994. pap. 295.00 (*0-7605-0087-8*) Rector Pr.

***British Vocational Qualifications.** Comp. by Kogan Page Ltd. Staff. 356p. 1994. 99.00x (*0-7494-1453-7*, Pub. by Kogan Page Educ UK) Taylor & Francis.

***British Vocational Qualifications.** Comp. by Kogan Page Ltd. Staff. 356p. 1994. pap. 65.00x (*0-7494-1454-5*, Pub. by Kogan Page Educ UK) Taylor & Francis.

British Voter. Michael Kinnear. 1981. text ed. 49.95 (*0-312-10563-0*) St Martin.

British War Budgets. (Economic & Social History of the World War Ser.). 1926. 150.00 (*0-686-83495-X*) Elliots Bks.

British War Finance, Nineteen Fourteen to Nineteen Nineteen. Henry F. Grady. LC 73-76688. (Columbia University. Studies in the Social Sciences: No. 279). reprint ed. 24.50 (*0-404-51279-8*) AMS Pr.

British Warbles. Eric Simms. 1987. 23.95 (*0-685-43765-5*) Viking Penguin.

British Warship Design in World War II: Selected Papers from the Transactions of the Royal Institution of Naval Architects. R. Baker et al. LC 83-61246. (Illus.). 214p. 1983. 24.95 (*0-87021-921-9*) Naval Inst Pr.

British Warships & Auxiliaries, 1990-91. Maritime Books Staff. (C). 1986. text ed. 59.00 (*0-907771-44-0*, Pub. by Maritime Bks UK) St Mut.

British Warships & Auxiliaries, 1994-95. 1989. pap. 18.00 (*0-907771-56-4*, Pub. by Maritime Bks UK) St Mut.

British Warships since Nineteen Forty-Five, Pt. 1. Maritime Books Staff. (C). 1986. text ed. 40.00 (*0-9506323-4-1*, Pub. by Maritime Bks UK) St Mut.

British Warships since Nineteen Forty-Five, Pt. 2. 1989. pap. 16.00 (*0-9503323-6-4*, Pub. by Maritime Bks UK) St Mut.

British Warships since Nineteen Forty-Five, Pt. 2. Maritime Books Staff. (C). 1986. text ed. 40.00 (*0-685-38788-7*, Pub. by Maritime Bks UK) St Mut.

British Warships since Nineteen Forty-Five, Pt. 4. Maritime Books Staff. (C). 1986. text ed. 40.00 (*0-907771-12-2*, Pub. by Maritime Bks UK) St Mut.

British Warships since Nineteen Forty-Five, Pt. 5. Maritime Books Staff. (C). 1986. text ed. 50.00 (*0-907771-13-0*, Pub. by Maritime Bks UK) St Mut.

British Water Plants. rev. ed. S. M. Haslam et al. (Illus.). 1982. pap. 14.50x (*0-916422-64-X*) Mad River.

British Watercolors: Drawings of the 18th & 19th Centuries from the Yale Center for British Art. Scott Wilcox. (Illus.). 240p. 1985. pap. 19.50 (*0-933920-68-7*) Am Fed Arts.

British Watercolors & Drawings: The Virginia & George Ablah Gift, Pt. 1. Howard E. Wooden. LC 86-50682. (Illus.). 68p. 1986. pap. 10.00 (*0-939324-25-3*) Wichita Art Mus.

British Watercolors & Drawings: The Virginia & George Ablah Gift, Pt. II. Howard E. Wooden. LC 87-50489. (Illus.). 62p. 1987. pap. 10.00 (*0-939324-29-6*) Wichita Art Mus.

British Watercolors from the West Foundation. Donald Rosenthal. Ed. by Kelly Morris & Amanda Woods. (Illus.). 56p. 1988. pap. 10.00 (*0-939802-47-3*) High Mus Art.

British Watercolours: The Great Age, 1750-1880. Anne Lyles. Ed. by Andrew Wilton. (Illus.). 340p. 1993. 70.00 (*3-7913-1254-5*, Pub. by Prestel) TeNeues.

British Way in Warfare, 1688-2000. David French. 288p. (C). 1990. text ed. 55.00 (*0-04-445789-8*); pap. text ed. 19.95 (*0-04-445791-X*) Routledge Chapman & Hall.

***British Welfare State: A Critical History.** John Brown. (Historical Association Studies). 192p. (C). 1995. 39.95 (*0-631-18044-3*); pap. 12.95 (*0-631-17192-4*) Blackwell Pubs.

British West Indian Slavery, 1750-1834: The Process of Amelioration. J. R. Ward. (Illus.). 336p. 1988. 74.00 (*0-19-820144-3*) OUP.

British West Indies. William L. Burn. LC 73-21259. (Illus.). 196p. 1975. reprint ed. text ed. 49.75 (*0-8371-6138-X*, BUBW, Greenwood Pr) Greenwood.

British Wild Flowers, 2 vols., Set. John Hutchinson. LC 72-6576. (Illus.). 947p. 1973. 50.00 (*0-685-01612-9*) Fairleigh Dickinson.

British Women Novelists, 1750-1850, 12 vols., Set. 1992. Boxed set. boxed 1,161.50 (*0-415-08103-3*, B0115, Pub. by Thoemmes Pr UK) Routledge.

British Women Poets, 1660-1800: An Anthology. Joyce Fullard. LC 88-51902. (Illus.). 618p. 1990. 55.00 (*0-87875-370-2*) Whitston Pub.

British Women Writers: A Critical Reference Guide. Ed. by Janet Todd. 688p. 1989. 59.50 (*0-8044-3334-8*) Continuum.

British Women Writers: An Anthology from the Fourteenth Century to the Present. Dale Spender & Janet Todd. LC 89-6572. 960p. 1989. 39.95 (*0-87226-326-6*) P Bedrick Bks.

British Women's Diaries: A Descriptive Bibliography of Selected Nineteenth Century Women's Manuscript Diaries. Cynthia Huff. LC 84-45280. (Studies in Social History: No. 4). 176p. (C). 1985. 37.50 (*0-404-61604-6*) AMS Pr.

***British Women's History: A Bibliographical Guide.** Comp. by June Hannam et al. LC 95-1038. (History & Related Disciplines Select Bibliographies Ser.). 1995. text ed. write for info. (*0-7190-4652-1*, Pub. by Manchester Univ Pr UK) St Martin.

British Words on Cassette. 2nd ed. 173p. 1992. pap. 45.00 (*1-85739-085-7*) Bowker-Saur.

British Work Studies: Original Anthology. Ed. by Leon Stein. LC 77-70550. (Work Ser.). 1977. lib. bdg. 58.95 (*0-405-10217-8*) Ayer.

British Working Class Reader Seventeen Ninety to Eighteen Forty-Eight: Literacy & Social Tension. Robert K. Webb. LC 55-27828. 1971. reprint ed. lib. bdg. 35.00 (*0-678-00578-8*) Kelley.

British Writers, Vol. I. Ed. by Ian Scott-Kilvert. LC 78-23483. 1979. 85.00 (*0-684-15798-5*, Scribners) S&S Trade.

British Writers, Vol. II. Ed. by British Council Staff & Ian Scott-Kilvert. LC 78-23483. (British Council Pamphlet Ser.). 1979. lib. bdg. 85.00 (*0-684-16407-8*, Scribners) S&S Trade.

British Writers, Vol. III. Ed. by Ian Scott-Kilvert. LC 78-23483. 1980. lib. bdg. 85.00 (*0-684-16408-6*, Scribners) S&S Trade.

British Writers, Vol. IV. Ed. by Ian Scott-Kilvert. LC 78-23483. 1981. lib. bdg. 85.00 (*0-684-16635-6*, Scribners) S&S Trade.

British Writers, Vol. V. Ed. by Ian Scott-Kilvert. LC 78-23483. 1982. lib. bdg. 85.00 (*0-684-16636-4*, Scribners) S&S Trade.

British Writers, Vol. VI. Ed. by Ian Scott-Kilvert. LC 78-23483. 1983. lib. bdg. 85.00 (*0-684-16637-2*, Scribners) S&S Trade.

British Writers, Vol. VII. Ed. by Ian Scott-Kilvert. LC 78-23483. 1984. lib. bdg. 85.00 (*0-684-16638-0*, Scribners) S&S Trade.

British Writers, Vol. 8. Ed. by Ian Scott-Kilvert. LC 78-23483. 1984. lib. bdg. 60.00 (*0-684-17417-0*, Scribners) S&S Trade.

British Writers: Kingsley Amis to J. R. R. Tolkien. Ed. by George Stade. 528p. 1987. text ed. 95.00 (*0-684-18612-8*, Scribners) S&S Trade.

British Writers: Kingsley Amis to J. R. R. Tolkien, Suppl. II. Ed. by George Stade. LC 87-16648. 672p. 1991. Supplement II. text ed. 95.00 (*0-684-19214-4*, Scribners) S&S Trade.

British Writers & Their Work, No. 10. British Writers & Their Work Staff. LC 63-63096. (Bison Book Ser.). 146p. reprint ed. pap. 39.50 (*0-7837-1764-4*, 2005768) Bks Demand.

British Writers & Their Work, No. 11. Philip Handerson. LC 63-63096. 188p. reprint ed. pap. 53.60 (*0-8357-7435-X*, 2025429) Bks Demand.

British Writers & Their Work, No. 1: Geoffrey Chaucer & Sir Thomas Malory. Nevill Coghill & M. C. Bradbrook. LC 63-63096. 115p. reprint ed. pap. 32.80 (*0-8357-7436-8*, 2023207) Bks Demand.

British Writers of the Thirties. Valentine Cunningham. 544p. 1990. reprint ed. pap. 22.50 (*0-19-282655-7*) OUP.

British Writers Series, 8 vols., Set. 1984. 625.00 (*0-684-18253-X*, Scribners) S&S Trade.

British Year Book of International Law, 1988, Vol. 59. 2nd ed. Derek W. Bowett. Ed. by Ian Brownlie. 616p. 1990. 135.00 (*0-19-825408-3*) OUP.

British Year Book of International Law, 1989: Sixtieth Year of Issue, Vol. 60. Ed. by Ian Brownlie & Derek W. Bowett. 744p. 1991. 165.00 (*0-19-825431-8*) OUP.

British Year Book of International Law, 1990, Vol. 61. Ed. by Ian Brownlie & Derek W. Bowett. (Illus.). 672p. 1992. 159.00 (*0-19-825726-0*) OUP.

British Year Book of International Law, 1992, Vol. 62. Ed. by Ian W. Brownlie & Derek W. Bowet. 760p. 1993. 169.00 (*0-19-825445-8*) OUP.

British Year Book of International Law, 1992, Vol. 63. Ed. by Ian W. Brownlie & Derek W. Bowett. 896p. (C). 1994. 135.00 (*0-19-825446-6*, 8191) OUP.

***British Year Book of International Law 1993 Vol. 64.** Ed. by Ian Brownlie & Derek Bowett. 800p. 1995. 145.00 (*0-19-825447-4*) OUP.

British Yearbook of International Law, 1920-1989, 1-46 Vols., Vols. 1-62. 3,680.00 (*0-8377-9029-8*); mic. film write for info. (*0-318-57418-7*) Rothman.

British Yearbook of International Law, 1983, Vol. 54. Ian Brownlie & Derek W. Bowett. 577p. 1985. 110.00 (*0-19-825508-X*) OUP.

British Yearbook of International Law, 1987, Vol. 58. Ian Brownlie. Ed. by Derek W. Bowett. 680p. 1988. 140.00 (*0-19-825619-1*) OUP.

Britishisms: A Dictionary of British English. rev. ed. Lawrence Holofcener. 164p. 1984. pap. 3.95 (*0-942676-78-5*) Partners Pr NJ.

Britny Fox - Boys in Heat. pap. 16.95 (*0-89524-604-X*) Cherry Lane.

Briton, Boer, & Yankee: The United States & South Africa, 1870-1914. Thomas J. Noer. LC 78-16749. 206p. reprint ed. pap. 58.80 (*0-7837-0296-5*, 2040617) Bks Demand.

Briton, British, Britisher see Metaphor

Briton Hadden: A Biography of the Co-Founder of Time. Noel F. Busch. LC 75-25253. 236p. 1975. reprint ed. text ed. 55.00 (*0-8371-8395-2*, BUBH, Greenwood Pr) Greenwood.

***Britons.** Colley. 1994. 12.99 (*0-517-13616-3*) Random Hse Value.

Britons: Forging the Nation, 1707-1837. Linda Colley. LC 92-13256. (Illus.). 432p. (C). 1992. 37.50 (*0-300-05737-7*) Yale U Pr.

Britons: Forging the Nation 1707-1837. Linda Colley. (Illus.). 432p. (C). 1994. pap. 14.00 (*0-300-05925-6*) Yale U Pr.

Britons & Anglo-Saxons in the Early Middle Ages. David N. Dumville. (Collected Studies: No. CS379). 352p. 1993. 95.00 (*0-86078-332-4*) Ashgate Pub Co.

Britons in American Labor: A History of the Influence of the United Kingdom Immigrants on American Labor, 1820-1914. Clifton K. Yearley. LC 78-64227. (Johns Hopkins University. Studies in the Social Sciences. Thirtieth Ser. 1912: 1). reprint ed. 24.50 (*0-404-61329-2*) AMS Pr.

Britons to Arms! The Story of the Volunteer Soldier. Glenn A. Steppler. (Illus.). 160p. 1992. 30.00 (*0-7509-0057-1*) A Sutton Pub.

Brittania Rules. C. Northcote Parkinson. 144p. 1992. reprint ed. pap. text ed. 12.00 (*0-86299-468-3*) A Sutton Pub.

Brittania Triumphans: Inigo Jones, Rubens & Whitehall Palace. Roy Strong. (Lectures). (Illus.). 72p. 1981. 10.95 (*0-500-55012-3*) Thames Hudson.

Brittanica's Typesetters: Women Compositors in Edwardian Edinburgh. Sian Reynolds. (Edinburgh Education & Society Ser.). (Illus.). 160p. 1989. 37.50 (*0-85224-634-X*, Pub. by Edinburgh U Pr UK); pap. 15.00 (*0-85224-652-8*, Pub. by Edinburgh U Pr UK) Col U Pr.

Brittany. (Insight Guides Ser.). 1993. pap. 21.95 (*0-395-66307-5*) HM.

Brittany. (Insight Pocket Guides Ser.). (Illus.). 133p. 1993. pap. 9.95 (*0-395-66909-X*) HM.

Brittany. Linda L. Bartell. 384p. 1989. pap. 3.95 (*0-380-75545-9*) Avon.

Brittany. Nicky Bissell. (Breed Bks.). (Illus.). 1995. write for info. (*0-87714-111-8*) Denlingers.

Brittany. Frank V. Dawes. 1990. pap. 16.95 (*0-8442-9941-3*, Passport Bks) NTC Pub Grp.

Brittany. Marie Delarue. 1990. 60.00 (*0-86565-123-X*) Vendome.

Brittany. Passport Staff. 120p. 1993. pap. 17.95 (*0-8442-9967-7*, Passport Bks) NTC Pub Grp.

Brittany. rev. ed. Comp. by Nelles Verlag. (Nelles Guides Ser.). (Illus.). 256p. 1993. pap. 14.95 (*3-88618-389-0*, Pub. by Nelles Verlag GW) Seven Hills Bk.

Brittany: Walks, Motor Tours, Gazetteer, Where to Stay, Where to Eat, What to See, Plus Large-Scale IGN Maps. Institute Geographic Nationale Staff. (IGN Touring & Leisure Guides to France Ser.). (Illus.). 144p. (Orig.). 1991. pap. 19.95 (*1-85365-242-3*, Pub. by McCarta UK) Seven Hills Bk.

Brittany & Channel Islands Cruising Guide: Cherbourg to St. Nazaire, the Channel Islands & Brittany Canals. 3rd ed. David Jefferson. (Illus.). 208p. 1991. 45.00 (*0-7136-3417-0*) Sheridan.

***Brittany & Normandy.** (Independent Travellers Ser.). (Illus.). 288p. (Orig.). 1995. pap. 9.95 (*0-86190-531-8*) Hunter NJ.

***Brittany Butterfield & the Back-to-School Blues.** Wendy C. Staub. (Angels Ser.: No. 2). 144p. 1995. pap. 3.50 (*0-8217-5057-7*) Zebra.

Brittany Champions, 1952-1981. Jan L. Pata. (Illus.). 280p. 1986. 36.95 (*0-940808-20-X*) Camino E E & Bk.

Brittany Champions, 1982-1986. Jan L. Freund & Camino E. E. & B. Co. Staff. (Illus.). 117p. 1987. pap. 28.95 (*0-940808-37-4*) Camino E E & Bk.

Brittany Champions, 1987-1993. Camino Book Co. Staff. (Illus.). 125p. 1995. pap. 32.95 (*1-55893-036-1*) Camino E E & Bk.

Brittany Green Guide. 2nd ed. Date not set. pap. 18.00 (*2-06-701314-9*, 314) Michelin.

***Brittany Green Guide English Edition.** Michelin Staff. Date not set. pap. 17.95 (*0-7859-7200-5*, 2067013149) Fr & Eur.

Brittany Spaniels. Ed. by Beverly Pisano & Evelyn Monte. (Illus.). 128p. 1989. 11.95 (*0-86622-223-5*, KW-092) TFH Pubns.

Brittany the Brontosaurus. Abbie Dee & Annie Scott. (Emergent Reader Ser.). 8p. (J). (ps-1). 1991. pap. text ed. 21.00 (*1-56843-032-9*); pap. text ed. 4.25 (*1-56843-080-9*) BGR Pub.

Britten. Christopher Headington. Ed. by John Lade. LC 82-1027. (Composer as Contemporary Ser.: No. 1). (Illus.). 166p. 1982. 18.95 (*0-8419-0802-8*); pap. 11.50 (*0-8419-0803-6*) Holmes & Meier.

Britten & Auden in the Thirties: The Year 1936. Donald Mitchell. LC 80-25980. (Illus.). 176p. 1981. 25.00 (*0-295-95814-6*) U of Wash Pr.

Britten's A Midsummer Night's Dream: Making An Opera from Shakespeare's Comedy. William H. L. Godsalve. LC 94-7296. 1995. write for info. (*0-8386-3551-2*) Fairleigh Dickinson.

Britten's Gloriana. Ed. by Paul Banks. (Aldeburgh Studies in Music: Vol. I). (Illus.). 224p. (C). 1993. text ed. 45.00 (*0-85115-340-2*) Boydell & Brewer.

Britten's Old Clock & Watches & Their Makers. 3rd ed. Antique Collector's Club Staff. (Illus.). 517p. 1978. reprint ed. 59.50 (*0-902028-69-3*) Antique Collect.

***Brittle Bondage.** Anne Mather. (Presents Ser.). 1995. pap. 3.25 (*0-373-11722-1*, 1-11722-5) Harlequin Bks.

Brittle-Ductile Transition in Rocks: The Heard Volume. Ed. by A. G. Duba et al. (Geophysical Monograph Ser.: Vol. 56). 243p. 1990. 42.00 (*0-87590-025-9*, GM0560259) Am Geophysical.

***Brittle Failure of Rock Materials: Test Results & Constitutive Models.** G. E. Andreev. 380p. 1995. 115.00 (*90-5410-602-6*, Pub. by A A Balkema NE) Ashgate Pub Co.

***Brittle Innings.** Michael Bishop. LC 93-31150. 1995. mass mkt. 5.99 (*0-553-56943-0*) Bantam.

Brittle Matrix Composites: Proceedings of the Second International Symposium Held at Cedzyna, Poland, 20-22 Sept., 1988. Ed. by A. M. Brandt. 1989. 135.00 (*1-85166-360-6*) Elsevier.

Brittle Matrix Composites - One: Proceedings of the European Mechanics Colloquium 204 "Structure & Crack Propagation in Brittle Matrix Composite Materials", September 12-15, 1985, Jablonna, Poland. European Mechanics Colloquium 204 Staff. Ed. by A. M. Brandt & I. H. Marshall. 590p. 1987. 158.50 (*1-85166-041-0*, Pub. by Elsevier Applied Sci UK) Elsevier.

Brittle Matrix Composites - Three: Proceedings of the Third International Symposium, 17-19 Sept., 1991, Warsaw, Poland. Ed. by A. M. Brandt & I. H. Marshall. 606p. 1991. 161.50 (*1-85166-687-7*) Elsevier.

Brittle Middle East: A Political & Internationally Legal Evaluation of Iran & the United States of America, 1979-1980. Albert Norman. 190p. 1981. 8.80 (*0-318-00824-6*) A Norman.

***Brittle Sword: The Kentucky Militia, 1776-1912.** Richard G. Stone. LC 77-76330. (Kentucky Bicentennial Bookshelf Ser.). (Illus.). reprint ed. pap. 38.80 (*0-7837-9587-4*, 2060336) Bks Demand.

Brittle Water. Sam Pereira. (Illus.). 1987. 50.00 (*0-318-41022-2*); pap. 27.50 (*0-318-41023-0*) Abattoir.

Brittlebrush: Arizona Through the Eyes of Its Elders - Memoirs, Stories, & Poems by Senior Citizens. Ed. by Nadine L. Smith & Elie Schultz. LC 93-34881. (Illus.). 1993. write for info. (*0-9617772-3-0*) Scottsdale Cmnty Coll.

Britton: The French Text Carefully Revised with an English Translation, Introduction & Notes, Vol. I. Francis M. Nichols. LC 83-80259. 419p. 1983. reprint ed. lib. bdg. 158.00 (*0-912004-49-5*) W W Gaunt.

Britton: The French Text Carefully Revised with an English Translation, Introduction & Notes, Vol. II. Francis M. Nichols. 398p. 1983. reprint ed. write for info. (*0-318-57311-3*) W W Gaunt.

Briulio Fiesco. Ed. by Jessie A. Owens. (Sixteenth Century Madrigal Ser.: Vol. 15). 1995. 86.00 (*0-8240-5512-8*) Garland.

BRM: The Saga of British Racing Motors, Vol. 1: The Front Engined Cars 1945-60. Doug Nye & Tony Rudd. (Illus.). 400p. 1994. 120.00 (*0-947981-37-3*, Pub. by Motor Racing UK) Motorbooks Intl.

An Asterisk (*) at the beginning of an entry indicates that the title is appearing in BIP for the first time. 917

Broaching: Tooling & Practice. Horace E. Linsley. LC 61-9128. 224p. reprint ed. pap. 63.90 (*0-8357-7437-6*, 2001909) Bks Demand.

Broad & Alien Is the World. Ciro Alegria. LC 62-17709. 1973. 40.00 (*0-85036-171-0*) Dufour.

Broad & Alien Is the World. Ciro Alegria. LC 62-17709. 1983. pap. 22.00 (*0-85036-282-2*) Dufour.

Broad & Alien Is the World. Ciro Alegria. 434p. 1987. 40.00 (*0-317-61293-X*); pap. 18.95 (*0-317-61294-8*) Dufour.

Broad & Narrow Interpretations of Philosophy of Technology. Ed. by Paul T. Durbin. (C). 1990. lib. bdg. 85.50 (*0-7923-0684-8*) Kluwer Ac.

Broad Axes. James D. Gamble. Ed. by Jane W. Gamble. (Illus.). 76p. (Orig.). 1986. pap. 7.95 (*0-9617220-0-2*) Tanro Co.

Broad Back of the Angel. Leon Rooke. LC 77-70901. 1977. 15.95 (*0-914590-42-1*); pap. 6.95 (*0-914590-43-X*) Fiction Coll.

Broad-Based Taxes: New Options & Sources. Ed. by Richard A. Musgrave. 302p. 1973. 3.00 (*0-317-33984-2*, 238) Comm Econ Dev.

Broad Bill off Conscience Bay see NEA Series

Broad Daylight (Poems) Beth Joselow. 68p. (Orig.). (C). 1989. pap. 8.95 (*0-934257-24-8*) Story Line.

Broad Economic Impact of Nuclear Power. OECD Staff. 244p. (Orig.). 1992. pap. 62.00 (*92-64-13789-0*) OECD.

***Broad Form Property Damage Coverage.** 3rd ed. Patrick J. Wielinski & Jack P. Gibson. 487p. 1992. pap. 49.50 (*1-886813-03-5*) Intl Risk Mgt.

Broad Grins: Comprising, with New Additional Tales in Verse, Those Formerly Published Under the Title of "My Nightgown & Slippers", Repr. Of 1802 Ed. George Colman. Bd. with Eccentricities for Edinburgh. LC 75-31180. LC 75-31180. (Romantic Context: Poetry 1789-1830 Ser.: Vol. 33). 1977. Set lib. bdg. 57.00 (*0-8240-2132-0*) Garland.

Broad Highway. Jeffrey Farnol. 1975. lib. bdg. 21.05 (*0-89966-085-1*) Buccaneer Bks.

Broad Highway. Jeffrey Farnol. 1976. 18.95 (*0-8488-0268-3*) Amereon Ltd.

Broad Players. Charlie A. Harris. (Orig.). 1983. pap. 2.25 (*0-87067-226-6*, BH226) Holloway.

Broad Reach. John E. McKelvy, Jr. 223p. 1991. 27.95 (*0-9635668-0-6*) Pilot Press.

Broad Shoulders & Tight Ends. Geraldine A. Broatz & Yvonne K. Ameche. (Illus.). (Orig.). 1995. pap. 14.95 (*0-9640964-0-4*) Fair Catch.

Broad Stone of Empire: Problems of Crown Colony Administration, 2 vols, Set. Charles Bruce. LC 70-179507. (Select Bibliographies Reprint Ser.). 1977. reprint ed. 75.95 (*0-8369-6636-8*) Ayer.

Broad Stripes & Bright Stars. Allegheny Trails Council, Boy Scouts of America & National Flag Foundation Staff. LC 73-95742. (Illus.). 61p. 1996. reprint ed. 4.95 (*0-934021-05-8*) Natl Flag Foun.

***Broadax & Bayonet: The Role of the United States Army in the Development of the Northwest, 1815-1860.** Francis P. Prucha. LC 94-44363. 1995. write for info. (*0-8032-8738-0*) U of Nebr Pr.

***Broadaxe & Bayonet: The Role of the U. S. Army in the Development of the Northwest, 1815-1860.** Francis P. Prucha. (Illus.). 304p. 1995. pap. 12.00 (*0-8032-5151-3*, Bison Books) U of Nebr Pr.

Broadband: Business Services, Technologies & Strategic Impact. David Wright. LC 93-28367. 1993. 79.00 (*0-89006-589-6*) Artech Hse.

***Broadband Coding, Modulation & Transmission Engineering.** 2nd ed. Ed. by Bernhard E. Keiser. (Illus.). 477p. (C). 1994. pap. text ed. 69.00 (*0-941893-06-5*) CEEPress Bks.

***Broadband Communications: A Professional's Guide to ATM, Fame Relay, SMDs, Sonet, & B-ISDN.** Balaji Kumar. 1994. text ed. 60.00 (*0-07-035968-7*) McGraw.

Broadband Communications: Proceedings of the IFIP TC6 Workshop on Broadband Communications, Estoril, Portugal, 20-22 January 1992. Ed. by A. Casaca. LC 92-2268. (IFIP Transactions C: Communication Systems Ser.: Vol. C-4). 1992. write for info. (*0-444-89464-0*, North Holland) Elsevier.

***Broadband Communications II: Proceedings of the IFIP TC6 Second Conference on Broadband Communications, Paris, France, 2-4 March, 1994.** Ed. by Samir Tohme & Augusto Casaca. LC 94-24484. (IFIP Transactions & Communications Systems Ser.). 1994. write for info. (*0-444-81834-0*, North Holland) Elsevier.

Broadband Communications Systems. Ed. by James Conard. 1993. pap. 49.00 (*0-685-69688-X*, HCOX) Warren Gorham & Lamont.

Broadband Islands-Towards Integration: Proceedings of the 2nd International Conference on Broadband Islands, Athens, Greece, 14-16 June 1993. Ed. by Otto Spaniol & Fiona Williams. LC 93-38722. 1993. 165.75 (*0-444-81710-7*, North Holland) Elsevier.

Broadband Islands '94: Connecting with the End User: Proceedings of the Third International Conference on Broadband Islands, Hamburg, Germany, 7-9 June 1994. Ed. by Wulf Bauerfeld et al. LC 94-13848. 1994. 171.50 (*0-444-81905-3*, North Holland) Elsevier.

Broadband LAN Technology. Gary Y. Kim. LC 88-24232. (Illus.). 224p. reprint ed. pap. 63.90 (*0-7837-1802-0*, 2042003) Bks Demand.

Broadband Matching: Theory & Implementation. Ed. by W. K. Chen. 744p. (C). 1988. text ed. 97.00 (*9971-5-0219-4*) World Scientific Pub.

Broadband Matching: Theory & Implementations. W. K. Chen. 350p. 1993. pap. text ed. 40.00 (*981-02-1453-7*) World Scientific Pub.

Broadband Microwave Applications of Fiber Optics. rev. ed. IGIC, Inc. Staff. (Fiber Optic Reprint Ser.: Vol. 33). (Illus.). 200p. 1994. pap. 75.00 (*1-56851-082-9*) Info Gatekeepers.

Broadband Network Analysis & Design. Daniel Minoli. LC 93-12353. 1993. write for info. (*0-89006-675-2*) Artech Hse.

Broadband Networking. Lawrence Gasman. 1994. pap. 44.95 (*0-442-01168-7*) Van Nos Reinhold.

Broadband Networking ABCs: ATM, BISDN, Cell-Frame Relay to SONET. 2nd ed. Robert P. Davidson. 1993. pap. 39.95 (*0-89435-459-0*) Wiley.

Broadband Networking ABCs for Managers: ATM, BISDN, Cell-Frame Relay Sonet. Robert P. Davidson. 176p. 1994. pap. text ed. 29.95 (*0-471-61954-X*) Wiley.

***Broadband Patch Antennas.** Jean-Francois Zurcher & Fred E. Gardiol. LC 94-23905. 1995. write for info. (*0-89006-777-5*) Artech Hse.

***Broadband Seismology & Small Regional Seismic Networks.** R. B. Hermann. LC 95-5245. (Investigations of the New Madrid Seismic Zone Ser.: Vol. S). 1996. write for info. (*0-615-00485-7*) US Geol Survey.

Broadband Switching: Architectures, Protocols, Design & Analysis. C. Dhas et al. LC 91-16306. 528p. 1991. 65.00 (*0-8186-8926-9*, 1926) IEEE Comp Soc.

Broadband Telecommunications Technology. Byeong G. Lee & Minho Kang. (Telecommunications Ser.). 600p. 1993. text ed. 84.00 (*0-89006-653-1*) Artech Hse.

Broadcast - Cable Regulation. Marvin R. Bensman. 184p. (Orig.). (C). 1990. pap. text ed. 20.00 (*0-8191-7661-3*) U Pr of Amer.

Broadcast Advertising: A Comprehensive Working Textbook. 3rd ed. Sherilyn K. Zeigler & Herbert H. Howard. LC 90-33584. (Illus.). 358p. (C). 1991. text ed. 34.95 (*0-8138-0072-2*) Iowa St U Pr.

Broadcast Advertising Copywriting. William L. Hagerman. 256p. 1989. pap. 32.95 (*0-240-80037-0*, Focal) Buttrwrth-Heinemann.

Broadcast & Be Damned. Alan Thomas. 242p. 1980. 29.95 (*0-522-84198-8*) Intl Spec Bk.

Broadcast & Cable Management. Norman Marcus. 368p. (C). 1986. text ed. 44.00 (*0-13-083577-3*) P-H.

Broadcast & Cable Programming: The Current Perspective. 2nd ed. Charles E. Clift et al. 256p. 1993. per. 22.95 (*0-8403-8422-X*) Kendall-Hunt.

Broadcast & Cable Selling. 2nd ed. Charles H. Warner & Joseph Buchman. 447p. (C). 1993. text ed. 38.95 (*0-534-19770-1*) Intl Thomson.

Broadcast Announcing. William L. Hagerman. LC 92-28940. 304p. (C). 1992. text ed. write for info. (*0-13-036872-5*) P-H.

Broadcast-Cable Copywriting. 5th ed. Peter B. Orlik. LC 93-27113. 540p. 1993. text ed. 50.00 (*0-205-15082-9*) Allyn.

Broadcast-Cable Programming: Strategies & Practices. 4th ed. Susan T. Eastman. 588p. (C). 1993. text ed. 41.95 (*0-534-16662-8*) Intl Thomson.

Broadcast Century: A Biography of American Broadcasting. Robert L. Hilliard & Michael C. Keith. (Illus.). 296p. 1992. 41.95 (*0-240-80046-X*, Focal) Buttrwrth-Heinemann.

Broadcast Clues. Dick Belsky. 256p. (Orig.). 1993. pap. 4.50 (*0-515-11153-8*) Jove Pubns.

Broadcast Communications Dictionary. 3rd ed. Lincoln Diamant. 1991. pap. 27.95 (*0-8442-3325-0*, Natl Textbk) NTC Pub Grp.

Broadcast Communications Dictionary. 3rd rev. ed. Ed. by Lincoln Diamant. LC 88-25093. 266p. 1989. text ed. 49.95 (*0-313-26502-X*, DBD/, Greenwood Pr) Greenwood.

Broadcast Data Systems: Teletext & RDS. Peter L. Mothersole & Norman W. White. (Illus.). 158p. 1990. pap. 29.95 (*0-240-51354-1*, Focal) Buttrwrth-Heinemann.

Broadcast Diversity in Eastern Europe: A Final Symposium Report of the Global Studio Project. (International Communications Report Ser.). 321p. 35.00 (*0-89206-194-4*) CSI Studies.

Broadcast Journalism: A Guide for the Presentation of Radio & Television News. 2nd ed. David K. Cohler. LC 93-17586. 1993. text ed. write for info. (*0-13-088659-9*) P-H Gen Ref & Trav.

Broadcast Journalism: Techniques of Radio & TV News. 2nd ed. Andrew Boyd. (Illus.). 390p. 1993. pap. 27.95 (*0-7506-0794-7*) Buttrwrth-Heinemann.

Broadcast Management: Radio & Television. 2nd ed. Ward L. Quaal & James A. Brown. (Illus.). 464p. 1976. pap. text ed. 15.00 (*0-8038-0764-3*) Hastings.

Broadcast Mandate: Bloodlines. Don Schroeder. 240p. (Orig.). 1993. pap. 12.95 (*0-943487-43-9*) Sevgo Pr.

Broadcast News. 2nd ed. Mitchell Stephens. 384p. (C). 1986. text ed. 29.50 (*0-03-071753-1*) HB Coll Pubs.

Broadcast News. 3rd ed. Mitchell Stephens. (Illus.). 384p. (C). 1993. pap. text ed. 26.75 (*0-03-079176-6*) HB Coll Pubs.

Broadcast News: Writing & Reporting. Peter Mayeux. 432p. (C). 1991. pap. write for info. (*0-697-05573-6*) Brown & Benchmark.

***Broadcast News: Writing & Reporting.** Peter Mayeux. 432p. (C). 1995. pap. write for info. (*0-697-20151-1*) Brown & Benchmark.

Broadcast News Handbook. Donald Miles. LC 75-2550. 1975. teacher ed 2.75 (*0-672-21198-X*, Bobbs); pap. 9.95 (*0-672-21183-1*, Bobbs) Macmillan.

Broadcast News Manual of Style. R. H. MacDonald. 202p. (C). 1987. pap. text ed. 25.50 (*0-582-99865-4*, 75290) Longman.

Broadcast News Manual of Style. 2nd ed. Ronald MacDonald. 384p. (C). 1994. pap. text ed. 14.95 (*0-8013-1110-1*, 79570) Longman.

Broadcast News Process. 4th ed. Fred Shook & Dan Lattimore. (Illus.). 376p. (C). 1992. pap. text ed. 32.95 (*0-89582-235-0*) Morton Pub.

Broadcast News Writing & Reporting. Ted White. LC 92-50053. (Illus.). 320p. (C). 1993. pap. text ed. 26.50 (*0-312-06150-1*) St Martin.

Broadcast News Writing, Reporting & Production. Ted White et al. 384p. (C). 1984. text ed. write for info. (*0-02-427010-5*) Macmillan.

***Broadcast News Writing Stylebook.** Robert A. Papper. LC 94-25081. 1994. pap. text ed. write for info. (*0-205-14693-7*) Allyn.

Broadcast Newswriting. David K. Cohler. 288p. (C). 1989. pap. text ed. write for info. (*0-13-083528-5*) P-H.

***Broadcast Newswriting: The RTNDA Reference Guide.** Mervin Block. LC 94-29925. 1994. 29.95 (*1-56625-017-X*) Bonus Books.

Broadcast Programming & Promotions Worktext. Marilyn J. Matelski. (Illus.). 202p. 1989. pap. 21.95 (*0-240-80025-7*, Focal) Buttrwrth-Heinemann.

Broadcast Sound Technology. Michael Talbot-Smith. 234p. 1990. 49.95 (*0-408-05442-5*) Buttrwrth-Heinemann.

Broadcast Studio Equipment: U.S. Markets, Technologies, & Opportunities: 1994-1999 Analysis & Forecasts. Stuart Hirschhorn. 200p. 1994. pap. text ed. 1,795.00 (*1-878218-50-6*) World Info Tech.

Broadcast Talk. Ed. by Paddy Scannell. (Media, Culture & Society Ser.). 224p. (C). 1992. text ed. 49.95 (*0-8039-8374-3*); pap. text ed. 19.95 (*0-8039-8375-1*) Sage.

Broadcast Technology Report, 1990. Michael Fitzmaurice. 56p. (Orig.). 1990. pap. 40.00 (*0-89324-082-6*) Natl Assn Broadcasters.

Broadcast Technology Worktext. Samuel Ebersole. (Illus.). 257p. 1992. pap. 28.95 (*0-240-80122-9*, Focal) Buttrwrth-Heinemann.

Broadcast Traffic Assistant. Jack Rudman. (Career Examination Ser.: C-96). 1994. pap. 29.95 (*0-8373-0096-7*) Nat Learn.

Broadcast Transmission Engineering Practice. Wharton et al. LC 92-13189. (Illus.). 279p. 1992. 125.00 (*0-240-51335-5*, Focal) Buttrwrth-Heinemann.

***Broadcast Voice Handbook.** Ann S. Utterback. (Illus.). 264p. 1995. text ed. 29.95 (*1-56625-022-6*) Bonus Books.

Broadcast Voice Handbook: How to Polish Your On-Air Delivery. Ann Utterback. (Illus.). 265p. 1990. 26.95 (*0-929387-16-3*) Bonus Books.

***Broadcast Voice Handbook: How to Polish Your On-Air Delivery.** Ann Utterback. (Illus.). 265p. 1990. pap. 19.95 (*1-56625-010-2*) Bonus Books.

***Broadcast Voice Handbook: How to Polish Your On-Air Delivery, Coping with Stress (50 mins.)** Ann Utterback. 1990. audio 19.95 (*1-56625-039-0*) Bonus Books.

Broadcast Voice Handbook: How to Polish Your On-Air Delivery, Vocal Exercises (50 mins.) Ann Utterback. (Illus.). 265p. 1990. audio 19.95 (*1-56625-037-4*) Bonus Books.

***Broadcast Voice Handbook: How to Polish Your On-Air Delivery, Vocal Expressiveness (50 mins.)** Ann Utterback. 1995. audio 19.95 (*1-56625-038-2*) Bonus Books.

Broadcast Voice Performance. Michael C. Keith. (Illus.). 192p. 1989. pap. 29.95 (*0-240-80003-6*, Focal) Buttrwrth-Heinemann.

Broadcast Writing. Daniel Garvey & William L. Rivers. LC 81-13745. 384p. (C). 1982. pap. text ed. 32.50 (*0-582-28173-3*, 71224); student ed, pap. text ed. 26.50 (*0-582-28171-7*, 71222) Longman.

Broadcast Writing: Drama, Comedies, & Documentaries. Ken Dancyger. (Electronic Media Guide Ser.). 96p. 1991. pap. 15.95 (*0-240-80054-0*, Focal) Buttrwrth-Heinemann.

Broadcast Writing: Principles & Practices. 2nd ed. Roger Walters. LC 93-32501. (Series in Mass Communication). 1993. pap. text ed. write for info. (*0-07-068031-0*) McGraw.

Broadcast Writing as a Liberal Art. Seth Finn. 224p. (C). 1991. pap. text ed. write for info. (*0-13-084609-0*) P-H.

Broadcasters. Red Barber. (Quality Paperbacks Ser.). (Illus.). 288p. 1986. pap. 8.95 (*0-306-80260-0*) Da Capo.

Broadcasters. William Russell. LC 93-44982. (J). 1994. write for info. (*1-57103-054-9*) Rourke Pr.

Broadcaster's Guide to Special Events & Sponsorship Risk Management. Ed. by Daryl Everett. 61p. 1991. 40.00 (*0-89324-115-6*) Natl Assn Broadcasters.

Broadcaster's Legal Guide for Conducting Contests & Promotions. James Albert. LC 85-60744. 237p. 1985. 34.95 (*0-933893-08-6*) Bonus Books.

Broadcasting. Central Office of Information HMSO Staff. (Aspects of Britain Ser.). 91p. 1993. pap. 9.00 (*0-11-701761-2*, HM17612, Pub. by HMSO UK) UNIPUB.

Broadcasting: Its New Day. Samuel L. Rothafel & Raymond F. Yates. LC 70-161153. (History of Broadcasting: Radio to Television Ser.). 1977. reprint ed. 31.95 (*0-405-03571-3*) Ayer.

Broadcasting: The New Law. Nicholas Reville. 1991. U.K. pap. 33.00 (*0-406-00137-5*) Butterworth Legal Pubs.

Broadcasting - Cable & Beyond: An Introduction to Modern Electronic Media. 2nd ed. Joseph R. Dominick et al. LC 92-30610. 1992. text ed. write for info. (*0-07-017817-8*) McGraw.

Broadcasting - Cable & Beyond: An Introduction to Modern Electronic Media. 4th ed. Joseph R. Dominick. 1994. text ed. write for info. (*0-07-072158-0*) McGraw.

Broadcasting & Bargaining: Labor Relations in Radio & Television. Ed. by Allen E. Koenig. LC 76-98123. 358p. reprint ed. pap. 102.10 (*0-8357-6779-5*, 2035456) Bks Demand.

Broadcasting & Cable Television: Policies for Diversity & Change. Committee for Economic Development. LC 75-6536. 120p. 1975. pap. 2.50 (*0-87186-058-9*) Comm Econ Dev.

Broadcasting & Cable Yearbook 1994, 2 vols., 1. Bowker, R. R., Staff. LC 71-649524. 2109p. 1994. write for info. (*0-8352-3439-8*) Bowker.

Broadcasting & Cable Yearbook 1994, 2 vols., 2. Bowker, R. R., Staff. LC 71-649524. 2109p. 1994. write for info. (*0-8352-3440-1*) Bowker.

Broadcasting & Cable Yearbook 1994, 2 vols., Set. Bowker, R. R., Staff. LC 71-649524. 2109p. 1994. pap. 169.95 (*0-8352-3438-X*) Bowker.

***Broadcasting & Cable Yearbook 1995, 2 volumes. Ed. by Bowker, R. R., Staff. 2109p. 1995. 169.95 (*0-8352-3601-3*) Bowker.**
"A comprehensive directory."-- ASSOCIATION TRENDS. For the latest & most comprehensive information on the radio, TV, & cable industries, the only place to turn is BROADCASTING & CABLE YEARBOOK 1995. Generation after generation has relied on the YEARBOOK to help them work more efficiently in the fast-paced radio, television, & cable industries. Whether it's contacting consultants or account representatives...or locating new program sources...or even finding a new niche for a radio station, the 1995 edition of BROADCASTING is the only resource you need for: * Thoroughly updated listings for all radio & tv stations in the U.S. & Canada, containing addresses, telephone & FAX numbers, frequencies, ownership, programming & more * Comprehensive cable coverage of multiple systems operators (MSOs) & independent owners with 1,000 subscribers or more * Index of radio & TV station call letters * Descriptions of radio formats & listing of stations which carry those formats * Station ownership & cross-ownership listings * Information on direct broadcast satellites, Multichannel Multipoint Distribution Services (MMDS), regional cable TV news program networks, wireless cable companies, & businesses that provide bartering services * Listings for key industry services--ad agencies... producers, distributors & production services...station reps...law firms...PR services...satellites...equipment manufacturers...programming services...& more * Current market statistics * Information about trade associations...trade shows...broadcasting education...awards...books & magazines on every aspect of communications...& videos * Yellow Pages of radio, TV & cable contact information in a separate volume. ***Publisher Provided Annotation.***

***Broadcasting & Cable Yearbook 1995, Vol. 1.** Ed. by Bowker, R. R., Staff. 1995. Not sold separately (*0-8352-3602-1*) Bowker.

***Broadcasting & Cable Yearbook 1995, Vol. 2.** Ed. by Bowker, R. R., Staff. 1995. Not sold separately (*0-8352-3603-X*) Bowker.

Broadcasting & Democracy in France. Ruth Thomas. 1976. 25.00 (*0-8464-0217-3*) Beekman Pubs.

Broadcasting & Democracy in West Germany. Arthur Williams. 1976. 25.00 (*0-8464-0218-1*) Beekman Pubs.

Broadcasting & Detente. Gerhard Wettig. LC 77-72285. 1977. text ed. 24.95 (*0-312-10588-6*) St Martin.

Broadcasting & Politics in Western Europe. Ed. by Raymond Kuhn. 184p. 1985. 35.00 (*0-7146-3274-0*, Pub. by F Cass Pubs UK) Intl Spec Bk.

Broadcasting & Telecommunication: An Introduction. 2nd ed. John R. Bittner. (Illus.). 544p. (C). 1985. text ed. write for info. (*0-13-083551-X*) P-H.

Broadcasting & Telecommunication: An Introduction. 3rd ed. John R. Bittner. 1990. text ed. 32.00 (*0-13-083239-1*, 640103) P-H.

Broadcasting Bibliography. rev. ed. National Association of Broadcasters Staff. Ed. by Suan M. Hill. 74p. 1989. 10.00 (*0-89324-076-1*) Natl Assn Broadcasters.

Broadcasting, Cable & Beyond: An Introduction to Modern Electronic Media. Jonathan Tankel. (McGraw-Hill Series in Mass Communication). 1990. pap. text ed. write for info. (*0-07-017549-7*) McGraw.

Broadcasting Finance in Transition: A Comparative Handbook. Ed. by Jay G. Blumler & T. J. Nossiter. (Communication & Society Ser.). 416p. 1991. 55.00 (*0-19-505089-4*) OUP.

Broadcasting from the High Seas, Eighteen Fifty-Eight to Nineteen Seventy-Six. Paul Harris. (Illus.). 1977. 29.00 (*0-8464-0219-X*) Beekman Pubs.

Broadcasting in America: A Survey of Electronic Media, 6 Vols. 6th ed. Head & Bruce Sterling. (C). 1989. text ed. 53.56 (*0-395-43253-7*) HM.

An Asterisk (*) at the beginning of an entry indicates that the title is appearing in BIP for the first time.

Broadcasting in America: A Survey of Electronic Media, 6 Vols. 6th ed. Head & Bruce Sterling. (C). 1990. pap. 2.76 (0-395-52668-X); student ed, pap. 16.76 (0-395-52936-0) HM.

Broadcasting in America, Brief. Sydney Head & Christopher Sterling. (C). 1991. write for info. (0-395-54445-9) HM Soft Schl Col Div.

Broadcasting in India. G. S. Awasthy. 270p. 1965. 7.95 (0-318-37276-2) Asia Bk Corp.

Broadcasting in India. 2nd ed. P. C. Chatterji. 228p. 1992. 29.95 (0-8039-9107-X) Sage.

Broadcasting in South Africa. Ruth Tomaselli et al. (Studies on the South African Media). 232p. 1990. text ed. 29.95 (0-941702-25-1); pap. text ed. 16.95x (0-85255-311-0) Lake View Pr.

Broadcasting in the Arab World: A Survey of the Electronic Media in the Middle East. 2nd ed. Douglas A. Boyd. LC 92-39984. (Illus.). 360p. (C). 1993. text ed. 39.95 (0-8138-0468-X) Iowa St U Pr.

Broadcasting in the Malay World: Radio, Television, & Video in Brunei, Indonesia, Malaysia, & Singapore. Drew O. McDaniel. LC 93-46297. (Communication & Information Science Ser.). 352p. 1994. 49.50 (1-56750-070-6); pap. 22.50 (1-56750-071-4) Ablex Pub.

Broadcasting in the Third World: Promise & Performance. Elihu Katz & George Wedell. 320p. 1978. 34.00 (0-674-08341-5) HUP.

Broadcasting in the United Kingdom: A Guide to Information Sources. 2nd ed. Barrie MacDonald. 304p. 1993. text ed. 100.00 (0-7201-2086-1, Mansell Pub) Cassell.

Broadcasting It! An Encyclopaedia of Homosexuality in Film, Radio, & TV in the U. K., 1923-1993. Keith Howes. LC 93-5198. (Lesbian & Gay Studies). 960p. 1993. 64.95 (0-304-32700-X, InBook); pap. text ed. 27.95 (0-304-32702-6, InBook) Cassell.

***Broadcasting Law: A Comparative Study.** Eric Barendt. 280p. 1995. pap. 29.95 (0-19-826021-0) OUP.

Broadcasting Law: A Comparative Study. Eric M. Barendt. 280p. (C). 1993. 49.95 (0-19-825254-4, 2001) OUP.

Broadcasting Propaganda: International Radio Broadcasting & the Construction of Political Reality. Philo C. Wasburn. LC 92-15783. (Praeger Series in Political Communication). 208p. 1992. text ed. 45.00 (0-275-93841-7, C3841, Praeger Pubs) Greenwood.

Broadcasting Studios. 1990. 36.00 (0-86022-245-4, Pub. by Build Servs Info Assn UK) St Mut.

***Broadcasting the Canadian Way.** fac. ed. Albert A. Shea. LC 63-19560. (Illus.). 143p. Date not set. pap. 40.80 (0-7837-7546-6, 2046923) Bks Demand.

***Broadcasting the Local News: The Early Years of Pittsburgh's KDKA - TV.** Lynn B. Hinds. LC 94-43060. (Illus.). 200p. 1995. 40.00 (0-271-01438-5); pap. 16.95 (0-271-01439-3) Pa St U Pr.

Broadcasting to the Soviet Union: International Politics & Radio. Maury Lisann. LC 74-14046. (Illus.). 224p. 1975. 34.95 (0-275-05590-6, Praeger Pubs) Greenwood.

Broadcloth & Britches: The Santa Fe Trade. Seymour V. Connor & Jimmy M. Skaggs. LC 76-17978. 252p. 1977. 19.50 (0-89096-022-4) Tex A&M Univ Pr.

Broadening Horizons: Transportation & Development Around the Pacific. Comp. by American Society of Civil Engineers Staff. LC 80-66122. 430p. 1980. pap. 36.00 (0-87262-244-4) Am Soc Civil Eng.

Broadening the Base of Treatment for Alcohol Problems. Institute of Medicine, Committee on Treatment of Alcohol Problems Staff. 644p. 1990. 49.95 (0-309-04038-8) Natl Acad Pr.

Broadening the Horizons of Linear Low Technology: Regional Technical Conference, October 1-2, 1985, Quaker Square Hilton, Akron, Ohio-SPE, Akron Section. Society of Plastics Engineers Staff. 214p. reprint ed. pap. 61.00 (0-8357-7438-4, 2027691) Bks Demand.

Broadening Your Biblical Horizons: New Testament Survey. LC 63-7410. 62p. 1983. teacher ed, ring bd. 10.95 (0-910566-19-4) Evang Trg Assn.

Broadening Your Biblical Horizons: New Testament Survey. Walter M. Dunnett. LC 63-7410. 96p. 1963. pap. text ed. 7.95 (0-910566-03-8) Evang Trg Assn.

Broadening Your Biblical Horizons: Old Testament Survey, Pt. I: Genesis - Esther. rev. ed. LC 64-10037. 62p. 1985. teacher ed, ring bd. 10.95 (0-910566-20-8) Evang Trg Assn.

Broadening Your Biblical Horizons: Old Testament Survey, Pt. I: Genesis - Esther. rev. ed. Samuel J. Schultz. LC 64-10037. 96p. 1968. pap. text ed. 7.95 (0-910566-01-1) Evang Trg Assn.

Broadening Your Biblical Horizons: Old Testament Survey, Pt. II: Job - Malachi. 74p. 1991. teacher ed, ring bd. 10.95 (0-910566-49-6) Evang Trg Assn.

Broadening Your Biblical Horizons: Old Testament Survey, Pt. II: Job - Malachi. Gary V. Smith. 96p. 1991. pap. text ed. 7.95 (0-910566-47-X) Evang Trg Assn.

Broader Implications of Ericksonian Therapy. Ed. by Stephen R. Lankton. LC 89-71310. (Ericksonian Monographs: No. 7). 128p. 1990. 26.95 (0-87630-582-6) Brunner-Mazel.

Broader Way: A Woman's Life in the New Japan. Sumio Mishima. LC 74-138596. vi, 247p. 1970. reprint ed. text ed. 35.00 (0-8371-5797-8, MIBW, Greenwood Pr) Greenwood.

Broadlooms & Businessmen: A History of the Bigelow-Sanford Carpet Company. John S. Ewing & N. P. Norton. LC 54-12236. (Studies in Business History: No. 17). (Illus.). 459p. 1955. 42.50 (0-674-08350-4) HUP.

Broadman Bible Commentary, 12 vols., Set. Ed. by Clifton J. Allen et al. Incl. General Articles, Genesis-Exodus rev. ed. LC 78-93918. 1969. lib. bdg. 24.99 (0-8054-1125-9); Vol. 2. LC 77-1665. lib. bdg. 24.99 (0-8054-1102-X); LC 77-1665. lib. bdg. 24.99 (0-8054-1103-8); LC 77-84583. lib. bdg. 24.99 (0-8054-1104-6); Vol. 5. LC 75-17091. lib. bdg. 24.99 (0-8054-1105-4); Vol. 6. LC 75-34953. (0-8054-1106-2); LC 58-1212. lib. bdg. 24.99 (0-8054-1107-0); General Articles, Matthew-Mark rev. ed. LC 78-93918. 1969. text ed. (0-8054-1108-9); 1969. (0-8054-1109-7); LC 58-1212. 1969. (0-8054-1110-0); (0-8054-1111-9); LC 58-1212. 1969. (0-8054-1112-7); General Articles, Matthew-Mark rev. ed. LC 78-93918. 1969. text ed. (0-8054-1108-9); General Articles, Genesis-Exodus rev. ed. LC 78-93918. 1969. lib. bdg. 24.99 (0-8054-1125-9); LC 78-93918. 1969. Set lib. bdg. 279.00 (0-8054-1100-3) Broadman.

Broadman Church Manual. Howard Foshee. LC 72-94629. 192p. 1973. 12.99 (0-8054-2525-X) Broadman.

Broadman Comments, 1994-95: Fifty-Two Ready-to-Teach Bible Study Lessons. Donald F. Ackland & Robert J. Dean. 400p. 1994. pap. 10.99 (0-8054-1727-3, 4217-27) Broadman.

Broadman Minister's Manual. Franklin M. Segler. LC 68-26920. 1968. 12.99 (0-8054-2307-9) Broadman.

Broadmoor: A History of Criminal Lunacy & Its Problems. Ralph Partridge. LC 75-31440. (Illus.). 278p. 1976. reprint ed. lib. bdg. 22.50 (0-8371-8520-3, PABRO, Greenwood Pr) Greenwood.

Broadmoor Memories: The History of the Broadmoor. Elena Bertozzi-Villa. LC 93-86687. (Illus.). 204p. 1993. 39.95 (0-929521-80-3) Pictorial Hist.

Broadribb's Introductory Pediatric Nursing. M. I. Marks. (Illus.). 592p. (C). 1994. pap. text ed. 25.95 (0-397-54946-6, Lippincott Nursing) Lippincott.

Broadsheet Collection of Thirteen Rare Crowley Items. Aleister Crowley. 1993. 16.95 (1-55818-326-4) Holmes Pub.

Broadside. 1988. 20.00 (0-317-90529-5) Inkblot Pubns.

Broadside. Thorne Smith. 20.95 (0-8488-1471-1) Amereon Ltd.

Broadside Authors & Artists. Ed. by Leaonead P. Bailey. LC 70-108887. 1974. 9.95 (0-910296-25-1) Broadside Pr.

Broadside Ballad: The Development of the Street Ballad from Traditional Song to Popular Newspaper. Leslie Shepard. LC 78-50797. (Illus.). 1978. 9.95 (0-913714-00-3); pap. 4.95 (0-913714-01-1) Legacy Books.

Broadside Ballads of Boston, 1813: The Isaiah Thomas Collection. Arthur F. Schrader. (Illus.). 42p. 1988. reprint ed. pap. 7.50 (0-944026-04-4) Am Antiquarian.

Broadside Series, No. 1. Ed. by Lee Engdahl. 300.00 (0-939489-11-2) Engdahl Typo.

***Broadsides: Indiana, the Early Years Resource Guide.** Dani B. Pfaff. 424p. Date not set. pap. 6.25 (1-885323-50-6) IN Hist Bureau.

Broadsides & Posters from the National Archives. Comp. by Nancy E. Allyn. LC 86-743. (Illus.). 32p. 1986. pap. text ed. 2.50 (0-911333-37-1, 200049) National Archives & Recs.

Broadsides from the Other Orders: A Book of Bugs. Sue Hubbell. LC 92-27165. 288p. 1993. 23.00 (0-679-40062-1) Random.

Broadsides from the Other Orders: A Book of Bugs. Sue Hubbell. 1994. pap. 12.00 (0-679-75300-1) Random.

Broadview Anthology of Poetry. Ed. by Herbert Rosengarten & Amanda Goldrick-Jones. 1993. pap. 17.95 (1-55111-006-7) Broadview Pr.

Broadview Guide to Writing. Doug Babington & Don LePan. 260p. 1991. pap. 8.95 (0-921149-76-X) Broadview Pr.

Broadway. Brooks Atkinson. LC 85-18197. (Illus.). 572p. 1985. reprint ed. pap. 19.95 (0-87910-047-8) Limelight Edns.

Broadway: An Encyclopedic Guide to the History, People & Places of Times Square. Ken Bloom. 400p. 1990. 50.00 (0-8160-1249-0) Facts on File.

Broadway & Hollywood: A History of Economic Interaction. Robert W. McLaughlin. LC 73-21606. (Dissertations on Film Ser.: Vol. 3). 322p. 1977. 23.95 (0-405-04873-4) Ayer.

Broadway & Hollywood Too. Andrew A. Aros. LC 80-67670. 60p. 1980. pap. 6.50 (0-932352-04-9) Applause Pubns.

Broadway Anecdotes. Peter Hay. 416p. 1990. reprint ed. pap. 8.95 (0-19-504620-X) OUP.

Broadway Babies: The People Who Made the American Musical. Ethan Mordden. 256p. 1988. pap. 10.95 (0-19-505425-3) OUP.

Broadway Ballads. 128p. 1992. pap. 12.95 (0-7935-1446-0, 00311570) H Leonard.

Broadway Below the Sidewalk: Concert Saloons of Old New York. Ed. by William L. Slout. LC 94-26402. (Clipper Studies in the Theatre: No. 4). xvi, 115p. 1994. lib. bdg. 27.00x (0-8095-0301-8); pap. 17.00x (0-8095-1301-3) Borgo Pr.

Broadway Belter's Songbook. (Piano-Vocal Ser.). 176p. (Orig.). 1993. pap. 16.95 (0-7935-2118-1, 00311608) H Leonard.

Broadway Bound. Neil Simon. 132p. (YA). (gr. 9-12). 1988. pap. 8.00 (0-452-26148-1, Plume) NAL-Dutton.

Broadway Bound. Neil Simon. 118p. 1991. pap. 7.95 (0-452-26718-8, Plume) NAL-Dutton.

Broadway Bound. Neil Simon. LC 87-42653. (Illus.). 128p. 1987. 13.95 (0-394-56395-6) Random.

Broadway by the Bay, Thirty Years at the Coconut Grove Playhouse. Carol Cohan. (Illus.). 128p. 1987. 22.95 (0-940495-00-7); pap. 12.95 (0-940495-01-5) Pickering Pr.

Broadway Chances. Elizabeth S. Hill. 160p. (J). (gr. 5 up). 1994. pap. 4.99 (0-14-034929-4) Puffin Bks.

***Broadway Chicken.** Jean-Luc Fromental. LC 94-35487. (Illus.). 40p. (J). (gr. 1-4). 1995. 14.95 (0-7868-0061-5); lib. bdg. 14.89 (0-7868-2048-9) Hyprn Child.

***Broadway Classics: YPL, No. 3B.** 24p. (Orig.). 1994. pap. 5.95 (0-89724-212-2) Warner Brothers.

Broadway Comedy Songs. 144p. (Orig.). 1993. pap. 12.95 (0-7935-2690-6, 00311630) H Leonard.

Broadway Day & Night. Ken Marsolais. Ed. by Bill Grose. 288p. 1992. 50.00 (0-671-74637-5) PB.

Broadway Deluxe. Hal Leonard Publishing Company Staff. 1987. pap. 22.95 (0-88188-306-9, HLP 00309245) H Leonard.

Broadway Down East. Elliot Norton. 1978. 10.00 (0-89073-055-5) Boston Public Lib.

Broadway Gold. (Ultimate Ser.). 272p. 1982. pap. 17.95 (0-88188-155-4, 00361396) H Leonard.

Broadway in the West End: An Index of Reviews of the American Theatre in London, 1950-1975. Comp. by William T. Stanley. LC 77-89108. 206p. 1978. text ed. 42.95 (0-8371-9852-6, STB/, Greenwood Pr) Greenwood.

Broadway Jazz. 128p. 1992. pap. 12.95 (0-7935-1445-2, 00311569) H Leonard.

Broadway Limited. Joel Rosenbaum & Tom Gallo. LC 88-32103. (Illus.). 96p. (C). 1988. pap. 18.00 (0-9621541-0-5) Railpace Co.

Broadway Love Songs. 176p. 1992. pap. 14.95 (0-7935-1249-2, 00311558) H Leonard.

Broadway Melody of Nineteen Ninety-Nine. Robert Steiner. 168p. 1993. 18.95 (0-932511-66-X); pap. 8.95 (0-932511-67-8) Fiction Coll.

Broadway, Mon Village. Damon Runyon. (FRE.). 1982. pap. 11.95 (0-7859-4165-7) Fr & Eur.

Broadway Musical: A Collaboration in Hits & Flops. Bernard Rosenberg & Ernest Harburg. (Illus.). 350p. 1993. 39.95 (0-8147-7433-4) NYU Pr.

Broadway Musical: A Critical & Musical Survey. Joseph P. Swain. (Illus.). 408p. 1990. 30.00 (0-19-505434-2) OUP.

Broadway Musical: A Critical & Musical Survey. Joseph P. Swain. (Illus.). 400p. 1992. pap. 11.95 (0-19-507482-3) OUP.

Broadway Musicals of the 30s. Stanley Green. LC 81-22127. (Quality Paperbacks Ser.). (Illus.). 383p. (C). 1982. reprint ed. pap. 14.95 (0-306-80165-5) Da Capo.

Broadway Musicals Show by Show. 3rd ed. Stanley Green. 372p. 1990. pap. 16.95 (0-88188-836-2, 00183121) H Leonard.

Broadway Musicals Show by Show. 4th ed. Stanley Green. (Illus.). 398p. 1994. pap. 16.95 (0-7935-3083-0, 00183121) H Leonard.

Broadway Musicals Show by Show, 1891-1916. Stanley Green. 160p. 1991. pap. 14.95 (0-7935-0777-4, 00311514) H Leonard.

Broadway Musicals Show by Show, 1917-1929. Stanley Green. 192p. 1991. pap. 14.95 (0-7935-0778-2, 00311515) H Leonard.

Broadway Musicals Show by Show, 1930-1939. Stanley Green. 176p. 1991. pap. 14.95 (0-7935-0779-0, 00311516) H Leonard.

Broadway Musicals Show by Show, 1940-1949. Stanley Green. 176p. 1991. pap. 14.95 (0-7935-0780-4, 00311517) H Leonard.

Broadway Musicals Show by Show, 1950-1959. Stanley Green. 192p. 1991. pap. 14.95 (0-7935-0781-2, 00311518) H Leonard.

Broadway Musicals Show by Show, 1960-1971. Stanley Green. 176p. 1991. pap. 14.95 (0-7935-0808-8, 00311521) H Leonard.

Broadway Musicals Show by Show, 1972-1988. Stanley Green. 176p. 1991. pap. 14.95 (0-7935-0782-0, 00311519) H Leonard.

Broadway on Record: A Directory of New York Cast Recordings of Musical Shows, 1931-1986. Comp. by Richard C. Lynch. LC 87-11822. (Discographies Ser.: No. 28). 357p. 1987. text ed. 45.00 (0-313-25523-7, LBR/, Greenwood Pr) Greenwood.

Broadway Overtures for Piano, No. 2. 1987. 9.95 (0-88188-544-4, 359442) H Leonard.

Broadway Overtures for Piano One. 1987. 9.95 (0-88188-543-6, 359441) H Leonard.

Broadway Scrapbook. J. Brooks Atkinson. LC 71-104221. 312p. 1970. reprint ed. text ed. 59.75 (0-8371-3331-9, ATBS, Greenwood Pr) Greenwood.

***Broadway Sheet Music: A Comprehensive Listing of Published Music from Broadway & Other Stage Shows, 1918-1993.** Donald J. Stubblebine. 256p. 1995. lib. bdg. 65.00x (0-7864-0047-1) McFarland & Co.

Broadway Showstoppers. (Piano-Vocal Ser.). 176p. (Orig.). 1994. pap. 14.95 (0-7935-2685-X, 00311629) H Leonard.

Broadway Talks: What Professionals Think about Commercial Theater in America. Arvid F. Sponberg. LC 90-37839. (Contributions in Drama & Theatre Studies: No. 31). 256p. 1990. text ed. 55.00 (0-313-26687-5, SBX/, Greenwood Pr) Greenwood.

Broadway Theatre. Andrew B. Harris. LC 93-19344. (Theatre Production Ser.). 1994. write for info. (0-415-06039-7) Routledge.

Broadway Theatre. Andrew B. Harris. 1994. pap. 16.95 (0-415-10520-X, Pub. by Tavistock UK) Routledge Chapman & Hall.

Broadway Theatre Posters. Wendy Nelson-Cave. (Illus.). 112p. 1993. 14.98 (0-8317-5166-5) Smithmark.

Broadway Today. (Listen & Play Ser.). 40p. (Orig.). 1994. audio, pap. 19.95 (0-89724-134-7) Warner Brothers.

Broadway Today. Ed. by Milton Okun. 1994. pap. 14.95 (0-89524-814-X) Cherry Lane.

Broadway Torch Songs. (Piano-Vocal Ser.). 128p. (Orig.). 1993. pap. 12.95 (0-7935-2654-X, 00311628) H Leonard.

Broadway Two. Ed. by Charles North & James Schuyler. 1989. pap. 15.00 (0-914610-70-8); boxed, pap. 25.00 (0-914610-71-6) Hanging Loose.

Broadway Waltzes. 144p. 1992. pap. 14.95 (0-7935-1444-4, 00311568) H Leonard.

Broadway's Prize-Winning Musicals: An Annotated Guide for Libraries & Audio Collectors. Leo N. Miletich. LC 92-4125. 255p. 1993. pap. 14.95 (1-56023-018-5) Harrington Pk.

Broadway's Prize-Winning Musicals: An Annotated Guide for Libraries & Audio Collectors. Leo N. Miletich. LC 92-4125. (Illus.). 222p. 1993. lib. bdg. 39.95 (1-56024-288-4) Haworth Pr.

Broc: The Littlest Champion. Timothy Baize. LC 89-92510. (Illus.). 185p. (Orig.). (J). (gr. 6-12). 1989. pap. 9.95 (0-9625193-0-8) T Baize.

Brocade. Grace Tseng. LC 94-9757. (J). 1994. write for info. (0-688-12515-8) Lothrop.

Brocade by Night: 'Kokin Wakashu' & the Court Style in Japanese Classical Poetry. Helen C. McCullough. LC 84-50637. 608p. 1985. 62.50 (0-8047-1246-8) Stanford U Pr.

Brocade of the Pen: The Art of Islamic Writing. Ulku Bates et al. Ed. by Carol G. Fisher. (Illus.). (Orig.). 1991. pap. 12.00 (1-879147-10-6) Kresge Art Mus.

Brocade Pillow: Azaleas of Old Japan. Ito Ihei. Tr. by Kaname Kato. (Illus.). 184p. 1984. 22.50 (0-8348-0191-4) Weatherhill.

Brocade River Poems: Selected Works of the Tang Bynasty Courtesan Xue Tao. Tr. by Jeanne Larsen. 116p. 1987. pap. text ed. 10.95 (0-691-01434-5) Princeton U Pr.

Brocade Valley. Anyi Wang. Tr. by Bonnie S. McDougall & Chen Maiping. LC 92-18529. 128p. (Orig.). 1992. 17.95 (0-8112-1224-6) New Directions.

Brocaded Slipper & Other Vietnamese Tales. Lynette D. Vuong. LC 81-19139. (Trophy Bk.). (Illus.). 128p. (J). (gr. 2-5). 1992. pap. 3.95 (0-06-440440-4, Trophy) HarpC Child Bks.

Broca's Brain. Carl Sagan. 384p. 1986. mass mkt. 5.99 (0-345-33689-5) Ballantine.

Broca's Brain: Reflections on the Romance of Science. Carl Sagan. LC 78-21810. (Illus.). 1979. 14.95 (0-394-50169-1) Random.

Broccoli & Company: Over 100 Healthy Recipes. Audra Hendrickson & Jack Hendrickson. LC 89-4533. (Illus.). 144p. 1989. pap. 9.95 (0-88266-558-8, Garden Way Pub) Storey Comm Inc.

***Broccoli-Banana Dilemma.** Amy B. Daniels. (Illus.). 32p. (J). (gr. 2-5). 1996. 12.95 (1-881519-06-6) WorryWart.

Broccoli by Brody. Lora Brody. LC 92-23442. 1993. 10.00 (0-688-12183-7) Morrow.

Broccoli Tapes. Jan Slepian. (J). (gr. 3-7). 1989. 14.95 (0-399-21712-6, Philomel Bks) Putnam Pub Group.

Broccoli Tapes. Jan Slepian. (J). (gr. 4-7). 1990. pap. 2.95 (0-590-43473-X) Scholastic Inc.

Broccoli Tapes. Jan Slepian. (J). (gr. 4-7). 1990. pap. 2.95 (0-590-44263-5) Scholastic Inc.

Broccoli Tapes. braille ed. Jan Slepian. 225p. (J). 1992. vinyl bd. 18.00 (1-56956-201-6, BR8145) W A T Braille.

Broceliande. Henry de Montherlant. 192p. (FRE.). 1956. pap. 10.95 (0-7859-1289-4, 2070245861) Fr & Eur.

Brochos Boy. Yocheved Ehrman. LC 85-71349. 1986. pap. 2.95 (0-8197-0500-4) Bloch.

Brochs of Scotland. N. G. Ritchie. 1989. pap. 25.00 (0-85263-928-7, Pub. by Shire UK) St Mut.

Brochure: Labels & Placards for the Carriage of Dangerous Goods (English Only) International Maritime Organization Staff. 1988. text ed. 45.00 (0-89771-871-2, Pub. by Intl Maritime Org UK) St Mut.

Brochure: Labels & Placards for the Carriage of Dangerous Goods (English Only) International Maritime Organization Staff. 1989. text ed. 50.00 (0-685-61552-9, Pub. by Intl Maritime Org UK) St Mut.

Brochure & Pamphlet Collection, No. 3. (Illus.). 224p. 1994. 79.95 (4-938586-45-2, Pub. by PIE Bks JA) Bks Nippan.

Brochure Design Forum, No. 2. P. I. E. Books Staff. (Illus.). 224p. 1993. 79.95 (4-938586-38-X, Pub. by PIE Bks JA) Bks Nippan.

Brochures for Book Publishers. 3rd ed. Dan Poynter. (Book Publishing Consultation with Dan Poynter Ser.). (Illus.). 50p. 1992. student ed 19.95 (0-915516-48-9) Para Pub.

Brock. large type ed. John Bingham. 352p. 1982. 15.95 (0-7089-0884-5) Ulverscroft.

Brock & the Defector. large type ed. John Bingham. 416p. 1984. 15.95 (0-7089-1082-3) Ulverscroft.

Brockhaus Dictionary in One Volume: Der Brockhaus in Einem Band Neu von A-Z. 2nd ed. Brockhaus. 1020p. (GER.). 1985. write for info. (0-8288-1967-X, M15502) Fr & Eur.

Brockhaus Enzklopaedie, 20 vols. & 5 suppl. vols., Set. 19th ed. Brockhaus. 19200p. (GER.). 1986. 3,995.00 (0-8288-1966-1, M7315) Fr & Eur.

Brockhaus of Natural Sciences: Brockhaus der Naturwissenschaften und der Technik, 5 vols., Set. Brockhaus. 832p. (GER.). 1983. 250.00 (0-7859-0845-5, M7314) Fr & Eur.

Brockhaus Riemann Musiklexikon, Vol. 1, A-K. Carl Dahlhaus & Hans H. Eggebrecht. (GER.). 1978. 175.00 (3-7653-0303-8) Eur-Am Music.

Brockhaus Riemann Musiklexikon, Vol. 1, A-K. deluxe ed. Carl Dahlhaus & Hans H. Eggebrecht. (GER.). 1978. 195.00 (0-685-73242-8) Eur-Am Music.

Brockington's Manual: What Every Pastor & Layman-Member Should Know about the Local Baptist Church. rev. ed. H. Frazier Brockington, II. (Illus.). 90p. 1989. reprint ed. pap. 6.95 (0-317-93031-1) Natl BIE Pub.

B

An Asterisk (*) at the beginning of an entry indicates that the title is appearing in BIP for the first time. 919

Brockington's Manual: What Every Pastor & Layman-Member Should Know about the Local Baptist Church: A Complete Outline of Church Structure with a Contemporary View. rev. ed. H. Frazier Brockington, II. Ed. & Illus. by Janice A. Brockington. 110p. 1991. pap. 6.95 (*0-685-48876-4*) Natl BIE Pub.

Brockman: Record of the Brockman & Drake-Brockman Family. D. H. Drake-Brockman. (Illus.). 158p. 1993. reprint ed. lib. bdg. write for info. (*0-318-70226-6*) Higginson Bk Co.

Brockman Scrapbook: Bell, Bledoe, Brockman, Burrus, Dickson, James, Pedan, et al. W. E. Brockman. (Illus.). 442p. 1993. reprint ed. lib. bdg. 77.50 (*0-8328-3651-6*); reprint ed. pap. 67.50 (*0-8328-3652-4*) Higginson Bk Co.

Brockport, New York: Beginning with "And" William Heyen. LC 88-19684. 50p. 1989. pap. 12.95 (*0-935061-27-4*) Contemp Res.

Brockton District Court Automation Requirements Analysis. Robert Lowe et al. 138p. 1989. 8.00 (*0-685-33609-3*, NERO-231) Natl Ctr St Courts.

Brockway Family, Descendants of Wolston Brockway. D. Williams Patterson. (Illus.). 167p. 1989. reprint ed. lib. bdg. 44.00 (*0-8328-0326-X*); reprint ed. pap. 34.00 (*0-8328-0327-8*) Higginson Bk Co.

***Broder le Linge De Maison.** Egle Salvy. (Illus.). 176p. 1993. write for info. (*2-200-21458-8*) Lacis Pubns.

B

Broderick's Bones. Russell Shorto. 1989. 11.95 (*0-943718-36-8*) Kipling Pr.

Broderie Anglaise. Violet Trefusis. Tr. by Barbara Bray. 144p. 1986. pap. 5.95 (*0-15-614167-1*, Harvest Bks) HarBrace.

Brodock's Designer Color Guide. Brodock Press Staff. (Illus.). 42p. 1990. 95.00 (*0-8230-6045-4*, Watsn-Guptill) Watsn-Guptill.

Brodsky's Poetics & Aesthetics. Ed. by Lev Loseff & Valentina Polukhina. LC 89-70322. 240p. 1990. text ed. 45.00 (*0-312-04511-5*) St Martin.

Brody Bates' Choice. Jacquelyn R. Thrash. 298p. (YA). 1992. 21.95 (*0-9635247-0-4*); pap. write for info. (*0-9635247-1-2*) Three Pines.

***Brody Reading Manual: An Implementation Guide for Teachers.** Sara Brody. (Brody Reading Method). 55p. 1987. teacher ed write for info. (*1-886042-02-0*) Larc Pubg.

***Brody Reading Method: Complete Set.** Sara Brody. (Brody Reading Method Ser.). Date not set. pap. text ed. write for info. (*1-886042-11-X*) Larc Pubg.

***Brogan: To Earn a Dollar.** large type ed. L. D. Tetlow. (Linford Western Library). 256p. 1995. pap. 14.95 (*0-7089-7687-5*, Linford) Ulverscroft.

Brogeen & the Green Shoes. Patricia Lynch. 208p. 1989. pap. 6.95 (*1-85371-051-2*, Pub. by Poolbeg Pr IE) Dufour.

Brogeen & the Princess of Sheen. Patricia Lynch. (J). (gr. 1 up). 1986. pap. 11.95 (*0-85105-905-8*, Pub. by Colin Smythe Ltd UK) Dufour.

Brogeen Follows the Magic Flute. Patricia Lynch. 191p. (J). (ps-8). 1988. pap. 6.95 (*1-85371-022-9*, Pub. by Poolbeg Pr IE) Dufour.

Broke Aide. Gail Sher. LC 85-4702. 80p. 1985. 15.00 (*0-930901-35-5*); pap. 7.00 (*0-930901-36-3*) Burning Deck.

Broke by the War: Letters of a Slave Trader. Ed. by Edmund L. Drago. LC 91-17887. (Illus.). 162p. 1991. text ed. 24.95 (*0-87249-763-1*) U of SC Pr.

***Broken Alliance.** Jonathan Kaufman. 1995. pap. text ed. 14.00 (*0-684-80096-9*, Touchstone Bks) S&S Trade.

Broken Alliance: The Turbulent Times Between Blacks & Jews in America. Jonathan Kaufman. LC 88-1948. 272p. 1988. text ed. 19.95 (*0-684-18699-3*, Scribners) S&S Trade.

Broken Anchor. Carolyn Keene. (Nancy Drew Files Ser.: No. 70). (J). 1991. pap. 3.50 (*0-671-74228-0*) PB.

***Broken & Whole: Essays on Religion & the Body.** annuals Ed. by Maureen A. Tilley & Susan A. Ross. (Annual Volume of the College Theology Society, 1993 Ser.). 340p. (C). 1994. lib. bdg. 49.50 (*0-8191-9746-7*, Pub. by College Theology Society) U Pr of Amer.

***Broken & Whole: Essays on Religion & the Body.** annuals Ed. by Maureen A. Tilley & Susan A. Ross. (Annual Volume of the College Theology Society, 1993 Ser.). 340p. (Orig.). (C). 1994. pap. 32.50 (*0-8191-9747-5*, Pub. by College Theology Society) U Pr of Amer.

Broken Angel: Myth & Method in Valery. Ursula Franklin. (Studies in the Romance Languages & Literatures: No. 222). 160p. 1984. pap. 17.50 (*0-8078-9226-2*) U of NC Pr.

Broken Apple: New York City in the 1980's. Herbert London. 256p. 1989. 34.95 (*0-88738-296-7*) Transaction Pubs.

Broken April. Ismail Kadare. 248p. (C). 1990. 17.95 (*0-941533-57-3*) New Amsterdam Bks.

Broken Armour. large type ed. Leila Mackinlay. 346p. 1989. 17.95 (*0-7089-1961-8*) Ulverscroft.

Broken Arrow Boy. Adam Moore. Ed. by Nancy R. Thatch. LC 90-5933. (Books for Students by Students Ser.). (Illus.). 26p. (J). (gr. 3-8). 1990. lib. bdg. 14.95 (*0-933849-24-9*) Landmark Edns.

Broken Arrows. Robert Smyth. 36p. 1982. 4.00 (*0-938756-05-2*) Yellow Moon.

***Broken Balance & the Wolves of Isle Royal.** Rolf Peterson. (Illus.). 160p. 1995. 29.50 (*1-57223-031-2*, WCP) Outlook Pubng.

Broken Bars: New Perspectives from Mexican Women Writers. Kay S. Garcia. LC 93-27814. 241p. 1994. 32.50x (*0-8263-1512-7*) U of NM Pr.

Broken Betrothal. Gao Xiaosheng. 1987. 6.95 (*0-8351-2051-1*) China Bks.

***Broken Blade.** Simon Hawke. (Chronicles of Athas Ser.). 320p. (Orig.). 1995. pap. 4.95 (*0-7869-0137-3*) TSR Inc.

Broken Boat. Mark Anderson. LC 78-14534. 75p. 1978. 3.50 (*0-87886-104-1*, Greenfld Rev Pr) Greenfld Rev Lit.

Broken Body. Jean Vanier. 160p. 1988. pap. 9.95 (*0-8091-2979-5*) Paulist Pr.

Broken Bonds: The Disintegration of Yugoslavia. Lenard J. Cohen. 299p. (C). 1993. pap. text ed. 19.95 (*0-8133-1854-8*) Westview.

***Broken Bonds: Yugoslavia's Disintegration & Balkan Politics in Transition.** 2nd ed. Lenard Cohen. LC 94-24015. (C). 1995. pap. text ed. 19.95 (*0-8133-2477-7*) Westview.

Broken Bottles, Broken Dreams: Understanding & Helping the Children of Alcoholics. Charles Deutsch. LC 81-5729. 232p. 1982. pap. text ed. 17.95 (*0-8077-2663-X*) Tchrs Coll.

Broken Bough. large type ed. Iris Bromige. 317p. 1977. 15.95 (*0-7089-0044-5*) Ulverscroft.

***Broken Bow.** Sherrie Johnson. (J). 1994. pap. 4.95 (*0-87579-768-7*) Deseret Bk.

Broken Bowl: New & Uncollected Poems. James A. Emanuel. LC 82-83858. 72p. 1983. per. 4.50 (*0-916418-42-1*) Lotus.

Broken Boys - Men: Recovery from Childhood Sexual Abuse. Stephen D. Grubman-Black. 1990. pap. 12.95 (*0-8306-3562-9*) TAB Bks.

Broken Boys - Mending Men: Recovery from Childhood Sexual Abuse. Stephen D. Grubman-Black. 1992. mass mkt. 4.99 (*0-8041-0940-0*) Ivy Books.

Broken Brain: The Biological Revolution in Psychiatry. Nancy C. Andreasen. LC 83-48782. (Illus.). 288p. 1985. pap. 13.00 (*0-06-091272-3*, PL 1272, PL) HarpC.

Broken Bread & Broken Bodies: The Lord's Supper & World Hunger. Joseph A. Grassi. LC 84-18888. 128p. reprint ed. pap. 36.50 (*0-8357-8545-9*, 2034876) Bks Demand.

***Broken Bridge.** Lynne R. Banks. LC 94-26636. 336p. (YA). (gr. 5 up). 1995. 15.00 (*0-688-13595-1*) Morrow Jr Bks.

Broken Bridge. Philip Pullman. LC 91-15893. 256p. (YA). (gr. 7 up). 1992. lib. bdg. 15.99 (*0-679-91972-4*) Knopf Bks Yng Read.

Broken Bridge. Philip Pullman. 224p. (YA). (gr. 7 up). 1994. pap. 4.99 (*0-679-84715-4*, Bullseye Bks) Random Bks Yng Read.

***Broken Butterfly: A Story to Help Children Understand Responsibility & Forgiveness.** Julie G. Dickerson. (Helping Children Understand Ser.). 32p. (J). (gr. k-6). 1996. pap. 11.95 (*0-964676-8-6*) Cherubic Pr.

***Broken Child.** Marcia Cameron. 384p. 1995. 20.00 (*0-8217-4826-2*) Zebra.

Broken Churches, Broken Nation: Denominational Schism & the Coming of the American Civil War. C. C. Goen. LC 85-7131. 208p. 1985. pap. 14.95 (*0-86554-187-6*, MUP-P17) Mercer Univ Pr.

Broken Circle: A True Story of Murder & Magic in Indian Country. Rodney Barker. 1993. mass mkt. 4.99 (*0-8041-1147-2*) Ivy Books.

Broken Cistern. Bonamy Dobree. LC 72-6790. (Studies in Comparative Literature: No. 35). 1972. reprint ed. lib. bdg. 58.95 (*0-8383-1664-6*) M S G Haskell Hse.

Broken Code: The Exploitation of DNA. Marc Lappe. LC 84-22190. (Illus.). 288p. (Orig.). 1985. 17.95 (*0-87156-835-7*) Sierra.

***Broken Code of Silence.** Joseph M. Gabriel, Jr. & John Yoder. 92p. (C). 1994. pap. text ed. 12.95 (*0-9643102-0-1*) J M Gabriel.

Broken Commandment. Ed. by Toson Shimazaki. Tr. & Intro. by Kenneth Strong. 249p. 1977. pap. 19.50 (*0-86008-191-5*, Pub. by U of Tokyo JA) Col U Pr.

Broken Compass: A Study of the Major Comedies of Ben Jonson. Edward B. Partridge. LC 75-38386. 254p. 1976. reprint ed. text ed. 59.75 (*0-8371-8662-5*, PABC, Greenwood Pr) Greenwood.

Broken Connection: Alzheimer's Disease. Liduin E. Souren & Emile H. Franssen. LC 93-25579. 325p. (DUT.). 1993. Pt. 2, Practical Guidelines for Caring for the Alzheimer Patient. pap. text ed. 30.00 (*90-265-1371-2*, Pub. by Swets Pub Serv NE) Swets North Am.

Broken Connection: Alzheimer's Disease, Pt. 1: Origin & Course. Liduin E. Souren & Emile H. Franssen. LC 93-25579. 325p. (DUT.). 1993. Pt. 1, Origin & Course. 50.00 (*90-265-1334-8*, Pub. by Swets Pub Serv NE) Swets North Am.

***Broken Connection: On Death & the Continuity of Life.** Robert J. Lifton. 500p. Date not set. pap. write for info. (*0-88048-874-3*, 8874) Am Psychiatric.

Broken Consort. large type ed. James Gollin. LC 90-35645. 322p. 1990. lib. bdg. 17.95 (*1-56054-012-5*) Thorndike Pr.

Broken Contract: A Memoir of Harvard Law School. Richard D. Kahlenberg. 250p. 1992. 22.00 (*0-8090-3165-5*) Hill & Wang.

Broken Contract: A Memoir of Harvard Law School. Richard D. Kahlenberg. 238p. reprint ed. pap. 11.95 (*0-571-19807-4*) Faber & Faber.

***Broken Cops: The Other Side of Policing.** William H. Kroes. 150p. 1988. pap. 19.95 (*0-398-06217-X*) C C Thomas.

Broken Cops: The Other Side of Policing. William H. Kroes. 150p. (C). 1988. text ed. 35.95x (*0-398-05400-2*) C C Thomas.

Broken Cord. M. Dorris. 1990. pap. 59.70 (*0-06-091980-9*, PL) HarpC.

Broken Cord. Michael Dorris. LC 88-45893. (Illus.). 288p. 1990. reprint ed. pap. 12.00 (*0-06-091682-6*, PL) HarpC.

Broken Cord: A Family's Ongoing Struggle with Fetal Alcohol Syndrome. Michael Dorris. 1989. 18.95 (*0-06-016071-3*, HarpT) HarpC.

Broken Cord: A Family's Ongoing Struggle with Fetal Alcohol Syndrome. large type ed. Michael Dorris. (Large Print Books General Ser.). 466p. 1990. lib. bdg. 21.95 (*0-8161-5018-4*) G K Hall.

Broken Country: Reflections from a War. Ted Grieder. 65p. (Orig.). 1989. 15.00 (*0-9621842-1-7*); pap. text ed. 7.00 (*0-9621842-0-9*) Strait Gate Pr.

***Broken Covenant.** Moshe Arens. 1995. 25.00 (*0-671-86964-7*) S&S Trade.

Broken Covenant. Charles M. Sennott. 1992. pap. 19.95 (*0-13-099508-8*) P-H.

Broken Covenant. Charles M. Sennott. (Illus.). 288p. 1992. pap. 23.00 (*0-671-76715-1*) S&S Trade.

Broken Covenant. Charles M. Sennott. 512p. 1994. mass mkt. 4.99 (*1-55817-755-8*, Pinnacle NY) Windsor NY.

Broken Covenant. Robert Todaro. 1992. mass mkt. 4.99 (*0-06-100440-5*, Harp PBks) HarpC.

Broken Covenant: American Civil Religion in Time of Trial. Robert N. Bellah. LC 74-19479. 204p. 1992. pap. text ed. 12.95 (*0-226-04199-9*) U Ch Pr.

Broken Covenants, No. NI1: Report of the Northern Ireland Human Rights Assembly, 6-8 April 1992. 245p. 1993. pap. 20.00 (*0-946088-40-3*, Pub. by NCCL UK) St Mut.

***Broken Crayons.** Robert Black. 112p. 1994. per., pap. text ed. 15.00 (*0-7872-0182-0*) Kendall-Hunt.

Broken Creek. large type ed. Lee Floren. (Nightingale Ser.). 240p. 1991. pap. 14.95 (*0-8161-4969-0*, Nightingale) Hall.

***Broken Creek.** large type ed. Lee Floren. (Western Library). 304p. 1995. pap. 14.95 (*0-7089-7692-1*, Linford) Ulverscroft.

Broken Creek; Gunsmoke Gambler, 2 vols. in 1. Lee Floren. 384p. 1992. pap. 4.50 (*0-8439-3344-5*) Dorchester Pub Co.

Broken Date. R. L. Stine. Ed. by Patricia MacDonald. 224p. (J). 1991. reprint ed. mass mkt. 3.99 (*0-671-69322-0*, Archway) PB.

***Broken Days.** Ann Rinaldi. LC 94-17665. (Quilt Trilogy Ser.: Vol. 2). (J). 1995. 13.95 (*0-590-46053-6*) Scholastic Inc.

Broken Dice: And Other Mathematical Tales of Chance. Ivar Ekeland. Tr. by Carol Volk. LC 93-19341. (Illus.). 192p. 1993. 19.95 (*0-226-19991-6*) U Ch Pr.

Broken Dolls. Von Amon. LC 81-14943. 1986. 22.95 (*0-87949-183-3*) Ashley Bks.

Broken Dreams. Bill Dodd. (Orig.). 1992. pap. 12.95 (*0-7022-2428-6*, Pub. by Univ Queensland Pr AT) Intl Spec Bk.

Broken Dreams Wounded Hearts. Greg Glassford. 160p. 1993. pap. 4.99 (*0-88368-244-3*) Whitaker Hse.

Broken Drought. Craig Dent. (C). 1990. 23.00 (*0-89771-039-8*, Pub. by Pascoe Pub AT) St Mut.

Broken E String: A Collection of Short Stories. Pierre Mande. (Illus.). 67p. 1988. 7.95 (*0-935087-17-6*) Wright Pub Co.

Broken Ear. Herge. (Adventures of Tintin Ser.). 1978. mass mkt. 7.95 (*0-316-35850-9*, Joy St Bks) Little.

Broken Earth: The Rural Chinese. Steven W. Mosher. LC 83-47982. 336p. (C). 1983. 27.95 (*0-02-921700-8*) Free Pr.

Broken Earth: The Rural Chinese. Steven W. Mosher. LC 84-47982. (Illus.). 317p. 1984. pap. 14.95 (*0-02-921720-2*) Free Pr.

Broken Engagement. large type ed. Hilda Perry. (Linford Romance Library). 1989. pap. 11.95 (*0-7089-6659-4*, Linford) Ulverscroft.

Broken English: Poetry & Partiality. Heather McHugh. LC 93-13612. (Illus.). 158p. 1993. text ed. 35.00 (*0-8195-5268-2*, Wesleyan Univ Pr); pap. 14.95 (*0-8195-6272-6*, Wesleyan Univ Pr) U Pr of New Eng.

Broken Face of Summer. Michael Hogan. Ed. by Kirk Robertson. LC 81-68829. (Windriver Ser.). 48p. (Orig.). (C). 1981. pap. 4.00 (*0-916918-16-5*) Duck Down.

Broken Fountain. Thomas Belmonte. LC 78-32167. 160p. 1980. text ed. 35.50 (*0-231-04542-5*); pap. text ed. 15.00 (*0-231-04543-3*) Col U Pr.

Broken Fountain. 2nd ed. Thomas Belmonte. 224p. 1989. pap. text ed. 15.00 (*0-231-07059-4*) Col U Pr.

Broken Fountain. 2nd enl. ed. Thomas Belmonte. 1989. text ed. 38.00 (*0-231-07058-6*) Col U Pr.

Broken Frame: Three Lectures. Karsten Harries. LC 88-18040. 99p. 1989. 23.95 (*0-8132-0672-3*) Cath U Pr.

***Broken Frame: Three Lectures.** Karsten Harries. LC 88-18040. (Illus.). reprint ed. pap. 36.20 (*0-7837-9189-5*, 2049889) Bks Demand.

Broken Glass. Arthur Miller. 1995. pap. 4.75 (*0-8222-1413-X*) Dramatists Play.

Broken Glass. Arthur Miller. 96p. 1994. pap. 7.95 (*0-14-048095-1*) Viking Penguin.

***Broken Glass & the Last Yankee: Two Plays by Arthur Miller.** Arthur Miller. 192p. 1994. 9.99 (*1-56865-104-X*, GuildAmerica) Dblday Bk Music.

Broken God: Power under Control. David E. Schroeder. (Master's Plan for Men Ser.). 144p. (Orig.). 1994. pap. 9.99 (*0-8010-8376-1*) Baker Bk.

Broken Goddess. Hans Bemmann. 1994. pap. 8.00 (*0-451-04534-3*, ROC) NAL-Dutton.

Broken Ground: John F. Kennedy & the Politics of Education. Laurence J. McAndrews. LC 91-14284. (Modern American History Ser.). 248p. 1991. 62.00 (*0-8240-1897-4*) Garland.

Broken Gun. Louis L'Amour. LC 85-2817. 1984. mass mkt. 3.99 (*0-553-24847-2*) Bantam.

Broken Gun. large type ed. Louis L'Amour. (Special Ser.). 213p. 1993. reprint ed. pap. 16.95 (*1-56054-649-2*) Thorndike Pr.

Broken Hand: The Life of Thomas Fitzpatrick, Mountain Man, Guide & Indian Agent. Leroy R. Hafen. LC 80-23451. (Illus.). xiv, 359p. 1981. reprint ed. pap. 9.95 (*0-8032-7208-1*, Bison Books) U of Nebr Pr.

Broken Heart. John Ford. Ed. by T. J. P. Spencer. (Revels Plays Ser.). 256p. 1981. 32.00 (*0-8018-2479-6*) Johns Hopkins.

Broken Heart. Meg Schneider. (You Choose the Romance Ser.: Bk. 4). 128p. (YA). 1994. write for info. (*0-307-22603-4*, Wave WI) Western Pub.

***Broken Heart.** fac. ed. John Ford. Ed. by Donald K. Anderson, Jr. LC 68-10354. (Regents Renaissance Drama Ser.). 141p. 1994. pap. 40.20 (*0-7837-7337-4*, 2047290) Bks Demand.

Broken Heart: A Tragedy. John Ford. LC 72-38184. (English Experience Ser.: No. 456). 80p. 1972. reprint ed. 25.00 (*90-221-0456-7*) Walter J Johnson.

Broken Heart: Applying the Atonement to Life's Experiences. Bruce C. Hafen. LC 89-34628. 212p. 1989. 12.95 (*0-87579-220-0*) Deseret Bk.

Broken Heart Whole Heart: A Family & Addiction. Pecki Sherman & Virginia S. Newlin. LC 89-11167. 192p. (Orig.). 1989. pap. 9.95 (*1-877674-01-X*) Hampshire Bks.

Broken-Hearted Detective. Milton Bass. Ed. by Dana Isaacson. 256p. (Orig.). 1994. mass mkt. 4.99 (*0-671-74243-4*) PB.

Broken Heartland: The Rise of America's Rural Ghetto. Osha G. Davidson. 224p. 1990. text ed. 24.95 (*0-02-907055-4*) Macmillan.

Broken Hearts. Gretta Berghammer & Rod Caspers. 1984. 3.75 (*0-87129-142-8*, B70) Dramatic Pub.

Broken Hearts. R. L. Stine. Ed. by Pat MacDonald. (Fear Street Super Chiller Ser.). 224p. (Orig.). 1993. mass mkt. 3.99 (*0-671-78609-1*, Archway) PB.

Broken Hill-Sydney-Tasman Sea Transect New South Wales, Eastern Australia. 1991. 95.00 (*0-87590-782-2*, GGT 5) Am Geophysical.

***Broken Hoe: Cultural Reconfiguration in Biase Southwest Nigeria.** David Uru Iyam. 1995. lib. bdg. 55.00 (*0-226-38848-4*); pap. text ed. 18.95 (*0-226-38849-2*) U Ch Pr.

***Broken Home: Lessons in Sorrow.** B. M. Palmer. Ed. by J. Ligon Duncan, 3rd. 112p. (C). 1995. reprint ed. pap. text ed. 6.95 (*1-884416-07-1*) A Press.

Broken Ice. Hap Gilliland. (Indian Culture Ser.). (J). (gr. 1-8). 1972. 5.95 (*0-89992-024-1*) Coun India Ed.

***Broken Image: Restoring Personal Wholeness Through Healing Prayer.** Leanne Payne. 192p. 1995. reprint ed. pap. 11.99 (*0-8010-5334-X*) Baker Bk.

Broken Images: A Study of The Waste Land. Robert L. Schwarz. LC 87-40502. 264p. 1989. 40.00 (*0-8387-5137-7*) Bucknell U Pr.

Broken Iris: Fifty Haiku. Tom Smith. (Persephone Press Poetry Ser.: No. 4). 32p. 1990. pap. 8.00 (*0-9624737-7-4*) S P-Persephone Pr.

Broken Juke. Don Revell. Ed. by Patricia Wilcox. LC 75-21920. (Iris Poets Ser.: Vol. 1). 55p. 1975. pap. 5.00 (*0-916078-00-0*) Iris Pr.

Broken K Pueblo: Prehistoric Social Organization in the American Southwest. James N. Hill. LC 70-111383. (Anthropological Papers of the University of Arizona: No. 18). 159p. reprint ed. pap. 45.40 (*0-8357-7439-2*, 2030980) Bks Demand.

Broken Lance. large type ed. Frank Gruber. (Linford Western Library). 1989. pap. 11.95 (*0-7089-6759-0*, Linford) Ulverscroft.

Broken Land. Ian McDonald. 1992. 22.50 (*0-553-08983-8*, Spectra); pap. 11.00 (*0-553-37054-5*, Spectra) Bantam.

Broken Land. Ian McDonald. 1993. mass mkt. 5.99 (*0-553-56324-6*, Spectra) Bantam.

Broken Laws Broken Bodies: Torture & the Right to Redress in Indonesia. 92p. (Orig.). 1993. pap. 8.00 (*0-934143-57-9*) Lawyers Comm Human.

Broken Letter. Carl Lawrence. 130p. 1993. 9.95 (*0-685-68151-3*); pap. 6.95 (*0-9638575-0-9*) Shannon Pubs.

Broken Lights & Mended Lives: Theology & Common Life in the Early Church. Rowan A. Greer. LC 85-21823. 251p. 1986. 30.00 (*0-271-00422-3*) Pa St U Pr.

Broken Lights & Mended Lives: Theology & Common Life in the Early Church. Rowan A. Greer. 256p. 1991. pap. 13.95 (*0-271-00786-9*) Pa St U Pr.

***Broken Lines-Emmy van Leersum, 1930-1984.** Ed. by Yvonne G. Joris. (Illus.). 232p. 1995. text ed. 49.95 (*90-5349-058-2*) U of Pa Pr.

Broken Lives: Separation & Divorce in England, 1660-1857. Lawrence Stone. LC 92-31576. 388p. 1993. 35.00 (*0-19-820254-7*) OUP.

Broken Lullaby. Sharon Green. (Intrigue Ser.). 1993. mass mkt. 2.99 (*0-373-22244-0*, 1-22244-7) Harlequin Bks.

Broken Lullaby. Sharon Green. (Harlequin Promo Ser.). 1994. mass mkt. 3.99 (*0-373-83305-9*, 1-83305-2) Harlequin Bks.

***Broken Memories: Case Studies in Memory Impairment.** Ed. by Ruth Campbell & Martin Conway. (Illus.). 496p. 1995. 64.95 (*0-631-18722-7*) Blackwell Pubs.

***Broken Memories: Case Studies in Memory Impairment.** Ed. by Ruth Campbell & Martin Conway. (Illus.). 496p. 1995. pap. 24.95 (*0-631-18723-5*) Blackwell Pubs.

Broken Middle: Out of Our Ancient History. Gillian Rose. 336p. 1992. text ed. 54.95 (*0-631-16359-X*); pap. text ed. 22.95 (*0-631-18221-7*) Blackwell Pubs.

Broken Mirror: China after Tiananmen. Ed. by George Hicks. 551p. 1990. lib. bdg. 45.00 (*1-55862-069-9*) St James Pr.

***Broken Mirrors - Broken Minds.** Maitland McDonagh. (Illus.). 293p. (Orig.). Date not set. pap. 19.95 (*0-9517012-4-X*, Pub. by Sun Tavern Flds UK) AK Pr Dist.

Broken Mirrors - Broken Minds: The Dark Dreams of Dario Angento. Maitland McDonagh. LC 93-45770. 1994. 18.95 (*0-8065-1514-7*, Citadel Pr) Carol Pub Group.

An Asterisk (*) at the beginning of an entry indicates that the title is appearing in BIP for the first time.

Broken Moon. Carole Satyamurti. 64p. 1988. pap. 8.95 (*0-19-282097-4*) OUP.

Broken Nest. Rabindranath Tagore. 104p. 1983. 5.50 (*0-318-37008-5*) Asia Bk Corp.

Broken Nuptials in Shakespeare's Plays. Carol T. Neely. LC 84-29947. 272p. reprint ed. pap. 77.60 (*0-7837-3325-9*, 2057731) Bks Demand.

Broken Nuptials in Shakespeare's Plays. Carol T. Neely. LC 93-24730. 264p. 1993. reprint ed. pap. 14.95 (*0-252-06362-7*) U of Ill Pr.

Broken off by the Music. John Yau. (Burning Deck Poetry Ser.). 56p. 1981. 15.00 (*0-930900-95-2*) Burning Deck.

Broken Pattern: Sunlight & Shadows of Hopi History. Vada Carlson. (Illus.). 208p. 1985. 16.95 (*0-87961-148-0*); pap. 8.95 (*0-87961-149-9*) Naturegraph.

***Broken Patterns: Professional Women & the Quest for a New Feminine Identity.** Anita M. Harris. 288p. 1995. 39.95 (*0-8143-2550-5*); pap. 17.95 (*0-8143-2551-3*) Wayne St U Pr.

Broken Penny. Julian Symons. 224p. 1988. pap. 3.95 (*0-88184-388-1*) Carroll & Graf.

Broken Pieces. (Illus.). 224p. 1979. 9.95 (*0-685-19261-X*) Shepherd-Moore Ed Foun.

Broken Pieces. Marie Shepherd-Moore. 1980. 8.95 (*0-9602670-2-6*, 112137) Assn Family Living.

Broken Pitcher: A Comedy. Heinrich Von Kleist. Tr. by B. A. Morgan. LC 77-181939. (North Carolina. University. Studies in the Germanic Languages & Literatures: No. 31). reprint ed. 27.00 (*0-404-50931-2*) AMS Pr.

Broken Place. Michael Shaara. 1994. mass mkt. 5.99 (*0-671-89865-5*) PB.

Broken Portraits: Personal Accounts of Chinese Students. David Kwon. 256p. (Orig.). 1990. 29.95 (*0-8351-2429-0*); pap. 12.95 (*0-685-32415-X*) China Bks.

Broken Pot Restored: Le Jeu de la Feuillee of Adam de la Halle. Gordon D. McGregor. LC 90-84433. (Edward C. Armstrong Monographs on Medieval Literature: No. 6). 185p. (Orig.). 1991. pap. 14.95 (*0-917058-76-3*) French Forum.

Broken Pots. Ossie Enekwe. 1977. 3.00 (*0-912678-31-3*, Greenfld Rev Pr) Greenfld Rev Lit.

Broken Promise. Kenneth A. McCormack. 99p. (C). 1989. text ed. 45.00 (*1-872795-65-X*, Pub. by Pentland Pr UK) St Mut.

***Broken Promise.** Theresa Scott. (Hunters of the Ice Age Ser.). 448p. (Orig.). 1995. mass mkt. 4.99 (*0-8439-3723-8*) Dorchester Pub Co.

***Broken Promise: The Subversion of U. S. Labor Relations, 1947-1994.** James A. Gross. LC 94-42510. (Labor & Social Change Ser.). 384p. (C). 1995. lib. bdg. 49.95 (*1-56639-325-6*) Temple U Pr.

Broken Promise: Why the Federal Election Commission Failed. Brooks Jackson. (Twentieth Century Fund Paper Ser.). 90p. 1990. 9.95 (*0-685-59484-X*) TCFP-PPP.

Broken Promise of Reclamation Reform. Hamilton Candee & Laura King. 1987. write for info. (*0-318-62598-9*) NRDC Newsletter.

Broken Promises. Judy Baer. (Cedar River Daydreams Ser.: Bk. 5). 128p. (Orig.). (J). (gr. 7 up). 1989. pap. 3.99 (*1-55661-087-4*) Bethany Hse.

Broken Promises. Henry Virkler. 1992. pap. write for info. (*0-8499-3374-9*) Word Inc.

***Broken Promises: Agrarian Reform.** William C. Thiesenhusen. 1995. text ed. 59.95 (*0-8133-8458-3*) Westview.

***Broken Promises: Agrarian Reform & the Latin American Campesino.** William C. Thiesenhusen. 226p. (C). 1995. pap. text ed. 19.95 (*0-8133-2401-7*) Westview.

Broken Promises: How Americans Fail Their Children. W. Norton Grubb & Marvin Lazerson. x, 389p. 1988. pap. text ed. 15.95 (*0-226-31004-3*) U Ch Pr.

Broken Promises: Popular Protest, Indian Nationalism & the Congress Party in Bihar, 1935-1946. Vinita Damodaran. 412p. (C). 1993. 35.00 (*0-19-562979-5*) OUP.

Broken Promises: Reading Instruction in Twentieth Century America. Patrick W. Shannon. LC 88-2797. (Critical Studies in Education). 208p. 1988. text ed. 55.00 (*0-89789-161-9*, H161, Bergin & Garvey); pap. text ed. 15.95 (*0-89789-160-0*, G160, Bergin & Garvey) Greenwood.

Broken Promises: Torture & Killings Continue in Turkey. Ed. by Human Rights Watch Staff. 86p. (Orig.). 1992. pap. 7.00 (*1-56432-092-8*) Hum Rts Watch.

Broken Promises Unfulfilled Dreams, Human Rights & Democracy In South Korea. Marcia Greenberg & Helet Merkling. Ed. by Kerry K. Cuomo et al. 42p. (Orig.). (C). 1992. pap. text ed. write for info. (*1-881055-01-9*) RFK Mem Ctr HR.

Broken Purse Strings: Congressional Budgeting, 1974-88. Rudolph G. Penner & Alan J. Abramson. LC 88-27801. (Illus.). 129p. (Orig.). (C). 1988. lib. bdg. 45.00 (*0-87766-453-6*); pap. text ed. 15.50 (*0-87766-424-2*) Urban Inst.

Broken Rebel: A Study in Culture, Politics, & Authoritarian Character. Rupert Wilkinson. 400p. reprint ed. pap. 114.00 (*0-8357-7440-6*, 2013988) Bks Demand.

***Broken Record.** H. Schipper. 1994. pap. 3.99 (*0-517-13184-6*) Random.

Broken Record: The Inside Story of the Grammy Awards. Henry Schipper. (Illus.). 224p. 1992. 17.95 (*1-55972-104-9*, Birch Ln Pr) Carol Pub Group.

Broken Record, Reminiscenses. Roy Campbell. LC 70-131657. 1971. reprint ed. 29.00 (*0-403-00544-2*) Scholarly.

Broken Ring: The Destruction of the California Indians. Van H. Garner. LC 80-52892. (Illus.). 1982. 26.95 (*0-87026-057-X*) Westernlore.

Broken Roots: A Collection of Stories. Osher J. Schuchinsky. 1993. 15.95 (*0-533-10452-1*) Vantage.

***Broken Saber Trail.** Manuel S. Borges. 300p. (Orig.). 1995. pap. 9.95 (*0-7610-0093-3*) NW Pub.

Broken Sands. Jordana Diengdoh. 1989. 17.50 (*81-224-0178-3*, Pub. by Wiley Eastern II) S Asia.

Broken Scale Variance & the Light Cone see Fundamental Interactions at High Energy Three: Tracts in Mathematics & Natural Sciences

***Broken Seals: A New Translation of the Shuibu Zhuan or Water Margin.** Tr. by John Dent-Young & Alex Dent-Young. (Marshes of Mount Liang Ser.: Pt. 1). 448p. 1994. pap. 47.50x (*962-201-602-2*, Pub. by Chinese Univ HK) Coronet Bks.

Broken Shore: The Marin Peninsula in California History. Arthur Quinn. (Illus.). 192p. 1987. reprint ed. pap. 9.95 (*0-939061-00-7*) Redwood Press.

Broken Silence: Conversations with 23 Silent Film Stars. Michael G. Ankerich. LC 92-50952. 331p. 1993. lib. bdg. 35.00x (*0-89950-835-9*) McFarland & Co.

***Broken Silence: Voices of Japanese Feminism.** Ed. by Sandra Buckley. (Illus.). 324p. 1996. 40.00x (*0-520-08513-2*); pap. 15.95 (*0-520-08514-0*) U CA Pr.

Broken Silences: Interviews with Black & White Women Writers. Ed. by Shirley M. Jordan. LC 92-28914. 325p. (C). 1993. 22.95 (*0-8135-1932-2*) Rutgers U Pr.

Broken Silences: Interviews with Black & White Women Writers. Ed. by Shirley M. Jordan. LC 92-28914. 325p. (C). 1995. pap. 16.95 (*0-8135-1933-0*) Rutgers U Pr.

Broken Spears: The Aztec Account of the Conquest of Mexico. Intro. by Miguel Leon-Portilla. LC 91-35657. (Illus.). 224p. 1992. pap. 14.00 (*0-8070-5501-8*) Beacon Pr.

Broken Spell: A Cultural & Anthropological History of Preindustrial Europe. Pieter Spierenburg. LC 90-19386. (Illus.). 320p. (C). 1991. text ed. 45.00 (*0-8135-1675-7*); pap. text ed. 15.00 (*0-8135-1676-5*) Rutgers U Pr.

Broken Sphere. Nigel Findley. (Cloakmaster Cycle Ser.: No. 5). 320p. (Orig.). 1993. pap. 4.95 (*1-56076-596-8*) TSR Inc.

Broken Spur. large type ed. Dudley Dean. (Linford Western Library). 304p. 1989. pap. 11.95 (*0-7089-6709-4*, Linford) Ulverscroft.

Broken Staff. Dorothy Wills & Mildred Wills. 1963. 4.25 (*0-685-68600-0*, MC-2) Lillenas.

Broken Staff: Judaism Through Christian Eyes. Frank E. Manuel. (Illus.). 363p. (C). 1992. 39.95 (*0-674-08370-9*) HUP.

Broken Strand. Betty Schilling. LC 94-42614. 1994. 12.50 (*0-943512-45-X*) Linwood Pub.

Broken String: Poems. Karla Andersdatter. (Illus.). 138p. (C). 1994. pap. 14.95 (*0-911051-63-5*) Plain View.

Broken Structures: Severe Personality Disorders & Their Treatment. Salman Akhtar. LC 91-47121. 440p. 1992. 50.00 (*0-87668-538-6*) Aronson.

Broken Sword: Policing France During the German Occupation. Yann Stephan. LC 91-51073. (Illus.). 130p. (Orig.). (C). 1992. pap. 9.50 (*0-942511-43-3*) OICJ.

Broken Symmetries. Paul Preuss. LC 83-4809. 333p. 1983. 25.00 (*0-89366-151-1*) Ultramarine Pub.

Broken Symmetries: A Study of Agency in Shakespeare's Plays. John Freund. LC 91-30845. (Worcester Polytechnic Institute Studies in Science, Technology, & Culture: Vol. 8). 214p. (C). 1992. text ed. 38.95 (*0-8204-1505-7*) P Lang Pubs.

Broken Tablets: The Cult of the Law in French Art from David to Delacroix. Jonathan P. Ribner. LC 92-23046. 1993. 50.00 (*0-520-07749-0*) U CA Pr.

Broken Taboo: Sex in the Family. Blair Justice & Rita Justice. LC 78-23720. 304p. 1979. 42.95 (*0-87705-389-8*); pap. 20.95 (*0-87705-482-7*) Human Sci Pr.

Broken Things. rev. ed. M. R. De Haan. 1988. 6.99 (*0-929239-00-8*) Discovery Hse Pubs.

Broken to Be Made Whole. Cheryl Bass-Foster. 170p. 1993. pap. 8.95 (*1-884687-01-6*) N Horzns Pub.

Broken Treaties. Victor Contoski. 1973. pap. 2.50 (*0-912284-42-0*) New Rivers Pr.

Broken Tree see Burning Dawn

Broken Triangle: Peking, Djakarta, & the PKI. Sheldon W. Simon. LC 68-22279. 223p. reprint ed. pap. 63.60 (*0-8357-7441-4*, 2020744) Bks Demand.

Broken Trust & Other Poems. Priscilla C. Staples. 1993. 12.95 (*0-533-10687-7*) Vantage.

***Broken Trust, Broken Land: Freeing Ourselves from the War over the Environment.** Robert G. Lee. 220p. (Orig.). 1994. pap. 14.95 (*1-885221-02-9*) BookPartners.

Broken Umbrellas. Kate Spohn. (Illus.). 32p. (J). (ps-3). 1994. lib. bdg. 14.99 (*0-670-85769-6*) Viking Child Bks.

Broken Vase. Rex Stout. (Mystery Ser.). 160p. (Orig.). 1995. mass mkt. 4.99 (*0-553-25632-7*) Bantam.

Broken Vessel. Kate Ross. 304p. 1994. 18.95 (*0-670-84999-5*, Viking) Viking Penguin.

***Broken Vessel.** Kate Ross. 304p. 1995. mass mkt. 5.95 (*0-14-023453-5*, Penguin Bks) Viking Penguin.

Broken Vessels. Andre Dubus. 195p. 1991. 19.95 (*0-87923-885-2*) Godine.

Broken Vessels. Andre Dubus. 195p. 1992. pap. 11.95 (*0-87923-948-4*) Godine.

Broken Vows. Stephanie Daniels. 224p. (Orig.). 1993. pap. 2.95 (*1-56597-107-8*, Kismet) Meteor Pub.

***Broken Vows.** Grove. 1995. mass mkt. 4.50 (*0-06-108304-6*, Harp PBks) HarpC.

***Broken Vows.** Shirl Henke. 448p. (Orig.). 1995. mass mkt., pap. 5.99 (*0-8439-3842-0*) Dorchester Pub Co.

Broken Voyages. Diana DeVere. 150p. (Orig.). 1990. pap. 9.95 (*0-9623686-6-0*) Castalia MN.

Broken Wall: Stories of the Mingling Folk. Edward A. Steiner. LC 73-152958. (Short Story Index Reprint Ser.). 1977. reprint ed. 19.95 (*0-8369-3873-9*) Ayer.

Broken Walls. Caleb Rosado. 160p. 1989. pap. 0.99 (*0-8163-0862-4*) Pacific Pr Pub Assn.

Broken Wave: The Chinese Communist Peasant Movement, 1922-1928. Roy Hofheinz, Jr. (East Asian Ser.: Vol. 90). 352p. 1977. 37.50 (*0-674-08391-1*) HUP.

Broken Waves: A History of the Fiji Islands in the Twentieth Century. Brij V. Lal. LC 92-17786. (Pacific Islands Monograph Ser.: No. 11). (Illus.). 424p. 1992. text ed. 38.00 (*0-8248-1418-5*) UH Pr.

Broken Web: The Educational Experience of Hispanic American Women. Ed. by Teresa McKenna & Flora I. Ortiz. (Mujer Latina Ser.). 262p. 1989. pap. 23.95 (*0-942177-00-2*) Floricanto Pr.

Broken Wheel: Chung Kuo, Bk. 2. David Wingrove. 1991. mass mkt. 5.99 (*0-440-20928-5*) Dell.

Broken Window: Beckett's Dramatic Perspective. Jane A. Hale. LC 86-9447. 192p. 1987. 17.95 (*0-911198-82-2*) Purdue U Pr.

Broken Wing, Broken Promise: A Season Inside the Philadelphia Eagles. Phil Anastasia. (Illus.). 200p. 1993. 18.00 (*0-940159-20-1*) Camino Bks.

Broken Wings. Kahlil Gibran. Tr. by Anthony R. Ferris. 1965. pap. 6.95 (*0-8065-0190-1*, 190, Citadel Pr) Carol Pub Group.

Broken Wings: Hollywood's Air Crashes. James H. Farmer. LC 84-60464. (Illus.). 120p. (Orig.). 1984. pap. 9.95 (*0-933126-46-8*) Pictorial Hist.

Broken Wings see Author of Beltraffio

Broken Wings of the Samurai: The Destruction of the Japanese Air Force. Robert C. Mikesh. (Illus.). 199p. 1993. 36.95 (*1-55750-083-5*) Naval Inst Pr.

Broken Wings Will Fly. Mick Blackistone. (Illus.). 32p. (J). (gr. 2-6). 1992. 10.95 (*0-87033-439-5*, Tidewtr Pubs) Cornell Maritime.

Broken Word: Communication Pathos in Modern Literature. Winston Weathers. (Communication & the Human Condition Ser.). 240p. 1981. 68.00 (*0-685-01947-0*) Gordon & Breach.

Broken World of Sacrifice: An Essay in Ancient Indian Ritual. J. C. Heesterman. LC 92-36751. 344p. (C). 1993. lib. bdg. 60.00 (*0-226-32300-5*); pap. text ed. 24.95 (*0-226-32301-3*) U Ch Pr.

Broken, Yet Never Sundered Orthodox Witness & the Ecumenical Movement. Gregory Wingenbach. 200p. 1987. pap. 12.95 (*0-917651-28-6*) Holy Cross Orthodox.

***Brokenburn: The Journal of Kate Stone, 1861-1868.** Anderson. 1995. pap. text ed. (*0-8071-2017-0*) La State U Pr.

Brokenburne: A Southern Auntie's War Tale. Virginia F. Boyle. LC 77-38642. (Black Heritage Library Collection). (Illus.). 1977. reprint ed. 18.95 (*0-8369-9000-5*) Ayer.

Brokenclaw. John Gardner. 1991. mass mkt. 5.50 (*0-425-12721-4*) Berkley Pub.

Brokenhearted. Nancy Weber. 1990. mass mkt. 4.50 (*1-55817-374-9*, Pinnacle NY) Windsor NY.

Brokenness, Discernment & Counseling see Lay Counseling Series

Broker. Lennart Bruce. 80p. 1984. pap. 5.00 (*0-915572-75-3*) Panjandrum.

***Broker-Dealer Operations under Securities & Commodities Law: Financial Responsibility, Credit Regulation, Customer Protection, 2 vols., Set.** Jerry W. Markham & Thomas L. Hazen. (Securities Ser.). 1995. ring bd. write for info. (*0-614-06263-2*) Clark Boardman Callaghan.

Broker-Dealer Regulation. David A. Lipton. (Securities Law Ser.). 1988. ring bd. 145.00 (*0-87632-599-1*) Clark Boardman Callaghan.

Broker-Dealers & Securities Markets. Sheldon M. Jaffe. 438p. 1977. text ed. 95.00 (*0-07-032218-X*) Shepards-McGraw.

Broker or Advocate? The U. S. Role in the Arab-Israeli Dispute, 1973-1978. Harvey Sicherman. LC 78-10438. (Foreign Policy Research Institute. Monograph Ser.: No. 25). 128p. reprint ed. pap. 36.50 (*0-7837-1778-4*, 2041976) Bks Demand.

Brokered Justice: Race, Politics, & Mississippi Prisons, 1798-1992. William B. Taylor. LC 93-32001. 300p. 1994. 49.50 (*0-8142-0621-2*) Ohio St U Pr.

Brokers, Bagmen, & Moles: Fraud & Corruption in the Chicago Futures Markets. David Greising & Laurie Morse. 337p. 1991. text ed. 24.95 (*0-471-53057-3*) Wiley.

***Broker's Edge: How to Sell Securities in Any Market.** Steven Drozdeck. 1995. pap. 27.95 (*0-13-311044-3*) P-H.

Brokers in Transportation: A Comprehensive History, Study & Guide on Motor Carrier Brokers of Property in the United States. rev. ed. John P. Martell. 198p. 1988. pap. text ed. 29.95 (*0-9621540-0-8*) Transmart.

Brokers Loans: A Study in the Relation Between Speculative Credits & the Stock Market, Business & Banking. Lewis H. Haney et al. LC 75-2638. (Wall Street & the Security Market Ser.). 1975. reprint ed. 23.95 (*0-405-06963-4*) Ayer.

Brokers of Morality: Thai Ethnic Adaptation in a Rural Malaysian Setting. Louis Golomb. LC 78-4141. (Asian Studies at Hawaii: No. 23). (Illus.). 254p. reprint ed. pap. 72.40 (*0-8357-6045-6*, 2034638) Bks Demand.

Bromberg & Ribstein on Partnership, 2 vols., Set. Alan R. Bromberg & Larry E. Ribstein. 1200p. 1988. 595.00 (*0-316-10925-8*) Little.

Bromeliaceae Andre Anae. deluxe ed. Edouard F. Andre. Ed. by Michael Rothenberg. Tr. by Doris Love. (Illus.). 211p. 1983. reprint ed. 150.00 (*0-685-31056-6*) Big Bridge Pr.

Bromeliaceae of Ecuador. Jean Gilmartin. (Monographiae Phanerogamarum Ser.: No. 4). (Illus.). 1972. 72.00 (*3-7682-0725-0*) Lubrecht & Cramer.

Bromeliads. Bill Wall. (Wisley Handbooks Ser.). (Illus.). 64p. (Orig.). 1990. pap. 5.95 (*0-304-32197-4*, Pub. by Cassell UK) Sterling.

Bromeliads: An Illustrated Dictionary. Clive Innes. (Illus.). 224p. 1995. 39.95 (*0-88192-291-9*) Timber.

Bromelioideae (Bromeliaceae) Lyman B. Smith & Robert J. Downs. LC 79-14114. (Flora Neotropica Monograph Ser.: Vol. 14, No. 3). (Illus.). 650p. 1983. reprint ed. pap. 65.00 (*0-89327-210-8*) NY Botanical.

Bromine. (Metals & Minerals Ser.). 1993. lib. bdg. 250.95 (*0-8490-8962-X*) Gordon Pr.

Bromine Compounds: Chemistry & Applications. Ed. by D. Price et al. 422p. 1988. 146.25 (*0-444-42982-4*) Elsevier.

Bromley Genealogy. Viola A. Bromley. (Illus.). 452p. 1989. reprint ed. lib. bdg. 79.50 (*0-8328-0328-6*); reprint ed. pap. 69.50 (*0-8328-0329-4*) Higginson Bk Co.

Brompton Hospital Guide to Chest Physiotherapy. 5th ed. B. Webber. 1988. pap. 29.95 (*0-632-01978-6*) Blackwell Sci.

Bronc People. William Eastlake. 254p. 1991. pap. 11.00 (*0-9627387-5-1*) Bamberger.

Bronc to Breakfast. Mike Logan. LC 88-91264. (Illus.). 80p. (Orig.). 1988. pap. 7.95 (*0-937959-53-7*) Falcon Pr MT.

Broncbuster. Mike Clumpner. 220p. (Orig.). 1980. pap. 1.95 (*0-89083-671-X*) Zebra.

Bronchial Asthma. 2nd ed. Ed. by M. Eric Gershwin. 656p. 1986. text ed. 125.00 (*0-8089-1814-1*, 791543, Grune) Saunders.

Bronchial Asthma: Genetic Population & Psychiatric Study. D. Leigh & E. Marley. LC 67-14544. 1967. 89.00 (*0-08-012167-5*, Pub. by Pergamon Repr UK) Franklin.

Bronchial Asthma: Mechanisms & Therapeutics. 3rd ed. Ed. by Earle B. Weiss & Myron Stein. LC 92-49468. (Illus.). 1300p. 1993. 210.00 (*0-316-92899-2*) Little.

Bronchial Asthma: Principles of Diagnosis & Treatment. Ed. by M. Eric Gershwin & Georges Halpern. LC 93-38240. (Illus.). 784p. 1994. text ed. 125.00 (*0-89603-253-1*) Humana.

Bronchial Carcinoma: An Integrated Approach to Diagnosis & Management. Ed. by M. Bates. (Illus.). 240p. 1985. 115.00 (*0-387-13234-1*) Spr-Verlag.

Bronchial Circulation. Ed. by Butler. (Lung Biology in Health & Disease Ser.: Vol. 57). 832p. 1992. 235.00 (*0-8247-8443-X*) Dekker.

Bronchial Hyperresponsiveness. Ed. by Hartmut Zwick. LC 92-49734. 100p. 1992. write for info. (*3-211-82375-1*); pap. 25.00 (*0-387-82375-1*) Spr-Verlag.

Bronchial Mucology & Related Diseases. Luigi Allegra & Pier C. Braga. (Bronchial Mucology Ser.). 224p. 1990. 76.50 (*0-88167-753-1*) Raven.

Bronchoalveolar Lavage. Baughman. 297p. 1991. 65.00 (*0-8151-0549-5*, Yr Bk Med Pubs) Mosby Yr Bk.

Bronchoalveolar Lavage: Cytology & Clinical Applications. Michael W. Stanley et al. LC 90-5064. (Illus.). 256p. 1991. 110.00 (*0-89640-189-8*) Igaku-Shoin.

Bronchogenic Carcinoma. Omar M. Salazar et al. (Oncologic Division of Radiation Oncology Ser.: Vol. 13). (Illus.). 384p. 1981. pap. 135.00 (*0-08-027464-1*, Pergamon Pr) Elsevier.

Bronchopulmonary Dysplasia. Ed. by Eduardo Bancalari & J. Thomas Stocker. (Aspen Seminars on Pediatric Disease Ser.). 441p. 1988. 110.00 (*0-89116-681-5*) Hemisp Pub.

Bronchopulmonary Dysplasia: Strategies for Total Patient Care. Carolyn Lund. 260p. 1990. text ed. 19.95 (*0-9622975-2-6*) NICU INK.

Bronchoscopy: A Text Atlas. Ed. by Udaya B. Prakash. LC 93-7652. 560p. 1994. 190.00 (*0-7817-0095-7*); sl. write for info. (*0-7817-0221-6*) Raven.

Bronco Brothers. abr. ed. Rocky Falls. 90p. 1995. pap. 6.95 (*1-56901-355-1*) NW Pub.

Bronco Junky. Willard Gellis. 80p. 1992. pap. write for info. (*0-917455-22-3*) Big Foot NY.

Bronco Trail. John Benteen. (Sundance Ser.: No. 6). 160p. 1981. pap. 1.75 (*0-8439-1045-3*) Dorchester Pub Co.

Bronco Trail: Sundance. large type ed. John Benteen. (Linford Western Library). 1991. pap. 13.95 (*0-7089-7121-0*) Ulverscroft.

Brone in the Parlor. Bettye Martin-McRae. Ed. by Carol Boyd. 120p. (Orig.). 1992. pap. 9.95 (*1-878162-03-9*) Unicorn Pr USA.

Bronislava Nijinska: A Dancer's Legacy. Nancy Van Norman Baer. LC 86-4384. (Illus.). 100p. (Orig.). 1986. pap. 14.95 (*0-88401-048-1*) Fine Arts Mus.

Bronislava Nijinska: Early Memoirs. Bronislava Nijinska. Ed. by Irina Nijinska & Jean Rawlinson. Tr. by Jean Rawlinson. LC 92-13666. (Illus.). 576p. 1992. pap. 18.95 (*0-8223-1295-6*) Duke.

Bronk: An Essay. Cid Corman. 112p. 1976. 4.00 (*0-916562-06-9*) Truck Pr.

Bronka Stooler Boo Boo Boo: Stories & Art of a Child Author. 3rd ed. Pablo Cuneo. (Mucho Somos Ser.: No. 5). (Illus.). 9p. (gr. 1-5). 1986. 1.25 (*0-914370-50-2*) Mothers Hen.

Bronsdon & Box Families. Lucius B. Marsh & Harriet F. Parker. (Illus.). 332p. 1989. reprint ed. lib. bdg. 63.00 (*0-8328-0330-8*); reprint ed. pap. 53.00 (*0-8328-0331-6*) Higginson Bk Co.

Bronson Alcott, Teacher. Dorothy McCuskey. LC 71-89201. (American Education: Its Men, Institutions & Ideas, Ser.). 1977. reprint ed. 21.95 (*0-405-01440-6*) Ayer.

Bronson Alcott's Life & Philosophy, 2 vols. Franklin B. Sanborn. 1972. 200.00 (*0-87968-794-0*) Gordon Pr.

Bronson M. Cutting: Progressive Politician. Richard Lowitt. LC 92-15345. (Illus.). 7432p. 1992. 55.00x (*0-8263-1347-7*) U of NM Pr.

Bronstein's Children. Jurek Becker. Tr. by Leila Vennewitz. 1988. pap. 19.95 (*0-15-114350-1*) HarBrace.

Bronte Bibliography. Ed. by G. Anthony Yablon & John Turner. LC 78-13504. 151p. 1978. text ed. 35.00 (*0-313-27711-7*) Greenwood.

B

An Asterisk (*) at the beginning of an entry indicates that the title is appearing in BIP for the first time. 921

Bronte Country. J. Stuart & A. Erskine. LC 71-179270. (English Literature Ser.: No. 33). 1971. lib. bdg. 69.95 (*0-8383-1252-7*) M S G Haskell Hse.

Bronte Family, 2 vols., Set. Francis A. Leyland. LC 70-157554. (English Literature Ser.: No. 33). 1971. reprint ed. lib. bdg. 150.00 (*0-8383-1256-X*) M S G Haskell Hse.

Bronte Sisters & George Eliot: A Unity of Difference. Barbara Prentis. 208p. 1987. 57.50 (*0-389-20756-X*, N8315) B&N Imports.

Bronte Story. Margaret Lane. LC 75-108394. (Illus.). 368p. 1971. reprint ed. text ed. 35.00 (*0-8371-3817-5*, LABS, Greenwood Pr) Greenwood.

***Bronte Wilde, Radical Love, Pt. 1.** Howe. 1995. pap. text ed. 12.95 (*1-55713-205-4*) Sun & Moon CA.

Bronteana: The Rev. Patrick Bronte, His Collected Works & Life. Patrick B. Bronte. LC 77-148320. reprint ed. 38.00 (*0-404-08920-8*) AMS Pr.

Brontes. P. Bentley. LC 75-30922. (Studies in the Brontes: No. 64). 1975. lib. bdg. 75.00 (*0-8383-2096-1*) M S G Haskell Hse.

Brontes. Intro. by Harold Bloom. (Modern Critical Views Ser.). 211p. 1987. 29.95 (*0-87754-687-8*) Chelsea Hse.

Brontes. C. Martin. (Life & Works). (Illus.). 112p. (J). (gr. 7 up). 1989. 14.95 (*0-685-58635-9*); lib. bdg. 19.94 (*0-86592-299-3*) Rourke Corp.

Brontes. Irene Willis. LC 76-52966. (Studies in the Brontes: No. 64). 1977. reprint ed. lib. bdg. 75.00 (*0-8383-2141-0*) M S G Haskell Hse.

Brontes: A Scene from the Childhood of Charlotte, Branwell, Emily, & Anne. Catherine Brighton. LC 93-26097. (J). 1994. 11.95 (*0-8118-0608-1*) Chronicle Bks.

Brontes: Branwell, Anne, Emily, Charlotte. Bettina L. Knapp. (Literature & Life Ser.). 192p. 1991. 19.95 (*0-8264-0514-2*, F Ungar Bks) Continuum.

Brontes: Charlotte Bronte & Her Family. Rebecca Fraser. 1988. 25.00 (*0-517-56438-6*, Crown) Crown Pub Group.

Brontes: Charlotte Bronte & Her Family. Rebecca Fraser. (Illus.). 560p. 1990. pap. 14.00 (*0-449-90465-2*, Columbine) Fawcett.

Brontes: Fact & Fiction. Angus MacKay. LC 70-148277. reprint ed. 16.00 (*0-404-08886-4*) AMS Pr.

Brontes: Life & Letters, 2 Vols. Clement Shorter. LC 68-24918. (English Biography Ser.: No. 31). 1969. reprint ed. lib. bdg. 75.00 (*0-8383-0186-X*) M S G Haskell Hse.

Brontes: Life & Letters, 2 vols., Set. Clement K. Shorter. (BCL1-PR English Literature Ser.). 1992. reprint ed. lib. bdg. 150.00 (*0-7812-7451-6*) Rprt Serv.

Brontes, & Other Essays. Godfrey F. Bradby. LC 67-30176. (Essay Index Reprint Ser.). 1977. 18.95 (*0-8369-0240-8*) Ayer.

Brontes in Ireland. William Wright. LC 70-160161. (English Literature Ser.: No. 33). 1971. lib. bdg. 54.95 (*0-8383-1257-8*) M S G Haskell Hse.

Brontes in Ireland: Where the Novels Came From. William Wright. LC 76-29146. (Illus.). 1985. 10.00 (*0-916620-12-3*) Portals Pr.

Brontes of Ballynaskeagh. W. Houghton Crowe. 180p. 1978. 17.95 (*0-85221-100-7*) Dufour.

Brontes: Three Great Novels: Jane Eyre, Wuthering Heights, The Tenant of Wildfell Hall. Charlotte Bronte et al. 944p. 1994. pap. text ed. 14.95 (*0-19-282285-3*) OUP.

Bronto Lost. Tiffany B. Eisberg et al. (Under Twenty Writing Society Ser.). (Illus.). 60p. (J). (gr. 3-5). 1994. pap. 6.95 (*1-56721-070-8*) Twnty-Fifth Cent Pr.

***Bronto's Brunch.** Jan Pienkowski. (Introducing Furrytails Ser.). (J). (ps). 1995. 19.99 (*0-525-45354-7*) Dutton Child Bks.

Brontosaur. Rupert Oliver. (J). (gr. 4-7). 1991. 4.95 (*0-8167-1303-0*) Troll Assocs.

Brontosaurus. Stuart A. Kallen. Ed. by Julie Berg. LC 94-1819. (If the Dinosaurs Could Talk Ser.). (J). 1994. lib. bdg. 14.96 (*1-56239-286-7*) Abdo & Dghtrs.

Brontosaurus. Sheehan. (Dinosaur Library: Set I). (Illus.). 24p. (J). 1981. lib. bdg. 14.00 (*0-86592-111-3*) Rourke Enter.

Brontosaurus. Lanford Wilson. 1978. pap. 2.75 (*0-8222-0157-7*) Dramatists Play.

Brontosaurus: Mini Dinos. David Hawcock. (Illus.). 10p. (J). (ps-2). 1993. 5.95 (*0-8050-2361-5*) H Holt & Co.

Bronwen, the Traw, & the Shape-Shifter. James Dickey. LC 85-27082. (Illus.). 32p. (J). (gr. k-3). 1986. 13.95 (*0-15-212580-9*, HB Juv Bks) HarBrace.

***Bronx Angel.** Ed Dee. 304p. 1995. 21.95 (*0-446-51774-7*) Warner Bks.

***Bronx Angel.** Ed Dee. 1996. mass mkt. write for info. (*0-446-60337-6*) Warner Bks.

Bronx Beat: Reflections of a Police Commander. Tony Bouza. 1990. 23.00 (*0-942511-29-8*); pap. 12.00 (*0-942511-27-1*) OICJ.

Bronx Bombers: Memories & Memorabilia of the New York Yankees. Bruce Chadwick. (Illus.). 132p. 1992. 24.95 (*1-55859-243-1*) Abbeville Pr.

Bronx Boy. Gerard Flynn. LC 92-91076. 224p. 1993. pap. 10.95 (*1-56002-246-9*, Univ Edtns) Aegina Pr.

Bronx in Print: An Annotated Catalogue of Books & Pamphlets about the Bronx. Candace Kuhtas & Narcisco Rodriguez. Ed. by Gary Hermalyn. 16p. (Orig.). 1981. pap. 11.00 (*0-685-65206-8*) Bronx County.

Bronx in the Frontier Era: From the Beginning to 1696. Lloyd Ultan. LC 92-42459. (Illus.). 152p. 1993. 20.00 (*0-941980-34-0*) Bronx County.

Bronx in the Frontier Era from the Beginning to 1696. BCHS (Bronx County Historical Society) Staff. 256p. 1994. boxed 20.00 (*0-8403-9215-X*) Kendall-Hunt.

Bronx in the Innocent Years: 1890-1925. Lloyd Ultan & Gary Hermalyn. (Life in the Bronx Ser.). (Illus.). 192p. (C). 1992. reprint ed. text ed. 25.00 (*0-941980-32-4*) Bronx County.

Bronx It Was Only Yesterday: 1935-1965. Lloyd Ultan & Gary Hermalyn. (Life in the Bronx Ser.). (Illus.). 192p. 1993. text ed. 25.00 (*0-941980-33-2*) Bronx County.

Bronx Remembered. Nicholasa Mohr. LC 75-6306. (Trophy Keypoint Bk.). 288p. (YA). (gr. 7 up). 1993. pap. 4.95 (*0-06-447100-4*, Trophy) HarpC Child Bks.

Bronx Triangle: A Portrait of Norwood. Edna Mead. Ed. by Gary Hermalyn & Lloyd Ultan. (Illus.). 141p. 1982. 12.00 (*0-941980-09-X*) Bronx County.

Bronx Walking Tours. Ed. by Siegel Associates Staff. (Walking Tours of the Cities Ser.: Vol. 1). (Illus.). 160p. 1988. 39.95 (*0-911963-00-6*); pap. 14.95 (*0-911963-01-4*) Siegel Bks.

Bronze. Georgia Johnson. LC 70-161267. (Black Heritage Library Collection). 1977. reprint ed. 15.95 (*0-8369-8826-4*) Ayer.

Bronze: A Book of Verse. Georgia D. Johnson. LC 73-18585. reprint ed. 27.50 (*0-404-11396-6*) AMS Pr.

Bronze Age. Vere G. Childe. LC 63-18050. 1930. 20.00 (*0-8196-0123-3*) Biblo.

Bronze Age. V. Gordon Childe. (Irvington Reprint Series in Anthropology). (C). 1991. reprint ed. pap. text ed. 1.00 (*0-8290-2604-5*, A-32) Irvington.

Bronze-Age America. Barry Fell. 1982. 22.50 (*0-316-27771-1*) Little.

Bronze Age Cemetery at Gibeon. James B. Pritchard. (University Museum Monographs: No. 25). (Illus.). x, 123p. 1963. pap. 20.00 (*0-934718-17-2*) U PA Mus Pubns.

Bronze Age Metalwork in Southern Britain. Susan M. Pearce. 1989. pap. 25.00 (*0-85263-680-6*, Pub. by Shire UK) St Mut.

Bronze Age Metalwork in Southern Sweden: Aspects of Social & Spatial Organization 1800-500 B. C. Thomas B. Larsson. (Illus.). xii, 200p. (Orig.). 1986. pap. text ed. 70.00x (*91-7174-229-8*) Coronet Bks.

Bronze & Iron: Ancient Near Eastern Artifacts in the Metropolitan Museum of Art. Oscar W. Muscarella. 1994. 75.00 (*0-8109-6450-3*) Abrams.

Bronze & Iron: Ancient Near Eastern Artifacts in the Metropolitan Museum of Art. Oscar W. Muscarella. (Illus.). 504p. 1989. 75.00 (*0-87099-525-1*) Metro Mus Art.

***Bronze Bow.** Estelle Kleinman. Ed. by J. Friedland & R. Kessler. (Novel-Ties Ser.). (J). (gr. 5-7). 1995. student ed, pap. text ed. 15.95 (*1-56982-310-3*) Lrn Links.

Bronze Bow. Elizabeth G. Speare. 256p. (J). (gr. 6 up). 1961. 14.95 (*0-395-07113-5*) HM.

Bronze Bow. Elizabeth G. Speare. LC 61-10640. (Illus.). 272p. (J). (gr. 6 up). 1973. pap. 7.95 (*0-395-13719-5*, Sandpiper) HM.

Bronze Bow. braille ed. Elizabeth G. Speare. 364p. 1993. Braille. vinyl bd. 29.12 (*1-56956-338-1*, BR9149) W A T Braille.

Bronze Casting & American Sculpture, 1850-1900. Michael E. Shapiro. LC 82-49307. (Illus.). 208p. 1985. 50.00 (*0-87413-218-5*) U Delaware Pr.

Bronze, Clay & Stone: Chinese Art in the C. C. Wang Family Collection. Annette L. Juliano. (Illus.). 184p. 1989. 45.00 (*0-295-96805-2*) U of Wash Pr.

Bronze Grimoire: New Magic for Elric! Chaosium, Inc. Staff. (Elric Roleplaying Game Ser.). (Illus.). 96p. (Orig.). 1994. pap. 12.95 (*1-56882-029-1*, 2905) Chaosium.

Bronze Hook of Pisces. Anthony P. Faretra. 96p. 1994. 9.00 (*0-8059-3546-0*) Dorrance.

Bronze Horseman. Aleksandr Pushkin. Ed. by E. Little. (Library of Russian Classics). 84p. pap. text ed. 15.95 (*0-631-14385-8*, Pub. by Duckworth UK) Focus Info Gr.

Bronze Horseman: Mednyi Vsadnik. Pushkin. Ed. by T. E. Little. (C). reprint ed. pap. text ed. 12.95 (*1-85399-245-3*, Pub. by Brstl Class Pr UK) Focus Info Gr.

Bronze Killer: The Story of a Family's Fight Against a Very Common Enemy - Hemochromatosis. Marie Warder. 134p. (Orig.). 1989. pap. 12.95 (*0-88925-885-6*) Gordon Soules Bk.

Bronze Liver of Piacenza: Analysis of a Polytheistic Structure. L. B. Van der Meer. (Dutch Monographs on Ancient History & Archaeology: Vol. II). (Illus.). 210p. (C). 1987. 83.00 (*90-70265-41-9*, Pub. by Gieben NE) Benjamins North Am.

Bronze Mystique. Barbara Delinsky. 1992. mass mkt. 4.50 (*0-373-83252-4*, 1-83252-6) Harlequin Bks.

Bronze Screen: Chicana & Chicano Film Culture. Rosa L. Fregoso. LC 93-7755. 182p. 1993. text ed. 39.95 (*0-8166-2135-7*); pap. 15.95 (*0-8166-2136-5*) U of Minn Pr.

Bronze Sculpture: Sculpture from 1500-1800 in the Collection of the Museum Boymans-van Beuningen. Emile Van Binnebeke. (Illus.). 200p. 1994. pap. 35.00 (*90-6918-126-6*, Pub. by Mus Boymans-van Beuningen NE) U of Wash Pr.

Bronze Statue of a Youth. David Rinne. (Illus.). 30p. (Orig.). 1975. pap. 5.95 (*0-89236-043-7*) J P Getty Trust.

Bronze Vessels of Ancient China in the Avery Brundage Collection. Rene-Yvon L. D'Argence. LC 77-71672. (Illus.). 144p. 1977. pap. 17.50 (*0-295-96648-3*) U of Wash Pr.

Bronze-Working Centres of Western Asia 1000-539 B.C. Ed. by John Curtis. (Studies in Egyptian Archaeology). (Illus.). 200p. 1988. text ed. 59.95 (*0-7103-0274-6*, Pub. by Kegan Paul Intl UK) Routledge Chapman & Hall.

Bronzegefasse Von Olympia: Mit Ausnahme der Geometrischen Dreifuesse nd der Kessel Des Orienta Lisierenden Stils. Werner Gauer. Ed. by German Archeological Institute Staff. (Olympische Forschungen Ser.: Vol. XX, Pt. 1). (Illus.). xv, 308p. (GER.). (C). 1991. lib. bdg. 246.15 (*3-11-012737-7*) De Gruyter.

***Bronzes: Sculptors & Founders, 1800-1930, Index.** Harold Berman. LC 94-23075. Date not set. 20.00x (*0-88740-704-8*) Schiffer.

***Bronzes: Sculptors & Founders, 1800-1930, Vol. I.** Harold Berman. LC 94-23075. (Illus.). 224p. Date not set. 79.95 (*0-88740-700-5*) Schiffer.

***Bronzes: Sculptors & Founders, 1800-1930, Vol. II.** Harold Berman. LC 94-23075. (Illus.). 272p. Date not set. 79.95 (*0-88740-701-3*) Schiffer.

***Bronzes: Sculptors & Founders, 1800-1930, Vol. III.** Harold Berman. LC 94-23075. (Illus.). 320p. Date not set. 79.95 (*0-88740-702-1*) Schiffer.

***Bronzes: Sculptors & Founders, 1800-1930, Vol. IV.** Harold Berman. LC 94-23075. (Illus.). 400p. Date not set. 79.95 (*0-88740-703-X*) Schiffer.

Bronzes from Achutrajpur Orissa. Debala Mitra. 1978. 50.00 (*0-8364-0136-0*) S Asia.

Bronzes of the 19th Century: A Dictionary of Sculptors. Pierre Kjellberg. Tr. by Leslie Bockol et al. LC 94-66376. (Illus.). 685p. 1994. 150.00 (*0-88740-629-7*) Schiffer.

Bronzes 1500-1650: The Robert H. Smith Collection. Anthony Radcliffe. (Illus.). 160p. 1994. 50.00 (*0-302-00636-2*, Pub. by P Wilson Pubs) Sothebys Pubns.

Bronzeville Boys & Girls. Gwendolyn Brooks. LC 56-8152. (Illus.). 48p. (J). (gr. 3-6). 1967. lib. bdg. 14.89 (*0-06-020651-9*) HarpC Child Bks.

Bronzeworkers in the Athenian Agora. Carol C. Mattusch. (Excavations of the Athenian Agora Picture Bks.: No. 20). (Illus.). 32p. 1982. pap. 3.00 (*0-87661-624-4*) Am Sch Athens.

Bronzino As Draughtsman: An Introduction. Craig H. Smyth. LC 74-178089. (Illus.). 8.00 (*0-685-71747-X*) J J Augustin.

Bronzino's Chapel of Eleonora in the Palazzo Vecchio. Janet Cox-Rearick. (California Studies in the History of Art: No. XXIX). (C). 1992. 75.00 (*0-520-07480-7*) U CA Pr.

Brood. Paul Mantell & Avery Hart. (X-Men Digest Novels Ser.). (Illus.). 112p. (Orig.). (J). (gr. 2 up). 1994. pap. 3.50 (*0-679-86568-3*, Bullseye Bks) Random Bks Yng Read.

***Brooding Angel.** Marie Ferrarella. (Special Edition Ser.). 1995. mass mkt. 3.75 (*0-373-09963-0*, 1-09963-9) Silhouette.

Broodmales. Nor Hall & Warren R. Dawson. LC 89-21777. 173p. (Orig.). 1989. pap. 13.50 (*0-88214-340-9*) Spring Pubns.

Broodstock Management & Egg & Larval Quality. N. Bromage & R. J. Roberts. 1994. pap. write for info. (*0-632-03591-9*) Blackwell Sci.

Broodthaers: Writings, Interviews, Photographs. Ed. by Benjamin H. Buchloh. (October Bks.). 175p. (Orig.). 1988. 30.00 (*0-262-02281-8*); pap. 12.50x (*0-262-52135-0*) MIT Pr.

Brook. Barbara Lyons. LC 75-42444. 1976. 10.00 (*0-914916-10-6*); pap. 1.95 (*0-914916-15-7*) Ku Paa.

Brook. Alfred Tennyson. LC 93-46404. (Illus.). 32p. (J). (ps-2). 1994. 14.95 (*0-531-06854-4*); lib. bdg. 14.99 (*0-531-08704-2*) Orchard Bks Watts.

Brook Farm. John T. Codman. 1972. 59.95 (*0-87968-795-9*) Gordon Pr.

Brook Farm. Lindsay Swift. 320p. 1973. reprint ed. pap. 4.95 (*0-8065-0358-0*, Citadel Pr) Carol Pub Group.

Brook Farm: Historic & Personal Memoirs. John T. Codman. LC 71-134371. reprint ed. 55.00 (*0-404-08419-2*) AMS Pr.

Brook of Our Own. M. G. Harkness. 1965. pap. 6.95 (*0-87233-820-7*) Bauhan.

Brook Taylor's Role in the History of Linear Perspective. K. Andersen. Ed. by G. J. Toomer. (Sources in the History of Mathematics & Physical Sciences Ser.: Vol. 10). (Illus.). 272p. 1991. 49.50 (*0-387-97486-5*) Spr-Verlag.

Brooke & Her Rock Star Mom. Francine Pascal. (Sweet Valley Twins & Friends Ser.: No. 55). (YA). 1992. pap. 3.25 (*0-553-15965-8*) Bantam.

Brooke & the Guilty Secret. Marti Plemons. (Grace Street Kids Ser.). (Illus.). 128p. (J). (gr. 3-6). 1992. pap. 4.99 (*0-87403-938-X*, 24-03768) Standard Pub.

Brooke Book. Brooke Shields. (Illus.). 128p. 1982. pap. 7.95 (*0-685-06960-5*) PB.

Brooke County Virginia-West Virginia Licenses & Marriages, 1797-1874. Renee B. Sherman. (Illus.). 349p. (Orig.). 1992. pap. 28.00 (*1-55613-534-3*) Heritage Bk.

Brooke, Fauquier, Loudoun & Alexandria Artillery. Michael J. Andrus. (Virginia Regimental Histories Ser.). (Illus.). 124p. 1990. 19.95 (*0-930919-92-0*) H E Howard.

Brooke Lawrence's Permanent Weight: I Lost 40 Pounds, You Can Too! Brooke Lawrence. Ed. by Dave Davies. 37p. (Orig.). 1989. pap. 29.95 (*1-56610-002-X*) Data Comms Grp.

Brooke Shields. Bob Italia. LC 92-13689. (Cover Girls Ser.). (J). 1992. lib. bdg. 12.94 (*1-56239-110-0*) Abdo & Dghtrs.

Brooke's Little Lies. Ann Norton. (Fifteen - Nickelodeon Bks.: No. 2). 112p. (J). (gr. 4-9). 1992. pap. 2.95 (*0-448-40491-5*, G&D) Putnam Pub Group.

Brooke's Romeus & Juliet, Being the Original of Shakespeare's Romeo & Juliet. Arthur Broke. Ed. by J. J. Munro. LC 74-134609. reprint ed. 21.50 (*0-404-04539-1*) AMS Pr.

Brookfield Zoo Connections: A Program to Enhance Classroom Studies. Ed. by Chicago Zoological Society Staff. (Orig.). (J). (gr. k-8). 1986. pap. text ed. 30.00 (*0-913934-03-8*) Chicago Zoo.

***Brookgreen Gardens Sculpture.** rev. ed. Beatrice G. Proske. (Illus.). 574p. (C). 1968. text ed. 15.00 (*0-9638206-0-5*) Brookgreen.

***Brookgreen Gardens Sculpture, Vol. II.** Robin S. Salmon. (Illus.). 311p. (C). 1993. text ed. 18.00 (*0-9638206-1-3*) Brookgreen.

***Brookgreen Gardens Sculpture & Brookgreen Gardens Sculpture Vol. II.** Beatrice G. Proske & Robin R. Salmon. (Illus.). 885p. (C). 1993. text ed. 30.00 (*0-9638206-2-1*) Brookgreen.

Brookhart Campaigns in Iowa, 1920-1926. Jerry A. Neprash. LC 68-58612. (Columbia University. Studies in the Social Sciences: No. 366). reprint ed. 20.00 (*0-404-51366-2*) AMS Pr.

Brookhaven Lectures: Vistas in Research. Brookhaven National Laboratory Staff. Incl. Vol. 1. 220p. 1967. text ed. 169.00 (*0-677-11550-4*); Vol. 2. 208p. 1968. text ed. 169.00 (*0-677-12950-5*); Vol. 3. 198p. 1968. text ed. 169.00 (*0-677-12990-4*); Vol. 4. 188p. 1969. text ed. 169.00 (*0-677-13500-9*); write for info. (*0-318-52697-2*) Gordon & Breach.

Brooking on Building Contracts. 2nd ed. Bennet. 1980. 69.00 (*0-409-43460-4*) Butterworth Legal Pubs.

Brookings at Seventy-Five. James A. Smith. 236p. 1991. 22.95 (*0-8157-8008-7*) Brookings.

Brookings Institution: A Fifty-Year History. Charles B. Saunders, Jr. LC 66-27855. 118p. 1966. 4.50 (*0-8157-7714-0*); pap. 2.00 (*0-8157-7713-2*) Brookings.

Brookings Institution, Nineteen Sixteen to Nineteen Fifty-Two: Expertise & the Public Interest in a Democratic Society. Donald T. Critchlow. LC 84-20699. (Illus.). 247p. 1985. 23.00 (*0-87580-103-X*) N Ill U Pr.

Brookings Papers on Economic Activity: No. 1-1978. Ed. by Arthur M. Okun & George L. Perry. LC 74-129564. 238p. reprint ed. pap. 67.90 (*0-8357-7442-2*, 2025394) Bks Demand.

Brookings Papers on Economic Activity: No. 2-1979. Ed. by Arthur M. Okun & George L. Perry. LC 74-129564. 226p. reprint ed. pap. 64.50 (*0-8357-7444-9*, 2025396) Bks Demand.

Brookings Papers on Economic Activity: No. 3-1978. Ed. by Arthur M. Okun & George L. Perry. LC 74-129564. 370p. reprint ed. pap. 105.50 (*0-8357-7443-0*, 2025395) Bks Demand.

***Brooklands Giants.** Bill Boddy. (Illus.). 160p. 1995. 42.95 (*0-85429-960-2*, Pub. by J H Haynes & Co UK) Motorbooks Intl.

Brookline: Evolution of an American Jewish Suburb. Bruce A. Philips. LC 90-23079. (European Immigrants & American Society Ser.). 200p. 1991. reprint ed. 15.00 (*0-8240-7428-9*) Garland.

Brooklyn. Frommer. Date not set. write for info. (*0-15-614175-2*) HarBrace.

Brooklyn: People & Places, Past & Present. Grace Glueck & Paul Gardner. (Illus.). 256p. 1991. 45.00 (*0-8109-3118-4*) Abrams.

Brooklyn: Where to Go, What to Do, How to Get There. Ellen Freudenheim. 1991. pap. 12.95 (*0-312-05395-9*) St Martin.

***Brooklyn - The Way It Was.** Brian Merlis. 250p. Date not set. 39.95 (*1-878741-21-7*); pap. 24.95 (*1-878741-20-9*) Israelowitz Pub.

Brooklyn Almanac. Ed. by Margaret Latimer. (Brooklyn Rediscovery Publication Ser.). (Illus.). 102p. 1984. pap. 7.95 (*0-933250-11-8*) Bklyn Educ.

Brooklyn & the World. Ed. by Martin Tucker. (Confrontation Special Anthology Issue Ser.). 352p. 1983. pap. 5.00 (*0-913057-00-2*) L I U Press.

Brooklyn at Play: A Social & Cultural History of Brooklyn at the Turn of the Century. Robert P. Smith. (Bicentennial Ser.). 1976. lib. bdg. 250.00 (*0-87700-226-6*) Revisionist Pr.

Brooklyn Book of the Dead. Stanley Nelson. 108p. pap. 6.00 (*0-912292-22-9*) The Smith.

Brooklyn Book of the Dead. Michael Stephens. LC 93-36135. 228p. 1994. 19.95 (*1-56478-037-6*) Dalkey Arch.

Brooklyn Book of the Dead. deluxe limited ed. Stanley Nelson. 108p. 50.00 (*1-882986-01-6*) The Smith.

***Brooklyn Botanic Garden.** RH Value Publishing Staff. Date not set. pap. 12.99 (*0-517-12139-5*) Random.

***Brooklyn Bounce.** Joe Poss & Henry R. Schlesinger. 240p. (Orig.). 1994. mass mkt. 4.99 (*0-380-77337-6*) Avon.

***Brooklyn Boy.** 1996. pap. 11.00 (*1-880909-43-X*, Basset Bks) Baskerville.

Brooklyn Branding Parlors. limited ed. James Purdy. Ed. by Josh Gosciak & Maurice Kenny. LC 85-18994. (Illus.). 24p. (Orig.). (C). 1986. pap. 10.00 (*0-936556-13-7*) Contact Two.

Brooklyn-Breukelen Poems. Leo Vroman. Ed. by Stanley H. Barkan. Tr. by Claire N. White. (Review Dutch Writers Chapbook Ser.). 48p. 1989. 15.00 (*0-89304-175-0*); 15.00 (*0-89304-177-7*); pap. 5.00 (*0-89304-176-9*); pap. 5.00 (*0-89304-178-5*); audio 10.00 (*0-89304-179-3*) Cross-Cultrl NY.

Brooklyn Bridge: A Novel. Leslie Kaplan. Tr. by Thomas Spear. 184p. 1992. 19.95 (*0-88268-112-5*); pap. 9.95 (*0-88268-113-3*) Station Hill Pr.

Brooklyn Bridge: Fact & Symbol. 2nd ed. Alan Trachtenberg. LC 78-68548. (Illus.). 1979. pap. text ed. 12.95 (*0-226-81115-8*, P828) U Ch Pr.

Brooklyn City Directory, 1859. J. Lain. 1972. 59.95 (*0-87968-796-7*) Gordon Pr.

Brooklyn College: The First Half Century. Murray M. Horowitz. LC 81-65408. (Studies on Society in Change: No. 22). 1981. 22.50 (*0-930888-11-1*) Brooklyn Coll Pr.

Brooklyn Cookbook. Lynn Stallworth. 1991. 25.00 (*0-394-58417-1*) Knopf.

***Brooklyn Dodger Baseball.** Historical Briefs, Inc. Staff. Ed. by Thomas Antonucci & Michael Antonucci. 200p. 1993. pap. 19.95 (*0-89677-048-6*) Hist Briefs.

Brooklyn Dodger Days. Richard Rosenblum. LC 90-36691. (Illus.). 32p. (J). (gr. 1-5). 1991. text ed. 13.95 (*0-689-31512-0*, Atheneum Bks Young) S&S Childrens.

An Asterisk (*) at the beginning of an entry indicates that the title is appearing in BIP for the first time.

B

An Asterisk (*) at the beginning of an entry indicates that the title is appearing in BIP for the first time.

923

Brotherhood of the Rosy Cross. A. E. Waite. (Illus.). 650p. (Orig.). 1992. pap. 36.00 (1-56459-100-X) Kessinger Pub.

Brotherhood of the Sea: The Sailors' Union of the Pacific, 1885-1985. Stephen Schwartz. 200p. 1986. boxed 44.95x (0-88738-121-9) Transaction Pubs.

Brotherhood of the Stars. Kirby Greene. 1994. mass mkt. 4.99 (0-553-29635-3, Spectra) Bantam.

Brotherhood of the Tomb. Daniel Easterman. 1991. mass mkt. 5.50 (0-06-100206-2, Harp PBks) HarpC.

Brotherhood of Thieves. Howard Pelham. 192p. 1994. 17.95 (0-8034-9049-6, Avalon Bks) Bouregy.

Brotherhood of Thieves: Or, A True Picture of the American Church & Clergy. Stephen S. Foster. LC 79-82190. (Anti-Slavery Crusade in America Ser.). 1970. reprint ed. 11.95 (0-405-00628-4) Ayer.

Brotherhood of Tyrants: Manic Depression & Absolute Power. D. Jablow Hershman & Julian Lieb. 220p. (C). 1994. 29.95 (0-87975-888-0) Prometheus Bks.

Brotherhood of War, 4 vols., Set. W. E. B. Griffin. 1992. boxed 23.96 (0-515-11024-8) Jove Pubns.

Brotherhood of War, 4 vols., Set: No. 2. W. E. B. Griffin. 1992. Set. boxed 23.96 (0-515-11026-4) Jove Pubns.

Brotherhood of War, Bk. 1: Lieutenants. W. E. B. Griffin. 416p. 1987. mass mkt. 5.99 (0-515-09021-2) Jove Pubns.

Brotherhood of War, Bk. 2: Captains. W. E. B. Griffin. 416p. 1987. mass mkt. 6.90 (0-515-09138-3) Jove Pubns.

Brotherhood of War, Bk. 3: The Majors. W. E. B. Griffin. 384p. 1987. mass mkt. 5.99 (0-515-08995-8) Jove Pubns.

Brotherhood of War, Bk. 4: Colonels. W. E. B. Griffin. 480p. 1987. mass mkt. 5.99 (0-515-09022-0) Jove Pubns.

Brotherhood of War, Bk. 5: Berets. W. E. B. Griffin. 416p. 1987. mass mkt. 5.99 (0-515-09020-4) Jove Pubns.

Brotherhood of War, Bk. 6: Generals. W. E. B. Griffin. 384p. 1987. mass mkt. 5.99 (0-515-08455-7) Jove Pubns.

Brotherhood of War, Bk. 8: Aviators. W. E. B. Griffin. 1989. mass mkt. 5.99 (0-515-10053-6) Jove Pubns.

Brotherkind. J. N. Williamson. 288p. 1987. reprint ed. pap. 3.50 (0-8439-2436-5) Dorchester Pub Co.

Brotherly Community, the Highest Command of Love: Two Anabaptist Documents of 1650 & 1560. Andreas Ehrenpreis & Claus Felbinger. LC 78-21065. 150p. 1979. pap. 6.50 (0-87486-190-X) Plough.

Brotherly Faithfulness: Epistles from a Time of Persecution. Jakob Hutter. LC 79-15886. 256p. 1979. pap. 7.50 (0-87486-191-8) Plough.

Brotherly House. Graces S. Richmond. 1988. pap. 2.95 (0-345-35555-5, Ballantine Epiphany) Ballantine.

Brotherly Love. Pete Dexter. 1993. pap. 4.99 (0-517-11207-8) Random Hse Value.

Brotherly Love. Pete Dexter. LC 91-52666. 274p. 1991. 22.00 (0-394-58573-9) Random.

Brotherly Love. Randye Lordon. 272p. 1993. 18.95 (0-312-09254-7) St Martin.

Brotherly Love. Randye Lordon. 272p. 1994. pap. 9.95 (0-312-10947-4, Stonewall Inn) St Martin.

Brotherly Love. Pete Dexter. (Contemporary American Fiction Ser.). 288p. 1992. reprint ed. pap. 10.00 (0-14-016773-0, Penguin Bks) Viking Penguin.

Brotherly Love: Murder & the Politics of Prejudice in Nineteenth-Century Rhode Island. Charles Hoffmann & Tess Hoffmann. LC 93-9959. (Illus.). 240p. (C). 1993. lib. bdg. 27.50 (0-87023-852-3) U of Mass Pr.

***Brotherly Love: The Story of Joseph.** Alyce Haramilio. Ed. by Alister MacLean. (Bible Cartoon Ser.: Vol. 1, Bk. II). (Illus.). 100p. (CHI, FRE, GER, JPN, KOR & SPA.). 1994. lib. bdg. 20.00 (0-940178-05-2) Sitare.

Brotherly Tomorrows: Movements for a Cooperative Society in America, 1820-1920. Edward K. Spann. (Illus.). 328p. 1989. text ed. 41.50 (0-231-06708-9) Col U Pr.

***Brotherman.** Herb Boyd & Robert Allen. Date not set. pap. write for info. (0-345-38317-6) Ballantine.

Brotherman: The Odyssey of Black Men in America - An Anthology. Herb Boyd & Robert L. Allen. 1995. 35.00 (0-345-37670-6) Ballantine.

Brothers. Debbie Bailey. (Talk About Ser.). 14p. (J). 1993. text ed. 4.95 (1-55037-274-2, Pub. by Annick CN) Firefly Bks Ltd.

Brothers. Michael Bar-Zohar. LC 92-52666. 400p. 1993. 21.00 (0-449-90511-X, Columbine) Fawcett.

***Brothers.** Michael Bar-Zohar. 1995. mass mkt. 5.99 (0-449-14678-2, GM) Fawcett.

Brothers. Robert De Maria. 352p. 1984. pap. 3.95 (0-345-90232-7) Ballantine.

Brothers. Terence. Tr. by Frank O. Copley. LC 62-18621. Orig. Title: Adelphoe. 1962. pap. 2.15 (0-672-60311-X, LLA112, Bobbs) Macmillan.

Brothers. Terence. Ed. by Gratwick. (Classical Texts Ser.). 1987. 49.95 (0-85668-315-9, Pub. by Aris & Phillips UK); pap. 28.00 (0-85668-316-7, Pub. by Aris & Phillips UK) David Brown.

Brothers. 2nd ed. Cynthia Cockburn. (C). 1983. pap. text ed. 21.50 (0-86104-384-7) Westview.

Brothers. Frederick Barthelme. 272p. 1994. reprint ed. pap. 10.95 (0-14-013209-0, Penguin Bks) Viking Penguin.

Brothers: A Novel of Supreme Seduction. Chayym Zeldis. LC 75-40555. 496p. 1986. reprint ed. pap. 5.99 (0-933503-60-1) Sure Sellers.

Brothers: A Protohistory. 2nd abr. rev. ed. Judi Beckley West. Ed. by Randall West. 85p. (Orig.). 1981. pap. 17.95 (0-942478-00-2) Photopia Pr.

Brothers: Black Soldiers in Nam. Stanley Goff et al. 248p. 1987. pap. 3.95 (0-425-10648-9) Berkley Pub.

***Brothers: Male Dominance.** 2nd ed. Cynthia Cockburn. (C). Date not set. text ed. 51.00 (0-7453-0582-2, Pub. by Pluto Pr UK) Westview.

***Brothers: Male Dominance.** 2nd ed. Cynthia Cockburn. (C). 1983. pap. text ed. 21.50 (0-7453-0583-0, Pub. by Pluto Pr UK) Westview.

***Brothers: The Hidden World of Japan's Richest Family.** Lesley Downer. 448p. 1995. 25.00 (0-679-42554-3) Random.

Brothers: The Origins of the Henry W. & Albert A. Berg Collection of English & American Literature, The New York Public Library. Lola L. Szladits. (Illus.). 76p. 1985. 10.00 (0-87104-281-9) NY Pub Lib.

Brothers: The Politics of Violence among the Sekani of Northern British Columbia. Guy Lanoue. 250p. 1992. 49.50 (0-85496-746-X) Berg Pubs.

Brothers: The Untold Story of Jesus's Evil Brother. Chayym Zeldis. 1992. pap. 5.99 (1-56171-098-9, S P I Bks) Sure Sellers.

Brothers see Phormio

Brothers Against the Raj. Leonard A. Gordon. 1990. text ed. 68.00 (0-231-07442-5); pap. text ed. 25.00 (0-231-07443-3) Col U Pr.

Brothers & Keepers. John E. Wideman. 1984. 22.50 (0-8050-3307-6) H Holt & Co.

Brothers & Keepers. John E. Wideman. 1992. 21.00 (0-8446-6603-3) Peter Smith.

***Brothers & Keepers.** John E. Wideman. 1995. pap. write for info. (0-679-75694-9) Random.

Brothers & Sinners. Rodman Philbrick. 352p. (Orig.). 1993. pap. 4.99 (0-451-17677-4, Onyx) NAL-Dutton.

Brothers & Sisters. Bebe M. Campbell. 480p. 1994. 21.95 (0-399-13929-X) Putnam Pub Group.

***Brothers & Sisters.** Bebe M. Campbell. 560p. Date not set. pap. text ed. 6.99 (0-425-14940-4) Berkley Pub.

Brothers & Sisters. Jane M. Leder. 1994. mass mkt. 5.99 (0-345-37995-0) Ballantine.

Brothers & Sisters. Maxine B. Rosenberg. (Illus.). 32p. (J). (gr. k-3). 1991. 14.95 (0-395-51121-6, Clarion Bks) HM.

Brothers & Sisters. Ellen Senisi. LC 92-42912. (J). 1993. 12.95 (0-590-46419-1) Scholastic Inc.

Brothers & Sisters. Debby Slier. (Hello Baby Bks.). 12p. (J). (ps). 1989. 2.95 (1-56288-146-9) Checkerboard.

***Brothers & Sisters.** large type ed. Bebe M. Campbell. LC 95-5418. (Large Print Book Ser.). 1995. 26.95 (1-56895-211-2) Wheeler Pub.

***Brothers & Sisters: A Guide for Families of Children with Epilepsy.** Epilepsy Foundation of America Staff. 95p. 1992. pap. 10.95 (0-916570-03-7) Epilepsy Foundation of America.

Brothers & Sisters: A Study in Child Psychology. 2nd ed. Karl Konig. 88p. 1992. pap. 8.00 (0-89345-271-8, Steinerbks) Garber Comm.

Brothers & Sisters: Getting Back Together with Your Adult Siblings. Barbara L. Johnson. 144p. 1991. 20.95 (0-87975-682-9) Prometheus Bks.

Brothers & Sisters: How They Shape Our Lives. Jane M. Leder. 304p. 1991. 19.95 (0-312-06312-1) St Martin.

Brothers & Sisters: Real Love Knows No Boundaries!, 2 bks. in 1. John Ballard. LC 93-12119. (MacBurnie King Soul to Soul Adventure Ser.: Bk. 2). (Illus.). 1995. pap. 14.95 (0-932279-11-2) World Citizens.

Brothers & Sisters - a Special Part of Exceptional Families. 2nd ed. Thomas H. Powell & Peggy A. Gallagher. LC 92-14205. 320p. (C). 1992. pap. text ed. 23.00 (1-55766-110-3) P H Brookes.

Brothers & Sisters of Retarded Children: An Exploratory Study. Frances K. Grossman. LC 73-170664. (Special Education & Rehabilitation Monograph Ser.: No. 9). 267p. reprint ed. pap. 76.10 (0-8357-3977-5, 2036675) Bks Demand.

Brothers & Strangers: The East European Jew in German & German Jewish Consciousness, 1800-1923. Steven E. Aschheim. LC 81-69812. 350p. 1982. text ed. 25.00 (0-299-09110-4) U of Wis Pr.

***Brothers, Are You Listening? A Success Guide for the 90's.** Michael Taylor. 140p. (Orig.). (C). 1994. pap. 15.95 (0-9641894-0-2) Creat Pub Grp.

Brothers Ashkenazi. I. J. Singer. Tr. by Joseph Singer. 448p. 1993. 11.95 (0-14-039086-3, Penguin Classics) Viking Penguin.

Brothers at War: Dissident & Rebel Activities in Southern Africa. Abiodun Alao. 224p. 1994. text ed. 59.50 (1-85043-816-1, Pub. by I B Tauris UK) St Martin.

Brothers Beyond Blood: A Battalion Surgeon in the South Pacific. George Sharpe. Ed. by Melissa Roberts. (Illus.). 352p. 1989. 18.95 (0-89015-689-1) Sunbelt Media.

Brothers: Black & Poor: A True Story of Courage & Survival. Sylvester Monroe & Peter Goldman. 288p. 1989. mass mkt. 4.95 (0-345-36156-3) Ballantine.

Brother's Country: Poems. Tom Andrews. (National Poetry Ser.: 1989). 76p. (Orig.). 1990. pap. 9.95 (0-89255-151-8) Persea Bks.

Brothers Don't Know Everything. Linda Lee Maifair. LC 93-4605. (Illus.). (J). 1993. pap. 3.99 (0-8066-2635-6, 9-2635, Augsburg) Augsburg Fortress.

Brothers Five: The Babbitts of Arizona. Dean E. Smith. (Illus.). 270p. (Orig.). 1989. 21.95 (0-910152-12-8); pap. 14.95 (0-910152-13-6) AZ Hist Foun.

Brothers from Bataan: POWs, 1942-1945. Adrian R. Martin. (Illus.). 334p. (Orig.). 1992. pap. 21.95 (0-89745-142-2) Sunflower U Pr.

Brothers Gant. large type ed. Elliot Long. (Dales Western Ser.). 194p. 1992. pap. 16.95 (1-85389-357-9, Dales) Ulverscroft.

***Brothers Gourmet Coffees.** 60p. (Orig.). 1995. pap. 595.00 (0-7605-2178-6) Rector Pr.

Brothers Grimm: From Enchanted Forest to Modern World. Jack D. Zipes. 1988. 35.00 (0-415-90081-6, A1389, Routledge NY) Routledge.

Brothers Grimm: From Enchanted Forests to the Modern World. Jack D. Zipes. 205p. 1989. pap. 14.95 (0-415-90209-6, A3802, Routledge NY) Routledge.

Brothers Grimm & Folktale. Ed. by James M. McGlathery et al. (Illus.). 280p. 1991. pap. 12.95 (0-252-06191-8) U of Ill Pr.

Brothers Grimm & Their Critics: Folktales & the Quest for Meaning. Christa Kamenetsky. (Illus.). 400p. (C). 1993. text ed. 45.00 (0-8214-1020-2) Ohio U Pr.

Brothers Grimm & Their Critics: Folktales & the Quest for Meaning. Christa Kamenetsky. LC 92-55. (Illus.). 384p. (C). 1994. reprint ed. pap. text ed. 26.95 (0-8214-1066-0) Ohio U Pr.

Brothers, I Loved You All. Hayden Carruth. LC 77-95138. 100p. 1978. pap. 8.95 (0-8180-1544-6) Sheep Meadow.

Brothers in Arms. Lois M. Bujold. 352p. (Orig.). 1989. mass mkt. 5.99 (0-671-69799-4) Baen Bks.

***Brothers in Arms.** William Davis. (Illus.). 144p. 1995. 15.98 (0-8317-0768-2) Smithmark.

Brothers-in-Arms. large type ed. Margaret Abbey. LC 92-43164. (Romance Ser.). 1993. 18.95 (1-56054-426-0) Thorndike Pr.

Brothers in Arms. Lee P. Huntington. (Illus.). 72p. (J). (gr. 3-8). 1991. reprint ed. pap. 8.00 (0-88150-214-6) Countryman.

Brothers in Arms: A Journey from War to Peace. William Broyles, Jr. 288p. 1987. mass mkt. 4.50 (0-380-70355-6) Avon.

Brothers in Blood. Clark Howard. 1994. mass mkt. 4.95 (0-312-92520-4) St Martin.

Brothers in Blood. large type ed. D. C. Brod. LC 93-40531. 1994. pap. 16.95 (0-7862-0150-9) Thorndike Pr.

Brothers in Blood: A Quint McCauley Mystery. D. C. Brod. LC 93-3636. 288p. 1993. 21.95 (0-8027-3239-9) Walker & Co.

Brothers in Christ: The History of the Oldest Anabaptist. Fritz Blanke. Tr. by Joseph Nordenhaug. LC 61-6723. 78p. reprint ed. pap. 25.00 (0-8357-7445-7, 2029246) Bks Demand.

Brothers in Clay: The Story of Georgia Folk Pottery. John A. Burrison. LC 82-14884. (Brown Thrasher Bks.). (Illus.). 352p. 1994. pap. 24.95 (0-8203-1696-2) U of Ga Pr.

Brothers in Crime. Georges Feydeau. 1993. 2.50 (0-87129-293-9, B76) Dramatic Pub.

Brothers in Crime. Clifford R. Shaw et al. 378p. reprint ed. pap. 107.80 (0-8357-7446-5, 2024104) Bks Demand.

Brothers in Deed to Brothers in Need. Ed. by Clarence Hiebert. LC 74-76588. (Illus.). 486p. 1974. 29.95 (0-87303-037-0) Faith & Life.

Brothers in Gray. R. W. Richards. Ed. by Jeff Boart. (Alternative History Trilogy Ser.: Bk. II). (Illus.). 313p. 1993. pap. 12.95 (0-9625502-1-3) RoKarn Pubns.

***Brothers in War.** Al Schock. 250p. Date not set. pap. write for info. (0-18-875200-5) Crescent MN.

Brothers K. David J. Duncan. 1993. mass mkt. 6.99 (0-553-56314-9) Bantam.

Brothers Karamazov. Fydor Dostoevsky. 1976. 36.95 (0-8488-0797-9) Amereon Ltd.

Brothers Karamazov. Fyodor Dostoyevsky. (Airmont Classics Ser.). (J). (gr. 11 up). 1966. pap. 3.95 (0-8049-0128-7, CL-128) Airmont.

Brothers Karamazov. Fyodor Dostoyevsky. 1984. mass mkt. 5.50 (0-553-21216-8, Bantam Classics) Bantam.

Brothers Karamazov. Fyodor Dostoyevsky. 1992. pap. 20.00 (0-679-41003-1) McKay.

Brothers Karamazov. Fyodor Dostoyevsky. Tr. by Constance Garnett. (Modern Library College Editions). (YA). 1951. pap. text ed. write for info. (0-07-553575-0, T12) McGraw.

Brothers Karamazov. Fyodor Dostoyevsky. Ed. by Manuel Komroff-Hill. 701p. 1986. pap. 5.95 (0-451-52388-1, CE1464, Sig Classics) NAL-Dutton.

Brothers Karamazov. Fyodor Dostoyevsky. (Classics Ser.). 1982. mass mkt. 6.95 (0-14-044416-5, Penguin Classics) Viking Penguin.

Brothers Karamazov. Fyodor Dostoyevsky. Ed. by Jan Van Der Eng & Jan M. Meijer. 1971. text ed. 33.85 (90-279-1758-2) Mouton.

Brothers Karamazov. Fyodor Dostoyevsky. Tr. by Constance Garnett. LC 38-5761. 822p. 1977. 17.00 (0-394-60415-6, Modern Lib) Random.

Brothers Karamazov. Fyodor Dostoyevsky. LC 91-50046. (Vintage Classics Ser.). 832p. 1991. pap. 16.00 (0-679-72925-9, Vin) Random.

Brothers Karamazov. Fyodor Dostoyevsky. Ed. by Ralph E. Matlaw. (Critical Editions Ser.). 1000p. (C). 1976. pap. text ed. 15.95 (0-393-09214-3) Norton.

Brothers Karamazov. Fyodor Dostoyevsky. 595p. 1983. reprint ed. lib. bdg. 44.95 (0-89966-315-X) Buccaneer Bks.

***Brothers Karamazov: A Dramatization.** Fyodor Dostoyevsky. 1995. pap. 5.95 (0-8222-1425-3) Dramatists Play.

Brothers Karamazov: A New Translation. Fyodor Dostoyevsky. Tr. & Intro. by David McDuff. 960p. 1993. 8.95 (0-14-044527-7, Penguin Classics) Viking Penguin.

Brothers Karamazov: Worlds of the Novel. Robin F. Miller. (Masterwork Studies). 160p. (C). 1992. text ed. 21.95 (0-8057-8060-2, Twayne) Macmillan.

Brothers Karamazov: Worlds of the Novel. Robin F. Miller. (Masterwork Studies: No. 83). 160p. (C). 1992. pap. 12.95 (0-8057-8118-8, Twayne) Macmillan.

Brothers Karamazov & the Poetics of Memory. Diane O. Thompson. (Cambridge Studies in Russian Literature). 373p. (C). 1991. 74.95 (0-521-34572-3) Cambridge U Pr.

Brothers Karamazov Notes. Gary Carey. 1967. pap. 4.25 (0-8220-0265-5) Cliffs.

Brother's Keeper, Sister's Child. Margaret Stephens. 183p. (Orig.). 1989. pap. 7.00 (0-932112-26-9) Carolina Wren.

Brothers Keepers. Donald E. Westlake. 272p. 1993. mass mkt. 4.99 (0-446-40135-8, Mysterious Paperbk) Warner Bks.

Brothers Like Friends. Klaus Kordon. Tr. by Elizabeth D. Crawford. 192p. (J). (gr. 5 up). 1992. 14.95 (0-399-22137-9, Philomel Bks) Putnam Pub Group.

Brothers Majere. Kevin Stein. LC 88-51720. (Dragonlance Preludes Trilogy Ser.: Vol. 3). (Illus.). 352p. (Orig.). (J). 1990. pap. 4.95 (0-88038-776-9) TSR Inc.

Brothers Mann: The Lives of Heinrich & Thomas Mann, 1871-1950 & 1875-1955. Nigel Hamilton. LC 78-15114. 432p. reprint ed. pap. 123.20 (0-8357-8050-3, 2033742) Bks Demand.

***Brothers No More.** William F. Buckley, Jr. 1995. 23.95 (0-385-47794-5) Doubleday.

Brothers of Dragons: Job Dolens & Francois Villon. Barbara N. Sargent-Baur. LC 89-23835. (Garland Monographs in Medieval Literature: Vol. 3). (Illus.). 150p. 1990. 15.00 (0-8240-4036-8, 1231) Garland.

Brothers of Gwynedd Quartet. Edith Pargeter. 822p. 1990. pap. 15.95 (0-7472-3267-9, Pub. by Headline UK) Trafalgar.

Brothers of Light, Brothers of Blood: The Penitentes of the Southwest. Marta Weigle. LC 88-72048. (Illus.). 320p. 1989. pap. 18.95 (0-941270-58-0) Ancient City Pr.

Brothers of Light, Brothers of Blood: The Penitentes of the Southwest. Marta Weigle. LC 75-21188. reprint ed. pap. 82.00 (0-8357-7447-3, 2024680) Bks Demand.

Brothers of No Kin: And Other Stories. Conrad Richter. LC 72-10812. (Short Story Index Reprint Ser.). 1977. reprint ed. 24.95 (0-8369-4225-6) Ayer.

Brothers of Silence. large type ed. Frank Gruber. (Linford Mystery Library). 416p. 1992. pap. 14.95 (0-7089-7219-5, Linford) Ulverscroft.

***Brothers of the Cosmos.** Takis G. Phylactou. 1994. pap. 10.00 (0-533-10793-8) Vantage.

Brothers of the Dragon. Robin W. Bailey. 320p. (Orig.). 1993. pap. 4.99 (0-451-45251-8, ROC) NAL-Dutton.

Brothers of the Heart. Joan Blos. LC 87-1089. 176p. (J). (gr. 7 up). 1987. reprint ed. pap. 3.95 (0-689-71166-2, Aladdin Paperbacks) S&S Childrens.

Brothers of the Heart: A Story of the Northwest, 1837-1838. Joan Blos. LC 85-40293. 176p. (YA). (gr. 5 up). 1985. text ed. 14.95 (0-684-18452-4, C Scribner Sons Young) S&S Childrens.

Brothers of the Heart: A Story of the Old Northwest, 1837-1838. 2nd ed. Joan W. Blos. LC 92-39668. 176p. (J). (gr. 3-7). 1993. reprint ed. pap. 3.95 (0-689-71724-5, Aladdin Paperbacks) S&S Childrens.

Brothers of the Pine. Tim Simmons. (Orig.). 1995. pap. 15.99 (1-881542-16-5) Blue Star Prodns.

***Brothers of the Sword.** Michael Reisig. 430p. 1995. pap. 12.95 (1-56901-715-8) NW Pub.

Brothers of the Trail. Max Brand. 1976. reprint ed. lib. bdg. 20.95 (0-88411-514-3, Aeonian Pr) Amereon Ltd.

Brothers of Uterica. Benjamin Capps. LC 87-23387. (Southwest Life & Letters Ser.). 320p. 1988. reprint ed. 22.50 (0-87074-257-4); reprint ed. pap. 10.95 (0-87074-258-2) SMU Press.

Brothers on the Range. large type ed. Burt Arthur. LC 92-46295. 1993. pap. 17.95 (0-7927-1571-3, Curley Lrg Print) Chivers N Amer.

Brothers on the Santa Fe & Chihuahua Trails: Edward James Glascow & William Henry Glasgow, 1846-1848. Mark L. Gardner. (Illus.). 224p. 1993. 24.95 (0-87081-291-2) Univ Pr Colo.

Brothers, Sisters & Special Needs: Information & Activities for Helping Young Siblings of Children with Chronic Illnesses & Developmental Disabilities. Lobato. LC 90-1518. 224p. 1990. pap. text ed. 30.00 (1-55766-043-3) P H Brookes.

Brothers Unite: An Account of the Uniting of Eberhard Arnold & the Rhoen Bruderhof with the Hutterian Church. Eberhard Arnold et al. Ed. & Tr. by Hutterian Brethren. LC 88-23560. (Illus.). 384p. 1988. 19.00 (0-87486-023-7) Plough.

Brothers, Very Far Away & Other Poems. Hans Christian Andersen. 44p. 1991. pap. 4.95 (1-880755-03-3) Mermaid Pr.

Brothers' War: Civil War Letters to Their Loved Ones from the Blue & Gray. Annette Tapert. 1989. pap. 10.00 (0-679-72211-4, Vin) Random.

Broto. Adele Ellis. 1987. pap. 2.95 (9971-972-61-1) OMF Bks.

Brough Superior. C. E. Allen. (Illus.). 88p. 1990. pap. 19.95 (1-870979-18-4, Pub. by Bay View Bks UK) Motorbooks Intl.

Brought Forward. Robert B. Graham. LC 77-169552. (Short Story Index Reprint Ser.). 1977. reprint ed. 19.95 (0-8369-4014-8) Ayer.

Brought in Dead. large type ed. Jack Higgins. LC 93-34639. 1994. 18.95 (0-7927-1823-2, Curley Lrg Print); pap. 17.95 (0-7927-1822-4, Curley Lrg Print) Chivers N Amer.

Brought to Bed: Childbearing in America, 1750-1950. Judith W. Leavitt. (Illus.). 304p. 1988. pap. 11.95 (0-19-505690-6) OUP.

Brought to Book: Censorship & School Libraries in Australia. Ken Dillon & Claire Williams. 1993. pap. 30.00 (1-875589-28-7) D W Thorpe.

Brought to Light: Thirty Years of Drug Smuggling, Arms Deals, & Covert Action. Alan Moore et al. (Illus.). 80p. 1989. 29.95 (0-913035-70-X); pap. 8.95 (0-913035-67-X) Eclipse Bks.

Brought up in Dublin. Derry Jeffares. LC 87-71416. 108p. 1987. 14.95 (0-86140-253-7, Pub. by Colin Smythe Ltd UK) Dufour.

Brought up to Leave. Derry Jeffares. LC 87-71415. 108p. 1987. 18.95 (0-86140-254-5, Pub. by Colin Smythe Ltd UK) Dufour.

***Broussard's Restaurant Cookbook.** Gunter Preuss & Evelyn Preuss. (Illus.). 256p. 1995. 22.95 (1-56554-139-1) Pelican.

Brouwer's Cambridge Lectures on Intuitionism. Ed. by D. Van Dalen. LC 80-41239. 100p. 1981. 42.95 (0-521-23441-7) Cambridge U Pr.

An Asterisk (*) at the beginning of an entry indicates that the title is appearing in BIP for the first time.

B

An Asterisk (*) at the beginning of an entry indicates that the title is appearing in BIP for the first time.

Browning's Ancient Classical Sources. Thurman L. Hood. LC 72-100765. (Studies in Browning: No. 4). 1922. reprint ed. pap. 75.00 (*0-8383-0045-6*) M S G Haskell Hse.

Browning's Beginnings: The Art of Disclosure. Herbert F. Tucker. LC 80-17727. 269p. reprint ed. pap. 76.70 (*0-7837-2913-8*, 2057541) Bks Demand.

Brownings' Correspondence: A Checklist. Ed. by Philip Kelley & Ronald Hudson. LC 77-93932. (Illus.). xxx, 498p. 1978. 95.00 (*0-911459-15-4*) Wedgestone Pr.

Brownings' Correspondence: 1809-1826, Vol. 1. Ed. by Philip Kelley & Ronald Hudson. LC 84-5287. (Illus.). xlviii, 383p. 1984. 65.00 (*0-911459-09-X*) Wedgestone Pr.

Brownings' Correspondence: 1827-1831, Vol. 2. Ed. by Philip Kelley & Ronald Hudson. LC 84-5287. (Illus.). xvi, 413p. 1984. 65.00 (*0-911459-10-3*) Wedgestone Pr.

Brownings' Correspondence: 1832-1837, Vol. 3. Ed. by Philip Kelley & Ronald Hudson. LC 84-5287. (Illus.). xvi, 446p. 1985. 65.00 (*0-911459-11-1*) Wedgestone Pr.

Brownings' Correspondence: 1838-1840, Vol. 4. Ed. by Philip Kelley & Ronald Hudson. LC 84-5287. (Illus.). xvi, 452p. 1986. 65.00 (*0-911459-12-X*) Wedgestone Pr.

Brownings' Correspondence, Vol. 11: Letters 1982-2177. Robert Browning et al. Ed. by Philip Kelley. LC 84-5287. (Illus.). xvi, 422p. 1993. 65.00 (*0-911459-22-7*) Wedgestone Pr.

Brownings' Correspondence, 1841-1842, Vol. 5. Robert Browning & Elizabeth Barrett Browning. Ed. by Philip Kelley & Ronald Hudson. LC 84-5287. (Illus.). xiv, 428p. 1987. 65.00 (*0-911459-16-2*) Wedgestone Pr.

Brownings' Correspondence, 1842-1843, Vol. 6. Robert Browning & Elizabeth Barrett Browning. Ed. by Philip Kelley & Ronald Hudson. LC 84-5287. (Illus.). xiv, 425p. 1988. 65.00 (*0-911459-17-0*) Wedgestone Pr.

Brownings' Correspondence, 1843, Vol. 7: Letters 1174-1406. Robert Browning & Elizabeth Barrett Browning. Ed. by Philip Kelley & Ronald Hudson. LC 84-5287. (Illus.). xiv, 429p. 1989. 65.00 (*0-911459-18-9*) Wedgestone Pr.

Brownings' Correspondence, 1843-1844, Vol. 8: Letters 1407-1617. Robert Browning & Elizabeth Barrett Browning. Ed. by Philip Kelley & Ronald Hudson. LC 84-5287. (Illus.). xiv, 447p. 1990. 65.00 (*0-911459-19-7*) Wedgestone Pr.

Brownings' Correspondence, 1844, Vol. 9: Letters 1618-1798. Robert Browning & Elizabeth Barrett Browning. Ed. by Philip Kelley & Scott Lewis. LC 84-5287. (Illus.). xvi, 423p. 1991. 65.00 (*0-911459-20-0*) Wedgestone Pr.

Brownings' Correspondence, 1845, Vol. 10: Letters 1799-1981. Robert Browning & Elizabeth Barrett Browning. Ed. by Philip Kelley & Scott Lewis. LC 84-5287. (Illus.). xiv, 422p. 1992. 65.00 (*0-911459-21-9*) Wedgestone Pr.

Browning's Dramatic Monologues & the Post-Romantic Subject. Loy D. Martin. LC 85-9796. 304p. 1985. text ed. 42.50 (*0-8018-2653-5*) Johns Hopkins.

Browning's England. H. Clarke. 1972. 59.95 (*0-87968-797-5*) Gordon Pr.

Browning's Essay on Chatterton. Robert Browning. Ed. by Donald Smalley. LC 79-100145. 194p. 1970. reprint ed. text ed. 49.75 (*0-8371-3257-6*, BRCH, Greenwood Pr) Greenwood.

Browning's Experiments with Genre. Donald S. Hair. LC 75-185715. (University of Toronto, Department of English Studies & Texts: No. 19). 220p. reprint ed. pap. 62.70 (*0-8357-8051-1*, 2033993) Bks Demand.

Browning's Hatreds. Daniel Carlin. LC 93-2907. 1993. 48.00 (*0-19-811229-7*, Clarendon Pr) OUP.

Browning's Italy. Helen A. Clarke. LC 72-3566. (Studies in Browning: No. 4). (Illus.). 1972. reprint ed. lib. bdg. 69.95 (*0-8383-1546-1*) M S G Haskell Hse.

Browning's Later Poetry, 1871-1889. Clyde de L. Ryals. LC 75-16927. 288p. 1975. 37.95 (*0-8014-0964-0*) Cornell U Pr.

Browning's Message to His Time. Edward Berdoe. LC 73-16003. (Studies in Browning: No. 4). 1974. reprint ed. lib. bdg. 75.00 (*0-8383-1724-3*) M S G Haskell Hse.

Brownings of Casa Guidi. Edward C. McAleer. LC 78-56858. (Illus.). 112p. 1979. 12.00 (*0-930252-04-7*); pap. 6.25 (*0-930252-03-9*) Browning Inst.

Browning's Parleyings; The Autobiography of a Mind. William C. DeVane. (BCL1-PR English Literature Ser.). 306p. 1992. reprint ed. lib. bdg. 89.00 (*0-7812-7462-1*) Rprt Serv.

Browning's Youth. John R. Maynard. (Illus.). 512p. 1977. 42.50 (*0-674-08441-1*) HUP.

Brownisme Turned the In-Side Out-Ward. Christopher Lawne. LC 76-6282. (English Experience Ser.: No. 74). 40p. 1968. reprint ed. 7.00 (*90-221-0074-X*) Walter J Johnson.

Brown's Alcohol Motor Fuel Cookbook: Make Your Own Alcohol for Any Gas-Powered Engine. M. Brown. 1986. lib. bdg. 250.00 (*0-8490-3698-4*) Gordon Pr.

***Brown's Boundary Control & Legal Principles.** 4th ed. Curtis M. Brown et al. 1995. text ed. 69.95 (*0-471-04312-5*) Wiley.

Brown's Completed Burdwood Azimuth Tables. Brown, Son & Ferguson Ltd. Staff. (C). 1987. 30.00 (*0-85174-078-2*, Pub. by Brwn Son Ferg) St Mut.

Brown's Encyclopedia of Television. 3rd ed. Les Brown. 723p. 1991. pap. 22.95 (*0-8103-9420-0*) Visible Ink Pr.

Brown's Encyclopedia of Television. 3rd ed. Les Brown. 723p. 1992. pap. 55.00 (*0-8103-8871-5*, 089165) Visible Ink Pr.

Browns Ferry Nuclear Plant Fire. Andrew J. Pryor. 1977. 4.25 (*0-686-22684-4*, TR 77-2) Society Fire Protect.

Brown's Guide to the Georgia Outdoors: Hiking, Biking & Canoeing Trips. Ed. & Intro. by John W. English. LC 86-26879. (Illus.). 272p. (Orig.). 1986. pap. 16.95 (*0-87797-128-5*) Cherokee.

Brown's Knots & Splices. S. Jutsum. (C). 1987. 35.00 (*0-85174-104-5*, Pub. by Brwn Son Ferg) St Mut.

Brown's Nautical Almanac. Brown, Son & Ferguson Ltd. Staff. (C). 1987. 150.00 (*0-85174-541-5*, Pub. by Brwn Son Ferg) St Mut.

Brown's Nautical Diary & Days Work Book. Ed. by Brown, Son & Ferguson Ltd. Staff. (C). 1987. 47.00 (*0-685-45090-2*, Pub. by Brwn Son Ferg) St Mut.

Brown's Nautical Star Chart. P. Clissold & A. J. Tweddell. (C). 1987. pap. 20.00 (*0-85174-435-4*, Pub. by Brwn Son Ferg) St Mut.

Brown's North Atlantic Track Chart. Brown, Son & Ferguson Ltd. Staff. (C). 1987. 22.00 (*0-85174-133-9*, Pub. by Brwn Son Ferg) St Mut.

Browns of Providence Plantations: The Colonial Years, Vol. 1. James B. Hedges. LC 52-5032. 419p. reprint ed. 119.50 (*0-8357-7449-X*, 2027510) Bks Demand.

Browns of Providence Plantations, Vol. 2: The Nineteenth Century. James B. Hedges. LC 68-23790. 345p. reprint ed. pap. 98.40 (*0-7837-0020-2*, 2027510) Bks Demand.

Brown's Park. Diana A. Kouris. (Illus.). 288p. (Orig.). 1988. pap. 12.95 (*0-941875-03-2*) Wolverine Gallery.

Brown's Pocket Book for Seamen. G. Forsberg. (C). 1987. 75.00 (*0-85174-391-9*, Pub. by Brwn Son Ferg) St Mut.

Brown's Requiem. James Ellroy. 256p. (Orig.). 1981. mass mkt. 4.99 (*0-380-78741-5*) Avon.

Brown's Requiem. limited ed. James Ellroy. (Armchair Detective Library). 256p. (Orig.). 1994. reprint ed. 75.00 (*1-56287-068-8*) Armchair Detective.

Brown's Requiem. James Ellroy. (Armchair Detective Library). 256p. (Orig.). 1994. reprint ed. 22.00 (*1-56287-067-X*) Armchair Detective.

Brown's Rule of the Road Manual. rev. ed. Rev. by H. H. Brown. (Illus.). (C). 1987. 75.00 (*0-85174-405-2*, Pub. by Brwn Son Ferg) St Mut.

Brown's Seamen's Wages Calculator from 1 Day to 12 Months, & from 1.00 Pound to 200.00 Pounds per Month. Brown, Son & Ferguson Ltd. Staff. (C). 1987. 22.00 (*0-85174-182-7*, Pub. by Brwn Son Ferg) St Mut.

Brown's Signal Reminder. Mead. (C). 1987. 22.00 (*0-85174-127-4*, Pub. by Brwn Son Ferg) St Mut.

Brown's Signalling: How to Learn the International Code of Signals. rev. ed. Rev. by J. E. Milligan. (C). 1987. 66.00 (*0-85174-350-1*, Pub. by Brwn Son Ferg) St Mut.

Brown's Star Atlas. Brown, Son & Ferguson Ltd. Staff. (C). 1987. 72.00 (*0-85174-271-8*, Pub. by Brwn Son Ferg) St Mut.

Browns Through the Years. Bill Borst & Jim Scott. 20p. 1987. pap. 7.95 (*0-9612260-2-1*) Krank Pr.

Brown's Tidal Streams: In Twelve Charts, for Each Hour of the Tide at Dover. Brown, Son & Ferguson Ltd. Staff. (C). 1987. 72.00 (*0-85174-170-3*, Pub. by Brwn Son Ferg) St Mut.

Brown's Vick Morse Cards. Brown, Son & Ferguson Ltd. Staff. (C). 1987. 22.00 (*0-85174-177-0*, Pub. by Brwn Son Ferg) St Mut.

Brown's Vick Semaphore Cards. Brown, Son & Ferguson Ltd. Staff. (C). 1987. 25.00 (*0-85174-178-9*, Pub. by Brwn Son Ferg) St Mut.

Brownsea Trail: A Brave, Clean, & Reverent Path. Ed. by Robert D. Neligh. LC 92-81312. (Illus.). 300p. 1993. 21.95 (*0-9631648-5-6*); pap. 12.95 (*0-9631648-6-4*) Ambush Pub.

Brownson Reader. Orestes A. Brownson. 1978. 34.95 (*0-405-10848-6*, 11851) Ayer.

Brownson's Quarterly Review, Set: Vol. 1-29. Orig. Title: Boston Quarterly Review. reprint ed. Set. lib. bdg. 1,305.00 (*0-404-19506-7*) AMS Pr.

Brownson's Quarterly Review, Vol. 1-29. Orig. Title: Boston Quarterly Review. reprint ed. lib. bdg. 45.00 (*0-685-73580-X*) AMS Pr.

Brownstone. J. Rubins et al. 101p. 1987. pap. 4.95 (*0-88145-054-5*) Broadway Play.

Brownstone Angel. large type ed. Norma Newcomb. 1992. 19.95 (*0-7927-0911-X*, Curley Lrg Print); pap. 17.95 (*0-7927-0912-8*, Curley Lrg Print) Chivers N Amer.

Brownstone Facade. large type ed. Catherine M. Rae. 240p. 1990. reprint ed. lib. bdg. 16.95 (*1-56054-027-3*) Thorndike Pr.

Brownstone Front. Guy Gilpatric. LC 75-37544. (Short Story Index Reprint Ser.). 1977. reprint ed. 26.95 (*0-8369-4103-9*) Ayer.

Brownsville. Alter F. Landesman. 430p. 1989. 27.50 (*0-8197-0151-3*); pap. 16.95 (*0-8197-0563-2*) Bloch.

Brownsville: Linn County's Oldest Town. Margaret S. Carey & Patricia H. Hainline. (Illus.). 48p. 1976. pap. 4.95 (*0-934784-01-9*) Calapooia Pubns.

Brownsville Raid. John D. Weaver. LC 92-14435. (Illus.). 344p. (C). 1992. pap. 12.95 (*0-89096-528-5*) Tex A&M Univ Pr.

Brownup. Ron Welburn. 1977. per. 3.00 (*0-912678-32-1*, Greenfld Rev Pr) Greenfld Rev Lit.

Browsing in Morgue. LC 86-72926. 96p. 1987. pap. 4.95 (*0-940755-00-9*) Barlow Pr.

***Browsing the World Wide Web with Word for Windows.** Ron Person & Tow. (Illus.). 384p. (Orig.). 1995. pap. 27.99 (*0-7897-0243-6*) Que.

***Brox's Ultimate Outlet Guide to New England: An Insider's Guide to the Region's Best Factory Outlet & Off-Price Shopping.** Andrea Brox. Ed. by Beverly J. Wood. LC 94-27142. (Illus.). 338p. (Orig.). 1994. per., pap. 12.95 (*0-9636123-1-X*) Pleasant St Pr.

Brrm! Brrm! see Man from Japan: A Novel

Brrr! James Stevenson. LC 89-34615. (Illus.). 32p. (J). (ps up). 1991. 13.95 (*0-688-09210-1*); lib. bdg. 13.88 (*0-688-09211-X*) Greenwillow.

***BRS-Seven: The Phase-Locked Loop with Experiments.** Howard M. Berlin. LC 78-6535. (Bugbook Reference Ser.). 1978. pap. text ed. 10.95 (*0-89704-017-1*) E&L Instru.

Bru Book. Francois Theimer. (Illus.). 200p. (FRE.). 1991. 63.95 (*0-912823-07-0*, BT-113) Gold Horse.

Bru Dolls: Magnificent French Dolls. Lydia Richter. (Illus.). 104p. 1989. 29.95 (*0-87588-357-5*) Hobby Hse.

Bruach Blend see Beautiful Just!

Bruce: Family Record of the Bruces & the Cumyns, with an History Introduction & Appendix. M. E. Bruce. (Illus.). 692p. 1991. reprint ed. lib. bdg. 109.00 (*0-8328-1760-0*); reprint ed. pap. 99.00 (*0-8328-1761-9*) Higginson Bk Co.

Bruce: Robertiking O'Scots. Robert S. Silver. 64p. 1986. 25.00 (*0-85411-035-6*, Pub. by Saltire Soc) St Mut.

***Bruce Beasley: Sculpture.** Peter Selz & Manfred Fath. (Illus.). 176p. 1995. pap. 25.00 (*3-89165-098-1*) U of Wash Pr.

Bruce Beaver: New & Selected Poems 1960-1990. Bruce Beaver. 1991. pap. 19.95 (*0-7022-2338-7*, Pub. by Univ Queensland Pr AT) Intl Spec Bk.

Bruce Beckons. 2nd ed. W. Sherwood Fox. (Illus.). 264p. 1988. pap. 16.95 (*0-8020-6007-2*) U of Toronto Pr.

Bruce Beresford: Instincts of the Heart. Peter Coleman. (Illus.). 168p. (Orig.). 1993. pap. 11.00 (*0-207-17526-8*, Pub. by Angus & Robertson AT) HarpC.

Bruce Brady's Game Trails. Bruce Brady. 1991. 21.95 (*1-879034-03-4*) MS River Pub.

Bruce Catton's America. Oliver E. Jensen. 1993. 12.50 (*0-88394-070-1*) Promntory Pr.

Bruce Chatwin. Nicholas Murray. (Illus.). 139p. 1993. 32.00 (*1-85411-079-9*, Pub. by Seren Bks UK); pap. 15.95 (*1-85411-080-2*, Pub. by Seren Bks UK) Dufour.

Bruce Cost's Asian Ingredients: Buying & Cooking the Staple Foods of China, Japan & Southeast Asia. Bruce Cost. LC 88-8943. 1988. 22.95 (*0-688-05877-9*) Morrow.

Bruce Coville's Book of Aliens: Tales to Warp Your Mind. Bruce Coville. (J). (gr. 4-7). 1994. pap. 2.95 (*0-590-46162-1*) Scholastic Inc.

***Bruce Coville's Book of Ghosts: Tales to Haunt You.** Bruce Coville. (J). (gr. 4-7). 1994. pap. 2.95 (*0-590-46160-5*) Scholastic Inc.

Bruce Coville's Book of Monsters: Tales to Give You the Creeps. Bruce Coville. (J). (gr. 4-7). 1993. pap. 2.95 (*0-590-46159-1*) Scholastic Inc.

***Bruce Covill's Book of Nightmares: Tales to Make You Scream.** Bruce Coville. (J). (gr. 4-7). 1995. pap. 3.50 (*0-590-46161-3*) Scholastic Inc.

Bruce Davidson Photographs. Bruce Davidson. LC 78-73352. 168p. 30.00 (*0-671-40067-3*); pap. text ed. 17.50 (*0-671-40068-1*) Agrinde Pubns.

Bruce Dorfman: Nightsongs & Placefields (Paintings) Contrib by Lois Katz. (Illus.). 32p. (Orig.). 1988. pap. write for info. (*0-9620831-0-0*) Arts East Fndtn.

***Bruce Family History, 1788 to 1992.** W. W. Denny & H. C. Bruce. (Illus.). 95p. 1995. reprint ed. lib. bdg. 29.00 (*0-8328-4583-3*); reprint ed. pap. 19.00 (*0-8328-4584-1*) Higginson Bk Co.

Bruce Goff, Architect. Bruce Goff. Ed. by Delton Ludwig. (Illus.). 1978. 47.50 (*0-685-47637-5*) Prairie Sch.

Bruce Gould on Commodities. Bruce G. Gould. (Illus.). 218p. 1983. write for info. (*0-318-56807-1*) B Gould Pubns.

Bruce Gould on Commodities, Vol. 1, Pt. 1. Bruce G. Gould. 213p. 1983. pap. 30.00 (*0-918706-05-X*) B Gould Pubns.

Bruce Gould on Commodities, Vol. 1, Pt. 2. Bruce G. Gould. 213p. 1983. pap. 30.00 (*0-918706-07-6*) B Gould Pubns.

Bruce Gould on Commodities, Vol. 1, Pts. 1 & 2. Bruce G. Gould. 213p. 1983. Vol. 1, Pt. 1 & 2. pap. write for info. (*0-318-56796-2*) B Gould Pubns.

Bruce Gould on Commodities, Vol. 2, Pt. 1. Bruce G. Gould. (Illus.). 218p. 1983. pap. 30.00 (*0-918706-08-4*) B Gould Pubns.

Bruce Gould on Commodities, Vol. 2, Pt. 2. Bruce G. Gould. (Illus.). 218p. 1983. pap. 30.00 (*0-918706-06-8*) B Gould Pubns.

Bruce Gould on Commodities, Vol. 3, Pt. 1. Bruce G. Gould. 231p. 1983. pap. 30.00 (*0-918706-10-6*) B Gould Pubns.

Bruce Gould on Commodities, Vol. 3, Pt. 2. Bruce G. Gould. 244p. 1983. pap. 12.95 (*0-918706-12-2*) B Gould Pubns.

Bruce Gould on Commodities, Vol. 2. Bruce G. Gould. 213p. 1977. 30.00 (*0-686-84395-9*) B Gould Pubns.

Bruce Gould on Commodities, Vol. 3. Bruce Gould. 213p. 1977. 30.00 (*0-686-84396-7*) B Gould Pubns.

Bruce Gould on Commodities, Vol. 4. Bruce Gould. 213p. 1978. 30.00 (*0-686-84397-5*) B Gould Pubns.

Bruce Gould on Commodities, Vol. 5. Bruce Gould. 213p. 1978. 30.00 (*0-686-84398-3*) B Gould Pubns.

Bruce Gould on Commodities, Vol. 6. Bruce Gould. 213p. 1979. 30.00 (*0-686-84399-1*) B Gould Pubns.

Bruce Helander: Curious Collage. Robert Mahoney. LC 93-80843. (Illus.). 112p. 1994. 50.00 (*0-9628514-6-9*) Grassfield Pr.

Bruce Hornsby - Harbor Lights. (Illus.). 92p. (Orig.). pap. 19.95 (*0-89724-059-6*) Warner Brothers.

Bruce Hornsby & the Range - A Night on the Town. Ed. by Milton Okun. pap. 14.95 (*0-89524-580-9*) Cherry Lane.

Bruce Hornsby & the Range - Five of the Best. Ed. by Milton Okun. pap. 7.95 (*0-89524-539-6*) Cherry Lane.

Bruce Hornsby & the Range - Scenes from the Southside (Piano - Vocal) Ed. by Milt Okun & Mark Phillips. (Illus.). 63p. (Orig.). 1990. pap. text ed. 12.95 (*0-89524-385-7*) Cherry Lane.

***Bruce Hornsby Anthology.** 256p. (Orig.). 1994. pap. 22.95 (*0-89724-425-7*) Warner Brothers.

Bruce Jenner's the Athletic Body: A Complete Fitness Guide for Teenagers. Bruce Jenner & Bill Dobbins. (Orig.). 1984. 17.95 (*0-685-08970-3*) S&S Trade.

Bruce Kurland: Watercolors & Paintings. Hugh Crean & Samuel Miller. LC 85-63887. (Illus.). 40p. 1986. pap. 12.00 (*0-936827-00-9*) C Bernard Gallery Ltd.

***Bruce Lee: Fighting Spirit.** Bruce Thomas. LC 94-25723. 329p. 1994. 25.00 (*1-883319-11-0*); pap. 14.95 (*1-883319-25-0*) Frog CA.

Bruce Lee: Fists of Fury. Edward Gross. 1990. pap. 14.95 (*1-55698-233-X*) Movie Pubs Servs.

Bruce Lee: The Untold Story. Unique Publications Staff. (Illus.). 80p. 1980. pap. 5.50 (*0-86568-009-4*, 401) Unique Pubns.

Bruce Lee - An Oral Biography. Jesse R. Glover. 150p. 1990. pap. 14.95 (*0-9602328-4-2*) Glover Pubns.

Bruce Lee, Between Wing Chun & Jeet Kune Do. 96p. 1976. pap. 9.95 (*0-9602328-0-X*) Glover Pubns.

Bruce Lee Story. Linda Lee. Ed. by Jack Vaughan. LC 88-63487. 192p. 1988. pap. text ed. 19.95 (*0-89750-121-7*, 460) Ohara Pubns.

Bruce Lee's Fighting Method: Advanced Techniques, Vol. 4, No. 405. Bruce Lee & Mitoshi Uyehara. LC 77-92737. (Specialties Ser.). (Illus.). 1977. pap. 8.95 (*0-89750-053-9*) Ohara Pubns.

Bruce Lee's Fighting Method: Basic Training, Vol. II, No. 403. Bruce Lee & Mitoshi Uyehara. Ed. by Doris Shelrud. LC 77-79057. (Specialties Ser.). (Illus.). 1977. pap. text ed. 8.95 (*0-89750-051-2*, Wehman) Ohara Pubns.

Bruce Lee's Fighting Method: Self-Defense Techniques, Vol. 1, No. 402. Bruce Lee & Mitoshi Uyehara. LC 76-51476. (Specialties Ser.). (Illus.). 1976. pap. text ed. 8.95 (*0-89750-050-4*, Wehman) Ohara Pubns.

Bruce Lee's Fighting Method: Skill in Techniques, Vol. 3, No. 404. Bruce Lee & Mitoshi Uyehara. LC 77-81831. (Specialties Ser.). (Illus.). 1977. pap. 8.95 (*0-89750-052-0*, Wehman) Ohara Pubns.

Bruce Lee's Non-Classical Gung Fu. Jesse R. Glover. 130p. 1978. pap. 14.95 (*0-9602328-1-8*) Glover Pubns.

Bruce Lee's Non-Classical Gung-Fu, Bk. II. Jesse R. Glover. 65p. 1980. pap. 14.95 (*0-9602328-2-6*) Glover Pubns.

Bruce Lee's Non-Classical Stickinghands. Jesse R. Glover. Ed. by Edward C. Hart. (Illus.). 200p. 1982. 25.00 (*0-9602328-3-4*) Glover Pubns.

Bruce Lee's One & Three Inch Power Punch. Bruce Lee. 1989. pap. 3.95 (*0-86568-112-0*) Unique Pubns.

***Bruce Mclaren - The Man & His Racing Team.** Erin S. Young. (Illus.). 232p. 1995. 24.95 (*1-85260-511-1*, Pub. by J H Haynes & Co UK) Motorbooks Intl.

Bruce McLean. 36p. 1980. 24.00 (*0-685-16967-7*, Pub. by Third Eye Centre UK) St Mut.

***Bruce Moose.** Wright & Oliver. 32p. (J). 1996. 7.99 (*1-56476-462-1*, 6-3462); audio 11.99 (*7-900881-93-X*, 3-1193) SP Pubns.

Bruce Nauman: Exhibition Catalogue & Raissone. Ed. by Joan Simon et al. LC 94-2902. 1994. write for info. (*0-935640-43-6*) Walker Art Ctr.

Bruce Nauman: Prints 1970-1989. Christopher Cordes & John Yau. Ed. by Debbie Taylor. (Illus.). 128p. 1989. write for info. (*0-318-66699-5*) Castelli Graphics.

Bruce Nauman: Twenty-Five Years. Susan Brundage. (Illus.). 64p. 1994. pap. 209.95 (*0-8478-1817-9*) Rizzoli Intl.

Bruce Nauman Prints 1970-89. Ed. by Christopher Cordes. (Illus.). 236p. 1989. text ed. 75.00 (*0-9625240-0-X*); pap. text ed. 40.00 (*0-685-40656-3*) Castelli Graphics.

Bruce Rogers: A Life in Letters, 1870-1957. Joseph Blumenthal. (Illus.). 200p. 1989. 95.00 (*0-935072-16-0*) W T Taylor.

Bruce Rogers: Selected Letters, 1915-1918. limited ed. (Illus.). 64p. 1988. 110.00 (*0-936897-09-0*) Caliban.

***Bruce Springsteen.** Andrews & McMeel Staff. 1994. 4.95 (*0-8362-3108-2*) Andrews & McMeel.

Bruce Springsteen. Ron Frankl. LC 93-1850. (Pop Culture Legends Ser.). (YA). (gr. 7 up). 1994. 18.95 (*0-7910-2327-3*, Am Art Analog); pap. write for info. (*0-7910-2352-4*, Am Art Analog) Chelsea Hse.

Bruce Springsteen: Our Reasons to Believe. Carole Tuszynski. (Illus.). 119p. (Orig.). 1986. pap. text ed. 14.00 (*0-9617170-0-9*) C Tuszynski.

Bruce Stuart & Kim Stuart's College 101. Bruce S. Stuart. LC 92-17425. 242p. 1993. pap. 14.00 (*0-02-015881-5*, Collier S&S) S&S Trade.

Bruce Tegner's Complete Book of Jujitsu. Bruce Tegner. LC 77-5023. (Illus.). 1978. pap. 12.00 (*0-87407-027-9*, T27) Thor.

Bruce Tegner's Complete Book of Self-Defense. Bruce Tegner. LC 74-28358. (Illus.). 223p. 1975. pap. 12.00 (*0-87407-030-9*, T-30) Thor.

Bruce Trilogy. Nigel Tranter. 1047p. 1989. pap. 22.95 (*0-340-37186-2*, Pub. by H & S UK) Trafalgar.

Brucella Melitensis. Ed. by J. M. Verger & M. Plommet. 1985. lib. bdg. 110.50 (*0-89838-742-6*) Kluwer Ac.

Brucellosis. Ed. by Lyon Valette & W. Hennessen. (Developments in Biological Standardization Ser.: Vol. 56). (Illus.). xiv, 782p. 1984. pap. 128.00 (*3-8055-3944-4*) S Karger.

Brucellosis: Clinical & Laboratory Aspects. Ed. by Edward J. Young & Michael J. Corbel. 240p. 1989. 191.00 (*0-8493-6661-5*, RC123) CRC Pr.

Brucellosis: Proceedings of the International Symposium on Standardization & Control of Vaccines & Reagents, 24, Tunise & Bourse du Travail, 1968. Ed. by Microbiological Standardization, Permanent Section Staff. (Immunobiological Standardization Symposia Ser.: Vol. 12). 1970. 24.00 (*3-8055-0634-1*) S Karger.

Brucellosis in Wild Animals. M. M. Rementsova. 1987. 35.00 (*81-7087-005-4*, Pub. by Oxford IBH II) S Asia.

Bruce's Story. Francine Pascal. (Sweet Valley High Super Star Ser.: No. 2). 1990. pap. 3.50 (*0-553-28464-9*) Bantam.

An Asterisk (*) at the beginning of an entry indicates that the title is appearing in BIP for the first time.

Bruchidae (Coleoptera) of Northwest India. G. L. Arora. (Oriental Insects Supplements Ser.: No. 7). 1977. 30.00 (1-877711-17-9) Assoc Pubs FL.

Bruchko. Bruce Olson. LC 73-81494. 208p. (Orig.). 1973. pap. 8.99 (0-88419-133-8, Creation Hse) Strang Comms Co.

*Bruchwaelder des Westlichen Rheinischen Schiefergebirges Vol. 228. T. Schoenert. (Dissertationes Botanicae Ser.). (Illus.). 143p. (GER.). 1994. text ed. 52.50x (3-443-64141-5) Lubrecht & Cramer.

Brucke: German Expressionist Prints from the Granvil & Marcia Specks Collection. Reinhold Heller. 400p. (Orig.). 1988. 50.00 (0-685-32945-3); pap. 24.95 (0-941680-08-8) M&L Block.

Brucke in Dschungel see Bridge in the Jungle

Bruckner. rev. ed. Hans-Hubert Schonzeler. (Illus.). 192p. 1978. pap. 7.95 (0-7145-0145-X) M Boyars Pubs.

Bruckner. Derek Watson. (Master Musicians Ser.: No. M171). (Illus.). 174p. 1975. reprint ed. pap. 13.00 (0-8226-0708-5) Littlefield.

Bruckner, 2 vols., Set. Ernst Kurth. 1971. reprint ed. write for info. (3-487-04110-3, Pub. by Georg Olms GW) Lubrecht & Cramer.

Bruckner-Mahler, Schoenberg: Music Book Index. Dika Newlin. 293p. 1993. reprint ed. lib. bdg. 79.00 (0-7812-9582-3) Rprt Serv.

Brudder & the Babe. Quincy D. Mathis. Ed. & Comp. by Danny E. Mathis. LC 93-60735. 92p. (Orig.). (J). (gr. 1-4). 1994. 8.95 (1-55523-636-7) Winston-Derek.

Bruder-Grimm-Symposion Zur Historischen Wortforschung: Beitrage Zu der Marburger Tagung Vom Juni 1985. Ed. by Hildebrandt & Knoop. (Historische Wortforschung, Untersuchungen Zur Sprach- und Kulturgeschichte des Deutschen in Seinen Europaischen Bezugen Ser.: Vol. 1). x, 299p. (C). 1986. lib. bdg. 126.95 (0-89925-315-6) De Gruyter.

*Bruder-Grimm-Symposion Zur Historischen Wortforschung: Beitrage Zu der Marburger Tagung Vom Juni 1985. Ed. by Hildebrandt & Knoop. (Historische Wortforschung, Untersuchungen Zur Sprach- und Kulturgeschichte des Deutschen in Seinen Europaischen Bezugen Ser.: Vol. 1). x, 299p. (C). 1986. lib. bdg. 126.95 (3-11-010673-6) De Gruyter.

Bruegel. Robert L. Delevoy. LC 90-50884. (Illus.). 1991. pap. 25.00 (0-8478-1349-5) Rizzoli Intl.

Bruegel. Walter S. Gibson. (World of Art Ser.). (Illus.). 216p. 1985. pap. 14.95 (0-500-20156-0) Thames Hudson.

Bruegel. Walter S. Gibson. (World of Art Ser.). (Illus.). 216p. 1985. 19.95 (0-500-18159-4) Thames Hudson.

Bruegel. Keith Roberts. (Color Library). (Illus.). 128p. (C). 1994. reprint ed. pap. 14.95 (0-7148-2239-6, Pub. by Phaidon Press UK) Chronicle Bks.

*Bruegel. Keith Roberts. (Color Library). (Illus.). 128p. (C). 1994. reprint ed. 19.95 (0-7148-3206-5, Pub. by Phaidon Press UK) Chronicle Bks.

Bruegel Masters of Art. Wolfgang Stechow. 1990. 22.95 (0-8109-3103-6) Abrams.

Bruegel, or the Workshop of Dreams. Claude-Henri Rocquet. Tr. by Nora Scott. (Illus.). 224p. 1991. 24.95 (0-226-72342-9) U Ch Pr.

Bruegel's Peasants: Art & Audience in the Northern Renaissance. Margaret A. Sullivan. (Illus.). 240p. (C). 1994. 60.00 (0-521-44150-1) Cambridge U Pr.

*Brueghel: A Gift for Telling Stories. Pierre Sterckx. Tr. by John Goodman. LC 94-47283. (Art for Children Ser.). (Illus.). 64p. (ENG & FRE.). (YA). (gr. 3 up). 1995. lib. bdg. 14.95 (0-7910-2806-2) Chelsea Hse.

Bruges Engagement. Madeleine Ker. 1994. 2.99 (0-373-11650-0) Harlequin Bks.

Bruges Flower Lace. Edna Sutton. 1987. 18.95 (0-85219-650-4) Robin & Russ.

Bruges-La-Morte. Georges Rodenbach. Tr. by Philip Mosley. LC 86-51023. 78p. (FRE.). 1986. pap. 12.95 (0-905075-23-4, Pub. by Wilfion Bks UK) Dufour.

*Bruise Theory. Natalie Kenvin. (New Poets of America Ser.: No. 16). 65p. 1995. 20.00 (1-880238-20-9); pap. 12.50 (1-880238-21-7) BOA Edns.

Bruised & Broken: Understanding & Healing Psychological Problems. Ed. by Paul Meier et al. LC 92-6988. 240p. 1992. 16.99 (0-8010-6292-6) Baker Bk.

Bruised but Not Broken: Finding Strength for Your Times. Stanley C. Baldwin. LC 85-2977. 209p. 1985. pap. 8.99 (0-88070-080-7, Multnomah Bks) Questar Pubs.

*Bruised but Not Broken: Studies in Coping for Today's Adult Groups. (LifeTopics Ser.). Date not set. 19.95 (1-55513-569-2, 75697) Cook.

*Bruised by Life: Turn Life's Wounds into Gifts. Kathleen R. O'Connell. 1994. pap. 10.95 (0-925190-32-2) Fairview Press.

*Bruised Hibiscus: A Novel. Elizabeth Nunez. LC 94-32697. 1994. 19.95 (1-56743-065-1) Amistad Pr.

Bruiser. Gordon Grice. (Widow Maker Bks.). 30p. 1993. pap. text ed. 5.00 (1-884438-03-2) Epiphany AR.

*Bruises of Satan. 77p. (Orig.). 1981. pap. 3.95 (1-879655-01-2) CTM Dallas.

Bruises of Satan. Carroll Thompson. 1981. per. 3.95 (0-89985-986-0) Christ for the Nations.

Bruising Apothecary: Images of Pharmacy & Medicine in Health Care. Arnold. 1989. pap. 24.95 (0-85369-223-8, Pub. by Pharmaceutical Pr UK) Rittenhouse.

*Bruising the Red Earth: Ochre Mining & Ritual in Aboriginal Tasmania. Anthony Sagona. 244p. Date not set. pap. 39.95 (0-522-84602-5) Intl Spec Bk.

Bruit et La Fureur. William Faulkner. 384p. (FRE.). 1972. pap. 11.95 (0-7859-2271-7, 2070361624) Fr & Eur.

Bruja En la Sopa. Marie-Francine Hebert. (Primeros Lectores Ser.). (Illus.). 60p. (SPA.). (J). (gr. 5 up). 1994. pap. 5.95 (958-07-0078-8) Firefly Bks Ltd.

Brujas de Barahona. Domingo Miras. Ed. by Virtudes Serrano. (Nueva Austral Ser.: Vol. 273). (SPA.). 1993. pap. text ed. 24.95x (84-239-7273-9) Elliots Bks.

*Brujo: Seduced by Evil. Jann A. Wolcott. LC 95-67555. 322p. (Orig.). 1994. pap. text ed. 6.95 (0-9644293-0-6) Route Sixty-Six.

Brulebois. Marcel Ayme. (FRE.). 1988. pap. 24.95 (0-7859-1669-5, 2070203859) Fr & Eur.

*Brules. Combs. 1995. mass mkt. 5.99 (0-440-21728-8) Dell.

Brules. Harry Combs. LC 93-37555. 1994. 22.95 (0-385-31195-8) Delacorte.

Brules. Zoe Oldenbourg. (FRE.). 1975. pap. 13.95 (0-7859-4043-X, 2070366855) Fr & Eur.

Brules: A Novel. Harry Combs. 1992. 19.95 (0-89141-455-X) TernStyle Pr.

Brum. Astrid Holm. LC 92-61952. (Chunky Shape Bks.). (Illus.). 22p. (J). (ps). 1993. 3.25 (0-679-84493-7) Random Bks Yng Read.

Brumaire: The Rise of Bonaparte. J. B. Morton. (Select Bibliographies Reprint Ser.). 1977. reprint ed. 25.95 (0-518-19075-7) Ayer.

Brumas. Joanna Freuh. LC 82-84279. (Illus.). 36p. (Orig.). 1983. pap. text ed. 6.95 (0-9605550-2-1) FreshCut.

Brumfield: Descendants of Thomas Brumfield of Berks County, Pennsylvania: Genealogy & Family History, 1720-1960. Ray C. Brumfield & Blackman O. Brumfield. 493p. 1992. reprint ed. lib. bdg. 86.00 (0-8328-2404-6); reprint ed. pap. 76.00 (0-8328-2405-4) Higginson Bk Co.

Brummer Collection of Medieval Art: Duke University Museum of Art. Ed. by Caroline Bruzelius & Jill Meredith. LC 90-30300. (Illus.). 318p. 1991. text ed. 68.00 (0-8223-1055-4) Duke.

Brunch. Christie Williams. LC 80-85004. (Illus.). 177p. (Orig.). 1981. pap. 6.95 (0-911954-59-7) Bristol Pub Ent CA.

Brunch Basket. Ed. by Janet M. George. LC 84-81269. (Illus.). 339p. 1985. 14.95 (0-9613563-0-8) Rockford Lea.

Brunch Menus. (Great Meals in Minutes Ser.). (Illus.). 104p. 1984. 15.93 (0-86706-170-7); lib. bdg. 21.93 (0-86706-171-5) Time-Life.

Brunches & Breakfasts. Better Homes & Gardens Editors. (Illus.). 80p. 1989. 9.95 (0-696-01858-6) Meredith Bks.

Brundtland Challenge & the Cost of Inaction. Ed. by Alex Davidson & Michael Dence. 159p. 1988. pap. text ed. 17.95 (0-88645-076-4, Pub. by Inst Res Pub CN) Ashgate Pub Co.

*Brunei. (American Geographical Society Around the World Program Ser.). 1995. lib. bdg. 17.95 (0-614-04864-8) Am Geographical.

*Brunei. (American Geographical Society Around the World Program Ser.). 1995. pap. 9.95 (0-614-04865-6) Am Geographical.

Brunei. S. Hassal & P. Hassal. (Let's Visit Places & Peoples of the World Ser.). (Illus.). 96p. (J). (gr. 5 up). 1988. 14.95 (0-7910-0158-X) Chelsea Hse.

Brunei. Sylvia C. Krausse & Gerald H. Krausse. (World Bibliographical Ser.: No. 93). 230p. 1989. lib. bdg. 65.00 (1-85109-029-0) ABC-CLIO.

Brunei. David K. Wright. LC 91-22511. (Enchantment of the World Ser.). 128p. (J). (gr. 5-9). 1991. lib. bdg. 20.55 (0-516-02602-X) Childrens.

*Brunei: Commercial Law. 300p. (Orig.). 1994. pap. 295.00 (0-7605-1234-5) Rector Pr.

Brunei: The Modern Southeast-Asian Islamic Sultanate. David Leake, Jr. LC 89-42730. 190p. 1989. lib. bdg. 27.50x (0-89950-434-5) McFarland & Co.

*Brunei Business Intelligence Handbook. (Illus.). 70p. (Orig.). 1994. pap. 295.00 (0-7605-1009-1) Rector Pr.

*Brunei Commercial Law. 150p. (C). 1994. pap. 295.00 (0-7605-0089-4) Rector Pr.

Brunei Rainforest Adventure. Peter Brown. (Illus.). 64p. (YA). 1993. 11.95 (0-563-36756-3, BBC-Parkwest) Parkwest Pubns.

*Brunei Tax Law. 150p. (C). 1994. pap. 295.00 (0-7605-0088-6) Rector Pr.

Brunelliaceae. Jose Cuatrecasas. LC 85-13613. (Flora Neotropica Monograph Ser.: No. 2S). (Illus.). 103p. 1985. pap. text ed. 21.00 (0-89327-265-5) NY Botanical.

Brunelliaceae. Jose Cuatrecasas. LC 72-91637. (Flora Neotropica Monograph Ser.: No. 2). (Illus.). 190p. 1984. reprint ed. 15.00 (0-89327-263-9) NY Botanical.

Brunetto Latini: The Book of the Treasure - Li Livres dou Tresor. Brunetto Latini. Tr. by Paul Barrette & Spurgeon Baldwin. LC 92-21785. (Library of Medieval Literature: Series B, Vol. 90). 440p. 1992. 63.00 (0-8153-0763-2) Garland.

Brunner & Suddarth's Textbook of Medical-Surgical Nursing. 7th ed. Suzanne C. Smeltzer & Brenda G. Bare. (Illus.). 2064p. 1992. text ed. 65.95 (0-397-54797-8) Lippincott.

Brunnstrom's Clinical Kinesiology. 4th ed. Rev. by L. Don Lehmkuhl & Laura K. Smith. LC 82-25249. (Illus.). 453p. (C). 1983. text ed. 29.95 (0-8036-5529-0) Davis Co.

*Brunnstrom's Clinical Kinesiology. 5th ed. Laura K. Smith et al. (Illus.). 550p. (C). 1995. text ed. 32.00 (0-8036-7916-5) Davis Co.

Brunnstrom's Movement Therapy in Hemiplegia: A Neurophysiologic Approach. 2nd ed. Kathryn A. Sawner & Jeanne M. LaVigne. (Illus.). 288p. 1992. text ed. 39.50 (0-397-54808-7) Lippincott.

Bruno. Alberto Guigou. LC 85-50670. (Senda Dramatica Ser.). (Illus.). 72p. (Orig.). (SPA.). 1985. pap. 7.95 (0-685-43160-6) Senda Nueva.

Bruno Bauer & Karl Marx. Rosen. (Studies in Social History: No. 2). 1977. lib. bdg. 99.00 (90-247-1948-8) Kluwer Ac.

Bruno Bruni. Ed. by Hanns T. Flemming. (Illus.). 159p. 1978. 25.00 (0-936598-00-X) J Szoke Graphics.

Bruno Bruni. Hans Redeker. Tr. by Helge Ayers. (Bibliophilen Taschenbucher Ser.). (Illus.). 247p. (Orig.). 1981. pap. 15.00 (3-921785-16-2) J Szoke Graphics.

Bruno Helps Out. Alan Parry & Linda Parry. LC 91-70401. (Bruno Bks.). (Illus.). 16p. (J). (ps-00). 1991. bds. 1.49 (0-8066-2528-7, 9-2528, Augsburg) Augsburg Fortress.

Bruno Is Sorry. Alan Parry & Linda Parry. LC 91-70402. (Bruno Bks.). (Illus.). 16p. (J). (ps-00). 1991. bds. 1.49 (0-8066-2529-5, 9-2529, Augsburg) Augsburg Fortress.

Bruno Kreisky: Chancellor of Austria: A Political Biography. H. Pierre Secher. 224p. 1994. 17.95 (0-8059-3451-0) Dorrance.

Bruno Lier: Ad Topica Carminum Amatorium Symbolae, Repr. Of 1914 Ed. Bruno Lier et al. Ed. by Steele Commager. Bd. with Keith Preston: Studies in the Diction of the Sermo Amatorius in Roman Comedy. Bruno Lier et al. Ed. by Steele Commager. LC 77-70837.; Alfons Spies: Militat Omnis Amons. Bruno Lier et al. Ed. by Steele Commager. LC 77-70837. LC 77-70837. (Latin Poetry Ser.). 1978. Set lib. bdg. 31.00 (0-8240-2973-9) Garland.

Bruno of Hollywood. Paul Mantee. LC 93-90462. 240p. 1994. 18.00 (0-345-38379-6) Ballantine.

Bruno: or On the Natural & Divine Principle of Things. F. W. Schelling. Tr. by Michael Vater. LC 83-5101. (Hegelian Studies). 269p. 1984. 64.50 (0-87395-793-8); pap. 21.95 (0-87395-792-X) State U NY Pr.

Bruno Sammartino: An Autobiography of Wrestling's Living Legend. Bruno Sammartino et al. LC 89-81625. (Illus.). 244p. 1990. pap. 14.95 (0-911137-14-9) Imagine.

Bruno Says Thanks. Alan Parry & Linda Parry. LC 91-70404. (Bruno Bks.). (Illus.). 16p. (J). (ps-00). 1991. bds. 1.49 (0-8066-2531-7, 9-2531, Augsburg) Augsburg Fortress.

Bruno's Dream. Iris Murdoch. 320p. 1976. pap. 10.95 (0-14-003176-6, Penguin Bks) Viking Penguin.

Brunovsky, Albin. L'udmila Peterajova. 44p. (C). 1985. 195.00 (0-685-22613-1, Pub. by Collets UK) Pro-Am Music.

*Brunschwig Style. Murray Douglas & Chippy Irvine. LC 94-40231. 208p. 1995. 45.00 (0-8212-2041-1) Little.

Brunswick: A Pictorial History. Ed. by Warren F. Broderick. (Illus.). (Orig.). 1978. pap. 9.95 (0-686-26173-9) Brunswick Hist Soc.

*Brunswick County: Virginia Publick Claims. Janice L. Abercrombie & Richard Slatten. (Virginia Publick Claims Ser.). ix, 58p. 1991. pap. 8.00x (0-8095-8517-0) Borgo Pr.

Brunswick County: Virginia Publick Claims. Janice L. Abercrombie & Richard Slatten. (Virginia Publick Claims Ser.). ix, 58p. (C). 1991. reprint ed. lib. bdg. 23.00x (0-8095-8308-9) Borgo Pr.

Brunswick County Marriages, 1450-1800. Catherine L. Knorr. 146p. 1982. reprint ed. 18.50 (0-89308-261-9, VA 24) Southern Hist Pr.

Brunswick County Marriages, 1750-1853. John Vogt & T. William Kethley. (Virginia Historic Marriage Register Ser.). (Illus.). xiii, 296p. (Orig.). 1988. pap. 15.00x (0-935931-40-6) Borgo Pr.

Brunswick County Marriages, 1750-1853. John Vogt & T. William Kethley. (Virginia Historic Marriage Register Ser.). xiii, 296p. (Orig.). (C). 1988. reprint ed. lib. bdg. 37.00x (0-8095-8238-4) Borgo Pr.

*Brunswick County, North Carolina Marriage Bonds & Certificates, 1804-1867. Francis T. Ingmire. 36p. 1994. lib. bdg. 27.00 (0-8095-8011-X); pap. 9.50 (0-8095-8516-2) Borgo Pr.

*Brunswick County, Virginia Court Order Books, 1737-1749. T.L.C. Genealogy Staff. 111p. (Orig.). 1992. spiral bd., pap. 12.00 (1-886633-48-7) TLC Genealogy.

*Brunswick County, Virginia Court Orders, 1732-1737. T. L.C. Genealogy Staff. LC 92-80169. 121p. (Orig.). 1992. spiral bd., pap. 15.00 (1-886633-47-9) TLC Genealogy.

*Brunswick County, Virginia Deeds, 1740-1744. T.L.C. Genealogy Staff. 75p. (Orig.). 1991. spiral bd., pap. 11.00 (1-886633-44-4) TLC Genealogy.

*Brunswick County, Virginia Deeds, 1745-1749. T.L.C. Genealogy Staff. LC 91-65010. 96p. (Orig.). 1991. spiral bd., pap. 11.00 (1-886633-45-2) TLC Genealogy.

*Brunswick County, Virginia Wills, 1739-1750. T.L.C. Genealogy Staff. LC 91-65972. 76p. (Orig.). 1991. spiral bd., pap. 14.00 (1-886633-46-0) TLC Genealogy.

Brunswick Deserter-Immigrants of the American Revolution. Clifford N. Smith. (German-American Genealogical Research Monograph: No. 1). 55p. (Orig.). 1974. pap. 15.00 (0-915162-00-8) Westland Pubns.

Brunswick Troops 1809-15. Otto Von Pivka. (Men-at-Arms Ser.: No. 167). (Illus.). 48p. pap. 11.95 (0-85045-613-4, 9099, Pub. by Osprey UK) Stackpole.

Brunus & the New Bear. Ellen S. Walsh. LC 92-29060. (J). 1993. pap. 4.95 (0-15-212675-9) HarBrace.

*Bruschetta: Crostoni & Crostini - over 1,000 Country Recipes from Italy. Anne Taruschio & Franco Taruschio. (Illus.). 160p. 1995. 24.95 (1-85793-474-1, Pub. by Pavilion UK) Trafalgar.

Brush. Pere Calders. Tr. by Marguerite Feitlowitz. LC 85-23873. (Illus.). 32p. (J). (ps-3). 1986. 10.95 (0-916291-05-7) Kane-Miller Bk.

Brush. Pere Calders. Tr. by Marguerite Feitlowitz. (Illus.). 32p. (J). (ps-3). 1988. reprint ed. pap. 6.95 (0-916291-16-2) Kane-Miller Bk.

Brush Calligraphy. Illus. by Arthur Baker. (Lettering, Calligraphy, Typography Ser.). 95p. (Orig.). 1984. pap. 6.95 (0-486-24533-0) Dover.

Brush, Comb, Scrub: Inventions to Keep You Clean. Vicki Cobb. LC 88-2930. (Trophy Nonfiction Bk.). (Illus.). 32p. (J). (gr. 1-4). 1993. pap. 3.95 (0-06-446107-6, Trophy) HarpC Child Bks.

Brush Country Woman. Ada M. Holland. LC 87-27941. (Centennial Series of the Association of Former Students: No. 26). (Illus.). 240p. 1988. 17.50 (0-89096-328-2) Tex A&M Univ Pr.

Brush Coyotes. Sigurd J. Simonsen. Ed. by Dan C. McCurry & Richard E. Rubenstein. LC 74-30653. (American Farmers & the Rise of Agribusiness Ser.). 1975. reprint ed. 23.95 (0-405-06829-8) Ayer.

Brush Decoration for Ceramics. Marc Bellaire. LC 64-8931. 1964. 3.95 (0-934706-02-6) Prof Pubns Ohio.

Brush Foundation Study of Child Growth & Development I: Psychometric Tests. Elizabeth Ebert & Katherine Simmons. (SRCD M: Vol. 8, No. 2). 1972. reprint ed. 12.00 (0-527-01527-X, SRCD.M 35) Periodicals Srv.

Brush Foundation Study of Child Growth & Development II: Physical Growth & Development. Katherine Simmons. (SRCD M: Vol. 9, No. 1). 1972. reprint ed. 16.00 (0-527-01530-X, SRCD.M 37) Periodicals Srv.

Brush Lettering. Eliza Schulte & Marilyn Reaves. (Illus.). 128p. 1992. pap. 16.95 (0-8306-3631-5, 4080, Design Pr) TAB Bks.

Brush Lettering: An Instructional Manual of Western Brush Lettering. Marilyn Reaves & Eliza Schulte. 128p. 1993. pap. 19.95 (1-55821-269-8) Lyons & Burford.

Brush Management: Principles & Practices for Texas & the Southwest. Charles J. Scifres. LC 79-7407. (Illus.). 376p. 1980. 24.50 (0-89096-080-1) Tex A&M Univ Pr.

Brush Mind. Kazuaki Tanahashi. LC 90-7398. (Illus.). 148p. (Orig.). 1990. per., pap. 15.00 (0-938077-29-5) Parallax Pr.

Brush of an Angel's Wing. Charlie Shedd. 220p. 1994. 14.99 (0-89283-854-X, Vine Bks) Servant.

*Brush of an Angel's Wing. large type ed. Charlie Shedd. 192p. 1995. pap. 9.95 (0-8027-2686-0) Walker & Co.

*Brush of Angel's Wings. Carolyn Blaylock. 160p. 1995. pap. 6.95 (1-57071-073-2) Sourcebks.

Brush of the Masters: Drawings from Iran & India. Esin Atil. LC 78-70427. (Illus.). 1978. pap. 20.00 (0-934686-29-7) Freer.

Brush-on Color Magic. Kay B. Weiner. (Illus.). 32p. (Orig.). 1994. pap. 12.95 (0-9625663-5-7) Eastman Pub.

Brush Strokes. Deborah Ford. 24p. (Orig.). 1991. pap. 4.00 (1-880286-02-5) Singular Speech Pr.

Brush up Your Bible! Michael Macrone. LC 93-4350. (Illus.). 368p. 1993. 20.00 (0-06-270024-3, Harper Ref) HarpC.

*Brush up Your Bible. Michael Macrone. (Illus.). 384p. 1995. pap. 10.00 (0-06-272020-1) HarpC.

Brush up Your Shakespeare! Michael Macrone. (Illus.). 256p. 1994. pap. 10.00 (0-06-272018-X, Harper Ref) HarpC.

Brush with Art. Alwyn Crawshaw. (Illus.). 96p. 1993. 19.95 (0-89134-536-1, 30547) North Light Bks.

Brush with Cats. Pam Martins. (Illus.). 48p. 1995. 14.95 (0-285-63087-3, Pub. by Souvenir UK) Atrium Pubs.

Brush with Life. Frank S. Smith & John Man. (Illus.). 160p. 1994. 45.00 (0-297-83231-X) Trafalgar.

Brush with Magic. William J. Brooke. LC 92-41744. (Illus.). 160p. (J). (gr. 3 up). 1993. 15.00 (0-06-022973-X); lib. bdg. 14.89 (0-06-022974-8) HarpC Child Bks.

*Brush with Magic. William J. Brooke. LC 92-41744. (Illus.). 144p. (J). (gr. 3 up). 1995. pap. 3.95 (0-06-440490-0, Trophy) HarpC Child Bks.

Brush with Nature, A. Jeff Kinzie & Sharon Kinzie. Ed. by Bill Thompson. LC 86-63833. 52p. 1987. pap. 8.95 (0-916809-14-5) Scott Pubns MI.

Brush with Shakespeare: The Bard in Painting, 1780-1910. Lucy Oakley et al. LC 85-29669. (Illus.). 140p. (Orig.). (ps-12). 1985. pap. 18.00 (0-89280-024-0) Montgomery Mus.

Brush Writing: Calligraphy Techniques for Beginners. Ryokushu Kuiseko. LC 87-82854. 96p. 1988. pap. 19.00 (0-87011-862-5) Kodansha.

Brush Your Teeth Please. Leslie McGuire. LC 92-85152. (Illus.). 10p. (J). (ps-k). 1993. 9.95 (0-89577-474-7) RD Assn.

Brushed with Elegance. Susan Scheewe. 36p. 1973. pap. 5.50 (1-56770-106-X) S Scheewe Pubns.

Brushes: A Handbook for Artists & Artisans. Jacques Turner. 1992. pap. 13.95 (0-07-065599-5) McGraw.

Brushes: A Handbook for Artists & Artisans. Jacques Turner. 96p. 1992. pap. 13.95 (0-8306-3975-6, 4157, Design Pr) TAB Bks.

Brushes with Power: Modern Politics & the Chinese Art of Calligraphy. Richard C. Kraus. LC 90-23590. (Illus.). 220p. 1991. 30.00 (0-520-07285-5) U CA Pr.

Brushes with the Literary: Letters of a Washington Artist, 1943-1959. Marcella C. Winslow. LC 92-18920. (Southern Literary Studies). (Illus.). 395p. 1993. 29.95 (0-8071-1761-7) La State U Pr.

Brushing Your Teeth. Don R. Horner et al. (Project MORE Daily Living Skills Ser.). (Illus.). 32p. 1979. reprint ed. pap. text ed. 5.95 (0-685-67488-6) PRO-ED.

Brushing Your Teeth, Set. Don R. Horner et al. (Project MORE Daily Living Skills Ser.). (Illus.). 32p. 1979. reprint ed. pap. text ed. 149.00 (0-685-05747-X) PRO-ED.

Brushlanders. Robert Winship. 144p. 1992. 18.95 (1-881515-00-1) TX Review Pr.

Brushless Permanent-Magnet & Reluctance Motor Drives. T. J. Miller. (Monographs in Electrical & Electronic Engineering: No. 21). (Illus.). 244p. 1989. 64.00 (0-19-859369-4) OUP.

Brushless Permanent-Magnet Motor Design. Duane C. Hanselman. LC 93-43581. 1994. text ed. 55.00 (0-07-026025-7) McGraw.

Brushless Servomotors: Fundamentals & Applications. Ed. by Yasuhiko Dote & Sakan Kinoshita. (Monographs in Electrical & Electronic Engineering: No. 23). (Illus.). 288p. 1990. 95.00 (0-19-859372-4) OUP.

B

An Asterisk (*) at the beginning of an entry indicates that the title is appearing in BIP for the first time. 927

Brushstrokes: A Novel. Gary Levine. 179p. 1982. pap. 5.95 (*0-940118-65-3*) Moznaim.

Brushstrokes: Styles & Techniques of Chinese Painting. So Kam Ng. (Illus.). 56p. 1992. pap. 14.95 (*0-295-97239-4*) U of Wash Pr.

Brushstrokes & Free-Style Alphabets: One Hundred Complete Fonts. Dan X. Solo. LC 77-70048. (Pictorial Archive Ser.). 1977. pap. 5.95 (*0-486-23488-6*) Dover.

Brushstrokes & Landscapes (from My Pen) Pinceladas y Paisajes (de Mi Pluma) Carmen D. Lucca. Ed. by Ediciones Mairena Staff. LC 89-92209. (Illus.). 130p. (Orig.). (ENG & SPA.). 1990. pap. 7.00 (*0-9623968-0-X*) Poets Refuge.

Brushstrokes on the Plateau. 321p. 1984. 4.95 (*0-89734-069-8*, PL56-1) Mus Northern Ariz.

Brushwork Basics. Evelyn Gildner. LC 84-40780. 52p. (Orig.). 1984. pap. text ed. 10.95 (*0-916809-10-2*) Scott Pubns MI.

Brushwork Diary: Watercolors of Early Nevada. Illus. by Walter S. Long. LC 91-12179. 136p. 1991. 24.95 (*0-87417-174-1*) U of Nev Pr.

Brushwork on Ceramics. John Sutton. LC 82-186799. (Illus.). 192p. 1980. pap. 5.98 (*0-686-36021-4*) Scott Pubns MI.

Brusilov's Break-Through, a Novel of the First World War. Sergei N. Sergeev-Tsienskii. Tr. by Allen Altschuler. LC 75-39014. (Soviet Literature in English Translation Ser.). 336p. 1978. reprint ed. 24.75 (*0-88355-416-X*) Hyperion Conn.

Brusque Transect from Atlantic Coast to Bolivian Border, Southern Brazil. 1991. 95.00 (*0-87590-781-4*, GGT 4) Am Geophysical.

Brussels. (Insight Guides Ser.). 1993. pap. 21.95 (*0-395-66430-6*) HM.

Brussels. (Insight Pocket Guides Ser.). (Illus.). 100p. 1993. pap. 9.95 (*0-395-66907-3*) HM.

Brussels. (American Express Travel Guides Ser.). (Illus.). 208p. 1993. pap. 13.00 (*0-671-84933-6*, P-H Travel) P-H Gen Ref & Trav.

Brussels. Ed. by Alexander B. Murphy. (World Cities Ser.). 224p. 1993. text ed. 49.95 (*0-470-22010-4*) Halsted Pr.

Brussels: With Bruges, Ghent, & Antwerp. Antony Mason. LC 93-47110. (Cadogan City Guides Ser.). (Illus.). 320p. (Orig.). 1995. pap. 14.95 (*1-56440-273-8*, Pub. by Cadogan Bks UK) Globe Pequot.

Brussels, Bruges, Ghent & Antwerp. Antony Mason. LC 93-47110. (Cadogan Guides Ser.). 1994. 10.99 (*0-947754-55-5*, Pub. by Cadogan Books UK) Macmillan.

Brussels Griffon Champions, 1952-1991. Camino E. E. & B. Co. Staff. (Illus.). 175p. 1993. pap. 36.95 (*1-55893-000-0*) Camino E E & Bk.

Brussels Horloge de Sapience: Iconography & Text of Brussels, Bibliotheque Royale, MS. IV 111. Peter R. Monks. LC 90-2215. (Litterae Textuales Ser.). (Illus.). viii, 223p. (ENG & FRE.). 1990. pap. 48.75 (*90-04-09088-6*) E J Brill.

Brussels Pocket Guide. rev. ed. Berlitz Editors. LC 80-69546. (Pocket Guides Ser.). (Illus.). 144p. 1994. pap. 7.95 (*2-8315-1589-0*) Berlitz.

Brussels Travel Guide. 1993. pap. 7.95 (*2-8315-2205-6*) Berlitz.

Brusski: A Story of Peasant Life in Soviet Russia. Fedor I. Panferov. LC 75-37341. (Early Soviet Literature Ser.). (Orig.). 1977. lib. bdg. 21.45 (*0-88355-414-3*) Hyperion Conn.

Brut. Lawman. Tr. & Intro. by Rosamund Allen. 528p. 1993. pap. 12.95 (*0-460-87021-1*, Everyman's Classic Lib) C E Tuttle.

Brut. Lawman. Tr. & Intro. by Rosamund Allen. LC 92-16866. 1992. text ed. 45.00 (*0-312-08576-1*) St Martin.

Brut: Part II. Chronicles of England Staff. (EETS, OS Ser.: No. 136). 1972. reprint ed. 45.00 (*0-527-00134-1*) Periodicals Srv.

Brut, or the Chronicle of England, Pt. 1. Ed. by F. Brie. (EETS, OS Ser.: Vol. 131). 1972. reprint ed. 42.00 (*0-8115-0151-5*) Periodicals Srv.

Brut Y Tywysogion or the Chronicle of the Princes: Peniarth MS. 20 Version. Thomas Jones. (History & Law Ser.: No. 11). 272p. 1952. 25.95 (*0-7083-0103-7*, Pub. by U of Wales UK) Bks Intl VA.

Brut y Tywysogion, or the Chronicle of the Princes of Wales (681-1281) Ed. by John Williams. (Rolls Ser.: No. 17). 1972. reprint ed. 45.00 (*0-8115-1022-0*) Periodicals Srv.

Brutal Castration of the Lady Doctor. Remy Theberge. Ed. by R. Moisan. 110p. 1990. 10.50 (*0-918862-04-3*) Golden Gambit.

Brutal Choreographies: Oppositional Strategies & Narrative Design in the Novels of Margaret Atwood. J. Brooks Bouson. LC 93-2964. 216p. (C). 1993. 27.50 (*0-87023-845-0*) U of Mass Pr.

Brutal Conquest. Jerry Ahern. (Survivalist Ser.: No. 22). 1991. pap. 3.50 (*0-8217-3538-1*) Zebra.

Brutal Intimates: Rapists. Zulma Gonzalez-Parker. (Orig.). 1989. pap. 2.50 (*1-878255-03-7*) Heartfelt Pr.

Brutal Justice: The Ordeal of an American City. Henry Cohen. LC 79-26797. 248p. 1980. lib. bdg. 10.00 (*0-89444-027-6*) John Jay Pr.

Brutal Need: Law, Lawyers, & the Welfare Rights Movement, 1960-1973. Martha F. Davis. LC 93-1313. 224p. Date not set. 26.50 (*0-300-05378-9*) Yale U Pr.

Brutalitarians & the Bomb. Lorin Peterson. LC 87-83304. (Illus.). 160p. 1988. 9.95 (*0-945690-00-2*) Hillside CA.

Brutality of Nations. Dan N. Jacobs. 1987. 22.95 (*0-394-47138-5*) Knopf.

Brutality Unchecked: Human Rights Abuses Along the U. S. Border with Mexico. Ed. by Human Rights Watch Staff. 88p. (Orig.). 1992. pap. 7.00 (*1-56432-075-8*) Hum Rts Watch.

Brute. Guy Des Cars. 304p. 1951. 10.95 (*0-686-55610-0*) Fr & Eur.

Brute. Guy Des Cars. 448p. (FRE.). 1960. pap. 6.95 (*0-8288-9552-X*, M5716) Fr & Eur.

Brute & Other Farces: Seven Short Plays. Anton Chekhov. Tr. by Eric Bentley & Theodore Hoffman. 96p. 1987. reprint ed. 19.95 (*1-55783-003-7*); reprint ed. pap. 5.95 (*1-55783-004-5*) Applause Theatre Bk Pubs.

Brute New World: The Rediscovery of Latin America in the Early 19th Century. Desmond Gregory. (Illus.). 240p. (C). 1993. text ed. 59.50 (*1-85043-567-7*, Pub. by I B Tauris UK) St Martin.

Bruton's Visit of Lord Jagannath 350 Years Ago: British Beginnings in Orissa. Ed. by P. T. Nair. 1986. 14.00 (*0-8364-1610-4*, Pub. by Minerva II) S Asia.

Brutus. M. Tullius Cicero. xxvi, 312p. 1964. write for info. (*3-296-11500-5*, Pub. by Georg Olms GW) Lubrecht & Cramer.

Brutus. Marcus T. Cicero. Bd. with Orator (Loeb Classical Library: No. 342). (ENG & LAT.). 15.50 (*0-674-99377-2*) HUP.

Brutus. Mark Dunster. (Antony Ser.: Pt. 6). (Orig.). 1980. pap. 4.00 (*0-89642-063-9*) Linden Pubs.

Brutus: or The Fall of Tarquin. John H. Payne. (BCL1-PS American Literature Ser.). 56p. 1992. reprint ed. lib. bdg. 59.00 (*0-7812-6828-1*) Rprt Serv.

Brutus Revival: Parricide & Tyrannicide During the Renaissance. Manfredi Piccolomini. LC 89-78134. (Illus.). 200p. (C). 1991. 24.95 (*0-8093-1649-8*) S Ill U Pr.

Brutus the Bear. Dave Sargent & Pat Sargent. (Animal Pride Ser.). 64p. (J). (gr. 2-6). 1992. pap. write for info. (*1-56763-006-5*) Ozark Pub.

Brutus the Wonder Poodle. Linda Gondosch. LC 89-39377. (Stepping Stone Bks.). (Illus.). 64p. (Orig.). (J). (gr. 2-4). 1990. lib. bdg. 5.99 (*0-679-90573-1*); pap. 1.95 (*0-679-80573-7*) Random Bks Yng Read.

Bruyers Moraliste: Quatre Etudes sur "Les Caracteres" Louis Van Delft. (Coll. Hist. des Idees et Crit. Litt.). 178p. (FRE.). 1971. pap. 49.95 (*0-7859-5302-7*) Fr & Eur.

Bryan Adams. Darlene Fredricks. (Orig.). 1987. pap. 2.95 (*0-345-33887-1*) Ballantine.

Bryan Adams: The Illustrated Biography. Sandy Robertson. (Illus.). 64p. 1992. pap. 10.95 (*0-7119-3101-1*, OP47086) Omnibus NY.

Bryan City Cemetery Brazos County Texas Books 1, 2, 3, & 4. Mary Collie-Cooper. 193p. (Orig.). 1987. pap. 10.00 (*0-943553-03-2*) Collie-Cooper Ent.

Bryan Ferry: Street Life. (Illus.). 88p. 1986. pap. 12.95 (*0-7119-1020-0*, AM64106) Music Sales.

Bryan Ferry Boys & Girls. (Illus.). 40p. 1985. pap. 11.95 (*0-7119-0792-7*, AM61466) Music Sales.

Bryan Hunt, No. 25. Ed. by Kyoichi Tsuzuki. (Art Random Ser.). (Illus.). 48p. 1990. 32.95 (*4-7636-8528-7*, Pub. by Kyoto Shoin JA) Bks Nippan.

Bryan Hunt: A Decade of Drawings. Museum Studies Class Staff. (Illus.). 61p. 1983. pap. 20.00 (*0-936270-20-9*) CA St U LB Art.

Bryan Hunt: Recent Drawings. (Illus.). 40p. (Orig.). 1989. pap. 10.00 (*0-924008-01-6*) Blum Helman.

Bryan Money. F. Zerbe. (Illus.). 1983. reprint ed. pap. 10.00 (*0-942666-00-3*) S J Durst.

Bryan on Imperialism. William J. Bryan. LC 71-111701. (American Imperialism: Viewpoints of United States Foreign Policy, 1898-1941 Ser.). 1976. reprint ed. 18.95 (*0-405-02005-8*) Ayer.

Bryan Robson's Soccer Skills. Bryan Robson. (Illus.). 128p. (Orig.). 1987. pap. 14.95 (*0-8069-6654-8*) Sterling.

Bryan's Sectional Maps of Oahu. rev. ed. John R. Clere. (Illus.). 204p. 1990. pap. 6.75 (*1-878536-00-1*) EMIC Graphics.

Bryan's Sectional Maps of Oahu. rev. ed. John R. Clere. (Illus.). 210p. 1991. pap. text ed. 7.00 (*1-878536-01-X*) EMIC Graphics.

Bryan's Sectional Maps of Oahu. rev. ed. John R. Clere. (Illus.). 208p. 1991. pap. text ed. 7.25 (*1-878536-02-8*) EMIC Graphics.

Bryan's Sectional Maps of Oahu. rev. ed. John R. Clere. (Illus.). 208p. 1992. pap. text ed. 7.50 (*1-878536-03-6*) EMIC Graphics.

Bryan's Sectional Maps of Oahu. rev. ed. John R. Clere. (Illus.). 212p. 1993. pap. text ed. 7.75 (*1-878536-04-4*) EMIC Graphics.

Bryant Family History, Ancestry & Descendants of David Bryant (1756) of Springfield, N. J., Washington Co., & Wolf Lake, Noble Co., Ind. C. V. Braiden. (Illus.). 270p. 1992. reprint ed. lib. bdg. 52.50 (*0-8328-2307-4*); reprint ed. pap. 42.50 (*0-8328-2308-2*) Higginson Bk Co.

Bryant's Law & Other Broadsides: Recent Controversial Writings of John Bryant. John Bryant. 1990. pap. 19.95 (*0-9617444-2-1*) Socratic Pr.

Bryce - Mount Dutton, UT. rev. ed. Ed. by Trails Illustrated Staff. (Illus.). 1992. Folded topographical map. 7.95 (*0-925873-72-1*) Trails Illustrated.

Bryce Canyon. Ed. by Jeff Nicholas. (Wish You Were Here Postcard Bks.). (Illus.). 32p. 1992. pap. 4.95 (*0-939365-06-5*) Sierra Pr CA.

Bryce Canyon: The Story Behind the Scenery. John Bezy. LC 79-93079. (Illus.). 48p. 1980. pap. 6.95 (*0-916122-69-7*) KC Pubns.

***Bryce Canyon National Park: A Visual Interpretation.** Nicky Leach. Ed. by Rose Houk & Jeff Nicholas. (Wish You Were Here Ser.). (Illus.). 48p. (Orig.). 1995. pap. 7.95 (*0-939365-42-1*) Sierra Pr CA.

Bryce Canyon National Park, UT. rev. ed. Ed. by Trails Illustrated Staff. (Illus.). 1994. Folded topographical map. 7.95 (*0-925873-19-5*) Trails Illustrated.

Bryggen Papers, Bryggen Pottery: Introduction & Pingsdorf Ware, No. 1. Hartwig Ludtke. (Supplementary Ser.: No. 4). (Illus.). 128p. (Orig.). 1989. pap. 59.50x (*82-00-02796-1*, Pub. by Almqv & Wiksell SW) Coronet Bks.

Brylcreem Boy. Bob Freeman. 262p. (C). 1989. text ed. 39.00 (*1-872795-60-9*, Pub. by Pentland Pr UK) St Mut.

Bryn & Llangattock-nigh-Usk: A Short History, Reminiscences & Photographs. Barbara Beck. 187p. (C). 1989. 59.00 (*0-905928-24-5*, Pub. by D Brown & Sons Ltd UK) St Mut.

Bryn Mawr Cookbook. limited ed. 300p. 1985. 20.00 (*0-317-39614-5*) Pubns Devl Co.

Bryn Mawr Memories. Elizabeth B. Kelley. (Illus.). 31p. (Orig.). (C). 1988. pap. 12.50 (*0-945677-05-7*) Riverby Bks.

Bryoflora of the Atolls of Micronesia. H. A. Miller et al. (Illus.). 1963. pap. 24.00 (*3-7682-5411-9*) Lubrecht & Cramer.

Bryogeographie-Du Mont Bokor (Cambodge) 1979. P. Tixier. (Bryophytorum Bibliotheca Ser.: No. 18). (Illus.). 1979. pap. text ed. 24.00 (*3-7682-1227-0*) Lubrecht & Cramer.

Bryogeography of Expedition Area, Axelberg Heiberg Island, N. W. T. Canada. M. Kuc. 1973. 25.00 (*3-7682-0912-1*) Lubrecht & Cramer.

Bryological Contributions: Presented in Celebration of the Distinguished Scholarship of Rudolf M. Schuster. Ed. by J. J. Engel & S. Hattori. (Nova Hedwigia Ser.: Beiheft 90). (Illus.). 402p. 1988. pap. 160.00 (*3-443-51012-4*) Lubrecht & Cramer.

Bryophyta of South Africa. T. R. Sim. (Illus.). 475p. 1973. reprint ed. 157.00 (*3-87429-053-0*) Koeltz Sci Bks.

Bryophyte Development: Physiology & Biochemistry. Ed. by R. N. Chopra & S. C. Bhatla. (Illus.). 320p. 1990. 205.00 (*0-8493-5289-4*, QK533) CRC Pr.

Bryophyte Ecology. Ed. by A. J. Smith. (Illus.). 472p. 1982. 89.95 (*0-412-22340-6*, NO. 6656) Chapman & Hall.

Bryophytes: Their Chemistry & Chemical Taxonomy. H. D. Zinsmeister & R. Mues. (Proceedings of the Phytochemical Society of Europe Ser.: No. 29). (Illus.). 488p. 1990. 125.00 (*0-19-857716-8*) OUP.

Bryophytes & Lichens in a Changing Environment. Ed. by Jeffrey W. Bates & Andrew M. Farmer. (Illus.). 416p. 1992. 125.00 (*0-19-854291-7*) OUP.

Bryophytes of the Palaeozoic & Mesozoic. Cora Oostendorp. (Bryophytorum Bibliotheca Ser.: Vol. 34). (Illus.). 208p. 1987. pap. 78.25 (*3-443-62006-X*) Lubrecht & Cramer.

Bryostephane Steereana. Ed. by W. R. Buck. (Memoirs Ser.: Vol. 45). (Illus.). 778p. 1987. pap. 130.00 (*0-89327-322-8*) NY Botanical.

Bryozoa: Present & Past. Ed. & Intro. by June R. Ross. (Illus.). 340p. (Orig.). 1987. pap. 60.00 (*0-930216-02-4*) West Wash Univ.

Bryozoan Evolution. F. K. McKinney & Jeremy B. Jackson. (Illus.). 256p. 1987. text ed. 55.00 (*0-04-560012-0*) Routledge Chapman & Hall.

Bryozoan Evolution. Frank K. McKinney & Jeremy B. Jackson. (Illus.). 252p. 1991. pap. text ed. 15.95 (*0-226-56047-3*) U Ch Pr.

Brzemie Krzyza. Joseph Cyrene. LC 85-62388. (Illus.). 80p. (Orig.). (POL.). 1985. pap. text ed. 8.00 (*0-930401-03-4*) Artex Pub.

BS Syndrome: How to Uncover It, Fight It, Master It. Victor Salupo. 258p. 1987. pap. 14.95 (*0-933219-00-8*) Bull Buster.

BS 1 Skillbooklet, No. I. Barbara J. Crane. (Crane Reading System-English Ser.). (Illus.). (J). (gr. k-2). 1982. pap. text ed. 2.49 (*0-89075-031-9*) Bilingual Ed Serv.

BS 7750: Implementing the Environment Management Standard. Brian Rothery. 200p. 1993. 59.95 (*0-566-07392-7*, Pub. by Gower UK) Ashgate Pub Co.

BSA. Don Morley. (Osprey Colour Library). (Illus.). 1991. pap. 15.95 (*1-85532-118-1*, Pub. by Osprey Pubng Ltd UK) Motorbooks Intl.

BSA: A Competition History. Norman Vanhouse. LC 86-81146. (Illus.). 345p. 1987. 29.95 (*0-85429-479-1*, F479, Pub. by G T Foulis Ltd) Haynes Pubns.

BSA Complete Story. Owen Wright. (Crowood Motoclassics Ser.). (Illus.). 160p. 1992. 29.95 (*1-85223-702-3*, Pub. by Crowood UK) Motorbooks Intl.

BSA Family Book. Boy Scouts of America Staff. (Illus.). 72p. (Orig.). (C). 1990. pap. 2.95 (*0-8395-3012-9*, 33012) BSA.

***BSA, Illustrated Motorcycle Legends.** Bacon. (Illus.). 1995. (*0-7858-0254-1*) Bk Sales Inc.

BSD-Lite 4.4 CD-ROM Companion: Domestic Edition. Computer Systems Research Group Staff. 112p. (Orig.). 1994. pap. 40.00 (*1-56592-081-3*) OReilly & Assocs.

***BSD-Lite 4.4 CD-ROM Companion: International Edition.** Computer Systems Research Group Staff. 112p. (Orig.). 1994. pap. 40.00 (*1-56592-092-9*) OReilly & Assocs.

***BSD 4.4 Vols. 1-5.** Computer Systems Research Group Staff. (Orig.). 1994. pap. 120.00 (*1-56592-077-5*); cd-rom, pap. 150.00 (*1-56592-082-1*) OReilly & Assocs.

BSD 4.4 Programmer's Reference Manual. Computer Systems Research Group Staff. 886p. (Orig.). 1994. pap. 30.00 (*1-56592-078-3*) OReilly & Assocs.

BSD 4.4 Programmer's Supplementary Documents. Computer Systems Research Group Staff. 596p. (Orig.). 1994. pap. 30.00 (*1-56592-079-1*) OReilly & Assocs.

BSD 4.4 System Manager's Manual. Computer Systems Research Group Staff. 804p. (Orig.). 1994. pap. 30.00 (*1-56592-080-5*) OReilly & Assocs.

BSD 4.4 User's Reference Manual. Computer Systems Research Group Staff. 905p. (Orig.). 1994. pap. 30.00 (*1-56592-075-9*) OReilly & Assocs.

BSD 4.4 User's Supplementary Documents. Computer Systems Research Group Staff. 712p. (Orig.). 1994. pap. 30.00 (*1-56592-076-7*) OReilly & Assocs.

bshru's Vision of Peace & Security in Nuclear Age. Ed. by P. N. Haksar. (C). 1988. 34.00 (*0-317-93110-5*) S Asia.

B.S.Ing: The Secrets of Success in the Business World. Len Matlick. 120p. 1987. pap. 14.00 (*0-87364-428-X*) Paladin Pr.

BT--Behavior Therapy. Spencer A. Rathus & Jeffrey Nevid. 1978. pap. 2.95 (*0-451-09949-4*, E9949, Sig) NAL-Dutton.

***BTEC First-Mathematics for Technicians.** A. Greer & G. W. Taylor. 352p. (C). 1982. pap. 30.00x (*0-85950-916-8*, Pub. by S Thornes Pubs UK) St Mut.

***BTEC National N11 Mathematics for Technicians.** 2nd ed. Stanley Thornes Publ. Ltd. Staff. 448p. (C). 1994. pap. 30.00x (*0-7487-1701-3*, Pub. by S Thornes Pubs UK) St Mut.

***BTEC National N111 Mathematics for Technicians.** A. Greer & G. W. Taylor. 352p. (C). 1989. pap. 30.00x (*0-85950-932-X*, Pub. by S Thornes Pubs UK) St Mut.

B'tween: Messages from Michael. Leo D. Hall. (Illus.). 180p. (Orig.). (YA). (gr. 6-12). 1992. pap. 8.75 (*0-914107-03-8*) Lion House Pr.

***Bua Luang Compact WYSIWYS English-Thai Dictionary.** E. G. Allyn. 349p. (Orig.). 1994. pap. 12.95 (*0-942777-13-1*) Bua Luang Pub.

Buarij: Portrait of a Lebanese Muslim Village. Anne H. Fuller. LC 61-14633. (Middle Eastern Monographs: No. 6). 106p. 1961. pap. 4.50 (*0-674-08550-7*) HUP.

Bub & Chub. Gina C. Erickson & Kelli C. Foster. (Get Ready...Get Set...Read! Ser.). (Illus.). 24p. (J). (ps-2). 1992. pap. 3.50 (*0-8120-4859-8*) Barron.

Bub or The Very Best Thing. Natalie Babbitt. LC 93-78758. (Michael di Capua Bks.). (Illus.). 32p. (J). (gr. k up). 1994. lib. bdg. 14.89 (*0-06-205045-1*) HarpC Child Bks.

Bub or The Very Best Thing. Natalie Babbitt. LC 93-78758. (Michael di Capua Bks.). (Illus.). 32p. (J). (gr. k up). 1994. 15.00 (*0-06-205044-3*) HarpC Child Bks.

Buba Leah & Her Paper Children. Lillian H. Ross. (Illus.). 32p. (J). (gr. k-3). 1991. 17.95 (*0-8276-0375-4*) JPS Phila.

Bubb Booklets Letters of Richard Aldington to Charles Clinch Bubb. Richard Aldington. (Illus.). 64p. 1988. 40.00 (*0-930126-25-4*) Typographeum.

Bubba. Sam Havens. (Illus.). 48p. 1973. pap. 4.00 (*0-88680-014-5*) I E Clark.

Bubba & Buddha: Fat People Are People Too! David Anderson & William Anderson. 50p. 1993. pap. 5.99 (*1-884382-00-2*) Know Sweatshop.

Bubba Bear. Bob Reese. (Yellowstone Ser.). (Illus.). (J). (gr. k-6). 1986. 7.95 (*0-89868-173-1*); pap. 2.95 (*0-89868-174-X*); pap. 20.00 (*0-685-50871-4*) ARO Pub.

***Bubba Gump Shrimp Co. Cookbook: Recipes & Reflections from Forrest Gump.** Oxmoor House Staff. 1994. 14.95 (*0-8487-1479-2*) Oxmoor Hse.

Bubba, Missy & Me. Eugene Platt. LC 92-64263. 128p. (Orig.). 1992. pap. 10.00 (*0-937684-29-5*) Tradd St Pr.

***Bubbas & Beaus: A Close Look at the Customs, Cuisine, & Culture of Southern Men.** Gail Gilchriest. (Illus.). 192p. 1995. pap. 10.95 (*0-7868-8055-4*) Hyperion.

***Bubba's Last Farewell.** Clarissa W. Adkinson. (J). (gr. 1-8). Date not set. pap. write for info. (*1-885005-07-5*) LynHawk Pubng.

Bubba's Truck. Tom Townsend. 128p. (YA). (gr. 6-12). 1992. 14.95 (*0-89015-857-6*) Sunbelt Media.

***Bubbe Hinda's Helper.** Rochel Sandman. Ed. by D. Rosenfeld. (Illus.). 32p. (J). 1995. write for info. (*0-922613-77-X*) Hachai Pubns.

Bubbe Meisehs by Shayneh Maidelehs: Poetry by Jewish Granddaughters about Our Grandmothers. Intro. by Leslea Newman. 112p. (Orig.). 1989. pap. text ed. 8.00 (*0-939821-00-1*) HerBooks.

Bubbee Bear Coloring Book. Arthur Von Wiesenberger. (Bubbee the Bear Stories Ser.). (Illus.). 10p. (Orig.). (J). (gr. k-2). 1995. pap. text ed. 0.99 (*0-9624574-9-3*) Best Cellar Bks.

Bubble. Anand Mulk-Raj. 604p. 1984. 19.90 (*0-86578-243-1*) Ind-US Inc.

Bubble & Burp Machine. E. Paul Braxton. 216p. (Orig.). 1986. pap. 3.95 (*0-939017-00-8*) Hermit Pr FL.

Bubble Bubble. rev. ed. Mercer Mayer. (Illus.). 48p. (J). 1992. reprint ed. pap. 5.95 (*1-879920-03-4*) Rain Bird Prods.

Bubble, Bubble, Toil & Trouble. Hans Carl. 254p. (C). 1991. 45.00 (*0-7223-2498-7*, Pub. by A H S Ltd UK) St Mut.

Bubble, Bubble, Toil & Trouble. Shirley Lueth. 264p. 1993. reprint ed. pap. 7.95 (*0-937911-03-8*) Lueth Hse Pub.

Bubble Chambers. Yu A. Aleksandrov. Tr. by William R. Frisken. LC 66-14342. 382p. reprint ed. pap. 108.90 (*0-8357-7451-1*, 2055192) Bks Demand.

Bubble Column Reactions. Wolf-Dieter Deckwer. 533p. 1991. text ed. 385.00 (*0-471-91811-3*) Wiley.

***Bubble Didn't Burst: The Story of Nathan Benderson.** Dick Hirsch. 1995. pap. 9.95 (*0-9647235-0-6*) Stonecroft Pub.

Bubble-Domain Memory Devices. Alan B. Smith. LC 73-89263. (Modern Frontiers in Applied Science Ser.). (Illus.). 270p. reprint ed. pap. 77.00 (*0-8357-7452-X*, 2010074) Bks Demand.

***Bubble Dynamics & Interface Phenomena: Proceedings IUTAM Symposium, Held in Birmingham, U. K., 6-9 September 1992.** Ed. by J. R. Blake. (Fluid Mechanics & Its Applications Ser.). 512p. (C). 1994. lib. bdg. 216.00 (*0-7923-3008-0*) Kluwer Ac.

Bubble Festival. Jacqueline Barber & Carolyn Willard. Ed. by Lincoln Bergman & Carl Babcock. (Great Explorations in Math & Science (GEMS) Ser.). (Illus.). 184p. (J). (gr. k-6). 1992. pap. 12.50 (*0-912511-80-X*) Lawrence Science.

928

An Asterisk (*) at the beginning of an entry indicates that the title is appearing in BIP for the first time.

Bubble Gum. Kate Noble. (Africa Stories Ser.). (Illus.). 32p. (J). (ps-4). 1995. 14.95 (*0-9631798-0-2*) Silver Seahorse.
Bubble Gum & Chalk Dust. Mary L. Carney. LC 82-4041. 96p. (Orig.). 1982. pap. 7.95 (*0-687-03987-8*) Abingdon.
Bubble Gum in the Sky. Louise Everett. LC 86-30859. (Illus.). 32p. (J). (gr. k-2). 1988. lib. bdg. 7.89 (*0-8167-0998-X*); pap. text ed. 1.95 (*0-8167-0999-8*) Troll Assocs.
Bubble Leak Testing HB see Leak Testing: Question & Answer Books H
***Bubble Most Firm.** M. Scott Pop. 2p. 1995. 5.95 (*0-89815-661-0*) Ten Speed Pr.
Bubble Noise & Cavitation Erosion in Fluid Systems 1993. Ed. by R. E. Arndt et al. LC 93-73593. 129p. Date not set. pap. 40.00 (*0-7918-1040-2*) ASME.
Bubble-ology. Jacqueline Barber. Ed. by Lincoln Bergman & Kay Fairwell. (Great Explorations in Math & Science (GEMS) Ser.). (Illus.). 53p. (J). (gr. 5-9). 1987. reprint ed. pap. 8.50 (*0-912511-11-7*) Lawrence Science.
Bubble Reputation. Cathie Pelletier. LC 92-25447. 1993. 21.00 (*0-517-59311-4*, Crown) Crown Pub Group.
Bubble Reputation. Cathie Pelletier. Ed. by Donna Ng. 304p. 1994. reprint ed. pap. 12.00 (*0-671-89010-7*, WSP) PB.
Bubble, the Birds, & the Noise. Cal Roy. (Illus.). (J). (gr. k-4). 1968. 8.95 (*0-8392-3069-9*) Astor-Honor.
Bubble Trouble. Mary Packard. LC 94-16975. (My First Hello Reader! Ser.). (Illus.). (J). 1995. 3.95 (*0-590-48513-X*) Scholastic Inc.
Bubble Trouble: And Other Poems & Stories. Margaret Mahy. LC 92-3540. (Illus.). 80p. (J). (gr. 3-7). 1992. text ed. 13.95 (*0-689-50557-4*, McElderry) S&S Childrens.
***Bubble Trouble Ghost.** Janet Craig. LC 94-12894. (Illus.). 32p. (J). (gr. k-2). 1994. lib. bdg. 11.59 (*0-8167-3586-7*); pap. text ed. 2.95 (*0-8167-3587-5*) Troll Assocs.
Bubble Wake Dynamics in Liquids & Liquid-Solid Suspensions. Liang-Shih Fan & Katsumi Tsuchiya. (Chemical Engineering Ser.). 384p. 1990. text ed. 110.00 (*0-409-90286-1*) Buttrwrth-Heinemann.
***Bubblemania.** Sheila Dalton. (Illus.). 32p. (Orig.). (J). (gr. 1-4). 1992. pap. 5.95 (*0-920501-75-3*) Orca Bk Pubs.
Bubblemania. Penny R. Durant. LC 93-38274. 96p. (J). (gr. 3 up). 1994. pap. 3.99 (*0-380-77373-2*, Camelot) Avon.
Bubbles: (Don't Place All Your Faith in This Here Earthly Basket) Victor Thasiah. (Illus.). (Orig.). 1988. pap. 3.99 (*0-9616644-0-1*) Vicris Pubn.
Bubbles: A Self-Portrait. Beverly Sills. LC 76-11606. 1976. 13.95 (*0-685-73303-3*, Bobbs) Macmillan.
Bubbles: A Thematic Unit. Kimberly Robinson. (Thematic Units Ser.). (Illus.). 80p. (gr. 1-3). 1991. student ed 8.95 (*1-55734-275-X*) Tchr Create Mat.
Bubbles: Poetry for Fun & Meaning. Ed. by Theodore E. Wade, Jr. LC 86-83029. (Illus.). 159p. 1987. 9.95 (*0-930192-17-6*) Gazelle Pubns.
Bubbles, Bubbles, Everywhere. Melvin Berger & Dwight Kuhn. Ed. by Lisa Trumbauer. (Early Science Big Bks.). (Illus.). 16p. (J). (ps-2). 1994. pap. text ed. 14.95 (*1-56784-017-5*) Newbridge Comms.
***Bubbles, Bubbles, Everywhere: Mini Books.** Melvin Berger & Dwight Kuhn. Ed. by Lisa Trumbauer. (Early Science Big Bks.). 16p. (J). (ps-2). Date not set. pap. text ed. 2.95 (*1-56784-041-8*) Newbridge Comms.
Bubbles, Drops & Particles in Non-Newtonian Fluids. Chhabra. 1992. 196.00 (*0-8493-6718-2*, QC189) CRC Pr.
***Bubbles in Polymeric Liquids.** Semyon P. Levitskiy & Zinoviy P. Shulman. LC 94-61880. 307p. 1995. pap. text ed. 85.00 (*1-56676-247-2*) Technomic.
Bubbles, Rainbows & Worms: Science Experiments for Pre-School Children. Sam E. Brown. LC 80-84598. (Illus.). 105p. (J). (ps-1). 1981. pap. 8.95 (*0-87659-100-4*) Gryphon Hse.
***Bubbles Tail.** Josephine Warrior. 1994. 7.95 (*0-533-10463-7*) Vantage.
Bubbles, Voids & Bumps in Time: The New Cosmology. Ed. by James Cornell. (Illus.). 203p. (C). 1992. pap. 16.95 (*0-521-42673-1*) Cambridge U Pr.
Bubblin' Over: Simple Ideas for Spectacular Parties. Ann Cain & Melisa Buchanan. (Illus.). 160p. (Orig.). 1991. pap. write for info. (*1-879129-01-9*) Oak Plantation.
Bubbling Brown Sugar. Loften Mitchell & Rosetta Le Noire. 33p. (Orig.). 1985. pap. 4.95 (*0-685-22962-9*) Broadway Play.
***Bubbling Cauldron: Race, Ethnicity & the Urban Crisis.** Ed. by Michael P. Smith & Joe R. Feagin. 360p. 1995. text ed. 49.95 (*0-8166-2331-7*) U of Minn Pr.
***Bubbling Cauldron: Race, Ethnicity & the Urban Crisis.** Ed. by Michael P. Smith & Joe R. Feagin. 360p. 1995. pap. 17.95 (*0-8166-2332-5*) U of Minn Pr.
Bubbling under the Hot One Hundred: 1959-1985. Joel Whitburn. (Illus.). 377p. 1992. text ed. 34.95 (*0-89820-082-2*) Record Research.
Bubblin's An' B'ilin's at the Center. Merle D. Graves. LC 75-122688. (Short Story Index Reprint Ser.). (Illus.). 1977. 18.95 (*0-8369-3552-7*) Ayer.
Bubby, Me & Memories. Barbara Pomerantz. LC 83-191743. (Illus.). 32p. (J). (ps up). 1983. 7.95 (*0-8074-0253-2*, 104025) UAHC.
Buber on God & the Perfect Man. Pamela Vermes. LC 94-1377. 1994. write for info. (*1-874774-22-6*, Pub. by Littman Lib Jew UK); pap. write for info. (*1-874774-23-4*, Pub. by Littman Lib Jew UK) Bnai Brith Bk.
Buber's Way to "I & Thou" Rivka Horwitz. 288p. 1988. text ed. 29.95 (*0-8276-0305-3*) JPS Phila.
Bubi. Henry H. Parr. 190p. 1995. pap. 7.95 (*1-56901-249-0*) NW Pub.
Bubishi: Martial Art Spirit. George Alexander & Ken Penland. (Illus.). 205p. (Orig.). 1993. pap. 34.95 (*0-9631775-1-6*) Yamazato Pubns.
Bubonic Plague in Early Modern Russia: Public Health & Urban Disaster. John T. Alexander. LC 79-3652. (Johns Hopkins University Studies in Historical & Political Science: Ser. 98, No. 1). (Illus.). 405p. reprint ed. pap. 115.50 (*0-7837-4783-7*, 2044539) Bks Demand.
***Bubsy One & Two Player's Guide.** Bradygames Staff. 1994. pap. 9.99 (*1-56686-220-5*) Brady Compu Bks.
***Buccaneer.** Donna Fletcher. 384p. (Orig.). Date not set. pap. text ed. 6.99 (*0-515-11652-1*) Jove Pubns.
Buccaneer. M. S. Hunter. LC 88-83329. 320p. (Orig.). 1989. pap. 9.95 (*1-55583-153-2*) Alyson Pubns.
Buccaneer. rev. ed. Anna M. Hall. LC 74-162904. (Bentley's Standard Novels Ser.: No. 79). reprint ed. 17.00 (*0-404-54479-7*) AMS Pr.
Buccaneer: HS Buccaneer S Mk 2. (Aeroguide Ser.: No. 5). write for info. (*0-918805-04-X*) Pac Aero Pr.
Buccaneer & Other Poems. Richard H. Dana, Sr. (Notable American Authors Ser.). 1992. reprint ed. lib. bdg. 75.00 (*0-7812-2610-4*) Rprt Serv.
Buccaneer Basketball: Eighty Years of Basketball History at East Tennessee State University. D. Chip Kessler. (Illus.). 198p. (Orig.). 1990. pap. 9.95 (*0-932807-57-7*) Overmountain Pr.
Buccaneer Bks. E. Porter. 1980. lib. bdg. 16.95 (*0-89968-252-9*, Lghtyr Pr) Buccaneer Bks.
Buccaneer Surgeon. Frank Slaughter. 1976. reprint ed. lib. bdg. 22.95 (*0-89190-533-2*, Rivercity Pr) Amereon Ltd.
Buccaneers. large type ed. Edith Wharton. Ed. by Marion Mainwaring. LC 94-1128. 1994. 25.95 (*1-56895-062-4*) Wheeler Pub.
Buccaneers. Edith Wharton. LC 93-13901. 384p. 1994. reprint ed. pap. 10.95 (*0-14-023202-8*, Penguin Bks) Viking Penguin.
***Buccaneers: Tie-in Edition.** Edith Wharton. (Illus.). 448p. 1995. 15.95 (*0-670-86645-8*, Viking) Viking Penguin.
Buccaneers & Marooners of America. Ed. by Howard Pyle. (Illus.). 420p. 1990. reprint ed. pap. 15.00 (*0-87380-173-3*) Rio Grande.
Buccaneer's Atlas: Basil Ringrose's South Sea Wagoner. Ed. by Derek Howse & Norman J. Thrower. (C). 1991. 75.00 (*0-520-05410-5*) U CA Pr.
Buccaneers Bride. Jean Innes. 1989. pap. 3.75 (*0-8217-2742-7*) Zebra.
Buccaneers, Bunnies & Battles. Dolly Khazar. 1991. 6.95 (*0-533-09166-7*) Vantage.
Buccaneers of America. John Esquemeling. 278p. 1988. 19.95 (*0-88029-149-4*) Dorset Pr.
Buccaneers of America. Alexander O. Exquelmelin. Ed. by Jack Sweetman. LC 92-31556. (Classics of Naval Literature Ser.). (Illus.). 365p. 1993. 32.95 (*1-55750-077-0*) Naval Inst Pr.
Buccaneers of America. John Esquemeling. 480p. 1976. reprint ed. 25.00 (*0-87928-071-9*) Corner Hse.
Buccaneers of America: A True Account of the Most Remarkable Assaults Committed of Late Years Upon the Coast of the West Indies by the Buccaneers of Jamaica & Tortuga. John Esquemeling. (Illus.). 488p. 1992. reprint ed. pap. 15.00 (*0-87380-176-8*) Rio Grande.
Bucchero Pottery from Southern Etruria. Tom Rasmussen. LC 78-13464. (Cambridge Classical Studies). (Illus.). 1979. 59.95 (*0-521-22316-4*) Cambridge U Pr.
Bucco. Gene E. Moore. (Illus.). 64p. 1992. pap. 6.95 (*0-9633267-0-8*) Greenhawk Bks.
Buch der ECK Parabeln, Band 1. Harold Klemp. 297p. 1989. pap. 11.00 (*1-57043-076-4*) ECKANKAR.
Buch der ECK Parabeln, Band 1. Harold Klemp. 297p. (GER.). 1988. 11.00 (*0-88155-072-8*) Illum Way Pub.
Buch der Schrift, Enthaltend die Schriftzeichen und Alphabete Aller Zeiten und Aller Volker des Erdkreises. Carl Faulmann. xii, 286p. 1986. reprint ed. write for info. (*3-487-07827-9*, Pub. by Georg Olms GW) Lubrecht & Cramer.
Buch und Bibliothekswissenschaft im Informationszeitalter: Eine Festschrift fur Paul Kaegbein. 485p. (GER.). 1990. lib. bdg. 86.00 (*3-598-10915-6*) K G Saur.
Buchanan Book: The Life of Alexander Buchanan. A. W. Buchanan. (Illus.). 501p. 1989. reprint ed. lib. bdg. 88.00 (*0-8328-0336-7*); reprint ed. pap. 78.00 (*0-8328-0337-5*) Higginson Bk Co.
Buchanan Calls the Shots. Jonas Ward. (Buchanan Ser.). 144p. 1981. pap. 1.95 (*0-449-14210-8*, GM) Fawcett.
Buchanan Calls the Shots. large type ed. Jonas Ward. 1990. pap. 12.95 (*0-7089-6943-7*, Linford) Ulverscroft.
Buchanan on the Prod. Jonas Ward. (Buchanan Ser.). 144p. 1981. pap. 1.95 (*0-449-14107-1*, GM) Fawcett.
Buchanan on the Prod. large type ed. Jonas Ward. (Linford Western Library). 304p. 1985. pap. 11.95 (*0-7089-6144-4*, Linford) Ulverscroft.
Buchanan Says No. large type ed. Jonas Ward. (Linford Western Library). 256p. 1985. pap. 11.95 (*0-7089-6140-1*, Linford) Ulverscroft.
Buchanan Says No. large type ed. Jonas Ward. Bd. with Buchanan's Range War. 1984. 12.00 (*0-685-29746-2*) Ulverscroft.
Buchanan Says No see Buchanan's Range War
Buchanan Takes Over. Jonas Ward. 1981. pap. 1.95 (*0-449-14063-6*, GM) Fawcett.
Buchanan Takes Over. large type ed. Jonas Ward. 1989. pap. 11.95 (*0-7089-6772-8*, Linford) Ulverscroft.
Buchanan's Big Fight. Jonas Ward. 1981. pap. 1.95 (*0-449-14406-2*) Fawcett.
Buchanan's Big Fight. large type ed. Jonas Ward. 1990. pap. 12.95 (*0-7089-6868-6*, Linford) Ulverscroft.
Buchanan's Big Showdown. Jonas Ward. (Buchanan Ser.). 176p. 1981. pap. 1.95 (*0-449-14109-8*, GM) Fawcett.
Buchanan's Black Sheep. Jonas Ward. (Buchanan Ser.). 176p. 1984. pap. 2.50 (*0-449-12412-6*, GM) Fawcett.
Buchanan's Black Sheep. large type ed. Jonas Ward. 1990. pap. 12.95 (*0-7089-6938-0*, Linford) Ulverscroft.
Buchanan's Gamble. large type ed. Jonas Ward. (Linford Western Library). 305p. 1989. pap. 11.95 (*0-7089-6683-7*, Linford) Ulverscroft.
Buchanan's Gun. Jonas Ward. (Buchanan Ser.). 160p. 1982. pap. 1.95 (*0-449-14211-6*, GM) Fawcett.
Buchanan's Manhunt. Jonas Ward. 1981. pap. 1.75 (*0-449-14119-5*, GM) Fawcett.
Buchanan's Manhunt. large type ed. Jonas Ward. (Linford Western Library). 1989. pap. 11.95 (*0-7089-6760-4*, Linford) Ulverscroft.
Buchanans of Ohio. Jim Buchanan. v, 170p. (Orig.). 1987. pap. 11.50 (*1-55613-036-8*) Heritage Bk.
Buchanan's Range War. large type ed. Jonas Ward. (Linford Western Library). 320p. 1987. pap. 11.95 (*0-7089-6351-X*, Linford) Ulverscroft.
Buchanan's Range War. large type ed. Jonas Ward. Bd. with Buchanan Says No. 1984. Set pap. 12.00 (*0-685-29747-0*) Ulverscroft.
Buchanan's Range War see Buchanan Says No
Buchanans' Revenge. large type ed. Jonas Ward. 496p. 1985. 15.95 (*0-7089-1291-5*) Ulverscroft.
Buchanan's Siege. Jonas Ward. 160p. 1982. pap. 2.25 (*0-449-14086-5*, GM) Fawcett.
Buchanan's Siege. large type ed. Jonas Ward. (Linford Western Library). 1990. pap. 12.95 (*0-7089-6804-X*, Linford) Ulverscroft.
Buchanan's Stage Line. large type ed. Jonas Ward. (Linford Western Library). 288p. 1987. pap. 11.95 (*0-7089-6427-3*, Linford) Ulverscroft.
Buchanan's Texas Treasure. Jonas Ward. (Buchanan Ser.). 160p. 1982. pap. 2.25 (*0-449-14175-6*, GM) Fawcett.
Buchanan's Texas Treasure. large type ed. Jonas Ward. 1991. pap. 13.95 (*0-7089-6960-7*) Ulverscroft.
Bucheinband: Ein Handbuch fur Buchbinder und Bucherfreunde. Gustav A. Bogeng et al. (Buchkunliche Arbeiten Ser.: Vol. V). viii, 198p. 1991. reprint ed. write for info. (*3-487-02552-3*, Pub. by Georg Olms GW) Lubrecht & Cramer.
***Buchenwald Report.** Tr. by David A. Hackett. 1995. text ed. 35.00 (*0-8133-1777-0*) Westview.
Bucher im Staube: Die Theologie Johann Arndts in ihrem Verhaltnis zur Mystik. Christian Braw. (Studies in Medieval & Reformation Thought: Vol. 39). (Illus.). ii, 236p. 1986. 48.00 (*90-04-07815-0*) E J Brill.
Bucher-Meyer Controversy: An Original Anthology. Ed. by Moses I. Finley. LC 79-4954. (Ancient Economic History Ser.). (GER.). 1979. lib. bdg. 35.95 (*0-405-12346-9*) Ayer.
Bucher und Schrifften, 6 vols., Set. Paracelsus Theophrastus. Ed. by K. Goldammer. xx, 4805p. 1977. reprint ed. write for info. (*3-487-03327-5*, Pub. by Georg Olms GW) Lubrecht & Cramer.
Bucherkunde Zur Geschichte und Literatur des Konigreichs Polen. Walther-Albert M. Recke. xi, 242p. reprint ed. write for info. (*0-318-71861-8*, Pub. by Georg Olms GW) Lubrecht & Cramer.
Bucherornamentik Der Renaissance see Handbook of Renaissance Ornament: 1290 Designs from Decorated Books
Bucherschatz der Deutschen Nationaliteratur des XVI und XVII Jahrunderts. Karl W. Heyse. viii, 186p. 1967. reprint ed. write for info. (*0-318-71800-6*, Pub. by Georg Olms GW) Lubrecht & Cramer.
Buchner: The Complete Plays. Georg Buchner. Ed. by Michael Patterson. Tr. by Howard Brenton et al. (Methuen World Dramatists Ser.). 1987. pap. 9.95 (*0-413-14090-3*, A0041, Pub. by Methuen UK) Heinemann.
Buchner: Woyzek. J. Guthrie. (Bristol German Texts Ser.). (GER.). 14.95 (*1-85399-347-6*, Pub. by Brstl Class Pr UK) Focus Info Gr.
Buchrolle in der Kunst. Theodor Birt. ix, 352p. 1976. reprint ed. write for info. (*3-487-05950-9*, Pub. by Georg Olms GW) Lubrecht & Cramer.
Buchsbaum Rings & Applications. J. Stuckrad & W. Vogel. 300p. 1987. 79.00 (*0-387-16844-3*) Spr-Verlag.
Buchsbaum's Complete Handbook of Practical Electronics Reference Data. 3rd ed. Walter H. Buchsbaum. Ed. by Robert C. Genn, Jr. 672p. 1987. 16.95 (*0-13-084641-4*, Busn); text ed. 39.95 (*0-13-084633-3*, Busn) P-H.
Buck. Alan Benjamin. LC 93-31161. (Illus.). (J). 1994. 15.00 (*0-671-88718-1*, S&S Bks Young Read) S&S Childrens.
Buck. Tamela Larimer. LC 86-90774. 176p. (Orig.). (J). (gr. 7 up). 1986. pap. 2.50 (*0-380-75172-0*, Flare) Avon.
Buck: A Life Sketch of James H. Harless. Robert B. Conner & Ruel Foster. (Illus.). 166p. 1992. 25.00 (*0-937058-30-0*) West Va U Pr.
Buck: Johannes Buck, 1747-1790; Christian & Catherine Buck & Their Descendants, 1754-1958. Fisher et al. (Illus.). xii, 138p. 1993. reprint ed. lib. bdg. 35.00 (*0-8328-3276-6*); reprint ed. pap. 25.00 (*0-8328-3277-4*) Higginson Bk Co.
Buck; a Tennessee Boy in Korea. Keller Cox & Raymond L. Frazier. 1982. 9.95 (*0-9610818-0-5*); pap. 4.95 (*0-9610818-1-3*) Chogie Pubs.
Buck Barry, Texas Ranger & Frontiersman. Ed. by James K. Greer. LC 84-11863. (Illus.). xviii, 262p. 1984. pap. 6.95 (*0-8032-7013-5*) U of Nebr Pr.
Buck Book: All Sorts of Things to Do with a Dollar Bill Besides Spend It. Anne A. Johnson. 88p. 1993. ring bd. 11.95 (*1-878257-51-X*) Klutz Pr.
Buck Brothers Chisels, Trade Catalogue 1890. pap. 7.00 (*1-879335-07-7*) Astragal Pr.
Buck-Buck the Chicken. Amy Ehrlich. LC 86-31639. (Step into Reading Bks.). (Illus.). 48p. (J). (gr. 1-3). 1987. pap. 3.50 (*0-394-88804-9*) Random Bks Yng Read.
Buck Family-Virginia. William P. Buck. Ed. by Janie B. Buck. (Orig.). 1985. pap. 10.00 (*0-934530-04-1*) Buck Pub.
Buck Fever. Bruce Cochran. 96p. 1994. pap. 7.95 (*1-57223-001-0*) Outlook Pubng.
Buck Fever: Deer Camp Cartoons. Bruce Cochran. Orig. Title: Buck Fever. 1991. pap. 7.95 (*1-55971-135-3*) NorthWord.
Buck Fever: The Deer Hunting Tradition in Pennsylvania. Mike Sajna. LC 90-30615. 256p. 1990. 29.95 (*0-8229-3645-3*); pap. 15.95 (*0-8229-5436-2*) U of Pittsburgh Pr.
Buck Fever see Buck Fever: Deer Camp Cartoons
Buck Fever see Deer Camp Cartoons
Buck Fever Papers. Sherwood Anderson. Ed. by Welford D. Taylor. LC 73-151252. (Illus.). 286p. reprint ed. pap. 81.60 (*0-8357-7453-8*, 2033116) Bks Demand.
Buck Godot: Psmith, No. 2. Phil Foglio. (Buck Godot Ser.). (Illus.). 72p. 1987. pap. 7.95 (*0-685-18868-X*, Starblaze) Donning Co.
Buck Godot, Zap Gun for Hire!, No. 1. Phil Foglio. LC 86-4498. (Buck Godot Ser.). (Illus.). 72p. (Orig.). 1986. pap. 7.95 (*0-89865-365-7*, Starblaze) Donning Co.
Buck Godot, Zap Gun for Hire!, No. 2. Phil Smith & Phil Fogilio. Ed. by Kay Reynolds. (Buck Godot Ser.). (Illus.). 64p. (Orig.). 1987. pap. 7.95 (*0-89865-459-9*, Starblaze) Donning Co.
Buck Leonard: In His Own Words. Buck Leonard. 1976. 29.95 (*0-8488-1544-0*) Amereon Ltd.
Buck Leonard: the Black Lou Gehrig: The Hall of Famers's Story in His Own Words. Buck Leonard & James Riley. 304p. 1995. 20.00 (*0-7867-0119-6*) Carroll & Graf.
Buck Peters, Ranchman. Clarence E. Mulford. 320p. 1993. mass mkt. 4.99 (*0-8125-2499-3*) Tor Bks.
Buck Peters, Ranchman. Clarence E. Mulford. 1973. reprint ed. lib. bdg. 24.95 (*0-88411-202-0*, Aeonian Pr) Amereon Ltd.
Buck Peterson's Complete Guide to Fishing. Buck Peterson. (Illus.). 144p. (Orig.). 1991. pap. 8.95 (*0-89815-405-7*) Ten Speed Pr.
Buck Peterson's Guide to Deer Hunting. B. R. Peterson. (Illus.). 132p. (Orig.). 1989. pap. 7.95 (*0-89815-291-7*) Ten Speed Pr.
Buck Peterson's Guide to Indoor Life. Brian Peterson. (Illus.). 96p. (Orig.). 1992. pap. 6.95 (*0-89815-468-5*) Ten Speed Pr.
***Buck Rogers: A Life in the Future.** Martin Caidin. (Buck Rogers Ser.). (Illus.). 320p. (Orig.). 1995. 19.95 (*0-7869-0144-6*) TSR Inc.
Buck Rogers: Introduction to the 25th Century. Jeff Grubb. (Illus.). 1993. 20.00 (*1-56076-636-0*) TSR Inc.
Buck Rogers: The First 60 Years in the 25th Century. Ed. by Lorraine D. Williams. LC 88-50400. (Buck Rogers Hardcover Collector's Volume Ser.). (Illus.). 368p. (J). 1988. 24.95 (*0-88038-604-5*) TSR Inc.
Buck Schiwetz' Memories. E. M. Schiwetz. LC 78-6370. (Joe & Betty Moore Texas Art Ser.: No. 3). (Illus.). 118p. 1978. 29.95x (*0-89096-053-4*) Tex A&M Univ Pr.
Buck Starts Here: Enterprise & the Arts. Ed. by Robert K. Manoff. 165p. 1984. 11.95 (*0-917103-00-9*) Vol Lawyers Arts.
***Buck Starts Here: How the Federal Reserve Can Make or Break Your Financial Future.** David M. Jones. 1995. pap. 24.95 (*0-13-180498-7*) P-H.
Buck Stops Here: The Executive's Guide to Bottom-Line Decisions & Actions. Carl Heyel. LC 93-12895. 1994. pap. 14.95 (*0-442-01721-9*) Van Nos Reinhold.
Buck Van Huss: The Legend. Willie J. Malone. 160p. 1989. 15.00 (*0-317-93444-9*); pap. 6.95 (*0-317-93445-7*) Willane Pub.
***Buck Wilders Small Fry Fishing Guide.** Tim Smith & Mark Herrick. LC 94-79423. (Illus.). 64p. Date not set. pap. 12.95 (*0-9643793-0-9*) A & S Pubng.
Buckaroo: Visions & Voices of the American Cowboy. Hal Cannon. 1993. 45.00 (*0-671-88054-3*) S&S Trade.
Buckaroo Banzai. Earl MacRauch. pap. 4.95 (*0-671-50574-2*) S&S Trade.
Buckaroos & Boxcars. Byron Grosfield. 136p. 1981. pap. 6.50 (*0-9613875-0-5*) Wild Horse Pubns.
Buckaroo's Code. Wayne D. Overholser. (Orig.). 1994. 14.95 (*0-7451-4594-9*, Gunsmoke) Chivers N Amer.
Buckaroo's Code. Wayne D. Overholser. 192p. (Orig.). 1992. reprint ed. pap. 3.50 (*0-8439-3290-2*) Dorchester Pub Co.
Buckaroos in Paradise: Cowboy Life in Northern Nevada. Howard W. Marshall & Richard E. Ahlborn. LC 81-10500. (Illus.). 112p. reprint ed. pap. 32.00 (*0-7837-6186-4*, 2045908) Bks Demand.
Buckdancer's Choice: Poems. James Dickey. LC 65-21079. (Wesleyan Poetry Program Ser.: Vol. 28). 79p. (C). 1965. pap. 10.95 (*0-8195-1028-9*, Wesleyan Univ Pr) U Pr of New Eng.
***Bucket.** Eric Forrer. (Illus.). 32p. (J). (gr. 3-8). 1993. 15.00 (*0-9632596-0-1*) McRoy & Blackburn.
Bucket Diagrams: A Problem-Solving Approach to Renal Physiology. Herbert F. Janssen. (Illus.). 144p. (C). 1993. pap. text ed. 17.50 (*0-89672-323-2*) Tex Tech Univ Pr.
Bucket Nut. Liza Cody. 224p. 1995. mass mkt. 5.50 (*0-446-40459-4*, Mysterious Paperbk) Warner Bks.
Bucket of Bones. John A. Walker. (Orig.). Date not set. pap. 7.95 (*0-9639798-1-7*) J A Walker Pub.
***Bucket of Eels & the Modern Husband.** Paul Godfrey. 128p. 1995. pap. 13.95 (*0-413-68830-5*, A0723) Heinemann.
Bucket of Nails. Elliott Richman. 20p. (Orig.). 1990. pap. 3.00 (*0-318-50052-3*) Samisdat.
Bucket of Tongues. Duncan McLean. 256p. 1994. pap. 15.95 (*0-436-27631-3*, Pub. by W Heinemann Ltd) Trafalgar.
Bucket Wheel Excavator. Walter Durst & Werner Vogt. 450p. 1988. text ed. 118.00 (*0-87849-075-2*, Pub. by Trans Tech GW) LPS Dist Ctr.

B

An Asterisk (*) at the beginning of an entry indicates that the title is appearing in BIP for the first time. 929

***Bucketful of Dreams: Contemporary Parables for All Ages.** Christopher Buice. 1995. pap. 10.00 (1-55896-288-3) Unitarian Univ.

Buckethead Bunch: Bossy, Loser, Show-off & Angry. Mike Epperley. LC 92-85592. (Illus.). 40p. (Orig.). (J). (gr. k-6). 1992. pap. 5.98 (1-882183-24-X) Computer Pr.

Buckethead Families: Givers & Takers. rev. ed. Mike Epperley. LC 92-85597. (Buckethead Ser.). (Illus.). 32p. (J). (gr. k-6). 1992. pap. 5.98 (1-882183-23-1) Computer Pr.

Buckets. Mark A. Krueger. 62p. 1991. pap. 10.95 (0-87868-410-7) Child Welfare.

Buckets & Brawn: The History of Sarasota & Its Fire Department. Wayne A. Welsh & Patrick B. Whelan. 120p. 1993. 24.95 (0-9638831-0-0); pap. 9.95 (0-9638831-1-9) W A Welsh.

Buckett: VAT Enforcement & Appeals Manual. 2nd ed. Alan Buckett. 1990. pap. 64.00 (0-406-51590-5) Butterworth Legal Pubs.

***Buckeye Blake: Art on the Western Front.** Sarah E. Boehme. (Illus.). 60p. 1995. pap. 15.00 (0-295-97327-7) U of Wash Pr.

Buckeye Cookery & Practical Housekeeping. Ed. by Estelle W. Wilcox. 536p. 1988. reprint ed. pap. 12.95 (0-87351-228-6, Borealis Book) Minn Hist.

Buckeye Country. Harlan Hatcher. 1993. reprint ed. lib. bdg. 89.00 (0-7812-5371-3) Rprt Serv.

Buckeye Football Fitness: Fourth Down & One Rep to Go. Steve Bliss. LC 83-81242. (Illus.). 368p. (Orig.). (C). 1986. pap. 15.95 (0-88011-214-X, PBLI0214) Human Kinetics.

Buckeye Heritage: Ohio's History in Song. Elizabeth A. Salt. 144p. 1992. pap. 13.95 (0-89804-813-3, Enthea Pr) Ariel GA.

Buckeye Legends: Folktales & Lore from Ohio. Michael J. Katz. LC 94-2379. 176p. 1994. text ed. 37.50 (0-472-09558-7); pap. text ed. 15.95 (0-472-06558-0) U of Mich Pr.

Buckeye Rovers in the Gold Rush: An Edition of Two Diaries. rev. ed. Ed. by H. Lee Scamehorn et al. LC 89-31054. 235p. 1989. 24.95 (0-8214-0922-0); pap. 13.95 (0-8214-0923-9) Ohio U Pr.

Buckeye Schoolmaster: A Chronicle of Midwestern Rural Life. Ed. by J. Merton England. LC 93-40591. (Illus.). 410p. 1994. text ed. 109.95 (0-7734-9415-4) E Mellen.

Buckeyes: A Collection of Verse. Margaret G. Wiliamson. Ed. by Margaret E. Burton. LC 90-12367. 52p. (Orig.). 1990. pap. 5.00 (0-938310-10-0) Volunteer Pubns.

Buckeyes: Ohio State Football. Wilbur Snypp & Bob Hunter. (College Sports Book Ser.). (Illus.). 352p. (YA). (gr. 6-12). 1988. 16.95 (0-87397-307-0) Strode.

Buckfang's LOGO Challenge: Shapes & Angles. T. M. Kemnitz. 1984. Apple & Texas Instrument. pap. 4.95 (0-89824-077-8) Trillium Pr.

Buckfang's LOGO Challenge: Words, Lists & Numbers. T. M. Kemnitz. 1985. IBM. pap. 4.95 (0-89824-099-9); Commodore. pap. 4.95 (0-89824-098-0) Trillium Pr.

Buckfang's Primary LOGO Activity Cards: Apple & IBM LOGO. Thomas M. Kemnitz & Barbara Romanowich. 32p. (J). (gr. k-3). 1985. 12.99 (0-89824-117-0) Trillium Pr.

Buckfang's Primary LOGO Activity Cards: Commodore & Apple Terrapin. Thomas M. Kemnitz & Barbara Romanowich. 32p. (J). (gr. k-3). 1985. 12.99 (0-89824-118-9) Trillium Pr.

Buckhorn Fires. Adair Anderson. LC 90-70671. 128p. (Orig.). 1990. pap. 7.00 (1-56002-012-1) Aegina Pr.

Buckingham Babylon: The Rise & Fall of the House of Windsor. Peter Fearon. (Illus.). 384p. 1993. 22.50 (1-55972-204-5, Birch Ln Pr) Carol Pub Group.

Buckingham Blowout. Axel Kilgore. (They Call Me the Mercenary Ser.: No. 17). 1984. pap. 2.25 (0-685-07894-9) Zebra.

***Buckingham County: Virginia Publick Claims.** Janice L. Abercrombie & Richard Slatten. (Virginia Publick Claims Ser.). ix, 37p. 1991. pap. 5.00x (0-8095-8524-3) Borgo Pr.

Buckingham County: Virginia Publick Claims. Janice L. Abercrombie & Richard Slatten. (Virginia Publick Claims Ser.). ix, 37p. (C). 1991. reprint ed. lib. bdg. 20.00 (0-8095-8309-7) Borgo Pr.

***Buckingham County, Virginia Board of Supervisors Minute Book, 1870-1887.** Jeanne Stinson. vi, 100p. 1994. lib. bdg. 33.00 (0-8095-8279-1); pap. 13.00 (0-8095-8520-0) Borgo Pr.

***Buckingham County, Virginia Church & Marriage Records, 1764-1822.** Mary B. Warren. 87p. 1993. lib. bdg. 27.00 (0-8095-8281-3); pap. 10.00 (0-8095-8521-9) Borgo Pr.

***Buckingham County, Virginia Extant Poll Lists (1788-1840, 1841 & 1848)** Jeanne Stinson. vi, 136p. 1994. lib. bdg. 33.00 (0-8095-8280-5); pap. 13.00 (0-8095-8522-7) Borgo Pr.

***Buckingham County, Virginia Land Tax Summaries & Implied Deeds Vol. 1: 1782-1814.** Roger G. Ward. 343p. 1993. lib. bdg. 47.00 (0-8095-8275-9); pap. 20.00 (0-8095-8523-5) Borgo Pr.

***Buckingham County, Virginia Undetermined Chancery Files Index.** Jeanne Stinson. vi, 121p. 1994. lib. bdg. 33.00 (0-8095-8278-3); pap. 13.00 (0-8095-8525-1) Borgo Pr.

***Buckingham County, Virginia 1850 U. S. Census.** Benjamin B. Weisiger, 3rd. 151p. 1984. lib. bdg. 27.00 (0-8095-8184-1); pap. 10.00 (0-8095-8518-9) Borgo Pr.

***Buckingham County, Virginia 1860 U. S. Census.** Randy Kidd. vi, 169p. 1994. lib. bdg. 43.00 (0-8095-8276-7); pap. 18.00 (0-8095-8519-7) Borgo Pr.

Buckingham Family, or the Descendants of Thomas Buckingham of Milford, CT. F. W. Chapman. (Illus.). 384p. 1989. reprint ed. lib. bdg. 65.50 (0-8328-0338-3); reprint ed. pap. 57.50 (0-8328-0339-1) Higginson Bk Co.

***Buckingham Palace: The Palace & Its Royal Circle in Photographs.** Hall. 1995. 7.99 (0-517-12158-1) Random Hse Value.

Buckinghamshire Village Book. Buckinghamshire Federation of Women's Institutes. 192p. 1987. 30.00 (0-905392-80-9) St Mut.

Buckland Abbey. National Trust Staff. (Illus.). 64p. 1991. pap. 9.95 (0-7078-0114-1, Pub. by Natl Trust UK) Trafalgar.

Buckland Bible Dictionary see Diccionario Biblico Universal

***Buckland Gypsies' Domino Divination Deck.** Buckland. 1995. pap. text ed. 12.95 (1-56718-094-9) Llewellyn Pubns.

Buckland's Complete Book of Witchcraft. Raymond Buckland. LC 85-45280. (Practical Magick Ser.). (Illus.). 272p. (Orig.). (C). 1986. student ed, pap. 14.95 (0-87542-050-8) Llewellyn Pubns.

Buckle down! on American Citizenship: Student Text. 2nd ed. Profiles Corporation Staff. (Illus.). 73p. (YA). (gr. 7-12). 1992. pap. text ed. 30.00 (0-7836-1302-4, ST BD01) Profiles Corp.

Buckle down! on American Citizenship: Teacher's Guide. 2nd ed. Profiles Corporation Staff. (Illus.). 73p. (YA). (gr. 7-12). 1992. Grades 7-12. 14.00 (0-7836-1303-2, ST BD02) Profiles Corp.

Buckle down on Ohio Mathematics: Student Workbook. Profiles Corporation Staff. (Illus.). 120p. (Orig.). (YA). (gr. 7-12). 1992. 30.00 (0-7836-1246-X, ST BD51) Profiles Corp.

Buckle down on Ohio Mathematics: Teacher's Guide. Profiles Corporation Staff. (Illus.). 120p. (Orig.). (YA). (gr. 7-12). 1992. 40.00 (0-7836-1248-6, ST BD52) Profiles Corp.

Buckle down! on Ohio Reading: Workbook & Diagnostic Tests. Profiles Corporation. (Illus.). 168p. 1994. 35.00 (0-7836-1316-4, BD15) Profiles Corp.

Buckle down! on Ohio Writing: Student Workbook. Profile Corporation Staff. 88p. 1994. 30.00 (0-7836-1313-X, BD21) Profiles Corp.

Buckledown, the Workhound. Danny Shanahan. LC 92-13433. (J). 1993. 14.95 (0-316-78276-9) Little.

Buckler's Hard. A. J. Holland. 236p. 1985. 65.00 (0-85937-328-2, Pub. by K Mason Pubns Ltd UK) St Mut.

Bucklett's Pursuit. James Workman. (Orig.). 1995. pap. 6.99 (1-881542-19-X) Blue Star Prodns.

Buckley on the Companies Acts. 15th ed. Ed. by Leonard Hoffman et al. 1993. student ed, ring bd. write for info. (0-318-67320-7) Butterworth Legal Pubs.

***Buckley, Stephen Many Angles.** Marco Livingstone. 84p. 1985. pap. 28.00 (0-905836-49-9, Pub. by Museum Modern Art UK) St Mut.

Buckling & Post-Buckling, Vol. 288. J. Arbocz et al. (Lecture Notes in Physics Ser.). vii, 246p. 1987. 34.00 (0-387-18312-4) Spr-Verlag.

***Buckling & Postbuckling of Composite Structures: 1994 International Mechanical Engineering Congress & Exposition, Chicago, Illinois - November 6-11, 1994.** Ed. by A. K. Noor. (AD - PVP Ser.: Vol. 41, Vol. 293). 140p. 1994. 60.00 (0-7918-1443-2, G00938) ASME.

Buckling of Offshore Structures. A. C. Walker et al. LC 83-83188. 472p. 1984. 69.00 (0-87201-067-8) Gulf Pub.

Buckling of Shells for Engineers. L. Kollar & E. Dulacsha. LC 83-1697. 303p. 1984. text ed. 135.00 (0-471-90328-0, Wiley-Interscience) Wiley.

Buckling of Structures. International Union of Theoretical & Applied Mechanics Staff. Ed. by B. Budiansky. LC 75-31726. (International Union of Theoretical & Applied Mechanics Symposia Ser.). (Illus.). 420p. 1976. 126.00 (0-387-07274-8) Spr-Verlag.

Buckling of Structures - Theory & Experiment: The Josef Singer Anniversary Volume. Ed. by I. Elishakoff et al. (Studies in Applied Mechanics: No. 19). 450p. 1988. 133.50 (0-444-70474-4) Elsevier.

Buckmaster. large type ed. Tex Larrigan. (Linford Western Library). 272p. 1993. pap. 14.95 (0-7089-7443-0, Linford) Ulverscroft.

Buckmaster & the Cattlelifters. large type ed. Tex Larrigan. (Linford Western Library). 272p. 1992. pap. 14.95 (0-7089-7176-8, Linford) Ulverscroft.

Buckminster Fuller. Martin Pawley. (Design Heroes Ser.). (Illus.). 192p. 1991. 24.95 (0-8008-1116-X) Taplinger.

Buckminster Fuller. Robert R. Potter. Ed. by Richard Gallin. (Pioneers in Change Ser.). (Illus.). 144p. (J). (gr. 5-9). 1990. lib. bdg. 13.95 (0-382-09967-2); pap. 6.95 (0-382-09972-9) Silver Burdett Pr.

Buckminster Fuller's Universe. Lloyd S. Sieden. 1987. 21.95 (0-317-62639-6) Freundlich.

Buckminster Fuller's Universe: An Appreciation. L. S. Seiden. (Illus.). 460p. 1989. 24.95 (0-306-43178-5, Plenum Pr) Plenum.

Buckminsterfullerene & Related Carbon Clusters. Ed. by W. Edward Billups & Marco A. Ciufolini. LC 93-3028. 339p. 1993. 59.00 (1-56081-608-2) VCH Pubs.

Bucknell University. Photos by Robert Krist. (First Edition Ser.). (Illus.). 112p. 1990. 39.00 (0-916509-29-X) Harmony Hse Pub LO.

Buckram Syndrome: A Critical Essay on Paperbacks in Public Libraries of the United States. Marie T. Curley. LC 68-31033. (Public Library Reporter: NO. 13). 79p. reprint ed. pap. 25.00 (0-8357-7454-6, 2024258) Bks Demand.

Buck's Book: A View of the Third Vermont Infantry Regiment. John E. Balzer. 80p. 1992. pap. 9.95 (0-9634722-2-4) Balzer & Assocs.

Bucks Camp Log: A Wisconsin Deer Camp Diary, 1916-1928. Marjorie Williams. 111p. 1974. 8.95 (0-932558-02-X) Wisconsin Sptmn.

Bucks County Blues. Sonia Raiziss. (Illus.). 1977. per. 2.50 (0-912284-90-0) New Rivers Pr.

***Bucks County, Pennsylvania Deed Book 5 (1713-1731)** T. L.C. Genealogy Staff. LC 91-65973. 89p. (Orig.). 1991. spiral bd., pap. 14.00 (1-886633-36-3) TLC Genealogy.

Bucks County Photographs of Early Architecture. Aaron Siskind. (Illus.). 112p. 1974. 12.95 (0-910302-02-2) Bucks Co Hist.

Bucks of Goober Hollow. Gilbert Morris. LC 94-7012. (Ozark Adventures Ser.: Vol. 1). (J). (gr. 3-7). 1994. pap. 4.99 (0-8423-4392-X) Tyndale.

Bucks Point Lace-Making. Pamela Nottingham. 1985. 18.50 (0-7134-2234-3) Robin & Russ.

Bucks Point Lace Patterns. Henk Hardeman. 1985. pap. 22.95 (0-7134-4868-7) Robin & Russ.

Bucks Start Here: How to Turn Your Hidden Assets into Money. Claude Olney. 1992. pap. 10.00 (0-688-11607-8, Quill) Morrow.

Buckskin & Homespun: Frontier Clothing in Texas, 1820-1870. David Holman & Billie Persons. (Illus.). 130p. 1979. 120.00 (0-685-00714-6) Wind River Pr.

Buckskin Brigades. L. Ron Hubbard. 315p. (Orig.). 1987. pap. 3.95 (0-88404-280-4) Bridge Pubns Inc.

Buckskin Brigades. L. Ron Hubbard. LC 86-33823. 256p. (Orig.). 1987. reprint ed. 16.95 (0-915463-46-6, Jameson Bks); reprint ed. pap. 5.95 (0-685-17493-X, Jameson Bks) Green Hill.

Buckskin, Calico & Lace: Oklahoma's Territorial Women. Glenda Carlile. Ed. by Clifton Warren. 116p. (Orig.). 1990. pap. text ed. 10.95 (0-9628214-0-3) Sthrn Hills Pub.

***Buckskin Challenge.** large type ed. Lee Floren. (Western Ser.). 1994. pap. 14.95 (0-7089-7588-7, Linford) Ulverscroft.

Buckskin Giant Special Edition. Kit Dalton. 368p. pap. 3.95 (0-8439-2777-1) Dorchester Pub Co.

Buckskin Joe: A Memoir. Edward J. Hoyt. Ed. by Glenn Shirley. LC 87-27364. (Illus.). xiv, 202p. 1988. reprint ed. pap. 6.95 (0-8032-7239-1) U of Nebr Pr.

Buckskin Mare. Baxter Black. (Illus.). 100p. (Orig.). 1989. 39.95 (0-939343-05-3); pap. 11.95 (0-939343-06-1) R Stockman & Coyote.

Buckskin No. 10: Bolt-Action. Roy LeBeau. 208p. (Orig.). 1986. pap. 2.50 (0-8439-2315-6) Dorchester Pub Co.

Buckskin No. 11: Trigger Guard. Roy LeBeau. 192p. 1986. pap. 2.50 (0-8439-2336-9) Dorchester Pub Co.

Buckskin No. 6: Trigger Spring. Roy LeBeau. 240p. (Orig.). 1985. pap. 2.50 (0-8439-2229-X) Dorchester Pub Co.

Buckskin No. 7: Cartridge Coast. Roy LeBeau. 240p. (Orig.). 1985. pap. 2.50 (0-8439-2252-4) Dorchester Pub Co.

Buckskin No. 8: Hangfire Hill. Roy LeBeau. 208p. (Orig.). 1985. pap. 2.50 (0-8439-2271-0) Dorchester Pub Co.

Buckskin No. 9: Crossfire Country. 208p. (Orig.). pap. 2.50 (0-8439-2294-X) Dorchester Pub Co.

Buckskin Rider. W. F. Bragg. 192p. 1986. reprint ed. pap. 2.50 (0-8439-2338-5) Dorchester Pub Co.

Buckskin Run. Louis L'Amour. 1984. mass mkt. 3.99 (0-553-24764-6) Bantam.

Buckskin Special Edition: The Bucksin Breed. Kit Dalton. (Buckskin Ser.). 368p. (Orig.). 1988. pap. 3.95 (0-8439-2587-6) Dorchester Pub Co.

***Buckskinner.** R. C. House. LC 94-49020. (Novel of the West Ser.). 210p. 1995. 19.95 (0-87131-783-4) M Evans.

Buckskins. Albert R. Booky. LC 90-33902. 312p. (Orig.). 1990. pap. 12.95 (0-86534-125-7) Sunstone Pr.

Buckskins & Blood. John Legg. 1994. mass mkt. 3.50 (0-06-100749-8) HarpC.

***Buckskins, Blades, & Biscuits.** Allen K. Johnston. 1995. pap. 24.95 (0-88839-363-6) Hancock House.

Buckskins, Bullets, & Business: A History of Buffalo Bill's Wild West. Sarah J. Blackstone. LC 85-17760. (Contributions to the Study of Popular Culture Ser.: No. 14). (Illus.). 167p. 1986. text ed. 42.95 (0-313-24596-7, BBU/, Greenwood Pr) Greenwood.

Bucksport Vital Records. Donna Hoffman. LC 82-73244. 125p. 1982. pap. 14.95 (0-941216-03-9) Cay-Bel.

Buckwalter: Geriatric Mental Health Nursing: Current & Future Challenges. 173p. 1991. 20.00 (1-55642-199-0) SLACK Inc.

Bucky Badger Story. Gwen Schultz. LC 80-82753. (Illus.). 96p. (Orig.). 1981. pap. 5.00 (0-915988-51-8) Reading Gems.

Bucky Follows a Cold Trail. large type ed. William M. Raine. LC 91-19656. 376p. 1991. reprint ed. lib. bdg. 15.95 (1-56054-214-4) Thorndike Pr.

Bucky for Beginners. Mary Laycock. (Illus.). 64p. (Orig.). (J). (gr. 4-12). 1984. pap. text ed. 7.95 (0-918932-82-3) Activity Resources.

Bucky Gets Busted. David B. Smith. LC 93-37921. (Bucky Stone Ser.: Vol. 7). (J). 1993. write for info. (0-8280-0807-8) Review & Herald.

Bucky Leaves Home. Carey E. Harbin. (Illus.). 26p. (Orig.). (J). (ps-1). 1991. pap. 2.95 (0-918995-02-7) Voc-Offers.

Bucolica: Concordantiae in Carmina Bucolica. Vol. CXIII. write for info. (0-318-71961-4, Pub. by Georg Olms GW) Lubrecht & Cramer.

Bucolica - Concordantiae in Carmina Bucolica. Ed. by Matthias Korn & Wolfgang Slaby. Bd. CXIII. Date not set. write for info. (0-318-71081-1, Pub. by Georg Olms GW) Lubrecht & Cramer.

Bucolici Graeci. Ed. by Andrew S. Gow. (Oxford Classical Texts Ser.). 1952. 19.95 (0-19-814517-9) OUP.

Bucoliques see Oeuvres

Bucoliques de Virgile. Paul Valery. Bd. with Variations sur les Bucoliques. Set pap. 3.95 (0-685-36607-3) Fr & Eur.

BUCOMCO: A Business Communication Simulation. 2nd ed. John Melrose & Krisan K. Melrose. LC 93-38289. 1993. write for info. (1-56118-530-2) Paradigm MN.

BUC's New Boat Price Guide, 1993. 31th ed. 1990. 19.95 (0-911778-23-3) BUC Intl.

BUC's Used Boat Price Guides, 3 vols., 1. 55th ed. 1989. 65.00 (0-911778-61-6) BUC Intl.

BUC's Used Boat Price Guides, 3 vols., 2. 55th ed. 1989. 55.00 (0-911778-62-4) BUC Intl.

BUC's Used Boat Price Guides, 3 vols., 3. 55th ed. 1989. 45.00 (0-911778-63-2) BUC Intl.

Bud: An Autobiography. David L. Furman. 1991. 16.95 (0-533-09292-2) Vantage.

Bud Collins' Modern Encyclopedia of Tennis. 2nd ed. Bud Collins & Zander Hollander. 500p. 1993. 37.95 (0-8103-8988-6, 101769) Gale.

Bud Collins' Modern Encyclopedia of Tennis. 2nd ed. Bud Collins & Zander Hollander. 600p. 1993. pap. 14.95 (0-8103-9443-X, 089154) Visible Ink Pr.

Bud Norton Story. Michael Goc. (Illus.). 168p. 1982. pap. 12.95 (0-939398-02-8) Fox River.

Bud Powell. Clifford J. Safane. (Jazz Masters Ser.). 40p. pap. 10.95 (0-8256-4082-2) Music Sales.

Bud Stewart, Michigan's Legendary Lure Maker: A Biography of Elman "Bud" Stewart. Frank R. Baron & Raymond L. Carver. Ed. by Milton M. Ferguson. (Illus.). 228p. 1991. 70.00 (0-917231-12-0) Ferguson Comns Pubs.

***Bud Wilkinson: An Intimate Portrait of an American Legend.** Jay Wilkinson. 1994. 19.95 (1-57167-001-7) Sagamore Pub.

Bud Wilkinson: An Intimate Portrait of an American Legend. Jay Wilkinson & Gretchen Hirsch. (Illus.). 250p. 1994. 19.95 (0-571-67001-6) Sagamore Pub.

***Budalex 88 Proceedings.** Ed. by T. Magay & J. Zigany. 580p. (C). 1990. pap. 180.00x (963-05-5863-7, Pub. by Akad Kiado HU) St Mut.

Budapest. (Berlitz Travel Guide Ser.). (Illus.). 1982. pap. 6.95 (0-02-969870-7) Macmillan.

Budapest. (Baedeker's Ser.). (Illus.). 1991. 16.95 (0-13-094723-7, P-H Travel) P-H Gen Ref & Trav.

Budapest. G. Szaras. (Illus.). (C). 1987. 115.00 (0-685-32395-1, Pub. by Collets) St Mut.

Budapest. Domokos Varga. (Illus.). 136p. 1988. 27.50 (0-87951-288-1) Overlook Pr.

Budapest. Domokos Varga. 136p. 1985. 59.00 (0-317-42872-1, Pub. by Collets) St Mut.

Budapest. 2nd ed. (Insight Guide Ser.). (Illus.). 350p. 1994. pap. 21.95 (0-395-71072-3) HM.

Budapest: A Complete Guide. I Wellner. (Illus.). 1982. pap. 18.00 (963-13-1489-8, Coutinho Pub) IBD Ltd.

Budapest: A Critical Guide. A. Torok. (Illus.). 178p. (C). 1989. pap. 80.00 (0-569-09207-8, Pub. by Collets) St Mut.

Budapest: A Critical Guide. Andras Torok. (Illus.). 180p. 1991. pap. 12.95 (1-55652-133-2) Chicago Review.

Budapest: A Critical Guide. 3rd ed. Andras Torok. (Illus.). 201p. 1992. pap. 14.95 (0-939010-24-0) Zephyr Pr.

Budapest: Critical Guide. A. Torok. 206p. (C). 1991. 50.00 (0-89771-849-6, Pub. by Collets) St Mut.

Budapest: The Complete Guide with Trips to Lake Balaton & Medieval Towns Along the Danube. 2nd ed. 1994. pap. 11.00 (0-679-02570-7) Fodors Travel.

***Budapest a Central European Capital.** Gyorgy Enyedi & Viktoria Szirmai. 1993. text ed. 64.95 (0-471-94596-X) Wiley.

Budapest: A City Set in Time. 69p. (C). 1991. 35.00 (0-89771-847-X, Pub. by Collets) St Mut.

Budapest & New York: Studies in Metropolitan Transformation, 1870-1930. Ed. by Thomas Bender & Carl E. Schorske. (Illus.). 416p. 1994. 39.95 (0-87154-113-0) Russell Sage.

***Budapest & Seine Geschichte.** M. Mohos. (Illus.). 32p. (ENG, GER & HUN.). 1993. pap. 18.00 (963-05-6624-9, Pub. by A K HU) Intl Spec Bk.

Budapest Atlas. A. Ajtay. (Illus.). 90p. (ENG, FRE, GER, HUN & RUS.). (C). 1989. pap. 40.00 (0-685-37545-5, Pub. by Collets) St Mut.

Budapest Atlas: Budapest Karto, Vallalat, 1987. A. Ajtay. (Illus.). (C). 1987. 40.00 (0-685-32397-8, Pub. by Collets UK) Pro-Am Music.

Budapest Ballet. K. Kortvelyes. 198p. 1981. 72.00 (0-317-57223-7, Pub. by Collets UK) St Mut.

Budapest City Map. Collets Staff. (Illus.). (ENG, FRE & GER.). (C). 1989. pap. 40.00 (0-569-09225-6, Pub. by Collets) St Mut.

Budapest City Plan. Collets Staff. (Illus.). (ENG, GER, HUN & RUS.). (C). 1990. pap. 40.00 (0-685-37544-7, Pub. by Collets) St Mut.

Budapest Danube. P. Buza. 174p. (C). 1991. 80.00 (0-89771-848-8, Pub. by Collets) St Mut.

Budapest for the Tournament Player. Mikhail Tseitlin & Igor Glaskov. 128p. 1992. pap. 14.95 (0-8050-2431-X, Pub. by Batsford Chess UK) H Holt & Co.

Budapest Gambit. A. C. Van der Tak. (Electronic Chessbooks Ser.). 1993. disk 25.00x (0-917237-01-3) Chess Combi.

Budapest Guide & Atlas. Collets Staff. (Illus.). 119p. (C). 1990. 60.00 (0-685-37551-X, Pub. by Collets) St Mut.

Budapest in Seventy-One Colour Photographs. Collets Staff. (Illus.). 66p. (C). 1980. 60.00 (0-569-08648-5, Pub. by Collets UK) Pro-Am Music.

Budapest Museum of Fine Art. A. Czobor. 116p. (C). 1988. 50.00 (0-685-34460-6, Pub. by Collets) St Mut.

Budapest Museum of Fine Arts. Collet's Staff. 128p. 1981. pap. 35.00 (0-317-57226-1, Pub. by Collets) St Mut.

Budapest Museum of Fine Arts. A. Czobor. (Illus.). 116p. (C). 1988. text ed. 50.00 (0-685-40302-5, Pub. by Collets) St Mut.

Budapest, Nineteen Hundred: A Historical Portrait of a City & Its Culture. John Lukacs. (Illus.). 1990. pap. 10.95 (0-8021-3250-2) Grove-Atltic.

Budapest Photoguide. P. Dobai. (Illus.). 64p. (C). 1988. 75.00 (0-685-47204-3, Pub. by Collets) St Mut.

Budapest Pocket Guide. Berlitz Editors. (Pocket Guides Ser.). 1994. pap. 7.95 (2-8315-2374-5) Berlitz.

B

An Asterisk (*) at the beginning of an entry indicates that the title is appearing in BIP for the first time.

Budapest Prestel Guide. Hella Markus. Ed. by Julia Kluge-Fabenyi. (Prestel Travel Guide Ser.). (Illus.). 192p. 1994. pap. 19.95 (3-7913-1329-0, Pub. by Prestel) TeNeues.

***Budapest 1896 International Chess Tournament: The First Great Chess Tournament in Hungary.** John C. Owen. (Great Tournament Ser.). (Illus.). 205p. 1994. 36.00 (0-939433-20-6) Caissa Edit.

Buddenbrooks. Thomas Mann. LC 92-52929. 1994. 20.00 (0-679-41737-0) Knopf.

Buddenbrooks. Thomas Mann. 1984. pap. 15.00 (0-394-72637-5) Random.

Buddenbrooks. Thomas Mann. 1994. pap. 15.00 (0-679-75260-9) Random.

Buddenbrooks. Thomas Mann. Tr. by H. T. Lowe-Porter. 644p. 1988. reprint ed. lib. bdg. 45.95 (0-89966-599-3) Buccaneer Bks.

Buddenbrooks: Family Life As the Mirror of Social Change. Martin Swales. (Twayne's Masterwork Studies: No. 79). 144p. 1991. text ed. 21.95 (0-8057-9402-6, Twayne); pap. 12.95 (0-8057-8551-5, Twayne) Macmillan.

Buddenbrooks: The Decline of a Family. Thomas Mann. Tr. by John E. Woods. LC 92-18990. 1993. 35.00 (0-679-41994-2) Knopf.

Buddha. 276p. 1987. 18.50 (3-87860-153-0, Pub. by Stiftung Gralsbotschaft GW) Grail Fndtn-Amer.

Buddha. Michael Carrithers. LC 83-8004. (Past Masters Ser.). 1984. 7.95 (0-19-287589-2) OUP.

Buddha. Susan L. Roth. LC 93-8240. (J). 1994. 15.95 (0-385-31072-2) Doubleday.

Buddha. Alistair Shearer. LC 91-67309. (Art & Imagination Ser.). (Illus.). 96p. 1992. pap. 14.95 (0-500-81038-9) Thames Hudson.

Buddha: A Pictorial History of His Life & Legacy. Jeannine Auboyer. Tr. by Nelly Marans. LC 83-10140. (Illus.). 272p. 1983. 100.00 (0-8245-0588-3) Crossroad NY.

Buddha: His Life, His Doctrine & His Order. Hermann Oldenberg. 1972. 59.95 (0-87968-800-9) Gordon Pr.

Buddha: His Life, His Doctrine, His Order. Herman Oldenverg. (C). 1992. 27.00 (81-7062-177-1, Pub. by Lancer II) S Asia.

Buddha: His Life Retold. R. A. Mitchell. 274p. (C). 1991. reprint ed. pap. 14.95 (1-55778-442-6) Paragon Hse.

Buddha: The Emptiness of the Heart. Osho Rajneesh. Ed. by Deva Sarito & Deva Ashik. (Zen Ser.). 288p. 1989. 12.95 (3-89338-055-8, Pub. by Rebel Hse GW) Osho Chidvilas.

Buddha & Buddhism. Maurice Percheron. Tr. by Edmund Stapleton. LC 82-3471. (Spiritual Masters Ser.). (Illus.). 192p. 1984. 18.95 (0-87951-157-5); pap. 9.95 (0-87951-193-1) Overlook Pr.

Buddha & Christ: Nativity Stories & Indian Traditions. Zacharias P. Thundy. LC 92-38855. (Numen Bookseries (Studies in the History of Religions): No. 60). x, 296p. 1992. 77.25 (90-04-09741-4) E J Brill.

Buddha & His Religion. J. B. Saint-Hilaire. 1972. 59.95 (0-87968-798-3) Gordon Pr.

Buddha & His Sayings. Hara C. Syama-Sankara. LC 78-70128. reprint ed. 18.00 (0-404-17387-X) AMS Pr.

Buddha & His Teachings. Narada Mahathera. 412p. (Orig.). 1988. pap. 10.50 (955-24-0025-2, Pub. by Buddhist Pubns Soc CE) Wisdom MA.

Buddha & Jesus: Conversations. Carrin Dunne. 1975. pap. 9.95 (0-87243-057-X) Templegate.

Buddha & Man. Eikichi Ikeyama. Tr. by Toshikazu Arai. LC 89-9763. 1989. pap. 7.95 (0-938474-09-X) Buddhist Study.

***Buddha & Mohammed - Why Not? The Awesome Impact of Jesus' Life on Earth.** Ed. by Michael Warden. (Real Life Bible Curriculum Ser.). (Illus.). 6p. 1995. pap. 2.99 (1-55945-526-8) Group Pub.

Buddha & the Christ. B. H. Streeter. 1972. 59.95 (0-87968-799-1) Gordon Pr.

Buddha & the Christ: Explorations in Buddhist & Christian Dialogue. Leo D. Lefebure. LC 93-7972. (Faith Meets Faith Ser.). 250p. (Orig.). 1993. pap. 18.95 (0-88344-924-2) Orbis Bks.

Buddha & the Gospel of Buddhism. Ananda K. Coomaraswamy. 1988. pap. 12.95 (0-8065-1101-X, Citadel Pr) Carol Pub Group.

Buddha & the Gospel of Buddhism. Ananda K. Coomaraswamy. (Illus.). 1975. text ed. 27.50 (0-685-13638-8) Coronet Bks.

Buddha-Dhamma or the Life & Teachings of the Buddha. Narada Thera. (C). 1991. 16.00 (81-206-0540-3, Pub. by Asian Educ Servs II) S Asia.

Buddha Eye: An Anthology of the Kyoto School. 2nd ed. Ed. by Frederick Franck. 256p. 1991. reprint ed. pap. 14.95 (0-8245-1071-2) Crossroad NY.

***Buddha Gaya Through the Ages.** D. C. Ahir. (C). 1995. 20.00x (81-7030-409-1, Pub. by Sri Satguru Pubns II) S Asia.

Buddha: His Quest for Serenity: A Biography. rev. ed. George N. Marshall. 264p. 1990. 29.95 (0-87047-048-5); pap. 15.95 (0-87047-049-3) Schenkman Bks Inc.

Buddha in the Crown: Avalokitesvara in the Buddhist Traditions of Sri Lanka. John C. Holt. (Illus.). 272p. 1991. 52.00 (0-19-506418-6) OUP.

Buddha in the Robot: A Robot Engineer's Thoughts on Science & Religion. Masahiro Mori. Tr. by Charles S. Terry. 192p. 1981. pap. 9.95 (4-333-01002-0, Pub. by Kosei Pub Co JA) C E Tuttle.

Buddha Mimansa. Maitriya. Ed. by Maharaja Yogiraja. LC 78-70098. reprint ed. 23.50 (0-404-17347-0) AMS Pr.

Buddha Nature. Sallie B. King. LC 89-77740. (SUNY Series in Buddhist Studies). 205p. (C). 1991. 59.50 (0-7914-0427-7); pap. 19.95 (0-7914-0428-5) State U NY Pr.

Buddha Nature: A Festschrift in Honor of Minoru Kiyota. Ed. by Paul J. Griffiths & John P. Keenan. 194p. (C). 1991. 39.50 (0-914910-77-9) Buddhist Bks.

Buddha Nature: A Study of the Tathagatagarbha. Brian E. Brown. 1991. 28.00 (81-208-0631-X, Pub. by Motilal Banarsidass II) S Asia.

Buddha-Nature, Mind & the Problem of Gradualism in a Comparative Perspective. David S. Ruegg. 1989. 50.00 (0-7286-0152-4, Pub. by Sch Orient & African Stud UK) S Asia.

Buddha of Suburbia. Hanif Kureishi. 288p. 1991. pap. 11.00 (0-14-013168-X, Penguin Bks) Viking Penguin.

Buddha of the Future: An Early Maitreya from Thailand. Nandana Chutiwongs & Denise P. Leidy. LC 94-70506. (Asia Society Galleries Ser.). (Illus.). 112p. 1994. pap. 25.00 (0-295-97368-4) U of Wash Pr.

Buddha Root Farm. Tripitaka Master Hua. Tr. by Buddhist Text Translation Society et al. (Illus.). 72p. (Orig.). 1976. pap. 4.00 (0-917512-08-1) Buddhist Text.

Buddha Sutra, a Dialogue with the Glorious One. Torkom Saraydarian. LC 93-94948. 400p. 1994. pap. write for info. (0-929874-35-8) TSG Pub Found.

Buddha Sutra, a Dialogue with the Glorious One. Torkom Saraydarian. LC 93-94948. 400p. 1994. write for info. (0-929874-36-6) TSG Pub Found.

Buddha Tree. Fumio Niwa. LC 74-15259. 380p. 1971. pap. 12.95 (0-8048-0995-X) C E Tuttle.

Buddha Tree. Fumio Niwa. Tr. by Kenneth Strong. 1966. 25.00 (0-7206-1125-3) Dufour.

Buddha, Truth & Brotherhood. Ed. by Dwight Goddard. 166p. 1995. pap. 12.00 (0-89540-292-0, SB-292) Sun Pub.

Buddha Way. Charles R. Woods. 8p. 1994. 8.00 (0-06-251139-4) Harper SF.

Buddha Within: Tathagatagarbha Doctrine According to the Shentong Interpretation of the Ratnagotravibhaga. S. K. Hookham. LC 89-49755. (SUNY Series in Buddhist Studies). 422p. 1991. 59.50 (0-7914-0357-2); pap. 19.95 (0-7914-0358-0) State U NY Pr.

Buddhacarita or Acts of the Buddha, 2 vols. in 1. Asvaghosa. Ed. & Tr. by E. H. Johnson. reprint ed. text ed. 29.50 (0-685-13633-7) Coronet Bks.

Buddhacarita or Acts of the Buddha. Tr. by E. H. Johnston. reprint ed. 24.00x (0-8364-0360-6) S Asia.

Buddhacarita or Acts of the Buddha. E. H. Johnston. (C). 1992. reprint ed. 27.50 (81-208-1029-5, Pub. by Motilal Banarsidass II) S Asia.

Buddhadatta's Manuals, 2 vols. in 1. Buddhadatta. Ed. by A. P. Buddhadatta. LC 78-72382. reprint ed. 47.50 (0-404-17244-X) AMS Pr.

***Buddhadhamma: Natural Laws & Values for Life.** Phra P. Payutto. Tr. by Grant A. Olson. (Buddhist Studies Ser.). 315p. 1995. text ed. 59.50x (0-7914-2631-9) State U NY Pr.

***Buddhadhamma: Natural Laws & Values for Life.** Phra P. Payutto. Tr. by Grant A. Olson. (SUNY Series in Buddhist Studies). 315p. (C). 1995. pap. text ed. 19.95x (0-7914-2632-7) State U NY Pr.

Buddhadharma in Blossom, No. III. Ven Shen Kai. LC 91-61485. 400p. (Orig.). (CHI.). 1992. lib. bdg. write for info. (1-56369-004-7) Jen Chen Buddhism.

Buddhadharma in Blossom, No. IV. Ven Shen Kai. LC 91-61485. (Orig.). (CHI.). 1992. write for info. (1-56369-006-3) Jen Chen Buddhism.

Buddhadharma in Blossom, Vol. V. Ven Shen Kai. LC 91-61485. 264p. (Orig.). (CHI.). 1991. pap. (1-56369-000-4) Jen Chen Buddhism.

Buddhaghosa's Parables. Buddhaghosa. Tr. by T. Rogers. LC 78-72384. reprint ed. 37.50 (0-404-17246-6) AMS Pr.

Buddhahood. P. D. Mehta. 200p. 1990. pap. 15.95 (1-85230-055-8) Element MA.

Buddhahood Without Meditation: A Visionary Account Known As Refining Apparent Phenomena, Nangjang. Dudjom Lingpa. Tr. by Richard Barron. LC 93-34038. (Illus.). 245p. 1994. reprint ed. 100.00 (1-881847-01-2) Chagdud Gonpa-Padma.

Buddha's Ancient Path. Piyadassi Thera. 240p. (Orig.). (C). 1987. pap. 12.00 (955-24-0024-4, Pub. by Buddhist Pubns Soc CE) Wisdom MA.

Buddha's Crown. Duncan Long. (Night Stalkers Ser.: No. 8). 1992. mass mkt. 3.99 (0-06-100346-8, Harp PBks) HarpC.

Buddhas' Doctrine of Truth: Dhamma & Buddhist Religion As Practiced by the Holy Brotherhood in Siam. Luang Suriyabongs. Tr. by Krachang Bunnag. LC 77-87512. reprint ed. 14.50 (0-404-16870-1) AMS Pr.

Buddha's Golden Path. Dwight Goddard. 214p. 1981. pap. 16.00 (0-89540-074-X, SB-074) Sun Pub.

Buddha's Golden Path. 2nd rev. ed. Dwight Goddard. LC 78-72435. reprint ed. 27.00 (0-404-17296-2) AMS Pr.

Buddha's Law among the Birds. Edward Conze. (Illus.). 65p. 1986. reprint ed. 8.00 (81-208-0198-9, Pub. by Motilal Banarsidass II) S Asia.

Buddha's Lions. Abhayadatta. Tr. by James Robinson. LC 79-12397. (Tibetan Translation Ser.). (Illus.). 1979. 32.00 (0-913546-60-7); pap. 17.95 (0-913546-61-5) Dharma Pub.

Buddha's Little Instruction Book. Jack Kornfield. LC 93-41545. 1994. mass mkt. 6.95 (0-553-37385-4) Bantam.

***Buddha's Path. Nina Van Gorkom. 160p. (Orig.). (C). 1995. pap. 11.95 (1-897633-12-2, Pub. by Triple Gem UK) Atrium Pubs.**
Why are we in this life? Why do we have to suffer? The Buddha gave his own unique answer to these questions. He taught that the cause of suffering is within man, namely his own faults & defilements, & not in the external situation. He explained that only profound knowledge of his own mind & of all phenomena of his life can lead to the end of suffering. Nina Van Gorkom expounds the basic principles of Buddhism for those who have no previous knowledge of experience of this way of life. The four noble truths - Suffering, the Origin of Suffering, the Cessation of Suffering - are explained as a philosophy & a practical guide which can be followed in today's world. Available through Atrium Distributors.
Publisher Provided Annotation.

Buddha's Path of Virtue. 2nd ed. Dhammapada. Tr. by F. L. Woodward. LC 78-72419. reprint ed. 21.50 (0-404-17283-0) AMS Pr.

Buddha's Philosophy of Man. Tr. & Intro. by Trevor Ling. 256p. 1993. pap. 6.95 (0-460-87207-9, Everyman's Classic Lib) C E Tuttle.

Buddha's Question. W. W. Rowe. LC 93-13993. (J). 1995. pap. 9.95 (1-55939-020-4) Snow Lion Pubns.

Buddha's Relics from Kapilvastu. K. M. Srivastava. (C). 1986. 40.00 (0-8364-2827-7, Pub. by Agam Kala Prakashan) S Asia.

Buddha's Sermon on the Mount. Manly P. Hall. pap. 4.00 (0-89314-307-3) Philos Res.

***Buddha's Socio-Political Ideas.** Phramaha C. Khongchinda. (C). 1993. 22.00x (81-7013-082-4, Pub. by Navrang) S Asia.

Buddha's System of Meditation: Phase (I-VIII), 4 vols., Set. Ayoda P. Pradhan. 1986. text ed. 150.00 (81-207-0140-2, Pub. by Sterling Pubs II) Apt Bks.

Buddha's Victory. Sangharakshita. 96p. (Orig.). 1991. pap. 9.95 (0-904766-50-0, Pub. by Windhorse UK) Windhorse Pubns.

Buddhavacana & Dei Verbum. Michael Fuss. LC 91-10070. (BIL Ser.: No. 3). xvi, 479p. 1991. 137.25 (90-04-08991-8) E J Brill.

Buddhavamsa & the Cariya-Pitaka, Pt. 1. Buddhavamsa. Ed. by Richard Morris. LC 78-72391. reprint ed. 17.00 (0-404-17249-0) AMS Pr.

Buddhism. Thomas Berry. LC 75-10518. 1967. pap. 9.95 (0-89012-017-X) Anima Pubns.

Buddhism. Holly Connolly & Peter Connolly. Ed. by W. Owen Cole. (World Religions Ser.). (Illus.). 140p. (Orig.). (YA). (gr. 9 up). 1992. pap. 14.95 (1-871402-07-7, Pub. by S Thornes UK) Dufour.

***Buddhism.** Catherine Hewitt. (World Religion's Ser.). (Illus.). 48p. (J). (gr. 5-7). Date not set. 15.95 (1-56847-375-3) Thomson Lrning.

Buddhism. Christmas Humphreys. (Pelican Ser.). 256p. (Orig.). 1951. mass mkt. 6.95 (0-14-020228-5, Penguin Bks) Viking Penguin.

Buddhism. Robert C. Lester. LC 86-43010. (Illus.). 144p. 1987. pap. 11.00 (0-06-065243-8) Harper SF.

Buddhism. Hans W. Schumann. 1987. pap. 8.95 (0-8356-0452-7, Quest) Theos Pub Hse.

Buddhism. Madhu B. Wangu. (World Religions Ser.). (Illus.). 128p. (YA). (gr. 7-12). 1992. bds. 17.95 (0-8160-2442-1) Facts on File.

Buddhism: A History. N. Ross Reat. LC 93-1792. (Religions of the World). 336p. (C). 1993. text ed. 60.00 (0-87573-001-9, Asian Human Pr); pap. text ed. 25.00 (0-87573-002-7, Asian Human Pr) Jain Pub Co.

Buddhism: A Modern Perspective. Ed. by Charles S. Prebish. LC 74-300085. 346p. 1975. pap. 14.95 (0-271-01195-5) Pa St U Pr.

Buddhism: A Religion of Infinite Compassion. Ed. by Clarence H. Hamilton. LC 52-1623. 1952. pap. 5.50 (0-672-60340-3, LLA133, Bobbs) Macmillan.

Buddhism: A Way of Life & Thought. Nancy W. Ross. LC 81-40081. (Illus.). 224p. 1981. pap. 12.00 (0-394-74754-2, Vin) Random.

Buddhism: Being a Sketch of the Life & Teachings of Gautama, the Buddha. T. Rhys Davids. LC 78-72417. reprint ed. 28.00 (0-404-17278-4) AMS Pr.

Buddhism: History & Diversity of a Great Tradition. Elizabeth Lyons & Heather Peters. (Illus.). 64p. 1985. pap. 9.95 (0-934718-76-8) U PA Mus Pubns.

Buddhism: Its Birth & Dispersal. rev. ed. Carolina A. Davids. LC 78-72407. reprint ed. 25.00 (0-404-17268-7) AMS Pr.

Buddhism: Its Essence & Development. Edward Conze. 1959. pap. text ed. 13.00 (0-06-130058-6, TB 58, Torch) HarpC.

Buddhism: Its Essence & Development. Edward Conze. 25.25 (0-8446-1889-6) Peter Smith.

Buddhism: Its History & Literature. Rhys Davids. 1972. lib. bdg. 250.00 (0-87968-510-7) Krishna Pr.

Buddhism: Primitive & Present in Magadha & in Ceylon. 2nd ed. Reginald S. Copleston. (C). 1984. reprint ed. 18.00 (0-8364-2412-3, Pub. by Asian Educ Servs II) S Asia.

Buddhism: A Study of the Buddhist Norm. Carolina A. Davids. LC 78-72408. reprint ed. 25.00 (0-404-17269-5) AMS Pr.

Buddhism after Patriarchy: A Feminist History, Analysis, & Reconstruction of Buddhism. Rita M. Gross. LC 92-9133. 365p. 1992. 49.50 (0-7914-1403-5); pap. 16.95 (0-7914-1404-3) State U NY Pr.

Buddhism & American Thinkers. Ed. by Kenneth K. Inada & Nolan P. Jacobson. LC 83-409. 180p. 1984. 64.50 (0-87395-753-9); pap. 21.95 (0-87395-754-7) State U NY Pr.

Buddhism & Asian History. Ed. by Joseph M. Kitagawa. (Readings from the Encyclopedia of Religion Ser.). 432p. (C). 1989. pap. 12.95 (0-02-897212-0) Macmillan.

Buddhism & Asoka. Balkrishna G. Gokhale. LC 78-72443. reprint ed. 41.50 (0-404-17298-9) AMS Pr.

***Buddhism & Bioethics.** Damien Keown. LC 95-5776. 1995. write for info. (0-312-12671-9) St Martin.

Buddhism & Buddhists in China. Lewis Hodous. LC 78-72440. reprint ed. 17.50 (0-404-17306-3) AMS Pr.

Buddhism & Christianity: Rivals & Allies. Ninian Smart. LC 92-29475. 176p. 1993. text ed. 27.95 (0-8248-1519-X); pap. text ed. 15.95 (0-8248-1520-3) UH Pr.

Buddhism & Christianity in Japan: From Conflict to Dialogue, 1854-1899. Notto R. Thelle. LC 86-16147. (Illus.). 368p. 1987. text ed. 30.00 (0-8248-1006-6) UH Pr.

Buddhism & Ethnicity: Social Organization of a Buddhist Temple in Kelantan. Mohamed Yusoff Ismail. 165p. 1993. 32.50 (981-3016-26-4, Pub. by Inst SE Asian Studies SI) Ashgate Pub Co.

Buddhism & Faith. Masatoshi G. Mori. LC 78-70102. reprint ed. 21.50 (0-404-17353-5) AMS Pr.

Buddhism & Immortality. William S. Bigelow. LC 78-72379. reprint ed. 16.50 (0-404-17228-8) AMS Pr.

***Buddhism & Interfaith Dialogue Pt. 1, 2 vols. Sequel to Zen & Western Thought.** Masao Abe. Ed. by Steven Heine. LC 95-6926. 1995. write for info. (0-8248-1751-6); pap. write for info. (0-8248-1752-4) UH Pr.

Buddhism & Its Christian Critics. Paul Caras. 316p. (C). 1987. 29.00 (81-85132-01-1) S Asia.

Buddhism & Its Christian Critics. Paul Carus. 1972. 250.00 (0-87968-801-7) Gordon Pr.

Buddhism & Its Place in the Mental Life of Mankind. Paul Dahlke. LC 78-72403. reprint ed. 29.00 (0-404-17265-2) AMS Pr.

***Buddhism & Jungian Psychology.** 2nd ed. J. Marvin Spiegelman & Mokusen Miyuki. LC 85-70850. 224p. (Orig.). 1987. pap. 12.95 (1-56184-111-0) New Falcon Pubns.

Buddhism & Lamaism. J. B. Ellam. 1984. reprint ed. pap. 9.95 (0-916411-79-6, Oriental Classics) Holmes Pub.

Buddhism & Language: A Study of Indo-Tibetan Scholasticism. Jose I. Cabezon. LC 93-23903. (SUNY Series, Toward a Comparative Philosophy of Religions). 299p. 1994. 64.50x (0-7914-1899-5); pap. 21.95x (0-7914-1900-2) State U NY Pr.

Buddhism & Nonviolent Global Problem-Solving: Ulan Bator Explorations. Ed. by Sarah Gilliatt & Glen D. Paige. 176p. 1991. pap. 10.00 (0-685-53745-5) S M Matsunaga.

Buddhism & Other Religious Cults of South-East India. S. S. Tripathy. (C). 1988. 120.00 (81-85067-15-5, Pub. by Sundeep II) S Asia.

Buddhism & Psychotherapy. Manly P. Hall. pap. 12.95 (0-89314-394-4) Philos Res.

Buddhism & Society: A Great Tradition & Its Burmese Vicissitudes. exp. ed. Melford E. Spiro. LC 81-18522. 530p. 1982. pap. 15.00 (0-520-04672-2) U CA Pr.

***Buddhism & Society in Southeast Asia.** Donald K. Swearer. (C). 1995. pap. text ed. 16.95x (0-7914-2460-X) State U NY Pr.

***Buddhism & Society in Southeast Asia.** expanded rev. ed. Donald K. Swearer. 224p. (C). 1995. text ed. 49.50x (0-7914-2459-6) State U NY Pr.

Buddhism & the Arts of Japan. rev. ed. Richard B. Pilgrim. LC 93-9361. 78p. (Orig.). 1993. pap. 9.95 (0-89012-069-2) Anima Pubns.

***Buddhism & the Baha'i Faith: An Introduction to the Baha'i Faith for Theravada Buddhists.** Moojan Momen. 128p. (Orig.). 1995. pap. 11.95 (0-85398-384-4) G Ronald Pub.

Buddhism & the Contemporary World: Change & Self Correction. Nolan P. Jacobson. LC 82-5909. 203p. 1982. 18.95 (0-8093-1052-X); pap. 14.95 (0-8093-1071-6) S Ill U Pr.

***Buddhism & the Emerging World Civilization: Essays in Honor of Nolan Pliny Jacobson.** Ed. by Ramakrishna Puligandla & David L. Miller. LC 93-3267. 256p. (C). 1995. 29.95 (0-8093-1842-3) S Ill U Pr.

Buddhism & the Race Question. George P. Malalasekera & K. N. Jayatilleke. LC 77-18853. (Race Question in Modern Thought). 73p. 1978. reprint ed. text ed. 49.50 (0-313-20208-7, MABU, Greenwood Pr) Greenwood.

Buddhism & the State in Sixteenth Century Japan. Neil McMullin. LC 84-42572. 452p. reprint ed. pap. 128.90 (0-8357-3390-4, 2039647) Bks Demand.

Buddhism & Whitehead's Process Philosophy. Anil K. Sarkar. LC 92-903203. 199p. reprint ed. pap. 56.80 (0-7837-5200-8, AU00438) Bks Demand.

Buddhism & Zen. Nyogen Senzaki & Ruth Strout-McCandless. LC 87-60884. 96p. 1988. reprint ed. pap. 7.95 (0-86547-315-3, North Pt Pr) FS&G.

***Buddhism as a Religion: Its Historical Development & Its Present Conditions.** H. Hackmann. (C). 1993. 8.50 (81-85557-70-5) S Asia.

Buddhism As Presented by the Brahmanical Systems. Chitrarekha V. Kher. (Bibliotheca Indo-Buddhica Ser.: No. 92). (C). 1992. 58.00 (81-7030-293-5) S Asia.

Buddhism Betrayed? Religion, Politics, & Violence in Sri Lanka. Stanley J. Tambiah. LC 91-38944. (Illus.). 238p. 1992. lib. bdg. 34.95 (0-226-78949-7); pap. text ed. 14.95 (0-226-78950-0) U Ch Pr.

Buddhism for Today. 2nd ed. Subhuti, pseud. (Illus.). 212p. 1988. reprint ed. pap. 12.95 (0-904766-34-9, Pub. by Windhorse UK) Windhorse Pubns.

Buddhism in America: The Social Organization of an Ethnic Religious Institution. Tetsuden Kashima. LC 76-57837. (Contributions in Sociology Ser.: No. 26). (Illus.). 272p. 1977. text ed. 29.95 (0-8371-9534-9, KSO/, Greenwood Pr) Greenwood.

Buddhism in Central Asia. B. N. Puri. (C). 1993. 25.00x (81-208-0372-8, Pub. by Motilal Banarsidass II) S Asia.

Buddhism in China. Samuel Beal. 1977. 19.95 (0-8369-7129-9, 7963) Ayer.

B

Buddhism in China. Samuel Beal. 1972. lib. bdg. 250.00 (*0-87968-479-8*) Krishna Pr.

Buddhism in China: A Historical Survey. Kenneth Ch'en. (Studies in History of Religion: Vol. 1). 1974. pap. 21.95 (*0-691-00015-8*) Princeton U Pr.

Buddhism in Chinese History. Arthur F. Wright. LC 59-7432. (Illus.). xiv, 144p. 1959. pap. 9.95 (*0-8047-0548-8*) Stanford U Pr.

Buddhism in Chinese History. Arthur F. Wright. (Illus.). 144p. reprint ed. pap. 15.00 (*957-9482-38-1*, PRE012, Pub. by SMC Pub CC) Oriental Bk Store.

***Buddhism in Chinese Society: An Economic History from the Fifth to the Tenth Centuries.** Jacques Gernet. Tr. by Franciscus Verellen. LC 94-42484. (ENG & FRE.). 1995. write for info. (*0-231-07380-1*) Col U Pr.

Buddhism in Comparative Light. Hijime Nakamura. 1986. 15.00 (*0-685-35378-8*, Pub. by Motilal Banarsidass II) S Asia.

Buddhism, in Its Connection with Brahmanism & Hinduism, & in Contrast with Christianity. 2nd ed. Monier-Williams. LC 78-70101. reprint ed. 57.50 (*0-404-17349-7*) AMS Pr.

Buddhism in Japan. K. Krishna Murthy. (C). 1989. 34.00 (*81-85067-25-2*, Pub. by Sundeep II) S Asia.

Buddhism in Karnataka. R. C. Kiremath. (C). 1994. text ed. 19.50 (*81-246-0013-9*, Pub. by DK Pubs Dist II) S Asia.

Buddhism in Kerala. P. C. Alexander. LC 78-72369. reprint ed. 37.50 (*0-404-17216-4*) AMS Pr.

Buddhism in Life: The Anthropological Study of Religion & the Sinhalese Practice of Buddhism. Martin Southwold. LC 83-9890. (Themes in Social Anthropology Ser.). 232p. 1983. 79.50 (*0-7190-0971-5*) Elliots Bks.

Buddhism in North India. D. C. Ahir. (Illus.). (C). 1989. 50.00 (*81-85132-09-7*, Pub. by Classics India Pubns II) S Asia.

***Buddhism in Practice.** Ed. by Donald S. Lopez, Jr. LC 94-48201. (Princeton Readings in Religion Ser.). 1995. write for info. (*0-691-04442-2*); pap. write for info. (*0-691-04441-4*) Princeton U Pr.

Buddhism in Pre-Christian Britain. Donald A. Mackenzie. 1977. lib. bdg. 59.95 (*0-8490-1558-8*) Gordon Pr.

Buddhism in Russia: The Story of Agvan Dorziev-Lhasa's Emissary to the Tsar. John Snelling. (Illus.). 256p. 1993. pap. 22.95 (*1-85230-332-8*) Element MA.

Buddhism in South India. D. C. Ahir. (Bibliotheca Indo-Buddhica Ser.: No. 112). (C). 1992. 22.00 (*81-7030-332-X*) S Asia.

Buddhism in the Classical Age (c. 400-750 A.D.) Sudha Sengupta. (C). 1985. 50.00 (*0-8364-2829-3*, Pub. by Sundeep II) S Asia.

Buddhism in the History of Indian Ideas. N. N. Bhattacharya. (C). 1993. 31.00 (*81-7304-017-6*, Pub. by Manohar II) S Asia.

Buddhism in the Twentieth Century. Peggy Morgan. (Illus.). 64p. 1985. pap. 8.95 (*0-7175-1394-7*, Pub. by S Thornes UK) Dufour.

Buddhism in Tibet. K. Krishna Murthy. (C). 1989. 28.50 (*81-85067-16-3*, Pub. by Sundeep Prakashan II) S Asia.

Buddhism in Tibet. Emil Schlagintweit. 1972. 69.95 (*0-87968-802-5*) Gordon Pr.

Buddhism in Translations. Henry C. Warren. LC 78-70138. reprint ed. 47.50 (*0-404-17408-6*) AMS Pr.

Buddhism in Translations. Henry C. Warren. (C). 1987. reprint ed. 22.50 (*81-208-0335-3*, Pub. by Motilal Banarsidass II) S Asia.

Buddhism in World Peace. Ed. by S. Narayan. 1990. 21.50 (*81-210-0251-6*, Pub. by Inter-India Pubns) S Asia.

***Buddhism Lt. of Asia.** Chen. 1977. pap. 7.95 (*0-8120-0272-5*) Barron.

Buddhism Made Plain: An Introduction for Christians & Jews. Antony Fernando & Leonard Swidler. LC 84-18880. 176p. (Orig.). 1985. pap. 14.95 (*0-88344-198-5*) Orbis Bks.

Buddhism of H. P. Blavatsky. H. J. Spierenburg. xiv, 335p. 1991. 12.50 (*0-913004-68-5*) Point Loma Pub.

Buddhism of Tibet. Tr. by J. Hopkins & L. Rimpoche. (C). 1987. 35.00 (*81-208-0375-2*, Pub. by Motilal Banarsidass II) S Asia.

Buddhism of Tibet. Dalai Lama. Ed. & Tr. by Jeffrey Hopkins. LC 87-13049. 219p. 1987. reprint ed. pap. 12.95 (*0-937938-48-3*) Snow Lion Pubns.

Buddhism of Tibet or Lamaism. L. A. Waddell. (C). 1991. reprint ed. 35.00 (*0-685-50014-4*, Pub. by Asian Educ Servs II) S Asia.

Buddhism of Tibet or Lamaism: Mystic Cults Symbolism & Mythology. 2nd ed. Waddell. (C). 1995. pap. 29.95 (*0-7007-0245-8*, Pub. by Curzon Pr UK) Humanities.

Buddhism, Primitive & Present in Magdha & in Ceylon. 2nd ed. Reginald S. Copleston. LC 78-72398. reprint ed. 28.00 (*0-404-17257-1*) AMS Pr.

Buddhism, Sexuality, & Gender. Ed. by Jose I. Cabezon. LC 90-46557. 241p. (C). 1992. 59.50 (*0-7914-0757-8*); pap. 19.95 (*0-7914-0758-6*) State U NY Pr.

Buddhism Through American Women's Eyes. 1994. pap. 14.00 (*0-938077-71-6*) Parallax Pr.

***Buddhism Through American Women's Eyes.** Ed. by Karma L. Tsomo. LC 95-10507. 175p. 1995. 12.95 (*1-55939-047-6*) Snow Lion Pubns.

Buddhism Transformed: Religious Change in Sri Lanka. Richard Gombrich & Gananth Obeyesekere. 500p. (C). 1990. pap. text ed. 17.95 (*0-691-01901-0*) Princeton U Pr.

Buddhism under Mao. Holmes Welch. LC 72-78428. (Harvard East Asian Ser.: No. 69). (Illus.). 684p. reprint ed. pap. 180.00 (*0-7837-1736-9*, 2057266) Bks Demand.

Buddhisme au Cambodge. Adhemard Leclere. LC 76-179215. reprint ed. 72.00 (*0-404-54843-1*) AMS Pr.

Buddhist: Art & Faith. Wladimir Zwalf. (Illus.). 300p. 1985. text ed. 19.95 (*0-02-934500-6*) Macmillan.

Buddhist Adhidhamma: Meditation & Concentration. U Kyaw Min. 192p. 1987. pap. 7.95 (*0-89346-287-X*) Heian Intl.

Buddhist & Hindu Art in the Collection of John H. Mann. Comp. by Doanda Randall. (Illus.). 285p. (Orig.). 1981. 65.00 (*0-940492-01-6*) Asian Conserv Lab.

Buddhist & Taoist Practice in Medieval Chinese Society: Buddhist & Taoist Studies II. Ed. by David W. Chappell. LC 86-30808. (Asian Studies at Hawaii: No. 34). 256p. 1987. pap. text ed. 18.00 (*0-8248-0957-2*) UH Pr.

Buddhist & Taoist Studies Number One. Ed. by Michael Saso & David W. Chappell. (Asian Studies at Hawaii: No. 18). (Illus.). 174p. 1977. pap. text ed. 10.50 (*0-8248-0420-1*) UH Pr.

***Buddhist & Vedic Studies: A Miscellany.** O. H. Wijesekera. (C). 1994. text ed. 27.00 (*81-208-1063-5*, Pub. by Motilal Banarsidass II) S Asia.

Buddhist Approach to Peace. Nikkyo Niwano. Tr. by Masuo Nezu. (Illus.). 162p. 1977. 10.95 (*4-333-00308-3*, Pub. by Kosei Pub Co JA) C E Tuttle.

Buddhist Art & Architecture. Robert E. Fisher. LC 92-62141. (World of Art Ser.). (Illus.). 216p. 1993. pap. 12.95 (*0-500-20265-6*) Thames Hudson.

Buddhist Art in India. Jas Burgess. 240p. 1988. 35.00 (*0-317-52134-9*, Pub. by S Chand II) St Mut.

Buddhist Art in India. enl. rev. ed. Albert Grunwedel. Ed. by James Burgess. Tr. by Agnes C. Gibson. LC 65-3064. (Illus.). 1965. reprint ed. 39.50 (*0-678-07260-4*) Kelley.

Buddhist Art in India. Albert Grunwedel. Tr. by Agnes C. Gibson. (Illus.). 236p. (GER.). reprint ed. text ed. 37.50 (*0-685-13649-3*) Coronet Bks.

Buddhist Art in India, Ceylon, & Java. J. P. Vogel. (Illus.). 187p. 1977. reprint ed. text ed. 23.50 (*0-685-13643-4*) Coronet Bks.

Buddhist Art of East Asia. Dietrich Seckel. Tr. by Ulrich H. Mammitzsch. (East Asian Research Aids & Translations Ser.: Vol. 2). (Illus.). 560p. 1989. 40.00 (*0-914584-97-9*) WWUCEAS.

Buddhist Art of Gandhara. John Marshall. (Illus.). 1981. reprint ed. text ed. 30.00 (*0-685-43580-6*) Coronet Bks.

***Buddhist Art of Nagarjunakonda.** K. Rama. (C). 1995. 88.00x (*81-85067-90-2*, Pub. by Sundeep II) S Asia.

Buddhist Art of the Tibetan Plateau. Liu Lizhong. (Illus.). 358p. 1988. 100.00 (*0-8351-2128-3*) China Bks.

***Buddhist Art of Tibet.** (Illus.). 60p. (Orig.). 1995. pap. 45.00 (*0-7605-1691-X*) Rector Pr.

Buddhist Behavioral Codes & the Modern World: An International Symposium. Ed. by Charles Fu & Sandra A. Wawrytko. LC 94-8355. (Contributions to the Study of Religion Ser.: No. 38). 352p. 1994. text ed. 59.95 (*0-313-28890-9*, Greenwood Pr) Greenwood.

Buddhist Bible. Ed. by Dwight Goddard. LC 93-36003. 720p. 1994. pap. 18.00 (*0-8070-5911-0*) Beacon Pr.

Buddhist Birth Stories; or Jataka Tales, Vol. 1. Ed. by V. Fausboll. Tr. by Rhys T. Davids. LC 78-72443. reprint ed. 42.50 (*0-404-17309-8*) AMS Pr.

Buddhist Birth Stories; or Jataka Tales: The Oldest Collection of Folklore Extant. Rhys Davids. Ed. by Richard M. Dorson. Tr. by Thomas Williams. LC 77-70620. (International Folklore Ser.). 1977. reprint ed. lib. bdg. 40.95 (*0-405-10090-6*) Ayer.

Buddhist Book Illuminations. Pratapaditya Pal & Julia Meech-Pekarik. LC 87-92183. (Illus.). 339p. 1988. lib. bdg. 225.00 (*0-318-40043-X*) Hacker.

Buddhist Catechism: An Outline of the Doctrine of the Buddha Gotama. Subhadra Bhikshu. 95p. 1995. pap. 8.00 (*0-89540-293-9*, SB-293) Sun Pub.

Buddhist Cave Temples of India. Owen C. Kail. (Illus.). xi, 138p. 1981. text ed. 25.00 (*0-86590-043-4*, Pub. by Taraporevala II) Apt Bks.

Buddhist Cave Temples of India. Robert S. Wauchope. LC 78-70139. reprint ed. 34.50 (*0-404-17409-4*) AMS Pr.

Buddhist-Christian Dialogue: Mutual Renewal & Transformation. Ed. by Paul O. Ingram & Frederick J. Streng. LC 85-24528. 254p. 1986. pap. text ed. 10.00 (*0-8248-0829-0*) UH Pr.

***Buddhist-Christian Synthesis.** D. B. Bakhroushin. 1994. 10.95 (*0-533-11042-4*) Vantage.

Buddhist Churches of America: Jodo Shinshu. Donald R. Tuck. LC 87-28931. (Studies in American Religion: Vol. 28). 350p. 1987. lib. bdg. 99.95 (*0-88946-672-6*) E Mellen.

Buddhist Conception of Spirits. 2nd enl. rev. ed. Bimala C. Law. LC 78-72462. reprint ed. 21.50 (*0-404-17334-9*) AMS Pr.

Buddhist Cosmology. W. Randolph Kloetzli. 1989. reprint ed. 21.00 (*81-208-0463-5*, Pub. by Motilal Banarsidass II) S Asia.

Buddhist Critique of the Christian Concept of God. Gunapala Dharmasiri. LC 87-11989. 357p. (C). 1988. 35.95 (*0-942353-01-3*); pap. 15.95 (*0-942353-00-5*) Gldn Leaves Pub.

Buddhist Dictionary. Nyanatiloka. LC 77-87508. reprint ed. 20.00 (*0-404-16846-9*) AMS Pr.

Buddhist Doctrine of Experience. Thomas A. Kockumutton. 1989. reprint ed. 18.00 (*81-208-0662-X*, Pub. by Motilal Banarsidass II) S Asia.

Buddhist Education in Ceylon, & Other Essays. Ginige Jinapriya. LC 78-72901. reprint ed. 18.50 (*0-404-17313-6*) AMS Pr.

Buddhist Emptiness & Christian Trinity: Essays & Explorations. Ed. by Roger J. Corless & Paul F. Knitter. 144p. 1990. pap. 8.95 (*0-8091-3131-5*) Paulist Pr.

Buddhist Essays. Paul Dahlke. Tr. by Bhikkhu Silicara. LC 78-72404. reprint ed. 37.50 (*0-404-17266-0*) AMS Pr.

Buddhist Ethics: A Cross Cultural Approach. Charles S. Prebish. 248p. 1992. per. 21.95 (*0-8403-7424-0*) Kendall-Hunt.

Buddhist Ethics: The Path to Nirvana. Hammalawa Saddhatissa. (Basic Book - Orange Ser.). 216p. (Orig.). 1994. pap. 12.95 (*0-86171-053-3*) Wisdom MA.

Buddhist Ethics: The Way to Salvation? Paul Tice. 12p. (Orig.). 1994. pap. 2.50 (*1-885395-03-5*) Book Tree.

Buddhist Ethics & Modern Society: An International Symposium. Ed. by Charles W. Fu & Sandra A. Wawrytko. LC 91-8237. (Contributions to the Study of Religion Ser.: No. 31). 472p. 1991. text ed. 55.00 (*0-313-27628-5*, FBE, Greenwood Pr) Greenwood.

Buddhist Experience: Sources & Interpretations. Ed. by Stephen Beyer. 274p. (C). 1974. pap. 19.95 (*0-8221-0127-0*) Intl Thomson.

Buddhist Faith & Sudden Enlightenment. Sung-Bae Park. LC 82-10459. 211p. 1983. 59.50 (*0-87395-673-7*); pap. 19.95 (*0-87395-674-5*) State U NY Pr.

Buddhist Feminine Ideal. Diana M. Paul. LC 79-12031. (American Academy of Religion. Dissertation Ser.: No. 30). 250p. reprint ed. pap. 71.30 (*0-7837-5404-3*, 2045168) Bks Demand.

Buddhist Festivals. John Snelling. (Holidays & Festivals Ser.). (Illus.). 48p. (J). (gr. 3-8). 1987. 11.95 (*0-685-67596-3*); lib. bdg. 15.94 (*0-86592-980-7*) Rourke Corp.

***Buddhist Forum, Vol. III.** Ed. by Tadeusz Skorupski. (C). 1994. 78.00 (*0-7286-0231-8*, Pub. by Sch Orient & African Stud UK) S Asia.

***Buddhist Forum, Vol. III.** Ed. by Tadeusz Skorupski & Ulrich Pagel. (C). 1994. 64.00 (*0-614-04125-2*, Pub. by Sch Orient & African Stud UK) S Asia.

***Buddhist Forum Vol. III: 1991-1993.** Ed. by Tadeusz Skorpski & Ulrich Pagel. (C). 1994. 68.00 (*0-614-04126-0*, Pub. by Sch Orient & African Stud UK) S Asia.

Buddhist Forum, Vol. 1: Seminar Papers, 1987-1988. Ed. by Tadeusz Skoupski. 1990. pap. 18.50 (*0-7286-0162-1*, Pub. by Sch Orient & African Stud UK) S Asia.

Buddhist Forum, Vol. 2: Seminar Papers, 1988-90. Ed. by Tadeusz Skorupski. (C). 1992. text ed. 30.00 (*0-7286-0719-0*, Pub. by Heritage IA) S Asia.

Buddhist Hand-Symbol. Aisaburo Akiyama. LC 78-72367. reprint ed. 22.50 (*0-404-17214-8*) AMS Pr.

Buddhist Handbook. Thru L. Lissi. (Salamander Ser.: No. 3). 32p. 1993. reprint ed. pap. 2.95 (*1-56640-593-9*) Pomegranate Calif.

Buddhist Handbook: A Complete Guide to the Buddhist Schools, Teaching, Practice, & History. John Snelling. 384p. (Orig.). 1991. pap. 14.95 (*0-89281-319-9*) Inner Tradit.

Buddhist Heritage in India & Abroad. Ed. by G. Kuppuram & K. Kumudamani. (C). 1992. 78.50 (*81-85067-78-3*, Pub. by Sundeep II) S Asia.

Buddhist Hermeneutics. Ed. by Donald S. Lopez, Jr. LC 87-30175. (Studies in East Asian Buddhism: No. 6). 320p. 1988. text ed. 35.00 (*0-8248-1161-5*) UH Pr.

Buddhist Hermeneutics. Ed. by Donald S. Lopez, Jr. (Studies in East Asian Buddhism: No. 6). 308p. (C). 1992. reprint ed. pap. text ed. 15.95 (*0-8248-1447-9*) UH Pr.

Buddhist Hybrid Sanskrit Grammar & Dictionary, 2 vols., Set. F. Edgerton. 1987. 125.00 (*0-8288-1781-2*, M15067) Fr & Eur.

Buddhist Hybrid Sanskrit Grammar & Dictionary, 2 vols., Set, Vol. 1: Grammar; Vol. 2: Dictionary. Franklin Edgerton. 1992. reprint ed. 76.00 (*81-208-0997-1*, Pub. by Motilal Banarsidass II) S Asia.

Buddhist I Ching. Ou-i Chih-hsu. Tr. by Thomas Cleary. LC 86-31460. (Dragon Editions Ser.). 240p. 1987. pap. 15.00 (*0-87773-408-9*) Shambhala Pubns.

Buddhist Iconography: Compact Edition. Lokesh Chandra. (C). 1991. 98.50 (*81-85179-71-9*, Pub. by Aditya Prakashan II) S Asia.

Buddhist Images of Human Perfection: The Arahant of the Suta Pitaka Compared with the Bodhisataya & Mahasiddha. Nathan Katz. 1989. reprint ed. 21.50 (*81-208-0647-6*, Pub. by Motilal Banarsidass II) S Asia.

Buddhist India. T. W. Rhys Davids. (C). 1993. reprint ed. 16.00x (*81-208-0424-4*, Pub. by Motilal Banarsidass II) S Asia.

Buddhist India. Thomas W. Davids. LC 78-38349. (Select Bibliographies Reprint Ser.). 1977. reprint ed. 30.95 (*0-8369-6766-6*) Ayer.

Buddhist Leader in Ming China: The Life & Thought of Han-shan Te-ch'ing, 1546-1623. Sung-Peng Hsu. LC 78-50068. (Institute for Advanced Study of World Religions Ser.). 1979. text ed. 32.50 (*0-271-00542-4*) Pa St U Pr.

Buddhist Legends, 3 vols. Tr. by E. W. Burlingame. (C). 1979. reprint ed. 84.00 (*0-86013-057-6*, Pub. by Pali Text) Wisdom MA.

Buddhist Legends, 3 vols., Set. Dhammapadatthakatha. Tr. by Eugene W. Burlingame. LC 78-72421. reprint ed. 105.00 (*0-404-17610-0*) AMS Pr.

Buddhist Literature. G. R. Sain. (C). 1992. 32.00 (*0-8364-2812-9*, Pub. by Atlantic Pubs II) S Asia.

Buddhist Logic, 2 Vols. T. Stcherbatsky. 1958. reprint ed. Set. text ed. 142.35 (*90-279-0060-4*) Mouton.

Buddhist Logic, 2 vols., Set. T. Stcherbatsky. (C). 1993. text ed. 32.00 (*81-208-1019-8*, Pub. by Motilal Banarsidass II) S Asia.

Buddhist Logic & Epistemology. Ed. by Evans & Bimal K. Matilal. 1986. lib. bdg. 104.50 (*90-277-2222-6*) Kluwer Ac.

Buddhist Lovers & Other Troubles. Jorn K. Bramann. LC 93-85864. 84p. (Orig.). 1994. pap. 8.00 (*0-945073-17-8*) Nightsun MD.

Buddhist Mahayana Texts. E. B. Crowell. 1972. lib. bdg. 250.00 (*0-87968-499-2*) Krishna Pr.

Buddhist Mahayana Texts. Ed. by E. B. Cowell et al. 448p. 1987. reprint ed. pap. 9.95 (*0-486-25552-2*) Dover.

Buddhist Manual of Psychological Ethics. Caroline A. Rhys Davids. 1975. reprint ed. 24.00 (*0-8364-2573-1*, Pub. by Munshiram Manoharial II) S Asia.

***Buddhist Meditation, Vol. 1.** St. Ruth. 1995. pap. 3.95 (*0-946672-01-6*, Pub. by Buddhist Pubng UK) Atrium Pubs.

Buddhist Meditation in Theory & Practice: A General Exposition According to the Pali Canon of the Theravada School. 3rd ed. Paravahera V. Mahathera. 496p. (C). 1987. text ed. 12.95 (*967-9920-41-0*, Buddhist Missionary Society) Wisdom MA.

Buddhist Meditation on China. Paul F. Schmidt. LC 84-81398. (Illus.). 74p. 1984. lib. bdg. 15.00 (*0-912998-06-7*); pap. 8.00 (*0-912998-07-5*) Hummingbird.

Buddhist Monasteries in Western Himalaya. Romi Khosla. 1979. 150.00 (*0-7855-0308-0*, Pub. by Ratna Pustak Bhandar) St Mut.

Buddhist Monasteries in Western Himalaya. Romi Khosla. 276p. (C). 1979. 290.00 (*0-89771-124-6*, Pub. by Ratna Pustak Bhandar) St Mut.

Buddhist Monastic Architecture in Sri Lanka. Anuradha Seneviratna & Benjamin Polk. (C). 1992. 67.50 (*81-7017-281-0*, Pub. by Abhinav II) S Asia.

Buddhist Monastic Life. Mohan Wijayaratna. Tr. by Claude Grangier & Steven Collins. 200p. (C). 1990. pap. 13.95 (*0-521-36708-5*) Cambridge U Pr.

Buddhist Monks & Monasteries of India: Their History & Their Contribution to Indian Culture. Sukumar Dutt. (C). 1989. 26.00 (*81-208-0498-8*, Pub. by Motilal Banarsidass II) S Asia.

Buddhist Monuments of China & South-East India. I. K. Sarma. (C). 1985. 54.00 (*0-8364-2184-1*, Pub. by Sundeep II) S Asia.

Buddhist Paintings-Japanese National Treasures: Restored Copies. Illus. by Miyahara Ryusen. 127p. 1981. 65.00 (*4-333-01039-X*, Pub. by Kosei Pub Co JA) C E Tuttle.

Buddhist Parables. E. W. Burlingame. 1972. 59.95 (*0-87968-803-3*) Gordon Pr.

Buddhist Parables. E. W. Burlingame. 1972. lib. bdg. 250.00 (*0-87968-494-1*) Krishna Pr.

Buddhist Parables. Eugene W. Burlingame. (C). 1991. reprint ed. 22.00 (*81-208-0738-3*, Pub. by Motilal Banarsidass II) S Asia.

Buddhist Path to Awakening: A Study of the Bodhi-Pakkhiya Dhamma. R. M. Gethin. LC 92-7819. (Brill's Indological Library: Vol. 7). (Illus.). xii, 382p. 1992. 111.50 (*90-04-09442-3*) E J Brill.

Buddhist Philosophy: A Historical Analysis. David J. Kalupahana. LC 75-20040. 212p. (C). 1976. pap. 11.95 (*0-8248-0392-2*, Eastwest Ctr Pr) UH Pr.

Buddhist Philosophy in India & Ceylon. A. Berriedale Keith. 1973. lib. bdg. 250.00 (*0-87968-181-0*) Krishna Pr.

Buddhist Philosophy in India & Ceylon. 2nd ed. A. Berriedale Keith. (C). 1979. 12.75 (*0-8364-2422-0*, Pub. by Munshiram Manoharial II) S Asia.

Buddhist Poetry of the Great Kamo Priestess: Daisaiin Senshi & "Hosshin Wakashu" Edward Kamens. LC 89-71219. (Michigan Monograph Series in Japanese Studies: No. 5). xiv, 171p. 1990. 32.95 (*0-939512-41-6*) U MI Japan.

Buddhist Praying Wheel. William Simpson. (C). 1991. reprint ed. 39.00 (*81-206-0647-7*, Pub. by Asian Educ Servs II) S Asia.

Buddhist Precept & Practice: Traditional Buddhism in the Rural Highlands of Ceylon. rev. ed. Richard Gombrich. (C). 1991. reprint ed. 27.50 (*81-208-0780-4*, Pub. by Motilal Banarsidass II) S Asia.

Buddhist Precepts & Practice. Richard F. Gombrich. 220p. 1992. 59.95 (*0-7103-0444-7*, A9510, Pub. by Kegan Paul Intl UK) Routledge Chapman & Hall.

Buddhist Priest Myoe: A Life of Dreams. Hayao Kawai. Tr. by Mark Unno. (Illus.). 237p. (C). 1992. 30.00 (*0-685-62265-7*) Lapis Pr.

Buddhist Priests Choose Christ. Kametani et al. Tr. by Satsuki Wakabayashi & John Terry. 140p. 1989. pap. 8.95 (*0-933704-77-1*) Dawn Pr.

Buddhist Psychological Ethics. 3rd ed. Tr. by Mrs. C. A. Davids. (C). 1974. reprint ed. 40.00 (*0-86013-062-2*, Pub. by Pali Text) Wisdom MA.

Buddhist Psychotherapy: An Eastern Therapeutical Approach to Mental Problems. H. S. Nissanka. 1993. 27.50 (*0-7069-6883-2*, Pub. by Vikas II) S Asia.

Buddhist Reflections: The Significance of the Teachings & Methods of Buddhism for the West. Lama A. Govinda. 272p. (Orig.). 1991. pap. 14.95 (*0-87728-714-7*) Weiser.

Buddhist Religion: A Historical Introduction. 3rd ed. Richard H. Robinson & Willard L. Johnson. 290p. (C). 1982. pap. 19.95 (*0-534-01027-X*) Intl Thomson.

Buddhist Remains in Afghanistan. R. B. Narain. 68p. 1991. 12.00 (*0-685-62631-8*, Pub. by Kala Prakashan) Nataraj Bks.

Buddhist Remains in Andhra & the History of Andhra Between 225 & 610 A.D. K. R. Subramanian. (C). 1989. reprint ed. 17.50 (*81-206-0444-X*, Pub. by Asian Educ Servs II) S Asia.

Buddhist Revival in China: With a Section of Photos by Henri Cartier-Bresson. Holmes Welch. LC 68-15645. (Harvard East Asian Ser.: Vol. 33). 424p. reprint ed. pap. 120.90 (*0-8357-7455-4*, 2017757) Bks Demand.

Buddhist Revival in Sri Lanka: Religious Tradition, Reinterpretation & Response. George D. Bond. Ed. by Frederick M. Denny. (Studies in Comparative Religion). 331p. (C). 1988. text ed. 34.95 (*0-87249-557-4*) U of SC Pr.

Buddhist Saints in India: A Study in Buddhist Values & Orientations. Reginald A. Ray. 528p. 1994. 49.95 (*0-19-507202-2*) OUP.

932

An Asterisk (*) at the beginning of an entry indicates that the title is appearing in BIP for the first time.

Buddhist Saints of the Forest & the Cult of Amulets: A Study in Charisma, Hagiography, Sectarianism & Millenial Buddhism. Stanley J. Tambiah. LC 83-15113. (Cambridge Studies in Social & Cultural Anthropology: No. 49). (Illus.). 432p. 1984. pap. 32.95 (*0-521-27787-6*) Cambridge U Pr.

Buddhist Sangha: Paradigm of the Ideal Human Society. Sunanda Putuwar. 136p. (C). 1991. lib. bdg. 34.00 (*0-8191-8279-6*); pap. text ed. 19.50 (*0-8191-7842-X*) U Pr of Amer.

Buddhist Savants of Kashmir - Their Contribution Abroad. A. Kaul. 167p. 1987. 30.95 (*0-318-36659-2*) Asia Bk Corp.

Buddhist Scriptures. Tr. by Edward Conze. (Classics Ser.). (Orig.). 1959. pap. 9.95 (*0-14-044088-7*, Penguin Classics) Viking Penguin.

Buddhist Sects in India. 2nd ed. Nalinaksha Dutt. 1977. 9.00 (*0-88386-971-3*) S Asia.

Buddhist Sects of Japan: Their Histories, Philosophical Doctrines & Sanctuaries. Emile Steinilber-Oberlin. Tr. by Marc Loge. 1977. lib. bdg. 39.95 (*0-8490-1559-6*) Gordon Pr.

Buddhist Sects of Japan, Their History, Philosophical Doctrines & Sanctuaries. Emile Steinilber-Oberlin. Tr. by Marc Loge. LC 78-109854. (Illus.). 303p. 1971. reprint ed. text ed. 35.00 (*0-8371-4349-7*, STBS, Greenwood Pr) Greenwood.

Buddhist Sociology. Nandasena Ratnapala. (Bibliotheca Indo-Buddhica Ser.: No. 117). 1993. 21.00 (*81-7030-363-X*) S Asia.

Buddhist Spirituality I: Indian, Southeast Asian, Tibetan, & Early Chinese. Ed. by Takeuchi Yoshinori et al. 440p. 1995. reprint ed. pap. 19.95 (*0-8245-1452-1*) Crossroad NY.

Buddhist Spirituality, Vol. 1: Indian, Southeast Asian, Tibetan, Early Chinese. Ed. by Takeuchi Yoshinori et al. LC 93-9360. (World Spirituality Ser.: Vol. 8). 500p. 1993. 49.50 (*0-8245-1277-4*) Crossroad NY.

Buddhist Stories. Paul Dahlke. Tr. by Bhikkhu Silacara. LC 71-106285. (Short Story Index Reprint Ser.). 1977. 21.95 (*0-8369-3322-2*) Ayer.

Buddhist Stories. Tr. by F. L. Woodward. LC 78-70141. reprint ed. 20.00 (*0-404-17414-0*) AMS Pr.

Buddhist Studies: Ancient & Modern. Philip Denwood & Alexander Piatigorsky. 220p. 1981. 45.00 (*0-7007-0153-2*, Pub. by Curzon Pr UK) Humanities.

Buddhist Studies in Honour of I. B. Horner. Ed. by L. Cousins et al. LC 74-77963. 275p. 1974. lib. bdg. 99.00 (*90-277-0473-2*) Kluwer Ac.

Buddhist Studies in the People's Republic of China, 1990-1991. Ed. & Tr. by Michael R. Saso. 1993. pap. text ed. 14.00 (*0-8248-1464-9*) UH Pr.

Buddhist Studies Nineteen Thirty-Four to Nineteen Seventy-Two. Edward Conze. 512p. 1977. reprint ed. 20.00 (*0-686-48400-2*) Wheelwright Pr.

Buddhist Sutras: Origin, Development, Transmission. Kogen Mizuno. (Illus.). 220p. 1982. pap. 10.95 (*4-333-01028-4*, Pub. by Kosei Pub Co JA) C E Tuttle.

Buddhist Suttas. Rhys Davids. 1972. lib. bdg. 250.00 (*0-87968-511-5*) Krishna Pr.

***Buddhist Symbols in Tibetan Culture.** Dagyab Rinpoche. Tr. by Maurice Walshe. (Illus.). 160p. (Orig.). 1995. pap. 14.95 (*0-614-07220-4*) Wisdom MA.

Buddhist Symbols on Japanese Swords. Hawley. 1986. reprint ed. pap. 4.95 (*0-910704-51-1*) Hawley.

Buddhist Tantras. Alex Wayman. (C). 1990. reprint ed. 21.00 (*81-208-0699-9*, Pub. by Motilal Banarsidass II) S Asia.

Buddhist Tantras: Light on Indo-Tibetan Esotericism. Alex Wayman. LC 91-22348. 247p. 1992. 49.95 (*0-7103-0445-5*, A6764, Pub. by Kegan Paul Intl UK) Routledge Chapman & Hall.

Buddhist Teaching of Totality. Garma C. Chang. LC 70-136965. 1971. 32.50 (*0-271-01142-4*); pap. 15.95 (*0-271-01179-3*) Pa St U Pr.

***Buddhist Terminological Dictionary: The Mongolian Mahavyutpatti.** Ed. by Alice Sarkozi. (Bibliotheca Orientalis Hungarica Ser.: Vol. XLII). 504p. 1995. 78.00 (*963-05-6871-3*, Pub. by A K HU) Intl Spec Bk.

Buddhist Texts from Japan, 3 pts. in 1 vol. Friedrich M. Mueller. LC 73-18824. (Illus.). reprint ed. 34.50 (*0-404-11430-X*) AMS Pr.

***Buddhist Texts Through the Ages.** Ed. by E. Conze et al. 323p. 1995. pap. 15.95 (*1-85168-107-8*) Onewrld Pubns.

Buddhist Texts Through the Ages. Ed. by Edward Conze et al. 323p. 1992. 42.50 (*0-685-68011-8*, Pub. by M Manoharial II) Coronet Bks.

Buddhist Texts Through the Ages. Edward Conze. (C). 1992. 28.00 (*81-215-0574-7*, Pub. by Munshiram Manoharial II) S Asia.

Buddhist Theory of Perception: With Special Reference to Pramana Varttika of Kharmakirti. C. S. Vyas. (C). 1991. 20.00 (*81-7013-083-2*, Pub. by Navarang II) S Asia.

Buddhist Thought & Ritual. Intro. by David J. Kalupahana. LC 90-7065. (C). 1990. 24.95 (*0-89226-088-2*, New Era Bks); pap. 12.95 (*0-89226-089-0*, New Era Bks) Paragon Hse.

Buddhist Thought in India. Edward Conze. 1967. pap. 17.95 (*0-472-06129-1*, 129, Ann Arbor Bks) U of Mich Pr.

Buddhist Tradition: In India, China & Japan. Ed. by William T. Debary. 448p. 1972. pap. 8.76 (*0-394-71696-5*, V702, Vin) Random.

Buddhist Trends in Southeast Asia. Ed. by Trevor Ling. 189p. 1993. 38.45 (*981-3035-80-3*, Pub. by Inst SE Asian Studies SI); pap. 25.00 (*981-3035-81-1*, Pub. by Inst SE Asian Studies SI) Ashgate Pub Co.

Buddhist View of the Future of Mankind. Kosho Ko-nyo Otani. 19p. (ENG & JPN.). 1988. pap. 3.50 (*0-914910-94-9*) Buddhist Bks.

Buddhist Vision. Alex Kennedy. (Illus.). 222p. (Orig.). 1987. pap. 8.95 (*0-87728-620-5*) Weiser.

Buddhist Vision for Renewing Society. S. Sivaraksa. 243p. 1981. 7.95 (*0-318-36653-3*) Asia Bk Corp.

Buddhist Wisdom. George Grimm. (C). 1989. 11.00 (*81-208-0510-0*) S Asia.

***Buddhist Writings on Meditation & Daily Practice: The Serene Reflection Meditation Tradition.** Ed. by P. T. Jiyu-Kennett & Daizui MacPhillamy. Tr. by Hubert Nearman. 382p. (Orig.). (C). 1994. pap. 12.00 (*0-930066-15-4*) Shasta Abbey.

***Buddhist Yoga: A Comprehensive Course.** Thomas Cleary. 1995. pap. 10.00 (*1-57062-018-0*) Shambhala Pubns.

Buddhistic Studies. Ed. by Bimala C. Law. LC 78-72463. reprint ed. 74.50 (*0-404-17335-7*) AMS Pr.

Buddhist's Shakespeare: Affirming Self-Deconstructions. James Howe. LC 93-31807. 1994. write for info. (*0-8386-3522-9*) Fairleigh Dickinson.

Buddie & I. Sallie Robinson. 54p. 1987. reprint ed. pap. 2.95 (*0-8341-1216-7*) Beacon Hill.

***Buddies.** Nancy H. Brewer. 200p. 1995. pap. 7.95 (*1-56901-796-4*) NW Pub.

Buddies. Mary Gallagher. 1982. pap. 2.75 (*0-8222-0160-7*) Dramatists Play.

***Buddies.** Peggy Lindt. (Illus.). 32p. (J). 1995. 9.95 (*0-87905-663-0*) Gibbs Smith Pub.

Buddies. Ethan Mordden. (Stonewall Inn Editions Ser.). 256p. 1987. pap. 8.95 (*0-312-01005-2*) St Martin.

Buddies. Barbara Park. (YA). (gr. 7 up). 1986. pap. 2.95 (*0-380-69992-3*, Flare) Avon.

Buddies & Bobtails. Bob Kornegay. 1990. 17.95 (*0-9617591-6-X*) MS River Pub.

Budding Botanist: Investigations with Plants. Evalyn Hoover et al. Ed. by Gretchen Winkleman & Judith Hillen. (Illus.). 109p. (Orig.). (J). (gr. 3-6). 1993. pap. text ed. 14.95 (*1-881431-40-1*, 1213) AIMS Educ Fnd.

Budding Fig Tree. Roy R. Newman & Pat Brooks. LC 87-62894. 1988. pap. text ed. 2.50 (*0-932050-39-5*) New Puritan.

Budding Prospects. T. Coraghessan Boyle. (Contemporary American Fiction Ser.). 336p. 1985. mass mkt. 6.95 (*0-14-008151-8*, Penguin Bks) Viking Penguin.

Budding Revolution in State Income Taxes. Steven D. Gold. (Legislative Finance Papers: No. 61). (C). 1987. pap. 10.00 (*1-55516-061-1*, 5101-0061) Natl Conf State Legis.

***Buddist Bible, the Favorite Scriptures of the Zen Sect.** Ed. by Dwight Goddard. LC 78-72434. reprint ed. 65.00 (*0-404-17297-0*) AMS Pr.

***Buddist Psychotherapy: An Eastern Approach to Mental Problems.** H. S. Nissanka. (C). 1995. 24.00x (*0-7069-9003-X*, Pub. by Vikas II) S Asia.

***Buddy: A Story about Tolerance & Understanding Differences.** Paulette Berube. 24p. (J). (gr. 1-4). 1994. 5.95 (*1-884063-24-1*) Mar Co Prods.

Buddy Badger. Dave Sargent & Pat Sargent. (Animal Pride Ser.). (Illus.). 48p. (Orig.). (J). (gr. k-8). 1993. text ed. 11.95 (*1-56763-036-7*); pap. text ed. 5.95 (*1-56763-037-5*) Ozark Pub.

Buddy DeFranco: A Biographical Portrait & Discography. John Kuehn & Arne Astrup. LC 93-19962. (Studies in Jazz: Vol. 12). (Illus.). 278p. 1993. 39.50 (*0-8108-2538-4*) Scarecrow.

Buddy Guy - Damn Right I've Got the Blues. (Illus.). 104p. (Orig.). 1994. pap. 18.95 (*0-7935-1918-7*, 00694854) H Leonard.

Buddy Holly Golden Anniversary Songbook. Leonard, Hal, Publishing Staff. 1991. 14.95 (*0-88188-557-6*, HL00383750) H Leonard.

Buddy Holly Is Alive & Well on Ganymede. Bradley Denton. 304p. 1992. mass mkt. 4.50 (*0-380-71876-6*, AvoNova) Avon.

***Buddy Holly Story.** Tobler. Date not set. per. 9.95 (*0-85965-035-9*, Pub. by Plexus Pub UK) InBook.

***Buddy Love Now on Video.** Ilene Cooper. LC 95-1767. 128p. (YA). (gr. 5 up). 1995. 13.95 (*0-06-024663-4*); lib. bdg. 13.89 (*0-06-024664-2*) HarpC Child Bks.

***Buddy Reading: Cross-Age Tutoring in a Multicultural, School.** Samway et al. 144p. 1995. pap. text ed. 16.00 (*0-435-08840-8*) Heinemann.

Buddy Rich's Modern Interpretation of Snare Drum Rudiments. Buddy Rich & Henry Adler. (Illus.). 100p. 1942. pap. 9.95 (*0-8256-1003-6*, AM36419) Music Sales.

Buddy Rock's Race. Kate Green. (Fossil Family Tales Ser.). (Illus.). 32p. (J). (gr. 1-4). 1992. lib. bdg. 22.79 (*0-89565-781-3*) Childs World.

Buddy Stall's Louisiana Potpourri. Gaspar J. Stall. 208p. write for info. (*0-8187-0142-0*) Harlo Press.

Buddy Stall's Louisiana Potpourri. Gasper J. Stall. LC 91-76491. (Illus.). 272p. 1991. 17.95 (*0-88289-913-9*) Pelican.

Buddy Stall's New Orleans. Gaspar J. Stall. LC 90-40789. (Illus.). 192p. 1990. 17.95 (*0-88289-813-2*) Pelican.

Buddy System. Diane Ames. (Camp Counselors Ser.: No. 2). (YA). 1992. mass mkt. 3.50 (*0-06-106075-5*, Harp PBks) HarpC.

Buddy the Beaver. Illus. by Bob Storms. (World of Animals Ser.). 24p. (Orig.). (J). (gr. k-4). 1993. pap. 4.95 (*0-89346-529-1*) Heian Intl.

***Buddy, the First Seeing Eye Dog.** Eva Moore. LC 95-6725. (Hello Reader! Ser., Level 4). (Illus.). (J). 1996. write for info. (*0-590-26585-7*) Scholastic Inc.

Buddy Trap. Sheri C. Sinykin. LC 90-49994. 144p. (J). (gr. 3-7). 1991. text ed. 13.95 (*0-689-31674-7*, Atheneum Bks Young) S&S Childrens.

***Buddy's: Meditations on Desire.** Persky. Date not set. per. 9.95 (*0-921586-19-1*, Pub. by New Star Bks CN) InBook.

Buddy's Shadow. Shirley Becker. (Illus.). 32p. (J). (ps-2). 1991. pap. 6.95 (*0-944727-08-5*) Jason & Nordic Pubs.

Buddy's Shadow. Shirley Becker. (Illus.). 32p. (J). (ps-2). 1992. reprint ed. 13.95 (*0-944727-19-0*) Jason & Nordic Pubs.

***Budgee Budgee Cottontail.** Jo Mora. Ed. by Steve Mitchell. (Illus.). (J). (gr. 3). 1994. 24.95 (*0-922029-23-7*) D Stoecklein Photo.

Budgerigar Handbook. Ernest Hart. 17.95 (*0-87666-414-1*, H-901) TFH Pubns.

Budgerigars. (Colorguide Ser.). 1982. pap. 6.95 (*0-940842-09-2*) South Group.

Budgerigars. Carol Kyle. (Illus.). 80p. 1989. pap. 5.95 (*0-86622-714-8*, PB-145) TFH Pubns.

Budgerigars. George A. Radtke. Orig. Title: Wellensittiche-Mein Hobby. (Illus.). 1979. 9.95 (*0-87666-984-4*, KW-011) TFH Pubns.

Budgerigars. Zuza Vrbova. (Junior Pet Care Ser.). (Illus.). 48p. (J). (gr. 2 up). 1990. lib. bdg. 9.95 (*0-86622-556-0*, J-006) TFH Pubns.

Budgerigars, Look & Learn. Tammy Halaburda. 64p. pap. 7.95 (*0-7938-0058-7*, KD018) TFH Pubns.

Budgerigars, Training. Risa Teitler. (Illus.). 96p. 1979. 9.95 (*0-87666-887-2*, KW-070) TFH Pubns.

Budget: A Translation. Rene Stourm. (Brookings Institution Reprint Ser.). reprint ed. lib. bdg. 39.00 (*0-697-00169-5*) Irvington.

Budget: On Commercial & Colonial Policy. Robert Torrens. LC 68-58032. (Reprints of Economic Classics Ser.). 427p. 1970. reprint ed. 45.00 (*0-678-00558-3*) Kelley.

Budget Access Europe: The Affordable Way to Tour Europe. Access Guides Staff. (Access Travel Guides Ser.). (Illus.). 224p. 1994. pap. 18.00 (*0-06-277120-5*, Harper Ref) HarpC.

Budget Analysis As a Monitoring Technique: Training Guide & Resource Materials. Joseph C. Henson. (Illus.). 120p. 1983. 12.00 (*0-941077-08-X*, 35,968) NCLS Inc.

Budget Analyst. Jack Rudman. (Career Examination Ser.: C-1143). 1994. pap. 34.95 (*0-8373-1143-8*) Nat Learn.

Budget Assistant (USPS) Jack Rudman. (Career Examination Ser.: C-848). 1994. pap. 29.95 (*0-8373-0848-8*) Nat Learn.

Budget Auto Restoration. Bert Mills. (Illus.). 288p. 1990. pap. 24.95 (*0-87938-405-0*) Motorbooks Intl.

Budget Book. Robert Koster. 89p. (Orig.). 1989. pap. text ed. 30.00 (*0-685-29030-1*) Quantum Films.

Budget Book. 2nd ed. John L. McCabe. 45p. (Orig.). 1987. pap. 3.95 (*0-945326-06-8*) Intrawest Pub.

Budget Builder. Lester J. Giese et al. (Orig.). 1989. pap. text ed. 34.95 (*0-910049-05-X*) Lateral Thinkers.

Budget Builder I for Community Associations. Lester J. Giese. LC 82-90784. 63p. 1982. 21.95 (*0-910049-01-7*) Lateral Thinkers.

***Budget Clerk.** (Career Examination Ser.: Series 1). Date not set. pap. 23.95 (*0-8373-3696-1*) Nat Learn.

Budget Deficit: The Causes, the Costs, the Outlook. Leonard J. Santow. 1988. 21.95 (*0-317-03939-3*) NY Inst Finance.

Budget Deficit: The Causes, the Costs, the Outlook. Leonard J. Santow. (Illus.). 320p. 1988. pap. 24.95 (*0-13-085085-3*) P-H.

Budget Deficit: The Crisis of the Eighties. Melvin Greenhut & Charles W. Smithson. Ed. by Steve Pejovich & Henry Dethloff. (Series on Public Issues: No. 13). 22p. 1984. pap. 2.00 (*0-86599-023-9*) PERC.

Budget Deficits & Economic Activity in Asia. Kanhaya L. Gupta. (Illus.). 224p. 1991. 74.50 (*0-415-05540-7*, A5831) Routledge.

Budget Deficits & Economic Performance. Richard C. Burdekin & Farrokh K. Langdana. LC 92-5393. 224p. 1992. 59.95 (*0-415-07262-X*, A9686) Routledge.

Budget Dining & Lodging in New England. 3rd ed. Fran Sullivan & Frank Sullivan. (Illus.). 304p. (Orig.). 1992. pap. 12.95 (*0-87106-190-2*) Globe Pequot.

Budget Director. Jack Rudman. (Career Examination Ser.: C-2648). 1994. pap. 39.95 (*0-8373-2648-6*) Nat Learn.

Budget Enforcement Act of Nineteen Ninety: One Year After. Susan M. Wolfe & Richard E. May. (State-Federal Issue Brief Ser.: Vol. 4, No. 4). 10p. 1991. pap. text ed. 6.50 (*1-55516-893-0*, 8500-0404) Natl Conf State Legis.

Budget Examiner. Jack Rudman. (Career Examination Ser.: C-97). 1994. pap. 29.95 (*0-8373-0097-5*) Nat Learn.

Budget Examining Trainee. Jack Rudman. (Career Examination Ser.: C-98). 1994. pap. 27.95 (*0-8373-0098-3*) Nat Learn.

Budget Flying: A Private Pilot's Guide. 2nd ed. Dan Ramsey. (Illus.). 192p. 1989. 24.95 (*0-8306-9448-X*) TAB Bks.

Budget Guide to Britain. American Automobile Assn. Staff. 1992. pap. 12.95 (*1-56251-006-1*) AAA.

Budget Guide to France. American Automobile Assn. Staff. 1992. pap. 12.95 (*1-56251-007-X*) AAA.

Budget Guide to Italy. American Automobile Assn. Staff. 1992. pap. 12.95 (*1-56251-008-8*) AAA.

***Budget Guide to Retail Store Planning & Design.** 2nd ed. Jeff Grant. (Illus.). 96p. 1995. pap. 24.95 (*0-944094-10-4*) ST Pubns.

Budget Imbalance & the External Influences: A Study of the Legislative Budget Board of Texas. Glen C. Cope & Thomas Keel. (Policy Research Project Report Ser.: No. 99). 46p. 1992. 8.00 (*0-89940-707-2*) LBJ Sch Pub Aff.

Budget in the American Commonwealths. Eugene E. Agger. LC 75-158232. (Columbia University. Studies in the Social Sciences: No. 66). reprint ed. 39.50 (*0-404-51066-3*) AMS Pr.

Budget Innovation in the States. Allen Schick. LC 76-161594. 235p. reprint ed. pap. 67.00 (*0-8357-7456-2*, 2025405) Bks Demand.

Budget Kit. Judy Lawrence. 97p. 1992. pap. 15.95 (*0-7931-0495-5*, 560874) Dearborn Finan.

***Budget Lodging Guide.** Orig. Title: U. S. & Worldwide Travel Accomodations Guide. 618p. 1995. pap. 14.95 (*0-945499-06-X*) B&J Pubns.

Budget Management: A Reader in Local Government Financial Management. Jack Rabin et al. (Public Budgeting Laboratory Ser.). 258p. (Orig.). 1983. pap. 16.95 (*0-89854-090-9*) U of GA Inst Govt.

Budget-Maximizing Bureaucrat: Appraisals & Evidence. Ed. by Andre Blais & Stephane Dion. LC 90-29888. (Policy & Institutional Studies). 384p. 1991. 49.95 (*0-8229-3679-8*) U of Pittsburgh Pr.

***Budget Object Classification: Origins & Recent Trends.** (Illus.). 74p. (Orig.). (C). 1995. pap. text ed. 35.00x (*0-7881-1702-5*) Diane Pub.

Budget of Paradoxes, 2 Vols, Set. Augustus De Morgan. Ed. by David E. Smith. (Select Bibliographies Reprint Ser.). 1977. 60.95 (*0-8369-5119-0*) Ayer.

Budget of the United Nations. Syracuse University Staff. LC 78-2451. (Carnegie Endowment for International Peace, United Nations Studies: No. 1). 63p. 1978. reprint ed. text ed. 45.00 (*0-313-20328-8*, BUUN, Greenwood Pr) Greenwood.

***Budget of the United States: Historical Tables.** 1995. lib. bdg. 251.99 (*0-8490-6736-7*) Gordon Pr.

Budget of the United States Government, Fiscal Year, 1991. (Illus.). 1583p. 1990. per., pap. 38.00 (*0-16-017723-5*, S/N 041-001-003) USGPO.

***Budget of U. S. Government: 1996 Analytical Perspectives.** 1996. pap. 24.00 (*0-16-045413-1*) Claitors.

***Budget of U. S. Government: 1996 Appendix.** 1996. pap. 42.00 (*0-16-045410-7*) Claitors.

***Budget of U. S. Government: 1996 Fiscal Year.** 1996. pap. 17.00 (*0-16-045409-3*) Claitors.

Budget Officer. Jack Rudman. (Career Examination Ser.: C-1144). 1994. pap. 29.95 (*0-8373-1144-6*) Nat Learn.

***Budget Policy: Issues in Capping Mandatory Spending.** (Illus.). 100p. (Orig.). (C). 1995. pap. text ed. 30.00x (*0-7881-1687-8*) Diane Pub.

Budget Policy: Prompt Action Necessary to Avert Long-Term Damage to the Economy. (Illus.). 116p. (Orig.). (C). 1993. pap. text ed. 30.00 (*1-56806-334-2*) Diane Pub.

Budget Processes in the States, 1992. Marcia Howard. 40p. (Orig.). 1992. pap. text ed. 20.00 (*1-55877-154-9*) Natl Governor.

Budget Puzzle: Understanding Federal Spending. John F. Cogan et al. 176p. (C). 1993. 32.50 (*0-8047-2091-6*); pap. 11.95 (*0-8047-2092-4*) Stanford U Pr.

Budget Puzzle: Understanding Federal Spending. John F. Cogan et al. LC 93-31627. 1994. 30.00 (*0-8047-2322-2*); pap. 12.95 (*0-8047-2323-0*) Stanford U Pr.

Budget Quartet: Critical Policy & Management Issues. Donald Axelrod. LC 88-6194. 204p. (Orig.). (C). 1989. pap. text ed. 16.00 (*0-312-02386-3*) St Martin.

Budget Reform for Government: A Comprehensive Allocation & Management System (CAMS) Michael Babunakis. LC 82-354. xviii, 231p. 1982. text ed. 49.95 (*0-89930-016-2*, BBG/, Quorum Bks) Greenwood.

Budget Repair Guide. Gene Constant. 1993. 13.95 (*0-533-10457-2*) Vantage.

Budget Shopper's Guide to the Delaware Valley. rev. ed. Thomas L. Widing. LC 80-84929. 160p. (Orig.). 1981. pap. 3.95 (*0-917908-03-1*) Hamilton Hse.

Budget Skiers Guidebook-Western U. S. rev. ed. Michael J. Studebaker. LC 84-62474. (Budget Travel Bks.: No. 1). 160p. 1985. pap. 6.95 (*0-932145-27-2*) Glastonbury Pr.

Budget Standards for the United Kingdom: Constructing the Budget Standards. Jonathan Bradshaw. (Studies in Cash & Care). 272p. 1993. 59.95 (*1-85628-591-X*, Pub. by Avebury Pub UK) Ashgate Pub Co.

Budget Supervisor. Jack Rudman. (Career Examination Ser.: C-2684). 1994. pap. 34.95 (*0-8373-2684-2*) Nat Learn.

Budget Technician. Jack Rudman. (Career Examination Ser.: C-2170). 1994. pap. 27.95 (*0-8373-2170-0*) Nat Learn.

Budget Traveler's Guide to Great Off-Beat Vacations in the United States & Canada. Paige Palmer. LC 90-48747. 64p. (Orig.). 1991. pap. 4.95 (*0-87576-149-6*) Pilot Bks.

Budget Vacationers Guidebook: Western U. S. rev. ed. Michael J. Studebaker. LC 85-80299. (Budget Travel Bks.: No. 2). 336p. 1986. pap. 8.95 (*0-932145-37-X*) Glastonbury Pr.

Budgetary & Economic Analysis of the North American Free Trade Agreement. (Illus.). 117p. (Orig.). (C). 1993. pap. text ed. 50.00 (*1-56806-545-0*) Diane Pub.

Budgetary Control in Academic Libraries. Murray S. Martin. LC 76-5648. (Foundations in Library & Information Science: Vol. 5). 219p. 1978. lib. bdg. 73.25 (*0-89232-010-9*) Jai Pr.

***Budgetary Decisions: A Public Choice Approach.** Dirk-Jan Kraan. 280p. (C). 1995. write for info. (*0-521-41871-2*); pap. write for info. (*0-521-55867-0*) Cambridge U Pr.

Budgetary Forecasting in Local Government: New Tools & Techniques. Howard Frank. LC 93-6765. 232p. 1993. text ed. 55.00 (*0-89930-725-6*, FBH/, Quorum Bks) Greenwood.

Budgetary Policy, International & Intertemporal Trade in the Global Economy. Ed. by W. H. Buiter. (Lectures in Economics Ser.: Vol. 10). 128p. 1989. 64.00 (*0-444-87135-7*, North Holland) Elsevier.

Budgetary Politics: The Finances of the European Communities. Helen Wallace. LC 81-141517. (Studies in Contemporary Europe: 1). 120p. reprint ed. pap. 34.20 (*0-8357-7457-0*, 2023262) Bks Demand.

Budgetary Politics in American Governments. James J. Gosling. 240p. (Orig.). (C). 1992. pap. text ed. 28.50 (*0-8013-0393-1*, 78172) Longman.

Budgeting: A Comparative Theory of Budgetary Processes. rev. ed. Aaron Wildavsky. 430p. (C). 1985. pap. 18.95 (*0-88738-604-0*) Transaction Pubs.

B

An Asterisk (*) at the beginning of an entry indicates that the title is appearing in BIP for the first time.

Budgeting: A Guide for Practising Managers. V. G. Murti. 188p. 1984. text ed. 27.50 (*0-86590-560-6*, Pub. by Sterling Pubs II) Apt Bks.

Budgeting: Profit Planning & Control. 4th ed. Glenn A. Welsch. (Illus.). 656p. 1976. text ed. write for info. (*0-13-085712-2*) P-H.

Budgeting: Profit Planning & Control. 5th ed. Glenn A. Welsch et al. 656p. (C). 1988. text ed. 75.00 (*0-13-085754-8*) P-H.

Budgeting & Cost Management for Medical Groups. Thomas A. Feuerstein & Craig A. Anderson. Ed. by Center for Research in Ambulatory Health Care Administration Staff. 176p. (Orig.). 1990. pap. 22.00 (*0-933948-22-0*, 2277) Ctr Res Ambulatory.

Budgeting & Financial Management Handbook. Edward J. McMillan. LC 94-20960. 1994. 48.00 (*0-88034-089-4*) Am Soc Assn Execs.

Budgeting & Profit Planning Manual. 2nd ed. James P. Willson. 1988. 145.00 (*0-7913-0073-0*) Warren Gorham & Lamont.

Budgeting & Profit Planning Manual. 2nd suppl. ed. James P. Willson. 1991. Supplemented annually, write for info. 51.50 (*0-7913-1003-5*) Warren Gorham & Lamont.

Budgeting & the Political Process in Libraries: Simulation Games. Peter Hamon et al. (Illus.). 70p. (Orig.). 1992. pap. text ed. 20.00 (*0-87287-855-4*) Libs Unl.

B

Budgeting At Your Finger Tips. Eric Gelb. 16p. (Orig.). 1994. pap. 2.95 (*0-9631289-4-9*) Career Advan.

***Budgeting at Your Finger Tips Lesson Plan.** Eric Gelb. (Illus.). 32p. (Orig.). (C). Date not set. teacher ed 10.00 (*0-9631289-5-7*) Career Advan.

Budgeting, Auditing, & Evaluation: Functions & Integration in Seven Governments. Ed. by Andrew Gray et al. LC 92-14731. 152p. (C). 1993. 39.95 (*1-56000-071-6*) Transaction Pubs.

***Budgeting Basics & Beyond: A Complete Step-by-Step Guide for Nonfinancial Managers.** Jae K. Shim & Joel G. Siegel. LC 94-21394. 1994. 49.95 (*0-13-085572-3*); pap. 19.95 (*0-13-312232-8*) P-H.

Budgeting Essentials: Personal Financing to Save Money Time & Effort. Cal Augusta. Ed. by Thomas Sliwiak. LC 94-76684. 64p. 1994. pap. 5.95 (*0-9638761-1-2*) Graphic Thought.

Budgeting for a Small Business. Terry Dickey. Ed. by Philip Gerould. LC 92-54352. (Small Business & Entrepreneurship Ser.). 175p. (Orig.). 1993. pap. 15.95 (*1-56052-171-6*) Crisp Pubns.

Budgeting for America. 2nd ed. John Cranford. 225p. 1989. pap. 19.95 (*0-87187-441-5*) Congr Quarterly.

Budgeting for Data Processing. Anker Andersen. 49p. pap. 7.95 (*0-86641-089-9*) Inst Mgmt Account.

***Budgeting for Disarmament: The Costs of War & Peace.** Michael Renner. 70p. (Orig.). 1994. pap. 5.00 (*1-878071-23-8*) Worldwatch Inst.

Budgeting for Financial Managers. Jae K. Shim & Joel G. Siegel. LC 93-35670. 1993. 69.95 (*0-13-085564-2*) P-H.

Budgeting for Higher Education at the State Level: Enigma, Paradox, & Ritual. Ed. by Daniel T. Layzell & Jan W. Lyddon. LC 90-63845. (ASHE-ERIC Higher Education Report Ser.: No. 4). 110p. 1990. pap. 17.00 (*1-878380-01-X*) GWU Schl E&HD.

***Budgeting for Modern Government.** 2nd ed. Donald Axelrod. 464p. (C). 1994. pap. text ed. 42.00 (*0-312-08417-X*) St Martin.

Budgeting for National Objectives. Committee for Economic Development. LC 66-17307. 72p. 1966. lib. bdg. 2.50 (*0-87186-721-4*); pap. 1.50 (*0-87186-021-X*) Comm Econ Dev.

Budgeting for Nebraska Local Governments. John W. Swain. 49p. (Orig.). 1983. pap. 3.50 (*1-55719-086-0*) U NE CPAR.

Budgeting for Newspapers. rev. ed. David Pew & Jay Matthews. (Illus.). 55p. 1989. pap. 49.95 (*1-877888-11-7*) Intl Newspaper.

***Budgeting for Non-Financial Managers: Prepare Effective Budgets & Stick to Them.** Ian Maitland. (Institute of Management Ser.). 275p. 1995. pap. 43.50 (*0-273-61712-5*, Pub. by Pitman Pub Ltd UK) Trans-Atl Phila.

Budgeting for Nonprofits. 2nd ed. Christian P. Frederiksen. LC 79-89135. 1980. ring bd. 59.00 (*0-916664-13-9*) Datarex Corp.

Budgeting for Not-for-Profit Organizations. Robert D. Vinter & Rhea K. Kish. LC 84-47855. 390p. 1984. text ed. 35.00 (*0-02-933410-1*) Free Pr.

Budgeting for Sustainability. John C. Honig. (Topics in Operations Research Ser.). v, 363p. 1986. pap. 12.50 (*1-877640-14-X*) Op Res Soc.

Budgeting for the Law School Library in the 1990's. 2nd ed. Betty W. Taylor & Dan F. Henke. (Law Library Information Reports: Vol. 2). (Illus.). 56p. 1993. pap. text ed. 100.00 (*0-87802-094-2*) Glanville.

Budgeting Guide for Nonprofit Administrators & Volunteers. Michael Burns. 64p. 1990. pap. text ed. 19.95 (*1-882445-04-X*) D A T A.

Budgeting in Texas: Process, Problems, Prospects. Ed. by Aman Khan. 232p. (C). 1991. lib. bdg. 47.50 (*0-8191-8305-9*) U Pr of Amer.

***Budgeting, Policy, Politics: An Appreciation of Aaron Wildavsky.** Ed. by Naomi Caiden & Joseph White. 148p. (C). 1994. 29.95 (*1-56000-192-5*) Transaction Pubs.

Budgeting Problems. G. Kenneth Nelson & Joe J. Cramer, Jr. LC 68-28845. (Illus.). 182p. reprint ed. 51.90 (*0-8357-9849-6*, 2012524) Bks Demand.

Budgeting Public Funds: The Decision Process in an Urban School District. Donald Gerwin. LC 69-17326. 184p. reprint ed. pap. 52.50 (*0-8357-7458-9*, 2023726) Bks Demand.

Budgeting Techniques for Libraries & Information Centers. Michael E. Koenig. LC 80-27698. (Professional Development Ser.: Vol. 1). (Illus.). 75p. reprint ed. pap. 25.00 (*0-8357-7459-7*, 2020935) Bks Demand.

Budgeting Your Cash: The Great Balancing Act. A. Jay Hirsch. (Illus.). 162p. (Orig.). 1983. pap. 29.95 (*0-9610920-0-9*) A J Hirsch.

Budgets: An Analytical & Procedural Handbook for Government & Non-Profit Organizations. Michael Babunakis. LC 76-5323. (Illus.). 257p. 1976. text ed. 69.50 (*0-8371-8900-4*, BBP/, Greenwood Pr) Greenwood.

Budgets & Strategy: The Road to Offtackle. Ed. by Steven T. Ross & David A. Rosenberg. (America's Plans for War Against the Soviet Union 1945-1950 Ser.). 432p. 1990. 50.00 (*0-8240-7161-1*) Garland.

Budgets for Acquisitions: Strategies for Serials, Monographs, & Electronic Formats. Ed. by Sul H. Lee. LC 91-12603. (Journal of Library Administration). (Illus.). 133p. 1991. lib. bdg. 29.95 (*1-56024-158-6*) Haworth Pr.

Budgie at Bendick's Point. Duchess of York, pseud. (Illus.). (J). (ps-1). 1989. pap. 13.00 (*0-671-67684-9*, S&S Bks Young Read) S&S Childrens.

Budgie Goes to Sea. Duchess of York, pseud. (Illus.). 40p. (J). (ps-1). 1991. pap. 13.00 (*0-671-73474-1*, S&S Bks Young Read) S&S Childrens.

Budgie the Little Helicopter. Duchess of York, pseud. (Illus.). (J). (ps-1). 1989. pap. 14.00 (*0-671-67683-0*, S&S Bks Young Read) S&S Childrens.

Budgies As a Hobby. Evelyn Miller. (Save Our Planet Ser.). (Illus.). 98p. 1991. pap. 7.95 (*0-86622-416-5*, TT002) TFH Pubns.

Budgies As a New Pet. Barry Martin. (Illus.). 64p. (Orig.). 1990. pap. 5.95 (*0-86622-611-7*, TU-004) TFH Pubns.

Budgies for Those Who Care. Oliver Denton. (Illus.). 32p. 1994. pap. 3.95 (*0-7938-1386-7*, B108) TFH Pubns.

Budo: The Teachings of Morihei Ueshiba, the Founder of Aikido. Morihei Ueshiba. (Illus.). 112p. 1991. 19.00 (*4-7700-1532-1*) Kodansha.

Budoshoshinshu: The Warrior's Primer. William S. Wilson. Ed. by Todd Henschell. (History & Philosophy Ser.). (Illus.). 180p. (Orig.). 1984. pap. 12.95 (*0-89750-096-2*, 433) Ohara Pubns.

Bud's Easy Note Taking Kit. James Roberts. 44p. (C). 1989. pap. text ed. write for info. (*0-9609436-5-X*) Lawrence Hse.

Bud's Easy Term Paper Kit. 9th ed. Alvin Baron. 1991. pap. text ed. 3.50 (*0-9609436-6-8*) Lawrence Hse.

Bud's Homespun Almost Poetry. V. A. Vaseen. 1991. 14.95 (*0-533-09624-3*) Vantage.

Buds of Ballybunion. John B. Keane. 1979. pap. 9.95 (*0-85342-610-4*) Dufour.

Buehler & Pearsons Survey of Organic Syntheses, Vol. 3. Williams. 1993. write for info. (*0-471-81944-1*) Wiley.

Buehler's Backyard Boatbuilding. George Buehler. (Illus.). 256p. 1990. pap. text ed. 24.95 (*0-87742-257-5*) Intl Marine.

Buehnenanweisung und Dramaturgie. Hinweise zu Interpretation und Inszenierung in Shakespeare's First Folio und den Quartoversionen. Margarete Munkelt. (Bochum Studies in English: No. 12). x, 346p. (Orig.). (GER.). 1981. pap. 37.00 (*90-6032-206-1*) Benjamins North Am.

Buel. Mark Dunster. 19p. 1991. pap. 4.00 (*0-89642-197-X*) Linden Pubs.

Buen Comienzo. (SPA.). 1993. 7.95 (*0-88336-552-9*) New Readers.

Buen Tiempo, Mal Tiempo: Teacher's Theme Guide. (Que Maravilla! Ser.). (Illus.). (Orig.). (SPA.). 1992. pap. 29.95 (*1-56334-165-4*) Hampton-Brown.

Buen Tiempo, Mal Tiempo, Que Tiempo Hace? Ina Cumpiano. (Que Maravilla! Ser.). (Illus.). 24p. (Orig.). (SPA.). (J). (gr. 1-3). 1992. pap. text ed. 29.95 (*1-56334-026-7*) Hampton-Brown.

Buen Tiempo, Mal Tiempo, Que Tiempo Hace? Level 2. Ina Cumpiano. (Que Maravilla! Ser.). 24p. (Orig.). (SPA.). 1992. pap. 6.00 (*1-56334-215-4*) Hampton-Brown.

Buena Familia Hace un Mundo Mejor. (SPA.). 3.50 (*0-318-02210-9*) Chrstphrs NY.

Buena Guarda. Lope De Vega. 125p. (SPA.). 1964. 7.95 (*0-8288-7162-0*, S9044) Fr & Eur.

***Buena Salud: 10 Pasos Simples para la Mujer.** Carolle Jean-Murat. LC 94-79750. (Illus.). 127p. (Orig.). (SPA.). 1994. pap. 14.95 (*1-886185-24-7*) Mosley Pubng.

Buena Vista: Estancia de Frutos Menores, Fabrica de Harinas y Hacienda Cafetalera (1833-1904) Guillermo A. Baralt. Tr. by CARIMAR Staff. (Illus.). 141p. (Orig.). (SPA.). (C). 1988. text ed. 35.00 (*0-9622083-0-2*); pap. 22.00 (*0-9622083-1-0*) Cnsrvation Trust PR.

Buenas Acciones de Clifford. Norman Bridwell. Tr. by Argentina Palacios. Orig. Title: Clifford's Good Deeds. 32p. (SPA.). (J). (gr. k-3). pap. 2.95 (*0-590-40179-3*) Scholastic Inc.

Buenas Noches, Gatito (Good Night, Little Kitten) (My First Reader Ser.). (Illus.). 28p. (SPA.). (J). (ps-2). 1991. pap. 3.95 (*0-516-55354-2*) Childrens.

Buenas Noches, Gatito (Good Night, Little Kitten) (My First Reader Ser.). (Illus.). 28p. (SPA.). (J). (ps-2). 1991. lib. bdg. 15.40 (*0-516-35354-3*) Childrens.

Buenas Noches, Irene. H. Ledbetter & John A. Lomax. Ed. by D. Pike. Tr. by Hector Pichardo. (Illus.). (SPA.). (J). (ps-2). 1993. pap. text ed. 15.00 (*0-922053-27-8*) N Edge Res.

***Buenas Noches, Luna.** Margaret W. Brown. LC 94-43633. (Illus.). 32p. (SPA.). (J). (ps-1). 1995. 12.95 (*0-06-026214-1*) HarpC Child Bks.

Buenas Nuevas. William MacDonald. Orig. Title: Good News. 96p. (SPA.). 1986. pap. 3.50 (*0-8254-1451-2*) Kregel.

Buenas Nuevas: Estudios En Galatas. Ellet J. Waggoner. 150p. (Orig.). (SPA.). 1993. pap. 6.95 (*0-9635077-1-0*) Glad Tidngs.

Buenas Nuevas para Todos. P. Frank. (SPA.). Date not set. 1.50 (*0-685-74905-3*, 490349) Editorial Unilit.

***Buenas Nuevas para Usted.** Charles Brock. Tr. by Ruby Vargas. 28p. (SPA.). Date not set. pap. 1.00 (*1-885504-05-5*) Church Gwth.

Buenos Aires. (Insight Guides Ser.). 1993. pap. 21.95 (*0-395-66279-6*) HM.

Buenos Aires: Four Hundred Years. Ed. by Stanley R. Ross & Thomas F. McGann. 204p. (C). 1982. text ed. 20.00 (*0-292-70738-X*) U of Tex Pr.

Buenos Aires Alive. Linda Tristan. (Alive Travel Ser.). (Illus.). 1990. 10.95 (*0-935572-20-1*) Alive Pubns.

***Buenos Airies Alive & the Best of Argentina.** Arnold Greenburg. (Alive Ser.). (Illus.). 440p. (Orig.). 1995. pap. 14.95 (*1-55650-680-5*) Hunter NJ.

Buenos Dias, Espiritu Santo. Benny Hinn. 1990. pap. 6.99 (*1-56063-081-7*, 498414) Editorial Unilit.

Buenos Vecinos Comunicandose con los Mexicanos. John Condon. Tr. by Carmen Deneve. 95p. (Orig.). (SPA.). 1994. pap. text ed. 13.95 (*1-877864-22-6*) Intercult Pr.

***Buerger Besonderer Art: Evangelische Pfarrer in Preussen 1850-1914.** Oliver Janz. (Veroeffentlichungen der Historischen Kommision Zu Berlin Ser.: Bd. 87). 632p. (GER.). (C). 1994. lib. bdg. 203.10 (*3-11-014140-X*) De Gruyter.

Buero Vallejo: Dreamer for the People. Ed. by Thompson. 1994. 49.95 (*0-85668-553-4*, Pub. by Aris & Phillips UK); pap. 22.00 (*0-85668-554-2*, Pub. by Aris & Phillips UK) David Brown.

Bueromaschinen Lexikon. 18th ed. (GER.). 1975. pap. 75.00 (*0-8288-5792-X*, M7316) Fr & Eur.

Bueschel's Saloon Series: B. A. Stevens - Billiard & Bar Goods. Richard M. Bueschel. (Illus.). 264p. (Orig.). (C). 1990. pap. 29.95 (*0-86667-049-1*) Coin Slot Bks.

Buff Runners. Jory Sherman. (Gunn Ser.: No. 14). 1982. pap. 2.25 (*0-8217-1093-5*) Zebra.

Buffa Buffalo. Bob Reese. (Yellowstone Ser.). (Illus.). (J). (gr. k-6). 1986. 7.95 (*0-89868-175-8*); pap. 2.95 (*0-89868-176-6*) ARO Pub.

Buffalo. Emilie U. Lepthien. LC 89-457. (New True Bks.). (Illus.). 48p. (J). (gr. k-4). 1989. lib. bdg. 12.90 (*0-516-01161-8*); pap. 4.95 (*0-516-41161-6*) Childrens.

Buffalo. Henry Inman & Buffalo Bill Cody. (Illus.). 1977. reprint ed. pap. 4.95 (*0-89646-028-2*) Vistabooks.

***Buffalo: Lake City in Niagara Land.** Richard C. Brown. 1984. 27.95 (*0-89781-036-8*) Preferred Mktg.

Buffalo Afternoon. Susan F. Schaeffer. 608p. 1990. mass mkt. 5.95 (*0-8041-0580-4*) Ivy Books.

Buffalo & Indians on the Great Plains. Noel Grisham & Betsy Warren. (Illus.). (J). (gr. k-4). 1985. 12.95 (*0-89015-470-8*) Sunbelt Media.

Buffalo & Other Stories. 2nd ed. Wayne Ude. LC 89-12215. 88p. 1990. 15.95 (*0-89924-067-4*); pap. 8.95 (*0-89924-066-6*) Lynx Hse.

***Buffalo & the Scorpion.** J. Hunter Downs. 270p. 1996. pap. 8.95 (*0-7610-0495-5*) NW Pub.

Buffalo Architecture: A Guide. Reyner Banham et al. (Illus.). 352p. 1981. pap. 17.95x (*0-262-52063-X*) MIT Pr.

Buffalo Are Coming. J. T. Edson. 1994. mass mkt. 4.50 (*0-440-21046-1*) Dell.

Buffalo Bill. Aurand Harris. (J). 1954. 5.00 (*0-87602-110-0*) Anchorage.

Buffalo Bill. Nancy Robison. LC 90-47221. (First Bks.). (Illus.). 64p. (J). (gr. 3-5). 1991. lib. bdg. 13.93 (*0-531-20007-8*) Watts.

Buffalo Bill: Frontier Daredevil. Augusta Stevenson. LC 90-23767. (Childhood of Famous Americans Ser.). (Illus.). 192p. (J). (gr. 3-7). 1991. reprint ed. pap. 3.95 (*0-689-71479-3*, Aladdin Paperbacks) S&S Childrens.

Buffalo Bill: His Adventures in the West. Ned Buntline. LC 74-15731. (Popular Culture in America Ser.). (Illus.). 320p. (YA). (gr. 7 up). 1975. reprint ed. 25.95 (*0-405-06366-0*) Ayer.

Buffalo Bill: Last of the Great Scouts. Helen C. Wetmore. LC 65-13258. 1994. 7.98 (*0-681-00457-6*) Longmeadow Pr.

Buffalo Bill: Last of the Great Scouts. Helen C. Wetmore. LC 65-13258. (Illus.). xvi, 318p. 1965. pap. 9.95 (*0-8032-5215-3*, Bison Books) U of Nebr Pr.

Buffalo Bill: Wild West Showman. Mary R. Davidson. (Discovery Biographies Ser.). (Illus.). 80p. (J). (gr. 2-6). 1993. reprint ed. lib. bdg. 12.95 (*0-7910-1432-0*) Chelsea Hse.

Buffalo Bill & His Wild West: A Pictorial Biography. Joseph G. Rosa & Robin May. LC 88-34426. (Illus.). xii, 244p. 1989. pap. 14.95 (*0-7006-0399-9*) U Pr of KS.

Buffalo Bill & the Pony Express. Eleanor Coerr. LC 93-24261. (I Can Read Book). (Illus.). 64p. (J). (gr. k-3). 1994. 14.00 (*0-06-023372-9*) HarpC Child Bks.

Buffalo Bill & the Pony Express. Eleanor Coerr. LC 93-24261. (Illus.). 64p. (J). (gr. k-3). 1995. lib. bdg. 13.89 (*0-06-023373-7*) HarpC Child Bks.

Buffalo Bill & the Pony Express. Debbie Dadey. (Disney's American Frontier Ser.: Bk. 13). 80p. (J). (gr. 1-4). 1994. lib. bdg. 12.89 (*0-7868-5004-3*); pap. 3.50 (*0-7868-4005-6*) Disney Pr.

Buffalo Bill Historical Center, Cody, Wyoming. LC 84-72062. (Illus.). 60p. 1989. pap. 6.95 (*0-917859-24-3*) Sunrise SBCA.

Buffalo Bill Remembers. William W. Quinn. LC 91-5063. 468p. 1991. boxed 18.95 (*0-923568-23-9*) Wilderness Adventure Bks.

Buffalo Bills. Steve Potts. (NFL Today Ser.). (J). (gr. 4 up). 1991. lib. bdg. 15.95 (*0-88682-360-9*) Creative Ed.

Buffalo Bills Official All-New Trivia Book II. Scott Pitoniak. (Illus.). 112p. (Orig.). 1992. pap. 8.99 (*0-312-08151-0*) St Martin.

Buffalo Bills Official Trivia Book. Scott Pitoniak. (Illus.). 128p. (Orig.). 1989. pap. 8.95 (*0-312-03737-6*) St Martin.

Buffalo Bill's True Tales. Buffalo Bill, pseud. (Illus.). 24p. 1977. reprint ed. pap. 3.95 (*0-89646-022-3*) Vistabooks.

Buffalo Bill's Wild West. Joseph J. Arpad & Kenneth R. Lincoln. LC 73-106990. (Wild & Woolly West Ser.: No. 19). (Illus.). (Orig.). 1971. pap. 3.00 (*0-910584-62-1*) Filter.

Buffalo Bird Woman's Garden: Agriculture of the Hidatsa Indians. Gilbert Wilson. LC 87-20355. (Illus.). xxiii, 129p. 1987. reprint ed. pap. 8.95 (*0-87351-219-7*, Borealis Book) Minn Hist.

Buffalo Black's Talking Proud. Eva Noles. 132p. (Orig.). 1986. pap. 9.95 (*0-9624731-0-3*) Noles Pub.

Buffalo Bluff. Brian Meyer. 1988. pap. 13.95 (*0-9620314-5-3*) Meyer Enter.

Buffalo Bones IV: Stories from Wyoming's Past. William H. Barton. (Illus.). 64p. 1984. pap. 2.50 (*0-943398-08-8*) Wyoming St Mus.

***Buffalo Box.** large type ed. Frank Gruber. 1994. 20.95 (*0-7089-3165-0*) Ulverscroft.

Buffalo Boys. Rick Cleveland. 59p. 1992. pap. 5.95 (*1-56850-008-4*) Chicago Plays.

Buffalo Breath. Frank J. Lombardo. (Illus.). 130p. (Orig.). 1988. 6.95 (*0-945702-01-9*) Vertizon Bks.

Buffalo Brenda. Jill Pinkwater. LC 88-31929. 208p. (J). (gr. 5-9). 1989. text ed. 14.95 (*0-02-774631-3*, Mac Bks Young Read) S&S Childrens.

Buffalo Brenda. Jill Pinkwater. LC 91-14806. 208p. (J). (gr. 3-7). 1992. reprint ed. pap. 3.95 (*0-689-71586-2*, Aladdin Paperbacks) S&S Childrens.

Buffalo Castle. Rick Loomis. (Illus.). 1982. 3.00 (*0-940244-01-2*) Flying Buffalo.

Buffalo Coat. Carol R. Brink. LC 93-17131. (Washington State University Press Reprint Ser.). 421p. 1993. reprint ed. pap. 17.95 (*0-87422-095-5*) Wash St U Pr.

Buffalo Cookbook. Judi Hebbring. 33p. 1981. pap. 2.25 (*0-318-02142-0*) Natl Buffalo Assn.

***Buffalo Cookbook: The Low Fat Solution to Eating Red Meat.** Ruth M. Johnston. 1995. 39.95 (*0-88839-345-8*) Hancock House.

Buffalo County: A Pictorial History. Mary Ann Pattison. LC 93-4366. 1993. write for info. (*0-89865-870-5*) Donning Co.

Buffalo Creek - Valley of Death. Dennis Deitz & Carlene Mowery. 25.00 (*0-938985-10-8*) Mntn Memories Bks.

Buffalo Creek & Gauley. William E. Warden. (Illus.). 80p. 1991. pap. 20.00 (*1-878343-03-3*) E Crist.

Buffalo Creek Disaster: The Story of the Survivors' Unprecedented Lawsuit. Gerald M. Stern. 1977. pap. 9.95 (*0-394-72343-0*, Vin) Random.

Buffalo Dance: A Blackfoot Legend. Illus. by Beatriz Vidal. LC 92-15444. 32p. 1993. 15.95 (*0-316-89728-0*, Joy St Bks) Little.

Buffalo Days: The Personal Narrative of a Cattleman, Indian Fighter & Army Officer. Homer W. Wheeler. LC 89-24967. (Illus.). xxxii, 400p. 1990. reprint ed. pap. 12.95 (*0-8032-9726-2*, Bison Books) U of Nebr Pr.

Buffalo Gal. Bill Wallace. LC 91-28243. 192p. (J). (gr. 5 up). 1992. 14.95 (*0-8234-0943-0*) Holiday.

Buffalo Gal. Bill Wallace. Ed. by Pat MacDonald. 192p. (J). 1993. reprint ed. pap. 3.50 (*0-671-79899-5*, Minstrel Bks) PB.

***Buffalo Gals: Women of the Old West.** Brandon M. Miller. (Illus.). 88p. (YA). (gr. 5 up). 1995. lib. bdg. 18.95 (*0-8225-1730-2*) Lerner Group.

Buffalo Gals & Other Animal Presences. Ursula K. Le Guin. 222p. 1994. pap. 8.95 (*0-451-45434-0*, ROC) NAL-Dutton.

Buffalo Gals, Won't You Come Out Tonight. Ursula K. Le Guin. LC 94-18443. (Illus.). 80p. 1994. 16.95 (*0-87654-071-X*) Pomegranate Calif.

***Buffalo Girls.** McMurtry. 1995. pap. 6.99 (*0-671-53615-X*) Silhouette.

Buffalo Girls. Larry McMurtry. 1990. 19.95 (*0-685-38917-0*) S&S Trade.

Buffalo Girls. large type ed. Larry McMurtry. (General Ser.). 436p. 1991. text ed. 14.95 (*0-8161-5242-X*, Large Print Bks) Hall.

Buffalo Grass & Tall Corn: Recollections of the Nebraska Family of Robert Garret Farritor & Anne Graham Farritor. Charles F. Farritor. (Illus.). 110p. (Orig.). 1987. pap. 10.00 (*0-9618054-0-4*) C F Farritor.

Buffalo Ground. large type ed. Stack Sutton. (Linford Western Library). 1991. pap. 13.95 (*0-7089-7127-X*, Linford) Ulverscroft.

Buffalo Guns & Barbed Wire: Two Frontier Accounts. Don H. Biggers. (Illus.). 280p. 1991. 39.95 (*0-89672-242-2*) Tex Tech Univ Pr.

***Buffalo Hair.** Carlyle Brown. 1995. 4.75 (*0-8222-1463-6*) Dramatists Play.

Buffalo Hearts. Sun Bear. 1976. pap. 5.95 (*0-943404-01-0*) Bear Tribe.

Buffalo Hiders. Judd Cole. (Cheyenne Ser.: No. 10). 176p. (Orig.). 1994. pap. 3.99 (*0-8439-3623-1*) Dorchester Pub Co.

Buffalo Hump & the Penateka Comanches. Jodye L. Schilz & Thomas F. Schilz. (Southwestern Studies: No. 88). (Illus.). 72p. 1989. pap. 10.00 (*0-87404-179-1*) Tex Western.

***Buffalo Hunt.** Freedman. 1995. pap. 8.95 (*0-8234-1159-1*) Holiday.

Buffalo Hunt. Russell Freedman. LC 87-35303. (Illus.). 52p. (J). (gr. 3-7). 1988. lib. bdg. 18.95 (*0-8234-0702-0*) Holiday.

Buffalo Hunter. Zane Grey. 224p. 1990. pap. 3.50 (*0-8439-2955-3*) Dorchester Pub Co.

***Buffalo Hunters.** Charles M. Robinson, III. LC 95-7590. 1995. write for info. (*1-880510-18-9*); pap. write for info. (*1-880510-19-7*) State House Pr.

An Asterisk (*) at the beginning of an entry indicates that the title is appearing in BIP for the first time.

Buffalo Hunters. Time-Life Books Editors. LC 92-39726. (American Indians Ser.). 1993. write for info. (*0-8094-9425-6*); lib. bdg. write for info. (*0-8094-9426-4*) Time-Life.

***Buffalo Hunters.** deluxe ed. Charles M. Robinson, III. LC 95-7590. 1995. lib. bdg. write for info. (*1-880510-20-0*) State House Pr.

Buffalo Hunters: The Story of the Hide Men. Mari Sandoz. LC 77-14079. x, 372p. 1978. pap. 11.95 (*0-8032-5883-6*, Bison Books) U of Nebr Pr.

Buffalo Jock Rap: The "Settle Your Bet" Pro Sports Trivia Book. Daniel A. Locche & Brenda C. Alesii. 264p. (Orig.). 1989. 8.95 (*1-877697-00-1*) Brendan Ventures.

Buffalo Knife. William O. Steele. 1992. 16.50 (*0-8446-6505-3*) Peter Smith.

Buffalo Knife. William O. Steele. 123p. (J). (gr. 3-7). 1990. pap. 3.95 (*0-15-213212-0*, Odyssey) HarBrace.

Buffalo Land. William D. Berry. (Illus.). 48p. (J). (gr. 5-8). 1985. reprint ed. pap. 9.95 (*0-938271-01-6*) Press N Amer.

Buffalo Man. Edward Todd. 1978. pap. 1.50 (*0-8439-0588-3*) Dorchester Pub Co.

***Buffalo McCloud.** Cassie Miles. (American Romance Ser.). 1995. pap. 3.50 (*0-373-16567-6*, 1-16567-9) Harlequin Bks.

Buffalo Medicine. Don Coldsmith. (Spanish Bit Saga Ser.: No. 4). 1988. mass mkt. 4.50 (*0-553-26938-0*) Bantam.

Buffalo National River, East, AR. (Illus.). 1993. 7.95 (*1-56695-000-7*) Trails Illustrated.

Buffalo Nickel. Annette R. Cohen & Ray M. Druley. (Illus.). 130p. (Orig.). 1979. pap. 7.50 (*0-939836-00-9*) Potomac Ent.

Buffalo Nickel. Floyd Salas. LC 91-48217. 347p. 1992. 19.95 (*1-55885-049-X*) Arte Publico.

Buffalo Nickel. C. W. Smith. Ed. by Julie Rubenstein. 512p. 1995. reprint ed. pap. 6.50 (*0-671-62446-6*) PB.

Buffalo Nickel Blues Band. Judie Angell. LC 91-3793. 192p. (J). (gr. 3-7). 1991. reprint ed. pap. 3.95 (*0-689-71448-3*, Aladdin Paperbacks) S&S Childrens.

***Buffalo, NY.** (Streetfinder Ser.). (Illus.). 1993. pap. 12.95 (*0-528-95267-6*) Rand McNally.

Buffalo Poem. Nathan Whiting. 65p. 1970. 4.00 (*0-913219-10-X*); pap. 2.00 (*0-913219-11-8*) Pym-Rand Pr.

Buffalo Poem. deluxe ed. Nathan Whiting. 65p. 1970. 7.50 (*0-913219-12-6*) Pym-Rand Pr.

Buffalo River: National River, West. Ed. by Trails Illustrated Staff. (Illus.). 1992. Folded topographical map. 8.99 (*0-925873-65-9*) Trails Illustrated.

Buffalo River Country. 3rd rev. ed. Kenneth L. Smith. LC 67-18813. (Illus.). 176p. 1976. pap. 12.95 (*0-912456-02-7*) Ozark Soc Bks.

Buffalo River Hiking Trails. Tim Ernst. 118p. 1991. pap. text ed. 12.95 (*1-882906-01-2*) Ernst Wilderness.

Buffalo River Hiking Trails. 2nd ed. Tim Ernst. (Illus.). 128p. 1994. pap. 14.95 (*1-882906-13-6*) Ernst Wilderness.

Buffalo Rochester & Pittsburgh Railway. 2nd ed. Paul Pietrak. LC 92-71876. (Illus.). (C). 1992. reprint ed. pap. 20.00 (*0-9620195-3-4*) S R Ames.

Buffalo Sabres. John Gilbert. LC 93-47952. (NHL Today Ser.). 32p. (J). 1995. 14.95 (*0-88682-670-5*) Creative Ed.

Buffalo Soldier. Charles Goodman. (Orig.). 1993. pap. 3.95 (*0-87067-373-4*) Holloway.

Buffalo Soldier. Clarence A. Mauge. 1993. 8.75 (*0-8062-4754-1*) Carlton.

Buffalo Soldiers. Robert Miller. (Reflections of a Black Cowboy Ser.). (Illus.). 104p. (J). (gr. 4-7). 1992. lib. bdg. 12.95 (*0-382-24080-4*); pap. 4.95 (*0-382-24085-5*) Silver Burdett Pr.

Buffalo Soldiers. Robert O'Connor. LC 93-43487. 1994. pap. 12.00 (*0-679-74203-4*, Vin) Random.

Buffalo Soldiers. Catherine Reef. (African-American Soldiers Ser.). (Illus.). 80p. (J). (gr. 4-7). 1993. lib. bdg. 14.98 (*0-8050-2372-0*) TFC Bks NY.

Buffalo Soldiers: A Narrative of the Negro Cavalry in the West. William H. Leckie. LC 67-15571. (Illus.). 1975. pap. 13.95 (*0-8061-1244-1*) U of Okla Pr.

Buffalo Soldiers: A Novel. Robert O'Connor. 1993. 22.00 (*0-679-41508-4*) Knopf.

***Buffalo Soldiers: The Story of Emanuel Stance.** Robert H. Miller. LC 94-28640. (Illus.). (J). 1994. 12.95 (*0-382-24395-1*); 12.95 (*0-382-24400-1*); lib. bdg. 14.95 (*0-382-24391-9*) Silver.

Buffalo Soldiers, Braves, & the Brass: The Story of Fort Robinson, Nebraska. Frank N. Schubert. LC 93-9262. (Illus.). 296p. (C). 1993. 27.95 (*0-942597-44-3*) White Mane Pub.

Buffalo Soldiers Coloring Book. Herschell Turner & G. L. Blanchard. 32p. (J). (gr. 4-6). 1992. pap. 3.95 (*1-882205-02-2*) All Media Prods.

Buffalo Soldiers in Italy: Black Americans in World War II. Hondon B. Hargrove. LC 84-42609. (Illus.). 223p. 1985. lib. bdg. 28.50x (*0-89950-116-8*) McFarland & Co.

Buffalo Soldier's Legacy: "Ready & Forward" 3rd ed. Lucille Ricks. (Illus.). 126p. 1993. pap. 12.00 (*0-929757-99-8*) Regt QM.

Buffalo Soldiers West. rev. ed. Carroll. (Illus.). 1995. 24.95 (*0-8488-1519-X*, J M C & Co); pap. 15.95 (*0-8488-1518-1*, J M C & Co) Amereon Ltd.

Buffalo Spring. large type ed. Fred Grove. (Linford Western Library). 368p. 1985. pap. 11.95 (*0-7089-6189-4*, Linford) Ulverscroft.

Buffalo Views: Twenty-Six Historic Postcards of Buffalo, New York. Ed. by Richard Kegler. (Illus.). (Orig.). 1991. pap. 9.95 (*0-9631082-0-4*) P Twenty-Two Pubns.

Buffalo War. Patrick E. Andrews. 256p. 1993. pap. 3.50 (*0-8217-4299-X*) Zebra.

Buffalo War. Peter McCurtin. (Sundance Ser.: No. 39). 192p. (Orig.). 1981. pap. 1.95 (*0-8439-0990-0*) Dorchester Pub Co.

Buffalo Waterfront: A Guidebook. Timothy Tielman. 1990. pap. 5.95 (*1-879201-00-3*) Meyer Enter.

Buffalo Woman. Paul Goble. LC 83-15704. (Illus.). 32p. (J). (gr. k up). 1984. text ed. 14.95 (*0-02-737720-2*, Bradbury S&S) S&S Childrens.

Buffalo Woman. Paul Goble. LC 86-20573. (Illus.). 32p. (J). (gr. k up). 1987. pap. 4.95 (*0-689-71109-3*, Aladdin Paperbacks) S&S Childrens.

Buffalo Woman Comes Singing: The Spirit Song of a Rainbow Medicine Woman. Brooke Medicine Eagle. 480p. (Orig.). 1991. pap. 12.50 (*0-345-36143-1*, Ballantine Trade) Ballantine.

***Buffalotarrak: An Anthology of the Basque People of Buffalo, Wyoming.** Ed. by Dollie Iberlin & David Romtvedt. (Illus.). 80p. (Orig.). 1995. pap. 10.00 (*0-9633755-1-2*) Ucross Fnd.

***Buffer Stock Models & the Demand for Money.** Paul Mizen. LC 94-20722. 1994. write for info. (*0-312-12318-3*) Macmillan.

Buffers for Pich & Metal Ion Control. D. D. Perrin & B. Dempsey. 1979. pap. 25.00 (*0-412-21890-9*, NO.6218) Chapman & Hall.

Buffet for Unwelcome Guests: The Best Short Mysteries of Christianna Brand. Ed. by Francis M. Nevins, Jr. & Martin H. Greenberg. LC 83-526. (Mystery Makers Ser.). 316p. 1983. 17.95 (*0-8093-1140-2*) S Ill U Pr.

Buffet on the Bayou: A Scrumptious Salute to Houston. LC 93-78576. 333p. 1993. 17.95 (*0-9637270-0-1*) Houston Jr Forum.

Buffets: A Guide for Professionals. Georges C. St. Laurent & Chet Holden. LC 85-22677. 368p. 1986. text ed. 49.95 (*0-471-83229-4*) Wiley.

Buffets & Potlucks. Canter. 159p. 1989. spiral bd. 5.50 (*0-941016-54-4*) Penfield.

Buffets, Cocktails & Receptions. Thuries. 1994. text ed. write for info. (*0-442-01688-3*) Van Nos Reinhold.

Buffet's Complete Engravings, 1948-1980. Maurice Rheims. (Illus.). 244p. 1983. 125.00 (*1-55660-046-1*) A Wofsy Fine Arts.

Buffet's Lithographs II, 1979-1986: With Three Original Lithographs. Charles Sorlier. 266p. 1987. 350.00 (*1-55660-047-X*) A Wofsy Fine Arts.

***Buffett: The Making of an American Capitalist.** Roger Lowenstein. LC 95-8494. 512p. 1995. 27.50 (*0-679-41584-X*) Random.

Buffo: The Genius of Vulgar Comedy. Anthony F. Caputi. LC 78-15992. (Illus.). 263p. reprint ed. pap. 75.00 (*0-8357-8820-2*, 2056745) Bks Demand.

Buffoons, Queens & Wooden Horsemen: The Dyo & Gouan Societies of the Bambara of Mali. Pascal J. Imperato. LC 82-82902. (Illus.). 77p. (Orig.). 1983. pap. 25.00 (*0-910385-00-9*) Kilima Hse Pubs.

Buffy the Vampire Slayer. Richie T. Cusick. Ed. by Pat MacDonald. 192p. (J). 1992. mass mkt. 3.99 (*0-671-79220-2*) PB.

Buford: True Story of "Walking Tall" Sheriff Buford Pusser. W. R. Morris. LC 83-62125. 215p. 1984. 14.95 (*0-915045-00-1*) Poplar Bks.

***Buford Bear.** Wright & Oliver. 32p. (J). 1996. 7.99 (*1-56476-461-3*, 6-3461); audio 11.99 (*7-900880-95-X*, 3-1095) SP Pubns.

Buford, the Little Bighorn. Bill Peet. (Illus.). 48p. (J). (gr. k-3). 1975. 13.95 (*0-395-20337-6*) HM.

Buford, the Little Bighorn. Bill Peet. (Illus.). 48p. (J). (gr. k-3). 1983. pap. 5.95 (*0-395-34067-5*) HM.

Bufotenin (Dimethylserotonin - Mappine) Index of New Information & Medical Research Bible. Patrick M. Pfeifer. 160p. 1994. 44.50 (*0-7883-0218-3*); pap. 39.50 (*0-7883-0219-1*) ABBE Pubs Assn.

Bug. (Ultimate Sticker Ser.). (Illus.). 20p. (J). 1994. 6.95 (*1-56458-480-1*) Dorling Kindersley.

***Bug & the Slug in the Rug.** Steve Allen. LC 95-78159. (Illus.). 1995. 16.95 (*1-880851-17-2*) Greene Bark Pr.

Bug Book. Katie Baldwin & Muffet Callender. (Illus.). 1974. pap. 0.75 (*0-914916-08-4*) Ku Paa.

Bug Book. Drescher. (J). Date not set. 14.95 (*0-06-022711-7*, HarpT); lib. bdg. 14.89 (*0-06-022712-5*, HarpT) HarpC.

Bug Book. Edward Gorey. (Illus.). (J). (gr. 4 up). 1987. 8.95 (*0-915361-69-8*) Modan-Adama Bks.

***Bug Book: Wireless Microphones & Surveillance Transmitters.** 3rd ed. M. L. Shannon. (Illus.). 122p. (Orig.). 1995. pap. text ed. 19.97 (*1-884451-06-3*) Lysias Pr.

Bug Book & the Bug Bottle. Hugh Danks. LC 86-40541. (Illus.). 64p. (Orig.). (J). (gr. k-5). 1987. pap. 9.95 (*0-89480-314-X*, 1314) Workman Pub.

Bug Busters: Poison Free Pest Controls for House & Garden. Bernice Lifton. LC 90-19678. (Illus.). 272p. 1991. pap. 9.95 (*0-89529-451-6*) Avery Pub.

Bug City. Fasa Corporation Staff. (Shadowrun Ser.). (Illus.). 148p. 1994. pap. 18.00 (*1-55560-253-3*) FASA Corp.

Bug Club. Gina C. Erickson & Kelli C. Foster. (Get Ready...Get Set...Read! Ser.). (Illus.). 24p. (J). (ps-2). 1991. pap. 3.50 (*0-8120-4730-3*) Barron.

***Bug Creek Problem & the Cretaceous-Tertiary Transition at McGuire Creek, Montana.** Donald L. Lofgren. LC 95-12046. (Geological Sciences Publications: Vol. 140). 1995. pap. write for info. (*0-520-09800-5*) U CA Pr.

Bug Death. 1988. 25.00 (*0-317-90525-2*) Inkblot Pubns.

Bug Hunt in Hawaii nei. Joy S. Au. (Illus.). 32p. 1993. 12.95 (*1-56647-046-3*) Mutual Pub HI.

Bug-Jargal: Avec: Le Dernier Jour d'un Condamme. Victor Hugo. (FRE.). 1989. pap. 10.95 (*0-7859-3221-6*, 2266023292) Fr & Eur.

Bug Making. C. Boyd Pfeiffer. (Illus.). 224p. 1993. 22.95 (*1-55821-258-2*) Lyons & Burford.

***Bug Making.** C. Boyd Pfeiffer. 224p. 1995. pap. 14.95 (*1-55821-414-3*) Lyons & Burford.

***Bug Off!** Terri Fields. (J). (gr. 4-7). 1995. pap. 2.99 (*0-590-48941-0*) Scholastic Inc.

Bug Off! Fifty Simple Ways to Protect Yourself from Burglars, Thieves, Muggers, Con-Artists, & Other Lowlifes. Jim Mantice. (Illus.). 96p. (Orig.). 1992. pap. 5.95 (*0-9631380-0-6*) Walnut Grove Pubs.

Bug Out Diary. Zachary Z. Kinney. (Illus.). 109p. (Orig.). (C). 1992. pap. text ed. 13.95 (*1-880047-10-1*) Creative Des.

Bug Riddles. Viki Woodworth. (Funny Side up Ser.). (Illus.). (J). (gr. 1-4). 1992. lib. bdg. 19.93 (*0-89565-864-X*) Childs World.

Bug Wars. Robert Asprin. 224p. 1993. mass mkt. 4.99 (*0-441-07373-5*) Ace Bks.

Bugaboo Rock: A Climber's Guide. Randall Green & Joe Bensen. LC 89-77605. (Illus.). 176p. (Orig.). 1990. vinyl bd. 16.95 (*0-89886-233-7*) Mountaineers.

Bugaboo Words. Noreen V. Briggs. (Illus.). 160p. (J). (gr. 3 up). 1989. 26.95 (*0-937857-13-0*, 1570) Speech Bin.

Bugaboos. Candace R. Curran. 12p. (Orig.). 1992. pap. 3.50 (*0-9626308-3-7*) Haleys.

Bugarstica: Bilingual Anthology of the Earliest Extant South Slavic Folk Narrative Song. John S. Miletich. (Illinois Medieval Monographs: No. III). 384p. 1990. 34.95 (*0-252-01711-0*) U of Ill Pr.

Bugatti. Hugh Conway. (Illus.). 500p. 1989. 225.00 (*0-87938-390-9*) Motorbooks Intl.

Bugatti. Jay Schleifer. LC 93-15491. (Cool Classics Ser.). (Illus.). 48p. (J). (gr. 6 up). 1994. text ed. 13.95 (*0-89686-813-3*, Crstwood Hse) Silver Burdett Pr.

Bugatti (Rembrandt) Catalogue Raisonne of the Sculptures. V. Chalom Des Cordes & J. Chalom Des Cordes. (Illus.). 336p. (FRE.). 1987. 250.00 (*1-55660-192-1*) A Wofsy Fine Arts.

Bugbear of Literacy. rev. ed. Ananda K. Coomaraswamy. 150p. 1979. pap. 17.95 (*0-900588-19-5*) S Perennis.

Bugby Hole, St. Croix, U. S. Virgin Islands: A Land Use Plan. Lou Borie. 41p. 1979. 7.50 (*0-318-14611-8*) Isl Resources.

Bugg Books Series. (Illus.). (J). (gr. 1 up). 1994. write for info. (*0-9638463-4-5*, Crtoon Mdia) Cethial Commns.

***Bugger Bucharest.** Maureen Martena. 192p. 1995. pap. 11.99 (*1-85594-126-0*) InBook.

Buggies. Phyllis H. Keaton. LC 88-5951. (Super-Charged Ser.). (Illus.). 48p. (J). (gr. 5-6). 1988. text ed. 11.95 (*0-89686-375-1*, Crstwood Hse) Silver Burdett Pr.

Buggies & Bad Times. Ed. by Eleanor Arnold. LC 87-401343. (Memories of Hoosier Homemakers Ser.). (Illus.). 170p. (Orig.). 1985. pap. 8.95 (*0-685-25999-4*) IN Extension.

Buggies & Bad Times see Memories of Hoosier Homemakers

Buggies, Blizzards, & Babies. Cora F. Hawkins. (Iowa Heritage Collection Ser.). (Illus.). 191p. 1994. reprint ed. pap. 8.95 (*0-8138-0183-4*) Iowa St U Pr.

Buggly Bear's Hiccup Cure. True Kelley. LC 81-16903. (Illus.). 48p. (J). (ps-3). 1982. 5.95 (*0-8193-1081-6*); lib. bdg. 5.95 (*0-8193-1082-4*) Parents.

Buggly Bear's Hiccup Cure. True Kelly. LC 94-11352. 1994. lib. bdg. 14.60 (*0-8368-0982-3*) Gareth Stevens Inc.

Buggy Bear Cleans Up. Robert Kraus. Ed. by Bonnie Brook. (Miss Gator's Schoolhouse Ser.). (Illus.). 48p. (J). (ps-3). 1989. lib. bdg. 5.95 (*0-671-68608-9*); pap. 2.95 (*0-671-68612-7*) Silver Pr.

Buggy Books: A Guide to Juvenile & Popular Books on Insects & Their Relatives. Gary A. Dunn. (YES Special Publication Ser.: No. 3). 120p. 1990. pap. text ed. 6.95 (*1-884256-02-3*) Yng Entomol.

Buggy Riddles. (J). 1992. pap. 4.99 (*0-14-036178-2*) Puffin Bks.

Buggy Riddles. Katy Hall & Lisa Eisenberg. LC 85-1450. (Easy-to-Read Bks.). (Illus.). 48p. (J). (ps-3). 1986. lib. bdg. 9.89 (*0-8037-0140-3*) Dial Bks Young.

Buggy Riddles. Katy Hall & Lisa Eisenberg. LC 85-1450. (Easy-to-Read Ser.). (Illus.). 48p. (J). (ps-3). 1988. pap. 4.95 (*0-8037-0554-9*) Dial Bks Young.

Buggy Riddles. Katy Hall & Lisa Eisenberg. (J). (gr. 2-5). 1989. audio, pap. 14.95 (*0-87499-118-8*) Live Oak Media.

Buggy Riddles. Katy Hall & Lisa Eisenberg. LC 93-6556. (Easy-to-Read Ser.: Level3). (Illus.). (J). (gr. 1-4). 1993. reprint ed. pap. 3.25 (*0-14-036543-5*) Puffin Bks.

Buggy Riddles, 4 bks., Set. Katy Hall & Lisa Eisenberg. (J). (gr. 2-5). 1989. audio, pap. 29.95 (*0-87499-120-X*) Live Oak Media.

Buggy Town: An Era in American Transportation. Charles M. Snyder. LC 84-2307. (Oral Traditions Projects Ser.). (Illus.). 84p. 1984. 12.50 (*0-271-00377-4*, Keystone Bks) Pa St U Pr.

Buggy Wheel Restaurant Cookbook, Vol. 1: Main Dishes & Vegetables. Ed. by Barbara Bontrager. 128p. 1989. spiral bd. write for info. (*0-318-64848-2*) Buggy Wheel.

Buggy Wheel Restaurant Cookbook, Vol. 2: Sweets & Such. Ed. by Barbara Bontrager. 128p. 1989. spiral bd. write for info. (*0-318-64849-0*) Buggy Wheel.

Buggy Wheel Restaurant Cookbook, Vol. 3: Salads, Dressings & Relishes. Ed. by Barbara Bontrager. 128p. 1990. Spiral bdg. spiral bd. write for info. (*0-318-64850-4*) Buggy Wheel.

Buggy Wheel Restaurant Cookbook, Vol. 4: Pies, Pastries & Breads. Ed. by Barbara Bontrager. 128p. 1990. spiral bd. write for info. (*0-318-64851-2*) Buggy Wheel.

Bugialli on Pasta. Giuliano Bugialli. (Illus.). 352p. 1988. 27.50 (*0-671-62024-X*) S&S Trade.

Buginese Language. U. Sirk. (Languages of Asia & Africa Ser.). 122p. 1983. 23.00 (*0-317-56602-4*, Pub. by Collets UK) Pro-Am Music.

Buginese Language: Languages of Asia & Africa. U. Sirk. 122p. 1983. 35.00 (*0-317-39481-9*, Pub. by Collets UK) St Mut.

Bugis Weddings: Rituals of Social Location in Modern Indonesia. Susan B. Millar. LC 89-62006. (Monograph Ser.: No. 29). (Illus.). 236p. (Orig.). (C). 1989. pap. 17.50 (*0-944613-06-3*); pap. 11.50 (*0-685-30762-X*) UC Berkeley Ctrs SE Asia.

Bugle Echoes. Ed. by Francis F. Browne. LC 75-116394. (Granger Index Reprint Ser.). 1977. 20.95 (*0-8369-6135-8*) Ayer.

Bugle Elk & Little Toot. Bob Reese. (Yellowstone Ser.). (Illus.). (J). (gr. k-6). 1986. 7.95 (*0-89868-177-4*); pap. 2.95 (*0-89868-178-2*) ARO Pub.

Bugle Remembered. J. W. Kingmann. LC 90-70456. 148p. (Orig.). 1991. pap. 7.00 (*1-56002-113-6*) Aegina Pr.

Bugler's Handbook. Date not set. 2.95 (*1-56222-212-0*, 93862) Mel Bay.

***Bugles Are Silent: A Novel of the Texas Revolution from the Alamo to San Jacinto.** 2nd ed. John R. Knaggs. 299p. Date not set. 19.95 (*1-881825-02-7*) Hist Pubns TX.

Bugles, Banners, & War Bonnets. Ernest L. Reedstrom. LC 77-165608. 384p. reprint ed. pap. 109.50 (*0-8357-7461-9*, 2023062) Bks Demand.

Bugles Blow No More. Clifford Dowdey. LC 90-30891. 512p. 1990. reprint ed. 34.95 (*0-87797-176-5*) Cherokee.

***Bugles Echo Across the Valley: Northern Oswego County, New York & the Civil War.** David K. Parsons. 250p. 1994. pap. 17.50 (*1-886303-04-5*) Write to Print.

***Bugles Echo Across the Valley: Oswego County, New York & the Civil War.** rev. ed. David K. Parsons. Ed. by Marie K. Parsons. (Illus.). 250p. 1995. pap. 17.50 (*1-886303-09-6*) Write to Print.

***Bugles Echo Across the Valley Vol. 2: Civil War Muster Rolls for Oswego County, New York.** David K. Parsons. (Illus.). 130p. (Orig.). 1995. pap. 12.50 (*1-886303-10-X*) Write to Print.

Bugles in the Afternoon. Ernest Haycox. 1976. 23.95 (*0-8488-1362-6*) Amereon Ltd.

Bugles in the Afternoon. Ernest Haycox. 1990. pap. 3.95 (*1-55817-455-9*, Pinnacle NY) Windsor NY.

Bugles in the Night. Burt Arthur. 1993. 14.95 (*0-7451-4580-9*, Gunsmoke) Chivers N Amer.

Bugles in the Valley: Garnett's Fort Simcoe. rev. ed. H. Dean Guie. LC 77-88149. (Illus.). 205p. 1977. pap. 5.95 (*0-87595-057-4*) Oregon Hist.

***Buglhat Motet Anthologies: Selections from Liber Cantus (Vocum Quatuor) Triginta Novem Motetos Habet.** Ed. by Mary Lewis. LC 95-5755. (Sixteenth-Century Motet Ser.: No. 14). 392p. 1995. 98.00 (*0-8240-7914-0*) Garland.

Bugling for Elk. Dwight Schuh. (Illus.). 164p. 1983. 17.95 (*0-912299-02-9*); pap. 12.95 (*0-912299-03-7*) Stoneydale Pr Pub.

Bugs. Heather Amery & Jane. (Discover Hidden Worlds Ser.). 48p. (J). 1994. write for info. (*0-307-15664-8*, Golden Bks) Western Pub.

***Bugs.** James E. Gerholdt. LC 95-1509. (Incredible Insects Ser.). (J). 1995. lib. bdg. 13.99 (*1-56239-480-0*) Abdo & Dghtrs.

Bugs! Patricia McKissack & Fredrick McKissack. LC 88-22875. (Rookie Reader Ser.). (Illus.). 32p. (J). (ps-2). 1988. lib. bdg. 10.35 (*0-516-02088-9*); pap. 2.95 (*0-516-42088-7*) Childrens.

Bugs. Nancy W. Parker & Joan R. Wright. LC 86-29387. (Illus.). 40p. (J). (gr. 1-4). 1987. 15.00 (*0-688-06623-2*); lib. bdg. 14.93 (*0-688-06624-0*) Greenwillow.

Bugs. Nancy W. Parker & Joan R. Wright. LC 86-29387. (Illus.). 40p. (J). (gr. k up). 1988. pap. 4.95 (*0-688-08296-3*, Mulberry) Morrow.

***Bugs: A Closer Look at the World's Tiny Creatures.** Jinny Johnson. LC 94-35361. (Illus.). 48p. (J). (gr. 2-7). 1995. 16.95 (*0-89577-677-4*, Readers Digest Kids) RD Assn.

Bugs: Stingers, Suckers, Sweeties, Swingers. Liz Greenbacker. LC 92-24963. (First Bks.). (Illus.). 64p. (J). (gr. 5-8). 1993. lib. bdg. 13.93 (*0-531-20072-8*) Watts.

Bugs: Stingers, Suckers, Sweeties, Swingers. Liz Greenbacker. (First Bks.). (Illus.). 64p. (J). (gr. 5-8). 1993. pap. 6.95 (*0-531-15673-7*) Watts.

Bugs - Bugs - Bugs, Vol. 10. Shirley A. Barone. (Illus.). 44p. (Orig.). (J). (ps-2). 1989. pap. write for info. (*0-318-66620-0*) Toad Hse Bks.

***Bugs & Beasties ABC.** Cheryl Nathan et al. LC 95-11534. 32p. (Orig.). (J). (gr. 1-4). 1995. 15.95 (*1-56790-516-1*, Cool Kids Pr) Cool Hand Comms.

***Bugs & Beasties ABC.** Cheryl Nathan. (Illus.). 32p. (Orig.). (J). (gr. 1-4). 1995. pap. 5.50 (*1-56790-515-3*) Cool Hand Comms.

Bugs & Critters. Brian Holly. (Discover Nature Ser.). (Illus.). 32p. (J). (gr. 3-7). 1985. pap. 3.50 (*0-88625-118-4*) Durkin Hayes Pub.

***Bugs & Other Insects.** Bobbie Kalman. LC 94-22904. (Crabapple Ser.). (Illus.). 32p. (Orig.). (J). (gr. k-3). 1994. lib. bdg. 14.95 (*0-86505-613-X*) Crabtree Pub Co.

***Bugs & Other Insects.** Bobbie Kalman. LC 94-22904. (Crabapple Ser.). (Illus.). 32p. (Orig.). (J). (gr. k-3). 1994. pap. 5.95 (*0-86505-713-3*) Crabtree Pub Co.

Bugs & Other Insects. Doris Roettger. 1991. 8.99 (*0-86653-992-1*) Fearon Teach Aids.

Bugs & Veronica: Two Plays. John White. 1966. pap. 4.75 (*0-8222-0161-5*) Dramatists Play.

Bugs, Beetles & Other Insects. 1989. pap. 0.71 (*0-394-82276-5*) Random.

***Bugs Bunny.** Golden Western Staff. (J). Date not set. pap. 1.59 (*0-307-08215-6*, Golden Pr) Western Pub.

Bugs Bunny: Fifty Years & Only One Grey Hare. Joe Adamson. (Illus.). 192p. 1991. pap. 19.95 (*0-8050-1855-7*, Owl) H Holt & Co.

Bugs Bunny: The Pirate Island. (Golden Story Book 'n Tape Ser.). (Illus.). 24p. (J). (ps-3). 1991. write for info. (*0-307-14176-4*, 14176) Western Pub.

B

An Asterisk (*) at the beginning of an entry indicates that the title is appearing in BIP for the first time.

Bugs Bunny Jubilee: Fifty Years & Only One Grey Hare. Text by Joe Adamson. 1990. 35.00 (*0-8050-1190-0*) H Holt & Co.

Bugs, Folks & Fun. Samuel Breeland. 93p. (Orig.). 1984. pap. 4.95 (*0-9615422-0-9*) S Breeland.

Bug's Gift. Scott Deschaine & Lynette Weisberg. (Illus.). 20p. (J). 1991. pap. 1.95 (*1-878181-01-7*) Discovery Comics.

***Bugs Go Marching.** Rozanne J. Williams. (Emergent Readers Ser.). 16p. (J). (gr. k-2). 1995. 2.49 (*0-916119-91-2*) Creat Teach Pr.

Bugs in the Program, Problems in Federal Government Computer Software Development & Regulation, Staff Study, September 1989. (Illus.). 42p. 1989. pap. 1.50 (*0-16-006364-7*, S/N 052-070-06604-1) USGPO.

Bugs in the System: Insects & Their Impact on Human Affairs. May Berenbaum. (C). 1995. 24.00 (*0-201-62499-0*) Addison-Wesley.

***BUGS in Writing: A Guide to Debugging Your Prose.** Lyn Dupre. LC 94-29807. (C). 1995. pap. text ed. 21.50 (*0-201-60019-6*) Addison-Wesley.

Bugs of the World. George C. McGavin. (Of the World Ser.). (Illus.). 192p. 1993. 25.95 (*0-8160-2737-4*) Facts on File.

Bugs, Slugs & Other Thugs: Controlling Garden Pests Organically. Rhonda M. Hart. LC 90-50607. (Illus.). 224p. 1991. pap. 9.95 (*0-88266-664-9*) Storey Comm Inc.

B

Bugs to Bunnies: Hands-on Animal Science Activities for Young Children. Kenn Goin et al. (Illus.). 192p. (Orig.). (J). (gr. k-2). 1989. pap. text ed. 14.95 (*0-943129-03-6*) Chatterbox Pr.

***Bugs' Woids of Wisdom.** Warner Brothers Staff. (Looney Tunes Pop-Up Ser.). 5p. (J). 1996. 4.95 (*0-446-91099-6*) Warner Bks.

Bugsy. James Toback. 1991. pap. 12.95 (*0-8065-1288-1*, Citadel Pr) Carol Pub Group.

Bugsy: The Bloodthirsty, Lusty Life of Bugsy Siegel. George Carpozi. 1992. pap. 4.99 (*1-56171-148-9*) Sure Sellers.

Bugsy Goes to Cork. Carolyn Swift. 1990. pap. 7.95 (*1-85371-071-7*, Pub. by Poolbeg Pr IE) Dufour.

Bugsy Goes to Limerick. Carolyn Swift. 170p. (J). 1990. pap. 6.95 (*1-85371-014-8*, Pub. by Poolbeg Pr IE) Dufour.

Bugsy's Baby: The Secret Life of Mob Queen Virginia Hill. Andy Edmonds. LC 92-35889. 1993. 19.95 (*1-55972-164-2*, Birch Ln Pr) Carol Pub Group.

Bugwise. Pamela M. Hickman. (J). 1991. pap. 9.57 (*0-201-57074-2*) Addison-Wesley.

Bugz: An Extraterrestrial Pop-up Book. Contrib by Ron Van der Meer. LC 93-85507. (Illus.). 10p. (YA). 1994. 12.95 (*1-56138-339-2*) Running Pr.

Buheler's Backyard Boatbuilding. George Buheler. 1991. pap. text ed. 24.95 (*0-07-158380-7*) McGraw.

Buhr-ool Juwahir (Bahr al-Gewahir) Muhammad Ibn-Jusuf Al-Herewi. Ed. by Hukem A. Mujeed. 294p. reprint ed. write for info. (*0-318-71535-X*, Pub. by Georg Olms GW) Lubrecht & Cramer.

Buick: A Complete History. 3rd ed. LC 85-60916. 442p. 39.95 (*0-915038-64-1*, 3-AQ-0042) Auto Quarterly.

Buick Free Spirit Power Manual. John Thawley. (Illus.). 112p. (Orig.). Date not set. pap. text ed. 9.95 (*0-936834-23-4*) S S Autosports.

Buick Muscle 1965-1970. Ed. by R. M. Clarke. (Brooklands Bks). (Illus.). 100p. 1984. pap. 16.95 (*0-946489-41-6*, Pub. by Brooklands Bks UK) Motorbooks Intl.

Buick-Olds Pontiac, 1975-90 Repair & Tune-up Guide. Chilton Staff. (Illus.). 464p. 1990. pap. text ed. 16.95 (*0-8019-8039-9*) Chilton.

Buick Stage II V-6 Racing Engine: The Complete Preparation Guide for NASCAR, Grand National, & Short Track Racing. Dave Emanuel. 36p. 1987. pap. 6.95 (*0-942099-00-1*) Performance Pub.

Buick Technical Tips. Jim Crame. 325p. 1993. 19.95 (*0-9636866-0-7*) W MI Buick.

Buick, 1946-1978: The Classic Postwar Years. Jan P. Norbye & Jim Dunne. LC 92-33314. (MBI Ser.). (Illus.). 200p. 1993. 24.95 (*0-87938-727-0*) Motorbooks Intl.

Buik of Alexander the Conqueror III. Gilbert Hay. Ed. by John Cartwright. 254p. 1988. text ed. 45.00 (*0-08-036999-5*, Pub. by Aberdeen U Pr) Macmillan.

Buik of the Most Noble & Vailzeand Conqueror Alexander the Great. John Barbour. Ed. by David Laing. LC 70-161748. (Bannatyne Club, Edinburgh. Publications: No. 46). reprint ed. 62.50 (*0-404-52756-6*) AMS Pr.

***Build a Better Life by Stealing Office Supplies: Dogbert's Big Book of Business.** Scott Adams. (Illus.). 111p. 1994. pap. 7.95 (*0-8362-1757-8*) Andrews & McMeel.

Build a Better Mousetrap. Susan Striker. (Anti-Coloring Bks.). (Illus.). 64p. (J). (gr. 2 up). 1983. pap. 6.95 (*0-8050-2615-0*, Owl) H Holt & Co.

Build a Better Staff: Hiring, Evaluating, & Firing Staff Members. Ed. by Darla Struck & Jeff Stratton. 119.00 (*0-8342-0403-7*, 04037) Aspen Pub.

Build-a-Board. Marilynn G. Barr. (Illus.). 128p. (J). (gr. 1-6). 1991. pap. 10.95 (*1-878279-32-7*) Monday Morning Bks.

Build-a-Book Geometry. Christopher C. Healy. 239p. (YA). (gr. 9-12). 1993. pap. 9.95 (*1-55953-066-9*) Key Curr Pr.

Build a Clancy: A Step-by-Step Guide to Your First Boat. J. D. Brown & Bob Pickett. 96p. 1992. pap. 13.95 (*0-87742-318-0*) Intl Marine.

Build a Classic Timber-Framed House: Planning & Design - Traditional Materials & Methods - Affordable Methods. Jack A. Sobon. LC 93-14118. (Illus.). 208p. 1994. 29.95 (*0-88266-842-0*, Garden Way Pub); pap. 19.95 (*0-88266-841-2*, Garden Way Pub) Storey Comm Inc.

Build a Doll's House. Michael Morse. LC 93-25460. 1993. reprint ed. 19.95 (*0-89024-188-0*) Kalmbach.

Build a Doodle, No. 1. B. Armstrong. (Holiday & Art Ser.). 32p. (J). (gr. k-4). 1985. 2.95 (*0-88160-124-1*, LW 133) Learning Wks.

Build a Doodle, No. 2. B. Armstrong. (Holiday & Art Ser.). 32p. (J). (gr. k-4). 1985. 2.95 (*0-88160-125-X*, LW 134) Learning Wks.

Build a Doodle Circus. Beverly Armstrong. (Holiday & Art Ser.). (Illus.). 32p. (J). (gr. k-4). 1986. 2.95 (*0-88160-133-0*, LW138) Learning Wks.

Build a Doodle City. Beverly Armstrong. (Enrichment & Gifted Ser.). (Illus.). 32p. (J). (gr. k-4). 1986. 2.95 (*0-88160-132-2*, LW136) Learning Wks.

Build a Doodle Farm. Beverly Armstrong. (Holiday & Art Ser.). (Illus.). 32p. (J). (gr. k-4). 1986. 2.95 (*0-88160-130-6*, LW135) Learning Wks.

Build a Doodle Kit. Linda Schwartz. (J). (gr. k-4). 1990. pap. 10.95 (*0-88160-198-5*, LW152) Learning Wks.

Build a Doodle Ocean. Beverly Armstrong. (Holiday & Art Ser.). (Illus.). 32p. (J). (gr. k-4). 1986. 2.95 (*0-88160-131-4*, LW137) Learning Wks.

Build a Great Future. Norman Vincent Peale. 1987. audio 8.95 (*0-943371-00-7*) Positive Comns.

***Build a Great Team: Pick the Right People for the Right Roles.** Ros Jay. (Institute of Management Ser.). 250p. 1995. pap. 36.50 (*0-273-61376-6*, Pub. by Pitman Pub Ltd UK) Trans-Atl Phila.

Build a Guidance Program Planning Model Module, Competency-Based Career Guidance (CBCG) - Category A: Guidance Program Planning. National Center for Research in Vocational Education Staff. 1985. 7.95 (*0-317-03856-7*, CG100A05) Ctr Educ Trng Employ.

Build a Literate Classroom. Donald H. Graves. LC 90-43879. (Reading-Writing Teacher's Companion Ser.). 198p. (Orig.). (C). 1991. pap. text ed. 14.00 (*0-435-08488-7*, 08488) Heinemann.

Build a Power Hacksaw with Vise. Vincent R. Gingery. LC 92-90772. (Illus.). 69p. (Orig.). 1992. pap. text ed. 8.95 (*1-878087-12-6*) D J Gingery.

Build a Two Cylinder Stirling Cycle Engine. David J. Gingery. LC 90-93266. (Illus.). 76p. (Orig.). 1991. pap. 9.95 (*1-878087-09-6*) D J Gingery.

***Build a View Camera: Metal & Wood Camera Construction.** James Tannehill & Ed Romney. 49p. 1995. pap. text ed. 16.00 (*1-886996-63-6*) Hillcrst Pub.

***Build a World Wide Web Site: The Programmers Guide to Creating Building & Maintaining a Web...** Gray. 1995. pap. (*0-7615-0064-2*) Prima Pub.

Build & Repair with Concrete: The Complete Do-It-Yourself Manual. Quikrete Companies Staff. LC 85-30139. (Illus.). 165p. 1986. 6.95 (*0-937558-16-8*) Scharff Ltd.

Build & Repair with Concrete: The Complete Do-It-Yourself Manual. 2nd ed. Quikrete Companies Staff. LC 85-30139. (Illus.). 165p. 1986. 7.95 (*0-937558-18-4*) Scharff Ltd.

Build Cell. Bill Steinbock. 1993. disk 69.00 (*1-56690-045-X*, OnWord Pr) High Mtn.

Build It: Out of Sight Sewing Center. Joseph D. D'Addario. 1972. pap. 5.95 (*0-686-01898-2*) Classic Furn Kits.

Build-It-Better-Yourself Woodworking Projects: Accents for the Country Home. Nick Engler. LC 89-35630. (Illus.). 128p. 1989. 19.95 (*0-87857-841-2*, 14-963-0); pap. 14.95 (*0-87857-842-0*, 14-963-1) Rodale Pr Inc.

Build-It-Better-Yourself Woodworking Projects: Benches, Swings & Gliders. 128p. 1991. 19.95 (*0-87857-943-5*) Rodale Pr Inc.

Build-It-Better-Yourself Woodworking Projects: Country Furniture: Cupboards, Cabinets & Shelves. Nick Engler. LC 90-35898. 128p. 1991. 19.95 (*0-87857-929-X*, 14-885-0); pap. 14.95 (*0-87857-953-2*, 14-885-1) Rodale Pr Inc.

Build-It-Better-Yourself Woodworking Projects: Country Furniture: Kitchens & Dining Rooms. Nick Engler. LC 88-26445. (Illus.). 128p. 1989. 19.95 (*0-87857-790-4*, 14-733-0); pap. 14.95 (*0-87857-852-8*, 14-733-1) Rodale Pr Inc.

Build-It-Better-Yourself Woodworking Projects: Country Furniture: Living Rooms & Dens. Nick Engler. LC 89-5956. (Illus.). 128p. 1989. 19.95 (*0-87857-838-2*, 14-019-0); pap. 14.95 (*0-87857-853-6*, 14-019-1) Rodale Pr Inc.

Build-It-Better-Yourself Woodworking Projects: Desks & Bookcases. Nick Engler. LC 89-70278. (Illus.). 128p. 1990. 19.95 (*0-87857-847-1*, 14-007-0); pap. 14.95 (*0-87857-848-X*, 14-007-1) Rodale Pr Inc.

Build-It-Better-Yourself Woodworking Projects: Display Cases, Frames, & Shelves. Nick Engler. LC 89-10876. (Illus.). 128p. 1990. 19.95 (*0-87857-843-9*, 14-449-0); pap. 14.95 (*0-87857-844-7*, 14-449-1) Rodale Pr Inc.

Build-It Book of Digital Clocks. 2nd ed. Robert Haviland. (Illus.). 350p. 1986. pap. 14.95 (*0-8306-1683-7*) TAB Bks.

Build it Right! How to Put Value & Quality in Your New Home. Myron Ferguson. (Illus.). 274p. (Orig.). 1994. pap. 16.95 (*0-931625-23-8*) DIMI Pr.

Build It Right: Supervising the Construction of Your Home. Kenneth L. Petrocelly. 1990. 24.95 (*0-07-156851-4*) McGraw.

Build It Right Supervising Company. Kenneth L. Petrocelly. (Illus.). 208p. 1990. 24.95 (*0-8306-7433-0*, 3433); pap. 14.95 (*0-8306-3433-9*) TAB Bks.

Build It Strong! Julian Rowe & Molly Perham. LC 94-16941. (First Science Ser.). (Illus.). 32p. (J). (gr. 1-4). 1994. lib. bdg. 13.95 (*0-516-08138-1*); pap. 4.95 (*0-516-48138-X*) Childrens.

Build It Together: Thirty Easy Woodworking Projects for Kids & Adults. Katie Hamilton & Gene Hamilton. (Illus.). 144p. 1994. pap. 16.95 (*0-8117-2421-2*) Stackpole.

Build It Together: Twenty-Seven Easy to Make Woodworking Projects for Adults & Children. Katie Hamilton & Gene Hamilton. (Illus.). 192p. 1984. 24.95 (*0-684-18125-8*, Scribners) S&S Trade.

***Build It with Bales: A Step-by-Step Guide to Straw-Bale Construction.** S. O. MacDonald & Matts Myhrman. 80p. 1994. write for info. (*0-9642821-0-0*) Inhabit Srvs.

Build It with Boxes. Joan Irvine. LC 91-45589. (Illus.). 96p. (J). (gr. 3 up). 1993. 14.00 (*0-688-12081-4*); lib. bdg. 13.93 (*0-688-11524-1*); pap. 6.95 (*0-688-11525-X*, Pub. by Beech Tree Bks) Morrow Jr Bks.

Build-It-Yourself Furniture Catalog. Franklynn Peterson. LC 76-6567. 1976. pap. 4.95 (*0-13-085902-8*, Reward) P-H.

Build Like Me. Jane L. Mills & Larry D. Johnson. LC 86-60362. (Building Set Ser.: Level 2). (Illus.). 13p. (Orig.). (J). (ps). 1986. pap. 4.00 (*0-938155-01-6*) Read A Bol.

Build Like Me, 3 vols., Set. Jane L. Mills & Larry D. Johnson. LC 86-60362. (Building Set Ser.: Level 2). (Illus.). 13p. (Orig.). (J). (ps). 1986. pap. 12.00 (*0-685-13524-1*) Read A Bol.

Build Me a Castle. David M. Pierce. 1995. write for info. (*0-89296-485-5*) Mysterious Pr.

Build or Buy a Loom, Pt. 1. Harriet Tidball. Bd. with Pt. 2. Patterns for Pick-Ups. LC 76-24013. LC 76-24013. (Guild Monographs: No. 23). (Illus.). 38p. 1968. Set pap. 7.95 (*0-916658-23-6*) Shuttle Craft.

***Build or Renovate Your Own Home.** David Pocock. 1995. 23.95 (*0-8062-5241-3*) Carlton.

Build the Alamo. Mark Wheatly. Ed. by Ed Eakin. (Illus.). 32p. (J). (gr. 4-5). 1989. 10.95 (*0-89015-721-9*) Sunbelt Media.

Build the Communist Party - the Party of the Working Class. Henry Winston. 1969. pap. 0.35 (*0-87898-039-3*) New Outlook.

Build the Homes Your Buyers Want: How to Add Value & Appeal to Your Homes. Michael Knorr. LC 91-35567. (Illus.). 112p. 1991. pap. 24.00 (*0-86718-371-3*) Home Builder.

Build the Instant Catboat. Harold H. Payson. (Illus.). 48p. 1987. pap. text ed. 12.95 (*0-87742-222-2*) Intl Marine.

Build the Instant Catboat. Harold H. Payson. 1987. pap. text ed. 12.95 (*0-07-155839-X*) McGraw.

Build the Market Offering: How to Take Your Products to Market. Richard H. Montgomery. (Illus.). 200p. 1989. ring bd. 34.95 (*0-915991-13-6*); ring bd. 39.95 (*0-915991-14-4*) R H Mont Assocs.

Build the Musashi: The Birth & Death of the World's Greatest Battleship. Akira Yoshimura. Tr. by Vincent Murphy. (Illus.). 160p. 1992. 19.95 (*4-7700-1579-8*) Kodansha.

Build the New Instant Boats. Harold H. Payson. LC 84-81554. (Illus.). 160p. 1987. pap. text ed. 19.95 (*0-87742-187-0*) Intl Marine.

Build the New Instant Boats. Harold H. Payson. 1987. pap. text ed. 19.95 (*0-07-155966-3*) McGraw.

Build unto My Holy Name: The Story of the Denver Temple. Twila Bird. Ed. by Breck England. LC 87-51134. (Illus.). 208p. 1987. 15.00 (*0-9619296-0-X*) DCAPCC.

Build-Up. William Carlos Williams. LC 52-5166. (Stecher Trilogy Ser.: Vol. 3). 1968. reprint ed. pap. 9.95 (*0-8112-0227-5*, NDP259) New Directions.

Build with Adobe. 3rd enl. rev. ed. Marcia Southwick. LC 73-1504. (Illus.). 235p. 1994. reprint ed. pap. 14.95 (*0-8040-0634-2*) Swallow.

***Build with Beakman: Bacteria Farm.** (J). 1994. pap. 12.95 (*0-8362-7013-4*) Andrews & McMeel.

***Build with Beakman: Electronic Intercom.** (J). 1994. pap. 12.95 (*0-8362-7012-6*) Andrews & McMeel.

***Build with Beakman: Hovercraft: From the Hit TV Show "Beakman's World"** Luann Colombo. (Illus.). 24p. (J). 1995. pap. 12.95 (*0-8362-7040-1*) Andrews & McMeel.

***Build with Beakman: Spud Watch: From the Hit TV Show "Beakman's World"** Luann Colombo. (Illus.). 24p. 1995. pap. 12.95 (*0-8362-7042-8*) Andrews & McMeel.

Build You Own Home, a Guide for Subcontracting the Easy Way, a System to Save Time & Money. 4th enl. ed. J. James Hasenau. (Illus.). 1992. pap. 12.95 (*0-913042-19-6*) Holland Hse Pr.

Build Your Bible Knowledge - Acts. John H. Tiner. 1988. pap. 4.50 (*0-89137-335-7*) Quality Pubns.

Build Your Brain Power. Arthur Winter & Ruth Winter. 224p. 1987. pap. 9.95 (*0-312-01006-0*) St Martin.

Build Your Case. Rodney E. Kleber. (ESOL College Ser.). (Illus.). 224p. (C). 1988. text ed. 21.94 (*0-201-16527-9*) Addison-Wesley.

Build Your Church Through Camping. Lloyd Mattson. 48p. (Orig.). 1984. pap. 1.95 (*0-942684-06-0*) Camp Guidepts.

***Build Your Dream Home for Less.** R. Dodge Woodson. 192p. (Orig.). 1995. pap. 18.99 (*1-55870-383-7*) Betterway Bks.

Build Your Home Darkroom. rev. ed. Lista Duren & Wil McDonald. (Illus.). 154p. (C). 1990. reprint ed. pap. 17.95 (*0-936262-04-4*) Amherst Media.

Build Your Own. R. Daley & S. Daley. 1991. 24.95 (*0-8306-6428-9*) TAB Bks.

Build Your Own Adobe. Paul Aller & Doris Aller. (Illus.). 111p. reprint ed. pap. 30.00 (*0-7837-1222-7*, 2041753) Bks Demand.

***Build Your Own Bugs Book & Kit: Learn All about Insects As You Stamp Together Real Bugs!** Dennis Schatz. (Illus.). 32p. (J). 1995. pap. 14.95 (*0-8362-4242-4*) Andrews & McMeel.

Build-Your-Own Cathedral of Learning. Illus. by Leonard G. Martin. 44p. (Orig.). 1991. pap. 20.00 (*1-878242-00-8*) Fourth River Pr.

***Build Your Own Climbing Wall.** Ramsay Thomas. (How to Rock Climb Ser.). (Illus.). 32p. 1995. pap. text ed. 5.95 (*0-934641-73-0*) Chockstone Pr.

***Build Your Own Computer.** 2nd ed. Kenneth L. Hughes. LC 95-14627. 1995. pap. write for info. (*1-55622-459-1*) Wordware Pub.

Build Your Own Computer Accessories & Save a Bundle. Bonnie J. Hargrave & Ted Dunning. 1992. text ed. 29.95 (*0-07-026380-9*); pap. text ed. 19.95 (*0-07-026381-7*) McGraw.

Build Your Own Computer Accessories & Save a Bundle. Bonnie J. Hargrave & Ted Dunning. LC 92-11594. (Illus.). 376p. 1992. 29.95 (*0-8306-3865-2*, 4134, Windcrest); pap. 19.95 (*0-8306-3866-0*, 4134, Windcrest) TAB Bks.

Build Your Own Contemporary Playhouse. Karen Dallago-Barnofsky & Sharon Dallago-Genden. (Build Your Own Playhouse Ser.: No. 2). (Illus.). 1991. pap. 18.95 (*1-879226-12-X*) Munchkin Pubns.

Build Your Own Deck Manual. Randy Byrne. Ed. & Illus. by David Sabotka. 64p. 1990. pap. 9.95 (*0-934039-28-3*, A200) Natl Plan Serv.

***Build Your Own Dinosaurs: Learn All about Dinosaurs As You Stamp Together Real Dinosaur Skeletons.** Dennis Schatz. (Illus.). 32p. (J). 1994. pap. 14.95 (*0-8362-4512-1*) Andrews & McMeel.

Build Your Own Electric Car. Bob Brant. (Illus.). 288p. 1993. 26.95 (*0-8306-4232-3*, 4283) TAB Bks.

Build Your Own Electric Guitar: Custom Guitar Assembly Made Easy. Bill Foley. 1986. pap. 19.95 (*0-9618361-0-5*) Bold Strummer Ltd.

Build Your Own Electric Power Plant: A Home Solar Electric Plant. rev. ed. Jack Hedger. (Illus.). 150p. 1993. 29.95 (*0-9634007-3-8*); pap. 24.95 (*0-9634007-2-X*) Akela West Pubs.

Build Your Own Empire State Building. Alan Rose. LC 94-2619. 1994. pap. 14.38 (*0-201-62705-1*) Addison-Wesley.

***Build Your Own Farm.** Random House Staff. (J). 1994. 5.99 (*0-517-10248-X*) Random Hse Value.

Build Your Own Furniture. Peter Stamberg. LC 81-66174. 1981. pap. 8.95 (*0-345-29553-6*) Ballantine.

Build Your Own Gabled-Front Playhouse. Karen Dallago-Barnofsky & Sharon Dallago-Genden. (Build Your Own Playhouse Ser.: No. 1). (Illus.). 1991. pap. 18.95 (*1-879226-11-1*) Munchkin Pubns.

Build Your Own Garage Manual. Ed. by National Plan Service, Inc. Staff. (Illus.). 88p. 1987. pap. 12.95 (*0-934039-26-7*, A270) Natl Plan Serv.

Build Your Own Grandfather Clock & Save. John A. Nelson. (Illus.). 144p. 1988. 19.95 (*0-8306-9053-0*, 3053); pap. 12.95 (*0-8306-9353-X*, 3053) TAB Bks.

Build Your Own Green PC. Wallace Wang. LC 94-7918. 1994. pap. text ed. 19.95 (*0-07-068156-2*) McGraw.

Build Your Own Home for Less Than 15,000 Dollars. Paul Bemish. LC 84-60483. (Illus.). 128p. (Orig.). 1984. pap. 9.95 (*0-688-02640-0*, Quill) Morrow.

Build Your Own Home Security System. Delton T. Horn. 1993. text ed. 27.95 (*0-07-030392-4*); pap. text ed. 16.95 (*0-07-030393-2*) McGraw.

Build Your Own Home Security System. Delton T. Horn. LC 92-41602. 1993. 27.95 (*0-8306-3870-9*); pap. 14.60 (*0-8306-3871-7*) TAB Bks.

Build Your Own Home Theater. Robert I. Wolenik. 212p. 1993. 16.95 (*0-672-30381-7*) Sams.

Build Your Own IBM Compatible & Save a Bundle. Aubrey Pilgrim. 224p. (Orig.). 1987. 22.95 (*0-8306-0231-3*, 2831); pap. 16.95 (*0-8306-2831-2*) TAB Bks.

Build Your Own IBM Compatible & Save a Bundle. 2nd ed. Aubrey Pilgrim. (Illus.). 272p. (Orig.). 1991. pap. 19.95 (*0-8306-3804-0*, 3804, Windcrest) TAB Bks.

Build Your Own Inexpensive Dollhouse: With One Sheet of 4 by 8 Plywood & Home Tools. E. J. Tangerman. LC 76-50272. (Illus.). 48p. 1978. pap. 3.50 (*0-486-23493-2*) Dover.

***Build Your Own Intelligent Mobile Space Robot.** Steven J. Montgomery. 1995. disk, pap. text ed. 29.95 (*0-07-042946-4*) McGraw.

Build Your Own Kit House. Jonathan Erickson. LC 87-29048. (Illus.). 288p. 1988. 22.95 (*0-8306-7873-5*, 2873); pap. 14.95 (*0-8306-2873-8*) TAB Bks.

Build Your Own LAN & Save a Bundle. Aubrey Pilgrim. 1992. 31.95 (*0-07-050107-6*); pap. 21.95 (*0-07-050108-4*) McGraw.

Build Your Own LAN & Save a Bundle. Aubrey Pilgrim. LC 92-5692. (Illus.). 256p. 1992. 31.95 (*0-8306-4088-6*, 4210, Windcrest); pap. 21.95 (*0-8306-4089-4*, 4210, Windcrest) TAB Bks.

Build Your Own Laser, Phaser, Ion Ray Gun & Other Working Space-Age Projects. Robert E. Iannini. 1983. pap. text ed. 17.95 (*0-07-156069-6*) McGraw.

Build Your Own Laser, Phaser, Ion Ray Gun & Other Working Space-Age Projects. Robert E. Iannini. (Illus.). 308p. 1983. pap. 17.95 (*0-8306-0604-1*, 1604) TAB Bks.

Build Your Own Log Home from Scratch. 2nd ed. S. Blackwell Duncan. (Illus.). 352p. 1988. 25.95 (*0-8306-9481-1*, 3081); pap. 16.95 (*0-8306-9081-6*, 3081) TAB Bks.

Build Your Own Low-Cost Data Acquisition & Display Devices. Jeffrey H. Johnson. 1993. text ed. 19.95 (*0-07-032618-5*) McGraw.

Build Your Own Low-Cost Data Acquisition & Display Devices. Jeffrey H. Johnson. 1993. pap. text ed. 23.95 (*0-8306-4348-6*) TAB Bks.

Build Your Own Low-Cost Hangar. Joe Christy. (Illus.). 126p. (Orig.). 1983. pap. 9.25 (*0-8306-2357-4*, 2357) TAB Bks.

Build Your Own Low Cost Home. L. O. Anderson & Harold F. Zornig. 204p. 1972. pap. 15.95 (*0-486-21525-3*) Dover.

Build Your Own Low-Cost Log Home. Roger Hard. LC 85-70197. (Illus.). 208p. 1985. pap. 16.95 (*0-88266-399-2*, Garden Way Pub) Storey Comm Inc.

An Asterisk (*) at the beginning of an entry indicates that the title is appearing in BIP for the first time.

Build Your Own Low-Cost PC & Save a Bundle. Aubrey Pilgrim. 1993. 29.95 (*0-07-050105-X*); pap. 19.95 (*0-07-050106-8*) McGraw.

Build Your Own Low-Cost PC & Save a Bundle. Aubrey Pilgrim. LC 92-26118. (Illus.). 224p. 1992. 29.95 (*0-8306-4086-X*, Windcrest); pap. 18.95 (*0-8306-4087-8*, Windcrest) TAB Bks.

Build Your Own Low-Cost PostScript Printer & Save a Bundle. 2nd ed. Horace LaBadie, Jr. 1993. pap. text ed. 19.95 (*0-07-035887-7*, Windcrest) TAB Bks.

***Build Your Own Low-Cost Signal Generator.** Delton T. Horn. 1994. pap. text ed. 19.95 (*0-07-030429-7*) McGraw.

Build Your Own Macintosh: The CAT Mac. Bob Brant. (Illus.). 100p. 1990. spiral bd. 24.95 (*0-9624249-0-0*) Brants Bks.

Build Your Own Macintosh & Save a Bundle. 2nd ed. Bob Brant. 376p. 1992. 29.95 (*0-8306-3973-X*, 4156, Windcrest); pap. 19.95 (*0-8306-3974-8*, 4156, Windcrest) TAB Bks.

Build Your Own Macintosh Compatible & Save A Bundle. Bob Brant. (Illus.). 224p. 1990. pap. 17.95 (*0-8306-3656-0*, 3656, Windcrest) TAB Bks.

Build Your Own Macintosh Compatible & Save a Bundle. Bob Brant. 1990. pap. 17.95 (*0-07-156888-3*) McGraw.

***Build Your Own Microcomputer Based on the Intel 8088.** Walter Fuller. 192p. 1995. pap. text ed. 28.95 (*0-8273-7069-5*) Delmar.

***Build Your Own Mobile Power Tool Centers.** John R. McPherson. (Illus.). 144p. (Orig.). 1995. pap. 19.99 (*1-55870-380-2*) Betterway Bks.

Build Your Own Multimedia PC. Aubrey Pilgrim. LC 93-21305. 1994. pap. text ed. 36.95 (*0-07-050113-0*, Windcrest) TAB Bks.

Build Your Own Multimedia PC with CD Rom. Aubrey Pilgrim. 1993. pap. text ed. 36.95 (*0-8306-4566-7*, Windcrest) TAB Bks.

***Build Your Own PC: A Complete Guide to Renovating & Constructing Personal Computers.** Ian Sinclair. (Illus.). 256p. 1994. pap. 29.95 (*0-7506-2006-4*) Buttrwrth-Heinemann.

Build Your Own Pentium Processor. Aubrey Pilgrim. LC 94-6945. 1994. text ed. 32.95 (*0-07-050163-7*, Windcrest) TAB Bks.

Build Your Own Pentium Processor PC. Aubrey Pilgrim. 1994. pap. text ed. 19.95 (*0-07-050164-5*) McGraw.

Build Your Own Polyhedra. Peter Hilton. 1994. pap. 27.50 (*0-201-49096-X*) Addison-Wesley.

Build Your Own Polyhedra. Peter J. Hilton & Jean Pedersen. 1988. spiral bd. 27.50 (*0-201-22060-1*) Addison-Wesley.

Build Your Own PostScript Laser Printer & Save a Bundle. Horace W. LaBadie. 1991. pap. text ed. 16.95 (*0-07-157701-7*) McGraw.

Build Your Own PostScript Laser Printer & Save a Bundle. Horace W. LaBadie, Jr. (Illus.). 144p. 1991. 24.95 (*0-8306-4738-4*, 3738, Windcrest); pap. 16.95 (*0-8306-3738-9*, Windcrest) TAB Bks.

Build Your Own PostScript Printer & Save a Bundle. 2nd ed. Horace W. LaBadie, Jr. LC 92-41245. 1993. 19.60 (*0-8306-4306-0*) TAB Bks.

Build Your Own Radio. Jim Becker & Andy Mayer. (Discovery Kit Ser.). (Illus.). 64p. (Orig.). (J). (gr. 3 up). 1992. 19.95 (*1-56138-071-7*) Running Pr.

Build Your Own Rainbow: A Workbook for Career & Life Management. Barrie Hopson & Mike Scally. LC 92-50992. 296p. 1993. pap. 12.95 (*0-89384-208-7*) Pfeiffer & Co.

Build Your Own Road. Lois Wolffe-Morgan. 1992. mass mkt. 4.99 (*0-425-13186-6*) Berkley Pub.

Build Your Own Road: Get Where You Want to Go - The Way You Want to Get There. Lois Wolf-Morgan. LC 89-85529. 169p. 1989. 19.95 (*0-939975-03-3*) Exec Pr NC.

Build Your Own Shed Manual: A210. Randy Byrne. Ed. by National Plan Service Staff. (Illus.). 64p. 1992. per. 9.95 (*0-934039-38-0*) Natl Plan Serv.

Build Your Own Shortwave Antennas. 2nd ed. Andrew Yoder. LC 94-10829. 1994. pap. text ed. 16.95 (*0-07-076534-0*) TAB Bks.

Build Your Own Stone House: Using the Easy Slipform Method. rev. ed. Karl Schwenke & Sue Schwenke. Ed. by Ben Watson. LC 90-50422. 160p. 1991. pap. 11.95 (*0-88266-639-8*) Storey Comm Inc.

Build Your Own Sukkah see Kadima Kesher Series

Build Your Own Telescope. Richard Berry. LC 93-39362. 1993. write for info. (*0-943396-42-5*) Willmann-Bell.

Build Your Own Telescope: Complete Plans for Five High-Quality Telescopes That Anyone Can Build. Richard Berry. (Illus.). 240p. 1985. 24.95 (*0-317-19458-5*, Scribners) S&S Trade.

Build Your Own Test Equipment. Homer L. Davidson. 1991. pap. text ed. 19.95 (*0-07-015559-3*) McGraw.

Build Your Own Test Equipment. Homer L. Davidson. (Illus.). 300p. 1991. 25.95 (*0-8306-8475-1*, 3475); pap. 17.95 (*0-8306-3475-4*) TAB Bks.

***Build Your Own Town.** Random House Staff. (J). 1994. 5.99 (*0-517-10249-8*) Random Hse Value.

Build Your Own Tudor Playhouse. Karen Dallago-Barnofsky & Sharon Dallago-Genden. (Build Your Own Playhouse Ser.: No. 3). (Illus.). 1991. pap. 18.95 (*1-879226-13-8*) Munchkin Pubns.

Build Your Own Universal Computer Interface. Bruce Chubb. 1989. pap. text ed. 21.95 (*0-07-155740-7*) McGraw.

Build Your Own Universal Computer Interface. Bruce Chubb. (Illus.). 288p. 1989. 27.95 (*0-8306-9422-6*, 3122); pap. 21.95 (*0-8306-3122-4*, 3122) TAB Bks.

***Build Your Own Web Site for Almost Free: Create a World Wide Web Site with HTML, Perl, & Linux.** Linus Paulson. 600p. 1995. cd-rom, pap. 36.96 (*1-57169-053-0*) Waite Group Pr.

Build Your Own Wood Toys. R. J. DeCristoforo. LC 88-33364. (Illus.). 364p. (Orig.). 1989. pap. 12.95 (*0-8069-6993-8*) Sterling.

Build Your Own Woodburning Furnace. Bill White. LC 78-66818. (Illus.). 1978. pap. 3.50 (*0-9601794-2-9*) FireBuilders.

Build Your Own Working Fiberoptic, Infrared, & Laser Space-Age Projects. Robert E. Iannini. (Illus.). 288p. 1987. 24.95 (*0-8306-0824-9*, NO. 2724); pap. 17.95 (*0-8306-2724-3*) TAB Bks.

Build Your Own Working Fiberoptic, Infrared & Laser Space-Age Projects. Robert E. Iannini. 1987. pap. text ed. 17.95 (*0-07-156282-6*) McGraw.

Build Your Own Working Robot: The Second Generation. David L. Heiserman. (Illus.). 140p. (Orig.). 1987. 18.95 (*0-8306-1181-9*, 2781) TAB Bks.

Build Your Own Z80 Computer. Steve Ciarcia. 473p. 1980. pap. text ed. 28.95 (*0-07-010962-1*, BYTE Bks) McGraw.

Build Your Own 386 - 386sx & Save a Bundle. 2nd ed. Aubrey Pilgrim. 1992. pap. 18.95 (*0-07-050089-4*) McGraw.

Build Your Own 486-486SX & Save a Bundle. 2nd ed. Aubrey Pilgrim. (Illus.). 256p. 1992. 29.95 (*0-8306-4217-X*, 4270, Windcrest); pap. 19.95 (*0-8306-4216-1*, 4270, Windcrest) TAB Bks.

Build Your Own 80286 IBM Compatible & Save a Bundle. Aubrey Pilgrim. (Illus.) 208p. 1988. 24.95 (*0-8306-0331-X*) TAB Bks.

Build Your Own 80386 Compatible & Save a Bundle. 2nd ed. Aubrey Pilgrim. 1991. write for info. (*0-8306-3752-4*, Windcrest); pap. 18.95 (*0-8306-3750-8*, Windcrest) TAB Bks.

Build Your Own 80386 IBM Compatble & Save a Bundle. Aubrey Pilgrim. 1988. pap. 17.95 (*0-07-155874-8*) McGraw.

Build Your Own 80386 IBM Compatible & Save a Bundle. Aubrey Pilgrim. (Illus.). 224p. 1988. 24.95 (*0-8306-9131-6*, 3131); pap. 17.95 (*0-8306-3131-3*, 3131) TAB Bks.

Build Your Own 80486 & Save a Bundle. Aubrey Pilgrim. 1992. pap. 19.95 (*0-07-050110-6*) McGraw.

Build Your Own 80486 & Save a Bundle. 2nd ed. Aubrey Pilgrim. 1992. 29.95 (*0-07-050109-2*) McGraw.

Build Your Own 80486 PC & Save a Bundle. Aubrey Pilgrim. (Illus.). 224p. 1991. pap. 16.95 (*0-8306-7628-7*, Windcrest) TAB Bks.

Builder Also Grows. Elizabeth Montgomery. Ed. by Sylvia Ashton. LC 77-82653. 1979. 19.95 (*0-87949-099-3*) Ashley Bks.

***Builder Illustrations Index.** Ruth Richardson & Robert Thorne. (Illus.). 846p. 1995. 230.00 (*0-907101-06-2*, Pub. by Hutton Plus UK) Antique Collect.

Builder Lite: Developing Dynamic Batch Files. Ronny Richardson. 1992. 44.95 (*0-07-052362-2*); pap. 32.95 (*0-07-052363-0*) McGraw.

Builder Lite: Developing Dynamic Batch Files. Ronny Richardson. (Illus.). 368p. 1992. 44.95 (*0-8306-4175-0*, 4248, Windcrest); pap. 32.95 (*0-8306-4176-9*, 4248, Windcrest) TAB Bks.

Builder of Bridges: The Biography of Dr. Bob Jones, Sr. R. K. Johnson. (Illus.). 383p. 1982. reprint ed. pap. 9.95 (*0-89084-157-8*) Bob Jones Univ Pr.

Builder of Men: Life in New Hampshire CCC Camps. David D. Draves. (Illus.). 432p. 1992. pap. 18.00 (*0-914339-39-7*) P E Randall Pub.

Builder of the Moon. Tim Wynne-Jones. LC 88-12703. (Illus.). 32p. (J). (ps-3). 1989. text ed. 14.95 (*0-689-50472-1*, McElderry) S&S Childrens.

Builder of the New South: Being the Story of the Life Work of Daniel Augustus Tompkins. George T. Winston. LC 75-38375. (Select Bibliographies Reprint Ser.). 1977. reprint ed. 23.95 (*0-8369-6792-5*) Ayer.

Builder of the West: The Life of General William Jackson Palmer. John S. Fisher. Ed. by Stuart Bruchey. LC 80-1306. (Railroads Ser.). (Illus.). 1981. reprint ed. lib. bdg. 38.95 (*0-405-13775-3*) Ayer.

Builder of the Year Plan Collection. Building News Staff. 1993. pap. 29.95 (*1-55701-082-X*) BNI Pubns.

Builder Through History. Richard Wood. LC 93-24398. (Journey Through History Ser.). (Illus.). 48p. (J). (gr. 5-8). 1994. 15.95 (*1-56847-102-5*) Thomson Lrning.

Builders: A Story & Study of Freemasonry. 9th ed. Joseph F. Newton. (Illus.). 345p. 1985. reprint ed. 16.95 (*0-88053-045-6*, M 301) Macoy Pub.

Builders: A Story & Study of Freemasonry. 10th ed. Joseph F. Newton. (Illus.). xxx, 315p. 1989. reprint ed. 16.95 (*0-318-42073-2*, M301) Macoy Pub.

Builders: Marvels of Engineering. National Geographic Society Book Division Staff. Ed. by Elizabeth L. Newhouse. LC 92-30615. (Illus.). 288p. 1992. 41.95 (*0-87044-837-4*) Natl Geog.

Builders: Marvels of Engineering. National Geographic Society Book Division Staff. Ed. by Elizabeth L. Newhouse. LC 92-30615. (Illus.). 288p. 1994. pap. 40.00 (*0-87044-836-6*) Natl Geog.

Builder's & Contractor's Guide to New Methods & Materials in Home Construction. Larry Emerson & Walter Oleksy. LC 82-23098. 283p. 1983. text ed. 45.00 (*0-13-086033-6*) P-H.

Builder's & Contractor's Handbook of Construction Claims. Philip R. McDonald & George C. Baldwin. 350p. 1989. text ed. 60.00 (*0-13-085796-3*) P-H.

Builder's & Contractor's Yearbook: The Construction Yearbook, 1987. Andrew M. Civitello, Jr. 704p. 1987. text ed. 59.95 (*0-13-085929-X*) P-H.

Builders & Dreamers: Habonin Labor Zionist Youth in North America: a Century in Memoir. Ed. by J. J. Goldberg & Elliot King. LC 91-58244. 1993. 29.95 (*0-8453-4839-6*, Cornwall Bks) Assoc Univ Prs.

Builders & Lenders Attitudes: The Nebraska Mortage Finance Fund Use of FHA 235 Housing. Jack Ruff & Peggy Hein. 32p. 1979. pap. 2.50 (*1-55719-097-6*) U NE CPAR.

Builders & Pioneers of Australia. Arthur Jose. LC 71-107720. (Essay Index Reprint Ser.). 1977. 20.95 (*0-8369-1522-4*) Ayer.

Builders, Brewers & Burghers: Germans of Washington State. Dale R. Wirsing. LC 77-71316. 1977. pap. 6.00 (*0-917048-03-2*) Wash St Hist Soc.

Builder's Comprehensive Dictionary. 2nd ed. Robert Putnam. (Illus.). 528p. 1989. reprint ed. pap. 24.95 (*0-934041-50-4*) Craftsman.

***Builders' Costs for Hundred Best-Selling Home Plans.** R. S. Means. 1994. pap. 34.95 (*0-87629-356-9*) R S Means.

Builder's Director. Batty Langley. LC 69-16324. (Illus.). 1972. reprint ed. 15.95 (*0-405-08730-6*, Pub. by Blom Pubns UK) Ayer.

Builders' Estimating Data. David Cross. 304p. 1990. 64.95 (*0-434-90250-0*) Buttrwrth-Heinemann.

Builder's Estimating Databook. Robert Taylor. (Illus.). 224p. 1988. pap. 17.95 (*0-8306-2768-5*, 2768) TAB Bks.

Builder's Guide to Accounting. rev. ed. Michael C. Thomsett. 304p. 1987. pap. 22.50 (*0-934041-18-0*) Craftsman.

***Builder's Guide to Foundations & Framing.** Dan Ramsey. LC 94-48314. 1995. text ed. 44.00 (*0-07-051814-9*) McGraw.

Builder's Guide to Running a Successful Construction Company. David Gerstel. 240p. 1992. 27.95 (*0-942391-36-5*) Taunton.

Builder's Guide: 1839 see Works of Asher Benjamin: Boston, 1806-1843

Builder's Jewel. Batty Langley. LC 69-16325. (Illus.). 1972. reprint ed. 12.95 (*0-405-08731-4*, Pub. by Blom Pubns UK) Ayer.

Builders' Liability. Mark L. Levine. 1980. write for info. (*0-318-02240-0*) Prof Pubns & Educ.

Builders Merchants (Scotland) Ed. by ICC Information Group Staff. 1987. 695.00 (*1-85036-953-4*, Pub. by ICC Info Group Ltd UK) St Mut.

Builders of Alaska: The Russian Governors, 1818-1867. Richard A. Pierce. (Alaska History Ser.: No. 28). (Illus.). 1985. 11.00 (*0-919642-07-1*) Limestone Pr.

Builders of Catholic America. Albert J. Nevins. LC 85-72363. 250p. (Orig.). 1985. pap. 7.95 (*0-87973-582-1*, 582) Our Sunday Visitor.

Builders of Latin America. Watt Stewart & Harold I. Peterson. LC 76-167425. (Essay Index Reprint Ser.). 1977. reprint ed. 38.95 (*0-8369-2724-9*) Ayer.

Builders of Maine. James M. Flanagan. LC 91-58091. 400p. (YA). 1994. pap. 10.00 (*0-932433-86-3*) Windswept Hse.

Builders of My Soul. Brian Arkins. 1990. lib. bdg. 69.00 (*0-389-20913-9*) B&N Imports.

Builders of the Ancient World: Marvels of Engineering. Ed. by Donald J. Crump. LC 86-5278. (Special Publications Series 21: No. 1). (Illus.). (YA). (gr. 8 up). 1986. 12.95 (*0-87044-585-5*) Natl Geog.

Builders of the Bay Colony. Samuel E. Morison. LC 75-41198. reprint ed. 26.45 (*0-404-14741-0*) AMS Pr.

Builders of the Bay Colony. Samuel E. Morison. LC 81-9649. (Illus.). 418p. 1982. reprint ed. pap. 15.95 (*0-930350-22-7*) NE U Pr.

Builders of the Bridge: The Story of John Roebling & His Son. David B. Steinman. LC 72-5074. (Technology & Society Ser.). (Illus.). 462p. 1980. reprint ed. 39.95 (*0-405-04724-X*) Ayer.

Builders of the Canadian Commonwealth. George H. Locke. LC 67-28755. (Essay Index Reprint Ser.). 1977. 21.95 (*0-8369-0621-7*) Ayer.

Builders of the Dawn. Corrine McLaughlin & Gordon Davidson. LC 89-29638. (Illus.). 372p. (Orig.). 1990. pap. 17.95 (*0-913990-68-X*) Book Pub Co.

Builders of the Nation. Helen Konz. LC 92-85407. 325p. 1993. pap. 9.95 (*1-55523-556-5*) Winston-Derek.

Builders of the Social Order. Joseph F. Thorning. LC 68-57340. (Essay Index Reprint Ser.). 1977. 19.95 (*0-8369-0936-4*) Ayer.

Builder's Office Manual. rev. ed. Michael C. Thomsett. 224p. 1987. pap. 15.50 (*0-934041-27-X*) Craftsman.

Building. Will Eisner. Ed. by Dave Schreiner & Denis Kitchen. (Illus.). 80p. 1987. 25.00 (*0-87816-024-8*); pap. 8.95 (*0-87816-025-6*) Kitchen Sink.

Building. David Glover. LC 94-1478. (Make It Work! Science Ser.). (Illus.). 48p. (J). (gr. 5-9). 1994. 15.95 (*1-56847-259-5*) Thomson Lrning.

Building. Mason Jackson. LC 86-24115. (Illus.). 128p. 1987. pap. 6.95 (*0-932334-85-7*, NY28037, Empire State Bks) Hrt of the Lakes.

Building. Illus. by Dave Lind & Meg Wright. (Visualized Songs Ser.). 20p. (J). (gr. 1-8). 1983. pap. 4.50 (*0-86508-135-2*) BCM Pubn.

***Building.** Wilkinson. 1995. 18.99 (*0-679-97256-0*) Random.

***Building.** Philip Wilkinson. (Eyewitness Bks.). (Illus.). (J). 1995. 17.00 (*0-679-87256-6*) Knopf.

Building: First Readers. Jacqueline Harding. (Series 929). (Illus.). 28p. (J). (ps-00). 1992. 3.50 (*0-7214-1491-5*) Ladybird Bks.

Building: The Process & the Product. Denis R. Harper. (Illus.). 428p. reprint ed. pap. 122.00 (*0-8357-7470-8*, 2030339) Bks Demand.

Building a Better Board, Book I: A Guide to Effective Leadership. 2nd ed. Andrew Swanson. 89p. 1992. 25.00 (*0-930807-28-6*, 600227) Fund Raising.

Building a Better Board, Book II: The Role of the Nonprofit Board in Strategic Planning, Vol. 2. Andrew Swanson. 75p. 1992. 25.00 (*0-930807-29-4*, 600319) Fund Raising.

Building a Better Bookshelf. Michael DeCristofaro. LC 75-733230. 1975. student ed 7.00 (*0-8064-0259-8*, 701); audio 459.00 (*0-8064-0260-1*) Bergwall.

Building a Better Hitter. Stephen Pecci. 160p. 1991. pap. write for info. (*0-697-11404-X*) Brown & Benchmark.

Building a Better Hospital Board. John A. Witt. LC 87-21226. 204p. 1987. 37.00 (*0-910701-29-6*, 0892) Health Admin Pr.

Building a Better Industry: Evaluating & Implementing Total Quality Management. 1993. pap. 15.00 (*1-879304-52-X*) AIA DC.

Building a Better Mousetrap: Programmer's Guide to Interfacing with the Mouse for IBM And... Jeffrey Donovan. 1993. pap. text ed. 39.95 (*0-07-881930-X*) Osborne-McGraw.

Building a Better Team: A Handbook for Managers & Facilitators. Peter Moxon. LC 93-20443. 208p. 1993. 55.95 (*0-566-07424-9*, Pub. by Gower UK) Ashgate Pub Co.

***Building a Biblical Faith: A Guide to Christian Theology.** Charles H. Bayer. LC 94-32750. 128p. (Orig.). 1995. pap. 11.99 (*0-8272-0220-2*) Chalice Pr.

Building a Birchbark Canoe: The Algonquin Wabanaki Tciman. David Gidmark. (Illus.). 208p. 1994. pap. 17.95 (*0-8117-2504-9*) Stackpole.

Building a Borough. Evelyn Gonzalez et al. 122p. 1986. 19.95 (*0-917535-09-X*) Bronx Mus.

Building a Bridge. Lisa S. Begaye. LC 92-82138. (Illus.). 32p. (J). (gr. k up). 1993. 14.95 (*0-87358-557-7*) Northland AZ.

Building a Bridge to Algebra. Barbara Adams. (C). Date not set. pap. text ed. 35.00 (*1-881592-30-8*) Hayden-McNeil.

***Building a Bridge to the Self: The Saddhuki Man Jivan Mukti.** Dyne N. Shaffron. Ed. by Nancy Earle. LC 95-75212. 160p. (Orig.). 1995. pap. 9.95 (*1-886836-10-8*) Black Diamnd.

Building a Canadian-American Free Trade Area. Ed. by Edward R. Fried et al. LC 87-71507. (Dialogues on Public Policy Ser.). 217p. 1987. pap. 10.95 (*0-8157-2973-1*) Brookings.

Building a Cancer Information Network in Texas: A Demonstration in the Heart of Texas Region. Contrib by Lonna Milburn. (Special Project Report Ser.). 277p. 1989. pap. 10.00 (*0-89940-864-8*) LBJ Sch Pub Aff.

Building a Career: The Effect of Initial Job Experiences & Related Work Attitudes on Later Employment. Joseph A. Raelin. LC 80-24848. 178p. 1980. pap. 4.00 (*0-911558-73-X*) W E Upjohn.

***Building a Caring, Cooperative Classroom: Integrating Social Skills Through Language Curriculum.** James Bellanca. LC 91-62547. 144p. 1991. pap. 17.95 (*0-932935-61-3*) IRI-Skylght.

Building a Caring-Sharing Community of Believers. Elvin M. Powers. 128p. 1983. pap. 3.95 (*0-8341-0822-4*) Beacon Hill.

Building a Chain of Customers. Richard J. Schonberger. 1990. text ed. 35.00 (*0-02-927991-7*) Free Pr.

Building a Champion: On Football & the Making of the 49ers. Bill Walsh & Glenn Dickey. (Illus.). 376p. 1991. mass mkt. 5.99 (*0-312-92579-4*) St Martin.

Building a Character. Constantin Stanislavski. 1977. 25.00 (*0-87830-012-0*, Theatre Arts Bks); pap. 14.95 (*0-87830-982-9*, Theatre Arts Bks) Routledge Chapman & Hall.

Building a Character. Constantin Stanislavski. 320p. 1989. pap. 14.95 (*0-685-45688-9*, A3322, Theatre Arts Bks) Routledge Chapman & Hall.

Building a Character. braille ed. Constantin Stanislavski. 529p. 1992. vinyl bd. 42.32 (*1-56956-203-2*, BR8492) W A T Braille.

Building a Christian World View, Vol. 1: God, Man, & Knowledge. Ed. by W. Andrew Hoffecker & Gary S. Smith. LC 86-91437. 368p. 1986. 14.99 (*0-87552-281-5*) Presby & Reformed.

Building a Christian World View, Vol. 2: The Universe, Society, & Ethics. Ed. by W. Andrew Hoffecker & Gary S. Smith. LC 86-91437. 496p. (C). 1988. 17.99 (*0-87552-282-3*) Presby & Reformed.

Building a Clancy: A Step-by-Step Guide to Your First Boat. J. D. Brown & Bob Pickett. 1992. pap. text ed. 13.95 (*0-07-008173-5*) McGraw.

Building a Classical Music Library: Makes Music Appreciation Approachable. 3rd rev. ed. Bill Parker. Ed. by Jack Caravella. (Illus.). 300p. 1995. pap. 14.95 (*0-9641332-0-2*) Jormax Pubng.

Building a Community of Citizens: Civil Society in the 21st Century. Ed. by Don E. Eberly. 550p. (C). 1994. lib. bdg. 75.00 (*0-8191-9613-4*); pap. text ed. 29.50 (*0-8191-9614-2*) U Pr of Amer.

Building a Competitive America: First Annual Report of the Competitiveness Policy Council. (Illus.). 52p. (Orig.). (C). 1992. pap. text ed. 27.95 (*1-56806-115-3*) Diane Pub.

Building a Consensus Toward Space: Proceedings of the Air War College 1988 Space Issue Symposium. Contrib by John B. Rhinelander et al. (Illus.). 138p. 1990. per., pap. 5.50 (*0-16-020920-X*, S/N 008-070-006) USGPO.

Building a Contract: Solicitations-Bids & Proposals - A Team Effort? Daniel M. Jacobs et al. Ed. by Keith A. Jacobson. (National Contract Management Association Workshop Ser.). 191p. (Orig.). 1990. per. 52.95 (*0-940343-20-7*) Natl Contract Mgmt.

Building a Database for Nursing Education Enrollment Management. American Association of Colleges of Nursing Staff. 175p. 1989. 18.00 (*0-922148-03-1*) AACN.

B

An Asterisk (*) at the beginning of an entry indicates that the title is appearing in BIP for the first time. 937

B

Building a Deductive Database. Miguel Nussbaum. Ed. by George W. Zobrist. (Computer Engineering & Computer Science Ser.). 172p. (C). 1992. text ed. 54.50 (*0-89391-768-0*) Ablex Pub.

Building a Defence Technology Base. B. D. Kapur. 1990. 29.50 (*81-7062-089-9*, Pub. by Lancer International II) S Asia.

***Building a Democratic Political Order: Reshaping American Liberalism in the 1930's & 1940's.** David Plotke. (Illus.). 320p. (C). 1995. write for info. (*0-521-42059-8*) Cambridge U Pr.

***Building a Diverse Faculty.** Ed. by Joanne Gainen & Robert Boice. LC 85-644763. (New Directions for Teaching & Learning Ser.: No. 53). 110p. (Orig.). 1993. pap. 16.95 (*1-55542-725-1*) Jossey-Bass.

Building a Dream: Mary Bethune's School. Richard Kelso. LC 92-18069. (Stories of America Ser.). (Illus.). 46p. (J). (gr. 2-5). 1992. lib. bdg. 21.36 (*0-8114-7217-5*) Raintree Steck-V.

Building a Dynamic Team: A Practical Guide to Maximizing Team Performance. Richard Y. Chang. (High Performance Team Ser.). Orig. Title: Effectiveness Through Team Building. (Illus.). 120p. 1994. pap. 12.95 (*1-883553-31-8*) R Chang Assocs.

Building a Fair Pay Program: A Step by Step Guide. Roger Plachy. LC 86-47595. 315p. 1986. 75.00 (*0-8144-7662-7*) AMACOM.

Building a Faith to Live By: Programs for Youth (Foundation for Discipleship) Bryon R. McCane & Preston C. VanLoon. 128p. 1987. pap. 11.00 (*0-8170-1107-2*) Judson.

Building a Financial Services Marketing Plan: Working Plans for Product & Segment Marketing. Bank Marketing Association Staff. LC 89-23301. 369p. 1989. pap. 49.95 (*0-942061-02-0*, Financial Sourcebks) Sourcebks.

Building a Fortune with Small Investment Groups. Greg James. 225p. (Orig.). 1983. pap. 23.95 (*0-910019-27-4*) United Support.

Building a Gas Fired Crucible Furnace. David J. Gingery. LC 88-91058. (Illus.). 108p. (Orig.). 1988. pap. 9.95 (*1-878087-08-8*) D J Gingery.

Building a Global Civic Culture: Education for an Independent World. Elise Boulding. (Syracuse Studies on Peace & Conflict Resolution). 192p. 1990. pap. text ed. 16.95x (*0-8156-2487-5*) Syracuse U Pr.

Building a Global Civic Culture: Education for an Interdependent World. Elise Boulding. (John Dewey Lecture Ser.). 208p. 1988. text ed. 18.95 (*0-8077-2867-5*) Tchrs Coll.

Building a Great Children's Ministry. Evelyn M. Johnson & Bobbie Bower. Ed. by Lyle E. Schaller. (Creative Leadership Ser.). 112p. (Orig.). 1992. pap. 10.95 (*0-687-03388-8*) Abingdon.

Building a Great Library: The Coolidge Years at Harvard. William Bentinck-Smith. (Illus.). 301p. 1976. 20.00 (*0-674-08578-7*) HUP.

Building a Great Marriage. Anne Ortlund. LC 84-16078. 192p. 1984. pap. 8.99 (*0-8007-5234-1*) Revell.

Building a Happy Marriage. Michael P. Pentar. LC 86-6349. 1988. pap. 2.95 (*0-8198-1114-9*) Pauline Bks.

Building a Healthy America: Conquering Disease & Disability. 2nd rev. ed. Ed. by Terry Lierman. 248p. 1987. 49.00 (*0-913113-12-3*) M Liebert.

***Building a Healthy Family: Practical Advice for Couples, Small Groups or Larger Classes.** Bill Flatt. 1993. pap. 12.99 (*0-89225-421-1*) Gospel Advocate.

Building a Healthy Lawn: A Safe & Natural Approach. Stuart Franklin. Ed. by Deborah Burns. LC 87-46446. (Illus.). 176p. 1988. pap. 9.95 (*0-88266-518-9*, Garden Way Pub) Storey Comm Inc.

Building a Home Darkroom (KW-14), KW-14. Ray Miller. LC 81-66622. (Kodak Workshop Ser.). (Illus.). 96p. 1991. pap. 13.95 (*0-87985-746-3*) Saunders Photo.

***Building a Home in a Pull-Apart World: Powerful Principles for a Happier Marriage: Four Steps That Work.** Bill Bright & Vonette Bright. LC 94-45053. 1995. write for info. (*1-56399-058-X*) NewLife Pubns.

Building a House. Byron Barton. LC 80-22674. (Illus.). 32p. (J). (ps-1). 1981. lib. bdg. 16.93 (*0-688-84291-7*) Greenwillow.

Building a House. Byron Barton. (ESL Theme Links Ser.). (Illus.). 32p. 1992. pap. 6.00 (*1-56334-200-6*); pap. text ed. 29.95 (*1-56334-182-4*) Hampton-Brown.

Building a House. Byron Barton. (ESL Theme Links Ser.). (Illus.). 32p. (J). (K-3). 1992. pap. text ed. 6.00 (*1-56334-185-9*) Hampton-Brown.

Building a House. Byron Barton. (ESL Theme Links Ser.). (Illus.). 1993. ring bd. 99.50 (*1-56334-298-7*); audio 10.50 (*1-56334-296-0*); 35.00 (*1-56334-297-9*) Hampton-Brown.

Building a House. Byron Barton. LC 80-22674. (Illus.). (J). (ps up). 1990. reprint ed. pap. 4.95 (*0-688-09356-6*, Mulberry) Morrow.

Building a House: Teacher's Guide. (ESL Theme Links Ser.). (Illus.). 1993. 15.00 (*1-56334-344-4*) Hampton-Brown.

Building a Jawbone Kayak. Zu Freeman. Ed. by Kathi DeFremery. LC 89-50508. (Illus.). 54p. (Orig.). 1989. pap. 8.95 (*0-917436-03-2*) Tamal Vista.

***Building a Language-Focused Curriculum for the Preschool Classroom Vol. I: A Foundation for Lifelong Communication.** Mabel L. Rice & Kim A. Wilcox. LC 94-49085. 248p. 1995. pap. 32.00 (*1-55766-177-4*) P H Brookes.

***Building a Language-Focused Curriculum for the Preschool Classroom Vol. II: A Planning Guide.** Bunce. 480p. 1995. pap. 55.00 (*1-55766-192-8*) P H Brookes.

***Building a Legacy: Voices Oncology Nurses.** Brenda Nevidjon. LC 95-4063. (Nursing Ser.). 500p. 1995. 49.95 (*0-86720-727-2*) Jones & Bartlett.

Building a Lima Locomotive. Scott D. Trostel. Ed. by Russell Heine. (Ohio Railroad Heritage Ser.). (Illus.). 88p. (Orig.). 1990. pap. text ed. 14.95 (*0-925436-05-4*) Cam-Tech Pub.

Building a Log Home From Scratch or Kit. 2nd ed. Dan Ramsey. (Illus.). 302p. (Orig.). 1987. pap. 16.95 (*0-8306-2858-4*) TAB Bks.

Building a Log Home from Scratch or Kit. 2nd ed. Dan Ramsey. 1987. pap. 16.95 (*0-07-155212-X*) McGraw.

Building a Mail Order Business: A Complete Manual for Success. 3rd ed. William A. Cohen. 608p. 1991. text ed. 37.95 (*0-471-52082-9*) Wiley.

Building a Meaningful Life with the Carpenter's Twenty Megatruths. Herb Miller. 108p. (Orig.). 1968. pap. write for info. (*0-937462-03-9*) Net Pr.

Building a Medical Vocabulary. 3rd ed. Peggy C. Leonard. (Illus.). 560p. 1992. pap. text ed. 27.95 (*0-7216-4690-5*) Saunders.

Building a Mini Stock Step-by-Step. Jean Genibrel. (Illus.). 128p. (Orig.). Date not set. pap. text ed. 10.95 (*0-936834-52-8*) S S Autosports.

Building a Model Black Community: The Roxbury Action Program. Stewart E. Perry. 100p. 1978. pap. text ed. 12.95 (*0-87855-773-3*) Transaction Pubs.

Building a Moral System. Robert B. Ashmore, Jr. 224p. (C). 1987. pap. text ed. 20.00 (*0-13-086265-7*) P-H.

Building a More Democratic United Nations: Proceedings of the First International Conference on a More Democratic UN. Frank Barnaby. 1991. text ed. 45.00 (*0-7146-3442-5*, Pub. by F Cass Pubs UK); pap. text ed. 19.50 (*0-7146-4080-8*, Pub. by F Cass Pubs UK) Intl Spec Bk.

Building a Mortgage Banking Team. MBA Staff. 160p. 1992. per. 40.00 (*0-8403-8227-8*) Kendall-Hunt.

Building a Mortgage Banking Team: Hiring & Managing Top Achievers. Anita Willis-Boyland. (Illus.). 150p. (Orig.). 1992. pap. 50.00 (*0-945359-13-6*) Mortgage Bankers.

Building a Multi-Use Barn: For Garage, Animals, Workshop, or Studio. John Wagner. (Illus.). 192p. (Orig.). 1994. pap. 19.95 (*0-913589-76-4*) Williamson Pub Co.

Building a Nation: Essays on India. Yogesh Atal. 1982. 20.00 (*0-8364-0843-8*, Pub. by Ranjan Pubs II) S Asia.

Building a National Health-Care System. Committee for Economic Development. LC 73-75244. 105p. 1973. pap. 2.00 (*0-87186-049-X*) Comm Econ Dev.

Building a National Image: Architectural Drawings for the American Democracy, 1789-1912. Bates Lowry. (Illus.). 1986. 75.00 (*0-8027-0873-0*) Walker & Co.

***Building a National Immunization System: A Guide to Immunization Services & Resources.** Children's Defense Fund Staff. 136p. 1994. pap. write for info. (*1-881985-06-7*) Childrens Defense.

Building a National Literature: The Case of Germany, 1830-1870. Peter U. Hohendahl. Tr. by Renate Franciscono. LC 89-899. 400p. 1989. reprint ed. 47.50 (*0-8014-1862-3*); reprint ed. pap. 17.95 (*0-8014-9622-5*) Cornell U Pr.

***Building a National System for School-to-Work Transition: Lessons from Britain & Australia.** Margaret Vickers. 64p. 1991. pap. 10.00 (*1-887410-71-6*) Jobs for Future.

Building a Network of Welcoming Services: Amerasian Resettlement - 1991 Conference Proceedings. 145p. (Orig.). (C). 1994. pap. text ed. 29.95 (*1-56806-158-7*) Diane Pub.

Building a New American State: The Expansion of National Administrative Capacities, 1877-1920. Stephen Skowronek. LC 81-15225. (Illus.). 400p. 1982. 74.95 (*0-521-23022-5*); pap. 18.95 (*0-521-28865-7*) Cambridge U Pr.

Building a New Boston: Politics & Urban Renewal, 1950-1970. Thomas H. O'Connor. 328p. 1993. text ed. 24.95 (*1-55553-161-X*) NE U Pr.

Building a New Dream: A Family Guide to Coping with Chronic Illness & Disability. Janet R. Maurer. 1990. pap. 9.57 (*0-201-55098-9*) Addison-Wesley.

Building a New Europe: The Challenge of System Transformation & Systemic Reform. Wolfgang H. Reinicke. 216p. (C). 1993. pap. 12.95 (*0-8157-7391-9*) Brookings.

Building a New Global Order: Emerging Trends in International Security. Ed. by David Dewitt et al. (Illus.). 440p. (C). 1994. pap. text ed. 19.95 (*0-19-540964-7*) OUP.

Building a New Heritage: Tourism, Culture & Identity in the New Europe. Ed. by G. J. Ashworth & Peter J. Larkham. LC 93-43216. 296p. 1994. 59.95x (*0-415-07931-4*, B3891, Routledge NY) Routledge.

Building a New India: An Agenda for National Renaissance. Subramanian Swamy. (C). 1992. 14.00 (*81-85674-21-3*, Pub. by UBS Pubs Dist II) S Asia.

Building a New South: A Guide to Southern Social Justice Organizations. Ed. by Hayward Wilkirson et al. 224p. (Orig.). 1994. pap. 40.00 (*0-938737-32-5*) Denali Press.

Building a New Stomach. V. G. Rocine. (Nutrition Ser.). 1991. lib. bdg. 75.00 (*0-8490-4260-7*) Gordon Pr.

Building a New Stomach. V. G. Rocine. reprint ed. spiral bd. 4.95 (*0-7873-0732-7*) Mokelumne.

***Building a New World.** Richard Sanchez. LC 94-21879. (J). 1994. lib. bdg. 14.96 (*1-56239-333-2*) Abdo & Dghtrs.

***Building a New World: Africans in America, 1500-1900.** Philip Koslow. (Kingdoms of Africa Ser.). (Illus.). 64p. (J). (gr. 3 up). 1995. 14.95 (*0-7910-3143-8*); pap. 7.95 (*0-7910-3144-6*) Chelsea Hse.

Building a Pacific Community. Ed. by Paul F. Hooper. LC 81-17252. (Addresses & Papers of the Community Lecture). 190p. reprint ed. pap. 54.20 (*0-7837-1311-8*, 2041459) Bks Demand.

Building a Peace System. Robert A. Irwin. 330p. (Orig.). 1989. pap. 12.95 (*0-936391-39-1*) Expro Pr.

Building a Pharmacist's Patient Data Base. Nancy A. Mason & Leslie A. Shimp. (Clinical Skills Program, Advancing Pharmaceutical Care Ser.). 96p. 1993. ring bd. 50.00 (*1-879907-32-1*) Am Soc Hlth-Syst.

***Building a Popular Science Library Collection for High School to Adult Learners: Issues & Recommended Resources.** Gregg Sapp. LC 94-46939. 328p. 1995. text ed. 45.00 (*0-313-28936-0*, Greenwood Pr) Greenwood.

Building a Positive Attitude: Toward Yourself, Others & Success. 2nd ed. Rich Wilkins. 1991. 9.95 (*0-9631968-1-2*) R Wilkins Co.

Building a Positive Attitude Toward Yourself, Others & Success. Rick Wilkins. 160p. 1991. pap. text ed. 9.95 (*0-9631968-0-4*) R Wilkins Co.

Building a Practice with Patterns of Excellence: For Counseling Practitioners, Therapists, & All Mental Health Practitioners. C. Rex Heisler. 357p. 1987. 39.95 (*0-929564-00-6*) Pneumatikos Counsel Inst.

Building a Profession: Autobiographical Perspectives on the Beginnings of Comparative Literature in the United States. Ed. by Lionel Gossman & Mihai I. Spariosu. LC 93-3458. (SUNY Series, The Margins of Literature). 234p. (C). 1994. 57.50 (*0-7914-1799-9*); pap. 18.95 (*0-7914-1800-6*) State U NY Pr.

Building a Professional Culture in Schools. Ed. by Ann Lieberman. (Series on School Reform). 248p. (C). 1988. text ed. 32.95 (*0-8077-2901-9*); pap. text ed. 18.95 (*0-8077-2900-0*) Tchrs Coll.

Building a Profitable Business: The Proven Step-by-Step Guide to Starting & Running Your Own Business. 2nd ed. Charles Chickadel & Greg Straughn. 320p. 1994. pap. 15.95 (*1-55850-272-6*) Adams Pubng.

Building a Program for Full Employment in New York. Sumner M. Rosen. LC 84-167076. 66p. 1983. pap. 6.00 (*0-88156-010-3*) Comm Serv Soc NY.

Building a Pyramid of Musicianship. Sally Herman. 28p. 1988. Student Pages, 28p. student ed, pap. text ed. 25.00 (*0-8497-4855-0*, C8829) Kjos.

Building a Quality Workforce. (Orig.). 1992. lib. bdg. 85.95 (*0-8490-8851-8*) Gordon Pr.

Building a Quality Workforce. 85p. (Orig.). 1988. pap. 4.50 (*0-16-003781-6*, S/N 029-000-00425-1) USGPO.

Building a Race Car Picture by Picture. Steve Smith. (Illus.). 56p. (Orig.). Date not set. pap. text ed. 6.95 (*0-936834-10-2*) S S Autosports.

***Building a Rainbow: Helping to Build Drug- & Violence-Free Communities Through the Arts.** Banner Staff. 32p. 1994. student ed, audio 275.00 (*0-9642274-0-1*) Banner Project.

Building a Recording Studio: The Complete Guide to Studio Design & Construction. rev. ed. Jeff Cooper. LC 84-90061. (Illus.). 209p. 1984. spiral bd. 30.00 (*0-916899-00-4*) Synergy Group.

Building a Robot: A Straightforward Approach. Kevin Nairon. 152p. 1993. spiral bd., pap. 19.95 (*0-9635636-1-0*) Humanform Robot.

***Building a Safer Society: Strategic Approaches to Crime Prevention.** Ed. by Michael Tonry & David P. Farrington. 700p. 1995. lib. bdg. 45.00 (*0-226-80824-6*) U Ch Pr.

Building a School System. Helen Praetz. 178p. 1980. 32.50 (*0-522-84213-5*) Intl Spec Bk.

Building a Shared Vision for Environmental Education: A Conference Sponsored by the Federal Task Force on Environmental Education. 305p. (Orig.). (C). 1993. pap. text ed. 60.00 (*1-56806-741-0*) Diane Pub.

Building a Speech. Sheldon Metcalfe. 416p. (C). 1991. pap. text ed. 21.50 (*0-03-023423-9*) HB Coll Pubs.

***Building a State: Ukraine in a Post-Soviet World.** Ed. by Sharon L. Wolchik & Vladimir Zviglyanich. (Central European University Press Book Ser.). 304p. 1995. 69.00 (*1-85866-029-7*); pap. 24.00 (*1-85866-030-0*) OUP.

Building a Street Stock Step by Step. Bob Emmons. (Illus.). 64p. (Orig.). Date not set. pap. text ed. 10.95 (*0-936834-44-7*) S S Autosports.

Building a Strip Canoe. rev. ed. Gil Gilpatrick. (Illus.). 128p. (Orig.). 1993. pap. 11.95 (*0-89933-026-6*) DeLorme Map.

Building a Strong Union. 56p. 1993. 0.35 (*0-318-59960-0*) Newspaper Guild.

***Building a Successful Accounting Practice.** William Conner. 288p. (Orig.). 1995. pap. text ed. 69.00 (*0-89447-312-3*) Cypress.

***Building a Successful Board-Test Strategy.** Stephen F. Scheiber. (Test & Measurement Ser.). 280p. 1994. 44.95 (*0-7506-9432-7*) Buttrwrth-Heinemann.

Building a Successful Medical Transcription Business. 196p. 1993. pap., vhs 495.00 (*0-934385-57-2*) Hlth Prof Inst.

Building a Successful Pharmacy Practice: A Case Study. D. C. Huffman. 94p. (Orig.). 1973. pap. 12.00 (*0-910769-10-9*) Am Coll Apothecaries.

Building a Successful Professional Practice with Advertising. Irwin Braun. LC 81-66214. 301p. reprint ed. pap. 85.80 (*0-8357-7462-7*, 2023499) Bks Demand.

Building a Successful Software Business. Dave Radin. Ed. by Mike Loukides. (Illus.). 394p. (Orig.). 1994. pap. 19.95 (*1-56592-064-3*) OReilly & Assocs.

Building a Supernatural Church. Mark T. Barclay. 50p. 1991. reprint ed. pap. 5.00 (*0-944802-11-7*) M Barclay Pubns.

Building a Sustainable Society. Lester R. Brown. 1982. pap. 11.95 (*0-393-30027-7*) Norton.

***Building a Three-Way Partnership: The Leader's Role in Linking School, Families & Community.** Kathy Barclay & Elizabeth Boone. (Illus.). 240p. 1995. 24.95x (*0-590-49720-0*) Scholastic Inc.

Building a Total Quality Culture. Joe Batten. Ed. by W. Philip Gerould. (Fifty-Minute Ser.). 100p. (Orig.). 1992. pap. 9.95 (*1-56052-176-7*) Crisp Pubns.

***Building a UNIX Internet Server.** George Eckel. (Illus.). 350p. (Orig.). 1995. pap. 38.00 (*1-56205-494-5*) New Riders Pub.

Building a Vertical Steam Engine from Castings. Andrew Smith. 9.00 (*0-85242-723-9*) Apple Blossom.

Building a Wilderness Retreat: The Wild 80. Glenn Devery. LC 89-35632. (Voyageur Naturalist Library). (Illus.). 240p. 1989. 3.99 (*0-89658-086-5*) Voyageur Pr.

***Building a Windows NT Internet Server.** Harper. 350p. 1995. 38.00 (*1-56205-484-8*) New Riders Pub.

***Building a Windows NT Internet Server.** Eric Harper. (Illus.). 350p. (Orig.). 1995. pap. 38.00 (*1-56205-447-3*) New Riders Pub.

Building a Winning Sales Force. George J. Lumsden. 300p. 1986. ring bd. 159.95 (*0-85013-157-X*) Dartnell Corp.

Building a Winning Sales Team: How to Recruit, Train & Motivate the Best. Gini G. Scott. (Entrepreneur's Guide Ser.). 200p. 1991. pap. 22.95 (*1-55738-209-3*) Probus Pub Co.

Building a Workforce Investment System for America. Thomas Lindsley. 42p. 1992. pap. text ed. 9.95 (*0-88713-654-0*) Nat Alliance.

Building a World Community: Humanism in the Twenty-First Century. Ed. by Paul Kurtz. 362p. (C). 1989. text ed. 35.95x (*0-87975-538-5*) Prometheus Bks.

Building a World of True Love. HSA Publications Staff. 42p. pap. 2.50 (*0-685-61697-5*) HSA Pubns.

***Building a 3D Game Engine in C++** Hook. Date not set. 34.95 (*0-471-12326-9*) Wiley.

Building Academic Fluency. Romstedt. 1992. pap. 18.95 (*0-8384-3412-6*) Heinle & Heinle.

Building Academic Fluency. Romstedt. 1992. teacher ed, pap. 7.95 (*0-8384-3988-8*) Heinle & Heinle.

Building Academic Skills: An ESL Workbook. G. T. Schwabe. (Illus.). 388p. (C). 1987. pap. text ed. write for info. (*0-318-61174-0*) P-H.

Building Access Applications: Using Point-&-Click Programming. John Dranchak. 416p. (Orig.). 1995. pap. text ed. 29.95 (*0-471-30361-5*) Wiley.

***Building Accounting Systems: A Transaction Cycle Approach.** James T. Perry & Gary P. Schneider. 1994. write for info. (*0-538-84454-X*) S-W Pub.

***Building Accounting Systems Access Ed. A Transaction Cycle Approach.** James T. Perry & Gary P. Schneider. LC 95-1160. 1996. pap. 37.95 (*0-538-84897-9*) S-W Pub.

Building Acoustics. B. F. Day et al. (Illus.). viii, 120p. 1969. 25.25 (*0-444-20047-9*, Pub. by Elsevier Applied Sci UK) Elsevier.

Building Adirondack Furniture: The Art, the History, & the How-To. John Wagner. (Illus.). 128p. (Orig.). 1994. pap. 12.95 (*0-913589-87-X*) Williamson Pub Co.

Building Air Change Rate & Infiltration Measurements-STP 719. Ed. by Hunt et al. 195p. 1980. 28.00 (*0-8031-0607-6*, 04-71900-10) ASTM.

Building Air Quality. U. S. Environmental Protection Agency Staff. 230p. 1992. pap. 55.00 (*0-86587-312-7*) Gov Insts.

***Building Air Quality: A Guide for Building Owners & Facility Managers.** (Illus.). 229p. (Orig.). (C). 1994. pap. text ed. 60.00x (*0-7881-1021-7*) Diane Pub.

***Building Air Quality: A Guide for Building Owners & Facility Managers.** 1995. lib. bdg. 252.95 (*0-8490-7427-4*) Gordon Pr.

Building Air Quality: A Guide for Building Owners & Facility Managers. U. S. Environmental Protection Agency Staff & National Institute for Occupational Safety & Health Staff. 244p. 1993. 59.50 (*0-912702-80-X*) Global Eng Doc.

Building Air Tightness & Ventilation: An Overview of International Practice. M. Liddament. 1986. 60.00 (*0-86022-143-1*, Pub. by Build Servs Info Assn UK) St Mut.

Building America: A Securities Industry Experience. Ed. by Ronald Vrana. (Illus.). 23p. (Orig.). 1990. teacher ed write for info. (*0-943447-09-7*) Free Ent Partner.

***Building American Submarines.** 1994. lib. bdg. 250.95 (*0-8490-6436-8*) Gordon Pr.

***Building American Submarines, 1914-1940.** (Illus.). 182p. (Orig.). (C). 1994. pap. text ed. 45.00x (*0-7881-1094-2*) Diane Pub.

Building American Submarines, 1914-1940. Gary E. Weir. (Contributions to Naval History Ser.: No. 3). (Illus.). 166p. (C). 1991. pap. 8.50 (*0-945274-04-1*) Naval Hist Ctr.

Building America's Health: A Report, 5 vols. in 2, 1-3. President's Commission on the Health Needs of the Nation. LC 75-17239. (Social Problems & Social Policy Ser.). (Illus.). 1976. reprint ed. 66.95 (*0-405-07509-X*) Ayer.

Building America's Health: A Report, 5 vols. in 2, Set. President's Commission on the Health Needs of the Nation. LC 75-17239. (Social Problems & Social Policy Ser.). (Illus.). 1976. reprint ed. 134.95 (*0-405-07508-1*) Ayer.

Building America's Health: A Report, 5 vols. in 2, Vols. 4-5. President's Commission on the Health Needs of the Nation. LC 75-17239. (Social Problems & Social Policy Ser.). (Illus.). 1976. reprint ed. 66.95 (*0-405-07510-3*) Ayer.

***Building an American Clock Movement.** Steven G. Conover. (Illus.). 88p. 1994. pap. 21.95 (*0-9624766-3-3*, 114) Clockmakers.

Building an Antislavery Wall: Black Americans in the Atlantic Abolitionist Movement, 1830-1860. R. J. Blackett. LC 89-42928. 238p. 1989. pap. 14.95 (*0-8014-9624-1*) Cornell U Pr.

An Asterisk (*) at the beginning of an entry indicates that the title is appearing in BIP for the first time.

B

An Asterisk (*) at the beginning of an entry indicates that the title is appearing in BIP for the first time.

Building Business Through Downtown Events: How to Use Special Events to Promote Downtown. Downtown Research & Development Center Staff. (Illus.). 56p. (Orig.). 1992. pap. 29.00 (*0-915910-34-9*) Downtown Res.

Building by the Book, No. 3. Ed. by Mario Di Valmarana. LC 84-2249. (Palladian Studies in America: No. I). (Illus.). 125p. 1990. 30.00 (*0-8139-1233-4*) U Pr of Va.

Building by the Book, Vol.2. Ed. by Mario Di Valmarana. LC 84-2249. (Palladian Studies in America: I). (Illus.). 150p. 1986. 30.00 (*0-8139-1072-2*) U Pr of Va.

Building by the Book: Pattern Book Architecture in New Jersey. Robert P. Guter. (C). 1992. 34.95 (*0-8135-1848-2*) Rutgers U Pr.

Building C Libraries: Windows. Len Dorfman. (Illus.). 512p. 1990. 36.95 (*0-8306-8418-2*, Windcrest); pap. 26.95 (*0-8306-3418-5*, Windcrest) TAB Bks.

Building California: The Story of the Carpenters' Union. Ed. by Paul Bullock. 388p. 1982. 15.00 (*0-89215-126-9*) U Cal LA Indus Rel.

Building Canada: A History of Public Works. Ed. by Norman R. Ball. (Illus.). 352p. 1988. pap. 24.95 (*0-8020-6898-7*) U of Toronto Pr.

Building Capitalism: Historical Change & the Labour Process in the Production of the Built Environment. Linda Clarke. (Illus.). 320p. 1991. 97.50 (*0-415-01552-9*, 9870); pap. 32.50 (*0-415-01553-7*, A6672) Routledge.

Building Care for Hospitality Operations. Bruce H. Axler. 1974. pap. 3.95 (*0-672-96124-5*, Bobbs) Macmillan.

***Building Chairs.** LC 94-30363. (Art of Woodworking Ser.). 1994. write for info. (*0-8094-9525-2*) Time-Life.

Building Character. Bonnie Budzowski. (NetWork Discussion Guides Ser.). 48p. 1994. pap. 4.99 (*0-87788-096-4*) Shaw Pubs.

Building Character. Gladys Hunt. (Discipleship Ser.). 48p. 1992. pap. 4.99 (*0-310-54711-3*) Zondervan.

Building Character: Tales from Montana, & Other Damn Lies. Dick Hoskins. (Orig.). Date not set. pap. 7.95 (*0-9639816-0-9*) Polecat Pr.

Building Character in the American Boy: The Boy Scouts, YMCA, & Their Forerunners, 1870-1920. David I. Macleod. LC 83-47763. 464p. 1983. text ed. 27.50 (*0-299-09400-6*) U of Wis Pr.

Building Character in Young People. Philip St. Romain. LC 85-12030. 96p. (Orig.). 1986. pap. 7.95 (*0-88289-483-8*) Pelican.

Building Chicago: Suburban Developers & the Creation of a Divided Metropolis. Ann D. Keating. (Urban Life & Urban Landscape Ser.: Vol. 1). (Illus.). 230p. 1988. text ed. 36.50 (*0-8142-0455-4*) Ohio St U Pr.

Building Children's Self-Esteem. Amy R. Vigilante. 20p. 1990. 2.95 (*1-56456-032-5*, 237) W Gladden Found.

Building Children's Self-Esteen: Spanish Version. Amy R. Vigilante. 20p. 1990. 2.95 (*1-56456-033-3*, 237S) W Gladden Found.

Building Children's Wooden Toys. Edward A. Baldwin & Verner W. Clapp. Ed. by Barbara Ferguson. LC 89-85928. (Illus.). 112p. (Orig.). 1990. pap. 9.95 (*0-89721-214-2*) Ortho Info.

Building Christian Character. Paul Anderson. (Building Bks.). 48p. 1984. reprint ed. student ed 6.99 (*0-87123-436-X*); reprint ed. teacher ed 7.99 (*0-87123-430-0*) Bethany Hse.

Building Christian Character: A Guidebook Through the Elements of Christian Character. Blair Adams & Joel Stein. LC 89-51225. 203p. (Orig.). 1988. pap. 19.95 (*0-916387-13-5*) Truth Forum.

Building Christian Commitment. Richard L. Dugan. (Building Bks.). 107p. (Orig.). 1982. student ed 6.99 (*0-87123-831-4*); teacher ed 7.99 (*0-87123-418-1*) Bethany Hse.

Building Christian Community Through Small Groups. Roberta Hestenes. 1985. audio, pap. 69.95 (*0-9602638-5-3*) Fuller Seminary.

Building Christian English Series. Lela Birky & Lucy Conley. (gr. 3-8). 1973. write for info. (*0-686-05606-X*); teacher ed write for info. (*0-686-05607-8*) Rod & Staff.

Building Christian Relationships. Neta Jackson. (Building Bks.). 64p. 1984. pap. 6.99 (*0-87123-407-6*); teacher ed, pap. 7.99 (*0-87123-429-7*) Bethany Hse.

Building Christian Values. Eva Gibson & Steve Price. (Building Bks.). (Orig.). 1989. teacher ed 7.99 (*1-55661-025-4*); student ed 6.99 (*1-55661-024-6*) Bethany Hse.

Building Cities That Work. Edmund P. Fowler. (Illus.). 320p. 1992. 49.95 (*0-7735-0820-1*, Pub. by McGill CN) U of Toronto Pr.

Building Cities That Work. Edmund P. Fowler. (Illus.). 336p. (C). 1994. pap. text ed. 19.95 (*0-7735-1183-0*, Pub. by McGill CN) U of Toronto Pr.

Building City Council Leadership Skills: A Casebook of Models & Methods. National League of Cities Staff. 158p. 1980. 20.00 (*0-317-35151-6*, 3504); 10.00 (*0-317-35152-4*) Natl League Cities.

***Building Classic Salmon Flies.** Ron Alcott. Ed. by Arleigh D. Richardson, 3rd. (Illus.). 176p. 1995. 35.00 (*0-88150-314-2*, Countryman Classics) Countryman.

Building Classic Small Craft, Vol. 1. John Gardner. 1991. pap. text ed. 27.95 (*0-07-022858-2*) McGraw.

Building Classic Small Craft, Vol. 1. John C. Gardner. LC 76-8778. (Illus.). 314p. 1987. text ed. 34.50 (*0-87742-065-3*) Intl Marine.

Building Classic Small Craft, Vol. I. John C. Gardner. (Illus.). 314p. 1991. pap. 24.95 (*0-87742-299-0*, 60240P) Intl Marine.

Building Classic Small Craft, Vol. 2. John C. Gardner. LC 82-80401. (Illus.). 256p. 1984. 35.00 (*0-87742-157-9*) Intl Marine.

Building Classical. Ed. by Richard Economakis. (Illus.). 300p. 1993. 115.00 (*1-85490-288-1*, Academy Edits) St Martin.

Building Classroom Discipline. 4th ed. C. M. Charles. 205p. (C). 1992. teacher ed write for info. (*0-8013-0942-5*, 79224); pap. text ed. 28.50 (*0-8013-0788-0*, 78842) Longman.

***Building Classroom Discipline.** 5th ed. C. M. Charles. LC 95-14822. (C). 1996. pap. text ed. 28.50 (*0-8013-1507-7*) Longman.

***Building Coalitions: Coalition Formation & Maintenance.** (Illus.). 68p. (Orig.). (C). 1995. reprint ed. pap. text ed. 45.00 (*0-7881-1581-2*) Diane Pub.

Building Coalitions: How to Link TQE Schools with Government, Business, & Community. Betty E. Steffy & Jane C. Lindle. (Total Quality Education for the World's Best Schools Ser.: Vol. 5). 128p. 1994. pap. 16.00 (*0-8039-6105-7*) Corwin Pr.

Building Coalitions in the Human Services: Guidelines for Practice. Milan J. Dluhy. (Human Services Guides Ser.: Vol. 60). (Illus.). 144p. (C). 1990. pap. text ed. 17.95 (*0-8039-2604-9*) Sage.

Building Code Primer. William H. Correale. (Illus.). 1979. text ed. write for info. (*0-07-013171-6*) McGraw.

Building Code Quick Reference Guide: A Schematic Building Design Timesaver. William J. Brummett & Alec W. Johnson. (Illus.). 128p. 1993. pap. 30.95 (*0-912045-58-2*) Prof Pubns CA.

Building Code Requirements for Masonry Structures (ACI 530-92 - ASCE 5-92 - TMS 402-92); Specifications for Masonry Structures (ACI 530.1-92 - ASCE 6-92 - TMS 602-92); Commentary on Building Code Requirements for Masonry Structures (ACI 530-92 - ASCE 5-92 - TMS 402-92); Commentary on Specifications for Masonry Structures (ACI 530.1-92 - ASCE 6-92 - TMS 602-92) American Concrete Institute Staff & American Society of Civil Engineers Staff. LC 92-33528. 88p. 1992. 65.00 (*0-87262-928-7*) Am Soc Civil Eng.

Building Code Requirements for Masonry Structures & Specifications for Masonry Structures, & Related Commentaries, 2 vols. 88p. 1992. 48.75 (*0-685-45553-X*, 530.1-92) ACI.

Building Code Requirements for Masonry Structures & Specifications for Masonry Structures, & Related Commentaries, 2 vols., Set. 88p. 1992. 68.25 (*0-685-45552-1*, 5301) ACI.

Building Code Requirements for Reinforced Concrete. rev. ed. 1986. 48.95 (*0-318-35473-X*, 318-83(86)) ACI.

Building Code Requirements for Reinforced Concrete, 1989, with Commentary: ACI 318-89(92). ANSI 318R-89. rev. ed. ACI Committee Staff. 1992. 89.25 (*0-317-99889-7*) ACI.

Building College Spelling Skills. Crosby et al. (C). 1987. pap. text ed. 23.00 (*0-673-39250-3*) HarpCollege.

Building College Writing. Marilyn Kok & Leah Schietinger. 450p. (C). 1992. pap. text ed. 18.75 (*0-15-505501-1*) HB Coll Pubs.

Building Communication Partnerships: A Professional's Guide. Yvonne Gillette. 256p. 1989. pap. 29.95 (*1-55990-011-3*) Special Pr TX.

Building Communication Theories: A Socio-Cultural Approach. Ed. by Fred L. Casmir. (LEA's Communication Ser.). 320p. 1994. text ed. 59.95 (*0-8058-1516-3*) L Erlbaum Assocs.

Building Communication Theory. 2nd rev. ed. Dominic Infante et al. (Illus.). 563p. (Orig.). (C). 1993. pap. text ed. 29.95 (*0-88133-709-9*) Waveland Pr.

Building Communities: A Vision for a New Century. Commission on Future of Comm Coll Staff. 1988. pap. 18.50 (*0-87117-182-1*) Am Assn Comm Coll.

***Building Communities from the Inside Out: A Path Toward Finding & Mobilizing a Community's Assets.** John P. Kretzmann & John L. McKnight. 376p. (Orig.). 1993. pap. 14.50x (*0-87946-108-X*) ACTA Pubns.

Building Communities of Difference: Higher Education in the 21st Century. William G. Tierney. LC 92-31297. (Critical Studies in Education & Culture). 184p. 1993. text ed. 49.95 (*0-89789-312-3*, H312, Bergin & Garvey); pap. text ed. 16.95 (*0-89789-313-1*, G313, Bergin & Garvey) Greenwood.

***Building Communities of Learners: A Collaboration Among Students, Teachers, Families & Community.** Sudia P. McCaleb. 240p. 1994. pap. text ed. 13.00 (*0-312-09163-X*) St Martin.

Building Communities That Work: Community Economic Development. (Capitols & Communities Ser.). 17p. 1991. 15.00 (*1-55516-800-0*, 3901) Natl Conf State Legis.

Building Communities Through Strategic Planning: A Guidebook for Community Colleges. Kay McClenney et al. 88p. 1991. 20.00 (*0-87117-230-5*) Am Assn Comm Coll.

Building Community: A Manual Exploring Issues of Women & Disability. Women & Disability Awareness Project Staff. 1984. teacher ed 15.00 (*0-931629-01-2*) Educ Equity Con.

***Building Community: Social Studies in the Middle School Years.** Ed. by Mary Burke-Hengen & Tim Gillespie. LC 95-8643. 1995. pap. text ed. write for info. (*0-435-08904-8*) Heinemann.

***Building Community: The Human Side of Work.** Manning. (GC-Principles of Management Ser.). 1996. text ed. 44.95 (*0-538-83586-9*) S-W Pub.

***Building Community: West African Style.** Arkansas International Center Staff & CTIR Staff. (J). (gr. 6-9). 1994. ring bd., sl. 35.95 (*0-614-06470-8*) U of Denver Teach.

Building Community in Schools. Thomas J. Sergiovanni. LC 93-19582. (Education-Higher Education Ser.). 242p. 1993. 28.95 (*1-55542-571-2*) Jossey-Bass.

Building Community in Youth Groups. Denny Rydberg. (Illus.). 179p. (Orig.). 1985. pap. 15.99 (*0-931529-06-9*) Group Pub.

Building Community Support for Schools. Peak Performance Associates Staff. 168p. (C). 1994. 49.95 (*0-8403-9289-3*) Kendall-Hunt.

Building Competences in the Firm: Lessons from Japanese & European Optoelectronics. Kumiko Miyazaki. LC 94-20757. 1994. write for info. (*0-312-12314-0*) St Martin.

***Building Competitiveness: United States Expatriate Management Strategies in Mexico.** rev. ed. Jane H. Stanford. LC 94-35672. (Garland Studies on Industrial Productivity). (Illus.). 224p. 1995. 59.00 (*0-8153-1939-8*) Garland.

Building Computer Literacy: Levels A thru I. Wesley A. Many & Walter Friker. (Illus.). 1985. teacher ed 9.50 (*0-932957-01-3*); pap. 6.75 (*0-932957-00-5*) Natl School.

Building Condition Assessment in the U. S. A. James Douglas. (C). 1992. text ed. 65.00 (*0-85406-548-2*, Pub. by R-I-C-S Bks UK) St Mut.

Building Confidence in Communication. Daniel M. Dunn. (C). 1988. pap. text ed. 32.00 (*0-673-39929-X*) HarpCollege.

Building Confidence, Resolving Conflicts: Proceedings of the Second Asia-Pacific Roundtable. Ed. by Muthiah Alagappa. 155p. 1990. 75.00 (*0-7103-0372-6*, A4534, Pub. by Kegan Paul Intl UK) Routledge Chapman & Hall.

Building Confidence with Human Problems: A Workbook. Gordon Burnand. 151p. 1991. pap. 75.00 (*0-907774-06-7*, Pub. by Ldrship Ltd UK) St Mut.

Building Consensus in Groups: A Guide to Participatory Decision Making. Sam Kaner et al. (Illus.). 224p. 1995. pap. 19.95 (*0-86571-310-3*) New Soc Pubs.

Building Consensus in Groups: A Guide to Participatory Decision Making. Sam Kaner et al. (Illus.). 224p. 1995. lib. bdg. 49.95 (*0-86571-309-X*) New Soc Pubs.

Building Construction. James E. Ambrose. 1990. text ed. 49.95 (*0-442-20755-7*) Chapman & Hall.

Building Construction, 4 vols., Set. James E. Ambrose. 1992. 187.80 (*0-442-01336-1*) Chapman & Hall.

Building Construction: Interior Systems. James E. Ambrose. (Illus.). 208p. 1991. text ed. 49.95 (*0-442-00292-0*) Chapman & Hall.

Building Construction: Service Systems. James E. Ambrose. (Illus.). 160p. 1992. text ed. 49.95 (*0-442-00294-7*) Chapman & Hall.

Building Construction: Site & Below-Grade Systems. James E. Ambrose. 1991. text ed. 49.95 (*0-442-00293-9*) Chapman & Hall.

Building Construction & Design. James E. Ambrose. 1992. pap. 49.95 (*0-442-00719-1*) Chapman & Hall.

Building Construction and Design Instructional Manual. J. Ambrose. 1992. text ed. write for info. (*0-442-01317-5*) Van Nos Reinhold.

Building Construction Before Mechanization. John Fitchen. (Illus.). 400p. 1989. pap. 17.50 (*0-262-56047-X*) MIT Pr.

Building Construction Codes, Specifications, & Regulations Sourcebook. Joseph Macdonald. 1992. text ed. 65.50 (*0-07-044334-3*) McGraw.

Building Construction Engineer. Jack Rudman. (Career Examination Ser.: C-3170). 1994. pap. 39.95 (*0-8373-3170-6*) Nat Learn.

Building Construction Estimating. Stephen D. Schuette & Roger W. Liska. LC 93-46813. 1994. text ed. write for info. (*0-07-911816-X*) McGraw.

Building Construction Estimator. Jack Rudman. (Career Examination Ser.: C-1145). 1994. pap. 34.95 (*0-8373-1145-4*) Nat Learn.

Building Construction for the Fire Service. 3rd ed. Francis L. Brannigan. Ed. by Gordon P. McKinnon & Debra Matson. (Illus.). 667p. 1992. 55.75 (*0-685-66127-X*); text ed. 55.75 (*0-685-59451-3*, BCFS-3) Natl Fire Prot.

Building Construction Handbook. Roy Chudley. 1988. pap. 32.95 (*0-7506-0115-9*) Buttrwrth-Heinemann.

Building Construction Illustrated. 2nd enl. ed. Frank Ching & Cassandra Adams. (Illus.). 400p. 1991. pap. 27.95 (*0-442-23498-8*) Van Nos Reinhold.

Building Construction in Mughal India: The Evidence from Painting. Ahsan J. Qaisar. (Illus.). 100p. 1989. 22.50 (*0-19-562260-X*) OUP.

Building Construction Inspection: A Guide for Architects. Jay Bannister. 1991. text ed. 64.95 (*0-471-53004-2*) Wiley.

Building Construction Inspector. Jack Rudman. (Career Examination Ser.: C-1146). 1994. pap. 29.95 (*0-8373-1146-2*) Nat Learn.

Building Construction Inspector I. Jack Rudman. (Career Examination Ser.: C-1831). 1994. pap. 29.95 (*0-8373-1831-9*) Nat Learn.

Building Construction Inspector II. Jack Rudman. (Career Examination Ser.: C-1832). 1994. pap. 34.95 (*0-8373-1832-7*) Nat Learn.

Building Construction Inspector III. Jack Rudman. (Career Examination Ser.: C-1833). 1994. pap. 34.95 (*0-8373-1833-5*) Nat Learn.

Building Construction Practice: Pratique de la Construction des Batiments. 11th ed. M. Mittag. 352p. (FRE.). 1983. write for info. (*0-7859-4923-2*) Fr & Eur.

***Building Construction Principles, Practices & Materials.** Glenn M. Hardie. LC 94-39073. 1995. text ed. 72.00 (*0-13-350570-7*) P-H.

Building Construction Program Manager. Jack Rudman. (Career Examination Ser.: C-3098). 1994. pap. 39.95 (*0-8373-3098-X*) Nat Learn.

Building Construction Related to the Fire Service. IFSTA Committee Staff. Ed. & Intro. by Gene P. Carlson. LC 86-80301. (Illus.). 166p. (Orig.). 1986. pap. text ed. 16.50 (*0-87939-059-X*) IFSTA.

Building Construction Trades. Michael Sumichrast. (Opportunities in...Ser.). (Illus.). 160p. 1991. 13.95 (*0-8442-8633-8*, VGM Career Bks) NTC Pub Grp.

Building Consultant: The Owner's Guide to Understanding Construction of His Home, What You Should Know about Building Specifications. enl. ed. J. James Hasenau. LC 77-89657. (Illus.). 1987. pap. 12.95 (*0-913042-11-0*) Holland Hse Pr.

Building Consultant: The Owner's Guide to Understanding Construction of His Home, What You Should Know about Building Specifications. 4th enl. ed. J. James Hasenau. LC 77-89657. (Illus.). 1987. 12.95 (*0-913042-08-0*) Holland Hse Pr.

Building Contract Dictionary. Vincent Powell-Smith & David Chappell. 464p. 1985. 94.95 (*0-85139-758-1*, Butterwrth Archit) Buttrwrth-Heinemann.

Building Contractor. R. Dodge Woodson. LC 93-18549. 1993. pap. write for info. (*0-8306-4321-4*) TAB Bks.

Building Contractor: Start & Run A Money-Making Business. R. Dodge Woodson. 1993. pap. text ed. 17.95 (*0-07-071770-2*) McGraw.

***Building Contracts & Practice.** 2nd ed. Justice Smellie. 454p. 1979. boxed 72.00 (*0-409-66785-4*, NZ) Butterworth Legal Pubs.

Building Control by Legislation: The U. K. Experience. J. H. Garnham Wright. LC 82-21762. (Theory & Practice of Building Control Ser.: No. 1). (Illus.). 255p. reprint ed. pap. 72.70 (*0-8357-4615-1*, 2037547) Bks Demand.

Building Control Systems. 2nd ed. Vaughn Bradshaw. LC 93-21609. (Illus.). 600p. 1993. text ed. 69.95 (*0-471-57378-7*) Wiley.

Building Controls into Structured Systems. Alan E. Brill. LC 82-70209. (Illus.). 168p. (Orig.). 1986. text ed. 49.00 (*0-13-086059-X*, Yourdon) P-H.

Building Cooperative Processing Applications Using SAA. John Tibbetts & Barbara Bernstein. 320p. 1992. pap. text ed. 39.95 (*0-471-55485-5*) Wiley.

Building Credibility with the Powers That Be. Marilyn MacKenzie & Gail Moore. 1990. pap. 7.95 (*0-911029-29-X*) Heritage Arts.

Building Custodian. Jack Rudman. (Career Examination Ser.: C-99). 1994. pap. 23.95 (*0-8373-0099-1*) Nat Learn.

Building Custodian-Maintenance Engineer. 8th ed. Frank R. Keating & Craig S. Herrman. 1988. pap. 9.95 (*0-13-085812-9*, Arco Test) P-H Gen Ref & Trav.

Building Custom Software Tools & Libraries. Martin Stitt. 304p. 1993. disk, pap. 72.90 (*0-471-57914-9*); pap. text ed. 32.95 (*0-471-57915-7*) Wiley.

Building Customer Loyalty. Barbara Glanz. LC 94-1234. (Business Skills Experience Ser.). 128p. 1994. pap. 10.00 (*0-7863-0253-4*) Irwin Prof Pubng.

Building Customer Loyalty. Ian Linton. 192p. (Orig.). 1993. pap. 39.50x (*0-273-60080-X*, Pub. by Pitman Pub Ltd UK) Trans-Atl Phila.

***Building Dances: A Guide to Putting Movements Together.** Susan McGreevy-Nichols & Helene Scheff. LC 95-8141. 128p. 1995. pap. write for info. (*0-87322-573-2*, BMCG 0573) Human Kinetics.

Building Data Networks. Bradner. 350p. 1993. boxed 44.00 (*0-13-087354-3*) P-H.

***Building Databases with Approach 3.** Elaine Marmel. 1994. text ed. 49.95 (*0-471-05252-3*) Wiley.

***Building Databases with Approach 3.** Elaine Marmel. LC 94-31731. 1994. pap. text ed. 24.95 (*0-471-05223-X*) Wiley.

Building dBase IV 2.0 Applications: A Hands-on Programming Guide. Martin L. Rinehart. LC 93-35644. 1993. pap. 34.95 (*0-201-62634-9*) Addison-Wesley.

Building Decision Support Systems. John L. Bennett. LC 82-1632. (Computer Science Ser.). 1983. text ed. 41.95 (*0-201-00563-8*) Addison-Wesley.

Building Deck Waterproofing, No. STP 1084. Ed. by Laura E. Gish. LC 90-30660. (Special Technical Publication (STP) Ser.). (Illus.). 150p. 1990. text ed. 52.00 (*0-8031-1384-6*, 04-010840-10) ASTM.

Building Decks. Cy De Cosse Incorporated Staff. LC 89-23708. (Black & Decker Home Improvement Library). 128p. 1990. 14.95 (*0-86573-708-8*); pap. 12.95 (*0-86573-709-6*) Cy De Cosse.

***Building Democracy: A Casebook of Community Architecture.** Graham Towers. 160p. 1995. 85.00x (*1-85728-088-1*, Pub. by UCL Pr UK); pap. 27.50x (*1-85728-089-X*, Pub. by UCL Pr UK) Taylor & Francis.

Building Democracy? The International Dimension of Democratisation in Eastern Europe. Ed. by Geoffrey Pridham et al. LC 94-10228. 1994. text ed. 45.00 (*0-312-12231-4*) St Martin.

Building Democracy & Free Enterprise in Nicaragua: Recommendations to the Chamorro Government. Intro. by Duncan W. Sellars. 88p. (Orig.). (ENG & SPA.). 1990. pap. 10.00 (*0-923128-03-4*) Intl Free Found.

Building Democracy in One-Party Systems: Theoretical Problems & Cross-Nation Experiences. Ed. by Gary Wekkin et al. LC 92-38234. 304p. 1993. text ed. 55.00 (*0-275-94551-0*, C4551, Praeger Pubs) Greenwood.

***Building Democratic Instutitions: Party Systems in Latin America.** Ed. by Scott Mainwaring & Timothy R. Scully. 600p. 1995. 65.00x (*0-8047-2307-9*) Stanford U Pr.

Building Democratic Instutitions: Party Systems in Latin America. Ed. by Scott Mainwaring & Timothy R. Scully. LC 93-46528. 600p. 1995. pap. 19.95 (*0-8047-2305-2*) Stanford U Pr.

Building Department Guide to Disaster Mitigation: 1991 Edition. 21.15 (*1-884590-23-3*, 218L91) Intl Conf Bldg Off.

Building Design & Construction Handbook. 5th ed. Frederick S. Merritt. 1994. text ed. 99.95 (*0-07-041596-X*) McGraw.

Building Design for Handicapped & Aged Persons. 1992. text ed. 49.00 (*0-07-012533-3*) McGraw.

An Asterisk (*) at the beginning of an entry indicates that the title is appearing in BIP for the first time.

*Building Design Vignette Primer & Mock Building Design Exam. 2nd ed. Ken Zinns & Barry Chin. (Illus.). 60p. (Orig.). 1994. pap. 42.00 (*0-933885-09-1*) Arcade Pubs.

Building Diversity: Recruitment & Retention in the '90s. 2nd ed. Ed. by Mary L. Santovec. LC 92-9586. 169p. 1992. pap. text ed. 69.50 (*0-912150-23-8*) Magna Pubns.

Building Domestic Liberty: Charlotte Perkins Gilman's Architectural Feminism. Polly W. Allen. LC 87-35311. (Illus.). 208p. (Orig.). (C). 1988. 27.50x (*0-87023-627-X*); pap. 14.95 (*0-87023-628-8*) U of Mass Pr.

Building Doors, Windows & Skylights. Ed. by Fine Homebuilding Magazine Staff. LC 88-50568. (Fine Homebuilding Builder's Library Ser.). (Illus.). 160p. 1989. 25.95 (*0-942391-14-4*) Taunton.

*Building Dreams. Dee Blassie & Mychal Wynn. Ed. by Denise Smith. (Illus.). (Orig.). (J). (gr. k up). Date not set. pap. 9.95 (*1-880463-45-8*) Rising Sun.

*Building Dreams: Helping Students Discover Their Potential. Mychal Wynn. Ed. by Denise Smith. (Orig.). 1994. student ed, pap. 9.95 (*1-880463-42-3*) Rising Sun.

*Building Dreams: Helping Students Discover Their Potential. Mychal Wynn. Ed. by Denise Smith. (Orig.). (C). 1995. pap. 15.95 (*1-880463-41-5*) Rising Sun.

Building Dynamic Churches. Medford Jones. (Orig.). 1991. pap. 12.99 (*0-89900-390-7*) College Pr Pub.

Building Early America. Ed. by Charles E. Peterson. (Illus.). 407p. 1992. reprint ed. 32.95 (*1-879335-30-1*); reprint ed. pap. 19.95 (*1-879335-31-X*) Astragal Pr.

Building Early Childhood Systems: A Resource Handbook. Jule M. Sugarman. 112p. 1991. pap. 13.95 (*0-87868-451-4*) Child Welfare.

*Building Early Intervention Teams: Working Together for Children & Families. Briggs. 250p. 1995. 48.00 (*0-8342-0638-2*) Aspen Pub.

Building Economics for Architects. Thorbjoern Mann. (Illus.). 224p. 1992. text ed. 39.95 (*0-442-00389-7*) Van Nos Reinhold.

Building Economics in Theory & Practice. Rosalie Ruegg. 1990. text ed. 62.95 (*0-442-26417-8*) Chapman & Hall.

Building Economy: Design, Production & Organization. 3rd ed. P. A. Stone. 280p. 1983. 111.00 (*0-08-028677-1*, Pub. by Pergamon Repr UK) Franklin.

*Building Effective Coalitions to Prevent the Spread of HIV: Planning Considerations. 1994. 15.50 (*0-917160-26-6*) Am Sch Health.

Building Effective Decision Support Systems. Ralph H. Sprague, Jr. & Eric D. Carlson. 304p. (C). 1982. text ed. 81.00 (*0-13-086215-0*) P-H.

Building Effective Mastery Learning Schools. Ed. by James H. Block et al. 240p. (C). 1989. pap. text ed. 26.50 (*0-582-28552-6*, 71580) Longman.

Building Effective Sentences: Grammar, Punctuation, & Writing Techniques. Judith L. White. LC 92-40028. 1992. write for info. (*0-02-800883-9*) Glencoe.

Building Effective Volunteer Committees. Nancy Macduff. Ed. by Janie Millgard. (Illus.). 82p. (C). 1986. pap. 11.95 (*0-945795-01-7*) MBA Pub.

Building Energy Efficiency. (Illus.). 85p. (Orig.). (C). 1992. pap. text ed. 25.00 (*0-941375-76-5*) Diane Pub.

*Building Energy Efficiency. 1994. lib. bdg. 250.00 (*0-8490-6452-X*) Gordon Pr.

Building Energy Efficiency Standards. (Illus.). 250p. (Orig.). (C). 1993. pap. text ed. 45.00 (*1-56806-887-5*) Diane Pub.

Building Energy Management: An Introduction. Ron L. Highnote. 240p. (C). 1990. student ed 89.95 (*1-880168-01-4*) Inst Applied Sci.

Building Energy Management--Conventional & Solar Approaches: Proceedings of the International Congress, 12-16 May 1980, Povoa de Varzim, Portugal. Fernandes E. De Oliveira et al. LC 80-40415. 800p. 1981. 471.00 (*0-08-026144-2*, Pub. by Pergamon Repr UK) Franklin.

Building Energy Management & Control Systems. 2nd ed. F. William Payne & John J. McGowan. (Illus.). 399p. 1988. text ed. 67.95 (*0-442-23734-0*) Chapman & Hall.

Building Energy Management Systems: The Basics. G. J. Levermore. (C). 1988. 140.00 (*0-86022-205-5*, Pub. by Build Servs Info Assn UK) St Mut.

Building Energy Management Systems for the Operator. G. J. Levermore. 1989. 80.00 (*0-86022-216-0*, Pub. by Build Servs Info Assn UK) St Mut.

Building Engineering & Systems Design. 2nd ed. Frederick S. Merritt & James E. Ambrose. (Illus.). 656p. 1989. text ed. 65.00 (*0-442-20668-2*) Chapman & Hall.

Building English Sentences, 10 bks. Eugene Hall. Incl. Alternates. 1985. pap. text ed. 7.95 (*0-8325-0482-3*); With Be. 1985. pap. text ed. 7.95 (*0-8325-0475-0*); With One Verb. 1985. pap. text ed. 7.95 (*0-8325-0476-9*); With Two Verbs. 1985. (*0-8325-0477-7*); With Verbals. 1985. (*0-8325-0480-7*); With Adverbs. 1986. (*0-8325-0478-5*); Building Complex English Sentences. 1985. (*0-8325-0485-8*); With Verbs & Verb Phrases. 1988. (*0-8325-0481-5*); With Adjectives. 1985. (*0-8325-0483-1*); With Auxiliary Verbs. 1985. (*0-8325-0479-3*); write for info. (*0-318-53534-3*) NTC Pub Grp.

Building English Skills. large type ed. Griffin. Incl. Pink Level, 2 vols. large type ed. 332p. (gr. 1). 1984. 68.53 (*0-317-02117-6*, 4-03210-00); Plum Level, 2 vols. large type ed. 442p. (J). (gr. 2). 1985. 84.15 (*0-317-02118-4*, 4-03220-00); (J). write for info. (*0-318-66086-5*) Am Printing Hse.

Building English Skills: The McDougal, Littell English Program. large type ed. J. Littell et al. Incl. Green Level, 3 vols. 725p. (J). (gr. 8). 1984. 209.00 (*0-317-02124-9*, J-03150-00); (J). 1984. 103.40 (*0-317-04890-2*) Am Printing Hse.

Building Envelope: Applications of New Technology Cladding. Alan Brookes & Chris Grech. (Illus.). 132p. 1990. text ed. 49.95 (*0-408-50030-1*, Butterwrth Archit) Buttrwrth-Heinemann.

Building Equipment & Energy Management Series. Center for Occupational Research & Development Staff. (Technology Ser.). (Illus.). 1646p. (C). 1981. pap. text ed. 138.00 (*1-55502-278-2*) CORD Commns.

Building Equipment Mechanic (U. S. P. S.) Jack Rudman. (Career Examination Ser.: C-1608). 1994. pap. 27.95 (*0-8373-1608-1*) Nat Learn.

Building Ethernet Networks: Installing, Maintaining, & Troubleshooting Ethernet Networks. Robert Chang. 1992. 34.95 (*1-55851-202-0*) M&T Bks.

Building European Society: Occupational Change & Social Mobility in Europe, 1840-1940. Ed. by David Vincent & Andrew Miles. LC 92-29423. 320p. (C). 1993. text ed. 69.95 (*0-7190-3499-X*, Pub. by Manchester Univ Pr UK) St Martin.

Building European Ventures: Proceedings of the Second Annual EFER Forum held at Insead, France, 14-15 Dec. 1989. Ed. by Sue Birley. 240p. 1990. 50.00 (*0-444-88746-6*, North Holland) Elsevier.

Building Evaluation. Ed. by Wolfgang F. Preiser. (Illus.). 344p. 1989. 89.50 (*0-306-43337-0*, Plenum Pr) Plenum.

Building Excellence: Selecting, Motivating & Retaining a Professional Foodservice Staff. 56p. 1984. pap. 17.25 (*0-914528-33-5*, MG865) Natl Restaurant Assn.

Building Expert Systems. Frederick Hayes-Roth et al. LC 82-24511. (Teknowledge Ser.). (Illus.). (C). 1983. text ed. 49.50 (*0-201-10686-8*) Addison-Wesley.

Building Expert Systems in Prolog. D. Merritt. (Compass International Ser.). (Illus.). xv, 358p. 1989. 52.00 (*0-387-97016-9*) Spr-Verlag.

Building Expert Systems in Training & Education. R. Scott Grabinger et al. LC 89-48609. (Illus.). 192p. 1990. text ed. 45.00 (*0-275-93491-8*, C3491, Greenwood Pr) Greenwood.

Building Expert Systems Prolog. D. Merritt. 1989. 169.00 (*0-387-97015-0*) Spr-Verlag.

Building Failures. 2nd ed. W. H. Ransom. 200p. 1981. text ed. 45.00 (*0-419-14260-6*, E & FN Spon); pap. text ed. 19.95 (*0-419-14270-3*, E & FN Spon) Routledge Chapman & Hall.

Building Failures: A Guide to Diagnosis, Remedy & Prevention. 3rd ed. Lyall Addleson. (Illus.). 120p. 1992. text ed. 77.95 (*0-7506-0226-0*, Butterwrth Archit) Buttrwrth-Heinemann.

Building Faith in Families. Frank G. Dunn. LC 86-21818. 160p. (Orig.). 1987. pap. 8.95 (*0-8192-1394-2*) Morehouse Pub.

Building Family Communication. J. Denis Mercier & Waln K. Brown. 20p. 1992. 2.95 (*1-56456-071-6*, 270) W Gladden Found.

Building Family Competence: Primary & Secondary Prevention Strategies. Luciano L'Abate. (Illus.). 240p. (C). 1990. text ed. 38.00 (*0-8039-3488-2*) Sage.

Building Family Faith: Weekly Lectionary-Based Activities, No. 1, Cycle A. Lisa Bellecci-St. Romain. (Illus.). 112p. (Orig.). 1993. spiral bd. 10.95 (*0-89243-542-9*) Liguori Pubns.

Building Family Faith: Weekly Lectionary-Based Activities, No. 2, Cycle B. Lisa Bellecci-St. Romain & Lisa Bellecci Stromain. (Illus.). 112p. (Orig.). 1995. pap. 10.95 (*0-89243-533-X*) Liguori Pubns.

Building Family Faith: Weekly Lectionary-Based Activities, No. 3, Cycle C. Lisa Bellecci-St. Romain. (Illus.). 112p. (Orig.). 1993. spiral bd. 10.95 (*0-89243-543-7*) Liguori Pubns.

*Building Family Faith Through Lent, Cycle A. Lisa M. St. Romain. 32p. 1994. pap. text ed. 1.95 (*0-89243-807-X*) Liguori Pubns.

*Building Family Faith Through Lent, Cycle B. Lisa M. St. Romain. 32p. 1994. pap. text ed. 1.95 (*0-89243-808-8*) Liguori Pubns.

*Building Family Faith Through Lent (Cycle C) Lectionary Based Activities. Lisa Bellecci-St. Romain. LC 94-79444. (Illus.). 32p. (Orig.). 1994. pap. 1.95 (*0-89243-772-3*) Liguori Pubns.

Building Family Strengths: Blueprints for Action. Ed. by Nick Stinnett et al. LC 79-51329. 461p. reprint ed. pap. 131.40 (*0-8357-7464-3*, 2033140) Bks Demand.

Building Family Strengths Five: Continuity & Diversity. Ed. by George Rowe et al. 505p. 1984. pap. 15.95 (*0-89292-090-4*) Educ Dev Ctr.

Building Family Strengths Four: Positive Support Systems. Sally Van Zandt. Ed. by Nick Stinnett et al. 601p. 1982. pap. 14.50 (*0-685-42770-6*) Educ Dev Ctr.

Building Family Values: Using the Tools of Bonding & Boundaries. Rodney Dean & Nancy Dean. LC 93-41667. 208p. (Orig.). 1994. pap. 9.95 (*0-941005-98-4*) Chrch Grwth VA.

Building Fences. (Illus.). 96p. 1974. 6.00 (*0-914452-41-X*, 405) Am Assn Voc Materials.

Building Fences of Wood, Metal, Stone & Plants. John Vivian. Ed. by Susan Williamson. LC 86-32489. (Illus.). 192p. (Orig.). 1987. pap. 13.95 (*0-913589-27-6*) Williamson Pub Co.

Building Financial Decision-Making Models: An Introduction to Principles & Procedures. Donald R. Moscato. LC 80-65704. 160p. reprint ed. pap. 45.60 (*0-8357-7465-1*, 2023581) Bks Demand.

Building Fine Furniture: A Simple, Uncomplicated Method. G. William Scherer. LC 92-21741. (Illus.). 288p. 1992. pap. 18.95 (*0-8069-8712-X*) Sterling.

Building Fine Furniture from Solid Wood. Ken Sadler. (Illus.). 160p. (Orig.). 1994. pap. 24.95 (*1-55870-327-6*) Betterway Bks.

Building Fire Service Training Centers. National Fire Protection Association Staff. 17p. 1992. 16.75 (*0-317-63544-1*, 1402-92) Natl Fire Prot.

Building Floors, Walls & Stairs. Ed. by Fine Homebuilding Magazine Staff. LC 88-50567. (Fine Homebuilding Builder's Library Ser.). (Illus.). 160p. 1989. 25.95 (*0-942391-12-8*) Taunton.

Building Fluency in English: Authentic Speech. Adolf E. Hieke & Ronald W. Dunbar. 200p. (C). 1985. pap. text ed. 12.25 (*0-13-086125-1*) P-H.

Building Fluency in English: Conversation Management. Ronald W. Dunbar & Adolf E. Hieke. (Illus.). 250p. (C). 1985. pap. text ed. 12.50 (*0-13-086117-0*) P-H.

Building Foodservice Sales: Instructors Guide. Educational Foundation of the National Restaurant Association Staff. (Illus.). 56p. (Orig.). 1993. pap. 25.00 (*0-915452-25-1*) Educ Found.

Building Foodservice Sales: Instructor's Guide. Educational Foundation of the NRA Staff. 56p. 1993. 4.69 (*0-8403-8642-7*) Kendall-Hunt.

Building Foodservice Sales: Leaders Guide. Educational Foundation of the National Restaurant Association Staff. (Illus.). 48p. (Orig.). 1993. pap. 25.00 (*0-915452-27-8*) Educ Found.

Building Foodservice Sales: Leader's Guide. Educational Foundation of the NRA Staff. 48p. 1993. 4.39 (*0-8403-8641-9*) Kendall-Hunt.

Building Foodservice Sales: Manager Handbook. Educational Foundation of the National Restaurant Association Staff. (Illus.). 64p. (Orig.). 1993. pap. 30.00 (*0-915452-24-3*) Educ Found.

Building Foodservice Sales: Manager Handbook. Educational Foundation of the NRA Staff. 64p. 1993. pap. text ed., spiral bd. 4.63 (*0-8403-8640-0*) Kendall-Hunt.

Building Foodservice Sales: Server Guide. Educational Foundation of the National Restaurant Association Staff. (Illus.). 32p. (Orig.). 1993. pap. 7.95 (*0-915452-26-X*) Educ Found.

Building Foodservice Sales: Server Guide. Educational Foundation of the NRA Staff. 32p. 1993. 1.17 (*0-8403-8643-5*) Kendall-Hunt.

Building for a Lifetime. Margaret Wylde. 272p. 1993. 44.95 (*1-56158-036-8*) Taunton.

Building for Books: The Architectural Evolution of the Advocates' Library, 1680-1925. I. G. Brown. 1989. text ed. 59.00 (*0-08-037968-0*, Pergamon Pr) Elsevier.

*Building for Effective Mission: A Complete Guide for Congregations on Bricks & Mortar Issues. Kennon L. Callahan. LC 95-11864. 1995. 16.00 (*0-06-061280-0*) Harper SF.

Building for Energy Conservation. P. W. O'Callaghan. 1978. 105.00 (*0-08-022120-3*, Pub. by Pergamon Repr UK) Franklin.

Building for God's Glory (Haggai & Zechariah) Michael Bentley. 1989. pap. 10.99 (*0-85234-259-4*, Pub. by Evangel Pr UK) Presby & Reformed.

Building for Modern Man. Ed. by Thomas H. Creighton. LC 74-80385. (Essay Index Reprint Ser.). 1977. 20.95 (*0-8369-1029-X*) Ayer.

Building for Peace at Home & Abroad. Maxwell S. Stewart. LC 71-134138. (Essay Index Reprint Ser.). 1977. reprint ed. 20.95 (*0-8369-2372-3*) Ayer.

Building for Safety Compendium: An Annotated Bibliography & Information Directory for Safe Building Programs in Disaster-Prone Areas. Yasmin Aysan et al. (Building for Safety Ser.). 80p. (Orig.). 1994. pap. 13.50 (*1-85339-181-6*, Pub. by Intermed Tech UK) Women Ink.

Building for South Asia: An Architectural Autobiography. Benjamin Polk. (C). 1993. 49.00 (*81-7017-300-0*, Pub. by Abhinav II) S Asia.

Building for the Arts: A Guidebook for the Planning & Design of Cultural Facilities. Catherine R. Brown et al. Ed. by Gina Briefs-Elgin. LC 89-40275. (Illus.). 1989. pap. 29.95 (*0-9611710-4-9*) Western States.

Building for the Centuries: Illinois, 1865-1898. John H. Keiser. LC 77-1764. (Sesquicentennial History of Illinois Ser.). 402p. 1977. 29.95 (*0-252-00617-8*) U of Ill Pr.

Building for the Future. Ed. by Geothermal Resources Council. (Transactions Ser.: Vol. 11). 1987. 40.00 (*0-934412-62-6*) Geothermal.

Building for the Garden. Michael Green. Ed. by John Patrick. (Lothian Australian Garden Ser.). (Illus.). 64p. (Orig.). 1995. pap. 9.95 (*0-85091-320-9*, Pub. by Lothian Pub AT) Seven Hills Bk.

Building for Tomorrow. Nicola Barber. LC 92-24925. (Facing the Future Ser.). (Illus.). 48p. (J). (gr. 5). 1992. lib. bdg. 22.80 (*0-8114-2805-2*) Raintree Steck-V.

Building for Tomorrow: Global Enterprise & the U. S. Construction Industry. 120p. 1988. pap. text ed. 14.95 (*0-309-03937-1*) Natl Acad Pr.

Building for Tomorrow: International Experience in Construction Industry Development. D. Miles & R. Neale. vii, 238p. (Orig.). 1991. pap. 24.00 (*92-2-107284-3*) Intl Labour Office.

Building for Women. Ed. by Suzanne Keller. LC 80-8783. (Lincoln Institute of Land Policy Book Ser.). 235p. reprint ed. pap. 67.00 (*0-7837-3267-8*, 2043286) Bks Demand.

Building Foundations: Housing & Federal Policy. Ed. by Denise DiPasquale & Langley C. Keyes. LC 90-30442. (Illus.). 512p. (C). 1990. 59.95 (*0-8122-8223-X*); pap. 27.95 (*0-8122-1309-2*) U of Pa Pr.

Building Foundations for Secondary School Mathematics. Hollowell et al. 281p. 1995. pap. 34.95 (*0-939765-63-2*, G154) Janson Pubns.

Building from Within: Alaskans Who Build Their Own. 2nd ed. Joan Koponen. (Illus.). 168p. 1983. pap. 14.00 (*0-9610356-0-9*) J Koponen.

*Building Functional Social Skills: Group Activities for Adults. Angela Dikengil & Monique Kaye. 211p. 1992. pap. text ed. 49.00 (*0-88450-595-2*, 4280) Commun Skill.

Building Future Security: Strategies for Restructuring the Defense Technology & Industrial Base. (Illus.). 160p. (Orig.). (C). 1993. pap. text ed. 75.00 (*0-7881-0051-3*) Diane Pub.

Building Garden Furniture: More Than Thirty Beautiful Outdoor Projects. Ray Martin & Lee Rankin. (Illus.). 160p. 1994. pap. 15.95 (*0-8069-8375-2*) Sterling.

Building Gender Fairness in Schools. Beverly A. Stitt. LC 88-2003. 230p. (Orig.). (C). 1988. pap. text ed. 16.95 (*0-8093-1474-6*) S Ill U Pr.

Building Geographic Literacy: An Interactive Approach. Charles A. Stansfield, Jr. 256p. (Orig.). (C). 1992. pap. write for info. (*0-02-415660-4*) Macmillan.

Building German Airpower, 1909-1914. John H. Morrow. LC 76-15287. 164p. reprint ed. pap. 46.80 (*0-8357-7466-X*, 2023171) Bks Demand.

Building Global Partnerships for Library Cooperation. Ruth Seidman. LC 92-44370. 1993. 28.00 (*0-87111-409-7*) SLA.

Building Global Security Through Cooperation: Annals of Pugwash 1989. Ed. by Joseph Rotblat & John P. Holdren. (Illus.). 320p. 1991. text ed. 83.00 (*0-387-52813-X*) Spr-Verlag.

Building God's House in the Roman World: Architectural Adaptation among Pagans, Jews, & Christians. L. Michael White. LC 89-32588. (ASOR Library of Biblical & Near Eastern Archaeology). (Illus.). 208p. 1990. text ed. 33.50x (*0-8018-3906-8*) Johns Hopkins.

B

Building Gold, Silver & Precious Stones: A Devotional Exposition of First Corinthians 3: 8-15. rev. ed. N. A. Woychuk. 196p. (Orig.). 1985. pap. 5.00 (*1-880960-02-8*) Script Memory Fl.

*Building Good Families in a Changing World. Elisabeth Porter. 224p. 1995. pap. 24.95 (*0-522-84648-3*) Paul & Co Pubs.

Building Guard. Jack Rudman. (Career Examination Ser.: C-2295). 1994. pap. 23.95 (*0-8373-2295-2*) Nat Learn.

Building Guitar Speed. David Coe. 1993. 8.95 (*1-56222-093-4*, 94399) Mel Bay.

Building Habitats for Reptiles: A Step by Step Guide. Don Adams. (Illus.). 40p. (Orig.). 1987. pap. 3.95 (*0-916005-07-0*) Silver Sea.

Building Hardwick: Community Histories in Landscape & Architecture. Claire W. Dempsey. (Illus.). viii, 64p. (Orig.). 1991. pap. 10.00 (*0-9631184-0-4*) Hardwick Hist.

Building Harmonica Technique. Date not set. 8.95 (*0-7866-0002-0*, 95167); audio 9.98 (*0-7866-0064-0*, 95167C) Mel Bay.

Building Health & Youthfulness. 13th rev. ed. Paul C. Bragg & Patricia Bragg. 1994. pap. 3.95 (*0-685-75252-6*) Hlth Sci.

Building Healthy Friendships: Teaching Friendship Skills to Young People. Terry Beck. Ed. by Diane Parker. LC 94-1691. 140p. 1994. 9.95 (*1-56875-073-0*) R & E Pubs.

Building Healthy Gardens: A Safe & Natural Approach. rev. ed. Catharine Osgood Foster. Ed. by Jeff Silva. LC 88-45486. Orig. Title: The Organic Gardener. (Illus.). 288p. 1989. reprint ed. pap. 11.95 (*0-88266-527-8*, Garden Way Pub) Storey Comm Inc.

*Building High Commitment in a Low-Commitment World. Bill Hull. 208p. 1995. text ed. 14.99 (*0-8007-1711-2*) Revell.

Building Homes. Graham Rickard. (Houses & Homes Ser.). (Illus.). 32p. (J). (gr. 2-5). 1989. 15.95 (*0-8225-2129-6*, Lerner Publctns) Lerner Group.

Building Hoover Dam: An Oral History of the Great Depression. Andrew Dunar & Dennis McBride. LC 92-44170. (Twayne's Oral History Ser.: No. 11). 350p. 1993. text ed. 27.95 (*0-8057-9110-8*, Twayne); pap. 15.95 (*0-8057-9133-7*, Twayne) Macmillan.

Building Hypermedia Applications: A Software Development Guide. Gary T. Howell. 1992. text ed. 43.00 (*0-07-030601-X*) McGraw.

*Building IBM: Shaping an Industry & Its Technology. Emerson W. Pugh. LC 94-21609. 432p. 1995. 30.00x (*0-262-16147-8*) MIT Pr.

Building Idaho: An Architectural History. Jennifer E. Attebery. LC 90-36717. (Illus.). 192p. (C). 1991. 29.95 (*0-89301-139-8*) U of Idaho Pr.

Building Implementable Marketing Models. P. A. Naert & P. S. Leeflang. 1974. pap. text ed. 44.50 (*90-207-0436-2*) Kluwer Ac.

Building in a Hot Climate. T. M. Stoll & G. I. Evstratov. 366p. (C). 1987. 100.00 (*0-685-36923-4*, Pub. by Collets) St Mut.

Building in a New Spain: Contemporary Spanish Architecture. Kenneth Frampton et al. Ed. by Pauline Saliga & Martha Thorne. Tr. by Kathryn J. Deiss. LC 92-53939. (Illus.). 188p. 1992. pap. 24.95 (*0-86559-098-2*) Art Inst Chi.

Building in a New Spain: Contemporary Spanish Architecture. Ed. by Pauline Saliga & Martha Throne. (Illus.). 188p. 1993. 45.00 (*84-252-1577-3*) Rizzoli Intl.

*Building in Big Brother: The Cryptographic Policy Debate. Ed. by Lance J. Hoffman. LC 95-3758. 1995. 29.95 (*0-387-94441-9*) Spr-Verlag.

*Building in Britain: The Origins of a Modern Industry. Akira Satoh. Tr. by Ralph Morton. (Illus.). 1995. 76.95 (*1-85928-084-6*, Pub. by Scolar Pr UK) Ashgate Pub Co.

Building in Egypt: Pharaonic Stone Masonry. Dieter Arnold. (Illus.). 336p. 1991. 80.00 (*0-19-506350-3*) OUP.

*Building in France, Building in Iron, Building in Ferroconcrete. Sigfried Giedion. Tr. by J. Duncan Berry. (Texts & Documents Ser.). 248p. 1995. 39.95 (*0-89236-319-3*, Getty Ctr Hist Art & Human); pap. 24.95 (*0-89236-320-7*, Getty Ctr Hist Art & Human) J P Getty Trust.

An Asterisk (*) at the beginning of an entry indicates that the title is appearing in BIP for the first time. 941

B

Building in Hot Dry Climates. Belwant S. Saini. LC 79-41777. 176p. reprint ed. pap. 50.20 (*0-8357-7467-8*, 2029265) Bks Demand.

Building in Pain. Anthony Vidler. (Swanson Lecture Ser.). 50p. 1991. pap. write for info. (*1-880337-03-7*) Cranbrook Acad.

Building in Quality. 60p. 1992. pap. 18.00 (*0-11-886083-6*, HM60836, Pub. by HMSO UK) UNIPUB.

Building in the Garden: The Architecture of Joseph Allen Stein in India & California. Stephen White. (Illus.). 384p. 1993. 55.00 (*0-19-562924-8*) OUP.

Building in the Garden: The Architecture of Joseph Allen Stein in India & California. Stephen White. (Illus.). 384p. 1994. reprint ed. pap. 15.95 (*0-19-563223-0*) OUP.

Building Industrial Competitiveness in Developing Countries. Sanjaya Lall. 75p. (Orig.). 1990. pap. 19.00 (*92-64-13397-6*) OECD.

Building Influence: How to Make an Impact on Local Laws That Affect Your Business. Jan Teague. Ed. by Sharon Costello. 118p. (Orig.). 1991. pap. 10.00 (*0-86718-373-X*) Home Builder.

Building Influence for the School Librarian. Gary Hartzell. (Professional Growth Ser.). 100p. 1994. pap. text ed. 28.95 (*0-938865-32-3*) Linworth Pub.

Building Information Literacy Using High Technology: A Guide for Schools & Libraries. Roxanne Mendrinos. (Illus.). 170p. 1994. pap. text ed. 25.00 (*1-56308-032-X*) Libs Unl.

Building Information Partnerships: Conference Proceedings, Anchorage, Alaska, May 5-9, 1990. Ed. by Mark Miller & Gerry Feinstein. 285p. (Orig.). 1991. pap. text ed. 20.00 (*1-55877-135-2*) Natl Governor.

Building Information Systems in the Islamic World. Ed. by Z. Sardar. 176p. 1988. text ed. 80.00 (*0-7201-1971-5*, Mansell Pub) Cassell.

Building Innovation into Program Reviews: Analysis of Service Delivery Alternatives. Harry P. Hatry et al. LC 89-8920. (Illus.). 126p. (Orig.). 1989. pap. text ed. 22.50 (*0-87766-465-X*) Urban Inst.

Building Inspector. Jack Rudman. (Career Examination Ser.: C-104). 1994. pap. 29.95 (*0-8373-0104-1*) Nat Learn.

Building Inspector II. Jack Rudman. (Career Examination Ser.: C-3077). 1994. pap. 34.95 (*0-8373-3077-7*) Nat Learn.

***Building Inspector Trainee.** (Career Examination Ser.: Series 1). Date not set. pap. 27.95 (*0-8373-3682-1*) Nat Learn.

***Building Intelligent Systems with Fuzzy Logic & Neurofuzzy Logic Networks.** T. A. Tilly. 69.95 (*0-471-94244-8*) Wiley.

Building Interactive Systems: Architectures & Tools. Ed. by P. Gray et al. (Workshops in Computing Ser.). viii, 243p. 1992. pap. 59.00 (*0-387-19736-2*) Spr-Verlag.

Building Internal Team-Partnerships: Engineers Guide to Business Series. Harry T. Roman. LC 93-2702. 1993. 19.95 (*0-7803-0365-2*, HL0465-5) Inst Electrical.

***Building International Community: Cooperating for Peace.** Ed. by Kevin Clements & Robin Ward. 328p. 1995. pap. 19.95 (*1-86373-800-2*) Paul & Co Pubs.

***Building Internet Applications with Visual Basic.** Programming Staff & Marchuk. (Illus.). 480p. (Orig.). 1995. pap. 39.99 (*0-7897-0214-2*) Que.

***Building Internet Applications with Visual C Plus Plus.** Markus W. Pope. (Illus.). 608p. (Orig.). 1995. pap. 49.99 (*0-7897-0213-4*) Que.

Building Interpersonal Relationships Through Talking, Listening, Communicating. 2nd ed. Jeffrey S. Bormaster & Carol L. Treat. (C). 1994. spiral bd. 29.00 (*0-89079-592-4*, 6690) PRO-ED.

Building James Coombes Table Engine. Andrew Smith. 7.00 (*0-905180-05-4*) Apple Blossom.

Building Japan: 1868-1876. Richard H. Brunton. (Illus.). 128p. (C). 1991. text ed. 60.00 (*1-873410-05-0*, Pub. by Japan Library) Humanities.

Building Jerusalem. Ed. by Yann Lovelock. (C). 1988. 25.00 (*0-904524-48-5*, Pub. by Rivelin Grapheme Pr) St Mut.

***Building Jerusalem: Jewish Architecture in Britain.** Ed. & Intro. by Sharman Kadish. LC 95-3374. 1995. write for info. (*0-85303-283-1*, Pub. by Vallentine Mitchell UK); pap. write for info. (*0-85303-309-9*, Pub. by Vallentine Mitchell UK) Intl Spec Bk.

Building Jewish Life: Hanukkah. Joel L. Grishaver. (Building Jewish Life Ser.). (Illus.). 48p. 1988. pap. text ed. 4.95 (*0-933873-15-8*) Torah Aura.

Building Jewish Life: Hanukkah Activity Book. Joel L. Grishaver. (Illus.). 31p. (J). 1988. pap. 1.85 (*0-933873-32-8*) Torah Aura.

Building Jewish Life: Passover. Joel L. Grishaver. (Building Jewish Life Ser.). (Illus.). 48p. 1988. pap. text ed. 4.95 (*0-933873-16-6*) Torah Aura.

***Building Jewish Life: Passover Activity Book.** Joel L. Grishaver. (Illus.). 26p. (Orig.). (J). (gr. k-2). 1992. pap. text ed. 1.95 (*0-933873-23-9*) Torah Aura.

Building Jewish Life: Purim. Joel L. Grishaver. (Building Jewish Life Ser.). (Illus.). 46p. 1988. pap. text ed. 4.95 (*0-933873-12-3*) Torah Aura.

Building Jewish Life: Purim Activity Book. Joel L. Grishaver. (Illus.). 31p. 1988. pap. 1.85 (*0-933873-31-X*) Torah Aura.

Building Jewish Life: Purim Megillah. Joel L. Grishaver. (Illus.). 32p. 1988. pap. 1.85 (*0-933873-36-0*) Torah Aura.

Building Jewish Life: Rosh Ha-Shanah & Yom Kippur. Joel L. Grishaver. LC 87-13949. (Illus.). 48p. (Orig.). (YA). (gr. k-3). 1987. pap. text ed. 4.95 (*0-933873-17-4*) Torah Aura.

Building Jewish Life: Rosh Ha-Shanah & Yom Kippur Activity Book. Joel L. Grishaver. (Illus.). 32p. (J). (gr. 1-2). 1988. student ed 1.85 (*0-933873-26-3*) Torah Aura.

Building Jewish Life: Rosh Ha-Shanah Mahzor. Joel L. Grishaver. (Illus.). 1988. pap. 2.50 (*0-933873-28-X*) Torah Aura.

***Building Jewish Life: Shabbat.** Joel L. Grishaver. (Illus.). 48p. (Orig.). (J). 1990. pap. text ed. 4.95 (*0-933873-51-4*) Torah Aura.

Building Jewish Life: Shabbat Activity Book. Joel L. Grishaver. (Illus.). 32p. (J). (gr. 1-2). 1990. student ed 1.85 (*0-933873-50-6*) Torah Aura.

Building Jewish Life: Siddur Commentary. Joel L. Grishaver. (Illus.). 48p. (Orig.). (J). (gr. 2-4). 1992. pap. text ed. 2.45 (*0-933873-74-3*) Torah Aura.

Building Jewish Life: Sukkot & Simhat Torah. Joel L. Grishaver. (Building Jewish Life Ser.). (Illus.). 48p. (J). 1988. pap. text ed. 4.95 (*0-933873-13-1*) Torah Aura.

Building Jewish Life: Sukkot & Simhat Torah Activity Book. Joel L. Grishaver. (Illus.). 32p. (J). (gr. 1-2). 1988. student ed 1.85 (*0-933873-27-1*) Torah Aura.

Building Jewish Life: Synagogue Activity Book. Joel L. Grishaver. (Illus.). (J). (gr. 1-2). 1991. pap. text ed. 1.85 (*0-933873-59-X*) Torah Aura.

Building Jewish Life: Yom Kippur Mahzor. Joel L. Grishaver. (Illus.). 1988. pap. 2.50 (*0-933873-29-8*) Torah Aura.

Building Jewish Life Passover Haggadah. Joel L. Grishaver. (Building Jewish Life Ser.). (Illus.). 48p. (Orig.). (ENG & HEB.). (J). (gr. 4-8). 1989. pap. 2.95 (*0-933873-41-7*) Torah Aura.

Building Jewish Life Prayers & Blessings. Melanie Berman. (Building Jewish Life Ser.). (Illus.). 32p. (Orig.). (J). (gr. k-2). 1991. pap. text ed. 1.85 (*0-933873-66-2*) Torah Aura.

***Building Kites: Flying High with Math.** Nancy A. Belsky. Ed. by Joan Gideon. (Math Projects Ser.). (Illus.). 65p. (Orig.). (J). (gr. 5-8). 1994. student ed, pap. 10.95 (*0-86651-918-1*) Seymour Pubns.

Building Knowledge-Based Systems. John Edwards. 224p. (C). 1990. pap. text ed. 165.00 (*0-273-03048-5*, Pub. by Pitman Pubng UK) St Mut.

Building Knowledge-Based Systems: Towards a Methodology. John Edwards. 1991. pap. text ed. 52.95 (*0-470-21756-1*) Halsted Pr.

Building Knowledge Systems: Developing & Managing Rule-Based Applications. John E. Girard & Jennifer P. Jones. 1989. text ed. 40.00 (*0-07-023437-X*) McGraw.

Building Language Power I: Lessons to Provide Experience, Study, & Observation for Skillful Use of the English Language. Linda N. Harst & Margaret S. Wiederhold. 96p. 1992. pap. text ed. 12.95 (*0-944459-51-X*) ECS Lrn Systs.

Building Language Power II: Lessons to Provide Experience, Study, & Observation for Skillful Use of the English Language. Linda N. Harst & Margaret S. Wiederhold. 96p. 1992. pap. text ed. 12.95 (*0-944459-52-8*) ECS Lrn Systs.

Building Language Power III: Lessons to Provide Experience, Study, & Observation for Skillful Use of the English Language. Linda N. Harst & Margaret S. Wiederhold. 96p. 1993. pap. 12.95 (*0-944459-68-4*) ECS Lrn Systs.

Building LANtastic Networks. Joseph R. Levy. 1994. pap. 29.95 (*1-55851-394-9*) M&T Bks.

Building Lapstrake Canoes. Walter J. Simmons. (Boatbuilding Ser.). (Illus.). 94p. 1981. pap. 22.50 (*0-924947-04-7*) Duck Trap Pr.

Building Law for Students. 2nd ed. Anne Galbraith. 336p. 1991. pap. 34.95 (*0-7506-0302-X*) Buttrwrth-Heinemann.

Building Layout. W. P. Jackson. LC 79-21174. (Illus.). 1979. pap. 15.00 (*0-910460-69-8*) Craftsman.

Building Leaders for Church Education. Kenneth O. Gangel. (C). 1981. 25.99 (*0-8024-1592-X*) Moody.

Building Leaders for Strategic Youth Ministry. Barry St. Clair. (Moving Toward Maturity Ser.). 128p. 1991. pap. 12.99 (*0-89693-288-5*) SP Pubns.

Building Leaders for the New Business Arena: How to Cultivate Strong Leadership for the New Corporate Environment. Bob Collins. LC 88-50555. 179p. 1988. 17.95 (*0-9620580-0-9*) Vision Pubs.

Building Lenin's Russia. Simon I. Liberman. LC 75-39057. (Russian Studies: Perspectives on the Revolution). 228p. 1977. reprint ed. lib. bdg. 23.10 (*0-88355-437-2*) Hyperion Conn.

Building Lexicons for Machine Translation: Papers from the 1993 Spring Symposium. Ed. by Bonnie Dorr. (Technical Reports). (Illus.). 139p. (Orig.). (C). 1993. spiral bd. 25.00 (*0-929280-39-3*) Amer Artificial.

Building Library Collections. 6th ed. Arthur Curley & Dorothy Broderick. LC 84-23665. 350p. 1985. 27.50 (*0-8108-1776-4*) Scarecrow.

Building Library Collections on Aging. Mary J. Brazil. 175p. 1990. lib. bdg. 45.00 (*0-87436-559-7*) ABC-CLIO.

Building Licensing Laws. Ronald Desiatnik. 1992. ring bd. 283.00 (*0-685-65886-4*, Pub. by Law Bk Co) W W Gaunt.

Building Life Skills. Louise A. Liddell. LC 93-26390. (Home Economics Ser.). (Illus.). 575p. 1994. 38.60 (*0-87006-094-5*) Goodheart.

Building Lifeskills (One, Two, Three) A Communication Workbook. K. Lynn Savage. (Illus.). 1989. student ed 5.95 (*0-685-28139-6*, 75253) Longman.

Building Lifeskills (One, Two, Three) A Communication Workbook, Level 1. K. Lynn Savage. (Illus.). 1989. pap. text ed. write for info. (*0-582-90744-6*, 75256) Longman.

Building Lifeskills (One, Two, Three) A Communication Workbook, Level 2. K. Lynn Savage. (Illus.). 1987. pap. text ed. 6.84 (*0-582-90747-0*, 75255) Longman.

Building Lifeskills (One, Two, Three) A Communication Workbook, Level 3. K. Lynn Savage. (Illus.). 1989. pap. text ed. 6.84 (*0-582-90746-2*) Longman.

Building Literacy. Barbara Gruber. (Instant Idea Bks.). (Illus.). 64p. (J). (gr. k-6). 1992. 7.95 (*0-86734-139-4*, FS-8323) Schaffer Pubns.

Building Literacy with Interactive Charts. Scholastic Books Staff. 1993. pap. 9.95 (*0-590-49234-9*) Scholastic Inc.

Building Living Relationships. Kenneth W. Tieman. LC 81-68570. (Illus.). 111p. (Orig.). 1981. pap. 5.95 (*0-9606474-0-6*) Centennial Repros.

Building Lobster, Crab, Shrimp, Eel & Other Fishtraps. Tom Bailey. (Illus.). 1985. 14.95 (*0-318-19504-6*); lib. bdg. 15.50 (*0-318-19503-8*) Comtech Pubns.

***Building Local Area Networks with Netware 4.X.** Patrick Corrigan. 1994. disk, pap. 39.95 (*1-55851-426-0*) M&T Bks.

Building Local Area Networks with Novell's Netware. Patrick H. Corrigan & Aisling Guy. (Illus.). 635p. (Orig.). 1989. disk 39.95 (*1-55851-025-7*); pap. 29.95 (*1-55851-010-9*) M&T Bks.

Building Local Area Networks with Novell's Netware, Versions 2.2 & 3.X. Patrick H. Corrigan & Aisling Guy. (Illus.). 665p. 1992. pap. 29.95 (*1-55851-237-3*); disk, pap. 39.95 (*1-55851-239-X*) M&T Bks.

Building Local Area Networks with Novell's NetWare Versions 2.2 to 3.12. 3rd ed. Patrick H. Corrigan & Aisling Guy. 655p. (Orig.). 1993. disk, pap. 39.95 (*1-55851-293-4*) M&T Bks.

Building LOGO Skills: Terrapin Book B. Steven L. Mandell. 376p. (gr. 4-6). 1986. pap. text ed. 28.75 (*0-314-89685-6*); teacher ed, pap. text ed. 35.00 (*0-314-88708-3*) West Pub.

***Building Lotus Notes X.0 AP.** Stephen D. McLeod. Date not set. write for info. (*0-679-76190-X*) Random.

***Building Love with Family Traditions.** Jeanne Yawney. 1995. pap. 7.98 (*0-88290-525-2*, 1054) Horizon Utah.

Building Low-Resistance Boats: Build Twenty Four Boats That Move Easily Through the Water. Thomas F. Jones. 240p. 1991. pap. 21.95 (*0-87742-284-2*) Intl Marine.

Building; Machines. Ed. by Robert McCarter et al. (Pamphlet Architecture Ser.: No. 12). (Illus.). 64p. (Orig.). 1987. pap. 10.95 (*0-910413-40-1*) Princeton Arch.

Building Machines & What They Do. Derek Radford. LC 91-71860. 32p. (J). (ps-3). 1994. pap. 4.99 (*1-56402-364-8*) Candlewick Pr.

Building Maintenance. Jack Rudman. (Occupational Competency Examination Ser.: OCE-8). 1994. pap. 23.95 (*0-8373-5708-X*) Nat Learn.

Building Maintenance & Preservation: A Guide for Design & Management. 2nd ed. Ed. by Edward D. Mills. LC 93-45309. (Illus.). 240p. 1994. 74.95 (*0-7506-0900-1*) Buttrwrth-Heinemann.

Building Maintenance Custodian (U.S.P.S.) (Career Examination Ser.: C-3430). 1994. pap. 23.95 (*0-8373-3430-6*) Nat Learn.

Building Maintenance Economics & Management. A. H. Spedding. 410p. 1987. text ed. 65.00 (*0-419-14290-8*, E & FN Spon) Routledge Chapman & Hall.

Building Maintenance Engineering Price Book 1985-86. Bernard T. Lewis. 300p. 1986. 39.95 (*0-412-01071-2*, 9666, Chap & Hall NY) Chapman & Hall.

Building Maintenance Foreman. Jack Rudman. (Career Examination Ser.: C-1147). 1994. pap. 27.95 (*0-8373-1147-0*) Nat Learn.

Building Maintenance Supervisor. Jack Rudman. (Career Examination Ser.: C-1148). 1994. pap. 27.95 (*0-8373-1148-9*) Nat Learn.

Building Maintenance Technician. William Thomas. (Illus.). 151p. (C). 1988. lib. bdg. 55.00 (*0-943863-13-9*) Marsh-Wentworth.

Building Management by Professionals: For Building Owners, Developers, Architects, & the Design & Construction Team. Ray Moxley. LC 92-2429. 144p. 1993. 49.95 (*0-7506-0443-3*, Butterwrth Archit) Buttrwrth-Heinemann.

Building Manager. Jack Rudman. (Career Examination Ser.: C-1149). 1994. pap. 29.95 (*0-8373-1149-7*) Nat Learn.

Building Managerial Effectiveness. J. T. McMahon. (Work in America Institute Studies in Productivity: No. 39). 56p. 1984. pap. 39.00 (*0-317-66816-1*, Pergamon Pr) Elsevier.

Building Managerial Effectiveness. J. Timothy McMahon. LC 85-9352. (Studies in Productivity: Highlights of the Literature Ser.: Vol. 39). 1985. 55.00 (*0-08-029512-6*) Work in Amer.

Building Marriages for Life. Jerry Jones & Sandy Jones. 112p. (Orig.). 1993. pap. 7.99 (*1-56043-764-2*) Destiny Image.

Building Marvelous Miami. Nicholas N. Patricios. (Illus.). 376p. 1994. 49.95 (*0-8130-1299-6*) U Press Fla.

Building Materials Directory 1994. (C). 1994. pap. text ed. 12.00 (*1-55989-525-X*) Underwrtrs Labs.

***Building Materials Directory 1995.** (C). 1995. pap. text ed. 12.50 (*1-55989-723-6*) Underwrtrs Labs.

Building Materials Evaluation Handbook. Forrest Wilson. 368p. 1984. text ed. 62.95 (*0-442-29325-9*) Chapman & Hall.

***Building Materials Prod. KNWLG.** National Retail Hardware Association Staff. 420p. 1995. 69.99 (*0-7872-0492-7*) Kendall-Hunt.

***Building Materials Technology: Structural Performance & Environmental Impact.** L. Reed Brantley & Ruth T. Brantley. 1995. write for info. (*0-07-007265-5*) McGraw.

Building Math Skills. Foley et al. Incl. Level 1. 1981. text ed. (*0-201-13350-4*); Level 1. 1981. (*0-201-13359-8*); Level 1. 1981. (*0-201-13360-1*); Level 2. 1981. text ed. (*0-201-13370-9*); Level 2. 1981. (*0-201-13379-2*); Level 2. 1981. (*0-318-50134-1*); 1981. write for info. (*0-318-50133-3*) Addison-Wesley.

Building Mechanical Engineer. Jack Rudman. (Career Examination Ser.: C-2571). 1994. pap. 34.95 (*0-8373-2571-4*) Nat Learn.

Building Mechanical Systems. 2nd ed. F. T. Andrews. LC 75-11895. 412p. 1976. 39.50 (*0-07-001847-2*) Krieger.

Building Model Cars, Vol. I: The Best of Scale Auto Enthusiast Magazine, 1979-1984. 96p. 1991. 21.95 (*0-9631279-1-8*); pap. 9.95 (*0-9631279-0-X*) Highland Prods.

Building Model Cars, Vol. II: The Best of Scale Auto Enthusiast Magazine, 1979-1984. 96p. 1992. 21.95 (*0-9631279-3-4*); pap. 9.95 (*0-9631279-2-6*) Highland Prods.

Building Morale... Motivating Staff: Problems & Solutions. American Association of School Administrators Staff. (Critical Issues Report Ser.). 1983. 11.95 (*0-318-01771-7*, 021-00834) Am Assn Sch Admin.

Building Motion in Wind: Proceedings. Ed. by N. Isyumov & T. Tschanz. 109p. 1986. 16.00 (*0-87262-434-X*) Am Soc Civil Eng.

Building Motivation in the Classroom: A Structured Approach to Improving Student Achievement. Robert C. Hawley & Isabel L. Hawley. LC 78-69902. 1979. pap. 17.95 (*0-913636-10-X*) Educ Res MA.

***Building Multimedia Applications with Visual Basic.** Michael Regelski. (Illus.). 512p. (Orig.). 1995. pap. text ed. 39.99 (*0-7897-0139-1*) Que.

Building Multimedia Performance Support Systems. Angus Reynolds. 1994. text ed., disk 45.00 (*0-07-911684-1*) McGraw.

Building Neighborhood Organizations. James V. Cunningham & Milton Kotler. LC 83-1182. 224p. 1983. pap. text ed. 9.95 (*0-268-00669-5*) U of Notre Dame Pr.

Building Networks: Cooperation As a Strategy for Success in a Changing World. Gilroy & Swan. 280p. (C). 1984. per. 6.95 (*0-8403-3254-8*) Kendall-Hunt.

***Building Neural Networks.** David M. Skapura. LC 94-39062. (C). 1996. text ed. write for info. (*0-201-53921-7*) Addison-Wesley.

Building New Communities: New Deal America & Fascist Italy. Diane Ghirardo. (Illus.). 240p. (C). 1989. text ed. 39.50 (*0-691-04067-2*) Princeton U Pr.

Building New Nursing Organizations: Visions & Realities. Cathleen K. Wilson. LC 91-22412. 240p. 1992. 48.00 (*0-8342-0307-3*, 20307) Aspen Pub.

Building New Orleans: The Engineer's Role. James S. Janssen. (Illus.). 132p. (Orig.). 1987. pap. 11.95 (*0-9619160-0-1*) W S Nelson & Co.

BNI Building News Electrical Costbook, 1994. BNI Building News Staff. 1993. 29.95 (*1-55701-096-X*) BNI Pubns.

Building News Electrical 1995 Costbook. 2nd ed. 1994. pap. 39.95 (*1-55701-114-1*) BNI Pubns.

***Building News Electrical 1996 Costbook.** 3rd ed. 1995. pap. 39.95 (*1-55701-139-7*) BNI Pubns.

Building News Facilities Manager's 1995 Costbook. 1994. pap. 59.95 (*1-55701-116-8*) BNI Pubns.

***Building News Facilities Manager's 1996 Costbook.** 2nd ed. 1995. pap. 69.95 (*1-55701-141-9*) BNI Pubns.

Building News General Construction 1995 Costbook. 5th ed. 1994. pap. 49.95 (*1-55701-109-5*) BNI Pubns.

***Building News General Construction 1996 Costbook.** 6th ed. 1995. pap. 54.95 (*1-55701-134-6*) BNI Pubns.

Building News General Contruction Costbook, 1994. 4th ed. BNI Building News Staff. 1993. 44.95 (*1-55701-091-9*) BNI Pubns.

Building News Home Builder's 1995 Costbook. 3rd ed. 1994. pap. 29.95 (*1-55701-113-3*) BNI Pubns.

***Building News Home Builder's 1996 Costbook.** 4th ed. 1995. pap. 29.95 (*1-55701-138-9*) BNI Pubns.

Building News Home Remodeler's 1995 Costbook. 1994. pap. 29.95 (*1-55701-117-6*) BNI Pubns.

***Building News Home Remodeler's 1996 Costbook.** 2nd ed. 1995. pap. 29.95 (*1-55701-142-7*) BNI Pubns.

Building News Homebuilder's Costbook, 1994. 2nd ed. BNI Building News Staff. 1993. 29.95 (*1-55701-095-1*) BNI Pubns.

***Building News Mechanical-Electrical 1995 Costbook.** 5th ed. BNI Building News Staff. 1994. pap. 49.95 (*1-55701-112-5*) BNI Pubns.

***Building News Mechanical-Electrical 1996 Costbook.** 6th ed. 1995. pap. 59.95 (*1-55701-137-0*) BNI Pubns.

Building News Public Works 1995 Costbook. 2nd ed. 1994. pap. 49.95 (*1-55701-115-X*) BNI Pubns.

***Building News Public Works 1996 Costbook.** 3rd ed. 1995. pap. 54.95 (*1-55701-140-0*) BNI Pubns.

Building News Remodeling 1995 Costbook. 5th ed. 1994. pap. 49.95 (*1-55701-110-9*) BNI Pubns.

***Building News Remodeling 1996 Costbook.** 6th ed. 1995. pap. 54.95 (*1-55701-135-4*) BNI Pubns.

Building News Square Foot 1995 Costbook. 5th ed. 1994. pap. 49.95 (*1-55701-111-7*) BNI Pubns.

***Building News Square Foot 1996 Costbook.** 6th ed. 1995. pap. 59.95 (*1-55701-136-2*) BNI Pubns.

Building Object-Oriented Systems: An Introduction from Concepts to Implementation in C Plus Plus. Robert E. Callan. LC 94-68194. 304p. (C). 1995. 69.00 (*1-56252-264-7*) Computational Mech MA.

***Building OCXs.** Toohey et al. (Illus.). 416p. (Orig.). 1995. pap. text ed. 39.99 (*0-614-07262-X*) Que.

***Building OCXs.** Toohey. (Orig.). 1995. pap. (*0-7897-0138-3*) Que.

Building of a Department: Chemistry at Southern Illinois University, 1927-1967. James W. Neckers. LC 78-13384. (Illus.). 197p. 1979. 12.95 (*0-8093-0901-7*) S Ill U Pr.

Building of British Social Anthropology. Ian G. Langham. 420p. 1981. lib. bdg. 136.50 (*90-277-1264-6*) Kluwer Ac.

Building of Castle Howard. Charles Saumarez Smith. LC 89-52015. (Illus.). xvii, 222p. 1990. 29.95 (*0-226-76403-6*) U Ch Pr.

An Asterisk (*) at the beginning of an entry indicates that the title is appearing in BIP for the first time.

An Asterisk (*) at the beginning of an entry indicates that the title is appearing in BIP for the first time.

943

Building Sentences. 3rd ed. Benita Mackie & Shirley J. Rompf. LC 94-16909. 384p. 1994. pap. text ed. write for info. (*0-13-150138-0*) P-H.
Building Sermons to Meet People's Needs. Harold T. Bryson & James C. Taylor. LC 78-74962. 1991. 10.99 (*0-8054-2109-2*) Broadman.
Building Services. P. R. Smith & W. G. Julian. (Illus.). 313p. 1976. 79.25 (*0-85334-657-7*, Pub. by Elsevier Applied Sci UK) Elsevier.
***Building Services Administrator.** (Career Examination Ser.: Series 1). Date not set. pap. 39.95 (*0-8373-3628-7*) Nat Learn.
Building Services & Environmental Issues: Interim Report. 1990. 90.00 (*0-86022-299-3*, Pub. by Build Servs Info Assn UK) St Mut.
Building Services & Environmental Issues: The Bibliography. 1992. 36.00 (*0-86022-360-4*, Pub. by Build Servs Info Assn UK) St Mut.
Building Services Engineering: A Review of Its Development. N. S. Billington & B. M. Roberts. LC 80-42036. (International Series on Building Environmental Engineering: Vol. 1). 537p. 1982. text ed. 227.00 (*0-08-026741-6*, Pub. by Pergamon Repr UK) Franklin.
Building Services Equipment-7. BSRIA Staff. (C). 1988. 1,050.00 (*0-685-33892-4*, Pub. by Build Servs Info Assn UK) St Mut.
Building Services for Old People. 1993. 36.00 (*0-86022-234-9*, Pub. by Build Servs Info Assn UK) St Mut.
Building Services for Swimming Pools: An Annotated Bibliography. S. Loyd. 1992. 100.00 (*0-86022-325-6*, Pub. by Build Servs Info Assn UK) St Mut.
Building Services Futures Workshops 1990-91. D. Gregory. 1991. 108.00 (*0-86022-289-6*, Pub. by Build Servs Info Assn UK) St Mut.
Building Services in the Middle East. 1991. 90.00 (*0-86022-282-9*, Pub. by Build Servs Info Assn UK) St Mut.
Building Services in the Year 2000. D. Gregory. 1985. 60.00 (*0-86022-157-1*, Pub. by Build Servs Info Assn UK) St Mut.
Building Services Industry: The Single European Market & 1992. 2nd ed. BSRIA Staff. (C). 1988. 150.00 (*0-86022-219-5*, Pub. by Build Servs Info Assn UK) St Mut.
Building Services Legislation Directory. 2nd ed. M. Johansson. 94p. (C). 1993. 110.00x (*0-86022-339-6*, Pub. by Build Servs Info Assn UK) St Mut.
Building Services Maintenance. S. Loyd. 1990. 60.00 (*0-86022-264-0*, Pub. by Build Servs Info Assn UK) St Mut.
Building Services Maintenance. S. R. Loyd. (C). 1987. 135.00 (*0-86022-129-6*, Pub. by Build Servs Info Assn UK) St Mut.
Building Services Materials Handbook: Heating, Sanitation & Fire Protection. Building Services Research & Development Association Staff. 704p. 1987. text ed. 110.00 (*0-419-14310-6*, E & FN Spon) Routledge Chapman & Hall.
Building Services Thesaurus. G. Beale. 1993. 100.00 (*0-86022-341-8*, Pub. by Build Servs Info Assn UK) St Mut.
Building Services Thesaurus. 5th ed. 1993. 75.00 (*0-86022-284-5*, Pub. by Build Servs Info Assn UK) St Mut.
***Building Sex: Men, Women, & the Construction of Sexuality.** Aaron Betsky. 1995. write for info. (*0-688-13167-0*) Morrow.
Building Simulation '89: Conference, 1989 (Vancouver, Canada) 380p. 1989. pap. 75.00 (*0-685-66779-0*, SPSA89-1) Soc Computer Sim.
Building Simulation '91: Conference, 1991. Clarke et al. 680p. 1991. pap. 90.00 (*0-911801-99-5*, SPSA91-1) Soc Computer Sim.
Building Sino-American Relations: An Analysis for the 1990s. Ed. by William T. Tow. LC 91-792. 327p. (C). 1989. pap. 18.95 (*0-88702-061-5*) Washington Inst Pr.
Building Skills TOEFL. 2nd ed. King & Stanley. 1989. 21.95 (*0-17-555729-2*); pap. 18.95 (*0-17-555730-6*) Heinle & Heinle.
Building Slavic Collections. Jurij A. Luciw. 63p. 1980. pap. text ed. 3.75 (*0-686-63318-0*) Slavia Lib.
Building Small Barns, Sheds & Shelters. Monte Burch. Ed. by Fred Stetson. LC 82-15439. (Illus.). 248p. 1983. pap. 12.95 (*0-88266-245-7*, Garden Way Pub) Storey Comm Inc.
***Building Small Church Coalitions: Learnings from the Northern Neck Project.** Roy W. Pneuman. 1993. pap. 8.75 (*1-56699-129-3*, OD104) Alban Inst.
***Building SMU: 1915-1957.** Ruth P. Maddox. 1995. pap. 27.00 (*1-884363-07-5*) Odenwald Pr.
Building Social Problem-Solving Skills: Guidelines from a School-Based Program. Maurice J. Elias & John F. Clabby. LC 91-41080. (Social & Behavioral Sciences Ser.). 348p. 1992. 36.95 (*1-55542-433-3*) Jossey-Bass.
***Building Socialism in Bolshevik Russia: Ideology & Industrial Organization, 1917-1921.** Thomas F. Remington. LC 84-3603. (Series in Russian & East European Studies: No. 6). 232p. 1984. pap. 66.20 (*0-7837-8543-7*, 2049358) Bks Demand.
Building Societies: Structure, Performance & Change. Donal McKillop. 272p. (C). 1993. lib. bdg. 69.00 (*1-85333-880-X*, Pub. by Graham & Trotman UK) Kluwer Ac.
Building Society Finance. Phillips. 1983. pap. 44.95 (*0-85258-231-5*) Chapman & Hall.
Building Soils for Better Crops: Organic Matter Management. Fred Magdoff. LC 92-2362. (Our Sustainable Future Ser.: Vol. 2). xii, 176p. 1993. 22.95 (*0-8032-3160-1*) U of Nebr Pr.
Building Sound Finance in Emerging Market Economies: Proceedings of a Conference Held in Washington, D.C., June 10-11,1993. Ed. by Gerard Caprio et al. LC 94-7903. 1994. 27.50 (*1-55775-380-6*) Intl Monetary.
Building Sound Self-Esteem: Instructor's Guide. Lilburn S. Barksdale. 145p. 1978. pap. 105.00 (*0-918588-04-9*) Barksdale Foun.
Building Sound Self-Esteem Facilitator's Kit. L. S. Barksdale. 1978. Incl. facilitators guide, participants manual, 8 audio cassette tapes, wall chart & transparency, le. pap., vinyl bd. 105.00 (*0-918588-14-6*, 200) Barksdale Foun.
Building Sound Self-Esteem Instructor's Kit. L. S. Barksdale. (Illus.). 1978. Incl. instructor's guide, 5 audio cassette tapes, participant's manual, wall chart & transparency, l. pap. 105.00 (*0-918588-13-8*, 201) Barksdale Foun.
Building Sound Self-Esteem Participant's Kit. L. S. Barksdale. 86p. 1978. Incl. manual for building self-esteem, 3 audio cassette tapes & lesson cards. pap. 39.95 (*0-918588-15-4*, 203) Barksdale Foun.
Building South. Ed. by Tom Schlesinger. (Southern Exposure Ser.). (Illus.). 128p. (Orig.). (C). 1980. pap. 4.00 (*0-943810-08-6*) Inst Southern Studies.
***Building Spec Homes Profitably.** R. S. Means. 1994. pap. 29.95 (*0-87629-357-7*) R S Means.
Building Staff - Volunteer Relations. rev. ed. Ivan H. Scheier. Ed. by Susan J. Ellis. LC 93-73624. (Volunteer Energy Ser.). (Illus.). 72p. 1993. pap. 16.75 (*0-940576-14-7*) Energize.
Building States & Nations: Models & Data Resources, Vol. 1. Ed. by Shmuel N. Eisenstadt & Stein Rokkan. LC 73-77873. 398p. reprint ed. pap. 113.50 (*0-8357-7469-4*, 2021891) Bks Demand.
Building Stone Walls. rev. ed. John Vivian. LC 75-20773. (Illus.). 112p. 1979. pap. 8.95 (*0-88266-074-8*, Garden Way Pub) Storey Comm Inc.
Building Stones for an Understanding of the Mystery of Golgotha. Rudolf Steiner. 240p. 1985. 13.95 (*0-85440-263-2*) Anthroposophic.
***Building Strategic Relationships: How to Extend Your Organization's Reach Through Partnerships, Alliances, & Joint Ventures.** William Bergquist et al. (Management Ser.). 272p. 1995. 28.95 (*0-7879-0092-3*) Jossey-Bass.
***Building Strategies for College Reading: A Text with Thematic Reader.** Jane L. McGrath. LC 94-32425. 448p. (C). 1994. pap. text ed. write for info. (*0-13-043894-4*) P-H.
Building Strength at the YMCA. Wayne L. Westcott. LC 86-20838. (Illus.). 104p. (Orig.). 1987. pap. text ed. 9.00 (*0-87322-082-X*, LWES4885, YMCA USA) Human Kinetics.
***Building Strong Brands.** Aaker. 1994. 28.00 (*0-02-900151-X*) Free Pr.
Building Strong Families with Proverbs. John L. Kachelman, Jr. 1994. 7.95 (*0-89137-141-9*) Quality Pubns.
Building Strong Foundations: Evaluation Strategies for Family Resource Programs. Julia Litell. 148p. 1986. pap. 30.00 (*1-885429-00-2*) Family Resource.
Building Strong Healthy Feet. 13th rev. ed. 1994. 5.95 (*0-685-75254-2*) Hlth Sci.
Building Strong Male Relationships. James Osterhaus. 1993. pap. 2.99 (*0-8024-3710-9*) Moody.
Building Stronger Families. Royce Money. LC 83-51300. 156p. 1984. pap. 7.99 (*0-88207-244-7*, Victor Books) SP Pubns.
Building Stronger Marriages & Families. Billy J. Daugherty. 175p. (Orig.). 1991. pap. 6.95 (*0-89274-858-3*, HH-858) Victory Ctr OK.
Building Structural Design Handbook. Ed. by Richard N. White & Charles G. Salmon. LC 86-15808. 1214p. 1987. text ed. 95.00 (*0-471-08150-7*) Krieger.
Building Structural Engineer. Jack Rudman. (Career Examination Ser.: C-2568). 1994. pap. 39.95 (*0-8373-2568-4*) Nat Learn.
Building Structures. Ed. by Donald R. Sherman. 596p. 1987. 55.00 (*0-87262-612-1*) Am Soc Civil Eng.
Building Structures. 2nd ed. James E. Ambrose. LC 92-16362. 725p. 1993. text ed. 84.95 (*0-471-54060-9*) Wiley.
Building Structures: Elementary Analysis & Design. Ronald E. Shaeffer. (Illus.). 1980. text ed. 50.00 (*0-13-086561-3*) P-H.
Building Subsidence Liability & Insurance. F. Eaglestone & J. Apted. (C). 1988. 265.00 (*0-685-33789-8*, Pub. by Witherby & Co UK) St Mut.
Building Success in Math. Langbort. 1985. pap. 17.25 (*0-534-03394-6*) Seymour Pubns.
***Building Successful Multicultural Organization: Challenges & Opportunities.** Marlene G. Fine. LC 94-39345. 232p. 1995. text ed. 55.00 (*0-89930-681-0*, Quorum Bks) Greenwood.
Building Successful Parent-Teacher Partnerships. R. Eleanor Duff et al. LC 79-91107. (Illus.). 84p. (Orig.). 1980. pap. 9.95 (*0-89334-053-7*) Humanics Ltd.
Building Successful Parent-Teacher Partnerships. R. Eleanor Duff et al. LC 79-91107. (Illus.). 84p. (Orig.). 1980. lib. bdg. 19.95 (*0-89334-188-6*, 188-6) Humanics Ltd.
Building "Sunshine" Walter J. Simmons. (Boatbuilding Ser.). (Illus.). 70p. 1981. 37.50 (*0-924947-07-1*); pap. 22.50 (*0-924947-03-9*) Duck Trap Pr.
Building Support for School Music: A Practical Guide. Ed. by National Coalition for Music Education Staff. 64p. (Orig.). (C). 1991. 8.00 (*0-940796-97-X*, 1004) Music Ed Natl.
Building Support Networks for Schools. Pat Wagner. 170p. 1991. pap. text ed. 35.00 (*0-87436-615-1*) ABC-CLIO.
Building Support Networks for the Elderly: Theory & Applications. David E. Biegel et al. LC 84-8337. (Sage Human Services Guides Ser.: No. 36). 160p. reprint ed. pap. 45.60 (*0-7837-4562-1*, 2044091) Bks Demand.
Building Surveys. 2nd ed. P. Glover & H. S. Staveley. (Illus.). 264p. 1991. text ed. 79.95 (*0-7506-1003-4*) Buttrwrth-Heinemann.
Building Sustainable Communities: An Environmental Guide for Local Government, Energy: Efficiency & Production. Center for the Study of Law & Politics Staff. 258p. 1991. 40.00 (*1-880386-06-2*) Ctr Study Law.
Building Sustainable Communities: An Environmental Guide for Local Government, Open Space: Preservation & Acquisition. Center for the Study of Law & Politics Staff. 162p. 1991. 40.00 (*1-880386-05-4*) Ctr Study Law.
Building Sustainable Communities: An Environmental Guide for Local Government, Solid Waste: Reduction, Reuse, & Recycling. Center for the Study of Law & Politics Staff. 144p. 1991. 40.00 (*1-880386-02-X*) Ctr Study Law.
Building Sustainable Communities: An Environmental Guide for Local Government, Toxics: Management & Reduction. Center for the Study of Law & Politics Staff. 182p. 1991. 40.00 (*1-880386-03-8*) Ctr Study Law.
Building Sustainable Communities: An Environmental Guide for Local Government, Toxics: Management & Reduction. Center for the Study of Law & Politics Staff. 92p. 1991. 40.00 (*1-880386-04-6*) Ctr Study Law.
Building Sustainable Communities: An Environmental Guide for Local Government, Urban Forestry. Center for the Study of Law & Politics Staff. 112p. 1991. 40.00 (*1-880386-07-0*) Ctr Study Law.
Building Sustainable Communities: An Environmental Guide for Local Government, Water: Conservation & Reclamation. Center for the Study of Law & Politics Staff. 135p. 1990. 40.00 (*1-880386-01-1*) Ctr Study Law.
Building Sustainable Communities: Tools & Concepts for Self-Reliant Economic Change. C. George Benello et al. Ed. by Ward Morehouse. LC 88-24123. 196p. (Orig.). 1989. pap. 13.50 (*0-942850-11-4*) Bootstrap Pr.
Building Sustainable Communities, an Environmental Guide for Local Government: Air Quality: Pollution Prevention & Mitigation. 228p. 1992. 40.00 (*1-880386-09-7*) Ctr Study Law.
Building Sustainable Communities, an Environmental Guide for Local Government: Land Use: Stewardship & the Planning Process. 126p. 1993. 40.00 (*1-880386-10-0*) Ctr Study Law.
Building Sustainable Communities, an Environmental Guide for Local Government: Water Quality: Protection & Remediation. 326p. 1991. 40.00 (*1-880386-08-9*) Ctr Study Law.
Building Systems: Room Air & Air Contaminant Distribution. Ed. by Mildred Geshwiler. 274p. (C). 1989. 70.00 (*0-910110-64-6*) Am Heat Ref & Air Eng.
Building Systems Evaluation Handbook. Charles J. McClain. (Illus.). 260p. 1991. pap. text ed. 69.00 (*0-86587-266-X*) Gov Insts.
Building Systems Integration Handbook. Ed. by Richard D. Rush. (Illus.). 1991. reprint ed. pap. text ed. 34.95 (*0-7506-9198-0*) Buttrwrth-Heinemann.
Building Systems Reference Guide. Tyler G. Hicks. (Engineering Reference Guide Ser.). 160p. 1987. text ed. 43.00 (*0-07-028802-X*) McGraw.
Building Team Power: How to Unleash the Collaborative Genius of Work Teams. Thomas A. Kayser & Tonya Mantooth. LC 93-48207. (Illus.). 304p. 1994. text ed. 25.00 (*0-7863-0302-6*) Irwin Prof Pubng.
Building Teams, Building People: Expanding the Fifth Resource. Bonita Drolet & Thomas Harvey. LC 93-61663. 220p. 1994. pap. text ed. 35.00 (*1-56676-084-4*) Technomic.
Building Technology: Mechanical & Electrical Systems. William J. McGuinness & Benjamin J. Stein. LC 76-14961. 596p. 1977. teacher ed 5.00 (*0-471-01601-2*); text ed. 79.95 (*0-471-58433-9*) Wiley.
Building Terminology: An Illustrated Guide for Students. Peter Brett. (Illus.). 304p. 1993. pap. write for info. (*0-7506-1724-1*) Buttrwrth-Heinemann.
Building Terminology: An Illustrated Guide for Students & Professionals. Peter Brett. (Illus.). 304p. 1989. 52.95 (*0-434-90176-8*) Buttrwrth-Heinemann.
Building the Allchin. W. J. Hughes. 25.00 (*0-85242-635-6*) Apple Blossom.
Building the American Community: The School Curriculum & the Search for Social Control. Barry Franklin. (Studies in Curriculum History Ser.: Vol. 4). 1986. 50.00 (*1-85000-075-1*, Falmer Pr); pap. 31.00 (*1-85000-076-X*, Falmer Pr) Taylor & Francis.
Building the Atlantic World. Robert Strausz-Hupe et al. LC 74-1517. 400p. 1974. reprint ed. text ed. 65.00 (*0-8371-7386-8*, STAW, Greenwood Pr) Greenwood.
Building the Balalaika, a Russian Folk Instrument. James H. Flynn, Jr. LC 84-90311. (Illus.). 55p. 1984. spiral bd. 9.95 (*0-9613258-0-1*) J H Flynn.
Building the Beam Engine Mary. Tubal Cain. (Illus.). 9.00 (*0-85242-754-9*) Apple Blossom.
Building the Beloved Community: Maurice McCrackin's Life for Peace & Civil Rights. Judith A. Bechtel & Robert M. Coughlin. (Illus.). 288p. 1991. 34.95 (*0-87722-783-7*) Temple U Pr.
Building the Blackfish. Dana Story. (Illus.). 192p. 1988. text ed. 24.95 (*0-87742-980-4*) Intl Marine.
Building the Blackfish. Dana Story & John Clayton. (Illus.). 192p. 1988. 24.95 (*0-938459-04-X*) Ten Pound Isl Bk.
Building the Burlington Northern RR in N Scale. Model Railroader Magazine Staff. Ed. by Michael Emmerich. (Illus.). 56p. (Orig.). 1990. pap. 8.95 (*0-89024-119-8*) Kalmbach.
***Building the Churches of Kievan Russia.** Pavela Rappoport. 300p. 1995. 59.50 (*0-86078-327-8*, Pub. by Variorum UK) Ashgate Pub Co.
Building the City Beautiful: The Benjamin Franklin Parkway & the Philadelphia Museum of Art. David B. Brownlee. LC 89-22806. (Illus.). 136p. (Orig.). 1989. pap. 18.95 (*0-87633-081-2*) Phila Mus Art.
Building the City of God: Community & Cooperation among the Mormons. 2nd ed. Leonard J. Arrington et al. (Illus.). 520p. 1992. pap. 16.50 (*0-252-06235-3*) U of Ill Pr.
Building the Cold from Memory. Jack Driscoll. (Ithaca House Poetry Ser.). 80p. (Orig.). (C). 1989. pap. 9.95 (*0-87886-130-0*) Greenfld Rev Lit.
Building the Competitive Workforce: Investing in Human Capital for Corporate Success. Philip Mirvis. 272p. 1993. text ed. 34.95 (*0-471-59257-9*) Wiley.
Building the Contest Oration. Ezra C. Buehler & Richard L. Johannesen. LC 65-11208. 202p. 1965. 24.00 (*0-8242-0008-X*) Wilson.
Building the Crosby Catboat. Barry Thomas. (Illus.). 60p. 1989. pap. 9.95 (*0-913372-48-X*) Mystic Seaport.
Building the Data Warehouse. W. H. Inmon. 1992. 39.95 (*0-89435-404-3*) Wiley.
Building the Data Warehouse. W. H. Inmon. 1993. text ed. 44.95 (*0-471-56960-7*, GD4043) Wiley.
Building the Death Railway: The Ordeal of American POWs in Burma, 1942-1945. Ed. by Ronald E. Marcello. LC 92-97641. 368p. 1993. 24.95 (*0-8420-2428-X*) Scholarly Res Inc.
Building the Dream: A Social History of Housing in America. Gwendolyn Wright. (Illus.). 352p. (C). 1983. reprint ed. pap. 18.50 (*0-262-73064-2*) MIT Pr.
***Building the E-Motive Industry.** Scott A. Cronk. 200p. 1995. 35.00 (*1-56091-560-9*, R148) Soc Auto Engineers.
Building the Earth. Teilhard De Chardin. 1965. pap. 14.95 (*0-87193-078-1*) Dimension Bks.
Building the Educational State: Canada West, 1836-1871. Bruce Crtis. 440p. 1988. 80.00 (*1-85000-275-4*, Falmer Pr) Taylor & Francis.
Building the Escorial. George Kubler. LC 87-47140. (Illus.). 360p. 1981. 65.00x (*0-691-03975-5*) Princeton U Pr.
Building the Flying Aces Moth. Bill Warner. (Doug Pratt's Modeling Guides Ser.). 120p. 1992. pap. 9.95 (*0-8306-2510-0*, 2094) TAB Bks.
Building the Free Society: Democracy Capitalism & Catholic Social Teaching. 1993. pap. 16.99 (*0-8028-0120-X*) Eerdmans.
***Building the Future: A Blueprint for Change, "By Our Homes You Will Know Us": Final Report of the Nat'l Commission on American Indian, Alaska Native, & Native Hawaiian Housing.** 1995. lib. bdg. 250.00 (*0-8490-6518-6*) Gordon Pr.
***Building the Future: K-12 Network Technology Planning Guide.** 188p. 1994. pap. 11.75 (*0-8011-1166-8*) Calif Education.
Building the Future Together Proceedings of the Symposium Organized. Commission of the European Communities Staff. 56p. 1991. pap. 8.00 (*92-826-0546-9*, CM-70-91-225-EN-C) UNIPUB.
Building the Good School: Participating Parents at Charquin. Gloria W. Fearn. LC 92-84077. (Illus.). 150p. (Orig.). 1993. pap. 14.95 (*0-9635804-0-X*) Ohlone Pr.
Building the Haven: A Keel-Centered Daysailer. Maynard Bray. 1987. pap. text ed. 15.00 (*0-07-156111-0*) McGraw.
Building the Healing Partnership: Parents, Professionals & Children with Chronic Illnesses & Disabilities. Patricia Taner-Leff & Elaine Walizer. (C). 1993. text ed. 34.95 (*0-914797-63-8*); pap. text ed. 24.95 (*0-914797-60-3*) Brookline Bks.
Building the Heisler. Kozo Hiraoka. LC 86-62912. 249p. 1986. 31.50 (*0-914104-09-8*) Wildwood Pubns MI.
Building the Herd. Wendy Woollett. (Illus.). 225p. (Orig.). 1989. pap. 14.95 (*0-9622317-0-3*) Tailight Studio.
Building the Herreshoff Dinghy: The Manufacturer's Method. Barry Thomas. (Illus.). vi, 50p. 1977. pap. 9.95 (*0-913372-33-1*) Mystic Seaport.
Building the High-Performance Sales Force. Joseph A. Petrone. 224p. 1994. 26.95 (*0-8144-0219-4*) AMACOM.
Building the Hobby Stock Car. Bob Emmons. (Illus.). 72p. (Orig.). Date not set. pap. text ed. 10.95 (*0-936834-26-9*) S S Autosports.
Building the Home. Larry Arrowood. LC 90-29298. 206p. (Orig.). 1991. pap. 7.99 (*0-932581-80-3*) Word Aflame.
Building the House: Essays on Christian Education. Ed. by James A. DeJong & Louis Y. Van Dyke. 153p. (Orig.). 1981. pap. 5.95 (*0-932914-05-5*) Dordt Coll Pr.
Building the House Church. Lois Barrett. LC 86-14324. 176p. (Orig.). 1986. pap. 9.95 (*0-8361-3415-X*) Herald Pr.
Building the House of Marriage. William K. Summers. Ed. by Claudette Wassil-Grimm. LC 89-84941. (Illus.). 242p. (Orig.). 1991. pap. 12.95 (*0-945339-06-2*) R Erdmann Pub.
Building the Independent Subway. Frederick Kramer. 1990. pap. 13.95 (*0-915276-50-X*) Quadrant Pr.
Building the Information-Age Organization: Structure Control & Information Technologies. James I. Cash. LC 93-40865. 512p. (C). 1994. text ed. 69.95 (*0-256-12458-2*) Irwin.
Building the Information Highway. Les Freed & Frank J. Derfler. (Illus.). (Orig.). 1994. pap. 24.95 (*1-56276-126-9*) Ziff-Davis.
Building the Kaiser's Navy: The Imperial Naval Office & German Industry in the Tirpitz Era, 1890-1919. Gary E. Weir. LC 90-19529. (Illus.). 289p. 1992. 36.95 (*1-55750-929-8*) Naval Inst Pr.

An Asterisk (*) at the beginning of an entry indicates that the title is appearing in BIP for the first time.

An Asterisk (*) at the beginning of an entry indicates that the title is appearing in BIP for the first time.

945

Building Your Own House. Robert Roskind. LC 83-40029. (Illus.). 448p. 1984. pap. 19.95 (0-89815-110-4) Ten Speed Pr.

Building Your Own House, Bk. II. Robert Roskind. (Illus.). 288p. 1991. pap. 14.95 (0-89815-358-1) Ten Speed Pr.

Building Your Own Kitchen Cabinets. Jere Cary. LC 82-51260. (Illus.). 152p. 1983. pap. 14.95 (0-918804-15-9) Taunton.

Building Your Own Rocket Motors. Teleflite Corporation. Incl. Incredible Five Cent Sugar Rocket. 1983. pap. 5.00 (0-317-29266-8); Microsond One. 1983. pap. 2.00 (0-317-29267-6); Homemade Hydrogen Report. 1983. pap. 5.00 (0-317-29268-4); (Illus.). 148p. (Orig.). 1983. Set pap. 21.95 (0-930387-00-7) Teleflite Corp.

***Building Your Own Theology, Vol. 1.** Richard S. Gilbert. 1995. pap. 6.00 (0-614-06536-4) Unitarian Univ.

***Building Your Own Theology, Vol. 2.** Richard S. Gilbert. 1995. pap. 6.00 (0-614-06537-2) Unitarian Univ.

***Building Your Own Theology Vol. 3: Ethics, an Exploration in Personal Morality.** Richard S. Gilbert. 64p. 1995. pap. 15.00 (1-55896-283-2) Unitarian Univ.

Building Your Own Toys. Sabine Lohf. LC 89-22276. (Craft Bks.). 64p. (J). (gr. 5 up). 1989. lib. bdg. 15.45 (0-516-09251-0); pap. 8.95 (0-516-49251-9) Childrens.

Building Your Relationship with Christ. Matthew S. Prince & New Life Inc. Staff. 1988. pap. text ed. 3.00 (0-942026-02-0) ATAP Corp.

Building Your Rheumatology Practice. Joseph J. Weiss. 140p. 1984. pap. 18.75 (0-9613906-0-3) Belleraphon.

Building Your Rheumatology Practice. Joseph J. Weiss. 1984. 18.50 (0-318-03666-5) J J Weiss.

Building Your School Public Relations Skills: A Guidebook for Professionals. (Public Relations Professional Development Ser.). 1987. 16.95 (0-317-59088-X, 411-13368) Natl Sch PR.

Building Your Self-Image. Josh McDowell. 220p. 1986. 4.99 (0-8423-1395-8) Tyndale.

Building Yourself: Putting Your Success Together One Piece at a Time. Elliot Essman. 240p. (Orig.). 1994. pap. 14.95 (0-9636451-3-7) Autonomy Pub.

Building Youth Ministry in the Parish. Jerome Finn. Ed. by Robert Stamschror. (Illus.). 117p. 1993. pap. 19.95 (0-88489-256-5) St Marys.

Buildings. LC 92-7673. (Eyewitness Visual Dictionaries Ser.). (Illus.). 64p. 1993. 14.95 (1-56458-102-0) Dorling Kindersley.

Buildings. K. S. Brown. (Illus.). 225p. 1988. 42.00 (0-387-96876-8) Spr-Verlag.

Buildings. Heather Govier. Ed. by Richard Young. LC 91-19816. (First Technology Library). (Illus.). 32p. (J). (gr. 3-5). 1991. lib. bdg. 15.93 (1-56074-007-8) Garrett Ed Corp.

Buildings. Hazel Harrison. (Painting Solution Ser.). 1991. 17.98 (1-55521-721-4) Bk Sales Inc.

***Buildings.** Iqbal Hussain. (Connections! Ser.). (Illus.). 32p. (YA). (gr. 4 up). 1995. 12.95 (1-56847-452-0) Thomson Lrning.

***Buildings.** Philip Wilkinson. LC 94-24705. (DK Pocket Ser.). (Illus.). 160p. (YA). (gr. 7 up). 1995. pap. 5.95 (1-56458-885-8) Dorling Kindersley.

Buildings: Their Uses & the Spaces about Them, Vol. 8. (Metropolitan America Ser.). 478p. 1974. 46.95 (0-405-05421-1) Ayer.

Buildings & Equipment for Home Economics in Secondary Schools. Melvin Brodshaug. LC 75-176592. (Columbia University. Teachers College. Contributions to Education Ser.: No. 502). reprint ed. 37.50 (0-404-55502-0) AMS Pr.

Buildings & Halls of the Hermitage. T. M. Sikolova. 1982. 65.00 (0-317-57317-9, Pub. by Collets UK) St Mut.

Buildings & Power: Freedom & Control in the Origin of Modern Building Types. Thomas A. Markus. LC 92-33282. (Illus.). 352p. 1993. 75.00 (0-415-07664-1, B2360, Routledge NY); pap. 29.95 (0-415-07665-X, B2364, Routledge NY) Routledge.

Buildings & Projects: 1933-1937, Vol. XII. Le Corbusier. Ed. by H. Allen Brooks. LC 82-24246. (Le Corbusier Archive Ser.). 632p. 1983. lib. bdg. 260.00 (0-8240-5061-4) Garland.

Buildings & Projects, 1926-1958. Ed. by Vincent Scully. LC 87-8754. (Louis I. Kahn Archive Ser.: Vol. 1). 592p. 1987. 335.00 (0-8240-1817-6) Garland.

Buildings & Projects, 1959-1961. Ed. by Vincent Scully. LC 87-8754. (Louis I. Kahn Archive Ser.: Vol. 2). 480p. 1988. 270.00 (0-8240-1818-4) Garland.

Buildings & Projects, 1962-1965. Ed. by Vincent Scully. LC 87-8754. (Louis I. Kahn Archive Ser.: Vol. 4). 496p. 1988. 280.00 (0-8240-1820-6) Garland.

Buildings & Projects, 1967-1969. Ed. by Vincent Scully. LC 87-8754. (Louis I. Kahn Archive Ser.: Vol. 6). 640p. 1988. 350.00 (0-8240-1822-2) Garland.

Buildings & Projects, 1970-1974. Ed. by Vincent Scully & Marshall D. Meyers. Tr. by Alexander Zonis. LC 87-8754. (Louis I. Kahn Archive Ser.: Vol. 7). 416p. 1988. 235.00 (0-8240-1823-0) Garland.

Buildings & Reality: Architecture in the Age of Information, Vol. 4. Ed. by Michael Benedikt. (Illus.). 128p. 1988. pap. 15.00 (0-8478-5484-1) Ctr Study of Amer Archit.

Buildings & Society: Essays on the Social Development of the Built Environment. Ed. by Anthony D. King. LC 80-40938. (Illus.). 329p. 1984. pap. 29.95 (0-7102-0234-2, 02342, RKP) Routledge.

Buildings & Structures of American Railroads. Alter G. Berg. 1976. lib. bdg. 134.95 (0-8490-1561-8) Gordon Pr.

Buildings & the Designs of Andrea Palladio. O. Bertotti-Scamozzi. 230p. reprint ed. pap. 65.60 (0-8357-7474-0, 2021770) Bks Demand.

Buildings & the Environment. Robert Goodland. LC 76-22811. (Illus.). 1976. pap. 10.00 (0-89327-052-0) NY Botanical.

Buildings & the Geometry of Diagrams. Ed. by L. A. Rosati. (Lecture Notes in Mathematics Ser.: Vol. 1181). vii, 277p. 1986. pap. 34.80 (0-387-16466-9) Spr-Verlag.

Buildings & Towns in Pastel. (Leisure Arts Ser.: No. 22). (Illus.). 32p. pap. 4.95 (0-85532-532-1, Pub. by Search Pr UK) A Schwartz & Co.

***Buildings Archaeology.** Ed. by Jason Wood. (Oxbow Monographs in Archaeology: No. 43). (Illus.). 272p. 1994. 49.50 (0-946897-75-1, Pub. by Oxbow Bks UK) David Brown.

Buildings, Bridges & Tunnels. Jackie Gaff. LC 91-212. (Tell Me about Bks.). (Illus.). 40p. (Orig.). (J). (gr. 2-5). 1991. pap. 3.99 (0-679-80865-5) Random Bks Yng Read.

Buildings for Hospitality. R. Fellows & J. Fellows. 224p. (Orig.). 1990. pap. 31.50 (0-273-03074-4, Pub. by Pitman Pub Ltd UK) Trans-Atl Phila.

Buildings for Industry. LC 72-142926. (Architectural Record Book). (Illus.). ix, 309p. 1972. reprint ed. text ed. 65.00 (0-8371-5928-8, ARBI, Greenwood Pr) Greenwood.

Buildings for Small Acreages: Farm, Ranch & Recreation. James S. Boyd. LC 77-80716. 1978. 33.25 (0-8134-1966-2); pap. text ed. 24.95 (0-685-02533-0) Interstate.

***Buildings for the Performing Arts: A Design & Development Guide.** Ian Appleton. (Illus.). 160p. 1995. text ed. 59.95 (0-7506-1276-2, Butterwrth Archit) Buttrwrth-Heinemann.

Buildings in Pencil. Gene Franks. (How to Draw & Paint Ser.). (Illus.). 32p. (Orig.). 1989. pap. 5.95 (1-56010-035-4, HT-217) W Foster Pub.

Buildings in Use Study: Part 1: Technical Factors; Part 2: Functional Factors; Appendix: Field Tests Manual, 2 pts. Harvey Z. Rabinowitz. (Publications in Architecture & Urban Planning: No. R75-1). (Illus.). v, 258p. 1985. reprint ed. 12.00 (0-938744-37-2) U of Wis Ctr Arch-Urban.

Buildings in Watercolor. Richard S. Taylor. (Illus.). 128p. 1991. pap. 24.95 (0-89134-415-2) North Light Bks.

Buildings in Watercolour. (Leisure Arts Ser.: No. 20). (Illus.). 32p. pap. 4.95 (0-85532-527-5, Pub. by Search Pr UK) A Schwartz & Co.

Buildings in Watercolour. Richard S. Taylor. (Illus.). 128p. 1990. 39.95 (0-7134-6178-0, Pub. by Batsford UK) Trafalgar.

Buildings Manager. Jack Rudman. (Career Examination Ser.: C-1153). 1994. pap. 29.95 (0-8373-1153-5) Nat Learn.

Buildings of Alaska. Alison K. Hoagland. (Buildings of the United States Ser.). (Illus.). 352p. 1993. 45.00 (0-19-507363-0) OUP.

Buildings of Alaska. Alison K. Hoagland. (Buildings of the United States Ser.). (Illus.). 352p. 1995. reprint ed. pap. 16.95 (0-19-509380-1) OUP.

Buildings of Bath. Richard K. Morriss. (Buildings of...Ser.). (Illus.). 128p. 1993. pap. 15.99 (0-7509-0256-6) A Sutton Pub.

Buildings of Berkeley. Robert Bernhardi. (Illus.). 116p. 1984. reprint ed. 10.95 (0-317-17550-5) Forest Hill.

Buildings of Berkeley: Phase Two. Robert Bernhardi. (Illus.). 142p. (Orig.). 1991. 15.00 (0-9605472-3-1) Forest Hill.

Buildings of Chester. Richard K. Morriss. (Buildings of... Ser.). (Illus.). 128p. 1993. pap. 15.99 (0-7509-0255-8) A Sutton Pub.

***Buildings of Early Everett: A Pictorial Survey of the Architecture of the Everett Boom, 1891-1894.** David Dilgard. (Illus.). 105p. 1994. pap. 16.95 (1-881147-12-6) Lowell Print.

Buildings of Iowa. David Gebhard. (Buildings of the United States Ser.). 565p. 1993. 45.00 (0-19-506148-9) OUP.

Buildings of Iowa. David Gebhard & Gerald Mansheim. (Buildings of the United States Ser.). (Illus.). 578p. 1995. reprint ed. pap. 18.95 (0-19-509378-X) OUP.

Buildings of Irish Towns. Ed. by Patrick Shaffrey & Maura Shaffrey. 1984. 19.95 (0-87243-126-6) Templegate.

Buildings of Ludlow. Richard K. Morriss. (Buildings of... Ser.). (Illus.). 128p. 1993. pap. 15.99 (0-7509-0254-X) A Sutton Pub.

Buildings of Michigan. Kathryn B. Eckert. (Buildings of the United States Ser.). (Illus.). 624p. 1993. 45.00 (0-19-506149-7) OUP.

Buildings of Michigan. Kathryn B. Eckert. (Buildings of the United States Ser.). (Illus.). 624p. 1995. reprint ed. pap. 18.95 (0-19-509379-8) OUP.

Buildings of Rhode Island. William H. Jordy. (Buildings of the United States Ser.). 512p. 1996. 45.00 (0-19-506147-0) OUP.

Buildings of Shrewsbury. Richard K. Morriss. (Buildings of. ..Ser.). (Illus.). 128p. 1993. pap. 15.99 (0-7509-0253-1) A Sutton Pub.

***Buildings of South Church, Bergenfield, New Jersey.** Adrian C. Leiby. (Illus.). 72p. 1992. pap. 9.95 (1-881576-10-8) Providence Hse.

Buildings of Spherical Type & Finite BN-Pairs. J. Tits. LC 74-5714. (Lecture Notes in Mathematics Ser.: Vol. 386). 229p. 1986. pap. 42.30 (0-387-06757-4) Spr-Verlag.

Buildings of Stratford-upon-Avon. Richard K. Morriss. (Buildings of...Ser.). (Illus.). 128p. (Orig.). 1994. pap. 16.00 (0-7509-0559-X) A Sutton Pub.

Buildings of the District of Columbia. Pamela Scott & Antoinette J. Lee. LC 93-9187. (Buildings of the United States Ser.). 480p. 1993. 45.00 (0-19-506146-2) OUP.

Buildings of the District of Columbia. Pamela Scott & Antoinette J. Lee. (Buildings of the United States Ser.). (Illus.). 480p. 1995. reprint ed. pap. 16.95 (0-19-509389-5) OUP.

***Buildings of the Historic New Orleans Collection.** Photos by Richard Sexton. LC 94-75847. (Illus.). 24p. 1994. pap. 9.00 (0-917860-35-7) Historic New Orleans.

Buildings of the Third Dynasty. Leonard Woolley. (Ur Excavations Ser.: Archaeology, No. 6). (Illus.). x, 110p. 1974. 60.00 (0-686-17772-X) U PA Mus Pubns.

***Buildings of Venice.** Richard Goy. 1994. 60.00 (0-7148-3005-4, Pub. by Phaidon Press UK) Chronicle Bks.

Buildings of Warwick. Richard K. Morriss. (Buildings of... Ser.). (Illus.). 128p. (Orig.). 1994. pap. 16.00 (0-7509-0558-1) A Sutton Pub.

Buildings of Worcester. Richard K. Morriss. (Buildings of... Ser.). (Illus.). 128p. (Orig.). 1994. pap. 16.00 (0-7509-0557-3) A Sutton Pub.

Buildings on the East Side of the Agora: Remains Beneath the Stoa of Attalos. Rhys Townsend. (Athenian Agora Ser.: Vol. 27). (Illus.). 300p. (C). 1994. text ed. 120.00 (0-87661-227-3) Am Sch Athens.

Buildup: The Politics of Defense in the Reagan Era. Daniel Wirls. LC 91-55075. 280p. 1992. 32.95 (0-8014-2442-9) Cornell U Pr.

Built by Japan: Competitive Strategies of the Japanese Construction Industry. Fumio Hasegawa. 1988. text ed. 44.95 (0-471-63254-6) Wiley.

Built Environment. Ed. by Tom Bartuska & Gerald Young. LC 92-54360. 250p. (C). 1994. pap. text ed. 25.95 (1-56052-187-2) Crisp Pubns.

Built Environment: A Subject Index, 1800-1960, 4 vols., Set. Terence Russell. 4450p. 1990. text ed. 700.00 (0-576-40006-8) Gregg Intl.

Built Environment: Present & Future Values. Ed. by Frederick Bonkovsky. (Illus.). 76p. (Orig.). 1986. pap. 5.95 (1-55630-000-X) Brentwood Comm.

***Built for a Better Future: The Brynmawr Rubber Factory.** Victoria Perry. (Illus.). 96p. 1995. pap. 25.00 (1-873487-04-5, Pub. by White Cockade UK) Paul & Co Pubs.

Built in Boston: City & Suburb, 1800-1950. Douglass Shand-Tucci. LC 88-14151. (Illus.). 304p. (C). 1988. reprint ed. pap. 20.95 (0-87023-649-0) U of Mass Pr.

Built in Fear of Heat. Ava L. Haymon. Ed. by Roy Zarucchi. (Chapbook Ser.). (Illus.). 36p. (Orig.). 1994. pap. text ed. 6.95 (1-879205-45-9) Nightshade Pr.

Built in Milwaukee. Randy Garber. LC 81-70932. (Illus.). 228p. 1983. pap. 19.95 (0-299-97015-9) U of Wis Pr.

Built-in Projects for the Home. Cy DeCosse Incorporated Staff. LC 93-8783. (Black & Decker Home Improvement Library). 128p. 1993. 14.95 (0-86573-730-4); pap. 12.95 (0-86573-731-2) Cy De Cosse.

Built-in Test. Robert W. Archbald. 442p. 1990. pap. 65.00 (0-9625300-0-X) Fellows Pub.

Built-In Test for VLSI: Pseudorandom Techniques. Paul H. Bardell et al. LC 87-23013. 354p. 1987. text ed. 115.00 (0-471-62463-2) Wiley.

Built in Texas. Ed. by Francis E. Abernethy. (Publications of the Texas Folklore Society: No. 42). (Illus.). 288p. 1979. 24.50 (0-935014-00-4) E-Heart Pr.

Built in U. S. A. Nineteen Thirty-Two to Nineteen Forty-Four. Ed. by Elizabeth B. Mock et al. Bd. with Post-War Architecture. LC 68-57299. LC 68-57299. (Museum of Modern Art Publications in Reprint). (Illus.). 260p. 1969. reprint ed. 24.95 (0-405-01526-7) Ayer.

Built-in U. S. War Drive. Vince Copeland. 106p. 4.00 (0-89567-038-0) World View Forum.

Built in Washington: Twelve Thousand Years of Pacific Northwest Archaeological Sites & Historic Buildings. Washington State Office of Archaeology & Historic Preservation Staff et al. LC 89-22823. (Illus.). 187p. (Orig.). 1990. pap. 11.95 (0-87422-065-3) Wash St U Pr.

Built-Ins. (Home Repair & Improvement Ser.). (Illus.). 136p. 1979. 14.60 (0-8094-2430-4); lib. bdg. 20.60 (0-8094-2431-2) Time-Life.

Built Like A Bear. James P. Dowd. 190p. 1979. 16.00 (0-87770-212-8) Ye Galleon.

Built of Earth & Song: Churches of Northern New Mexico. Marie R. Cash. (Illus.). 184p. 1993. pap. 14.95 (1-878610-30-9) Red Crane Bks.

Built on Balance. Carol Emich. (Illus.). 150p. (Orig.). 1991. pap. 14.95 (0-9631211-0-3) Emich Ensembles.

Built on Honor, Sailed with Skill: The American Coasting Schooner. Frederick F. Kaiser. LC 89-39925. (Illus.). 320p. 1989. 48.00 (0-931781-05-1) Jennings Pr.

Built on the Banks of the Kalamazoo. Kit Lane. LC 93-83589. (Saugatuck Maritime Ser.). (Illus.). 288p. 1993. pap. 17.50 (1-877703-00-1) Pavilion Pr.

Built, the Unbuilt & the Unbuildable: In Pursuit of Architectural Meaning. Robert Harbison. (Illus.). 192p. (C). 1993. pap. 12.95x (0-262-58122-1) MIT Pr.

Built, the Unbuilt, the Unbuildable: In Pursuit of Architectural Meaning. Robert Harbison. (Illus.). 192p. 1991. 32.50x (0-262-08204-7) MIT Pr.

Built to Last. Leigh Roberts. (Superromance Ser.). 1993. mass mkt. 3.39 (0-373-70543-3, 1-70543-3) Harlequin Bks.

Built to Last: Successful Habits of Visionary Companies. James C. Collins & Jerry I. Porras. LC 94-20571. 1994. 25.00 (0-88730-671-3) Harper Busn.

Built to Last: The Grateful Dead 25th Anniversary Tour Book. Jamie Jensen. (Illus.). 96p. 1990. pap. 8.95 (0-452-26478-2, Plume) NAL-Dutton.

Built-up Ship Model. Charles G. Davis. 1990. pap. 5.95 (0-486-26174-3) Dover.

Builth Wells. R. W. Fenn & J. B. Sinclair. (Towns & Villages of Wales Ser.). (Illus.). 1993. pap. 15.50 (0-7509-0490-9) A Sutton Pub.

Buitenaardse Beschaving see UFO Contact from Planet Iarga

Bujh Niranjan: An Ismaili Mystical Poem. Ali S. Asani. (Orig.). 1992. pap. 14.95 (0-932885-08-X) Harvard CMES.

Buke of the Howlat. Richard Holland. LC 78-169476. (Bannatyne Club, Edinburgh. Publications: No. 3). reprint ed. 18.50 (0-404-52703-5) AMS Pr.

Bukhara. Intro. by Dmitriy Arapov. (Great Photographic Archives Ser.). (Illus.). 160p. 1995. 35.00 (1-873938-07-1, Pub. by Ithaca UK) Paul & Co Pubs.

Bukharans: A Dynastic, Diplomatic & Commercial History. Audrey Burton. (Illus.). 360p. 1990. 75.00 (0-7103-0382-3, A4532, Pub. by Kegan Paul Intl UK) Routledge Chapman & Hall.

Bukharin & the Bolshevik Revolution: A Political Biography, 1888-1938. Stephen F. Cohen. (Illus.). 1980. reprint ed. pap. 15.95 (0-19-502697-7) OUP.

Bukharin in Retrospect. Ed. by Theodor Bergmann et al. 256p. 1994. 49.95 (0-87332-691-1) M E Sharpe.

Bukkyo No Genten see Beginnings of Buddhism

Bukkyo No Inochi Hokekyo see Shakyamuni Buddha: A Narrative Biography

Buku Pegangan Sistem Unix Dan Internet. Budi Rahardjo. 266p. (IND.). 1994. pap. 19.95 (1-885130-11-2) Open Pathways.

***Buky Schwartz Videoconstructions.** Ed. by Bill Judson. (Illus.). 142p. 1995. 50.00 (0-88039-023-9) Academy Chi Pubs.

***Bulb Expert: A Complete Guide to Indoor & Outdoor Bulbs for Color All Year Round.** D. G. Hessayon. (Expert Ser.). (Illus.). 128p. 1995. pap. 10.95 (0-903505-42-8, Pub. by Expert Bks UK) Sterling.

Bulb for All Seasons: In Which a Flower Is Grown Indoors Every Month of the Year. Quin Ellis. LC 93-12437. 1994. 13.00 (0-688-12412-7) Hearst Bks.

***Bulb to Tulip.** Oliver S. Owen. (Lifewatch Ser.). (J). 1995. write for info. (1-56239-488-6) Abdo & Dghtrs.

***Bulbs.** Editors of Time-Life Books. Ed. by Janet Cave. LC 95-9168. (Time Life Complete Gardener Ser.). (Illus.). 160p. 1995. write for info. (0-7835-4112-0) Time-Life.

Bulbs. Ed. by James Fanning. (Plants & Gardens Ser.). (Illus.). 1989. ring bd. 3.95 (0-945352-39-5, Sterling) Bklyn Botanic.

Bulbs. Derek Fell. (American Garden Association's Garden Guides Ser.). (Illus.). 192p. 1993. 9.98 (0-8317-6939-4) Smithmark.

***Bulbs.** Ryan. 1994. pap. 12.99 (0-517-13454-3) Random.

Bulbs: Four Seasons of Beautiful Blooms. Lewis Hill & Nancy Hill. Ed. by Gwen Steege. LC 94-14240. (Illus.). 224p. 1994. 28.95 (0-88266-878-1, Garden Way Pub); pap. text ed. 18.95 (0-88266-877-3, Garden Way Pub) Storey Comm Inc.

Bulbs: How to Select, Grow & Enjoy. George H. Scott. LC 81-84156. 160p. 1982. pap. 16.95 (0-89586-146-1) Price Stern.

***Bulbs For All Seasons.** 208p. 1994. pap. 17.95 (0-696-20371-5) Meredith Bks.

Bulbs for All Seasons. Better Homes & Gardens Staff. 1994. 24.95 (0-696-00081-4) Meredith Bks.

Bulbs for All Seasons. 4th ed. Sunset Magazine & Book Editors. LC 85-50846. (Illus.). 96p. 1985. pap. 8.99 (0-376-03086-0) Sunset Menlo Pk.

Bulfinch Guide to Carpets: How to Identify, Classify, & Evaluate Antique Carpets & Rugs. Enza Milanesi. (Illus.). 192p. 1993. 19.95 (0-8212-2057-8) Bulfinch Pr.

***Bulfinch Illustrated Encyclopedia of Antiques Vol. 1.** Paul Atterbury & Lars Tharp. (Illus.). 332p. 1994. 50.00 (0-8212-2077-2) Bulfinch Pr.

Bulfinch Pocket Dictionary of Art Terms. 3rd rev. ed. Rev. by David Diamond. (Illus.). 144p. 1992. pap. 8.95 (0-8212-1905-7) Bulfinch Pr.

Bulfinch Solution: Teaching the Ancient Classics in American Schools. Marie S. Cleary. LC 90-36454. (Illus.). 160p. (Orig.). (C). 1990. pap. text ed. 19.95 (0-88143-112-5) Ayer.

Bulfinch's Mythology. 1988. 12.99 (0-517-27415-9) Random Hse Value.

Bulfinch's Mythology. Thomas Bulfinch. LC 90-55347. 288p. 1990. 5.98 (0-89471-881-9) Courage Bks.

Bulfinch's Mythology. Thomas Bulfinch. LC 34-27086. 778p. 1978. 15.00 (0-394-60437-7, Modern Lib) Random.

Bulfinch's Mythology. Thomas Bulfinch. LC 92-35376. 1993. 20.00 (0-679-60046-9, Modern Lib) Random.

Bulfinch's Mythology, 3 vols. Incl. Vol. 1. Age of Fable. 408p. 1962. pap. 3.95 (0-451-62444-0, ME2230); Vols 2 & 3. Age of Chivalry & Legends of Charlemagne. 608p. pap. 4.95 (0-451-62252-9); (YA). (gr. 7). 1962. Set pap. 4.95 (0-451-62659-1, Ment) NAL-Dutton.

Bulfinch's Mythology. abr. ed. Thomas Bulfinch. Ed. by Edmund Fuller. 448p. 1959. mass mkt. 5.95 (0-440-30845-3, LE) Dell.

***Bulfinch's Mythology: The Age of Chivalry & the Legends of Charlemagne.** Bulfinch. 1995. pap. (0-452-01153-1, Mer) NAL-Dutton.

Bulfinch's Mythology: The Age of Fable. Thomas Bulfinch. 408p. 1962. pap. 5.99 (0-451-62799-7, Ment) NAL-Dutton.

***Bulfinch's Mythology: The Age of Fable.** Norma L. Goodrich. 416p. 1995. 12.95 (0-452-01152-3, Plume) NAL-Dutton.

Bulfinch's Mythology: The Age of Fable, Vol. 1. Thomas Bulfinch. 1962. pap. 5.99 (0-451-62814-4) NAL-Dutton.

Bulfinch's Mythology: The Age of Fable, the Age of Chivalry, Legends of Charlemagne. Ed. by Richard P. Martin. LC 91-55002. (Illus.). 640p. 1991. 37.50 (0-06-270025-1, Harper Ref) HarpC.

Bulgakov: Six Plays. Mikhail Bulgakov. Tr. by Michael Glenny et al. (Methuen World Dramatists Ser.). 416p. (Orig.). (C). 1991. pap. 13.95 (0-413-64530-4, A0496, Pub. by Methuen UK) Heinemann.

Bulgaria. (Essential Guides Ser.). 1994. 7.95 (0-8442-8901-9, Passport Bks) NTC Pub Grp.

***Bulgaria.** Ed. by Caroline Aldrich. (C). 1995. 50.00 (0-929851-35-8) Am Assn Coll Registrars.

An Asterisk (*) at the beginning of an entry indicates that the title is appearing in BIP for the first time.

Bulgaria. Julian Popescu. (Let's Visit Places & Peoples of the World Ser.). (Illus.). 96p. (J). (gr. 5 up). 1988. 14.95 (*1-55546-177-8*) Chelsea Hse.

***Bulgaria.** Abraham Resnick. LC 94-37948. (Enchantment of the World Ser.). 172p. (J). (gr. 5-9). 1995. lib. bdg. 20.55 (*0-516-02631-3*) Childrens.

Bulgaria. annot. ed. Ed. by Richard J. Crampton. (World Bibliographical Ser.: No. 107). 234p. 1989. lib. bdg. 65.00 (*1-85109-104-1*) ABC-CLIO.

Bulgaria: A Bibliographic Guide. Marin V. Pundeff. LC 65-60006. (Bibliographic Guides Ser.). 1968. reprint ed. 12.95 (*0-405-00059-6*) Ayer.

Bulgaria: A Travel Guide. Philip Ward. LC 90-45357. 1990. pap. 17.95 (*0-88289-827-2*) Pelican.

Bulgaria: An Economic Assessment. OECD Staff. 152p. (Orig.). 1992. pap. 23.00 (*92-64-13753-X*) OECD.

Bulgaria: Country Reporter. Lewis B. Sckolnick. (Illus.). 60p. 1994. pap. 895.00 (*1-57205-208-2*) Rector Pr.

Bulgaria: Crisis & Transition to a Market Economy, 2 vols., Vol. I: The Main Report. 216p. 1991. 11.95 (*0-8213-1894-2*, 11894) World Bank.

Bulgaria: Crisis & Transition to a Market Economy, 2 vols., Vol. II: Sectoral Analysis. 236p. 1991. 13.95 (*0-8213-1895-0*, 11895) World Bank.

***Bulgaria: Human Rights & Democracy.** (Illus.). 60p. (Orig.). 1994. pap. 125.00 (*0-7605-0017-7*) Rector Pr.

Bulgaria: Imprisonment of Ethnic Turks. Amnesty International Staff. 40p. (Orig.). 1986. pap. 5.00 (*0-86210-097-6*, Pub. by Amnesty Intl Pubns UK) Amnesty Intl USA.

Bulgaria: Mediaeval Wall Paintings. K. Mijatev. (UNESCO World Art Ser.). (Illus.). 96p. (C). 1961. text ed. 300.00 (*0-685-47837-8*, Pub. by Collets) St Mut.

Bulgaria: Past & Present. George C. Logio. LC 73-480409. reprint ed. 42.00 (*0-404-56133-0*) AMS Pr.

Bulgaria: Politics, Economics & Society. Robert J. McIntyre. (Marxist Regimes Ser.). 225p. 1988. text ed. 49.00 (*0-86187-398-X*, Pub. by Pinter Pubs UK); text ed. 17.50 (*0-86187-399-8*, Pub. by Pinter Pubs UK) St Martin.

***Bulgaria: U. S. Non Profit Aid.** 70p. (Orig.). 1995. pap. 125.00 (*0-7605-1537-9*) Rector Pr.

Bulgaria Business Forecaster. Ed. by Lewis B. Sckolnick. 70p. (Orig.). (C). 1994. pap. 675.00 (*1-57205-354-2*) Rector Pr.

***Bulgaria Business Intelligence Handbook.** (Illus.). 70p. (Orig.). 1994. pap. 295.00 (*0-7605-1042-3*) Rector Pr.

***Bulgaria Business Risk Outlook.** 70p. (Orig.). 1994. pap. 495.00 (*0-7605-1424-0*) Rector Pr.

Bulgaria Country Studies: Area Handbook. 2nd ed. Ed. by Glenn E. Curtis. LC 93-10955. (Area Handbook Ser.). 1993. 27.00 (*0-8444-0751-8*) Lib Congress.

Bulgaria During the Second World War. Marshall L. Miller. LC 74-82778. 304p. 1975. 37.50 (*0-8047-0870-3*) Stanford U Pr.

Bulgaria, Eighteen Seventy-Eight to Nineteen Eighteen: A History. Richard J. Crampton. (East European Monographs: No. 138). 580p. 1983. text ed. 60.00 (*0-88033-029-5*) East Eur Quarterly.

***Bulgaria in American Perspective: Political & Cultural Issues.** Marin Pundeff. 350p. 1994. 49.00 (*0-88033-295-6*) East Eur Quarterly.

Bulgaria in Pictures. LC 93-23080. (Visual Geography Ser.). (Illus.). 64p. (YA). (gr. 5 up). 1994. lib. bdg. 18.95 (*0-8225-1890-2*, Lerner Publctns) Lerner Group.

***Bulgaria: International Customs Journal, 1993-1994.** 8th ed. 262p. (Orig.). (C). 1994. pap. text ed. 95.00x (*0-7881-1220-1*) Diane Pub.

Bulgaria Legal Texts. Ed. by Lewis B. Sckolnick. 225p. (Orig.). (C). 1994. pap. text ed. 595.00 (*1-57205-445-X*) Rector Pr.

Bulgaria Pocket Guide. Berlitz Editors. (Pocket Guides Ser.). 1995. pap. 7.95 (*2-8315-1374-X*) Berlitz.

Bulgarian-Americans. Nikolay G. Altankov. LC 78-1012. 1979. per. 10.00 (*0-918660-09-2*) Ragusan Pr.

Bulgarian Americans. Claudia Carlson & David Allen. (Peoples of North America Ser.). (Illus.). 112p. 1990. lib. bdg. 17.95 (*0-87754-865-X*) Chelsea Hse.

Bulgarian Basic Course. Foreign Service Institute Staff. 487p. 1980. audio 245.00 (*0-88432-089-8*, AFL450); 34.95 (*0-88432-749-3*, AFL990) Audio-Forum.

Bulgarian Cinema. Ronald Holloway. LC 84-49318. (Illus.). 216p. 1986. 40.00 (*0-8386-3183-5*) Fairleigh Dickinson.

Bulgarian Communism: The Road to Power 1934-1944. Nissan Oren. LC 84-25247. xiv, 290p. (C). 1985. reprint ed. text ed. 69.50 (*0-313-24741-2*, 0RBC, Greenwood Pr) Greenwood.

Bulgarian Communist Party from Blagoev to Zhivkov. John D. Bell. LC 85-17744. (Publication Ser.: No. 320). 202p. (Orig.). 1985. pap. text ed. 9.95 (*0-8179-8202-7*) Hoover Inst Pr.

Bulgarian Complete Course. 1994. 14.95 (*0-8442-3753-1*, NTC Busn Bks) NTC Pub Grp.

Bulgarian Economy in the Twentieth Century. John R. Lampe. 256p. 1986. text ed. 45.00 (*0-312-10785-4*) St Martin.

Bulgarian-English - English-Bulgarian Pocket Dictionary. E. Stankowa & I. Harlakowa. 287p. 1993. reprint ed. pap. 24.00 (*954-02-0001-6*) IBD Ltd.

***Bulgarian-English--English-Bulgarian Pocket Dictionary.** E. Stankowa. 287p. (BUL & ENG.). 1993. pap. text ed. write for info. (*0-7859-8764-9*) Fr & Eur.

Bulgarian-English & English-Bulgarian Dictionary. E. Stankowa & I. Harlakowa. 288p. (C). 1991. 170.00 (*0-569-09301-5*, Pub. by Collets) St Mut.

Bulgarian-English Dictionary. R. Russev. 1990. lib. bdg. 39.95 (*0-8288-2627-7*) Fr & Eur.

Bulgarian-English Dictionary. R. Russev. (BUL & ENG.). 42.50 (*0-685-04461-0*, 006-2) Saphrograph.

Bulgarian-English Dictionary. 2nd ed. T. Atanassova et al. 1050p. (BUL & ENG.). 1990. 85.00 (*0-8288-0447-8*, M9829) Fr & Eur.

Bulgarian-English Dictionary, 2 vols. 3rd ed. T. Atanassova. 1050p. 1990. 94.00 (*0-88431-074-4*) IBD Ltd.

Bulgarian-English Dictionary, 2 vols., Set. T. Atanassova. 1050p. (C). 1988. 295.00 (*0-89771-904-2*, Pub. by Collets) St Mut.

Bulgarian-English English-Bulgarian Concise Dictionary. Ivan Tchomakov. 400p. (Orig.). 1991. pap. 11.95 (*0-87052-145-4*) Hippocrene Bks.

Bulgarian Folk Costumes. Maria Veleva. 30p. (Orig.). 1982. pap. 5.00 (*0-936922-06-0*) Tamburitza.

Bulgarian-German Pocket Dictionary: Taschenwoerterbuch Bulgarisch-Deutsch. 11th ed. P. Rankoff. 367p. (BUL & GER.). 1987. 14.95 (*0-8288-0999-2*, F34910) Fr & Eur.

Bulgarian-Hindi Dictionary. deluxe ed. B. Kanti Varma. 706p. (BUL & HIN.). 1978. 95.00 (*0-8288-4866-1*, M9836) Fr & Eur.

***Bulgarian-Hungarian Pocket Dictionary.** J. Bodey. 560p. (BUL & HUN.). 1985. pap. 15.00x (*963-205-132-7*, Pub. by Akad Kiado HU) St Mut.

***Bulgarian-Hungarian Pocket Dictionary.** J. Bodey. 560p. (BUL & HUN.). (C). 1985. 39.00x (*0-614-00654-6*, Pub. by Akad Kiado HU) St Mut.

Bulgarian Icons. Atanas Bozhdov. 528p. 1984. 420.00 (*0-317-61243-3*, Pub. by Collets UK) Pro-Am Music.

Bulgarian Icons Through the Centuries. K. Paskaleva. (Illus.). 332p. (C). 1987. text ed. 350.00 (*0-685-40245-2*, Pub. by Collets) St Mut.

Bulgarian Monasteries: Monuments of History, Culture & Art. Georgi Charukov. 382p. 1981. 149.00 (*0-569-08507-1*, Pub. by Collets UK) St Mut.

Bulgarian Mural Paintings of the 14th Century. Dora Panayotova. Tr. by Marguerite Alexieva & Theodora Athanassova. (Illus.). 37.50 (*0-8057-5003-7*) Irvington.

Bulgarian Mythology. I. Georgieva. 212p. (C). 1985. 195.00 (*0-685-31465-0*, Pub. by Collets UK) Pro-Am Music.

Bulgarian Phrasebook. (Hugo Ser.). 128p. (Orig.). 1994. pap. 4.95 (*0-85285-216-9*) Hunter NJ.

Bulgarian-Russian Dictionary. 519p. (BUL & RUS.). 1977. 29.95 (*0-8288-5294-4*, M9095) Fr & Eur.

Bulgarian Travel Pack. (Hugo Ser.). 128p. (Orig.). 1994. 14.95 (*0-85285-217-7*) Hunter NJ.

Bulgarian Umbrella. Vladimir Kostov. Tr. by Ben Reynolds. 256p. 1988. text ed. 39.95 (*0-312-02387-1*) St Martin.

Bulgarian Voices: Letting the People Speak. Philip Ward. (Illus.). 352p. (Orig.). 1992. pap. 21.95 (*0-906672-64-3*) Oleander Pr.

Bulgarians in the Past: Pages from the Bulgarian Cultural History. D. Mishew. LC 74-135823. (Eastern Europe Collection Ser.). 1971. reprint ed. 29.95 (*0-405-02766-4*) Ayer.

Bulgarians in the Seventeenth Century: Slavic Orthodox Society & Culture under Ottoman Rule. Dennis P. Hupchick. LC 92-50889. 342p. 1993. lib. bdg. 45.00 (*0-89950-822-7*) McFarland & Co.

Bulgaria's Agriculture: Situation Trends & Prospects. 220p. 1991. pap. 35.00 (*92-826-2922-8*, CM-71-91-283-EN-C) UNIPUB.

Bulgarich-Deutsches Phraseologisches Worterbuch: Bulgarian-German Phraseology Dictionary. J. Nikolowa et al. 1088p. (BUL & GER.). 1977. 95.00 (*0-8288-5295-2*, M9833) Fr & Eur.

Bulgarisch-Byzantinische Aufsatze. Veselin Besevliev. (Collected Studies: No. CS80). (Illus.). 370p. (C). 1978. reprint ed. lib. bdg. 124.95 (*0-86078-024-4*, Pub. by Variorum UK) Ashgate Pub Co.

***Buli-English Dictionary.** Franz Kroger. (Researches on African Languages & Cultures Ser.). 572p. (C). 1994. pap. text ed. 54.00 (*3-88660-821-2*) Westview.

Bulimarexia. Marlene Boskind-White. 1991. pap. 10.95 (*0-393-30117-6*) Norton.

Bulimarexia: The Binge-Purge Cycle. 2nd ed. Marlene Boskind-White & William C. White, Jr. 1987. 19.95 (*0-393-02368-0*) Norton.

Bulimia. Cheryl G. Mercier. 20p. 1990. 2.95 (*1-56456-024-4*, 226) W Gladden Found.

Bulimia: A Guide for Family & Friends. Robert T. Shermand & Ronald A. Thompson. 160p. 1990. text ed. 18.95 (*0-669-24503-8*) Free Pr.

Bulimia: A Systems Approach to Treatment. Maria P. Root et al. (Professional Bks.). (Illus.). 1986. 34.95 (*0-393-70024-0*) Norton.

Bulimia: Book for Therapist & Client. Barbara G. Bauer et al. LC 85-72774. 210p. (Orig.). 1986. pap. text ed. 19.95 (*0-915202-56-5*) Accel Devel.

***Bulimia: Disease of Addiction.** 12p. (Orig.). 1993. pap. 2.00 (*0-9638074-1-2*) Food Addicts.

Bulimia: Psychoanalytic Treatment & Theory. Ed. by Harvey J. Schwartz. 564p. 1988. text ed. 70.00x (*0-8236-0605-8*, BN 00605) Intl Univs Pr.

Bulimia: The Binge-Eating & Purging Syndrome. Gretchen Goff. 16p. 1983. pap. 1.15 (*0-89486-204-9*, 1416B) Hazelden.

Bulimia: a Guide to Recovery: Understanding & Overcoming the Binge-Purge Syndrome. rev. ed. Lindsey Hall & Leigh Cohn. LC 86-45375. 192p. 1992. pap. 12.95 (*0-936077-17-4*) Gurze Bks.

Bulimia! Help Me, Lord! Molly Saunders. 196p. (Orig.). 1988. pap. 7.99 (*0-914903-53-5*) Destiny Image.

Bulimia Nervosa. James Mitchell. 188p. (C). 1989. text ed. 24.95 (*0-8166-1626-4*) U of Minn Pr.

Bulimia Nervosa: Basic Research, Diagnosis & Therapy. Ed. by Manfred M. Fichter. 364p. 1990. text ed. 106.95 (*0-471-92405-9*) Wiley.

***Bulimia Nervosa & Binge-Eating: A Guide to Recovery.** Peter J. Cooper. LC 95-8359. (Illus.). 160p. 1995. 35.00 (*0-8147-1522-2*); pap. 12.95 (*0-8147-1523-0*) NYU Pr.

Bulimic College Student: Evaluation, Treatment, & Prevention. Ed. by Leighton C. Whitaker & William N. Davis. LC 88-34725. (Journal of College Student Psychotherapy: Vol. 3, Nos. 2-4). 340p. 1989. 49.95 (*0-86656-874-3*) Haworth Pr.

Bulimic College Student: Evaluation, Treatment, & Prevention. Ed. by Leighton C. Whitaker & William N. Davis. LC 88-34725. (Journal of College Student Psychotherapy: Vol. 3, Nos. 2-4). 340p. 1989. pap. 19.95 (*0-86656-832-8*) Haworth Pr.

Bulk Acoustic Wave Theory & Devices. Joel Rosenbaum. (Acoustics Library). 400p. 1988. text ed. 49.00 (*0-89006-265-X*) Artech Hse.

Bulk Crystal Growth Technology. Shin-ichi Akai et al. (Japanese Technology Reviews Ser.: Vol. 4). 192p. 1989. pap. text ed. 95.00 (*2-88124-289-8*) Gordon & Breach.

Bulk Handling & Transport Conference, Vol. I. Ed. by Cargo Systems Staff. 1977. 195.00 (*0-317-89778-0*, Pub. by Cargo Systs UK) St Mut.

Bulk Handling & Transport Conference, Vol. II. Ed. by Cargo Systems Staff. 1979. 195.00 (*0-317-89779-9*, Pub. by Cargo Systs UK) St Mut.

Bulk Handling & Transport Conference, Vol. III. Ed. by Cargo Systems Staff. 1981. 195.00 (*0-907499-13-9*, Pub. by Cargo Systs UK) St Mut.

Bulk Handling & Transport Conference, Vol. IV. Ed. by Cargo Systems Staff. 1983. 195.00 (*0-907499-36-8*, Pub. by Cargo Systs UK) St Mut.

Bulk Handling & Transport Conference, Vol. V. Cargo Systems Staff. 1985. 195.00 (*0-907499-48-1*, Pub. by Cargo Systs UK) St Mut.

Bulk Handling of Paddy & Rice in Malaysia: An Economic Analysis. G. J. Ryland & K. M. Menz. (C). 1989. text ed. 58.00 (*0-949511-86-2*, Pub. by ACIAR) St Mut.

Bulk in ISO Containers. John Agnew & Gerry Askham. (C). 1978. 60.00 (*0-906297-01-X*, Pub. by ICHCA UK) St Mut.

Bulk in ISO Containers, No. 1. ICHCA Staff. (C). 1988. 90.00 (*0-685-46502-0*, Pub. by ICHCA UK) St Mut.

Bulk Materials Handling Handbook. Jacob Fruchtbaum. (Illus.). 512p. 1988. text ed. 89.95 (*0-442-22684-5*) Chapman & Hall.

Bulk Materials Storage, Handling & Transportation: 4th International Conference, 1992, 2 vols., Set. Intro. by Peter Arnold. (Illus.). 599p. (Orig.). 1992. pap. 119.00 (*0-85825-554-5*) Accents Pubns.

Bulk-Mineable Gold Resources, 2 vols., Vol. I: North, Central & South America. LC 91-60229. 1991. 245.00 (*0-942218-26-4*) Minobras.

Bulk-Mineable Gold Resources, 2 vols., Vol. II: Europe, Africa, Asia, Oceania, Australia. LC 91-60229. 1991. 215.00 (*0-685-51894-9*) Minobras.

Bulk of the Chronicles of Scotland: Or, a Metrical Version of the History of Hector Boece, 3 vols., Set. William Stewart. Ed. by W. B. Turnbull. (Rolls Ser.: No. 6). 1972. reprint ed. 180.00 (*0-8115-1007-7*) Periodicals Srv.

***Bulk Oil Storage Plant License.** (Career Examinations Ser.: Series 1). Date not set. pap. 23.95 (*0-8373-3762-3*) Nat Learn.

Bulk Oxygen Systems at Consumer Sites. (Fifty Ser.). 1990. pap. 16.75 (*0-685-58094-6*, 50-90) Natl Fire Prot.

Bulk Solids Handling: An Introduction to the Practice & Technology. J. S. Mason & A. S. Goldberg. 384p. 1986. text ed. 110.00 (*0-412-01251-0*, 9889, Chap & Hall NY) Chapman & Hall.

Bulk-Tonnage Metal Deposits. LC 82-62928. 1983. 97.40 (*0-942218-20-5*) Minobras.

Bulk Vending Machines: Your Route to Success. Dick McNicholas. (Illus.). 35p. 1985. pap. 6.95 (*0-943592-01-1*) Publishers Pr.

Bulkeley Family: Or, The Descendants of Rev. Peter Bulkeley Who Settled at Concord, MA in 1636. F. W. Chapman. (Illus.). 289p. 1989. reprint ed. lib. bdg. 53.50 (*0-8328-0342-1*); reprint ed. pap. 43.50 (*0-8328-0343-X*) Higginson Bk Co.

Bulkington. Louis Phillips. (Hollow Spring Poetry Ser.). (Illus.). 32p. (Orig.). 1982. pap. 4.00 (*0-936198-08-7*) Hollow Spring Pr.

Bulktrans Eighty-Five. Ed. by Cargo Systems International Staff. (C). 1985. 150.00 (*0-685-55018-4*, Pub. by Cargo Systs UK) St Mut.

Bulktrans Eighty-Nine. Ed. by Cargo Systems International Staff. (C). 1989. 150.00 (*0-907499-64-3*, Pub. by Cargo Systs UK) St Mut.

Bulktrans Eighty-One. Ed. by Cargo Systems International Staff. (C). 1981. 150.00 (*0-907499-15-5*, Pub. by Cargo Systs UK) St Mut.

Bulktrans Eighty-Three. Ed. by Cargo Systems International Staff. (C). 1983. 150.00 (*0-685-55017-6*, Pub. by Cargo Systs UK) St Mut.

Bulktrans Ninety-One. Ed. by Cargo Systems International Staff. (C). 1991. 450.00 (*0-907499-73-2*, Pub. by Cargo Systs UK) St Mut.

Bull: A Religious & Secular History of Phallus Worship & Male Homosexuality. Georgia Pesek-Marous. (Illus.). 185p. (Orig.). 1984. pap. 9.95 (*0-916453-01-4*) TAU Pr.

Bull: The Family of Stephen Bull of Kinghurst Hall, County Warwick, England & Ashley Hall, South Carolina, 1600-1960. H. D. Bull. 161p. 1994. reprint ed. lib. bdg. 35.00 (*0-8328-4145-5*); reprint ed. pap. 25.00 (*0-8328-4146-3*) Higginson Bk Co.

Bull by the Horns. Irwin Parnes & Joy Parnes. LC 88-50419. 1988. pap. 10.50 (*0-685-45839-3*) World Univ AZ.

Bull Connor. William A. Nunnelley. 240p. 1990. pap. 21.95 (*0-8173-0495-9*) U of Ala Pr.

***Bull Cook & Authentic Historical Recipes & Practices.** George L. Herter & Berthe E. Herter. LC 94-42189. 1995. pap. text ed. 14.00 (*0-88001-390-7*) Ecco Pr.

Bull Creek. Jesse D. Jennings & Dorothy Sammons-Lohse. (Anthropological Papers: No. 105). (Orig.). 1982. pap. 17.50 (*0-87480-201-6*) U of Utah Pr.

Bull Dancing, Vol. 5. Paul Lake. 1977. pap. 3.95 (*0-685-50008-X*) New Poets Chestnut Hills.

Bull Dog Faith. Marilyn Hickey. 28p. (Orig.). pap. write for info. (*1-56441-122-2*) M Hickey Min.

Bull from the Sea. Mary Renault. 1975. pap. 7.00 (*0-394-71504-7*, Vin) Random.

Bull Halsey: A Biography. E. B. Potter. LC 85-15419. (Illus.). 421p. 1985. 34.95 (*0-87021-146-3*) Naval Inst Pr.

Bull-Hunchers. Howard A. Hanlon. (Illus.). 1970. 10.00 (*0-87012-042-5*) McClain.

Bull of Minos. Leonard Cottrell. 23.95 (*0-88411-469-4*, Aeonian Pr) Amereon Ltd.

Bull Run. Paul Fleischman. LC 92-14745. (Laura Geringer Bk.). (Illus.). 112p. (J). (gr. 5 up). 1993. 14.95 (*0-06-021446-5*); lib. bdg. 14.89 (*0-06-021447-3*) HarpC Child Bks.

***Bull Run.** Paul Fleischman. LC 92-14745. (Illus.). 128p. (YA). (gr. 5 up). 1995. pap. 4.95 (*0-06-440588-5*, Trophy) HarpC Child Bks.

Bull Run: Its Strategy & Tactics. Robert M. Johnston. 1977. 20.95 (*0-8369-6944-8*, 7825) Ayer.

Bull Run to Bull Run: Four Years in the Army of Northern Virginia. George Baylor. 1983. reprint ed. 29.95 (*0-89201-106-8*) Zenger Pub.

Bull Session: Courtside Stories about the Chicago Bulls from Kerr to Jordan. Johnny Kerr & Terry Pluto. LC 89-61556. (Illus.). 276p. 1989. 17.95 (*0-929387-01-5*) Bonus Books.

Bull Terrier Champions, 1952-1981. Jan L. Freund. (Illus.). 104p. 1984. pap. 36.95 (*0-940808-16-1*) Camino E E & Bk.

Bull Terrier Champions, 1982-1986. Camino E. E. & B. Co. Staff. (Illus.). 62p. 1987. pap. 28.95 (*0-940808-58-7*) Camino E E & Bk.

Bull Terriers. Martin Weil. (Illus.). 128p. 1990. 11.95 (*0-86622-781-4*, KW-112) TFH Pubns.

Bull Terriers: An Owner's Companion. Robin Salyn. (Illus.). 192p. 1989. 39.95 (*1-85223-142-4*, Pub. by Crowood Pr UK) Trafalgar.

Bull Threshers & Bindlestiffs: Harvesting & Threshing on the North American Plains. Thomas D. Isern. LC 90-11967. (Illus.). xiv, 250p. 1990. 29.95 (*0-7006-0468-5*) U Pr of KS.

Bullaire Du Pape Calixte the Second, 2 vols. in 1. Ulysse Robert. (Illus.). c, 931p. 1979. reprint ed. write for info. (*3-487-06765-X*, Pub. by Georg Olms GW) Lubrecht & Cramer.

Bulldog: A Compiler for VLIW Architecture. John R. Ellis. (Association of Computing Machinery Doctoral Dissertation Award Ser.). (Illus.). 250p. 1986. 42.50x (*0-262-05034-X*) MIT Pr.

Bulldog: The Bristol Bulldog Fighter. David Luff. LC 88-60697. (Illus.). 188p. 1988. 29.95 (*0-87474-648-5*) Smithsonian.

Bulldog: The World's Most Famous Truck. John B. Montville. (Illus.). 1979. pap. 19.95 (*0-89404-008-1*) Aztex.

Bulldog Champions, 1952-1987. Camino E. E. & B. Co. Staff. (Illus.). 320p. 1988. pap. 36.95 (*0-940808-78-1*) Camino E E & Bk.

Bulldog Drummond. H. C. McNeile. 1976. 18.95 (*0-8488-1151-8*) Amereon Ltd.

Bulldog Drummond. Sapper. 180p. 1989. pap. 3.50 (*0-88184-453-5*) Carroll & Graf.

Bulldog Drummond Returns. H. C. McNeile. 1976. reprint ed. lib. bdg. 18.95 (*0-89190-841-2*, Rivercity Pr) Amereon Ltd.

Bulldog Drummond Strikes Back. H. C. McNeile. 1976. reprint ed. lib. bdg. 22.95 (*0-89190-842-0*, Rivercity Pr) Amereon Ltd.

Bulldog George. Max Bannah. LC 93-20807. (J). 1994. 4.25 (*0-383-03739-5*) SRA Schl Grp.

***Bulldogs.** Forbush. 1994. (*0-7938-1071-X*) TFH Pubns.

Bulldogs. T.F.H. Publications Staff. (Illus.). 160p. 1989. 11.95 (*0-86622-164-6*, KW-101) TFH Pubns.

Bulldogs & All about Them. Henry S. Cooper & F. Barrett Fowler. 1992. lib. bdg. 88.95 (*0-8490-5207-6*) Gordon Pr.

Bulldozer. Sam Sargent & Micheal Alves. (Illus.). 96p. 1994. pap. text ed. 12.95 (*0-87938-887-0*) Motorbooks Intl.

***Bulldozers.** LC 94-41309. (Look Inside Cross-Sections Ser.). (Illus.). 32p. (J). (gr. 1-4). 1995. pap. 5.95 (*0-7894-0012-X*) Dorling Kindersley.

Bulldozers & Fables & Fantasies for Adults. Manoj Das. (New World Literature Ser.: No. 26). 1990. 19.50 (*81-7018-604-8*, Pub. by BR Pub II) S Asia.

Bulleins Bulwarke of Defence Against All Sickness, Sorness & Woundes. William Bullein. LC 73-37139. (English Experience Ser.: No. 350). (Illus.). 488p. 1971. reprint ed. 125.00 (*90-221-0350-1*) Walter J Johnson.

Bullein's Dialogue Against the Fever Pestilence. Mark W. Bullen. Ed. by A. H. Bullen. (EETS, ES Ser.: No. 52). 1972. reprint ed. 29.00 (*0-527-00258-5*) Periodicals Srv.

Buller: the Scapecoat? A History of General Sir Redvers Buller, V. C. Geoffrey S. Powell. (Illus.). 256p. 1994. 42.50 (*0-85052-279-X*, Pub. by L Cooper Bks UK) Trans-Atl Phila.

Buller's Professional Course in Bartending for Home Study. Jon Buller. LC 82-23309. (Illus.). 160p. 1983. pap. 7.95 (*0-916782-33-6*) Harvard Common Pr.

Bulles Bleues. Maurice Maeterlinck. 236p. (FRE.). 1948. 14.95 (*0-7859-0014-4*, F66680) Fr & Eur.

Bullet. Robert Kammen. 224p. 1994. mass mkt. 3.99 (*0-8217-4751-7*) Zebra.

B

Bullet & Shell: The Civil War As the Soldier Saw It. George F. Williams. (Illus.). 480p. 1992. 9.98 (*0-681-41497-9*) Longmeadow Pr.

Bullet-Brand Empire. William Hopson. 1993. 14.95 (*0-7451-4573-6*, Gunsmoke) Chivers N Amer.

Bullet Breed. large type ed. Lloyd Madison. (Linford Western Library). 304p. 1986. pap. 11.95 (*0-7089-6291-2*, Linford) Ulverscroft.

Bullet for a Star. Stuart M. Kaminsky. 192p. 1991. mass mkt. 4.99 (*0-446-40061-0*, Mysterious Paperbk) Warner Bks.

Bullet for a Widow. large type ed. Marshall Grover. (Linford Western Library). 224p. 1989. pap. 11.95 (*0-7089-6714-0*, Linford) Ulverscroft.

Bullet for Betty. large type ed. Cyril Joyce. 1991. pap. 13.95 (*0-7089-7002-8*) Ulverscroft.

Bullet for Lincoln. Benjamin King. LC 92-40408. 352p. 1993. 19.95 (*0-88289-927-9*) Pelican.

Bullet for Stonewall. Benjamin King. LC 89-25552. 272p. 1990. 19.95 (*0-88289-768-3*) Pelican.

Bullet Heart. Michael Doane. LC 93-37263. 1994. 23.00 (*0-679-42507-1*) Knopf.

Bullet in the Ballet. Caryl Brahms & S. J. Simon. LC 84-80237. 159p. 1984. reprint ed. pap. 5.95 (*0-930330-12-9*) Intl Polygonics.

Bullet Manager: How to Shoot from the Hip Without Shooting Yourself in the Foot. Paul Kaufman & Cindy Wetmore. LC 93-7098. 1994. 9.99 (*0-385-47055-X*) Doubleday.

Bullet Park. John Cheever. LC 91-55304. (Vintage International Ser.). 256p. 1992. pap. 10.00 (*0-679-73787-1*, Vin) Random.

Bullet Park. large type ed. John Cheever. LC 93-35696. 1993. 20.95 (*0-7862-0082-0*) Thorndike Pr.

***Bullet Penetration: Modeling the Dynamics & the Incapacitation Resulting from Wound Trauma.** Duncan Macpherson. LC 94-79577. (Illus.). 303p. 1994. 39.95 (*0-9643577-0-4*) Ballistic Pubns.

Bullet Proof. W. F. Bragg. 1981. pap. 1.95 (*0-8439-0909-9*) Dorchester Pub Co.

Bullet Range - Iron Man, Iron Horse. Will Cook. 320p. 1993. pap. 4.99 (*0-8439-3534-0*) Dorchester Pub Co.

Bullet Song. W. F. Bragg. 1981. pap. 1.75 (*0-8439-0880-7*) Dorchester Pub Co.

Bullet Train. large type ed. Joseph Rance & Arei Kato. 410p. 1980. 12.00 (*0-7089-0697-4*) Ulverscroft.

Bullet Welcome. Steven C. Lawrence. 1992. 14.95 (*0-7451-4547-7*, Gunsmoke) Chivers N Amer.

Bulletboys (Guitar - Vocal) Ed. by John Chappell & Mark Phillips. (Illus.). 62p. (Orig.). 1990. pap. text ed. 14.95 (*0-89524-453-5*) Cherry Lane.

Bulletin, Vol. 1, No. 1. Benton, William, Museum of Art Staff. 28p. 1972. write for info. (*0-918386-07-1*) W Benton Mus.

Bulletin, Vol. 1, No. 2. Benton, William, Museum of Art Staff. 24p. 1973. 1.00 (*0-918386-10-1*) W Benton Mus.

Bulletin, Vol. 1, No. 3. Benton, William, Museum of Art Staff. 32p. 1974. 1.00 (*0-918386-14-4*) W Benton Mus.

Bulletin, Vol. 1, No. 4. Benton, William, Museum of Art Staff. 38p. 1976. 1.00 (*0-918386-19-5*) W Benton Mus.

Bulletin, Vol. 1, No. 5. Benton, William, Museum of Art Staff. 48p. 1977. 1.00 (*0-918386-24-1*) W Benton Mus.

Bulletin, Vol. 1, No. 6. Benton, William, Museum of Art Staff. 32p. 1978. 1.00 (*0-918386-25-X*) W Benton Mus.

Bulletin, Vol. 1, No. 7. Benton, William, Museum of Art Staff. 31p. 1979. 1.00 (*0-918386-30-6*) W Benton Mus.

Bulletin, Vols. 4-6 In 1 Vol. Mongolia Society Staff. 1966. pap. 5.00 (*0-910980-02-0*) Mongolia.

Bulletin: Council for Research in Music Education. Ed. by Marilyn P. Zimmerman. 96p. 1963. 18.00 (*0-686-37032-5*) U IL Sch Music.

Bulletin Board Basics: Hands on Science. Jeannine Perez. Ed. by Helen Stranich & Eric Hogan. (Illus.). 96p. 1991. pap. 9.95 (*1-878727-09-5*) First Teacher.

Bulletin Board Bonanza. Dorothy Michener & Beverly Muschlitz. (Illus.). 96p. (J). (gr. 2-6). 1981. pap. 7.95 (*0-86530-028-3*, IP-283) Incentive Pubns.

Bulletin Board Book for All Seasons. Susanne Glover et al. 64p. (J). (gr. k-6). 1980. 7.95 (*0-916456-79-X*, GA 160) Good Apple.

Bulletin Board Brighteners. Roberta C. Dishman. 56p. 1987. ring bd. 12.95 (*0-89265-121-0*) Randall Hse.

Bulletin Board Designs for the Christian Classroom. Carolyn Berg. 1984. teacher ed. pap. 6.95 (*0-570-03930-4*, 12-2866) Concordia.

Bulletin Board Extravaganzas. Barbra Glickstein. 80p. (gr. k-8). 1981. 8.95 (*0-86653-002-9*, GA229) Good Apple.

Bulletin Board Ideas. Mary Currier. 128p. (Orig.). 1990. pap. 12.99 (*0-8010-2555-9*) Baker Bk.

Bulletin Board Ideas. Bonnie Morris. 48p. (Orig.). 1991. pap. 6.95 (*0-687-04553-3*) Abingdon.

Bulletin Board Ideas. James H. Robinson & Rowena D. Robinson. LC 72-94108. 80p. 1981. pap. 5.95 (*0-570-03141-9*, 12-2525) Concordia.

Bulletin Board Ideas: Creative Ways to Communicate the Gospel. Sandra Sorlien. (Illus.). 40p. (Orig.). 1980. pap. 6.99 (*0-8066-1778-0*, 10-0949, Augsburg) Augsburg Fortress.

Bulletin Board Quotes, 5 vols., Set. Gayle T. Watts. (Orig.). 1992. pap. 49.95 (*0-945772-09-2*) Clarkston Pub.

Bulletin Board Quotes for Business People. Gayle T. Watts. 54p. (Orig.). 1992. pap. 12.95 (*0-945772-04-1*) Clarkston Pub.

Bulletin Board Quotes for Sports Lovers. Gayle T. Watts. 54p. (Orig.). 1992. pap. 12.95 (*0-945772-12-2*) Clarkston Pub.

Bulletin Board Quotes for Teachers. Gayle T. Watts. 54p. (Orig.). 1992. pap. 12.95 (*0-945772-05-X*) Clarkston Pub.

Bulletin Board Quotes of the Bible. Gayle T. Watts. 54p. (Orig.). 1992. pap. 12.95 (*0-945772-06-8*) Clarkston Pub.

Bulletin Board Quotes of Wisdom & Vision. Gayle T. Watts. 54p. (Orig.). 1992. pap. 12.95 (*0-945772-07-6*) Clarkston Pub.

Bulletin Board Sketches. Rachel L. Weaver. 1980. pap. 4.05 (*0-686-32319-X*) Rod & Staff.

Bulletin Board Smorgasbord. Susanne Glover & Georgeann Grewe. (Teacher Time-Savers Ser.). (J). (gr. 2-6). 1982. 9.95 (*0-88160-091-1*, LW 233) Learning Wks.

Bulletin Board Systems for Business. Lamont Wood & Dana Blankenhorn. 384p. 1992. disk 34.95 (*0-471-55348-4*) Wiley.

Bulletin Boards: For Reading, Spelling & Language Skills. Robyn Spizman. 64p. (J). (gr. k-6). 1984. student ed 7.95 (*0-86653-210-2*, GA 574) Good Apple.

Bulletin Boards: Ideas for Holidays & Special Days. Robyn Spizman. 64p. (J). (gr. k-6). 1984. student ed 7.95 (*0-86653-211-0*, GA 567) Good Apple.

Bulletin Boards: Seasonal Ideas & Activities. Robyn Spizman. 64p. (J). (gr. k-6). 1984. student ed 7.95 (*0-86653-218-8*, GA 568) Good Apple.

Bulletin Boards: To Reinforce Basic Math Skills. Robyn Spizman. 64p. (J). (gr. k-6). 1984. student ed 7.95 (*0-86653-208-0*, GA 573) Good Apple.

Bulletin Boards & Displays: Good Ideas for Librarians & Teachers. Gayle Skaggs. LC 92-56694. (Illus.). 168p. 1993. pap. 21.95 (*0-89950-884-7*) McFarland & Co.

Bulletin Boards for All Occasions. Donna Rushing. Ed. by Karen Brewer. (Illus.). 48p. (Orig.). 1994. pap. 6.49 (*0-7847-0227-6*, 14-03317) Standard Pub.

Bulletin Boards for Every Month. Jeanne Cheyney & Arnold Cheyney. (Illus.). 112p. (Orig.). (J). (gr. k-3). 1990. pap. 9.95 (*0-673-38828-X*) GdYrBks.

Bulletin Boards for Reinforcing Positive Behavior. Lee Canter. (Illus.). 46p. 1986. student ed 7.95 (*0-939007-00-2*) Lee Canter & Assocs.

Bulletin Boards for Reinforcing Positive Behavior: Primary Grades 1-3. Lee Canter. (Illus.). 48p. 1986. student ed 7.95 (*0-9608978-9-5*) Lee Canter & Assocs.

Bulletin Boards Plus. Robyn Spizman. 112p. (J). (gr. k-6). 1989. 9.95 (*0-86653-510-1*, GA1080) Good Apple.

Bulletin Boards Should Be More Than Something to Look At. Esther Finton. 64p. (J). (gr. k-6). 1979. 7.95 (*0-916456-32-3*, GA97) Good Apple.

Bulletin Boards That Bless. Tom Orange & Nancee McClure. (Helping Hand Ser.). 48p. (YA). (gr. 4-8). 1984. student ed 7.95 (*0-86653-201-3*, SS 821, Shining Star Pubns) Good Apple.

Bulletin Boards That Communicate: Creative Ideas for the Congregation. Sandra Sorlien. 48p. (Orig.). 1984. pap. 6.99 (*0-8066-2073-0*, 10-0950, Augsburg) Augsburg Fortress.

Bulletin Boards that Teach: One Hundred-Twenty Creative Ideas for the Classroom. Sandra Sorlien. (Illus.). 48p. (Orig.). 1988. pap. 6.99 (*0-8066-2407-8*, 10-0951) Augsburg Fortress.

Bulletin Boards Through the Year. Pat Spencer. (Illus.). 96p. (J). (gr. k-4). 1988. student ed 10.95 (*1-55734-062-5*) Tchr Create Mat.

Bulletin Boards to Brag About, Grades K - 6: Delightfully Dimensional Displays. Barbara Black. (Illus.). 58p. (Orig.). 1985. pap. 8.95 (*0-673-18280-0*) GdYrBks.

Bulletin Boards to Promote Good Study Skills & Positive Self-Concept. Robyn Spizman. 48p. (J). (gr. k-6). 1984. student ed 6.95 (*0-86653-261-7*, GA 575) Good Apple.

Bulletin Boards to Teach the Bible. Susan Julio. (Bulletin Board Ser.). (Illus.). 96p. (J). (gr. 3-7). 1994. 9.95 (*1-56417-003-9*, SS3825, Shining Star Pubns) Good Apple.

Bulletin du Centre D'Hydrogeologie, Vol. 4. 270p. (GER.). 1983. 15.40 (*3-261-03335-5*) P Lang Pubs.

Bulletin Interviews: Reprints of the 32 Interviews with Eminent Personalities in Meteorology & Hydrology That Appeared in the WMO Bulletin Between 1981 & 1988. World Meteorological Organization Staff. (WMO Ser.: No. 708). (Illus.). 405p. 1988. pap. 30.00 (*92-63-10708-4*, Pub. by Wrld Meteorological SZ) Am Meteorological.

Bulletin of Energy Prices see Energy Prices: 1973-1992

Bulletin of Far Eastern Bibliography, Set: Vol. 1-5. reprint ed. Set. 225.00 (*0-404-19507-5*) AMS Pr.

Bulletin of Information Nos. 13, 14, 15 & 16, the Arkansas History Commission. Dallas T. Herndon. 168p. 1977. reprint ed. 20.00 (*0-89308-077-2*, AR 8) Southern Hist Pr.

Bulletin of Religion, ISPP Vol. 1, No. 4. M. A. Barth. 60p. 1974. reprint ed. 2.00 (*0-88065-050-8*, Messers Today & Tomorrow) Scholarly Pubns.

Bulletin of Statistics on World Trade in Engineering Products. 413p. (ENG, FRE & RUS.). 1988. pap. 46.00 (*92-1-016221-8*, EFR.88.II.E.14) UN.

Bulletin of Statistics on World Trade in Engineering Products: 1971-1980. Incl. pap. 9.50 (*0-686-93344-3*, E.73.11.E.10); 1972pap. 14.50 (*0-686-93345-1*, E.74.11.E.5); 1973 pap. 17.00 (*0-686-93346-X*, E.75.11.E.7); Standard 1974. pap. 17.00 (*0-686-93347-8*, E.76.11.E.7); 1975 pap. 26.00 (*0-686-93348-6*, E.77.11.E.4); 1976 pap. 23.00 (*0-686-93349-4*, E.78.11.E.7); 1977pap. 19.00 (*0-686-93350-8*, E.79.11.E.4); 1978. pap. 22.00 (*0-685-12599-8*, E.80.11.E.9); 1979 pap. 26.00 (*0-685-12600-5*, E.81.11.E.13); 1980 pap. 26.00 (*0-685-12601-3*, E.82.11.E.5); 1982 (ENG, FRE & RUS.). 401p. 1984. pap. 38.00 (*0-685-12603-X*, E.84.11.E.5); 1982 (ENG, FRE & RUS.). 401p. 1984. pap. 38.00 (*0-685-12603-X*, E.84.11.E.5); 1976 pap. 23.00 (*0-686-93349-4*, E.78.11.E.7); 1975 pap. 26.00 (*0-686-93348-6*, E.77.11.E.4); 1972pap. 14.50 (*0-686-93345-1*, E.74.11.E.5); (ENG, FRE & RUS.). write for info. (*0-318-60531-7*) UN.

Bulletin of Statistics on World Trade in Engineering Products, 1988. 535p. 1990. 55.00 (*92-1-016245-5*, 90.II.E.20) UN.

Bulletin of Statistics on World Trade in Engineering Products, 1989. 1991. 55.00 (*92-1-016254-4*, 91.II.E.9) UN.

Bulletin of Statistics on World Trade in Engineering Products, 1987. 417p. 55.00 (*92-1-016229-3*, EFR.89.II.E.5) UN.

Bulletin of the Boston Museum of Fine Arts, 1903-1942, 8 vols. & index. Boston Museum of Fine Arts Staff. LC 71-119596. (Illus.). 1971. reprint ed. 44.00 (*0-685-73166-9*); reprint ed. 49.50 (*0-685-03214-0*) Ayer.

Bulletin of the Boston Museum of Fine Arts, 1903-1942, 8 vols. & index, Set. Boston Museum of Fine Arts Staff. LC 71-119596. (Illus.). 1971. reprint ed. 401.00 (*0-405-01242-X*) Ayer.

Bulletin of the European Communities, No. 1. European Communities Staff. 68p. 1993. pap. 9.00 (*92-826-5358-7*, CM-NF-93-001-EN-C, Pub. by Europ Com) UNIPUB.

Bulletin of the European Communities No. 3-1991, Vol. 24. European Communities Staff. 103p. 1991. pap. 9.00 (*0-685-49250-8*, CM-AA-91-003-EN-C) UNIPUB.

Bulletin of the European Communities, Supplement 2, 1993: The Challange of Enlargement Commission Opinion on Norway's. 68p. 1993. pap. 9.00 (*92-826-5932-1*, CM-NF-93-002-EN-C) UNIPUB.

Bulletin of the European Communities (Supplements Only) Development & Future of the Common Agricultural Policy. European Communities Staff. (Bulletin of European Communities Ser.: No. 5). 68p. 1992. pap. 6.00 (*92-826-3547-3*, CM-NF-91-005-EN-C, Pub. by Europ Com) UNIPUB.

Bulletin of the Metropolitan Museum of Art: Old Series 1905-1942, 37 vols, Set. 1,100.00 (*0-685-27565-5*) Ayer.

Bulletin of the Metropolitan Museum of Art, New York: Old Series, Nov. 1905-June 1942. Metropolitan Museum of Art Staff. 1968. 7.78 (*0-405-02357-X*, 16013) Ayer.

Bulletin of the Museum of Modern Art. Metropolitan Museum of Art Staff. 1967. 15.95 (*0-405-18720-3*, 15626) Ayer.

Bulletin of the Museum of Modern Art, 1933-1963, 7 Vols. Museum of Modern Art Library Staff. LC 38-43. 1967. reprint ed. 35.00 (*0-685-06505-7*) Ayer.

Bulletin of the Museum of Modern Art, 1933-1963, 7 Vols. Museum of Modern Art Library Staff. LC 38-43. 1967. reprint ed. 203.95 (*0-405-01500-3*) Ayer.

Bulletin of the Nuttall Ornithological Club: A Quarterly Journal of Ornithology, 8 vols. in 3, 1. Nuttall Ornithological Club Staff. LC 73-17834. (Natural Sciences in America Ser.). (Illus.). 1826p. 1974. reprint ed. 45.95 (*0-405-05755-5*) Ayer.

Bulletin of the Nuttall Ornithological Club: A Quarterly Journal of Ornithology, 8 vols. in 3, 2. Nuttall Ornithological Club Staff. LC 73-17834. (Natural Sciences in America Ser.). (Illus.). 1826p. 1974. reprint ed. 45.95 (*0-405-05756-3*) Ayer.

Bulletin of the Nuttall Ornithological Club: A Quarterly Journal of Ornithology, 8 vols. in 3, 3. Nuttall Ornithological Club Staff. LC 73-17834. (Natural Sciences in America Ser.). (Illus.). 1826p. 1974. reprint ed. 44.95 (*0-405-05757-1*) Ayer.

Bulletin of the Nuttall Ornithological Club: A Quarterly Journal of Ornithology, 8 vols. in 3, Set. Nuttall Ornithological Club Staff. LC 73-17834. (Natural Sciences in America Ser.). (Illus.). 1826p. 1974. reprint ed. 134.95 (*0-405-05754-7*) Ayer.

Bulletin of the Opposition, 1929-1941, 4 vols. Leon Trotsky et al. Ed. by Carol Lisker. LC 72-89901. 1904p. (RUS.). 1973. lib. bdg. 325.00 (*0-913460-01-X*) Pathfinder NY.

Bulletin, Vol. 17: John Taylor Arms: His World & Work. S. William Pelletier & Patricia Phagan. 1993. 10.00 (*0-685-66927-0*) Georgia Museum of Art.

Bulletin, Vol. 18: Annual Report 1990-1991. 1991. 3.00 (*0-685-66928-9*) Georgia Museum of Art.

Bulletins from a War. Helen Webster. (Illus.). 46p. (Orig.). 1980. pap. 8.00 (*0-915380-11-0*) Word Works.

Bulletins from the Home Front. Carolyn Kennedy. (Illus.). 140p. 1992. pap. 7.00 (*0-9634387-0-0*) Cherry Tree Pr.

Bulletins of American Paleontology, Set. 25.00 (*0-87710-256-2*); 25.00 (*0-87710-258-9*); 25.00 (*0-87710-257-0*); 25.00 (*0-87710-259-7*); 25.00 (*0-87710-260-0*); 25.00 (*0-87710-261-9*); 25.00 (*0-87710-262-7*); 25.00 (*0-87710-263-5*); 25.00 (*0-87710-264-3*); 25.00 (*0-87710-265-1*); 25.00 (*0-87710-266-X*); 25.00 (*0-87710-267-8*); 25.00 (*0-87710-268-6*); 25.00 (*0-87710-269-4*); 25.00 (*0-87710-271-6*); 25.00 (*0-87710-272-4*); 25.00 (*0-87710-273-2*); 25.00 (*0-87710-274-0*); 25.00 (*0-87710-275-9*); 25.00 (*0-87710-276-7*); 25.00 (*0-87710-277-5*); 25.00 (*0-87710-278-3*); 25.00 (*0-87710-279-1*); 25.00 (*0-87710-281-3*); 25.00 (*0-87710-282-1*); 25.00 (*0-87710-283-X*); 25.00 (*0-87710-298-8*); 25.00 (*0-87710-301-1*); 25.00 (*0-87710-302-X*); 25.00 (*0-87710-303-8*); 25.00 (*0-87710-304-6*); 25.00 (*0-87710-305-4*); 25.00 (*0-87710-306-2*); 25.00 (*0-87710-381-X*); 25.00 (*0-87710-382-8*); 25.00 (*0-87710-385-2*); 25.00 (*0-87710-388-7*) Paleo Res.

Bulletins of American Paleontology, Vol. 41. 25.00 (*0-87710-270-8*) Paleo Res.

***Bulletins of American Paleontology: Vol. 55.** Incl. Some Late Cenozoic Stony Corals from Northern Venezuela No. 246. N. E. Weisbord. 1968. pap. 8.00 (*0-87710-184-1*); Miocene & Pliocence Mollusks from Trinidad No. 247. Peter Jung. 1968. pap. (*0-615-00780-5*); 25.00 (*0-87710-284-8*) Paleo Res.

***Bulletins of American Paleontology: Vol. 56.** Incl. Names of & Variation in Central American Larger Foraminifera, Particularly the Eocene Pseudophragminids- No. 4 No. 248. W. S. Cole. 1969. pap. 3.00 (*0-87710-186-8*); Report of the North Carolina Geological Survey No. 249. Emmons. 1970. pap. 3.00 (*0-87710-187-6*); Revision of R. P Whitfield's Types of Rugose & Tabulate Corals in the Museum of Paleontology, University of California, & in the United States National Museum No. 250. E. Stumm. 1969. pap. 1.50 (*0-87710-188-4*); Catalogue of Type Specimens of the Belanski Collection No. 251. C. O. Levorson. 1969. pap. 0.75 (*0-87710-189-2*); Some Late Cenozoic Echinoidea from Cabo Blanco, Venezuela No. 252. N.E. Weisbord. 1969. pap. 3.50 (*0-87710-190-6*); Neosciadiocapsidae, a New Family of Upper Cretaceous Radiolaria No. 253. E. A. Pessagno. 1969. pap. 4.00 (*0-87710-191-4*); Taxonomy, Distribution, & Phylogeny of the Cymatiid Gastropods Argobuccinum, Fusitriton, Mediargo & Priene No. 254. Judith T. Smith. 1970. 8.00 (*0-87710-192-2*); 25.00 (*0-87710-285-6*) Paleo Res.

***Bulletins of American Paleontology: Vol. 57.** Incl. Ammonite Fauna of the Kialagvik Formation at Wide Bay, Alaska Penninsula No. 255. G. E. Westermann. 1969. pap. 9.00 (*0-87710-193-0*); New Middle Jurassic Ammonitina from New Guinea No. 256. T. A. Getty. 1970. pap. 6.00 (*0-87710-194-9*); 25.00 (*0-87710-286-4*) Paleo Res.

***Bulletins of American Paleontology: Vol. 59.** N. E. Weisbord. Incl. Bibliography of Cenozoic Echinoidea No. 263: Including Some Mesozoic & Paleozoic Titles. 1971. (*0-615-00779-1*); 25.00 (*0-87710-288-0*) Paleo Res.

***Bulletins of American Paleontology: Vol. 60.** Incl. Jurassic & Cretaceous Hagiastridae from the Blake-Bahama Basin & the Great Valley Sequence, California Coast Ranges No. 264. E. A. Pessagno. 3.75 (*0-87710-202-3*); New Species of Coronula (Cirripedia) from the Lower Pliocene of Venezuela No. 265. N. E. Weisbord. 1971. 0.80 (*0-87710-203-1*); Trepostomatus Ectoprocta (Bryozoa) from the Lower Chickamauga Group, Wills Valley, Alabama No. 267. F.K. McKinney. 1971. 8.00 (*0-87710-205-8*); Palynology & the Independence Shale of Iowa No. 266. J.B. Urban. 1971. (*0-615-00771-6*); 25.00 (*0-87710-289-9*) Paleo Res.

***Bulletins of American Paleontology: Vol. 61.** Incl. Catalogue of Murex No. 268. Emily Vokes. 1971. pap. 15.00 (*0-87710-206-6*); Fossill Mollusks from Carriarou, West Indies No. 269. Peter Jung. 1971. pap. 10.00 (*0-87710-207-4*); Cretaceous Radiolaria No. 270. E.A. Pessagno. 1972. pap. 15.00 (*0-87710-208-2*); 25.00 (*0-87710-290-2*) Paleo Res.

***Bulletins of American Paleontology: Vol. 62.** Incl. Mature Modification & Dimorphism in Selected Late Paleozoic Ammonoids No. 272. R. A. Davis. 1972. 7.50 (*0-87710-210-4*); Siluro-Devonian Microfaunal Biostratigraphy in Nevada No. 274. W.A. McClellan. 1973. pap. 6.00 (*0-87710-212-0*); 25.00 (*0-87710-291-0*) Paleo Res.

***Bulletins of American Paleontology: Vol. 63.** Incl. Reexamination of Chitinozoa from the Cedar Valley Formation of Iowa with Observations on their Morphology & Distribution No. 275. J. B. Urban. 1972. pap. 3.00 (*0-87710-213-9*); Upper Cretaceous Spumellariina from the Great Valley Sequence, California Coast Ranges No. 276. E. A. Pessagno. 1973. pap. 4.00 (*0-87710-214-7*); Tithonian (Jurassic) Ammonite Fauna & Stratigraphy of Sierra Catroce, San Luis Potosi, Mexico Vol. 277. H. M. Verna. Ed. by G. E. Westermann. 1973. pap. 10.00 (*0-87710-215-5*); 25.00 (*0-87710-292-9*) Paleo Res.

***Bulletins of American Paleontology: Vol. 64.** Incl. Palynology of the Almond Formation, Rock Springs Uplift, Wyoming No. 278. J.F. Stone. 1793. pap. 10.00 (*0-87710-216-3*); Tabulate Corals & Echinoderms from the Pennsylvanian Winterset Limestone, Hogshooter Formation, Northeastern Oklahoma No. 279. H.L. Strimple & J.M. Cocke. 1973. pap. (*0-615-00781-3*); Stratigraphy & Genera of Clacerous Foraminifera of the Fraileys Facies of Central Kentucky No. 280. R.G. Browne & E.R. Pohl. 1973. pap. 3.50 (*0-87710-218-X*); Crinoid Studies No. 281, Pt. I: Some Pennsylvanian Crinoids from Nebraska. H.L. Strimple. 1974. pap. 4.00 (*0-87710-219-8*); Crinoid Studies No. 281, Pt. II: Some Permian Crinoids from Nebraska, Kansas & Oklahoma. H.L. Strimple. 1974. pap. 4.00 (*0-615-00790-2*); 25.00 (*0-87710-293-7*) Paleo Res.

***Bulletins of American Paleontology: Vol. 66.** Incl. Middle-Ordovician Crinoids from Southwestern Virginia & Eastern Tennessee No. 283. Julia Veinus. 1974. pap. 5.00 (*0-87710-221-X*); Gastropoda of the Fox Hill Formation of North Dakota No. 284. J.M. Erikson. pap. 4.50 (*0-87710-222-8*); Late Cenozoic Corals of South Florida No. 285. N.E. Weisbord. 1974. pap. 10.50 (*0-87710-223-6*); Neogene Biostratigraphy of Southern Hispaniola No. 286. W.A. Van Den Bold. 1974. pap. 4.25 (*0-87710-224-4*); 25.00 (*0-87710-295-3*) Paleo Res.

***Bulletins of American Paleontology: Vol. 68.** Incl. North American Paracrinoidea No. 288: Ordovician Echinodermata. R.L. Parsley & L.W. Mintz. 1975. pap. 4.50 (*0-87710-226-0*); Ostracodes from the Late Neogene of Cuba No. 289. W.A. Van Den Bold. 1975. pap. 2.50 (*0-87710-227-9*); Vol. 290. Cirripedia of Florida & Surrounding Waters. pap. 2.50 (*0-87710-228-7*); 25.00 (*0-87710-297-X*) Paleo Res.

An Asterisk (*) at the beginning of an entry indicates that the title is appearing in BIP for the first time.

---

personal photos, cartoons, artwork, cowboy quips, & original definitions of terminology. A tribute has been paid to friends & acquaintances of the author by including their livestock brands throughout the book. Humor, entwined with thought provoking entities that make up this diversified country collection, will enhance & delight the senses. Fannye Lovelady, Dewey, Arizona, Honoree of the National Cowboy Hall of Fame, Oklahoma City, Oklahoma, Past Secretary & Historian of the Cowboy's Turtle Association - From piggin' strings to the artist's paint brush makes Rodeo one of the world's greatest sports. Lewis Bowman's 500 plus quips & Western phrases are hilarious, i.e.: "the worst trouble with loafing is, ya never know when yer done!" Margie Geenough Henson, Tucson, Arizona, Honoree of seven National & State Cowgirl Halls of Fame - This book makes me wish I were back in the saddle again. Lewis Bowman has captured the spirit of early day Rodeo & Western ranch family history along with a lot of western humor i.e. "If yer gonna kill time, work it to death!" BUMFUZZLED at $15.95 a copy, plus shipping & handling, will be distributed through Copper Queen Publishing, Inc. P.O. Box Drawer 48, Bisbee, AZ, 85603. Fax: 521-532-2247, Phone: 521-432-2244. *Publisher Provided Annotation.*

B

An Asterisk (*) at the beginning of an entry indicates that the title is appearing in BIP for the first time.

949

Bumper-to-Bumper: The Diesel Mechanics Student's Guide to Tractor-Trailer Operations. Mike Brynes & Associates Staff. (Illus.). x, 242p. (Orig.). (C). 1993. pap. text ed. 21.90 (*0-9621687-4-2*, B2BMSG) M Byrnes & Assocs.

Bumper-to-Bumper: The Instructor's Guide. Mike Byrnes & Associates Staff. (Illus.). xii, 448p. (C). 1992. Incls. The complete Guide to Tractor-Trailer Operations, 545p. 110.00 (*0-9621687-2-6*, B2BIG) M Byrnes & Assocs.

Bumpety Bump. Kathy Henderson. LC 93-3541. (Illus.). 24p. (J). (ps). 1994. 9.95 (*1-56402-312-5*) Candlewick Pr.

Bumping & Bouncing. Alison Lester. (Illus.). 16p. (J). (ps-00). 1989. pap. 3.50 (*0-670-81991-3*) Viking Child Bks.

Bumps Are What You Climb On. Warren W. Wiersbe. 1980. pap. 5.99 (*0-8010-9629-4*) Baker Bk.

Bumps in the Night. Harry Allard. (Illus.). (J). (gr. k-3). 1984. pap. 3.25 (*0-553-15711-6*, Skylark) Bantam.

***Bumps in the Road: Overcoming Obstacles on the Journey to Success.** Joseph L. Neely. 64p. 1995. 5.95 (*1-56245-192-8*) Great Quotations.

Bump's Umbrella. Christopher James. (Illus.). 24p. (J). (ps-3). 1990. 6.95 (*0-88625-277-6*) Durkin Hayes Pub.

***Bump's Umbrella.** Christopher James. 24p. (J). (ps). 1992. 6.49 (*1-881445-09-7*) Sandvik Pub.

Bumptious Buncombe. Franklin H. Stover. Tr. by Hans Ziegmar. 40p. (Orig.). 1989. pap. 7.00 (*0-931553-06-7*) Oneiric Pr.

Bumpy Johnson & Lumumba Odingo: Two Uncompromised Black Men in the Slavery Society Called the United States of America. Lumumba Odingo & H. Khalif Khalifah. (Illus.). 82p. (Orig.). Date not set. pap. 7.95 (*1-56411-013-3*) Untd Bros & Sis.

Bums: An Oral History of the Brooklyn Dodgers. Peter Golenbock. 1986. mass mkt. 4.95 (*0-671-55455-7*) PB.

Bums, Beatniks & Hippies. Ernie Bushmiller. Ed. by James Kitchen. LC 90-5155. (Ernie Bushmiller's Nancy Ser.). (Illus.). 1990. pap. 8.95 (*0-87816-113-9*) Kitchen Sink.

Bums Eat Shit & Other Poems. Sparrow Thirteen. 16p. (Orig.). 1990. pap. 3.00 (*0-916397-05-X*) Manic D Pr.

***Bums No More! The Championship Season of the 1955 Brooklyn Dodgers.** Stewart Wolpin. LC 94-48467. 1995. 25.00 (*0-312-11576-8*, Pub. by Thomas Dunne Bks) St Martin.

Bum's Rush: Phrases & Fallacies of Rush Limbaugh, the Selling of Environmental Backlash. Don T. Jacobs. Ed. by Beatrice Jacobs. LC 94-75645. 184p. 1994. pap. text ed. 12.00 (*0-9625040-5-X*) Legendary Pub.

Bun. William Maxwell. LC 93-42390. (J). 1995. 16.00 (*0-679-86053-3*); lib. bdg. 17.99 (*0-679-96053-8*) Knopf Bks Yng Read.

Buna-Kima or Theologia Africana, Vol. I. Omenana Staff. 200p. (Orig.). 1982. pap. 9.95 (*0-943324-03-3*) Omenana.

Bunch Grass: A Chronicle of Life on a Cattle Ranch. Horace A. Vachell. LC 75-178467. (Short Story Index Reprint Ser.). 1977. reprint ed. 21.95 (*0-8369-4068-7*) Ayer.

Bunch Grass Pioneer. Joe Smith. (Illus.). 79p. 1987. 12.00 (*0-87770-393-0*) Ye Galleon.

Bunch of Balloons: A Book - Workbook for Grieving Children. Dorothy Ferguson. (Illus.). (Orig.). (J). (gr. 1-6). 1992. pap. 5.95 (*1-56123-054-5*) Centering Corp.

Bunch of Fun Dramas. Wanda Pearce. LC 89-33094. (Orig.). 1990. pap. 6.99 (*0-8054-7528-1*) Broadman.

Bunches & Bunches of Bunnies. Louise Mathews. (Illus.). 32p. (J). (gr. k-3). 1991. reprint ed. pap. 3.95 (*0-590-44766-1*) Scholastic Inc.

Bunchies. Nancy Smith & Lynda Milligan. Ed. by Sharon Holmes. (Illus.). 1992. pap. 7.95 (*1-880972-03-4*) Pssblts Denver.

Bunco Book. Walter B. Gibson. 1986. pap. 9.95 (*0-8065-0990-2*, Citadel Pr) Carol Pub Group.

Bunco Kelly & Other Yarns of Portland & NW Oregon. Thomas K. Worcester. (Illus.). 80p. (Orig.). 1983. pap. 7.95 (*0-911518-66-5*) Touchstone Oregon.

Buncombe County, North Carolina, Index to Deeds, 1783-1850. James E. Wooley. 565p. 1983. 38.50 (*0-89308-294-5*) Southern Hist Pr.

Bundelkhand Kshetr Ke Krishi Padarth Vipanan Ka Vivechanatmak Mulyankan. D. C. Aggarwal. 331p. (HIN.). 1990. 44.00 (*81-7041-199-8*, Pub. by Scientific Pubs II) St Mut.

Bundes-Immissionsschutzgesetz. Klaus Hansmann. 511p. 1993. pap. 26.00 (*3-7890-3133-X*, Pub. by Nomos Verlags GW) Intl Bk Import.

Bundesanstalt fuer Geowissenschaften und Rohstoffe. Hermann Wagner. (Rohstoffwirtschaftliche Laenderberichte, No. XXX: U. S. A.-Stahlveredlerl, Molybdaen-Wolfram). 171p. (GER.). 1985. pap. text ed. 55.00 (*0-317-44695-9*) Lubrecht & Cramer.

Bundesarchiv of the Federal Republic of Germany, Koblenz. Ed. by Henry Friedlander & Sybil Milton. LC 89-16915. (Archives of the Holocaust Ser.: Vol. 20). 600p. 1993. 140.00 (*0-8240-5577-2*) Garland.

Bundesbank: Germany's Central Bank in the International Monetary System. Ellen Kennedy. (Chatham House Papers). 144p. 1991. pap. 14.95 (*0-87609-099-4*) Coun Foreign.

Bundesbuch (Ex 20,22-23,33) Studien zu Seiner Entstehung und Theologie. Ludger Schwienhorst-Schonberger. (Beiheft zur Zeitschrift fuer die Alttestamentliche Wissenschaft Ser.: Band 188). xiv, 468p. (C). 1990. lib. bdg. 129.25 (*3-11-012404-1*) De Gruyter.

Bundeswehr & Western Security. Ed. by Stephen F. Szabo. LC 89-24299. 288p. 1990. text ed. 59.95 (*0-312-04139-X*) St Martin.

Bundi: The Culture of a Papua New Guinea People. David G. Fitz-Patrick & John Kimbuna. (Illus.). 178p. 1983. 35.00 (*0-295-96233-X*) U of Wash Pr.

Bundle. Edward Bond. 98p. 1978. pap. 9.95 (*0-413-39360-7*, A0042, Pub. by Methuen UK) Heinemann.

Bundle from Britain. Alistair Horne. (Illus.). 352p. 1994. 23.95 (*0-312-11136-3*, Pub. by Thomas Dunne Bks) St Martin.

Bundle of Beasts. Patricia Hooper. LC 86-34413. (Illus.). 64p. (J). (gr. 3-7). 1987. 14.95 (*0-395-44259-1*) HM.

Bundle of Beasts. Patricia Hooper. (J). (gr. 4-7). 1992. pap. 3.95 (*0-395-61620-4*) HM.

Bundle of Elder Sticks. Helen G. Slonaker. 93p. 1984. 4.95 (*0-89697-169-4*) Intl Univ Pr.

Bundle of Grief...a Shovel of Stars: Collections of Poems by Writers in Maryland, Virginia, & the District of Columbia. Comp. & Pref. by Joseph D. Adams. (Poet's Domain Ser.: Vol. 4). xii, 84p. (Orig.). 1991. pap. 6.95 (*1-880016-07-9*) Road Pubs.

Bundle of Joy. Barbara Bretton. (American Romance Ser.: No. 393). 1991. mass mkt. 3.25 (*0-373-16393-2*) Harlequin Bks.

***Bundle of Joy.** large type ed. Barbara Bretton. (Sensation Ser.). 1994. 17.95 (*0-373-58868-2*, Silhouette Lrg Print) Chivers N Amer.

***Bundle of Joy: A Precious Gift.** Illus. by Murray Callahan. (Petites Ser.). 80p. 1995. 4.95 (*0-88088-772-9*) Peter Pauper.

Bundle of Letters see Lady Barbarina

Bundle of Nebraska Memories. enl. rev. ed. Patricia A. Schneider. (Illus.). 114p. 1991. 13.95 (*0-9624560-1-2*) P A Schneider.

Bundle of Nebraska Memories. exp. rev. ed. Patricia A. Schneider. Ed. by Clare S. Harkins. LC 89-92202. 72p. 1989. 12.95 (*0-9624560-0-4*) P A Schneider.

Bundle of Papyrus. Moelwyn Merchant. 124p. (C). 1989. pap. 22.00x (*0-86383-544-9*, Pub. by Gomer Pr UK) St Mut.

Bundle of Sticks. Pat R. Mauser. (J). 1994. 17.50 (*0-8446-6770-6*) Peter Smith.

Bundle of Sticks. Pat R. Mauser. LC 87-1074. (Illus.). 176p. (J). (gr. 3-6). 1987. reprint ed. pap. 3.95 (*0-689-71169-7*, Aladdin Paperbacks) S&S Childrens.

Bundling. H. R. Stiles. 1973. 59.95 (*0-87968-804-1*) Gordon Pr.

Bundling: Its Origin, Progress & Decline in America. Henry R. Stiles. LC 89-28243. 146p. 1992. 45.00 (*1-55888-893-4*) Omnigraphics Inc.

Bundling: Its Origin, Progress & Decline in America. Henry R. Stiles. LC 72-9681. reprint ed. 31.00 (*0-404-57499-8*) AMS Pr.

Bundling: Its Origins, Progress, & Decline in America. Henry R. Stiles. 146p. 1985. reprint ed. pap. 7.95 (*0-918222-72-9*) Applewood.

Bundt Cakes. Herbert & Plageman. LC 73-76681. (Illus.). 1973. pap. 2.95 (*0-915942-00-3*) SF Design.

Bungalow: A Novel. Lynn Freed. LC 92-24814. 1993. 21.00 (*0-671-75587-0*) S&S Trade.

***Bungalow: America's Arts & Crafts Home.** Paul Duchscherer. (Illus.). 128p. 1995. 27.95 (*0-670-86353-X*, Viking Studio); pap. 21.95 (*0-14-025156-1*, Viking Studio) Studio Bks.

***Bungalow: The Production of a Global Culture.** 2nd ed. Anthony D. King. (Illus.). 400p. 1995. pap. 19.95 (*0-19-509523-5*) OUP.

Bungalows, Camps & Mountain Houses. William P. Comstock & Clarence Schermerhorn. (Illus.). 151p. 1990. pap. 19.95 (*1-55835-063-2*) AIA Press.

Bungee Jumping. Bob Italia. LC 93-15331. (Action Sports Library). (J). (gr. 6 up). 1993. lib. bdg. 13.99 (*1-56239-230-1*) Abdo & Dghtrs.

Bungee Jumping for Fun & Profit. Nancy Frase. Ed. by Thomas Todd. LC 92-7104. (Illus.). 216p. (Orig.). 1992. pap. 12.99 (*0-934802-81-5*) ICS Bks.

Bungle Family: An Original Compilation. First Collection of One Year from the Daily Strip, 1928. Harry J. Tuthill. Ed. by Bill Blackbeard. LC 76-53057. (Classic American Comic Strips Ser.). (Illus.). 1977. 18.00 (*0-88355-669-3*) Hyperion Conn.

Bungle in the Jungle. John Bush & Paul Geraghty. (Illus.). 32p. (J). (ps-2). 1992. 17.95 (*0-09-174056-8*, Pub. by Hutchinson UK) Trafalgar.

Bungling in Kashmir. Balraj Madhok. 178p. 1975. pap. 2.85 (*0-88253-695-8*) Ind-US Inc.

Bungo Manual: Selected Reference Materials for Students of Classical Japanese. Helen C. McCullough. (Cornell East Asia Ser.: No. 48). 104p. 1993. reprint ed. 10.00 (*0-939657-03-1*) Cornell East Asia Pgm.

Bunk: Prelude to Depression. William E. Woodward. LC 76-22715. (Social & Intellectual History of American 1920's Ser.). 1976. reprint ed. lib. bdg. 35.00 (*0-306-70846-9*) Da Capo.

Bunk One. Donald R. Stoltz. Ed. by Gwen Costa. LC 90-22976. 100p. (Orig.). (YA). 1991. pap. 13.95 (*0-87949-346-1*) Ashley Bks.

Bunker & Me: Summer Adventures of Best Friends, Vol. I. Marta Effinger. Ed. by Lawrence & Penny. (Illus.). 30p. (J). (gr. 3-5). 1990. 12.95 (*0-929917-02-2*) Magnolia PA.

Bunker Archeology. Paul Virilio. (Illus.). 216p. (Orig.). 1994. pap. 34.95 (*1-56898-015-9*) Princeton Arch.

Bunker Climate Atlas of the North Atlantic Ocean: Observations, Vol. 1. H. J. Isemer. Ed. by L. Hasse. (Topics in Atmospheric & Oceanographic Sciences Ser.). (Illus.). 225p. 1985. 178.00 (*0-387-15568-6*) Spr-Verlag.

Bunker Family, Branches Early Identified with Charlestown & Nantucket, Mass., & Delaware & Maryland, As Well As Early Bunkers & Those in Europe. C. W. Bunker. 797p. 1993. reprint ed. lib. bdg. 125.00 (*0-8328-3556-0*); reprint ed. pap. 115.00 (*0-8328-3557-9*) Higginson Bk Co.

Bunker Genealogy, Ancestry & Descendants of Benjamin 3 (James 2, James 1) E. C. Moran, Jr. 232p. 1993. reprint ed. lib. bdg. 47.50 (*0-8328-3560-9*); reprint ed. pap. 37.50 (*0-8328-3561-7*) Higginson Bk Co.

Bunker Genealogy, Dover Branch, Vol. III. Edward C. Moran, Jr. 389p. 1993. reprint ed. lib. bdg. 69.50 (*0-8328-3554-4*); reprint ed. pap. 59.50 (*0-8328-3555-2*) Higginson Bk Co.

Bunker Genealogy, The Charlestown & Nantucket, Mass., Branches, & Some Unconnected Groups. E. C. Moran, Jr. 302p. 1993. reprint ed. lib. bdg. 56.50 (*0-8328-3558-7*); reprint ed. pap. 46.50 (*0-8328-3559-5*) Higginson Bk Co.

Bunker Hill: Notes & Queries on a Famous Battle, Notes & Queries on a Famous Battle. Harold Murdock. LC 68-58328. (Illus.). 1969. reprint ed. 15.00 (*0-87152-054-0*) Reprint.

***Bunker Hill Story.** Turner Publishing Company Staff. LC 94-61336. 128p. 1994. 48.00 (*1-56311-168-3*) Turner Pub KY.

Bunker Papers: Reports to the President from Vietnam, 1967-1973, 3 vols., Set. Ed. by Douglas Pike. (Indochina Research Monograph). 902p. 1990. pap. 35.00 (*1-55729-019-9*) IEAS.

***Bunkers.** 2nd ed. Christopher Fisher & Jonathan Lux. 1994. 105.00 (*1-85044-522-2*) Lloyds London Pr.

Bunkhouse Journal. Diane J. Hamm. LC 90-8062. 96p. (YA). (gr. 7 up). 1990. text ed. 13.95 (*0-684-19206-3*, C Scribner Sons Young) S&S Childrens.

Bunkhouse Man: A Study of Work & Play in the Camps of Canada, 1903-1914. Edmund W. Bradwin. LC 68-57564. (Columbia University. Studies in the Social Sciences: No. 296). reprint ed. 20.00 (*0-404-51296-8*) AMS Pr.

Bunnicula: A Rabbit Tale of Mystery. Deborah Howe & James Howe. LC 78-11472. (Illus.). 112p. (J). (gr. 4-6). 1979. text ed. 14.00 (*0-689-30700-4*, Atheneum Bks Young) S&S Childrens.

Bunnicula: A Rabbit-Tale of Mystery. Deborah Howe & James Howe. (Illus.). 100p. (J). (gr. 3-7). 1980. pap. 3.99 (*0-380-51094-4*, Camelot) Avon.

Bunnicula: A Study Guide. Barbara Reeves. Ed. by Joyce Friedland & Rikki Kessler. (Novel-Ties Ser.). (J). (gr. 2-5). 1991. pap. text ed. 15.95 (*0-88122-572-X*) Lrn Links.

Bunnicula: The Vampire Bunny & His Friends, 4 vols. James Howe. 1986. pap. 14.00 (*0-380-70910-4*, Camelot) Avon.

Bunnicula: The Vampire Bunny & His Friends, 4 vols., Set. James Howe. 1986. boxed, pap. 10.00 (*0-380-70281-9*, Camelot) Avon.

Bunnicula Escapes! A Pop-Up Adventure. James Howe. (Illus.). 12p. (J). (ps up). 1995. 14.95 (*0-688-13212-X*, Tupelo Bks) Morrow Jr Bks.

Bunnicula Fun Book. James Howe. LC 92-34561. (Illus.). 176p. (J). 1993. pap. 9.95 (*0-688-11952-2*) Morrow Jr Bks.

Bunnies. Illus. by Pat Paris. (Baby Animal Pop-Up Bks.). 10p. (J). (ps). 1989. 4.95 (*0-8120-5990-5*) Barron.

Bunnies & Their Hobbies. Nancy Carlson. LC 83-23161. (Illus.). 32p. (J). (ps-3). 1984. lib. bdg. 14.95 (*0-87614-257-9*, Carolrhoda) Lerner Group.

Bunnies & Their Sports. Nancy Carlson. (Illus.). 32p. (J). (ps-3). 1989. pap. 4.99 (*0-14-050617-9*, Puffin) Puffin Bks.

Bunnies' Ball. Annie Ingle. LC 93-8536. (Pictureback Ser.). (Illus.). (J). 1994. pap. 2.50 (*0-685-70891-8*) Random Bks Yng Read.

Bunnies' Ball. Katharine Ross. LC 92-29930. (Pictureback Ser.). (Illus.). (J). 1994. 2.50 (*0-679-83503-2*) Random Bks Yng Read.

Bunnies, Bears & Birthdays. Marti Abbott & Betty J. Polk. 1991. 10.99 (*0-8224-0638-1*) Fearon Teach Aids.

Bunnies, Bunnies, Bunnies. Retan. (J). 1995. pap. 7.95 (*0-671-88247-3*, S&S Bks Young Read) S&S Childrens.

Bunnies, Bunnies, Bunnies. Ed. by Walter Retan. LC 90-41486. (Illus.). 96p. (J). (ps-2). 1991. pap. 14.95 (*0-671-73221-8*, S&S Bks Young Read) S&S Childrens.

Bunnies Count to Ten. (Through the Window Ser.). (Illus.). 10p. (J). 1994. write for info. (*0-307-16352-0*) Western Pub.

Bunnies' Easter Bonnet. Nan Roloff & Amy Flynn. LC 94-6728. (Illus.). (J). 1994. 2.25 (*0-448-40739-6*, G&D) Putnam Pub Group.

Bunnies Love. Illus. by Lisa McCue. LC 90-61307. 24p. (J). (ps-1). 1991. 4.95 (*0-679-80385-8*) Random Bks Yng Read.

Bunnies on Their Own. Amy Ehrlich. LC 85-20467. (Illus.). 32p. (J). (ps-2). 1992. pap. 3.99 (*0-8037-1138-7*, Puff Pied Piper) Puffin Bks.

Bunnikin's Picnic Party. (Rhyming Stories Ser.: No. 401-1). (Illus.). (J). (ps-k). pap. 3.50 (*0-7214-0206-2*) Ladybird Bks.

Bunny. Anne T. Perkins. (Big Books - Mini Bks.). (Illus.). 8p. (J). 1993. 12.00 (*1-884204-02-3*) Teach Nxt Door.

Bunny: A Bio-Discography of Jazz Trumpeter Bunny Berigan. Vince Danca. (Illus.). (Orig.). 1978. pap. 5.50 (*0-9602390-1-4*) V Danca.

Bunny: A Storybook for Children Who Have a Parent with Multiple Personalities. Lauren Lund. (Illus.). 36p. (Orig.). (J). 1993. pap. text ed. 5.95 (*0-9637149-1-0*) Soft Words.

Bunny Berigan: Elusive Legend of Jazz. Robert Dupuis. LC 99-21408. (Illus.). xxii, 392p. 1993. 24.95 (*0-8071-1648-3*) La State U Pr.

Bunny Big & Little. Gorbaty. (Pet Parade Bks.). (J). 1995. 4.50 (*0-671-89837-X*, Litl Simon S&S) S&S Childrens.

Bunny Book. John D'Hondt. (Illus.). 276p. (Orig.). 1991. pap. 11.95 (*1-879194-05-8*) GLB Pubs.

Bunny Book. Richard Scarry. (Golden Super Shape Bks.). (Illus.). 24p. (J). (ps-00). 1987. pap. write for info. (*0-307-10048-0*, Golden Bks) Western Pub.

Bunny Book. 3rd ed. Susan O. Higgins. Ed. by V. I. Wexner. (Holiday Ser.). (Illus.). 76p. (J). (ps-3). 1985. reprint ed. pap. 3.95 (*0-939973-03-0*) Pumpkin Pr Pub Hse.

Bunny Books. Laura C. Busch. (Little Readers Ser.). (J). (ps-2). 1990. 13.95 (*1-880642-06-9*) Little Read.

Bunny Box. Lena Anderson. (Bunny Ser.). (Illus.). 20p. (J). (ps). 1991. bds. 3.95 (*91-29-59858-3*) FS&G.

Bunny, Bunny. K. Hall. (My First Reader Ser.). (Illus.). 28p. (J). (ps-2). 1990. 10.50 (*0-516-05352-3*); pap. 3.95 (*0-516-45352-1*) Childrens.

Bunny Bunny: Gilda Radner: A Sort of Love Story. Alan Zweibel. 1994. 14.95 (*0-679-43085-7*, Villard Bks) Random.

Bunny Butz Sings the Blues. Sha Gaff. LC 91-67753. (Illus.). 70p. (J). 1993. pap. 7.00 (*1-56002-161-6*, Univ Edtns) Aegina Pr.

Bunny Days. Marilynn G. Barr. (Illus.). 48p. (J). (ps-1). 1993. pap. 5.95 (*1-878279-54-8*) Monday Morning Bks.

Bunny Fun. Lena Anderson. (Bunny Ser.). (Illus.). 20p. (J). (ps). 1991. bds. 3.95 (*91-29-59860-5*) FS&G.

Bunny Honey Springtime Search. Tony Tallarico. (Where Are They? Ser.). (Illus.). 24p. (J). 1992. pap. 3.95 (*1-56156-099-5*) Kidsbks.

Bunny Hop. Teddy Slater. (Illus.). 32p. (J). 1992. pap. 2.95 (*0-590-45354-8*, Cartwheel) Scholastic Inc.

Bunny Lake Is Missing. large type ed. Evelyn Piper. LC 92-28645. (Nightingale Ser.). 320p. 1993. pap. 15.95 (*0-8161-5634-4*, Nightingale) Hall.

Bunny Magic. Chris Cahill. LC 89-61633. (Rhyme-Fingerplay-Puppet Book Ser.). (Illus.). 12p. (J). (ps-1). 1990. bds. 5.95 (*1-877779-02-4*) Schneider Educational.

Bunny Mitten's Book. Judith Blau. (Illus.). 7p. (J). (ps). 1991. 5.95 (*0-679-81315-2*) Random Bks Yng Read.

Bunny Party. Illus. by Lena Anderson. (Bunny Ser.). (J). (ps). 1989. bds. 3.95 (*91-29-59134-1*, Pub. by R & S Bks) FS&G.

Bunny Play. Loreen Leedy. LC 87-17793. (Illus.). 32p. (J). (ps-3). 1988. lib. bdg. 12.95 (*0-8234-0679-2*) Holiday.

Bunny Rabbit Birthday Stickers. Susan W. Labelle. (Illus.). (J). (gr. k-3). 1992. pap. 1.00 (*0-486-27326-1*) Dover.

Bunny Rabbits in Mother Gooseland. Ruth Waldrop. LC 86-61389. (Illus.). (Orig.). (J). (ps-3). 1987. pap. 4.95 (*0-317-59032-4*); audio 4.95 (*0-317-59033-2*) RuSK Inc.

Bunny Rattle. Illus. by Cheryl Harte. (Learning Ladders Ser.). 12p. (J). (ps). 1989. 5.99 (*0-394-89956-3*) Random Bks Yng Read.

Bunny Riddles. Katy Hall & Lisa Eisenberg. LC 93-13241. (Illus.). (J). (ps-4). 1995. write for info. (*0-8037-1519-6*); lib. bdg. write for info. (*0-8037-1521-8*) Dial Bks Young.

Bunny Runs Away. Bernice Chardiet & Grace Maccarone. (J). 1992. pap. 2.50 (*0-590-44932-X*) Scholastic Inc.

Bunny Story. Illus. by Lena Anderson. (Bunny Ser.). (J). (ps). 1989. bds. 3.95 (*91-29-59132-5*, Pub. by R & S Bks) FS&G.

Bunny Trouble. Hans Wilhelm. (Illus.). 40p. (Orig.). (J). (ps-3). 1987. pap. 6.95 (*0-590-63198-5*) Scholastic Inc.

Bunny Trouble. Hans Wilhelm. (Illus.). 40p. (Orig.). (J). (ps-3). 1991. 3.95 (*0-590-45042-5*); Book & cassette. audio 6.95 (*0-590-63153-5*) Scholastic Inc.

Bunny Who Found Easter. Charlotte Zolotow. (Illus.). 32p. (J). (gr. k-3). 1983. 14.95 (*0-395-27677-2*); pap. 5.95 (*0-395-34068-3*) HM.

Bunnykins in the Kitchen. Warrener. (J). 1987. 4.95 (*0-670-80569-6*) Viking Child Bks.

Bunny's ABC Box. Maida Silverman. (Little Poke & Look Bks.). (Illus.). 24p. (J). (ps-1). 1986. pap. 3.95 (*0-448-01464-5*, G&D) Putnam Pub Group.

Bunny's Alphabet Eggs. Lisa Bassett. LC 92-37987. (Illus.). (J). (gr. 2 up). 1993. 3.99 (*0-517-08153-9*) Random Hse Value.

Bunny's Birthday. Michelle Cartlidge. (Chunky Bks.). (Illus.). 24p. (J). (ps). 1992. bds. 2.95 (*0-525-44843-8*, DCB) Dutton Child Bks.

Bunny's Easter Basket. Stephanie St. Pierre. (Pudgy Pop-up Board Bks.). (Illus.). 12p. (J). (ps). 1994. bds. 4.95 (*0-448-40461-3*, G&D) Putnam Pub Group.

Bunny's Hungry. Muff Singer. LC 93-85485. (Squeeze-&-Squeak Bks.). (J). (ps). 1994. 4.99 (*0-89577-566-2*) RD Assn.

Bunny's Night Out. Roni Schotter. (Illus.). 32p. (J). (ps-3). 1989. 13.95 (*0-316-77465-0*, Joy St Bks) Little.

Bunny's Numbers. Dick McCue. (Animal Shape Board Bks.). (Illus.). 24p. (J). (ps). 1984. pap. 2.95 (*0-671-50944-6*, Litl Simon S&S) S&S Childrens.

Bunny's Nutshell Library, 4 bks., Set. Robert Kraus. Incl. First Robin. LC 65-11450. 1965. (*0-06-023285-4*); Juniper. LC 65-11450. 1965. (*0-06-023295-1*); Silver Dandelion. LC 65-11450. 1965. (*0-06-023300-1*); Springfellow's Parade. LC 65-11450. 1965. (*0-318-52914-9*); LC 65-11450. (Illus.). (J). (gr. 1 up). 1965. 10.95 (*0-06-023225-0*) HarpC Child Bks.

***Bunny's Treehouse Tales.** 1995. 7.99 (*0-88705-856-6*) Joshua Morris.

Bunnysitters. Kate Banks. LC 90-27441. (Stepping Stone Bks.). (Illus.). 80p. (Orig.). (J). (gr. 2-4). 1991. pap. 2.50 (*0-679-81232-6*) Random Bks Yng Read.

***Bunratty: Rebirth of a Castle.** Bernard Share. 190p. Date not set. pap. 11.95 (*0-86322-206-4*, Pub. by Brandon Bk Pubs IE) Irish Bks Media.

Buns & Puns. Rebecca Brown. (Illus.). 144p. (Orig.). 1995. pap. 14.95 (*1-884415-00-8*) Amber Pubng.

Buns of Steel Total Body Workout. Leisa Hart & Liz Neporent. (Illus.). 272p. (Orig.). 1995. pap. 13.99 (*0-446-67089-8*) Warner Bks.

Buns Travels Across America. Cottonpaw. (Illus.). 48p. (J). (gr. k-5). 1992. pap. 7.95 (*1-881274-01-2*) Cotton Tale.

An Asterisk (*) at the beginning of an entry indicates that the title is appearing in BIP for the first time.

B

An Asterisk (*) at the beginning of an entry indicates that the title is appearing in BIP for the first time.

951

Bureaucracy, Economy, & Leadership in China: The Institutional Origins of the Great Leap Forward. David Bachman. 1991. 54.95 (*0-521-40275-1*) Cambridge U Pr.

Bureaucracy, Economy, & Leadership in China: The Institutional Origins of the Great Leap Forward. David Bachman. 242p. (C). 1991. write for info. (*0-521-40269-7*) Cambridge U Pr.

Bureaucracy in a Democracy. Charles Hyneman. LC 74-6023. reprint ed. 34.50 (*0-404-11549-7*) AMS Pr.

Bureaucracy in Modern Society. 2nd ed. Peter M. Blau. (Orig.). 1971. pap. text ed. write for info. (*0-394-31452-2*) Random.

Bureaucracy in Modern Society. 3rd ed. Peter M. Blau & Marshall W. Meyer. 180p. (Orig.). (C). 1987. pap. text ed. write for info. (*0-07-555033-4*) McGraw.

Bureaucracy in Pakistan. Charles H. Kennedy. 268p. 1988. 24.00 (*0-19-577364-0*) OUP.

Bureaucracy in the Modern State: An Introduction to Comparative Public Administration. Ed. by Jon Pierre. LC 94-6261. 1995. 69.95 (*1-85278-725-2*, Pub. by E Elgar Pub UK) Ashgate Pub Co.

Bureaucracy of the "Statist Reserve" The Case of the U. S. A. Stephan Leibfried. (Western Societies Papers). 117p. 1979. 11.95 (*0-8014-9634-9*) Cornell U Pr.

Bureaucracy on Trial: Policy Making by Government Agencies. William W. Boyer. LC 63-16942. 1964. 19.95 (*0-672-51129-0*) Irvington.

Bureaucracy, Organisational Behaviour, & Development. Prayag Mehta. 188p. (C). 1989. text ed. 24.00 (*0-8039-9614-4*) Sage.

Bureaucracy, Politics, & Decision Making in Post-Mao China. Ed. by Kenneth G. Lieberthal & David M. Lampton. LC 91-9476. (Studies on China: Vol. 14). (Illus.). 384p. 1992. 45.00 (*0-520-07356-8*) U CA Pr.

Bureaucracy, Politics & Public Policy. 3rd ed. Francis E. Rourke. (C). 1987. pap. text ed. 15.50 (*0-673-39475-1*) HarpCollege.

Bureaucracy Problem. James Q. Wilson. (Reprint Series in Political Science). (C). 1993. reprint ed. pap. text ed. 1.00 (*0-8290-3686-5*, PS-578) Irvington.

Bureaucracy, Technology, Ideology: Quality of Life East & West. Bogdan Mieczkowski & Oleg Zinam. LC 84-71093. (Issue Studies (U. S. S. R. & East Europe): No. 5). 463p. (Orig.). 1984. pap. 28.00 (*0-910895-02-3*) Assn Study Nat.

Bureaucracy vs Creativity: The Dilemna of Modern Leadership. Frederick C. Dyer & John M. Dyer. LC 65-25638. (Business & Economics Ser.: No. 9). 1965. 10.95 (*0-87024-134-6*) U of Miami Pr.

Bureaucracy vs. Environment: The Environmental Costs of Bureaucratic Governance. Ed. by John Baden & Richard L. Stroup. 248p. (C). 1981. text ed. 27.50 (*0-472-10010-6*) U of Mich Pr.

Bureaucrat & Intellectual in the Ottoman Empire: The Historian Mustafa Ali (1541-1600) Cornell H. Fleischer. LC 85-43277. (Near East Studies). (Illus.). 368p. 1986. text ed. 59.50x (*0-691-05464-9*) Princeton U Pr.

Bureaucrat & Intellectual in the Ottoman Empire: The Historian Mustafa Ali (1541-1600) Cornell H. Fleischer. LC 85-43277. (Princeton Studies on the Near East). 406p. reprint ed. pap. 115.80 (*0-7837-6770-6*, 2046600) Bks Demand.

Bureaucratic & Governmental Reform. Donald J. Calista. LC 86-27482. (Public Policy Studies: Vol. 9). 1986. 73.25 (*0-89232-375-2*) Jai Pr.

Bureaucratic Authoritarianism: Argentina, 1966-1973 - In Comparative Perspective. Guillermo O'Donnell. 1988. 52.50 (*0-520-04260-3*) U CA Pr.

Bureaucratic Blunder World: A Behaviorial Profile of the Indian Bureaucracy. K. K. Khanna. 1985. 17.50 (*0-8364-1473-X*, Pub. by National Sahitya Akademi) S Asia.

Bureaucratic Culture in India. Damyanti Bhatnager. (C). 1989. 26.00 (*81-7033-066-1*, Pub. by Rawat II) S Asia.

Bureaucratic Democracy: The Search for Democracy & Efficiency in American Government. Douglas Yates. (C). 1982. pap. text ed. 9.95 (*0-685-48475-0*) HUP.

Bureaucratic Democracy: The Search for Democracy & Efficiency in American Government. Douglas Yates. LC 81-7235. (Illus.). 288p. 1982. 32.00 (*0-674-08611-2*) HUP.

Bureaucratic Democracy: The Search for Democracy & Efficiency in American Government. Douglas Yates. LC 81-7235. 288p. 1987. pap. text ed. 11.95 (*0-674-08612-0*) HUP.

Bureaucratic Discretion: Law & Policy in Federal Regulatory Agencies. Gary C. Bryner. (Government & Politics Ser.). 240p. 1987. 50.00 (*0-08-034494-1*, Pergamon Pr); pap. 18.95 (*0-08-034493-3*, Pergamon Pr) Elsevier.

***Bureaucratic Dynamics: The Roles.** B. Dan Wood. (Transforming American Politics Ser.). (C). 1994. pap. text ed. 19.95 (*0-8133-1847-5*) Westview.

***Bureaucratic Dynamics: The Roles.** B. Dan Wood. (Transforming American Politics Ser.). (C). 1994. text ed. 59.95 (*0-8133-1846-7*) Westview.

Bureaucratic Encounters: A Pilot Study in the Evaluation of Government Services. Daniel Katz et al. LC 74-620202. 270p. 1975. 16.00 (*0-87944-173-9*) Inst Soc Res.

Bureaucratic Encounters: A Pilot Study in the Evaluation of Government Services. Daniel Katz et al. LC 74-620202. 280p. reprint ed. pap. 79.80 (*0-7837-5280-6*, 2045018) Bks Demand.

***Bureaucratic Experience: A Critique of Life in the Modern Organization.** 4th ed. Ralph P. Hummel. 304p. 1994. pap. text ed. 17.50 (*0-312-09554-6*) St Martin.

Bureaucratic Government: U. S. A. David Nachmias & David H. Rosenbloom. 269p. (Orig.). 1980. pap. text ed. 16.00 (*0-312-10806-0*) St Martin.

Bureaucratic Justice. Jerry L. Mashaw. LC 82-17506. 242p. 1983. text ed. 45.00 (*0-300-02808-3*) Yale U Pr.

Bureaucratic Justice: Managing Social Security Disability Claims. Jerry L. Mashaw. LC 82-17506. 242p. 1985. reprint ed. pap. 16.00 (*0-300-03403-2*, Y-526) Yale U Pr.

Bureaucratic Labor Market: The Case of the Federal Civil Service. T. A. DiPrete. (Studies & Work & Industry). (Illus.). 358p. 1989. 49.50 (*0-306-43184-X*, Plenum Pr) Plenum.

Bureaucratic Malpractice: Hospital Regulation in N. J. 120p. 1974. 17.00 (*0-943136-03-2*) Ctr Analysis Public Issues.

Bureaucratic Mercy: The Home Office & the Treatment of Capital Cases in Victorian Britain. Roger Chadwick. LC 91-45919. (Modern European History Ser.). 432p. 1992. 104.00 (*0-8153-0740-3*) Garland.

***Bureaucratic Merry-Go-Round: Manipulating the Transfer of Indian Civil Servants.** Frank De Zwart. 250p. 1994. pap. 39.50 (*90-5356-132-3*) IBD Ltd.

Bureaucratic Personality & Organization Structure. Christopher Allinson. LC 84-18680. 168p. 1984. text ed. 65.00 (*0-566-00712-6*) Ashgate Pub Co.

Bureaucratic Policy Making in a Technological Society. Gerard S. Gryski. 241p. 1981. 18.95 (*0-87073-831-5*); pap. text ed. 11.95 (*0-87073-829-1*) Schenkman Bks Inc.

***Bureaucratic Politics: Executive Reorganization During the Truman Administration.** William E. Pemberton. LC 78-2990. 270p. 1979. reprint ed. pap. 77.00 (*0-7837-8850-9*, AU00454) Bks Demand.

Bureaucratic Politics & Foreign Policy. Morton H. Halperin et al. LC 73-22384. 340p. 1974. pap. 14.95 (*0-8157-3407-7*) Brookings.

Bureaucratic Politics & Regulatory Reform: The EPA & Emissions Trading. Brian J. Cook. LC 87-15032. (Contributions in Political Science Ser.: No. 196). 181p. 1988. text ed. 45.00 (*0-313-25493-1*, CBC/, Greenwood Pr) Greenwood.

Bureaucratic Reform in Provincial China: Ting Jih-ch'ang in Restoration Kiangsu, 1867-1870. Jonathan K. Ocko. (East Asian Monographs: No. 103). 316p. 1983. 28.00 (*0-674-08617-1*) HUP.

Bureaucratic Reform in the Ottoman Empire: The Sublime Porte, 1789-1922. Carter V. Findley. LC 79-22162. (Princeton Studies on the Near East). 493p. reprint ed. pap. 140.60 (*0-7837-0232-9*, 2040540) Bks Demand.

Bureaucratic Responsibility. John P. Burke. LC 85-45866. 288p. 1986. text ed. 45.00x (*0-8018-3009-5*) Johns Hopkins.

Bureaucratic Transition in Malaya. Robert O. Tilman. LC 64-20418. 187p. reprint ed. pap. 53.30 (*0-8357-7477-5*, 2026216) Bks Demand.

Bureaucratisation in Northwestern Europe 1880-1985: Domination & Governance. Rolf Torstendahl. 272p. (C). 1991. text ed. 75.00 (*0-415-00026-2*, A4916) Routledge.

Bureaucratization of Socialism. Donald C. Hodges. LC 80-23253. 224p. 1981. lib. bdg. 27.50 (*0-87023-138-3*) U of Mass Pr.

Bureaucratization of the World. Henry Jacoby. LC 74-166224. 1973. pap. 15.00 (*0-520-03044-3*) U CA Pr.

Bureaucratization of the World. Bruno Rizzi. Tr. by Adam Westoby. 272p. (C). 1985. 19.95 (*0-02-927140-1*) Free Pr.

Bureaucratizing the Muse: Public Funds & the Cultural Worker. Steven C. Dubin. LC 86-30862. (Illus.). 248p. (C). 1987. 28.50 (*0-226-16748-8*) U Ch Pr.

Bureaucrats. Honore De Balzac. Tr. by Charles Foulkes. (European Classics Ser.). 300p. 1993. 39.95 (*0-8101-0973-5*); pap. 14.95 (*0-8101-0987-5*) Northwestern U Pr.

Bureaucrats & Beggars: French Social Policy in the Age of the Enlightenment. Thomas M. Adams. (Illus.). 364p. 1991. 49.95 (*0-19-505168-8*) OUP.

Bureaucrats & Brainpower: Government Regulation of Universities. Paul Seabury et al. LC 79-51328. 171p. 1979. pap. text ed. 18.95 (*0-917616-35-9*) Transaction Pubs.

Bureaucrats & Ministers in Contemporary Japanese Government. Yung H. Park. LC 85-82273. (Japan Research Monograph: No. 8). 192p. 1986. pap. 7.50 (*0-912966-84-X*) IEAS.

Bureaucrats & People: Grassroots Participation in Third World Development. John D. Montgomery. LC 87-15344. (Studies in Development). 160p. 1988. text ed. 28.00 (*0-8018-3541-0*) Johns Hopkins.

Bureaucrats & Policy Making: A Comparative Overview. Ed. by Ezra N. Suleiman. LC 83-17171. 320p. 1985. 39.95 (*0-8419-0847-8*); pap. 18.95 (*0-8419-1021-9*) Holmes & Meier.

Bureaucrats & Politicians in Western Democracies. Joel D. Aberbach et al. 322p. 1982. pap. 15.95 (*0-674-08627-9*) HUP.

Bureaucrats, Clients, & Geography: The Bailly Nuclear Power Plant Battle in Northern Indiana. Nancy J. Obermeyer. (Research Papers Ser.: No. 216). (Illus.). 140p. 1989. pap. write for info. (*0-89065-121-3*) U Chicago Comm Geo.

Bureaucrats of Buenos Aires, 1769-1810: Amor al Real Servicio. Susan M. Socolow. (Illus.). xxi, 356p. (C). 1987. lib. bdg. 48.00 (*0-8223-0753-7*) Duke.

Bureaucrats, Planters, & Workers: The Making of the Tobacco Monopoly in Bourbon Mexico. Susan Deans-Smith. 384p. (C). 1992. text ed. 40.00x (*0-292-70786-X*) U of Tex Pr.

***Bureaucrat's Yarns.** Sayan Chatterjee. (C). 1994. text ed. 15.00 (*81-241-0228-7*, Pub. by Har-Anand Pubns II) S Asia.

Burebs l'Epoque de Philippe II. Francis Brumont. Ed. by Stuart Bruchey. LC 77-81824. (Dissertations in European Economic History Ser.). (Illus.). (FRE.). 1978. lib. bdg. 29.95 (*0-405-10776-5*) Ayer.

Burelain. Richard Jorif. 222p. (FRE.). 1991. pap. 10.95 (*0-7859-2614-3*, 2070383733) Fr & Eur.

Burford NDU Model: Caring in Practice. Ed. by Christopher Johns. LC 94-12532. 1994. write for info. (*0-632-03886-1*) Blackwell Sci.

Burg: An Italian-American Community at Bay in Trenton. Peter A. Peroni. LC 79-63258. 1979. pap. text ed. 19.00 (*0-8191-0724-7*) U Pr of Amer.

Burgage Tenure in Mediaeval England. Morley de Wolf Hemmeon. (Harvard Historical Studies). ix, 234p. 1986. reprint ed. 32.50 (*0-8377-2233-0*) Rothman.

Burgano Bride. large type ed. Nina Shaldon. (Linford Romance Library). 304p. 1992. pap. 14.95 (*0-7089-7137-7*, Linford) Ulverscroft.

***Burgee: Premier Northwest Marina Guide.** David Kutz. LC 94-99234. (Illus.). 190p. 1994. pap. 19.95 (*0-9641934-9-3*) Pierside Pub.

Burger Book. Larry Zisman & Honey Zisman. 128p. 1994. mass mkt. 3.99 (*0-312-95274-0*) St Martin.

Burger Book: Dozens of Recipes for Juicy Burgers & Delicious Side Dishes. rev. ed. Larry Zisman & Honey Zisman. 128p. (Orig.). 1993. pap. 10.95 (*0-312-09256-3*) St Martin.

Burger Court: Political & Judicial Profiles. Ed. by Charles M. Lamb & Stephen C. Halpern. (Illus.). 528p. 1991. 49.95 (*0-252-01733-1*); pap. 19.95 (*0-252-06135-7*) U of Ill Pr.

Burger Court: The Counter-Revolution That Wasn't. Vincent Blasi. LC 83-5828. 320p. 1986. pap. 17.00 (*0-300-03620-5*) Yale U Pr.

Burger, Fries & a Friend to Go. Fran Sciacca & Jill Sciacca. (Lifelines Ser.). (YA). (gr. 7 up). 1987. pap. 3.95 (*0-89066-097-2*) World Wide Pubs.

Burger Meisters. Marcel Desaulniers. LC 93-13662. 1994. 20.00 (*0-671-86538-2*) S&S Trade.

Burger Time. Carol Taylor. LC 93-9281. (Voyages Ser.). (Illus.). (J). 1994. pap. write for info. (*0-383-03678-X*) SRA Schl Grp.

Burger's Daughter. Nadine Gordimer. 362p. 1980. pap. 11.95 (*0-14-005593-2*, Penguin Bks) Viking Penguin.

Burgers, Fries, & a Friend to Go: Making Friends. Fran Sciacca & Jill Sciacca. (Lifelines Ser.). 64p. (YA). 1992. pap. 3.99 (*0-310-48041-8*) Zondervan.

Burger's Medicinal Chemistry & Drug Discovery. 5th ed. Ed. by Manfred E. Wolff. LC 94-12687. 1994. text ed. 195.00 (*0-471-57556-9*) Wiley.

Burgers 'N Fries 'N Cinnamon Buns. Bobbie E. Hinman. 56p. 1992. pap. 5.00 (*0-9632524-0-2*) B E Hinman.

Burgers 'N Fries 'N Cinnamon Buns: Low Fat, Meatless Versions of Fast Food Favorites. rev. ed. Bobbie Hinman. LC 93-26027. 80p. 1993. pap. 6.95 (*0-913990-16-7*) Book Pub Co.

Burgers on the Moon. Benjamin K. Bennett. (Illus.). 10p. (Orig.). (J). 1990. pap. 2.00 (*0-935350-21-7*) Luna Bisonte.

Burgess: Colonists of New England & Nova Scotia. Kenneth F. Burgess. (Illus.). 134p. 1991. reprint ed. lib. bdg. 34.00 (*0-8328-2213-2*); reprint ed. pap. 24.00 (*0-8328-2214-0*) Higginson Bk Co.

Burgess Animal Book for Children. Thornton W. Burgess. (J). 28.95 (*0-8488-0716-2*) Amereon Ltd.

Burgess Bird Book for Children. Thornton W. Burgess. (J). 24.95 (*0-8488-0404-X*) Amereon Ltd.

***Burgess Book of Lies.** Adrian Burgess & Alan Burgess. (Illus.). 480p. 1994. 30.00 (*0-938567-38-1*) Cloudcap.

Burgess Families in the Nineteen Hundred Soundex. Susan Mortensen. (Borgo Family Histories Ser.: No. 5). 160p. Date not set. lib. bdg. write for info. (*0-89370-823-2*); pap. write for info. (*0-89370-923-9*) Borgo Pr.

Burgess Flower Book for Children. Thornton W. Burgess. 21.95 (*0-8488-0717-0*) Amereon Ltd.

Burgess Genealogy: Kings Co., Nova Scotia Branch of the Descendants of Thomas & Dorothy Burgess. B. H. Burgess. (Illus.). 99p. 1990. reprint ed. lib. bdg. 28.50 (*0-8328-1450-4*); reprint ed. pap. 18.50 (*0-8328-1451-2*) Higginson Bk Co.

Burgess Genealogy Memorial of the Family of Thomas & Dorothy Burgess, Who Were Settled at Sandwich, in the Plymouth Colony in 1637. Ebenezer Burgess. (Illus.). 212p. 1989. reprint ed. lib. bdg. 36.50 (*0-8328-0344-8*); reprint ed. pap. 26.50 (*0-8328-0345-6*) Higginson Bk Co.

Burgess, Mullins, Browning, Brown, & Allied Families. James A. Burgess. LC 78-59336. vi, 262p. 1985. reprint ed. lib. bdg. 23.00x (*0-89370-870-4*) Borgo Pr.

Burgess Sea Shore Book for Children. Thornton W. Burgess. (J). 24.95 (*0-8488-0403-1*) Amereon Ltd.

Burgess Shale. Harry B. Whittington. LC 85-2297. 166p. reprint ed. pap. 47.40 (*0-7837-3332-1*, 2057739) Bks Demand.

Burgess Shale Book. Lisa W. Peters. (J). 1995. 15.95 (*0-8050-2419-0*) H Holt & Co.

Burgess Unabridged: A New Dictionary of Words You Have Always Needed. Gelett Burgess. LC 83-46013. (Classics of Modern American Humor Ser.). (Illus.). reprint ed. 27.50 (*0-404-19928-3*) AMS Pr.

Burgh Records of the City of Glasgow. Ed. by John Smith. LC 71-168149. (Maitland Club, Glasgow. Publications: No. 16). reprint ed. 20.00 (*0-404-52952-6*) AMS Pr.

Burgher & Peasant. Catherine Rapp. LC 75-140039. (Catholic University Studies in German: No. 7). reprint ed. 37.50 (*0-404-50227-X*) AMS Pr.

Burglar. David Goodis. LC 90-50598. 160p. 1991. pap. 8.00 (*0-679-73472-4*, Vin) Random.

Burglar. David Goodis. LC 88-71698. 160p. 1989. reprint ed. pap. 7.95 (*0-88739-131-1*, Blk Lizard) Creat Arts Bk.

Burglar Alarm Systems. Capel. 1979. pap. 22.95 (*0-408-00405-3*) Buttrwrth-Heinemann.

Burglar Alarm Systems, 1995. American Business Directories Staff. 1995. spiral bd., pap. 980.00 (*1-56105-598-0*) Am Busn Direct.

Burglar Alarm Trade: Systems, Equipment & Installation Methods. 1991. lib. bdg. 79.95 (*0-8490-4757-9*) Gordon Pr.

Burglar Bill. Allan Ahlberg. (Picture Puffins Ser.). (Illus.). (J). 1992. pap. 3.99 (*0-14-050301-3*) Viking Child Bks.

***Burglar in the Closet: A Bernie Rhodenbarr Mystery.** Lawrence Block. LC 95-9857. 256p. 1995. 20.95 (*0-525-93993-8*, Dutton) NAL-Dutton.

***Burglar Who Thought He Was Bogart: A Bernie Rhodenbarr Mystery.** Lawrence Block. LC 95-1969. 1995. 20.95 (*0-525-94016-2*, Dutton) NAL-Dutton.

***Burglar Who Traded Ted Williams.** Lawrence Block. 384p. 1995. mass mkt. 5.99 (*0-451-18426-2*, Onyx) NAL-Dutton.

Burglar Who Traded Ted Williams: A Bernie Rhodenbarr Mystery. Lawrence Block. LC 93-40191. 1994. 19.95 (*0-525-93807-9*, Dutton) NAL-Dutton.

***Burglar Who Traded Ted Williams: A Bernie Rhodenbarr Mystery.** large type ed. Lawrence Block. LC 94-19549. (Cloak & Dagger Ser.). 452p. 1994. 21.95 (*0-7862-0299-8*) Thorndike Pr.

Burglaries & Celebrations. Naomi Clark. 1977. 6.95 (*0-685-80001-6*); 2.95 (*0-685-80002-4*) Oyez.

Burglars Can't Be Choosers. Lawrence Block. LC 94-16720. 1995. 19.95 (*0-525-93943-1*, Dutton) NAL-Dutton.

***Burglars Can't Be Choosers: A Bernie Rhodenbarr Mystery.** large type ed. Lawrence Block. LC 95-7911. 331p. 1995. 23.95 (*0-7862-0468-0*) Thorndike Pr.

Burglars on the Job: Streetlife & Residential Break-Ins. Richard T. Wright & Scott Decker. 224p. 1994. text ed. 37.50 (*1-55553-185-7*) NE U Pr.

Burglary: The Victim & the Public. Irvin Waller & Norman Okihiro. LC 78-5720. (Canadian Studies in Criminology: No. 4). 204p. reprint ed. pap. 58.20 (*0-8357-7478-3*, 2023677) Bks Demand.

Burglary Protection & Insurance Surveys. D. E. Bugg et al. (C). 1985. 150.00 (*0-685-33788-X*, Pub. by Witherby & Co UK) St Mut.

Burgoo Stew. Susan Patron. LC 90-43791. (Illus.). 32p. (J). (ps-1). 1991. 14.95 (*0-531-05916-2*); 14.99 (*0-531-08516-3*) Orchard Bks Watts.

Burgoyne Diller. Barbara Haskell. (Illus.). 180p. 1992. pap. 35.00 (*0-8109-6801-0*) Abrams.

Burgoyne Diller: The Early Geometric Work: Paintings, Constructions & Drawings. Ed. by K. R. Eagles-Smith. (Illus.). (C). 1990. pap. text ed. write for info. (*0-941576-14-0*) Harcourts Contemporary.

Burgoyne Surrounded Quilt in a Day. Eleanor Burns. (Illus.). 64p. 1992. 8.95 (*0-922705-36-4*) Quilt Day.

Burgoyne's Invasion of Nineteen Seventy-Seven: Etc. Samuel A. Drake. 1988. reprint ed. lib. bdg. 49.00 (*0-7812-0035-0*) Rprt Serv.

Burgoyne's Invasion of Seventeen Seventy-Seven, Etc. Samuel A. Drake. 1977. reprint ed. 49.00 (*0-403-06301-9*) Scholarly.

Burgraves. Victor Hugo. (FRE.). 1985. pap. 10.95 (*0-7859-2665-8*) Fr & Eur.

Burgundian Code: Book of Constitutions or Law of Gundobad Additional Enactments. Tr. by Katherine F. Drew. LC 70-182499. (Middle Ages Ser.). 128p. (Orig.). 1972. pap. text ed. 15.95 (*0-8122-1035-2*) U of Pa Pr.

Burgundian Court Song in the Time of Binchois: The Anonymous Chansons of El Escorial, MS V. III. 24. Walter H. Kemp. (Oxford Monographs on Music). (Illus.). 176p. 1990. 55.00 (*0-19-816135-2*) OUP.

Burgundian Gothic Architecture. Robert Branner. Ed. by John Harris & Alastair Laing. (Studies in Architecture: No. III). (Illus.). 206p. 1986. pap. 39.95 (*0-302-02751-3*, Pub. by Zwemmer Bks UK) Sothebys Pubns.

Burgundian Netherlands. Walter Prevenier & W. M. Blockmans. (Illus.). 420p. 1986. 125.00 (*0-521-30611-6*) Cambridge U Pr.

Burgundy. (Insight Guides, Windows on the World Ser.). (Illus.). 350p. 1993. pap. 21.95 (*0-395-65986-8*) HM.

***Burgundy.** Hubrecht Duijker. (Wine Lover's Touring Guides Ser.). (Illus.). 144p. (Orig.). 1995. pap. 15.95 (*1-85365-306-3*, Pub. by Spectrum UK) Seven Hills Bk.

Burgundy. Anthony Hanson. (Books on Wine Ser.). 354p. (Orig.). 1982. pap. 13.95 (*0-571-11798-8*) Faber & Faber.

Burgundy. Robert M. Parker, Jr. write for info. (*0-318-69054-3*) S&S Trade.

***Burgundy.** 2nd ed. Anthony Hanson. (Books on Wine Ser.). (Illus.). 432p. (Orig.). 1995. 40.00 (*0-571-15389-5*); pap. 24.95 (*0-571-15178-7*) Faber & Faber.

Burgundy & Beavjolais on a Budget. D. Delaforce. (C). 1989. text ed. 29.95 (*0-948032-82-0*, Pub. by Rosters Ltd) St Mut.

Burgundy Fields. Tom Saber. Ed. by John Shapiro. (Illus.). 20p. 1992. reprint ed. 9.00 (*1-880537-51-6*) Dimension.

Burgundy Green Guide. 2nd ed. Date not set. pap. 18.00 (*2-06-701308-4*, 308) Michelin.

***Burgundy Green Guide English Edition.** Michelin Staff. Date not set. pap. 17.95 (*0-7859-7201-3*, 2067013084) Fr & Eur.

***Burgundy Stars: A Year in the Life of a Great Burgundy Restaurant.** William Echikson. LC 94-24260. 1995. 22.95 (*0-316-19993-1*) Little.

Burhans: Descendants from the First Ancestor in America, Jacob Burhans, 1660, & His Son, Jan Burhans, 1663. S. Burhans, Jr. (Illus.). 799p. 1991. reprint ed. lib. bdg. 124.00 (*0-8328-1895-X*); reprint ed. pap. 114.00 (*0-8328-1896-8*) Higginson Bk Co.

Burial. Graham Masterton. 384p. 1994. 22.95 (*0-312-85681-4*) Tor Bks.

B

952

An Asterisk (*) at the beginning of an entry indicates that the title is appearing in BIP for the first time.

An Asterisk (*) at the beginning of an entry indicates that the title is appearing in BIP for the first time.

953

Burma: From Monarchy to Dictatorship. Aung Chin Win Aung. Ed. by Don Lee. 220p. (C). 1994. 44.50 (*0-939758-28-8*) Eastern Pr.

Burma: Insurgency & the Politics of Ethnicity. Martin Smith. LC 91-5031. (Illus.). 512p. (C). 1991. text ed. 69.95 (*0-86232-868-3*, Pub. by Zed Books UK); pap. 29.95 (*0-86232-869-1*, Pub. by Zed Books UK) Humanities.

Burma: Literature, Historiography, Scholarship, Language, Life & Buddhism. Hla Pe. 224p. 1986. pap. text ed. 19.75 (*9971-988-00-3*, Pub. by Inst SE Asian Studies SI) Ashgate Pub Co.

Burma: Military Rule & the Politics of Stagnation. Josef Silverstein. LC 77-3127. (Politics & International Relations of Southeast Asia Ser.). (Illus.). 239p. reprint ed. pap. 68.20 (*0-8357-5607-6*, 2056847) Bks Demand.

Burma: Military Technical Atlas Scale: 1: 200000. Ed. by Lewis B. Sckolnick. 75p. (Orig.). (RUS.). (C). 1994. pap. text ed. 2,000.00 (*1-57205-458-1*) Rector Pr.

Burma: The Next Killing Fields? Alan Clements. (Real Story Ser.). 96p. 1992. pap. 5.00 (*1-878825-21-6*) Odonian Pr.

Burma: The Untold Story. Won-Loy Chan. (Illus.). 160p. 1986. 14.95 (*0-89141-266-2*) Presidio Pr.

Burma & Beyond. James G. Scott. LC 77-87054. reprint ed. 62.50 (*0-404-16856-6*) AMS Pr.

***Burma Business Executive Outlook.** 70p. (Orig.). 1994. pap. 295.00 (*0-7605-1377-5*) Rector Pr.

***Burma Commercial Law.** 150p. 1994. pap. 295.00 (*0-7605-0095-9*) Rector Pr.

Burma Delta: Economic Development & Social Change on an Asian Rice Frontier, 1852-1941. Michael Adas. LC 73-15256. 272p. reprint ed. 77.60 (*0-8357-9772-4*, 2015350) Bks Demand.

Burma in Revolt: Opium & Insurgency since 1948. Bertil Lintner. LC 94-25846. 1994. text ed. 59.95 (*0-8133-2344-4*) Westview.

Burma Interlude. Marjorie C. Nickerson. Ed. by Thomas Nickerson. (Illus.). 128p. 1981. 3.00 (*0-914916-55-6*) Ku Paa.

Burma Nineteen Forty-Two to Nineteen Forty-Five. Raymond A. Callahan. Ed. by Noble Frankland & Christopher Dowling. LC 79-52240. (Politics & Strategy of the Second World War Ser.). 192p. 1979. 18.50 (*0-87413-162-6*) U Delaware Pr.

Burma Railway Artist: An Artist at War in Singapore, Thailand & Burma, 1942-45. Jack Chalker. (Illus.). 176p. 1994. 42.50 (*0-85052-337-0*, Pub. by L Cooper Bks UK) Trans-Atl Phila.

Burma Road to Poverty. Mya Maung. LC 90-27555. 360p. 1991. text ed. 69.50 (*0-275-93613-9*, C3613, Praeger Pubs) Greenwood.

Burma Roadsters: The 464th in China-Burma-India. Eric R. Craine. LC 92-33293. 1992. write for info. (*0-934525-21-8*) West Research.

***Burma Tax Law.** 150p. (C). 1994. pap. 295.00 (*0-7605-0090-8*) Rector Pr.

Burma Thailand Frontier Over. Wilson. (C). 1985. pap. 11.00 (*0-89680-124-1*, Ohio U Ctr Intl) Ohio U Pr.

Burma-Thailand Railway. Hank Nelson & Gavan McCormack. 192p. 1994. pap. 17.95 (*1-86373-577-1*, Pub. by Allen Unwin AT) Paul & Co Pubs.

Burma Today. Sekhar Bandyopadhyay. 120p. 1987. 19.95 (*0-318-37226-6*) Asia Bk Corp.

Burmah: A Photographic Journey. Noel F. Singer. (Illus.). 140p. (C). 1995. 55.00 (*1-870838-26-2*, Pub. by Kiscadale UK) Weatherhill.

Burman: His Life & Notions. James G. Scott, pseud. LC 77-87055. reprint ed. 67.50 (*0-404-16857-4*) AMS Pr.

Burma's Foreign Relations: Neutralism in Theory & Practice. Chi-Shad Liang. LC 90-31953. 288p. 1990. text ed. 55.00 (*0-275-93455-1*, C3455, Praeger Pubs) Greenwood.

Burma's Revolution of the Spirit: The Struggle for Democratic Freedom & Dignity. Alan Clements & Leslie Kean. (Illus.). 128p. 1994. 35.00 (*0-89381-580-2*) Aperture.

Burmese: An Introduction to the Literary Style. John Okell. (Southeast Asian Language Text Ser.). Date not set. write for info. (*1-877979-44-9*) North Ill U Ctr SE Asian.

Burmese: An Introduction to the Script. John Okell. (Southeast Asian Language Text Ser.). Date not set. write for info. (*1-877979-43-0*) North Ill U Ctr SE Asian.

Burmese: An Introduction to the Spoken Language, Bk. 1. John Okell. (Southeast Asian Language Text Ser.). Date not set. write for info. (*1-877979-41-4*) North Ill U Ctr SE Asian.

Burmese: An Introduction to the Spoken Language, Bk. 2. John Okell. (Southeast Asian Language Text Ser.). Date not set. write for info. (*1-877979-42-2*) North Ill U Ctr SE Asian.

***Burmese Administrative Cycles: Anarchy & Conquest, c. 1580-1760.** Victor B. Lieberman. LC 83-13716. reprint ed. pap. 101.80 (*0-7837-9376-6*, 2060126) Bks Demand.

Burmese Administrative Cycles: Anarchy & Conquest, Fifteen Eighty to Seventeen Sixty. Victor B. Lieberman. LC 83-13716. (Illus.). 275p. 1984. 57.50x (*0-691-05407-X*) Princeton U Pr.

Burmese Arcady. Collin M. Enriquez. LC 77-87075. reprint ed. 25.50 (*0-404-16814-0*) AMS Pr.

Burmese Buddhist Law. E Maung. LC 77-87483. reprint ed. 25.00 (*0-404-16812-4*) AMS Pr.

Burmese Buddhist Sculpture. Otto Karow. (Illus.). 164p. 1991. 47.50 (*1-879155-04-4*); pap. 39.60 (*1-879155-05-2*) Lotus WA.

Burmese Caper. A. J. Greenspan & Iris W. Collet. 1990. pap. 9.95 (*0-913878-44-8*) T Horton & Dghts.

Burmese Communist Party in the 1980's. Charles B. Smith. 136p. 1985. pap. text ed. 22.75 (*9971-902-76-1*, Pub. by Inst SE Asian Studies SI) Ashgate Pub Co.

Burmese Crafts: Past & Present. Sylvia Fraser-Lu. (Illus.). 372p. 1994. 150.00 (*0-19-588608-9*) OUP.

***Burmese Dance & Theatre.** Noel F. Singer. (Images of Asia Ser.). 120p. 1995. 16.95 (*967-65-3086-7*) OUP.

Burmese Days. George Orwell. 21.95 (*0-8488-0602-6*) Amereon Ltd.

Burmese Days. George Orwell. LC 34-35694. 288p. 1950. 8.95 (*0-15-114975-5*) HarBrace.

Burmese Days. George Orwell. LC 73-12947. 287p. 1974. reprint ed. pap. 8.95 (*0-15-614850-1*, Harvest Bks) HarBrace.

Burmese Drama: A Study of Burmese Plays. U. Htin Aung. LC 77-87015. reprint ed. 21.50 (*0-404-16827-2*) AMS Pr.

Burmese Drama, A Study with Translations of Burmese Plays. Maung A. Htin. LC 78-6062. xx, 266p. 1978. reprint ed. text ed. 59.75 (*0-313-20381-4*, AUBD, Greenwood Pr) Greenwood.

Burmese-English Dictionary. R. C. Judson. 860p. (BUR & ENG.). 1992. 95.00 (*0-8288-7249-X*) Fr & Eur.

Burmese-English Dictionary. A. Judson. 643p. 1989. reprint ed. 54.00 (*0-88431-046-9*) IBD Ltd.

Burmese Entrepreneurship: Creative Response in the Colonial Economy. Aung T. Thet. (Beitrage Zur Sudasien Ser.: Band 126). 213p. (Orig.). 1989. pap. 39.50x (*3-515-05339-5*) Coronet Bks.

Burmese Family. Daw Mi Mi Khaing. LC 76-6607. (Illus.). reprint ed. 22.50 (*0-404-15291-0*) AMS Pr.

Burmese Folk-Tales. U. Htin Aung. LC 77-87016. reprint ed. 22.00 (*0-404-16828-0*) AMS Pr.

Burmese Journey. Norma Bixler. LC 67-11440. 246p. reprint ed. pap. 70.20 (*0-8357-7480-5*, 2016111) Bks Demand.

Burmese Kitchen. Copeland Marks & Aung Thein. LC 87-22242. (Illus.). 288p. 1987. 19.95 (*0-87131-524-6*) M Evans.

Burmese Kitchen. Copeland Marks. 1994. pap. 12.95 (*0-87131-768-0*) M Evans.

Burmese Loneliness: A Tale of Travel in Burma, the Southern Shan States & Keng Tung. Collin M. Enriquez. LC 77-87076. reprint ed. 26.00 (*0-404-16815-9*) AMS Pr.

Burmese Looking Glass: A Human Rights Adventure & a Jungle Revolution. Edith T. Mirante. 352p. 1994. pap. 11.00 (*0-87113-570-1*) Grove-Atltic.

Burmese Nationalist Movements, 1940-1949. U. Maung Maung. LC 90-11053. 416p. (C). 1991. text ed. 39.00 (*0-8248-1342-1*) UH Pr.

Burmese Phrasebook. David Bradley. (Illus.). 128p. (Orig.). 1988. pap. 2.95 (*0-86442-026-9*) Lonely Planet.

Burmese Political Values: The Socio-Political Roots of Authoritarianism. Maung Gyi. LC 83-2169. 288p. 1983. text ed. 59.95 (*0-275-90993-X*, C0993, Praeger Pubs) Greenwood.

Burmese Politics: The Dilemma of National Unity. Josef Silverstein. LC 80-200. 274p. reprint ed. pap. 78.10 (*0-7837-5683-6*, 2059111) Bks Demand.

Burmese Polity, 1752-1819: Politics, Administration, & Social Organization in the Early Kon-baung Period. William J. Koenig. LC 88-63416. (Michigan Papers on South & Southeast Asia: No. 34). 332p. 1990. 31.95 (*0-89148-056-0*); pap. 17.95 (*0-89148-057-9*) Ctr S&SE Asian.

Burmese Puppets. Noel F. Singer. (Images of Asia Ser.). (Illus.). 126p. 1993. 16.95 (*0-19-588589-9*) OUP.

***Burmese Pythons.** Coborn. 1995. pap. text ed. (*0-7938-0263-6*) TFH Pubns.

Burmese Self-Taught. R. F. St. John. 168p. 1992. 9.95 (*0-7818-0053-6*) Hippocrene Bks.

Burmese Self-Taught. A. St. John. (C). 1991. reprint ed. text ed. 12.50 (*0-8364-2653-3*, Pub. by Asian Educ Servs II) S Asia.

Burmese Supernaturalism. enl. ed. Melford E. Spiro. LC 77-17280. 336p. reprint ed. pap. 95.80 (*0-8357-8901-2*, 2025708) Bks Demand.

Burmese Way: To Where?: Report of a Mission to Myanmar (Burma) Makhdoom A. Khan. LC 92-217192. (Illus.). 95p. reprint ed. pap. 27.10 (*0-7837-5225-3*, 2044958) Bks Demand.

Burn. Vassily Aksyonov. Tr. by Michael Glenny. LC 84-42521. 528p. 1985. 18.95 (*0-394-52492-6*); pap. 10.95 (*0-394-74174-9*) Random.

Burn. Bob Judd. 1993. mass mkt. 4.99 (*0-425-13946-8*) Berkley Pub.

***Burn.** John Lutz. LC 94-32187. (Henry Holt Mystery Ser.). 1995. 22.50 (*0-8050-3480-3*) H Holt & Co.

***Burn.** Bill Ransom. LC 95-9747. 320p. (Orig.). 1995. text ed. 19.95 (*0-441-00246-3*) Ace Bks.

Burn: Late 60's-Early 70's, 3 bks., Set. Vassily Aksyonov. Tr. by Michael Glenny. 528p. (RUS.). 1984. 19.95 (*0-317-07248-X*) HM.

Burn after Reading. Leo Hamalian. LC 78-67678. 1979. 8.95 (*0-933706-02-2*); pap. 4.95 (*0-933706-03-0*) Ararat Pr.

Burn All Your Bridges. large type ed. Eleanor Drew. 288p. 1987. 16.95 (*0-7089-1583-3*) Ulverscroft.

Burn Care. 32p. 1985. 6.00 (*0-912452-51-X*, P-50) Am Phys Therapy Assn.

Burn Care: An Anthology. 1985. pap. 6.00 (*0-912452-50-1*) Am Phys Therapy Assn.

Burn Care & Rehabilitation: Principles & Practice. Ed. by Reginald L. Richard & Marlys J. Staley. LC 93-8304. (Contemporary Perspectives in Rehabilitation Ser.: Vol. 12). (Illus.). 711p. (C). 1993. 90.00 (*0-8036-7361-2*) Davis Co.

***Burn Care Products Market.** 241p. (Orig.). 1995. pap. 2,795.00 (*0-7605-2319-3*) Rector Pr.

Burn-in: An Engineering Approach to the Design & Analysis of Burn-In Procedures. Finn Jensen & Niels E. Petersen. LC 82-1952. 167p. 1982. text ed. 190.00 (*0-471-10215-6*, Wiley-Interscience) Wiley.

Burn Marks. Sara Paretsky. 1991. mass mkt. 5.99 (*0-440-20845-9*) Dell.

Burn Marks. large type ed. Sara Paretsky. (Large Print Books General Ser.). 533p. 1990. lib. bdg. 19.95 (*0-8161-5004-4*) G K Hall.

Burn, Missouri, Burn. Randall Greenwood. 320p. (Orig.). 1995. mass mkt. 4.99 (*0-8125-3455-7*) Tor Bks.

Burn on, Sweet Fire. Sandra Dubay. 480p. 1991. pap. 4.50 (*0-8439-3032-2*) Dorchester Pub Co.

***Burn Out: A Case for Dr. Anne Vernon.** Alan Scholefield. LC 95-14711. 1995. write for info. (*0-312-13035-X*) St Martin.

***Burn-Out: A Commander Shaw Novel.** Philip McCutchan. 224p. 1995. 27.00 (*0-340-60096-9*, Pub. by H & S UK) Trafalgar.

Burn-Out: Renewing Your Energy. Lura J. Geiger. (Orig.). 1987. pap. 24.95 (*0-931055-32-6*); audio (*0-318-61668-8*) LuraMedia.

Burn-Out: Stages of Disillusionment in the Helping Professions. Jerry Edelwich & Archie Brodsky. LC 79-27412. 255p. 1980. pap. 19.95 (*0-89885-035-5*) Human Sci Pr.

Burn Patient. Burke & Tompkins. Date not set. 45.00 (*0-8151-1333-1*, Yr Bk Med Pubs) Mosby Yr Bk.

Burn Patient: Anesthetic Management & Immediate Care. Zauder & Stehling. 1991. write for info. (*0-8151-9860-4*, Yr Bk Med Pubs) Mosby Yr Bk.

Burn Reconstruction. Bruce M. Achauer. (Illus.). 210p. 1990. text ed. 95.00 (*0-86577-341-6*) Thieme Med Pubs.

Burn Season. John Lantigua. 1990. mass mkt. 4.50 (*0-06-100097-3*, Harp PBks) HarpC.

Burn Therapy & Research. Witold Rudowski et al. LC 74-29339. (Illus.). 351p. reprint ed. pap. 100.10 (*0-8357-7481-3*, 2020752) Bks Demand.

Burn This. Lanford Wilson. 1988. pap. 9.95 (*0-374-52158-1*) FS&G.

***Burn This Gossip: The True Story of George Benjamin of Belleville.** Sheldon Godfrey & Judith Godfrey. 160p. 1991. 26.50 (*0-9695102-0-9*) Dun.

Burn Trauma. Robert Demling & Cheryl LaLonde. (Trauma Management Ser.). (Illus.). 320p. 1989. text ed. 87.00 (*0-86577-281-9*) Thieme Med Pubs.

Burn Up. Anne Bailey. 144p. (YA). (gr. 7 up). 1992. pap. 4.95 (*0-571-16504-4*) Faber & Faber.

Burn Wound Coverings, Vol. I. Ed. by Donald L. Wise. 192p. 1984. 119.00 (*0-8493-5706-3*, RD96) CRC Pr.

Burn Wound Coverings, Vol. II. Ed. by Donald L. Wise. 176p. 1984. 168.00 (*0-8493-5707-1*, RD96, CRC Reprint) Franklin.

Burne-Jones. William Waters. 1989. pap. 25.00 (*0-85263-199-5*, Pub. by Shire UK) St Mut.

Burne-Jones -- A Quest for Love: Works by Sir Edward Burne-Jones BT & Related Works by Contemporary Artists. Peter Nahum Ltd. Staff. (Illus.). (C). 1993. pap. 60.00 (*1-872508-03-0*) St Mut.

Burne-Jones Talking, His Conversations, 1895-1898: Preserved by His Studio Assistant, Thomas Rooke. Edward C. Burne-Jones. Ed. by Mary Lago. LC 81-51062. 231p. reprint ed. pap. 65.90 (*0-7837-2358-X*, AU00423) Bks Demand.

Burne-Jones, the Pre-Raphaelites & Their Century, 2 Vols., Set. Hilary Morgan. (Illus.). (C). 1989. 195.00 (*0-685-75371-9*) St Mut.

Burne-Jones, the Pre-Raphaelites & Their Century, 2 Vols., Vol. 1: The Text. Hilary Morgan. (Illus.). (C). 1989. write for info. (*1-872508-01-4*) St Mut.

Burne-Jones, the Pre-Raphaelites & Their Century, 2 Vols., Vol. 2: The Plates. Hilary Morgan. (Illus.). (C). 1989. write for info. (*1-872508-02-2*) St Mut.

Burned Alive! Jerry Golden. 176p. 1987. pap. text ed. 5.95 (*0-939079-01-1*) ChristLife Pubs.

Burned & Beautiful. Katy Tartakoff. (Illus.). 54p. (Orig.). (J). Date not set. student ed 14.95 (*0-9629365-1-0*) Childrens Lgcy.

Burned at the Stake. Henry S. Westbrook. Ed. by Al I. Obaba. 124p. (Orig.). (YA). 1991. pap. text ed. 9.95 (*0-916157-88-1*) African Islam Miss Pubns.

Burned Books. Ken A. Smith. 56p. 1981. pap. 11.95 (*0-906427-23-1*, Pub. by Bloodaxe Bks UK) Dufour.

Burned Bramble. Manes Sperber. Tr. by Constantine Fitzgibbon. LC 87-27545. (Like a Tear in the Ocean Trilogy Ser.: Vol. 1). 432p. 1988. 39.50 (*0-8419-1051-0*) Holmes & Meier.

***Burned County Data, 1809-1848: As Found in the Virginia Contested Election Files.** Benjamin B. Weisiger, III. 100p. 1986. pap. 15.00x (*0-935931-76-7*) Borgo Pr.

Burned County Data, 1809-1848: As Found in the Virginia Contested Election Files. Benjamin B. Weisiger, III. 100p. (C). 1986. reprint ed. lib. bdg. 35.00x (*0-8095-8155-8*) Borgo Pr.

Burned Out: A Teacher Speaks Out. Jack Dewey. LC 86-60763. (Illus.). 96p. (Orig.). 1986. pap. 6.95 (*0-933050-37-2*) New Eng Pr VT.

Burned-over District: The Social & Intellectual History of Enthusiastic Religion in Western New York, 1800-1850. Whitney R. Cross. LC 50-12161. 382p. 1982. pap. 16.95 (*0-8014-9232-7*) Cornell U Pr.

Burnett: The Family of Burnett of Leys, with Collateral Branches. Ed. by J. Allardyce. xxii, 367p. 1992. reprint ed. lib. bdg. 71.00 (*0-8328-2309-0*); reprint ed. pap. 61.00 (*0-8328-2310-4*) Higginson Bk Co.

Burnett-Baker-Beaman. Blanche M. Burnett. LC 85-71711. 218p. reprint ed. pap. 30.00 (*0-916497-55-0*); reprint ed. fiche 6.00 (*0-916497-54-2*) Burnett Micro.

Burnham: Genealogical Records of Thomas Burnham. 2nd ed. R. H. Burnham. 292p. 1991. reprint ed. lib. bdg. 55.50 (*0-8328-2106-3*); reprint ed. pap. 45.50 (*0-8328-2107-1*) Higginson Bk Co.

Burnham Family; or Genealogical Records of the Descendants of the Four Emigrants of the Name, Who Were among the Early Settlers in America. Roderick H. Burnham. (Illus.). 546p. 1989. reprint ed. lib. bdg. 94.00 (*0-8328-0350-2*); reprint ed. pap. 84.00 (*0-8328-0351-0*) Higginson Bk Co.

Burnham Index to Architectural Literature, Vol. 1. Ed. by Art Institute of Chicago Staff. LC 89-16850. 532p. 1990. 216.00 (*0-8240-2661-6*) Garland.

Burnham Index to Architectural Literature, Vol. 2. Ed. by Art Institute of Chicago Staff. LC 89-16850. 518p. 1990. 216.00 (*0-8240-2662-4*) Garland.

Burnham Index to Architectural Literature, Vol. 3. Ed. by Art Institute of Chicago Staff. LC 89-16850. 510p. 1990. 216.00 (*0-8240-2663-2*) Garland.

Burnham Index to Architectural Literature, Vol. 4. Ed. by Art Institute of Chicago Staff. LC 89-16850. 508p. 1990. 216.00 (*0-8240-2664-0*) Garland.

Burnham Index to Architectural Literature, Vol. 5. Ed. by Art Institute of Chicago Staff. LC 89-16850. 506p. 1990. 216.00 (*0-8240-2665-9*) Garland.

Burnham Index to Architectural Literature, Vol. 6. Ed. by Art Institute of Chicago Staff. LC 89-16850. 514p. 1990. 216.00 (*0-8240-2666-7*) Garland.

Burnham Index to Architectural Literature, Vol. 7. Ed. by Art Institute of Chicago Staff. LC 89-16850. 514p. 1990. 216.00 (*0-8240-2667-5*) Garland.

Burnham Index to Architectural Literature, Vol. 8. Ed. by Art Institute of Chicago Staff. LC 89-16850. 516p. 1990. 216.00 (*0-8240-2668-3*) Garland.

Burnham Index to Architectural Literature, Vol. 9. Ed. by Art Institute of Chicago Staff. LC 89-16850. 578p. 1990. 216.00 (*0-8240-2669-1*) Garland.

Burnham Index to Architectural Literature, Vol. 10. Ed. by Art Institute of Chicago Staff. LC 89-16850. 658p. 1990. 216.00 (*0-8240-2670-5*) Garland.

Burnham of Chicago: Architect & Planner. Thomas S. Hines. LC 74-79625. 1979. pap. 19.95 (*0-226-34171-2*, P835) U Ch Pr.

Burnham's Celestial Handbook: An Observer's Guide to the Universe Beyond the Solar System, 1. Robert Burnham, Jr. & Herbert A. Luft. LC 77-82888. (Illus.). 1978. reprint ed. pap. 13.95 (*0-486-23567-X*) Dover.

Burnham's Celestial Handbook: An Observer's Guide to the Universe Beyond the Solar System, 2. Robert Burnham, Jr. & Herbert A. Luft. LC 77-82888. (Illus.). 1978. reprint ed. pap. 13.95 (*0-486-23568-8*) Dover.

Burnham's Celestial Handbook: An Observer's Guide to the Universe Beyond the Solar System, Vol. 3. Robert Burnham, Jr. (Illus.). 1979. pap. 13.95 (*0-486-23673-0*) Dover.

***Burning.** Jane Chambers. (Classic Novels Ser.). 160p. 1995. pap. 9.95 (*1-886586-00-4*) T n T Class.

Burning. Jeff Fain. 288p. 1984. pap. 2.95 (*0-8439-2160-9*) Dorchester Pub Co.

***Burning.** Frank Norwood. LC 94-40987. 1995. 21.95 (*0-385-31380-2*, Dial) Doubleday.

Burning. Jay A. Parry. LC 91-11107. 208p. (Orig.). 1991. pap. 8.95 (*0-87579-521-8*) Deseret Bk.

Burning: New & Selected Poems, 1970-1990. Laurel A. Bogen. 85p. (Orig.). (C). 1991. pap. text ed. 9.95 (*0-9622847-4-2*) Red Wind Bks.

Burning Air & a Clear Mind: Contemporary Israeli Women Poets. Ed. by Myra Glazer. LC 80-22487. (Illus.). 163p. 1981. 17.95 (*0-8214-0572-1*) Ohio U Pr.

Burning & a Shining Light: English Spirituality in the Age of Wesley. Ed. by David L. Jeffrey. LC 86-29085. 527p. (Orig.). reprint ed. pap. 150.20 (*0-7837-3181-7*, 2042785) Bks Demand.

Burning & Other Stories: The 1972 Iowa Short Fiction Award. Jack Cady. LC 72-76304. (Iowa Short Fiction Award Ser.). 157p. 1972. 19.95 (*0-87745-030-7*) U of Iowa Pr.

***Burning Angel.** James L. Burke. 352p. 1995. 22.95 (*0-7868-6082-0*) Hyperion.

Burning at Stake in the United States. 20p. 1986. reprint ed. pap. 3.00 (*0-933121-13-X*) Black Classic.

Burning Baby & Other Ghosts. John Gordon. LC 92-54579. 112p. (YA). (gr. 7-11). 1993. 14.95 (*1-56402-067-3*) Candlewick Pr.

Burning Bed. Faith McNulty. 288p. 1981. pap. 3.95 (*0-05-024747-6*) Bantam.

Burning Bed: The True Story of an Abused Wife. Faith McNulty. 320p. 1989. mass mkt. 4.50 (*0-380-70771-3*) Avon.

Burning Beds & Mermaids: Stories for Advanced Listening & Conversation. Gail Forman. 192p. 1994. pap. text ed. 18.75 (*0-13-101189-8*) P-H.

Burning Behaviour of Textiles & Its Assessment by Oxygen-Index Methods, Vol. 18, No. 1-3. A. R. Horrocks et al. 205p. (C). 1989. pap. 168.00 (*1-870812-10-7*, Pub. by Textile Institue UK) St Mut.

Burning Brambles: Selected Poems 1944-1979. Roland Mathias. 163p. (C). 1983. 22.00x (*0-85088-728-3*, Pub. by Gomer Pr UK) St Mut.

Burning Bright. Tom Dowd. (Shadowrun Ser.: No. 15). 288p. (Orig.). 1994. pap. 4.99 (*0-451-45368-9*, ROC) NAL-Dutton.

Burning Bright. Melissa Scott. 352p. 1993. 21.95 (*0-312-85502-8*) Tor Bks.

Burning Bright. Melissa Scott. 1994. mass mkt. 4.99 (*0-8125-2175-7*) Tor Bks.

Burning Bright. John Steinbeck. 128p. 1994. 8.95 (*0-14-018742-1*, Penguin Classics) Viking Penguin.

Burning Bright. Edward Wharton-Tigar & A. J. Wilson. 280p. 1987. text ed. 36.00 (*0-947671-11-0*) Metal Bulletin.

Burning Bright: A Play in Story Form. John Steinbeck. 112p. 1979. mass mkt. 6.00 (*0-14-004999-1*, Penguin Bks) Viking Penguin.

An Asterisk (*) at the beginning of an entry indicates that the title is appearing in BIP for the first time.

***Burning Bright: An Anthology of Sacred Poetry.** Ed. by Patricia Hampl. 192p. 1995. 20.00 (*0-345-38029-0*) Ballantine.

Burning Bright: The Genesis of an Opera. Frank Lewin & Louis E. Auld. (Monograph: No. 1). (Illus.). 100p. (Orig.). 1985. pap. 15.00 (*0-937129-00-3*) Lyrica.

Burning Bush. Lev Gillet. 1975. pap. 6.95 (*0-87243-063-4*) Templegate.

Burning Bush: A Fire History of Australia. Stephen J. Pyne. (Illus.). 520p. 1992. pap. 15.95 (*0-8050-2101-9*, Owl) H Holt & Co.

Burning Bush: Jewish Symbolism & Mysticism. Etan Levine. LC 81-52463. (Illus.). 123p. (Orig.). 1982. pap. 10.00 (*0-87203-105-5*) Hermon.

Burning Bush: Poems & Other Writings of Jewish Content, 1940 to 1980. Aaron Kramer. LC 81-68624. 256p. 1983. 14.95 (*0-8453-4706-3*, Cornwall Bks) Assoc Univ Prs.

Burning Bush Patrol. Richard J. Marshall. 1991. pap. 7.95 (*0-88494-804-8*) Bookcraft Inc.

Burning Caldron of North-East India. G. S. Ghurye. 163p. 1980. 18.95 (*0-318-36866-8*) Asia Bk Corp.

Burning Chrome. William Gibson. 208p. 1987. mass mkt. 5.50 (*0-441-08934-8*) Ace Bks.

Burning Court. John D. Carr. 215p. 1985. pap. 4.95 (*0-930330-27-7*) Intl Polygonics.

Burning Dawn. large type ed. Elspeth Sandys. Orig. Title: The Broken Tree. 640p. 1983. 15.95 (*0-7089-1008-4*) Ulverscroft.

Burning Daylight. Jack London. (Illus.). 362p. 1991. pap. 9.95 (*0-932458-34-3*) Star Rover.

Burning Desire: A Play in Three Acts. William Mastrosimone. 256p. Date not set. pap. 11.95 (*1-880399-54-7*) Smith & Kraus.

Burning Dog. John M. Bennett. 24p. 1983. pap. 4.00 (*0-935350-09-8*); audio (*0-318-57236-2*) Luna Bisonte.

Burning Dog. deluxe limited ed. John M. Bennett. 24p. 1983. 9.00 (*0-935350-10-1*) Luna Bisonte.

Burning Douglas-Fir Slash: Physical, Chemical & Microbial Effects in the Soil. John L. Neal et al. (Oregon State University, Forest Research Laboratory, Research Papers: No. 1). 35p. reprint ed. pap. 25.00 (*0-8357-7482-1*, 2026109) Bks Demand.

Burning down the House. Merry McInerney. 256p. 1994. 17.95 (*0-312-85698-9*) Forge NYC.

***Burning down the House.** Merry McInerney. 320p. 1995. mass mkt. 5.99 (*0-8125-3651-7*) Forge NYC.

Burning Evidence: A Mystery Jigsaw Puzzle. John Lutz. (BePuzzled Ser.). (Orig.). (C). 1993. 20.00 (*0-922242-53-4*) Lombard Mktg.

Burning Fields. David Middleton. LC 90-49724. 64p. 1991. pap. 7.95 (*0-8071-1639-4*) La State U Pr.

Burning Fiery Furnace: Shadrach, Meshach, & Abednego. Guy Williams. LC 91-52608. (Orig.). (YA). 1991. pap. 5.00 (*0-88734-413-5*) Players Pr.

Burning Flesh. Kanta Grover. 1990. text ed. 12.95 (*0-7069-4985-4*, Pub. by Vikas II) S Asia.

Burning Forest. Tr. & Frwd. by Adam Czerniawski. LC 87-73053. (Illus.). 192p. (Orig.). 1988. pap. 18.95 (*1-85224-009-1*, Pub. by Bloodaxe Bks UK) Dufour.

Burning Fountain: A Study in the Language of Symbolism. rev. ed. Philip Wheelwright. 12.50 (*0-8446-4469-2*) Peter Smith.

Burning Garbage in the U. S. Practice vs. State of the Art. Marjorie J. Clarke et al. LC 91-28771. 288p. 1991. pap. 47.00 (*0-918780-49-7*) INFORM NY.

Burning Glass, Stories. Helen Norris. LC 91-10557. 192p. 1992. 19.95 (*0-8071-1790-0*) La State U Pr.

Burning Grass. Cyprian Ekwensi. (African Writers Ser.). 118p. (C). 1962. pap. 9.95 (*0-435-90669-0*) Heinemann.

***Burning Ground.** Jo Clayton. (Shadowsong Trilogy Ser.: Bk. 2). 400p. 1995. pap. 4.99 (*0-88677-663-5*) DAW Bks.

Burning-Ground. Lawrence Russ. (Poetry Chapbook Ser.). 32p. (Orig.). 1981. pap. 4.00 (*0-937669-01-6*) Owl Creek Pr.

Burning Hills. Louis L'Amour. (Orig.). 1985. pap. 3.99 (*0-553-28210-7*) Bantam.

Burning House. Ann Beattie. 256p. 1987. mass mkt. 4.95 (*0-345-35182-7*) Ballantine.

***Burning Hunger: Three Decades of Personal Struggles Against Poverty: a West African Experience.** Derrick Knight. (Illus.). 208p. 1995. pap. 16.95 (*1-870670-32-9*, Pub. by Panos Bks UK) Paul & Co Pubs.

Burning in Water, Drowning in Flame. Charles Bukowski. LC 74-8125. 236p. 1994. reprint ed. 25.00 (*0-87685-192-8*); reprint ed. pap. 12.50 (*0-87685-191-X*) Black Sparrow.

Burning Island: A Journey Through Myth & History in the Volcano Country, Hawai'i. Pamela Frierson. LC 90-46398. (Illus.). 256p. 1991. 22.50 (*0-87156-794-6*) Sierra.

Burning Issues in Centre-State Financial Relations. G. Thimmaiah. 1985. 18.50 (*0-8364-1510-8*, Pub. by Ashish II) S Asia.

Burning Issy. Melvin Burgess. LC 93-32430. (YA). (gr. 5 up). 1994. 15.00 (*0-671-89003-4*, S&S Bks Young Read) S&S Childrens.

Burning Land. large type ed. Emma Drummond. 624p. 1987. 17.95 (*0-7089-8379-0*, Charnwood) Ulverscroft.

Burning Library: Essays. Edmund White. Ed. by David Bergman. LC 94-6575. 1994. 25.00 (*0-679-43475-5*) Knopf.

Burning Man. Michael Hammonds. 1991. mass mkt. 4.50 (*1-55817-490-7*, Pinnacle NY) Windsor NY.

Burning March. Neil Albert. 256p. 1994. 18.95 (*0-525-93718-8*, Dutton) NAL-Dutton.

***Burning March.** Neil Albert. 256p. 1995. pap. 4.50 (*0-451-17860-2*, Sig) NAL-Dutton.

Burning Memory: Times of Testing & Reckoning. Alice L. Eckardt. LC 92-40203. (Holocaust Ser.). 1993. 88.00 (*0-08-041931-3*, Pergamon Pr) Elsevier.

Burning Money. Grace. 1984. 14.95 (*0-02-544930-3*) Macmillan.

Burning Mouth Syndrome. Isaac Van der Waal. (Illus.). 95p. 1990. 24.00 (*87-16-10381-5*, Yr Bk Med Pubs) Mosby Yr Bk.

Burning Obsession. Robert A. Walker. 1989. pap. 3.95 (*1-55817-214-9*, Pinnacle NY) Windsor NY.

Burning of a Strange Fire. Barney Fuller. LC 93-78567. 224p. 1993. pap. 9.99 (*1-56384-049-9*) Huntington Hse.

Burning of Brinsley MacNamara. Padraic O'Farrell. (Illus.). 176p. 1990. pap. 11.95 (*0-946640-56-4*, Pub. by Lilliput Pr Ltd IE) Irish Bks Media.

Burning of Rome. Alfred J. Church. 20.00 (*0-8196-1252-9*) Biblo.

Burning of the Convent. Louise G. Whitney. LC 70-90196. (Mass Violence in America Ser.). 1969. reprint ed. 22.95 (*0-405-01341-8*) Ayer.

Burning of the Ships. Douglas Scott. 344p. 1982. pap. 2.75 (*0-345-29549-8*) Ballantine.

Burning of Troy: Essays on Catastrophe & Chronology. Alfred De Grazia. (Quantavolution Ser.: No. 12). 300p. (Orig.). 1984. pap. 17.00 (*0-940268-07-8*) Metron Pubns.

***Burning Passions: An Introduction to the Study of Silent Cinema.** Paolo C. Usai. (Illus.). 128p. 1994. text ed. 39.95 (*0-85170-407-7*) Ind U Pr.

***Burning Passions: An Introduction to the Study of Silent Cinema.** Paolo C. Usai. (Illus.). 128p. 1994. pap. 19.95 (*0-85170-408-5*, Pub. by British Film Inst UK) Ind U Pr.

Burning Patience. Antonio Skarmeta. Tr. by Katherine Silver. LC 86-25285. (Discovery Ser.). 128p. 1994. reprint ed. pap. 10.00 (*1-55597-197-0*) Graywolf.

Burning Place: Poems. Judith Bishop. 80p. (Orig.). 1994. pap. 8.50 (*1-56474-110-9*) Fithian Pr.

Burning Plain & Other Stories. Juan Rulfo. Tr. by George D. Schade. LC 67-25698. (Texas Pan American Ser.). (Illus.). 191p. 1967. pap. 10.95 (*0-292-70132-2*) U of Tex Pr.

Burning Point. Merry McInerney. 1996. 20.95 (*0-312-85699-7*) Forge NYC.

Burning Quest. large type ed. Clare F. Holmes. LC 93-32285. 1994. write for info. (*0-8161-5843-6*) G K Hall.

Burning Question of Trades Unionism. Daniel De Leon. 1977. pap. 0.50 (*0-935534-32-6*) NY Labor News.

Burning Questions of Bingo Brown. Betsy C. Byars. 176p. (J). (gr. 3 up). 1990. pap. 3.99 (*0-14-032479-8*, Puffin) Puffin Bks.

Burning Questions of Bingo Brown. Betsy C. Byars. LC 87-21022. 160p. (J). (gr. 3-7). 1988. pap. 14.00 (*0-670-81932-8*) Viking Child Bks.

***Burning Questions of Bingo Brown.** Carol Klitzner. Ed. by J. Friedland & R. Kessler. (Novel-Ties Ser.). (J). (gr. 4-6). 1992. student ed, pap. text ed. 15.95 (*0-88122-729-3*) Lrn Links.

Burning Questions of Bingo Brown. large type ed. Betsy Byars. 232p. (J). (gr. 3-7). 1989. 14.95 (*0-8161-4770-1*, Large Print Bks) Hall.

Burning Ring of Fire Cycle: or Welcome to Sinland, Welcome to Pair o' Dice. David Sandlin. 1992. 35.00 (*0-932526-40-3*) Nexus Pr.

Burning Sandlewood. Constance Hester. 20p. (Orig.). 1992. pap. 5.00 (*1-883348-03-X*) Fresh Ink.

***Burning Season: The Murder of Chico Mendes & the Fight for the Amazon Rain Forest.** Andrew Revkin. LC 94-30091. 1994. 10.95 (*0-452-27405-2*, Plume) NAL-Dutton.

Burning Shore. Wilbur Smith. 1987. mass mkt. 4.95 (*0-449-21189-4*, Crest) Fawcett.

***Burning Sky.** Ron Faust. 256p. 1995. mass mkt. 5.99 (*0-8125-3532-4*) Forge NYC.

Burning Springs. Louis Reed. LC 85-51953. 280p. 1987. pap. 9.95 (*0-916383-05-9*, Univ Edtns) Aegina Pr.

Burning Springs & Other Tales of the Little Kanawha. 3rd ed. Howard B. Lee. 160p. 1991. reprint ed. pap. 8.00 (*0-87012-016-6*) McClain.

Burning Tears of Sassurum. Sharon Baker. 288p. (Orig.). 1988. pap. 3.50 (*0-380-75113-5*) Avon.

Burning the Apostle. Bill Granger. 368p. 1993. mass mkt. 5.99 (*0-446-36499-1*) Warner Bks.

Burning the Apostle. large type ed. Bill Granger. LC 93-21869. 592p. 1993. reprint ed. lib. bdg. 21.95 (*1-56054-692-1*) Thorndike Pr.

Burning the Box of Beautiful Things: ARK Magazine & the Development of a Postmodern Sensibility at the Royal College of Art, 1950-1962. Alex Seago. LC 93-25909. (Illus.). 256p. (C). 1995. 55.00 (*0-19-817221-4*, Clarendon Pr) OUP.

***Burning the Box of Beautiful Things: The Development of a Postmodern Sensibility.** Alex Seago. (Illus.). 244p. 1995. pap. 26.95 (*0-19-817405-5*) OUP.

Burning the Curtain: Four Spanish Plays. Intro. by Gwynne Edwards. 240p. (Orig.). 1995. pap. 21.95 (*0-7145-2983-4*) M Boyars Pubs.

Burning the Fence. Walter McDonald. LC 80-54792. 58p. (Orig.). 1981. 7.95 (*0-89672-088-8*); pap. 4.95 (*0-89672-087-X*) Tex Tech Univ Pr.

***Burning the Flag: The Great 1989-1990 American Flag Desecration Controversy.** Robert J. Goldstein. LC 95-5541. 544p. 1995. text ed. 39.00x (*0-87338-526-8*) Kent St U Pr.

Burning the Hymnal: The Uncollected Poems of William Koefkorn. William Koefkorn. Ed. by Ted Genoways. 104p. 1994. pap. 12.95 (*0-9635559-3-6*) Slow Tempo.

Burning the Iceberg: The Alaskan Fisherman's Novel. 2nd ed. White Deschner. LC 90-71536. 260p. (Orig.). 1992. pap. 12.95 (*0-9605388-3-6*) Tern Pr.

Burning the Knife: New & Selected Poems. Robin Magowan. LC 84-23671. (Poets Now Ser.: No. 8). 134p. 1985. 13.50 (*0-8108-1777-2*) Scarecrow.

Burning the Old Year. Steven F. White. (Illus.). 64p. (Orig.). 1984. 17.50 (*0-87775-160-9*); pap. 7.95 (*0-87775-162-5*) Unicorn Pr.

Burning the Prairie. John Reinhard. 96p. 1988. pap. 5.00 (*0-89823-104-3*) New Rivers Pr.

Burning the Snow. Finvola Drury. Ed. by Wendy Low. (Orig.). 1989. pap. 10.00 (*1-877664-02-2*) Landers & Francis Pubs.

Burning the Trees. Margaret Shipley. Ed. by Nancy Andrews. LC 85-71013. 74p. (Orig.). 1985. pap. 7.50 (*0-9614643-0-5*) James Andrews Co.

Burning the Year-Lobo: Poems 1962-1975. William Childress. LC 86-81734. 1986. 15.00 (*0-9607958-4-7*); pap. 10.00 (*0-9607958-5-5*) Essai Seay Pubns.

Burning Time. Leslie Glass. LC 93-627. 1993. 18.50 (*0-385-46933-0*) Doubleday.

Burning Time. Carol Matas. LC 94-443. (YA). (gr. 6 up). 1994. 15.95 (*0-385-32097-3*) Delacorte.

Burning Times. Evelyn Vaughn. (Shadows Ser.). 1994. mass mkt. 3.50 (*0-373-27039-9*, 1-27039-6) Harlequin Bks.

Burning Tree: Poems from the First Thousand Years of Welsh Verse. Comp. by Gwyn Williams. LC 78-11853. 234p. 1979. reprint ed. text ed. 55.00 (*0-313-21185-X*, WIBT, Greenwood Pr) Greenwood.

Burning Valley. large type ed. J. L. Bouma. (Linford Western Library). 384p. 1986. pap. 11.95 (*0-7089-6210-6*, Linford) Ulverscroft.

Burning Velocities of Hydrocarbon Flames. S. A. Weil. (Research Bulletin Ser.: No. 30). iv, 48p. 1961. 5.00 (*0-317-56879-5*) Inst Gas Tech.

Burning Village. Menke Katz. LC 75-190721. (Illus.). 136p. 1973. 10.00 (*0-912292-28-8*) The Smith.

Burning Water. Mercedes Lackey. 320p. 1992. mass mkt. 4.99 (*0-8125-2485-3*) Tor Bks.

Burning with a Vision: Poetry of Science & the Fantastic. Thomas Disch et al. Ed. & Illus. by Robert Frazier. 138p. 1984. 14.75 (*0-913896-22-5*); pap. 8.75 (*0-913896-23-3*) Owlswick Pr.

***Burning with Passion: (Valentine)** Emma Darcy. (Presents Ser.). 1995. pap. 3.25 (*0-373-11721-3*, 1-11721-7) Harlequin Bks.

Burning Within: The Story of My Life & Death. Wallace RaNelle & Curtis Taylor. LC 94-260. 218p. 1994. 16.95 (*1-882723-05-8*) Gold Leaf Pr.

Burning Wood. David Williams. 204p. 1975. 6.95 (*0-88784-435-9*, Pub. by Hse of Anansi Pr CN) Genl Dist Srvs.

Burnish Me Bright. Julia Cunningham. 18.25 (*0-8446-6252-6*) Peter Smith.

Burnout: Funny Car Races. Jay Denan. LC 79-64700. (Illus.). 32p. (J). (gr. 4-9). 1980. lib. bdg. 10.79 (*0-89375-256-8*); pap. 2.95 (*0-89375-257-6*) Troll Assocs.

Burnout: What You Can Do to End the Suffering. Janet Buell. LC 88-71772. (Illus.). 162p. (Orig.). 1988. pap. 16.95 (*0-929551-01-X*) Ability Workshop Pr.

Burnout among Social Workers. Ed. & Intro. by David F. Gillespie. LC 87-14930. (Journal of Social Service Research: Vol. 10, No. 1). 105p. 1987. 29.95 (*0-86656-666-X*) Haworth Pr.

Burnout & Stress Management Handbook: Professional Handbook Ser. Pref. by James J. Messina. 78p. (Orig.). 1982. pap. text ed. 11.00 (*0-931975-14-X*) Advanced Dev Sys.

Burnout in Blue: Managing the Police Marginal Performer. Hillary M. Robinette. LC 87-14581. 173p. 1987. text ed. 55.00 (*0-275-92687-7*, C2687, Praeger Pubs); pap. text ed. 22.95 (*0-275-92688-5*, B2688, Praeger Pubs) Greenwood.

Burnout in HIV - AIDS Health Care & Support: Impact for Professionals & Volunteers. Huib Van Dis & Emma Van Dongen. 79p. 1993. pap. 25.00 (*90-5356-042-4*) IBD Ltd.

Burnout in Probation & Corrections. John T. Whitehead. LC 88-28776. (Illus.). 184p. 1989. text ed. 49.95 (*0-275-92959-0*, C2959, Praeger Pubs) Greenwood.

Burnout Syndrome: Current Research, Theory, Interventions. John W. Jones. LC 81-84967. 179p. (Orig.). 1981. pap. 12.95 (*0-930171-00-4*) London Hse.

Burns. W. E. Henley. LC 74-6451. (English Literature Ser.: No. 33). 1974. lib. bdg. 49.95 (*0-8383-1891-6*) M S G Haskell Hse.

Burns. L. M. Watts. LC 73-21618. (English Biography Ser.: No. 31). 1974. lib. bdg. 49.95 (*0-8383-1803-7*) M S G Haskell Hse.

Burns. Principal Shairp. LC 73-164626. (Select Bibliographies Reprint Ser.). 1977. reprint ed. 20.95 (*0-8369-5909-4*) Ayer.

Burns: A Study of the Poems & Songs. Thomas Crawford. xv, 400p. 1960. 49.50 (*0-8047-0055-9*); pap. 16.95 (*0-8047-0056-7*) Stanford U Pr.

Burns: Anthentic Likenesses. Basil Skinner. (C). 1989. pap. text ed. 20.00 (*0-907526-48-9*, Alloway Pub) St Mut.

Burns: Therapy & Psychology with Subject Analysis & Research Bibliography. Lynn P. Chenn. LC 84-45661. 150p. 1985. 44.50 (*0-88164-208-8*); pap. 39.50 (*0-88164-209-6*) ABBE Pubs Assn.

Burns: Treatment & Research. Ed. by Peter C. Leung et al. 324p. (C). 1991. text ed. 104.00 (*9971-5-0674-2*) World Scientific Pub.

Burns Almanac. John D. Ross. LC 72-144474. reprint ed. 27.50 (*0-404-08534-2*) AMS Pr.

Burns & His Poetry. Henry A. Kellow. LC 70-120983. (Poetry & Life Ser.). reprint ed. 27.50 (*0-404-52525-3*) AMS Pr.

Burns & Their Treatment. 3rd ed. I. F. Muir et al. (Illus.). 192p. 1987. pap. text ed. 95.00 (*0-407-00333-9*) Buttrwrth-Heinemann.

Burns As Others Saw Him. W. L. Renwick. 52p. 1982. 30.00 (*0-686-87372-6*, 085411015, Pub. by Saltire Soc) St Mut.

Burns at Mossgiel. William R. Jolly. LC 76-52433. (English Literature Ser.: No. 33). 1977. lib. bdg. 47.95 (*0-8383-2144-5*) M S G Haskell Hse.

Burns Braille Transcription Dictionary. Mary F. Burns. LC 91-40378. 96p. 1992. 14.95 (*0-89128-232-7*) Am Foun Blind.

Burns Calendar. Comp. by James Gibson. LC 70-144555. (Illus.). reprint ed. 27.50 (*0-404-08513-X*) AMS Pr.

Burns Companion. Alan N. Bold. LC 89-70109. 196p. 1991. text ed. 39.95 (*0-312-04500-X*) St Martin.

Burns Federation: Song Book. Alloway Publishing Staff. (C). 1989. pap. text ed. 30.00 (*0-902320-10-6*, Alloway Pub) St Mut.

Burns for Bairns. Irving Miller. (Illus.). (C). 1989. pap. text ed. 35.00 (*0-907526-46-2*, Alloway Pub) St Mut.

Burns Handbook. John D. Ross. LC 76-144475. reprint ed. 24.50 (*0-404-08535-0*) AMS Pr.

Burns in Children: Pediatric Burn. Ed. by Hugo F. Carvajal. (Illus.). 352p. 1987. 79.00 (*0-8151-1442-7*, GKC-1, Yr Bk Med Pubs) Mosby Yr Bk.

Burns in Dumfriesshire. 3rd ed. William McDowall. LC 74-144516. reprint ed. 14.50 (*0-404-08518-0*) AMS Pr.

***Burns Indiana Statutes.** annot. ed. Date not set. write for info. (*0-614-05786-8*) Michie Butterworth.

Burns Indiana Statutes Annotated, 37 vols. write for info. (*0-672-83879-6*); (*0-318-54326-5*) Michie Butterworth.

Burns Lore of Dumfries & Galloway. M. Mackay. (C). 1988. 75.00 (*0-907526-36-5*, Alloway Pub) St Mut.

Burns Mantle Best Plays of Nineteen Forty-Nine to Nineteen Fifty. Ed. by John Chapman. LC 75-19860. (Best Plays Series). 1978. 30.95 (*0-405-09177-X*) Ayer.

Burnsiana. James A. Mackay. (C). 1988. 150.00 (*0-907526-35-7*, Alloway Pub) St Mut.

Burnside. William Marvel. LC 91-8419. (Illus.). xiv, 538p. (C). 1991. 32.50 (*0-8078-1983-2*) U of NC Pr.

Burnside Biographical Dictionary. Laverne Galeener-Moore. x, 236p. (Orig.). 1991. pap. 19.50 (*1-55613-488-6*) Heritage Bk.

Burnside Breech Loading Carbines. Edward A. Hull. LC 86-60682. (Illus.). 95p. 1986. 16.00 (*0-917218-22-1*) A Mowbray.

Burnside Problem & Identities in Groups. S. I. Adian. Tr. by John C. Lennox & J. Wiegold. (Ergebnisse der Mathematik und Ihrer Grenzgebiete Ser.: Vol. 95). 1979. 65.00 (*0-387-08728-1*) Spr-Verlag.

Burnside's Medical Examination Review. Ed. by John W. Burnside. (Illus.). 833p. 1986. pap. 47.00 (*0-443-08265-0*) Churchill.

***Burnt Book: Reading the Talmud.** Marc-Alain Quaknin. Tr. by Llewellyn Brown. LC 94-39674. (ENG & FRE.). 1995. write for info. (*0-691-03729-9*) Princeton U Pr.

Burnt Bridges: A Souvenir of the Singing Sixties & Beyond. Charles Marowitz. (Illus.). 245p. 1992. 34.95 (*0-340-49659-2*, Pub. by H & S UK) Trafalgar.

***Burnt Cork & Tambourines: A Source Book of Negro Ministrelsy.** William L. Slout. LC 95-3717. (Clipper Studies in the Theater: No. 11). 1995. lib. bdg. write for info. (*0-89370-358-3*); pap. write for info. (*0-89370-458-X*) Borgo Pr.

***Burnt Offerings.** Timothy Liu. 84p. (Orig.). 1995. pap. 12.00 (*1-55659-104-7*) Copper Canyon.

Burnt Offerings. Robert Marasco. 1993. reprint ed. lib. bdg. 18.95x (*0-89968-437-8*, Lghtyr Pr) Buccaneer Bks.

Burnt Offerings: Parables for Twentieth Century Christians. E. T. Eberhart. LC 77-23158. 1977. pap. 5.95 (*0-687-04375-1*) Pilgrim Hse.

Burnt Offerings & the Bloodstained Sands: Psychopolitics & the Sacrifice of the Phoenix. Gyeorgos C. Hatonn. Tr. by Dharma. 218p. (Orig.). (C). 1991. pap. 10.00 (*0-922356-33-5*) Amer West Pubs.

Burnt Orange Heresy. Charles Willeford. LC 90-50253. (Vintage Crime - Black Lizard Ser.). 160p. 1990. 7.95 (*0-679-73252-7*, Vin) Random.

Burnt Orange Heresy. Charles Willeford. LC 77-167708. 160p. 1987. reprint ed. pap. 3.95 (*0-88739-025-0*, Blk Lizard) Creat Arts Bk.

Burnt-out Case. Graham Greene. 1977. mass mkt. 4.95 (*0-14-001894-8*, Penguin Bks) Viking Penguin.

Burnt-out Case. Graham Greene. (Twentieth-Century Classics Ser.). 200p. 1992. pap. 9.95 (*0-14-018539-9*, Penguin Classics) Viking Penguin.

Burnt out Incense: The Saga of Citeaux America Epoch. M. Raymond. 445p. 1988. reprint ed. write for info. (*0-8198-1117-3*); reprint ed. pap. write for info. (*0-8198-1118-1*) Pauline Bks.

***Burnt Pearls: Ghetto Poems.** Abraham Sutzkever. Tr. by Seymour Mayne. 52p. 1995. lib. bdg. 20.00 (*0-8095-4528-4*) Borgo Pr.

***Burnt Stick.** Anthony Hill. LC 95-2698. (Illus.). 1995. write for info. (*0-395-73974-8*) Ticknor & Flds Bks Yng Read.

Burnt Tavern Road. I. Yevish. 224p. (Orig.). 1992. 15.95 (*0-9626330-5-4*); pap. 11.95 (*0-9626330-4-6*) I Yevish Bks.

Burnt Toast. Richard Roe. LC 79-87687. (Orig.). pap. 7.95 (*0-9602100-2-4*) St Wrks Cooperative.

Burnt Toast & Other Recipes. 2nd ed. Susan H. Sibbet. (Illus.). 80p. 1990. reprint ed. pap. 9.95 (*0-9625104-3-2*) White Mtn Pr.

Burnt Water. Carlos Fuentes. Tr. by Margaret S. Peden. 1986. pap. 12.00 (*0-374-51988-9*) FS&G.

Burnton Widows: A Nyla Wade Mystery. Vicki P. McConnell. LC 94-42465. (Orig.). 1994. pap. 10.95 (*0-9630822-7-2*) Madwoman Pr.

Burodyssey of H. O. M. E. R. Hebron E. Adams. LC 93-90932. (Illus.). 96p. (Orig.). 1994. pap. 9.95 (*0-9632919-1-2*) Foxon Pr.

Buros Desk Reference: Psychological Assessment in the Schools. Ed. by James C. Impara & Linda U. Murphy. 454p. (C). 1994. pap. text ed. 39.95 (*0-910674-37-X*) Buros Inst Mental.

B

An Asterisk (*) at the beginning of an entry indicates that the title is appearing in BIP for the first time. 955

BURP: A Journal about Food & How to Enjoy It. John R. Parker. (Illus.). 190p. (Orig.). 1986. pap. 8.95 (*0-912095-01-6*) Johmax Bks Inc.

Burpee American Garden Perennials. Suzanne F. Bales. 1991. pap. 9.00 (*0-671-86393-2*, P-H Gardening) P-H Gen Ref & Trav.

***Burpee Complete Gardener.** Maureen Heffernan et al. LC 95-13141. 1995. text ed. write for info. (*0-02-860378-8*) Macmillan.

Burpee Container Gardening. Suzanne F. Bales. (Burpee American Gardening Ser.). (Illus.). 96p. 1993. pap. 9.00 (*0-671-84648-5*, P-H Gardening) P-H Gen Ref & Trav.

Burpee Flowering Shrubs. Burpee Staff. 1992. pap. 9.00 (*0-671-87144-7*, P-H Gardening) P-H Gen Ref & Trav.

Burpee Groundcovers. Margaret Roach. (Burpee American Gardening Ser.). (Illus.). 96p. 1993. pap. 9.00 (*0-671-84647-7*, P-H Gardening) P-H Gen Ref & Trav.

Burpee Ornamental Trees. Charles O. Cresson. (Burpee American Gardening Ser.). (Illus.). 96p. 1993. pap. 9.00 (*0-671-84646-9*, P-H Gardening) P-H Gen Ref & Trav.

Burpee Water Gardening. Ken Druse. (Burpee American Gardening Ser.). (Illus.). 96p. 1993. pap. 9.00 (*0-671-84645-0*, P-H Gardening) P-H Gen Ref & Trav.

Burpee's American Harvest Cookbooks: The Spring Garden. Perla Meyers. 1988. 8.95 (*0-317-64461-0*, Fireside) S&S Trade.

Burr. Gore Vidal. 1986. mass mkt. 5.95 (*0-345-33921-5*) Ballantine.

Burr Bibliography: A List of Books Relating to Aaron Burr. Hamilton B. Tompkins. LC 76-177470. reprint ed. 21.50 (*0-404-06497-3*) AMS Pr.

Burrage Memorial: A Genealogical History of the Descendants of John Burrage. A. A. Burrage. (Illus.). 265p. 1989. reprint ed. lib. bdg. 49.50 (*0-8328-1292-7*); reprint ed. pap. 39.50 (*0-8328-1293-5*) Higginson Bk Co.

***Burrelle's Media Directory Volume 3: Broadcast Media: Part Two; Television & Cable.** annuals 290p. 1993. pap. write for info. (*1-885601-05-0*) Burrelles Info.

***Burrelle's Media Directory 1994.** annuals 4702p. 1993. pap. 500.00 (*1-885601-00-X*) Burrelles Info.

***Burrelle's Media Directory-1994 Vol. 2: Magazines & Newsletters.** annuals 1310p. 1993. pap. 200.00 (*1-885601-03-4*) Burrelles Info.

***Burrelle's Media Directory 1994 Newspaper & Related Media: Non-Daily Newspaper, 2 vols., Set.** annuals 1150p. 1993. pap. write for info. (*1-885601-02-6*) Burrelles Info.

***Burrelle's Media Directory 1994 Newspapers & Related Media: Part One: Daily Newspapers, 2 vols., Set.** annuals 606p. 1993. pap. 200.00 (*1-885601-01-8*) Burrelles Info.

***Burrelle's Media Directory 1994 Volume 3; Broadcast Media: Part One; Radio Stations.** annuals 1346p. 1993. pap. 250.00 (*1-885601-04-2*) Burrelles Info.

***Burrelle's Media Directory-1995.** annuals Ed. by James L. Hayes & Kathleen M. Guindon. 5209p. 1994. pap. 500.00 (*1-885601-12-3*) Burrelles Info.

***Burrelle's Media Directory-1995 Broadcast Media: Radio.** annuals Ed. by James L. Hayes & Kathleen M. Guindon. 1512p. 1994. pap. 250.00 (*1-885601-16-6*) Burrelles Info.

***Burrelle's Media Directory-1995 Broadcast Media: Television & Cable, 2, set.** annuals Ed. by James L. Hayes & Kathleen M. Guindon. 605p. 1994. pap. write for info. (*1-885601-17-4*) Burrelles Info.

***Burrelle's Media Directory-1995 Newspapers & Related Media: Daily Newspapers.** annuals Ed. by James L. Hayes & Kathleen M. Guindon. 749p. 1994. pap. 200.00 (*1-885601-13-1*) Burrelles Info.

***Burrelle's Media Directory 1995 Newspapers & Related Media: Non-Daily Newspapers, 2, set.** annuals Ed. by James L. Hayes & Kathleen M. Guindon. 1207p. 1994. pap. write for info. (*1-885601-14-X*) Burrelles Info.

***Burrelle's Media Directory 1996.** annuals Ed. by James L. Hayes & Kathleen M. Guindon. 1995. pap. 500.00 (*1-885601-24-7*) Burrelles Info.

***Burrelle's Media Directory-1996 Broadcast Media: Radio.** annuals Ed. by James L. Hayes & Kathleen M. Guindon. 1512p. 1995. pap. 250.00 (*1-885601-32-8*) Burrelles Info.

***Burrelle's Media Directory 1996 Broadcast Media: Television & Cable, 2, set.** annuals Ed. by James L. Hayes & Kathleen M. Guindon. 608p. 1995. pap. write for info. (*1-885601-33-6*) Burrelles Info.

***Burrelle's Media Directory-1996 Magazines & Newsletters.** annuals Ed. by James L. Hayes & Kathleen M. Guindon. 1440p. 1995. pap. 200.00 (*1-885601-31-X*) Burrelles Info.

***Burrelle's Media Directory-1996 Newspapers & Related Media: Daily Newspapers.** annuals 752p. 1995. pap. 200.00 (*1-885601-29-8*) Burrelles Info.

***Burrelle's Media Directory-1996 Newspapers & Related Media: Non-Daily Newspapers.** annuals Ed. by James L. Hayes & Kathleen M. Guindon. 1208p. 1995. pap. write for info. (*1-885601-30-1*) Burrelles Info.

***Burrelle's Minnesota Media Directory-1996.** Ed. by James L. Hayes & Kathleen M. Guindon. 1996. pap. write for info. (*1-885601-41-7*) Burrelles Info.

***Burrelle's New England Media Directory-1995.** annuals Ed. by James L. Hayes & Kathleen M. Guindon. 376p. 1995. pap. 95.00 (*1-885601-28-X*) Burrelles Info.

***Burrelle's New England Media Directory-1996.** rev. ed. Ed. by James L. Hayes & Kathleen M. Guindon. 376p. 1996. pap. 95.00 (*1-885601-40-9*) Burrelles Info.

***Burrelle's New Jersey Media Directory-1995.** Ed. by James L. Hayes & Kathleen M. Guindon. 185p. 1995. pap. 60.00 (*1-885601-25-5*) Burrelles Info.

***Burrelle's New Jersey Media Directory-1996.** rev. ed. Ed. by James L. Hayes & Kathleen M. Guindon. 185p. 1996. pap. 60.00 (*1-885601-37-9*) Burrelles Info.

***Burrelle's New York Media Directory-1995.** Ed. by James L. Hayes & Kathleen M. Guindon. 432p. 1995. pap. 95.00 (*1-885601-26-3*) Burrelles Info.

***Burrelle's New York Media Directory-1996.** rev. ed. Ed. by James L. Hayes & Kathleen M. Guindon. 432p. 1996. pap. 95.00 (*1-885601-38-7*) Burrelles Info.

***Burrelle's Pennsylvania Media Directory-1995.** Ed. by James L. Hayes & Kathleen M. Guindon. 236p. 1995. pap. 85.00 (*1-885601-27-1*) Burrelles Info.

***Burrelle's Pennsylvania Media Directory-1996.** rev. ed. Ed. by James L. Hayes & Kathleen M. Guindon. 236p. 1996. pap. 85.00 (*1-885601-39-5*) Burrelles Info.

***Burrell's Patent Law Reports Vols. 1-13: 1953-1990, Set.** Date not set. 520.00 (*0-614-00835-2*, Pub. by Juta SA) W W Gaunt.

Burrillville (Rhode Island) As It Was & As It Is. Horace A. Keach. iv, 100p. (Orig.). 1992. pap. 12.00 (*1-55613-536-X*) Heritage Bk.

Burrito Book. P. J. Birosik. 160p. (Orig.). 1991. pap. 8.95 (*0-380-76428-8*) Avon.

Burrito de Belen (The Bethlehem Donkey) Dowley & Bishop. (SPA.). Date not set. 2.99 (*1-56063-223-2*, 490389) Editorial Unilit.

Burro Bill & Me. 2nd ed. Edna C. Price. (Illus.). 300p. (C). 1993. reprint ed. pap. 9.95 (*1-878900-28-5*) DVNH Assn.

Burros & Paintbrushes: A Mexican Adventure. Everett G. Jackson. LC 84-40558. (Wardlaw Bk.). (Illus.). 170p. 1985. 13.95 (*0-89096-229-4*) Tex A&M Univ Pr.

Burros of Mavrick Gulch. Lou Ray. (Illus.). 44p. (Orig.). (J). (gr. k-5). 1983. pap. 7.95 (*0-9612346-0-1*, 83-090410) Ray-Foster.

Burroughs Dictionary: An Alphabetical List of Proper Names, Word, Phrases & Concepts Contained in the Published Works of Edgar Rice Burroughs. George T. McWhorter. LC 87-14266. (Illus.). 462p. 1987. lib. bdg. 65.00 (*0-8191-6512-3*) U Pr of Amer.

Burroughs File. William S. Burroughs. 1984. pap. 11.95 (*0-87286-152-X*) City Lights.

Burrough's Kankakee's Earliest Settlers. Burroughs. 1986. 24.95 (*0-917914-54-6*); pap. 11.95 (*0-685-18891-4*) Lindsay Pubns.

Burrowers Beneath. limited ed. Brian Lumley. (Illus.). 192p. 1988. reprint ed. 22.50 (*0-932445-30-6*) Ganley Pub.

Burrows. Shirley Greenway. (Animal Homes Ser.). (Illus.). 24p. (J). (gr. k-4). 1991. lib. bdg. 10.40 (*1-878137-11-5*) Newington.

Burrows: The Law of Restitution. Andrew Burrows. 608p. 1993. pap. 52.00 (*0-406-01019-6*, U.K.) Butterworth Legal Pubs.

Burrows Textbook of Microbiology. 22th ed. Bob A. Freeman. (Illus.). 1100p. 1985. text ed. 105.00 (*0-7216-3868-6*) Saunders.

Burr's Hill: A Seventeenth Century Wampanoag Burial Ground in Warren, Rhode Island, Vol. 2. Ed. by Susan G. Gibson. LC 80-81354. (Illus.). 182p. 1980. pap. 10.00 (*0-317-55200-7*) Haffenreffer Mus Anthro.

Burs under the Saddle: A Second Look at Books & Histories of the West. Ramon F. Adams. LC 64-13593. 624p. 1989. pap. 19.95 (*0-8061-2170-X*) U of Okla Pr.

***Burst: Les Paul Standard.** 1994. 24.95 (*0-8256-9388-8*, LA10008) Music Sales.

Burst into Music: Teaching Music to Young Children. Jennifer A. Townsend. (Illus.). 112p. 1993. pap. 12.95 (*1-877969-25-7*) J & S Pub.

***Burst of Brilliance: Germantown, Pennsylvania, & Navajo Weaving.** Dilys Winegrad. (Illus.). 72p. 1995. pap. text ed. 19.95 (*0-8122-0990-7*) U of Pa Pr.

Burst of Light. Audre Lorde. LC 88-3924. 134p. (Orig.). 1988. lib. bdg. 18.95 (*0-932379-40-0*); pap. 8.95 (*0-932379-39-7*) Firebrand Bks.

Burst of Speed: Five Proven Techniques to Increase Your Speed. Joe Miller. (Illus.). 144p. 1984. 15.95 (*0-89651-705-5*); pap. 8.95 (*0-89651-706-3*) B L Pub.

Burst out Laughing. Barry Stevens. LC 84-45365. (Illus.). 192p. (Orig.). 1985. pap. 9.95 (*0-89087-410-7*) Celestial Arts.

Bursting Bonds: The Heir of Slaves - The Autobiography of a "New Negro" enl. ed. William Pickens. Ed. by William L. Andrews. LC 91-6847. (Blacks of the Diaspora Ser.). (Illus.). 112p. 1991. 25.00 (*0-253-34496-4*); pap. 8.95 (*0-253-20671-5*, MB-671) Ind U Pr.

Bursting of New Wineskins: Reflection on Religion & Culture at the End of Affluence. Carl A. Raschke. LC 78-16604. (Pittsburgh Theological Monographs: No. 24). 1978. 10.75 (*0-915138-34-4*) Pickwick.

Bursting the Bonds? A Jewish-Christian Dialogue on Jesus & Paul. Leonard Swidler et al. LC 90-39046. (Faith Meets Faith Ser.). 1990. 39.95 (*0-88344-713-4*); pap. 16.95 (*0-88344-712-6*) Orbis Bks.

Bursting the Foundations: A Bibliographical Primer on the Criticism of Culture. Tom Morris. LC 81-82009. (Paunch Ser.: No. 55-56). (Illus.). 164p. 1981. pap. 7.00 (*0-9602478-5-8*) Paunch.

Bursting with Joy - Una Celebracion! Gino Aisenberg & Elizabeth Montes. (Illus.). (Orig.). (J). (gr. 1-8). 1992. teacher ed 15.95 (*1-55944-025-2*) Franciscan Comns.

Burt Affair. R. B. Joynson. (General Psychology Ser.). 400p. 1989. 35.00 (*0-415-01039-X*, A3371) Routledge.

***Burt & Me: My Days & Nights with Burt Reynolds.** Elaine B. Hall. 352p. 1994. mass mkt. 5.99 (*0-7860-0117-8*, Pinnacle NY) Windsor NY.

Burt Bacharach Anthology. 1992. pap. 19.95 (*0-943351-43-X*, XW1504) Astor Bks.

Burt Dow: Deep-Water Man. Robert McCloskey. LC 68-364. (Illus.). 64p. (J). (gr. 4-6). 1963. pap. 16.99 (*0-670-19748-3*) Viking Child Bks.

Burt Dow, Deep-Water Man. Robert McCloskey. (Illus.). 64p. (J). (ps-3). 1989. pap. 4.99 (*0-14-050978-X*, Puffin) Puffin Bks.

Burt Reynolds. Lisa Smith. LC 92-61597. (Illus.). 128p. 1994. 27.50 (*0-9633808-0-X*) Magic Light.

Burt Rutan: Reinventing the Airplane. Vera F. Rollo. LC 91-52844. (Illus.). 300p. 1991. 24.50 (*0-917882-33-4*) MD Hist Pr.

Burt Shotton, Dodgers Manager: A Baseball Biography. David Gough. 151p. 1994. pap. 23.95 (*0-89950-981-9*) McFarland & Co.

***Burt Wolf's Menu Cookbook.** Burt Wolf. LC 95-13791. 1995. write for info. (*0-385-47273-0*) Doubleday.

Burt Wolf's Table. Burt Wolf. LC 93-43380. 1994. 20.00 (*0-385-47274-9*) Doubleday.

Burton: A Biography of Sir Richard Francis Burton. Byron Farwell. 464p. 1990. pap. 9.95 (*0-14-012068-8*, Penguin Bks) Viking Penguin.

Burton & Cyb, No. 1. Antonio Segura. Ed. by Bernd Metz. Tr. by David Rosenthal. (Illus.). 49p. (Orig.). 1991. pap. 9.95 (*0-87416-101-0*) Catalan Communs.

Burton & Stanley. Frank O'Rourke. (J). (gr. 4-7). 1993. 15.95 (*0-87923-824-0*) Godine.

Burton & the Giggle Machine. Dorothy Haas. LC 91-25411. (Illus.). 160p. (J). (gr. 5-8). 1992. text ed. 13.95 (*0-02-738203-6*, Bradbury S&S) S&S Childrens.

Burton Joyce & Bulcote. Bulcote Local History Society Staff & Burton Joyce. (Towns & Villages of England Ser.). (Illus.). 1994. pap. 10.00 (*0-7509-0599-9*) A Sutton Pub.

Burton Lazars Cartulary: A Medieval Leicestershire Estate. Terry Bourne & David Marcombe. (C). 1987. text ed. 30.00 (*0-685-22184-9*, Pub. by Univ Nottingham UK) St Mut.

Burton on Burton. Tim Burton & Mark Salisbury. (Directors on Directors Ser.). (Illus.). 200p. 1995. 22.95 (*0-571-17392-6*) Faber & Faber.

Burton Rascoe. Donald M. Hensley. LC 77-110361. (Twayne's United States Authors Ser.). 155p. 1970. lib. bdg. 17.95 (*0-8057-0608-9*) Irvington.

Burtonian Melancholy in the Plays of John Ford. S. Blaine Ewing. 122p. (C). 1940. reprint ed. pap. 39.95 (*0-8383-0027-8*) M S G Haskell Hse.

Burton's Zoom Zoom Va-room Machine. Dorothy Haas. Ed. by Pat MacDonald. 144p. (J). (gr. 4-7). 1993. pap. 2.99 (*0-671-74702-9*, Minstrel Bks) PB.

Burton's Zoom Zoom Va-Rooom Machine. Dorothy Haas. LC 89-77426. (Illus.). 144p. (J). (gr. 5-8). 1990. text ed. 13.95 (*0-02-738201-X*, Bradbury S&S) S&S Childrens.

Burundi. Morna Daniels. (World Bibliographical Ser.). 1992. lib. bdg. 63.50 (*1-85109-194-7*) ABC-CLIO.

***Burundi.** Karen L. Niesen et al. LC 95-15771. (OIES Country Guide Ser.). 1995. write for info. (*0-929851-44-7*) Am Assn Coll Registrars.

Burundi. Marian T. Wolbers. (Places & Peoples of the World Ser.). (Illus.). 120p. (YA). (gr. 6 up). 1989. lib. bdg. 14.95 (*1-55546-785-7*) Chelsea Hse.

Burundi. Allan Carpenter & Matthew Maginnis. Ed. by John Rowe. LC 73-4971. (Enchantment of Africa Ser.). 93p. (YA). (gr. 6-12). reprint ed. pap. 26.60 (*0-8357-2700-9*, 2039764) Bks Demand.

Burundi: Civil Rights Reporter. Lewis B. Scholnick. (Illus.). 60p. (Orig.). (C). 1994. pap. 45.00 (*1-57205-086-1*) Rector Pr.

Burundi: Ethnocide As Discourse & Practice. Rene Lemarchand. (Woodrow Wilson Center Press Ser.). 200p. (C). 1994. 54.95 (*0-521-45176-0*) Cambridge U Pr.

Burundi: The Tragic Years. Thomas P. Melady. LC 73-89357. (Illus.). 128p. reprint ed. pap. 36.50 (*0-8357-8822-9*, 2033470) Bks Demand.

Burundi Ethnic Massacres, 1988. David Ress. LC 91-45122. 136p. 1992. lib. bdg. 69.95 (*0-7734-9878-8*) E Mellen.

Burwell & Metcalfe's Heart Disease & Pregnancy: Physiology & Management. 2nd ed. James Metcalfe et al. 408p. 1986. 125.00 (*0-316-56797-3*) Little.

***Burwell Directory of Information Brokers - 1994.** Helen P. Burwell. 600p. 1994. 79.50 (*0-938519-10-7*) Burwell Ent.

***Burwell World Directory of Information Brokers 1995.** Ed. by Helen P. Burwell. 800p. 1995. pap. text ed. 99.50 (*0-938519-11-5*) Burwell Ent.

Bury Him Kindly. large type ed. Pat Burden. 296p. 1992. 21.95 (*0-7505-0368-8*, Pub. by Magna Print Bks) Ulverscroft.

Bury it Deep. Sam Reaves. LC 93-3242. 272p. 1993. 21.95 (*0-399-13870-6*, Putnam) Putnam Pub Group.

***Bury It Deep.** Sam Reaves. 272p. 1994. mass mkt. 4.99 (*0-380-72266-6*) Avon.

Bury Love Deep. large type ed. Rosemary A. Sisson. 352p. 1986. 15.95 (*0-7089-1451-9*) Ulverscroft.

Bury Me Deep. Christopher Pike. Ed. by Patricia MacDonald. 224p. (Orig.). (J). 1991. mass mkt. 3.99 (*0-671-69057-4*, Archway) PB.

Bury Me Deep. large type ed. H. Lloyd Ingham. (Linford Mystery Library). 304p. 1987. pap. 11.95 (*0-7089-6458-3*, Linford) Ulverscroft.

***Bury Me in a Free Land: The Abolitionist Movement in Indiana, 1816-1865.** Gwendolyn J. Crenshaw. 69p. 1993. pap. 3.00 (*1-885323-48-4*) IN Hist Bureau.

Bury Me in a Pot Bunker: A Personal Golf Odyssey. Pete Dye & Mark Shaw. LC 94-18252. 1995. 22.12 (*0-201-40769-8*) Addison-Wesley.

Bury Me Sioux. Ed. by Arnold Perrin. 1982. pap. 2.00 (*0-939736-46-2*) Wings ME.

***Bury Me Standing: The Gypsies & Their Journey.** Isabel Fonseca. LC 95-14272. 1995. write for info. (*0-679-40678-6*) Knopf.

Bury Me with Balloons. Pat Postlewaite. 250p. 1991. pap. 9.95 (*0-938577-06-9*) St Johns Pub.

Bury My Bones but Keep My Words: African Tales for Retelling. Illus. by Meshack Asare. 192p. (J). (gr. 5 up). 1994. pap. 4.99 (*0-14-036889-2*) Puffin Bks.

Bury My Bones but Keep My Words: African Tales for Retelling. Tony Fairman. (Illus.). 192p. (YA). 1992. 15.95 (*0-8050-2333-X*, Bks Young Read) H Holt & Co.

Bury My Heart at Fun-Fun Mountain. Bill Amend. (Foxtrot Collection Ser.). (Illus.). 128p. 1993. pap. 8.95 (*0-8362-1706-3*) Andrews & McMeel.

Bury My Heart at Wounded Knee. Dee Brown. 1992. reprint ed. lib. bdg. 32.95 (*0-89966-975-1*) Buccaneer Bks.

Bury My Heart at Wounded Knee: An Indian History of the American West. Dee Brown. LC 70-121633. (Illus.). 512p. 1971. 27.50 (*0-8050-1045-9*) H Holt & Co.

Bury My Heart at Wounded Knee: An Indian History of the American West. Dee Brown. 512p. (C). 1991. pap. 14.95 (*0-8050-1730-5*, Owl) H Holt & Co.

Bury My Heart at Wrigley Field: When the Cubs Were the White Socks. Larry D. Names. (History of the Chicago Cubs Ser.: Pt. 1). (Illus.). 280p. 1989. 18.95 (*0-9621684-0-8*) G K Scott Pub.

Bury St. Edmunds & the Urban Crisis, 1290-1539. Robert S. Gottfried. LC 81-11984. (Illus.). 324p. 1981. 49.50 (*0-691-05340-5*) Princeton U Pr.

***Bury St. Edmunds & the Urban Crisis, 1290-1539.** Robert S. Gottfried. LC 81-11984. reprint ed. pap. 94.40 (*0-7837-9345-6*, 2060086) Bks Demand.

***Bury the Bishop.** Kate Gallison. 1995. pap. 4.99 (*0-440-21854-3*) Dell.

Bury the Dead. Peter Carter. LC 85-45995. 374p. (J). (gr. 6 up). 1987. 17.00 (*0-374-31011-4*) FS&G.

Bury the Dead. Irwin Shaw. 1970. pap. 2.75 (*0-8222-0165-8*) Dramatists Play.

Burying Grounds of Sharon, Conn., Amenia & North East, New York. L. Van Alystyne. LC 84-125476. 268p. 1983. reprint ed. 15.00 (*0-932334-47-4*, NY14030) Hrt of the Lakes.

Burying Lenin: The Revolution in Soviet Ideology & Foreign Policy. Steven Kull. 219p. 1992. text ed. 46.50 (*0-8133-1501-8*) Westview.

Burying Lenin: The Revolution in Soviet Ideology & Foreign Policy. Steven Kull. 219p. (C). 1992. pap. text ed. 19.95 (*0-8133-1500-X*) Westview.

Burying Mao: Chinese Politics in the Age of Deng Xiaoping. Richard Baum. LC 94-9892. 1994. 35.00 (*0-691-03639-X*) Princeton U Pr.

Burying Place of Gov. Arnold: An Account of the Establishment, Destruction & Restoration of the Burying Place of Benedict Arnold. Alice Brayton. (Illus.). 135p. (Orig.). 1960. pap. 4.75 (*0-917012-21-6*) Preserv Soc Newport.

Burying Point. Ann Brahms. 320p. 1991. mass mkt. 4.99 (*0-8217-3892-5*) Zebra.

Burying SM: The Politics of Knowledge & the Sociology of Power in Africa. David W. Cohen & E. S. Odhiambo. (Social History of Africa Ser.). 168p. (C). 1992. pap. 19.95 (*0-435-08063-6*, 08063) Heinemann.

Burying Uncertainty: Risk & the Case Against Geological Disposal of Nuclear Waste. Kristin S. Shrader-Frechette. LC 92-35083. 1993. 40.00 (*0-520-08244-3*); pap. 15.00 (*0-520-08301-6*) U CA Pr.

***Bus.** Chris L. Demarest. LC 95-6623. (J). 1996. write for info. (*0-15-200810-1*, Red Wagon Bks) HarBrace.

Bus Deregulation in the Metropolitan Areas. Laurie Pickup et al. Ed. by Francesca Kenny. (Oxford Studies in Transport). 278p. 1991. text ed. 59.95 (*1-85628-198-1*, Pub. by Avebury Pub UK) Ashgate Pub Co.

Bus Driver. Jack Rudman. (Career Examination Ser.: C-2197). 1994. pap. 19.95 (*0-8373-2197-2*) Nat Learn.

Bus Driver's Guide to Commercial Drivers License. Robert M. Calvin. Ed. by Marilyn M. Martin. 19.50 (*0-89262-177-X*) Career Pub.

Bus Fare to Kentucky: The Autobiography of Skeeter Davis. Skeeter Davis. LC 93-8841. (Illus.). 288p. 1993. 19.95 (*1-55972-191-X*, Birch Ln Pr) Carol Pub Group.

Bus Home: Poems. Shirley B. Anders. LC 85-24644. (Breakthrough Ser.: No. 49). 64p. 1986. pap. 9.95 (*0-8262-0603-4*) U of Mo Pr.

Bus Inspection Guidelines. (National Cooperative Transit Research Program Synthesis Ser.: No. 10). 73p. 1987. 9.20 (*0-309-04405-7*) Transport Res Bd.

Bus Maintainer, Group A. Jack Rudman. (Career Examination Ser.: C-100). 1994. pap. 19.95 (*0-8373-0100-9*) Nat Learn.

Bus Maintainer, Group B. Jack Rudman. (Career Examination Ser.: C-101). 1994. pap. 19.95 (*0-8373-0101-7*) Nat Learn.

Bus Maintenance Improvement. (Special Report Ser.: No. 198). 59p. 1983. 8.60 (*0-309-03521-X*) Transport Res Bd.

Bus Nine to Paradise. Leo F. Buscaglia. LC 85-63187. 276p. 1986. 16.95 (*0-943432-67-7*) SLACK Inc.

Bus Nine to Paradise. Leo F. Buscaglia. 1987. reprint ed. pap. 10.00 (*0-449-90222-6*, Columbine) Fawcett.

Bus of My Own. Jim Lehrer. LC 92-7526. (Illus.). 256p. 1992. 24.95 (*0-399-13765-3*, Putnam) Putnam Pub Group.

Bus Operator. Jack Rudman. (Career Examination Ser.: C-102). 1994. pap. 19.95 (*0-8373-0102-5*) Nat Learn.

Bus Operator - Conductor: (NYCTA-MABSTOA) 7th ed. Ed. by Hy Hammer. LC 93-6817. 1993. pap. 12.00 (*0-671-87134-X*) P-H.

Bus Operator-Conductor. Jack Rudman. (Career Examination Ser.: C-3383). 1994. pap. 19.95 (*0-8373-3383-0*) Nat Learn.

Bus People. Rachel Anderson. LC 92-1506. 112p. (YA). (gr. 5 up). 1992. 13.95 (*0-8050-2297-X*, Bks Young Read) H Holt & Co.

Bus Planning & Operation in Urban Areas: A Practical Guide. G. A. Giannopoulos. (Illus.). 384p. 1989. text ed. 84.95 (*0-566-05673-9*, Pub. by Gower UK) Ashgate Pub Co.

***Bus Ride to Justice: Changing the System by the System the Life & Works of Fred D. Gray Preacher - Attorney - Politician.** Fred D. Gray. LC 94-41805. (Illus.). 416p. 1995. 25.00 (*1-881320-23-5*) Black Belt Pr.

B

956

An Asterisk (*) at the beginning of an entry indicates that the title is appearing in BIP for the first time.

Bus Riders. Sharon P. Denslow. LC 92-14109. (Illus.). 32p. (J). (ps-2). 1993. text ed. 14.95 (*0-02-728682-7*, Four Winds Pr) S&S Childrens.

Bus Ridership: An Analysis of a Survey in the Omaha Metropolitan Area. Murray Frost. 78p. (Orig.). 1984. pap. 6.50 (*1-55719-045-3*) U NE CPAR.

Bus Ride...(s) Scott Shaw. 35p. (Orig.). 1990. pap. 5.95 (*1-877792-23-3*) Buddha Rose.

Bus Station Mystery. Gertrude C. Warner. LC 74-8293. (Boxcar Children Mysteries Ser.: No. 18). (Illus.). 128p. (J). (gr. 2-7). 1974. lib. bdg. 10.95 (*0-8075-0975-2*); pap. 3.50 (*0-8075-0976-0*) A Whitman.

Bus Stop. William Inge. 1956. pap. 4.75 (*0-8222-0166-6*) Dramatists Play.

Bus Stops. Taro Gomi. LC 88-10193. (Illus.). 32p. (J). (ps-1). 1988. 10.95 (*0-87701-551-1*) Chronicle Bks.

Bus Touring: A Guide to Charter Vacations, USA. Stuart Warren. 160p. (Orig.). 1989. pap. 9.95 (*0-912528-95-8*) John Muir.

Bus Transit Accessibility for the Handicapped in Urban Areas. (National Cooperative Highway Research Program Report Ser.: No. 83). 73p. 1981. 7.60 (*0-309-03272-5*) Transport Res Bd.

Bus Transport in India: The Structure, Management & Performance of Road Transport Corporation. Sundarsanam Padam. 1990. 32.50 (*81-202-0222-8*, Pub. by Ajanta II) S Asia.

Bus Transportation Technician. Jack Rudman. (Career Examination Ser.: C-3321). 1994. pap. 27.95 (*0-8373-3321-0*) Nat Learn.

***Bus Trip.** 1995. pap. text ed. 16.95 (*1-884832-07-5*) JTG Nashville.

***Bus Trip.** Sandviks Bokforlag. (Illus.). 8p. (J). (ps). 1993. 11.49 (*1-881445-23-2*) Sandvik Pub.

Bus Trip Handbook. Earl Borders, Jr. LC 84-60654. (Illus.). 112p. (Orig.). 1985. pap. 8.95 (*0-917125-00-2*) Home Run Pr.

Busca Da Excelencia. Ted Engstrom & Alec Mackenzie. 96p. (POR.). 1990. 3.95 (*0-8297-1632-7*) Life Pubs Intl.

Buscadero. Bill Brooks. LC 93-6523. (Novel of the West Ser.). 210p. 1993. 16.95 (*0-87131-728-1*) M Evans.

Buscadero. large type ed. Bill Brooks. LC 93-20784. 1993. 18.95 (*0-8161-5858-4*, Large Print Bks) Hall.

Buscadero. large type ed. Tex Larrigan. (Linford Western Library). 288p. 1994. pap. 14.95 (*0-7089-7496-1*, Linford) Ulverscroft.

Buscaglia: Born for Love. LC 91-51071. 298p. 1992. 19.00 (*1-55642-213-X*) SLACK Inc.

Buscaglia: Love. 150p. 1972. 15.00 (*0-685-72905-2*) SLACK Inc.

Buscapade: Plain Talk Across the U. S. A. Allen H. Neuharth. 1987. 16.95 (*0-944347-00-2*) USA Today Bks.

BusCapade: Plain Talk Across the USA. 320p. 1987. 16.95 (*0-318-23485-8*) USA Today Bks.

Busch-Reisinger Museum: Harvard University. Charles Haxthausen. LC 80-65261. (Illus.). 156p. 1980. pap. 34.95 (*0-89659-138-7*) Abbeville Pr.

***Busch-Reisinger Museum: History & Holdings.** Peter Nisbet & Emilie Norris. (Illus.). 125p. 1995. pap. 9.95 (*0-916724-79-4*, 4794) Harvard Art Mus.

Buschsbaum's Complete Handbook of Practical Electronic Reference Date. 3rd ed. Walter H. Buschsbaum & Robert C. Genn, Jr. 672p. 1987. pap. 16.95 (*0-317-65985-5*) P-H.

Buses Roll. Carol Baldwin. Ed. by Linn Underhill. (Illus.). 112p. (C). 1974. pap. text ed. 4.95 (*0-393-05535-3*) Norton.

***Bush: A Guide to the Vegetated Landscapes of Australia.** Ian G. Read. (Illus.). 1995. pap. 22.95 (*0-86840-254-0*, Pub. by New South Wales Univ Pr AT) Intl Spec Bk.

Bush Administration's Record on Human Rights in 1989. Human Rights Watch Staff. 296p. 1990. pap. 15.00 (*0-929692-41-1*) Hum Rts Watch.

Bush & Gorbachev. Michael R. Beschloss & Strobe Talbott. 1989. write for info. (*0-318-65992-1*, E Burlingame Bks) HarpC.

***Bush Animals.** Kathie Atkinson. (J). (ps-3). 1994. pap. 3.95 (*1-86373-589-5*) IPG Chicago.

Bush Base, Forest Farm: Culture, Environment & Development. Ed. by Elisabeth Croll & David Parkin. (European Inter-University Development Opportunity Study Group Ser.). (Illus.). 224p. 1992. 65.00 (*0-415-06656-5*, A7299); pap. 17.95 (*0-415-06657-3*, A7340) Routledge.

Bush Flying. Steven Levi & Jim O'Meara. 1992. pap. text ed. 16.95 (*0-07-157163-9*) McGraw.

Bush Flying. Steven Levi & Jim O'Meara. (Practical Flying Ser.). 168p. 1992. pap. 16.95 (*0-8306-3462-2*, 1037) TAB Bks.

***Bush Flying: The Romance of the North.** Robert S. Grant. 1995. pap. 24.95 (*0-88839-350-4*) Hancock House.

Bush for the Bushman: Need "The Gods Must Be Crazy" Kalahari People Die? John Perrott. LC 92-11105. (Illus.). 222p. (Orig.). 1993. pap. 14.95 (*1-881399-04-4*) Beaver Pond P&P.

Bush Is Still Burning see Zarza Sique Ardiendo

Bush Paths. Keith Arrowsmith. 177p. (C). 1989. text ed. 60.00 (*1-872795-24-2*, Pub. by Pentland Pr UK) St Mut.

Bush Pilot with a Briefcase: The Happy-Go-Lucky Story of Grant McConachie. Ronald Keith. (Airlines History Project Ser.). (Illus.). reprint ed. 39.50 (*0-404-19326-9*) AMS Pr.

Bush Pilots of Alaska. Frwd. by Fred Hirschmann. LC 89-83730. (Illus.). 144p. 1989. 39.95 (*1-55868-012-8*) Gr Arts Ctr Pub.

Bush Presidency: First Appraisals. Colin Campbell et al. LC 91-18333. 320p. (Orig.). (C). 1991. 25.00 (*0-934540-90-X*); pap. text ed. 19.95x (*0-934540-91-8*) Chatham Hse Pubs.

Bush Presidency: Triumphs & Adversities. Ed. by Dilys M. Hill & Phil Williams. LC 93-42731. 1994. text ed. 35.00 (*0-312-12102-4*) St Martin.

Bush-Quayle: The Reagan Legacy. Arthur F. Ide. (Illus.). xiv, 136p. (Orig.). (C). 1989. pap. 9.00 (*0-938659-03-0*) Scholars Bks.

Bush Savings Plan. Aldona Robbins & Gary Robbins. 1990. pap. 10.00 (*0-943802-55-5*, 152) Natl Ctr Pol.

Bush Studies. Barbara Baynton. 140p. (Orig.). 1994. pap. 9.00 (*0-207-17794-5*, Pub. by Angus & Robertson AT) HarpC.

Bush vs. the Congressional Democrats, Whose Tax Plan Is Better? John C. Goodman et al. (Illus.). 19p. (C). 1992. pap. 5.00 (*0-943802-95-4*, BG116) Natl Ctr Pol.

Bushels of Rubles: Soviet Youth in Transition. Kitty Weaver. LC 92-15987. 224p. 1992. text ed. 45.00 (*0-275-93844-1*, C3844, Praeger Pubs) Greenwood.

Bushes. Cass R. Sandak. LC 91-11153. (First Families Ser.). (Illus.). 48p. (J). (gr. 5). 1991. text ed. 4.95 (*0-89686-632-7*, Crstwood Hse) Silver Burdett Pr.

Bushfire. James Preston. 1993. 17.00 (*0-86025-258-2*, Pub. by Ian Henry Pubns UK) Empire Pub Srvs.

Bushfire: Stories of Lesbian Desire. Ed. by Karen Barber. 206p. (Orig.). 1991. pap. 8.95 (*1-55583-312-8*, Lace MA) Alyson Pubns.

Bushido: The Soul of Japan. Inazo Nitobe. 228p. 1994. pap. 8.95 (*0-8048-1961-0*) C E Tuttle.

Bushido Incident. Betty A. Crawford. 320p. (Orig.). 1992. mass mkt. 4.99 (*0-88677-517-5*) DAW Bks.

Bushido, The Warrior's Code. Inazo Nitobe. Ed. by Charles Lucas. LC 75-21718. (History & Philosophy Ser.). (Illus.). 1975. pap. text ed. 9.95 (*0-89750-031-8*, 303, Wehman) Ohara Pubns.

Bushido Thing. Jack Morris. (Illus.). 350p. 1994. 25.00 (*0-912479-08-6*) Palmer Pr.

Bushisms: "His World New Order...Thing": The Deep Deep Thoughts of Bush & Friends. Larry Engelmann. Ed. by Diane Parker. LC 92-50171. (Illus.). 60p. 1992. pap. 3.50 (*0-88247-934-2*) R & E Pubs.

Bushman Myth: The Making of a Namibian Underclass. Robert J. Gordon. 304p. 1992. text ed. 67.00 (*0-8133-1173-X*) Westview.

Bushman Myth: The Making of a Namibian Underclass. Robert J. Gordon. 304p. (C). 1992. pap. text ed. 19.95 (*0-8133-1381-3*) Westview.

Bushman of the Kalahari, Reading Level 5. Steyn. (Original People Ser.: Set II). (Illus.). 48p. (J). (gr. 4-8). 1989. 12.50 (*0-685-58810-6*); lib. bdg. 16.67 (*0-86625-267-3*) Rourke Corp.

Bushman Who Came Back. Arthur W. Upfield. 192p. 1989. pap. 5.95 (*0-02-025911-5*, Collier S&S) S&S Trade.

Bushmaster Fall. Carl Posey. 1992. 19.95 (*1-55611-245-9*) D I Fine.

Bushmasters: America's Jungle Warriors of World War II. Anthony Arthur. 1988. mass mkt. 4.95 (*0-312-91358-3*) St Martin.

Bushmen. Alf Wannenburgh. (Illus.). 192p. (C). 1988. 180.00 (*1-85368-036-2*, Pub. by New Holland Pubs UK) St Mut.

Bushmen Brouhaha. J. Bianchi. (Illus.). 24p. (J). (ps-8). 1987. 12.95 (*0-921285-10-8*, Pub. by Bungalo Bks CN); pap. 4.95 (*0-921285-08-6*, Pub. by Bungalo Bks CN) Firefly Bks Ltd.

Bushmills Irish Pub Guide. Sybil Taylor. (Illus.). 224p. (Orig.). 1994. pap. 14.95 (*0-86281-385-9*, Pub. by Appletree Pr IE) Irish Bks Media.

Bushranger of the Skies. large type ed. Arthur Upfield. 1978. 21.95 (*0-7089-0132-8*) Ulverscroft.

Bushu: Radicals of the Japanese Script. Olov B. Anderson. (Scandinavian Institute of Asian Studies Monograph). 87p. (C). 1981. pap. 15.00 (*0-7007-0127-3*, Pub. by Curzon Pr UK) Humanities.

***Bushwacked by Bushmasters: Waco, the Raw Truth. Ronald R. Davidson. 208p. (Orig.). 1995. pap. 19.95 (*0-9645223-0-6*) Watchman Davidson.**
On February 26, 1993, the World Trade Center was bombed. Less than 44 hours later the Treasury Department raided the Branch Davidian church/home in Waco, Texas. The resulting 51-day stand-off captured the attention of the American public & the entire world. BUSHWACKED BY BUSHMASTERS, WACO THE RAW TRUTH, shows the connection between the WORLD TRADE CENTER bombing & the resulting raid on the Waco Branch Davidians. It explores the connection between the build-up of the Iraqi military preceding OPERATION: DESERT STORM & the retaliatory strike by the Iraqis against the WORLD TRADE CENTER. By clear & convincing evidence, the reader will see how innocent victims of the LARGEST civilian law enforcement action in U.S. history, were railroaded into prison to cover up the American government's evil deeds. This book has a foreign flavor as well, clearly showing the Italian government's clandestine use of the American banking system to hide the secret financing of the Iraqi military build-up. To order direct, contact: Watchman Publishing, (800) 699-WACO or write to: Watchman Publishing, Box 301, Miranda, CA 95553. *Publisher Provided Annotation.*

Bushwacked Piano. Thomas McGuane. 1994. pap. 11.00 (*0-394-25886-X*) Random.

Bushwalking in Australia. 2nd ed. John Chapman & Monica Chapman. (Illus.). 224p. (Orig.). 1992. pap. 12.95 (*0-86442-171-0*) Lonely Planet.

Bushwalking in Papua New Guinea. 2nd ed. Yvon Perusse. (Illus.). 208p. 1993. pap. 14.95 (*0-86442-052-8*) Lonely Planet.

Bushwhacked Piano. Thomas McGuane. LC 84-40014. (Vintage Contemporaries Ser.). 224p. 1984. pap. 11.00 (*0-394-72642-1*, Vin) Random.

***Bushwhackers.** large type ed. Frank Gruber. (Linford Western Ser.). 1994. pap. 14.95 (*0-7089-7641-7*, Linford) Ulverscroft.

Bushwhackers. Lee Floren. 192p. (Orig.). 1986. reprint ed. pap. 2.50 (*0-8439-2385-7*) Dorchester Pub Co.

Bushwhackers: The Civil War in North Carolina - The Mountains. William Trotter. LC 90-28760. (Civil War in North Carolina Ser.). (Illus.). 338p. 1991. reprint ed. pap. 12.95 (*0-89587-087-8*) Blair.

Bushwhackers see Bitter Sage

Bushwhackers - Ride the Wild Country. Lee Floren. 368p. 1992. pap. 4.50 (*0-8439-3277-5*) Dorchester Pub Co.

Bushwhackers & Other Stories. Mary N. Murfree. LC 73-90588. (Short Story Index Reprint Ser., Vol. 1). 1977. 20.95 (*0-8369-3071-1*) Ayer.

***Bushwhacker's View of the Adirondacks.** John E. Winkler. Ed. by Nea S. Burdick. LC 94-44156. 1995. pap. 27.50 (*0-925168-37-8*) North Country.

Bushwick Human Services Directory. Gail Harris. 84p. 1984. pap. text ed. 7.50 (*0-88156-071-5*) Comm Serv Soc NY.

Bushworkers & Bosses: Logging in Northern Ontario, 1900-1980. Ian Radforth. 367p. 1987. 45.00 (*0-8020-2639-7*); pap. 20.95 (*0-8020-6653-4*) U of Toronto Pr.

Bushy Bride: Norwegian Fairy Tale. Illus. by Seymour Chwast. LC 83-71174. (Creative's Collection of Fairy Tales). 32p. (J). (gr. 6 up). 1983. lib. bdg. 13.95 (*0-87191-952-4*) Creative Ed.

Business. Incl. Introduction to Business & Stock Market. Leon C. Megginson et al. LC 84-81087. (C). 1987. Not sold separately (*0-669-12927-5*); Test Item File. Leon C. Megginson et al. LC 84-81087. (C). 1987. 2.00 (*0-669-05879-3*); Instruction Manual. Leon C. Megginson et al. LC 84-81087. (C). 1987. 2.00 (*0-669-05881-5*); Users Guide. Leon C. Megginson et al. LC 84-81087. (C). 1987. 2.00 (*0-669-07611-2*); AV Guide. Leon C. Megginson et al. LC 84-81087. (C). 1987. 2.00 (*0-669-07612-0*); Stock Market. Leon C. Megginson et al. LC 84-81087. (C). 1987. 10.50 (*0-669-07616-3*); Business Supply Topics. Leon C. Megginson et al. LC 84-81087. (C). 1987. 2.00 (*0-669-07618-X*); Three Ring Binder. Leon C. Megginson et al. LC 84-81087. (C). 1987. 3.00 (*0-669-07622-8*); Business Step Savers. Leon C. Megginson et al. LC 84-81087. (C). 1987. 50.00 (*0-669-07755-0*); LC 84-81087. 670p. (C). 1987. Set text ed. 32.00 (*0-669-05878-5*); Incl. Not sold separately (*0-669-12927-5*); 2.00 (*0-669-05879-3*); 2.00 (*0-669-05881-5*); 2.00 (*0-669-07611-2*); 2.00 (*0-669-07612-0*); 10.50 (*0-669-07616-3*); 2.00 (*0-669-07618-X*); 3.00 (*0-669-07622-8*); 50.00 (*0-669-07755-0*); Study guide. Set student ed 14.00 (*0-669-05880-7*); Incl. Not sold separately (*0-669-12927-5*); 2.00 (*0-669-05879-3*); 2.00 (*0-669-05881-5*); 2.00 (*0-669-07611-2*); 2.00 (*0-669-07612-0*); 10.50 (*0-669-07616-3*); 2.00 (*0-669-07618-X*); 3.00 (*0-669-07622-8*); 50.00 (*0-669-07755-0*); Instr.'s resources. Set teacher ed 2.00 (*0-669-07613-9*); Incl. Not sold separately (*0-669-12927-5*); 2.00 (*0-669-05879-3*); 2.00 (*0-669-05881-5*); 2.00 (*0-669-07611-2*); 2.00 (*0-669-07612-0*); 10.50 (*0-669-07616-3*); 2.00 (*0-669-07618-X*); 3.00 (*0-669-07622-8*); 50.00 (*0-669-07755-0*); Software pkg. Apple. Set Apple II 80.00 (*0-669-10254-7*); Incl. Not sold separately (*0-669-12927-5*); 2.00 (*0-669-05879-3*); 2.00 (*0-669-05881-5*); 2.00 (*0-669-07611-2*); 2.00 (*0-669-07612-0*); 10.50 (*0-669-07616-3*); 2.00 (*0-669-07618-X*); 3.00 (*0-669-07622-8*); 50.00 (*0-669-07755-0*); Busn. profiles. 2.00 (*0-669-07615-5*); Incl. Not sold separately (*0-669-12927-5*); 2.00 (*0-669-05879-3*); 2.00 (*0-669-05881-5*); 2.00 (*0-669-07611-2*); 2.00 (*0-669-07612-0*); 10.50 (*0-669-07616-3*); 2.00 (*0-669-07618-X*); 3.00 (*0-669-07622-8*); 50.00 (*0-669-07755-0*); Archive testing prog. 150.00 (*0-669-09489-7*); Incl. Not sold separately (*0-669-12927-5*); 2.00 (*0-669-05879-3*); 2.00 (*0-669-05881-5*); 2.00 (*0-669-07611-2*); 2.00 (*0-669-07612-0*); 10.50 (*0-669-07616-3*); 2.00 (*0-669-07618-X*); 3.00 (*0-669-07622-8*); 50.00 (*0-669-07755-0*); Software pkg. IBM PC. 80.00 (*0-669-09001-8*); Incl. Not sold separately (*0-669-12927-5*); 2.00 (*0-669-05879-3*); 2.00 (*0-669-05881-5*); 2.00 (*0-669-07611-2*); 2.00 (*0-669-07612-0*); 10.50 (*0-669-07616-3*); 2.00 (*0-669-07618-X*); 3.00 (*0-669-07622-8*); 50.00 (*0-669-07755-0*); Archive test prog. IBM PC. 150.00 (*0-669-11561-4*) Heath.

Business. William Naumes & Margaret J. Naumes. (Illus.). 704p. 1987. text ed. write for info. (*0-13-091307-3*) P-H.

Business. David L. Riley, Sr. LC 89-91725. (Illus.). 60p. (Orig.). 1989. pap. 12.50 (*0-9618976-3-5*) EBI.

Business. Jack Rudman. (Undergraduate Program Field Test Ser.: UPFT-3). 1994. pap. 23.95 (*0-8373-6003-X*) Nat Learn.

Business. 2nd ed. Incl. Instructor's Resource Manual. Samuel C. Certo et al. 1987. Pt. A. (*0-205-11452-0*, H1452-5); Instructor's Resource Manual. Samuel C. Certo et al. 1987. Pt. B. (*0-205-11453-9*, H1453-3); Instructor's Resource Manual. Samuel C. Certo et al. 1987. Pt. C. (*0-205-11454-7*, H1454-1); Instructor's Resource Manual. Samuel C. Certo et al. 1987. Pt. D. (*0-205-11455-5*, H1455-8); Instructor's Resource Manual. Samuel C. Certo et al. 1987. Pt. E. (*0-205-11456-3*, H1456-6); Instructor's Resource Manual. Samuel C. Certo et al. 1987. Pt. F. (*0-205-11457-1*, H1457-4); 672p. 1987. Set text ed. 36.00 (*0-205-11450-4*, H1450-9) Allyn.

Business. 2nd ed. Ricky W. Griffin & Ronald J. Ebert. 720p. (C). 1990. text ed. write for info. (*0-13-092123-8*) P-H.

Business, 2 Vols. 2nd ed. Robert Kreitner et al. (C). 1989. text ed. 53.16 (*0-395-43360-6*) HM.

Business, 2 Vols. 2nd ed. Robert Kreitner et al. (C). 1989. student ed, pap. 17.56 (*0-395-52354-0*) HM.

Business, 2 Vols. 2nd ed. Robert Kreitner et al. (C). 1990. pap. 5.16 (*0-395-52352-4*); 101.56 (*0-395-52952-2*) HM.

Business, 2 Vols. 2nd ed. Robert Kreitner et al. (C). 1990. pap. 5.56 (*0-395-52353-2*) HM.

Business, 2 Vols. 2nd ed. Robert Kreitner et al. (C). 1991. 24.76 (*0-395-52953-0*) HM.

Business. 2nd ed. Fred Luthans & Richard M. Hodgetts. LC 91-11117. 651p. (C). 1992. text ed. 50.00 (*0-03-054624-9*) Dryden Pr.

Business. 2nd ed. Fred Luthans & Richard M. Hodgetts. 864p. 1993. pap. text ed. 29.50 (*0-03-097378-3*) Dryden Pr.

Business. 3rd ed. Ricky W. Griffin & Ronald J. Ebert. 832p. (C). 1992. text ed. write for info. (*0-13-094434-3*) P-H.

Business. 3rd ed. William Pride et al. (C). 1991. write for info. (*0-395-47308-X*) HM Soft Schl Col Div.

Business, Bk. 2. Harris Winitz. (All about Language Ser.). (Illus.). 50p. (Orig.). (YA). (gr. 7 up). 1986. audio, pap. text ed. 22.00 (*0-939990-46-6*) Intl Linguistics.

Business: A Changing World. O. C. Ferrell & Geoffrey A. Hirt. LC 92-20222. 784p. (C). 1992. text ed. 31.95 (*0-256-11683-0*) Irwin.

Business: A Student's Guide. Desmond W. Evans. 448p. (Orig.). 1993. pap. 43.50 (*0-273-60085-0*, Pub. by Pitman Pub Ltd UK) Trans-Atl Phila.

Business: Contemporary Concepts & Practices. John H. Jackson & Vernon A. Musselman. (Illus.). 672p. (C). 1987. text ed. write for info. (*0-13-091430-4*); student ed write for info. (*0-318-61353-0*) P-H.

Business: Foundations of Our Business System. 3rd annot. ed. Samuel C. Certo et al. 720p. 1989. teacher ed write for info. (*0-318-66328-7*, H22189) Allyn.

Business: Foundations of Our Business System. 3rd ed. Samuel C. Certo et al. 720p. 1989. write for info. (*0-318-66329-5*, H23500); student ed 17.00 (*0-685-29825-6*, H23559); vhs write for info. (*0-318-66331-7*, H23518); write for info. (*0-318-66330-9*, H22189); write for info. (*0-318-66332-5*, H23534) Allyn.

Business: Gaining the Competitive Edge. Norman M. Scarborough. 704p. (C). 1992. pap. write for info. (*0-318-68763-1*) Allyn.

Business: Its Legal, Ethical & Global Environment. 3rd ed. Marianne M. Jennings. 941p. (C). 1994. text ed. 60.95 (*0-534-20695-6*) Intl Thomson.

Business: The American Challenge for Global Competitiveness. William G. Zikmund et al. LC 94-10914. 608p. (C). 1994. 61.95 (*0-256-11412-9*) Irwin.

Business: The Owner's Manual. Ted J. Solomon. 1994. 12.95 (*0-8062-4808-4*) Carlton.

Business--Education Partnerships for 21st Century. Kochhar. 250p. 1993. 79.00 (*0-8342-0503-3*, S31) Aspen Pub.

Business: a Philosophical Perspective. Thomas E. Schaefer. 148p. 1974. pap. 3.00 (*0-8477-2616-9*) U of PR Pr.

Business Accounting, No. 1. F. Wood. 576p. (C). 1989. 100.00 (*0-685-39827-7*, Inst Pur & Supply) St Mut.

Business Accounting, No. 2. F. Wood. 640p. (C). 1989. 115.00 (*0-685-39826-9*, Inst Pur & Supply) St Mut.

Business Accounting, 2 vols., Set. 6th ed. Frank Wood. 1216p. 1993. pap. 87.50 (*0-317-05412-0*, Pub. by Pitman Pub Ltd UK) Trans-Atl Phila.

Business Accounting, Vol. 1. 6th ed. Frank Wood. 1216p. 1993. pap. write for info. (*0-273-03912-1*, Pub. by Pitman Pub Ltd UK) Trans-Atl Phila.

Business Accounting, Vol. 2. 6th ed. Frank Wood. 1216p. 1993. pap. write for info. (*0-273-03914-8*, Pub. by Pitman Pub Ltd UK) Trans-Atl Phila.

Business Accounting & Finance Blueprint. Ian R. Davidson & Chris A. Mallin. LC 92-38569. 250p. 1993. 29.95 (*0-631-18687-5*) Blackwell Pubs.

Business, Accounting & Finance Problem Solver. rev. ed. Research & Education Association Staff. LC 78-64582. (Illus.). 862p. 1994. pap. text ed. 23.95 (*0-87891-516-8*) Res & Educ.

Business Acronyms. Ed. by Julie E. Towell. 1988. 75.00 (*0-8103-2549-7*) Gale.

***Business Across Cultures.** Laura M. English & Sarah Lynn. LC 94-35166. 192p. 1995. pap. text ed. write for info. (*0-201-82532-5*) Addison-Wesley.

Business Administration. Josephine Shaw. 352p. (Orig.). 1991. pap. 32.50 (*0-273-03213-5*, Pub. by Pitman Pub Ltd UK) Trans-Atl Phila.

Business Administration: An Introductory Study. Owen S. Hiner. LC 74-465152. (Longman Business Ser.). 314p. reprint ed. pap. 89.50 (*0-8357-7483-X*, 2022531) Bks Demand.

B

An Asterisk (*) at the beginning of an entry indicates that the title is appearing in BIP for the first time. 957

Business Administration for NVQ: A Complete Introduction to Office Management. Leanne M. Ansell. LC 94-6151. (Illus.). 288p. 1994. pap. 34.95 (0-631-19365-0) Blackwell Pubs.

Business Administration for the Dental Assistant. 4th ed. Ann Ehrlich. (Illus.). 185p. 1991. pap. text ed. 23.95 (0-940012-33-2) Colwell Syst.

Business Administration for the Medical Assistant. 4th ed. Ann Ehrlich et al. LC 81-67045. (Illus.). 1991. pap. text ed. 23.95 (0-940012-32-4) Colwell Syst.

Business Advocate Or Corporate Policeman? Stephen F. Jablonsky et al. LC 92-70834. 40p. 1993. pap. 15.00 (0-910586-86-1) Finan Exec.

***Business Agreements Kit.** Ted Nicholass. 1995. pap. 19.95 (0-936894-90-3) Upstart Pub.

Business Alliances Guide: The Hidden Competitive Weapon. Robert P. Lynch. LC 92-15341. 352p. 1993. text ed. 29.95 (0-471-57030-3) Wiley.

Business Analysis & Decision Making with Spreadsheet Software. William E. Leigh. 1991. pap. 14.95 (0-89600-017-6) IE Pasadena.

Business Analysis & Graphics with Lotus 1-2-3. Lawrence H. Nitz. (Illus.). 176p. 1985. pap. 32.95 (0-13-091604-8) P-H.

Business Analysis & Graphics with Lotus 1-2-3. Lawrence H. Nitz. write for info. (0-318-59621-0) S&S Trade.

B

Business Analysis with Spreadsheets Using VP Planner Plus. Patrick McKlown & Robert D. Brown. 464p. (Orig.). (C). 1988. pap. text ed. 34.95 (0-8162-5543-1) Holden-Day.

Business & Accounting Ethics in Islam. Treevor Gambling & Rifaat A. Karim. 160p. 1991. text ed. 70.00 (0-7201-2074-8, Mansell Pub) Cassell.

Business & Administrative Communication. 2nd ed. Kitty Locker. 704p. (C). 1991. text ed. 58.95 (0-256-08747-4, 12-2304-02) Irwin.

Business & Administrative Communication. 3rd ed. Kitty O. Locker. LC 94-17702. 720p. (C). 1994. text ed. 58.95 (0-256-14064-2) Irwin.

Business & Administrative Correspondence under the Kings of Ur. Edmond Sollberger. LC 66-25697. 18.00 (0-685-71738-0) J J Augustin.

Business & Banking: Political Change & Economic Integration in Western Europe. Paulete Kurzer. LC 92-56780. (Cornell Studies in Political Economy). 280p. 1993. 39.95 (0-8014-2798-3) Cornell U Pr.

Business & Beyond, Vol. 1: The Best of the Best of America. Peter Finkbeiner-Zellmann & Jane Michael-Rushmer. Ed. by Mathews, Walter, Associates Inc. Staff. (Signum Guides Ser.). (Illus.). 192p. 1989. 30.00 (0-9622133-0-6) Signum Pub Inc.

Business & Bureaucracy in a Chinese City: An Ethnography of Private Business Households in Contemporary China. Ole Bruun. LC 93-31927. (China Research Monographs: No. 43). 1993. pap. 20.00 (1-55729-042-3) IEAS.

Business & Capitalism: An Introduction to Business History. Norman S. Gras. LC 68-55720. (Reprints of Economic Classics Ser.). (Illus.). xxii, 408p. 1971. reprint ed. 45.00 (0-678-00747-0) Kelley.

Business & Career Planning Workbook. Kumiko Watanuki. 1990. pap. 8.95 (0-533-08567-5) Vantage.

Business & Careers in Marine Sciences. James S. McNutt, Jr. 332p. 1993. pap. text ed. 24.00 (1-884104-02-9) Hydrodyne Marine.

Business & Commercial Laws of Russia: Translations with Expert Commentary, 3 vols. Ed. by John P. Hupp. Tr. by Russica Information, Inc. Staff. LC 93-12865. 1993. text ed. 600.00 (0-07-172479-6) Shepards-McGraw.

Business & Consumer Mathematics. 5th ed. Walter H. Lange et al. 752p. (C). 1991. pap. text ed. 51.95 (0-256-09135-8) Irwin.

Business & Corporate Taxation: A Handbook, with Supplement Containing 7 New Chapters on Tax Planning for Partnership Firms. Ed. by H. P. Ranina. (C). 1990. 175.00 (0-89771-265-X) St Mut.

Business & Culture of the Enterprise Society. John Deeks. LC 92-34951. 272p. 1993. text ed. 57.95 (0-89930-791-4, DBU, Quorum Bks) Greenwood.

Business & Democracy in Latin America. Ed. by Ernest Bartell & Leigh A. Payne. (Pitt Latin American Ser.). 240p. (C). 1995. 49.95 (0-8229-3853-7); pap. 19.95 (0-8229-5537-7) U of Pittsburgh Pr.

Business & Democracy in Spain. Robert E. Martinez. LC 92-31845. 344p. 1993. text ed. 59.95 (0-275-94391-7, C4391, Praeger Pubs) Greenwood.

Business & Economic Forecasting: Decision Support System Software. Leroy F. Simmons & George Wright. 1990. Net. text ed. write for info. (0-471-51369-5) Wiley.

Business & Economic Laws. S. Saharay & S. Saha. (C). 1989. 100.00 (0-89771-454-7, Current Dist) St Mut.

***Business & Economic Statistics.** Robert D. Mason. 1970. 4.50 (0-256-01268-7) Irwin Prof Pubng.

Business & Economic Statistics. 4th ed. Robert D. Mason. (Plaid Ser.). 166p. 1983. pap. 11.95 (0-87094-334-0) Irwin Prof Pubng.

Business & Economics see Comprehensive Dissertation Index 1861-1972

Business & Economics see Comprehensive Dissertation Index: Ten Year Cumulation, 1973-1982

Business & Economics see Comprehensive Dissertation Index: Five-Year Cumulation, 1983-1987

Business & Economics Books 1876-1983, 5 vols., Set. 5256p. 1983. 199.00 (0-8352-1614-4) Bowker.

Business & Economics Funding Guide. Carolyn Looff. Ed. by Christina Bitting. 134p. (Orig.). (C). 1987. lib. bdg. 34.75 (0-88044-087-2); pap. text ed. 17.75 (0-88044-088-0) AASCU Press.

Business & Economics Statistics with Computer Applications. William E. Becker & Donald L. Harnett. LC 85-9025. (C). 1987. teacher ed write for info. (0-201-10957-3); text ed. 39.16 (0-201-10956-5) Addison-Wesley.

Business & Education. Frank A. Vanderlip. LC 73-2537. (Big Business; Economic Power in a Free Society Ser.). 1973. reprint ed. 39.95 (0-405-05115-8) Ayer.

Business & Environment in India. Ed. by Shamim Ahmad & Khaliq Ahmad. (C). 1990. 22.00 (81-7024-298-3, Pub. by Ashish II) S Asia.

***Business & Environmental Accountability.** Lesley Grayson et al. (C). 1994. 150.00x (0-946655-82-0, Pub. by S Thornes Pubs UK) St Mut.

Business & Finance Career Directory. R. Fry. 1992. pap. 29.95 (0-685-59977-9) Visible Ink Pr.

Business & Finance Career Directory. R. Fry. 1992. pap. 17.95 (0-8103-9428-6) Visible Ink Pr.

Business & Finance Career Directory. 2nd ed. Ed. by Bradley J. Morgan. (Career Advisor Ser.). 300p. 1992. 39.00 (0-8103-5604-X, 101576) Gale.

Business & Finance Workbook in Spanish. Ana C. Jarvis. 246p. (ENG & SPA.). (C). 1981. pap. 19.95 (0-8288-1413-9, S39175) Fr & Eur.

Business & Financial Management. 6th ed. B. K. Watts. (Illus.). 312p. 1988. pap. text ed. 24.50 (0-7121-0792-4) Trans-Atl Phila.

Business & Financial Record of World War Years. Seibert, Herbert D., & Co. Staff. LC 75-2670. (Wall Street & the Security Market Ser.). 1975. reprint ed. 46.95 (0-405-07233-3) Ayer.

***Business & General Aviation Aircraft Pilot Reports.** Aviation Staff. 1995. pap. text ed. 19.95 (0-07-003092-8) TAB Bks.

Business & Government. Ronald H. Wolf & Vernon A. Mund. 434p. (C). 1980. text ed. 19.95 (0-89894-006-0) Advocate Pub Group.

Business & Government. 3rd ed. H. Craig Petersen. 560p. (C). 1990. text ed. 39.00 (0-06-045157-2) HarpCollege.

Business & Government. 4th ed. H. Craig Petersen. LC 92-11252. (C). 1992. 63.00 (0-06-501101-5) HarpCollege.

Business & Government: Essays in 20th Century Cooperation & Confrontation. Ed. by Joseph R. Frese & Jacob Judd. LC 82-5590. (American Economic Enterprise Ser.: Vol. 4). 248p. 1985. 25.00 (0-912882-52-2) Sleepy Hollow.

Business & Government in Industrializing Asia. Ed. by Andrew MacIntyre. LC 94-1663. 1994. write for info. (0-8014-8227-5) Cornell U Pr.

Business & Government in the Oil Industry: A Case Study of Sun Oil, 1876 to 1945, Vol. 5. August W. Giebelhaus. Ed. by Glenn Porter. LC 77-7795. (Industrial Development & the Social Fabric Ser.). 425p. (Orig.). 1980. 73.25 (0-89232-089-3) Jai Pr.

Business & Health. (Business Strategy Ser.: Vol. 9). 78p. 1991. 26.00 (0-88406-239-2) GA St U Busn Pr.

Business & Industrial Park Development Handbook. Michael D. Beyard. (Community Builders Handbook Ser.). 380p. 1988. 64.95 (0-87420-678-2, I11) Urban Land.

Business & Industry: Partners in Education. American Association of School Administrators Staff. 9p. (Orig.). 1984. pap. 0.60 (0-87652-067-0, 021-00114) Am Assn Sch Admin.

Business & Its Beliefs: The Ideas That Helped Build IBM. Thomas J. Watson. LC 62-20813. (McKinsey Foundation Lecture Ser.). 117p. reprint ed. pap. 33.40 (0-8357-7484-8, 2055974) Bks Demand.

Business & Its Environment. David P. Baron. 768p. 1992. text ed. write for info. (0-13-092511-X) P-H.

Business & Its Environment: Essays for Thomas C. Cochran. Ed. by Harold I. Sharlin. LC 82-6143. (Contributions in American Studies: No. 63). (Illus.). 264p. 1983. text ed. 55.00 (0-313-21438-7, SHB/, Greenwood Pr) Greenwood.

Business & Its Legal Environment. David E. Brody. LC 85-60976. 857p. (C). 1986. text ed. 34.00 (0-669-07306-7); Study guide. student ed write for info. (0-669-11147-3); Instr.'s guide. teacher ed 2.00 (0-669-07307-5) Heath.

Business & Its Legal Environment. 3rd ed. Thomas W. Dunfee et al. 832p. (C). 1991. text ed. write for info. (0-13-092305-2) P-H.

Business & Jobs in the Rural World: Local Initiatives for Job Creation. OECD Staff. 203p. (Orig.). 1992. pap. 41.00 (92-64-13630-4) OECD.

Business & Law for the Shipmaster. rev. ed. F. N. Hopkins. (C). 1987. 216.00 (0-85174-456-7, Pub. by Brwn Son Ferg) St Mut.

Business & Law for the Shipmaster. 7th ed. F. N. Hopkins. 908p. 1989. text ed. 160.00 (0-85174-537-7) Sheridan.

Business & Law in Saudi Arabia. G. Mutawakil. 220p. (C). 1990. 125.00 (0-907151-18-3, Pub. by IMMEL Pubng UK) St Mut.

Business & Legal Aspects of Representing Talent in the Entertainment Industry. University of California at Los Angeles, School of Law Staff et al. (Illus.). 564p. 1984. write for info. (0-318-57534-5) UCLA Law.

Business & Legal CD-ROMS in Print. 275p. 1994. pap. 55.00 (0-88736-970-7) Mecklermedia.

***Business & Legal CD-ROMs in Print 1995.** 400p. 1995. pap. 59.95 (0-614-01337-2) Mecklermedia.

Business & Legal Forms for Authors & Self-Publishers. Tad Crawford. LC 89-80740. 176p. 1990. pap. 15.95 (0-927629-03-8, 10167) Allworth Pr.

***Business & Legal Forms for Authors & Self-Publishers.** Tad Crawford. 176p. 1995. pap. 15.95 (1-880559-37-4) Allworth Pr.

Business & Legal Forms for Fine Artists. Tad Crawford. LC 89-80742. 128p. 1990. pap. 12.95 (0-927629-01-1, 30197) Allworth Pr.

***Business & Legal Forms for Fine Artists.** Tad Crawford. LC 95-766695. 144p. 1995. reprint ed. pap. 16.95 (1-880559-30-7) Allworth Pr.

Business & Legal Forms for Graphic Designers. Tad Crawford & Eva D. Bruck. LC 90-80447. 208p. 1990. pap. 19.95 (0-927629-07-0, 30239) Allworth Pr.

***Business & Legal Forms for Graphic Designers.** rev. ed. Tad Crawford & Eva D. Bruck. LC 95-75287. 224p. 1995. pap. 22.95 (1-880559-26-9) Allworth Pr.

Business & Legal Forms for Illustrators. Tad Crawford. LC 89-80741. 160p. 1990. pap. 15.95 (0-927629-02-X, 30206) Allworth Pr.

Business & Legal Forms for Photographers. Tad Crawford. LC 90-85554. 192p. (Orig.). 1991. pap. 18.95 (0-9607118-2-1) Allworth Pr.

***Business & Macroeconomics.** Christopher Pass et al. LC 94-42204. (Elements of Business Ser.). 1995. write for info. (0-415-12399-2) Routledge.

***Business & Macroeconomics.** Christopher L. Pass et al. LC 94-42204. (Elements of Business Ser.). 1995. pap. text ed. write for info. (0-415-12400-X) Routledge.

Business & Management Careers, 6 vols., Set. 98.00 (0-685-23033-3, CG106S) Ready Ref Pr.

Business & Management Courses. Brian Heap. 60p. (C). 1991. pap. 40.00 (1-85352-885-4, Pub. by HLT Pubns UK) St Mut.

Business & Management Principles. John A. Guerrieri, Jr. 143p. 1971. pap. 5.00 (0-318-13879-4, D6) Data Process Mgmt.

Business & Management Studies. (Higher Education in the Polytechnics & Colleges Ser.). 50p. 1990. pap. 11.00 (0-11-270698-3, HM6983) UNIPUB.

Business & Managerial Communication. Linda P. Driskill et al. 830p. (C). 1992. text ed. 49.25 (0-15-505589-5) Dryden Pr.

Business & Managerial Occupations: The Employment Outlook. 1994. lib. bdg. 256.95 (0-8490-9021-0) Gordon Pr.

Business & Marketing for Engineering & Scientists. Tony Curtis. LC 93-49026. 1994. 16.95 (0-07-707868-3) McGraw.

Business & Microeconomics: An Introduction to the Market Environment. Christopher Pass & Bryan Lowes. LC 93-39826. (Elements of Business Ser.). 224p. 1994. 59.95x (0-415-06845-2, B3534) Routledge.

***Business & Microeconomics: An Introduction to the Market Environment.** Christopher Pass & Bryan Lowes. LC 93-39826. (Elements of Business Ser.). 1994. pap. 19.95 (0-415-06846-0, B0184) Routledge.

Business & Office Education: Instructor Resource Guide. Center for Occupational Research & Development Staff. (Job Safety & Health Instructional Materials Ser.). (Illus.). 70p. (C). 1981. pap. text ed. 20.00 (1-55502-035-6) CORD Commns.

Business & Office Safety. Center for Occupational Research & Development Staff. (Job Safety & Health Instructional Materials Ser.). (Illus.). 28p. (C). 1981. pap. text ed. 2.50 (1-55502-089-5) CORD Commns.

Business & Personal Privacy: How to Protect Yourself. 1991. lib. bdg. 300.00 (0-8490-4779-X) Gordon Pr.

Business & Politics: A Comparative Introduction. 2nd ed. Graham K. Wilson. LC 90-35022. 240p. (C). 1990. pap. text ed. 17.95x (0-934540-82-9) Chatham Hse Pubs.

Business & Politics: A Study of Collective Action. William D. Coleman. 352p. 1988. 55.00 (0-7735-0648-9, Pub. by McGill CN); pap. 24.95 (0-7735-0664-0, Pub. by McGill CN) U of Toronto Pr.

Business & Politics in America from the Age of Jackson to the Civil War: The Career Biography of W. W. Corcoran. Henry Cohen. LC 79-98708. (Illus.). 409p. 1971. text ed. 39.95 (0-8371-3300-9, CBP/, Greenwood Pr) Greenwood.

Business & Politics in India: A Historical Perspective. Dwijendra Tripathi. (C). 1991. 26.50 (81-85425-59-0, Pub. by Manohar II) S Asia.

Business & Politics in Indonesia. Andrew MacIntyre. 176p. 1991. pap. 24.95 (0-04-442330-6, Pub. by Allen & Unwin Aust Pty AT) Paul & Co Pubs.

Business & Politics in Peru: The State & the National Bourgeoisie. Ed. by Francisco Durand. 230p. (C). 1993. pap. text ed. 39.50 (0-8133-8472-9) Westview.

Business & Professional Communication: A Resource Text. James W. Ward. 192p. (C). 1993. pap. text ed., spiral bd. 14.95 (0-8403-8646-X) Kendall-Hunt.

Business & Professional Communication: Concepts & Practices. James Benjamin & Raymie E. McKerrow. LC 93-4747. (C). 1993. 32.50 (0-673-18560-5) HarpCollege.

***Business & Professional Communication: Managing Information in an Information Age.** Wallace V. Schmidt & Greg H. Gardner. 1995. text ed. 30.95 (0-538-83250-9) S-W Pub.

Business & Professional Communication Workbook. Joe Martinez. 96p. (C). 1992. pap. text ed. write for info. (0-8403-7563-8) Kendall-Hunt.

Business & Professional Communications. Curtis et al. (C). 1991. text ed. 31.50 (0-673-38095-5) HarpCollege.

Business & Professional Income under the Personal Income Tax. C. H. Kahn. (National Bureau of Economic Research Ser.: No. D.8). 1964. 35.00 (0-691-04107-5) Princeton U Pr.

Business & Professional Writing: A Guide to the Process. 2nd ed. Gerald Siegel. 96p. (C). 1994. per., pap. text ed. 17.95 (0-8403-9196-X) Kendall-Hunt.

Business & Public Policy. John T. Dunlop. LC 80-81866. (Harvard Business School Publications). 135p. (C). 1980. 11.00 (0-87584-119-8) HUP.

Business & Religion in Britain, Vol. 5. David Jeremy. (Business & History Ser.). 220p. 1988. text ed. 76.95 (0-566-05096-X) Ashgate Pub Co.

Business & Religion in the American 1920s. Rolf Lunden. LC 87-17597. (Contributions in American Studies: No. 91). (Illus.). 220p. 1988. text ed. 55.00 (0-313-25151-7, LBU/, Greenwood Pr) Greenwood.

***Business & Social Etiquette with Disabled People: A Guide to Getting along with Persons Who Have Impairments of Mobility, Vision, Hearing or Speech.** Chalda Maloff & Susan M. Wood. 162p. 1988. pap. 24.95 (0-398-06266-8) C C Thomas.

Business & Social Etiquette with Disabled People: A Guide to Getting along with Persons Who Have Impairments of Mobility, Vision, Hearing or Speech. Chalda Maloff & Susan M. Wood. 162p. (C). 1988. 39.95 (0-398-05463-0) C C Thomas.

Business & Social Progress. Ed. by Clarence C. Walton. LC 78-104393. 157p. 1970. 5.95 (0-87186-323-5) Comm Econ Dev.

Business & Society. Thomas Kempner et al. 288p. (C). 1974. text ed. 25.00 (0-8464-1161-X) Beekman Pubs.

Business & Society. Edmund Marshall. LC 92-32042. (Elements of Business Ser.). 1993. write for info. (0-415-06849-5); pap. 26.00 (0-415-06850-9, B0109) Routledge.

Business & Society. Donna J. Wood. (C). 1990. text ed. 54.50 (0-673-39937-0) HarpCollege.

Business & Society. 2nd ed. Wood. (C). 1994. text ed. 61.00 (0-673-52263-6) HarpCollege.

Business & Society: A Managerial Approach. 4th ed. Frederick A. Sturdivant & Heidi Vernon-Wortzel. 544p. (C). 1990. text ed. 55.95 (0-256-07036-9) Irwin.

Business & Society: A Managerial Approach. 5th ed. Heidi Vernon-Wortzel. LC 93-38861. 592p. (C). 1994. text ed. 61.95 (0-256-11589-3) Irwin.

***Business & Society: A Reader in the History, Sociology, & Ethics of Business.** Barry Castro. (Illus.). 304p. 1996. pap. text ed. 24.95 (0-19-509566-9) OUP.

Business & Society: Corporate Strategy, Public Policy, Ethics. 7th ed. William C. Frederick et al. 1992. text ed. write for info. (0-07-015613-1) McGraw.

Business & Society: Ethics & Stakeholder Management. 2nd ed. Archie B. Carroll. LC 92-12942. 1993. text ed. 54.95 (0-538-82296-1) S-W Pub.

Business & Society: Ethics, Government, & the World Economy. Alfred A. Marcus. LC 92-23081. 704p. (C). 1992. text ed. 60.95 (0-256-08866-7) Irwin.

Business & Society: 1976-2000. John L. Paluszek. LC 75-44485. (AMA Survey Report Ser.). 46p. reprint ed. pap. 25.00 (0-8357-7485-6, 2050198) Bks Demand.

Business & Society Dimensions of Conflict & Cooperation. Ed. by S. Prakash Sethi & Cecilia M. Falbe. LC 86-45548. 672p. 1987. text ed. 29.95 (0-669-13207-1) Free Pr.

Business & Society in a Changing World Order. Ed. by Dean C. Ludwig. LC 93-18882. 312p. 1993. text ed. 99.95 (0-7734-9267-4) E Mellen.

Business & Society in Japan: Fundamentals for Businessmen. East Asian Studies Program-Ohio State University. Ed. by Bradley M. Richardson. LC 81-2710. 334p. 1981. text ed. 75.00 (0-275-91701-0, C1701, Praeger Pubs) Greenwood.

Business & Society Review: 1972-1987, Set: Vols. 1-15. Bound Set. 600.00 (0-8377-9031-X) Rothman.

Business & Technical Communication: A Bibliography, 1975-1985. Debra L. Hull. LC 87-4749. 243p. 1987. 25.00 (0-8108-1971-6) Scarecrow.

Business & Technical Writing: An Annotated Bibliography of Books, 1880-1980. Gerald J. Alred et al. LC 80-29211. 249p. 1981. 20.00 (0-8108-1397-1) Scarecrow.

Business & Technological Dynamics in Newly Industrializing Asia. Wenlee Ting. LC 84-8387. (Illus.). xv, 199p. 1985. text ed. 65.00 (0-89930-073-1, TII/, Quorum Bks) Greenwood.

Business & Technology. Ed. by Terry Page. 154p. (C). 1987. 75.00 (1-85184-027-3) St Mut.

Business & the Environment. Twyla Dell. Ed. by W. Philip Gerould. LC 93-72978. (Fifty-Minute Ser.). (Illus.). 100p. (Orig.). 1995. pap. 9.95 (1-56052-253-4) Crisp Pubns.

***Business & the Environment.** Ed. by Michael D. Rogers. LC 94-48399. 1995. write for info. (0-312-12573-9) St Martin.

Business & the Environment: A Resource Guide. Ed. by Allison A. Pennell et al. LC 91-38369. 364p. 1992. text ed. 55.00 (1-55963-159-7) Island Pr.

Business & the Environment: Implications of the New Environmentalism. Ed. by Denis Smith. 192p. 1992. pap. 32.50 (1-85396-159-0) St Martin.

***Business & the Environment Vol. 1.** Denis Smith. 1994. pap. 16.95 (0-312-12297-7) St Martin.

Business & the Legal Environment. 2nd ed. Marianne M. Jennings. 774p. (C). 1991. text ed. 59.95 (0-534-92499-9); student ed 19.95 (0-534-92502-2) Intl Thomson.

Business Annals. Willard L. Thorp. (General Ser.: No. 8). 381p. 1926. reprint ed. 99.10 (0-87014-007-8); reprint ed. mic. film 49.60 (0-685-61139-6) Natl Bur Econ Res.

Business Application Software. PC-SIG, Inc. Staff. 1991. pap. 29.95 (0-07-157861-7) McGraw.

Business Application Software: An IBM PC Lab Manual. Mary L. McElroy et al. (Orig.). (C). 1986. pap. text ed. 12.95 (0-938188-34-8); disk write for info. (0-318-61046-9) Mitchell Pub.

Business Application Software: Lotus 1-2-3 (Version 2.4) Lon Ingalsbe. LC 93-35639. (Illus.). 304p. (C). 1994. pap. write for info. (0-02-359766-6) Macmillan.

Business Application Software for IBM Alternate, with 3.5 Disk. 3rd ed. Lon Ingalsbe. (C). 1991. pap. write for info. (0-02-359701-1, Merrill Pub Co) Macmillan.

An Asterisk (*) at the beginning of an entry indicates that the title is appearing in BIP for the first time.

Business Application Software for IBM & Compatible Microcomputer Alternate. 3rd ed. Lon Ingalsbe. 1991. pap. write for info. (*0-675-22389-X*, Merrill Pub Co) Macmillan.

Business Application Software for IBM & Microcomputer Alternate, with 5.25 Disk. 3rd ed. Lon Ingalsbe. 1991. pap. write for info. (*0-675-22388-1*, Merrill Pub Co) Macmillan.

Business Applications for Lotus 123 Macros. David Whigham. (Illus.). 224p. 1992. pap. 34.95 (*0-12-746150-7*) Acad Pr.

Business Applications for the IBM PC with Lotus, dBASE III-III Plus & Wordperfect. Lon Ingalsbe. (C). 1988. pap. write for info. (*0-675-21042-9*, Merrill Pub Co) Macmillan.

Business Applications for the IBM PC with VP-Planner, dBASE III-III Plus & Wordperfect with Software. Lon Ingalsbe. (C). 1988. pap. write for info. (*0-675-21035-6*, Merrill Pub Co) Macmillan.

Business Applications Shareware. PC-SIG, Inc. Staff. 304p. 1991. pap. 29.95 (*0-8306-2490-2*, Windcrest) TAB Bks.

Business Applications Software: dBase IV 2.2. Lon Ingalsbe. (Illus.). 224p. (Orig.). (C). 1994. pap. write for info. (*0-02-359631-7*) Macmillan.

Business Applications Software: DOS (6.0) Lon Ingalsbe. LC 93-40555. 160p. (C). 1994. pap. write for info. (*0-02-359781-X*) Macmillan.

Business Applications Software: Wordperfect. Lon Ingalsbe. LC 93-49659. 288p. (C). 1994. pap. write for info. (*0-02-359791-7*) Macmillan.

Business Applications Software for the IBM & Compatible Microcomputers. 3rd ed. Lon Ingalsbe. 848p. (C). 1990. pap. write for info. (*0-675-21175-1*, Merrill Pub Co) Macmillan.

Business Applications Software for the IBM-PC. 2nd ed. Lon Ingalsbe. 544p. (C). 1987. pap. write for info. (*0-675-20936-6*, Merrill Pub Co); pap. write for info. (*0-675-20760-6*, Merrill Pub Co) Macmillan.

Business Applications Software Workbook. Gerald A. Silver & Myrna L. Silver. LC 91-92961. (Illus.). 96p. (C). 1991. pap. 21.50 (*1-880472-01-5*) Edit Enter.

Business Applications Using the IBM PC: Wordperfect, dBaseII-III, Lotus 1-2-3, & Data Transfer Between Applications. Carolyn Meinhardt & Ralph Verno. 384p. (C). 1987. pap. text ed. 26.95 (*0-685-14442-9*) McGraw.

Business Applications with Microcomputers: A Guidebook for Building Your Own Systems. Jeanne M. Follman. 348p. 1989. 24.95 (*0-13-039471-8*) P-H.

Business Arbitration - What You Need to Know. 4th ed. Robert Coulson. LC 85-48286. 180p. 1991. pap. 10.00 (*0-943001-25-0*) Am Arbitration.

Business Architectural Imagery in America, 1870-1930. Kenneth T. Gibbs. LC 84-2743. (Architecture & Urban Design Ser.: No. 10). (Illus.). 210p. reprint ed. pap. 59.90 (*0-8357-1575-2*, 2070443) Bks Demand.

Business As a Humanity. Ed. by Thomas Donaldson & R. Edward Freeman. (Ruffin Series in Business Ethics). 256p. 1994. 34.95 (*0-19-507156-5*) OUP.

Business As a Learning Community. Ronnie Lessem. LC 92-44981. 1993. 19.95 (*0-07-707787-3*) McGraw.

Business As a System of Power. Robert A. Brady. LC 76-167311. (Essay Index Reprint Ser.). 1977. reprint ed. 25.95 (*0-8369-2753-2*) Ayer.

***Business As Unusual: The Handbook for Managing & Supervising Organizational Change.** Price Pritchett & Ron Pound. 27p. 1988. pap. 5.95 (*0-944002-01-3*) Pritchett Assocs.

Business As Unusual: The People & Principles of Herman Miller. Hugh De Pree. 280p. 1986. text ed. 9.95 (*0-87911-005-8*) Herman Miller.

Business Aspects of Medical Practice. rev. ed. Hoyt W. Torras & James R. Lyle. 1992. pap. 49.95 (*1-879249-05-7*) HlthCare Consult.

Business Aspects of Medical Practice. 2nd ed. Hoyt W. Torras & James R. Lyle. 1992. pap. 49.95 (*1-879249-10-3*) HlthCare Consult.

Business Aspects of Technology Transfer: Marketing & Acquisition. William M. Watkins. LC 89-8736. 271p. 1990. 45.00 (*0-8155-1206-6*) Noyes.

Business Assistant. Jack Rudman. (Career Examination Ser.: C-2885). 1994. pap. 29.95 (*0-8373-2885-3*) Nat Learn.

Business Associations. Clement Shum. 88p. (C). 1991. pap. text ed. 22.00 (*962-209-308-6*, Pub. by Hong Kong U Pr HK) St Mut.

Business Associations. 2nd ed. Ribstein. 1990. write for info. (*0-8205-0271-5*, 481); teacher ed write for info. (*0-8205-0276-6*); Documents Supplement. write for info. (*0-8205-0275-8*) Bender.

Business Associations: Agency, Partnerships & Corporations: Cases & Materials. 2nd ed. William A. Klein & J. Mark Ramseyer. (University Casebook Ser.). 865p. 1994. text ed. 42.50 (*1-56662-146-1*); teacher ed, pap. text ed. write for info. (*1-56662-176-3*) Foundation Pr.

Business Associations: Cases & Materials on Agency, Partnership, & the Legal Problems of Business Enterprise. Andrew Beckerman-Rodau. 592p. (C). 1993. ring bd. 48.00 (*1-879581-01-9*) Lupus Pubns.

Business Associations - Agency, Partnerships, & Corporations, Cases & Materials On. William A. Klein & J. Mark Ramseyer. (University Casebook Ser.). 763p. 1991. text ed. 37.50 (*0-88277-878-1*) Foundation Pr.

Business Associations - Agency, Partnerships, & Corporations, Revised Teacher's Manual for Cases & Materials On. William A. Klein & J. Mark Ramseyer. (University Casebook Ser.). 376p. (C). 1992. pap. text ed. write for info. (*1-56662-012-0*) Foundation Pr.

Business Associations - Agency, Partnerships, & Corporations, 1993: Supplement to Cases & Materials On. William A. Klein & J. Mark Ramseyer. (University Casebook Ser.). 108p. (C). 1992. pap. text ed. 6.95 (*1-56662-057-0*) Foundation Pr.

Business Atlas of Great Britain, 1974. Ed. by Gower Publications Staff. 1974. 40.00 (*0-8464-0223-8*) Beekman Pubs.

Business Atlas of Western Europe in English, French, German & Spanish Languages. Ed. by Gower Economic Publications Staff. (Illus.). 144p. 1974. 40.00 (*0-8464-0224-6*) Beekman Pubs.

Business Auto & Travel: Tax Guide 102. Holmes F. Crouch. Ed. by Irma J. Crouch. LC 92-73881. (One Hundred: Individuals & Families Ser.). (Illus.). 224p. 1992. pap. text ed. 16.95 (*0-944817-07-6*) Allyear Tax.

Business Auto Coverage. Diane H. Swiesz. 1991. 39.50 (*1-56461-008-X*, 46030) Rough Notes.

Business Babble: A Cynic's Dictionary of Corporate Jargon. David Olive. 192p. 1991. text ed. 14.95 (*0-471-54789-1*) Wiley.

Business, Banking, & Politics: The Case of British Steel, 1918-1939, Vol, 39. Steven Tolliday. LC 78-23826. (Studies in Business History). (Illus.). 448p. 1987. 42.00 (*0-674-08725-9*) HUP.

Business BASIC. Penny Fanzone et al. LC 86-60093. (Illus.). 525p. (Orig.). (C). 1986. teacher ed write for info. (*0-938188-46-1*); pap. text ed. 28.95 (*0-938188-41-0*); disk write for info. (*0-318-61047-7*) Mitchell Pub.

Business BASIC -- What Do You Say After It Says: READY: How to Develop & Maintain "Plain Vanilla"-Transportable Business BASIC Application Software. rev. ed. Scott B. Ryan. Ed. by Starla J. Ryan. (C). 1990. pap. 65.00 (*0-9621699-1-9*) Busn Basic Servs.

Business Basics: An Outline of Business Theory & Practice. Wayne L. McNaughton. (Quality Paperback Ser.: No. 317). 344p. (Orig.). 1976. pap. 13.00 (*0-8226-0317-9*) Littlefield.

Business Basics in Hawaii: Secrets of Starting Your Own Business in Our State. Dennis K. Kondo. LC 88-20296. 288p. 1988. pap. 14.95 (*0-8248-1193-3*) UH Pr.

Business Behavior & Management Structure. A. L. Minkes & C. S. Nutall. LC 84-27687. 221p. 1985. text ed. 32.50 (*0-312-10895-8*) St Martin.

***Business Benchmarking Handbook.** 210p. (Orig.). 1994. pap. 295.00 (*0-7605-0774-0*) Rector Pr.

Business Bible: Ten Commandments for Creating an Ethical Workplace. Wayne Dosick. LC 94-16474. 1994. pap. 10.00 (*0-88730-708-8*) Harper Busn.

Business Bible: Ten Commandments for Creating an Ethical Workplace. Wayne Dosick. LC 93-15976. 1993. 18.00 (*0-688-12237-X*) Morrow.

Business Biography Master Index. Ed. by Barbara McNeil. 652p. 1987. 189.00 (*0-8103-1499-1*) Gale.

Business Biography of John Wanamaker. Joseph H. Appel. reprint ed. lib. bdg. 32.50 (*0-404-00365-6*) AMS Pr.

Business, Bk. 1. Harris Winitz. (All about Language Ser.). 50p. (Orig.). 1986. audio 22.00 (*0-939990-41-5*) Intl Linguistics.

Business Blindspots: Replacing Your Company's Entrenched & Outdated Myths & Beliefs. Benjamin Gilad. 1993. 24.95 (*1-55738-536-X*) Probus Pub Co.

Business Borrowers Complete Success Kit. 4th ed. Tyler G. Hicks. 596p. 1990. pap. 99.50 (*0-934311-54-4*) Intl Wealth.

Business Borrowers Complete Success Kit. 5th ed. Tyler G. Hicks. 596p. 1992. pap. 99.50 (*1-56150-005-4*) Intl Wealth.

Business Borrowers Complete Success Kit. 6th ed. Tyler G. Hicks. 596p. 1993. pap. 99.50 (*1-56150-055-0*) Intl Wealth.

Business Borrowers Complete Success Kit. 7th ed. Tyler G. Hicks. 596p. 1994. pap. 99.50 (*1-56150-105-0*) Intl Wealth.

Business Broker's Manual. rev. ed. Gene C. Carpenter. LC 86-50900. (Illus.). 250p. (Orig.). 1995. pap. text ed. 39.95 (*0-940867-00-1*) Trend Pubns.

***Business Builders: Success Strategies to Get Clients to Come to You.** Harold Metz. (Illus.). 208p. (Orig.). 1995. pap. text ed. 30.00 (*0-89447-314-X*) Cypress.

Business Building Ideas for Franchises & Small Business. rev. ed. Med Serif. LC 85-601. 46p. 1985. pap. 3.50 (*0-87576-119-4*) Pilot Bks.

Business Building in the Nineties. Douglas J. Swanson. 117p. (Orig.). 1993. pap. text ed. 29.95 (*0-9634368-1-3*) Swanson Grp.

Business Building Letters. 20.00 (*1-877723-75-4*, 30010) Rough Notes.

Business Buy-Sell Agreements. Ed. by Edward D. Giacomini. LC 91-72877. 460p. 1991. ring bd. 110.00 (*0-88124-411-2*, BU31490) Cont Ed Bar-CA.

Business Buying Basics. Martin Bloom. 180p. (Orig.). 1992. pap. 12.95 (*0-945339-54-2*) R Erdmann Pub.

***Business Buzzwords: Everything You Need to Know to Speak the Lingo of the 90's.** Charles B. Wendel & Elaine Svennson. 166p. 1995. pap. 16.95 (*0-8144-7894-8*) AMACOM.

***Business Buzzwords: Walking the Talk from Adhocracy to Zero Defectors.** Charles B. Wendel. 1995. 18.95 (*0-8144-0263-1*) AMACOM.

Business Calculations: Model Answers. F. Fitzer. (C). 1989. 59.00 (*0-85297-276-8*, Pub. by Inst Bankers UK) St Mut.

Business Calculator Operations. 2nd ed. Joan E. Warner. LC 82-510. (C). 1983. write for info. (*0-8359-0577-2*, Reston) P-H.

Business Calculus. Ronald Smith. LC 91-58276. (Outline Ser.). (Illus.). 352p. (Orig.). (C). 1993. pap. 13.00 (*0-06-467136-4*, Harper Ref) HarpC.

Business Capital Sources. 150p. 1995. 35.00 (*0-685-56477-0*) B Klein Pubns.

Business Capital Sources. 4th ed. Tyler G. Hicks. 150p. 1990. pap. 15.00 (*0-934311-57-9*) Intl Wealth.

Business Capital Sources. 5th ed. Tyler G. Hicks. 150p. 1992. pap. 15.00 (*1-56150-008-9*) Intl Wealth.

Business Capital Sources. 6th ed. Tyler G. Hicks. 150p. 1993. pap. 15.00 (*1-56150-058-5*) Intl Wealth.

Business Capital Sources. 7th ed. Tyler G. Hicks. 150p. 1994. pap. 15.00 (*1-56150-098-4*) Intl Wealth.

Business Card Design. 1990. 29.50 (*0-88108-066-7*) Art Dir.

Business Card Graphics Two. P. I. E. Books Editors. (Illus.). 224p. 1993. 79.95 (*4-938586-31-2*, Pub. by PIE Bks JA) Bks Nippan.

Business Cards Dynamic Graphic Design. PBC International, Inc. Editors. 1993. pap. 29.95 (*0-86636-239-8*) PBC Intl Inc.

Business Cards, No. 2: A Collection from Around the World. Takenobu Igarashi. (Illus.). 224p. 1994. 89.95 (*4-7661-0758-6*, Pub. by Graphic Sha JA) Bks Nippan.

Business Career Planning Guide. Jim Porterfield. 1993. pap. 9.95 (*0-538-82039-X*) S-W Pub.

Business Career Planning Series, 5 bks. Frank Gilabert. (Orig.). (YA). (gr. 12). 1993. The Biz Careers Finance Guide: How to Improve Your Business Knowledge about Finance, 100p. pap. 14.95 (*1-884194-02-8*); The Biz Careers Accounting Guide: How to Improve Your Business Knowledge about Accounting, 100p. pap. 14.95 (*1-884194-01-X*); The Biz Careers Planning Guide: How to Prepare for Your Business Career, 70p. pap. 9.95 (*1-884194-00-1*); The Business Careers Information Systems Guide: How to Improve Your Business Knowledge about Informa. pap. 14.95 (*1-884194-03-6*); The Biz Careers Marketing Guide: How to Improve Your Business Knowledge about Marketing, 100p. pap. 14.95 (*1-884194-04-4*) Biz Careers.

Business Career Planning Series, 5 bks., Set. Frank Gilabert. (Orig.). (YA). (gr. 12). 1993. pap. 55.00 (*1-884194-05-2*) Biz Careers.

Business Case Studies: An Integrated Skills Approach. Ian Spurr et al. 112p. (Orig.). (C). 1987. pap. text ed. 23.95 (*0-273-02600-3*) Trans-Atl Phila.

Business Case Studies: French. Roderick Paton. 124p. (ENG & FRE.). 1980. pap. 19.95 (*0-8288-0986-0*, M 14377) Fr & Eur.

Business Case Studies: German. R. Paton. 124p. (ENG & GER.). 1980. pap. 17.95 (*0-8288-0991-7*, M 9204) Fr & Eur.

Business Cases in Statistical Decision Making: Computer Based Applications. Lawrence H. Peters & J. Brian Gray. LC 93-5828. 1993. text ed. write for info. (*0-13-285834-7*) P-H.

Business Cash Books Made Easy. Max Pullen. (Business Basics Ser.). pap. text ed. write for info. (*0-7494-0735-2*, Pub. by Kogan Page Educ UK) Taylor & Francis.

Business Checking Account. Jerry Belch. Ed. by Valerie Harris. (Simulating the Medical Office). 76p. 1993. Business Checking Account, 76p. 7.98 (*0-89262-316-0*) Career Pub.

Business China: A Practical Guide to Understanding Chinese Business Culture. Peggy Kenna & Sondra Lacy. LC 93-42811. 1994. 5.95 (*0-8442-3556-3*, NTC Busn Bks) NTC Pub Grp.

***Business City to City Atlas U. S. A.** (Illus.). 210p. (Orig.). 1994. pap. 135.00 (*0-7605-0841-0*) Rector Pr.

Business Civilization in Decline. Robert L. Heilbroner. 127p. (C). 1976. pap. text ed. 3.95 (*0-393-09184-8*) Norton.

Business Commercial Poster Session Miscellaneous: Contains Sections 19, Posters 23. Karl W. Boer. (Sharing the Sun Solar Technology in the Seventies Ser.: Vol. 10). 1977. 120.00 (*0-08-021706-0*, Pub. by Pergamon Repr UK) Franklin.

Business Communication. William V. Ruch. 624p. (C). 1990. write for info. (*0-675-21314-2*, Merrill Pub Co) Macmillan.

Business Communication. Stallard et al. (C). 1988. write for info. (*0-256-06063-0*) Irwin.

Business Communication. Gretchen N. Vik & Jeannette W. Gilsdorf. LC 93-22405. 640p. (C). 1993. text ed. 58.95 (*0-256-11376-9*) Irwin.

Business Communication. Chester L. Wolford & Gretchen Vanneman. LC 91-73616. 603p. (C). 1993. text ed. 35.25 (*0-15-505492-9*) Dryden Pr.

Business Communication. 2nd ed. Deborah C. Andrews & William D. Andrews. (Illus.). 656p. (C). 1992. text ed. write for info. (*0-02-303541-2*) Macmillan.

Business Communication. 2nd ed. Larry R. Andrews. (Illus.). 288p. (C). 1992. student ed, pap. write for info. (*0-02-303551-X*) Macmillan.

***Business Communication.** 3rd ed. Jules Harcourt et al. LC 94-35088. 1996. text ed. 49.95 (*0-538-71170-1*) S-W Pub.

***Business Communication: A Case Method Approach.** LC 94-21339. 1989. student ed 10.00 (*1-56118-678-3*) Paradigm MN.

***Business Communication: A Case Method Approach.** Roy W. Poe & Rosemary T. Fruehling. LC 94-21339. 1989. teacher ed, text ed. 8.00 (*1-56118-338-5*) Paradigm MN.

Business Communication: A Case Method Approach. 5th ed. Roy W. Poe & Rosemary T. Fruehling. LC 94-21339. 425p. 1989. text ed. 25.95 (*1-56118-337-7*) Paradigm MN.

Business Communication: A Classroom Simulation. James B. Stull & John W. Baird. LC 92-14971. 192p. (C). 1992. pap. text ed. write for info. (*0-13-092503-9*) P-H.

Business Communication: A Functional Perspective. Gary F. Kohut & Carol M. Baxter. 480p. (C). 1987. pap. write for info. (*0-675-20456-9*, Merrill Pub Co) Macmillan.

Business Communication: A Functional Perspective. Gary F. Kohut & Carol M. Baxter. 480p. (C). 1988. write for info. (*0-675-20455-0*, Merrill Pub Co) Macmillan.

Business Communication: A Problem-Solving Approach. 4th ed. Roy W. Poe & Rosemary T. Fruehling. 416p. (C). 1989. text ed. 29.95 (*0-07-050443-1*) McGraw.

Business Communication: A Problem-Solving Approach. 4th ed. Roy W. Poe & Rosemary T. Fruehling. 406p. 1989. teacher ed 8.00 (*1-56118-318-0*); student ed 8.45 (*1-56118-313-X*); pap. text ed. 26.50 (*1-56118-317-2*) Paradigm MN.

Business Communication: A Process Approach. Caroline L. Bloomfield & Irene R. Fairley. 549p. (C). 1990. text ed. 45.25 (*0-15-505668-9*) HB Coll Pubs.

Business Communication: An Audience-Centered Approach. Paul V. Anderson. 775p. (C). 1989. text ed. 40.00 (*0-15-505597-6*); pap. text ed. 4.00 (*0-15-505598-4*) HB Coll Pubs.

Business Communication: Concepts & Applications in an Electronic Age. 5th rev. ed. Ed. by Randolph H. Hudson & Bernard J. Selzler. (Illus.). (C). 1994. pap. text ed. write for info. (*0-935732-48-9*) Roxbury Pub Co.

Business Communication: High Tech - High Touch. Berle Haggblade & Marie Flatley. 1990. pap. text ed. write for info. (*0-07-025437-0*) McGraw.

Business Communication: Principles & Applications. 2nd ed. Glenn C. Pearce et al. 1988. text ed. 41.50 (*0-471-84851-4*) P-H.

Business Communication: Principles & Processes. Mary P. Cullinan. 688p. (C). 1989. text ed. 38.00 (*0-03-011869-7*) HB Coll Pubs.

Business Communication: Principles & Processes. 2nd ed. Mary P. Cullinan. 320p. (C). 1993. 24.00 (*0-03-096784-8*) HB Coll Pubs.

Business Communication: Principles & Processes. 5th ed. Mary P. Cullinan. 320p. (C). 1993. pap. text ed. write for info. (*0-03-079098-0*) HB Coll Pubs.

Business Communication: Process & Practice. Arthur H. Bell. (C). 1987. text ed. 29.50 (*0-673-18326-2*) HarpCollege.

Business Communication: Process & Product. Mary E. Guffey. 558p. (C). 1994. text ed. 50.95 (*0-534-92898-6*) S-W Pub.

Business Communication: Strategy & Skill. Mary Munter. (Illus.). 448p. 1987. text ed. write for info. (*0-13-091919-5*) P-H.

Business Communication: Systems & Applications. Betty R. Ricks & Kay F. Gow. LC 86-26747. 479p. 1987. text ed. 34.50 (*0-471-81824-0*) P-H.

Business Communication: Ten Steps to Success. L. Longheed. (Business for Career Success Ser.). 1994. pap. text ed. 12.00 (*0-201-51676-4*) Longman.

Business Communication: Theory & Practice, Study Guide. 2nd ed. Pearce et al. 1988. pap. text ed. 17.95 (*0-471-60168-3*) P-H.

Business Communication: Toward 2000. Arthur H. Bell. 640p. (C). 1992. text ed. 54.95 (*0-538-81673-2*, EC61AA) S-W Pub.

Business Communication Casebook, No. 3. Ed. by G. Pepper Holland et al. 1980. pap. text ed. 6.90 (*0-931874-10-6*) Assn Busn Comm.

Business Communication Casebook, No. 2. Ed. by G. Pepper Holland & Donald J. Leonard. 1977. pap. text ed. 6.90 (*0-931874-06-8*) Assn Busn Comm.

***Business Communication (CIM Workbook)** Misiura. 1995. pap. write for info. (*0-7506-1995-3*, Focal) Buttrwrth-Heinemann.

Business Communication Fundamentals. Bobbye D. Sorrels. (Illus.). 480p. (C). 1984. pap. write for info. (*0-675-20096-2*, Merrill Pub Co) Macmillan.

Business Communication II Workbook: COM 122. Linda S. Wilkinson. 188p. 1992. spiral bd. 19.95 (*0-8403-8148-4*) Kendall-Hunt.

Business Communication, Study Guide. William V. Ruch. 256p. (C). 1990. pap. write for info. (*0-675-22197-8*, Merrill Pub Co) Macmillan.

***Business Communication That Really Works.** Bonnie Lund & Office Depot Staff. Ed. by Anne Knudsen. (Small Business Solutions Ser.). (Orig.). 1995. pap. 13.95 (*0-8442-2997-0*, NTC Busn Bks) NTC Pub Grp.

***Business Communication That Really Works! Technology for Business.** Bonnie Lund. Ed. by Peter H. Engel. (Office Depot's Small Business Solutions Ser.). (Illus.). 128p. (Orig.). 1995. pap. 13.95 (*1-886111-24-3*) Affinity CA.

Business Communication Today. 3rd ed. Courtland L. Bovee. 1992. text ed. write for info. (*0-07-006746-5*) McGraw.

Business Communication Today. 4th ed. Courtland L. Bovee & John V. Thill. LC 94-4095. 1994. write for info. (*0-07-006876-3*) McGraw.

Business Communication with Contemporary Issues & Microcomputer Applications. 2nd ed. Marth H. Rader & Linda A. Kurth. LC 92-17795. 1994. text ed. 55.95 (*0-538-70665-1*) S-W Pub.

Business Communication with Writing Improvement Exercises. 4th ed. Phyllis D. Hemphill. 356p. (C). 1991. pap. text ed. write for info. (*0-13-092255-2*) P-H.

***Business Communication with Writing Improvement Exercises.** 5th ed. Phyllis D. Hemphill & Donald W. McCormick. LC 95-16084. 1995. pap. text ed. 41.33 (*0-13-317224-4*) P-H.

Business Communications. C. Chappell & W. L. Read. 216p. (Orig.). (C). 1984. 90.00 (*0-685-39847-1*, Inst Pur & Supply) St Mut.

Business Communications. R. T. Chappell & W. L. Read. 216p. (Orig.). (C). 1989. 80.00 (*0-685-36149-7*, Inst Pur & Supply) St Mut.

***Business Communications.** CUNA Staff. 208p. 1995. per., pap. text ed. 25.70 (*0-7872-0981-3*, VL02) Kendall-Hunt.

An Asterisk (*) at the beginning of an entry indicates that the title is appearing in BIP for the first time. 959

Business Communications. Himstreet et al. (gr. 9-12). 1982. teacher ed 8.64 (*0-02-831550-2*); text ed. 26.64 (*0-02-831290-2*); 5.96 (*0-02-831300-3*) Glencoe.

Business Communications. Claudia Rawlins. LC 92-54688. (Outline Ser.). 256p. 1993. pap. 12.00 (*0-06-467155-0*, Harper Ref) HarpC.

Business Communications. deluxe ed. Ray E. Barfield & Sylvia S. Titus. Ed. by George T. Friedlob. (Business Library). 320p. (Orig.). 1992. text ed. 14.95 (*0-8120-4639-0*) Barron.

Business Communications. 2nd ed. Michael E. Adelstein & W. Keats Sparrow. 480p. (C). 1990. text ed. 40.00 (*0-15-505608-5*); teacher ed, pap. text ed. 4.00 (*0-15-505609-3*) Dryden Pr.

Business Communications. 3rd ed. Raymond A. Dumont & John M. Lannon. (C). 1990. text ed. 37.50 (*0-673-52045-5*) HarpCollege.

Business Communications. 5th ed. R. T. Chappell & W. L. Read. LC 84-670120. 216p. (Orig.). 1984. 24.50 (*0-7121-2403-9*) Trans-Atl Phila.

Business Communications. 10th ed. William C. Himstreet et al. LC 92-26389. 791p. 1993. text ed. 53.95 (*0-534-92897-8*) Intl Thomson.

***Business Communications.** 11th ed. Carol M. Lehman et al. LC 95-12251. 1996. pap. 53.95 (*0-538-84778-6*) S-W Pub.

Business Communications: A Managerial Approach. Bernard H. Newman & Mary E. Oliverio. LC 76-21593. 1976. pap. 4.95 (*0-686-17616-2*) Monong Pub.

Business Communications: A Problem-Solving Approach. 3rd ed. Roy W. Poe. 416p. (C). 1984. teacher ed 12.10 (*1-56118-316-4*); student ed 8.25 (*1-56118-314-8*); pap. text ed. 27.95 (*1-56118-315-6*) Paradigm MN.

Business Communications: An Annotated Bibliography. Ed. by Stanley J. Birkin. LC 79-8296. 686p. 1980. text ed. 59.95 (*0-313-20923-5*, WBW/, Greenwood Pr) Greenwood.

***Business Communications: BUS 320.** California College for Health Sciences Staff. 95p. (C). 1995. student ed write for info. (*0-933195-61-3*) Allied Hlth Pubns.

Business Communications: Skills & Strategies. Jane W. Gibson & Richard M. Hodgetts. 640p. (C). 1990. text ed. 64.50 (*0-06-042307-2*) HarpCollege.

Business Communications: Speaking & Writing Effectively. Flora Reia. (Illus.). 250p. (C). 1987. pap. text ed. 13.95 (*0-935920-47-1*, Ntl Pubs Blck) P-H.

Business Communications: Strategies & Skills. 4th rev. ed. Richard C. Huseman & James M. Lahiff. Ed. by John Penrose. (Illus.). 677p. (C). 1991. text ed. 51.25 (*0-03-033067-X*) Dryden Pr.

Business Communications: Strategies for Success. Burnett & Dollar. LC 88-5197. 550p. 1989. 39.95 (*0-87393-090-8*); student ed 13.95 (*0-685-24301-X*) Dame Pubns.

Business Communications: Writing, Interviewing, & Speaking at Work. Randall E. Majors. 352p. (C). 1990. pap. text ed. 46.50 (*0-06-044183-6*) HarpCollege.

Business Communications at Work. Brian D. Bakos. (Illus.). 192p. (C). 1987. pap. text ed. write for info. (*0-13-091752-4*) P-H.

Business Communications, No. 1: Grammar, Resumes, Cover Letters, & Thank You Letters. Eleanor M. Saris. 225p. (C). 1989. ring bd. 19.95 (*0-318-43230-7*) EIT VA.

Business Communities of India. Dwijendra Tripathi. 1985. 26.00 (*0-8364-1276-1*, Pub. by Manohar II) S Asia.

***Business Community of Seventeenth-Century England.** Richard Grassby. 624p. (C). 1995. write for info. (*0-521-43450-5*) Cambridge U Pr.

Business Computations. Kathleen Harcharik & Moses A. Armijo. (Illus.). 320p. (C). 1982. pap. text ed. write for info. (*0-13-093104-7*) P-H.

Business Computer Applications. Lewis M. Elia & Zalondek. 1987. 10.00 (*0-87350-191-8*); teacher ed, disk 59.95 (*0-87350-781-9*); disk 59.95 (*0-87350-790-8*); Apple II 59.95 (*0-87350-789-4*) Milady Pub.

Business Computer Systems: An Introduction. 2nd ed. David M. Kroenke. LC 83-17381. (Illus.). 689p. 1984. text ed. 26.95 (*0-938188-07-0*); student ed, boxed 8.50 (*0-938188-12-7*); disk write for info. (*0-318-57706-2*); 5.95 (*0-685-08270-9*) Mitchell Pub.

Business Computer Systems: An Introduction. 3rd ed. David M. Kroenke & Dolan. 752p. (C). 1986. student ed 10.50 (*0-685-14445-3*) McGraw.

Business Computer Systems: Special Edition Using Applications Software. David M. Kroenke et al. 577p. (Orig.). (C). 1986. pap. text ed. 28.95 (*0-938188-36-4*); teacher ed write for info. (*0-938188-09-7*); student ed 8.50 (*0-685-14447-X*); disk write for info. (*0-318-61049-3*) Mitchell Pub.

Business Computer Systems Design. Kathleen Dolan. 336p. 1984. pap. text ed. 13.95 (*0-938188-20-8*) Mitchell Pub.

Business Computers: Planning, Selecting, Implementing Your First Computer System. Robert T. Keim. 384p. (C). 1985. write for info. (*0-675-20286-8*, Merrill Pub Co) Macmillan.

Business Computing. Steve Skidmore. 232p. (C). 1987. pap. text ed. 24.95 (*0-7131-3633-2*, Pub. by E Arnold UK) Routledge Chapman & Hall.

Business Computing Primer. John Edwards & Colin Lewis. 240p. 1994. pap. 44.50 (*0-273-60005-2*, Pub. by Pitman Pub Ltd UK) Trans-Atl Phila.

Business Concentration & Price Policy. Universities-National Bureau Staff. (Conference Ser.: No. 5). 519p. 1955. reprint ed. 135.00 (*0-87014-196-1*) Natl Bur Econ Res.

Business Concentration & Price Policy: Proceedings. Conference of the Universities. LC 75-19699. (National Bureau of Economic Research Ser.). 1975. reprint ed. 42.95 (*0-405-07579-0*) Ayer.

Business Concepts: A Text for English Practice. 2nd rev. ed. Barbara T. Dowling & Marianne M. Arden. LC 92-31120. Orig. Title: Business Concepts for English Practice. 1993. pap. 20.95 (*0-8384-4077-0*) Heinle & Heinle.

Business Concepts for English Practice see Business Concepts: A Text for English Practice

Business Confidential. Boardroom's Experts & Editors Staff. LC 86-30963. 520p. 1987. 50.00 (*0-932648-82-7*) Boardroom.

Business Consultant. Jack Rudman. (Career Examination Ser.: C-1962). 1994. pap. 34.95 (*0-8373-1962-5*) Nat Learn.

Business Contract Forms. Robert J. English. LC 83-23312. (Business Practice Library: 1-692). 574p. 1993. text ed. 115.00 (*0-471-80162-3*) Wiley.

Business Contracts: Forms & Tax Analysis, Vol. 1. 2nd ed. Robert J. English et al. LC 94-762. (Business Practice Library). 1994. Volume 1. write for info. (*0-471-59813-5*) Wiley.

Business Contracts: Forms & Tax Analysis, Vol. 2. 2nd ed. Robert J. English et al. LC 94-762. (Business Practice Library). 1994. Volume 2. write for info. (*0-471-59814-3*) Wiley.

Business Contracts: Forms & Tax Analysis, Vol. 2. 2nd ed. Robert J. English et al. LC 94-762. (Business Practice Library). 1994. Set. text ed. 232.00 (*0-471-59815-1*) Wiley.

Business Contracts & the Sale of Goods. Roger J. Leo. Ed. by Alan L. Schneider. (Business Law Ser.). 69p. (Orig.). 1987. pap. 25.75 (*0-685-28082-9*) BLI Inc.

Business Corporation in the Democratic Society. Wolfgang Dorow. Orig. Title: Die Unternehmung in der Demokratischen Gesellschaft. (Illus.). 388p. (C). 1987. lib. bdg. 112.00 (*0-89925-295-8*) De Gruyter.

Business Corporation Law, BCL. Martin Fogelman. write for info. (*0-318-59329-7*) West Pub.

Business Correspondence: Letters, Faxes & Memos. L. Longheed. (English for Business Success Ser.). (Illus.). 143p. 1993. pap. text ed. 12.00 (*0-201-55537-9*) Addison-Wesley.

Business Correspondence Essentials. 4th ed. Rosemary T. Fruehling & Sharon Bouchard. 208p. 1986. text ed. 10.96 (*0-07-022515-X*) McGraw.

Business Correspondence for Today: Letters, Memos & Short Reports. Jeanette Gilsdorf. 400p. 1989. pap. text ed. 26.50 (*0-471-83246-4*) P-H.

Business Correspondence in English. M. G. Calasso. 247p. (ENG & SPA.). 1980. pap. 20.75 (*0-8288-1548-8*, S35380) Fr & Eur.

***Business Crime: Cases & Materials, Supplement for 1994-1995 with Problems.** Harry First. (University Casebook Ser.). (Illus.). 137p. 1994. pap. text ed. 9.50 (*1-56662-219-0*) Foundation Pr.

Business Crime: Criminal Liability of the Business Community, 7 vols. Stanley S. Arkin & Earl C. Dudley. 1981. Updates. ring bd. write for info. (*0-8205-1265-6*) Bender.

Business Crime: Its Nature & Control. Michael Clarke. LC 89-77988. 250p. 1990. text ed. 49.95 (*0-312-04633-2*) St Martin.

Business Crime, Case & Materials. Harry First. (University Casebook Ser.). 850p. 1989. text ed. 40.95 (*0-88277-732-7*) Foundation Pr.

Business Crime, Cases & Materials Teacher's Manual. Harry First. (University Casebook Ser.). 97p. 1990. pap. text ed. write for info. (*0-88277-857-9*) Foundation Pr.

***Business Crisis Planning.** (Illus.). 300p. (Orig.). 1994. pap. 295.00 (*0-7605-0606-X*) Rector Pr.

***Business Culture in France.** Colin Gordon. 288p. 1995. pap. 24.95 (*0-7506-1832-9*) Buttrwrth-Heinemann.

***Business Culture in Germany.** Collin Randlesome. 288p. 1994. pap. 24.95 (*0-7506-1833-7*) Buttrwrth-Heinemann.

***Business Culture in Spain.** Kevin Bruton. 288p. 1994. pap. 24.95 (*0-7506-1831-0*) Buttrwrth-Heinemann.

Business Cultures in Europe. 2nd ed. Ed. by Collin Randlesome. 320p. 1993. pap. 34.95 (*0-7506-0872-2*) Buttrwrth-Heinemann.

Business Cycle: Growth & Crisis under Capitalism. Howard J. Sherman. (Illus.). 466p. 1992. text ed. 60.00 (*0-691-04262-4*); pap. text ed. 19.95 (*0-691-02721-8*) Princeton U Pr.

Business Cycle: Theories & Evidence, Proceedings of the Sixteenth Annual Economic Policy Conference of the Federal Reserve Bank of St. Louis. Ed. by Michael T. Belongia & Michelle R. Garfinkel. LC 92-11616. 240p. (C). 1992. lib. bdg. 57.00 (*0-7923-9239-6*) Kluwer Ac.

Business Cycle after Keynes: A Contemporary Analysis. A. W. Mullineux. LC 83-27160. 132p. 1984. 45.00 (*0-389-20453-6*, 08014) B&N Imports.

Business Cycle Analysis: Papers Presented at the Fourteenth CIRET Conference Proceedings - Lisbon 1979. W. Strigel. 456p. 1984. text ed. 93.95 (*0-566-00368-6*) Ashgate Pub Co.

Business Cycle Analysis by Means of Economic Surveys, Pt. II: Papers Presented at the 20th CIRET Conference Proceedings, Budapest 1991. Karl H. Oppenlander & Gunter Poser. 480p. 1993. 75.95 (*1-85628-429-8*, Pub. by Avebury Pub UK) Ashgate Pub Co.

Business Cycle Analysis by Means of Economic Surveys, Pt. 1: Papers Presented at the 20th CIRET Conference Proceedings, Budapest 1991. Oppenlander & Poser. 453p. 1992. 93.95 (*1-85628-260-0*, Pub. by Avebury Pub UK) Ashgate Pub Co.

Business Cycle in a Changing World. Arthur F. Burns. LC 69-12462. (Business Cycles Ser.: No. 18). 366p. 1969. 95.70 (*0-87014-200-3*, 67) Natl Bur Econ Res.

Business Cycle in a Changing World. Arthur F. Burns. LC 69-12462. (National Bureau of Economic Research, Studies in Business Cycles: Vol. 18). 368p. reprint ed. pap. 104.90 (*0-8357-2601-0*, 2015967) Bks Demand.

Business Cycle Indicators, 1. Ed. by Geoffrey H. Moore. LC 60-14062. (National Bureau of Economic Research Ser.: Vol. 10). 793p. reprint ed. pap. 180.00 (*0-8357-7486-4*, 2005917) Bks Demand.

Business Cycle Indicators, 2. Ed. by Geoffrey H. Moore. LC 60-14062. (National Bureau of Economic Research Ser.: Vol. 10). 197p. reprint ed. pap. 56.20 (*0-8357-7487-2*, 2019644) Bks Demand.

Business Cycle Indicators & Measures: A Complete Guide to Using & Interpreting the Key Economic Indicators. George Hildebrand. 300p. 1992. 50.00 (*1-55738-410-X*) Probus Pub Co.

Business Cycle Surveys in the Assessment of Economic Activity: Papers Presented at the 17th Ciret Conference Proceedings Vienna 1985. K. H. Oppenlander & G. Poser. 674p. 1986. text ed. 99.95 (*0-566-05108-7*) Ashgate Pub Co.

Business Cycle Surveys with Special Reference to the Pacific Basin Economies: Papers Presented at the 19th CIRET Conference Proceedings, OSaka, 1989. Karl H. Oppenlander & Gunter Poser. (CIRET Conference Proceedings Ser.). 761p. 1990. text ed. 119.95 (*1-85628-123-X*, Pub. by Avebury Pub UK) Ashgate Pub Co.

Business Cycle Theory. G. Gabisch & Hans-Walter Lorenz. (Lecture Notes in Economics & Mathematical Systems Ser.: Vol. 283). vii, 229p. 1986. pap. 23.30 (*0-387-17188-6*) Spr-Verlag.

Business Cycle Theory. 2nd ed. G. Gabisch & Hans-Walter Lorenz. (Universitext Ser.). (Illus.). 260p. 1989. pap. 39.00 (*0-387-51059-1*) Spr-Verlag.

Business-Cycle Theory: Its Development & Present Status. Alvin H. Hansen. LC 79-1578. 1980. reprint ed. 18.50 (*0-88355-884-X*) Hyperion Conn.

Business Cycles: A Theoretical, Historical & Statistical Analysis of the Capitalist Process. abr. ed. Joseph A. Schumpeter. LC 86-8183. vii, 461p. 1989. reprint ed. pap. text ed. 24.95 (*0-87991-263-4*) Porcupine Pr.

Business Cycles: Indicators & Forecasting. Mark W. Watson. Ed. by James H. Stock. LC 93-19498. (Studies in Business Cycles: Vol. 28). (Illus.). 320p. 1993. lib. bdg. 49.95 (*0-226-77488-0*) U Ch Pr.

Business Cycles: Inflation & Forecasting. 2nd ed. Geoffrey H. Moore. LC 83-3829. (National Bureau of Economic Research, Studies in Business Cycles: No. 24). 499p. reprint ed. pap. 142.30 (*0-8357-6986-0*, 2057069) Bks Demand.

Business Cycles: The Nature & Causes of Economic Fluctuations. Thomas E. Hall. LC 89-70955. 256p. 1990. text ed. 45.00 (*0-275-93085-8*, C3085, Praeger Pubs) Greenwood.

Business Cycles: The Problem & Its Setting. Wesley C. Mitchell. LC 75-19730. (National Bureau of Economic Research Ser.). (Illus.). 1975. reprint ed. 41.95 (*0-405-07608-8*) Ayer.

Business Cycles: The Problem & Its Setting. Wesley C. Mitchell. (Studies in Business Cycles: No. 1). 519p. 1927. reprint ed. 135.00 (*0-87014-084-1*) Natl Bur Econ Res.

Business Cycles: Theory & Empirical Methods. Ed. by Willi Semmler. LC 93-49662. (Recent Economic Thought Ser.). 416p. (C). 1994. lib. bdg. 125.00 (*0-7923-9448-8*) Kluwer Ac.

Business Cycles: Theory & Evidence. Andy Mullineux et al. LC 92-26627. 208p. 1993. 44.95 (*0-631-18566-6*); pap. 19.95 (*0-631-18567-4*) Blackwell Pubs.

Business Cycles: Theory, History, Indications, & Forecasting. Victor Zarnowitz. (National Bureau of Economic Research Conference Report Ser.). 552p. 1992. 70.00 (*0-226-97890-7*) U Ch Pr.

***Business Cycles: Theory, History, Indicators & Forecasting.** Victor Zarnowitz. xx, 594p. 1996. pap. 32.50x (*0-226-97891-5*) U Ch Pr.

Business Cycles & Depressions: An Encyclopedia. Ed. by David Glasner. 900p. Date not set. 95.00 (*0-8240-0944-4*) Garland.

Business Cycles & Equilibrium. Fischer Black. 200p. 1987. pap. 19.95 (*0-631-17493-1*) Blackwell Pubs.

Business Cycles & Financial Crisis. A. W. Mullineux. 200p. 1990. reprint ed. text ed. 42.50 (*0-472-10181-1*) U of Mich Pr.

***Business Cycles & Forecasting.** Howard J. Sherman & David X. Kolk. LC 95-5180. (C). 1995. 62.50 (*0-06-501139-2*) HarpCollege.

Business Cycles & Forecasting. 8th ed. Lloyd M. Valentine. (C). 1991. text ed. 59.95 (*0-538-80575-7*, HG65HA) S-W Pub.

Business Cycles & Their Causes. Wesley C. Mitchell. LC 86-8182. (Illus.). xii, 226p. 1989. reprint ed. pap. text ed. 12.95 (*0-87991-262-6*) Porcupine Pr.

Business Cycles & Unemployment: Proceedings. President's Conference on Unemployment Committee. LC 75-19697. (National Bureau of Economic Research Ser.). (Illus.). 1975. reprint ed. 36.95 (*0-405-07577-4*) Ayer.

Business Cycles in the Postwar World: Some Reflections on Recent Research. Philip A. Klein. LC 76-316. (Domestic Affairs Studies: No. 42). 57p. reprint ed. pap. 25.00 (*0-8357-4442-6*, 2037277) Bks Demand.

Business Cycles in Yugoslavia. Branko Horvat. LC 72-105544. 261p. reprint ed. pap. 74.40 (*0-8357-9433-4*, 2015410) Bks Demand.

Business Data & Market Information Source Book for the Forest Products Industry. Edwin Kallio & Edward Dickerhoof. LC 79-63022. 215p. 1979. 30.00 (*0-935018-02-6*); 20.00 (*0-685-01662-5*) Forest Prod.

Business Data Communication. 3rd rev. ed. David A. Stamper. Ed. by Michelle Baxter. 500p. (C). 1992. text ed. 53.75 (*0-8053-7720-4*) Benjamin-Cummings.

Business Data Communications. 2nd ed. William Stallings & Richard Van Slyke. 658p. (C). 1994. write for info. (*0-02-415433-4*) Macmillan.

***Business Data Communications.** 4th ed. David A. Stamper. LC 94-3572. (C). 1995. text ed. 53.75 (*0-8053-7715-8*) Benjamin-Cummings.

Business Data Communications: Basic Concepts, Security, & Design. 4th ed. Jerry Fitzgerald. 722p. (C). 1993. Net. text ed. write for info. (*0-471-54845-6*) Wiley.

Business Data Processing. Robert Jacobs. (Core Business Program Ser.). (Illus.). 128p. 1985. 7.95 (*0-8160-0051-4*) Facts on File.

Business Data Systems. 4th ed. H. D. Clifton. 480p. 1990. pap. text ed. 58.00 (*0-13-091695-1*) P-H.

Business Dateline Controlled Vocabulary. Ed. by V. MacLeod & S. Thornberry. 1990. 25.00 (*0-914604-41-4*) UMI Louisville.

Business Decision Making with 1-2-3. Mark Albion & Edward Hoff. (Illus.). 336p. (C). 1988. 40.95 (*0-13-094178-6*) P-H.

Business Decisions with Computers. Daniel Schutzer. 1991. text ed. 49.95 (*0-442-31879-0*) Van Nos Reinhold.

Business Demography: A Guide & Reference for Business Planners & Marketers. Louis G. Pol. LC 87-2494. 312p. 1987. text ed. 59.95 (*0-89930-218-1*, PDY/, Quorum Bks) Greenwood.

Business Depressions & Financial Panics: Collected Essays in American Business & Economic History. Samuel Rezneck. LC 68-28644. 201p. 1969. text ed. 49.95 (*0-8371-1501-9*, REB/, Greenwood Pr) Greenwood.

Business Desktop Publishing Applications: Job-Based Tasks. V. Lyons & C. Ziegler. 200p. (C). 1994. teacher ed write for info. (*1-56118-399-7*); disk, pap. text ed. 15.95 (*1-56118-398-9*); 3.5 hd, pap. text ed. 15.95 (*1-56118-400-4*) Paradigm MN.

Business Diaries of Sir Alexander Grant. James S. Adam. 144p. (C). 1989. 38.00 (*0-85976-349-8*, Pub. by J Donald) St Mut.

Business Dictionary. William Selden & Louis C. Nanassy. (Illus.). 224p. (C). 1984. text ed. 23.00 (*0-13-094680-X*); pap. 10.50 (*0-13-094672-9*) P-H.

Business Dictionary of Computers. 3rd ed. Jerry M. Rosenberg. (Business Dictionaries Ser.). 416p. 1993. text ed. 45.00 (*0-471-58575-0*); pap. text ed. 14.95 (*0-471-58574-2*) Wiley.

***Business Directory & Buyer's Guide: Orange County, NY.** Comp. by Emily O'Connor & Mary Fenelon. 400p. (Orig.). Date not set. pap. write for info. (*0-945965-02-8*) Centers Composition.

Business Directory of Industry & Service: The Big Green Book. 1984. 95.00 (*0-940640-02-3*) Registry Pubns.

Business Directory of Industry & Service: The Big Green Book. 1985. 95.00 (*0-940640-03-1*) Registry Pubns.

Business Directory of Poland. 1993. 197.00 (*0-9632313-0-8*) Global Comm Netwk.

Business Directory of the New Independent States. 1200p. 1992. 295.00 (*1-880141-35-3*) Triumph Bks.

Business Disability Insurance. Jeff Sadler. 1992. 29.50 (*1-56461-109-4*, 46180) Rough Notes.

Business Disasters Book of Days: The World's Greatest Financial Mishaps, Follies & Remarkable Events. Jill Herbers. LC 94-17247. 1994. 9.95 (*0-8065-1585-6*) Carol Pub Group.

Business Doctor. Arnold S. Goldstein. Ed. by Mark T. Lauer. 240p. (Orig.). 1994. pap. 19.95 (*1-880539-25-X*) Garrett FL.

***Business Documentation Handbook.** 90p. (Orig.). 1995. pap. 145.00 (*0-7605-1514-X*) Rector Pr.

Business Documents: Their Origins, Sources & Uses in Historical Research. J. Armstrong & S. Jones. 224p. 1987. text ed. 90.00 (*0-7201-1846-8*, Mansell Pub) Cassell.

Business Documents of Murashu Sons of Nippur: Dated in the Reign of Darius II (424-404 B. C.) Albert T. Clay. LC 08-33650. (University of Pennsylvania, Babylonian Expedition, Series A: Cuneiform Texts: Vol. 10). 207p. reprint ed. pap. 59.00 (*0-8357-7488-0*, 2052021) Bks Demand.

Business Documents of Murashu Sons of Nippur Dated in the Reign of Artaxerxes I, (464-424 B. C.) Hermann V. Hilprecht & A. T. Clay. LC 08-33650. (University of Pennsylvania, Babylonian Expedition, Series A: Cuneiform Texts: Vol. 9). 185p. reprint ed. pap. 52.80 (*0-8357-7490-2*, 2052015) Bks Demand.

Business Documents of Murashu Sons of Nippur Dated in the Reign of Darius II. Albert T. Clay. LC 13-1107. (University of Pennsylvania, The Museum, Publications of the Babylonian Section: Vol. 2, No. 1). 180p. reprint ed. pap. 51.30 (*0-8357-7489-9*, 2052016) Bks Demand.

Business Documents of the Hammurapi Period from the British Museum. Leroy Waterman. LC 78-72773. (Ancient Mesopotamian Texts & Studies). reprint ed. 22.50 (*0-404-18229-1*) AMS Pr.

Business Dynamics. Hobart Conover et al. 481p. 1982. teacher ed write for info. (*0-672-97978-0*); text ed. write for info. (*0-672-97973-X*); student ed write for info. (*0-672-97977-2*) Macmillan.

Business Earth Stations for Telecommunications. Walter L. Morgan & Denis Rouffet. (Telecommunications Ser.). 234p. 1988. text ed. 79.95 (*0-471-63556-1*) Wiley.

Business Economics. Maria Moschandreas. LC 93-38120. 1994. write for info. (*0-415-10909-4*); pap. write for info. (*0-415-10910-8*) Routledge.

***Business Economics.** Comp. by Richard Schwindt. (Business Administration Reading Lists & Course Outlines Ser.: 17). (Illus.). 232p. (Orig.). (C). 1995. pap. text ed. 25.00 (*0-88024-177-2*) Eno River Pr.

An Asterisk (*) at the beginning of an entry indicates that the title is appearing in BIP for the first time.

961

B

Business for Profits. Ed. by Allan H. Smith. LC 86-61837. (Illus.). 288p. (Orig.). 1987. pap. 10.00 (*0-931113-04-0*) Success Publ.

***Business for the Twenty-First Century.** Steven Skinner & John Ivancevich. 232p. (C). 1992. student ed, text ed. 18.95 (*0-256-09691-0*) Irwin.

Business for the Twenty-First Century. Steven J. Skinner & John M. Ivancevich. 864p. (C). 1991. text ed. 53.95 (*0-256-09222-2*) Irwin.

Business Forecasting. Wilford J. Eiteman. 1954. 4.50 (*0-912164-40-9*) Masterco Pr.

Business Forecasting. 2nd ed. J. Holton Wilson & Barry Keating. LC 93-3729. 496p. (C). 1993. text ed. 66.95 (*0-256-11871-X*) Irwin.

Business Forecasting. 3rd ed. John E. Hanke & Arthur G. Reitsch. 544p. 1989. teacher ed write for info. (*0-318-63856-8*, H18112) Allyn.

Business Forecasting. 3rd suppl. ed. John E. Hanke & Arthur G. Reitsch. 544p. 1989. disk write for info. (*0-685-22007-9*, H18138) Allyn.

Business Forecasting. 4th ed. John E. Hanke & Arthur G. Reitsch. 544p. (C). 1992. text ed. 43.00 (*0-205-13349-5*) Allyn.

***Business Forecasting.** 5th ed. John E. Hanke & Arthur G. Reitsch. LC 94-36217. 1994. text ed. 68.00 (*0-205-16005-0*) P-H Gen Ref & Trav.

Business Forecasting: Concepts & Microcomputer Applications. Neil E. Seitz. (C). 1984. teacher ed write for info. (*0-8359-0605-1*, Reston); pap. text ed. 35.00 (*0-8359-0604-3*, Reston) P-H.

Business Forecasting & Economic Cycles. S. G. Karsten. 308p. (Orig.). (C). 1990. pap. text ed. 32.00 (*0-8191-7911-6*) U Pr of Amer.

***Business Forecasting & Planning.** Peter Shearer. LC 93-43160. 1994. 33.90 (*0-13-094962-0*) P-H Intl.

Business Forecasting for Management. Branko Pecar. Ed. by Glyn Davis & Simon Lillystone. LC 93-47175. 1994. 14.95 (*0-07-707865-9*) McGraw.

Business Forecasting in a Lotus 1-2-3 Environment. Colin Lewis. 1989. disk, pap. text ed. 53.50 (*0-471-92357-5*) Wiley.

Business Forecasting Revolution. F. Gerard Adams. (Wharton Executive Library). (Illus.). 256p. 1986. 25.00 (*0-19-503700-6*) OUP.

Business Forecasting Using Financial Models: How to Use the Key Techniques of Financial Modelling to Interpret Business Proposals. Ed. by Neil Hogg. (Financial Times Management Ser.). 224p. 1994. 105.00x (*0-273-60529-1*, Pub. by Pitman Pubng UK) St Mut.

***Business Form Market.** 400p. (Orig.). 1994. pap. 1,295.00 (*1-57205-947-8*) Rector Pr.

Business Forms & Contracts in Plain English for Craftspeople. 2nd ed. Leonard D. DuBoff. 128p. 1993. reprint ed. pap. 14.95 (*0-934026-83-1*) Interweave.

Business Forms & Systems - Wholesale, 1995. American Business Directories Staff. 1995. spiral bd., pap. 715.00 (*1-56105-599-9*) Am Busn Direct.

Business Forms for Galleries & Frame Shops. Ed. by Vivian C. Kistler. 32p. (Orig.). 1989. pap. text ed. 12.00 (*0-938655-26-4*) Columba Pub.

Business Forms for Managing a Small Business. Ed. by J. K. Lasser Staff. 1994. pap. 29.95 (*0-671-88328-3*, J K Lasser) P-H Gen Ref & Trav.

***Business Forms for Paralegals.** Charles P. Nemeth. LC 94-41808. (Paralegals Law Library). 1995. text ed. 98.00 (*0-471-01998-4*) Wiley.

Business Forms for the Fax & Copier. Sharon Aselin-Kerr. Ed. by Michael G. Crisp. LC 90-64140. (Illus.). 122p. (Orig.). 1991. pap. 9.95 (*1-56052-074-4*) Crisp Pubns.

Business Forms from ALI-ABA Course Materials. 373p. 1983. Set including 1984, 1985, 1987 & 1988 supplements. ring bd. 140.00 (*0-317-30789-4*, F302/F304/F306/F307/F309) Am Law Inst.

Business Forms from ALI-ABA Course Materials. 2nd ed. Frwd. by Paul A. Wolkin. LC 91-71725. 332p. 1991. ring bd. 100.00 (*0-8318-0669-9*, B669); 3.5 hd, 5.25 hd 140.00 (*0-685-59034-8*, B669/B676) Am Law Inst.

Business Forms from ALI-ABA Course Materials, No. 1. suppl. ed. 200p. 1984. 23.00 (*0-685-53940-7*, F304) Am Law Inst.

Business Forms from ALI-ABA Course Materials, No. 2. suppl. ed. 210p. 1985. 28.50 (*0-685-53941-5*, F306) Am Law Inst.

Business Forms from ALI-ABA Course Materials, No. 3. suppl. ed. 209p. 1987. 30.00 (*0-685-53942-3*, F307) Am Law Inst.

Business Forms from ALI-ABA Course Materials, No. 4. suppl. ed. 182p. 1988. 30.00 (*0-685-53943-1*, F309) Am Law Inst.

***Business Forms on File Collection: 1995 Edition.** Ed. by Facts of File Staff. 312p. 1995. ring bd. 125.00x (*0-8160-3191-6*) Facts on File.

***Business Forms on File Collection: 1995 Update.** Ed. by Facts on File Staff. 1995. ring bd. 40.00x (*0-8160-3190-8*) Facts on File.

Business France: A Practical Guide to Understanding French Business Culture. Peggy Kenna & Sondra Lacy. LC 93-40572. 1994. 5.95 (*0-8442-3554-7*, NTC Busn Bks) NTC Pub Grp.

Business Gaining the Competition. Norman M. Scarborough. 1993. text ed. 39.00 (*0-205-15796-3*) Allyn.

Business Game. Larry W. Mills & Danny B. McDowell. (C). 1987. 20.25 (*0-673-39026-8*) HarpCollege.

Business Games. Martin G. Groder. LC 80-19095. 260p. 1980. 50.00 (*0-932648-14-2*) Boardroom.

***Business German Dictionary: English-German - German-English.** rev. ed. P. H. Collin et al. 676p. 1994. 52.50 (*0-948549-50-5*) IBD Ltd.

Business Germany: A Practical Guide to Understanding German Business Culture. Peggy Kenna & Sondra Lacy. LC 93-40566. 1994. 5.95 (*0-8442-3555-5*, NTC Busn Bks) NTC Pub Grp.

***Business Global Competition: Organizing the New Global Competitor.** (Illus.). 128p. (Orig.). 1995. pap. 495.00 (*0-7605-1877-7*) Rector Pr.

Business, Government, & Society. 3rd ed. Douglas F. Greer. (Illus.). 604p. (C). 1992. teacher ed write for info. (*0-318-69280-5*) Macmillan.

Business, Government, & Society. 3rd ed. Douglas F. Greer. (Illus.). 604p. (C). 1993. text ed. write for info. (*0-02-347150-6*) Macmillan.

Business, Government, & Society: A Managerial Perspective: Text & Cases. 7th ed. George A. Steiner & John F. Steiner. LC 93-9105. (Series in Management). 1993. text ed. write for info. (*0-07-061226-9*) McGraw.

Business, Government, & Society: Managing Competitiveness, Ethics & Social Issues. Newman S. Perry. (Illus.). 825p. (C). 1994. text ed. write for info. (*0-02-393401-8*) Macmillan.

Business-Government Cooperation, 1917-1932: The Rise of Corporatist Policies. Intro. by Robert F. Himmelberg. LC 93-47242. (Business & Government in America since 1870 Ser.: Vol. 5). 440p. 1994. 62.00 (*0-8153-1407-8*) Garland.

Business-Government Relations & Interdependence: A Managerial & Analytic Interdependence. John M. Stevens et al. LC 87-32279. 175p. 1988. text ed. 45.00 (*0-89930-310-2*, SVB/, Quorum Bks) Greenwood.

***Business, Government, Society: The Global Political Economy.** Arthur A. Goldsmith. LC 95-13447. 720p. (C). 1995. text ed. 56.25 (*0-256-12833-2*) Irwin.

Business Grammar Handbook. Scott R. Pancoast & Lance M. White. LC 85-20248. (Illus.). 210p. 1992. pap. 9.95 (*0-87131-709-5*) M Evans.

Business Graphics: A C Plus Plus Toolkit for Windows Applications. John Levine. 1993. disk, pap. 39.95 (*1-55851-330-2*) M&T Bks.

Business Graphics: Concepts & Applications. Coburn. 320p. 1991. 18.50 (*0-87835-520-0*) Boyd & Fraser.

Business Graphics, 1976: Advance Printing of Papers Summaries. Fall Symposium on Business Graphics Staff. Ed. by Shou L. Hou. LC 76-46764. 112p. reprint ed. pap. 32.00 (*0-8357-7492-9*, 2025039) Bks Demand.

Business Groups in Thailand. Krirkkiat Phipatseritham & Kunio Yoshihara. 39p. (Orig.). 1984. pap. text ed. 16.95 (*9971-902-69-9*, Pub. by Inst SE Asian Studies SI) Ashgate Pub Co.

Business Guide: Plan Every Day with Positive Expectancy. 1991. 14.95 (*0-911703-34-9*) CDS Assocs.

Business Guide for Interior Designers: A Practical Checklist for Analyzing the Various Conditions of a Design Project & the Related Clauses for a Letter of Agreement. Harry Siegel. 48p. 1976. pap. 7.95 (*0-8230-7460-9*, Whitney Lib) Watsn-Guptill.

Business Guide for the Home Based Commercial Artist. J. F. Jones. 50p. (Orig.). 1989. pap. 10.00 (*0-9617813-3-5*) Drakestone Pub.

Business Guide for the Professional Home-Based Photographer. J. F. Jones. 50p. (Orig.). 1989. pap. 10.00 (*0-9617813-2-7*) Drakestone Pub.

Business Guide to a California Small Claims Court. Douglas G. Carnahan. 1992. pap. 44.00 (*1-55943-162-8*) Butterworth Legal Pubs.

Business Guide to Avoiding Environmental Liability. Thomas M. Downs. 174p. 1993. pap. text ed. 85.00 (*0-86587-349-6*) Gov Insts.

Business Guide to European Community Legislation. Ed. by Stanbrook & Hooper. 800p. 1993. text ed. 325.00 (*0-471-93698-7*) Wiley.

***Business Guide to European Community Legislation.** 2nd ed. Stanbrook et al. Ed. by Bernard O'Connor. LC 95-5155. 1995. text ed. 145.00 (*0-471-95341-5*, Pub. by Wiley Chancery Law UK) Wiley.

Business Guide to Japan: Opening Doors & Closing Deals! Boye De Mente. LC 89-50662. 125p. (Orig.). 1989. pap. 5.95 (*0-8048-1613-1*) C E Tuttle.

Business Guide to Local Area Network. William Stallings. 1990. pap. 24.95 (*0-672-22728-2*, Bobbs) Macmillan.

***Business Guide to Modern China.** Jon P. Alston & Stephen Y. He. LC 95-1342. 1995. write for info. (*0-88406-269-4*) GA St U Busn Pr.

Business Guide to Print Promotion. Marlene Miller. LC 87-83397. (Illus.). 224p. (Orig.). 1988. pap. 19.95 (*0-945372-03-5*) Iris Comn Grp.

***Business Guide to Privacy & Data Protection Legislation.** Ed. by Charles Franklin. LC 94-42196. (ICC Publications: Vol. 498). 1995. write for info. (*92-842-1131-X*); pap. text ed. write for info. (*90-6544-724-5*) Kluwer Law Tax Pubs.

Business Guide to Selling Information by Mail. E. R. Jones. (Illus.). 110p. 1982. 15.00 (*0-9600934-4-3*) E R Jones.

Business Guide to Small Computers. Lawrence Calmus. LC 82-10080. 240p. reprint ed. pap. 68.40 (*0-8357-3249-5*, AU00411) Bks Demand.

Business Guide to the XENIX System. Rebecca Thomas et al. (Illus.). 488p. 1984. pap. 19.95 (*0-201-08847-9*) Addison-Wesley.

Business Guide to Tosca: Effects & Actions. George S. Dominguez. LC 79-20054. 383p. reprint ed. pap. 109.20 (*0-8357-7493-7*, 2025187) Bks Demand.

Business Guide to Waste Reduction & Recycling: A Step-by-Step Guide to Saving Resources & Money by Reducing Waste. (Illus.). 111p. (Orig.). (C). 1993. pap. text ed. 60.00 (*1-56806-318-0*) Diane Pub.

***Business Guidebook to Law & Leading Attorneys - Minnesota Edition: Minnesota Business Guidebook to Law & Leading Attorneys.** American Research Corporation Staff. Ed. by Joseph P. Mitzel. (Guidebooks to Law & Leading Attorneys Ser.). 526p. (Orig.). 1994. pap. 49.95 (*1-885573-01-4*) Am Research.

Business Handbook on Terrorism, Security & Survival: A Proactive Guide for Personal Security in Today's Business Environment. Gerry S. Thomas. 1994. pap. text ed. 29.95 (*0-9640570-0-X*) Vance Brook.

Business Handbook on Terrorism, Security & Survival: A Proactive Guide for Personal Security in Today's Business Environment. 2nd ed. Gerry S. Thomas. (Illus.). 176p. 1995. pap. text ed. 29.95 (*0-9640570-1-8*) Vance Brook. Protecting businesses & their personnel against increasing threats of terrorism, mob violence & crime requires an informed methodical & consistent approach to personal safety. Prepared by a career professional in military intelligence, the BUSINESS HANDBOOK ON TERRORISM, SECURITY & SURVIVAL provides comprehensive guidelines for the individual business person to establish a complete program for effective personal, family & office security. Designed as both a planning & reference tool, this easy-to-read, up-to-date handbook addresses: assessing the threat at home & overseas; developing a system of "defense in depth" for business & residential security; minimizing office vulnerability; family security with special considerations for children; vehicle safety & defensive driving; security for rail, air, & sea travel; hotel security; planning for survival as a hostage; bomb threat planning with complete guidelines for recognition of vehicle, mail & parcel bombs; dealing safely with civil disturbances; comprehensive profiles of domestic & foreign terrorist groups & their American business targets; a resource guide covering the full range of equipment, supporting materials & training that business persons may require. Comprehensive reproducible checklists are also provided. "Terrific..a must for modern, global business." (The Book Reader) VISA/MC accepted for direct orders. From: Vance Brook Publishing, (800) 824-5810 or FAX (802) 429-2279, P.O. Box 35, West Newbury, VT 05085.** ***Publisher Provided Annotation.

Business History: Concepts & Measurement. Ed. by Charles Harvey. 150p. 1990. text ed. 35.00 (*0-7146-3366-6*, Pub. by F Cass Pubs UK) Intl Spec Bk.

Business History: Selected Readings. Ed. by Kenneth A. Tucker. 442p. 1977. 42.00 (*0-7146-3030-6*, Pub. by F Cass Pubs UK) Intl Spec Bk.

Business History of Atlantic Steel Company, Nineteen Hundred One to Nineteen Sixty-Eight. Harry R. Kuniansky. LC 75-41767. (Companies & Men: Business Enterprises in America Ser.). 1976. 31.95 (*0-405-08082-4*) Ayer.

Business History of General Trading Companies: The International Conference on Business History 13. Ed. by Shin'ichi Yonekawa & Nideki Yoshihara. 300p. 1987. 49.50 (*0-86008-408-6*, Pub. by U of Tokyo JA) Col U Pr.

Business History of Shipping. Ed. by Keiichiro Nakagawa & Tsunehiko Yui. 300p. 1985. 37.50 (*0-86008-367-5*, Pub. by U of Tokyo JA) Col U Pr.

Business History of the World: A Chronology. Richard B. Robinson, Jr. LC 93-25476. 576p. 1993. text ed. 79.50 (*0-313-26094-X*, Greenwood Pr) Greenwood.

Business Houses in Western India: A Study in Entreprenurial Response, 1850-1956. Dwijendra Tripathi & Makrand Mehta. 1990. 30.00 (*81-85054-83-5*, Pub. by Manohar II) S Asia.

Business Idea Greetings: Letters for Gifts, Mailing, Faxing. Data Notes Staff. (Illus.). 70p. 1992. 49.95 (*0-911569-16-2*) Prosperity & Profits.

Business Idea Publications, Bylaw Ideas, & More. Data Notes Staff. 138p. 1993. ring bd. 79.95 (*0-911569-89-8*) Prosperity & Profits.

Business Impact on Education & Child Development Reform. 52p. 1991. 11.00 (*0-87186-251-4*) Comm Econ Dev.

Business in a Changing World. 3rd ed. William H. Cunningham et al. LC 92-16799. 1993. text ed. 51.95 (*0-538-81391-1*) S-W Pub.

Business in Accountancy. Hutchinson. 1987. 498.95 (*0-442-31753-0*) Chapman & Hall.

Business in Action. 3rd ed. Lester R. Bittel et al. 608p. 1987. text ed. 31.95 (*0-07-005565-3*) McGraw.

Business in Action: An Introduction to Business. 2nd ed. Lester R. Bittel et al. 1984. text ed. 38.95 (*0-07-005515-7*) McGraw.

Business in American Life: A History. Thomas C. Cochran. LC 78-38740. 416p. 1974. 6.95 (*0-07-011520-6*, Prof & Ref Bk Div); pap. text ed. 6.95 (*0-07-011525-7*) McGraw.

Business in an Information Economy. David K. Graf et al. 416p. 1989. pap. text ed. 20.72 (*0-07-010900-1*) McGraw.

Business in an Information Economy. David K. Graf et al. 1990. Computer Activities, Apple. teacher ed, disk write for info. (*0-07-838529-6*); Computer Activities, IBM. teacher ed, disk write for info. (*0-07-838531-8*) McGraw.

Business in Context. D. Needle. 384p. 1990. pap. 34.50 (*0-412-02661-9*, A4463, Chap & Hall NY) Chapman & Hall.

Business in English. A. Jack Hacikyan & Marilyn Gill. 232p. (C). (gr. 10-12). 1987. pap. text ed. 10.00 (*0-13-095472-1*); audio 25.00 (*0-686-66150-8*) Prentice ESL.

Business in France. Joseph Szarka. 224p. (Orig.). 1992. pap. 52.50 (*0-273-03630-0*, Pub. by Pitman Pub Ltd UK) Trans-Atl Phila.

Business in French: Les Affaires En Francais. Jean-Pierre Bajard & C. Sibieude. 224p. (FRE.). 1988. pap. 29.95 (*0-8288-1550-X*, F14960); teacher ed, pap. write for info. (*0-8288-1551-8*, F16350) Fr & Eur.

Business in Japan: A Guide to Japanese Business Practice & Procedure. 2nd rev. ed. Paul Norbury & Geoffrey Bownas. 226p. 1985. 100.00 (*0-317-39059-7*, Pub. by P Norbury Pubns Ltd UK) St Mut.

Business in Literature. rev. ed. Ed. by Charles A. Burden & Valerie E. Mock. 345p. 1988. pap. 29.95 (*0-88406-206-6*) GA St U Busn Pr.

Business in Mexico: Managerial Behavior, Protocol, & Etiquette. Candace B. McKinnis & Arthur A. Natella, Jr. LC 93-23222. (Illus.). 159p. 1994. lib. bdg. 39.95 (*1-56024-406-2*) Haworth Pr.

Business in Nineteen Ninety: A Look to the Future. Adam Starchild. LC 79-114257. 254p. reprint ed. pap. 72.40 (*0-8357-5495-2*, AU00383) Bks Demand.

Business in Society: An Introduction to Business. William Withers. LC 66-16635. (Illus.). 1966. 26.50 (*0-89197-055-X*); teacher ed write for info. (*0-89197-057-6*); pap. text ed. 14.95 (*0-89197-056-8*) Irvington.

Business in the Age of Depression & War. Ed. by R. P. Davenport-Hines. 326p. 1990. text ed. 35.00 (*0-7146-3387-9*, Pub. by F Cass Pubs UK) Intl Spec Bk.

Business in the Age of Reason. Ed. by R. P. Davenport-Hines & Jonathan Liebenau. 224p. 1987. 35.00 (*0-7146-3306-2*, Pub. by F Cass Pubs UK) Intl Spec Bk.

Business in the Contemporary World. Ed. by Herbert L. Sawyer. (Illus.). 256p. (Orig.). (C). 1988. pap. text ed. 24.00 (*0-8191-7114-X*) U Pr of Amer.

Business in the Public Eye. Gerrit A. Wagner. Tr. by Theodore Plantinga. LC 81-19486. 129p. reprint ed. pap. 36.80 (*0-8357-7494-5*, 2023225) Bks Demand.

***Business in the Russian Free Market.** Mikhail C. Lapidus et al. Tr. by Leonid Jezmir. LC 95-94101. 244p. (Orig.). (C). 1995. pap. 18.00 (*0-9645464-1-8*) MIR Hse.

Business in the Shadow of Apartheid: U. S. Firms in South Africa. Ed. by Jonathan Leape et al. LC 84-47741. 288p. 1984. text ed. 35.00 (*0-669-08404-2*) Free Pr.

Business in Today's World. James Lowry & Bernard Weinrich. 812p. (C). 1989. pap. text ed. write for info. (*0-538-80255-3*, BGB75LA) S-W Pub.

Business in Today's World. 13th ed. James Lowry & Weinrich. (C). 1994. text ed. 31.95 (*0-538-82806-4*, GB75MA) S-W Pub.

Business Income & Price Levels: The Accounting, Legal, & Political Views. Barbara Merino. Ed. by Richard P. Brief. LC 80-1460. (Dimensions of Accounting Theory & Practice Ser.). 1980. lib. bdg. 31.95 (*0-405-13482-7*) Ayer.

Business Income Coverage. Virginia M. Bates. 1991. 39.50 (*1-56461-032-2*, 46050) Rough Notes.

Business Incorporations in the United States, 1800-1943. George H. Evans, Jr. (General Ser.: No. 49). 192p. 1948. reprint ed. 50.00 (*0-87014-048-5*) Natl Bur Econ Res.

Business-Industry Hazardous Materials Program Employee Training Manual. Mike Rager. (Illus.). (Orig.). (C). 1989. pap. write for info. (*0-318-65930-1*) Amer Hazmat.

Business Information: How to Find It, How to Use It. 2nd ed. Michael R. Lavin. 512p. 1992. 49.95 (*0-89774-556-6*); pap. 38.50 (*0-89774-643-0*) Oryx Pr.

Business Information Desk Reference. Melvyn N. Freed & Virgil P. Diodato. 528p. 1991. text ed. 90.00 (*0-02-910651-6*) Macmillan.

Business Information Desk Reference: Where to Find Answers to Business Questions. Melvyn N. Freed. 528p. 1992. pap. 20.00 (*0-02-897141-8*) Macmillan.

Business Information Guide. American Institute of Certified Public Accountants Staff. LC 85-118541. (Illus.). 135p. reprint ed. pap. 38.50 (*0-8357-4596-1*, 2037528) Bks Demand.

Business Information Hungary: A Four Dimension Guide. Attila Becskehazi & Jason McDonald. LC 92-74249. (Illus.). 204p. (Orig.). 1992. pap. 30.00 (*1-882482-00-X*) Cent Europ Res.

***Business Information Libraries International.** 800p. (C). 1994. 595.00 (*1-57205-792-0*) Rector Pr.

Business Information on Beijing. China Machine Pr. Staff. (C). 1988. 90.00 (*0-685-30211-3*, Pub. by China Machine Pr CH) St Mut.

B

An Asterisk (*) at the beginning of an entry indicates that the title is appearing in BIP for the first time.

Business Information Processing with BASIC. George W. Struble. LC 79-1423. 1980. text ed. write for info. (*0-201-07640-3*); trans. write for info. (*0-201-07643-8*) Addison-Wesley.

Business Information Resource Directory 1994. Ed. by Lewis B. Sckolnick. 450p. (Orig.). (C). 1994. pap. 225.00 (*1-57205-326-7*) Rector Pr.

Business Information Services: Building Your Organization with Interactive Technology. Ed. by Bruce K. Cole. Tr. by Philipe Met. 200p. (Orig.). (C). 1992. pap. text ed. 21.95 (*0-9632631-0-2*) Diaspora Pr.

***Business Information Services: Some Aspects of Structure, Organisation, & Problems.** 2nd fac. ed. Malcolm J. Campbell. LC 82-125825. 179p. 1981. reprint ed. pap. 51.10 (*0-7837-8148-2*, 2047956) Bks Demand.

Business Information Sources. 3rd rev. ed. Lorna M. Daniells. LC 92-41827. 1993. 35.00 (*0-520-08180-3*) U CA Pr.

Business Information Systems: An Introduction. 5th ed. David Kroenke & Richard Hatch. 1993. text ed. write for info. (*0-07-035871-0*) McGraw.

Business Information Systems: An Introduction. 5th ed. David Kroenke & Richard Hatch. 1993. Study guide. student ed, pap. text ed. write for info. (*0-07-035873-7*) McGraw.

Business Information Systems: Analysis, Design & Practice. G. Curtis. (Illus.). 450p. (C). 1990. text ed. 27.95 (*0-201-17523-1*) Addison-Wesley.

Business Information Systems: The New Edition of Clifton's Business Data Systems. 5th ed. Dennis Clifton & Alistair Sutcliffe. 500p. 1994. pap. text ed. 35.00 (*0-13-107970-0*) P-H.

Business Innovation & Competitiveness in the 1990s. Henry Kyambalesa. LC 93-3200. 191p. 1993. 59.95 (*1-85628-504-9*, Pub. by Avebury Pub UK) Ashgate Pub Co.

Business Insurance. 5th ed. Edwin H. White & Herbert Chasman. 564p. 1986. 24.95 (*0-13-100867-6*, Busn) P-H.

***Business Insurance.** 6th ed. LC 95-16210. 1995. pap. 49.95 (*0-7931-1403-9*, R & R Newkirk) Dearborn Finan.

Business Insurance Guide, 1993-1994: How to Purchase the Best & Most Affordable Coverage. Jamie McLeroy. Ed. by Les Abromovitz. LC 93-39676. 416p. 1993. ring bd. 89.50 (*1-56759-009-8*) Summers Pr.

Business Insurance Law & Practice Guide. Bender's Editorial Staff. 1989. Updates. ring bd. write for info. (*0-8205-1591-4*) Bender.

Business Intelligence: Putting It All Together. Kirk W. Tyson. LC 86-27309. 288p. 1986. text ed. 30.00 (*0-941101-00-2*) Lead Edge IL.

Business Intelligence Investigations. Ralph D. Thomas. 125p. (Orig.). 1992. pap. 38.00 (*0-918487-48-X*) Thomas Pubns TX.

Business Intelligence System: A New Tool for Competitive Advantage. Tamar Gilad & Benjamin Gilad. LC 88-47707. 256p. 1988. 24.95 (*0-8144-5929-3*) AMACOM.

Business Interactions. Candace Matthews. (Illus.). 224p. (C). 1987. pap. text ed. 17.25 (*0-13-100876-5*) P-H.

Business Interest Groups in Nineteenth Century Brazil. Eugene Ridings. LC 93-32152. (Latin American Studies: Vol. 78). 304p. (C). 1994. 59.95 (*0-521-45485-9*) Cambridge U Pr.

Business Interests, Organizational Development & Private Interest Government: An International Comparative Study of the Food Processing Industry. Ed. by Wyn Grant. (European University Institute, Series C (Political & Social Science): No. 8). viii, 232p. (C). 1987. lib. bdg. 75.40 (*0-89925-380-6*) De Gruyter.

***Business Interests, Organizational Development & Private Itnerest Government: An International Comparative Study of the Food Processing Industry.** Ed. by Wyn Grant. (European University Institute, Series C (Political & Social Science): No. 8). viii, 232p. (C). 1987. lib. bdg. 75.40 (*3-11-011395-3*) De Gruyter.

Business International Almanac 1994. 660p. (C). 1994. 225.00 (*1-57205-713-0*) Rector Pr.

***Business International Atlas.** (Illus.). 300p. (Orig.). 1994. pap. 195.00 (*0-7605-0842-9*) Rector Pr.

***Business International Payment & Risk Handbook 1994.** (Illus.). 115p. (Orig.). 1994. pap. 295.00 (*0-7605-1165-9*) Rector Pr.

***Business International: Transforming the Global Corporation: How the World's Leading Companies Create & Manage Continuous Change.** (Illus.). 125p. (Orig.). 1995. pap. 495.00 (*0-7605-1879-3*) Rector Pr.

Business International's Global Management Desk Reference. Shirley B. Dreifus. 1992. text ed. 49.95 (*0-07-009333-4*) McGraw.

Business Internationals Guide to Doing Business in Mexico. Gray Newman. 1992. text ed. 34.95 (*0-07-009339-3*) McGraw.

Business International's Guide to International Licensing. Thomas J. Ehrbar. 1993. text ed. 39.95 (*0-07-009332-6*) McGraw.

Business Interruption Coverage. ABA, Tort & Insurance Practice Section Staff. LC 87-71809. 165p. 1987. pap. 29.95 (*0-89707-318-5*, 519-0070) Amer Bar Assn.

Business Investment & Loan Agreements: Forms & Authorities. suppl. ed. Herbert B. Max. 1985. Supplements avail. 75.00 (*0-317-29386-9*, #H43902) HarBrace.

Business Is Business...Right? Evelyn Crabtree. 150p. (Orig.). 1996. pap. 5.95 (*0-945969-06-6*) Kohinoor Bks.

Business Is Looking Up: Featuring Renaldo Rodriguez. Barbara Aiello & Jeffrey Shulman. (Kids on the Block Book Ser.). (Illus.). 48p. (J). (gr. 3-6). 1991. lib. bdg. 13.98 (*0-8050-3136-7*) TFC Bks NY.

Business Italy: A Practical Guide to Understanding Italian Business Culture. Peggy Kenna & Sondra Lacy. LC 94-16181. (Orig.). 1994. pap. 5.95 (*0-8442-3557-1*, NTC Busn Bks) NTC Pub Grp.

Business Japan: A Practical Guide to Understanding Japanese Business Culture. Peggy Kenna & Sondra Lacy. LC 93-42809. 1994. 5.95 (*0-8442-3552-0*, NTC Busn Bks) NTC Pub Grp.

Business Japanese: A Guide to Communicating in Japanese. Nissan Motor Company Staff. 300p. (ENG & JPN.). 1988. pap. 39.95 (*0-8288-0992-5*, M 900) Fr & Eur.

Business Jokes. Bill Stott. Ed. by Helen Exley & Samantha Armstrong. (Joke Bks.). (Illus.). 60p. 1991. 6.99 (*1-85015-259-4*) Exley Giftbooks.

Business Journalism: Management Cases & Notes. Albert N. Greco. (Business Magazine Publishing Ser.). 200p. 1988. 40.00x (*0-8147-3014-0*); pap. 27.50x (*0-8147-3015-9*) NYU Pr.

Business Journals of the United States: Historical Guides to the World's Periodicals & Newspapers. Ed. by William Fisher. LC 90-38420. 328p. 1991. text ed. 69.50 (*0-313-25292-0*, FBJ/, Greenwood Pr) Greenwood.

Business Judgement Rule: Fiduciary Duties of Corporate Directors & Officers. Dennis J. Block. write for info. (*0-318-66842-4*) P-H.

Business Judgment Rule: Fiduciary Duties of Corporate Directors. 4th ed. Dennis J. Block et al. LC 93-39489. 1993. 150.00 (*0-13-299744-4*) Aspen Law.

Business Justification of IT. Robert Zmud & V. Sambamurthy. 100p. 1994. 15.00 (*1-885065-02-7*) Finan Exec.

Business Kit. Business Kids Staff. (Illus.). 129p. (YA). (gr. 8-12). 1989. teacher ed 14.95 (*0-9625075-1-2*); 49.95 (*0-9625075-0-4*) Lemonade Kids.

Business Knowledge Investment: The Building Globally-Architected Information. Jack French. 1990. text ed. 50.00 (*0-13-091000-7*) P-H.

Business Korea: A Practical Guide to Understanding South Korean Busines Culture. Peggy Kenna & Sondra Lacy. LC 94-16182. (Orig.). 1994. pap. 5.95 (*0-8442-3559-8*, NTC Busn Bks) NTC Pub Grp.

Business Korea Yearbook, 1993-94. (Illus.). 1312p. (Orig.). (C). 1994. pap. text ed. 495.00 (*0-7881-0282-6*) Diane Pub.

Business Korea Yearbook, 1993-94. (Illus.). 436p. (Orig.). 1993. 695.00 (*0-934393-27-3*) Rector Pr.

Business Law. 228p. pap. write for info. (*0-926709-27-5*) MicroMash.

Business Law. A. Abbott & P. Pendlebury. 591p. (C). 1988. 135.00 (*0-685-39838-2*, Inst Pur & Supply) St Mut.

Business Law. Helen J. Bond & Peter Kay. 332p. (C). 1990. text ed. 35.00 (*1-85431-110-7*, Pub. by Blackstone Pr UK) W W Gaunt.

Business Law. Scott Failing. 298p. (C). 1991. pap. text ed. 69.95 (*1-878025-22-8*) Western Schls.

Business Law. K. Keenan & Riches. 322p. (C). 1990. 120.00 (*0-685-39839-0*, Inst Pur & Supply) St Mut.

Business Law. Anthony King & John Barlow. 200p. 1993. 34.00 (*1-85431-291-X*, Pub. by Blackstone Pr UK) W W Gaunt.

Business Law. M. Marsha & S. Soulsby. 292p. (C). 1989. 115.00 (*0-685-39840-4*, Inst Pur & Supply) St Mut.

Business Law. P. Palfreman. (C). 1990. 130.00 (*0-7487-0406-X*, Pub. by S Thornes Pubs UK) St Mut.

Business Law. Jack Rudman. (DANTES Ser.: No. 7). 1994. pap. 23.95 (*0-8373-6607-0*) Nat Learn.

***Business Law.** Jack Rudman. (DANTES Ser.: No. 7). 1994. 39.95 (*0-8373-6507-4*) Nat Learn.

Business Law. John Scura. 960p. (C). 1993. per., pap. text ed. 58.95 (*0-8403-8735-0*) Kendall-Hunt.

Business Law. Peter J. Shedd & Robert N. Corley. LC 92-13227. 1200p. (C). 1992. text ed. write for info. (*0-13-108127-6*) P-H.

Business Law. J. Singh. 1985. 75.00 (*0-317-61967-5*) St Mut.

Business Law. Darryl L. Webb. LC 83-22473. (College Outline Ser.). 244p. (C). 1984. pap. text ed. 12.50 (*0-15-600003-2*) HB Coll Pubs.

Business Law. deluxe ed. Christopher Dungan & Donald Ridings. (Business Library). 320p. 1990. 16.95 (*0-8120-4189-5*) Barron.

Business Law. 2nd ed. John W. Hardwicke. 1992. pap. 11.95 (*0-8120-1385-9*) Barron.

Business Law. 2nd ed. R. G. Lawson & D. Smith. 208p. 1992. pap. 29.95 (*0-7506-0375-5*) Buttrwrth-Heinemann.

Business Law. 2nd ed. Nigel Savage & Robert Bradgate. 1993. U. K. pap. 40.00 (*0-406-00620-2*) Butterworth Legal Pubs.

Business Law. 2nd ed. William T. Schantz & Janice E. Jackson. (Illus.). 1295p. (C). 1987. text ed. 67.00 (*0-314-26205-9*) West Pub.

Business Law. 3rd ed. S. B. Marsh & J. Soulsby. LC 85-11331. 6.50 (*0-07-084876-9*) McGraw.

Business Law. 5th alternate ed. John R. Allison & Robert A. Prentice. Ed. by Rate A. Howell. 1088p. (C). 1992. text ed. 43.00 (*0-03-073153-4*) Dryden Pr.

Business Law. 5th ed. Robert T. Cheng & Robert D. Upp. 781p. (C). 1989. text ed. 63.00 (*0-314-66495-5*) West Pub.

Business Law. 5th ed. George Getz. (gr. 9-12). 1977. student ed 8.64 (*0-02-831110-8*); teacher ed 7.28 (*0-02-831120-5*); text ed. 25.32 (*0-02-831100-0*) Glencoe.

Business Law. 5th ed. Peter Gillies. 861p. 1993. 63.00 (*1-86287-097-7*, Pub. by Federation Pr AU) W W Gaunt.

Business Law. 6th ed. Peter Gillies. 884p. 1994. pap. 54.00 (*1-86287-119-1*, Pub. by Federation Pr AU) W W Gaunt.

***Business Law.** 7th ed. Peter Gillies. 900p. 1995. pap. 54.00 (*1-86287-155-8*, Pub. by Federation Pr AU) W W Gaunt.

Business Law: An Introduction. Victor D. Lopez. LC 92-28448. 400p. (C). 1992. text ed. 34.95 (*0-256-12389-6*) Irwin.

Business Law: Comprehensive. 14th ed. Ronald A. Anderson et al. (C). 1989. pap. text ed. write for info. (*0-538-80222-7*, LA68NA) S-W Pub.

Business Law: Part One Syllabus. Singleton et al. 1973. pap. text ed. 8.25 (*0-89420-042-9*, 146755); audio 471.20 (*0-89420-128-X*, 146700) Natl Book.

Business Law: Part Two Syllabus. Singleton et al. 1973. pap. text ed. 8.25 (*0-89420-054-2*, 146757); audio 471.20 (*0-685-03485-2*, 146700) Natl Book.

Business Law: Principles & Cases. 4th ed. Daniel V. Davidson et al. LC 92-26530. 1199p. 1993. text ed. 60.95 (*0-534-93280-0*) Intl Thomson.

Business Law: Principles & Cases. 4th ed. Daniel V. Davidson et al. LC 92-26530. 1199p. 1993. student ed, pap. 19.95 (*0-534-93284-3*) Intl Thomson.

Business Law: Principles & Cases, Sixth Edition. Study Guide. 6th ed. John W. Wyatt & Madie B. Wyatt. 1979. pap. text ed. write for info. (*0-07-072163-7*) McGraw.

Business Law: Principles & Practice, 2 Vols. 2nd ed. Arnold J. Goldman & William D. Sigismond. (C). 1987. teacher ed, pap. 5.56 (*0-395-44970-7*); student ed, pap. 14.36 (*0-395-44971-5*) HM.

Business Law: Principles, Cases, & Policy. 2nd ed. Mark E. Roszkowski et al. (C). 1989. text ed. 43.25 (*0-673-39927-3*) HarpCollege.

Business Law: Principles, Cases & Policy. 3rd ed. Mark E. Roszkowski. (C). 1991. text ed. 73.00 (*0-673-52130-3*) HarpCollege.

Business Law: Principles, Cases & Policy. 3rd ed. Mark E. Roszkowski. (C). 1991. 25.50 (*0-673-52219-9*) HarpCollege.

Business Law: Principles, Cases, Legal Environment. 11th ed. Ronald A. Anderson et al. 1264p. (C). 1991. text ed. write for info. (*0-538-81270-2*, LA70KA) S-W Pub.

Business Law: Selected Questions & Unofficial Answers Indexed to Content Specification Outline. American Institute of Certified Public Accountants Staff. Ed. by James D. Blum & Mark S. Goldstein. LC 84-189048. 151p. reprint ed. pap. 43.10 (*0-8357-7496-1*, 2025095) Bks Demand.

Business Law: Text & Cases. 2nd ed. Virginia G. Maurer. 1228p. (C). 1987. text ed. 59.00 (*0-15-505648-4*); student ed, pap. text ed. 20.50 (*0-15-505649-2*) Dryden Pr.

Business Law: Text & Cases. 3rd ed. Cameron & Phillip J. Scaletta, Jr. 1312p. (C). 1989. text ed. 64.95 (*0-256-07131-4*); student ed 21.95 (*0-256-07245-0*) Irwin.

Business Law: Text & Cases. 4th ed. Townes L. Dawson & Earl W. Mounce. 1979. teacher ed 2.00 (*0-669-01691-8*); text ed. 38.00 (*0-669-01690-X*) Heath.

Business Law: Text & Cases. 5th rev. ed. John R. Allison et al. 1344p. (C). 1991. text ed. 59.00 (*0-03-031049-0*) Dryden Pr.

Business Law: Text with Cases. Arthur R. Miller & Thomas L. Gossman. (C). 1989. text ed. 66.50 (*0-673-38413-6*) HarpCollege.

Business Law: The Legal Environment, Text & Cases. 4th ed. Joseph L. Frascona et al. (Illus.). 1200p. 1990. text ed. 50.00 (*0-205-12566-2*, H25661) Allyn.

Business Law: The Legal, Ethical & International Environment. Henry R. Cheeseman. 1520p. (C). 1991. text ed. write for info. (*0-13-094095-X*) P-H.

***Business Law: The Legal, Ethical, & International Environment.** 2nd ed. Henry R. Cheeseman. LC 94-29244. 1994. text ed. 45.00 (*0-13-309758-7*) P-H.

Business Law: UCC Applications. 6th ed. R. Robert Rosenberg et al. LC 82-13001. 640p. 1983. text ed. 33.50 (*0-07-053901-4*) McGraw.

Business Law: With UCC Applications. 8th ed. Gordon W. Brown et al. LC 92-30558. 1992. 38.00 (*0-02-800653-4*) Glencoe.

***Business Law Vol. 1: 1994-95.** Anthony King & John Barlow. (Legal Practice Course Guides Ser.). 332p. Date not set. pap. 34.00 (*1-85431-366-5*, Pub. by Blackstone Pr UK) W W Gaunt.

***Business Law - Legal Studies.** Irvin N. Gleim & Jordan B. Ray. LC 94-78213. 786p. (Orig.). (C). 1994. pap. text ed. 16.95 (*0-917537-73-4*) Gleim Pubns.

***Business Law - Legal Studies Objective Questions & Explanations: Objective Questions & Explanations.** 4th ed. Irvin N. Gleim & Jordan B. Ray. LC 94-78214. 736p. (C). 1994. pap. text ed. 16.95 (*0-917537-72-6*) Gleim Pubns.

***Business Law & Professional Responsibilities.** (CPA Review Ser.: Vol. 1). 592p. 1995. pap. 32.95 (*0-538-84715-8*) S-W Pub.

Business Law & Professional Responsibilities. Nathan M. Bisk. (CPA Comprehensive Exam Review Ser.). 1994. pap. 31.95 (*0-88128-641-9*) Totaltape.

***Business Law & Professional Responsibilities: Campbell Williams CPA Review.** H. James Williams & Carole C. Williams. (C). 1994. 35.00 (*0-9635927-4-2*) C Williams Pub.

Business Law & the Legal Environment. 2nd ed. Alvin. 1226p. (C). 1988. student ed 14.75 (*0-15-505660-3*) HB Coll Pubs.

Business Law & the Legal Environment. 2nd ed. Jethro K. Lieberman. 1226p. (C). 1988. text ed. 56.00 (*0-15-505659-X*) HB Coll Pubs.

Business Law & the Legal Environment. 3rd ed. Burt A. Leete & Karla H. Fox. 1216p. 1989. teacher ed write for info. (*0-318-63874-6*, H1842-9); trans. write for info. (*0-318-63877-0*, H88008); write for info. (*0-318-63876-4*, H18658); write for info. (*0-318-63876-2*, H1843-7); write for info. (*0-318-63878-9*, H88016) Allyn.

Business Law & the Legal Environment. 3rd ed. Jethro K. Lieberman & George J. Siedel, III. 1400p. (C). 1993. pap. text ed. 11.50 (*0-15-505519-4*) Dryden Pr.

Business Law & the Legal Environment. 3rd ed. Jethro K. Lieberman & George J. Siedel, III. 1400p. (C). 1993. text ed. 57.25 (*0-15-505516-X*); teacher ed, pap. text ed. 11.00 (*0-15-505518-6*) Dryden Pr.

Business Law & the Legal Environment. 15th ed. Ronald A. Anderson et al. LC 92-29951. 1993. text ed. 65.95 (*0-538-81985-5*) S-W Pub.

Business Law & the Regulation of Business. 4th ed. Len Y. Smith et al. Ed. by Fenton. LC 92-30209. 1200p. (C). 1993. text ed. 68.50 (*0-314-01185-4*) West Pub.

Business Law & the Regulatory Environment: Concepts & Cases. 8th ed. Michael Metzger et al. 1792p. (C). 1991. text ed. 69.95 (*0-256-08700-8*, 02-0405-08) Irwin.

Business Law & the Regulatory Environment: Concepts & Cases. 9th ed. Michael B. Metzger et al. LC 94-12503. (Irwin Legal Studies in Business Ser.). 1408p. (C). 1994. 69.95 (*0-256-14103-7*) Irwin.

Business Law & the Regulatory Environment: Concepts & Cases. 9th ed. Michael B. Metzger et al. LC 94-12503. (Legal Studies in Business). 1995. pap. write for info. (*0-256-17191-2*) Irwin.

Business Law & the Regulatory Environment: Principles & Cases. 12th ed. Ronald A. Anderson et al. LC 94-826. 1264p. 1995. text ed. 61.95 (*0-538-84228-8*) S-W Pub.

***Business Law & the Regulatory Environment - College of Charleston: Concepts & Cases.** 8th ed. Michael Metzger et al. (C). 1992. text ed. 38.95 (*0-256-12138-9*) Irwin.

Business Law for CPA Candidates. Mark E. Roszkowski. (C). 1992. text ed. 40.00 (*0-673-52218-0*) HarpCollege.

Business Law Guide to Switzerland. Pestalozzi et al. 690p. 1992. 112.50 (*0-685-67808-3*, 5593) Commerce.

***Business Law in California.** 12th ed. Beller et al. 100p. (C). Date not set. student ed 14.00 (*0-914504-13-4*) General Educ.

***Business Law in California.** 12th ed. Beller et al. (Illus.). 516p. (C). 1995. 37.50x (*0-914504-12-6*) General Educ.

Business Law in Egypt. Michael H. Davis. 350p. 1983. 123.00 (*90-6544-086-0*) Kluwer Law Tax Pubs.

Business Law in Europe. Ed. by Paul Storm & Maarten Ellis. 1990. ring bd. 206.00 (*90-6544-978-7*) Kluwer Law Tax Pubs.

***Business Law in Spain.** 2nd ed. Bernardo M. Cremades. 716p. 1992. pap. text ed. 110.00 (*0-406-02003-5*, UK) Butterworth Legal Pubs.

Business Law in Zimbabwe. R. H. Christie. 632p. 1985. pap. write for info. (*0-7021-1573-8*, Pub. by Juta SA) W W Gaunt.

***Business Law Made Simple.** Stephen G. Christianson. LC 94-41819. 1995. 12.00 (*0-385-47557-8*) Doubleday.

Business Law Monographs, 34 vols., Set. 1984. write for info. (*0-8205-1080-7*) Bender.

Business Law of Australia. 7th ed. R. B. Vermeesch & K. E. Lindgren. 1991. Australia. 59.00 (*0-409-30359-3*) Butterworth Legal Pubs.

***Business Law of Australia Workbook.** 2nd ed. A. Ardagh. 296p. 1994. pap. 35.00 (*0-409-31036-0*, Austral) Butterworth Legal Pubs.

***Business Law of China: Cases, Texts, & Commentary.** Guigup Wang. 590p. 1993. boxed 125.00 (*0-614-05485-0*, SI) Butterworth Legal Pubs.

***Business Law of China: Cases, Texts & Commentary.** Gulguo Wang. 1994. boxed 125.00 (*0-409-99645-9*, SI) Butterworth Legal Pubs.

Business Law Series, 6 vols., Set. Ed. by Alan L. Schneider. (Orig.). 1988. pap. 145.10 (*0-685-28078-0*) BLI Inc.

Business Law Text. Poust. 1991. pap. text ed. 22.75 (*0-314-70828-6*) West Pub.

Business Law the Easy Way. Robert W. Emerson. LC 93-21028. (Easy Way Ser.). 1994. pap. 11.95 (*0-8120-4760-5*) Barron.

Business Law-Thirty. 2nd ed. R. Robert Rosenberg & Joseph G. Bonnice. (C). 1976. 7.72 (*0-07-053670-8*) McGraw.

Business Law-Thirty. 3rd ed. Joseph G. Bonnice & R. Robert Rosenberg. 1982. text ed. 14.88 (*0-07-006472-5*) McGraw.

Business Law Today. 2nd ed. Roger L. Miller & Gaylord A. Jentz. Ed. by Clyde Perlee. 894p. (C). 1991. text ed. 60.25 (*0-314-74269-7*) West Pub.

Business Law Today: Text, Summarized Cases, Legal, Ethical, Regulatory, & International Environment. 3rd ed. Roger L. Miller & Gaylord A. Jentz. Ed. by Perlee. LC 93-25927. 850p. (C). 1993. text ed. 67.00 (*0-314-02582-0*) West Pub.

Business Law Today, Comprehensive Edition: Text, Cases, Legal, Ethical, Regulatory, & International Environment. 3rd ed. Roger L. Miller & Gaylord A. Jentz. Ed. by Perlee. 620p. (C). Date not set. text ed. 70.75 (*0-314-02851-X*) West Pub.

Business Law Today, the Essentials: Text, Summarized Cases, Legal, Ethical, Regulatory, & International Environment. 3rd ed. Roger L. Miller & Gaylord A. Jentz. Ed. by Perlee. LC 93-37600. 620p. (C). 1993. text ed. 49.25 (*0-314-02852-8*) West Pub.

Business Law with UCC Applications. 7th ed. Gordon W. Brown et al. 704p. 1989. text ed. 30.55 (*0-07-053919-7*) McGraw.

Business Laws of Egypt, 3 vols., Set: Vols. 1-3. N. H. Karam. (C). 1988. Set. lib. bdg. 560.00 (*1-85333-000-0*, Pub. by Graham & Trotman UK) Kluwer Ac.

Business Laws of Egypt: Basic Work & Supplement Service, 1990, Vols. 1-3. N. H. Karam. (C). 1990. 371.00 (*1-85333-342-5*, Pub. by Graham & Trotman UK); lib. bdg. 632.00 (*1-85333-327-1*, Pub. by Graham & Trotman UK) Kluwer Ac.

B

An Asterisk (*) at the beginning of an entry indicates that the title is appearing in BIP for the first time.

963

Business Laws of Egypt: Basic Work 1991 & 1991 Supplement Services, Se: Vols. 1-3. N. H. Karam. (Arab Business Laws Ser.). 150p. 1991. Set. ring bd. 1, 260.00 (*1-85333-497-9*, Pub. by Graham & Trotman UK) Kluwer Ac.

Business Laws of Egypt, Basic Work, 1992, Set: Vols. 1-3. N. H. Karam. 950p. 1992. Set. ring bd. 1,195.00 (*1-85333-645-9*, Pub. by Graham & Trotman UK) Kluwer Ac.

Business Laws of Egypt, Vols. 1-3: Basic Work, 1989 & 1989 Supplement Service. N. H. Karam. (C). 1989. ring bd. 612.00 (*1-85333-233-X*, Pub. by Graham & Trotman UK) Kluwer Ac.

Business Laws of Iran: Basic Work 1994. Tr. by Habib Shirazi. LC 93-23157. (Middle East Business Law Ser.). 600p. (C). 1993. ring bd. 330.00 (*1-85333-953-9*, Pub. by Graham & Trotman UK) Kluwer Ac.

Business Laws of Iraq, Set: Vols. 1-3. N. H. Karam. (C). 1988. Set. lib. bdg. 560.00 (*1-85333-002-7*, Pub. by Graham & Trotman UK) Kluwer Ac.

Business Laws of Iraq, Set: Vols. 1-3. N. H. Karam. (C). 1990. Set. ring bd. 371.00 (*1-85333-343-3*, Pub. by Graham & Trotman UK) Kluwer Ac.

Business Laws of Iraq, Vols. 1-3. N. H. Karam. (C). 1990. lib. bdg. 818.00 (*1-85333-328-X*, Pub. by Graham & Trotman UK) Kluwer Ac.

Business Laws of Iraq: Basic Work Plus Four Nineteen Eighty-Two Updating Supplements, Vol. 1. Tr. by N. H. Karam. 400p. 1982. 1,020.00 (*0-86010-379-X*, Pub. by Graham & Trotman UK) St Mut.

Business Laws of Iraq: Basic Work 1991. N. H. Karam. (Arab Business Laws Ser.). 1200p. 1991. ring bd. 840.00 (*1-85333-557-6*, Pub. by Graham & Trotman UK) Kluwer Ac.

Business Laws of Iraq, Vols. 1-3: Basic Work, 1989 & 1989 Supplement Service. N. H. Karam. (C). 1989. ring bd. 612.00 (*1-85333-228-3*, Pub. by Graham & Trotman UK) Kluwer Ac.

Business Laws of Kuwait, 3 vols., Set: Vols. 1-3. N. H. Karam. (C). 1988. Set. lib. bdg. 560.00 (*1-85333-004-3*, Pub. by Graham & Trotman UK) Kluwer Ac.

Business Laws of Kuwait: Basic Work & Supplement Service, 1990, Set: Vols. 1-3. N. H. Karam. (C). 1990. Set. ring bd. 371.00 (*0-685-31781-1*, Pub. by Graham & Trotman UK) Kluwer Ac.

Business Laws of Kuwait: Basic Work & Supplement Service, 1990, Vols. 1-3. N. H. Karam. (C). 1990. lib. bdg. 911.00 (*1-85333-329-8*, Pub. by Graham & Trotman UK) Kluwer Ac.

Business Laws of Kuwait: Basic Work 1991. N. H. Karam. (Arab Business Laws Ser.). 1200p. 1991. ring bd. 840.00 (*1-85333-556-8*, Pub. by Graham & Trotman UK) Kluwer Ac.

Business Laws of Kuwait, Vols. 1-3: Basic Work, 1989 & 1989 Supplement Service. N. H. Karam. (C). 1989. ring bd. 612.00 (*1-85333-165-1*, Pub. by Graham & Trotman UK) Kluwer Ac.

Business Laws of Kuwait, Vols. 1-3: Basic Work 1991 & 1991 Supplement Service, Set. N. H. Karam. 1600p. (C). 1991. lib. bdg. 914.00 (*0-86010-954-2*, Pub. by Graham & Trotman UK) Kluwer Ac.

Business Laws of Kuwait, Vols. 1-4: Basic Work 1992 & 1992 Supplement Service. N. H. Karam. (Arab Business Laws Ser.). 1800p. 1992. 935.00 (*1-85333-641-6*, Pub. by Graham & Trotman UK) Kluwer Ac.

Business Laws of Kuwait, Vols. 1-4: Basic Work 1993 & 1993 Supplement Service. N. H. Karam. (Arab Business Laws Ser.). 2000p. (C). 1993. ring bd. 977.00 (*1-85333-816-8*, Pub. by Graham & Trotman UK) Kluwer Ac.

Business Laws of Oman: Basic Work 1989, Set: Vols. 1-2. M. Hall. (Arab Business Laws Ser.). (C). 1990. Set. lib. bdg. 780.00 (*1-85333-377-8*, Pub. by Graham & Trotman UK) Kluwer Ac.

Business Laws of Oman, Vols. 1 & 2: Basic Work, 1988 & 1988 Supplement Service. M. Hall. (C). 1988. (*0-318-64521-1*, Pub. by Graham & Trotman UK) Kluwer Ac.

Business Laws of Oman, Vols. 1 & 2: Basic Work, 1988 & 1988 Supplement Service, Set. M. Hall. (C). 1988. ring bd. 560.00 (*1-85333-006-X*, Pub. by Graham & Trotman UK) Kluwer Ac.

Business Laws of Saudi Arabia, Set: Vols. 1-3. N. H. Karam. (C). 1988. Set. lib. bdg. 560.00 (*1-85333-008-6*, Pub. by Graham & Trotman UK) Kluwer Ac.

Business Laws of Saudi Arabia, Set: Vols. 1-3. N. H. Karam. (C). 1990. Set. ring bd. 457.00 (*1-85333-346-8*, Pub. by Graham & Trotman UK) Kluwer Ac.

Business Laws of Saudi Arabia, Vols. 1-3. N. H. Karam. (C). 1990. lib. bdg. 938.00 (*1-85333-331-X*, Pub. by Graham & Trotman UK) Kluwer Ac.

Business Laws of Saudi Arabia, Vols. 1-3: Basic Work 1991. N. H. Karam. (Arab Business Laws Ser.). 1500p. 1991. ring bd. 1,250.00 (*1-85333-507-X*, Pub. by Graham & Trotman UK) Kluwer Ac.

Business Laws of Saudi Arabia, Vols. 1-4: Basic Work 1992. N. H. Karam. (Arab Business Laws Ser.). 1800p. 1992. 1,255.00 (*1-85333-647-5*, Pub. by Graham & Trotman UK) Kluwer Ac.

Business Laws of Saudi Arabia, Vols. 1-4: Basic Work 1993 & 1993 Supplement Service. N. H. Karam. (Arab Business Laws Ser.). 2100p. (C). 1993. ring bd. 682.00 (*1-85333-798-6*, Pub. by Graham & Trotman UK) Kluwer Ac.

Business Laws of the U. A. E. Fed. Law, 1983: Insurance Companies & Insurance Agents Law. Ed. by Witherby's Editorial Staff. (C). 1985. 480.00 (*0-685-33787-1*, Pub. by Witherby & Co UK) St Mut.

Business Laws of the United Arab Emirates, Set: Vols. 1-3. M. Hall. (C). 1988. Set. lib. bdg. 560.00 (*1-85333-010-8*, Pub. by Graham & Trotman UK) Kluwer Ac.

Business Laws of the United Arab Emirates, Set: Vols. 1-3. M. Hall. (C). 1990. Set. ring bd. 371.00 (*1-85333-347-6*, Pub. by Graham & Trotman UK) Kluwer Ac.

Business Laws of the United Arab Emirates, Vols. 1-3. M. Hall. (C). 1990. lib. bdg. 725.00 (*1-85333-332-8*, Pub. by Graham & Trotman UK) Kluwer Ac.

Business Laws of the United Arab Emirates Vols. 1-4: Basic Work 1993 & 1993 Supplement Service. D. El-Alami. Ed. by Arab Business Laws Staff. (Arab Business Laws Ser.). 1700p. 1995. ring bd. 342.00 (*1-85333-806-0*, Pub. by Graham & Trotman UK) Kluwer Ac.

Business Laws of the United Arab Emirates, Vols. 1-3: Basic Work, 1989 & 1989 Supplement Service. M. Hall. (C). 1989. ring bd. 588.00 (*1-85333-243-7*, Pub. by Graham & Trotman UK) Kluwer Ac.

Business Laws of the United Arab Emirates, Vols. 1-3: Basic Work 1991, Set. Ed. by M. Hall. (Arab Business Laws Ser.). 1000p. 1991. rig bd. 525.00 (*1-85333-503-7*, Pub. by Graham & Trotman UK) Kluwer Ac.

Business Laws of the United Arab Emirates, Vols. 1-4: Basic Work 1992 & 1992 Supplement Service. M. Hall. 1400p. 1992. ring bd. 695.00 (*1-85333-643-2*, Pub. by Graham & Trotman UK) Kluwer Ac.

***Business Laws of Yemen.** (Arab & Islamic Law Ser.). 312p. (C). 1995. lib. bdg. 270.00 (*1-85966-112-2*, Pub. by Graham & Trotman UK) Kluwer Ac.

Business Lawyer: 1964-1993, 48 vols., Set. 2,245.00 (*0-8377-9032-8*) Rothman.

Business Lawyer's Handbook: What Business Lawyers Do. Clifford R. Ennico. LC 91-12602. 1992. pap. 29.95 (*0-87632-824-9*) Clark Boardman Callaghan.

Business Leaders Who Built Financial Empires. Jodine Mayberry. (Twenty Events Ser.). (Illus.). 48p. (J). (gr. 4-8). 1994. lib. bdg. 22.80 (*0-8114-4934-3*) Raintree Steck-V.

***Business Leadership.** Viv Shackleton. LC 94-39924. (Essential Business Psychology Ser.). 208p. 1995. 49.95x (*0-415-12678-9*, C0548); pap. 15.95 (*0-415-10330-4*, C0025) Routledge.

Business Leases - Termination & Renewal. Michael Haley. 264p. (C). 1991. 130.00 (*1-85190-136-1*, Pub. by Tolley Pubng UK) St Mut.

***Business, Legal, & Tax Planning for Dental Practices.** William P. Prescott. LC 94-30140. 1994. write for info. (*0-87814-424-2*) PennWell Bks.

Business Legal Forms Disk Library. Wiley Law Publications Editorial Staff. (Business Practice Library). 80p. 1992. 3.5 hd, ring bd. 325.00 (*0-471-57784-7*); 5.25 hd, ring bd. 325.00 (*0-471-57786-3*) Wiley.

Business Legal Forms Disk Library. suppl. ed. Wiley Law Publications Editorial Staff. (Business Practice Library). 88p. 1993. ring bd. 95.00 (*0-471-30514-6*); ring bd. 95. 00 (*0-471-30513-8*) Wiley.

Business Legal Guide for Computer Entrepreneurs. John C. Yates. 288p. 1985. 24.95 (*0-13-104175-4*); pap. 14.95 (*0-13-104167-3*) P-H.

Business Letter Handbook: Spanish-English, English-Spanish. Barbara S. De Meza. (gr. 12 up). 1987. pap. text ed. 8.00 (*0-13-104183-5*, 17765) Prentice ESL.

***Business Letter Writing.** Lindsell-Roberts. 1995. pap. 11. 95 (*0-02-860014-2*) Macmillan.

Business Letter Writing. Sheryl Lindsell-Roberts. LC 94-18524. 1994. write for info. (*0-671-88637-1*) Macmillan.

Business Letters. John J. Astor. LC 91-77181. 178p. 1991. 35.00 (*1-56541-214-1*) Chalidze.

Business Letters: A No-Nonsense Guide to Writing & Revising Them Including a Chapter on Memos. John Hyland. 56p. 1992. pap. 8.00 (*1-881779-00-9*) Short St Pr.

Business Letters for Artists. M. Stephen Doherty. 128p. 1993. pap. 12.95 (*0-8230-0302-7*, Watsn-Guptill) Watsn-Guptill.

Business Letters for Busy People. Jim Dugger. 1991. pap. 12.95 (*1-55852-059-7*) Natl Pr Pubns.

***Business Letters for Busy People.** 3rd ed. Jim Dugger. 256p. 1995. pap. 15.99 (*1-56414-196-9*) Career Pr Inc.

Business Letters for Busy People: More Than 200 Time-Saving, Ready-to-Use Business Letters for Any Occasion. Jim Dugger. 224p. 1993. pap. 14.95 (*1-56414-103-9*) Career Pr Inc.

Business Letters for Publishers: Creative Correspondence Outlines. 2nd rev. ed. Dan Poynter. 82p. 1985. disk 29. 95 (*0-915516-47-0*) Para Pub.

Business Letters Made Simple. Betty Hutchinson & Warner A. Hutchinson. LC 84-24717. (Made Simple Ser.). (Illus.). 192p. 1985. pap. 12.00 (*0-385-19427-7*) Doubleday.

Business Letters Made to Measure. Domino Books Ltd Staff. (C). 1988. 60.00 (*1-85122-047-X*, Pub. by Domino Bks Ltd UK) St Mut.

Business Letters That Get Results. J. Hamilton Jones. 228p. 1991. pap. 9.95 (*1-55850-042-1*) Adams Pubng.

Business Letters the Easy Way. 2nd ed. Andrea B. Geffner. 1991. pap. 10.95 (*0-8120-4626-9*) Barron.

Business Liability Insurance: Litigation, Arbitration & Settlement. Edward J. Zulkey. 450p. 1994. ring bd. 105.00 (*0-88063-708-0*) Michie Butterworth.

Business Library & How to Use It. Ed. by Ernest Maier et al. 300p. 1995. lib. bdg. 45.00 (*0-7808-0026-5*) Omnigraphics Inc.

Business Life & Public Policy: Essays in Honour of D. C. Coleman. Ed. by Neil McKendrick & R. B. Outhwaite. 256p. 1986. 74.95 (*0-521-26275-5*) Cambridge U Pr.

Business Listening Tasks. P. Hanks & J. Corbett. (Cambridge Professional English Ser.). 1986. teacher ed, pap. 12.95 (*0-521-27327-7*) Cambridge U Pr.

Business Listening Tasks. P. Hanks & J. Corbett. (Cambridge Professional English Ser.). 1986. student ed, pap. 11.95 (*0-521-27326-9*) Cambridge U Pr.

Business Listening Tasks. P. Hanks & J. Corbett. (Cambridge Professional English Ser.). 1986. pap. 29.95 (*0-521-25345-4*) Cambridge U Pr.

***Business Litigation in Florida.** Florida Bar Staff. LC 95-60229. 684p. 1995. disk, ring bd. 75.00 (*0-945979-69-X*, 226) FL Bar Legal Ed.

***Business, Loan & Real Property Forms, 3 vols., Set.** Mark Mullins. 1994. 375.00 (*1-55834-140-4*) Michie Butterworth.

Business Loan Costs & Bank Market Structure: An Empirical Estimate of Their Relations. Donald P. Jacobs. LC 72-171571. (National Bureau of Economic Research, Occasional Paper Ser.: No. 115). 115p. reprint ed. pap. 32.80 (*0-8357-7497-X*, 2006219) Bks Demand.

Business Loan Costs & Bank Market Structure: An Empirical Estimate of Their Relations. Donald P. Jacobs. (Occasional Papers: No. 115). 115p. 1971. reprint ed. 28.80 (*0-87014-239-9*) Natl Bur Econ Res.

Business Loan Workouts, 1988. Albert F. Reisman. (Commercial Law & Practice Course Handbook Ser.). 1073p. 1988. 17.50 (*0-685-69387-2*) PLI.

Business Loans: Guide to Money Sources & How to Approach Them. rev. ed. Rick S. Hayes. 1989. pap. text ed. 17.95 (*0-471-61129-8*) Wiley.

Business Lobbies: The Public Good & the Bottom Line. Sar A. Levitan & Martha Cooper. LC 83-48071. 168p. 1983. text ed. 20.00 (*0-8018-3108-3*) Johns Hopkins.

Business Location Decisions & Cities. 120p. 1982. 20.00 (*0-318-17706-4*, IB 82-907) Pub Tech Inc.

Business Logistics. 3rd ed. Nicholas A. Glaskowsky, Jr. et al. 600p. (C). 1992. text ed. 50.00 (*0-15-505652-2*) Dryden Pr.

Business Logistics: Independent Study Manual. 2nd ed. John J. Coyle. 272p. (C). 1993. per., pap. text ed. 20.95 (*0-8403-8836-5*) Kendall-Hunt.

Business Logistics Management. 3rd ed. Ronald H. Ballou. 704p. 1991. text ed. 70.00 (*0-13-105545-3*, 140801) P-H.

Business Machine Maintainer & Repairer. Jack Rudman. (Career Examination Ser.: C-1155). 1994. pap. 23.95 (*0-8373-1155-1*) Nat Learn.

Business Machine Operator. Jack Rudman. (Career Examination Ser.: C-1895). 1994. pap. 23.95 (*0-8373-1895-5*) Nat Learn.

Business Machine Supervisor. Jack Rudman. (Career Examination Ser.: C-1897). 1994. pap. 27.95 (*0-8373-1897-1*) Nat Learn.

Business Machines Practice Set: RPM Unlimited. 3rd ed. Dorothy L. Albertson & Cathy Fillmore-Hoyt. 240p. 1989. pap. text ed. 10.60 (*0-07-000962-7*) McGraw.

Business Man in the Amusement World: A Volume of Progress in the Field of the Theatre. Robert Grau. LC 73-160233. (Moving Pictures Ser.). xiv, 362p. 1971. reprint ed. lib. bdg. 42.95 (*0-89198-034-2*) Ozer.

Business Management. (VGM Career Planner Ser.). 7.95 (*0-8442-8689-3*, VGM Career Bks) NTC Pub Grp.

Business Management. PMA, Ltd. Staff. 160p. 1991. pap. text ed. 55.00 (*0-8403-6727-9*) Kendall-Hunt.

Business Management & Policies. B. M. Wali & Y. B. Yalawar. 480p. 1989. text ed. 45.00 (*81-207-0719-2*, Pub. by Sterling Pubs II) Apt Bks.

Business Management & Systems Analysis. Eddie Moynihan. (Information Systems Ser.). (Illus.). 240p. 1993. write for info. (*0-632-03168-9*) Blackwell Sci.

***Business Management & Systems Analysis.** Eddie Moynihan. 500p. Date not set. pap. 26.00 (*1-872474-05-5*, Pub. by Alfred Waller UK) Paul & Co Pubs.

Business Management for Contractors: How to Make Profits in Today's Market. Paul J. Cook. Orig. Title: Business Management for the General Contractor. (Illus.). 229p. 1991. pap. 35.95 (*0-87629-269-4*, 67250) R S Means.

Business Management for Farmers. J. W. Looney. LC 80-67888. (Illus.). 739p. 1983. 42.00 (*0-932250-11-4*) Red Wing Busn.

Business Management for Independent Schools. 4th ed. 1990. ring bd. 50.00 (*0-934338-72-8*) NAIS.

Business Management for the General Contractor see Business Management for Contractors: How to Make Profits in Today's Market

Business Management Guide for Arizona Contractors. Ed. by Builders' Publishing Co., Staff. 247p. 1986. 23.95 (*0-941385-00-0*) Builders AZ.

Business Management Guide for Arizona Contractors. 5th rev. ed. Builder's Publishing Company Staff. 284p. 1993. reprint ed. spiral bd. 29.95 (*0-941385-03-5*) Builders AZ.

***Business Management Guide for Arizona Contractors.** 6th rev. ed. Builders' Publishing Company Staff. (Illus.). 290p. 1995. spiral bd. 29.95 (*0-931385-04-0*) Builders AZ.

Business Management in School Systems of Different Sizes. Max R. Brunstetter. LC 76-176607. (Columbia University. Teachers College. Contributions to Education Ser.: No. 455). reprint ed. 37.50 (*0-404-55455-5*) AMS Pr.

Business Management in the Local Church. David R. Pollock. 1992. student ed 11.99 (*0-8024-0933-4*) Moody.

Business Management Laboratory. 3rd ed. Ronald Jensen & David J. Cherrington. 248p. (C). 1983. pap. text ed. 28.95 (*0-256-02699-8*) Irwin.

Business Management Laboratory. 4th ed. Ronald Jensen. 176p. (C). 1991. pap. text ed. 31.95 (*0-256-10184-1*, 11-3504-04) Irwin.

Business Management of General Consumer Magazines. 2nd ed. William P. Rankin & Eugene S. Waggaman, Jr. LC 84-1908. 208p. 1984. text ed. 55.00 (*0-275-91745-2*, C1745, Praeger Pubs) Greenwood.

Business Management of Institutional Homes for Children. Leonard B. Job. LC 72-176910. (Columbia University. Teachers College. Contributions to Education Ser.: No. 215). reprint ed. 37.50 (*0-404-55215-3*) AMS Pr.

Business Management of Interior Design. Dennis G. Murphy. (Orig.). (C). 1988. pap. text ed. write for info. (*0-938614-05-3*) Stratford Hse.

Business Management Software Directory for IBM & Compatible DOS Computers. ICP Staff & Larry A. Welke. Ed. by Sheila Cunningham & Marilyn Law. 1990. pap. 19.95 (*0-88094-174-X*) Intl Computer.

Business Management with Lotus Agenda. George Geis. (Illus.). 352p. (C). 1991. 5.25 hd, pap. text ed. 59.95 (*1-878748-23-8*); 3.5 hd, pap. text ed. 59.95 (*1-878748-24-6*) Course Tech.

Business Manager. Jack Rudman. (Career Examination Ser.: C-1898). 1994. pap. 34.95 (*0-8373-1898-X*) Nat Learn.

Business Manager's Guide to Controlling Legal Costs. Carl S. Pavetto. LC 89-90688. (Business Managers Ser.: Vol. 1). (Orig.). 1989. pap. 34.00 (*0-925997-00-5*) CSP Assocs Inc.

Business Managers in Ancient Rome: A Social & Economic Study of Institores. LC 94-17201. (Columbia Studies in the Classical Tradition: Vol. 21). 114.50 (*90-04-10038-5*) E J Brill.

Business Map of Nigeria. Oxford University Press Staff & Graham & Trotman Ltd. Staff. 1980. pap. text ed. 17.00 (*0-86010-194-0*) G & T Inc.

Business Map of the Arab World. Oxford University Press Staff. 1980. pap. text ed. 17.00 (*0-86010-211-4*) G & T Inc.

***Business Market Atlas International.** (Illus.). 400p. (Orig.). 1995. pap. 795.00 (*0-7605-1673-1*) Rector Pr.

***Business Market Insiders: Going Local: How Global Companies Become Market Insiders.** 125p. (Orig.). 1995. pap. 495.00 (*0-7605-1878-5*) Rector Pr.

Business Marketing. Andrew C. Gross et al. Ed. by Diane L. McOscar. 763p. (C). 1992. text ed. 63.16 (*0-395-56083-7*) HM.

***Business Marketing: A Managerial Approach.** 6th rev. ed. Robert W. Haas. LC 94-42374. 1995. pap. 58.95 (*0-538-84752-2*) S-W Pub.

***Business Marketing: An Interaction & Network Perspective.** Ed. by Kristian Moller & David T. Wilson. LC 94-29887. 1995. lib. bdg. write for info. (*0-7923-9504-2*) Kluwer Ac.

Business Marketing Management. Frank G. Bingham, Jr. & Barney T. Raffield, III. LC 94-4271. 1995. text ed. 55.95 (*0-538-83678-4*) S-W Pub.

Business Marketing Management. Robert Eckles. 250p. (C). 1989. Casebound. boxed, text ed. write for info. (*0-13-105396-5*) P-H.

Business Marketing Management: A Strategic View of Industrial & Organizational Markets. 4th ed. Michael Hutt & Thomas Speh. 800p. (C). 1992. text ed. 58.00 (*0-03-054167-0*) Dryden Pr.

Business Marketing Management: Text & Cases. 5th ed. Robert W. Haas. 700p. 1992. text ed. 59.95 (*0-534-92976-1*) Intl Thomson.

***Business Marketing Strategy: Cases, Concepts, & Applications.** Ed. by Kasturi Rangan et al. LC 94-22561. (Marketing Ser.). 864p. (C). 1994. text ed. 70.95 (*0-256-16911-X*) Irwin.

***Business Marketing Strategy: Concepts & Applications.** Ed. by V. K. Rangan et al. LC 94-22562. (Marketing Ser.). 192p. (C). 1995. 38.95 (*0-256-16910-1*) Irwin.

Business Mastery: A Business Planning Guide for Creating a Fulfilling Thriving Business & Keeping it Successful. 2nd ed. Cherie M. Sohnen-Moe. LC 91-90322. 256p. (C). 1991. pap. 19.95 (*0-9621265-3-5*) Sohnen-Moe Assocs.

Business Math. 3rd ed. G. C. Alvey & R. Robert Rosenberg. 1984. text ed. 11.56 (*0-07-053823-9*) McGraw.

Business Math: Practical Applications. Cheryl Cleaves et al. LC 92-24687. 1993. write for info. (*0-13-105784-7*) P-H.

Business Math: Practical Applications. 3rd ed. Cheryl Cleaves et al. LC 92-24686. 712p. 1992. pap. text ed. write for info. (*0-13-105735-9*) P-H.

Business Math: Practical Applications. 3rd ed. Cheryl Cleaves et al. 1993. write for info. (*0-318-69557-X*) Prentice ESL.

Business Math: Practical Applications, Brief Edition. 3rd ed. Cheryl Cleaves et al. 432p. (C). 1992. pap. text ed. write for info. (*0-13-092685-X*) P-H.

Business Math: The Bottom Line. 3rd ed. Lloyd D. Brooks. 450p. 1994. teacher ed 35.00 (*1-56118-658-9*); student ed 7.25 (*1-56118-662-7*); pap. text ed. 35.00 (*1-56118-657-0*); student ed, 5.25 hd 150.00 (*1-56118-660-0*); student ed, 3.5 hd 150.00 (*1-56118-659-7*) Paradigm MN.

Business Math Basics. 4th ed. Robert E. Swindle. 350p. (C). 1990. pap. 49.95 (*0-534-91995-2*) PWS Pubs.

Business Math Concepts. rev. ed. Raymond Cote. 408p. (C). 1986. 22.50 (*0-89702-047-2*) Irwin.

Business Math Concepts. 4th rev. ed. Raymond Cote. 408p. (C). 1988. 33.50 (*0-89702-045-6*) Irwin.

Business Math Electronic Calculations: Advanced Business Problem Solving. Albert G. Giordano & Pauline K. Palmen. 160p. (C). 1992. pap. text ed. write for info. (*0-13-107962-X*) P-H.

Business Math Essentials. Robert J. Hughes. LC 92-38454. 300p. (C). 1993. text ed. 15.50 (*0-256-13056-6*) Irwin.

Business Math Is Easy. Stephen Scarpitta. 165p. (Orig.). 1992. pap. text ed. 18.50 (*1-878038-11-7*) Multi-Services.

Business Math on the Job: Practice Set. R. Robert Rosenberg & J. E. Sexton. 1969. text ed. 12.96 (*0-07-053770-4*) McGraw.

An Asterisk (*) at the beginning of an entry indicates that the title is appearing in BIP for the first time.

Business of Sewing: How to Start, Maintain & Achieve Success. Barbara W. Sykes. LC 92-81282. 192p. 1992. pap. 14.95 (*0-9632857-5-0*) Collins Pubns.
Business of Shipping. 6th ed. Lane C. Kendall & James J. Buckley. (Illus.). 455p. 1994. text ed. 45.00x (*0-87033-454-9*) Cornell Maritime.
Business of Show Business. Gail Plummer. LC 72-6180. (Illus.). 238p. 1973. reprint ed. text ed. 35.00 (*0-8371-6485-0*, PLSB, Greenwood Pr) Greenwood.
Business of State Trial Courts. LC 83-17436. 158p. 1983. pap. write for info. (*0-89656-070-8*, R-083) Natl Ctr St Courts.
*__Business of Talk: Organizations in Action.__ Ed. by Deirdre Boden. 280p. 1995. text ed. 52.95 (*0-7456-0291-6*) Blackwell Pubs.
*__Business of Talk: Organizations in Action.__ Ed. by Deirdre Boden. 280p. (C). 1995. pap. text ed. 19.95 (*0-7456-1356-X*) Blackwell Pubs.
Business of Tanks, 1933 to 1945. G. MacLeod Ross. 340p. (C). 1989. 75.00 (*0-685-36176-4*, Pub. by A H S Ltd UK) St Mut.
Business of Tanks, 1933-1945. G. MacLeod Ross. 340p. (C). 1990. 35.00 (*0-685-49137-4*, Pub. by A H S Ltd UK) St Mut.
Business of the Japanese State: Energy Markets in Comparative & Historical Perspective. Richard J. Samuels. LC 87-5230. (Cornell Studies in Political Economy). (Illus.). 376p. (C). 1987. pap. 16.95 (*0-8014-9462-1*) Cornell U Pr.
Business of the Supreme Court: A Study in the Federal Judicial System. Felix Frankfurter & James M. Landis. LC 92-75951. 362p. 1993. reprint ed. 75.00 (*1-56169-025-2*) W W Gaunt.
Business of the Theatre. Alfred L. Bernheim. LC 64-14693. 1972. 24.95 (*0-405-08266-5*, Pub. by Blom Pubns UK) Ayer.
Business of Tour Operations. 3rd ed. Pat Yale. 256p. (Orig.). 1995. pap. 36.50 (*0-273-60177-6*, Pub. by Pitman Pub Ltd UK) Trans-Atl Phila.
Business of Tourism. 4th ed. J. C. Holloway. 200p. 1994. pap. 33.50 (*0-273-60130-X*, Pub. by Pitman Pub Ltd UK) Trans-Atl Phila.
Business of Trading in Stocks. John Durand & A. T. Miller. LC 67-28631. 1967. reprint ed. 12.00 (*0-87034-019-0*) Fraser Pub Co.
Business of Travel: Agency Operations & Administration. Dennis L. Foster. 1990. 33.50 (*0-02-680869-2*) Macmillan.
Business of Veterinary Practice. Ed. by John Sheridan & Owen McCafferty. LC 92-41236. (Veterinary Handbook Ser.). 1993. pap. text ed. 39.00 (*0-08-040846-X*, Pergamon Pr) Elsevier.
Business of Woodwork. Bill Norlin. 326p. 1992. text ed. 75.00 (*0-9635117-7-7*) Woodwork Pr.
Business of Writing & Speaking: A Managerial Communication Manual. L. Robbins. 224p. 1985. text ed. write for info. (*0-07-053089-0*) McGraw.
Business Office Manager. Jack Rudman. (Career Examination Ser.: C-1964). 1994. pap. 34.95 (*0-8373-1964-1*) Nat Learn.
Business Office Recycling Guide. John P. Allison. 24p. (Orig.). (C). 1992. pap. 7.95 (*0-9632789-8-3*) RMC Pub Grp.
Business Officer. Jack Rudman. (Career Examination Ser.: C-2076). 1994. pap. 34.95 (*0-8373-2076-3*) Nat Learn.
*__Business Officers in Higher Education: History of NACUBO.__ 2nd ed. Neal O. Hines & Abbott Wainwright. LC 94-46392. 1995. write for info. (*0-915164-99-X*) NACUBO.
Business One Irwin Banker's Guide to Online Databases. Monk et al. 300p. 1988. text ed. 60.00 (*0-87094-749-4*) Irwin Prof Pubng.
Business One Irwin Business & Investment Almanac 1994. 18th ed. Ed. by Summer N. Levine & Caroline Levine. 750p. 1994. 75.00 (*1-55623-926-2*) Irwin Prof Pubng.
Business One Irwin Guide to Using the Wall Street Journal. 4th rev. ed. Michael B. Lehmann. LC 92-39045. (Illus.). 416p. 1992. write for info. (*1-55623-840-1*) Irwin Prof Pubng.
Business Online: Professionals Guide to Electronic Information. Jean M. Scanlon et al. 400p. 1989. text ed. 65.00 (*0-471-60838-6*) Wiley.
*__Business Online Searching: The Basics & Beyond.__ Marydee Ojala. 250p. 1996. pap. 39.95 (*0-910965-16-1*) Online.
Business Operations Guidebook: "The How-to Guide for Start-up Entrepreneurs" Robert Haiber. Ed. by W. P. Haiber. LC 91-70719. (Illus.). 150p. (Orig.). 1993. per., pap. 19.99 (*0-944089-18-6*) Info Devels.
Business Opinions: Recent Developments in Opinion Practice. Donald W. Glazer & Arthur N. Field. 788p. 1991. pap. text ed. 70.00 (*0-685-49909-X*, B4-6960) PLI.
Business Opinions, 1992: The Use & Implications of the ABA Accord & Guidelines. (Corporate Law & Practice Course Handbook, 1985-86 Ser.). 381p. 1992. pap. 70.00 (*0-685-69388-0*) PLI.
*__Business Opportunities in a Free Cuba.__ Alexander Franco. 180p. 1995. pap. 19.95 (*0-9645329-0-5*) Amer Growth Partners.
Business Opportunities in the Far East: The Complete Reference Guide to Practices & Procedures. Ed. by Lawrence Chimerine et al. 528p. 1990. text ed. 80.00 (*1-55623-197-0*) Irwin Prof Pubng.
*__Business Opportunities in the Russian Far Northeast Commonwealth of Independent States.__ Lawrence Williams. Date not set. 19.95 (*0-9643746-0-9*) Polar Pubng.
Business Opportunities in the United States: The Complete Reference Guide to Practices & Procedures. Ed. by Robert F. Cushman & R. Lawrence Soares. 600p. 1992. 90.00 (*1-55623-493-7*) Irwin Prof Pubng.
Business Opportunities Workbook: A Rural Revitalization Program for Community Leaders. 2nd ed. (Illus.). 98p. (C). 1993. pap. text ed. 45.00 (*0-7881-0061-0*) Diane Pub.
Business Opportunity Appraiser. Wilfred F. Tetreault & Robert W. Clements. (Illus.). 50p. 1980. text ed. 4.95 (*0-937152-03-X*) Am Busn Consult.
Business or Hobby? How to Prove a Profit Motive In Horsebreeding. Lee D. Kersten. LC 83-72627. 77p. 1983. pap. text ed. 12.95 (*0-914669-00-1*) Agri Pub Co.
Business Organisation. Lawrence R. Dicksee. Ed. by Richard P. Brief. LC 80-1488. (Dimensions of Accounting Theory & Practice Ser.). 1980. reprint ed. lib. bdg. 31.95 (*0-405-13518-1*) Ayer.
Business Organisation: A System Framework. B. Vardharajan & J. P. Mahajan. 1084p. 1986. 42.50 (*81-209-0001-4*, Pub. by Pitambar Pub II) St Mut.
Business Organisations & Insolvency. Ed. by Elmer Doonan et al. 210p. (C). 1990. 60.00 (*1-85352-086-1*, Pub. by HLT Pubns UK) St Mut.
Business Organization Agencies & Publications. 7th ed. Estell. 1993. 345.00 (*0-8103-8355-1*) Gale.
Business Organization & Combination. Lewis H. Haney. LC 73-2511. (Big Business; Economic Power in a Free Society Ser.). 1973. reprint ed. 36.95 (*0-405-05092-5*) Ayer.
Business Organization & the Myth of the Market Economy. William Lazonick. (Illus.). 350p. (C). 1992. 49.95 (*0-521-39419-8*) Cambridge U Pr.
Business Organization & the Myth of the Market Economy. William Lazonick. (Illus.). 396p. (C). 1993. pap. 16.95 (*0-521-44788-7*) Cambridge U Pr.
Business Organization in Great Britain: Eighteen Fifty-Six to Nineteen Fourteen. James B. Jefferys. Ed. by Stuart Bruchey. LC 77-77176. (Dissertations in European Economic History Ser.). 1978. lib. bdg. 47.95 (*0-405-10789-7*) Ayer.
Business Organizations & Finance: Legal & Economic Principles. 5th ed. William A. Klein & John C. Coffee, Jr. (University Textbook Ser.). Date not set. pap. text ed. 19.95 (*1-56662-047-3*) Foundation Pr.
Business Organizations in Papua New Guinea. Peter C. Tashjian. xvi, 282p. 1989. pap. 33.00 (*0-455-20828-X*, Pub. by Law Bk Co) W W Gaunt.
*__Business Organizations in Tennessee.__ Richard R. Spore, III. 432p. 1995. 137.00 (*0-925773-19-0*) M Lee Smith.
Business Organizations with Tax Planning, 16 vols. Zolman Cavitch. 1963. Updates. ring bd. write for info. (*0-8205-1165-X*) Bender.
*__Business Outlook International 1994.__ (Illus.). 400p. (Orig.). 1995. pap. 595.00 (*0-7605-1674-X*) Rector Pr.
Business Owner's Guide to Accounting & Bookkeeping. Placencia, Oliver & Welge Staff. Ed. by Scott D. Crawford. (Successful Business Library). 145p. 1991. pap. 19.95 (*1-55571-156-1*) Oasis Pr OR.
Business Owners Guide to Achieving Financial Success. David Duryee. 168p. 1994. text ed. 20.00 (*0-7863-0228-3*) Irwin Prof Pubng.
Business Owner's Operating Manual: A Step-by-Step Guide to Planning, Operating, & Evaluating Your Business. James Burton & W. Blan McBride. (Modern Accounting Perspectives & Practices Ser.). 352p. 1991. text ed. 69.95 (*0-471-87927-4*) Wiley.
Business Papers to Accompany Contemporary Business. 7th ed. Louis E. Boone & David L. Kurtz. Ed. by Nikki Paahana. 32p. (C). 1993. 14.50 (*0-03-074698-1*) Dryden Pr.
Business Parks, Office Parks, Plazas & Centers: A Study of Development Practices & Procedures. James R. McKeever. LC 72-127217. (Urban Land Institute Series Technical Bulletin: No. 65). (Illus.). 128p. reprint ed. pap. 36.50 (*0-8357-7500-3*, 2011369) Bks Demand.
Business Participation Rates & Self-Employed Incomes: Analysis of the Fifty Largest U. S. Ancestry Groups. Frank A. Fratoe & Ronald L. Meeks. (Minority Economic Development Ser.: No. 3). 81p. 1988. pap. 5.95 (*0-318-39973-3*) UCLA CAAS.
Business Partnering for Continuous Improvement: How to Forge Enduring Alliances among Employees, Suppliers & Customers. Charles C. Poirier & William F. Houser. LC 92-23473. 256p. 1994. pap. 19.95 (*1-881052-39-7*) Berrett-Koehler.
Business Partners: The Best Pistol - Ammunition Combinations for Personal Defense. Peter A. Kasler. (Illus.). 200p. 1991. text ed. 22.95 (*0-87364-609-6*) Paladin Pr.
Business People in the News: A Compilation of News Stories & Feature Articles from American Newspapers & Magazines Covering People in Industry, Finance & Labor, Vol. 1. Ed. by Barbara Nykoruk. LC 76-4617. (Illus.). xl, 412p. 1976. 85.00 (*0-8103-0044-3*) Gale.
*__Business Performance Appraisals.__ 400p. (Orig.). 1995. pap. 295.00 (*0-7605-1454-2*) Rector Pr.
Business Performance in the Retail Sector: The Experience of the John Lewis Partnership. Keith R. Bradley & Simon Taylor. 160p. 1992. 59.00 (*0-19-825694-9*) OUP.
Business Periodical Index, 1958-59 thru 1989-90. annuals 225.00 (*0-685-05414-4*) Wilson.
Business Periodical Index, 1990-91 thru 1993-94. annuals write for info. (*0-685-22242-X*) Wilson.
Business Persons' Guide to Taxation in the 90's: Starting & Running Your Business. Harry R. Oliver, III. 212p. 1990. 19.95 (*0-9622569-1-9*) El Dorado Pr.
Business Perspective on Industry & Health Care. W. B. Goldbeck. LC 77-7982. (Springer Series in Industry & Health Care: Vol. 2). 1978. pap. 42.00 (*0-387-90298-8*) Spr-Verlag.
Business Plan. Center for Innovation & Business Development Staff. 200p. 1988. 29.95 (*0-930204-26-3*) Lord Pub.
*__Business Plan.__ Alan West. 196p. (C). 1991. pap. 36.00x (*0-273-03628-9*, Pub. by Pitman Pubng UK) St Mut.
Business Plan: First Step to Success. rev. ed. Erwin C. Busse. LC 93-80683. (Illus.). 39p. (C). 1994. pap. text ed. 14.95 (*0-9623557-1-2*) Haldon Mktg Servs.
Business Plan: Planning for the Small Business. Alan West. 208p. (Orig.). 1988. 21.95 (*0-89397-288-6*) Nichols Pub.
Business Plan - Approved. G. Nigel Cohen. 192p. 1994. pap. 19.95 (*0-566-07453-2*, Pub. by Gower UK) Ashgate Pub Co.

Business Plan & Evaluation: Simple As One-Two-Three - Three Easy Steps for a Do-It-Yourself Business Plan - Just Fill in the Blanks. rev. ed. William L. Mazzo. LC 85-62990. 254p. (C). 1986. reprint ed. pap. text ed. 19.95 (*0-936257-00-8*) Busn Plan Pub.
A business plan guidebook in three easy steps, just fill in the blanks. This guidebook marks the first time a step-by-step guide on creating a business plan for new & expanding businesses & their owners has been developed. Combining "what-to" with "how-to," the guidebook is designed to give "hands-on" guidance that will help readers prepare an effective business plan. It is already in its third edition. "If you want lenders to take you seriously, but you don't know how to write a business plan, Mazzo's book makes it as easy as 1-2-3." New Business Opportunities. "Unpretentious & direct, it's actually more of a detailed outline than a book, but that's where its beauty lies. It's simple."--The Security Traders Handbook. A BUSINESS PLAN & EVALUATION is distributed by Baker & Taylor, Ingram. ***Publisher Provided Annotation.***

Business Plan Guide for Independent Consultants. Herman Holtz. LC 94-6924. 1994. text ed. 59.95 (*0-471-59736-8*); pap. text ed. 17.95 (*0-471-59735-X*) Wiley.
*__Business Plan Handbook.__ 225p. (Orig.). 1995. pap. 395.00 (*0-7605-1709-6*) Rector Pr.
*__Business Plan into Action Handbook.__ 225p. (Orig.). 1995. pap. 295.00 (*0-7605-1710-X*) Rector Pr.
Business Plan Workbook. Gary A. Cooper. 448p. 1989. ring bd. 69.95 (*0-13-106767-2*) P-H.
Business Plan Workbook: A Step-By-Step Guide for Developing & Writing a Business Plan. Jeri Sutton & Christine L. Cannon. 65p. (Orig.). 1987. student ed 18.00 (*0-945233-00-0*) Kelson Pub.
Business Plan Workbook & Outline. Date not set. 29.95 (*0-685-69349-X*); disk 39.95 (*0-685-69350-3*) Lord Pub.
Business Planner: A Complete Guide to Raising Finance for Your Business. Iain Maitland. 200p. 1992. pap. 29.95 (*0-7506-0136-1*) Buttrwrth-Heinemann.
Business Planning. Franklin A. Gevurtz. (University Casebook Ser.). 1075p. 1991. text ed. 43.95 (*0-88277-868-4*) Foundation Pr.
*__Business Planning.__ 2nd ed. Franklin A. Gevurtz. (University Casebook Ser.). 1083p. (C). 1995. text ed. 47.95 (*1-56662-241-7*) Foundation Pr.
Business Planning: A Approach to Strategic Management. Bill Richardson & Roy Richardson. 288p. (Orig.). 1992. pap. 36.50 (*0-273-03720-X*, Pub. by Pitman Pub Ltd UK) Trans-Atl Phila.
Business Planning: Adaptable to Courses Utilizing Herwitz' Casebook on Planning of Corporate Transactions. Casenotes Publishing Co., Inc. Staff. Ed. by Norman S. Goldenberg et al. (Legal Briefs Ser.). 1984. pap. write for info. (*0-87457-011-5*, 1440) Casenotes Pub.
Business Planning: Materials on the Planning of Corporate Transactions Including the Revised Business Planning Problems & the Model Business Corporation Act. 2nd rev. ed. David R. Herwitz. (University Casebook Ser.). 851p. 1990. reprint ed. pap. text ed. 28.95 (*0-88277-210-4*) Foundation Pr.
Business Planning: Problems & Materials. 2nd ed. William H. Painter. LC 84-2186. (American Casebook Ser.). 1008p. (C). 1989. reprint ed. text ed. 47.00 (*0-314-80258-4*) West Pub.
*__Business Planning: 1994 Supplement.__ Franklin A. Geourtz. (University Casebook Ser.). 85p. 1994. pap. text ed. 6.95 (*1-56662-195-X*) Foundation Pr.
Business Planning - an Approach to Strategic Management. R. Richardson. 236p. (C). 1989. 145.00 (*0-685-39854-4*, Inst Pur & Supply) St Mut.
Business Planning for Healthcare Organizations: The Experts' Guide to Creating & Maintaining a Competitive Advantage. Jeff Rogers. (Illus.). 102p. (C). 1988. student ed 87.00 (*0-923680-00-4*) Amer ComVision Inc.
Business Planning for Scientists & Engineers. (Illus.). 155p. (Orig.). (C). 1993. pap. text ed. 40.00x (*1-56806-077-7*) Diane Pub.
Business Planning for the Board. Ed. by Hugh Buckner. (Director's Bookshelf Ser.). 256p. 1971. 32.00 (*0-8464-0227-0*) Beekman Pubs.
*__Business Planning for the First Time.__ David Irwin. 256p. (C). 1995. 54.00x (*0-273-61086-4*, Pub. by Pitman Pubng UK) St Mut.
Business Planning Guide. 6th ed. David H. Bangs, Jr. 1992. pap. 19.95 (*0-936894-39-3*) Upstart Pub.
*__Business Planning Guide.__ 7th ed. 1996. pap. 22.95 (*0-936894-96-2*, 6100-2407) Upstart Pub.
Business Planning, Teachers Manual For. Franklin A. Gevurtz. (University Casebook Ser.). 111p. (C). 1991. pap. text ed. write for info. (*0-88277-948-6*) Foundation Pr.
Business Planning, Teacher's Manual to Accompany. 3rd ed. William H. Painter. (American Casebook Ser.). 137p. 1994. pap. text ed. write for info. (*0-314-04066-8*) West Pub.
Business Planning, 1990 Supplement: Problems & Materials In. 2nd ed. William H. Painter. (American Casebook Ser.). 256p. 1990. pap. text ed. 15.50 (*0-314-72204-1*) West Pub.
Business Plans & Loan Applications That Work: A Book of Models Based on Real Documents. John R. Taylor. 250p. 1993. pap. 34.95 (*1-883671-00-0*); Model Business Plans Software Template. disk 24.95 (*1-883671-03-5*) Taylor-Gray.
Business Plans Handbook. Ed. by Karin E. Koek. 1000p. 1994. 99.00 (*0-8103-9222-4*, 101951) Gale.
Business Plans That Win: Lessons from the MIT Enterprise Forum. Stanley R. Rich & David E. Gumpert. LC 84-48617. (Illus.). 224p. 1987. pap. 12.00 (*0-06-091391-6*, PL 1391, PL) HarpC.
Business Plans That Win Venture Capital. Terrence B. McGarty. 1989. text ed. 94.95 (*0-471-50180-8*) Wiley.
Business Plans to Game Plans. Jan B. King. 1994. 29.95 (*1-56343-071-1*) Merritt Co.
Business Plans to Manage Day to Day Operations: Real-Life Results for Small Business Owners & Operators. Christopher R. Malburg. LC 92-34809. 288p. 1993. disk 85.00 (*0-471-57296-9*); pap. 39.95 (*0-471-57299-3*) Wiley.
*__Business Plus Strategy Equals Success: Business Plannign Made Easier.__ M. Nadine Lynch. (Illus.). 203p. (Orig.). Date not set. pap. 19.95 (*0-9645674-0-7*) MNL Pub.
Business Policies & Decision Making. Ed. by Raymond J. Ziegler. LC 66-11454. 1966. pap. text ed. 7.95 (*0-89197-688-4*) Irvington.
Business Policy. Jack Rudman. (ACT Proficiency Examination Program Ser.: PEP-23). 1994. pap. 23.95 (*0-8373-5523-0*) Nat Learn.
Business Policy: An Analytical Introduction. 2nd ed. George Luffman et al. 208p. (Orig.). (C). 1991. pap. text ed. 24.95 (*0-631-18195-4*) Blackwell Pubs.
*__Business Policy: Managing Strategic Processes.__ 8th ed. Joseph L. Bower et al. LC 95-2575. 912p. (C). 1995. 66.95 (*0-256-11591-5*) Irwin.
Business Policy: Principles & Practices, 1989. D. Thakur. (C). 1989. 300.00 (*0-685-36465-8*) St Mut.
Business Policy: Text & Cases. 7th ed. C. Roland Christensen et al. 928p. (C). 1990. text ed. 66.95 (*0-256-08602-8*) Irwin.
Business Policy & Strategic Management. 5th rev. ed. Lawrence R. Jauch & William F. Glueck. 960p. 1988. text ed. write for info. (*0-07-032347-X*) McGraw.
Business Policy & Strategic Management: Planning, Strategy, & Action. George C. Sawyer. 528p. (C). 1990. text ed. 49.00 (*0-15-505680-8*) Dryden Pr.
*__Business Policy & Strategy.__ Comp. by Richard Schwindt. (Business Administration Reading Lists & Course Outlines Ser.: 12). (Illus.). 246p. (C). 1995. pap. text ed. 25.00 (*0-88024-172-1*) Eno River Pr.
Business Policy & Strategy. Shrivastava. (C). 1994. text ed. 57.95 (*0-538-81749-6*, GH63AA) S-W Pub.
Business Policy Game. rev. ed. Richard Lindhe et al. LC 84-73026. 112p. 1985. pap. 16.95 (*0-931920-98-1*) Dame Pubns.
*__Business Policy Game: An International Simulation: Player's Manual.__ 4th ed. Richard V. Cotter & David J. Fritzsche. LC 94-44025. 1995. pap. text ed. write for info. (*0-13-339144-2*) P-H.
*__Business, Politics, & Cigarettes: Multiple Levels, Multiple Agendas.__ Richard McGowan. LC 95-7279. 184p. 1995. text ed. 55.00 (*0-89930-964-X*, Quorum Bks) Greenwood.
Business, Politics, & International Relations (Industrielle Interessenpolitik und Staat) Steel, Cotton, & International Cartels in British Politics, 1924-1939. Clemens A. Wurm. LC 92-30239. (Illus.). 400p. (ENG & GER.). (C). 1993. 84.95 (*0-521-40520-3*) Cambridge U Pr.
Business Possibilities: A Series of Suggestions. Ed. by Bibliotheca Press Research Division Staff. 300p. 1983. text ed. 75.00 (*0-939476-92-4*, Biblio Pr) Prosperity & Profits.
Business Power & Public Policy. Alfred C. Neal. LC 81-7348. 176p. 1981. text ed. 45.00 (*0-275-90686-8*, C0686, Praeger Pubs) Greenwood.
Business Practices in India. Khaliq Ahmad. 1989. 30.00 (*0-8364-2571-5*, Pub. by Popular Prakashan II) S Asia.
Business Presentations Using Harvard Graphics. Lloyd D. Brooks & Bryant Brooks. LC 92-33029. 1993. 19.50 (*0-02-800407-8*) Glencoe.
Business Presentations Workbook. Clark Lambert. 264p. 1988. spiral bd. 39.95 (*0-13-107467-9*) P-H.
Business Presentations Workbook. Clark Lambert. 264p. 1989. pap. 12.95 (*0-13-107518-7*) P-H.
Business Press Editor. Edgar A. Grunwald. (Business Magazine Publishing Ser.). 200p. 1988. 40.00x (*0-8147-3016-7*); pap. 17.50x (*0-8147-3017-5*) NYU Pr.
Business Pricing & Inflation. Malcolm C. Sawyer. LC 83-3121. 175p. 1984. text ed. 25.00 (*0-312-10908-3*) St Martin.
Business Principles: Syllabus. Ronald W. Singleton. 1976. pap. text ed. 9.25 (*0-89420-002-X*, 102100); audio 240.40 (*0-89420-129-8*, 102000) Natl Book.

B

966
An Asterisk (*) at the beginning of an entry indicates that the title is appearing in BIP for the first time.

***Business Principles & Management.** 10th ed. Kenneth E. Everard & Jim Burrow. LC 94-47501. 1996. 36.95 (*0-538-62466-3*) S-W Pub.

Business Problems & Solutions for Proprietors & Partnerships. Luanna C. Blagrove. LC 81-65224. 160p. (C). 1981. 24.95 (*0-9604466-8-0*); pap. 19.95 (*0-9604466-9-9*) Blagrove Pubns.

Business Problems of the Eighties. Jules Backman. (ITT Key Issues Lecture Ser.). 1980. pap. write for info. (*0-672-97499-1*) Macmillan.

***Business Process Benchmarking: Finding & Implementing Best Practices.** Robert C. Camp. LC 94-34028. 1994. 35.00 (*0-87389-296-8*) ASQC Qual Pr.

***Business Process Change: Reengineering Concepts, Methods, & Technologies.** Ed. by William Kettinger & Varun Grover. 704p. (C). 1995. 84.95 (*1-878289-29-2*) Idea Group Pub.

***Business Process Engineering: ARIS-Navigator for Reference Models for Industrial Enterprises.** Ed. by A. W. Scheer. 100p. 1995. 125.00 (*3-540-14511-7*) Spr-Verlag.

***Business Process Engineering: Reference Models for Industrial Enterprises.** 2nd enl. rev. ed. August-Wilhelm Scheer. LC 94-31047. 1994. 89.00 (*0-387-58234-7*) Spr-Verlag.

Business Process Improvement: The Breakthrough Strategy for Total Quality, Productivity, & Competitiveness. H. James Harrington. 288p. 1991. text ed. 26.95 (*0-07-026768-5*) McGraw.

Business Process Re-Engineering: Breakpoint Strategies for Market Dominance. Henry J. Johansson et al. LC 93-7341. 250p. 1993. text ed. 37.95 (*0-471-93883-1*) Wiley.

***Business Process Re-Engineering - Information Systems Opportunities & Challenges: Proceedings of the IFIP TC8 Open Conference on Business Process Re-engineering: Information Systems Opportunities & Challenges, Queensland Gold Coast, Australia, 8-11 May 1994.** Ed. by Bernard C. Glasson. LC 94-34772. (IFIP Transactions, Computer Science & Technology Ser.: Vol. A-54). 1994. write for info. (*0-444-82062-0*) Elsevier.

***Business Process Reengineering: Breakpoint Strategies for Market Dominance.** Henry J. Johannson et al. 1994. pap. text ed. 19.95 (*0-471-95088-2*) Wiley.

Business Process Reengineering: Current Issues & Applications. LC 93-13268. 1993. 35.95 (*0-89806-133-4*) Ind Eng Mgmt Pr.

***Business Processes: Modelling & Analysis for Re-Engineering & Improvement.** Martyn A. Ould. LC 95-3608. 1995. text ed. 45.00 (*0-471-95352-0*) Wiley.

Business Profitability Data. John B. Walton. 170p. (Orig.). 1983. pap. 15.00 (*0-939356-03-1*) Weybridge.

Business Profitability Data. John B. Walton. 170p. (Orig.). 1985. pap. 15.00 (*0-939356-04-X*) Weybridge.

Business Profitability Data. John B Walton. 170p. (Orig.). 1987. pap. 15.00 (*0-939356-05-8*) Weybridge.

Business Profitability Data. John B. Walton. 170p. (Orig.). 1990. pap. 15.00 (*0-939356-06-6*) Weybridge.

Business Profitability Data. John B. Walton. 170p. (Orig.). 1991. pap. 40.00 (*0-939356-07-4*) Weybridge.

Business Profitability Data, 1980. John B. Walton. (Biennial Publication Ser.). 158p. (Orig.). 1981. pap. 12.00 (*0-939356-01-5*) Weybridge.

Business Profitability Data 1982. John B. Walton. (Annual Publication Ser.). 170p. (Orig.). 1982. pap. 15.00 (*0-939356-02-3*) Weybridge.

Business Programming in C for DOS-Based Systems. A. C. Millspaugh. 482p. (C). 1993. pap. text ed. 35.75 (*0-15-500139-6*) Dryden Pr.

Business Programming Logic. 4th ed. Jay Singelmann & Jean Longhurst. 432p. 1990. pap. text ed. write for info. (*0-13-092065-7*) P-H.

Business Programming Logic: A Structured Approach. 2nd ed. Jay Singlemann & Jean Longhurst. (Illus.). 288p. (C). 1982. text ed. 18.95 (*0-685-03776-6*) P-H.

Business Programming Logic & Design. Russell. (C). 1994. text ed. 37.50 (*0-673-46840-2*) HarpCollege.

Business Programming Using dBase IV. Sudesh Duggal. (C). 1991. write for info. (*0-675-21137-9*, Merrill Pub Co) Macmillan.

Business Promotion Coordinator. Jack Rudman. (Career Examination Ser.: C-2527). 1994. pap. 34.95 (*0-8373-2527-7*) Nat Learn.

Business Protocol: How to Survive & Succeed in Business. Jan Yager. 246p. 1991. text ed. 34.95 (*0-471-54259-8*); pap. text ed. 14.95 (*0-471-51234-6*) Wiley.

***Business Quality: Making Quality Work with TQ.** (Illus.). 125p. (Orig.). 1995. pap. 495.00 (*0-7605-1876-9*) Rector Pr.

Business Quotations. Helen Exley. (Best of Quotations Ser.). (Illus.). 60p. 1993. 6.99 (*1-85015-266-7*) Exley Giftbooks.

Business Quotes. Ed. by Mac Anderson. 77p. (Orig.). 1988. pap. 7.50 (*1-880461-16-1*) Celebrat Excell.

Business Rankings Annual 1990. Brooklyn Public Library Business Staff. 650p. 1990. 170.00 (*0-8103-4293-6*) Gale.

Business Rankings Annual 1991. Brooklyn Bus Libr Staff. 1991. 170.00 (*0-8103-4294-4*) Gale.

Business Rankings Annual 1992. Brooklyn Bus Libr Staff. 1992. 170.00 (*0-8103-4295-2*) Gale.

Business Rankings Annual 1993. Brooklyn Bus Libr Staff. 1993. 170.00 (*0-8103-5347-4*) Gale.

***Business Rankings Annual 1995: Lists of Companies, Products, Services, & Activities Compiled from a Variety of Published Sources.** Brooklyn Business Library Staff. 800p. 1995. 170.00 (*0-8103-8953-3*) Gale.

Business Ratios - A New Guide to Interpretation. Ed. by ICC Information Group Staff. 1988. 425.00 (*0-86261-763-4*, Pub. by ICC Info Group Ltd UK) St Mut.

Business Re-Engineering in Financial Services: Strategies for Designing Processes & Developing New Products. Stephen Drew. (Financial Times Management Ser.). 288p. 1994. 135.00x (*0-273-60456-2*, Pub. by Pitman Pubng UK) St Mut.

***Business Re-Engineering in Financial Services: Strategies for Designing Processes & Developing New Products.** Stephen Drew. 288p. 1994. 135.00 (*0-614-04100-7*, Pub. by Pitman Pubng UK) St Mut.

Business Readings (in Chinese) Chin-ming Ch'ian et al. Ed. by Chen-ch'ing Li & Te-ming Yeh. (Mandarin Training Center Ser.). 229p. (Orig.). (CHI.). 1991. pap. text ed. 13.95 (*0-88710-171-2*) Yale Far Eastern Pubns.

Business Recipes: Workbook for Homemade Money. Lenea Howe. 190p. (Orig.). (C). 1988. student ed 19.00 (*0-685-22579-8*) Scandia Pub.

Business Records Control. 7th ed. Joseph S. Fosegan. LC 94-4122. 1995. text ed. 23.95 (*0-538-62363-2*) S-W Pub.

Business Recycling Manual. INFORM, Inc. Staff & Recourse Systems, Inc. Staff. LC 90-23341. 202p. 1991. ring bd. 42.50 (*0-918780-57-8*) INFORM NY.

Business Recycling of Business Going Out of Business, Bankrupt Business, etc. rev. ed. 1991. 17.95 (*0-913597-94-5*) Prosperity & Profits.

***Business Reference & Investment Guide to the Commonwealth of the Northern Mariana Islands.** 3rd ed. William H. Stewart et al. (Illus.). 232p. (C). 1994. pap. text ed. 95.00x (*0-7881-1049-7*) Diane Pub.

Business Relocation: A Guide to Moving a Business. V. G. Haines. 1970. 22.00 (*0-8464-0229-7*) Beekman Pubs.

Business Reorganizations. Gerber. 1986. write for info. (*0-8205-0041-0*, 078) Bender.

Business Report: Writer, Reader & Text. James Van Oosting. (Illus.). 320p. 1983. pap. write for info. (*0-13-107581-0*) P-H.

Business Report Writing. 2nd rev. ed. Joel P. Bowman & Bernadine P. Branchaw. (Illus.). 599p. (C). 1988. text ed. 50.00 (*0-03-013244-4*) Dryden Pr.

Business Reports: Samples from the "Real World" William E. Rivers. (Illus.). 272p. 1981. pap. text ed. write for info. (*0-13-107656-6*) P-H.

Business Reports in English. J. M. Comfort et al. (Illus.). 128p. 1985. pap. 11.95 (*0-521-27294-7*) Cambridge U Pr.

Business Rescue: How to Fix a Company That's Losing Money. Al Rosen. 1989. pap. 11.95 (*0-9620675-0-4*) Busn Univ Pr.

Business Research: An Informal Guide. Paul Timm & Rick Farr. Ed. by W. Philip Gerould. LC 93-73200. (Illus.). 100p. (Orig.). 1994. pap. 9.95 (*1-56052-249-6*) Crisp Pubns.

Business Research for Decision Making. 3rd ed. Duane Davis & Robert M. Cosenza. LC 92-30553. 622p. 1993. text ed. 56.95 (*0-534-93249-5*) Intl Thomson.

Business Research Methods. Charles H. Fay et al. Ed. by Paul S. Donnelly. 448p. (C). 1986. teacher ed write for info. (*0-318-57301-6*) McGraw.

Business Research Methods. 3rd rev. ed. William G. Zikmund. (Illus.). 742p. (C). 1991. text ed. 56.00 (*0-03-033078-5*) Dryden Pr.

Business Research Methods. 4th ed. C. William Emory & Donald R. Cooper. 784p. (C). 1991. text ed. 65.95 (*0-256-09265-6*) Irwin.

Business Research Methods. 4th ed. William G. Zikmund. LC 93-2283. 776p. (C). 1994. text ed. 65.25 (*0-03-097585-9*) Dryden Pr.

***Business Research Methods.** 4th ed. William G. Zikmund. LC 93-2283. 873p. (C). 1994. teacher ed, pap. text ed. 70.00 (*0-03-097855-6*) Dryden Pr.

***Business Research Methods.** 5th ed. Donald R. Cooper & C. William Emory. LC 95-5000. (Statistics Ser.). 681p. (C). 1994. text ed. 65.95 (*0-256-13777-3*) Irwin Prof Pubng.

Business Research Projects for Students. D. Jankowicz. 296p. 1991. pap. 25.00 (*0-412-36820-X*, A6194) Chapman & Hall.

Business Research Yearbook: Global Business Perspectives. Ed. by Abbass F. Alkhafaji. 1146p. (C). 1994. pap. text ed. 95.00 (*0-8191-9531-6*) U Pr of Amer.

Business Researcher's Handbook: The Comprehensive Guide for Research Professionals. 2nd ed. LC 80-54127. 250p. 1983. 175.00 (*0-934940-18-5*) Wash Res.

Business Response to Keynes, Nineteen Twenty-Nine to Nineteen Sixty-Four. Robert M. Collins. LC 81-3898. (Contemporary American History Ser.). 320p. 1981. text ed. 47.50 (*0-231-04486-0*) Col U Pr.

***Business Resumption Planning.** Edward S. Derlin et al. 592p. 1994. 132.00 (*0-7913-2127-4*) Warren Gorham & Lamont.

Business Retention Strategies. Sarah Eilers. Ed. by Jenny Murphy. 26p. (Orig.). 1988. pap. 18.00 (*0-317-04813-9*) Natl Coun Econ Dev.

***Business Risk & Payment International Handbook, 12 vols., Set.** (Illus.). 1400p. (Orig.). 1995. pap. 1,495.00 (*0-7605-1600-6*) Rector Pr.

***Business Risk International Country Handbook, 12 vols., Set.** (Illus.). 1200p. (Orig.). 1994. pap. 3,995.00 (*0-7605-1330-9*) Rector Pr.

Business Roundtable Participation Guide: A Primer for Business on Education. 2nd ed. (Illus.). 117p. (C). 1993. pap. text ed. 50.00 (*0-7881-0067-X*) Diane Pub.

Business Russian. 180p. 1993. 16.00 (*1-880100-14-2*) Russian Info Srvs.

Business Russian. Siegfried Kohls. 232p. 1991. pap. 16.95 (*0-8442-4220-9*, Passport Bks) NTC Pub Grp.

Business Russian: Self Instruction Course (For English-Speaking Specialists) I. F. Zhdanova. 378p. (C). 1992. pap. text ed. 12.95 (*0-8285-4996-6*) Firebird NY.

Business Russian Complete Course. 1994. 14.95 (*0-8442-3784-1*, NTC Busn Bks) NTC Pub Grp.

***Business Savvy.** Oak Associates Staff. 160p. 1995. pap. 11.95 (*4-89684-244-8*, Pub. by Yohan Pubns JA) Weatherhill.

Business Scenarios for the Nineties: Strategic Perspectives. Ed. by Y. R. Reddy & Dharni P. Sinha. 168p. (C). 1992. 25.00 (*0-7069-5876-4*, Pub. by Vikas II) S Asia.

Business School in the Nineteen Eighties: Liberialism Versus Vocationalism. Paul Hugstad. LC 82-16601. 172p. 1983. text ed. 45.00 (*0-275-91014-8*, C1014, Praeger Pubs) Greenwood.

***Business Security K-9.** George Duet & Karen F. Duet. (Illus.). 256p. 1995. 22.00 (*0-87605-439-4*) Howell Bk.

Business Self: The Recovery of Public Esteem. Benjamin DeMott. (Philip Morris Lectures on Business & Society Ser.). 54p. 1993. pap. write for info. (*1-884663-01-X*) Baruch Coll Cty U.

Business Sense: Exercising Management's Five Freedoms. Dan Thomas. 224p. 1993. 28.00 (*0-02-932444-0*) Free Pr.

Business Sense: For Budding Entrepreneurs. Carlita Faxton. 64p. (Orig.). 1994. pap. write for info. (*0-9636553-6-1*) C Faxton.

Business Serials: An International Guide to Periodicals in Business, Marketing & Advertising. 1000p. 1994. write for info. (*0-929976-01-0*) Blue Ridge Int.

Business Serials of the U. S. Government. 2nd ed. Ed. by Priscilla C. Geahigan & Robert Rose. LC 88-3428. 96p. 1988. pap. text ed. 10.00 (*0-8389-3349-1*) ALA.

***Business Services in Europe.** European Commission Staff. 259p. 1995. pap. 25.00 (*92-826-9660-X*, CA-86-94-222-EN, Pub. by Europ Com) UNIPUB.

Business Services Specialist. Jack Rudman. (Career Examination Ser.: C-3611). 1994. 34.95 (*0-8373-3611-2*, C-3611) Nat Learn.

Business Side of Geology: A Collection of Articles Reprinted from the AAPG Explorer, 1987-1988. Robert E. Megill. (Illus.). v, 48p. 1989. ring bd. 15.00 (*0-89181-812-X*) AAPG.

Business Side of Medical Practice. 1988. pap. 44.95 (*0-89970-003-9*, OP-410/8) AMA.

Business Side of Writing. Russell A. Stultz. (Illus.). 144p. 1984. text ed. write for info. (*0-13-107822-4*); pap. 15.50 (*0-13-107814-3*) P-H.

Business Side of Writing. Russell A. Stultz. (Business-Professional Ser.). (Illus.). 208p. 1989. pap. 15.95 (*1-55622-157-6*) Wordware Pub.

Business Situation German. Andrew Castley. 97p. (ENG & GER.). 1980. pap. 19.95 (*0-8288-4685-5*, M9206) Fr & Eur.

Business Skills for Young Dentists: A Hands-on Guide for the Young Professional. rev. ed. John P. Sullivan. 125p. 1993. pap. 29.95 (*0-9638856-0-X*) Pronet Pr.

Business Small Talk: Five Steps to Success. L. Longheed. (Business for Career Success Ser.). (YA). 1995. pap. text ed. 12.00 (*0-201-54261-7*); audio write for info. (*0-201-54262-5*) Longman.

***Business Social Skills.** rev. ed. Ed. by Harold Almon. 102p. 1995. pap. 10.95 (*0-917921-09-7*) Bee At Ease Ent.

Business Software Applications: DOS, WordPerfect, Lotus dBASE IV. Edward J. Coburn et al. 256p. (C). 1990. teacher ed 5.80 (*1-56118-055-6*); pap. text ed. 19.95 (*1-56118-054-8*) Paradigm MN.

Business Software Catalog. 1987. pap. 39.95 (*0-942093-00-3*) Intl Database Mgmt.

Business Software Companion. Corey Sandler & Tom Badgett. 412p. 1993. pap. text ed. 22.95 (*0-471-56940-2*) Wiley.

Business Software Directory, 2 vols., Set. 4th ed. Comp. by Information Sources, Inc. Staff. 2186p. 1990. 295.00 (*0-938734-42-3*) Learned Info.

Business Spain: A Practical Guide to Understanding Spanish Business Culture. Peggy Kenna & Sondra Lacy. LC 94-17746. (Orig.). (SPA.). 1995. pap. 5.95 (*0-8442-3563-6*, NTC Busn Bks) NTC Pub Grp.

Business Spanish. Roberto R. Saona & Anne White. (Made Simple Ser.). (Illus.). 250p. 1993. audio write for info. (*0-7506-1732-2*); audio write for info. (*0-7506-1734-9*); audio write for info. (*0-7506-1733-0*) Buttrwrth-Heinemann.

Business Spanish. Roberto R. Saona & Anne White. (Made Simple Ser.). 250p. 1994. pap. write for info. (*0-7506-1735-7*) Buttrwrth-Heinemann.

Business Speaker's Almanac. Jack Griffin. 1994. 39.95 (*0-13-177544-8*) P-H.

Business Speaker's Humor Handbook. Michael Iapoce. LC 88-10612. (Orig.). 1988. pap. text ed. 14.95 (*0-471-63649-5*) Wiley.

Business Speaking. Paula B. Becker & Dennis Becker. LC 92-27382. 200p. (C). 1992. text ed. 17.95 (*0-256-12630-5*) Irwin.

Business Spelling & Word Power. 2nd ed. Abraham H. Lass. 1961. teacher ed 6.67 (*0-672-96013-3*, Bobbs) Macmillan.

Business Spelling & Word Power. 2nd ed. Rosemarie McCauley & Keith Slocum. 336p. (C). 1983. teacher ed write for info. (*0-672-97976-4*); pap. text ed. write for info. (*0-672-97975-6*) Macmillan.

Business Spelling & Word Power. 7th ed. Abraham H. Lass. 1961. pap. text ed. 9.95 (*0-672-96012-5*, Bobbs); 3.95 (*0-672-96015-X*, Bobbs) Macmillan.

Business Sponsorship. Caroline Gillies. 192p. 1991. text ed. 51.95 (*0-7506-0012-8*) Buttrwrth-Heinemann.

Business Start-up & Management Reference Directory: A Guide to Doing Business in California. Myrna Sison. (Illus.). 240p. (C). 1994. pap. 30.00 (*1-883614-50-3*) CA Kit Direct.

***Business Start-Up & Management Reference Directory: A Guide to Doing Business in California 1995.** (Illus.). 240p. 1995. pap. 40.00 (*1-883614-52-X*) CA Kit Direct.

Business Start-up Fees: An International Directory. Alpha Pyramis Research Division Staff. 100p. 1983. text ed. 119.95 (*0-913597-01-5*) Prosperity & Profits.

Business Start-up Fees: U. S. Edition. Ed. by Frieda Carrol. LC 83-90726. 50p. 1983. text ed. 59.95 (*0-911569-13-8*); pap. text ed. 29.95 (*0-911569-08-1*) Prosperity & Profits.

Business Start-up Practice. Dana Shilling. 144p. 1987. text ed. 29.95 (*0-13-107749-X*) P-H.

Business Start-ups: The Professional's Guide to Tax & Financial Strategies. David Minars. 300p. 1987. text ed. 49.95 (*0-13-107707-4*) P-H.

***Business Starter Handbook.** 70p. (Orig.). (RUS.). 1995. pap. 45.00 (*0-7605-1479-8*) Rector Pr.

***Business Stat Companion.** Stergios Fotopoulos. 60p. (C). 1995. 12.95 (*0-7872-0606-7*) Kendall-Hunt.

Business Stationary Graphics, No. 2. (Illus.). 224p. 1994. 79.95 (*4-938586-48-7*, Pub. by PIE Bks JA) Bks Nippan.

Business Statistics. Harper. 1136p. 1996. 46.95 (*0-8016-6825-5*) Mosby Yr Bk.

Business Statistics. Lawrence L. Lapin. LC 84-6690. (College Outline Ser.). 341p. (C). 1984. pap. text ed. 12.50 (*0-15-601553-6*) HB Coll Pubs.

Business Statistics. Gary E. Meek et al. 800p. 1986. write for info. (*0-685-17397-6*) Allyn.

Business Statistics. N. K. Nag. Ed. by J. C. Maity. 1985. 79.00 (*0-317-38754-5*, Current Dist) St Mut.

Business Statistics. Suranjan Saha. (C). 1989. 60.00 (*0-89771-398-2*, Current Dist) St Mut.

Business Statistics. G. V. Shenoy et al. (C). 1988. pap. 14.00 (*81-224-0011-6*, Pub. by Wiley Eastern II) S Asia.

Business Statistics. 2nd ed. Douglas Downing & Jeffrey Clark. LC 92-14114. (Business Review Ser.). 1992. pap. 11.95 (*0-8120-1384-0*) Barron.

Business Statistics, 6 Vols. 6th ed. Wayne W. Daniel & James C. Terrell. (C). 1991. text ed. 61.16 (*0-395-47270-9*) HM.

***Business Statistics: A Computer-Assisted Workbook.** Douglas Bonett. 260p. (C). 1994. per., pap. text ed. 28.95 (*0-8403-9657-0*) Kendall-Hunt.

Business Statistics: A Decision Making Approach. 4th ed. David F. Groebner & Patrick W. Shannon. (Illus.). 900p. (C). 1993. text ed. write for info. (*0-02-347841-1*) Macmillan.

Business Statistics: A Decision Making Approach. 4th ed. David F. Groebner & Patrick W. Shannon. (Illus.). 900p. (C). 1993. student ed, pap. write for info. (*0-02-339931-7*) Macmillan.

Business Statistics: A First Course. John E. Freund & Benjamin M. Perles. (Quantitative Analysis for Business Ser.). 368p. 1974. pap. text ed. write for info. (*0-13-107714-7*) P-H.

Business Statistics: A Problem-Solving Approach. Herbert F. Spirer. LC 74-31598. (Irwin Series in Quantitative Analysis for Business). 400p. reprint ed. pap. 114.00 (*0-8357-7501-1*, 2055675) Bks Demand.

Business Statistics: An Introductory Course. Ken Black. Ed. by Leyh. 654p. (C). 1992. text ed. 61.00 (*0-314-92219-9*) West Pub.

Business Statistics: Basic Concepts & Methodology. 4th ed. Wayne W. Daniel & James C. Terrell. 800p. 1986. disk write for info. (*0-318-60186-9*) HM.

Business Statistics: Basic Concepts & Methodology. 5th ed. Wayne W. Daniel & James C. Terrell. 1988. Incl. solns. manual & study guide. teacher ed write for info. (*0-318-63306-X*); student ed 16.76 (*0-318-36888-9*) HM.

Business Statistics: Contemporary Decision Making. Ken Black. Ed. by Leyh. LC 93-34134. 1000p. (C). 1993. text ed. 65.25 (*0-314-02474-3*) West Pub.

Business Statistics: Elements & Application. Mario J. Picconi et al. (C). 1992. 12.50 (*0-06-500723-9*); 12.50 (*0-06-500724-7*) HarpCollege.

Business Statistics: Elements & Application. Mario J. Picconi et al. (C). 1992. student ed 25.00 (*0-06-500175-3*) HarpCollege.

Business Statistics: Elements & Application, Minitab Manual IBM. Mario J. Picconi et al. (C). 1992. 21.00 (*0-06-501667-X*) HarpCollege.

Business Statistics: Elements & Applications. Mario J. Picconi et al. LC 92-16383. (C). 1993. text ed. 70.50 (*0-06-500174-5*) HarpCollege.

Business Statistics: Fundamentals & Applications. Moshe Ben-Horim & Haim Levy. Ed. by Paul S. Donnelly. LC 82-15060. (Random House Business Division Ser.). 564p. (C). 1982. text ed. 39.50 (*0-394-33022-6*) Random.

Business Statistics: Nineteen Sixty-One to Nineteen Eighty-Eight. 328p. 1990. per., pap. 16.00 (*0-16-019795-3*, S/N 003-010-001) USGPO.

Business Statistics: Text, Cases & Software. Owen P. Hall, Jr. & Harvey E. Adelman. 768p. (C). 1991. text ed. 73.95 (*0-256-06089-4*, 10-2510-01) Irwin.

Business Statistics: The Essentials. suppl. ed. David F. Groebner & Patrick W. Shannon. 576p. (C). 1987. write for info. (*0-318-61565-7*, Merrill Pub Co) Macmillan.

***Business Statistics by Example.** 5th ed. Sincich. 1995. text ed., disk 74.00 (*0-02-410441-8*) P-H.

Business Statistics for Quality & Productivity. David M. Levine et al. LC 94-16360. 1994. write for info. (*0-13-841719-9*) P-H.

Business Statistics TA. Harper. 1996. write for info. (*0-8016-6830-1*) Mosby Yr Bk.

Business Statistics TB. Harper. 1996. write for info. (*0-8016-6826-3*) Mosby Yr Bk.

Business Statistics with Computer Applications. Archie W. Earl, Sr. (Probability & Statistics Ser.). 580p. 1994. pap. text ed. 47.95 (*1-884169-03-1*) Intl Educ Improve.

Business Statistics with Computer Applications. Archie W. Earl, Sr. (Probability & Statistics Ser.). 580p. 1995. lib. bdg. 62.95 (*1-884169-02-3*) Intl Educ Improve.

An Asterisk (*) at the beginning of an entry indicates that the title is appearing in BIP for the first time. 967

Business Statistics, 1986. 25th ed. (Illus.). 264p. 1987. pap. 16.00 (0-16-000379-2, S/N 003-010-00181-0) USGPO.

Business Step Savers see Business

Business Stories - Business Savvy: How to Compile & Publish Your Business History. Cynthia B. Chapman. (Orig.). 1992. pap. 15.00 (1-881611-02-7) Authors & Editors.

Business Strategies for a Caring Profession: A Practitioner's Guidebook. APA Practice Directorate Staff. LC 94-13771. 170p. 1994. 24.95 (1-55798-254-6) Am Psychol.

Business Strategies for the Ex-U. S. S. R. Guide. Igor Tsigelny. 250p. 1993. 39.95 (0-9636817-0-2); pap. 29.95 (0-9636817-1-0) Intl Univ Line.

Business Strategies for Tough Times. reprint ed. 9.95 (0-685-71682-1, 807) Inst Real Estate.

Business Strategy. 2nd ed. John Grieve-Smith. (Illus.). (C). 1991. pap. text ed. 21.95 (0-631-17738-8) Blackwell Pubs.

Business Strategy & Ethnic Identity. Knut Opsal. (Bergen Studies in Social Anthropology: No. 44). 127p. (Orig.). 1989. pap. text ed. 13.95 (0-936508-73-6) Barber Pr.

Business Strategy & Information Technology. Ed. by Ewan Sutherland & Yves Morieux. 240p. (C). 1991. text ed. 74.00 (0-415-04336-0, A5334) Routledge.

Business Strategy & Planning: A Strategic Management Approach. A. R. Morden. LC 92-40088. 1993. write for info. (0-07-707718-0) McGraw.

Business Strategy & Policy. 3rd ed. Garry Smith et al. (C). 1991. write for info. (0-395-43367-3); boxed write for info. (0-395-56735-1) HM Soft Schl Col Div.

Business Strategy & Public Policy: Perspectives from Industry & Academia. Ed. by Alfred A. Marcus et al. LC 86-30388. 334p. 1987. text ed. 75.00 (0-89930-172-X, MBS/, Quorum Bks) Greenwood.

Business Strategy & Retailing. Ed. by Gerry Johnson. LC 86-23404. 300p. 1987. text ed. 93.50 (0-471-91337-5) Wiley.

*Business Strategy & Security Analysis: The Key to Long Term Investment Profits. Raymond K. Suutari. 320p. 1995. 70.00 (0-7863-0409-X) Irwin Prof Pubng.

*Business Strategy for Sustainable Development: Leadership & Accountability for the 90's. (Illus.). 127p. (Orig.). (C). 1994. pap. text ed. 75.00x (0-7881-1048-9) Diane Pub.

Business Strategy for the Political Arena. Frank Shipper & Marianne M. Jennings. LC 83-13838. (Illus.). xx, 177p. 1984. text ed. 49.95 (0-89930-037-5, JPO/, Quorum Bks) Greenwood.

Business Strategy Game - A Global Industry Simulation, Player's Manual. 6th ed. Arthur A. Thompson, Jr. & Gregory J. Stappenbeck. 144p. (C). 1992. pap. text ed. 24.50 (0-256-09724-0, 21-1284-42); pap. text ed. 25.95 (0-256-09723-2, 31-1284-42) Irwin.

*Business Strategy Handbook 1995. (Illus.). 300p. (Orig.). 1994. pap. 295.00 (0-7605-0633-7) Rector Pr.

Business Strategy in Practice. Bengt Karlof. 1987. text ed. 61.95 (0-471-91620-X) Wiley.

Business Student's Guide to Course Assignments. 2nd ed. Norma Carr-Ruffino. LC 90-80849. (Illus.). 425p. (C). 1991. pap. text ed. 15.95 (0-9625889-0-3) Carlyle Pr.

Business Studies. Alan Hosking. 318p. (C). 1990. pap. 44.00 (1-85352-572-3, Pub. by HLT Pubns UK) St Mut.

Business Studies. Alan Hoskins. 318p. (C). 1990. pap. 44.00 (1-85352-530-8, Pub. by HLT Pubns UK) St Mut.

*Business Studies. 2nd ed. Robert Dransfield & David Needham. LC 94-21705. 1994. write for info. (0-07-707954-X) McGraw.

*Business Studies: 1500 Questions & Answers for Tutorial Teaching, Self Study & Revision. Christopher Sivewright. 128p. 1995. pap. 9.95 (1-898563-07-1, Pub. by Albion Pubng UK) Paul & Co Pubs.

Business Studies "A" Level Workbook. David Needham & Robert Dransfield. LC 92-43624. 1993. 10.99 (0-07-707607-9) McGraw.

*Business Success from Seizing the Environmental Initiative. Christine Hemming. (Business & the Environment Practitioner Ser.). (C). 1994. 150.00x (0-946655-93-6, Pub. by S Thornes Pubs UK) St Mut.

Business Success in Mental Health Practice: Modern Marketing, Management, & Legal Strategies. Robert H. Woody. LC 89-11046. (Social & Behavioral Sciences Ser.). 244p. 1989. 32.95x (1-55542-168-7) Jossey-Bass.

Business Success in the Countryside. HMSO Staff. 56p. 1992. pap. 19.00 (0-11-752663-0, HM26630, Pub. by HMSO UK) UNIPUB.

Business Success Skills. Jim Rohrbach. 100p. (Orig.). 1994. pap. 19.95 (0-9627754-1-X) J M Rohrbach.

Business Success Start-up Kit, 8 bklts., Set. Laurence J. Pino. 1990. 99.95 (1-56354-000-2) Open U FL.

Business Supply Topics see Business

Business Systems: The Fabric of Management. Richard C. Anderson. LC 73-17244. (Illus.). 124p. 7.95 (0-913842-06-0) Correlan Pubns.

Business Systems Analysis & Design. William S. Davis. 534p. 1994. text ed. 48.95 (0-534-18954-7) Boyd & Fraser.

Business Systems Design. Bartow K. Hodge & James P. Clements. LC 85-8216. (C). 1986. teacher ed write for info. (0-8359-0520-9, Reston) P-H.

Business Systems Development Process: A Management Perspective. Roger E. Walters. LC 86-20483. 175p. 1987. text ed. 49.95 (0-89930-125-8, WSY/, Quorum Bks) Greenwood.

*Business Systems Engineering: Managing Breakthrough Changes for Productivity & Profit. Gregory H. Watson. LC 94-32752. 1994. text ed. 29.95 (0-471-01884-8) Wiley.

Business Systems in East Asia: Firms, Markets & Societies. Richard Whitley. 288p. 1993. 45.00 (0-685-75076-0) Sage.

Business Systems in East Asia: Firms, Markets & Societies. Richard Whitley. 288p. 1994. pap. 21.94 (0-685-75077-9) Sage.

Business Taiwan: A Practical Guide to Understanding Taiwan's Business Culture. Peggy Kenna & Sondra Lacy. LC 93-42810. 1994. 5.95 (0-8442-3553-9, NTC Busn Bks) NTC Pub Grp.

Business Taxation. 4th ed. Neil Stein. 440p. 1991. pap. 37.95 (0-7506-0515-4) Buttrwrth-Heinemann.

*Business Taxation on the European Union. Gloria Teixeira. 1995. 235.00 (0-471-95157-9) Wiley.

Business Technology for Managers: An Office Automation Handbook. Neil Perlin. LC 85-223. (Professional Librarian Ser.). 206p. 1986. pap. 24.95 (0-86729-123-0, Hall Reference) Macmillan.

Business Telcommunications see Telecommunications for Managers

Business Telecommunications. Edward Roche. 512p. (C). 1991. text ed. 51.00 (0-03-032914-0) Dryden Pr.

Business Telecommunications. 2nd ed. Stanford H. Rowe. 688p. (C). 1991. write for info. (0-02-404104-1) Macmillan.

*Business Telephone Number & Addresses U. S. A. (Illus.). 240p. (Orig.). 1994. pap. 195.00 (0-7605-0959-X) Rector Pr.

Business Television Directory, 1991. Warren Publishing, Inc. Staff. Ed. by Susan Irwin. 300p. 1990. write for info. (0-911486-59-3) Warren Pub Inc.

Business Television Directory, 1992. 4th rev. ed. Warren Publishing, Inc. Staff. Ed. by Susan Irwin. 236p. 1992. write for info. (0-911486-63-1) Warren Pub Inc.

Business Theatre: Skits & Plays for Meetings, Conferences, Schools, Etc. Lamp Light Press Staff. 70p. 1993. ring bd. 19.95 (0-917593-32-4, Lamp Light Pr) Prosperity & Profits.

Business Theory for Secretaries. Wilford J. Eiteman. 1968. 6.95 (0-912164-04-2) Masterco Pr.

Business Thinking in Not-for-Profit Organizations. Walraven. 39.00 (0-8342-0424-X) Aspen Pub.

Business Through the Eyes of Faith. Richard C. Chewning et al. 1989. write for info. (0-318-64590-4) Harper SF.

Business Thru the Eyes of Faith. Chewning. 1990. pap. text ed. 11.00 (0-06-061350-5, PL) HarpC.

Business-to-Business Advertising: A Marketing Management Approach. Charles H. Patti et al. LC 90-47970. (Illus.). 320p. 1991. 39.95 (0-8442-3471-0, NTC Busn Bks) NTC Pub Grp.

Business-to-Business Communications Handbook. Fred Messner. 1991. 59.95 (1-56318-001-4) Assn Natl Advertisers.

Business-to-Business Direct Marketing. 2nd ed. Bernie Goldberg & Tracy Emerick. (Illus.). 490p. 1991. 79.00 (1-879644-00-2) Direct Mktg.

Business to Business Direct Marketing: Proven Direct Response Methods to Generate More Leads & Sales. Robert Bly. 220p. 1993. 39.95 (0-8442-3472-9, NTC Busn Bks) NTC Pub Grp.

Business to Business in German. Charles Berlitz. 208p. (Orig.). (GER.). 1994. pap. 10.95 (0-399-51832-0, Perigree Bks) Berkley Pub.

Business to Business in Russian. Charles Berlitz. 224p. (Orig.). (RUS.). 1994. pap. 12.95 (0-399-51831-2, Perigree Bks) Berkley Pub.

Business-to-Business Market Research: Identifying, Qualifying & Understanding Your Customers. Martin P. Block & Tamara S. Block. 1994. 37.50 (1-55738-559-9) Probus Pub Co.

*Business to Business Marketing. Daragh O'Reilly & Julian Gibas. (Pitman Marketing Ser.). 250p. 1995. pap. 47.50 (0-273-61692-7, Pub. by Pitman Pub Ltd UK) Trans-Atl Phila.

Business to Business Marketing Management. Frank Bingham. 744p. (C). 1989. text ed. 61.95 (0-256-07975-7) Irwin.

Business to Business Negotiation. George Holmes et al. 120p. 1991. 30.95 (0-7506-0300-3) Buttrwrth-Heinemann.

Business Today. 5th ed. David J. Rachman. 1986. 14.95 (0-685-25735-5) McGraw.

Business Today. 7th ed. David J. Rachman et al. LC 92-17433. 1992. 43.95 (0-685-59721-0) McGraw.

*Business Tool: A Business Start-up & Reference Guide. Raymond Lopez & Miriam E. Aguilar. (Illus.). 221p. (Orig.). 1994. pap. 42.00 (0-9643887-3-1) West Comm Tech.

*Business Tool: A Business Start-up & Reference Guide. Raymond Lopez & Miriam E. Aguilar. (Illus.). 246p. (Orig.). 1994. pap. 21.00 (0-9643887-1-5) West Comm Tech.

*Business Tort of Fraud & Misrepresentation. Warren Freedman. 660p. 1994. ring bd. 180.00 (0-614-05981-X) Michie Butterworth.

Business Tort of Fraud & Misrepresentation, 1989-1991, 2 vols. suppl. ed. Warren Freedman. 660p. 1991. Latest suppl. 12/91. 70.00 (0-88063-763-3) Butterworth Legal Pubs.

Business Tort of Fraud & Misrepresentation, 1989-1991, 2 vols., Set. Warren Freedman. 660p. 1991. ring bd. 180.00 (0-88063-251-8) Butterworth Legal Pubs.

Business Torts, 4 vols. Joseph D. Zamore. 1989. Updates available. ring bd. write for info. (0-8205-1143-9) Bender.

Business Torts & Competitor Litigation. Richard A. Givens. 1989. text ed. 95.00 (0-07-172135-5) Shepards-McGraw.

Business Training & Technical Assistance Providers in New York City. Coy M. La Sister. 41p. 1985. pap. text ed. 4.75 (0-88156-070-7) Comm Serv Soc NY.

Business Transaction Forms. 3rd rev. ed. Stuart J. Faber. 300p. 1986. pap. text ed. 38.50 (0-318-40133-9) Lega Bks.

Business Transactions in Germany, 4 vols. Bernard Ruster & Volker Bringezu. (Illus.). 1983. Updates available. ring bd. write for info. (0-8205-1394-6) Bender.

Business Transactions Law. 3rd ed. R. Sharrock. 499p. 1992. pap. 45.00 (0-7021-2921-6, Pub. by Juta SA) W W Gaunt.

Business Transfers & Employee Rights. 2nd ed. John McMullen. 1992. 90.00 (0-406-00084-0, U.K.) Butterworth Legal Pubs.

Business Travel. Rob Davidson. 256p. (Orig.). 1994. pap. 42.50 (0-273-60415-5, Pub. by Pitman Pub Ltd UK) Trans-Atl Phila.

Business Travel Guide To Europe. Berlitz Editors. (Pocket Guides Ser.). (Illus.). 384p. 1994. pap. 8.95 (2-8315-2480-6) Berlitz.

*Business Travel Policies & Costs. 350p. (Orig.). 1994. pap. text ed. 995.00 (0-7605-0907-7) Rector Pr.

Business Travel Survival Guide. Jack Cummings. 396p. 1991. pap. text ed. 14.95 (0-471-53075-1) Wiley.

Business Traveler's Atlas. Chris Miles. (Illus.). 208p. 1992. pap. 12.95 (0-13-095217-6, H M Gousha) P-H Gen Ref & Trav.

Business Traveler's Guide to Good Health on the Road: The Nation's Leading Health, Travel, & Business Experts Tell How to Maximize Your Health While Traveling. Ed. by Karl Neumann & Maury Rosenbaum. 212p. 1994. pap. 12.95 (1-56561-036-9, 004233) Chronimed.

*Business Traveler's Road Atlas, 1996. Rand McNally Staff. 216p. 1995. ring bd. 9.95 (0-528-81480-X) Rand McNally.

*Business Trust. Ted DeLong. 86p. 1995. 25.00 (1-885661-08-8) Estate Protection.

Business Typing. Speedwriting Institute Staff. 1976. pap. 5.95 (0-671-18137-8, Arco Test) P-H Gen Ref & Trav.

*Business U. S. A. Directory of Addresses & Telephone Geographic Edition 1995. 1000p. (Orig.). 1995. pap. 295.00 (0-7605-1616-2) Rector Pr.

*Business U. S. A. Directory of Addresses & Telephones 1995. 1800p. (Orig.). 1995. pap. 295.00 (0-7605-1615-4) Rector Pr.

Business under the Balls: How to Be a Successful Pawnbroker. 4th ed. P. Taylor Fletcher. (Illus.). 267p. 1993. 89.95 (1-883103-01-0) United NC.

Business Unit & Divisional Performance Measurement. Mahmoud Ezzamel. (Advanced Management Accounting & Finance Ser.). (Illus.). 152p. 1992. pap. text ed. 19.95 (0-12-245670-X) Acad Pr.

Business United Kingdom: A Practical Guide to Understanding British Business Culture. Peggy Kenna & Sondra Lacy. LC 94-17745. (Orig.). 1995. pap. 5.95 (0-8442-3560-1, NTC Busn Bks) NTC Pub Grp.

*Business User's Guide to the Internet. Sam Sternberg. (Computer Science Ser.). 350p. 1995. pap. 34.95 (0-442-01937-8) Van Nos Reinhold.

Business Uses of the Freedom of Information Act, No. 14. 2nd ed. Thomas C. Papson & Charlotte D. Young. (Corporate Practice Ser.). 1991. ring bd. 95.00 (1-55871-231-3) BNA.

Business Valuation Handbook. Glenn M. Desmond & Richard E. Kelley. 322p. 1988. 54.50 (0-930458-03-6) Valuation.

Business Valuation Handbook. rev. ed. Glenn M. Desmond et al. 322p. 1988. 49.50 (0-930458-02-8) Appraisal Inst.

Business Valuation Manual: An Understandable, Step-by-Step Guide to Finding the Value of a Business. rev. ed. Thomas W. Horn. LC 89-903. (Illus.). 233p. 1990. 29.95 (0-87521-015-5) Charter Oak Pr.

*Business Valuation Practice. Lloyd Callard & William J. Pallot. 420p. 1994. pap. 75.00 (0-455-21213-9, Pub. by Law Bk Co) W W Gaunt.

Business Valuations for Lawyers. Andrew J. Duncan & Raymond E. McKay, Jr. 1991. 75.00 (0-943856-34-5, 455) SC Bar CLE.

Business Value of Computers: An Executive's Guide. Paul A. Strassmann. (Illus.). 530p. 1990. 49.00 (0-9620413-2-7) Info Econ Pr.

Business Ventures for Physicians. Lee S. Kolczun et al. 208p. 1989. 45.00 (0-87489-479-4) Med Economics.

Business Ventures in Eastern Europe & Russia, 2 vols. 2nd ed. David E. Birenbaum. 1526p. 1993. ring bd. 185.00 (0-13-291394-1) Aspen Law.

*Business Ventures in the Former Soviet Union: Negotiation & Protocol, Do's & Don'ts. Joseph A. Kliger. LC 94-70713. 1994. write for info. (0-87814-428-5) PennWell Bks.

*Business Week Guide: Small Business Trends & Entrepreneurship Are Reshaping the Economy. Business Week Editors. 1995. pap. text ed. 12.95 (0-07-009424-1) McGraw.

Business Week Guide: The Quality Imperative. Business Week Editors. 1994. pap. text ed. 12.95 (0-07-009345-8) McGraw.

*Business Week Guide to the Information Highway: Strategies & Solutions. Lindstrom. 1995. pap. text ed. 21.95 (0-07-882124-X) Osborne-McGraw.

Business Week Readings in Strategic Management: Strategy Formulation & Implementation. 2nd ed. John A. Pearce, II & Richard B. Robinson, Jr. 1988. pap. write for info. (0-318-62544-X) McGraw.

Business Weeks Guide to Global Investments Using Electronic Tools. Robert Schwabach. 1994. disk, pap. text ed. 39.95 (0-07-882055-3) Osborne-McGraw.

Business Weeks Guide to Multimedia Presentations. Glenn Collyer. 1994. cd-rom, pap. text ed. 34.95 (0-07-882057-X) Osborne-McGraw.

Business Week's Guide to Mutual Funds. 4th ed. Jeffrey M. Laderman. 1994. pap. text ed. 14.95 (0-07-035961-X) McGraw.

Business Week's Guide to Mutual Funds. 4th ed. Jeffrey M. Laderman. 1994. text ed. 24.95 (0-07-035960-1) McGraw.

*Business Week's Guide to Mutual Funds. 5th ed. Laderman. 1995. pap. text ed. 14.94 (0-07-035216-X) McGraw.

*Business Week's Guide to Mutual Funds. 5th ed. Laderman. 1995. 24.95 (0-07-035215-1) McGraw.

Business Week's Guide to the Best Business Schools. 3rd ed. John A. Byrne. 1993. text ed. 24.95 (0-07-009336-9); pap. text ed. 14.95 (0-07-009337-7) McGraw.

*Business Week's Guide to the Best Business Schools. 4th ed. Ed. by John A. Byrne et al. LC 94-41147. 1995. pap. text ed. 14.95 (0-07-009422-5) McGraw.

Business Week's Guide to the Best Executive Education Programs. Cynthia Greene. 1992. pap. text ed. 14.95 (0-07-009335-0) McGraw.

Business Within Europe. Anthony Scott. 1994. pap. 37.50 (0-273-60475-9, Pub. by Pitman Pub Ltd UK) Trans-Atl Phila.

Business Without Bosses: How Self-Managing Teams are Building High Performance Companies. Charles C. Manz & Henry P. Sims, Jr. LC 93-7864. 256p. 1993. text ed. 24.95 (0-471-57700-6) Wiley.

Business Workout Strategies: Tax & Legal Aspects. Lewis D. Solomon & Lewis J. Saret. LC 92-15947. (Business Practice Library). 376p. 1992. text ed. 138.00 (0-471-55872-9) Wiley.

Business Workouts Manual. 2nd ed. Donald L. Rome et al. (Bankruptcy Law Ser.). 736p. 1992. 130.00 (0-7913-1014-0) Warren Gorham & Lamont.

Business Workouts Manual. 2nd suppl. ed. Donald L. Rome et al. (Bankruptcy Law Ser.). 736p. 1992. Supplemented annually, write for info. 50.00 (0-685-56392-8) Warren Gorham & Lamont.

Business Worksheets for Lotus 1-2-3. Jack Grushcow. (Illus.). 1986. 18.95 (0-8359-0547-0, Reston); Diskette. disk 49.00 (0-685-08098-6, Reston) P-H.

Business World. Roger Speegle & William B. Giesecke. (Illus.). (Orig.). (C). 1983. pap. text ed. 12.95 (0-19-434109-7) OUP.

Business Writer's Handbook. 3rd ed. Charles T. Brusaw et al. LC 86-60634. 832p. (C). 1987. 19.95 (0-312-00571-7) St Martin.

Business Writer's Handbook. 4th ed. Charles T. Brusaw et al. LC 92-50042. (Illus.). 784p. (C). 1992. pap. text ed. 17.00 (0-312-05734-2) St Martin.

Business Writer's Handbook. 4th rev. ed. Charles T. Brusaw et al. LC 92-36034. 1993. 24.95 (0-312-08715-2) St Martin.

Business Writer's Quick Reference Guide. Shipley Associates. LC 85-29533. 319p. 1986. pap. text ed. 60.00 (0-471-84541-8) Wiley.

Business Writing: Cases & Problems. Daphne Jameson et al. 200p. (Orig.). (C). 1987. pap. text ed. 9.60 (0-87563-308-0) Stipes.

Business Writing: Integrating Process & Purpose. 5th ed. Rosemary T. Fruehling & Sharon Bouchard. 288p. 1993. teacher ed 8.00 (1-56118-499-3); pap. text ed. 16.95 (1-56118-498-5) Paradigm MN.

Business Writing: Process & Forms. Richard P. Batteiger. 467p. (C). 1985. pap. 38.95 (0-534-04620-7) Intl Thomson.

Business Writing: Strategies & Samples. Jeanne W. Halpern et al. 608p. (C). 1987. pap. write for info. (0-02-349310-0) Macmillan.

Business Writing - What Works, What Won't: Proven Techniques for Writing Business Memos, Letters, Reports & Copy That Gets Results. Wilma Davidson. (Illus.). 288p. (Orig.). 1994. pap. 13.95 (0-312-10948-2) St Martin.

Business Writing, a Gregg Text-Kit in Adult Education. Jeanne Reed & R. Finch. 1970. text ed. 24.75 (0-07-051480-1) McGraw.

*Business Writing at Its Best. Minerva Neiditz. 240p. (C). 1993. text ed. 22.95 (0-256-14855-4) Irwin.

Business Writing at Its Best. Minerva H. Neiditz. 288p. 1993. text ed. 20.00 (0-7863-0137-6) Irwin Prof Pubng.

Business Writing at Work. Eleanor J. Davidson. LC 93-29856. 272p. (C). 1993. 28.50 (0-256-14220-3) Irwin Prof Pubng.

Business Writing Essentials. Michael H. Markel. LC 87-60507. 224p. (C). 1987. pap. text ed. 13.00 (0-312-00737-X); Instr's. manual. teacher ed write for info. (0-318-62508-3); Instr's. ed. teacher ed write for info. (0-318-62509-1) St Martin.

Business Writing for Adults. Jack Little. 137p. 1983. pap. 5.00 (0-934768-02-1) Altair Pr.

Business Writing Handbook. William C. Paxson. 288p. 1984. mass mkt. 5.99 (0-553-27041-9, Bantam Classics) Bantam.

Business Writing Made Easy: An Executive Study Guide. James E. Vincler & Nancy H. Vincler. 220p. (Orig.). 1985. pap. text ed. 19.95 (0-911395-00-8) Persuasive.

Business Writing Made Simple: A Manager's Handbook. Ed. by Stephen D. Bruce. 1986. pap. 24.95 (1-55645-421-X) Busn Legal Reports.

Business Writing Quick & Easy. 2nd ed. Laura Brill. LC 89-45447. 256p. 1989. 16.95 (0-8144-5979-X) AMACOM.

Business Writing Style Book. John S. Fielden & Jean D. Fielden. 152p. 1986. 6.95 (0-13-108290-6, Busn) P-H.

Business Writing the Modular Way. Harley Bjelland. 300p. 1991. 26.95 (0-8144-5034-2, 040545) AMACOM.

*Business Writing the Modular Way: How to Research, Organize & Compose Effective Memos, Letters, Articles, Reports, Proposals, Manuals, Specifications & Books. fac. ed. Harley Bjelland. LC 91-53049. (Illus.). 283p. 1992. pap. 80.70 (0-7837-8358-2, 2049148) Bks Demand.

Business Writing with Style: Strategies for Success. John Tarrant. 1991. text ed. 37.50 (0-471-53211-8); pap. text ed. 10.95 (0-471-53212-6) Wiley.

B

An Asterisk (*) at the beginning of an entry indicates that the title is appearing in BIP for the first time.

B

An Asterisk (*) at the beginning of an entry indicates that the title is appearing in BIP for the first time.

969

Busy Year. Leo Lionni. LC 91-29149. (Illus.). 36p. (J). (ps-2). 1992. 7.99 (*0-679-82464-2*); lib. bdg. 10.99 (*0-679-92464-7*) Knopf Bks Yng Read.

Busy Year. Leo Lionni. 1992. pap. 10.99 (*0-685-52501-5*) McKay.

Busybody Brandy. Jessie Haas. LC 93-29569. (Illus.). 24p. (J). 1994. 14.00 (*0-688-12792-4*); lib. bdg. 13.93 (*0-688-12793-2*) Greenwillow.

Busybody Nora. Johanna Hurwitz. (Illus.). 64p. (J). (gr. 2-5). 1991. pap. 3.99 (*0-14-034592-2*, Puffin) Puffin Bks.

Busybody Nora. Johanna Hurwitz. LC 89-13649. (Illus.). 64p. (J). (ps up). 1990. reprint ed. 12.95 (*0-688-09092-3*); reprint ed. lib. bdg. 12.88 (*0-688-09093-1*) Morrow Jr Bks.

Busybody Nora: A Study Guide. Joyce Friedland & Rikki Kessler. (Novel-Ties Ser.). (J). (gr. 2-4). 1982. student ed, teacher ed 15.95 (*0-88122-002-7*) Lrn Links.

But - He Was Good to His Mother: The Lives & Crimes of Jewish Gangsters. Robert A. Rockaway. (Illus.). 272p. 1993. 24.95 (*0-317-05837-1*, Pub. by Gefen Pub Hse IS) Gefen Bks.

***But - He Was Good to His Mother: The Lives & Times of Jewish Gangsters.** Robert A. Rockaway. (Illus.). 272p. (Orig.). 1994. pap. 8.95 (*965-229-092-0*) Gefen Bks.

But a Brown Bird Sang. Evelyn Copeland. 1993. 16.95 (*0-533-10562-5*) Vantage.

But Also Good Business: Texas Commerce Banks & the Financing of Houston & Texas, 1886-1986. Walter L. Buenger & Joseph A. Pratt. LC 86-40215. (Illus.). 468p. 1986. 32.50 (*0-89096-280-4*) Tex A&M Univ Pr.

***But Beautiful: A Book about Jazz.** Geoff Dyer. 205p. Date not set. 21.00 (*0-86547-490-7*) FS&G.

***But Can the Phoenix Sing?** Christa Laird. LC 94-28422. (YA). (gr. 7 up). 1995. 15.00 (*0-688-13612-5*) Greenwillow.

But, Daddy, Did You See Shoshoni? Pebbles, Rocks, & Steppingstones. Joseph P. Murphy. 256p. 1991. pap. 17.95 (*0-9631361-0-0*) An Tostal Pr.

But Do They Have Field Experience! Ed. by Elayne Clift. (Illus.). x, 165p. (Orig.). 1993. pap. 14.95 (*0-9634827-0-X*, Kumarian Pr) OGN Pubns.

But Doctor, What Should I Eat? Isadore Rosenfeld. LC 94-8942. 1994. 25.00 (*0-679-42818-6*) Random.

But Enough About You. Cynthia Heimel. 256p. 1986. 11.95 (*0-685-16661-9*) S&S Trade.

But Everybody Does It: Peer Pressure. Mary B. Christian. LC 85-17112. (Christian Reader Ser.). (Illus.). 72p. (Orig.). (J). (gr. 4-7). 1986. pap. 3.99 (*0-570-03636-4*, 39-1098) Concordia.

But Everyone Else Looks So Sure of Themselves: A Guide to Surviving the Teen Years. Denise V. Lang. LC 90-39087. (Illus.). 160p. (Orig.). (YA). (gr. 7 up). 1991. pap. 9.95 (*1-55870-177-X*) Shoe Tree Pr.

But for the Grace of God. Peter G. Cranford. (Illus.). 200p. 1982. pap. 8.95 (*0-9605822-1-5*) Great Pyramid.

But for the Grace of God.... Martin. (Orig.). 1984. pap. 1.00 (*0-914733-02-8*) Desert Min.

But for the Lovers. Wilfrido D. Nolledo. LC 94-9184. 325p. 1994. reprint ed. pap. 12.95 (*1-56478-067-8*) Dalkey Arch.

But Gentlemen Marry Brunettes. Anita Loos. 96p. 1994. 7.95 (*0-14-018488-0*, Penguin Classics) Viking Penguin.

***But God Remembered: Stories of Women from Creation to the Promised Land.** Sandy E. Sasso. LC 94-18262. (Illus.). 32p. (J). (gr. k-5). 1995. 16.95 (*1-879045-43-5*) Jewish Lights.

But Gosh Honey, There's a Possum in the John! And Other Humorous Incidents Retold in Verse & Song. Vada L. Jones. LC 91-72942. (Illus.). 96p. (Orig.). 1991. pap. 7.50 (*0-944104-01-0*) Calico Paws. RECEIVED NATIONAL RECOGNITION FOR EXCELLENCE AT ANNUAL BOOK AWARDS CEREMONY SPONSORED BY THE NATIONAL ASSOCIATION OF INDEPENDENT PUBLISHERS. Thirty-seven rhymed & metered illustrated verses full of hilarious fun & unusual insight. "G" rated humor all members of the family will enjoy. Title poem is based on the author's surprise encounter with a possum in the master bathroom of her home. "Each page is a delight...honest & tuneful, reveling in the small thrill of everyday wonder. A great poem, He's Not A Pretty Monster, But He's Ours! begins, There's a spoon-bending monster/ Who lives at our place,/ Existing among us,/ Occupying no space... Before you take yourself too seriously...Jones has something whimsical that will break a mood or lighten a load."--THE BOOK READER. "...light, bouncy...hilarious... poetry..."--VELMA DANIELS, WINTER HAVEN NEWS CHIEF. "Jones uses simple rhymes & metaphors in her short, rhythmic verses: I like a fresh & gentle rain/ That stops awhile, then starts again./ Flowers bounce on a nimble stem,/ And laugh when raindrops tickle them."--K.K.

ZULEGER, BEST OF TIMES. ***Publisher Provided Annotation.***

But Granny Did! Margaret Wild. LC 92-31906. (Voyages Ser.). (Illus.). (J). 1993. 3.75 (*0-383-03559-7*) SRA Schl Grp.

***But I Am a Black Cartoonist.** John Slade. 112p. 1995. per., pap. text ed. 14.95 (*0-7872-1052-8*) Kendall-Hunt.

But I Can't Eat That: Kitchen Tested Recipes for People with Multiple Allergies. Heidi Passow. (Illus.). 240p. 1993. pap. 19.99 (*0-9637260-9-9*) Dragon Express.

But I Didn't Want a Divorce. Andre Bustanoby. 1978. pap. 8.99 (*0-310-22171-4*, 9207P) Zondervan.

But I Digress: The Exploitation of Parentheses in English Printed Verse. John Lennard. (Illus.). 344p. 1992. 69.00 (*0-19-811247-5*) OUP.

***But I Don't Want to Cook!Book: Do-Able Dishes for the "Who, Me??" Cook.** Dottie Haynes. (Illus.). 274p. (Orig.). 1994. pap. 19.95 (*0-9641312-1-8*) Goldberry Pubng.

But I Love Fruits. Georges Ohsawa & Jacques De Langre. (Illus.). 1993. pap. 4.50 (*0-916508-32-3*) Happiness Pr.

But I Never Thought He'd Die: Practical Help for Widows. Miriam B. Nye. LC 78-9644. 150p. 1978. pap. 9.99 (*0-664-24208-1*, Westminster) Westminster John Knox.

But I Played It Perfectly in the Practice Room. Charlotte S. Whitaker & Donald R. Tanner. 82p. (Orig.). (C). 1987. pap. text ed. 21.00 (*0-8191-5702-3*) U Pr of Amer.

But "I" Say unto You. John G. Reisinger. 112p. (Orig.). 1989. pap. write for info. (*0-925703-04-4*) Crown MA.

But I Thought You Really Loved Me. Evelyn W. Minshull. LC 76-14992. 150p. (YA). (gr. 7 up). 1976. 8.00 (*0-664-32600-5*, Westminster) Westminster John Knox.

But I Won't Go Out in a Boat: A Collection of Poems. Sharon Chmielarz. 1991. pap. 6.00 (*0-89823-119-1*) New Rivers Pr.

But I Wouldn't Want to Die There. Nancy Pickard. Ed. by Linda Marrow. 256p. 1994. reprint ed. mass mkt. 5.50 (*0-671-72331-6*, Pocket Star Bks) PB.

But I Wouldn't Want to Die There: A Jenny Cain Mystery. large type ed. Nancy Pickard. LC 93-33294. 1993. 19.95 (*0-7862-0080-4*) Thorndike Pr.

But I Wouldn't Want to Live There. Michael Cader. LC 93-83913. (Illus.). 160p. 1993. 12.95 (*1-56138-280-9*) Running Pr.

But I'll Be Back Again. Cynthia Rylant. LC 93-16188. (Illus.). 80p. (YA). (gr. 7 up). 1993. pap. 4.95 (*0-688-12653-7*, Pub. by Beech Tree Bks) Morrow.

But I'll Be Back Again: An Album. Cynthia Rylant. LC 88-17860. (Illus.). 80p. (J). (gr. 5-7). 1989. 15.95 (*0-531-05806-9*); lib. bdg. 15.99 (*0-531-08406-X*) Orchard Bks Watts.

But, I'm Different: Third Grade Student Book see Philosophy for Young Thinkers Program

But Is It Art? The Spirit of Art as Activism. Ed. by Nina Felshin. LC 94-36846. (Illus.). 416p. (Orig.). 1995. pap. 18.95 (*0-941920-29-1*) Bay Pr.

But Is It Art? The Value of Art & the Temptation of Theory. B. R. Tilghman. (Modern Revivals in Philosophy Ser.). 206p. 1994. 51.95 (*0-7512-0293-2*, Pub. by Gregg Revivals UK) Ashgate Pub Co.

But Is It Science? The Philosophical Question in the Evolution-Creation Controversy. Ed. by Michael Ruse. LC 87-35818. (Frontiers of Philosophy Ser.). (Illus.). 375p. 1988. 29.95x (*0-87975-439-7*) Prometheus Bks.

***But Is It True? A Citizen's Guide to Environmental Health & Safety Issues.** Aaron Wildavsky. (Illus.). 704p. 1995. text ed. 35.00x (*0-674-08922-7*, WILBUT) HUP.

But It Is in Brevard. Patti Kornberg. Ed. by Sally A. Stewart & Nanci Hellmich. (Illus.). 216p. (Orig.). 1982. pap. 4.95 (*0-686-82539-X*) P Kornberg.

But It Was Just a Joke ... ! Theater Scenes & Monologues for Eliminating Sexual Harassment: A Performance Manual & Workshop Guide. Dorene Ludwig. 170p. 1991. student ed 17.50 (*0-89215-170-6*) U Cal LA Indus Rel.

But Jesus. James L. Berkman. (Patriot Ser.: Vol. 7, No. 1). (Orig.). 1990. pap. 10.00 (*0-943662-13-3*, 2-870-544) Runaway Pubns.

But Ky Irina, Vol. 2. Irina Zisman. 126p. 1994. pap. write for info. (*0-9635574-3-2*) Alpha Bks VA.

***But Listen!** Susan C. Cottrell. 1976. 3.00 (*0-87129-405-2*, B35) Dramatic Pub.

But Names Will Never Hurt Me. Bernard Waber. LC 75-40473. (Illus.). 32p. (J). (gr. k-3). 1976. 14.95 (*0-395-24383-1*) HM.

But No Candy. Gloria Houston. (Illus.). 32p. (J). (ps-3). 1992. lib. bdg. 14.95 (*0-399-22142-5*, Philomel Bks) Putnam Pub Group.

But No Elephants. (Parents Magazine Press Read-Aloud Library). (Illus.). 42p. (J). (ps-3). 1992. lib. bdg. 14.60 (*0-8368-0875-4*); lib. bdg. 13.26 (*0-685-61510-3*) Gareth Stevens Inc.

But No Elephants. Jerry Smath. LC 79-16136. (Illus.). 48p. (J). (ps-3). 1979. 5.95 (*0-8193-1007-7*); lib. bdg. 5.95 (*0-8193-1008-5*) Parents.

But No Elephants. Jerry Smath. (Sunny Day Bks.). (Illus.). 48p. (J). (ps-2). 1991. pap. 2.95 (*0-448-41078-8*, G&D) Putnam Pub Group.

But Not a Drop to Drink: The Lifesaving Guide to Good Water. Steve Coffel. 352p. 1991. mass mkt. 4.95 (*0-8041-0811-0*) Ivy Books.

But Not for Love: Stories of Majorie Barnard & M. Barnard Eldershaw. Ed. by Robert Darby. 240p. (Orig.). 1989. pap. text ed. 12.95 (*0-04-351070-1*) Routledge Chapman & Hall.

But Not Forgotten: The Adventure of the University Players. Norris Houghton. LC 79-136071. (Illus.). 1971. reprint ed. text ed. 69.50 (*0-8371-5221-6*, HONF, Greenwood Pr) Greenwood.

But Not Forsaken. Helen G. Brenneman. 1983. pap. 3.50 (*0-87813-954-0*) Christian Light.

But Not Kate. Marissa Moss. Ed. by Melanie Donovan. LC 90-25751. (Illus.). 32p. (J). (ps-3). 1992. 14.00 (*0-688-10600-5*); lib. bdg. 13.93 (*0-688-10601-3*) Lothrop.

***But Not Nate! A Book about Opposites.** Andrew M. Gutelle. Ed. by Jean Crawford. (Snugglebug Bks.). (Illus.). 24p. (J). (ps). 1994. write for info. (*0-7835-4501-0*) Time-Life.

But Not Next Door. Harry Rosen & David Rosen. 1962. 12.95 (*0-8392-1007-8*) Astor-Honor.

But Not the Hippopotamus. Sandra Boynton. Ed. by Kate Klimo. (Boynton Board Bks.). (Illus.). 14p. (J). (ps-00). 1982. 3.95 (*0-671-44904-4*, Litl Simon S&S) S&S Childrens.

***But Ossifer, It's Not My Fault.** Mark. 1994. pap. 4.99 (*0-918259-62-2*) CCC Pubns.

But Seriously, Folks! Pat Oliphant. (Orig.). 1983. pap. 6.95 (*0-8362-1199-5*) Andrews & McMeel.

But She Said: Feminist Practices of Biblical Interpretation. Elizabeth S. Fiorenza. LC 92-9. (Illus.). 272p. 1993. 24.00 (*0-8070-1214-9*); pap. 14.00 (*0-8070-1215-7*) Beacon Pr.

But She's Still My Grandma! Doreen Rappaport. LC 81-20236. (Illus.). 32p. (J). (gr. 1-5). 1982. 16.95 (*0-89885-072-X*) Human Sci Pr.

But, That's Another Story. Harriotte B. Smith. 1993. 18.95 (*0-533-10160-3*) Vantage.

But the Crackling Is Superb: An Anthology on Food & Drink by Fellows & Foreign Members of the Royal Society of London. Nicholas Kurti & Giana Kurti. (Illus.). 280p. 1988. 29.90 (*0-85274-301-7*) IOP Pub.

But the People's Creatures: The Philosophical Basis of the English Civil War. John Sanderson. LC 88-8519. 256p. 1989. text ed. 59.95 (*0-7190-2765-9*, Pub. by Manchester Univ Pr UK) St Martin.

But Then I Remembered. Chaya L. Rothstein. 1991. 10.95 (*0-87306-558-1*) Feldheim.

But Theriously Folkth. Johnny Hart. (B.C. Ser.: No. 25). 128p. (Orig.). 1982. pap. 1.95 (*0-449-14485-2*, GM) Fawcett.

But Theriously Folkth. Johnny Hart. (Orig.). 1987. pap. 2.25 (*0-449-13197-1*) Fawcett.

But Thinking Makes It So: Conformity & Deviance in Social Problems. Ed. by Marcia Gillespie et al. LC 76-41779. 208p. (C). 1977. pap. text ed. 8.95 (*0-8422-5250-9*) Irvington.

But This Night Is Different. Raymond A. Zwerin & Audrey F. Marcus. (Illus.). 48p. (J). (gr. k-3). 1981. pap. 10.95 (*0-8074-0032-7*, 102561) UAHC.

But Time & Chance: The Biography of Padre Martinez of Taos. Fray A. Chavez. LC 81-27. 176p. 1981. 35.00 (*0-913270-96-2*); pap. 11.95 (*0-913270-95-4*) Sunstone Pr.

But We Were Born Free. Elmer H. Davis. LC 73-138585. 229p. 1971. reprint ed. text ed. 55.00 (*0-8371-5784-6*, DABF, Greenwood Pr) Greenwood.

But What Does the Hippopotamus Say? Francesca Simon. LC 93-32297. (Illus.). (J). 1994. 11.95 (*0-15-200029-1*, Gulliver Bks) HarBrace.

***But What If? Writing Reversal Scripts.** Carolyn W. Greenlee. 34p. (YA). (gr. 7-12). 1994. pap. text ed. 8.50 (*1-887400-03-6*) Earthen Vessel Prodns.

But What If I Don't Want to Go to College? Harlow Unger. 176p. 1992. pap. 10.95 (*0-8160-2836-2*) Facts on File.

But What If I Don't Want to Go to College? A Guide to Successful Careers Through Alternative Education. Harlow G. Unger. 176p. (YA). 1992. lib. bdg. 19.95 (*0-8160-2534-7*) Facts on File.

But What, My Dear, Do You Know about Hotels? And Other Stories about Old Times in Colorado. Florence G. Means. Ed. by Lorna C. Mason. (Illus.). 144p. (Orig.). 1992. pap. 8.95 (*0-944720-02-1*) Greenridge Pr.

But What of Earth? Piers Anthony. 1989. mass mkt. 4.95 (*0-8125-3098-5*) Tor Bks.

But What: Selected Poems. Judith Herzberg. Tr. by Shirley Kaufman. LC 87-43198. (Field Translation Ser.). 120p. 1988. 15.00 (*0-932440-24-X*); pap. 9.00 (*0-932440-23-1*) Oberlin Coll Pr.

But When She Was Bad, Pt. 1. Marlene Matthews. (Road to Avonlea Ser.: No. 23). (J). (gr. 4-7). 1994. mass mkt. 3.99 (*0-553-48122-3*) Bantam.

But When You Are Older: Reflections on Coming to Age. Donald X. Burt. 112p. (Orig.). 1992. pap. text ed. 5.95 (*0-8146-2030-2*) Liturgical Pr.

But Where Is Love? Abbe Lane. 512p. 1994. mass mkt. 5.99 (*0-446-60035-0*) Warner Bks.

But Why Don't We Go to War? Finding Jesus' Path to Peace. Susan M. Landis. 224p. (Orig.). 1993. pap. 9.95 (*0-8361-3647-0*) Herald Pr.

But Will It Bite Me? A Reference Book of Insects for Children & Their Grownups. Edith G. Bailes. 112p. (Orig.). (J). (gr. 1-6). 1985. pap. 9.95 (*0-9611118-1-X*) Cardamom.

***But Will They Use It? Social Service Utilization by Rural Elderly.** rev. ed. Linda M. Havir. LC 95-13768. (Garland Studies on the Elderly in America). (Illus.). 240p. 1995. 60.00 (*0-8153-1964-9*) Garland.

But with Respect: Memorable Interviews with Statesmen & Parliamentarians. Robin Day. (Illus.). 320p. Date not set. 39.95 (*0-297-81302-1*) Trafalgar.

But Yet a Woman: A Novel. Arthur S. Hardy. LC 70-164562. (American Fiction Reprint Ser.). 1977. reprint ed. 29.95 (*0-8369-7039-X*) Ayer.

But You Can Feel It. Emil B. Fries. LC 80-65108. (Illus.). 424p. 1980. pap. 12.50 (*0-8323-0354-2*) Binford Mort.

But You Can't Leave Shirley. Shirley A. Porter. LC 92-64097. 176p. (Orig.). 1992. pap. 9.95 (*0-936029-28-5*) Western Bk Journ.

Butadiene & Styrene: Assessment of Health Hazard. Ed. by M. Sorsa et al. (IARC Scientific Publications: Vol. 127). 440p. 1994. pap. 95.00 (*92-832-2127-3*) OUP.

Butanols: Four Isomers, 1-Butanol, 2-Butanol, Tert-Butanol, Isobutanol. (Environmental Health Criteria Ser.: No. 65). 141p. 1987. pap. 7.80 (*0-318-23396-7*) World Health.

Butch. Jay Rayn. 194p. (Orig.). 1992. pap. text ed. 10.95 (*0-9633031-0-4*) RMG Ent.

Butch. Jay Rayn. LC 93-29580. 160p. (Orig.). 1993. reprint ed. pap. 7.95 (*1-55583-316-0*) Alyson Pubns.

***Butch - Femme.** Ed. by M. G. Soares. 1995. write for info. (*0-517-70222-3*, Crown) Crown Pub Group.

Butch & the Bad Baloney. Bruce Porter. (Illus.). 40p. (Orig.). (J). (gr. 1 up). 1987. pap. 3.95 (*0-939925-15-X*) R C Law & Co.

Butch Beards Basic Basketball: The Complete Player. Butch Beard et al. LC 85-18108. (Illus.). 144p. 1985. 14.95 (*0-935576-14-2*) Kesend Pub Ltd.

***Butch Cassidy.** Carl R. Green & William R. Sanford. LC 94-24844. (Outlaws & Lawmen of the Wild West Ser.). (Illus.). 48p. (J). (gr. 4-10). 1995. lib. bdg. 14.95 (*0-89490-587-2*) Enslow Pubs.

Butch Cassidy, My Brother. Lula P. Betenson & Dora Flack. LC 75-2332. (Illus.). 281p. reprint ed. 80.10 (*0-8357-9044-4*, 2015648) Bks Demand.

Butch II. Jay Rayn. 190p. (Orig.). 1994. pap. 8.95 (*1-55583-317-9*, Lace MA) Alyson Pubns.

Butcher. Rex Miller. Ed. by Doug Grad. 320p. (Orig.). 1994. mass mkt. 5.50 (*0-671-86882-9*) PB.

Butcher. Jack Rudman. (Career Examination Ser.: C-1156). 1994. pap. 27.95 (*0-8373-1156-X*) Nat Learn.

***Butcher: A Novel.** Alina Reyes. Tr. by David Watson. 192p. 1994. 15.00 (*0-8021-1571-3*, Grove) Grove-Atltic.

Butcher, Baker: A True Account of a Serial Murderer. Walter Gilmour & Leland E. Hale. 352p. (Orig.). 1991. pap. 4.99 (*0-451-40276-6*, Onyx) NAL-Dutton.

Butcher Bird. Dean Ing. 352p. 1993. 21.95 (*0-312-85397-1*) Forge NYC.

Butcher Bird. Dean Ing. 432p. 1994. mass mkt. 5.99 (*0-8125-2241-9*) Tor Bks.

Butcher Boy. Patrick McCabe. LC 93-2831. 224p. 1993. 19.95 (*0-88064-147-9*) Fromm Intl Pub.

Butcher Boy. Patrick Mccabe. 1994. mass mkt. 9.95 (*0-385-31237-7*) Doubleday.

Butcher Workmen: A Study of Unionization. David Brody. LC 64-21240. (Wertheim Publications in Industrial Relations). 332p. 1964. 29.95 (*0-674-08925-1*) HUP.

Butchering Livestock at Home. 1982. pap. 2.95 (*0-88266-279-1*) Storey Comm Inc.

Butchering, Processing & Preservation of Meat. Frank G. Ashbrook. (Illus.). 336p. 1973. reprint ed. pap. 23.95 (*0-442-20377-2*) Chapman & Hall.

Butchers & Other Stories of Crime. Peter Lovesey. LC 87-42706. 208p. 1987. 15.95 (*0-89296-195-3*) Mysterious Pr.

Butchers & Other Stories of Crime. Peter Lovesey. LC 87-7718. 208p. 1988. pap. 9.95 (*0-89296-960-1*) Mysterious Pr.

Butcher's Broom. Neil Gunn. 432p. 1994. 25.95 (*0-8027-1291-6*) Walker & Co.

Butcher's Crossing. John E. Williams. LC 87-28735. (Reprint Ser.). 275p. 1988. reprint ed. pap. 11.95 (*1-55728-030-4*) U of Ark Pr.

Butcher's Dozen: Thirteen Famous Michigan Murders. Larry Wakefield. 192p. 1991. pap. 13.95 (*1-878005-17-0*) Northmont Pub.

Butchers' Grand Ball: Meditations on Goree Island in Photographs & Carefully Chosen Words. Kiarri T. Cheatwood. LC 93-84326. (Illus.). 96p. (Orig.). 1993. pap. 14.50 (*1-879289-03-2*) Native Sun Pubs.

Butchers of Hull. Peter Didsbury. 1982. pap. 12.95 (*0-906427-42-8*, Pub. by Bloodaxe Bks UK) Dufour.

Butchers Theatre. Jonathan Kellerman. 1989. mass mkt. 6.50 (*0-553-27510-0*) Bantam.

Butcher's Wife. Li Ang. Tr. by Howard Goldblatt & Ellen Yeung. LC 89-46060. (Asian Voices Ser.). 142p. 1990. reprint ed. pap. 9.95 (*0-8070-8323-2*) Beacon Pr.

***Butcher's Wife & Other Stories.** Li Ang. Ed. by Howard Goldblatt. 300p. 1995. pap. text ed. 18.95 (*0-88727-222-3*) Cheng & Tsui.

Butch's Biscuit Book: Homemade Delectables for Your Dog. rev. ed. Charlotte L. Anderson & Donna S. Thalheimer. (Illus.). 20p. (Orig.). 1986. pap. 3.25 (*0-9617468-1-5*) Lovin Ovens.

Bute Broadsides in the Houghton Library Harvard University, Guide & Index to the Microfilm Collection. Hugh Amory. LC 81-11939. 98p. 1981. 60.00 (*0-89235-025-3*) Res Pubns CT.

***Butler: Butleriana, Genealogica et Biographica, or Genealogical Notes Concerning Mary Butler & Her Descendants, As Well As the Bates, Harris, Sigourney & Other Families with Which They Have Intermarried.** J. D. Butler. 162p. 1994. reprint ed. lib. bdg. 35.00 (*0-8328-4303-2*); reprint ed. pap. 25.00 (*0-8328-4304-0*) Higginson Bk Co.

Butler: Butlers & Kinsfolk. Elmer E. Butler. (Illus.). 362p. 1991. reprint ed. lib. bdg. 66.00 (*0-8328-2108-X*); reprint ed. pap. 56.00 (*0-8328-2109-8*) Higginson Bk Co.

Butler: Hydra Conspiracy. Philip Kirk. (Butler Ser.). 208p. 1983. pap. 2.50 (*0-8439-2038-6*) Dorchester Pub Co.

Butler: Smart Bombs. Philip Kirk. 208p. 1983. pap. 2.50 (*0-8439-2049-1*) Dorchester Pub Co.

Butler: The Slayboys. Philip Kirk. 208p. 1983. pap. 2.50 (*0-8439-2056-4*) Dorchester Pub Co.

An Asterisk (*) at the beginning of an entry indicates that the title is appearing in BIP for the first time.

An Asterisk (*) at the beginning of an entry indicates that the title is appearing in BIP for the first time.

***Butterfly & Hellflower, 3 vols. in 1.** Eluki bes Shahar. 640p. 1993. 12.98 (*1-56865-048-5*, GuildAmerica) Dblday Bk Music.

Butterfly & Life Span Nutrition. Majid Ali. 419p. (Orig.). 1995. pap. 16.99 (*1-879131-01-3*) Inst of Prev Med.

Butterfly & Moth. Paul Whalley. LC 88-1574. (Eyewitness Bks.). (Illus.). 64p. (J). (gr. 5 up). 1988. 16.00 (*0-394-89618-1*); lib. bdg. 16.99 (*0-394-99618-6*) Knopf Bks Yng Read.

***Butterfly & Other Stories.** Wang Meng. 215p. 1995. lib. bdg. 23.00 (*0-8095-4504-7*) Borgo Pr.

Butterfly & the Stone. Lucretia Fisher. LC 80-29260. (Illus.). 48p. (Orig.). (J). (ps up). 1981. pap. 3.95 (*0-916144-69-0*) Stemmer Hse.

Butterfly As Companion: Meditations on the First Three Chapters of the Chuang Tzu. Kuang-Ming Wu. LC 87-17986. (SUNY Series in Religious Studies). 512p. 1990. 59.50 (*0-88706-685-2*); pap. 19.95 (*0-88706-686-0*) State U NY Pr.

***Butterfly Bandit.** Ester H. Prudlo. LC 95-78162. (Illus.). (J). (gr. 1-4). 1995. 14.95 (*1-880851-19-9*) Greene Bark Pr.

Butterfly Book. Donald W. Stokes. 1991. pap. 11.95 (*0-316-81780-5*) Little.

Butterfly Books. Laura C. Busch. (Little Readers Ser.). (J). (ps-2). 1989. 13.95 (*1-880642-03-4*) Little Read.

Butterfly Boy. Laurence Yep. (J). (ps-3). 1993. 16.00 (*0-374-31003-3*) FS&G.

Butterfly Caste: A Social History of Pellagra in the South. Elizabeth W. Etheridge. LC 70-176431. (Contributions in American History Ser.: No. 17). 278p. 1972. text ed. 59.95 (*0-8371-6276-9*, EHP/, Greenwood Pr) Greenwood.

Butterfly Charted Designs. Lindberg Press Staff. (Illus.). 48p. (Orig.). 1988. pap. 2.95 (*0-486-25639-1*) Dover.

Butterfly Children. Adell Palmer. 1974. pap. 3.95 (*0-89036-050-2*) Hawkes Pub Inc.

Butterfly Conservation. T. R. New. (Illus.). 230p. 1992. pap. 29.95 (*0-19-553228-7*) OUP.

Butterfly Effect: A Helen Keremos Detective Novel. Eva Zaremba. 200p. 1994. pap. 9.95 (*0-929005-56-2*, Pub. by Second Story Pr CN) InBook.

Butterfly Express. Jane B. Moncure. LC 88-22944. (Magic Castle Readers Ser.). (Illus.). 32p. (ENG & SPA.). (J). (ps-2). 1989. lib. bdg. 21.36 (*0-89565-392-3*) Childs World.

***Butterfly Express: Magic Castle Reader.** (Magic Castle Ser.). 1993. pap. text ed. 3.95 (*1-56189-377-3*) Amer Educ Pub.

***Butterfly Garden.** Judith Levicoff et al. (Illus.). 48p. (Orig.). (J). (gr. 1-4). 1994. pap. 10.95 (*1-880812-17-7*) S Ink WA.

Butterfly Garden. Mathew Tekulsky. LC 85-8609. (Illus.). 144p. 1985. 16.95 (*0-916782-70-0*); pap. 9.95 (*0-916782-69-7*) Harvard Common Pr.

Butterfly Gardening: Creating Summer Magic in Your Garden. Xerces Society Staff. LC 90-30362. 1990. pap. 20.00 (*0-87156-615-X*) Sierra.

Butterfly Gardening for the South. Geyata Ajilvsgi. LC 90-20565. 360p. 1991. 29.95 (*0-87833-738-5*) Taylor Pub.

***Butterfly Gardens: Luring Nature's Loveliest Pollinators to Your Yard.** Ed. by Alcinda Lewis. (21st-Century Gardening Ser.). (Illus.). 1995. per., pap. 6.95 (*0-945352-88-3*) Bklyn Botanic.

Butterfly Greetings Directory: Butterfly Greetings to Duplicate & Use. Greetings Etc. by Alfreda Staff. 1984. pap. text ed. 23.95 (*0-318-04376-9*, Greetings) Prosperity & Profits.

Butterfly Hunt. Yoshi. LC 90-7361. (Illus.). 32p. (J). (gr. k up). 1991. pap. 14.95 (*0-88708-137-1*, Picture Book Studio) S&S Childrens.

Butterfly Hunt. Yoshi. LC 92-6631. (Illus.). 28p. (J). (gr. k). 1993. reprint ed. Mini-bk. 4.95 (*0-88708-270-X*, Picture Book Studio) S&S Childrens.

Butterfly in the Garden. Mary Whalley & Paul Whalley. LC 86-5705. (Animal Habitats Ser.). (Illus.). 32p. (J). (gr. 4-6). 1986. lib. bdg. 17.27 (*1-55532-068-6*) Gareth Stevens Inc.

Butterfly in the Greenhouse. John V. Aho. (Orig.). 1984. pap. 4.95 (*0-9613629-0-1*) Townsend Harbor.

Butterfly Iron-on Transfer Patterns. Barbara Christopher. (Illus.). 48p. (Orig.). 1991. pap. 2.95 (*0-486-26908-6*) Dover.

Butterfly Is Born. Melvin Berger. (Early Science Big Bks.). (Illus.). 16p. (J). (ps-2). 1993. pap. text ed. 14.95 (*1-56784-012-4*) Newbridge Comms.

***Butterfly Is Born: Mini Books.** Melvin Berger. Ed. by Lisa Trumbauer. (Early Science Big Bks.). 16p. (J). (ps-2). Date not set. pap. text ed. 2.95 (*1-56784-037-X*) Newbridge Comms.

Butterfly Jar. Jeffrey Moss. (Illus.). (J). (ps up). 1989. 15.95 (*0-553-05704-9*) Bantam.

***Butterfly Kiss.** Marcial Boo. LC 94-41940. (Illus.). (J). 1995. write for info. (*0-15-200841-1*) HarBrace.

Butterfly Kisses: Little Intimacies That Can't Be Bought; Sometimes Noticed Sometimes Not. Terry Kellogg & Marvel E. Harrison. 48p. 1991. 12.95 (*1-880257-02-5*) BRAT Pub.

Butterfly League. Helen P. Swope. (Illus.). 128p. (Orig.). 1994. 9.25 (*0-9639938-0-1*) Lodestar CA.

***Butterfly Magic.** Melissa Getzoff. LC 95-4870. (First-Start Science Ser.). (Illus.). 32p. (J). (gr. k-2). 1995. lib. bdg. 8.50 (*0-8167-3862-9*) Troll Assocs.

***Butterfly Magic.** Melissa Getzoff. LC 95-4870. (First-Start Science Ser.). (Illus.). 32p. (J). (gr. k-2). 1995. pap. text ed. 2.50 (*0-8167-3863-7*) Troll Assocs.

Butterfly Mazes: An Educational-Activity Coloring Book. Spizzirri Publishing Inc Staff. Ed. by Linda Spizzirri. (Illus.). 32p. (J). (gr. 1-8). 1989. pap. 1.00 (*0-86545-146-X*) Spizzirri.

Butterfly Mobile. Ed. by Amy Cohn. (Book Mobiles Ser.). (Illus.). 22p. (J). (ps up). 1994. bds. 5.95 (*0-688-13588-9*, Tupelo Bks) Morrow.

Butterfly Montane. large type ed. Dorothy Cork. 1990. 21.95 (*0-7089-2294-5*) Ulverscroft.

Butterfly Net & A Kingdom: And Other Stories. Blair Fuller. LC 88-12082. 192p. (Orig.). 1989. pap. 8.95 (*0-88739-065-X*) Creat Arts Bk.

Butterfly Night of Old Brown Bear. Nicolas Van Pallandt. (J). (ps-3). 1992. bds. 15.00 (*0-374-31009-2*) FS&G.

***Butterfly of Dinard.** Eugenio Montale. Tr. by G. Singh. LC 72-160048. reprint ed. pap. 53.10 (*0-7837-9584-X*, 2060333) Bks Demand.

Butterfly on Wall Street. Henry Filbert. LC 94-68458. 64p. 1994. pap. 9.95 (*0-9637515-2-2*) Dageforde Pub.

Butterfly Pattern Collection. Ed. by Sandra Hatch. (Illus.). 168p. (Orig.). 1992. pap. text ed. 14.95 (*1-882138-04-X*) Hse White Birches.

***Butterfly Powder & the Mountains of Iowa.** Erich Eipert. LC 94-60785. 283p. (Orig.). 1994. pap. 12.00 (*0-9642349-3-9*) Turnbuckle Pr.

Butterfly Revolution. William Butler. LC 67-10948. 224p. 1986. pap. 3.95 (*0-345-33182-6*) Ballantine.

Butterfly Rises. Kit Tremaine. LC 87-24969. 216p. 1987. pap. 12.95 (*0-931892-15-5*) B Dolphin Pub.

Butterfly Secret. Toni Tucci. (Orig.). 1978. pap. 2.50 (*0-89083-394-X*) Zebra.

Butterfly Secret: I Am Special Childrens Story Books. Carol T. Plum. 32p. (J). (ps-3). 1989. lib. bdg. 9.95 (*0-87973-017-X*, 17); pap. text ed. 5.95 (*0-87973-014-5*, 14) Our Sunday Visitor.

***Butterfly Seeds.** Mary Watson. LC 95-13250. (J). 1995. write for info. (*0-688-14132-3*, Tambourine Bks); lib. bdg. write for info. (*0-688-14133-1*, Tambourine Bks) Morrow.

Butterfly Stained Glass Coloring Book. Ed Sibbett. (Illus.). (J). (gr. k-3). 1985. pap. 3.95 (*0-486-24820-8*) Dover.

Butterfly Stories: A Novel. William T. Vollmann. LC 93-2489. 288p. 1993. 21.00 (*0-8021-1502-0*); pap. 11.00 (*0-8021-3400-9*) Grove-Atltic.

***Butterfly Story.** Anca Hariton. LC 94-19377. (Illus.). (J). 1995. 14.99 (*0-525-45212-5*) Dutton Child Bks.

Butterfly Tree. Ed. by Conrad Balfour. 1985. pap. 7.50 (*0-89823-068-3*) New Rivers Pr.

Butterfly Tree. Robert E. Bell. (Library of Alabama Classics). 248p. 1991. pap. 15.95 (*0-8173-0560-2*) U of Ala Pr.

Butterflyfishes: Success on the Coral Reef. Philip J. Motta. (Developments in Environmental Biology of Fishes Ser.). (C). 1989. lib. bdg. 140.50 (*0-7923-0168-4*) Kluwer Ac.

Butterfly's Dream: In Search of the Spiritual Roots of Zen. Albert Low. 160p. 1993. pap. 14.95 (*0-8048-1822-3*) C E Tuttle.

***Butterfly's Surprise.** Muff Singer. (Illus.). 18p. (J). (ps-3). 1995. bds. 3.99 (*0-89577-670-7*) RD Assn.

Butterick's Eighteen Ninety-Two Metropolitan Fashions. Butterick Publishing Co. Staff. LC 94-13379. (Illus.). 160p. 1994. reprint ed. pap. 11.95 (*0-486-27983-9*) Dover.

Buttermilk. Stephen Cosgrove. (Serendipity Bks.). (Illus.). 32p. (Orig.). (J). (gr. 1-4). 1986. pap. 2.95 (*0-8431-1565-3*) Price Stern.

Buttermilk Bear. Stephen Cosgrove. (Serendipity Bks.). (Illus.). 32p. (J). (gr. 1-4). 1987. pap. 3.95 (*0-8431-1908-X*) Price Stern.

***Buttermilk Bear.** Stephen Cosgrove. (Serendipity Ser.). (Illus.). 32p. (J). (ps-4). 1995. pap. 3.95 (*0-8431-3828-9*) Price Stern.

Buttermilk Book. Lee E. Benning. 1995. 25.00 (*0-8050-3118-9*) H Holt & Co.

Buttermilk Bottoms: A Novel. Kenn Robbins. LC 87-4997. 268p. reprint ed. pap. 76.40 (*0-7837-1625-7*, 2041918) Bks Demand.

Buttermilk Curve. Deana L. Jensen. (Illus.). 1991. pap. 13.95 (*0-9615793-3-1*) D L Jensen.

***Butternut Guerillas: A Story of Grierson's Raid.** Larry D. Underwood. LC 94-68459. 208p. 1994. pap. 14.95 (*0-9637515-8-1*) Dageforde Pub.

***Butter's Goat.** T. S. Frank. 1994. 3.00 (*0-87129-430-3*, B27) Dramatic Pub.

Butterscotch. Milo Manara. 64p. 1994. pap. 12.95 (*1-56163-109-4*, Eurotica) NBM.

Butterscotch: The Flavor of the Invisible. Milo Manara. Ed. by Bernd Metz. Tr. by Tom Leighton. (Illus.). 72p. 1988. pap. 10.95 (*0-87416-047-2*) Catalan Communs.

Butterscotch Dreams: Chants for Fun & Learning. Sonja Dunn. LC 89-30384. 111p. (Orig.). 1987. pap. text ed. 14.00 (*0-435-08497-6*, 08497) Heinemann.

Butterwings. Robin James. (Serendipity Bks.). (Illus.). 32p. (Orig.). (J). (gr. 1-4). 1993. pap. 3.95 (*0-8431-3494-1*) Price Stern.

***Butterworth Landlord & Tenant Handbook.** 4th ed. Butterworths Editors. 949p. 1992. pap. text ed. 66.00 (*0-406-01028-5*, UK) Butterworth Legal Pubs.

Butterworth Lectures, 1990-91. 120p. 1992. pap. 40.00 (*0-406-00982-1*, U.K.) Butterworth Legal Pubs.

***Butterworth Lectures, 1991-92.** 55p. 1993. pap. 40.00 (*0-406-01611-9*, U.K.) Butterworth Legal Pubs.

***Butterworth Scottish Family Law Service.** David Nichols et al. 1994. ring bd. 275.00 (*0-406-01356-X*, UK) Butterworth Legal Pubs.

***Butterworth Selection of Statutes: Constitutional Law.** J. C. Bekker. 158p. 1990. pap. 35.00 (*0-409-01219-X*, SA) Butterworth Legal Pubs.

***Butterworths Accountants' Legal Service.** 1056p. 1993. ring bd. 240.00 (*0-406-00859-0*, UK) Butterworth Legal Pubs.

***Butterworths Accountants' Legal Service.** Denis Keenan. Date not set. ring bd. 120.00 (*0-615-00251-X*) Butterworth Legal Pubs.

***Butterworths Annotated Acts: Copyright Act.** J. Lahore & W. Rothnie. Date not set. write for info. (*0-409-31001-8*, Austral) Butterworth Legal Pubs.

***Butterworths Annotated Acts: Trade Practices Act.** L. Layton & R. Steinwall. 550p. 1994. pap. 30.00 (*0-409-30968-0*, Austral) Butterworth Legal Pubs.

***Butterworths Annotations of the New Zealand Statutes.** 2nd ed. Date not set. ring bd. 365.00 (*0-409-79311-6*, UK) Butterworth Legal Pubs.

***Butterworths Australian Corporations Legislation 1994, Vol. 1.** 1994. boxed 51.00 (*0-409-30939-7*, Austral) Butterworth Legal Pubs.

***Butterworths Australian Corporations Legislation 1994, Vol. 2.** 1994. boxed 17.00 (*0-409-30948-6*, Austral) Butterworth Legal Pubs.

Butterworths Australian Taxation Handbook, 1992. R. L. Deutsch et al. 1992. pap. 44.00 (*0-00-014438-X*) Butterworth Legal Pubs.

Butterworths Banking Law Handbook. Ed. by Graham McBain. 1989. U.K. pap. 84.00 (*0-406-18130-6*) Butterworth Legal Pubs.

Butterworths Banking Law Handbook. 2nd ed. Graham S. McBain. 730p. 1993. pap. 110.00 (*0-406-02005-1*, UK) Butterworth Legal Pubs.

Butterworths Budget Tax Tables, 1992. 27th ed. Ed. by Butterworths Staff. 12p. 1992. pap. 10.00 (*0-406-50847-X*, U.K.) Butterworth Legal Pubs.

Butterworths Budget Tax Tables, 1993. 29th ed. Butterworths Editorial Staff. 12p. 1993. pap. 10.00 (*0-406-01606-2*, U.K.) Butterworth Legal Pubs.

***Butterworths Budget Tax Tables, 1994-95.** 1994. pap. write for info. (*0-406-50799-6*) Butterworth Legal Pubs.

***Butterworths Budget Tax Tables 1994-95.** 1994. 4.95 (*0-406-05054-6*) Butterworth Legal Pubs.

Butterworths Business Tax Service. John Wosner et al. 1990. ring bd. 300.00 (*0-406-50451-2*) Butterworth Legal Pubs.

Butterworths Central & East European Business Law Bulletin. Cole, Corette & Abrotyn & Abrutyn. 1991. 385.00 (*0-406-12150-8*, U.K.) Butterworth Legal Pubs.

Butterworths Commercial Law Handbook. Gwyneth Pitt. 1989. U.K. pap. 41.00 (*0-406-54722-X*) Butterworth Legal Pubs.

***Butterworths Commercial Law in New Zealand.** John Farrar. 1008p. 1992. boxed 162.00 (*0-409-78964-X*, NZ) Butterworth Legal Pubs.

***Butterworths Commercial Law in New Zealand.** 2nd ed. John Farrar. 1008p. 1992. pap. 140.00 (*0-409-78900-3*, NZ) Butterworth Legal Pubs.

***Butterworths Commercial Service, 2 vols., Set.** Michael Midgley & Lee Andrew. Date not set. ring bd. write for info. (*0-409-68100-8*, NZ) Butterworth Legal Pubs.

Butterworths Company Forms Manual. Ed. by S. W. Magnus. 1988. U.K. pap. 110.00 (*0-406-01630-5*) Butterworth Legal Pubs.

Butterworths Company Law Cases. Ed. by D. D. Prentice & Mary Stokes. 1988. U.K. 1,260.00 (*0-406-07650-2*) Butterworth Legal Pubs.

Butterworths Company Law Guide. 2nd ed. Ed. by Michael Renshall & Keith Walmsley. 1990. U.K. pap. 47.00 (*0-406-19702-4*) Butterworth Legal Pubs.

Butterworths Company Law Service, 2 vols., Set. Ed. by Philip L. Mitchell et al. 1991. ring bd. 440.00 (*0-406-19570-6*, U.K.) Butterworth Legal Pubs.

Butterworths Company Secretarial Practice Manual. David Venus. 1990. U.K. pap. 64.00 (*0-406-50502-0*) Butterworth Legal Pubs.

***Butterworths Company Secretarial Practice Manual.** 2nd ed. 1994. pap. write for info. (*0-406-02881-8*) Butterworth Legal Pubs.

Butterworths Company Secretarial Procedures & Precedents. 1993. U.K. ring bd. 220.00 (*0-406-00570-2*, UK) Butterworth Legal Pubs.

Butterworths Competition Law, 3 vols. Ed. by Peter Freeman et al. 1991. U.K. ring bd. 1,190.00 (*0-406-16500-9*) Butterworth Legal Pubs.

Butterworths Competition Law Handbook. 3rd ed. Garth Lindrup. 826p. 1993. pap. 100.00 (*0-406-02280-1*, UK) Butterworth Legal Pubs.

Butterworths Construction Law Manual. Redmond Cooper. 342p. 1993. 96.00 (*0-406-00635-0*, UK) Butterworth Legal Pubs.

Butterworths Costs Service, 2 vols. Ed. by Michael Cook et al. 1991. Set, U.K. ring bd. 390.00 (*0-406-10749-1*) Butterworth Legal Pubs.

Butterworths County Court Precedents & Pleadings. Ed. by C. Oddie et al. U.K. ring bd. 370.00 (*0-406-29211-6*) Butterworth Legal Pubs.

***Butterworths Court Tariffs & Fees.** Butterworths Editorial Staff. Date not set. pap. write for info. (*0-409-01562-8*, SA) Butterworth Legal Pubs.

***Butterworths Current Law Digest 1984-1988.** Christine O'Brien. 1104p. 1990. boxed write for info. (*0-409-78879-1*, NZ) Butterworth Legal Pubs.

***Butterworths Current Law Digest 1989-1992.** Christine O'Brien. 1000p. 1993. boxed 243.00 (*0-408-71356-9*, NZ) Butterworth Legal Pubs.

***Butterworths District Court Reports.** Robert Kerr. Date not set. write for info. (*0-409-68407-4*, NZ) Butterworth Legal Pubs.

Butterworths EC Brief Annual Volume 1991. 1992. U. K. pap. 390.00 (*0-406-00878-7*) Butterworth Legal Pubs.

***Butterworths EC Case Citator & Service.** Ed. by Stuart Issacs. 1994. write for info. (*0-406-04120-2*) Butterworth Legal Pubs.

***Butterworths EC Legislation Implementation Service.** 1994. write for info. (*0-406-00594-X*) Butterworth Legal Pubs.

Butterworths Employment Law Guide. Ed. by Christopher Osman. 1990. U.K. pap. 84.00 (*0-406-13579-7*) Butterworth Legal Pubs.

***Butterworths Employment Law Guide: New Zealand Edition.** Gordon Anderson. 863p. 1993. pap. 90.00 (*0-409-47051-1*, NZ) Butterworth Legal Pubs.

Butterworths Employment Law Handbook. 5th ed. Ed. by Peter Wallington. 1990. U.K. pap. 52.00 (*0-406-50870-4*) Butterworth Legal Pubs.

***Butterworths Environmental Law Handbook.** Andrew Waite. 1040p. 1994. pap. text ed. 99.00 (*0-406-04471-6*, UK) Butterworth Legal Pubs.

***Butterworths European Court Practice.** David Vaughan. 750p. 1993. boxed 390.00 (*0-406-02346-8*, UK) Butterworth Legal Pubs.

Butterworths Family Law Act, Rules & Regulations Student Edition. Butterworths Staff. 1989. ring bd. 43.00 (*0-409-30322-4*) Butterworth Legal Pubs.

Butterworths Family Law Handbook. C. M. Lyon & Adrian Lyon. 1991. pap. 48.00 (*0-406-60980-2*, U.K.) Butterworth Legal Pubs.

***Butterworths Family Law Journal.** Roger Chapman. Date not set. ring bd. write for info. (*0-409-78999-2*, NZ) Butterworth Legal Pubs.

Butterworths Family Law Service, 3 vols. Ed. by P. M. Bromley et al. 1991. Set, U.K. ring bd. 520.00 (*0-406-10720-3*) Butterworth Legal Pubs.

***Butterworths Family Law Statutes.** 5th ed. 9480p. 1993. pap. 81.00 (*0-409-79049-4*, NZ) Butterworth Legal Pubs.

***Butterworths Finance Bill Act 1994 Handbook.** 244p. 1994. pap. text ed. 60.00 (*0-406-03618-7*, UK) Butterworth Legal Pubs.

Butterworths Financial & Tax Planning Through Pensions. 2nd ed. Peter Smith. 1992. pap. 70.00 (*0-406-00580-X*) Butterworth Legal Pubs.

***Butterworths Financial Services Law Handbook.** Deborah A. Sabalot. 1030p. 1994. pap. text ed. 110.00 (*0-406-02461-8*, UK) Butterworth Legal Pubs.

Butterworths Food Law. Anthony Painter. 618p. 1992. U.K. pap. 75.00 (*0-406-00642-3*) Butterworth Legal Pubs.

***Butterworths Guide to International Money Laundering Laws.** Richard Parlour. 223p. 1994. pap. text ed. 176.00 (*0-406-03494-X*, UK) Butterworth Legal Pubs.

Butterworths Guide to Legal Aid in Scotland. Ed. by Butterworths Staff. 1989. pap. 40.00 (*0-406-16901-2*) Butterworth Legal Pubs.

***Butterworths Guide to the Council Tax in Scotland.** Butterworths Editors. 260p. 1993. pap. text ed. 53.00 (*0-406-02453-7*, UK) Butterworth Legal Pubs.

***Butterworths Guide to the European Communities.** 2nd ed. Rebecca Wallace & William Stewart. 300p. 1992. pap. text ed. 54.00 (*0-406-00624-5*, UK) Butterworth Legal Pubs.

***Butterworth's Handbook of Consolidated VAT Legislation.** Frwd. by David Milne. 1994. pap. write for info. (*0-406-04554-2*) Butterworth Legal Pubs.

Butterworths Handbook of Singapore Land Law. Butterworths Staff. 917p. 1986. pap. 98.00 (*0-409-99516-9*) Butterworth Legal Pubs.

Butterworths Immigration Law Service. Eugene Cotran et al. 1991. U.K. ring bd. 290.00 (*0-406-11650-4*) Butterworth Legal Pubs.

Butterworths Insolvency Law Handbook. 2nd ed. Ed. by Michael Crystal. 1990. U.K. pap. 70.00 (*0-406-50065-7*) Butterworth Legal Pubs.

***Butterworths Insolvency Law Handbook.** 3rd ed. Ed. by Michael Crystal & Mark Phillips. 1994. write for info. (*0-406-02262-3*) Butterworth Legal Pubs.

Butterworths Insurance Law Handbook. 3rd ed. Ed. by Digby C. Jess. 1992. U. K. pap. 79.00 (*0-406-00575-3*) Butterworth Legal Pubs.

Butterworths Intellectual Property Law Handbook. Jeremy Phillips. 1990. U.K. pap. 60.00 (*0-406-50471-7*) Butterworth Legal Pubs.

Butterworths International Insolvency Law. Ed. by Allen & Overy. 1460p. 1993. U.K. boxed 338.00 (*0-406-00085-9*) Butterworth Legal Pubs.

Butterworths International Taxation of Financial Instruments & Transactions. 2nd ed. Geoffrey Pennells. 610p. 1994. boxed write for info. (*0-406-10660-6*, U.K.) Butterworth Legal Pubs.

***Butterworths International Taxation of Financial Instruments & Transactions: Your Definitive International Guide to the Tax Treatment of Financial Instruments, 3 Vols.** 2nd ed. Geoff Pennells & Jeremy Bradburne. 1994. write for info. (*0-406-00855-8*) Butterworth Legal Pubs.

***Butterworths Ireland Capital Tax Acts 1993-94.** Alan Moore et al. 1993. pap. text ed. 99.00 (*0-614-05555-5*, IE) Butterworth Legal Pubs.

***Butterworths Ireland Companies Act.** Lyndon MacCann. 1993. pap. text ed. 120.00 (*1-85475-148-4*, IE) Butterworth Legal Pubs.

***Butterworths Ireland Guide to the European Communities.** 1989. pap. text ed. 24.00 (*1-85475-192-1*, IE) Butterworth Legal Pubs.

***Butterworths Ireland Tax Acts 1993-94.** Alan Moore et al. 1993. pap. text ed. 126.00 (*1-85475-631-1*, IE) Butterworth Legal Pubs.

***Butterworths Ireland Tax Guide 1993-94.** Mel O'Cuinneagain et al. 1993. pap. text ed. 99.00 (*1-85475-626-5*, IE) Butterworth Legal Pubs.

***Butterworths Ireland Vat Acts 1993-94.** Alan Moore & James D. Somers. 1993. pap. text ed. 99.00 (*1-85475-636-2*, IE) Butterworth Legal Pubs.

***Butterworths Law Diary & Directory 1995.** Butterworths Editorial Staff. 1995. write for info. (*0-614-05466-4*) Butterworth Legal Pubs.

Butterworths Law Digest Yearbook, 2 vols., Set, 1987/88 & 1989. Teo & Woon. Complete Set 1987/88 & 1989. 196.00 (*0-409-99579-7*) Butterworth Legal Pubs.

An Asterisk (*) at the beginning of an entry indicates that the title is appearing in BIP for the first time.

An Asterisk (*) at the beginning of an entry indicates that the title is appearing in BIP for the first time.

Buyer Beware: Safeguarding Consumer Rights. Binah B. Taylor. LC 92-5493. (Human Rights Ser.). (YA). 1992. 22.60 (*0-86593-172-0*); 16.95 (*0-685-59286-3*) Rourke Corp.

Buyer Beware: Step-by-Step Guide for the First Time Home Buyer. Paige McClinte. LC 94-65053. 320p. (Orig.). 1997. 29.95 (*1-884573-01-0*); pap. 19.95 (*1-884573-18-5*) S-By-S Pubns.

Buyer Brokerage Made Easy. Jack Gale. Ed. by Christopher Bettin. 100p. (Orig.). (C). 1991. pap. 17.00 (*0-913652-75-X*) Realtors Natl.

Buyer Brokering. James B. Warkentin. 1991. 24.95 (*0-9614681-0-6*) Charter Pr.

Buyer One. Jack Rudman. (Career Examination Ser.: C-1845). 1994. pap. 23.95 (*0-8373-1845-9*) Nat Learn.

Buyer, Seller & Broker's Guide to Creative Home Finance. Norman G. Miller & Paul R. Goebel. (Illus.). 464p. 1986. 14.95 (*0-13-109413-0*) P-H.

Buyer-Seller Interactions: Empirical Research & Normative Issues. Ed. by Peter H. Reingen & Arch G. Woodside. LC 81-855. (Proceedings Ser.). (Illus.). 189p. 1982. pap. text ed. 12.00 (*0-87757-149-X*) Am Mktg.

Buyer Two. Jack Rudman. (Career Examination Ser.: C-1846). 1994. pap. 27.95 (*0-8373-1846-7*) Nat Learn.

Buyerism: How to Buy a Franchise or Small Business. Ed. by Robert A. Fowler & T. W. Hummel. 1979. pap. 5.95 (*0-685-48362-2*) WWWWW Info Serv.

Buyerism: How to Buy or Start & Successfully Run Your Own Small Business. Ed. by Robert A. Fowler. 1971. pap. 5.95 (*0-317-11969-9*) WWWWW Info Serv.

Buyerism: Survival & Tactics to Help You Buy or Start & Successfully Run Your Own Small Business. Ed. by Robert A. Fowler. 1982. pap. 2.95 (*0-317-11982-6*) WWWWW Info Serv.

Buyers. Gerald Toy. Ed. by Shelia Lenahan. (Illus.). 28p. (Orig.). 1983. pap. text ed. 2.95 (*0-911017-01-1*) Seacliffe.

Buyers & Borrowers: The Application of Consumer Theory to the Study of Library Use. Charles D. Emery. LC 91-23991. (Illus.). 182p. 1992. lib. bdg. 39.95 (*1-56024-183-7*) Haworth Pr.

Buyers Are Liars & Sellers Are Too! Richard Courtney. 1992. pap. 6.95 (*0-9635026-0-3*) Eggman Pub.

Buyer's Book of Solar Water Heaters. 4th ed. Kaiman Lee & Michael Silverstein. LC 79-104450. (Illus.). 1979. 50.00 (*0-915250-30-6*) Environ Design.

Buyer's Guide: An Analysis of Selected U. S. Stamps. Stephen R. Datz. 176p. (Orig.). 1992. pap. 14.95 (*0-88219-026-1*) General Trade.

Buyer's Guide: 1992. 312p. 1992. pap. 66.00 (*0-318-12148-4*) AATCC.

***Buyer's Guide for Office Products & Stationery.** 2nd ed. 190p. 1992. pap. 35.00 (*0-909532-91-5*) D W Thorpe.

Buyer's Guide for Office Products & Stationery 1994. 190p. 1994. pap. 30.00 (*1-875589-50-3*) D W Thorpe.

Buyers Guide, Nineteen Eighty Eight. 200p. 1987. pap. 5.00 (*0-935297-06-5*) Titanium.

Buyer's Guide to Affordable Antique Jewelry: How to Find, Buy, & Care for Fabulous Antique Jewelry. Anna M. Miller. LC 92-37557. 1993. 9.95 (*0-8065-1411-6*) Carol Pub Group.

Buyer's Guide to American Wines: The Right Wine for the Right Price. rev. ed. Anthony D. Blue. LC 91-58283. 304p. 1992. reprint ed. pap. 15.00 (*0-06-273158-0*, PL) HarpC.

Buyer's Guide to Business Insurance. Don Bury & Larry Heischman. Ed. by Camille Akin. 312p. 1994. pap. 19.95 (*1-55571-162-6*); ring bd. 39.95 (*1-55571-310-6*) Oasis Pr OR.

Buyer's Guide to Cosmetics. Patricia Boughton & Martha E. Hughes. 1981. pap. 6.95 (*0-394-74859-X*) Random.

Buyer's Guide to Dentistry. Christensen. 195p. 1994. 49.00 (*0-8016-6776-3*) Mosby Yr Bk.

Buyer's Guide to Diabetes Products 1995. American Diabetes Association Staff. 40p. 1994. pap. 4.95 (*0-945448-20-1*, CMISBUY) Am Diabetes.

Buyers Guide to Risk Management Services. 400p. 1993. write for info. (*0-318-72430-8*) Risk Mgmt Magzne.

Buyer's Guide to Sheltered Housing. Age Concern England Staff. (C). 1989. 35.00 (*0-86242-063-6*, Pub. by Age Concern Eng UK) St Mut.

Buyer's Guide to Software for the IBM Personal Computer. Phillip Lemmons. 1983. pap. 18.95 (*0-07-037150-4*, BYTE Bks) McGraw.

Buyer's Guide to the Rare Coin Market. Q. David Bowers. 372p. (Orig.). 1990. pap. text ed. 14.95 (*0-943161-26-6*) Bowers & Merena.

Buyer's Guide to the Rare Coin Market. 2nd ed. Q. David Bowers. (Illus.). 372p. (Orig.). 1992. pap. text ed. 19.95 (*0-943161-47-9*) Bowers & Merena.

Buyer's Guide to the Supply of Goods & Service Act, 1982. Ed. by Geoffrey Woodroffe. 68p. (C). 1988. 35.00 (*0-685-29257-6*, Inst Pur & Supply) St Mut.

Buyer's Guide to the Supply of Goods & Service Act, 1982. Geoffrey Woodroffe. 68p. (C). 1989. 45.00 (*0-685-36155-1*) St Mut.

Buyer's Guide to the Supply of Goods & Service Act, 1982. G. Woodroofe. 68p. (C). 1983. 45.00 (*0-685-39830-7*, Inst Pur & Supply) St Mut.

Buyer's Guide to United States Gold Coins. Q. David Bowers. (Illus.). 122p. (Orig.). 1989. text ed. 19.95 (*0-943161-22-3*); pap. text ed. 12.95 (*0-943161-17-7*) Bowers & Merena.

Buyer's Manual. (C). 22.00 (*0-87102-010-6*, 45-9410) Natl Ret Merch.

Buying a Bargain Home. (Illus.). 128p. (Orig.). 1989. pap. 34.95 (*1-879562-02-2*) Info Servs CA.

Buying a Bargain Home. rev. ed. (Illus.). 144p. (Orig.). 1990. pap. 34.95 (*1-879562-03-0*) Info Servs CA.

Buying a Better Environment: Cost-Effective Regulation Through Permit Trading. Ed. by Erhard F. Joeres & Martin H. David. LC 83-47673. (Land Economics Monographs: No. 6). 296p. 1983. pap. 9.95 (*0-299-95044-1*) U of Wis Pr.

Buying a Business. Ronald J. McGregor. Ed. by Philip Gerould. LC 92-82770. (Small Business & Entrepreneurship Ser.). 200p. (Orig.). 1993. pap. 15.95 (*1-56052-166-X*) Crisp Pubns.

Buying a Business. 2nd ed. Mike Allen & Robert Hodgkinson. 208p. 1989. lib. bdg. 78.50 (*1-85333-277-1*, Pub. by Graham & Trotman UK) Kluwer Ac.

Buying a Business in Russia: A Handbook for Westerners on Russian Privatization. Youry Petchenkine. 182p. 1993. 89.00 (*0-9637388-0-1*) D N Yng & Assocs.

Buying a Cellular-Mobile Telephone. S. K. Brown. (Illus.). 1988. pap. 5.95 (*0-943927-00-5*) S K Brown Pub.

Buying a Company in Trouble. Ian Walker & Cork Gully. 144p. 1992. 57.95 (*0-566-07289-0*, Pub. by Gower UK) Ashgate Pub Co.

Buying a Computer Micro-Mini or Main Frame. T. J. Sorger. (Illus.). pap. 12.95 (*0-9604072-1-9*) Sorger Assocs.

Buying a Home in Northern Virginia, 1994 Edition. David Rathgeber. 184p. 1994. pap. 9.95 (*0-9635337-1-1*) Rathco Realty Res.

***Buying a Home in the Washington, D. C. Metropolitan Area.** David Rathgeber. 164p. 1995. pap. 9.95 (*0-9635337-3-8*) Rathco Realty Res.

Buying a Home When You're Single. Donna G. Albrecht. 1994. pap. text ed. 12.95 (*0-471-02499-6*) Wiley.

Buying a House, Buying a Mobile Home. Northwest Regional Educational Laboratory Staff. (Illus.). 1979. text ed. 13.96 (*0-07-047302-1*) McGraw.

Buying a Shop. A. St. J. Price. 128p. (Orig.). 1990. pap. text ed. 20.95 (*0-8464-1373-6*) Beekman Pubs.

Buying Actuals: An Investor's Manual for Evaluating Gold & Silver. Jack N. Moneyhon. (Illus.). 80p. (Orig.). 1984. pap. 16.95 (*0-930907-00-0*) Great & Sm Pubs.

Buying America Back. Ed. by Jonathan Greenberg & William Kistler. LC 92-72317. 621p. 1993. 27.95 (*0-933031-69-6*); pap. 16.95 (*0-933031-85-8*) Coun Oak Bks.

Buying & Caring for Your Car & Insurance for Your Life, Health & Possessions. Northwest Regional Educational Laboratory Staff. (Lifeworks Ser.). (Illus.). 1980. text ed. 13.96 (*0-07-047307-2*) McGraw.

Buying & Goodbying of Behaviorism's Way: Confessions & Perspectives of an Ex-Behaviorist. Jon R. Davidson. LC 76-52140. 1978. 16.95 (*0-87212-079-1*) Libra.

Buying & Installing Generic Software for Library Use see Essential Guide to the Library IBM PC

Buying & Managing Residential Real Estate. Andrew J. McLean. 208p. (Orig.). 1989. pap. 12.95 (*0-8092-4412-8*) Contemp Bks.

Buying & Owning Your Own Airplane. 2nd ed. James E. Ellis. LC 91-13494. (Illus.). 304p. 1991. 29.95 (*0-8138-0168-0*); pap. 20.95 (*0-8138-0170-2*) Iowa St U Pr.

***Buying & Selling a Business.** Mark T. Lauer. Ed. by Debra L. Franco. 250p. (Orig.). 1995. pap. 24.95 (*1-880539-33-0*) Garrett FL.

Buying & Selling a Business: A Step-by-Step Guide. Robert F. Klueger. 236p. 1988. pap. text ed. 19.95 (*0-471-60312-0*) Wiley.

***Buying & Selling a Car for Dummies.** David Solomon. 1995. pap. 16.99 (*1-56884-380-1*) IDG Bks.

Buying & Selling a Home. Changing Times Staff. 320p. 1990. pap. 10.95 (*0-938721-12-7*) Kiplinger Bks.

***Buying & Selling a Home: A Homeowner's Guide to Survival.** Tom Tynan. Ed. by Pete Billac. (Illus.). 144p. 1994. pap. write for info. (*0-943629-13-6*) Swan Pub.

Buying & Selling a Home in California: A Complete Guide. Diane Hymer. 230p. 1994. pap. 16.95 (*0-8118-0433-X*) Chronicle Bks.

Buying & Selling a Horse. Cherry Hill. 1991. pap. 2.95 (*0-88266-654-1*, Garden Way Pub) Storey Comm Inc.

Buying & Selling a Residence in France. Keith F. Baker & Georges Daublon. 130p. (C). 1993. 195.00 (*0-85459-809-X*, Pub. by Tolley Pubng UK) St Mut.

Buying & Selling a Small Business. 3rd ed. Michael M. Coltman. (Business Ser.). 168p. (Orig.). 1991. pap. 8.95 (*0-88908-988-4*) Self-Counsel Pr.

Buying & Selling a Small Business. Verne A. Bunn. Ed. by Stuart Bruchey & Vincent P. Carosso. LC 78-18955. (Small Business Enterprise in America Ser.). (Illus.). 1979. reprint ed. lib. bdg. 17.95 (*0-405-11459-1*) Ayer.

Buying & Selling Antiques: A Dealer's Inside View. Don Cline & Sara Pitzer. LC 85-61478. 112p. (Orig.). 1986. pap. 11.95 (*0-88266-406-9*, Storey Pub) Storey Comm Inc.

Buying & Selling Antiques & Collectibles: For Fun & Profit. Joan Bingham & Don Bingham. LC 94-7707. 224p. 1994. pap. 16.95 (*0-8048-1986-6*) C E Tuttle.

Buying & Selling Business Opportunities. Wilfred F. Tetreault & Robert W. Clements. LC 80-66117. (Illus.). 232p. 1980. text ed. 35.00 (*0-937152-00-5*) Am Busn Consult.

Buying & Selling Business Opportunities: A Sales Transaction Handbook. Wilfred F. Tetreault. LC 80-18771. 208p. 1981. 37.95 (*0-201-07711-6*) Addison-Wesley.

Buying & Selling Businesses. Alan L. Schneider. (Business Law Ser.). 53p. (Orig.). 1987. pap. 24.75 (*0-685-28080-2*) BLI Inc.

***Buying & Selling Businesses & Companies.** D. R. Magarey. 316p. 1989. boxed 69.00 (*0-409-49535-2*, Austral) Butterworth Legal Pubs.

Buying & Selling Country Land. Daniel Reisman & Sanford J. Durst. (Illus.). 1981. lib. bdg. 19.95 (*0-915262-40-1*) S J Durst.

***Buying & Selling Gas: A Practical Guide for Operators, Non-Operators, & Royalty Owners.** Ed. by Paul Strohl. 1994. pap. text ed. 59.95 (*0-471-11269-0*) Wiley.

Buying & Selling Gas: A Practical Guide for Operators, NonOperators & Royalty Owners. Paul Strohl. 232p. 1991. 59.95 (*1-55840-438-4*, P7407) Exec Ent Pubns.

Buying & Selling in Furniture. 1980. 190.00 (*0-317-43754-2*) St Mut.

Buying & Selling Medical Practices: A Valuation Guide. 1990. 52.00 (*0-685-45433-9*, OP370089) AMA.

Buying & Selling of America's Newspapers. Ed. by Loren Ghiglione. 200p. 1984. 21.95 (*0-89730-109-9*) Blue-Rib Grp.

Buying & Selling Private Companies & Businesses. 4th ed. Humphrey Wine & Simon Beswick. 300p. 1992. U.K. pap. 55.00 (*0-406-00487-0*) Butterworth Legal Pubs.

***Buying & Selling Real Estate.** Everett L. Gracey. 40p. (Orig.). 1994. pap. 9.95 (*1-56167-189-4*) Am Literary Pr.

***Buying & Selling Small Business.** 4th ed. Michael M. Coltman. 1994. pap. 9.95 (*0-88908-842-X*) Self-Counsel Pr.

Buying & Setup Guide to High-Tech Electronics. William Barden, Jr. Ed. by Janet K. Barden. (Illus.). 1988. write for info. (*0-318-63255-1*) W Barden Inc.

Buying & Supplying Quality. 2nd ed. Richard T. Weber & Ross H. Johnson. LC 93-24982. 264p. 1993. 36.95 (*0-87389-253-4*) ASQC Qual Pr.

Buying Antique Furniture: An Advisory. Lew Larason. Ed. by Pattie Guthrie. (Illus.). 174p. (Orig.). 1992. pap. text ed. 14.95 (*0-936099-02-X*) Scorpio Pubns.

Buying Antique Jewelry: Skipping the Mistakes. Karen Lorene. (Illus.). 164p. (Orig.). 1987. pap. 19.95 (*0-9618302-0-4*) Lorene Pubns.

***Buying Book Printing.** 4th ed. Dan Poynter. (Book Publishing Consultation with Dan Poynter Ser.). (Illus.). 35p. 1994. student ed 14.95 (*0-568-60013-4*) Para Pub.

Buying Books: A How-to-Do-It Manual for Librarians. Audrey Eaglen. (How-to-Do-It Ser.). 166p. 1989. pap. text ed. 39.95 (*1-55570-013-6*) Neal-Schuman.

Buying Breakfast for My Kamikaze Pilot. Norman Stock. LC 94-4868. (Peregrine Smith Poetry Ser.). 64p. 1994. pap. 9.95 (*0-87905-601-0*) Gibbs Smith Pub.

Buying Equipment & Programs for Home or Office. Ed. by C. J. McDonald. (M.D. Computing: Benchmark Papers). (Illus.). 205p. 1987. 54.00 (*0-387-96455-X*) Spr-Verlag.

Buying for Armageddon: Business, Society, & Military Spending since the Cuban Missile Crisis. John L. Boies. 1994. write for info. (*0-318-72414-6*) Rutgers U Pr.

Buying for Armageddon: Society, Economy, & the State since the Cuban Missile Crisis. John L. Boies. LC 93-41777. (Arnold & Caroline Rose Monograph Series of the American Sociological Association). 200p. (C). 1994. text ed. 40.00 (*0-8135-2082-7*) Rutgers U Pr.

Buying Foreclosures Before the Auction. Reis Network Staff. (Home Study Book & Cassette Tapes Ser.). 62p. 1985. 69.95 (*0-9616384-1-9*) Reis Network.

***Buying French Wine from the Chateau & Vineyard: An Explorer's Guide.** Hilary Wright. (Illus.). 208p. 1994. 9.95 (*0-7493-1819-8*) Antique Collect.

Buying Game: Fashion Buying & Merchandising. Sidney Packard & Miriam Guerreiro. (Illus.). (C). 1979. student ed 17.50 (*0-87005-315-9*); teacher ed 2.50 (*0-87005-331-0*) Fairchild.

Buying Greenhouse Insurance: The Economic Costs of CO2 Emission Limits. Alan Manne & Richard Richels. (Illus.). 192p. 1992. 29.95x (*0-262-13280-X*) MIT Pr.

Buying Guide for Fresh Fruits, Vegetables, Herbs & Nuts. 7th rev. ed. Hugh Oakley. (Illus.). 136p. (C). 1980. pap. text ed. 4.00 (*0-9611512-0-X*) Castle & Cooke.

Buying Guide to California Wines. 3rd ed. Ed. by John M. Brennan. (Illus.). 1986. 29.95 (*0-916040-53-4*) Wine Consul Calif.

Buying, Handling & Using Fresh Fruits. 20p. 1984. pap. 5.00 (*0-317-57879-0*, PB180) Natl Restaurant Assn.

Buying, Handling & Using Fresh Vegetables. 20p. 1984. pap. 5.00 (*0-317-57880-4*, PB210) Natl Restaurant Assn.

Buying Happiness. Edgar J. Goodspeed. LC 68-29207. (Essay Index Reprint Ser.). 1977. reprint ed. 18.95 (*0-8369-0483-4*) Ayer.

Buying In: A Complete Guide to Acquiring A Business or Professional Practice. Lawrence W. Tuller. 340p. 1990. 24.95 (*0-8306-7061-0*, 30061) TAB Bks.

Buying In: A Complete Guide to Acquiring a Business or Professional Practice. Lawrence W. Tuller. 1991. text ed. 24.95 (*0-07-156115-3*) McGraw.

Buying Insurance: Maximum Protection at Minimum Cost. Wilson J. Humber. 80p. 1994. pap. 3.99 (*0-8024-1212-2*) Moody.

Buying into America: How Foreign Money Is Changing the Face of Our Nation. Martin Tolchin & Susan J. Tolchin. LC 87-40198. 402p. 1988. 19.95 (*0-8129-1667-0*, Times Bks) Random.

Buying into America: How Foreign Money Is Changing the Face of Our Nation. rev. ed. Martin Tolchin & Susan Tolchin. LC 93-14624. 400p. 1993. reprint ed. pap. 14.95 (*0-918535-17-4*) Farragut Pub.

Buying Jewelry. Bingham. Date not set. pap. 5.99 (*0-685-69319-8*, Harp PBks) HarpC.

Buying Lots from Developers. 1986. lib. bdg. 79.95 (*0-8490-3535-X*) Gordon Pr.

Buying More House for Less Money. Ceil Lohmar. 1990. pap. 9.95 (*1-55738-162-3*) Probus Pub Co.

Buying or Building a Broadcast Station in the 1990s. Erwin G. Krasnow et al. 108p. 1991. write for info. (*0-318-68496-9*) Natl Assn Broadcasters.

Buying or Selling a Business. Dana Herbison. (Illus.). 68p. (Orig.). 1990. pap. 7.00 (*0-931113-35-0*) Success Publ.

Buying or Selling a Home: Tax Breaks. 32p. (Orig.). 1993. pap. 6.50 (*0-685-66961-0*, 5412) Commerce.

Buying or Selling an Insurance Broker. Michael G. Collins. (C). 1986. 250.00 (*0-685-33786-3*, Pub. by Witherby & Co UK) St Mut.

Buying or Selling Your Home. 32p. 1991. pap. 2.00 (*0-685-07104-9*, 417-0007) Amer Bar Assn.

***Buying Power: The Political Economy of Japanese Foreign Aid.** David Arase. LC 94-34471. 307p. 1995. lib. bdg. 49.95 (*1-55587-447-9*) Lynne Rienner.

Buying Power of Labor & Post-War Cycles. Asher Achinstein. LC 68-57563. (Columbia University. Studies in the Social Sciences: No. 292). reprint ed. 20.00 (*0-404-51292-5*) AMS Pr.

***Buying Power Survey.** 225p. (Orig.). 1994. pap. 195.00 (*0-7605-0276-5*) Rector Pr.

Buying Real Estate Foreclosures. Melissa S. Kollen. 224p. 1992. pap. text ed. 14.95 (*0-07-035818-4*) McGraw.

Buying Real Estate Super-Bargains at California Tax Sales. Ronald Starr. 78p. (Orig.). 1991. pap. 20.00 (*0-934521-11-5*) Unlimited Golden Pr.

Buying, Renting & Borrowing in Texas: The Rules of the Game. H. Clyde Farrell & Paul Kens. LC 80-52895. (Illus.). 278p. 1980. 10.95 (*0-937606-00-6*); pap. 6.95 (*0-937606-01-4*) Tex Consumer.

Buying, Renting & Borrowing in Texas: The Rules of the Game. 3rd rev. ed. H. Clyde Farrell & Joe Fiore. (Illus.). Date not set. pap. 10.95 (*0-937606-02-2*) Tex Consumer.

***Buying Retail Is Stupid! Southern California's Discount Guide to Buying Everything at up to 80 Percent off Retail.** 4th expanded rev. ed. Trisha King & Deborah Newmark. LC 94-68715. 528p. 1994. pap. 16.95 (*0-932767-06-0*) Newmark Mgmt Inst.

Buying Right. John W. Schaub. Ed. by Valerie D. Schaub. (Orig.). 19.95 (*0-936177-01-2*, BF673.N4C55); pap. 16.95 (*0-936177-00-4*) Pro Serve Corp.

Buying, Selling & Merging Businesses. 2nd ed. Jere D. McGaffey. LC 89-84075. 579p. 1989. text ed. 99.00 (*0-8318-0519-6*, B519) Am Law Inst.

Buying, Selling, Starting a Business. Ray L. Gustafson. LC 82-90702. 152p. 1982. pap. text ed. 20.00 (*0-9609046-0-3*) GHC.

Buying Serials: A How-to-Do-It Manual for Librarians. N. Bernard Basch & Judy McQueen. (How-to-Do-It Ser.). 198p. 1990. pap. text ed. 39.95 (*1-55570-058-6*) Neal-Schuman.

Buying Short-Haul Microwave. Steve Ditto. 1988. 19.95 (*0-936648-24-4*) Telecom Lib.

Buying Smart: How to Buy a Used Car. Marc Beauparlant. 1994. pap. 3.99 (*0-9641886-6-X*) Bee Pubng.

Buying Stocks Without a Broker. Charles B. Carlson. 304p. 1992. text ed. 29.95 (*0-07-009951-0*); pap. text ed. 16.95 (*0-07-009952-9*) McGraw.

Buying Surplus Property from the U. S. Government. Barry L. McVay. 20p. (Orig.). 1987. pap. 12.50 (*0-912481-04-8*) Panoptic Ent.

***Buying the Best.** 1995. pap. text ed. write for info. (*1-886312-00-1*) Buying Best.

Buying the Wind: Regional Folklore in the United States. Richard M. Dorson. LC 63-13010. 573p. 1972. pap. text ed. 18.95 (*0-226-15862-4*) U Ch Pr.

Buying Time. Peter Elvy. 160p. (C). 1988. 30.00 (*0-85597-385-4*, Pub. by McCrimmon Pub) St Mut.

Buying Time. Joe W. Haldeman. 304p. 1990. pap. 3.95 (*0-380-70439-0*) Avon.

Buying Time: An Anthology Celebrating Twenty Years of the Literature Program of the National Endowment for the Arts. Ed. by Scott Walker. LC 85-80545. 312p. 1985. 20.00 (*0-915308-72-X*) Graywolf.

Buying Treasury Securities at Federal Reserve Banks. James F. Tucker. 79p. 1989. pap. 4.50 (*0-317-02697-6*) FRB Richmond.

Buying Trouble? National Security & Reliance on Foreign Industry. James F. Miskal. LC 92-42182. 1993. 44.50 (*0-8191-9012-8*); pap. 19.50 (*0-8191-9013-6*) U Pr of Amer.

Buying TV & Radio Airtime: A Money-Saving Method That Puts You in Control. Timothy J. Scanlan. LC 91-91004. 80p. 1991. 85.00 (*1-880112-01-9*) Evergr Media.

Buying Your First Cellular Mobile Telephone. Chris Stevens. 25p. (Orig.). 1990. pap. (*0-943927-01-3*) S K Brown Pub.

Buying Your First Franchise: The Least You Need to Know. Rebecca Luhn. Ed. by Philip Gerould. (Small Business & Entrepreneurship Ser.). 175p. (Orig.). 1994. pap. 15.95 (*1-56052-190-2*) Crisp Pubns.

***Buying Your First Home for Dummies.** 1995. pap. 16.99 (*1-56884-385-2*) IDG Bks.

***Buying Your Next Car.** White. Date not set. 5.99 (*0-517-12412-2*) Random.

Buying Your Next Car: How to Stick It to the Dealer Before the Dealer Can Stick It to You. J. Michel White. LC 92-47125. 144p. (Orig.). 1993. pap. 8.95 (*0-943173-79-5*) Harbinger AZ.

Buyout! Employee Ownership as an Alternative to Plant Shutdowns: The Ohio Experience. John Logue et al. LC 86-623028. (Illus.). 104p. (Orig.). 1986. pap. text ed. 9.95 (*0-933522-15-0*) Kent Popular.

Buz. Richard Egielski. LC 94-36033. (Laura Geringer Book Ser.). (Illus.). 32p. (J). (ps-2). 1995. 14.95 (*0-06-023566-7*); lib. bdg. 14.89 (*0-06-023567-5*) HarpC Child Bks.

Buzandaran Patmutiwn: The Epic Histories. Faustos of Buzand. Ed. by Nina G. Garsoian. LC 83-14297. (Classical Armenian Texts Ser.). 1984. 50.00 (*0-88206-033-3*) Caravan Bks.

Buzbee. Joe W. Cates. (Illus.). 96p. (J). (gr. 3-8). 1987. lib. bdg. write for info. (*0-942403-04-5*) J Barnaby Dist.

Buzby. Julia Hoban. LC 89-29408. (I Can Read Bk.). (Illus.). 64p. (J). (gr. k-3). 1990. lib. bdg. 14.89 (*0-06-022398-7*) HarpC Child Bks.

An Asterisk (*) at the beginning of an entry indicates that the title is appearing in BIP for the first time.

An Asterisk (*) at the beginning of an entry indicates that the title is appearing in BIP for the first time.

B

By-Laws of the International Development Association. 8p. English. write for info. (0-8213-1480-7, 11480); French. write for info. (0-8213-1481-5, 11481); Spanish. write for info. (0-8213-2042-4, 12042) World Bank.
By-Laws of the International Finance Corporation. 12p. English. write for info. (0-8213-1478-5, 11478); French. write for info. (0-8213-1479-3, 11479); Spanish. write for info. (0-8213-2037-8, 12037) World Bank.
By-Laws of the Multilateral Investment Guarantee Agency. 12p. English. write for info. (0-8213-1484-X, 11484); French. write for info. (0-8213-1485-8, 11485); Spanish. write for info. (0-8213-1486-6, 11486) World Bank.
By Life's Grace: Musings on the Essence of Social Change. Fran Peavey. 192p. 1994. 39.95 (0-86571-284-0); pap. 14.95 (0-86571-285-9) New Soc Pubs.
By-Line: Ernest Hemingway. Ernest Hemingway. Ed. by William White. LC 67-15483. 512p. 1981. text ed. 50.00 (0-684-16600-3, Scribners); pap. 16.95 (0-684-13685-6, Scribners) S&S Trade.
By Line Ernest Hemingway. Ernest Hemingway. 1981. 27. 50 (0-685-45828-8, Scribners) S&S Trade.
By Lock & Pound. Vivian Bird. 208p. (C). 1989. 69.00 (0-947712-06-2, Pub. by S A Baldwin UK) St Mut.
By Love Beguiled. Sandra DuBay. 480p. (Orig.). 1986. pap. 3.95 (0-8439-2818-2) Dorchester Pub Co.
By Love Betrayed. Sandra DuBay. 432p. (Orig.). 1993. pap. 4.99 (0-8439-3282-1) Dorchester Pub Co.
By Love Compelled: The Life of Fr. Philip Rinaldi. Peter M. Rinaldi. (Illus.). 228p. (Orig.). 1973. pap. 6.95 (0-89944-032-0) Don Bosco Multimedia.
By Love Divided. Rebecca Burton. 1978. pap. 1.95 (0-8439-0558-1) Dorchester Pub Co.
By Love Possessed. James G. Cozzens. LC 57-10062. 1957. 8.50 (0-15-115113-X) HarBrace.
***By Love Possessed.** James G. Cozzens. 1994. reprint ed. lib. bdg. 21.95x (1-56849-549-8) Buccaneer Bks.
By Love Unveiled. Deborah Martin. 384p. (Orig.). 1993. pap. 4.99 (0-451-40362-2, Topaz) NAL-Dutton.
***By Love's Command.** Helen Carras. 384p. 1995. mass mkt. 4.99 (0-8217-4901-3) Windsor NY.
***By Lunar Light: A Novel.** Joyce Frazeur. 240p. (Orig.). 1995. pap. 12.95 (1-56474-129-X) Fithian Pr.
By Many Infallible Proofs. F. Von Kietzell. 76p. pap. 4.95 (0-88172-137-9) Believers Bkshelf.
By Means of Performance: Intercultural Studies of Theatre & Ritual. Ed. by Richard Schechner & Willa Appel. (Illus.). (C). 1990. pap. 22.95 (0-521-33915-4) Cambridge U Pr.
By My Lady's Honor. Joanna McGuaran. 1994. mass mkt. 4.99 (0-440-21368-1) Dell.
By My Spirit. R. W. Stringfield & Tom Keene. 1974. 5.25 (0-685-74870-7, MB-348) Lillenas.
By Myself. David Kherdian. LC 92-44366. (Illus.). 32p. (J). (ps-2). 1993. 14.95 (0-8050-2386-0, Bks Young Read) H Holt & Co.
By Myself But Not Alone: A Prayer Journal for Divorced Moms. Barbara Owen. LC 93-42901. 1994. pap. 10.00 (0-8170-1201-X) Judson.
***By-Name Index to the Centennial History of Arkansas.** Lewis E. Roberts. 1994. pap. 28.50 (0-941765-97-0) Arkansas Res.
***By-Name Index to the Centennial History of Arkansas.** 2nd ed. Lewis E. Roberts. 260p. 1994. 38.50 (0-941765-96-2) Arkansas Res.
By Nature's Design: An Exploratorium Book. Pat Murphy. Ed. by Judith Dunham. LC 92-41313. (Illus.). 120p. 1993. 29.95 (0-8118-0444-5); pap. 18.95 (0-8118-0329-5) Chronicle Bks.
By Night Unstarred: An Autobiographical Novel. Patrick Kavanagh. LC 76-57462. 1978. 50.00 (0-914612-07-7) Kavanagh.
By Nile & Tigris, 2 vols., Set. Ernest A. Budge. LC 75-28120. (Illus.). reprint ed. 75.00 (0-404-11312-5) AMS Pr.
By No Extraordinary Means. Joanne Lynn. 1986. 35.00 (0-253-31287-6) Ind U Pr.
By No Extraordinary Means: The Choice to Forgo Life-Sustaining Food & Water. Ed. by Joanne Lynn. LC 85-45781. (Medical Ethics Ser.). 323p. 1986. 35.00 (0-253-33659-7); pap. 16.95 (0-253-20517-4, MB-517) Ind U Pr.
***By Oak, Ash & Thorn: Modern Celtic Shamanism.** D. J. Conway. LC 94-40820. (Illus.). 288p. 1995. pap. 12.95 (1-56718-166-X) Llewellyn Pubns.
By One Spirit. Karl A. Olsson. (Illus.). 1962. pap. 12.95 (0-910452-10-5) Covenant.
By Order of Adoption. Jean Downie. LC 91-41048. 80p. 1992. pap. 9.95 (0-942963-18-0) Distinctive Pub.
By Parked Cars. J. D. Woolery. 48p. 1986. pap. 5.95 (0-917658-23-X) BPW & P.
By-Paths in Hebraic Bookland. Israel Abrahams. LC 77-174368. 1977. reprint ed. 19.95 (0-405-08177-4, Pub. by Blom Pubns UK) Ayer.
By Post to the Apostles. Helen Homan. LC 74-148219. (Biography Index Reprint Ser.). 1977. 23.95 (0-8369-8066-2) Ayer.
By-Products & Waste Materials in Fat Technology. Henryk Niewiadomski & Hanna Szczepanska. 352p. 1995. text ed. 69.95 (0-13-109547-1) P-H.
By-Products of the Cane Sugar Industry: An Introduction to Their Industrial Utilization. 3rd rev. ed. J. M. Paturau. (Sugar Ser.: No. 11). 436p. 1989. 146.25 (0-444-88214-6) Elsevier.
By Rail Through the Heart of Ireland. Padraic O'Farrell. (Illus.). 1990. pap. 16.95 (0-85342-948-0, Pub. by Mercier Pr IE) Dufour.
By Reason Of... M. R. Henderson. 224p. 1987. pap. 3.95 (0-380-70374-2) Avon.
By Reason of Insanity. James N. Harvey. 352p. 1991. mass mkt. 5.99 (0-312-92533-6) St Martin.
By Reason of Insanity. Shane Stevens. 540p. 1990. pap. 5.95 (0-88184-609-0) Carroll & Graf.
By Reason of Insanity: Essays on Psychiatry & the Law. Ed. by Lawrence Z. Freedman. LC 83-3314. 256p. 1983. lib. bdg. 40.00 (0-8420-2203-1) Scholarly Res Inc.
By Reason of Mercy. Tom Tiemens. 64p. 1993. pap. 5.00 (1-884212-00-X) T Tiemens Minist.
By Reason or Force: Chile & the Balancing of Power in South America, 1830-1905. Robert N. Burr. (University of California Publications in Social Welfare: No. 77). 332p. reprint ed. pap. 94.70 (0-7837-4802-7, 2044449) Bks Demand.
***By Recommendation Only: Party & Wedding Guide to San Francisco, Marin, & the Central Peninsula.** 2nd expanded ed. Johanna Kaestner. (Party & Wedding Guides Ser.). 320p. (Orig.). 1995. pap. 15.95 (0-9627482-5-0) Adobe Creek.
By Recommendation Only: Party & Wedding Guide to the Greater East Bay. Johanna Kaestner. (Party & Wedding Guides Ser.). 300p. (Orig.). 1994. pap. 15.95 (0-9627482-3-4) Adobe Creek.
By Recommendation Only: Party & Wedding Guide to the Southern Peninsula. 2nd rev. ed. Johanna Kaestner. (Party & Wedding Guides Ser.). 288p. (Orig.). 1993. pap. 15.95 (0-9627482-4-2) Adobe Creek.
By Reef & Palm. Louis Becke. LC 75-116938. (Short Story Index Reprint Ser.). 1977. 19.95 (0-8369-3440-7) Ayer.
By Request. D. W. Sutherland. 24p. 1987. pap. 35.00 (0-317-59398-6, Pub. by Witherby & Co UK) St Mut.
By Request: Baby On the Way. 1994. mass mkt. 5.50 (0-373-20104-4) Harlequin Bks.
By Request: Father Knows Last! 1994. mass mkt. 5.50 (0-373-20101-X) Harlequin Bks.
By Request: Lover, Come Back. 1994. mass mkt. 5.50 (0-373-20098-6) Silhouette.
By Request: Men in Uniform. 1994. mass mkt. 5.50 (0-373-20100-1) Silhouette.
***By Request: Stranded!** 1995. pap. 5.50 (0-373-20108-7) Harlequin Bks.
By Request: Temperature Rising. 1994. mass mkt. 5.50 (0-373-20099-4) Harlequin Bks.
***By Request: There's Something about a Cowboy.** 1995. mass mkt. 5.50 (0-373-20113-3) Harlequin Bks.
***By Request: Thieves, Spies & Other Lovers.** 1995. pap. 5.50 (0-373-20109-5) Harlequin Bks.
By Request: Undercover Lovers. 1994. mass mkt. 5.50 (0-373-20102-8) Harlequin Bks.
By Request; Conveniently Yours. 1994. mass mkt. 5.50 (0-373-20103-6) Harlequin Bks.
By Right of Sword. Arthur W. Marchmont. 1976. lib. bdg. 15.30 (0-89968-064-X, Lghtyr Pr) Buccaneer Bks.
By Rope & Lead. Ernest Haycox. 1976. 22.95 (0-89190-972-9) Amereon Ltd.
By Royal Command. Curtis P. Iaukea & Lorna K. Watson. Ed. by Niklaus R. Schweizer. LC 87-14111. (Illus.). 240p. 1988. pap. 5.00 (0-9616738-5-0) Hui Hanai.
By Sanction of Law. Joshua H. Jones. LC 73-144643. reprint ed. 47.50 (0-404-00179-3) AMS Pr.
***By Sea, Air, & Land: An Illustrated History of the U. S. Navy & the War in Southeast Asia.** Edward J. Marolda. (Illus.). 410p. (Orig.). 1995. pap. text ed. 43.00 (0-945274-10-6) Naval Hist Ctr.
By Sea & by River: A Naval History of the Civil War. Bern Anderson. (Quality Paperbacks Ser.). (Illus.). 344p. 1989. pap. 13.95 (0-306-80367-4) Da Capo.
By Searching. Isobel Kuhn. 1959. pap. 4.50 (0-8024-0053-1) Moody.
By Shaker Hands. June Sprigg. LC 90-50316. (Illus.). 234p. 1990. pap. 19.95 (0-87451-542-4) U Pr of New Eng.
By Ships Alone: Churchill & the Dardanelles. Jeffrey D. Wallin. LC 79-51940. 232p. 1981. lib. bdg. 18.75 (0-89089-034-X) Carolina Acad Pr.
By Shore & Sedge. Bret Harte. LC 72-121560. (Short Story Index Reprint Ser.). 1977. 20.95 (0-8369-3517-9) Ayer.
By Special Request. Piggly Wiggly Carolina Company Staff. 1993. write for info. (0-9637716-0-4) Piggly Wiggly.
By Special Request. large type ed. Antonia Ridge. 235p. 1981. 12.00 (0-7089-0573-0) Ulverscroft.
By Special Request: Old Recipes for a New Generation. Leu Wilder. 160p. 1993. 12.95 (0-9638840-0-X) L&W Enter.
By Standing Stone & Elder Tree: Ritual & the Unconscious. rev. ed. William G. Gray. LC 90-43188. (New World Magic Ser.). (Illus.). 208p. 1990. reprint ed. pap. 9.95 (0-87542-299-3) Llewellyn Pubns.
***By Stealth.** Colin Forbes. 536p. 1993. pap. 14.95 (0-330-32947-2, Pub. by Pan Books UK) Trans-Atl Phila.
By Still Waters. rev. ed. John M. Drescher. (Visitation Pamphlet Ser.). 1988. 1.95 (0-8361-3477-X) Herald Pr.
By Streamliner, New York to Florida. Joe Welsh. (Illus.). 144p. (Orig.). 1994. pap. 39.95 (0-944119-14-X) Andover Junction.
By Study & Also by Faith Vol. 1: Essays in Honor of Hugh W. Nibley. Ed. by John M. Lundquist & Stephen D. Ricks. LC 89-77960. 704p. 1990. 21.95 (0-87579-339-8) Deseret Bk.
By Study & Also by Faith Vol. 2: Essays in Honor of Hugh W. Nibley. Ed. by John M. Lundquist & Stephen D. Ricks. LC 89-77960. 676p. 1990. 21.95 (0-87579-340-1) Deseret Bk.
By Surprise. Henri Michaux. Tr. by Randolph Hough. 112p. (Orig.). 1987. pap. 5.95 (0-937815-05-5) Hanuman Bks.
By the Banks of the Thames: Russians in Eighteenth Century Britain. A. G. Cross. (Illus.). 356p. 1980. 38.00 (0-89250-085-9) Orient Res Partners.
By the Beautiful Sea: The Rise & High Times of That Great American Resort, Atlantic City. Charles E. Funnell. 1983. 15.95 (0-8135-0986-6) Rutgers U Pr.
***By the Bias of Sound: Selected Poems: 1974-1994.** Gustaf Sobin. 200p. (Orig.). 1995. pap. 13.95 (1-883689-20-1) Talisman Hse.
***By the Bias of Sound: Selected Poems: 1974-1994.** Gustaf Sobin. 200p. 1995. lib. bdg. 33.95 (1-883689-21-X) Talisman Hse.
By the Body of the Earth: The Sannyasi. 2nd ed. SATPREM Staff. Tr. by Luc Venet. 387p. 1991. pap. text ed. 12.00 (0-938710-08-7) Inst Evolutionary.
By the Body of the Earth or the Sanngasi. Satprem. (Works of Satprem-Institute for Evolutionary Research). 377p. 12.00 (0-685-65587-3) Aurobindo Assn.
By the Bomb's Early Light: American Thought & Culture at the Dawn of the Atomic Age. Paul Boyer. LC 94-4241. (Illus.). 470p. 1994. reprint ed. pap. text ed. 16.95 (0-8078-4480-2) U of NC Pr.
By the Book. Christine Dorsey. 224p. (Orig.). 1990. pap. 2.75 (1-878702-10-6, Kismet) Meteor Pub.
By the Book. Susan M. Malone. LC 92-74829. 256p. 1993. 18.00 (1-880909-00-6) Baskerville.
By the Candelabra's Glare. L. Frank Baum. LC 80-28443. 1981. reprint ed. 50.00 (0-8201-1361-1) Schol Facsimiles.
By the Content of Their Character. Myron E. Gruenwald. (Illus.). 80p. 1986. pap. 5.00 (0-9601536-5-9) M E Gruenwald.
By the Cut of Your Clothes. Richards. Ed. by Doug Grad. 224p. (Orig.). 1995. mass mkt. 4.99 (0-671-87242-7) PB.
By the Cypress Swamp: The Arkansas Stories of Octave Thanet. Michael B. Dougan & Carol W. Dougan. 232p. 1980. 14.95 (0-686-47044-3) J W Bell.
By the Dawn's Early Light: Al Amanecer. Karen Ackerman. Tr. by Alma F. Ada. LC 93-34815. (Illus.). 40p. (ENG & SPA.). (J). (ps-3). 1994. English ed. text ed. 14.95 (0-689-31788-3, Atheneum Bks Young); Spanish ed. text ed. 14.95 (0-689-31917-7, Atheneum Bks Young) S&S Childrens.
By the Dawn's Early Light: The Story of the Star Spangled Banner. Steven Kroll. LC 92-27101. (Illus.). 40p. (J). (ps-5). 1994. 14.95 (0-590-45054-9) Scholastic Inc.
By the Dim & Flaring Lamps: The Civil War Diaries of Samuel McIlvaine. Intro. by Clayton E. Cramer. LC 89-12579. (Illus.). 157p. 1990. 28.95 (0-912526-46-7) Lib Res.
By the Far Collins. Martin T. Borrell. (C). 1989. text ed. 39.00 (1-85821-012-7, Pub. by Pentland Pr UK) St Mut.
By the Finger of God: Demon Possession & Exorcism in Early Christianity in the Light of Modern Views of Mental Illness. Selby V. McCasland. LC 79-8111. reprint ed. 23.50 (0-404-18425-1) AMS Pr.
***By the Fruit of Her Own Hands: The Life & Times of Julia Tutwiler.** Garland Reeves. 1995. pap. write for info. (1-878561-35-9) Seacoast AL.
By the Good People of Virginia: Our Commonwealth's Government. 2nd ed. Paul C. Cline & Daniel B. Fleming, Jr. (Virginia Government Textbook Ser.). (Illus.). 1986. 6.00 (0-318-01330-4) VA Chamber Com.
By the Grace of Guile: The Role of Deception in Natural History & Human Affairs. Loyal Rue. LC 93-32877. (Illus.). 368p. 1994. 27.50 (0-19-507508-0) OUP.
By the Great Horn Spoon. Sid Fleischman. (Illus.). (J). (gr. 4-6). 1963. 16.95 (0-316-28577-3, Joy St Bks) Little.
By the Great Horn Spoon. Sid Fleischman. (Illus.). (J). (gr. 4-6). 1988. mass mkt. 5.95 (0-316-28612-5, Joy St Bks) Little.
By the Gun. Richard Matheson. 192p. 1994. pap. 4.50 (0-425-14099-7) Berkley Pub.
By the Gun. Richard Matheson. 1994. 18.95 (0-87131-747-8) M Evans.
By the Harbour Wall. Kim Taplin. 1990. pap. 12.95 (1-870612-75-2, Pub. by Enitha Pr UK) Dufour.
By the Holy Tetraktys: Symbol & Reality in Man & Universe. L. Gordon Plummer. (Study Ser.: No. 9). (Illus.). 96p. (Orig.). (C). 1982. pap. 6.50 (0-913004-44-8) Point Loma Pub.
By the Ionian Sea: Notes of a Ramble in Southern Italy. George Gissing. LC 90-63812. 176p. 1991. reprint ed. pap. 9.95 (0-910395-71-3) Marlboro Pr.
By the Law of Nature: Form & Value in Nineteenth-Century America. Howard Horwitz. (Illus.). 336p. 1991. 52.00 (0-19-506227-2) OUP.
***By the Light.** Lionel C. Bascom & Barbara Loecher. 224p. (Orig.). 1995. mass mkt. 4.99 (0-380-77801-7) Avon.
By the Light of His Lamp. John F. Marshall. (Spirit & Life Ser.). 1967. 2.00 (0-686-11574-0) Franciscan Inst.
By the Light of the Halloween Moon. Caroline Stutson. LC 92-10258. (Illus.). 1993. 16.00 (0-688-12045-8); lib. bdg. 15.93 (0-688-12046-6) Lothrop.
By the Light of the Halloween Moon. Caroline Stutson. (Illus.). 32p. (J). (ps-3). 1994. pap. 4.99 (0-14-055305-3) Puffin Bks.
***By the Light of the Moon.** Gina Erickson & Kelli C. Foster. (Get Ready-Get Set-Read! Ser.). 24p. (J). (gr. k-3). 1995. pap. 3.50 (0-8120-1027-2) Barron.
***By the Light of the Moon.** Marcia Evanick. 1995. mass mkt. 3.75 (0-373-07676-2) Silhouette.
By the Light of the North Star. Hua-Ching Ni. (Orig.). 1994. pap. write for info. (0-937064-62-9) SevenStar Comm.
***By the Light of the Silvery Moon.** Ed. by Ruth Petrie. 192p. 1995. pap. 9.95 (1-85381-775-9, Pub. by Virago Pr UK) Trafalgar.
By the London Post. John Lister. Ed. by Arnold S. Relman. 248p. (Orig.). 1985. pap. text ed. 13.95 (0-910133-13-1) MA Med Soc.
By the Marshes of Minas. Charles G. Roberts. LC 74-178456. (Short Story Index Reprint Ser.). 1977. reprint ed. 21.95 (0-8369-4057-1) Ayer.
***By the Numbers: A Guide to Using Economic Data to Improve Investing.** Stan Carnes & Stephen Slifer. (Practical Investing Ser.). 200p. 1995. pap. text ed. write for info. (1-887147-03-9) Intl Finan Pr.
By the Numbers: Principles of Automotive Parts Management. Gary J. Naples. 200p. 1994. 29.00 (1-56091-520-X, R140) Soc Auto Engineers.
By The Numbers Series. 1994. pap. 24.90 (0-9631961-5-4) Sibylline Bks.
By the Open Sea. August Strindberg. Tr. by Mary Sandbach. 208p. 1987. pap. 8.95 (0-14-044488-2, Penguin Classics) Viking Penguin.
By the Open Sea. August Strindberg. LC 72-3561. (Studies in Fiction: No. 34). (C). 1972. reprint ed. lib. bdg. 75.00 (0-8383-1547-X) M S G Haskell Hse.
By the Orders of the Great White Queen: An Anthology of Campaigning in Zululand, 1879. Ed. by Ian Knight. 276p. 1992. 37.50 (1-85367-122-3) Stackpole.
By the Patient & Not by the Book: Constancy & Change in Small Town Doctoring, 1893-1987. Paul I. Crellin & John K. Crellin. (Illus.). xi, 76p. (Orig.). 1988. pap. 12.95 (0-89386-021-2) Acorn NC.
By the People: A History of Americans as Volunteers. rev. ed. Susan J. Ellis & Katherine H. Noyes. LC 89-43301. (Nonprofit Sector Ser.). 454p. 1990. 32.95x (1-55542-217-9) Jossey-Bass.
***By the People, for the People: U. S. Government & Citizenship, Set.** Deborah Short et al. (Illus.). 174p. 1995. reprint ed. pap. text ed. 12.50 (0-937354-69-4) Delta Systems.
By the People, for the People Vol. 2: U. S. Government & Citizenship. Deborah Short et al. 224p. (C). 1991. pap. text ed. write for info. (0-13-105149-0) P-H.
By the People, U. S. Government Structure: An English As a Second Language Text. (Illus.). 172p. (Orig.). (C). 1994. pap. text ed. 21.95 (0-7881-0542-6) Diane Pub.
By the Pool of Bethesda. Floyd Thompkins. (Illus.). 108p. (Orig.). 1993. per. 6.95 (0-9636064-0-9) Genesis One Twnty-Six.
By the Power of Their Dreams: Songs, Prayers, & Sacred Shields of the Plains Indians. Maureen E. Mansell. LC 93-8148. (Illus.). 96p. 1994. 16.95 (0-8118-0460-7) Chronicle Bks.
By the Pricking of My Thumbs: A Tommy & Tuppence Mystery. Agatha Christie. 1992. mass mkt. 4.99 (0-06-100335-2, Harp PBks) HarpC.
By the Prophet of the Earth: Ethnobotany of the Pima. L. S. Curtin. LC 83-24334. (Illus.). 156p. 1984. reprint ed. pap. 8.95 (0-8165-0854-2) U of Ariz Pr.
By the River of Life. Scott Carneal. LC 91-75094. 158p. 1992. pap. 7.95 (1-55523-460-7) Winston-Derek.
By the River of No Return. Don I. Smith. LC 85-60311. (Illus.). 112p. 1985. reprint ed. pap. 7.99 (0-932773-00-1) High Country Bks.
By the Rivers of Babylon. Nelson DeMille. 432p. 1990. mass mkt. 6.99 (0-446-35859-2) Warner Bks.
By the Rivers of Babylon. large type ed. Nelson De Mille. 624p. 1983. 23.95 (0-7089-8091-0, Charnwood) Ulverscroft.
By the Rivers of Babylon & Other Stories. Jorge De Sena. Ed. by Daphne Patai. 1989. 19.95 (0-8135-1388-X) Rutgers U Pr.
By the Rivers of Babylon & Other Stories. Jorge De Sena. Ed. by Daphne Patai. LC 88-21100. (Fiction Ser.). 155p. 1991. pap. 10.95 (0-8135-1688-9) Rutgers U Pr.
***By the Rules: The NCAA.** Ted Weissberg. LC 95-14676. (Illus.). (YA). (gr. 8-12). 1995. lib. bdg. 14.21 (0-531-11235-7) Watts.
By the Sea. Robert Farber. (Illus.). 160p. 1987. 49.95 (0-317-64598-6) Melrose Pub Inc.
By the Sea. Mary Hofstrand. (Illus.). 32p. (J). (ps-3). 1990. pap. 3.95 (0-14-054208-6, Puffin) Puffin Bks.
By the Sea. Michelle Koch. LC 89-23344. (Illus.). 24p. (J). (ps up). 1991. 13.95 (0-688-09549-6); lib. bdg. 13.88 (0-688-09550-X) Greenwillow.
By the Seat of My Pants: My Life in Country Music. Buddy Killen & Tom Carter. (Illus.). 288p. 1993. 22.00 (0-671-79540-6) S&S Trade.
***By the Seat of Your Pants.** Ruth McCarthy. 60p. 1994. per., pap. text ed. 4.95 (0-7872-0054-9) Kendall-Hunt.
By the Shores of Silver Lake. rev. ed. Laura Ingalls Wilder. LC 52-7529. (Little House Bks.). (Illus.). 304p. (J). (gr. 3-7). 1953. 15.95 (0-06-026416-0) HarpC Child Bks.
By the Shores of Silver Lake. rev. ed. Laura Ingalls Wilder. LC 52-7529. (Little House Bks.). (Illus.). 304p. (J). (gr. 3-7). 1961. lib. bdg. 15.89 (0-06-026417-9) HarpC Child Bks.
By the Shores of Silver Lake see Little House Books
By the Sound. Edward Dorn. LC 91-19033. 228p. (Orig.). 1991. 25.00 (0-87685-841-8); pap. 12.50 (0-87685-840-X) Black Sparrow.
By the Sound, signed ed. deluxe ed. Edward Dorn. LC 91-19033. 228p. (Orig.). 1991. 30.00 (0-87685-842-6) Black Sparrow.
By the Stream of Antique Song. Tr. & Intro. by David Cloutier. 40p. (Orig.). (C). 1988. pap. 6.00 (0-9607756-8-4) Singular Speech Pr.
By the Sweat of My Brow. Wheless. 2.50 (0-685-02583-7) Outlook.
By the Sweat of the Brow: Literature & Labor in Antebellum America. Nicholas K. Bromell. LC 93-17247. 272p. 1993. 29.95 (0-226-07554-0) U Ch Pr.
***By the Sweat of the Brow: Literature & Labor in Antebellum America.** Nicholas K. Bromell. (Literary Studies). 286p. 1995. pap. text ed. 15.95 (0-226-07555-9) U Ch Pr.
By the Sweat of Their Brow: Mexican Immigrant Labor in the United States, 1900-1940. Mark Reisler. LC 76-5329. 304p. (Orig.). 1976. text ed. 59.95 (0-8371-8894-6, RPE/, Greenwood Pr) Greenwood.

B

An Asterisk (*) at the beginning of an entry indicates that the title is appearing in BIP for the first time.

An Asterisk (*) at the beginning of an entry indicates that the title is appearing in BIP for the first time.

B

Byron & the Ruins of Paradise. Robert F. Gleckner. LC 80-11656. (Illus.). xxiv, 365p. 1980. reprint ed. text ed. 65.00 (*0-313-22421-8*, GLBR, Greenwood Pr) Greenwood.

Byron & the Spoiler's Art. rev. ed. Paul West. 280p. 1992. pap. 10.95 (*0-930829-13-1*) Lumen Inc.

***Byron & the Victorians.** Andrew Elfenbein. (Cambridge Studies in Nineteenth-Century Literature & Culture: 4). 292p. (C). 1995. 54.95 (*0-521-45452-2*) Cambridge U Pr.

Byron & Tragedy. Martyn Corbett. LC 87-20301. 192p. 1988. text ed. 39.95 (*0-312-01338-8*) St Martin.

Byron As Critic. Clement Goode. LC 65-15893. (Studies in Byron: No. 5). 1969. reprint ed. lib. bdg. 49.95 (*0-8383-0696-9*) M S G Haskell Hse.

Byron at Southwell. Willis W. Pratt. LC 72-6745. (Studies in Byron: No. 5). 1972. reprint ed. lib. bdg. 51.95 (*0-8383-1646-8*) M S G Haskell Hse.

Byron Birdsall's Alaska & Other Exotic Worlds. Byron Birdsall. Ed. by Lael Morgan & Kent Sturgis. LC 92-40095. (Illus.). 80p. 1993. 32.95 (*0-945397-16-X*); pap. 22.95 (*0-945397-15-1*) Epicenter Pr.

Byron Browne: Studies in Gouache from the 1940's. Richard W. Lizza & Alain G. Joyaux. 16p. (Orig.). 1987. pap. 3.50 (*0-915511-06-1*) Ball State Art.

Byron Browne: Ten Paintings of the 1950's. Intro. by Stephen B. Browne & Stephen L. Schlesinger. (Illus.). (Orig.). 1986. pap. 5.00 (*0-9614661-1-1*) Gallery Schlesinger Boisante.

B

Byron Chronology. Norman Page. 144p. 1988. text ed. 38.50 (*0-8161-8952-8*, Hall Reference) Macmillan.

Byron Dairymple on Trout Fishing: 50 Years of Success. Byron W. Dairymple. LC 91-9164. 192p. 1990. 17.95 (*0-8329-0460-0*, Winchester Pr) New Win Pub.

Byron Haskin. Ed. by Joe Adamson. LC 84-14080. (Directors Guild of American Oral History Ser.: No. 1). (Illus.). 334p. 1984. 27.50 (*0-8108-1740-3*) Scarecrow.

Byron in England: His Fame & After-Fame. Samuel C. Chew. LC 79-115233. (Illus.). 420p. 1972. reprint ed. 9.00 (*0-403-00475-6*) Scholarly.

Byron in England: His Fame & After-Fame. Samuel C. Chew. (BCL1-PR English Literature Ser.). 415p. 1992. reprint ed. lib. bdg. 99.00 (*0-7812-7475-3*) Rprt Serv.

Byron in Italy. Peter Quennell. 1977. 18.95 (*0-8369-7147-7*, 7979) Ayer.

Byron Mystery. John C. Fox. (BCL1-PR English Literature Ser.). 248p. 1992. reprint ed. lib. bdg. 79.00 (*0-7812-7478-8*) Rprt Serv.

Byron Mystery. John C. Fox. LC 72-131707. (Illus.). 262p. 1972. reprint ed. 29.00 (*0-403-00594-9*) Scholarly.

***Byron Nelson: The Little Black Book: Anecdotes, Memories & Lessons on the 50th Anniversary of One Man's Greatest Year in Golf.** Byron Nelson. LC 95-15760. 1995. write for info. (*1-56530-180-3*) Summit TX.

Byron Nelson's Winning Golf. limited ed. Byron Nelson. 192p. 1992. reprint ed. 50.00 (*0-87833-021-6*) Taylor Pub.

Byron Nelson's Winning Golf. Byron Nelson. 192p. 1992. reprint ed. 18.95 (*0-87833-800-4*); reprint ed. pap. 9.95 (*0-87833-801-2*) Taylor Pub.

Byron, the Bible, & Religion: Essays from the Twelfth International Byron Seminar. Ed. by Wolf Z. Hirst. LC 89-40786. 200p. 1991. 32.50 (*0-87413-401-3*) U Delaware Pr.

Byron, the Last Journey, April 1823-April 1824. Harold G. Nicolson. (BCL1-PR English Literature Ser.). 288p. 1992. reprint ed. lib. bdg. 79.00 (*0-7812-7481-8*) Rprt Serv.

Byron, the Last Phase. Richard Edgcumbe. LC 72-1332. (Studies in Byron: No. 5). 1972. reprint ed. lib. bdg. 65.95 (*0-8383-1441-4*) M S G Haskell Hse.

Byron the Man. Robert L. Bellamy. 1972. 59.95 (*0-87968-808-4*) Gordon Pr.

Byron the Poet: A Collection of Essays & Addresses by Contemporary Critics. Walter A. Briscoe. LC 67-30803. (Studies in Byron: No. 5). (Illus.). 1969. reprint ed. lib. bdg. 75.00 (*0-8383-0694-2*) M S G Haskell Hse.

Byron the Satirist. Frederick L. Beaty. LC 85-2943. 236p. 1985. 25.00 (*0-87580-109-9*) N Ill U Pr.

Byron White. Bob Italia. Ed. by Paul Deegan. LC 92-13714. (Supreme Court Justices Ser.). (J). 1992. lib. bdg. 13.99 (*1-56239-095-3*) Abdo & Dghtrs.

Byron's Bulldog: The Letters of John Cam Hobhouse to Lord Byron. Peter W. Graham. LC 84-5250. (Illus.). 375p. 1984. 49.50 (*0-8142-0367-1*) Ohio St U Pr.

Byron's Child. Carola Dunn. 224p. 1991. 18.95 (*0-8027-1132-4*) Walker & Co.

Byron's Dialectic: Skepticism & the Critique of Culture. Terence A. Hoagwood. LC 93-54880. 1993. 33.50 (*0-8387-5245-4*) Bucknell U Pr.

Byron's "Don Juan" & Eighteenth-Century Literature: A Study of Some Rhetorical Continuities & Discontinuities. A. B. England. LC 73-16943. 197p. 1975. 29.50 (*0-8387-1417-X*) Bucknell U Pr.

Byron's Double Discovery. Pamela A. Braithwaite. (Illus.). 120p. (Orig.). (J). (gr. 4-10). 1991. pap. 4.00 (*1-880960-00-1*) Script Memory Fl.

Byron's Heroines. Caroline Franklin. (Illus.). 296p. 1992. 59.00 (*0-19-811230-0*) OUP.

Byron's Historical Dramas. Richard Lansdown. (Illus.). 272p. 1992. 59.00 (*0-19-811252-1*) OUP.

Byron's Letters & Journals, 12 vols. George G. Byron. Ed. by Leslie A. Marchand. Incl. Vol. I. In My Hot Youth: Seventeen Ninety-Eight to Eighteen Ten. 288p. 1973. 25.00 (*0-674-08940-5*); Vol. IV. Wedlock's the Devil: Eighteen Fourteen to Eighteen Fifteen. 369p. 1975. 29.95 (*0-674-08944-8*); Vol. V. So Late into the Night: Eighteen Fifteen to Eighteen Eighteen. 320p. 1990. 25.00 (*0-674-08945-6*); Vol. VI. Flesh Is Frail: Eighteen Eighteen to Eighteen Nineteen. 289p. 1990. 25.00 (*0-674-08946-4*); Vol. VII. Between Two Worlds: Eighteen Twenty. 282p. 1990. 25.00 (*0-674-08947-2*); Vol. VIII. Born for Opposition: Eighteen Twenty-One. 384p. 1990. 29.95 (*0-674-08948-0*); Vol. IX. In the Wind's Eye: Eighteen Twenty One to Eighteen Twenty Two. 248p. 1990. 25.00 (*0-674-08949-9*); Vol. XI. For Freedom's Battle. 256p. 1990. 25.00 (*0-674-08953-7*); Vol. XII. Trouble of an Index. 176p. 1990. 25.00 (*0-674-08954-5*); Vol. V. So Late into the Night: Eighteen Fifteen to Eighteen Eighteen. 320p. 1990. 25.00 (*0-674-08945-6*); Vol. IX. In the Wind's Eye: Eighteen Twenty One to Eighteen Twenty Two. 248p. 1990. 25.00 (*0-674-08949-9*); write for info. (*0-318-53015-5*) HUP.

Byron's Letters & Journals, Vol. 2: Famous in My Time, 1810-1812. George G. Byron. Ed. by Leslie A. Marchand. LC 74-160825. 308p. 1973. reprint ed. pap. 87.80 (*0-7837-1680-X*, 2057212) Bks Demand.

Byron's Letters & Journals, Vol. 3: Alas! the Love of Women. George G. Byron. Ed. by Leslie A. Marchand. LC 74-160825. 385p. reprint ed. pap. 81.30 (*0-7837-1681-8*, 2057212) Bks Demand.

Byron's Letters & Journals Vol. 10: A Heart for Every Fate, 1822-1823. George G. Byron. Ed. by Leslie A. Marchand. LC 73-81853. 245p. 1973. reprint ed. pap. 69.90 (*0-7837-4085-9*, 2057212) Bks Demand.

Byron's Poetry. George G. Byron. Ed. by Frank D. McConnell. (Critical Editions Ser.). (C). 1978. pap. text ed. 12.95 (*0-393-09152-X*) Norton.

Byron's Politics. Malcolm Kelsall. 224p. 1987. 57.50 (*0-389-20715-2*, N8273) B&N Imports.

***Byron's Shadow.** Jason Foss. 1995. lib. bdg. 20.00 (*0-7278-4700-7*) Severn Hse.

Byssinosis-Causative Agent & Clinical Aspects. Shirley Institute Staff. (C). 1982. 395.00 (*0-685-36021-0*, Pub. by British Textile Tech UK) St Mut.

Bystander. Muriel K. Zager. (Illus.). 192p. (Orig.). 1993. pap. 9.95 (*0-89407-109-2*) Strawberry Hill.

Bystander: A History of Street Photography. Colin Westerbeck & Joel Meyerowitz. LC 93-14900. (Illus.). 432p. 1994. 60.00 (*0-8212-1755-0*) Bulfinch Pr.

Byt. T. William Fuller. LC 89-61549. 80p. 1989. 7.50 (*1-882022-01-7*) O Bks.

Byte Brothers Input an Investigation. Lois McCoy et al. (Illus.). (J). 1983. pap. 2.25 (*0-380-85571-2*, 85571, Camelot) Avon.

Byte Guide to CD ROM. Michael Nadeau. 1994. cd-rom, pap. text ed. 39.95 (*0-07-881982-2*) Osborne-McGraw.

***Byte Guide to CD-ROM, Second Edition.** 2nd ed. Michael Nadeau. 1995. cd-rom, pap. text ed. 39.95 (*0-07-882104-5*) Osborne-McGraw.

Byte Guide to CP-M. Mark Dahmke & Steve Ciarcia. 216p. 1984. pap. text ed. 21.95 (*0-07-015072-9*, BYTE Bks) McGraw.

***Byte Guide to OpenDoc.** David Berkowitz. 1995. pap. text ed. 29.95 (*0-07-882118-5*) Osborne-McGraw.

***Byte Guide to Optimizing Windows 95.** Craig Menefee & Lenny Bailes. 1995. pap. text ed. 29.95 (*0-07-882120-7*) Osborne-McGraw.

***Byte Guide to Telescript.** Cronder Concepcion & Paul Staniforth. 1995. pap. text ed. 29.95 (*0-07-882119-3*) Osborne-McGraw.

Byte of the Apple: A Beginner's Guide. Linda Hyler et al. (Illus.). 250p. 1984. 18.95 (*0-8359-0543-8*, Reston); disk 25.00 (*0-8359-0546-2*, Reston) P-H.

Bytes & Bites: With a Bark or Two for Good Measure. Tom C. Armstrong. LC 93-73192. 56p. (Orig.). 1993. pap. 5.99 (*0-9638661-0-9*) AD HOC Bks.

Bytes DOS Programmers Cookbook. Keith Graham. 1994. cd-rom, pap. text ed. 34.95 (*0-07-882048-0*) Osborne-McGraw.

Bytes Mac Programmers Cookbook. Rob Terrell. 1994. disk, pap. text ed. 29.95 (*0-07-882062-6*) Osborne-McGraw.

***Bytes of Faith.** Robert Hauff. 176p. Date not set. 18.95 (*1-56167-194-0*) Noble Hse MD.

***Bytes of Passion.** Gregg Goodrich. 238p. 1994. pap. 8.95 (*1-56901-421-3*) NW Pub.

Bytes OS 2 Programmers Cookbook. Kathy Ivens. 1994. pap. text ed. 34.95 (*0-07-882039-1*) Osborne-McGraw.

Bytes Windows Programmers Cookbook. John Ribar. 1994. cd-rom, pap. text ed. 34.95 (*0-07-882037-5*) Osborne-McGraw.

BYW, Who Are We? (30 Devotions for Baptist Young Women) Deborah P. Brunt. (Illus.). 96p. (Orig.). 1989. pap. text ed. 3.95 (*0-936625-58-9*) Womans Mission Union.

Byway to Love. Margaret SeBastian. (Regency Love Story Ser.). 224p. (Orig.). 1980. pap. 1.75 (*0-449-50044-6*, Coventry) Fawcett.

Byways in Bookland. James W. Thompson. LC 73-88033. (Essay Index Reprint Ser.). 1977. 19.95 (*0-8369-1158-X*) Ayer.

Byways in Handweaving. Mary M. Atwater. LC 88-18432. (Illus.). 128p. 1988. pap. 13.95 (*0-916658-47-3*) Shuttle Craft.

Byways of America. Ed. by Ideals Publications Staff. (Illus.). 1994. 22.95 (*0-8249-4053-9*) Ideals.

Byways of Blessedness. James Allen. 202p. 1992. pap. 20.00 (*0-89540-202-5*, SB-202) Sun Pub.

Byworlder. Poul Anderson. 224p. 1993. mass mkt. 3.99 (*0-671-72178-X*) Baen Bks.

Byzance: Etat - Societe - Economie. Dionysios Zakythinos. (Collected Studies: No. CS25). 440p. (C). 1973. reprint ed. lib. bdg. 109.95 (*0-902089-59-5*, Pub. by Variorum UK) Ashgate Pub Co.

Byzance et la Formation de L'Etate Russe. Alexandre Soloviev. (Collected Studies: No. CS92). (Illus.). 334p. (C). 1979. reprint ed. lib. bdg. 99.50 (*0-86078-037-6*, Pub. by Variorum UK) Ashgate Pub Co.

Byzantine see Greek Museums

Byzantine Achievement. Robert Byron. 352p. 1988. 24.95 (*0-7102-1392-1*, RKP) Routledge.

Byzantine Altar Gospel. Joseph Raya & Jose De Vinck. 350p. 1979. 87.50 (*0-911726-35-7*, CODE AGU); 127.50x (*0-911726-34-9*, CODE AGC); 187.50x (*0-911726-51-9*, CODE AGL) Alleluia Pr.

Byzantine & Early Islamic Near East: (I) Problems in the Literary Source Material. Ed. by Lawrence I. Conrad. LC 92-352. (Studies in Late Antiquity & Early Islam). (Illus.). 428p. 1992. text ed. 29.95 (*0-87850-080-4*) Darwin Pr.

***Byzantine & Early Islamic Near East No. II: Land Use & Settlement Patterns.** Ed. by Averil Cameron & G. R. King. LC 92-352. (Studies in Late Antiquity & Early Islam). (Illus.). 320p. 1994. 35.00x (*0-87850-106-1*) Darwin Pr.

Byzantine & Medieval Greece: Churches, Castles & Art. Paul Hetherington. (Illus.). 224p. 1992. 39.95 (*0-7195-4725-3*, Pub. by John Murray UK); pap. 24.95 (*0-7195-5080-7*, Pub. by John Murray UK) Trafalgar.

Byzantine & Turkish Sardis. Clive Foss. LC 75-14017. (Archaeological Exploration of Sardis, Monograph Ser.: No. 4). (Illus.). 232p. reprint ed. pap. 67.30 (*0-7837-1697-4*, 2057226) Bks Demand.

Byzantine Architecture. Cyril Mango. LC 85-62749. (History of World Architecture Ser.). (Illus.). 224p. 1985. pap. 29.95 (*0-8478-0615-4*) Rizzoli Intl.

Byzantine Architecture & Decoration. John A. Hamilton. LC 77-39658. (Select Bibliographies Reprint Ser.). 1977. reprint ed. 25.95 (*0-8369-9937-1*) Ayer.

***Byzantine Armies 1118-1462 AD.** Ian Health. (Men-at-Arms Ser.). (Illus.). 48p. 1995. pap. 12.95 (*1-85532-347-8*, Pub. by Osprey UK) Stackpole.

Byzantine Armies 886-1118. Ian Heath. (Men-at-Arms Ser.: No. 89). (Illus.). 48p. pap. 11.95 (*0-85045-306-2*, 9027, Pub. by Osprey UK) Stackpole.

***Byzantine Art & Architecture.** Estela Echevarria. (World Heritage Ser.). (J). 1995. lib. bdg. 15.00 (*0-516-08395-3*) Childrens.

***Byzantine Art & Architecture.** Estela Echevarria. (World Heritage Ser.). 36p. (YA). (gr. 3 up). 1995. lib. bdg. 20.00 (*0-614-07382-0*) Childrens.

Byzantine Art & Architecture: An Introduction. Lyn Rodley. LC 92-33797. (Illus.). 320p. (C). 1992. pap. write for info. (*0-521-35724-1*) Cambridge U Pr.

Byzantine Art & Architecture: An Introduction. Lyn Rodley. LC 92-33797. (Illus.). 320p. (C). 1994. 79.95 (*0-521-35440-4*) Cambridge U Pr.

Byzantine Art in the Collections of Soviet Museums. Alice Bank. 338p. 1985. 340.00 (*0-317-61244-1*, Pub. by Collets UK) Pro-Am Music.

Byzantine Art in the Making: Main Lines of Stylistic Development in Mediterranean Art, 3rd-7th Century. Ernst Kitzinger. 183p. 1980. pap. text ed. 16.95 (*0-674-08956-1*) HUP.

Byzantine Aspects of Italy. Daniel Crena De Iongh. LC 67-19211. (Illus.). 1967. 7.50 (*0-393-04134-4*) Norton.

***Byzantine Butterflies: The Folk Paintings of Peter & Helen Contis.** Richard Armstrong. LC 95-10591. (Illus.). 160p. 1995. 40.00 (*0-87951-612-7*) Overlook Pr.

Byzantine Church & Culture. Joseph Raya. Ed. by Jose M. De Vinck. LC 91-77254. 72p. (Orig.). 1992. 9.75 (*0-911726-54-3*, CODE CCC); pap. 6.75 (*0-911726-55-1*, CODE CCB) Alleluia Pr.

Byzantine Churches of Greece & Cyprus. Elias Mastrogiannopoulos. 136p. 1984. 16.00 (*0-917651-06-5*); pap. 10.00 (*0-917651-07-3*) Holy Cross Orthodox.

Byzantine Coins & Their Values: Coins Listed 2250, rev. ed. David R. Sear et al. (Illus.). 526p. 1987. 100.00 (*0-900652-71-3*, Pub. by Seaby UK) Trafalgar.

Byzantine Commonwealth: Eastern Europe, 500-1453. Dimitri Obolensky. LC 82-16970. (Illus.). 552p. 1983. reprint ed. pap. 16.95 (*0-913836-98-2*) St Vladimirs.

Byzantine Daily Worship. 2nd ed. Joseph Raya & Jose De Vinck. 1050p. 1992. Black imitation morocco. 48.75 (*0-911726-07-1*, CODE BDW) Alleluia Pr.

Byzantine Decorative Art. Peter Vaboulis. (Illus.). 250p. 200.00 (*0-89241-035-3*, D139) Caratzas.

Byzantine Diplomacy. Ed. by Simon Franklin & Jonathan Shepard. 288p. 1992. 87.50 (*0-86078-338-3*, Pub. by Variorum UK) Ashgate Pub Co.

***Byzantine East, Latin West: Art-Historical Studies in Honor of Kurt Weitzmann.** Ed. by Doula Mouriki. LC 94-22518. 1995. write for info. (*0-691-04339-6*) Princeton A & A.

Byzantine Ecclesiastical Personalities. Pref. by Nomikos M. Vaporis. (Byzantine Fellowship Lectures: No. 2). 107p. 1975. pap. 2.95 (*0-916586-04-9*) Holy Cross Orthodox.

Byzantine Empire. rev. ed. Robert Browning. LC 91-25402. 310p. 1992. pap. text ed. 19.95 (*0-8132-0754-1*) Cath U Pr.

Byzantine Empire. Norman H. Baynes. LC 75-41020. reprint ed. 21.50 (*0-404-14641-4*) AMS Pr.

Byzantine Epistles Lectionary: Apostolos. Joseph Raya & Jose De Vinck. 550p. 1981. Unsewn folded sheets. 67.50 (*0-911726-38-1*, CODE AEU); Red cloth. 87.50 (*0-911726-37-3*, CODE AEC); Silk Moire end-sheets. 105.00 (*0-911726-50-0*, CODE AEL) Alleluia Pr.

Byzantine Eye: Studies in Art & Patronage. Robin Cormack. (Collected Studies: No. CS296). (Illus.). 350p. (C). 1989. lib. bdg. 106.50 (*0-86078-244-1*, Pub. by Variorum UK) Ashgate Pub Co.

Byzantine Fellowship Lectures, No. One, No. 1. Ed. by N. M Vaporis. (Illus.). 1974. pap. 2.95 (*0-916586-02-2*) Holy Cross Orthodox.

***Byzantine Figural Processional Crosses.** John A. Cotsonis. LC 94-29675. (Byzantine Collection Publications: 10). (Illus.). 1994. pap. 20.00x (*0-88402-228-5*) Dumbarton Oaks.

***Byzantine Gospel: Maximus the Confessor in Modern Scholarship.** Aidan Nichols. 280p. 1993. text ed. 39.95 (*0-567-09651-3*, Pub. by T & T Clark UK) Bks Intl VA.

Byzantine Grammarians: Their Place in History. Robert H. Robins. LC 92-47496. (Trends in Linguistics, Studies & Monographs: Vol. 70). xi, 278p. (C). 1993. lib. bdg. 129.25 (*3-11-013574-4*) Mouton.

Byzantine Heroic Poetry. David Ricks. 192p. (ENG & GRE.). (C). 1990. text ed. 45.00 (*0-89241-498-7*) Caratzas.

Byzantine History: 324-610, Vol. 1. A. Christophilopoulou. Tr. by W. W. Phelps. viii, 411p. (ENG.). 1986. text ed. 87.50 (*0-317-57955-X*, Pub. by A M Hakkert SP) Coronet Bks.

Byzantine History in the Early Middle Ages: The Rede Lecture Delivered in Senate House, Cambridge, June 12, 1900. Frederic Harrison. LC 78-38357. (Select Bibliographies Reprint Ser.). 1977. reprint ed. 13.95 (*0-8369-6774-7*) Ayer.

Byzantine History, Vol. II: 610-867. Aikaterina Christophilopoulou. Tr. by Timothy Cullen. xxii, 534p. 1993. pap. 99.00 (*90-256-1044-7*, Pub. by A M Hakkert NE) Benjamins North Am.

Byzantine Hymnography & Byzantine Chant. Dimitri Conomos. (Nicholas E. Kulukundis Lectures in Hellenism). 56p. (Orig.). 1984. pap. text ed. 4.95 (*0-917653-04-1*) Hellenic Coll Pr.

Byzantine Hymnology. Christos Vrionides. 268p. 1980. 10.00 (*0-916586-33-2*) Holy Cross Orthodox.

Byzantine Inheritance of Eastern Europe. Dimitri Obolensky. (Collected Studies: No. CS156). (Illus.). 300p. (C). 1982. reprint ed. lib. bdg. 87.95 (*0-86078-102-X*, Pub. by Variorum UK) Ashgate Pub Co.

Byzantine Lady: Ten Portraits, 1250-1500. Donald M. Nicol. LC 93-35728. (Illus.). 168p. (C). 1994. 39.95 (*0-521-45531-6*) Cambridge U Pr.

Byzantine Lead Seals. Nicolas Oikonomides. (Byzantine Collection Publications Ser.: No. 7). (Illus.). 28p. (Orig.). 1985. pap. 6.00 (*0-88402-144-0*) Dumbarton Oaks.

Byzantine Lead Seals, Set. G. Zacos & A. Veglery. Incl. Imperial Seals Vth to XVth Cent., Non-Imperial Seals VIth to IX Cent.,Pt. 1. (*0-685-71727-5*); Non-Imperial Seals VIth to IXth Cent., Pt. II. (*0-685-71728-3*); Imperial & Allied Seals Vth to XIVth Cent., Non-Imperial Seals VIth to IXth Cent., Pt. III. (*0-685-71729-1*); Two-Hundred Sixty Plates Illustrate Ten Gold Bullae; Two Bulloteria, Four Thousand Fifty Lead Seals & Eight Hundred Eighty-Four Monograms, Pt. IV. (*0-685-71730-5*); 250.00 (*0-685-71726-7*) J J Augustin.

***Byzantine Legacy in Eastern Europe.** Ed. by Lowell Clucas. (East European Monographs). 1988. 44.50 (*0-88033-127-5*) East Eur Quarterly.

Byzantine Legacy in the Orthodox Church. John Meyendorff. LC 82-797. 268p. (Orig.). 1982. pap. 10.95 (*0-913836-90-7*) St Vladimirs.

Byzantine Liturgy. Hans-Joachim Schulz. 284p. 1992. pap. 17.50 (*0-8146-6072-X*, Pueblo Bks) Liturgical Pr.

***Byzantine Liturgy: Hymnology & Order.** Theodore Bogdanos. 490p. 1993. 60.00 (*1-884432-00-X*) Greek Orthodox.

***Byzantine Magic.** Ed. by Henry Maguire. LC 94-33501. (Dumbarton Oaks Ser.). (Illus.). 216p. (C). 1995. text ed. 30.00 (*0-88402-230-7*) HUP.

Byzantine Masterpiece Recovered, the Thirteenth-Century Murals of Lysi, Cyprus. Annemarie W. Carr. (Illus.). 159p. (C). 1991. text ed. 37.50 (*0-292-78117-2*); pap. 19.95 (*0-292-78118-0*) U of Tex Pr.

Byzantine Military Unrest 471-843. W. E. Kaegi, Jr. xii, 393p. 1981. lib. bdg. 87.50 (*0-317-54435-7*, Pub. by A M Hakkert SP) Coronet Bks.

Byzantine Military Unrest 471-843: An Interpretation. Walter E. Kaegi, Jr. xii, 373p. 1981. pap. 81.00 (*90-256-0902-3*, Pub. by A M Hakkert NE) Benjamins North Am.

Byzantine Monuments & Topography of the Pontos, 2 vols., Set. Anthony Bryer & David Winfield. LC 84-1661. (Dumbarton Oaks Studies: Vol. 20). (Illus.). 752p. 1985. 80.00 (*0-88402-122-X*) Dumbarton Oaks.

Byzantine Mosaic Decoration: Aspects of Monumental Art in Byzantium. Otto Demus. (Illus.). 162p. (C). 1993. lib. bdg. 40.00 (*0-89241-018-3*) Caratzas.

Byzantine Music & Hymnography. Henry J. Tillyard. LC 74-24242. reprint ed. 31.50 (*0-404-13116-6*) AMS Pr.

Byzantine Music Theory & Practice. 1989. write for info. (*0-318-64507-6*) Holy Cross Orthodox.

Byzantine Patriarchate, Four Hundred Fifty-One to Twelve Hundred Four. 2nd rev. ed. George Every. LC 78-63340. (Crusades & Military Orders Ser.: Second Series). reprint ed. 45.00 (*0-404-17015-3*) AMS Pr.

Byzantine Philanthropy & Social Welfare, Vol. I. 2nd enl. rev. ed. Demetrios J. Constantelos. (Studies in the Social & Religious History of the Mediaeval Greek World). (Illus.). 300p. (C). 1991. lib. bdg. 60.00 (*0-89241-402-2*) Caratzas.

Byzantine Pilgrimage Art. Gary Vikan. (Byzantine Collection Publications Ser.: No. 5). (Illus.). 52p. 1982. pap. 6.00 (*0-88402-113-0*) Dumbarton Oaks.

An Asterisk (*) at the beginning of an entry indicates that the title is appearing in BIP for the first time.

An Asterisk (*) at the beginning of an entry indicates that the title is appearing in BIP for the first time.

979

C. E. L. Green, Shore & Landscape Painter of Lynn & Newlyn. Frederic A. Sharf & John H. Wright. LC 80-66234. (Illus.). 47p. 1980. pap. 4.00 (*0-88389-103-4*, Essx Institute) Peabody Essex Mus.

C. E. O. L. Forman & B. Shir-Cliff. 1991. write for info. (*0-936614-13-7*) Forman Pub.

C Elements of Style: The Programming Guide to Developing Well-Written C & C Plus Plus Programs. Steve Oualline. LC 92-33734. 200p. (Orig.). 1992. pap. 26.95 (*1-55851-291-8*) M&T Bks.

C. Everett Koop: The Health of a Nation. Anne Bianchi. LC 92-1230. (New Directions Ser.). (Illus.). 104p. (YA). (gr. 7 up). 1992. lib. bdg. 15.40 (*1-56294-103-8*) Millbrook Pr.

C. F. A. Voysey. Stuart Durant. (Architectural Monographs). (Illus.). 128p. 1992. 55.00 (*0-312-05199-9*) St Martin.

***C. F. A. Voysey.** Wendy Hitchmough. (Illus.). 280p. 1995. pap. 75.00 (*0-7148-3003-8*, Pub. by Phaidon Press UK) Chronicle Bks.

C. F. G. Masterman. L. Masterman. (Illus.). 400p. 1968. 25.00 (*0-7146-1565-X*, Pub. by F Cass Pubs UK) Intl Spec Bk.

C. F. G. Masterman: A Biography. Lucy B. Masterman. LC 68-88329. (Illus.). 1968. reprint ed. 45.00 (*0-678-05187-9*) Kelley.

C. F. Rehnborg: A Collection of His Essays, Speeches, & Writings. C. F. Rehnborg. Ed. by Lee Johnson. (Illus.). 300p. (Orig.). 1985. pap. write for info. (*0-9606564-2-1*) C F Rehnborg.

C-F, What Else Is New? Timothy J. Tynan. (Illus.). 384p. (Orig.). 1991. pap. 9.95 (*0-9630615-6-9*) T J Tynan.

C for BASIC Programmers. T. D. Brown, Jr. 210p. (Orig.). (C). 1987. pap. 22.95 (*0-9615336-1-7*) Silicon Pr.

***C for Business Programming.** John C. Molluzzo. LC 94-40848. 1995. pap. text ed. 44.00 (*0-13-482282-X*) P-H.

C for COBOL Programmers. Jim Gearing. (C). 1996. pap. text ed. write for info. (*0-8053-1660-4*) Benjamin-Cummings.

C for Corporate Programmers: A No-Nonsense Guide for Experienced Business Programmers. J. Inglis. LC 93-45016. 1994. pap. text ed. 32.95 (*0-471-93965-X*) Wiley.

C for Engineers & Scientists: An Introduction to Programming with ANSI C. Gary Bronson. Ed. by Mixter. LC 92-21688. 500p. (C). 1993. pap. text ed. 41.75 (*0-314-00816-0*) West Pub.

C for FORTRAN Programmers. T. D. Brown, Jr. 220p. 1990. 22.95 (*0-929306-01-5*) Silicon Pr.

C for FORTRAN Programmers. James F. Kerrigan. (Illus.). 304p. 1991. 33.95 (*0-8306-8661-4*, 3661, Windcrest); pap. 24.95 (*0-8306-7661-9*, Windcrest) TAB Bks.

C for Fun & Profit. Steve Schustack. 608p. 1993. disk 29.95 (*0-672-30365-5*) Sams.

C for Non-C Programmers. 2nd ed. Anthony S. Rudd. 1993. pap. 39.95 (*0-89435-468-X*) Wiley.

C for Pascal & Fortran Programmers. Gerald J. Lemay. 114p. (C). 1993. student ed 15.00 (*1-883496-02-0*); pap. text ed. 25.00 (*1-883496-01-2*) P S Melvil Pr.

C for Pascal Programmers. T. D. Brown, Jr. 215p. (C). 1987. pap. 22.95 (*0-9615336-4-1*) Silicon Pr.

C for Professional Programmers. 2nd ed. Keith Tizzard. LC 92-22197. (Ellis Horwood Series in Computers & their Applications). 250p. 1992. pap. 29.00 (*0-13-116997-1*, Tavistock-E Horwood) Routledge Chapman & Hall.

C for Programmers. Walter A. Burkhard. 562p. (C). 1988. pap. 42.95 (*0-534-08856-2*) PWS Pubs.

C for Programmers: A Complete Tutorial Based on the ANSI Standard. 2nd ed. Leendert Ammeraal. 1991. pap. text ed. 32.95 (*0-471-92851-8*) Wiley.

C for Rookies. Paul J. Perry. (Illus.). 250p. (Orig.). 1993. Incl. disk. disk, pap. 19.95 (*1-56529-280-4*) Que.

C for RPG Programmers. Jennifer Hamilton. 320p. (Orig.). 1992. pap. 69.00 (*0-9628743-6-1*) Duke Commns Intl.

C for the Microprocessor Engineer. S. J. Cahill. LC 93-38106. 340p. 1994. pap. text ed. 51.00 (*0-13-115825-2*) P-H Gen Ref & Trav.

C for Windows Animation Graphics Programming. Lee A. Adams. 1993. pap. text ed. 39.95 (*0-07-000409-9*) TAB Bks.

C for Windows Animation Programming. Lee Adams. (Illus.). 768p. 1992. pap. 39.95 (*0-8306-3810-5*, 4114, Windcrest) TAB Bks.

C from BASIC. Robert J. Traister, Sr. 64p. 1985. disk (*0-318-59139-1*) P-H.

C from the Ground Up. Herbert Schildt. 1994. pap. text ed. 27.95 (*0-07-881969-5*) McGraw.

C. G. Jung. Elie Humbert. Tr. by Ronald G. Jalbert. LC 88-2582. 168p. 1988. 19.95 (*0-933029-26-8*); pap. 14.95 (*0-933029-18-7*) Chiron Pubns.

C. G. Jung: Lord of the Underworld. Colin Wilson. (Illus.). 160p. (Orig.). 1988. pap. 9.95 (*0-85030-716-3*, Pub. by Aquarian Pr UK) Thorsons SF.

C. G. Jung: Word & Image. G. G. Jung. Ed. by Aniela Jaffe. LC 78-17319. (Bollingen Ser.: Vol. XCVII, No. 2). (Illus.). 252p. 1979. 49.50 (*0-691-09942-1*); pap. 19.95 (*0-691-01847-2*) Princeton U Pr.

C. G. Jung & the Humanities: Toward a Hermeneutics of Culture. Ed. by Karin Barnaby & Pellegrino D'Acierno. (Illus.). 338p. (C). 1989. text ed. 49.50 (*0-691-08616-8*) Princeton U Pr.

C. G. Jung As I Knew Him, Set. Kitty Kurti. Bd. with Bk. 2. Journey Across the World & Beyond. LC 87-80056. 254p. 1987. Set pap. 12.00 (*0-935886-03-6*) East & West Pubns.

C. G. Jung, Emma Jung, Toni Wolff. Ed. by Ferne Jensen & Sidney Mullen. (Illus.). 131p. (Orig.). 1982. pap. 8.95 (*0-685-07805-1*) Analyt Psych SF.

C. G. Jung Speaking: Interviews & Encounters. Carl G. Jung. Ed. by William McGuire. Tr. by R. F. Hull & Ralph Manheim. LC 77-71985. (Bollingen Ser.: No. 97). 1986. text ed. 49.50 (*0-691-09894-8*); pap. 17.95 (*0-691-01871-5*) Princeton U Pr.

C. G. Jung's Psychology of Religion & Synchronicity. Robert Aziz. LC 89-30039. (Transpersonal & Humanistic Psychology Ser.). 269p. 1990. 59.50 (*0-7914-0166-9*); pap. 19.95 (*0-7914-0167-7*) State U NY Pr.

***C-Glycoside Synthesis.** Maarten H. Postema. 400p. 1995. 99.50 (*0-8493-9150-4*, 9150) CRC Pr.

C Graphics. B. Korites & M. Novack. 1988. 18.50 (*0-685-24877-1*, 206-B); disk 18.50 (*0-685-24878-X*, 206-ID) Kern Intl.

C. H. Graun & Lotti. John H. Roverts. (Handel Sources Ser.). 1987. 30.00 (*0-8240-6479-8*) Garland.

C. H. Spurgeon & the Modern Church. Robert Sheehan. 1985. pap. 3.99 (*0-946462-05-4*, Pub. by Evangel Pr UK) Presby & Reformed.

C. H. Spurgeon's Autobiography, Set. Mrs. C. H. Spurgeon & J. W. Harrald. 1992. 80.00 (*1-56186-103-0*) Pilgrim Pubns.

C. H. Spurgeon's Prayers. C. H. Spurgeon. 192p. 1990. reprint ed. pap. 4.95 (*1-56186-349-1*) Pilgrim Pubns.

C Handbook: CAD, CAM, CAE, CIM. Carl Machover. (Computer Graphics Technology & Management Ser.). (Illus.). 400p. 1989. 44.50 (*0-8306-9398-X*, 3098) TAB Bks.

C. Hubert H. Parry: His Life & Music. Jeremy Dibble. (Illus.). 594p. 1992. 95.00 (*0-19-315330-0*) OUP.

C. I. A. - Cocaine in America? A Veteran of the C. I. A. Drug War Tells All. Kenneth C. Bucchi. 1994. pap. 5.99 (*1-56171-322-8*, S P I Bks) Sure Sellers.

C I B A Collection of Medical Illustrations, 12 bks., Set. Illus. by Frank H. Netter. Incl. Vol. 1, Pt. 1. Nervous System: Anatomy & Physiology. LC 53-2151. (Illus.). 1983. 50.00 (*0-914168-10-X*); Vol. 1, Pt. 2. Nervous System: Neurologic & Neuromuscular Disorders. LC 53-2151. 1986. 52.00 (*0-914168-11-8*); Vol. 2. Reproductive System. LC 53-2151. 1974. 47.50 (*0-914168-02-9*); Vol. 3, Pt. 1. Digestive System: Upper Digestive Tract. LC 53-2151. 1974. 39.00 (*0-914168-03-7*); Vol. 3, Pt. 2. Digestive System: Lower Digestive Tract. LC 53-2151. 1974. 41.00 (*0-914168-04-5*); Vol. 3, Pt. 3. Digestive System: Liver, Biliary Tract & Pancreas. LC 53-2151. 1974. 38.00 (*0-914168-05-3*); Vol. 4. Endocrine System & Selected Metabolic Diseases. LC 53-2151. 1974. 47.50 (*0-914168-06-1*); Vol. 5. Heart. LC 53-2151. 1974. 55.00 (*0-914168-07-X*); Vol. 6. Kidneys, Ureters & Urinary Bladder. LC 53-2151. 1974. 55.00 (*0-914168-08-8*); Vol. 7. Respiratory System. LC 53-2151. 1974. 55.00 (*0-914168-09-6*); Vol. 8, Pt. 1. Musculoskeletal System: Anatomy, Physiology & Metabolic Disorders. LC 53-2151. 1974. 55.00 (*0-914168-14-2*); Musculoskeletal System - Developmental Disorders, Tumors, Rheumatic Diseases & Joint Replacement. LC 53-2151. 1974. 58.50 (*0-914168-15-0*); Musculoskeletal System - Developmental Disorders, Tumors, Rheumatic Diseases & Joint Replacement. LC 53-2151. 1974. 58.50 (*0-914168-15-0*); LC 53-2151. (Illus.). 1974. Complete set. 475.00 (*0-914168-00-2*) CIBA Med.

C. I. C. D. Collegium Internationale Chirurgiae Digestive: Abstracts-9th World Congress, Jerusalem, Aug.-Sept. 1986. Ed. by M. M. Feuchtwanger. (Journal: Digestive Surgery: Vol. 3, No. 2). 140p. 1986. pap. 58.50 (*3-8055-4466-9*) S Karger.

C. I. D. Room. large type ed. Peter Alding. (Linford Mystery Library). 1991. pap. 13.95 (*0-7089-7153-9*) Ulverscroft.

C. I. I. Aviation Claims, No. 200A. B. G. Jervis. (C). 1981. 240.00 (*0-685-33777-4*, Pub. by Witherby & Co UK) St Mut.

C. I. I. Aviation Law, No. 180A/063. B. G. Jervis. (C). 1983. 240.00 (*0-685-33776-6*, Pub. by Witherby & Co UK) St Mut.

C. I. I. Aviation Underwriting, No. 190A/073. B. G. Jervis. (C). 1981. 230.00 (*0-685-33775-8*, Pub. by Witherby & Co UK) St Mut.

C. I. I. Economic Organisation, No. 820. S. R. Diacon. (C). 1981. 230.00 (*0-685-33774-X*, Pub. by Witherby & Co UK) St Mut.

C. I. I. Economics, No. 030. S. R. Diacon. (C). 1981. 230.00 (*0-685-33773-1*, Pub. by Witherby & Co UK) St Mut.

C. I. I. English Law, No. 020. G. D. James. (C). 1983. 230.00 (*0-685-33772-3*, Pub. by Witherby & Co UK) St Mut.

C. I. I. Financial Aspects of Life Business, No. 140-081. W. E. Blunden. (C). 1987. 230.00 (*0-685-33771-5*, Pub. by Witherby & Co UK) St Mut.

C. I. I. Financial Aspects of Pension Business, No. 150-082. L. W. Tutt & S. I. Tutt. (C). 1986. 230.00 (*0-685-33770-7*, Pub. by Witherby & Co UK) St Mut.

C. I. I. Insurances of Liability, No. 070. C. Smythe. (C). 1988. 230.00 (*0-685-33769-3*, Pub. by Witherby & Co UK) St Mut.

C. I. I. Insurances of the Person, No. 050. G. C. Evans. (C). 1985. 230.00 (*0-685-33768-5*, Pub. by Witherby & Co UK) St Mut.

C. I. I. Interruption Insurance, No. 260. J. H. Phillips. (C). 1981. 230.00 (*0-685-33767-7*, Pub. by Witherby & Co UK) St Mut.

C. I. I. Introduction to Insurance, No. 010. G. C. Dickson. (C). 1984. 230.00 (*0-685-33766-9*, Pub. by Witherby & Co UK) St Mut.

C. I. I. Legal Liabilities, No. 210. A. J. Peck. (C). 1987. 240.00 (*0-685-33765-0*, Pub. by Witherby & Co UK) St Mut.

C. I. I. Legal Principles, No. 021. G. D. James. (C). 1981. 230.00 (*0-685-33764-2*, Pub. by Witherby & Co UK) St Mut.

C. I. I. Liability Insurance, No. 220. D. S. McCallum. (C). 1981. 230.00 (*0-685-33763-4*, Pub. by Witherby & Co UK) St Mut.

C. I. I. Life Assurance Law & Practice, No. 090. C. Marshall. (C). 1984. 230.00 (*0-685-33762-6*, Pub. by Witherby & Co UK) St Mut.

C. I. I. Life Assurance Law & Taxation, No. 130-071. C. Marshall. (C). 1984. 230.00 (*0-685-33761-8*, Pub. by Witherby & Co UK) St Mut.

C. I. I. Life Assurance Practice, No. 120-061. F. Thornber. (C). 1981. 230.00 (*0-685-33760-X*, Pub. by Witherby & Co UK) St Mut.

C. I. I. Life Assurance Salesmanship & Marketing, No. 910. D. J. Dwyer. (C). 1981. 230.00 (*0-685-33759-6*, Pub. by Witherby & Co UK) St Mut.

C. I. I. Management, 2 vols., Set: No. 300. Ed. by M. White. (C). 1981. Set. 230.00 (*0-685-33758-8*, Pub. by Witherby & Co UK) St Mut.

C. I. I. Management Eleven Insurance Broking, No. 311. B. E. Bone. (C). 1983. 240.00 (*0-685-33757-X*, Pub. by Witherby & Co UK) St Mut.

C. I. I. Management Eleven Insurance Companies, No. 310. Witherby's Editorial Staff. (C). 1981. 230.00 (*0-685-33756-1*, Pub. by Witherby & Co UK) St Mut.

C. I. I. Management Eleven Lloyd's, No. 312. Witherby's Editorial Staff. (C). 1981. 230.00 (*0-685-33755-3*, Pub. by Witherby & Co UK) St Mut.

C. I. I. Management Eleven Risk Management, No. 313. R. L. Carter. (C). 1981. 230.00 (*0-685-33754-5*, Pub. by Witherby & Co UK) St Mut.

C. I. I. Marine & Aviation Insurance, No. 051. Witherby's Editorial Staff. (C). 1988. 230.00 (*0-685-33753-7*, Pub. by Witherby & Co UK) St Mut.

C. I. I. Marine Claims, No. 200M/083. Witherby's Editorial Staff. (C). 1981. 230.00 (*0-685-33752-9*, Pub. by Witherby & Co UK) St Mut.

C. I. I. Marine Law, No. 180M/063. D. Lee. (C). 1986. 230.00 (*0-685-33751-0*, Pub. by Witherby & Co UK) St Mut.

C. I. I. Marine Underwriting, No. 190-073. Witherby's Editorial Staff. (C). 1985. 230.00 (*0-685-33750-2*, Pub. by Witherby & Co UK) St Mut.

C. I. I. Motor Insurance, No. 080. R. Ellis & D. M. Mitchell. (C). 1988. 230.00 (*0-685-33749-9*, Pub. by Witherby & Co UK) St Mut.

C. I. I. Motor Insurance: Underwriting & Claims, No. 230. M. A. Freeman & A. H. Pellatt. (C). 1986. 230.00 (*0-685-33748-0*, Pub. by Witherby & Co UK) St Mut.

C. I. I. Pension Law & Taxation, No. 160-072. L. W. Tutt & S. I. Tutt. (C). 1988. 240.00 (*0-685-33747-2*, Pub. by Witherby & Co UK) St Mut.

C. I. I. Pension Scheme Design & Administration, No. 170-060. D. A. Reeve. (C). 1984. 240.00 (*0-685-33746-4*, Pub. by Witherby & Co UK) St Mut.

C. I. I. Pensions & Related Benefits, No. 100-041. D. Trebilcock. (C). 1988. 230.00 (*0-685-33745-6*, Pub. by Witherby & Co UK) St Mut.

C. I. I. Practice of Reinsurance, No. 280. R. L. Carter. (C). 1981. 250.00 (*0-685-33744-8*, Pub. by Witherby & Co UK) St Mut.

C. I. I. Principles & Practice of Insurance, No. 040. J. T. Steele. (C). 1984. 230.00 (*0-685-33743-X*, Pub. by Witherby & Co UK) St Mut.

C. I. I. Principles of Reinsurance, No. 270. Ed. by Witherby's Editorial Staff. (C). 1981. 230.00 (*0-685-33742-1*, Pub. by Witherby & Co UK) St Mut.

C. I. I. Property & Pecuniary Insurance, No. 060. C. E. Hall. (C). 1985. 230.00 (*0-685-33741-3*, Pub. by Witherby & Co UK) St Mut.

C. I. I. Property Insurance Risk Assessment & Control, No. 240. Martin Way. (C). 1987. 230.00 (*0-685-33740-5*, Pub. by Witherby & Co UK) St Mut.

C. I. I. Property Insurance Underwriting & Claims, No. 250. F. H. Jones. (C). 1987. 230.00 (*0-685-33739-1*, Pub. by Witherby & Co UK) St Mut.

C. I. I. Quantitive Methods As Applied to Insurance, No. 110. G. C. Dickson. (C). 1982. 230.00 (*0-685-33737-5*, Pub. by Witherby & Co UK) St Mut.

C. I. I. Reinsurance Market, No. 290. R. L. Carter. (C). 1981. 230.00 (*0-685-33738-3*, Pub. by Witherby & Co UK) St Mut.

C. I. I. Use of Business English, No. 810. M. Barnes. (C). 1981. 230.00 (*0-685-33736-7*, Pub. by Witherby & Co UK) St Mut.

C. I. Lewis & the Social Theory of Conceptualistic Pragmatism: The Individual & the Good Social Order. C. Paul Colella. LC 92-1107. 232p. 1992. lib. bdg. 89.95 (*0-7734-9800-1*) E Mellen.

***C. I. R. C. U. S. R. I. N. G. of Relationships.** (K. I. D. S. Church Ser.: Vol. 4). 160p. (J). (gr. 1-6). 1992. ring bd. 119.00 (*1-57405-038-9*) CharismaLife Pub.

C. I. S., Telephone Area Code & Information Directory. 24p. (Orig.). (RUS.). 1992. Russian text. pap. 25.00 (*0-685-59555-2*) Rector Pr.

***C in Plain English.** Brian Overland. LC 95-18697. 1995. pap. 19.95 (*1-55828-430-3*) H Holt & Co.

C. Inkpen: The Case of the Dangling Ribbon. Robert D. Halpert. 1992. 14.95 (*0-533-10109-3*) Vantage.

***C Is for Cajun Coloring Book.** 8th ed. J. A. Allen. 1993. pap. 2.95 (*0-87511-652-3*) Claitors.

***C Is for Cat.** Pamela Prince. 1994. pap. 5.99 (*0-517-13139-0*) Random.

***"C" Is for City.** Nikki Grimes. LC 94-46794. (Illus.). (J). 1995. write for info. (*0-688-11808-9*); lib. bdg. write for info. (*0-688-11809-7*) Lothrop.

C Is for Clown. Stan Berenstain & Janice Berenstain. (Bright & Early Bks.: No. 14). (Illus.). (J). (ps-1). 1972. lib. bdg. 7.99 (*0-394-92492-4*) Random Bks Yng Read.

***C Is for Colorado.** Gayle Shirley. LC 89-83793. 40p. (Orig.). (J). (gr. k-3). 1989. 7.95 (*0-937959-81-2*) Falcon Pr MT.

C Is for Cookie. Joe Raposo. (Xylotone Fun! Ser.). (Illus.). 16p. (J). 1993. spiral bd. 9.95 (*0-7935-2155-6*, 00824048) H Leonard.

C Is for Cookie & Other Kids' Favorites. Joe Raposo. (Sing 'n' Color Fun! Ser.). (Illus.). (J). 1993. spiral bd. 6.95 (*0-7935-1954-3*, 00823016) H Leonard.

C Is for Corpse. Sue Grafton. 1987. mass mkt. 5.99 (*0-553-28036-8*) Bantam.

C Is for Corpse. Sue Grafton. (Paperback Ser.). 371p. 1991. pap. 14.95 (*0-8161-5146-6*) G K Hall.

C Is for Corpse. Sue Grafton. 1986. 21.95 (*0-8050-2818-8*) H Holt & Co.

C Is for Cowboy: (Love Letters) Lisa Jackson. (Special Edition Ser.). 1994. mass mkt. 3.50 (*0-373-09926-6*, 1-09926-6) Silhouette.

C Is for Coyote. Douglas Stinson. (Special Species Ser.). (Illus.). 40p. (J). (gr. 1 up). 1993. 15.95 (*1-879244-04-7*) Windom Bks.

C Is for Curious: An ABC of Feelings. Woodleigh Hubbard. (Illus.). 40p. (J). (ps-1). 1990. 13.95 (*0-87701-679-8*) Chronicle Bks.

C Is For Curious: An Emotional Address Book. Woodleigh Hubbard. 1993. 14.95 (*0-8118-0347-3*) Chronicle Bks.

***C Is for Curious 2 Is for Dancing: An ABC of Feelings - A 123 of Actions.** Woodleigh Hubbard. (J). (ps-3). 1995. pap. 8.95 (*0-8118-1078-X*) Chronicle Bks.

C. Iuli Caesaris de Bello Gallico, 7 vols. in 1. Julius Caesar. Ed. by W. R. Connor. LC 78-67135. (Latin Texts & Commentaries Ser.). (ENG & LAT.). 1979. reprint ed. lib. bdg. 63.95 (*0-405-11607-1*) Ayer.

C. J. Thornton, Entrepreneur: Agriculture, Business, Politics. Ed. by Mary E. Glass. 287p. 1983. lib. bdg. 42.00 (*1-56475-240-2*); fiche write for info. (*1-56475-241-0*) U NV Oral Hist.

C. J.'s Defense. Carolyn Andrews. (Temptation Ser.). 1994. pap. 2.99 (*0-685-71209-5*, 1-25598-3) Harlequin Bks.

C. K. & the Time She Quit the Family. Patricia L. Gauch. (Sandcastle Ser.). (Illus.). 32p. (J). (ps-3). 1992. pap. 5.95 (*0-399-22405-X*, Putnam) Putnam Pub Group.

C. K. Ogden: A Bio-Bibliographic Study. W. Terrence Gordon. 166p. 1990. 22.50 (*0-8108-2317-9*) Scarecrow.

C. Konkordanz Zur Naturalis Historia Des C. Plinius Secundus, 3 vols. Plinius Secundus. Ed. by Peter Rosumek & Dietmar Najock. Bd. LV. 1750p. (GER.). Date not set. Set. write for info. (*0-318-70605-9*, Pub. by Georg Olms GW) Lubrecht & Cramer.

C. L. A. Handbook & Membership Directory. Catholic Library Association. 35.00 (*0-318-51303-X*) Cath Lib Assn.

C. L. A. S. S. - College Learning & Study Skills. 3rd ed. Debbie G. Longman & Rhonda H. Atkinson. Ed. by Baxter. LC 92-30204. 450p. (C). 1993. pap. text ed. 31.50 (*0-314-01231-1*) West Pub.

***C. L. R. James: A Political Biography.** Kent Worcester. LC 95-6899. (SUNY Series, INTERRUPTIONS). 304p. 1995. text ed. 59.50 (*0-7914-2751-X*); pap. 19.95 (*0-7914-2752-8*) State U NY Pr.

C. L. R. James: His Intellectual Legacies. Ed. by William E. Cain & Selwyn R. Cudjoe. LC 94-4518. 488p. (C). 1995. lib. bdg. 55.00 (*0-87023-906-6*); pap. 19.95 (*0-87023-907-4*) U of Mass Pr.

C. L. R. James & Revolutionary Marxism: Selected Writings 1939-1949. Ed. by Scott McLemee & Paul Le Blanc. LC 92-20631. (Revolutionary Studies). 264p. (C). 1993. pap. 18.50 (*0-391-03824-9*) Humanities.

C. L. R. James & Revolutionary Marxism: Selected Writings 1939-1949. Ed. by Scott McLemee & Paul Le Blanc. LC 92-20631. (Revolutionary Studies). 264p. (C). 1993. text ed. 49.95 (*0-391-03786-2*) Humanities.

***C. L. R. James & the "Negro Question"** Ed. by Scott McLemee. 224p. 1996. lib. bdg. 40.00 (*0-87805-807-9*); pap. 16.95 (*0-87805-823-0*) U Pr of Miss.

C. L. R. James & the Struggle for Happiness. Anna Grimshaw & Keith Hart. 60p. (Orig.). 1991. pap. 5.00 (*0-918266-27-0*) Smyrna.

C. L. R. James Archive: A Reader's Guide. Anna Grimshaw. 110p. (Orig.). 1991. pap. 10.00 (*0-918266-30-0*) Smyrna.

C. L. R. James Reader. C. L. James. 1992. pap. 19.95 (*0-631-18495-3*) Blackwell Pubs.

C. L. R. James's Caribbean. Ed. by Paget Henry & Paul Buhle. LC 91-42237. 304p. 1992. lib. bdg. 48.00 (*0-8223-1231-X*); pap. text ed. 18.95 (*0-8223-1244-1*) Duke.

C. L. Sonnichsen. Joyce G. Roach. LC 79-53653. (Western Writers Ser.: No. 40). (Illus.). 48p. (Orig.). 1979. pap. 3.95 (*0-88430-064-1*) Boise St U W Writ Ser.

C. L. Sonnichsen: A Grassroots Historian. Dale L. Walker. (Southwestern Studies: No. 34). 1972. pap. 10.00 (*0-87404-141-4*) Tex Western.

C Language Algorithms for Digital Signal Processing. Paul Embree. 1990. text ed. 69.00 (*0-13-133406-9*) P-H.

C Language for Beginners. rev. ed. Charles A. Stanley. Ed. by Deanna Dahl & Elise Colson. 200p. 1985. pap. 19.95 (*0-9614857-0-1*) Pressure Appli.

C Language Interfaces AT&T. 1988. 26.95 (*0-13-109661-3*) P-H.

C Language on the IBM PC. Microtrend, Inc. Staff. 1984. 14.95 (*0-685-08090-0*) P-H.

C Language Scientific Subroutine Library Version 2.0. Peerless Engineering Service Staff. 428p. 1988. text ed. 65.00 (*0-471-61233-2*) Wiley.

C-LECT Jr. rev. ed. Ed. by Paul Downes. 6p. (Orig.). (J). (gr. 7-10). 1992. teacher ed write for info. (*1-55631-201-6*); student ed 1.25 (*1-55631-202-4*) Chron Guide.

C Library Reference for Standard System V. Specialized Systems Consultants, Inc. Staff. 32p. (Orig.). 1985. pap. 6.00 (*0-916151-11-5*) Specialized Sys.

An Asterisk (*) at the beginning of an entry indicates that the title is appearing in BIP for the first time.

C

An Asterisk (*) at the beginning of an entry indicates that the title is appearing in BIP for the first time.

981

C. S. Lewis. 2nd ed. Catherine Swift. LC 89-82261. (Men of Faith Ser.). 128p. (Orig.). 1990. 4.99 (*1-55661-126-9*) Bethany Hse.

C. S. Lewis: A Biography. A. N. Wilson. 1991. pap. 14.00 (*0-449-90609-4*) Fawcett.

C. S. Lewis: A Biography. A. N. Wilson. 1990. 25.00 (*0-393-02813-5*) Norton.

C. S. Lewis: A Biography. Roger L. Green & Walter Hooper. LC 75-29425. 320p. 1994. reprint ed. pap. 12.95 (*0-15-623205-7*, Harvest Bks) HarBrace.

C. S. Lewis: A Critical Essay. rev. ed. Peter Kreeft. 72p. 1988. reprint ed. pap. 5.95 (*0-931888-26-3*) Christendom Pr.

C. S. Lewis: A Reference Guide, 1972-1988. Susan Lowenberg. LC 92-42316. (Reference Guide to Literature Ser.). 320p. 1993. text ed. 55.00 (*0-8161-1846-9*) G K Hall.

C. S. Lewis: An Annotated Checklist of Writings about Him & His works. Joe R. Christopher & Joan K. Ostling. LC 73-76556. (Serif Series: Bibliographies & Checklists: No. 30). 407p. reprint ed. pap. 116.00 (*0-7837-0567-0*, 2040911) Bks Demand.

C. S. Lewis: His Literary Achievement. C. N. Manlove. LC 87-4775. 224p. 1987. text ed. 39.95 (*0-312-00899-6*) St Martin.

C. S. Lewis: Images of His World. Douglas Gilbert & Clyde S. Kilby. LC 73-8697. 192p. reprint ed. pap. 54.80 (*0-317-30141-1*, 2025324) Bks Demand.

C. S. Lewis: The Man & His God. Richard Harries. LC 87-25678. 1987. pap. 5.95 (*0-8192-1416-7*) Morehouse Pub.

C. S. Lewis: Writings from the Shadowlands. Henry W. Griffin. (Spiritual Legacy Ser.). 160p. (Orig.). 1995. pap. 9.95 (*0-8245-2506-X*) Crossroad NY.

***C. S. Lewis a Study Guide: The Screwtape Letters for Individuals & Groups.** Frank S. Kastor. (Orig.). Date not set. pap. 9.95 (*0-9618112-1-8*) St Marks Pr.

C. S. Lewis at the Breakfast Table. Como. 1992. pap. 12.95 (*0-15-623207-3*, Harvest Bks) HarBrace.

C. S. Lewis at the Breakfast Table. Como. 1985. 10.95 (*0-02-570620-9*) Macmillan.

***C. S. Lewis for the Third Millenium.** Peter Kreeft. 190p. (Orig.). 1994. pap. 11.95 (*0-89870-523-1*) Ignatius Pr.

C. S. Lewis Handbook: A Comprehensive Guide to His Life, Thought, & Writings. Comp. by Colin Duriez. LC 90-20228. 256p. 1990. reprint ed. pap. 9.99 (*0-8010-3001-3*) Baker Bk.

C. S. Lewis in Context. Doris T. Myers. LC 94-7537. 264p. 1994. 28.00x (*0-87338-497-0*) Kent St U Pr.

C. S. Lewis Letters to Children. Lyle W. Dorsett & Marjorie L. Mead. 124p. 1988. pap. 7.00 (*0-02-031741-7*, Collier S&S) S&S Trade.

C. S. Lewis Letters to Children. C. S. Lewis. (J). 1985. 9.95 (*0-02-570830-9*) Macmillan.

C. S. Lewis: Man of Letters: A Reading of His Fiction. Thomas Howard. LC 90-81993. 259p. 1990. reprint ed. pap. 11.95 (*0-89870-305-0*) Ignatius Pr.

C. S. Lewis, Spinner of Tales: A Guide to His Fiction. Evan K. Gibson. LC 80-10754. 294p. reprint ed. pap. 83.80 (*0-317-30140-3*, 2025323) Bks Demand.

C. S. Lewis Through the Shadowlands: The Real Story of His Life with Joy Davidman. Brian Sibley. LC 86-13096. 192p. 1994. reprint ed. pap. 7.99 (*0-8007-5534-0*) Revell.

C. S. Lovett: Maranatha Man. C. S. Lovett. (Illus.). 1978. pap. 2.95 (*0-938148-02-8*) Prsnl Christianity.

C. S. Peirce: Logic & the Classification of the Sciences. Beverley E. Kent. (C). 1986. text ed. 44.95 (*0-7735-0562-8*, Pub. by McGill CN) U of Toronto Pr.

C. Sallusti Crispi: Catilina, Iugurtha, Historiarum Fragmenta Selecta: Appendix Sallustiana. Sallust. Ed. by L. D. Reynolds. (Oxford Classical Texts Ser.). 280p. 1991. 35.00 (*0-19-814667-1*, 1507) OUP.

C-Set Kit. Myers. (C). 1995. pap. text ed. write for info. (*0-7167-2117-1*) W H Freeman.

C Seven Plus Fraction Characterization. Ed. by G. Ali Mansoori & Larry Chorn. (Advances in Thermodynamics Ser.). (Illus.). 240p. (C). 1989. text ed. 83.00 (*0-8448-1565-9*) Taylor & Francis.

C-SPAN in the Communication Classroom: Theories & Application. Ed. by Janette K. Muir. LC 92-61675. 112p. (C). 1992. pap. text ed. 17.95 (*0-944811-09-4*) Speech Commun Assn.

C Squared Compiler Concepts. B. Teufel et al. 188p. 1993. pap. 29.00 (*0-387-82431-6*) Spr-Verlag.

C Standard Library Handbook. Robert Del Rossi. Ed. by Lance A. Leventhal. (Lance A. Leventhal Microtrend Ser.). 500p. (Orig.). 1992. pap. 29.95 (*0-915391-50-3*, Microtrend) Slawson Comm.

C Style: Standards & Guidelines. David Straker. 180p. 1991. pap. text ed. 41.00 (*0-13-116898-3*) P-H.

C. Suetoni Tranquilli de Vita Caesarum: Libri VII-VIII. Suetonius. Ed. by W. R. Connor & George W. Mooney. LC 78-67142. (Latin Texts & Commentaries Ser.). (ENG & LAT.). 1979. reprint ed. lib. bdg. 48.95 (*0-405-11611-X*) Ayer.

C. Suetoni Tranquilli Divus Augustus. Suetonius. Ed. by W. R. Connor. LC 78-67149. (Latin Texts & Commentaries Ser.). (ENG & LAT.). 1979. reprint ed. lib. bdg. 19.95 (*0-405-11617-9*) Ayer.

C. Suetonii Tranquilli Vita Tiberii & C. Suetonii Tranquilli Vita Tiberi: C-24-C-40. Suetonius. Ed. by W. R. Connor. LC 78-67161. (Latin Texts & Commentaries Ser.). (ENG, GER & LAT.). 1979. reprint ed. lib. bdg. 21.95 (*0-405-11625-X*) Ayer.

C. T. Studd. Norman P. Grubb. 1991. pap. 6.95 (*0-87508-202-5*) Chr Lit.

C. T. the Living Christmas Tree. Darrel W. Dewoody & Betty N. Dewoody. (Illus.). (J). (gr. k-6). 1989. write for info. (*0-318-64917-9*) Old Amer Pr.

C Through Design. George Defenbaugh, Jr. & Richard Smedley. LC 88-11222. (Computer Scientist Ser.). (Illus.). 648p. (C). 1988. pap. text ed. 40.95 (*0-938661-10-8*) Franklin Beedle.

C Toolbox: Ready-to-Run Programs in Turbo C, Microsoft C, & Quick C. 2nd ed. William J. Hunt. 496p. 1989. pap. 24.95 (*0-201-51815-5*) Addison-Wesley.

C-Tools for Scientists & Engineers. Louis Baker. (Illus.). 320p. 1989. pap. text ed. 34.95 (*0-07-003355-2*) McGraw.

C Trainer. Alan R. Feuer. 288p. 1986. pap. text ed. 24.33 (*0-13-109752-0*) P-H.

C Traps & Pitfalls. Andrew Koenig. (Illus.). 144p. (C). 1989. pap. text ed. 21.50 (*0-201-17928-8*) Addison-Wesley.

C Trillogy: A Complete Library for C Programmers. Eric P. Bloom. 600p. 1987. 34.95 (*0-8306-7890-5*, 2890H) TAB Bks.

C Trilogy. 2nd ed. Eric P. Bloom. 1992. pap. 26.95 (*0-07-157889-7*) McGraw.

C Trilogy. 2nd ed. Eric P. Bloom. (Illus.). 624p. 1992. pap. 26.95 (*0-8306-2533-X*, 3946, Windcrest) TAB Bks.

C-Types of N-Dimensional Lattices & Five- Dimensional Primitive Parallelohedra with Application to the Theory of Coverings. S. S. Ryskov & E. P. Baranovskii. LC 78-21923. (Proceedings of the Steklov Institute of Mathematics Ser.). 140p. 1978. 83.00 (*0-8218-3037-6*, STEKLO-137) Am Math.

C-Unit: Search for Community in Prison. Elliot Studt et al. LC 67-31158. 354p. 1968. 35.00 (*0-87154-850-X*) Russell Sage.

C User Interface Library. Ted Pugh. 356p. (Orig.). 1993. pap. 49.50 (*1-85058-295-5*, Pub. by Sigma Press UK) Coronet Bks.

C User's Group Library: A Directory of Public Domain C Source Code, 1. Ed. by Donna S. Ward. 200p. (Orig.). 1989. pap. 10.00 (*0-923667-00-8*, C Users Group) R & D Pubns KS.

C User's Group Library: A Directory of Public Domain C Source Code, Set: Vol. 1. Ed. by Donna S. Ward. 200p. (Orig.). 1989. Set. pap. write for info. (*0-923667-01-6*, C Users Group) R & D Pubns KS.

C Users' Group Library: A Directory of User Supported C Source Code, Vol. II. Ed. by Kenji Hino. 220p. (Orig.). 1989. pap. 10.00 (*0-923667-02-4*, C Users Group) R & D Pubns KS.

C Users' Group Library, Vol. III: A Directory of User Supported C Source Code. Ed. by Bernard Williams et al. (Illus.). 300p. (Orig.). 1992. pap. 10.00 (*0-923667-03-2*, C Users Group) R & D Pubns KS.

C User's Guide to ANSIC. Ken Arnold & John Peyton. (Illus.). 96p. 1992. pap. 20.95 (*0-201-56331-2*) Addison-Wesley.

C. Valerius Flaccus: Argonautica Book II. H. M. Poortvliet. 357p. (Orig.). 1992. pap. text ed. 49.50 (*90-5383-022-7*, Pub. by VU Univ Pr NE) Paul & Co Pubs.

C. Vann Woodward, Southerner. John H. Roper. LC 86-25020. 398p. 1987. 30.00 (*0-8203-0933-8*) U of Ga Pr.

C. W. Judge Vernon: Early Life in Tahoe City, California, 1906-1980. Intro. by Ann Tiller. (Illus.). 100p. 1980. lib. bdg. 27.00 (*1-56475-203-8*); fiche write for info. (*1-56475-204-6*) U NV Oral Hist.

C. W. von Gluck: "Orfeo" Ed. by Patricia Howard. (Cambridge Opera Handbooks Ser.). (Illus.). 200p. 1981. pap. 19.95 (*0-521-29664-1*) Cambridge U Pr.

C Word: Teenagers & Their Families Living with Cancer. Elena Dorfman. 1994. pap. 16.95 (*0-939165-21-X*) NewSage Press.

C Workbook. Sathis Menon. 288p. 1993. pap. text ed. write for info. (*0-07-041576-5*) McGraw.

C Workbook. Richard S. Wiener & Lewis J. Pinson. (Illus.). 352p. (C). 1990. pap. text ed. 34.50 (*0-201-50930-X*) Addison-Wesley.

C. Wright Mills. Ed. by John Eldridge. (Key Sociologists Ser.). 128p. 1983. pap. 5.95 (*0-85312-534-1*, NO. 3466, Tavistock-E Horwood) Routledge Chapman & Hall.

C. Wright Mills: A Native Radical & His American Intellectual Roots. Rick Tilman. LC 83-43034. 240p. 1984. 30.00 (*0-271-00360-X*) Pa St U Pr.

C. Wright Mills: An American Utopian. Irving L. Horowitz. LC 83-5619. 348p. (C). 1983. 29.95 (*0-02-914970-3*) Free Pr.

C. Wright Mills: An American Utopian. Irving L. Horowitz. 1985. pap. 16.95 (*0-02-915010-8*) Free Pr.

C-XSC: A C Plus Plus Class Library for Extended Scientific Computing. R. Klatte et al. Tr. by G. F. Corliss et al. LC 92-46681. 1993. 49.95 (*0-387-56328-8*) Spr-Verlag.

C. Z. Guest's Five Seasons of Gardening. C. Z. Guest. (Illus.). 176p. 1992. 29.95 (*0-8212-1897-2*) Bulfinch Pr.

C. Z. Guest's Five Seasons of Gardening Planner. C. Z. Guest. LC 93-26354. (Illus.). 96p. 1994. 14.95 (*0-8212-2039-X*) Bulfinch Pr.

C Zone: Peak Performance Under Pressure. Robert Kriegel & Marilyn H. Kriegel. 1985. pap. 9.95 (*0-449-90164-5*, Columbine) Fawcett.

C-7 Caribou in Action. Wayne Mutza. (Aircraft in Action Ser.). (Illus.). 50p. Date not set. pap. 8.95 (*0-89747-292-6*, 1132) Squad Sig Pubns.

C-119 Flying Boxcar. A. T. Lloyd. 228p. 1992. 41.95 (*0-918805-37-6*); pap. 29.95 (*0-918805-38-4*) Pac Aero Pr.

C-123 Provider in Action. Al Adcock. (Aircraft in Action Ser.). (Illus.). 50p. 1992. pap. 8.95 (*0-89747-276-4*, 1124) Squad Sig Pubns.

C-128 Programming in Machine Language. Gerd Mollmann. Ed. by Susan Dorn. Tr. by Ludwig J. Prazak. 250p. (Orig.). 1987. pap. 19.95 (*0-941689-02-6*) Prog Peripherals.

***C-17 Aircraft: Cost & Performance Issues.** (Illus.). 50p. (Orig.). (C). 1995. pap. text ed. 35.00x (*0-7881-1673-8*) Diane Pub.

***C-47 Skytrain in Action.** Larry Davis. (Aircraft in Action Ser.). (Illus.). 58p. 1995. pap. 8.95 (*0-89747-329-9*) Squad Sig Pubns.

CA Attorney General Opinions. Warren L. Hanna. 1989. write for info. (*0-8205-1978-2*, 978) Bender.

***CA-Clipper Developer's Library.** James Occhiogrosso. 1995. pap. text ed. 44.95 (*0-07-911883-6*, Windcrest) TAB Bks.

***CA-Clipper Interface Handbook.** 2nd ed. John P. Mueller & B. J. Walsh. LC 95-2754. 1995. pap. text ed. 44.95 (*0-07-911919-0*) McGraw.

CA-Clipper 5.2: Step-by-Step. Dan Gutierrez. 448p. 1994. pap. text ed. 29.95 (*0-471-55499-5*) Wiley.

CA Compensation Cases, 54 vols. Ryan & Robinson. 1989. write for info. (*0-8205-1979-0*) Bender.

Ca Dao Vietnam: Bilingual Anthology of Vietnamese Folk Poetry. Ed. & Tr. by John Balaban. (Illus.). (ENG & VIE.). 1980. 19.95 (*0-87775-128-5*); pap. 13.95 (*0-87775-129-3*) Unicorn Pr.

CA Employer's Guide to Employee Handbook & Personnel Policy Manual. Morrison & Foerster Staff. 1989. write for info. (*0-8205-1072-6*) Bender.

CA Employment Law, 4 vols. Wilcox et al. 1989. Updates. spiral bd. write for info. (*0-8205-1282-6*, 282) Bender.

CA Environmental Law, 4 vols., Set. Selmi & Manaster. 1989. write for info. (*0-8205-1102-1*) Bender.

Ca Marche! Cours de Francais Communicatif. Karl C. Sandberg et al. (Illus.). 480p. (ENG & FRE.). (C). 1990. Incl. instr's. manual, recordings, tapescript, CAI software, transparency masters & videos. text ed. write for info. (*0-13-033861-3*) P-H.

Ca Marche! Cours de Francais Communicatif. Karl C. Sandberg et al. (Illus.). 480p. (ENG & FRE.). (C). 1992. pap. text ed. write for info. (*0-13-033879-6*) P-H.

CA Public Agency Practice, 3 vols. Gregory L. Ogen. 1988. ring bd. write for info. (*0-8205-1141-2*) Bender.

CA Public Sector Labor Relations. Zerger et al. 1989. write for info. (*0-8205-1176-5*) Bender.

CA 2 Plus Plus Antagonists in CNS: Proceedings of Investigators' Meeting. Ed. by R. A. Janis & D. J. Triggle. (Drugs in Development Ser.). (Illus.). 520p. (Orig.). 1994. pap. text ed. 75.00 (*0-9637603-1-9*) Neva Pr.

CA 2 Plus Pump of Plasma Membrane. Alcides F. Rega. Ed. by Patricio J. Garrahan. 184p. 1986. 102.00 (*0-8493-6253-9*, QH601, CRC Reprint) Franklin.

***CA-Visual Objects Interface Handbook.** Mueller & Walsh. 1995. disk, pap. text ed. 44.95 (*0-07-912089-X*) McGraw.

CA 90s: Computing Architecture for the '90s. 3rd ed. (Illus.). 178p. (C). 1993. 54.95 (*0-923108-08-4*) Comp Assocs NY.

CAAD Futures '87: Proceedings of the 2nd International Conference on Computer-Aided Architectural Design Futures, Eindhoven, the Netherlands, 20-22 May, 1987. Ed. by T. Maver & H. Wagter. 262p. 1988. 87.25 (*0-444-42916-6*) Elsevier.

CAAD Futures '91: Computer Aided Architectural Design Futures Education, Research, Applications. Ed. by Gerhard N. Schmitt. 596p. 1992. 84.00 (*3-528-08821-4*, Pub. by Vieweg & Sohn GW) Ballen Bkslr.

CAAD Futures '93: Proceedings of the International Conference on Computer-Aided Architectural Design Futures, Pittsburgh, PA, U. S. A., 7-10 July 1993. Ed. by Ulrich Flemming & Skip Van Wyk. LC 93-4829. 1993. write for info. (*0-444-89922-7*, North Holland) Elsevier.

CAAP 1981 Trees in Algebra & Programming: Proceedings. Ed. by E. Astesiano & C. Boehm. (Lecture Notes in Computer Science Ser.: Vol. 112). 364p. 1981. pap. 23.10 (*0-387-10828-9*) Spr-Verlag.

CAAP 1983. Ed. by G. Ausiello & M. Protasi. (Lecture Notes in Computer Science Ser.: Vol. 159). 416p. (ENG & FRE.). 1983. pap. 40.00 (*0-387-12727-5*) Spr-Verlag.

CAAP '86, Vol. 214. Ed. by P. Franchi-Zannettacci. (Lecture Notes in Computer Science Ser.). vi, 306p. 1986. pap. 39.00 (*0-387-16443-X*) Spr-Verlag.

CAAP '88. Ed. by M. Dauchet & Maurice Nivat. (Lecture Notes in Computer Science Ser.: Vol. 299). viii, 304p. 1988. pap. 39.00 (*0-387-19021-X*) Spr-Verlag.

CAAP '90: Fifteenth Colloquium on Trees in Algebra & Programming Copenhagen, Denmark, May 15-18, 1990 Proceedings. Ed. by A. Arnold et al. (Lecture Notes in Computer Science Ser.: Vol. 431). vi, 285p. 1990. pap. 32.70 (*0-387-52590-4*) Spr-Verlag.

CAAP '92. Ed. by J. C. Raoult et al. (Lecture Notes in Computer Science Ser.: Vol. 581). 361p. 1992. pap. 52.00 (*0-387-55251-0*) Spr-Verlag.

CAB Abstracts Online Manual. 1,989th ed. CABI Staff. 384p. (Orig.). 1989. pap. text ed. 69.50 (*0-85198-597-1*) CAB Intl.

Cab at the Door & Midnight Oil. V. S. Pritchett. 1994. 16.00 (*0-679-60103-1*, Modern Lib) Random.

CAB International Serials Checklist 1988. CABI Staff. 511p. (Orig.). 1988. pap. text ed. 66.50 (*0-85198-606-4*) CAB Intl.

CAB Thesaurus, 1990, 2 vols. 1,990th ed. CABI Staff. 1227p. (Orig.). 1990. pap. text ed. 190.00 (*0-85198-687-0*) CAB Intl.

***Cabal: An Aurelio Zen Mystery.** Michael Dibdin. (Aurelio Zen Mystery Ser.). 1994. pap. 4.99 (*0-553-56173-1*) Bantam.

Cabal Nightbreed. Clive Barker. 1991. mass mkt. 5.99 (*0-671-74288-4*) PB.

Cabal of Zealots. Vincent Katz. 106p. (Orig.). 1988. 5.95 (*0-937815-16-0*) Hanuman Bks.

Cabal Seminar, 76-77: Proceedings, Caltech-UCLA Logic Seminar 1976-1977. Ed. by A. S. Kechris & Y. N. Moschovakis. (Lecture Notes in Mathematics Ser.: Vol. 689). 1978. pap. 24.00 (*0-387-09086-X*) Spr-Verlag.

Cabal Seminar, 79-81. Ed. by A. S. Kechris et al. (Lecture Notes in Mathematics Ser.: Vol. 1019). 284p. 1983. pap. 35.30 (*0-387-12688-0*) Spr-Verlag.

Cabala: Its Influence on Judaism & Christianity. Bernard Pick. 1991. lib. bdg. 75.00 (*0-8490-4257-7*) Gordon Pr.

Cabala: Its Influence on Judaism & Christianity. Bernhard Pick. 115p. 1993. pap. 9.00 (*0-89540-287-4*, SB-287) Sun Pub.

Cabalah Primer: Introduction to English-Hebrew Cabalah. Henrietta Bernstein. 192p. 1984. pap. 11.00 (*0-87516-526-5*) DeVorss.

Cabale. Enzo Cormann. Tr. by Gideon Y. Schein. (Publications Ser.: No. 12). 122p. (Orig.). 1985. pap. text ed. 8.95 (*0-913745-09-X*) Ubu Repertory.

***Cabaleta.** limited ed. Joan Brossa. (Illus.). (CAT.). 1993. 3,750.00 (*0-614-00246-X*) Elliots Bks.

***Cabaleta: Con Doce Litografias Originales Firmados por Moises Villelia.** limited ed. Joan Brossa. (Illus.). (CAT.). 1993. 3,750.00 (*0-614-00141-2*) Elliots Bks.

***Caballero de las Espuelas de Oro - Retablo Jovial.** Alejandro Casona. 216p. 1991. pap. 12.95 (*0-7859-5209-8*) Fr & Eur.

Caballero de las Espuelas de Oro. Retablo Jovial. Alejandro Casona. Ed. by Maria D. Marcos Sanchez. (Nueva Austral Ser.: Vol. 223). (SPA.). 1991. pap. text ed. 15.95 (*84-239-7223-2*) Elliots Bks.

***Caballero de Olmedo.** 6th ed. Lope De Vega. 168p. 1991. pap. write for info. (*0-7859-5205-5*) Fr & Eur.

Caballeros. Ruth L. Barker. Ed. by Carlos E. Cortes. Tr. by Norma Van Sweringen. LC 76-1237. (Chicano Heritage Ser.). (Illus.). 1977. reprint ed. lib. bdg. 33.95 (*0-405-09484-1*) Ayer.

Caballito Blanco y Otras Poesias Favoritas. (Dias y Dias de Poesia (Green Small Book) Ser.). (Illus.). 40p. (Orig.). (SPA.). (J). (gr. 1-4). 1991. pap. text ed. 7.00 (*1-56334-062-3*) Hampton-Brown.

Caballito Blanco y Otras Poesias Favoritas: Green Small Book Set, 6 bks., Set. Alma F. Ada. (Dias y Dias de Poesia Ser.). (Illus.). 40p. (Orig.). (SPA.). (J). (gr. 1-3). 1992. pap. 42.00 (*1-56334-118-2*) Hampton-Brown.

Caballos, Caballos, Caballos: Horses, Horses, Horses. Allan Fowler. LC 91-35063. (Rookie Read-about Science Ser.). (Illus.). 32p. (SPA.). (J). (ps-2). 1992. lib. bdg. 11.10 (*0-516-34921-X*); pap. 3.95 (*0-516-54921-9*); 23.48 (*0-516-59622-5*) Childrens.

Caballos (Horses) L. Stone. (Spanish Language Books, Set 1: Animales de Granja (Farm Animals)). (J). 1991. 8.95 (*0-86592-987-4*) Rourke Enter.

Cabanatuan. Vince Taylor. 1985. 16.95 (*0-87244-069-9*) Texian.

Cabanis: Enlightenment & Medical Philosophy in the French Revolution. Martin S. Staum. LC 79-3231. 1980. 62.50 (*0-691-05301-4*) Princeton U Pr.

Cabanocey: The History, Customs & Folklore of St. James Parish. Lillian Bourgeois. 211p. 1990. 28.00 (*0-88289-104-9*) Pelican.

Cabaret. (Illus.). 32p. 1983. pap. 8.95 (*0-88188-440-5*, 00359453); pap. 35.00 (*0-88188-469-3*, 00362105) H Leonard.

Cabaret Performance: Sketches, Songs, Monologues, Memoirs, Vol. I. - Europe 1890-1925. Ed. & Tr. by Laurence Senelick. (Illus.). 1989. pap. 14.95 (*1-55554-043-0*) PAJ Pubns.

Cabaret Performance Vol. II: Europe, 1920-1940 Sketches, Songs, Monologues, Memoirs. Ed. & Tr. by Laurence Senelick. (PAJ Bks.). (Illus.). 288p. 1992. text ed. 45.00 (*0-8018-4378-2*); pap. text ed. 15.95 (*0-8018-4543-2*) Johns Hopkins.

Cabaret Songbook. Intro. by Ronny Schiff. (Piano-Vocal-Guitar Music Bk.). 224p. (Orig.). 1991. pap. 15.95 (*0-7935-0086-9*, HL00490488) H Leonard.

***Cabarrus County, North Carolina Marriage Bonds & Certificates, 1793-1868.** Francis T. Ingmire. 164p. 1994. lib. bdg. 47.00 (*0-8095-8015-2*); pap. 20.00 (*0-8095-8527-8*) Borgo Pr.

Cabbage: Cures to Cuisine. Judith Hiatt. (Illus.). 80p. 1989. 14.95 (*0-87961-188-X*); pap. 6.95 (*0-87961-189-8*) Naturegraph.

Cabbage Moon. Tim Chadwick. LC 93-28952. (Illus.). 32p. (J). (ps-2). 1994. 14.95 (*0-531-06827-7*) Orchard Bks Watts.

Cabbage Moth & the Shamrock. Ethel Marbach. LC 91-575. (Illus.). 32p. (J). (ps-2). 1991. 9.00 (*0-671-74864-5*, Green Tiger S&S) S&S Childrens.

Cabbage Patch Kids Visit the Doctor. M. J. Carr. (J). (ps-3). 1993. pap. 2.50 (*0-685-64929-6*) Scholastic Inc.

Cabbage Patch Kids Visit the Doctor. M. J. Carr. (J). (ps-3). 1993. pap. 2.50 (*0-590-46631-3*) Scholastic Inc.

Cabbage Rose. M. C. Helldorfer. LC 91-9833. (Illus.). 32p. (J). (ps-3). 1993. text ed. 14.95 (*0-02-743513-X*, Bradbury S&S) S&S Childrens.

***Cabbage Soup: Knitting Patterns for Soft-Sculptured Dolls.** Janet W. Mysse. (Illus.). Date not set. spiral bd., pap. 6.95 (*0-9623098-0-X*) Janknits.

Cabbage Syndrome. C. Barnes. 1990. 70.00 (*1-85000-757-8*, Falmer Pr); pap. 33.00 (*1-85000-758-6*, Falmer Pr) Taylor & Francis.

Cabbages & Geraniums: Memories of the Holocaust. Valerie Furth. (Atlantic Studies on Society in Change, Social Science Monographs). (Illus.). 80p. 1989. text ed. 60.00 (*0-88033-962-4*) East Eur Quarterly.

Cabbages & Kings. O. Henry. LC 92-40936. (Twentieth-Century Classics Ser.). 288p. 1993. 10.95 (*0-14-018689-1*, Penguin Classics) Viking Penguin.

Cabbages Are Chasing the Rabbits. Arnold Adoff. LC 85-893. (Illus.). 32p. (J). (gr. k-3). 1985. 15.95 (*0-15-213875-7*, HB Juv Bks) HarBrace.

Cabbagetown Cafe Cookbook. Julie Jordan. LC 86-2306. (Illus.). 228p. (Orig.). 1986. pap. 12.95 (*0-89594-192-9*) Crossing Pr.

C

An Asterisk (*) at the beginning of an entry indicates that the title is appearing in BIP for the first time.

Cabbie. Marti Riera. Ed. by Bernd Metz. Tr. by Jeff Lisle. (Illus.). 80p. 1987. pap. 10.95 (*0-87416-042-1*) Catalan Communs.
Cabell - the Cabells & Their Kin: A Memorial Volume of History, Biography & Genealogy. A. Brown. (Illus.). 708p. 1991. reprint ed. lib. bdg. 109.00 (*0-8328-1703-1*); reprint ed. pap. 99.00 (*0-8328-1704-X*) Higginson Bk Co.
Cabell Scene. Robert Canary. (James Branch Cabell Ser.). 300p. 1975. lib. bdg. 250.00 (*0-87700-236-3*) Revisionist Pr.
Cabell under Fire. Geoffrey Morley-Mower. 1974. lib. bdg. 250.00 (*0-87700-214-2*) Revisionist Pr.
Cabell's Directory of Publishing Opportunities in Management & Marketing. 6th ed. Ed. by David W. Cabell. 1400p. (C). 1994. pap. 59.95 (*0-911753-08-7*) Cabell Pub.
Cabell's Directory of Publishing Opportunities in Accounting, Economics & Finance. 6th ed. Ed. by David W. Cabell. 900p. (C). 1994. pap. 59.95 (*0-911753-07-9*) Cabell Pub.
Cabell's Directory of Publishing Opportunities in Education. 4th ed. Ed. by David W. Cabell. (C). 1995. pap. text ed. write for info. (*0-911753-05-2*) Cabell Pub.
Cabell's Directory of Publishing Opportunities in Nursing. Ed. by David W. Cabell & Deborah L. English. 448p. (Orig.). 1993. pap. text ed. 29.95 (*0-911753-06-0*) Cabell Pub.
Cabeza De Vaca: Conquistador Who Cared. Mary D. Wade. (Illus.). 64p. (J). (gr. 3-5). 1994. 10.95 (*1-882539-14-1*); pap. 4.95 (*1-882539-15-X*) Colophon Hse.
Cabeza de Vaca: His Relation of the Journey Florida to the Pacific 1528-1536. Haniel Long. (Illus.). 40p. 1988. reprint ed. 60.00 (*0-942067-00-2*) Okeanos Pr.
Cabeza de Vaca: New World Explorer. Keith Brandt. LC 92-36960. (Illus.). 48p. (J). (gr. 4-6). 1993. lib. bdg. 10.79 (*0-8167-2829-1*); 3.50 (*0-8167-2830-5*) Troll Assocs.
Cabildo on Jackson Square. rev. ed. Samuel Wilson, Jr. & Leonard V. Huber. LC 70-117643. 1973. pap. 8.95 (*0-911116-41-9*) Pelican.
Cabin. Thomas B. Baldwin. 120p. 1993. 12.00 (*0-9636032-0-5*) Baldwin PA.
Cabin: Reminiscence & Diversions. David Mamet. 1992. 20.00 (*0-679-41558-0*) Random.
Cabin: Reminiscence & Diversions. David Mamet. LC 93-10493. 1993. pap. 10.00 (*0-679-74720-6*, Vin) Random.
Cabin, a Mountain Adventure. Barbara Hallowell. LC 86-7981. 1986. pap. 8.95 (*0-913239-42-9*) Appalach Consortium.
Cabin & Parlor: Or, Slaves & Masters. J. Thornton Randolph. LC 77-149876. (Black Heritage Library Collection). 1977. 28.95 (*0-8369-8756-X*) Ayer.
Cabin & Plantation Songs. Comp. by Thomas P. Fenner. LC 74-24079. reprint ed. 29.50 (*0-404-12908-0*) AMS Pr.
Cabin at Singing River: Building a Home in the Wilderness. Chris Czajkowski. (Illus.). 176p. 1991. pap. 12.95 (*0-921820-31-3*, Pub. by Camden Hse CN) Firefly Bks Ltd.
Cabin Boy's Story. LC 70-83935. (Black Heritage Library Collection). 1977. 21.95 (*0-8369-8527-3*) Ayer.
Cabin Cars of the Pennsylvania & Long Island Railroads. Illus. by Alan B. Chesley. LC 82-81756. (Caboose Data Bk.: No. 2). 64p. 1982. pap. 14.95 (*0-685-08288-1*) NJ Intl Inc.
Cabin Comments: A Journal of Life in Jackson Hole. Elisabeth Anderson et al. LC 80-53090. (Illus.). 286p. (gr. 7-12). 1980. 14.75 (*0-933160-08-9*); pap. 7.75 (*0-933160-09-7*) Teton Bkshop.
Cabin Faced West. Jean Fritz. (Classics Ser.). (Illus.). (J). (gr. 1-7). 1987. pap. 4.99 (*0-14-032256-6*, Puffin) Puffin Bks.
Cabin Faced West. Jean Fritz. (Illus.). (J). (gr. 4-7). 1958. 13.95 (*0-698-20016-0*, Coward) Putnam Pub Group.
Cabin Faced West: A Study Guide. Dina Claydon. Ed. by Joyce Friedland & Rikki Kessler. (Novel-Ties Ser.). 21p. (YA). (gr. 9-12). 1990. pap. text ed. 15.95 (*0-88122-409-X*) Lrn Links.
Cabin Fever. Anne French. 52p. 1991. pap. 9.95 (*1-86940-050-X*) OUP.
Cabin Fever. Anne French. 1991. pap. 9.95 (*0-19-694005-2*) OUP.
***Cabin Fever.** Donald Vining. (Orig.). 1995. pap. text ed. 5.95 (*1-56333-338-4*) Masquerade.
Cabin Fever. B. M. Bower. 290p. (J). 1981. reprint ed. lib. bdg. 16.35 (*0-89966-017-7*) Buccaneer Bks.
Cabin Fever. Elizabeth Jolley. LC 90-55966. 224p. 1992. reprint ed. pap. 10.00 (*0-06-092151-X*, PL) HarpC.
Cabin Fever: A Centennial Collection of Stories about the Seeley Lake Area. rev. ed. Seeley Lake Writers Club Staff. Ed. by Suzanne M. Vernon. 296p. 1990. pap. 15.95 (*0-9620902-4-7*) Vernon Print & Pub.
***Cabin Fever: A Laney Samms Mystery.** Carol Schmidt. 1995. pap. 10.95 (*1-56280-098-1*) Naiad Pr.
***Cabin Fever: Dialogues with Nature.** Richard E. Carter. LC 95-12551. 1995. write for info. (*1-880090-20-1*) Galde Pr.
Cabin Fever: Sheds & Shelters, Huts & Hideaways. Marie-France Boyer. LC 93-60122. (Illus.). 112p. 1993. 19.95 (*0-500-01575-9*) Thames Hudson.
Cabin Fever: Two Hundred-Two Activities for Turning Your Child's Rainy Days, Sick Days, & Snow Days into Great Days. Steve Bennett & Ruth Bennett. (Illus.). 240p. (Orig.). 1994. mass mkt. 6.95 (*0-14-023909-X*, Penguin Bks) Viking Penguin.
Cabin Fever on Noah's Ark. Brooks R. Faulkner. (Orig.). 1991. pap. 5.99 (*0-8054-6046-2*) Broadman.
Cabin Full of Mice. Janet Foster. (True Adventure Bks.). (Illus.). 36p. (J). (gr. 2 up). 1992. pap. 4.95 (*0-919872-66-2*, Pub. by Greey dePencier CN) Firefly Bks Ltd.
Cabin Key. Gloria Rand. LC 93-10398. (Illus.). (J). 1994. 14.95 (*0-15-213884-6*) HarBrace.
***Cabin 102.** Sherry Garland. LC 95-13414. (Illus.). (J). 1995. write for info. (*0-15-200663-X*); pap. write for info. (*0-15-200662-1*) HarBrace.
Cabin Six Plays Cupid. Marilyn Kaye. (Camp Sunnyside Friends Ser.: No. 2). 128p. (Orig.). (J). (ps-8). 1989. pap. 2.95 (*0-380-75701-X*, Camelot) Avon.
***Cabin Surprise.** Judy Delton. (Lottery Luck Ser.: Bk. 8). (Illus.). 96p. (Orig.). (J). (gr. 2-5). 1995. pap. 3.95 (*0-7868-1025-4*) Hyprn Ppbks.
Cabin Twelve: A One Act Play. John Bishop. 1978. pap. 2.75 (*0-8222-0171-2*) Dramatists Play.
***Cabinet.** Barbara S. Feinberg. (Inside Government Ser.). (Illus.). 64p. (J). (gr. 5-8). 1995. lib. bdg. 14.98 (*0-8050-3421-8*) TFC Bks NY.
Cabinet. Peter Hennessy. 240p. 1986. pap. 21.95 (*0-631-14969-4*) Blackwell Pubs.
Cabinet & Political Power in New Zealand. Elizabeth McLeay. (Readings in New Zealand Politics Ser.: No. 5). (Illus.). 192p. 1995. pap. 35.00 (*0-19-558312-4*) OUP.
Cabinet d'Amateur. Georges Perec. (FRE.). 1989. pap. 6.95 (*0-7859-3151-1*, 2253050598) Fr & Eur.
Cabinet Decisions on Foreign Policy: The British Experience, October 1938-June 1941. Christopher Hill. (London School of Economics Monographs in International Studies). (Illus.). 368p. (C). 1991. 64.95 (*0-521-39195-4*) Cambridge U Pr.
Cabinet des Antiques. Honore De Balzac. Ed. by Pierre-Georges Castex. (Coll. Prestige). 1958. 49.95 (*0-685-34071-6*); pap. 29.95 (*0-8288-9361-6*) Fr & Eur.
Cabinet Des Manuscrits De la Bibliotheque Imperiale. Leopold V. Delisle. lvi, 1654p. 1978. reprint ed. write for info. (*3-487-06485-5*, Pub. by Georg Olms GW) Lubrecht & Cramer.
Cabinet Du Duc D'Aumont: A Facsimile of the 1870 Edition Recording the Auction of 1782. Charles Davilier. Ed. by Edgar Munhall. (Reprint Series of Historical Auction Catalogues). (Illus.). 256p. (FRE.). 1986. reprint ed. text ed. 50.00 (*0-317-93172-5*) Acanthus Pr.
Cabinet Government in Australia. 2nd rev. ed. S. Encel. (Illus.). viii, 255p. 1974. pap. 19.95 (*0-522-84063-9*) Intl Spec Bk.
Cabinet Government in India. Madhu Limaye. 135p. 1989. text ed. 35.00 (*81-7027-138-X*, Pub. by Radiant Pubs II) S Asia.
Cabinet Government in Ontario: A View from Inside. Edward E. Stewart. 104p. 1990. pap. text ed. 17.95 (*0-88645-098-5*, Pub. by Inst Res Pub CN) Ashgate Pub Co.
Cabinet in the Commonwealth: Post-War Developments in Africa, the West Indies & South East Asia. H. V. Wiseman. LC 74-10379. 364p. 1976. reprint ed. text ed. 65.00 (*0-8371-7681-6*, WICO, Greenwood Pr) Greenwood.
Cabinet-Maker & Upholsterer's Drawing Book. Thomas Sheraton. (Illus.). 352p. 1972. pap. 12.95 (*0-486-22255-1*) Dover.
Cabinet-Maker & Upholsterer's Guide. George Hepplewhite. LC 69-19164. 1969. reprint ed. pap. 9.95 (*0-486-22183-0*) Dover.
Cabinet Making & Millwork. John L. Feirer. 1977. 39.95 (*0-684-14914-1*, Scribners) S&S Trade.
Cabinet-Making & Millwork. 5th ed. John L. Feirer. 1989. text ed. 50.00 (*0-02-537355-2*) Macmillan.
Cabinet Making & Millwork. 5th ed. Fierer. 1987. 33.32 (*0-02-675950-0*) Macmillan.
Cabinet Ministers & Parliamentary Government. Ed. by Kenneth A. Shepsle & Michael Laver. (Political Economy of Institutions & Decisions Ser.). (Illus.). 352p. (C). 1994. 59.95 (*0-521-43246-4*); pap. 21.95 (*0-521-43837-3*) Cambridge U Pr.
Cabinet of Curiosities: Natural, Artificial, & Historical. Charles A. Goodrich. (Notable American Authors Ser.). 1992. reprint ed. lib. bdg. 75.00 (*0-7812-2930-8*) Rprt Serv.
***Cabinet of Curiousities: Inquiries into Museums & Their Prospects.** Stephen E. Weil. LC 94-30993. 1995. write for info. (*1-56098-511-9*) Smithsonian.
Cabinet of Dr. Caligari. Robert Weine. (Illus.). 90p. (Orig.). 1988. pap. 8.95 (*0-571-12567-0*) Faber & Faber.
Cabinet of Dr. Caligari: Texts, Contexts, Histories. Michael Budd. LC 89-70309. (Illus.). 280p. (Orig.). (C). 1990. text ed. 40.00 (*0-8135-1570-X*); pap. 14.95 (*0-8135-1571-8*) Rutgers U Pr.
Cabinet of Natural History & American Rural Sports, 3 vols. in one. Ed. by Keir B. Sterling. LC 77-81115. (Biologists & Their World Ser.). (Illus.). 1978. reprint ed. lib. bdg. 77.95 (*0-405-10704-8*) Ayer.
Cabinet of Reed-Warblers. Lawrence Courtney-Haines. 94p. (C). 1992. pap. text ed. 65.00 (*0-949324-39-6*, Pub. by Surrey Beatty & Sons AT) St Mut.
Cabinet Politician: The Postmasters General, 1829-1909. Dorothy G. Fowler. reprint ed. 26.00 (*0-404-02542-0*) AMS Pr.
Cabinet Reform in Britain, 1914-1963. Hans Daalder. x, 381p. 1963. 47.50 (*0-8047-0139-3*) Stanford U Pr.
Cabinetmaker's Guide to the Router. Doug Geller. pap. write for info. (*0-671-60723-5*) S&S Trade.
Cabinetmaker's Notebook. James Krenov. LC 91-20083. (Illus.). 136p. 1991. pap. 12.95 (*0-8069-8470-8*) Sterling.
Cabinetmakers of America. 2nd ed. Ethel H. Bjerkoe. LC 57-7278. (Illus.). 272p. 1978. 22.50 (*0-685-04519-6*) Schiffer.
Cabinetmaking. LC 92-11188. (Art of Woodworking Ser.). 1992. write for info. (*0-8094-9904-5*); lib. bdg. write for info. (*0-8094-9905-3*) Time-Life.
Cabinetmaking. Ken Calhoun. (Illus.). 304p. (C). 1984. text ed. 51.00 (*0-13-110064-5*) P-H.
Cabinetmaking. Peters. 1986. 29.95 (*0-684-18520-2*, Scribners) S&S Trade.
Cabinetmaking: Building Drawers. Raymond L'Hevreux. LC 81-730635. 1981. student ed 5.00 (*0-8064-0267-9*, 705); audio 109.00 (*0-8064-0268-7*) Bergwall.
Cabinetmaking: Design & Construction. William P. Spence & Duane Griffiths. 432p. 1991. pap. text ed. 47.00 (*0-13-109489-0*) P-H.
Cabinetmaking: From Design to Finish. Byron W. Maguire. (Illus.). 416p. 1986. pap. 15.50 (*0-13-109737-7*) P-H.
Cabinetmaking: From Design to Finish. 2nd ed. Byron W. Maguire. 416p. 1990. reprint ed. pap. 22.00 (*0-934041-62-8*) Craftsman.
Cabinetmaking: Rod Layout. Raymond L'Hevreux. LC 80-730671. 1981. student ed 7.00 (*0-8064-0265-2*, 704); audio 189.00 (*0-8064-0266-0*) Bergwall.
Cabinetmaking & Millwork. John L. Feirer. 1982. teacher ed 4.72 (*0-02-662770-1*); text ed. 31.36 (*0-02-662760-4*); student ed 7.40 (*0-02-662740-X*) Bennett IL.
Cabinetmaking & Millwork. Jack Rudman. (Occupational Competency Examination Ser.: OCE-9). 1994. pap. 23.95 (*0-8373-5709-8*) Nat Learn.
Cabinetmaking & Millwork: Tools, Materials, Layout. Alf A. Dahl & J. Douglas Wilson. LC 53-11586. (Books of the Building Trade). 359p. reprint ed. pap. 102.40 (*0-8357-7955-6*, 2006111) Bks Demand.
Cabinetmaking, Patternmaking & Millwork. Gaspar Lewis. LC 79-50917. (Carpentry-Cabinetmaking Ser.). 438p. (C). 1981. teacher ed 12.00 (*0-8273-1815-4*) Delmar.
Cabinetmaking the Professional Approach. John L. Feirer. 1986. text ed. 29.95 (*0-02-596200-0*) Macmillan.
Cabinetry: The Woodworkers Guide to Building Professional-Looking Cabinets & Shelves. Ed. by Robert A. Yoder. LC 91-23894. (Illus.). 448p. 1991. 26.95 (*0-87857-981-8*, 14-379-0) Rodale Pr Inc.
Cabinetry Basics. Sam Allen. LC 91-12939. (Basics Ser.). (Illus.). 128p. 1991. pap. 9.95 (*0-8069-8290-X*) Sterling.
Cabinetry Basics. Sam Allen. 128p. 1991. reprint ed. lib. bdg. 27.00x (*0-8095-7607-4*) Borgo Pr.
Cabinets & Bookcases. (Art of Woodworking Ser.). 1994. 18.95 (*0-8094-9945-2*) Time-Life.
***Cabinets & Built-Ins.** Ed. by Konm Oberrecht. LC 94-6950. 1995. pap. 14.95 (*1-880029-41-3*) Creative Homeowner.
Cabinets & Built-Ins: A Practical Guide to Building Professional Quality Cabinetry. Paul Levine. (Illus.). 384p. 1994. 27.95 (*0-87596-590-3*) Rodale Pr Inc.
Cabinets & Counselors: The President & the Executive Branch. CQ Inc. Staff. 163p. 1989. 20.95 (*0-87187-519-5*) Congr Quarterly.
Cabinets, Bookcases & Closets. Tom Philbin. Ed. by Shirley M. Horowitz. LC 80-69620. (Illus.). 160p. (Orig.). 1980. pap. 9.95 (*0-932944-22-1*) Creative Homeowner.
Cabinets, Lost & Found. S. Dillon Ripley. (Connecticut Academy of Arts & Sciences Ser., Trans.: Vol. 46). 1975. pap. 29.50 (*0-685-22883-5*) Elliots Bks.
Cabins & Cottages. (Home Repair & Improvement Ser.). (Illus.). 136p. 1978. 14.60 (*0-8094-2412-6*); lib. bdg. 20.60 (*0-8094-2411-8*) Time-Life.
Cabins, Cottages & Mansions: Homes of the Presidents of the United States. Nancy D. Benbow & Christopher H. Benbow. (Illus.). 248p. (C). 1993. pap. text ed. 16.95 (*0-939631-61-X*) Thomas Publications.
Cabins, Cottages, & Resorts of Northern California. Tom Thompson & Marthea Thompson. (Illus.). 170p. (Orig.). 1994. pap. 9.95 (*0-9641409-0-X*) Rustic Getaways.
Cabins Crummies & Hacks. John Henderson. LC 91-90580. (South Ser.: Vol. 2). (Illus.). 84p. (Orig.). 1991. pap. 29.95 (*0-9629037-2-8*) H & M Prods.
Cabins Crummies & Hacks. John Henderson. LC 92-72661. (North & West Ser.: Vol. 3). (Illus.). 80p. (Orig.). 1992. pap. 29.95 (*0-9629037-3-6*) H & M Prods.
Cabins Crummies & Hacks Vol. 1: North & East. John Henderson. LC 90-93655. (Illus.). 128p. 1991. pap. 39.95 (*0-9629037-1-X*) H & M Prods.
Cabins Crummies & Hacks Vol. 4: South & West. LC 92-72611. (Illus.). 84p. 1993. pap. 29.95 (*0-9629037-4-4*) H & M Prods.
Cabins in the Laurel. Muriel E. Sheppard. LC 91-2943. (Chapel Hill Bks.). (Illus.). xv, 287p. (C). 1991. reprint ed. 29.95 (*0-8078-1986-7*); reprint ed. pap. 16.95 (*0-8078-4328-8*) U of NC Pr.
CABIS: Computer-Aided Bookkeeping Instruction System. Robin Cooper & Michael Vitale. LC 86-32148. 80p. (C). 1987. 25.00 (*0-201-11306-6*); teacher ed, text ed. 30.00 (*0-317-60800-2*) Addison-Wesley.
Cable. Louise Simonson et al. 176p. 1992. pap. 13.95 (*0-87135-937-5*) Marvel Entmnt.
Cable Advertiser's Handbook. 2nd ed. Ronald B. Kaatz. (Illus.). 262p. 1985. 29.95 (*0-8442-3131-2*, NTC Busn Bks) NTC Pub Grp.
***Cable & Satellite Carrier Compulsory Licenses: An Overview & Analysis.** 1995. lib. bdg. 256.95 (*0-8490-6752-9*) Gordon Pr.
Cable & Station Coverage Atlas, 1991 Edition. Warren Publishing, Inc. Staff. Ed. by Albert Warren. (Illus.). 628p. 1991. reprint ed. 345.00 (*0-911486-45-3*) Warren Pub Inc.
Cable & Station Coverage Atlas, 1992 Edition. 26th rev. ed. Warren Publishing, Inc. Staff. Ed. by Albert Warren. (Illus.). 650p. 1992. write for info. (*0-911486-55-0*) Warren Pub Inc.
Cable & Station Coverage Atlas, 1993 Edition. rev. ed. Warren Publishing, Inc. Staff. Ed. by Michael Taliaferro. (Illus.). 1993. 360.00 (*0-911486-68-2*) Warren Pub Inc.
Cable & Station Coverage Atlas, 1994 Edition. rev. ed. Warren Publishing, Inc. Staff. Ed. by Michael Taliaferro. (Illus.). 1994. 375.00 (*0-911486-79-8*) Warren Pub Inc.
***Cable & Station Coverage Atlas, 1995.** rev. suppl. ed. Warren Publishing, Inc. Staff. Ed. by Michael Taliaferro. (Illus.). 1995. 395.00 (*0-911486-90-9*) Warren Pub Inc.
Cable & Wire Network Markets. Market Intelligence Staff. 250p. 1993. 3,900.00 (*1-56753-535-6*) Frost & Sullivan.
***Cable-Car.** June Drummond. 160p. 1995. 16.95 (*0-7451-8651-3*, Black Dagger) Chivers N Amer.
Cable Car. Christopher Swan. LC 73-77725. (Illus.). 1978. pap. 9.95 (*0-89815-145-7*) Ten Speed Pr.
Cable Car & the Dragon. Herb Caen. LC 85-32004. (Illus.). 40p. (J). 1986. 10.95 (*0-87701-390-X*) Chronicle Bks.
***Cable Car & the Dragon.** Herb Caen. (J). (ps-3). 1995. pap. 5.95 (*0-8118-1054-2*) Chronicle Bks.
Cable Car Murder. Elizabeth A. Taylor. (Northern California Mysteries Ser.). 240p. 1988. reprint ed. mass mkt. 4.99 (*0-8041-0281-3*) Ivy Books.
Cable Cars: A Traveler's Guide to Europe's Fascinating Cable Railways. Bernard C. Winn. LC 90-81304. (Illus.). 128p. (Orig.). 1990. pap. 8.95 (*0-9615161-5-1*) Incline Pr.
Cable Communication. 2nd ed. Thomas F. Baldwin & D. Stevens McVoy. (Illus.). 464p. (C). 1988. text ed. 82.00 (*0-13-110263-X*) P-H.
Cable Communication Policy Act of 1984. Jay Ricks & Richard E. Wiley. 1985. 35.00 (*0-317-29482-2*, #CO3360) HarBrace.
***Cable Communications: Building the Information Infrastructure.** Bartlett. 1995. 50.00 (*0-07-005355-3*) McGraw.
Cable Contacts Yearbook Directory, 1988. Ed. by Bob Del Pazzo. 1988. 184.00 (*0-935224-32-7*) Larimi Comm.
Cable Distribution & Interconnection Systems for Telephone Wire Center Modernization U. S. Markets, Competitors, Customers & Technologies: 1993-1998 Analysis & Forecasts. Amadee Bender. 250p. 1993. pap. text ed. 2,850.00 (*1-878218-40-9*) World Info Tech.
Cable for Information Delivery: A Guide for Librarians, Educators & Cable Professionals. Ed. by Brigitte L. Kenney. LC 83-19892. (Professional Librarian Ser.). 172p. 1984. pap. 30.50 (*0-86729-055-2*) G K Hall.
Cable Franchising & Regulation: A Local Government Guide to the New Law. 400p. 1985. 50.00 (*0-933729-00-6*); 35.00 (*0-317-36782-X*) Natl League Cities.
Cable Harbor. Donald Bowie. 336p. 1982. pap. 3.50 (*0-380-59493-5*, 59493-5, Flare) Avon.
Cable, Inside & Out. rev. ed. Frank W. Horn. LC 74-21671. (ABC of the Telephone Ser.: Vol. 5). (Illus.). 100p. (C). 1988. pap. text ed. 13.95 (*1-56016-004-7*) ABC TeleTraining.
Cable Laying: Guidelines to Exposures & Insurance. A. S. Bashford. 1990. 39.00 (*1-85609-015-9*, Pub. by Witherby & Co UK) St Mut.
Cable Logging Systems. Studier. 1974. pap. 9.95 (*0-88246-015-3*) Oreg St U Bkstrs.
Cable Management Systems. E. A. Reeves. (Illus.). 336p. 1992. 76.95 (*0-632-02808-4*) Blackwell Sci.
Cable on Academe. Carole Cable. LC 93-48668. (Illus.). 128p. (C). 1994. pap. 8.95 (*0-292-71170-0*) U of Tex Pr.
Cable Programming Resource Directory 1987: A Guide to Community TV Production Facilities & Programming Sources & Outlets. Ed. by Gregory Epler-Wood & Paul D'Ari. 240p. (Orig.). 1987. pap. text ed. 34.95 (*0-89461-047-3*) Broadcasting Pubns.
***Cable Shielding for Electromagnetic Compatibility.** Tsaliovich. (Electrical Engineering Ser.). 1994. text ed. 69.95 (*0-442-01425-2*) Van Nos Reinhold.
Cable Splicer. Jack Rudman. (Career Examination Ser.: C-1624). 1994. pap. 20.00 (*0-8373-1624-3*) Nat Learn.
Cable Statistics Book: 1993 Edition. rev. suppl. ed. Warren Publishing, Inc. Staff. Ed. by Michael Taliaferro. (Television & Cable Factbook Ser.: No. 61). (Illus.). 1993. 95.00 (*0-911486-71-2*) Warren Pub Inc.
Cable-Stayed Bridges. Ed. by Carl C. Ulstrup. (Sessions Proceedings Ser.). 72p. 1988. 15.00 (*0-87262-647-4*) Am Soc Civil Eng.
Cable Stayed Bridges. Rene Walther et al. 208p. 1988. 115.50 (*0-7277-1321-3*, Pub. by T Telford UK) Am Soc Civil Eng.
Cable Structures. Max Irvine. (Illus.). 272p. 1992. reprint ed. pap. 8.95 (*0-486-67127-5*) Dover.
Cable Supported Bridges: Concept & Design. Niels J. Gimsing. LC 82-23748. (Illus.). 410p. reprint ed. pap. 116.90 (*0-7837-6376-X*, 2046089) Bks Demand.
Cable Television. 1973. 2.00 (*0-686-09554-5*) Network Project.
Cable Television: A Reference Guide to Information. Ronald Garay. LC 87-24955. 192p. 1988. text ed. 49.95 (*0-313-24751-X*, GCT/, Greenwood Pr) Greenwood.
Cable Television: A Source Guide. 1991. lib. bdg. 75.00 (*0-8490-4911-3*) Gordon Pr.
Cable Television: Handbook & Forms. Ira C. Stein. 942p. 1985. text ed. 95.00 (*0-07-060989-6*) Shepards-McGraw.
Cable Television: Media & Copyright Law Aspects, 1983. Ed. by Herman C. Jehoram. 300p. 1982. pap. 24.00 (*0-686-40978-7*) Kluwer Ac.
Cable Television: Strategy for Penetrating Key Urban Markets. James D. Scott. LC 76-367151. (Michigan Business Papers: No. 58). 144p. reprint ed. pap. 41.10 (*0-317-28862-8*, 2022081) Bks Demand.
Cable Television & Other Nonbroadcast Media: Law & Policies. Daniel L. Brenner et al. LC 85-30946. (Entertainment & Communications Law Ser.). 1986. ring bd. 145.00 (*0-87632-489-8*) Clark Boardman Callaghan.
Cable Television & the First Amendment. Patrick Parsons. LC 86-45883. 176p. 1987. text ed. 35.00 (*0-669-14459-2*) Free Pr.
***Cable Television Consumer Services Specialist.** (Career Examination Ser.: Series 1). Date not set. pap. 29.95 (*0-8373-3683-X*) Nat Learn.
Cable Television Law: A Video Communications Practice Guide, 3 vols. Charles D. Ferris & Frank W. Lloyd. 1983. Updates available. ring bd. write for info. (*0-8205-1148-X*) Bender.

C

An Asterisk (*) at the beginning of an entry indicates that the title is appearing in BIP for the first time.

Cable Television Law Nineteen Ninety-Two: Cable Faces Congress, the Courts & Competition, 2 vols., Set. Frank W. Llyod. (Patents, Copyrights, Trademarks, & Literary Property Ser.). 1743p. 1992. pap. text ed. 80.00 (*0-685-56909-8*, G4-3877) PLI.

Cable Television Law 1993: Learning to Live with the 1992 Cable Act, 2 vols., Set. (Patents, Copyrights, Trademarks, & Literary Property Ser.). 1824p. 1993. 80.00 (*0-685-65518-0*, G4-3895) PLI.

***Cable Television Specialist.** (Career Examination Ser.: Series 1). Date not set. pap. 29.95 (*0-8373-3684-8*) Nat Learn.

Cable Television Technical Handbook. Bobby Harrell. LC 84-72796. (Artech House Telecom Library). 330p. reprint ed. pap. 94.10 (*0-7837-1333-9*, 2041481) Bks Demand.

Cable Television Technology. K. Deschler. 352p. 1987. pap. text ed. 18.95 (*0-07-027378-2*) McGraw.

Cable Television Technology & Operations. Eugene R Bartlett. 1990. text ed. 50.00 (*0-07-003957-7*) McGraw.

Cable Television U. S. A. An Analysis of Government Policy. Martin H. Seiden. LC 72-76453. (Special Studies in U. S. Economic, Social & Political Issues). 1972. 46.50 (*0-275-28634-7*) Irvington.

Cable Tool Fishing. 72p. 1968. 10.00 (*1-56034-001-0*, T010) Natl Water Well.

Cable TV Advertising: In Search of the Right Formula. Ed. by Rajeev Batra & Rashi Glazer. LC 88-37395. 199p. 1989. text ed. 55.00 (*0-89930-406-0*, BTA, Quorum Bks) Greenwood.

Cables & Wiring. AVO Multi-Amp Institute Staff. LC 92-31886. 196p. 1993. pap. text ed. 27.95 (*0-8273-5460-6*) Delmar.

Cables to the Ace. Thomas Merton. 100p. 1986. 8.95 (*0-87775-192-7*) Unicorn Pr.

Cableviewing. Carrie Heeter & Bradley S. Greenberg. Ed. by Brenda Dervin. LC 88-10450. (Communication & Information Science Ser.). 336p. 1988. text ed. 57.50 (*0-89391-466-5*); pap. text ed. 27.50 (*0-89391-467-3*) Ablex Pub.

***CABNIS Guidelines & Application Kit.** 75p. (Orig.). 1994. pap. 75.00 (*0-7605-0340-0*) Rector Pr.

***Cabo Handbook: La Paz to Cabo San Lucas.** Joe Cummings. (Moon Travel Handbooks Ser.). (Illus.). 275p. 1995. pap. 14.95 (*1-56691-028-5*) Moon Pubns CA.

CABO Model Energy Code. 1992. 10.80 (*1-884590-03-9*, 125S92) Intl Conf Bldg Off.

CABO One & Two Family Dwelling Code. 1992. pap. 31.00 (*1-884590-35-7*, 111S92); ring bd. 37.00 (*1-884590-04-7*, 111L92) Intl Conf Bldg Off.

Cabo San Lucas. Susan H. Crow. LC 83-80309. (Illus.). 112p. (Orig.). 1984. pap. 8.95 (*0-912457-00-7*) Graphic Image.

Caboose. Joanne Barkan. (Come Aboard Bks.). (Illus.). 12p. (J). (ps-00). 1992. pap. 3.50 (*0-689-71574-9*, Aladdin Paperbacks) S&S Childrens.

Caboose Mystery. Gertrude C. Warner. LC 66-10791. (Boxcar Children Mysteries Ser.: No. 11). (Illus.). 128p. (J). (gr. 2-7). 1966. lib. bdg. 10.95 (*0-8075-1008-4*); pap. 3.50 (*0-8075-1009-2*) A Whitman.

Caboose Who Got Loose. Bill Peet. LC 79-155554. (Illus.). 48p. (J). (gr. k-3). 1980. 14.95 (*0-395-14805-7*); pap. 5.95 (*0-395-28715-4*) HM.

Cabooses of the New Haven & New York Central Railroads. Illus. by Alan B. Chesley. (Caboose Data Bk.: No. 1). 48p. 1989. pap. 14.95 (*0-934088-04-7*) NJ Intl Inc.

***Cabooses of the Norfolk & Western.** Robert G. Bowers & James F. Brewer. Ed. by James F. Brewer & Laura S. Hughes. LC 94-65928. (Illus.). 248p. 1994. text ed. 49.95 (*0-9633254-1-8*) Norfolk & Wstrn HS.

Cabot: History & Genealogy of the Cabot Family, 1475-1927. L. Vernon Briggs. (Illus.). 885p. 1992. reprint ed. lib. bdg. 145.00 (*0-8328-2277-9*); reprint ed. pap. 135.00 (*0-8328-2278-7*) Higginson Bk Co.

Cabot Station. William S. Schaill. 240p. 1992. mass mkt. 4.99 (*0-380-71714-X*) Avon.

Cabot Voyages & Bristol Discovery under Henry VII: With Cartography of the Voyages by R. A. Skelton. James A. Williamson. (Halkuyt Society Works Ser.: No. 2, Vol. 120). 1972. reprint ed. 50.00 (*0-8115-0406-9*) Periodicals Srv.

Cabot Wright Begins. James Purdy. 228p. 1986. pap. 4.50 (*0-88184-196-X*) Carroll & Graf.

Cabrera Infante in the Menippean Tradition. Ardis Nelson. Ed. by Thomas Lathrop et al. 123p. Date not set. 15.75 (*0-936388-20-X*); pap. 10.75 (*0-936388-15-3*) Juan de la Cuesta.

Cabrillo. Nancy Lemke. (Illus.). 128p. (Orig.). 1991. pap. 8.95 (*0-945092-19-9*) EZ Nature.

Cabrillo's Ships. C. A. Stern. (Illus.). 30p. (Orig.). 1992. pap. write for info. (*0-9632944-0-7*) C A Stern.

Cacahuatl Eater: Ruminations of an Unabashed Chocolate Addict. Jonathan Ott. (Illus.). 128p. (Orig.). 1985. 15.00 (*0-9614234-0-4*); pap. 7.50 (*0-9614234-1-2*) Natural Prod.

Cacao: A Novel on Migrants & Their Problem of Adaptation. 2nd ed. Jose Morales. Ed. by Mario Uceda. 114p. (SPA.). reprint ed. pap. 4.95 (*0-938693-01-8*) Maya Pubns.

Cacao Biotechnology Symposium Proceedings. Ed. by Paul S. Dimick. (Illus.). 154p. (Orig.). 1986. pap. text ed. 25.00 (*0-9616407-0-7*) Penn State Food.

Cacciatore: Three Short Plays. Joseph Pintauro. 1980. pap. 4.75 (*0-8222-0172-0*) Dramatists Play.

Cacciotti Method. Tony Cacciotti. 1985. pap. write for info. (*0-345-30717-8*) Ballantine.

***Cachalot.** Alan D. Foster. (Orig.). 1994. reprint ed. lib. bdg. 20.00 (*0-7278-4617-5*) Severn Hse.

Cache. Philip Jose Farmer. 288p. 1986. pap. 2.95 (*0-8125-3755-6*) Tor Bks.

Cache & Curry: The Sportsman's Cookbook. rev. ed. Anne S. Sidwell. LC 83-150968. (Illus.). 222p. 1983. pap. 12.00 (*0-9612022-0-3*) Travfunish Pub.

Cache & Interconnect Architectures in Multiprocessors. Ed. by Michel Dubois & Shreekant S. Thakkar. (C). 1990. lib. bdg. 90.00 (*0-7923-9074-1*) Kluwer Ac.

Cache & Memory Hierarchy: A Performance Directed Approach. Steven Przybylski. 223p. 1990. 49.95 (*1-55860-136-8*) Morgan Kaufmann.

Cache-Coherence Problem in Shared-Memory Multiprocessors: Hardware Solutions. Milo Tomasevic & Veljko Milutinovic. LC 93-18273. 431p. 1993. text ed. 62.00 (*0-8186-4092-8*, 4092) IEEE Comp Soc.

***Cache Coherence Problem in Shared-Memory Multiprocessors: Software Solutions (7-95)** Ed. by I. Tartalja & Veljko Milutinovic. 1996. pap. text ed. write for info. (*0-8186-7096-7*, BP07096) IEEE Comp Soc.

Cache Hunting I. H. G. Carson. 112p. (Orig.). 1984. pap. text ed. 7.95 (*0-941620-32-8*) Carson Ent.

Cache Hunting II. H. Glenn Carson. 96p. (Orig.). 1988. pap. 8.95 (*0-941620-39-5*) Carson Ent.

Cache la Poudre: The Natural History of a Rocky Mountain River. Howard E. Evans. 1993. pap. 13.95 (*0-87081-301-3*) Univ Pr Colo.

Cache La Poudre - Big Thompson, CO. (Illus.). 1994. 7.95 (*1-56695-002-3*) Trails Illustrated.

Cache Memory Book. Jim Handy. LC 93-6652. (Illus.). 269p. 1993. text ed. 44.95 (*0-12-322985-5*) Acad Pr.

Cache-Memory Management Data Book. Texas Instruments Engineering Staff. 668p. 1991. 19.95 (*0-685-62496-X*, SCAD002) Tex Instr Inc.

Cache of Jewels & Other Collective Nouns. Ruth Heller. (J). (ps-3). 1989. 13.95 (*0-448-19211-X*, G&D) Putnam Pub Group.

Cache Poor. Margaret St. George. (Intrigue Ser.). 1993. mass mkt. 2.99 (*0-373-22230-0*, 1-22230-6) Harlequin Bks.

Cache Tours. Ann Schimpf & Scott Datwyler. (Illus.). 1977. pap. 2.50 (*0-915272-11-3*) Wasatch Pubs.

Cachet. large type ed. Jane Ashford. 464p. (Orig.). 1988. 15.95 (*0-7089-1754-2*) Ulverscroft.

Cachet d'Onyx. Lea. Jules Barbey d'Aurevilly. (FRE.). 1991. pap. 15.95 (*0-7859-3331-X*, 2905964553) Fr & Eur.

Cachet Identifier of U. S. Cacheted First Day Covers. Michael Mellone. (Illus.). 1977. pap. 6.95 (*0-89794-004-0*) FDC Pub.

***Cachet Makers Directory, 1995.** Comp. by Betty Hindley. 16p. 1994. pap. 3.25 (*1-879390-20-5*) Am First Day.

***Cachetmaker Index & Scott Number Index for First Days Vols. 1-38.** Ed. by Wayne Gasper. 44p. (Orig.). 1994. pap. text ed. 8.95 (*1-879390-17-5*) Am First Day.

Cachoritos. (SPA.). (J). (ps-3). 1993. pap. 2.25 (*0-307-70078-X*, Golden Pr) Western Pub.

***Caciques & Their People: A Volume in Honor of Ronald Spores.** Ed. by Joyce Marcus & Judith F. Zeitlin. LC 94-34805. (Anthropological Papers:Museum of Anthropology: No. 89). 1995. write for info. (*0-915703-37-8*) U Mich Mus Anthro.

Cackle Goes A-Courting. Mecka Lind. (J). (ps-3). 1992. 18.95 (*0-87614-715-5*, Carolrhoda) Lerner Group.

Cactaceae: Descriptions & Illustrations of Plants of the Cactus Family, 4 Vols in 2, 1. 2nd ed. Nathaniel L. Britton & J. N. Rose. (Illus.). 1937. 37.50 (*0-486-21191-6*) Dover.

Cactaceae: Descriptions & Illustrations of Plants of the Cactus Family, 4 Vols in 2, 2. 2nd ed. Nathaniel L. Britton & J. N. Rose. (Illus.). 1937. 37.50 (*0-486-21192-4*) Dover.

Cacti. W. Barthlott. (C). 1979. text ed. 125.00 (*0-85950-416-6*, Pub. by S Thornes Pubs UK) St Mut.

Cacti. Innes Glass. 1991. 24.99 (*0-517-05650-X*) Random Hse Value.

Cacti. Clive Innes. (Wisley Handbooks: The Royal Horticultural Society Ser.). (Illus.). 64p. (Orig.). 1992. pap. 5.95 (*0-304-32030-7*, Pub. by Cassell UK) Sterling.

Cacti. Marcus Schneck. 1992. 12.99 (*0-517-07321-8*) Random Hse Value.

***Cacti: The Illustrated Dictionary.** Rod Preston-Mafham & Ken Preston-Mafham. (Illus.). 224p. 1995. pap. 19.95 (*0-304-34616-0*, Pub. by Cassell UK) Sterling.

Cacti & Other Succulents. Wendy Madgwick. LC 91-14934. (Green World Ser.). (Illus.). 48p. (J). (gr. 5-9). 1992. lib. bdg. 22.13 (*0-8114-2737-4*) Raintree Steck-V.

Cacti & Succulents. Hans Hecht. LC 93-44069. (Illus.). 160p. 1994. 24.95 (*0-8069-0548-4*) Sterling.

Cacti & Succulents: Step-by-Step to Growing Success. Bill Keen. (Crowood Gardening Guides Ser.). (Illus.). 128p. 1991. pap. 16.95 (*1-85223-264-1*, Pub. by Crowood Pr UK) Trafalgar.

Cacti & Succulents in Habitat. Ken Preston-Mafham. (Illus.). 160p. 1994. 24.95 (*0-304-34294-7*, Pub. by Cassell UK) Sterling.

***Cacti & Succulents in Habitat.** Ken Preston-Mafham. (Illus.). 160p. 1995. pap. 19.95 (*0-304-34551-2*, Pub. by Cassell UK) Sterling.

Cacti & Succulents of El Paso. Clark Champie. (Illus.). 100p. 1974. pap. text ed. 10.00 (*0-318-23616-8*) Abbey Garden.

Cacti of Arizona. 3rd ed. Lyman D. Benson. LC 70-77802. (Illus.). 238p. reprint ed. pap. 67.90 (*0-8357-3178-2*, 2039443) Bks Demand.

Cacti of Texas & Neighboring States: A Field Guide. Del Weniger. (Illus.). 366p. (C). 1984. pap. 22.95 (*0-292-71063-1*) U of Tex Pr.

Cacti of the United States & Canada. Lyman Benson. LC 73-80617. (Illus.). xii, 1104p. 1982. 99.50 (*0-8047-0863-0*) Stanford U Pr.

***Cacti, Shrubs & Trees of Anza-Borrego: An Amateur's Key to Identifying Desert Plants.** Paul R. Johnson. (Illus.). 30p. 1990. pap. 3.50 (*0-910805-06-7*) Anza-Borrego.

Cactos (Cactus) J. Cooper. (Spanish Language Books, Set 3: Los Jardines de la Tierra (The Earth's Garden)). (J). 1991. 8.95 (*0-86592-546-1*) Rourke Enter.

Cactus. J. Cooper. (Earth's Garden Ser.). (J). 1991. 8.95 (*0-86592-622-0*) Rourke Enter.

Cactus. Carol Lerner. LC 91-35678. (Illus.). 32p. (J). 1992. 15.00 (*0-688-09636-0*); lib. bdg. 14.93 (*0-688-09637-9*) Morrow Jr Bks.

***Cactus.** Peter Murray. (Nature Bks.). (Illus.). 32p. (J). (gr. 2-6). 1995. lib. bdg. 22.79 (*1-56766-191-2*) Childs World.

Cactus. Cynthia Overbeck. LC 82-211. (Natural Science Bks.). (Illus.). 48p. (J). (gr. 4 up). 1982. lib. bdg. 19.95 (*0-8225-1469-9*, Lerner Publctns); pap. 5.95 (*0-8225-9556-7*, Lerner Publctns) Lerner Group.

***Cactus: A Prickly Portrait of a Desert Eccentric.** Linda Hinrichs & Nikolay Zurek. LC 94-37782. 1995. 16.95 (*0-00-638288-6*) Collins SF.

Cactus Air Force. deluxe ed. Thomas G. Miller, Jr. LC 69-15320. (Illus.). 242p. 1990. reprint ed. 55.00 (*0-934841-17-9*) Adm Nimitz Foun.

Cactus Air Force. Thomas G. Miller, Jr. LC 69-15320. (Illus.). 242p. 1990. reprint ed. 15.00 (*0-934841-18-7*) Adm Nimitz Foun.

Cactus & Pine. Sharlot M. Hall. (Illus.). 250p. 1989. reprint ed. 22.00 (*0-317-93874-6*); reprint ed. pap. 15.50 (*0-317-93875-4*) Sharlot Hall Mus Pr.

***Cactus Blood: A Mystery Novel.** Lucha Corpi. LC 94-38164. 200p. 1995. 18.95 (*1-55885-134-8*) Arte Publico.

Cactus Caprice. Robert King. 4.95 (*0-89741-001-7*) Roadrunner Tech.

***Cactus Cavalier.** Fox. 1995. mass mkt. (*0-440-21062-3*) Dell.

Cactus Country: A Friendly Introduction to Cacti of the Southwest Deserts. Jim Willoughby & Sue Willoughby. LC 92-44836. (Illus.). 128p. (Orig.). 1993. pap. 6.95 (*0-914846-71-X*) Golden West Pub.

***Cactus Desert.** Donald M. Silver. (One Square Mile Ser.). (Illus.). 48p. (J). (gr. 2-7). 1995. text ed. 14.95 (*0-7167-6573-X*, Sci Am Yng Rdrs) W H Freeman.

Cactus Fence. Anne B. Brauer. 234p. (Orig.). 1994. pap. 18.50 (*0-9632718-4-9*) A-A Bks.

Cactus Flower Bakery. Harry Allard. LC 90-36565. (Trophy Picture Bk.). (Illus.). 32p. (J). (ps-3). 1993. pap. 4.95 (*0-06-443297-1*, Trophy) HarpC Child Bks.

Cactus Flowers. Ed. by Jeff Nicholas. (Wish You Were Here Postcard Bks.). 32p. (Orig.). 1994. pap. 4.95 (*0-939365-39-1*) Sierra Pr CA.

Cactus Flowers: A Wild Horizons Postcard Book. Thomas A. Wiewandt. (Postcard Book Ser.). (Illus.). 52p. 1992. pap. 8.95 (*1-879728-01-X*) Wild Horizons.

***Cactus Garden.** Robert Ward. LC 95-2809. 1995. 22.00 (*0-671-88265-1*) PB.

Cactus Hotel. Brenda Z. Guiberson. LC 90-41748. (Illus.). 32p. (J). (ps-2). 1991. 15.95 (*0-8050-1333-4*, Bks Young Read) H Holt & Co.

Cactus Hotel. Brenda Z. Guiberson. LC 90-41748. (Illus.). 32p. (J). (ps-3). 1993. pap. 4.95 (*0-8050-2960-5*, Bks Young Read) H Holt & Co.

Cactus Jack. O. C. Fisher. 1982. 15.95 (*0-87244-066-4*) Texian.

Cactus Love. Samuel B. Lall. 4.80 (*0-89253-578-4*) Ind-US Inc.

Cactus Love. Lee Lynch. 240p. 1994. pap. 9.95 (*1-56280-071-X*) Naiad Pr.

Cactus Primer. Arthur C. Gibson & Park S. Noble. (Illus.). 296p. 1986. 54.00 (*0-674-08990-1*) HUP.

Cactus Primer. Arthur C. Gibson & Park S. Nobel. (Illus.). 296p. 1990. pap. 23.00 (*0-674-08991-X*) HUP.

Cactus War. R. E. Cochrane. LC 86-72017. 176p. (Orig.). 1987. pap. 4.95 (*0-916383-19-9*) Aegina Pr.

Cactus Wren. Anders H. Anderson & Anne Anderson. LC 72-77133. (Illus.). 240p. reprint ed. pap. 68.40 (*0-8357-7957-2*, 2029647) Bks Demand.

Cacus & Marsyas in Etrusco-Roman Legend. Jocelyn P. Small. LC 82-47614. (Monographs in Art & Archaeology: No. 45). (Illus.). 208p. 1982. 45.00 (*0-691-03562-8*) Princeton U Pr.

Cad: A Handbook for Heels. Charles Schneider. 1992. pap. 14.95 (*0-922915-09-1*) Feral Hse.

CAD - CAM: From Principles to Practice. Chris McMahon & James J. Browne. LC 93-16384. 508p. (C). 1993. text ed. 69.95 (*0-201-56502-1*) Addison-Wesley.

CAD - CAM: Computer Aided Design & Computer Aided Manufacture: A Source Guide. 1991. lib. bdg. 250.00 (*0-8490-4865-6*) Gordon Pr.

***CAD - CAM Handbook.** Machover. 1995. 69.50 (*0-07-039375-3*) McGraw.

CAD - CAM Integration & Innovation. Ed. by Khalil Taraman. LC 84-52278. (Manufacturing Update Ser.). (Illus.). 474p. reprint ed. pap. 135.10 (*0-7837-6279-8*, 2045994) Bks Demand.

CAD - CAM Strategic Planning Guide. 1991. 75.00 (*0-934869-13-8*) Cad-Cam Pub.

CAD Accelerators: Proceedings of the International Workshop on Hardware Accelerators for CAD, Oxford, U. K., 20-21 Sept., 1989. Ed. by T. Ambler et al. 300p. 1991. 100.00 (*0-444-88964-7*, North Holland) Elsevier.

CAD & Robotics in Architecture & Construction. 290p. 1991. pap. 57.50 (*0-87683-608-2*) GP Pub.

CAD Applications: Architectural. David L. Goetsch. 256p. 1986. teacher ed 12.00 (*0-8273-2633-5*); pap. text ed. 22.95 (*0-8273-2632-7*) Delmar.

CAD Applications: Electronics. Gerry Hansen. 256p. 1986. teacher ed 12.00 (*0-8273-2547-9*) Delmar.

CAD Applications: Mechanical. Gary Bertoline. 256p. 1986. teacher ed 14.00 (*0-8273-2549-5*); pap. text ed. 26.95 (*0-8273-2548-7*) Delmar.

CAD Assignments. Paul Whelan. (Illus.). 352p. (Orig.). 1994. pap. 39.50 (*0-7487-7784-9*, Pub. by Stanley Thornes UK) Trans-Atl Phila.

CAD Based Programming for Sensory Robots. Ed. by B. Ravani. (NATO Asi Series F: Vol. 50). 580p. 1988. 118.00 (*0-387-50415-X*) Spr-Verlag.

CAD-Based Vision Workshop: Proceedings. 2nd ed. LC 93-80368. 320p. 1994. pap. text ed. 60.00 (*0-8186-5310-8*, 5310) IEEE Comp Soc.

CAD, CAE, CAM, CID Lexikon. 3rd ed. Gerhard Klause. 399p. (ENG & GER.). 1992. lib. bdg. 85.00 (*0-8288-3615-9*, F93200) Fr & Eur.

CAD-CAE Descriptive Geometry. Ed. by Daniel Ryan. 1991. 49.95 (*0-8493-4273-2*, TA345) CRC Pr.

CAD-CAM: Computer-Aided Design & Manufacturing. Mikell P. Groover, Jr. & Emory W. Zimmers, Jr. LC 83-11132. (Illus.). 489p. (C). 1983. text ed. 92.00 (*0-13-110130-7*) P-H.

CAD-CAM: Design & Drafting CAD-CAM Systems, NC Tape Prep, Software Packages, CRTs, Workstations, Recording Systems, Plotters & Printers, Digitizers, Computers. 2nd ed. Society of Manufacturing Engineers Staff. LC 84-52371. (Productivity Equipment Ser.). 640p. reprint ed. pap. 180.00 (*0-8357-3045-X*, 2039300) Bks Demand.

CAD-CAM: Design & Drafting Systems, CAD-CAM Systems, Graphic Systems, NC Tape Prep, Software Packages, CRTs, Workstations, Plotters & Printers, Digitizers. Society of Manufacturing Engineers Staff. LC 83-50894. (Productivity Equipment Ser.). 598p. reprint ed. pap. 170.50 (*0-8357-7959-9*, 2025353) Bks Demand.

CAD-CAM: Meeting Today's Productivity Challenge. K. Taraman. 296p. (C). 1982. text ed. 48.00 (*0-13-110122-6*) P-H.

CAD-CAM: Meeting Today's Productivity Challenge, First Edition. Ed. by Khalil Taraman. LC 80-69006. 291p. reprint ed. pap. 83.00 (*0-8357-7960-2*, 2026158) Bks Demand.

CAD-CAM Abstracts Annual 1990. 947p. 1991. 250.00 (*0-8352-2978-5*, Bowker A&I Pub) Bowker.

CAD-CAM & FEM in Metal Working. Ed. by A. Niku-Lari & S. K. Ghosh. LC 88-19669. (Technology Transfer Handbook Ser.). (Illus.). 300p. 1988. 116.00 (*0-08-035917-5*, Pub. by Pergamon Repr UK) Franklin.

CAD-CAM & MIS in Japan: Computer Applications in Japanese Industry. Noboru Takagi et al. 1987. text ed. 152.00 (*0-12-682580-7*) Acad Pr.

CAD-CAM & the Computer Revolution: Selected Papers from CAD-CAM I & CAD-CAM II. Society of Manufacturing Engineers Staff. LC 74-21735. 363p. reprint ed. pap. 103.50 (*0-8357-7958-0*, 2013132) Bks Demand.

CAD-CAM, CAE. Richard K. Miller & Terri C. Walker. LC 88-81648. (Survey on Technology & Markets Ser.: No. 57). 50p. 1989. pap. text ed. 200.00 (*1-55865-056-3*) Future Tech Surveys.

CAD-CAM, CAE: Evaluating Today's Systems. Charles M. Foundyller. Ed. by Bruce L. Jenkins. (Series in CAD-CAM, CAE). (Illus.). 120p. 1984. ring bd. 99.00 (*0-938484-18-4*) Daratech.

CAD-CAM, CAE: Survey, Review & Buyers' Guide. Charles M. Foundyller. Ed. by Bruce L. Jenkins. (Series in CAD-CAM, CAE). Orig. Title: U. S. Directory of Vendors. (Illus.). 745p. 1986. ring bd. 428.00 (*0-938484-20-6*) Daratech.

***CAD-CAM, CAE: Survey, Review & Buyers' Guide 1994.** Charles M. Foundyller. Ed. by Bruce L. Jenkins. (Daratech Series in CAD-CAM, CAE). (Illus.). 1994. ring bd. 972.00x (*0-938484-34-6*) Daratech.

CAD-CAM, CAE: The Contemporary Technology. Charles M. Foundyller. Ed. by Bruce L. Jenkins. (Series in CAD-CAM, CAE). (Illus.). 260p. 1984. ring bd. 127.00 (*0-938484-17-6*) Daratech.

CAD CAM CAE for Industrial Progress: Proceedings of the IFIP TC 5 International Fonference, Bangalore, India, 29-30 June 1985. Ed. by V. Rajaraman. 298p. 1986. 72.00 (*0-444-70000-5*) Elsevier.

CAD-CAM-CAE Hardware Products Database. Ed. by Philip C. Flora. 1988. 49.00 (*0-929076-08-7*); 5.25 hd 124.00 (*0-929076-09-5*) TecSpec.

CAD-CAM, CAE: Purchase Specification Templates. William G. Beazley. Ed. by Bruce L. Jenkins. (Series in CAD-CAM, CAE). 230p. 1987. ring bd. 240.00 (*0-938484-22-2*) Daratech.

CAD-CAM-CAE Software Products Database. Ed. by Philip C. Flora. 1988. 49.00 (*0-929076-10-9*); 5.25 hd 124.00 (*0-929076-11-7*) TecSpec.

CAD-CAM Data Management Systems: A Buyer's Guide. Robert H. Johnson et al. 200p. 1988. ring bd. 795.00 (*0-685-44397-3*) Mgmt Roundtable.

CAD-CAM Databases: Implementation & Planning Strategies. Ed. by Management Roundtable, Inc. Staff. (Illus.). 350p. 1986. spiral bd. 295.00 (*0-932007-08-2*, B00045) Mgmt Roundtable.

CAD-CAM Dictionary. Preston & Crawford. 224p. 1985. 99.75 (*0-8247-7524-4*) Dekker.

CAD-CAM for Production Tooling. Ed. by Thomas J. Drozda. 272p. 1989. 44.00 (*0-87263-348-9*) SME.

CAD-CAM Glossary. 19.25 (*0-686-40545-5*) C I M Systems.

CAD-CAM International Software Directory. Flora. 1991. write for info. (*0-8306-5464-X*) TAB Bks.

CAD-CAM Manager's Complete Anthology. Management Roundtable, Inc. Staff. (Illus.). 176p. (Orig.). 1987. per. 75.00 (*0-932007-11-2*, B54) Mgmt Roundtable.

CAD-CAM, Robotics, & Factories of the Future, Vols. 1-2: Proceedings of the International Conference, 5th, 2 vols. Ed. by S. N. Dwivedi et al. (Illus.). 1991. 110.00 (*0-685-74373-X*) Spr-Verlag.

C

An Asterisk (*) at the beginning of an entry indicates that the title is appearing in BIP for the first time.

CAD-CAM, Robotics, & Factories of the Future, Vols. 1-2: Proceedings of the International Conference, 5th, 2 vols., Set. Ed. by S. N. Dwivedi et al. (Illus.). 1991. 198.00 (*0-685-50989-3*) Spr-Verlag.

CAD-CAM, Robotics, & Factories of the Future, Vols. 1-2: Proceedings of the International Conference, 5th, 2 vols., Vol. 1: Concurrent Engineering. Ed. by S. N. Dwivedi et al. (Illus.). xxxi, 584p. 1991. Vol. 1, Concurrent Engineering, xxxi, 584p. 110.00 (*0-387-53399-0*) Spr-Verlag.

CAD-CAM, Robotics, & Factories of the Future, Vols. 1-2: Proceedings of the International Conference, 5th, 2 vols., Vol. 2: Flexible Automation. Ed. by S. N. Dwivedi et al. (Illus.). xxxii, 637p. 1991. Vol. 2, Flexible Automation, xxxii, 637p. 110.00 (*0-387-53400-8*) Spr-Verlag.

CAD-CAM Systems Planning & Implementation. C. S. Knox. (Mechanical Engineering Ser.: Vol. 22). 328p. 1983. 99.75 (*0-8247-7041-2*) Dekker.

Cad-Cam Theory & Practice. Ibrahim Zeid. 1991. text ed. write for info. (*0-07-072857-7*) McGraw.

CAD Cookbook Collection. Phil Kreiker. LC 93-72760. 328p. (C). 1993. disk, pap. 34.95 (*0-929870-22-0*) Advanstar Commns.

CAD Design Studio: 3D Modeling As a Fundamental Design Skill. Stephen Jacobs. 128p. 1991. text ed. 34.00 (*0-07-032227-9*); pap. text ed. 22.95 (*0-07-032228-7*) McGraw.

CAD for Control Systems. Linkens. 600p. 1993. 165.00 (*0-8247-9060-X*) Dekker.

***CAD Frameworks: Principles & Architecture.** Pieter Van der Wolf. LC 94-31394. (SECS Ser.). 236p. (C). 1994. lib. bdg. 92.50 (*0-7923-9501-8*) Kluwer Ac.

CAD Geometry Data Exchange Using STEP: Realization of Interface Processors. Ed. by H. J. Helpenstein. (Research Reports ESPRIT). 460p. 1994. pap. 58.00 (*0-387-56902-2*) Spr-Verlag.

CAD-I Database: An Approach to an Engineering Database, Version 4.0. Ed. by M. Raflik et al. (Research Reports ESPRIT, Project 322, CAD Interfaces: Vol. 5). x, 147p. 1990. pap. 29.00 (*0-387-53383-4*) Spr-Verlag.

CAD in Clothing & Textiles: A Collection of Expert Views. Ed. by Winifred Aldrich. (Illus.). 192p. 1991. 44.95 (*0-632-02977-3*) Blackwell Sci.

CAD in Clothing & Textiles: A Collection of Expert Views. 2nd ed. Ed. by Winifred Aldrich. LC 94-19280. 1994. write for info. (*0-632-03893-4*) Blackwell Sci.

CAD in Reinforced Concrete Detailing & Structural Steelwork. (Conference Proceedings Ser.). 112p. 1988. 59.00 (*0-7277-1340-X*) Am Soc Civil Eng.

Cad in the European Textiles. Shirley Inst. Staff. (C). 1980. 90.00 (*0-685-36023-7*, Pub. by British Textile Tech UK) St Mut.

CAD Layer Guidelines: Recommended Designations for Architecture, Engineering, & Facility Management Computer Aided Design. Ed. by CAD Layer Guidelines Task Force Staff. (Illus.). 40p. 1990. 20.00 (*1-55835-058-6*) AIA Press.

CAD of Wire Antennas & Related Radiating Structures. B. D. Popovic. (Electronic & Electrical Research Studies: Antenna Ser.: No. 1641). 324p. 1991. text ed. 145.00 (*0-471-93067-9*) Wiley.

CAD on a Personal Computer: Technology & Applications, Software & Systems, Suppliers & Costs. Krouse Association Staff. 121p. (C). 1985. 179.00 (*0-914849-03-4*) TBC Inc.

CAD Rating Guide: A Tool for the Evaluation of Computer-Aided Design (Including FEM, GIS, & Animation) 4th ed. W. Bradley Holtz. LC 94-60711. (Illus.). 620p. (Orig.). 1994. pap. 150.00 (*0-9634168-1-2*) ZEM Pr.

CAD Systems: Proceedings of the IFIP Working Conference on Computer Aided Design Systems, Austin, Texas, February 12-14, 1976. John J. Allan, 3rd. 458p. 1976. 77.00 (*0-7204-0472-X*, North Holland) Elsevier.

CAD Systems Framework: Proceedings of the WG 5.2 Working Conference, Roros, June 1982. Ed. by Ketil Bo & Frank M. Lillehagen. x, 342p. 1983. 59.00 (*0-444-86604-3*, I-172-83, North Holland) Elsevier.

CAD Systems in Mechanical & Production Engineering. Peter Ingham. 180p. 1990. pap. text ed. 18.95 (*0-8311-3008-3*) Indus Pr.

CAD Systems Using AI Techniques: Proc. of the IFIP TC10-WG10.2 Working Conf., Tokyo, Japan, 6-7 June 1989. Ed. by G. Odawara. 230p. 1989. 64.00 (*0-444-88319-3*, North Holland) Elsevier.

CAD Training Handbook Series. Christian Bohler & Hans Frommer. (C). 1990. pap. text ed. 175.50 (*1-56990-122-8*) Hanser-Gardner.

Cad Tutor Versacad Design. J. Sunyogh et al. 1987. pap. 26.80 (*0-02-668071-8*) Macmillan.

Cada Celebracion. Emilio Muller. LC 89-50924. 72p. 1989. 5.95 (*0-88177-078-7*, DR078) Discipleship Res.

***Cada Dia un Nuevo Comienzo.** 400p. (SPA.). 1994. pap. 15.50 (*968-39-0794-6*) Hazelden.

Cada Muchacho Necesita un Modelo Vivo. Jorge A. Leon. 96p. (SPA.). 1988. reprint ed. pap. 4.25 (*0-311-46087-9*) Casa Bautista.

Cada Nuevo Dia. Corrie Ten Boom. Tr. by Alejandro Clifford. (Each New Day Ser.). 224p. 1987. reprint ed. pap. 6.50 (*0-311-40043-4*, Edit Mundo) Casa Bautista.

Cada Vez Mejor. Maria P. Haro et al. (Illus.). 512p. (C). 1990. pap. text ed. write for info. (*0-13-087800-6*) P-H.

Cada Vez Mejor. Maria P. Haro et al. (Illus.). 512p. (C). 1992. text ed. write for info. (*0-13-087792-1*) P-H.

Cadastral Map in the Service of the State: A History of Property Mapping. Roger J. Kain & Elizabeth Baigent. LC 92-10661. (Illus.). 416p. 1992. 49.95 (*0-226-42261-5*) U Ch Pr.

Cadastre. Aime Cesaire. Tr. by Emile Snyder. LC 75-169155. 160p. 1973. 15.95 (*0-89388-070-1*); pap. 9.95 (*0-89388-085-X*) Okpaku Communications.

Cadastre. Aime Cesaire. Bd. with Soleil Cou Coupe.; Corps Perdu. Set pap. 8.95 (*0-8288-9082-X*, 2020016672) Fr & Eur.

Cadaver. Mary Kittredge. 1993. mass mkt. 3.99 (*0-312-95002-0*) St Martin.

Cadaver: An Edwina Crusoe Medical Mystery. large type ed. Mary Kittredge. LC 92-11069. 308p. 1992. reprint ed. 16.95 (*1-56054-448-1*) Thorndike Pr.

Cadbury, Knox, & Talbert: American Contributions to the Study of Acts. Mikeal Parsons. (Biblical Scholarship in North America Ser.). 274p. 1992. 39.95 (*1-55540-653-X*, 061118); pap. 24.95 (*1-55540-654-8*) Scholars Pr GA.

Cadcam Process. Ed. by Barry Hawkes. 288p. (C). 1988. pap. text ed. 150.00 (*0-685-47904-8*, Pub. by Pitman Pubng UK) St Mut.

Cad/Cam/Cae Systems: Justification, Implementation, Productivity Measurement. Mark E. Coticchia et al. LC 92-22195. (Computer-Aided Engineering Ser.: Vol. 2). 352p. 1993. Alk. paper. disk 150.00 (*0-8247-8961-X*) Dekker.

CADD Department. Katherine Panchyk & Richard Panchyk. (Illus.). 200p. 1991. pap. 32.95 (*0-442-00509-1*) Chapman & Hall.

Caddie Woodlawn. Carol R. Brink. 256p. (J). 1970. pap. 3.95 (*0-02-041880-9*, Collier Bks Young) S&S Childrens.

Caddie Woodlawn. Carol R. Brink. LC 73-588. (Illus.). 288p. (J). (gr. 4-6). 1973. text ed. 15.95 (*0-02-713670-1*, Mac Bks Young Read) S&S Childrens.

Caddie Woodlawn. Carol R. Brink. LC 89-18357. (Illus.). 288p. (J). (gr. 4-6). 1990. pap. 3.95 (*0-689-71370-3*, Aladdin Paperbacks) S&S Childrens.

Caddie Woodlawn: A Study Guide. Carol Fuhler. (Novel-Ties Ser.). (J). (gr. 4-7). 1988. student ed, teacher ed 15.95 (*0-88122-079-5*) Lrn Links.

Caddie's Disciple. James L. Ives. Ed. by Marion Ransom et al. LC 93-91527. 335p. (C). 1993. pap. 10.50 (*0-9635962-0-9*) Anabest.

Caddis Larvae: Larvae of the British Trichoptera. Norman E. Hickin. LC 68-58408. (Illus.). 480p. 1975. 42.50 (*0-8386-6945-X*) Fairleigh Dickinson.

Caddisflies. Gary LaFontaine. (Illus.). 336p. 1989. 35.00 (*0-941130-98-3*) Lyons & Burford.

Caddmania: Causes & Cure, CEPA 1985 Spring Conference Proceedings. Ed. by Patricia Johnson. 1985. 30.00 (*0-933007-10-8*) Natl Soc Comp Eng.

Caddo-Hollywood Conflict: The Public & Private Letters of Franklin Jones, Sr., 1985-1988, Vol. IV. Franklin Jones, Sr. Ed. by Ann Adams. LC 84-27375. 300p. 1989. 29.95 (*0-915433-16-8*) Packrat WA.

***Caddo Indians: Tribes at the Convergence of Empires, 1542-1854.** F. Todd Smith. (Centennial Series of the Association of Former Students: No. 56). (Illus.). 256p. 1995. 24.50x (*0-89096-642-7*) Tex A&M Univ Pr.

***Caddo Indians: Where We Come From.** Cecile E. Carter. LC 95-3395. 1995. write for info. (*0-8061-2747-3*) U of Okla Pr.

Caddo Nation: Archaeological & Ethnohistoric Perspectives. Timothy K. Perttula. LC 91-46225. (Texas Archaeology & Ethnohistory Ser.). (Illus.). 344p. 1992. text ed. 40.00x (*0-292-71150-6*) U of Tex Pr.

***Caddo Parish, Louisiana Newspaper Gleanings 1844-1865.** Wanda V. Head. 98p. (Orig.). 1992. pap. text ed. 18.00 (*1-57088-000-X*) J&W Ent.

***Caddo Parish, Louisiana Newspaper Gleanings 1866-1868.** Wanda V. Head. 121p. (Orig.). 1994. pap. text ed. 18.00 (*1-57088-001-8*) J&W Ent.

Caddo Was-- A Short History of Caddo Lake. Fred Dahmer. LC 94-17945. 1995. pap. 8.95 (*0-292-71576-5*) U of Tex Pr.

Caddoan Saltmakers in the Ouachita Valley: The Hardman Site. Ed. by Ann M. Early. LC 93-43986. (Arkansas Archeological Survey Research Ser.: No. 43). 1994. 25.00 (*1-56349-074-9*) AR Archaeol.

Caddoan Texts, Pawnee, South Band Dialect. Gene Weltfish. LC 73-3553. (American Ethnological Society Publications: No. 17). reprint ed. 32.00 (*0-404-58167-6*) AMS Pr.

Caddy. Bert D'Anza. (Illus.). 88p. 1994. pap. 9.00 (*0-8059-3658-0*) Dorrance.

Caddy Spoons: An Illustrated Guide. John Norie. (Illus.). 282p. 1989. 110.00 (*0-7195-4439-4*, Pub. by John Murray UK) Trafalgar.

Cadeau de Cesar. Rene De Goscinny & M. Uderzo. (Illus.). (FRE.). (J). 1990. 19.95 (*0-8288-4959-5*) Fr & Eur.

***Caden Walaa!** Karin Calley & Noel Pearson. (Jam Roll Picture Bks.). 32p. (J). 1995. 19.95 (*0-7022-2704-8*, Pub. by Univ Queensland Pr AT) Intl Spec Bk.

Cadena Perpetua. Charles W. Colson. 304p. (Orig.). (SPA.). 1983. pap. 9.25 (*0-89922-221-8*) Edit Caribe.

Cadenas De Gozo: Bound for Joy. Stuart Briscoe. (SPA.). 5.50 (*84-7228-373-9*, 220124, Pub. by Edit Clie SP) TSELF.

***Cadence Count.** Ray Bradley. 270p. (Orig.). (C). 1995. pap. text ed. 9.95 (*1-884707-13-0*) Golden Lifestyles.

Cadences. F. S. Flint. LC 78-64026. (Des Imagistes: Literature of the Imagist Movement Ser.). (Illus.). reprint ed. 29.50 (*0-404-17099-4*) AMS Pr.

Cadences: Icon & Abstraction in Context. Gary Sangster et al. Ed. by Alice Yang. (Illus.). 111p. 1991. 18.00 (*0-915557-72-X*) New Mus Contemp Art.

Cadenza. Ruth K. Noack. 30p. 1991. vhs 14.95 (*0-942229-04-5*); spiral bd. 4.95 (*0-942229-03-7*) Video Album.

Cadenza. Ralph Cusack. LC 84-21372. 228p. 1984. reprint ed. 20.00 (*0-916583-04-X*); reprint ed. pap. 7.95 (*0-916583-05-8*) Dalkey Arch.

Cadenza for Caruso. Barbara Paul. Date not set. pap. 5.95 (*1-55882-134-1*) Intl Polygonics.

Cadenzas for Violoncello. Sanos Starker & Janos. 1976. pap. 5.00 (*0-318-19425-2*, 60117-906) Peer-Southrn.

Cades Cove: The Life & Death of a Southern Appalachian Community, 1818-1937. Durwood Dunn. LC 87-18212. (Illus.). 288p. 1988. lib. bdg. 30.00x (*0-87049-554-2*); pap. 14.95 (*0-87049-559-3*) U of Tenn Pr.

Cades Cove Story. 3rd ed. A. Randolph Shields. Ed. by Paula A. Degen. 116p. reprint ed. pap. 4.50 (*0-937207-07-1*) GSMNH.

Cadet Gray: Your Guidebook to Military Schools, Military Colleges, & Cadet Programs. Valentine DelVecchio. (Illus.). 212p. (Orig.). (YA). (gr. 7-12). 1990. pap. 11.95 (*0-9625749-0-2*) Ref Desk Bks.

Cadet Rousseau. Illus. by Jerry Blanton. 32p. (Orig.). 1988. pap. 5.00 (*0-929436-05-9*) Eyesburg Pr.

Cadets: Code Name: Snowball, No. 1. Ned Bannister. (J). (gr. 3 up). 1988. pap. 2.95 (*0-345-35115-0*) Ballantine.

Cadets at War: The True Story of Teenage Heroism at the Battle of New Market. Susan P. Beller. LC 90-21952. (Illus.). 96p. (J). (gr. 8-12). 1991. 9.95 (*1-55870-196-6*) Shoe Tree Pr.

Cadets in Gray: The Story of the Cadets of the South Carolina Military Academy & Cadet Rangers in the Civil War. Gary R. Baker. LC 89-61483. (Illus.). 242p. 1990. 21.95 (*0-9623065-0-9*) Palmetto Bookworks.

Cadette & Senior Girl Scout Handbook. (Illus.). 176p. (J). (gr. 6-12). 1987. pap. 7.25 (*0-88441-342-X*, 20-791) Girl Scouts USA.

Cadette & Senior Girl Scout Interest Projects. (Illus.). 160p. (J). (gr. 6-12). 1987. pap. 6.00 (*0-88441-343-8*, 20-792) Girl Scouts USA.

Cadette & Senior Girl Scouts Leaders' Guide. braille ed. Girl Scouts of the U. S. A. Staff. 178p. 1992. vinyl bd. 14.24 (*1-56956-204-0*, BR7563) W A T Braille.

***Cadette Girl Scout Handbook.** Girl Scouts of the U. S. A. Staff. (Illus.). 144p. (J). (gr. 6-9). 1995. pap. 9.95 (*0-88441-283-0*) Girl Scouts USA.

Cadfael Companion. Robin Whiteman. 1995. write for info. (*0-89296-513-4*) Mysterious Pr.

Cadiens d'Asteur-Today's Cajuns. 3rd ed. Philip Gould. Ed. by Sandy Hebert. Tr. by Barry Ancelet. LC 84-80584. (Illus.). 144p. (ENG & FRE.). reprint ed. 23.95 (*0-917541-00-6*) Galerie Pr.

Cadiens d'Asteur-Today's Cajuns: A Bilingual Edition. Photos by Philip Gould. LC 91-26881. (Illus.). 144p. 1991. pap. 19.95 (*0-8071-1736-6*) La State U Pr.

Cadillac. David Featherston. (Color Library). (Illus.). 128p. 1993. pap. 15.95 (*1-85532-328-1*, Pub. by Osprey Pubng Ltd UK) Motorbooks Intl.

Cadillac. Charles Temple. LC 93-42387. (Illus.). (J). 1995. write for info. (*0-399-22654-0*) Putnam Pub Group.

Cadillac: Standard of the World. Shirley Haines & Harry Haines. LC 92-42305. (J). 1993. 17.26 (*0-86593-252-2*); 12.95 (*0-685-66358-2*) Rourke Corp.

Cadillac: Standard of the World. Maurice D. Hendry. (Illus.). 504p. 1990. 49.95 (*0-915038-75-7*, 3-AQ-0005) Auto Quarterly.

Cadillac & the Dawn of Detroit. Annick H. Carthew. LC 94-19472. (Illus.). 320p. (Orig.). 1994. pap. 14.95 (*0-923568-38-7*) Wilderness Adventure Bks.

Cadillac & the Founding of Detroit: Commemorating the 275th Anniversary of the Founding of the City of Detroit. Detroit Historical Society. LC 76-25500. (Illus.). 116p. 1976. pap. 10.95 (*0-8143-1571-2*) Wayne St U Pr.

***Cadillac Cowboy.** Michael Collins. 272p. 1995. 20.95 (*1-55611-461-3*) D I Fine.

Cadillac Desert: The American West & Its Disappearing Water. Marc Reisner. 592p. 1987. pap. 13.00 (*0-14-010432-1*, Penguin Bks) Viking Penguin.

Cadillac Desert: The American West & Its Disappearing Water. rev. ed. Marc Reisner. (Illus.). 624p. 1993. pap. 14.95 (*0-14-017824-4*, Penguin Bks) Viking Penguin.

Cadillac Eldorado. James W. Howell & Jeanna Swanson-Howell. (Illus.). 160p. Date not set. pap. 21.95 (*0-87938-879-X*) Motorbooks Intl.

Cadillac Flight. Marshall Harrison. 352p. 1993. mass mkt. 5.50 (*0-515-11232-1*) Jove Pubns.

Cadillac FWD, 1990-93. Ed. by Chilton Staff. (Total Car Care Ser.). 1994. pap. 21.95 (*0-8019-8420-3*) Chilton.

Cadillac Jack. Larry Mcmurtry. Ed. by Bill Grose. 1990. pap. 6.50 (*0-671-73902-6*) PB.

Cadillac Jack. Larry McMurtry. 1987. pap. 10.00 (*0-671-63720-7*, Fireside Bks) S&S Trade.

Cadillac the Heartbreak of America: Fifteen Years of Consumer Disillusionment. James Musselman. 140p. (Orig.). 1988. pap. 12.95 (*0-9621259-0-3*) Essential Info Inc.

Cadillac 1967-89 Repair & Tune-up Guide. Chilton Automotives Editorial Staff. LC 88-43187. (Illus.). 512p. 1989. pap. text ed. 16.95 (*0-8019-7943-9*) Chilton.

Cadillacs & Dinosaurs. Frank S. Chadwick. (Xenozoic Tales Ser.). (Illus.). 144p. (Orig.). (YA). (gr. 9-12). 1990. pap. 18.00 (*1-55878-073-4*) Game Designers.

Cadillacs & Dinosaurs. Mark Schultz. Ed. by Dave Schreiner. (Illus.). 136p. 1989. pap. 12.95 (*0-87816-071-X*) Kitchen Sink.

Cadillacs & Dinosaurs. deluxe limited ed. Mark Schultz. Ed. by Dave Schreiner. (Illus.). 136p. 1989. 25.00 (*0-87816-070-1*) Kitchen Sink.

Cadillacs & Dinosaurs. Mark Schultz. Ed. by Davd Schreiner. (Illus.). 136p. (J). (gr. 3 up). 1994. reprint ed. pap. 14.95 (*0-87816-261-5*) Kitchen Sink.

Cadillacs & Dinosaurs, Set. Mark Schultz. Ed. by Dave Schreiner. (Illus.). 392p. (J). (gr. 3 up). 1993. Boxed set. boxed, pap. 39.95 (*0-87816-259-3*) Kitchen Sink.

Cadillacs & Dinosaurs: Time in Overdrive. Mark Schultz. Ed. by Dave Schreiner. (Cadillacs & Dinosaurs Ser.). (Illus.). 128p. 1993. pap. 14.95 (*0-87816-214-3*) Kitchen Sink.

Cadiz Experiment in Central America, 1808 to 1826. Mario Rodriquez. LC 76-50256. 328p. reprint ed. pap. 93.50 (*0-7837-4844-2*, 2044491) Bks Demand.

***CADKey Companion.** John G. Cherng. LC 95-13811. (Graphics Ser.). 728p. (C). 1995. 26.95 (*0-256-17142-4*) Irwin.

Cadkey Light: A Handbook. Clifford E. Horton. 224p. (Orig.). (C). 1992. pap. write for info. (*0-02-357195-0*) Macmillan.

CADKEY Light: Computer Aided Design & Drafting for Engineers & Technology. Jon M. Duff. 1991. pap. text ed. 55.00 (*0-13-117383-9*, 340401) P-H.

***Cadkey Seven Workbook.** Leonard O. Nasman. (Illus.). 110p. 1994. student ed 19.95 (*1-880544-49-0*, CAD7-1) Micro Educ.

***Cadkey 107: The Complete Cadkey 7 Textbook.** Leonard O. Nasman. (Illus.). 330p. 1995. pap. text ed. 43.95 (*1-880544-51-2*, CAD7-2) Micro Educ.

Cadmean Letters: The Transmission of the Alphabet to the Aegean & Further West Before 1400 B.C. Martin Bernal. LC 90-2977. xiii, 156p. 1990. text ed. 19.50 (*0-931464-47-1*) Eisenbrauns.

Cadmium. (Metals & Minerals Ser.). 1994. lib. bdg. 250.99 (*0-8490-9027-X*) Gordon Pr.

Cadmium. D. Chizhikov & D. Hayler. LC 66-14655. 1966. 112.00 (*0-08-011611-6*, Pub. by Pergamon Repr UK) Franklin.

Cadmium. Ed. by E. C. Foulkes. (Handbook of Experimental Pharmacology Ser.: Vol. 80). (Illus.). 450p. 1986. 327.00 (*0-387-16025-6*) Spr-Verlag.

Cadmium. Ed. by S. Safe & O. Hutzinger. (Environmental Toxin Ser.: Vol. 2). (Illus.). 270p. 1988. 115.00 (*0-387-15551-1*) Spr-Verlag.

Cadmium & Health: A Toxicological & Epidemiological Appraisal, Vol. I. Ed. by Lars F. Friberg et al. 224p. 1985. Exposure, Dose, & Matabolism. 168.00 (*0-8493-6690-9*, RA1231, CRC Reprint) Franklin.

Cadmium & Health: A Toxicological & Epidemiological Appraisal Effects Response, Vol. II. Ed. by Lars Friberg et al. 320p. 1986. Effects & Response. 187.00 (*0-8493-6691-7*, RA1231, CRC Reprint) Franklin.

Cadmium in the Aquatic Environment. Ed. by Jerome O. Nriagu & John B. Sprague. (Advances in Environmental Science & Technology Ser.). 272p. 1987. text ed. 115.00 (*0-471-85884-6*, Wiley-Interscience) Wiley.

Cadmium in the Environment. Mislin & O. Ravera. (Experientia Supplementa Ser.: Vol. 50). 148p. 1986. 59.00 (*0-8176-1760-4*, Pub. by Birkhauser Vlg SZ) Birkhauser.

Cadmium in the Environment: Ecological Cycling, Pt. I. Jerome O. Nriagu. LC 79-25087. (Environmental Science & Technology A Wiley-Interscience Ser. of Texts & Monographs). 696p. 1980. 120.00 (*0-471-06455-6*, Wiley-Interscience) Krieger.

Cadmium in the Environment: Health Effects, Pt. II. Jerome O. Nriagu. (Environmental Science & Technology Ser.). 920p. 1981. 158.00 (*0-471-05884-X*, Wiley-Interscience) Krieger.

Cadmium in the Human Environment: Toxicity & Carcinogenicity. Ed. by G. F. Nordberg et al. (IARC Scientific Publications: No. 118). (Illus.). 496p. 1993. pap. 125.00 (*92-832-2118-4*) OUP.

Cadmium, Nickel, Some Epoxides, Miscellaneous Industrial Chemicals & General Considerations of Volatile Anaesthetics. IARC Working Group on the Evaluation of the Carcinogenic Risk of Chemicals to Man (1975: Lyon, France) Staff. (IARC Monographs on the Evaluation of Carcinogenic Risk of Chemicals to Man: No. 11). 308p. reprint ed. pap. 87.80 (*0-8357-6461-3*, 2035832) Bks Demand.

Cadmium Pigments: An Encouraging Outlook. Cadmium Pigments Subcommittee. 21p. 1983. write for info. (*0-318-61698-X*) Dry Color Mfrs.

Cadmium Toxicity. Mennear. (Modern Pharmacology-Toxicology Ser.: Vol. 15). 240p. 1979. 125.00 (*0-8247-6766-7*) Dekker.

Cadmus & Europa. C. Herbert Oliver. 1994. pap. 10.95 (*0-533-10989-2*) Vantage.

Cadmus et Hermione. Jean-Baptiste Lully. Ed. by Theodore De Lajarte. (Chefs-d'oeuvre classiques de l'opera francaise Ser.: Vol. 20). (Illus.). 274p. (FRE.). 1970. reprint ed. pap. 32.50 (*0-8450-1120-0*) Broude.

Cadomian Orogeny. Ed. by R. S. D'Lemos et al. (Geological Society Special Publications: No. 51). (Illus.). 242p. 1990. 94.00 (*0-903317-47-8*, Pub. by Geol Soc Pub Hse UK) AAPG.

Cadre School Life. Yang Jiang. Tr. by Geremie Barme & Bennett Lee. 90p. 1984. 12.50 (*0-930523-01-6*) Readers Intl.

Cadres, Bureaucracy, & Political Power in Communist China. A. Doak Barnett. LC 67-15895. (Studies of the East Asian Institute). 565p. 1967. text ed. 54.00 (*0-231-03035-5*) Col U Pr.

Cadres Sociaux de la Memoire: The Social Framework of Memory. Maurice Halbwachs. LC 74-25758. (European Sociology Ser.). 310p. 1975. reprint ed. 25.95 (*0-405-06512-4*) Ayer.

Cadron Creek: A Photographic Narrative. Lil Junas. LC 79-90495. (Illus.). 96p. 1979. 13.95 (*0-912456-05-1*) Ozark Soc Bks.

C.A.D.S. John Sievert. 400p. 1986. pap. 3.50 (*0-8217-1641-7*) Zebra.

C.A.D.S., No. 11: Death Zone Attack. John Sievert. 176p. 1991. pap. 3.50 (*0-8217-3374-5*) Zebra.

C.A.D.S., No. 3: Tech Commando. John Sievert. 400p. 1986. pap. 2.95 (*0-8217-1893-2*) Zebra.

C.A.D.S., No. 4: Tech Strike Force. John Sievert. 288p. 1987. pap. 2.95 (*0-8217-1993-9*) Zebra.

C.A.D.S. No. 5: Tech Satan. John Sievert. 1988. pap. 2.95 (*0-8217-2313-8*) Zebra.

C.A.D.S., No. 6: Tech Inferno. John Sievert. 288p. 1988. pap. 2.95 (*0-8217-2410-X*) Zebra.

C.A.D.S., Vol. 10: Recon by Fire. John Sievert. 1990. pap. 2.95 (*0-8217-3147-5*) Zebra.

C

An Asterisk (*) at the beginning of an entry indicates that the title is appearing in BIP for the first time.

CADSES: Computer Aided Design of Scientific & Engineering Systems. Joseph Chi. 268p. (Orig.). 1984. pap. text ed. 24.95 (*0-930945-01-8*) HCP Systems.

Cadwallader Colden: A Representative Eighteenth Century Official. Alice M. Keys. LC 73-181938. reprint ed. 39. 50 (*0-404-03666-X*) AMS Pr.

Cadwallader Colden: A Representative Eighteenth Century Official. Alice M. Keys. (BCL1 - United States Local History Ser.). 375p. 1991. reprint ed. lib. bdg. 89.00 (*0-7812-6274-7*) Rprt Serv.

***CAE - CAD Application to Electronic Packaging: 1994 International Mechanical Engineering Congress & Exposition, Chicago, Illinois - November 6-11, 1994.** (Electrical & Electronics Packaging Ser.: Vol. 9). 96p. 1994. 48.00 (*0-7918-1460-2*, G00955) ASME.

CAE-CAD-CAM Markets: A State of the Industry Report. (Illus.). 255p. 1987. ring bd. 1,800.00 (*0-317-65741-0*) Busn Trend.

Caedmon: The First English Poet. Robert T. Gaskin. 64p. (C). 1902. reprint ed. pap. 39.95 (*0-8383-0033-2*) M S G Haskell Hse.

Caedmon's Song. large type ed. Peter Robinson. 419p. 1993. 21.95 (*0-7505-0347-5*, Pub. by Magna Print Bks) Ulverscroft.

Caen: The Brutal Battle & Breakout from Normandy. Henry Maule. LC 89-893. (Battle Standards Ser.). (Illus.). 176p. (C). 1989. reprint ed. lib. bdg. 25.00x (*0-8095-7502-7*) Borgo Pr.

***Caerns: Places of Power.** (Werewolf). Date not set. 15.00 (*1-56504-066-X*) White Wolf.

Caesar. Mark Dunster. (Borgia Ser.: Pt. 3). 1979. pap. 4.00 (*0-89642-049-3*) Linden Pubs.

Caesar. Alan Massie. 228p. 1994. 20.00 (*0-7867-0121-8*) Carroll & Graf.

Caesar, 2 vols., Set. Theodore A. Dodge. LC 63-12453. (Illus.). 1968. 42.00 (*0-8196-0122-5*) Biblo.

***Caesar: A History of the Art of War among the Romans down to the End of the Roman Empire, with a Detailed Account of the Campaigns of Caius Julius Caesar.** Theodore A. Dodge. (Illus.). 816p. 1995. 59.95 (*1-85367-216-5*, Pub. by Greenhill Bks UK) Stackpole.

Caesar: De Bello Gallico - Index Verborum. Ed. by Rene Lecrompe. Vol. XI. xvi, 373p. 1968. write for info. (*0-318-71972-X*, Pub. by Georg Olms GW) Lubrecht & Cramer.

Caesar: Invasion of Britain. W. Welch & C. G. Duffield. (Illus.). 97p. pap. text ed. 10.00x (*0-86516-008-2*) Bolchazy-Carducci.

Caesar: Politician & Statesman. Matthias Gelzer. 368p. 1985. pap. 15.50 (*0-674-09001-2*) HUP.

Caesar: The Wars of Julius Caesar, A Module for Ancient Empires. Scott Bowden & Greg Pitts. (Ancient Empires Ser.). (Illus.). 48p. (Orig.). 1991. pap. 10.00 (*0-9626655-4-1*) Emperors Pr.

Caesar - Concordantia et Index Caesaris, 2 vols., Set. Ed. by Cordelia M. Birch. (Alpha Omega, Reihe A Ser.: Bd. C). 1550p. (GER.). 1989. 374.40 (*3-487-07991-7*, Pub. by Georg Olms GW) Lubrecht & Cramer.

Caesar - De Bello Gallico - Index Verborum. Ed. by Rene Lecrompe. Bd. XI. xvi, 373p. 1968. write for info. (*0-318-71084-6*, Pub. by Georg Olms GW) Lubrecht & Cramer.

Caesar - De Bello Gallico. Index Verborum. Ed. by Rene Lecrompe. Bd. XI. xvi, 373p. 1968. write for info. (*0-318-70657-1*, Pub. by Georg Olms GW) Lubrecht & Cramer.

Caesar - Lexicon Caesarianum, Vol. I. Ed. by Heinrich Meusel. vi, 772p. 1958. write for info. (*3-296-11201-4*, Pub. by Georg Olms GW) Lubrecht & Cramer.

Caesar - Lexicon Caesarianum, Vol. II, 1. Ed. by Heinrich Meusel. xi, 648p. 1958. write for info. (*3-296-11202-2*, Pub. by Georg Olms GW) Lubrecht & Cramer.

Caesar - Lexicon Caesarianum, Vol. II, 2. Ed. by Heinrich Meusel. 674p. 1958. write for info. (*3-296-11203-0*, Pub. by Georg Olms GW) Lubrecht & Cramer.

***Caesar Against the Celts.** Ramon Jimenez. (Illus.). 276p. 1995. 27.50 (*1-885119-19-4*); pap. 14.95 (*1-885119-20-8*) Sarpedon.

Caesar & Christ, Vol. III. Will Durant. (Story of Civilization Ser.: Vol. 3). (Illus.). 1994. 17.98 (*1-56731-014-1*, MJF Bks) Fine Comms.

Caesar & Christ: A History of Roman Civilization from Its Beginnings to A.D. 337. Will Durant. (Story of Civilization Ser.: Vol. 3). 1983. 35.00 (*0-671-11500-6*) S&S Trade.

Caesar & Pompey. Caesar & Pompey. LC 77-133642. (Tudor Facsimile Texts. Old English Plays Ser.: No. 114). reprint ed. 49.50 (*0-404-53414-7*) AMS Pr.

Caesar & Roman Politics Sixty to Fifty B.C. J. A. Sabben-Clare. 222p. 1981. reprint ed. 17.95 (*0-906515-94-7*, Pub. by Brstl Class Pr UK) Focus Info Gr.

Caesar & the Crisis of the Roman Aristocracy: A Civil War Reader. Sel. by James S. Ruebel. LC 93-21007. (Oklahoma Series in Classical Culture: Vol. 18). (Illus.). 216p. 1994. 18.95 (*0-8061-2590-X*) U of Okla Pr.

Caesar Antichrist. Alfred Jarry. Tr. by Antony Melville & Alastair Brotchie. 120p. (Orig.). 1992. pap. 13.99 (*0-947757-46-5*) Serpents Tail.

Caesar, Christ & Constantine: A History of the Early Church in Rome. Desmond O'Grady. LC 90-61060. (Orig.). 1991. pap. 7.95 (*0-87973-456-6*, 456) Our Sunday Visitor.

Caesar of Santa Fe: A Novel from History. Tim MacCurdy. LC 89-85379. 246p. (Orig.). 1993. pap. 11.95 (*0-938513-07-9*) Amador Pubs.

Caesar of the East. Afonso De Albuquerque. Ed. by J. Villiers & T. F. Earle. (Hispanic Classics Ser.). 320p. (C). 1991. text ed. 55.00 (*0-85668-487-2*, Pub. by Aris & Phillips UK); pap. text ed. 25.00 (*0-85668-488-0*, Pub. by Aris & Phillips UK) David Brown.

Caesar or Nothing. Pio Baroja. Tr. by Louis How. 337p. 1976. reprint ed. 45.00 (*0-86527-224-7*) Fertig.

Caesarian Section & Birth Factors: Subject Index with Bibliography. Sherry A. Walker. LC 88-47551. 150p. 1988. 44.50 (*0-88164-608-3*); pap. 39.50 (*0-88164-609-1*) ABBE Pubs Assn.

Caesaris Augusti Res Gestae et Fragmenta. rev. ed. Herbert W. Benario. LC 89-25021. (Classical Studies: Pedagogy Ser.). (Illus.). 135p. (C). 1990. reprint ed. text ed. 32.50 (*0-8143-2137-2*); reprint ed. pap. text ed. 15.95 (*0-8143-2138-0*) Wayne St U Pr.

Caesarius of Arles: Life, Testament, Letters. Tr. & Intro. by William Klingshirn. (Translated Texts for Historians Ser.). 288p. (Orig.). 1994. pap. text ed. 15.95 (*0-85323-368-3*, Pub. by Liverpool Univ Pr UK) U of Pa Pr.

Caesarius of Arles: The Making of a Christian Community in Late Antique Gaul. William E. Klingshirn. (Studies in Medieval Life & Thought Ser.: No. 22). (Illus.). 352p. (C). 1994. 59.95 (*0-521-43095-X*) Cambridge U Pr.

Caesar's Army: A Study of the Military Art of the Romans in the Last Days of the Republic. H. P. Judson. (Illus.). x, 131p. (C). 1993. text ed. 25.00 (*0-89005-539-4*) Ares.

Caesar's Army: A Study of the Military Art of the Romans in the Last Days of the Republic. Harry P. Judson. LC 61-12877. (Illus.). 127p. (J). (gr. 7 up). 1888. 24.00 (*0-8196-0113-6*) Biblo.

Caesar's Column. Ignatius Donnelly. 318p. 1993. reprint ed. lib. bdg. 35.00 (*0-8328-3174-3*) Higginson Bk Co.

Caesar's Column: A Story of the Twentieth Century. Ignatius Donnelly. LC 76-42811. reprint ed. 42.50 (*0-404-60060-3*) AMS Pr.

Caesar's Column: A Story of the Twentieth Century. Ignatius Donnelly. (Notable American Authors Ser.). 1992. reprint ed. lib. bdg. 75.00 (*0-7812-2670-8*) Rprt Serv.

***Caesar's Conquest of Gaul.** Don Nardo. LC 95-16225. (World History Ser.). 1996. lib. bdg. write for info. (*1-56006-301-7*) Lucent Bks.

Caesar's Conquest of Gaul. 2nd rev. ed. Thomas R. Holmes. LC 78-137242. (BCL Ser.). reprint ed. 49.50 (*0-404-03317-2*) AMS Pr.

Caesars Dialogue. Edith Nesbit. LC 73-38215. (English Experience Ser.: No. 480). 154p. 1972. reprint ed. 14.00 (*90-221-0480-X*) Walter J Johnson.

Caesar's Due: Loyalty & King Charles, 1642-1646. J. L. Malcolm. (Royal Historical Society Ser.: No. 38). 256p. 1983. 63.00 (*0-901050-90-3*) Boydell & Brewer.

Caesars Fall: Antony, Pt. 3. Mark Dunster. 1978. pap. text ed. 4.00 (*0-89642-045-0*) Linden Pubs.

***Caesar's Invasion of Britain.** Peter B. Ellis. (Illus.). 144p. 1994. 37.50x (*0-09-473850-5*, Pub. by Constable Pubs UK) Trans-Atl Phila.

Caesars of the Wilderness: Medard Chouart, Sieur des Groseilliers & Pierre Espirt Radisson, 1618-1710. Grace Lee Nute. Ed. by Mira Wilkins. LC 76-29750. (European Business Ser.). (Illus.). 1977. reprint ed. lib. bdg. 35.95 (*0-405-09766-2*) Ayer.

Caesars of the Wilderness: Medard Chouart, Sieur des Groseilliers & Pierre Espirt Radisson, 1618-1710. Grace L. Nute. LC 78-811. (Publications of the Minnesota Historical Society). 428p. reprint ed. pap. 122.00 (*0-8357-3319-X*, 2039543) Bks Demand.

Caesars of the Wilderness: The Story of the Hudson's Bay Company. Peter C. Newman. 480p. 1988. pap. 10.95 (*0-14-011456-4*, Penguin Bks) Viking Penguin.

Caesars Palace Book of Sports Betting. Bert R. Sugar. 256p. (Orig.). 1992. pap. 14.95 (*0-312-05058-5*, Pub. by Thomas Dunne Bks) St Martin.

Caesar's Rise. Mark Dunster. (Antony Ser.: Pt. 1). 40p. (Orig.). 1986. pap. 5.00 (*0-89642-134-1*) Linden Pubs.

Caesar's Time. Silverberg. (Time Tours Ser.: No. 6). 1991. mass mkt. 3.50 (*0-06-106017-8*, Harp PBks) HarpC.

Caesar's War in Alexandria: Caesar, Bellum Civile, III, 102-112 & Bell. Alex. 1-33. Gavin Townend. 66p. (LAT.). 1989. pap. 10.00 (*0-86516-219-0*) Bolchazy-Carducci.

Caeser's Centurion. abr. ed. James Ellis. 310p. 1995. pap. 9.95 (*1-56901-519-8*) NW Pub.

Caete de Gusto Hacid el Otono con las Matematicas y Ciencias. R. Adair et al. 116p. (ENG & SPA.). (J). (gr. k-1). 1988. pap. text ed. 16.95 (*1-881431-19-3*, 1401) AIMS Educ Fnd.

Cafe at Saint Marks. Ed. by Van K. Brock et al. 1973. pap. 5.00 (*0-938078-03-8*) Anhinga Pr.

Cafe Au Lait. George S. Elias. LC 76-18449. 1976. 7.50 (*0-87881-050-1*); pap. 4.50 (*0-87881-051-X*) Mojave Bks.

Cafe Beaujolais. Margaret S. Fox & John Bear. LC 84-51172. (Illus.). 224p. (Orig.). 1984. 19.95 (*0-89815-150-3*); pap. 16.95 (*0-89815-134-1*) Ten Speed Pr.

Cafe Berlin. Harold Nebenzal. 288p. 1994. pap. 10.00 (*0-380-72169-4*) Avon.

Cafe Brenda Cookbook: Redefining Seafood & Vegetarian Cuisine. Brenda Langton & Margaret Stuart. (Illus.). 240p. (Orig.). 1992. pap. 17.95 (*0-89658-205-1*) Voyageur Pr.

Cafe Con Leche: Race, Class, & National Image in Venezuela. Winthrop R. Wright. (Illus.). 184p. (Orig.). (C). 1993. pap. 11.95 (*0-292-79080-5*) U of Tex Pr.

Cafe Cong. Niall Quinn. 164p. (Orig.). 1991. pap. 14.95 (*0-86327-303-3*, Pub. by Wolfhound Pr IE) Dufour.

Cafe des Artistes Cookbook: Favorite Recipes from One of New York's Most Romantic Restaurants. George Lang. (Illus.). 96p. 1984. 14.00 (*0-517-55307-4*, C P Pubs) Crown Pub Group.

Cafe Isotope. Alan Bernheimer. 1980. per. 7.50 (*0-935724-00-1*) Figures.

***Cafe Oklahoma: Casual Recipes for the Casual Sooner Lifestyle.** 350p. 1994. write for info. (*0-9641096-0-3*) JSL of Midwest.

Cafe Pasqual's Cookbook: Spirited Recipes from Santa Fe. Katherine Kagel. Ed. by Bill LeBlond. LC 92-41350. (Illus.). 160p. 1993. pap. 18.95 (*0-8118-0293-0*) Chronicle Bks.

Cafe Purgatorium. Dana M. Anderson & Charles De Lint. 288p. 1993. mass mkt. 3.99 (*0-8125-1512-9*) Tor Bks.

Cafe Royal: Ninety Years of Bohemia. Guy Deghy. LC 79-8061. reprint ed. 25.00 (*0-404-18372-7*) AMS Pr.

Cafe U. S. A.: Where to Go for the Best Cup of Joe! Your Ultimate Annual Guide to Massachusetts. Lou Nicolaides. 1994. pap. 12.95 (*0-9637060-1-2*) Ludwig CA.

Cafe U. S. A.: Where to Go for the Best Cup of Joe! Your Ultimate Annual Guide to the Coffee State. Lou Nicolaides. 1994. pap. 11.95 (*0-9637060-2-0*) Ludwig CA.

Cafe Wisconsin. Joanne R. Stuttgen. LC 92-42346. (Orig.). 1993. pap. 11.95 (*1-55971-157-4*) NorthWord.

Cafes of Childhood. R. Nikolas Macioci. 52p. (Orig.). 1992. pap. 6.95 (*0-9627501-9-0*) Event Horizon.

Cafes of Childhood. R. Nikolas Macioci. 44p. (Orig.). 1991. pap. 7.00 (*0-9628094-2-X*) Pearl Edit.

Cafeteria America: New Identities in Contemporary Life. June Sochen. LC 87-35378. 146p. 1988. 19.95 (*0-8138-0255-5*) Iowa St U Pr.

Cafeteria Plans...A Win-Win Employee Fringe Benefit. Andrew J. Bedsole & Irving L. Blackman. (Special Report Ser.: No. 23). 65p. 1988. pap. 25.00 (*0-916181-29-4*) Blackman Kallick Bartelstein.

Cafeteria Supervisor. Jack Rudman. (Career Examination Ser.: C-1157). 1994. pap. 29.95 (*0-8373-1157-8*) Nat Learn.

Caffe' L.A. The Coffeehouse Directory for L.A. County. Louis Nicolaides. 1993. pap. 9.95 (*0-9637060-0-4*) Ludwig CA.

***Caffe U. S. A. Ventura, Santa Barbara & Central Coast Edition; Your Ultimate Guide to the Coffee.** Louis Nicolaides. 1994. pap. 12.95 (*0-9637060-3-9*) Ludwig CA.

Caffeine: A Medical & Scientific Subject Analysis & Research Index with Bibliography. Hanna U. Tyler. LC 83-71650. 150p. 1985. 44.50 (*0-941864-95-2*); pap. 39.50 (*0-941864-94-4*) ABBE Pubs Assn.

Caffeine: Perspectives from Recent Research. Ed. by P. B. Dews. (Illus.). 260p. 1987. 88.00 (*0-387-13532-4*) Spr-Verlag.

Caffeine: The Most Popular Stimulant. Richard Gilbert. (Encyclopedia of Psychoactive Drugs Ser.: No. 1). (Illus.). 1992. lib. bdg. 19.95 (*0-685-52239-3*) Chelsea Hse.

Caffeine & Health. Jack E. James. (Illus.). 432p. 1991. text ed. 72.00 (*0-12-380105-2*) Acad Pr.

Caffeine & Nicotine. Richard S. Lee & Mary P. Lee. LC 94-2279. (Drug Abuse Prevention Library). (J). (gr. 7 up). 1994. 15.95 (*0-8239-1701-0*) Rosen Group.

Caffeine, Coffee, & Health. Ed. by Silvio Garattini. LC 92-49681. (Monographs of the Mario Negri Institute for Pharmacological Research). 432p. 1993. 104.00 (*0-88167-961-5*) Raven.

Caffey's Pediatric X-Ray Diagnosis. 8th ed. Silverman. 1985. 295.00 (*0-8151-7681-3*, Yr Bk Med Pubs) Mosby Yr Bk.

Caffey's Pediatric X-ray Diagnosis: An Integrated Imaging Approach. 9th ed. Ed. by Frederic N. Silverman. LC 92-18838. 2147p. 1992. 325.00 (*0-8151-1462-1*) Mosby Yr Bk.

CAFM Systems Buyer's Guide, 1992. rev. ed. Ed. by Larry Yu. (GSI Management Resource Ser.). 175p. 1992. 65. 00 (*0-9625154-4-2*) Graphic Systs.

Cage. Alberts Bels. Tr. by Ojars Kratins. 149p. 1990. 35.00 (*0-7206-0802-3*, Pub. by Peter Owen Ltd UK) Dufour.

Cage. Peter McCurtin. (Sundance Ser.: No. 41). 208p. 1982. pap. 2.25 (*0-8439-1077-1*) Dorchester Pub Co.

Cage. Audrey Schulman. LC 93-37907. 1994. write for info. (*1-56512-035-3*) Algonquin Bks.

***Cage.** Audrey Schulman. 272p. 1995. mass mkt. 5.99 (*0-380-72473-1*) Avon.

Cage. Ruth M. Sender. LC 86-8562. 252p. (YA). (gr. 7 up). 1986. text ed. 16.95 (*0-02-781830-6*, Mac Bks Young Read) S&S Childrens.

Cage. Ruth M. Senderowicz. (J). (gr. 5 up). 1988. mass mkt. 3.99 (*0-553-27003-6*, Starfire) Bantam.

***Cage.** Cal Skinner. 340p. (Orig.). 1995. pap. 9.95 (*0-7610-0167-0*) NW Pub.

Cage. S. M. Stirling & Shirley Meier. 416p. 1991. mass mkt. 4.50 (*0-671-72047-3*) Baen Bks.

Cage. large type ed. Audrey Schulman. LC 94-15398. 1994. 22.95 (*0-7927-2078-4*, Curley Lrg Print); pap. 21.95 (*0-7927-2077-6*, Curley Lrg Print) Chivers N Amer.

Cage. Charlotte T. Hirsch. LC 74-22788. (Labor Movement in Fiction & Non-Fiction Ser.). reprint ed. 45.00 (*0-404-58442-X*) AMS Pr.

Cage & Aviary Birds. Dennis Kelsey-Wood. (Colorguide Ser.). 1982. pap. 6.95 (*0-940842-11-4*) South Group.

Cage & Aviary Birds. Martin & Albert Ellis. 1980. pap. 16. 95 (*0-685-43766-3*) Viking Penguin.

Cage Aux Folles. (Illus.). 1983. 9.95 (*0-88188-555-X*, 00384040) H Leonard.

Cage Eleven. Gerry Adams. LC 93-12851. (Orig.). 1993. 11.45 (*1-879823-04-7*); pap. 7.45 (*1-879823-05-5*) Sheridan Sq Pr.

Cage Five is Going to Break. E. Richard Johnson. LC 89-85726. 156p. 1989. reprint ed. pap. 5.95 (*1-55882-024-8*, Lib Crime Classics) Intl Polygonics.

***Cage for Loulou: Poems.** Rudolph R. Von Abele. LC 77-17394. 61p. 1978. pap. 25.00 (*0-7837-8505-4*, 2049313) Bks Demand.

Cage Hydrocarbons. Ed. by George A. Olah. 432p. 1990. text ed. 99.95 (*0-471-62292-3*) Wiley.

Cage of Fireflies: Modern Japanese Haiku. Ed. & Tr. by Lucien Stryk. LC 93-15212. 122p. 1993. 24.95 (*0-8040-0976-7*); pap. 11.95 (*0-8040-0977-5*) Swallow.

Cage of Ice. large type ed. Sally Wentworth. 263p. 1992. 21.95 (*0-7505-0251-7*, Pub. by Magna Print Bks) Ulverscroft.

Cage of Melancholy: Identity & Metamorphosis in the Mexican Culture. Roger Bartra. Tr. by Christopher J. Hall. LC 91-16813. (Illus.). 180p. (C). 1992. text ed. 40. 00 (*0-8135-1749-4*) Rutgers U Pr.

***Cage of Shadows.** Meg Griffin. 352p. 1995. mass mkt. 4.99 (*0-8217-4940-4*) Windsor NY.

Cage of Wild Cries. Claudia Menza. 1991. pap. 12.95 (*0-88962-445-3*) Riverrun NY.

Cage Your Rage: An Inmate's Guide to Anger Control. Murray Cullen. (Illus.). 94p. 1992. pap. 12.00 (*0-929310-76-4*) Am Correctional.

Cagebirds. David Campton. 1977. 2.50 (*0-87129-274-2*, C44) Dramatic Pub.

***Caged Birds.** Constance Vogel. Ed. by Carol Spelius & Wayne Spelius. 89p. (Orig.). 1994. pap. 9.95 (*0-941363-28-7*) Lake Shore Pub.

Caged Dragons: An American POW in WWII Japan. Robert E. Haney. (Illus.). 267p. 1991. 19.95 (*1-879094-06-1*) Momentum Bks.

Caged Eagles: Downed American Fighter Pilots, 1940-1945. Vern Haugland. 288p. 1991. pap. 16.95 (*0-8306-2147-4*, TAB-Aero) TAB Bks.

Caged-In. Zita Sodeika. LC 92-72478. 94p. (Orig.). (ENG & LIT.). (YA). 1992. pap. 15.00 (*0-9617756-2-9*) Galerija.

***Caged Innocence.** Sherry L. Rock. LC 94-60632. 192p. 1994. text ed. 14.95 (*1-884570-07-0*) Research Triangle.

Cages. Paul Covert. (New Writers Ser.). 1971. 3.95 (*0-87140-531-8*) Liveright.

Cages. Ruth Fainlight. 1966. 13.95 (*0-8023-1129-6*) Dufour.

Cages. Peg Kehret. LC 90-21230. 160p. (J). (gr. 5 up). 1991. 14.99 (*0-525-65062-8*, Cobblehill Bks) Dutton Child Bks.

Cages. Dave McKean. (Illus.). 48p. (Orig.). 1991. pap. 3.50 (*1-879450-17-8*) Tundra MA.

Cages. Dave McKean. (Illus.). 48p. (Orig.). 1991. pap. 3.50 (*1-879450-18-6*) Tundra MA.

Cages. Peg Kehret. Ed. by Pat MacDonald. 160p. (J). 1993. reprint ed. pap. 3.50 (*0-671-75879-9*, Minstrel Bks) PB.

***Cages: Short Fiction by Ed Gorman.** Ed Gorman. 370p. 1995. 35.00 (*0-9631367-6-3*) Deadline Pr.

Cages: Snowangel & Epiphany. Lewis J. Carlino. 1964. pap. 4.75 (*0-8222-0174-7*) Dramatists Play.

Cages & Aviaries. Curt A. Enehjelm. Tr. by U. Erich Friese. Orig. Title: Kafige und Volieren. (Illus.). 160p. 1981. 12. 95 (*0-87666-840-6*, H-1039) TFH Pubns.

Cages of Reason: The Rise of the Rational State in France, Japan, the United States, & Great Britain. Bernard S. Silberman. LC 92-31653. (Illus.). 408p. (C). 1993. lib. bdg. 65.00 (*0-226-75736-6*); pap. text ed. 19.95 (*0-226-75737-4*) U Ch Pr.

Cages of Steel: The Politics of Imprisonment in America. Ed. by J. J. Vander Wall. (Illus.). ix, 445p. (Orig.). 1992. pap. 16.95 (*0-944624-17-0*) Maisonneuve Pr.

Cages on Opposite Shores. Janset B. Shami. LC 94-9347. (Emerging Voices - New International Fiction Ser.). 256p. 1994. 24.95 (*1-56656-165-5*); pap. 11.95 (*1-56656-157-4*) Interlink Pub.

Cages to Jump Shots: Pro Basketball's Early Years. Robert W. Peterson. (Illus.). 240p. 1991. reprint ed. pap. 9.95 (*0-19-507261-8*) OUP.

Caging the Bear: Containment & the Cold War. Charles Gati. LC 73-19522. (C). 1974. pap. text ed. write for info. (*0-672-61351-4*, Bobbs) Macmillan.

Caging the Lion: Cross-Cultural Fictions. Bruce E. Fleming. LC 92-5799. (New Studies in Aesthetics: Vol. 13). 232p. 1992. 29.95 (*0-8204-1912-5*) P Lang Pubs.

Cagle's NCLEX-RN Comprehensive Review. Toni J. Cagle. (Illus.). 310p. 1989. pap. 24.95 (*0-685-30453-1*) Cagles Nursing.

Cagliostro. Vincente Huidobro. 1974. lib. bdg. 59.95 (*0-87968-809-2*) Gordon Pr.

Cagliostro. W. Trowbridge. 1974. 250.00 (*0-87968-106-3*) Gordon Pr.

Cagliostro. W. R. Trowbridge. 312p. 1992. reprint ed. pap. 22.50 (*1-56459-063-1*) Kessinger Pub.

***Cagliostro & the Egptian Rite of Freemasonry.** Henry R. Evans. 1994. pap. 9.95 (*1-55818-308-6*, Sure Fire) Holmes Pub.

Cagliostro Tarot. Stuart R. Kaplan. 68p. 1981. 16.00 (*0-913866-70-9*) US Games Syst.

Cagliostro's Egyptian Rite of Freemasonry Rituals. Compte De Cagliostro. 60p. 1993. pap. 14.95 (*1-56459-321-5*) Kessinger Pub.

Cagney: The Actor As Auteur. Patrick McGilligan. (Quality Paperbacks Ser.). (Illus.). 1980. reprint ed. pap. 6.95 (*0-306-80120-5*) Da Capo.

Cagnotte. Eugene Labiche. 182p. (FRE.). 1990. pap. 9.95 (*0-7859-1257-6*, 2038712123) Fr & Eur.

Cahaba Prison & the Sultana Disaster. William O. Bryant. LC 89-33833. (Illus.). 192p. 1990. 21.95 (*0-8173-0468-1*) U of Ala Pr.

Cahal Pech, the Ancient Maya, & Modern Belize: The Story of an Archaeological Park. Joseph W. Ball. (University Research Lecture Ser.: No. 9). (Illus.). 116p. 1994. 30.00 (*1-879691-17-5*) SDSU Press.

Cahier De Georges Braque see Illustrated Notebooks, 1917-1955

Cahier d'ombres see Notebook of Shadows: Selected Poems, 1974-1980

Cahier d'un Retour au Pays Natal: Return to My Native Land. Aime Cesaire. (Livre-Poche Bilingue Ser.). pap. 8.95 (*0-7859-0622-3*, F92379) Fr & Eur.

An Asterisk (*) at the beginning of an entry indicates that the title is appearing in BIP for the first time.

***Cahier 1: Mutti-Vati Kultur.** Ed. by Witte de With Staff. (Cahiers Ser.). 196p. 1995. pap. 29.95 (*90-73362-27-X*) Dist Art Pubs.

***Cahier 2: Mutti-Vati Kultur.** Ed. by Witte de With Staff. (Cahiers Ser.). 210p. 1995. pap. 29.95 (*90-73362-28-8*) Dist Art Pubs.

Cahiers de l'Institut de Science Economique Appliquee: Bibliographie Marxologique. Liste Complementaire. Incl. Avant-Propos. M. Rubel. (*0-318-58728-9*); Critique de la Dialectique et de la Philosophie de Hegel (D'Apres les Manuscrits Parisiens de 1844. Karl Marx. 1962. (*0-318-58729-7*); Circulaire Contre Kriege. Karl Marx & F. Engels. 1962. (*0-318-58730-0*); Socialisme Britannique et Marxisme Vers la Fin du XIX Siecle. L. Epsztein. 1962. (*0-318-58731-9*); Apercus Sur Les-Utopies. G. Sorel. 1962. (*0-318-58732-7*); Marx et Keynes. P. Mattick. 1962. (*0-318-58733-5*); (Economies et Societes Series S: No. 5). 1962. Set pap. 26.00 (*0-8115-0792-0*) Periodicals Srv.

Cahiers du Cinema: The 1950s: Neo-Realism, Hollywood, New Wave. Ed. by Jim Hillier. (Harvard Film Studies). 320p. 1985. 36.00 (*0-674-09060-8*); pap. text ed. 15.50 (*0-674-09061-6*) HUP.

Cahiers du Cinema: The 1960s: New Wave, New Cinema, Reevaluating Hollywood. Ed. by Jim Hillier. (Film Studies Ser.). 368p. 1987. text ed. 38.00 (*0-674-09062-4*) HUP.

Cahiers du Cinema Vol. 2: The Nineteen Sixties: New Wave, New Cinema, Reevaluating Hollywood. Jim Hillier. (Film Studies Ser.). 384p. (C). 1992. pap. 14.95 (*0-674-09065-9*) HUP.

Cahiers du Cinema, 1969-1972: The Politics of Representation. Ed. by Nick Browne. (Harvard Film Studies). 384p. 1989. 38.00 (*0-674-09063-2*) HUP.

Cahiers Elisabethains: Etudes sur la Pre-Renaissance et la Renaissance Anglaises, 3 vols., Set. Incl. Vol. 1. Nos. 1-6, 1972-74. 47.50 (*0-685-73107-3*); Vol. 2. Nos. 7-10, 1975-76. 47.50 (*0-685-73108-1*); Vol. 3. Nos. 11-15, 1977-79. 47.50 (*0-685-73109-X*); 142.50 (*0-404-19303-X*) AMS Pr.

Cahiers et les Poesies d'Andre Walter. Andre Gide. (FRE.). 1986. pap. 18.95 (*0-7859-2801-4*) Fr & Eur.

Cahiers et les Poesies d'Andre Walter. Andre Gide. (Poesie Ser.). 224p. (FRE.). 1952. 14.95 (*2-07-032360-9*) Schoenhof.

Cahiers Mathematiques, 4 tomes. Incl. Tome 1-Exercises Corriges sur des Structures Elementaires. J. Bentz. 1966. pap. 4.40 (*90-279-6317-7*); Tome 2-Exercises Corriges sur des Structures Elementaires. A. M. Decaillot. 1969. pap. 6.40 (*90-279-6321-5*); Tome 3-Morceaux Choisis D'algebre et de Combinatoire pour les Sciences Humaines. 1970. pap. 5.60 (*90-279-7008-4*); No. 15. Tome 4-Distributions Statistiques et Lois de Probabilite. Bruno Leclerc. 1972. pap. 9.20 (*0-686-22161-3*); (Mathematische Lehrbucher und Monographien). Set pap. 6.67 (*0-685-03426-7*) Mouton.

Cahiers, Vol. 1. Paul Valery. Ed. by J. Robinson. (FRE.). 1973. lib. bdg. 115.00 (*0-7859-3817-6*) Fr & Eur.

Cahiers, Vol. 2. Paul Valery. Ed. by Judith Robinson. (FRE.). 1988. lib. bdg. 125.00 (*0-7859-3821-4*) Fr & Eur.

***Cahiers 3: L'Oeuvre a-t-Elle Lieu?** Micheal Asher et al. (Illus.). 172p. Date not set. pap. 29.95 (*3-928762-29-X*) Dist Art Pubs.

Cahokia & Surrounding Mound Groups. D. I. Bushnell, Jr. (Harvard University Peabody Museum of Archaeology & Ethnology Papers: Vol. 3, No. 1). 1972. reprint ed. pap. 14.00 (*0-527-01192-4*) Periodicals Srv.

Cahokia & the Hinterlands: Middle Mississippian Cultures of the Midwest. Ed. by Thomas E. Emerson & R. Barry Lewis. (Illus.). 376p. 1991. 49.95 (*0-252-01705-6*) U of Ill Pr.

Cahokia Atlas: A Historical Atlas of Cahokia Archaeology. Melvin Fowler. Ed. by Thomas E. Emerson & Evelyn Taylor. (Studies in Illinois Archaeology: No. 6). (Illus.). 245p. 1989. pap. 20.00 (*0-942579-06-2*) IHPA.

Cahokia: City of the Sun: Prehistoric Urban Center in the American Bottom. Claudia G. Mink. LC 92-81951. (Illus.). 80p. (Orig.). 1992. pap. text ed. 10.00 (*1-881563-00-6*) Cahokia MMS.

***Cahokia's Countryside: Household Archaeology, Settlement Patterns, & Social Power.** Mark W. Mehrer. LC 94-45750. (Illus.). 225p. (Orig.). 1995. pap. 29.00 (*0-87580-565-5*) N Ill U Pr.

Cahoon's Formulating X-Ray Techniques. 9th ed. Thomas T. Thompson. LC 79-87805. xii, 322p. 1979. 27.95 (*0-8223-0431-7*) Duke.

Cahoots. Rick Johnston. 1990. pap. 4.75 (*0-8222-0173-9*) Dramatists Play.

Cahuachi in the Ancient Nasca World. Helaine Silverman. LC 92-42223. (Illus.). 376p. 1993. text ed. 59.95 (*0-87745-407-8*) U of Iowa Pr.

Cahuilla. Craig A. Doherty & Katherine M. Doherty. LC 93-31863. (Native American People Ser.). (J). (gr. 4 up). 1994. write for info. (*0-86625-527-3*) Rourke Corp.

Cahuilla - California. Frank W. Porter, 3rd et al. (Indians of North American Ser.). (Illus.). 144p. (YA). (gr. 5 up). 1989. 18.95 (*1-55546-693-1*) Chelsea Hse.

Cahuilla Dictionary. Hansjakob Seiler & Kojiro Hioki. LC 78-71635. 1979. pap. 14.95 (*0-939046-04-0*) Malki Mus Pr.

Cahuilla Dictionary. Hansjacob Seiller & Kojiro Hioki. 291p. (C). 1993. reprint ed. lib. bdg. 37.00x (*0-8095-6203-0*) Borgo Pr.

Cahuilla Grammar. Hansjakob Seiler. LC 76-52060. 1977. pap. 12.00 (*0-939046-05-9*) Malki Mus Pr.

Cahuilla Grammar. Hansjakob Seiler. x, 361p. (C). 1993. reprint ed. lib. bdg. 31.00x (*0-8095-6206-5*) Borgo Pr.

Cahuilla Indians. Harry C. James. 1969. pap. 10.00 (*0-939046-06-7*) Malki Mus Pr.

Cahuilla Indians. Harry C. James. (Illus.). xx, 185p. (C). 1993. reprint ed. lib. bdg. 27.00x (*0-8095-6211-1*) Borgo Pr.

Cahuilla Indians of Southern California. L. John Bean & Harry W. Lawton. 1965. 2.00 (*0-939046-08-3*) Malki Mus Pr.

Cahuilla Landscape: The Santa Rosa & San Jacinto Mountains. Lowell J. Bean et al. Ed. by Sylvia B. Vane. LC 91-8148. (Anthropological Papers: No. 37). 1991. text ed. 19.95 (*0-87919-121-X*); pap. text ed. 14.95 (*0-87919-120-1*) Ballena Pr.

CAI Author-Instructor: An Introduction & Guide to the Preparation of Computer-Assisted Instruction Materials. Joseph C. Meredith. LC 70-125876. 144p. 1971. 24.95 (*0-87778-014-5*) Educ Tech Pubns.

CAI Network Evaluation Criteria & Methodology (Seattle, Wash. Nov., 1973) 2nd ed. 76p. 1976. 6.00 (*0-917054-10-5*) Med Communications.

CAI Sourcebook. Robert L. Burke. (Illus.). 224p. (C). 1982. 17.50 (*0-13-110148-X*) P-H.

CAI Study Skills Notebook. William F. Brown et al. 30p. (Orig.). (C). 1987. pap. text ed. 5.00 (*1-881936-02-3*) WFB Ent.

Caillebotte: The Impressionist. M. Berhaut. (Rhythm & Color Two Ser.). 1970. 9.95 (*0-8288-9517-1*) Fr & Eur.

Caillebotte & His Garden at Yerres. Pierre Wittmer. 1991. 95.00 (*0-8109-3167-2*) Abrams.

Caiman - Cartas Boca Abajo. 2nd ed. A. Buero Vallejo. 198p. (SPA.). 1984. pap. 8.95 (*0-7859-5131-8*) Fr & Eur.

Caiman Ante el Espejo: Un Ensayo de Interpretacion De lo Cubano. Uva De Aragon Clavijo. LC 93-70718. (Coleccion Cuba y Sus Jueces Ser.). 112p. (Orig.). (SPA.). 1993. pap. 13.00 (*0-89729-676-1*) Ediciones.

Cain: A Mystery. Adapt. by I. E. Clark. (Illus.). 40p. 1970. pap. 10.00 (*0-88680-017-X*); pap. 2.00 (*0-88680-016-1*) I E Clark.

Cain: Son of the Serpent. David M. Eichhorn. (Limited Editions Reprints Ser.). 160p. 1985. reprint ed. 14.95 (*0-940646-24-2*); reprint ed. pap. 8.95 (*0-940646-19-6*) Rossel Bks.

Cain: The Biography of James M. Cain. Roy Hoopes. LC 86-27926. (Illus.). 704p. 1987. pap. 16.95 (*0-8093-1361-8*) S Ill U Pr.

Cain Adamnain. Ed. by Kuno Meyer. (Anecdota Oxoniensia Ser.: No. 12). 1988. reprint ed. 37.50 (*0-404-63962-3*) AMS Pr.

Cain & Abel. Mel L. Piper. 48p. 1987. pap. 2.95 (*0-88144-103-1*) Christian Pub.

Cain & Abel. Joyce Raub. (Arch Bks.). (Illus.). 24p. (J). (gr. k-4). 1986. pap. 1.99 (*0-570-06199-7*, 59-1422) Concordia.

Cain & Beowulf: A Study in Secular Allegory. David E. Williams. LC 82-165351. (Illus.). 127p. reprint ed. pap. 36.20 (*0-8357-6372-2*, 2035726) Bks Demand.

Cain Conversion. Richard Aellen. LC 92-54460. 1993. 21.95 (*1-55611-348-X*) D I Fine.

***Cain Conversion.** Richard Aellen. 1994. pap. 5.50 (*0-06-100711-0*, Harp PBks) HarpC.

***Cain His Brother.** Anne Perry. LC 95-8680. 1995. 22.95 (*0-449-90847-X*) Fawcett.

Cain on Screen: Contemporary Spanish Cinema. Thomas G. Deveny. LC 93-39695. (Illus.). 352p. (ENG & SPA.). 1993. 39.50 (*0-8108-2707-7*) Scarecrow.

***Caine Mutiny.** Herman Wouk. 1994. lib. bdg. 27.95x (*1-56849-443-2*) Buccaneer Bks.

Caine Mutiny. Herman Wouk. 560p. 1992. pap. 10.95 (*0-316-95510-8*) Little.

Caine Mutiny. Herman Wouk. LC 51-9977. 1954. 27.50 (*0-385-04053-9*) Doubleday.

Caine Mutiny. braille ed. Herman Wouk. 1276p. 1990. vinyl bd. 102.08 (*1-56956-205-9*, BR8215) W A T Braille.

Caine Mutiny. Herman Wouk. (Classics of Naval Literature Ser.). 648p. 1987. reprint ed. 32.95 (*0-87021-010-6*) Naval Inst Pr.

Caine Mutiny Court-Martial. Herman Wouk. LC 54-5354. 1954. reprint ed. 14.95 (*0-385-04054-7*) Doubleday.

Caine's Trail. large type ed. Cameron Judd. LC 91-18385. 261p. 1991. reprint ed. lib. bdg. 15.95 (*1-56054-212-8*) Thorndike Pr.

Cain's Book. Alexander Trocchi. LC 92-24900. (Orig.). 1992. 9.95 (*0-8021-3314-2*) Grove-Atltic.

Cain's Craft. David Madden. LC 84-20215. 176p. 1985. 20.00 (*0-8108-1750-0*) Scarecrow.

Cain's Keeper. Dennis W. Krabbenhoft. LC 88-92299. 240p. (Orig.). 1989. pap. 9.95 (*0-9621962-0-7*) Cortina Pubns.

Caio Manhattan. Rebecca Wright. Ed. by Maureen Owen. LC 76-23323. (Illus.). (Orig.). 1977. pap. 4.00 (*0-916382-11-7*) Telephone Bks.

Cairene Egyptian Colloquial Arabic. J. Olmsted Gary & S. Gamal-Eldin. (Descriptive Grammars Ser.). 152p. 1986. pap. 72.50 (*0-7099-3815-2*, Pub. by Croom Helm UK) Routledge Chapman & Hall.

Cairn Terrier Champions: 1952-1986. Camino E. E. & B. Co. Staff. (Illus.). 229p. 1987. pap. 36.95 (*0-940808-47-1*) Camino E E & Bk.

Cairn Terriers. Erliss McCormack. (Illus.). 160p. 1989. lib. bdg. 11.95 (*0-86622-871-3*, KW169) TFH Pubns.

Cairngorms. Desmond Nethersole-Thompson & Adam Watson. 324p. (C). 1986. 40.00 (*0-906664-12-8*, Pub. by Mercat Pr Bks UK) St Mut.

Cairns of British Columbia & Washington. Harlan I. Smith & Gerard Fowke. LC 73-3517. (Jesup North Pacific Expedition. Publications: Vol. 2, Pt. 2). reprint ed. 22.50 (*0-404-58118-8*) AMS Pr.

Cairo. (Insight Guides Ser.). 1993. pap. 21.95 (*0-395-66431-4*) HM.

Cairo: A Critical Analysis of Microsoft's Object-Oriented Strategy. Computer Technology Research Corp. Staff. (Illus.). 184p. (Orig.). 1994. 280.00 (*1-56607-032-5*) Comput Tech Res.

Cairo: A Practical Guide. 6th ed. Ed. by Cassandra Vivian. (Illus.). 300p. 1988. pap. 25.00 (*977-424-190-8*, Pub. by Am Univ Cairo Pr UA) Col U Pr.

Cairo: A Practical Guide with Directory & Maps. 5th ed. Ed. by Deborah Cowley & Aleya Serour. 1987. pap. 15.00 (*977-424-136-3*, Pub. by Am Univ Cairo Pr UA) Col U Pr.

Cairo: Sketches of Its History, Monuments & Social Life. Stanley Lane-Poole. LC 73-6286. (Middle East Ser.). 1979. reprint ed. 33.95 (*0-405-05345-2*) Ayer.

Cairo: Tales of the City. Ed. by John Miller & Kirsten Miller. LC 93-1815. (Chronicles Abroad Ser.). 192p. 1994. 12.95 (*0-8118-0492-5*) Chronicle Bks.

Cairo: The Site & the History. Morsi Saad El-Din et al. LC 87-82873. (Illus.). 104p. 1988. 24.95 (*0-8071-1472-3*) La State U Pr.

Cairo Calls: Sketchbook Street Views from the African Metropolis of Araby (Including an Alexandrian Supplement) Dickinson Weber. LC 90-60954. (Downtown (the Great Capitals) Ser.: No. 3). (Illus.). 68p. (Orig.). (C). 1990. pap. 10.00 (*0-936721-02-2*) Sandscape Pr.

Cairo Cats. Dawn A. Poore. 256p. 1994. mass mkt. 3.99 (*0-8217-4571-9*) Zebra.

Cairo, City of Art & Commerce. Gaston Wiet. Tr. by Seymour Feiler. LC 83-5620. xiii, 170p. (C). 1983. reprint ed. text ed. 49.75 (*0-313-24010-8*, WCCA, Greenwood Pr) Greenwood.

Cairo Community Heritage. Cairo Roots Society Staff. (Illus.). 317p. 1986. 42.00 (*0-88107-055-6*) Curtis Media.

***Cairo Compact & Panel Reports.** John C. Topping, Jr. & Climate Institute Staff. 34p. 1989. pap. 10.00 (*0-614-06733-2*) Climate Inst.

Cairo Geniza. 2nd ed. Paul E. Kahle. LC 60-14602. 407p. reprint ed. pap. 116.00 (*0-8357-7961-0*, 2056072) Bks Demand.

Cairo Geniza. P. E. Kahle. (British Academy, London, Schweich Lectures on Biblical Archaeology Series, 1930). 1972. reprint ed. pap. 30.00 (*0-8115-1283-5*) Periodicals Srv.

Cairo Guide. Federal Writers' Project. Illinois. LC 73-3613. (American Guide Ser.). reprint ed. 37.50 (*0-404-57916-7*) AMS Pr.

Cairo Guidebook: A 1920s Guide for Call of Cthulhu. Chaosium, Inc. Staff. Ed. by Lynn Willis. (Call of Cthulhu Roleplaying Game Ser.). (Illus.). 96p. (Orig.). (YA). 1995. pap. 10.95 (*1-56882-025-9*, 2351) Chaosium.

Cairo, Jerusalem, & Damascus, Three Chief Cities of the Egyptian Sultans. David S. Margoliouth. LC 80-1918. (Illus.). reprint ed. 54.50 (*0-404-18980-6*) AMS Pr.

Cairo Nilometer: Studies in Ibn Iaghri Birdi's Chronicles of Egypt. William Popper. LC 51-9495. (University of California Publications in Social Welfare: Vol. 12). 282p. reprint ed. pap. 80.40 (*0-8357-7962-9*, 2021491) Bks Demand.

Cairo Notebooks. Ammiel Alcalay. 76p. (Orig.). 1994. pap. 9.50 (*0-935162-13-5*) Singing Horse.

Cairo University & the Making of Modern Egypt. Donald M. Reid. (Cambridge Middle East Library: No. 23). (Illus.). 320p. (C). 1990. 64.95 (*0-521-36641-0*) Cambridge U Pr.

Caissons Across Europe: An Artillery Captain's Personal War. Richard M. Hardison. Ed. by Ed Eakin. (Illus.). 320p. 1990. 18.95 (*0-89015-758-8*) Sunbelt Media.

Caithness & Sutherland Records. Ed. by Alfred W. Johnston & Amy Johnston. (Viking Society for Northern Research: Old Lore Ser.). reprint ed. 27.50 (*0-404-60238-X*) AMS Pr.

***Caitlin.** Catherine Dunphy. (Degrassi Book Ser.). (YA). 1995. pap. 4.95 (*1-55028-255-7*); bds. 16.95 (*1-55028-253-0*) Formac Dist Ltd.

***Caitlin: The Life of Caitlin Thomas.** Paul Ferris. (Illus.). 288p. 1995. pap. 16.95 (*0-7126-6290-1*, Pub. by Pimlico) Trafalgar.

***Caitlin's Big Idea.** Gloria Skurzynski. LC 94-27622. 64p. (J). (gr. 2-5). 1994. pap. text ed. 2.50 (*0-8167-3592-1*, Little Rainbow) Troll Assocs.

***Caitlin's Big Idea.** Gloria Skurzynski. (Illus.). (J). 1995. lib. bdg. 9.79 (*0-8167-3814-9*, Little Rainbow) Troll Assocs.

Caitlin's Holiday. Helen V. Griffith. LC 89-27228. (Illus.). 96p. (J). (gr. 1 up). 1990. 12.95 (*0-688-09470-8*) Greenwillow.

Caius Geht Ein Licht Auf see Mystery of the Roman Ransom

Caius Marius. P. A. Kildahl. LC 67-28862. (Twayne's Rulers & Statesmen of the World Ser.). 191p. (C). 1968. lib. bdg. 17.95 (*0-8290-1756-9*) Irvington.

Caja de Botones. Frances Sainz. (Cityscapes Ser.). 23p. (J). (ps-1). 1992. pap. text ed. 23.00 (*1-56843-045-0*); pap. text ed. 4.50 (*1-56843-092-2*) BGR Pub.

***Caja de los Botones.** Margarette S. Reid. LC 89-38566. (Illus.). 24p. (SPA.). (J). (ps-2). 1995. 14.99 (*0-525-45445-4*, DCB) Dutton Child Bks.

***Caja de los Botones.** Margarette S. Reid. (Illus.). 24p. (SPA.). (J). (ps-2). 1995. pap. 4.99 (*0-14-055642-7*, Puff Unicorn) Puffin Bks.

Caja de Zapatos Vacia. Virgilio Pinera & Luis F. Gonzales-Cruz. LC 86-80352. (Coleccion Teatro). 83p. (Orig.). (SPA.). 1986. pap. 7.95 (*0-89729-390-8*) Ediciones.

Cajal on the Cerebral Cortex: An Annotated Translation of the Complete Writings. Ed. by Javier DeFelipe & Edward G. Jones. (History of Neuroscience Ser.: No. 1). (Illus.). 672p. 1988. 75.00 (*0-19-505280-3*) OUP.

Cajal's Degeneration & Regeneration of the Nervous System. Ed. by Javier DeFelipe & Edward G. Jones. Tr. by Raoul M. May. (History of Neuroscience Ser.: No. 5). (Illus.). 1168p. 1991. 65.00 (*0-19-506516-6*, 11153) OUP.

Cajal's Histology of the Nervous System, 2 vols. Santiago Ramon y Cajal. Ed. by Larry W. Swanson. Tr. by Neely Swanson. LC 93-35437. (History of Neuroscience Ser.: No. 6). (Illus.). 1664p. 1995. 195.00 (*0-19-507401-7*) OUP.

Cajetan: Commentary on St. Thomas Aquinas on Being & Essence. Tr. by Lottie Kendzierski & S. J. Wade. LC 64-7794. (Medieval Philosophical Texts in Translation Ser.). 1965. 2.00 (*0-87462-214-X*) Marquette.

Cajetan Responds: A Reader in Reformation Controversy. Tommaso De Vio. Ed. by Jared Wicks. LC 77-22666. 300p. reprint ed. pap. 85.50 (*0-8357-7963-7*, 2029507) Bks Demand.

Cajita de Musica. 2nd rev. ed. Ester Feliciano-Mendoza. LC 82-4910. (Ninos y Letras Ser.). (Illus.). 61p. (gr. 8-12). 1983. pap. 5.00 (*0-8477-3525-7*) U of PR Pr.

Cajon: A Pictorial Album. Chard Walker. LC 90-34707. (Illus.). 184p. 1991. 53.95 (*0-87046-095-1*, Trans-Anglo) Interurban.

Cajun: A Novel. Elizabeth N. Dubus. (Arcadia Ser.). 394p. 1994. reprint ed. pap. 11.95 (*0-9636307-2-5*) Levee Pr LA.

***Cajun: Cuisine of the Bayou.** Ed. by G & R Publishing Staff. (Uni-Book Ser.). 160p. (Orig.). 1994. pap. text ed. 3.00 (*1-56383-028-0*, 3700) G & R Pub.

Cajun Accent: Recipe Collection in Acadian Tradition. 4th rev. ed. Mary A. Fontenot. (Illus.). 152p. 1990. pap. write for info. (*0-9614245-2-4*) Swallow Pubns.

Cajun Alphabet: Full-Color Edition. James Rice. LC 90-39342. (Illus.). 64p. (J). (ps-8). 1991. 16.95 (*0-88289-822-1*) Pelican.

Cajun & Creole Folktales: The French Oral Tradition of South Louisiana. Anno. by Barry J. Ancelet. LC 93-31848. (World Folktale Library: Vol. 1). (Illus.). 296p. 1994. 40.00 (*0-8153-1498-1*, H1792) Garland.

Cajun & Creole Folktales: The French Oral Tradition of South Louisiana. Ed. by Barry Jean Ancelet. LC 93-46885. 296p. 1994. reprint ed. pap. 18.95 (*0-87805-709-9*) U Pr of Miss.

Cajun Caress. Ashland Price. 1990. mass mkt. 4.25 (*0-8217-3109-2*) Zebra.

Cajun Columbus. rev. ed. Alice D. Hughes. LC 91-16783. (Illus.). 40p. (J). 1991. 12.95 (*0-88289-875-2*) Pelican.

Cajun Cooks. Lillie P. Gallagher. 9.95 (*0-9610174-3-0*) Petit Press.

Cajun Country. Barry J. Ancelet et al. Ed. by Lynwood Montell. LC 90-28931. (Folklife in the South Ser.). 1991. pap. 15.95 (*0-87805-467-7*) U Pr of Miss.

Cajun Country Cookin' Cookbook. John Uhler & Glenna Uhler. 1989. pap. 6.95 (*0-87511-124-6*) Claitors.

Cajun Country Guide. Macon Fry & Julie Posner. LC 92-17360. (Illus.). 272p. 1992. pap. 14.95 (*0-88289-831-0*) Pelican.

Cajun Country Tour Guide & Festival Guide. Ed. by Trent Angers. (Illus.). 124p. 1991. per. 5.00 (*0-925417-07-6*) Acadian Hse Pub.

Cajun-Creole Cooking. Terry Thompson. 288p. 1987. mass mkt. 4.95 (*0-345-34260-7*) Ballantine.

Cajun-Creole Cooking. Terry L. Thompson. LC 86-80061. (Illus.). 160p. 1986. 14.95 (*0-89586-371-5*) Price Stern.

Cajun Cuisine. Beau Bayou. 19.95 (*0-8488-0285-3*) Amereon Ltd.

Cajun Cuisine: Authentic Cajun Recipes from Louisiana's Bayou Country. W. Thomas Angers. Ed. by Sue McDonough. Tr. by Randy Herpin. (Illus.). 224p. 1985. 17.95 (*0-935619-00-3*) Beau Bayou. CAJUN CUISINE is the most attractive, authentic & available Cajun cookbook in print with 130,000 copies sold through 17 printings. The book is widely acclaimed for quality & authenticity by Louisiana food writers & has been featured by the AP & UPI & hundreds of publications. Four career Cajun home economists & more than ten practitioners of traditional, authentic Cajun cooking & a former President of the Louisiana Press Association all served as advisors in the production of the book. CAJUN CUISINE offers exotic & succulent dishes which are Cajun classics, such as couche-couche, pain perdue, maque choux, gumbos, etoufees, fricasses & jambalayas. ("Jomba" was originally a native method of cooking meat & fish, & was shared with Acadian homemakers who added rice & produced jambalaya). "The 'Key' word here is 'authentic' & this cookbook contains true Cajun recipes; ones that have been handed down through the years in old Acadian families. These are the foods that you will find on the tables in real Cajun homes, not just recipes some chef calls 'Cajun cooking'."--Betty Bernard, Lake Charles, Louisiana, THE LAKE CHARLES AMERICAN PRESS. Available through Baker & Taylor, Forrest Sales, 2616 Spain Street, New Orleans, LA 70117 (1-800-346-2106 nationwide, in Louisiana 1-800-349-

An Asterisk (*) at the beginning of an entry indicates that the title is appearing in BIP for the first time. 987

2106) or direct from Beau Bayou Publishing Company, P.O. Box 53089, Laffayette, LA 70505 (1-318-5991); $17. 95 plus $2.00 shipping & handling. State of Louisiana residents add 4% sales tax.
Publisher Provided Annotation.

Cajun Dancing. Rand Speyrer. LC 92-44209. 192p. 1993. pap. 14.95 (*0-88289-970-8*) Pelican.

Cajun Dictionary: A Collection of Commonly Used Words & Phrases by the People of South Louisiana. rev. ed. James M. Sothern. (Illus.). 50p. 1986. pap. text ed. 5.95 (*0-934114-79-X*) Marine Educ.

Cajun Families of the Atchafalaya: Their Ways & Words. Greg Guirard. (Illus.). 88p. (Orig.). 1989. pap. 14.00 (*0-685-29428-5*) G Guirard.

Cajun Fiddle Tune Book. Deborah Greenblatt. 64p. 1985. pap. text ed. 12.95 (*0-931759-03-X*) Centerstream Pub.

Cajun Folktales. J. J. Reneaux. 176p. (J). (gr. 5 up). 1992. 19.95 (*0-87483-283-7*); pap. 9.95 (*0-87483-282-9*) August Hse.

Cajun Foodways. C. Paige Gutierrez. LC 92-9963. (Illus.). 256p. 1992. 35.00 (*0-87805-562-2*); pap. 15.95 (*0-87805-563-0*) U Pr of Miss.

Cajun French Language, Vol. I. Raymond L. Landreneau, Jr. LC 89-71246. 112p. 1990. pap. 19.95 (*0-913845-03-5*) Chicot Pr.

***Cajun Gingerbread Boy.** Berthe Amoss. LC 94-78160. (Illus.). 20p. (J). (ps-2). 1995. 12.95 (*0-7868-0114-X*) Hyprn Child.

Cajun Gourmet Afloat & on the Road: For a Society on the Move! Carlo DiNapoli. Ed. by Renee C. DiNapoli. (Illus.). 272p. (Orig.). 1991. pap. 14.95 (*0-9627946-1-9*) Hawk FL.

Cajun Healthy. Jude W. Theriot. LC 94-18499. 1994. 22.95 (*1-56554-085-9*) Pelican.

***Cajun Hidden Word Puzzle.** J. A. Allen. 1983. pap. 2.95 (*0-87511-644-2*) Claitors.

***Cajun Household Wisdom: You Know You Still Alive If It's Costin' You Money.** Kenneth A. Atchity. 1994. 9.95 (*0-681-00772-9*) Longmeadow Pr.

Cajun Humor, A Little. 2nd ed. Lyle E. Bergeron. (Illus.). 35p. (Orig.). 1993. pap. text ed. 6.95 (*0-9636785-0-7*) L E Bergeron.

Cajun Music: A Reflection of a People, Vol. 1. 2nd ed. Ann A. Savoy. LC 84-70917. (Illus.). 418p. 1984. reprint ed. pap. text ed. 32.00 (*0-930169-00-X*) Bluebird Pr.

Cajun Music: Its Origins & Development. Barry J. Ancelet. (Louisiana Life Ser.). 58p. (Orig.). 1989. pap. 5.00 (*0-940984-48-2*) U of SW LA Ctr LA Studies.

Cajun Music & Zydeco: Photographs. Photos by Philip Gould. LC 91-44353. (Illus.). 144p. 1992. 39.95 (*0-8071-1769-2*); cd-rom 49.95 (*0-8071-1818-4*) La State U Pr.

Cajun Night Before Christmas. Trosclair. Ed. by Howard Jacobs. LC 74-151725. (Illus.). 48p. (YA). (gr. 6-12). 1973. 12.95 (*0-88289-002-6*) Pelican.

Cajun Night Before Christmas: Full-Color Edition. Trosclair. Ed. by Howard Jacobs. LC 92-8375. (Illus.). 48p. (J). (gr. k-3). 1992. 14.95 (*0-88289-940-6*); audio 9.95 (*0-88289-914-7*); boxed 25.00 (*0-88289-947-3*) Pelican.

Cajun Night Before Christmas Coloring Book. James Rice. 32p. (J). (gr. k-4). 1976. pap. 2.75 (*0-88289-138-3*) Pelican.

Cajun Odyssey: From Nova Scotia to Louisiana ... with Love. Beryl S. Stiles. (Illus.). 200p. 1982. pap. 8.99 (*0-686-37651-X*) Thomson-Shore.

Cajun Odyssey II: The Acadian Story Continues . . . in South Louisiana. Beryl S. Stiles. (Illus.). 190p. 1986. 9.99 (*0-318-22556-5*) Thomson-Shore.

Cajun Pecan House Cookbook. Carolyn Angelette. 164p. 1989. 9.95 (*0-9629822-0-2*) Cajun Pecan.

Cajun Quick. Jude W. Theriot. LC 92-20868. (Illus.). 288p. 1993. 21.95 (*0-88289-841-8*) Pelican.

Cajun Reunion. Bernard Broussard & Raymond Broussard. 143p. (Orig.). 1989. write for info. (*0-318-64550-5*) Cypress Bks.

***Cajun Revelation: Cooking Secrets from Acadiana's Award-Winning Chefs.** 224p. 1995. 15.95 (*1-879958-25-2*) Tradery Hse.

Cajun Sketches: From the Prairies of Southwest Louisiana. Lauren C. Post. LC 90-31294. (Illus.). 215p. 1990. pap. 11.95 (*0-8071-1605-X*) La State U Pr.

Cajuns: Essays on Their History & Culture. Ed. by Glenn R. Conrad. LC 83-70891. (U. S. L. History Ser.). 280p. (C). 1983. 20.00 (*0-940984-10-5*) U of SW LA Ctr LA Studies.

Cajuns: From Acadia to Louisiana. William F. Rushton. (Illus.). 352p. 1980. pap. 15.00 (*0-374-51557-3*) FS&G.

Cajuns Images: Images Cadiennes. Beverly Matherne. 36p. (Orig.). 1994. pap. text ed. 6.00x (*1-56439-032-2*) Ridgeway.

***Cajuns of George Rodrigue.** 1976. 24.95 (*0-8487-0443-6*) Claitors.

Cajuns of Louisiana Bayous. Josef. LC 85-116811. (Illus.). 55p. (Orig.). 1985. reprint ed. pap. 12.95 (*0-9614524-0-4*) Authentic Am Art.

Cajuns of the German Coast. Olympe LaReine. LC 91-67752. 126p. 1993. pap. 8.00 (*1-56002-160-8*, Univ Edtns) Aegina Pr.

Cajun's Persuasions. Beryl S. Stiles. (Illus.). 326p. 1986. reprint ed. 12.00 (*0-318-22557-3*) Thomson-Shore.

***Cake & Candles.** Andrews & McMeel Staff. 1994. 4.95 (*0-8362-3110-4*) Andrews & McMeel.

Cake Bible. Rose L. Beranbaum. LC 88-1369. (Illus.). 420p. 1988. 27.95 (*0-688-04402-6*) Morrow.

Cake Decorating. Elaine Macgregor. 1990. 5.00 (*0-517-03164-7*) Random Hse Value.

***Cake Decorating Simplified.** Lawrence M. Rosenberg & David Gamon. (Illus.). 168p. 1995. 24.95 (*0-8317-1187-6*) A D Bragdon.

Cake Design & Decoration. 4th ed. L. J. Hanneman & G. I. Marshall. (Illus.). viii, 262p. 1979. 43.25 (*0-85334-793-X*, Pub. by Elsevier Applied Sci UK) Elsevier.

Cake Formation in Panticulate Systems. Edward J. Griffith. 237p. 1991. lib. bdg. 65.00 (*0-89573-748-5*) VCH Pubs.

***Cake in a Jar.** Jackie Gannaway. 30p. 1995. pap. 3.95 (*1-885597-06-1*) Cookbook Cup.

Cake in the Hat Box. Arthur Upfield. (Bon Mystery Ser.). 18.95 (*0-89190-567-7*, Am Repr) Amereon Ltd.

Cake in the Hat Box. large type ed. Arthur Upfield. 1979. 12.00 (*0-7089-0335-5*) Ulverscroft.

***Cake Mix Cakes.** 30p. 1995. pap. 3.95 (*1-885597-10-X*) Cookbook Cup.

Cake Sculpture & Sculptured Figure Piping. Roland A. Winbeckler. (Illus.). 35p. (Orig.). 1986. pap. 10.95 (*0-930113-06-3*) Winbeckler.

Cake Styling: Presenting & Photographing Your Cakes. Nicholas Lodge & Graham Tann. (Illus.). 90p. 1992. 14. 95 (*1-85238-137-X*, Pub. by New Holland Pubs UK) Sterling.

Cake That Mack Ate. Rose Robart. LC 86-47709. (Joy Street Bks.). (Illus.). (J). (ps-3). 1987. 14.95 (*0-316-74890-0*) Little.

Cake That Mack Ate. Rose Robart. (Illus.). (J). (ps-3). 1991. mass mkt. 4.95 (*0-316-74891-9*) Little.

Cakes: Delicious New Low-Fat Recipes. Donna Deane & Minnie Bernardino. LC 92-40573. (Simply Healthful Ser.). (Illus.). 96p. (Orig.). 1993. pap. 9.95 (*1-881527-07-7*) Chapters Pub.

Cakes: From Amish & Mennonite Kitchens. Ed. by Phyllis P. Good & Rachel T. Pellman. (Pennsylvania Dutch Cookbooks Ser.). (Illus.). 32p. (Orig.). 1983. pap. 2.95 (*0-934672-12-1*) Good Bks PA.

Cakes & Ale. W. Somerset Maugham. 208p. 1993. 9.95 (*0-14-018588-7*, Penguin Classics) Viking Penguin.

Cakes & Cookies. Norwalk. 1986. 4.98 (*0-671-07752-X*) S&S Trade.

***Cakes & Cowpokes: New Desserts from the Old West.** Wayne Harley Brachman. 1995. write for info. (*0-688-13091-7*) Morrow.

Cakes & Miracles: A Purim Tale. Barbara D. Goldin. LC 92-25848. (Illus.). (J). 1993. reprint ed. pap. 4.99 (*0-14-054871-8*) Puffin Bks.

Cakes & Miracles: A Purin Tale. Barbara D. Goldin. (Illus.). (J). (ps-3). 1991. 15.00 (*0-670-83047-X*) Viking Child Bks.

Cakes & Pastries. (Good Cooks Library). 1989. 9.99 (*0-517-67102-6*) Random Hse Value.

Cakes & Pastries. Christian Teubner et al. LC 85-60081. (Illus.). 192p. 1985. 30.00 (*0-688-04218-X*) Hearst Bks.

Cakes & Pastries at the Academy. 2nd ed. Olivia Erschen & Patricia Babrant. LC 92-44172. (California Culinary Academy Ser.). 128p. 1993. reprint ed. pap. 11.95 (*1-56426-039-9*, Calif Culinary Acad) Cole Group.

***Cakes, Cupcakes & Cheesecakes.** Ed. by Chuck Williams. (Williams-Sonoma Kitchen Library). (Illus.). 108p. Date not set. write for info. (*0-7835-0304-0*) Time-Life.

Cakes for the Queen of Heaven. Shirley A. Ranck. 176p. (Orig.). 1995. pap. 13.95 (*1-878980-10-6*) Delphi IL.

Cakes from the Amish & Mennonite Kitchen. Phyllis P. Good. 1991. pap. 2.95 (*1-56148-042-8*) Good Bks PA.

Cakes Men Like: Fifty Fun-Filled Recipes. Benjamin Darling. 60p. 1992. 9.95 (*0-8118-0007-5*) Chronicle Bks.

Cakes You Can Make: A Step-by-Step Illustrated Cookbook. Sachiko Moriyama. (Illus.). 48p. (Orig.). 1989. pap. 10.95 (*0-87040-800-3*) Japan Pubns USA.

Cakes...Cakes...& More Cakes. Martwyn M. Smith. 1991. spiral bd., pap. 8.00 (*0-87012-491-9*) McClain.

Cakewalk. Lee Smith. 240p. 1986. mass mkt. 5.99 (*0-345-33950-9*) Ballantine.

Cakewalk: Loving Spoonfuls from a Southern Kitchen : 25 Cake Recipes. Robbin Gourley. LC 94-15251. 1994. 15. 00 (*0-385-47174-2*) Doubleday.

Cal: A Guide to the World's Largest University & Its Environment. Ed. by David Warshaw. LC 82-12788. (Illus.). 256p. 1982. 7.95 (*0-87297-055-8*) Diablo.

***Cal: A Novel.** Bernard MacLaverty. 160p. 1995. pap. 11.00 (*0-393-31332-8*, Norton Paperbks) Norton.

***Cal Coolidge Doesn't Life Here Anymore: Glimpses of Northhampton MA.** Teddy Milne. LC 94-74079. 1994. pap. 12.95 (*0-938875-33-7*) Pittenbruach Pr.

CAL for Europe-Computer Assisted Learning for Europe: Proceedings of a Conf. of the European Commission on the Development of Educational Software, Eschede, The Netherlands 25-28- May 1986. Ed. by T. Plomp et al. 176p. 1987. 46.25 (*0-444-70258-X*, North Holland) Elsevier.

***Cal Look VW.** Keith Seume. (Illus.). 128p. 1995. pap. text ed. 17.95 (*0-7603-0028-3*) Motorbooks Intl.

Cal-Oregon-Revegetation Notes: U. S. National Forests - Utilizing Locally Collected Seeds for Revegetation of Dry Forest Soils in California or Oregon. 3rd ed. Craig C. Dremann. (Illus.). 57p. (Orig.). (C). 1993. pap. 7.50 (*0-933421-40-0*) Redwood Seed.

***Cal-OSHA Handbook.** Joel M. Cohen & Robert D. Peterson. Ed. by James T. Dufour. 349p. (Orig.). (C). 1994. pap. text ed. 45.00 (*1-878630-60-1*) CA Chamber Commerce.

Cal-OSHA Organizer. Ed. by James T. Dufour. (Orig.). (C). 1992. pap. text ed. 25.00 (*1-878630-28-8*) CA Chamber Commerce.

Cal Ripken. Richard Rambeck. (Sports Biographies Ser.). (ENG & SPA.). (J). (gr. 2-6). 1992. lib. bdg. 21.36 (*0-89565-867-4*) Childs World.

***Cal Ripken.** Richard Rambeck. (ENG & SPA.). (J). (gr. 2-6). 1992. lib. bdg. 21.36 (*1-56766-052-5*) Childs World.

Cal Ripken, Jr: Oriole Ironman. Stew Thornley. (J). (gr. 4-9). 1992. pap. 4.95 (*0-8225-9624-5*, Lerner Publctns) Lerner Group.

Cal Ripken, Jr. Oriole Ironman. Stew Thornley. (J). (gr. 4-9). 1992. 13.50 (*0-8225-0547-9*, Lerner Publctns) Lerner Group.

Cal Ripken, Jr. Quiet Hero. Lois Nicholson. LC 93-22741. (Illus.). 112p. (J). (gr. 4-8). 1993. bds. 12.95 (*0-87033-445-X*, Tidewtr Pubs) Cornell Maritime.

Cal Ripken, Jr. Star Shortstop. Jeff Savage. LC 94-5544. (Sports Reports Ser.). (Illus.). 104p. (J). (gr. 4-10). 1994. lib. bdg. 17.95 (*0-89490-485-X*) Enslow Pubs.

Cal Ripken Jr. The Authorized Political History. Summit Group Staff. 1993. 39.95 (*1-56530-098-X*) Summit TX.

Cal Rodgers & the Vin Fiz: The First Transcontinental Flight. Eileen F. Lebow. (Illus.). 264p. 1989. 29.95 (*0-87474-704-X*) Smithsonian.

Cal y Canto. 2nd ed. Rafael Alberti. 112p. (SPA.). 1988. pap. 9.95 (*0-7859-5146-6*, S19846) Fr & Eur.

Calabash: A Guide to the History, Culture, & Art of African Americans in Seattle & King County, Washington. Esther H. Mumford. (Illus.). 158p. (Orig.). 1993. pap. 9.95 (*0-9605670-7-0*) Ananse Pr.

Calabash of Wisdom & Other Igbo Stories. Romanus Egudu. LC 73-85560. 141p. 1973. text ed. 12.95 (*0-88357-005-X*); pap. 4.95 (*0-88357-004-1*) NOK Pubs.

Calabazas Opuestas, Vol. 5: Pasitos Spanish Language Development Books. Darlyne F. Schott. (Pasitos Hacia la Lectura Ser.). 16p. (J). (gr. k-1). 1990. pap. text ed. 11.00 (*1-56537-054-6*) D F Schott Educ.

Calabi-Yau Manifolds: A Bestiary for Physicists. T. Hubsch. 400p. (C). 1992. text ed. 74.00 (*981-02-0662-3*) World Scientific Pub.

Calaboose Express. large type ed. Marshall Grover. (Linford Western Library). 288p. 1989. pap. 11.95 (*0-7089-6721-3*, Linford) Ulverscroft.

Calamari Cookbook. Joseph Schultz & Beth Regardz. LC 87-10073. 132p. 1987. 9.95 (*0-89087-365-8*) Celestial Arts.

Calamidadien el Caribe: Las Bombas en Puerto Rico. Louise Cripps. Tr. by Blanca L. Paniague. 178p. (SPA.). 1989. pap. 6.96 (*0-942423-02-X*) Borinquen Bks.

Calamities. Jamestown Editorial Group Staff. (Critical Reading Ser.). 158p. (J). (gr. 6-8). 1994. pap. 8.75 (*0-89061-748-1*) Jamestown Pubs.

Calamities, Catastrophies, & Chaos. Peter Popoff. Ed. by Don Tanner. LC 80-69974. (Illus.). 108p. 1980. pap. 2.50 (*0-938544-01-2*) Faith Messenger.

Calamities of Jane. 1993. pap. 5.95 (*1-56201-039-5*) Blue Moon Bks.

***Calamitous Courting of Hetty King.** McHugh. 1995. pap. 3.99 (*0-553-48127-4*) Bantam.

Calamity. Camilla Ashforth. LC 92-54956. (Illus.). 32p. (J). (ps up). 1993. 15.95 (*1-56402-252-8*) Candlewick Pr.

Calamity: A Speak Piece for Mixed Voices. Gerald Kaminski. LC 84-1843. 45p. 1984. pap. 6.95 (*0-931896-04-5*) Cove View.

***Calamity at the Circus.** Jerry Jerman. 132p. 1996. pap. 4.99 (*1-56476-551-2*, 6-3351) SP Pubns.

Calamity in the Caribbean: Puerto Rico & the Bomb. L. L. Cripps. 185p. 1987. pap. 11.95 (*0-87047-035-3*) Schenkman Bks Inc.

***Calamity Jane: A Study in Historical Criticism.** rev. ed. Roberta B. Sollid. LC 94-48732. 256p. 1995. 16.95 (*0-917298-33-0*) MT Hist Soc.

Calamity Jane: Her Life & Her Legend. Doris Faber. LC 91-40050. (Illus.). 80p. (J). (gr. 5-9). 1992. 14.95 (*0-395-56396-8*) HM.

Calamity Jane & the Lady Wildcats. Duncan Aikman. LC 86-25022. (Illus.). xviii, 384p. 1987. reprint ed. pap. 12. 95 (*0-8032-5911-5*) U of Nebr Pr.

Calamity Jane at Fort Sanders. Ron Fontes & Justine Korman. LC 92-52976. (Disney's American Frontier Ser.: Bk. 8). (Illus.). 80p. (J). (gr. 1-4). 1992. lib. bdg. 12. 89 (*1-56282-265-9*); pap. 3.50 (*1-56282-264-0*) Disney Pr.

Calamity Mom. Diana Palmer. (To Mother with Love Ser.). 1993. mass mkt. 4.99 (*0-373-48254-X*, 5-48254-2) Silhouette.

Calamity of the Realm, No. 2: The Commonwealth of Both Nations. Pawel Jasienica. Tr. by Alexander Jordan. LC 92-81364. 1992. write for info. (*1-881284-03-4*) Am Inst Polish.

Calamity Trail. Gary D. Trump. (Illus.). 220p. (Orig.). 1988. pap. 3.95 (*0-944540-05-8*) West Side Bks.

Calamity Trail. 2nd rev. ed. Gary D. Trump. Ed. by Ann Cross. 233p. (Orig.). 1989. reprint ed. pap. 4.95 (*0-9622856-6-8*) Tag Bks.

Calamityville Terror. William Gleason. 73p. 1981. pap. 4.95 (*0-87129-156-8*, C51) Dramatic Pub.

Calamus: A Series of Letters Written During the Years 1868-1880 to a Young Friend (Peter Doyle) Walt Whitman. (American Biography Ser.). 173p. 1991. reprint ed. lib. bdg. 59.00 (*0-7812-8415-5*) Rprt Serv.

Calamus Lovers: Walt Whitman's Working-Class Camerados. Peter Doyle et al. Ed. by Charley Shively. (Illus.). 224p. (Orig.). 1987. lib. bdg. 25.00 (*0-917342-17-8*); pap. 10.00 (*0-917342-18-6*) Gay Sunshine.

Calatrava Berlin: Five Projects funf Projekte. Tr. by John D. Gartrell. LC 93-45912. (Illus.). 1994. 59.50 (*0-8176-2985-8*, Pub. by Birkhauser Vlg SZ) Birkhauser.

Calavar. Robert M. Bird. (Works of Robert Montgomery Bird). 1989. reprint ed. lib. bdg. 79.00 (*0-7812-1988-4*) Rprt Serv.

Calavar; or The Knight of the Conquest: A Romance of Mexico, 2 vols., Set. Robert M. Bird. LC 78-64061. reprint ed. 75.00 (*0-404-17070-6*) AMS Pr.

Calaveras County Illustrated & Described, 1885. Ed. by Charles Clough. (Illus.). 112p. reprint ed. 13.45 (*0-944194-28-1*); reprint ed. pap. 8.95 (*0-944194-27-3*) Linrose Pub.

***Calawba County, North Carolina Will Bk. 1.** Elizabeth B. Sherrill. 126p. (Orig.). 1994. pap. 15.50 (*0-7884-0042-8*) Heritage Bk.

Calbert & His Adventures. Carolee W. Henney. LC 90-83140. (Illus.). 104p. (Orig.). (J). (gr. 2-5). 1990. pap. 9.95 (*0-9626580-0-6*) Aton Pr.

Calbert & His Adventures. deluxe limited ed. Carolee W. Henney. LC 90-83140. (Illus.). 104p. (Orig.). (J). (gr. 2-5). 1990. 24.95 (*0-9626580-1-4*) Aton Pr.

Calc - Spreadsheet Planner: Lab Pack. Diane Roberts & Bonnie Schroeder. (Illus.). 199.95 (*1-56177-095-7*, L394-3); 199.95 (*1-56177-047-7*, L194-3); disk 8.95 (*1-56177-094-9*, D394-3); Apple II 8.95 (*1-56177-046-9*, D194-3) CES Compu-Tech.

Calc - Spreadsheet Planner: Lab Pack. Diane Roberts et al. (Illus.). 5 vols. 1990. student ed, teacher ed 179.95 (*1-56177-145-7*, L494-3) CES Compu-Tech.

Calc I Helper. Robert Miller. 1991. pap. text ed. 8.95 (*0-07-042257-5*) McGraw.

Calc II Helper. Robert Miller. 1991. pap. text ed. 8.95 (*0-07-042258-3*) McGraw.

Calcareous Algae & Stromatolites. Ed. by R. Riding. (Illus.). 544p. 1990. 148.00 (*0-387-52373-1*) Spr-Verlag.

Calcareous Foraminifera in the Brownwood Shale Near Bridgeport, Texas, H. J. Plummer & Foraminifera of the Cisco Group in Texas. J. A. Cushman & J. A. Waters. (Bulletin Ser.: BULL 3019). (Illus.). 90p. 1930. 1.00 (*0-318-03305-4*) Bur Econ Geology.

Calcareous Nannoplankton Biocoenosis: Sediment Trap Studies in the Equatorial Atlantic, Central Pacific, & Panama Basin. John C. Steinmetz. Ed. by Susumu Honjo. (Ocean Biocoenosis Ser.: No. 1). (Illus.). 85p. 1991. pap. text ed. 10.00 (*1-880224-00-3*) Woods Hole Ocean.

Calcification in Biological Systems. Bonucci. 1992. 225.00 (*0-8493-5735-7*, QP535) CRC Pr.

Calcified Tissue. Hukins. 1989. 83.95 (*0-8493-7115-5*, QP88) CRC Pr.

Calciotropic Hormones & Calcium Metabolism. Ed. by M. Cecchettin & G. Sergre. 238p. 1986. 106.25 (*0-444-80771-3*, Excerpta Medica) Elsevier.

Calcitonin Gene-Related Peptide: The First Decade of a Novel Pleiotropic Neuropeptide. Ed. by Yvette Tache et al. LC 92-13110. (Annals Ser.: Vol. 657). 1992. write for info. (*0-89766-713-1*); pap. write for info. (*0-89766-714-X*) NY Acad Sci.

Calcitonin 1984. Ed. by W. Doepfner. 199p. 1987. 88.75 (*0-444-90463-8*) Elsevier.

Calcitonin '84: Chemistry, Physiology, Pharmacology & Clincial Aspects: Proceedings of the International Symposium Calcitonin 1984, Milian, 2-4 October 1984. Ed. by A. Pecile. (International Congress Ser.: No. 663). 498p. 1986. 153.50 (*0-444-80690-3*, Excerpta Medica) Elsevier.

Calcitonine: Fisiologia e Farmacologia. M. Azria. (Illus.). x, 152p. 1990. 78.50 (*3-8055-5088-X*) S Karger.

Calcitonins: Physiology & Pharmacology. M. Azria. (Illus.). x, 152p. 1989. 78.50 (*3-8055-4851-6*) S Karger.

Calcium - Sequestering Cell Organelles: In Situ Localization, Morphological & Functional Characterization. Ed. by Bernd Walz & Otto Baumann. (Progress in Histochemistry & Cytochemistry Ser.: Vol. 20, No. 2). 47p. 1989. pap. text ed. 45.00 (*0-89574-300-0*, Pub. by Gustav Fischer Verlag); pap. text ed. 40.00 (*0-685-31390-5*, Pub. by Gustav Fischer Verlag) VCH Pubs.

Calcium & Cell Function, Vol. 6. Wai Y. Cheung. (Molecular Biology Ser.). 1986. text ed. 143.00 (*0-12-171406-3*) Acad Pr.

Calcium & Cell Function, Vol. 7. Ed. by Wai Y. Cheung. (Molecular Biology Ser.). 182p. 1987. text ed. 124.00 (*0-12-171407-1*) Acad Pr.

Calcium & Cellular Secretion. Ed. by Ronald P. Rubin. LC 82-7489. 288p. 1982. 65.00 (*0-306-40978-X*, Plenum Pr) Plenum.

Calcium & Contractility: Smooth Muscle. Ed. by A. K. Grover & E. E. Daniel. LC 84-28841. (Contemporary Biomedicine Ser.). (Illus.). 512p. 1985. 99.50 (*0-89603-066-0*) Humana.

Calcium & Hypertension. Ed. by C. Gennari & S. G. Massry. (Journal: American Journal of Nephrology: Vol. 6, Suppl. 1, 1986). (Illus.). vi, 166p. 1987. pap. 46.50 (*3-8055-4370-0*) S Karger.

Calcium & Ion Channel Modulation. Ed. by A. D. Grinnell et al. LC 88-5928. (Illus.). 458p. 1988. 115.00 (*0-306-42834-2*, Plenum Pr) Plenum.

Calcium & Its Role in Biology. Helmut Sigel. (Metal Ions in Biological Systems Ser.: Vol. 17). 560p. 1984. 190.00 (*0-8247-7172-9*) Dekker.

***Calcium & Magnesium in Early Life.** Ed. by Reginald Tsang. LC 94-21058. 1995. write for info. (*0-8493-4613-4*) CRC Pr.

Calcium & Phosphorus in Health & Disease. Ed. by John J. Anderson & Sanford C. Garner. (Modern Nutrition Ser.). 432p. 1995. 139.95 (*0-8493-7845-1*, 7845) CRC Pr.

Calcium & the Cell. CIBA Foundation Staff. LC 86-9246. (CIBA Foundation Symposia Ser.: No. 122). 300p. 1986. text ed. 75.00 (*0-471-91088-0*, Wiley-Interscience) Wiley.

Calcium & the Heart. Glenn A. Langer. 400p. 1990. 98.50 (*0-88167-617-9*) Raven.

Calcium & Your Health. Takuo Fujita. LC 87-80495. (Illus.). 144p. 1987. pap. 9.95 (*0-87040-691-4*) Japan Pubns USA.

Calcium Antagonists. H. Lydtin & P. Trenkwalder. (Illus.). 272p. 1989. 70.00 (*0-387-51372-8*, 3257) Spr-Verlag.

An Asterisk (*) at the beginning of an entry indicates that the title is appearing in BIP for the first time.

C

An Asterisk (*) at the beginning of an entry indicates that the title is appearing in BIP for the first time.

989

*Calculations for A-Level Physics. 2nd ed. T. L. Lowe & J. F. Rounce. 452p. (C). 1994. pap. 33.00x (0-7478-1452-X, Pub. by S Thornes Pubs UK) St Mut.

Calculations for Agriculture & Horticulture. Graham Boatfield. Ed. by Iar Hamilton. (Illus.). 120p. pap. 16.95 (0-85236-145-9, Pub. by Farming Pr UK) Diamond Farm Bk.

Calculations for Examination Physics. G. Miller. (C). 1985. text ed. 65.00 (0-85950-212-0, Pub. by S Thornes Pubs UK) St Mut.

Calculations for GCSE Chemistry. E. N. Ramsden. (C). 1987. text ed. 40.00 (0-85950-667-3, Pub. by S Thornes Pubs UK) St Mut.

Calculations for the Electrical Exam. Tom Henry. (Illus.). 297p. (Orig.). (C). 1993. pap. text ed. 28.00 (0-945495-37-4) T Henrys CECB.

Calculations of Medications: Using the Proportion. 2nd ed. Mary A. Scott. 226p. 1989. pap. text ed. 25.95 (0-8385-1019-1, A1019-7) Appleton & Lange.

Calculator-Based Trigonometry with Applications. Newcomb Greenleaf. LC 87-17934. 301p. (C). 1988. text ed. 50.95 (0-534-08178-9) Brooks-Cole.

Calculator Enhancement for Differential Equations. T. Proctor & D. R. LaTorre. (Clemson Calculator Enhancement Ser.). 140p. (C). 1992. pap. text ed. 12.00 (0-03-092730-7) SCP.

Calculator Enhancement for Differential Equations. T. G. Proctor. 105p. (C). 1990. pap. text ed. 8.00 (0-15-505673-5) HB Coll Pubs.

Calculator Enhancement for Introductory Statistics. Iris B. Fetta. 160p. (C). 1990. pap. text ed. 12.00 (0-15-505678-6) Dryden Pr.

Calculator Enhancement for Introductory Statistics. Iris B. Fetta. (Clemson Calculator Enhancement Ser.). 280p. (C). 1992. pap. text ed. 15.00 (0-03-092726-9) SCP.

Calculator Enhancement for Linear Algebra. D. R. LaTorre. 130p. (C). 1990. pap. text ed. 8.00 (0-15-505674-3) HB Coll Pubs.

Calculator Enhancement for Linear Algebra. D. R. LaTorre. (Clemson Calculator Enhancement Ser.). 192p. (C). 1992. pap. text ed. 12.00 (0-03-092729-3) SCP.

Calculator Enhancement for Multivariable Calculus. J. A. Reneke. (Clemson Calculator Enhancement Ser.). 144p. (C). 1992. pap. text ed. 12.00 (0-03-092731-5) SCP.

Calculator Enhancement for Multivariate Calculus. J. A. Reneke. 94p. (C). 1990. pap. text ed. 8.00 (0-15-505675-1) HB Coll Pubs.

Calculator Enhancement for Precalculus. Iris B. Fetta. (Clemson Calculator Enhancement Ser.). 224p. (C). 1992. pap. text ed. 15.00 (0-03-092727-7) SCP.

Calculator Enhancement for Single-Variable Calculus. James H. Nicholson. 99p. (C). 1990. pap. text ed. 8.00 (0-15-505676-X) HB Coll Pubs.

Calculator Enhancement for Single Variable Calculus. James H. Nicholson & John Kenelly. (Clemson Calculator Enhancement Ser.). 196p. (C). 1992. pap. text ed. 12.00 (0-03-092728-5) SCP.

Calculator Explorations & Problems. Don Miller. (J). 1992. pap. 10.95 (0-201-48038-7) Addison-Wesley.

Calculator Explorations & Problems. Don Miller. 108p. (J). (gr. 5-12). 1979. pap. text ed. 10.95 (0-914040-75-8) Cuisenaire.

*Calculator Fun. Wishing Well Staff. Date not set. 9.99 (0-88705-643-1) Joshua Morris.

Calculator Layout: The Numerical Concept, Vol. 1. 2nd rev. ed. Ralph E. Shaeffer. Ed. by Jean Dale. LC 83-90855. (Illus.). 135p. 1991. pap. text ed. 35.95 (0-9611418-2-4) R Shaeffer.

Calculator Layout: The Numerical Concept, Vol. 2. Ralph E. Shaeffer. Ed. by Dennis Gibson. LC 83-90855. (Illus.). 144p. 1989. pap. text ed. 39.95 (0-9611418-1-6) R Shaeffer.

Calculator Logic Systems & Mathematical Understandings. Enid R. Burrows. LC 90-6090. (Illus.). 133p. (Orig.). 1990. pap. 22.50 (0-87353-295-3) NCTM.

*Calculator Mania: 101 Ways to Enjoy a Calculator Without Throwing It. (Planet Dexter's Ser.). (J). 1995. pap. 14.99 (0-201-40932-1) Addison-Wesley.

Calculator Math, 3 vols. Vervoort & Mason. (Makemaster Bk.). (J). (gr. 7-12). 1980. Beginning Grades 5-7. pap. 10.99 (0-8224-1200-4); Intermediate Grades 6-8. pap. 10.99 (0-8224-1201-2); Advanced Grades 8-10. pap. 10.99 (0-8224-1202-0) Fearon Teach Aids.

Calculator Math Problems, Examples & Activities. Kenneth Goldberg. 208p. 1982. 18.95 (0-13-743310-7) P-H.

Calculator Proficiency. Ronald Merchant. 144p. 1989. pap. text ed. 14.95 (0-89863-123-8) Star Pub CA.

Calculator Programs for Chemical Engineers, Vol. 2. Chemical Engineering Magazine Editors. 300p. 1984. text ed. 40.00 (0-07-010849-8) McGraw.

Calculator Programs for Classical Algebra. Charles W. Young. LC 86-28400. 340p. (Orig.). 1987. pap. 19.95 (0-9617321-0-5) C & R Pr.

Calculator Programs for the Health Sciences. J. H. Abramson & E. Peritz. (Illus.). 1983. pap. text ed. 32.50 (0-19-503188-1) OUP.

*Calculator Programs for the Hydrocarbon Processing Industries. fac. ed. S. Jagannath. LC 80-18679. 430p. Date not set. pap. 122.60 (0-7837-7419-2, 2047214) Bks Demand.

Calculator Puzzles, Tricks & Games. Norvin Pallas. 1991. pap. 3.95 (0-486-26670-2) Dover.

Calculator Quest: Exploring Number Concepts. Bright et al. 96p. 1994. pap. 19.95 (0-939765-64-0, G164) Janson Pubns.

*Calculator Riddles. David A Adler. LC 94-41874. (Illus.). 32p. (J). 1995. pap. 12.95 (0-8234-1186-9) Holiday.

*Calculator Tutorial. William L. Merril. (Illus.). 1994. pap. text ed. 8.95 (0-914534-11-4) Stokes.

Calculator View of Essentials of Precalculus Algebra & Trigonometry Using the Casio FX-7700G. 5th ed. Dennis T. Christy & John Paulling. 116p. (C). 1992. spiral bd. write for info. (0-697-17096-9) Wm C Brown Pubs.

Calculator View of Precalculus Using the Casio FX-7700G. 2nd ed. Dennis T. Christy & John Paulling. 116p. (C). 1992. spiral bd. write for info. (0-697-17097-7) Wm C Brown Pubs.

*Calculators. Marion Smoothey. (Let's Investigate Ser.). (Illus.). (YA). 1994. lib. bdg. 16.95 (1-68543-577-7) Marshall Cavendish.

Calculators in Mathematics Education: 1992 Yearbook. Ed. by James T. Fey. LC 91-47745. (Illus.). 248p. 1992. 20.00 (0-87353-342-9) NCTM.

Calculators, Number Patterns, & Magic. Morris Bureloff & Connie Johnson. (Illus.). (J). (gr. 4-12). 1977. pap. text ed. 7.95 (0-918932-49-1) Activity Resources.

Calculi of Symbolic Logic I. Steklov Institute of Mathematics, Academy of Sciences, U. S. S. R. Staff. Ed. by V. P. Orevkov. (Proceedings of the Steklov Institute of Mathematics Ser.: No. 98). 229p. 1971. 62.00 (0-8218-1898-8, STEKLO-98) Am Math.

Calculo de los Precios de Cuenta en la Evaluacion de Proyectos: Estudios de Casos con Base en el Metodo Little-Mirrlees - Squire van der Tak. Ed. by Terry A. Powers. 482p. 1981. write for info. (0-940602-01-6) IADB.

*Calculus. William Adams. 275p. (C). 1995. per., pap. text ed. 29.95 (0-7872-1115-X) Kendall-Hunt.

Calculus. K. G. Binmore. LC 82-19728. (London School of Economics Mathematics Ser.). 450p. 1983. pap. 37.95 (0-521-28952-1) Cambridge U Pr.

Calculus. William E. Boyce & Richard C. DePrima. LC 87-27943. 1055p. 1988. Net. text ed. write for info. (0-471-09333-5) Wiley.

*Calculus. Gerald Bradley & Karl Smith. LC 94-27258. 1995. text ed. 82.00 (0-13-178617-2) P-H.

*Calculus. Thomas P. Dick et al. LC 94-39281. 1995. text ed. 78.95 (0-534-94452-3) PWS Pubs.

Calculus. Scott Farrand & Nancy J. Poxon. (College Outline Ser.). 462p. (C). 1984. pap. text ed. 12.50 (0-15-601556-0) HB Coll Pubs.

Calculus. Ross L. Finney & George B. Thomas, Jr. (Illus.). 1044p. (C). 1990. text ed. 61.25 (0-201-19343-4) Addison-Wesley.

Calculus. Harley Flanders. LC 84-18773. (Illus.). 984p. (C). 1995. text ed. write for info. (0-7167-1643-7) W H Freeman.

Calculus. Leonard Gillman & Robert H. McDowell. (Illus.). (C). 1979. pap. text ed. 8.95 (0-393-09054-X) Norton.

Calculus. Stanley I. Grossman & Richard B. Lane. LC 92-17664. 1993. text ed. 73.25 (0-03-096420-2) SCP.

Calculus. Deborah Hughes-Hallett et al. LC 93-32103. 1993. text ed. 39.50 (0-471-58621-8); pap. text ed. 32.00 (0-471-31055-7) Wiley.

Calculus. Gerald J. Janusz. 768p. (C). 1994. text ed. write for info. (0-697-15374-6) Wm C Brown Pubs.

Calculus. Gerald J. Janusz. 768p. (C). 1994. Solutions manual. write for info. (0-697-16312-1) Wm C Brown Pubs.

Calculus. Lynn H. Loomis. LC 81-14937. (Mathematics Ser.). (Illus.). 1000p. 1982. student ed write for info. (0-201-05046-3) Addison-Wesley.

Calculus. Jack Rudman. (DANTES Ser.: No. 8). 1994. pap. 23.95 (0-8373-6608-9) Nat Learn.

*Calculus. Jack Rudman. (DANTES Ser.: No. 8). 1994. 39.95 (0-8373-6508-2) Nat Learn.

Calculus. John Saxon et al. (C). 1988. 48.00 (0-939798-34-4); teacher ed, disk 200.00 (1-56577-012-9); 17.00 (0-939798-35-2); 39.00 (0-939798-36-0) Saxon Pubs OK.

Calculus. Robert Seeley. 962p. (C). 1990. text ed. 61.25 (0-15-505681-6); disk write for info. (0-318-67040-2); disk write for info. (0-318-67041-0); write for info. (0-318-67042-9) SCP.

Calculus. Gilbert Strang. (Illus.). 672p. (C). 1991. teacher ed 12.50 (0-9614088-3-9); text ed. 57.50 (0-9614088-2-0) Wellesley-Cambridge Pr.

Calculus. Donald Trim. (C). 1993. text ed. 45.00 (0-13-117276-X) P-H.

Calculus. Dennis H. Wortman & Robert Seeley. 962p. (C). 1990. By Dennis H. Wortman. pap. text ed. 18.75 (0-15-505685-9); By Dennis H. Wortman. write for info. (0-15-505682-4) SCP.

Calculus. 2nd ed. Ross L. Finney. (Illus.). 976p. (C). 1994. text ed. 72.25 (0-201-54977-8) Addison-Wesley.

Calculus. 2nd ed. Leonard Gillman & Robert H. McDowell. (Illus.). (C). 1978. text ed. 48.95 (0-393-09051-5) Norton.

Calculus. 2nd ed. Leonard I. Holder et al. LC 94-6514. 1994. text ed. 75.95 (0-534-23304-X) Brooks-Cole.

Calculus. 2nd ed. Richard A. Hunt. (C). 1994. text ed. 78.50 (0-06-043046-X) HarpCollege.

Calculus. 2nd ed. M. A. Munem & D. J. Foulis. LC 83-50583. (Illus.). 1048p. 1984. text ed. 69.95x (0-87901-236-6); Brief ed., 738p. text ed. 59.95x (0-87901-254-4) Worth.

Calculus. 2nd ed. James Stewart. 1056p. (C). 1991. text ed. 74.95 (0-534-13212-X) Brooks-Cole.

Calculus. 3rd ed. Dennis D. Berkey & Paul Blanchard. 1200p. (C). 1992. teacher ed write for info. (0-03-076153-0); text ed. 73.25 (0-03-046927-9); text ed. 56.00 (0-03-076154-9) SCP.

Calculus. 3rd ed. Ralph L. Jeffery. 307p. reprint ed. pap. 87.50 (0-8357-7969-6, 2014259) Bks Demand.

Calculus. 3rd ed. Lynn H. Loomis. LC 81-14937. (Mathematics Ser.). (Illus.). 1000p. (C). 1982. text ed. 73.25 (0-201-05045-5) Addison-Wesley.

*Calculus. 3rd ed. Michael Spivak. (Illus.). xiv, 670p. (C). 1994. text ed. 50.00x (0-914098-89-6) Publish or Perish.

*Calculus. 3rd ed. James Stewart. LC 94-29764. 1120p. (C). 1995. text ed. 75.95 (0-534-21798-2) Brooks-Cole.

Calculus. 3rd ed. Dennis Zill. 1051p. (C). 1992. text ed. 78.95 (0-534-92793-9) PWS Pubs.

Calculus. 4th ed. Stanley I. Grossman. 896p. (C). 1988. text ed. 64.00 (0-15-505759-6); Instr's. sol. manual. teacher ed 16.75 (0-15-505761-8) SCP.

Calculus. 4th ed. Protter. 1000p. (C). 1988. boxed 30.00 (0-86720-093-6); 12.50 (0-86720-174-6); 13.75 (0-86720-115-0) Jones & Bartlett.

Calculus. 5th ed. Marvin L. Bittinger. (Illus.). 560p. (C). 1992. text ed. 58.25 (0-201-53056-2) Addison-Wesley.

Calculus. 5th ed. Earl W. Swokowski. 1168p. (C). 1991. text ed. 78.95 (0-534-92492-1) PWS Pubs.

*Calculus. 6th ed. Marvin L. Bittinger. LC 95-12150. (C). 1996. text ed. write for info. (0-201-59338-6) Addison-Wesley.

Calculus. 6th ed. Earl W. Swokowski et al. LC 93-35389. (Series in Calculus & Upper-Division Mathematics). 1994. text ed. 78.95 (0-534-93624-5) PWS Pubs.

Calculus. Gordon M. Peterson & R. F. Graesser. (Quality Paperback Ser.: No. 51). 321p. (Orig.). 1974. reprint ed. pap. 7.95 (0-8226-0051-X) Littlefield.

Calculus. Atherton H. Sprague. LC 52-6205. 587p. reprint ed. 167.30 (0-8357-9850-X, 2012416) Bks Demand.

Calculus, 1. 2nd ed. M. A. Munem & D. J. Foulis. LC 83-50583. (Illus.). 1984. student ed 11.95x (0-87901-237-4) Worth.

Calculus, 1. 4th ed. Protter. 1000p. (C). 1988. 12.50 (0-86720-111-8) Jones & Bartlett.

Calculus, 2. 2nd ed. M. A. Munem & D. J. Foulis. LC 83-50583. (Illus.). 1984. student ed 11.95x (0-87901-253-6) Worth.

*Calculus, No. 111. Anthony Nicolaides. (C). 1990. pap. 39.95x (1-872684-12-2, Pub. by P A S S Pubns UK) St Mut.

Calculus, Pt. 1. Ross L. Finney & George B. Thomas, Jr. (Illus.). 1044p. (C). 1990. student ed, pap. text ed. 18.25 (0-201-19346-9) Addison-Wesley.

Calculus, Pt. 2. Ross L. Finney & George B. Thomas, Jr. (Illus.). 1044p. (C). 1990. Student study guide, Pt. II. student ed, pap. text ed. 16.25 (0-201-53246-8) Addison-Wesley.

Calculus: A First Course. Ransom V. Lynch & Donald R. Ostberg. LC 82-23300. 704p. (C). 1983. reprint ed. text ed. 49.50 (0-89874-597-7) Krieger.

Calculus: A Graphing Approach. Ross L. Finney. (Illus.). 1040p. (C). 1994. text ed. 69.95 (0-201-56901-9) Addison-Wesley.

Calculus: A Graphing Approach, Preliminary,, Pt. I. Ross L. Finney et al. (Illus.). 400p. (C). 1993. pap. text ed. 16.25 (0-201-56903-5) Addison-Wesley.

Calculus: A Modeling Approach. 3rd ed. Marvin L. Bittinger. LC 83-6334. (Illus.). 544p. 1984. write for info. (0-201-11217-5); teacher ed write for info. (0-201-11219-1); student ed write for info. (0-201-11218-3) Addison-Wesley.

Calculus: A Modeling Approach. 4th ed. Marvin L. Bittinger. (Illus.). 560p. (C). 1988. text ed. 56.95 (0-201-12216-2) Addison-Wesley.

Calculus: A Practical Approach. 2nd ed. Kenneth Kalmanson & Patricia C. Kenschaft. LC 77-81756. (Illus.). 429p. (C). 1978. text ed. 59.95x (0-87901-083-5) Worth.

Calculus: A Short Course with Applications. 2nd ed. Gerald Freilich & Frederick P. Greenleaf. 436p. (C). 1985. text ed. 56.00 (0-15-505746-4) SCP.

Calculus: An Historical Approach. W. M. Priestley. (Undergraduate Texts in Mathematics Ser.). (Illus.). 1984. 39.00 (0-387-90349-6) Spr-Verlag.

Calculus: An Integrated Approach. Donald B. Small & John M. Hosack. 768p. (C). 1990. teacher ed write for info. (0-318-65613-2); text ed. write for info. (0-07-058264-5) McGraw.

Calculus: An Introduction to Applied Mathematics. 2nd ed. Harvey P. Greenspan et al. 1986. text ed. write for info. (0-07-082101-1) McGraw.

*Calculus: Derive Calculus Workbook. Kulich & Victor. (C). 1994. text ed. 16.50 (0-673-99455-4) HarpCollege.

Calculus: Differential & Integral-Combined Syllabus. Lloyd B. Williams & Allan W. Gray. 1976. text ed. 12.95 (0-89420-059-3, 122210); audio 140.95 (0-89420-130-1, 350500) Natl Book.

Calculus: Differential Syllabus, Pt. 1. Lloyd B. Williams & Allan W. Gray. 1976. text ed. 9.25 (0-89420-057-7, 122202); audio 89.20 (0-89420-131-X, 350510) Natl Book.

*Calculus: Early Transcendental Functions. Roland E. Larson et al. 1128p. (C). 1995. text ed. write for info. (0-669-39349-5) Heath.

*Calculus: Early Transcendentals. 3rd ed. James Stewart. LC 94-32714. 1120p. 1995. text ed. 75.95 (0-534-25158-7) Brooks-Cole.

Calculus: Early Transcendentals Version. 2nd ed. James Stewart. 1104p. (C). 1991. text ed. 74.95 (0-534-13830-6) Brooks-Cole.

Calculus: Graphical, Numerical, Algebraic, of a Single Variable. Ross L. Finney et al. LC 93-37037. 962p. (C). 1994. text ed. 59.25 (0-201-56902-7) Addison-Wesley.

Calculus: Integral Syllabus, Pt. 2. Lloyd B. Williams & Allan W. Gray. 1976. text ed. 6.75 (0-89420-058-5, 122208); audio 56.70 (0-89420-132-8, 350516) Natl Book.

Calculus: Late Trigonometry Version. 5th ed. Earl W. Swokowski. 1184p. 1992. text ed. 78.95 (0-534-92937-0) PWS Pubs.

Calculus: Multi-Variable Calculus & Linear Algebra with Applications, Vol. 2. 2nd ed. Tom M. Apostol. LC 67-14605. 673p. (C). 1969. Net. text ed. write for info. (0-471-00007-8) Wiley.

Calculus: One & Several Variables. Robert Ellis & Denny Gulick. 1133p. (C). 1990. text ed. 40.00 (0-15-505692-1) SCP.

Calculus: One & Several Variables. 6th ed. Santurnino L. Salas. 1232p. 1990. Net. text ed. write for info. (0-471-61195-6); Net. write for info. (0-471-61198-0) Wiley.

Calculus: One-Variable Calculus with an Introduction to Linear Algebra, Vol. 1. 2nd ed. Tom M. Apostol. LC 73-20899. 666p. (C). 1967. Net. text ed. write for info. (0-471-00005-1) Wiley.

Calculus: Preliminary Edition. Deborah Hughes-Hallett et al. 743p. 1992. Net. pap. text ed. write for info. (0-471-57723-5) Wiley.

Calculus: Pure & Applied. A. J. Sherlock et al. (Illus.). 534p. (Orig.). 1982. pap. text ed. 19.95 (0-7131-3446-1, Pub. by E Arnold UK) Routledge Chapman & Hall.

Calculus: Single Variable. 6th ed. Santurnino L. Salas & Einar Hille. 800p. 1990. Net. text ed. write for info. (0-471-61626-5) Wiley.

*Calculus: Visual Calculus. Scheider. (C). 1993. text ed. 15.50 (0-673-99015-X) HarpCollege.

Calculus: With Analytic Geometry. Edward M. Pease & George P. Wadsworth. LC 68-56150. 1087p. reprint ed. pap. 180.00 (0-8357-7971-8, 2012457) Bks Demand.

Calculus Activities for Graphic Calculators. Dennis Pence. 280p. (C). 1990. pap. 27.95 (0-534-92431-X) PWS Pubs.

Calculus Activities for Graphic Calculators. 2nd ed. Dennis Pence. 1994. pap. 27.95 (0-534-93267-3) PWS Pubs.

Calculus Activities for the TI-81 Graphic Calculator. Dennis Pence. 280p. (C). 1992. pap. 22.95 (0-534-92709-2) PWS Pubs.

Calculus Affair. Herge. (Illus.). 62p. (J). 19.95 (0-8288-5014-3) Fr & Eur.

Calculus Algebra Laboratories Using Derive. Phil DeMarois. 120p. (Orig.). (C). 1992. pap. text ed. 16.95 (0-9623629-1-3) MathWare.

Calculus & Analytic Geometry. Lynn E. Garner. (C). 1988. text ed. write for info. (0-02-340590-2) Macmillan.

Calculus & Analytic Geometry. H. Schachter. 1972. text ed. 46.95 (0-07-055056-5) McGraw.

Calculus & Analytic Geometry. alternate ed. Douglas F. Riddle. 1110p. (C). 1984. text ed. 78.95 (0-534-01198-5) PWS Pubs.

Calculus & Analytic Geometry. 2nd ed. C. H. Edwards, Jr. & David E. Penney. (Illus.). 1088p. (C). 1986. text ed. write for info. (0-318-59385-8) P-H.

Calculus & Analytic Geometry. 3rd ed. Henry Edwards & David E. Penney. 1216p. (C). 1989. text ed. write for info. (0-13-111204-X) P-H.

Calculus & Analytic Geometry. 3rd ed. Philip W. Gillett. LC 87-81231. 965p. (C). 1988. text ed. 44.50 (0-669-13100-8); text ed. write for info. (0-318-62455-9); Selected solutions. 11.50 (0-669-13104-0) Heath.

Calculus & Analytic Geometry. 4th ed. Douglas F. Riddle. 1172p. (C). 1984. text ed. 78.95 (0-534-01468-2) PWS Pubs.

Calculus & Analytic Geometry. 5th ed. Sherman K. Stein & Anthony Barcellos. 1992. text ed. write for info. (0-07-061175-0) McGraw.

Calculus & Analytic Geometry. 5th ed. George B. Thomas, Jr. & Ross L. Finney. LC 78-55832. (Illus.). 1979. student ed write for info. (0-201-07543-1); student ed write for info. (0-201-07655-1) Addison-Wesley.

Calculus & Analytic Geometry. 6th ed. George B. Thomas, Jr. & Ross L. Finney. LC 83-2569. (Illus.). 1100p. 1984. write for info. (0-201-16290-3) Addison-Wesley.

*Calculus & Analytic Geometry. 9th ed. George B. Thomas & Ross L. Finney. LC 94-30543. (C). 1996. text ed. write for info. (0-201-53174-7) Addison-Wesley.

Calculus & Analytic Geometry, 1. 7th ed. George B. Thomas, Jr. & Ross L. Finney. LC 87-14422. (Illus.). 1136p. (C). 1988. text ed. 61.25 (0-201-16321-7) Addison-Wesley.

Calculus & Analytic Geometry, I. 4th ed. Al Shenk. (C). 1987. text ed. 61.50 (0-673-16725-9) HarpCollege.

Calculus & Analytic Geometry, II. 4th ed. Al Shenk. (C). 1987. text ed. 56.50 (0-673-16726-7) HarpCollege.

Calculus & Analytic Geometry, Pt. 1. George B. Thomas, Jr. & Ross L. Finney. LC 78-55832. (Illus.). 1979. 24.95 (0-201-07541-5) Addison-Wesley.

Calculus & Analytic Geometry, Pt. I. 8th ed. George B. Thomas, Jr. & Ross L. Finney. (Illus.). 750p. (C). 1992. text ed. 62.50 (0-201-53286-7) Addison-Wesley.

Calculus & Analytic Geometry, Pt. 2. George B. Thomas, Jr. & Ross L. Finney. LC 78-55832. (Illus.). 1979. 26.95 (0-201-07542-3) Addison-Wesley.

Calculus & Analytic Geometry, Pt. II. 8th ed. George B. Thomas, Jr. & Ross L. Finney. (Illus.). 750p. (C). 1992. text ed. 41.95 (0-201-53287-5) Addison-Wesley.

Calculus & Analytic Geometry, Set. 7th ed. George B. Thomas, Jr. & Ross L. Finney. LC 87-14422. (Illus.). 1136p. (C). 1988. text ed. 73.25 (0-201-16320-9) Addison-Wesley.

Calculus & Analytic Geometry, Set. 8th ed. George B. Thomas, Jr. & Ross L. Finney. (Illus.). 976p. (C). 1992. text ed. 73.25 (0-201-52929-7) Addison-Wesley.

Calculus & Analytic Geometry, Vol. I. 3rd ed. Philip W. Gillett. LC 87-81231. 424p. (C). 1988. text ed. 12.50 (0-669-13101-6) Heath.

Calculus & Analytic Geometry, Vol. II. 3rd ed. Philip W. Gillett. LC 87-81231. 356p. (C). 1988. text ed. 12.50 (0-669-13102-4) Heath.

Calculus & Analytic Geometry, Vol. III. 3rd ed. Philip W. Gillett. LC 87-81231. 371p. (C). 1988. text ed. 12.50 (0-669-13103-2) Heath.

Calculus & Analytic Geometry: Brief Version. 5th ed. Sherman K. Stein & Anthony Barcellos. 1992. text ed. write for info. (0-07-061199-8) McGraw.

C

An Asterisk (*) at the beginning of an entry indicates that the title is appearing in BIP for the first time.

An Asterisk (*) at the beginning of an entry indicates that the title is appearing in BIP for the first time.

*Calculus Reader, 3 vols., Vol. I. rev. ed. David A. Smith & Lawrence C. Moore. 428p. (C). 1994. text ed. write for info. (0-669-33303-4) Heath.

*Calculus Reader, 3 vols., Vol. II. rev. ed. David A. Smith & Lawrence C. Moore. 360p. (C). 1994. text ed. write for info. (0-669-35386-8) Heath.

*Calculus Reader, 3 vols., Vol. III. rev. ed. David A. Smith & Lawrence C. Moore. 290p. (C). 1994. text ed. write for info. (0-669-35387-6) Heath.

Calculus Refresher for Technical People. A. Albert Klaf. 1957. pap. text ed. 7.95 (0-486-20370-0) Dover.

Calculus Review for Engineers, Vols. 1 & 2. David Ullrich. (Illus.). 648p. (Orig.). (C). 1991. pap. text ed. 50.00 (1-56049-018-7) NCSU CE IES.

Calculus Single Variable. 2nd ed. Richard A. Hunt. (C). 1994. text ed. 46.00 (0-673-46927-1) HarpCollege.

Calculus Single Variable. 2nd ed. Richard A. Hunt. (C). 1994. Solutions manual. 18.50 (0-06-501450-2) HarpCollege.

Calculus Single Variable with Analytic Geometry. 6th ed. Louis Leithold. 900p. (C). 1990. text ed. 74.50 (0-06-043930-0) HarpCollege.

*Calculus: Student Solution Manual. Deborah Hughes-Hallett et al. 1994. pap. text ed. write for info. (0-471-04645-0) Wiley.

Calculus T - L. J. Douglas Child. (C). 1990. disk, pap. text ed. 59.95 (0-534-11815-1) Brooks-Cole.

Calculus T - L II. rev. ed. J. Douglas Child. 1993. disk, pap. text ed. 69.95 (0-534-17341-1) Brooks-Cole.

Calculus the Easy Way. 2nd ed. Douglas Downing. (Easy Way Ser.). (Illus.). 320p. 1988. pap. 10.95 (0-8120-4078-3) Barron.

Calculus Three Exam File. Ed. by David R. Arterburn. (Exam File Ser.). 282p. (Orig.). 1986. pap. 14.50 (0-910554-63-3) Engineering.

Calculus Tutoring Book. Carol Ash & Robert B. Ash. 533p. 1986. pap. 34.95 (0-7803-1044-6) Inst Electrical.

Calculus Tutoring Book. Robert Ash & Carol Ash. LC 85-23049. 544p. 1986. 44.95 (0-87942-183-5, PC01776) Inst Electrical.

Calculus Two Exam File. Ed. by David R. Arterburn. (Exam File Ser.). 282p. (Orig.). 1986. pap. 14.50 (0-910554-62-5) Engineering.

C

Calculus Unveiled. Annette Sinclair. (Illus.). 192p. 1994. text ed. 24.50 (0-931541-53-0) Mancorp Pub.

Calculus Using Mathematica. Keith D. Stroyan. (Illus.). 270p. 1993. Macintosh pkg. mac hd 59.95 (0-12-672976-X); IBM/DOS pkg. 59.95 (0-12-672977-8); NeXT pkg. 59.95 (0-12-672978-6) Acad Pr.

Calculus Using Mathematica: Scientific Projects & Mathematical Background. Keith D. Stroyan. LC 93-29546. 1993. pap. text ed. 9.95 (0-12-672975-1) Acad Pr.

Calculus Virgin: An Artist's View of the Language of Calculus. D'Arcy Hayman & Louis Leithold. (Illus.). 128p. (Orig.). 1992. pap. 14.75 (0-9632435-1-9) Tortue Pubns.

Calculus with Analytic Geometry. Karen Benbury & Rebecca Lee. LC 92-53287. (College Outline Ser.). 448p. (C). 1993. pap. 13.00 (0-06-467161-5, Harper Ref) HarpC.

Calculus with Analytic Geometry. Richard H. Crowell & William E. Slesnick. (Illus.). (C). 1968. text ed. 35.95 (0-393-09782-X) Norton.

Calculus with Analytic Geometry. John B. Fraleigh. LC 79-18693. (Illus.). 1980. text ed. write for info. (0-201-03041-1); student ed write for info. (0-201-03042-X); write for info. (0-318-50135-X) Addison-Wesley.

Calculus with Analytic Geometry. Leonard I. Holder. 839p. (C). 1988. text ed. 72.95 (0-534-08202-5) PWS Pubs.

Calculus with Analytic Geometry. Mervin L. Keedy et al. 1050p. (C). 1987. teacher ed write for info. (0-201-15043-3); text ed. write for info. (0-201-15040-9); student ed write for info. (0-201-15041-7) Addison-Wesley.

Calculus with Analytic Geometry. Joseph Repka. (Illus.). 1344p. (C). 1993. text ed. write for info. (0-697-06918-4) Wm C Brown Pubs.

Calculus with Analytic Geometry. Joseph Repka. (Illus.). 1344p. (C). 1993. Calculator View of Calculus Using the TI-81, TI-85. write for info. (0-697-16777-1); Calculator View of Calculus Using the Casio. write for info. (0-697-16778-X); Calculator View of Calculus Using the HP486. write for info. (0-697-21296-3) Wm C Brown Pubs.

Calculus with Analytic Geometry. Joseph Repka. (Illus.). 1344p. (C). 1994. Solutions manual, Part 1. write for info. (0-697-11365-5); Solutions manual, Part 2. write for info. (0-697-12197-6) Wm C Brown Pubs.

Calculus with Analytic Geometry. Richard Silverman. (Illus.). 448p. 1985. student ed (0-13-111642-8) P-H.

Calculus with Analytic Geometry. George F. Simmons. LC 84-14359. 1056p. 1985. text ed. write for info. (0-07-057419-7) McGraw.

Calculus with Analytic Geometry. Arthur B. Simon. (C). 1982. text ed. 67.50 (0-673-16044-0) HarpCollege.

Calculus with Analytic Geometry. 2nd ed. John B. Fraleigh. LC 79-18693. (C). 1985. text ed. write for info. (0-201-12010-0); write for info. (0-201-12011-9) Addison-Wesley.

Calculus with Analytic Geometry. 2nd ed. Nathan O. Niles & George E. Haborak. (Illus.). 640p. 1982. text ed. write for info. (0-13-112011-5) P-H.

Calculus with Analytic Geometry. 3rd ed. John B. Fraleigh. (Illus.). 953p. (C). 1990. write for info. (0-201-50366-2); text ed. 73.25 (0-201-50363-8) Addison-Wesley.

Calculus with Analytic Geometry, 3 vols. 3rd ed. Roland E. Larson & Robert P. Hostetler. LC 85-80719. 1013p. (C). 1986. text ed. 45.50 (0-669-09568-0); Study & soln. guide. student ed 12.00 (0-669-10098-6); Transparencies. trans. 50.00 (0-669-10102-8); Vol. I, sol. guide. 10.50 (0-669-10099-4); Vol. II, sol. guide. 10.50 (0-669-10100-1); Vol. III, sol. guide. 10.50 (0-669-10101-X) Heath.

Calculus with Analytic Geometry, 2 vols. 3rd ed. Louis Leithold. (C). 1976. (0-06-363953-X); write for info. (0-06-363954-8) HarpCollege.

Calculus with Analytic Geometry. 3rd ed. Edwin J. Purcell. (Illus.). 1978. 36.95 (0-13-112052-2); Solutions manual. pap. 6.95 (0-13-112037-9); Linear algebra supp. pap. text ed. write for info. (0-13-112029-8) P-H.

Calculus with Analytic Geometry. 4th ed. Howard Anton. 1408p. (C). 1991. Net. text ed. write for info. (0-471-50901-9) Wiley.

*Calculus with Analytic Geometry. 4th ed. Howard Anton & Albert Herr. 1994. text ed. write for info. (0-471-10771-9) Wiley.

Calculus with Analytic Geometry. 4th ed. C. H. Edwards, Jr. & David E. Penney. LC 93-41257. 1994. text ed. write for info. (0-13-457912-7) P-H Gen Ref & Trav.

Calculus with Analytic Geometry. 4th ed. Roland E. Larson et al. 1083p. (C). 1993. text ed. write for info. (0-669-16406-2); Study & solutions guide. write for info. (0-669-16407-0); Complete solutions guide, Vol. I. write for info. (0-669-16408-9); Solutions, Vol. II. write for info. (0-669-16409-7); Solutions, Vol. III. write for info. (0-669-16411-9); Test item file. write for info. (0-669-21828-6); Computer Projects for Calculus. write for info. (0-669-28499-8) Heath.

Calculus with Analytic Geometry, 2 vols. 4th ed. Louis Leithold. (C). 1981. write for info. (0-06-363958-0); Set, 2 vols. in 1. text ed. 34.00 (0-06-043935-1) HarpCollege.

*Calculus with Analytic Geometry. 5th alternate ed. Roland E. Larson & Robert P. Hostetler. 1123p. (C). 1994. text ed. write for info. (0-669-34227-0) Heath.

*Calculus with Analytic Geometry. 5th ed. Howard Anton. 1994. text ed. 70.95 (0-471-07653-8) Wiley.

*Calculus with Analytic Geometry. 5th ed. Howard Anton. 1994. text ed. 84.95 (0-471-59495-4) Wiley.

Calculus with Analytic Geometry. 5th ed. A. W. Goodman. (Illus.). (C). 1993. text ed. 49.50 (0-931541-29-8) Mancorp Pub.

*Calculus with Analytic Geometry. 5th ed. Roland E. Larson et al. 1127p. (C). 1994. text ed. write for info. (0-669-35335-3) Heath.

Calculus with Analytic Geometry. 6th ed. Louis Leithold. 1400p. (C). 1990. text ed. 81.50 (0-06-044107-0) HarpCollege.

Calculus with Analytic Geometry. 6th ed. Dale E. Varberg & Edwin J. Purcell. 944p. (C). 1991. text ed. write for info. (0-13-117755-9) P-H.

Calculus with Analytic Geometry: A First Course. 3rd ed. Murray H. Protter & Charles B. Morrey, Jr. LC 76-12801. (Mathematics Ser.). (C). 1977. teacher ed write for info. (0-201-06031-0); text ed. 34.36 (0-201-06037-X); student ed write for info. (0-318-50136-8) Addison-Wesley.

*Calculus with Analytic Geometry: A Problem Solving & Graphical Approach. Ravindra N. Kalia. 200p. (C). 1996. pap. text ed. write for info. (0-9638155-2-0) Global Pubng.

Calculus with Analytic Geometry: Alternate Edition. 2nd ed. Earl W. Swokowski. 1089p. (C). 1988. text ed. 78.95 (0-87150-008-6) PWS Pubs.

Calculus with Analytic Geometry: Brief Edition. 4th ed. Sherman K. Stein. 768p. 1987. text ed. write for info. (0-07-061162-9) McGraw.

Calculus with Analytic Geometry: Early Transcendentals Version. 4th ed. C. H. Edwards, Jr. & David E. Penney. LC 94-1432. 1994. text ed. write for info. (0-13-300575-5); pap. text ed. 35.00 (0-13-300591-7) P-H.

Calculus with Analytic Geometry: Student Solutions Manual. 2nd ed. John B. Fraleigh. (C). 1985. write for info. (0-201-12012-7) Addison-Wesley.

*Calculus with Analytic Geometry: With Calculus Companion-Vol. 1, Student Solutions Manual, & Discovering Calculus with Derivatives. 4th ed. Howard Anton et al. 61994p. 1994. text ed. write for info. (0-471-10772-7) Wiley.

*Calculus with Analytic Geometry: With Maple Discovering Calculus & Students Solutions Manual. 4th ed. Howard Anton et al. 1994. text ed. write for info. (0-471-10168-0) Wiley.

*Calculus with Analytic Geometry Vol. 1. 4th ed. Howard Anton et al. 1994. text ed. write for info. (0-471-10621-6) Wiley.

Calculus with Analytic Geometry Alternate with Late Trigonometry. 4th alternate ed. Roland E. Larson & Robert P. Hostetler. 1113p. (C). 1990. text ed. 44.50 (0-669-17843-8); Instr.'s guide. teacher ed 2.00 (0-669-21738-7); Transparencies. trans. 60.00 (0-669-16412-7); Study & solutions guide. 12.00 (0-669-17844-6); Complete Solutions Guide, Vol. I. 10.50 (0-669-17845-4); Solutions, Vol. II. 10.50 (0-669-17846-2); Solutions, Vol. III. 10.50 (0-669-17847-0); Test item file. 2.00 (0-669-21817-0) Heath.

*Calculus with Analytic Geometry & Students Solutions Manual to Accompany Anton Set. 4th ed. Howard Anton. 1993. text ed. write for info. (0-471-01992-5) Wiley.

Calculus with Analytic Geometry, Brief Edition. 4th ed. Howard Anton. 1008p. (C). 1991. Net. text ed. write for info. (0-471-54805-7) Wiley.

Calculus with Analytic Geometry for the Technologies. Lawrence M. Clar & James A. Hart. (Technological Mathematics Ser.). (Illus.). 1980. text ed. write for info. (0-13-111856-0) P-H.

Calculus with Analytical Geometry. Jack Rudman. (College Level Examination Ser.: CLEP-43). 1994. 39.95 (0-8373-5393-9); pap. 23.95 (0-8373-5343-2) Nat Learn.

Calculus with Analytical Geometry. 4th ed. Robert Ellis & Denny Gulick. 996p. (C). 1990. write for info. (0-318-67039-9); text ed. 66.50 (0-15-505687-5); pap. text ed. 28.50 (0-15-505689-1); student ed, pap. text ed. 18.75 (0-15-505691-3); disk write for info. (0-318-67037-2); disk write for info. (0-318-67038-0); 5.00 (0-15-505688-3) HB Coll Pubs.

Calculus with Analytical Geometry: Late Trigonometry Version. 3rd ed. Howard Anton. LC 88-23349. 752p. 1989. Net. text ed. write for info. (0-471-62211-7); write for info. (0-471-50263-4) Wiley.

Calculus with Application to the Management, Social, Behaviorial & Biomedical Sciences. Geoffrey Berresford. 608p. (C). 1988. Casebound. boxed, text ed. write for info. (0-13-110628-7) P-H.

Calculus with Applications. Daniel L. Auvil. LC 81-14914. 1982. student ed write for info. (0-201-10064-9) Addison-Wesley.

Calculus with Applications. James L. Burgmeier et al. 640p. (C). 1990. teacher ed write for info. (0-318-65085-1); student ed 19.95 (0-07-557357-1) McGraw.

Calculus with Applications. James L. Burgmeier et al. 700p. (C). 1989. text ed. write for info. (0-394-36277-2) Random.

Calculus with Applications. Ronald J. Harshbarger & James J. Reynolds. 800p. (C). Instr.'s guide. teacher ed write for info. (0-669-32636-4); Study & Solutions guide. write for info. (0-669-32637-2); Test item file. write for info. (0-669-32639-9) Heath.

Calculus with Applications. Ronald J. Harshbarger & James J. Reynolds. LC 89-85548. 752p. (C). 1990. teacher ed 2.00 (0-669-21148-6); text ed. 37.00 (0-669-21145-1); 7.50 (0-669-21146-X); 2.00 (0-669-21429-9) Heath.

Calculus with Applications. Claudia Taylor & Lawrence Gilligan. 700p. (C). 1989. text ed. 62.95 (0-534-10272-7) Brooks-Cole.

Calculus with Applications. Rosario Urso. LC 94-1803. 1994. write for info. (0-07-066651-2) McGraw.

Calculus with Applications. Dale E. Varberg & Walter Fleming. 496p. (C). 1991. text ed. write for info. (0-13-110826-3) P-H.

Calculus with Applications. 2nd ed. Ronald J. Harshbarger & James J. Reynolds. 800p. (C). text ed. write for info. (0-669-32635-6) Heath.

Calculus with Applications. 2nd ed. Karl J. Smith. 496p. (C). 1992. text ed. 62.95 (0-534-16884-1) Brooks-Cole.

Calculus with Applications. 4th ed. Margaret L. Lial & Charles D. Miller. (C). 1988. text ed. 43.75 (0-673-38251-6) HarpCollege.

Calculus with Applications. 5th abr. ed. Margaret L. Lial et al. LC 92-27441. (C). 1992. 47.00 (0-673-46725-2) HarpCollege.

Calculus with Applications. 5th ed. Margaret L. Lial et al. LC 92-27440. (C). 1992. 48.00 (0-673-46726-0) HarpCollege.

Calculus with Applications: Brief Version. 4th ed. Margaret L. Lial & Charles D. Miller. (C). 1989. text ed. 42.75 (0-673-38465-9) HarpCollege.

Calculus with Applications & Computing, Vol. 1. Peter D. Lax et al. (Illus.). 600p. 1983. 51.00 (0-387-90179-5) Spr-Verlag.

Calculus with Applications for Business & the Social & Natural Sciences. Chester Piascik. Ed. by Pullins. LC 92-29638. 900p. (C). 1993. text ed. 66.00 (0-314-01270-2) West Pub.

Calculus with Applications to Management, Economics, & the Social & Natural Sciences. Chester Piascik. 500p. (C). 1987. write for info. (0-675-20440-2, Merrill Pub Co) Macmillan.

Calculus with Applications to the Management, Life & Social Sciences. Charles L. Vanden Eynden & Lawrence E. Spence. (C). 1990. text ed. 61.50 (0-673-18838-8) HarpCollege.

Calculus, with Computer Applications. Ransom V. Lynch et al. LC 72-86514. 975p. reprint ed. pap. 180.00 (0-8357-7972-6, 2055979) Bks Demand.

Calculus with Elementary Functions (Introductory Calculus). Jack Rudman. (College Level Examination Ser.: CLEP-21). 1994. 39.95 (0-8373-5371-8); pap. 23.95 (0-8373-5321-1) Nat Learn.

Calculus with Hewlett Packard Symbol Manipulating Calculator HP-285 & HP-48SX. Lynn E. Garner. (Illus.). 120p. (Orig.). (C). 1990. pap. write for info. (0-02-340599-6) Dellen Pub.

Calculus with Maple V. John S. Devitt. LC 93-10291. 1993. pap. 27.95 (0-534-16362-9) Brooks-Cole.

Calculus with MathCAD. R. J. Miech. 183p. (C). 1991. pap. 27.95 (0-534-15481-6) PWS Pubs.

*Calculus with the Hewlett-Packard 48. 3rd ed. Lynn E. Garner. (Illus.). 160p. 1994. pap. write for info. (0-02-340585-6, Merrill Pub Co) Macmillan.

Calculus Workbook Using Maple. Loren N. Argabright & Robert C. Busby. 128p. (C). 1993. pap. text ed., spiral bd. 14.95 (0-8403-8993-0) Kendall-Hunt.

Calcutta. (Insight Guides Ser.). 1993. pap. 21.95 (0-395-66323-7) HM.

Calcutta. Ed. by Martha Hanna. (Illus.). 72p. (C). 1993. pap. 30.00 (0-88884-563-4, Pub. by CN Mus Contemporary Photo CN) U Ch Pr.

Calcutta: An Annotated Bibliography. Amalendu Ray. 1990. 17.50 (0-8364-2626-6, Pub. by Asiatic Bk Agency JA) S Asia.

Calcutta: The Home & the Street. Photos by Raghubir Singh. LC 88-50224. (Illus.). 112p. 1988. 45.00 (0-500-24133-3) Thames Hudson.

Calcutta: The Living City, Vol. I: The Past. Ed. by Sukanta Chaudhuri. (Illus.). 232p. 1991. 65.00 (0-19-562585-4) OUP.

Calcutta: The Living City, Vol. II: The Present & the Future. Ed. by Sukanta Chaudhuri. (Illus.). 400p. 1991. 65.00 (0-19-562586-2) OUP.

Calcutta: The Profile of a City. Nisith R. Ray. 1986. 11.50 (0-317-56328-9, Pub. by KP Bagchi IA) S Asia.

Calcutta Cycle Rickshaw Pullers: A Sociological Study. Subir Bandyopadhyay. 1990. 14.50 (81-85195-27-7, Pub. by Minerva II) S Asia.

Calcutta Diary. Ashok Mitra. 206p. 1977. 32.50 (0-7146-3082-9, Pub. by F Cass Pubs UK) Intl Spec Bk.

Calcutta, Eighteen Fifty-One. Henry Scholberg. (Writers Workshop Bluebird Ser.). 78p. 1976. 12.00 (0-86578-098-6); 8.00 (0-86578-097-8) Ind-US Inc.

Calcutta in the Eighteenth Century. P. Thankappan Nair. 1984. 22.50 (0-8364-1232-X, Pub. by Mukhopadhyaya II) S Asia.

Calcutta in the Seventeenth Century. P. Thankappan Nair. 1986. 38.00 (0-8364-1619-8, KL Mukhopadhyay) S Asia.

Calcutta in the Twentieth Century: An Urban Disaster. Manimanjari Mitra. 1990. 27.50 (0-8364-2627-4, Pub. by Asiatic Bk Agency JA) S Asia.

Calcutta Journal of Natural History, 5 vols., Set. J. Clelland. (C). 1988. text ed. 800.00 (0-685-22120-2) St Mut.

Calcutta Journal of Natural History, Set: Vols. 1-5. J. M'Clelland. 5645p. 1985. reprint ed. Set. 2,500.00 (81-7089-030-6, Pub. by Intl Bk Distr II) St Mut.

Calcutta on the Eve of Her Tercentenary. Asok Mitra. 1990. 23.00 (81-7017-270-5, Pub. by Abhinav II) S Asia.

Calcutta Psyche. Gèeti Sen. Ed. by Rupa. (C). 1991. text ed. 27.00 (0-8364-2651-7, Pub. by Ajanta II) S Asia.

Calcutta, Society & Change, 1690-1990. Samaren Roy. (C). 1991. 31.50 (81-7167-046-6, Pub. by Rupa II) S Asia.

*Calcutta: The Living City Vol. I & II: The Past; The Present & Future, 2 vols., Set. Ed. by Sukanta Chaudhuri. (Illus.). 676p. 1995. pap. 39.95 (0-19-563698-8) OUP.

Calcutta Three Hundred - Kolkata Memoirs of a Diverse City: Overseas Tribute to Calcutta on Her Tercentenary. Ed. by Sachi G. Dastidar. (Illus.). 157p. (Orig.). 1993. pap. text ed. 10.00 (0-9634363-0-9) S Asia Forum.

Caldaire Holdings Ltd & Bluebird Securities Ltd Command Paper. (Monopolies & Mergers Commission Report Ser.: No. 1403). 86p. 1991. pap. 25.00 (0-10-114032-0, HM0032) UNIPUB.

Calde of the Long Sun. Gene Wolfe. 384p. 1994. 22.95 (0-312-85583-4) Tor Bks.

*Calde of the Long Sun. Gene Wolfe. 1995. mass mkt. 6.99 (0-8125-3420-4) Tor Bks.

Caldecott. Frank Jakubowsky. 78p. (Orig.). 1985. pap. 6.95 (0-932588-09-3) Jesus Bks.

Caldecott, a Speed-Read Book. Frank Jakubowsky. 78p. (Orig.). 1990. pap. 100.00 (0-932588-16-6) Jesus Bks.

Caldecott & Co. Maurice Sendak. 1990. pap. 8.95 (0-374-52218-9, Noonday) FS&G.

Caldecott Honor Books Search-a-Word Learning Guide: The First Twenty-Five Years, 1938-1962. Irene W. Bell. 300p. 1990. lib. bdg. 24.00 (0-87287-593-8) Libs Unl.

Caldecott Search-A-Word Learning Guide. Irene W. Bell. 257p. 1988. lib. bdg. 23.50 (0-87287-592-X) Libs Unl.

Calder: With Eight Original Lithographs. Giovanni Carandente & Jacques Dupin. (Illus.). 24p. 1968. With eight orig. lithographs. pap. 300.00 (1-55660-138-7) A Wofsy Fine Arts.

Calder: With Five Original Lithographs. Carlos Franqui. (Illus.). 26p. 1971. With five orig. lithographs. pap. 250. 00 (1-55660-137-9) A Wofsy Fine Arts.

Calder Born, Calder Bred. Dailey. (Orig.). 1993. mass mkt. 5.99 (0-671-87500-0) PB.

Calder Born, Calder Bred see Stands A Calder Man

Calder Range. Janet Dailey. 1993. mass mkt. 5.99 (0-671-87517-5) PB.

Calderas & Associate Igneous Rocks. (Reprint Volumes Ser.). 622p. 1984. reprint ed. pap. 20.00 (0-685-11742-1, 0-148-0227D) Am Geophysical.

Calderon. R. C. Trench. LC 70-128409. (Studies in Spanish Literature: No. 36). 1970. reprint ed. lib. bdg. 39.95 (0-8383-1151-2) M S G Haskell Hse.

Calderon: Plays One. Pedro Calderon de la Barca. Tr. & Intro. by Gwynne Edwards. (Methuen World Dramatists Ser.). 304p. (Orig.). 1991. pap. 14.95 (0-413-63460-4, A0538, Pub. by Methuen UK) Heinemann.

Calderon: The Imagery of Tragedy. Charlene E. Suscavage. LC 91-16880. (Iberica Ser.: Vol. 1). 225p. 1992. 39.95 (0-8204-1396-8) P Lang Pubs.

Calderon: The Secular Plays. Robert Ter Horst. LC 82-4747. 264p. 1982. 29.00 (0-8131-1440-3) U Pr of Ky.

Calderon - Konkordanz Zu Calderon Part II: Koncordanz Zu Den Comedias y Dramas, Vol. VI. Date not set. write for info. (0-318-71615-1, Pub. by Georg Olms GW) Lubrecht & Cramer.

Calderon & the Seizures of Honor. Edwin Honig. LC 78-186674. 285p. 1972. 29.95 (0-674-09075-6) HUP.

Calderon de la Barca: Imagery, Rhetoric & Drama. John V. Bryans. (Serie A: Monagrafias, LXIV). 207p. (C). 1977. pap. 45.00 (0-7293-0047-1, Pub. by Tamesis Bks Ltd UK) Boydell & Brewer.

Calderon de la Barca: Six Plays. Edwin Honig. 400p. (Orig.). (C). Date not set. pap. 21.95 (1-882763-05-X) IASTA.

An Asterisk (*) at the beginning of an entry indicates that the title is appearing in BIP for the first time.

An Asterisk (*) at the beginning of an entry indicates that the title is appearing in BIP for the first time.

Calendar of Wills Relating to the Counties of Northampton & Rutland. Ed. by W. P. Phillimore. Bd. with Calendar of Chancery Proceedings, Bills & Answers.; Index Nominum to the Royalist Composition Papers. (British Record Society Index Library Ser.: Vols. 1,2 & 3). 1972. reprint ed. 67.00 (0-8115-1452-8) Periodicals Srv.

Calendar of Writs of Privy Seal: 1601-1603 see Index to Bills of Privy Signet, Commonly Called Signet Bills: 1584 -1596 & 1603-1624

Calendar Quilts. Joan Hanson. Ed. by Liz McGehee & Shellie Tucker. LC 90-28085. (Illus.). 88p. (Orig.). 1991. pap. 16.95 (0-943574-77-3) That Patchwork.

Calendar Status Study: 1974. 50p. 3.50 (0-318-14430-1) IJA NYU.

Calendario Manual y Guia de Forasteros de La Isla de Cuba Para el Ano de 1795. 2nd ed. 146p. (SPA.). reprint ed. text ed. 9.00 (0-89729-392-4) Ediciones.

Calendars, No. 1460. (Illus.). 48p. 1989. 9.95 (1-878259-15-6) Neibauer Pr.

Calendars of Administrations in the Consistory Court of Lincoln: A. D. 1540-1659. Ed. by C. W. Foster. (British Record Society Index Library Ser.: Vol. 52). 1972. reprint ed. pap. 52.00 (0-685-09953-9) Periodicals Srv.

Calendars of Huntingdonshire Wills: 1479-1652. Comp. by W. N. Nobel. (British Record Society Index Library Ser.: Vol. 42). 1972. reprint ed. pap. 19.00 (0-8115-1487-0) Periodicals Srv.

Calendars of the World: A Look at Calendars & the Ways We Celebrate. Margo Westrheim. 1994. pap. 11.95 (1-85168-051-9) Onewrld Pubns.

Calendars of Wills & Administrations at Lincoln, Vol. 4: Archdeaconry of Stow. Peculiar Courts & Miscellaneous Courts. Ed. by C. W. Foster. (British Record Society Index Library Ser.: Vol. 57). 1972. reprint ed. pap. 35.00 (0-8115-1502-8) Periodicals Srv.

Calendars of Wills & Administrations in the Consistory Court of the Bishop of Lichfield & Coventry, 1516-1652. Ed. by W. P. Phillimore. (British Record Society Index Library Ser.: Vol. 7). 1972. reprint ed. pap. 53.00 (0-8115-1454-4) Periodicals Srv.

Calendars of Wills & Administrations Relating to the County of Dorset. Ed. by George S. Fry. (British Record Society Index Library Ser.: Vol. 53). 1972. reprint ed. pap. 25.00 (0-8115-1498-6) Periodicals Srv.

Calendars Unlimited. Methods & Solutions Staff. 1988. 49. 95 (0-87280-544-1, 574, Asher-Gallant) Caddylak Systs.

Calender of Letters Relating to North Wales, 1533-c. 1700. Ed. by B. E. Howells. (History & Law Ser.). 287p. 1967. text ed. 22.50 (0-7083-0106-1, Pub. by U of Wales UK) Bks Intl VA.

Calendering & Winding Seminar, 1989: Holiday Inn - Hobby Airport, Houston, TX, April 30-May 3. Technical Association of the Pulp & Paper Industry Staff. (TAPPI Notes Ser.). (Illus.). 145p. pap. 41.40 (0-8357-6319-6, 2035593) Bks Demand.

Calendering & Winding Short Course, 1992: Marriott Executive Park Hotel, Charlotte, NC, May 3-6. Technical Association of the Pulp & Paper Industry Staff. (TAPPI Notes Ser.). reprint ed. pap. 50.00 (0-7837-2438-1, 2042590) Bks Demand.

Calendering & Winding Technology. Technical Association of the Pulp & Paper Industry Staff. 119p. reprint ed. pap. 34.00 (0-8357-7973-4, 2025294) Bks Demand.

Calendrier De la Vie et Des Ecrits De Louis-Claude de Saint-Martin, Vol. III. Robert Amadou. 350p. write for info. (0-318-71424-8, Pub. by Georg Olms GW) Lubrecht & Cramer.

Calends: Poems from Hollywood. Mark Dunster. 28p. (Orig.). 1992. pap. 5.00 (0-89642-203-8) Linden Pubs.

Calenhad: A Beacon of Gondor. Tim Cooke. Ed. by Jessica Ney. (Fortresses of Middle Earth Ser.). (Illus.). 48p. (Orig.). (YA). (gr. 12). 1990. pap. 9.00 (1-55806-097-9, 8203) Iron Crown Ent Inc.

Calf. Mary Ling. LC 92-53486. (See How They Grow Ser.). (Illus.). 24p. (J). (ps-1). 1993. 7.95 (1-56458-205-1) Dorling Kindersley.

Calf. 5th ed. J. H. Roy. 350p. 1990. text ed. 89.95 (0-407-00520-X) Blackwell Sci.

Calf Care: And Raising Young Stock. 2nd ed. W. D. Hoard & Sons Co. Staff. (Illus.). 48p. 1990. pap. text ed. 3.00 (0-932147-11-9, Hoards Dairyman) Hoard & Sons Co.

***Calf Care: And Raising Your Stock.** rev. ed. W. D. Hoard & Sons Company Staff. (Illus.). 48p. (C). 1994. pap. text ed. 3.50 (0-932147-23-2, Hoards Dairyman) Hoard & Sons Co.

Calf for Christmas. Astrid Lindgren. Tr. by Barbara Lucas. (Illus.). 32p. (J). (ps up). 1991. bds. 13.95 (91-29-59920-2, Pub. by R & S Bks) FS&G.

Calf Fries to Caviar. Janel Franklin. 1984. pap. 13.95 (0-9610956-0-1) JAN-SU Pubns.

***Calf Grows Up: The Story of Dairying with a Guide to Teaching & Learning.** Betty A. Lockhart. Ed. by Donald G. Lockhart. (Illus.). 1992. teacher ed 7.00 (1-880327-23-6) Perceptions.

Calf Love. large type ed. Joyce Fussey. 168p. (Orig.). 1990. 9.97 (1-85089-466-3, Pub. by ISIS UK) Transaction Pubs.

Calf Rearing. 2nd ed. Bill Thickett et al. (Illus.). 176p. 1988. 27.95 (0-85236-180-7, Pub. by Farming Pr UK); text ed. 21.95 (0-685-49181-1, Pub. by Farming Pr UK) Diamond Farm Bk.

Calf Roping. Roy Cooper. Ed. by Randy Witte. (Illus.). 144p. (Orig.). 1984. pap. 12.95 (0-911647-04-X) Western Horseman.

Calf to Dolphin. Oliver S. Owen. LC 94-19967. (Lifewatch Ser.). (Illus.). (J). 1994. lib. bdg. 14.96 (1-56239-292-1) Abdo & Dghtrs.

Calgary: Canada's Frontier Metropolis. Max Foran & Heather M. Foran. (Illus.). 368p. 1982. 29.95 (0-89781-055-4) Preferred Mktg.

***Calgary Architecture: The Boom Years, 1972-1982.** Pierre Guimond & Brian Sinclair. (Illus.). 1984. 23.95 (0-920490-38-7) Temeron Bks.

***Calgary Architecture: The Boom Years, 1972-1982.** Pierre Guimond & Brian Sinclair. (Illus.). 309p. (Orig.). 1984. pap. 14.95 (0-920490-39-5) Temeron Bks.

Calgary Flames. Terry Jones. LC 93-48431. (NHL Today Ser.). 32p. (J). 1995. 14.95 (0-88682-671-3) Creative Ed.

Calhoon. Thorne Douglas. 1980. pap. 1.75 (0-449-13935-2, GM) Fawcett.

Calhoun & the South Carolina Nullification Movement. Frederic Bancroft. 1966. 10.75 (0-8446-1052-6) Peter Smith.

Calhoun Plantation Songs. 2nd ed. Emily Hallowell. LC 74-24103. reprint ed. 34.50 (0-404-12945-5) AMS Pr.

Caliban. Isaac Asimov & Roger M. Allen. 320p. (Orig.). 1993. pap. 9.95 (0-441-09079-6) Ace Bks.

Caliban. Ed. by Harold Bloom. (Major Literary Characters Ser.). 280p. (C). 1992. lib. bdg. 34.95 (0-7910-0914-9) Chelsea Hse.

Caliban. Ernest Renan. Tr. by Eleanor G. Vickery. LC 70-169928. (Shakespeare Society of New York. Publications: No. 9a). reprint ed. 27.50 (0-404-54209-3) AMS Pr.

Caliban & Other Essays. Roberto F. Retamar. Tr. by Edward Baker. 168p. (Orig.). 1989. text ed. 34.95 (0-8166-1742-2); pap. text ed. 14.95 (0-8166-1743-0) U of Minn Pr.

Caliban in Blue. Walter McDonald & Miller Williams. 51p. (Orig.). 1976. 4.50 (0-89672-054-3); pap. 2.25 (0-89672-053-5) Tex Tech Univ Pr.

Caliban in Exile: The Outsider in Caribbean Fiction. Margaret P. Joseph. LC 91-44509. (Contributions to the Study of World Literature Ser.: No. 43). 160p. 1992. text ed. 45.00 (0-313-28107-6, JCE/, Greenwood Pr) Greenwood.

Caliban Poems. Richard O'Connell. 1992. pap. 10.00 (0-685-55467-8) Atlantis Edns.

Caliban Reborn: Renewal in Twentieth-Century Music. Wilfrid Mellers. LC 79-14238. (Music Reprint Ser.). 1979. reprint ed. lib. bdg. 29.50 (0-306-79569-8) Da Capo.

***Calibans.** Williams. Date not set. pap. write for info. (0-09-926361-0) Random Hse Value.

***Caliban's Hour.** Tad Williams. LC 94-5399. 1994. 14.99 (0-06-105204-3) HarpC.

***Caliban's Kingdom: Stanford's Experiment with Multiculturalism.** David Sacks. 200p. 1995. 19.95 (1-882926-08-0) Intercoll Studies.

***Calibration: Philosophy in Practice.** 2nd ed. (Illus.). 528p. 1994. reprint ed. 69.00 (0-9638650-0-5) Fluke.

***Calibration & Applictions of Satellite Sensors.** Becker & Tsuchiya. (Advances in Space Research Ser.: No. 17-1). 1995. pap. text ed. write for info. (0-08-042640-9, Pergamon Pr) Elsevier.

***Calibration Guide from the First International Airborne Imaging Spectrometer Calibration Workshop, 1994.** 38p. 1994. 25.00 (0-614-02692-X) ASP & RS.

Calibration in Air Monitoring-STP 598. 356p. 1976. 33.00 (0-8031-0297-6, 04-598000-17) ASTM.

Calibration of Fundamental Stellar Quantities. Ed. by D. S. Hayes et al. 1985. lib. bdg. 162.50 (90-277-2109-2) Kluwer Ac.

Calibration of Passive Remote Observing Optical & Microwave Instrumentation, Vol. 1493. B. W. Guenther. 1991. 62.00 (0-8194-0602-3) SPIE.

Calibration of Photon Personal Dosemeter in Terms of ICRU Operational Quantity. P. J. Dimbylow et al. (National Radiological Protection Board Ser.: No. NRBP-R230). 94p. 1990. pap. 25.00 (0-85951-317-3, HM7331) UNIPUB.

Calibration of Response-Type Road Roughness Measuring Systems. (National Cooperative Highway Research Program Report Ser.: No. 228). 81p. 1980. 7.60 (0-309-03034-X) Transport Res Bd.

Calibration of Stellar Ages. Ed. by A. G. Davis Philip. 250p. 1988. 25.00 (0-933485-09-3) L Davis Pr.

Calibration of Survey Instruments Used in Radiation Protection for the Assessment of Ionizing Radiation Fields & Radioactive Surface Contamination. LC 91-38019. (Report Ser.: No. 112). 1991. 25.00 (0-929600-23-1) NCRP Pubns.

Calibrations. David Lunde. LC 79-16512. 1980. 8.00 (0-931588-07-3); pap. 3.50 (0-931588-08-1) Allegany Mtn Pr.

Caliche-Origin Classification, Morphology & Uses. C. C. Reeves, Jr. LC 76-2234. 1976. text ed. 39.95 (0-686-16733-3) Estacado Bks.

Calico. Raine Cantrell. 336p. (Orig.). 1993. mass mkt. 4.99 (1-55773-913-7) Diamond.

Calico & Beyond: The Use of Patterned Fabric in Quilts. Roberta M. Horton. LC 85-72039. (Illus.). 80p. (Orig.). 1985. pap. 16.95 (0-914881-03-5) C & T Pub.

Calico & Tin Horns. Candace Christiansen. LC 91-3706. (Illus.). 32p. (J). 1992. 16.00 (0-8037-1179-4); lib. bdg. 15.89 (0-8037-1180-8) Dial Bks Young.

Calico Bear. Angela E. Hunt. 1991. 8.99 (0-8423-0302-2) Tyndale.

Calico Birthday Book. (Illus.). 96p. 9.95 (1-897954-46-8) Sterling.

Calico Bush. Rachel Field. (J). (gr. 4-8). 1988. pap. 3.50 (0-440-40100-3, YB) Dell.

Calico Bush. Rachel Field. LC 66-19095. (Illus.). 224p. (J). (gr. 5-9). 1987. text ed. 14.95 (0-02-734610-2, Mac Bks Young Read) S&S Childrens.

Calico Bush. Rachel Field. (J). 1990. reprint ed. mass mkt. 3.99 (0-440-40368-5, Yearling Classics) Dell.

Calico Captive. Elizabeth G. Speare. (J). (gr. k-6). 1973. mass mkt. 3.99 (0-440-41156-4, YB) Dell.

Calico Captive. Elizabeth G. Speare. (Illus.). 288p. (J). (gr. 7-9). 1957. 15.95 (0-395-07112-7) HM.

Calico Chronicle: Texas Women & Their Fashions, 1830-1910. Betty J. Mills. LC 84-52249. (Illus.). 192p. 1985. 25.95 (0-89672-129-9); pap. 15.95 (0-89672-128-0) Tex Tech Univ Pr.

Calico Cows. Arlene Dubanevich. (Illus.). 32p. (J). (ps-3). 1993. lib. bdg. 13.50 (0-670-84436-5) Viking Child Bks.

Calico Cupboards. 352p. 1980. 16.95 (0-918544-54-8) Wimmer Bks.

Calico Families. Ann M. Martin. LC 76-20575. 48p. 1977. 9.95 (0-88289-118-9) Pelican.

***Calico House.** Joanna Brazier. Ed. by Kerry Hoffman. (International Quilt Shop Ser.). (Illus.). 88p. (Orig.). 1995. pap. 19.95 (1-56477-093-1, B213) That Patchwork.

Calico Kitchen Muffins. large type ed. Bonnie Cready & Peggy Brough. 48p. 3.95 (0-9613908-0-8) Bennett Enter.

Calico's Country Cats. Ruth C. Lembke. LC 82-80861. (Illus.). 64p. 1982. 5.95 (0-686-39811-4) R C Lembke.

CALICO's LION User's Manual. Carol O. Daniel & T. David Daniel. 1985. ring bd. 35.00 (0-916625-16-8) Computer Assis.

Caliente Gold Robbery. J. R. Roberts. (Gunsmith Ser.: No. 128). 192p. (Orig.). 1992. pap. 3.99 (0-515-10903-7) Jove Pubns.

Calif of Fornia. Pat'rick N. Pugh. LC 93-92578. 216p. 1993. pap. 9.95 (1-883184-08-8) PNP.

Califate of the West. D. Mackenzie. 368p. 1987. 290.00 (1-85077-163-4, Darf Pubs Ltd) St Mut.

***Califobia: Adventures in LaLa Land.** Colin White & Laurie Boucke. Ed. by David Cleveland. (Illus.). 260p. (Orig.). (C). 1995. pap. 12.25 (0-9625006-4-X) White-Boucke.

Califonia Paisano: The Life of William McPherson. Don Meadows. 1972. 10.00 (0-87093-163-6) Dawsons.

California. (RAC Travel Guides Ser.). (Illus.). 96p. 1991. pap. 6.95 (0-7117-0481-3) Hunter NJ.

California. (Visitor's Guides Ser.). (Illus.). 256p. 1994. pap. 13.95 (0-86190-464-8) Hunter NJ.

California. (Bed & Breakfast Ser.). (Illus.). 144p. 1991. pap. 15.00 (0-13-068412-0, P-H Travel) P-H Gen Ref & Trav.

California. (Insider's Guide Ser.). 1989. pap. 14.95 (1-55650-163-3) Hunter NJ.

California, 12 vols. Incl. Vol. 1. Golden Days. 44p. pap. 2.50 (0-317-05956-4); Vol. 2. Mighty Land. 44p. pap. 2.50 (0-89167-012-2); Vol. 3. Discovery Trails. 44p. pap. 2.50 (0-89167-013-0); Vol. 4. Roads to Castles. 44p. pap. 2.50 (0-89167-014-9); Vol. 5. Avenues to Progress. 44p. pap. 2.50 (0-89167-015-7); Vol. 6. Outdoor Adventures. 44p. pap. 2.50 (0-89167-016-5); Vol. 7. Wilderness Byways. 44p. pap. 2.50 (0-89167-017-3); Vol. 8. Briny Blue. 36p. pap. 2.50 (0-89167-018-1); Vol. 9. Growing Metropolis. 36p. pap. 2.50 (0-317-05957-2); Vol. 10. Capital Scenes. 52p. pap. 2.50 (0-89167-020-3); Vol. 11. Great Fifty-Eight: Counties A-M. 36p. pap. 2.50 (0-89167-021-1); Vol. 12. Great Fifty-Eight: Counties N-Y. 44p. pap. 2.50 (0-89167-022-X); (Heritage Ser.). 44p. Set pap. write for info. (0-89167-011-4) E V Salitore.

California. Gunther Barth. (Windsor Destination Guides Ser.). (Illus.). 64p. 1992. pap. 12.95 (1-874111-06-5, Pub. by Windsor Bks UK) Seven Hills Bk.

California. Marcello Bertinetti & Valeria M. De Fabianis. (Illus.). 128p. 1993. 14.98 (0-8317-1155-8) Smithmark.

***California.** CMAM Staff. Date not set. write for info. (1-878867-77-6) Fodors Travel.

California. Thomas Cook. (Passport's Illustrated Travel Guides from Thomas Cook Ser.). (Illus.). 192p. 1993. pap. 12.95 (0-8442-9032-7, Passport Bks) NTC Pub Grp.

California. Janet Greenberg. LC 94-1038. (American Food Library). (J). 1994. write for info. (0-86625-511-7) Rourke Pubns.

California. Ed. by Robert F. Heizer. LC 77-17162. (Handbook of North American Indians Ser.: Vol. 8). (Illus.). 800p. 1978. text ed. 25.00 (0-87474-188-2, HEV8) Smithsonian.

***California.** David Lantis et al. 544p. (C). 1995. per., pap. text ed. 45.95 (0-7872-1018-8) Kendall-Hunt.

***California.** Pelta. 1995. pap. text ed. (0-8225-9668-7) Lerner Group.

California. Kathy Pelta. LC 93-1497. (Hello U. S. A. Ser.). (Illus.). 72p. (J). (gr. 3-6). 1993. lib. bdg. 17.50 (0-8225-2738-3, Lerner Publctns) Lerner Group.

California. R. Conrad Stein. LC 87-37948. (America the Beautiful Ser.). (Illus.). 144p. (J). (gr. 4 up). 1988. lib. bdg. 20.55 (0-516-00451-4) Childrens.

California. Ed. by Suntree Publishing Staff. (Travel Bug Ser.). (Illus.). 1994. pap. 18.00 (0-671-87906-5, P-H Travel) P-H Gen Ref & Trav.

California. Kathleen Thompson. LC 87-16395. (Portrait of America Library). 48p. (J). 1987. 21.36 (0-8174-4621-4) Raintree Steck-V.

California. braille ed. R. Conrad Stein. 209p. (J). 1993. vinyl bd. 15.40 (1-56956-174-5, BR9031) W A T Braille.

California. rev. ed. (Baedeker's Ser.). (Illus.). 1991. 22.95 (0-13-094731-8, P-H Travel) P-H Gen Ref & Trav.

California. rev. ed. Illus. by Greg Lawson. LC 82-90775. (ENG, FRE, GER, JPN & SPA.). 1989. pap. 11.95 (0-916251-33-0) Sunbelt Pubns.

California. 4th rev. ed. (Insight Guide Ser.). (Illus.). 336p. 1994. pap. 21.95 (0-395-71073-1) HM.

California: A Bibliography of Theses & Dissertations in Geography, No. 753. Sandra J. Lemprecht. 1975. 5.50 (0-686-20344-5) CPL Biblios.

California: A Guide to the Golden State. Federal Writers' Project Staff & Writers Program-WPA Staff. (American Guide Ser.). 1989. reprint ed. lib. bdg. 79.00 (0-7812-1005-4, 1005) Rprt Serv.

California: A Guide to the Golden State. Federal Writers' Project Staff. LC 72-84461. (American Guidebook Ser.). 1980. reprint ed. lib. bdg. 89.00 (0-403-02157-X) Somerset Pub.

California: A History. 4th ed. Andrew Rolle. LC 86-4790. (Illus.). 600p. (C). 1987. text ed. write for info. (0-88295-839-9) Harlan Davidson.

California: A History of Upper & Lower California. Alexander Forbes. LC 72-9443. (Far Western Frontier Ser.). (Illus.). 384p. 1973. reprint ed. 26.95 (0-405-04972-2) Ayer.

California: A Picture Memory. 1990. 7.99 (0-517-01746-6) Random Hse Value.

California: An Environmental Atlas. Bern Kreissman. 1991. pap. 19.95 (0-9627489-9-4) Bear Klaw Pr.

California: An Illustrated History. T. H. Watkins. (Illus.). 1983. 17.95 (0-685-07114-6) Random Hse Value.

California: An Intimate History. rev. ed. Gertrude F. Atherton. LC 74-152969. (Select Bibliographies Reprint Ser.). 1977. reprint ed. 31.95 (0-8369-5721-0) Ayer.

***California: Earthquakes & Jews.** Ed. by William M. Kramer. (Western American Ethnic Studies Book). 272p. 1995. pap. text ed. 24.00 (0-914615-15-7) I Nathan Pub Co.

California: Its Government & Politics. 4th ed. Michael J. Ross. LC 91-18891. 272p. (C). 1992. pap. 24.95 (0-534-16434-X) Intl Thomson.

California: Land of Contrast. 3rd ed. David W. Lantis et al. 496p. 1981. per. 16.95 (0-8403-2493-6) Kendall-Hunt.

California: Land of New Beginnings. David Lavender. LC 86-30929. x, 480p. 1987. reprint ed. 33.00 (0-8032-2874-0); reprint ed. pap. 17.95 (0-8032-7924-8) U of Nebr Pr.

***California: Nelles Guide.** rev. ed. (Nelles Guides Ser.). (Illus.). 256p. 1995. pap. 14.95 (3-88618-406-4, Pub. by Nelles Verlag GW) Seven Hills Bk.

California: People of a Region. 4th ed. J. Chapin et al. (Our Nation, Our World Ser.). 288p. 1983. text ed. 23.52 (0-07-010561-8) McGraw.

California: Raices Nativas. 8p. (Orig.). (SPA.). 1990. reprint ed. teacher ed 3.95 (0-911981-68-3) Cloud Pub.

California: Raices Nativas. (Illus.). 64p. (Orig.). (SPA.). (J). (gr. 4-6). 1990. reprint ed. pap. text ed. 12.45 (0-911981-09-8) Cloud Pub.

California: Roots. Michael McCabe & Virginia Brew. (Illus.). 59p. (J). (gr. 4-6). 1983. student ed 5.25 (0-911981-05-5) Cloud Pub.

California: Roots. Charles Lavaroni. 144p. (J). (gr. 4-6). 1984. reprint ed. pap. text ed. 11.45 (0-911981-04-7) Cloud Pub.

California: Roots. Michael McCabe & Virginia Brew. 28p. (J). (gr. 4-6). 1991. reprint ed. teacher ed 7.95 (0-911981-07-1) Cloud Pub.

California: The Geography of Diversity. Crane S. Miller & Richard S. Hyslop. LC 82-73744. (Illus.). 255p. 1983. pap. 29.95 (0-87484-441-X) Mayfield Pub.

California: The Golden Shore by the Sundown Sea. 2nd ed. William Hutchinson. 430p. 1988. pap. 22.95 (0-89863-140-8) Star Pub CA.

California: The Irish Dream. Patrick J. Dowling. (Illus.). xxx, 429p. (Orig.). 1989. 25.00 (0-9620974-1-1); pap. 17. 00 (0-9620974-0-3) Gold Gate Pubs.

California: The Irish Dream. 2nd ed. Patrick J. Dowling. (Illus.). xxxi, 442p. (Orig.). 1989. write for info. (0-9620974-3-8) Gold Gate Pubs.

California: The Pacific Connection. David W. Lantis et al. (Illus.). 595p. (C). 1988. 35.00 (0-9629915-1-1); pap. text ed. 29.95 (0-9620015-2-X) Creekside Pr.

***California: The Politics of Diversity.** David Lawrence. LC 94-35221. 250p. 1994. pap. text ed. 23.25 (0-314-04600-3) West Pub.

California: The Rush for Gold. L. Wade. (Doors to America's Past Ser.). (J). 1991. 11.95 (0-86592-467-8) Rourke Enter.

California: The State & Its Education System. Harold L. Hodgkinson. (Orig.). 1986. pap. 5.50 (0-937846-90-2) Inst Educ Lead.

California: Trip Planner & Guide. Passport Books Staff. 1994. pap. 14.95 (0-8442-9216-8, Passport Bks) NTC Pub Grp.

California: Triumph of the Entrepreneurial Spirit. Bob Shallit. 376p. 1989. 32.95 (0-89781-293-X, 5217) Preferred Mktg.

California: Vanishing Habitats & Wildlife. Photos & Intro. by B. Moose Peterson. (Illus.). 144p. 1993. pap. 21.95 (0-89802-589-3) Beautiful Am.

California - De Mar a Mar: (California - From Sea to Shining Sea) Dennis B. Fradin. LC 92-12944. (From Sea to Shining Sea Ser.). (Illus.). 64p. (SPA.). (J). (gr. 3-5). 1993. lib. bdg. 16.50 (0-516-33805-6); pap. 5.95 (0-516-53805-5) Childrens.

California - Early History. Randy L. Womack. (Illus.). 96p. (gr. 4 up). 1989. student ed 10.95 (1-56500-027-7) Gldn Educ.

California - from Sea to Shining Sea. Dennis B. Fradin. LC 92-12944. (From Sea to Shining Sea Ser.). (Illus.). 64p. (J). (gr. 3-5). 1992. lib. bdg. 16.50 (0-516-03805-2); pap. 5.95 (0-516-43805-0) Childrens.

California - Geography. Randy L. Womack. (Illus.). 80p. (gr. 4 up). 1989. student ed 8.95 (1-56500-028-5) Gldn Educ.

***California - Northern State Business Handbook.** 400p. (C). 1995. text ed. 795.00 (0-7605-1920-X) Rector Pr.

***California - Southern State Business Handbook.** 400p. (C). 1995. text ed. 895.00 (0-7605-1921-8) Rector Pr.

California--Collected Works of Federal Writers Project: Northern Edition. Federal Writers Project Staff. 1991. reprint ed. text ed. 98.00 (0-7812-5510-4) Rprt Serv.

California--Collected Works of Federal Writers Project: Southern Edition. Federal Writers Project Staff. 1991. reprint ed. lib. bdg. 98.00 (0-7812-5518-X) Rprt Serv.

California Achievement Test (CAT) (Admission Test Ser.: ATS-101). 39.95 (0-8373-5851-5, ATS-101); pap. 23.95 (0-8373-5801-9, ATS-101) Nat Learn.

An Asterisk (*) at the beginning of an entry indicates that the title is appearing in BIP for the first time.

An Asterisk (*) at the beginning of an entry indicates that the title is appearing in BIP for the first time.

995

California College Cookbook. UCLA Students. Ed. by Jennifer Openshaw & Karen Friedman. (Illus.). 147p. (C). 1988. 8.95 (0-317-91326-3) UCLA Gov Intern Assn.

California College Review. William Ott. 80p. (C). 1994. 7.16 (0-8403-9217-6) Kendall-Hunt.

California Commercial Industrial Directories, 60 Vols., No. 32. Jacques Melek. (Plumas Ser.). 200p. (Orig.). 1982. pap. write for info. (0-942330-53-6) J Melek.

California Commercial Industrial Directories, No. 33. Jacques Melek. (Riverside Ser.). 200p. (Orig.). 1983. 96.00 (0-686-35962-3); pap. write for info. (0-942330-54-4) J Melek.

California Commercial Industrial Directories: Alamedia, No. 1. Jacques Melek. 200p. (Orig.). 1983. 96.00 (0-942330-22-6) J Melek.

California Commercial Industrial Directories: Alamedia, Set. Jacques Melek. 200p. (Orig.). 1983. pap. 48.00 (0-686-35979-8) J Melek.

California Commercial Industrial Directories: Alpine, No. 2. Jacques Melek. 150p. (Orig.). 1983. 96.00 (0-942330-23-4) J Melek.

California Commercial Industrial Directories: Amador, No. 3. Jacques Melek. 200p. (Orig.). 1983. 96.00 (0-942330-24-2) J Melek.

California Commercial Industrial Directories: Butte, Vol 4. Jacques Melek. 200p. (Orig.). 1983. 96.00 (0-942330-25-0) J Melek.

California Commercial Industrial Directories: Calaveras, Vol. 5. Jacques Melek. 150p. (Orig.). 1983. 96.00 (0-942330-27-7) J Melek.

California Commercial Industrial Directories: Central Sierra Counties, Vol. 7. Jacques Melek. 200p. (Orig.). 1983. 96.00 (0-686-35977-1) J Melek.

California Commercial Industrial Directories: Contra Costa, Vol. 6. Jacques Melek. 200p. (Orig.). 1983. 96.00 (0-942330-28-5) J Melek.

California Commercial Industrial Directories: Del Norte, Vol. 8. Jacques Melek. 200p. (Orig.). 1983. 96.00 (0-942330-29-3) J Melek.

California Commercial Industrial Directories: El Dorado, Vol. 9. Jacques Melek. 150p. (Orig.). 1983. 96.00 (0-942330-30-7) J Melek.

California Commercial Industrial Directories: Fresno, No. 10. Jacques Melek. 200p. (Orig.). 1982. pap. write for info. (0-942330-31-5) J Melek.

California Commercial Industrial Directories: Fresno, Set. Jacques Melek. 200p. (Orig.). 1982. pap. 48.00 (0-685-05927-8) J Melek.

California Commercial Industrial Directories: Glenn, No. 11. Jacques Melek. 200p. (Orig.). 1983. 96.00 (0-942330-32-3) J Melek.

California Commercial Industrial Directories: Humboldt, No. 12. Jacques Melek. 200p. (Orig.). 1983. 96.00 (0-942330-33-1) J Melek.

California Commercial Industrial Directories: Imperial, No. 13. Jacques Melek. 200p. (Orig.). 1983. 96.00 (0-942330-34-X) J Melek.

California Commercial Industrial Directories: Inyo, No. 14. Jacques Melek. 200p. (Orig.). 1983. 96.00 (0-942330-35-8) J Melek.

California Commercial Industrial Directories: Kern, No. 15. Jacques Melek. 200p. (Orig.). 1983. 96.00 (0-942330-36-6) J Melek.

California Commercial Industrial Directories: Kings, No. 16. Jacques Melek. 200p. (Orig.). 1983. 96.00 (0-942330-37-4) J Melek.

California Commercial Industrial Directories: Lake, No. 17. Jacques Melek. 200p. (Orig.). 1983. 96.00 (0-942330-38-2) J Melek.

California Commercial Industrial Directories: Lassen, No. 18. Jacques Melek. 200p. (Orig.). 1983. pap. 96.00 (0-685-05926-X) J Melek.

California Commercial Industrial Directories: Los Angeles, No. 19. Jacques Melek. 200p. (Orig.). 1983. pap. write for info. (0-942330-40-4) J Melek.

California Commercial Industrial Directories: Madera, No. 20. Jacques Melek. 200p. (Orig.). 1983. 96.00 (0-942330-41-2) J Melek.

California Commercial Industrial Directories: Marin, No. 21. Jacques Melek. 200p. (Orig.). 1983. 96.00 (0-686-98669-5); pap. write for info. (0-942330-42-0) J Melek.

California Commercial Industrial Directories: Mariposa, No. 22. Jacques Melek. 200p. (Orig.). 1983. pap. write for info. (0-942330-43-9) J Melek.

California Commercial Industrial Directories: Mendocino, No. 23. Jacques Melek. 200p. (Orig.). 1983. pap. write for info. (0-318-56681-8) J Melek.

California Commercial Industrial Directories: Merced, No. 24. Jacques Melek. 200p. (Orig.). 1983. pap. write for info. (0-318-56680-X) J Melek.

California Commercial Industrial Directories: Modoc, No. 25. Jacques Melek. 200p. (Orig.). 1983. pap. write for info. (0-942330-46-3) J Melek.

California Commercial Industrial Directories: Mono, No. 26. Jacques Melek. 200p. (Orig.). 1983. pap. write for info. (0-942330-47-1) J Melek.

California Commercial Industrial Directories: Monterey, No. 27. Jacques Melek. 200p. (Orig.). 1983. pap. write for info. (0-942330-48-X) J Melek.

California Commercial Industrial Directories: Napa, No. 28. Jacques Melek. 200p. (Orig.). 1983. 96.00 (0-685-05925-1) J Melek.

California Commercial Industrial Directories: Nevada, No. 29. Jacques Melek. 150p. 1983. pap. write for info. (0-942330-50-1) J Melek.

California Commercial Industrial Directories: Northern Sierra Counties, No. 59. Jacques Melek. 200p. (Orig.). 1983. 96.00 (0-942330-80-3) J Melek.

California Commercial Industrial Directories: Northern State Counties, No. 58. Jacques Melek. 200p. (Orig.). 1983. 96.00 (0-686-98787-X); pap. write for info. (0-942330-79-X) J Melek.

California Commercial Industrial Directories: Orange, No. 30. Jacques Melek. 200p. (Orig.). 1983. 96.00 (0-942330-51-X) J Melek.

California Commercial Industrial Directories: Placer, No. 31. Jacques Melek. 150p. (Orig.). 1983. pap. write for info. (0-942330-52-8) J Melek.

California Commercial Industrial Directories: San Benito, No. 35. Jacques Melek. 200p. 1983. pap. write for info. (0-942330-56-0) J Melek.

California Commercial Industrial Directories: San Bernardino, No. 36. Jacques Melek. 200p. (Orig.). 1983. pap. write for info. (0-942330-57-9) J Melek.

California Commercial Industrial Directories: San Diego, No. 37. Jacques Melek. 200p. 1983. pap. write for info. (0-942330-58-7) J Melek.

California Commercial Industrial Directories: San Francisco, No. 38. Jacques Melek. 200p. (Orig.). 1983. pap. write for info. (0-942330-59-5) J Melek.

California Commercial Industrial Directories: San Joaquin, Vol. 39. Jacques Melek. 200p. (Orig.). 1983. 96.00 (0-942330-60-9) J Melek.

California Commercial Industrial Directories: San Luis Obispo, No. 40. Jacques Melek. 200p. (Orig.). 1983. pap. 96.00 (0-942330-61-7) J Melek.

California Commercial Industrial Directories: San Mateo, No. 41. Jacques Melek. 200p. (Orig.). 1983. 96.00 (0-942330-62-5) J Melek.

California Commercial Industrial Directories: Sanislaus, No. 50. Jacques Melek. 200p. (Orig.). 1983. 96.00 (0-942330-71-4) J Melek.

California Commercial Industrial Directories: Santa Barbara, No. 42. Jacques Melek. 200p. (Orig.). 1983. pap. 96.00 (0-942330-63-3) J Melek.

California Commercial Industrial Directories: Santa Clara, No. 43. Jacques Melek. 200p. (Orig.). 1983. 96.00 (0-942330-64-1) J Melek.

California Commercial Industrial Directories: Santa Cruz, No. 44. Jacques Melek. 200p. (Orig.). 1983. 96.00 (0-942330-65-X) J Melek.

California Commercial Industrial Directories: Shasta, No. 45. Jacques Melek. 200p. (Orig.). 1983. 96.00 (0-942330-66-8) J Melek.

California Commercial Industrial Directories: Sierra, No. 46. Jacques Melek. 150p. 1982. 96.00 (0-942330-67-6) J Melek.

California Commercial Industrial Directories: Siskiyou, No. 47. Jacques Melek. 200p. 1983. 96.00 (0-942330-68-4) J Melek.

California Commercial Industrial Directories: Solano, No. 48. Jacques Melek. 200p. (Orig.). 1983. pap. 96.00 (0-942330-69-2) J Melek.

California Commercial Industrial Directories: Sonoma, No. 49. Jacques Melek. 200p. (Orig.). 1983. 96.00 (0-942330-70-6) J Melek.

California Commercial Industrial Directories: Tehama, No. 51. Jacques Melek. 200p. (Orig.). 1983. 96.00 (0-942330-72-2) J Melek.

California Commercial Industrial Directories: Trinity, No. 52. Jacques Melek. 200p. 1983. 96.00 (0-942330-73-0) J Melek.

California Commercial Industrial Directories: Tulane, No. 53. Jacques Melek. 150p. (Orig.). 1983. 96.00 (0-942330-74-9) J Melek.

California Commercial Industrial Directories: Tuolumne, No. 54. Jacques Melek. 200p. (Orig.). 1983. 96.00 (0-942330-75-7) J Melek.

California Commercial Industrial Directories: Ventura, No. 55. Jacques Melek. 200p. (Orig.). 1983. 96.00 (0-942330-76-5) J Melek.

California Commercial Industrial Directories: Yuba, No. 54. Jacques Melek. 200p. (Orig.). 1983. 96.00 (0-942330-78-1) J Melek.

California Commercial Law: June 1992 Update, 2 vols., Set. James E. Crawford & Neil B. Martin. Ed. by Christopher D. Dworin. LC 65-63004. 261p. 1992. pap. 43.00 (0-88124-513-5, BU-30044) Cont Ed Bar-CA.

California Commodity Cuisine Recipe Collection. California Department of Education Staff. (Illus.). 100p. 1986. pap. 13.00 (0-8011-0274-X) Calif Education.

California Community Association Reference Guide, 1993. James P. Lingl. 356p. 1993. text ed. 40.00 (0-9629533-2-6) CAPCO.

California Community Association Reference Guide, 1993. 2nd ed. James P. Lingl. 360p. 1993. text ed. 40.00 (0-9629533-3-4) CAPCO.

***California Community Association Reference Guide, 1994.** James P. Lingl. 366p. 1994. text ed. 40.00 (0-9629533-4-2) CAPCO.

California Community Property, Cases & Materials. 5th ed. Harold E. Verrall & Gail B. Bird. (American Casebook Ser.). 604p. 1993. reprint ed. text ed. 44.50 (0-314-41163-1) West Pub.

California Community Property Handbook. 3rd ed. William W. Bassett. LC 91-75064. 540p. 1991. pap. 25.00 (1-55943-124-5) Michie Butterworth.

California Community Property with Tax Analysis. Joseph A. Stein & Jack Zuckerman. LC 85-71220. 1985. ring bd. write for info. (0-8205-1113-7) Bender.

California Complex Litigation Manual. Michael I. Greer et al. 430p. 1993. ring bd. 115.00 (1-55943-068-0) Michie Butterworth.

California Complex Litigation Manual. suppl. ed. Michael I. Greer et al. 1993. 45.00 (0-685-74321-7) Butterworth Legal Pubs.

California Compliance Calendar. 1991. write for info. (1-55871-263-1) BNA.

California Condition: A Pregnant Architecture. LC 82-83257. (Illus.). 104p. 1982. 14.85 (0-934418-15-2) Mus Contemp Art.

California Condominium & Planned Development Practice. Richard C. Smith. 844p. 1984. 115.00 (0-88124-127-X, RE-38870) Cont Ed Bar-CA.

California Condominium Handbook, 2 vols. 2nd ed. John P. Hanna. LC 75-7623. 420p. 1986. 150.00 (0-317-00608-8) Lawyers Cooperative.

California Condominium Handbook, 2 vols. 2nd suppl. ed. John P. Hanna. LC 75-7623. 420p. 1993. Suppl. 1993. 39.00 (0-317-03218-6) Lawyers Cooperative.

California Condominium Handbook: Law & Practice, Residential & Commercial, Common Interest Development, 2 vols. 2nd ed. John Paul Hanna. write for info. (0-318-61717-X) Bancroft Whitney Co.

California Condor. Alison Tibbitts & Alan Roocroft. (Animals, Animals, Animals Ser.). (Illus.). 32p. (J). (ps-2). 1992. lib. bdg. 12.95 (1-56065-107-5) Capstone Pr.

California Connection: Sixteen Paintings from the Gifford & Joann Phillips Collections. Anne C. Edgerton. (Illus.). 32p. 1983. pap. 9.95 (0-89013-145-7) Museum NM Pr.

California Conquered: War & Peace on the Pacific, 1846-1850. Neal Harlow. LC 81-7588. (Illus.). 544p. 1982. 45.00 (0-520-04430-4); pap. 16.00 (0-520-06605-7) U CA Pr.

California Conservatorships & Guardianships, Set: Vols. 1 & 2. William S. Johnstone, Jr. & Susan T. House. Ed. by Pamela J. Jester. LC 90-80562. 1378p. 1990. Set. ring bd. 145.00 (0-88124-175-X, ES-31500) Cont Ed Bar-CA.

California Conservatorships & Guardianships: March 1993 Update. William S. Johnstone, Jr. et al. Ed. by Carine Archer. LC 90-80562. 296p. 1993. ring bd. 47.00 (0-88124-608-5, ES-31502) Cont Ed Bar-CA.

California Consolidated Court Services Project. National Center for State Courts Staff. 65p. 1975. pap. write for info. (0-318-61188-0, MAB-019) Natl Ctr St Courts.

California Construction Defect Litigation: Residential & Commercial. 2nd ed. Thomas E. Miller. (Construction Law Library). 760p. 1992. text ed. 128.00 (0-471-57266-7) Wiley.

California Construction Law. 15th ed. Kenneth C. Gibbs & Gordon Hunt. (Construction Law Library). 336p. 1992. text ed. 118.00 (0-471-55911-3); pap. text ed. 60.00 (0-471-55910-5) Wiley.

California Construction Law Digests. James Acret. LC 93-2786. (Construction Law Ser.). 551p. 1993. text ed. 65.00 (0-07-172375-7) McGraw.

California Construction Law Manual. James Acret. LC 93-39597. (Construction Law Ser.). 1990. text ed. 45.00 (0-07-172581-4) Shepards-McGraw.

California Construction Law Manual. 4th ed. James Acret. 584p. 1990. text ed. 110.00 (0-07-172212-2) Shepards-McGraw.

California Construction Law Manual: Contractors Edition 1990. James Acret. 1990. 45.00 (0-07-172279-3) Shepards-McGraw.

California Consumer Cooperative Incorporation Sourcebook. 88p. 1984. pap. text ed. 6.50 (0-317-19723-1) Calif Dept Co.

California Continuing Judicial Studies Program. National Center for State Courts Staff. (Paul Reardon Ser.). 31p. 1981. 1.86 (0-685-15085-2, PRS-013) Natl Ctr St Courts.

California Contractors' Exam, No. 10. Harry Koch. 1989. pap. 10.95 (0-910553-22-X) Ken-Bks.

California Controversies: Major Issues in the History of the State. 2nd ed. Ed. by Leonard Pitt. (Illus.). 384p. 1990. pap. text ed. write for info. (0-88295-879-8) Harlan Davidson.

California Cook: Casually Elegant Recipes with Exhilarating Taste. Diane R. Worthington. LC 93-40445. 1994. 27.95 (0-553-09179-4) Bantam.

California Cookbook. Betty Evans. LC 94-9732. 288p. 1994. 21.95 (0-88415-197-2) Gulf Pub.

California Cooking with Betty Evans. Betty Evans. LC 85-62457. (Illus.). (Orig.). 1985. pap. 6.95 (0-931104-16-5) Sunflower Ink.

California Cool. (Illus.). 128p. (GER.). Date not set. write for info. (3-283-00259-2, Pub. by Georg Olms GW) Lubrecht & Cramer.

California Cool: West Coast Jazz of the 50s & 60s, the Album Cover Art. Ed. by Graham Marsh & Glyn Callingham. LC 92-14118. (Illus.). 112p. 1992. 24.95 (0-8118-0275-2) Chronicle Bks.

California Copper. Joan Hohl. 1994. mass mkt. 4.50 (0-373-48283-3, 5-48283-1) Silhouette.

California Corporate Practice Guide. rev. ed. Morgan D. King. 760p. 1987. 75.00 (0-915544-10-5) Lawpress CA.

California Corporate Securities Law Notebook. California Continuing Education of the Bar Staff. 356p. 1973. 50.00 (0-88124-024-9, BU-71010) Cont Ed Bar-CA.

California Corporation: Legal Aspects of Organization & Operation. 2nd ed. Herbert Kraus. (Corporate Practice Ser.: No. 31). 1993. 92.00 (1-55871-294-1) BNA.

California Corporation Formation Package & Minute Book. rev. ed. Kevin W. Finch. Ed. by Scott Crawford. (Successful Business Library). 284p. mac hd, ring bd. 69.95 (1-55571-318-1); disk, ring bd. 69.95 (1-55571-317-3) Oasis Pr OR.

California Corporation Formation Package & Minute Book. rev. ed. Kevin W. Finch. Ed. by Scott Crawford. (Successful Business Library). 284p. 1992. ring bd. 39.95 (1-55571-189-8) Oasis Pr OR.

California Corporation Formation Package & Minute Book. 7th rev. ed. Kevin W. Finch. Ed. by Scott Crawford. (Successful Business Library). 284p. 1992. pap. 29.95 (1-55571-185-5) Oasis Pr OR.

***California Corporation Formation Package & Minute Book.** 8th ed. Kevin Finck. (Successful Business Library). 284p. 1995. ring bd. 39.95 (1-55571-368-8) Oasis Pr OR.

***California Corporation Formation Package & Minute Book.** 8th ed. Kevin Finck. (Successful Business Library). 284p. 1995. pap. 29.95 (1-55571-369-6) Oasis Pr OR.

California Corporations Code & Corporate Securities Rules. 1993. pap. 33.00 (1-55943-192-X) Parker Pubns.

California Corporations Code & Corporate Securities Rules. Bender's Editorial Staff. 1972. write for info. (0-8205-1191-9) Bender.

California Corporations Code, 1993. 1992. pap. 33.00 (1-55943-139-3) Butterworth Legal Pubs.

California Counties on the Fiscal Fault Line. 1992. 30.00 (0-685-53198-8) CA State Assn.

California Country: Interior Design, Architecture & Style. Diane D. Saeks. Ed. by Nion McEvoy. (Illus.). 144p. 1992. 35.00 (0-8118-0016-4) Chronicle Bks.

***California Country: Interior Design, Architecture, & Style.** Diane D. Saeks. (Illus.). 208p. 1994. pap. 22.95 (0-8118-0772-X) Chronicle Bks.

California County Fact Book. (Illus.). 235p. (C). 1989. 26.95 (0-685-18794-2) CA State Assn.

California County Projections, 1991: Regional Market Update & Projections. 102p. 1991. pap. write for info. (0-318-69703-3) CCSCE.

California County Projections, 1992: Regional Market Update & Projections. 102p. 1992. 195.00 (1-878316-14-1) CCSCE.

California County Summits. Gary Suttle. Ed. by Thomas Winnett. LC 93-46432. (Illus.). 192p. (Orig.). 1994. pap. 14.95 (0-89997-164-4) Wilderness Pr.

California Court of Appeals: Executive Summary. National Center for State Courts Staff. 40p. 1974. pap. write for info. (0-318-61310-7, R-013A) Natl Ctr St Courts.

California Court of Appeals: Full Report. National Center for State Courts Staff. 344p. 1974. pap. write for info. (0-318-61311-5, R-013) Natl Ctr St Courts.

California Courtroom Evidence. 3rd ed. Joseph W. Cotchett & Fulton Haight. 1988. ring bd. 85.00 (1-55943-171-7) Parker Pubns.

California Courtroom Evidence, No. 1. 3rd suppl. ed. Joseph W. Cotchett & Fulton Haight. 1990. Suppl. 1, 1/90. 30.75 (0-685-66638-7) Parker Pubns.

California Courtroom Evidence, No. 2. 3rd suppl. ed. Joseph W. Cotchett & Fulton Haight. 1990. Suppl. 2, 9/90. 31.50 (0-685-66639-5) Parker Pubns.

California Courtroom Evidence, No. 3. 3rd suppl. ed. Joseph W. Cotchett & Fulton Haight. 1991. Suppl. 3 9/91. 34.75 (0-685-66640-9) Parker Pubns.

California Courtroom Evidence, No. 4. 3rd suppl. ed. Joseph W. Cotchett & Fulton Haight. 1992. Suppl. 4, 9/92. 48.50 (0-685-66641-7) Parker Pubns.

California Courtroom Evidence, No. 5. 3rd suppl. ed. Joseph W. Cotchett & Fulton Haight. 1993. Suppl. 5, 8/93. write for info. (0-318-70319-X) Parker Pubns.

California Courtroom Evidence Foundations. Joseph W. Cotchett & Gerald F. Uelmen. 220p. 1994. spiral bd. 39.50 (0-250-47229-5) Michie Butterworth.

California Courtroom Evidence, 1988-93. 3rd ed. Joseph W. Cotchett & Fulton Haight. 670p. 1994. ring bd. 115.00 (1-55943-122-9) Michie Butterworth.

California Courtroom Evidence, 1988-93. 3rd suppl. ed. Joseph W. Cotchett & Fulton Haight. 1993. 51.00 (0-911110-60-7) Parker Pubns.

***California Courts.** Vena Garrett. 1995. pap. 11.95 (0-929563-25-5) Pearson Pubns.

California Coven Project. Bob Stickgold. 192p. 1981. pap. 2.50 (0-345-28677-4, Del Rey) Ballantine.

California Cowboys. Dane Coolidge. LC 84-28001. 190p. 1985. reprint ed. pap. 9.95 (0-8165-0862-3) U of Ariz Pr.

California Crazy: Roadside Vernacular Architecture. Rip Georges & Jim Heimann. LC 79-24181. (Illus.). 144p. (Orig.). 1980. pap. 12.95 (0-87701-171-0) Chronicle Bks.

California Crime Perspective, 1994. Ed. by Kathleen O. Morgan et al. 24p. 1994. 18.00 (1-56692-254-2) Morgan Quitno Corp.

***California Crime Perspective 1995.** Ed. by Kathleen O. Morgan et al. 24p. 1995. 18.00 (1-56692-354-9) Morgan Quitno Corp.

California Criminal Defense Practice, 6 vols. Richard Erwin & Michael Millman. 1981. Updates. ring bd. write for info. (0-8205-1171-4, 171) Bender.

***California Criminal Evidence Guide: A Handbook for the Criminal Justice Student.** 4th ed. Raymond M. Hill. 260p. (C). 1988. pap. text ed. 16.50 (0-614-04718-8) Halleck Creek Pub.

California Criminal Evidence Workbook. Marvin G. Engquist. 240p. (C). 1994. spiral bd. 23.95 (0-8403-9501-9) Kendall-Hunt.

California Criminal Law. 2nd ed. Judy H. Kaci. LC 93-81037. 600p. 1994. pap. 50.00 (1-884439-01-2) Infotronix.

***California Criminal Law.** 3rd ed. Judy H. Kaci. 636p. (C). 1995. pap. 60.00 (1-884439-03-9) Infotronix.

California Criminal Law & Procedure for Security Officers. Lawrence C. Waddington. (Illus.). (Orig.). 1988. pap. 7.95 (0-87084-124-6) Anderson Pub Co.

California Criminal Law Manual. 8th rev. ed. Derald D. Hunt. 242p. 1991. pap. text ed. write for info. (0-8087-5159-X) Burgess MN Intl.

***California Criminal Law Trial Guide.** Ellen Krietzberg & John J. E. Markham, II. LC 94-38296. 1994. write for info. (0-8205-1164-1) Bender.

California Criminal Law 2D, 6 vols. B. E. Witkin & N. L. Epstein. 1988. 595.00 (0-318-40086-3) Lawyers Cooperative.

An Asterisk (*) at the beginning of an entry indicates that the title is appearing in BIP for the first time.

An Asterisk (*) at the beginning of an entry indicates that the title is appearing in BIP for the first time.

California Girls! Ann M. Martin. (Baby-Sitters Club Super Special Ser.: No. 5). 240p. (J). (gr. 3-7). 1990. pap. 3.95 (*0-590-43575-2*) Scholastic Inc.

California Girls Paper Dolls. Robbins. 1990. pap. 5.95 (*0-913035-57-2*) Eclipse Bks.

California Glory. Dana F. Ross. (Holts Ser.: No. 4). 1991. mass mkt. 4.99 (*0-553-28970-5*) Bantam.

California Glory. large type ed. Dana F. Ross. (General Ser.). 476p. 1992. text ed. 21.95 (*0-8161-5310-8*, Large Print Bks) Hall.

California Gold. California State Grange Staff. LC 92-32005. 1992. write for info. (*0-87197-355-3*) Favorite Recipes.

California Gold. John Jakes. 768p. 1990. mass mkt. 5.95 (*0-345-36943-2*) Ballantine.

California Gold. John Jakes. 1989. 19.95 (*0-394-56106-6*) Random.

California Gold. Phyllis Zauner. (Western Mini-Histories Ser.). (Illus.). 64p. (Orig.). 1980. pap. 5.95 (*0-936914-00-9*) Zanel Pubns.

California Gold: Selected Source Materials for College Research Papers. Ed. by Edwin R. Bingham. LC 81-2001. ix, 117p. 1981. reprint ed. text ed. 35.00 (*0-313-22776-4*, BICAG, Greenwood Pr) Greenwood.

California Gold: The Beginning of Mining in the Far West. Rodman W. Paul. LC 47-54111. (Bison Book Ser.). (Illus.). 400p. reprint ed. pap. 114.00 (*0-8357-7974-2*, 2029161) Bks Demand.

California Gold & the Highgraders. F. D. Calhoon. (Illus.). 375p. (Orig.). 1988. pap. 10.00 (*0-945862-00-8*) Cal Con Pubs.

California Gold Rush. LC 61-10677. 1988. 14.95 (*0-8167-1518-1*) Troll Assocs.

***California Gold Rush.** Andrew Bronin. (Jackdaws Ser.). (Illus.). 1991. 24.95 (*1-56696-067-3*); student ed 32.00 (*0-614-07311-1*) Golden Owl NY.

***California Gold Rush.** R. Conrad Stein. LC 94-38651. (Cornerstones of Freedom Ser.). (Illus.). 32p. (J). (gr. 3-6). 1995. lib. bdg. 12.30 (*0-516-06691-9*) Childrens.

California Gold Rush. May McNeer. LC 87-4685. (Landmark Bks.: No. 6). 160p. (J). (gr. 5-9). 1987. reprint ed. pap. 4.99 (*0-394-89177-5*) Random Bks Yng Read.

California Gold Rush: A Guide to the California Gold Rush. Eugene R. Hart. Ed. by Joette Judkins. (Illus.). 128p. (Orig.). 1993. pap. 14.95 (*0-9634197-1-4*, GR1) FreeWheel CA.

California Gold Rush: Search for Treasure. Catherine E. Chambers. LC 83-18280. (Adventures in Frontier America Ser.). (Illus.). 32p. (J). (gr. 5-9). 1984. lib. bdg. 11.59 (*0-8167-0051-6*); pap. text ed. 2.95 (*0-8167-0052-4*) Troll Assocs.

California Gold Rush: West with the Forty-Niners. Elizabeth Van Steenwyk. (First Bks.). (Illus.). 64p. (J). (gr. 5-8). 1991. lib. bdg. 13.93 (*0-531-20032-9*) Watts.

California Gold Rush Merchant: The Journal of Stephen Chapin Davis. Stephen C. Davis. Ed. by Benjamin B. Richards. LC 73-21490. (Illus.). 124p. (C). 1974. reprint ed. text ed. 49.75 (*0-8371-6408-7*, DAGR, Greenwood Pr) Greenwood.

California Gold Rush Merchant: The Journal of Stephen Chapin Davis. Stephen C. Davis. (American Biography Ser.). 124p. 1991. reprint ed. lib. bdg. 59.00 (*0-7812-8103-2*) Rprt Serv.

California Gold-Rush Plays. Ed. by Glenn Loney. LC 83-61191. Orig. Title: American Pioneer Drama. 1983. 34.00 (*0-933826-34-6*); pap. 12.95 (*0-933826-35-4*) PAJ Pubns.

California Gold Rush Trail. Lynda Hatch. (Pathways of America Ser.). (Illus.). 96p. (J). (gr. 4-8). 1994. 9.95 (*0-86653-810-0*, GA1502) Good Apple.

California Gold Wine List, 1994. Tracy Hamilton. 50p. 1993. pap. 5.95 (*0-9639241-0-9*) Calif Gold.

***California Gold Wine List 1995.** Tracy Hamilton. (Orig.). 1994. pap. 7.95 (*0-9639241-1-7*) Calif Gold.

California Golf: The Complete Guide. 3rd ed. Ed. by Ray March. (Illus.). 608p. 1991. 16.95 (*0-935701-16-8*) Foghorn Pr.

California Golf: The Complete Guide. 5th ed. Ed. by Mark Soltau. 860p. 1994. 17.95 (*0-935701-79-6*) Foghorn Pr.

***California Golf: The Complete Guide.** 6th ed. Ed. by Mark Soltau. 86p. 1996. 19.95 (*0-935701-90-7*) Foghorn Pr.

***California Gothic.** Etchison. 1995. mass mkt. (*0-440-21726-1*) Dell.

California Government & Politics Annual, 1978-79. Ed. by Gary L. Wilhelm et al. (Illus.). 1978. pap. text ed. 3.50 (*0-930302-17-6*) Cal Journal.

California Government & Politics Annual, 1979-1980. Ed. by Thomas R. Hoeber et al. (Illus.). (C). 1979. pap. text ed. 3.50 (*0-930302-22-2*) Cal Journal.

California Government & Politics Annual, 1980-81. Ed. by Thomas R. Hoeber et al. (Illus.). 128p. (Orig.). (C). 1980. pap. text ed. 3.95 (*0-930302-24-9*) Cal Journal.

California Government & Politics Annual, 1981-82. Ed. by Thomas R. Hoeber et al. (Annual Ser.). (Illus.). 128p. (Orig.). (C). 1981. pap. 4.50 (*0-930302-50-8*) Cal Journal.

California Government & Politics Annual, 1982-83. Thomas R. Hoeber et al. (Annual Ser.). (Illus.). 128p. (Orig.). (C). 1982. pap. text ed. 4.95 (*0-930302-44-3*) Cal Journal.

California Government & Politics Annual, 1983-1984. Ed. by Thomas R. Hoeber & Charles Price. (Illus.). 128p. (C). 1983. pap. text ed. 4.95 (*0-930302-53-2*) Cal Journal.

California Government & Politics Annual, 1984-85. Ed. by Thomas R. Hoeber & Charles Price. (Illus.). 128p. 1984. pap. text ed. 4.95 (*0-930302-54-0*) Cal Journal.

California Government & Politics Annual, 1985-1986. Ed. by Thomas R. Hoeber & Charles Price. (Illus.). 128p. (Orig.). (C). 1985. pap. text ed. 5.95 (*0-930302-56-7*) Cal Journal.

California Government & Politics Annual, 1986-87. Thomas R. Hoeber & Charles Price. (Illus.). 128p. (Orig.). (C). 1986. pap. text ed. 5.95 (*0-930302-58-3*) Cal Journal.

California Government & Politics Annual, 1987-88. Thomas R. Hoeber & Charles Price. (Illus.). 128p. (Orig.). 1987. pap. 5.95 (*0-930302-61-3*) Cal Journal.

California Government & Politics Annual, 1988-89. Thomas R. Hoeber & Charles Price. (Illus.). 128p. (Orig.). 1988. pap. 6.95 (*0-930302-62-1*) Cal Journal.

California Government & Politics Annual, 1989-90. Thomas R. Hoeber & Charles Price. (Illus.). 128p. (Orig.). 1989. pap. 7.95 (*0-930302-69-9*) Cal Journal.

California Government & Politics Annual, 1990-91. Thomas R. Hoeber & Charles Price. (Illus.). 128p. (Orig.). 1990. pap. 7.95 (*0-930302-72-9*) Cal Journal.

California Government & Politics Today. 5th ed. Charles P. Sohner & Mona Field. (C). 1989. pap. text ed. 4.50 (*0-673-39894-3*) HarpCollege.

California Government Today: Politics of Reform. 4th ed. Charles G. Bell & Charles M. Price. LC 91-8880. 336p. (C). 1992. pap. 29.95 (*0-534-16458-7*) Intl Thomson.

***California Government Today: Politics of Reform.** 5th ed. Charles M. Price & Charles G. Bell. LC 95-13452. 1996. pap. 25.95 (*0-534-25998-7*) Intl Thomson.

California Government Tort Liability Practice. 3rd ed. Ed. by Lawrence M. Freiser. LC 92-52724. 1034p. 1992. 150.00 (*0-88124-465-1*, TO-31690) Cont Ed Bar-CA.

California Governments Performance Standards, 1990. Ed. by Greg Michels. (Governments Performance Standards Ser.). (Illus.). 150p. 1990. text ed. 125.00 (*1-55507-476-6*) Municipal Analysis.

California Grandeur & Genre: From the Collection of James L. Coran & Walter A. Nelson-Rees. Iona M. Chelette et al. LC 91-28616. (Illus.). 108p. 1992. 50.00 (*0-295-97188-6*); pap. 29.95 (*0-295-97189-4*) U of Wash Pr.

California Grassland Restoration Literature. Halverson & Keeley. 35p. (Orig.). (C). reprint ed. pap. 5.00 (*0-933421-44-3*) Redwood Seed.

California Green Guide. Date not set. pap. 18.00 (*2-06-159801-3*, 1598) Michelin.

***California Green Guide English Edition.** Michelin Staff. Date not set. pap. 17.95 (*0-7859-7177-7*, 2061598013) Fr & Eur.

California Grizzly. Tracy I. Storer & Lloyd P. Tevis, Jr. LC 78-17671. (Illus.). xii, 359p. 1978. reprint ed. pap. 9.95 (*0-8032-9101-9*) U of Nebr Pr.

California Groundwater & Soil Contamination: Technical Preparation & Litigation Management. Thomas J. Bois, II & Bernard J. Luther. LC 94-7250. (Environmental Law Library). 1994. text ed. 128.00 (*0-471-01996-8*) Wiley.

California Guide to Motel-Hotel Discounts. Ruth Callarman. 104p. (Orig.). 1985. pap. 6.98 (*0-9613087-1-0*) Potter Pubns.

California Guide to Reporting Hazardous Releases: Rules & Procedures. Albert M. Cohen. LC 92-11436. 1992. write for info. (*0-8205-1359-8*) Bender.

California Guide to Restaurant Discounts. Ruth Callarman. 160p. (Orig.). 1985. pap. 8.98 (*0-9613087-2-9*) Potter Pubns.

California Gunsmiths. Lawrence P. Shelton. (Illus.). 302p. 1977. boxed 29.65 (*0-87387-081-6*) Shumway.

California Handbook: A Comprehensive Guide to Sources of Current Information & Action. 7th ed. Thaddeus C. Trzyna. (California Information Guides Ser.). 258p. (Orig.). 1994. pap. 35.00 (*1-880028-01-8*) Cal Inst Public.

***California Handbook of Social Intercourse.** Patrick Grates. 260p. 1994. pap. 5.95 (*0-9642693-0-9*) Accordion Creations.

California Hazardous Waste Directory, 1991-1992. David Ronce. 482p. 1991. pap. text ed. 199.00 (*1-880720-00-0*) In Media Res.

***California Health Bar Drink Guide.** Berk. 1995. 9.98 (*1-884822-27-4*) Blck Dog & Leventhal.

California Health Care Perspective, 1994. Ed. by Kathleen O. Morgan et al. 24p. 1994. 18.00 (*1-56692-154-6*) Morgan Quitno Corp.

***California Health Care Perspective 1995.** Ed. by Kathleen O. Morgan et al. 24p. 1995. 18.00 (*1-56692-404-9*) Morgan Quitno Corp.

California Heartland: A Pictorial History & Tour Guide of Eight Northern California Counties. Sandra B. Shepherd. (Illus.). 208p. 1993. 27.95 (*0-942087-07-0*) Scottwall Assocs.

***California Heartland Recipes.** (Illus.). 192p. 1994. text ed. 19.95 (*0-9643181-0-5*) KXTV.

California Herbal Remedies: The History & Uses of Native Medicinal Plants. Lolo Westrich. (Illus.). 180p. 1989. pap. 14.95 (*0-87201-457-6*) Gulf Pub.

California Heritage Continues. 1991. pap. 15.95 (*0-385-41759-4*) Doubleday.

California Heritage Cookbook. Pasadena Junior League Staff. 1990. pap. 19.95 (*0-385-41677-6*) Doubleday.

California High: Warbirds of the West Coast. Michael O'Leary. (Wings Ser.: No. 3). (Illus.). 96p. (Orig.). 1992. pap. 17.95 (*1-872004-37-7*) Specialty Pr.

California High School Proficiency Examination. Jack Rudman. (Admission Test Ser.: ATS-39). 1994. pap. 23.95 (*0-8373-5039-5*) Nat Learn.

California Highway Patrol...Yesterday & Today. Robert A. Wick. (Illus.). 224p. (Orig.). 1990. pap. 18.95 (*0-926480-01-4*) Phase Three Pub.

California Hiking: The Complete Guide. Tom Stienstra & Michael Hodgson. 832p. 1994. pap. 17.95 (*0-935701-69-9*) Foghorn Pr.

***California Hiking: The Complete Guide.** 2nd ed. Tom Stienstra & Michael Hodgson. 856p. 1995. pap. 18.95 (*0-935701-93-1*) Foghorn Pr.

***California Hiring & Termination Guide: Forms & Procedures.** Ellen S. Savage. 220p. (Orig.). (C). 1994. pap. text ed. 79.00 (*1-878630-59-8*) CA Chamber Commerce.

California Historic Sites. Ed. by Old California Preservation Society Staff. (Illus.). 1986. pap. 4.95 (*0-913290-69-6*) Camaro Pub.

California Historical & Biographical Index., Vol. 1. Ronald V. Jackson. LC 78-53687. (Illus.). 1984. lib. bdg. 30.00 (*0-89593-172-9*) Accelerated Index.

California Hit. Don Pendleton. (Executioner Ser.: No. 11). 1989. pap. 3.50 (*1-55817-070-7*, Pinnacle NY) Windsor NY.

California Homeowner's Guidebook: How to Deal with Home Alteration Contractors. Clifford W. Pool. Ed. by Keith I. F'Mayer. 106p. (Orig.). 1992. pap. 19.95 (*0-9635362-1-4*, TX3 401 617) Courier Pub.

California Hot Air Balloon Mystery. Carole Marsh. (Carole Marsh California Bks.). (Illus.). (J). (gr. 2-9). 1994. 24.95 (*0-7933-2354-1*); pap. 14.95 (*0-7933-2355-X*); disk 29.95 (*0-7933-2356-8*) Gallopade Pub Group.

California Human Resources Forecast 1993. Susan Way-Smith & Daniel J. Mitchell. 35p. 1993. pap. 15.00 (*0-89215-181-1*) U Cal LA Indus Rel.

California Impressions. J. W. Morgan. Ed. by David Perkins. (Illus.). 1886. 71.00 (*0-937048-46-1*) CSUN.

California in Depth: A Stereoscopic Look at the Nineteenth Century. Jim Crain. LC 93-44431. (Illus.). 112p. 1994. 24.95 (*0-8118-0423-2*) Chronicle Bks.

California in Perspective 1994. Ed. by Kathleen O. Morgan et al. 26p. 1994. 18.00 (*1-56692-204-6*) Morgan Quitno Corp.

***California in Perspective 1995.** Ed. by Kathleen O. Morgan et al. 26p. 1995. pap. 18.00 (*1-56692-454-5*) Morgan Quitno Corp.

California in Prose & Verse see Works of Benjamin Parke Avery, 1828-1875

California in the Making. Rockwell D. Hunt. LC 73-20904. 325p. 1974. reprint ed. 69.50 (*0-8371-5866-4*, HUCM, Greenwood Pr) Greenwood.

California in the Year Two Thousand: A Look into the Future of the Golden State As It Approaches the Millennium. Charles F. Adams. LC 92-29085. (Illus.). 256p. 1992. 21.95 (*0-87015-263-7*) Pacific Bks.

California in 1792: A Spanish Naval Visit. Donald C. Cutter. LC 90-50231. (American Exploration & Travel Ser.: Vol. 71). (Illus.). 192p. 1990. 24.95 (*0-8061-2306-0*) U of Okla Pr.

***California in 1792: A Spanish Naval Visit.** Donald C. Cutter. LC 90-50231. (American Exploration & Travel Ser.: Vol. 71). (Illus.). 192p. 1995. pap. 12.95 (*0-8061-2731-7*) U of Okla Pr.

California Income Tax Laws. Prentice-Hall Editorial Staff. 1100p. 1989. pap. text ed. 41.50 (*0-13-112285-1*, Busn) P-H.

California Income Tax Laws: 1993 Edition. rev. ed. RIA In-House Professional Staff. 1000p. 1992. pap. text ed. 64.50 (*0-7811-0064-X*) Res Inst Am.

California Incorporation System. Bender's Editorial Staff. 1985. Incl. disks. disk write for info. (*0-8205-1638-4*) Bender.

California Incorporator: 1.0. Anthony Mancuso. 336p. 1990. disk 129.00 (*0-87337-027-9*) Nolo Pr.

California Indian Country: The Land & the People. Dolan H. Eargle, Jr. LC 91-67406. (Illus.). (J). (gr. 4). 1992. pap. 10.00 (*0-937401-20-X*) Trees Co Pr.

California Indian Nights Entertainments. Comp. by Edward W Gifford & Gwendoline H. Block. LC 76-43713. reprint ed. 52.50 (*0-404-15546-4*) AMS Pr.

California Indian Shamanism. Ed. by Lowell J. Bean. LC 92-6167. (Anthropological Papers: No. 39). (Illus.). 274p. 1992. text ed. 33.00 (*0-87919-125-2*); pap. text ed. 27.50 (*0-87919-124-4*) Ballena Pr.

California Indian Tribes: Northern, Vol. 1. Bellerophon Books Staff. (J). (gr. 1-9). 1995. pap. 3.95 (*0-88388-153-5*) Bellerophon Bks.

California Indian Tribes: Southern, Vol. 2. Bellerophon Books Staff. (J). (gr. 4-7). 1995. pap. 3.95 (*0-88388-184-5*) Bellerophon Bks.

California Indian Watercraft. Richard W. Cunningham. LC 88-24426. (Illus.). (Orig.). 1988. pap. 12.95 (*0-945092-01-6*) EZ Nature.

California Indians. C. L. Keyworth. (First Americans Ser.). (Illus.). 96p. (J). (gr. 5-8). 1990. 18.95 (*0-8160-2386-7*) Facts on File.

California Indians: A Source Book. 2nd enl. rev. ed. Ed. by Robert F. Heizer & M. A. Whipple. LC 72-122951. (Illus.). 1971. 42.50 (*0-520-01770-6*); pap. 22.50 (*0-520-02031-6*) U CA Pr.

California Indians: An Educational Coloring Book. Spizzirri Publishing Co. Staff. Ed. by Linda Spizzirri. (Illus.). 32p. (J). (gr. 1-8). 1986. pap. 1.75 (*0-86545-080-3*) Spizzirri.

California Indians: An Illustrated Guide. George Emanuels. (Illus.). 172p. (J). (gr. 4-8). 1990. reprint ed. pap. 14.95 (*0-9607520-3-X*) Diablo Bks.

California Indians: Primary Resources. Sylvia B. Vane & Lowell J. Bean. LC 90-40604. (Anthropological Papers: No. 36). (C). 1990. text ed. 45.00 (*0-87919-119-8*); pap. text ed. 33.00 (*0-87919-118-X*) Ballena Pr.

***California Indians & the Environment.** (News from Native California Special Report Ser.: No. 1). 24p. 1992. lib. bdg. 17.00 (*0-8095-4986-7*) Borgo Pr.

California Initiatives & Referendums, 1912-1990: A Survey & Guide to Research. John M. Allswang. 220p. 1991. lib. bdg. 29.95 (*1-878644-02-5*) Regina Bks.

California Insects. Jerry A. Powell & Charles L. Hogue. LC 78-62876. (California Natural History Guides Ser.: No. 44). (Illus.). 1980. pap. 15.00 (*0-520-03782-0*) U CA Pr.

California Insects. Jerry A. Powell & Charles L. Hogue. LC 78-62876. (California Natural History Guides Ser.: No. 44). (Illus.). 398p. reprint ed. pap. 113.50 (*0-7837-4692-X*, 2044439) Bks Demand.

California Institute of Psychology Modern Guide to Psychotherapy. John F. Fielder et al. 1991. pap. 13.95 (*0-9631938-5-6*) CIP Comms.

California Insurance Code & Ethics Prelicense Course. Anthony Schools Corporation Staff. 102p. (Orig.). 1992. pap. text ed. 20.00 (*0-941833-42-9*) Anthony Schools.

California Insurance Code, 1993. 1993. pap. 32.00 (*1-55943-189-X*) Butterworth Legal Pubs.

California Insurance Disputes. Robert C. Clifford. LC 91-62069. 480p. 1993. ring bd. 115.00 (*1-55943-114-8*) Michie Butterworth.

California Insurance Disputes, No. 1. suppl. ed. Robert C. Clifford. LC 91-62069. 1993. 48.00 (*0-685-70035-6*) Butterworth Legal Pubs.

California Insurance Disputes, Rev. 1. Robert C. Clifford. ring bd. 90.00 (*1-55943-197-0*) Parker Pubns.

California Insurance Law & Practice, 4 vols. Bender's Editorial Staff. LC 86-71788. (Illus.). 1986. Updates. ring bd. write for info. (*0-8205-1155-2*) Bender.

California Insurance Law Digest. John DiMugno. LC 93-37974. 1994. text ed. 60.00 (*0-07-172544-X*) Shepards-McGraw.

California Intellectual Property Handbook. 1991. write for info. (*0-8205-1855-7*) Bender.

California Inter Pocula. fac. ed. Hubert H. Bancroft. LC 67-29422. (Works of Hubert Howe Bancroft Ser.). 1967. reprint ed. 40.00 (*0-914888-28-5*) Bancroft Pr.

California International Trade Register, 1994. 6th ed. 784p. 1994. disk write for info. (*0-318-72185-6*) Database Pub Co.

California International Trade Register, 1994. 6th ed. 784p. 1995. pap. 125.00 (*0-929695-62-3*) Database Pub Co.

California Interpretive History. 6th ed. J. James Rawls. 1993. pap. text ed. write for info. (*0-07-004269-1*) McGraw.

California Jeopardy! Answers & Questions about Our State! Carole Marsh. (Carole Marsh California Bks.). (Illus.). (J). (gr. 3-12). 1994. lib. bdg. 24.95 (*0-7933-4091-8*); pap. 14.95 (*0-7933-4092-6*); disk 29.95 (*0-7933-4093-4*) Gallopade Pub Group.

California Job Journal. Allison-Garrett. 91p. 1990. pap. 29.99 (*1-878235-04-4*) Taylor Pub MI.

California Joe: Noted Scout & Indian Fighter. Joe E. Milner & Earle R. Forrest. LC 87-5908. (Illus.). viii, 396p. 1987. reprint ed. pap. 9.95 (*0-8032-8150-1*) U of Nebr Pr.

California "Jography" A Fun Run Thru Our State! Carole Marsh. (Carole Marsh California Bks.). (Illus.). (YA). (gr. 3-12). 1994. lib. bdg. 24.95 (*1-55609-511-2*); pap. 14.95 (*1-55609-510-4*); disk 29.95 (*0-685-45935-7*) Gallopade Pub Group.

California Judges' Benchbook: Criminal Posttrial Proceedings 1991, 4 vols., Set. Intro. by Paul M. Li. LC 90-82513. 368p. 1991. pap. text ed. 65.00 (*0-88124-382-5*, CR-31791) Cont Ed Bar-CA.

California Judges' Benchbook: Criminal Pretrial Proceedings 1991, 4 vols., Set. Intro. by Paul M. Li. LC 90-82514. 253p. 1991. pap. text ed. 65.00 (*0-88124-380-9*, CR-31791) Cont Ed Bar-CA.

California Judges' Benchbook: Criminal Trials 1991, Set. Intro. by Paul M. Li. LC 90-82512. 266p. 1991. pap. text ed. 65.00 (*0-88124-381-7*, CR-31791) Cont Ed Bar-CA.

California Judges Benchbook: Nineteen Ninety-One Edition, 4 vols., Set. Intro. by Paul M. Li. 1342p. 1991. pap. text ed. 65.00 (*0-88124-379-5*, CR-31791) Cont Ed Bar-CA.

California Judges Benchbook: Search & Seizure 1991, 4 vols., Set. George Brunn. LC 90-86111. 455p. 1991. pap. text ed. 65.00 (*0-88124-366-3*, CR-31791) Cont Ed Bar-CA.

California Judicial Council Forms Manual, 3 vols. California Continuing Education of the Bar Staff. LC 81-65171. 350p. 1981. 80.00 (*0-88124-081-8*, CP-74000) Cont Ed Bar-CA.

California Judicial Retirement Study. Sheila D'Amico et al. 134p. 1988. 8.00 (*0-685-33610-7*, WRO-097) Natl Ctr St Courts.

California Jurisprudence 3d, 66 vols. suppl. ed. 1993. Suppl. 1993. write for info. (*0-318-57172-2*) Lawyers Cooperative.

California Jury Instructions - Civil. 7th ed. 1056p. 1986. 120.00 (*0-317-52098-9*) West Pub.

California Jury Selection & Management Survey. National Center for State Courts Staff. 81p. 1976. pap. write for info. (*0-318-61289-5*, MAB-020) Natl Ctr St Courts.

California Juvenile Court Practice, 2 vols., 1. 2nd ed. California Continuing Education of the Bar Staff. 1122p. 1981. 75.00 (*0-88124-083-4*, CR-35520) Cont Ed Bar-CA.

California Juvenile Court Practice, 2 vols., 2. 2nd ed. California Continuing Education of the Bar Staff. 1122p. 1981. 75.00 (*0-88124-084-2*, CR-35530) Cont Ed Bar-CA.

California Juvenile Court Practice, 2 vols., Set. 2nd ed. California Continuing Education of the Bar Staff. 1122p. 1981. 125.00 (*0-88124-085-0*) Cont Ed Bar-CA.

California Kid's Cookbook: Recipes, How-to, History, Lore & More! Carole Marsh. (Carole Marsh California Bks.). (Illus.). (YA). (gr. 3-12). 1994. lib. bdg. 24.95 (*0-7933-0178-5*); pap. 14.95 (*0-7933-0177-7*); disk 29.95 (*0-7933-0179-3*) Gallopade Pub Group.

California Kill. George G. Gilman. (Edge Ser.: No. 7). 1989. pap. 3.50 (*1-55817-250-5*, Pinnacle NY) Windsor NY.

An Asterisk (*) at the beginning of an entry indicates that the title is appearing in BIP for the first time.

California Politics: Economics, Power, & Policy. James W. Lamare. Ed. by Perlee. LC 93-25933. 250p. (C). 1993. pap. text ed. 27.75 (0-314-02677-0) West Pub.

California Politics & Government: A Practical Approach. 2nd ed. Larry N. Gerston & Terry Christensen. 130p. (C). 1993. pap. 8.95 (0-534-20190-3) Intl Thomson.

*California Politics & Government: A Practical Approach. 3rd ed. Larry N. Gerston & Terry Christensen. 129p. 1995. pap. 9.95 (0-534-21768-0) Intl Thomson.

California Politics & Government, 1970-1983: A Selected Bibliography. Jack Leister et al. LC 84-23492. (Occasional Bibliographies Ser.: No. 3). 86p. reprint ed. pap. 25.00 (0-7837-2135-8, 2042417) Bks Demand.

California Politics, Eighteen Forty-Six to Nineteen Twenty: The Emerging Corporate State. Spencer C. Olin, Jr. Ed. by Norris Hundley, Jr. & John A. Schutz. (Golden State Ser.). (Illus.). 96p. 1981. pap. 10.00 (0-87835-114-0) MTL.

California Poppy. limited ed. Judy Sutcliffe. (Illus.). 1984. 25.00 (0-943164-04-4) Geronima.

California Population Characteristics, 1991. rev. ed. Stephen Levy. LC 90-660112. 1991. pap. 195.00 (1-878316-09-5) CCSCE.

California Population Characteristics, 1992. rev. ed. Stephen Levy. LC 90-660112. 1992. pap. 195.00 (1-878316-13-3) CCSCE.

California Population Trends. LC 88-189799. 30p. (Orig.). 1988. reprint ed. pap. 50.00 (0-923172-00-9) West Econ Rsch.

*California Potteries: The Complete Book. Michael Schneider. (Illus.). 256p. 1995. 49.95 (0-88740-877-X) Schiffer.

California Practice Handbook: Attorney Ethics. Stanley W. Lamport. Ed. by Profesional Responsibility & Ethics Committee, Los Angeles County Bar Association Staff et al. LC 93-6043. Date not set. write for info. (0-8205-1091-2) Bender.

California Practice Handbook: Depositions. Ed. by Los Angeles County Bar Association, Litigation Section Staff et al. LC 92-29942. 1992. write for info. (0-8205-1782-8) Bender.

California Practice Handbook: General Discovery Principles. Ed. by Los Angeles County Bar Association, Litigation Section Staff et al. LC 92-2455. 1992. write for info. (0-8205-1784-4) Bender.

California Practice Handbook: Pretrial Disposition. Jill Sellers. Date not set. write for info. (0-8205-1785-2) Bender.

California Practice Handbook: Provisional Remedies. Ed. by Edythe Bronston et al. LC 92-44096. 1993. write for info. (0-8205-1973-1) Bender.

California Practice with Forms, 22 vols. suppl. ed. 1991. Suppl. 1991. write for info. (0-318-57173-0) Lawyers Cooperative.

*California Predator. Eric Anderson. 180p. 1995. pap. 7.95 (1-56901-588-0) NW Pub.

*California Preliminary Examinations. Mark B. Simons. 196p. 1994. pap. 42.50 (0-250-47239-2) Michie Butterworth.

California Preliminary Examinations. 7th ed. Mark B. Simons. 1993. pap. 39.50 (1-55943-173-3) Butterworth Legal Pubs.

*California Private School Directory. California Department of Education Staff. 304p. 1994. pap. 16.00 (0-8011-1170-6) Calif Education.

California Probate Code, 1993. 1992. pap. 24.00 (1-55943-188-1) Butterworth Legal Pubs.

California Probate Practice, 4 vols. 1991. write for info. (0-8205-1015-7) Bender.

*California Probate Procedure, 2 vols., Set. 5th ed. Arthur K. Marshall & Andrew S. Garb. 480p. 1994. ring bd. 160.00 (1-55943-089-3) Michie Butterworth.

*California Probate Procedures, Suppl. 1, 4/91. Arthur K. Marshall & Andrew S. Garb. Date not set. 71.50 (1-55943-087-7) Butterworth Legal Pubs.

*California Probate Procedures, Suppl. 2, 11/93. Arthur K. Marshall & Andrew S. Garb. Date not set. 55.00 (1-55943-088-5) Butterworth Legal Pubs.

*California Probate Procedures, Vol. 1. Arthur K. Marshall & Andrew S. Garb. Date not set. 71.50 (0-614-00282-6) Butterworth Legal Pubs.

California Probate Workflow Manual, 2 vols. rev. suppl. ed. California Continuing Education of the Bar Staff. Ed. by William L. Blaine. LC 79-53359. 1990. Aug. '90 suppl. 32.00 (0-88124-314-0, ES-31561) Cont Ed Bar-CA.

California Probate Workflow Manual, 2 vols., Set. rev. ed. California Continuing Education of the Bar Staff. Ed. by William L. Blaine. LC 79-53359. 1989. 120.00 (0-88124-072-9, ES-31560) Cont Ed Bar-CA.

California Probate Workflow Manual Vols. 1 & 2: March 1993 Update. rev. ed. Valerie J. Merritt. Ed. by Janette Tom. LC 79-53359. 268p. 1993. ring bd. 40.00 (0-88124-600-X, ES-31563) Cont Ed Bar-CA.

California Probate Workflow Manual Vols. 1 & 2: October 1991 Update. rev. ed. Valerie J. Merritt. Ed. by Christopher D. Dworin. LC 79-53359. 275p. 1991. ring bd. 45.00 (0-88124-437-6, ES-31562) Cont Ed Bar-CA.

California Procedure. B. E. Witkin. write for info. (0-318-59786-1) Bancroft Whitney Co.

California Procedure, 10 vols. 3rd ed. B. E. Witkin. LC 70-146142. 1985. 900.00 (0-317-03220-8) Lawyers Cooperative.

California Procedure, 10 vols. 3rd suppl. ed. B. E. Witkin. LC 70-146142. 1991. Suppl. 1991. 134.00 (0-317-04335-8) Lawyers Cooperative.

California Products & Liability Actions. Bender's Editorial Staff & Joseph W. Cochett. 1975. Updates. ring bd. write for info. (0-8205-1189-7) Bender.

California Professional Corporation Handbook. 5th ed. Anthony Mancuso. LC 93-40930. 1993. pap. 34.95 (0-87337-234-4) Nolo Pr.

California Progressivism Revisited. Ed. by William Deverell & Tom Sitton. LC 93-11110. 240p. 1994. 40.00 (0-520-08469-1); pap. 15.00 (0-520-08470-5) U CA Pr.

California Property & Casualty Course. James J. Smith. Date not set. 50.00 (1-56461-077-2, 26972) Rough Notes.

California Property Management. Donna Grogan. 1989. pap. 27.95 (0-915799-56-1) Rockwell WA.

California Psychological Inventory Handbook. Edwin I. Megargee. LC 76-186581. (Jossey-Bass Behavioral Science Ser.). (Illus.). 324p. reprint ed. pap. 92.40 (0-7837-2503-5, 2042662) Bks Demand.

California Public Administration. 2nd ed. T. A. Quinn & Ed Salzman. (Illus.). 120p. 1982. pap. 4.95 (0-930302-51-6) Cal Journal.

*California Public Construction Contract Manual. James Acret. LC 95-1310. (Construction Law Ser.). 1995. write for info. (0-07-172725-6) Shepards-McGraw.

California Public Gardens: A Visitor's Guide. Eric Sigg. (Illus.). 304p. (Orig.). 1991. pap. 16.95 (0-945465-56-4) John Muir.

*California Public School Directory. California Department of Education Staff. 768p. 1994. pap. 16.00 (0-8011-1091-2) Calif Education.

California Public Sector: Directory of Official Personnel in Federal, State & Local Governments in California. Ed. by Christie Glenneys. (Illus.). 1088p. 1993. 195.00 (0-9634402-1-7) CA Public Sector.

California Publishing Marketplace: A Comprehensive Directory of Markets, Opportunities, & Resources for Writers. Ed. by Marjorie Gersh. 256p. (Orig.). 1989. pap. 14.95 (0-9622592-0-9) Writers Connection.

California Publishing Marketplace: A Comprehensive Directory of Markets, Opportunities, & Resources for Writers. Ed. by Marjorie Gersh. (Orig.). 1990. pap. 16.95 (0-9622592-1-7) Writers Connection.

California Quail. A. Starker Leopold. LC 76-48003. (Illus.). 1978. pap. 15.00 (0-520-05456-3) U CA Pr.

California Quarry. Jon Sharpe. (Trailsman Ser.: No. 148). 176p. (Orig.). 1994. pap. 3.50 (0-451-17883-1, Sig) NAL-Dutton.

California Quiz Bowl Crash Course! Carole Marsh. (Carole Marsh California Bks.). (Illus.). (YA). (gr. 3-12). 1994. lib. bdg. 24.95 (1-55609-519-8); pap. 14.95 (1-55609-518-X); disk 29.95 (0-7933-1400-3) Gallopade Pub Group.

California Radio Guide. Patrick J. Cooper. LC 90-93565. (Illus.). 124p. (Orig.). 1991. pap. 9.95 (0-9628118-2-3) CA Radio Guide.

California Radiocarbon Dates. 6th ed. Gary S. Breschini et al. vi, 148p. 1990. pap. 9.50 (0-685-46945-X) Coyote Press.

California Radiocarbon Dates. 7th ed. Gary S. Breschini et al. vi, 120p. (C). 1992. pap. 9.50 (1-55567-011-3) Coyote Press.

California Railroads: An Encyclopedia of Cable Car, Common Carrier, Horsecar, Industrial Interurban, Logging, Monorail, Motor Road, Shortlines, Streetcar, Switching & Terminal Railroads in California (1851-1992) Alvin A. Fickewirth. LC 92-12495. 1992. 46.95 (0-87095-106-8) Gldn West Bks.

California Rancho Cooking. Jacqueline H. McMahan. LC 83-72309. (Illus.). 248p. 1983. 14.95 (0-9612150-0-3) Olive Pr.

California Rancho Cooking. rev. ed. Jacqueline H. McMahan. (Illus.). 1988. pap. 12.95 (0-9612150-7-0) Olive Pr.

California Ranchos: Patented Private Land Grants Listed by County. Burgess M. Shumway. Ed. by Mary A. Burgess & Michael Burgess. LC 87-11696. (Stokvis Studies in Historical Chronology & Thought: No. 11). 144p. 1988. reprint ed. lib. bdg. 27.00x (0-89370-835-6, Sidewinder Press); reprint ed. pap. 17.00x (0-89370-935-2, Sidewinder Press) Borgo Pr.

California Range Brushlands & Browse Plants. Arthur W. Sampson & Beryle S. Jespersen. (Illus.). 162p. 1963. pap. text ed. 8.00 (0-931876-54-0, 4010) ANR Pubns CA.

California Real Estate. Joseph Newton et al. 576p. 1988. text ed. 53.00 (0-13-112442-0) P-H.

California Real Estate Appraisal. 2nd ed. Martha R. Williams. LC 92-38128. 450p. 1993. pap. 36.95 (0-7931-0580-3, 152307, Real Estate Ed) Dearborn Finan.

California Real Estate Appraisal: Residential Properties. 3rd ed. George H. Miller et al. (Illus.). 304p. (C). 1987. text ed. 50.00 (0-13-112558-3) P-H.

*California Real Estate Appraisal: Residential Properties. 4th rev. ed. George H. Miller et al. LC 94-40190. 1995. text ed. 42.67 (0-13-312067-8) P-H.

California Real Estate Economics. Anthony Schools Corporation Staff. (Real Estate College-Level Ser.). (Illus.). 320p. (C). 1988. pap. text ed. 39.95 (0-941833-14-3) Anthony Schools.

California Real Estate Escrow. Lois Kadosh & Gary Beckner. 250p. 1988. pap. text ed. 36.95 (0-88462-762-4, 1523-05, Real Estate Ed) Dearborn Finan.

California Real Estate Finance. 2nd ed. Roger Bernhardt. LC 90-71016. 528p. 1990. lib. bdg. 45.00 (0-89089-433-7) Carolina Acad Pr.

California Real Estate Finance. 2nd rev. ed. Anthony Schools Corporation Staff. (Real Estate College-Level Ser.). (Illus.). 320p. (C). 1990. pap. text ed. 39.95 (0-941833-25-9) Anthony Schools.

California Real Estate Finance. 2nd suppl. ed. Roger Bernhardt. 528p. 1993. write for info. (0-318-67286-3) Carolina Acad Pr.

California Real Estate Finance. 3rd ed. Minnie Lush & David Sirota. LC 94-5784. 1994. pap. 36.95 (0-7931-1043-2, Real Estate Ed) Dearborn Finan.

California Real Estate Finance. 5th ed. Robert J. Bond et al. 416p. 1994. text ed. 34.67 (0-13-117987-X) P-H.

California Real Estate Finance, 1993. 4th ed. Robert J. Bond et al. 416p. (C). 1993. text ed. 30.75 (0-13-117318-9) P-H.

California Real Estate Law. Philip B. Bergfield. (Illus.). 480p. (C). 1983. text ed. write for info. (0-07-004896-7) McGraw.

California Real Estate Law. Roger Bernhardt. LC 67-5714. 1992. 60.00 (0-317-03214-3) Lawyers Cooperative.

California Real Estate Law. Erin Riley. 1991. pap. 32.95 (0-915799-85-5) Rockwell WA.

California Real Estate Law. 3rd ed. William H. Pivar & Robert J. Bruss. 528p. 1994. text ed. 39.95 (0-7931-0731-8, 1523-02, Real Estate Ed) Dearborn Finan.

California Real Estate Law: Text & Cases. 2nd ed. Theodore H. Gordon. (Illus.). 304p. 1985. student ed, pap. text ed. 15.67 (0-317-11404-2) P-H.

California Real Estate Law: Text & Cases. 3rd ed. Theodore H. Gordon. 368p. (C). 1990. pap. text ed. 44.00 (0-13-116476-7) P-H.

California Real Estate Law & Practice, 17 vols. Bender's Editorial Staff & Don Augustine. 1973. ring bd. write for info. (0-8205-1271-0) Bender.

California Real Estate Law & Practice, 17 vols. Bender's Editorial Staff & Don Augustine. 1986. write for info. (0-318-67983-3) Bender.

California Real Estate Laws. 3rd rev. ed. Anthony Schools Corporation Staff. (Real Estate College-Level Ser.). (Illus.). 320p. (C). 1990. pap. text ed. 39.95 (0-941833-29-1) Anthony Schools.

California Real Estate License Examinations. 3rd ed. Harry W. Koch. 1988. pap. 10.00 (0-910553-16-5) Ken-Bks.

California Real Estate License Preparation Text. 6th rev. ed. William H. Pivar. (Illus.). 320p. (C). 1984. student ed 17.95 (0-685-08873-1) P-H.

California Real Estate License Preparation Text. 9th ed. William H. Pivar. LC 93-3893. 1993. pap. text ed. 41.00 (0-13-220013-9) P-H.

California Real Estate Practice. William L. Mansfield. 480p. 1994. text ed. 34.80 (0-13-121187-0) P-H.

California Real Estate Practice. 3rd rev. ed. Lowell Anderson et al. 476p. (C). 1994. pap. text ed. 39.95 (0-7931-0730-X, 1523-0103, Real Estate Ed) Dearborn Finan.

California Real Estate Practice. 3rd rev. ed. Anthony Schools Corporation Staff. (Real Estate College-Level Ser.). (Illus.). 320p. (C). 1990. pap. text ed. 39.95 (0-941833-31-3) Anthony Schools.

California Real Estate Practice. 5th ed. Hyman M. Berston. (C). 1988. text ed. 38.95 (0-256-03477-X) Irwin.

California Real Estate Practice. 6th ed. Hyman M. Berston. LC 93-30798. 560p. (C). 1993. text ed. 44.95 (0-256-08288-X) Irwin.

California Real Estate Practices. 5th ed. Kathryn Haupt. (Illus.). 564p. (Orig.). 1991. pap. 27.95 (0-915799-88-X) Rockwell WA.

California Real Estate Primer. 41th rev. ed. Ray D. Westcott. Ed. by David D. Westcott. Orig. Title: The Real Estate Primer. (Illus.). 383p. 1992. pap. text ed. 18.95 (0-940745-03-8) REP Pubs CA.

*California Real Estate Primer. 42th rev. ed. Ray D. Westcott. Ed. by David D. Westcott. Orig. Title: The Real Estate Primer. (Illus.). 380p. 1995. pap. text ed. 19.95 (0-940745-04-6) REP Pubs CA.

*California Real Estate Principles. Sherry Shindler. (Illus.). (Orig.). (C). 1995. pap. text ed. 39.95 (0-934772-03-7) Ashley Crown Systems Inc.

California Real Estate Principles. 3rd rev. ed. Anthony Schools Corporation Staff. (Real Estate College-Level Ser.). (Illus.). 320p. (C). 1990. pap. text ed. 39.95 (0-941833-28-3) Anthony Schools.

California Real Estate Principles. 3rd rev. ed. Dennis J. McKenzie et al. LC 88-17172. 388p. 1988. text ed. 38.95 (0-471-62140-4) P-H.

California Real Estate Principles. 3rd rev. ed. Charles Stapleton et al. 516p. (C). 1994. pap. text ed. 37.95 (0-7931-0729-6, 1510-5403, Real Estate Ed) Dearborn Finan.

California Real Estate Principles. 4th ed. Dennis J. McKenzie et al. LC 93-25065. (California Real Estate Ser.). 1993. text ed. 49.00 (0-13-117979-9) P-H.

California Real Estate Principles. 6th ed. Hyman Berston. 544p. (C). 1991. text ed. 40.95 (0-256-07940-4, 04-821-06) Irwin.

*California Real Estate Principles. 7th ed. Hyman M. Berston. LC 94-22609. 544p. (C). 1994. 43.95 (0-256-13597-5) Irwin.

California Real Estate Register. 2nd ed. Linda M. Lowson. 1991. ring bd. 195.00 (0-944354-01-7); disk 425.00 (0-317-94093-7) Global Infonet.

California Real Property Financing: Volume One: Basic Loan Documentation. 475p. 1988. 100.00 (0-685-20221-6, RE-30970) Cont Ed Bar-CA.

California Real Property Practice Forms Manual: January 1992 Update. Ed. by John K. Chapin. LC 88-61368. 130p. 1992. ring bd. 25.00 (0-88124-462-7, RE30923) Cont Ed Bar-CA.

California Real Property Practice Forms Manual: March 1991 Update. Ed. by John K. Chapin. LC 88-61368. 150p. 1991. ring bd. 22.00 (0-88124-370-1, RE-30922) Cont Ed Bar-CA.

California Real Property Practice Forms Manual: March 1993 Update. Ed. by John K. Chapin. LC 88-61368. 125p. 1993. ring bd. 25.00 (0-88124-597-6, RE-30924) Cont Ed Bar-CA.

California Real Property Remedies Practice. Ed. by Craig H. Scott et al. LC 81-70784. 506p. 1982. 95.00 (0-88124-098-2, RE-38860) Cont Ed Bar-CA.

California Real Property Sales Transactions. 2nd ed. Ed. by Gordon L. Graham. LC 93-70989. 1007p. 1993. text ed. 130.00 (0-88124-619-0, RE-32090) Cont Ed Bar-CA.

California Reapportionment & the Chicano Community: An Historical Overview, 1960-1980. Richard Santillan. 45p. 1981. pap. text ed. 10.50 (1-883638-04-6) Rose Inst.

California Red: A Life in the American Communist Party. Dorothy R. Healey & Maurice Isserman. LC 92-38430. (Illus.). 280p. (C). 1993. reprint ed. pap. 12.95 (0-252-06278-7) U of Ill Pr.

California Red Wine Book. Paul Gillette. (Wine Library: Vol. 1). (Illus.). 1984. pap. 6.95 (0-913290-76-9) Camaro Pub.

California Redwoods & the North Coast. Bob Von Normann. Ed. by George Castaldo. (Illus.). 32p. (Orig.). 1984. 5.95 (0-915687-00-3) FVN Corp.

California Redwoods Color Book. Ed. by Tammy L. Anderson. 26p. (J). (ps-8). 1988. pap. 1.95 (0-915687-03-8) FVN Corp.

California Reefs. Chuck Davis. (Illus.). 120p. (Orig.). 1991. 29.95 (0-8118-0072-5); pap. 16.95 (0-87701-787-5) Chronicle Bks.

California Rental Housing Reference Book. 5th ed. California Apartment Association Staff. 431p. 1992. pap. 24.95 (1-882243-00-5) CA Apt Assn.

California Residential Landlord-Tenant Practice. 950p. 1986. 105.00 (0-88124-138-5, RE-37730) Cont Ed Bar-CA.

California Residential Property Management. 3rd rev. ed. Anthony Schools Corporation Staff. (Real Estate College-Level Ser.). (Illus.). 320p. (C). 1990. pap. text ed. 39.95 (0-941833-32-1) Anthony Schools.

California Retail Liquor Store. Guideline Publishing Co. Staff. 54p. (Orig.). 1972. pap. 9.95 (0-917474-00-7) Guideline Pub.

California Riparian Systems: Proceedings of a Conference on Their Ecology, Conservation, & Productive Management. Ed. by Richard E. Warner. 1983. pap. 45.00 (0-520-05035-5) U CA Pr.

*California Rivers & Streams: The Conflict Between Fluvial Process & Land Use. Jeffrey F. Mount. LC 95-10822. (Illus.). 1995. write for info. (0-520-20192-2); pap. write for info. (0-520-22502-3) U CA Pr.

California Road Atlas. Susan Farewell et al. (State Road Atlases Ser.). 56p. 1990. pap. 4.95 (0-13-110891-3, H M Gousha) P-H Gen Ref & Trav.

California Road Atlas: 1991 Edition. Thomas Bros. Maps Staff. (Illus.). 286p. 1991. pap. 18.95 (0-88130-491-3) Thomas Bros Maps.

California Road Atlas & Driver's Guide: 1994 Edition. (Illus.). 320p. 1994. pap. 18.95 (0-88130-625-8) Thomas Bros Maps.

*California Road Atlas & Driver's Guide: 1995 Edition. Thomas Bros. Maps Staff. (Illus.). 320p. 1995. pap. 18.95 (0-88130-688-6) Thomas Bros Maps.

California Road Atlas & Driver's Guide, 1990. Thomas Bros. Maps Staff. (Illus.). 286p. 1990. pap. 17.95 (0-88130-418-2) Thomas Bros Maps.

California Road Riders. J. J. Scot. LC 78-66958. (Illus.). 1978. 18.00 (0-9601946-1-4) Harvestman.

California Rollercoasters! Carole Marsh. (Carole Marsh California Bks.). (Illus.). (YA). (gr. 3-12). 1994. lib. bdg. 24.95 (0-7933-5236-3); pap. 14.95 (0-7933-5237-1); disk 29.95 (0-7933-5238-X) Gallopade Pub Group.

California Romantics: Harbingers of Watercolorism. Robert Perine. LC 86-73257. (Illus.). 96p. 1987. 18.95 (0-936725-01-X) Artra Pub.

California Rush. Sherwood Kiraly. 288p. 1990. text ed. 17.95 (0-02-563570-0) Macmillan.

California Sand Wasps of the Subtribe Stictiellina. Richard M. Bohart & J. E. Gillaspy. (Bulletin of the California Insect Survey Ser.: Vol. 27). 1986. pap. 35.00 (0-520-09697-5) U CA Pr.

California Scenic Drives. Stewart Green. (Falcon Guidebook Ser.). (Illus.). 240p. (Orig.). 1993. pap. 11.95 (1-56044-162-3) Falcon Pr MT.

California Scheming. Beth Cruise. LC 92-2739. (Saved by the Bell Ser.: No. 3). 144p. (Orig.). (YA). (gr. 5 up). 1992. pap. 2.95 (0-02-042776-X, Collier Bks Young) S&S Childrens.

California School Accounting Manual. California Department of Education Staff. 240p. 1992. pap. 12.00 (0-8011-1025-4) Calif Education.

California School Trivia: An Amazing & Fascinating Look at Our State's Teachers, Schools & Students! Carole Marsh. (Carole Marsh California Bks.). (Illus.). (YA). (gr. 3-12). 1994. lib. bdg. 24.95 (0-7933-0175-0); pap. 14.95 (0-7933-0174-2); disk 29.95 (0-7933-0176-9) Gallopade Pub Group.

California Screamin' The Glory Days of Corvette Road Racing. Michael Antonick. (Illus.). 160p. 1990. pap. 19.95 (0-933534-31-0) M Bruce Assocs.

California Sculpture Show. California-International Arts Foundation Staff. Ed. by Barbara McAlpine. Tr. by Jeanne Hart et al. (Illus.). 168p. 1984. pap. 6.00 (0-917571-00-2) CA Intl Arts.

California Seafood Cookbook: A Cook's Guide to the Fish & Shellfish of California, the Pacific Coast & Beyond. Isaac Cronin et al. LC 82-24450. (Illus.). 288p. 1983. 20.00 (0-943186-04-8); pap. 12.95 (0-943186-03-X) Aris Bks.

California Search & Seizure Practice. 2nd ed. Marshall W. Krause. LC 77-71392. (Illus.). 260p. 1977. 70.00 (0-88124-050-8, CR-31320) Cont Ed Bar-CA.

California Search & Seizure Practice: April 1993 Update. 2nd ed. Robert N. Waxman. LC 77-71392. 229p. 1993. pap. text ed. 65.00 (0-88124-613-1, CR-31321) Cont Ed Bar-CA.

An Asterisk (*) at the beginning of an entry indicates that the title is appearing in BIP for the first time.

C

C

*California Water. Arthur L. Littleworth & Eric L. Garner. (Orig.). 1995. pap. 47.50 (0-923956-25-5) Solano Pr.

*California Water Law & Policy, 2 vols., Set. Scott Slater. 1000p. 1995. ring bd. 160.00 (0-250-47246-5) Michie Butterworth.

California Water Resources Directory: A Guide to Organizations & Information Resources. 2nd ed. Ed. by Roberta Childers. LC 90-1636. (California Information Guides Ser.). 120p. (Orig.). 1991. pap. 25.00 (0-912102-93-4) Cal Inst Public.

*California Wax Museum. Renon Blum. LC 94-30507. 16p. (J). (gr. 4-8). 1994. pap. 5.00 (0-88734-518-2) Players Pr.

California Weekender: Northern California, Vol. 2. Ed. by California Travel Association Staff. (Illus.). 1987. pap. 4.95 (0-913290-74-2) Camaro Pub.

California Weekender: Southern California, Vol. 1. Ed. by California Travel Association Staff. (Illus.). 1987. pap. 4.95 (0-913290-73-4) Camaro Pub.

California Welfare Reform: Recycling the 1601 Elizabethan Poor Law. Harold E. Simmons. (C). 1975. pap. 10.00 (0-87312-006-X) Gen Welfare Pubns.

California Western International Law Journal: 1970-1992, 23 vols., Set. 862.50 (0-8377-9035-2) Rothman.

California Western Law Review: 1965-1992, 29 vols. mic. film write for info. (0-318-57420-9) Rothman.

California Western Law Review: 1965-1992, 29 vols., Set. 1,105.00 (0-8377-9036-0) Rothman.

California White Cap Murders: An Episode in Vigilantism. limited ed. Helen R. Goss. (Illus.). 132p. 1969. 20.00 (0-910740-16-X) Holmes.

California White Wine Book. Paul Gillette. (Wine Library: Vol. 2). (Illus.). 1984. pap. 6.95 (0-913290-77-7) Camaro Pub.

California Whitewater: A Guide to the Rivers. 3rd rev. ed. Jim Cassady et al. (Illus.). 336p. 1995. pap. 19.95 (0-9613650-2-1) North Fork Pr.

California Wildfire Landscaping. Maureen Gilmer. LC 94-8523. 176p. 1994. pap. 10.95 (0-87833-864-0) Taylor Pub.

California Wildflower Drawings: A Coloring Book. Judy Sutcliffe. (Illus.). 1993. pap. 3.95 (0-943164-19-2) Geronima.

California Wildflowers. Beverly Magley. LC 88-83883. (Interpreting the Great Outdoors Ser.). (Illus.). 32p. (Orig.). (J). (gr. 3-6). 1989. pap. 5.95 (0-937959-58-8) Falcon Pr MT.

California Wildlands. George Wuerthner. (Illus.). 104p. (Orig.). 1994. pap. 14.95 (1-56037-051-3) Am Wrld Geog.

California Wildlife. Bernard Shanks. (California Geographic Ser.). (Illus.). 128p. 1989. pap. 9.95 (0-937959-47-2) Falcon Pr MT.

California Wildlife Viewing Guide. Jeanne Clark. Ed. by Chris Cauble. (Watchable Wildlife Ser.). (Illus.). 160p. (Orig.). 1993. pap. 7.95 (1-56044-068-6) Falcon Pr MT.

California Will Drafting, 3 vols. 3rd ed. Ed. by Pamela J. Jester. 1992. Vol. 2, 571p. write for info. (0-318-69586-3); Vol. 3, 427p. write for info. (0-318-69587-1) Cont Ed Bar-CA.

California Will Drafting, 3 vols., Set. 3rd ed. Ed. by Pamela J. Jester. LC 92-70205. 1992. ring bd. 210.00 (0-88124-477-5, ES-30320) Cont Ed Bar-CA.

California Will Drafting, 3 vols., Vol. 1. 3rd ed. Ed. by Pamela J. Jester. 512p. 1992. write for info. (0-318-69585-5) Cont Ed Bar-CA.

California Wills & Probate. 3rd ed. (Ken-Books California Ser.). 1987. 8.00 (0-910553-11-4) Ken-Bks.

California Wills & Trust-Forms, Vol. 3. Bender Editorial Staff. 1991. write for info. (0-8205-1893-X) Bender.

California Wills & Trusts, Vol. 3. Bender Editorial Staff. 1991. write for info. (0-8205-1034-3) Bender.

California Wind Atlas. California Energy Commission. (Illus.). 216p. 1985. pap. 39.50 (0-88016-065-9) WindBks.

California Wind Energy Projects. California Energy Commission Staff. 110p. 1993. pap. 75.00 (0-88016-066-7) WindBks.

California Wine Country: Cooking with Betty Evans. Betty Evans. LC 92-64301. (Illus.). 120p. (Orig.). 1992. pap. 7.95 (0-931104-34-3) Sunflower Ink.

California Wine Country: Picture Memory. 1992. 7.99 (0-517-07273-4) Random Hse Value.

California Wine Country Cookbook: Fifty-Eight Chefs, Winemakers & Wineries Share 162 of Their Favorite Recipes with You. Ed. by Robert P. Hoffman & Virginia M. Hoffman. (Illus.). 192p. (Orig.). 1991. pap. 12.95 (0-9629927-4-7) Hoffman CA.

California Wine Country Cookbook, No. Two: 102 Chefs, Winemakers, & Wineries Share 172 of Their Best Recipes with You. 2nd rev. ed. Ed. by Virginia M. Hoffman & Robert P. 116 Intro. by Hoffman. (Illus.). 208p. 1993. pap. 12.95 (0-9629927-6-3) Hoffman CA.

California Wine Country Cooking Secrets: Starring the Best Restaurants & Wineries of Napa - Sonoma. 2nd rev. ed. Kathleen D. Fish. Ed. by Fred Hernandez. (Illus.). 272p. 1993. pap. 13.95 (0-9620472-8-7) Bon Vivant Pr.

California Wine Country Herbs & Spices Cookbook: 72 Chefs, Winemakers, & Wineries Share 188 of Their Best Recipes Featuring Herbs & Spices. Ed. by Virginia M. Hoffman & Robert P. Hoffman. (Illus.). 224p. (Orig.). 1994. pap. 12.95 (0-9629927-5-5) Hoffman CA.

California Wine Drinks. William I. Kaufman. Ed. by M. T. Sullivan. 128p. 1982. pap. 4.95 (0-932664-19-9) Wine Appreciation.

California Wine Pages 1987. Michael H. Clinton. (Illus.). 504p. (Orig.). 1987. pap. 19.95 (0-940597-00-4) B Jackson Pub.

California Wine Tour, Sierra Foothills & Central Valley. Vintage Image Staff. 128p. 1988. pap. 5.95 (0-932664-37-7) Wine Appreciation.

California Wine Winners, 1983. Trudy H. Ahlstrom & J. T. Devine. 72p. (Orig.). 1984. pap. 4.95 (0-9614025-0-4) Varietal Fair.

California Wine Winners, 1984. Trudy H. Ahlstrom & J. T. Devine. 96p. (Orig.). 1984. pap. 4.95 (0-9614025-1-2) Varietal Fair.

California Wine Winners, 1985. Trudy H. Ahlstrom & J. T. Devine. 104p. (Orig.). 1985. pap. 5.95 (0-9614025-2-0) Varietal Fair.

California Wine Winners, 1986. Trudy H. Ahlstrom & J. T. Devine. (Orig.). 1986. pap. 5.95 (0-9614025-3-9) Varietal Fair.

California Wine Winners, 1987. Trudy H. Ahlstrom & J. T. Devine. (Illus.). (Orig.). 1987. pap. 5.95 (0-9614025-4-7) Varietal Fair.

California Wine Winners, 1988. Trudy Ahlstrom & J. T. Devine. (Illus.). 128p. (Orig.). 1988. pap. 5.95 (0-9614025-5-5) Varietal Fair.

California Wine Winners, 1989. Trudy H. Ahlstrom & J. T. Devine. (Illus.). 128p. (Orig.). 1989. pap. 5.95 (0-9614025-6-3) Varietal Fair.

California Wine Winners, 1991. Trudy H. Ahlstrom & J. T. Devine. (Illus.). 160p. (Orig.). 1990. pap. 5.95 (0-9614025-7-1) Varietal Fair.

California Wine Winners, 1992: The Best from the 1991 Competitions. Trudy H. Ahlstrom & J. T. Devine. (Illus.). 160p. (Orig.). 1991. pap. 6.95 (0-9614025-8-X) Varietal Fair.

California Wine Winners, 1993: The Best of the 1992 Judgings. Ed. by Trudy Ahlstrom & J. T. Devine. (Illus.). 160p. (Orig.). 1992. pap. 6.95 (0-9614025-9-8) Varietal Fair.

California Wine Winners, 1994: The Best of the 1993 Competitions. Ed. by J. T. Devine. (Illus.). 176p. (Orig.). 1993. pap. 6.95 (1-881796-00-0) Varietal Fair.

California Wine Winners, 1995: The Best of the 1994 Judgings. Ed. by Trudy Ahlstrom & J. T. Devine. (Illus.). 176p. (Orig.). 1994. pap. 6.95 (1-881796-01-9) Varietal Fair.

*California Wine Winners, 1996: The Best of the 1995 Judgings. Ed. by Trudy Ahlstrom & J. T. Devine. (Illus.). 176p. (Orig.). 1995. pap. 8.95 (1-881796-02-7) Varietal Fair.

*California Winemaker's Cook Book. Ed. by Ken Parry. 180p. 1994. pap. text ed. 13.95 (1-886026-00-9) Wine Grape.

California Women. Joan M. Jensen & Gloria R. Lothrop. Ed. by Norris Hundley, Jr. & John A. Schutz. (Golden State Ser.). (Illus.). 200p. 1987. pap. 10.00 (0-929651-15-4) MTL.

California Women Speak: Speeches by California Women in Elected Public Office. Ed. by Doris Earnshaw. 122p. 1994. pap. 12.50 (0-9640574-0-9) Alta Vista Pr.

California Workers' Compensation Citator. C. Duke Marsh. (Personal Injury Library). 296p. 1993. text ed. 138.00 (0-471-59539-X) Wiley.

California Workers' Compensation Claims & Benefits. 9th ed. David O'Brien. 1100p. 1993. ring bd. 125.00 (0-250-47224-4) Michie Butterworth.

California Workers' Compensation Forms. 230p. 1993. disk, pap. 65.00 (0-250-47226-0) Butterworth Legal Pubs.

*California Workers' Compensation Handbook. Stanford D. Herlick. 550p. 1994. pap. 59.00 (0-250-47234-1) Michie Butterworth.

California Workers' Compensation Handbook. 13th ed. Stanford D. Herlick. 500p. 1993. pap. 55.00 (1-55943-202-0) Butterworth Legal Pubs.

California Workers' Compensation Law, 2 vols., No. 1. 4th suppl. ed. Stanford D. Herlick. 1991. Suppl. 1, 7/91. 47.50 (0-685-66646-8) Butterworth Legal Pubs.

California Workers' Compensation Law, 2 vols., No. 2. 4th suppl. ed. Stanford D. Herlick. 1992. Suppl. 2, 11/92. 48.00 (0-685-70880-2) Butterworth Legal Pubs.

California Workers' Compensation Law, 2 vols., No. 3. 4th suppl. ed. Stanford D. Herlick. 1993. 58.50 (0-685-74586-4) Butterworth Legal Pubs.

*California Workers' Compensation Law, 2 vols., Set. Stanford D. Herlick. 1100p. 1994. ring bd. 175.00 (0-250-47257-0) Michie Butterworth.

California Workers' Compensation Law, 2 vols., Set. 4th ed. Stanford D. Herlick. 1990. ring bd. 160.00 (1-55943-170-9) Butterworth Legal Pubs.

California Workers' Compensation Law & Practice: With Forms, Vols. 1 & 2. 3rd ed. Sheldon C. St. Clair. write for info. (0-318-63651-4) Lega Bks.

*California Workers Rights: A Manual of Job Rights, Protections & Remedies. 2nd ed. Joan M. Braconi et al. LC 94-49150. 1995. pap. write for info. (0-937817-08-2) CLRE UCAL Berk.

California Zip Code Guide, 1988. rev. ed. Western Economic Research Co. Inc. Staff. 227p. 1988. 100.00 (0-685-23267-0) West Econ Rsch.

California Zoning Practice. Donald G. Hagman et al. 592p. 1969. 75.00 (0-88124-009-5, RE-30510) Cont Ed Bar-CA.

*California 1995. Frommer Staff. (Frommer's Travel Guides Ser.). 592p. 1995. pap. 16.95 (0-02-860057-6) Macmillan.

California, 1995: The Complete Guide with the Best of the Wine Country & the National Parks. Fodor's Travel Staff. (Illus.). 1994. pap. 17.00 (0-679-02701-7) Fodors Travel.

*California 1995: With Las Vegas & the Grand Canyon. Berkeley Staff. (Berkeley Guides Ser.). 1994. pap. 17.50 (0-679-02778-5) Fodors Travel.

California '46 to '48. Jacob W. Harlan. 1992. reprint ed. lib. bdg. 75.00 (0-7812-5047-1) Rprt Serv.

Californial Poly-Technic State University. Photos by Dan Budnick. (Illus.). 112p. 1987. 37.50 (0-916509-25-7) Harmony Hse Pub LO.

*Californian. Todhunter Ballard. 368p. 1995. mass mkt. 4.99 (0-8439-3836-6) Dorchester Pub Co.

Californian, Vol. 1. George P. Hammond. LC 65-27831. 208p. 1971. 30.00 (0-685-02681-7) Brick Row.

Californian Architecture in Santa Barbara. H. Philip Staats. (Illus.). 144p. 1990. pap. 24.50 (0-942655-02-8) Archit CT.

*Californian Bungalow in Australia: Origins-Revival-Source Ideas for Restoration. Graeme Butler. (Illus.). 154p. (Orig.). 1995. pap. 24.95 (0-85091-355-1, Pub. by Lothian Pub AT) Seven Hills Bk.

Californian Catholicism. Kay Alexander. Ed. by Phillip Hammond. (Religious Contours of California: Window to the World's Religions: Vol. I). 128p. (Orig.). 1993. pap. 9.95 (1-56474-062-5) Fithian Pr.

Californian Indian Nights. Edward W. Gifford & Gwendoline H. Block. LC 90-33808. (Illus.). x, 323p. 1990. reprint ed. pap. 10.95 (0-8032-7031-3, Bison Books) U of Nebr Pr.

Californian Shell Artifacts. E. W. Gifford. Ed. by A. L. Kroeber et al. (University of California Anthropological Records Ser.: Vol. 9, No. 1). (Illus.). iii, 132p. (C). 1985. reprint ed. pap. 9.70 (1-55567-013-X) Coyote Press.

Californian Wildlife Region. rev. ed. Vinson Brown & George Lawrence. (Illus.). 224p. (J). (gr. 4 up). 1995. pap. 8.95 (0-87961-201-0) Naturegraph.

Californians. Gertrude F. Atherton. LC 68-23712. (Americans in Fiction Ser.). reprint ed. lib. bdg. 19.00 (0-8398-0063-0); reprint ed. pap. text ed. 6.95 (0-89197-689-2) Irvington.

Californians. James D. Houston. LC 84-70423. 304p. 1985. reprint ed. pap. 8.95 (0-916870-84-7) Creat Arts Bk.

Californians: Searching for the Golden State. 10th ed. James D. Houston. 290p. 1992. reprint ed. pap. 10.95 (0-9617681-6-9) Otter B Bks.

Californians: The Best of the West. large type ed. Ed. by Bill Pronzini & Martin H. Greenberg. 1990. 19.50 (0-8161-4975-5, Large Print Bks) Hall.

California's Amazing Agriculture. Margaret R. Sherman. LC 76-134229. 287p. (gr. 3-6). 1979. text ed. 14.95 (0-87015-229-7) Pacific Bks.

*California's Best Bed & Breakfasts: Delightful Places to Stay & Great Things to Do When You Get There. Fodor's Staff. 1995. 15.50 (0-679-02696-7) Fodors Travel.

California's Changing Environment. Raymond F. Dasmann. Ed. by Norris Hundley, Jr. & John A. Schutz. (Golden State Ser.). (Illus.). 96p. 1981. pap. 10.00 (0-929651-16-2) MTL.

California's Changing Landscape: The Diversity, Ecology & Conservation of California Vegetation. Michael Barbour et al. (Illus.). 1991. pap. write for info. (0-943460-17-4) Calif Native.

California's Changing Landscapes. 2nd ed. Gordon B. Oakeshott. (Illus.). 1978. text ed. write for info. (0-07-047584-9) McGraw.

California's Channel Islands - One Thousand One Questions Answered. Marla Daily. (Illus.). 284p. 1990. reprint ed. pap. 15.00 (0-945092-13-X) EZ Nature.

California's Chumash Indians. rev. ed. Santa Barbara Museum of Natural History. (Illus.). 72p. (J). (ps-4). 1988. reprint ed. pap. 5.95 (0-945092-00-8) EZ Nature.

California's Contractor's Examination. 9th ed. Harry W. Koch. 1983. pap. 9.00 (0-318-40126-6) Ken-Bks.

California's Daughter: Gertrude Atherton & Her Times. Emily W. Leider. LC 90-32410. 425p. 1991. 35.00 (0-8047-1820-2) Stanford U Pr.

California's Daughter: Gertrude Atherton & Her Times. Emily W. Leider. (Illus.). 425p. (C). 1993. pap. 14.95 (0-8047-2219-6) Stanford U Pr.

California's Disappearing Coast: A Legislative Challenge. Gilbert E. Bailey & Paul S. Thayer. LC 74-170336. 115p. (Orig.). reprint ed. pap. 32.80 (0-7837-2134-X, 2042416) Bks Demand.

California's Early Documents: Treaty of Guadalupe Hidalgo & Original Constituiton. 68p. (ENG & SPA.). pap. 3.95 (0-686-09017-9) E V Salitore.

California's Eastern Sierra: A Visitor's Guide. Sue Irwin. (Illus.). 144p. (Orig.). (C). 1992. pap. 15.95 (0-9628505-0-0) Cachuma Pr.

California's "Employer Sanctions" The Case of the Disappearing Law. Kitty Calavita. (Research Report Ser.: No. 39). 64p. (Orig.). (C). 1982. pap. 5.00 (0-935391-38-X, RR-39) UCSD Ctr US-Mex.

California's Fourteeners: A Hiking & Climbing Guide. Stephen F. Porcella. 1993. pap. 9.95 (0-9630490-0-3) Palisades.

California's Gabrielino Indians. Bernice E. Johnston. LC 62-52618. (Frederick Webb Hodge Anniversary Publication Fund Ser.: Vol. 8). 208p. reprint ed. pap. 59.30 (0-8357-2758-0, 2039882) Bks Demand.

California's Gold Rush Days: A Contemporaneous Account of a Visit to Northern California in 1851. Alexandre Holinski. Tr. by Mary T. Corea. (West Coast Studies: No. 7). 96p. Date not set. lib. bdg. write for info. (0-8095-2800-2, Sidewinder Press); pap. write for info. (0-8095-3800-8, Sidewinder Press) Borgo Pr.

California's Gold, 1991. Calif. Dept. of Educ. Staff et al. (Two Hundred Ser.). 172p. (Orig.). 1992. teacher ed, pap. text ed. 12.00 (0-929722-54-X) CA State Library Fndtn.

California's Gold 1992 (Three Hundred Series) Teacher's Guide. Calif. Dept. of Educ. Staff et al. (Orig.). 1993. teacher ed, pap. text ed. 12.00 (0-929722-55-8) CA State Library Fndtn.

California's Gold, 1993. Dept. of Educ. Staff et al. (Four Hundred Ser.). (Orig.). 1994. teacher ed, pap. text ed. 12.00 (0-929722-77-9) CA State Library Fndtn.

*California's Gold 1994. California Department of Education Staff et al. (500 Ser.). 113p. 1995. teacher ed, pap. text ed. 12.00 (0-929722-84-1) CA State Library Fndtn.

California's Great Cabernets: The Wine Spectator's Guide for Consumers. James Laube. 1989. 29.95 (0-918076-71-4, Wine Spectator) M Shanken Comm.

*California's Great Outdoor Events: One-Thousand Wild & Wonderful Things to Do in California's Parks & Public Lands. Ken McKowen. (Illus.). 576p. (Orig.). 1995. pap. 16.95 (0-935701-50-8) Foghorn Pr.

California's Immigrant Children: Theory, Research, & Implications for Educational Policy. Ed. by Wayne A. Cornelius & Ruben Rumbaut. (Contemporary Perspectives Ser.: No. 8). 1995. pap. 21.95 (1-878367-17-X) UCSD Ctr US-Mex.

California's Indians & the Gold Rush. Clifford E. Trafzer. LC 89-64434. (Illus.). 61p. (Orig.). (J). (gr. 4-7). 1990. pap. 10.95 (0-940113-21-X) Sierra Oaks Pub.

California's Latinos: A Research Bibliography. Comp. by Richard Santillan. 27p. 1988. pap. text ed. 8.50 (1-883638-08-9) Rose Inst.

California's Latinos, 1988: An Opinion Survey. 184p. 1988. pap. text ed. 20.00 (1-883638-10-0) Rose Inst.

California's Maritime Heritage. Martin P. Riegel. LC 87-62442. (California Heritage Ser.: Vol. I). (Illus.). 88p. (Orig.). (C). 1987. 15.00 (0-944871-01-1); pap. 9.00 (0-944871-00-3) Riegel Pub.

*California's Mission la Purisima Concepcion: The Hageman & Ewing Reports. Fred C. Hageman & Russell C. Ewing. Ed. by Richard S. Whitehead. LC 90-63872. (Illus.). 307p. 1991. pap. 19.95 (1-879208-00-8) SB Trust Hist.

California's Mission Revival. Karen Weitze. LC 83-22580. (California Architecture & Architects Ser.: Vol. 3). (Illus.). 176p. 1984. 22.50 (0-912158-89-1) Hennessey.

California's (Most Devastating!) Disasters & (Most Calamitous!) Catastrophies! Carole Marsh. (Carole Marsh California Bks.). (Illus.). (YA). (gr. 3-12). 1994. lib. bdg. 24.95 (0-7933-0163-7); pap. 14.95 (0-7933-0162-9); disk 29.95 (0-7933-0164-5) Gallopade Pub Group.

California's National Parks. (Windsor Destination Guides Ser.). (Illus.). 56p. 1992. pap. 12.95 (1-874111-05-7, Pub. by Windsor Bks UK) Seven Hills Bk.

California's Native American Tribes, No. 1: Achumawi Tribe. Mary N. Boule. (Illus.). 40p. (Orig.). (J). (gr. 2-3). 1992. pap. 4.50 (1-877599-25-5) Merryant Pubs.

California's Native American Tribes, No. 10: Maidu-KonKow Tribe. Mary N. Boule. (Illus.). 40p. (Orig.). (J). (gr. 4-5). 1992. pap. 4.50 (1-877599-34-4) Merryant Pubs.

California's Native American Tribes, No. 11: Coast Miwok. Mary N. Boule. (Illus.). 40p. (Orig.). (J). (gr. 2-4). 1992. pap. 4.50 (1-877599-35-2) Merryant Pubs.

California's Native American Tribes, No. 12: Eastern Miwok Tribe. Mary N. Boule. (Illus.). 40p. (Orig.). (J). (gr. 3-5). 1992. pap. 4.50 (1-877599-36-0) Merryant Pubs.

California's Native American Tribes, No. 13: Lake Miwok Tribe. Mary N. Boule. (Illus.). 40p. (Orig.). (J). (gr. 3-5). 1992. pap. 4.50 (1-877599-37-9) Merryant Pubs.

California's Native American Tribes, No. 14: Ohlone Tribe. Mary N. Boule. (Illus.). 40p. (Orig.). (J). (gr. 4-5). 1992. pap. 4.50 (1-877599-38-7) Merryant Pubs.

California's Native American Tribes, No. 15: Patwin Tribe. Mary N. Boule. (Illus.). 60p. (Orig.). (J). (gr. 3-5). 1992. pap. text ed. 4.50 (1-877599-49-2) Merryant Pubs.

California's Native American Tribes, No. 16: Western & N. E. Pomo Tribe. Mary N. Boule. (Illus.). 40p. (Orig.). (J). (gr. 2-3). 1992. pap. 4.50 (1-877599-39-5) Merryant Pubs.

California's Native American Tribes, No. 17: East & S. E. Pomo Tribe. Mary N. Boule. (Illus.). 40p. (Orig.). (J). (gr. 3-4). 1992. pap. 4.50 (1-877599-40-9) Merryant Pubs.

California's Native American Tribes, No. 18: Salinan Tribe. Mary N. Boule. (Illus.). 40p. (Orig.). (J). (gr. 4-5). 1992. pap. 4.50 (1-877599-41-7) Merryant Pubs.

California's Native American Tribes, No. 19: Shasta Tribe. Mary N. Boule. (Illus.). 40p. (Orig.). (J). (gr. 2-4). 1992. pap. 4.50 (1-877599-42-5) Merryant Pubs.

California's Native American Tribes, No. 2: Atsugewi Tribe. Mary N. Boule. (Illus.). 40p. (Orig.). (J). (gr. 2-3). 1992. pap. 4.50 (1-877599-26-3) Merryant Pubs.

California's Native American Tribes, No. 20: Tolowa Tribe. Mary N. Boule. (Illus.). 40p. (Orig.). (J). (gr. 2-3). 1992. pap. 4.50 (1-877599-43-3) Merryant Pubs.

California's Native American Tribes, No. 21: Tubatulabal Tribe. Mary N. Boule. (Illus.). 60p. (J). (gr. 2-4). 1992. pap. 4.50 (1-877599-24-7) Merryant Pubs.

California's Native American Tribes, No. 22: Wintu Tribe. Mary N. Boule. (Illus.). 40p. (Orig.). (J). (gr. 4-5). 1992. pap. 4.50 (1-877599-44-1) Merryant Pubs.

California's Native American Tribes, No. 23: Valley Yokuts Tribe. Mary N. Boule. (Illus.). 40p. (Orig.). (J). (gr. 4-5). 1992. pap. 4.50 (1-877599-45-X) Merryant Pubs.

California's Native American Tribes, No. 24: Foothill Yokuts Tribe. Mary N. Boule. (Illus.). 40p. (Orig.). (J). (gr. 3-5). 1992. pap. 4.50 (1-877599-46-8) Merryant Pubs.

California's Native American Tribes, No. 25: Yuki Tribe. Mary N. Boule. (Illus.). 40p. (Orig.). (J). (gr. 2-3). 1992. pap. 4.50 (1-877599-47-6) Merryant Pubs.

California's Native American Tribes, No. 26: Yurok Tribe. Mary N. Boule. (Illus.). 40p. (Orig.). (J). (gr. 2-3). 1992. pap. 4.50 (1-877599-48-4) Merryant Pubs.

California's Native American Tribes, No. 3: Cahuilla Tribe. Mary N. Boule. (Illus.). 40p. (Orig.). (J). (gr. 2-4). 1992. pap. 4.50 (1-877599-27-1) Merryant Pubs.

1002

An Asterisk (*) at the beginning of an entry indicates that the title is appearing in BIP for the first time.

C

An Asterisk (*) at the beginning of an entry indicates that the title is appearing in BIP for the first time.

1003

Call of Earth. Orson S. Card. LC 92-36971. (Homecoming Saga Ser.: No. 2). 304p. 1992. 21.95 (0-312-93037-2) Tor Bks.

Call of Earth. Orson S. Card. (Homecoming Saga Ser.: No. 2). 352p. 1994. mass mkt. 5.99 (0-8125-3261-9) Tor Bks.

Call of Earth. deluxe ed. Orson S. Card. LC 92-36971. (Homecoming Saga Ser.: No. 2). 304p. 1993. 200.00 (0-312-85477-3) Tor Bks.

Call of Glengarron. large type ed. Nancy Buckingham. 1991. 21.95 (0-7089-2425-5) Ulverscroft.

Call of God: The Theme of Vocation in the Poetry of Donne & Herbert. Robert B. Shaw. LC 81-66126. (Cowley Lectures). 123p. (Orig.). 1981. pap. 6.00 (0-936384-04-2) Cowley Pubns.

Call of Gold. Newell D. Chamberlain. LC 81-50164. (Illus.). 187p. 1981. reprint ed. pap. 4.95 (0-934136-12-2) Western Tanager.

Call of Honor. David Bannerman. 1985. pap. 2.50 (0-8217-1593-3) Zebra.

Call of Human Nature: The Role of Scatology in Modern German Literature. Dieter Rollfinke & Jacqueline Rollfinke. LC 86-1490. (Illus.). 256p. 1986. lib. bdg. 30.00 (0-87023-536-2) U of Mass Pr.

Call of Kolea. Maura O'Connor. Tr. by Keola Wong. 24p. 1993. pap. text ed. write for info. (1-882163-08-7) Moanalua Grdns Fnd.

Call of Mother Africa. Stan Grant. (Illus.). reprint ed. 10.00 (0-686-24749-3) Courier Pr FL.

***Call of Our Blood: The Wisdom of the Hispanic People.** Ed. & Tr. by Nick Kanellos. (Classic Wisdom Collection). 128p. (Orig.). (ENG & SPA.). 1995. 12.95 (1-880032-58-9) New Wrld Lib.

Call of Service. Robert Coles. 384p. 1994. pap. 10.95 (0-395-71084-7) HM.

Call of Service: A Witness to Idealism. Robert Coles. LC 93-2317. 1993. 22.95 (0-395-63647-7) HM.

Call of Service: A Witness to Idealism. large type ed. Robert Coles. LC 94-10670. 482p. 1994. 22.95 (0-8161-7404-0) Hall.

Call of Stories: Stories & the Moral Imagination. Robert Coles. 256p. 1990. pap. 10.95 (0-395-52815-1) HM.

***Call of the Ages.** Thomas W. Petrisko. LC 95-69033. 509p. 1995. pap. 11.95 (1-882972-59-7) Queenship Pub.

Call of the Brotherhood of the Rosycross: Esoteric Analysis of the Fama Fraternitatis R. C of 1615 see Secrets of the Rosicrucian Brotherhood

Call of the Canyon. Zane Grey. 1992. mass mkt. 3.99 (0-06-100342-5, Harp PBks) HarpC.

***Call of the Canyon - Mysterious Rider.** Grey. 1995. mass mkt. 4.99 (0-06-100919-9, Harp PBks) HarpC.

Call of the Colorado. Ray Webb. 184p. 1994. pap. 23.95 (0-89301-161-4) U of Idaho Pr.

Call of the Cuckoo. Norman Lang. 1993. mass mkt. 4.99 (0-06-100622-X, Harp PBks) HarpC.

Call of the Daimon. Aldo Carotenuto. Tr. by Charles Nobar. (Orig.). (ITA.). 1994. pap. 19.95 (0-933029-83-7) Chiron Pubns.

Call of the Deep. Linda Piazza. 160p. (Orig.). 1994. pap. 3.50 (0-380-77330-9, Flare) Avon.

Call of the Dervish. Pir V. Khan. 1993. pap. 12.00 (0-930872-44-4) Omega Pubns NY.

Call of the Earth. Evangelos Averoff-Tossizza. Tr. by Andre Michalopoulos. 300p. 1988. 12.50 (0-89241-134-1) Caratzas.

Call of the Fife & Drum: Three Novels of the American Revolution. Howard Fast. 640p. 1987. pap. 9.95 (0-8065-1027-7, Citadel Pr) Carol Pub Group.

***Call of the Game: What Really Goes On in the Broadcast Booth.** Gary Bender & Michael L. Johnson. LC 94-26463. (Illus.). 263p. 1994. 19.95 (1-56625-013-7) Bonus Books.

Call of the Gita. R. K. Math. 192p. 1987. pap. 2.95 (0-87481-537-1, Pub. by Ramakrishna Math II) Vedanta Pr.

Call of the Goddess: Seven Lives of an Androgyne. Hymen W. Picard. 1992. 18.95 (0-533-09692-8) Vantage.

Call of the High Plains. Charles Hancock. Ed. by Harry Chrisman. 250p. (Orig.). 1989. pap. 12.00 (1-882021-23-1) Salt River Pr.

***Call of the Horned Piper.** Nigel Jackson. 1990. pap. 17.95 (1-898307-09-1, Pub. by Capall Bann Pubng UK) Holmes Pub.

Call of the Jungle. (Amazing Mazes Story Ser.). (Illus.). 48p. (Orig.). (J). (gr. k-3). 1989. pap. 2.95 (0-8431-2705-8) Price Stern.

***Call of the Loon.** Paul Strong. (Camp & Cottage Ser.). (Illus.). 144p. (Orig.). 1995. pap. write for info. (1-55971-458-1) NorthWord.

Call of the Minaret. 2nd enl. rev. ed. Kenneth Cragg. LC 85-7107. 386p. 1985. pap. 16.95 (0-88344-207-8) Orbis Bks.

***Call of the Peacock.** Susan Udy. (Rainbow Romances Ser.). 160p. 1995. 14.95 (0-7090-5488-2, 923) Parkwest Pubns.

Call of the Phoenix. Dorothy Thomas. 287p. 1974. reprint ed. spiral bd. 11.00 (0-7873-0864-1) Mokelumne.

Call of the Phoenix Vignettes of Old & New China. Robert M. Bartlett. (Illus.). 150p. 1987. 12.95 (0-914339-19-2) P E Randall Pub.

Call of the Rainbow Warrior: An Environmental Fable. Twyla Dell. 96p. 1990. 12.95 (0-9626197-0-1) Foresight Inst.

Call of the Range: The Story of the Nebraska Stock Growers Association. Nellie S. Yost. LC 66-30428. (Illus.). 437p. 1966. 17.95 (0-8040-0028-X) Swallow.

Call of the Running Tide: A Portrait of an Island Family. Nancy P. Graff. (Illus.). (J). (gr. 3-7). 1991. 16.95 (0-316-32278-4) Little.

Call of the Sea & Other Verse. Robert A. Bowen. (Illus.). 1969. pap. 2.00 (0-912462-01-9) Foun Hist Rest.

Call of the Ships & the Sea. (Shorewood Art Programs for Education Ser.). 8p. 1983. teacher ed 107.00 (0-88185-018-7); 143.00 (0-685-42754-4) Shorewood Fine Art.

Call of the Siren: Manatees & Dugongs. Tim Dietz. LC 92-53036. (Illus.). 224p. (Orig.). 1992. pap. 15.95 (1-55591-104-8) Fulcrum Pub.

Call of the Spirit: Conversion with Swami Akhandananda. Niramayananda. 170p. 1987. pap. 2.95 (0-87481-538-X, Pub. by Ramakrishna Math II) Vedanta Pr.

Call of the Toad. Gunter Grass. Tr. by Ralph Manheim. LC 92-20233. 1992. 19.95 (0-15-125743-4) HarBrace.

Call of the Toad. Gunter Grass. Tr. by Ralph Manheim. 1993. pap. 10.95 (0-15-615340-8) HarBrace.

Call of the Torah: Bamidbar. E. Munk. 1993. 20.95 (0-89906-046-3); 17.95 (0-89906-047-1) Mesorah Pubns.

***Call of the Torah: Bereishis - Genesis.** E. Munk. 1994. 20.95 (0-89906-040-4); pap. 17.95 (0-89906-041-2) Mesorah Pubns.

***Call of the Torah: Shimos - Exodus.** E. Munk. 1994. 20.95 (0-89906-042-0); pap. 17.95 (0-89906-043-9) Mesorah Pubns.

Call of the Torah: Vayikra. E. Munk. 1992. 20.95 (0-89906-044-7); pap. 17.95 (0-89906-045-5) Mesorah Pubns.

Call of the Wendigo. Hardy Robin. (YA). 1994. pap. 3.50 (0-553-29828-3) Bantam.

Call of the Wild. (Illustrated Junior Library). (Illus.). (J). (gr. 3-12). 1965. 12.95 (0-448-06027-2, G&D) Putnam Pub Group.

Call of the Wild. Jack London. 14.95 (0-8488-0106-7, Amereon Hse) Amereon Ltd.

Call of the Wild. Jack London et al. (Classics Illustrated Ser.). (Illus.). 52p. (YA). Date not set. pap. 4.95 (1-57209-010-3) Classics Int Ent.

Call of the Wild. Jack London. 64p. 1990. pap. 1.00 (0-486-26472-6) Dover.

Call of the Wild. Jack London. (Illustrated Classics Collection 1). 64p. (J). (gr. 6-12). 1994. pap. 3.60 (1-56103-417-7) Lake Pub Co.

Call of the Wild. Jack London. LC 94-13622. (Illus.). 1994. pap. 2.95 (0-681-00695-1) Longmeadow Pr.

Call of the Wild. Jack London. LC 93-18409. (Illus.). (J). 1994. text ed. 19.95 (0-02-759455-6) Macmillan.

Call of the Wild. Jack London. Ed. by Kin Platt. LC 73-75461. (Now Age Illustrated Ser.). (Illus.). 64p. (J). (gr. 5-10). 1973. pap. 2.95 (0-88301-095-X) Pendulum Pr.

Call of the Wild. Jack London. (Classics Ser.). 128p. (J). (gr. 3-7). 1983. pap. 2.99 (0-14-035000-4, Puffin) Puffin Bks.

Call of the Wild. Jack London. (Classics Ser.). 128p. (J). (gr. 5 up). 1994. pap. 2.99 (0-14-036669-5) Puffin Bks.

Call of the Wild. Jack London. LC 79-24464. (Short Classics Ser.). (Illus.). 48p. (J). (gr. 4 up). 1980. Pub. 1980. lib. bdg. 22.80 (0-8172-1656-1) Raintree Steck-V.

Call of the Wild. Jack London. (Children's Classics Ser.). (J). 1991. 12.99 (0-517-06003-5) Random Hse Value.

Call of the Wild. Jack London. LC 90-50182. (Vintage-Library of America Ser.). 1990. pap. 8.50 (0-679-72535-0, Vin) Random.

Call of the Wild. Jack London. LC 63-14831. (Illus.). 144p. (YA). (gr. 6 up). 1970. 13.95 (0-02-759510-2, Mac Bks Young Read) S&S Childrens.

Call of the Wild. Jack London. Bd. with White Fang. 1984. Set pap. 2.95 (0-671-53147-6, WSP) PB.

Call of the Wild. Jack London. Bd. with White Fang. LC 85-60633. LC 85-60633. (Illus.). 304p. 1985. 12.95 (0-89577-211-6) RD Assn.

Call of the Wild. Jack London. Bd. with White Fang (Classics Ser.). 293p. (gr. 7-12). 1991. 3.95 (0-553-21233-8) Bantam.

***Call of the Wild.** Jack London & Daniel Dyer. LC 95-15717. (Illus.). 1995. write for info. (0-8061-2757-0) U of Okla Pr.

Call of the Wild. Jack London. 271p. 1983. reprint ed. lib. bdg. 19.95 (0-89966-473-3) Buccaneer Bks.

***Call of the Wild: A Naturalistic Romance.** Jacqueline Tavernier-Courbin. (Twayne's Masterwork Studies Ser.: No. 142). 128p. (Orig.). 1994. text ed. 22.95x (0-8057-8081-5, Twayne); pap. 12.95 (0-8057-4458-4, Twayne) Macmillan.

Call of the Wild: A Study Guide. Scott Gifford. (Novel-Ties Ser.). (YA). (gr. 9-12). 1990. pap. text ed. 15.95 (0-88122-411-1) Lrn Links.

Call of the Wild & Selected Stories. Jack London. 176p. (J). (gr. 6). 1960. pap. 3.95 (0-451-52390-3, Sig Classics) NAL-Dutton.

Call of the Wild & White Fang Notes. Samuel J. Umland. 70p. (Orig.). 1982. pap. text ed. 3.75 (0-8220-0279-5) Cliffs.

Call of the Wild Readalong. Jack London. (Illustrated Classics Collection 1). 64p. 1994. audio, pap. 13.50 (1-56103-419-3) Lake Pub Co.

Call of the Wild Student Activity Book. Marcia Sohl & Gerald Dackerman. (Now Age Illustrated Ser.). (Illus.). 16p. (J). (gr. 4-10). 1976. pap. 1.25 (0-88301-182-4) Pendulum Pr.

Call of the Wild, White Fang, & Other Stories. Jack London. Ed. by Robert C. Leitz, III. (World's Classics Ser.). 400p. 1990. pap. 5.95 (0-19-282709-X) OUP.

Call of the Wild, White Fang, & Other Stories. Jack London. Ed. by Andrew Sinclair. 416p. 1993. 7.95 (0-14-018651-4, Penguin Classics) Viking Penguin.

***Call of the Wolves.** Melvin Berger. (Ranger Rick Science Spectacular Ser.). 16p. (J). (gr. 2-4). 1995. pap. text ed. 14.95 (1-56784-216-X) Newbridge Comms.

***Call of the Wolves.** Jim Murphy. (J). (ps-3). 1994. pap. 4.95 (0-590-41940-4) Scholastic Inc.

Call of the Wood Pigeon: A Day in the Life of a Monk in Pre-Viking Ireland. Richard Roche. 1989. pap. 30.00 (0-685-65152-5, Pub. by Veritas IE) St Mut.

Call of the Wood Pigeon - Glaoch an Choluir Choille: A Day in the Life of a Monk in Pre-Viking Ireland. Richard Roche. (Illus.). (Orig.). (J). (gr. 1-8). 1990. pap. 9.95 (1-85390-047-8, Pub. by Veritas Pubns IE) Irish Bks Media.

Call of Trumpets. large type ed. Jane Lane. (Shadows of the Crown Ser.). 1974. 15.95 (0-85456-615-5) Ulverscroft.

Call of Zion: The Story of the First Welsh Mormon Emigration. Ronald C. Dennis. (Specialized Monograph Ser.: Vol. 2). 10.95 (0-88494-628-2) Bookcraft Inc.

***Call School: Rural Education in the Midwest to 1918.** Paul Theobald. LC 94-6920. 264p. (C). 1995. 29.95x (0-8093-1859-8) S Ill U Pr.

Call Steps: Plains, Camps, Stations, Consistories. Kenneth Irby. 1992. pap. 12.95 (0-88268-090-0) Station Hill Pr.

Call the Darkness Light. Nancy Zaroulis. LC 78-74714. (Hera Ser.). 560p. 1993. pap. 15.00 (0-939149-98-2) Soho Press.

Call the Next Witness. Philip P. Mason. LC 86-7122. xii, 208p. 1986. pap. 5.95 (0-226-50955-9) U Ch Pr.

Call the Roll: The First 150 Years of the Arkansas Legislature. Jerry E. Hinshaw. LC 86-60243. 256p. 1986. 22.95 (0-914546-66-X) Rose Pub.

Call the Sabbath a Delight. Walter J. Chantry. 112p. (Orig.). 1991. pap. 5.95 (0-85151-588-6) Banner of Truth.

Call to Action: An Analysis & Overview of the United States Criminal Justice System, with Recommendations. National Commission on Crime & Justice Staff. Ed. by Linda M. Thurston. LC 91-68516. 102p. (Orig.). 1993. pap. 8.00 (0-88378-067-4) Third World.

Call to Action: An Interpretation of the Great Uprising, Its Source & Causes. James B. Weaver. LC 73-36. (Gold Ser.: Vol. 2). 445p. 1974. reprint ed. 36.95 (0-405-05924-8) Ayer.

Call to Action: Handbook for Ecology, Peace & Justice. Ed. by Brad Erickson. LC 89-29296. (Illus.). 288p. 1990. pap. 14.95 (0-87156-611-7) Sierra.

Call to Action: Killing Giants & Subduing Kingdoms. rev. ed. Roberts Liardon. 108p. 1985. pap. 5.99 (1-879993-12-0) Embassy Pub.

Call to America to Build Zion: An Original Anthology. Ed. by Moshe Davis. LC 77-70723. (America & the Holy Land Ser.). 1977. lib. bdg. 23.95 (0-405-10306-9) Ayer.

Call to Arms. Alan D. Foster. (Damned Ser.: Bk. 1). 1992. mass mkt. 5.99 (0-345-37574-2, Del Rey) Ballantine.

***Call to Arms.** Thomas K. Martin. 240p. (Orig.). 1995. pap. text ed. 4.99 (0-441-00242-0) Ace Bks.

Call to Assembly: The Autobiography of a Musical Storyteller. Willie Ruff. LC 90-50514. (Illus.). 384p. 1991. 24.95 (0-670-83800-4) Viking Penguin.

Call to Authenticity: The Essays of Ezequiel Martinez Estrada. James Maharg. LC 77-7175. (Romance Monographs: No. 26). 1977. 26.00 (84-399-7352-7) Romance.

Call to Awaken, Vol. I. Karl G. Kamper & Karen M. Carson. 269p. 1986. text ed. 15.00 (0-9616739-1-5) Atonement Ent.

Call to Battle. Jerry Ahern. (Survivalist Ser.: No. 23). 1992. pap. 3.50 (0-8217-3698-1) Zebra.

***Call to Character: A Family Treasury.** Ed. by Colin Greer & Herbert Kohl. 1995. 25.00 (0-06-017339-4, HarpT) HarpC.

Call to Civic Service: National Service for Country & Community. Charles C. Moskos. 224p. 1988. text ed. 29.95 (0-02-921991-4) Free Pr.

Call to Comfort: A Counseling Manual for Every Christian. Tom Yarbrough. LC 88-6711. 144p. (Orig.). 1988. pap. 7.95 (0-89390-119-9) Resource Pubns.

Call to Conscience: Jews, Judaism, & Conscientious Objection. Albert S. Axelrad. LC 85-24010. 207p. 1986. text ed. 25.00 (0-88125-092-9); pap. 16.95 (0-88125-081-3) Ktav.

Call to Danger. large type ed. Christopher Coram. (Linford Mystery Library). 304p. 1988. pap. 11.95 (0-7089-6621-7, Linford) Ulverscroft.

Call to Die. large type ed. Christopher Coram. (Linford Mystery Library). 1990. pap. 12.95 (0-7089-6842-2, Linford) Ulverscroft.

Call to Discipleship. Juan Carlos Ortiz & Jamie Buckingham. LC 75-7476. 136p. 1975. pap. 5.95 (0-88270-122-3) Bridge Pub.

Call to Duty. Richard Herman, Jr. 432p. 1994. mass mkt. 5.50 (0-380-71831-6) Avon.

Call to Duty. Richard Herman, Jr. LC 92-19121. 1993. 20.00 (0-688-11438-5) Morrow.

Call to Excellence: Stories of Eight West Coast Churches. Alfred H. Smith. 108p. (Orig.). 1993. pap. 4.00 (0-88028-137-5, 1196) Forward Movement.

Call to Faith & Morality: A Time for Revolution. W. B. Carraway. LC 92-90301. (Illus.). 360p. (Orig.). 1993. pap. 14.95 (0-9633855-0-X) BAC Pubns.

Call to Follow Jesus. Kay Arthur. (International Inductive Study Ser.). 1994. pap. 4.99 (1-56507-221-9) Harvest Hse.

Call to Greatness: A Spiritual Journey of Self-Discovery & Self-Awareness. IsanaMada. LC 93-72543. (Illus.). 408p. (Orig.). 1994. pap. 19.95 (0-9635218-1-0) Dhyana Pr.

Call to Holiness: New Frontiers in Spirituality for Today's Religious. Renato Perino. LC 85-28621. 160p. (Orig.). 1986. pap. 7.95 (0-8189-0493-5) Alba.

Call to Holy Living: Walking with God in Joy, Praise, & Gratitude. Bruce Larson. LC 87-34579. (Christian Growth Bks.). (Illus.). 128p. (Orig.). 1988. pap. 9.99 (0-8066-2305-5, 10-0963, Augsburg) Augsburg Fortress.

Call to Honor. Gilbert Morris & Bobby Funderburk. LC 92-44517. (Price of Liberty Ser.: No. 1). 224p. (Orig.). 1993. pap. 8.99 (0-8499-3494-X) Word Inc.

Call to Humanity. Swami Rama. LC 88-211010. 150p. (Orig.). 1988. pap. 8.95 (0-89389-111-8) Himalayan Pubs.

Call to Islam. Muhammad Siddiqi. 40p. (Orig.). 1985. pap. 3.00 (1-56744-250-1) Kazi Pubns.

Call to Love. Chiara Lubich. Tr. by Jerry Hearne. 166p. 1989. pap. 8.95 (0-911782-67-2) New City.

Call to Love see Way to Love: The Last Meditations of Anthony de Mello

Call to Manhood: In a Fatherless Society. David E. Long. LC 92-78464. 208p. 1994. pap. 9.99 (1-56384-047-2) Huntington Hse.

***Call to Ministry: The Vision of Bishop John J. Sullivan.** Julie Sly. 176p. (Orig.). 1995. pap. 9.95 (1-55612-718-9) Sheed & Ward MO.

***Call to Ministry - from Dream to Reality.** Ting W. Lee. 137p. (CHI.). 1989. pap. 5.00 (1-56582-023-1) Christ Renew Min.

Call to Order. Jean Cocteau. LC 74-30365. (Studies in French Literature: No. 45). 1974. lib. bdg. 75.00 (0-8383-2056-2) M S G Haskell Hse.

Call to Order: Floor Politics in the House & Senate. Steven S. Smith. 270p. 1989. 34.95 (0-8157-8014-1); pap. 14.95 (0-8157-8013-3) Brookings.

Call to Organize! How to Wage War on Chaos & Clutter...& Win. Valerie Titlow. 111p. 1992. spiral bd. 9.95 (0-9633085-0-5) Organizers.

Call to Personhood: A Christian Theory of the Individual in Social Relationships. Alistair I. McFadyen. 336p. (C). 1990. 74.95 (0-521-38471-0); pap. 19.95 (0-521-40929-2) Cambridge U Pr.

Call to Prayer. Germaine Copeland. 160p. (Orig.). 1991. pap. 6.95 (0-89274-855-9, HH-855) Harrison Hse.

Call to Prayer. rev. ed. Comp. by David Butts. 112p. 1993. pap. 5.99 (0-87403-999-1, 11-03011) Standard Pub.

Call to Prayer: Public Worship Through the Christian Year. Ed. by Caryl Micklem. 176p. (Orig.). 1993. pap. 12.99 (0-8028-1523-5) Eerdmans.

Call to Prophethood. Saida Chaudhry. (Illus.). (J). (gr. 2-5). pap. 4.00 (0-89259-046-7) Am Trust Pubns.

***Call to Purpose: How Men Make Sense of Life-Changing Experiences.** Richard Solly. LC 94-46389. 225p. (Orig.). 1995. pap. 11.95 (1-56838-045-3) Hazelden.

Call to Reason: An Introduction to Atheism. 2nd ed. Intro. by Mary DeYoung. 1979. reprint ed. 12.50 (0-936128-01-1) De Young Pr.

Call to Remembrance: Connecting the Heart to Baha'u'llah. Comp. by Geoffry W. Marks. 308p. 1992. 30.00 (0-87743-237-6) Bahai.

Call to Responsible Freedom. Lud Golz. 126p. (Orig.). 1993. pap. 7.99 (1-56043-753-7) Destiny Image.

Call to Revolution: The Mystical Anarchism of Gustav Landauer. Charles B. Maurer. LC 75-14827. 219p. reprint ed. pap. 62.50 (0-8357-7976-9, 2027659) Bks Demand.

Call to Righteousness. Paul A. Tanner. 1984. pap. 0.95 (0-87162-404-4, D3012) Warner Pr.

Call to Spiritual Reformation: Encouragement from Paul & His Prayers. D. A. Carson. LC 92-11392. 256p. 1992. pap. 11.99 (0-8010-2569-9) Baker Bk.

***Call to Teach.** Hansen. 208p. (C). 1995. text ed. 39.00x (0-8077-3469-1); pap. text ed. 17.95x (0-8077-3468-3) Tchrs Coll.

***Call to the American People.** Hector C. Borghetty. LC 94-90160. 344p. (Orig.). 1995. pap. 7.95 (1-56002-462-3) Aegina Pr.

Call to the Center: The Gospel's Invitation to Deeper Prayer. 2nd ed. Basil Pennington. 168p. 1995. reprint ed. pap. 9.95 (1-56548-070-8) New City.

Call to the Church from Wang Ming-Dao. Ming-Dao Wang. 1983. pap. 4.95 (0-87508-094-4) Chr Lit.

Call to the Heights. Geoffrey Hodson. LC 75-30656. 224p. (Orig.). 1975. pap. 6.95 (0-8356-0477-2, Quest) Theos Pub Hse.

Call to the Infinite. Aryeh Kaplan. 257p. (C). 1986. 15.95 (0-940118-10-6) Moznaim.

Call to the Ministry. C. H. Spurgeon. pap. 0.99 (1-56632-076-3) Revival Lit.

Call to the Sky: The Decoy Collection of James M. McCleery. (Illus.). 120p. 1992. 24.95 (0-88415-057-7, 5-57); pap. 14.95 (0-88415-047-X, 5047) Gulf Pub.

Call to Wholeness. Kenneth L. Bakken. LC 84-23837. 128p. (Orig.). 1985. pap. 9.95 (0-8245-0683-9) Crossroad NY.

Call to Witness: Reflections on the Gospel of Matthew. Oliver McTernan. 120p. 1989. pap. 4.95 (0-8146-1838-3) Liturgical Pr.

***Call to Write: An Invitation for Aspiring Writers.** William L. White & Pamela Woll. 237p. (Orig.). 1995. pap. 12.95 (0-938475-05-3) Lighthouse Trg Inst.

Call up the Wind. Anne McAllister. (Presents Ser.). 1994. mass mkt. 2.99 (0-373-11620-9, 1-11620-1) Harlequin Bks.

Call up the Wind. large type ed. Anne McAllister. (Harlequin Ser.). 1993. reprint ed. lib. bdg. 18.95 (0-263-13268-4, Pub. by Mills & Boon UK) Thorndike Pr.

Call Waiting. R. L. Stine. (YA). 1994. pap. 3.99 (0-590-47480-4) Scholastic Inc.

Call Yourself Alive? Nina Cassian. LC 87-83570. 1989. pap. 16.95 (0-948259-38-8) Dufour.

Calla Handbook. Anna Chamot. (Illus.). 353p. 1993. write for info. (0-201-53963-2) Addison-Wesley.

Callachaca: Style & Status in an Inca Community. Susan A. Niles. LC 87-16782. (Illus.). 264p. 1987. text ed. 32.95 (0-87745-177-X) U of Iowa Pr.

Callaghan's Appellate Advocacy Manual (Lawyer's Edition), 2 vols., Set. John Cooley. 1989. 160.00 (0-318-41453-8) Clark Boardman Callaghan.

Callaghan's Way: American Hero. Marie Ferrarella. 1994. mass mkt. 3.50 (0-373-07601-0, 1-07601-7) Harlequin Bks.

An Asterisk (*) at the beginning of an entry indicates that the title is appearing in BIP for the first time.

Callaghen. Louis L'Amour. 192p. 1984. mass mkt. 3.99 (*0-553-24759-X*) Bantam.

***Callaham's Russian-English Dictionary of Science & Technology.** 4th ed. Ludmilla I. Callaham et al. (ENG & RUS.). 1995. text ed. 95.00 (*0-471-61139-5*) Wiley.

***Callahan in New England.** Harry Callahan & Diana L. Johnson. (Illus.). 52p. (Orig.). 1994. pap. 16.00 (*0-933519-28-1*) D W Bell Gallery.

Callahan Incorporates. Irene W. Ames. 169p. 1992. pap. 10.00 (*1-883166-00-4*) Frst Edition.

Callahan, the Last War Bird. Marvin L. Skelton. (Illus.). 156p. (Orig.). 1980. pap. 25.00 (*0-89126-081-1*) MA-AH Pub.

Callahan Touch. Spider Robinson. LC 92-21155. (Orig.). 1993. 18.95 (*0-441-09075-3*) Ace Bks.

***Callahan Touch.** Spider Robinson. 240p. (Orig.). 1995. pap. text ed. 5.50 (*0-441-00133-5*) Ace Bks.

Callahan's Crosstime Saloon. Spider Robinson. 192p. 1989. pap. 4.50 (*0-441-09043-5*) Ace Bks.

Callahan's Lady. Spider Robinson. 1990. mass mkt. 4.99 (*0-441-09072-9*) Ace Bks.

Callahan's Secret. 1989. pap. 4.50 (*0-441-09074-5*) Ace Bks.

Callaloo, Calypso & Carnival: The Cuisines of Trinidad & Tobago. Dave DeWitt & Mary J. Wilan. 120p. 1993. pap. 10.95 (*0-89594-638-6*) Crossing Pr.

Callander Square. Anne Perry. 256p. 1985. mass mkt. 4.95 (*0-449-20999-7*, Crest) Fawcett.

Callander Square. large type ed. Anne Perry. 1981. 12.00 (*0-7089-0718-0*) Ulverscroft.

Callanetics: Ten Years Younger in Ten Hours. Callan Pinckney. 208p. 1987. pap. 12.50 (*0-380-70261-4*) Avon.

Callanetics Countdown: Thirty Days to a Beautiful Body. Callan Pinckney. 192p. 1991. pap. 12.00 (*0-380-71453-1*) Avon.

Callanetics Countdown: Thirty Days to a Beautiful Body. Callan Pinckney. 1990. 19.95 (*0-394-58613-1*) Random.

Callanetics for Your Back. Callan Pinckney. 192p. 1990. pap. 11.95 (*0-380-70506-0*) Avon.

Callas: Portrait of a Prima Donna. George Jellinek. LC 75-179728. (Biography Index Reprint Ser.). 1977. reprint ed. 31.95 (*0-8369-8096-4*) Ayer.

Callas: Portrait of a Prima Donna. George Jellinek. 416p. 1986. reprint ed. pap. 8.95 (*0-486-25047-4*) Dover.

Callas Legacy. John Ardoin. 1979. 3.95 (*0-684-16343-8*, Scribners); 5.50 (*0-684-15297-5*, Scribners) S&S Trade.

Callas Legacy: A Biography of a Career. rev. ed. John Ardoin. (Illus.). 256p. 1982. 5.50 (*0-684-17450-2*, Scribners) S&S Trade.

Callas Legacy: The Complete Guide to Her Recordings. rev. ed. John Ardoin. (Illus.). 320p. 1991. pap. 16.95 (*0-684-19306-X*, Scribners) S&S Trade.

***Callas Legacy: The Complete Guide to Her Recordings on Compact Disc.** 4th ed. John Ardoin. (Illus.). 254p. Date not set. pap. 19.95 (*0-931340-90-X*, Amadeus Pr) Timber.

Callback: NASA's Aviation Safety Reporting System. Rex Hardy. LC 89-600326. (Illus.). 208p. 1990. 24.95 (*0-87474-463-6*) Smithsonian.

***Callbook Supplement, 1994.** Watson-Guptill Publications Staff. 1994. pap. 19.95 (*0-8230-8723-9*) Watsn-Guptill.

Called: New Thinking on Christian Vocation. M. Basil Pennington. 128p. 1983. pap. 7.95 (*0-8164-2472-1*) Harper SF.

Called & Accountable. Henry Blackaby & Joyce Mitchell. Ed. by Cathy Butler. 62p. (Orig.). 1991. pap. text ed. 3.95 (*1-56309-000-7*) Womans Mission Union.

Called & Accountable. Henry Blackaby & Joyce Mitchell. Ed. by Cathy Butler. 62p. (Orig.). (SPA.). 1991. pap. text ed. 3.95 (*1-56309-038-4*) Womans Mission Union.

Called & Committed: World-Changing Discipleship. David Watson. LC 82-824. 240p. 1982. pap. 8.99 (*0-87788-101-4*) Shaw Pubs.

Called & Empowered: Global Mission in Pentecostal Perspective. Ed. by Murray W. Dempster et al. LC 91-32846. 368p. 1991. pap. 14.95 (*0-943575-47-8*) Hendrickson MA.

Called & Gifted: The American Catholic Laity: Reflections of the American Bishops Commemorating the Fifteenth Anniversary of the Issuance of the "Decree on the Apostolate of the Laity" National Conference of Catholic Bishops Staff. 4p. 1980. pap. 0.75 (*1-55586-727-8*) US Catholic.

Called, Appointed, Annointed. Janny Grein. 95p. (Orig.). 1985. pap. 5.95 (*0-89274-354-9*) Harrison Hse.

Called by a Panther. Michael Z. Lewin. 1991. 17.95 (*0-89296-439-1*) Mysterious Pr.

Called by God: A Theology of Vocation & Lifelong Commitment. Marie T. Hermit & Francis K. Nemeck. 160p. (Orig.). 1992. pap. text ed. 11.95 (*0-8146-5909-8*, M Glazier) Liturgical Pr.

Called by Name. Peter G. Van Breemen. 1978. pap. 14.95 (*0-87193-094-3*) Dimension Bks.

Called by Name: A Program & Resource Guide. Bishops' Committee on Vocations. 84p. (Orig.). (ENG & SPA.). 1988. pap. 4.95 (*1-55586-183-0*) US Catholic.

***Called by Name: Discovering Your Unique Purpose in Life.** Robert J. Furey. 160p. (Orig.). 1995. pap. 11.95 (*0-8245-1484-X*) Crossroad NY.

Called from Within: Early Women Lawyers of Hawaii. Ed. by Mari J. Matsuda. LC 92-11002. (Biography Monographs). 400p. 1992. text ed. 45.00 (*0-8248-1430-4*); pap. 26.95 (*0-8248-1448-7*) UH Pr.

Called Home. Robert Irvine. Ed. by Dana Isaacson. 256p. 1993. reprint ed. mass mkt. 4.99 (*0-671-74929-3*) PB.

Called in Christ: Our Privileges & Opportunities As God's Children. Robert Folkenberg. LC 93-21392. 1993. 4.99 (*0-8163-1203-6*) Pacific Pr Pub Assn.

Called into Her Presence: Praying with Feminine Images of God. Virginia A. Froehle. LC 91-75852. 136p. 1992. spiral bd. 9.95 (*0-87793-470-3*) Ave Maria.

Called Out. A. G. Mojtabai. LC 93-32776. 1994. 22.00 (*0-385-47430-X*, N A Talese) Doubleday.

Called to Account. Sarah Spencer. (C). 1988. 21.00 (*0-946088-12-8*, Pub. by NCCL UK) St Mut.

Called to Account. M'Liss Switzer & Katherine Hale. LC 87-16675. (New Leaf Ser.). 145p. 1987. pap. 8.95 (*0-931188-55-5*) Seal Pr Feminist.

Called to Account. Frank H. Taylor. (C). 1989. text ed. 59.00 (*1-85821-045-3*, Pub. by Pentland Pr UK) St Mut.

Called to Action: The Knights of Columbus in Louisiana, 1962-1992. Barbara B. Lacour. Ed. by Irvon J. Gomez et al. LC 94-76030. (Illus.). 480p. 1994. 28.00 (*0-9640808-1-8*) LA St Council.

Called to Africa: Thirty-Five Years in Central Africa: a Missionary Building Schools, Hospitals, & Churches. Chester D. Scott & William D. Scott. LC 92-33473. 1993. 24.95 (*0-87483-297-7*) August Hse.

Called to Be a Layman: Ever Expanding Circles of Christian Witness. rev. ed. Gus Gustafson. LC 89-61586. 160p. 1989. pap. 6.95 (*0-917851-36-6*) Bristol Hse.

Called to Be a Layman Study Guide. 20p. 1993. pap. 2.95 (*0-917851-90-0*) Bristol Hse.

Called to Be Champions. J. J. Turner. 1988. pap. 4.75 (*0-89137-825-1*) Quality Pubns.

Called to Be Faithful: Reflections on Cycle B Readings for the Sundays of Lent. Catherine Nerney. 1985. 2.50 (*0-8091-9339-6*) Paulist Pr.

Called to Be Friends: A How-To Guide for Inviting & Incorporating Friends into Your Church. Nicholas B. Van Dyck & G. Edwin Bontrager. (Illus.). 42p. (Orig.). 1990. pap. write for info. (*0-318-66980-3*) MB Missions.

Called to Be Peacemakers: A New Call to Peacemaking Workbook. John K. Stoner. 98p. 1993. reprint ed. 5.00 (*0-9619012-0-9*) New Call Peacemkng.

Called to Be Saints. Fay E. Butler. 140p. 1993. pap. 10.00 (*1-883483-00-X*) Ellis-Butler Minist.

Called to Be Saints: Christian Living in First Century Rome. Michael Mullins. 576p. 1989. 60.00 (*1-85390-177-6*, Pub. by Veritas IE) St Mut.

Called to Be Warriors. Fay E. Butler. 160p. (Orig.). 1993. pap. 10.00 (*1-883483-02-6*) Ellis-Butler Minist.

Called to Care: A Training Manual for Small Group Leaders. Palmer Becker. 144p. (Orig.). 1993. pap. 6.95 (*0-8361-3622-5*) Herald Pr.

Called to Care: Biblical Images for Social Ministry. Robert Kysar. 176p. (Orig.). 1991. pap. 13.00 (*0-8006-2470-X*, 1-2470) Augsburg Fortress.

Called to Caregiving. Ed. by June A. Gibble & Fred W. Swartz. 175p. (Orig.). 1987. pap. 12.95 (*0-87178-150-6*) Brethren.

Called to Create. Ed. by Carol Walden. LC 86-62617. 104p. (Orig.). 1986. pap. 7.95 (*0-89390-070-2*) Resource Pubns.

***Called to Darkness.** J. V. Lewton. 224p. 1995. mass mkt. 3.99 (*0-8217-4914-5*) Zebra.

Called to Equip: A Training & Resource Manual for Pastors. Palmer Becker. 120p. (Orig.). 1993. pap. 6.95 (*0-8361-3623-3*) Herald Pr.

Called to Full Unity: Documents on Anglican-Roman Catholic Relations 1966-1983. Ed. by Joseph W. Witmer & J. Robert Wright. 360p. 1986. pap. 14.95 (*1-55586-937-8*) US Catholic.

Called to His Supper. Jeannine T. Leichner. (Illus.). 64p. (Orig.). (J). (gr. 1-3). 1990. pap. 3.95 (*0-87973-138-9*, 138) Our Sunday Visitor.

Called to Holiness. Bernard Haring. (C). 1988. 39.00 (*0-685-22289-6*, Pub. by St Paul Pubns UK) St Mut.

Called to Holiness. Bernard Haring. 104p. (C). 1990. 29.00 (*0-85439-199-1*, Pub. by St Paul Pubns UK) St Mut.

Called to Intimacy. George A. Maloney. LC 83-3782. 164p. 1983. pap. 6.95 (*0-8189-0452-6*) Alba.

Called to Jerusalem: Sent to the World. Theodore F. Schneider. 1992. pap. 14.50 (*1-55673-429-8*, 9232) CSS OH.

Called to Life. Yves Congar. 160p. (Orig.). 1987. pap. 12.95 (*0-8245-0835-1*) Crossroad NY.

Called to Life. Yves Congar. (Orig.). (C). 1988. 39.00 (*0-85439-265-3*, Pub. by St Paul Pubns UK) St Mut.

Called to Live Justly Social Justice in Luke-Acts. Anne M. Reardon & Kate Chambers. (Illus.). 36p. 1984. 2.95 (*0-934134-20-0*) Sheed & Ward MO.

Called to Love: A Discussion Program for the Newly Married. Francis J. Schweigert. 58p. (Orig.). 1982. pap. 7.00 (*0-936098-41-4*) Intl Marriage.

***Called to Parish Ministry: Identity, Challenges & Spirituality of Lay Ministers.** Greg Dues & Barbara Walkley. LC 94-62158. 176p. (Orig.). 1995. pap. 12.95 (*0-89622-649-2*) Twenty-Third.

Called to Pray. Wim Malgo. 3.95 (*0-937422-19-3*) Midnight Call.

Called to Preach, Condemned to Survive: The Education of Clayton Sullivan. Clayton Sullivan. LC 85-13654. xiv, 237p. 1985. 19.95 (*0-86554-173-6*, MUP-H163) Mercer Univ Pr.

Called to Serve: A Guidebook for Altar Servers. Albert J. Nevins. LC 81-82546. 48p. (J). (gr. 4 up). 1981. pap. 14.95 (*0-87973-663-1*, 663) Our Sunday Visitor.

Called to Serve Him. Elaine Cannon & Ed J. Pinegar. 1991. 11.95 (*0-88494-806-4*) Bookcraft Inc.

Called to Spiritual Maturity, Hebrews, Chapters 1-4, Pt. 1. Eva Gibson. (Discovering the Heart of God Ser.). 112p. 1993. pap. 5.95 (*1-56616-007-3*, 524001) Aglow Communs.

Called to the Hard Places: Biography - Missionary Pioneer China, Indonesia. Grace Chang. 1990. pap. 5.95 (*0-87508-093-6*) Chr Lit.

Called to the Ministry. Edmund Clowney. 1976. pap. 4.99 (*0-87552-144-4*) Presby & Reformed.

Called to Witness: A Manual for Congregational Outreach. Jerry L. Schmalenberger. LC 92-32743. 1992. pap. 8.25 (*1-55673-558-8*, 9306) CSS OH.

Called Together: Building a Foundation for a Christian Marriage. Steve Prokopchak & Mary Prokopchak. 160p. 1992. pap. text ed. write for info. (*0-9634951-0-0*) S&M Prokopchak.

Called unto Holiness, Vol. 1. Timothy L. Smith. LC 62-11409. 416p. 1962. 19.95 (*0-8341-0282-X*) Beacon Hill.

Called unto Holiness, Vol. 2. W. T. Purkiser. 368p. 1983. 19.95 (*0-8341-0868-2*) Beacon Hill.

Called unto Liberty! On Language & Nationalism. Colin H. Williams. LC 93-30787. (Multilingual Matters Ser.: Vol. 97). 270p. 1994. 99.00 (*1-85359-198-X*, Pub. by Multilingual Matters UK); pap. 39.95 (*1-85359-197-1*, Pub. by Multilingual Matters UK) Taylor & Francis.

Callender Papers. Cynthia Voigt. (J). (gr. 6 up). 1994. pap. 3.95 (*0-449-70184-0*, Juniper) Fawcett.

Callender Papers. Cynthia Voigt. LC 82-13797. 224p. (J). (gr. 4-8). 1983. text ed. 15.95 (*0-689-30971-6*, Atheneum Bks Young) S&S Childrens.

Caller. Chris Ahlemann. Ed. by James B. Van Treese. 390p. 1993. pap. 9.95 (*1-56901-014-5*) NW Pub.

Caller. abr. ed. Chris Ahlemann. 390p. 1995. pap. 9.95 (*1-56901-466-3*) NW Pub.

Calles de la Habana Intramuros. Manuel F. Santalices. (Illus.). 168p. (SPA.). 1989. 40.00 (*0-917049-22-5*); pap. 25.00 (*0-917049-17-9*) Saeta.

Calles Rectas, Sendero Torcido (Straight Sts, Crooked Path) A. H. Mottesi. (SPA.). Date not set. 1.79 (*0-685-74906-1*, 498505) Editorial Unilit.

Callico Tree. Juanitta Baldwin. 280p. 1992. lib. bdg. 19.95 (*1-880308-02-9*); pap. 13.95 (*1-880308-03-7*) Suntop.

***Callicross: An Original Calligraphy Alphabet Charted for Cross-Stitch & Needlepoint.** Elizabeth West. 16p. (Orig.). 1995. pap. 5.00 (*0-9636135-1-0*) SBC Pubns.

Callie. Dave Sargent. 160p. (YA). 1992. pap. write for info. (*1-56763-002-2*) Ozark Pub.

Callie's Way Home. Michael Knoedler. (Destination Ser.). 160p. (YA). (gr. 6-12). 1991. per., pap. 3.95 (*0-89486-729-6*, 5116A) Hazelden.

Calligram: Essays in New Art History from France. Ed. by Norman Bryson. (Cambridge New Art History & Criticism Ser.). (Illus.). 224p. 1988. 65.00 (*0-521-35046-8*); pap. 18.95 (*0-521-35927-9*) Cambridge U Pr.

Calligrammes. Guillaume Apollinaire. 192p. (FRE.). 1970. pap. 11.95 (*0-7859-2754-9*, F82072) Fr & Eur.

Calligrammes. Guillaume Apollinaire. (Poesie Ser.). (FRE.). 1964. pap. 9.95 (*2-07-030008-0*) Schoenhof.

Calligrammes: Poems of Peace & War (1913-1916) Guillaume Apollinaire. Tr. & Notes by Anne H. Greet. 525p. (ENG & FRE.). 1991. pap. 16.00 (*0-520-07390-8*) U CA Pr.

Calligrams. 2nd ed. Guillaume Apollinaire. Tr. by Anne H. Greet. LC 69-13012. (French Ser.). (ENG & FRE.). 1973. 17.50 (*0-87775-010-6*); pap. 7.50 (*0-87775-068-8*) Unicorn Pr.

Calligraphers & Painters: A Treatise by Qadi Ahmad, Son of Mir-Munshi. Tr. by V. Minorsky. (Occasional Papers Ser.: Vol. 3, No. 2). (Illus.). 1959. pap. 6.00 (*0-934686-06-8*) Freer.

Calligraphers Handbook. 1988. 4.99 (*0-517-66664-2*) Random Hse Value.

Calligrapher's Handbook. 2nd ed. Ed. by Heather Child. (Illus.). 272p. 1986. pap. 15.95 (*0-8008-1198-4*) Taplinger.

Calligrapher's Project Book. Susanne Haines. 144p. 1993. pap. 18.00 (*0-00-412483-9*, Pub. by HarpC UK) HarpC.

Calligraphic Alphabets. Arthur Baker. LC 79-8223. (Pictorial Archive Ser.). (Illus.). 153p. (Orig.). 1974. pap. 7.95 (*0-486-21045-6*) Dover.

Calligraphic Bookplates & Monograms. Villu Toots. Tr. by Ago Ambre. (Illus.). 144p. (Orig.). 1992. pap. write for info. (*0-9623131-1-4*) Intl Letter Arts.

Calligraphic Designs. Mimi Armstrong. (International Design Library). (Illus.). 48p. (Orig.). 1983. pap. 5.95 (*0-88045-031-2*) Stemmer Hse.

***Calligraphic Flourishes: A New Approach to an Ancient Art.** William Hildebrandt. (Illus.). 128p. 1995. pap. 15.95 (*1-56792-033-0*) Godine.

Calligraphic Initials. Arthur Baker. LC 78-56108. (Illus.). 1978. 12.50 (*0-910158-44-4*); pap. 8.95 (*0-910158-48-7*) Art Dir.

Calligraphic Lettering. 3rd enl. rev. ed. Ralph Douglass. 112p. 1967. spiral bd. 14.95 (*0-8230-0551-8*, Watsn-Guptill) Watsn-Guptill.

Calligraphic State: Textual Domination & History in a Muslim Society. Brinkley Messick. (Comparative Studies on Muslim Societies: No. 16). (C). 1992. 40.00 (*0-520-07605-2*) U CA Pr.

Calligraphic Styles. Tom Gourdie. LC 78-52316. (Illus.). 106p. 1982. pap. 9.95 (*0-8008-1181-X*) Taplinger.

Calligraphic Swash Initials. Arthur Baker. (Illus.). 96p. (Orig.). (gr. 7 up). 1984. pap. 4.95 (*0-486-24427-X*) Dover.

Calligraphotechnia, Or, the Art of Faire Writing. Richard Gething. LC 73-6134. (English Experience Ser.: No. 599). 1973. reprint ed. 14.00 (*90-221-0599-7*) Walter J Johnson.

Calligraphy. Arthur Baker. (Pictorial Archive Ser.). (Illus.). 160p. (Orig.). 1973. pap. 7.95 (*0-486-22895-9*) Dover.

***Calligraphy.** Evans. 1995. (*0-7858-0332-7*) Bk Sales Inc.

Calligraphy. C. Evans. (Practical Guides Ser.). (Illus.). 48p. (J). (gr. 6 up). 1990. lib. bdg. 14.96 (*0-88110-432-9*, Usborne); pap. 7.95 (*0-7460-0426-5*, Usborne) EDC.

***Calligraphy.** Michael Gullick. Ed. by Stephen Calloway. (Illus.). 64p. 1995. pap. 9.95 (*1-55921-152-0*) Moyer Bell.

Calligraphy. Manda Hanson. (Workstations Ser.). (Illus.). 48p. (J). (gr. 9 up). 1993. 21.95 (*0-8431-3664-2*) Price Stern.

Calligraphy. David Harris. 1991. 14.99 (*0-517-06700-5*) Random Hse Value.

Calligraphy. Ed. by Natalie J. Hartman. (Illus.). 100p. (Orig.). 1989. pap. write for info. (*0-318-64660-9*) Art Print Binding.

Calligraphy. Arthur Newhall. (How to Draw & Paint Ser.). (Illus.). 32p. (Orig.). 1990. pap. 5.95 (*1-56010-064-8*, HT-227) W Foster Pub.

Calligraphy. George Schwandner. 1958. pap. 9.95 (*0-486-20475-8*) Dover.

Calligraphy: A Practical Handbook for the Beginner. Muriel M. Parker. 1982. 6.98 (*0-517-38135-4*) Random Hse Value.

***Calligraphy: Art & Colour.** Peter Halliday. (Illus.). 96p. 1995. 29.95 (*0-7134-6483-6*, Pub. by Batsford UK) Trafalgar.

Calligraphy: Elegant & Easy. Joyce Ryan. LC 94-94049. (Illus.). 104p. (Orig.). 1994. pap. 12.95 (*0-939077-04-3*) Butterfly Bks.

Calligraphy: The Art of Beautiful Writing. Katherine Jeffares. 1978. pap. 7.00 (*0-87980-356-8*) Wilshire.

Calligraphy: The Art of Beautiful Writing. Elizabeth Lucas. (Illus.). 1984. pap. 18.50 (*0-13-112269-X*) P-H.

Calligraphy: The Art of Lettering with the Broad Pen. Byron J. MacDonald. pap. 5.95 (*0-8008-1182-8*) Taplinger.

Calligraphy: The Art of Written Forms. unabridged ed. Donald M. Anderson. LC 92-12563. Orig. Title: The Art of Written Forms. (Illus.). 368p. 1992. reprint ed. pap. text ed. 17.95 (*0-486-27212-5*) Dover.

Calligraphy: The Italic Alphabet for Right & Left-Handed Writers. 2nd rev. ed. Mary J. Gormley. LC 83-90347. (Illus.). 85p. 1983. pap. 8.95 (*0-9611590-0-6*) Inkspot Pr.

Calligraphy, A to Z. David Stuart. LC 84-16380. (Illus.). 208p. (YA). (gr. 9-12). 1985. 17.95 (*0-87396-088-2*) Stravon.

Calligraphy Alphabets Made Easy. Margaret Shepherd. (Illus.). 1986. pap. 10.00 (*0-399-51257-8*, Perigree Bks) Berkley Pub.

Calligraphy & Islamic Culture. Annemarie Schimmel. (Hagop Kevorkian Series on Near Eastern Art & Civilization). 1984. 60.00 (*0-8147-7830-5*); pap. 30.00 (*0-8147-7896-8*) NYU Pr.

Calligraphy & Lettering Design. Arthur Newhall. (Artist's Library). (Illus.). 64p. (Orig.). 1990. pap. 6.95 (*1-56010-031-1*, AL15) W Foster Pub.

Calligraphy & Lettering, No. 2. Al Mack. (How to Draw & Paint Ser.). (Illus.). 32p. (Orig.). 1989. pap. 5.95 (*1-56010-024-9*, HT211) W Foster Pub.

Calligraphy & Ornamental Lettering. Lance Martin & Robert Dicke, Jr. Ed. by E. Cooper. (Illus.). 1979. 12.95 (*0-8024-9953-8*) Pleasure Trove.

Calligraphy & Painting in the Wu-tsa-tsu: Conservative Aesthetics in Seventeenth Century China. Sewall J. Oertling, II. (Michigan Monographs in Chinese Studies: No. 66). 1994. write for info. (*0-89264-098-7*); pap. write for info. (*0-89264-099-5*) Ctr Chinese Studies.

Calligraphy & Palaeography. A. S. Osley. (Illus.). 1966. 25.00 (*0-8079-0020-6*) October.

Calligraphy & Related Ornamentation. Lance Martin & Scott Aagre. (Illus.). 98p. (Orig.). 1982. lib. bdg. 12.95 (*0-317-57776-X*); pap. 5.95 (*0-685-18122-7*) Pleasure Trove.

Calligraphy As a Home Business. rev. ed. Carroll, Frieda, Research Division Staff. 78p. 1992. 19.95 (*0-911569-74-X*) Prosperity & Profits.

Calligraphy Book. Peter Grislis. 64p. (J). (gr. 4 up). 1990. pap. 5.95 (*0-590-42546-3*) Scholastic Inc.

Calligraphy Book Companion. Peter Grislis. (J). (gr. 4-7). 1994. pap. 4.95 (*0-590-46152-4*) Scholastic Inc.

Calligraphy for Fun & Profit. Anne Leptich & Jacque Evans. 1982. pap. 7.00 (*0-87980-385-1*) Wilshire.

Calligraphy for Kids. William A. Bostick. (Illus.). 32p. (Orig.). (J). (gr. 3-12). 1991. student ed 9.95 (*0-9606630-1-0*) La Stampa Calligrafica.

Calligraphy for the Beginner. Tom Gourdie. LC 79-63439. (Illus.). 64p. 1983. reprint ed. pap. 6.95 (*0-8008-1188-7*) Taplinger.

Calligraphy in the Arts of the Muslim World. Anthony Welch. LC 78-11796. (Illus.). 216p. 1979. text ed. 39.95 (*0-292-73818-8*) U of Tex Pr.

Calligraphy in the Copperplate Style. Herb Kaufman & Geri Homelsky. (Illus.). 50p. (Orig.). 1981. pap. 2.95 (*0-486-24037-1*) Dover.

Calligraphy in the Graphic Arts. Michael Harvey. 1989. pap. 16.95 (*0-370-31139-6*) Random.

Calligraphy Is Fun. Abraham Lincoln. 80p. (Orig.). 1990. pap. 12.95 (*0-943295-13-0*) Graphics Plus FL.

***Calligraphy Made Easy.** Gaynor Goffe. 1994. 12.99 (*0-517-10203-X*) Random Hse Value.

Calligraphy Made Easy. Tina Serafini. LC 81-50781. 1984. pap. 7.00 (*0-87980-388-6*) Wilshire.

Calligraphy Made Easy. Margaret Shepherd. 1989. pap. 8.95 (*0-399-50964-X*, Perigree Bks) Berkley Pub.

Calligraphy Masterclass. Ed. by Peter Halliday. LC 89-71018. (Illus.). 128p. 1990. 25.00 (*0-87951-400-0*) Overlook Pr.

Calligraphy of Lloyd J. Reynolds: A Contemporary American Writing Master. 2nd rev. ed. William Gunderson & Charles Lehman. (Illus.). 80p. 1989. pap. 17.95 (*0-87595-208-9*) Oregon Hist.

***Calligraphy Projects.** F. Watt & A. Rowley. (Practical Guides Ser.). (Illus.). 32p. (YA). (gr. 5 up). 1995. lib. bdg. 13.96 (*0-88110-742-5*, Usborne); pap. 5.95 (*0-7460-1733-2*, Usborne) EDC.

Calligraphy Skills & Techniques. Judy Martin & Miriam Strimbley. LC 94-15246. 1994. pap. 18.00 (*0-02-022655-1*) Macmillan.

C

An Asterisk (*) at the beginning of an entry indicates that the title is appearing in BIP for the first time. 1005

Calligraphy Source Book. Miriam Stribley. LC 86-10190. 160p. 1986. 19.95 (0-89471-468-6) Running Pr.

Calligraphy Techniques. John Lancaster. (Illus.). 144p. 1992. pap. 22.95 (0-7134-4370-7, Pub. by Batsford UK) Trafalgar.

Calligraphy Techniques. Karen McMannon. (Illus.). 192p. 1990. 8.99 (0-517-69910-9) Random Hse Value.

Calligraphy Techniques & Uses. Eugene Metcalf. (Artist's Library). (Illus.). 64p. (Orig.). 1989. pap. 6.95 (0-929261-10-0, AL10) W Foster Pub.

Calligraphy Tips. Bill Gray. 1989. pap. text ed. 12.95 (0-07-157369-0) McGraw.

Calligraphy Tips. Bill Gray. (Illus.). 128p. 1986. pap. 12.95 (0-13-112673-3) P-H.

Calligraphy Tips. Bill Gray. (Illus.). 128p. 1989. pap. 12.95 (0-8306-5501-8, Design Pr) TAB Bks.

Calligraphy Today: Twentieth Century Tradition & Practice. Heather Child. (Illus.). 128p. 1988. bds. 22.95 (0-8008-1206-9) Taplinger.

Calligraphy with Class. Sylvia Diamond. (Illus.). 105p. 1988. pap. 14.95 (0-932906-23-0) Pan-Am Publishing Co.

Calligraphy's Flowering, Decay & Restoration. Paul Standard. 1977. pap. 3.95 (0-8008-1183-6) Taplinger.

Callimachus, 2 vols. in 1. Callimachus. Ed. by Rudolfus Pfeiffer & W. R. Connor. LC 78-18592. (Greek Texts & Commentaries Ser.). 1979. reprint ed. lib. bdg. 71.95 (0-405-11433-8) Ayer.

Callimachus: Hymns, Epigrams, Select Fragments. Tr. by Stanley Lombardo & Diane Rayor. LC 87-45479. 144p. 1987. pap. text ed. 12.95x (0-8018-3281-0) Johns Hopkins.

Callimachus: Proceedings of the Groningen Workshops on Hellenistic Poetry. Ed. by M. A. Harder et al. (Hellenistica Groningana Ser.: No. I). ii, 229p. 1993. pap. 45.00 (90-6980-064-0, Pub. by Egbert Forsten NE) Benjamins North Am.

*Callimachus & His Critics. Alan Cameron. LC 95-2674. 1995. write for info. (0-691-04367-1) Princeton U Pr.

Callimachus' Hymns One, Two, Five, Six. Robert Schmiel. (Greek Commentaries Ser.). 51p. (Orig.). (C). 1984. pap. text ed. 6.00 (0-929524-05-5) Bryn Mawr Commentaries.

Calling. Tom Absher. LC 87-70542. 72p. (Orig.). 1987. 15.95 (0-914086-72-3); pap. 9.95 (0-914086-73-1) Alicejamesbooks.

*Calling. Brother Andrew. 256p. 1995. 18.99 (0-345-39753-3, Moorings) Ballantine.

Calling. Kathryn M. Griffith. 384p. 1994. mass mkt. 4.50 (0-8217-4659-6) Zebra.

Calling. James D. Kath. Ed. by James B. Van Treese. 282p. 1994. pap. 8.95 (1-56901-061-7) NW Pub.

*Calling. Meredith. 124p. Date not set. pap. 5.99 (1-886820-03-1) Meredith WA.

Calling. Lewis P. Stanek. 71p. (Orig.). 1991. pap. 8.14 (0-685-48269-3) Dayspring Pr.

*Calling. Walter York. Ed. by M. L. Jones. 700p. (Orig.). 1995. pap. 9.95 (1-882270-30-4) Old Rugged Cross.

*Calling: A Journey Within Your Own Being. Steven S. Sadleir. 108p. (Orig.). 1995. pap. 12.95 (1-883544-02-5) Self Awareness.

*Calling: A Song for the Baptized. Caroline A. Westerhoff. LC 94-27023. 172p. 1994. pap. 10.95 (1-56101-101-0) Cowley Pubns.

Calling: Essays on Teaching in the Mother Tongue. Gail Griffin. LC 91-68032. 272p. (Orig.). 1992. pap. 14.95 (0-9623879-2-4) Trilogy Bks.

Calling a Pastor to a Baptist Church. rev. ed. Allix B. James. Ed. by Amos Jones, Jr. 50p. (Orig.). 1983. pap. 4.95 (0-910683-00-X) Townsnd-Pr.

Calling a Truce to Terror: The American Response to International Terrorism. Ernest Evans. LC 78-22722. (Contributions in Political Science Ser.: No. 29). (Illus.). 180p. 1979. text ed. 49.95 (0-313-21140-X, EIT/, Greenwood Pr) Greenwood.

Calling All Elk. Jim Zumbo. Ed. by Jeri D. Walton. (Illus.). 200p. (Orig.). 1989. pap. 14.95 (0-685-27819-0) Wapiti Valley Pub Co.

Calling All Heroes. Paco I. Taibo, 2nd. Tr. by John Mitchell & Ruth M. de Aguilar. LC 90-32134. 128p. 1990. 16.95 (0-917635-08-6); pap. 8.95 (0-917635-09-4) Plover Pr.

Calling All Horses: And Other Favorite Essays & Poems from the Syndicated Newspaper Column Looking in, Looking Out 1989-1993. Gail Grenier. 100p. 1993. 8.00 (0-9639343-0-9) Little Syndicate.

Calling All Monsters. Chris Westwood. LC 91-19601. 224p. (YA). (gr. 7 up). 1993. lib. bdg. 14.89 (0-06-022462-2) HarpC Child Bks.

Calling & Separation: Opening the Door to Your Ministry. Bob Yandian. 64p. (C). 1991. pap. 4.95 (1-880089-00-9) Pillar OK.

Calling & Veiled Threat, 2 bks. in 1. Jerry B. Jenkins. (Jennifer Grey Mystery Collections: No. 3). 7.95 (1-55748-168-7) Barbour & Co.

Calling B for Butterfly. Louise Lawrence. LC 81-48648. (Trophy Starwanderer Bk.). 224p. (YA). (gr. 7 up). 1988. pap. 3.95 (0-06-447036-9, Trophy) HarpC Child Bks.

*Calling Church & Seminary into the 21st Century. Donald E. Messer. 176p. 1995. 15.95 (0-687-01351-8) Abingdon.

*Calling Crow. Paul Clayton. 320p. (Orig.). 1995. pap. text ed. 4.99 (0-425-14532-8) Berkley Pub.

Calling Disciples. John Colligan et al. 54p. (Orig.). 1984. 1.95 (0-911905-22-7) Past & Mat Rene Ctr.

Calling Disciples, Mentality. John Colligan et al. LC 84-60459. (Calling Disciples Ser.: Bk. 2). 67p. (Orig.). 1984. pap. text ed. 2.95 (0-911905-21-9) Past & Mat Rene Ctr.

Calling Disciples: Outlines. Chuck Gallagher et al. LC 84-60459. (Calling Disciples Ser.: Bk. 1). 64p. (Orig.). 1984. pap. text ed. 2.95 (0-911905-23-5) Past & Mat Rene Ctr.

Calling Dr. Kildare. large type ed. Max Brand. LC 92-41195. (General Ser.). 1993. pap. 14.95 (0-8161-5717-0, Large Print Bks) Hall.

Calling His Children Home: Poems. Gregory Donovan. LC 93-4057. 64p. (Orig.). (C). 1993. text ed. 18.95 (0-8262-0895-9); pap. 9.95 (0-8262-0896-7) U of Mo Pr.

Calling Home. Michael Cadnum. 144p. (J). (gr. 7 up). 1993. pap. 3.99 (0-14-034569-8, Puffin) Puffin Bks.

Calling Home. Michael Cadnum. 192p. (J). (gr. 7 up). 1991. 14.95 (0-670-83566-8) Viking Child Bks.

Calling Home: Working Class Women's Writings. Ed. by Janet Zandy. LC 89-39328. (Illus.). 340p. (C). 1990. text ed. 40.00 (0-8135-1527-0); pap. 13.95 (0-8135-1528-9) Rutgers U Pr.

Calling in Sick. William Talcott. (End of the Century Bks.). 60p. (Orig.). 1989. pap. 5.00 (0-926664-02-6) Bay Area Ctr Art & Tech.

Calling Jesus Names: The Social Value of Labels in Matthew. Bruce J. Malina & Jerome H. Neyrey. LC 88-5821. (Foundations & Facets: Social Facets Ser.). 192p. 1988. pap. 15.95 (0-944344-05-4) Polebridge Pr.

Calling of a Rock Star. Beth Whitaker. (Illus.). 68p. (Orig.). 1988. pap. 7.99 (0-914903-63-2) Destiny Image.

Calling of an Angel. Gary L. Glum. 247p. (C). 1988. 45.00 (0-9620364-0-4) Silent Walker Pub.

Calling of Cable. Brian R. Tinsley. Ed. & Illus. by Alexis Satchell. 125p. (Orig.). 1987. pap. 5.95 (0-931841-08-9) Satchells Pub.

Calling of Dan Matthews. Harold B. Wright. LC 93-41972. 368p. (Orig.). 1995. pap. 4.95 (1-56554-048-4) Pelican.

Calling of Elizabeth Courtland & Honor Bound, 2 bks. in 1. Colleen Reece. (Romance Reader Ser.: No. 1). 7.95 (1-55748-089-3) Barbour & Co.

Calling of Emily Evans. Janette Oke. LC 89-78543. 224p. (Orig.). 1990. pap. 7.99 (1-55661-118-8) Bethany Hse.

Calling of Emily Evans. large type ed. Janette Oke. 222p. (Orig.). 1990. 9.99 (1-55661-121-8) Bethany Hse.

Calling of Sociology: And Other Essays on the Pursuit of Learning. Edward Shils. LC 79-15048. 1980. lib. bdg. 27.50 (0-226-75323-9) U Ch Pr.

Calling of the Church in a Changing World. Paul G. Schrotenboer. (Lecture Ser.). 50p. (Orig.). 1989. pap. 1.75 (0-932914-19-5) Dordt Coll Pr.

Calling of the Laity. Ed. by Verna Dozier. LC 88-70761. 157p. (Orig.). 1988. pap. 12.95 (1-56699-027-0, AL106) Alban Inst.

Calling on Dragons. Patricia C. Wrede. LC 92-35469. (Enchanted Forest Chronicles Ser.: Bk. 3). (J). 1993. 16.95 (0-15-200950-7, J Yolen Bks) HarBrace.

*Calling on Dragons. Patricia C. Wrede. (YA). 1994. pap. 3.95 (0-590-48467-2) Scholastic Inc.

Calling the Circle: The First & Future Culture. Christina Baldwin. 258p. 1994. pap. 14.95 (0-9632310-8-1) Swan Raven.

Calling the Dead. C. G. Hanzlicek. LC 82-70743. 1982. 16.95 (0-915604-70-1); pap. 9.95 (0-915604-71-X) Carnegie-Mellon.

*Calling the Doves: Canto por las Palomas. Juan F. Herrera. LC 94-45901. (Illus.). (ENG & SPA.). (J). 1995. write for info. (0-89239-132-4) Childrens Book Pr.

Calling the Equality Bluff: Women in Israel. Ed. by Barbara Swirski & Marilyn P. Safir. (Athene Ser.). 320p. (C). 1993. reprint ed. text ed. 44.00 (0-8077-6251-2); reprint ed. pap. text ed. 21.95 (0-8077-6250-4) Tchrs Coll.

Calling the Police: Citizen Reporting of Serious Crime. (Illus.). 203p. (Orig.). (C). 1993. pap. text ed. 35.00 (1-56806-812-3) Diane Pub.

Calling the Police: The Interpretation of, & Response to, Calls for Assistance from the Public. P. A. Waddington. LC 93-1211. 231p. 1993. 59.95 (1-85628-527-8, Pub. by Avebury Pub UK) Ashgate Pub Co.

Calling the Shots: Profiles of Women Filmmakers. Janis Cole. 1994. pap. 16.95 (1-55082-085-0, Pub. by Quarry Pr CN) InBook.

Calling the Shots: The Memoirs of an NHL Referee. Bruce Hood & Murray Townsend. (Illus.). 256p. 1988. 22.95 (0-7737-2209-2, Pub. by Stoddart Pubng CN) Genl Dist Srvs.

Calling the Wind: Twentieth Century African-American Short Stories. Ed. by Clarence Major. LC 92-52620. 1993. pap. 13.00 (0-06-098201-2, PL) HarpC.

Calling to Mind: An Account of the First Hundred Years of Steel Brothers & Company Ltd. Ed. by H. E. Braund. (Illus.). 1975. 72.00 (0-08-017415-9, Pub. by Pergamon Repr UK) Franklin.

Calling Tracy: Six Decades of Dick Tracy. James Van Hise. 1990. pap. 14.95 (1-55698-241-0) Movie Pubs Servs.

Calling up the Reserves: Work & Family Considerations for Employers. (BNA Special Report Series on Work & Family: No. 35). 32p. 1990. 35.00 (1-55871-189-9, BSP198) BNA.

Calling upon the Name of the Lord. Bill Freeman. 125p. (Orig.). Date not set. pap. 3.50 (0-914271-59-8) Mnstry Wrd.

Calling Woods. James L. Davis. LC 85-72742. 80p. 1986. reprint ed. 25.00 (0-937653-00-4) Bollenbaugh Hill.

Calling Yourself Home. Michael Rattee. 67p. (Orig.). 1986. pap. 6.00 (0-914946-59-5) Cleveland St Univ Poetry Ctr.

*Callings: A Gathering of Autobiographical Stories by Northwest Nazarene College Faculty & Staff. Ed. by Gaymon Bennett. (Illus.). 137p. (Orig.). 1994. pap. 5.00 (1-880899-01-9) Melville & Co.

Callings: The Gospel in the World. Paul Helm. 143p. (C). 1987. pap. 7.50 (0-85151-512-6) Banner of Truth.

Calliope. Robert Crosson. 60p. (Orig.). 1988. pap. 7.95 (0-89807-257-3) Illuminati.

Calliope. Greta Lipson & Jane Romantowski. 160p. (gr. 4-8). 1981. 12.95 (0-86653-025-8, GA230) Good Apple.

Calliope Garden. Kathleen L. Mendel. Ed. by Candy K. Brethauer. LC 91-77829. 40p. (Orig.). (C). 1992. pap. 5.20 (1-878142-25-9) Telstar TX.

Calliope's Sisters. Richard L. Anderson. 320p. 1989. pap. text ed. 33.33 (0-13-155425-5) P-H.

Callirhoe: Love Story in Syracuse. Chariton. Ed. & Tr. by G. P. Goold. LC 94-6918. (Loeb Classical Library: Vol. 481). 1995. text ed. 16.95 (0-674-99530-9, L481) HUP.

Callis. Mark Dunster. 39p. (Orig.). 1994. pap. 5.00 (0-89642-247-X) Linden Pubs.

Callista Roy: An Adaptation Model. Louette R. Lutjens. (Notes on Nursing Theories Ser.: Vol. 3). (Illus.). 68p. (C). 1991. 18.95 (0-8039-4577-9); pap. 8.95 (0-8039-4228-1) Sage.

*Callisto Group. Michael Westheim. (The Callisto Ser.). (Illus.). 192p. (J). (gr. 4-7). 1995. 15.95 (0-9647507-9-1) Dolphin Bks.

Callisto Myth from Ovid to Atwood. Kathleen Wall. 240p. 1988. 44.95 (0-7735-0640-3, Pub. by McGill CN) U of Toronto Pr.

Callmann Unfair Competition, Trademarks & Monopolies: 1981-1989, 9 vols., Set. 4th ed. Louis Altman & Rudolf Callman. LC 81-7639. (IP Ser.). 1981. ring bd. 1,195.00 (0-685-24625-6) Clark Boardman Callaghan.

Callot's Graphic Work: A Catalogue Raisonne, 2 vols. Jules Lieure. (Illus.). (FRE.). 1989. reprint ed. Set, Vol. 1, 368p, Vol. 2, 364p. 295.00 (1-55660-028-3) A Wofsy Fine Arts.

Callous Problem. G. Kuntscher. (Illus.). 160p. 1974. 8.00 (0-87527-133-2) Green.

*Calloway's Castle. 24p. (J). 1994. 12.95 (0-910523-15-0) Grandin Bk Co.

Calls of Frogs & Toads. Lang Elliott. (Illus.). 28p. Date not set. 13.95 (1-878194-04-6) Nature Sound Studio.

Callvac Directory. 700p. 1993. 30.00 (0-9639379-0-1) Firstlink.

Callville: Head of Navigation, Arizona Territory. Ed. by Stanley W. Paber. (Illus.). 40p. 1981. pap. 4.95 (0-913814-39-3) Nevada Pubns.

Cally's Enterprise. Claudia Mills. 128p. (J). (gr. 5 up). 1989. pap. 2.75 (0-380-70693-8, Camelot) Avon.

Calm & Clear. Lama Mi-pham. LC 73-79058. (Tibetan Translation Ser.: Vol. 1). (Illus.). 128p. 1973. pap. 12.95 (0-913546-02-X) Dharma Pub.

Calm & Insight: A Buddhist Manual for Meditators. Khantipalo. (C). 1987. pap. 17.50 (0-7007-0141-9, Pub. by Curzon Pr UK) Humanities.

Calm at Sunset, Calm at Dawn. Paul Watkins. 1991. pap. 8.95 (0-380-71222-9) Avon.

Calm Beneath the Storm: Reflections & Prayers for Young People. Donal Neary. 80p. 1984. pap. 4.95 (0-8294-0470-8) Loyola Univ Pr.

Calm Beneath the Storm: Reflections & Prayers for Young People. Donal Neary. 77p. 1989. pap. 22.00 (0-86217-096-6, Pub. by Veritas IE) St Mut.

Calm Down: Stress Control. Frank J. McGuigan. 256p. 1992. per. 32.00 (0-8403-7172-1) Kendall-Hunt.

Calm Ocean. Gerhard Roth. Tr. by Helga Schreckenberger & Jacqueline Vansant. LC 92-45048. (Studies in Austrian Literature, Culture, & Thought. Translation Ser.). 238p. 1993. pap. 20.50 (0-929497-64-3) Ariadne CA.

Calm Out of the Storms. Benny B. Bristow. 1987. pap. 5.75 (0-89137-321-7) Quality Pubns.

Calm Weather: A Volume of Essays. Gilbert Thomas. LC 67-22121. (Essay Index Reprint Ser.). 1977. reprint ed. 19.95 (0-8369-0931-3) Ayer.

Calming the Mind & Discerning the Real. Tr. by Alex Wayman. 1979. reprint ed. 24.00 (0-8364-2519-7, Pub. by Motilal Banarsidass II) S Asia.

*Calming the Roller Coaster Relationship. Janet A. Blue. 92p. (Orig.). 1995. pap. 12.98 (1-882786-27-0) New Dawn NY.

*Calming the Roller Coaster Ride. Janet A. Blue. 1995. 10.98 (0-614-04157-0) New Dawn NY.

Calming the Storm. Carrin Dunne. 1994. pap. 10.95 (0-87243-205-X) Templegate.

Calming Upset Customers. Rebecca Morgan. Ed. by Michael G. Crisp. LC 88-72256. (Fifty-Minute Ser.). (Illus.). 96p. (Orig.). 1989. pap. 9.95 (0-931961-65-3) Crisp Pubns.

*Calmly Plotting the Resurrection: Lenten Reflections for Individuals & Groups. Donna E. Schaper. 120p. (Orig.). 1995. pap. 6.95 (0-8298-1067-6) Pilgrim OH.

Calmodulin. Ed. by P. Cohen & C. B. Klee. 400p. 1988. 166.75 (0-444-80945-7) Elsevier.

Calmodulin & Cell Functions, Vol. 356. Ed. by D. Martin Watterson & Frank F. Vincenzi. LC 80-29310. (Annals Ser.). 446p. 1980. 88.00 (0-89766-101-X); pap. 88.00 (0-89766-102-8) NY Acad Sci.

Calo Arbis: Semiotic Aspects of a Chicano Language Variety. Adolfo Ortega. LC 90-25441. (American University Studies: Linguistics: Ser. XIII, Vol. 21). 264p. (C). 1991. text ed. 45.95 (0-8204-1542-1) P Lang Pubs.

Calor. Amado Pena & Juanita Alba. (Illus.). 32p. 1994. 19.95 (1-56796-069-3) WRS Group.

Caloric Equivalents for Investigations in Ecological Energetics. Ed. by Kenneth W. Cummins & John C. Wuycheck. (Communications of the International Association of Theoretical & Applied Limnology: No. 18). 158p. (Orig.). 1971. pap. text ed. 27.50 (3-510-52018-1, Pub. by E Schweizerbartsche GW) Lubrecht & Cramer.

Caloric Microwave Cookbook. LC 82-72355. 1982. write for info. (0-87502-105-0) Benjamin Co.

Calorie-Carbohydrate Controlled Diet. rev. ed. Clara L. Gerwick. Ed. by Nutrition Education Center Staff. (Orig.). reprint ed. pap. text ed. 4.75 (0-915187-02-7) Nutrition Ed.

Calorie Cost Tables. Craige Schensted. 100p. 1971. pap. 4.00 (0-911014-14-4) Neo Pr.

Calorie Counter for Six Quick-Loss Diets. William I. Kaufman. 64p. 1992. pap. 3.50 (0-515-08920-6) Jove Pubns.

Calorie Guide to Brand Names. William I. Kaufman. 64p. 1992. pap. 3.99 (0-515-08921-4) Jove Pubns.

Calorie Points for Weight Control. rev. ed. Clara L. Gerwick. Ed. by Nutrition Education Center Staff. Orig. Title: Stucky Points for Weight Control. 40p. (Orig.). pap. text ed. 3.95 (0-915187-04-3) Nutrition Ed.

Calorie Register. Jim Bennett. 72p. 1991. pap. 7.95 (1-879031-03-5) JBBA Pub.

Calorie-Sodium Controlled Diet. rev. ed. Clara L. Gerwick. Ed. by Nutrition Education Center Staff. (Orig.). reprint ed. pap. text ed. 4.75 (0-915187-03-5) Nutrition Ed.

Caloriechex. Lois M. Darley. 80p. (Orig.). 1988. student ed 6.95 (0-939909-02-2) Scribe Write.

Calories & Carbohydrates. Barbara Kraus. 1987. pap. 7.95 (0-452-25953-3, Plume) NAL-Dutton.

Calories & Carbohydrates. 5th rev. ed. Barbara Kraus. 1985. mass mkt. 6.95 (0-452-25663-1, Plume) NAL-Dutton.

Calories & Carbohydrates. 7th rev. ed. Barbara Kraus. 1973. pap. 3.95 (0-451-14914-9, Sig) NAL-Dutton.

Calories & Carbohydrates. 8th rev. ed. Barbara Kraus. 400p. 1973. pap. 3.95 (0-451-15849-0, Sig) NAL-Dutton.

Calories & Carbohydrates. 8th rev. ed. Barbara Kraus. 366p. 1989. pap. 8.95 (0-452-26176-7, Plume) NAL-Dutton.

Calories & Carbohydrates. 9th ed. Barbara Kraus. 385p. 1991. 9.95 (0-452-26559-2, Plume) NAL-Dutton.

Calories & Carbohydrates. 9th ed. Barbara Kraus. 1991. pap. 4.99 (0-451-16923-9, Sig) NAL-Dutton.

Calories & Carbohydrates. 10th ed. Barbara Kraus. 448p. 1993. pap. 11.00 (0-452-26936-9, Plume) NAL-Dutton.

Calories & Carbohydrates. 10th rev. ed. Barbara Kraus. 448p. 1993. pap. 5.99 (0-451-17532-8, Sig) NAL-Dutton.

*Calories & Carbohydrates. 11th rev. ed. Barbara Kraus. 1995. 5.99 (0-451-18335-5, ROC) NAL-Dutton.

Calories & Weight. 1991. lib. bdg. 150.00 (0-8490-5139-8) Gordon Pr.

Calories & Weight: The USDA Pocket Guide. (Illus.). 114p. 1990. pap. 1.75 (0-16-020335-X, S/N 001-000-04556-3) USGPO.

Calorimetry: Fundamentals and Practice. Wolfgang Hemminger & Guenther Hohne. (Illus.). 310p. 1984. lib. bdg. 100.00 (0-89573-056-1) VCH Pubs.

Calorimetry & Thermal Analysis of Polymers. Ed. by Vincent B. F. Mathot. LC 93-48558. 369p. 1994. write for info. (1-56990-126-0) Hanser-Gardner.

Calorimetry in High Energy Physics: International Conference. Ed. by D. Anderson et al. 600p. (C). 1991. text ed. 151.00 (981-02-0562-7) World Scientific Pub.

Calorimetry in High Energy Physics: Proceedings. A. Menzione & A. Scribano. 696p. 1994. text ed. 124.00 (981-02-1672-6) World Scientific Pub.

Calorimetry in High Energy Physics: Proceedings of the 3rd International Conference. J. Siegrist. 816p. 1993. text ed. 161.00 (981-02-1303-4) World Scientific Pub.

Calov Bible of J. S. Bach. Johann Sebastian Bach. Ed. by Howard H. Cox. LC 85-24557. (Studies in Musicology: No. 92). 470p. reprint ed. pap. 134.00 (0-8357-1706-2, 2070540) Bks Demand.

Calquhoun - Calhoun & Their Ancestral Homelands. Ellen R. Johnson. 250p. (Orig.). 1993. pap. text ed. 21.00 (1-55613-873-3) Heritage Bk.

*CALS & Concurrent Engineering Handbook. (Illus.). 240p. (Orig.). 1994. pap. 595.00 (0-7605-1156-X) Rector Pr.

CALS Collection, 3 vols. Global Staff. 1993. lib. bdg., ring bd. 559.00 (0-912702-77-X) Global Eng Doc.

Calthorpe: Notes on the Calthore & Calthrop in the Counties of Norfold & Lincolnshire & Elsewhere. C. W. Carr-Calthrop. 151p. 1994. reprint ed. lib. bdg. 34.00 (0-8328-4136-6); reprint ed. pap. 24.00 (0-8328-4137-4) Higginson Bk Co.

Calumet & Fleur-de-Lys: Archaeology of Indian & French Contact in the Midcontinent. Ed. by John A. Walthall & Thomas E. Emerson. LC 91-37953. (Illus.). 320p. (C). 1992. text ed. 45.00 (1-56098-158-X) Smithsonian.

Calumet "K" Merwin-Webster. LC 90-63345. (Illus.). 345p. 1993. reprint ed. 24.95 (1-56114-145-3) Second Renaissance.

Calumet Region: A Master Bibliography. Ed. by Lance Trusty. 121p. (Orig.). (C). 1985. pap. write for info. (0-943766-01-X) Regional Study.

Calumet Region Historical Guide. Writers' Program, Indiana Staff. LC 73-3619. (American Guide Ser.). reprint ed. 29.00 (0-404-57921-3) AMS Pr.

*Calumet Region, Indiana's Last Frontier. Powell A. Moore. 685p. 1991. pap. 21.00 (1-885323-16-6) IN Hist Bureau.

Calumet Theatre. (Copper Country Local History Ser.: Vol. 14). (Illus.). 95p. 1979. 3.00 (0-942363-13-2) C J Monette.

*Calum's Way of It. Willie Robertson. 144p. (C). 1994. pap. 32.00x (1-874640-75-0, Pub. by Argyll Pubng UK) St Mut.

Calvaire. Octave Mirbeau. Tr. by Christine Donougher. (Dedalus European Classics Ser.). 268p. (Orig.). 1994. pap. 12.95 (0-7818-0106-0) Hippocrene Bks.

C

An Asterisk (*) at the beginning of an entry indicates that the title is appearing in BIP for the first time.

C

An Asterisk (*) at the beginning of an entry indicates that the title is appearing in BIP for the first time.

1007

CaMaPe: An Organizational & Educational Systems Approach to Secondary School Development. Mart Petri & Gina Burkhardt. 100p. (Orig.). (C). 1992. pap. text ed. 15.00 (*1-878234-04-8*) Reg Lab Educ IOT NE Isls.

Camarades, 2 vols. Erich-Maria Remarque. 1976. pap. 11.95 (*0-7859-4070-7*); pap. 11.95 (*0-7859-4071-5*) Fr & Eur.

Camaro. Jay Schleifer. LC 92-3809. (Cool Classics Ser.). (Illus.). 48p. (J). (gr. 5). 1993. text ed. 13.95 (*0-89686-696-3*, Crstwood Hse) Silver Burdett Pr.

Camaro! Chevy's Classy Chassis. Ray Miller. (Chevy Chase Ser.: Vol. 4). (Illus.). 320p. 1981. 44.95 (*0-913056-10-3*) Evergreen Pr.

Camaro! From Challenger to Champion: The Complete History. Gary L. Witzenburg. LC 81-70135. (Marque History Bks). (Illus.). 216p. 1982. 29.95 (*0-915038-33-1*, 3-AQ-0001) Auto Quarterly.

Camaro: Style, Speed, & Spirit. Consumer Guide Auto Editors & James M. Flammang. (Illus.). 128p. 1993. 12.95 (*1-56173-538-8*, 1012200) Pubns Intl Ltd.

Camaro: 1967-1981. Chilton Automotives Editorial Staff. LC 78-7168. (Illus.). 360p. 1981. pap. 16.95 (*0-8019-7045-8*) Chilton.

Camaro & Firebird Performance Handbook. Peter C. Sessler. LC 92-33695. (Performance Handbook Ser.). (Illus.). 176p. 1993. pap. 18.95 (*0-87938-711-4*) Motorbooks Intl.

Camaro City. Alan Sternberg. LC 94-5118. 1994. 19.95 (*0-15-115373-6*) HarBrace.

***Camaro Muscle.** Bill Holder & Phil Kunz. LC 95-5978. (Enthusiast Color Ser.). (Illus.). 96p. 1995. pap. 12.95 (*0-7603-0092-5*) Motorbooks Intl.

Camaro Muscle Portfolio, 1967-73. R. M. Clarke. (Illus.). 140p. 1992. pap. 18.95 (*1-85520-145-3*) Motorbooks Intl.

Camaro Performance. David Shelby. (Illus.). 176p. 1993. pap. 16.95 (*1-55788-057-3*, HP Books) Berkley Pub.

Camaro Restoration. Tom Currao & Ron Sessions. (Illus.). 208p. 1990. pap. 16.00 (*0-89586-375-8*, HP Books) Berkley Pub.

Camaro Restoration Tips & Techniques. Ed. by R. M. Clarke. (Illus.). 164p. (Orig.). 1988. pap. 17.95 (*1-869826-86-8*, Pub. by Brooklands Bks UK) Motorbooks Intl.

Camaro SS & Z-28 Nineteen Sixty-Six to Seventy Three. R. M. Clarke. (Illus.). 100p. 1990. pap. 16.95 (*1-85520-042-2*, Pub. by Brooklands Bks UK) Motorbooks Intl.

Camaro White Book, 1967-93. rev. ed. Michael Antonick. (Illus.). 128p. 1993. pap. 11.95 (*0-933534-34-5*) M Bruce Assocs.

Camas Prairie: Idaho's Railroad on Stilts. Hal Riegger. Ed. by Pacific Fast Mail Staff. (Illus.). 160p. 1986. 32.50 (*0-915713-13-6*) Pac Fast Mail.

Camba & Kolla: Migration & Development in Santa Cruz, Bolivia. Allyn M. Stearman. LC 84-26978. (Illus.). xii, 228p. 1985. pap. 24.00 (*0-8130-0802-6*) U Press Fla.

Camber of Culdi. Katherine Kurtz. (Legends of Camber of Culdi Ser.: Bk. 1). 1987. mass mkt. 4.95 (*0-345-34767-6*, Del Rey) Ballantine.

Camber the Heretic. Katherine Kurtz. (Legends of Camber of Culdi Ser.: Bk. 3). 1987. mass mkt. 4.95 (*0-345-34754-4*, Del Rey) Ballantine.

Camberwell Beauty. large type ed. Frances Melvin. 352p. 1984. 15.95 (*0-7089-1105-6*) Ulverscroft.

Camberwell Beauty & Other Stories. Victor S. Pritchett. LC 74-5215. 1974. 9.95 (*0-394-49222-6*) Random.

***Camberwell School of Arts & Crafts: 1943-1960, Its Students & Teachers.** Geoff Hassell. (Illus.). 250p. 1995. 59.50 (*1-85149-180-5*) Antique Collect.

Cambia tu Mundo! - Change Your World! Comp. by David Fajardo. (Juventud en Accion - Youth in Action Ser.). 64p. (SPA.). 1992. pap. 2.65 (*0-311-12256-6*) Casa Bautista.

Cambiame, Senor! Evelyn Christenson. 224p. 1980. 4.95 (*0-88113-035-4*) Edit Betania.

Cambie el Mundo a Traves de la Oracion. Wesley L. Duewel. Tr. by Juan S. Araujo. 192p. (SPA.). (C). 1988. pap. 4.95 (*0-88113-045-1*) Edit Betania.

Cambio Chameleon. Mauro Magellan. LC 89-19995. (Illus.). 32p. (J). 1990. 10.95 (*0-89334-118-5*) Humanics Ltd.

Cambio Tecnologico y Desarrollo Industrial. Simon Teitel & Larry E. Westphal. 1990. write for info. (*950-557-099-6*) IADB.

Cambio y Desarrollo en Puerto Rico: La Transformacion Ideologic del Partido Popular Democratico. Gerardo N. Davil. 214p. (SPA.). 1985. 6.50 (*0-8477-2435-2*) U of PR Pr.

Cambios: Descubriendo lo Mejor Que Hay en Ti. Bill Cosby et al. Ed. by Juan Callejas et al. Tr. by Pierre Trevant. (Destrezas para la Adolescencia Ser.). (Illus.). 192p. (Orig.). (SPA.). (YA). (gr. 6-8). 1987. pap. text ed. 6.85 (*0-933419-21-X*) Quest Intl.

Cambios: La Cultura Hispanica. J. Wilhite & E. Coughlin. 1983. pap. 28.95 (*0-8384-1183-5*) Heinle & Heinle.

Cambios: The Spirit of Transformation in Spanish Colonial Art. Ed. by Donna Pierce. LC 92-16521. (Illus.). 152p. 1992. 50.00 (*0-8263-1408-2*); pap. 29.95 (*0-8263-1409-0*) U of NM Pr.

Cambios en Politicas Internacionales Dirigidas Hacia Centroamerica: Conferencia de ONGs Centroamericanos y de los Estados Unidos Realizada en Washington, D. C. del 10-12 Junio, 1991. Ed. by Washington Office on Latin America Staff. 43p. (Orig.). (SPA.). (C). 1991. pap. text ed. 5.00 (*0-929513-21-5*) WOLA.

Cambises. Thomas Preston. LC 74-133723. (Tudor Facsimile Texts. Old English Plays Ser.: No. 44). reprint ed. 49.50 (*0-404-53344-2*) AMS Pr.

Cambodge: Fetes Civiles et Religieuses. Adhemard Leclere. LC 77-87040. reprint ed. 47.50 (*0-404-16832-9*) AMS Pr.

Cambodge et Cambodgiens: Metamorphose du Royaume Khmer par une Methode Francaise de Protectorat. Paul M. Collard. LC 77-87068. reprint ed. 25.50 (*0-404-16806-X*) AMS Pr.

Cambodia. Claudia Canesso. (Places & Peoples of the World Ser.). (Illus.). 96p. (YA). (gr. 6 up). 1989. lib. bdg. 14.95 (*1-55546-798-9*) Chelsea Hse.

Cambodia. Brian Fawcett. 224p. 1989. pap. 8.95 (*0-02-032150-3*, Collier S&S) S&S Trade.

***Cambodia.** Mariam Greenblatt. LC 94-37949. (Enchantment of the World Ser.). 172p. (J). (gr. 5-9). 1995. lib. bdg. 20.55 (*0-516-02632-1*) Childrens.

Cambodia: A Country Study. 3rd ed. Russell R. Ross. LC 89-600150. (Area Handbook Ser.). (Illus.). 398p. 1990. Individual mailing box. per. 18.00 (*0-16-020838-6*, S/N 008-020-01203-3) USGPO.

Cambodia: A Matter of Survival. Ed. by Martin Wright. 1989. 25.00 (*1-55862-047-8*) St James Pr.

Cambodia: A Shattered Society. Marie A. Martin. Tr. by Mark W. Mcleod. LC 93-31837. 383p. 1994. 40.00 (*0-520-07052-6*) U CA Pr.

Cambodia: A Travel Survival Kit. Daniel Robinson & Tony Wheeler. (Illus.). 132p. (Orig.). 1992. pap. 12.95 (*0-86442-174-5*) Lonely Planet.

Cambodia: Its People, Its Society, Its Culture. David J. Steinberg & Herbert H. Vreeland. LC 59-13226. (Survey of World Cultures Ser.). 365p. reprint ed. pap. 104.10 (*0-8357-7978-5*, 2005433) Bks Demand.

Cambodia: Justice System & Human Rights Violations. James D. Ross. Ed. by William G. O'Neill & Michael J. Posner. 74p. (Orig.). 1992. pap. 10.00 (*0-934143-53-6*) Lawyers Comm Human.

Cambodia: Military Technical Atlas Scale: 1: 200000. Ed. by Lewis B. Sckolnick. 60p. (Orig.). (RUS.). (C). 1994. pap. text ed. 600.00 (*1-57205-459-X*) Rector Pr.

Cambodia: Military Technical Atlas Scale: 1: 50000. Ed. by Lewis B. Sckolnick. 400p. (Orig.). (RUS.). (C). 1994. pap. text ed. 8,000.00 (*1-57205-460-3*) Rector Pr.

Cambodia: Post-Settlement Reconstruction & Development. Robert J. Muscat & Jonathan Stromseth. (Occasional Papers of the East Asian Institute). 143p. 1989. pap. 9.00 (*0-913418-04-8*) Columbia U E Asian Inst.

Cambodia: Starvation & Revolution. George C. Hildebrand & Gareth Porter. LC 76-1646. 124p. reprint ed. pap. 35.40 (*0-8357-7979-3*, 2019474) Bks Demand.

Cambodia: The Legacy & Lessons of UNTAC. Trevor Findlay. (SIPRI Peacekeeping Ser.: No. 1). 150p. 1995. 45.00 (*0-19-829186-8*); pap. 28.00 (*0-19-829185-X*) OUP.

***Cambodia: Vote for Peace.** 110p. 1994. pap. text ed. 14.95 (*92-1-100670-8*) UN.

Cambodia & the Dilemmas of U. S. Policy. F. Brown. (Critical Issues 1991 Ser.: Nos. 2 & 3). 64p. 1991. pap. 8.95 (*0-87609-111-7*) Coun Foreign.

Cambodia, Laos. Nelles Verlag. (Nelles Guides Ser.). 1994. pap. 14.95 (*3-88618-396-3*, Pub. by Nelles Verlag GW) Seven Hills Bk.

Cambodia, Pol Pot, & the United States: The Faustian Pact. Michael Haas. LC 90-27548. 184p. 1991. text ed. 45.00 (*0-275-94005-5*, C4005, Praeger Pubs) Greenwood.

***Cambodia Tax Law.** 150p. (C). 1994. pap. 295.00 (*0-7605-0091-6*) Rector Pr.

Cambodia, 1975-1978: Rendezvous with Death. Ed. by Karl D. Jackson. (Illus.). 344p. 1992. text ed. 55.00 (*0-691-07807-6*); pap. text ed. 17.95 (*0-691-02541-X*) Princeton U Pr.

Cambodia 1975-1982. Michael Vickery. LC 83-61478. 361p. 1984. 40.00 (*0-89608-190-7*); pap. 16.00 (*0-89608-189-3*) South End Pr.

Cambodian Agony. 2nd ed. Ed. by David A. Ablin & Marlowe Hood. LC 90-21763. 496p. (C). 1990. pap. text ed. 23.95 (*0-87332-754-3*) M E Sharpe.

Cambodian Campaign: 29 April-30 June 1970. David I. Folkman, Jr. & Philip D. Caine. 132p. 1993. reprint ed. pap. 15.00 (*0-923135-60-X*) Dalley Bk Service.

Cambodian Crisis & the U. S. Policy Dilemmas. Robert G. Sutter. 135p. (C). 1990. pap. text ed. 35.50 (*0-8133-8047-2*) Westview.

Cambodian Culture since Nineteen Seventy-Five: Homeland & Exile. Ed. by May M. Ebihara et al. (Asia East by South Ser.). (Illus.). 216p. 1994. 32.95 (*0-8014-2967-6*); pap. 12.95 (*0-8014-8173-2*) Cornell U Pr.

Cambodian-English - English-Cambodian Dictionary. 355p. (CAM & ENG.). 1990. reprint ed. 28.00 (*0-88431-057-4*) IBD Ltd.

Cambodian-English-Cambodian Dictionary: Bilingual General Dictionary. rev. ed. 355p. (CAM & ENG.). 1990. 49.95 (*0-8288-4006-7*, F44450) Fr & Eur.

Cambodian-English Dictionary, 2 vols., Vol. 1. Robert K. Headley et al. LC 77-8913. (Publications in the Languages of Asia: No. 3). (Illus.). 736p. reprint ed. pap. 180.00 (*0-7837-1103-4*, 2041633) Bks Demand.

Cambodian-English Dictionary, 2 vols., Vol. 2. Robert K. Headley et al. LC 77-8913. (Publications in the Languages of Asia: No. 3). (Illus.). 818p. reprint ed. pap. 180.00 (*0-7837-1104-2*, 2041633) Bks Demand.

Cambodian-English English-Cambodian Dictionary. (Concise Dictionary of American Literary Biography Ser.). 355p. 1989. pap. 16.95 (*0-87052-818-1*) Hippocrene Bks.

Cambodian-English Glossary. Franklin E. Huffman & Im Proum. (Linguistic Ser.). 160p. (CAM & ENG.). (C). 1981. pap. 15.00 (*0-300-02070-8*) Yale U Pr.

***Cambodian-English Picture Dictionary.** Claudia Schwalm. (Illus.). 89p. (J). (gr. k-6). 1995. audio 20.00 (*1-57371-005-9*) Cult Connect.

Cambodian Folk Stories: From the Gatiloke. Muriel P. Carrison. 140p. 1993. pap. 12.95 (*0-8048-1905-X*) C E Tuttle.

Cambodian Incursion. Tran Dinh Tho. 245p. 1989. reprint ed. pap. 24.50x (*0-923135-10-3*) Dalley Bk Service.

Cambodian (Khmer)-German Dictionary: Woerterbuch Khmer-Deutsch, 2 vols., Set. R. Gaudes. 1330p. (CAM & GER.). 1985. 195.00 (*0-8288-1096-6*, F67990) Fr & Eur.

Cambodian Literary Reader & Glossary. Franklin E. Huffman & Im Proum. LC 76-50538. (Yale Linguistic Ser.). 491p. reprint ed. pap. 140.00 (*0-8357-8052-X*, 2033762) Bks Demand.

Cambodian Literary Reader & Glossary. Ed. by Franklin E. Huffman & Im Proum. 596p. 1988. reprint ed. pap. text ed. 16.00 (*0-300-02069-4*) Cornell SE Asia.

Cambodian Refugees in Long Beach, California: The Definitive Study. Scott Shaw. LC 89-22148. (Illus.). 103p. (C). 1989. pap. 11.95 (*1-877792-02-0*, F869. L7S53) Buddha Rose.

Cambodian System of Writing & Beginning Reader. Franklin E. Huffman. 365p. (C). 1987. reprint ed. pap. text ed. 14.00 (*0-300-01314-0*) Cornell SE Asia.

***Cambodian Teenage Refugees.** (Illus.). 70p. (YA). 1995. lib. bdg. 45.00 (*0-7605-1524-7*) Rector Pr.

Cambodian Writing System & Reader. Frank E. Huffman. LC 78-104614. (Spoken Language Ser.). 377p. (Orig.). (C). 1982. pap. text ed. 16.00 (*0-87950-470-6*) Spoken Lang Serv.

Cambodians in America: Courageous People from a Troubled Country. Alice Lucas. (New Faces of Liberty Background Essays Ser.). (Illus.). 25p. 1993. pap. text ed. 5.00 (*0-936434-70-8*) SF Study Ctr.

Cambodians in Thailand: People on the Edge. Ed. by Virginia L. Hamilton. 27p. 1985. 2.00 (*0-317-40511-X*) US Comm Refugees.

Cambodia's Economy & Industrial Development. Samphan Khieu. Tr. by Laura Summers. LC 79-113666. (Southeast Asia Program, Department of Asian Studies, Cornell University - Data Paper: No. 111). (Illus.). 139p. reprint ed. pap. 39.70 (*0-7837-1768-7*, 2041962) Bks Demand.

Cambodia's Lament: A Selection of Cambodian Writing. Ed. by George Chigas. LC 91-62374. 112p. 1991. pap. 7.00 (*0-9630295-0-9*) Rev of Asian.

Cambodia's New Deal: A Report. William Shawcross. LC 94-15976. (Contemporary Issue Paper Ser.: No. 1). 1994. 9.95 (*0-87003-051-5*) Carnegie Endow.

Camborne Play: A Verse Translation of Beunans Meriasek. Myrna Combellack. (C). 1989. text ed. 70.00 (*1-85022-039-5*, Pub. by Dyllansow Truran UK) St Mut.

***Cambria County, PA Cemeteries, Vol. 1.** Des Warzel. Date not set. pap. 10.95 (*1-55856-192-7*) Closson Pr.

***Cambria County, PA Cemeteries, Vol. 2.** Des Warzel. 250p. 1995. pap. 19.95 (*1-55856-193-5*) Closson Pr.

Cambria County, PA Willbook Index. Patricia W. Collins. 59p. 1984. pap. text ed. 9.50 (*0-933227-08-6*) Closson Pr.

***Cambria Forest: Reflections on Its Native Pines & Its Eventful Past.** Taylor Coffman. LC 95-69476. (Illus.). xv, 80p. (Orig.). 1995. pap. 12.95 (*0-9647195-0-9*) Coast Herit Pr.

Cambria Tribune Marriages & Deaths, Vol. 5. Ed. by Patricia W. Collins. 302p. per., pap. text ed. 23.00 (*0-933227-58-2*) Closson Pr.

Cambrian & Early Ordovician Stratigraphy & Paleontology of the Basin & Range Province, Western United States, No. T125. Ed. by Taylor. (IGC Field Trip Guidebooks Ser.). 96p. 1989. 21.00 (*0-87590-662-1*) Am Geophysical.

Cambric Poetry Project One. Ed. by Joel Rudinger. 1978. pap. 6.95 (*0-918342-06-6*) Cambric.

***Cambridge.** (Pevensey Heritage Guides Ser.). (Illus.). 112p. 1994. pap. 9.95 (*0-907115-63-2*); pap. 9.95 (*0-907115-80-2*); pap. 9.95 (*0-907115-81-0*) Sterling.

Cambridge. Ed. by Alan Nelson. (Records of Early English Drama Ser.). 1100p. 1989. 175.00 (*0-8020-5751-9*) U of Toronto Pr.

Cambridge. Pevensey Pr. Staff. (C). 1987. text ed. 60.00 (*0-907115-39-X*, Pub. by Pevensey UK); pap. text ed. 40.00 (*0-907115-40-3*, Pub. by Pevensey UK) St Mut.

Cambridge: A Living Tradition. Michael Grant & Ernest Frank. (C). 1987. text ed. 95.00 (*0-907115-45-4*, Pub. by Pevensey UK) St Mut.

Cambridge: A Novel. Caryl Phillips. LC 92-56359. 1993. pap. 10.00 (*0-679-73689-1*) Random.

Cambridge Air & Space Dictionary. Ed. by Peter M. Walker. (Illus.). 336p. (C). 1990. pap. 14.95 (*0-521-39763-4*) Cambridge U Pr.

***Cambridge Ancient History: Volume of Plates, Vols. 5-6.** Ed. by John Boardman. (Illus.). 276p. (C). 1995. 70.00 (*0-521-23349-6*) Cambridge U Pr.

Cambridge & Clare. Harry Godwin. 230p. 1985. 64.95 (*0-521-30765-1*) Cambridge U Pr.

Cambridge & the Monetary Theory of Production: The Collapse of Marshallian Macroeconomics. Robert J. Bigg. LC 89-28767. 220p. 1990. text ed. 49.95 (*0-312-04072-5*) St Martin.

Cambridge Annotated Study Bible. rev. ed. Ed. by Howard C. Kee. 1250p. Date not set. pap. 34.95 (*0-521-50777-4*) Cambridge U Pr.

Cambridge "Apostles" Frances M. Brookfield. LC 70-148758. reprint ed. 34.50 (*0-404-08729-9*) AMS Pr.

Cambridge Architecture. Tim Rawle. (Illus.). 224p. 1993. pap. 29.95 (*0-233-98818-1*, Pub. by A Deutsch UK) Trafalgar.

Cambridge Architecture: A Concise Guide. Nicholas Ray. (Illus.). 125p. (C). 1994. pap. 18.95 (*0-521-45855-2*) Cambridge U Pr.

Cambridge Architecture: A Concise Guide. Nicholas Ray. (Illus.). 125p. (C). 1994. 54.95 (*0-521-45222-8*) Cambridge U Pr.

Cambridge Astronomy Guide: A Practical Introduction to Astronomy. William Liller & Ben Mayer. (Illus.). 170p. (C). 1990. pap. 22.95 (*0-521-39915-7*) Cambridge U Pr.

Cambridge Atlas of Astronomy. 3rd ed. Ed. by Jean Audouze et al. (Illus.). 472p. (C). 1994. 75.00 (*0-521-43438-6*) Cambridge U Pr.

Cambridge Atlas of Medieval Warfare. Nicholas Hooper & Matthew Bennett. (Illus.). 208p. (C). 1994. write for info. (*0-521-44049-1*) Cambridge U Pr.

Cambridge Australian English Style Guide. Pam Peters. (Illus.). 864p. (C). 1995. 79.95 (*0-521-43401-7*) Cambridge U Pr.

Cambridge Before Darwin: The Ideal of a Liberal Education, 1800-1860. Martha M. Garland. LC 80-40327. 206p. reprint ed. pap. 58.80 (*0-8357-7980-7*, 2031655) Bks Demand.

Cambridge Bibliography of English Literature, 5 vols, 1. 1972. 145.00 (*0-521-04499-5*) Cambridge U Pr.

Cambridge Bibliography of English Literature, 5 vols, 2. 1972. 140.00 (*0-521-04500-2*) Cambridge U Pr.

Cambridge Bibliography of English Literature, 5 vols, 4. 1972. 160.00 (*0-521-08535-7*) Cambridge U Pr.

Cambridge Bibliography of English Literature, 5 vols, 5. 1972. 105.00 (*0-521-04503-7*) Cambridge U Pr.

Cambridge Biographical Dictionary see Larousse Biographical Dictionary

Cambridge Biographical Encyclopedia. Ed. by David Crystal. (Illus.). 1280p. (C). 1994. 49.95 (*0-521-43421-1*) Cambridge U Pr.

Cambridge Book of Poetry. Charlotte F. Bates. LC 72-80371. (Granger Index Reprint Ser.). 1977. 31.95 (*0-8369-6052-1*) Ayer.

Cambridge Book of Prose & Verse in Illustration of English Literature: From the Beginnings to the Cycles of Romance. Ed. by George Sampson. (BCL1-PR English Literature Ser.). 438p. 1992. reprint ed. lib. bdg. 99.00 (*0-7812-7127-4*) Rprt Serv.

Cambridge Brick Details. Philip A. Rizzo. LC 83-63460. 128p. 1984. 13.95 (*0-9613164-0-3*) Rotunda Bks.

Cambridge Buses. Mark Seal. (Cambridge Town, Gown & County Ser.: Vol. 21). 1978. pap. 4.95 (*0-900891-24-6*) Oleander Pr.

Cambridge Castle. rev. ed. William M. Palmer. (Cambridge Town, Gown & County Ser.: Vol. 5). (Illus.). 1976. pap. 4.95 (*0-902675-67-2*) Oleander Pr.

Cambridge Characters. Irene Lister. (Cambridge Town, Gown & County Ser.: Vol. 20). (Illus.). 1978. pap. 4.95 (*0-900891-25-4*) Oleander Pr.

Cambridge Chaucer Companion. Ed. by Piero Boitani & Jill Mann. 300p. 1986. pap. 16.95 (*0-521-31689-8*) Cambridge U Pr.

***Cambridge College Ghosts.** (Jarrold Ghost Ser.). (Illus.). 144p. (Orig.). 1994. pap. 8.95 (*0-7117-0675-1*) Seven Hills Bk.

Cambridge College Walks. Frank A. Reeve. (Cambridge Town, Gown & County Ser.: Vol. 25). (Illus.). 1978. pap. 4.95 (*0-900891-42-4*) Oleander Pr.

Cambridge College Walks French Edition. Frank A. Reeve. (Cambridge Town, Gown & County Ser.: Vol. 25). (Illus.). 1978. pap. 4.95 (*0-685-55599-2*) Oleander Pr.

Cambridge College Walks German. Frank A. Reeve. (Cambridge Town, Gown & County Ser.: Vol. 25). (Illus.). 1978. pap. 4.95 (*0-685-55600-X*) Oleander Pr.

Cambridge Colleges Cookbook. Ed. by Rebecca Freeman. 1993. pap. 21.00 (*1-85183-060-X*, Silent Bks) St Mut.

Cambridge Commemorated: An Anthology of University Life. Ed. by Helen Fowler. 398p. (C). 1989. pap. 29.95 (*0-521-38910-0*) Cambridge U Pr.

***Cambridge Companion to American Realism & Naturalism: From Howells to London.** Ed. by Donald Pizer. (Cambridge Companions to Literature Ser.). 320p. (C). 1995. 59.95 (*0-521-43300-2*); pap. 17.95 (*0-521-43876-4*) Cambridge U Pr.

Cambridge Companion to Aquinas. Ed. by Norman Kretzmann & Eleonore Stump. LC 92-31977. (Companions to Philosophy Ser.). 320p. (C). 1993. pap. 18.95 (*0-521-43769-5*) Cambridge U Pr.

Cambridge Companion to Aquinas. Ed. by Norman Kretzmann & Eleonore Stump. LC 92-31977. (Companions to Philosophy Ser.). 320p. (C). 1993. 64.95 (*0-521-43195-6*) Cambridge U Pr.

Cambridge Companion to Aristotle. Ed. by Jonathan Barnes. (Cambridge Companions to Philosophy Ser.). 416p. (C). 1995. 59.95 (*0-521-41133-5*); pap. 17.95 (*0-521-42294-9*) Cambridge U Pr.

Cambridge Companion to Beckett. Ed. by John Pilling. LC 92-47287. (Cambridge Companions to Literature Ser.). (Illus.). 272p. (C). 1994. 59.95 (*0-521-41366-4*) Cambridge U Pr.

Cambridge Companion to Beckett. Ed. by John Pilling. LC 92-47287. (Cambridge Companions to Literature Ser.). (Illus.). 272p. (C). 1994. pap. 16.95 (*0-521-42413-5*) Cambridge U Pr.

Cambridge Companion to Brecht. Ed. by Peter Thomson & Glendyr Sacks. LC 93-18181. (Cambridge Companions to Literature Ser.). (Illus.). 334p. (C). 1994. 59.95 (*0-521-41446-6*); pap. 16.95 (*0-521-42485-2*) Cambridge U Pr.

Cambridge Companion to British Romanticism. Ed. by Stuart M. Curran. (Cambridge Companions to Literature Ser.). 300p. (C). 1993. 54.95 (*0-521-33355-5*); pap. 16.95 (*0-521-42193-4*) Cambridge U Pr.

Cambridge Companion to Chopin. Ed. by Jim Samson. (Illus.). 288p. (C). 1992. 64.95 (*0-521-40490-8*) Cambridge U Pr.

C

An Asterisk (*) at the beginning of an entry indicates that the title is appearing in BIP for the first time.

Cambridge Companion to Dante. Ed. by Rachel Jacoff. LC 92-17126. (Cambridge Companions to Literature Ser.). (Illus.). 292p. (C). 1993. 59.95 (0-521-41748-1); pap. 19.95 (0-521-42742-8) Cambridge U Pr.

Cambridge Companion to Descartes. Ed. by John G. Cottingham. (Companions to Philosophy Ser.). 624p. (C). 1992. 59.95 (0-521-36623-2); pap. 18.95 (0-521-36696-8) Cambridge U Pr.

***Cambridge Companion to Edith Wharton.** Ed. by Millicent Bell. 240p. (C). 1995. write for info. (0-521-45358-5) Cambridge U Pr.

***Cambridge Companion to Edith Wharton.** Ed. by Millicent Bell. 240p. (C). 1995. pap. write for info. (0-521-48513-4) Cambridge U Pr.

Cambridge Companion to English Poetry, Donne to Marvell. Ed. by Thomas N. Corns. LC 92-44508. (Cambridge Companions to Literature Ser.). 250p. (C). 1993. 64.95 (0-521-41147-5); pap. 17.95 (0-521-42309-0) Cambridge U Pr.

Cambridge Companion to English Renaissance Drama. Ed. by A. R. Braunmuller & Michael Hattaway. (Cambridge Companions to Literature Ser.). (Illus.). 380p. (C). 1990. 59.95 (0-521-34657-6); pap. 17.95 (0-521-38662-4) Cambridge U Pr.

Cambridge Companion to Foucault. Ed. by Gary Gutting. LC 93-26634. (Companions to Philosophy Ser.). 416p. (C). 1994. pap. 17.95 (0-521-40887-3) Cambridge U Pr.

Cambridge Companion to Foucault. Ed. by Gary Gutting. LC 93-26634. (Companions to Philosophy Ser.). 416p. (C). 1994. 59.95 (0-521-40332-4) Cambridge U Pr.

Cambridge Companion to Freud. Ed. by Jerome Neu. (Companions to Philosophy Ser.). 350p. (C). 1991. pap. 18.95 (0-521-37779-X) Cambridge U Pr.

***Cambridge Companion to Habermas.** Ed. by Stephen K. White. (Cambridge Companions to Philosophy Ser.). 352p. (C). 1995. 59.95 (0-521-44120-X) Cambridge U Pr.

***Cambridge Companion to Habermas.** Ed. by Stephen K. White. (Cambridge Companions to Philosophy Ser.). 352p. (C). 1995. pap. 17.95 (0-521-44666-X) Cambridge U Pr.

Cambridge Companion to Hegel. Ed. by Frederick C. Beiser. LC 92-15572. (Cambridge Companions to Philosophy Ser.). 592p. (C). 1993. 64.95 (0-521-38274-2); pap. 19.95 (0-521-38711-6) Cambridge U Pr.

Cambridge Companion to Heidegger. Ed. by Charles Guignon. LC 92-22753. (Companions to Philosophy Ser.). 432p. (C). 1993. 64.95 (0-521-38570-9); pap. 18.95 (0-521-38597-0) Cambridge U Pr.

***Cambridge Companion to Henry David Thoreau.** Ed. by Joel Myerson. (Cambridge Companions to Literature Ser.). 304p. (C). 1995. 59.95 (0-521-44037-8); pap. 16.95 (0-521-44594-9) Cambridge U Pr.

Cambridge Companion to Hume. Ed. by David F. Norton. LC 92-47406. (Companions to Philosophy Ser.). 448p. (C). 1993. 64.95 (0-521-38273-4); pap. 18.95 (0-521-38710-8) Cambridge U Pr.

***Cambridge Companion to Husserl.** Ed. by Barry Smith & David W. Smith. (Cambridge Companions to Philosophy Ser.). 496p. (C). 1995. 59.95 (0-521-43023-2) Cambridge U Pr.

***Cambridge Companion to Husserl.** Ed. by Barry Smith & David W. Smith. (Cambridge Companions to Philosophy Ser.). 496p. (C). 1995. pap. 17.95 (0-521-43616-8) Cambridge U Pr.

Cambridge Companion to Ibsen. Ed. by James McFarlane. (Companions to Literature Ser.). (Illus.). 304p. (C). 1994. 59.95 (0-521-41166-1); pap. 16.95 (0-521-42321-X) Cambridge U Pr.

Cambridge Companion to James Joyce. Ed. by Derek Attridge. (Cambridge Companions to Literature Ser.). 288p. (C). 1990. pap. 16.95 (0-521-37673-4) Cambridge U Pr.

Cambridge Companion to Kant. Ed. by Paul Guyer. (Companions to Philosophy Ser.). 400p. (C). 1992. 69.95 (0-521-36587-2); pap. 18.95 (0-521-36768-9) Cambridge U Pr.

Cambridge Companion to Locke. Ed. by Vere Chappell. LC 93-33190. (Companions to Philosophy Ser.). 384p. (C). 1994. 59.95 (0-521-38371-4); pap. 17.95 (0-521-38772-8) Cambridge U Pr.

***Cambridge Companion to Mark Twain.** Ed. by Forrest G. Robinson. LC 94-24658. (Cambridge Companions to Literature Ser.). 288p. (C). 1995. 59.95 (0-521-44036-X); pap. 16.95 (0-521-44593-0) Cambridge U Pr.

Cambridge Companion to Marx. Ed. by Terrell Carver. (Companions to Philosophy Ser.). 400p. (C). 1991. pap. 18.95 (0-521-36694-1) Cambridge U Pr.

Cambridge Companion to Marx. Ed. by Terrell Carver. (Companions to Philosophy Ser.). 400p. (C). 1991. 69.95 (0-521-36625-9) Cambridge U Pr.

Cambridge Companion to Medieval English Theatre. Ed. by Richard Beadle. (Companions to Literature Ser.). (Illus.). 400p. (C). 1994. 59.95 (0-521-36670-4); pap. 16.95 (0-521-45916-8) Cambridge U Pr.

Cambridge Companion to Milton. Ed. by Dennis Danielson. (Cambridge Companions to Literature Ser.). (Illus.). (C). 1989. 59.95 (0-521-33402-0); pap. 16.95 (0-521-36885-5) Cambridge U Pr.

Cambridge Companion to Plato. Ed. by Richard Kraut. (Companions to Philosophy Ser.). 817p. (C). 1992. 59.95 (0-521-43018-6); pap. 18.95 (0-521-43610-9) Cambridge U Pr.

Cambridge Companion to Sartre. Ed. by Christina Howells. (Companions to Philosophy Ser.). 448p. (C). 1992. 59.95 (0-521-38114-2); pap. 18.95 (0-521-38812-0) Cambridge U Pr.

Cambridge Companion to Shakespeare Studies. Ed. by Stanley Wells. (Cambridge Companions to Literature Ser.). (Illus.). 340p. 1986. 59.95 (0-521-26737-4); pap. 17.95 (0-521-31841-6) Cambridge U Pr.

***Cambridge Companion to Spinoza.** Ed. by Don Garrett. (Cambridge Companions to Philosophy Ser.). 528p. (C). 1993. write for info. (0-521-39235-7); pap. write for info. (0-521-39865-7) Cambridge U Pr.

Cambridge Companion to T. S. Eliot. Ed. by A. David Moody. LC 93-43558. (Cambridge Companions to Literature Ser.). 300p. (C). 1995. 59.95 (0-521-42080-6) Cambridge U Pr.

Cambridge Companion to T. S. Eliot. Ed. by A. David Moody. LC 93-43558. (Companions to Literature Ser.). 300p. (C). 1995. pap. 16.95 (0-521-42127-6) Cambridge U Pr.

***Cambridge Companion to the Clarinet.** Colin Lawson. (Cambridge Companions to Music Ser.). (Illus.). 300p. (C). 1995. write for info. (0-521-47066-8); pap. write for info. (0-521-47668-2) Cambridge U Pr.

***Cambridge Companion to the Recorder.** Ed. by John M. Thomson & Anthony Rowland-Jones. (Cambridge Companions to Music Ser.). (Illus.). 275p. (C). 1992. write for info. (0-521-35269-X); pap. write for info. (0-521-35816-7) Cambridge U Pr.

Cambridge Companion to the Violin. Ed. by Robin Stowell. (Illus.). 288p. (C). 1993. pap. 19.95 (0-521-39923-8) Cambridge U Pr.

***Cambridge Companion to Walt Whitman.** Ed. by Ezra Greenspan. LC 94-12452. (Cambridge Companions to Literature Ser.). (Illus.). 256p. (C). 1995. 59.95 (0-521-44343-1); pap. 16.95 (0-521-44807-7) Cambridge U Pr.

Cambridge Companions to Philosophy. Ed. by Nicholas Jolley. (Cambridge Companions to Philosophy Ser.). (Illus.). 528p. (C). 1994. pap. 18.95 (0-521-36769-7) Cambridge U Pr.

Cambridge Companions to Philosophy. Ed. by Nicholas Jolley. (Cambridge Companions to Philosophy Ser.). (Illus.). 528p. (C). 1994. 59.95 (0-521-36588-0) Cambridge U Pr.

Cambridge Concise Encyclopedia. Ed. by David Crystal. LC 92-27407. 1991. 37.95 (0-521-41614-0) Cambridge U Pr.

Cambridge Coordinated Science: Biology. Mary Jones & Geoff Jones. (Coordinated Science Ser.). (Illus.). 200p. (C). 1993. pap. 17.50 (0-521-45944-3) Cambridge U Pr.

Cambridge Coordinated Science: Chemistry. 2nd ed. Mary Jones et al. (Coordinated Science Ser.). (Illus.). 208p. (C). 1993. pap. 17.50 (0-521-45945-1) Cambridge U Pr.

Cambridge Coordinated Science: Physics. 2nd ed. Mary Jones et al. (Coordinated Science Ser.). (Illus.). 247p. (C). 1993. pap. 17.50 (0-521-45943-5) Cambridge U Pr.

***Cambridge Dictionary of American Biography.** Ed. by John S. Bowman. 896p. (C). 1995. 44.95 (0-521-40258-1) Cambridge U Pr.

Cambridge Dictionary of Australian Places. Richard Appleton & Barbara Appleton. (Illus.). 386p. (C). 1993. 65.00 (0-521-39506-2) Cambridge U Pr.

***Cambridge Dictionary of Philosophy.** Ed. by Robert Audi. 944p. (C). 1995. 89.95 (0-521-40224-7); pap. 27.95 (0-521-48328-X) Cambridge U Pr.

***Cambridge Dictionary of Statistics in the Medical Sciences.** B. S. Everitt. (Illus.). 200p. (C). 1995. write for info. (0-521-47382-9); pap. write for info. (0-521-47928-2) Cambridge U Pr.

Cambridge Eclipse Photography Guide: How & Where to Observe & Photograph Solar & Lunar Eclipses. Jay M. Pasachoff & Michael A. Covington. (Illus.). 96p. (C). 1993. pap. 16.95 (0-521-45651-7) Cambridge U Pr.

Cambridge Economic History of Europe, 8 vols. Incl. Vol. 1. Agrarian Life of the Middle Ages. 1966. 165.00 (0-521-04505-3); Vol. 2. Trade & Industry in the Middle Ages. 1987. 175.00 (0-521-08709-0); Vol. 3. Economic Organization & Policies in the Middle Ages. 1963. 135.00 (0-521-04506-1); Vol. 4. Economy of Expanding Europe in the 16th & 17th Centuries. 1967. 135.00 (0-521-04507-X); Vol. 7, Pt. 1. Industrial Economies--Britain, France, Germany & Scandinavia. 1978. pap. 24.95 (0-685-42028-0); Vol. 7, Pt. 2. Industrial Economies--United States, Japan & Russia. 1978. pap. 24.95 (0-685-42029-9); Industrial Economies--Development of Economic & Social Policies. 1989. 185.00 (0-521-22504-3); Pt. 2: The United States, Japan & Russia. Industrial Economies: Capital, Labour & Enterprise. Ed. by Peter Mathias & Michael Postan. 1982. pap. 44.95 (0-521-28801-0); write for info. (0-318-51268-8) Cambridge U Pr.

Cambridge Economic History of India: Volume 1, c. 1200 - c. 1750. Ed. by Tapan Raychaudhuri & Irfan Habib. LC 80-40454. (Illus.). 600p. 1982. 125.00 (0-521-22692-9) Cambridge U Pr.

Cambridge Economic History of India: Volume 2, c. 1757 - c. 1970. Ed. by Dharma Kumar & Meghnad Desai. LC 80-49697. (Illus.). 600p. 1983. 150.00 (0-521-22802-6) Cambridge U Pr.

***Cambridge Economic History of the United States Vol. 1: The Colonial Era.** Ed. by Stanley L. Engerman & Robert E. Gallman. (Illus.). 560p. (C). 1995. write for info. (0-521-39442-2) Cambridge U Pr.

Cambridge Encyclopedia. Ed. by David Crystal. (Illus.). 1528p. (C). 1994. 49.95 (0-521-44429-2) Cambridge U Pr.

Cambridge Encyclopedia of Australia. Ed. by Susan Bambrick. (Illus.). 400p. (C). 1994. 54.95 (0-521-36511-2) Cambridge U Pr.

Cambridge Encyclopedia of China. 2nd ed. Ed. by Brian Hook & Denis C. Twitchett. (Illus.). 492p. (C). 1991. 64.95 (0-521-35594-X) Cambridge U Pr.

Cambridge Encyclopedia of Human Evolution. Ed. by Stephen Jones et al. (Illus.). 512p. (C). 1993. 100.00 (0-521-32370-3) Cambridge U Pr.

***Cambridge Encyclopedia of Human Evolution.** Ed. by Steve Jones et al. (Illus.). 512p. (C). 1994. pap. 34.95 (0-521-46786-1) Cambridge U Pr.

Cambridge Encyclopedia of India, Pakistan, Bangladesh, Sri Lanka, Nepal, Bhutan & the Maldives. Ed. by Francis Robinson. (Illus.). (C). 1989. 64.95 (0-521-33451-9) Cambridge U Pr.

Cambridge Encyclopedia of Japan. Ed. by Richard J. Bowring & Peter Kornicki. (Illus.). 352p. (C). 1993. 54.95 (0-521-40352-9) Cambridge U Pr.

Cambridge Encyclopedia of Language. David Crystal. (Illus.). 440p. 1987. 54.95 (0-521-26438-3) Cambridge U Pr.

Cambridge Encyclopedia of Language. David Crystal. (Illus.). 470p. (C). 1991. pap. 27.95 (0-521-42443-7) Cambridge U Pr.

Cambridge Encyclopedia of Latin America & the Caribbean. 2nd ed. Ed. by Simon Collier et al. (Illus.). 500p. (C). 1992. 64.95 (0-521-41322-2) Cambridge U Pr.

Cambridge Encyclopedia of Russia: And the Former Soviet Union. Ed. by Archie Brown et al. (Illus.). 616p. (C). 1994. 49.95 (0-521-35593-1) Cambridge U Pr.

***Cambridge Encyclopedia of the English Language.** David Crystal. (Illus.). 500p. (C). 1995. 49.95 (0-521-40179-8) Cambridge U Pr.

Cambridge Encyclopedia of the Middle East & North Africa. Ed. by Trevor Mostyn & Albert Hourani. (Illus.). 456p. 1988. 64.95 (0-521-32190-5) Cambridge U Pr.

Cambridge English Course. Michael Swan & C. Walter. 1988. pap. write for info. (0-318-63780-4) Cambridge U Pr.

Cambridge English Course, Bk. 3A. Michael Swan & C. Walter. 1988. student ed, pap. 5.50 (0-521-35737-3) Cambridge U Pr.

Cambridge English Course, Bk. 3B. Michael Swan & C. Walter. 1988. student ed, pap. 5.50 (0-521-35738-1) Cambridge U Pr.

Cambridge English Course, Bk. 3C. Michael Swan & C. Walter. 1988. student ed, pap. 5.50 (0-521-35739-X) Cambridge U Pr.

Cambridge Essays 1888-1889, Vol. 1. Bertrand Russell. Ed. by Kenneth Blackwell et al. (Collected Papers of Bertrand Russell). 588p. 1988. text ed. 130.00 (0-04-920067-4, A9409) Routledge Chapman & Hall.

***Cambridge Factfinder.** Ed. by David Crystal. 1994. pap. 14.95 (0-521-46991-0) Cambridge U Pr.

Cambridge Gardens. Pevensey Pr. Staff. (C). 1987. text ed. 65.00 (0-907115-20-9, Pub. by Pevensey UK) St Mut.

***Cambridge Gazetteer of the United States & Canada: A Dictionary of Places.** Archie Hobson. (Illus.). 784p. (C). 1994. 49.95 (0-521-41579-9) Cambridge U Pr.

Cambridge GED Program: Interpreting Arts & Literature. 2nd ed. Jerry Howett. (C). 1991. pap. write for info. (0-318-68299-0) P-H.

Cambridge GED Program: Science. 2nd rev. ed. Cambridge Staff. 448p. (C). 1992. pap. text ed. 7.65 (0-13-116427-9) P-H.

Cambridge GED Program: Social Science. 2nd rev. ed. Cambridge Staff. 384p. (C). 1992. pap. text ed. 7.65 (0-13-116435-X) P-H.

Cambridge GED Program in Math. 2nd ed. Jerry Howett. (C). 1993. pap. text ed. 7.65 (0-13-126616-0) P-H.

Cambridge Glass, 1949-1953. Bill Smith. 1986. pap. 14.95 (0-89145-079-3) Collector Bks.

Cambridge Guide to African & Caribbean Theatre. Ed. by Martin Banham et al. LC 93-36900. (Illus.). 224p. (C). 1994. 49.95 (0-521-41139-4) Cambridge U Pr.

Cambridge Guide to American Theatre. Ed. by Don B. Wilmeth & Tice L. Miller. (Illus.). 504p. (C). 1993. 49.95 (0-521-40134-8) Cambridge U Pr.

Cambridge Guide to Asian Theatre. Ed. by James R. Brandon & Martin Banham. LC 93-22340. (Illus.). 220p. (C). 1993. 49.95 (0-521-41623-X) Cambridge U Pr.

Cambridge Guide to Astronomical Discovery. William Liller. (Illus.). 240p. (C). 1992. 29.95 (0-521-41839-9) Cambridge U Pr.

Cambridge Guide to Literature in English. 2nd ed. Ed. by Ian Ousby. (Illus.). 1061p. (C). 1994. 49.95 (0-521-44086-6) Cambridge U Pr.

***Cambridge Guide to the Constellations.** Michael E. Bakich. (Illus.). 320p. (C). 1995. 49.95 (0-521-46520-6); pap. 19.95 (0-521-44921-9) Cambridge U Pr.

Cambridge Guide to the Museums of Britain & Ireland. Kenneth Hudson & Ann Nicholls. (Illus.). 464p. (C). 1989. pap. 19.95 (0-521-37892-3) Cambridge U Pr.

***Cambridge Guide to Theatre.** 2nd ed. Ed. by Martin Banham. (Illus.). 1250p. (C). 1994. 49.95 (0-521-43437-8) Cambridge U Pr.

Cambridge Guide to World Theatre. Ed. by Martin Banham. (Illus.). 1000p. (C). 1989. 74.95 (0-521-26595-9) Cambridge U Pr.

Cambridge Guide to World Theatre. Ed. by Martin Banham. (Illus.). 1110p. (C). 1992. pap. 24.95 (0-521-42903-X) Cambridge U Pr.

Cambridge Handbook of American Literature. Jack Salzman. 320p. 1986. 32.95 (0-521-30703-1) Cambridge U Pr.

Cambridge Handbook of Contemporary China. Colin Mackerras & Amanda Yorke. (Illus.). 280p. (C). 1992. pap. 22.95 (0-521-38755-8) Cambridge U Pr.

Cambridge Historical Encyclopedia of Great Britain & Ireland. Ed. by Christopher Haigh. (Illus.). 392p. (C). 1990. pap. 27.95 (0-521-39552-6) Cambridge U Pr.

Cambridge Historical Society Proceedings, 44 vols., Set. 1989. reprint ed. pap. 440.00 (1-878284-00-2) Cmbrdg Hist.

Cambridge History of Africa, 8 vols., Set. Incl. Vol. 1. From the Earliest Times to ca. 500 B. C. Ed. by J. D. Clark. LC 76-2261. 1982. 190.00 (0-521-22215-X); Vol. 2. From ca. 500 B.C. to A.D. 1050. Ed. by J. D. Fage. LC 76-2261. 1979. 170.00 (0-521-21592-7); Vol. 3. ca. 1050-1600. Ed. by R. Oliver. LC 76-2261. 1977. 185.00 (0-521-20981-1); Vol. 4. Ed. by R. Gray. LC 76-2261. 700p. 1975. 145.00 (0-521-20413-5); Vol. 5. Ed. by J. E. Flint. LC 76-2261. 700p. 1977. 135.00 (0-521-20701-0); Vol. 6. From 1870 to 1905. Ed. by Roland Oliver & G. N. Sanderson. LC 76-2261. (Illus.). 952p. 1985. 130.00 (0-512-22803-5); Vol. 7. From 1905 to 1940. Ed. by Andrew Roberts. LC 76-2261. (Illus.). 1000p. 1986. 155.00 (0-521-22505-1); Vol. 8. From 1940 to 1975. Ed. by Michael Crowder. LC 76-2261. (Illus.). 800p. 1985. 150.00 (0-521-22409-8); Vol. 8. From 1940 to 1975. Ed. by Michael Crowder. LC 76-2261. (Illus.). 800p. 1985. pap. 22.95 (0-685-08824-3); LC 76-2261. (Illus.). 1986. 821.00 (0-521-33460-8) Cambridge U Pr.

Cambridge History of American Foreign Relations, 4 vols., Set. (C). 1993. 99.95 (0-521-44988-X) Cambridge U Pr.

Cambridge History of American Foreign Relations: The American Search for Opportunity, 1865-1913. Walter LaFeber. LC 92-36165. 1993. 27.95 (0-521-38185-1) Cambridge U Pr.

Cambridge History of American Foreign Relations: The Creation of a Republican Empire, 1776-1865, Vol. 1. Bradford Perkins. LC 92-36165. 1993. 27.95 (0-521-38209-2) Cambridge U Pr.

***Cambridge History of American Foreign Relations Vol. 1: The Creation of a Republican Empire, 1776-1865.** Bradford Perkins. (Illus.). 272p. (C). 1995. pap. 15.95 (0-521-48384-0) Cambridge U Pr.

***Cambridge History of American Foreign Relations Vol. 2: The American Search for Opportunity, 1865-1913.** Walter LaFeber. (Illus.). 272p. (C). 1995. pap. 15.95 (0-521-48383-2) Cambridge U Pr.

Cambridge History of American Foreign Relations Vol. 3: The Globalizing of America, 1913-1945. Akira Iriye. (Illus.). 240p. (C). 1993. 27.95 (0-521-38206-8) Cambridge U Pr.

***Cambridge History of American Foreign Relations Vol. 3: The Globalizing of America, 1913-1945.** Akira Iriye. (Illus.). 254p. (C). 1995. pap. 15.95 (0-521-48382-4) Cambridge U Pr.

Cambridge History of American Foreign Relations Vol. 4: America in the Age of Soviet Power, 1945-1991. Warren I. Cohen. (Illus.). 272p. (C). 1993. 27.95 (0-521-38193-2) Cambridge U Pr.

***Cambridge History of American Foreign Relations Vol. 4: America in the Age of Soviet Power, 1945-1991.** Warren I. Cohen. (Illus.). 304p. (C). 1995. pap. 15.95 (0-521-48381-6) Cambridge U Pr.

Cambridge History of American Literature, Vol. 1, 1590-1820. Ed. by Sacvan Bercovitch & Cyrus Patell. LC 92-42479. 880p. (C). 1994. 69.95 (0-521-30105-X) Cambridge U Pr.

Cambridge History of American Literature: Prose Writing - 1820-1865, Vol. 2. Ed. by Sacvan Bercovitch. 800p. (C). 1995. 69.95 (0-521-30106-8) Cambridge U Pr.

Cambridge History of Central Asia Vol. 1: From Earliest Times to the Rise of the Mongols. Ed. by Denis Sinor. (Illus.). 504p. (C). 1990. 105.00 (0-521-24304-1) Cambridge U Pr.

Cambridge History of China Vol. 1: The Ch'in & Han Empires, 221 BC-AD 220. Ed. by Denis C. Twitchett & Michael Loewe. (Illus.). 752p. 1986. 155.00 (0-521-24327-0) Cambridge U Pr.

Cambridge History of China Vol. 3: Sui & T'ang China: 589-906 A.D. Ed. by Denis C. Twitchett. LC 76-29852. (Illus.). 1979. 155.00 (0-521-21446-7) Cambridge U Pr.

Cambridge History of China Vol. 6: Alien Regimes & Border States, 710-1368. Ed. by Denis C. Twitchett & Herbert Franke. (Illus.). 816p. (C). 1994. 120.00 (0-521-24331-9) Cambridge U Pr.

Cambridge History of China Vol. 7: The Ming Dynasty, 1368-1644. Ed. by Frederick W. Mote & Denis C. Twitchett. (Illus.). 752p. 1988. 155.00 (0-521-24332-7) Cambridge U Pr.

Cambridge History of China Vol. 10: Late Ch'ing 1800-1911. Ed. by John K. Fairbank. LC 76-29852. (Cambridge History of China Ser.). 1978. 155.00 (0-521-21447-5) Cambridge U Pr.

Cambridge History of China Vol. 11: Late Ch'ing 1800-1911. Ed. by John K. Fairbank & Kwang-Ching Liu. LC 76-29852. (Illus.). 1980. 155.00 (0-521-22029-7) Cambridge U Pr.

Cambridge History of China Vol. 12: Republican China 1912-1949. Ed. by John K. Fairbank. LC 76-29852. (Illus.). 1002p. 1983. 165.00 (0-521-23541-3) Cambridge U Pr.

Cambridge History of China Vol. 13: Republican China 1912-1949. Ed. by John K. Fairbank & Albert Feuerwerke. (Illus.). 1000p. 1986. 155.00 (0-521-24338-6) Cambridge U Pr.

Cambridge History of China Vol. 14: The People's Republic of China, Pt. 1: The Emergence of Revolutionary China, 1949-1965. Ed. by Roderick MacFarquhar & John K. Fairbank. LC 76-29852. (Illus.). 680p. 1987. 130.00 (0-521-24336-X) Cambridge U Pr.

Cambridge History of China Vol. 15: The People's Republic, Pt. 2: Revolutions Within the Chinese Revolution, 1966-1982. Ed. by Roderick MacFarquhar & John K. Fairbank. (Illus.). 1024p. (C). 1991. 135.00 (0-521-24337-8) Cambridge U Pr.

Cambridge History of Classical Literature: Greek Literature, Vol. I. Ed. by P. E. Easterling & Bernard M. Knox. LC 82-22048. (Illus.). 936p. 1985. 120.00 (0-521-21042-9) Cambridge U Pr.

An Asterisk (*) at the beginning of an entry indicates that the title is appearing in BIP for the first time. 1009

Cambridge History of Classical Literature Vol. 1, Pt. 1: Early Greek Poetry. P. E. Easterling. 1989. pap. 21.95 (*0-521-35981-3*) Cambridge U Pr.

Cambridge History of Classical Literature Vol. 1, Pt. 2: Greek Drama. P. E. Easterling. 1989. pap. 21.95 (*0-521-35982-1*) Cambridge U Pr.

Cambridge History of Classical Literature Vol. 1, Pt. 3: Philosophy, History, & Oratory. P. E. Easterling. 1989. pap. 21.95 (*0-521-35983-X*) Cambridge U Pr.

Cambridge History of Classical Literature Vol. 1, Pt. 4: The Hellenistic Period & the Empire. P. E. Easterling. 1989. pap. 21.95 (*0-521-35984-8*) Cambridge U Pr.

Cambridge History of Classical Literature Vol. II: Latin Literature. Ed. by Edwin J. Kenney & W. V. Clausen. LC 79-121. (Illus.). 960p. 1982. 120.00 (*0-521-21043-7*) Cambridge U Pr.

Cambridge History of Classical Literature Vol. II: Latin Literature - Pt. 1, The Early Republic. Ed. by Edwin J. Kenney & W. V. Clausen. LC 82-19780. 223p. 1983. pap. 21.95 (*0-521-27375-7*) Cambridge U Pr.

Cambridge History of Classical Literature Vol. II: Latin Literature - Pt. 2, The Late Republic. Ed. by Edwin J. Kenney & W. V. Clausen. LC 82-19781. 153p. 1983. pap. 21.95 (*0-521-27374-9*) Cambridge U Pr.

Cambridge History of Classical Literature Vol. II: Latin Literature - Pt. 3, The Age of Augustus. Ed. by Edwin J. Kenney & W. V. Clausen. LC 82-19783. 239p. 1983. pap. 21.95 (*0-521-27373-0*) Cambridge U Pr.

Cambridge History of Classical Literature Vol. II: Latin Literature - Pt. 4, The Early Principate. Ed. by Edwin J. Kenney & W. V. Clausen. LC 82-19782. 204p. 1983. pap. 21.95 (*0-521-27372-2*) Cambridge U Pr.

Cambridge History of Classical Literature Vol. II: Latin Literature - Pt. 5, The Later Principate. Ed. by Edwin J. Kenney & W. V. Clausen. LC 82-19784. 154p. 1983. pap. 21.95 (*0-521-27371-4*) Cambridge U Pr.

Cambridge History of English Literature, Vol. 1-15. Ed. by Adolphus W. Ward & A. R. Waller. LC 07-40856. reprint ed. write for info. (*0-8357-7981-5*, 2029226) Bks Demand.

Cambridge History of Iran, Vol. 1: The Land of Iran. Ed. by W. B. Fisher & Stanley I. Grossman. LC 67-12845. (Illus.). 804p. 1968. Vol. 1 - The Land of Iran (ed. by W. B. Fisher), 804p., 1968. 140.00 (*0-521-06935-1*) Cambridge U Pr.

Cambridge History of Iran, Vol. 2: The Median & Archaemenian Periods. Ed. by Ilya Gershevitch & Stanley I. Grossman. LC 67-12845. (Illus.). 963p. 1985. Vol. 2 - The Median & Archaemenian Periods (ed. by Ilya Gershevitch), 963p., 1985. 145.00 (*0-521-20091-1*) Cambridge U Pr.

Cambridge History of Iran, Vol. 3, Pt. 2. LC 67-12845. (Illus.). 720p. 1983. 140.00 (*0-521-24693-8*) Cambridge U Pr.

Cambridge History of Iran, Vol. 3: The Seleucid, Parthian & Sasanid Periods. Ed. by Ehsan Yarshater & Stanley I. Grossman. LC 67-12845. (Illus.). 680p. 1983. Vol. 3 - The Seleucid, Parthian & Sasanid Periods (ed. by Ehsan Yarshater), Pt.1, 680p., 1983. 130.00 (*0-521-20092-X*) Cambridge U Pr.

Cambridge History of Iran, Vol. 4: From the Arab Invasion to the Saljugs. Ed. by R. N. Frye & Stanley I. Grossman. LC 67-12845. (Illus.). 747p. 1975. Vol. 4 - From the Arab Invasion to the Saljuqs (ed. by R. N. Frye), 747p., 1975. 130.00 (*0-521-20093-8*) Cambridge U Pr.

Cambridge History of Iran, Vol. 5: The Saljuq & Mongol Periods. Ed. by J. A. Boyle & Stanley I. Grossman. LC 67-12845. (Illus.). 778p. 1968. Vol. 5 - The Saljuq & Mongol Periods (ed. by J. A. Boyle), 778p., 1968. 130.00 (*0-521-06936-X*) Cambridge U Pr.

Cambridge History of Iran, Vol. 6: The Timurid & Sefavid Periods. Ed. by Peter Jackson et al. LC 67-12845. (Illus.). 1120p. 1986. Vol.6 - The Timurid & Sefavid Periods (ed. by Peter Jackson & Laurence Lockhart), 1120p., 1986. 150.00 (*0-521-20094-6*) Cambridge U Pr.

Cambridge History of Iran, Vol. 7: From Nadir Shah to the Islamic Republic. Ed. by Peter Avery & Stanley I. Grossman. LC 67-12845. (Illus.). 1088p. 1991. Vol. 7 - From Nadir Shah to the Islamic Republic (ed. by Peter Avery, et al), 1088p., 1991. 150.00 (*0-521-20095-4*) Cambridge U Pr.

Cambridge History of Islam, 4 Vols. Incl. Vol. 1A. Central Islamic Lands from Pre-Islamic Times to the First World War. Ed. by P. M. Holt et al. 1977. pap. 47.95 (*0-521-29135-6*); Vol. 1B. Central Islamic Lands Since 1918. Ed. by P. M. Holt et al. 1977. pap. 47.95 (*0-521-29136-4*); Vol. 2A. Indian Subcontinent, Southeast Asia, Africa & the Muslim West. Ed. by P. M. Holt et al. 1977. pap. 47.95 (*0-521-29137-2*); Vol. 2B. Islamic Society & Civilization. Ed. by P. M. Holt et al. 1978. 105.00 (*0-521-21949-3*); Vol. 2B. Islamic Society & Civilization. Ed. by P. M. Holt et al. 1977. pap. 47.95 (*0-521-29138-0*); 1977. Set. Set pap. 99.95 (*0-521-08755-4*) Cambridge U Pr.

Cambridge History of Japan Vol. 1: Ancient Japan. Ed. by Delmer M. Brown. (Illus.). 700p. (C). 1993. 115.00 (*0-521-22352-0*) Cambridge U Pr.

Cambridge History of Japan Vol. 3: Medieval Japan. Ed. by Kozo Yamamura. (Illus.). 992p. (C). 1990. 120.00 (*0-521-22354-7*) Cambridge U Pr.

Cambridge History of Japan Vol. 4: Early Modern Japan. Ed. by John W. Hall. (Illus.). 896p. (C). 1991. 120.00 (*0-521-22355-5*) Cambridge U Pr.

Cambridge History of Japan Vol. 5: The Nineteenth Century. Ed. by Marius B. Jansen. (Illus.). 992p. (C). 1989. 120.00 (*0-521-22356-3*) Cambridge U Pr.

Cambridge History of Japan Vol. 6: The Twentieth Century. Ed. by Peter Duus. (Illus.). 1989. 120.00 (*0-521-22357-1*) Cambridge U Pr.

Cambridge History of Judaism Vol. 1: Introduction, The Persian Period. Ed. by W. D. Davies & Louis Finkelstein. LC 77-85704. 461p. 1984. 94.95 (*0-521-21880-2*) Cambridge U Pr.

Cambridge History of Judaism Vol. 2: The Hellenistic Age. Ed. by W. D. Davies & Louis Finkelstein. (Illus.). 756p. 1990. 115.00 (*0-521-21929-9*) Cambridge U Pr.

Cambridge History of Later Greek & Early Medieval Philosophy. D. M. Armstrong. 1967. 120.00 (*0-521-04054-X*) Cambridge U Pr.

Cambridge History of Later Medieval Philosophy: From the Rediscovery of Aristotle to the Disintegration of Scholasticism 1100-1600. Norman Kretzman et al. LC 81-10086. 1050p. 1988. pap. 39.95 (*0-521-36933-9*) Cambridge U Pr.

Cambridge History of Latin America: Bibliographical Essays, Vol. 11. Ed. by Leslie Bethell. 760p. (C). 1995. 89.95 (*0-521-39525-9*) Cambridge U Pr.

Cambridge History of Latin America: Colonial Latin America, 5 vols. Ed. by Leslie Bethell. Incl. Vol. 1. Colonial Latin America. 600p. 1985. 115.00 (*0-521-23223-6*); Vol. 2. Colonial Latin America. 850p. 1985. 130.00 (*0-521-24516-8*); Vol. 3. From Independence to 1870. 961p. 1985. 130.00 (*0-521-23224-4*); Vol. 4. 1870-1930. 704p. 1986. 120.00 (*0-521-23225-2*); Vol. 5. 1870-1930. 976p. 1986. 130.00 (*0-521-24517-6*); (Illus.). write for info. (*0-318-57955-3*) Cambridge U Pr.

Cambridge History of Latin America Pt. 1: Latin America since 1930, Economy, Society & Politics, Vol. 6. Ed. by Leslie Bethell. 607p. (C). 1995. 79.95 (*0-521-23226-0*) Cambridge U Pr.

Cambridge History of Latin America Pt. 2: Latin America since 1930, Economy, Society & Politics, Vol. 6. Ed. by Leslie Bethell. 798p. (C). 1995. 79.95 (*0-521-46556-7*) Cambridge U Pr.

Cambridge History of Latin America Vol. 7: Latin America since 1930. Ed. by Leslie Bethell. (Illus.). (C). 1990. 120.00 (*0-521-24518-4*) Cambridge U Pr.

Cambridge History of Latin America Vol. 8: Latin America since 1930. Ed. by Leslie Bethell. 656p. (C). 1991. 110.00 (*0-521-26652-1*) Cambridge U Pr.

***Cambridge History of Latin America Vol. 10: Latin America since 1930, Ideas, Culture, & Society.** Ed. by Leslie Bethell. 600p. (C). 1995. write for info. (*0-521-49594-6*) Cambridge U Pr.

Cambridge History of Latin American Literature, Vol. 1: Discovery to Modernism. Ed. by Roberto G. Echevarria & Enrique Pupo-Walker. LC 93-37750. 1995. write for info. (*0-521-34069-1*) Cambridge U Pr.

Cambridge History of Latin American Literature, Vol. 2: The Twentieth Century. Ed. by Roberto G. Echevarria & Enrique Pupo-Walker. LC 93-37750. 1995. write for info. (*0-521-34070-5*) Cambridge U Pr.

Cambridge History of Latin American Literature, Vol. 3: Brazilian Literature. Ed. by Roberto G. Echevarria & Enrique Pupo-Walker. LC 93-37750. 1995. write for info. (*0-521-41035-5*) Cambridge U Pr.

Cambridge History of Literary Criticism Vol. 1: Classical Criticism. Ed. by George A. Kennedy. (C). 1990. 69.95 (*0-521-30006-1*) Cambridge U Pr.

Cambridge History of Literary Criticism Vol. 1: Classical Criticism. Ed. by George A. Kennedy. 400p. (C). 1993. pap. 24.95 (*0-521-31717-7*) Cambridge U Pr.

***Cambridge History of Literary Criticism Vol. 8: From Formalism to Poststructuralism.** Ed. by Raman Selden. 550p. (C). 1995. write for info. (*0-521-30013-4*) Cambridge U Pr.

Cambridge History of Medieval Political Thought c. 350-c. 1450. Ed. by J. H. Burns. 832p. 1988. 125.00 (*0-521-24324-6*) Cambridge U Pr.

Cambridge History of Medieval Political Thought c. 350-c. 1450. Ed. by J. H. Burns. 832p. (C). 1991. pap. 39.95 (*0-521-42388-0*) Cambridge U Pr.

Cambridge History of Political Thought, 1450-1700. Ed. by J. H. Burns & Mark Goldie. 800p. (C). 1991. 125.00 (*0-521-24716-0*) Cambridge U Pr.

Cambridge History of Political Thought 1450-1700. Ed. by J. H. Burns. 816p. (C). 1995. pap. 37.95 (*0-521-47772-7*) Cambridge U Pr.

Cambridge History of Renaissance Philosophy. Ed. by C. B. Schmitt et al. 900p. 1988. 125.00 (*0-521-25104-4*) Cambridge U Pr.

Cambridge History of Renaissance Philosophy. Ed. by C. B. Schmitt et al. 992p. (C). 1991. pap. 37.95 (*0-521-39748-0*) Cambridge U Pr.

Cambridge History of Russian Literature. Ed. by Charles A. Moser. 628p. (C). 1992. pap. 29.95 (*0-521-42567-0*) Cambridge U Pr.

Cambridge History of Russian Literature. Ed. by Charles A. Moser. 628p. (C). 1992. 94.95 (*0-521-41554-3*) Cambridge U Pr.

Cambridge History of Southeast Asia Vol. 1: From Early Times to c. 1800. Ed. by Nicholas Tarling. (Illus.). 520p. (C). 1993. 79.95 (*0-521-35505-2*) Cambridge U Pr.

Cambridge History of Southeast Asia Vol. 2: The Nineteenth & Twentieth Centuries. Ed. by Nicholas Tarling. (Illus.). 520p. (C). 1993. 79.95 (*0-521-35506-0*) Cambridge U Pr.

Cambridge History of the Bible, 3 Vols. Incl. Vol. 1. From the Beginnings to Jerome. Ed. by P. R. Ackroyd & C. F. Evans. LC 63-24435. 1975. pap. 54.95 (*0-521-09973-0*); Vol. 2. West from the Fathers to the Reformation. Ed. by G. W. Lampe. LC 63-24435. 1975. 84.95 (*0-521-04255-0*); Vol. 2. West from the Fathers to the Reformation. Ed. by G. W. Lampe. LC 63-24435. 1975. pap. 49.95 (*0-521-29017-1*); LC 63-24435. 1975. Set. 155.00 (*0-521-08778-3*); Incl. Vol. 1. pap. 54.95 (*0-521-09973-0*); Vol. 2. 84.95 (*0-521-04255-0*); Vol. 2. pap. 49.95 (*0-521-29017-1*); Set pap. 120.00 (*0-521-29018-X*) Cambridge U Pr.

Cambridge History of the English Language Vol. 1: The Beginnings to 1066. Ed. by Richard M. Hogg. (Illus.). 616p. (C). 1992. 120.00 (*0-521-26474-X*) Cambridge U Pr.

Cambridge History of the English Language Vol. 2: 1066-1476. Ed. by N. F. Blake. (Illus.). 692p. (C). 1992. 130.00 (*0-521-26475-8*) Cambridge U Pr.

Cambridge History of the English Language Vol. 5: English in Britain & Overseas: Origins & Development, Vol. 5. Ed. by Robert Burchfield. (Illus.). 692p. (C). 1995. 110.00 (*0-521-26478-2*) Cambridge U Pr.

Cambridge Illustrated Dictionary of Natural History. R. J. Lincoln & G. A. Boxshall. (Illus.). 408p. 1987. 39.95 (*0-521-30551-9*) Cambridge U Pr.

Cambridge Illustrated Dictionary of Natural History. R. J. Lincoln & G. A. Boxshall. (Illus.). 420p. (C). 1990. pap. 19.95 (*0-521-39941-6*) Cambridge U Pr.

Cambridge Illustrated History of British Theatre. Simon Trussler. (Cambridge Illustrated Histories Ser.). (Illus.). 400p. (C). 1994. 39.95 (*0-521-41913-1*) Cambridge U Pr.

Cambridge Illustrated History of France. Colin Jones. (Cambridge Illustrated Histories Ser.). (Illus.). 352p. (C). 1995. 39.95 (*0-521-43294-4*) Cambridge U Pr.

Cambridge Illustrated History of the Middle Ages, Vol. 1: 350-950. Ed. by Robert Fossier. Tr. by Janet Sondheimer. (Illus.). 587p. (C). 1989. 69.95 (*0-521-26644-0*) Cambridge U Pr.

Cambridge Illustrated History of the Middle Ages, Vol. 3: 1250-1520. Ed. by Robert Fossier. Tr. by Sarah Hanbury-Tenison. (Illus.). 528p. 1986. 69.95 (*0-521-26646-7*) Cambridge U Pr.

***Cambridge Illustrated History of Warfare.** Ed. by Geoffrey Parker. (Cambridge Illustrated Histories Ser.). (Illus.). 416p. (C). 1995. 39.95 (*0-521-44073-4*) Cambridge U Pr.

Cambridge in the Age of Enlightenment: Science, Religion & Politics from the Restoration to the French Revolution. John Gascoigne. 1989. 64.95 (*0-521-35139-1*) Cambridge U Pr.

***Cambridge International Dictionary of English.** Ed. by Paul Proctor. (Illus.). 1792p. (C). 1995. 24.95 (*0-521-48236-4*) Cambridge U Pr.

***Cambridge International Dictionary of English.** Ed. by Paul Proctor. 1995. pap. 22.95 (*0-521-48469-3*) Cambridge U Pr.

***Cambridge International Dictionary of English.** Ed. by Paul Proctor. (Illus.). 1792p. (C). 1995. pap. 19.95 (*0-521-48421-9*) Cambridge U Pr.

Cambridge Latin Course, Unit I. 3rd ed. Ed Phinney. LC 87-10281. 1988. 18.95 (*0-521-34379-8*) Cambridge U Pr.

Cambridge Latin Course, 3 bklts, Unit 5, Pupils Books. Cambridge School Classics Project Foundation Staff. Incl. Dido et Aeneas. 1974. (*0-318-51271-8*); Nero et Agrippina. 1974. (*0-318-51272-6*); Words & Phrases. 1974. (*0-318-51273-4*); (Illus.). 1974. Set pap. 5.95 (*0-521-08545-4*) Cambridge U Pr.

***Cambridge Latin Course Unit 1.** 3rd ed. Ed Phinney. 232p. (C). 1988. teacher ed, pap. 13.50 (*0-521-34853-6*) Cambridge U Pr.

***Cambridge Latin Course Unit 2.** 3rd ed. Ed Phinney. (C). 1988. teacher ed, pap. 14.95 (*0-521-34855-2*) Cambridge U Pr.

Cambridge Latin Course, Unit 2: North American Edition. 1988. 19.95 (*0-521-34381-X*) Cambridge U Pr.

Cambridge Latin Course, Unit 4: North America. 3rd ed. Ed. by Ed Phinney. 1991. 38.95 (*0-521-34380-1*) Cambridge U Pr.

Cambridge Latin Course, Unit 4: North American. 3rd ed. Ed Phinney. (C). 1992. student ed, pap. 8.95 (*0-521-34860-9*) Cambridge U Pr.

Cambridge Lectures. Arthur T. Quiller-Couch. LC 72-4723. (Essay Index Reprint Ser.). 1977. reprint ed. 20.95 (*0-8369-2970-5*) Ayer.

***Cambridge Love & Relationships Test.** Dan Pape. 33p. (Orig.). (C). 1995. write for info. (*1-882330-41-2*) Magni Co.

Cambridge Medical Reviews: Haematological Oncology, Vol. 1. Ed. by Adrian C. Newland et al. (Illus.). 260p. (C). 1991. 89.95 (*0-521-40193-3*) Cambridge U Pr.

Cambridge Medical Reviews: Haematological Oncology, Vol. 2. Ed. by Armand Keating et al. (Illus.). 228p. (C). 1993. 84.95 (*0-521-43190-5*) Cambridge U Pr.

Cambridge Medical Reviews: Haematological Oncology, Vol. 3. Ed. by Alan Burnett et al. (Illus.). 200p. (C). 1994. 89.95 (*0-521-44208-7*) Cambridge U Pr.

Cambridge Medical Reviews Vol. 1: Neurobiology & Psychiatry. Ed. by Robert Kerwin et al. (Illus.). 176p. (C). 1992. 74.95 (*0-521-39542-9*) Cambridge U Pr.

Cambridge Medical Reviews Vol. 2: Neurobiology & Psychiatry. Ed. by Robert Kerwin. (Illus.). 150p. (C). 1993. 74.95 (*0-521-43483-1*) Cambridge U Pr.

***Cambridge Medical Reviews Vol. 4: Haematological Oncology.** Ed. by James Armitage et al. (Cambridge Medical Reviews Ser.: No. 4). (Illus.). 250p. (C). 1994. write for info. (*0-521-46169-3*) Cambridge U Pr.

***Cambridge Medical Reviews: Neurobiology & Psychiatry Vol. 3: Neuroimaging.** Ed. by Robert Kerwin et al. (Cambridge Medical Reviews Ser.: No. 3). (Illus.). 150p. (C). 1995. 89.95 (*0-521-45365-8*) Cambridge U Pr.

Cambridge Medieval History, 9 vols. Incl. Vol. 6. Victory of the Papacy. 1929. 185.00 (*0-521-04538-X*); write for info. (*0-318-51274-2*) Cambridge U Pr.

Cambridge Minds. Richard Mason. 240p. (C). 1994. 39.95 (*0-521-45405-0*); pap. 19.95 (*0-521-45625-8*) Cambridge U Pr.

Cambridge Multisectoral Dynamic Model. Ed. by Terry Barker & William Peterson. (Cambridge Studies in Applied Econometrics: No. 5). (Illus.). 400p. 1988. 79.95 (*0-521-33004-1*) Cambridge U Pr.

Cambridge Music: From the Middle Ages to Modern Times. Frida Knight. (Cambridge Town, Gown & County Ser.: Vol. 29). (Illus.). 1980. 25.00 (*0-900891-51-3*) Oleander Pr.

Cambridge Music Manuscripts 900-1700. Ed. by Iain Fenlon. LC 81-17059. 174p. 1982. 79.95 (*0-521-24452-8*) Cambridge U Pr.

Cambridge New Bibliography of English Literature, 4 vols., Set. Incl. Vol. 1. 600-1660. Ed. by George Watson. LC 73-82455. 1282p. 1974. 150.00 (*0-521-20004-0*); Vol. 2. 1660-1800. Ed. by George Watson. LC 73-82455. xxii, 1072p. 1971. 160.00 (*0-521-07934-9*); Vol. 3. 1800-1900. Ed. by George Watson. LC 73-82455. xxiv, 1956p. 1969. 140.00 (*0-521-07255-7*); Vol. 4. 1900-1950. Ed. by I. R. Willison & George Watson. LC 73-82455. xix, 1414p. 1972. 125.00 (*0-685-42032-9*); Index. Ed. by George Watson. LC 73-82455. 285p. 1977. 49.95 (*0-521-21310-X*); Vol. 1. 600-1660. Ed. by George Watson. LC 73-82455. 1282p. 1974. 150.00 (*0-521-20004-0*); Vol. 2. 1660-1800. Ed. by George Watson. LC 73-82455. xxii, 1072p. 1971. 160.00 (*0-521-07934-9*); Vol. 3. 1800-1900. Ed. by George Watson. LC 73-82455. xxiv, 1956p. 1969. 140.00 (*0-521-07255-7*); Vol. 4. 1900-1950. Ed. by I. R. Willison & George Watson. LC 73-82455. xix, 1414p. 1972. 125.00 (*0-685-42032-9*); LC 73-82455. (Illus.). 1987. 470.00 (*0-521-34378-X*) Cambridge U Pr.

Cambridge Newspapers & Opinion, 1780-1850. Michael J. Murphy. (Cambridge Town, Gown & County Ser.: Vol. 12). (Illus.). 1977. 21.95 (*0-900891-15-7*) Oleander Pr.

Cambridge Nobody Knows. Frank A. Reeve. (Cambridge Town, Gown & County Ser.: Vol. 14). (Illus.). 1977. pap. 4.95 (*0-900891-10-6*) Oleander Pr.

Cambridge Orations 1982-1993: A Selection. James Diggle. (Illus.). 128p. (C). 1994. pap. 13.95 (*0-521-46618-0*) Cambridge U Pr.

Cambridge Paperback Encyclopedia. Ed. by David Crystal. (Illus.). 972p. (C). 1994. pap. 19.95 (*0-521-47733-6*) Cambridge U Pr.

***Cambridge Paperback Encyclopedia.** 2nd ed. Ed. by David Crystal. (Illus.). 1100p. (C). 1995. pap. 19.95 (*0-521-55968-5*) Cambridge U Pr.

Cambridge Platonists. Frederick J. Powicke. viii, 219p. (GER.). 1970. reprint ed. write for info. (*0-318-70503-6*, Pub. by Georg Olms GW); reprint ed. write for info. (*0-318-71273-3*, Pub. by Georg Olms GW) Lubrecht & Cramer.

Cambridge Platonists: A Study. Frederick J. Powicke. (Illus.). viii, 219p. 1970. reprint ed. 32.37 (*0-685-66505-4*, 05102832, Pub. by Georg Olms GW) Lubrecht & Cramer.

Cambridge Pre-Ged Program in Math. 2nd ed. Cambridge. 1988. pap. text ed. 9.00 (*0-13-113762-X*) P-H.

Cambridge Pre-Ged Program in Reading. Cambridge Staff. 1988. pap. text ed. 9.00 (*0-13-114265-8*) P-H.

Cambridge Pre-Ged Program in Writing. 2nd ed. M. Keller. 1988. pap. text ed. 9.00 (*0-13-114240-2*) P-H.

Cambridge Preparation for the TOEFL Test. Jolene Gear. 512p. (C). 1993. pap. 19.95 (*0-521-36745-X*) Cambridge U Pr.

Cambridge Preparation for the TOEFL Test. Jolene Gear. 512p. (C). 1993. pap. 39.95 (*0-521-36539-2*) Cambridge U Pr.

Cambridge Preparation for the TOEFL Test. Jolene Gear. 512p. (C). 1993. pap. 55.00 (*0-521-42191-8*) Cambridge U Pr.

Cambridge Press, Sixteen Thirty-Eight to Sixteen Ninety-Two. George P. Winship. LC 68-57346. (Essay Index Reprint Ser.). 1977. 24.95 (*0-8369-1004-4*) Ayer.

Cambridge Program for the GED Mathematics Test. Jerry Howett. (GED Preparation Ser.). (Illus.). 352p. (Orig.). 1988. student ed, pap. text ed. 4.20 (*0-8428-9393-8*) Cambridge Bk.

Cambridge Program for the GED Reading Skills Test. Ed. by Brian Schenk. (GED Preparation Ser.). 256p. (Orig.). 1988. pap. text ed. 6.90 (*0-8428-9390-3*) Cambridge Bk.

Cambridge Program for the GED Science Test. Ed. by Brian Schenk. (GED Preparation Ser.). (Illus.). 224p. (Orig.). 1988. pap. text ed. write for info. (*0-8428-9389-X*) Cambridge Bk.

Cambridge Program for the GED Social Studies Test. Rosendo Abreu. (GED Preparation Ser.). (Illus.). 272p. (Orig.). 1988. Cambridge Exercise Book for the Social Studies Test. student ed 3.30 (*0-8428-9394-6*) Cambridge Bk.

Cambridge Program for the GED Writing Skills Test. Aaron Percefull. (GED Preparation Ser.). 304p. (Orig.). 1988. pap. text ed. 6.45 (*0-8428-9387-3*) Cambridge Bk.

Cambridge Program for the High School Equivalency Examination. Jerry Long & Jeff Tenzer. Ed. by Brian Schenk. (GED Preparation Ser.). (Illus.). 816p. (Orig.). 1988. pap. text ed. write for info. (*0-8428-9385-7*) Cambridge Bk.

Cambridge Readings in Dante's Comedy. Ed. by Kenelm Foster & Patrick Boyde. LC 81-3861. 220p. 1982. 69.95 (*0-521-24140-5*) Cambridge U Pr.

Cambridge Reflections. Helen K. Wilson. (C). 1989. 65.00 (*1-85183-041-3*, Silent Bks) St Mut.

An Asterisk (*) at the beginning of an entry indicates that the title is appearing in BIP for the first time.

An Asterisk (*) at the beginning of an entry indicates that the title is appearing in BIP for the first time.

1011

Camera Lucida. Roland Barthes. 1982. pap. 9.95 (*0-374-52134-4*) FS&G.

Camera Maintenance & Repair. Thomas Tomosy. (Illus.). 160p. 1993. pap. 24.95 (*0-936262-09-5*) Amherst Media.

Camera Never Blinks Twice: The Further Adventures of a Television Journalist. Dan Rather. 1994. 23.00 (*0-688-09748-0*) Morrow.

***Camera Never Blinks Twice: The Further Adventures of a Television Journalist.** large type ed. Dan Rather & Mickey Herskowitz. LC 94-48913. 1995. write for info. (*0-7862-0414-1*) Thorndike Pr.

Camera Notes: The Official Organ of the Camera Club of New York, 6 vols. in 3, Set. (Photography Ser.). 1978. 395.00 (*0-306-77553-0*) Da Capo.

Camera Notes: The Official Organ of the Camera Club of New York, 6 vols. in 3, Vol. 1: 1897-1899. (Photography Ser.). 1978. Vol. 1, 1897-1899. 165.00 (*0-306-77554-9*) Da Capo.

Camera Notes: The Official Organ of the Camera Club of New York, 6 vols. in 3, Vol. 2: 1899-1901. (Photography Ser.). 1978. Vol. 2, 1899-1901. 165.00 (*0-306-77555-7*) Da Capo.

Camera Notes: The Official Organ of the Camera Club of New York, 6 vols. in 3, Vol. 3: 1901-1903. (Photography Ser.). 1978. Vol. 3, 1901-1903. 165.00 (*0-306-77556-5*) Da Capo.

Camera Obscura. Hans Knuchel. (Illus.). 80p. 1992. 35.00 (*3-906700-49-6*, Pub. by Lars Muller SZ) Dist Art Pubs.

Camera on the Crags. Alan Hankinson. 176p. (C). 1989. text ed. 89.00 (*1-85183-018-9*, Silent Bks) St Mut.

Camera on the Waterfront: A Maritime Pictorial. (Illus.). 1985. pap. 11.95 (*0-9607530-2-8*) Seacoast CA.

***Camera Picta: Sarai Sherman.** Rolando Bellini et al. (Illus.). 84p. 1995. pap. 29.95 (*0-295-97411-7*) U of Wash Pr.

Camera Politica: The Politics & Ideology of Contemporary Hollywood Film. Michael Ryan & Douglas M. Kellner. LC 86-45477. (Illus.). 346p. (Orig.). 1988. 47.95 (*0-253-31334-1*); pap. 14.95 (*0-253-20604-9*, MB-604) Ind U Pr.

Camera Profits & Photo Market Guide. 1987. lib. bdg. 39.00 (*0-8490-3906-1*) Gordon Pr.

Camera Ready with QuarkXPress: A Practical Guide to Creating Direct-to-Press Documents from the Desktop. Cyndie Klopfenstein. (Illus.). 216p. (Orig.). 1993. disk, pap. 35.00 (*1-56609-089-X*) Peachpit Pr.

Camera Repair, Restoration & Adaptation. Mark Baczynsky. (Illus.). 52p. 1982. pap. 24.95 (*0-89816-009-X*) Embee Pr.

Camera Repairman's Guide to Practical Photography. Ray Oberreuter. 178p. 1991. pap. 15.95 (*0-9630169-0-3*) Grassroots.

Camera Security Manual: How to Outwit Camera Thieves & Damage Gremlins. Ron Swartley. (Illus.). 64p. (Orig.). 1994. pap. 7.95 (*0-9634309-2-0*) Frontier Image.

***Camera Smart Screen Actor.** Richard Brestoff. LC 94-34487. (Career Resource Book Ser.). 1994. 14.95 (*1-880399-76-8*) Smith & Kraus.

Camera, Spade & Pen: An Inside View of Southwestern Archaeology. Marc Gaede. LC 80-23751. (Illus.). 160p. reprint ed. pap. 45.60 (*0-8357-7984-X*, 2029652) Bks Demand.

Camera Technology: The Dark Side of the Lens. Norman Goldberg. (Illus.). 309p. 1992. text ed. 29.95 (*0-12-287570-2*) Acad Pr.

Camera Terms & Concepts. David E. Elkins. (Illus.). 144p. 1993. pap. 19.95 (*0-240-80150-4*, Focal) Buttrwrth-Heinemann.

Camera Work: A Pictorial Guide. Alfred Stieglitz. Ed. by Marianne F. Margolis. LC 77-85410. (Illus.). 1978. pap. 13.95 (*0-486-23591-2*) Dover.

Cameral Analysis: A Method of Treating the Psychoneuroses Using Hypnosis. David L. Pedersen. LC 93-37852. (Illus.). 224p. 1994. 59.95x (*0-415-10424-6*, B3806, Routledge NY); pap. 18.95 (*0-415-10425-4*, B3910, Routledge NY) Routledge.

Cameraready. Kenneth A. Caird. (Illus.). 400p. 1973. ring bd. 60.00 (*0-87703-066-9*) Univelt Inc.

Cameras at the Zoo. James Arrabito. (Cameras at . . . Ser.: Vol. I). (Illus.). 16p. (Orig.). (J). (gr. 3-10). 1991. pap. 4.95 (*0-9622596-0-8*) Arraster Pub.

Cameras for Image Intensifier Fluorography, No. 15. International Commission on Radiation Units & Measurements. LC 73-97641. 1969. 25.00 (*0-913394-08-4*) Intl Comm Rad Meas.

Camerer Cuss Book of Antique Watches. T. P. Camerer. (Illus.). 336p. 1976. 69.50 (*0-902028-33-2*) Antique Collect.

Cameron. Beverly Barton. (Silhouette Desire Ser.). 1993. mass mkt. 2.99 (*0-373-05796-2*, 5-05796-3) Silhouette.

Cameron Aurameter in Action: Step-by-Step Method for Use of the Aurameter in Dowsing. Bill Cox. (Illus.). 48p. 1982. per. 8.75 (*0-88234-008-5*) Life Understanding.

Cameron Solid State Stereophonic Phonograph, 1968-71. rev. ed. Ed. by Frank Adams. (Illus.). 11p. reprint ed. spiral bd. 15.00 (*1-56642-166-7*, R-33) AMR Pub Co.

Cameron Story. William T. Cameron. LC 90-81754. (Illus.). 200p. Date not set. 69.95 (*0-9626599-1-6*) Aztex.

Cameron Volume on Unconventional Mineral Deposits. Wayne C. Shanks. LC 83-71422. (Illus.). 223p. 1983. 10.00 (*0-89520-414-2*, 414-2) SMM&E Inc.

***Cameron Volume on Unconventional Mineral Deposits.** fac. ed. Wayne C. Shanks. LC 83-71422. (Illus.). 260p. 1983. reprint ed. pap. 74.10 (*0-7837-7871-6*, 2047628) Bks Demand.

Cameron's Architectural Complex at Pushkin. G. D. Khodasevich & M. G. Voronov. 102p. (RUS.). 1982. pap. 30.00 (*0-317-57230-X*, Pub. by Collets UK) St Mut.

Cameron's Closet. Gary Brandner. 1987. pap. 3.50 (*0-449-13068-1*) Fawcett.

Cameron's Closet. Gary Brandner. 1987. pap. 3.95 (*0-449-13400-8*, GM) Fawcett.

Cameron's Crossing. Philip McCutchan. 176p. 1993. 17.95 (*0-312-09762-X*) St Martin.

Cameroon. Mark W. DeLancey & Peter J. Schraeder. (World Bibliographical Ser.: No. 63). 202p. 1986. lib. bdg. 55.00 (*1-85109-006-1*) ABC-CLIO.

***Cameroon.** Jasmin Saidi & AACRAO-AID Project Staff. LC 95-15776. (OIES Country Guide Ser.). 1995. write for info. (*0-929851-43-9*) Am Assn Coll Registrars.

Cameroon. Loreto Todd. (Varieties of English Around the World Text Ser.: Vol. T1). (Illus.). 180p. (Orig.). 1982. pap. 44.00 (*3-87276-261-3*); audio 51.00 (*0-318-41845-2*) Benjamins North Am.

Cameroon & Chad in Historical & Contemporary Settings. Ed. by Mario Azevedo. LC 88-27652. (African Studies: Vol. 10). (Illus.). 212p. 1989. lib. bdg. 89.95 (*0-88946-191-0*) E Mellen.

Cameroon & Its National Character. Ed. by Mario Azevedo. LC 84-80033. (Illus.). 105p. (Orig.). 1984. pap. text ed. 8.50 (*0-317-04155-X*) Educ Awareness.

Cameroon Business Forecaster. Ed. by Lewis B. Sckolnick. 70p. (Orig.). (C). 1994. pap. 675.00 (*1-57205-400-X*) Rector Pr.

***Cameroon Business Intelligence Handbook.** (Illus.). 70p. (Orig.). 1994. pap. 295.00 (*0-7605-1096-2*) Rector Pr.

***Cameroon Business Risk Outlook.** 70p. (Orig.). 1994. pap. 495.00 (*0-7605-1413-5*) Rector Pr.

Cameroon, CAR, Chad: Business Risk Overview. Ed. by Lewis B. Sckolnick. 125p. (Orig.). (C). 1994. pap. text ed. 495.00 (*1-57205-530-8*) Rector Pr.

Cameroon Federation: Political Integration in a Fragmentary Society. Willard R. Johnson. 1970. 65.00 (*0-691-03081-2*) Princeton U Pr.

Cameroon in Pictures. Ed. by Lerner Publications, Department of Geography Staff. (Visual Geography Ser.). (Illus.). 64p. (YA). (gr. 5 up). 1989. lib. bdg. 18.95 (*0-8225-1857-0*, Lerner Publctns) Lerner Group.

***Cameroon Tax Law.** 150p. (C). 1994. pap. 295.00 (*0-7605-0092-4*) Rector Pr.

Cameroon with Egbert. Dervla Murphy. (Illus.). 282p. 1991. 21.95 (*0-87951-415-9*) Overlook Pr.

Cameroon with Egbert. Dervla Murphy. (Illus.). 282p. 1992. pap. 13.95 (*0-87951-476-0*) Overlook Pr.

Cameroons. Albert F. Calvert. 1976. lib. bdg. 59.95 (*0-8490-1564-2*) Gordon Pr.

Camfield No. 113: Walking to Wonderland. Barbara Cartland. 176p. (Orig.). 1993. pap. 3.99 (*0-515-11021-3*) Jove Pubns.

Camfield No. 114: Terror from the Throne. Barbara Cartland. 176p. (Orig.). 1993. pap. 3.99 (*0-515-11046-9*) Jove Pubns.

Camfield No. 116: Peaks of Ecstasy. Barbara Cartland. 176p. (Orig.). 1993. pap. 3.99 (*0-515-11085-X*) Jove Pubns.

Camfield No. 117: Luck Logan Finds Love. Barbara Cartland. 176p. (Orig.). 1993. pap. 3.99 (*0-515-11106-6*) Jove Pubns.

Camfield No. 118: The Angel & the Rake. Barbara Cartland. 176p. (Orig.). 1993. pap. 3.99 (*0-515-11122-8*) Jove Pubns.

Camfield No. 119: The Queen of Hearts. Barbara Cartland. 176p. (Orig.). 1993. pap. 3.99 (*0-515-11139-2*) Jove Pubns.

Camfield No. 120: The Wicked Widow. Barbara Cartland. 176p. (Orig.). 1993. pap. 3.99 (*0-515-11169-4*) Jove Pubns.

Camfield No. 122: Love at the Ritz. Barbara Cartland. 1993. pap. 3.99 (*0-515-11219-4*) Jove Pubns.

Camfield No. 125: This Is Love. Barbara Cartland. 176p. (Orig.). 1994. pap. 3.99 (*0-515-11286-0*) Jove Pubns.

***Camfield No. 137: The Incomparable.** Barbara Cartland. (Camfield Ser.: No. 137). 176p. (Orig.). 1995. pap. text ed. 3.99 (*0-515-11531-2*) Jove Pubns.

***Camfield No. 138: The Innocent Imposter.** Barbara Cartland. 176p. (Orig.). 1995. pap. text ed. 3.99 (*0-515-11554-1*) Jove Pubns.

***Camfield No. 140: A Magical Moment.** Barbara Cartland. 176p. (Orig.). 1995. pap. text ed. 3.99 (*0-515-11594-0*) Jove Pubns.

Cami & Other Familiar Friends. Della Dockery. (Illus.). 20p. (J). (ps). 1987. pap. 2.95 (*0-943487-05-6*) Sevgo Pr.

Camila. Madeleine L'Engle. Tr. by Pedro Barbadillo. 197p. (SPA.). (YA). (gr. 9-12). 1992. pap. write for info. (*84-204-4555-X*) Santillana.

Camilla. Fanny Burney. Ed. by Edward A. Bloom & Lillian D. Bloom. (World's Classics Paperback Ser.). 1983. pap. 10.95 (*0-19-281662-4*) OUP.

Camilla. Madeleine L'Engle. (Young Love Romance Ser.). 288p. (YA). (gr. 7 up). 1982. pap. 3.99 (*0-440-91171-0*, LFL) Dell.

***Camilla.** Madeleine L'Engle. 1995. 17.25 (*0-8446-6833-8*) Peter Smith.

Camilla: A Novella. Dorothea Schlegel. Ed. by Ruth Richardson. Tr. by Edwina Lawler. LC 89-13623. (Schlegel Translations Ser.: Vol. 2). 96p. 1990. lib. bdg. 49.95 (*0-88946-367-0*) E Mellen.

Camilla: C. H. Wedgwood, 1901-1955 - A Life. C. Carr-Gregg & D. Wetherell. 242p. 1990. pap. 24.95 (*0-86840-387-3*, Pub. by New South Wales Univ Pr AT) Intl Spec Bk.

***Camilla: The King's Mistress: A Love Story.** Caroline Graham. LC 94-24235. (Illus.). 256p. 1994. 19.95 (*0-8092-3407-6*) Contemp Bks.

***Camilla's Conscience.** Sandra Heath. (Regency Romance Ser.). 224p. (Orig.). 1995. pap. 3.99 (*0-451-18259-6*, Sig) NAL-Dutton.

Camilla's New Hairdo. Tricia Tusa. (Illus.). 32p. (J). (ps-3). 1991. 14.95 (*0-374-31021-1*) FS&G.

***Camilla's New Hairdo.** Tricia Tusa. (Illus.). 32p. (J). (ps-3). 1994. pap. text ed. 4.95 (*0-374-41040-2*, Sunburst Bks) FS&G.

Camille & Other Plays. Incl. Camille. Alexandre Dumas, fils. (*0-318-53310-3*); Peculiar Position. Augustin Scribe. 1957. (*0-318-53311-1*); Glass of Water. Augustin Scribe. 1957. (*0-318-53312-X*); Scrap of Paper. Victorien Sardou. 1957. (*0-318-53313-8*); Olympe's Marriage. Emile Augier. 1957. (*0-318-53314-6*); (Mermaid Dramabook Ser.). 306p. (Orig.). 1957. Set pap. 10.95 (*0-8090-0706-1*) Hill & Wang.

Camille & the Sunflowers. Laurence Anholt. (Illus.). 32p. (J). (ps-2). 1994. 13.95 (*0-8120-6409-7*) Barron.

Camille Claudel. Reine-Marie Paris. LC 88-1759. (Illus.). 114p. 1988. Dist. by NE U Pr. pap. 24.95 (*0-940979-04-7*) Natl Museum Women.

Camille Claudel: Une Femme. Anne Delbee. Tr. by Carol Cosman. LC 92-11176. (Illus.). 320p. 1992. 20.00 (*1-56279-026-9*) Mercury Hse Inc.

Camille Pissaro at Crystal Palace. Nicholas Reed. 1993. pap. 29.95 (*0-9515258-2-4*, Pub. by Lilburne Pr UK) St Mut.

Camille Pissarro. Joachim Pissarro. LC 93-12280. 1993. 75.00 (*0-8109-3724-7*) Abrams.

Camille Pissarro. Joachim Pissarro. LC 92-15547. (Rizzoli Art Ser.). (Illus.). 24p. 1992. 7.95 (*0-8478-1582-X*) Rizzoli Intl.

Camille Pissarro. Richard Thomson. (Illus.). 128p. (C). 1990. 30.00 (*0-941533-90-5*) New Amsterdam Bks.

***Camille Pissarro & His Family.** Anne Thorold & Kristen Erickson. (Illus.). 80p. 1995. 19.95 (*1-85444-032-2*, 0322, Pub. by Ashmolean Mus UK) A Schwartz & Co.

Camille Saint-Saens: His Life & Art. Watson Lyle. 210p. 1990. reprint ed. lib. bdg. 69.00 (*0-7812-9083-X*) Rprt Serv.

Camille Silvy: River Scene, France. Mark Haworth-Booth. LC 91-44136. (Getty Museum Studies on Art). (Illus.). 121p. 1992. pap. 15.95 (*0-89236-205-7*) J P Getty Trust.

Camille St. Saens & the French Solo Concerto from 1850-1920. Michael Stegemann. Tr. by Ann C. Sherwin. LC 90-40053. 1991. 21.95 (*0-931340-35-7*, Amadeus Pr) Timber.

Camillo Renato: Opere, Documenti E Testimonianze. Ed. by Antonio Rotondo. LC 72-3454. (Corpus Reformatorum Italicorum & Biblioteca Ser.). (Illus.). 353p. (ITA & LAT.). 1968. 25.00 (*0-87580-034-3*) N Ill U Pr.

Camilo Jose Cela. D. W. McPheeters. LC 74-75876. (Twayne's World Authors Ser.). 1969. lib. bdg. 17.95 (*0-8057-2204-1*) Irvington.

Caminamos Por una Senda Marcada: We Travel an Appointed Way. A. W. Tozer. (SPA.). 3.95 (*84-7645-364-7*, 223513, Pub. by Edit Clie SP) TSELF.

Caminando Con Dios: Walking with God. Perez de Emde. (SPA.). 4.95 (*84-7228-812-9*, 220130, Pub. by Edit Clie SP) TSELF.

***Caminemos Con Jesus: Toward a U. S. Hispanic Theology of Accompaniment.** Roberto S. Goizueta. 196p. (Orig.). 1995. pap. 16.95 (*1-57075-034-3*) Orbis Bks.

Camino: Su Guia a Paso II de Legalizacion. Thomas Esparza, Jr. (Illus.). 80p. (Orig.). 1990. reprint ed. pap. text ed. 6.95 (*1-879817-04-7*) Star Light Pr.

Camino a la Oracion Ferviente. A. W. Pink & Tell. 200p. 1994. 8.00 (*0-939125-68-4*) Evangelical Lit.

Camino-Abundancia Juan Jose (Path-Success Juan Jose), No. 1. (Illus.). (SPA.). Date not set. 0.39 (*0-685-74907-X*, 496101) Editorial Unilit.

Camino-Abundancia Juan Jose (Path-Success Juan Jose), No. 2. (Illus.). (SPA.). Date not set. 0.39 (*0-685-74908-8*, 496102) Editorial Unilit.

Camino-Abundancia Juan Jose (Path-Success Juan Jose), No. 3. (Illus.). (SPA.). Date not set. 0.39 (*0-685-74909-6*, 496103) Editorial Unilit.

Camino-Abundancia Juan Jose (Path-Success Juan Jose), No. 4. (Illus.). (SPA.). Date not set. 0.39 (*0-945792-08-5*, 496104) Editorial Unilit.

Camino-Abundancia Juan Jose (Path-Success Juan Jose), No. 5. (Illus.). (SPA.). Date not set. 0.39 (*0-945792-09-3*, 496105) Editorial Unilit.

Camino-Abundancia Juan Jose (Path-Success Juan Jose), No. 6. (Illus.). (SPA.). Date not set. 0.39 (*0-945792-10-7*, 496106) Editorial Unilit.

Camino-Abundancia Juan Jose (Path-Success Juan Jose), No. 7. (Illus.). (SPA.). Date not set. 0.39 (*0-945792-11-5*, 496107) Editorial Unilit.

***Camino Biblico.** John A. Hash. (Illus.). 403p. (Orig.). 1993. pap. 8.95 (*1-879595-01-X*) Bible Path Minist.

Camino de Amelia. Linda J. Altman. Tr. by Daniel Santacruz. (Illus.). 32p. (SPA.). (J). (gr. k-5). 1994. 14.95 (*1-880000-07-5*); pap. 5.95 (*1-880000-10-5*) Lee & Low Bks.

Camino De Jesus: Jesus People Maturity Manual. David Wilkerson. (SPA.). 3.25 (*84-7228-230-9*, 220131, Pub. by Edit Clie SP) TSELF.

Camino de la Rosacruz En Nuestra Epoca. Jan Van Rijckenborgh. 70p. (SPA.). 1986. pap. 2.00 (*84-87055-00-1*) Rosycross Pr.

Camino De la Salvacion: The Way of Salvation. Gordon Girod. (SPA.). 4.95 (*84-7228-104-3*, 220134, Pub. by Edit Clie SP) TSELF.

Camino De la Vida: The Way to Life. J. E. Davis. (SPA.). 4.95 (*84-7645-041-9*, 223099, Pub. by Edit Clie SP) TSELF.

Camino De la Vida Eterna: The Hearth of the Gospel. A. T. Pierson. (SPA.). 4.95 (*84-7228-978-8*, 223054, Pub. by Edit Clie SP) TSELF.

Camino de Occidente: Introduccion a las Humanidades. Hector O. Ciarlo. LC 82-7003. 258p. (Orig.). (SPA.). (C). 1984. pap. 5.00 (*0-8477-3504-4*) U of PR Pr.

Camino de Perfeccion. Teresa de Jesus. Ed. by Maria J. Mancho Duque. (Nueva Austral Ser.: Vol. 246). (SPA.). 1991. pap. text ed. 24.95x (*84-239-7246-1*) Elliots Bks.

***Camino de Santiago.** I. G. Bango Torviro. (Illus.). 368p. (SPA.). 1993. 295.00x (*84-239-5294-0*) Elliots Bks.

Camino del Calvario (Calvary Road) Roy Hession. (SPA.). 1993. 3.50 (*958-9149-11-1*, 494028) Editorial Unilit.

Camino Hacia Dios. Dwight L. Moody. Orig. Title: The Way to God. 128p. (SPA.). 1983. pap. 3.99 (*0-8254-1490-3*) Kregel.

Camino Hacia el Amor. rev. ed. Donald A. Dohr. LC 81-71328. Orig. Title: Beginning Your Marriage. 128p. 1982. pap. 4.25 (*0-915388-14-6*, 152, Buckley Pubns) ACTA Pubns.

Camino Hacia el Cielo: Heaven & How to Get There. D. L. Moody. (SPA.). 3.95 (*84-7228-945-1*, 223019, Pub. by Edit Clie SP) TSELF.

Camino Hacia el Lugar Santisimo: The Way to the Holiest. F. B. Meyer. (SPA.). 6.95 (*84-7645-261-6*, 223319, Pub. by Edit Clie SP) TSELF.

Camino Real Activity Book: Spanish Settlers in the Southwest. Walter D. Yoder. (Illus.). 48p. (Orig.). (J). (gr. 3-9). 1994. pap. 7.95 (*0-86534-218-0*) Sunstone Pr.

Camino Real de Tierra Adentro. Comp. by Gabriella G. Palmer. (Cultural Resources Ser.: No. 11). (Illus.). 200p. (Orig.). 1992. 8.00 (*1-878178-12-1*) Bureau of Land Mgmt NM.

Camino (The Road) A Guide to Phase II with Forms. Thomas Esparza, Jr. 80p. (Orig.). 1990. reprint ed. lib. bdg. 19.95 (*1-879817-03-9*) Star Light Pr.

Caminos Por Que Debe Andar Cristiano: Roads a Christian Must Travel. Merrill C. Tenney. (SPA.). 3.95 (*84-7228-773-4*, 220135, Pub. by Edit Clie SP) TSELF.

Camiones. Harry McNaught. (Spanish Translations Picturebacks Ser.). (Illus.). 32p. (SPA.). (J). (ps-3). 1993. 2.25 (*0-394-85220-6*) Random Bks Yng Read.

Camiones (Trucks) J. Cooper. (Spanish Language Books, Set 5: Maquinas de Viaje (Traveling Machines)). (J). 1991. 8.95 (*0-86592-509-7*) Rourke Enter.

***Camisa English Spoken - S. Garcia.** 3rd ed. Lauro Olmo. 234p. 1986. pap. 9.95 (*0-7859-5184-9*) Fr & Eur.

CAMM Program: Creating a Mature Marriage. Ann M. Ruben. 162p. (C). 1980. 29.95 (*0-9608400-0-1*) Women Are Wonderful.

Cammy Takes a Bow. Karen S. Dean. (J). (gr. 3-7). 1988. pap. 2.50 (*0-380-75400-2*, Camelot) Avon.

Camomile Lawn. Mary Wesley. 224p. 1990. pap. 11.00 (*0-14-012392-X*, Penguin Bks) Viking Penguin.

Camoniana Californiana: Commemorating the Quadricentennial of the Death of Luis Vaz de Camoes. Ed. by Maria D. Belchior & Enrique Martinez-Lopez. LC 85-82255. 266p. (Orig.). (ENG & POR.). 1985. pap. 20.00 (*0-942208-21-8*) Bandanna Bks.

Camouflage. Otto. (J). Date not set. 14.00 (*0-06-023342-7*, Festival); lib. bdg. 13.89 (*0-06-023343-5*, Festival) HarpC Child Bks.

Camouflage: Concealing & Disguising Troops, Weapons, & Field Installations. 1986. lib. bdg. 250.00 (*0-8490-3588-0*) Gordon Pr.

Camouflage: A Soviet View Pts. 1 & 2: Operational Camouflage of the Troops & Camouflage of Actions by Ground Force Subunits. V. A. Matsulenko & A. A. Beketov. LC 88-600452. (Soviet Military Thought Ser.: No. 22). (Illus.). 295p. (Orig.). 1989. pap. 12.00 (*0-16-002258-4*, S/N 008-070-006) USGPO.

Camouflage & Mimicry. Denis Owen. LC 82-2566. (Phoenix Ser.). (Illus.). 160p. (C). 1982. pap. text ed. 12.50 (*0-226-64188-0*) U Ch Pr.

Camourade: Selected Poems of Paul Laraque. Tr. by Rosemary Manno. LC 87-71704. 116p. 1988. pap. 9.95 (*0-915306-71-9*) Curbstone.

***Camp: North of 55.** Carole O. Cole. (Illus.). 128p. (Orig.). 1995. pap. 16.95 (*0-945767-02-1*) Write Place.

***Camp: The Lie that Tells the Truth.** Core. Date not set. per. 14.95 (*0-85965-044-8*, Pub. by Plexus Pub UK) InBook.

Camp Adventure. Mary E. Fearnehough. LC 92-59948. 108p. (J). (gr. 4-8). 1993. pap. 5.95 (*1-55523-576-X*) Winston-Derek.

Camp & Battle with Washington Artillery. W. M. Owen. 36.50 (*0-8488-1120-8*) Amereon Ltd.

Camp & Community: Manzanar & the Owens Valley. Ed. by Jessie A. Garrett & Ronald C. Larson. 1977. pap. 7.95 (*0-930046-00-5*) CSUF Oral Hist.

***Camp & Cottage Log.** NorthWord Press, Inc. Staff. (Illus.). 128p. 1995. write for info. (*1-55971-459-X*) NorthWord.

Camp & Field Life of the Fifth New York Volunteer Infantry. Alfred Davenport. 485p. 1989. reprint ed. 32.50 (*0-942211-77-4*) Olde Soldier Bks.

Camp & Prison Journal. Griffin Frost. LC 94-96080. (Illus.). 325p. 1994. reprint ed. 32.00 (*0-9628936-5-X*) Pr Camp Pope.

Camp & Trail. S. E. White. (Illus.). 280p. 1987. reprint ed. 25.00 (*0-935632-53-0*) Wolfe Pub Co.

Camp & Trail Cooking Techniques: A Treasury of Skills & Recipes for All Outdoor Chefs. Jim Capossela. (Illus.). 320p. (Orig.). 1994. kivar 20.00 (*0-88150-282-0*) Countryman.

Camp & Trail Methods. E. Kreps. (Illus.). 273p. pap. 4.00 (*0-936622-01-6*) A R Harding Pub.

Camp Beale's Springs & the Hualpai Indians. Dennis G. Casebier. LC 79-92835. (Illus.). 240p. (Orig.). 1980. 18.50 (*0-914224-08-5*) Tales Mojave Rd.

Camp Big Paw. Doug Cushman. LC 89-26867. (I Can Read Bk.). (Illus.). 64p. (J). (gr. k-3). 1990. lib. bdg. 14.89 (*0-06-021368-X*) HarpC Child Bks.

Camp Big Paw. Doug Cushman. LC 89-26867. (Trophy I Can Read Bk.). (Illus.). 64p. (J). (gr. k-3). 1993. pap. 3.50 (*0-06-444166-0*, Trophy) HarpC Child Bks.

An Asterisk (*) at the beginning of an entry indicates that the title is appearing in BIP for the first time.

An Asterisk (*) at the beginning of an entry indicates that the title is appearing in BIP for the first time.

1013

Campaign of Trafalgar, 2 vols. in 1. Julian S. Corbett. LC 70-154131. (Illus.). reprint ed. 44.50 (0-404-09234-9) AMS Pr.

***Campaign of 1776: The Road to Trenton.** Gregory T. Edgar. 422p. (Orig.). 1995. pap. text ed. 30.00 (0-7884-0185-8) Heritage Bk.

Campaign of 1812 in Russia. Carl Von Clausewitz. write for info. (0-9628715-7-5) Blue Crane Bks.

***Campaign of 1812 in Russia.** Carl Von Clausewitz. Date not set. write for info. (0-9628715-8-3) Blue Crane Bks.

Campaign of 1812 in Russia. Carl Von Clausewitz. 288p. 1992. 37.50 (1-85367-114-2, 5480) Stackpole.

***Campaign of 1812 in Russia.** Carl Von Clausewitz. (Illus.). 272p. 1995. reprint ed. pap. 13.95 (0-306-80650-9) Da Capo.

***Campaign of 1866 in Germany.** Prussian General Staff. (European War Ser.: No. 2). (Illus.). 672p. 1994. write for info. (0-89839-201-2) Battery Pr.

Campaign on New Britain. Frank Hough & John Crown. (Elite Unit Ser.: No. 31). (Illus.). 264p. reprint ed. 32.50 (0-89839-172-5) Battery Pr.

Campaign Organization. Xandra Kayden. 192p. (C). 1978. pap. text ed. 13.00 (0-669-01782-5) Heath.

Campaign Ribbons. John R. Simmons. (Illus.). 188p. (Orig.). 1990. pap. 14.95 (0-89745-132-5) Sunflower U Pr.

Campaign Savvy-School Support. 2nd rev. ed. Jean W. Huyler. LC 81-9397. (Illus.). 57p. (C). 1981. pap. 5.95 (0-941554-02-3, LB2825.H87) EdCom.

Campaign Seventy Eight: A Comprehensive Political Handbook to the Vote Returns & Candidates. Warren J. Mitofsky & Martin Plissner. 1980. 51.95 (0-405-12517-8) Ayer.

Campaign Seventy-Six. Ed. by Martin Plissner et al. LC 77-78784. (Individual Publications). (Illus.). 1977. lib. bdg. 51.95 (0-405-10515-0) Ayer.

Campaign Seventy-Two: The Managers Speak. Ernest R. May & Janet Fraser. LC 73-85182. 224p. 1973. 25.00 (0-674-09141-8); pap. 13.50 (0-674-09143-4) HUP.

Campaign Sketches of the War with Mexico. William S. Henry. LC 72-9448. (Far Western Frontier Ser.). (Illus.). 354p. 1973. reprint ed. 24.95 (0-405-04976-5) Ayer.

Campaign That Won America: The Story of Yorktown. Burke Davis. (Illus.). 319p. 1979. reprint ed. pap. 4.95 (0-915992-01-9) Eastern Acorn.

Campaign to Valley Forge. John F. Reed. 1980. reprint ed. 12.95 (0-913150-42-8) Pioneer Pr.

Campaign, 1932: An Analysis. Roy V. Peel. (History - United States Ser.). 242p. 1993. reprint ed. lib. bdg. 79.00 (0-7812-4926-0) Rprt Serv.

Campaigning. large type ed. Jim Miller. (Linford Western Library). 304p. (Orig.). 1988. pap. 11.95 (0-7089-6487-7, Linford) Ulverscroft.

Campaigning Against the Sioux. A. N. Judd. (Illus.). 1906. 15.00 (0-914074-05-9, J M C & Co) Amereon Ltd.

Campaigning for Office: A Woman Runs. Jewel Lansing. LC 91-52962. 200p. 1991. pap. 9.95 (0-88247-887-7) R & E Pubs.

Campaigning for the Massachusetts Senate: Electioneering Outside the Political Limelight. Jerome M. Mileur & George T. Sulzner. LC 73-85898. 208p. 1974. pap. 14.95 (0-87023-140-5) U of Mass Pr.

Campaigning in America: A History of Election Practices. Robert J. Dinkin. LC 88-29627. 243p. 1989. text ed. 55.00 (0-313-26167-9, DCE/, Greenwood Pr) Greenwood.

Campaigning in the Philippines. Karl I. Faust. LC 72-111740. (American Imperialism: Viewpoints of United States Foreign Policy, 1898-1941 Ser.). 1970. reprint ed. 25.95 (0-405-02017-1) Ayer.

Campaigning on the Oxus & the Fall of Khiva. J. A. MacGahan. LC 78-115561. (Russia Observed Ser.). 1970. reprint ed. 28.95 (0-405-03047-9) Ayer.

Campaigning with Crook. Charles King. LC 64-11332. (Western Frontier Library: Vol. 25). (Illus.). 192p. 1983. pap. 9.95 (0-8061-1377-4) U of Okla Pr.

Campaigning with Custer & the Nineteenth Kansas Volunteer Cavalry on the Washita Campaign, 1868-69. David L. Spotts. LC 87-30204. (Illus.). xii, 215p. 1988. reprint ed. pap. 6.95 (0-8032-9174-4) U of Nebr Pr.

Campaigning with Grant. Horace Porter. 632p. 1986. pap. 12.95 (0-306-80277-5) Da Capo.

***Campaigning with King: Charles King, Chronicler of the Old Army.** Don Russell. Ed. by Paul L. Hedren. LC 90-12335. (Illus.). 241p. 1991. reprint ed. pap. 68.70 (0-7837-8912-2, 2049623) Bks Demand.

Campaigning with the Fighting Ninth. C. M. Wrench. 642p. (C). 1990. 135.00 (0-9589855-0-2, Pub. by Boolarong Pubns AT) St Mut.

Campaigning with the Roundheads. William G. Gavin. 1989. 50.00 (0-89029-531-X) Morningside Bkshop.

Campaigns Against Corporal Punishment: Prisoners, Sailors, Women, & Children in Antebellum America. Myra C. Glenn. LC 84-8476. (American Social History Ser.). 221p. 1984. 74.50 (0-87395-812-8); pap. 24.95 (0-87395-813-6) State U NY Pr.

Campaigns Against Hunger. Elvin C. Stakman et al. LC 67-20882. (Illus.). 344p. reprint ed. pap. 98.10 (0-7837-1728-8, 2057258) Bks Demand.

Campaigns Against Western Defense: NATO's Adversaries & Critics. Clive Rose. LC 84-18067. 320p. 1985. text ed. 32.50 (0-312-11469-9) St Martin.

Campaigns & Conscience: The Ethics of Political Journalism. Philip Seib. LC 93-37023. (Series in Political Communication). 176p. 1994. text ed. 49.95 (0-275-94623-1, Praeger Pubs); pap. text ed. 16.95 (0-275-94624-X, Praeger Pubs) Greenwood.

Campaigns & Elections. George Sullivan. (Ballots & Bandwagons Ser.). (Illus.). 128p. (J). (gr. 5 up). 1991. lib. bdg. 12.95 (0-382-24315-3); pap. 7.95 (0-382-24321-8) Silver Burdett Pr.

Campaigns & Elections: A Reader in Modern American Politics. Larry J. Sabato. (C). 1988. pap. text ed. 32.00 (0-673-39912-5) HarpCollege.

***Campaigns & Elections American Style.** Ed. by James A. Thurber & Candice J. Nelson. LC 94-32609. (C). 1995. text ed. 65.00 (0-8133-1966-8); pap. text ed. 19.95 (0-8133-1967-6) Westview.

Campaigns, Congress & the Courts: The Making of Federal Campaign Finance Laws. Robert E. Mutch. LC 87-30874. 237p. 1988. text ed. 49.95 (0-275-92784-9, C2784, Praeger Pubs) Greenwood.

Campaigns in Kentucky & Tennessee, 1862-1864. (Papers of the Military Historical Society of Massachusetts: Vol. 7). (Illus.). 1990. reprint ed. 40.00 (1-56837-011-3) Broadfoot.

Campaigns in Palestine from Alexander the Great. I. Abrahams. (British Academy, London, Schweich Lectures on Biblical Archaeology Series, 1930). 1972. reprint ed. pap. 19.00 (0-8115-1264-9) Periodicals Srv.

Campaigns in the News: Mass Media & Congressional Elections. Ed. by Jan P. Vermeer. LC 87-8423. (Contributions in Political Science Ser.: No. 187). 240p. 1987. text ed. 49.95 (0-313-25187-8, VCN/, Greenwood Pr) Greenwood.

***Campaigns in the West: American Autobiography.** John DuBois. 120p. 1995. lib. bdg. 69.00 (0-7812-8506-2) Rprt Serv.

Campaigns in Virginia, Maryland, Pennsylvania, 1862-1863. (Papers of the Military Historical Society of Massachusetts: Vol. 3). 509p. 1989. reprint ed. 40.00 (1-56837-007-5) Broadfoot.

Campaigns in Virginia 1861-1862. Ed. by Theodore F. Wright. (Papers of the Military Historical Society of Massachusetts: Vol. 1). 369p. 1989. reprint ed. 40.00 (1-56837-005-9) Broadfoot.

Campaigns of a Non-Combatant. George Townsend. LC 82-10757. (Collector's Library of the Civil War). (gr. 7 up). 1983. 26.60 (0-8094-4250-7) Time-Life.

Campaigns of a Non-Combatant. George A. Townsend. LC 73-125720. (American Journalists Ser.). 1971. reprint ed. 20.95 (0-405-01703-0) Ayer.

Campaigns of Alexander. Arriam. Tr. by Aubrey De Selincourt. 430p. 1986. 16.95 (0-88029-079-X) Dorset Pr.

Campaigns of Alexander. Arrian. Tr. by Aubrey De Selincourt. (Classics Ser.). 1976. pap. 10.95 (0-14-044253-7, Penguin Classics) Viking Penguin.

Campaigns of Napoleon: The Mind & Method of History's Greatest Soldier. David G. Chandler. 1182p. 1973. text ed. 75.00 (0-02-523660-1) Macmillan.

Campaigns of Stuart's Cavalry. H. B. McClellan. 1993. 9.98 (1-55521-971-3) Bk Sales Inc.

Campaigns of the Civil War, 16 vols., Set. (Illus.). 1990. reprint ed. 300.00 (0-916107-76-0) Broadfoot.

Campaigns of the Seventeenth Maine. Edwin B. Houghton. 333p. 1985. reprint ed. 30.00 (0-942211-51-0) Olde Soldier Bks.

Campaigns of Walker's Texas Division. Joseph P. Blessington. LC 93-43423. (Illus.). 332p. 1994. 29.95 (1-880510-04-9) State House Pr.

Campaigns of Walker's Texas Division. limited ed. Joseph P. Blessington. LC 93-43423. (Illus.). 332p. 1994. 60.00 (1-880510-05-7) State House Pr.

Campamentos y Retiros Cristianos - Christian Camps & Retreats. Hugo Redmon. 128p. (Orig.). (SPA.). 1992. pap. 3.85 (0-311-11051-7) Casa Bautista.

Campanas Al Viento. Guillermo De Bango. 384p. (Orig.). 1992. pap. 18.00 (0-9631736-1-8) Ediciones Cambio.

Campanerito Azul: Poemas para Ninos. Vizcarrondo Carmelinc. LC 84-28124. (Ninos y Letras Ser.). (Illus.). 72p. (C). 1985. pap. 5.00 (0-8477-3528-1) U of PR Pr.

Campanian Coinages, Four Eighty-Five to Three Eighty-Five B. C. K. Rutter. 200p. 1980. 60.00 (0-85224-345-6, Pub. by Edinburgh U Pr UK) Col U Pr.

Campanulas. H. Clifford Crook. LC 76-46559. (Illus.). 1977. reprint ed. 12.50 (0-913728-18-7) Theophrastus.

Campanus of Novara & Medieval Planetary Theory: "Theorica planetarum" Ed. by Francis S. Benjamin, Jr. & G. J. Toomer. (Medieval Science Publications: No. 16). (Illus.). 508p. 1972. 45.00 (0-299-05960-X) U of Wis Pr.

Campaspe & Sappho & Phao. John Lyly. Ed. by George K. Hunter et al. LC 90-13563. (Revels Plays Ser.). (Illus.). 352p. 1992. text ed. 59.95 (0-7190-1550-2, Pub. by Manchester Univ Pr UK) St Martin.

Campbell. M. C. Pilcher. 444p. 1991. reprint ed. lib. bdg. 78.50 (0-8328-2043-1); reprint ed. pap. 68.50 (0-8328-2044-X) Higginson Bk Co.

Campbell: Earliest Campbell Families in Maine. L. A. Campbell. 77p. 1994. reprint ed. lib. bdg. 25.00 (0-8328-4179-X); reprint ed. pap. 15.00 (0-8328-4180-3) Higginson Bk Co.

Campbell: International Corporate Insolvency Law. Dennis Campbell. 1992. pap. 220.00 (0-406-00901-5) Butterworth Legal Pubs.

Campbell Chronicles: Samuel Campbell of Lancaster County, Pennsylvania, & His Descendants. Mary W. Burgess. LC 87-6311. (Borgo Family Histories Ser.: No. 3). (Illus.). 128p. Date not set. lib. bdg. write for info. (0-89370-378-8); pap. write for info. (0-89370-478-4) Borgo Pr.

Campbell Chronicles & Family Sketches. Ruth H. Early. LC 77-93960. (Illus.). 554p. 1978. reprint ed. 30.00 (0-8063-0798-6) Regional.

***Campbell Chronicles & Family Sketches: Embracing the History of Campbell County, Virginia 1782-1926.** Ruth H. Early. (Illus.). 578p. 1994. pap. 39.95 (0-614-00902-2, 1560) Clearfield Co.

Campbell Contacts in America, 1979-1985, 7 vols. Ed. by Frances Nelson & Sheila Hardy. 1986. lib. bdg. write for info. (0-318-60841-3) Borgo Pr.

Campbell Contacts in America, 1979-1985, Vol. 1. Ed. by Frances Nelson & Sheila Hardy. LC 85-642854. 1986. lib. bdg. 22.00x (0-8095-6900-0) Borgo Pr.

Campbell Contacts in America, 1979-1985, Vol. 2. Ed. by Frances Nelson & Sheila Hardy. LC 85-642854. 1986. lib. bdg. 22.00x (0-8095-6901-9) Borgo Pr.

Campbell Contacts in America, 1979-1985, Vol. 3. Ed. by Frances Nelson & Sheila Hardy. LC 85-642854. 1986. lib. bdg. 22.00x (0-8095-6902-7) Borgo Pr.

Campbell Contacts in America, 1979-1985, Vol. 4. Ed. by Frances Nelson & Sheila Hardy. LC 85-642854. 1986. lib. bdg. 22.00x (0-8095-6903-5) Borgo Pr.

Campbell Contacts in America, 1979-1985, Vol. 5. Ed. by Frances Nelson & Sheila Hardy. LC 85-642854. 1986. lib. bdg. 22.00x (0-8095-6904-3) Borgo Pr.

Campbell Contacts in America, 1979-1985, Vol. 6. Ed. by Frances Nelson & Sheila Hardy. LC 85-642854. 1986. lib. bdg. 22.00x (0-8095-6905-1) Borgo Pr.

Campbell Contacts in America, 1979-1985, Vol. 7. Ed. by Frances Nelson & Sheila Hardy. LC 85-642854. 1986. lib. bdg. 22.00x (0-8095-6906-X) Borgo Pr.

Campbell Contacts in America, 1979-1987, Vol. 8. Ed. by Frances Nelson & Sheila Hardy. 1986. lib. bdg. 22.00 (0-685-73969-4) Borgo Pr.

Campbell Contacts in America, 1979-1987, Vol. 8. Ed. by Frances Nelson & Sheila Hardy. 1987. Vol. 9, 1987. lib. bdg. 22.00x (0-8095-6946-9) Borgo Pr.

Campbell Contacts in America, 1979-1987, Vol. 9. Ed. by Frances Nelson & Sheila Hardy. 1986. lib. bdg. 22.00x (0-8095-6947-7) Borgo Pr.

***Campbell County: Virginia Publick Claims.** Janice L. Abercrombie & Richard Slatten. (Virginia Publick Claims Ser.). ix, 28p. 1991. pap. 5.00x (0-8095-8528-6) Borgo Pr.

Campbell County: Virginia Publick Claims. Janice L. Abercrombie & Richard Slatten. (Virginia Publick Claims Ser.). ix, 28p. (C). 1991. reprint ed. lib. bdg. 20.00 (0-8095-8310-0) Borgo Pr.

***Campbell County, Georgia Superior Court Deeds & Mortgages Grantee-Grantor Index 1829-1931.** Ed. by LaGroon Redmond. LC 94-60683. 1078p. 1994. text ed. 53.25 (1-883793-04-1) W H Wolfe.

***Campbell County, Virginia Deeds, 1782-1784.** T.L.C. Genealogy Staff. LC 91-65289. 52p. (Orig.). 1991. spiral bd., pap. 9.00 (1-886633-49-5) TLC Genealogy.

***Campbell County, Virginia Deeds, 1784-1790.** T.L.C. Genealogy Staff. LC 91-65289. 112p. (Orig.). 1991. spiral bd., pap. 14.00 (1-886633-50-9) TLC Genealogy.

***Campbell County, Virginia Deeds, 1790-1796.** T.L.C. Genealogy Staff. 141p. (Orig.). 1991. spiral bd., pap. 15.00 (1-886633-51-7) TLC Genealogy.

***Campbell County, Virginia Wills & Inventories, 1782-1847.** William L. Hopkins. 232p. 1989. lib. bdg. 57.00 (0-8095-8282-1); pap. 30.00 (0-8095-8529-4) Borgo Pr.

***Campbell County, Virginia Wills, 1782-1800.** T.L.C. Genealogy Staff. LC 91-75279. 129p. (Orig.). 1991. spiral bd., pap. write for info. (1-886633-52-5) TLC Genealogy.

Campbell Hollow Archaic Occupations. Ed. by C. Russell Stafford. LC 85-16682. (Kampsville Archeological Center Research Ser.: No. 4). (Illus.). 280p. (Orig.). 1985. pap. 9.95 (0-942118-21-9) Ctr Amer Arche.

***Campbell, Ken a Few Ways Through the Window.** Des. by Robert Burn. (Illus.). 1990. pap. 52.00 (0-905836-69-3, Pub. by Museum Modern Art UK) St Mut.

***Campbell, Ken a Few Ways Through the Window.** deluxe limited ed. Des. by Robert Burn. (Illus.). 1990. pap. 80.00 (0-614-03381-0, Pub. by Museum Modern Art UK) St Mut.

Campbell Machine Shorthand Dictionary. 2nd ed. Bill Campbell. 558p. (C). 1989. spiral bd. 29.95 (1-881069-00-1) Obsidian Pub.

***Campbell Soup Company: A Report on the Company's Environmental Policies & Practices.** (Illus.). 52p. (C). 1994. reprint ed. pap. text ed. 200.00x (0-7881-0935-9, Coun on Econ) Diane Pub.

Campbell-Stone Movement in Ontario: Christian Church (Disciples of Christ), Churches of Christ, Independent Christian Churches-Churches of Christ. Ed. by Claude E. Cox. LC 93-45602. (Illus.). 484p. 1994. 109.95 (0-7734-9421-9) E Mellen.

Campbellism: Its History & Heresies. Bob L. Ross. 1962. pap. 3.50 (1-56186-502-8) Pilgrim Pubns.

Campbellites, Cow-Bells, Rosary Beeds, & Snake-Handlers. Bob Ross. 1994. 3.95 (1-56186-522-2) Pilgrim Pubns.

Campbell's Best-Ever Recipes One Hundred Twenty-Fifth Anniversary Edition. Better Homes & Gardens Staff. 1994. 12.95 (0-696-20324-3) Meredith Bks.

Campbell's Cooking in Minutes. (Favorite All Time Recipes Ser.). (Illus.). 96p. 1993. 7.98 (1-56173-967-7, 2010305) Pubns Intl Ltd.

Campbell's Creative Cooking with Soup. Campbells Soup Company Staff. 1988. 10.99 (0-517-69881-1) Random Hse Value.

Campbell's Creative Cooking with Soup Cookbook. Consumer Guide Editors. 1985. 12.95 (0-517-45250-2) Random Hse Value.

Campbell's Deliciously Easy Recipes. (Favorite All Time Recipes Ser.). (Illus.). 96p. 1993. 7.98 (1-56173-891-3, 2014700); spiral bd. 3.50 (1-56173-544-2, 2014701) Pubns Intl Ltd.

Campbell's Elementary Quiz Book, No. 2. John P. Campbell. (Elementary School Ser.). 247p. (Orig.). 1993. pap. 12.95 (0-944322-15-8) Patricks Pr.

Campbell's Elementary School Quiz Book, Bk. II. rev. ed. John P. Campbell. (Elementary School Ser.). 161p. 1993. pap. 12.95 (0-944322-00-X) Patricks Pr.

Campbell's English-Santali Dictionary. Ed. by R. M. MacPhail. 1984. 40.00 (0-8364-1137-4, Pub. by Mukhopadhyaya II) S Asia.

Campbell's Fabulous One-Dish Meals. (Favorite All Time Recipes Ser.). (Illus.). 96p. 1993. 7.98 (0-7853-0078-3, 2019401); spiral bd. 3.50 (1-56173-858-1, 2019401) Pubns Intl Ltd.

Campbell's Great American Cookbook: A Culinary Treasury of More Than 500 Best-Loved Recipes from Colonial Times to the Present. Campbells Soup Company Staff. (Illus.). 352p. 1989. 12.99 (0-517-69241-4) Random Hse Value.

Campbell's High School-College Quiz Book: The Quiz Contestant's Vade Mecum. rev. ed. John P. Campbell. LC 84-19012. 524p. (YA). (gr. 9 up). 1984. reprint ed. pap. 16.95 (0-9609412-3-1) Patricks Pr.

Campbell's List: A Directory of Selected Lawyers Since 1879. rev. ed. Ed. by John A. Campbell, Jr. LC 34-11733. 320p. 1989. pap. 10.00 (0-933089-00-7) Campbells List.

Campbell's Mastering the Myths Quiz Book. John P. Campbell. 400p. (Orig.). 1995. pap. 16.95 (0-944322-20-4) Patricks Pr.

Campbell's Microwave Cookbook. Campbells Soup Company Staff. 1988. 9.99 (0-517-65522-5) Random Hse Value.

Campbell's Middle School Quiz Book, No. 2. John P. Campbell. 332p. (Orig.). (J). (gr. 5-8). 1986. pap. 14.95 (0-9609412-6-6) Patricks Pr.

Campbell's Middle School Quiz Book, No. 3. John P. Campbell. (Middle School Ser.). 280p. (Orig.). 1990. pap. 14.95 (0-944322-05-0) Patricks Pr.

Campbell's Middle School Quiz Book No. 1. John P. Campbell. (Middle School Ser.). 326p. (Orig.). (J). (gr. 5-8). 1985. pap. 14.95 (0-9609412-4-X) Patricks Pr.

Campbell's One Hundred Seventy-Five Lightning Rounds. John P. Campbell. (Lightning Rounds Ser.). 185p. (Orig.). 1992. pap. 14.95 (0-944322-08-5) Patricks Pr.

Campbell's One Hundred Seventy-Six Lightning Rounds. John P. Campbell. (Lightning Rounds Ser.). 182p. (Orig.). 1994. pap. 14.95 (0-944322-18-2) Patricks Pr.

Campbell's Operative Orthopedics. 8th ed. A. H. Crenshaw. 3870p. 1991. 450.00 (0-8016-1096-6) Mosby Yr Bk.

***Campbell's Potpourri, Vol. V.** John P. Campbell. (Quiz Bowl Questions Ser.: Vol. V). 280p. 1995. pap. 14.95 (0-944322-21-2) Patricks Pr.

Campbell's Potpourri II of Quiz Bowl Questions. rev. ed. John P. Campbell. LC 84-61238. (Campbell's Potpourri Ser.). 354p. (YA). (gr. 9 up). 1991. pap. 14.95 (0-9609412-2-3) Patricks Pr.

Campbell's Potpourri III of Quiz Bowl Questions. John P. Campbell. (Campbell's Potpourri Ser.). 288p. (Orig.). (J). (gr. 7-12). 1985. pap. 14.95 (0-9609412-5-8) Patricks Pr.

Campbell's Potpourri IV of Quiz Bowl Questions. John P. Campbell. (Campbell's Potpourri Ser.). 280p. (Orig.). 1990. pap. 14.95 (0-944322-03-4) Patricks Pr.

Campbell's Quick & Easy Recipes. Patricia Teberg. 1994. pap. 9.99 (0-517-10337-0) Random Hse Value.

Campbell's Simply Delicious Recipes. Patricia Teberg. 1992. pap. 9.99 (0-517-08757-X) Random Hse Value.

Campbell's Two Hundred Eleven Lightning Rounds. John P. Campbell. (Lightning Rounds Ser.). 216p. (Orig.). 1992. pap. 14.95 (0-944322-09-3) Patricks Pr.

Campbell's Two Hundred Ten Lightning Rounds. John P. Campbell. (Lightning Rounds Ser.). 215p. 1991. pap. 14.95 (0-944322-07-7) Patricks Pr.

Campbell's Two Hundred Thirteen Lightning Rounds. John P. Campbell. (Lightning Rounds Ser.). 218p. (Orig.). 1994. pap. 14.95 (0-944322-19-0) Patricks Pr.

Campbell's Two-Hundred Twelve Lightning Rounds. John P. Campbell. (Lightning Rounds Ser.). 217p. (Orig.). 1993. pap. 14.95 (0-944322-14-X) Patricks Pr.

Campbell's Two Thousand Four Quiz Questions. John P. Campbell. (Two Thousand Ser.). 232p. (Orig.). 1993. pap. 14.95 (0-944322-13-1) Patricks Pr.

Campbell's Two Thousand One Quiz Questions. John P. Campbell. (Two Thousand Ser.). 232p. (Orig.). 1990. pap. 14.95 (0-944322-01-8) Patricks Pr.

Campbell's Two Thousand Three Quiz Questions. John P. Campbell. (Two Thousand Ser.). 260p. (Orig.). 1992. pap. 14.95 (0-944322-10-7) Patricks Pr.

Campbell's Two Thousand Two Quiz Questions. John P. Campbell. (Two Thousand Ser.). 253p. (Orig.). 1991. pap. 14.95 (0-944322-06-9) Patricks Pr.

***Campbell's Urology: Review & Assessment.** Donald L. Lamm & Angelo S. Paola. 304p. 1995. pap. text ed. 49.00 (0-7216-5158-5) Saunders.

Camper Critters. Bob Reese. (Yellowstone Ser.). (Illus.). (J). (gr. k-6). 1986. 7.95 (0-89868-169-3); pap. 2.95 (0-89868-170-7) ARO Pub.

Camper of the Week. Amy Schwartz. LC 90-23033. (Illus.). 32p. (J). (gr. k-2). 1991. 15.95 (0-531-05942-1); 15.99 (0-531-08542-2) Orchard Bks Watts.

***Camper's & Backpacker's Bible.** Tom Huggler. LC 94-24426. (Illus.). 1995. 12.95 (0-385-47194-7) Doubleday.

Camper's Companion: The Pack-along Guide for Better Outdoor Trips. 2nd ed. Rick Greenspan & Hal Kahn. 464p. 1994. pap. 12.95 (0-935701-72-9) Foghorn Pr.

Camper's Guide to British Columbia Parks, Lakes, & Forests, Vol. 1: Vancouver, Lower Mainland, Cariboo-Shuswap-Okanagan. Lillian B. Morava. 152p. 1992. pap. 16.95 (0-87201-208-5) Gulf Pub.

Camper's Guide to British Columbia Parks, Lakes, & Forests, Vol. 2: Kootenay & Northern British Columbia. Lillian B. Morava. 152p. 1992. pap. 16.95 (0-87201-215-8) Gulf Pub.

Camper's Guide to California, Northern California, Vol. 1. (Illus.). 176p. 1988. pap. 12.95 (0-87201-152-6) Gulf Pub.

Camper's Guide to California, Southern California, Vol. 2. 176p. 1988. pap. 12.95 (0-87201-153-4) Gulf Pub.

An Asterisk (*) at the beginning of an entry indicates that the title is appearing in BIP for the first time.

An Asterisk (*) at the beginning of an entry indicates that the title is appearing in BIP for the first time.

Campus Pursuit: How to Make the Most of the College Visit & Interview. 5th ed. G. Gary Ripple. 32p. 1993. 4.00 (0-945981-78-3) Octameron Assocs.

Campus Security & Law Enforcement. 2nd ed. John W. Powell et al. LC 93-21319. 272p. 1994. 44.95 (0-7506-9441-6) Buttrwrth-Heinemann.

Campus Security Guard I. Jack Rudman. (Career Examination Ser.: C-565). 1994. pap. 23.95 (0-8373-0565-9) Nat Learn.

Campus Security Guard II. Jack Rudman. (Career Examination Ser.: C-566). 1994. pap. 27.95 (0-8373-0566-7) Nat Learn.

Campus Security Guard III. Jack Rudman. (Career Examination Ser.: C-567). 1994. pap. 129.95 (0-8373-0567-5) Nat Learn.

Campus Security Officer. Jack Rudman. (Career Examination Ser.: C-2260). 1994. pap. 23.95 (0-8373-2260-X) Nat Learn.

Campus Security Officer I. Jack Rudman. (Career Examination Ser.: C-2261). 1994. pap. 23.95 (0-8373-2261-8) Nat Learn.

Campus Security Officer II. Jack Rudman. (Career Examination Ser.: C-1700). 1994. pap. 27.95 (0-8373-1700-2) Nat Learn.

Campus Security Officer Trainee. Jack Rudman. (Career Examination Ser.: C-2081). 1994. pap. 23.95 (0-8373-2081-X) Nat Learn.

Campus Security Specialist. Jack Rudman. (Career Examination Ser.: C-1701). 1994. 45.95 (0-685-03518-2); pap. 29.95 (0-8373-1701-0) Nat Learn.

Campus Site: A Prehistoric Site at Fairbanks, Alaska. Charles M. Mobley. LC 90-29894. (Illus.). xx, 104p. 1991. 30.00 (0-912006-48-X); pap. 20.00 (0-912006-52-8) U of Alaska Pr.

Campus Strategies for Libraries & Electronic Information. Ed. by Caroline R. Arms. (Illus.). 404p. 1990. text ed. 34.95 (1-55558-036-X, EY-C185E-DP, Digital DEC) Buttrwrth-Heinemann.

Campus Survival Cookbook, No. 1. Joelyn S. Gilchrist & Jacqueline Wood. LC 72-100. (Illus.). 160p. 1977. pap. 9.25 (0-688-05030-1, Quill) Morrow.

Campus Survival Cookbook: No. 2. Jacqueline Wood & Joelyn S. Gilchrist. LC 81-38387. 1981. pap. 9.45 (0-688-00568-3, Quill) Morrow.

Campus Vacations Directory. 4th rev. ed. Ed. by Joan Beers. 45p. 1989. pap. 10.75 (0-317-93127-X) Campus Vacations.

Campus Violence: Kinds, Causes, & Cures. Ed. by Jeffrey W. Pollard. LC 93-35657. (Journal of College Student Psychotherapy). (Illus.). 314p. 1994. lib. bdg. 49.95 (1-56024-568-9) Haworth Pr.

Campus Visits & College Interviews. Zola D. Schneider. 130p. 1987. 9.95 (0-87447-260-1) College Bd.

***Campus Wars: Multiculturalism & the Politics of Difference.** LC 94-29253. (C). 1994. pap. text ed. 17.95 (0-8133-2481-5) Westview.

***Campus Wars: Multiculturalism & the Politics of Difference.** Ed. by John Arthur & Amy Shapiro. LC 94-29253. (C). 1994. text ed. 55.00 (0-8133-2480-7) Westview.

Campus Wars: The Peace Movement at American State Universities in the Vietnam Era. Kenneth J. Heineman. 1994. pap. 18.95 (0-8147-3512-6) NYU Pr.

Campus Wars: The Peace Movement in American State Universities in the Vietnam Era. Kenneth Heineman. 368p. (C). 1993. text ed. 50.00 (0-8147-3490-1) NYU Pr.

Campuses Respond to Violent Tragedy. Dorothy Siegel. LC 94-21315. (American Council on Education-Oryx Press Series on Higher Education). 1994. 34.95 (0-89774-825-5) Oryx Pr.

Campustown in the Throes of the Counterculture. Mark Graubard. 420p. 1974. pap. 6.95 (0-915858-00-2) Campus Scope.

Campustown U. S. A. at Midcentury. Mark Graubard. 308p. 1971. pap. 5.95 (0-915858-01-0) Campus Scope.

Campylobacter: Progress in Research. Ed. by D. G. Newell. (Illus.). 400p. 1982. lib. bdg. 121.00 (0-85200-455-9) Kluwer Ac.

Campylobacter Infection in Man & Animals. Ed. by Jean-Paul Butzler. 256p. 1984. 119.00 (0-8493-5446-3, QR201, CRC Reprint) Franklin.

Campylobacter Jejuni: Current Status & Future Trends. Ed. by Irving Nachamkin et al. (Illus.). 312p. 1992. text ed. 79.00 (1-55581-042-X) Am Soc Microbio.

Campylobacter Pylori. Marshall. 1991. 65.00 (0-86542-108-0) Mosby Yr Bk.

Camus. rev. ed. Germaine Bree. LC 72-178591. 289p. reprint ed. pap. 82.40 (0-8357-7554-2, 2052318) Bks Demand.

Camus: "The Stranger" Patrick McCarthy. (Landmarks of World Literature Ser.). 128p. 1988. pap. 10.95 (0-521-33851-4) Cambridge U Pr.

Camus: A Critical Examination. David Sprintzen. 368p. 1991. pap. 22.95 (0-87722-827-2) Temple U Pr.

Camus' Imperial Vision. Anthony Rizzuto. LC 81-1370. 160p. 1981. 15.00 (0-8093-1002-3) S Ill U Pr.

Camus's L'Etranger: Fifty Years On. Adele King. 1992. text ed. 45.00 (0-312-06858-1) St Martin.

Camus's Recit, La Chute: A Rewriting Through Dante's Commedia. Jacqueline G. Roston. (Studies in the Humanities: Literature-Politics-Society: Vol. 5). 188p. 1985. text ed. 26.75 (0-8204-0269-9) P Lang Pubs.

Camwood on the Leaves & Before the Blackout: Plays. Wole Soyinka. LC 73-92792. Date not set. 8.95 (0-89388-150-3); pap. 5.95 (0-89388-151-1) Okpaku Communications.

Camworth Cameo. large type ed. Delia Foster. (Linford Romance Library). 272p. 1989. pap. 11.95 (0-7089-6646-2, Linford) Ulverscroft.

Can a Believer Be Lost? 2nd ed. Ralph V. Reynolds. 118p. (C). 1986. pap. 5.50 (1-877917-00-1) Alpha Bible Pubns.

Can a Busy Christian Develop Her Spiritual Life? Answers to Questions Women Ask About... Kay Arthur. 1994. pap. 8.99 (1-55661-518-3) Bethany Hse.

Can a Christian Be a Nationalist? Isabelo F. Magalit. 35p. (Orig.). 1993. pap. 3.75 (971-10-0517-4, Pub. by New Day Pub PH) Cellar.

Can a Christian Have a Demon. Don Basham. 128p. 1991. pap. 5.95 (0-89228-015-8) Impact Christian.

Can a Gluten-Free Diet Help You...How? Lloyd Rosenvold. 224p. (Orig.). 1990. pap. 9.95 (0-87983-538-9) Keats.

Can a Seed Grow Here? My Intimate Story of the Struggle to Become a Medical Doctor, to Minister to Those in Need of Assistance While Overcoming the Ghetto & the Resistance of the Establishment. Wilbert Williams, Jr. 160p. (Orig.). Date not set. pap. text ed. write for info. (0-9627257-6-5) Aye Aye Pr.

***Can a Woman Minister, or Teach God's Word to Men?** Izora Taylor. 1995. 9.95 (0-8062-5355-X) Carlton.

Can a Woman Over Forty? Lynne Norris. LC 79-12587. 1979. 10.95 (0-933380-41-0); pap. 5.95 (0-933380-47-X) Olive Pr Pubns.

***Can-Am History.** Pete Lyons. (Illus.). 256p. 1995. 39.95 (0-7603-0017-8) Motorbooks Intl.

Can America Afford to Grow Old? Paying for Social Security. Henry J. Aaron et al. 144p. 1989. pap. 9.95 (0-8157-0043-1) Brookings.

***Can America Be Saved?** Franklin W. Dunbar. Date not set. pap. 7.95 (0-9643937-8-6) Rutledge Bks.

Can America Compete? Robert Z. Lawrence. LC 84-9401. 156p. 1984. 28.95 (0-8157-5176-1); pap. 10.95 (0-8157-5175-3) Brookings.

Can America Last? From the Wilderness to World-Power. Ed. by William G. Fitzgerald. LC 73-13131. (Foreign Travelers in America, 1810-1935 Ser.). 324p. 1974. reprint ed. 26.95 (0-405-05453-X) Ayer.

Can America Remain Committed? U. S. Security Horizons in the 1990s. Ed. by David G. Haglund. LC 92-26325. 306p. (C). 1992. pap. text ed. 54.50 (0-8133-1691-X) Westview.

***Can an Educated Workforce Be a "Business Necessity"?** Douglas S. McDowell. 33p. 1991. pap. 10.00 (0-614-06155-5, 2025-PP-4040) EPF.

Can & Bottle Bills. rev. ed. 195p. 1981. pap. 12.00 (0-318-11818-1) Stanford Enviro.

Can Animals & Machines Be Persons? A Dialogue. Justin Leiber. LC 85-21888. 88p. (C). 1985. lib. bdg. 21.50 (0-87220-003-5); pap. 3.95 (0-87220-002-7) Hackett Pub.

Can Anyone Help my Child? Therapies & Treatment for Attention Deficit & Other Learning & Behavioral Disorders in Children, Adolescents, & Adults. rev. ed. Guy D. Ogan. 186p. (Orig.). 1991. pap. 9.95 (0-9631880-1-1) Faith Pub & Media.

Car Birds Get Lost? And Other Questions about Animals. Jack Myers. LC 90-85911. (Illus.). 64p. (J). (gr. 1-5). 1991. 12.95 (1-878093-32-0) Boyds Mills Pr.

Can Birds Get Lost? And Other Questions about Animals. Jack Myers. (Illus.). 64p. (J). (gr. 1-7). 1994. 7.95 (1-56397-401-0) Boyds Mills Pr.

Can California Be Competitive & Caring? Ed. by Daniel J. Mitchell & Jane Wildhorn. LC 89-11126. (Monograph & Research Ser.: No. 49). 389p. 1989. pap. 17.00 (0-89215-152-8) U Cal LA Indus Rel.

Can-Can. (Illus.). 1981. 8.95 (0-88188-065-5, 00312065); pap. 35.00 (0-88188-009-4, 00312066) H Leonard.

Can Capitalism Survive? Benjamin A. Rogge. LC 78-17378. 1979. 12.00 (0-913966-46-0) Liberty Fund.

Can Christ Become Good News Again? John B. Cobb, Jr. 200p. (Orig.). 1991. pap. 15.99 (0-8272-0456-6) Chalice Pr.

Can Christians Be Educated? Morton T. Kelsey. Ed. by Harold W. Burgess. LC 77-3691. 154p. (Orig.). 1977. pap. 11.95 (0-89135-008-X) Religious Educ.

Can Christians Have Fun? Steve Wamberg & Annie Wamberg. (Active Bible Curriculum Ser.). (Illus.). 48p. 1992. pap. 9.99 (1-55945-134-3) Group Pub.

Can Civil Wars Be Avoided? Electoral & Constitutional Models for Ethnically Divided Countries. David Chapman. 151p. (C). 1991. pap. 50.00 (0-948826-26-6, Pub. by Inst Social Invent UK) St Mut.

***Can Congress Be Fixed (& Is It Broken)? Five Essays on Congressional Reform.** Ed. by Peter Robinson. LC 95-5853. (Publication Ser.: Vol. 428). 1995. write for info. (0-8179-9362-2) Hoover Inst Pr.

***Can Cuba Survive? An Interview with Fidel Castro.** Beatriz Pages. 105p. 1993. pap. 9.95 (1-875284-58-3, Pub. by Ocean Pr AT) Talman.

Can Dead People Speak to Us? Kingdom Quotes Staff. Date not set. pap. write for info. (0-930179-42-0) Johns Enter.

Can Delinquency Be Measured? Sophia Robison. LC 75-129307. (Criminology, Law Enforcement, & Social Problems Ser.: No. 129). (Illus.). 312p. 1972. reprint ed. 24.00 (0-87585-129-0) Patterson Smith.

***Can Democracy Fly in Space? The Challenge of Revitalizing the U. S. Space Program.** W. D. Kay. LC 95-13917. 1995. text ed. write for info. (0-275-95254-1, Praeger Pubs) Greenwood.

***Can Do.** Bob Reese. (Ten Word Book Ser.). (Illus.). (J). (gr. k-3). 1994. lib. bdg. 9.25 (0-89868-247-9, Read Res) ARO Pub.

***Can Do.** Bob Reese. (Ten Word Book Ser.). (Illus.). (J). (gr. k-3). 1994. pap. 3.50 (0-89868-248-7, Read Res) ARO Pub.

***Can Do! The Story of the Seabees.** William B. Huie. 1994. reprint ed. lib. bdg. 29.95x (1-56849-534-X) Buccaneer Bks.

Can Do Art. Steven Snyder. (Illus.). 200p. 1981. pap. 19.95 (0-9603530-1-1) US Screen.

Can Do DOS. Neil Rubenking. 1993. pap. 12.95 (1-56276-147-1) Ziff-Davis.

Can Do, Jenny Archer. Ellen Conford. (J). (gr. 4-7). 1993. mass mkt. 3.95 (0-316-15372-9) Little.

Can-Do Manager: How to Get Your Employees to Take Risks, Take Action, & Get Things Done. Tess Kirby. LC 89-45453. 192p. 1989. 19.95 (0-8144-5887-4) AMACOM.

Can Do (Said Sue) A Rich Life Helping the Poor. Sue Sadow. LC 90-83463. (Illus.). 266p. (Orig.). 1991. pap. 9.95 (0-9616108-5-9) Beaumont Bks.

Can Do Thoughts in a "Can't Do" World: Ideas of Leaders. Bob E. Couch. (Illus.). 160p. (Orig.). 1993. pap. 13.95 (1-882555-00-7) Town Creek Pubns.

Can Do Thoughts in a "Can't Do" World, Vol. 2: More Ideas of Leaders. Bob E. Couch. LC 93-94097. (Illus.). 160p. (Orig.). 1994. pap. 14.95 (1-882555-07-4) Town Creek Pubns.

Can Do Windows. Neil Rubenking. 1993. pap. 5.95 (1-56276-163-3) Ziff-Davis.

***Can Dogs Fly? Fido's Book of Pop-Up Transportation Surprises.** Martin Chatterton. LC 94-49613. (Illus.). (J). 1995. 9.95 (0-8037-1776-8) Dial Bks Young.

Can Dogs Talk?, Vol. 1. Mary Shields. (Happy Dog Trilogy from Alaska Ser.). (Illus.). 32p. (Orig.). (J). (ps-3). 1991. audio 13.00 (0-9618348-4-6); pap. 10.00 (0-9618348-1-1) Pyrola Pub.

Can Drowning Be Fun? A Nonsense Book. Stella Snead. (Illus.). 64p. (Orig.). 1992. pap. write for info. (1-878635-01-8) Pont La Vue Pr.

Can Elephants Drink Through Their Noses? The Strange Things People Say about Animals at the Zoo. Deborah Dennard. LC 92-9956. (Question of Science Book Ser.). (Illus.). (J). (gr. k-3). 1992. 19.95 (0-87614-720-1, Carolrhoda) Lerner Group.

***Can Employee Involvement Be Mandated?** Daniel V. Yager & Scott C. Ehrlich. 58p. 1992. pap. 10.00 (0-614-06152-0, 2037-PP-4040) EPF.

Can Ethics Be Christian? James M. Gustafson. LC 74-11622. 1977. reprint ed. pap. text ed. 13.95 (0-226-31102-3, P734) U Ch Pr.

Can Ethics Be Taught? Perspectives, Challenges & Approaches at Harvard Business School. Thomas R. Piper et al. 1993. text ed. 19.95 (0-07-103417-X) McGraw.

Can Ethics Be Taught? Perspectives, Challenges, & Approaches at the Harvard Business School. Thomas R. Piper et al. LC 92-27077. 208p. 1993. 19.95 (0-87584-400-6) Harvard Busn.

***Can Europe Work? Germany & the Reconstruction of Postcommunist Societies.** Ed. by Stephen Hanson & Willfried Spohn. (Jackson School Publications in International Studies). 1995. pap. 17.50 (0-295-97461-3) U of Wash Pr.

***Can Europe Work? Germany & the Reconstruction of Postcommunist Societies.** Ed. by Stephen Hanson & Willfried Spohn. (Jackson School Publications in International Studies). 248p. (C). 1995. 35.00 (0-295-97460-5) U of Wash Pr.

***Can Fallen Pastors Be Restored? The Churches Response to Sexual Misconduct.** Armstrong. 1995. pap. 9.99 (0-8024-1412-5) Moody.

***Can Families Survive in Pagan America.** Samuel Dresner. LC 94-72828. 350p. 1995. pap. 15.99 (1-56384-080-4) Huntington Hse.

Can God see Apprenticeship of Faith

Can Gorbachev's Reforms Succeed? Victoria Bonnell et al. 136p. (Orig.). (C). 1990. pap. 12.95 (0-9622629-1-9) UCB CFSEES.

Can Governments Learn? Comparative Perspectives on Evaluation & Organizational Learning. Ed. by Frans L. Leeuw et al. 270p. (C). 1994. text ed. 34.95 (1-56000-130-5) Transaction Pubs.

Can Grande's Castle. Amy Lowell. LC 71-131771. 232p. 1918. reprint ed. 29.00 (0-403-00658-9) Scholarly.

Can Have Diet: The Easy Guide to Informed Food Choices. 3rd rev. ed. Patricia M. Stein & Norma J. Winn. 96p. 1988. pap. 5.50 (0-9620965-0-4) Nutrit Coun-Educ.

Can Have Diet & More! The Easy Guide to Informed Exercise & Food Choices. 4th ed. Patricia M. Stein & Norma J. Winn. 80p. 1990. pap. 5.95 (0-318-50014-0) Nutrit Coun-Educ.

Can Health Care Costs Be Controlled? A Study in Production & Development in Health Care. Ingemar Stahl. (Illus.). 164p. (Orig.). 1986. pap. text ed. 50.00x (91-7504-048-4) Coronet Bks.

Can Hitler Invade America? A Myth Exposed. John T. Flynn. 1984. lib. bdg. 79.95 (0-87700-593-1) Revisionist Pr.

Can Homophobia Be Cured? Wrestling with Questions That Challenge the Church. Bruce Hilton. 144p. (Orig.). 1992. pap. 10.95 (0-687-04631-9) Abingdon.

Can I Afford Retirement? An Easy-to-Understand Source & Planning Book. J. G. Krane. 225p. 1993. 19.95 (0-9633581-0-3) New Leaf Comms.

Can I Afford Time for Friendship? Answers to Questions Women Ask about Friends. Stormie Omartian. 1994. pap. 8.99 (1-55661-517-5) Bethany Hse.

Can I Be a Christian Without Being Weird? Kevin Johnson. LC 92-15804. (YA). 1992. pap. 6.99 (1-55661-281-8) Bethany Hse.

Can I Be Good? Livingston Taylor & Maggie Taylor. LC 92-23193. (Illus.). (J). 1993. 14.95 (0-15-200436-X) HarBrace.

Can I Call after Midnight. Leonard VanderZee. 76p. (Orig.). (YA). (gr. 10-12). 1989. teacher ed, pap. text ed. 17.95 (0-930265-70-X) CRC Pubns.

Can I Control My Changing Emotion? Answers to Question Women Ask about Their Moods. Annie Chapman. 1994. pap. 8.99 (1-55661-519-1) Bethany Hse.

***Can I Go Home Now?** Ann Orsini. 237p. (Orig.). 1994. pap. 14.95 (0-9642267-0-7) Phoenix Sparks.

Can I Have a Cookie. Bill Keane. (Illus.). 1985. mass mkt. 3.99 (0-449-12972-1) Fawcett.

Can I Have a Stegosaurus, Mom? Can I!? Please? Lois G. Grambling. LC 93-39178. (Illus.). 32p. (J). (gr. k-3). 1995. lib. bdg. 14.95 (0-8167-3386-4) BrdgeWater.

Can I Have Five Minutes of Your Time? A No-Nonsense, Fun Approach to Sales. Hal Becker & Florence Mustric. 158p. (Orig.). 1993. pap. 12.95 (0-9619590-7-X) Oakhill Pr.

Can I Help? Helping the Hearing Impaired in Emergency Situations. S. Harold Collins. (Beginning Sign Language Ser.). (Illus.). 32p. (Orig.). 1993. pap. text ed. 2.95 (0-931993-57-1, GP-057) Garlic Pr OR.

Can I Just Do It Till I Need Glasses? And Other Lies Grown-Ups Told You. Ludlow Porch. LC 85-61976. 219p. 1985. 12.95 (0-931948-81-9) Peachtree Pubs.

Can I Keep Him. Lynn Joseph. (J). (gr. 4 up). 1992. pap. 4.99 (0-14-054527-1) Puffin Bks.

Can I Keep Him? Steven Kellogg. LC 72-142453. (Pied Piper Bks.). (Illus.). (J). (ps-3). 1971. 13.99 (0-8037-0988-9); lib. bdg. 12.89 (0-8037-0989-7) Dial Bks Young.

Can I Keep Him. Kellog Steven. (J). 1992. pap. 4.99 (0-14-054867-X, Puffin) Puffin Bks.

Can I Look Now? Recovery from Multiple Personality Disorder. Rachel Downing. 36p. 1992. pap. 5.00 (0-9633913-0-5) Educ Rec Comm.

Can I Make a Difference? Christian Family Life Today. Albert S. Rossi. LC 89-38001. 128p. (Orig.). 1990. pap. 5.95 (0-8091-3125-0) Paulist Pr.

Can I Play Too? Physical Education for Physically Disabled Children in Mainstream Schools. Sheila E. Jowsey. 112p. 1992. pap. 25.00 (1-85346-217-9, Pub. by D Fulton UK) Taylor & Francis.

Can I Play You My Song? The Compositions & Invented Notations of Children. Rena Upitis. LC 92-4674. 187p. 1992. pap. text ed. 18.00 (0-435-08705-3, 08705) Heinemann.

***Can I Really Believe?** Howard Vos. (World Classic Reference Library). 188p. (Orig.). 1995. pap. 7.99 (0-529-10254-4) World Bible.

Can I Really Sell? Jeff T. Pignato. 72p. (Orig.). 1987. pap. 6.95 (0-936029-07-2) Western Bk Journ.

Can I Speak for You Brother? A One-Man Show Depicting Black Leaders. Philip E. Walker. LC 83-50187. (Illus.). 80p. 1983. pap. 6.50 (0-918270-13-8) That New Pub.

Can I Talk to You? Puedo Charlar Contigo? Elizabeth Skoglund. (SPA.). 4.95 (84-7228-511-1, 220730, Pub. by Edit Clie SP) TSELF.

Can Ice Cream & Oranges Prevent the Common Cold & Influenza? Stanley J. Goodwin. (Illus.). 1979. pap. 2.40 (0-686-24961-5) Northland Pubns WA.

Can Information Technology Result in Benevolent Bureaucracies? Proceedings of the IFIP TC9-WG 9.2 Working Conference, Namur, Belgium 3-6 Jan., 1985. Ed. by L. Ynstrom et al. 240p. 1986. 48.75 (0-444-87873-4, North Holland) Elsevier.

Can Irrigated Agriculture Survive the Groundwater Crisis? Ed. by Joseph B. Summers & Darla G. Leslie. 140p. (Orig.). 1991. pap. 36.00 (0-9618257-7-4) US Comm Irrigation.

Can Israel Survive in a Hostile World? David A. Lewis. LC 93-87251. 352p. (Orig.). 1994. pap. 11.95 (0-89221-260-8) New Leaf.

Can It Be? A Different Problem Resource Book. William L. Swart. 36p. 1990. pap. text ed. 6.00 (1-883547-02-4) Tricon Pub.

***Can It Happen Again? Chronicles of the Holocaust.** Ed. by Jack Spencer & Roselle K. Chartock. LC 95-12348. 1995. 9.98 (1-884822-26-6) Blck Dog & Leventhal.

Can "IT" Happen Again? Essays on Instability & Finance. Hyman P. Minsky. LC 82-10789. 320p. 1984. pap. text ed. 25.95 (0-87332-305-X) M E Sharpe.

Can Kids Save the Earth? Melvin Berger. (Ranger Rick Science Spectacular Ser.). 16p. (J). (gr. 2-4). 1994. pap. 14.95 (1-56784-209-7) Newbridge Comms.

Can Kill You But Can't Eat You. Dawn Steel. 1994. mass mkt. 5.99 (0-671-73833-X) PB.

Can Language Be Planned: Sociolinguistic Theory & Practice for Developing Nations. Ed. by Joan Rubin & Bjorn H. Jernudd. LC 70-129618. (Illus.). 368p. 1971. pap. text ed. 6.95 (0-8248-0358-2) UH Pr.

Can Literacy Lead to Development: A Case Study in Literacy, Adult Education, & Economic Development in India. Uwe Gustafsson. LC 91-65025. (Publications in Linguistics: No. 97). 172p. (Orig.). 1991. pap. 12.00 (0-88312-804-7); fiche 12.00 (0-88312-938-8) Summer Instit Ling.

***Can Mainline Denominations Make a Comeback?** Tony Campolo. 224p. 1995. pap. 15.00 (0-8170-1234-6) Judson.

Can Man Be Civilized? Harry E. Barnes. 1971. 250.00 (0-87700-028-X) Revisionist Pr.

***Can Man Live Without God.** Ravi Zacharias. 1994. 17.99 (0-8499-1173-7) Word Inc.

Can Mankind Survive? Morrison I. Swift. 1977. lib. bdg. 250.00 (0-8490-1565-0) Gordon Pr.

Can Meditation Be Done? Thomas Hora. (Discourses in Metapsychiatry Ser.). 33p. 1984. pap. 6.00 (0-913105-09-0) PAGL Pr.

Can Men & Women Be Just Friends? rev. ed. Andre Bustanoby. Orig. Title: Just Friends. 144p. 1993. pap. 7.99 (0-310-58891-X) Zondervan.

Can Men Become Gods? Spiros Zodhiates. 1992. pap. 4.99 (0-89957-494-7) AMG Pubs.

Can Modern War Be Just? James T. Johnson. LC 84-3523. 240p. 1984. 32.00 (0-300-03165-3) Yale U Pr.

C

An Asterisk (*) at the beginning of an entry indicates that the title is appearing in BIP for the first time.

C

An Asterisk (*) at the beginning of an entry indicates that the title is appearing in BIP for the first time.

Can You Imagine? Joseph Linn. (J). 1983. 5.95 (*0-8341-9273-X*, BCMB-519); ring bd. 0.75 (*0-685-68207-2*, MU-728); audio 12.98 (*0-685-68208-0*, TA-9045C) Lillenas.

Can You Imagine? Creative Drawing Adventures for the Jewish Holidays. Marji Gold-Vukson & Micheal Gold-Vukson. LC 91-42842. 48p. (J). (ps-5). 1991. pap. 3.95 (*0-929371-31-3*) Kar Ben.

Can You Jump Like a Frog? Illus. by Marc T. Brown. 8p. (J). (ps-00). 1989. 5.95 (*0-525-44463-7*, DCB) Dutton Child Bks.

Can You Know God's Will for Your Life? Charles R. Smith. 1979. pap. 1.50 (*0-88469-044-X*) BMH Bks.

***Can You Make a Living Doing That?** Brad Kearns. 200p. 1996. pap. 9.95 (*0-9634568-8-1*) Trimarket.

Can You Match This? Jokes about Unlikely Pairs. Rick Walton & Ann Walton. (Make Me Laugh! Joke Bks.). (Illus.). 32p. (J). (gr. 1-4). 1989. 11.95 (*0-8225-0973-3*, Lerner Publctns) Lerner Group.

Can You Match This? Jokes about Unlikely Pairs. Rick Walton & Ann Walton. (Make Me Laugh! Joke Bks.). (Illus.). 36p. (J). reprint ed. pap. 2.95 (*0-8225-9565-6*, Lerner Publctns) Lerner Group.

Can You Name That Team? A Guide to Professional Baseball, Football, Soccer, Hockey, & Basketball Teams & Leagues. David B. Biesel. LC 91-26356. 240p. 1991. 37.50 (*0-8108-2458-2*) Scarecrow.

Can You Play. Harriet Ziefert. LC 88-24025. (Pictureback Ser.). (Illus.). 24p. (Orig.). (J). (ps-2). 1989. pap. 2.25 (*0-394-82001-0*) Random Bks Yng Read.

***Can You Really Know Your Future?** Robert Lindsted. 100p. (Orig.). 1992. pap. 7.95 (*1-879366-32-0*) Hearthstone OK.

Can You Remember to Forget: And 32 Other Questions for Tomorrow's Leaders. James Moore. 1991. 8.95 (*0-687-04628-9*) Abingdon.

Can You Retire? D. Dixon. 1968. 48.00 (*0-08-012725-8*, Pub. by Pergamon Repr UK) Franklin.

Can You Say a Few Words? Joan Detz. 1991. pap. 10.95 (*0-312-05830-6*) St Martin.

Can You See Me? Shirley Greenway. LC 92-5215. (Animals Q & A Ser.). (Illus.). 32p. (J). (ps-2). 1992. lib. bdg. 11.00 (*0-8249-8575-3*, Ideals Child); pap. 3.95 (*0-8249-8560-5*, Ideals Child) Hambleton-Hill.

***Can You See Me Yet?** Findley. Date not set. per. 14.95 (*0-88922-119-7*, Pub. by Talonbooks CN) InBook.

C

Can You Solve These?, No. 1: Mathematical Problems to Test Your Thinking Powers. David Wells. (Illus.). 80p. 1985. pap. 6.95 (*0-906212-22-7*, Pub. by Tarquin UK) Parkwest Pubns.

Can You Solve These?, No. 2: Mathematical Problems to Test Your Thinking Powers. David Wells. (Illus.). 80p. (Orig.). (J). (gr. 5 up). 1985. pap. 6.95 (*0-906212-34-0*, Pub. by Tarquin UK) Parkwest Pubns.

Can You Solve These?, No. 3. David Wells. (Tarquin Can You Solve These Ser.). (Illus.). 56p. (Orig.). 1986. pap. 6.95 (*0-685-13308-7*, Pub. by Tarquin UK) Parkwest Pubns.

Can You Stand Forgiveness? Tom Cutting. Ed. by Sherry Jacks. LC 90-71174. 160p. 1990. write for info. (*0-9627096-0-3*) Whitehead TX.

Can You Stand to Be Blessed? T. D. Jakes. 196p. (Orig.). 1994. pap. 9.99 (*1-56043-801-0*) Destiny Image.

Can You Stand to Be Blessed? T. D. Jakes. 48p. (Orig.). 1994. student ed, pap. 6.99 (*1-56043-812-6*) Destiny Image.

Can You Sue Your Parents for Malpractice? Paula Danziger. 144p. (YA). (gr. 7 up). 1980. mass mkt. 3.99 (*0-440-91066-8*, LFL) Dell.

Can You Take It Like a Man: A Poetic Vision of Masculinity. H. Christian Green. Ed. by Julie A. Houser. (Illus.). 174p. Date not set. 19.95 (*0-9634943-0-9*) Truth Quest.

Can You Teach Me to Pick My Nose. Martyn N. Godfrey. 128p. (Orig.). 1990. pap. 3.50 (*0-380-75915-2*, Flare) Avon.

Can You Tell Me How What You Are Doing Now Is to Do Something Philosophical? Peter H. Barnett. pap. 5.00 (*0-915066-40-8*) Assembling Pr.

Can You Trust a Tomato in January. Vince Staten. 1994. pap. 10.00 (*0-671-88578-2*, Touchstone Bks) S&S Trade.

Can You Trust a Tomato in January? Everything You Wanted to Know - & a Few Things You Didn't - about Food in the Grocery Store. Vince Staten. 208p. 1993. 19.00 (*0-671-76941-3*) S&S Trade.

Can You Trust the Bible? Frances Hogan. 252p. 1991. pap. 8.99 (*0-89283-694-6*) Servant.

Can You Win? Orkin. (C). 1995. pap. text ed. write for info. (*0-7167-2155-4*) W H Freeman.

***Can Your Cat Do That? A Whimsical Aid to Expanding a Child's Imagination.** Galen K. Lillethorup. Ed. & Illus. by Kragh Lillethorup. LC 95-92189. 32p. (J). (ps). 1995. pap. 8.95 (*0-9646015-0-8*) Sibling Pr.

Can Your Child Read? Is He Hyperactive? rev. ed. William G. Crook. 1977. pap. 6.95 (*0-933478-01-1*) Prof Bks Future Health.

Can Your Faith Fail? Charles Capps. 1978. pap. 2.95 (*0-89274-105-8*) Harrison Hse.

Cana Roja. Eutimio Alonso. LC 80-65446. (Coleccion Polymita Ser.). 348p. (Orig.). (SPA.). 1982. pap. 14.95 (*0-89729-251-0*) Ediciones.

Canaan. Jose P. Aranha. Tr. by Mariano J. Lorente. 1977. lib. bdg. 59.95 (*0-8490-1566-9*) Gordon Pr.

Canaan: A Small New England Town During the American Revolutionary War. Harold W. Felton. LC 90-84951. (Illus.). 180p. (Orig.). 1990. pap. 10.95 (*0-9626184-0-3*, Bramble Bks) Bramble Co.

Canaan Valley & the Black Bear. 3rd ed. Ruth C. Allman. 1988. reprint ed. pap. 8.00 (*0-87012-220-7*) McClain.

Canaanite God Reshep. William J. Fullo. (Essays Ser.: No. 8). 1976. pap. 8.00 (*0-940490-98-6*) Am Orient Soc.

Canaanite Myth & Hebrew Epic: Essays in the History of the Religion of Israel. Frank M. Cross. LC 72-76564. 394p. 1973. 35.00 (*0-674-09175-2*) HUP.

Canaanite Myths & Legends. John C. Gibson. (Illus.). 208p. 1978. 39.95 (*0-567-02351-6*, Pub. by T & T Clark UK) Bks Intl VA.

***Canada.** (American Geographical Society Around the World Program Ser.). 1994. lib. bdg. 17.95 (*0-614-04850-8*) Am Geographical.

***Canada.** (American Geographical Society Around the World Program Ser.). 1994. pap. 9.95 (*0-614-04851-6*) Am Geographical.

Canada. Elizabeth Ayer. (World Partners Ser.). (Illus.). 64p. (YA). (gr. 7 up). 1990. lib. bdg. 17.27 (*0-86593-091-0*); lib. bdg. 12.95 (*0-685-36363-5*) Rourke Corp.

Canada. Donna Bailey. LC 91-21292. (Where We Live Ser.). (Illus.). 32p. (J). (gr. 1-4). 1992. lib. bdg. 19.97 (*0-8114-2568-1*); pap. 3.95 (*0-8114-7181-0*) Raintree Steck-V.

Canada. Lionel Bender. (People & Places Ser.). (Illus.). 48p. (J). (gr. 4-8). 1987. lib. bdg. 12.95 (*0-382-09508-1*) Silver Burdett Pr.

Canada. Ed. by George W. Brown. LC 71-134059. (Essay Index Reprint Ser.). 1977. 44.95 (*0-8369-2147-X*) Ayer.

Canada. Jean Bruchesi. (Merveilles de la France et du Monde Ser.). (Illus.). 190p. (FRE.). 1952. lib. bdg. 9.95 (*0-8288-3993-X*) Fr & Eur.

Canada. Elizabeth Duthie. 1994. 12.98 (*0-8317-1556-1*) Smithmark.

Canada. Harald R. Fabien & Karl Teuschl. (Windsor Destination Guides Ser.). (Illus.). 56p. 1992. pap. 12.95 (*1-874111-00-6*, Pub. by Windsor Bks UK) Seven Hills Bk.

Canada. David Flint. LC 92-43923. (On the Map Ser.). (Illus.). 32p. (J). (gr. 3-4). 1993. lib. bdg. 19.97 (*0-8114-2939-3*) Raintree Steck-V.

Canada. Ed. by Ernest Ingles. (World Bibliographical Ser.: No. 62). (Illus.). 350p. 1990. lib. bdg. 92.00 (*1-85109-005-3*, Pub. by Clio Pr UK) ABC-CLIO.

Canada. Kevin J. Law. (Let's Visit Places & Peoples of the World Ser.). (Illus.). (J). (gr. 5 up). 1988. 14.95 (*0-222-00912-8*) Chelsea Hse.

Canada. Kevin J. Law. (Places & Peoples of the World Ser.). (Illus.). 128p. (YA). (gr. 5 up). 1990. lib. bdg. 14. 95 (*0-7910-1101-1*) Chelsea Hse.

Canada. Pang Guek Cheng. LC 93-11018. (Cultures of the World Ser.). (J). (gr. 5 up). 1993. 21.95 (*1-85435-579-1*) Marshall Cavendish.

Canada. Lewis K. Parker. LC 93-42778. (Dropping in On Ser.). (J). 1994. write for info. (*1-55916-002-0*) Rourke Bk Co.

Canada. Louis Sabin. LC 84-40437. (Illus.). 32p. (J). (gr. 3-6). 1985. lib. bdg. 9.49 (*0-8167-0302-7*); pap. text ed. 2.95 (*0-8167-0303-5*) Troll Assocs.

Canada. Elma Schemenauer. LC 94-11943. (New True Bks.). (Illus.). 48p. (J). (gr. k-4). 1994. pap. 4.95 (*0-516-41065-2*) Childrens.

Canada. Elma Schemenaur. LC 94-11943. (New True Bks.). (Illus.). 48p. (J). (gr. k-4). 1994. lib. bdg. 12.90 (*0-516-01065-4*) Childrens.

Canada. J. Shepherd. LC 87-14626. (Enchantment of the World Ser.). (Illus.). 128p. (J). (gr. 5-9). 1987. lib. bdg. 20.55 (*0-516-02757-3*) Childrens.

Canada. Jane Sunday. LC 92-10767. (World in View Ser.). 96p. (J). 1992. lib. bdg. 24.26 (*0-8114-2455-3*) Raintree Steck-V.

Canada. Nelles Verlag. (Nelles Guides Ser.). 1993. pap. 14. 95 (*3-88618-394-7*, Pub. by Nelles Verlag GW) Seven Hills Bk.

Canada. Ed. by Mel Watkins & James Warren. (Handbooks to the Modern World Ser.). 512p. 1992. lib. bdg. 60.00 (*0-8160-1831-6*) Facts on File.

Canada. David K. Wright. LC 89-43197. (Children of the World Ser.). (Illus.). 64p. (J). (gr. 5-6). 1991. lib. bdg. 21. 26 (*0-8368-0256-X*) Gareth Stevens Inc.

Canada: A Story of Challenge. J. M. Careless. (Illus.). 449p. 1991. pap. 7.95 (*0-7736-7354-7*, Pub. by Stoddart Pubng CN) Genl Dist Srvs.

Canada: A Travel Survival Kit. 5th ed. Mark Lightbody & Tom Smallman. (Illus.). 936p. 1994. pap. 19.95 (*0-86442-216-4*) Lonely Planet.

Canada: An American Nation. John W. Dafoe. LC 71-110739. reprint ed. 20.00 (*0-404-00616-7*) AMS Pr.

Canada: An International Power. Andre Siegfried. Tr. by Doris Hemming. LC 72-4299. (World Affairs Ser.: National & International Viewpoints). 288p. 1972. reprint ed. 21.95 (*0-405-04590-5*) Ayer.

***Canada: Business Financing Handbook.** (Illus.). 70p. (Orig.). 1994. pap. 295.00 (*0-7605-1184-5*) Rector Pr.

Canada: Business Risk Overview. Ed. by Lewis B. Sckolnick. 125p. (Orig.). (C). 1994. pap. text ed. 495.00 (*1-57205-598-7*) Rector Pr.

***Canada: Commercial Law.** 300p. (Orig.). 1994. pap. 295.00 (*0-7605-1236-1*) Rector Pr.

Canada: Country Reporter. Lewis B. Sckolnick. (Illus.). 60p. 1994. pap. 895.00 (*1-57205-171-X*) Rector Pr.

Canada: Facts & Figures. Suzanne LeVert. (Let's Discover Canada Ser.). (Illus.). (J). (gr. 3 up). 1992. lib. bdg. 16.95 (*0-7910-1035-X*) Chelsea Hse.

Canada: Foreign Financing Reporter. Ed. by Lewis B. Sckolnick. (Illus.). 60p. (Orig.). 1994. pap. 225.00 (*1-57205-243-0*) Rector Pr.

Canada: In Celebration of Commerce. Michael F. Harrington et al. 1991. 37.95 (*0-89781-372-3*) Preferred Mktg.

Canada: North of Sixty. Brian Lewis et al. (Illus.). 304p. 1991. 50.00 (*0-7710-1581-X*, Pub. by McClelland & Stewart CN) Firefly Bks Ltd.

Canada: OECD Economic Survey. Ed. by Lewis B. Sckolnick. (Illus.). 200p. (Orig.). (C). 1994. pap. text ed. 165.00 (*1-57205-633-9*) Rector Pr.

Canada: Ontario Census Index 1848-50, (Upper Canada), Vols. 1 & 2. Ronald V. Jackson. (Illus.). lib. bdg. 99.00 (*0-89593-762-X*) Accelerated Index.

Canada: Ontario 1800-1842 Census Index, Vol. 1. (Illus.). 1985. lib. bdg. 54.00 (*0-89593-234-2*) Accelerated Index.

Canada: Photographic Journey. Bill Harris. (Illus.). 1991. 12.99 (*0-517-05373-X*) Random Hse Value.

***Canada: Reclaiming the Middle Ground.** Donald G. Lenihan et al. 162p. 1994. pap. 16.95 (*0-88645-167-1*) Ashgate Pub Co.

Canada: Ron Martin & Henry Saxe. (Illus.). 114p. (Orig.). 1978. pap. text ed. 5.00 (*0-89192-236-9*, Ctr Inter-Am Rel) Interbk Inc.

***Canada: The Land.** Lynda Sorensen. LC 94-46853. (North of the Border Ser.). (J). 1995. write for info. (*1-55916-106-X*) Rourke Bk Co.

Canada: The Strategic & Military Pawn. Gerard S. Vano. LC 87-22887. 163p. 1988. text ed. 45.00 (*0-275-92876-4*, C2876, Praeger Pubs) Greenwood.

Canada: Trade, Licensing & Investing Rules & Regulations. Ed. by Lewis B. Sckolnick. (Illus.). 80p. (Orig.). (C). 1994. pap. 225.00 (*1-57205-056-X*) Rector Pr.

Canada: Unity in Diversity. Charles F. Doran & Puay Tang. LC 89-81592. (Headline Ser.: No. 291). 62p. 1990. pap. 5.95 (*0-87124-131-5*) Foreign Policy.

Canada see American Nations Past & Present

Canada see MacDonald Countries

Canada see American Dissertations on Foreign Education: A Bibliography with Abstracts

***Canada - An American Nation? Essays on Continentalism, Identity, & the Canadian Frame of Mind.** Allan Smith. 400p. 1994. 55.00 (*0-7735-1229-2*, Pub. by McGill CN); pap. 24.95 (*0-7735-1252-7*, Pub. by McGill CN) U of Toronto Pr.

Canada - the Culture. Bobbie Kalman. LC 93-34384. (Lands, Peoples, & Cultures Ser.). (Illus.). 32p. (Orig.). (J). (gr. 3-6). 1993. lib. bdg. 15.95 (*0-86505-219-0*); pap. 7.95 (*0-86505-299-9*) Crabtree Pub Co.

Canada - the Land. Bobbie Kalman. LC 93-23516. (Lands, Peoples, & Cultures Ser.). (Illus.). 32p. (Orig.). (J). (gr. 3-6). 1993. lib. bdg. 15.95 (*0-86505-217-4*); pap. 7.95 (*0-86505-297-2*) Crabtree Pub Co.

Canada - the People. Bobbie Kalman. LC 93-34328. (Lands, Peoples, & Cultures Ser.). (Illus.). 32p. (Orig.). (J). (gr. 3-6). 1993. lib. bdg. 15.95 (*0-86505-218-2*); pap. 7.95 (*0-86505-298-0*) Crabtree Pub Co.

Canada - U. S. Relations & Canadian Foreign Policy. W. J. Stankiewicz. (Illus.). 1973. 50.00 (*0-686-09046-2*) Girs Pr.

Canada - United States Relationship: The Politics of Energy & Environmental Coordination. Ed. by Jonathan Lemco. LC 91-34774. 240p. 1992. text ed. 47. 95 (*0-275-94239-2*, C4239, Praeger Pubs) Greenwood.

Canada, Adieu? Quebec Debates its Future. Tr. by Richard Fidler. 328p. 1991. pap. text ed. 19.95 (*0-88645-130-2*, Pub. by Inst Res Pub CN) Ashgate Pub Co.

Canada after the War. Ed. by Alexander Brady & Francis R. Scott. LC 75-128212. (Essay Index Reprint Ser.). 1977. 23.95 (*0-8369-1867-3*) Ayer.

Canada & Asia: A Guide to Archives & Manuscripts. G. Raymond Nunn. 800p. 1995. text ed. 240.00 (*0-7201-2110-8*, Mansell Pub) Cassell.

Canada & Collective Security: Odd Man Out. Joseph T. Jockel & Joel J. Sokolsky. LC 86-5041. (Washington Papers: No. 121). 133p. 1986. text ed. 45.00 (*0-275-92217-0*, C2217, Praeger Pubs) Greenwood.

Canada & Her People. 1990. 29.99 (*0-517-05412-4*) Random Hse Value.

Canada & Immigration: Public Policy & Public Concern. Freda Hawkins. (Canadian Public Administration Ser.). 1972. 16.50 (*0-7735-0128-2*, Pub. by McGill CN); pap. 4.95 (*0-7735-0160-6*) U of Toronto Pr.

Canada & Immigration: Public Policy & Public Concern. 2nd ed. Freda Hawkins. 496p. 1989. pap. 24.95 (*0-7735-0633-0*, Pub. by McGill CN) U of Toronto Pr.

Canada & Imperial Defense: A Study of the Origins of the British Commonwealth's Defense Organization, 1867-1919. Richard A. Preston. LC 66-29550. (Duke University, Commonwealth-Studies Center, Publication Ser.: No. 29). reprint ed. pap. 149.50 (*0-8357-7987-4*, 2023435) Bks Demand.

Canada & International Civil Aviation 1932-1948. David MacKenzie. 228p. 1989. text ed. 40.00 (*0-8020-5828-0*) U of Toronto Pr.

Canada & International Peacekeeping. Joshua T. Jockel. LC 94-1903. (Significant Issues Ser.: Vol. 16, No. 3). 88p. (Orig.). 1994. pap. 9.50 (*0-89206-245-2*) CSI Studies.

Canada & Its Provinces: History of the Canadian People & Their Institutions, 23 vols., Set. Adam Shortt & Doughty Shortt. (BCL1 - History - Canada Ser.). 1991. reprint ed. text ed. 1,725.00 (*0-7812-6349-2*) Rprt Serv.

Canada & Japan in the Twentieth Century. Ed. by John Schultz & Kimitada Miwa. (Illus.). 320p. 1992. pap. 21. 95 (*0-19-540860-8*) OUP.

***Canada & Quebec: One Country, Two Histories.** Robert Bothwell. (Illus.). 288p. 1995. 34.95 (*0-7748-0524-2*) U of Wash Pr.

Canada & South Asia: Political & Strategic Relations. Arthur G. Rubinoff. (C). 1992. text ed. 32.00 (*1-895214-02-5*, Pub. by Centre S Asian Studies CN); pap. text ed. 23.00 (*1-895214-01-7*, Pub. by Centre S Asian Studies CN) S Asia.

Canada & South Asian Development: Trade & Aid. Ed. by Nanda K. Choudhry. LC 91-2773. (International Studies in Sociology & Social Anthropology: No. 57). 163p. 1991. pap. 34.50 (*90-04-09416-4*) E J Brill.

Canada & the Age of Conflict: A History of Canadian External Policies, 1867-1921, Vol. I. C. P. Stacey. 420p. 1984. pap. text ed. 20.95 (*0-8020-6560-0*) U of Toronto Pr.

Canada & the Age of Conflict: A History of Canadian External Policies, 1921-48--the Mackenzie King Era, Vol. II. C. P. Stacey. 480p. 1981. pap. 22.95 (*0-8020-6420-5*) U of Toronto Pr.

Canada & the American Revolution: The Disruption of the First British Empire. George M. Wrong. LC 68-31300. reprint ed. 72.50 (*0-8154-0261-9*) Cooper Sq.

Canada & the American Revolution; the Disruption of the First British Empire. George M. Wrong. (History - United States Ser.). 497p. 1993. reprint ed. lib. bdg. 99. 00 (*0-7812-4875-2*) Rprt Serv.

Canada & the Birth of Israel: A Study in Canadian Foreign Policy. David J. Bercuson. 302p. reprint ed. pap. 86.10 (*0-7837-1045-3*, 2041357) Bks Demand.

Canada & the British Army, 1846-1871: A Study in the Practice of Responsible Government. rev. ed. Charles P. Stacey. LC 64-7285. 312p. reprint ed. pap. 89.00 (*0-8357-7988-2*, 2055481) Bks Demand.

Canada & the Canadian Question. Goldwin Smith. LC 70-163837. (Social History of Canada Ser.). 256p. reprint ed. pap. 73.00 (*0-8357-6367-6*, 2035721) Bks Demand.

Canada & the Crisis in Central America. Jonathan Lemco. LC 90-43134. 208p. 1991. text ed. 49.95 (*0-275-93718-6*, C3718, Praeger Pubs) Greenwood.

Canada & the Fight for Freedom. William L. King. LC 76-37835. (Essay Index Reprint Ser.). 1977. reprint ed. 26. 95 (*0-8369-2601-3*) Ayer.

Canada & the French. Ed. by Donald J. Riseborough. LC 74-75155. 274p. reprint ed. pap. 78.10 (*0-8357-7989-0*, 2022901) Bks Demand.

Canada & the Gold Standard: Balance of Payments Adjustment under Fixed Exchange Rates, 1871-1913. Trevor J. Dick & John E. Floyd. (Studies in Monetary & Financial History). (Illus.). 304p. (C). 1992. 64.95 (*0-521-40408-8*) Cambridge U Pr.

Canada & the Grand Trunk, 1829-1924. H. A. Lovett. Ed. by Stuart Bruchey. LC 80-1328. (Railroads Ser.). 1981. reprint ed. lib. bdg. 24.95 (*0-405-13802-4*) Ayer.

Canada & the International Seabed: Domestic Determinants & External Constraints. Elizabeth Riddell-Dixon. 240p. (C). 1989. text ed. 55.00 (*0-7735-0694-2*, Pub. by McGill CN) U of Toronto Pr.

Canada & the Metis, 1869-1885. D. N. Sprague. 200p. (C). 1988. pap. 18.50 (*0-88920-964-2*, Pub. by Wilfrid Laurier CN) Humanities.

***Canada & the Middle East: The Foreign Policy of a Client State.** Tareq Y. Ismael. (Contemporary Issues: American-Arab Institute for Strategic Studies). 126p. (Orig.). (C). 1994. pap. text ed. 16.95x (*1-55059-076-6*) Temeron Bks.

Canada & the New Constitution: The Unfinished Agenda, 2 Vols., Vol. 1. Ed. by Stanley M. Beck & Ivan Bernier. 399p. 1983. pap. text ed. 16.95 (*0-920380-73-5*, Pub. by Inst Res Pub CN) Ashgate Pub Co.

Canada & the New International Law of the Sea, Vol. 54. Douglas M. Johnston. (Collected Research Studies of the Royal Commission on the Economic Union & Development Prospects for Canada: No. 54). 152p. 1985. 15.95 (*0-8020-7301-8*) U of Toronto Pr.

Canada & the United Nations. Frederic H. Soward & Edgar McInnis. LC 74-6712. (National Studies on International Organization-Carnegie Endowment for International Peace). 285p. 1975. reprint ed. text ed. 59.75 (*0-8371-7546-1*, SOCU, Greenwood Pr) Greenwood.

Canada & the United States: Ambivalent Allies. John H. Thompson & Stephen J. Randall. LC 93-29652. (United States & the Americas Ser.). (Illus.). 352p. 1994. 45.00 (*0-8203-1618-0*); pap. 18.95 (*0-8203-1619-9*) U of Ga Pr.

Canada & the United States: Ambivalent Allies. John H. Thompson & Stephen J. Randall. 352p. (C). 1994. 49.00 (*0-7735-1208-X*, Pub. by McGill CN); pap. text ed. 22. 95 (*0-7735-1209-8*, Pub. by McGill CN) U of Toronto Pr.

Canada & the United States: Differences That Count. Ed. by David Thomas. 420p. 1993. pap. 19.95 (*1-55111-018-0*) Broadview Pr.

Canada & the United States: Enduring Friendship, Persistant Stress. Charles F. Doran & John H. Sigler. 264p. 1985. pap. 15.95 (*0-13-113812-X*); pap. 7.95 (*0-13-113804-9*) Am Assembly.

Canada & the United States: The Civil War Years. Robin W. Winks. 450p. (C). 1988. reprint ed. pap. text ed. 34. 00 (*0-8191-7116-6*) U Pr of Amer.

Canada & the United States: The Politics of Partnership. Robert Bothwell. (Twayne's International History Ser.: No. 10). 200p. (C). 1992. text ed. 27.95 (*0-8057-7914-0*, Twayne); pap. 14.95 (*0-8057-9213-9*, Twayne) Macmillan.

Canada & the United States: Transnational & Transgovernmental Relations. Hero N. Fox et al. LC 75-45495. (Illus.). 443p. 1976. pap. text ed. 19.50 (*0-231-04026-1*) Col U Pr.

Canada & the United States in the 1990s: An Emerging Partnership. William C. Winegard & J. J. Sokolsky. (Institute for Foreign Policy Analysis Ser.). 113p. 1991. 11.95 (*0-08-040584-3*) Brasseys Inc.

Canada As a Borderlands Society. Roger Gibbins. (Borderlands Ser.: No. 2). 18p. 1989. write for info. (*0-9625055-0-1*) Canadian-Amer Ctr.

Canada at the Polls, Nineteen Seventy-Nine & Nineteen Eighty: A Study of the General Elections. Ed. by Howard R. Penniman. LC 81-19144. (Illus.). 448p. reprint ed. pap. 127.70 (*0-8357-4443-4*, 2037278) Bks Demand.

Canada at the Polls, 1984: A Study of the Federal General Elections. Ed. by Howard Penniman. LC 87-27252. (At the Polls Ser.). xiii, 218p. (C). 1988. lib. bdg. 62.95 (*0-8223-0805-3*); pap. text ed. 21.95 (*0-8223-0821-5*) Duke.

An Asterisk (*) at the beginning of an entry indicates that the title is appearing in BIP for the first time.

Canada Business Corporations Act. 3rd ed. Price Waterhouse Staff. 136p. 1987. pap. 25.00 (0-409-80656-0) Butterworth Legal Pubs.

*Canada Business Directory - Massachusetts. 200p. (Orig.). 1994. pap. 125.00 (0-7605-0897-6) Rector Pr.

*Canada Business Executive Outlook. 70p. (Orig.). 1994. pap. 295.00 (0-7605-1345-7) Rector Pr.

*Canada Business Intelligence Handbook. (Illus.). 70p. (Orig.). 1994. pap. 295.00 (0-7605-1072-5) Rector Pr.

Canada Celebrates Multiculturalism. Bobbie Kalman. LC 93-34136. (Lands, Peoples, & Cultures Ser.). (Illus.). 32p. (Orig.). (J). (gr. 3-6). 1993. lib. bdg. 15.95 (0-86505-220-4); pap. 7.95 (0-86505-300-6) Crabtree Pub Co.

Canada Census Index, 1881 British Columbia. Ronald V. Jackson. (Illus.). 1986. lib. bdg. 129.00 (0-89593-543-0) Accelerated Index.

*Canada Commercial Law. 210p. (C). 1994. pap. 295.00 (0-7605-0093-2) Rector Pr.

Canada Company Handbook, 1993. 5th ed. Ed. by David Curry et al. 590p. 1993. pap. 39.95 (0-921925-45-X) Ref Press.

*Canada Company Handbook, 1994. 6th ed. 600p. 1994. pap. 39.95 (0-614-02587-7) Ref Press.

*Canada Company Handbook, 1995. 7th ed. 600p. 1995. pap. 39.95 (0-921925-78-6) Ref Press.

Canada Country Notes. Ed. by World Eagle Staff. (Country Notes Ser.). (Illus.). 40p. (Orig.). 1990. teacher ed, pap. 14.95 (0-930141-33-4) World Eagle.

*Canada Dry: Temperance Crusades Before Confederation. Jan Noel. (Illus.). 296p. 1994. 50.00 (0-8020-0552-7); pap. 19.95 (0-8020-6976-2) U of Toronto Pr.

Canada East. (Insider's Guides Ser.). (Illus.). 256p. (Orig.). 1993. pap. 15.95 (1-55650-581-7) Hunter NJ.

*Canada Fire: Radical Evangelicalism in British North America, 1775-1812. G. A. Rawlyk. 272p. 1994. 49.95 (0-7735-1221-7, Pub. by McGill CN); pap. 18.95 (0-7735-1277-2, Pub. by McGill CN) U of Toronto Pr.

Canada Firsts. Ralph Nader. LC 91-77176. 165p. 1992. pap. 12.00 (0-936758-25-2) Country Rds.

Canada Gazetteer Atlas. (Illus.). 174p. (C). 1980. lib. bdg. 75.00 (0-226-09259-3) U Ch Pr.

*Canada Geese. Roger Ethier. (Classic Ser.). (YA). 1994. pap. 9.95 (0-9644924-0-7) Folklore VA.

Canada Geese Quilt. Natalie Kinsey-Warnock. (Illus.). 60p. (YA). (gr. 5 up). 1992. pap. 3.50 (0-440-40719-2, YB) Dell.

Canada Geese Quilt. Natalie Kinsey-Warnock. LC 88-32661. (Illus.). 64p. (J). (gr. 4 up). 1989. 13.00 (0-525-65004-0, Cobblehill Bks) Dutton Child Bks.

Canada Goose. Mark Ahlstrom. LC 83-24015. (Wildlife Habits & Habitats Ser.). (Illus.). 48p. (J). (gr. 5). 1984. lib. bdg. 12.95 (0-89686-243-7, Crstwood Hse) Silver Burdett Pr.

Canada Goose. Kit H. Breen. LC 89-70600. (Voyageur Wilderness Ser.). (Illus.). 96p. (Orig.). 1990. reprint ed. 24.95 (1-85310-173-7) Voyageur Pr.

Canada Green Guide. 5th ed. Date not set. pap. 19.00 (2-06-151705-6, 517) Michelin.

*Canada Green Guide English Edition. Michelin Staff. Date not set. pap. 17.95 (0-7859-7176-9, 2061517056) Fr & Eur.

*Canada Green Guide French Edition. Michelin Staff. (FRE.). Date not set. pap. 17.95 (0-7859-7209-9, 2067005162) Fr & Eur.

Canada in a Wider Economic Community. Harry E. English et al. LC 72-9739. (Canada in the Atlantic Economy Ser.: No. 13). 164p. reprint ed. pap. 46.80 (0-8357-7990-4, 2026520) Bks Demand.

Canada in Pictures. Lerner Publications, Department of Geography Staff. (Visual Geography Ser.). (Illus.). 64p. (YA). (gr. 5 up). 1989. lib. bdg. 18.95 (0-8225-1870-8, Lerner Publctns) Lerner Group.

Canada in Space. Lydia Dotto. (Illus.). 371p. 1987. 24.95 (0-7725-1657-X, Pub. by Stoddart Pubng CN) Genl Dist Srvs.

Canada in the Changing World Economy. B. W. Wilkinson. LC 80-80329. (Canadian-U. S. Prospect Ser.). 180p. 1980. 10.00 (0-88806-067-X) Natl Planning.

Canada in the Classroom: Content & Strategies for the Social Studies. Ed. by William W. Joyce. LC 85-61551. (Bulletin Ser.: No. 76). 119p. (Orig.). 1985. pap. text ed. 8.95 (0-87986-050-2, 498-15324) Nat Coun Soc Studies.

Canada in the World Economy. John A. Stovel. LC 59-7663. (Economic Studies: No. 108). (Illus.). 379p. 1959. 25.00 (0-674-09250-3) HUP.

Canada in Transition. Ed. by Grant McClellan. (Reference Shelf Ser.). 1977. 15.00 (0-8242-0603-7) Wilson.

Canada Investigates Industrialism: The Royal Commission on the Relations of Labor & Capital, 1989. abr. ed. Ed. by Gregory S. Kealey. LC 70-189604. (Social History of Canada Ser.). 491p. reprint ed. pap. 140.00 (0-8357-3765-9, 2036494) Bks Demand.

Canada Is My Home. Photos & Adapt. by David Wright. LC 92-17726. (My Home Country Ser.). (Illus.). (J). 1992. lib. bdg. 21.26 (0-8368-0846-0) Gareth Stevens Inc.

Canada-Japan: Policy Issues for the Future. Ed. by K. Lorne Brownsey. 222p. 1989. pap. text ed. 23.95 (0-88645-086-1, Pub. by Inst Res Pub CN) Ashgate Pub Co.

Canada Je T'Aime - I Love You. Roch Carrier. LC 90-70137. (Illus.). 72p. (J). 1991. 29.95 (0-88776-253-0) Tundra Bks.

Canada Jewish Travel Guide. Oscar Israelowitz. (Illus.). 196p. 1992. 9.95 (1-878741-10-1) Israelowitz Pub.

Canada Labour Code: An Office Consolidation, 3 pts. 860p. 1991. Pt. III: Standard Hours, Wages, Vacations & Holidays, 144p. pap. 18.00 (0-409-90055-9) Butterworth Legal Pubs.

Canada Labour Code: An Office Consolidation, 3 pts., Pt. I: Industrial Relations. 104p. 1991. pap. 17.00 (0-409-90053-2) Butterworth Legal Pubs.

Canada Labour Code: An Office Consolidation, 3 pts., Pt. II: Occupational Safety & Health. 612p. 1991. pap. 43. 00 (0-409-90054-0) Butterworth Legal Pubs.

Canada Labour Code: An Office Consolidation, 3 pts., Set. 860p. 1991. pap. 65.00 (0-409-90056-7) Butterworth Legal Pubs.

Canada Labour Relations Board Policies & Procedures. Foisy et al. 608p. 1986. 125.00 (0-409-81975-1) Butterworth Legal Pubs.

Canada Naturally: The Book. Richard West. (Illus.). 120p. 1993. pap. text ed. 24.95 (0-9636805-0-1) Events Unltd.

Canada Nineteen Hundred to Nineteen Forty-Five. Robert Bothwell et al. 1987. pap. 21.95 (0-8020-6801-4) U of Toronto Pr.

Canada North: Journey to the High Arctic. J. K. Stager & Harry Swain. LC 92-11925. (Touring North America Ser.). (Illus.). 160p. 1992. 25.00 (0-8135-1890-3); pap. 9.95 (0-8135-1891-1) Rutgers U Pr.

*Canada Northern Social Concerns Vol. II. 435p. (Orig.). 1995. pap. 195.00 (0-7605-1865-3) Rector Pr.

*Canada Northern Social Concerns Vol. III, Pt. 1. 160p. (Orig.). 1995. pap. 195.00 (0-7605-1862-9) Rector Pr.

Canada Nursing Job Guide, 1989. Ed. by Martha J. Denney. 166p. 1989. pap. 50.00 (0-932834-06-X) Prime Natl Pub.

Canada Occupational Safety & Health Regulations & Safety & Health Committees & Representatives Regulations: Consolidated Working Copy. 134p. (Orig.). 1992. pap. 11.65 (0-660-14419-0, Pub. by Canada Commun Grp CN) Accents Pubns.

Canada on the Threshold of the 21st Century: European Reflections upon the Future of Canada. Selected Papers of the First All-European Studies Conference, The Hague, The Netherlands, Oct 24-27, 1990. Ed. by Cornelius H. Remie & Jean-Michel Lacroix. LC 91-20633. xx, 565p. 1991. 50.00x (1-55619-124-3) Benjamins North Am.

Canada Pocket Guide. Berlitz Editors. (Pocket Guides Ser.). (Illus.). 1988. pap. 10.95 (2-8315-2375-3) Berlitz.

Canada Post Offices, 1755-1895. Frank Campbell. LC 72-77023. (Illus.). 191p. 1972. 35.00 (0-88000-008-2) Quarterman.

*Canada Postal Code Directory. 600p. (Orig.). 1994. pap. 45.00 (0-7605-0544-6) Rector Pr.

Canada Province Studies. Randy L. Womack. 96p. (gr. 4 up). 1991. student ed 10.95 (1-56500-026-9) Gldn Educ.

*Canada, Provinces & Territories. Lynda Sorensen. LC 94-38248. (North of the Border Ser.). (J). 1995. write for info. (1-55916-105-1) Rourke Bk Co.

*Canada Remapped. Reid. 1994. per. 14.95 (0-88978-249-0, Pub. by Arsenal Pulp CN) InBook.

Canada since Nineteen Forty-Five. 2nd ed. Robert Bothwell et al. (Illus.). 512p. 1989. 45.00 (0-8020-2647-8); pap. 21.95 (0-8020-6672-0) U of Toronto Pr.

Canada since Nineteen Forty-Five: Power, Politics, & Provincialism. Robert Bothwell et al. LC 81-152041. (Illus.). 515p. reprint ed. pap. 146.80 (0-7837-0537-9, 2040865) Bks Demand.

Canada Southern Country. R. D. Tennant, Jr. Ed. by Noel Hudson. (Illus.). 208p. 35.00 (1-55046-007-2, Pub. by Boston Mills Pr CN) Genl Dist Srvs.

Canada Stamp Album. Ed. by David S. Macdonald. (Illus.). 416p. 1984. pap. 21.95 (0-937458-08-2) Harris & Co.

Canada Studies Program: Activity Manual. Stan Garrod. Ed. by John Chalk & Elizabeth Yockstick. (Illus.). 105p. (gr. 4). 1981. 85.00 (0-943068-27-4); teacher ed 12.00 (0-943068-26-6) Graphic Learning.

Canada, the Commonwealth & the Common Market: A Report of the 1962 Summer Institute, Mount Allison University. Ed. by William B. Cunningham. LC 63-25277. 150p. reprint ed. pap. 42.80 (0-8357-7991-2, 2023825) Bks Demand.

Canada, the GATT, & the International Trade System. 2nd ed. Frank Stone. 276p. 1992. pap. text ed. 26.95 (0-88645-145-0, Pub. by Inst Res Pub CN) Ashgate Pub Co.

Canada, the Missing Years: The Lost Images of Our Heritage. Patricia Pierce. (Illus.). 160p. 1987. 19.95 (0-7737-5120-3, Pub. by Stoddart Pubng CN) Genl Dist Srvs.

*Canada, the People. Lynda Sorensen. LC 94-48246. (J). 1995. write for info. (1-55916-108-6) Rourke Bk Co.

Canada Travellers Guide. 6th ed. Berlitz Staff. 752p. 1994. pap. 16.95 (2-8315-1711-7) Berlitz.

Canada: U. S. Capital Market. Robert M. Dunn, Jr. LC 78-71657. (Canadian-U. S. Prospect Ser.). 148p. 1978. 6.00 (0-88806-046-7) Natl Planning.

Canada-U. S. Employment Transfers: A Guide to Personal Planning. 4th ed. Levine et al. 304p. 1992. pap. 30.50 (0-685-67171-2, 4045) Commerce.

*Canada-U. S. Free Trade: The Faltering Impetus for a Historic Reversal. D. L. McLachlan. 62p. (Orig.). (C). 1987. pap. text ed. 7.95x (0-920490-74-3) Temeron Bks.

Canada-U. S. Free Trade Agreement: Implications, Opportunities, & Challenges. Ed. by Daniel E. Nolle. 208p. 1989. 40.00x (0-8147-5764-2) NYU Pr.

Canada-U. S. Relations: Perceptions & Misperceptions. Ed. by Dorothy Robins-Mowry. 64p. (Orig.). (C). 1988. pap. text ed. 9.00 (0-8191-6873-4, Aspen Inst for Humanistic Studies) U Pr of Amer.

Canada: U. S. Relations: Policy Environments, Issues & Prospects. Harald Von Riekoff et al. LC 79-91042. (Canadian-U. S. Prospect Ser.). 156p. 1979. 6.00 (0-88806-059-9) Natl Planning.

Canada-U. S. Tax Comparisons. Ed. by John B. Shoven & John Whalley. LC 92-13915. (National Bureau of Economic Research Project Report Ser.). (Illus.). 392p. (C). 1992. 55.00 (0-226-75483-9) U Ch Pr.

Canada under Siege. Pierre Berton. (Illus.). 88p. (J). (gr. 5-8). 1992. pap. 5.99 (0-7710-1431-7, Pub. by McClelland & Stewart CN) Firefly Bks Ltd.

Canada-United States Free Trade Agreement & the Cultural Industries. Annette B. Fox. (Pew Case Studies in International Affairs). 62p. (C). 1994. pap. text ed. 2.50 (1-56927-137-2) Geo U Inst Dplmcy.

Canada: United States Trade & Economic Interdependence. Peter Morici & Laura L. Megna. (Canadian-U. S. Prospect Ser.). 64p. (Orig.). 1980. pap. 5.00 (0-88806-072-6) Natl Planning.

Canada Votes, Nineteen Thirty-Five to Nineteen Eighty-Eight. Frank Feigert. LC 88-33541. (Illus.). 352p. 1989. 82.50 (0-8223-0894-0) Duke.

Canada West. (Insider's Guides Ser.). (Illus.). 320p. (Orig.). 1993. pap. 15.95 (1-55650-580-9) Hunter NJ.

Canada with Love: Canada Avec Amour. Prod. by Lorraine Monk. (Illus.). 112p. 1992. 29.95 (1-895565-00-6) Firefly Bks Ltd.

Canada with Love - Canada Avec Amour. Lorraine Monk. 1993. pap. 19.95 (1-895565-27-8) Firefly Bks Ltd.

Canada Year Book, 1994. Ed. by Jonina Wood. (Illus.). 720p. 1993. 72.00 (0-660-15186-3, Pub. by Canada Commun Grp CN) Accents Pubns.

Canada Yearbook. Incl. 1975(Illus.). 1977. 18.50 (0-685-12913-6, SSC17); 1976-1977. 1977. pap. 23.00 (0-660-00761-4, SSC106); 1980-1981. 31.50 (0-685-12915-2, SSC169); write for info. (0-318-60602-X) UNIPUB.

Canada 1770-1777 Census Index Nova Scotia. (Illus.). lib. bdg. 33.00 (0-89593-233-4) Accelerated Index.

Canada 1825 Census Index Quebec. (Illus.). 1986. lib. bdg. write for info. (0-89593-235-0) Accelerated Index.

Canada 1842 Census Index Ontario. (Illus.). lib. bdg. write for info. (0-89593-236-9) Accelerated Index.

Canada 1848-1850 Census Index Upper Canada. (Illus.). lib. bdg. 80.00 (0-89593-237-7) Accelerated Index.

Canada 1851 Census Index New Brunswick. (Illus.). 1986. lib. bdg. 83.00 (0-89593-239-3) Accelerated Index.

Canada 1851 Census Index Nova Scotia. (Illus.). 1986. lib. bdg. 83.00 (0-89593-241-5) Accelerated Index.

Canada 1881 Census Index Manitoba. (Illus.). 1986. lib. bdg. 111.00 (0-89593-238-5) Accelerated Index.

Canada 1881 Census Index New Brunswick. (Illus.). lib. bdg. write for info. (0-89593-242-3) Accelerated Index.

Canada 1881 Census Index Northwest Territory (Includes Alberta, Sasawatchen, & Yukon Territory) (Illus.). lib. bdg. 120.00 (0-89593-240-7) Accelerated Index.

Canada 1985. Robert Turnbull. Ed. by Robert C. Fisher. (Fisher Annotated Travel Guides Ser.). 336p. 1984. 13. 95 (0-8116-0072-6) NAL-Dutton.

Canada, 1989. Stephen Birnbaum. (Birnbaum's Travel Guides Ser.). 624p. 1988. pap. 12.95 (0-318-35548-5) HM.

*Canada 1994. OECD Staff. (Development Cooperation Review Ser.: No. 5). 64p. (Orig.). 1994. pap. 9.00x (92-64-14221-5) OECD.

*Canada 1995. 11th ed. Wayne C. Thompson. 148p. 1995. pap. 9.50 (0-943448-90-5) Stryker-Post.

*Canada, 1995: An International Regulatory & Strategy Report. Ed. by Mary Collins. 312p. 1994. pap. 275.00 (1-882615-09-3) Parexel Intl.

Canada, 1995: The Complete Guide to Cities, Parks & Outdoor Adventures. Fodor's Travel Staff. (Illus.). 1994. pap. 18.00 (0-679-02702-5) Fodors Travel.

Canada's Balance of International Indebtedness: 1900-1913. Jacob Viner. Ed. by Mira Wilkins. LC 78-3953. (International Finance Ser.). (Illus.). 1979. reprint ed. lib. bdg. 33.95 (0-405-11254-8) Ayer.

Canada's Balance of International Indebtedness, 1900-1913: An Inductive Study in the Study of International Trade. Jacob Viner. LC 78-15119. (Illus.). x, 318p. 1979. reprint ed. lib. bdg. 39.50 (0-87991-855-1) Porcupine Pr.

Canada's Bishops: Sixteen Fifty-Eight to Nineteen Seventy-Five. Clarence A. Liederbach. LC 73-94082. 1976. pap. 2.95 (0-913228-10-9) R J Liederbach.

*Canada's Century: Governance in a Maturing Society. Ed. by C. E. Franks et al. 400p. 1995. 49.95 (0-7735-1293-4) U of Toronto Pr.

Canada's Cold Environments. Ed. by Hugh M. French & Olav Slaymaker. 336p. 1992. 45.00 (0-7735-0925-9, Pub. by McGill CN) U of Toronto Pr.

*Canada's Department of External Affairs Vol. 2: Coming of Age, 1946-1968. John Hiliker & Donald Barry. (Canadian Public Administration Ser.). (Illus.). 528p. 1995. 49.95 (0-7735-0738-8); pap. 24.95 (0-7735-0752-3) U of Toronto Pr.

Canada's Department of External Affairs, Vol. 1: The Early Years, 1909-1946. John F. Hilliker. (Canadian Public Administration Ser.). (Illus.). 440p. (C). 1990. text ed. 49.95 (0-7735-0736-1, Pub. by McGill CN); pap. text ed. 19.95 (0-7735-0751-5, Pub. by McGill CN) U of Toronto Pr.

Canada's Financial System in War. Benjamin H. Higgins. (Occasional Papers: No. 19). 93p. 1944. reprint ed. 24. 20 (0-87014-334-4) Natl Bur Econ Res.

Canada's First Nations: A History of Founding Peoples from Earliest Times. Olive P. Dickason. LC 91-50884. (Civilization of the American Indian Ser.: Vol. 208). (Illus.). 624p. (C). 1992. 42.95 (0-8061-2438-5); pap. 24. 95 (0-8061-2439-3) U of Okla Pr.

Canada's Flying Heritage. Frank H. Ellis. 1980. reprint ed. pap. 20.95 (0-8020-6417-5) U of Toronto Pr.

Canada's Great Highway: From the First Stake to the Last Spike. J. H. Secretan. Ed. by Stuart Bruchey. LC 80-1344. (Railroads Ser.). (Illus.). 1981. reprint ed. lib. bdg. 27.95 (0-405-13815-6) Ayer.

Canada's Health Care System: Bordering on the Possible. Jane Fulton. (Illus.). 300p. (Orig.). 1993. pap. text ed. 95.00 (1-881393-08-9) Faulkner & Gray.

Canada's Hollywood: The Canadian State & Feature Films. Ted Magder. (State & Economic Life Ser.). 368p. 1993. 50.00 (0-8020-2970-1); pap. 22.95 (0-8020-7433-2) U of Toronto Pr.

Canada's Incredible Coast. Ed. by William R. Gray. LC 91-19420. (Special Publications Series 26: No. 2). (Illus.). 1991. 12.95 (0-87044-829-3) Natl Geog.

Canadas Indians. Lewis B. Sckolnick. (Civil Rights Reporter Ser.). (Illus.). 60p. (Orig.). (C). 1994. pap. 45. 00 (1-57205-168-X) Rector Pr.

Canada's Indians: Contemporary Conflicts. James Frideres. 1974. text ed. 12.95 (0-13-112763-2); pap. text ed. 12.95 (0-13-112755-1) P-H.

Canada's Jews: A Social & Economic Study of Jews in Canada in the 1930s. Louis Rosenberg. (McGill-Queen's Studies in Ethnic History). (Illus.). 464p. 1993. 49.95 (0-7735-0997-6, Pub. by McGill CN); pap. 24.95 (0-7735-1109-1, Pub. by McGill CN) U of Toronto Pr.

*Canada's Money. Ed. by John M. Kleeberg. (Illus.). 155p. 1994. 25.00 (0-89722-252-0) Am Numismatic.

Canada's Official Languages. Richard Joy. 160p. (Orig.). 1992. 45.00 (0-8020-5007-7); pap. 18.95 (0-8020-6938-X) U of Toronto Pr.

Canada's RMC: A History of the Royal Military College. Richard A. Preston. LC 77-413015. (Illus.). 467p. reprint ed. pap. 133.10 (0-8357-4027-7, 2036719) Bks Demand.

Canada's Salesman to the World: The Department of Trade & Commerce, 1892-1939. O. Mary Hill. LC 77-371641. (Canadian Public Administration Ser.). (Illus.). 647p. reprint ed. pap. 180.00 (0-7837-1167-0, 2041696) Bks Demand.

*Canada's Undeclared War: Fighting Words from the Literary Trenches. Kenneth McGoogan. 277p. (Orig.). 1991. pap. 18.95 (1-55059-032-4) Temeron Bks.

Canada's Unity Crisis: Implications for U. S.-Canadian Economic Relations. Earl H. Fry. LC 92-32165. 1992. 8.95 (0-87078-335-1) TCFP-PPP.

*Canada's Vegetation: A World Perspective. Geoffrey A. Scott. (Illus.). 408p. 1995. 65.00 (0-7735-1240-3); pap. 29.95 (0-7735-1241-1) U of Toronto Pr.

Canada's War: The Politics of the Mackenzie King Government, 1939-1945. J. L. Granatstein. 435p. 1990. reprint ed. pap. 24.95 (0-8020-6797-2) U of Toronto Pr.

Canada's Wilderness Lands. Ed. by Donald J. Crump. LC 81-48074. (Special Publications Series 17: No. 2). 200p. 1982. 12.95 (0-87044-413-1); lib. bdg. 12.95 (0-87044-418-2) Natl Geog.

Canadian - U. S. Telecommunications in a Global Context. Ed. by William F. Averyt. 159p. (Orig.). 1986. pap. text ed. 18.00 (0-944799-00-0) U VT Schl Busn Admin.

Canadian ABC: An Alphabet Book for Kids. Lynn Cook. (Illus.). 60p. (J). 1990. pap. 8.95 (0-921254-24-5, Pub. by Penumbra Pr CN) U of Toronto Pr.

Canadian Agricultural Trade: Disputes, Actions & Prospects. Ed. by G. E. Lerner & K. K. Klein. 300p. 1990. pap. 24.95 (0-919813-90-9, Pub. by Univ Calgary CN) Paul & Co Pubs.

Canadian Agriculture. M. J. Troughton. 356p. 1982. 193.00 (0-569-08705-8) St Mut.

Canadian Agriculture in War & Peace, 1935-1950. George E. Britnell & V. C. Fowke. (Illus.). 518p. 1962. 60.00 (0-8047-0089-3) Stanford U Pr.

*Canadian Airborne Insignia, 1942-Present. Harry Pugh & Thomas Clark. LC 94-70190. (Elite Insignia Guides Ser.). (Illus.). 160p. (Orig.). 1994. pap. 16.00 (0-9633231-3-X) C&D Ent.

Canadian Airmen & the First World War: The Official History of the Royal Canadian Air Force, Vol. 1. S. F. Wise. 980p. 1980. 49.95 (0-8020-2379-7) U of Toronto Pr.

Canadian Almanac & Directory 1989. 142th ed. 1283p. 1988. 80.00 (0-7730-4912-6) Gale.

Canadian Almanac & Directory 1991. 144th ed. Walters. 1990. 102.00 (1-895021-04-9) Gale.

Canadian Almanac & Directory 1993. 146th ed. 1992. 145. 00 (1-895021-09-X, 071036, Pub. by CN Almanac & Dir CN) Gale.

*Canadian Almanac & Directory 1994. 147th ed. 1993. 159.95 (1-895021-12-X, Pub. by CN Almanac & Dir CN) Gale.

*Canadian Almanac & Directory 1995. 148th ed. Ed. by Susan Bracken. 1450p. 1995. 167.95 (1-895021-15-4, Pub. by CN Almanac & Dir CN) Gale.

Canadian-American Economic Relations: Conflict & Cooperation on a Continental Scale. Ed. by David L. McKee. LC 88-6610. 245p. 1988. text ed. 55.00 (0-275-92836-5, C2836, Praeger Pubs) Greenwood.

Canadian-American Free Trade (The Sequel) Historical, Political & Economic Dimensions. Ed. by A. R. Riggs & Tom Velk. 113p. 1989. pap. text ed. 18.00 (0-88645-073-X, Pub. by Inst Res Pub CN) Ashgate Pub Co.

Canadian-American Relations, 1849-1874. Lester B. Shippee. (History - United States Ser.). 514p. 1993. reprint ed. lib. bdg. 99.00 (0-7812-4861-2) Rprt Serv.

Canadian-American Trade & Investment under the Free Trade Agreement. Harold Crookell. LC 90-32922. 240p. 1990. text ed. 55.00 (0-89930-481-8, CCF/, Quorum Bks) Greenwood.

Canadian & American Constitutions in Comparative Perspective. Marian C. McKenna. LC 93-91361. 250p. (Orig.). 1993. pap. text ed. 18.95 (1-895176-26-3, Pub. by Univ Calgary CN) Paul & Co Pubs.

Canadian & Mexican Softgoods Buyers. Ed. by Edgar Adcock et al. 155p. (Orig.). 1993. pap. 117.00 (0-87228-039-X) Salesmans.

Canadian Annual Review of Politics & Public Affairs, 1971. Ed. by John T. Saywell. LC 72-96452. 1972. 55.00 (0-8020-1887-4) U of Toronto Pr.

An Asterisk (*) at the beginning of an entry indicates that the title is appearing in BIP for the first time. 1019

Canadian Annual Review of Politics & Public Affairs, 1971. John T. Saywell. LC 72-96452. 406p. reprint ed. pap. 115.80 (*0-8357-4012-9*, 2036705) Bks Demand.
Canadian Annual Review of Politics & Public Affairs, 1972. Ed. by John T. Saywell. LC 72-96452. 1974. 55.00 (*0-8020-1990-0*) U of Toronto Pr.
Canadian Annual Review of Politics & Public Affairs, 1973. Ed. by John T. Saywell. LC 72-96452. 1975. 55.00 (*0-8020-2154-9*) U of Toronto Pr.
Canadian Annual Review of Politics & Public Affairs, 1973. John T. Saywell. LC 72-96452. 377p. reprint ed. pap. 107.50 (*0-8357-4013-7*, 2036705) Bks Demand.
Canadian Annual Review of Politics & Public Affairs, 1974. Ed. by John T. Saywell. LC 72-96452. 1976. 55.00 (*0-8020-2196-4*) U of Toronto Pr.
Canadian Annual Review of Politics & Public Affairs, 1974. John T. Saywell. LC 72-96452. 454p. reprint ed. pap. 129.40 (*0-8357-4014-5*, 2036705) Bks Demand.
Canadian Annual Review of Politics & Public Affairs, 1975. John T. Saywell. LC 72-96452. 420p. reprint ed. pap. 119.70 (*0-8357-4015-3*, 2036705) Bks Demand.
Canadian Annual Review of Politics & Public Affairs, 1976. Ed. by John T. Saywell. 1977. 55.00 (*0-8020-2279-0*) U of Toronto Pr.
Canadian Annual Review of Politics & Public Affairs, 1977. Ed. by John T. Saywell. LC 72-96452. 1979. 55.00 (*0-8020-2313-4*) U of Toronto Pr.
Canadian Annual Review of Politics & Public Affairs 1978: A Reference Guide & Record. Ed. by John T. Saywell. 391p. 1979. 55.00 (*0-8020-2347-9*) U of Toronto Pr.
Canadian Annual Review of Politics & Public Affairs, 1979. Ed. by R. B. Byers. 1981. 55.00 (*0-8020-2407-6*) U of Toronto Pr.
Canadian Annual Review of Politics & Public Affairs, 1980. Ed. by R. B. Byers. 400p. 1982. 55.00 (*0-8020-2462-9*) U of Toronto Pr.
Canadian Annual Review of Politics & Public Affairs 1981. Ed. by R. B. Byers. 489p. 1984. 55.00 (*0-8020-2500-5*) U of Toronto Pr.
Canadian Annual Review of Politics & Public Affairs, 1982. Ed. by R. B. Byers. (Canadian Annual Review Ser.). 368p. 1984. 55.00 (*0-8020-2533-1*) U of Toronto Pr.
Canadian Annual Review of Politics & Public Affairs 1984. Ed. by R. B. Byers. 344p. 1987. 55.00 (*0-8020-2591-9*) U of Toronto Pr.
Canadian Annual Review of Politics & Public Affairs 1985. Ed. by R. B. Byers. 428p. 1988. 55.00 (*0-8020-5722-5*) U of Toronto Pr.
Canadian Annual Review of Politics & Public Affairs 1987. Ed. by R. B. Byers. 350p. 1991. 60.00 (*0-8020-5851-5*) U of Toronto Pr.
***Canadian Annual Review of Politics & Public Affairs, 1988.** Ed. by David Leyton-Brown. 352p. 1994. 70.00 (*0-8020-5849-3*) U of Toronto Pr.
***Canadian Annual Review of Politics & Public Affairs, 1989.** Ed. by David Leyton-Brown. 320p. (C). 1995. 70.00 (*0-8020-0714-7*) U of Toronto Pr.
Canadian Annual Review of Politics & Publics Affairs 1975. Ed. by John T. Saywell. LC 76-96452. 1976. 55.00 (*0-8020-2245-6*) U of Toronto Pr.
Canadian Annual Review 1960: A Reference Guide & Record. Ed. by John T. Saywell. 401p. 1961. 55.00 (*0-8020-1150-0*) U of Toronto Pr.
Canadian Annual Review 1961: A Reference Guide & Record. Ed. by John T. Saywell. 476p. 1962. 55.00 (*0-8020-1196-9*) U of Toronto Pr.
Canadian Annual Review, 1962. John T. Saywell. LC 61-3380. 501p. reprint ed. pap. 142.80 (*0-8357-4003-X*, 2036704) Bks Demand.
Canadian Annual Review 1962: A Reference Guide & Record. Ed. by John T. Saywell. 485p. 1963. 55.00 (*0-8020-1246-9*) U of Toronto Pr.
Canadian Annual Review, 1963. John T. Saywell. LC 61-3380. 586p. reprint ed. pap. 167.10 (*0-8357-4004-8*, 2036704) Bks Demand.
Canadian Annual Review 1963: A Reference Guide & Record. Ed. by John T. Saywell. 568p. 1964. 55.00 (*0-8020-1289-2*) U of Toronto Pr.
Canadian Annual Review, 1964. John T. Saywell. LC 61-3380. 549p. reprint ed. pap. 156.50 (*0-8357-4005-6*, 2036704) Bks Demand.
Canadian Annual Review 1964: A Reference Guide & Record. Ed. by John T. Saywell. 531p. 1965. 55.00 (*0-8020-1331-7*) U of Toronto Pr.
Canadian Annual Review, 1965. John T. Saywell. LC 61-3380. 585p. reprint ed. pap. 166.80 (*0-8357-4006-4*, 2036704) Bks Demand.
Canadian Annual Review 1965: A Reference Guide & Record. Ed. by John T. Saywell. 568p. 1966. 55.00 (*0-8020-1401-1*) U of Toronto Pr.
Canadian Annual Review, 1966. John T. Saywell. LC 61-3380. 537p. reprint ed. pap. 153.10 (*0-8357-4007-2*, 2036704) Bks Demand.
Canadian Annual Review 1966: A Reference Guide & Record. Ed. by John T. Saywell. 521p. 1967. 55.00 (*0-8020-1442-9*) U of Toronto Pr.
Canadian Annual Review, 1967. John T. Saywell. LC 61-3380. 552p. reprint ed. pap. 157.40 (*0-8357-4008-0*, 2036704) Bks Demand.
Canadian Annual Review 1967: A Reference Guide & Record. Ed. by John T. Saywell. 536p. 1968. 55.00 (*0-8020-1549-2*) U of Toronto Pr.
Canadian Annual Review, 1968. John T. Saywell. LC 61-3380. 550p. reprint ed. pap. 156.80 (*0-8357-4009-9*, 2036704) Bks Demand.
Canadian Annual Review 1968: A Reference Guide & Record. Ed. by John T. Saywell. 536p. 1969. 55.00 (*0-8020-1649-9*) U of Toronto Pr.
Canadian Annual Review, 1969. Ed. by John T. Saywell & Donald F. Forster. LC 61-3380. 55.00 (*0-8020-1736-3*) U of Toronto Pr.
Canadian Annual Review, 1969. John T. Saywell. LC 61-3380. 532p. reprint ed. pap. 151.70 (*0-8357-4010-2*, 2036704) Bks Demand.
Canadian Annual Review, 1970. Ed. by John T. Saywell & Donald F. Forster. LC 61-3380. xvi, 618p. 55.00 (*0-8020-1818-1*) U of Toronto Pr.
Canadian Annual Review, 1970. John T. Saywell. LC 61-3380. 634p. reprint ed. pap. 180.00 (*0-8357-4011-0*, 2036704) Bks Demand.
Canadian Anti-Combines Administration, 1952-1960. Gideon Rosenbluth & H. G. Thorburn. LC 64-982. 114p. reprint ed. pap. 32.50 (*0-8357-7992-0*, 2026535) Bks Demand.
Canadian Archival Studies & the Rediscovery of Provenance. Ed. by Tom Nesmith. (Society of American Archivists & Association of Canadian Archivists Ser.). (Illus.). 526p. 1993. 59.50 (*0-8108-2660-7*) Scarecrow.
Canadian Army & the Normandy Campaign: A Study of Failure in High Command. John A. English. LC 90-48955. 376p. 1991. text ed. 49.95 (*0-275-93019-X*, C3019, Praeger Pubs) Greenwood.
Canadian Army at War. Mike Chappell. (Men-at-Arms Ser.: No. 164). (Illus.). 48p. pap. 11.95 (*0-85045-600-2*, 9096, Pub. by Osprey UK) Stackpole.
***Canadian Art Vol. II (G-K) Catalogue of the National Gallery of Canada.** Ed. by Pierre B. Landry & Claire Champ. 416p. 1995. pap. 74.95 (*0-88884-638-X*) U Ch Pr.
Canadian Artists' Survival Manual. Rosemary Gahlinger-Beaune. (Illus.). 119p. 1987. 21.95 (*0-920806-99-6*, Pub. by Penumbra Pr CN) U of Toronto Pr.
Canadian Banks & Global Competitiveness. James L. Darroch. 304p. 1994. 34.95 (*0-7735-1138-5*, Pub. by McGill CN) U of Toronto Pr.
Canadian Baptists & Christian Higher Education. Ed. by G. A. Rawlyk. 142p. (C). 1988. text ed. 39.95 (*0-7735-0677-2*, Pub. by McGill CN); pap. text ed. 17.95 (*0-7735-0684-5*, Pub. by McGill CN) U of Toronto Pr.
Canadian Ben. Steven L. Carson. LC 79-51132. (Illus.). 238p. 1979. 9.95 (*0-918628-25-3*); pap. 5.95 (*0-918628-26-1*) Congeros Pubns.
Canadian Bibliography of International Law. Ed. by Christian L. Wiktor. 800p. 1984. 95.00 (*0-8020-5615-6*) U of Toronto Pr.
Canadian Bicycle Tours: Twelve Breathtaking Tours Through Quebec, Ontario, Newfoundland, Nova Scotia, New Brunswick, & Prince Edward Island. Jerry Dennis. (Illus.). 240p. 1992. pap. 14.95 (*0-8050-1492-6*, Owl) H Holt & Co.
Canadian Biennial of Contemporary Art. Diana Nemiroff. (Illus.). 188p. 1990. pap. 24.95 (*0-88884-595-2*) U Ch Pr.
Canadian Books for Young People. 4th ed. Andre Gagnon & Ann Gagnon. 188p. 1988. pap. 18.95 (*0-8020-6662-3*) U of Toronto Pr.
Canadian Books in Print Author and Title Index 1993. Ed. by Marian Butler. LC 70-418272. 1235p. 1993. 145.00 (*0-8020-4667-3*) U of Toronto Pr.
Canadian Books in Print Subject Index. Ed. by Marian Butler. LC 73-76124. 698p. 1993. 125.00 (*0-8020-4668-1*) U of Toronto Pr.
Canadian Books in Print 1994: Author - Title Index. Ed. by Marian Butler. 1235p. 1994. 150.00 (*0-8020-4674-6*) U of Toronto Pr.
Canadian Books in Print 1994: Subject Index. Ed. by Marian Butler. 698p. 1994. text ed. 130.00 (*0-8020-4675-4*) U of Toronto Pr.
***Canadian Books in Print 1995: Author - Title Index.** Ed. by Marian Butler. 1250p. (C). 1995. 150.00 (*0-8020-4682-7*) U of Toronto Pr.
***Canadian Books in Print 1995: Subject Index.** Ed. by Marian Butler. 700p. (C). 1995. 130.00 (*0-8020-4683-5*) U of Toronto Pr.
Canadian Brass: The Making of a Professional Army, 1860-1939. Stephen J. Harris. (Illus.). 296p. 1988. 35.00 (*0-8020-5765-9*) U of Toronto Pr.
Canadian Brass Book: The Story of the World's Favorite Brass Ensemble. Rick Walters. 224p. 1992. pap. 14.95 (*0-7935-1665-X*, 00183007) H Leonard.
Canadian Bureaucracy & Federalism, Nineteen Forty-Seven to Sixty-Five. Taylor Cole. (Monograph Series in World Affairs: Vol. 3, 1965-66, Bk. 3). (Orig.). pap. 3.95 (*0-87940-009-9*) Monograph Series.
Canadian Business Reader. 272p. 1986. pap. 15.95 (*0-7737-2079-0*, Pub. by Stoddart Pubng CN) Genl Dist Srvs.
Canadian Campaigns 1860-70. Rene Chartrand. (Men-at-Arms Ser.: No. 249). (Illus.). 48p. pap. 11.95 (*1-85532-226-9*, 9220, Pub. by Osprey UK) Stackpole.
Canadian Cancer Conference: Proceedings of the Sixth Canadian Cancer Research Conference 1964, Vol. 6. R. W. Begg & C. P. Leblond. LC 55-8263. 1966. 222.00 (*0-08-011410-5*, Pub. by Pergamon Repr UK) Franklin.
Canadian Cancer Conference: Proceedings of the 8th Canadian Cancer Res. Conference Saskatoon Saskatch 1969, No. 8. J. Morgan. LC 55-8263. 1969. 189.00 (*0-08-006791-3*, Pub. by Pergamon Repr UK) Franklin.
Canadian Canons: Essays in Literary Value. Ed. by Robert Lecker. 288p. 1992. 35.00 (*0-8020-5826-4*); pap. 16.95 (*0-8020-6770-X*) U of Toronto Pr.
Canadian Cases in the Philosophy of Law. 2nd ed. Ed. by Jerome E. Bickenbach. 260p. 1993. pap. text ed. 17.95 (*1-55111-026-1*) Broadview Pr.
Canadian Center for Architecture: Building & Gardens. Ed. by Larry Richards. (Illus.). 156p. (Orig.). 1989. pap. 17.95x (*0-262-68058-0*) MIT Pr.
Canadian Challenge. Christian DuFour. 1990. pap. text ed. 23.95 (*0-88645-113-2*, Pub. by Inst Res Pub CN) Ashgate Pub Co.
***Canadian Challenge: Le Defi Quebecois.** Dufour. Date not set. per. 12.95 (*0-88982-105-4*, Pub. by Oolichan Bks CN) InBook.
Canadian Childhoods: A Tundra Anthology. LC 88-50262. (Illus.). (J). (gr. 4-8). 1989. 24.95 (*0-88776-208-5*) Tundra Bks.
Canadian CIM Markets. Richard K. Miller & Terri C. Walker. LC 88-84067. (Survey on Technology & Markets Ser.: No. 72). 50p. 1989. pap. text ed. 200.00 (*1-55865-119-5*) Future Tech Surveys.
Canadian Coastal & Inland Steam Vessels, 1809-1930. John M. Mills. LC 79-91504. 135p. 1979. 28.00 (*0-913423-01-7*) Steamship Hist Soc.
Canadian Company Law: Cases, Notes & Materials. 3rd ed. Palmer & Welling. 592p. 1986. pap. 65.00 (*0-409-80510-6*) Butterworth Legal Pubs.
Canadian Competition Law & Policy at the Centenary. Ed. by R. S. Khemani & W. T. Stanbury. 669p. 1991. pap. text ed. 34.95 (*0-88645-135-3*, Pub. by Inst Res Pub CN) Ashgate Pub Co.
Canadian Conflict of Laws. 2nd ed. Castel. 824p. 1986. 162.00 (*0-409-89939-9*) Butterworth Legal Pubs.
Canadian Conflict of Laws. 2nd suppl. ed. Castel. 824p. 1986. pap. 50.00 (*0-409-89377-3*) Butterworth Legal Pubs.
***Canadian Conflict of Laws.** 3rd ed. 730p. 1994. boxed 145.00 (*0-409-91182-8*, CN) Butterworth Legal Pubs.
Canadian Constitution & the Courts: The Function & Scope of Judicial Review. 3rd ed. Strayer. 400p. 1988. 108.00 (*0-409-80631-5*) Butterworth Legal Pubs.
Canadian Constitutional Law: Cases, Notes & Materials. 3rd ed. Whyte et al. 1808p. 1992. pap. 100.00 (*0-409-87605-4*) Butterworth Legal Pubs.
Canadian Constitutional Law in a Modern Perspective. Ed. by J. Noel Lyon & Ronald G. Atkey. LC 78-18165. 1403p. reprint ed. pap. 180.00 (*0-8357-7993-9*, 2014276) Bks Demand.
Canadian Contributions to the International Congress of Slavists, 7th International Congress. Ed. by Zbigniew Folejewski. (Slavistic Printings & Reprintings Ser.: No. 285). 1973. 88.50 (*90-279-2543-7*) Mouton.
Canadian Controls on Natural Gas Exports. G. C. Watkins. 20p. 1990. pap. 10.00 (*0-918714-23-0*) Intl Res Ctr Energy.
Canadian Corporate Directors on the Firing Line. Murray G. Ross. LC 80-154129. 146p. 1980. 26.95 (*0-07-092422-8*) McGraw.
Canadian Cowboy: Stories of Cows, Cowboys, & Cayuses. Andy Russell. 1994. 21.95 (*0-7710-7880-3*, Pub. by McClelland & Stewart CN) Firefly Bks Ltd.
Canadian Criminal Justice. Griffiths. 1989. pap. 53.00 (*0-409-83453-X*, Pub. by Buttrwrth Can Acad CN) Buttrwrth-Heinemann.
Canadian Criminal Justice. 2nd ed. Griffiths. 1993. write for info. (*0-409-89871-6*, Pub. by Buttrwrth Can Acad CN) Buttrwrth-Heinemann.
Canadian Criminal Justice History: An Annotated Bibliography. Russell C. Smandych et al. 332p. 1987. 65.00 (*0-8020-5720-9*) U of Toronto Pr.
Canadian Criminal Law Cases & Comments. 5th ed. Schmeiser. 848p. 1985. pap. 113.00 (*0-409-86538-9*) Buttrwrth-Heinemann.
Canadian Crisis. Don Pendleton. (Executioner Ser.: No. 24). 1989. pap. 3.50 (*1-55817-267-X*, Pinnacle NY) Windsor NY.
Canadian Crisis: A Guide for American Media. Ed. by Sol W. Sanders & William T. Alpert. 208p. 1992. pap. 9.95 (*0-9632125-0-8*) W H Donner Fnd.
Canadian Culture at the Crossroads: Film, Television, & the Media in the 1960's. Wendy Michener Symposium Staff. 64p. (C). 1989. pap. text ed. 7.00 (*1-55022-091-8*, Pub. by ECW Press CN) Genl Dist Srvs.
Canadian Customs Invoice: A Program for the IBM PC & Compatibles. Daniel M. Sivilich. (Orig.). 1990. 19.95 (*0-945510-03-9*) Intl Info Assocs.
Canadian Dakota. Wilson D. Wallis. LC 76-43887. (AMNH. Anthropological Papers: Vol. 41, Pt. 1). reprint ed. 57.50 (*0-404-15746-7*) AMS Pr.
***Canadian Defence Industries in the New Global Environment.** Alistair D. Edgar & David G. Haglund. 216p. 1995. 44.95 (*0-7735-1272-1*); pap. 17.95 (*0-7735-1273-X*) U of Toronto Pr.
Canadian Demand for Household Furniture & Anticipated Trends: Handbook of Furniture Manufacturing & Retailing. 3rd ed. Thomas W. McCormack. LC 93-43951. (Illus.). 60p. 1993. pap. 280.00 (*0-921577-39-7*) AKTRIN.
***Canadian Demand for Office Furniture & Anticipated Trends.** 3rd ed. Thomas W. McCormack. LC 94-45282. 76p. (Orig.). 1995. pap. text ed. 280.00 (*0-921577-48-6*) AKTRIN.
Canadian Dental Law. Rozovsky. 152p. 1987. 55.00 (*0-409-86335-1*) Butterworth Legal Pubs.
Canadian Diaries & Autobiographies. William Matthews. LC 50-62732. 144p. reprint ed. pap. 41.10 (*0-8357-7994-7*, 2052054) Bks Demand.
Canadian Dictionary of Business & Economics. David Crane. 416p. 1993. 45.00 (*0-7737-2691-8*, Pub. by Stoddart Pubng CN) Genl Dist Srvs.
Canadian Dictionary of Labor Relations: Dictionnaire Canadien des Relations du Travail. 2nd ed. Gerard Dion. 993p. (ENG & FRE.). 1987. 95.00 (*0-8288-0416-8*, M6163) Fr & Eur.
Canadian Dominion: A Chronicle of Our Northern Neighbor. Oscar D. Skelton. (BCL1 - History - Canada Ser.). 296p. 1991. reprint ed. lib. bdg. 79.00 (*0-7812-6358-1*) Rprt Serv.
Canadian Dreams & American Control: The Political Economy of the Canadian Film Industry. Manjunath Pendakur. LC 90-12144. (Contemporary Film & Television Ser.). 331p. (C). 1991. 49.95 (*0-8143-1998-X*); pap. 19.95 (*0-8143-1999-8*) Wayne St U Pr.
Canadian Drug Identification Code. Health Protection Branch, National Health & Welfare Canada Staff. 1023p. (Orig.). 1993. pap. 97.50 (*0-660-57987-1*, Pub. by Canada Commun Grp CN) Accents Pubns.
Canadian Economic Forecasting: In a World Where All's Unsure. Mervin Daub. 264p. 1987. 44.95 (*0-7735-0621-7*, Pub. by McGill CN) U of Toronto Pr.
Canadian Economic History. W. T. Easterbrook & Hugh G. Aitken. 606p. 1988. reprint ed. pap. 24.95 (*0-8020-6696-8*) U of Toronto Pr.
Canadian Economic Policy & the Impact of International Capital Flows. Richard E. Caves & Grant L. Reuber. LC 77-443977. (Canada in the Atlantic Economy Ser.: No. 10). 92p. reprint ed. pap. 26.30 (*0-8357-4018-8*, 2036708) Bks Demand.
Canadian Economic Thought: The Political Economy of a Developing Nation, 1814-1914. Craufurd D. Goodwin. LC 61-6223. (Duke University, Commonwealth-Studies Center, Publication Ser.: No. 15). 230p. reprint ed. pap. 65.60 (*0-8357-7995-5*, 2023387) Bks Demand.
Canadian Economics. Shedd et al. (C). 1993. 64.00 (*0-06-046097-0*) HarpCollege.
Canadian Economics Macro. Shedd et al. (C). 1993. 35.50 (*0-06-046099-7*) HarpCollege.
Canadian Economics Micro. Shedd et al. (C). 1993. 35.50 (*0-06-046098-9*) HarpCollege.
Canadian Education: A Sociological Analysis. W. Martin & A. Macdonell. 1978. pap. 13.33 (*0-13-113092-7*) P-H.
***Canadian Education: Historical Themes & Contemporary Issues.** Ed. & Intro. by E. Brian Titley. 216p. (Orig.). (C). 1990. pap. text ed. 18.95x (*1-55059-007-3*) Temeron Bks.
Canadian Employee Benefit Plans, 1991. Ed. by Mary E. Brennan. 392p. (Orig.). 1992. pap. 42.00 (*0-89154-436-4*) Intl Found Employ.
Canadian Employee Benefit Plans, 1992. Ed. by Mary Brennan. LC 92-75625. 393p. 1993. pap. 42.00 (*0-89154-458-5*) Intl Found Employ.
Canadian Employee Benefit Plans, 1993. Ed. by Mary E. Brennan. 162p. (Orig.). 1994. pap. 45.00 (*0-89154-477-1*) Intl Found Employ.
Canadian Encyclopedia, 3 vols., Set. 175.00 (*0-317-14672-6*) Ency Brit Inc.
***Canadian Entertainers of World War II.** Ray Stephens. (Illus.). 160p. 1995. lib. bdg. 47.00 (*0-8095-4805-4*) Borgo Pr.
Canadian Entry. Christilot Hanson. (Illus.). 140p. 1972. pap. 3.95 (*0-7720-0519-2*, Pub. by Stoddart Pubng CN) Genl Dist Srvs.
Canadian Environmental Directory, 1992. 1992. 175.00 (*1-895021-08-1*, Pub. by CN Almanac & Dir CN) Gale.
Canadian Environmental Directory, 1993. 1993. pap. 197.50 (*1-895021-11-1*, 101550, Pub. by CN Almanac & Dir CN) Gale.
***Canadian Environmental Directory 1994.** 4th ed. 1400p. 1994. 225.00 (*1-895021-14-6*, Pub. by CN Almanac & Dir CN) Gale.
Canadian Environmental Policy: Ecosystems, Politics, & Process. Robert Boardman. 240p. 1992. pap. 31.00 (*0-19-540774-1*) OUP.
***Canadian Environmental Protection Act Priority Substances List Assessment Report: Inorganic Fluorides.** (Illus.). 80p. (Orig.). (C). 1994. pap. text ed. 50.00x (*0-7881-1262-7*) Diane Pub.
***Canadian Environmental Protection Act Priority Substances List Assessment Report: Mineral Fibers (Man-Made Vitreous Fibers)** (Illus.). 59p. (Orig.). (C). 1994. pap. text ed. 50.00x (*0-7881-1261-9*) Diane Pub.
Canadian Evangelicalism in the Twentieth Century. John G. Stackhouse, Jr. (Illus.). 328p. 1993. 55.00 (*0-8020-0509-8*); pap. 19.95 (*0-8020-7468-5*) U of Toronto Pr.
Canadian Family Law. C. Malcolm Kronby. 224p. 1991. pap. 12.95 (*0-7737-5424-5*, Pub. by Stoddart Pubng CN) Genl Dist Srvs.
***Canadian Family Policies: Cross-National Comparisons.** Maureen Baker. 480p. (C). 1995. 60.00 (*0-8020-2963-9*); pap. 25.00 (*0-8020-7786-2*) U of Toronto Pr.
Canadian Federalism: From Crisis to Constitution. Ed. by Harold Waller et al. (Publius Bks.). 282p. (Orig.). (C). 1987. lib. bdg. 49.50 (*0-8191-6560-3*) U Pr of Amer.
Canadian Federalism: Meeting Global Economic Challenges? Douglas M. Brown & Murray G. Smith. 300p. 1991. pap. 15.00 (*0-88911-574-5*, Pub. by Inst Res Pub CN) Ashgate Pub Co.
Canadian Federation, Its Origin & Achievement: A Study in Nation Building. Reginald G. Trotter. (BCL1 - History - Canada Ser.). 348p. 1991. reprint ed. lib. bdg. 89.00 (*0-685-41298-9*) Rprt Serv.
Canadian Fighter Pilot. John McQuarrie. 1992. 34.95 (*0-07-551480-X*, Pub. by McGrw-Hill Ryerson CN) Howell Pr VA.
Canadian Film Technology. Gerald G. Graham. LC 87-40704. (Illus.). 272p. 1990. 48.50 (*0-87413-347-5*) U Delaware Pr.
Canadian Financial Management. 2nd ed. Davis & George E. Pinches. (C). 1991. text ed. 54.50 (*0-06-041563-0*) HarpCollege.
Canadian Financial Management: Study Guide. 2nd ed. Davis. (C). 1993. 21.50 (*0-06-041559-2*) HarpCollege.
Canadian Financial Markets. 3rd ed. W. T. Hunter. 275p. 1992. pap. text ed. 18.95 (*0-921149-48-4*) Broadview Pr.
***Canadian First Day Cover Handbook, 1950-1959.** Bruce Perkins. 172p. (Orig.). 1994. pap. 16.95 (*1-879390-18-3*) Am First Day.

An Asterisk (*) at the beginning of an entry indicates that the title is appearing in BIP for the first time.

Canadian Fishing Trip: A Guidebook. John Harschutz. Ed. by Richard Harschutz. LC 92-73117. (Illus.). 144p. (Orig.). 1993. pap. 7.95 (*0-9630638-4-7*) Barker & North.

Canadian Folklore: Perspectives on Canadian Literature. Edith Fowke. 160p. 1989. pap. 9.95 (*0-19-540671-0*) OUP.

***Canadian Football League Facts, Figures, & Records 1995.** rev. ed. Canadian Football League Staff. (Illus.). 272p. 1995. pap. 16.95 (*1-57243-031-1*) Triumph Bks.

Canadian Football League Facts, Figures & Record Book. 2nd ed. Canadian Football Leagues Staff. 240p. 1994. 14.95 (*1-880141-71-X*) Triumph Bks.

***Canadian Football League Facts, Figures & Record Book, 1994.** 1994. pap. 14.95 (*1-880141-72-8*) Triumph Bks.

***Canadian Foreign Direct Investment in the United States 1974-1994.** Francis M. Jeffries. 400p. (Orig.). 1995. pap. 250.00 (*1-878974-17-3*) Jeffries & Assocs.

***Canadian Forms & Precedents: Banking & Finance, 4 vols., Set.** Date not set. ring bd. 595.00 (*0-409-89842-2*, CN) Butterworth Legal Pubs.

Canadian Frontier: Fifteen Thirty-Four to Eighteen Twenty-One. rev. ed. W. J. Eccles. LC 83-5753. (Histories of the American Frontier Ser.). (Illus.). 257p. 1983. pap. 14.95 (*0-8263-0706-X*) U of NM Pr.

Canadian Fur Trade in the Industrial Age. Arthur J. Ray. 284p. 1990. 40.00 (*0-8020-2699-0*); pap. 19.95 (*0-8020-6743-3*) U of Toronto Pr.

Canadian Gothic & American Modern: Two Plays. Joanna M. Glass. 1977. pap. 4.75 (*0-8222-0178-X*) Dramatists Play.

Canadian Grain Trade. Duncan A. MacGibbon. LC 32-18135. 237p. reprint ed. pap. 67.60 (*0-8357-7996-3*, 2014307) Bks Demand.

Canadian Guide to Campus & Non-Profit Meeting Facilities. 3rd ed. 44p. 1993. write for info. (*1-881761-07-X*) AMARC.

Canadian Guide to International Adoptions: How to Find, Adopt, & Bring Home Your Child. John Bowen. (Reference Ser.). 160p. (Orig.). 1992. Canadian ed. pap. 11.95 (*0-88908-538-2*) Self-Counsel Pr.

Canadian Guidelines for the Prevention, Diagnosis, Management & Treatment of Sexually Transmitted Diseases in Neonates, Children, Adolescents & Adults, April 1992, Vol. 18S1. Health & Welfare Canada Staff. 213p. (Orig.). 1992. pap. 25.95 (*0-660-14767-X*, Pub. by Canada Commun Grp CN) Accents Pubns.

Canadian Health Care: Is It the Right Approach for U. S. Reform? 15.00 (*0-317-05098-2*, PR-119); 10.00 (*0-317-05099-0*, PR-119) Manu All Prod & Innov.

Canadian Health Care & the State: A Century of Evolution. Ed. by C. David Naylor. 288p. 1992. 49.95 (*0-7735-0934-8*, Pub. by McGill CN); pap. 22.95 (*0-7735-0949-6*, Pub. by McGill CN) U of Toronto Pr.

Canadian Health Care System: Lessons for the United States. Ed. by Susan B. Eve et al. 300p. 1994. pap. text ed. write for info. (*1-885196-02-4*) Ctr Tex Studies.

Canadian Health Information: A Legal & Risk Management Guide. 2nd ed. Lorne A. Rozovsky & Fay A. Rozovsky. 216p. text ed. 45.95 (*0-409-90618-2*) Butterworth Legal Pubs.

Canadian High-Tech in a World Economy: A Case Study of Information Technology. David W. Conklin & France St. Hilaire. 392p. 1988. pap. text ed. 25.00 (*0-88645-054-3*, Pub. by Inst Res Pub CN) Ashgate Pub Co.

Canadian History; A Reader's Guide Vol. 1: Beginnings to Confederation, Vol. I: Pre-Confederation. Ed. by M. Brook Taylor & Doug Owram. 304p. 1994. 55.00 (*0-8020-5016-6*) U of Toronto Pr.

Canadian History: A Reader's Guide Vol. 2: Confederation to the Present, I. Ed. by M. Brook Taylor & Doug Owram. 1994. pap. 18.95 (*0-8020-6826-X*) U of Toronto Pr.

Canadian History: A Reader's Guide Vol. 2: Confederation to the Present, II. Ed. by M. Brook Taylor & Doug Owram. 1994. pap. 19.95 (*0-8020-7676-9*) U of Toronto Pr.

Canadian History: A Reader's Guide Vol. 2: Confederation to the Present, Vol. II: Post-Confederation. Ed. by M. Brook Taylor & Doug Owram. 384p. 1994. 47.50 (*0-8020-2801-2*) U of Toronto Pr.

Canadian History & Literature: Classified, Alphabetical & Chronological Listings. Harvard University Library Staff. LC 68-22417. (Widener Library Shelflist: No. 20). 419p. 1968. text ed. 20.00 (*0-674-09351-8*) HUP.

Canadian History Before Confederation: Essays & Interpretations. Ed. by J. M. Bumsted. LC 77-187766. 522p. reprint ed. pap. 148.80 (*0-8357-7997-1*, 2055804) Bks Demand.

Canadian Hospitals, Nineteen Twenty to Nineteen Seventy: A Dramatic Half Century. George Agnew. LC 73-78942. 320p. reprint ed. pap. 91.20 (*0-8357-7998-X*, 2023486) Bks Demand.

Canadian Identity. 2nd ed. William L. Morton. 1972. 13.95 (*0-8020-6139-7*) U of Toronto Pr.

Canadian Import File: Trade, Protection & Adjustment. G. E. Salembier & Andrew R. Moroz. Ed. by Frank Stone. 4197. pap. text ed. 20.00 (*0-88645-046-2*, Pub. by Inst Res Pub CN) Ashgate Pub Co.

Canadian Impressionism. P. Duval. (Illus.). 176p. 1990. 50.00 (*0-7710-2964-0*, Pub. by McClelland & Stewart CN) Firefly Bks Ltd.

Canadian Indian Bibliography, 1960-1970. Thomas S. Abler et al. LC 75-300070. 748p. reprint ed. pap. 180.00 (*0-8357-7999-8*, 2026481) Bks Demand.

Canadian Industrial Policy. Peter Moriei et al. LC 82-81566. 116p. (Orig.). 1982. pap. 10.00 (*0-89068-063-9*) Natl Planning.

Canadian Inland Seas. Ed. by I. P. Martini. 512p. 1986. 95.00 (*0-444-42683-3*) Elsevier.

***Canadian Insurance Claims Directory 1995.** annuals 63th ed. Ed. by Gwen Peroni. 400p. (C). 1995. pap. 37.00 (*0-8020-4042-X*) U of Toronto Pr.

Canadian International Development Assistance Policies: An Appraisal. Ed. by Cranford Pratt. 432p. 1994. 39.95 (*0-7735-1180-6*, Pub. by McGill CN) U of Toronto Pr.

Canadian Ironies: Politics & Play. Linda Hutcheon. (Illus.). 208p. 1991. pap. 22.50 (*0-19-540830-6*) OUP.

Canadian ISBN Publishers' Directory. National Library Canada Staff. 473p. (Orig.). 1992. pap. 77.35 (*0-660-57481-0*, Pub. by Canada Commun Grp CN) Accents Pubns.

Canadian Issues: Essays in Honour of Henry F. Angus. Robert M. Clark. LC 62-53358. 393p. reprint ed. pap. 112.10 (*0-8357-6358-7*, 2035712) Bks Demand.

Canadian Japanese & World War II. Forrest E. LaViolette. LC 48-11190. 332p. reprint ed. pap. 94.70 (*0-317-09537-4*, 2055473) Bks Demand.

Canadian Jazz Discography. Jack Litchfield. 945p. 1982. 40.00 (*0-8020-2448-3*) U of Toronto Pr.

Canadian Jewish Outlook Anthology. Ed. by Henry M. Rosenthal & S. Cathy Berson. 325p. (C). 1988. pap. 5.00 (*0-685-30699-2*) Left Bank.

Canadian Kiss. Christine Carson. 1990. mass mkt. 4.25 (*0-8217-3135-1*) Zebra.

Canadian Labor Laws & the Treaty. Bryce M. Stewart. LC 77-76689. (Columbia University. Studies in Social Sciences: No. 278). 1969. reprint ed. 32.50 (*0-404-51278-X*) AMS Pr.

Canadian Labour in Politics. Gad Horowitz. LC 68-101781. (Studies in the Structure of Power Decision-Making in Canada: No. 4). 285p. reprint ed. pap. 81.30 (*0-8357-8053-8*, 2034041) Bks Demand.

Canadian Labour Relations Board Reports, Ser. 2. Ed. by Roy C. Filion & Marcia D. McNeil. 1993. 120.00 (*0-409-90270-5*) Butterworth Legal Pubs.

***Canadian Law Dictionary.** 3rd ed. John A. Yogis. 1995. pap. 12.95 (*0-8120-1887-7*) Barron.

Canadian Law of Architecture & Engineering. McLachlin & Wallace. 512p. 1987. 115.00 (*0-409-80481-9*) Butterworth Legal Pubs.

Canadian Law of Consent to Treatment. Rozovsky. 176p. 1989. 53.00 (*0-409-80630-7*) Butterworth Legal Pubs.

Canadian Law of Mortgages of Land. Joseph E. Roach. 592p. 1993. text ed. 95.00 (*0-409-90349-3*) Butterworth Legal Pubs.

Canadian Law of Nuisance. Bilson. 232p. 1991. 57.00 (*0-409-80573-4*) Butterworth Legal Pubs.

Canadian Law of Wills, 2 vols., 1. 3rd ed. Feeney. 880p. 1987. write for info. (*0-409-80607-2*) Butterworth Legal Pubs.

Canadian Law of Wills, 2 vols., 2. 3rd ed. Feeney. 880p. 1987. write for info. (*0-409-80608-0*) Butterworth Legal Pubs.

Canadian Law of Wills, 2 vols., Set. 3rd ed. Feeney. 880p. 1987. 200.00 (*0-409-81000-2*) Butterworth Legal Pubs.

Canadian Left: A Critical Analysis. N. Penner. 1977. pap. 13.67 (*0-13-113126-5*) P-H.

Canadian Legal Directory. Henry J. Morgan. (Biographical Reference Work Ser.). xii, 279p. 1989. reprint ed. 59.00 (*0-7812-0696-0*, Am Repr Serv) Rprt Serv.

Canadian Life & Health Insurance Law. Harriett E. Jones. (FLMI Insurance Education Program Ser.). 502p. (C). 1992. text ed. 83.00 (*0-939921-30-8*) LOMA.

Canadian Life & Health Insurance Law: Student Guide. Ed. by Dani L. Long. (FLMI Insurance Education Program Ser.). (Orig.). (C). 1992. pap. text ed. 17.00 (*0-939921-31-6*) LOMA.

Canadian Literary Prose: A Preliminary Stylistic Atlas. Robert Cluett. 200p. (C). 1990. text ed. 26.00 (*1-55022-096-9*, Pub. by ECW Press CN); pap. text ed. 16.00 (*1-55022-098-5*, Pub. by ECW Press CN) Genl Dist Srvs.

***Canadian Literature: Recent Essays.** Ed. by Manorama Trikha. (C). 1994. 24.00 (*81-85753-05-9*, Pub. by Radiant Pubs II) S Asia.

Canadian Literature Index, 1985. Ed. by Janet Fraser. 404p. (C). 1987. text ed. 195.00 (*1-55022-013-6*, Pub. by ECW Press CN) Genl Dist Srvs.

Canadian Literature Index, 1986. Ed. by Janet Fraser. 480p. (C). 1991. text ed. 195.00 (*1-55022-078-0*, Pub. by ECW Press CN) Genl Dist Srvs.

Canadian Literature Index, 1987. Ed. by Janet Fraser. 530p. (C). 1991. text ed. 195.00 (*1-55022-084-5*, Pub. by ECW Press CN) Genl Dist Srvs.

Canadian Literature Index, 1988. Ed. by Janet Fraser & Allan Weiss. 500p. (C). 1992. text ed. 195.00 (*1-55022-144-2*, Pub. by ECW Press CN) Genl Dist Srvs.

Canadian Manor & Its Seigneurs: The Story of a Hundred Years, 1761-1861. George M. Wrong. 1977. 19.95 (*0-8369-6996-0*, 7873) Ayer.

Canadian Manuscripts in the Boston Public Library: A Descriptive Catalog. Boston Public Library Staff. 1971. lib. bdg. 75.00 (*0-8161-0930-3*, Hall Library) G K Hall.

***Canadian Marc Communication Format for Bibliographic Data.** National Library Staff. 1993. 123.50x (*0-660-15355-6*, Pub. by Canada Commun Grp CN) Accents Pubns.

Canadian Marine Policy & Strategy Project Phase One Report on National Requirements. 65p. (Orig.). (C). 1993. pap. text ed. 30.00 (*1-56806-412-8*) Diane Pub.

Canadian Maritimes: Images & Encounters. Ed. by Peter Ennals. (Pathways in Geography Ser.: No. 6). (Illus.). 52p. 1993. pap. text ed. 5.00 (*0-9627379-8-4*) NCFGE.

Canadian Master Tax Guide, 1993. 48th ed. 1000p. 1993. pap. 33.00 (*0-685-67170-4*, 1016) Commerce.

Canadian Microeconomics. McCready. (C). Date not set. 32.50 (*0-06-044348-0*, HarpT) HarpC.

Canadian Millionaire: The Life & Business Times of Sir Joseph Flavelle, Bart., 1858-1939. Michael Bliss. (Reprints in Canadian History Ser.). 582p. 1992. reprint ed. pap. 24.95 (*0-8020-7351-4*) U of Toronto Pr.

Canadian Minerals Yearbook, 1991: Review & Outlook. Energy, Mines, & Resources Canada Staff. 735p. (Orig.). 1992. pap. 51.95 (*0-660-14678-9*, Pub. by Canada Commun Grp CN) Accents Pubns.

***Canadian Minerals Yearbook, 1992: Review & Outlook.** (Minerals Report Ser.: No. 41). 735p. (Orig.). 1993. pap. 55.25x (*0-660-15180-4*, Pub. by Canada Commun Grp CN) Accents Pubns.

***Canadian Mines: Perspective: Production, Reserves, Development, Exploration-1991.** Andre Lemieux. (Mineral Bulletin Ser.: No. 233). 42p. (Orig.). 1993. pap. 24.65x (*0-660-58966-4*, Pub. by Canada Commun Grp CN) Accents Pubns.

Canadian Mines Directory. 245p. (C). 1994. lib. bdg. 75.00 (*1-57205-012-8*) Rector Pr.

Canadian Mining Taxation. 2nd ed. Parsons. 272p. 1990. 82.00 (*0-409-89384-6*) Butterworth Legal Pubs.

Canadian Mortgage Payments. 2nd ed. Clifford Marshall & Stephen S. Solomon. 320p. 1993. pap. 8.95 (*0-8120-1617-3*) Barron.

***Canadian Motor Carrier Directory.** 2nd ed. 1994. ring bd. 95.00 (*1-880701-16-2*) Trans Tech Srvs.

Canadian Multinationals & International Finance. Ed. by Gregory P. Marchildon & Duncan McDowall. LC 92-12975. 185p. 1992. text ed. 37.50 (*0-7146-3481-6*, Pub. by F Cass Pubs UK) Intl Spec Bk.

Canadian Music: A Selected Checklist, 1950-1973. Ed. by Lynne Jarman. LC 76-55840. 1976. 30.00 (*0-8020-5327-0*) U of Toronto Pr.

Canadian Music of the Twentieth Century. George A. Proctor. LC 81-143054. (Illus.). 323p. reprint ed. pap. 92.10 (*0-7837-0531-X*, 2040859) Bks Demand.

Canadian National Election Study, 1965. Philip Converse et al. 1972. write for info. (*0-89138-058-2*) ICPSR.

Canadian National Election Study, 1974. Harold Clarke et al. 1977. write for info. (*0-89138-156-2*) ICPSR.

Canadian National Theatre on the Air, 1925-1961: A Descriptive Bibliography & Union List. Howard Fink & Brian Morrison. 48p. 1983. fiche 75.00 (*0-8020-0358-3*) U of Toronto Pr.

Canadian National's Western Depots. Charles Bohi. (Illus.). 128p. 20.00 (*0-317-06119-4*, Pub. by Boston Mills Pr CN) Genl Dist Srvs.

Canadian Native Literature. Ed. by Penny Petrone. 316p. 1990. pap. 19.95 (*0-19-540796-2*) OUP.

Canadian Nights. Albert Hickman. LC 74-144157. (Short Story Index Reprint Ser.). 1977. reprint ed. 23.95 (*0-8369-3772-4*) Ayer.

Canadian North: Source of Wealth or Vanishing Heritage. J. Benedickson et al. 1977. pap. 7.40 (*0-13-112912-0*) P-H.

Canadian Novel: A Search for Identity. M. F. Salat. (New World Literature Ser.: No. 68). (C). 1993. 16.00 (*81-7018-751-6*, Pub. by BR Pub II) S Asia.

Canadian Novel: Beginnings, Vol. 2. Ed. by John Moss. (Illus.). 216p. Date not set. text ed. 17.95 (*0-920053-15-7*, Pub. by NC Press CN); pap. 12.95 (*0-920053-17-3*, Pub. by NC Press CN) U of Toronto Pr.

Canadian Novel: Here & Now, Vol. 1. Ed. by John Moss. (Illus.). 204p. Date not set. text ed. 17.95 (*0-920053-06-8*, Pub. by NC Press CN); pap. 12.95 (*0-920053-04-1*, Pub. by NC Press CN) U of Toronto Pr.

Canadian Novel: Modern Times, Vol. 3. Ed. by John Moss. (Illus.). 204p. Date not set. pap. 12.95 (*0-919601-90-1*, Pub. by NC Press CN) U of Toronto Pr.

Canadian Novel: Present Tense, Vol. 4. Ed. by John Moss. (Illus.). 224p. Date not set. text ed. 17.95 (*0-919601-67-7*, Pub. by NC Press CN); pap. 12.95 (*0-919601-65-0*, Pub. by NC Press CN) U of Toronto Pr.

Canadian Nuclear Fuel Waste Management Program: Special Issue of the Journal Radioactive Waste Management & the Nuclear Fuel Cycle. K. W. Dormuth. 190p. 1987. pap. text ed. 135.00 (*3-7186-0414-0*) Gordon & Breach.

Canadian Nurses & the Law. Morris. 256p. 1991. 49.00 (*0-409-80190-9*) Butterworth Legal Pubs.

Canadian Nursing: Issues & Perspectives. Kerr. 1990. write for info. (*0-8016-2632-3*) Mosby Yr Bk.

Canadian Nursing: Issues & Perspectives. 2nd ed. Kerr. 416p. 1990. pap. 32.50 (*0-8016-6274-5*) Mosby Yr Bk.

Canadian Nursing Faces the Future, No. 2: Development & Change. Baumgart. 680p. 1992. pap. 27.50 (*0-8016-6330-X*) Mosby Yr Bk.

Canadian Occasions. John Buchan. LC 70-90618. (Essay Index Reprint Ser.). 1977. 21.95 (*0-8369-1275-6*) Ayer.

Canadian Ocean Law & Policy. VanderZwagg. 584p. 1991. 120.00 (*0-409-80664-1*) Butterworth Legal Pubs.

Canadian Office Management Manual: An on-the-Job Guide for Office Professionals. 2nd ed. Anne Morton. (Reference Ser.). 288p. 1993. Canadian ed. pap. 9.95 (*0-88908-537-4*) Self-Counsel Pr.

Canadian Official Publications. Olga B. Bishop. (Guides to Official Publications: Vol. 9). 308p. 1981. 123.00 (*0-08-024697-4*, Pub. by Pergamon Repr UK) Franklin.

Canadian Pacific: A Brief History. John McDougall. LC 68-23392. 212p. reprint ed. pap. 60.50 (*0-317-26031-6*, 2023833) Bks Demand.

Canadian Pacific Diagrams & Data: Steam Locomotives. Ed. by Omer Lavallee. (Illus.). 10.00 (*0-317-06120-8*, Pub. by Boston Mills Pr CN) Genl Dist Srvs.

Canadian Pacific Line. G. Munk. 1990. 75.00 (*0-9516038-5-X*, Pub. by Ship Pictorial Pubng UK) St Mut.

Canadian Pacific Railroad & the Development of Western Canada, 1896-1914. John A. Eagle. (Illus.). 352p. (C). 1989. text ed. 49.95 (*0-7735-0674-8*, Pub. by McGill CN) U of Toronto Pr.

Canadian Pacific's Western Depots: The Country Station in Western Canada. Charles W. Bohi & Leslie S. Kozma. (Illus.). 168p. 1993. 44.95 (*0-942035-25-9*) South Platte.

Canadian Painters Eleven (1953-1960) from the Robert McLaughlin Gallery. Ross Fox. (Illus.). 63p. (Orig.). 1994. pap. text ed. 12.00 (*0-914337-17-3*) Mead Art Mus.

Canadian Perspectives on Air Pollution. J. Hillborn & M. Still. (Illus.). 81p. (Orig.). (C). 1994. pap. text ed. 40.00 (*0-7881-0636-8*) Diane Pub.

Canadian Perspectives on International Law & Organization. Ed. by Ronald S. Macdonald et al. LC 72-98024. 992p. reprint ed. pap. 180.00 (*0-317-27016-8*, 2023647) Bks Demand.

Canadian Philosophers. Ed. by David Copp. 421p. 1993. pap. 20.00 (*0-919491-16-2*, Pub. by Univ Calgary CN) Paul & Co Pubs.

Canadian Poetry. Ed. by Jack David & Robert Lecker. 320p. 1982. pap. 5.95 (*0-7736-7036-X*, Pub. by Stoddart Pubng CN); pap. 5.95 (*0-7736-7037-8*, Pub. by Stoddart Pubng CN) Genl Dist Srvs.

Canadian Political Life: An Alberta Perspective. Gibbins et al. 256p. (C). 1990. pap. text ed. 19.95 (*0-8403-5882-2*) Kendall-Hunt.

Canadian Political Party Systems. 376p. 1992. pap. text ed. 19.95 (*0-921149-90-5*) Broadview Pr.

Canadian Politics: An Introduction to the Discipline. 2nd ed. Ed. by James P. Bickerton & Alain G. Gagnon. 400p. 1994. pap. 26.95 (*1-55111-023-7*) Broadview Pr.

Canadian Polity: A Comparative Introduction. 3rd ed. Ronald G. Landes. 450p. 1991. pap. text ed. 45.00 (*0-13-116740-5*) P-H.

Canadian Post-Modern Performance. Leabhart et al. Ed. by Thomas Leabhart. (Mime Journal Ser.). (Illus.). 91p. (Orig.). 1986. pap. 12.00 (*0-9611066-4-6*) Pomona Coll.

Canadian Postmodern: A Study of Contemporary English-Canadian Fiction. Linda Hutcheon. 248p. 1989. pap. 19.95 (*0-19-540668-0*) OUP.

Canadian Practical Stylist with Reading. 2nd ed. Sheridan Baker et al. 432p. (C). 1990. pap. text ed. 25.00 (*0-06-040466-3*) HarpCollege.

Canadian Prairie West & the Ranching Frontier. David H. Breen. 312p. 1983. 35.00 (*0-8020-5548-6*) U of Toronto Pr.

Canadian Prairies: A History. Gerald Friesen. (Illus.). 540p. 1987. pap. 21.95 (*0-8020-6648-8*) U of Toronto Pr.

Canadian Prairies: A History. Gerald Friesen. (Illus.). 560p. reprint ed. pap. 159.60 (*0-8357-3777-2*, 2036507) Bks Demand.

Canadian Protestant & Catholic Missions, 1820-1960: Historical Essays in Honor of Webster. John S. Moir & C. T. McIntire. (Toronto Studies in Religion: Vol. 3). 266p. 1988. text ed. 39.00 (*0-8204-0465-9*) P Lang Pubs.

Canadian Protestant Experience, 1760-1990. Ed. by George A. Rawlyk. 254p. 1990. pap. 19.95 (*0-7735-1132-6*, Pub. by McGill CN) U of Toronto Pr.

Canadian Provincial Politics. 2nd ed. M. Robin. 1978. pap. write for info. (*0-13-113233-4*) P-H.

***Canadian Public Education System: Issues & Prospects.** Ed. by Y. L. Lam. 337p. (Orig.). (C). 1990. pap. text ed. 21.95x (*1-55059-019-7*) Temeron Bks.

Canadian Public Sector Case. McCready. 1985. 50.00 (*0-409-84816-6*, Pub. by Buttrwrth Can Acad CN) Buttrwrth-Heinemann.

Canadian Readings in Personnel & Human Resource Management. Shimon L. Dolan & Randall S. Schuler. 467p. (C). 1987. pap. text ed. 34.25 (*0-314-32487-9*) West Pub.

Canadian Real Estate: Canada's Bestselling & Most Comprehensive Real Estate Guide for Buyers, Sellers & Professionals. 456p. 1987. 29.95 (*0-7737-2114-2*, Pub. by Stoddart Pubng CN) Genl Dist Srvs.

Canadian Real Estate Guide. Richard Steacy. 456p. 1992. 19.95 (*0-7737-2567-9*, Pub. by Stoddart Pubng CN) Genl Dist Srvs.

Canadian Reciprocity Treaty of Eighteen Fifty-Four. Charles C. Tansill. LC 78-63976. (Johns Hopkins University. Studies in the Social Sciences. Thirtieth Ser. 1912: 2). 96p. 1983. reprint ed. 37.50 (*0-404-61221-0*) AMS Pr.

Canadian Relations with South Africa: A Diplomatic History. Brian D. Tennyson. 254p. (Orig.). (C). 1982. pap. text ed. 24.50 (*0-8191-2633-0*) U Pr of Amer.

Canadian Rights Reporter, Series 2. 1993. 120.00 (*0-409-88230-5*) Butterworth Legal Pubs.

Canadian Rockies Access Guide. John Dodd & Gail Helgason. (Illus.). 360p. (Orig.). 1991. pap. 15.95 (*0-919433-92-8*) Hunter NJ.

Canadian Science Fiction & Fantasy. David Ketterer. LC 91-25710. 228p. 1992. text ed. 27.50 (*0-253-33122-6*) Ind U Pr.

Canadian Sea Ice Atlas from Microwave Remotely Sensed Imagery, July 1987-June 1990. Ed. by Ellsworth Ledrew. (Climatological Studies: No. 44). (Illus.). 80p. (Orig.). 1993. pap. 32.45 (*0-660-57966-9*, Pub. by Canada Commun Grp CN) Accents Pubns.

Canadian Selection: Book & Periodicals for Libraries. 2nd ed. Ed. by Mavis Cariou et al. 517p. 1986. 85.00 (*0-8020-4630-4*) U of Toronto Pr.

Canadian Selection: Books & Periodicals for Libraries. Edith T. Jarvi et al. LC 78-312410. 1072p. reprint ed. pap. 180.00 (*0-8357-3993-7*, 2036693) Bks Demand.

Canadian Short Stories. Ed. by Raymond Knister. LC 79-160938. (Short Story Index Reprint Ser.). 1977. reprint ed. 20.95 (*0-8369-3917-4*) Ayer.

Canadian Sioux. James H. Howard. LC 83-23506. (Studies in the Anthropology of North American Indians). xvi, 207p. 1984. 25.00 (*0-8032-2327-7*) U of Nebr Pr.

C

An Asterisk (*) at the beginning of an entry indicates that the title is appearing in BIP for the first time. 1021

Canadian Small & Medium-Sized Enterprise: Situation & Challenges. Gerald D'Amboise. 230p. 1991. pap. text ed. 23.00 (*0-88645-121-3*, Pub. by Inst Res Pub CN) Ashgate Pub Co.

Canadian Social Policy. 2nd rev. ed. Ed. by Shankar A. Yelaja. 442p. (C). 1987. pap. 25.00 (*0-88920-961-8*, Pub. by Wilfrid Laurier CN) Humanities.

Canadian Social Welfare Policy: Federal & Provincial Dimensions. Jacqueline S. Ismael. (Canadian Public Administration Ser.). 208p. 1985. 44.95 (*0-7735-0579-2*, Pub. by McGill CN); pap. 24.95 (*0-7735-0612-8*, Pub. by McGill CN) U of Toronto Pr.

Canadian Society: A Macro Analysis. 2nd ed. Harry Hiller. 1991. pap. text ed. 28.00 (*0-13-116757-X*, 680201) P-H.

Canadian Society: A Sociological Analysis. M. Hiller. 1976. pap. 16.00 (*0-13-113324-1*) P-H.

Canadian Society During the French Regime. William J. Eccles. LC 68-27288. (E. R. Adair Memorial Lectures). 178p. reprint ed. pap. 50.80 (*0-317-28412-6*, 2022294) Bks Demand.

***Canadian-Soviet Relations, 1936-1980.** Ed. by Aloysius Balawyder. 222p. 1995. lib. bdg. 37.00 (*0-8095-4933-6*) Borgo Pr.

Canadian Spiders, No. II. James H. Emerton. (Connecticut Academy of Arts & Sciences Ser., Trans.: Vol. 20). 1916. pap. 49.50 (*0-685-22846-0*) Elliots Bks.

Canadian State: Political Economy & Political Power. Ed. by Leo Panitch. 1977. pap. 18.95 (*0-8020-6322-5*) U of Toronto Pr.

Canadian Telecommunication Equipment & Service Markets: Digital Wireless Communications Take Off. Market Intelligence Staff. 340p. 1994. 2,295.00 (*1-56753-989-0*) Frost & Sullivan.

Canadian Tort Law. 4th ed. Linden. 840p. 1988. 150.00 (*0-409-80191-7*) Butterworth Legal Pubs.

Canadian Tort Law. 5th ed. Allen M. Linden. 864p. 1993. text ed. 155.00 (*0-409-90596-8*); student ed. pap. text ed. 80.00 (*0-409-91429-0*) Butterworth Legal Pubs.

Canadian Tort Law: Cases, Notes & Materials. 9th ed. Wright et al. 928p. 1990. pap. 108.00 (*0-409-88898-2*) Butterworth Legal Pubs.

***Canadian Tort Law: Cases, Notes & Materials.** 10th ed. Allen Linden & Lewis Klar. 864p. 1994. pap. 85.00 (*0-409-91188-7*, CN) Butterworth Legal Pubs.

Canadian Treasures: Twenty Five Artists, Twenty Five Paintings, 25 Years. Brad Blain & John H. Panabaker. (C). 1981. pap. 9.95 (*0-919423-36-1*, Pub. by Wilfrid Laurier CN) Humanities.

Canadian Treaty Calendar: Repertoire des Traites du Canada, 1928-1978, Set: Vols. 1 & 2. Christian L. Wiktor. LC 82-12462. (ENG & FRE.). 1983. Set. lib. bdg. 150.00 (*0-379-20600-5*) Oceana.

Canadian-United States Tariff & Canadian Industry: Multisectoral Analysis. James R. Williams. LC 78-316454. 185p. reprint ed. pap. 52.80 (*0-685-15914-0*, 2056123) Bks Demand.

***Canadian War Posters.** Marc Choko. (Illus.). 192p. (Orig.). 1994. pap. 51.95x (*0-614-00437-3*, Pub. by Canada Commun Grp CN) Accents Pubns.

Canadian West Gifset, 4 bks., Set. Janette Oke. (Orig.). 1986. pap. 27.99 (*0-87123-972-8*) Bethany Hse.

***Canadian West Saga.** Oke. 1995. 12.98 (*0-88486-112-0*) Arrowood Pr.

Canadian Who's Who. (BCL1 - History - Canada Ser.). 1991. reprint ed. lib. bdg. 99.00 (*0-7812-6346-8*) Rprt Serv.

***Canadian Who's Who, Vol. XXX.** Ed. by Kieran Simpson. 1300p. (C). 1995. 160.00 (*0-8020-4685-1*) U of Toronto Pr.

Canadian Who's Who Index 1898-1984: Incorporating Men & Women of the Time. Evelyn McMann. 528p. 1986. 125.00 (*0-8020-4633-9*) U of Toronto Pr.

Canadian Who's Who, 1992, Vol. XXVII. Ed. by Kieran Simpson. 1150p. 1992. 155.00 (*0-8020-4664-9*) U of Toronto Pr.

Canadian Who's Who 1994, No. XXIX. Ed. by Kieran Simpson. 1253p. 1994. text ed. 160.00 (*0-8020-4677-0*) U of Toronto Pr.

Canadian Wilds. Martin Hunter. 277p. pap. 4.00 (*0-936622-02-4*) A R Harding Pub.

Canadian Wing Commanders of Fighter Command in WW Two. George Brown & Michel Lavigne. 324p. (C). 1987. 105.00 (*0-317-90383-7*, Pub. by Picton UK) St Mut.

Canadian Women Writing Fiction. Ed. by Mickey Pearlman. LC 92-44969. 288p. 1993. text ed. 32.50 (*0-87805-636-X*) U Pr of Miss.

Canadian Women's Movement, 1960-1990: A Guide to Archival Resources. Ed. by Margaret Fulford. 380p. (C). 1992. text ed. 70.00 (*1-55022-156-6*, Pub. by ECW Press CN) Genl Dist Srvs.

Canadian Woods: Their Properties & Uses. 3rd ed. Ed. by E. J. Mullins & T. S. McKnight. 400p. 1981. 40.00 (*0-8020-2430-0*) U of Toronto Pr.

Canadian Writers. Arthur L. Phelps. LC 73-38030. (Essay Index Reprint Ser.). 1977. reprint ed. 16.95 (*0-8369-2617-X*) Ayer.

Canadian Writers & Their Works: Cumulated Index, Fiction Series. Ed. by Donald W. McLeod. 102p. (C). 1993. pap. text ed. 20.00 (*1-55022-142-6*, Pub. by ECW Press CN) Genl Dist Srvs.

Canadian Writers & Their Works: Cumulated Index, Poetry Series. Ed. by Donald W. McLeod. 137p. (C). 1993. pap. text ed. 20.00 (*1-55022-143-4*, Pub. by ECW Press CN) Genl Dist Srvs.

Canadian Writers & Their Works, Vol. 1: Fiction. Ed. by Robert Lecker et al. (Illus.). 256p. (C). 1983. text ed. 45.00 (*0-920802-45-1*, Pub. by ECW Press CN) Genl Dist Srvs.

Canadian Writers & Their Works, Vol. 1: Poetry. Ed. by Robert Lecker et al. (Illus.). 250p. (C). 1988. text ed. 45.00 (*0-920763-69-3*, Pub. by ECW Press CN) Genl Dist Srvs.

Canadian Writers & Their Works, Vol. 10: Fiction. Ed. by Robert Lecker et al. (Illus.). 294p. (C). 1989. text ed. 45.00 (*0-920763-85-5*, Pub. by ECW Press CN) Genl Dist Srvs.

Canadian Writers & Their Works, Vol. 10: Poetry. Ed. by Robert Lecker et al. (Illus.). 395p. (C). 1992. text ed. 45.00 (*1-55022-069-1*, Pub. by ECW Press CN) Genl Dist Srvs.

Canadian Writers & Their Works, Vol. 2: Fiction. Ed. by Robert Lecker et al. (Illus.). 270p. (C). 1989. text ed. 45.00 (*1-55022-046-2*, Pub. by ECW Press CN) Genl Dist Srvs.

Canadian Writers & Their Works, Vol. 2: Poetry. Ed. by Robert Lecker et al. (Illus.). 289p. (C). 1983. text ed. 45.00 (*0-920802-46-X*, Pub. by ECW Press CN) Genl Dist Srvs.

Canadian Writers & Their Works, Vol. 3: Poetry. Ed. by Robert Lecker et al. (Illus.). 200p. (C). 1987. text ed. 45.00 (*0-920763-19-7*, Pub. by ECW Press CN) Genl Dist Srvs.

Canadian Writers & Their Works, Vol. 4: Fiction. Ed. by Robert Lecker et al. (Illus.). 298p. (C). 1991. text ed. 45.00 (*1-55022-052-7*, Pub. by ECW Press CN) Genl Dist Srvs.

Canadian Writers & Their Works, Vol. 4: Poetry. Ed. by Robert Lecker et al. (Illus.). 286p. (C). 1990. text ed. 45.00 (*1-55022-021-7*, Pub. by ECW Press CN) Genl Dist Srvs.

Canadian Writers & Their Works, Vol. 5: Fiction. Ed. by Robert Lecker et al. (Illus.). 257p. (C). 1990. text ed. 45.00 (*1-55022-027-6*, Pub. by ECW Press CN) Genl Dist Srvs.

Canadian Writers & Their Works, Vol. 5: Poetry. Ed. by Robert Lecker et al. (Illus.). 329p. (C). 1985. text ed. 45.00 (*0-920802-90-7*, Pub. by ECW Press CN) Genl Dist Srvs.

Canadian Writers & Their Works, Vol. 6: Fiction. Ed. by Robert Lecker et al. (Illus.). 272p. (C). 1985. text ed. 45.00 (*0-920802-86-9*, Pub. by ECW Press CN) Genl Dist Srvs.

Canadian Writers & Their Works, Vol. 6: Poetry. Ed. by Robert Lecker et al. (Illus.). 316p. (C). 1989. text ed. 45.00 (*1-55022-007-1*, Pub. by ECW Press CN) Genl Dist Srvs.

Canadian Writers & Their Works, Vol. 7: Fiction. Ed. by Robert Lecker et al. (Illus.). 310p. (C). 1985. text ed. 45.00 (*0-920802-88-5*, Pub. by ECW Press CN) Genl Dist Srvs.

Canadian Writers & Their Works, Vol. 7: Poetry. Ed. by Robert Lecker et al. (Illus.). 316p. (C). 1990. text ed. 45.00 (*1-55022-057-8*, Pub. by ECW Press CN) Genl Dist Srvs.

Canadian Writers & Their Works, Vol. 8: Fiction. Ed. by Robert Lecker et al. (Illus.). 283p. (C). 1989. text ed. 45.00 (*1-55022-032-2*, Pub. by ECW Press CN) Genl Dist Srvs.

Canadian Writers & Their Works, Vol. 8: Poetry. Ed. by Robert Lecker et al. (Illus.). 412p. (C). 1992. text ed. 45.00 (*1-55022-063-2*, Pub. by ECW Press CN) Genl Dist Srvs.

Canadian Writers & Their Works, Vol. 9: Fiction. Ed. by Robert Lecker et al. (Illus.). 373p. (C). 1987. text ed. 45.00 (*0-920763-79-0*, Pub. by ECW Press CN) Genl Dist Srvs.

Canadian Writers & Their Works, Vol. 9: Poetry. Ed. by Robert Lecker et al. (Illus.). 271p. (C). 1985. text ed. 45.00 (*0-920802-47-8*, Pub. by ECW Press CN) Genl Dist Srvs.

Canadian Writers & Thier Works, Vol. 3: Fiction. Ed. by Robert Lecker et al. (Illus.). 276p. (C). 1988. text ed. 45.00 (*0-920763-74-X*, Pub. by ECW Press CN) Genl Dist Srvs.

Canadian Writer's Market: An Extensive Guide for Freelance Writers. 11th ed. Jem Bates. 1994. pap. 14.95 (*0-7710-8795-0*, Pub. by McClelland & Stewart CN) Firefly Bks Ltd.

Canadian Writers, Nineteen Twenty to Nineteen Fifty-Nine, Vol. 68. W. H. New. (Dictionary of Literary Biography Ser.: Vol. 68). 1988. 128.00 (*0-8103-1746-X*) Gale.

Canadian Writers since 1960, 2nd Series, Vol. 60. Ed. by W. H. New. (Dictionary of Literary Biography Ser.). 416p. 1987. 128.00 (*0-8103-1738-9*) Gale.

Canadian Yiddish Writings. Ed. by Abraham Bovarsky & Lazar Sarna. LC 77-362060. 150p. reprint ed. pap. 42.80 (*0-317-10945-6*, 2022287) Bks Demand.

Canadians. (Old West Ser.). (Illus.). 240p. 1977. 19.93 (*0-8094-1543-7*); lib. bdg. 25.93 (*0-8094-1542-9*) Time-Life.

Canadians. Andrew H. Malcolm. (Illus.). 416p. 1991. pap. 13.95 (*0-312-06921-9*) St Martin.

Canadians. George Woodcock. LC 79-3176. (Illus.). 301p. 1980. 32.00x (*0-674-09335-6*) HUP.

Canadians: Eighteen Sixty-Seven to Nineteen Sixty-Seven, Pt. 1. James M. Careless & R. Craig Brown. (Illus.). 1995. pap. 14.95 (*0-312-11795-7*) St Martin.

Canadians at Last: The Integration of Newfoundland As a Province. Raymond B. Blake. (Illus.). 272p. (C). 1994. 55.00 (*0-8020-0554-3*); pap. 19.95 (*0-8020-6978-9*) U of Toronto Pr.

Canadians in the Making: A Social History of Canada. Arthur R. Lower. LC 81-4142. (Illus.). xxiv, 475p. 1981. reprint ed. text ed. 89.50 (*0-313-23037-4*, LOCAN, Greenwood Pr) Greenwood.

***Canadians on Everest.** Bruce Patterson. (Illus.). 241p. 1990. 29.95 (*1-55059-015-4*) Temeron Bks.

Canadians with Custer in Eighteen Seventy-Six. Bernie Rosevear & Stephen Rosevear. (Illus.). 24p. (Orig.). 1992. pap. 8.95 (*0-940696-32-0*) Monroe County Lib.

Canadienne: Memories of a Vanishing Culture. Gabrielle L. Caffee. 254p. (Orig.). (C). 1992. pap. text ed. 24.00 (*0-8191-8796-8*) U Pr of Amer.

Canadiens, Canadians & Quebecoi's. B. Hodgins et al. 1974. pap. text ed. 7.40 (*0-13-112888-4*) P-H.

Canaima. Romulo Gallegos. Ed. by Charles Minguet. (Coleccion Archivos). 522p. (SPA.). 1991. 34.95 (*84-00-07120-4*) U of Pittsburgh Pr.

***Canaima.** Romulo Gallegos. Tr. by Will Kirkland. LC 95-10682. (Pittsburgh Editions of Latin American Literature Ser.). 1995. write for info. (*0-8229-3883-9*); pap. write for info. (*0-8229-5561-X*) U of Pittsburgh Pr.

Canaima. Romulo Gallegos. Tr. by Jaime Tello. LC 84-2096. (Illus.). 360p. 1986. reprint ed. 22.95 (*0-8061-9928-8*); reprint ed. pap. 10.95 (*0-8061-2119-X*) U of Okla Pr.

Canal & River Cruising: The IWA Manual. Sheila Davenport. (C). 1990. text ed. 59.00 (*0-906754-49-6*, Pub. by Fernhurst Bks UK) St Mut.

Canal & River Levees. P. Peter. (Developments in Geotechnical Engineering Ser.: Vol. 29). 540p. 1982. 148.75 (*0-444-99726-1*) Elsevier.

***Canal Architecture.** Peter L. Smith. (C). 1989. pap. 25.00x (*0-7478-0169-X*, Pub. by Shire UK) St Mut.

Canal Bed. Helena Minton. LC 84-72463. 1985. 15.95 (*0-914086-52-9*); pap. 9.95 (*0-914086-53-7*) Alicejamesbooks.

Canal Bibliography: With a Primary Emphasis on the United States & Canada. Albright G. Zimmerman. 187p. (C). 1991. pap. text ed. 24.95 (*0-930973-11-9*) Canal Hist Tech.

Canal Boat to Freedom. 2nd ed. Thomas Fall. (Illus.). (YA). (gr. 4-6). reprint ed. pap. write for info. (*0-9636532-0-2*) Neversink Valley.

Canal Boatman: My Life on Upstate Waterways. Richard Garrity. LC 77-21909. (New York State Bks.). (Illus.). 240p. 1984. pap. 14.95 (*0-8156-0191-3*) Syracuse U Pr.

Canal Capers: Pun-ting about the English Midlands. A. L. Christopherson. (Illus.). 42p. (Orig.). 1991. pap. text ed. 2.95 (*0-9601372-0-3*) Christopherson.

Canal Country. Emily Williams. (Illus.). 120p. 1982. 16.95 (*0-9608330-1-3*) H M Cardamone.

Canal Electrical Supervisor. Jack Rudman. (Career Examination Ser.: C-3301). 1994. pap. 29.95 (*0-8373-3301-6*) Nat Learn.

Canal for All Seasons: The Romance of Ohio's Canal Era. M. Ruth Norton. (Illus.). 85p. (Orig.). Date not set. pap. 4.00 (*1-880443-07-4*) Roscoe Village.

Canal History & Technology Proceedings, Vol. XII. 1993. pap. 15.00 (*0-685-36265-5*) Canal Hist Tech.

Canal Irrigation in Prehistoric Mexico: The Sequence of Technological Change. William E. Doolittle. (Illus.). 219p. (C). 1990. text ed. 32.50x (*0-292-71558-7*) U of Tex Pr.

Canal Irrigation in the Punjab. Paul W. Paustian. LC 68-58614. (Columbia University. Studies in the Social Sciences: No. 322). reprint ed. 20.00 (*0-404-51322-0*) AMS Pr.

Canal Maintenance Shop Supervisor I. Jack Rudman. (Career Examination Ser.: C-3015). 1994. pap. 29.95 (*0-8373-3015-7*) Nat Learn.

Canal Maintenance Shop Supervisor II. Jack Rudman. (Career Examination Ser.: C-3016). 1994. pap. 29.95 (*0-8373-3016-5*) Nat Learn.

Canal Maintenance Supervisor I. Jack Rudman. (Career Examination Ser.: C-3141). 1994. pap. 29.95 (*0-8373-3141-2*) Nat Learn.

Canal Maintenance Supervisor II. Jack Rudman. (Career Examination Ser.: C-3142). 1994. pap. 29.95 (*0-8373-3142-0*) Nat Learn.

Canal Priests of Mars. Marcus L. Rowland. (Space: Eighteen Eighty-Nine Ser.). (Illus.). 64p. (Orig.). (YA). 1990. pap. 8.00 (*1-55878-039-4*) Game Designers.

***Canal Section Superintendent.** (Career Examination Ser.: Series 1). Date not set. pap. 29.95 (*0-8373-3661-9*) Nat Learn.

Canal Structure Operator. Jack Rudman. (Career Examination Ser.: C-3133). 1994. pap. 29.95 (*0-8373-3133-1*) Nat Learn.

Canal Systems Automation Manual. USDI Staff. (C). 1992. text ed. 235.00 (*81-7233-045-6*, Pub. by Scientific Pubs II) St Mut.

Canal Town. Samuel H. Adams. Ed. by Frank Bergmann. 476p. 1988. pap. 15.95 (*0-8156-0228-6*) Syracuse U Pr.

***Canal Town & Country Seat: The Historical Geography of Morris.** Ed. by Michael P. Conzen & Valerie M. Mckay. LC 94-3798. (Studies on the Illinois & Michigan Canal Corridor: Vol. 8). 1994. 15.00 (*0-89065-143-4*) U Chicago Comm Geo.

Canal Walks of England & Wales. Ray Quinlan. (Illus.). 576p. 1994. boxed 50.00 (*0-7509-0608-1*) A Sutton Pub.

Canal Walks, Vol. 1: Derbyshire & Nottinghamshire. John Merrill. 1986. 25.00 (*0-907496-30-X*, Pub. by JNM Pubns UK) St Mut.

Canal Water & Whiskey: Tall Tales of the Erie Canal Country. rev. ed. Marvin A. Rapp. (Illus.). 398p. (C). 1992. pap. 19.95 (*1-878097-07-5*) Canisius Coll Pr.

Canalboat Primer. Erie Canal Museum Staff. 57p. 1981. pap. 4.95 (*1-883582-01-6*) Erie Canal Mus.

Canales (Canals) J. Cooper. (Maravillas de la Humanidad (Man-Made Wonders) Ser.: Set VI). (SPA.). (J). 1991. 8.95 (*0-86592-923-8*) Rourke Enter.

***Canaletto.** Christopher Baker. (Color Library). (Illus.). 128p. (C). 1994. 19.95 (*0-7148-3207-3*, Pub. by Phaidon Press UK) Chronicle Bks.

***Canaletto.** Christopher Baker. (C). 1994. pap. 14.95 (*0-7148-3249-9*, Pub. by Phaidon Press UK) Chronicle Bks.

Canaletto. J. G. Links & Katherine Baetjer. (Illus.). 384p. 1990. 45.00 (*0-8109-3155-9*, Abrams); pap. 35.00 (*0-87099-561-8*, Abrams) Metro Mus Art.

***Canaletto.** rev. ed. J. G. Links. (Illus.). 240p. (C). 1994. reprint ed. 49.95 (*0-7148-3170-0*, Pub. by Phaidon Press UK) Chronicle Bks.

Canaletto: Giovanni Antonio Canal, 1697-1768, 2 vols., Set. 2nd rev. ed. W. G. Constable. Ed. by J. G. Links. (Illus.). 1126p. 1989. 285.00 (*0-19-817389-X*) OUP.

Canaletto: Selected Drawings. Terisio Pignatti. LC 74-104778. (Illus.). 200p. 1970. Individually boxed. boxed 160.00 (*0-271-00105-4*) A Wofsy Fine Arts.

Canaletto & England. Michael Liversidge et al. (Illus.). 192p. 1994. 50.00 (*1-85894-002-8*) U of Wash Pr.

Canaletto Drawings: Forty-Seven Works. Canaletto. 1991. pap. 3.95 (*0-486-26647-8*) Dover.

Canaletto's Complete Etchings. Harry Salamon. (Illus.). 104p. (ITA.). 1971. 135.00 (*1-55660-158-1*) A Wofsy Fine Arts.

Canaletto's Etchings: Catalogue Raisonne. rev. ed. Ruth Bromberg. (Illus.). 244p. 1993. 150.00 (*1-55660-214-6*) A Wofsy Fine Arts.

Canalgate: A Panama Canal Brief for the American People. rev. ed. Samuel J. Stoll. (Illus.). 616p. 1989. 24.95 (*0-9623409-0-1*); pap. 19.95 (*0-9623409-1-X*) Policy Pr.

Canaller's Songbook. William Hullfish. (Illus.). 88p. 1993. 6.00 (*0-933788-44-4*) Am Canal & Transport.

Canals. J. Cooper. (Man-Made Wonders Ser.). (J). 1991. 8.95 (*0-86592-638-7*) Rourke Enter.

Canals - a New Look. Ed. by Mark Baldwin & Tony Burton. 198p. (C). 1989. 70.00 (*0-85033-516-7*, Pub. by S A Baldwin UK) St Mut.

Canals & American Cities: Assessing the Impact of Canals on the Course of American Urban Life. Scott F. Anfinson et al. (Illus.). 112p. 1994. pap. 15.00 (*0-930973-14-3*) Canal Hist Tech.

Canals & Industry: Engineering in Lowell, 1821-1880. Patrick M. Malone. (Illus.). 27p. (Orig.). 1983. pap. 2.50 (*0-942472-07-1*) Lowell Museum.

Canals & Railroads of the Mid-Atlantic States, 1800-1860. Christopher T. Baer. 80p. 1981. pap. 15.00 (*0-914650-19-X*) Hagley Museum.

Canals & Waterways. Chris Oxlade. LC 93-49749. (Technology Craft Topics Ser.). (Illus.). (J). 1994. 12.60 (*0-531-14331-7*) Watts.

Canals & Waterways. Michael E. Ware. 1989. pap. 25.00 (*0-85263-878-7*, Pub. by Shire UK) St Mut.

Canals Are My Home. Iris Bryce. 142p. 1987. 50.00 (*0-685-21018-9*, Pub. by K Mason Pubns Ltd UK) St Mut.

Canals Are My Home. large type ed. Iris Bryce. 1991. 21.95 (*0-7089-2511-1*) Ulverscroft.

Canals Are My Life. Iris Bryce. 104p. 1987. 50.00 (*0-85937-277-4*, Pub. by K Mason Pubns Ltd UK) St Mut.

Canals Are My Life. large type ed. Iris A. Bryce. (Non-Fiction Ser.). 224p. 1992. 21.95 (*0-7089-2762-9*) Ulverscroft.

Canals for a Nation: A History of the Canal Era in the United States, 1790-1860. Ronald E. Shaw. LC 90-42008. 304p. 1991. text ed. 30.00 (*0-8131-1701-1*) U Pr of Ky.

Canals for a Nation: The Canal Era in the United States, 1790-1860. Ronald E. Shaw. LC 90-42008. (Illus.). 304p. 1993. reprint ed. pap. text ed. 15.00 (*0-8131-0815-2*) U Pr of Ky.

Canals of England. Martin M. Evans. (Country Ser.). (Illus.). 160p. 1994. 24.95 (*0-297-83261-1*) Trafalgar.

***Canals of England.** Martin M. Evans. (Country Ser.). (Illus.). 160p. 1995. pap. 16.95 (*0-297-83471-1*, Pub. by Orion) Trafalgar.

Canals of England. Eric De Mare. (Illus.). 144p. 1991. reprint ed. pap. 20.00 (*0-86299-418-7*) A Sutton Pub.

Canals of Mid-America. Leslie C. Swanson. (Illus.). 1986. 4.00 (*0-911466-16-9*) Swanson.

Canals of New York State: 1991 Edition. American Canal Society Staff. (Illus.). 1991. 6.00 (*0-933788-82-7*) Am Canal & Transport.

Canals of South & Southeast England. Ellis C. Hadfield. LC 78-78974. (Illus.). 393p. 1969. 29.95 (*0-678-05552-1*) Kelley.

Canals of South West England. Charles Hadfield. LC 68-71608. (Illus.). 206p. 1967. 24.95 (*0-678-05699-4*) Kelley.

Canapes & Frivolities: Recipes from the Savoy, London. Anton Edelmann & Jane Suthering. (Illus.). 144p. pap. 24.95 (*1-85145-824-7*, Pub. by Pavilion UK) Trafalgar.

Canard: A Revolution in Flight. Frwd. by Andy Lennon & Burt Rutan. LC 84-71364. (AV Bk.: No. 8). (Illus.). 200p. 1984. pap. 19.95 (*0-938716-18-2*) Markowski Intl.

Canard et la Panthere. Marcel Ayme. (Folio - Cadet Bleu Ser.: No. 128). (Illus.). 63p. (FRE.). (J). (gr. 1-5). 1991. pap. 9.95 (*2-07-031128-7*) Schoenhof.

***Canarias y America.** F. Morales Padron. (Gran Enciclopedia de Espana y America Ser.). (Illus.). (SPA.). 1989. 200.00x (*84-87053-12-2*) Elliots Bks.

Canaries. George C. Lynch. (Colorguide Ser.). 1982. pap. 6.95 (*0-940842-10-6*) South Group.

Canaries. Paul R. Paradise. (Illus.). 1979. 9.95 (*0-86622-725-3*, KW-004) TFH Pubns.

Canaries. 2nd rev. ed. (Canaries for Pleasure & Profit Ser.). (Illus.). 80p. 1984. pap. 5.95 (*0-86622-236-7*, PB-102) TFH Pubns.

Canaries: A Complete Pet Owner's Manual. Otto Von Frisch. 64p. 1991. pap. 5.95 (*0-8120-4611-0*) Barron.

Canaries: Look & Learn. T. Halaburda. (Illus.). 64p. 1993. 7.95 (*0-7938-0068-4*, KD007) TFH Pubns.

Canaries & Related Birds. Horst Bielfeld. (Illus.). 200p. 1988. 34.95 (*0-86622-646-X*, H-1089) TFH Pubns.

Canaries As a Hobby. Anmarie Barrie. 1992. pap. 7.95 (*0-86622-433-5*) TFH Pubns.

C

An Asterisk (*) at the beginning of an entry indicates that the title is appearing in BIP for the first time.

An Asterisk (*) at the beginning of an entry indicates that the title is appearing in BIP for the first time.

1023

C

Cancer Biology Reviews, Vol. 1. Ed. by John J. Marchalonis et al. LC 80-644712. (Illus.). 368p. 1980. reprint ed. pap. 99.40 (*0-7837-0741-X*, 2041063) Bks Demand.

Cancer Biology Reviews, Vol. 2. Ed. by John J. Marchalonis et al. LC 80-644712. (Illus.). 294p. 1981. reprint ed. pap. 83.80 (*0-7837-0742-8*) Bks Demand.

Cancer Biology Reviews, Vol. 3. Ed. by John J. Marchalonis et al. LC 80-644712. (Illus.). 223p. 1982. reprint ed. pap. 63.60 (*0-7837-0743-6*) Bks Demand.

Cancer-Birth Control Pills: Cause & Effect, Relationship, Benefits vs. Risks. American Medical Association Staff & Jacques Melek. (Illus.). 500p. (Orig.). 1984. pap. 19.85 (*0-685-09135-X*, Sunbright Bks) J Melek.

Cancer Book: A Guide to Understanding the Causes, Prevention, & Treatment of Cancer. Geoffrey M. Cooper. LC 93-16282. 256p. 1993. pap. text ed. 14.95 (*0-86720-770-1*) Jones & Bartlett.

Cancer Care: A Personal Guide. Harold Glucksberg & Jack W. Singer. LC 79-16930. 1980. 45.00 (*0-8018-2255-6*) Johns Hopkins.

Cancer Care: An International Survey. Ronald W. Raven et al. LC 86-9247. 340p. reprint ed. pap. 96.90 (*0-7837-4506-0*, 2044283) Bks Demand.

***Cancer Care: Prevention, Treatment & Palliation.** Ed. by J. David & Marie Curie. (Illus.). 444p. 1994. pap. text ed. 54.25 (*1-56593-288-9*, 0612) Singular Publishing.

Cancer Care & Cost: DRGs & Beyond. Ed. by Richard M. Scheffler & Neil C. Andrews. LC 89-19803. 260p. 1989. pap. text ed. 28.00 (*0-910701-45-8*, 0895) Health Admin Pr.

Cancer Care Protocols for Hospital & Home Care Use. 2nd ed. Doris Ahana & Marilyn Kunishi. 368p. 1986. pap. 35.95 (*0-8261-3293-6*) Springer Pub.

Cancer Causes & Natural Controls. Lynn Dallin. LC 82-13765. 374p. 1984. 24.95 (*0-87949-224-4*) Ashley Bks.

Cancer Causes & Prevention. Ed. by Swedish Cancer Committee Staff. 500p. 1992. 200.00 (*0-85066-344-X*) Taylor & Francis.

Cancer Cell. Ed. by K. Sikora et al. (British Medical Bulletin Ser.: Vol. 47, No. 1). (Illus.). 1991p. 1991. text ed. write for info. (*0-443-04489-9*) Churchill.

Cancer Cell Adhesion & Tumor Invasion. P. Brodt. (Medical Intelligence Unit Ser.). write for info. (*1-57059-082-6*) R G Landes.

***Cancer Cell Metastasis.** Ed. by R. G. Vile. (Molecular Medical Science Ser.). 1995. text ed. 49.95 (*0-471-95266-4*) Wiley.

Cancer Chemo-& Immunopharmacology Part 1: Chemopharmacology. Ed. by G. Mathe & Franco M. Muggia. (Recent Results in Cancer Research Ser.: Vol. 74). (Illus.). 315p. 1980. 77.00 (*0-387-10162-4*) Spr-Verlag.

Cancer Chemoprevention. Wattenberg. 1992. 161.00 (*0-8493-4715-7*, RC268) CRC Pr.

***Cancer Chemotherapeutic Agents.** Ed. by William O. Foye. LC 94-39366. (Professional Reference Book Ser.). 1995. write for info. (*0-8412-2920-1*) Am Chemical.

Cancer Chemotherapy. Barton & Burke. 480p. 1991. boxed 50.00 (*0-86720-434-6*) Jones & Bartlett.

Cancer Chemotherapy. Ed. by F. Homburger. (Karger Highlights, Oncology One Ser.). (Illus.). 1979. pap. 12.00 (*3-8055-3026-9*) S Karger.

Cancer Chemotherapy. 3rd ed. T. J. Priestman. 225p. 1989. pap. 44.00 (*0-387-19551-3*) Spr-Verlag.

Cancer Chemotherapy: A Veterinary Handbook. Kevin A. Hahn & Richardson. 1994. 29.50 (*0-683-03837-0*) Williams & Wilkins.

Cancer Chemotherapy: A Veterinary Handbook. Ed. by Kevin A. Hahn & Ralph C. Richardson. LC 94-4930. 1994. write for info. (*0-8121-1693-3*) Williams & Wilkins.

Cancer Chemotherapy: Challenges for the Future. Ed. by K. Kimura et al. (International Congress Ser.: No. 776). 356p. 1988. 108.75 (*0-444-80942-2*, Excerpta Medica) Elsevier.

Cancer Chemotherapy: Concepts, Clinical Investigations & Therapeutic Advances. Ed. by Franco M. Muggia. (Cancer Treatment & Research Ser.). (C). 1988. lib. bdg. 107.00 (*0-89838-381-1*) Kluwer Ac.

***Cancer Chemotherapy: Nursing Process.** 2nd ed. Margaret B. Burke et al. (Nursing Ser.). 470p. 1995. 54.95 (*0-86720-718-3*) Jones & Bartlett.

Cancer Chemotherapy: Principles & Practice. B. A. Chabner & Collins. (Illus.). 576p. 1990. text ed. 105.00 (*0-397-50900-6*) Lippincott.

Cancer Chemotherapy - Challenges for the Future, Vol. 8: Proceedings of the Eighth Nagoya International, Symposium on Cancer Treatmenet, Nagoya, Japan, 16-17 October 1992, Vol. 1048. Ed. by K. Kimura et al. (International Congress Ser.). 336p. 1993. 200.00 (*0-444-81694-1*, Excerpta Medica) Elsevier.

Cancer Chemotherapy - Challenges for the Future, Volume 3: Proceedings of the 3rd Nagoya International Symposium on Cancer Treatment, Nagoya, Japan, Sept. 28-30, 1987. Ed. by K. Kimura et al. (International Congress Ser.: NO. 838). 324p. 1989. 92.50 (*0-444-81037-4*, Excerpta Medica) Elsevier.

***Cancer Chemotherapy & Biological Response Modifiers.** Ed. by H. M. Pineso et al. 732p. 1994. 285.75 (*0-444-82056-6*) Elsevier.

Cancer Chemotherapy & Biological Response Modifiers, Vol. 12. Ed. by H. M. Pindeo et al. 700p. 1991. 214.50 (*0-444-81443-4*) Elsevier.

Cancer Chemotherapy & Biological Response Modifiers, Vol. 14. Ed. by H. M. Pinedo et al. 692p. 1993. 268.50 (*0-444-81509-0*) Elsevier.

Cancer Chemotherapy & Biotherapy: The Reference Guide. 2nd ed. Linda Tenenbaum. LC 94-6844. (Illus.). 640p. 1994. pap. text ed. 41.95 (*0-7216-6720-1*) Saunders.

Cancer Chemotherapy & Selective Drug Development: Proceedings of the Tenth Anniversary Meeting of the Coordination Committee for Human Tumor Investigations, Brighton, England (24-28 October, 1983) K. R. Harrap et al. (Developments in Oncology Ser.). 615p. 1984. lib. bdg. 94.50 (*0-89838-673-X*) Kluwer Ac.

Cancer Chemotherapy by Infusion. 2nd Ed. Ed. by Jacob J. Lokich. LC 90-61367. 712p. 1990. 129.00 (*0-944496-14-8*) Precept Pr.

Cancer Chemotherapy: Challenges for the Future: Proceedings of the Nagoya International Symposium on Cancer Treatment, 1st, Nagoya, Japan, 14-16 October, 1985. Ed. by K. Kimura et al. (International Congress Ser.: No. 729). 374p. 1986. 80.00 (*0-317-55282-1*, Excerpta Medica) Elsevier.

Cancer Chemotherapy: Challenges for the Future, Vol. 4: Proc. of the 4th Nagoya Internat. Symp. on Cancer Treatment, Nagoya, Japan, Oct. 11-13, 1988. Ed. by K. Kimura et al. (International Congress Ser.: No. 904). 372p. 1990. 113.00 (*0-444-81189-3*, Excerpta Medica) Elsevier.

Cancer Chemotherapy: Challenges for the Future, Vol. 5: Proceedings of the 5th Nagoya International Symposium on Cancer Treatment, Nagoya, Japan, Oct. 2-4 1989. Ed. by K. Kimura et al. (International Congress Ser.: No. 945). 364p. 1990. 125.50 (*0-444-81381-0*, Excerpta Medica) Elsevier.

Cancer Chemotherapy Handbook. 2nd ed. Robert T. Dorr & Daniel D. Von Hoff. 1368p. 1993. text ed. 99.00 (*0-8385-1036-1*, A1036-1) Appleton & Lange.

Cancer Chemotherapy Handbook. 3rd ed. Fischer & Knobf. 656p. 1989. 39.00 (*0-8151-5115-2*, Yr Bk Med Pubs) Mosby Yr Bk.

Cancer Chemotherapy Handbook. 4th ed. David S. Fischer et al. LC 93-14659. 544p. 1993. 39.95 (*0-8016-6882-4*) Mosby Yr Bk.

Cancer Chemotherapy I. Franco M. Muggia. 1983. lib. bdg. 125.00 (*90-247-2713-8*) Kluwer Ac.

Cancer Chemotherapy in Small Animal Practice. Jane M. Dobson & Neil T. Gorman. LC 93-3434. (Library of Veterinary Practice). 1994. pap. 34.95 (*0-632-03694-X*) Blackwell Sci.

Cancer Chemotherapy: Reprinted Selected Top Articles Published 1976 - 1978. Ed. by F. Homburger. (Karger Highlights, Oncology Two Ser.). (Illus.). 1979. pap. 12.00 (*3-8055-3029-3*) S Karger.

Cancer Conqueror: An Incredible Journey to Wellness. Greg Anderson. 156p. 1990. pap. 7.95 (*0-8362-2415-9*) Andrews & McMeel.

Cancer Control: International Cancer Congress, 12th, Buenos Aires, 1978, Vol. 2. Ed. by A. Canonico et al. LC 79-40704. (Advances in Medical Oncology, Research & Education Ser.: Vol. II). (Illus.). 1979. 140.00 (*0-08-024385-1*, Pub. by Pergamon Repr UK) Franklin.

Cancer Control in the Countries of the Council of Mutual Economic Assistance. N. P. Napalkov & S. Eckhardt. 742p. 1982. 177.00 (*0-569-08718-X*) St Mut.

***Cancer Control in the Countries of the Council of Mutual Economic Assistance.** Ed. by N. P. Napalkov & S. Eckhardt. 741p. (C). 1982. 105.00x (*963-05-3036-8*) St Mut.

Cancer Cure that Works. 1991. lib. bdg. 250.00 (*0-8490-5033-2*) Gordon Pr.

***Cancer Curers - or Quacks? The Story of a Secret Herbal Remedy.** Ed. by T. Llew Jones & Safydd W. Jones. 128p. 1993. pap. 21.00 (*1-85902-023-2*, Pub. by Gomer Pr UK) St Mut.

Cancer Cytogenetics. Ed. by Sverre Heim & Felix Mitelman. 1987. text ed. 69.95 (*0-471-63816-1*) Wiley.

***Cancer Cytogenics.** 2nd ed. Ed. by Heim & Mitelman. Date not set. text ed. 59.95 (*0-471-12052-9*) Wiley.

Cancer Del Ano 2000: las Sectas: The Cults-Cancer for the Year 2000. C. Ramon Valles. (SPA.). 10.95 (*84-7645-330-2*, 223502, Pub. by Edit Clie SP) TSELF.

Cancer Dermatology. Ed. by Frederick Helm. LC 78-10586. 519p. reprint ed. pap. 148.00 (*0-685-20933-4*, 2056513) Bks Demand.

Cancer Diagnosis: Early Detection. Ed. by P. Bannasch. (Illus.). 272p. 1992. pap. 69.00 (*0-387-54503-4*) Spr-Verlag.

Cancer Diagnosis in Children. L. D. Samuels. (CRC Uniscience Ser). 1972. 46.00 (*0-87819-009-0*, R) CRC Pr.

Cancer Diagnosis in Vitro Monoclonal Antibodies. Kupchik. (Immunology Ser.: No. 39). 400p. 1988. 140.00 (*0-8247-7809-X*) Dekker.

Cancer Diagnostic & Treatment Products. Business Communications Co., Inc. Staff. 225p. 1987. pap. 1,950.00 (*0-89336-584-X*, C-047R) BCC.

***Cancer Diagnostic Imaging Markets.** Market Intelligence Staff. 410p. 1994. 2,295.00 (*0-7889-0139-7*) Frost & Sullivan.

Cancer, Diagnostics, & Chemotherapy: A Reference Manual. Cynthia C. Chernecky. 1991. pap. text ed. 29.50 (*0-7216-3187-8*) Saunders.

Cancer Diagnostics & Therapeutic Markets. (Market Research Reports: No. 376). (Illus.). 170p. 1994. 795.00 (*0-317-04983-6*) Theta Corp.

Cancer Dictionary. Roberta Altman & Michael J. Sarg. (Illus.). 352p. 1992. lib. bdg. 40.00 (*0-8160-2608-4*) Facts on File.

Cancer Dictionary. Roberta Altman & Michael Sarg. (Illus.). 352p. 1994. reprint ed. pap. 16.95 (*0-8160-3027-8*) Facts on File.

Cancer Epidemic: Shadow of the Conquest of Nature. Gotthard Booth. LC 59-7362. (Illus.). 277p. 1980. 89.95 (*0-88946-625-4*) E Mellen.

***Cancer Epidemiology & Prevention.** 2nd ed. Joseph F. Fraumeni, Jr. Ed. by David Schottenfeld. (Illus.). 1500p. 1996. 195.00 (*0-19-505354-0*) OUP.

Cancer Experience: Nursing Diagnosis & Management. Doris L. Carnevali & Ann C. Reiner. 483p. 1990. text ed. 33.50 (*0-397-54726-9*) Lippincott.

Cancer Factories: America's Tragic Quest for Uranium Self-Sufficiency. Howard Ball. LC 92-32225. (Contributions in Medical Studies: No. 37). 216p. 1993. text ed. 52.95 (*0-313-27566-1*, BFJ, Greenwood Pr) Greenwood.

***Cancer Free.** Sidney Winawer. 1995. 25.00 (*0-671-79967-3*) S&S Trade.

Cancer-Free: Thirty-Five Who Triumphed over Cancer Naturally. East West Foundation Staff & Ann Fawcett. (Illus.). 256p. (Orig.). 1991. pap. 18.00 (*0-87040-794-5*) Japan Pubns USA.

Cancer from Beef: The DES Controversy, Federal Food Regulation, & Consumer Confidence in Modern America. Alan I. Marcus. LC 93-21505. 1994. text ed. 38.50 (*0-8018-4700-1*) Johns Hopkins.

Cancer Genetics in Women, 2 vols., Set. Ed. by Lynch. 1987. 220.00 (*0-8493-5180-4*, RC281, CRC Reprint) Franklin.

***Cancer Handbook.** 940p. (Orig.). 1995. pap. 195.00 (*0-7605-1641-3*) Rector Pr.

Cancer Handbook. Mary B. Cook. (Nursing Ser.). 250p. (C). 1995. pap. 40.00 (*0-86720-676-4*) Jones & Bartlett.

***Cancer Handbook: A Guide for the Non-Specialist.** Darrell E. Ward. LC 95-8318. (Illus.). 1995. pap. write for info. (*0-8142-0675-1*) Ohio St U Pr.

Cancer, HIV & AIDS. Ed. by V. Beral et al. (Cancer Surveys Ser.: Vol. 10). (Illus.). 250p. (C). 1991. text ed. 60.00 (*0-87969-362-2*) Cold Spring Harbor.

Cancer Imaging Manual. Stomper. (Illus.). 288p. 1992. text ed. 89.50 (*0-397-51252-X*) Lippincott.

Cancer Imaging with Radiolabeled Antibodies. Ed. by David M. Goldenberg. (Cancer Treatment & Research Ser.). (C). 1990. lib. bdg. 185.00 (*0-7923-0631-7*) Kluwer Ac.

Cancer Immunoembryotherapy: A New Weapon Against Cancer. Ed. by F. Columbus. 72p. (Orig.). 1994. pap. 27.00 (*1-56072-107-3*) Nova Sci Pubs.

Cancer Immunology: Innovative Approaches to Therapy. Ed. by Ronald B. Herberman. (Cancer Treatment & Research Ser.). 1986. lib. bdg. 94.50 (*0-89838-757-4*) Kluwer Ac.

Cancer in Atomic Bomb Survivors. Ed. by Itsuzo Shigematsu & Abraham Kagan. (GANN Monographs on Cancer Research: No. 32). 204p. 1986. 79.50 (*0-306-42501-7*, Plenum Pr) Plenum.

Cancer in Childhood. Ed. by John O. Godden. LC 73-15003. 259p. reprint ed. pap. 73.90 (*0-317-30343-0*, 2024715) Bks Demand.

Cancer in Children. 2nd enl. rev. ed. Ed. by P. A. Voute et al. (Current Treatment of Cancer Ser.). (Illus.). 400p. 1986. pap. 64.00 (*0-387-15342-X*) Spr-Verlag.

Cancer in Children: Clinical Management. 3rd rev. ed. Ed. by P. A. Voute et al. (Current Treatment of Cancer Ser.). (Illus.). 352p. 1992. 100.00 (*0-387-55186-7*) Spr-Verlag.

Cancer in Italian Migrant Populations. Ed. by M. Geddes et al. (IARC Scientific Publications: No. 123). (Illus.). 302p. (C). 1993. pap. 75.00 (*92-832-2123-0*) OUP.

Cancer in Organ Transplant Recipients. Ed. by D. Schmahl & I. Penn. (Illus.). 184p. 1991. pap. 89.00 (*0-387-53020-7*) Spr-Verlag.

Cancer in the Community: Class & Medical Authority. Martha Balshem. LC 92-48963. (Ethnographic Inquiry Ser.). (Illus.). 192p. 1993. 42.00 (*1-56098-250-0*); pap. 15.95 (*1-56098-251-9*) Smithsonian.

Cancer in the Elderly. Ed. by F. I. Caird & T. B. Brewin. (Illus.). 295p. 1990. text ed. 185.00 (*0-7236-0972-1*, Pub. by John Wright UK) Buttrwrth-Heinemann.

Cancer in the Elderly: Approaches to Early Detection & Treatment. Ed. by Jerome W. Yates. LC 89-21664. 272p. 1989. 44.95 (*0-8261-6930-9*) Springer Pub.

***Cancer in the Elderly: Directions for Research.** Ed. by Ian S. Fentiman & Silvio Monfardini. (Illus.). 192p. 1994. text ed. 92.00 (*0-19-262200-5*) OUP.

Cancer in the First Year of Life: Leukemia, Neuroblastomas, Soft Tissue Sarcomas. Ed. by F. Lampert et al. (Beitraege zur Onkologie, Contributions to Oncology Ser.: Vol. 41). (Illus.). viii, 174p. 1991. 57.00 (*3-8055-5233-5*) S Karger.

Cancer in the Netherlands, 2 vols., Set. Ed. by F. J. Cleton & J. W. Coebergh. (C). 1988. pap. text ed. 68.00 (*0-89838-400-1*) Kluwer Ac.

Cancer in the United States. Abraham M. Lilienfeld et al. LC 72-80658. (Vital & Health Statistics Monographs, American Public Health Association). (Illus.). 572p. 1972. 47.50 (*0-674-09425-5*) HUP.

Cancer in the Young: A Sense of Hope. Margaret O. Hyde & Lawrence E. Hyde. LC 84-27126. 96p. (YA). (gr. 9 up). 1985. 10.00 (*0-664-32722-2*, Westminster) Westminster John Knox.

Cancer in Two Voices. Sandra Butler & Barbara Rosenblum. LC 91-18052. 208p. (Orig.). 1991. pap. 12.95 (*0-933216-84-X*) Spinsters Ink.

Cancer Incidence in Defined Populations. Ed. by John Cairns et al. LC 80-7676. (Banbury Report Ser.: Vol. 4). (Illus.). 458p. 1980. 52.00 (*0-87969-203-0*) Cold Spring Harbor.

Cancer Incidence in Five Continents, Vol. 3. International Agency for Research on Cancer Staff. Ed. by John Waterhouse. LC 77-354964. 606p. 1976. reprint ed. pap. 157.60 (*0-8357-6448-6*, 2035820) Bks Demand.

Cancer Incidence in Five Continents, Vol. 4. International Agency for Research on Cancer Staff. Ed. by John Waterhouse. LC 77-354964. 820p. 1982. reprint ed. pap. 180.00 (*0-8357-6449-4*) Bks Demand.

Cancer Incidence in Five Continents, Vol. V. Ed. by Calum S. Muir et al. (IARC Scientific Publications: No. 88). 1010p. 1988. 120.00 (*92-832-1188-X*) OUP.

Cancer Incidence in Five Continents, Vol. 6. Ed. by D. M. Parkin et al. (IARC Scientific Publications: No. 120). (Illus.). 1076p. 1993. 185.00 (*92-832-2120-6*) OUP.

Cancer Incidence in Jewish Migrants to Israel, 1961-1981. Ruth Steinitz et al. (IARC Scientific Publications: No. 98). (Illus.). 328p. 1990. pap. 65.00 (*92-832-1198-7*) OUP.

Cancer Incidence in Singapore, 1968-1977. K. Shanmugaratnam et al. LC 83-166286. (IARC Scientific Publications: No. 47). (Illus.). 187p. reprint ed. pap. 53.30 (*0-8357-6453-2*, 2035824) Bks Demand.

Cancer Incidence in the U. S. S. R. Supplement To Cancer Incidence in Five Continents, Vol. 3. 2nd rev. ed. International Agency for Research on Cancer Staff. Ed. by N. P. Napalkov & D. M. Parkin. LC 83-138474. (IARC Scientific Publications: No. 48). 83p. reprint ed. pap. 25.00 (*0-7837-4004-2*, 2043834) Bks Demand.

Cancer Industry: The Classic Expose on the Cancer Establishment. Ralph W. Moss. pap. 14.95 (*1-55778-439-6*); pap. 19.95 (*1-881025-09-8*) Equinox Pr.

***Cancer Information Service: A 15-Year History of Service & Research.** 1995. lib. bdg. 251.95 (*0-8490-6728-6*) Gordon Pr.

Cancer Invasion & Metastasis: Biologic Mechanisms & Therapy. Ed. by Stacey B. Day et al. LC 77-83695. (Progress in Cancer Research & Therapy Ser.: No. 5). (Illus.). 540p. reprint ed. pap. 153.90 (*0-7837-7099-5*, 2046928) Bks Demand.

Cancer Is Good for You. Richard Gioeli. (Illus.). 1981. pap. text ed. 3.95 (*0-933278-11-X*) Twen Fir Cent.

Cancer, Its Cause, Prevention & Cure. Edward H. Smalpage. 127p. 1972. reprint ed. spiral bd. 5.50 (*0-7873-0800-5*) Mokelumne.

Cancer Journals. 2nd ed. Audre Lorde. LC 80-53110. 77p. 1980. pap. 7.00 (*1-879960-26-5*) Aunt Lute Bks.

Cancer Journals & Serials: An Analytical Guide. Ed. by Pauline M. Vaillancourt. LC 87-29580. (Annotated Bibliographies of Serials: A Subject Approach Ser.: No. 11). 288p. 1988. text ed. 55.00 (*0-313-24055-8*, VCC/, Greenwood Pr) Greenwood.

Cancer Management in Man: Biological Response Modifiers, Chemotherapy, Antibiotics, Hyperthermia Supporting Measures. Paul V. Woolley. (C). 1989. lib. bdg. 137.00 (*0-89838-999-2*) Kluwer Ac.

Cancer Management in Man: Detection, Diagnosis, Surgery, Radiology, Chronobiology, Endocrine Therapy. Ed. by Alfred L. Goldson. (C). 1989. lib. bdg. 137.00 (*0-89838-998-4*) Kluwer Ac.

Cancer Markers: Diagnostic & Developmental Significance. Ed. by Stewart Sell. LC 79-91071. (Contemporary Biomedicine Ser.). 541p. 1980. 89.50 (*0-89603-009-1*) Humana.

Cancer Medicine. 3rd ed. James F. Holland & Emil Frei. (Illus.). 2600p. 1993. text ed. 198.50 (*0-8121-1422-1*) Williams & Wilkins.

Cancer Metastasis. Ed. by V. Schirrmacher & R. Schwartz-Albiez. (Illus.). 290p. 1989. pap. 56.00 (*0-387-50471-0*, 2962) Spr-Verlag.

Cancer Metastasis: Biological & Biochemical Mechanisms & Clinical Aspects. Ed. by G. Prodi et al. (Advances in Experimental Medicine & Biology Ser.: Vol. 233). (Illus.). 504p. 1988. 125.00 (*0-306-42907-1*, Plenum Pr) Plenum.

Cancer Microbe. Alan Cantwell, Jr. Ed. by Suzanne Henig. (Illus.). 281p. 1990. pap. 18.95 (*0-917211-01-4*) Aries Rising.

Cancer Modeling. Thompson & Brown. (Statistics: Textbooks & Monographs: Vol. 83). 440p. 1987. 140.00 (*0-8247-7773-5*) Dekker.

Cancer Monographs on the Evaluation of Carcinogenic Risk of Chemicals to Man. International Agency for Research on Cancer Staff. Incl. Vol. 1. 1972. 4.80 (*0-686-16797-X*); Vol. 2. Some Inorganic & Organometallic Compounds. 1973. 4.80 (*0-686-16798-8*); Vol. 3. Certain Polycyclic Aromatic Hydrocarbons & Heterocyclic Compounds. 1973. 7.20 (*0-686-16799-6*); Vol. 4. Some Aromatic Amines, Hydrazine & Related Substances, N-Nitrose Compounds & Miscellaneous Alkylating Agents. 1974. 7.20 (*0-686-16800-3*); Vol. 5. Some Organochlorine Pesticides. 1974. 7.20 (*0-686-16801-1*); Vol. 6. Sex Hormones. 1974. 7.20 (*0-686-16802-X*); Vol. 7. Some Anti-Thyroid & Related Substances, Nitrofurens & Industrial Chemicals. 1974. 12.80 (*0-686-16803-8*); Vol. 8. Some Aromatic Azo Compounds. 1975. 14.40 (*0-686-16804-6*); Vol. 9. Some Aziridines, N-, S-, & O- Mustards & Selemium. 1975. 10.80 (*0-686-16805-4*); Vol. 10. Some Naturally Occurring Substances. 1976. 15.20 (*0-686-16806-2*); write for info. (*0-318-56473-4*) World Health.

Cancer Mortality & Morbidity Statistics: Japan & the World, 1993. Ed. by Suketami Tominaga et al. LC 93-35677. (Gann Monograph on Cancer Research: No. 41). 1994. 89.95 (*0-8493-7748-X*, RC271) CRC Pr.

Cancer Nursing. Belcher. 288p. 1992. 29.95 (*0-685-65102-9*) Mosby Yr Bk.

Cancer Nursing. Susan L. Groenwald. (C). 1987. pap. text ed. 75.00 (*0-86720-403-6*); boxed 110.00 (*0-86720-351-X*) Jones & Bartlett.

Cancer Nursing. 2nd ed. Susan L. Groenwald et al. 1376p. 1990. boxed 125.00 (*0-86720-435-4*) Jones & Bartlett.

Cancer Nursing. 3rd ed. Susan L. Groenwald. (Illus.). 1350p. 1993. text ed. 125.00 (*0-86720-640-3*) Jones & Bartlett.

Cancer Nursing: A Comprehensive Textbook. Baird et al. (Illus.). 1104p. 1991. text ed. 125.00 (*0-7216-2698-X*) Saunders.

An Asterisk (*) at the beginning of an entry indicates that the title is appearing in BIP for the first time.

C

An Asterisk (*) at the beginning of an entry indicates that the title is appearing in BIP for the first time.

1025

Cancionero de las Obras de Juan del Enzina, Salamanca, 1496. Ed. by J. C. Temprano. (Spanish Ser.: No. 13). 6p. 1984. fiche 10.00 (*0-942260-39-2*) Hispanic Seminary.

Cancionero de Onate-Castaneda. Ed. by Dorothy S. Severin et al. (Spanish Ser.: No. 36). xxxiv, 436p. 1990. 40.00 (*0-942260-92-9*) Hispanic Seminary.

Cancionero para Preescolares. Ed. by Salomon R. Mussiett. 54p. (SPA.). (J). (ps). 1989. pap. 3.50 (*0-311-32226-3*) Casa Bautista.

Cancionero, Sonetos y Canciones. Francesco Petratca. Tr. & Intro. by Angel Crespo. (Nueva Austral Ser.: Vol. 42). (SPA.). 1991. pap. text ed. 24.95x (*84-239-1842-4*) Elliots Bks.

Cancionero y Romancero de Ausencias. Miguel Hernandez. Ed. by Jose C. Rovira. (Nueva Austral Ser.: Vol. 154). (SPA.). 1991. pap. text ed. 24.95x (*84-239-1954-4*) Elliots Bks.

Canciones. Antonio Machado. Tr. by Robert Bly. LC 80-27641. 15p. 1980. pap. 4.00 (*0-915124-46-7*) Coffee Hse.

Canciones de Nuestra Cabana: Songs of Our Cabana. rev. ed. World Association of Girl Guides Girl Scouts, Our Cabana Committee Staff. 112p. (Orig.). (ENG & SPA.). 1980. pap. 5.50 (*0-88441-366-7*, 23-113) Girl Scouts USA.

Canciones de un Febrero. Roberto B. Alberty. Ed. by Carlos R. Alberty & Sofia Cardona. (Illus.). 60p. (Orig.). (SPA.). 1987. pap. 7.00 (*0-317-52541-7*) C R Alberty.

Canciones Espanolas: Seleccion III y IV. Federico De Onis & Emilio De Torre. 75p. (SPA.). 1952. 2.00 (*0-318-14244-9*) Hispanic Inst.

Canciones Espanolas (Seleccion II) 39p. 1946. 1.00 (*0-317-04060-X*) Hispanic Inst.

Canciones Mexicanas. Vicente T. Mendoza. 126p. 1948. 3.00 (*0-318-14245-7*) Hispanic Inst.

***Canciones-Montsalv-Voice.** 1994. 9.95 (*0-614-01276-7*, UM20507) Omnibus NY.

Cancun & Cozumel Guide. Berlitz Editors. (Travellers Guides Ser.). (Illus.). 144p. 1993. pap. 7.95 (*2-8315-0705-7*) Berlitz.

Cancun, Cozumel, Yucatan Peninsula, 1995: From the Best Beaches to the Maya Ruins. Fodor's Travel Staff. (Illus.). 1994. pap. 12.00 (*0-679-02703-3*) Fodors Travel.

Cancun Handbook & Mexico's Caribbean Coast. 4th ed. Chicki Mallan. LC 94-4896. 260p. 1994. pap. 13.95 (*1-56691-050-1*) Moon Pubns CA.

CANDA Conference Proceedings '93. Ed. by Stefan Schuber. LC 92-73669. 157p. pap. 54.00 (*0-943330-37-8*) Advanstar Commns.

Candaules' Wife, & Other Old Stories. Emily J. Putnam. LC 72-169559. (Short Story Index Reprint Ser.). 1977. reprint ed. 19.95 (*0-8369-4022-9*) Ayer.

Candee Genealogy, with Notices of Allied Families. C. Baldwin. (Illus.). 240p. 1989. reprint ed. lib. bdg. 42.00 (*0-8328-1302-8*); reprint ed. pap. 32.00 (*0-8328-1303-6*) Higginson Bk Co.

Candelario Soleda-Guaracha y Latigo: Poemas de Guao y Caimito. LC 86-81115. (Coleccion Espejo de Paciencia Ser.). 71p. (Orig.). (SPA.). 1986. pap. 6.95 (*0-89729-427-0*) Ediciones.

C&H Complete Dessert Cookbook. LC 80-69641. 1981. 7.95 (*0-87502-087-9*) Benjamin Co.

Candice & Edgar Bergen. Skip Press. LC 94-20395. (Star Families Ser.). (J). 1995. text ed. 13.95 (*0-89686-878-8*, Crstwood Hse) Silver Burdett Pr.

***Candice & Edgar Bergen.** Skip Press. (Star Families Ser.). (Illus.). (YA). (gr. 5 up). 1995. pap. 7.95 (*0-382-24940-2*, Crstwood Hse) Silver Burdett Pr.

Candice Is Dead. large type ed. Alan S. Well. (Linford Mystery Library). 1989. pap. 11.95 (*0-7089-6744-2*, Linford) Ulverscroft.

Candiciform & Pachycaul Succulents. Gorden Rowley. Ed. by Herman Schwartz & Ron LaFon. (Illus.). 282p. 1980. 80.00 (*0-912647-03-5*) Strawberry.

Candid. Mark Dunster. 14p. (Orig.). 1991. pap. 4.00 (*0-89642-193-7*) Linden Pubs.

Candid Camera in General Psychology. Allen Funt. 1993. text ed. write for info. (*0-07-022801-9*) McGraw.

Candid Camera in Social Psychology. Allen Funt. 1993. text ed. write for info. (*0-07-022804-3*) McGraw.

Candid Classroom. Gilbert E. Dannenberg. 150p. 1992. pap. 6.95 (*0-9631427-0-4*) Candid Pub.

Candid History of the Jesuits. Joseph McCabe. 1977. lib. bdg. 59.95 (*0-8490-1567-7*) Gordon Pr.

Candid-Impartial Narrative of the Transactions of the Fleet Under the Command of Lord Howe. Thomas O'Beirne. LC 75-77108. (Eyewitness Accounts of the American Revolution Ser., No. 1). 1969. reprint ed. 11.95 (*0-405-01170-9*) Ayer.

Candid Questions Concerning Gospel Form Criticism: A Methodological Sketch of Fundamental Problematics of Form & Redaction Criticism. 2nd ed. Erhard T. Guttgemans. Tr. by William G. Doty. LC 79-10167. (Pittsburgh Theological Monographs: No. 26). 1979. pap. 15.00 (*0-915138-24-7*) Pickwick.

Candid Thoughts in Poetry. Mildred L. White-Kaufman. 1992. 6.95 (*0-533-09353-8*) Vantage.

Candida. George Bernard Shaw. Ed. by Raymond S. Nelson. LC 79-190706. 1973. pap. 3.70 (*0-672-61088-4*, Bobbs) Macmillan.

Candida. George Bernard Shaw. LC 91-51110. (Shaw Ser.). 60p. 1992. pap. 6.00 (*0-88734-235-3*) Players Pr.

Candida. George Bernard Shaw. 1950. pap. 7.00 (*0-14-045037-8*, Penguin Bks) Viking Penguin.

Candida: A Nutritional Approach. Louise Tenney. (Todays Health Ser.: No. 1). 1988. pap. 3.95 (*0-913923-28-1*) Woodland UT.

Candida: A Twentieth Century Disease. Shirley Lorenzani. LC 85-81549. (Pivot Original Health Bks.). 176p. (Orig.). 1986. pap. 4.95 (*0-87983-375-0*) Keats.

Candida: Treating It Successfully. rev. ed. Bruce R. Blinzler. (Illus.). 43p. 1987. pap. write for info. (*0-943761-04-2*) Creative ID.

Candida Adherence to Epithelial Cells. Ed. by Ghannoum. 1990. 217.00 (*0-8493-5979-1*, QR201) CRC Pr.

Candida Albicans. Ray C. Wunderlich & Dwight K. Kalita. Ed. by Richard A. Passwater & Earl Mindell. (Good Health Guide Ser.). 32p. (Orig.). 1984. pap. 2.50 (*0-87983-364-5*) Keats.

Candida Albicans: Cellular & Molecular Biology. Ed. by R. Prasad. (Illus.). 296p. 1991. 149.00 (*0-387-51926-2*) Spr-Verlag.

Candida Albicans: Could Yeast Be Your Problem? Leon Chaitow. (Orig.). 1989. pap. 7.95 (*0-89281-247-8*, Heal Arts VT) Inner Tradit.

Candida Albicans: The Pathogenic Fungus. Ed. by Cora G. Saltarelli. (Illus.). 270p. 1989. 88.00 (*0-89116-897-4*) Hemisp Pub.

Candida Albicans Epidemic. 1992. lib. bdg. 75.00 (*0-8490-8706-6*) Gordon Pr.

Candida Albicans Yeast-Free Cookbook. Associates of Price Pottinger Nutrition Foundation Staff & Pat Connolly. LC 85-9730. 168p. (Orig.). 1985. pap. 10.95 (*0-87983-409-9*) Keats.

Candida & Candidamycosis. Ed. by E. Tumbay et al. (FEMS Symposium Ser.: No. 50). (Illus.). 308p. 1991. 85.00 (*0-306-43829-1*, Plenum Pr) Plenum.

Candida & Candidosis. 2nd ed. Odds. 448p. 1988. text ed. 105.00 (*0-7020-1265-3*) Saunders.

Candida & How She Lied to Her Husband. George Bernard Shaw. LC 79-56703. (Bernard Shaw Early Texts: Play Manuscripts in Facsimile). 1981. lib. bdg. 20.00 (*0-8240-4579-3*) Garland.

Candida Control Cookbook: What You Should Know & What You Should Eat to Manage Yeast Infections. rev. ed. Gail Burton. LC 92-33404. 256p. 1993. reprint ed. pap. 12.95 (*0-944031-49-8*) Aslan Pub.

Candida Diet Against It: What You Eat Can Help Direct Your Immune System to Help You. Luc De Schepper. 1994. pap. 9.95 (*0-572-01501-1*, Pub. by W Foulsham UK) Trans-Atl Phila.

Candida Directory: The Comprehensive Guide to Yeast-Free Living. Helen Gustafson & Maureen O'Shea. LC 93-50920. 192p. 1994. pap. 11.95 (*0-89087-714-9*) Celestial Arts.

Candida Hofer. (Illus.). 80p. 1991. 35.00 (*3-88375-155-3*, Pub. by Walther Konig GW) Dist Art Pubs.

Candida, Silver (Mercury) Fillings & the Immune System. rev. ed. Ed. by Betsy Russell-Manning. LC 85-80413. 1990. Incl. companion bk. - Home Remedies for Candida. pap. 16.95 (*0-930165-10-1*) Greenswrd Pr.

Candida, the Epidemic of This Century: Solved. Luc De Schepper. (Medical Sciences, General Medicine Ser.). (Illus.). 147p. 1986. 10.00 (*0-9614734-1-X*) LDS Pubns.

Candida Yeast: The Battle in Your Body. Jonathon D. Miller. (Orig.). 1986. pap. 2.50 (*0-935815-03-1*) Lifecircle.

Candidate. Gustave Flaubert. Bd. with Castle of Hearts. LC 76-6879. LC 76-6879. 311p. 1978. reprint ed. 45.00 (*0-86527-225-5*) Fertig.

Candidate: The Truth Behind the Presidential Campaign. Emily O'Reily. 160p. (Orig.). (C). 1991. pap. 13.99 (*1-85594-021-3*, Pub. by Attic IE) InBook.

Candidate for Murder. Joan L. Nixon. (YA). 1992. pap. 3.99 (*0-440-21212-X*) Dell.

Candidate for Murder. large type ed. Joan L. Nixon. LC 93-42058. 1994. pap. 15.95 (*0-7862-0142-8*) Thorndike Pr.

***Candidate Images in Presidential Elections.** Kenneth L. Hacker. (Political Communications Ser.). 224p. 1995. text ed. 59.95 (*0-275-94714-9*, Praeger Pubs); pap. text ed. 18.95 (*0-275-95161-8*, Praeger Pubs) Greenwood.

Candidate Selection in Comparative Perspective: The Secret Garden of Politics. Ed. by Michael Gallagher & Michael Marsh. (Modern Politics Ser.: Vol. 18). 288p. (C). 1988. text ed. 45.00 (*0-8039-8124-4*) Sage.

Candidates Biblical Scoreboard. David W. Balsiger. (Biblical News Ser., 1986: No. 1). 1986. 2.25 (*0-89921-015-5*) Biblical News Serv.

Candidates Biblical Scoreboard, 1986 California, No. 1. 1.00 (*0-89921-016-3*) Biblical News Serv.

Candidates Biblical Scoreboard, 1986 California, No. 2. 1.00 (*0-89921-019-8*) Biblical News Serv.

Candidates Biblical Scoreboard, 1986 California, No. 3. 1.00 (*0-89921-020-1*) Biblical News Serv.

Candidates Biblical Scoreboard, 1986 National, No. 2. 2.25 (*0-89921-017-1*) Biblical News Serv.

Candidates Biblical Scoreboard, 1986 National, No. 3. 2.25 (*0-89921-018-X*) Biblical News Serv.

Candidates, Congress, & the American Democracy. Linda L. Fowler. (Analytical Perspectives on Politics Ser.). 220p. (C). 1993. pap. text ed. 16.95 (*0-472-06473-8*) U of Mich Pr.

Candidates Defeated in Roman Elections: Some Ancient Roman "Also-Rans" T. Robert Broughton. LC 90-56339. (Transactions Ser.: Vol. 81, Pt. 4). 64p. (Orig.). (C). 1991. pap. 10.00 (*0-87169-814-5*, T814-BRT) Am Philos.

Candidates for Europe: The British Experience. Martin Holland. 180p. 1986. text ed. 55.95 (*0-566-00871-8*) Ashgate Pub Co.

Candidates for Office: Beliefs & Strategies. John W. Kingdon. 9.00 (*0-8446-2377-6*) Peter Smith.

Candidates for the European Parliament, April-May 1979. Jacques-Rene Rabier et al. LC 84-62936. 1985. write for info. (*0-89138-893-1*) ICPSR.

***Candidate's Formation Journal.** Thomas Zanzig. Ed. by Robert Stamschror. (Confirmed in a Faithful Community Ser.). (Illus.). 64p. (Orig.). (YA). (gr. 9-12). 1995. pap. text ed. 3.70 (*0-88489-313-8*) St Marys.

Candidate's Handbook for Winning Local Elections. Harvey Yorke & Liz Doherty. LC 81-90654. 168p. (Orig.). (C). 1982. pap. 11.00 (*0-9607598-0-8*) Harvey Yorke.

Candidates, Parties, & Campaigns. 2nd ed. Barbara G. Salmore & Stephen A. Salmore. 302p. 1989. pap. text ed. 22.95 (*0-87187-484-9*) Congr Quarterly.

***Candidate's Reflection & Mission Journal.** Thomas Zanzig. Ed. by Robert Stamschror. (Confirmed in a Faithful Community Ser.). (Illus.). 64p. (Orig.). (YA). (gr. 9-12). 1995. pap. text ed. 3.70 (*0-88489-342-1*) St Marys.

Candidates: See How They Run: An Insider's View of the New Hampshire Presidential Primary. Hugh Gregg. (Illus.). 304p. 1990. 22.95 (*0-914339-29-X*) P E Randall Pub.

Candidate's Wife. Virginia Coffman. 1991. 18.95 (*0-7278-4114-9*) Severn Hse.

Candidate's Wife. large type ed. Virginia Coffman. LC 91-29409. 295p. 1992. reprint ed. lib. bdg. 18.95 (*1-56054-255-1*) Thorndike Pr.

Candidate's Wife. Patricia O'Brien. 1993. reprint ed. mass mkt. 5.99 (*0-312-95021-7*) St Martin.

Candidates '88. Marvin Kalb & Hendrik Hertzberg. LC 88-16603. 300p. 1988. text ed. 49.95 (*0-86569-186-X*, Auburn Hse) Greenwood.

Candide. Voltaire. 15.95 (*0-8488-0656-5*) Amereon Ltd.

Candide. Voltaire. 1985. 2.50 (*0-8120-3505-4*) Barron.

Candide. Voltaire. 1991. pap. 1.00 (*0-486-26689-3*) Dover.

Candide. Voltaire. Bd. with Zadig. (Airmont Classics Ser.). 1966. Set pap. 1.50 (*0-8049-0117-1*, CL-117) Airmont.

Candide. Francois Voltaire. Ed. by Norman L. Torrey. (Crofts Classics Ser.). 128p. 1946. pap. text ed. write for info. (*0-88295-100-9*) Harlan Davidson.

Candide. Francois-Marie de Voltaire & Roger Pearson. LC 92-52911. 384p. 1992. 17.00 (*0-679-41746-X*, Everymans Lib) Knopf.

Candide. Francois-Marie de Voltaire. 288p. (FRE.). 1901. pap. 10.95 (*0-7859-1262-2*, 2038715505) Fr & Eur.

Candide. Francois-Marie de Voltaire. Ed. by J. H. Brumfitt. 1972. pap. 13.95 (*0-19-832372-7*) OUP.

Candide. Francois-Marie de Voltaire. LC 84-25512. 1985. pap. 7.95 (*0-394-60522-5*, Modern Lib) Random.

Candide. Francois-Marie de Voltaire. Tr. by John Butt. (Classics Ser.). 1950. pap. 4.95 (*0-14-044004-6*, Penguin Classics) Viking Penguin.

Candide. 2nd ed. Francois Voltaire. (C). 1991. pap. text ed. 6.95 (*0-393-96058-7*) Norton.

Candide, Vol. 1. Francois-Marie de Voltaire. 1984. pap. 2.95 (*0-553-21166-8*, Bantam Classics) Bantam.

Candide: A Dual-Language Book. Voltaire & Shane Weller. LC 92-37473. 208p. (Orig.). (ENG & FRE.). 1993. pap. 7.95 (*0-486-27625-2*) Dover.

Candide: And, Philosophical Letters. Francois-Marie de Voltaire. Ed. by Haskell M. Block. LC 92-50226. 1992. 13.50 (*0-679-60003-5*, Modern Lib) Random.

Candide: Optimism Demolished. Haydn Mason. (MWS Ser.). 170p. 1992. text ed. 21.95 (*0-8057-8085-8*, Twayne); pap. 12.95 (*0-8057-8559-0*, Twayne) Macmillan.

Candide & Other Stories. Francois-Marie de Voltaire. Tr. & Intro. by Roger Pearson. (World's Classics Ser.). 384p. 1990. pap. 4.95 (*0-19-281730-2*) OUP.

Candide & Other Writings. Francois-Marie de Voltaire. Ed. by Haskell M. Block. (Modern Library College Editions). 1965. pap. text ed. write for info. (*0-07-553646-3*, T64) McGraw.

Candide Notes. James K. Lowers. 1965. pap. 3.95 (*0-8220-0283-3*) Cliffs.

Candide; or, All for the Best, 1759 see Prince of Abissinia: A Tale, 1759

Candide ou l'Optimisme. Francois-Marie de Voltaire. 79p. (FRE.). 1990. pap. 10.95 (*0-7859-1441-2*, 2091878340) Fr & Eur.

Candide, Zadig & Selected Stories. Francois-Marie A. De Voltaire. Tr. by Donald M. Frame. 1989. pap. 2.50 (*0-451-52357-1*) NAL-Dutton.

Candide, Zadig & Selected Stories. Francois-Marie de Voltaire. Tr. by Donald M. Frame. 1961. pap. 3.95 (*0-451-52426-8*, Sig Classics) NAL-Dutton.

Candideces-Versos Spanish Poetry. N. P. Cartwright. LC 83-76. 91p. (ENG & SPA.). 1983. pap. text ed. 5.00 (*0-9601482-3-X*) N P Cartwright.

***Candidiasis.** fac. ed. Ed. by Gerald P. Bodey. LC 84-22342. (Illus.). 293p. Date not set. pap. 83.60 (*0-7837-7283-1*, 2047023) Bks Demand.

Candidiasis: Pathogenesis, Diagnosis, & Treatment. 2nd ed. Ed. by Gerald Bodey. LC 92-21810. 432p. 1993. 100.00 (*0-88167-954-2*) Raven.

Candidly, Allen Funt: A Million Smiles Later. Allen Funt. LC 93-44936. 1994. 22.00 (*1-56980-008-1*) Barricade Bks.

Candidly Yours. John Cherrington. (Illus.). 256p. 1989. 27.95 (*0-85236-200-5*, Pub. by Farming Pr UK) Diamond Farm Bk.

Candids of the King: Rare Photographs of Elvis Presley by Friends & Fans. Comp. by Jim E. Curtin. (Illus.). 208p. 1993. pap. 14.95 (*0-8212-2065-9*) Bulfinch Pr.

Candie for the Foundling. Anne Gordon. 731p. (C). 1989. text ed. 75.00 (*1-872795-75-7*, Pub. by Pentland Pr UK) St Mut.

Candies, Beverages & Snacks: From Amish & Mennonite Kitchens. Ed. by Phyllis P. Good & Rachel T. Pellman. (Pennsylvania Dutch Cookbooks Ser.). (Illus.). 32p. (Orig.). 1983. pap. 2.95 (*0-934672-15-6*) Good Bks PA.

Candies, Beverages & Snacks from the Amish & Mennonite Kitchen. Phyllis P. Good. 1991. pap. 2.95 (*1-56148-045-2*) Good Bks PA.

Candle: A Story of Light & Love. Nathaniel R. Gorham. LC 86-81545. (Illus.). 1986. 7.95 (*0-939303-00-0*) Educ Lrn Syst.

Candle, a Story of Love & Faith. Sally Ann Smith. Ed. by Luana Luther. LC 91-72745. (Illus.). 32p. (J). (gr. 3-6). 1991. pap. 9.95 (*0-944875-22-X*) Doral Pub.

Candle Burning Magic. Anna Riva. 96p. 1980. pap. 4.50 (*0-943832-06-3*) Intl Imports.

Candle Burning Magic with the Psalms. William A. Oribello. 100p. 1988. pap. 5.00 (*0-938294-58-X*) Glob Comm-Inner Lght.

Candle Corner. large type ed. Frances Turk. 416p. 1986. 15.95 (*0-7089-1411-X*) Ulverscroft.

Candle for D'Artagnan. Chelsea Q. Yarbro. 1994. pap. 13.95 (*0-312-89019-2*) Orb NYC.

Candle for D'Artagnan. Chelsea Q. Yarbro. 512p. 1989. pap. 22.95 (*0-312-93202-2*) St Martin.

Candle for Grandpa: A Guide to the Jewish Funeral for Children & Parents. David Techner & Judith Hirt-Manheimer. (Illus.). (J). (gr. k-3). 1993. 10.95 (*0-8074-0507-8*, 123070) UAHC.

Candle for Poland: Four Hundred Sixty-Nine Days of Solidarity. Leszek Szymanski. LC 82-1231. (Stokvis Studies in Historical Chronology & Thought: Vol. 2). 128p. 1982. lib. bdg. 25.00x (*0-89370-166-1*); pap. 15.00x (*0-89370-266-8*) Borgo Pr.

***Candle for the Devil.** Susanne McCarthy. (Presents Ser.). 1995. mass mkt. 3.25 (*0-373-11748-5*, 1-11748-0) Harlequin Bks.

Candle in Darkness: A Novel. June Livesay. 280p. 1990. pap. 8.95 (*0-914984-22-5*) Starburst.

Candle in Her Heart. Emilie Loring. 1976. reprint ed. lib. bdg. 20.95 (*0-88411-353-1*, Aeonian Pr) Amereon Ltd.

Candle in the Dark. Ruth Blake. LC 88-17302. (Illus.). 176p. (Orig.). 1988. pap. 6.99 (*0-932581-36-6*) Word Aflame.

Candle in the Dark. Megan Chance. 1993. mass mkt. 4.99 (*0-440-21487-4*, Dell Trade Pbks) Dell.

***Candle in the Darness: Celtic Spirituality from Wales.** Patrick Thomas. 151p. 1993. pap. 21.00 (*0-86383-974-6*, Pub. by Gomer Pr UK) St Mut.

Candle in the Rain. Andy Ray. 179p. (Orig.). 1990. pap. 9.95 (*0-9621856-0-4*) Panther Pr.

Candle in the Wind. George Bernau. 1990. 19.95 (*0-446-51499-3*) Warner Bks.

Candle in the Wind. George Bernau. 544p. 1992. mass mkt. 5.99 (*0-446-36128-3*) Warner Bks.

Candle in the Wind. Aleksandr Solzhenitsyn. Tr. by Keith Armes & Arthur Hudgins. LC 73-77712. 149p. 1973. text ed. 11.95 (*0-8166-0681-1*) U of Minn Pr.

Candle in the Wind: My Thirty Years in Book Publishing. Thomas P. Coffey. 222p. 1985. pap. 5.95 (*0-87193-212-1*) Dimension Bks.

Candle in the Wind: Religion in Soviet Union. Eugene Shirley. 1990. 43.50 (*0-89633-135-0*); pap. 21.95 (*0-89633-136-9*) Ethics & Public Policy.

Candle in the Window. Christina Dodd. 1991. mass mkt. 3.95 (*0-06-104026-6*, Harp PBks) HarpC.

Candle in the Window. large type ed. Christina Dodd. LC 92-1179. 641p. 1992. reprint ed. lib. bdg. 17.95 (*1-56054-383-3*) Thorndike Pr.

***Candle in Wind.** Wartski. Date not set. mass mkt. 4.50 (*0-449-70442-4*) Fawcett.

Candle-Lightin' Time. Paul L. Dunbar. LC 76-164797. (Illus.). reprint ed. 19.50 (*0-404-00030-4*) AMS Pr.

***Candle Lighting.** David J. Eveleigh. (C). 1989. pap. 25.00x (*0-85263-726-8*, Pub. by Shire UK) St Mut.

Candle Magick Workbook. Kala Pajeon & Ketz Pajeon. (Illus.). 256p. 1991. pap. 9.95 (*0-8065-1268-7*, Citadel Pr) Carol Pub Group.

Candle of the Lord. William C. De Pauley. LC 75-107693. (Essay Index Reprint Ser.). 1977. 18.95 (*0-8369-1496-1*) Ayer.

Candle of the Lord. Elfrida V. Foulds. LC 82-63176. 1983. pap. 3.00 (*0-87574-248-3*) Pendle Hill.

Candle of the Lord. Robert B. Mussman. 1992. pap. 5.99 (*0-88019-292-5*) Schmul Pub Co.

Candle of Vision. A. E. 175p. 1994. pap. 14.00 (*0-89540-298-X*, SB-298) Sun Pub.

Candle on the Hill: Images of Camphill Life. Ed. by Cornelius Pietzner. (Illus.). 174p. 1990. reprint ed. 31.50 (*0-88010-296-9*); reprint ed. pap. 19.95 (*0-88010-297-7*) Anthroposophic.

Candle Opera. Richard W. Sparks. (Illus.). 54p. (J). (gr. 1-10). 1983. pap. 5.95 (*0-9614185-0-8*) S J F Co.

Candle or the Sun. Gopal Baratham. 224p. (Orig.). 1992. pap. 15.99 (*1-85242-225-4*) Serpents Tail.

Candle Power: A Game of Light. Dorothee L. Mella. 48p. 1992. pap. 4.95 (*0-9636345-0-X*) Domel.

Candle Revisited: Essays on Science & Technology. Peter Day. Ed. by Richard Catlow. (Illus.). 144p. 1994. pap. 14.95 (*0-19-855835-X*) OUP.

Candle Talk. Barbara Birenbaum. LC 90-33299. (Kindl Adventure Ser.: No. 7). (Illus.). 54p. (J). (gr. 2-5). 1991. lib. bdg. 10.95 (*0-935343-10-5*); pap. 5.95 (*0-935343-15-6*) Peartree.

Candle, the Lantern, the Daylight. Mildred B. Young. LC 61-15103. (Orig.). 1961. pap. 3.00 (*0-87574-116-9*) Pendle Hill.

Candle Therapy. Catherine Riggs-Bergesen. (Illus.). 153p. (Orig.). 1992. pap. 16.95 (*0-9640440-1-3*) Other Worldly.

***Candle Within Her Soul: Mary Elizabeth Mahnkey & Her Ozarks (1877-1948)** Ellen G. Massey. (Illus.). 344p. 1996. lib. bdg. 42.95 (*0-944436-51-X*) Univ Central AR Pr.

***Candlebox.** (Guitar Super-Tab Ser.). 84p. (Orig.). 1994. pap. 18.95 (*0-89724-234-3*) Warner Brothers.

Candleflame. David Hilton. LC 76-30374. (Illus.). 20p. 1976. pap. 3.00 (*0-915124-20-3*, Toothpaste) Coffee Hse.

Candleford Green. large type ed. Flora Thompson. Bd. with Over to Candleford. 1978. 12.50 (*0-685-29748-9*) Ulverscroft.

Candleford Green see Over to Candleford

An Asterisk (*) at the beginning of an entry indicates that the title is appearing in BIP for the first time.

C

An Asterisk (*) at the beginning of an entry indicates that the title is appearing in BIP for the first time.

1027

Cannabis, Alcohol, & the South African Student: Adolescent Drug Use, 1974-1985. Brian M. Du Toit. (Monographs in International Studies, Africa Ser.: No. 59A). 176p. (Orig.). (C). 1991. pap. text ed. 17.00 (*0-89680-166-7*) Ohio U Pr.

Cannabis & Culture. Ed. by Vera Rubin. (World Anthropology Ser.). (Illus.). xiv, 598p. 1975. 53.10 (*90-279-7669-4*) Mouton.

Cannabis (Marijuana) & Cannabinoids: Medical Subject Research Directory with Bibliography. American Health Research Institute Staff. Ed. by John C. Bartone. LC 82-72018. 105p. 1982. 44.50 (*0-941864-52-9*); pap. 39.50 (*0-941864-53-7*) ABBE Pubs Assn.

Cannabis Now. James D. Graham. (Illus.). 128p. reprint ed. pap. 36.50 (*0-8357-6434-6*, 2035805) Bks Demand.

Cannaways. Graham Shelby. 1982. pap. 3.50 (*0-8217-1019-2*) Zebra.

Cannaways Concern. Graham Shelby. 1983. pap. 3.50 (*0-8217-1124-5*) Zebra.

Canned Code for DOS & Windows. Steve Rimmer. 1994. pap. text ed. 29.95 (*0-07-053003-3*) McGraw.

Canned Code for DOS & Windows. Steve Rimmer & LeRoy Cooke. LC 93-34624. 1994. disk 39.95 (*0-8306-4511-X*, Windcrest); disk, pap. 29.95 (*0-8306-4512-8*, Windcrest) TAB Bks.

Canned Foods: Principles of Thermal Process Control, Acidification & Container Closure Evaluation. 5th ed. Food Processors Institute Staff. 231p. 1988. pap. text ed. 75.00 (*0-937774-20-0*) Food Processors.

Canned Goods As Caviar: American Film Comedies of the 1930s. Gerald Weales. LC 84-28132. x, 386p. 1985. pap. 12.95 (*0-226-87664-0*) U Ch Pr.

Canned Laughter: The Best Stories from Radio & Television. Peter Hay. 272p. 1992. 25.00 (*0-19-506836-X*) OUP.

Canned Lit. Allan Gould. (Illus.). 227p. 1991. pap. 14.95 (*0-7737-5433-4*, Pub. by Stoddart Pubng CN) Genl Dist Srvs.

***Cannen County, TN: Family History.** Turner Publishing Company Staff. LC 94-61463. (Illus.). 208p. 1994. 48.00 (*1-56311-171-3*) Turner Pub KY.

***Canneries of the Eastern Shore: With Photographs Made Especially for This Book by A. Vernon Taylor.** R. Lee Burton. LC 85-41006. (Illus.). reprint ed. pap. 58.80 (*0-7837-9074-0*, 2049823) Bks Demand.

Cannery Boat & Other Japanese Short Stories. Takiji Kobayashi. LC 70-122589. reprint ed. 12.50 (*0-404-03736-4*) AMS Pr.

Cannery Boat & Other Japanese Short Stories. Takiji Kobayashi. LC 68-30823. (Illus.). 271p. 1969. reprint ed. text ed. 35.00 (*0-8371-0133-6*, KOCB, Greenwood Pr) Greenwood.

Cannery Captives: Women Workers in the Produce Processing Industry (an Original Press Anthology) Ed. by Dan C. McCurry & Richard E. Rubenstein. LC 74-30623. (American Farmers & the Rise of Agribusiness Ser.). (Illus.). 1975. 46.95 (*0-405-06770-4*) Ayer.

Cannery Row. John Steinbeck. 208p. 1993. pap. 4.50 (*0-14-017738-8*, Penguin Bks) Viking Penguin.

Cannery Row. John Steinbeck. LC 93-11713. 224p. 1994. pap. 8.95 (*0-14-018737-5*, Penguin Classics) Viking Penguin.

Cannery Row: The History of Old Ocean View Avenue. Michael K. Hemp. LC 86-32023. (Illus.). 128p. 1993. reprint ed. pap. 16.95 (*0-941425-00-2*) History Co.

Cannery Row see Short Novels of John Steinbeck

Cannery Row see Of Mice & Men

Cannery Women, Cannery Lives: Mexican Women, Unionization, & the California Food Processing Industry, 1930-1950. Vicki L. Ruiz. LC 87-13878. (Illus.). 212p. 1987. pap. 14.95 (*0-8263-0988-7*) U of NM Pr.

Canniatura, the Crevice: The Crevice. Achille Serrao. Tr. by Luigi Bonaffini. LC 94-15600. (Studies in Southern Italian & Italian-American Culture: Vol. 6). 136p. (C). 1995. text ed. 38.95 (*0-8204-2517-6*) P Lang Pubs.

Cannibal. John Hawkes. LC 49-48130. 1949. pap. 9.95 (*0-8112-0063-9*, NDP123) New Directions.

***Cannibal.** Terese Svoboda. LC 94-34305. 138p. 1995. 19.95 (*0-8147-8012-1*) NYU Pr.

Cannibal Eliot & the Lost Histories of San Francisco. Hilton Obenzinger. LC 93-12722. 256p. (Orig.). 1993. pap. 12.95 (*1-56279-047-1*) Mercury Hse Inc.

Cannibal Encounters: Europeans & Island Caribs, 1492-1763. Philip P. Boucher. (Studies in Atlantic History & Culture). 232p. 1992. text ed. 33.50x (*0-8018-4365-0*) Johns Hopkins.

Cannibal Eyes. Ron Platt. LC 91-51145. (Illus.). 24p. (Orig.). 1992. pap. 7.00 (*0-938437-40-2*) MIT List Visual Arts.

Cannibal Flower. Alice Joanou. (Orig.). 1991. pap. 4.95 (*1-878320-72-6*) Masquerade.

Cannibal Galaxy. Cynthia Ozick. 1984. pap. 7.95 (*0-525-48133-8*, Obelisk) NAL-Dutton.

***Cannibal Galaxy.** Cynthia Ozick. (Library of Modern Jewish Literature). 162p. 1995. pap. 14.95 (*0-8156-0354-1*) Syracuse U Pr.

Cannibal Grisly True Story. Mel Helmer. 1991. pap. 3.95 (*1-55817-501-6*, Pinnacle NY) Windsor NY.

Cannibal Heart. Margaret Millar. 207p. 1985. pap. 4.95 (*0-930330-32-3*) Intl Polygonics.

Cannibal Killers: The History of Impossible Murders. Moira Martingale. 192p. 1994. pap. 10.95 (*0-7867-0096-3*) Carroll & Graf.

Cannibal Owl. Chad Oliver. 1994. 4.99 (*0-553-29656-6*) Bantam.

Cannibal Queen. Stephen Coonts. Ed. by Paul McCarthy. 392p. 1993. pap. 6.50 (*0-671-74885-8*) PB.

***Cannibal Tours & Glass Boxes: The Anthropology of Museums.** Michael M. Ames. 238p. 1992. pap. 19.95 (*0-7748-0483-1*) U of Wash Pr.

Cannibal Who Overate. Hugh Pentecost. 191p. 1990. pap. 3.95 (*0-88184-614-7*) Carroll & Graf.

Cannibalism: Ecology & Evolution among Diverse Taxa. Ed. by Mark A. Elgar & Bernard J. Crespi. (Illus.). 376p. 1992. 75.00 (*0-19-854650-5*) OUP.

***Cannibalism: From Sacrifice to Survival.** Hans Askenasy. (Illus.). 268p. (C). 1994. 25.95 (*0-87975-906-2*) Prometheus Bks.

Cannibalism: Human Aggression & Cultural Form. Eli Sagan. 148p. 1993. pap. 8.00 (*1-882231-00-7*) FishDrum Mag.

Cannibalism in China. Key R. Chong. LC 90-5997. 350p. 1990. 36.00 (*0-89341-618-5*, Longwood Academic) Hollowbrook.

Cannibals. Thurman Hoskins. (Orig.). (J). (ps-12). 1988. pap. 2.95 (*0-87067-350-5*) Holloway.

Cannibals All!, or, Slaves Without Masters. George Fitzhugh. Ed. by C. Vann Woodward. LC 60-5400. (John Harvard Library). 303p. 1960. pap. 13.95 (*0-674-09451-4*) HUP.

Cannibals & Condos: Texans & Texas along the Gulf Coast. Robert L. Maril. LC 86-5759. (Tarleton State University Southwestern Studies in the Humanities: No. 3). 136p. 1986. 13.95 (*0-89096-276-6*) Tex A&M Univ Pr.

Cannibals & Kings. Marvin Harris. LC 90-55701. 368p. 1991. pap. 12.00 (*0-679-72849-X*, Vin) Random.

Cannibals & Kings: The Origins of Cultures. Marvin Harris. 1978. pap. 8.95 (*0-394-72700-2*) Random.

Cannibals & Missionaries. Mary McCarthy. LC 79-4869. 384p. 1979. 10.95 (*0-15-115387-6*, Harvest Bks) HarBrace.

Cannibals & Missionaries. Mary McCarthy. 1991. pap. 10.95 (*0-15-615386-6*) HarBrace.

Cannibals in Sicily & the Bathing Huts. Monique Lange. Tr. by Barbara Beaumont. (Iris Ser.). 112p. 1988. 18.95 (*0-7145-2879-X*) M Boyars Pubs.

Cannibals in the Midst. Adrian Harris. Ed. by James B. Van Treese. 357p. 1993. pap. 9.95 (*1-56901-032-3*) NW Pub.

Cannibals of Sunset Drive. Dan K. Carlsruh. LC 92-40568. 143p. (J). (gr. 3-7). 1993. text ed. 13.95 (*0-02-717110-8*, Mac Bks Young Read) S&S Childrens.

Cannibals, Witches, & Divorce: Estranging the Renaissance. Ed. by Marjorie Garber. LC 86-45472. (Selected Papers from the English Institute; 1982-83, New Ser.: No. 11). 256p. 1987. text ed. 33.50x (*0-8018-3405-8*) Johns Hopkins.

Cannibis in Amsterdam: A Geography of Hashish & Marijuana. A. C. Jansen. (Illus.). 168p. 1991. pap. 26.00 (*90-6283-802-2*, Coutinho Pub) IBD Ltd.

Canning & Preserving. Linda Ferrari. LC 94-7799. 1994. pap. write for info. (*1-56799-098-3*, Friedman-Fairfax) M Friedman Pub Grp Inc.

Canning & Preserving Without Sugar. 3rd ed. Norma M. MacRae. LC 92-21478. (Illus.). 240p. (Orig.). 1993. pap. 12.95 (*1-56440-163-4*) Globe Pequot.

Canning, Freezing, Curing, & Smoking of Meat, Fish, & Game. Wilbur F. Eastman, Jr. LC 75-16830. (Illus.). 208p. 1975. pap. 9.95 (*0-88266-045-4*) Storey Comm Inc.

Canning Handbook: Surface Finishing Technology, Integrated Design. Canning, W., & Co., Ltd. Staff. (Illus.). 1060p. 1982. 69.95 (*0-419-12900-6*, NO. 5031, E & FN Spon) Routledge Chapman & Hall.

Cannon the Librarian. Mike Thaler. (Illus.). 32p. (Orig.). (J). 1993. pap. 3.50 (*0-380-76964-6*, Camelot Young) Avon.

Cannonball Chris. Jean Marzollo. LC 86-31512. (Stepping into Reading Bks.). (Illus.). 48p. (J). (gr. 2-3). 1987. pap. 3.50 (*0-394-88512-0*) Random Bks Yng Read.

Cannonball Run. Michael Avallone. 1981. pap. 2.50 (*0-8439-0993-5*) Dorchester Pub Co.

Cannonball Simp. John Burningham. LC 93-32369. (Illus.). 32p. (J). (ps up). 1994. 15.95 (*1-56402-338-9*) Candlewick Pr.

***Cannonball Simp.** John Burningham. LC 93-32369. 1995. pap. 5.99 (*1-56402-366-4*) Candlewick Pr.

Cannoneer in Navajo Country: Journal of Private Josiah M. Rice, 1851. limited ed. Ed. by Richard H. Dillon. (Illus.). 1970. 25.00 (*0-912094-15-X*) Old West.

Cannoneers: GI Life in a World War II Cannon Company. W. Stanford Smith. (Illus.). 136p. 1993. pap. 16.95 (*0-89745-164-3*) Sunflower U Pr.

Cannoneers in Gray: The Field Artillery of the Army of Tennessee, 1861-1865. Larry J. Daniel. LC 83-17899. (Illus.). 248p. 1989. pap. 19.50 (*0-8173-0481-9*) U of Ala Pr.

Cannons: An Introduction to Civil War Artillery. Dean S. Thomas. (Illus.). 72p. 1985. pap. 5.95 (*0-939631-03-2*) Thomas Publications.

Cannons & Sails: Meeting the Challenges to Marriage. Bill Doskocil. 164p. (Orig.). (C). 1989. pap. 5.95 (*0-9629600-0-4*) Rock Cornerstone.

***Cannon's Concise Guide to Rules of Order.** Hugh Cannon. 1995. pap. 9.95 (*0-395-73326-X*) HM.

Cannon's Guide to Freshwater Fishing with Downriggers. Tom Huggler. (Orig.). 1986. pap. text ed. 8.95 (*0-9616991-0-8*) Cannon-S & K.

Cannons of the Comstock. Brock Thoene & Bodie Thoene. (Saga of the Sierras Ser.). 224p. (YA). 1992. pap. 7.99 (*1-55661-166-8*) Bethany Hse.

Cannon's Point Plantation, 1794-1860: Living Conditions & Status Patterns in the Old South. John S. Otto. LC 83-15784. (Studies in Historical Archaeology). 1984. text ed. 47.00 (*0-12-531060-9*) Acad Pr.

***Cannon's Revenge.** W. W. Lee. LC 94-22437. 171p. 1995. 19.95 (*0-8027-4147-9*) Walker & Co.

Cannot Plead Black Anymore. Harold E. Byrd. LC 78-67830. (Illus.). 1978. 9.95 (*0-9601972-0-6*); pap. 6.95 (*0-9601972-1-4*) Byrd.

Cann's Keys to Better Meetings: An Authoritative New Guide to Parliamentary Procedure. Marjorie M. Cann. 80p. 1990. pap. 7.95 (*0-940882-17-5*) HB Pubns.

Canny Mr. Glencannon. Guy Gilpatric. 1976. 18.95 (*0-88411-574-7*, Aeonian Pr) Amereon Ltd.

Canny wi' the Sugar: A Collection of Scottish-American Poems. Wilma H. Clements. Ed. by Mildred W. Westburg. LC 84-52299. (Illus.). 88p. 1984. pap. 10.00 (*0-87423-034-9*) Westburg.

Canoe & White Water: From Essential to Sport. C. E. Franks. LC 77-2611. 1977. 25.00 (*0-8020-2236-7*) U of Toronto Pr.

Canoe & White Water: From Essential to Sport. C. E. Franks. LC 77-2611. (Illus.). 245p. reprint ed. pap. 69.90 (*0-8357-4137-0*, 2036910) Bks Demand.

Canoe Camping Vermont & New Hampshire Rivers. 2nd ed. Roioli Schweiker. LC 85-3870. (Canoe Camping Ser.). (Illus.). 128p. 1985. pap. 9.00 (*0-942440-22-6*, Backcountry) Countryman.

***Canoe Club, Vol. 1.** Thomas M. Tomlinson. LC 95-94412. (Illus.). 336p. (Orig.). 1995. pap. 11.95 (*0-9645199-0-9*) Billingsgate Pub.

Canoe Country. David J. Backes. 272p. 1991. pap. 14.95 (*1-55971-112-4*) NorthWord.

Canoe Country. Florence P. Jaques. LC 89-2524. (Illus.). 78p. 1989. reprint ed. pap. 7.50 (*0-87351-235-9*) Minn Hist.

Canoe Country Camping: Wilderness Skills for the Boundary Waters & Quetico. Michael Furtman. LC 92-70989. (Illus.). 208p. (Orig.). 1992. pap. 14.95 (*0-938586-66-1*) Pfeifer-Hamilton.

Canoe Country Reflections. Larry Rice. (Illus.). 64p. (Orig.). 1993. pap. 11.99 (*0-934802-85-8*) ICS Bks.

Canoe Country Wildlife: A Field Guide to the Boundary Waters & Quetico. Mark Stensaas. LC 92-70991. (Illus.). 224p. (Orig.). 1992. pap. 14.95 (*0-938586-65-3*) Pfeifer-Hamilton.

***Canoe-Fishing New York Rivers & Streams.** M. Paul Keesler. 176p. 1995. 24.95 (*0-9645372-0-6*); pap. 19.95 (*0-9645372-1-4*) Mid-York Sports.

Canoe Guide's Handbook: How to Plan & Guide a Trip for 2-12 People. Gil Gilpatrick. (Illus.). 160p. (Orig.). 1983. pap. 10.95 (*0-89933-011-8*) DeLorme Map.

Canoe Handbook: Techniques for Mastering the Sport of Canoeing. Slim Ray. LC 91-16032. (Illus.). 224p. 1992. pap. 15.95 (*0-8117-3032-8*) Stackpole.

Canoe Racing: The Competitor's Guide to Marathon & Downriver Racing. Peter Heed & Dick Mansfield. (Illus.). 256p. 1992. pap. 14.95 (*0-937921-52-1*) Acorn Pub.

Canoe Routes: Northwest Oregon. Philip Jones. LC 81-18860. (Illus.). 160p. (Orig.). 1982. pap. 8.95 (*0-89886-043-1*) Mountaineers.

Canoe Routes of Ontario: Published in Cooperation with the Ministry of Natural Resources. (Illus.). 112p. 1992. pap. 19.95 (*0-7710-6068-8*, Pub. by McClelland & Stewart CN) Firefly Bks Ltd.

Canoe Touring in East Anglia. Wilson Ltd. Staff & Imray L. Norie. (C). 1986. 50.00 (*0-85288-121-5*, Pub. by Imray Laurie Norie & Wilson UK) St Mut.

Canoe Trails of the Deep South. Chuck Estes et al. (Illus.). 304p. 1992. pap. 14.95 (*0-89732-066-2*) Menasha Ridge.

***Canoe Trip.** Bobbie Kalman. (Crabapple Ser.). (Illus.). 32p. (J). (ps-3). 1995. lib. bdg. 14.95 (*0-86505-619-6*); pap. 5.95 (*0-86505-719-2*) Crabtree Pub Co.

Canoe Trip Mystery. Gertrude C. Warner. (Boxcar Children Mysteries Ser.: No. 40). (J). (gr. 4-7). 1994. 10.95 (*0-8075-1058-0*); pap. 3.50 (*0-8075-1059-9*) A Whitman.

Canoe Tripping with Children: Unique Advice to Keeping Kids Comfortable. David Harrison & Judy Harrison. LC 90-30901. (Illus.). 160p. (Orig.). 1990. pap. 9.95 (*0-934802-60-2*) ICS Bks.

Canoe Voyage up the Minnay Sotor, 2 Vols. George W. Featherstonhaugh. LC 71-111618. 1970. reprint ed. Vol. 1, 416p. Vol. 2, 372p. 20.00 (*0-87351-057-7*) Minn Hist.

Canoe Voyage up the Mississippi & Around Lake Superior in 1846. Charles Lanman. LC 77-85592. 1978. reprint ed. 17.50 (*0-912382-22-8*); reprint ed. 8.00 (*0-912382-23-6*) Black Letter.

Canoecraft, Woodstrip Construction. T. Moores & M. Mohr. (Illus.). 148p. 1988. pap. 16.95 (*0-920656-24-2*, Pub. by Camden Hse CN) Firefly Bks Ltd.

Canoeing. (Teach Yourself Ser.). 184p. 1993. pap. 9.95 (*0-8442-3912-7*) NTC Pub Grp.

Canoeing. Donna Bailey. LC 90-23055. (Sports World Ser.). (Illus.). 32p. (J). (gr. 1-4). 1991. lib. bdg. 19.97 (*0-8114-2903-2*); pap. 3.95 (*0-8114-4706-5*) Raintree Steck-V.

Canoeing. Norman S. Barrett. Ed. by Franklin Watts Ltd. LC 86-51222. (Picture Library). (Illus.). 32p. (J). (ps-3). 1988. lib. bdg. 12.53 (*0-531-10349-8*) Watts.

Canoeing. Boy Scouts of America Staff. (Illus.). 88p. (J). (gr. 6-12). 1989. pap. 1.85 (*0-8395-3308-X*, 33308) BSA.

Canoeing. Laurie Gullion. LC 93-5599. (Outdoor Pursuits Ser.). (Illus.). 152p. 1994. pap. 12.95 (*0-87322-443-4*, PGUL0443) Human Kinetics.

Canoeing: A Beginner's Guide to the Kayak. Nigel Foster. 64p. (C). 1990. text ed. 65.00 (*0-906754-50-X*, Pub. by Fernhurst Bks UK) St Mut.

Canoeing: Coastal & Eastern Rivers, Vol. 1. Zip Kellogg. (Maine Geographic Ser.). (Illus.). 48p. 1993. pap. 4.95 (*0-89933-060-6*) DeLorme Map.

Canoeing: Northern Rivers, Vol. 3. Zip Kellogg. (Maine Geographic Ser.). (Illus.). 48p. 1986. pap. 4.95 (*0-89933-062-2*) DeLorme Map.

Canoeing: Trips in Connecticut. Pamela Detels & Janet Harris. (Illus.). 1977. pap. 3.95 (*0-931964-03-2*) Birch Run Pub.

Canoeing: Trips in Western Mass. Deborah Thomas & Suzanne S. Clauser. Ed. by P. Detels. (Illus.). 1979. 4.95 (*0-685-95410-2*) Birch Run Pub.

Canoeing: Western Rivers, Vol. 2. Zip Kellogg. (Maine Geographic Ser.). (Illus.). 48p. 1985. pap. 4.95 (*0-89933-061-4*) DeLorme Map.

Canoeing & Camping: Beyond the Basics. Cliff Jacobson. LC 92-4582. (Illus.). 196p. (Orig.). 1992. pap. 11.99 (*0-934802-80-7*) ICS Bks.

Canoeing & Kayaking: Instruction Manual. Laurie Gullion et al. Ed. by Thomas Foster. (Illus.). 116p. (Orig.). 1987. pap. 15.95 (*0-89732-136-7*) Am Canoe Assn.

Canoeing & Kayaking: Techniques, Tactics, Training. Marcus Bailie. (Crowood Sports Guides Ser.). (Illus.). 128p. 1992. pap. 19.95 (*1-85223-528-4*, Pub. by Crowood Pr UK) Trafalgar.

Canoeing & Kayaking for Persons with Physical Disabilities: Instruction Manual. Anne W. Webre & Janet A. Zeller. Ed. by Laurie Gullion. (Illus.). 112p. (Orig.). (C). 1990. pap. 14.95 (*0-943117-02-X*) Am Canoe Assn.

Canoeing & Kayaking Guide to the Streams of Florida, Vol. I: North Central Peninsula & Panhandle. Elizabeth Carter & John L. Pearce. LC 85-11596. (Illus.). 216p. (Orig.). 1985. pap. 12.95 (*0-89732-033-6*) Menasha Ridge.

Canoeing & Kayaking Guide to the Streams of Florida, Vol. II: Central & South Peninsula. Lou Glaros & Doug Sphar. LC 85-11596. 144p. 1987. pap. 11.95 (*0-89732-067-0*) Menasha Ridge.

Canoeing & Kayaking Guide to the Streams of Kentucky. rev. ed. Bob Sehlinger. LC 78-9837. (Illus.). 336p. 1978. pap. 14.95 (*0-89732-140-5*) Menasha Ridge.

Canoeing & Kayaking Ohio Streams: An Access Guide for Paddlers & Anglers. Steve Gillen & Richard Combs. (Illus.). 208p. 1994. pap. 17.00 (*0-88150-252-9*, Backcountry) Countryman.

Canoeing Central New York. William P. Ehling. LC 82-4018. (Canoeing Ser.). (Illus.). 176p. (Orig.). 1982. pap. 12.00 (*0-942440-01-3*, Backcountry) Countryman.

Canoeing Florida, Vol. 1: The Panhandle. Robert Anderson. (Illus.). 76p. (Orig.). 1990. pap. 4.95 (*0-932855-36-9*) Winner Enter.

Canoeing Florida, Vol. 2: Northern Peninsula. Robert Anderson. (Illus.). 84p. (Orig.). 1990. pap. 4.95 (*0-932855-37-7*) Winner Enter.

Canoeing Florida, Vol. 3: Southern Peninsula. Robert Anderson. (Illus.). 64p. (Orig.). 1990. pap. 4.95 (*0-932855-38-5*) Winner Enter.

Canoeing for Everyone. E. M. Harris. (C). 1987. 42.00 (*0-85174-311-0*, Pub. by Brwn Son Ferg) St Mut.

Canoeing in the Rain: Poems for My Aleut-Athabascan Son. Ann F. Chandonnet. (Illus.). 38p. (Orig.). 1990. pap. 10.00 (*0-9622738-2-1*) M Bliss.

Canoeing in the Rain: Poems for My Aleut-Athabascan Son. Ann F. Chandonnet. (Poetry Chapbook Ser.). (Illus.). 40p. (Orig.). 1990. pap. 10.00 (*0-317-99720-3*) Mr Cogito Pr.

Canoeing Made Easy: A Manual for Beginners with Tips for the Experienced. I. Herbert Gordon. LC 91-44664. (East Woods Book Ser.). (Illus.). 208p. (Orig.). 1992. pap. 16.95 (*0-87106-199-6*) Globe Pequot.

Canoeing Massachusetts, Rhode Island & Connecticut. Ken Weber. LC 79-90812. (Canoeing Ser.). (Illus.). 160p. 1987. pap. 11.00 (*0-942440-14-5*, Backcountry) Countryman.

Canoeing Michigan Rivers. Jerry Dennis & Craig Date. (Illus.). 152p. (Orig.). 1986. pap. 12.95 (*0-9608588-4-9*) Friede Pubns.

Canoeing the Adirondacks with Nessmuk: The Adirondack Letters of George Washington Sears. 2nd ed. Ed. by Dan Brenan. (Illus.). 180p. (C). 1993. pap. text ed. 14.95 (*0-8156-2594-4*) Syracuse U Pr.

Canoeing the Boundary Waters: The Account of One Family's Explorations. Marion Stresau. LC 78-68660. (Illus.). (Orig.). 1979. pap. 5.95 (*0-913140-28-7*) Signpost Bk Pub.

Canoeing the Delaware: A Guide to the River & Shore. Gary Letcher. (Illus.). 170p. 1985. pap. 10.95 (*0-8135-1077-5*) Rutgers U Pr.

Canoeing the Indian Way: Straight Talk for Modern Paddlers from the Dean of American Canoeists. Pierre Pulling. LC 88-19206. (Illus.). 128p. 1989. reprint ed. pap. 8.95 (*0-8117-2241-4*) Stackpole.

Canoeing the Jersey Pine Barrens. 4th ed. Robert Parnes. (East Woods Book Ser.). (Illus.). 256p. 1994. pap. 11.95 (*1-56440-373-4*) Globe Pequot.

Canoeing Whitewater. 8th rev. ed. Randy Carter. LC 67-23733. (Illus.). 1974. lib. bdg. 10.00 (*0-912660-00-7*); pap. 5.95 (*0-912660-02-3*) Appalachian Bks.

Canoeing Wild Rivers. 2nd expanded ed. Cliff Jacobson. LC 89-7601. (Illus.). 355p. (Orig.). 1989. pap. 19.95 (*0-934802-52-1*) ICS Bks.

Canoeing with the Cree. Eric Sevareid. LC 68-63520. (Illus.). 206p. 1968. reprint ed. pap. 8.95 (*0-87351-152-2*) Minn Hist.

Canoeist's Sketchbook. Robert Kimber. LC 91-18227. (Illus.). 202p. (Orig.). 1991. pap. 12.95 (*0-930031-45-8*) Chelsea Green Pub.

Canoer's Bible. rev. ed. Robert D. Mead. LC 74-33610. 1989. pap. 12.00 (*0-385-24578-5*) Doubleday.

Canoes & Kayaks for the Backyard Builder. Skip Snaith. (Illus.). 186p. 1988. pap. text ed. 19.95 (*0-87742-242-7*) Intl Marine.

Canoes & Kayaks for the Backyard Builder. Skip Snaith. 1988. pap. text ed. 21.95 (*0-07-156495-0*) McGraw.

Canoes of Oceania. A. C. Haddon & J. Hornell. (Special Publication Ser.: Nos. 27, 28, 29). (Illus.). 897p. 1975. reprint ed. pap. 45.00 (*0-910240-19-1*) Bishop Mus.

Canola & Rapeseed. F. Shahidi. 1990. text ed. 76.95 (*0-442-00295-5*) Chapman & Hall.

C

An Asterisk (*) at the beginning of an entry indicates that the title is appearing in BIP for the first time.

An Asterisk (*) at the beginning of an entry indicates that the title is appearing in BIP for the first time.

1029

C

Cantatas of Luigi Rossi: Analysis & Thematic Index, 2 vols., 1. Eleanor Caluori. LC 81-4749. (Studies in Musicology: No. 41). 311p. reprint ed. pap. 88.70 (*0-685-20840-0*, 2070067) Bks Demand.

Cantatas of Luigi Rossi: Analysis & Thematic Index, 2 vols., 2. Eleanor Caluori. LC 81-4749. (Studies in Musicology: No. 41). 218p. reprint ed. pap. 62.20 (*0-685-20841-9*, 2070067) Bks Demand.

Cantate: Responsorial Psalms for Sundays of the Year B. Margaret Daly. 161p. 1993. 59.00 (*1-85390-280-2*, Pub. by Veritas IE) St Mut.

Cantate du Narcisse see Poesies

Cantates see Oeuvres Completes de Jean-Philippe Rameau

Cantatrice Chauve: Including Lecon. Eugene Ionesco. write for info. (*0-318-63441-4*) Fr & Eur.

Cantatrice Chauve: La Lecon. Eugene Ionesco. (FRE.). 1972. pap. 10.95 (*0-8288-3690-6*, F105890) Fr & Eur.

Cantatrice Chauve see Theatre

Cantatrice Chauve - la Lecon. Eugene Ionesco. Ed. by Bulwa & March. (FRE.). (C). 1976. pap. text ed. 25.50 (*0-03-013731-4*) HB Coll Pubs.

Cantatrice Chauve & la Lecon. Eugene Ionesco. (Folio Ser.: No. 236). (FRE.). pap. 8.95 (*2-07-036236-1*) Schoenhof.

Cantatrice Chauve d'E. Ionesco. Michel Bigot. 243p. (FRE.). 1991. pap. 14.95 (*0-7859-2160-5*, 2070383474) Fr & Eur.

***Cantece de Mahala: Poeme.** Florentin Smarandache. Ed. by R. Muller. (Illus.). 120p. (C). 1995. pap. 9.99 (*1-879585-40-5*) Xiquan Pubng.

***Canted Antiferromagnetism: Hematite.** Allan H. Morrish. LC 94-35067. 200p. 1995. text ed. 46.00 (*981-02-2007-3*) World Scientific Pub.

***Cantemos Chiquitos No. I: Songs & Fingerplays from Mexico & South America.** Georgette Baker. (Illus.). 20p. (Orig.). (J). (gr. k-3). 1994. pap. 9.95 (*0-9623930-1-0*) Talented.

***Cantemos Chiquitos No. II: More Traditional Songs from South of the Border.** Georgette Baker. (Illus.). 30p. (Orig.). (J). (gr. k-3). Date not set. pap. 12.95 (*0-614-00850-6*) Talented.

Canten Navidad. Barbara MacArthur. (Illus.). 15p. (Orig.). (ENG & SPA.). (J). (ps-12). 1993. audio, pap. 12.95 (*1-881120-09-0*) Frog Pr WI.

***Canteras de Mitla, Oaxaca Tecnologia para la Arquitectura Monumental.** Nelly M. Robles-Garcia. (Vanderbilt University Publications in Anthropology: No. 47). (Illus.). 66p. (Orig.). (SPA.). 1994. pap. 12.00 (*0-935462-38-4*) Vanderbilt Pubns.

***Canterbury.** (Pevensey Heritage Guides Ser.). (Illus.). 112p. 1994. pap. 9.95 (*0-907115-64-0*) Sterling.

Canterbury: Its Rise, Ruin & Restoration. G. F. Maclear. 1976. lib. bdg. 34.95 (*0-8490-1568-5*) Gordon Pr.

***Canterbury Benedictional.** R. M. Woolley. (Henry Bradshaw Society). 204p. (C). 1995. text ed. 45.00 (*1-870252-10-1*) Boydell & Brewer.

***Canterbury Cathedral.** Ed. by Jonathan Keates & Angelo Hornak. (Illus.). 96p. Date not set. pap. 13.50 (*0-85667-069-3*) Scala Books.

Canterbury Cathedral & Its Romanesque Sculpture. Deborah Kahn. (Illus.). 230p. 1991. 45.00 (*0-292-71137-9*) U of Tex Pr.

Canterbury Folk. John M. Couper. ix, 58p. 1984. 19.95 (*0-522-84272-0*) Intl Spec Bk.

Canterbury Hall & Theatre of Varieties. John Earl & John Stanton. (Theatre in Focus Ser.). (Illus.). 63p. 1982. sl., pap. 105.00 (*0-85964-116-3*) Chadwyck-Healey.

Canterbury History & Guide. Tim Tatton-Brown. (History & Guide Ser.). (Illus.). 130p. 1994. 16.00 (*0-7509-0265-5*) A Sutton Pub.

Canterbury Law Review, Vols. 1-4: 1980-1991, Set. lib. bdg. 520.00 (*0-685-70504-8*) W W Gaunt.

Canterbury Pilgrimages. Henry S. Ward. 1972. 59.95 (*0-87968-811-4*) Gordon Pr.

Canterbury Pilgrims: Poems. Edwin F. Piper. 128p. 1989. 14.95 (*0-944266-06-1*) Maecenas Pr.

Canterbury Quadrangle, St. John's College, Oxford. Howard Colvin. (Illus.). 144p. 1988. 58.00 (*0-19-920159-5*) OUP.

Canterbury Tale from the Wife of Bath. Herman Ammann. (Illus.). 33p. 1970. pap. 7.50 (*0-88680-019-6*); pap. 2.50 (*0-88680-018-8*) I E Clark.

Canterbury Tales. Illus. by Victor G. Ambrus. LC 85-60147. 128p. (J). (gr. 4 up). 1985. 14.95 (*1-56288-259-7*) Checkerboard.

Canterbury Tales. Geoffrey Chaucer. Ed. by A. Kent Hieatt & Constance B. Hieatt. 448p. (gr. 9-12). 1982. mass mkt. 4.50 (*0-553-21082-3*, Bantam Classics) Bantam.

Canterbury Tales. Geoffrey Chaucer. Tr. by Ronald L. Ecker & Eugene J. Crook. LC 93-77730. 592p. (C). 1993. pap. text ed. 17.95 (*0-9636512-3-4*) Hodge & Braddock.
This is the first complete new translation of Chaucer's 14th-century Middle English classic to be published in over half a century. According to CHOICE, "It is difficult to imagine anyone doing a better job." As faithful to the original as a modern- English rendering permits, Ecker & Cook's translation includes the long-neglected prose tales (The Tale of Melibee & The Parson's Tale) in addition to the General Prologue & the 22 rhymed verse tales. Line numbers, corresponding to those found in Robinson, Benson, & other editions of the original text are included for the student's ease in locating particular lines or passages. Adding to the volume's value both to students & the general reader is a glossary of people, places & terms. With Ecker & Crook's translation, students & general readers alike may now gain a more balanced view of Chaucer's genius by having in modern English his complete masterpiece--what the poet John Dryden described as "God's plenty"--in all its variety. ***Publisher Provided Annotation.***

Canterbury Tales. Geoffrey Chaucer. Ed. by John Halverson. LC 79-153880. (Library of Literature: No. 27). 1971. pap. text ed. 12.19 (*0-672-61006-X*, Bobbs) Macmillan.

Canterbury Tales. Geoffrey Chaucer. Ed. & Tr. by David Wright. (World's Classics Paperback Ser.). 528p. 1986. pap. 4.95 (*0-19-281597-0*) OUP.

Canterbury Tales. Geoffrey Chaucer. LC 80-22141. (Short Classics Ser.). (Illus.). 48p. (J). (gr. 4 up). 1983. lib. bdg. 22.80 (*0-8172-1666-9*) Raintree Steck-V.

Canterbury Tales. Derek Pearsall. 380p. 1985. pap. 19.95 (*0-415-09444-5*, A8672) Routledge.

***Canterbury Tales.** Voelker. (Max Notes Ser.). 128p. 1995. pap. text ed. 3.95 (*0-87891-994-5*) Res & Educ.

Canterbury Tales. 2nd ed. Hopper. 1977. pap. 9.95 (*0-8120-0039-0*) Barron.

Canterbury Tales. Geoffrey Chaucer. 496p. (J). (ps-8). 1990. reprint ed. lib. bdg. 29.95 (*0-89966-671-X*) Buccaneer Bks.

Canterbury Tales, 2 Vols, 1. rev. ed. Ed. by Sophia Lee. LC 71-162886. (Illus.). reprint ed. write for info. (*0-404-54412-6*) AMS Pr.

Canterbury Tales, 2 Vols, 2. rev. ed. Ed. by Sophia Lee. LC 71-162886. (Illus.). reprint ed. write for info. (*0-404-54413-4*) AMS Pr.

Canterbury Tales, 2 Vols, Set. rev. ed. Ed. by Sophia Lee. LC 71-162886. (Illus.). reprint ed. 90.00 (*0-404-54550-5*) AMS Pr.

Canterbury Tales: A Facsimile & Transcription of the Hengwrt Manuscript with Variants from the Ellesmere Manuscript. Geoffrey Chaucer. Ed. by Paul G. Ruggiers. LC 77-18611. (Illus.). 1078p. 1979. 185.00 (*0-8061-1416-9*) U of Okla Pr.

Canterbury Tales: A Literary Pilgrimage. David Williams. (Masterwork Studies: No. 4). 128p. 1987. text ed. 21.95 (*0-8057-7952-3*, Twayne); pap. 12.95 (*0-8057-8004-1*, Twayne) Macmillan.

Canterbury Tales: A Reading. Derek Traversi. LC 83-1121. 256p. 1983. 36.50 (*0-87413-246-0*) U Delaware Pr.

Canterbury Tales: A Selection. Geoffrey Chaucer. Ed. by Donald R. Howard & James M. Dean. 1988. pap. 4.95 (*0-451-52400-4*, CE1514, Sig Classics) NAL-Dutton.

Canterbury Tales: Fifteenth-Century Continuations & Additions. Ed. by John M. Bowers. LC 92-22583. 1992. pap. 8.95 (*1-879288-23-0*) Medieval Inst.

Canterbury Tales: Nine Tales & the General Prologue. Geoffrey Chaucer. Ed. by V. A. Kolve & Glending Olson. (Critical Editions Ser.). 400p. (Orig.). (C). 1989. pap. text ed. 9.95 (*0-393-95245-2*) Norton.

Canterbury Tales & the Good Society. Paul A. Olson. (Illus.). 320p. 1987. text ed. 49.50x (*0-691-06693-0*) Princeton U Pr.

Canterbury Tales (Chaucer) Werthamer. (Book Notes Ser.). (C). 1984. pap. 2.95 (*0-8120-3406-6*) Barron.

Canterbury Tales Literature Guide. Johanna Wrinkle. 80p. 1992. pap. text ed. 10.95 (*0-944459-54-4*) ECS Lrn Systs.

Canterbury Tales Notes. 1964. pap. 3.95 (*0-8220-0292-2*) Cliffs.

Canterbury Tales of Chaucer, 5 Vols, 1. Geoffrey Chaucer. Ed. by Thomas Tyrwhitt. LC 74-39160. reprint ed. write for info. (*0-404-01551-4*) AMS Pr.

Canterbury Tales of Chaucer, 5 Vols, 2. Geoffrey Chaucer. Ed. by Thomas Tyrwhitt. LC 74-39160. reprint ed. write for info. (*0-404-01552-2*) AMS Pr.

Canterbury Tales of Chaucer, 5 Vols, 3. Geoffrey Chaucer. Ed. by Thomas Tyrwhitt. LC 74-39160. reprint ed. write for info. (*0-404-01553-0*) AMS Pr.

Canterbury Tales of Chaucer, 5 Vols, 4. Geoffrey Chaucer. Ed. by Thomas Tyrwhitt. LC 74-39160. reprint ed. write for info. (*0-404-01554-9*) AMS Pr.

Canterbury Tales of Chaucer, 5 Vols, 5. Geoffrey Chaucer. Ed. by Thomas Tyrwhitt. LC 74-39160. reprint ed. write for info. (*0-404-01555-7*) AMS Pr.

Canterbury Tales of Chaucer, 5 Vols, Set. Geoffrey Chaucer. Ed. by Thomas Tyrwhitt. LC 74-39160. reprint ed. 385.00 (*0-404-01550-6*) AMS Pr.

Canterbury Tales Prologue: Complete Study Guide. Sidney Lamb. 1966. pap. 4.95 (*0-8220-1404-1*) Cliffs.

Canterbury Tales, The Wife of Bath: Complete Study Guide. Sidney Lamb. 1983. pap. 4.95 (*0-8220-1408-4*) Cliffs.

Canters & Chronicles: The Use of Narrative in the Plays of Samuel Beckett & Harold Pinter. Kristin Morrison. LC 82-16086. viii, 228p. (C). 1986. pap. text ed. 9.95 (*0-226-54131-2*) U Ch Pr.

Canterville. Mark Dunster. 19p. (Orig.). 1985. pap. 4.00 (*0-89642-122-8*) Linden Pubs.

Canterville Ghost. Oscar Wilde. (Illus.). pap. 3.95 (*0-8283-1429-2*, 27, Intl Pocket Lib) Branden Pub Co.

Canterville Ghost. Oscar Wilde. LC 86-8179. (Illus.). (J). (gr. 4 up). 1991. pap. 15.95 (*0-88708-027-8*, Picture Book Studio) S&S Childrens.

Canterville Ghost. Darwin R. Payne. 49p. 1963. reprint ed. pap. 3.45 (*0-87129-044-8*, C71) Dramatic Pub.

Canterville Ghost: The Star Child. Oscar Wilde. Ed. by Geeta Seshamani. (Illus.). 72p. 1982. pap. text ed. 3.95 (*0-86131-295-3*, Pub. by Orient Longman Ltd II) Apt Bks.

Canterville Ghost & Other Stories. Oscar Wilde. (Classics Ser.). (Illus.). (YA). 1991. pap. text ed. 6.50 (*0-582-03589-9*, 79118) Longman.

Canti C No Cento Cinquanta. Ottaviano Petrucci. (Monuments of Music & Music Literature in Facsimile: Series I, Vol. 25). (Illus.). 1978. reprint ed. lib. bdg. 60.00 (*0-8450-2025-0*) Broude.

Canti Orphici: Orphic Songs & Other Poems. Dino Campana. Tr. by Luigi Bonaffini. LC 91-34869. (Studies in Southern Italian & Italian American Culture: Vol. 3). 277p. (ENG & ITA.). (C). 1992. text ed. 56.95 (*0-8204-1738-6*) P Lang Pubs.

Cantiaci. A. Detsicas. (Peoples of Roman Britain Ser.). (Illus.). 230p. 1991. text ed. 30.00 (*0-86299-117-X*) A Sutton Pub.

Canticle: Forgotten Realms. R. A. Salvatore. LC 90-71503. (Cleric Quintet Ser.: Bk. 1). 320p. (Orig.). 1991. pap. 4.95 (*1-56076-119-9*) TSR Inc.

Canticle for Leibowitz. Walter M. Miller, Jr. 320p. 1984. mass mkt. 5.99 (*0-553-27381-7*, Bantam Classics) Bantam.

Canticle for Leibowitz. Walter M. Miller. 1993. reprint ed. lib. bdg. 18.95 (*0-89968-353-3*, Lghtyr Pr) Buccaneer Bks.

Canticle for the Dead. Stephen C. Spry. Tr. by Ingram. 340p. 1995. pap. 9.95 (*1-56901-344-6*) NW Pub.

Canticle of Christmas. Tom Fettke & Camp Kirkland. 1991. spiral bd. 6.50 (*0-685-68435-0*, MC-75); audio 10.98 (*0-685-68436-9*, TA-9135C); cd-rom 14.98 (*0-685-68437-7*, DC-9135) Lillenas.

Canticle of Jack Kerouac. Lawrence Ferlinghetti. 16p. (Orig.). 1993. pap. 15.00 (*0-931659-14-0*) Limberlost Pr.

Canticle of Jack Kerouac. deluxe ed. Lawrence Ferlinghetti. 16p. (Orig.). 1993. 30.00 (*0-931659-15-9*) Limberlost Pr.

***Canticle of Love: Directed Journaling for Life's Singers.** Patsy R. Booth. 170p. 1993. pap. 12.95 (*0-614-04903-2*) Cedar Tree.

Canticles & Gathering Prayers. John Mossi & Suzanne Toolan. 148p. 1989. spiral bd. 9.95 (*0-88489-228-X*) St Marys.

Canticles of Joy: Christmas Poems 1966-1986. June A. Geissler. LC 87-32373. 38p. 1987. pap. 3.95 (*0-942179-04-8*) Shelby Hse.

Canticos De Navidad: Songs for Christmas. (SPA.). 6.25 (*84-7228-192-2*, 226076, Pub. by Edit Clie SP) TSELF.

Canticum Magnificat see Complete Works of Philippe de Monte

Cantilenes en Gelee. Boris Vian. 256p. 1970. 4.95 (*0-686-55685-2*) Fr & Eur.

***Cantina Cookery: Hot Stuff from Corpus Christi, Texas!** Maxine Sommers. (Illus.). 22p. (Orig.). 1995. pap. 4.95 (*0-943991-43-9*) Pound Sterling Pub.

Cantine Family: Descendants of Moses Cantine. Alice C. Huntington. 82p. 1982. reprint ed. pap. 9.50 (*1-56012-058-4*) Kinship Rhinebeck.

Canting Crew: London's Criminal Underworld, 1550-1700. John McMullen. 192p. 1984. text ed. 40.00 (*0-8135-1022-8*) Rutgers U Pr.

Cantiones see Complete Works of Philippe de Monte

Cantique des Cantiques see Theatre

Canto a la Raza: Composicion Sangvinea De Estudiantes De la Universidad De Puerto Rico. Angel Rodriguez Olleros. 94p. 1974. 2.00 (*0-8477-2314-3*) U of PR Pr.

***Canto Al Senor En la Isla Del Encanto.** Olga Serrano. 1992. pap. 4.95 (*0-87178-510-2*) Brethren.

Canto De Mi Tierra. Evaristo Ribera Chevremont. 97p. (C). 1971. 2.00 (*0-8477-3213-4*) U of PR Pr.

Canto del Viento. Raquel Fundora de Rodriguez Aragon. LC 82-62050. (Senda Poetica Ser.). 96p. (Orig.). 1983. pap. 6.95 (*0-918454-31-X*) Senda Nueva.

Canto E Bel Canto P.F. Tosi: Opinioni De Cantori Antchi E Moderni 1723. Ed. by Andrea D. Corte. LC 80-2268. reprint ed. 31.50 (*0-404-18823-0*) AMS Pr.

***Canto for the Birds.** Julia Connor. (Illus.). 38p. 1995. pap. write for info. (*0-914485-14-8*) Trill Pr.

Canto General. Pablo Neruda. (SPA.). 1968. 12.50 (*0-8288-2532-7*) Fr & Eur.

Canto General. Pablo Neruda. Tr. by Jack Schmitt. LC 90-39070. (Latin American Literature & Culture Ser.: No. 7). 418p. 1991. 38.00 (*0-520-05433-4*) U CA Pr.

Canto General. Pablo Neruda. 1993. pap. 15.00 (*0-520-08279-6*) U CA Pr.

***Canto General.** 2nd ed. Pablo Neruda. 496p. 1988. pap. 13.95 (*0-7859-5186-5*) Fr & Eur.

Canto Indispensable (Poesias) Roberto Ponciano. LC 87-81864. (Coleccion Espejo de Paciencia Ser.). 112p. (Orig.). (SPA.). 1987. pap. 9.00 (*0-89729-446-7*) Ediciones.

***Canto Latino: Spanish Songs for Children.** Illus. by Angelo Lopez. (Orig.). (J). (gr. k-5). 1995. audio 5.95 (*0-9638395-0-0*) Bi-Lateral Pr.

***Canto Latino: Spanish Songs for Children.** Illus. by Angelo Lopez. 36p. (Orig.). (J). (gr. k-5). 1995. audio, pap. text ed. 12.95 (*0-9638395-1-9*) Bi-Lateral Pr.

Canto Latinoamericano. Mario A. Uceda. Ed. by Flor A. Llanes. 108p. (Orig.). 1986. pap. 4.95 (*0-938693-02-6*) Maya Pubns.

Canto Moreno - Poems. Manfred Von Pentz. (Orig.). 1993. pap. 12.95 (*1-85756-001-9*, Pub. by Janus Pub UK) Intl Spec Bk.

Canto real das rodas rolantes see Real Chant of the Rolling Wheels

Cantonese, Vol. I. Foreign Service Institute Staff. 392p. (CHI.). 1979. audio 185.00 (*0-88432-020-0*, AFC131); 24.95 (*0-88432-799-X*, AFC991) Audio-Forum.

Cantonese, Vol. II. Foreign Service Institute Staff. 410p. (CHI.). 1980. audio 225.00 (*0-88432-033-2*, AFC140); 34.95 (*0-88432-581-4*, AFC992) Audio-Forum.

Cantonese: A Comprehensive Grammar. Stephen Matthews & Virginia Yip. LC 93-36173. 1994. pap. write for info. (*0-415-08945-X*, Routledge NY) Routledge.

***Cantonese - English Picture Dictionary.** Claudia Schwalm. (Illus.). 89p. (J). (gr. k-6). 1995. audio 20.00 (*1-57371-000-8*) Cult Connect.

Cantonese & Mandarin Phrase Book: Speaking Chinese in the Two Major Dialects. Rita M. Choy. 1991. pap. 16.95 (*0-941340-12-0*) China West.

Cantonese Ballads: Chinese. Wolfram Eberhard. (Asian Folklore & Social Life Monographs: No. 30). 1972. 14.00 (*0-89986-030-3*) Oriental Bk Store.

***Cantonese Basic Course.** 288p. 1995. pap. 16.95 (*0-7818-0289-X*) Hippocrene Bks.

Cantonese, Basic Course, V. 1: Includes Lessons 1-15 of Course in Cantonese. (Foreign Service Institute Basic Course Ser.). 408p. (Orig.). 1970. reprint ed. pap. text ed. 9.50 (*0-16-004371-9*, S/N 044-000-01268-5) USGPO.

Cantonese for Foreigners. Luk Ming. 1984. audio 29.95 (*962-14-0069-4*, CAFOFO) China Bks.

Cantonese Love Songs: An English Translation of Jiu Jiyung's Cantonese Songs of the Early 19th Century. Ed. by Peter Morris. 216p. (C). 1992. pap. text ed. 72.00 (*962-209-284-5*, Pub. by Hong Kong U Pr HK) St Mut.

Cantonese Phrasebook. Kam Lau. (Illus.). 180p. (Orig.). 1994. pap. 6.95 (*0-86442-217-2*) Lonely Planet.

***Cantonese Phrasebook.** Kam Lau. (Illus.). 224p. (Orig.). 1995. pap. 5.95 (*0-86442-340-3*) Lonely Planet.

Cantonese Sounds & Tones. Po-Fei Huang. 1965. 6.95 (*0-88710-005-8*); audio write for info. (*0-88710-006-6*) Yale Far Eastern Pubns.

Cantor Basics. James Hansen. 130p. (Orig.). 1991. pap. 9.95 (*0-912405-81-3*) Pastoral Pr.

Cantora: A Novel. Silvia Lopez-Medina. LC 91-43406. 317p. 1992. 19.95 (*0-8263-1375-2*) U of NM Pr.

Cantora: A Novel. Sylvia Lopez-Medina. 320p. 1993. pap. 10.00 (*0-345-38166-1*, One World) Ballantine.

Cantorian Set Theory & Limitation of Size. Michael Hallett. (Oxford Logic Guides Ser.: No. 10). 343p. 1986. reprint ed. pap. 27.50 (*0-19-853283-0*) OUP.

Cantor's Dilemma. Carl Djerassi. 240p. 1991. pap. 10.00 (*0-14-014359-9*, Penguin Bks) Viking Penguin.

Cantor's Manual of Jewish Law. Walter Orenstein. LC 94-9953. 200p. 1994. pap. 24.95 (*1-56821-258-5*) Aronson.

***Cantos.** Alfred Arteaga. (Illus.). 49p. 1991. pap. 7.95 (*0-9624536-2-5*) Chusma Hse.

Cantos de los Rios (Songs of the River) (SPA.). Date not set. 4.99 (*0-685-74910-X*, 490184) Editorial Unilit.

Cantos de Verdes Pastos (Salmos) (Songs of Green Pastures (Psalms)) (SPA.). Date not set. 4.99 (*0-685-74911-8*, 490187) Editorial Unilit.

***Cantos de Vida y Esperanza.** R. Dario. 148p. 1983. pap. 9.95 (*0-7859-5207-1*) Fr & Eur.

Cantos North. Henry Beissel. 63p. 1982. 6.95 (*0-920806-41-4*, Pub. by Penumbra Pr CN) U of Toronto Pr.

Cantos of Ezra Pound: No. 1-117. Ezra Pound. LC 70-117217. 1970. 31.95 (*0-8112-0350-6*) New Directions.

***Cantos Para Pedir Posadas y Otras Canciones de Navidad.** M. A. C. C. Team Staff. 24p. (SPA.). 1982. write for info. (*0-614-04893-1*) Mex Am Cult.

Cantos, Rimos y Rimas. Lonnie D. Zovi. 67p. (Orig.). (SPA.). (J). (gr. 5 up). 1990. pap. 22.95 (*0-935301-60-7*) Vibrante Pr.

Cantos y Rimas. Ivette Lopez & Dwight Garcia. (Lecturas Faciles). 68p. (SPA.). 1983. pap. text ed. 3.75 (*0-88345-524-2*, 21282) Prentice ESL.

Cantos y Rimas. Ivette Lopez & Dwight Garcia. 1987. pap. text ed. 7.00 (*0-13-113507-4*) Prentice ESL.

***Cantos (121-150)** Ezra Pound. Ed. by Michael Andre. Tr. by Sol LeWitt. 120p. Date not set. 69.95 (*0-934450-56-0*) Unmuzzled Ox.

Cantos (125-143) Ezra Pound. Allen Ginsberg & Robert Creeley. Ed. by Michael Andre. (Unmuzzled Ox Anthologies). (Illus.). 64p. (Orig.). 1986. pap. 12.00 (*0-934450-11-0*) Unmuzzled Ox.

Cantrell Family: A Biographical Album & History of the Descendants of Zebulen Cantrell, the Immigrant, with Data Concerning the Families Who Have Allied Themselves by Marriage, 1700-1898. C. G. Cantrell. (Illus.). 156p. 1989. reprint ed. lib. bdg. 35.00 (*0-8328-1306-0*); reprint ed. pap. 25.00 (*0-8328-1307-9*) Higginson Bk Co.

Cantrill-Cantrell Genealogy. Susan Cantrill Christie. LC 85-73793. 271p. 1986. reprint ed. 135.00 (*0-916497-69-0*); reprint ed. fiche 6.00 (*0-916497-68-2*) Burnett Micro.

Cantus: Piacenza, Biblioteca Capitolare 65. Keith Glaeske et al. (Wissenschaftliche Abhandlungen-Musicological Studies: Vol. 55, Pt. 2). xix, 178p. 1993. 100.00 (*0-931902-79-7*) Inst Mediaeval Mus.

Cantus - An Aquitanian Antiphoner: Toledo, Biblioteca Capitular, 44.2. Ronald T. Olexy et al. (Wissenschaftliche Abhandlungen-Musicological Studies: Vol. 55, Pt. 1). 185p. 1992. 80.00 (*0-931902-71-1*) Inst Mediaeval Mus.

Cantus Cunarum: English Nursery Rhymes in Latin. Bonnie Barrett. (Illus.). 30p. (Orig.). (LAT.). (YA). (gr. 6-12). 1991. spiral bd. 2.10 (*0-939507-00-5*, B707) Amer Classical.

Cantus Firmus. Aleksis Rannit. Tr. by Henry Lyman. 1978. 50.00 (*0-685-90033-9*) Elizabeth Pr.

Cantus Firmus in Mass & Motet Fourteen Twenty to Fifteen Twenty. Edgar H. Sparks. LC 74-31190. (Music Reprint Ser.). (Illus.). xi, 504p. 1975. reprint ed. lib. bdg. 65.00 (*0-306-70720-9*) Da Capo.

An Asterisk (*) at the beginning of an entry indicates that the title is appearing in BIP for the first time.

Canute the Great, Nine Ninety-Five to Ten Thirty-Five. Laurence M. Larson. LC 71-111764. (Heroes of the Nations Ser.). reprint ed. 30.00 (*0-404-03879-4*) AMS Pr.

Canvas. Adam Zagajewski. Tr. by Renata Gorczynski & Benjamin Ivry. 96p. 1992. 20.00 (*0-374-11867-1*) FS&G.

Canvas: Poems. Adam Zagajewski. 1994. pap. 8.00 (*0-374-52398-3*, Noonday) FS&G.

Canvas & the Brush. Romen Basu. 116p. 1970. 5.95 (*0-317-00320-8*, Pub. by Filma K L Mukhopadhyay II) R Basu.

***Canvas Decoys of North America.** Archie Johnson. LC 94-68902. (Illus.). 192p. 1994. pap. 29.95 (*0-9631815-3-X*) Decoy Mag.

Canvas Embroidery. Diana Springall. (Illus.). 192p. 1980. 19.95 (*0-8231-3298-6*) Branford.

Canvas Work. Jeremy Howard-Williams. (Illus.). 144p. (Orig.). 1993. pap. 11.95 (*0-924486-60-0*) Sheridan.

Canvasback on a Prairie Marsh. H. Albert Hochbaum. LC 80-22699. (Illus.). xxii, 207p. 1981. reprint ed. pap. 5.95 (*0-8032-7200-6*) U of Nebr Pr.

Canvasbacks: A Pictorial Study. Tricia Veasey. LC 88-63993. (Illus.). 96p. 1989. pap. 12.95 (*0-88740-154-6*) Schiffer.

Canvases & Careers: Institutional Change in the French Painting World. Harrison C. White & Cynthia A. White. LC 65-19469. (Illus.). 216p. 1993. pap. text ed. 11.95 (*0-226-89487-8*) U Ch Pr.

Canvassing L.A., an Artful Guide to Galleries, Museums, & Restaurants. Pasadena Art Alliance Staff. (Illus.). 80p. 1988. pap. text ed. 12.95 (*0-937042-07-2*) Pasadena Art.

***Canvassing the Health Needs of a Community.** Deanne Gaskill. (Research Paper: No. 7). 1992. pap. 21.00 (*0-7300-1522-X*, Pub. by Deakin Univ AT) St Mut.

Canyon. Michael P. Ghiglieri. LC 91-29222. 310p. (Orig.). 1992. pap. 15.95 (*0-8165-1286-8*) U of Ariz Pr.

Canyon Country. Helmut Friedrich & Witold Sartorius. (Windsor Destination Guides Ser.). (Illus.). 56p. 1992. pap. 12.95 (*1-874111-03-0*, Pub. by Windsor Bks UK) Seven Hills Bk.

Canyon Country. Wayne Ranney. (Plateau Ser.). 32p. 1993. pap. 6.95 (*0-89734-113-9*) Mus Northern Ariz.

Canyon Country: Mountain Biking. F. A. Barnes & Tom Kuehne. LC 87-73014. (Canyon Country Ser.: No. 17). (Illus.). 144p. (Orig.). 1988. pap. 8.00 (*0-9614586-5-8*) Canyon Country Pubns.

Canyon Country Arches & Bridges. F. A. Barnes. LC 86-50825. (Canyon Country Ser.: No. 15). (Illus.). 416p. (Orig.). 1987. pap. 9.95 (*0-9614586-1-5*) Canyon Country Pubns.

Canyon Country Camping. rev. ed. F. A. Barnes. (Illus.). 128p. 1991. pap. 6.00 (*0-915272-34-2*) Wasatch Pubs.

***Canyon Country Explorer, No. 1.** F. A. Barnes. LC 94-94154. (Canyon Country Ser.: No. 33). (Illus.). 112p. 1994. pap. 12.50 (*0-925685-07-0*) Canyon Country Pubns.

***Canyon Country Explorer, No. 2.** F. A. Barnes. (Canyon Country Ser.: No. 40). 112p. 1995. pap. 12.50 (*0-925685-18-6*) Canyon Country Pubns.

Canyon Country Geology for the Layman & Rockhound. F. A. Barnes. LC 77-95050. (Illus.). 1978. pap. 5.00 (*0-915272-17-2*) Wasatch Pubs.

Canyon Country Hiking & Natural History. F. A. Barnes. LC 76-58119. (Canyon Country Ser.). (Illus.). 1977. pap. 7.00 (*0-915272-07-5*) Wasatch Pubs.

Canyon Country Off-Road Vehicle Trails: Arches & la Sals Areas. F. A. Barnes. LC 77-95043. (Canyon Country Ser.). (Illus.). 1978. pap. 4.50 (*0-915272-13-X*) Wasatch Pubs.

Canyon Country Off-Road Vehicle Trails: Canyon Rims & Needles Areas. F. A. Barnes. LC 89-92058. (Canyon Country Ser.: No. 8). (Illus.). 96p. 1990. pap. 6.00 (*0-9614586-7-4*) Canyon Country Pubns.

Canyon Country Off-Road Vehicle Trails: Canyon Rims & Needles Areas. F. A. Barnes. LC 77-95043. (Canyon Country Ser.). (Illus.). 1978. pap. 4.50 (*0-915272-14-8*) Wasatch Pubs.

Canyon Country Off-Road Vehicle Trails: Island Area. F. A. Barnes. LC 77-95043. (Canyon Country Ser.). (Illus.). 1978. pap. 4.00 (*0-915272-15-6*) Wasatch Pubs.

Canyon Country Off-Road Vehicle Trails - Arches & La Sals Areas. rev. ed. F. A. Barnes. (Canyon Country Ser.: No. 6). (Illus.). 96p. 1989. reprint ed. pap. 6.00 (*0-9614586-0-7*) Canyon Country Pubns.

Canyon Country Off-Road Vehicle Trails - Island Area. rev. ed. F. A. Barnes. LC 88-70881. (Canyon Country Ser.: No. 4). (Illus.). 80p. (Orig.). 1988. reprint ed. pap. 6.00 (*0-9614586-6-6*) Canyon Country Pubns.

Canyon Country Off-Road Vehicle Trails - Maze Area. Jack Bickers. Ed. by F. A. Barnes. LC 88-70882. (Canyon Country Ser.: No. 18). (Illus.). 80p. (Orig.). 1988. pap. 6.00 (*0-9614586-3-1*) Canyon Country Pubns.

Canyon Country ORV Trails - Canyon Rims Recreation Area. F. A. Barnes. LC 90-86115. (Canyon Country Ser.: No. 25). (Illus.). 112p. (Orig.). 1991. pap. 6.00 (*0-925685-01-1*) Canyon Country Pubns.

Canyon Country Parklands: Treasures of the Great Plateau. Scott Thybony. Ed. by Margaret Sedeen. LC 93-3517. (Special Publications Series 28: No. 1). (Illus.). 1993. 12.95 (*0-87044-907-9*) Natl Geog.

Canyon Country Prehistoric Indians. Michalene Pendleton & F. A. Barnes. (Canyon Country Ser.). (Illus.). (Orig.). 1979. pap. 7.50 (*0-915272-24-5*) Wasatch Pubs.

Canyon Country Prehistoric Rock Art. F. A. Barnes. LC 82-60129. (Canyon Country Ser.). (Illus.). 304p. 1982. pap. 8.50 (*0-915272-25-3*) Wasatch Pubs.

Canyon Country Slickrock Hiking & Biking. F. A. Barnes. LC 88-62755. (Canyon Country Ser.: No. 21). (Illus.). 288p. (Orig.). 1990. pap. 12.00 (*0-9614586-4-X*) Canyon Country Pubns.

Canyon Country's Canyon Rims Recreation Area. F. A. Barnes & M. M. Barnes. LC 89-62344. (Canyon Country Ser.: No. 23). (Illus.). 216p. (Orig.). 1992. pap. 13.50 (*0-925685-00-3*) Canyon Country Pubns.

***Canyon Country's La Sal Mountains Hiking & Nature Handbook.** Jose Knighton. LC 94-71310. (Canyon Country Ser.: No. 34). (Illus.). 144p. 1995. pap. 11.00 (*0-925685-17-8*) Canyon Country Pubns.

Canyon De Chelly: Its People & Rock Art. Campbell Grant. LC 75-8455. 290p. 1978. pap. 16.95 (*0-8165-0523-3*) U of Ariz Pr.

Canyon de Chelly: The Story Behind the Scenery. rev. ed. Anderson & Supplee. LC 90-60035. (Illus.). 48p. 1990. pap. 6.95 (*0-88714-042-4*) KC Pubns.

Canyon de Chelly: The Story of Its Ruins & People. Zorro A. Bradley. (Illus.). 60p. 1973. pap. 3.00 (*0-16-003493-0*, S-N 024-005-00909-4) USGPO.

Canyon De Chelly: The Timeless Fold. Conger Beasley, Jr. (Illus.). 128p. 1988. per. 8.95 (*0-9604462-4-9*) Sweetlight.

***Canyon Door.** Kevin Boos. (Illus.). 148p. (Orig.). (J). (gr. 4-6). 1993. pap. 3.95 (*1-885101-00-7*) Writers Pr Srv.

***Canyon Door Resource Guide.** Kevin Boos et al. (Illus.). 40p. (Orig.). (J). (gr. 4-8). 1994. 7.99 (*1-885101-03-1*) Writers Pr Srv.

***Canyon Echoes: Recipes & Remembrances from Prairie Dog Pete.** Kevin Welch. (Illus.). 192p. 1994. 12.50 (*0-9645176-0-4*) Tex Pan Star.

***Canyon Hiking Guide to the Colorado Plateau.** 3rd ed. Michael R. Kelsey. (Illus.). 288p. (Orig.). 1995. pap. 12.95 (*0-944510-11-6*) Kelsey Pub.

Canyon Kill. Jack Slade. (Sundance Ser.: No. 24). 1979. pap. 1.75 (*0-8439-0618-9*) Dorchester Pub Co.

***Canyon Moon.** Carol Finch. 384p. 1995. pap. 4.99 (*0-8217-5036-4*) Zebra.

Canyon of the Gun. T. Olsen. 1983. pap. 2.95 (*0-449-13943-3*) Fawcett.

Canyon of the Gun - Haven of the Hunted, 2 vols. in 1. T. V. Olsen. 304p. 1993. pap. 4.99 (*0-8439-3545-6*) Dorchester Pub Co.

Canyon Passage. Ernest Haycox. 256p. 1992. pap. 3.50 (*1-55817-651-9*, Pinnacle NY) Windsor NY.

Canyon Revisited: A Rephotography of the Grand Canyon, 1923-1991. Donald L. Baars & Rex C. Buchanan. (Illus.). 160p. (Orig.). 1994. pap. 19.95 (*0-87480-458-2*) U of Utah Pr.

Canyon Visions: Photographs & Pastels of the Texas Plains. Dan Flores & Amy G. Winton. LC 89-4982. (Illus.). 113p. 1989. 29.00 (*0-89672-193-0*); pap. 20.00 (*0-89672-194-9*) Tex Tech Univ Pr.

Canyon Voyage: The Narrative of the Second Powell Expedition down the Colorado River from Wyoming, & the Explorations on Land, in the Years 1871 & 1872. Frederick S. Dellenbaugh. LC 84-8648. (Illus.). 277p. 1984. reprint ed. pap. 13.95 (*0-8165-0880-1*) U of Ariz Pr.

Canyon Winter. Walt Morey. 208p. (J). (gr. 5 up). 1994. pap. 3.99 (*0-14-036856-6*) Puffin Bks.

Canyoneering: The San Rafael Swell. Steve Allen. LC 91-24599. (Illus.). 320p. (Orig.). (C). 1992. pap. 14.95 (*0-87480-372-1*) U of Utah Pr.

***Canyoneering 2: Technical Loop Hikes in Southern Utah.** Steve Allen. LC 94-31739. (Illus.). 248p. (Orig.). 1995. pap. 19.95 (*0-87480-467-1*) U of Utah Pr.

Canyonlands: The Story Behind the Scenery. David W. Johnson. LC 89-45018. (Illus.). 48p. 1989. pap. 6.95 (*0-88714-034-3*) KC Pubns.

Canyonlands County: Geology of Canyonlands & Arches National Park. rev. ed. Donald L. Baars. LC 93-23140. (Illus.). 156p. 1993. pap. 12.95 (*0-87480-432-9*) U of Utah Pr.

***Canyonlands Maze - NE Glen Canyon, UT.** Ed. by Trails Illustrated Staff. 1994. 8.99 (*1-56695-019-8*) Trails Illustrated.

Canyonlands National Park. David Petersen. LC 91-35274. (New True Bks.). (Illus.). 48p. (J). (gr. k-4). 1992. lib. bdg. 12.90 (*0-516-01132-4*); pap. 4.95 (*0-516-41132-2*) Childrens.

Canyonlands National Park: Early History & First Descriptions. F. A. Barnes. LC 87-72287. (Canyon Country Ser.: No. 16). (Illus.). 160p. (Orig.). 1988. pap. 5.00 (*0-9614586-2-3*) Canyon Country Pubns.

Canyonlands National Park Needle - Island, UT. rev. ed. Ed. by Trails Illustrated Staff. (Illus.). 1994. Folded topographical map. 8.99 (*0-925873-10-1*) Trails Illustrated.

Canyonlands of Utah: A Pictorial of the Needles District. Aileen Maxwell & Thomas Maxwell. (Illus.). 32p. (Orig.). 1985. pap. 4.95 (*0-9614389-0-8*) Rigelle Pubns.

Canyonlands River Guide. Bill Belknap & Buzz Belknap. (Illus.). 14.95 (*0-916370-11-9*) Westwater.

Canyonlands River Guide: Westwater, Lake Powell, Canyonlands National Park. Bill Belknap & Buzz Belknap. LC 74-80876. (Illus.). 64p. 1974. 10.95 (*0-916370-08-9*); pap. 6.95 (*0-916370-07-0*) Westwater.

Canyons. Randy Frahm. LC 94-3156. (Images Ser.). 40p. (J). 1994. 16.95 (*0-88682-707-8*) Creative Ed.

Canyons. Gary Paulsen. (J). 1990. 15.95 (*0-385-30153-7*) Delacorte.

Canyons. Gary Paulsen. 1991. mass mkt. 3.99 (*0-440-21023-2*) Dell.

Canyons. Gary Paulsen. (J). (gr. 4-8). 1992. 17.25 (*0-8446-6590-8*) Peter Smith.

***Canyons of Color: Utah's Slickrock Wildland.** Gary P. Nabhan & Caroline Wilson. (Genesis Ser.). 1995. 37.50 (*0-06-258571-1*, HarpT); pap. 25.00 (*0-06-258560-6*, HarpT) HarpC.

Canyons of Dinosaur National Monument. Bob Gernant et al. Ed. by Don Baars. (Waterproof River Runners' Guides Ser.). (Illus.). 96p. 1992. pap. text ed. 15.95 (*0-9616591-3-0*) Canon Pubs.

Canyons of the Southwest: A Tour of the Great Canyon Country from Colorado to Northern Mexico. John Annerino. LC 93-18403. (Illus.). 160p. 1993. 25.00 (*0-87156-552-8*) Sierra.

***Canzonas & Capricio from the Seconda Aggiunta Alli Concerti Raccolti Dal Molto Reverendo Don Francesco Lucino a Due, Tre e Quattro Voci, di Diversi Eccellenti Autori...Novamente Raccolta, & Data in Luce Da Filippo Lomazzo, (Milan, 1617) & Nicolo Corradini il Primo Libro De Canzoni Francese a 4. & Alcune Suonate (Venice, 1624)** Ed. by James Ladewig. LC 94-43627. (Italian Instrumental Music of the Sixteenth & Seventeenth Centuries Ser.: Vol. 29). 224p. 1995. 78.00 (*0-8240-4528-9*) Garland.

Canzoni. Thomas A. Daly. (Classics of Modern American Humor. Second Ser.). (Illus.). reprint ed. 26.00 (*0-404-19929-1*) AMS Pr.

Canzoni: Testi E Commento a Cura Di Mauro Braccini. Rigaut de Barbezieux. LC 80-2188. reprint ed. 26.00 (*0-404-19017-0*) AMS Pr.

Canzoniere of Dante: A Contribution to Its Critical Edition. Aluigi Cossio. 1977. lib. bdg. 59.95 (*0-8490-1569-3*) Gordon Pr.

Canzoniere of Dante Alighieri. Dante Alighieri. xxxvi, 467p. 1985. reprint ed. lib. bdg. 79.00 (*0-7812-0560-3*) Rprt Serv.

***Caodaiism an Introduction: Cao Dai Indigenous Vietnamese Religion.** Merdeka Thien-Ly Huong Do. LC 94-74876. 106p. 1994. pap. text ed. write for info. (*0-9644543-0-0*) Cao Dai Temple.

Caos de las Sectas. J. Van Baalen. 375p. (SPA.). 1990. pap. 8.00 (*0-939125-45-5*) Evangelical Lit.

Cap. large type ed. Jim Bowden. (Linford Western Library). 1991. pap. 13.95 (*0-7089-7089-3*) Ulverscroft.

Cap - Cash-On-Cash: A Program for the HP 17BII & HP 19BII Financial Calculators. Edric Cane. 34p. (Orig.). 1991. disk, pap. 25.00 (*0-916785-10-6*) E Cane Sem.

Cap & Bells. Luigi Pirandello. 1974. 4.00 (*0-87141-048-6*) Manyland.

Cap & Gown. Ed. by Frederic L. Knowles. LC 70-116410. (Granger Index Reprint Ser.). 1977. 23.95 (*0-8369-6151-X*) Ayer.

Cap & Gown: Some College Verse. Joseph Harrison. LC 79-109140. (Granger Index Reprint Ser.). 1893. 10.00 (*0-685-39841-2*) Ayer.

Cap & Gown: Some College Verse. Joseph Harrison. LC 79-109140. (Granger Index Reprint Ser.). 1977. 19.95 (*0-8369-6124-2*) Ayer.

Cap & Gown: Third Series. R. L. Paget. LC 78-74825. (Granger Poetry Library). 1979. reprint ed. 24.50 (*0-89609-144-9*) Roth Pub Inc.

Cap Badges & Insignia of the Canadian Army, 1953-1973. rev. ed. Roy Thompson. (Military Reference Ser.). (Illus.). 220p. reprint ed. pap. text ed. 13.00 (*1-878973-05-3*) Hse History.

Cap Badges & Insignia of the RCN-RCAF & CAF 1953-1977. Roy Thompson. (Illus.). 76p. (Orig.). 1990. pap. 8.00 (*1-878973-01-0*) Hse History.

Cap de Bonne Esperance. Jean Cocteau. (Poesie Ser.). 247p. (FRE.). 1967. pap. 11.95 (*2-07-030076-5*) Schoenhof.

Cap de Bonne Esperance: Le Discours du Grand Sommeil. Jean Cocteau. (FRE.). 1991. pap. 14.95 (*0-7859-2760-3*) Fr & Eur.

Cap d'Erquy to Ile De Batz. Imray Laurie Norie & Wilson Ltd. Staff. (Illus.). (C). 1989. text ed. 60.00 (*0-685-40222-3*, Pub. by Imray Laurie Norie & Wilson UK) St Mut.

CAP GEMINI Reference to Expert Systems. Rex Maus & Susan Huggard. (CAP GEMINI America Ser.). 256p. 1990. text ed. 24.95 (*0-07-040981-1*) McGraw.

***Cap It off with a Smile: A Guide for Making & Keeping Friends.** Robin Inwald. LC 94-77395. (Illus.). 32p. (J). (gr. k-4). 1995. pap. 9.95 (*1-885738-01-3*) LIFETIME.

***Cap It off with a Smile: A Guide for Making & Keeping Friends.** Robin Inwald. LC 94-77395. (Illus.). 32p. (J). (gr. k-4). 1995. 16.95 (*1-885738-00-5*) Hilson Res.

Capabilities, Allocation & Earnings. Joop Hartog. 336p. (C). 1992. lib. bdg. 78.00 (*0-7923-9173-X*) Kluwer Ac.

Capability Brown. Joan Clifford. 1989. pap. 25.00 (*0-85263-274-6*, Pub. by Shire UK) St Mut.

Capability Maturity Model: Guidelines in Improving the Software Process. Mark Paulk et al. (SEI Series Software Engineering). (Illus.). 416p. (C). 1995. text ed. 49.50 (*0-201-54664-7*) Addison-Wesley.

Capability Problem in Contract Law: Further Readings on Well-Known Cases. Danzig. 1978. pap. text ed. 12.50 (*0-88277-501-4*) Foundation Pr.

Capablanca: A Compendium of Games, Notes, Articles, Correspondence, Illustrations & Other Rare Archival Materials on the Cuban Chess Genius Jose Raul Capablanca, 1888-1942. Edward Winter. LC 89-42761. 359p. 1989. lib. bdg. 45.00 (*0-89950-455-8*) McFarland & Co.

Capablanca's Best Chess Endings: 60 Complete Games. Irving Chernev. (Illus.). 288p. (C). 1982. pap. 5.95 (*0-486-24249-8*) Dover.

***Capable Cruiser.** Lin Pardey & Larry Pardey. (Illus.). 400p. 1987. 32.00 (*0-9646036-2-4*) Pardey Prods.

Capable of Honor. Allen Drury. 1993. reprint ed. lib. bdg. 24.95 (*1-56849-150-6*) Buccaneer Bks.

Capacious Hold-All: An Anthology of Englishwomen's Diary Writings. Ed. by Harriet Blodgett. (Feminist Issues: Practice, Politics, Theory Ser.). 431p. (Orig.). (C). 1991. text ed. 45.00 (*0-8139-1317-9*); pap. text ed. 14.95 (*0-8139-1318-7*) U Pr of Va.

Capacitacion De Maestros en ETE. W. V. Gritter. (SPA.). 1981. 4.90 (*1-55955-055-4*) CITE MI.

Capacitado para Orientar. Jay E. Adams. Orig. Title: Competent to Counsel. 328p. (SPA.). 1981. pap. 9.99 (*0-8254-1000-2*) Kregel.

Capacitados Para Restaurar: Ready to Restore. Jay E. Adams. (SPA.). 4.95 (*84-7645-083-4*, 223132, Pub. by Edit Clie SP) TSELF.

Capacitance, Inductance, & Crosstalk Analysis. Charles Walker. (Microwave Library). 230p. 1990. text ed. 69.00 (*0-89006-392-3*) Artech Hse.

Capacitandose: Analisis de las Necesidades. Gary Teja. (SPA Ser.). 1990. 0.35 (*1-55955-123-2*) CITE MI.

Capacitandose: Confeccion de Preguntas. W. V. Gritter. (SPA.). Date not set. write for info. (*0-318-70337-8*) CITE MI.

Capacitandose: Elaboracion De Libros De Ensenanza Biblica. Carlos Sandoval. (SPA.). 1986. 0.25 (*1-55955-064-3*) CITE MI.

Capacitandose: Los Pasos Para Elaborar un Programa De Instruccion. W. V. Gritter & Gary Teja. (SPA.). 1986. 0.60 (*1-55955-066-X*) CITE MI.

Capacitandose: Niveles de Aprendizaje. W. V. Gritter. (SPA.). 1990. 0.40 (*1-55955-124-0*) CITE MI.

Capacitandose: Objectivos. W. V. Gritter & Gary Teja. (SPA.). 1989. 0.85 (*1-55955-065-1*) CITE MI.

Capacitandose: Principios Basicos De la Ensenanza Programada. W. V. Gritter. (SPA.). 1986. 0.25 (*1-55955-107-0*) CITE MI.

Capacitandose: Reglas Generales De Construccion. W. V. Gritter. (SPA.). 1988. 0.45 (*1-55955-067-8*) CITE MI.

Capacitandose: Tipos De Textos. W. V. Gritter. (SPA.). 1986. 0.35 (*1-55955-068-6*) CITE MI.

Capacitese Como Lider. LeRoy Ford. Tr. by Guillermo Blair. 64p. (SPA.). 1986. reprint ed. pap. 2.75 (*0-311-17023-4*, Edit Mundo) Casa Bautista.

Capacities of the Human Spirit: Spirituality for Humanists. James Park. 1983. pap. 1.00 (*0-89231-021-9*) Existential Bks.

Capacitive & Resistive Electronic Components. D. S. Campbell & J. A. Hayes. LC 93-23721. (Electrocomponent Science Monographs: Vol. 8). 1994. text ed. 110.00 (*2-88124-845-4*) Gordon & Breach.

Capacitor Handbook. Cletus J. Kaiser. LC 90-85846. (Illus.). 126p. (Orig.). (C). 1990. pap. text ed. write for info. (*0-9628525-0-3*) C J Kaiser.

***Capacitor Handbook.** 2nd ed. Cletus J. Kaiser. LC 94-94595. (Illus.). 134p. (Orig.). (C). 1995. pap. text ed. 14.95 (*0-9628525-3-8*) C J Kaiser.

Capacitor Handbook. Cletus J. Kaiser. LC 92-35798. (Orig.). 1993. reprint ed. text ed. 29.95 (*0-442-01558-5*) Van Nos Reinhold.

Capacitor Market - Ceramic, Film, Paper, & Variable (U. S.) 1992. 1,500.00 (*0-685-61896-X*, A2548) Frost & Sullivan.

Capacitor Market - Tantalum, Aluminum & Other (U. S.) 320p. 1992. 1,500.00 (*0-685-61897-8*, A2549) Frost & Sullivan.

Capacity Aspect of Inventories. R. Bemelmans. (Lecture Notes in Economics & Mathematical Systems Ser.: Vol. 267). ix, 165p. 1986. pap. 25.30 (*0-387-16449-9*) Spr-Verlag.

Capacity for Agricultural Change: Indigenous Technical Knowledge & the New York State Agricultural Society in the Transformation of U. S. Agriculture, 1830-1862. Gregory A. Sanford. (Studies in Technology & Social Change: No. 4). 94p. (Orig.). (C). 1988. pap. 10.00 (*0-945271-04-2*) ISU-TSCP.

Capacity for Emotional Growth. Elizabeth R. Zetzel. LC 71-126355. 316p. 1971. text ed. 42.50 (*0-8236-0650-3*) Intl Univs Pr.

Capacity for Outrage: The Judicial Odyssey of J. Skelly Wright. Arthur S. Miller. LC 83-22761. (Contributions in American Studies: No. 74). (Illus.). xiv, 242p. 1984. text ed. 59.95 (*0-313-23304-7*, MSW/, Greenwood Pr) Greenwood.

Capacity for Wonder: Preserving National Parks. William R. Lowry. 380p. (C). 1994. 28.95 (*0-8157-5298-9*) Brookings.

Capacity for Work in the Tropics. Ed. by K. J. Collins & D. F. Roberts. (Society for the Study of Human Biology Symposium Ser.: No. 26). (Illus.). 300p. 1988. 64.95 (*0-521-30935-2*) Cambridge U Pr.

Capacity Management. John H. Blackstone. 384p. (C). 1989. text ed. 26.95 (*0-538-80277-4*, GF60AA) S-W Pub.

Capacity Management Techniques for Manufacturing Companies with MRP Systems. Urban Wemmerlov. LC 84-70268. 88p. 1984. pap. 15.00 (*0-935406-44-1*, 40644) Am Prod & Inventory.

Capacity Management Training Aid. Ashok Rao. LC 82-72090. 39p. 1982. 35.00 (*0-935406-18-2*) Am Prod & Inventory.

Capacity of Negroes for Religious & Moral Improvement Considered. Richard Nisbet. LC 73-100295. 207p. 1970. reprint ed. text ed. 45.00 (*0-8371-2940-0*, NIC&, Negro U Pr) Greenwood.

Capacity Oriented Analysis & Design of Production Systems. M. B. De Koster. (Lecture Notes in Economics & Mathematical Systems Ser.: Vol. 323). xii, 245p. 1989. pap. 39.30 (*0-387-50692-6*) Spr-Verlag.

Capacity Planning: A Practical Approach. Daniel A. Menasce. 1993. disk 44.00 (*0-685-70954-X*) P-H.

Capacity Planning & Performance Modeling: From Mainframes to Client-Server Systems. Daniel A. Menasce et al. LC 93-43464. 432p. 1994. 50.33 (*0-13-035494-5*) P-H.

Capacity Planning for Computer Systems. Tim Browning. (Illus.). 216p. 1994. pap. 34.95 (*0-12-136490-9*, AP Prof) Acad Pr.

Capacity Theory on Algebraic Curves. R. S. Rumely. (Lecture Notes in Mathematics Ser.: Vol. 1378). iii, 437p. 1989. pap. 50.30 (*0-387-51410-4*, 3278) Spr-Verlag.

C

An Asterisk (*) at the beginning of an entry indicates that the title is appearing in BIP for the first time. 1031

Capacity to Budget. Allen Schick. LC 89-25003. (Illus.). 244p. (Orig.). (C). 1990. lib. bdg. 52.00 (*0-87766-438-2*); pap. text ed. 18.50 (*0-87766-439-0*) Urban Inst.

Capacity to Respond: California Political Institutions Face Change. Ed. by Ted K. Bradshaw & Charles G. Bell. 113p. 1987. pap. 9.95 (*0-87772-313-3*) UCB IGS.

Capacity Utilization: A Theoretical & Empirical Analysis. Roger Betancourt & Christopher Clague. LC 80-22410. (Illus.). 320p. 1981. 59.95 (*0-521-23583-9*) Cambridge U Pr.

Capacity X. Bill DiMichele. (Illus.). 38p. (Orig.). 1988. pap. 3.00 (*0-926935-08-9*) Runaway Spoon.

Capasheea's Leadmine: A Novel. Foster Mullenax. 200p. (Orig.). 1989. pap. 9.95 (*0-87012-484-6*) McClain.

CAPD: A Decade of Experience. Ed. by G. La Greca et al. (Contributions to Nephrology Ser.: Vol. 89). (Illus.). x, 288p. 1991. 198.50 (*3-8055-5307-2*) S Karger.

CAPD: Host Defence, Nutrition & Ultrafiltration. Ed. by G. A. Coles et al. (Contributions to Nephrology Ser.: Vol. 85). (Illus.). viii, 172p. 1990. 134.50 (*3-8055-5215-7*) S Karger.

Cape & Islands Locater. John W. Davenport. (Illus.). 144p. (Orig.). 1989. pap. 12.95 (*0-934794-06-5*) First Impressions.

Cape Ann. Faith Sullivan. 342p. 1989. pap. 11.00 (*0-14-011979-5*, Penguin Bks) Viking Penguin.

***Cape Breton, 1952: The Photographic Vision of Timothy Asch.** Douglas Harper. (Illus.). 112p. 1994. 30.00 (*0-9644562-0-6*); pap. 20.00 (*0-9644562-1-4*) Intl Visual Sociol.

Cape Buffalo. William R. Sanford & Carl R. Green. LC 86-32859. (Wildlife Habits & Habitats Ser.). (Illus.). 48p. (J). (gr. 5). 1987. text ed. 12.95 (*0-89686-321-2*, Crstwood Hse) Silver Burdett Pr.

Cape Bulbs: Their Collection, Cultivation & Conservation. Richard L. Doutt. LC 93-17655. (Illus.). 180p. 1994. 34.95 (*0-88192-245-5*) Timber.

Cape Canaveral: Cape of Storms & Wild Cane Fields. Harriett Carr. 1974. pap. 5.00 (*0-912760-01-X*) Valkyrie Pub Hse.

Cape Cod. William Martin. 672p. 1991. 21.95 (*0-446-51510-8*) Warner Bks.

Cape Cod. William Martin. 736p. 1992. mass mkt. 5.99 (*0-446-36317-0*) Warner Bks.

Cape Cod. Photos by Alan Nyiri. LC 91-77669. (Illus.). 112p. 1992. 35.00 (*0-89272-303-3*) Down East.

Cape Cod: A Guide. Donald Wood. (Illus.). 1973. pap. 8.95 (*0-316-95164-1*) Little.

Cape Cod: An Artist's Sketchbook. Richard W. Rourke. (Illus.). 48p. 1992. pap. 8.50 (*1-884824-01-3*) Tryon Pubng.

Cape Cod: Gardens & Houses. Catherine Fallin. LC 93-40741. 1995. 45.00 (*0-671-86859-4*) S&S Trade.

Cape Cod: Its Natural & Cultural History: a Guide to Cape Cod National Seashore, Massachusetts. Robert Finch. LC 92-40414. (Official National Park Handbook, Cape Cod National Seashore Ser.: No. 148). 1993. write for info. (*0-912627-56-5*) Natl Park Serv.

Cape Cod: Its People & Their History. Henry C. Kittredge. 368p. 1987. reprint ed. pap. 12.50 (*0-940160-35-8*) Parnassus Imprints.

Cape Cod: Martha's Vineyard & Nantucket. Access Guides Staff. (Access Travel Guides Ser.). (Illus.). 192p. (Orig.). 1994. pap. 18.00 (*0-06-277123-X*, Harper Ref) HarpC.

Cape Cod: The Story Behind the Scenery. Glen Kaye. LC 80-81370. (Illus.). 48p. 1980. pap. 6.95 (*0-916122-73-5*) KC Pubns.

Cape Cod: The Writings of Henry D. Thoreau. Ed. by Joseph J. Moldenhauer & Elizabeth H. Witherell. 400p. 1988. 49.50 (*0-691-06532-2*) Princeton U Pr.

Cape Cod, & All Along Shore: Stories. Charles Nordhoff. LC 72-116964. (Short Story Index Reprint Ser.). 1977. 19.95 (*0-8369-3468-7*) Ayer.

Cape Cod & Islands Atlas & Guide Book, Vol. 8. Butterworth Company of Cape Cod, Inc. staff. (Illus.). 120p. 1988. pap. 12.95 (*0-937338-05-2*) Buttrwrth of Cape Cod.

Cape Cod & Plymouth Colony in the Seventeenth Century. H. Roger King. LC 93-13880. 320p. (Orig.). (C). 1993. lib. bdg. 57.50 (*0-8191-9185-X*); pap. text ed. 28.50 (*0-8191-9186-8*) U Pr of Amer.

Cape Cod & the Islands. Barbara P. Thrasher. (Illus.). 128p. 1993. 14.98 (*0-8317-0804-2*) Smithmark.

Cape Cod & the Islands: An Artist's Sketchbook. rev. ed. Richard W. Rourke. (Illus.). 52p. 1994. pap. 8.50 (*1-884824-08-0*) Tryon Pubng.

***Cape Cod & the Islands: An Explorer's Guide.** Kimberly Grant. (Explorer's Guide Ser.). (Illus.). 340p. (Orig.). 1995. pap. 17.00 (*0-88150-323-1*) Countryman.

Cape Cod & the Islands: The Geologic Story. Robert Oldale. (Orig.). 1992. pap. 12.95 (*0-940160-53-6*) Parnassus Imprints.

Cape Cod Annals. Marise Fawsett. (Illus.). 192p. (Orig.). 1990. pap. 12.50 (*1-55613-321-9*) Heritage Bk.

Cape Cod Architecture. Clair Baisly. LC 89-60503. (Illus.). 224p. 1989. 18.50 (*0-940160-43-9*) Parnassus Imprints.

Cape Cod Bed & Breakfast Guide & Innkeepers Recipes: Including Martha's Vineyard & Nantucket. Bobbi Cox & Beth Flanagan. Ed. by Brian F. Shortsleeve & Colleen M. McEwen. (Illus.). 225p. (Orig.). 1989. pap. 12.95 (*0-317-94010-4*) Cape Cod Life Mag.

Cape Cod Bed & Breakfast Guide & Innkeepers' Recipes Including Martha's Vineyard & Nantucket. 2nd ed. Beth Flanagan. 261p. Date not set. pap. 12.95 (*0-9622782-0-3*) Cape Cod Life Mag.

***Cape Cod Bed & Breakfast Guide & Innkeepers' Recipes Including Martha's Vineyard & Nantucket.** 3rd ed. Beth Flanagan. (Illus.). 1995. pap. 12.95 (*0-9622782-2-X*) Cape Cod Life Mag.

Cape Cod Blues. David L. Ulin. 16p. 1992. 3.00 (*0-87376-072-7*) Red Dust.

Cape Cod Calamities, No. 20. Noel W. Beyle. (Illus.). 48p. (Orig.). 1984. pap. 0.95 (*0-912609-03-6*) First Encounter.

Cape Cod Canal. 2nd rev. ed. Robert H. Farson. LC 77-74558. (Illus.). 180p. 1993. pap. 13.95 (*0-9616740-0-8*) Cape Cod Hist Pubns.

Cape Cod Caper. Margot Arnold, pseud. 192p. 1988. pap. 6.00 (*0-88150-116-6*, Foul Play) Countryman.

***Cape Cod Cocktail: And Other Poetry.** Peter Saunders. 80p. (Orig.). 1995. pap. 5.95 (*1-884482-04-X*) Stepngstone.

Cape Cod Conundrum. Margot Arnold. (Penny Spring & Sir Toby Glendower Mystery Ser.). 240p. 1993. 20.00 (*0-88150-244-8*, Foul Play) Countryman.

Cape Cod Conundrum. Margot Arnold. (Penny Spring & Sir Toby Glendower Mystery Ser.). 224p. 1994. reprint ed. pap. 6.50 (*0-88150-293-6*, Foul Play) Countryman.

Cape Cod Cookbook. Suzanne C. Gruver. (Cookbook Ser.). 1977. pap. 4.95 (*0-486-23564-5*) Dover.

Cape Cod House. Stanley Schuler. LC 82-80857. (Illus.). 144p. 1982. 25.00 (*0-916838-63-3*) Schiffer.

Cape Cod Jokes (Illustrated), No. 21. Noel W. Beyle. (Illus.). 48p. (Orig.). 1984. pap. 0.95 (*0-912609-04-4*) First Encounter.

Cape Cod Library of Local History & Genealogy: A Facsimile Edition of 108 Pamphlets Published in the Early 20th Century, 2 vols. Leonard H. Smith. 2066p. 1992. Vol. Vol. II. write for info. (*0-8063-1326-9*, 5473) Genealog Pub.

Cape Cod Library of Local History & Genealogy: A Facsimile Edition of 108 Pamphlets Published in the Early 20th Century, 2 vols., I. Leonard H. Smith. 2066p. 1992. write for info. (*0-8063-1325-0*, 5473) Genealog Pub.

Cape Cod Library of Local History & Genealogy: A Facsimile Edition of 108 Pamphlets Published in the Early 20th Century, 2 vols., Set. Leonard H. Smith. 2066p. 1992. 125.00 (*0-8063-1324-2*, 5473) Genealog Pub.

***Cape Cod, MA.** Historical Briefs, Inc. Staff. Ed. by Thomas Antoucci & Michael Antonucci. 176p. 1990. pap. 13.95 (*0-89677-010-9*) Hist Briefs.

Cape Cod Maritime Disasters. William P. Quinn. LC 90-91663. 240p. 1990. 35.00 (*0-936972-13-0*) Lower Cape.

Cape Cod Mystery. Phoebe A. Taylor. (Asey Mayo Cape Cod Mystery Ser.). 192p. 1985. pap. 6.00 (*0-88150-046-1*, Foul Play) Countryman.

Cape Cod Pilot. Josef Berger. (Illus.). 417p. 1985. reprint ed. pap. 14.95 (*0-930350-72-3*) NE U Pr.

Cape Cod Poems. Herman M. Ward. 36p. 1982. pap. 4.00 (*0-9610346-2-9*) Belle Mead Pr.

Cape Cod Railroads, Including Martha's Vineyard & Nantucket. Robert H. Farson. LC 90-82323. (Illus.). 336p. 1990. 39.95 (*0-9616740-1-6*) Cape Cod Hist Pubns.

Cape Cod Seafood Cookbook. Margaret D. Murphy. (Illus.). 172p. 1985. 14.95 (*0-940160-30-7*) Parnassus Imprints.

Cape Cod Seafood Cookbook, No. 29. Noel W. Beyle. (Illus.). 48p. (Orig.). 1987. pap. 0.95 (*0-912609-12-5*) First Encounter.

Cape Cod Sketchbook. 2nd ed. Jack Frost. (Illus.). 96p. 1994. reprint ed. pap. 12.95 (*0-940160-59-5*) Parnassus Imprints.

Cape Cod Skiing: And Other Poetry. Peter Saunders. 64p. (Orig.). 1993. pap. 5.95 (*1-884482-00-7*) Stepngstone.

Cape Cod Stories. Joseph C. Lincoln. 1976. reprint ed. lib. bdg. 21.95 (*0-88411-791-X*, Aeonian Pr) Amereon Ltd.

Cape Cod to the Rescue!, No. 22. Noel W. Beyle. (Illus.). 48p. (Orig.). 1984. pap. 0.95 (*0-912609-05-2*) First Encounter.

Cape Cod Wanderings: And Other Poetry. Peter Saunders. 80p. (Orig.). 1994. pap. 5.95 (*1-884482-03-1*) Stepngstone.

Cape Cod Years of John Fitzgerald Kennedy. Leo Damore. LC 93-20153. 260p. 1993. 12.95 (*0-941423-81-6*) FWEW.

Cape Cod's Cooking Secrets: Starring the Best Restaurants & Inns in Cape Cod, Martha's Vineyard & Nantucket. Kathleen D. Fish. Ed. by Fred Hernandez. (Illus.). 256p. (Orig.). 1993. pap. 14.95 (*0-9620472-9-5*) Bon Vivant Pr.

Cape Coloured People, Sixteen Fifty-Two to Nineteen Thirty-Seven. Johannes S. Marais. LC 74-15065. reprint ed. 44.00 (*0-404-12106-3*) AMS Pr.

***Cape Cooper Company Limited Medal for the Defence of O'Kiep.** Roberts Staff. (C). 1989. 90.00x (*1-873058-30-6*, Pub. by Roberts UK) St Mut.

***Cape Discovery: The Provincetown Fine Arts Work Center Anthology.** Ed. by Bruce Smith & Catherine Gammon. 459p. Date not set. pap. 15.95 (*1-878818-25-2*) Sheep Meadow.

Cape Education Ordinance 1956, No. 20: Onderwysordonnansie Nr. 20 van 1956. Ed. by Adv J. Cavvadas. (AFR & ENG.). ring bd. write for info. (*0-7021-0291-1*, Pub. by Juta SA) W W Gaunt.

Cape Fear. John D. MacDonald. 1986. mass mkt. 5.99 (*0-449-13190-4*, GM) Fawcett.

Cape Fear. John D. MacDonald. 1994. reprint ed. lib. bdg. 27.95 (*1-56849-304-5*) Buccaneer Bks.

Cape Fear Rising. Philip Gerard. LC 93-41369. 416p. 1994. 18.95 (*0-89587-108-4*) Blair.

Cape Girardeau: Biography of a City. Felix E. Snider & Earl A. Collins. (Illus.). 1956. 13.00 (*0-911208-02-X*) Ramfre.

Cape Hatteras Lighthouse: Sentinel of the Shoals. Dawson Carr. LC 90-50716. (Illus.). x, 143p. (Orig.). (C). 1991. pap. 8.95 (*0-8078-4319-9*) U of NC Pr.

Cape Henry Threshold. John R. Kight. (Illus.). 33p. 1990. pap. 5.00 (*1-878515-87-X*) W S Dawson.

Cape Horn. Felix Riesenberg. LC 94-11744. (Illus.). xvi, 500p. 1994. reprint ed. 39.95 (*1-881987-04-3*) Ox Bow.

Cape Horn: One Man's Dream, One Woman's Nightmare. Reanne Hemingway-Douglass. Ed. by Alice Klein. (Illus.). 288p. (Orig.). 1994. pap. 22.50 (*0-938665-29-4*) Fine Edge Prods.

Cape Horn & Other Stories from the End of the World. Francisco Coloane. Tr. by David A. Petreman. LC 90-19924. 192p. 1991. pap. 14.95 (*0-935480-50-1*) Lat Am Lit Rev Pr.

Cape Horn to Starboard. John Kretschmer. (Illus.). 160p. 1986. pap. 12.95 (*0-87742-207-9*) Intl Marine.

Cape Island. I. Yevish. LC 90-93097. 288p. (Orig.). 1990. 15.95 (*0-9626330-0-3*); pap. 11.95 (*0-9626330-1-1*) I Yevish Bks.

Cape Itself. Robert Finch. 1991. 39.95 (*0-393-02994-8*) Norton.

Cape Light: Color Photgraphs by Joel Meyerowitz. Joel Meyerowitz. Ed. by Bruce K. MacDonald & Clifford Ackley. 1979. pap. 29.95 (*0-87846-131-0*) Bulfinch Pr.

Cape May. Michael Biggs & Tom Carroll. 1991. 37.50 (*0-89802-614-8*) Beautiful Am.

Cape May County, New Jersey: The Making of an American Resort Community. Jeffrey M. Dorwart. LC 91-29058. (Illus.). 385p. (C). 1992. text ed. 40.00 (*0-8135-1783-4*); pap. 12.95 (*0-8135-1784-2*) Rutgers U Pr.

Cape May Ghost Stories. David J. Seibold. 1988. pap. 6.95 (*0-9610008-7-2*) Exeter Hse.

Cape Municipal Ordinance, 1974, No. 20: Munisipale Ordonnansie Nr. 20 van 1974. Ed. by Adv J. Cavvadas. (AFR & ENG.). ring bd. write for info. (*0-7021-0622-4*, Pub. by Juta SA) W W Gaunt.

Cape of Adventure. Ed. by Ian D. Colvin. LC 76-94309. (Illus.). 1969. reprint ed. 32.50 (*0-404-01638-3*) AMS Pr.

***Cape of Good Hope Medal 1880-1897.** Roberts Staff. (C). 1993. 90.00x (*1-873058-25-X*, Pub. by Roberts UK) St Mut.

Cape of Misfortune. large type ed. Yvonne Whittal. 296p. 1993. 21.95 (*0-7505-0410-2*, Pub. by Magna Print Bks) Ulverscroft.

Cape of Storms: A Personal History of the Crisis in South Africa. Anthony H. Heard. LC 90-11022. (Illus.). 295p. 1990. 21.95 (*1-55728-167-X*); pap. 11.95 (*1-55728-168-8*) U of Ark Pr.

Cape of Storms: The First Life of Adamastor. Andre Brink. LC 92-39321. 141p. 1993. 16.00 (*0-671-79907-X*) S&S Trade.

Cape Perpetua Shell Middens: Late Prehistoric Subsistence on the Central Oregon Coast. Rick Minor et al. (Illus.). 115p. 1989. write for info. (*0-318-64856-3*) NW Herit Pr.

Cape Route: Imperiled Western Lifeline. Robert J. Hanks. LC 81-80472. (Special Report Ser.). 80p. 1981. 11.95 (*0-685-05974-X*) Inst Foreign Policy Anal.

Cape Run. W. H. Mitchell & L. A. Sawyer. 214p. (C). 1988. 150.00 (*0-86138-030-4*, Pub. by T Dalton UK) St Mut.

Cape Sable Nova Scotia: Vital Records Seventeen Ninety-Nine to Eighteen Forty-One. Leonard H. Smith, Jr. LC 79-66242. 1979. text ed. 22.50 (*0-932022-13-8*) L H Smith.

***Cape Town: City Guide.** Jon Murray. (Illus.). 240p. 1996. pap. 9.95 (*0-86442-325-X*) Lonely Planet.

Cape Town Coolie. Reshard Gool. (African Writers Ser.). 183p. (Orig.). 1990. pap. 7.95 (*0-435-90568-6*, 90568) Heinemann.

Cape Verde. (Let's Visit Places & Peoples of the World Ser.). (Illus.). (J). (gr. 5 up). 1989. 14.95 (*0-7910-0145-8*) Chelsea Hse.

***Cape Verde.** Joseph Sevigny. Ed. by Dale E. Gough. (OIES Country Guide Ser.). (C). 1995. write for info. (*0-929851-33-1*) Am Assn Coll Registrars.

Cape Verde. Caroline S. Shaw. (World Bibliographical Ser.). 1991. lib. bdg. 68.50 (*1-85109-119-X*) ABC-CLIO.

***Cape Verde: Criulo Colony to Independent Nation.** Richard A. Lobban, Jr. LC 94-45454. (Nations of the Modern World Ser.). 1995. text ed. 55.00 (*0-8133-8451-6*) Westview.

Cape Verde & Sao Tome & Principe. Colm Foy et al. (Marxist Regimes Ser.). 250p. 1988. text ed. 49.00 (*0-86187-483-8*, Pub. by Pinter Pubs UK); text ed. 17.50 (*0-86187-484-6*, Pub. by Pinter Pubs UK) St Martin.

***Cape Verdean-American Coloring Book.** Ronald Barboza. (Illus.). 1995. write for info. (*0-9647284-1-9*) Barika Photo & Prodns.

***Cape Verdean Coloring Book.** Ronald Barboza. (Illus.). 1995. write for info. (*0-9647284-0-0*) Barika Photo & Prodns.

Cape Verdeans in Rhode Island: A Brief History. Waltraud B. Coli & Richard A. Lobban. (Rhode Island Ethnic Heritage Pamphlet Ser.). (Illus.). 52p. (Orig.). 1990. pap. 4.75 (*0-917012-94-1*) RI Pubns Soc.

Cape York: A Four W Experience. Lynn Fraser & Yvonne Fraser. 160p. (C). 1990. 75.00 (*0-86439-136-6*, Pub. by Boolarong Pubns AT) St Mut.

Capehart Amperion Service, Parts, Mechanical Amperion Record Changer Service Manual. rev. ed. Ed. by Frank Adams. (Illus.). 48p. reprint ed. spiral bd. 32.50 (*1-56642-164-0*, R-402) AMR Pub Co.

Capehart Model C10-20, 1935-1938: Service Manual. rev. ed. Ed. by Frank Adams. (Illus.). 52p. reprint ed. spiral bd. 29.50 (*1-56642-165-9*, R-438) AMR Pub Co.

Capehart Model 28-F of Circa 1928 Service Manual & Parts Catalog. 36p. 1983. reprint ed. spiral bd. 21.50 (*0-913698-79-2*, R-165) AMR Pub Co.

Capehart Model 28-GB, 1930: Service & Parts Manual. rev. ed. Ed. by Frank Adams. (Illus.). 32p. reprint ed. spiral bd. 24.95 (*1-56642-163-2*, R-313) AMR Pub Co.

Capehart's Packard Adapter for Wurlitzer Twin 2-16's & 2-12's: Installation Instructions. 16p. 1983. reprint ed. spiral bd. 12.50 (*0-913698-82-2*, R-166) AMR Pub Co.

Caper. Lawrence Sanders. 368p. 1991. pap. text ed. 6.50 (*0-425-12722-2*) Berkley Pub.

Caper the Kid. Jane Burton. LC 89-11566. (Baby Animals Growing up Ser.). (Illus.). 32p. (J). (gr. 2-3). 1989. lib. bdg. 17.27 (*0-8368-0203-9*) Gareth Stevens Inc.

Capers. Mark Dunster. (Poems from Hollywood Ser.). 64p. (Orig.). 1986. pap. 6.00 (*0-89642-131-7*) Linden Pubs.

Capers Papers. Charlotte Capers. LC 81-22013. 128p. 1992. pap. 14.95 (*0-87805-601-7*) U Pr of Miss.

Capers Papers. Charlotte Capers. LC 81-22013. 122p. reprint ed. pap. 34.80 (*0-7837-1062-3*, 2041584) Bks Demand.

Caperucita Roja. (Spanish Well Loved Tales Ser.: No. 700-1). (SPA.). (J). (gr. 2). 1990. boxed 3.50 (*0-7214-1409-5*) Ladybird Bks.

Caperucita Roja. (SPA.). (J). (ps-3). 1993. pap. 2.25 (*0-307-70098-4*, Golden Pr) Western Pub.

***Caperucita Roja.** rev. ed. Hanna Hutchinson. (Interlingo Ser.). Orig. Title: Red Ridinghood. (Illus.). 18p. (SPA.). (J). (gr. k-12). 1995. pap. 2.95 (*0-922852-00-6*, J063) Another Lang Pr.

Caperucita Roja y la Luna de Papel. Aida E. Marcuse. (Illus.). 24p. (Orig.). (SPA.). (J). (gr. k-6). 1993. lib. bdg. 7.50 (*1-56492-103-4*) Laredo.

Capes & Captains: An Anthology of the Australian Coast. Rainer Radok. 308p. (C). 1990. text ed. 79.00 (*0-949324-28-0*, Pub. by Surrey Beatty & Sons AT) St Mut.

Capetian France, 987-1328. Elizabeth M. Hallam. 366p. (FRE.). (C). 1983. pap. text ed. 25.50 (*0-582-48910-5*, 73393) Longman.

Capex: A Knowledge-Based Expert System for Substantive Audit Planning. J. Efrim Boritz & K. P. Wensley. (Rutgers Series in Accounting Research). 260p. (C). 1995. text ed. 49.95 (*1-55876-056-3*) Wiener Pubs Inc.

Caphne: A Portrait of Daphne Du Maurier. large type ed. Judith A. Cook. (Charnwood Library). 448p. 1992. 23.95 (*0-7089-8659-5*, Charnwood) Ulverscroft.

Capillarity Today: Proceedings of an Advanced Workshop on Capillarity Held In Memoriam Raymond Defay at Brussels, Belgium, 7-10 May 1990. Ed. by G. Petre et al. (Lecture Notes in Physics Ser.: Vol. 386). xi, 384p. 1991. 50.00 (*0-387-54367-8*) Spr-Verlag.

Capillary Crime, & Other Stories. Francis D. Millet. LC 72-157793. (Short Story Index Reprint Ser.). 1977. reprint ed. 20.95 (*0-8369-3905-0*) Ayer.

Capillary Electrophoresis. Dale Baker. 1994. text ed. 40.50 (*0-13-300070-2*) P-H.

***Capillary Electrophoresis.** Dale R. Baker. LC 94-3553. 1995. text ed. 49.95 (*0-471-11763-3*) Wiley.

Capillary Electrophoresis. Norberto A. Guzman. 200p. 1993. boxed write for info. (*0-13-117136-4*) P-H.

Capillary Electrophoresis: Principles & Practice. Reinhard C. Kuhn & Sabrina Hoffstetter-Kuhn. LC 93-19399. 375p. 1993. 69.00 (*0-387-56434-9*) Spr-Verlag.

Capillary Electrophoresis: Principles, Practice, & Applications. S. F. Li. LC 92-14151. (Journal of Chromatography Library: Vol. 52). 1992. write for info. (*0-444-89433-0*) Elsevier.

Capillary Electrophoresis: Principles, Practice, & Applications. S. F. Li. (Journal of Chromatography Library: Vol. 52). 608p. 1993. pap. 114.25 (*0-444-81590-2*) Elsevier.

Capillary Electrophoresis: Theory & Practice. Camilleri. 1993. 89.95 (*0-8493-7862-1*, QP519) CRC Pr.

Capillary Electrophoresis: Theory & Practice. Ed. by Paul D. Grossman & Joel C. Colburn. (Illus.). 352p. 1992. text ed. 69.95 (*0-12-304250-X*) Acad Pr.

***Capillary Electrophoresis in Analytical Biotechnology.** Georgio Righetti. 400p. 1995. write for info. (*0-8493-7825-7*, 7825) CRC Pr.

Capillary Electrophoresis of Small Molecules & Ions. Peter Jandik. LC 93-18350. 1993. 65.00 (*1-56081-533-7*) VCH Pubs.

Capillary Electrophoresis Technology. Guzman. (Chromatographic Science Ser.: Vol. 64). 880p. 1993. 175.00 (*0-8247-9042-1*) Dekker.

Capillary Functions & White Cell Interaction. Ed. by K. Messmer. (Progress in Applied Microcirculation Ser.: Vol. 18). (Illus.). x, 138p. 1991. 114.50 (*3-8055-5397-8*) S Karger.

Capillary Gas Chromatography in Food Control & Research. Ed. by R. Wittkowski & R. Matissek. LC 92-62247. 300p. 1992. pap. text ed. 75.00 (*1-56676-006-2*) Technomic.

Capillary Joining: Brazing & Soft-Soldering. Colin J. Thwaites. (Materials Science Research Studies: No. 2). (Illus.). 223p. reprint ed. pap. 63.60 (*0-8357-6046-4*, 2034240) Bks Demand.

Capillary Liquid Chromatography. Ed. by B. G. Belenkii et al. (Macromolecular Compounds Ser.). (Illus.). 262p. 1987. 85.00 (*0-306-10994-8*, Consultants) Plenum.

***Capillary Zone Electrophoresis.** F. Foret et al. LC 94-145941. (Electrophoresis Library). 346p. 1994. 145.00 (*1-56081-765-8*) VCH Pubs.

Capirotada: Eight El Paso Artists. Ed. by Kevin Donovan. (Illus.). 80p. 1992. 20.00 (*0-9630816-0-8*) El Paso Mus.

Capitaine de Quinze Ans. Jules Verne. pap. 8.95 (*0-685-37137-9*) Fr & Eur.

Capitaine de Quinze Ans. Jules Verne. (Illus.). 443p. (FRE.). 1978. reprint ed. pap. 17.95 (*0-7859-1219-3*, 2010050096) Fr & Eur.

Capitaine Fracasse. Theophile Gautier. write for info. (*0-318-63442-2*) Fr & Eur.

Capitaine Fracasse. Theophile Gautier. (Folio Ser.: No. 204). pap. 10.95 (*0-685-11060-5*) Schoenhof.

Capitaine Fracasse. Theophile Gautier. 576p. (FRE.). 1972. pap. 11.95 (*0-7859-2279-2*, 2070362043) Fr & Eur.

Capitaine Lightfoot. William R. Burnett. (FRE.). 1984. pap. 15.95 (*0-7859-2002-1*, 2070376141) Fr & Eur.

An Asterisk (*) at the beginning of an entry indicates that the title is appearing in BIP for the first time.

Capitaine Pamphile. Alexandre Dumas. 230p. (FRE.). 1977. pap. 24.95 (*0-7859-5519-4*) Fr & Eur.

Capitaine, Voyage Ton Flag: The Traditional Cajun Country Mardi Gras. Barry J. Ancelet. (Louisiana Life Ser.: No. 1). 38p. 1989. pap. 5.00 (*0-940984-46-6*) U of SW LA Ctr LA Studies.

Capitaines Courageux. Rudyard Kipling. 256p. (FRE.). 1989. pap. 10.95 (*0-7859-2255-5*, 2070335569) Fr & Eur.

Capital. Karl Marx. Ed. by Frederick Engels. 870p. (C). 1992. reprint ed. lib. bdg. 49.00 (*1-877767-76-X*) Univ Publng Hse.

Capital, Vol. 1. Karl Marx. Tr. by Ben Fowkes. 1152p. 1992. 14.95 (*0-14-044568-4*, Penguin Classics) Viking Penguin.

Capital, Vol. 2. Karl Marx. Tr. by David Fernbach. 624p. 1993. 13.95 (*0-14-044569-2*, Penguin Classics) Viking Penguin.

Capital, Vol. 3. Karl Marx. 1993. 14.95 (*0-14-044570-6*, Penguin Classics) Viking Penguin.

Capital: A Critique of Political Economy, Vol. 1. Karl Marx. Tr. by Ben Fowkes. 1977. pap. 15.16 (*0-394-72657-X*, Vin) Random.

Capital: A Moral Instrument? Centre for Theology & Public Issues Staff. 96p. (C). 1992. pap. 35.00 (*0-86153-149-3*, Pub. by St Andrew UK) St Mut.

***Capital: A New Abridgment.** Karl Marx. Ed. by David McLellan. (The World's Classics Ser.). (Illus.). 640p. 1995. pap. 14.95 (*0-19-283122-4*) OUP.

Capital: The Biography of Mexico City. Jonathan Kandell. LC 89-38908. 656p. 1990. pap. 19.95 (*0-8050-1267-2*, Owl) H Holt & Co.

Capital: The Biography of Mexico City. Jonathan Kandell. LC 88-42667. (Illus.). 704p. 1988. 24.95 (*0-394-54069-7*) Random.

Capital: The Process of Capital Production, Vol. 1. LC 67-19754. 768p. 1987. pap. text ed. 12.95 (*0-7178-0621-9*) Intl Pubs Co.

Capital: Vol. 2-The Process of Circulation of Capital. Karl Marx. Ed. by Friedrich Engels. LC 67-19764. 558p. 1985. pap. text ed. 7.50 (*0-7178-0622-7*) Intl Pubs Co.

Capital Accumulation & Income Distribution. Donald J. Harris. LC 76-54097. xii, 313p. 1978. 39.50 (*0-8047-0947-5*) Stanford U Pr.

Capital Accumulation & Worker's Struggle. Satya B. Datta. (C). 1990. 29.60 (*81-7074-038-X*, Pub. by KP Bagchi IA) S Asia.

Capital Accumulation & Workers Struggle in Indian Industrialization: The Case of the Tata Iron & Steel Company, 1900-1970. Satya B. Datta. 295p. (Orig.). 1986. pap. text ed. 48.00x (*91-7146-457-3*) Coronet Bks.

Capital Accumulation in a Corporatist Economy: In Association with "The Labour Institute for Economic Research," Helsinki, Finland. Juhana Vartiainen. Ed. by W. Krelle. LC 92-13497. (Lecture Notes in Economics & Mathematical Systems Ser.: Vol. 383). (Illus.). vii, 177p. 1992. pap. 48.00 (*0-387-55467-X*) Spr-Verlag.

***Capital Acquisitions Tax.** Brian Bohan. 1993. pap. text ed. 121.00 (*1-85475-607-9*, IE) Butterworth Legal Pubs.

Capital Address Book. Illus. by Lelia Hendren. 120p. 1989. 14.95 (*0-912347-37-6*) Fulcrum Pub.

Capital Adjustments. 1987. write for info. (*0-318-57363-6*); ring bd. 657.00 (*0-685-07439-0*); ring bd. 588.00 (*0-685-07440-4*) P-H.

Capital & Communities in Black & White: The Intersections of Race, Class, & Uneven Development. Gregory D. Squires. LC 93-30567. (SUNY Series, the New Inequalities). 185p. (C). 1994. 49.50x (*0-7914-1987-8*); pap. 16.95x (*0-7914-1988-6*) State U NY Pr.

Capital & Credit: A New Formulation of General Equilibrium Theory. Michio Morishima. 270p. (C). 1992. 54.95 (*0-521-41840-2*) Cambridge U Pr.

Capital & Credit: A New Formulation of General Equilibrium Theory. Michio Morishima. 224p. (C). 1994. pap. 19.95 (*0-521-46638-5*) Cambridge U Pr.

Capital & Credit in British Overseas Trade: The View from the Chesapeake 1770-1776. Jacob M. Price. LC 80-13815. 233p. 1980. 32.00 (*0-674-09480-8*) HUP.

Capital & Distribution of Labour Earnings. M. J. Sattinger. (Contributions to Economic Analysis Ser.: Vol. 126). 282p. 1980. 89.75 (*0-444-85397-9*, North Holland) Elsevier.

Capital & Employment. Ed. by Murray Milgate. (Studies Political Economy Ser.). 1983. text ed. 85.00 (*0-12-496250-5*) Acad Pr.

Capital & Entrepreneurship in South-East Asia. Rajeswary A. Brown. LC 93-40401. (Studies in the Economies of East & Southeast Asia). 1994. text ed. 75.00 (*0-312-12096-6*) St Martin.

Capital & Exploitation. John Weeks. LC 81-47163. 224p. 1981. pap. 12.95x (*0-691-00366-1*) Princeton U Pr.

Capital & Finance in the Age of the Renaissance: A Study of the Fuggers & Their Connections. Richard Ehrenberg. Tr. by H. M. Lucas. LC 85-170. (Reprints of Economic Classics Ser.). 390p. 1985. reprint ed. 45.00 (*0-678-00015-8*) Kelley.

Capital & Interest, 3 vols., Set. Eugen Von Bohm-Bawerk. Incl. Vol. 1. History & Critique of Interest Theories. LC 58-5555. 490p. 1959. (*0-910884-09-9*); Vol. 2. Positive Theory of Capital. LC 58-5555. 466p. 1959. (*0-910884-10-2*); Vol. 3. Further Essays on Capital & Interest. LC 58-5555. 246p. 1959. (*0-910884-11-0*); LC 58-5555. 1959. 47.50 (*0-910884-07-2*) Libertarian Press.

Capital & Its Earnings. John B. Clark. Ed. by Richard P. Brief. (Foundations of Accounting Ser.: No. 4). 80p. 1988. 10.00 (*0-8240-6123-3*) Garland.

Capital & Labor. 7th ed. Arnold Petersen. 1975. pap. text ed. 0.50 (*0-935534-06-7*) NY Labor News.

Capital & Labor: Including the Results of Machinery. Charles Knight. LC 76-38272. (Evolution of Capitalism Ser.). 254p. 1972. reprint ed. 26.95 (*0-405-04125-X*) Ayer.

Capital & Labor in American Copper, 1845-1990: A Study of the Linkages Between Product & Labor Markets. George H. Hildebrand & Garth L. Mangum. (Wertheim Publications in Industrial Relations). 332p. (C). 1992. 25.00 (*0-674-09481-6*) HUP.

Capital & Labor under Fascism. Carmen Haider. LC 68-58586. (Columbia University. Studies in the Social Sciences: No. 318). reprint ed. 28.50 (*0-404-51318-2*) AMS Pr.

Capital & Labour in South Africa. Darcy Du Toit. (Monographs from the African Studies Centre, Leiden). 480p. 1981. 75.00 (*0-7103-0001-8*, 00018, Pub. by Kegan Paul Intl UK) Routledge Chapman & Hall.

Capital & Labour on the Kimberley Diamond Fields, 1871-1890. Robert V. Turrell. (African Studies: No. 54). (Illus.). 320p. 1987. 69.95 (*0-521-33354-7*) Cambridge U Pr.

Capital & Lower Case Letters see Let's Learn Set

Capital & Output Trends in Manufacturing Industries, 1880-1948. Daniel Creamer & Martin Bernstein. (Occasional Papers: No. 41). 112p. 1954. reprint ed. 29.20 (*0-87014-355-7*); reprint ed. mic. film 20.00 (*0-685-61292-9*) Natl Bur Econ Res.

Capital & Output Trends in Mining Industries, 1870-1948. Israel Borenstein. (Occasional Papers: No. 45). 96p. 1954. reprint ed. 25.00 (*0-87014-359-X*); reprint ed. mic. film 20.00 (*0-685-61296-1*) Natl Bur Econ Res.

Capital & Politics in Western Europe. Ed. by David Marsh. (Illus.). 200p. 1983. 35.00 (*0-7146-3225-2*, Pub. by F Cass Pubs UK) Intl Spec Bk.

Capital & Population: A Study of the Economic Effects of Their Relations to Each Other. Frederick B. Hawley. LC 68-30525. (Reprints of Economic Classics Ser.). iv, 267p. 1972. reprint ed. 35.00 (*0-678-00904-X*) Kelley.

Capital & Power: Political Economy & Social Transformation. John Girling. 240p. 1987. lib. bdg. 58.50 (*0-7099-3850-0*, Pub. by Croom Helm UK) Routledge Chapman & Hall.

Capital & Rates of Return in Manufacturing Industries. George J. Stigler. LC 75-19736. (National Bureau of Economic Research Ser.). (Illus.). 1975. reprint ed. 21.95 (*0-405-07613-4*) Ayer.

Capital & Rates of Return in Manufacturing Industries. George J. Stigler. (General Ser.: No. 78). 242p. 1963. reprint ed. 65.30 (*0-87014-078-7*) Natl Bur Econ Res.

Capital & Steam Power: 1750-1800. 2nd ed. John Lord. 253p. 1966. 32.00 (*0-7146-1339-8*, Pub. by F Cass Pubs UK) Intl Spec Bk.

Capital & Technological Progress in the Indian Economy, 1950-51-1980-81. Birla Institute of Scientific Research, Staff. xvi, 198p. 1986. text ed. 25.00 (*81-7027-080-4*, Pub. by Radiant Pubs II) S Asia.

Capital & the Kingdom: Theological Ethics & Economic Order. Timothy J. Gorringe. LC 93-41999. 250p. (Orig.). 1994. pap. 18.95 (*0-88344-944-7*) Orbis Bks.

Capital & the State in Nigeria. John F. Ohiorhenuan. LC 88-7710. (Contributions in Afro-American & African Studies). 280p. 1989. text ed. 59.95 (*0-313-26460-0*, OCN, Greenwood Pr) Greenwood.

Capital & Wages: A Lakatosian History of the Wages Fund Doctrine. John Vint. 288p. 1994. 67.95 (*1-85278-864-X*, Pub. by E Elgar Pub UK) Ashgate Pub Co.

Capital Baby: The Resource Guide for New Parents in the Greater Washington Area. Lisa K. Friedman. 171p. (Orig.). 1990. pap. 12.95 (*0-9626564-0-2*) L K Friedman.

***Capital Berlin - Buildings for the Government on the Spreeinsel: International Competition for Urban Design Ideas, 1994.** LC 94-28460. 1994. pap. 59.00 (*0-8176-5040-7*) Birkhauser.

***Capital Berlin - Buildings for the Government on the Spreeinsel: International Competition for Urban Design Ideas, 1994.** Ed. by Arbeitsgruppe Berlin-Wettbewerbe Staff et al. LC 94-28460. 1994. 89.00 (*0-8176-5041-5*) Birkhauser.

Capital Berlin - Parliament District at the Spreebogen: International Competition for Urban Design Ideas, 1993. (Illus.). 256p. (ENG & GER.). 1993. 84.50 (*0-8176-2892-4*); pap. 64.50 (*0-8176-2893-2*) Spr-Verlag.

Capital Budget. Robert DeVoy & Harold Wise. Ed. by Michael Barker. LC 79-67387. (Studies in State Development Policy: Vol. 9). 73p. 1979. pap. 11.95 (*0-934842-08-6*) CSPA.

Capital Budgeting. Robert N. Holt. 90p. 1986. 295.00 (*0-934427-03-8*) Ivy Soft.

Capital Budgeting: Top Management Policy on Plant, Equipment, & Product Development. Joel Dean. LC 51-11344. (Illus.). 174p. 1951. text ed. 49.00 (*0-231-01847-9*) Col U Pr.

Capital Budgeting & Infrastructure in American Cities. 92p. 1983. 15.00 (*0-317-36616-5*, 5502); 10.00 (*0-317-36617-3*) Natl League Cities.

Capital Budgeting & Long-Term Financing Decisions. Neil E. Seitz. 632p. (C). 1990. text ed. 53.00 (*0-03-009989-7*) Dryden Pr.

Capital Budgeting Decision: Economic Analysis of Investment Projects. 8th ed. Harold Bierman, Jr. & Seymour Smidt. (Illus.). 608p. (C). 1992. teacher ed write for info. (*0-318-69338-0*) Macmillan.

Capital Budgeting Decision: Economic Analysis of Investment Projects. 8th ed. Harold Bierman, Jr. & Seymour Smidt. (Illus.). 608p. (C). 1993. text ed. write for info. (*0-02-309943-7*) Macmillan.

Capital Budgeting Handbook. Mike Kaufman. LC 85-70803. 1985. 60.00 (*0-87094-522-X*) Irwin Prof Pubng.

Capital Budgeting Techniques. 2nd ed. F. M. Wilkes. 409p. 1984. text ed. 94.95 (*0-471-90184-9*) Wiley.

Capital Budgeting under Uncertainty. Raj K. Aggarwal. 304p. 1993. text ed. 70.00 (*0-13-117250-6*) P-H.

Capital Cafe: Poems of Redneck, U. S. A. Louis D. Brodsky. 111p. 1993. 18.95 (*1-877770-48-5*); pap. 12.50 (*1-877770-49-3*) Time Being Bks.

Capital Campaign Handbook: How to Maximize Your Fund Raising Campaign. David J. Hauman. 224p. 1987. write for info. (*0-914756-40-0*, 600013) Taft Group.

***Capital Campaign in Higher Education: A Practical Guide for College & University Advancement.** G. David Gearhart. LC 94-44547. 1995. write for info. (*0-915164-98-1*) NACUBO.

Capital Capital City, 1790-1814. Suzanne Hilton. LC 91-31340. (Illus.). 160p. (J). (gr. 4 up). 1992. text ed. 14.95 (*0-689-31641-0*, Atheneum Bks Young) S&S Childrens.

Capital Case Sentencing: How to Protect Your Client. LC 88-71736. 48p. 1988. pap. 20.00 (*0-89707-384-3*, 509-0028-01) Amer Bar Assn.

***Capital Cases Benchbook.** National Judicial College Staff & ABA-JAD National Conference of State Trial Judges Staff. 383p. 1994. ring bd. 35.00 (*0-614-06244-6*) Natl Judicial Coll.

Capital Cities of Arab Islam. Philip K. Hitti. LC 72-92335. 184p. reprint ed. pap. 52.50 (*0-317-42319-3*, 2055877) Bks Demand.

Capital City. Omar Tyree. 400p. (Orig.). 1993. pap. 12.95 (*1-56411-075-3*) Untd Bros & Sis.

Capital City. Mari Sandoz. LC 81-14656. viii, 343p. 1982. reprint ed. 30.00 (*0-8032-4130-5*); reprint ed. pap. 6.95 (*0-8032-9126-4*) U of Nebr Pr.

Capital City: New York after the Revolution. Robert I. Goler. LC 86-81926. (Illus.). 52p. (Orig.). 1987. pap. text ed. 5.00 (*0-9616415-2-5*) Fraunces Tavern.

Capital Classics: Recipes from the Junior League of Washington. LC 89-5079. 160p. 1989. 24.95 (*0-934738-60-2*) Thomasson-Grant.

Capital Coefficients & Dynamic Input-Output Models. Ed. by W. F. Gossling. (Illus.). xvi, 157p. 1975. lib. bdg. 35.00 (*0-678-08073-9*) Kelley.

Capital, Competition, & Constraints: Managing Healthcare Technology in the 1990s - a Guide for Hospital Executive. ECRI Staff. (Illus.). 24p. 1992. pap. text ed. write for info. (*0-941417-25-5*) ECRI.

Capital Connection: Business, Science & Government. Peter Caws. (Philip Morris Lectures on Business & Society Ser.). 108p. 1993. pap. write for info. (*1-884663-00-1*) Baruch Coll Cty U.

Capital Connoisseur. Ed. by Sharon A. Burstein et al. (Illus.). 252p. 1988. 19.95 (*0-9620894-0-0*) LCIH.

Capital Consumption & Adjustment. Solomon Fabricant. (General Ser.: No. 35). 291p. 1938. reprint ed. 76.70 (*0-87014-034-5*); reprint ed. mic. film 38.40 (*0-685-61188-4*) Natl Bur Econ Res.

***Capital Controls, Exchange Rates & Monetary Policy in the World Economy.** Ed. by Sebastian Edwards. (Illus.). 384p. (C). 1995. 54.95 (*0-521-47228-8*) Cambridge U Pr.

***Capital Controls in Emerging.** Ed. by Christine Ries. (Political Economy of Global Interdependence Ser.). (C). 1995. text ed. 49.95 (*0-8133-8907-0*) Westview.

Capital Corruption: The New Attack on American Democracy. Amitai Etzioni. 357p. 1988. pap. 21.95 (*0-88738-708-X*) Transaction Pubs.

Capital Cost Estimating in the Process Industries. O. M. Kharbanad & E. A. Stallworthy. 304p. 1988. pap. text ed. 130.00 (*0-408-02660-X*) Buttrwrth-Heinemann.

Capital Cost Recovery & Leasing. E. F. Davis. 1987. 90.00 (*0-07-172041-3*) McGraw.

Capital, Courthouse & City Hall. 7th ed. David L. Martin. 360p. (C). 1988. pap. text ed. 24.95 (*0-582-28686-7*, 71699) Longman.

Capital Crime: Black Infant Mortality in America. Margaret S. Boone. (Frontiers of Anthropology Ser.: Vol. 4). 256p. (C). 1989. text ed. 49.95 (*0-8039-3373-8*); pap. text ed. 24.00 (*0-8039-3374-6*) Sage.

Capital Crimes. Lawrence Sanders. 352p. 1990. pap. text ed. 5.95 (*0-425-12164-X*) Berkley Pub.

Capital Crimes. large type ed. Lawrence Sanders. (General Ser.). 432p. 1990. lib. bdg. 20.95 (*0-8161-4924-0*); pap. 12.95 (*0-8161-4929-1*) G K Hall.

Capital Cubans: Refugee Adaptation in Washington, D. C. Margaret S. Boone. LC 88-35145. (Immigrant Communities & Ethnic Minorities in the U. S. & Canada Ser.: No. 40). 1989. 54.00 (*0-404-19450-8*) AMS Pr.

Capital, Distribution & Effective Demand: Studies in the "Classical" Approach to Economic Theory. Heinz D. Kurz. 200p. 1991. 44.95 (*0-7456-0629-6*) Blackwell Pubs.

Capital Dredging. 192p. 1991. text ed. 76.00 (*0-7277-1654-9*, Pub. by T Telford UK) Am Soc Civil Eng.

Capital Elites: High Society in Washington, D. C. after the Civil War. Kathryn A. Jacob. LC 94-11050. (Illus.). 344p. 1994. 35.00 (*1-56098-354-X*) Smithsonian.

Capital, Enterpreneurs & Profits. Ed. by R. T. Davenport-Hines. 305p. 1990. text ed. 34.00 (*0-7146-3386-0*, Pub. by F Cass Pubs UK) Intl Spec Bk.

Capital Equipment Purchases, No. 108. 700p. 1992. 115.00 (*0-929576-86-1*) Busn Laws Inc.

Capital Expansion, Employment & Economic Stability. Harold G. Moulton et al. LC 75-2655. (Wall Street & the Security Market Ser.). 1975. reprint ed. 35.95 (*0-405-06980-4*) Ayer.

Capital Expenditure Decision. Arthur V. Corr. 107p. 16.95 (*0-86641-091-0*, 83142) Inst Mgmt Account.

Capital Expenditures in the Steel Industry, Nineteen Hundred - Nineteen Fifty Three: Investigation of Economic Factors Influencing Their Timing & Magnitude. Eldon S. Hendriksen. Ed. by Richard P. Brief. LC 77-87300. (Development of Contemporary Accounting Thought Ser.). 1978. lib. bdg. 24.95 (*0-405-10939-3*) Ayer.

Capital Exports to Less Developed Countries. rev. ed. W. Guth. Tr. by F. B. Catty. 162p. 1963. lib. bdg. 37.50 (*90-277-0095-8*) Kluwer Ac.

Capital Facilities Planning: A Tactical Approach. Joseph Brevard. LC 85-70761. (Illus.). 408p. 1985. 42.95 (*0-918286-40-9*) Planners Pr.

Capital Financing. 64p. 1990. pap. 12.50 (*0-89867-543-X*, 20259) Am Water Wks Assn.

Capital Financing Strategies for Local Governments. Ed. by John Matzer, Jr. (Practical Management Ser.). (Illus.). 208p. (Orig.). 1983. pap. 23.95 (*0-87326-037-6*) Intl City-Cnty Mgt.

Capital Flight: Estimates, Issues, & Explanations. John T. Cuddington. LC 86-21386. (Studies in International Finance: No. 58). 1986. pap. text ed. 11.00 (*0-88165-230-X*) Princeton U Int Finan Econ.

Capital Flight: The Problem & Policy Responses. Donald R. Lessard & John Williamson. LC 87-17279. (Policy Analyses in International Economics Ser.: No. 23). 77p. reprint ed. pap. 25.00 (*0-7837-6407-3*, 2046387) Bks Demand.

Capital Flight: Theory, Measurement, & Policy Issues. Rudiger Dornbusch. 37p. 1990. pap. text ed. write for info. (*0-940602-31-8*) IADB.

Capital Flight & Economic Crisis: Mexican Post-Devaluation Exiles in a California Community. Valdemar De Murguia. (Research Report Ser.: No. 44). 27p. (Orig.). (C). 1986. pap. 5.00 (*0-935391-66-5*, RR-44) UCSD Ctr US-Mex.

Capital Flight & the Latin American Debt Crisis. Manuel Pastor, Jr. 45p. 1990. 12.00 (*0-944826-19-9*) Economic Policy Inst.

Capital Flight & Third World Debt. Donald R. Lessard & John Williamson. LC 87-17279. 271p. reprint ed. pap. 77.30 (*0-7837-4222-3*, 2043911) Bks Demand.

Capital Flows & International Policy Harmonization: Comprising Two Studies of the "Canada in the Atlantic Economy" Series. Harry E. English. LC 73-79292. (Canada in the Atlantic Economy Ser.: No. 4). 200p. reprint ed. pap. 57.00 (*0-8357-8054-6*, 2034054) Bks Demand.

Capital for Canada: Conflict & Compromise in the Nineteenth Century. David B Knight. LC 77-1154. (Research Papers Ser.: No. 182). 341p. 1977. pap. 12.00 (*0-89065-089-6*) U Chicago Comm Geo.

Capital for Canada: Conflict & Compromise in the Nineteenth Century. David B. Knight. LC 77-1154. (University of Chicago, Department of Geography, Research Paper Ser.: No. 182). (Illus.). 363p. reprint ed. pap. 103.50 (*0-7837-0408-9*, 2040729) Bks Demand.

Capital for Productivity & Jobs. Ed. by Eli Shapiro & William L. White. LC 77-23330. 1977. 11.95 (*0-13-113498-1*) Am Assembly.

Capital for Shipping. Lloyd's of London Press Staff. (Orig.). 1994. pap. 60.00 (*1-85044-504-4*) Lloyds London Pr.

Capital Formatic & Investment Incentives Around the World, 2 vols. Walter H. Diamond & Dorothy B. Diamond. 1981. Updates. ring bd. write for info. (*0-8205-1195-1*) Bender.

Capital Formation Alternatives in Higher Education. Ed. by Yamile Kahn. 118p. 1988. 20.00 (*0-915164-41-8*) NACUBO.

Capital Formation & Debt Financing for Hospitals. Saul, Ewing, Remick & Saul Staff. LC 92-25257. (Primer Series for Health Care Professionals). 30p. 1992. pap. 19.95 (*0-934753-76-8*) LRP Pubns.

Capital Formation & Economic Growth. Universities-National Bureau Staff. (Conference Ser.: No. 6). 690p. 1955. reprint ed. 160.00 (*0-87014-197-X*) Natl Bur Econ Res.

Capital Formation & Economic Growth: Proceedings. Conference of the Universities. LC 75-19700. (National Bureau of Economic Research Ser.). (Illus.). 1975. reprint ed. 54.95 (*0-405-07580-4*) Ayer.

Capital Formation by Expenditures on Formal Education: 1880 & 1890. Lewis C. Solmon. LC 75-2597. (Dissertations in American Economic History Ser.). (Illus.). 1975. 23.95 (*0-405-07218-X*) Ayer.

Capital Formation in Mainland China, 1952-1965. Kang Chao. LC 72-85526. (Michigan Studies on China). 192p. reprint ed. pap. 54.80 (*0-685-44488-0*, 2031502) Bks Demand.

Capital Formation in Residential Real Estate: Trends & Prospects. Leo Grebler et al. (Studies in Capital Formation & Financing: No. 1). 549p. 1956. reprint ed. 142.80 (*0-87014-099-X*) Natl Bur Econ Res.

Capital Formation in West Germany. Karl W. Roskamp. LC 64-22331. (Wayne State University, Center for Economic Studies, Monograph: No. 3). 288p. reprint ed. pap. 82.10 (*0-7837-3683-5*, 2043557) Bks Demand.

***Capital Gains Controversy: A Tax Analysts Reader.** 2nd ed. Ed. by Andrew J. Hoerner. 1992. pap. 34.95 (*0-918255-14-7*) Tax Analysts.

Capital Gains Tax. Anthony Sumption. Ed. by Giles Clarke. 1981. U.K. ring bd. 310.00 (*0-406-53882-4*) Butterworth Legal Pubs.

***Capital Gains Tax: Business Assets & Entities.** C. J. Taylor. 420p. 1994. pap. 75.00 (*0-455-21256-2*, Pub. by Law Bk Co) W W Gaunt.

Capital Games: An Activity Book about Raleigh, North Carolina. Louise Jordan & Jo Ramsay. 32p. (J). (gr. 3-5). 1984. pap. 2.50 (*0-9631710-2-X*) Jr League Raleigh.

Capital Goods Production in the Third World: An Economic Study of Technology Acquisition. Daniel Chudnovsky et al. LC 83-11059. 236p. 1984. text ed. 35.00 (*0-312-11927-5*) St Martin.

Capital Horse Country: A Rider's & Spectator's Guide. Jackie C. Burke. LC 94-6658. (Illus.). 294p. 1994. pap. 14.95 (*0-939009-80-3*) EPM Pubns.

An Asterisk (*) at the beginning of an entry indicates that the title is appearing in BIP for the first time. 1033

Capital Ideas: The Improbable Origins of Modern Wall Street. Peter L. Bernstein. 300p. 1991. text ed. 27.95 (0-02-903011-0) Free Pr.

Capital Ideas: The Improbable Origins of Modern Wall Street. Peter L. Bernstein. 340p. 1993. pap. 14.95 (0-02-903012-9) Free Pr.

Capital Imports & the American Balance of Payments, 1934-39: A Study in Abnormal International Capital Transfers. Arthur I. Bloomfield. LC 66-23017. (Reprints of Economic Classics Ser.). (Illus.). 1966. reprint ed. 39.50 (0-678-00165-0) Kelley.

Capital Improvement Programming Handbook for Small Cities & Other Governmental Units. Municipal Finance Officers Association Staff. LC 78-71712. (Illus.). 80p. 1978. 15.00 (0-686-84280-4) Municipal.

Capital in Agriculture: Its Formation & Financing since 1870. Alvin S. Tostlebe. (Studies in Capital Formation & Financing: No. 2). 258p. 1957. reprint ed. 68.70 (0-87014-100-7); reprint ed. mic. film 34.40 (0-685-61311-9) Natl Bur Econ Res.

Capital in Economic Theory: Neo-Classical Cambridge & Chaos. Syed N. Ahmad. 528p. 1991. text ed. 112.95 (1-85278-201-3, Pub. by E Elgar Pub UK) Ashgate Pub Co.

Capital in Manufacturing & Mining: Its Formation & Financing. Daniel Creamer et al. (Studies in Capital Formation & Financing: No. 6). 398p. 1960. reprint ed. 103.50 (0-87014-104-X); reprint ed. mic. film 51.80 (0-685-61324-0) Natl Bur Econ Res.

Capital in the American Economy: Its Formation & Financing. Simon Kuznets. LC 75-19717. (National Bureau of Economic Research Ser.). (Illus.). 1975. reprint ed. 53.95 (0-405-07596-0) Ayer.

Capital in the American Economy: Its Formation & Financing. Simon Kuznets & Elizabeth Jenks. (Studies in Capital Formation & Financing: No. 9). 694p. 1961. reprint ed. 160.00 (0-87014-107-4) Natl Bur Econ Res.

Capital in Transportation, Communications, & Public Utilities: Its Formation & Financing. Melville J. Ulmer. (Studies in Capital Formation & Financing: No. 4). 588p. 1960. reprint ed. 152.90 (0-87014-102-3) Natl Bur Econ Res.

Capital Income Taxation & Resource Allocation. Hans-Werner Sinn. LC 87-9126. (Studies in Mathematical & Managerial Economics: No. 35). 1988. 60.00 (0-444-70208-3, North Holland) Elsevier.

***Capital Inflows in the APEC Region.** Ed. by Mohsin S. Khan & Carmen M. Reinhart. LC 95-6419. (Occasional Papers: No. 122). 1995. write for info. (1-55775-466-7) Intl Monetary.

***Capital Inflows Problem: Concepts and Issues.** Guillermo A. Calvo et al. LC 94-33340. (Occassional Papers: Vol. 56). 1994. pap. 6.95 (1-55815-344-6) ICS Pr.

***Capital Intensity & Development Policy.** I. Berend. 265p. (C). 1985. 87.00x (963-05-3930-6, Pub. by Akad Kiado HU) St Mut.

Capital-Intensive Industries in Newly Industrializing Countries: The Case of the Brazilian Automobile & Steel Industries. Bernhard Fischer et al. xvii, 325p. 1988. lib. bdg. 67.50 (3-16-345445-3, Pub. by J C B Mohr GW) Coronet Bks.

Capital, Investment, & Development: Essays in Honor of Sukhamoy Chakravarty. Ed. by Kaushik Basu et al. LC 93-2938. (Illus.). 288p. 1993. 54.95 (1-55786-308-3) Blackwell Pubs.

Capital Investment & Financial Decisions. 5th ed. Levy & Sarnat. 1994. pap. text ed. 47.00 (0-13-300112-1) P-H.

Capital Investment & Financial Decisions. 5th ed. Haim Levy & Marshall Sarnat. LC 93-25792. 1994. pap. text ed. 20.00 (0-13-115882-1) P-H Gen Ref & Trav.

Capital Investment Control in the Air Transport Industry. Robert G. Vambery. LC 76-49506. 395p. 1977. lib. bdg. 50.00 (0-379-00588-3) Oceana.

Capital Investment Decision Making. Deryl Northcott. (Advanced Management Accounting & Finance Ser.). (Illus.). 92p. 1992. pap. text ed. 14.95 (0-12-521685-8) Acad Pr.

Capital Investment in Semiconductors: The Lifeblood of the U. S. Semiconductor Industry. (Illus.). 25p. (Orig.). (C). 1993. pap. text ed. 30.00 (1-56806-633-3) Diane Pub.

Capital Investment in Steel: A Plan for the 90s. William T. Hogan. LC 92-18730. 1992. text ed. 40.00 (0-669-27791-6) Free Pr.

Capital Investment Models of the Oil & Gas Industry: A Systems Approach. Louis J. Allain. Ed. by Stuart Bruchey. LC 78-22654. (Energy in the American Economy Ser.). (Illus.). 1979. lib. bdg. 46.95 (0-405-11959-3) Ayer.

Capital Issues Committee & War Finance Corporation. Woodbury Willoughby. LC 78-64154. (Johns Hopkins University. Studies in the Social Sciences. Thirtieth Ser. 1912: 2). 136p. 1983. reprint ed. 37.50 (0-404-61264-4) AMS Pr.

Capital-Labor Relations in the U. S. Textile Industry. Barry E. Truchil. LC 88-11755. 209p. 1988. text ed. 55.00 (0-275-92262-6, C2262, Praeger Pubs) Greenwood.

Capital Labor Substitutability in Malaysian Manufacturing. Maisom Abdullah. LC 91-25120. (Developing Economies of the Third World Ser.). 176p. 1991. 46.00 (0-8153-0627-X) Garland.

Capital Letters. Barbara Gregorich. (Horizons II Ser.). (Illus.). 24p. (J). (gr. 3-4). 1980. student ed 3.50 (0-89403-604-1) EDC.

Capital Libraries & Librarians: A Brief History of the District of Columbia Library Association. John Y. Cole. LC 94-12277. 1994. write for info. (0-8444-0837-9) Lib Congress.

Capital Maintenance for Colleges & Universities. Daniel Robinson. Ed. by Lanora Weizenbach. 35p. 1986. write for info. (0-915164-34-5) NACUBO.

Capital Management of Health Care Organizations. Kenneth Kaufman & Mark L. Hall. LC 90-4718. 163p. 1990. text ed. 37.00 (0-910701-55-5, 0890) Health Admin Pr.

Capital Market Effects of International Accounting Diversity. Frederick D. Choi. 132p. 1990. text ed. 40.00 (1-55623-429-5) Irwin Prof Pubng.

Capital Market Equilibria. Ed. by G. Bamberg & K. Spremann. (Illus.). x, 228p. 1986. pap. 59.00 (0-387-16248-8) Spr-Verlag.

Capital Market Equilibrium & Corporate Financial Decisions. Richard Stapleton. Ed. by Edward I. Altman & Ingo Walter. LC 76-52021. (Contemporary Studies in Economic & Financial Analysis: Vol. 13). 1980. lib. bdg. 73.25 (0-89232-054-0) Jai Pr.

Capital Markets. Bernard J. Foley. LC 90-28661. 320p. 1991. text ed. 69.95 (0-312-06163-3) St Martin.

Capital Markets & Corporate Governance. Ed. by Nicholas Dimsdale & Martha Prevezer. 360p. 1994. 60.00 (0-19-828788-7) OUP.

Capital Markets & Development. Steve H. Hanke. 1991. 29.95 (1-55815-073-0); pap. 12.95 (1-55815-091-9) ICS Pr.

***Capital Markets & Financial Intermediation.** Ed. by Colin Mayer & Xavier Vives. (Illus.). 384p. (C). 1995. pap. write for info. (0-521-55853-0) Cambridge U Pr.

Capital Markets & Institutions. 5th ed. Herbert E. Dougall & Jack E. Gaumnitz. (Illus.). 256p. (C). 1985. pap. text ed. 41.00 (0-13-113713-1) P-H.

Capital Markets & Prices: Valuing Uncertain Income Streams. C. G. Krouse. 606p. 1986. 49.00 (0-444-87931-5, North Holland) Elsevier.

Capital Markets & Trade: The United States Faces a United Europe. Ed. by Claude E. Barfield & Mark Perlman. 323p. (C). 1991. text ed. 35.00 (0-8447-3751-8) Am Enterprise.

***Capital Markets Forum Yearbook Vol. 1: 1993.** Ed. by Stephen Revell. (International Bar Association Ser.). 370p. (C). 1994. lib. bdg. 100.00 (1-85966-066-5, Pub. by Graham & Trotman UK) Kluwer Ac.

Capital Markets, Institutions & Instruments. Frank J. Fabozzi & Franco Modigliani. 640p. 1992. text ed. 71.00 (0-13-601436-4) P-H.

Capital Markets on the Development Process: The Case of Brazil. John Welch. LC 91-8338. (Latin American Ser.). 248p. (C). 1992. text ed. 49.95 (0-8229-1163-9) U of Pittsburgh Pr.

Capital Markets under Inflation. Ed. by Nicholas Bruck. LC 82-16623. 456p. 1982. text ed. 45.00 (0-275-90768-6, C0768, Praeger Pubs) Greenwood.

Capital Markets under Inflation. Ed. by Nicholas Bruck. LC 82-83150. 435p. 1982. write for info. (0-940602-03-2) IADB.

Capital Medicine: A Tradition of Excellence. Nancy B. Paull. (Illus.). 128p. 1994. 29.95 (1-882933-02-8) Cherbo Pub Grp.

Capital Mobility: The Impact on Consumption, Investment & Growth. Ed. by Leonardo Leiderman & Assaf Razin. (Illus.). 275p. (C). 1994. 54.95 (0-521-45438-7) Cambridge U Pr.

Capital Mobilization & Regional Financial Markets: The Pacific Coast States, 1850-1920. rev. ed. Kerry A. Odell. LC 92-27793. (Financial Sector of the American Economy Ser.). 240p. 1992. 60.00 (0-8153-0959-7) Garland.

Capital Needs in the Seventies. Barry Bosworth et al. LC 75-5157. 97p. reprint ed. pap. 27.70 (0-317-30182-9, 2025364) Bks Demand.

Capital of Solitude. Gregory Orfalea. LC 87-81729. (Ithaca House Ser.). 84p. 1988. pap. 9.95 (0-87886-129-7, Greenfld Rev Pr) Greenfld Rev Lit.

Capital of the American Century: The National & International Influence of New York City. Ed. by Martin Shefter. LC 92-43045. 256p. 1993. 29.95 (0-87154-768-6) Russell Sage.

Capital of the Tycoon, 2 vols., Set. Rutherford Alcock. 1863. 35.00 (0-403-00241-9) Scholarly.

Capital Outlay in Relation to a State's Minimum Educational Program. Foster E. Grossnickle. LC 72-176823. (Columbia University. Teachers College. Contributions to Education Ser.: No. 464). reprint ed. 37.50 (0-404-55464-4) AMS Pr.

Capital Output Employment Rations in Industrial Programming. W. Lissowski & J. Syskind. LC 64-195890. 1965. 102.00 (0-08-010732-X, Pub. by Pergamon Repr UK) Franklin.

Capital Output Ratio in the Indian Economy. V. P. Chitale. 120p. (C). 1986. text ed. 15.95 (81-7027-099-5, Pub. by Radiant Pubs II) S Asia.

Capital Planning: A Leadership Tool for Chief Financial Officers. Kenneth Kaufman. 15p. 1988. 20.00 (0-930228-66-9) Hlthcare Fin Mgmt.

Capital Police Officer. Jack Rudman. (Career Examination Ser.: C-2264). 1994. pap. 23.95 (0-8373-2264-2) Nat Learn.

***Capital, Power & Inequality.** Ed. by Halebsky. (Latin American Perspectives Ser.). (C). 1995. text ed. 66.00 (0-8133-2116-6); pap. text ed. 22.00 (0-8133-2117-4) Westview.

Capital Product Ratio & Size of Establishment for Manufacturing Industries. Stanley S. Schor. Ed. by Stuart Bruchey & Vincent P. Carosso. LC 78-18976. (Small Business Enterprise in America Ser.). (Illus.). 1979. lib. bdg. 17.95 (0-405-11479-6) Ayer.

Capital Projects: New Strategies for Planning, Management, & Finance. Ed. by John Matzer, Jr. LC 89-27321. (Practical Management Ser.). 230p. 1989. pap. 23.95 (0-87326-059-7) Intl City-Cnty Mgt.

Capital Punishment. Paul Almonte & Theresa Desmond. (Facts About Ser.). (Illus.). 48p. (J). (gr. 5-6). 1991. text ed. 4.95 (0-89686-660-2, Crstwood Hse) Silver Burdett Pr.

Capital Punishment. Stephen A. Flanders. (Library in a Book Ser.). 240p. (YA). (gr. 9-12). 1991. 22.95 (0-8160-1912-6) Facts on File.

Capital Punishment. Scott Hays. (Troubled Society Ser.). (Illus.). 64p. (YA). (gr. 7 up). 1990. lib. bdg. 17.27 (0-86593-074-0); lib. bdg. 12.95 (0-685-36322-8) Rourke Corp.

Capital Punishment. Michael Kronenwetter. (Contemporary World Issues Ser.). 242p. 1993. lib. bdg. 39.50 (0-87436-718-2) ABC-CLIO.

Capital Punishment. Joseph S. Roucek. Ed. by D. Steve Rahmas. (Topics of Our Times Ser.: No. 15). 32p. (YA). (gr. 7-12). 1975. lib. bdg. 4.95 (0-87157-816-6) SamHar Pr.

Capital Punishment. Ed. by Julia E. Johnson. LC 82-45668. (Capital Punishment Ser.). reprint ed. 32.50 (0-404-62421-9) AMS Pr.

Capital Punishment. U. S. Congress House. Committee on the Judiciary. LC 82-45651. (Capital Punishment Ser.). reprint ed. 49.50 (0-404-62431-6) AMS Pr.

Capital Punishment, No. 30. pap. 0.15 (0-87377-155-9) GAM Pubns.

Capital Punishment: A World View. James A. Joyce. LC 82-45669. (Capital Punishment Ser.). (Illus.). reprint ed. 34.50 (0-404-62422-7) AMS Pr.

***Capital Punishment: An Effective Punishment?** Ed. by Mark Siegel et al. (Compact Reference Ser.). 64p. (YA). 1994. pap. text ed. 11.95 (1-878623-86-9) Info Plus TX.

Capital Punishment: Criminal Law & Social Evolution. Jan Gorecki. LC 83-1875. 165p. 1986. pap. text ed. 15.50 (0-231-05659-1) Col U Pr.

***Capital Punishment: Cruel & Unusual.** rev. ed. Carol D. Foster et al. (Reference Ser.). 108p. 1994. pap. text ed. 20.95 (1-878623-66-4) Info Plus TX.

Capital Punishment: Nineteenth-Century Arguments. Ed. by Robert M. Folgelson. LC 74-3834. (Criminal Justice in America Ser.). 1977. reprint ed. 23.95 (0-405-06138-2) Ayer.

Capital Punishment: The Inevitability of Caprice & Mistake. rev. ed. Charles L. Black, Jr. (C). 1982. pap. text ed. 6.95 (0-393-95289-4) Norton.

Capital Punishment & British Politics. James B. Christoph. LC 62-12630. 200p. reprint ed. 57.00 (0-8357-9644-2, 2015752) Bks Demand.

Capital Punishment & the American Agenda. Franklin E. Zimring & Gordon J. Hawkins. (Illus.). 1987. 42.95 (0-521-33033-5) Cambridge U Pr.

Capital Punishment & the American Agenda. Franklin E. Zimring & Gordon J. Hawkins. (Illus.). 1989. pap. 17.95 (0-521-37863-X) Cambridge U Pr.

Capital Punishment & the Judicial Process: Cases & Materials. Randall Coyne & Lyn Entzeroth. LC 94-70568. 720p. 1994. lib. bdg. 75.00 (0-89089-581-3) Carolina Acad Pr.

Capital Punishment Anthology. Ed. by Victor L. Streib. LC 93-20676. 1993. write for info. (0-87084-007-X) Anderson Pub Co.

Capital Punishment As a Deterrent, & the Alternative. Gerald A. Gardiner. LC 82-45876. reprint ed. 19.50 (0-404-62415-4) AMS Pr.

Capital Punishment Dilemma, 1950-1977. Charles W. Trich, III. xiv, 278p. 1979. 18.50 (0-87875-163-7) Whitston Pub.

Capital Punishment in the Twentieth Century: With Intro. & Index Added. 5th rev. ed. E. Roy Calvert. Bd. with Death Penalty Enquiry. LC 73-172571. LC 73-172571. (Criminology, Law Enforcement, & Social Problems Ser.: No. 153). 1973. reprint ed. 30.00 (0-87585-153-3) Patterson Smith.

Capital Punishment in the United States. Ed. by Chester M. Pierce. LC 76-5828. (Studies in Modern Society: Political & Social Issues: No. 10). lib. bdg. 42.50 (0-404-10325-1) AMS Pr.

Capital Punishment in the United States. Raymond T. Bye. LC 82-45658. (Capital Punishment Ser.). 1983. reprint ed. 22.50 (0-404-62405-7) AMS Pr.

Capital Punishment Plus. J. Wilhelm Gaston. 1994. 16.95 (0-533-10816-0) Vantage.

Capital Run. (Endworld Ser.: No. 9). 224p. (Orig.). 1988. pap. 2.95 (0-8439-2584-1) Dorchester Pub Co.

Capital Run - New York Run, 2 vols. in 1. David Robbins. (Endworld Ser.). 432p. 1991. pap. 4.50 (0-8439-3173-6) Dorchester Pub Co.

Capital Scenes see California

Capital Ship Briefing: Leviathan. FASA Staff. (Renegade Legion Ser.). (Illus.). 1989. pap. 12.00 (1-55560-098-0, 5304) FASA Corp.

Capital Shortage & Unemployment in the World Economy. Ed. by Herbert Giersch. 360p. 1978. pap. text ed. 46.50 (0-685-43643-8, Pub. by J C B Mohr GW) Coronet Bks.

Capital Sources Digest: Commercial Finance & Leasing. Ed. by Robert C. Weaver, Jr. (Capital Sources Digest Ser.). 359p. 1987. 49.95 (0-935389-15-6) Sundance Vent.

Capital Sources Digest: Corporate Banking. Ed. by Robert C. Weaver, Jr. (Capital Sources Digest Ser.). 403p. 1987. 49.95 (0-935389-14-8) Sundance Vent.

Capital Sources Digest: Investment Banking. Ed. by Robert C. Weaver, Jr. (Capital Sources Digest Ser.). 359p. 1987. 49.95 (0-935389-13-X) Sundance Vent.

Capital Sources Digest: Venture Capital. Ed. by Robert C. Weaver, Jr. (Capital Sources Digest Ser.). 915p. 1987. 89.95 (0-935389-12-1) Sundance Vent.

Capital Sources Digest: Venture Capital, Vol 1 & 1A. Ed. by Robert C. Weaver, Jr. et al. (Capital Sources Digest Ser.). 1032p. 1986. 89.95 (0-685-43520-2) Sundance Vent.

Capital Sources Digest - Master Index. Ed. by Robert C. Weaver, Jr. (Capital Sources Digest Ser.). 163p. 1987. 29.95 (0-935389-11-3) Sundance Vent.

Capital Stock Conversion of State Chartered Savings Bank. Stephanie Tsacounmis. 34p. (Orig.). 1987. pap. 12.50 (0-936093-34-X) Packard Pr Fin.

Capital Stock Without Par Value. John R. Wildman & Weldon Powell. Ed. by Richard P. Brief. LC 80-1530. (Dimensions of Accounting Theory & Practice Ser.). 1980. reprint ed. lib. bdg. 61.95 (0-405-13551-3) Ayer.

Capital Taxation. Martin Feldstein. (Illus.). 504p. 1983. 50.00 (0-674-09482-4) HUP.

Capital, Taxes & Growth. Aldona Robbins & Gary Robbins. (Illus.). 45p. (C). 1992. pap. 10.00 (0-943802-72-5, 169) Natl Ctr Pol.

***Capital, the State, & Labour: A Global Perspective.** Ed. by Juliet Schor & Jong-Il You. LC 95-15673. 1995. write for info. (1-85898-295-2) Ashgate Pub Co.

***Capital Times: Tales from the Conquest of Time.** Eric Alliez. Tr. by Georges Van Den Abbeele. (Theory out of Bounds Ser.: Vol. 6). 408p. 1995. pap. text ed. 24.95 (0-8166-2260-4) U of Minn Pr.

Capital Transfer Tax. 2nd ed. Morcom & Parry. 336p. 1981. 65.00 (0-85941-055-2) St Mut.

Capital Transfers & Economic Policy: Canada, 1951-1962. Richard E. Caves & Grant L. Reuber. LC 79-129123. (Economic Studies: No. 135). 452p. 1971. 27.50 (0-674-09485-9) HUP.

Capital Value & Relative Wage Effects of Immigration into the United States, 1870-1930. Joseph Schachter. Ed. by Stuart Bruchey. LC 76-45112. (Nineteen Seventy-Seven Dissertations Ser.). (Illus.). 1977. lib. bdg. 23.95 (0-405-09923-1) Ayer.

***Capital View: A New Panorama of Washington, D.C.** Mark Klett & Merry Foresta. (Illus.). 26p. 1994. pap. text ed. 19.95 (0-9640305-0-0) Book Studio.

***Capital Views: A Photographic History of Concord, N.H., 1850-1930.** Elizabeth D. Hengen & Gary Samson. (Illus.). ix, 150p. (Orig.). 1994. 32.95 (0-915916-21-5); pap. 19.95 (0-915916-20-7) NH Hist Soc.

***Capital Visions: Reflections on a Decade of Urban Design & a Look Ahead.** Ed. by Iris Miller & Ronald Grim. (Illus.). v, 52p. (Orig.). (C). 1995. pap. text ed. write for info. (0-8444-0882-4) Lib Congress.

Capital, Vol. 1: The Process of Capitalist Production. Karl Marx. 820p. 1988. reprint ed. lib. bdg. 49.95 (0-89966-641-8) Buccaneer Bks.

Capital, Vol. 2: The Process of Circulation of Capital. Karl Marx. 558p. 1988. reprint ed. lib. bdg. 39.95 (0-89966-642-6) Buccaneer Bks.

Capital, Vol. 3: The Process of Capitalist Production As a Whole. Karl Marx. 960p. 1988. reprint ed. lib. bdg. 59.95 (0-89966-643-4) Buccaneer Bks.

Capital Wisdom: Papers from the Principals Academy. Ed. by Anne Walsh & Patricia Feistritzer. (Illus.). 67p. (Orig.). 1992. pap. 6.00 (0-685-60848-4) Natl Cath Educ.

Capitale de la Douleur: Avec: L'Amour la Poesie. Paul Eluard. 256p. 1970. 8.95 (0-686-55966-5) Fr & Eur.

Capitale de la Douleur & l'Amour la Poesies. Paul Eluard. (Poesie Ser.). (FRE.). pap. 9.95 (2-07-030095-1) Schoenhof.

Capitale de la Douleur, l'Amour de Poesie. Paul Eluard. (FRE.). 1970. pap. 10.95 (0-8288-3853-4, F99922) Fr & Eur.

Capitalism. Campbell McGrath. LC 89-24962. (Wesleyan New Poets Ser.). 64p. 1990. 22.50 (0-8195-2193-0, Wesleyan Univ Pr); pap. 10.95 (0-8195-1195-1, Wesleyan Univ Pr) U Pr of New Eng.

***Capitalism.** Peter Saunders. LC 95-16275. (Concepts in Social Thought Ser.). 1995. text ed. 37.95 (0-8166-2798-3); pap. text ed. 14.95 (0-8166-2799-1) U of Minn Pr.

Capitalism: A Celebration. Arthur Seldon. 288p. 1990. text ed. 34.95 (0-631-12558-2) Blackwell Pubs.

Capitalism: In Spite of It All. E. C. Sims. xviii, 408p. 1989. pap. text ed. 27.00 (2-88124-387-8) Gordon & Breach.

Capitalism: Opposing Viewpoints. rev. ed. Ed. by Bruno Leone. LC 86-3079. (IMS Ser.). (Illus.). 150p. (Orig.). (YA). (gr. 9-12). 1986. pap. text ed. 11.55 (0-89908-359-5) Greenhaven.

***Capitalism: The Economic Solution or the Political Illusion.** Date not set. pap. write for info. (0-614-05024-3) Gldn Obelisk.

Capitalism: The Technological Revolution & the Working Class. A. Galkin. 264p. (C). 1988. 60.00 (0-685-31592-4) St Mut.

Capitalism: The Unknown Ideal. Ayn Rand. 1986. pap. 5.99 (0-451-14795-2, Sig) NAL-Dutton.

Capitalism & a New Social Order: The Republican Version of the 1790's. Joyce Appleby. (Anson G. Phelps Lectureship on Early American History Ser.). 132p. 1984. 40.00 (0-8147-0581-2); pap. 15.00 (0-8147-0583-9) NYU Pr.

Capitalism & Agriculture in the Haouz of Marrakesh. Paul Pascon. Ed. by John R. Hall. Tr. by C. Edwin Vaughan & Veronique Ingham. 300p. 1986. 59.95 (0-7103-0189-8, 01898) Routledge Chapman & Hall.

Capitalism & Arithmetic: The New Math of the Fifteenth Century. Frank J. Swetz. LC 85-21694. 376p. (C). 1987. pap. 17.95 (0-8126-9014-1) Open Court.

Capitalism & Automation: Revolution in Technology & Capitalist Breakdown. Ramin Ramtin. 211p. (C). 1991. text ed. 73.50 (0-7453-0370-6, Pub. by Pluto Pr UK) Westview.

Capitalism & Catastrophe. S. Rousseas. LC 78-11996. (Illus.). 1979. 29.95 (0-521-22333-4) Cambridge U Pr.

Capitalism & Christians: Tough Gospel Challenges in a Troubled World Economy. Arthur Jones. LC 92-26350. 112p. 1993. pap. 6.95 (0-8091-3345-8) Paulist Pr.

An Asterisk (*) at the beginning of an entry indicates that the title is appearing in BIP for the first time.

Capitalism & Class in Colonial India. Salim Lakha. 240p. 1988. text ed. 25.00 (*81-207-0842-3*, Pub. by Sterling Pubs II) Apt Bks.

Capitalism & Communication: Global Culture & the Economics of Information. Nicholas Garnham. (Media, Culture & Society Ser.). (Illus.). 224p. (C). 1990. 45.00 (*0-8039-8257-7*); pap. 18.95 (*0-8039-8258-5*) Sage.

Capitalism & Confrontation in Sumatra's Plantation Belt 1870-1979. Ann L. Stoler. LC 84-17331. 228p. 1985. text ed. 32.00 (*0-300-03189-0*) Yale U Pr.

Capitalism & Confrontation in Sumatra's Plantation Belt, 1870-1979. 2nd ed. Ann L. Stoler. (Illus.). 300p. 1993. pap. text ed. 17.95 (*0-472-08219-1*) U of Mich Pr.

Capitalism & Culture. Ian Jamieson. 256p. 1980. text ed. 65.00 (*0-566-00356-2*) Ashgate Pub Co.

Capitalism & Dependence: Agrarian Politics in Western Uttar Pradesh, 1951-1991. Jagpal Singh. (C). 1992. 21.00 (*81-7304-026-5*, Pub. by Manohar II) S Asia.

Capitalism & Development. Leslie Sklair. LC 93-49038. 384p. 1994. 69.95x (*0-415-07546-7*, B3445, Routledge NY); pap. 22.95 (*0-415-07547-5*, B3449, Routledge NY) Routledge.

Capitalism & Fascism: Three Right-Wing Tracts, 1937-1941. LC 73-38475. (Evolution of Capitalism Ser.). 258p. 1978. reprint ed. 23.95 (*0-405-04115-2*) Ayer.

Capitalism & Freedom: Problems & Prospects; Proceedings of a Conference in Honor of Milton Friedman. Ed. by Richard T. Selden. LC 74-5333. 343p. reprint ed. pap. 97.80 (*0-8357-2728-9*, 2039838) Bks Demand.

Capitalism & Freedom: With a New Preface. Milton Friedman. LC 81-69810. 202p. (C). 1963. reprint ed. pap. text ed. 9.95 (*0-226-26401-7*) U Ch Pr.

Capitalism & Individualism: Reframing the Argument for a Free Society. Tibor R. Machan. LC 90-32882. 208p. 1990. text ed. 35.00 (*0-312-04766-5*) St Martin.

Capitalism & Leisure Theory. Chris Rojek. LC 85-2869. 224p. (Orig.). 1985. 45.00 (*0-422-79060-5*, 9558, Pub. by Tavistock UK); pap. 14.95 (*0-422-79070-2*, 9559, Pub. by Tavistock UK) Routledge Chapman & Hall.

Capitalism & Modern Social Theory: An Analysis of the Writings of Marx, Durkheim & Max Weber. Anthony Giddens. LC 70-161291. 1973. pap. 16.95 (*0-521-09785-1*) Cambridge U Pr.

Capitalism & Modernity: An Excursus on Marx & Weber. Derek Sayer. 176p. 1991. pap. 15.95 (*0-415-01728-9*, A5059) Routledge.

Capitalism & Nationalism in Prewar Japan: The Ideology of the Business Elite, 1868-1941. Byron K. Marshall. viii, 163p. 1967. 25.00 (*0-8047-0325-6*) Stanford U Pr.

***Capitalism & Organized Crime: Towards a Marxist History of the Mafia.** John Lea. 1996. pap. 16.50 (*1-899438-10-6*, Pub. by Porcupine Bks UK) Humanities.

Capitalism & Politics in Russia: A Social History of the Moscow Merchants, 1855 to 1905. Thomas C. Owen. LC 80-11279. (Illus.). 352p. 1981. 44.50 (*0-521-23173-6*) Cambridge U Pr.

Capitalism & Slavery. Eric Williams. LC 94-8722. 310p. 1994. reprint ed. 34.95 (*0-8078-2175-6*); reprint ed. pap. 14.95 (*0-8078-4488-8*) U of NC Pr.

Capitalism & Social Democracy. Adam Przeworski. (Studies in Marxism & Social Theory). 277p. 1986. pap. 19.95 (*0-521-33656-2*) Cambridge U Pr.

Capitalism & Social Theory: The Science of Black Holes. Rajani K. Kanth. LC 91-36533. (Studies in Institutional Economics Ser.). 256p. 1992. 54.95 (*1-56324-069-6*); pap. text ed. 25.95 (*1-56324-070-X*) M E Sharpe.

Capitalism & Socialism: A Theological Inquiry. Ed. by Michael Novak. 193p. 1979. 38.50 (*0-8447-2153-0*); pap. 19.50 (*0-8447-2154-9*) Am Enterprise.

Capitalism & Socialism on Trial. Fritz Sternberg. Tr. by Edward Fitzgerald. LC 68-8744. (Illus.). 603p. 1968. reprint ed. text ed. 85.00 (*0-8371-0237-5*, STCS, Greenwood Pr) Greenwood.

Capitalism & the American Political Ideal. Ed. by Edward Greenberg. LC 84-27722. 256p. 1985. pap. 25.95 (*0-87332-293-2*) M E Sharpe.

Capitalism & the Ecological Crisis. B. Gorizontov. 160p. 1985. pap. 30.00 (*0-317-89620-2*) St Mut.

Capitalism & the "Evil Empire" Reducing Superpower Conflict Through American Economic Reform. Ed. by Kenneth B. Taylor. LC 88-25315. 194p. (Orig.). 1988. pap. 17.50 (*0-945257-01-5*) Apex Pr.

Capitalism & the Historians. Ed. by Friedrich A. Hayek. 1963. pap. text ed. 12.95 (*0-226-32072-3*, P120) U Ch Pr.

***Capitalism & the Myth of the Individual in the Market.** Allan Engler. LC 94-49044. (C). 1995. text ed. 63.00 (*0-7453-0949-6*, Pub. by Pluto Pr UK) Westview.

***Capitalism & the Myth of the Individual in the Market, Vol. 2.** Allan Engler. LC 94-49044. (C). 1901. pap. text ed. 17.95 (*0-7453-0905-4*, Pub. by Pluto Pr UK) Westview.

Capitalism & the National Question in Canada. Ed. by Gary Teeple. LC 72-91690. 1972. pap. 12.95 (*0-8020-6171-0*) U of Toronto Pr.

Capitalism & the National Question in Canada. Ed. by Gary Teeple. LC 72-91690. 272p. reprint ed. pap. 77.60 (*0-8357-8055-4*, 2034025) Bks Demand.

Capitalism & the State in U. S.-Latin American Relations. Ed. by Richard R. Fagen. LC 78-65394. x, 446p. 1979. 47.50 (*0-8047-1020-1*) Stanford U Pr.

Capitalism & the Third World: Development, Dependence & the World System. Wil Hout. LC 93-16075. 240p. 1993. 62.95 (*1-85278-785-6*, Pub. by E Elgar Pub UK) Ashgate Pub Co.

Capitalism & the Welfare State: Dilemmas of Social Benevolence. Neil Gilbert. LC 83-42872. 1985. pap. 12.00 (*0-300-03477-6*) Yale U Pr.

Capitalism & Underdevelopment in Latin America. rev. ed. Andre G. Frank. LC 65-14271. 1969. reprint ed. pap. 12.00 (*0-85345-093-5*) Monthly Rev.

Capitalism & Unfree Labor: Anomaly or Necessity. Robert Miles. 256p. 1989. 55.00 (*0-422-79250-0*, A0712); pap. 18.95 (*0-685-26092-5*, A3795) Routledge Chapman & Hall.

Capitalism & Unfree Labour: Anomaly or Necessity? Robert Miles. 256p. 1987. lib. bdg. 49.50 (*0-422-61730-X*, Routledge NY) Routledge Chapman & Hall.

Capitalism As a Moral System: Adam Smith's Critique of the Free Market Economy. Spencer J. Pack. 320p. 1991. text ed. 59.95 (*1-85278-442-3*, Pub. by E Elgar Pub UK) Ashgate Pub Co.

Capitalism Conflict & Inflation. Bob Rowthorn. (C). 1980. pap. 18.50 (*0-85315-539-9*, Pub. by Lawrence & Wishart UK) Humanities.

Capitalism, Culture & Decline in Britain: 1750-1990. W. D. Rubenstein. 240p. 1992. 59.95 (*0-415-03718-2*, A6023); pap. 14.95 (*0-415-03719-0*, A6027) Routledge.

Capitalism for Beginners. Lekachman. (Documentary Comic Bks.). (Illus.). 1986. 6.95 (*0-317-03094-9*) Writers & Readers.

Capitalism for Kids: Growing Up to be Your Own Boss. Karl Hess. (J). (gr. 5 up). 1992. 12.95 (*0-942103-03-3*, 5615-34, Enter-Dearbrn); pap. 8.95 (*0-942103-06-8*, 5615-35, Enter-Dearbrn) Dearborn Finan.

Capitalism from Within: Economy, Society, & the State in a Japanese Fishery. David L. Howell. LC 94-11838. 1995. 38.00 (*0-520-08629-5*) U CA Pr.

***Capitalism, Genetics & the Natural Order.** David Perez. 26p. 1993. pap. 2.50 (*0-89567-121-2*) World View Forum.

Capitalism in a Mature Economy. Jean-Jacques Van Helten. 500p. 1990. text ed. 69.95 (*1-85278-318-4*, Pub. by E Elgar Pub UK) Ashgate Pub Co.

Capitalism in Amsterdam in the Seventeenth Century. Violet Barbour. LC 78-64208. (Johns Hopkins University. Studies in the Social Sciences. Thirtieth Ser. 1912: 1). reprint ed. 24.50 (*0-404-61313-6*) AMS Pr.

Capitalism in Colonial Puerto Rico: Central San Vicente in the Late Nineteenth Century. Teresita Martinez-Vergne. (Illus.). 208p. (C). 1992. lib. bdg. 29.95 (*0-8130-1110-8*) U Press Fla.

Capitalism in Context: Essays on Economic Development & Cultural Change in Honor of R. M. Hartwell. Ed. by John A. James & Mark F. Thomas. LC 94-1617. 1994. 31.00 (*0-226-39198-1*) U Ch Pr.

Capitalism in Contrasting Cultures. Ed. by Stewart R. Clegg & S. Gordon Redding. (Studies in Organization: No. 20). viii, 451p. (C). 1990. lib. bdg. 62.95 (*3-11-011857-2*) De Gruyter.

Capitalism in Crisis. James H. Rogers. 1938. 59.50 (*0-686-83499-2*) Elliots Bks.

Capitalism in Crisis: An International Perspective on the 1930's. Ed. by W. R. Garside. 224p. 1993. text ed. 39.95 (*0-312-04178-0*) St Martin.

Capitalism in Pakistan: A History of Socio-Economic Development. Tr. by Vyacheslav Belokrenitsky. (C). 1991. 12.50 (*81-7050-130-X*, Patriot) S Asia.

Capitalism in the Risorgimento: Joint-Stock Banking & Economic Development in the Kingdom of Sardinia, 1843-1859. rev. ed. Paul Howell. LC 91-38331. (Modern European History Ser.). 285p. 1992. 64.00 (*0-8153-0675-X*) Garland.

Capitalism Means War! 3rd ed. Daniel De Leon. 1970. pap. 0.50 (*0-935534-33-4*) NY Labor News.

Capitalism, Morality & Democracy. Scott R. Stripling. 240p. (Orig.). (C). 1994. pap. 24.95 (*0-87411-684-8*) Copley Pub.

Capitalism on the Frontier: Billings & the Yellowstone Valley in the Nineteenth Century. Carroll V. West. LC 92-15982. (Illus.). xiv, 297p. 1993. 37.95 (*0-8032-4755-9*) U of Nebr Pr.

Capitalism or Socialism: An Economic Critique for Christians. Enrique M. Urena. 1988. pap. 5.95 (*0-8199-0922-X*, Frncscn Herld) Franciscan Pr.

Capitalism, Patriarchy & Crime: Toward a Socialist Feminist Criminology. James Messerschmidt. LC 86-15608. 224p. 1986. 56.00 (*0-8476-7496-7*) Rowman.

Capitalism, Primitive & Modern: Some Aspects of Tolai Economic Growth. T. Scarlett Epstein. 182p. 1980. 34.95x (*0-87855-397-5*) Transaction Pubs.

Capitalism since Nineteen Forty-Five. Philip Armstrong et al. 352p. (C). 1991. pap. 26.95 (*0-631-17935-6*) Blackwell Pubs.

Capitalism, Socialism & Democracy. Joseph A. Schumpeter. 1962. pap. text ed. 14.00 (*0-06-133008-6*, TB 3008, Torch) HarpC.

Capitalism, Socialism & Democracy. Joseph A. Schumpeter. 1983. 26.75 (*0-8446-6027-2*) Peter Smith.

Capitalism, Socialism, & Democracy Revisited. Ed. by Larry Diamond & Marc F. Plattner. LC 93-4362. (Journal of Democracy Book Ser.). 152p. (C). 1993. text ed. 38.50 (*0-8018-4746-X*); pap. text ed. 12.95 (*0-8018-4747-8*) Johns Hopkins.

Capitalism, Socialism & Planning. B. Misra. (C). 1988. 11.00 (*81-204-0306-1*, Pub. by Oxford IBH II) S Asia.

***Capitalism, Socialism & Post-Keynesianism: Selected Essays of G. C. Harcourt.** G. C. Harcourt. LC 94-42154. (Economists of the Twentieth Century Ser.). 240p. 1995. 79.95 (*1-85898-079-8*, Pub. by E Elgar Pub UK) Ashgate Pub Co.

Capitalism, Socialism & Scientific Technical Revolution. Ed. by Collet's Holdings, Ltd. Staff. (Library of Political Knowledge: No. 9). 182p. 1983. 30.00 (*0-317-39484-3*, Pub. by Collets UK) St Mut.

Capitalism, Socialism, & Serfdom: Essays. Evsey D. Domar. (C). 1989. 74.95 (*0-521-37091-4*) Cambridge U Pr.

Capitalism, Socialism & the Development Crisis in Tanzania. Norman O'Neill. (Illus.). 295p. 1990. text ed. 78.95 (*0-566-05598-8*) Ashgate Pub Co.

Capitalism, Socialism, Ecology. Andre Gorz. Tr. by Chris Turner. LC 94-4430. 1994. pap. 59.95 (*0-86091-477-1*, Pub. by Verso UK) Routledge Chapman & Hall.

***Capitalism, Socialism, Transformation.** Leszek Balcerowicz. (Central European University Press Book Ser.). 304p. 1995. 55.00 (*1-85866-025-4*); pap. 19.95 (*1-85866-026-2*) OUP.

Capitalism, State Formation & Marxist Theory. Ed. by Phillip Corrigan. 9.95 (*0-7043-3311-2*, Pub. by Quartet UK) Charles River Bks.

Capitalism the Creator: The Economic Foundations of Modern Industrial Society. Carl Snyder. LC 70-172231. (Right Wing Individualist Tradition in America Ser.). 1972. reprint ed. 31.95 (*0-405-00439-7*) Ayer.

Capitalism Unmasked: How International Capitalism Is Stripping Our Jobs & Shipping Them to Foreign Lands for a Profit. 1992. lib. bdg. 75.00 (*0-8490-8717-1*) Gordon Pr.

Capitalism vs. Anti-Capitalism: The Triumph of Ricardian over Marxian Political Economy. Paul Fabra. 345p. (C). 1992. pap. 22.95 (*1-56000-644-7*) Transaction Pubs.

Capitalism vs. Capitalism: How America's Obsession with Individual Achievement & Short-Term Profit Has Led It to the Brink of Collapse. Michel Albert. Tr. by Paul Haviland. LC 93-4542. 288p. (Orig.). 1993. reprint ed. 25.95 (*1-56858-004-5*); reprint ed. pap. 12.95 (*1-56858-005-3*) FWEW.

Capitalism vs. Pragmatic Market Socialism: A General Equilibrium Evaluation. James A. Yunker. LC 93-23360. 1993. lib. bdg. 65.00 (*0-7923-9399-6*) Kluwer Ac.

Capitalism Wakes Up! Ali Shariati. Tr. by Mahmoud Mohseni. 32p. (Orig.). 1989. pap. text ed. 2.25 (*1-871031-33-8*) Abjad Bk.

***Capitalism with a Human Face.** Samuel Brittan. LC 94-28484. 304p. 1995. 69.95 (*1-85278-446-6*, Pub. by E Elgar Pub UK); pap. 23.95 (*1-85278-449-0*, Pub. by E Elgar Pub UK) Ashgate Pub Co.

Capitalism with Morality. David W. Haslett. LC 93-44416. 320p. (C). 1994. 49.95 (*0-19-828553-1*, Clarendon Pr) OUP.

Capitalisme dans le monde antique: Etudes sur l'histoire de l'economie romaine. G. Salvioli. Ed. by Moses Finley. Tr. by Alfred Bonnet. LC 79-5004. (Ancient Economic History Ser.). (FRE.). 1979. reprint ed. lib. bdg. 29.95 (*0-405-12393-0*) Ayer.

Capitalismo en Camino hacia el Olvido: La Lucha del Pueblo por un Nuevo Comienzo. Gus Hall. 96p. (SPA.). 1972. pap. 0.50 (*0-87898-090-3*) New Outlook.

Capitalist & Collective Action: Conflict & Cooperation in the Coal Industry. John R. Bowman. (Studies in Marxism & Social Theory). 288p. (C). 1989. 64.95 (*0-521-36265-2*) Cambridge U Pr.

Capitalist & Socialist Economies. 2nd ed. 114p. 1963. pap. 10.00 (*0-9601374-0-8*) R B Driscoll.

Capitalist City: Global Restructuring & Community Politics. Ed. by Michael P. Smith & Joe R. Feagin. 288p. 1987. pap. 21.95 (*0-631-15618-6*) Blackwell Pubs.

Capitalist Class: An International Study. Ed. by Tom Bottomore & Robert Brym. 320p. 1989. 45.00x (*0-8147-1110-3*) NYU Pr.

Capitalist Control & Workers' Struggle in the Brazilian Auto Industry. J. Humphrey. 1982. 39.50 (*0-691-09400-4*) Princeton U Pr.

Capitalist Democracy in Britain. Ralph Miliband. (C). 1984. pap. 12.95 (*0-19-285137-3*) OUP.

Capitalist Democracy on Trial: The Transatlantic Debate from Tocqueville to the Present. Dennis Smith. 208p. 1990. 55.00 (*0-415-04044-2*, A3708); pap. 17.95 (*0-415-04188-0*, A3712) Routledge.

Capitalist Development: Critical Essays. Ed. by Ghanshyam Shah. (C). 1990. 54.00 (*0-86132-270-3*, Pub. by Popular Prakashan II) S Asia.

Capitalist Development & Class Capacities: Marxist Theory & Union Organization. Jerry Lembcke. LC 87-37546. (Contributions in Labor Studies: No. 25). 213p. 1988. text ed. 55.00 (*0-313-26209-8*, LCD/, Greenwood Pr) Greenwood.

Capitalist Development & Crisis Theory: Accumulation, Regulation & Spatial Restructuring. Ed. by M. Gottdiener & Nicos Komninos. LC 88-15848. 280p. 1989. text ed. 49.95 (*0-312-02102-X*) St Martin.

Capitalist Development & Democracy. Dietrich Rueschemeyer et al. (Illus.). 385p. 1992. lib. bdg. 45.00 (*0-226-73142-1*); pap. text ed. 19.95 (*0-226-73144-8*) U Ch Pr.

Capitalist Development & the Peasant Economy of Peru. Adolfo Figueroa. LC 83-18861. (Cambridge Latin American Studies: No. 47). (Illus.). 168p. 1984. 64.95 (*0-521-25397-7*) Cambridge U Pr.

Capitalist Economies: Prospects for the 1990's. John Cornwall. 256p. 1991. text ed. 67.95 (*1-85278-378-8*, Pub. by E Elgar Pub UK) Ashgate Pub Co.

Capitalist Enterprise & Social Progress. Maurice H. Dobb. LC 79-1577. 1981. reprint ed. 31.00 (*0-88355-883-1*) Hyperion Conn.

Capitalist Form of Production in South Asia: Consequences of British Policies. Ed. by Franco Farinelli. (C). 1991. 17.00 (*81-85425-49-3*, Pub. by Manohar II) S Asia.

Capitalist Goals, Socialist Past: The rise of the Private Sector in Command Economies. Ed. by Perry L. Patterson. LC 93-20305. (C). 1993. pap. text ed. 41.50 (*0-8133-8402-8*) Westview.

Capitalist Imperative: Territory, Technology, & Industrial Growth. Michael Storper & Richard Walker. (Illus.). 352p. 1989. pap. text ed. 21.95 (*0-631-16533-9*) Blackwell Pubs.

Capitalist Imperialism, Crisis & the State. John Willoughby. (Fundamentals of Pure & Applied Economics Ser.: Vol. 7). 101p. 1986. pap. text ed. 27.00 (*3-7186-0322-5*) Gordon & Breach.

Capitalist Manifesto. Louis O. Kelso & Mortimer J. Adler. LC 75-14280. 265p. 1975. reprint ed. text ed. 55.00 (*0-8371-8210-7*, KECM, Greenwood Pr) Greenwood.

Capitalist Patriarchy & the Case for Socialist Feminism. Ed. by Zillah R. Eisenstein. LC 77-76162. 408p. reprint ed. pap. 116.30 (*0-7837-6984-9*, 2046796) Bks Demand.

Capitalist Property & Financial Power: A Comparative Study of Britain, the United States & Japan. John Scott. LC 86-2361. 256p. 1986. pap. 18.50 (*0-8147-7921-2*) NYU Pr.

Capitalist Revolution: Fifty Propositions about Prosperity, Equality & Liberty. Peter L. Berger. LC 85-73882. 288p. 1988. pap. text ed. 14.00 (*0-465-00868-2*) Basic.

***Capitalist Revolution in Eastern Europe: A Contribution to the Economic Theory of System Change.** Laszlo Csaba. 336p. 1995. 79.95 (*1-85278-672-8*, Pub. by E Elgar Pub UK) Ashgate Pub Co.

Capitalist Schools: Explanation & Ethics in Radical Studies of Schooling. Daniel P. Liston. (Critical Social Thought Ser.). 208p. 1988. text ed. 35.00 (*0-415-90044-1*, A1561, Routledge NY); pap. 12.95 (*0-415-90341-6*, A4779, Routledge NY) Routledge.

Capitalist Society: Readings for a Critical Sociology. Ed. by Richard Quinney. LC 78-70955. (Dorsey Series in Sociology). 450p. reprint ed. pap. 128.30 (*0-317-09052-6*, 2055673) Bks Demand.

Capitalist Space Economy: Analysis after Ricardo, Marx & Sraffa. Eric Sheppard & Trevor J. Barnes. 320p. 1990. text ed. 75.00 (*0-04-330401-X*) Routledge Chapman & Hall.

Capitalist Spirit: Toward a Religious Ethic of Wealth Creation. Ed. by Peter L. Berger. 180p. 1990. 18.95 (*1-55815-112-5*) ICS Pr.

Capitalist Welfare Systems: A Comparison of Japan, Britain, & Sweden. Arthur Gould. LC 92-38228. 288p. (C). 1994. pap. text ed. 28.50 (*0-582-08349-4*, 76451, Pub. by Longman UK) Longman.

Capitalist World Development: A Critique of Radical Development. Stuart Corbridge. 310p. (C). 1986. 57.00 (*0-8476-7509-2*, R7509); pap. 22.50 (*0-8476-7510-6*, R7510) Rowman.

Capitalist World Economy. Immanuel Wallerstein. LC 78-1161. (Studies in Modern Capitalism). 1979. pap. 19.95 (*0-521-29358-8*) Cambridge U Pr.

Capitalists & Columbia. J. Fred Rippy. Ed. by Stuart Bruchey & Eleanor Bruchey. LC 76-5031. (American Business Abroad Ser.). (Illus.). 1976. reprint ed. 26.95 (*0-405-09298-9*) Ayer.

C

Capitalists & Revolution in Nicaragua: Opposition & Accomodation. Rose J. Spalding. LC 93-38430. 340p. 1994. lib. bdg. 45.00 (*0-8078-2150-0*); pap. text ed. 15.95 (*0-8078-4456-X*) U of NC Pr.

***Capitalists, Caciques, & Revolution: The Native Elite & Foreign Enterprise in Chihuahua, Mexico, 1854-1911.** Mark Wasserman. LC 83-12481. reprint ed. pap. 69.60 (*0-7837-9030-9*, 2049781) Bks Demand.

Capitalists Without Capitalism: The Jains of India & the Quakers of the West. Balwant S. Nevaskar. LC 72-98709. (Contributions in Sociology Ser.: No. 6). 252p. 1971. text ed. 59.95 (*0-8371-3297-5*, NCA/, Greenwood Pr) Greenwood.

Capitalization of Cultural Production. Bernard Miege. 168p. 1989. pap. 13.95 (*0-88477-025-7*) Intl General.

Capitalization of Goodwill. Kemper Simpson. LC 78-63972. (Johns Hopkins University. Studies in the Social Sciences. Thirtieth Ser. 1912: 1). 112p. (C). reprint ed. 37.50 (*0-404-61218-0*) AMS Pr.

Capitalization Requirements for Multiple Line Property Liability Insurance Companies. Intro. by James E. Bachman & J. David Cummins. LC 78-57297. (S. S. Huebner Foundation Monographs: No. 6). (Illus.). 94p. (C). 1978. pap. 14.50 (*0-918930-06-5*) Huebner Foun Insur.

Capitalization Theory & Techniques Study Guide. Charles B. Akerson. 258p. 1984. student ed, spiral bd. 20.00 (*0-911780-73-4*) Appraisal Inst.

Capitalizing on Aseptic: Proceedings. Food Processors Institute Staff. 96p. (Orig.). 1984. pap. 25.00 (*0-937774-09-X*) Food Processors.

Capitalizing on Aseptic II: Proceedings. Food Processors Institute Staff. (Orig.). 1985. pap. text ed. 25.00 (*0-937774-15-4*) Food Processors.

***Capitalizing on Workplace Diversity: A Practical Guide to Organizational Success Through Diversity.** Richard Y. Chang. (Workplace Diversity Ser.). (Illus.). 120p. 1995. pap. 12.95 (*1-883553-66-0*) R Chang Assocs.

Capitals of Spanish America. William E. Curtis. 1976. lib. bdg. 59.95 (*0-8490-1570-7*) Gordon Pr.

Capitan Veneno; El Sombrero de Tres Picos. Pedro Antonio de Alarcon. (SPA.). 9.95 (*0-8288-2548-3*, S9860) Fr & Eur.

Capitan Veneo, No. 37. Pedro A. De Alarcon. 150p. (SPA.). 1978. write for info. (*0-8288-8575-3*) Fr & Eur.

***Capitation: New Opportunities & Risks in Managing Healthcare.** David I. Samuels. 250p. 1995. 45.00 (*1-55738-640-4*) Probus Pub Co.

Capitation Du Bas-Empire. Andre Deleage. LC 75-7313. (Roman History Ser.). (Illus.). (FRE.). 1975. reprint ed. 25.95 (*0-405-07195-7*) Ayer.

Capitein: A Critical Study of an 18th Century African. Kwesi K. Prah. LC 91-78314. 175p. 1992. 29.95 (*0-86543-331-3*); pap. 8.95 (*0-86543-332-1*) Africa World.

***Capitol.** Andrew Santella. LC 95-825. (Cornerstones of Freedom Ser.). (J). 1995. write for info. (*0-516-06626-9*) Childrens.

Capitol: A Pictorial History of the Capitol & of the Congress. rev. ed. (Illus.). 192p. 1988. pap. 10.00 (*0-16-006381-7*, S/N 052-071-00687-7) USGPO.

An Asterisk (*) at the beginning of an entry indicates that the title is appearing in BIP for the first time.

***Capitol - Capital: Government Resources for High-Technology Companies.** William A. Delphos. Ed. by Alan J. Beard et al. 228p. 1994. pap. 49.95 (*1-883917-01-8*) Venture Pub NA.

Capitol Advantage - Congress Directory, 103rd Congress, 1st Session: Congress at Your Fingertips. Ed. by John E. Hansan. (Illus.). 190p. 1993. 8.95 (*1-879617-10-2*); spiral bd. 7.50 (*1-879617-08-0*); per. 7.50 (*1-879617-09-9*) Capitol Advantage.

Capitol Advantage - Congress Directory, 103rd Congress, 1st Session: Congress at Your Fingertips. exp. ed. Ed. by John E. Hansan. 96p. 1993. 4.95 (*1-879617-11-0*) Capitol Advantage.

Capitol Advantages Congressional Directory. 6th ed. 188p. 1991. spiral bd., pap. 7.50 (*1-879617-00-5*); pap. 7.50 (*1-879617-01-3*) Capitol Advantage.

Capitol City Kidnapping. David Avon. 1992. 16.95 (*0-533-10134-4*) Vantage.

***Capitol Games.** T. Phelps. 1994. pap. 4.99 (*0-517-13213-3*) Random Hse Value.

Capitol Games: The Inside Story of Clarence Thomas, Anita Hill, & a Supreme Court Nomination. Timothy M. Phelps & Helen Winternitz. LC 92-54850. 464p. 1993. pap. 14.00 (*0-06-097553-9*, PL) HarpC.

Capitol Hill Manual. 2nd ed. Frank Cummings. LC 83-21048. (Illus.). 338p. reprint ed. pap. 96.40 (*0-7837-4598-2*, 2044317) Bks Demand.

Capitol Hit. 1993. mass mkt. 3.50 (*0-373-61173-0*, 1-61173-0) Harlequin Bks.

Capitol Ideas, an SHRM Guide to the Federal & State Legislative Process. 20p. 1992. 20.00 (*0-685-56808-3*, PB16) Soc Human Resc Mgmt.

Capitol in Albany. Photos by William Clift et al. 48p. 1985. pap. 12.50 (*0-89381-209-9*) Aperture.

Capitol Names: Individuals Woven into Oregon's History. Philip Cogswell, Jr. LC 76-56657. (Illus.). 133p. 1977. pap. 2.95 (*0-87595-054-X*) Oregon Hist.

Capitol of Virginia. Fiske Kimball. Ed. by Jon Kukla et al. 110p. 1989. reprint ed. text ed. 20.00 (*0-88490-154-8*); reprint ed. pap. text ed. 4.95 (*0-88490-155-6*) VA State Lib.

Capitol Offense. Tony Gibbs. 368p. 1995. 19.95 (*0-89296-474-X*) Mysterious Pr.

***Capitol Offense.** Tony Gibbs. 1996. mass mkt. write for info. (*0-446-40109-9*, Mysterious Paperbk) Warner Bks.

Capitol Press Corps: Newsmen & the Governing of New York State. David Morgan. LC 77-84771. (Contributions in Political Science Ser.: No. 2). 177p. 1978. text ed. 49.95 (*0-8371-9883-6*, MCP/, Greenwood Pr) Greenwood.

C

Capitol Punishment. Linda Proaps. (Illus.). 295p. 1991. 24.95 (*1-879563-03-7*) Lexicon CA.

Capitol Punishment: A Thriller. LC 93-47456. 1995. write for info. (*0-688-12983-8*) Morrow.

Capitol Reef: The Story Behind the Scenery. rev. ed. Virgil J. Olson & Helen Olson. LC 90-60036. (Illus.). 48p. 1990. pap. 6.95 (*0-88714-043-2*) KC Pubns.

Capitol Region: Day Trips in Maryland, Virginia, Pennsylvania, & Washington, D.C. Ed. by Anthony R. De Souza & Cotton Mather. LC 92-10412. (Touring North America Ser.). (Illus.). 220p. 1992. 25.00 (*0-8135-1870-9*); pap. 9.95 (*0-8135-1871-7*) Rutgers U Pr.

***Capitol Women: An Interpretive History of Women in Sacramento from 1850-1920.** Elaine Connolly & Dian Self. 185p. 1995. pap. text ed. 12.95 (*0-9645485-1-8*) Capito Womens.

Capitols of Texas. (Illus.). 1970. 20.00 (*0-318-41799-5*) Texian.

Capitols of Texas: A Visual History. Sara Clark. (Illus.). 130p. 1975. 20.00 (*0-88426-046-1*) Encino Pr.

Capitols of West Virginia: A Pictorial History. Stan B. Cohen & Richard Andre. LC 89-50354. (Illus.). 112p. (Orig.). 1989. pap. 9.95 (*0-929521-18-8*) Pictorial Hist.

Capitulatory Regime of Turkey: Its History, Origin, & Nature. Nasim Susa. LC 78-64288. (Johns Hopkins University. Studies in the Social Sciences. Thirtieth Ser. 1912: 18). reprint ed. 31.00 (*0-404-61388-8*) AMS Pr.

***CAPM Controversy: Policy & Strategy Implications for Investment Management.** 1993. write for info. (*0-614-03023-4*) Assn I M&R.

Cap'n Eri. Joseph C. Lincoln. 1976. reprint ed. lib. bdg. 25.95 (*0-88411-792-8*, Aeonian Pr) Amereon Ltd.

Cap'n Happy's Shot Guide: Recipes for "Shots" Slammed Around the World. Mark McKee & Pat Boppart. (Illus.). 128p. (Orig.). 1994. pap. 9.95 (*1-882907-02-7*) Old Market.

Capnography in Clinical Practice. J. S. Gravenstein & D. A. Paulus. 112p. 1988. text ed. 29.95 (*0-7506-9388-6*) Buttrwrth-Heinemann.

Capnography in the Operating Room: An Introductory Directory. W. Samuel May, Jr. et al. LC 85-18261. (Illus.). 64p. 1985. spiral bd. 18.00 (*0-88167-128-2*) Raven.

Capo Ha: Dizionario Dei Modi di Dire, Proverbi e Locuzioni. Giuseppe Pittano & Frase Fatta. 352p. (ITA.). 1993. 75.00 (*0-8288-9428-0*) Fr & Eur.

***Capoeira: African Brazilian Karate.** Yusef A. Salaam. (Illus.). 29p. (Orig.). 1990. pap. 5.95 (*1-56411-110-5*) Untd Bros & Sis.

Capoeira - A Brazilian Art Form: History, Philosophy, & Practice. Bira Almeida. (Illus.). 224p. 1986. pap. 12.95 (*0-938190-29-6*); 39.95 (*0-685-10441-9*) North Atlantic.

Capon Valley Sampler: Sketches of Appalachia from George Washington to Caudy Davis. Willard Wirtz. LC 89-29144. (Illus.). 240p. 1990. 14.95 (*0-910155-14-3*) Bartleby Pr.

Capone. Laurence Bergreen. 1994. 30.00 (*0-671-74456-9*) S&S Trade.

Capone: The Life & World of Al Capone. John Kobler. (Illus.). 431p. 1992. reprint ed. pap. 14.95 (*0-306-80499-9*) Da Capo.

Capone's Chicago. rev. ed. R. T. Enright. Ed. by Ray R. Cowdery. 96p. 1987. reprint ed. pap. 10.00 (*0-910667-13-6*) Northstar Bks.

Caporal Epingle. Jacques Perret. (FRE.). 1972. pap. 17.95 (*0-7859-3993-8*) Fr & Eur.

Caporetto. Agatha D. Anastasi. (Orig.). 1979. pap. 2.75 (*0-89083-543-8*) Zebra.

Capo's Revenge. Robert Cain. (Cybernarc Ser.: No. 4). 1992. mass mkt. 3.99 (*0-06-100461-8*, Harp PBks) HarpC.

Capote: A Biography. Gerald Clarke. 1989. pap. 12.95 (*0-345-36078-8*, Ballantine Trade) Ballantine.

Capote: A Biography. Gerald Clarke. (Illus.). 632p. 1991. 5.99 (*0-517-05541-4*) Random Hse Value.

Capote: A Biography. Gerald Clarke. 480p. 1986. 18.45 (*0-685-09993-8*) S&S Trade.

Capote Reader. Truman Capote. LC 86-10128. 736p. 1987. 35.00 (*0-394-55647-X*) Random.

Capp: From Design to Production. Ed. by J. Tulkoff. LC 88-62240. (Illus.). 270p. 1988. 44.00 (*0-87263-332-2*) SME.

Capped Langur in Bangladesh: Behavioral Ecology & Reproductive Tactics. C. B. Stanford. (Contributions to Primatology Ser.: Vol. 26). (Illus.). xviii, 180p. 1991. 98.50 (*3-8055-5396-X*) S Karger.

Cappella: Thirty Settings, Unaccompanied, Mixed Chorus, 3 to 8 Parts. Ed. by John C. Gardner & Simon Harris. 144p. 1992. pap. 17.95 (*0-19-336199-X*) OUP.

Cappella Giulia Chansonnier, Pt. 1. Alan Atlas. (Wissenschaftliche Abhandlungen-Musicological Studies: Vol. 27). 220p. 1976. lib. bdg. 74.00 (*0-912024-23-2*) Inst Mediaeval Mus.

Cappella Giulia Chansonnier, Pt. 2. Alan Atlas. (Wissenschaftliche Abhandlungen-Musicological Studies: Vol. 27). 220p. 1976. lib. bdg. 60.00 (*0-912024-24-0*) Inst Mediaeval Mus.

Cappuccino - Espresso: The Book of Beverages. Christie Katona & Thomas Katona. (Illus.). 176p. (Orig.). 1993. pap. 8.95 (*1-55867-099-8*, Nitty Gritty Ckbks) Bristol Pub Ent CA.

Cappy: Rollicking Rancher Atop Arizona's Mighty Rim. Vienna I. Curtiss. LC 79-84471. (Illus.). 1979. 12.00 (*0-9602742-0-0*) Collectors Choice.

Cappy Claus. Ann Robinson. (Illus.). 16p. (J). (ps-6). 1992. pap. 4.95 (*0-9633373-0-0*) Chameleon FL.

Cappy Ricks: The Subjugation of Matt Peasley. Peter B. Kyne. reprint ed. lib. bdg. 23.95 (*0-88411-690-5*, Aeonian Pr) Amereon Ltd.

Cappy Ricks Comes Back. Peter B. Kyne. reprint ed. lib. bdg. 23.95 (*0-88411-691-3*, Aeonian Pr) Amereon Ltd.

Cappy Ricks Retires. Peter B. Kyne. reprint ed. lib. bdg. 22.95 (*0-88411-692-1*, Aeonian Pr) Amereon Ltd.

***Cappy the Lonely Camel.** Donald Rubinetti. LC 95-9690. (Illus.). (J). 1995. write for info. (*0-382-39150-0*); lib. bdg. write for info. (*0-382-39151-9*); pap. write for info. (*0-382-39152-7*) Silver Burdett Pr.

Capri. (Panorama Books Collection). (FRE.). 3.95 (*0-685-36095-4*) Fr & Eur.

Capri. Old Vicarage Publications Staff. (C). 1982. pap. text ed. 60.00 (*0-685-22065-6*, Pub. by Old Vicarage UK) St Mut.

Capri. Alberto Savinio. Tr. by John Shepley. LC 89-62013. 80p. 1989. pap. 7.25 (*0-910395-49-7*) Marlboro Pr.

Capri: Guide to Purchase & Restoration. Kim Henson. (Illus.). 256p. 1989. 29.95 (*0-85429-644-1*, Pub. by G T Foulis Ltd) Haynes Pubns.

Capri: The Development & Competition History of Ford's European GT Car. Jeremy Walton. 205p. 31.95 (*0-85429-863-0*, F548, Pub. by G T Foulis Ltd) Haynes Pubns.

Capri Affair. David Hanna. (Crime Court Mystery Ser.). 256p. (Orig.). 1986. pap. 2.95 (*0-8439-5004-8*) Dorchester Pub Co.

Caprial's Cafe Favorites. Caprial Pence. 1994. 21.95 (*0-89815-600-9*) Ten Speed Pr.

Caprial's Seasonal Kitchen: An Innovative Chef's Menus & Recipes for Easy Home Cooking. Caprial Pence. LC 91-3274. (Illus.). 240p. (Orig.). 1991. pap. 19.95 (*0-88240-417-2*) Alaska Northwest.

Caprial's Seasonal Kitchen: An Innovative Chef's Menus & Recipes for Easy Home Cooking. Caprial Pence. (Orig.). 1992. pap. 12.95 (*0-88240-418-0*) Alaska Northwest.

Caprice. Laura Parker. 1994. mass mkt. 4.99 (*0-440-21238-3*) Dell.

Caprice. Ronald Firbank. LC 93-16388. (Bibelot Ser.). 96p. 1993. reprint ed. pap. 5.00 (*0-8112-1243-2*, NDP764) New Directions.

Caprice: A Slockman's Daughter. Doris Pilkington. (Orig.). 1991. pap. 12.95 (*0-7022-2400-6*, Pub. by Univ Queensland Pr AT) Intl Spec Bk.

Caprice, for Solo Bass Viola da Gamba. Rudolph Dolmetsch. Ed. by Adrian Rose. (Contemporary Instrumental Ser.: No. 7). (Illus.). i, 2p. 1994. 8.00 (*1-56571-082-7*, CI007) PRB Prods.

Capriceio. Leonard Salzedo. (Just Brass Ser.: No. 54). (C). 1991. pap. write for info. (*0-8464-3191-2*) Beekman Pubs.

Caprices of Goya. Jean Adhemar. (Illus.). 1951. 7.95 (*0-8288-3975-1*) Fr & Eur.

Caprichos. Francisco Goya. 1970. pap. 6.95 (*0-486-22384-1*) Dover.

Capricious Cosmos: Universe Beyond Law. Joe Rosen. 192p. 1992. text ed. 19.95 (*0-02-604931-7*) Macmillan.

***Capricorn.** 272p. (Orig.). Date not set. pap. text ed. 6.50 (*0-515-11670-X*) Jove Pubns.

***Capricorn.** 208p. (Orig.). 1995. pap. text ed. 4.50 (*0-425-14895-5*) Berkley Pub.

***Capricorn.** 256p. (Orig.). 1995. pap. text ed. 4.99 (*0-425-14911-0*) Berkley Pub.

Capricorn. Berkley Publshing Staff. (Day by Day Horoscopes, 1995 Ser.). 208p. (Orig.). 1994. pap. text ed. 3.99 (*0-425-15819-5*) Berkley Pub.

Capricorn. Lucille Callard. (Astro-Pups: Your Sign, Your Dogs Ser.). (Illus.). 60p. 1991. pap. 9.95 (*1-881038-09-2*) Penzance Pr.

Capricorn. Derek Parker & Julia Parker. LC 92-52793. (Sun & Moon Signs Library). (Illus.). 64p. 1992. 8.95 (*1-56458-093-8*) Dorling Kindersley.

Capricorn. Paula Taylor. (Sun Sign Ser.). 40p. (J). (gr. 4). 1989. lib. bdg. 13.95 (*0-88682-256-4*) Creative Ed.

Capricorn: Astro-Numerology. 2nd ed. Michael J. Kurban. (Illus.). 50p. 1991. pap. 8.00 (*0-938863-18-5*) Libra Press Chi.

Capricorn: Little Birth Sign. Andrews & McMeel. 1994. 4.95 (*0-8362-3072-8*) Andrews & McMeel.

Capricorn: The Artful Astrologer. Lee Holloway. 1993. 4.99 (*0-517-08259-4*) Random Hse Value.

Capricorn: Through the Numbers. Paul Rice & Valeta Rice. 64p. 1983. pap. 3.95 (*0-87728-574-8*) Weiser.

Capricorn see Sun Sign Diet

Capricorn People. Aaron Fletcher. 512p. 1983. pap. 3.95 (*0-8439-2012-2*) Dorchester Pub Co.

Capricorn Quadrant. Charles Ryan. 384p. 1991. pap. 4.99 (*0-451-17034-2*, Sig) NAL-Dutton.

Capricorn Stone. Madeleine Brent. 1983. pap. 3.50 (*0-449-20149-X*) Fawcett.

Capricornia Country. Barry Slade. (Illus.). 136p. 1993. 30.00 (*0-207-17484-9*, Pub. by Angus & Robertson AT) HarpC.

Capricornio: Astro-Numerogia. Michael J. Kurban. Tr. by Loretta H. Kurban. LC 86-91276. (Illus.). (Orig.). (SPA.). 1992. pap. 8.00 (*0-938863-54-1*) Libra Press Chi.

Caprock Canyonlands: Journeys into the Heart of the Southern Plains. Dan Flores. (M. K. Brown Range Life Ser.: No. 18). (Illus.). 212p. 1990. 22.95 (*0-292-71121-2*) U of Tex Pr.

Caprolen Captivity. Zeal I. Fisher. 1992. 16.95 (*0-533-10261-8*) Vantage.

Caps & Helmets of the American Revolution, Set I. Bellerophon Staff. (J). (gr. 1-9). 1992. pap. 5.95 (*0-88388-029-6*) Bellerophon Bks.

Caps & Helmets of the American Revolution, Set II. Bellerophon Staff. (J). (gr. 1-9). 1992. pap. 5.95 (*0-88388-040-7*) Bellerophon Bks.

Caps & Helmets of the American Revolution, Set III. Bellerophon Staff. (J). (gr. 1-9). 1992. pap. 5.95 (*0-88388-041-5*) Bellerophon Bks.

Caps, Commas, & Other Things. Sheryl Pastorek. 264p. 1982. pap. 18.00 (*0-87879-325-9*) Acad Therapy.

Caps for Sale. Esphyr Slobodkina. LC 84-43122. (Illus.). (J). 1947. 12.95 (*0-201-09147-X*); lib. bdg. 12.89 (*0-06-025778-4*) HarpC Child Bks.

Caps for Sale. Esphyr Slobodkina. LC 84-43122. (Trophy Picture Bk.). (Illus.). 48p. (J). (ps-2). 1987. pap. 3.95 (*0-06-443143-6*, Trophy) HarpC Child Bks.

Caps for Sale. Esphyr Slobodkina. (Illus.). (J). (gr. k-3). 1987. audio 22.95 (*0-87499-059-9*); audio, pap. 14.95 (*0-87499-058-0*) Live Oak Media.

Caps for Sale. Esphyr Slobodkina. 32p. (J). (gr. k-3). 1989. Big Book. 28.67 (*0-590-64643-5*); pap. 2.95 (*0-590-71775-8*) Scholastic Inc.

***Caps for Sale.** Esphyr Slobodkina. (Illus.). (J). (ps-2). 1995. audio, pap. 7.95 (*0-694-70004-5*) HarperAudio.

Caps for Sale, 4 bks., Set. Esphyr Slobodkina. (Illus.). (J). (gr. k-3). 1987. audio, pap. 29.95 (*0-87499-060-2*) Live Oak Media.

Caps for Sale: A Study Guide. Garrett Christopher. Ed. by Joyce Friedland & Rikki Kessler. (Little Novel-Ties Ser.). (J). (gr. k-3). 1991. pap. text ed. 14.95 (*0-88122-587-8*) Lrn Links.

Caps, Hats, Socks, & Mittens. Louise Bordon. (Big Book Ser.). (J). (ps-3). 1992. pap. 19.95 (*0-590-72429-0*) Scholastic Inc.

Caps, Hats, Socks, & Mittens: A Book about the Four Seasons. Louise Borden. (Illus.). (J). 1992. pap. 3.95 (*0-590-44872-2*, Blue Ribbon Bks) Scholastic Inc.

Capsaicin in the Study of Pain. Ed. by John N. Wood. (Neuroscience Perspectives Ser.). (Illus.). 304p. 1993. text ed. 69.95 (*0-12-762855-X*) Acad Pr.

Capsicum. John R. Christopher. Ed. by Lotus Bailey. LC 81-204342. (Illus.). 166p. 1980. pap. 6.95 (*1-879436-09-4*, 99109) Dr Chris Pubns.

Capsize! A Story of Survival in the North Atlantic. Nicolas Angel. Tr. by Alan Wakeman. LC 81-389. (Illus.). 178p. 1981. 15.95 (*0-393-03264-7*) Norton.

Capsized. James Nalepka. 1993. mass mkt. 5.50 (*0-06-109090-5*, Harp PBks) HarpC.

Capsized. large type ed. James Nalepka & Steven Callahan. LC 92-47254. 1993. 24.95 (*0-7927-1544-6*, Curley Lrg Print); pap. 22.95 (*0-7927-1543-8*, Curley Lrg Print) Chivers N Amer.

***Capstone of Faith.** Robert Moss. 176p. 1995. pap. 10.95 (*1-55517-174-5*) CFI Dist.

Capstone of Our Religion: Insights into the Doctrine & Covenants. Millet & Dahl. 11.95 (*0-88494-684-3*) Bookcraft Inc.

Capsule Comments on the Cults. Ross Rainey. 1988. pap. 2.50 (*0-937396-72-9*) Walterick Pubs.

Capsule Course in Black Poetry Writing. Gwendolyn Brooks et al. 64p. (YA). (gr. 12). 1975. pap. 6.00 (*0-910296-32-4*) Broadside Pr.

Capsule of the Mind: Chapters in the Life of Emily Dickinson. Theodore Van Ward. LC 61-13746. 217p. reprint ed. pap. 61.90 (*0-317-09654-0*, 2006437) Bks Demand.

Capsule View of the Bible. Russell Ogden. 1979. pap. 1.50 (*0-88469-045-8*) BMH Bks.

Capsuled in Summer. Everett A. Gillis. (Illus.). 64p. (Orig.). 1985. pap. 9.95 (*0-938328-03-4*) Pisces Pr TX.

Capt. Gougar & His Steamboats. T. J. Linosay. 1987. pap. 5.95 (*0-917914-67-8*) Lindsay Pubns.

Captain. Jan De Hartog. LC 88-23866. (Great War Stories Ser.). (Illus.). 431p. 1988. reprint ed. 24.95 (*0-933852-83-5*) Nautical & Aviation.

Captain. Ambrose E. Gonzales. LC 78-37593. (Black Heritage Library Collection). 1977. reprint ed. 22.95 (*0-8369-8969-4*) Ayer.

Captain Abdul's Pirate School. Colin McNaughton. LC 93-21293. (Illus.). 40p. (J). (ps up). 1994. 16.95 (*1-56402-429-6*) Candlewick Pr.

Captain Africa: The Battle for Egyptica. Dwayne Ferguson. (Illus.). 120p. 1990. pap. 7.95 (*0-9627483-0-7*) African Prince.

Captain Africa: The Battle for Egyptica. Dwayne J. Ferguson. LC 92-78316. (Young Reader's Ser.). (Illus.). 156p. (YA). (gr. 7-10). 1992. reprint ed. 24.95 (*0-86543-335-6*); reprint ed. pap. 9.95 (*0-86543-336-4*) Africa World.

Captain Africa & the Fury of Anubis: The Graphic Novel. Dwayne Ferguson. (Illus.). 96p. (YA). (gr. 4-11). 1994. 29.95 (*0-86543-397-6*); pap. 9.95 (*0-86543-398-4*) Africa World.

Captain Al's Inboard Boat Manual: A Complete Guide to Electric & Mechanical Systems. Al Meads. 1993. pap. 24.95 (*1-883177-51-0*) Phoenix Florida.

Captain America. Lee et al. (Marvel Masterworks Ser.: Vol. 14). 232p. 1990. 34.95 (*0-87135-630-9*) Marvel Entmnt.

Captain America: Bloodstone Hunt. Mark Gruenwald. (Illus.). 1993. pap. 15.95 (*0-87135-972-3*) Marvel Entmnt.

Captain America: Deathlok Lives. 64p. 1993. 4.95 (*0-7851-0019-9*) Marvel Entmnt.

Captain America: Streets of Poison. Mark Gruenwald et al. 128p. 1994. 15.95 (*0-7851-0057-1*) Marvel Entmnt.

Captain America: The Classic Years, 2 vols., 1. Joe Simon & Jack Kirby. (Illus.). 1990. write for info. (*0-87135-647-3*) Marvel Entmnt.

Captain America: The Classic Years, 2 vols., 2. Joe Simon & Jack Kirby. (Illus.). 1990. write for info. (*0-87135-648-1*) Marvel Entmnt.

Captain America: The Classic Years, 2 vols., Set. Joe Simon & Jack Kirby. (Illus.). 1990. boxed 75.00 (*0-87135-649-X*) Marvel Entmnt.

Captain & Joey & the Tumbled down Cabin. Mary J. Joachim. LC 89-81198. (Illus.). 47p. (Orig.). (J). 1990. pap. 4.95 (*0-916383-99-7*) Aegina Pr.

Captain & the Enemy. Graham Greene. 208p. 1989. pap. 7.95 (*0-14-012418-7*, Penguin Bks) Viking Penguin.

Captain & the Enemy. large type ed. Graham Greene. (General Ser.). 256p. 1989. 19.95 (*0-8161-4799-X*, Large Print Bks) Hall.

Captain & the Widow. Donna Winters. Ed. by Anne Severance. LC 89-82617. (Great Lakes Romances Ser.). 192p. (Orig.). 1990. pap. 6.95 (*0-923048-76-6*) Bigwater Pub.

Captain Bennett's Folly. Berry Fleming. 1989. 22.00 (*0-932966-93-4*) Permanent Pr.

Captain Bill McDonald Texas Ranger. Albert B. Paine. LC 86-61298. (Illus.). 454p. 1986. reprint ed. pap. 14.95 (*0-938349-03-1*) State House Pr.

Captain Blackman. John A. Williams. (Classic Reprint Ser.). 348p. 1988. reprint ed. pap. 10.95 (*0-938410-68-7*) Thunders Mouth.

Captain Blood. Rafael Sabatini. 1990. reprint ed. lib. bdg. 21.95 (*0-89968-546-3*) Buccaneer Bks.

Captain Blood - His Odyssey. Raphael Sabatini. 22.95 (*0-8488-1147-X*) Amereon Ltd.

***Captain Blood Returns.** Rafael Sabatini. 1994. lib. bdg. 21.95x (*1-56849-481-5*) Buccaneer Bks.

Captain Blood Returns. Raphael Sabatini. 1976. reprint ed. lib. bdg. 21.95 (*0-89190-742-4*, Rivercity Pr) Amereon Ltd.

Captain Boycott. Philip Rooney. 190p. 1966. reprint ed. 13.95 (*0-900068-90-6*, Pub. by Anvil Bks Ltd IE); reprint ed. pap. 4.95 (*0-900068-27-2*) Irish Bks Media.

Captain Boz & the Rusty Bicycle. Charles Leeuwenburg. (J). 1994. 7.95 (*0-533-10818-7*) Vantage.

Captain Brassbound's Conversion. George Bernard Shaw. Ed. by Rodelle Weintraub. LC 79-56711. (Bernard Shaw Early Texts: Play Manuscripts in Facsimile). 1981. lib. bdg. 20.00 (*0-8240-4586-6*) Garland.

***Captain Brenton's Heritage: The Gospel Message for Southwest Mexico.** Marguerite P. Boyce. (Illus.). 96p. (Orig.). 1994. pap. 10.95 (*1-881576-34-5*) Providence Hse.

Captain Britain. Alan Davis & Jamie Delano. (Illus.). 196p. 1988. pap. 15.95 (*1-85400-020-9*) Marvel Entmnt.

Captain Butterfly. Bob Leuci. 240p. 1987. 16.95 (*0-317-58348-4*) Freundlich.

Captain C. B. McKinney: The Law in South Texas. Chuck Parsons & Gary P. Fitterer. (Illus.). 160p. 1993. 29.95 (*0-9614936-0-7*) C Parsons.

Captain Canot, or Twenty Years of an African Slaver. Ed. by Brantz Mayer. LC 68-29011. (American Negro: His History & Literature, Ser. No. 1). 1969. reprint ed. 32.95 (*0-405-01830-4*) Ayer.

Captain Cat. Syd Hoff. LC 91-27518. (I Can Read Bk.). (Illus.). 48p. (J). (ps-2). 1993. 14.95 (*0-06-020527-X*); lib. bdg. 14.89 (*0-06-020528-8*) HarpC Child Bks.

Captain Cat. Syd Hoff. LC 91-27518. (I Can Read Bk.). (Illus.). 48p. (J). (ps-2). 1994. pap. 3.50 (*0-06-444176-8*, Trophy) HarpC Child Bks.

Captain Caution. Kenneth Roberts. 224p. 1982. pap. 2.95 (*0-449-24509-8*, Crest) Fawcett.

Captain Cavalier. Jackson Gregory. 1976. reprint ed. lib. bdg. 22.95 (*0-88411-281-0*, Aeonian Pr) Amereon Ltd.

An Asterisk (*) at the beginning of an entry indicates that the title is appearing in BIP for the first time.

Captain Charles Stuart: Anglo-American Abolitionist. Anthony J. Barker. LC 85-23703. 328p. 1986. text ed. 42.50 (*0-8071-1256-9*) La State U Pr.

Captain Chip & the March to Victory. Gilbert Morris. (Captain Chip & His Rag Tag Band Ser.). (J). (gr. 4-7). 1994. pap. 5.99 (*0-8024-1584-9*) Moody.

Captain Clapperton's Last Expedition to Africa, 2 vols., Set. Richard Lander. (Illus.). 1967. 65.00 (*0-7146-1827-6*, Pub. by F Cass Pubs UK) Intl Spec Bk.

Captain COMAL Gets Organized. Len Lindsay. (Amazing Adventures of Captain COMAL Ser.). (Illus.). 102p. 1984. pap. 14.95 (*0-928411-01-X*) COMAL Users.

Captain Cook. Jon Noonan. LC 92-8231. (Explorers Ser.). (Illus.). 48p. (J). (gr. 5). 1993. text ed. 12.95 (*0-89686-709-9*, Crstwood Hse) Silver Burdett Pr.

Captain Cook. Mark O'Flynn. 143p. (C). 1990. 30.00 (*0-947087-05-2*, Pub. by Pascoe Pub AT) St Mut.

Captain Cook & the Pacific. David W. Sylvester. Ed. by Marjorie Reeves. (Then & There Ser.). (Illus.). 92p. (YA). (gr. 7-12). 1971. reprint ed. pap. text ed. 4.75 (*0-582-20462-3*) Longman.

Captain Cook Cookbook. Robert Steffy. 1979. 2.50 (*0-915696-11-8*) Determined Prods.

Captain Cook in the Pacific. Robert D. Craig. (Pamphlets Polynesia Ser.: No. 1). (Illus.). 1978. pap. 3.50 (*0-939154-00-5*) Inst Polynesian.

Captain Cook, R. N. The Resolute Mariner. Thomas Vaughan & C. M. Murray-Oliver. LC 74-82649. (Illus.). 113p. 1974. 11.95 (*0-87595-049-3*) Oregon Hist.

***Captain Cook's Endeavour.** Karl H. Marquardt. (Anatomy of the Ship Ser.). (Illus.). 138p. 1995. 36.95 (*1-55750-118-1*) Naval Inst Pr.

Captain Coranto. large type ed. Julian Spilsbury. 448p. 1988. 15.95 (*0-7089-1807-7*) Ulverscroft.

Captain Cox, His Ballads & Books, or Robert Laneham's Letter. Robert Laneham. Ed. by Frederick J. Furnivall. LC 68-57998. (Ballad Society, London. Publications: No. 7). reprint ed. 30.00 (*0-404-50823-5*) AMS Pr.

Captain Cut-Throat. John D. Carr. 306p. 1988. pap. 3.95 (*0-88184-437-3*) Carroll & Graf.

Captain David. Miriam Klugman. 100p. (J). 1991. 9.95 (*1-56062-095-1*) CIS Comm.

Captain David Grief. Jack London. Orig. Title: Son of the Sun. 332p. 1987. reprint ed. pap. 5.95 (*0-935180-34-6*) Mutual Pub HI.

Captain Ding, the Double-Decker Pirate. David Cox. (Illus.). 32p. (J). (ps-1). 1993. 17.95 (*0-09-176365-7*, Pub. by Hutchinson UK) Trafalgar.

Captain Drowns. Preston A. Pairo, III. (Ocean City Mysteries Ser.). 177p. (Orig.). 1986. pap. 2.95 (*0-9616584-0-1*) Maryland Locale.

Captain Eco & the Fate of the Earth. Jonathon Porritt & Ellis Nadler. LC 91-60142. (Illus.). 48p. (J). (gr. 3 up). 1991. 13.95 (*1-879431-12-2*); lib. bdg. 14.99 (*1-879431-27-0*) Dorling Kindersley.

Captain Elias Pelletreau, Long Island Silversmith. M. C. Weaks. 1966. pap. 8.95 (*0-911660-04-6*) Yankee Peddler.

Captain Fiddle's Tune Book. Ryan J. Thomson. (Illus.). 45p. (Orig.). 1988. pap. 7.95 (*0-931877-09-1*) Captain Fiddle Pubns.

Captain, Fire Department. Jack Rudman. (Career Examination Ser.: C-120). 1994. pap. 39.95 (*0-8373-0120-3*) Nat Learn.

Captain Flounder, His Sole Brothers & Friends. Tony L. Bozanich. Ed. by Patricia Isaksen. (Illus.). 16p. (J). (ps-4). 1984. pap. 4.95 (*0-930655-00-1*) Antarctic Pr.

Captain from Connecticut: The Life & Naval Times of Isaac Hull. Linda M. Maloney. (Illus.). 540p. 1986. text ed. 47.50 (*0-930350-90-1*) NE U Pr.

Captain Grey. Avi. LC 92-37643. 160p. (J). 1993. 15.00 (*0-688-12233-7*) Morrow Jr Bks.

Captain Grey. Avi. LC 76-41182. (Illus.). (J). (gr. 5 up). 1977. 5.95 (*0-394-83484-4*) Pantheon.

Captain Grey. Avi. LC 92-37643. 160p. (J). (gr. 5 up). 1993. pap. 3.95 (*0-688-12234-5*, Pub. by Beech Tree Bks) Morrow.

Captain Hardscratch & Others: A Norwegian Immigrant's Recollections of Growing up on a Remote Island in Alaska. Ralph Soberg. LC 92-71217. (Illus.). 72p. (Orig.). 1992. pap. 10.50 (*0-9625429-3-8*) Hardscratch Pr.

Captain Harlock Returns. Robert W. Gibson. Ed. by Chris Ulm. (Illus.). 86p. (J). 1991. pap. 9.95 (*0-944735-75-4*) Malibu Graphics.

Captain Harlock Television Scripts, Vol. 1. Leiji Matsumoto. Ed. by Mickie Villa & Tom Mason. (Illus.). 135p. (YA). 1990. pap. 19.95 (*0-944735-63-0*) Malibu Graphics.

Captain Hawaii. Anthony D. Arkin. LC 94-2683. 256p. (J). (gr. 6-9). 1994. 15.00 (*0-06-021508-9*) HarpC Child Bks.

Captain Hawaii. Anthony D. Arkin. 224p. (J). (gr. 3-7). 1994. lib. bdg. 14.89 (*0-06-021509-7*) HarpC Child Bks.

Captain Hook: A Pilot's Tragedy & Triumph in the Vietnam War. Wynn F. Foster. LC 92-5089. (Illus.). 242p. 1992. 28.95 (*1-55750-256-0*) Naval Inst Pr.

Captain Hook Affair. Humphrey Carpenter. (J). write for info. (*0-318-59418-8*) HM.

Captain Jack Crawford: Buckskin Poet, Scout, & Showman. Darlis A. Miller. LC 93-8611. (Illus.). 384p. 1993. 45.00x (*0-8263-1449-X*) U of NM Pr.

Captain Jack, Modoc Renegade. Doris P. Payne. (Illus.). 272p. 1979. pap. 9.95 (*0-8323-0340-2*) Binford Mort.

Captain Jack Zodiac. Michael Kandel. 224p. 1991. 13.95 (*0-9623824-6-9*) Broken Mirrors Pr.

Captain Jack Zodiac. limited ed. Michael Kandel. 224p. 1991. 50.00 (*0-9623824-7-7*) Broken Mirrors Pr.

Captain Jack's Almanac: Puget Sound Edition, 1993. Jeff Renner & Joseph Kawaky. (Illus.). 432p. (Orig.). 1993. pap. 11.95 (*1-878258-32-X*) Marine Trade.

Captain Jack's Almanac: 1992 Puget Sound Edition. Ed. by Joseph Kawaky. (Illus.). 416p. (Orig.). 1992. pap. 9.95 (*1-878258-25-7*) Marine Trade.

Captain Jack's Pocket Almanac: 1990 Pacific Northwest Edition. Ed. by Joseph Kawaky. (Illus.). 408p. (Orig.). 1989. pap. 4.95 (*0-685-28983-4*) Marine Trade.

Captain James Cook. Ruth Harley. LC 78-18044. (Illus.). 48p. (J). (gr. 4-7). 1979. lib. bdg. 10.59 (*0-89375-177-4*); pap. 3.50 (*0-89375-169-3*) Troll Assocs.

***Captain James Cook.** Aldyth Morris. LC 94-48698. (Illus.). 1995. pap. 8.95 (*0-8248-1670-6*) UH Pr.

Captain James Cook: A Biography. Richard Hough. 500p. 1995. 29.95 (*0-393-03680-4*) Norton.

Captain James Cook & the Explorers of the Pacific. David Haney. Ed. by William H. Goetzmann. (World Explorers Ser.). (Illus.). 112p. (YA). (gr. 5 up). 1992. lib. bdg. 18.95 (*0-7910-1310-3*) Chelsea Hse.

Captain Jason & Other Poems. Louise F. Underhill. 52p. 1979. 10.00 (*0-685-55377-9*) Underhill Ent.

***Captain Jim & the Killer Whales.** Carol A. Amato. LC 95-13657. (Young Readers Ser.). (Illus.). (J). 1995. write for info. (*0-8120-9289-9*) Barron.

Captain Jinks, Hero. Ernest H. Crosby. LC 68-57519. (Muckrakers Ser.). reprint ed. lib. bdg. 18.75 (*0-8398-0282-X*) Irvington.

Captain John McCall, Seventeen Twenty-Six to Eighteen Twelve: His Ancestors & His Descendants. Clare M. McCall. LC 85-18767. (Illus.). 185p. 1985. lib. bdg. 40.00 (*0-88082-012-8*) New Eng Hist.

Captain John Smith. rev. ed. Everett Emerson. (Twayne's United States Authors Ser.). 180p. 1993. text ed. 21.95 (*0-8057-3989-0*, Twayne) Macmillan.

Captain John Smith: A Reference Guide. Kevin J. Hayes. (Reference Guides to Literature Ser.). 304p. (C). 1991. text ed. 45.00 (*0-8161-7275-7*, Hall Reference) Macmillan.

Captain John Smith: A Select Edition of His Writings. John Smith. Ed. by Karen O. Kupperman. LC 87-21485. (Institute of Early American History & Culture Ser.). (Illus.). xiv, 290p. (C). 1988. 39.95 (*0-8078-1778-3*); pap. 12.95 (*0-8078-4208-7*) U of NC Pr.

Captain John Sutter: Sacramento Valley's Sainted Sinner. Richard Dillon. LC 67-21511. (Illus.). 380p. 1981. reprint ed. pap. 12.95 (*0-934136-15-7*) Western Tanager.

Captain Joshua Slocum: The Life & Voyages of America's Best Known Sailor. Victor Slocum. (Illus.). 384p. 1993. pap. 16.50 (*0-924486-52-X*) Sheridan.

Captain Kidd & the War Against the Pirates. Robert C. Ritchie. 320p. 1989. reprint ed. pap. text ed. 14.95 (*0-674-09502-2*) HUP.

Captain Kidd's Cat. Robert Lawson. (Illus.). (J). (gr. 2-4). 1984. mass mkt. 7.95 (*0-316-51735-6*) Little.

***Captain Lavender.** Medbh McGuckian. LC 94-61972. 83p. 1994. 15.95 (*0-916390-67-5*); pap. 9.95 (*0-916390-66-7*) Wake Forest.

Captain Lee Hall of Texas. Dora N. Raymond. LC 73-5131. (Illus.). 384p. 1982. 29.95 (*0-8061-0086-9*) U of Okla Pr.

Captain Lightfoot. W. R. Burnett. 224p. reprint ed. lib. bdg. 19.95 (*0-89190-495-6*, Rivercity Pr) Amereon Ltd.

Captain Mansana & Other Stories. Bjornstjerne Bjornson. Tr. by Rasmos B. Anderson. LC 79-103494. (Short Story Index Reprint Ser.). 1977. 20.95 (*0-8369-3236-6*) Ayer.

Captain Matthew Arbuckle: A Documentary Biography. Joseph C. Jefferds. LC 80-68333. (Illus.). 112p. 1981. 15.00 (*0-914498-03-7*) WV Hist Ed Found.

Captain Maximus: Short Stories & Screen Treatment. Barry Hannah. Ed. by Gordon Lish. LC 84-48738. 128p. 1985. 11.95 (*0-394-54458-7*) Knopf.

Captain Miraculous & the Bound for Glory Kid. Sterling Beasley. (Illus.). 32p. (Orig.). (J). 1993. pap. 4.95 (*0-8059-3421-9*) Dorrance.

Captain Monsoon. large type ed. Victor Suthren. LC 93-10505. 1993. 17.95 (*1-56054-746-4*) Thorndike Pr.

Captain Moroni & the Title of Liberty. Sherrie Johnson. 1994. pap. 4.95 (*0-87579-813-6*) Deseret Bk.

***Captain Moses Rich Colman: Master Mariner: American Autobiography.** Moses Coleman. 119p. 1995. lib. bdg. 69.00 (*0-7812-8486-4*) Rprt Serv.

Captain Murrells Savory Seafood Recipes. William H. Martin & Wilma D. Martin. (Illus.). 133p. 1990. spiral bd. 13.95 (*0-9630689-0-3*) Rum Gully.

Captain Nathan Hale..., Major John Palsgrave Wyllys... Friends & Yale Classmates, Who Died in Their Country's Service. George Dudley Seymour. LC 33-36986. (Illus.). 296p. 1933. 15.00 (*0-318-16564-3*) Anderson Hse Mus.

Captain Nemo Cookbook Papers. Hal Painter. (Illus.). 144p. 1986. 10.95 (*0-87742-206-0*) Intl Marine.

Captain Noah. Hindi Brooks. (Illus.). 36p. (Orig.). (J). (gr. 1 up). 1989. pap. 4.00 (*0-88680-317-9*); 15.00 (*0-88680-318-7*) I E Clark.

Captain of All These Men of Death. J. Arthur Myers. 300p. 1977. 14.80 (*0-87527-160-X*) Green.

Captain of Cavalry. large type ed. Vivian Stuart. (Ulverscroft Ser.). 496p. 1994. 21.95 (*0-7089-3031-X*) Ulverscroft.

Captain of My Heart. Danelle Harmon. 432p. (Orig.). 1992. mass mkt. 4.50 (*0-380-76676-0*) Avon.

Captain of Our Salvation: A Study in the Patristic Exegesis of Hebrews. Rowan Greer. 325p. 1973. lib. bdg. 67.50 (*3-16-134822-2*, Pub. by J C B Mohr GW) Coronet Bks.

Captain of the Gray-Horse Troop. Hamlin Garland. LC 73-104460. reprint ed. lib. bdg. 16.00 (*0-8398-0653-1*) Irvington.

Captain of the Grayhorse Troop. Hamlin Garland. (Collected Works of Hamlin Garland). 1988. reprint ed. lib. bdg. 79.00 (*0-7812-1231-6*) Rprt Serv.

Captain of the Grayhorse Troop see Collected Works of Hamlin Garland

Captain of the Phantom: The Story of Henry Jackson Sargent, Jr., 1834-1862, As Revealed in Family Letters. Henry J. Sargent, Jr. (Illus.). xviii, 72p. 1967. 5.95 (*0-913372-00-5*) Mystic Seaport.

Captain of the Phantom Presidio: A History of the Presidio of Fronteras, Sonora, New Spain, 1686-1735, Including the Inspection by Brig. Pedro de Rivera, 1726. Fay J. Smith. LC 91-78370. (Spain Ser.: Vol. 14). (Illus.). 217p. 1993. 29.50 (*0-87062-216-1*) A H Clark.

Captain of the Polestar, & Other Tales. Arthur Conan Doyle. LC 70-116950. (Short Story Index Reprint Ser.). 1977. 12.95 (*0-8369-3453-9*) Ayer.

Captain or Colonel: The Soldier in Milton's Life & Art. Robert T. Fallon. LC 84-2308. (Illus.). 288p. 1985. 29.00 (*0-8262-0447-3*) U of Mo Pr.

Captain Orinoco's Onion. Cecily Matthews. LC 93-2802. (J). 1994. write for info. (*0-383-03680-1*) SRA Schl Grp.

Captain Orkle's Treasure. Harriet Micocci. (Illus.). (J). (gr. 3-7). 1961. 10.95 (*0-8392-3003-6*) Astor-Honor.

Captain Pantoja & Special Services. Mario Vargas Llosa. 1990. pap. 12.00 (*0-374-52236-7*, Noonday) FS&G.

Captain Pease: U. S. Coast Guard Pioneer. Florence Kern. 1982. 7.95 (*0-913377-10-4*) Alised.

Captain, Police Department. Jack Rudman. (Career Examination Ser.: C-121). 1994. pap. 39.95 (*0-8373-0121-1*) Nat Learn.

Captain Remembers. Sandra Russell. (Illus.). 141p. (Orig.). 1993. pap. 12.95 (*0-910303-42-8*) Writers Pub Serv.

***Captain Salvation: Jesus the Light of the World.** Bruce Yeo. 32p. (J). (gr. 4-12). 1994. pap. 1.95 (*0-9644578-0-6*) Strtlight Christ Comics.

Captain Sam. Vanessa Vargo. 1991. 2.99 (*0-517-06078-7*) Random Hse Value.

Captain Sam Grant, 1822-1861. Lloyd Lewis. 1991. pap. 13.95 (*0-316-52348-8*) Little.

Captain Samuel Tucker: Continental Navy 1747-1833. Philip C. Smith. LC 76-17150. 1976. 12.50 (*0-88389-058-5*, Essx Institute) Peabody Essex Mus.

***Captain Scott Moore's Snook Fishing Secrets.** G. B. Knowles. LC 94-96379. (Illus.). (Orig.). 1994. pap. text ed. 12.95 (*0-9642942-0-6*) Seven Pines.

Captain Scruffy. Tom Allen & Patsy Allen. (Illus.). 32p. (J). (ps-1). 1993. 15.95 (*0-460-88104-3*, J M Dent & Sons) Trafalgar.

Captain Sebastian: Fifty-Two Talks to Boys & Girls. F. Chenhalls Williams. 96p. 1961. reprint ed. pap. 3.50 (*0-87921-007-9*) Attic Pr.

Captain Shakespear. H. V. Winstone. 9.95 (*0-7043-2201-3*, Pub. by Quartet UK) Charles River Bks.

Captain Simon Metcalfe, Pioneer Fur Trader on the Northwest Coast, 1787-1794. Rhys Richards. (Alaska History Ser.: No. 37). 1991. 18.00 (*0-919642-37-3*) Limestone Pr.

Captain Sinbad. Graham Diamond. 250p. 1980. pap. 2.25 (*0-449-14341-4*, GM) Fawcett.

Captain Singleton. Daniel DeFoe. 1976. 22.95 (*0-8488-0978-5*) Amereon Ltd.

Captain Singleton. Daniel Defoe. Ed. by Shiv K. Kumar. (World's Classics Ser.). 320p. 1990. pap. 6.95 (*0-19-282200-4*) OUP.

Captain Sir Richard Francis Burton: The Secret Agent Who Made the Pilgrimage to Mecca, Discovered the Kama Sutra, & Brought the Arabian Nights to the West. Edward Rice. 512p. 1990. text ed. 35.00 (*0-684-19137-7*, Scribners) S&S Trade.

Captain Snap & the Children of Vinegar Lane. Roni Schotter. LC 88-22489. (Illus.). 32p. (J). (ps-3). 1989. 15.95 (*0-531-05797-6*); lib. bdg. 15.99 (*0-531-08397-7*) Orchard Bks Watts.

Captain Snap & the Children of Vinegar Lane. Roni Schotter. LC 88-22489. (Illus.). 32p. (J). (ps-3). 1993. pap. 5.95 (*0-531-07038-7*) Orchard Bks Watts.

Captain Steele: The Early Career of Richard Steele. Calhoun Winston. LC 64-16314. 235p. reprint ed. pap. 67.00 (*0-317-42061-5*, 2025881) Bks Demand.

Captain Stern: Running Out of Time, No. 3. Bernie Wrightson. Ed. by Phil Amara. (Illus.). 48p. (YA). (gr. 6 up). 1994. pap. 4.95 (*0-87816-230-5*) Kitchen Sink.

Captain Stern: Running Out of Time, No. 4. Bernie Wrightson. Ed. by Phil Amara. (Illus.). 48p. (J). (gr. 4 up). 1994. pap. 4.95 (*0-87816-231-3*) Kitchen Sink.

Captain Sternn: Running Out of Time. Bernie Wrightson. Ed. by Mark Martin. (Illus.). 48p. 1993. 4.95 (*1-56862-007-1*) Tundra MA.

Captain Stormfield's Visit to Heaven. Samuel L. Clemens. (Works of Samuel Clemens). 1989. reprint ed. lib. bdg. 79.00 (*0-685-28378-X*) Rprt Serv.

Captain Swing. Larry Duplechan. LC 93-28812. 184p. 1993. 15.95 (*1-55583-234-2*) Alyson Pubns.

Captain, the Countess & Cobbie the Swabby. Mary Hollingsworth. LC 92-4714. (J). (ps-3). 1992. pap. 8.99 (*0-7814-0967-5*, Chariot Bks) Chariot Family.

Captain, the Gypsy & the Giant Bird. Larry Cormier. Ed. by Mary-Ann S. Bruni. (Texas Ser.: Vol. 3). (Illus.). 48p. (J). (gr. k-8). 1986. 12.95 (*0-935857-07-9*); pap. write for info. (*0-935857-08-7*) Texart.

Captain Thomas Macdonough: Delaware Born Hero of the Battle of Lake Champlain. Virginia M. Burdick. (Illus.). 100p. (Orig.). 1991. pap. write for info. (*0-924117-04-4*) Delaware HP.

Captain Thomas Stukeley. LC 70-133643. (Tudor Facsimile Texts. Old English Plays Ser.: No. 109). reprint ed. 49.50 (*0-404-53409-0*) AMS Pr.

Captain Thunder & Blue Bolt, Bk. 1. Roy Thomas & Dann Thomas. (Illus.). 80p. (Orig.). 1988. pap. 9.95 (*0-317-91225-9*) Heroic Pub CA.

Captain Trips: A Biography of Jerry Garcia. Sandy Troy. 352p. 1994. 24.95 (*1-56025-076-3*) Thunders Mouth.

***Captain Trips: A Biography of Jerry Garcia.** Sandy Troy. (Illus.). 352p. 1995. pap. 13.95 (*1-56025-090-9*) Thunders Mouth.

Captain Video Book: The Du Mont Television Network Story. Neil Sullivan. (Illus.). 288p. 1992. 22.95 (*0-9625493-0-4*) Loosestrife Pr.

***Captain Visual's Big Book of Balloon Art! A Complete Book of Balloonology for Beginners & Advanced Twisters.** Captain Visual. (Illus.). 144p. 1995. pap. 9.95 (*0-8065-1641-0*, Citadel Pr) Carol Pub Group.

Captain Whiz-Bang. Diane Stanley. LC 86-16432. (Illus.). 32p. (J). (ps-2). 1987. 14.00 (*0-688-06226-1*); lib. bdg. 13.93 (*0-688-06227-X*) Morrow Jr Bks.

Captain Whopper. Albert G. Miller. (Illus.). (J). (gr. 3-7). 1968. 10.95 (*0-8392-3058-3*) Astor-Honor.

Captain Zomo. Alta M. Rymer. LC 79-67651. (Tales of Planet Artembo Ser.: Bk. 2). (Illus.). 48p. (Orig.). (J). (gr. 5-7). 1993. 20.00 (*0-9600792-2-X*) Rymer Bks.

Captains. Robert Brewer. 1993. pap. 9.95 (*1-878901-46-X*) Hampton Roads Pub Co.

Captains All. William W. Jacobs. LC 71-86147. (Short Story Index Reprint Ser.). 1977. 19.95 (*0-8369-3051-7*) Ayer.

Captains & Mariners of Early Maryland. Raphael Semmes. 1979. 66.95 (*0-405-10626-2*) Ayer.

Captains & the Kings. Taylor Caldwell. 1983. mass mkt. 5.95 (*0-449-20562-2*, Crest) Fawcett.

Captains & the Kings. Taylor Caldwell. 1994. reprint ed. lib. bdg. 37.95 (*1-56849-258-8*) Buccaneer Bks.

Captains & the Kings Depart: Life in India, 1928-1946. Jack Bazalgette. 1984. 35.00 (*0-317-43638-4*, Pub. by Amate Pr Ltd UK) St Mut.

Captain's Angel. large type ed. Marie-Louise Hall. 1993. 18.95 (*0-263-13548-9*, Pub. by Mills & Boon Ltd UK) Chivers N Amer.

Captain's Atlas: Jet Route Two Edition. Mark Map Co. Staff. (Illus.). 80p. 1994. pap. 15.95 (*0-916413-24-1*) Aviation.

***Captain's Beard.** Laura J. Bobrow. (Illus.). 32p. (J). (gr. k-3). 1995. pap. 3.99 (*0-87406-730-8*) Willowisp Pr.

Captain's Best Mate: The Journal of Mary Chipman Lawrence on the Whaler Addison, 1856-1860. Mary C. Lawrence. Ed. by Stanton Garner. LC 83-40018. (Illus.). 335p. 1986. pap. 16.95 (*0-87451-366-9*) U Pr of New Eng.

Captain's Bride: A Tale of the War & the Deserter's Daughter. William D. Herrington. Ed. by W. Keats Sparrow. (Illus.). xi, 80p. 1990. pap. 4.00 (*0-86526-247-0*) NC Archives.

Captain's Captive. Christine Dorsey. 1991. mass mkt. 4.50 (*0-8217-3508-X*) Zebra.

Captain's Coastal Directions: Port to Port Course Plans for Ocean Going Vessels. Doug Hines. 416p. 1992. pap. 64.95 (*0-9632803-0-9*) D Hines Assocs.

Captain's Conquest. Christine Elliot. 1989. pap. 3.95 (*0-8217-2620-X*) Zebra.

Captains Courageous. Rudyard Kipling. (Airmont Classics Ser.). (J). (gr. 6 up). 1964. pap. 1.75 (*0-8049-0027-2*, CL-27) Airmont.

Captains Courageous. Rudyard Kipling. 160p. 1985. pap. 2.50 (*0-553-21190-0*, Bantam Classics) Bantam.

Captains Courageous. Rudyard Kipling. (Illustrated Classics Collection 3). 64p. 1994. pap. 3.60 (*1-56103-522-X*) Lake Pub Co.

Captains Courageous. Rudyard Kipling. 176p. (J). (gr. 6). 1964. pap. 2.95 (*0-451-52381-4*, CJ1751, Sig Classics) NAL-Dutton.

Captains Courageous. Rudyard Kipling. 192p. 1992. pap. 2.50 (*0-8125-0438-0*) Tor Bks.

Captains Courageous. Rudyard Kipling. pap. 2.95 (*0-89375-607-5*) Troll Assocs.

***Captains Courageous.** Rudyard Kipling. Ed. by Leonee Ormond. (World's Classics Ser.). 224p. 1995. 8.95 (*0-19-282929-7*) OUP.

Captains Courageous. abr. ed. Rudyard Kipling. Ed. by John N. Fago. (Now Age Illustrated III Ser.). (Illus.). (J). (gr. 4-12). 1977. pap. text ed. 2.95 (*0-88301-262-6*) Pendulum Pr.

Captains Courageous. large type ed. Rudyard Kipling. (Classics Ser.). 227p. 1982. 23.95 (*0-7089-8032-5*, Charnwood) Ulverscroft.

Captains Courageous. Rudyard Kipling. reprint ed. lib. bdg. 18.95 (*0-88411-818-5*, Aeonian Pr) Amereon Ltd.

Captains Courageous. Rudyard Kipling. 1991. reprint ed. lib. bdg. 21.95 (*1-56849-080-1*) Buccaneer Bks.

Captains Courageous: Student Activity Book. Marcia Sohl & Gerald Dackerman. (Now Age Illustrated Ser.). (Illus.). 1976. student ed 1.25 (*0-88301-286-3*) Pendulum Pr.

Captains Courageous Readalong. Rudyard Kipling. (Illustrated Classics Collection 3). 64p. 1994. audio, pap. 13.50 (*1-56103-524-6*) Lake Pub Co.

Captain's Craps Revolution. 2nd ed. Frank Scoblete. 160p. 1995. pap. text ed. 21.95 (*1-882173-03-1*) Paone Pr.

Captains, Curates & Cockneys: The English in the Pacific Northwest. Frank L. Green. LC 81-620029. (Illus.). 105p. 1982. pap. 6.00 (*0-917048-52-0*) Wash St Hist Soc.

Captain's Daughter. Ed. by Aleksandr Pushkin. 248p. 1987. 30.00 (*0-317-92449-4*) St Mut.

Captain's Daughter: Kapitanskaya Dochka. Pushkin. Ed. by Fruma Gottschalk. (C). reprint ed. pap. text ed. 17.95 (*0-900186-12-7*, Pub. by Duckworth UK) Focus Info Gr.

Captain's Daughter & Other Stories. Aleksandr Pushkin. 1957. pap. 8.00 (*0-394-70714-1*, Vin) Random.

Captain's Daughter & Other Stories. Aleksandr Pushkin. 1992. 15.00 (*0-679-41331-6*, Everymans Lib) Knopf.

Captain's Daughter & Other Stories. Alexander Pushkin. 22.95 (*0-89190-231-7*, Am Repr) Amereon Ltd.

Captain's Daughters of Martha's Vineyard. Eliot E. Macy. LC 78-62650. (How We Lived Ser.: No. 1). 1979. 12.95 (*0-85699-141-4*); pap. 7.95 (*0-85699-142-2*) Chatham Pr.

C

Captain's Death Bed & Other Essays. Virginia Woolf. LC 50-7411. 248p. 1973. reprint ed. pap. 9.95 (*0-15-615395-5*, Harvest Bks) HarBrace.

Captain's Doxy. Lafayette Hammet. 480p. 1991. reprint ed. pap. 4.95 (*0-8439-3081-0*) Dorchester Pub Co.

Captains from Devon: The Great Elizabethan Seafarers Who Won the World for England. Helen H. Miller. LC 85-15712. (Illus.). 256p. 1985. 16.95 (*0-912697-27-X*) Algonquin Bks.

Captain's Guide to Liferaft Survival. Michael Cargal. (Illus.). 200p. 1990. 24.95 (*0-924486-00-7*) Sheridan.

Captain's Honor. braille ed. David Dvorkin & Daniel Dvorkin. 359p. 1990. vinyl bd. 28.72 (*1-56956-206-7*, BR8235) W A T Braille.

Captain's Honour. Daniel Dvorkin & David Dvorkin. (Star Trek: The Next Generation Ser.: No. 8). (Orig.). 1991. mass mkt. 5.50 (*0-671-74140-3*) PB.

Captain's Inheritance. Carola Dunn. 256p. 1994. mass mkt. 3.99 (*0-8217-4665-0*) Zebra.

Captain's Ladies. Sandra Riley. 384p. 1985. reprint ed. pap. 3.75 (*0-8439-2258-3*) Dorchester Pub Co.

Captain's Lady. Rachel Edwards. 240p. (Orig.). 1980. pap. 1.95 (*0-89083-640-X*) Zebra.

***Captain's Lady.** large type ed. Paula Marshall. (Legacy of Love Ser.). 1994. 18.95 (*0-263-14011-3*, Pub. by Mills & Boon Ltd UK) Chivers N Amer.

Captain's Lady: Cookbook-Personal Journal Circa Massachusetts 1837-1917, Vol. I: The Early Years. Barbara D. Jasmin. (Illus.). 192p. 1986. pap. write for info. (*0-9609534-1-8*) Captains Lady.

Captain's Lady: Cookbook-Personal Journal Circa Massachusetts 1837-1917, Vol. II. Ed. by Barbara D. Jasmin. LC 82-90816. (Illus.). 178p. 1982. pap. 10.95 (*0-9609534-0-X*) Captains Lady.

Captains of Consciousness. Stuart Ewen. LC 75-34432. 1977. pap. text ed. 6.95 (*0-07-019846-2*) McGraw.

Captains of Industry: Or, Men of Business Who Did Something Besides Making Money; a Book for Young Americans. James Parton. LC 72-2660. (Essay Index Reprint Ser.). 1977. reprint ed. 27.95 (*0-8369-2853-9*) Ayer.

Captains of the Civil War: Chronicle of the Blue & the Gray. William C. Wood. (History - United States Ser.). 424p. 1992. reprint ed. lib. bdg. 99.00 (*0-7812-6175-9*) Rprt Serv.

Captains of the Old Steam Navy: Makers of the American Naval Tradition, 1840-1880. Ed. by James C. Bradford. LC 86-16399. (Illus.). 356p. 1986. 35.00 (*0-87021-013-0*) Naval Inst Pr.

Captains of the Sands. Jorge Amado. 256p. 1988. pap. 7.95 (*0-380-89718-0*) Avon.

Captains of the Wilderness. Carl R. Baldwin. 317p. 1986. 21.95 (*0-318-22522-0*) Tiger Rose Pub.

Captain's Orders. Susan Connell. (Loveswept Ser.: No. 697). 1994. pap. 3.50 (*0-553-44439-5*, Loveswept) Bantam.

Captains Outrageous - For Doom the Bell Tolls. Roy V. Young. 320p. (Orig.). 1994. pap. 4.95 (*1-56076-855-X*) TSR Inc.

Captain's Table. large type ed. Alex Stuart. 416p. 1988. 21.95 (*0-7089-1823-9*) Ulverscroft.

Captain's Tale. Harold Taylor. 176p. (C). 1988. 40.00 (*0-86138-031-2*, Pub. by T Dalton UK) St Mut.

Captain's Verses. Pablo Neruda. Tr. & Intro. by Donald D. Walsh. LC 72-80977. 160p. (ENG & SPA.). 1972. pap. 8.95 (*0-8112-0457-X*, NDP345) New Directions.

Captain's Vixen. Wanda Owen. 400p. (Orig.). 1981. pap. 2.50 (*0-89083-709-0*) Zebra.

Captain's War: The Letters & Diaries of William H. S. Burgwyn, 1861-1865. Ed. by Herbert M. Schiller. LC 93-29312. (Illus.). 240p. (C). 1994. 24.95 (*0-942597-52-4*) White Mane Pub.

Captain's Wife: The South American Journals of Mario Graham 1821-23. Elizabeth Mavor. 208p. 1993. 39.95 (*0-297-81296-3*) Trafalgar.

Captif d'Yvoire. Steven Estvanik. (Illus.). 1984. 5.95 (*0-940244-19-5*) Flying Buffalo.

Caption Workbook. Nan Decker. (Caption Kit Ser.). (Illus.). 27p. (J). (gr. 5-8). 1984. pap. text ed. 1.95 (*0-913072-61-3*) Natl Assn Deaf.

Captions & Graphics for Low Budget Video. Robin Blythe-Lor. (Illus.). 123p. 1992. pap. 39.95 (*0-240-51312-6*, Focal) Buttrwrth-Heinemann.

Captivated. Nora Roberts. 1992. mass mkt. 3.39 (*0-373-09768-9*, 5-09768-8) Silhouette.

Captivated. large type ed. Nora Roberts. LC 93-620. 1993. pap. 17.95 (*1-56054-714-6*) Thorndike Pr.

Captivated Hearts. Valerie King. 320p. 1993. mass mkt. 3.99 (*0-8217-4139-X*) Zebra.

Captivating Cats. James Armstrong. 1991. pap. 14.95 (*1-55912-150-5*) CEDCO Pub.

Captive. 208p. 1993. pap. 5.95 (*1-56201-025-5*) Blue Moon Bks.

Captive. Parris A. Bonds. 384p. (Orig.). 1993. pap. 4.99 (*0-8439-3491-3*) Dorchester Pub Co.

Captive. Colleen Faulkner. 416p. 1994. mass mkt. 4.99 (*0-8217-4683-9*) Zebra.

***Captive.** Hansen. 1995. mass mkt. (*0-590-41624-3*) Scholastic Inc.

Captive. Joyce Hansen. LC 93-83134. (Illus.). 128p. (J). (gr. 3 up). 1994. 13.95 (*0-590-41625-1*, Scholastic Hardcover) Scholastic Inc.

Captive. Clint Hawkins. (Saddle Tramp Ser.: No. 2). (Orig.). 1992. mass mkt. 3.50 (*0-06-100332-8*, Harp PBks) HarpC.

Captive. Victoria Holt. 1990. mass mkt. 5.95 (*0-449-21817-1*, Crest) Fawcett.

Captive. Scott O'Dell. 244p. (J). (gr. 7 up). 1979. 14.95 (*0-395-27811-2*) HM.

Captive. L. J. Smith. (Secret Circle Ser.: No. 2). (YA). 1992. mass mkt. 3.99 (*0-06-106715-6*, Harp PBks) HarpC.

Captive. large type ed. Victoria Holt. LC 90-34617. 609p. 1990. reprint ed. lib. bdg. 20.95 (*1-56054-022-2*) Thorndike Pr.

Captive. Marcel Proust. 1987. reprint ed. lib. bdg. 22.95 (*0-89966-582-9*) Buccaneer Bks.

Captive: The True Story of the Captivity of Mrs. Mary Rowlandson among the Indians & God's Faithfulness to Her in Her Time of Trial. rev. ed. Mary Rowlandson. (Illus.). 96p. 1988. reprint ed. 14.95 (*0-929408-00-4*, E87R895R69) Amer Eagle Pubns Inc.

Captive: The True Story of the Captivity of Mrs. Mary Rowlandson among the Indians & God's Faithfulness to Her in Her Time of Trial. rev. ed. Mary Rowlandson. (Illus.). 44p. 1991. pap. 4.95 (*0-929408-03-9*) Amer Eagle Pubns Inc.

Captive - The Fugitive, Vol. 5. Marcel Proust. 1993. 19.50 (*0-679-42477-6*, Modern Lib) H Leonard.

Captive American: How to Stop Being a Political Prisoner in Your Own Country. Lee H. Brandenburg. 304p. 1988. 13.95 (*0-929158-00-8*) Hampton Bks.

Captive Americans: Prisoners During the American Revolution. Larry G. Bowman. LC 75-36984. viii, 146p. 1976. pap. 4.50 (*0-8214-0229-3*) Ohio U Pr.

Captive & the Free. Joyce Cary. 24.95 (*0-88411-309-4*, Aeonian Pr) Amereon Ltd.

Captive Angel. Elaine Crawford. (Wildflower Ser.). 352p. (Orig.). 1992. mass mkt. 4.99 (*1-55773-766-5*) Diamond.

Captive Angel. Deana James. 1989. mass mkt. 4.50 (*0-8217-2524-6*) Zebra.

Captive Audience. Bob Perelman. 1988. per. 6.00 (*0-935724-36-2*) Figures.

***Captive Bold.** Judie Kleng. LC 94-90115. 128p. (Orig.). 1995. pap. 8.00 (*1-56002-448-8*, Univ Edtns) Aegina Pr.

Captive Bride. Carol Finch. 496p. 1987. pap. 3.95 (*0-8217-1984-X*) Zebra.

Captive Bride. Johanna Lindsey. 1977. mass mkt. 5.99 (*0-380-01697-4*, 88799-1) Avon.

Captive Bride. Gilbert Morris. LC 87-15782. (House of Winslow Ser.: Bk. 2). 228p. (Orig.). 1987. pap. 8.99 (*0-87123-978-7*) Bethany Hse.

Captive Bride. large type ed. Johanna Lindsey. (General Ser.). 342p. 1992. text ed. 19.95 (*0-8161-5291-8*, Large Print Bks); pap. 15.95 (*0-8161-5292-6*, Large Print Bks) Hall.

Captive Caress. Sonya T. Pelton. 496p. 1986. pap. 3.95 (*0-8217-1923-8*) Zebra.

Captive Chains. Sonya T. Pelton. 1988. pap. 3.95 (*0-8217-2304-9*) Zebra.

Captive Cities: Studies in the Political Economy of Cities & Regions. Michael Harloe. LC 76-44297. 228p. reprint ed. 65.00 (*0-8357-9851-8*, 2051227) Bks Demand.

Captive City. Ovid Demaris. 1993. reprint ed. lib. bdg. 18.95 (*1-56849-014-3*) Buccaneer Bks.

Captive Community: Life in a Japanese Internment Camp, 1941-1945. Fern H. Miles. LC 87-61092. viii, 192p. (Orig.). 1987. pap. 8.95 (*0-9618895-0-0*) Mossy Creek Pr.

Captive Continent: The Stockholm Syndrome in European-Soviet Relations. Philip Pilevsky. LC 88-26573. 170p. 1989. text ed. 45.00 (*0-275-93064-5*, C3064, Praeger Pubs) Greenwood.

Captive Court: A Study of the Supreme Court of Canada. Ian Bushnell. 624p. 1993. 90.00 (*0-7735-0851-1*, Pub. by McGill CN) U of Toronto Pr.

Captive Desire. Jane Archer. 1989. pap. 3.75 (*0-8217-2612-9*) Zebra.

Captive Dove. Sonya T. Pelton. 448p. 1991. mass mkt. 4.95 (*0-8217-3332-X*) Zebra.

Captive Ecstasy. Elaine Barbieri. 1981. pap. 2.75 (*0-89083-738-4*) Zebra.

Captive Embrace. Sylvie F. Sommerfield. 1986. pap. 3.95 (*0-317-39259-X*) Zebra.

Captive Embraces. Fern Michaels. 1983. mass mkt. 4.95 (*0-345-31353-4*) Ballantine.

Captive Enchantress. Gina Robins. 448p. 1989. pap. 3.95 (*0-8217-2678-1*) Zebra.

Captive Flame. Catherine Creel. 512p. 1988. pap. 3.95 (*0-8217-2401-0*) Zebra.

***Captive Flesh.** Cleo Cordeli. (Black Lace Ser.). Date not set. pap. 5.95 (*0-352-32872-X*, London Bridge) Genl Dist Srvs.

Captive Heart. Phoebe Conn. 1985. pap. 3.95 (*0-8217-1569-0*) Zebra.

***Captive Heart.** Anita Gordon. 384p. (Orig.). 1995. pap. text ed. 4.99 (*0-515-11699-8*) Jove Pubns.

***Captive Heart.** Keene. (Illus.). (YA). 1995. mass mkt. 3.99 (*0-671-88199-X*, Archway) PB.

Captive Hearts, Captive Minds: Freedom & Recovery from Cults & Other Abusive Relationships. Madeleine L. Tobias & Janja Lalich. LC 93-33938. 288p. 1994. 24.95 (*0-89793-145-9*); pap. 14.95 (*0-89793-144-0*) Hunter Hse.

***Captive Husbandry & Propagation of the Boa Constrictors & Other Boine Snakes.** David Fogel. 1996. write for info. (*0-89464-921-3*) Krieger.

Captive II. (Victorian Era Ser.). 1993. pap. 5.95 (*0-929654-81-1*, 98) Blue Moon Bks.

Captive Imagination: A Casebook on "The Yellow Wallpaper" Ed. by Catherine Golden. (Illus.). 360p. (C). 1992. 35.00 (*1-55861-047-2*); pap. 14.95 (*1-55861-048-0*) Feminist Pr.

***Captive in the Virtual World.** Cathy E. Dubowski. LC 94-68250. (VR Troopers Ser.). 144p. (J). (gr. 2 up). 1994. pap. 3.95 (*0-8431-3843-2*) Price Stern.

Captive in Time. Sarah Dreher. LC 90-31304. 256p. (Orig.). 1990. pap. 9.95 (*0-934678-22-7*) New Victoria Pubns.

Captive Innocence. Fern Michaels. 1982. mass mkt. 5.95 (*0-345-30804-2*) Ballantine.

Captive Innocence. large type ed. Fern Michaels. (General Ser.). 425p. 1991. lib. bdg. 19.95 (*0-8161-5122-9*) G K Hall.

Captive Innocent. Allison Knight. 1989. pap. 3.75 (*0-8217-2745-1*) Zebra.

Captive Insurance Companies. P. A. Bawcutt. (C). 1987. 550.00 (*0-685-33785-5*, Pub. by Witherby & Co UK) St Mut.

Captive Invertebrates: A Guide to Their Biology & Husbandry. Fredric L. Frye. 160p. (C). 1992. lib. bdg. 29.50 (*0-89464-555-2*) Krieger.

***Captive IV: The Eyes Behind the Mask.** (Captive Ser.: No. 4). 1994. pap. 5.95 (*1-56201-067-0*) Blue Moon Bks.

Captive Kiss. Amy Christopher. 1992. mass mkt. 4.25 (*0-8217-3673-6*) Zebra.

Captive Land: The Politics of Agrarian Reform in the Philippines. James Putzel. LC 92-12667. 1992. pap. 18.00 (*0-85345-842-1*) Monthly Rev.

Captive Lion & Other Poems. William H. Davies. 1921. 39.50 (*0-685-89738-9*) Elliots Bks.

Captive Love. Lauren Wilde. 512p. 1988. pap. 3.95 (*0-8217-2375-8*) Zebra.

Captive Love - the Face of Love, 2 vols. in 1. Anne N. Reisser. 368p. 1990. reprint ed. pap. 3.95 (*0-8439-2939-1*) Dorchester Pub Co.

Captive Maidens. rev. ed. 1992. pap. 4.95 (*1-56333-014-8*) Masquerade.

***Captive Management Conservation of Amphibians & Reptiles.** Murphy et al. 1994. write for info. (*0-916984-33-8*) SSAR.

Captive Mind. Czeslaw Milosz. 1992. 21.00 (*0-8446-6615-7*) Peter Smith.

Captive Mind. Czeslaw Milosz. LC 89-40503. 272p. 1990. pap. 11.00 (*0-679-72856-2*, Vin) Random.

Captive Mind. Czeslaw Milosz. 1981. pap. 6.95 (*0-394-74724-0*) Random.

Captive Mistress. Deborah LeVarre. 1983. pap. 3.75 (*0-8217-1282-9*) Zebra.

Captive Moments. Amaresh Datta. (Redbird Ser.). 1976. 8.00 (*0-89253-528-8*); 4.00 (*0-89253-082-0*) Ind-US Inc.

Captive Nations: Eastern Europe, 1945-1990. Patrick Brogan. 1990. pap. 8.95 (*0-380-76304-4*) Avon.

Captive Nations: Nationalism of the Non-Russian Nations & Peoples of the Soviet Union. Roman Smal-Stocki. 1960. pap. 13.95x (*0-8084-0068-1*) NCUP.

Captive of Desire. Becky L. Weyrich. 1988. pap. 3.50 (*0-449-14448-8*) Fawcett.

Captive of Desire. 2nd ed. Becky L. Weyrich. 288p. 1987. pap. write for info. (*0-449-44446-5*, GM) Fawcett.

Captive of Kensington Palace. large type ed. Jean Plaidy. (Shadows of the Crown Ser.). 1975. 21.95 (*0-85456-599-X*) Ulverscroft.

Captive of Love. large type ed. Caroline Ross. (Linford Romance Library). 272p. 1988. pap. 11.95 (*0-7089-6463-X*, Linford) Ulverscroft.

***Captive of Pittsford Ridge.** Janice Ovecka. LC 94-24533. 128p. (Orig.). (YA). 1994. pap. 10.95 (*1-881535-11-8*) New Eng Pr VT.

Captive of the Castle of Sennaar: An African Tale. George Cumberland. Ed. by G. E. Bentley, Jr. 1991. 55.00 (*0-7735-0742-6*, Pub. by McGill CN) U of Toronto Pr.

Captive of the Caucasus. Andrei Bitov. Tr. by Susan Brownsberger. 352p. 1992. 23.00 (*0-374-11883-3*) FS&G.

Captive of the Caucasus. Andrei Bitov. 323p. 1994. pap. 15.00 (*0-00-271668-2*, Pub. by HarpC UK) HarpC.

***Captive of the Cheyenne: The Story of Nancy Jane Morton & the Plum Creek Massacre.** Russ Czaplewski. Ed. by Bob Wallace. LC 93-72732. (Illus.). 230p. (Orig.). (C). 1993. 17.95 (*0-9637898-1-3*); pap. 12.95 (*0-9637898-0-5*) Daw Cnty Hist Mus.

Captive of the Nootka Indians: The Northwest Coast Adventure of John R. Jewitt, 1802-1806. Ed. by Alice W. Shurcliff & Sarah S. Ingelfinger. LC 92-11915. 160p. 1992. 24.95 (*1-55553-131-8*) NE U Pr.

Captive of the Rising Sun: The POW Memoirs of Rear Admiral Donald T. Giles. Ed. by Donald T. Giles, Jr. LC 93-37042. 256p. 1994. 27.95 (*1-55750-320-6*) Naval Inst Pr.

Captive of the Vision of Paradise. Ivan Arguelles. 75p. 1982. pap. 5.95 (*0-915868-02-4*) Hartmus Pr.

Captive Passions. Fern Michaels. LC 76-56142. 1987. mass mkt. 5.95 (*0-345-34683-1*) Ballantine.

Captive Passions. Fern Michaels. 448p. 1992. reprint ed. 22.00 (*0-7278-4384-2*) Severn Hse.

Captive Populations: Caring for the Young, the Sick, the Imprisoned, & the Elderly. Jennie J. Kronenfeld & Marcia L. Whicker. LC 89-72125. 208p. 1990. text ed. 55.00 (*0-275-92723-7*, C2723, Praeger Pubs) Greenwood.

***Captive Press: Foreign Policy Crises & the First Amendment.** Carpenter. 1995. 24.95 (*1-882577-22-1*) Cato Inst.

***Captive Press: Foreign Policy Crises & the First Amendment.** Carpenter. 1995. pap. text ed. 14.95 (*1-882577-23-X*) Cato Inst.

Captive Press in the Third Reich. Oron J. Hale. LC 64-12182. (Illus.). 368p. 1964. 55.00x (*0-691-05109-7*); pap. 17.95 (*0-691-00770-5*) Princeton U Pr.

Captive Rose. Miriam Minger. 384p. 1991. pap. 3.95 (*0-380-76311-7*) Avon.

Captive Seawater Fishes: Science & Technology. Stephen Spotte. 976p. 1991. text ed. 115.00 (*0-471-54554-6*) Wiley.

Captive Secrets. Fern Michaels. (Orig.). 1991. mass mkt. 5.95 (*0-345-34123-6*) Ballantine.

Captive Secrets. large type ed. Fern Michaels. (General Ser.). 415p. (Orig.). 1992. text ed. 20.95 (*0-8161-5360-4*, Large Print Bks) Hall.

Captive Souls. abr. ed. Cheri Stow. 260p. 1995. 7.95 (*1-56901-490-6*) NW Pub.

Captive Splendor. Rochelle Wayne. 512p. 1993. mass mkt. 4.99 (*1-55817-701-9*, Pinnacle NY) Windsor NY.

Captive Splendors. Fern Michaels. 1983. mass mkt. 5.99 (*0-345-31648-7*) Ballantine.

Captive Splendors. Fern Michaels. 1994. 22.00 (*0-685-73092-1*) Severn Hse.

Captive Spriit: Selected Prose. Marina Tsvetaeva. 1994. pap. 16.00 (*0-679-75618-3*, Vin) Random.

Captive Sultan. Avigail Teichman. Ed. by Y. Y. Reinman. LC 85-72403. (Yom Tov Ser.: No. 1). (Illus.). 128p. (J). (gr. 7-11). 1985. 7.95 (*0-935063-12-9*); pap. 5.95 (*0-935063-04-8*) CIS Comm.

Captive Surrender. Michalann Perry. 496p. 1987. pap. 3.95 (*0-8217-1986-6*) Zebra.

Captive the Fugitive Time, Vol. III. Marcel Proust. 1982. pap. 22.00 (*0-394-71184-X*, Vin) Random.

Captive to a Dream. Susan Tanner. 448p. (Orig.). 1991. pap. 4.50 (*0-8439-3162-0*) Dorchester Pub Co.

Captive to His Kiss. Paige Brantley. 1992. mass mkt. 4.25 (*0-8217-3788-0*) Zebra.

Captive Treasure. Tena Carlyle. 1992. mass mkt. 4.25 (*0-8217-3762-7*) Zebra.

Captive Treasure. Milly Howard. (Light Line Ser.). 167p. (Orig.). 1988. pap. 5.95 (*0-89084-440-2*) Bob Jones Univ Pr.

Captive Victors: Shakespeare's Narrative Poems & Sonnets. Heather Dubrow. LC 86-19627. 288p. (C). 1987. 36.50 (*0-8014-1975-1*) Cornell U Pr.

Captive Vocabulary. Robert Greenman. (Illus.). 187p. 1980. pap. text ed. 4.50 (*0-912853-01-8*) NY Times.

Captive Voice: The Liberation of Preaching. David Buttrick. LC 93-31034. 176p. (Orig.). 1994. pap. 12.99 (*0-664-25540-X*) Westminster John Knox.

Captive Warriors: A Vietnam POW's Story. Sam Johnson & Jan Winebrenner. (Military History Ser.: No. 23). (Illus.). 310p. 1992. 24.50 (*0-89096-496-3*) Tex A&M Univ Pr.

***Captives.** Hoh. (Nightmare Hall Ser.: No. 25). 1995. mass mkt. (*0-590-25081-7*) Scholastic Inc.

Captives. Ralph L. Sides, Jr. 167p. (Orig.). (C). 1988. pap. text ed. 7.50 (*0-317-93317-5*) Yeshua Bks.

Captives. Don Wright. (Woodsman Ser.: No. 1). 448p. 1988. mass mkt. 5.99 (*0-8125-8991-2*) Tor Bks.

Captives: Australian Army Nurses in Japanese Prison Camps. Catherine Kenny. (Illus.). 173p. (Orig.). 1987. pap. 14.95 (*0-7022-1926-6*, Pub. by Univ Queensland Pr AT) Intl Spec Bk.

Captives see Amphitryon

Captives & Hostages in the Peloponnesian War. Andreas Panogopoulos. 296p. 1989. pap. 42.00 (*90-256-0935-X*, Pub. by A M Hakkert NE) Benjamins North Am.

***Captive's Journey.** (Orig.). 1994. pap. 5.95 (*1-56201-056-5*) Blue Moon Bks.

Captives of Korea: An Unofficial White Paper on the Treatment of War Prisoners; Our Treatment of Theirs: Their Treatment of Ours. William L. White. LC 78-14347. 347p. 1979. reprint ed. text ed. 35.00 (*0-313-20631-7*, WHCK, Greenwood Pr) Greenwood.

Captives of Shanghai, the Story of the President Harrison. David H. Grover & Gretchen G. Grover. (Illus.). 202p. (Orig.). 1989. pap. 11.95 (*0-9623935-0-9*) West Maritime Pr.

Captives of the Desert. Zane Grey. 1991. mass mkt. 3.99 (*0-06-100292-5*, Harp PBks) HarpC.

Captives of the Night. Loretta Chase. 416p. (Orig.). 1994. mass mkt. 4.99 (*0-380-76648-5*) Avon.

Captivi of Plautus. Plautus. Ed. by W. R. Connor & Wallace M. Lindsey. LC 78-67134. (Latin Texts & Commentaries Ser.). (ENG & LAT.). 1979. reprint ed. lib. bdg. 30.95 (*0-405-11608-X*) Ayer.

Captivite et Derniers Moments de Louis-Seize, 2 Vols. Gaston L. Beaucourt. LC 71-161732. reprint ed. 18.00 (*0-685-73111-1*) AMS Pr.

Captivite et Derniers Moments de Louis-Seize, 2 Vols, 1. Gaston L. Beaucourt. LC 71-161732. reprint ed. 18.00 (*0-404-07623-8*) AMS Pr.

Captivite et Derniers Moments de Louis-Seize, 2 Vols, 2. Gaston L. Beaucourt. LC 71-161732. reprint ed. 18.00 (*0-404-07624-6*) AMS Pr.

Captivite et Derniers Moments de Louis-Seize, 2 Vols, Set. Gaston L. Beaucourt. LC 71-161732. reprint ed. 35.00 (*0-404-07622-X*) AMS Pr.

Captivity. Toi Derricotte. LC 89-31840. (Poetry Ser.). 74p. 1989. 19.95 (*0-8229-3628-3*); pap. 10.95 (*0-8229-5422-2*) U of Pittsburgh Pr.

Captivity Captive. Rodney Hall. 192p. 1988. 15.95 (*0-374-11889-2*) FS&G.

Captivity Narrative of Hannah Duston. limited ed. Ed. & Intro. by Glenn R. Todd. (Illus.). 56p. 1987. 485.00 (*0-910457-12-3*) Arion Pr.

Captivity of Mahram. Shmuel Argaman. LC 90-83947. (Illus.). 120p. (J). (gr. 3-5). 1990. 11.95 (*1-56062-045-5*); pap. 8.95 (*0-685-46904-2*) CIS Comm.

Captivity of Pixie Shedman. Romulus Linney. 1981. pap. 4.75 (*0-8222-0180-1*) Dramatists Play.

Captivity of the Oatman Girls. R. B. Stratton. LC 76-104572. (Illus.). 294p. reprint ed. lib. bdg. 26.75 (*0-8398-1877-7*) Irvington.

Captivity of the Oatman Girls. R. B. Stratton. LC 83-1315. (Illus.). xvi, 294p. 1983. reprint ed. pap. 9.95 (*0-8032-9139-6*, Bison Books) U of Nebr Pr.

Captivity of the Oatman Girls among the Apache & Mohave Indians. Lorenzo D. Oatman & Olive A. Oatman. LC 94-4747. Orig. Title: Life among the Indians: or the Captivity of the Oatman Girls among the Apache & Mohave Indians. (Illus.). 240p. 1994. reprint ed. pap. 6.95 (*0-486-28078-0*) Dover.

Captivity Tales: An Original Anthology. LC 74-15729. (Popular Culture in America Ser.). (Illus.). 1975. reprint ed. 23.95 (*0-405-06365-2*) Ayer.

C

An Asterisk (*) at the beginning of an entry indicates that the title is appearing in BIP for the first time.

An Asterisk (*) at the beginning of an entry indicates that the title is appearing in BIP for the first time.

1039

C

Car Theft: The Offender's Perspective. Roy Light et al. (Home Organist Library: No. 130). 100p. 1993. pap. 15. 00 (*0-11-341069-7*, HM10697, Pub. by HMSO UK) UNIPUB.

Car Theft Kidnapping. Haji U. Hutchinson. Ed. by Zeba Siddiqui. (Invincible Abdullah Ser.: Vol. 2). (Illus.). 152p. (YA). (gr. 6-12). 1992. pap. 5.95 (*0-89259-123-4*) Am Trust Pubns.

Car Travel Games. T. Potter. (Travel Games Ser.). (Illus.). 32p. (J). (gr. 2 up). 1986. pap. 4.95 (*0-86020-926-1*) EDC.

Car Trip. Helen Oxenbury. (Out & about Bk.). (Illus.). 24p. (J). (ps-1). 1983. 3.95 (*0-8037-0009-1*, 0383-120) Dial Bks Young.

Car Trip. Helen Oxenbury. (Out & about Bks.). (Illus.). 24p. (J). (ps-1). 1994. pap. 3.99 (*0-14-050377-3*, Puff Pied Piper) Puffin Bks.

Car Trip for Mole & Mouse. Illus. by David Prebenna. 32p. (J). (ps-3). 1991. pap. 3.50 (*0-14-054392-9*, Puffin) Puffin Bks.

Car Trouble: How New Technology, Clean Fuels, & Creative Thinking Can Revive the Auto Industry & Save Our Cities from Smog & Gridlock. Ed. by World Resources Institute Staff. (Guide to the Environment Ser.). (Illus.). 224p. 1993. 27.50 (*0-8070-8522-7*); pap. 12.00 (*0-8070-8523-5*) Beacon Pr.

Car Tunes. Pat Lakin. 32p. (J). (gr. 1-6). 1987. 6.95 (*0-394-88771-9*) Random Bks Yng Read.

Car Use: A Social & Economic Study. M. C. Dix et al. LC 83-14177. 265p. 1983. text ed. 85.95 (*0-566-00666-9*) Ashgate Pub Co.

Car Wars. (Report on the Americas: Vol. XIII, No. 4). 52p. 2.50 (*0-317-34956-2*) NA Cong Lat Am.

Car Washing for Car Lovers: A Guidebook to Proper Car Washing, Waxing, & Other Maintenance Procedures to Keep Your Car Beautiful. Thomas A. DiCandia. Ed. by Ann R. Goldstein & Doreen S. Berne. (Illus.). 96p. 1990. per., pap. 13.95 (*0-9626744-0-0*) CA Bound Bks.

Car Washing Street. Denise L. Patrick. LC 92-9229. (Illus.). 32p. (J). (ps up). 1993. 14.00 (*0-688-11452-0*, Tambourine Bks); lib. bdg. 13.93 (*0-688-11453-9*, Tambourine Bks) Morrow.

Cara: Growing with a Retarded Child. Martha M. Jablow. LC 82-3283. 250p. 1982. pap. 12.95 (*0-87722-269-X*) Temple U Pr.

C

Cara a Cara: A Basic Reader for Communication. 2nd ed. William F. Ratliff et al. 240p. (SPA.). (C). 1982. pap. text ed. 21.00 (*0-03-057597-4*) HB Coll Pubs.

Cara A Cara: Face to Face. Jessie Penn-Lewis. (SPA.). 3.25 (*84-7645-115-6*, 223169, Pub. by Edit Clie SP) TSELF.

Cara a Cara Software. Ariew. 1987. 175.00 (*0-8384-1543-1*); write for info. (*0-318-66661-8*) Heinle & Heinle.

Cara Descubierta (Time to Stop Pretending) Palau. (SPA.). Date not set. write for info. (*1-56063-116-3*, 498016) Editorial Unilit.

Carabid Beetles. Ed. by Terry L. Erwin & Donald R. Whitehead. 1979. lib. bdg. 234.50 (*90-6193-596-2*) Kluwer Ac.

Carabid Beetles: Ecology & Evolution. Ed. by Konjev Desender et al. LC 93-31137. (Series Entomologica: Vol. 51). 492p. (C). 1994. lib. bdg. 257.00 (*0-7923-2464-1*) Kluwer Ac.

Carabid Beetles: Their Adaptations & Dynamics. Den Boer et al. 350p. 1987. pap. text ed. 110.00 (*0-89574-209-8*, Pub. by Gustav Fischer Verlag) VCH Pubs.

Carabid Beetles (Insecta: Coleoptera: Carabidae) of the Queen Charlotte Islands, British Columbia. David H. Kavanaugh. LC 91-58794. (Memoirs of the California Academy of Sciences Ser.: No. 16). (Illus.). 1992. pap. 25.00 (*0-940228-17-3*) Calif Acad Sci.

Carabidae, Coleoptera, Larvae of Fennoscandia & Denmark. Martin L. Luff. LC 93-3419. (Fauna Entomologica Scandinavica Ser.: Vol. 27). (Illus.). 187p. 1993. 54.50 (*90-04-09836-4*) E J Brill.

Carabidae (Coleoptera) of Fennoscandia & Denmark, Pt. 1. Carl H. Lindroth. (Fauna Entomologica Scandinavica Ser.: No. 15-1). (Illus.). 226p. 1985. text ed. 64.00 (*90-04-07727-8*) Lubrecht & Cramer.

Carabidae (Coleoptera) of Fennoscandia & Denmark, Pt. 2. Carl H. Lindroth. (Fauna Entomologica Scandinavica Ser.: Vol. 15/2). (Illus.). 274p. 1986. 45.75 (*90-04-08182-8*) Lubrecht & Cramer.

Carabidos de Navarra Espana: The Carabid Beetles of Navarra Spain (Coleoptera, Carabidae) L. Herrera & F. J. Arricibita. LC 88-25086. (Entomonograph: Vol. 12). (Illus.). 241p. (ENG & SPA.). 1990. 91.50 (*90-04-08980-2*) E J Brill.

***Caraboo: The Servant Girl Princess: The Real Story of the Grand Hoax.** Jennifer Raison & Michael Goldie. LC 94-42794. 1995. pap. write for info. (*1-56656-179-5*) Interlink Pub.

Caracas Alive. 3rd rev. ed. Harriet Greenberg & Arnold L. Greenberg. 1979. pap. 4.95 (*0-935572-01-5*) Alive Pubns.

Caracas Company, 1728-1784: Study in the History of Spanish Monopolistic Trade. Roland D. Hussey. Ed. by Mira Wilkins. LC 76-29752. (European Business Ser.). 1977. reprint ed. lib. bdg. 33.95 (*0-405-09768-9*) Ayer.

Caracter y Personalidad: Character & Personality. Salvador Iserte. (SPA.). 3.25 (*84-7228-405-0*, 220138, Pub. by Edit Clie SP) TSELF.

Caracteres. Jean D. La Bruyere. (Folio Ser.: No. 693). (FRE.). 1962. pap. 9.95 (*2-07-036693-6*) Schoenhof.

Caracteres: Avec: Caracteres de Theophraste. Jean De La Bruyere & Robert Pignarre. 668p. (FRE.). 1962. 10.95 (*0-7859-0065-9*, M1573) Fr & Eur.

Caracteres de Theophrastre, traduits du grec avec Les Caracteres, ou Les Moeurs de ce siecle. Jean De La Bruyere. Ed. by Garagon. (Class. Garnier Ser.). pap. 24. 95 (*0-685-34227-1*) Fr & Eur.

Caracteres de Theophrastre, traduits du grec avec Les Caracters, ou Les Moeurs de ce siecle. Jean De La Bruyere. Ed. by Garpon. (Coll. Prestige). 49.95 (*0-685-34228-X*) Fr & Eur.

***Caracterisation et les Modes de la Narration Dans le Roman Moderne: Theorie de Narratologie Caracterologique.** Frederic Fladenmuller. (Reading Plus Ser.: No. 14). 152p. (C). 1994. text ed. 42.95 (*0-8204-2267-3*) P Lang Pubs.

Caracteristicas Nacionales de la Literatura Cubana. Marcy Ares et al. (Patronato Ramon Guiteras Intercultural Center Ser.). 92p. (Orig.). (SPA.). 1985. pap. 6.95 (*0-89729-404-1*) Ediciones.

Carafa Chapel, Renaissance Art in Rome. Gail Geiger. (Sixteenth Century Essays & Studies: Vol. V). (Illus.). 210p. 1985. 50.00 (*0-940474-05-0*) Sixteenth Cent.

Caraga Antigua, 1521-1910: The Hispanization & Christianization of Agusan, Surigao & East Davao. Peter Schreuers. (San Carlos Humanities Ser.: No. 18). (Illus.). 475p. (Orig.). (C). 1990. 30.00 (*971-10-0055-5*, Pub. by San Carlos Univ PH); pap. 20.00 (*0-318-67305-3*) Cellar.

***Carambola Cultivation.** V. G. Sauco et al. (Plant Production & Protection Paper Ser.: 108). 80p. 1993. pap. write for info. (*92-5-103043-X*, F3043x) UNIPUB.

Carapace. Henry Kanabus. LC 77-13815. 1978. pap. 2.50 (*0-916328-09-0*) Yellow Pr.

Cara's Beach Party. Elaine Schulte. (Twelve Candles Club Ser.). 144p. (Orig.). (J). 1993. pap. 4.99 (*1-55661-252-4*) Bethany Hse.

Cara's Beloved. Laurie Paige. (Silhouette Romance Ser.). 1993. pap. 2.69 (*0-373-08917-1*, 5-08917-2) Silhouette.

Cara's Story. Maureen A. Burns & Cara M. Burns. (Illus.). 54p. 1987. pap. 8.00 (*0-9613084-2-7*) Empey Ent.

Carattaco. Ed. by Ernest Warburton. (Johann Christian Bach, 1735-1782 The Collected Works). 1986. 132.00 (*0-8240-6055-5*) Garland.

Caravaggio. John Gash. LC 94-16263. (Art Ser.). 24p. 1994. 7.95 (*0-8478-1784-9*) Rizzoli Intl.

Caravaggio. Howard Hibbard. LC 78-2145. (Icon Editions Ser.). (Illus.). 304p. 1985. pap. text ed. 30.00 (*0-06-430128-1*, Icon Edns) HarpC.

Caravaggio. Alfred Moir. (Masters of Art Ser.). (Illus.). 128p. 1989. 22.95 (*0-8109-3150-8*) Abrams.

Caravaggio. Michael Straight. LC 79-17678. (In Great Decades Ser.: Vol. II). 1979. pap. 4.95 (*0-934160-02-3*) Devon Pr.

Caravaggio. Giorgio Bonsanti. Tr. by Paul Blanchard. (Library of Great Masters). (Illus.). 80p. 1990. reprint ed. pap. 12.99 (*1-878351-07-9*) Riverside NY.

Caravaggio, Set. Michael Straight. LC 79-17678. (In Great Decades Ser.: Vol. II). 1979. boxed 30.00 (*0-685-01436-3*) Devon Pr.

Caravaggio & His Two Cardinals: Method & Meaning. Creighton E. Gilbert. LC 93-44381. 392p. 1995. 85.00 (*0-271-01312-5*) Pa St U Pr.

Caravaggio Rediscovered: The Lute Player. Keith Christiansen. (Illus.). 96p. 1990. 16.95 (*0-87099-575-8*) Metro Mus Art.

Caravaggio Studies. Walter F. Friedlaender. LC 74-5641. 486p. reprint ed. pap. 138.60 (*0-7837-1403-3*, 2041757) Bks Demand.

Caravaggio's Death of the Virgin. Pamela Askew. (Illus.). 208p. 1990. text ed. 50.00 (*0-691-03983-6*) Princeton U Pr.

Caravan. Dorothy Gilman. 1993. mass mkt. 5.99 (*0-449-22175-X*) Fawcett.

***Caravan.** Lawrence McKay, Jr. LC 95-2037. (Illus.). 32p. (J). (gr. k-4). 1995. 14.95 (*1-880000-23-7*) Lee & Low Bks.

Caravan. Ethna McKiernan. LC 89-71292. (Illus.). 80p. (Orig.). 1989. pap. 5.95 (*0-935697-04-7*) Midwest Villages.

Caravan. Ethna McKiernan. (Orig.). (C). 1990. pap. 15.00 (*0-948268-55-7*, Pub. by Dedalus Pr IE) St Mut.

Caravan. large type ed. Dorothy Gilman. 403p. 1992. reprint ed. lib. bdg. 19.95 (*1-56054-528-3*) Thorndike Pr.

Caravan. large type ed. Dorothy Gilman. 403p. 1993. pap. 13.95 (*1-56054-896-7*) Thorndike Pr.

Caravan Across China: An American Geologist Explores the Northwest, 1937-1938. J. Marvin Weller. Ed. by Harriet Weller. LC 84-23367. 1984. pap. 12.95 (*0-918295-00-9*) March Hare.

Caravan Cities. Mikhail I. Rostovtsev. LC 75-137287. reprint ed. 37.50 (*0-404-05445-5*) AMS Pr.

Caravan of Dreams. Idries Shah. 207p. 1988. 25.00 (*0-900860-14-6*, Pub. by Octagon Pr UK); pap. 12.50 (*0-86304-043-8*, Pub. by Octagon Pr UK) ISHK Bk Service.

***Caravan of Shadows.** White Wolf Staff. 1995. pap. 5.99 (*1-56504-831-8*, 04831) White Wolf.

Caravan Puppets. Michael Bond. LC 85-109047. (Illus.). 130p. (J). (gr. 3 up). 1983. write for info. (*0-00-184135-1*) Harper SF.

Caravan to Tiern. Andrea Mills. (Illus.). 1989. 8.95 (*0-940244-22-5*) Flying Buffalo.

Caravan to Vaccares. large type ed. Alistair MacLean. 1972. 12.00 (*0-85456-099-8*) Ulverscroft.

***Caravans.** Kurtz. 1994. pap. 18.00 (*1-56076-903-3*) TSR Inc.

Caravans. James A. Michener. 1986. mass mkt. 6.95 (*0-449-21380-3*, Crest) Fawcett.

Caravans. James A. Michener. 1963. 29.95 (*0-394-41849-2*) Random.

Caravans: Three Books of Poems. Mark Dunster. 57p. (Orig.). 1981. pap. 4.00 (*0-89642-071-X*) Linden Pubs.

Caravans of Mars. Ed Andrews. (Space: Eighteen Eighty-Nine Ser.). (Illus.). 64p. (Orig.). (YA). 1989. pap. 8.00 (*1-55878-023-8*) Game Designers.

***Caravans of the Himalaya.** Diane Summers & Eric Valli. LC 94-8139. (Illus.). 236p. 1994. 34.95 (*0-7922-2793-X*) Natl Geog.

Caravans To Tartary. Roland & Sabrina Michaud. LC 84-51676. (Illus.). 104p. 1990. pap. 17.95 (*0-500-27359-6*) Thames Hudson.

Caravansary & Conversation. Richard Curle. LC 73-134070. (Essay Index Reprint Ser.). 1977. 21.95 (*0-8369-2151-8*) Ayer.

***Caravanserai: Journeys among Australian Muslims.** Hanifa Deen. 208p. 1995. pap. 19.95 (*1-86373-865-7*) Paul & Co Pubs.

Carbamate Pesticides: A General Introduction. (Envrionmental Health Criteria Ser.: No. 64). 136p. 1987. pap. 7.80 (*92-4-154264-0*) World Health.

***Carbaryl.** Ed. by World Health Organization Staff. (Environmental Health Criteria Ser.). 358p. 1994. 45.90 (*92-4-157153-5*) World Health.

Carbenes, 2 vols., Set. Ed. by Robert A. Moss & Maitland Jones. LC 80-11836. (Reactive Intermediates in Organic Chemistry Ser.). 368p. 1983. reprint ed. Vol. 1. lib. bdg. 72.50 (*0-89874-620-5*) Krieger.

Carbenes, Vol. 1. Ed. by Robert A. Moss & Maitland Jones. LC 80-11836. (Reactive Intermediates in Organic Chemistry Ser.). 368p. 1983. reprint ed. Set. lib. bdg. 41. 00 (*0-89874-216-1*) Krieger.

Carbenes, Vol. 2. Ed. by Robert A. Moss & Maitland Jones. LC 80-11836. (Reactive Intermediates in Organic Chemistry Ser.). 390p. 1983. reprint ed. lib. bdg. 35.00 (*0-89874-160-2*) Krieger.

Carbine & Lance: The Story of Old Fort Sill. enl. rev. ed. Wilbur S. Nye. LC 79-13137. (Illus.). 448p. 1983. pap. 17.95 (*0-8061-1856-3*) U of Okla Pr.

Carbines of the Civil War, 1861-1865. John D. McAulay. 1981. 8.95 (*0-913150-45-2*) Pioneer Pr.

Carbocation Chemistry. P. Vogel. (Studies in Organic Chemistry: 21). 596p. 1985. 195.00 (*0-444-42522-5*) Elsevier.

Carbocationic Polymerization. Joseph P. Kennedy & Ernest Marechal. 532p. (C). 1991. reprint ed. lib. bdg. 94.50 (*0-89464-509-9*) Krieger.

Carbocyclic Cage Compounds: Chemistry & Applications. Eiji Osawa & Osamu Yonemitsu. (Methods in Stereochemical Analysis Ser.). (Illus.). 409p. 1992. text ed. 95.00 (*0-89573-728-0*) VCH Pubs.

Carbocyclization: Implications in Terpene Synthesis. Tse-Lok Ho. LC 87-21626. 768p. 1988. lib. bdg. 155.00 (*0-89573-279-3*) VCH Pubs.

Carbohydrate Addict's Diet: The Lifelong Solution to Yo-Yo Dieting. Rachael F. Heller & Richard F. Heller. 336p. 1993. pap. 5.99 (*0-451-17339-2*, Sig) NAL-Dutton.

Carbohydrate Addict's Diet; The Carbohydrate Addict's Program for Success, 2 vols., Set. Rachael F. Heller & Richard F. Heller. 1993. pap. 17.99 (*0-451-92689-7*, Sig) NAL-Dutton.

Carbohydrate Addict's Gram Counter. Rachael F. Heller & Richard F. Heller. 96p. (Orig.). 1993. pap. 2.99 (*0-451-17717-7*, Sig) NAL-Dutton.

Carbohydrate Addict's Program for Success: Taking Charge of Your Life & Your Weight. Rachael F. Heller & Richard F. Heller. 304p. (Orig.). 1993. pap. 12.00 (*0-452-26933-4*, Plume) NAL-Dutton.

Carbohydrate Analysis. Ed. by M. F. Chaplin & J. F. Kennedy. LC 94-11640. (Practical Approach Ser.: No. 143). (Illus.). 240p. 1994. pap. 50.00 (*0-19-963449-1*, IRL Pr) OUP.

Carbohydrate Analysis. 2nd ed. Ed. by M. F. Chaplin & J. F. Kennedy. LC 94-11640. (Practical Approach Ser.: No. 143). (Illus.). 240p. 1994. 93.00 (*0-19-963450-5*, IRL Pr) OUP.

Carbohydrate Antigens. Ed. by Per Garegg & Alf Lindberg. LC 92-39537. (Symposium Ser.: No. 516). 200p. 1992. 49.95 (*0-8412-2531-1*) Am Chemical.

Carbohydrate Chemistry. Ed. by John F. Kennedy. (Illus.). 696p. 1988. 175.00 (*0-19-855177-0*) OUP.

Carbohydrate Chemistry. Ed. by J. Thiem. (Topics in Current Chemistry Ser.: Vol. 154). (Illus.). 320p. 1990. 139.00 (*0-387-51576-3*, 3413) Spr-Verlag.

Carbohydrate Chemistry, Vol 9. A. B. Foster. 1979. 65.00 (*0-08-022354-0*, Pub. by Pergamon Repr UK) Franklin.

Carbohydrate Chemistry, Vols. 1-11. Ed. by J. S. Brimacombe. Incl. 1967 LiteratureLC 79-67610. 1968. 31.00 (*0-85186-002-8*); 1968 LiteratureLC 79-67610. 1969. 31.00 (*0-85186-012-5*); 1969 LiteratureLC 79-67610. 1970. 34.00 (*0-85186-022-2*); 1970 LiteratureLC 79-67610. 1971. 34.00 (*0-85186-032-X*); 1971 LiteratureLC 79-67610. 1972. 36.00 (*0-85186-042-7*); 1972 LiteratureLC 79-67610. 1973. 38.00 (*0-85186-052-4*); 1973 LiteratureLC 79-67610. 1975. 56. 00 (*0-85186-062-1*); 1974 LiteratureLC 79-67610. 1976. 61.00 (*0-85186-072-9*); 1975-76 LiteratureLC 79-67610. 1977. 82.00 (*0-85186-082-6*); 1976-77 LiteratureLC 79-67610. 1978. 82.00 (*0-85186-092-3*); 1977-78 LiteratureLC 79-67610. 1979. 97.00 (*0-85186-102-4*); LC 79-67610. write for info. (*0-318-50464-2*, Pub. by Royal Soc Chem UK) Am Chemical.

Carbohydrate Chemistry: Monosaccharides & Their Oligomers. Hassan S. El Khadem. 256p. 1988. text ed. 69.00 (*0-12-236870-3*) Acad Pr.

Carbohydrate Chemistry see Rodd's Chemistry of Carbon Compounds

Carbohydrate Chemistry Six: Plenary Lecture 6th International Symposium Carbohydrate Chemistry, Madison 8-72. W. Doane. (IUPAC, Organic Chemistry Division Ser.). 1973. 96.00 (*0-08-020730-8*, Pub. by Pergamon Repr UK) Franklin.

Carbohydrate Counting: Adding Flexibility to Your Food Choices. Barbara Barry & Gay Castle. Ed. by Karol Carstensen. (Illus.). 1994. pap. write for info. (*1-885115-06-7*) Intl Diabetes.

Carbohydrate Economy: Making Chemicals & Industrial Materials from Plant Matter. David Morris & Irshad Ahmed. LC 92-18177. (Illus.). 70p. 1992. pap. text ed. 25.00 (*0-917582-25-X*) Inst Local Self Re.

Carbohydrate Histochemistry of Epithelial Glycoproteins. Philip E. Reid & Carol M. Park. (Progress in Histochemistry & Cytochemistry Ser.: Vol. 21-4). 170p. 1990. 95.00 (*0-685-48103-4*); pap. 110.00 (*0-89574-323-X*) G F Verlag.

Carbohydrate Intolerance in Infancy. Ed. by Fima Lifshitz. LC 82-5107. (Clinical Disorders in Pediatric Nutrition SEr.: No. 1). 271p. reprint ed. pap. 77.30 (*0-318-35011-4*, 2030871) Bks Demand.

Carbohydrate Metabolism: Quantitative Physiology & Mathematical Modelling. C. Cobelli. Ed. by R. N. Bergman. LC 80-41383. 458p. pap. 130.60 (*0-685-20736-6*, 2030374) Bks Demand.

Carbohydrate Metabolism see Methods in Enzymology

Carbohydrate Metabolism & Its Disorders, Vol. 3. Ed. by P. J. Randle et al. LC 68-17670. 1981. text ed. 220.00 (*0-12-579703-6*) Acad Pr.

Carbohydrate Metabolism in Cultured Cells. Ed. by Michael J. Morgan. LC 86-12170. 536p. 1986. 125.00 (*0-306-42240-9*, Plenum Pr) Plenum.

Carbohydrate Metabolism in Pregnancy & the Newborn IV. Ed. by H. W. Sutherland et al. (Illus.). 390p. 1989. 148. 00 (*0-387-19547-5*, 2660) Spr-Verlag.

***Carbohydrate Metabolism of Tissues.** I. Krompecher & M. B. Laszlo. 214p. (C). 1983. 72.00x (*963-05-3229-8*, Pub. by Akad Kiado HU) St Mut.

Carbohydrate Metabolism, Part C see Methods in Enzymology

***Carbohydrate Modifications in Antisense Research.** Ed. by Yogesh S. Sanghvi & P. Dan Cook. LC 94-38930. (Symposium Ser.: No. 580). (Illus.). 240p. 1994. 69.95 (*0-8412-3056-0*) Am Chemical.

Carbohydrate Polyesters As Fat Substitutes. Ed. by Akoh & Swanson. LC 94-577. (Food Science & Technology Ser.: Vol. 62). 280p. 1994. 125.00 (*0-8247-9062-6*) Dekker.

Carbohydrate-Protein Interaction. Ed. by Irwin J. Goldstein. LC 78-25788. (ACS Symposium Ser.: No. 88). 223p. 1979. 29.95 (*0-8412-0466-7*) Am Chemical.

Carbohydrate-Protein Interaction: A Symposium Sponsored by the Division of Carbohydrate Chemistry at the 174th Meeting of the American Chemical Society, Chicago, Illinois, August 31-September 1, 1977. Ed. by Irwin J. Goldstein. LC 78-25788. (ACS Symposium Ser.: No. 88). (Illus.). 234p. reprint ed. pap. 66.70 (*0-7837-1964-7*, 2052442) Bks Demand.

Carbohydrate Recognition in Cellular Function. CIBA Foundation Symposium Staff. (CIBA Foundation Symposia Ser.: No. 145). 1989. text ed. 76.00 (*0-471-92307-9*) Wiley.

Carbohydrate Sulfates: A Symposium Sponsored by the ACS Division of Carbohydrate Chemistry at the 174th Meeting of the American Chemical Society, Chicago, Illinois, August 30-31, 1977. Richard G. Schweiger. LC 78-17918. (American Chemical Society Symposium Ser.: No. 77). 304p. reprint ed. pap. 86.70 (*0-685-15526-9*, 2052175) Bks Demand.

Carbohydrates. Alvin Silverstein et al. LC 91-41245. (Food Power Ser.). (Illus.). 48p. (J). (gr. 3-6). 1992. lib. bdg. 14. 90 (*1-56294-207-7*) Millbrook Pr.

Carbohydrates, 3 Vols. 2nd ed. Ward Pigman & Derek Horton. Incl. Vol. 1A. 1972. text ed. 198.00 (*0-12-556301-9*); Vol. 2A. 1970. text ed. 164.00 (*0-12-556302-7*); Vol. 2B. 1970. text ed. 179.00 (*0-12-556352-3*); write for info. (*0-318-50238-0*) Acad Pr.

Carbohydrates: Chemistry & Biochemistry, Vol. IB. 2nd ed. Ward Pigman. LC 68-26647. 1980. text ed. 163.00 (*0-12-556351-5*) Acad Pr.

Carbohydrates: Synthetic Methods & Applications in Medicinal Chemistry. Ed. by Haruo Ogura et al. LC 92-49258. 408p. 1993. 140.00 (*1-56081-701-1*) VCH Pubs.

Carbohydrates & Carbohydrate Polymers: Analysis, Biotechnology, Conformation, Modification, Antiviral & Other Commercial Applications. Ed. by Manssur Yalpani. 320p. (C). 1993. 167.00 (*1-882360-40-0*) ATL Pr Sci.

Carbohydrates & Weight Reduction: The Intermediate Plan. S. Mikielle Chatman. (Fat Chance Series Book Group: No. 12). 43p. 1992. pap. 3.99 (*1-881146-10-3*) Fat Chance.

Carbohydrates As Organic Raw Materials. Ed. by W. Lichtenthaler. (Illus.). 370p. 1991. lib. bdg. 125.00 (*1-56081-131-5*) VCH Pubs.

Carbohydrates in Solution. Ed. by Horace S. Isbell. LC 73-81038. (Advances in Chemistry Ser.: No. 117). 421p. 1973. 36.95 (*0-8412-0178-1*) Am Chemical.

Carbohydrates, Lipids & Accessory Growth Factors. Ed. by M. Rechcigl, Jr. (Comparative Animal Nutrition Ser.: Vol. 1). (Illus.). 1976. 78.50 (*3-8055-2268-1*) S Karger.

Carbolic & Leeches. Janet Wilks. 154p. (C). 1990. 30.00 (*0-7223-2472-3*, Pub. by A H S Ltd UK) St Mut.

Carbon: Electrochemical & Physicochemical Properties. Kim Kinoshita. LC 87-14180. 533p. 1988. text ed. 150. 00 (*0-471-84802-6*) Wiley.

Carbon Adsorption for Pollution Control. Nicholas P. Cheremisinoff & Paul N. Cheremisinoff. LC 92-23500. 208p. 1992. text ed. 70.00 (*0-13-393331-8*) P-H.

Carbon & Carbro Tissue: You Can Make It! Tracy Diers. (Illus.). 72p. (Orig.). 1986. 19.95 (*0-9617656-0-7*) Tracy Diers.

Carbon & Coal Gasification: Science & Technology. Ed. by J. L. Figueiredo & J. A. Moulijn. 1986. lib. bdg. 193.50 (*90-247-3286-7*) Kluwer Ac.

An Asterisk (*) at the beginning of an entry indicates that the title is appearing in BIP for the first time.

Carbon & the Biosphere: Proceedings. Ed. by George M. Woodwell & Erene Pecan. LC 73-600092. (AEC Symposium Ser.). 400p. 1973. pap. 18.00 (*0-87079-006-4*, CONF-720510); fiche 9.00 (*0-87079-156-7*, CONF-720510) DOE.

Carbon Black: Physics, Chemistry, & Elastomer Reinforcement. Jean B. Donnet et al. LC 75-16753. (Illus.). 363p. reprint ed. pap. 103.50 (*0-317-08000-8*, 2020283) Bks Demand.

Carbon Black: Science & Technology. 2nd rev. ed. Ed. by Jean-Baptiste Donnet et al. LC 93-16640. 488p. 1993. 199.00 (*0-8247-8975-X*) Dekker.

Carbon Black-Polymer Composites: The Physics of Electrically Conducting Composites. Ed. by Enid K. Sichel. LC 82-10032. (Plastics Engineering Ser.: No. 3). (Illus.). 224p. reprint ed. pap. 63.90 (*0-685-44446-5*, 2052256) Bks Demand.

Carbon-Carbon & Carbon-Proton NMR Couplings: Applications to Organic Stereochemistry & Conformational Analysis. James L. Marshall. LC 82-16117. (Methods in Stereochemical Analysis Ser.: Vol. 2). (Illus.). 241p. 1983. lib. bdg. 80.00 (*0-89573-113-4*) VCH Pubs.

Carbon-Carbon Bond Formation. Augustine. (Techniques & Applications in Organic Synthesis Ser.: Vol. 6). 464p. 1979. 175.00 (*0-8247-6787-X*) Dekker.

Carbon-Carbon Composites. G. M. Savage. (Illus.). 300p. 1992. 99.95 (*0-412-36150-7*, A9470) Chapman & Hall.

Carbon-Carbon Materials & Composites. Ed. by John D. Buckley & D. D. Edie. LC 92-35012. (Illus.). 281p. 1993. 54.00 (*0-8155-1324-0*) Noyes.

Carbon Catcher Program: Using the Earth to Take Carbon from the Sky. Ed. by Gerry Wass. (Illus.). 32p. (Orig.). 1993. pap. text ed. 4.95 (*0-9639534-0-0*) W A T E R Fnd.

Carbon Connection. Leonard Ridzon & Charles Walters, Jr. LC 90-61305. 112p. 1990. pap. 12.00 (*0-911311-24-6*) Halcyon Hse.

Carbon Copy Plus 6.0 Companion. David Angell. (Illus.). (Orig.). 1991. pap. 24.95 (*0-13-772344-X*) Brady Compu Bks.

***Carbon Cycle.** Leonard Ridzon & Charles Walters. LC 94-70735. 143p. 1994. 15.00 (*0-911311-46-7*) Halcyon Hse.

Carbon Cycling in the Glacial Ocean: Constraints on the Ocean's Role in Global Change: Quantitative Approaches in Paleoceanography. Ed. by Rainer Zahn et al. LC 93-49420. (NATO ASI Series I: Global Environmental Change: Vol. 17). (Illus.). 593p. 1994. 240.00 (*0-387-57594-4*) Spr-Verlag.

Carbon Dioxide. A. S. Young. 1993. 105.31 (*0-08-029196-1*, Pergamon Pr) Elsevier.

Carbon Dioxide: Current Views & Developments in Energy-Climate Research. Ed. by I. W. Bach et al. 1983. lib. bdg. 164.00 (*90-277-1485-1*) Kluwer Ac.

Carbon Dioxide: Friend or Foe? Sherwood B. Idso. (Illus.). xiii, 92p. (Orig.). 1982. pap. 9.95 (*0-9623489-0-2*) IBR Pr.

Carbon Dioxide Activation by Metal Complexes. Arno Behr. LC 88-14873. 161p. 1988. lib. bdg. 130.00 (*0-89573-826-0*) VCH Pubs.

Carbon Dioxide & Climate: Dedicated to Williard F. Libby & Hans E. Suss. L. M. Libby. (Illus.). 270p. 1980. pap. 48.00 (*0-08-026240-6*, Pergamon Pr) Elsevier.

Carbon Dioxide & Global Change: Earth in Transition. Sherwood B. Idso. (Illus.). viii, 292p. (Orig.). (C). 1989. pap. 19.95 (*0-9623489-1-0*) IBR Pr.

Carbon Dioxide As a Source of Carbon: Chemical & Biochemical Uses. Ed. by M. Aresta & G. Forti. (C). 1987. lib. bdg. 144.00 (*90-277-2444-6*) Kluwer Ac.

***Carbon Dioxide Chemistry: Environmental Issues.** Ed. by Jan & Claire-Marie. 405p. 1994. 129.95 (*0-85186-634-4*) Royal Soc CN.

Carbon Dioxide, Climate & Society: Proceedings of an IIASA Workshop, Feb. 1978. Ed. by J. Williams. 1978. 141.00 (*0-08-023252-3*, Pub. by Pergamon Repr UK) Franklin.

***Carbon Dioxide Corrosion in Oil & Gas Production.** Ed. by B. Kermani. (EFC Report Ser.: 13). 182p. 1994. 100.00 (*0-901716-58-8*, Pub. by Inst Materials UK) Ashgate Pub Co.

Carbon Dioxide Enrichment of Greenhouse Crops: Status & Carbon Dioxide Sources. Ed. by Herbert Z. Enoch & Bruce A. Kimball. 208p. 1986. 259.90 (*0-8493-5610-5*, SB415, CRC Reprint) Franklin.

Carbon Dioxide Enrichment of Greenhouse Crops, Vol. 1: Status & CO2 Sources. H. Enoch & B. Kimball. LC 85-16648. 1986. 106.00 (*0-8493-5611-3*, CRC Reprint) Franklin.

Carbon Dioxide Enrichment of Greenhouse Crops, Vol. 2: Physiology Yield Economics. H. Enoch & B. Kimball. LC 85-16648. 1986. 130.00 (*0-8493-5612-1*, CRC Reprint) Franklin.

Carbon Dioxide Equilibria & Their Applications. J. N. Butler. 1982. pap. write for info. (*0-201-10100-9*) Addison-Wesley.

Carbon Dioxide Equilibria & Their Applications. James N. Butler. 250p. 1991. 79.95 (*0-87371-624-8*, QD181) Lewis Pubs.

Carbon Dioxide Extinguishing Systems. National Fire Protection Association Staff. 46p. 1993. 2.25 (*0-317-63044-X*, 12-93) Natl Fire Prot.

Carbon Dioxide Fixation & Reduction in Biological & Model Systems. Ed. by Carl-Ivar Branden & Gunter Schneider. LC 93-45258. (Illus.). 320p. 1994. 135.00 (*0-19-854782-X*) OUP.

Carbon Dioxide Flooding. Klins. 267p. 1988. text ed. 94.00 (*0-13-115064-2*) P-H.

Carbon Dioxide Flooding: Basic Mechanisms & Project Design. Mark A. Klins. LC 83-6494. (Illus.). 267p. 1984. 36.00 (*0-934634-44-0*) Intl Human Res.

***Carbon Dioxide in Mississippi Rocks of the Paradox Basin & Adjacent Areas, Colorado, Utah, New Mexico, & Arizona.** James A. Cappa & Dudley D. Rice. LC 95-2. (Evolution of Sedimentary Basins, Vol. H; Bulletin Ser.: Vol. 2000). 1995. write for info. (*0-615-00474-1*) US Geol Survey.

Carbon Dioxide Lasers: Effects & Applications. Ed. by Walter W. Duley. 1976. text ed. 151.00 (*0-12-223350-6*) Acad Pr.

***Carbon Dioxide Removal from Coal-Fired Power Plants.** Chris Hendriks. LC 94-43111. (Energy & Environment Ser.: Vol. 1). 1995. write for info. (*0-7923-3269-5*) Kluwer Ac.

Carbon Dioxide Review, 1982. William C. Clark. (Illus.). 1982. pap. 52.00 (*0-19-855368-4*) OUP.

Carbon Dioxide (11-MO-594) & the Robert Schneider (11-MS-1177) Sites: Late Woodland, Emergent Mississippian, & Mississippian Occupations. Fred A. Finney & Andrew C. Fortier. (American Bottom Archaeology Ser.: Selected FAI-270 Site Reports: Vol. 11). (Illus.). 328p. 1985. pap. 19.50 (*0-252-01073-6*) U of Ill Pr.

Carbon Dynamics in Eutrophic, Temperate Lakes. Ed. by B. Riemann & M. Sondergaard. 296p. 1987. 84.75 (*0-444-42736-8*) Elsevier.

Carbon Emissions Control Strategies: Case Studies in International Cooperation. Ed. by William U. Chandler. LC 90-19136. (Illus.). 263p. 1990. pap. 25.00 (*0-942635-19-1*) World Wildlife Fund.

***Carbon Fiber Composites.** Deborah D. Chung. 288p. 1994. 89.95 (*0-7506-9145-X*) Buttrwrth-Heinemann.

Carbon Fibers. 2nd ed. Donnet & Bansal. (International Fiber Science & Technology Ser.: Vol. 10). 496p. 1990. 190.00 (*0-8247-7865-0*) Dekker.

Carbon Fibers: Information, Structure, & Properties. L. H. Peebles, Jr. LC 94-7765. 1994. write for info. (*0-8493-2450-5*) CRC Pr.

Carbon Fibers: Technology Uses & Prospects. Ed. by Plastics & Rubber Institute Staff. LC 86-5155. (Illus.). 217p. 1986. 36.00 (*0-8155-1079-9*) Noyes.

Carbon Fibers Filaments & Composites. Ed. by J. L. Figueiredo et al. (Proceedings of the NATO Advanced Study Institute on Carbon Fibers & Filamets Held in Alvor, Portugal, May 15-27, 1989 Ser.). (C). 1990. lib. bdg. 196.50 (*0-7923-0602-3*) Kluwer Ac.

Carbon Fibres & Their Composites. E. Fitzer. (Illus.). 309p. 1986. 106.00 (*0-387-15804-9*) Spr-Verlag.

Carbon-Fluorine Compounds: Chemistry, Biochemistry & Biological Activities. Ciba Foundation Staff. LC 72-76005. (Ciba Foundation Symposium: New Ser.: No. 2). 425p. reprint ed. pap. 121.20 (*0-317-28328-6*, 2022135) Bks Demand.

Carbon Fourteen. Ann Deagon. LC 74-79483. 72p. 1974. 15.00 (*0-87023-170-7*); pap. 8.95 (*0-87023-171-5*) U of Mass Pr.

Carbon-Fourteen Dating of Iron. Nikolas J. Van der Merwe. LC 75-76206. 149p. reprint ed. pap. 42.50 (*0-317-08213-2*, 2020171) Bks Demand.

Carbon-Functional Organosilicon Compounds. Ed. by Vaclav Chvalovsky & J. M. Bellama. LC 84-3438. (Modern Inorganic Chemistry Ser.). 318p. 1984. 69.50 (*0-306-41671-9*, Plenum Pr) Plenum.

Carbon-Graphite Fibers, No. YGB-165A: Highlighting New Applications, U. S. & Global Markets, Players & New Developments. Thomas Abraham. 1994. 2,650.00 (*0-89336-203-4*) BCC.

Carbon Isotope Techniques. Ed. by David C. Coleman & Brian Fry. (Isotopic Techniques in Plant, Soil, & Aquatic Biology Ser.: Vol. 1). (Illus.). 274p. 1991. text ed. 89.00 (*0-12-179730-9*); pap. 44.95 (*0-12-179731-7*) Acad Pr.

Carbon Monoxide, No. 43. Ed. by R. W. Cargill. (Solubility Data Ser.). (Illus.). 330p. 1990. 120.00 (*0-08-030733-7*, 1901; 1906; 2303; 1502, Pergamon Pr) Elsevier.

Carbon Monoxide & Human Lethality: Fire & Non-Fire Studies. Ed. by Marcelo M. Hirschler et al. LC 93-3411. vi, 424p. 1993. 160.00 (*1-85861-015-X*, Pub. by Elsevier Applied Sci UK) Elsevier.

Carbon Monoxide, Industry & Performance. Ed. by W. H. Walton. 1976. pap. 26.00 (*0-08-019966-6*, Pergamon Pr) Elsevier.

Carbon Monoxide Poisoning. K. K. Jain. 200p. (Orig.). 1990. 37.50 (*0-87527-258-4*) Green.

Carbon, Nitrogen & Sulfur Pollutants & Their Determination in Air & Water. Greyson. 416p. 1990. 165.00 (*0-8247-8235-6*) Dekker.

Carbon-Nitrogen-Sulfur: Human Interference in the Grand Biospheric Cycles. Vaclav Smil. LC 85-25758. (Modern Perspectives in Energy Ser.). 476p. 1985. 110.00 (*0-306-42026-0*, Plenum Pr) Plenum.

Carbon Partitioning Within & Between Organisms. Ed. by C. J. Pollock et al. (Environmental Plant Biology Ser.). (Illus.). 258p. 1992. 147.50x (*1-872748-95-3*, Pub. by Bios Scientific UK) Coronet Bks.

Carbon Reinforced Epoxy Systems, Vol. 15. Ed. by Kier M. Finlayson. LC 74-83231. (Materials Technology Ser.). 448p. 1989. pap. 34.00 (*0-87762-649-9*) Technomic.

Carbon Reinforced Epoxy Systems, Vol. 16. Ed. by Kier M. Finlayson. LC 74-83231. (Materials Technology Ser.). 556p. 1989. pap. 38.00 (*0-87762-650-2*) Technomic.

Carbon Stars. rev. ed. Z. K. Alksne & Ya Y. Ikaunieks. Ed. by J. H. Baumert. (Astronomy & Astrophysics Ser.: Vol. 11). Orig. Title: Uglerodnye Zvezdy. (Illus.). 192p. pap. 24.00 (*0-912918-16-0*, 0016) Pachart Pub Hse.

Carbon Steel Pipe, Structural Tubing, Line Pipe, Oil Country Tubular Goods. 40p. 1982. 10.00 (*0-685-56512-2*) Iron & Steel.

Carbon Steel, Wire & Rods. LC 92-75013. 136p. 1993. 35.00 (*0-932897-80-0*) Iron & Steel.

Carbon Substrates in Biotechnology. J. D. Stowell et al. Ed. by A. J. Beardsmore et al. (Society for General Microbiology Special Publications: Vol. 21). 220p. (C). 1987. 80.00 (*1-85221-021-4*, IRL Pr); pap. text ed. 50.00 (*1-85221-020-6*, IRL Pr) OUP.

Carbon-Thirteen in Organic Chemistry. Ed. by E. Buncel & C. C. Lee. (Isotopes in Organic Chemistry Ser.: Vol. 3). 288p. 1977. 113.00 (*0-444-41472-X*) Elsevier.

Carbon-Thirteen NMR Spectral Problems. Robert B. Bates & William A. Beavers. LC 79-92216. (Organic Chemistry Ser.). 288p. 1981. text ed. 49.50 (*0-89603-010-5*) Humana.

***Carbon 13 NMR Chemical Shifts in Structural & Stereochemical Analysis.** Kalevi Pihlaja & Erich Kleinpeter. LC 94-5420. (Methods in Stereochemical Analysis). 1994. write for info. (*0-89573-332-3*) VCH Pubs.

Carbon-13 NMR in Polymer Science. Ed. by Wallace M. Pasika. LC 79-13384. (ACS Symposium Ser.: No. 103). 344p. 1979. 38.95 (*0-8412-0505-1*) Am Chemical.

Carbon-13 NMR of Flavonoids. Ed. by P. K. Agrawal. (Studies in Organic Chemistry). 574p. 1989. 179.50 (*0-444-87449-6*) Elsevier.

Carbon-13 NMR Spectral Data: A "Living" COM-Microfiche Collection of Reference Material. 4th ed. Ed. by W. Bremser et al. 1987. 3,265.00 (*0-89573-419-2*) VCH Pubs.

Carbon-13 NMR Spectroscopy. Hans-Otto Kalinowski et al. LC 86-26767. 730p. 1988. text ed. 415.00 (*0-471-91306-5*) Wiley.

Carbon-13 NMR Spectroscopy: High-Resolution Methods & Applications in Organic Chemistry & Biochemistry. 3rd rev. ed. Eberhard Breitmaier & Wolfgang Voelter. LC 86-28098. (Illus.). 515p. 1987. 220.00 (*0-89573-493-1*) VCH Pubs.

***Carbon-13 NMR Spectroscopy in Biological Systems.** Ed. by Nicolau Beckmann. (Illus.). 334p. 1995. boxed 69.95 (*0-12-084370-6*) Acad Pr.

Carbon-13 Nuclear Magnetic Resonance Spectroscopy. 2nd ed. George C. Levy et al. 352p. (C). 1993. reprint ed. lib. bdg. 59.95 (*0-89464-796-2*) Krieger.

Carbon-14 in the Environment. National Council on Radiation Protection & Measurements Staff. LC 84-29586. (Report Ser.: No. 81). 65p. 1985. pap. text ed. 25.00 (*0-913392-73-1*) NCRP Pubns.

Carbonaceous Adsorbents for the Treatment of Ground & Surface Waters. James W. Neely & Eric G. Isacoff. LC 82-8930. (Pollution Engineering & Technology Ser.: No. 21). (Illus.). 240p. reprint ed. pap. 68.40 (*0-7837-5373-X*, 2045137) Bks Demand.

Carbonate Additions to Cement. Ed. by Paul Klieger & R. Douglas Hooton. LC 90-21. (Special Technical Publication Ser.: No. 1064). (Illus.). 88p. 1990. text ed. 39.00 (*0-8031-1454-0*, 04-010640-07) ASTM.

Carbonate Buildups: A Core Workshop. Paul M. Harris. (SEPM Core Workshop Ser.: No. 4). (Illus.). 599p. reprint ed. pap. 170.80 (*0-7837-5986-X*, 2045793) Bks Demand.

Carbonate Cements. Ed. by Nahum Schneidermann & Paul M. Harris. (Special Publications Ser.: No. 36). 408p. 1985. 49.00 (*0-918985-37-4*) SEPM.

Carbonate-Clastic Transitions. Ed. by L. J. Doyle & H. H. Roberts. (Developments in Sedimentology Ser.: Vol. 42). 300p. 1988. 97.50 (*0-444-42904-2*) Elsevier.

Carbonate Concepts from the Maldives, Indian Ocean. Edward G. Purdy & George T. Bertram. (Studies in Geology: No. 34). (Illus.). 56p. (Orig.). 1993. pap. 27.00 (*0-89181-042-0*) AAPG.

***Carbonate Depositional Environments.** Ed. by Peter A. Scholle et al. (AAPG Memoir Ser.: No. 33). (Illus.). xi, 708p. 1983. 78.00 (*0-89181-310-1*) AAPG.

Carbonate Depositional Environments - Modern & Ancient, Pt. 5: Diagenesis I. R. C. Bathurst & L. S. Land. Ed. by J. E. Warme & K. W. Shanley. LC 85-22384. (Colorado School of Mines Quarterly Ser.: Vol. 81, No. 4). (Illus.). 50p. 1987. pap. text ed. 15.00 (*0-918062-72-1*) Colo Sch Mines.

Carbonate Depositional Environments - Modern & Ancient, Pt. 6: Diagenesis II. R. B. Halley & R. K. Matthews. Ed. by J. E. Warme & K. W. Shanley. LC 85-22384. (Colorado School of Mines Quarterly Ser.: Vol. 82, No. 1). (Illus.). 1987. pap. text ed. 15.00 (*0-918062-73-X*) Colo Sch Mines.

Carbonate Depositional Environments--Modern & Ancient: Part 1: Reefs--Zonation, Depositional Facies, & Diagenesis. Noel P. James & Ian G. Macintyre. Ed. by John E. Warme et al. LC 85-22384. (Colorado School of Mines Quarterly Ser.: Vol. 80, No. 3). (Illus.). 80p. (C). 1985. pap. text ed. 15.00 (*0-918062-64-0*) Colo Sch Mines.

Carbonate Depositional Environments-Modern & Ancient: Part 2: Carbonate Platforms. P. M. Harris et al. Ed. by J. W. Warme & K. W. Shanley. LC 85-22384. (Colorado School of Mines Quarterly Ser.: Vol. 80, No.4, 1985). (Illus.). 70p. (C). 1986. pap. 15.00 (*0-918062-65-9*) Colo Sch Mines.

Carbonate Depositional Environments-Modern & Ancient: Part 3: Tidal Flats. E. A. Shinn & L. A. Hardie. Ed. by J. E. Warme & K. W. Shanley. (Colorado School of Mines Quarterly Ser.: Vol. 81, No. 1, 1986). (Illus.). 100p. (C). 1986. pap. 20.00 (*0-918062-66-7*) Colo Sch Mines.

Carbonate Depositional Environments-Modern & Ancient: Pt. 4: Periplatform Carbonates. Henry T. Mullins. Ed. by John E. Warme & Keith W. Shanley. LC 85-22384. (Colorado School of Mines Quarterly Ser.: Vol. 81, No. 2, 1986). (Illus.). 63p. 1986. pap. text ed. 20.00 (*0-918062-69-1*) Colo Sch Mines.

Carbonate Diagenesis As a Control on Stratigraphic Traps: With Examples from the Williston Basin. Mark W. Longman. (Education Course Note Ser.: No. 21). 166p. reprint ed. pap. 47.40 (*0-7837-3974-5*, 2043803) Bks Demand.

Carbonate Environments & Sequences of Caicos Platform, No. T374. Ed. by Wanless. (IGC Field Trip Guidebooks Ser.). 1989. 21.00 (*0-87590-598-6*) Am Geophysical.

Carbonate Microfabrics. Ed. by R. Rezak & D. L. Lavoie. LC 93-3272. (Frontiers in Sedimentary Geology Ser.). 1993. Acid-free paper. 79.00 (*0-387-94035-9*) Spr-Verlag.

***Carbonate Mud-Mounds: Their Origins & Evolution.** Ed. by C. L. Monty et al. LC 94-41305. (Special Publications of the International Association of Sedimentologists: No. 23). 1995. write for info. (*0-86542-933-2*) Blackwell Sci.

Carbonate Petroleum Reservoir. P. O. Roehl & P. W. Choquette. (Casebooks in Earth Sciences Ser.). (Illus.). 480p. 1985. 119.00 (*0-387-96012-0*) Spr-Verlag.

Carbonate Reservoir Rocks. Ed. by Robert B. Halley & Robert G. Loucks. (Core Workshop Notes Ser.: No. 1). 183p. 1980. 14.00 (*0-918985-23-4*) SEPM.

Carbonate Rock Depositional Models: A Microfacies Approach. Albert V. Carozzi. (Advanced Reference Ser.). 576p. 1988. reprint ed. text ed. 99.00 (*0-13-114398-0*) P-H.

Carbonate Rock Sequences from the Cretaceous of Texas, No. T376. Ed. by Moore. (IGC Field Trip Guidebooks Ser.). 56p. 1989. 21.00 (*0-87590-656-7*) Am Geophysical.

***Carbonate Rocks I: Classifications-Dolomite-Dolomitization.** Ed. by Peggy Rice et al. (AAPG Reprint Ser.: No. 4). (Illus.). 237p. 1972. pap. 6.00 (*0-89181-528-7*) AAPG.

***Carbonate Rocks III: Organic Reefs.** Ed. by R. H. Dott, Sr. et al. (AAPG Reprint Ser.: No. 15). (Illus.). 190p. 1975. pap. 6.00 (*0-89181-540-6*) AAPG.

Carbonate Sands. Ed. by Paul M. Harris. (Core Workshop Notes Ser.: No. 5). 464p. 1984. pap. 28.00 (*0-918985-27-7*) SEPM.

Carbonate Sedimentation & Petrology, Vol. 4. Ed. by P. A. Scholle et al. 160p. 1989. 24.00 (*0-87590-700-8*) Am Geophysical.

Carbonate Sediments & Their Diagenesis. 2nd ed. R. G. Bathurst. (Developments in Sedimentology Ser.: Vol. 12). 608p. 1975. pap. 39.00 (*0-444-41353-7*) Elsevier.

Carbonate Sequence Stratigraphy Recent Developments & Applications. Ed. by Robert G. Loucks & J. Frederick Sarg. (AAPG Memoir Ser.: No. 57). (Illus.). vi, 545p. 1993. 78.00 (*0-89181-336-5*) AAPG.

Carbonate-Siliciclastic Mixtures. Ed. by David A. Budd & Paul M. Harris. (Reprint Ser.: No. 14). (Illus.). 271p. (Orig.). 1990. pap. 29.50 (*0-918985-85-4*) SEPM.

Carbonates: Mineralogy & Chemistry. Ed. by R. J. Reeder. (Reviews in Mineralogy Ser.: Vol. 11). 394p. 1983. 17.00 (*0-939950-15-4*) Mineralogical Soc.

Carbonatite-Nephelinite Volcanism: An African Case History. Michael J. Le Bas. LC 76-21090. (Illus.). 401p. reprint ed. pap. 114.30 (*0-685-24171-8*, 2033049) Bks Demand.

***Carbonatite Volcanism: Oldoinyo Lengai & the Petrogenesis of Natrocarbonatites.** Ed. by K. Bell & J. Keller. 224p. 1995. 128.00 (*0-387-58299-1*) Spr-Verlag.

***Carbondale: A Pictorial History.** Betty Mitchell. (Illinois Pictorial History Ser.). (Illus.). 1992. write for info. (*0-943963-20-6*) G Bradley.

Carbondale Dreams. Steven Sater. 1991. pap. 4.75 (*0-8222-0181-X*) Dramatists Play.

Carbonic Anhydrase: From Biochemistry & Genetics to Physiology & Clinical Medicine: Proceedings of the International Workshop on Carbonic Anhydrase Held in Spoleto, Italy in March 1990. Ed. by F. Botre et al. (Illus.). 467p. 1991. text ed. 140.00 (*1-56081-179-X*) VCH Pubs.

Carbonic Anhydrases: Cellular Physiology & Molecular Genetics. Ed. by S. J. Dodgson et al. (Illus.). 385p. 1991. 95.00 (*0-306-43636-1*, Plenum Pr) Plenum.

Carboniferous Crinoids of Texas with Stratigraphic Implications see Palaeontographica Americana: No. 2

Carboniferous Geology of the Eastern United States. Ed. by Cecil. (IGC Field Trip Guidebooks Ser.). 168p. 1989. 35.00 (*0-87590-647-8*, T143) Am Geophysical.

Carbonylation: Direct Synthesis of Carbonyl Compounds. H. M. Colquhoun et al. LC 91-10817. (Illus.). 320p. 1991. 69.50 (*0-306-43747-3*, Plenum Pr) Plenum.

Carboplatin: Present Status & Future Directions. Ed. by D. Khayat. (Journal: Oncology: Vol. 50, Suppl. 2, 1993). (Illus.). iv, 54p. 1993. pap. 23.25 (*3-8055-5891-0*) S Karger.

Carburetors, Pistons, Piston Rings & Engine Valves - Markets & Opportunities: 1990-1995 Analysis. rev. ed. Dennis M. Zogbi. (Illus.). 200p. (Orig.). 1990. pap. text ed. 995.00 (*1-878218-12-3*) World Info Tech.

Carburizing & Carbonitriding. American Society for Metals Staff. LC 76-55702. 233p. reprint ed. pap. 66.50 (*0-317-20679-6*, 2025145) Bks Demand.

Carbyne Complexes. Ed. by H. Fischer et al. LC 88-39162. 236p. 1988. lib. bdg. 125.00 (*0-89573-849-X*) VCH Pubs.

***Carcajou.** Richard Holst. 200p. (Orig.). 1994. pap. 10.00 (*0-9643280-0-3*) Cape Elizabeth.

Carcajou. Rutherford G. Montgomery. LC 36-6665. (Illus.). (J). (gr. 6-8). 1936. 4.95 (*0-87004-105-3*) Caxton.

Carcass Trade. Noreen Ayers. 1994. 20.00 (*0-688-10875-X*) Morrow.

***Carcass Trade.** Noreen Ayres. 352p. 1995. reprint ed. mass mkt. 4.99 (*0-380-71572-4*) Avon.

Carcel. 4th ed. Jesus Zarate. 291p. (SPA.). 1972. 9.95 (*84-320-5269-8*) Ediciones.

An Asterisk (*) at the beginning of an entry indicates that the title is appearing in BIP for the first time. 1041

Carcellini Emerald with Other Tales. Constance C. Harrison. LC 79-98574. (Short Story Index Reprint Ser.). 1977. 20.95 (*0-8369-3148-3*) Ayer.

Carcino-Embryonic Proteins: Chemistry, Biology, Clinical Application, 2 vols., Set. Ed. by F. G. Lehmann. 1979. 236.00 (*0-444-80097-2*, North Holland) Elsevier.

Carcinoembryonic Antigen Gene Family. A. Yachi & J. E. Shively. 1989. 77.00 (*0-444-81089-7*) Elsevier.

Carcinofetal Proteins: Biology & Chemistry, Vol. 259. Ed. by Hidematsu Hirai & Elliot Alpert. (Annals Ser.). 452p. 1975. 54.50 (*0-89072-013-4*) NY Acad Sci.

Carcinogen Risk Assessment. Ed. by C. C. Travis. LC 87-37403. (Contemporary Issues in Risk Analysis Ser.: Vol. 3). (Illus.). 220p. 1988. 65.00 (*0-306-42848-2*, Plenum Pr) Plenum.

Carcinogen Risk Assessment: New Directions in the Qualitative & Quantitative Aspects. Ed. by Ronald W. Hart & Fred D. Hoerger. (Banbury Report Ser.: No. 31). (Illus.). 356p. 1988. 85.00 (*0-87969-231-6*) Cold Spring Harbor.

Carcinogenesis. Jerrold M. Ward. Ed. by Michael P. Waalkes. LC 93-28927. (Target Organ Toxicology Ser.). 496p. 1994. 100.00 (*0-7817-0124-4*) Raven.

Carcinogenesis, Vol. 1. Ed. by A. Canonico & G. P. Margison. (Illus.). 1979. 139.00 (*0-08-024379-7*, Pub. by Pergamon Repr UK) Franklin.

Carcinogenesis: Fundamental Mechanisms & Environmental Effects. Ed. by Bernard Pullman et al. (Jerusalem Symposia on Quantum Chemistry & Biochemistry Ser.: No. 13). 560p. 1980. lib. bdg. 126.50 (*90-277-1171-2*) Kluwer Ac.

Carcinogenesis: Proceedings of the Symposium Biology of Skin, University of Oregon Medical School, 1965. W. Montagna & R. Dobson. LC 60-10839. (Advances in Biology of Skin Ser.: Vol. 7). 1966. 153.00 (*0-08-011576-4*, Pub. by Pergamon Repr UK) Franklin.

Carcinogenesis & Adducts in Animals & Humans. Ed. by Miriam C. Poirier & F. A. Beland. (Progress in Experimental Tumor Research Ser.: Vol. 31). (Illus.). viii, 116p. 1987. 95.25 (*3-8055-4457-X*) S Karger.

Carcinogenesis & Aging, 2 vols. Ed. by Anisimou. 1987. 348.00 (*0-8493-6277-6*, RC268) CRC Pr.

Carcinogenesis & Dietary Fat. Ed. by S. Abraham. (Prostaglandins, Leukotrienes, & Cancer Ser.). (C). 1989. lib. bdg. 152.50 (*0-7923-0117-X*) Kluwer Ac.

Carcinogenesis & Mutagenesis. LC 77-91833. 388p. 39.00 (*0-930376-02-1*) Chem-Orbital.

Carcinogenesis & Mutagenesis Testing. Ed. by J. Fielding Douglas. LC 84-12820. (Contemporary Biomedicine Ser.). 352p. 1984. 89.50 (*0-89603-042-3*) Humana.

Carcinogenesis As a Biological Problem. I. Berenblum. 1975. 131.00 (*0-444-10628-6*) Elsevier.

Carcinogenic & Mutagenic Effects of Diesel Engine Exhaust: Proceedings of the International Symposium, Tsukuba, Japan, July 26-28, 1986. Ed. by N. Ishinishi et al. (Developments in Toxicology & Environmental Science Ser.: No. 13). 540p. 1987. 176.00 (*0-444-80854-X*) Elsevier.

Carcinogenic & Mutagenic Metal Compounds: Environmental & Analytical Chemistry & Biological Effects. E. Merian et al. (Current Topics In Environmental & Toxicological Chemistry Ser.: Vol. 8). 537p. 1985. text ed. 197.00 (*2-88124-022-4*) Gordon & Breach.

Carcinogenic & Mutagenic Metal Compounds 2. E. Merian et al. 544p. 1988. text ed. 125.00 (*2-88124-663-X*) Gordon & Breach.

Carcinogenic Risks: Strategies for Intervention: Risques Cancerogenes: Strategies d'Intervention: Proceedings of a Symposium Organized by IARC & L'Institute National de la Sante et de la Recherche Medicale... Held at Lyon, France, 30 November-2 December 1977. International Agency for Research on Cancer Staff. LC 81-463382. (IARC Scientific Publications: No. 25). 311p. reprint ed. pap. 88.70 (*0-8357-6450-8*, 2035821) Bks Demand.

Carcinogenically Active Chemicals. N. Irving Sax & Richard J. Lewis. 1991. text ed. 149.95 (*0-442-31875-8*) Van Nos Reinhold.

Carcinogenicity & Pesticides: Principles, Issues, & Relationships. Ed. by Nancy N. Ragsdale & Robert E. Menzer. LC 89-18052. (Symposium Ser.: No. 414). (Illus.). 237p. 1989. 54.95 (*0-8412-1703-3*) Am Chemical.

Carcinogens: Identification & Mechanisms of Action. Symposium on Fundamental Cancer Research Staff. Ed. by A. Clark Griffin & Charles R. Shaw. LC 78-23366. (Illus.). 505p. reprint ed. pap. 144.00 (*0-7837-7095-2*, 2046920) Bks Demand.

Carcinogens: Index of Modern Information. American Health Research Institute Staff. LC 88-47988. 150p. 1990. 44.50 (*1-55914-196-4*); pap. 39.50 (*1-55914-197-2*) ABBE Pubs Assn.

Carcinogens & Mutagens in the Environment: Food Products, Vol. 1. Ed. by Hans F. Stich. 320p. 1982. 191.00 (*0-8493-5881-7*, RC268, CRC Reprint) Franklin.

Carcinogens & Mutagens in the Environment: Naturally Occurring Compounds: Endogenous Formation & Modulation, Vol. II. Ed. by Hans F. Stich. 192p. 1983. 156.00 (*0-8493-5882-5*, RC268, CRC Reprint) Franklin.

Carcinogens & Mutagens in the Environment: Naturally Occurring Compounds: Epidemiology & Distribution, Vol. III. Ed. by Hans F. Stich. 208p. 1983. 156.00 (*0-8493-5883-3*, RC268, CRC Reprint) Franklin.

Carcinogens & Mutagens in the Environment: The Workplace, Vol. V. Hans F. Stich. 192p. 1985. 144.00 (*0-8493-5885-X*, RC268, CRC Reprint) Franklin.

Carcinogens & Mutagens in the Environment: The Workplace: Monitoring & Prevention of Occupational Hazards, Vol. IV. Ed. by Hans F. Stitch. 216p. 1985. 110.00 (*0-8493-5884-1*, RC268, CRC Reprint) Franklin.

Carcinogens & Related Substances: Analytical Chemistry for Toxicological Research. Malcolm C. Bowman. LC 79-20476. (Illus.). 328p. reprint ed. pap. 93.50 (*0-7837-0861-0*, 2041169) Bks Demand.

Carcinogens in Industry & the Environment. Sontag. (Pollution Engineering & Technology Ser.: Vol. 16). 776p. 1981. 210.00 (*0-8247-1021-5*) Dekker.

***Carcinoid Tumors.** Ed. by R. Arnold et al. (Journal: Digestion: Vol. 55, Suppl. 3, 1994). (Illus.). iv, 116p. 1994. pap. 45.75 (*3-8055-6121-0*) S Karger.

Carcinoma Corporis Uteri. E. Held et al. Ed. by A. Reist. (Fortschritte der Geburtshilfe & Gynaekologie Ser.: Vol. 49). (Illus.). 150p. 1973. 38.50 (*3-8055-1564-2*) S Karger.

Carcinoma of the Breast. I. K. Dhawan & V. K. Kapoor. (C). 1987. 170.00 (*81-85017-37-9*, Pub. by Interprint II) St Mut.

Carcinoma of the Colon & Rectum. Ed. by Warren E. Enker. LC 78-52538. (Illus.). 432p. reprint ed. pap. 123.20 (*0-685-23360-X*, 2032296) Bks Demand.

Carcinoma of the Esophagus & Gastric Cardia. Ed. by Guo J. Huang & Ying K'Ai Wu. (Illus.). 429p. 1984. 229.00 (*0-387-12535-3*) Spr-Verlag.

Carcinoma of the Oral Cavity & Oropharynx. Ed. by H. D. Pape et al. LC 93-30355. (Recent Results in Cancer Research Ser.: Vol. 134). 1994. 98.00 (*0-387-56819-0*) Spr-Verlag.

Carcinoma of the Supraglottic Larynx. James H. Boyd et al. (Self-Instructional Package Ser.). (Illus.). 77p. (Orig.). (C). 1993. pap. text ed. 25.00 (*1-56772-008-0*) AAO-HNS.

Carcinomas of Esophagus & Colon. M. Webber & L. Sekely. LC 84-1838. (In Vitro Models Cancer Research Ser.). 1985. 134.00 (*0-8493-5581-8*, CRC Reprint) Franklin.

Carcinomas of Liver & Pancreas. M. Webber & L. Sekely. LC 84-1838. (In Vitro Models Cancer Research Ser.: Vol. 2). 1984. 138.00 (*0-8493-5582-6*, CRC Reprint) Franklin.

Carcinomas of the Head & Neck. Ed. by Charlotte Jacobs. (C). 1990. lib. bdg. 144.50 (*0-7923-0668-6*) Kluwer Ac.

Carciofo: Strategie di Lettura e Proposte di Attivia. D. Musumeci. 1990. pap. text ed. write for info. (*0-07-557836-0*) McGraw.

***Carciovascular Disease Risk Factors: New Areas pf Research.** Ed. by World Health Organization Staff. (Technical Report Ser.). 53p. 1994. pap. 9.00 (*92-4-120841-4*) World Health.

Card. Arnold Bennett. (Twentieth-Century Classics Ser.). 224p. 1991. 7.95 (*0-14-018017-6*, Penguin Classics) Viking Penguin.

Card. Arnold Bennett. 21.95 (*0-8488-0736-7*) Amereon Ltd.

Card Book. Abigail Tom & Heather McKay. 160p. (C). 1991. pap. write for info. (*0-13-115767-1*) P-H.

***Card Bus System Architecture.** MindShare, Inc. Staff. 1995. pap. write for info. (*0-201-40997-6*) Addison-Wesley.

Card-Carrying Americans: Privacy, Security & the National ID Card Debate. Joseph W. Eaton. 240p. (C). 1986. 59.50 (*0-8476-7424-X*) Rowman.

Card Catalog: Current Issues. Ed. by Cynthia C. Ryans. LC 81-720. 336p. 1981. 25.00 (*0-8108-1417-X*) Scarecrow.

Card Catalog of the Manuscript Collections of the Archives of American Art, 11 Vols., Set. 5500p. 1981. lib. bdg. 750.00 (*0-8420-2174-4*) Scholarly Res Inc.

Card Catalog of the Manuscript Collections of the Archives of American Art: 1981-84 Supplement. Intro. by Archives of American Art Staff. LC 84-20203. 542p. 1985. lib. bdg. 75.00 (*0-8420-2235-X*) Scholarly Res Inc.

Card Catalog of the Oral History Collections of the Archives of American Art. Intro. by Garnett McCoy. LC 83-27098. 343p. 1984. lib. bdg. 75.00 (*0-8420-2216-3*) Scholarly Res Inc.

Card Catalog of the Rubel Asiatic Research Collection: Harvard University Fine Arts Library, 7 Vols. Intro. by Yenshew Lynn Chao. 3680p. 1989. lib. bdg. 2,010.00 (*0-86291-852-9*) U Pubns Amer.

***Card College, Vol. 1.** Roberto Giobbi. Tr. by Richard Hatch. (Illus.). 252p. 1995. 30.00 (*0-945296-13-4*) Hermetic Pr.

Card Control: Practical Methods & Forty Original Card Experiments. Arthur H. Buckley. (Illus.). 224p. 1993. reprint ed. pap. text ed. 8.95 (*0-486-27757-7*) Dover.

Card-Counting Guide to Winning Blackjack. Jack Black. Ed. by John Valente. (Illus.). 80p. (Orig.). 1983. 14.95 (*0-914087-00-2*) Consumer Pubn.

Card Crafting: Over Forty-Five Ideas for Making Greeting Cards & Stationery. Gillian Souter. (Illus.). 128p. (J). (gr. 6 up). 1993. pap. 9.95 (*0-8069-8683-2*) Sterling.

Card, Cross & Jones: Criminal Law. 12th ed. Richard Card et al. 570p. 1992. U.K. pap. 36.00 (*0-406-00086-7*, U.K.) Butterworth Legal Pubs.

Card Engineering. Ian Honeybone. (On the Spot Guides Ser.). (Illus.). 96p. 1994. 7.95 (*1-56970-501-1*, Nippan Pubns) Bks Nippan.

Card Fortune-Telling. Foulsham Editors. 96p. 1995. pap. 7.95 (*0-572-01541-0*, Pub. by Foulsham UK) Atrium Pubs.

Card Games. rev. ed. Michael Johnstone. (Family Matters Ser.). (Illus.). 96p. (Orig.). 1994. pap. 6.95 (*0-7063-7225-5*, Pub. by Ward Lock UK) Sterling.

Card Games: An Expert Guide to More Than 100 Card Games. LC 93-85519. (Gem Ser.). (Illus.). 256p. 1994. pap. 5.95 (*1-56138-380-5*) Running Pr.

Card Games: Victorian Patience & Other Games for One or More Participants. Anness Publishing Staff. (Illus.). 96p. 1992. 8.95 (*0-8212-1973-1*) Bulfinch Pr.

Card Games Around the World. Sid Sackson. LC 94-18073. Orig. Title: Playing Cards Around the World. (Illus.). 146p. 1994. reprint ed. pap. 6.95 (*0-486-28100-0*) Dover.

Card Games for Children. Len Collis. (Illus.). 96p. (J). (ps up). 1989. pap. 5.95 (*0-8120-4290-5*) Barron.

Card Games for One. rev. ed. Michael Johnstone. (Family Matters Ser.). (Illus.). 96p. 1994. pap. 6.95 (*0-7063-7224-7*, Pub. by Ward Lock UK) Sterling.

***Card Games for One or Two.** Consumer Guide Editors. 128p. 1995. pap. 6.99 (*0-451-82300-1*, Sig) NAL-Dutton.

Card Games for Two. rev. ed. Sean Callery. (Family Matters Ser.). (Illus.). 96p. 1994. pap. 6.95 (*0-7063-7223-9*, Pub. by Ward Lock UK) Sterling.

***Card Guide to New Testament Greeek.** Benjamin Chapman & Gary S. Shogren. 2p. (C). 1995. 2.95 (*1-887070-01-X*) Stylus Publ.

Card Index. Rozewicz. 11.95 (*0-7145-0061-5*); pap. 6.95 (*0-7145-0062-3*) M Boyars Pubs.

***Card Industry Directory: 1995 Edition.** Ed. by John Stewart. 800p. 1994. pap. 360.00 (*1-881393-28-3*) Faulkner & Gray.

***Card Is in the Mail.** Kosta Kontoyiannaki. (Illus.). 18p. (J). (gr. k-3). 1995. pap. 10.95 (*1-56606-035-4*) Bradley Mann.

Card Manipulations. Jean Hugard. LC 73-81508. 160p. 1973. reprint ed. pap. 5.95 (*0-486-20539-8*) Dover.

Card Modeling: The Art of Creating Scale Models in Paper. Eric S. Peterson. (Illus.). 56p. (Orig.). 1994. pap. 14.95 (*0-9637100-0-1*) Caltrop Pub.

C.A.R.D. Monterey Bay Area: Bicycle Books & Information. Martin Krieg & Sally Vantress. (Cycle America Ser.: No. 3). (Illus.). 96p. (Orig.). 1990. pap. 4.95 (*0-9611490-2-7*) Cycle Amer.

Card Photographs, a Guide to Their History & Value. Lou W. McCulloch. LC 81-51444. (Illus.). 235p. 1981. 30.00 (*0-916838-56-0*) Schiffer.

***Card-Placing for You.** Andrew Kambites. 96p. 1995. pap. 11.95 (*0-575-05943-5*, Pub. by V Gollancz UK) Trafalgar.

Card Play Technique. rev. ed. Victor Mollo & Nico Gardener. 384p. 1981. pap. 12.95 (*0-571-11759-7*) Faber & Faber.

Card Play Technique: Contract Bridge. Norman Squire. 1976. 19.95 (*0-8464-1458-9*) Beekman Pubs.

Card Player. Bernard G. Lovett. LC 84-61984. 250p. (Orig.). 1984. pap. 8.00 (*0-9613960-0-8*) Nike Pr.

***Card Player Digest: 1988-1994.** Ed. by Dana Smith. (Illus.). 256p. (Orig.). 1995. pap. 24.95 (*1-884466-23-0*) Poker & Plus.

Card Punch-Key Punch Operator (Alphabetic) Jack Rudman. (Career Examination Ser.: C-124). 1994. pap. 23.95 (*0-8373-0124-6*) Nat Learn.

Card Punch Operator. Jack Rudman. (Career Examination Ser.: C-125). 1994. pap. 23.94 (*0-8373-0125-4*) Nat Learn.

Card Sharks. Roger Zelazny et al. Ed. by George R. Martin. (Wild Cards Ser.: Bk. I). 512p. (Orig.). 1993. mass mkt. 5.99 (*0-671-72159-3*) Baen Bks.

***Card Sharks: How Upper Deck Turned an Innocent Child's Hobby into a High-Stakes, Billion-Dollar Business.** Pete Williams. LC 95-4183. 1995. write for info. (*0-02-629061-8*) Macmillan.

Card Sharps, Dream Books & Bucket Shops: Gambling in 19th-Century America. Ann Fabian. LC 90-55121. (Illus.). 296p. 1990. 27.50 (*0-8014-2501-8*) Cornell U Pr.

***Card Tricks.** June Ford. (You Can Do It! Ser.). (Illus.). 80p. (Orig.). (J). (ps up). Date not set. pap. 12.95 (*1-56530-074-2*) Summit TX.

Card Weaving. Candace Crockett. LC 91-24156. 144p. (Orig.). 1991. pap. 19.95 (*0-934026-61-0*) Interweave.

Card Weaving or Tablet Weaving. Russell E. Groff. (Illus.). 1992. pap. 7.00 (*1-56659-008-6*) Robin & Russ.

Card Wizard see How to Do Tricks with Cards

Cardanus Comforte. Girolamo Cardano. Ed. by T. Bedingfield. LC 77-6565. (English Experience Ser.: No. 82). 204p. 1969. reprint ed. 25.00 (*90-221-0082-0*) Walter J Johnson.

Cardboard Carpentry. Janet D'Amato & Alex D'Amato. (Activity Bks.). (Illus.). (J). (gr. 2-5). lib. bdg. 13.95 (*0-87460-085-5*) Lion Bks.

Cardboard Crown. Martin Boyd. (Fiction Ser.). 272p. 1986. mass mkt. 4.95 (*0-14-006904-6*, Penguin Bks) Viking Penguin.

Cardboard House. Martin Adan. (Palabra Sur Ser.). 110p. (C). 1990. 17.95 (*1-55597-129-6*) Graywolf.

Cardenio: or the Second Maiden's Tragedy. William Shakespeare et al. LC 93-73354. (Illus.). 275p. 1994. text ed. 25.00 (*0-944435-24-6*) Glenbridge Pub.

Carderock: Past & Present, a Climber's Guide. Hanel. LC 90-61742. 125p. 1990. pap. 7.00 (*0-915746-40-9*) Potomac Appalach.

***Cardiac Adaptation & Failure.** Ed. by M. Hori et al. LC 94-40505. 1995. 195.00 (*0-387-70133-8*) Spr-Verlag.

Cardiac Anaesthesia: Problems & Innovations. Ed. by S. De Lange et al. (Developments in Critical Care, Medicine, & Anesthesiology Ser.). 1986. lib. bdg. 92.50 (*0-89838-794-9*) Kluwer Ac.

Cardiac & Noncardiac Complications of Open Heart Surgery: Prevention, Diagnosis, & Treatment. Ed. by Morris N. Kotler & Anthony D. Alfieri. (Illus.). 432p. 1992. 62.00 (*0-87993-524-3*) Futura Pub.

Cardiac & Pulmonary Management. M. Gabriel Khan et al. LC 92-11602. (Illus.). 977p. 1992. pap. text ed. 49.50 (*0-8121-1494-9*) Williams & Wilkins.

Cardiac & Vascular Diseases, 2 vols. Ed. by Hadley L. Conn & Orville Horwitz. LC 71-98493. reprint ed. pap. 160.00 (*0-685-73701-2*, 2055998); reprint ed. pap. 160.00 (*0-685-73702-0*) Bks Demand.

Cardiac Anesthesia. 3rd ed. Ed. by Joel A. Kaplan. LC 92-24342. (Illus.). 1376p. 1993. text ed. 185.00 (*0-7216-6707-4*) Saunders.

Cardiac Anesthesia for Infants & Children. Jay Kamban. 400p. 1994. 70.00 (*0-8016-7289-9*) Mosby Yr Bk.

Cardiac Angiography. Stephen W. Miller. (Library of Radiology). 430p. 1984. 105.00 (*0-316-57367-1*) Little.

Cardiac Applications of Digital Angiography. Ed. by Alan G. Wasserman & Allan M. Ross. (Illus.). 320p. 1989. 53.00 (*0-87993-332-1*) Futura Pub.

***Cardiac Arrest: The Pathophysiology & Therapy of Sudden Death.** Ed. by Norman A. Paradis et al. LC 95-14196. (Illus.). 1995. write for info. (*0-683-06765-6*) Williams & Wilkins.

Cardiac Arrhythmia: Mechanisms, Diagnosis, & Management. Philip J. Podrid & Peter Kowey. 1472p. 1994. 159.00 (*0-683-06905-5*) Williams & Wilkins.

Cardiac Arrhythmias. 3rd ed. Ed. by David Bennett. 206p. 1989. text ed. 59.95 (*0-7236-1595-0*, Pub. by John Wright UK) Buttrwrth-Heinemann.

Cardiac Arrhythmias. 3rd ed. Mandel. 860p. 1995. write for info. (*0-397-51185-X*) Lippincott.

Cardiac Arrhythmias. 4th ed. David H. Bennett. LC 93-15125. (Illus.). 248p. 1993. pap. 45.00 (*0-7506-1638-5*) Buttrwrth-Heinemann.

Cardiac Arrhythmias: A Bedside Guide to Diagnosis & Treatment. Martin A. Alpert. LC 79-28272. (Illus.). 303p. reprint ed. pap. 86.40 (*0-8357-6763-9*, 2035424) Bks Demand.

Cardiac Arrhythmias: A Practical Approach. Ed. by Gerald V. Naccarelli. (Clinical Cardiovascular Therapeutics Ser.: Vol. 2). (Illus.). 600p. 1991. 70.00 (*0-87993-373-9*) Futura Pub.

Cardiac Arrhythmias: A Practical Guide for the Clinician. 2nd ed. Ed. by Robert A. Waugh et al. (Illus.). 448p. (C). 1994. text ed. 75.00 (*0-8036-9114-9*) Davis Co.

Cardiac Arrhythmias: An Approach to Their Electrocardiographic Recognition. 2nd ed. Alan E. Lindsay & Alberto Budkin. (Illus.). 178p. 1975. pap. 26.50 (*0-8151-5428-3*, Yr Bk Med Pubs) Mosby Yr Bk.

Cardiac Arrhythmias: An Integrated Approach for the Clinician. Eric N. Prystowsky & George Klein. (Illus.). 452p. 1994. text ed. 60.00 (*0-07-050984-0*) Hlth Prof Div.

Cardiac Arrhythmias: Diagnosis & Treatment. Ed. by J. Cosin et al. LC 88-25310. 650p. 1988. 268.00 (*0-08-034878-5*, Pub. by Pergamon Repr UK) Franklin.

Cardiac Arrhythmias: Electrophysiologic Techniques & Management. Ed. by Leonard S. Dreifus & Albert N. Brest. LC 70-6558. (Cardiovascular Clinics Ser.: Vol. 16, No. 1). (Illus.). 370p. 1985. 50.00 (*0-8036-2903-6*) Davis Co.

Cardiac Arrhythmias: New Therapeutic Drugs & Devices. Ed. by Joel Morganroth & E. Neil Moore. (Developments in Cardiovascular Medicine Ser.). 1985. lib. bdg. 88.00 (*0-89838-716-7*) Kluwer Ac.

Cardiac Arrhythmias: Recent Progress in Investigation & Management. Ed. by T. Iwa & G. Fontaine. 386p. 1988. 100.00 (*0-444-80912-0*) Elsevier.

Cardiac Arrhythmias: The Management of Atrial Fibrillation. Ed. by Ronald W. Campbell & Michiel J. Janse. LC 92-49869. 1992. write for info. (*3-540-55588-9*) Spr-Verlag.

Cardiac Arrhythmias: Triggered Activity & Related Mechanisms. Ed. by Paul F. Cranefield & Ronald S. Aronson. (Illus.). 720p. 1988. 125.00 (*0-87993-327-5*) Futura Pub.

Cardiac Arrhythmias for the Clinical Cardiologist: Proceedings, Workshop on Cardiac Arrhythmias, Mallorca, October 18-19, 1985. Ed. by E. Andries & R. Stroobandt. (International Congress Ser.: No. 724). 253p. 1987. 130.25 (*0-444-80826-4*, Excerpta Medica) Elsevier.

Cardiac Arrhythmias: From Diagnosis to Therapy. Ed. by Samuel Levy & Melvin Scheinman. (Illus.). 415p. 1984. 59.50 (*0-87993-213-9*) Futura Pub.

***Cardiac Auscultation.** Antonio C. deLeon. 29p. Date not set. 9.75 (*1-886128-00-6*) Laennec Pub.

Cardiac Biopsy. Ed. by Robert E. Fowles. (Illus.). 224p. 1992. 47.00 (*0-87993-366-6*) Futura Pub.

***Cardiac Catherization Handbook.** 2nd ed. Ed. by Morton J. Kern. LC 94-19485. 1994. write for info. (*0-8151-5036-9*) Mosby Yr Bk.

Cardiac Catherization Laboratory Policy & Procedures. Judith Smith. 1993. 130.00 (*1-879575-40-X*) Acad Med Sys.

***Cardiac Catheterization.** Ed. by Kirk L. Peterson & Pascal Nicod. LC 95-3944. 1995. write for info. (*0-7216-3064-2*) Saunders.

Cardiac Catheterization. rev. ed. Julia A. Purcell. Ed. by Nancy R. Hull. LC 82-10133. (Illus.). 36p. 1987. 3.75 (*0-939838-10-9*) Pritchett & Hull.

Cardiac Catheterization, Angiography & Intervention. 4th ed. William Grossman & Donald S. Baim. LC 90-5835. (Illus.). 698p. 1991. text ed. 79.00 (*0-8121-1342-X*) Williams & Wilkins.

***Cardiac Catheterization, Angiography & Intervention.** 5th ed. William Grossman & Donald S. Balm. LC 95-13453. 1995. write for info. (*0-683-03645-9*) Williams & Wilkins.

Cardiac Catheterization Handbook. Kern. (Illus.). 512p. 1991. 37.95 (*0-8016-6265-6*) Mosby Yr Bk.

Cardiac Catheters: Forecasts for 22 Products in an Evolving Market. Market Intelligence Staff. 413p. 1993. 1,995.00 (*1-56753-426-0*) Frost & Sullivan.

***Cardiac Catheters Market.** 445p. (Orig.). 1995. pap. 2,295.00 (*0-7605-2308-8*) Rector Pr.

Cardiac Colloquy: The First Comprehensive Video Textbook of Cardiac Surgery Technique. Ed. by Ann S. Adams & Arthur J. Roberts. (Illus.). 205p. 1988. 595.00 (*0-944903-00-2*) Adams Pub Group.

Cardiac Conduction System in Unexplained Sudden Death. Saroja Bharati & Maurice Lev. (Illus.). 416p. 1990. 115.00 (*0-87993-362-3*) Futura Pub.

Cardiac Contraction & the Pressure-Volume Relationship. Kiichi Sagawa et al. (Illus.). 496p. 1988. 75.00 (*0-19-504320-0*) OUP.

An Asterisk (*) at the beginning of an entry indicates that the title is appearing in BIP for the first time.

C

An Asterisk (*) at the beginning of an entry indicates that the title is appearing in BIP for the first time.

1043

Cardinal Meaning: Essays in Comparative Hermeneutics, Buddhism & Christianity. Ed. by Michael Pye & Robert Morgan. (Religion & Reason Ser.: No. 6). 203p. 1973. text ed. 29.35 (*90-279-7228-1*) Mouton.

***Cardinal Mine: A Ghost of the Past.** Signe E. Nakashima. 120p. 1995. pap. text ed. 9.95 (*0-9646928-0-5*) S E Nakashima.

Cardinal Newman. Susan Foister. (Illus.). 88p. 29.50 (*1-85514-023-3*, Pub. by Natl Port Gall UK) Antique Collect.

Cardinal Newman. Richard H. Hutton. LC 75-30029. reprint ed. 40.00 (*0-404-14033-5*) AMS Pr.

Cardinal Newman: Seeker of Truth. Thomas O'Loughlin. 1989. pap. 22.00 (*1-85390-096-6*, Pub. by Veritas IE) St Mut.

Cardinal Newman Prayerbook: Kindly Light. Comp. by Daniel M. O'Connell. 352p. 1985. pap. 14.95 (*0-87193-220-2*) Dimension Bks.

Cardinal of Lorraine & the Council of Trent: A Study in the Counter-Reformation. Henry O. Evennett. LC 83-45592. reprint ed. 57.50 (*0-404-19885-6*) AMS Pr.

Cardinal of the Kremlin. 1988. 15.95 (*0-671-66074-8*) PB.

Cardinal of the Kremlin. Tom Clancy. 1989. pap. 6.99 (*0-425-11684-0*) Berkley Pub.

Cardinal of the Kremlin. Tom Clancy. 544p. 1988. 19.95 (*0-399-13345-3*, Putnam) Putnam Pub Group.

***Cardinal Offense.** large type ed. Ralph McInerny. LC 94-47945. 694p. 1995. 22.95 (*0-7862-0402-8*) Thorndike Pr.

Cardinal Offense: A Father Dowling Mystery. Ralph McInerny. 384p. 1994. 21.95 (*0-312-11283-1*) St Martin.

Cardinal Pirelli see Five Novels

Cardinal Points: Cowinner of the 1987 Iowa Poetry Prize. Michael Pettit. LC 88-14797. (Iowa Poetry Prize Ser.). 96p. (Orig.). 1988. pap. 10.95 (*0-87745-206-7*) U of Iowa Pr.

Cardinal Points & Other Poems. Eugene Haun. LC 81-82658. 85p. (YA). (gr. 9-12). 1981. per., pap. 5.00 (*0-916418-32-4*) Lotus.

Cardinal Richelieu. Pat Glossop. (World Leaders - Past & Present Ser.). (Illus.). 112p. (YA). (gr. 5 up). 1990. 17.95 (*1-55546-822-5*) Chelsea Hse.

Cardinal Richelieu: Power & the Pursuit of Wealth. Joseph Bergin. 1990. pap. 18.00 (*0-300-04860-2*) Yale U Pr.

Cardinal Richelieu & Development of Absolutism. Geoffrey Treasure. (Illus.). 316p. 1982. pap. 11.95 (*0-85683-065-8*) Dufour.

C

***Cardinal Rules.** Barbara Delinsky. (Mira Bks.). 1995. mass mkt. 4.99 (*1-55166-068-7*, 1-66068-7, Mira Bks) Harlequin Bks.

Cardinal Sins. Terence Reese & David Bird. (Master Bridge Ser.). 128p. 1991. 24.95 (*0-575-04997-9*, Pub. by V Gollancz UK) Trafalgar.

Cardinal Spline Interpolation. I. J. Schoenberg. (CBMS-NSF Regional Conference Ser.: No. 12). vi, 125p. 1973. pap. text ed. 19.25 (*0-89871-009-X*) Soc Indus-Appl Math.

Cardinal Stickler: Salesian, Erudite & Librarian of the Holy Catholic Church. Joao S. Cla Dias. (Illus.). 46p. (Orig.). (C). 1987. pap. 5.00 (*1-877905-03-8*) Am Soc Defense TFP.

Cardinal Virtues. Andrew M. Greeley. 1991. mass mkt. 5.95 (*0-446-36094-5*) Warner Bks.

Cardinal Virtues. large type ed. Andrew M. Greeley. 1992. pap. 16.95 (*0-7927-0650-1*, Paragon Lrg Print) Chivers N Amer.

Cardinal Winds. limited ed. Michael G. Michaud. LC 92-81452. (Illus.). 28p. (Orig.). (C). 1992. 24.00 (*0-9620574-6-0*) MGM Pr.

Cardinal Wolsey: Church, State & Art. S. J. Gunn. Ed. by P. G. Lindley. (Illus.). 368p. (C). 1991. 64.95 (*0-521-37568-1*) Cambridge U Pr.

Cardinalism: A Fundamental Approach. Ed. by Maurice Allais. LC 93-8838. (Theory & Decision Library Series A). 320p. (C). 1994. lib. bdg. 134.00 (*0-7923-2398-X*) Kluwer Ac.

Cardinals & Heraldry. Mark T. Elvins. 128p. (C). 1988. 75.00 (*0-7212-0788-X*, Pub. by Regency Press) St Mut.

Cardinals & Saints. Arlene Zekowski & Stanley Berne. LC 58-11713. (Illus.). 1958. 100.00 (*0-913844-08-X*) Am Canadian.

Cardinals Fan's Little Book of Wisdom. Rob Rains. 1994. pap. 5.95 (*0-912083-77-8*) Diamond Communications.

Cardinals in the Ice Age. John Engels. LC 86-80012. (National Poetry Ser.). 72p. (Orig.). 1987. pap. 8.00 (*0-915308-91-6*) Graywolf.

***Cardinal's Sin: Psychic Defenders Uncover Evil in the Vatican.** Raymond Buckland. 336p. 1995. pap. 5.99 (*1-56718-102-3*) Llewellyn Pubns.

Cardinal's Snuffbox. Kenneth Roseman. (Illus.). 128p. (J). (gr. 4-6). 1982. pap. text ed. 7.95 (*0-8074-0059-9*, 140060) UAHC.

Cardington Crescent. Anne Perry. 304p. 1988. reprint ed. mass mkt. 5.99 (*0-449-21442-7*, Crest) Fawcett.

Cardio-Pulmonary Technician. Jack Rudman. (Career Examination Ser.: C-1159). 1994. pap. 39.95 (*0-8373-1159-4*) Nat Learn.

Cardio-Thoracic Surgery: What Is New in Current Practice, Proceedings of the Second International Symposium, Bad Deynhausen, 5-7 September 1991. Ed. by K. Minami et al. LC 92-9994. (International Congress Ser.: No. 985). 1992. write for info. (*0-444-89267-2*, Excerpta Medica) Elsevier.

Cardiocirculatory Function in Renal Disease. Ed. by H. Jahn et al. (Contributions to Nephrology Ser.: Vol. 41). (Illus.). xii, 460p. 1985. 131.25 (*3-8055-3914-2*) S Karger.

***Cardiogenic Embolism.** Ed. by Werner G. Daniel et al. LC 95-12357. 1995. write for info. (*0-683-02359-4*) Williams & Wilkins.

Cardiogenic Reflexes. Ed. by R. Hainsworth et al. (Illus.). 480p. 1987. 80.00 (*0-19-857630-7*) OUP.

Cardiograms: Theory & Applications. Ed. by D. N. Ghista et al. (Advances in Cardiovascular Physics Ser.: Vol. 2). (Illus.). 1979. 78.50 (*3-8055-2851-5*) S Karger.

Cardiologist's Painless Prescription for a Healthy Heart & a Longer Life. Joe D. Goldstrich. LC 93-92831. 416p. 1994. 19.95 (*0-9639877-0-4*) Nine-Heart-Nine.

Cardiology. Ed. by John D. Bonagura. (Contemporary Issues in Small Animal Practice Ser.: Vol. 7). (Illus.). 352p. 1987. text ed. 50.00 (*0-443-08474-2*) Churchill.

Cardiology. Andrew A. Grace et al. LC 92-49844. (Colour Guide Ser.). (Illus.). 128p. 1993. spiral bd. 19.95 (*0-443-04592-5*) Churchill.

Cardiology, 2 vols. Ed. by William W. Parmley et al. (Illus.). 2500p. Date not set. Set, Annual new page service. ring bd. 225.00 (*0-685-61017-9*, H3192S1) Lippincott.

Cardiology. 3rd ed. LC 92-48257. (Regents - Prentice-Hall Medical Assistant Kit Ser.). 112p. 1993. pap. 10.20 (*0-13-146598-8*) P-H.

Cardiology. 3rd ed. Joel W. Heger et al. LC 92-48965. (House Officer Ser.). 416p. 1993. pap. 20.00 (*0-683-03949-0*) Williams & Wilkins.

Cardiology: A Clinical Approach. 2nd ed. Ronald J. Vandenbelt. (Illus.). 516p. 1987. pap. text ed. 34.95 (*0-8151-8966-4*, Yr Bk Med Pubs) Mosby Yr Bk.

Cardiology: Evolution of Ideas. Richard J. Bing. LC 92-1542. 1992. text ed. 50.00 (*3-7186-0549-X*) Gordon & Breach.

Cardiology: Fundamentals & Practice. 2nd ed. Giuliani et al. 2416p. 1991. 129.00 (*0-8016-2006-6*) Mosby Yr Bk.

Cardiology: Fundamentals & Practice, 1986. R. O. Brandenburg. 2000p. 1987. 110.00 (*0-318-32737-6*, Yr Bk Med Pubs) Mosby Yr Bk.

Cardiology: Fundamentals & Practice, 1986, 2 vols., Set. R. O. Brandenburg. 2000p. 1987. Two vol. set. 150.00 (*0-8151-1139-8*, Yr Bk Med Pubs) Mosby Yr Bk.

Cardiology: Peterborough Symposium. Ed. by F. J. Fawcett. 1975. pap. 14.95 (*0-8464-1081-8*) Beekman Pubs.

Cardiology: The Evolution of the Science & the Art. Ed. by Richard J. Bing. LC 92-1542. 319p. 1992. pap. text ed. 20.00 (*3-7186-0554-6*) Gordon & Breach.

Cardiology & Cardiac Surgery: Current Topics. Ed. by Adalberto Grossi et al. LC 92-49291. (Illus.). 464p. 1992. 90.00 (*0-87993-540-5*) Futura Pub.

Cardiology & Co-Existing Disease. Ed. by Elliot Rapaport. (Illus.). 352p. 1994. 85.00 (*0-443-08887-X*) Churchill.

Cardiology for Nurses. Nanette K. Wenger et al. Ed. by Mildred C. McIntyre. 1980. text ed. 49.95 (*0-07-069290-4*) McGraw.

Cardiology Handbook for Health Professionals. M. Wayne Cooper. (Illus.). 186p. 1988. 22.50 (*0-87527-366-1*) Green.

Cardiology in Transition. Intro. by John O. Goodman & Vincent Siragusa. 175p. 1989. 39.95 (*0-9625207-0-5*) J Goodman & Assocs.

***Cardiology Medical Transcription.** S. Turley. 176p. (C). 1993. ring bd. write for info. (*0-933195-59-1*) Allied Hlth Pubns.

Cardiology of the Dog & Cat. M. Martin & B. Corcoran. (Library of Veterinary Practice). (Illus.). 224p. 1994. pap. 39.95 (*0-632-03298-7*, Pub. by Blckwell Sci Pubns UK) Blackwell Sci.

Cardiology Pearls. Ed. by Blase Carabello. (Illus.). 256p. (Orig.). 1993. pap. text ed. 39.00 (*0-932883-96-6*) Hanley & Belfus.

Cardiology Pocket Consultant. 3rd ed. H. R. Swanton. (Illus.). 608p. 1994. pap. write for info. (*0-632-03654-0*) Blackwell Sci.

Cardiology Problems in Primary Care. Thomas H. Lee, Jr. 320p. 1989. 39.95 (*0-87489-463-8*) Med Economics.

Cardiology Reviews 1: Human Atherosclerosis. Ed. by E. I. Chazov & V. N. Smirnov. (Soviet Medical Reviews Ser., Section A). 384p. 1987. text ed. 337.00 (*3-7186-0349-7*) Gordon & Breach.

Cardiology Secrets: Questions You Will Be Asked on Rounds, in the Clinic, on Oral Exams. Ed. by Olivia Adair & Edward P. Havranek. (Secrets Ser.). (Illus.). 300p. (Orig.). 1994. pap. text ed. 29.95 (*1-56053-104-5*) Hanley & Belfus.

Cardiology Today. Ed. by B. Guggenheim. (Illus.). xii, 396p. 1984. 131.25 (*3-8055-3761-1*) S Karger.

Cardiology Update: Reviews for Physicians. 1,990th ed. Ed. by Elliot Rapaport. 400p. 1990. 85.00 (*0-444-01517-5*) Elsevier.

Cardiology Update, 1983: Reviews for Physicians. Elliot Rapaport. 360p. 1983. 47.50 (*0-318-32521-7*) Elsevier.

***Cardiology Words & Phrases.** 2nd ed. 600p. 1995. pap. text ed. 39.00 (*0-934385-63-7*) Hlth Prof Inst.

Cardiology Words & Phrases: A Quick-Reference Guide. 196p. 1989. pap. 25.00 (*0-934385-16-5*) Hlth Prof Inst.

Cardiology 1986. Williams C. Roberts. (Illus.). 444p. 1986. text ed. 80.00 (*0-914316-52-4*, Yorke Med Bks) Buttrwrth-Heinemann.

Cardiology, 1992. Ed. by William C. Roberts et al. (Illus.). 1992. 95.00 (*0-7506-9318-5*) Buttrwrth-Heinemann.

Cardiology, 1993. William C. Roberts. Ed. by James T. Willerson et al. LC 93-71211. (Illus.). 490p. 1993. 95.00 (*0-7506-9451-3*) Buttrwrth-Heinemann.

***Cardiology 1995.** William C. Roberts. (Illus.). 528p. 1995. 69.00 (*0-87993-617-7*) Futura Pub.

Cardiomyopathic Heart. Ed. by Makoto Nagano et al. LC 93-4656. 480p. 1994. 100.00 (*0-7817-0092-2*) Raven.

Cardiomyopathies. Ed. by J. F. Goodwin & E. G. Olsen. LC 92-49589. 1993. write for info. (*3-540-55608-7*); 109.00 (*0-387-55608-7*) Spr-Verlag.

Cardiomyopathies: Clinical Presentation, Differential Diagnosis, & Management, Vol. 19, No. 1. Ed. by James A. Shaver. LC 70-6558. (Illus.). 288p. 1988. text ed. 75.00 (*0-8036-7821-5*) Davis Co.

Cardiomyopathies & Heart-Lung Transplantation. Amar S. Kapoor et al. 832p. 1991. text ed. 165.00 (*0-07-033570-2*) Hlth Prof Div.

Cardiomyopathy & Mycarditis: Cardiomyopathy Update Three. Ed. by Morie Sekiguchi & E. G. Olsen. 350p. 1990. text ed. 145.00 (*0-86008-458-2*, Pub. by U of Tokyo JA) Col U Pr.

Cardiomyoplasty. Ed. by Alain Carpentier et al. (Bakken Research Center Ser.). (Illus.). 296p. 1991. 85.00 (*0-87993-395-X*) Futura Pub.

Cardiopathies Valvulaires Acquises. J. Acar et al. (Illus.). 656p. (FRE.). 1985. 130.00 (*2-257-10441-2*) S M P F Inc.

Cardioplegia: Current Concepts & Controversies. R. J. Chiu. (Medical Intelligence Unit Ser.). 1993. 89.95 (*1-879702-54-1*, R) R G Landes.

Cardiopulmonary Anatomy & Physiology. L. R. Matthews. (Illus.). 352p. (C). 1994. pap. text ed. 24.95 (*0-397-54954-7*, Lippincott Medical) Lippincott.

Cardiopulmonary Anatomy & Physiology: Essentials for Respiratory Care. 2nd ed. Terry Des Jardins. LC 92-14625. 454p. 1993. pap. text ed. 28.95 (*0-8273-5007-4*) Delmar.

Cardiopulmonary Bypass: Anesthesia & Perioperat. Ross et al. 550p. Date not set. 80.00 (*0-8016-4178-0*) Mosby Yr Bk.

Cardiopulmonary Bypass: Current Concepts & Controversies. Tinker. 160p. 1989. text ed. 65.00 (*0-7216-8831-4*) Saunders.

Cardiopulmonary Bypass: Index of Modern Information. Samuel M. Morris. LC 88-47962. 150p. 1988. 44.50 (*0-88164-970-8*); pap. 39.50 (*0-88164-971-6*) ABBE Pubs Assn.

Cardiopulmonary Bypass: Physiology, Related Complications & Pharmacology. Ed. by Pierre A. Casthely & David Bregman. (Illus.). 552p. 1991. 85.00 (*0-87993-396-8*) Futura Pub.

Cardiopulmonary Bypass: Principles & Management. Kenneth M. Taylor. (Illus.). 440p. 1987. 74.00 (*0-683-08105-5*) Williams & Wilkins.

Cardiopulmonary Bypass: Principles & Practice. Ed. by Glenn P. Gravlee et al. LC 92-48697. (Illus.). 832p. 1993. 139.00 (*0-683-03720-X*) Williams & Wilkins.

***Cardiopulmonary Bypass: Principles & Techniques of Extracorporeal Circulation.** Ed. by Christina T. Mora et al. LC 94-29083. 535p. 1995. text ed. 139.00 (*0-387-94242-4*) Spr-Verlag.

Cardiopulmonary Bypass Bibliography. Howard D. Johnson & Marc S. Morgan. Ed. by Joe R. Utley et al. LC 89-80769. (Cardiothoracic Surgery Monographs). 610p. 1990. text ed. 50.00 (*0-9623617-8-X*) Cardiothoracic Rsch.

Cardiopulmonary Bypass in Neonates, Infants, & Young Children. Ed. by Richard A. Jonas & Martin J. Elliott. LC 94-8439. 1994. write for info. (*0-7506-1230-4*) Buttrwrth-Heinemann.

Cardiopulmonary Cerebral Resuscitation. 3rd ed. Peter Safar & Nicholas G. Bircher. (Illus.). 400p. 1988. pap. text ed. 29.50 (*0-7216-2156-2*, Bailliere-Tindall) Saunders.

Cardiopulmonary Critical Care. 2nd ed. Dantzker. (Illus.). 864p. 1991. text ed. 115.00 (*0-7216-2942-3*) Saunders.

Cardiopulmonary Critical Care Management. Ed. by Robert J. Fallat & John M. Luce. (Clinics in Critical Care Medicine Ser.: Vol. 14). (Illus.). 230p. 1988. text ed. 45.00 (*0-443-08564-1*) Churchill.

Cardiopulmonary Emergencies. 1990. 32.95 (*0-87434-269-4*) Springhouse Pub.

Cardiopulmonary Interactions in Acute Respiratory Failure. J. L. Vincent & P. M. Suter. (Update in Intensive Care & Emergency Medicine Ser.: Vol. 2). (Illus.). 290p. 1987. pap. 69.30 (*0-387-17474-5*) Spr-Verlag.

Cardiopulmonary Nursing. Martha Judson & Geneva Lamm. 116p. (C). 1994. pap. text ed., spiral bd. 8.76 (*0-8403-9241-9*) Kendall-Hunt.

Cardiopulmonary Pharmacology. Cynthia L. Howder. (Illus.). 302p. 1992. 34.00 (*0-683-04175-4*) Williams & Wilkins.

Cardiopulmonary Physical Therapy. 2nd ed. Irwin & Tecklin. (Illus.). 600p. 1990. 55.95 (*0-8016-2907-1*) Mosby Yr Bk.

Cardiopulmonary Physical Therapy. 3rd ed. Irwin & Techlin. 1995. 54.95 (*0-8016-7926-5*) Mosby Yr Bk.

***Cardiopulmonary Physical Therapy: A Clinical Manual.** Joanne Watchie. 368p. 1995. pap. text ed. 25.95 (*0-7216-6709-0*) Saunders.

Cardiopulmonary Physiology. Youtsey & Pilbeam. Date not set. 25.00 (*0-8016-3925-5*) Mosby Yr Bk.

Cardiopulmonary Physiology in Anesthesiology. Michael G. Levitzky. LC 94-2822. 384p. 1995. text ed. 49.00 (*0-07-037534-8*) Hlth Prof Div.

Cardiopulmonary Physiology in Critical Care. Ed. by Scharf. (Fundamental & Clinical Cardiology Ser.: Vol. 7). 464p. 1992. 85.00 (*0-8247-8649-1*) Dekker.

Cardiopulmonary Policy & Procedure Guideline Manual. Lora E. Burke. 1990. 65.00 (*1-879575-05-1*) Acad Med Sys.

Cardiopulmonary Rehabilitation. Ed. by Ciro Rampulla et al. LC 93-13742. (Current Topics in Rehabilitation Ser.). 1993. 45.00 (*0-387-19836-9*) Spr-Verlag.

Cardiopulmonary Rehabilitation: Basic Theory & Application. 2nd rev. ed. Frances J. Brannon et al. Ed. by Steven L. Wolf. LC 92-18329. (Contemporary Perspectives in Rehabilitation Ser.: Vol. 10). (Illus.). 450p. 1992. 39.00 (*0-8036-1122-6*) Davis Co.

Cardiopulmonary Resuscitation. Ed. by P. J. F. Baskett. (Monographs in Anaesthesiology: Vol. 17). 416p. 1989. 179.50 (*0-444-81051-X*) Elsevier.

Cardiopulmonary Resuscitation. David V. Skinner & Richard Vincent. LC 92-22057. (Oxford Handbooks in Emergency Medicine Ser.: No. 4). 224p. (C). 1993. 56.00 (*0-19-262286-2*); pap. 26.00 (*0-19-261940-3*) OUP.

Cardiopulmonary Resuscitation: Scientific Basis, Current Standards & Future Trends. Ed. by William Kaye & Nicholas G. Bircher. (Clinics in Critical Care Medicine Ser.: Vol. 16). (Illus.). 232p. 1989. text ed. 49.50 (*0-443-08557-9*) Churchill.

Cardiopulmonary Symptoms in Physical Therapy Practice. Meryl Cohen & Theresa Hoskins-Michel. (Illus.). 288p. 1988. pap. text ed. 36.95 (*0-443-08558-7*) Churchill.

Cardiorenal Disease. (Contributions to Nephrology Ser.: Vol. 106). (Illus.). x, 206p. 1994. 158.50 (*3-8055-5830-9*) S Karger.

CardioRenal Disorders & Diseases. 2nd rev. ed. Carl V. Leier & Harisios Boudoulas. (Illus.). 608p. 1992. 96.00 (*0-87993-517-0*) Futura Pub.

Cardiorespiratory & Cardiosomatic Psychophysiology. Ed. by P. Grossman et al. LC 86-21252. (NATO ASI Series A, Life Sciences: Vol. 114). 376p. 1986. 95.00 (*0-306-42395-2*, Plenum Pr) Plenum.

Cardiorespiratory & Motor Coordination. Ed. by H. P. Koepchen & T. Huopaniemi. (Illus.). 161p. 1991. pap. 117.00 (*0-387-52279-4*) Spr-Verlag.

Cardiorespiratory Disorders During Sleep. 2nd rev. ed. Ed. by Richard J. Martin. (Illus.). 408p. 1990. 55.00 (*0-87993-380-1*) Futura Pub.

Cardiorespiratory Intensive Care. A. Hedley Brown & Fernando Guzman. 288p. 1989. pap. text ed. 75.00 (*0-407-01253-2*) Buttrwrth-Heinemann.

Cardiothoracic Handbook: A Pocket Companion. A. Hedley Brown & Fernando Guzman. 192p. 1989. pap. text ed. 45.00 (*0-407-01743-7*) Buttrwrth-Heinemann.

Cardiothoracic Trauma. Symbas. 448p. 1989. text ed. 125.00 (*0-7216-2827-3*) Saunders.

Cardiotonic Drugs: A Clinical Review. 2nd rev. ed. Ed. by Carl V. Leier. (Fundamental & Clinical Cardiology Ser.: Vol. 2). 384p. 1991. 140.00 (*0-8247-8471-5*) Dekker.

Cardiovascular Actions of Anesthetics & Drugs Used in Anesthesia, Set: Vols. 1 & 2. Ed. by B. M. Altura & S. Halevy. (Illus.). xx, 570p. 1987. Set. 328.00 (*3-8055-4159-7*) S Karger.

Cardiovascular Actions of Anesthetics & Drugs Used in Anesthesia: Basic Aspects, Vol. 1. Ed. by B. M. Altura & S. Halevy. (Illus.). viii, 268p. 1986. 156.00 (*3-8055-4157-0*) S Karger.

Cardiovascular & Musculoskeletal Systems. Ed. by Thomas C. Jones et al. (Monographs on Pathology of Laboratory Animals). (Illus.). xvii, 312p. 1991. 289.00 (*0-387-53876-3*) Spr-Verlag.

Cardiovascular & Pulmonary Word Book. Littrell. (Word Book Ser.). 1991. 17.95 (*0-87434-415-8*) Springhouse Pub.

Cardiovascular & Pulmonary Word Book. 2nd ed. Littrell. 1993. 18.95 (*0-87434-519-7*) Springhouse Pub.

Cardiovascular & Renal Actions of Dopamine. Ed. by P. Soares-de-Silva. (Advances in the Biosciences Ser.: Vol. 88). 240p. 1993. 180.00 (*0-08-042209-8*, Pergamon Pr) Elsevier.

Cardiovascular & Respiratory Disease Therapy. Petrie. (Clinically Important Adverse Drug Interactions Ser.: Vol. 1). 244p. 1981. 84.75 (*0-444-80233-9*) Elsevier.

Cardiovascular Anesthesia. Estafanous. (Illus.). 1993. text ed. 125.00 (*0-397-51088-8*) Lippincott.

Cardiovascular Anesthesia. Carol L. Lake. (Illus.). 480p. 1984. 98.00 (*0-387-96028-7*) Spr-Verlag.

Cardiovascular Anesthesia & Postoperative Care. 2nd ed. Tarhan. 670p. 1988. 95.00 (*0-8151-8704-1*, Yr Bk Med Pubs) Mosby Yr Bk.

Cardiovascular Applications of Doppler Ultrasound. Ed. by Abdul-Majeed Salmasi & Andrew N. Nicolaides. (Illus.). 388p. 1989. text ed. 150.00 (*0-443-03592-X*) Churchill.

Cardiovascular Applications of Magnetic Resonance. Ed. by Gerald M. Pohost. LC 92-48279. (American Heart Association Monograph Ser.). (Illus.). 480p. 1993. 86.00 (*0-87993-548-0*) Futura Pub.

***Cardiovascular Aspects of Marfan Syndrome.** Ed. by R. Hetzer et al. 120p. 1995. 46.00 (*0-387-91465-X*) Spr-Verlag.

Cardiovascular Biomaterials. Ed. by G. W. Hastings. (Illus.). xiv, 198p. 1991. 135.00 (*0-387-19666-8*) Spr-Verlag.

Cardiovascular Biomechanics. K. B. Chandran. (Biomedical Engineering Ser.). (Illus.). 300p. (C). 1992. text ed. 80.00 (*0-8147-1471-4*) NYU Pr.

Cardiovascular Care Handbook. Ed. by Regina D. Ford. (Illus.). 500p. 1986. pap. 23.95 (*0-916730-98-0*) Springhouse Pub.

Cardiovascular Care of the Elderly. Ed. by T. Strasser. 174p. 1987. pap. text ed. 17.40 (*92-4-156098-3*) World Health.

Cardiovascular Complications of Liver Disease. Ed. by Arieh Bomzon & Laurence M. Blendis. 1990. 190.00 (*0-8493-4735-1*, RC848) CRC Pr.

Cardiovascular Critical Care Nursing. Diane K. Dressler. LC 93-22631. (Plans of Care for Specialty Practice Ser.). 315p. 1994. pap. text ed. 27.95 (*0-8273-5712-5*) Delmar.

Cardiovascular Devices & Their Applications. Leslie A. Geddes. LC 83-16746. 407p. reprint ed. pap. 116.00 (*0-7837-2827-1*, 2057645) Bks Demand.

Cardiovascular Diagnosis by Ultrasound. P. Hanrath. 1982. lib. bdg. 84.00 (*90-247-2692-1*) Kluwer Ac.

Cardiovascular Diagnostic Testing: A Nursing Guide. Susan L. Zorb. LC 90-14525. 206p. 1991. text ed. 49.00 (*0-8342-0204-2*, 20204) Aspen Pub.

Cardiovascular Disease. A. R. Lorimer & W. S. Hillis. (Treatment in Clinical Medicine Ser.). (Illus.). 300p. 1985. pap. 43.00 (*0-387-15426-4*) Spr-Verlag.

An Asterisk (*) at the beginning of an entry indicates that the title is appearing in BIP for the first time.

Cardiovascular Disease. Wrynn Smith. (Profile of Health & Disease in America Ser.). 144p. 1986. 40.00 (*0-8160-1025-0*) Facts on File.

Cardiovascular Disease: Assessment & Intervention. 3rd ed. Kathy Templin & Mary Stein. LC 94-60261. 240p. (C). 1993. pap. text ed. 49.95 (*1-878025-58-9*) Western Schls.

Cardiovascular Disease: Molecular & Cellular Mechanisms, Prevention, & Treatment. Ed. by L. L. Gallo. LC 87-20224. (GWUMC Department of Biochemistry Annual Spring Symposia Ser.). (Illus.). 608p. 1987. 135.00 (*0-306-42537-8*, Plenum Pr) Plenum.

Cardiovascular Disease: Nutrition for Prevention & Treatment. American Dietetic Association, Sports & Cardiovascular Nutritionists Staff. Ed. by Penny M. Kris-Etherton. LC 90-1031. (Illus.). 349p. (Orig.). 1990. pap. text ed. 42.00 (*0-88091-078-X*, 0104) Am Dietetic Assn.

***Cardiovascular Disease: Risk Factors & Intervention.** Ed. by Neil Poulter et al. 1993. 99.00 (*1-870905-54-7*) Scovill Paterson.

Cardiovascular Disease, Aging & Behavior. Ed. by Jeffrey W. Elias & Philip H. Marshall. (Series in Health Psychology & Behavioral Medicine). 196p. 1987. 63.00 (*0-89116-401-4*) Hemisp Pub.

Cardiovascular Disease in Diabetes. Ed. by Makoto Nagano et al. (Developments in Cardiovascular Medicine Ser.). 416p. (C). 1992. lib. bdg. 125.00 (*0-7923-1554-5*) Kluwer Ac.

Cardiovascular Disease in the Elderly. Ed. by Franz H. Messerli. (Developments in Cardiovascular Medicine Ser.). 1984. lib. bdg. 94.50 (*0-89838-596-2*) Kluwer Ac.

Cardiovascular Disease in the Elderly Patient. Ed. by Tresch & Aronow. LC 93-25822. (Fundamental & Clinical Cardiology Ser.: Vol. 17). 664p. 1994. 150.00 (*0-8247-8864-8*) Dekker.

Cardiovascular Disease in Women. Ed. by R. C. Becker & J. S. Alpert. (Journal: Cardiology, 1990: Vol. 77, Suppl. 2). (Illus.). iv, 140p. 1990. pap. 40.00 (*3-8055-5222-X*) S Karger.

***Cardiovascular Disease in Women: Journal: Cardiology, 1995.** Ed. by R. C. Becker & J. S. Alpert. (Journal: Cardiology Ser.: Vol. 86, No. 4, 1995). (Illus.). 98p. 1995. pap. 22.75 (*3-8055-6197-0*) S Karger.

***Cardiovascular Disease 2: Cellular & Molecular Mechanisms, Prevention, & Treatment: Proceedings of the Fourteenth Washington International Spring Symposium at the George Washington University Held in Washington, DC, June 6-10, 1994.** Ed. by Linda L. Gallo. (GWUMC Department of Biochemistry Annual Spring Symposium Ser.). 375p. 1995. 110.00 (*0-306-44992-7*) Plenum.

Cardiovascular Diseases. Ed. by H. S. Rosenberg & J. Bernstein. (Perspectives in Pediatric Pathology Ser.: Vol. 12). (Illus.). x, 162p. 1988. 158.50 (*3-8055-4716-1*) S Karger.

Cardiovascular Diseases: Genetics, Epidemiology & Prevention. James J. Nora et al. (Oxford Monographs on Medical Genetics: No. 22). (Illus.). 208p. 1991. 39.95 (*0-19-506032-6*, 2924) OUP.

***Cardiovascular Diseases & Disorders Sourcebook.** Ed. by Karen Bellenir & Peter D. Dresser. 1995. lib. bdg. 80.00x (*0-7808-0032-X*) Omnigraphics Inc.

Cardiovascular Diseases & Pregnancy. O. M. Eliseev. 200p. 1988. 83.00 (*0-387-19174-7*) Spr-Verlag.

Cardiovascular Diseases in Blacks. Ed. by Elijah Saunders. (Cardiovascular Clinics Ser.: Vol. 21, No. 3). (Illus.). 406p. 1991. text ed. 75.00 (*0-8036-7726-X*) Davis Co.

Cardiovascular Diseases in the United States. Iwao Moriyama et al. LC 73-154498. (Vital & Health Statistics Monographs, American Public Health Association). (Illus.). 524p. 1971. 45.00 (*0-674-09640-1*) HUP.

Cardiovascular Disorders. LC 93-24341. (Nursing Timesavers Ser.). 1993. write for info. (*0-87434-657-6*) Springhouse Pub.

Cardiovascular Disorders. Canobbio. (Illus.). 320p. 1990. 29.95 (*0-8016-1405-8*) Mosby Yr Bk.

Cardiovascular Disorders: Pathogenesis & Pathophysiology. Michael B. Gravanis. 576p. 1992. 95.00 (*0-8016-6336-9*) Mosby Yr Bk.

Cardiovascular Disorders & Behavior Vol. 3: Handbook of Psychology & Health. David S. Krantz et al. 400p. 1981. text ed. 79.95 (*0-89859-185-6*) L Erlbaum Assocs.

Cardiovascular Drug Therapy - Current Concepts: Journal: Cardiology, Vol. 72, Nos. 5 & 6. Ed. by E. A. Amsterdam. (Illus.). 164p. 1985. pap. 57.75 (*3-8055-4081-7*) S Karger.

Cardiovascular Drug Therapy in the Elderly. Adam Schneeweiss & Gotthard Schettler. (Developments in Cardiovascular Medicine Ser.). 400p. (C). 1988. lib. bdg. 117.50 (*0-89838-883-X*) Kluwer Ac.

Cardiovascular Drugs & the Management of Heart Disease. 2nd ed. Gordon A. Ewy & Rubin Bressler. 512p. 1992. 110.50 (*0-88167-850-3*) Raven.

Cardiovascular Drugs Market. (Market Research Reports: No. 382). 139p. 1994. 795.00 (*0-317-05455-4*) Theta Corp.

Cardiovascular Dynamics: A Psycholphysiological Study Behavioral Control, Type A, Task Performance, Test Anxiety, & Cardiovascular Responses. M. W. Van Schijndel. 166p. 1987. pap. 14.80 (*90-265-0793-3*, Pub. by Swets Pub Serv NE) Taylor & Francis.

Cardiovascular Education Course. Competence Assurance Systems Staff. (Illus.). 1984. pap. text ed. 60.00 (*0-89147-055-7*) CAS.

Cardiovascular Education Course: Acute Care. Competence Assurance Systems Staff. (Illus.). 195p. pap. text ed. 75.00 (*0-89147-112-X*) CAS.

Cardiovascular Effects of Dihydropyridine Type Calcium Antagonists & Agonists. Ed. by A. Fleckenstein et al. (Bayer Symposium Ser.: No. 9). (Illus.). 530p. 1986. 99.00 (*0-387-15455-8*) Spr-Verlag.

Cardiovascular Effects of Verapamin. (Landmark Ser.). 1979. 34.00 (*0-8422-4112-4*) Irvington.

Cardiovascular Emergencies. Ed. by Joseph P. Ornato. LC 86-17130. (Clinics in Emergency Medicine Ser.: No. 9). (Illus.). 272p. reprint ed. pap. 77.60 (*0-7837-6250-X*, 2045962) Bks Demand.

Cardiovascular Emergencies: Current Therapy. E. K. Chung. (Illus.). xii, 244p. 1985. 135.25 (*3-8055-3679-8*) S Karger.

Cardiovascular Engineering. Ed. by D. N. Ghista et al. (Advances in Cardiovascular Physics Ser.: Pt. I-IV). (Illus.). xxxxviii, 960p. 1983. 347.25 (*3-8055-3613-5*) S Karger.

Cardiovascular Engineering: Prostheses, Assist & Artificial Organs, Pt. IV. Ed. by D. N. Ghista et al. (Advances in Cardiovascular Physics Ser.: Vol. 5). (Illus.). viii, 292p. 1983. 114.50 (*3-8055-3612-7*) S Karger.

Cardiovascular Engineering, Part I: Modelling. Ed. by D. N. Ghista et al. (Advances in Cardiovascular Physics Ser.: Vol. 5). (Illus.). xiv, 230p. 1983. 114.50 (*3-8055-3609-7*) S Karger.

Cardiovascular Engineering, Part II: Monitoring. Ed. by D. N. Ghista et al. (Advances in Cardiovascular Physics Ser.: Vol. 5). (Illus.). viii, 280p. 1983. 114.50 (*3-8055-3610-0*) S Karger.

Cardiovascular Engineering, Part III: Diagnosis. Ed. by D. N. Ghista et al. (Advances in Cardiovascular Physics Ser.: Vol. 5). (Illus.). x, 158p. 1983. 91.25 (*3-8055-3611-9*) S Karger.

***Cardiovascular Evaluation of Athletes.** Bruce F. Waller & W. Proctor Harvey. 213p. Date not set. 74.00 (*1-886128-02-2*) Laennec Pub.

Cardiovascular Fluid Dynamics. Uri Dinnar. 264p. 1981. 168.00 (*0-8493-5573-7*, QP105, CRC Reprint) Franklin.

Cardiovascular Function of Peripheral Dopamine Receptors. Hieble. (Clinical Pharmacology Ser.: Vol. 15). 384p. 1990. 175.00 (*0-8247-8100-7*) Dekker.

Cardiovascular Health & Disease in Women. Ed. by Pamela S. Douglas. LC 92-48884. (Illus.). 368p. 1993. text ed. 68.50 (*0-7216-4567-4*) Saunders.

Cardiovascular Health & Risk Management: The Role of Nutrition & Medication in Clinical Practice. Sylvia Wassertheil-Smoller et al. (Illus.). 228p. 1988. pap. 44.95 (*0-8151-9179-0*, Yr Bk Med Pubs) Mosby Yr Bk.

Cardiovascular Hemorheology. Sheoten Oka. LC 80-41338. 220p. reprint ed. pap. 62.70 (*0-318-34831-4*, 2031702) Bks Demand.

Cardiovascular Imaging by Ultrasound. Ed. by P. Hanrath et al. LC 92-13423. (Developments in Cardiovascular Medicine Ser.: Vol. 134). 500p. 1992. lib. bdg. 237.50 (*0-7923-1755-6*) Kluwer Ac.

Cardiovascular Implants - Cardiac Valve Prostheses. 9p. 1991. 44.00 (*0-910275-06-8*, CV5840-113) Assn Adv Med Instrn.

***Cardiovascular Implants-Vascular Prostheses: VP20-1994.** rev. ed. AAMI Staff. (ANSI-AAMI American National Standard Ser.). (Illus.). 30p. 1994. pap. 49.00 (*1-57020-025-4*) Assn Adv Med Instrn.

Cardiovascular Intensive Care Nursing. Ed. by Pat M. Ashworth & Cilla Clarke. (Illus.). 272p. (Orig.). 1992. pap. text ed. 48.00 (*0-443-03356-0*) Churchill.

Cardiovascular-Interventional Technology Exam Review. Richard R. Carlton & Deborah Phlipot. (Illus.). 210p. 1992. pap. 15.95 (*0-397-54945-8*) Lippincott.

Cardiovascular Laser Therapy. Jeffrey M. Isner & Richard H. Clarke. 316p. 1989. 108.50 (*0-88167-484-2*) Raven.

Cardiovascular Magnetic Resonance Imaging. Gutierrez. 233p. 1991. 99.00 (*0-8151-4024-X*) Mosby Yr Bk.

Cardiovascular Magnetic Resonance Spectroscopy. Ed. by Saul Schaefer & Robert S. Balaban. (C). 1992. lib. bdg. 114.50 (*0-7923-1686-X*) Kluwer Ac.

Cardiovascular Medications for Cardiac Nursing. Sandra L. Underhill et al. (Illus.). 347p. 1990. text ed. 28.95 (*0-397-54790-0*) Lippincott.

***Cardiovascular Medicine Vol. 1.** fac. ed. Cardiovascular Medicine Staff & Herbert Y. Kressel. LC 81-48504. 388p. Date not set. pap. 110.60 (*0-7837-7224-6*, 2047074) Bks Demand.

Cardiovascular Nuclear Medicine. Ed. by A. Donath & A. Righetti. (Progress in Nuclear Medicine Ser.: Vol. 6). (Illus.). viii, 228p. 1980. 118.50 (*3-8055-0618-X*) S Karger.

Cardiovascular Nuclear Medicine. Kenneth P. Lyons. (Illus.). 334p. 1988. boxed 99.95 (*0-8385-1052-3*, A1052-8) Appleton & Lange.

Cardiovascular Nuclear Medicine & MRI. Ed. by Johan H. Reiber & Ernst E. Van Der Wall. (Developments in Cardiovascular Medicine Ser.). 384p. (C). 1992. lib. bdg. 162.50 (*0-7923-1467-0*) Kluwer Ac.

Cardiovascular Nursing. Evans. (Clinical Rotation Guide Ser.). 1989. pap. 14.95 (*0-87434-166-3*) Springhouse Pub.

Cardiovascular Nursing. Jeanne Holland. 1977. pap. text ed. 10.95 (*0-316-36998-5*, Little Med Div) Little.

Cardiovascular Nursing. Marjorowicz & Christiansen. 443p. 1989. 26.95 (*0-87434-167-1*) Springhouse Pub.

***Cardiovascular Nursing.** 2nd ed. Mary J. Evans. (Clinical Rotation Guides Ser.). 1994. pap. 15.95 (*0-87434-735-1*) Springhouse Pub.

Cardiovascular Nursing: Assessment & Intervention, No. 1. Guzzetta. (Illus.). 816p. 1992. 43.95 (*0-8016-2784-2*) Mosby Yr Bk.

Cardiovascular Pathology. Virmani & Fenoglio. (Illus.). 480p. 1990. text ed. 79.50 (*0-7216-3232-7*) Saunders.

Cardiovascular Pathology, 2 vols., Set. 2nd ed. Ed. by Malcolm D. Silver. (Illus.). 2043p. 1991. text ed. 325.00 (*0-443-08664-8*) Churchill.

Cardiovascular Pathology, Vol. 1. Ed. by Malcolm D. Silver. LC 82-12973. 725p. reprint ed. pap. 180.00 (*0-7837-1379-7*, 2041527) Bks Demand.

Cardiovascular Pathology, Vol. 2. Ed. by Malcolm D. Silver. LC 82-12973. 767p. reprint ed. pap. 180.00 (*0-7837-1380-0*) Bks Demand.

Cardiovascular Pathology: Clinicopathologic Correlations & Pathogenetic Mechanisms, Vol. 3. Frederick J. Schoen et al. 229p. 1995. 75.00 (*0-683-07600-0*) Williams & Wilkins.

Cardiovascular Pathology in Infants & Children. James B. Arey. (Illus.). 392p. 1984. text ed. 121.00 (*0-7216-1395-0*) Saunders.

Cardiovascular Pathophysiology. Gail G. Ahumada. (Illus.). 288p. 1986. 45.00 (*0-19-503703-0*); pap. 22.50 (*0-19-503704-9*) OUP.

Cardiovascular Pathophysiology. Ed. by Michael B. Gravanis. (Illus.). 400p. (C). 1987. pap. text ed. 35.00 (*0-07-024131-7*) McGraw.

Cardiovascular Pathophysiology. Kaplinsky et al. 560p. 1993. pap. 26.95 (*0-8016-2555-6*) Mosby Yr Bk.

Cardiovascular Pathophysiology: A Problem-Oriented Approach. John T. Fallon. (Illus.). 250p. 1994. pap. 24.95 (*0-397-51409-3*) Lippincott.

Cardiovascular Patient Education Resource Manual. Aspen Reference Group Staff. Ed. by Dwayne E. Eutsey. LC 93-48636. 1994. 179.00 (*0-8342-0542-4*) Aspen Pub.

Cardiovascular Pharmacology. 3rd ed. Michael J. Antonaccio. 576p. 1990. 96.50 (*0-88167-644-6*) Raven.

Cardiovascular Pharmacology & Therapeutics. Ed. by Bramah N. Singh et al. (Illus.). 1264p. 1993. text ed. 149.95 (*0-443-08814-4*) Churchill.

***Cardiovascular Pharmacology of the Prostaglandins.** fac. ed. Ed. by Arnold G. Herman et al. LC 80-5912. (Illus.). 472p. Date not set. pap. 134.60 (*0-7837-7201-7*, 2047098) Bks Demand.

Cardiovascular Pharmacology of 5-Hydroxytryptamine: Prospective Therapeutic Applications. Ed. by P. R. Saxena et al. (Developments in Cardiovascular Medicine Ser.). (C). 1990. lib. bdg. 205.00 (*0-7923-0502-7*) Kluwer Ac.

***Cardiovascular Pharmacology '87.** J. Gy. Papp. 649p. (C). 1986. 210.00x (*963-05-4651-5*) St Mut.

Cardiovascular Physiology. H. S. Badeer. (Continuing Education Ser.: Vol. 6). (Illus.). xvi, 276p. 1984. 46.50 (*3-8055-3796-4*) S Karger.

Cardiovascular Physiology. William R. Milnor. (Illus.). 520p. 1990. 37.95 (*0-19-505884-4*) OUP.

Cardiovascular Physiology. 2nd ed. Jon Goerke & Allan H. Mines. (Physiology Ser.). (Illus.). 232p. 1995. pap. text ed. 36.00 (*0-88167-387-0*) Raven.

Cardiovascular Physiology. 3rd ed. David E. Mohrman & Lois J. Heller. 224p. 1991. pap. text ed. 25.50 (*0-07-027999-3*) Hlth Prof Div.

Cardiovascular Physiology. 6th ed. Robert M. Berne & Levy. 298p. 1991. pap. 26.95 (*0-8016-6314-8*) Mosby Yr Bk.

Cardiovascular Physiology: An Integrated Approach. Evelyn M. Scott. 192p. 1988. text ed. 49.95 (*0-7190-1776-9*, Pub. by Manchester Univ Pr UK) St Martin.

Cardiovascular Physiology, Heart, Peripheral Circulation & Methodology: Proceedings of the 28th International Congress of Physiological Sciences, Budapest, Hungary, 1980. Ed. by A. G. Kovach et al. LC 80-41875. (Advances in Physiological Sciences Ser.: Vol. 8). (Illus.). 400p. 1981. 166.00 (*0-08-026820-X*, Pub. by Pergamon Repr UK) Franklin.

Cardiovascular Physiology, Microcirculation & Capillary Exchange: Proceedings of the 28th International Congress of Physiological Sciences, Budapest, 1980. Ed. by A. G. Kovach et al. LC 80-41873. (Advances in Physiological Sciences Ser.: Vol. 7). (Illus.). 400p. 1981. 155.00 (*0-08-026819-6*, Pub. by Pergamon Repr UK) Franklin.

Cardiovascular Physiology-Neural Control Mechanisms: Proceedings of the 28th International Congress of Physiological Sciences, Budapest, 1980. Ed. by A. G. Kovach et al. LC 80-41927. (Advances in Physiological Sciences Ser.: Vol. 9). (Illus.). 400p. 1981. 166.00 (*0-08-026821-8*, Pub. by Pergamon Repr UK) Franklin.

Cardiovascular Problems in Pediatric Critical Care. Ed. by David B. Swedlow & Russell C. Raphaely. (Clinics in Critical Care Medicine Ser.: Vol. 10). (Illus.). 311p. 1986. text ed. 48.00 (*0-443-08321-5*) Churchill.

Cardiovascular Procedures: Diagnostic Techniques & Therapeutic Procedures. Tilkian et al. (Illus.). 516p. 1986. 61.95 (*0-8016-4965-X*) Mosby Yr Bk.

Cardiovascular Psychophysiology: A Perspective. Paul A. Obrist. LC 80-28582. 246p. 1981. 45.00 (*0-306-40599-7*, Plenum Pr) Plenum.

Cardiovascular Radiology. Eugene Gedgaudas et al. (Illus.). 269p. 1985. text ed. 96.50 (*0-7216-1084-6*) Saunders.

Cardiovascular Reactivity & Stress: Patterns of Physiological Response. J. R. Turner. (Illus.). 200p. 1994. 34.50 (*0-306-44612-X*, Plenum Pr) Plenum.

Cardiovascular Reactivity to Psychological Stress & Disease. Ed. by Jim Blascovich & Edward S. Katkin. (Illus.). 258p. 1993. text ed. 40.00 (*1-55798-192-2*) Am Psychol.

Cardiovascular Response to Exercise. Ed. by Gerald F. Fletcher. LC 93-22393. (American Heart Association Monograph Ser.). (Illus.). 464p. 1993. 75.00 (*0-87993-559-6*) Futura Pub.

Cardiovascular Review. 7th ed. Gerald C. Timmis et al. 320p. 1986. text ed. 70.00 (*0-8089-1805-2*, 794596, Grune) Saunders.

Cardiovascular Review 1985. 6th ed. Gerald C. Timmis et al. 768p. 1985. text ed. 97.00 (*0-8089-1950-4*, 794595, Grune) Saunders.

Cardiovascular Risk Factors in Childhood: Epidemiology & Prevention. Ed. by Basil S. Hetzel & G. S. Berenson. (Major Health Issues Ser.: No. 1). 284p. 1987. 114.50 (*0-444-80813-2*) Elsevier.

***Cardiovascular Science & Technology Conference Proceedings: CSP93.** AAMI Staff. (Illus.). 248p. Date not set. pap. 80.00 (*1-57020-008-4*) Assn Adv Med Instrn.

Cardiovascular Shunts: Phylogenetic, Ontogenetic, & Clinical Aspects. Ed. by Kjell Johansen & Warren Burggren. (Alfred Benzon Symposium Ser.: Vol. 21). 492p. 1985. text ed. 70.00 (*0-88167-135-5*) Raven.

Cardiovascular Significance of Endothelium-Derived Vasoactive Factors. Ed. by Gabor M. Rubanyi. (Illus.). 384p. 1991. 85.00 (*0-87993-359-3*) Futura Pub.

Cardiovascular Surgery: A Handbook of Operative Surgery. 2nd ed. Ormand Julian et al. LC 78-119579. 365p. reprint ed. pap. 104.10 (*0-317-28226-3*, 2022731) Bks Demand.

***Cardiovascular Surgery--Thoracic Surgery.** Ed. by G. Schlag et al. LC 94-36670. (Fibrin Sealing in Surgical & Nonsurgical Fields: 6). 1994. write for info. (*0-387-58381-5*) Spr-Verlag.

Cardiovascular Survey Methods. G. A. Rose & H. Blackburn. (Monograph Ser.: No. 56). 188p. (ENG, FRE, RUS & SPA.). 1968. 11.20 (*92-4-140056-0*) World Health.

Cardiovascular System. Glenn F. Bastian. (C). 1993. 5.25 (*0-06-501707-2*) HarpCollege.

Cardiovascular System: General Considerations & Congenital Malformations. 3rd ed. Ed. by William B. Robertson. LC 92-20957. (Systemic Pathology Ser.: Vol. 10, Pt. A). 1993. pap. text ed. 139.00 (*0-443-03096-0*) Churchill.

Cardiovascular System: The Initial Examination. Hurst. 624p. 1993. 65.00 (*1-55664-392-6*) Mosby Yr Bk.

Cardiovascular System see Anatomy & Physiology: A Programmed Approach

Cardiovascular System & Physical Exercise. Victor L. Karpman. 240p. 1987. 168.00 (*0-8493-6528-7*, QP114) CRC Pr.

Cardiovascular Therapy. Donald G. Vidt. LC 81-9683. (Cardiovascular Clinics Ser.: Vol. 12, No. 2). (Illus.). 212p. 1981. 35.00 (*0-8036-8931-4*) Davis Co.

Cardiovascular Therapy & Drug Market. Ed. by Peter Allen. 300p. 1988. pap. 1,495.00 (*0-941285-38-3*) FIND-SVP.

Cardiovascular Toxicity of Cocaine. 1993. lib. bdg. 265.95 (*0-8490-8911-5*) Gordon Pr.

***Cardiovascular Toxicology.** fac. ed. Ed. by Ethard W. Van Stee. LC 80-5546. (Target Organ Toxicology Ser.). (Illus.). 400p. Date not set. pap. 114.00 (*0-7837-7166-5*, 2047131) Bks Demand.

Cardiovascular Toxicology. 2nd ed. Ed. by Daniel Acosta, Jr. (Target Organ Toxicology Ser.). 576p. 1992. 104.00 (*0-88167-937-2*) Raven.

***Cardiovascular Transformation: A Business Guide for Successful Growth.** John O. Goodman & Conrad Vernon. LC 94-29406. 175p. 1994. ring bd. 15.00 (*0-8342-0642-0*) Aspen Pub.

***Cardoso-Suite - Sudamer-Guitar.** 1994. 15.95 (*0-614-01278-3*, UM22457) Omnibus NY.

***Cardoso-Twenty Four Piezas Suda-AM-GT.** 1994. 19.95 (*0-614-01281-3*, UM22448) Omnibus NY.

Cardozo: A Study in Reputation. Richard A. Posner. LC 90-35479. 176p. 1990. 18.95 (*0-226-67555-6*) U Ch Pr.

Cardozo: A Study in Reputation. Richard A. Posner. (Illus.). xii, 156p. 1993. pap. 10.95 (*0-226-67556-4*) U Ch Pr.

Cardozo Law Review: 1979-1988, 14 vols., Set. 740.00 (*0-8377-9224-X*) Rothman.

Cardozo Studies in Law & Literature. Richard H. Weisberg & Jacob Burns Institute for Advanced Legal Studies Yeshiva University Staff. 1989. 15.00 (*0-685-29558-3*) Yeshiva U Lib.

Cards As Weapons. Ricky Jay. 96p. 1988. pap. 9.99 (*0-446-38756-8*) Warner Bks.

***Cards at Play.** Freddie North. (Illus.). 144p. 1995. pap. 16.95 (*0-7134-7644-3*, Pub. by Batsford UK) Trafalgar.

Cards, Cups & Crystal Ball. David Campton. 1987. 2.75 (*0-87129-337-4*, C67) Dramatic Pub.

C.A.R.D.S., Deck 1: Common Words & Phrases. 1993. 2.50 (*0-88336-181-7*); teacher ed 3.00 (*0-88336-187-6*) New Readers.

C.A.R.D.S., Deck 2: Word Patterns. 1993. 2.50 (*0-88336-182-5*); teacher ed 3.00 (*0-88336-188-4*) New Readers.

C.A.R.D.S., Deck 3: Compound Words. 1993. 2.50 (*0-88336-183-3*); 3.00 (*0-88336-189-2*) New Readers.

C.A.R.D.S., Deck 4: Homonyms & Word Patterns. 1993. 2.50 (*0-88336-184-1*); teacher ed 3.00 (*0-88336-190-6*) New Readers.

C.A.R.D.S., Deck 5: Prefixes, Suffixes, & Root Words. 1993. 2.50 (*0-88336-185-X*); teacher ed 3.00 (*0-88336-191-4*) New Readers.

C.A.R.D.S., Deck 6: Practical Words & Phrases. 1993. 2.50 (*0-88336-186-8*); teacher ed 3.00 (*0-88336-192-2*) New Readers.

Cards for Kids: Games, Tricks & Amazing Facts. Elin McCoy. LC 91-11373. (Illus.). 160p. (J). (gr. 1-7). 1991. text ed. 13.95 (*0-02-765461-3*, Mac Bks Young Read) S&S Childrens.

Cards of Winds & Changes. Judith Pintar. 24p. 1990. 12.95 (*0-88079-467-4*) US Games Syst.

Cards of Your Destiny. Robert Camp. Ed. by Lene Whitley & Katherine Ranft. 334p. (Orig.). 1992. pap. 24.95 (*1-88915-08-8*) Seven Thunders.

Cards on the Table. Agatha Christie. 240p. 1987. pap. text ed. 4.99 (*0-425-10567-9*) Berkley Pub.

C

An Asterisk (*) at the beginning of an entry indicates that the title is appearing in BIP for the first time.

Cards on the Table. Agatha Christie. LC 68-6254. (Agatha Christie Ser.). 1968. 14.95 (*0-396-09010-9*, Putnam) Putnam Pub Group.

C.A.R.D.S. Starter Pack. 1993. 26.00 (*0-88336-198-1*) New Readers.

Cardsearch 91. Robert B. McKinley. 32p. (Orig.). (gr. 12). 1991. pap. text ed. 25.00 (*0-943329-77-9*) RAM Res Pub.

Cardsearch 91. rev. ed. Robert B. McKinley. 32p. (Orig.). 1991. pap. text ed. 25.00 (*0-943329-78-7*) RAM Res Pub.

Cardsearch 92. Robert B. McKinley. 1991. pap. text ed. 39.95 (*0-943329-79-5*) RAM Res Pub.

Cardsearch 93. Robert B. McKinley. 100p. 1993. pap. text ed. 50.00 (*0-943329-81-7*) RAM Res Pub.

Carducci: His Critics & Translators in England & America, 1881-1932. S. Eugene Scalia. 1937. 9.50 (*0-913298-59-X*) S F Vanni.

Cardydd a Thu Hwnt see Cardiff & Beyond

Care: Discovery & Uses in Clinical & Community Nursing. Ed. by Madeleine M. Leininger. LC 88-10804. (Human Care & Health Ser.). 202p. 1988. pap. 19.95 (*0-8143-1997-1*) Wayne St U Pr.

Care: The Essence of Nursing & Health. Ed. by Madeleine M. Leininger. LC 87-30043. (Human Care & Health Ser.). 276p. (C). 1988. reprint ed. pap. 19.95 (*0-8143-1995-5*) Wayne St U Pr.

Care & Adjustment of Estey (Reed) Organs. (Illus.). 1982. pap. 3.00 (*0-913746-18-5*) Organ Lit.

Care & Breeding of Laboratory Animals. Ed. by Edmond J. Farris. LC 50-10593. 530p. reprint ed. pap. 151.10 (*0-8357-9852-6*, 2011871) Bks Demand.

Care & Commitment: Foster Parent Adoption Decisions. William Meezan & Joan F. Shireman. LC 85-2730. 247p. 1985. 64.50 (*0-88706-103-6*); pap. 21.95 (*0-88706-104-4*) State U NY Pr.

Care & Commitment: Taking the Personal Point of View. Jeffrey Blustein. 288p. 1991. 42.00 (*0-19-506799-1*) OUP.

***Care & Community in Modern Society: Passing on the Tradition of Service to Future Generations.** Margaret Gates & Associates Staff et al. LC 95-13733. (Nonprofit Sector Ser.). 1995. 39.95 (*0-7879-0109-1*) Jossey-Bass.

Care & Concern of the Churches. Edwin Groenhoff. LC 81-69760. (Heritage Ser.: Vol. 8). 1984. 8.95 (*0-911802-59-2*) Free Church Pubns.

Care & Conservation of Geological Material, Vol. 1: Minerals, Rocks, Meteorites & Lunar Finds. Frank M. Howie. (Illus.). 128p. 1992. 74.95 (*0-7506-0371-2*) Buttrwrth-Heinemann.

Care & Conservation of Georgian Houses. 3rd ed. 1986. 52.95 (*0-85139-787-5*) Buttrwrth-Heinemann.

***Care & Conservation of Georgian Houses: A Maintenance Manual of Edinburgh New Town.** 4th ed. Andy Davey. LC 94-25926. 1994. write for info. (*0-7506-1860-4*, Butterwrth Archit) Buttrwrth-Heinemann.

Care & Conservation of Palaeontological Material. Chris Collins. (B-H Series in Conservation & Museology). (Illus.). 168p. 1995. write for info. (*0-7506-1742-X*) Buttrwrth-Heinemann.

Care & Cost: Current Issues in Health Policy. Committee for Economic Development Staff. 231p. 1989. lib. bdg. 24.50 (*0-87186-344-8*) Comm Econ Dev.

Care & Counseling of the Aging. William M. Clements. LC 78-54547. (Creative Pastoral Care & Counseling Ser.). 96p. reprint ed. pap. 27.40 (*0-685-44052-4*, 2030562) Bks Demand.

Care & Counseling of Youth in the Church. Paul B. Irwin. LC 74-26334. (Creative Pastoral Care & Counseling Ser.). 96p. reprint ed. pap. 27.40 (*0-318-34892-6*, 2031269) Bks Demand.

Care & Cure of Crippled Children. Gathrone R. Giralestone. Ed. by William R. Phillips & Janet Rosenberg. LC 79-6900. (Physically Handicapped in Society Ser.). (Illus.). 1980. reprint ed. lib. bdg. 15.95 (*0-405-13111-9*) Ayer.

Care & Education of America's Young Children: Obstacles & Opportunities. Sharon L. Kagan. (National Society for the Study of Education Publication Ser.: No. 90, Pt. 1). 275p. 1991. 26.00 (*0-226-60154-4*) U Ch Pr.

Care & Education of Crippled Children in the United States. Edith R. Sollenberger. LC 74-1706. (Children & Youth Ser.: Vol. 21). (Illus.). 270p. 1974. reprint ed. 28.95 (*0-405-05983-3*) Ayer.

Care & Education of Young Children: Expanding Contexts, Sharpening Focus. Ed. by Frances O. Rust & Leslie Williams. 168p. (C). 1989. pap. text ed. 16.95 (*0-8077-2984-1*) Tchrs Coll.

Care & Education of Young Children in America: Policy, Politics & Social Science. Ed. by Ron Haskins & James J. Gallagher. LC 80-11788. (Illus.). 224p. (C). 1980. text ed. 35.00 (*0-89391-040-6*) Ablex Pub.

Care & Feeding of a Large Family. Eugene F. Diamond & Rosemary Diamond. 200p. 1989. 6.00 (*0-685-26276-6*) Liferose Pr.

Care & Feeding of a Visiting Author: Tips for Successful Personal Appearances. 1986. write for info. (*0-318-63132-6*) AAP.

Care & Feeding of Baskets: A Book on Basketry Conservation. 4th ed. Emily Hartley. (Illus.). 44p. 1987. pap. 8.95 (*0-943993-00-8*) Procrastination Pr.

Care & Feeding of Bonsai: A Basic Manual. Charles Anderson & Ruth Anderson. (Illus.). 21p. (Orig.). 1988. pap. 3.50 (*0-9621310-1-6*) HarborCrest.

Care & Feeding of Dirt Archaeologists. Melvin K. Lyons. x, 76p. 1978. pap. text ed. 5.95 (*0-685-66562-3*) Am Sch Orient Res.

Care & Feeding of Dirt Archaeologists: A Manual of Sanitation, Hygiene, & Medicine for Archaeological Field Expeditions in the Near East. Melvin K. Lyons. x, 76p. 1978. pap. text ed. 5.95 (*0-317-04130-4*) Am Schls Oriental.

***Care & Feeding of Fish.** Sarajo Frieden. LC 94-38738. (J). 1995. write for info. (*0-395-71251-3*) Ticknor & Flds Bks Yng Read.

Care & Feeding of Ideas. Bill Backer. Date not set. 12.00 (*0-8129-6358-X*) Random.

Care & Feeding of Ideas: A Guide to Encouraging Creativity. James L. Adams. LC 86-10895. 240p. 1986. pap. 12.50 (*0-201-10087-8*) Addison-Wesley.

Care & Feeding of Power Grid Tubes. Robert I. Sutherland & EIMAC Division of Varian Laboratory Staff. LC 67-30070. (Illus.). 166p. 1967. 10.95 (*0-933616-06-6*) Radio Pubns.

Care & Feeding of Sailing Crew. 2nd ed. Lin Pardey et al. (Illus.). 500p. 1995. 35.00 (*0-393-03726-6*) Norton.

Care & Feeding of Southern Men. Claudia Greco. (Illus.). 144p. 1987. 6.95 (*0-912697-60-1*) Algonquin Bks.

Care & Feeding of Spinning Wheels. Karen Pauli. LC 81-80903. (Illus.). 84p. 1986. pap. 7.50 (*0-934026-04-1*) Interweave.

***Care & Feeding of Support Groups.** Vickie Kaczmarek. 34p. 1993. pap. text ed. 18.50 (*1-882472-10-1*) Comm Grief Ctr.

Care & Feeding of Tenants. Andy Kane. (Illus.). 120p. 1981. pap. 10.00 (*0-87364-240-6*) Paladin Pr.

Care & Feeding of the Autoharp, Vol. 1. 2nd ed. Ed. by Becky Blackley. LC 82-108061. 100p. (Orig.). 1991. 10.00 (*0-912827-15-7*) I A D Pubns.

Care & Feeding of the Autoharp, Vol. 2. 2nd ed. Ed. by Becky Blackley. LC 82-108061. (Illus.). 88p. (Orig.). 1991. 10.00 (*0-912827-16-5*) I A D Pubns.

Care & Feeding of the Autoharp, Vol. 3. Ed. by Becky Blackley. LC 82-108061. (Illus.). 93p. (Orig.). 1984. pap. 10.00 (*0-912827-03-3*) I A D Pubns.

Care & Feeding of the Autoharp, Vol. 4. Ed. by Becky Blackley. LC 82-108061. (Illus.). 89p. (Orig.). 1986. pap. 10.00 (*0-912827-07-6*) I A D Pubns.

Care & Feeding of the Autoharp, Vol. 5. Ed. by Becky Blackley. LC 82-108061. (Care & Feeding of the Autoharp Ser.). (Illus.). 89p. (Orig.). 1986. pap. 10.00 (*0-912827-08-4*) I A D Pubns.

Care & Feeding of the Autoharp, Vol. 6. Ed. by Becky Blackley. LC 82-108061. (Illus.). 82p. (Orig.). 1989. pap. 10.00 (*0-912827-12-2*) I A D Pubns.

Care & Feeding of the Autoharp, Vol. 7. Ed. by Becky Blackley. LC 82-108061. (Illus.). 68p. (Orig.). 1991. pap. 10.00 (*0-912827-13-0*) I A D Pubns.

Care & Feeding of the Autoharp, Vol. 8. Ed. by Becky Blackley. LC 82-108061. (Illus.). 82p. (Orig.). 1991. 10.00 (*0-912827-14-9*) I A D Pubns.

Care & Feeding of the Autoharp, Vol. 9. Ed. by Becky Blackley. LC 82-108061. (Illus.). 94p. (Orig.). 1991. pap. 12.00 (*0-912827-17-3*) I A D Pubns.

Care & Feeding of the Autoharp, Vol. 11. Ed. by Becky Blackley. LC 82-108061. (Illus.). 112p. (Orig.). 1993. pap. text ed. 12.00 (*0-912827-19-X*) I A D Pubns.

Care & Feeding of the Autoharp, Vol. 12. Ed. by Becky Blackley. LC 82-108061. (Illus.). 142p. (Orig.). 1993. pap. text ed. 15.00 (*0-912827-22-X*) I A D Pubns.

Care & Feeding of the Autoharp, Vols. 9 & 10. Ed. by Becky Blackley. LC 82-108061. (Illus.). (Orig.). 1991. pap. 10.00 (*0-685-71877-8*); Vol. 10, 122p. write for info. (*0-912827-18-1*) I A D Pubns.

Care & Feeding of the Beast. E. D. Santos. (Orig.). Date not set. pap. write for info. (*0-9621831-2-1*) La Sombra Pub.

***Care & Feeding of the Long White Cane: Instructions in Care Travel for Blind People.** braille ed. Thomas Bickford. 104p. 1994. text ed. 8.32 (*1-56956-458-2*, BR9342) W A T Braille.

Care & Feeding of the Prostate. Arnold Perrin. 1980. pap. 1.00 (*0-939736-49-7*) Wings ME.

Care & Handling of Active Microform Files: AIIM TR13-1988. Association for Information & Image Management Staff. 1988. pap. 30.00 (*0-89258-128-X*, TR13) Assn Inform & Image Mgmt.

Care & Handling of Art Objects. Marjorie Shelley. 1990. pap. 12.95 (*0-8109-2446-3*) Abrams.

Care & Handling of Art Objects: Practices in the Metropolitan Museum of Art. Marjorie Shelley et al. (Illus.). 112p. 1987. pap. 7.95 (*0-87099-318-6*, Abrams) Metro Mus Art.

Care & Handling of Australian Native Animals. Ed. by Suzanne Hand. 210p. (C). 1990. text ed. 120.00 (*0-949324-29-9*, Pub. by Surrey Beatty & Sons AT) St Mut.

Care & Handling of Salmon: The Key to Quality. John P. Doyle. (Marine Advisory Bulletin Ser.: No. 45). 66p. (Orig.). 1992. pap. text ed. 5.00 (*1-56612-010-1*) AK Sea Grant CP.

Care & Identification of Nineteenth Century Photographic Prints (G-2S) James M. Reilly. LC 85-81727. (Illus.). 116p. (Orig.). 1986. pap. 29.95 (*0-87985-365-4*) Saunders Photo.

***Care & Maintenance of Sprinkler Systems.** 1994. pap. 22.25 (*0-614-03110-9*, 25-94) Natl Fire Prot.

Care & Operation of a Lathe. Sheldon Machine Co., Inc. Staff. (Illus.). 1988. pap. 11.95 (*0-930163-18-4*) Arlington Bk.

Care & Operation of Small Engines Gasoline. (Illus.). 72p. 1986. 10.00 (*0-89606-208-2*, 108) Am Assn Voc Materials.

Care & Operation of Small Engines Gasoline. (Illus.). 13p. 1986. teacher ed 3.00 (*0-89606-318-6*, 108TK) Am Assn Voc Materials.

Care & Preservation of Textiles. Karen Finch & Greta Putnam. (Illus.). 144p. (C). 1991. reprint ed. 35.00 (*0-916896-37-4*, LA77) Lacis Pubns.

Care & Punishment: The Dilemmas of Prison Medicine. Curtis Prout & Robert N. Ross. LC 87-35331. (Contemporary Community Health Ser.). (Illus.). 272p. (Orig.). 1988. 49.95 (*0-8229-3581-3*); pap. 14.95 (*0-8229-5403-6*) U of Pittsburgh Pr.

Care & Repair of Antiques. 1989. 12.99 (*0-517-00190-X*) Random Hse Value.

Care & Repair of Books. 4th rev. ed. Harry M. Lydenberg & John Archer. LC 60-11980. 128p. reprint ed. pap. 36.50 (*0-317-10303-2*, 2013679) Bks Demand.

***Care & Repair of Furniture.** Albert Jackson & David Day. LC 94-31332. 160p. 1994. 27.95 (*1-56158-096-1*) Taunton.

Care & Repair of Japanese Prints. Carl Schraubstadtler. (Orig.). 1978. reprint ed. pap. 8.00 (*0-940492-00-8*) Asian Conserv Lab.

Care & Repair of Lawn & Garden Tools. Homer L. Davidson. 272p. 1992. 26.95 (*0-8306-3898-9*, 3753); pap. 14.95 (*0-8306-3897-0*, 3753) TAB Bks.

Care & Repair of Small Marine Diesels. Chris Thompson. 132p. 1987. pap. text ed. 15.95 (*0-87742-953-7*) Intl Marine.

***Care & Training of Parents.** Melissa Whitehouse. LC 94-90534. 64p. (J). 1995. pap. 6.00 (*1-56002-499-2*, Univ Edtns) Aegina Pr.

Care & Training of the Mentally Handicapped: A Manual for the Caring Professionals. 7th ed. Charles H. Hallas et al. (Illus.). 409p. 1982. pap. text ed. 30.00 (*0-7236-0624-2*, Pub. by John Wright UK) Buttrwrth-Heinemann.

Care & Training of the Trotter & Pacer. James C. Harrison. 1985. 7.50 (*0-686-20618-5*) US Trotting.

Care & Use of Amphibians, Reptiles & Fish in Research. Ed. by Dorcas Shaeffer et al. LC 92-61834. 195p. 1992. 55.00 (*0-685-65156-8*) Scientists Ctr.

Care & Use of Japanese Woodworking Tools. Kip Mesirow. LC 78-60055. (Illus.). 1982. reprint ed. pap. 9.95 (*0-918036-08-9*) Woodcraft Supply.

Care-Cloth: Or, a Treatise of the Cumbers & the Troubles of Marriage. LC 76-57421. (English Experience Ser.: No. 835). 1977. reprint ed. lib. bdg. 20.00 (*90-221-0835-X*) Walter J Johnson.

Care, Cure, & Education of the Crippled Child: A Study of American Social & Professional Facilities to Care for, Cure, & Educate Crippled Children. Henry E. Abt. LC 74-1659. (Children & Youth Ser.). (Illus.). 240p. 1974. reprint ed. 24.95 (*0-405-05941-8*) Ayer.

Care Exam Guide. 2nd ed. 1994. pap. 21.95 (*0-7931-1106-4*, 197007-02, Real Estate Ed) Dearborn Finan.

Care for Frail Elders: Developing Community Solutions. Walter N. Leutz et al. LC 92-11506. 315p. 1992. text ed. 45.00 (*0-86569-029-4*, T029, Auburn Hse) Greenwood.

Care for the Caregiver: A Guide for Staff in the Helping Professions. Terrance P. McGuire & Kathleen McGowan. LC 90-62085. 64p. (Orig.). (C). 1991. pap. 8.95 (*1-55612-400-7*) Sheed & Ward MO.

Care for the Disabled: Family & Public Responsibilities. Francis G. Caro. 14p. 1980. pap. 1.50 (*0-88156-073-1*) Comm Serv Soc NY.

Care for the Elderly: Significant Innovations in Three European Countries. 248p. (C). 1991. pap. text ed. 59.50 (*0-8133-8293-9*) Westview.

Care for the Home Bound Patient. 5.00 (*0-318-19101-6*) Am Dental Hygienists.

Care for Your Body. Rhoda Nottridge. LC 92-13917. (Staying Healthy Ser.). (Illus.). 32p. (J). (gr. 6). 1993. text ed. 13.95 (*0-89686-787-0*, Crstwood Hse) Silver Burdett Pr.

Care Gaps. W. Halamandaris. (Illus.). 114p. (Orig.). (C). 1992. pap. text ed. 14.50 (*0-8191-8659-7*) U Pr of Amer.

Care Gaps. W. Halamandaris. (Illus.). 114p. (Orig.). (C). 1992. lib. bdg. 39.75 (*0-8191-8658-9*) U Pr of Amer.

***Care, Gender, & Justice.** Diemut Bubeck. 280p. 1995. 45.00 (*0-19-827990-6*) OUP.

Care-Giving in Dementia: Research & Applications. Ed. by Gemma M. Jones & Bere M. Miesen. (Illus.). 432p. 1991. 106.00 (*0-415-04265-8*, A6189, Tavistock) Routledge.

Care-Giving in Dementia: Research & Applications. Ed. by Gemma M. Jones & Bere M. Miesen. (Illus.). 432p. 1993. pap. 22.50 (*0-415-10168-9*, B0868) Routledge.

CARE Group Leader's Handbook. Chester M. Wright & David A. Huston. (Illus.). 202p. 1990. student ed, ring bd. 24.95 (*0-932345-04-2*) Antioch Publishes.

Care in the Community: Challenge & Demonstration. Martin Knapp et al. 385p. 1992. 55.95 (*1-85742-071-3*, Pub. by Ashgate UK); pap. 25.95 (*1-85742-069-1*, Pub. by Ashgate UK) Ashgate Pub Co.

***Care in the Community: Five Years On: Life in the Community for People with Learning Disabilities.** Paul Cambridge et al. LC 94-28012. 122p. 1994. 47.95 (*1-85742-273-2*, Pub. by Ashgate UK) Ashgate Pub Co.

***Care in the Community: Fives Years On: Life in the Community for People with Learning Disabilities.** Paul Cambridge et al. 122p. 1994. 51.95 (*1-85742-282-1*, Pub. by Ashgate UK) Ashgate Pub Co.

***Care in the Community for Young People with Learning Disabilities: The Client's Voice.** Janice Sinson. 250p. 1995. pap. 24.95x (*1-85302-310-8*, Pub. by J Kingsley Pubs UK) Taylor & Francis.

Care Log: A Planning & Organizing Aid for Long Distance Caregivers. Angela Heath. LC 93-71895. (Working Caregiver Ser.). 72p. (Orig.). 1993. student ed 15.95 (*0-9621333-2-9*, Amrcn Source Bks) Impact Pubs CA.

***Care Management & Health Care of Older People: The Darlington Community Care Project.** David Challis et al. 380p. 1995. 54.95 (*1-85742-184-1*, Pub. by Arena UK) Ashgate Pub Co.

***Care Management & Health Care of Older People: The Darlington Community Care Project.** David Challis et al. 380p. 1995. pap. 25.95 (*1-85742-190-6*, Pub. by Ashgate UK) Ashgate Pub Co.

Care Management Standards: Guidelines for Practice. 1988. pap. text ed. 10.00 (*0-910883-44-0*) Natl Coun Aging.

***Care Messages.** Mike El. 72p. 1994. pap. 6.00 (*1-57087-065-9*) Prof Pr NC.

Care of Books. J. Clark. 1976. lib. bdg. 59.95 (*0-8490-1572-3*) Gordon Pr.

Care of Children in Hospital: A Study. Else Stenbak. (Illus.). 68p. 1986. pap. 7.20 (*92-890-1033-9*) World Health.

Care of Children with Long-Term Tracheostomies. Ed. by Ken M. Bleile. LC 93-3951. (Illus.). 304p. (Orig.). (C). 1993. pap. text ed. 45.00 (*1-56593-094-0*, 0398) Singular Publishing.

Care of Chronically & Severely Ill: Comparative Social Policies. Ed. by J. Rogers Hollingsworth & Ellen J. Hollingsworth. LC 93-38398. (Social Institutions & Social Change Ser.). 256p. 1994. 42.95 (*0-202-30485-X*); pap. 21.95 (*0-202-30486-8*) Aldine de Gruyter.

***Care of Collections.** Ed. by Simon Knell. LC 94-11659. (Leicester Readers in Museums Studies). 276p. 1994. 65.00x (*0-415-11284-2*, B4528) Routledge.

***Care of Collections.** Ed. by Simon Knell. LC 94-11659. (Leicester Readers in Museums Studies). 1994. pap. 25.00 (*0-415-11285-0*, B4532) Routledge.

Care of Congenital Hand Anomalies. 2nd ed. Adriann Flatt. LC 94-20707. 1994. 89.00 (*0-942219-35-X*) Quality Med Pub.

Care of Converts. Keith M. Baily. 95p. (Orig.). 1979. teacher ed 1.99 (*0-87509-157-1*); pap. 1.99 (*0-87509-156-3*) Chr Pubns.

Care of Dependent Children in the Late Nineteenth & Early Twentieth Century. Ed. by Robert H. Bremner. LC 74-1670. (Children & Youth Ser.). 203p. 1979. reprint ed. 25.95 (*0-405-05950-7*) Ayer.

Care of Dependent, Neglected & Wayward Children: Report, Second Section of the International Congress of Charities, Correction & Philanthropy Chicago, June, 1893. Ed. by Anna G. Spencer & Charles W. Birtwell. LC 74-1707. (Children & Youth Ser.: Vol. 20). 163p. 1974. reprint ed. 20.95 (*0-405-05984-1*) Ayer.

Care of Destitute, Neglected, & Delinquent Children. Homer Folks. LC 72-137167. (Poverty U. S. A. Historical Record Ser.). 1975. reprint ed. 16.95 (*0-405-03105-X*) Ayer.

Care of Destitute, Neglected, & Delinquent Children. Homer Folks. LC 78-51849. (American Philanthropy of the Nineteenth Century Ser.). 272p. reprint ed. pap. 77.60 (*0-7837-6535-5*, 2045672) Bks Demand.

Care of Fine Books. Jane Greenfield. (Illus.). 224p. 1988. pap. 16.95 (*1-55821-003-2*) Lyons & Burford.

***Care of Frail Elderly People in the United Kingdom.** A. Tinker et al. 114p. 1994. pap. 20.00 (*0-11-321610-6*, HM16106, Pub. by HMSO UK) UNIPUB.

Care of Handicapped Children, Vol. 7. Ed. by Robert H. Bremner. LC 74-1671. (Children & Youth Ser.). 1978. 20.95 (*0-405-05951-5*) Ayer.

Care of Individuals with Cancer. Groenwald. 1991. pap. 49.95 (*0-86720-305-6*) Jones & Bartlett.

Care of Mind-Care of Spirit: A Psychiatrist Explores Spiritual Direction. Gerald G. May. 192p. 1992. reprint ed. pap. 11.00 (*0-06-065567-4*) Harper SF.

Care of Patients: Perspectives & Practices. rev. ed. Mack Lipkin. LC 86-24599. 235p. 1987. text ed. 14.00 (*0-300-03771-6*) Yale U Pr.

Care of Patients with Emotional Problems. 4th ed. Dolores F. Saxton & Phyllis W. Haring. (Illus.). 192p. 1984. pap. text ed. 17.95 (*0-8016-4330-9*) Mosby Yr Bk.

Care of Patients with Urologic Problems. Edwina A. McConnell & Mary F. Zimmerman. (Illus.). 309p. 1982. text ed. 22.50 (*0-397-54402-2*, 64-03430, Lippincott Nursing) Lippincott.

Care of People with Diabetes: A Manual of Nursing Practice. Trisha Dunning. LC 93-46697. 288p. 1994. pap. 26.95 (*0-632-03876-4*) Blackwell Sci.

Care of Persons, Care of Worlds: A Psychosystems Approach to Pastoral Care & Counseling. Larry K. Graham. 1992. pap. 16.95 (*0-687-04675-0*) Abingdon.

Care of Photographs. Siegfried Rempel. (Illus.). 192p. (Orig.). 1987. pap. 16.95 (*0-941130-48-7*) Lyons & Burford.

Care of Pictures. George L. Stout. LC 74-25487. (Illus.). 176p. 1975. reprint ed. pap. 6.95 (*0-486-23165-8*) Dover.

Care of Redundant Churches. Richard Wilding. 76p. 1990. pap. 16.00 (*0-11-752304-6*, HM0643) UNIPUB.

Care of Reptiles & Amphibians in Captivity. Chris Mattison. (Illus.). 336p. 1992. pap. 17.95 (*0-7137-2338-6*, Pub. by Blandford Pr UK) Sterling.

***Care of Strangers: The Rise of America's Hospital System.** Charles E. Rosenberg. LC 94-36036. (Illus.). 448p. 1994. pap. text ed. 16.95x (*0-8018-5082-7*) Johns Hopkins.

Care of Tanned Skins in Mammal Research Collections. Catharine A. Hawks et al. (Museology Ser.: No. 6). (Illus.). 32p. 1984. pap. 4.00 (*0-89672-130-2*) Tex Tech Univ Pr.

Care of the Acutely Ill & Injured: Proceedings of the Fifth International Congress of Emergency Surgery, Brighton, 1981. International Congress of Emergency Surgery, 5th: 1981: Brighton, Sussex. Ed. by David H. Wilson & Andrew K. Marsden. LC 82-1836. 480p. reprint ed. pap. 136.80 (*0-317-58717-X*, 2029644) Bks Demand.

An Asterisk (*) at the beginning of an entry indicates that the title is appearing in BIP for the first time.

Care of the Aged. Ed. by Isaac M. Rubinow & Leon Stein. LC 79-8683. (Growing Old Ser.). (Illus.). 1980. reprint ed. lib. bdg. 17.95 (*0-405-12800-2*) Ayer.

Care of the Aged see Aged & the Depression

Care of the Aged Persons in the United States. Florence E. Parker & Estelle M. Stewart. LC 75-17235. (Social Problems & Social Policy Ser.). 1976. reprint ed. 25.95 (*0-405-07504-9*) Ayer.

Care of the Aged, the Dying, & the Dead. 2nd ed. Ed. by Robert Kastenbaum. LC 76-19596. (Death & Dying Ser.). 1977. reprint ed. lib. bdg. 15.95 (*0-405-09590-2*) Ayer.

Care of the Aging: Report of a Macy Conference. Ed. by Carolyn Spieler. LC 78-54173. 126p. reprint ed. pap. 36. 00 (*0-317-19844-0*, 2023015) Bks Demand.

***Care of the Arthritic & Rheumatoid Hand.** 3rd ed. Adrian Flatt. 1995. 89.00 (*0-942219-83-X*) Quality Med Pub.

Care of the Baby under One Thousand Grams. David Harvey et al. 1989. text ed. 190.00 (*0-7236-0952-7*, Pub. by John Wright UK) Buttrwrth-Heinemann.

Care of the Burn Wound. Ed. by S. R. May & G. Dogo. (Illus.). xiv, 246p. 1985. 176.00 (*3-8055-3991-6*) S Karger.

Care of the Competition Horse: Prepare to Win. Sarah Pilliner. (Illus.). 176p. 1994. 24.95 (*0-7134-7090-9*, Pub. by Batsford UK) Trafalgar.

Care of the Critically Ill. 3rd ed. Ed. by Stephen M. Ayres et al. (Illus.). 500p. 1988. 39.95 (*0-8151-0349-2*, CMA-3, Yr Bk Med Pubs) Mosby Yr Bk.

Care of the Critically Ill Patient. Ed. by J. Tinker & M. Rapin. (Illus.). 1150p. 1982. 305.00 (*0-387-11289-8*) Spr-Verlag.

Care of the Critically Ill Patient. 2nd ed. Ed. by J. Tinker & Warren M. Zapol. (Illus.). 1504p. 1991. 148.00 (*0-387-19617-X*) Spr-Verlag.

Care of the Dying: A Catholic Perspective. 82p. 1993. pap. 9.00 (*0-87125-213-9*, 130) Cath Health.

Care of the Dying Child. Ed. by Ann Goldman. (Illus.). 222p. 1994. 65.00 (*0-19-262503-9*); pap. 27.95 (*0-19-261983-7*) OUP.

Care of the Dying Child: A Practical Guide for Those Who Help Others. Robert W. Buckingham. 192p. 1989. 17. 95 (*0-8245-1294-4*) Crossroad NY.

Care of the Elderly. Gail H. Maguire. 321p. 1985. 51.00 (*0-316-54380-2*) Little.

Care of the Elderly. Pinkston. (C). 1984. pap. 19.95 (*0-205-14449-7*, H4449) Allyn.

***Care of the Elderly.** R. B. Shukla. 60p. 1994. pap. 19.00 (*0-11-701845-7*, HM18457, Pub. by HMSO UK) UNIPUB.

Care of the Elderly: Policy & Practice. D. J. Hunter et al. 224p. 1988. pap. text ed. 29.90 (*0-08-036416-0*, Pub. by Aberdeen U Pr) Macmillan.

Care of the Elderly Patient: Policy Issues & Research Opportunities. Institute of Medicine Staff. 152p. 1989. pap. text ed. 18.00 (*0-309-04097-3*) Natl Acad Pr.

Care of the High-Risk Neonate. 4th ed. Ed. by Marshall H. Klaus & Avroy A. Fanaroff. LC 92-20397. (Illus.). 560p. 1993. text ed. 49.95 (*0-7216-3709-4*) Saunders.

Care of the Horse. British Horse Society Staff. (British Horse Society Manual of Stable Management Ser.: Bk. 2). (Illus.). 160p. 1988. pap. 11.95 (*0-939481-07-3*) Half Halt Pr.

***Care of the Horse at Grass.** Zoe Davies. (Illus.). 176p. 1995. 35.00 (*0-7134-7570-6*, Pub. by Batsford UK) Trafalgar.

Care of the Low Back: A Patient Guide. Garth S. Russell & Thomas R. Highland. (Illus.). 196p. (C). 1991. pap. 19. 95 (*0-8036-7674-3*) Davis Co.

Care of the Mentally Retarded. Marian Blackwell. 1979. 19.50 (*0-316-09890-6*) Little.

***Care of the Mother Grieving a Baby Relinquished for Adoption.** Rosemary Mander. 228p. 1995. 59.95 (*1-85628-597-9*, Pub. by Avebury Pub UK) Ashgate Pub Co.

Care of the Neurologically Handicapped Child. Arthur L. Prensky & Helen Palkes. (Illus.). 1982. 32.95 (*0-19-502917-8*) OUP.

Care of the Newborn. 2nd ed. Ed. by Richard L. Schreiner & Niceta C. Bradburn. (Illus.). 216p. 1987. text ed. 50. 00 (*0-88167-360-9*) Raven.

***Care of the Ophthalmic Patient.** 2nd ed. Perry. 480p. 1995. pap. 79.75 (*1-56593-334-6*, 0664) Singular Publishing.

Care of the Patient in Radiotherapy. Lochhead. (Illus.). 186p. 1984. pap. 36.95 (*0-632-01138-6*, B30312) Blackwell Sci.

Care of the Patient with Previous Coronary Bypass Surgery. David Waters & Martial G. Bourassa. LC 70-6558. (Cardiovascular Clinics Ser.: Vol. 21, No. 2). (Illus.). 287p. (C). 1991. 75.00 (*0-8036-9085-1*) Davis Co.

Care of the Post-Operative Surgical Patient. J. A. Smith & J. Watkins. LC 85-3811. 272p. 1985. pap. text ed. 90.00 (*0-407-00286-3*) Buttrwrth-Heinemann.

Care of the Renal Patient. 2nd ed. Levine. (Illus.). 336p. 1991. text ed. 49.50 (*0-7216-3056-1*) Saunders.

Care of the Self: The History of Sexuality, Vol. III. Michel Foucault. 1988. pap. 11.00 (*0-394-74155-2*, Vin) Random.

Care of the Seriously Mentally Ill: A Rating of State Programs. E. Fuller Torrey et al. 192p. 1990. 10.00 (*0-685-49406-3*) Pub Citizen Inc.

Care of the Skin. 3rd ed. Audrey Goldberg & Lucy Goldberg. 1988. pap. 27.95 (*0-434-90674-3*) Buttrwrth-Heinemann.

Care of the Soul: A Guide for Cultivating Depth & Sacredness in Everyday Life. Thomas Moore. 1992. 25. 00 (*0-06-016597-9*, HarpT) HarpC.

Care of the Soul: A Guide for Cultivating Depth & Sacredness in Everyday Life. Thomas Moore. 336p. 1994. pap. 13.00 (*0-06-092224-9*, PL) HarpC.

Care of the Soul: A Guide for Cultivating Depth & Sacredness in Everyday Life. large type ed. Thomas Moore. LC 93-13239. 496p. 1993. pap. 16.95 (*0-8027-2674-7*) Walker & Co.

***Care of the Soul & Soul Mates, 2 vols.** Thomas Moore. 656p. 1994. 39.95 (*0-06-017173-1*, HarpT) HarpC.

Care of the Stabled Horse. David Hamer. (Illus.). 176p. 1993. 27.50 (*0-7134-6998-6*, Pub. by Batsford UK) Trafalgar.

***Care of the Twenty Four-Twenty Five Week Gestational Age Infant: Small Baby Protocol.** 2nd rev. ed. Ed. by Laurie P. Gunderson & Carole Kenner. (Illus.). 230p. 1994. pap. text ed. 24.95 (*0-9622975-6-9*) NICU INK.

Care of the Wild: First Aid for Wild Creatures. William J. Jordan & John Hughes. (Illus.). 240p. 1991. reprint ed. lib. bdg. 27.50 (*0-299-13180-7*); reprint ed. pap. 12.95 (*0-299-13184-X*) U of Wis Pr.

Care of the Wild Feathered & Furred: Treating & Feeding Injured Birds & Animals. 20th anniversary rev. ed. Maxine Guy & Mae Hickman. (Illus.). 144p. 1993. pap. 14.95 (*0-935576-45-2*) Kesend Pub Ltd.

Care of the Wounded in Vietnam. Robert M. Hardaway. (Illus.). 244p. 1988. pap. 15.00 (*0-89745-106-6*) Sunflower U Pr.

***Care of Troublesome People.** Wayne E. Oates. Date not set. 10.95 (*1-56699-133-1*, AL154) Alban Inst.

Care of Wounds. Jane L. Garr & Barbara Kirk. 68p. 1993. spiral bd. 8.46 (*0-8403-8555-2*) Kendall-Hunt.

Care Planning: Chronic Problem- STAT Solution. Annita Watson & Marlene Mayers. 1976. pap. 6.95 (*0-686-18879-9*) KP Med.

Care Planning for the Older Adult: Nursing Diagnosis in Long-Term Care. Richard S. Ferri. (Illus.). 384p. 1994. pap. text ed. 26.50 (*0-7216-2132-5*) Saunders.

Care Planning Pocket Guide. 3rd ed. Janet R. Lederer. 1990. spiral bd. 13.56 (*0-201-58298-8*) Addison-Wesley.

Care Planning Pocket Guide: A Nursing Diagnosis Approach. 4th ed. Janet R. Lederer. 288p. (C). 1991. spiral bd. 21.50 (*0-8053-4103-X*) Addison-Wesley.

Care Planning Pocket Guide: A Nursing Diagnosis Approach. 5th ed. Janet R. Lederer et al. LC 92-48222. (C). 1993. spiral bd. 26.95 (*0-8053-4104-8*) Benjamin-Cummings.

Care Planning Pocket Guide: A Nursing Diagnosis Approach. 22th ed. Janet R. Lederer. LC 87-28987. 1988. pap. 17.50 (*0-201-16399-3*) Addison-Wesley.

Care Plans That Work with the MDS. Mattie Locke et al. 190p. (C). 1992. pap. text ed. 54.45 (*1-877735-03-5*, 104) M&H Pub Co TX.

Care Staff in Transition. 170p. 1990. pap. 24.00 (*0-11-321209-7*, HM9027) UNIPUB.

Care Staff Management: A Practitioner's Guide. John Clements & Ewa Zarkowska. LC 93-39531. 1994. pap. text ed. 37.95 (*0-471-94395-9*) Wiley.

CARE Team Model: How to Get Everyone Involved in Your Student Assistance Program, Grades 7-12. Richard Zimman. LC 92-40064. 144p. 1993. pap. 24.95 (*1-56246-061-7*, P235) Johnsn Inst.

Care, Use, & Maintenance of Fire Hose Including Connections & Nozzles. National Fire Protection Association Staff. 19p. 1993. 20.25 (*0-317-63566-2*, 1962-93) Natl Fire Prot.

Carebook: A Workbook for Caregiver Peace of Mind. Joyce Beedle. Ed. by Louise Dunn. 51p. 1991. ring bd. 24.50 (*0-9630730-5-2*) Lady Bug.

Carebook: A Workbook for Caregiver Peace of Mind. rev. ed. Joyce Beedle. 51p. 1993. reprint ed. student ed, ring bd. 24.50 (*0-9630730-8-7*) Lady Bug.

Careen: The Third Geologic Revolution. Charles L. Eserhut. LC 86-51063. (Illus.). 132p. (Orig.). 1986. pap. text ed. 10.00 (*0-9618481-0-3*) Southgate Pub.

Careen: The Third Geologic Revolution. Charles L. Eserhut. 131p. (Orig.). 1986. pap. 12.95 (*0-317-52325-2*) Writers Pub Serv.

Career. James Lee. LC 57-13380. 175p. 1957. 16.95 (*0-910278-34-2*) Boulevard.

Career Academies: Partnerships for Reconstructing American High Schools. David Stern et al. LC 92-21021. (Education-Higher Education Ser.). 216p. 1992. 28.95 (*1-55542-488-0*) Jossey-Bass.

Career Accounting Fundamentals. Melvin Morgenstein. 559p. (C). 1988. text ed. 44.00 (*0-15-505778-2*); disk write for info. (*0-318-64533-5*); disk write for info. (*0-318-64534-3*); 5.50 (*0-15-505782-0*) Dryden Pr.

Career Action Plan. William M. Bloomfield. 1989. 9.95 (*0-936007-15-X*, 3300) Meridian Educ.

Career Action Plan: Implementation Guide. William Bloomfield. (YA). (gr. 9 up). 1989. 12.95 (*0-936007-16-8*, 3301) Meridian Educ.

Career Actualization & Life Planning. Donald H. Blocher. LC 88-82697. 212p. 1989. pap. text ed. 16.95 (*0-89108-206-9*) Love Pub Co.

Career Advancement for Women in the Federal Service: An Annotated Bibliography & Resource Book. Lynn C. Ross. LC 93-19100. (Public Affairs & Administration Ser.: Vol. 28). 280p. 1993. 40.00 (*0-8153-1058-7*, SS867) Garland.

***Career Advancement Networking.** Winthrop W. Hamilton. 220p. Date not set. pap. 8.95 (*0-7610-0321-5*) NW Pub.

***Career Adventure: Your Guide to Personal Assessment, Career Exploration, & Decision Making.** Susan Johnston. 216p. (C). 1995. per. write for info. (*0-89787-823-X*) Gorsuch Scarisbrick.

Career after Cosmetology School: Step-by-Step Guide to a Lucrative Career & Salon Ownership. Jessica Brooks. LC 94-65047. 320p. (Orig.). 1995. 29.95 (*1-884573-07-X*); pap. 19.95 (*1-884573-12-6*) S-By-S Pubns.

Career Alternatives for Bankers: How to Use Your Background in Banking to Find Another Job. William B. King et al. LC 92-61912. 306p. 1992. pap. 24.95 (*0-9634403-0-6*) Magellan Pr.

Career Anchors: Discovering Your Real Values. rev. ed. Edgar H. Schein. LC 90-70227. (Illus.). 67p. 1990. pap. 9.95 (*0-88390-030-0*) Pfeiffer & Co.

Career Anchors: Discovering Your Real Values. rev. ed. Edgar H Schein. LC 92-40385. (Illus.). 87p. 1993. pap. 9.95 (*0-89384-210-9*) Pfeiffer & Co.

Career Anchors: Trainer's Manual. rev. ed. Edgar H. Schein. 87p. 1990. pap. 24.95 (*0-88390-256-7*) Pfeiffer & Co.

Career & Life Planning: A Developmental Approach. 2nd ed. Steven H. Eichmeier. 288p. 1993. spiral bd. 26.95 (*0-8403-8674-5*) Kendall-Hunt.

Career & Motherhood: Struggles for a New Identity. Ed. by Alan Roland & Barbara Harris. LC 78-8026. 212p. 1979. 35.95 (*0-87705-372-3*) Human Sci Pr.

***Career & Self Exploration.** Grace Hansen. (C). Date not set. pap. text ed. write for info. (*1-884155-07-3*) Day & Nite Pub.

***Career & Vocational Education for the Mildly Handicapped.** Rhoda W. Cummings & Cleborne D. Maddux. (Illus.). 262p. 1987. pap. 29.95 (*0-398-06080-0*) C C Thomas.

Career & Vocational Education for the Mildly Handicapped. Rhoda W. Cummings & Cleborne D. Maddux. (Illus.). 262p. 1987. 48.95x (*0-398-05344-8*) C C Thomas.

Career Angel: Female Version. Gerard M. Murray. 1945. pap. 13.00 (*0-8222-0183-6*) Dramatists Play.

Career Angel: Male Version. Gerard M. Murray. 1944. pap. 4.75 (*0-8222-0182-8*) Dramatists Play.

Career Applications for Word Processing. 2nd ed. Patricia A. Custer. 288p. (C). 1992. pap. text ed. write for info. (*0-13-963802-4*) P-H.

***Career Assessment Study Guide: HP 616.** Eberhart. 14p. (C). 1989. spiral bd. write for info. (*0-931657-09-1*) Learning Proc Ctr.

***Career at Any Cost.** Lilian White. 210p. (Orig.). 1995. pap. 8.95 (*1-56901-836-7*) NW Pub.

Career Awareness Day: A Prescription for Creating Job Awareness in Elementary & Intermediate School Students. Patricia A. Ciabotti & Herbert L. Crocker. 1981. pap. 10.95 (*0-936386-15-0*) Creative Learning.

Career Beginnings: Helping Disadvantaged Youth Achieve Their Potential. William M. Bloomfield. LC 89-61964. (Fastback Ser.: No. 293). 40p. (Orig.). (C). 1989. pap. 1.25 (*0-87367-293-3*) Phi Delta Kappa.

Career Burnout. Ayala Pines. 1989. pap. 12.95 (*0-02-925353-5*) Free Pr.

Career Burnout: Causes & Cures. Ayala Pines & Elliot Aronson. 240p. 1988. 27.95 (*0-02-925351-9*) Free Pr.

Career Caravan. John Ourth & Kathie T. Tamarri. 64p. (J). (gr. 4-8). 1979. 7.95 (*0-916456-52-8*, GA121) Good Apple.

Career Cartoonist: A Step-by-Step Guide to Presenting & Selling Your Artwork. Dick Gautier. 128p. (Orig.). (YA). 1992. pap. 10.95 (*0-399-51732-4*, Perigree Bks) Berkley Pub.

Career Challenge. Henry J. Opperman. LC 84-73103. 300p. (Orig.). 1988. 27.95 (*0-318-03059-4*) BJIS Pub.

***Career Change.** David P. Helfand. 1994. pap. 12.95 (*0-8442-4274-8*, VGM Career Bks) NTC Pub Grp.

Career Change: A Planning Book. J. Michael Adams. (Illus.). 208p. 1983. pap. text ed. 12.75 (*0-07-000401-3*) McGraw.

Career Change: Everything You Need to Know to Meet New Challenges & Take Control of Your Career. 1995. 12.95 (*0-8442-4276-4*, VGM Career Bks) NTC Pub Grp.

***Career Change: Everything You Need to Know to Meet New Challenges & Take Control of Your Career.** David Helfand. Ed. by Sarah Kennedy. (Orig.). 1994. pap. 12. 95 (*0-8442-4376-0*, VGM Career Bks) NTC Pub Grp.

Career Change in Midlife: Stress, Social Support & Adjustment. John R. French, Jr. et al. (Illus.). 152p. (Orig.). 1983. pap. text ed. 15.00 (*0-87944-290-5*) Inst Soc Res.

Career Change in Midlife: Stress, Social Support, & Adjustment. John R. French et al. LC 83-18643. (Institute for Social Research, Research Report Ser.). (Illus.). 156p. reprint ed. pap. 44.50 (*0-7837-5279-2*, 2045017) Bks Demand.

Career Changer's Guide to Training in the Bay Area. Kate Frazier. (Illus.). (Orig.). (C). 1989. pap. write for info. (*0-318-65403-2*) Frazier CA.

Career-Changer's Sourcebook. Gene R. Hawes. LC 82-5194. 176p. reprint ed. pap. 50.20 (*0-7837-1568-4*, 2041860) Bks Demand.

Career Choice & Development. Duane Brown et al. LC 83-49258. (Jossey-Bass Social & Behavioral Science Ser.). (Illus.). 527p. reprint ed. pap. 150.20 (*0-8357-4870-7*, 2037802) Bks Demand.

Career Choice & Development: Applying Contemporary Theories to Practice. 2nd ed. Duane Brown et al. LC 89-28868. (Management-Social & Behavioral Science Ser.). 648p. 1990. 30.95 (*1-55542-196-2*) Jossey-Bass.

Career Choice & Job Search. Jay Como. 96p. (Orig.). (YA). (gr. 9-12). 1986. student ed 5.95 (*0-936007-01-X*, 3070); teacher ed 3.95 (*0-936007-02-8*, 3070) Meridian Educ.

Career Choices: A Guide for Teens & Young Adults: Who Am I? What Do I Want? How Do I Get It? Mindy Bingham & Sandy Stryker. Ed. by Robert Shafer. LC 90-81785. (Illus.). 288p. (Orig.). (YA). (gr. 9 up). 1990. pap. 19.95 (*1-878787-02-0*) Acad Innovat.

Career Choices & Changes: A Guide for Discovering Who You Are, What You Want, & How to Get It. Mindy Bingham & Sandy Stryker. Ed. by Robert Shafer. (Illus.). 304p. (Orig.). (C). 1994. pap. 22.95 (*1-878787-06-3*) Acad Innovat.

Career Choices for Students Considering an MBA. rev. ed. (Career Choices for the Nineties Ser.). 166p. 1990. pap. 8.95 (*0-8027-7336-2*) Walker & Co.

Career Choices for Students of Art. rev. ed. (Career Choices for the Nineties Ser.). 166p. 1990. pap. 9.95 (*0-8027-7324-9*) Walker & Co.

Career Choices for Students of Business. rev. ed. (Career Choices for the Nineties Ser.). 166p. 1990. pap. 9.95 (*0-8027-7325-7*) Walker & Co.

Career Choices for Students of Communications & Journalism. rev. ed. (Career Choices for the Nineties Ser.). 166p. 1990. pap. 8.95 (*0-8027-7326-5*) Walker & Co.

Career Choices for Students of Computer Science. rev. ed. (Career Choices for the Nineties Ser.). 166p. 1990. pap. 8.95 (*0-8027-7327-3*) Walker & Co.

Career Choices for Students of Economics. rev. ed. (Career Choices for the Nineties Ser.). 166p. 1990. pap. 8.95 (*0-8027-7328-1*) Walker & Co.

Career Choices for Students of English. rev. ed. (Career Choices for the Nineties Ser.). 166p. 1990. pap. 8.95 (*0-8027-7330-3*) Walker & Co.

Career Choices for Students of History. rev. ed. (Career Choices for the Nineties Ser.). 166p. 1990. pap. 8.95 (*0-8027-7337-0*) Walker & Co.

Career Choices for Students of Law. rev. ed. (Career Choices for the Nineties Ser.). 166p. 1990. pap. 8.95 (*0-8027-7335-4*) Walker & Co.

Career Choices for Students of Mathematics. rev. ed. (Career Choices for the Nineties Ser.). 166p. 1990. pap. 8.95 (*0-8027-7331-1*) Walker & Co.

Career Choices for Students of Political Science & Government. rev. ed. (Career Choices for the Nineties Ser.). 166p. 1990. pap. 8.95 (*0-8027-7333-8*) Walker & Co.

Career Choices for Students of Psychology. rev. ed. (Career Choices for the Nineties Ser.). 166p. 1990. pap. 9.95 (*0-8027-7334-6*) Walker & Co.

Career Coach: Carol Kleiman's Inside Tips. 1995. pap. 15. 95 (*0-7931-1088-2*, 568006-01) Dearborn Finan.

Career Connection for College Education: A Guide to College Majors & Related Career Opportunities. Fred Rowe. 272p. (Orig.). 1994. pap. 16.95 (*1-56370-142-1*, CCCE) JIST Works.

Career Connection for Technical Education: A Guide to Technical Education & Related Career Opportunities. Fred Rowe. 190p. (Orig.). 1994. pap. 14.95 (*1-56370-143-X*, CCTE) JIST Works.

***Career Connections, 6 Vols.** (Series 2: Communications, the Art & Entrepreneurship). 288p. 1994. 89.95 (*0-8103-9962-8*, UXL) Gale.

Career Connections Series, 6 Vols., Vol. 6. (Illus.). 288p. (J). (gr. 6-9). 1993. Set. 89.95 (*0-8103-9384-0*, 102102, UXL) Gale.

Career Counseling: A Developmental Approach. Robert J. Drummond & Charles W. Ryan. LC 94-16162. 544p. (C). 1994. write for info. (*0-02-330675-0*, Merrill Pub Co) Macmillan.

Career Counseling: A Psychological Approach. Elizabeth B. Yost & M. Anne Corbishley. LC 86-46335. (Jossey-Bass Social & Behavioral Science Ser.). (Illus.). 281p. reprint ed. pap. 80.10 (*0-7837-2547-7*, 2042706) Bks Demand.

Career Counseling: A Psychological Approach. Elizabeth B. Yost & Anne M. Corbishley. LC 86-46335. (Social & Behavioral Science Ser.). 283p. 1992. reprint ed. pap. 14. 95 (*1-55542-420-1*) Jossey-Bass.

Career Counseling: Applied Concepts of Life Planning. 3rd ed. Vernon G. Zunker. LC 89-35346. 545p. (C). 1989. text ed. 47.95 (*0-534-12108-X*) Brooks-Cole.

Career Counseling: Applied Concepts of Life Planning. 4th ed. Vernon G. Zunker. LC 93-31419. 1994. text ed. 50. 95 (*0-534-21205-0*) Brooks-Cole.

Career Counseling: Contemporary Topics in Vocational Psychology. Ed. by W. Bruce Walsh & Samual H. Osipow. 312p. (C). 1990. text ed. 59.95 (*0-8058-0266-5*) L Erlbaum Assocs.

Career Counseling: Models, Methods & Materials. John O. Crites. (Illus.). 240p. 1981. text ed. write for info. (*0-07-013781-1*) McGraw.

Career Counseling: Skills & Techniques for Practitioners. Norman C. Gysbers & Earl J. Moore. (Illus.). 176p. 1986. text ed. write for info. (*0-13-114562-2*) P-H.

Career Counseling for Women. Ed. by W. Bruce Walsh & Samuel Osipow. (Contemporary Topics in Vocational Psychology Ser.). 392p. 1993. 79.95 (*0-8058-1035-8*); pap. 34.50 (*0-8058-1401-9*) L Erlbaum Assocs.

Career Counseling of Older Adults: Pioneers & Prophets - A Special Issue of Journal of Career Development. Ed. by Sandra Olson. 69p. 1987. pap. 14.95 (*0-89885-347-8*) Human Sci Pr.

Career Counseling Skills see Productive Supervisor: A Program of Practical Managerial Skills

Career Counseling Techniques. Duane Brown & Linda Brooks. 308p. 1990. text ed. 40.00 (*0-205-12874-2*, H28749) Allyn.

Career Counselling in Practice. Robert Nathan & Linda Hill. (Counselling in Practice Ser.). (Illus.). 160p. (C). 1992. 44.00 (*0-8039-8695-5*); pap. 19.95 (*0-8039-8696-3*) Sage.

***Career Counselor.** (Career Examination Ser.: Series 1). Date not set. pap. 29.95 (*0-8373-3698-8*) Nat Learn.

***Career Counselor.** Parrot. 1995. pap. text ed. (*0-8499-3677-2*) Word Inc.

***Career Counselor: Guidance for Planning Careers & Managing Career Crises.** Leslie Parrott & Les Parrott, III. LC 95-3274. (Contemporary Christian Counseling Ser.: Vol. 11). 1995. 16.99 (*0-8499-1074-9*); pap. 10.99 (*0-614-03764-6*) Word Inc.

Career Crash: The End of America's Love Affair with Work. Barry Glassner. 1994. 21.00 (*0-671-69026-4*) S&S Trade.

C

An Asterisk (*) at the beginning of an entry indicates that the title is appearing in BIP for the first time. 1047

Career Criminal Apprehension Program: Annual Report. 66p. (Orig.). (C). 1993. pap. text ed. 25.00 (*1-56806-802-6*) Diane Pub.

Career Crossroads: A Job Hunter's Guide. Mary A. Hogue & Liz Willison. 154p. (C). 1991. pap. 12.95 (*1-881457-02-8*) Cont Mgmt Cnslts.

Career, Culture, & Social Psychology in a Variety Art: The Magician. Robert A. Stebbins. 180p. (C). 1993. reprint ed. lib. bdg. 25.50 (*0-89464-731-8*) Krieger.

***Career Decision Making.** Calvin Tolar et al. 128p. (C). 1994. 14.95 (*0-8403-9619-8*) Kendall-Hunt.

Career Decision Making. Ed. by W. Bruce Walsh & Samuel H. Osipow. 280p. 1988. text ed. 39.95 (*0-89859-756-0*) L Erlbaum Assocs.

Career Decisions Planner: When to Move, When to Stay, & When to Go Out on Your Own. Joan Lloyd. 272p. 1992. text ed. 49.95 (*0-471-54733-6*); pap. text ed. 14.95 (*0-471-54732-8*) Wiley.

Career Design. Eric Sandburg. 57p. (C). 1993. 3.5 hd 31.00 (*0-03-098013-5*) Dryden Pr.

Career Development. Ed. by Douglas T. Hall. (International Library of Management). 528p. 1994. text ed. 172.95 (*1-85521-509-8*, Pub. by Dartmth Pub UK) Ashgate Pub Co.

Career Development. Richard Harvey & Patrick Schutz. 256p. (C). 1992. teacher ed. 7.10 (*1-56118-369-5*); pap. text ed. 13.95 (*1-56118-368-7*) Paradigm MN.

Career Development: A Life-Span Developmental Approach. Ed. by Fred W. Vondracek et al. (Vocational Psychology Ser.). 232p. (C). 1986. text ed. 39.95 (*0-89859-828-1*) L Erlbaum Assocs.

Career Development: A Plan for All Seasons. Thomas P. Ference & James A. Stoner. (Illus.). 1978. teacher ed, text ed. 10.00 (*0-07-020452-7*); student ed, text ed. 6.95 (*0-07-020451-9*) McGraw.

Career Development: Contemporary Readings. Ed. by Artis Palmo. LC 77-2721. (Illus.). 367p. (C). 1977. text ed. 36.50 (*0-8422-5270-3*) Irvington.

Career Development: Designing Our Career Machines. David V. Tiedeman. LC 79-14183. 256p. 1979. 14.95 (*0-910328-27-7*); pap. 10.95 (*0-910328-28-5*) Sulzburger & Graham Pub.

Career Development: Taking Charge of Your Career. 2nd ed. Monica E. Breidenbach. 288p. 1992. pap. text ed. 33.60 (*0-13-119132-2*) P-H.

Career Development: Theory & Practice. Ed. by David H. Montross & Christopher J. Shinkman. (Illus.). 442p. (C). 1992. text ed. 67.95x (*0-398-05764-8*) C C Thomas.

***Career Development: Theory & Practice.** Ed. by David H. Montross & Christopher J. Shinkman. (Illus.). 442p. 1992. pap. 37.95 (*0-398-06294-3*) C C Thomas.

Career Development Activities. Larry J. Kenneke. 1973. pap. 6.00 (*0-672-97621-8*, Bobbs) Macmillan.

Career Development & Job Training: A Manager's Handbook. James G. Stockard. LC 77-12978. 446p. reprint ed. pap. 127.20 (*0-317-27061-3*, 2023542) Bks Demand.

Career Development & Services: A Cognitive Approach. Gary W. Peterson et al. LC 90-39581. 496p. (C). 1991. text ed. 49.95 (*0-534-14496-9*) Brooks-Cole.

Career Development & Transition Education for Adolescents with Disabilities. 2nd ed. Gary M. Clark & Oliver P. Kolstoe. LC 94-347. 1994. text ed. write for info. (*0-205-14788-7*) Allyn.

Career Development & Vocational Behavior of Racial & Ethnic Minorities. Ed. by Frederick Leong. (Vocational Psychology Ser.). 304p. 1995. text ed. 59.95 (*0-8058-1303-9*) L Erlbaum Assocs.

Career Development Education in the Federal Republic of Germany. FESC. 1985. 24.00 (*0-907659-17-9*) St Mut.

Career Development for Teachers. Jim Donnelly. (Books for Teachers Ser.). 160p. 1992. pap. 23.00 (*0-7494-0645-3*, Pub. by Kogan Page Educ UK) Taylor & Francis.

***Career Development for the College Student.** Margie Sherman. (Illus.). 8p. 1994. pap. 2.50 (*1-884241-23-9*) Energeia Pub.

Career Development for the College Student. 5th ed. Ed. by Philip W. Dunphy. LC 80-26933. 128p. 1981. pap. 7.50 (*0-910328-02-1*) Sulzburger & Graham Pub.

Career Development in Adult Basic Education Programs. Richard S. Deems. 43p. 1983. 4.95 (*0-318-22057-1*, IN263) Ctr Educ Trng Employ.

Career Development in Organizations. Douglas T. Hall et al. LC 86-2932. (Management Ser.). 391p. 1986. 36.95x (*0-87589-681-2*) Jossey-Bass.

Career Development of Engineers & Scientists: Organizational Programs & Individual Choices. Robert Morrison & Richard Vosburgh. (Professional Bks.). (Illus.). 288p. (C). 1987. text ed. 59.95 (*0-442-26351-1*) Van Nos Reinhold.

Career Development of Single Parents. Penny L. Burge. 40p. 1987. 5.25 (*0-318-35274-5*, IN 324) Ctr Educ Trng Employ.

Career Development Programs in the Workplace. Lynn Slavenski & Marilyn Buckner. (Information Ser.: No. 333). 49p. 1988. 6.00 (*0-318-42050-3*) Ctr Educ Trng Employ.

Career Development Workbook. Kathleen B. LeBlanc & Sylvia R. De Gale. 96p. 1991. per. 11.95 (*0-8403-7188-8*) Kendall-Hunt.

Career Developments: Preparing for the 21st Century. Ed. by Robert Hanson. 170p. 1990. pap. 16.95 (*1-56109-032-8*) ERIC Clearinghouse.

Career Dimensions I: Personal Planning Guide. rev. ed. Walter D. Storey. LC 86-50206. 144p. 1986. pap. text ed. 14.95 (*0-88390-193-5*) Pfeiffer & Co.

Career Dimensions II: Manager's Guide. rev. ed. Walter D. Storey. LC 86-50206. 86p. 1986. pap. text ed. 14.95 (*0-88390-194-3*) Pfeiffer & Co.

Career Dimensions III: Trainer's Guide. rev. ed. Walter D. Storey. LC 86-50206. 68p. 1986. pap. text ed. 19.95 (*0-88390-195-1*) Pfeiffer & Co.

Career Diplomat, the Third Chapter: The Third Reich. Hugh R. Wilson, Jr. LC 72-11747. (Illus.). 112p. 1973. reprint ed. text ed. 35.00 (*0-8371-6702-7*, WICD, Greenwood Pr) Greenwood.

Career Direction: A Practical Guide for Planning Your Future. James C. Shafe & A. G. Strickland. (Illus.). 32p. 1987. student ed 1.79 (*1-877846-06-6*); 0.50 (*0-685-26568-4*) Sales & Mgmt Trg.

Career Direction: Facilitator's Guide. James C. Shafe & A. G. Strickland. (Illus.). 100p. (YA). (gr. 11 up). 1987. teacher ed 25.00 (*0-685-26165-4*) Sales & Mgmt Trg.

***Career Directions.** Donna Yena. 160p. (C). 1989. text ed. 17.95 (*0-256-10387-9*) Irwin.

Career Directions. 2nd ed. Donna J. Yena. LC 92-41863. 288p. (C). 1993. pap. text ed. 19.50 (*0-256-13145-7*) Irwin.

Career Directions for Dental Hygienists. rev. ed. Regina A. Dreyer. LC 87-71570. 220p. (Orig.). 1987. pap. text ed. 12.50 (*0-933163-01-0*) Career Directions.

Career Directions for Dental Hygienists. 3rd ed. Regina D. Thomas. (Illus.). 224p. (C). 1992. pap. text ed. 16.50 (*0-933163-03-7*) Career Directions.

Career Discovery. rev. ed. Elwood N. Chapman. LC 85-72809. (Fifty-Minute Ser.). (Illus.). 64p. (Orig.). (C). 1988. pap. 9.95 (*0-931961-07-6*) Crisp Pubns.

Career Discovery Encyclopedia, 6 vols. Ed. by C. J. Summerfield. (Illus.). (J). (gr. 3 up). 1993. 129.95 (*0-89434-144-8*) Ferguson.

Career Doctor: Preventing, Diagnosing & Curing Fifty Ailments That Can Threaten Your Career. Neil M. Yeager. 272p. 1991. text ed. 37.95 (*0-471-54497-3*); pap. text ed. 12.95 (*0-471-54496-5*) Wiley.

Career Drive: How to Arrive at the Job You Really Want. rev. ed. Carol J. Haack. Orig. Title: Points, Plugs & a Roadmap. (Illus.). 77p. (C). 1985. per., pap. text ed. 7.25 (*0-934635-36-6*) Voc Pub.

Career Dynamics: Matching Individual & Organizational Needs. Edgar H. Schein. (C). 1978. pap. text ed. 26.95 (*0-201-06834-6*) Addison-Wesley.

Career Education: A Curriculum Manual for Students with Handicaps. Baumgart. 444p. 1990. 119.00 (*0-8342-0131-3*, 20131) Aspen Pub.

***Career Education: Functional Life Skills Approach.** 3rd ed. Donn Brolin. (Illus.). 480p. 1994. write for info. (*0-02-315062-9*, Merrill Pub Co) Macmillan.

Career Education see Your Working Life: A Guide to Getting & Holding a Job

Career Education Cookbook. Diane Hodges. LC 79-84492. 130p. (Orig.). 1979. pap. text ed. 12.95 (*0-918452-21-X*, 392) Learning Pubns.

Career Education for Handicapped Individuals. 2nd ed. Charles J. Kokaska & Donn E. Brolin. 464p. (C). 1985. write for info. (*0-675-20282-5*, Merrill Pub Co) Macmillan.

Career Education For Physically Disabled Students: A Bibliography. Maria N. Stieglitz & James S. Cohen. LC 79-89057. 152p. 1980. 2.00 (*0-686-42978-8*) Human Res Ctr.

Career Education For Physically Disabled Students: Career Awareness Curriculum. Maria Stieglitz. LC 80-83986. (Illus.). 100p. (J). (gr. k-8). 1981. 2.00 (*0-686-38797-X*) Human Res Ctr.

Career Education For Physically Disabled Students: Classroom Business Ventures. James S. Cohen & Maria N. Stieglitz. LC 79-91614. (Illus.). 50p. 1980. 2.00 (*0-686-38798-8*) Human Res Ctr.

Career Education For Physically Disabled Students: Development As A Lifetime Activity. John T. Palmer. LC 80-82642. 64p. 1980. 2.00 (*0-686-38799-6*) Human Res Ctr.

Career Education For Physically Disabled Students: Self-Concept Curriculum. Maria Stieglitz. LC 80-82643. (Illus.). 96p. (J). (gr. k-3). 1981. 2.00 (*0-686-38800-3*) Human Res Ctr.

Career Education For Physically Disabled Students: Speaker's Bureau. Maria Stieglitz & James S. Cohen. LC 79-93340. (Illus.). 62p. 1980. 2.00 (*0-686-38801-1*) Human Res Ctr.

Career Education for Teachers & Counselors: A Practical Approach. Larry J. Bailey. LC 85-13959. 204p. 1985. pap. 13.50 (*0-910328-41-2*) Sulzburger & Graham Pub.

Career Education for the Handicapped Child in the Elementary Classroom. Gary M. Clark. LC 78-78028. 1979. pap. 16.95 (*0-89108-092-9*) Love Pub Co.

Career Education in Transition: Trends & Implications for the Future. Kenneth B. Hoyt & Karen R. Shylo. 68p. 1987. 7.00 (*0-318-35273-7*, IN 323) Ctr Educ Trng Employ.

Career Education: Nature & Status: A Special Issue of Journal of Career Development. Ed. by Kenneth B. Hoyt. 91p. 1987. pap. 16.95 (*0-89885-363-X*) Human Sci Pr.

Career Education Potpourri. Diane Hodges. LC 80-81946. 160p. (Orig.). 1980. teacher ed, pap. text ed. 9.95 (*0-918452-22-8*, 393) Learning Pubns.

Career Employment Opportunities Directory, 4 vols. 2nd ed. Incl. Vol. 1. Liberal Arts & Social Sciences. (*0-916270-43-2*); Vol. 2. Business Administration. (*0-916270-44-0*); Vol. 3. Engineering & Computer Science. (*0-916270-45-9*); Vol. 4. Sciences. (*0-916270-46-7*); 47.50 (*0-685-73548-6*) Ready Ref Pr.

Career Employment Opportunities Directory, 4 vols., Set. 2nd ed. Incl. Vol. 1. Liberal Arts & Social Sciences. (*0-916270-43-2*); Vol. 2. Business Administration. (*0-916270-44-0*); Vol. 3. Engineering & Computer Science. (*0-916270-45-9*); Vol. 4. Sciences. (*0-916270-46-7*); 190.00 (*0-916270-42-4*) Ready Ref Pr.

Career English Agricultural: Field Crops, Bk. 2. ELS, Inc. Staff. 1984. pap. 13.95 (*0-8384-3277-8*) Heinle & Heinle.

Career English Agricultural: Horticulture & Livestock. ELS, Inc. Staff. 1984. audio 20.00 (*0-8384-3304-9*) Heinle & Heinle.

Career English Agricultural: Horticulture & Livestock, Bk. 3. ELS, Inc. Staff. 1984. pap. 13.95 (*0-8384-3303-0*) Heinle & Heinle.

Career English Agricultural: Soils. ELS, Inc. Staff. 1984. audio 20.00 (*0-8384-3295-6*) Heinle & Heinle.

Career English Agricultural: Soils, Bk. 1. ELS, Inc. Staff. 1984. pap. 13.95 (*0-8384-3294-8*) Heinle & Heinle.

Career English Aviation: International Jet Aircraft. ELS, Inc. Staff. 1984. pap. 13.95 (*0-8384-3290-5*); audio 20.00 (*0-8384-3291-3*) Heinle & Heinle.

Career English Aviation: International Traffic Control. ELS, Inc. Staff. 1984. pap. 13.95 (*0-8384-3309-X*) Heinle & Heinle.

Career English Aviation: Maintenance. ELS, Inc. Staff. 1984. pap. 13.95 (*0-8384-3301-4*) Heinle & Heinle.

Career English Business. ELS, Inc. Staff. 1984. pap. 13.95 (*0-8384-3271-9*) Heinle & Heinle.

Career English Business: Banking. ELS, Inc. Staff. 1984. pap. 13.95 (*0-8384-3317-0*) Heinle & Heinle.

Career English Business: International Trade. ELS, Inc. Staff. 1984. pap. 13.95 (*0-8384-3284-0*) Heinle & Heinle.

Career English Composition for Business. ELS, Inc. Staff. 1989. pap. 15.95 (*0-8384-3335-9*); audio 20.00 (*0-8384-3336-7*) Heinle & Heinle.

Career English Composition Science. ELS, Inc. Staff. 1984. pap. 13.95 (*0-8384-3313-8*) Heinle & Heinle.

Career English Engineering: Civil & Mechanical. ELS, Inc. Staff. 1984. pap. 13.95 (*0-8384-3275-1*); audio 20.00 (*0-8384-3276-X*) Heinle & Heinle.

Career English Engineering: Electrical. ELS, Inc. Staff. 1984. pap. 13.95 (*0-8384-3269-7*); audio 20.00 (*0-8384-3270-0*) Heinle & Heinle.

Career English Hotel Personnel. ELS, Inc. Staff. 1984. pap. 13.95 (*0-8384-3305-7*) Heinle & Heinle.

Career English Practical Medicine, Bk. 1. ELS, Inc. Staff. 1984. pap. 13.95 (*0-8384-3292-1*) Heinle & Heinle.

Career English Practical Medicine, Bk. 1. ELS, Inc. Staff. 1984. audio 20.00 (*0-8384-3293-X*) Heinle & Heinle.

Career English Practical Surgery, Bk. 2. ELS, Inc. Staff. 1984. pap. 13.95 (*0-8384-3315-4*) Heinle & Heinle.

Career English Restaurant Employees. ELS, Inc. Staff. 1984. pap. 13.95 (*0-8384-3307-3*); audio 20.00 (*0-8384-3308-1*) Heinle & Heinle.

Career English Secretaries. ELS, Inc. Staff. 1984. pap. 13.95 (*0-8384-3319-7*) Heinle & Heinle.

Career English Tourism: Charters, Etc. ELS, Inc. Staff. 1984. audio 20.00 (*0-8384-3312-X*) Heinle & Heinle.

Career English Tourism: Charters, Etc., Bk. 1. ELS, Inc. Staff. 1984. pap. 13.95 (*0-8384-3311-1*) Heinle & Heinle.

Career English Tourism: Managers, Etc. ELS, Inc. Staff. 1984. audio 15.00 (*0-685-59487-4*) Heinle & Heinle.

Career English Tourism: Managers, Etc., Bk. 2. ELS, Inc. Staff. 1984. pap. 13.95 (*0-8384-3267-0*) Heinle & Heinle.

Career Examination Series. Jack Rudman. (Entire Ser.). Orig. Title: Civil Service Examination Passbook Series. 1994. pap. write for info. (*0-8373-0000-2*) Nat Learn.

Career Exploration. Catherine Patty. (Social Studies Ser.). 24p. (gr. 9-12). 1979. student ed 5.00 (*0-8209-0260-8*, SS-27) ESP.

Career Exploration. Catherine Patty. (Sound Filmstrip Kits Ser.). (gr. 5-8). 1981. teacher ed 34.00 (*0-8209-0440-6*, FCW-17) ESP.

Career Exploration: A Self-Paced Approach. 2nd ed. Charlie Mitchell et al. 128p. (C). 1992. spiral bd. 14.95 (*0-8403-8105-0*) Kendall-Hunt.

Career Exploration Activities Booklet: 25 Activities to Help Explore Occupations. Barbara Parramore & William E. Hopke. 48p. (Orig.). (J). (gr. 6 up). 1989. pap. text ed. 17.75 (*0-685-31414-6*) Careers Inc.

Career Explorations in Human Services. Ed. by William G. Emener & Margaret A. Darrow. (Illus.). 338p. (C). 1991. text ed. 56.95x (*0-398-05733-8*) C C Thomas.

***Career Explorations in Human Services.** Ed. by William G. Emener & Margaret A. Darrow. (Illus.). 338p. 1991. pap. 34.95 (*0-398-06108-4*) C C Thomas.

Career Fastrax: Your Personal Roadmap for Success. George E. Bartuska. 12p. 1993. 19.95 (*1-57005-000-7*) Tech Res Grp.

Career Finder. Lester Schwartz & Irv Brechner. 1990. pap. 16.00 (*0-345-36716-2*, Ballantine Trade) Ballantine.

Career Finder: Pathways to over 1500 Entry-Level Jobs. Lester Schwartz & Irv Brechner. LC 82-90224. 352p. 1986. pap. 9.95 (*0-345-33679-8*, Ballantine Trade) Ballantine.

***Career Fitness: How to Get & Keep the Job You Want in the 1990s.** Peter D. Weddle. LC 94-15761. 208p. 1994. 19.95 (*1-56977-850-7*) Cadell & Davies.

Career Fitness Program: Exercising Your Options. 3rd rev. ed. Diane Sukiennik et al. 272p. (C). 1992. pap. text ed. 20.50 (*0-89787-816-7*) Gorsuch Scarisbrick.

***Career Fitness Program: Exercising Your Options.** 4th ed. Diane Sukiennik et al. LC 94-45891. 288p. (C). 1995. per. write for info. (*0-89787-825-6*) Gorsuch Scarisbrick.

Career Focus: One Day at a Time. Colleen A. McEvoy. 369p. 1992. pap. text ed. 8.95 (*0-9633810-0-8*) C A McEvoy.

Career for the Nineties & Beyond: How to Acquire Everything You Want Now! Paul Stemborowski. 1994. pap. 12.95 (*0-533-10911-6*) Vantage.

Career Growth & Human Resource Strategies: The Role of the Human Resource Professional. Ed. by Manuel London & Edward M. Mone. LC 87-32281. 357p. 1988. text ed. 65.00 (*0-89930-229-7*, LHR/, Quorum Bks) Greenwood.

Career Guidance & Counseling Through the Life Span. 4th ed. Herr & Cramer. (C). 1992. text ed. 59.50 (*0-673-52196-6*) HarpCollege.

Career Guidance Inventory. enl. rev. ed. Des. by James E. Oliver. 1989. 3.00 (*0-933510-85-3*); 35.00 (*0-933510-86-1*) Wintergrn-Orchard Hse.

Career Guidance Technician. Jack Rudman. (Career Examination Ser.: C-3104). 1994. pap. 29.95 (*0-8373-3104-8*) Nat Learn.

Career Guide: Dun's Employment Opportunities Directory, 1994. Dun & Bradstreet Information Services Staff. 1993. 475.00 (*1-56203-271-2*, 01222834) Dun & Bradstreet.

***Career Guide: Road Maps to Meaning in the World of Work.** Gary L. Harr. 384p. 1995. pap. 27.95 (*0-534-21942-X*) Brooks-Cole.

***Career Guide for Creative & Unconventional People.** Carol Eikleberry. 192p. (Orig.). 1995. pap. 11.95 (*0-89815-757-9*) Ten Speed Pr.

Career Guide for Jobs in Communications. Ed. by Center for Communication, Inc. Staff. (Orig.). 1990. pap. 15.00 (*0-9625891-0-1*) Ctr Communication.

Career Guide for PhDs & PhD Candidates in English & Foreign Languages. English Showalter. vi, 87p. 1985. pap. text ed. 8.50 (*0-87352-146-3*) Modern Lang.

Career Guide for Women Scholars. Suzanna Rose. 224p. 1986. pap. 27.95 (*0-8261-5411-5*) Springer Pub.

Career Guide: Opportunities and Resources for You see Ebony Success Library

Career Guide to America's Top Industries: Essential Information on Opportunities & Trends in All Major Industries. JIST Editorial Staff. (America Ser.). 220p. (Orig.). 1993. pap. 11.95 (*1-56370-111-1*, CGTI) JIST Works.

***Career Guide to Industries: Supplement to Occupational Outlook Handbook.** 1992. pap. 12.00 (*0-614-06316-7*) Claitors.

Career Guide to Professional Associations: A Directory of Organizations by Occupational Field. 2nd ed. Carroll Staff. LC 80-13268. 288p. 1980. 19.95 (*0-910328-06-4*) Sulzburger & Graham Pub.

***Career Guide to Top Industries.** 2nd ed. J. Michael Farr & U. S. Department of Labor Staff. (America's Ser.). Date not set. pap. 14.95 (*1-56370-185-5*) JIST Works.

Career Imaging. rev. ed. Dahk Knox & Jan Knox. 140p. (Orig.). (C). 1993. pap. text ed. 14.95 (*1-881116-08-5*) Black Forrest Pr.

Career in Accountancy. Brian Heap. 60p. (C). 1991. pap. 40.00 (*1-85352-881-1*, Pub. by HLT Pubns UK) St Mut.

Career in C Major & Other Fiction. James M. Cain. Ed. by Roy Hoopes. 288p. 1986. pap. 6.95 (*0-07-009594-9*) McGraw.

Career in Crime. Sid Rowland. (Illus.). 75p. (Orig.). 1987. pap. 7.00 (*0-937158-03-8*) Del Valley.

Career in Law. Jim Corkery. 270p. 1989. pap. 25.00 (*1-86287-017-9*, Pub. by Federation Pr AU) W W Gaunt.

Career in Law. Brian Heap. 60p. (C). 1991. pap. 30.00 (*0-7510-0018-3*, Pub. by HLT Pubns UK) St Mut.

Career in Theoretical Physics. Philip Anderson. (Series in Twentieth Century Physics). 696p. 1994. text ed. 99.00 (*981-02-1717-X*); pap. text ed. 48.00 (*981-02-1718-8*) World Scientific Pub.

Career Index: A Selective Bibliography for Elementary Schools. Comp. by Gretchen S. Baldauf. LC 89-28611. (Bibliographies & Indexes in Education Ser.: No. 7). 224p. 1990. text ed. 55.00 (*0-313-24832-X*, BCX/, Greenwood Pr) Greenwood.

Career Information. Ronald H. Fredrickson. (Illus.). 416p. (C). 1981. text ed. write for info. (*0-13-114744-7*) P-H.

Career Information, Career Counseling, & Career Development: An Integrated Approach. 5th ed. Lee E. Isaacson & Duane Brown. LC 92-1610. 1993. text ed. write for info. (*0-205-14645-7*) Allyn.

Career Information Center, 13 vols., Set. 5th ed. Visual Education Center Staff. 1992. text ed. 229.00 (*0-02-897452-2*) Macmillan.

Career Information Coordinator. (Career Examination Ser.: C-3576). 1994. 34.95 (*0-8373-3576-0*) Nat Learn.

***Career Inside the World of Sales.** Carlienne Frisch. LC 94-22143. (Careers & Opportunities Ser.). (YA). (gr. 7 up). 1994. 14.95 (*0-8239-1895-5*) Rosen Group.

Career Interventions with Women: A Special Issue of Journal of Career Development. Linda Brooks & Marilyn Haring-Hidor. 68p. 1988. pap. 14.95 (*0-89885-431-8*) Human Sci Pr.

Career Inventories for the Learning Disabled (CAI) Carol Weller & Mary Buchanan. 1983. 50.00 (*0-87879-350-X*); 20.00 (*0-87879-351-8*); 10.00 (*0-685-44966-1*) Acad Therapy.

Career Karate. Steve Tomkins. LC 91-61142. (Illus.). 125p. (Orig.). 1991. pap. text ed. 15.00 (*0-945846-01-0*, R542) Realistic Syst.

Career Ladders for Challenged Youths in Transition from School to Adult Life. Shepherd Siegel et al. LC 91-48273. 182p. (Orig.). 1992. pap. text ed. 24.00 (*0-89079-546-0*, 6546) PRO-ED.

Career Legal Secretary. rev. ed. (C). 1993. reprint ed. pap. text ed. 10.95 (*0-314-64789-9*) West Pub.

Career Legal Secretary. National Association of Legal Secretaries Staff. 770p. 1993. reprint ed. text ed. 30.50 (*0-314-32237-X*) West Pub.

Career Literature, Software, & Video Review Guidelines. 15.00 (*0-685-75347-6*, 72225) Am Coun Assn.

Career Makers: America's Top One Hundred Fifty Executive Recruiters. exp. rev. ed. John Sibbald. LC 91-47692. (Illus.). 432p. 1993. reprint ed. pap. 12.00 (*0-88730-628-4*) Harper Busn.

Career Management. Jeffrey H. Greenhaus. (Illus.). 366p. (C). 1987. pap. text ed. 39.00 (*0-03-070446-4*) Dryden Pr.

C

An Asterisk (*) at the beginning of an entry indicates that the title is appearing in BIP for the first time.

C

An Asterisk (*) at the beginning of an entry indicates that the title is appearing in BIP for the first time.

1049

Careers & Couples: An Academic Question. Ed. by Leonore Hoffmann & Gloria DeSole. 63p. reprint ed. pap. 25.00 (*0-8357-8571-8*, 2034937) Bks Demand.

Careers & Creativity: Social Forces in the Arts. Harrison C. White. LC 93-19815. (Social Inequality Ser.). 219p. 1993. text ed. 58.00 (*0-8133-1543-3*) Westview.

Careers & Creativity: Social Forces in the Arts. Harrison C. White. LC 93-19815. (Social Inequality Ser.). 219p. (C). 1993. pap. text ed. 20.95 (*0-8133-1544-1*) Westview.

Careers & Identities. Michael A. Banks et al. 224p. 1991. 85.00 (*0-335-09715-4*, Open Univ Pr); pap. 27.00 (*0-335-09714-6*, Open Univ Pr) Taylor & Francis.

Careers & the Study of Political Science: A Guide for Undergraduates. 5th rev. ed. M. Hepburn et al. Ed. by Mary Curzan. 51p. 1994. pap. text ed. 3.50 (*1-878147-07-2*) Am Political.

Careers & Training in Hotels, Catering & Journalism. Hayler. 1993. pap. 29.95 (*0-7506-0166-3*) Buttrwrth-Heinemann.

Careers As a Flight Attendant. rev. ed. Catherine O. Lobus. Ed. by Ruth Rosen. (Careers in Depth Ser.). (YA). (gr. 7-12). 1994. lib. bdg. 14.95 (*0-8239-1179-9*) Rosen Group.

Careers As a Rock Musician. Del Hopkins & Margaret Hopkins. Ed. by Ruth Rosen. (Careers in Depth Ser.). (YA). (gr. 7-12). 1993. lib. bdg. 14.95 (*0-8239-1518-2*); pap. 9.95 (*0-8239-1725-8*) Rosen Group.

Careers As an Animal Rights Activist. Shelly Field. Ed. by Ruth Rosen. (Careers in Depth Ser.). (YA). (gr. 7-12). 1993. lib. bdg. 14.95 (*0-8239-1465-8*); pap. 9.95 (*0-8239-1722-3*) Rosen Group.

Careers As an Electrician. Elizabeth S. Lytle. LC 93-12776. (YA). 1993. 14.95 (*0-8239-1513-1*) Rosen Group.

Careers by Design: A Headhunter's Secrets for Success & Survival in Graphic. Roz Goldfarb. LC 92-75527. 224p. 1993. pap. 16.95 (*1-880559-05-6*) Allworth Pr.

Careers Checklists. Arlene S. Hirsch. 128p. 1991. pap. 9.95 (*0-8442-8557-9*, VGM Career Bks) NTC Pub Grp.

Careers, Colleagues, & Conflicts: Understanding Gender, Race, & Ethnicity in the Workplace. Armand Lauffer. LC 85-14276. (Sage Human Services Guides Ser.: No. 43). 182p. reprint ed. pap. 51.90 (*0-7837-6580-0*, 2046145) Bks Demand.

Careers Encyclopedia. 13th ed. Audrey Segal. Ed. by Katherine Lea. 800p. 1992. text ed. 80.00 (*0-304-31675-X*) Cassell.

Careers for Animal Lovers. Russell Shorto. (YA). 1992. pap. 5.00 (*0-395-63571-3*) HM.

Careers for Animal Lovers. Russell Shorto. LC 91-27657. (Choices Ser.). (Illus.). 64p. (YA). (gr. 7 up). 1992. lib. bdg. 14.40 (*1-56294-160-7*); pap. 4.95 (*1-56294-767-2*) Millbrook Pr.

Careers for Animal Lovers: And Other Zoological Types. Louise Miller. LC 90-50725. (Careers for You Ser.). 160p. (Orig.). (YA). (gr. 7 up). 1991. pap. 9.95 (*0-8442-8125-5*, VGM Career Bks) NTC Pub Grp.

Careers for Animal Lovers & Other Zoological Types. (Careers for You Ser.). 128p. 1991. 12.95 (*0-8442-8107-7*, VGM Career Bks) NTC Pub Grp.

Careers for Artistic Types. Andrew Kaplan. (Choices Ser.). (Illus.). 64p. (YA). (gr. 7 up). 1991. lib. bdg. 14.40 (*1-878841-20-3*); pap. 4.95 (*1-878841-46-7*) Millbrook Pr.

Careers for Bookworms & Other Literary Types. (Careers for You Ser.). 128p. 1990. 12.95 (*0-8442-8111-5*, VGM Career Bks) NTC Pub Grp.

Careers for Bookworms & Other Literary Types. Marjorie Eberts & Margaret Gisler. 160p. 1990. pap. 9.95 (*0-8442-8618-4*, VGM Career Bks) NTC Pub Grp.

***Careers for Bookworms & Other Literary Types.** Marjorie Eberts & Margaret Gisler. LC 95-3219. (Careers for You Ser.). 1995. write for info. (*0-8442-4335-3*); pap. write for info. (*0-8442-4336-1*) NTC Pub Grp.

***Careers for Caring People.** Ed. by Sarah Kennedy. 1995. 12.95 (*0-8442-4475-9*, VGM Career Bks) NTC Pub Grp.

***Careers for Caring People.** Ed. by Sarah Kennedy. (Orig.). 1995. pap. 9.95 (*0-8442-4476-7*, VGM Career Bks) NTC Pub Grp.

Careers for Computer Buffs. Andrew Kaplan. (YA). 1992. pap. 5.00 (*0-395-63560-8*) HM.

Careers for Computer Buffs. Andrew Kaplan. (Choices Ser.). (Illus.). 64p. (YA). (gr. 7 up). 1991. lib. bdg. 14.40 (*1-56294-021-X*); pap. 4.95 (*1-56294-768-0*) Millbrook Pr.

Careers for Computer Buffs & Other Technological Types. Marjorie Eberts & Margaret Gisler. LC 93-10584. 1994. 12.95 (*0-8442-1404-3*, VGM Career Bks); pap. 9.95 (*0-8442-4105-9*, VGM Career Bks) NTC Pub Grp.

Careers for Crafty People & Other Dexterous Types. Mark Rowh. LC 93-16030. 1994. 12.95 (*0-8442-4106-7*, VGM Career Bks); pap. 9.95 (*0-8442-4107-5*, VGM Career Bks) NTC Pub Grp.

Careers for Culture Lovers & Other Artsy Types. Marjorie Eberts. 1992. pap. 9.95 (*0-8442-8135-2*, VGM Career Bks) NTC Pub Grp.

Careers for Culture Lovers & Other Artsy Types. Marjorie Eberts & Margaret Gisler. (Careers for You Ser.). 130p. 1992. 12.95 (*0-8442-8134-4*, VGM Career Bks) NTC Pub Grp.

Careers for Dreamers & Doers: A Guide to Management Careers in the Nonprofit Sector. Lilly Cohen & Dennis R. Young. LC 89-38376. (Orig.). 1989. pap. 24.95 (*0-87954-294-2*) Foundation Ctr.

Careers for Environmental Types & Others Who Respect the Earth. Jane Kinney & Mike Fasulo. LC 92-47379. 160p. 1993. 12.95 (*0-8442-4102-4*, VGM Career Bks); pap. 9.95 (*0-8442-4103-2*, VGM Career Bks) NTC Pub Grp.

Careers for Film Buffs & Other Hollywood Types. Jaq Greenspon. 160p. 1993. 12.95 (*0-8442-4100-8*, VGM Career Bks); pap. 9.95 (*0-8442-4101-6*, VGM Career Bks) NTC Pub Grp.

Careers for Foreign Language Aficionados & Other Multilingual Types. H. Ned Seelye. (Careers for You Ser.). 160p. 1992. pap. 9.95 (*0-8442-8129-8*, VGM Career Bks) NTC Pub Grp.

Careers for Foreign Language Aficionados & Other Multilingual Types. H. Ned Seelye & J. Laurence Day. LC 91-24617. (Careers for You Ser.). 114p. 1992. 12.95 (*0-8442-8130-1*, VGM Career Bks) NTC Pub Grp.

Careers for Foreign Language Experts. Russell Shorto. (YA). 1992. pap. 5.00 (*0-395-63572-1*) HM.

Careers for Foreign Language Experts. Russell Shorto. LC 91-27661. (Choices Ser.). (Illus.). 64p. (YA). (gr. 7 up). 1992. lib. bdg. 14.40 (*1-56294-159-3*); pap. 4.95 (*1-56294-769-9*) Millbrook Pr.

Careers for Good Samaritans: And Other Humanitarian Types. Marjorie Eberts & Margaret Gisler. LC 90-50724. (Careers for You Ser.). 160p. (Orig.). (YA). (gr. 7 up). 1991. pap. 9.95 (*0-8442-8126-3*, VGM Career Bks) NTC Pub Grp.

Careers for Good Samaritans & Other Humanitarian Types. (Careers for You Ser.). 128p. 1991. 12.95 (*0-8442-8108-5*, VGM Career Bks) NTC Pub Grp.

Careers for Gourmets & Others Who Relish Food. Mary D. Donovan. LC 92-18846. (Careers for You Ser.). 1992. 12.95 (*0-8442-8138-7*, VGM Career Bks); pap. 9.95 (*0-8442-8139-5*, VGM Career Bks) NTC Pub Grp.

Careers for Hands-on Types. Russell Shorto. LC 91-47146. (Choices Ser.). (Illus.). 64p. (YA). (gr. 7 up). 1992. lib. bdg. 14.40 (*1-56294-065-1*) Millbrook Pr.

Careers for History Buffs & Others Who Learn from the Past. Blythe Camenson. LC 93-46827. (Illus.). 1994. pap. 12.95 (*0-8442-4108-3*, VGM Career Bks) NTC Pub Grp.

Careers for History Buffs & Others Who Learn from the Past. Blythe Camenson. 1994. pap. 9.95 (*0-8442-4109-1*, VGM Career Bks) NTC Pub Grp.

Careers for Horse Lovers. Ronald Trahan. (Illus.). 288p. 1981. 22.95 (*0-395-31331-7*) HM.

Careers for Kids at Heart & Others Who Adore Children. Marjorie Eberts & Margaret Gisler. LC 93-48703. 1994. 12.95 (*0-8442-4110-5*, VGM Career Bks); pap. 9.95 (*0-8442-4111-3*, VGM Career Bks) NTC Pub Grp.

Careers for Nature Lovers & Other Outdoor Types. Louise Miller. (Careers for You Ser.). 130p. 1992. 12.95 (*0-8442-8132-8*, VGM Career Bks); pap. 9.95 (*0-8442-8133-6*, VGM Career Bks) NTC Pub Grp.

Careers for Night Owls & Other Insomniacs. (Careers for You Ser.). 1994. 12.95 (*0-8442-4115-6*, VGM Career Bks); pap. 9.95 (*0-8442-4116-4*, VGM Career Bks) NTC Pub Grp.

Careers for Number Lovers. Andrew Kaplan. (Choices Ser.). (Illus.). 64p. (YA). (gr. 7 up). 1991. lib. bdg. 14.40 (*1-878841-21-1*); pap. 4.95 (*1-878841-47-5*) Millbrook Pr.

Careers for Numbers Crunchers & Other Quantitative Types. Rebecca E. Burnett. LC 92-24334. (Careers for You Ser.). 1993. 12.95 (*0-8442-8136-0*, VGM Career Bks); pap. 9.95 (*0-8442-8137-9*, VGM Career Bks) NTC Pub Grp.

Careers for Outdoor Types. Andrew Kaplan. (YA). 1992. pap. 5.00 (*0-395-63561-6*) HM.

Careers for Outdoor Types. Andrew Kaplan. (Choices Ser.). (Illus.). 64p. (YA). (gr. 7 up). 1991. lib. bdg. 14.40 (*1-56294-022-8*); pap. 4.95 (*1-56294-770-2*) Millbrook Pr.

Careers for People Who Like People. Russell Shorto. (YA). 1992. pap. 5.00 (*0-395-63573-X*) HM.

Careers for People Who Like People. Russell Shorto. LC 91-27662. (Choices Ser.). (Illus.). 64p. (YA). (gr. 7 up). 1992. lib. bdg. 14.40 (*1-56294-157-7*); pap. 4.95 (*1-56294-771-0*) Millbrook Pr.

Careers for People Who Like to Perform. Russell Shorto. (YA). 1992. pap. 5.00 (*0-395-63574-8*) HM.

Careers for People Who Like to Perform. Russell Shorto. LC 91-27660. (Choices Ser.). (Illus.). 64p. (YA). (gr. 7 up). 1992. lib. bdg. 14.40 (*1-56294-158-5*); pap. 4.95 (*1-56294-772-9*) Millbrook Pr.

***Careers for Plant Lovers & Other Green Thumb Types.** Blythe Camenson. (Orig.). 1995. 12.95 (*0-8442-4119-9*, VGM Career Bks); pap. write for info. (*0-8442-4120-2*, VGM Career Bks) NTC Pub Grp.

***Careers for Shutterbugs: And Other Candid Types.** Cheryl McLean. 1994. pap. 9.95 (*0-8442-4114-8*, VGM Career Bks) NTC Pub Grp.

Careers for Speech Communication Graduates. Al R. Weitzel. 80p. (Orig.). 1987. pap. text ed. 9.50 (*0-88133-256-9*) Sheffield WI.

Careers for Sports Fans. Andrew Kaplan. (YA). 1992. pap. 5.00 (*0-395-63562-4*) HM.

Careers for Sports Fans. Andrew Kaplan. (Choices Ser.). (Illus.). 64p. (YA). (gr. 7 up). 1991. lib. bdg. 14.40 (*1-56294-023-6*); pap. 4.95 (*1-56294-773-7*) Millbrook Pr.

Careers for Sports Nuts. William R. Heitzmann. 160p. 1991. pap. 9.95 (*0-8442-8570-6*, VGM Career Bks) NTC Pub Grp.

Careers for Sports Nuts & Other Athletic Types. W. Ray Heitzmann. (Careers for You Ser.). 128p. 1991. 12.95 (*0-8442-8110-7*, VGM Career Bks) NTC Pub Grp.

Careers for Students of History. Barbara J. Howe. 94p. 1989. 8.00 (*0-87229-044-1*) Am Hist Assn.

Careers for the Curious. Russell Shorto. LC 91-47145. (Choices Ser.). (Illus.). 64p. (YA). (gr. 7 up). 1992. lib. bdg. 14.40 (*1-56294-064-3*) Millbrook Pr.

***Careers for the Nineties & Beyond.** Rea Staff. 1994. pap. 17.95 (*0-87891-959-7*) Res & Educ.

Careers for Travel Buffs & Other Restless Types. Paul Plawin. (Careers for You Ser.). 160p. 1992. 12.95 (*0-8442-8109-3*, VGM Career Bks); pap. 9.95 (*0-8442-8127-1*, VGM Career Bks) NTC Pub Grp.

Careers for Women. Catherine Filene. LC 74-3948. (Women in America Ser.). 592p. 1974. reprint ed. 45.95 (*0-405-06094-7*) Ayer.

Careers for Women As Clergy. Julie F. Parker. Ed. by Ruth Rosen. (Careers in Depth Ser.). (YA). (gr. 7-12). 1993. lib. bdg. 14.95 (*0-8239-1424-0*); pap. 9.95 (*0-8239-1727-4*) Rosen Group.

Careers for Women in Politics. Richard S. Lee & Mary P. Lee. Ed. by Ruth Rosen. (YA). (gr. 7-12). 1989. lib. bdg. 14.95 (*0-8239-0966-2*) Rosen Group.

Careers for Wordsmiths. Andrew Kaplan. (YA). 1992. pap. 5.00 (*0-395-63563-2*) HM.

Careers for Wordsmiths. Andrew Kaplan. (Choices Ser.). (Illus.). 64p. (YA). (gr. 7 up). 1991. lib. bdg. 14.40 (*1-56294-024-4*); pap. 4.95 (*1-56294-774-5*) Millbrook Pr.

***Careers for Writers.** Ed. by Sarah Kennedy. 1995. 12.95 (*0-8442-4333-7*, VGM Career Bks) NTC Pub Grp.

***Careers for Writers.** Ed. by Sarah Kennedy. (Orig.). 1995. pap. text ed. 9.95 (*0-8442-4334-5*, VGM Career Bks) NTC Pub Grp.

Careers in a Corporate Hierarchy: Structural Timetables & Historical Effects (Monograph) James E. Rosenbaum. LC 83-22406. 1984. text ed. 55.00 (*0-12-597080-3*) Acad Pr.

Careers in Accounting. Gloria L. Gaylord & Glenda E. Ried. 128p. text ed. 16.95 (*0-8442-6120-3*, VGM Career Bks); pap. 11.95 (*0-8442-6121-1*, VGM Career Bks) NTC Pub Grp.

Careers in Accounting. Gloria L. Gaylord & Glenda E. Ried. LC 90-50729. (Professional Careers Ser.). 128p. (YA). (gr. 9 up). 1991. 16.95 (*0-8442-8140-9*, VGM Career Bks); pap. 12.95 (*0-8442-8141-7*, VGM Career Bks) NTC Pub Grp.

Careers in Advertising. S. William Pattis. 1990. pap. 12.95 (*0-8442-8697-4*, VGM Career Bks) NTC Pub Grp.

Careers in Advertising. S. William Pattis. 160p. 1991. 16.95 (*0-8442-8696-6*, VGM Career Bks) NTC Pub Grp.

Careers in Agribusiness & Industry. 4th ed. Marcella Smith et al. LC 76-106341. (Illus.). 395p. (YA). (gr. 9-12). 1991. 34.60 (*0-8134-2898-X*); teacher ed 6.95 (*0-8134-2899-8*); text ed. 25.95 (*0-685-54235-1*) Interstate.

Careers in Art. Gerald F. Brommer & Joseph Gatto. LC 83-73179. (Illus.). 256p. 1984. 23.95 (*0-87192-149-9*) Davis Mass.

Careers in Art. rev. ed. National Art Education Association Staff. (C). 1971. pap. 2.00 (*0-937652-14-8*) Natl Art Ed.

Careers in Art & Design. 6th rev. ed. Linda Ball. pap. text ed. write for info. (*0-7494-0674-7*, Pub. by Kogan Page Educ UK) Taylor & Francis.

Careers in Aviation. Sharon Carter. Ed. by Ruth Rosen. (Careers in Depth Ser.). (YA). (gr. 7-12). 1989. lib. bdg. 14.95 (*0-8239-0965-4*) Rosen Group.

Careers in Banking & Finance. Patricia Haddock. Ed. by Ruth Rosen. (Careers in Depth Ser.). (YA). (gr. 7-12). 1989. lib. bdg. 14.95 (*0-8239-0962-X*) Rosen Group.

Careers in Banking & Finance: How to Achieve Your Professional Goal. Donald Mayall. Ed. by American Institute of Banking Staff & Joseph Lubow. LC 85-18691. 143p. (Orig.). 1985. pap. 10.50 (*0-935183-00-0*) Amer Inst Bank.

Careers in Beauty Culture. Barbara L. Johnson. Ed. by Ruth Rosen. (Careers in Depth Ser.). (YA). (gr. 7-12). 1989. lib. bdg. 14.95 (*0-8239-1002-4*) Rosen Group.

Careers in Business. Lila B. Stair & Dorothy Domkowski. 208p. text ed. 16.95 (*0-8442-6117-3*, VGM Career Bks); pap. 11.95 (*0-8442-6118-1*, VGM Career Bks) NTC Pub Grp.

Careers in Business. Lila B. Stair. 176p. 1992. 16.95 (*0-8442-8144-1*, VGM Career Bks); pap. 12.95 (*0-8442-8146-8*, VGM Career Bks) NTC Pub Grp.

Careers in Business & the Public Sector: An Annotated Bibliography. Michael Parrish. 34p. 1986. pap. text ed. 8.00 (*0-9617990-0-5*) Ars Biblio.

Careers in Child Care. Marjorie Eberts. Ed. by Margaret Gisler. LC 93-47486. 1994. 16.95 (*0-8442-4191-1*, VGM Career Bks); pap. 12.95 (*0-8442-4193-8*, VGM Career Bks) NTC Pub Grp.

Careers in City Politics: The Case for Urban Democracy. Timothy Bledsoe. LC 92-36908. (Series in Policy & Institutional Studies). 256p. (C). 1993. text ed. 39.95 (*0-8229-3743-3*) U of Pittsburgh Pr.

Careers in Civil Litigation. LC 90-80004. 60p. 1990. pap. 14.95 (*0-89707-524-2*, 527-0031) Amer Bar Assn.

Careers in Clinical Research: Obstacles & Opportunities. Institute of Medicine, Committee on Addressing Career Paths for Clinical Research Staff. 344p. (C). 1994. text ed. 39.95 (*0-309-04890-7*) Natl Acad Pr.

Careers in Comedy. Sharon Menzel-Gerrie. LC 93-4962. (J). 1993. 14.95 (*0-8239-1517-4*); pap. 9.95 (*0-8239-1713-4*) Rosen Group.

Careers in Communication Arts & Sciences. (Illus.). 12p. 1987. pap. 1.00 (*0-318-40105-3*) ACA VA.

Careers in Communications. Shonan Noronha. LC 93-25152. (VGM Professional Careers Ser.). 1993. write for info. (*0-8442-4182-2*, VGM Career Bks); pap. write for info. (*0-8442-4183-0*, VGM Career Bks) VCH Pubs.

Careers in Communications. Shonan F. Noronha. 208p. text ed. 16.95 (*0-8442-6115-7*, VGM Career Bks); pap. 12.95 (*0-8442-6116-5*, VGM Career Bks) NTC Pub Grp.

Careers in Computer Field. rev. ed. Joseph Weintraub. 1993. 14.95 (*0-8239-1601-4*); pap. 9.95 (*0-8239-1723-1*) Rosen Group.

***Careers in Computers.** Ed. by Sarah Kennedy. 1995. 16.95 (*0-8442-4481-3*, VGM Career Bks) NTC Pub Grp.

***Careers in Computers.** Ed. by Sarah Kennedy. 1995. pap. 12.95 (*0-8442-4482-1*, VGM Career Bks) NTC Pub Grp.

Careers in Computers. Lila B. Stair. (Illus.). 168p. 1984. pap. 9.95 (*0-8442-6126-2*) NTC Pub Grp.

Careers in Computers. Lila B. Stair. 160p. 1991. 16.95 (*0-8442-8552-8*, VGM Career Bks); pap. 12.95 (*0-8442-8553-6*, VGM Career Bks) NTC Pub Grp.

Careers in Conservation. John McCormick. 112p. (Orig.). 1989. pap. 17.95 (*0-8464-1402-3*) Beekman Pubs.

Careers in Dentistry: Is It for You. S. Adele Doherty. (Illus.). 104p. (C). 1992. text ed. 25.00 (*0-9630511-4-8*) DSH Pub.

Careers in Diving. Steve Barksky et al. (Illus.). 309p. 1993. 19.95 (*0-941332-37-3*) Best Pub Co.

Careers in Education. Roy Edelfelt. (Professional Careers Ser.). 160p. 1988. 16.95 (*0-8442-6104-1*, VGM Career Bks); pap. 12.95 (*0-8442-6114-9*, VGM Career Bks) NTC Pub Grp.

Careers in Education. Roy A. Edelfelt & Blythe Camenson. LC 92-24710. (Professional Careers Ser.). 1993. 16.95 (*0-8442-4176-8*, VGM Career Bks); pap. 12.95 (*0-8442-4177-6*, VGM Career Bks) NTC Pub Grp.

Careers in Engineering. Geraldine O. Gardner. 150p. 1993. 16.95 (*0-8442-4184-9*, VGM Career Bks); pap. 12.95 (*0-8442-4185-7*, VGM Career Bks) NTC Pub Grp.

Careers in Engineering. Elliott S. Kanter. (Professional Careers Ser.). 1989. 16.95 (*0-8442-6311-7*, VGM Career Bks); pap. 12.95 (*0-8442-6312-5*, VGM Career Bks) NTC Pub Grp.

Careers in Engineering & Technology. 4th ed. George C. Beakley et al. (Illus.). 677p. (C). 1987. pap. write for info. (*0-02-307620-8*) Macmillan.

Careers in Entertainment Law. LC 90-80003. 119p. 1990. pap. 14.95 (*0-89707-525-0*, 527-0032) Amer Bar Assn.

Careers in Film & Video Production. Michael Horwin. (Illus.). 206p. 1989. pap. 25.00 (*0-240-80049-4*, Focal) Buttrwrth-Heinemann.

Careers in Finance. Trudy Ring. 150p. 1993. 16.95 (*0-8442-4186-5*, VGM Career Bks); pap. 12.95 (*0-8442-4187-3*, VGM Career Bks) NTC Pub Grp.

Careers in Firefighting. Mary P. Lee & Richard S. Lee. Ed. by Ruth Rosen. (Careers in Depth Ser.). (YA). (gr. 7-12). 1993. lib. bdg. 14.95 (*0-8239-1515-8*); pap. 9.95 (*0-8239-1724-X*) Rosen Group.

Careers in Foreign Languages: A Handbook. rev. ed. June L. Sherif. 228p. (C). (gr. 9-12). 1975. pap. 3.95 (*0-88345-250-2*) Prentice ESL.

Careers in Geography. 6th rev. ed. Ed. by Salvatore J. Natoli. LC 74-77075. (Illus.). 1994. 3.00 (*0-89291-184-0*) Assn Am Geographers.

Careers in Government. Mary E. Pitz. 1994. pap. 12.95 (*0-8442-4195-4*) NTC Pub Grp.

Careers in Graphic Arts. rev. ed. Virginia L. Roberson. (Careers in Depth Ser.). (Illus.). (YA). (gr. 7-12). 1993. lib. bdg. 14.95 (*0-8239-1349-X*); pap. 9.95 (*0-8239-1715-0*) Rosen Group.

Careers in Hazardous Waste Management: A Job Hunter's Guide to the Hazardous Waste Management Field. Jacalyn Spiszman. LC 89-83956. 69p. (Orig.). 1989. pap. text ed. 12.95 (*0-9622606-0-6*) EEC.

Careers in Health & Fitness. rev. ed. Jackie Heron. Ed. by Ruth Rosen. (Careers in Depth Ser.). (Illus.). 160p. (J). (gr. 7 up). 1990. 14.95 (*0-8239-1162-4*) Rosen Group.

Careers in Health Care. (Professional Careers Ser.). 1994. 16.95 (*0-8442-4198-9*, VGM Career Bks); pap. 12.95 (*0-8442-4199-7*, VGM Career Bks) NTC Pub Grp.

Careers in Health Care. Rachel Epstein. (Medical Issues Ser.). (Illus.). 112p. (YA). (gr. 6-12). 1989. 18.95 (*0-7910-0081-8*) Chelsea Hse.

Careers in Health Care. Barbara M. Swanson. LC 83-73721. 350p. 1984. text ed. 14.95 (*0-87094-443-6*) Irwin Prof Pubng.

Careers in Health Care. Barbara M. Swanson. 288p. text ed. 12.95 (*0-8442-6129-7*, VGM Career Bks); pap. 9.95 (*0-8442-6130-0*, VGM Career Bks) NTC Pub Grp.

Careers in Health Care. Barbara M. Swanson. 1989. pap. 12.95 (*0-8442-8699-0*, VGM Career Bks) NTC Pub Grp.

Careers in Health Care. 2nd ed. Barbara M. Swanson. 288p. 1991. 16.95 (*0-8442-8698-2*, VGM Career Bks) NTC Pub Grp.

Careers in High Tech. Nick Basta. 150p. 1992. 16.95 (*0-8442-4180-6*, VGM Career Bks); pap. 12.95 (*0-8442-4181-4*, VGM Career Bks) NTC Pub Grp.

Careers in Industrial Research & Development. James H. Saunders. LC 73-82193. 270p. reprint ed. pap. 77.00 (*0-8357-6049-9*, 2034567) Bks Demand.

Careers in International Affairs. rev. ed. Ed. by Maria Pinto Carland & Daniel H. Spatz, Jr. 307p. 1991. 15.00 (*0-934742-50-2*, GU Schl Foreign) Geo U Inst Dplmcy.

Careers in International Law. 240p. 1993. 19.99 (*0-89707-822-5*, 527-0026) Amer Bar Assn.

Careers in Journalism. (Professional Careers Ser.). 1994. 16.95 (*0-8442-4196-2*, VGM Career Bks); pap. 12.95 (*0-8442-4197-0*, VGM Career Bks) NTC Pub Grp.

Careers in Labor Law. Ellen K. Wayne. LC 85-71531. x, 100p. 1985. 14.95 (*0-89707-180-8*, 527-0025) Amer Bar Assn.

Careers in Law. Gary Munneke. 160p. 1992. 16.95 (*0-8442-8554-4*, VGM Career Bks); pap. 12.95 (*0-8442-8555-2*, VGM Career Bks) NTC Pub Grp.

***Careers in Law Enforcement: Interviewing for Results.** Jim Nelson. 1995. pap. 27.50 (*0-614-06593-3*) Graduate Group.

Careers in Law Enforcement & Security. rev. ed. Payl Cohen & Shari Cohen. Ed. by Ruth Rosen. (Careers in Depth Ser.). (YA). (gr. 7-12). 1994. lib. bdg. 14.95 (*0-8239-1878-5*); pap. 9.95 (*0-8239-1908-0*) Rosen Group.

Careers in Local Government. Felicity Taylor. 96p. (Orig.). 1990. pap. 17.95 (*0-8464-1403-1*) Beekman Pubs.

An Asterisk (*) at the beginning of an entry indicates that the title is appearing in BIP for the first time.

C

An Asterisk (*) at the beginning of an entry indicates that the title is appearing in BIP for the first time.

1051

CarePooling: How to Get the Help You Need to Care for the Ones You Love. Paula C. Lowe. LC 93-26746. 320p. (Orig.). 1993. pap. 14.95 (1-881052-16-8) Berrett-Koehler.

Carer Support in the Community. HMSO Staff. 116p. 1991. pap. 14.00 (0-11-321365-4, HM5364) UNIPUB.

Carers: Research & Practice. Julia Twigg. 154p. 1993. pap. 25.00 (0-11-701693-4, HM16934, Pub. by HMSO UK) UNIPUB.

Carers & Services. Julia Twigg et al. 90p. 1990. pap. 17.00 (0-11-701494-X, HM494X) UNIPUB.

Carer's Guide to Good Health. Sheryl Navin & Lynette Cusack. 61p. (Orig.). 1994. pap. 6.95 (0-85572-207-X, Pub. by Hill Content Pubng AT) Seven Hills Bk.

Carers Perceived: Policy & Practice in Informal Care. Julia Twigg & Karl Atkin. LC 93-15944. 1993. 90.00 (0-335-19112-6, Open Univ Pr); pap. 27.50 (0-335-19111-8, Open Univ Pr) Taylor & Francis.

***Cares of the Day.** Ivan Webster. 1994. pap. 8.95 (0-932511-90-2) Fiction Coll.

Cares That Infest. Cecil A. Poole. Ed. by AMORC Staff. LC 77-91873. 120p. 1978. 15.95 (0-912057-28-9, 501730) AMORC.

Caresharing: How to Relate to the Frail Elderly. V. Katherine Gray. 80p. (Orig.). 1984. pap. 8.00 (0-938846-15-9) Ebenezer Ctr.

Caress. Rosanne Bittner. 480p. 1992. mass mkt. 5.99 (0-8217-3791-0) Zebra.

Caress & Conquer. Connie Mason. 480p. (Orig.). 1993. pap. 4.99 (0-8439-3532-4) Dorchester Pub Co.

Caress & the Hurt: Prose & Verse. Clarine C. Gren Fell. (Illus.). 126p. reprint ed. pap. 8.50 (0-9612766-0-6) Gren Fell Read Ctr.

Caress of Fire. Martha Hix. 1992. mass mkt. 4.50 (0-8217-3718-X) Zebra.

Caress of Silk. Mary Martin. 496p. 1986. pap. 3.95 (0-8217-1842-8) Zebra.

Caress Softly Thy Love. S. Bradford Williams, Jr. LC 82-8141. 80p. (Orig.). 1982. pap. 4.00 (0-9608522-0-4) Copper Orchid.

Caresse. Joyce Wilson. 368p. 1989. reprint ed. pap. 3.95 (0-8439-2880-8) Dorchester Pub Co.

Caresses. Dorothy Fletcher. 1981. pap. 2.50 (0-89083-831-3) Zebra.

Caretaker. Jerry Evans. LC 92-62258. 128p. (Orig.). (YA). (gr. 11 up). 1992. pap. 7.59 (0-9623698-3-7) Magnum Pr.

***Caretaker.** L. A. Graf. Ed. by John Ordover. (Star Wars Book Ser.). 288p. 1995. mass mkt. 5.50 (0-671-51914-X, Pocket Star Bks) PB.

Caretaker. Harold Pinter. 1962. pap. 4.75 (0-8222-0184-4) Dramatists Play.

Caretaker & the Dumbwaiter. Harold Pinter. (Illus.). 121p. 1989. pap. 8.95 (0-8021-5087-X) Grove-Atltic.

Caretakers. Tabitha King. 352p. 1984. pap. 5.99 (0-451-16169-6, Sig) NAL-Dutton.

Caretakers: The Forgotten People. Maita Floyd. Ed. by Dorothy Tegeler. LC 88-16564. (Illus.). 120p. (Orig.). 1988. pap. 9.95 (0-9620599-0-0) Eskualdun Pubs Ltd.

Caretakers of Creation: Farmers Reflect on Their Faith & Work. Patrick Slattery. LC 90-45288. (Christian at Work in the World Ser.). 116p. (Orig.). 1991. pap. 8.95 (0-87946-051-2, 121) ACTA Pubns.

Caretakers of Creation: Farmers Reflect on Their Faith & Work. Patrick Slattery. LC 90-45288. (Christian at Work in the World Ser.). 128p. (Orig.). 1991. pap. 9.99 (0-8066-2505-8, 9-2505, Augsburg) Augsburg Fortress.

Caretakers of the Earth. Kathlyn Gay. LC 92-23048. (Better Earth Ser.). (Illus.). 104p. (J). (gr. 6 up). 1993. lib. bdg. 17.95 (0-89490-397-7) Enslow Pubs.

Caretakers of Wonder. Cooper Edens. (J). 1987. pap. 4.95 (0-671-97231-6, Green Tiger S&S) S&S Childrens.

Caretakers of Wonder. Cooper Edens. LC 91-24035. (Illus.). 40p. (J). (gr. 3 up). 1991. 11.95 (0-671-75193-X, Green Tiger S&S) S&S Childrens.

Caretakers of Wonder. 2nd ed. Cooper Edens. (Illus.). 40p. (J). (ps up). 1991. pap. 4.95 (0-671-76052-1, Green Tiger S&S) S&S Childrens.

Carevision: The Why & How of Christian Caregiving. Jerry K. Robbins. LC 93-23840. 176p. 1993. pap. 13.00 (0-8170-1195-1) Judson.

Carew Manor: A Short Guide. John Phillips. (C). 1985. pap. 30.00 (0-907335-21-7, Pub. by Sutton Libs & Arts) St Mut.

***Carewise Guide: Self-Care from Head to Toe.** Acamedica Press Staff. 448p. 1995. pap. 19.95 (1-886444-00-5) Employee Managed.

Carews of Beddington. Ronald Michell. 129p. 1989. pap. 29.00 (0-317-47426-X, Pub. by Sutton Libs & Arts) St Mut.

Carews of Beddington. Ronald H. Michell. (C). 1985. pap. 29.00 (0-907335-02-0, Pub. by Sutton Libs & Arts) St Mut.

Cargese Lecture Notes 1964: Vol. 1, Statistical Mechanics, Vol. 64. Ed. by Maurice Levy & B. Jancovici. 244p. (Orig.). (C). 1966. text ed. 218.00 (0-677-10980-6) Gordon & Breach.

Cargese Lecture Notes, 1965: Application of Mathematics to Problems in Theoretical Physics, Vol. 65. Ed. by Maurice Levy & F. Lurcat. 516p. 1967. text ed. 304.00 (0-677-11660-8) Gordon & Breach.

Cargese Lectures in Physics: 1970 Lectures, Vol. 5. Ed. by Maurice Levy & D. Bessis. 556p. (C). 1972. text ed. 331.00 (0-677-15180-2) Gordon & Breach.

Cargese Lectures in Physics, Vol. 6: 1971 Lectures, Vol. 6. Ed. by Evry L. Schatzman. viii, 732p. 1973. text ed. 497.00 (0-677-15320-1) Gordon & Breach.

Cargese Lectures in Physics, 1966-1968, Vol. 1. Ed. by Maurice Levy & M. Jean. 438p. (Orig.). 1967. text ed. 342.00 (0-677-11650-0) Gordon & Breach.

Cargese Lectures in Physics, 1966-1968, Vol. 2. Ed. by Maurice Levy & M. Jean. 432p. (Orig.). 1968. 175.00 (0-677-12720-0) Gordon & Breach.

Cargese Lectures in Physics, 1966-1968, Vol. 3. Ed. by Maurice Levy & M. Jean. 686p. (Orig.). 1969. text ed. 407.00 (0-677-13580-7) Gordon & Breach.

Cargese Lectures in Physics, 1969, Vol. 4. Ed. by Maurice Levy & D. Kastler. 398p. 1970. text ed. 292.00 (0-677-13910-1) Gordon & Breach.

Cargese Lectures in Physics, 1972, Vol. 7. Ed. by Maurice Levy. x, 502p. 1977. text ed. 241.00 (0-677-15750-9) Gordon & Breach.

Cargese Lectures in Theoretical Physics: High Energy Electromagnetic Interactions & Field Theory, Vol. 64. 334p. 1967. text ed. 272.00 (0-677-10990-3) Gordon & Breach.

Cargese Lectures Notes, 1963: Elementary Particles & High Energy Physics, Vol. 63. Ed. by Maurice Levy & P. Meyer. 370p. 1965. text ed. 267.00 (0-677-10590-8) Gordon & Breach.

***Cargill: A Report on the Company's Environmental Policies & Practices.** (Illus.). 51p. (C). 1994. reprint ed. pap. text ed. 200.00x (0-7881-0936-7, Coun on Econ) Diane Pub.

Cargill: Trading the World's Grain. Wayne Broehl. LC 91-31608. 1027p. 1992. 35.00 (0-87451-572-6) U Pr of New Eng.

Cargo. Jack London. 42p. 1992. 1.95 (0-932458-45-9) Star Rover.

Cargo Access Equipment for Merchant Ships. I. L. Buxton et al. 366p. (C). 1978. 110.00 (0-685-46525-X, Pub. by ICHCA UK) St Mut.

Cargo Access Equipment for Merchant Ships. I. L. Buxton et al. (C). 1989. 160.00 (0-685-37337-1, Pub. by ICHCA UK) St Mut.

Cargo Access Equipment for Merchant Ships. ICHCA Staff. (C). 1988. 110.00 (0-685-46497-0, Pub. by ICHCA UK) St Mut.

Cargo Carriers of the Great Lakes. 3rd ed. Jacques Les Strang. (Illus.). 193p. 1985. reprint ed. pap. 10.50 (0-937360-06-6) Harbor Hse MI.

Cargo Cult. John Thorpe. (Orig.). 1971. 4.00 (0-929844-00-9) Big Sky Bolinas.

Cargo Cult: Strange Stories of Desire from Melanesia & Beyond. Lamont Lindstrom. LC 93-5399. (Illus.). 288p. (C). 1993. lib. bdg. 36.00 (0-8248-1526-2); pap. text ed. 14.95 (0-8248-1563-7) UH Pr.

Cargo Cults & Millennarian Movements: Transoceanic Comparisons of New Religious Movements. Ed. by G. W. Trompt. (Religion & Society Ser.: No. 29). xvii, 459p. (C). 1990. lib. bdg. 129.25 (0-89925-601-5) Mouton.

Cargo Firefighting on Liquified Gas Carriers. Sigtto Staff. 1986. 120.00 (0-948691-01-8, Pub. by Witherby & Co UK) St Mut.

Cargo Handlers: Liability & Insurance. Bain Dawes. (C). 1982. 60.00 (0-906297-22-2, Pub. by ICHCA UK) St Mut.

Cargo Handlers, No. Five: Liabilities & Insurance. ICHCA Staff. (C). 1988. 90.00 (0-685-46499-7, Pub. by ICHCA UK) St Mut.

Cargo Handling. Ed. by ICHCA Staff. (C). 1988. 165.00 (0-685-46493-8, Pub. by ICHCA UK) St Mut.

Cargo Handling. J. R. Immer. 300p. (C). 1984. 165.00 (0-914501-03-8, Pub. by ICHCA UK) St Mut.

***Cargo Handling.** John R. Immer. (Illus.). 316p. (C). 1984. pap. text ed. 40.85 (1-879778-06-8) Marine Educ.

Cargo Handling Abstracts. ICHCA Staff. (C). 1988. 140.00 (0-685-46482-2, Pub. by ICHCA UK) St Mut.

Cargo Handling in a Modern Port. R. B. Oram. 1964. pap. 82.00 (0-08-011305-2, Pub. by Pergamon Repr UK) Franklin.

Cargo Handling in the High Tech Age. ICHCA Staff. 163p. (C). 1986. 500.00 (0-685-37353-3, Pub. by ICHCA UK) St Mut.

Cargo Handling in the High Tech Age. ICHCA Staff. (C). 1988. 300.00 (0-685-54104-5, Pub. by ICHCA UK) St Mut.

Cargo Handling into the Nineties, Vol. 11. ICHCA-Cargo Systems Editors. (C). 1992. text ed. 210.00 (0-907499-76-7, Pub. by Cargo Systs UK) St Mut.

Cargo Machines & What They Do. Derek Radford. LC 91-71823. (Illus.). 32p. (J). (ps up). 1992. 8.95 (1-56402-005-3) Candlewick Pr.

***Cargo Machines & What They Do.** Derek Radford. LC 91-71823. 1995. pap. 4.99 (1-56402-434-2) Candlewick Pr.

Cargo Marking. ICHCA Staff. (C). 1969. 25.00 (0-685-37341-X, Pub. by ICHCA UK) St Mut.

Cargo of Eagles. Margery Allingham. 18.95 (0-685-10847-3, Aeonian Pr) Amereon Ltd.

Cargo of Eagles. Margery Allingham. 206p. 1993. 19.95 (1-56723-003-2) Yestermorrow.

Cargo of Eagles. Margery Allingham. 224p. 1990. reprint ed. mass mkt. 3.99 (0-380-70576-1) Avon.

Cargo of Memories: Saga of the Majestic Showboat. Catherine R. King. (Illus.). 32p. (Orig.). 1992. pap. 16.95 (0-941092-24-0) Mtn St Pr.

Cargo of Spice: or Exploring Borneo. R. A. Wilson. 224p. 1994. text ed. 39.50 (1-85043-793-9, Pub. by I B Tauris UK) St Martin.

Cargo of Women: Susannah Watson & the Convicts of the Princess Royal. Babette Smith. 1988. 29.95 (0-86840-067-X, Pub. by New South Wales Univ Pr AT) Intl Spec Bk.

Cargo Pavements. Robert West. (C). 1980. 45.00 (0-906297-07-9, Pub. by ICHCA UK) St Mut.

Cargo Pavements, No. 3. ICHCA Staff. (C). 1988. 125.00 (0-685-46500-4, Pub. by ICHCA UK) St Mut.

***Cargo Preference Requirements: Objectives Not Significantly Advanced When Used in U. S. Food Aid Programs.** (Illus.). 160p. (Orig.). (C). 1995. pap. text ed. 45.00x (0-7881-1718-1) Diane Pub.

Cargo Routes: Truck Roads & Networks. (Road Transport Research Ser.). 133p. (Orig.). 1992. pap. 46.00 (92-64-13635-5) OECD.

Cargo Security: A Nuts & Bolts Approach. Lawrence S. Jones. 1983. text ed. 36.95 (0-409-95095-5) Buttrwrth-Heinemann.

Cargo Security in Transport Systems: Pt. 1 Pilferage & Cargo Security, Pt. 2 Major Theft & Cargo Security, 2 pts., Set, Pts. 1-2. ICHCA Staff. (C). 1976. Set, pts. 1-2. 100.00 (0-685-37346-0, Pub. by ICHCA UK) St Mut.

Cargo Security in Transport Systems, Part 1: Pilferage & Cargo Security. ICHCA Staff. (C). 1976. 36.00 (0-685-46484-9, Pub. by ICHCA UK) St Mut.

Cargo Security in Transport Systems, Part 2: Major Theft & Cargo Security. ICHCA Staff. (C). 1976. 65.00 (0-685-46483-0, Pub. by ICHCA UK) St Mut.

Cargo Work: The Care, Handling & Carriage of Cargoes. 11th rev. ed. L. G. Taylor. (C). 1987. 216.00 (0-85174-474-5, Pub. by Brwn Son Ferg) St Mut.

Cargoes: Famous Stories of the Sea. W. W. Jacobs. (Orig.). pap. 4.95 (0-8283-1430-6, 26, Intl Pocket Lib) Branden Pub Co.

Cargoes: Matson's First Century in the Pacific. William L. Worden. LC 80-21666. (Illus.). 204p. reprint ed. pap. 58.20 (0-8357-6050-2, 2034645) Bks Demand.

***Cargoes, Embargoes & Emissaries: The Commercial & Political Interaction of England & the German Hanse, 1450-1510.** John D. Fudge. 280p. 1995. 60.00 (0-8020-0559-4) U of Toronto Pr.

Cargoes for Crusoes. Grant M. Overton. LC 72-1316. (Essay Index Reprint Ser.). 1977. reprint ed. 30.95 (0-8369-2851-2) Ayer.

Caribbean. (Baedeker's Ser.). (Illus.). 620p. 1992. pap. 23.00 (0-13-063579-0, P-H Travel) P-H Gen Ref & Trav.

Caribbean. Frank Hill. (Pocket Pac Ser.). 1986. Incl. guide & phrasecard. 4.00 (0-88699-056-4) Travel Sci.

Caribbean. Photos by Bob Krist. LC 91-71226. (Illus.). 144p. 1991. 39.95 (1-55868-062-4) Gr Arts Ctr Pub.

Caribbean. Jean Martin. 1990. 12.98 (0-8317-1188-4) Smithmark.

Caribbean. Antony Mason. (People & Places Ser.). (Illus.). 48p. (J). (gr. 4-8). 1989. lib. bdg. 12.95 (0-382-09823-4) Silver Burdett Pr.

Caribbean. James A. Michener. 832p. 1992. mass mkt. 6.95 (0-449-21749-3, Crest) Fawcett.

Caribbean. W. Roberts. 1976. lib. bdg. 59.95 (0-8490-1574-X) Gordon Pr.

Caribbean. Cas Walker. (Focus On Ser.). (Illus.). 32p. (J). (gr. 4-6). 1991. 17.95 (0-237-60189-3, Pub. by Evans Bros Ltd UK) Trafalgar.

Caribbean. rev. ed. Frank Hill. (TravelCard Pac Ser.). 1992. Incl. 7 language cards, 1 phrasecard. 4.00 (0-88699-010-6) Travel Sci.

Caribbean. rev. ed. Eintou P. Springer. (Countries Ser.). (Illus.). 48p. (J). (gr. 5 up). 1987. lib. bdg. 14.95 (0-382-09469-7) Silver Burdett Pr.

Caribbean. 3rd ed. James Henderson. LC 94-3020. (Cadogan Guides Ser.). (Illus.). 720p. 1994. pap. 17.95 (1-56440-465-X) Globe Pequot.

Caribbean: A Novel. James A. Michener. 1989. 22.95 (0-394-56561-4) Random.

Caribbean: Culture of Resistance, Spirit of Hope. Ed. by Oscar Bolioli. LC 92-43635. 1993. pap. 7.95 (0-377-00254-2) Friendship Pr.

Caribbean: Its Implications for the United States. Virginia R. Dominguez & Jorge I. Dominguez. LC 81-65441. (Headline Ser.: No. 253). (Illus.). 80p. (Orig.). 1981. pap. 5.95 (0-87124-068-8) Foreign Policy.

Caribbean: Making Our Own Choices. Neil MacDonald. (C). 1990. pap. text ed. 30.00 (0-85598-086-9, Pub. by Oxfam Pubns UK) St Mut.

Caribbean: New Dynamics in Trade & Political Economy. Ed. by Anthony T. Bryan. 225p. (C). 1994. pap. 19.95 (1-56000-751-6, U Miami North-South Ctr) Transaction Pubs.

Caribbean: Survival, Struggle & Sovereignty. Catherine A. Sunshine. (Illus.). 232p. (Orig.). 1988. pap. 19.95 (0-918346-07-X) EPICA.

Caribbean: The Genesis of a Fragmented Nationalism. 2nd ed. Franklin W. Knight. (Latin American Histories Ser.). 416p. (C). 1990. 45.00 (0-19-505440-7); pap. text ed. 17.95 (0-19-505441-5) OUP.

Caribbean: The Lesser Antilles. rev. ed. Comp. by Nelles Verlag. (Nelles Guides Ser.). (Illus.). 256p. 1992. pap. 14.95 (3-88618-380-7, Pub. by Nelles Verlag GW) Seven Hills Bk.

***Caribbean: The Windward Islands.** James Henderson. (Cadogan Island Guides Ser.). (Illus.). 288p. 1994. pap. 12.95 (0-947754-77-6) Globe Pequot.

Caribbean ABC. Marion Rogers. (Illus.). 26p. (Orig.). (J). (ps-1). 1992. reprint ed. pap. 3.50 (0-935357-02-5) CRIC Prod.

***Caribbean Access.** 2nd rev. ed. (Access Travel Guides Ser.). (Illus.). 288p. (Orig.). 1994. pap. 18.00 (0-06-277128-0, Harper Ref) HarpC.

Caribbean Adventures: Classic Cajun Cooking & Tales from the Reign of the Pirates. Ed Landry. (Illus.). 128p. 1994. pap. 11.95 (0-9630244-1-8) Adlai Hse.

Caribbean Adventures: Extracts from Missionary Journals. Ed. by David U. Farquhar. (Illus.). 216p. 1993. 22.00 (0-913619-00-0) Mt Prospect Pr.

Caribbean Afoot! A Walking & Hiking Guide to Twenty-Nine of the Caribbean's Best Islands. M. Timothy O'Keefe. (Illus.). 224p. 1993. pap. 14.95 (0-89732-110-3) Menasha Ridge.

Caribbean after Grenada: Revolution, Conflict, & Democracy. Ed. by Scott B. MacDonald et al. LC 88-11986. 304p. 1988. text ed. 65.00 (0-275-92722-9, C2722, Praeger Pubs) Greenwood.

Caribbean Alphabet. Frane Lessac. LC 93-15833. (Illus.). 32p. (J). 1994. 15.00 (0-688-12952-8, Tambourine Bks); lib. bdg. 14.93 (0-688-12953-6, Tambourine Bks) Morrow.

Caribbean-American Trade Connection: Green Pages. Austin Tuitt. Date not set. lib. bdg. write for info. (0-944981-06-2) Unicullink.

Caribbean & African Cooking. Rosamund Grant. LC 92-6380. (Illus.). 168p. 1993. pap. 14.95 (0-940793-94-6) Interlink Pub.

Caribbean & Central American Databook, 1990: 1988. rev. ed. Caribbean Central American Action Staff. Ed. by Lisa Koukal. (Illus.). 383p. (C). 1987. pap. text ed. 53.50 (0-944804-00-4) Caribbean Central.

***Caribbean & Its People.** T. W. Mayer. (People & Places Ser.). (Illus.). 48p. (J). (gr. 5-8). 1995. 15.95 (1-56847-338-9) Thomson Lrning.

Caribbean & U. S. Robert F. Smith. (Twayne's International History Ser.: No. 11). 144p. 1994. text ed. 26.95 (0-8057-7925-6, Twayne); pap. 15.95 (0-8057-9220-1, Twayne) Macmillan.

Caribbean & World Politics: Cross Currents & Cleavages. Ed. by Jorge Heine & Leslie F. Manigat. LC 86-29466. 400p. (C). 1988. 49.50 (0-8419-1000-6) Holmes & Meier.

***Caribbean Baroque.** Pamela Gosner. (Illus.). 328p. 1996. 40.00 (0-89410-560-4); pap. 22.00 (0-89410-561-2) Three Continents.

Caribbean Basin Financing Opportunities: A Guide to Financing Trade & Investment in Central America & the Caribbean. 110p. (C). 1992. pap. text ed. 40.00 (0-941375-58-7) Diane Pub.

Caribbean Basin Financing Opportunities: A Guide to Financing Trade & Investment in Central America & the Caribbean. 1992. lib. bdg. 95.00 (0-8490-5510-5) Gordon Pr.

Caribbean Basin Financing Opportunities: A Guide to Financing Trade & Investment in Central America & the Caribbean. Julie N. Rauner. 118p. 1990. per., pap. 5.50 (0-16-022051-3, S/N 003-009-005) USGPO.

Caribbean Basin Initiative Guidebook, 1990. 7th ed. Jim Philips. (Illus.). 76p. 1990. per., pap. 4.00 (0-16-028050-8) USGPO.

Caribbean Basin Initiative Guidebook, 1992. (Illus.). 70p. (Orig.). (C). 1992. pap. text ed. 40.00 (0-941375-70-6) Diane Pub.

Caribbean Bound! Culture Roots, Places, & People. Linda Cousins. 160p. (Orig.). 1994. pap. 9.95 (0-930569-02-4) Univ Black Pr.

***Caribbean Business Handbook.** (Illus.). 240p. (Orig.). 1994. pap. 125.00 (1-57205-769-6) Rector Pr.

***Caribbean Business Telephone Book.** 300p. (Orig.). 1994. pap. 195.00 (0-7605-0590-X) Rector Pr.

Caribbean Call: The Missionary Story of Glen & Rachel Smith. David K. Bernard. LC 91-24607. (Illus.). 224p. (Orig.). 1991. pap. 7.99 (0-932581-88-9) Word Aflame.

Caribbean Canvas. Frane Lessac. LC 93-61864. (Illus.). 32p. 1994. 15.95 (1-56397-390-1, Wordsong) Boyds Mills Pr.

Caribbean Carnival: Songs of the West Indies. Irving Burgie. LC 91-760838. (Illus.). 32p. (J). (gr. 1 up). 1992. 15.00 (0-688-10779-6, Tambourine Bks); lib. bdg. 14.93 (0-688-10780-X, Tambourine Bks) Morrow.

Caribbean Choice. Michele Evans. 1989. pap. 14.95 (0-446-38716-9) Warner Bks.

Caribbean Collections: Recession Management Strategies for Libraries. Ed. by Mina J. Grothey. (Papers of the Seminar on the Acquisition of Latin American Library Materials: No. 32). 1989. 50.00 (0-917617-22-3) SALALM.

Caribbean Confederation: A Plan for the Union of the Fifteen British West Indian Colonies. Charles S. Salmon. LC 73-89057. 175p. 1970. reprint ed. text ed. 45.00 (0-8371-1833-6, SAD&, Negro U Pr) Greenwood.

Caribbean Conflict: Jamaica & the U. S. (Report on the Americas: Vol. XII, No. 3). 52p. 2.50 (0-317-34957-0) NA Cong Lat Am.

Caribbean Connections: Jamaica. Ed. by Catherine A. Sunshine & Deborah Menkart. LC 90-63270. (Caribbean Connections: Classroom Resources for Secondary Schools Ser.). (Illus.). (Orig.). 1991. pap. text ed. 12.00 (1-878554-05-0) Netwrk of Educ.

Caribbean Connections: Overview of Regional History. Ed. by Catherine H. Sunshine & Deborah Menkart. (Caribbean Connections: Classroom Resources for Secondary Schools Ser.). (Illus.). (Orig.). (YA). (gr. 7-12). 1991. pap. text ed. 16.00 (1-878554-06-9) Netwrk of Educ.

Caribbean Connections: Puerto Rico. Ed. by Deborah Menkart & Catherine A. Sunshine. LC 90-62779. (Caribbean Connections: Classroom Resources for Secondary Schools Ser.). (Illus.). 108p. (Orig.). 1990. pap. text ed. 12.00 (1-878554-04-2) Netwrk of Educ.

Caribbean Connoisseur. rev. ed. Michele Evans. 384p. 1995. pap. 17.99 (0-312-11251-3) St Martin.

Caribbean Connoisseur: An Insider's Guide to the Islands' Best Hotels, Resorts, & Inns. Michele Evans. (Illus.). 384p. (Orig.). 1991. pap. 17.95 (0-312-06315-6) St Martin.

Caribbean Contraceptive Prevalence Surveys. St. Kitts Nevis & Tirbani P. Jagdeo. 1985. write for info. (0-916683-16-8) Intl Plan Parent.

Caribbean Contraceptive Prevalence Surveys-2 Moutserrat. Tirbani Jagdeo. 1985. write for info. (0-916683-12-5) Intl Plan Parent.

Caribbean Cookbook. Denton S. Harewood. LC 85-80694. 150p. (Orig.). 1986. pap. 12.95 (0-934789-00-2) Hands-On Pub Co.

An Asterisk (*) at the beginning of an entry indicates that the title is appearing in BIP for the first time.

Caribbean Cookery. P. De Brissiere. (CHI & ENG.). pap. 4.95 (*0-87557-100-X*, 100-X) Saphrograph.

Caribbean Cooking. Devinia Sookia. 1994. 17.98 (*0-7858-0024-7*) Bk Sales Inc.

Caribbean Coral Reef Fishery Resources. 2nd ed. Ed. by J. L. Munro. (ICLARM Studies & Reviews: No. 7). (Illus.). 276p. 1983. text ed. 37.00 (*971-10-2200-1*, Pub. by ICLARM PH); pap. text ed. 33.00 (*971-10-2201-X*, Pub. by ICLARM PH) Intl Spec Bk.

Caribbean Countries: Economic Situation, Regional Issues, & Capital Flows. 84p. 1988. 7.95 (*0-8213-1143-3*, 11143) World Bank.

Caribbean Crosswords. A. L. Anduze. LC 93-70926. (Illus.). 64p. (YA). (gr. 5-12). 1993. pap. 8.95 (*0-932831-10-9*) Eastern Caribbean Inst.

Caribbean Crusade. James F. Mitchell. Ed. by Jill Bobrow. (Orig.). 1989. pap. write for info. (*0-9611712-0-0*) Concepts Pub.

Caribbean Cultural Identity: The Case of Jamaica. Rex Nettleford. (Afro-American Culture & Society Monograph Ser.: Vol. 1). (Illus.). 239p. 1978. 15.95 (*0-934934-00-2*) UCLA CAAS.

***Caribbean Currents: Caribbean Music from Rumba to Reggae.** Peter Manuel et al. LC 95-3152. (Illus.). 288p. (C). 1995. lib. bdg. 39.95 (*1-56639-338-8*); pap. 18.95 (*1-56639-339-6*) Temple U Pr.

Caribbean Dependence on the United States Economy. Ransford W. Palmer. LC 78-19770. (Praeger Special Studies). 192p. 1979. text ed. 38.95 (*0-275-90406-7*, C0406, Praeger Pubs) Greenwood.

Caribbean Desire. large type ed. Cathy Williams. 1992. reprint ed. lib. bdg. 18.95 (*0-263-12896-2*, Pub. by Mills & Boon UK) Thorndike Pr.

Caribbean Desserts. John Demers. LC 92-11267. 1992. pap. 10.95 (*0-89594-557-6*) Crossing Pr.

***Caribbean Development Bank.** Chandra Hardy. LC 94-45003. 135p. 1995. lib. bdg. 35.00 (*1-55587-469-X*); pap. text ed. 19.95 (*1-55587-495-9*) Lynne Rienner.

***Caribbean Development Bank.** Chandra Hardy. (Multilateral Development Banks Ser.: Vol. 3). 200p. 1995. pap. text ed. 19.95 (*1-55587-485-1*) Lynne Rienner.

Caribbean Discourse: Selected Essays. Edouard Glissant. Ed. by A. J. Arnold & Kandioura Drame. Tr. & Intro. by J. Michael Dash. LC 89-5469. (CARAF Bks.). 274p. 1992. reprint ed. 35.00 (*0-8139-1219-9*); reprint ed. pap. text ed. 14.95x (*0-8139-1373-X*) U Pr of Va.

Caribbean Dozen: Poems from Caribbean Poets. Ed. by John Agard & Grace Nichols. LC 93-47272. 96p. (J). (ps up). 1994. 19.95 (*1-56402-339-7*) Candlewick Pr.

Caribbean Dreams. Robert Friedman. 1989. 18.95 (*0-945167-21-0*) British Amer Pub.

Caribbean East Indians in American Assimilation, Adaptation & Group Experience. Mahin Gosine. 1990. write for info. (*0-9639318-2-2*) M Gosine.

Caribbean Echoes. J. P. Gimenez. 1977. lib. bdg. 59.95 (*0-8490-1575-8*) Gordon Pr.

Caribbean Economic Handbook. 350p. 1985. 80.00 (*0-86338-089-1*, 073073, Pub. by Euromonitor Pubns UK) Gale.

Caribbean Economic Handbook. 2nd ed. 1995. 80.00 (*0-685-58989-7*, 073060, Pub. by Euromonitor Pubns UK) Gale.

Caribbean Economies. Ed. by Vincent R. McDonald. LC 72-8622. 196p. 1972. pap. text ed. 8.95 (*0-8422-0258-7*) Irvington.

Caribbean Ethnicity Revisited: A Special Issue of the Journal Ethnic Groups. Ed. by Stephan D. Glazier. 168p. 1985. pap. text ed. 51.00 (*0-677-06615-5*) Gordon & Breach.

Caribbean Exodus. Ed. by Barry Levine. LC 86-21217. 300p. 1986. pap. text ed. 18.95 (*0-275-92183-2*, B2183, Praeger Pubs) Greenwood.

Caribbean Exodus. Ed. by Barry Levine. LC 86-21217. 300p. 1987. text ed. 55.00 (*0-275-92182-4*, C2182, Praeger Pubs) Greenwood.

Caribbean Exporters, Importers & Business Services Directory. Lloyd P. Spooner. 250p. 1989. 50.00 (*0-685-26558-7*) Caribbean Busn Dev.

Caribbean Family Planning Guide: A Self Instruction Manual for Health Professionals. Parris O'Neeall et al. 432p. 1990. 25.00 (*0-916683-24-9*) Intl Plan Parent.

Caribbean Fishermen Farmers: A Social Assessment of Smithsonian King Crab Mariculture. Richard W. Stoffle. LC 86-219094. 152p. (Orig.). (ENG & SPA.). 1986. pap. text ed. 15.00 (*0-87944-318-9*) Inst Soc Res.

Caribbean Fishermen Farmers: A Social Assessment of Smithsonian King Crab Mariculture. Richard W. Stoffle. (Institute for Social Research, Research Report Ser.). (Illus.). 151p. (Orig.). reprint ed. pap. 43.10 (*0-7837-5278-4*, 2045016) Bks Demand.

Caribbean Folk Legends. Theresa Lewis. LC 89-81981. (Young Reader's Ser.). 90p. (YA). (gr. 6-12). 1990. 19.95 (*0-86543-158-2*); pap. 7.95 (*0-86543-159-0*) Africa World.

Caribbean Geological Investigations. Harry H. Hess et al. LC 66-22403. (Geological Society of America, Memoir Ser.: No. 98). 429p. reprint ed. pap. 122.30 (*0-318-34698-2*, 2031801) Bks Demand.

Caribbean Geophysical, Tectonic & Petrologic Studies: Proceedings of the Caribbean Geological Conference, 5th, St. Thomas, Virgin Islands, 1968. Caribbean Geological Conference Staff. Ed. by Thomas W. Donnelly. LC 74-165441. (Geological Society of America, Memoir Ser.: No. 130). 274p. reprint ed. pap. 78.10 (*0-317-29126-2*, 2025025) Bks Demand.

Caribbean Geopolitics: Toward Security Through Peace? Andres Serbin. Tr. by Sabet Ramirez. LC 90-33398. (LACC Studies on Latin America & the Caribbean). 131p. 1990. lib. bdg. 32.00 (*1-55587-213-1*) Lynne Rienner.

Caribbean Georgian: The Great & Small Houses of the Caribbean. Pamela Gosner. LC 78-72966. (Illus.). 324p. (Orig.). 1982. 40.00 (*0-89410-011-4*); pap. 22.00 (*0-89410-012-2*) Three Continents.

Caribbean Gravity Field & Plate Tectonics. Carl Bowin. LC 76-16261. (Geological Society of America, Special Paper Ser.: No. 169). 135p. reprint ed. pap. 38.50 (*0-317-29080-0*, 2023738) Bks Demand.

Caribbean Growing-up As It Is Portrayed in Modern West Indian Novels: A Literary Sociology Instructional Unit. Frank A. Stone. 16p. 1984. 2.00 (*0-685-10185-1*) I N Thut World Educ Ctr.

***Caribbean Handbook: The Virgin, Leeward, & Windward Islands.** Karl Luntta. (Moon Travel Handbooks Ser.). (Illus.). 330p. 1995. pap. 16.95 (*1-56691-027-7*) Moon Pubns CA.

Caribbean Hideaways. Ian Keown. 1993. pap. 16.00 (*0-671-84921-2*, P-H Travel) P-H Gen Ref & Trav.

Caribbean Highlights. Berlitz Editors. (Pocket Guides Ser.). 1991. pap. 9.95 (*2-8315-0544-5*) Berlitz.

Caribbean Hoops: The Development of West Indian Basketball. Jay R. Mandle & Joan D. Mandle. LC 94-4491. (Caribbean Studies: Vol. 8). 1994. text ed. 31.00 (*2-88449-106-6*); pap. text ed. 16.00 (*2-88449-107-4*) Gordon & Breach.

Caribbean in Europe: Aspects of the West Indian Experience in Britain, France & the Netherlands. Ed. by Colin Brock. (Legacies of West Indian Slavery Ser.: No. 4). 224p. 1987. 35.00 (*0-7146-3263-5*, Pub. by F Cass Pubs UK) Intl Spec Bk.

Caribbean in the Global Political Economy. Ed. by Hilbourne Watson. LC 93-33333. 272p. 1994. pap. text ed. 19.95 (*1-55587-408-8*) Lynne Rienner.

Caribbean in the Global Political Economy. Ed. by Hilbourne A. Watson. LC 93-33333. 272p. 1994. lib. bdg. 40.00 (*1-55587-407-X*) Lynne Rienner.

Caribbean in the Pacific Century: Prospects for Caribbean-Pacific Cooperation. Jacqueline A. Braveboy-Wagner et al. LC 92-17082. 232p. 1993. lib. bdg. 36.50 (*1-55587-195-X*) Lynne Rienner.

Caribbean in the Wider World, 1492-1992: A Regional Geography. Bonham C. Richardson. (Geography of the World Economy Ser.). (Illus.). 240p. (C). 1992. 54.95 (*0-521-35186-3*); pap. 18.95 (*0-521-35977-5*) Cambridge U Pr.

Caribbean Interests of the United States. Chester L. Jones. 1976. lib. bdg. 59.95 (*0-87968-812-2*) Gordon Pr.

Caribbean Interests of the United States. Chester L. Jones. LC 73-111719. (American Imperialism: Viewpoints of United States Foreign Policy, 1898-1941 Ser.). 1970. reprint ed. 25.95 (*0-405-02029-5*) Ayer.

Caribbean Islands. Thomas D. Boswell & Dennis Conway. LC 92-11579. (Touring North America Ser.). (Illus.). 220p. (C). 1992. 25.00 (*0-8135-1894-6*); pap. 9.95 (*0-8135-1895-4*) Rutgers U Pr.

Caribbean Islands. 6th ed. (Handbooks of the World Ser.). 1994. 21.95 (*0-8442-8975-2*, Passport Bks) NTC Pub Grp.

Caribbean Islands Handbook, 1994. Joshua Eliot. 816p. 1994. 21.95 (*0-8442-9975-8*, Passport Bks) NTC Pub Grp.

***Caribbean Journal: Notes in the Sun.** Samuel J. Addeo. 35p. 1994. pap. text ed. 7.95 (*0-9642774-0-9*) BSP.

***Caribbean Journal: This Land Bonaire.** Samuel J. Addeo. Tr. by James Ashby. (Illus.). 100p. 1995. pap. 8.99 (*0-9642774-1-7*) BSP.

Caribbean Kill. Don Pendleton. (Executioner Ser.: No. 10). 1989. pap. 3.50 (*1-55817-069-3*, Pinnacle NY) Windsor NY.

Caribbean Law Librarian, Vol. 4. 1987. ring bd. 25.00 (*0-685-70503-X*) W W Gaunt.

Caribbean Law Librarian, 1984-86, 3 vols. in 1, Vols. 1-3. 85.00 (*0-685-70502-1*) W W Gaunt.

***Caribbean Legion: Patriots, Politicians, Soldiers of Fortune, 1946-1950.** Charles D. Ameringer. LC 94-39178. 184p. 1995. 28.50 (*0-271-01451-2*); pap. 15.95 (*0-271-01452-0*) Pa St U Pr.

Caribbean Life in New York City: Sociocultural Dimensions. Ed. by Constance R. Sutton & Elsa M. Chaney. (CMS Migration & Ethnicity Ser.). 250p. 1993. pap. 14.50 (*0-913256-92-7*) Ctr Migration.

Caribbean Literature, Vol. 18. Carrol F. Coates. Date not set. 25.00 (*0-918680-54-9*) Bagehot Council.

Caribbean Maritime Security. Michael A. Morris. LC 93-3841. 270p. 1994. text ed. 65.00 (*0-312-12057-5*) St Martin.

Caribbean Medicine Forward to Eden: A Source Book on the Healing Modalities of Guyana, The Caribbean & The Americas. Cwolde Kyte. (Illus.). 190p. (Orig.). 1988. 28.90 (*0-936901-07-1*); pap. 14.90 (*0-936901-06-3*) Ctr Sacred Healing.

Caribbean Migrants: Environment & Human Survival on St. Kitts & Nevis. Bonham C. Richardson. LC 82-7078. (Illus.). 224p. (C). 1983. text ed. 31.00x (*0-87049-360-4*); pap. text ed. 17.95 (*0-87049-361-2*) U of Tenn Pr.

Caribbean Mission. C. G. Oldendorp. Ed. by Johann J. Bossard. Tr. by Arnold R. Highfield & Valdimir Barac. 1987. 30.00 (*0-89720-075-6*) Karoma.

Caribbean Music History: A Selective Annotated Bibliography with Musical Supplement. Robert Stevenson et al. (Inter-American Music Review Ser.: Vol. IV, no. 1). 112p. (Orig.). 1981. pap. 12.00 (*0-685-55754-5*) Theodore Front.

Caribbean Mystery. Agatha Christie. 1992. mass mkt. 4.99 (*0-06-100365-4*, Harp PBks) HarpC.

Caribbean Mystery. large type ed. Agatha Christie. (Agatha Christie Ser.). 273p. 1989. lib. bdg. 16.95 (*0-8161-4537-7*) G K Hall.

Caribbean Neptune: The Maritime Postal Communications of the Greater & Lesser Antilles in the 19th Century. Robert G. Stone. LC 90-63101. (Illus.). 396p. 1993. 65.00 (*0-911989-22-6*) Philatelic Found.

***Caribbean New Voices 1.** Ed. by Stewart Brown. 192p. (Orig.). (C). 1996. pap. text ed. 9.95 (*0-582-23702-5*) Longman.

Caribbean New Wave: Contemporary Short Stories. Ed. by Stewart Brown. (Caribbean Writers Ser.). 181p. (Orig.). (C). 1990. pap. 9.95 (*0-435-98814-X*, 98814) Heinemann.

Caribbean New York: Black Immigrants & the Politics of Race. Philip Kasinitz. LC 91-55539. (Anthropology of Contemporary Issues Ser.). (Illus.). 296p. 1992. 42.95 (*0-8014-2651-0*); pap. 14.95 (*0-8014-9951-8*) Cornell U Pr.

Caribbean Perspectives: The Social Structure of a Region. Ed. by Joseph Lisowski. 224p. (C). 1990. pap. 21.95 (*0-88738-838-8*) Transaction Pubs.

Caribbean Pink. large type ed. Kathleen McBrearty. 1991. pap. 13.95 (*0-7089-6983-6*) Ulverscroft.

Caribbean Poetry Now. 2nd ed. Ed. by Stewart Brown. 224p. 1992. pap. 10.95 (*0-340-57379-1*, A9675, Pub. by E Arnold UK) Routledge Chapman & Hall.

Caribbean Popular Culture. Ed. by John A. Lent. LC 90-83084. (Illus.). 156p. (C). 1990. text ed. 26.95 (*0-87972-499-4*); pap. text ed. 13.95 (*0-87972-500-1*) Bowling Green Univ.

Caribbean Ports of Call: A Guide for Today's Cruise Passenger. 3rd ed. Kay Showker. LC 93-36229. (Voyager Book Ser.). (Illus.). 576p. 1993. pap. 18.95 (*1-56440-248-7*) Globe Pequot.

Caribbean Reef Fish. Steve Blount. (Pisces Photo Pak Ser.). 1991. pap. 13.95 (*1-55992-049-1*, Pisces Bks) Gulf Pub.

Caribbean Reef Invertebrates. Nancy Sefton & Steven K. Webster. LC 85-50789. 112p. 1989. pap. 19.95 (*0-930118-12-X*) Sea Chall.

Caribbean Region. Ed. by G. Dengo & J. Case. (DNAG, Geology of North America Ser.: Vol. H). (Illus.). 538p. 1990. 80.00 (*0-8137-5212-4*) Geol Soc.

Caribbean Region: Access, Quality, & Efficiency in Education. LC 93-389. (Country Study Ser.). 318p. 1993. 17.95 (*0-8213-2377-6*, 12377) World Bank.

Caribbean Region: Current Economic Situation, Regional Issues, & Capital Flows. World Bank Staff. LC 93-19951. (Country Study Ser.). 190p. 1993. 10.95 (*0-8213-2330-X*, 12330) World Bank.

Caribbean Research Center: Occasional Paper, No. 1. Martin Afflick et al. 90p. (Orig.). 1989. pap. text ed. write for info. (*0-318-66546-8*) Caribbean Rsch Ctr.

Caribbean Research Center: Occasional Paper, No. 2. Bolarinde Obebe et al. Ed. by Velta Clarke. 70p. (Orig.). 1989. pap. text ed. write for info. (*0-318-66547-6*) Caribbean Rsch Ctr.

Caribbean Seashells: A Guide to the Marine Mollusks of Puerto Rico & Other West Indian Islands, Bermuda & the Lower Florida Keys. Germaine L. Warmke & R. Tucker Abbott. LC 74-20443. (Illus.). 352p. 1975. reprint ed. pap. 7.95 (*0-486-21359-5*) Dover.

***Caribbean Sexuality.** Neilson A. Waithe. LC 93-77809. 104p. (Orig.). 1993. pap. 12.00 (*1-878422-10-3*) Moravian Ch in Amer.

Caribbean Slave: A Biological History. Kenneth F. Kiple. LC 84-19865. (Studies in Environment & History). 302p. 1985. 49.95 (*0-521-26874-5*) Cambridge U Pr.

Caribbean Slave Society & Economy. Hilary Beckles. 496p. 1994. 40.00 (*1-56584-085-2*) New Press NY.

Caribbean Slave Society & Economy: A Student Reader. Ed. by Hilary Beckles & Verene Shepherd. LC 93-6739. 496p. 1994. pap. 20.00 (*1-56584-086-0*) New Press NY.

Caribbean-South American Plate Boundary & Regional Tectonics. Ed. by William E. Bonini et al. (Memoir Ser.: No. 162). (Illus.). 432p. 1984. 19.00 (*0-8137-1162-2*) Geol Soc.

Caribbean Souvenir Songbook. Irving Burgie. Ed. by Milton Okun. pap. 5.95 (*0-685-75219-4*); audio 10.00 (*0-685-75220-8*) Cherry Lane.

Caribbean Stories. Robert Hull. (Tales from Around the World Ser.). (Illus.). 48p. (J). (gr. 5-9). 1994. 15.95 (*1-56847-190-4*) Thomson Lrning.

***Caribbean Stories: Supernatural Tales of Guyana.** Andrew A. Munroe. 145p. (Orig.). 1994. pap. 9.95 (*0-9643010-0-8*) Golden Grove.

Caribbean Story, Bk. 1: Foundations. William Claypole & John Robottom. (Longman Caribbean Ser.). (Illus.). (Orig.). (C). 1980. Bk. 1 Foundations. pap. text ed. 15.95 (*0-582-76534-X*) Longman.

Caribbean Story, Bk. 2: The Inheritors. William Claypole & John Robottom. (Longman Caribbean Ser.). (Illus.). (Orig.). (C). 1980. Bk. 2, The Inheritors. pap. text ed. 15.95 (*0-582-76533-1*) Longman.

Caribbean Story, Bk. One: Foundations. 2nd rev. ed. William Claypole & John Robottom. (Illus.). 198p. (C). 1989. pap. text ed. 20.95 (*0-582-03984-3*, 78486) Longman.

Caribbean Story, Bk. Two: The Inheritors. 2nd rev. ed. William Claypole & John Robottom. (Illus.). 218p. (C). 1989. pap. text ed. 20.50 (*0-582-03985-1*, 78487) Longman.

Caribbean Style. Suzanne Slesin et al. LC 84-26470. 290p. 1985. 45.00 (*0-517-55611-1*, C P Pubs) Crown Pub Group.

Caribbean Style: A Little Style Book. Suzanne Sleskin. 1994. pap. 12.00 (*0-517-88216-7*, C P Pubs) Crown Pub Group.

Caribbean Style Postcards. Suzanne Slesin. 1990. pap. 7.95 (*0-87701-655-0*) Chronicle Bks.

***Caribbean Telephone Yellow Pages.** (Illus.). 240p. (Orig.). 1994. pap. 125.00 (*1-57205-768-8*) Rector Pr.

Caribbean Tempest: The Dominican Republic Intervention of 1965. 65p. (Orig.). (C). 1994. pap. text ed. 35.00 (*0-7881-0263-X*) Diane Pub.

Caribbean Theology. Lewin L. Williams. LC 93-16707. (Research in Family & Religion Ser.: Vol. 2). 248p. (C). 1994. text ed. 43.95 (*0-8204-1859-5*) P Lang Pubs.

Caribbean Time Bomb: The United States' Complicity in the Corruption of Antigua. Robert Coram. LC 92-39969. 1993. 25.00 (*0-688-11543-8*) Morrow.

Caribbean Transformations. Sidney Mintz. 384p. 1989. text ed. 57.00 (*0-231-07114-0*); pap. text ed. 17.00 (*0-231-07115-9*) Col U Pr.

Caribbean Transformations. Sidney W. Mintz. LC 83-19997. 367p. reprint ed. pap. 104.60 (*0-8357-8057-0*, 2034113) Bks Demand.

Caribbean Travellers Guide. 6th ed. Berlitz Editors. (Travellers Guides Ser.). (Illus.). 440p. 1993. pap. 14.95 (*2-8315-1700-1*) Berlitz.

Caribbean Trivia. Chaitram Aklu. 96p. 1993. pap. 7.95 (*1-880365-39-1*) Prof Pr NC.

Caribbean Visions. Ed. by S. B. Jones-Hendrickson. LC 90-71043. (Illus.). 257p. 1990. 25.95 (*0-932831-06-0*) Eastern Caribbean Inst.

Caribbean Ways: A Cultural Guide. Chelle K. Walton. LC 92-64032. 299p. 1993. pap. 19.95 (*0-913215-57-0*) Riverdale Co.

Caribbean Women Novelists: An Annotated Critical Bibliography. Ed. by Olga Torres-Seda. LC 92-37915. (Bibliographies & Indexes in World Literature Ser.: No. 36). 442p. 1993. text ed. 69.95 (*0-313-28342-7*, PGD/, Greenwood Pr) Greenwood.

Caribbean Women Writers: Essays from the First International Conference. Ed. by Selwyn R. Cudjoe. LC 90-80896. 400p. (C). 1990. lib. bdg. 37.50 (*0-87023-731-4*) U of Mass Pr.

Caribbean World: A Complete Geography. Neil E. Sealey. (Illus.). 256p. (C). 1994. pap. 16.95 (*0-521-37764-1*) Cambridge U Pr.

Caribbean Writers: A Bio-Bibliographical Critical Encyclopedia. Ed. by Donald E. Herdeck et al. LC 77-3841. (Illus.). 963p. (gr. 9-12). 1979. lib. bdg. 70.00 (*0-914478-74-5*) Three Continents.

***Caribbean Yellow Pages 1995.** 1408p. (Orig.). 1995. pap. 59.75 (*976-8088-08-7*) Carib Imprint.

Caribbean, 1975-1980: A Bibliography of Economic & Rural Development. Manuel J. Carvajal. LC 91-39695. 897p. 1993. 89.50 (*0-8108-2422-1*) Scarecrow.

Caribbean, 1985. Steve Birnbaum. (Birnbaum's Travel Guides Ser.). pap. 11.95 (*0-685-42766-8*) HM.

Caribbean, 1995: The Complete Guide to Choosing & Enjoying the Perfect Island Vacation. Fodor's Travel Staff. (Illus.). 1994. pap. 18.00 (*0-679-02705-X*) Fodors Travel.

Caribbeans: Greater Antilles, Bermuda, Bahamas. (Nelles Guides Ser.). (Illus.). 256p. 1992. pap. 14.95 (*3-88618-379-3*, Pub. by Nelles Verlag GW) Seven Hills Bk.

Caribbee. Thomas Hoover. 512p. 1987. mass mkt. 4.50 (*0-8217-2400-2*) Zebra.

Cariboo Gold Rush Story. Don Waite. Ed. by Diane Brown. 96p. (Orig.). 1987. pap. 7.95 (*0-88839-202-8*) Hancock House.

Caribou. Martin Evans. (Illus.). 10.00 (*0-85242-500-7*) Apple Blossom.

Caribou. Lorle K. Harris. LC 88-18953. (Remarkable Animals Ser.). (Illus.). 60p. (J). (gr. 3 up). 1989. text ed. 13.95 (*0-87518-391-3*, Dillon Silver Burdett) Silver Burdett Pr.

Caribou. Jerolyn Nentl. LC 83-26254. (Wildlife Habits & Habitats Ser.). (Illus.). 48p. (J). (gr. 5). 1984. text ed. 12.95 (*0-89686-244-5*, Crstwood Hse) Silver Burdett Pr.

Cariboo: The Newly Discovered Gold Fields of British Columbia, Fully Described by a Returned Digger Who Made His Fortune There, & Who Advises Others to Go & Do Likewise. 76p. 1975. reprint ed. 12.00 (*0-87770-131-8*) Ye Galleon.

Caribou Alphabet. Mary B. Owens. (Illus.). 40p. (J). (ps-3). 1990. pap. 4.95 (*0-374-41043-7*, Sunburst Bks) FS&G.

Caribou Alphabet. Mary B. Owens. (Illus.). 40p. (J). (gr. k-6). 1988. 16.95 (*0-937966-25-8*) Tilbury Hse.

Caribou & the Stone Man. John E. Smelcer. 82p. 1991. pap. 7.95 (*0-9634000-1-0*) Salmon Run.

Caribou Country: From an Original Article Which Appeared in Ranger Rick Magazine, Copyright National Wildlife Federation. Illus. by Alton Langford. LC 92-7732. (Adventures of Ranger Rick Ser.). 20p. (J). (gr. k-3). 1992. 6.95 (*0-924483-53-9*); audio 35.95 (*0-924483-50-4*); 21.95 (*0-924483-51-2*); audio 9.95 (*0-924483-52-0*); audio write for info. (*0-924483-80-6*) Soundprints.

Caribou Eskimos. Kaj Birket-Smith. LC 76-21702. (Thule Expedition Ser.: Vol. 5). reprint ed. 137.50 (*0-404-58316-4*) AMS Pr.

Caribou Journey. Debbie S. Miller. LC 93-9777. (Illus.). (J). (gr. 2-5). 1994. 15.95 (*0-316-57380-9*) Little.

Caricature & Its Role in Graphic Satire. Ed. by Juergen Schulz. (Illus.). 120p. (Orig.). 1971. pap. 14.00 (*0-933519-15-X*) D W Bell Gallery.

Caricature History of the Georges. Thomas Wright. LC 68-56479. (Illus.). 1972. reprint ed. 38.95 (*0-405-09106-0*) Ayer.

Caricature of Love: A Discussion of Social, Psychiatric, & Literary Manifestations of Pathologic Sexuality. Hervey M. Cleckley. LC 57-8292. 319p. (C). 1967. reprint ed. 21.95 (*0-685-48777-6*); reprint ed. text ed. 21.95 (*0-685-48778-4*) E S Cleckley.

Caricature Relief Carving with Larry Green. Larry Green. (Illus.). 64p. 1993. pap. 12.95 (*0-88740-542-8*) Schiffer.

C

An Asterisk (*) at the beginning of an entry indicates that the title is appearing in BIP for the first time.

An Asterisk (*) at the beginning of an entry indicates that the title is appearing in BIP for the first time.

*__Caring for Older People.__ Jacci Stoyle. 128p. (C). 1991. pap. 35.00x (*0-7478-0451-6*, Pub. by S Thornes Pubs UK) St Mut.

__Caring for Older People: A Multi-Cultural Approach.__ Jacci Stoyle. 160p. (Orig.). 1991. pap. 24.50 (*0-7487-0451-5*, Pub. by Stanley Thornes UK) Trans-Atl Phila.

*__Caring for Older People in the Community.__ 3rd ed. Idris Williams. 1995. pap. 29.50 (*1-85775-025-X*) Scovill Paterson.

__Caring for Other People's Children: A Complete Guide to Family Day Care.__ Frances K. Alston. LC 92-17036. (Early Childhood Education Ser.). (Illus.). 320p. (C). 1992. pap. 18.95 (*0-8077-3218-4*) Tchrs Coll.

__Caring for Others.__ Brenda Clarke. LC 89-26296. (Tales of Courage Ser.). (Illus.). 48p. (J). (gr. 4-8). 1990. lib. bdg. 11.95 (*0-8114-2751-X*) Raintree Steck-V.

__Caring for Our Air.__ Carol Greene. LC 91-9236. (Caring for Our Earth Ser.). (Illus.). 32p. (J). (gr. k-3). 1991. lib. bdg. 12.95 (*0-89490-351-9*) Enslow Pubs.

__Caring for Our Animals.__ Carol Greene. LC 91-9237. (Caring for Our Earth Ser.). (Illus.). 32p. (J). (gr. k-3). 1991. lib. bdg. 12.95 (*0-89490-352-7*) Enslow Pubs.

__Caring for Our Built Heritage: Conservation Schemes Carried Out by County Councils in England & Wales in Association with District Councils & Other Agencies.__ Ed. by Tony Haskell. LC 92-24192. 1992. write for info. (*0-442-31547-3*, E & FN Spon) Routledge Chapman & Hall.

__Caring for Our Children: National Health & Safety Performance Standards: Guidelines for Out-of-Home Child Care Programs.__ American Academy of Pediatrics Staff & American Public Health Association Staff. 410p. 1992. pap. 34.95 (*0-87553-205-5*) Am Pub Health.

__Caring for Our Earth Series, 6 bks., Set.__ Carol Greene. (Illus.). (J). (gr. k-3). lib. bdg. 77.70 (*0-89490-377-2*) Enslow Pubs.

__Caring for Our Forests.__ Carol Greene. LC 91-4703. (Caring for Our Earth Ser.). (Illus.). 32p. (J). (gr. k-3). 1991. lib. bdg. 12.95 (*0-89490-353-5*) Enslow Pubs.

__Caring for Our Land.__ Carol Greene. LC 91-10613. (Caring for Our Earth Ser.). (Illus.). 32p. (J). (gr. k-3). 1991. lib. bdg. 12.95 (*0-89490-354-3*) Enslow Pubs.

__Caring for Our People.__ Carol Greene. LC 91-9235. (Caring for Our Earth Ser.). (Illus.). 32p. (J). (gr. k-3). 1991. lib. bdg. 12.95 (*0-89490-355-1*) Enslow Pubs.

__Caring for Our Water.__ Carol Greene. LC 91-2683. (Caring for Our Earth Ser.). (Illus.). 32p. (J). (gr. k-3). 1991. lib. bdg. 12.95 (*0-89490-356-X*) Enslow Pubs.

*__Caring for Ourselves: Hope for Healthy Relationships.__ Melody Beattie. 1991. vhs 29.95 (*0-89486-638-9*) Hazelden.

*__Caring for Patients: A Critique of the Medical Model.__ Allen Barbour. LC 94-27113. 1995. 45.00 (*0-8047-2389-3*) Stanford U Pr.

__Caring for Patients from Different Cultures: Case Studies from American Hospitals.__ Geri-Ann Galanti. LC 90-13173. 144p. (C). 1991. pap. text ed. 15.95x (*0-8122-1344-0*) U of Pa Pr.

__Caring for People.__ Jenny Rogers. 192p. 1990. 75.00 (*0-335-09430-9*, Open Univ Pr); pap. 22.00 (*0-335-09429-5*, Open Univ Pr) Taylor & Francis.

__Caring for People in Conflict.__ Phyllis J. Le Peau. (Caring People Bible Studies). 96p. (Orig.). 1991. pap. 4.99 (*0-8308-1192-3*, 1192) InterVarsity.

__Caring for People in Grief.__ Phyllis J. Le Peau. (Caring People Bible Studies). 96p. (Orig.). 1991. pap. 4.99 (*0-8308-1193-1*, 1193) InterVarsity.

__Caring for People in the Community: The New Agenda for Welfare.__ Ed. by Michael Titterton. 160p. 1994. pap. 36. 00 (*1-85302-112-1*, Pub. by J Kingsley Pubs UK) Taylor & Francis.

*__Caring for People with Alzheimer's Disease: A Training Manual for Direct Care Providers.__ Gayle Andresen. LC 94-31057. 208p. 1995. pap. 23.00 (*1-878812-22-X*) Hlth Prof Pr.

__Caring for People with Multiple Disabilities: An Interdisciplinary Guide for Caregivers.__ Cindy French et al. 128p. 1991. pap. text ed. 29.95 (*0-88450-394-1*, 4705) Commun Skill.

__Caring for People with Physical Impairment: The Journey Back.__ Group for the Advancement of Psychiatry, Committee on Handicaps Staff. LC 92-22055. (GAP Report Ser.: No. 135). 208p. 1992. text ed. 27.50 (*0-87318-203-0*) Am Psychiatric.

__Caring for People with Severe Mental Disorders: A National Plan of Research to Improve Services.__ 80p. (Orig.). (C). 1993. pap. text ed. 35.00 (*1-56806-885-9*) Diane Pub.

__Caring for Persons at the End of Life: A Facilitator's Guide to Educational Modules for Healthcare Leaders.__ 211p. 1993. ring bd. 25.00 (*0-87125-217-1*, 135) Cath Health.

__Caring for Physical Needs.__ Phyllis J. Le Peau. (Caring People Bible Studies). 96p. (Orig.). 1991. pap. 4.99 (*0-8308-1196-6*, 1196) InterVarsity.

__Caring for Quality in Day Services.__ 103p. 1992. pap. 18.00 (*0-11-321530-4*, HM15304, Pub. by HMSO UK) UNIPUB.

__Caring for School Age Children.__ Phyllis Click. 213p. 1994. pap. text ed. 18.95 (*0-8273-5411-8*) Delmar.

__Caring for Someone in Your Home.__ K. N. Tigges et al. LC 92-81466. (Illus.). 172p. (Orig.). 1992. pap. 11.95 (*0-9633017-0-5*) Mast Hlth Grp.

__Caring for Someone with AIDS.__ (Illus.). 52p. (Orig.). (C). Date not set. pap. 14.95 (*1-57205-009-8*) Rector Pr.

__Caring for Spiritual Needs.__ Phyllis J. Le Peau. (Caring People Bible Studies). 96p. (Orig.). 1991. pap. 4.99 (*0-8308-1194-X*, 1194) InterVarsity.

__Caring for the Alzheimer Patient: A Practical Guide.__ rev. ed. Ed. by Raye L. Dippel & J. Thomas Hutton. (Golden Age Books - Perspectives on Aging Ser.). 187p. (C). 1991. reprint ed. pap. 16.95 (*0-87975-663-2*) Prometheus Bks.

__Caring for the Burned: Life & Death in a Hospital Burn Center.__ James M. Mannon. 274p. (C). 1985. 44.95x (*0-398-05089-9*) C C Thomas.

__Caring for the Burned: Life & Death in a Hospital Burn Center.__ James M. Mannon. 1985. 42.50 (*0-318-23303-7*) Phoenix Soc.

__Caring for the Caregiver: A Nurse's Journey to Health & Inner Peace.__ Roberta M. Jarrett. 200p. 1993. pap. 12.95 (*0-9635191-0-7*) Pacific Edits.

__Caring for the Caregiver: Growth Models for Professional Leaders & Congregations.__ Gary L. Harbaugh. LC 92-72793. 1992. pap. 12.95 (*1-56699-059-9*, AL138) Alban Inst.

__Caring for the Children: Challenge to America.__ Ed. by Jeffery Lande et al. 336p. (C). 1989. text ed. 69.95 (*0-8058-0255-X*); pap. 29.95 (*0-8058-0256-8*) L Erlbaum Assocs.

__Caring for the Chronic Mentally Ill.__ Ursula C. Gerhart. LC 89-61482. 356p. (C). 1990. text ed. 42.00 (*0-87581-333-X*) Peacock Pubs.

__Caring for the Commonweal: Education for Religious & Public Life.__ Ed. by Parker J. Palmer et al. LC 89-78103. 272p. (C). 1990. 30.00 (*0-86554-358-5*, MUP-H286) Mercer Univ Pr.

__Caring for the Coronary Patient.__ David R. Thompson & Rosemary A. Webster. (Illus.). 280p. 1992. pap. 60.00 (*0-7506-0397-6*) Buttrwrth-Heinemann.

__Caring for the Countryside: The Proceedings of a Conference Held at Oxford Polytechnic in Conjunction with the Oxfordshire Countryside Group.__ Ed. by M Breakell et al. (C). 1984. 50.00 (*0-685-30267-9*, Pub. by Oxford Polytechnic UK) St Mut.

__Caring for the Developing Child.__ 2nd ed. Patricia E. Marhoefer & Lisa A. Vadnais. 1992. teacher ed 13.00 (*0-8273-4682-4*); text ed. 29.95 (*0-8273-4681-6*) Delmar.

__Caring for the Developing Child Workbook.__ 2nd ed. Patricia E. Marhoefer. 1992. 13.95 (*0-8273-4902-5*) Delmar.

__Caring for the Developmentally Disabled Child at Home: The Experiences of Low-Income Families.__ Michael J. Smith et al. LC 88-211256. 75p. 1987. pap. text ed. 7.00 (*0-88156-063-4*) Comm Serv Soc NY.

__Caring for the Disabled Elderly: Who Will Pay?__ Alice M. Rivlin & Joshua M. Wiener. LC 88-10528. 318p. 1988. pap. 16.95 (*0-8157-7497-4*) Brookings.

__Caring for the Dying Patient & His Family.__ Austin H. Kutscher & Michael Goldberg. LC 72-4350. 54p. 1973. pap. 3.95 (*0-930194-77-2*) Ctr Thanatology.

*__Caring for the Dying Patient & the Family.__ 3rd ed. J. Robbins & J. E. Moscrop. 304p. 1995. pap. 47.75 (*1-56593-328-1*, 0658) Singular Publishing.

*__Caring for the Earth: A Strategy for Survival.__ (Illus.). 159p. (Orig.). 1993. 29.95 (*1-85732-168-5*, Pub. by IUCN SZ) Island Pr.

__Caring for the Elderly.__ Veronica Windmill. 256p. (Orig.). 1992. pap. 36.50 (*0-273-03871-0*, Pub. by Pitman Pub Ltd UK) Trans-Atl Phila.

__Caring for the Elderly: Reshaping Health Policy.__ Ed. by Carl Eisdorfer et al. LC 89-2199. 544p. 1989. text ed. 55.00 (*0-8018-3810-X*) Johns Hopkins.

__Caring for the Elderly at Home: A Policy Perspective on Consumer Experiences with Publicly-Funded Home Care Programs in New York City.__ Francis G. Caro & Arthur E. Blank. LC 89-105204. 143p. 1987. pap. text ed. 12.00 (*0-88156-052-9*) Comm Serv Soc NY.

*__Caring for the Elderly Client.__ Mary A. Anderson et al. (Illus.). 470p. (C). 1995. pap. text ed. 19.95 (*0-8036-0009-7*) Davis Co.

__Caring for the Elderly in Diverse Care Settings.__ Charlotte Eliopoulos. (Illus.). 439p. 1989. text ed. 24.50 (*0-397-54671-8*) Lippincott.

__Caring for the Exercising Woman.__ Ed. by R. W. Hale & Morton A. Stenchever. (Current Topics in Obstetrics & Gynecology Ser.). 160p. 1991. 55.00 (*0-444-01568-X*) Elsevier.

__Caring for the Flock: Pastoral Ministry in the Local Congregation.__ David L. Larsen. LC 91-2175. 256p. (Orig.). 1991. pap. 10.99 (*0-89107-609-3*) Crossway Bks.

*__Caring for the Future: Report of the Independent Commission on Population & Quality of Life.__ Ed. by Paul Harrison. (Illus.). 320p. 1995. pap. 14.95 (*0-19-286186-7*) OUP.

__Caring for the Healing Heart: An Eating Plan for Recovery from Heart Attack.__ Eleanor Cousins. 160p. 1989. pap. 3.95 (*0-380-70744-6*) Avon.

__Caring for the Hungry & Homeless.__ 135p. 1985. 20.00 (*0-685-30545-7*) Pub Tech Inc.

__Caring for the Least of These.__ David Caes. 176p. (Orig.). 1992. pap. 9.95 (*0-8361-3594-6*) Herald Pr.

*__Caring for the Mind: The Comprehensive Guide to Mental Health.__ Dianne Hales. 1995. 39.95 (*0-553-09146-8*) Bantam.

__Caring for the Nursing Home Patient: Clinical & Managerial Challenges for Nurses.__ Charlotte Eliopoulos. 262p. (C). 1989. 52.00 (*0-8342-0047-3*, 20047) Aspen Pub.

__Caring for the Older Woman.__ Ed. by Morton A. Stenchever & G. A. Aagaard. (Current Topics in Obstetrics & Gynecology Ser.). 256p. 1991. 59.00 (*0-444-01549-3*) Elsevier.

__Caring for the Parkinson Patient: A Practical Guide.__ Ed. by Raye L. Dippel & J. Thomas Hutton. (Golden Age Books - Perspectives on Aging Ser.). (Illus.). 180p. 1989. 22.95x (*0-87975-478-8*); pap. 16.95 (*0-87975-562-8*) Prometheus Bks.

*__Caring for the Poor: A Strategy for Self-Empowerment.__ Horace R. Pratt. 124p. (Orig.). (C). 1994. pap. write for info. (*1-885591-10-1*) Morris Pubng.

__Caring for the Psychogeriatric Client.__ Priscilla Ebersole. LC 89-11516. 304p. 1989. 33.95 (*0-8261-6420-X*) Springer Pub.

__Caring for the Retarded in America: A History.__ Peter L. Tyor & Leland V. Bell. LC 84-6575. (Contributions in Medical History Ser.: No. 15). (Illus.). xvi, 215p. 1984. text ed. 49.95 (*0-313-20977-4*, TVS/, Greenwood Pr) Greenwood.

*__Caring for the Rural Community: An Interdisciplinary Curriculum.__ Ed. by American Psychological Association, Office of Rural Health. LC 94-49194. 1995. write for info. (*1-55798-288-0*) Am Psychol.

__Caring for the Sick at Home.__ Tieneke Van Bentheim et al. 160p. 1987. pap. 12.95 (*0-88010-254-3*) Anthroposophic.

__Caring for the Small Church: Insights from Women in Ministry.__ Nancy T. Foltz. LC 93-15844. (Small Church in Action Ser.). 80p. 1993. pap. 8.00 (*0-8170-1175-7*) Judson.

__Caring for the Working Man: The Rise & Fall of the Dispensary.__ Ed. by Charles E. Rosenberg. (Medical Care in the United States Ser.). 304p. 1989. reprint ed. lib. bdg. 20.00 (*0-8240-8341-5*) Garland.

*__Caring for the World: A Christian Religious Experience.__ fac. ed. J. Edward Carothers. LC 82-195056. (Illus.). 146p. 1994. pap. 41.70 (*0-7837-7709-4*, 2047468) Bks Demand.

__Caring for Those Who Can't.__ Carol Dettoni. 192p. (Orig.). 1993. pap. 1.60 (*1-56476-063-4*, Victor Books) SP Pubns.

__Caring for Those with Alzheimer's: A Pastoral Approach.__ Joan D. Roberts. LC 90-26574. 94p. (Orig.). 1991. pap. 4.95 (*0-8189-0593-X*) Alba.

__Caring for Those You Love: A Guide to Compassionate Care for the Aged.__ Bethany Chaffin. LC 84-63125. 107p. 1985. 10.98 (*0-88290-270-9*) Horizon Utah.

__Caring for Troubled Children.__ James K. Whittaker et al. LC 78-24750. (Jossey-Bass Social & Behavioral Science Ser.). 288p. reprint ed. pap. 82.10 (*0-7837-0188-8*, 2040484) Bks Demand.

__Caring for Widows: You & Your Church Can Make a Difference.__ Wesley M. Teterud. LC 93-1763. 128p. (Orig.). 1993. pap. 9.99 (*0-8010-8909-3*) Baker Bk.

__Caring for Young Children: Signing for Day Care Providers & Sitters.__ S. Harold Collins. (Beginning Sign Language Ser.). (Illus.). 32p. (Orig.). (J). (gr. 1-8). 1993. pap. text ed. 2.95 (*0-931993-58-X*, GP-058) Garlic Pr OR.

__Caring for Your Adolescent: Ages 12 to 21.__ American Academy of Pediatrics Staff. Ed. by Donald E. Greydanus. 326p. 1991. 19.95 (*0-553-07556-X*) Am Acad Pediat.

__Caring for Your Aging Parents.__ Robert R. Cadmus. 253p. 1984. 17.95 (*0-13-114786-2*) P-H.

__Caring for Your Aging Parents.__ Barbara Deane. LC 89-62760. 276p. 1989. pap. 10.00 (*0-89109-578-0*) NavPress.

__Caring for Your Aging Parents.__ Judy Hamlin. (Searching for Answers Ser.: No. 2). 64p. 1992. pap. 4.99 (*0-89693-098-X*) SP Pubns.

*__Caring for Your Aging Parents: A Planning & Action Guide.__ Cohen. 1995. pap. text ed. 10.95 (*0-87477-799-2*) J P Tarcher.

*__Caring for Your Aging Parents: A Planning & Action Guide.__ Donna Cohen & Carl Eisdorfer. 1995. pap. 10.95 (*0-399-07992-0*) Pub Group.

__Caring for Your Aging Parents: A Sourcebook of Timesaving Techniques & Tips.__ Kerri S. Smith. LC 91-33909. (Working Caregiver Ser.). 120p. (Orig.). 1992. pap. 8.95 (*0-9621333-8-8*, Amrcn Source Bks) Impact Pubs CA.

*__Caring for Your Aging Parents: A Sourcebook of Timesaving Techniques & Tips.__ Kerri S. Smith. LC 91-33909. (Working Caregiver Ser.). 120p. (Orig.). 1992. pap. 9.95 (*0-915166-90-9*, Amrcn Source Bks) Impact Pubs CA.

__Caring for Your Art: A Guide for Artists, Collectors, Galleries, & Art Institutions.__ Jill Snyder. LC 90-85555. (Illus.). 176p. (Orig.). 1991. pap. 14.95 (*0-9607118-1-3*) Allworth Pr.

__Caring for Your Baby & Young Child: Birth to Age 5.__ Steven P. Shelov. 676p. 1993. pap. 11.95 (*0-553-37184-3*) Bantam.

__Caring for Your Baby & Young Child - Birth to Age 5.__ American Academy of Pediatrics Staff. 676p. 1993. 19. 95 (*0-553-07186-6*) Am Acad Pediat.

__Caring for Your Cat.__ Paddy Cutts. 1994. 14.98 (*0-8317-1302-X*) Smithmark.

__Caring for Your Cat.__ Elza Dinwiddie-Boyd. (No Nonsense Pet Care Guide Ser.). (Orig.). 1991. pap. 4.95 (*0-681-41043-4*) Longmeadow Pr.

__Caring for Your Cat.__ Mark McPherson. LC 84-223. (Pet Library Ser.). (Illus.). 48p. (J). (gr. 3-7). 1985. lib. bdg. 9.89 (*0-8167-0115-6*); pap. text ed. 2.95 (*0-8167-0116-4*) Troll Assocs.

__Caring for your Cherished Possessions.__ Mary K. Levenstein & Cordelia F. Biddle. (Illus.). 160p. 1989. 14.95 (*0-517-57087-4*, Crown) Crown Pub Group.

__Caring for Your Cherished Possessions.__ Mary K. Levenstein. 1994. pap. 12.00 (*0-517-88226-4*, Crown) Crown Pub Group.

__Caring for Your Child: Questions Parents Ask.__ Marion Marshall & Lorraine Schapiro. 1981. pap. 2.95 (*0-88409-042-6*) Borden.

__Caring for Your Collections: Preserving & Protecting Your Art & Other Collectibles.__ National Committee to Save America's Cultural Collections Staff. (Illus.). 208p. 1992. 39.95 (*0-8109-3174-5*) Abrams.

__Caring for Your Dog.__ Dorian Breedlove. (No Nonsense Pet Care Guide Ser.). (Orig.). 1991. pap. 4.95 (*0-681-41044-2*) Longmeadow Pr.

__Caring for Your Dog.__ Mark McPherson. LC 84-222. (Pet Library Ser.). (Illus.). 48p. (J). (gr. 3-7). 1985. lib. bdg. 9.89 (*0-8167-0113-X*); pap. 2.95 (*0-8167-0114-8*) Troll Assocs.

__Caring for Your Elderly at Home: How to Give Good Health Care.__ Frida C. Adams et al. LC 89-51145. (Illus.). xxx, 179p. (Orig.). 1990. 21.95 (*0-685-27236-2*); pap. 14.95 (*0-685-27237-0*) Wasa-Trends Pub.

__Caring for Your Elderly Parents: The Help, Hope, & Cope Book.__ rev. ed. Patricia H. Rushford. LC 92-47073. 224p. 1993. pap. 8.99 (*0-8007-9207-6*) Revell.

__Caring for Your Fish.__ Mark McPherson. LC 84-8563. (Pet Library Ser.). (Illus.). 48p. (J). (gr. 3-7). 1985. lib. bdg. 9.89 (*0-8167-0109-1*); pap. text ed. 2.95 (*0-8167-0110-5*) Troll Assocs.

__Caring for Your Newborn Baby.__ Glenn R. Stoutt. 132p. 1990. 12.95 (*0-932471-12-9*) Falsoft.

__Caring for Your Old House: A Guide for Owners & Residents.__ Judith L. Kitchen. (Respectful Rehabilitation Ser.). (Illus.). 220p. (Orig.). 1991. pap. 16.95 (*0-89133-160-3*) Preservation Pr.

*__Caring for Your Older Dog.__ Chris C. Pinney. LC 95-6756. 1995. write for info. (*0-8120-9149-3*) Barron.

__Caring for Your Own Dead: A Final Act of Love.__ Lisa Carlson. Ed. by Barbara Agnew & Thomas Gray. (Illus.). 343p. (Orig.). 1987. 17.95 (*0-942679-00-8*); pap. 12.95 (*0-942679-01-6*) Upper Access.

__Caring for Your Pet Lobster: A Complete Guide.__ Weston Arey. (Illus.). 80p. 1991. pap. 5.95 (*0-89272-293-2*) Down East.

__Caring for Your Plants.__ Reader's Digest Editors. (Successful Gardening Ser.). (Illus.). 176p. 1994. 18.98 (*0-89577-603-0*) RD Assn.

__Caring for Your School-Age Child: Ages 5 to 12.__ American Academy of Pediatrics Staff. 1995. write for info. (*0-553-08982-X*) Am Acad Pediat.

*__Caring for Your School-Age Child: Ages 5 to 12.__ Ed. by Edward L. Schor. LC 95-15018. 1995. write for info. (*0-553-09981-7*) Bantam.

__Caring for Your Sick Cat.__ Carol A. Himsel. 192p. 1994. pap. 8.95 (*0-8120-1726-9*) Barron.

*__Caring for Your Wife in Sickness & in Health: A Husband's Guide to Understanding the Special Health Needs of a Woman.__ Richard H. Dominguez. LC 94-43736. 1995. 10.95 (*0-929239-68-7*) Discovery Hse Pubs.

__Caring for Yourself When Caring for Others.__ Margot Hover. LC 92-60890. 80p. (Orig.). 1993. pap. 7.95 (*0-89622-533-X*) Twenty-Third.

__Caring for Youth in Shelters: A Training Manual from Boys Town.__ Father Flanagan's Boys' Home Staff. Ed. by Boys Town Press Staff. 219p. (C). 1993. pap. text ed. 24.95 (*0-938510-41-X*, 63-001) Boys Town Pr.

__Caring God: Biblical Models of Discipleship.__ David M. Scholer. 64p. 1989. pap. 7.00 (*0-8170-1152-8*) Judson.

*__Caring Hands: Planning & Implementing a Caregiver Retreat.__ Joyce Bryan & Thomas F. Edson. 63p. (Orig.). 1995. pap. 25.00 (*0-9644874-0-3*) Orange Caregiver.

__Caring Heart.__ large type ed. I. M. Fresson. (Linford Romance Library). 1991. pap. 13.95 (*0-7089-7116-4*) Ulverscroft.

__Caring Imperative in Education.__ Ed. by Madeleine Leininger & Jean Watson. 316p. 1990. 22.95 (*0-88737-470-0*) Natl League Nurse.

*__Caring in an Unjust World: Negotiating Borders & Barriers in Schools.__ Ed. by Deborah Eaker & Jane Van Galen. 288p. (C). 1996. text ed. 59.50 (*0-7914-2799-4*); pap. text ed. 19.95x (*0-7914-2800-1*) State U NY Pr.

__Caring in Crisis: A Handbook of Intervention Skills for Nurses.__ 2nd ed. Bob Wright. LC 92-49335. (Orig.). 1993. 31.00 (*0-443-04599-2*) Churchill.

__Caring in Crisis: An Oral History of Critical Care Nursing.__ Jacqueline Zalumas. (Studies in Health, Illness, & Caregiving). 240p. (Orig.). (C). 1994. text ed. 36.95 (*0-8122-3255-0*); pap. text ed. 14.95 (*0-8122-1510-9*) U of Pa Pr.

__Caring in Emergencies.__ Sandra Mallan. (Skills for Caring Ser.). (Illus.). 48p. (Orig.). 1993. pap. text ed. 12.00 (*0-443-04622-0*) Churchill.

__Caring in Homes Initiative: A Policies & Foundation Training.__ Comp. by George Mabon. (C). 1991. 55.00 (*0-7855-0083-9*, Pub. by Natl Inst Soc Work) St Mut.

__Caring in Homes Initiative: An Induction Programme.__ Comp. by George Mabon. (C). 1991. 35.00 (*0-7855-0082-0*, Pub. by Natl Inst Soc Work) St Mut.

*__Caring in Our Communities: The Management Agenda.__ Norman Flynn & Clive Miller. 1991. pap. 35.00 (*0-902789-72-4*, Pub. by Natl Inst Soc Work) St Mut.

__Caring in Our Communities: The Management Agenda.__ Norman Flynn & Clive Miller. (C). 1991. 60.00 (*0-7855-0097-9*, Pub. by Natl Inst Soc Work) St Mut.

__Caring Is God.__ Bill Willis. 152p. (Orig.). 1994. pap. 11.95 (*1-880837-83-8*) Smyth & Helwys.

__Caring Kitchen Recipes.__ Gloria Lawson. LC 93-61485. 229p. (Orig.). ring bd. 12.95 (*0-945383-63-0*) Teach Servs.

__Caring One by One.__ Duane Ewers. LC 88-71581. 60p. (Orig.). 1988. pap. 4.95 (*0-88177-064-7*, DR064) Discipleship Res.

__Caring Parent.__ Henry Draper. 1983. text ed. 21.00 (*0-02-662850-3*) Bennett IL.

__Caring People Bible Studies, 8 titles, Set.__ Phyllis J. LePeau. 1991. 39.92 (*0-8308-1190-7*, 1190) InterVarsity.

__Caring Person's Guide to Handling the Severely Multiply Handicapped.__ Rachel Golding & Liz Goldsmith. (Illus.). 96p. 1986. pap. text ed. 15.00 (*0-88167-399-4*) Raven.

__Caring Prescriptions: Comprehensive Health Care Strategies for Young Children in Poverty.__ Karen N. Bell & Linda S. Simkin. LC 92-48194. (Illus.). 96p. (Orig.). 1993. pap. 15.95 (*0-926582-09-7*) NCCP.

C

***Caring Quotes: A Compendium of Caring Thoughts.** Ed. by Brothers Halamandaris Staff. 465p. 1994. per. 15.00 (*1-886450-00-5*) Caring Pub.

Caring Relationship: Elderly People & Their Families. Hazel Qureshi & Alan Walker. (Health, Society, & Policy Ser.). (C). 1990. 34.95 (*0-87722-663-6*) Temple U Pr.

Caring Services. Bill Clarke. (Skills for Caring Ser.). (Illus.). 48p. (Orig.). 1993. pap. text ed. 12.00 (*0-443-04527-5*) Churchill.

Caring, Sharing, & Getting Along: Children's Activities in Social Responsibility. Mary D. Johnson. LC 92-36341. 1993. write for info. (*1-56071-119-1*) ETR Assocs.

Caring Spaces, Learning Places: Children's Environments That Work. Jim Greenman. (Illus.). 217p. (Orig.). (C). 1988. pap. 29.00 (*0-942702-04-2*) Child Care.

Caring Systems. HMSO Staff. 75p. 1992. pap. 12.00 (*0-11-886090-9*, HM60909, Pub. by HMSO UK) UNIPUB.

Caring That Enables: A Manual for Developing Parish Family Ministry. Leif Kehrwald. 1991. pap. 7.95 (*0-8091-3240-0*) Paulist Pr.

Caring That Makes a Difference. Marilyn Cleland. 187p. (Orig.). 1990. text ed. 45.00 (*1-877592-15-3*) GSH&MC.

Caring Voices & Women's Moral Frames: Gilligan's View. Ed. by Bill Puka. LC 94-462. (Moral Development: a Compendium Ser.: No. 6). (Illus.). 544p. 1994. reprint ed. 79.00 (*0-8153-1553-8*) Garland.

Carino. Frances Sainz. (Cityscapes Ser.). 23p. (J). (ps-1). 1992. pap. text ed. 23.00 (*1-56843-047-7*); pap. text ed. 4.50 (*1-56843-094-9*) BGR Pub.

Carinthia. (Panorama Books Collection). (FRE.). 3.95 (*0-685-33965-3*) Fr & Eur.

Carinthian Love Songs. Margarethe Herzele. Tr. by Herbert Kuhner. LC 78-56886. (Bilingual Poetry Ser.: No. 2). (Illus.). 64p. (GER.). 1978. 15.00 (*0-89304-025-8*, CCC113); pap. 7.50 (*0-89304-026-6*) Cross-Cultrl NY.

Carinthian Slovenian Poetry. Ed. by Feliks J. Bister & Herbert Kuhner. (Illus.). 216p. (ENG & SLV.). 1984. 12.95 (*3-85013-029-0*) Slavica.

Carioca Fletch. Gregory McDonald. LC 85-16378. 288p. (Orig.). 1988. mass mkt. 4.99 (*0-446-34899-6*) Warner Bks.

Cariology. 3rd ed. Newbrun. (Illus.). 392p. 1989. text ed. 58.00 (*0-86715-205-2*) Quint Pub Co.

Cariology for the Nineties. Ed. by William H. Bowen & Lawrence A. Tabak. LC 92-48515. (Illus.). 470p. (C). 1993. text ed. 75.00 (*1-878822-17-9*) Univ Rochester Pr.

Carisma. Carlos Gonzalez. (SPA.). 1986. write for info. (*1-56491-005-9*) Imagine Pubs.

Carismas de Dios. Gerda Brown. (Illus.). 589p. (Orig.). (SPA.). (C). 1983. pap. 8.95 (*0-939868-98-9*) Chr Intl Pubs.

Carissima: A Lyric Drama. rev. ed. Benedict Markowski. LC 81-479565. (Illus.). 140p. 1980. ring bd. 25.00 (*0-9614820-0-1*) Poets Mark.

Carl: Portrait of an Artist. George Johnston. 144p. 1986. pap. 15.95 (*0-920806-77-5*, Pub. by Penumbra Pr CN) U of Toronto Pr.

Carl: Portrait of an Artist. limited ed. George Johnston. 144p. 1986. 47.50 (*0-920806-67-8*, Pub. by Penumbra Pr CN) U of Toronto Pr.

Carl A. Spaatz & the Air War in Europe. Richard G. Davis. LC 92-14889. (General Histories Ser.). 1992. boxed write for info. (*0-912799-75-7*); per. write for info. (*0-912799-77-3*) Off Air Force.

Carl A. Spaatz & the Air War in Europe. Richard G. Davis. (History of Aviation Ser.). (Illus.). 762p. 1993. 49.95 (*1-56098-254-3*) Smithsonian.

***Carl A. Spaatz & the Air War in Europe, 2 vols., Set.** 1994. lib. bdg. 600.00 (*0-8490-5814-7*) Gordon Pr.

Carl & Martha Shaw Family: Reminiscences by Their Children. Everett H. Shaw et al. 530p. 1994. pap. write for info. (*0-9641039-0-7*) J M Shaw.

Carl Andre: Qunicy Book. (Illus.). 1973. pap. 2.00 (*0-910663-03-3*) ICA Inc.

Carl Barks & the Art of the Comic Book. Michael Barrier. LC 81-20899. (Illus.). 228p. 1982. 70.00 (*0-9607652-0-4*); pap. 20.00 (*0-9607652-1-2*) M Lilien.

Carl Bornemann's Regiment: The Forty-First New York Infantry (DeKalb Regt.) in the Civil War. David G. Martin. LC 86-82998. (Illus.). 322p. (C). 1987. 24.00 (*0-944413-03-X*) Longstreet Hse.

***Carl Caught a Flying Fish.** Kevin O'Malley. LC 95-1756. (J). 1996. 12.00 (*0-689-80098-3*, S&S Bks Young Read) S&S Childrens.

Carl Cheng - John Doe Co: Twenty-Five Year Survey. Michael Hall & Betty Klausner. 58p. 1991. pap. write for info. (*1-880658-02-X*) San Barb CAF.

Carl De Keyser: God Inc. Carl De Keyser. (Illus.). 106p. 1992. pap. 40.00 (*90-72216-22-9*, Pub. by Focus NE) Dist Art Pubs.

Carl Dreyer. Marianne Helweg. (Film Ser.). 1979. lib. bdg. 59.95 (*0-8490-2880-9*) Gordon Pr.

***Carl E. Heffley's the Road Less Traveled: Form Poetry & How to Write It.** Carl E. Heffley. 188p. (Orig.). 1994. pap. text ed. 19.95 (*1-883331-07-2*) Anderie Poetry.

Carl Ernst Von Baer on the Study of Man & Nature. Carl E. Von Baer & William Coleman. LC 80-2105. (Illus.). 1981. lib. bdg. 60.95 (*0-405-13870-9*) Ayer.

Carl F. Gould: A Life in Architecture & the Arts. T. William Booth & William H. Wilson. (Illus.). 288p. 1995. 40.00 (*0-295-97360-9*) U of Wash Pr.

Carl Faberge. Habsburg Geza von. LC 93-26856. (First Impressions Ser.). (J). 1994. 19.95 (*0-8109-3324-1*) Abrams.

Carl Faberge: Goldsmith to the Imperial Court of Russia. A. K. Snowman. (Illus.). 1983. 12.99 (*0-517-40502-4*) Random Hse Value.

Carl Friedrich Gauss: A Bibliography. Comp. by Uta C. Merzbach. LC 83-20345. 551p. 1984. lib. bdg. 100.00 (*0-8420-2169-8*) Scholarly Res Inc.

Carl Goes Shopping. Alexandra Day. (Illus.). (J). (gr. 3 up). 1989. 12.95 (*0-374-31110-2*) FS&G.

Carl Goes to Daycare. Alexandra Day. (J). (ps). 1993. 12.95 (*0-374-31093-9*) FS&G.

***Carl Goes to Daycare.** Alexandra Day. 32p. (J). Date not set. 5.95 (*0-374-31145-5*) FS&G.

Carl Gustav Jung: Critical Assessments, 4 vol. set. Ed. by Renos Papadopoulos. LC 92-1044. 1650p. 1993. 499.00 (*0-415-04830-3*, A7769) Routledge.

Carl Hayden: Builder of the American West. Ross R. Rice. LC 93-43763. 372p. (C). Date not set. lib. bdg. 48.50 (*0-8191-9399-2*) U Pr of Amer.

Carl Jung & Christian Spirituality: A Reader. Ed. by Robert A. Moore. (Jung & Spirituality Ser.). 272p. 1988. pap. 12.95 (*0-8091-2950-7*) Paulist Pr.

Carl Jung & Soul Psychology. Karen Gibson & Donald Lathrop. (Orig.). 1991. pap. 12.95 (*1-56023-001-0*) Harrington Pk.

Carl Jung & Soul Psychology. Ed. by Gibson. LC 86-29497. 192p. (Orig.). 1987. reprint ed. text ed. 39.95 (*0-86656-632-5*) Haworth Pr.

Carl Laemmle & Universal Pictures: A Tribute. R. Gordon. 1976. lib. bdg. 69.95 (*0-8490-1579-0*) Gordon Pr.

Carl Larsson: Fifty Paintings. Karl R. Langewiesche. Tr. by Alan L. Rice. (Illus.). 104p. 1985. 19.95 (*0-940607-05-0*) Pictura NJ.

Carl Larsson: On the Sunny Side. Karl R. Langewiesche. Tr. by Alan L. Rice. (Illus.). 62p. 1984. reprint ed. 19.95 (*0-940607-06-9*) Pictura NJ.

Carl Larsson: The Autobiography of Sweden's Most Beloved Artist. (Illus.). 208p. 1992. pap. 16.95 (*0-941016-91-9*) Penfield.

Carl Lewis. Wayne Coffey. (Olympic Gold! Ser.). (Illus.). 64p. (J). (gr. 3-7). 1993. pap. 7.95 (*1-56711-052-5*) Blackbirch.

Carl Lewis. Wayne Coffey. (Olympic Gold! Ser.). (Illus.). 64p. (J). (gr. 3-7). 1993. lib. bdg. 14.95 (*1-56711-006-1*) Blackbirch.

***Carl Lewis: Champion Athlete.** Ed. by Nathan I. Huggins. (Black Americans of Achievement Ser.). (Illus.). 144p. (YA). (gr. 5 up). Date not set. 18.95 (*0-7910-2164-5*) Chelsea Hse.

Carl Lewis: Legend Chaser. Nathan Aaseng. LC 84-23348. (Sports Achievers Ser.). (Illus.). 56p. (J). (gr. 4-9). 1985. lib. bdg. 13.50 (*0-8225-0496-0*, Lerner Publctns) Lerner Group.

Carl Lotus Becker. Carl L. Becker. (BCL1 - U. S. History Ser.). 279p. 1991. reprint ed. lib. bdg. 79.00 (*0-7812-6095-7*) Rprt Serv.

***Carl Makes a Scrapbook.** Alexandra Day. (Illus.). 32p. 1994. 12.95 (*0-374-31129-3*) FS&G.

Carl Maria Von Weber. Julius Benedict. LC 74-24040. reprint ed. 38.50 (*0-404-12863-7*) AMS Pr.

Carl Maria Von Weber: A Guide to Research. Donald Henderson. LC 89-17159. (Composer Resource Manuals Ser.). 416p. 1990. 57.00 (*0-8240-4118-6*, H1006) Garland.

Carl Maria Von Weber: The Life of an Artist, 2 vols. Max M. Von Weber. 1990. reprint ed. lib. bdg. 140.00 (*0-7812-9099-6*) Rprt Serv.

Carl Maria Von Weber: The Life of an Artist, 2 Vols, Set. Max M. Von Weber. Ed. by J. Palgrave Simpson. LC 68-25305. 1969. reprint ed. lib. bdg. 79.95 (*0-8383-0190-8*) M S G Haskell Hse.

Carl Maria Von Weber, the Life of an Artist, 2 vols., Set. Max M. Weber. LC 68-31013. (Illus.). 1970. reprint ed. text ed. 65.00 (*0-8371-1931-6*, WECW, Greenwood Pr) Greenwood.

Carl Menger & His Legacy in Economics. Ed. by Bruce J. Caldwell. 407p. (C). 1990. text ed. 37.00 (*0-8223-1087-2*) Duke.

Carl Menger & the Origins of Austrian Economics. Max Alter. 256p. (C). 1990. text ed. 92.50 (*0-8133-0945-X*) Westview.

Carl Menger (1840-1921) Mark Blaug. (Pioneers in Economics Ser.: No. 26). 240p. 1992. 84.95 (*1-85278-489-X*, Pub. by E Elgar Pub UK) Ashgate Pub Co.

Carl Menger's Lectures to Crown Prince Rudolf of Austria. Ed. by Erich W. Streissler & Monika Streissler. LC 94-4584. 1994. 79.95 (*1-85898-075-5*, Pub. by E Elgar Pub UK) Ashgate Pub Co.

Carl Mydans: Photojournalist. Carl Mydans. LC 84-24349. (Illus.). 208p. 1993. 39.95 (*0-8109-1323-2*) Abrams.

Carl Nielsen, Symphonist. Robert Simpson. (Illus.). 260p. 1989. reprint ed. pap. 12.95 (*0-912483-50-4*) Pro-Am Music.

Carl Nielsen, Symphonist, 1865-1931. Robert W. Simpson. LC 78-59043. (Encore Music Editions Ser.). (Illus.). 236p. 1989. reprint ed. 26.50 (*0-88355-715-0*) Hyperion Conn.

Carl O. Sauer: A Tribute. Ed. by Martin Kenzer. LC 86-19184. (Illus.). 248p. 1987. 25.00 (*0-87071-249-7*); pap. text ed. 13.95 (*0-87071-248-9*) Oreg St U Pr.

Carl Oman Remembers: Early Episodes for Sharing. Carl Oman & Ida M. Culler. (Illus.). 229p. 1987. 14.95 (*0-87770-422-8*) Ye Galleon.

Carl Philipp Emanuel Bach: Thematic Catalogue. E. Eugene Helm. LC 86-36771. 408p. (C). 1989. text ed. 95.00 (*0-300-02654-4*) Yale U Pr.

Carl Philipp Emanuel Bach Edition, Series I, Vol. 24: (Eight) Keyboard Sonatas (1763-6): H. 176-8, 189, 92, 211-13. Carl P. Bach. Ed. by Claudia Wiggery et al. 127p. 1990. 125.00 (*0-19-324008-4*) OUP.

Carl Philipp Emanuel Bach Edition: Series II, Vol. 15: Keyboard Concerto No. 38 in C minor, H 448, Keyboard Concerto No. 39 in F major, H 454. Carl P. Bach. Ed. by Elias N. Kulukundis et al. (Illus.). 112p. 1989. 125.00 (*0-19-324001-7*) OUP.

Carl Philipp Emanuel Bach Edition: Series II, Vol. 23: 23 Sonatinas. Carl P. Bach. Ed. by Paul G. Wiley, II & Claudia Widgery. 1992. 100.00 (*0-19-324011-4*) OUP.

Carl Pops Up. Day. (J). 1994. 14.95 (*0-671-87105-6*, Green Tiger S&S) S&S Childrens.

Carl Rakosi: Man & Poet. Ed. by Michael Heller. (Man & Poet Ser.). 511p. 1993. 32.00 (*0-943373-22-0*); pap. 19.95 (*0-943373-23-9*) Natl Poet Foun.

Carl Rogers. Brian Thorne. (Key Figures in Counselling & Psychotherapy Ser.). (Illus.). 160p. (C). 1992. text ed. 44.00 (*0-8039-8462-6*); pap. text ed. 18.95 (*0-8039-8463-4*) Sage.

Carl Rogers Reader. Ed. by Howard Kirschenbaum & Valerie L. Henderson. 512p. 1989. pap. 14.95 (*0-395-48357-3*) HM.

Carl Ruggles: Composer, Painter, & Storyteller. Marilyn J. Ziffrin. LC 93-9914. (Music in American Life Ser.). (Illus.). 280p. (C). 1994. 37.50 (*0-252-02042-1*) U of Ill Pr.

***Carl Sagan & Immanuel Velikovsky.** Charles Ginenthal. 343p. (Orig.). Date not set. text ed. 21.49 (*0-9639759-0-0*) C Ginenthal Ivy Pr.

***Carl Sagan & Immanuel Velikovsky.** Charles Ginenthal. (Illus.). 448p. (Orig.). 1995. pap. 16.95 (*1-56184-075-0*) New Falcon Pubns.

Carl Sandburg. Richard Crowder. (United States Authors Ser.: No. 47). 176p. 1964. text ed. 20.95 (*0-8057-0648-8*, Twayne) Macmillan.

Carl Sandburg. Harry Golden. LC 88-14416. (Prairie State Bks.). 304p. 1988. pap. 9.95 (*0-252-06006-7*) U of Ill Pr.

***Carl Sandburg.** Carl Sandburg. Ed. by Frances S. Bolin. LC 94-30777. (Poetry for Young People Ser.). (Illus.). 48p. (J). (gr. 1-8). 1995. 14.95 (*0-8069-0818-1*) Sterling.

Carl Sandburg: A Biography. Penelope Niven. (Illus.). 864p. 1994. 19.95 (*0-252-02115-0*) U of Ill Pr.

Carl Sandburg: A Reference Guide. Dale Salwak. 1988. text ed. 40.00 (*0-8161-8821-1*, Hall Reference) Macmillan.

Carl Sandburg: His Life & Works. North Callahan. LC 86-43031. (Illus.). 320p. 1987. 29.75 (*0-271-00486-X*) Pa St U Pr.

Carl Sandburg: Poet & Historian. Lucas Longo. Ed. by D. Steve Rahmas. LC 73-185665. (Outstanding Personalities Ser.: No. 9). 32p. (YA). (gr. 7-12). 1972. lib. bdg. 4.95 (*0-87157-509-4*) SamHar Pr.

Carl Sandburg at the Movies: A Poet in the Silent Era 1920-1927. Ed. by Dale Fetherling & Doug Fetherling. LC 84-14068. 207p. 1985. 20.00 (*0-8108-1738-1*) Scarecrow.

Carl Sandburg Home. LC 82-600299. (National Park Service Handbook Ser.: No. 117). (Illus.). 128p. 1983. pap. 6.50 (*0-16-003450-7*, 024-005-00835-7) USGPO.

Carl Sandburg, Philip Green Wright, & the Asgard Press, 1900-1910: A Descriptive Catalogue of Early Books, Manuscripts, & Letters in the Clifton Waller Barrett Library. Clifton Waller Barrett Library Staff & Joan S. Crane. LC 75-6824. 158p. reprint ed. pap. 45.10 (*0-8357-2729-7*, 2039839) Bks Demand.

Carl Sandburg Remembered. William A. Sutton. LC 78-31298. 312p. 1979. 22.50 (*0-8108-1202-9*) Scarecrow.

Carl Sanders: Spokesman of the New South. James F. Cook. LC 93-36314. (C). 1994. 24.99 (*0-86554-433-6*) Mercer Univ Pr.

Carl Sauer's Fieldwork in Latin America. Robert C. West. LC 79-27117. (Dellplain Latin American Studies: No. 3). 183p. reprint ed. pap. 52.20 (*0-317-28164-X*, 2022588) Bks Demand.

***Carl Schlechter! Life & Times of the Austrian Chess Wizard.** Warren Goldman. (Great Masters Ser.). (Illus.). xiv, 537p. 1994. 46.00 (*0-939433-18-4*) Caissa Edit.

Carl Schmitt: Politics & Theory. Paul E. Gottfried. LC 90-36630. (Contributions in Political Science Ser.: No. 264). 168p. 1990. text ed. 49.95 (*0-313-27209-3*, GVC, Greenwood Pr) Greenwood.

***Carl Schmitt & Leo Strauss: The Hidden Dialogue; Including Strauss's Notes on Schmitt's Concept of the Political & Three Letters from Strauss to Schmitt.** Heinrich Meier. Tr. by J. Harvey Lomax. LC 95-8803. 1995. 18.95 (*0-226-51889-2*) U Ch Pr.

Carl Schmitt, Theorist for the Reich. Joseph W. Bendersky. LC 82-61353. 336p. 1983. 49.50 (*0-691-05380-4*) Princeton U Pr.

Carl Sternheim: A Critical Study. Rhys W. Williams. (British & Irish Studies in German Language & Literature: Vol. 5). 282p. 1982. pap. 45.40 (*3-261-04992-8*) P Lang Pubs.

Carl the Cactus. Joe W. Cates. (Illus.). 64p. (Orig.). (J). (gr. k-6). 1986. lib. bdg. 9.95 (*0-942403-03-7*); pap. 7.00 (*0-942403-01-0*) J Barnaby Dist.

Carl Van Vechten. Edward Lueders. (Twayne's United States Authors Ser.). 1964. pap. 13.95x (*0-8084-0070-3*, T74) NCUP.

Carl van Vechten & the Irreverent Decades. Bruce Kellner. 440p. reprint ed. pap. 125.40 (*0-317-27968-8*, 2052155) Bks Demand.

Carl Von Clausewitz: Historical & Political Writings. Ed. by Peter Paret & Daniel Moran. Tr. by Daniel Moran. (Illus.). 422p. 1992. text ed. 35.00 (*0-691-03192-4*) Princeton U Pr.

Carl Wimar: Chronicler of the Missouri River Frontier. Rick Stewart et al. (Illus.). 264p. 1991. 49.95 (*0-8109-3958-4*) Abrams.

Carl Yastrzemski. Sheppard Long. (Baseball Legends Ser.). (Illus.). 64p. (J). (gr. 3 up). 1994. lib. bdg. 14.95 (*0-7910-1195-X*, Am Art Analog) Chelsea Hse.

***Carl Zuckmayer Criticism: Tracing Endangered Fame.** Hans Wagener. (Literary Criticism in Perspective Ser.). 196p. 1995. 55.95 (*1-57113-064-0*) Camden Hse.

Carla & Annie. Susan K. Smith. 1989. pap. 5.95 (*0-913543-13-6*) African Am Imag.

Carla Goes to Court. Jo Beaudry & Lynne Ketchum. LC 82-2854. (Illus.). 32p. (J). (gr. 1-5). 1982. 16.95 (*0-89885-088-6*); pap. 10.95 (*0-89885-354-0*) Human Sci Pr.

Carla the Carpenter. Cathy E. Dubowski. (Busy Beavers, S9215 Ser.). (Illus.). 28p. (J). (ps-2). 1992. 3.95 (*0-7214-5339-2*) Ladybird Bks.

Carleman's Formulas in Complex Analysis. Lev Aizenberg. LC 92-43813. (Mathematics & Its Applications Ser.: No. 244). 316p. (C). 1993. lib. bdg. 137.00 (*0-7923-2121-9*) Kluwer Ac.

Carleton E. Watkins: A Listing of Photographs in the Collection of the California State Library. Richard Terry. (Illus.). 102p. 1984. pap. 9.50 (*0-929722-01-9*) CA State Library Fndtn.

Carleton E. Watkins: Photographs 1861-1874. Ed. by Jeffrey Fraenkel. (Illus.). 222p. 1989. 75.00 (*0-938491-27-X*) Fraenkel Gal.

Carleton Watkins: Selected Texts & Bibliography. Ed. by Amy Rule. LC 92-42581. 200p. 1993. text ed. 85.00 (*0-8161-0578-2*, Hall Reference) Macmillan.

Carleton's 'Traits & Stories' & the 19th Century Anglo-Irish Tradition. Barbara Hayley. LC 82-6847. (Irish Literary Studies: No. 12). 446p. (C). 1983. text ed. 44.00 (*0-389-20308-4*, 07143) B&N Imports.

Carlin School, A History Book: The Story of a School in Ravenna, Ohio, U. S. A. Lois F. Lewis. (Illus.). 28p. (Orig.). (J). (gr. 5). 1989. pap. text ed. write for info. (*0-9620136-3-3*) L F Lewis.

Carlisle, History & Guide. Michael R. McCarthy. LC 93-33707. 1993. pap. 16.00 (*0-7509-0236-1*) A Sutton Pub.

Carlisle's Guide to Government. Ed. by Richard C. Moore. LC 93-85942. (Orig.). 1993. pap. 12.95 (*0-9639034-0-3*) Univ Wholesale.

Carlisle's Guide to Government. Ed. by Richard C. Moore. 256p. (Orig.). 1994. pap. 12.95 (*0-9639034-4-6*) Univ Wholesale.

Carlito en el Parque una Tarde: Carl's Afternoon in the Park. Alexandra Day. (Illus.). 32p. (SPA.). (J). 1992. bds. 12.95 (*0-374-31100-5*, Mirasol) FS&G.

Carlito's Way. Edwin Torres. 1993. mass mkt. 5.99 (*0-380-72287-9*) Avon.

Carlitos y Snoopy. Charles M. Schulz. (Peanuts Ser.). 64p. (SPA.). (J). 1971. 4.95 (*0-8288-4512-3*) Fr & Eur.

Carlo A. Sperati: Grand Old Maestro. Camilla S. Strom. (Illus.). 200p. (Orig.). 1988. write for info. (*0-9620861-0-X*) Luther Coll Pr.

Carlo Abarth Foto Storia. Alfred S. Cosentino. 384p. 1989. 49.00 (*0-929991-16-8*) A S Cosentino Bks.

Carlo Capellini (Before 1650-1683) - Giovanni Battista Pederzuli (before 1650-after1692?) - Antonio Draghi (probably 1636-1700) - Filippo Vismarri (1635-1706?) - Carlo Agostino Badia (1672-1738), Vol. 16. Ed. by Lawrence Bennet. LC 85-752834. (Italian Cantata in the Seventeenth Century Ser.). 1986. lib. bdg. 25.00 (*0-8240-8890-5*) Garland.

Carlo Carra: The Complete Paintings, 1900-1966, 3 vols. Massimo Carra. (Illus.). (ITA.). 1968. Set: Vol. 1 606p., Vol. 2 718p., Vol. 3 638p. 795.00 (*1-55660-082-8*) A Wofsy Fine Arts.

Carlo Carra's Graphic Work. Massimo Carra. 150p. (ITA.). 1976. 120.00 (*1-55660-116-6*) A Wofsy Fine Arts.

Carlo Carretto Selected Writings. Carlo Carretto. Ed. by Robert Ellsberg. LC 93-42722. 200p. (Orig.). 1994. pap. 12.95 (*0-88344-956-0*) Orbis Bks.

***Carlo Collodi's Pinocchio.** Carlo Collodi. LC 95-10127. (Illus.). (J). 1995. write for info. (*0-399-22941-8*, Philomel Bks) Putnam Pub Group.

Carlo Fontana: The Drawings at Windsor Castle. Allan Braham & Hellmut Hager. Ed. by John Harris & Alastair Laing. (Studies in Architecture: No. XVIII). (Illus.). 222p. 1986. 125.00 (*0-302-02780-7*, Pub. by Zwemmer Bks UK) Sothebys Pubns.

Carlo Gesualdo, Prince of Venosa, Musician & Murderer. Cecil Gray. LC 76-104268. (Illus.). 145p. 1971. reprint ed. text ed. 35.00 (*0-8371-3934-1*, GRCG, Greenwood Pr) Greenwood.

Carlo Gesualdo, Prince of Venosa, Musician & Murderer. Cecil Gray & Philip Heseltine. 145p. 1990. reprint ed. lib. bdg. 59.00 (*0-7812-9063-5*) Rprt Serv.

Carlo Gozzi: Translations of "The Love of Three Oranges", "Turandot", & "The Snake Lady" with a Bio-critical Introduction. John L. DiGaetani. LC 87-17676. (Contributions in Drama & Theatre Studies: No. 24). 168p. 1988. text ed. 39.95 (*0-313-25676-4*, DCG/) Greenwood.

Carlo Michelstaedter & the Failure of Language. Daniela Bini. (Illus.). 314p. (C). 1992. lib. bdg. 42.95 (*0-8130-1111-6*) U Press Fla.

Carlo Pedretti: A Bibliography of His Work on Leonardo Da Vinci & the Renaissance, 1944-1984. In Celebration of His Twenty Five Years at the University of California, Los Angeles. Joyce P. Ludmer. (Illus.). 144p. (Orig.). 1987. pap. write for info. (*0-9617550-0-8*) E Belt Lib.

Carlo Scarpa. (Architecture & Urbanism Extra Edition Ser.). (Illus.). (Orig.). (ENG & JPN.). (C). pap. text ed. 76.95 (*4-900211-12-5*, Pub. by Japan Architect JA) Gingko Press.

Carlo Scarpa: Architecture in Details. Bianca Albertini & Alessandra Bagnoli. Tr. by Donald Mills. (Illus.). 240p. 1989. 75.00x (*0-262-01107-7*) MIT Pr.

Carlo Scarpa & the Castelvecchio. Richard Murphy. (Illus.). 224p. 1991. text ed. 99.95 (*0-408-50052-2*, Butterwrth Archit) Buttrwrth-Heinemann.

C

1056 An Asterisk (*) at the beginning of an entry indicates that the title is appearing in BIP for the first time.

C

Carmody-Wait: Cyclopedia of New York Practice with Forms, 35 vols., Set. 2nd suppl. ed. 1991. Suppl. 1991; set. write for info. (*0-318-57152-8*) Lawyers Cooperative.

Carn Brea. Michael Tangye. (C). 1989. 30.00 (*0-907566-11-1*, Pub. by Dyllansow Truran UK) St Mut.

Carna & the Boots of Seven Strides. Bill Harley. 80p. (J). (gr. 2-5). 1994. pap. 3.50 (*0-87406-681-6*) Willowisp Pr.

Carnaby & the Assassins. large type ed. Peter N. Walker. (Linford Mystery Library). 304p. 1988. pap. 11.95 (*0-7089-6619-5*, Linford) Ulverscroft.

Carnaby & the Conspirators. large type ed. Peter N. Walker. 1990. pap. 12.95 (*0-7089-6907-0*, Linford) Ulverscroft.

Carnaby & the Demonstrators. large type ed. Peter N. Walker. (Linford Mystery Library). 1991. pap. 13.95 (*0-7089-7080-X*, Linford) Ulverscroft.

Carnaby & the Eliminators. large type ed. Peter N. Walker. (Linford Mystery Library). 1991. pap. 13.95 (*0-7089-7068-0*, Linford) Ulverscroft.

Carnaby & the Hijackers. Peter N. Walker. (Black Dagger Crime Ser.). 200p. 1993. 16.50 (*0-7451-8614-9*, Black Dagger) Chivers N Amer.

Carnaby & the Hijackers. large type ed. Peter N. Walker. (Linford Mystery Library). 272p. 1988. pap. 11.95 (*0-7089-6507-5*, Linford) Ulverscroft.

Carnaby & the Infiltrators. Peter N. Walker. 192p. 1994. 16.95 (*0-7451-8641-6*, Black Dagger) Chivers N Amer.

Carnaby & the Jailbreakers. large type ed. Peter N. Walker. (Linford Mystery Library). 358p. 1988. pap. 11.95 (*0-7089-6567-9*, Linford) Ulverscroft.

Carnaby & the Kidnappers. large type ed. Peter N. Walker. (Linford Mystery Library). 384p. 1993. pap. 14.95 (*0-7089-7352-3*, Linford) Ulverscroft.

Carnaby & the Saboteurs. large type ed. Peter N. Walker. 1990. pap. 12.95 (*0-7089-6899-6*, Linford) Ulverscroft.

Carnaby Curse. large type ed. Daoma Winston. 132p. 1992. reprint ed. lib. bdg. 17.95 (*1-56054-515-1*) Thorndike Pr.

Carnage Again: Preliminary Report on Violations of the Laws of War by Both Sides in the November 1989 Offensive in El Salvador. Americas Watch Staff. 50p. 1989. 7.00 (*0-929692-86-1*, Am Watch) Hum Rts Watch.

Carnahan Conference on Crime Countermeasures, 1978: Proceedings. Ed. by R. William De Vore & John S. Jackson. LC 76-63633. 176p. 1978. pap. text ed. 22.50 (*0-89779-000-6*) OES Pubns.

Carnahan Conference on Crime Countermeasures, 1979: Proceedings. J. S. Jackson. Ed. by R. William De Vore. LC 79-64890. (Illus.). 182p. (Orig.). 1979. pap. 22.50 (*0-89779-018-9*, UKY BU117) OES Pubns.

Carnahan Conference on Crime Countermeasures, 1980: Proceedings. Ed. by R. William De Vore & J. S. Jackson. LC 79-644630. (Illus.). 160p. (Orig.). 1980. pap. 22.50 (*0-89779-030-8*, UKY BU120) OES Pubns.

Carnahan Conference on Security Technology, 1982: Proceedings. Ed. by R. William De Vore & J. S. Jackson. LC 79-64463. (Illus.). 194p. (Orig.). 1982. pap. 22.50 (*0-89779-052-9*, UKY BU127) OES Pubns.

Carnahan Conference on Security Technology, 1985: Proceedings. Ed. by R. William DeVore & J. S. Jackson. LC 82-64615. (Illus.). 181p. 1985. pap. 22.50 (*0-89779-061-8*, UKY BU137) OES Pubns.

Carnahan Conference on Security Technology, 1986: Proceedings. Ed. by R. William DeVore & J. S. Jackson. LC 82-64615. (Illus.). 159p. 1986. pap. 22.50 (*0-89779-065-0*, UKY BU140) OES Pubns.

Carnahan Conference on Security Technology, 1988: Proceedings. Ed. by R. William De Vore. LC 82-646157. (Illus.). 108p. 1988. pap. 22.50 (*0-89779-071-5*, UKY BU146) OES Pubns.

Carnal Christian: What Should We Think of the Carnal Christian? Ernest C. Reisinger. 75p. 1992. reprint ed. 1.95 (*0-85151-389-1*) Banner of Truth.

Carnal Christians: And Other Words That Don't Go Together. Rich Wilkerson. 176p. (Orig.). 1986. pap. 2.99 (*0-88368-188-9*) Whitaker Hse.

Carnal Cornucopia. 1993. pap. 4.95 (*0-8216-5101-3*, Univ Books) Carol Pub Group.

Carnal Days of Helen Seferis. Alexander Trocchi. (Orig.). 1993. pap. text ed. 4.95 (*1-56333-086-5*) Masquerade.

***Carnal Hours.** Max A. Collins. (Nathan Heller Novel Ser.). 400p. 1995. mass mkt. 5.99 (*0-451-17975-7*, Sig) NAL-Dutton.

Carnal Hours: A Nate Heller Novel. Max A. Collins. LC 93-30349. 352p. 1994. 20.95 (*0-525-93758-7*, Dutton) NAL-Dutton.

Carnal Innocence. Nora Roberts. 1992. 5.99 (*0-553-29597-7*) Bantam.

Carnal Israel: Reading Sex in Talmudic Culture. Daniel Boyarin. LC 92-9507. 1993. 35.00 (*0-520-08012-2*) U CA Pr.

***Carnal Israel: Reading Sex in Talmudic Culture.** Daniel Boyarin. 1993. pap. 14.95 (*0-520-20336-4*) U CA Pr.

Carnal Knowing: Female Nakedness & Religious Meaning in the Christian West. Margaret Miles. LC 90-55679. 272p. 1991. pap. 15.00 (*0-679-73401-5*, Vin) Random.

Carnal Knowledge: Manuscript Edition. Jules Feiffer. 1993. pap. 13.00 (*0-8222-0185-2*) Dramatists Play.

Carnal Musings of Sylvia Savage. Ruth M. Kempher. 1980. 2.00 (*0-686-71050-9*) Windless Orchard.

***Carnal Prayer Mat.** Li Yu. (Orig.). 1994. pap. 9.95 (*1-56201-081-6*, North Star Line) Blue Moon Bks.

Carnal Professor - Christ Set Forth. Robert Bolton & Thomas Goodwin. 484p. 1992. reprint ed. 23.95 (*1-877611-47-6*) Soli Deo Gloria.

Carnal Refreshment. James Camp. (Burning Deck Poetry Ser.). 1975. 15.00 (*0-930900-02-2*); pap. 4.00 (*0-930900-03-0*) Burning Deck.

***Carnal Rhetoric: Milton's Iconoclasm & the Poetics of Desire.** Lana Cable. LC 94-38249. 248p. 1995. lib. bdg. 44.95 (*0-8223-1560-2*); pap. text ed. 17.95 (*0-8223-1573-4*) Duke.

Carnal Sin. Edward Le Comte. 1994. 15.95 (*0-8313-5002-4*) Lantern.

Carnap on Meaning & Analyticity. Richard Butrick, Jr. LC 78-106469. (Janua Linguarum, Ser. Minor: No. 85). (Orig.). 1970. pap. text ed. 9.25 (*3-11-000277-9*) Mouton.

Carnatic Music & the Tamils. T. V. Kuppuswami. xix, 334p. 1992. 42.00 (*81-85163-25-1*, Pub. by Kalinga Pubns) Nataraj Bks.

Carnation Production, No. II. Holley & Baker. 176p. (C). 1991. pap. text ed. 25.50 (*0-8403-6308-7*) Kendall-Hunt.

Carnations: A One-Act Play. Raymond Carver. (Illus.). 1992. 95.00 (*0-939489-14-7*) Engdahl Typo.

Carnations: A One-Act Play. deluxe ed. Raymond Carver. (Illus.). 1992. 300.00 (*0-939489-13-9*) Engdahl Typo.

Carnations & Pinks: The Complete Guide. Sophie Hughes. (Illus.). 208p. 1993. pap. 19.95 (*1-85223-744-9*, Pub. by Crowood Pr UK) Trafalgar.

Carnaval. LeRoy Neiman. (Illus.). 1981. 100.00 (*0-937608-01-7*) Knoedler.

Carnaval de Venise: Comedie Lyrique, Vol. XVII. Andre Campra. LC 89-753010. (French Opera in the 17th & 18th Centuries Ser.: No. 5). (Illus.). 300p. (ENG & FRE.). 1990. lib. bdg. 86.00 (*0-945193-07-6*) Pendragon NY.

Carnaval Perpetuel. H. H. Cooper. (Illus.). 160p. 1987. 50.00 (*0-920668-44-5*) Firefly Bks Ltd.

Carnaval y Revolucion y Diecinueve Ensayos Mas. Miguel De Ferdinandy. Tr. by Magdalena De Ferdinandy et al. (Coleccion Mente y Palabra). 380p. (SPA.). 1977. 5.00 (*0-8477-0544-7*); pap. 4.00 (*0-8477-0545-5*) U of PR Pr.

Carnavalia! African-Brazilian Folklore & Crafts. Liza Papi. LC 93-38451. (Illus.). 48p. (J). 1994. 16.95 (*0-8478-1779-2*) Rizzoli Intl.

Carnegie. Ed. by Ellen Wilson. LC 91-65314. (Illus.). 72p. (Orig.). 1992. pap. 14.95 (*0-500-27642-0*) Thames Hudson.

Carnegie Atlas of Galaxies, 2 vols. Allan Sandage & John Bedke. LC 93-71702. (Publication 638 Ser.). (Illus.). 760p. (C). 1994. text ed. 92.00 (*0-87279-667-1*, 638) Carnegie Inst.

Carnegie Council on Policy Studies in Higher Education: A Summary of Reports & Recommendations. Carnegie Council on Policy Studies in Higher Education Staff. LC 80-7999. 503p. reprint ed. pap. 143.40 (*0-8357-4871-5*, 2037803) Bks Demand.

Carnegie Denied: Communities Rejecting Carnegie Library Construction Grants, 1898-1925. Robert S. Martin. LC 92-25741. (Beta Phi Mu Monograph: No. 3). 200p. 1993. text ed. 47.95 (*0-313-28609-4*, MNY, Greenwood Pr) Greenwood.

Carnegie Hall: The First Hundred Years. Richard Schickel & Michael Walsh. (Illus.). 256p. 1987. 49.50 (*0-8109-0773-9*) Abrams.

Carnegie Institution of Washington Year Book. Incl. Vol. 76. (Illus.). 1014p. 1977. 16.50 (*0-87279-649-3*); Vol. 77. (Illus.). 1032p. 1978. 16.50 (*0-87279-650-7*); Vol. 78. (Illus.). 893p. 1979. 16.50 (*0-87279-651-5*); Vol. 79. (Illus.). 740p. 1980. 16.50 (*0-87279-653-1*); Vol. 80. (Illus.). 784p. 1981. 16.50 (*0-87279-654-X*); Vol. 81. (Illus.). 786p. 1982. 16.50 (*0-87279-655-8*); Vol. 82. (Illus.). 789p. 1983. 16.50 (*0-87279-657-4*); Vol. 83. (Illus.). 195p. 1984. 7.00 (*0-87279-658-2*); Vol. 84. (Illus.). 206p. 1985. 7.00 (*0-87279-659-0*); Vol. 85. (Illus.). 198p. 1986. 7.00 (*0-87279-660-4*); Vol. 86. (Illus.). 206p. 1987. 7.00 (*0-87279-661-2*); Vol. 87. (Illus.). 235p. 1988. 7.00 (*0-87279-662-0*); Vol. 88. (Illus.). 208p. 1989. 7.00 (*0-685-42044-2*); Vol. 89. (Illus.). 208p. 1990. 7.00 (*0-87279-664-7*); Vol. 90. (Illus.). 183p. 1991. 7.00 (*0-87279-665-5*); Vol. 91. (Illus.). 200p. 1992. 7.00 (*0-87279-670-1*); write for info. (*0-318-51300-5*) Carnegie Inst.

Carnegie International, 1985. Ed. by John R. Lane et al. LC 85-25870. (Illus.). 256p. (Orig.). 1985. pap. 10.00 (*0-88039-011-5*) Mus Art Carnegie.

***Carnegie International, 1988.** Ed. by Sarah McFadden & Joan Simon. LC 88-30021. (Illus.). 202p. 1988. pap. 22.95 (*0-88039-019-0*) Mus Art Carnegie.

Carnegie International 1991: Carnegie Museum of Art, 2 vols. Francis M. Cookel et al. (Illus.). (Orig.). 1992. pap. 65.00 (*0-8478-1499-8*) Rizzoli Intl.

Carnegie International 1991: Carnegie Museum of Art, Vol. I. Francis M. Cookel et al. (Illus.). 144p. (Orig.). 1992. pap. write for info. (*0-318-68980-4*) Rizzoli Intl.

Carnegie International 1991: Carnegie Museum of Art, Vol. II. Francis M. Cookel et al. (Illus.). 96p. (Orig.). 1992. pap. write for info. (*0-318-68981-2*) Rizzoli Intl.

Carnegie Libraries: Restoration & Expansion. Lonn Frye. LC 92-33751. 1992. write for info. (*0-942579-17-8*) IHPA.

Carnegie Library in Illinois. Raymond Bial & Linda L. Bial. (Visions of Illinois Ser.). (Illus.). 192p. 1991. text ed. 39.95 (*0-252-01822-2*) U of Ill Pr.

Carnegie Mellon Anthology of Poetry. Ed. by Gerald Costanzo & Jim Daniels. LC 92-74533. 1993. 29.95 (*0-88748-162-0*); pap. 16.95 (*0-88748-163-9*) Carnegie-Mellon.

Carnegie Mellon University. Photos by Scott Goldsmith. (Illus.). 112p. 1990. 39.00 (*0-916509-53-2*) Harmony Hse Pub LO.

Carnegie Museum Collection from Southeastern Utah. Floyd W. Sharrock & Edward G. Keane. (Glen Canyon Ser.: No. 16). reprint ed. 31.50 (*0-404-60657-1*) AMS Pr.

Carnegie Nobody Knows. George Swetnam & Helene Smith. LC 89-60700. 186p. 1993. pap. 14.95 (*0-945437-07-2*) MacDonald-Sward.

Carnegie Series on Egypt, 9 vols., Set. (Illus.). (Orig.). 1990. boxed 49.95 (*0-911239-33-2*) Carnegie Mus.

Carnegie's Dinosaurs. Helen J. McGinnis. LC 82-70212. (Illus.). 120p. (Orig.). 1982. pap. 15.95 (*0-911239-00-6*) Carnegie Mus.

Carnegie's Excuse. Peter O'Donnell. LC 92-17617. (Illus.). 32p. (J). (ps-3). 1993. 14.95 (*0-590-46435-3*) Scholastic Inc.

Carnet de Croquis Asteriz Chez Rahazade. Rene Goscinny & Uderzo Goscinny. 64p. (FRE.). 1993. lib. bdg. 19.95 (*0-7859-3654-8*, 2865030085) Fr & Eur.

Carnet de Notes. 2nd ed. Jacques Maritain. (Illus.). 424p. (FRE.). 1965. 34.95 (*0-8288-9887-1*, F11670) Fr & Eur.

Carnet De Notes Spiritual. Paul Twitchell. 1978. pap. 5.00 (*0-914766-40-6*) Illum Way Pub.

Carnet De Notes Spirituel. Paul Twitchell. 248p. 1982. pap. 5.00 (*1-57043-072-1*); audio 25.00 (*1-57043-044-6*) ECKANKAR.

Carnet des Miserables Octobre-Decembre 1860. Victor Hugo. Ed. by Jean B. Barrere. 283p. (FRE.). 1965. pap. 41.95 (*0-7859-5342-6*) Fr & Eur.

Carnets. Albert Camus. Incl. I. Mai 1935 a Fevrier 1942. 37.95 (*2-07-021219-X*); Tome II, Janvier 1942-Mars 1951. 44.95 (*2-07-021220-3*); (Gallimard Ser.). (FRE.). write for info. (*0-318-51941-0*) Schoenhof.

Carnets, 4 tomes. Henri De Montherlant. Incl. 1942-1943(FRE.). 236p. 1948. pap. 26.95 (*0-7859-5308-6*); 1932-1934(FRE.). 224p. 1956. pap. 26.95 (*0-7859-5309-4*); 1930-1932(FRE.). 216p. 1956. pap. 26.95 (*0-7859-5310-8*); 1968. Set pap. write for info. (*0-318-51942-9*) Fr & Eur.

Carnets. rev. ed. Antoine De Saint-Exupery. 296p. (FRE.). 1975. pap. 19.95 (*0-7859-1280-0*, 2070108449) Fr & Eur.

Carnets d'Enquetes. Une Ethnographie Inedite de la France. Emile Zola. (FRE.). 1991. pap. 32.95 (*0-7859-3247-X*, 2266045695) Fr & Eur.

Carnets du Bon Dieu. Pierre Daninos. (FRE.). pap. 10.95 (*0-8288-9174-5*, F97920) Fr & Eur.

Carnets du Major Thompson. Pierre Daninos. 244p. (FRE.). 1968. 10.95 (*0-8288-9175-3*, F97931) Fr & Eur.

Carnets Du Major W. Marmaduke Thompson, Decouverte de la France et des Francais. Pierre Daninos. 1960. 11.95 (*0-685-11065-6*) Fr & Eur.

Carney's House Party. Maud H. Lovelace. 1976. 20.95 (*0-8488-1084-8*) Amereon Ltd.

Carnitine, Enzymes & Isoenzymes in Disease. Ed. by D. M. Goldberg et al. (Advances in Clinical Enzymology Ser.: Vol. 4). viii, 190p. 1986. 143.25 (*3-8055-4322-0*) S Karger.

Carnitine: Its Role in Lung & Heart Disorders. Ed. by E. Kaiser. (Illus.). x, 140p. 1987. 53.75 (*3-8055-4438-3*) S Karger.

***Carnitine System: A New Therapeutical Approach to Cardiovascular Diseases.** Ed. by J. W. De Jong & R. Ferrari. LC 94-46324. (Developments in Cardiovascular Medicine Ser.: Vol. 162). 1995. lib. bdg. 163.00 (*0-7923-3318-7*) Kluwer Ac.

Carnival. (Key Words Readers Ser.: B Series, No. 641-11b). (Illus.). (J). (ps-5). 3.50 (*0-7214-0634-3*) Ladybird Bks.

***Carnival.** (Best of Broadway Ser.). 1993. pap. 10.95 (*0-89724-498-2*, XW1657) Astor Bks.

Carnival! Robin Ballard. LC 94-6267. (Illus.). 24p. (J). (ps up). 1995. 15.00 (*0-688-13237-5*) Greenwillow.

Carnival. Denise Burden-Patmon & Kathryn D. Jones. (Illus.). 32p. (J). (gr. 2-5). 1993. pap. 4.95 (*0-671-79840-5*, S&S Bks Young Read) S&S Childrens.

Carnival. Illus. by CBS Masterworks Staff. (All Time Favorites Ser.). 128p. (Orig.). 1989. pap. 16.95 (*0-8258-0402-7*, ATF114) Fischer Inc NY.

Carnival! V. V. Eco et al. viii, 169p. 1984. text ed. 65.40 (*3-11-009589-0*) Mouton.

Carnival. Dave Etter. 1990. pap. 5.95 (*0-944024-19-X*) Spoon Riv Poetry.

Carnival. Alexander Galin. Tr. by Tom Cole. (Orig.). 1992. pap. 4.95 (*0-87129-161-4*, C84) Dramatic Pub.

***Carnival.** Roderick Hunt. (Oxford Reading Tree Ser.). (Illus.). 16p. (J). (gr. k-k). 1994. pap. 1.99 (*0-19-916303-0*) OUP.

Carnival. William W. Johnstone. 1989. pap. 3.95 (*0-8217-2576-9*) Zebra.

Carnival. Deborah J. Spence. 63p. 1987. 6.00 (*0-9615502-2-8*) Southern Inst Pr.

Carnival: Entertainments & Posthumous Tales. Isak Dinesen. LC 77-5666. xii, 338p. 1979. pap. 14.95 (*0-226-15304-5*) U Ch Pr.

Carnival: Poems. Seamus Cashman. 64p. 1988. pap. 6.95 (*0-86327-129-4*, Pub. by Wolfhound Pr IE) Dufour.

Carnival, American Style: Mardi Gras at New Orleans & Mobile. Samuel Kinser. LC 89-30476. (Illus.). 448p. 1990. 39.95 (*0-226-43729-9*) U Ch Pr.

Carnival & Theatre: Plebian Culture & the Structure of Authority in Renaissance England. Michael D. Bristol. 256p. 1989. pap. 13.95 (*0-415-90138-3*, A2730, Routledge NY) Routledge.

Carnival Aptitude. Greg Boyd. LC 93-70302. (Illus.). 120p. (Orig.). 1993. pap. 9.95 (*1-878580-47-7*) Asylum Arts.

Carnival at the River. Robert Greacen. (C). 1990. 30.00 (*0-948268-86-7*, Pub. by Dedalus Pr IE); pap. 15.00 (*0-948268-85-9*, Pub. by Dedalus Pr IE) St Mut.

Carnival Caper: Teenage Mutant Ninja Turtles. Stephen Murphy. (Sound Doodles Ser.). 16p. (J). (ps-2). 1994. write for info. (*1-883366-49-6*) YES Ent.

Carnival Comedy & Sacred Play: The Renaissance Dramas of Giovan Maria Cecchi. Douglas Radcliff-Umstead. LC 85-999. 200p. 1986. text ed. 22.50 (*0-8262-0462-7*) U of Mo Pr.

Carnival Culture: The Trashing of Taste in America. James B. Twitchell. (Illus.). 320p. 1992. 24.95 (*0-231-07830-7*) Col U Pr.

Carnival Culture: The Trashing of Taste in America. James B. Twitchell. 306p. 1993. pap. 14.95 (*0-231-07831-5*) Col U Pr.

Carnival Ghost. Francine Pascal. (Sweet Valley Twins Super Chiller Ser.: No. 3). (J). (gr. 3-7). 1990. mass mkt. 3.99 (*0-553-15859-7*) Bantam.

Carnival, Hysteria, & Writing: Collected Essays & Autobiography of Allon White. Allon White. LC 92-44198. 208p. 1993. 38.00 (*0-19-811296-3*); pap. 16.95 (*0-19-812287-X*) OUP.

Carnival in Romans. Emmanuel L. Ladurie. LC 79-52163. 426p. 1979. pap. 8.95 (*0-8076-0991-9*) Braziller.

Carnival of Destiny, Vol. 1. Vance Thompson. LC 72-4415. (Short Story Index Reprint Ser.). 1977. reprint ed. 21.95 (*0-8369-4191-8*) Ayer.

Carnival of Destruction. Brian Stableford. 448p. 1994. 21.95 (*0-7867-0122-6*) Carroll & Graf.

Carnival of Fear. J. Robert King. (Ravenloft Ser.: Bk. 5). 320p. (Orig.). 1993. pap. 4.95 (*1-56076-628-X*) TSR Inc.

Carnival of Fury: Robert Charles & the New Orleans Race Riot of 1900. William I. Hair. LC 75-34586. 216p. 1986. pap. text ed. 11.95 (*0-8071-1348-4*) La State U Pr.

Carnival of Images: Brazilian Television Fiction. Michele Mattelart & Armand Mattelart. LC 90-36026. 140p. 1990. text ed. 42.95 (*0-89789-212-7*, H212, Bergin & Garvey) Greenwood.

Carnival of Innocence. Andre Grill. LC 82-682. 1989. 13.95 (*0-87949-215-5*) Ashley Bks.

Carnival of Love. Paige Brantley. 416p. 1993. mass mkt. 4.50 (*0-8217-4343-0*) Zebra.

Carnival of Monsters. 1993. pap. 5.95 (*0-426-11025-0*, Dr Who) Carol Pub Group.

Carnival of Parting: The Tales of King Bharthari & King Gopi Chand As Sung & Told by Madhu Natisar Nath of Ghatiyali, Rajasthan. Ann G. Gold. (C). 1992. 45.00 (*0-520-07533-1*); pap. 17.00 (*0-520-07535-8*) U CA Pr.

Carnival of Repetition: Gaddis's The Recognitions & Postmodern Theory. John Johnston. LC 89-40397. (Pennsylvania Studies in Contemporary American Fiction). 184p. (C). 1989. text ed. 29.95 (*0-8122-8179-9*) U of Pa Pr.

Carnival of Saints. George Herman. LC 92-54989. 432p. 1994. 22.00 (*0-345-38150-5*) Ballantine.

Carnival of Souls: Herk Harvey's Classic Chiller. Michael H. Price. (Illus.). 56p. 1991. pap. 4.95 (*1-56398-019-3*) Malibu Graphics.

***Carnival of the Oppressed: Lula & the Brazilian Workers' Party.** Sue Branford & Bernardo Kucinski. (Illus.). 100p. 1995. pap. 10.00 (*0-85345-959-2*, PB9592) Monthly Rev.

Carnival of the Spirit: Seasonal Celebrations & Rites of Passage. Luisah Teish. LC 90-55784. 240p. 1994. pap. 12.00 (*0-06-250868-7*) Harper SF.

Carnival Secrets. Matthew Gryczan. 224p. 1994. pap. 10.00 (*0-941599-24-8*) Players Pr.

Carnival Stage: Vicentine Comedy Within the Serio-Comic Mode. Jose I. Suarez. LC 91-58948. 176p. 1993. 29.50 (*0-8386-3491-5*) Fairleigh Dickinson.

Carnival Time. Vivian Sathre. LC 91-4442. (J). (ps-3). 1992. pap. 14.00 (*0-671-76963-4*, S&S Bks Young Read) S&S Childrens.

Carnival Trilogy: Carnival, The Infinite Rehersal, & The Four Banks of the River of Space. Wilson Harris. 464p. (Orig.). 1994. pap. 15.95 (*0-571-15435-2*) Faber & Faber.

Carnivals & Commonplaces: Bakhtin's Chronotope, Cultural Studies & Film. Michael V. Montgomery. LC 93-8772. (American University Studies, IV: English Language & Literature: Vol. 173). 142p. (C). 1994. text ed. 43.95 (*0-8204-2194-4*) P Lang Pubs.

Carnivals, Rogues, & Heroes: An Interpretation of the Brazilian Dilemma. Roberto DaMatta. Tr. by John Drury. LC 90-70861. 296p. (C). 1991. text ed. 24.95 (*0-268-00780-2*) U of Notre Dame Pr.

Carnivals, Rogues, & Heroes: An Interpretation of the Brazilian Dilemma. Roberto DaMatta. Tr. by John Drury. LC 90-70861. (From the Helen Kellogg Institute for International Studies). (C). 1992. pap. text ed. 14.95 (*0-268-00794-2*) U of Notre Dame Pr.

Carnivora of the Edson Local Fauna (Late Hemphillian) Kansas. Jessica A. Harrison. LC 83-600029. (Smithsonian Contributions to Paleobiology Ser.: No. 54). 46p. reprint ed. pap. 25.00 (*0-317-29737-6*, 2022200) Bks Demand.

Carnivore Behavior, Ecology, & Evolution. Ed. by John L. Gittleman. LC 88-47725. 624p. 1989. 68.50 (*0-8014-2190-X*); pap. 27.50 (*0-8014-9525-3*) Cornell U Pr.

Carnivores. R. F. Ewer. LC 72-6263. (Comstock Book Ser.). 504p. 1986. pap. 24.95 (*0-8014-9351-X*) Cornell U Pr.

Carnivores. Penelope B. Kreps. 352p. 1993. mass mkt. 4.50 (*0-8217-4225-6*) Zebra.

Carnivorous Plants. Barrie E. Juniper et al. 353p. 1989. text ed. 196.00 (*0-12-392170-8*) Acad Pr.

Carnivorous Plants. Nancy J. Nielsen. LC 91-34422. (First Bks.). (Illus.). 64p. (J). (gr. 3-6). 1992. lib. bdg. 13.93 (*0-531-20056-6*) Watts.

Carnivorous Plants. Nancy J. Nielsen. (First Bks.). (Illus.). 64p. (J). (gr. 5-8). 1992. pap. 5.95 (*0-531-15644-3*) Watts.

Carnivorous Plants. Cynthia Overbeck. LC 81-17234. (Natural Science Bks.). (Illus.). 48p. (J). (gr. 4 up). 1982. lib. bdg. 19.95 (*0-8225-1470-2*, Lerner Publctns); pap. 5.95 (*0-8225-9535-4*, Lerner Publctns) Lerner Group.

Carnivorous Plants. Paul Temple. (Wisley Handbooks Ser.). (Illus.). 64p. (Orig.). 1990. pap. 5.95 (*0-304-31145-6*, Pub. by Cassell UK) Sterling.

Carnivorous Plants of Australia, Vol. 1. Allen Lowrie. (Illus.). 226p. 1987. 38.50 (*0-85564-253-X*, Pub. by Univ of West Aust Pr AT) Intl Spec Bk.

1058 An Asterisk (*) at the beginning of an entry indicates that the title is appearing in BIP for the first time.

An Asterisk (*) at the beginning of an entry indicates that the title is appearing in BIP for the first time.

1059

C

Carolina Lowcountry April 1775-June 1776 & the Battle of Fort Moultrie. rev. ed. Terry W. Lipscomb. Ed. by Judith M. Andrews. (South Carolina Revolutionary War Studies: No. 1). 56p. 1994. pap. write for info. (*1-880067-25-0*) SC Dept of Arch & Hist.

Carolina on My Mind. Anne M. Winston. (Silhouette Desire Ser.). 1994. mass mkt. 2.99 (*0-373-05845-4*, 5-05845-8) Silhouette.

*__Carolina Passion.__ Beth Griffin. 370p. 1995. pap. 9.95 (*0-7610-0142-5*) NW Pub.

*__Carolina Pirates & Colonial Commerce, 1670-1740.__ Shirley C. Hughson. LC 70-149345. 134p. 1992. pap. 20.00 (*0-87152-460-0*) Reprint.

Carolina Pirates & Colonial Commerce, 1670-1740. Shirley C. Hughson. LC 78-63831. (Johns Hopkins University. Studies in the Social Sciences. Thirtieth Ser. 1912: 5-7). reprint ed. 11.50 (*0-404-61091-9*) AMS Pr.

*__Carolina Quaker Experience, 1665-1985: An Interpretation.__ Seth B. Hinshaw. 342p. 1984. 16.00 (*0-614-04673-4*) NC Frnds Hist Soc.

Carolina Quakers. Seth B. Hinshaw. (Illus.). 74p. (Orig.). (YA). (gr. 5-7). 1971. pap. 1.50 (*0-942727-15-0*) NC Yrly Pubns Bd.

Carolina Quakers - Our Heritage, Our Hope: Tercentenary, 1672-1972. Seth B. Hinshaw & Mary E. Hinshaw. (Illus.). 160p. (Orig.). 1972. pap. 6.50 (*0-942727-14-2*) NC Yrly Pubns Bd.

Carolina Quest. Thomas C. Parramore. (gr. 7-8). 1978. text ed. 22.80 (*0-13-114900-8*) P-H.

Carolina Rice Kitchen: The African Connection. Karen Hess. LC 91-46341. (Illus.). 229p. 1992. 24.95 (*0-87249-666-X*) U of SC Pr.

Carolina Rocks! The Geology of South Carolina. Carolyn H. Murphy. Ed. by Tiger Creek Productions Staff. LC 94-20979. (Illus.). 250p. (Orig.). 1995. pap. 19.95 (*0-87844-121-2*) Sandlapper Pub Co.

Carolina Seashells. Nancy Rhyne. (Illus.). 1989. pap. 6.95 (*0-87844-077-1*) Sandlapper Pub Co.

*__Carolina Shout!__ Alan Schroeder. LC 94-17125. (Illus.). (J). 1995. 14.99 (*0-8037-1676-1*); lib. bdg. 14.89 (*0-8037-1678-8*) Dial Bks Young.

Carolina Sports by Land & Water: Incidents of Devil-Fishing, Wild-Cat, Deer & Bear Hunting. William Elliott. (Illus.). 292p. 1977. reprint ed. 12.50 (*0-87921-040-0*) Attic Pr.

Carolina Watermen: Bughunters & Boat Builders. Richard Kelly & Barbara Kelly. LC 93-17464. (Illus.). (Orig.). 1993. pap. 14.95 (*0-89587-104-1*) Blair.

Carolina Whitewater: A Canoeist's Guide to the Western Carolinas. Bob Benner & David Benner. LC 84-115920. (Illus.). 262p. 1977. pap. 14.95 (*0-89732-132-4*) Menasha Ridge.

Carolinas. Mary T. Mulkerin. (Road Atlas Ser.). (Illus.). 64p. 1992. pap. 5.95 (*0-13-117722-2*, H M Gousha) P-H Gen Ref & Trav.

Carolina's Courage. Elizabeth Yates. (Light Line Ser.). 131p. (J). (gr. 2-4). 1989. pap. 5.95 (*0-89084-482-8*) Bob Jones Univ Pr.

Carolinas Governments Performance Standards, 1990. Ed. by Greg Michels. (Governments Performance Standards Ser.). (Illus.). 150p. 1990. text ed. 125.00 (*1-55507-508-8*) Municipal Analysis.

Caroline. Cynthia Wright. 1991. mass mkt. 5.99 (*0-345-29196-4*) Ballantine.

*__Caroline.__ Cynthia Wright. 1994. pap. 8.95 (*0-345-38669-8*) Ballantine.

Caroline. large type ed. Jasmine Cresswell. (Nightingale Ser.). 282p. 1990. pap. 14.95 (*0-8161-5043-5*, Nightingale) Hall.

Caroline & the Raider. Linda L. Miller. Ed. by Linda Marrow. 368p. (Orig.). 1992. mass mkt. 5.99 (*0-671-67638-5*) PB.

Caroline Captivity of the Church: Charles I & the Remoulding of Anglicanism, 1625- 1641. Julian Davies. (Oxford Historical Monographs). 424p. 1992. 89.00 (*0-19-820311-X*) OUP.

Caroline Cherie, 4 vols., Tome I. Cecill Saint-Laurent. 1976. pap. 11.95 (*0-7859-4047-2*) Fr & Eur.

Caroline Cherie, 4 vols., Tome II. Cecill Saint-Laurent. 1976. pap. 11.95 (*0-7859-4048-0*) Fr & Eur.

Caroline Cherie, 4 vols., Tome III. Cecill Saint-Laurent. 1976. pap. 11.95 (*0-7859-4049-9*) Fr & Eur.

Caroline Cherie, 4 vols., Tome IV. Cecill Saint-Laurent. 1976. pap. 11.95 (*0-7859-4050-2*) Fr & Eur.

Caroline Chisholm. Margaret Kiddle. 208p. (Orig.). 1992. pap. 19.95 (*0-522-84428-6*) Intl Spec Bk.

Caroline Chisholm: The Emigrant's Friend. Joanna Bogle. 1994. pap. 14.95 (*0-85244-205-X*, Pub. by Gracewing UK) Morehouse Pub.

*__Caroline County: Virginia Publick Claims.__ Janice L. Abercrombie & Richard Slatten. (Virginia Publick Claims Ser.). ix, 100p. 1991. pap. 13.00x (*0-8095-8530-8*) Borgo Pr.

Caroline County: Virginia Publick Claims. Janice L. Abercrombie & Richard Slatten. (Virginia Publick Claims Ser.). ix, 100p. (C). 1991. reprint ed. lib. bdg. 33.00x (*0-8095-8311-9*) Borgo Pr.

*__Caroline County, Virginia Land Tax Lists, 1787-1799.__ T. L.C. Genealogy Staff. LC 91-65370. 175p. (Orig.). 1991. spiral bd., pap. 14.00 (*1-886633-54-1*) TLC Genealogy.

Caroline Drama: A Bibliographic History of Criticism. 2nd ed. Ed. by Rachel Fordyce. 332p. 1992. text ed. 55.00 (*0-8161-1835-3*, Hall Reference) Macmillan.

Caroline Feller Bauer's New Handbook for Storytellers. Caroline F. Bauer. LC 93-14959. (Illus.). 670p. 1993. lib. bdg. 44.00 (*0-8389-0613-3*) ALA.

*__Caroline Feller Bauer's New Handbook for Storytellers.__ Caroline F. Bauer. (Illus.). 550p. 1995. reprint ed. pap. text ed. 30.00x (*0-8389-0664-8*) ALA.

Caroline Fox 1819-1871. Robert Tod. (C). 1988. 23.00 (*0-900657-54-5*, Pub. by W Sessions UK) St Mut.

Caroline Gordon. Frederick P. McDowell. LC 66-64592. (University of Minnesota Pamphlets on American Writers Ser.: No. 59). 48p. (Orig.). reprint ed. pap. 25.00 (*0-7837-2874-3*, 2057581) Bks Demand.

Caroline Gordon: A Biography. Veronica A. Makowsky. (Illus.). 276p. 1989. 25.00 (*0-19-505718-X*) OUP.

Caroline Hunt: Philosopher for Home Economics. Marjorie East. 1982. write for info. (*0-8461-5049-2*) Am Home Eco.

Caroline, Light, Parker & Stafford Light Virginia Artillery. Homer D. Musselman. (Virginia Regimental Histories Ser.). (Illus.). 144p. 1992. 19.95 (*1-56190-036-2*) H E Howard.

Caroline Lockhart. Norris Yates. (Western Writers Ser.: No. 116). (Illus.). 48p. 1994. pap. 3.95 (*0-88430-115-X*) Boise St U W Writ Ser.

Caroline Lockhart: Her Life & Legacy. Necah S. Furman. LC 93-44383. (Illus.). 264p. (C). 1994. 35.00 (*0-295-97346-3*); pap. 18.95 (*0-295-97347-1*) U of Wash Pr.

Caroline M. Hewins: Her Book: A Mid-Century Child & Her Books (by Caroline M. Hewlins) & Caroline M. Hewins & Books for Children (by Jennie D. Lindquist) Ed. by Caroline M. Hewins. (American Biography Ser.). 107p. 1991. reprint ed. lib. bdg. 59.00 (*0-7812-8180-6*) Rprt Serv.

*__Caroline Miniscule.__ large type ed. Andrew Taylor. 1994. 21.95 (*0-7089-2288-0*) Ulverscroft.

Caroline Moves In. Lene Mayer-Skumanz. (Illus.). 96p. (J). (gr. 1-3). 1988. pap. 2.95 (*0-8120-3938-6*) Barron.

Caroline Norton's Defense: English Laws for Women in the 19th Century. Caroline Norton. 208p. 1982. 17.95 (*0-915864-87-8*); pap. 8.95 (*0-915864-88-6*) Academy Chi Pubs.

Caroline of England: An Augustan Portrait. Peter Quennell. 1977. 21.95 (*0-8369-7148-5*, 7980) Ayer.

Caroline Professional Playwrights: Massinger, Ford, Shirley, & Brome. Ira Clark. LC 91-45853. 240p. 1992. lib. bdg. 27.00 (*0-8131-1787-9*) U Pr of Ky.

Caroline Quest. large type ed. Barbara Whitnell. (Romance Ser.). 208p. 1993. 21.95 (*0-7089-2924-9*) Ulverscroft.

Caroline the Queen. large type ed. Jean Plaidy. (Shadows of the Crown Ser.). 1974. 21.95 (*0-85456-595-7*) Ulverscroft.

Caroline Zucker & the Birthday Disaster. Jan Bradford. LC 90-11159. (Caroline Zucker Ser.). (Illus.). 96p. (J). (gr. 2-5). 1991. lib. bdg. 9.89 (*0-8167-2021-5*); pap. text ed. 2.95 (*0-8167-2022-3*) Troll Assocs.

Caroline Zucker Gets Even. Jan Bradford. LC 89-20630. (Caroline Zucker Ser.). (Illus.). 96p. (J). (gr. 2-5). 1991. lib. bdg. 9.89 (*0-8167-2015-0*); pap. text ed. 2.95 (*0-8167-2016-9*) Troll Assocs.

Caroline Zucker Gets Her Wish. Jan Bradford. LC 90-31549. (Caroline Zucker Ser.). (Illus.). 96p. (J). (gr. 2-5). 1991. lib. bdg. 9.89 (*0-8167-2019-3*); pap. text ed. 2.95 (*0-8167-2020-7*) Troll Assocs.

Caroline Zucker Helps Out. Jan Bradford. LC 90-11156. (Illus.). 96p. (J). (gr. 2-5). 1991. lib. bdg. 9.89 (*0-8167-2025-8*); pap. text ed. 2.95 (*0-8167-2026-6*) Troll Assocs.

Caroline Zucker Makes a Big Mistake. Jan Bradford. LC 90-11160. (Illus.). 96p. (J). (gr. 2-5). 1991. lib. bdg. 9.89 (*0-8167-2023-1*); pap. text ed. 2.95 (*0-8167-2024-X*) Troll Assocs.

Caroline Zucker Meets Her Match. Jan Bradford. LC 90-10813. (Caroline Zucker Ser.). (Illus.). 96p. (J). (gr. 2-5). 1991. lib. bdg. 9.89 (*0-8167-2017-7*); pap. text ed. 2.95 (*0-8167-2018-5*) Troll Assocs.

Caroline's Contract. Lizbeth Dusseau. (Orig.). 1993. pap. text ed. 4.95 (*1-56333-122-5*) Masquerade.

Caroline's Daughters. Alice Adams. 1993. pap. write for info. (*0-449-22144-X*); mass mkt. 5.99 (*0-449-14876-9*, GM) Fawcett.

Caroline's Daughters. large type ed. Alice Adams. 432p. 1991. text ed. 22.95 (*0-8161-5302-7*) G K Hall.

Caroline's Halloween Spell. Francine Pascal. (Sweet Valley Kids Ser.: No. 33). (J). (ps-3). 1992. pap. 2.99 (*0-553-48006-5*) Bantam.

Caroling Dusk: An Anthology of Verse by Black Poets of the Twenties. Intro. by Countee Cullen. 240p. 1993. pap. 10.95 (*0-8065-1349-7*, Citadel Pr) Carol Pub Group.

Carolingian & Romanesque Architecture: 800-1200. 4th ed. Kenneth J. Conant. (Pelican History of Art Ser.). (Illus.). 522p. (C). 1959. reprint ed. text ed. 55.00 (*0-300-05297-9*); reprint ed. pap. text ed. 26.50 (*0-300-05298-7*) Yale U Pr.

Carolingian Chronicles: Royal Frankish Annals & Nithard's Histories. Tr. by Bernard W. Scholz & Barbara Rogers. 1970. pap. 13.95 (*0-472-06186-0*, 186, Ann Arbor Bks) U of Mich Pr.

Carolingian Civilization: A Reader. Ed. by Paul Dutton. 360p. 1993. pap. text ed. 21.95 (*1-55111-003-2*) Broadview Pr.

Carolingian Culture: Emulation & Innovation. Ed. by Rosamond McKitterick. LC 92-36984. (Illus.). 352p. (C). 1993. 69.95 (*0-521-40524-6*); pap. 22.95 (*0-521-40586-6*) Cambridge U Pr.

Carolingian Empire. Heinrich Fichtenau. Tr. by Peter Munz. (Medieval Academy Reprints for Teaching Ser.). 1979. reprint ed. pap. 11.95 (*0-8020-6367-5*) U of Toronto Pr.

Carolingian Learning, Masters & Manuscripts. John J. Contreni. (Collected Studies: No. CS363). 350p. 1992. text ed. 89.95 (*0-86078-317-0*, Pub. by Variorum UK) Ashgate Pub Co.

*__Carolingian, Ottonian, & Romanesque Buildings, 760-1130: A Graphic Introduction.__ William W. Clark & Warren Sanderson. (Illus.). 256p. (Orig.). (C). 1995. pap. 24.95 (*1-884470-07-6*) Astrion Pubng.

Carolingian Painting. Florentine Mutherich & J. E. Gaehde. LC 76-15908. 127p. 1977. pap. 11.95 (*0-8076-0852-1*) Braziller.

Carolingian Pastoral: Seven Versions. R. P. Green. 150p. 1980. 13.75 (*0-7049-0527-2*, Pub. by Brstl Class Pr UK) Focus Info Gr.

Carolingian Portraits: A Study in the Ninth Century. Eleanor S. Duckett. (Ann Arbor Paperbacks Ser.). 320p. 1988. pap. text ed. 16.95x (*0-472-06157-7*, Ann Arbor Bks) U of Mich Pr.

Carolingian Renewal: Sources & Heritage. Donald Bullough. 240p. 1992. text ed. 79.95 (*0-7190-3354-3*, Pub. by Manchester Univ Pr UK) St Martin.

Carolingians: A Family Who Forged Europe. Pierre Riche. Tr. by Michael I. Allen. LC 91-303532. (Middle Ages Ser.). 424p. (Orig.). (C). 1993. text ed. 49.95 (*0-8122-3062-0*); pap. text ed. 19.95 (*0-8122-1342-4*) U of Pa Pr.

Carolingians & the Written Word. Rosamond McKitterick. (Illus.). 296p. (C). 1989. 69.95 (*0-521-30539-X*); pap. 24.95 (*0-521-31565-4*) Cambridge U Pr.

Carolinian-English Dictionary. Frederick H. Jackson & Jeffrey C. Marck. LC 91-3220. 480p. (C). 1992. pap. text ed. 24.00 (*0-8248-1411-8*) UH Pr.

Carolinian Goes to War: The Civil War Narrative of Arthur Middleton Manigault, Brigadier General, C. S. A. Ed. by R. Lockwood Tower. LC 83-1063. (Illus.). 360p. (Orig.). 1992. pap. 14.95 (*0-87249-839-5*) U of SC Pr.

Carols Alive! Contrib by Tom Fettke. 1978. 5.95 (*0-685-68469-5*, MC-41); audio 12.98 (*0-685-68470-9*, TA-9001C) Lillenas.

Carols Alive Program Resources. Vann Trapp. 1980. 6.00 (*0-685-68471-7*, MC-41A) Lillenas.

Carols & Christmas Songs: Colinde, Vol. 4. Bartok. (Rumanian Folk Music Ser). 1975. lib. bdg. 147.50 (*90-247-1737-X*) Kluwer Ac.

Carols & Classics: For Choir & Congregation. Des. by Tom Fettke. 1994. 5.95 (*0-8341-9094-X*, MC-85) Lillenas.

*__Carols & Classics: For Choir & Congregation.__ Des. by Tom Fettke. 1994. digital audio 10.98 (*0-614-01738-6*, TA-9167C) Lillenas.

*__Carols & Classics: For Choir & Congregation.__ Des. by Tom Fettke. 1994. digital audio 60.00 (*0-614-01739-4*, MU-9167C) Lillenas.

*__Carols & Classics: For Choir & Congregation.__ Des. by Tom Fettke. 1994. cd-rom 60.00 (*0-614-01740-8*, MU-9167T) Lillenas.

*__Carols & Classics: For Choir & Congregation.__ suppl. ed. Des. by Tom Fettke. 1994. digital audio 45.00 (*0-614-01741-6*, MU-9167R) Lillenas.

*__Carols & Classics: For Choir & Congregation.__ suppl. ed. Des. by Tom Fettke. 1994. 6.00 (*0-614-01742-4*, L-9167C) Lillenas.

*__Carols & Classics: For Choir & Congregation.__ suppl. ed. Des. by Tom Fettke. 1994. 8.00 (*0-614-01743-2*, MC-85SF) Lillenas.

*__Carols & Classics: For Choir & Congregation.__ suppl. ed. Des. by Tom Fettke. 1994. write for info. (*0-614-01744-0*, OR-9167) Lillenas.

Carols by Candlelight. Floyd Hawkins. 1961. 1.50 (*0-8341-9153-9*, MC-3) Lillenas.

Carols for Choirs: Bk. 4, Fifty Carols for Sopranos & Altos. David Willcocks & John Rutter. (Orig.). 1980. pap. 16.95 (*0-19-353573-4*) OUP.

Carols for Choirs: Fifty Carols, Bk. 3. Ed. by David Willcocks. 1978. pap. text ed. 13.95 (*0-19-353570-X*) OUP.

Carols for Choirs: Fifty Carols for Christmas & Advent. Ed. by David Willcocks & John Ruttner. 1972. pap. 13.95 (*0-19-353565-3*) OUP.

Carols for Choirs: Fifty Christmas Carols, Bk. 1. Reginald Jacques & David Willcocks. (YA). (gr. 9 up). 1968. pap. 11.95 (*0-19-353222-0*) OUP.

Carols for Christmas. Ed. by David Willcocks. (Illus.). 96p. 1983. 27.00 (*0-8050-1235-4*) H Holt & Co.

Carols for Keyboard. Contrib by John Innes. 1980. 7.95 (*0-685-68555-1*, BCMC-255) Lillenas.

*__Carol's Kitchen.__ Carol J. Moore. (Illus.). 421p. (Orig.). 1993. ring bd. 27.00 (*0-9645003-0-2*) C J Moore.

*__Carols of Christmas.__ Ideals Publications Staff. 1994. 22.95 (*0-8249-4054-7*) Ideals.

Carols of Christmas. Rod McKuen. 1971. 3.95 (*0-394-47420-1*) Random.

Carols of Cornwall. Kenneth Pelmear. (C). 1989. 40.00 (*0-907566-22-7*, Pub. by Dyllansow Truran UK) St Mut.

Carols of the British Isles. Date not set. 6.95 (*1-56222-896-X*, 95038); audio 9.98 (*1-56222-912-5*, 95038C) Mel Bay.

Carols of Thomas Merritt. Dyllansow Truran Staff. (C). 1989. 40.00 (*0-9506431-7-3*, Pub. by Dyllansow Truran UK) St Mut.

Carols, Their Origin, Music, & Connection with Mystery-Plays: A Greenwood Archival Edition. William J. Phillips. LC 75-109821. (Illus.). 134p. 1971. reprint ed. text ed. 45.50 (*0-8371-4312-8*, PHCA, Greenwood Pr) Greenwood.

Carols to Sing, Clap & Play: A Companion to the Soprano Recorder Tuition Books. Heather Cox & Garth Rickard. (Illus.). 48p. 1984. pap. 6.50 (*0-918812-36-4*) MMB Music.

Carols We Play & Sing, Bk. 1. Contrib by Myra Schubert. 1989. 4.50 (*0-685-68320-6*, MC-272) Lillenas.

Carols We Play & Sing, Bk. 2. Myra Schubert. 1989. 4.50 (*0-685-71341-5*, MC-273) Lillenas.

Carolyn & Jack Farris Collection: Selected Contemporary Works. Robert McDonald. LC 82-81520. (Illus.). 68p. 1982. 13.50 (*0-934418-13-6*) Mus Contemp Art.

*__Carolyn G. Hart Presents Malice Domestic No. 4.__ Ed. by Greenberg. (Illus.). (J). 1995. mass mkt. 5.50 (*0-671-89631-8*) PB.

Carolyn Graham Turn-of-the-Century Songbook. Carolyn Graham. (Illus.). 95p. (gr. 7-12). 1987. pap. text ed. write for info. (*0-13-115189-4*, 21129); 12.00 (*0-685-05726-7*, 40143) Prentice ESL.

Carolyn Taylor's Home Haircuts & Styles for Men & Boys. Carolyn Taylor. (Illus.). 96p. pap. 9.95 (*0-9620272-2-7*, AE2) Anderson ID.

Carolyn Taylor's Home Haircuts & Styles for Women & Girls. Carolyn Taylor. (Illus.). 128p. pap. 12.95 (*0-9620272-1-9*, AE1) Anderson ID.

Carolyn Wyeth: A Retrospective Exhibition. Norton, R. W., Art Gallery Staff. LC 75-43579. (Contemporary Realists Ser.). (Illus.). 1976. pap. 2.50 (*0-913060-08-9*) Norton Art.

Carolyn's Mystery Dolls. Francine Pascal. (Sweet Valley Kids Ser.: No. 17). (J). (gr. 4-7). 1991. pap. 2.99 (*0-553-15870-8*) Bantam.

Carolyn's Revenge. large type ed. Flora Sinclair. (Linford Romance Library). 320p. 1987. pap. 11.95 (*0-7089-6449-4*, Linford) Ulverscroft.

Caron-Nadeau Family History: 1612-1986. Joanne L. Brooks. (Illus.). 380p. 1987. lib. bdg. 45.00 (*0-941216-35-7*); pap. 30.00 (*0-941216-36-5*) Cay-Bel.

Caron, Phillipe De: Oeuvres Completes, Pt. 1. Ed. by James Thomson. (Gesamtausgaben - Collected Works Ser.: Vol. VI). 120p. (ENG & GER.). 1970. lib. bdg. 4.00 (*0-912024-66-6*) Inst Mediaeval Mus.

Caron, Phillipe De: Oeuvres Completes, Pt. 2. Ed. by James Thomson. (Gesamtausgaben - Collected Works Ser.: Vol. VI). 130p. (ENG & GER.). 1970. lib. bdg. 4.00 (*0-912024-67-4*) Inst Mediaeval Mus.

Caro's Fundamental Secrets of Poker. Mike Caro. (Illus.). (Orig.). 1991. pap. 12.95 (*1-880069-00-8*) Mad Genius.

*__Caro's Fundamental Secrets of Winning Poker.__ 3rd ed. Mike Caro. LC 95-68284. (Illus.). 160p. 1995. pap. 9.95 (*0-940685-57-4*) Cardoza Pub.

Carotenoid As Colorants & Vitamin A Precursors: Technological & Nutritional Applications. Ed. by Jack C. Bauerfeind. LC 80-984. (Food Science & Technology Ser.). 1981. text ed. 174.00 (*0-12-082850-2*) Acad Pr.

Carotenoids: Chemistry & Biology. Ed. by N. I. Krinsky et al. (Illus.). 390p. 1989. 95.00 (*0-306-43607-8*, Plenum Pr) Plenum.

*__Carotenoids: Volumes 1A & Volumes 1B & "Key to Carotenoids", 3 vols.__ Ed. by G. Britton et al. 1995. text ed. 234.00 (*0-8176-2936-X*) Birkhauser.

*__Carotenoids: Volumes 1A & 1B, 2 vols.__ Incl. Carotenoids Vols. 1A & 1B: Isolation & Analysis; Spectroscopy. Ed. by G. Britton et al. LC 94-40358. (Illus.). 368p. 1994. text ed. 109.00 (*0-8176-2908-4*); Carotenoids Vol. 1B: Spectroscopy. Ed. by G. Britton et al. (Illus.). 384p. 1994. text ed. 109.00 (*0-8176-2909-2*); 179.00 (*0-8176-2910-6*) Birkhauser.

*__Carotenoids Vols. 1A & 1B: Isolation & Analysis; Spectroscopy.__ Ed. by G. Britton et al. LC 94-40358. (Carotenoids). (Illus.). 368p. 1994. text ed. 109.00 (*0-8176-2908-4*) Birkhauser.

Carotenoids Chemistry & Biochemistry: Proceedings of the International Symposium on Carotenoids, 6th, Liverpool, U. K., July 26-31, 1981. International Symposium on Carotenoids Staff. Ed. by T. W. Goodwin & G. Britton. (IUPAC Symposium Ser.). (Illus.). 320p. 1982. 164.00 (*0-08-026224-4*, E115, Pub. by Pergamon Repr UK) Franklin.

Carotenoids Five: Proceedings of the International Symposium on Carotenoids, 5th, Madison, U. S. A., July 23-28, 1978. International Symposium on Carotenoids Staff. Ed. by T. W. Goodwin. (IUPAC Symposium Ser.). (Illus.). 1979. 367.00 (*0-08-022359-1*, Pub. by Pergamon Repr UK) Franklin.

Carotenoids-Four: Proceedings. Ed. by Basil C. Weedon et al. 1976. 68.00 (*0-08-020974-2*, Pub. by Pergamon Repr UK) Franklin.

Carotenoids in Human Health. Ed. by Louise M. Canfield et al. LC 93-43193. (Annals Ser.: Vol. 691). 300p. 1993. 80.00 (*0-89766-827-8*); pap. write for info. (*0-89766-828-6*) NY Acad Sci.

Carotenoids Other Than Vitamin A 2: International Symposium on Carotenoids Other Than Vitamin A, Las Cruces, NM 5-69. IUPAC Staff & New Mexico State University Staff. (International Union of Pure & Applied Chemistry Ser.). 1969. 62.00 (*0-08-020731-6*, Pub. by Pergamon Repr UK) Franklin.

Carotid & the Eye. Ed. by Ramon Berguer & Harold Weiss. LC 85-6336. 238p. 1985. text ed. 49.95 (*0-275-91332-5*, C1332, Praeger Pubs) Greenwood.

Carotid Artery Disease. Larry J. Robson & Dorothy W. Bouwman. Ed. by Dorothy W. Bouwman & Oliver D. Grin. (Patient Education Ser.). (Illus.). 26p. (Orig.). 1990. pap. text ed. 3.00 (*0-929689-39-9*) Ludann Co.

Carotid Artery Plaques. Ed. by M. Hennerici et al. viii, 200p. 1988. 64.00 (*3-8055-4715-3*) S Karger.

Carotid Endarterectomy: Principles & Technique. Christopher Loftus. 1995. 130.00 (*0-942219-69-4*) Quality Med Pub.

Carotte. Illus. by Gilbert Houbre. (Gallimard - Mes Premieres Decouvertes Ser.: No. 4). (FRE.). (J). (ps-1). 1989. 13.95 (*2-07-035711-2*) Schoenhof.

Carotte et le Baton. Michel Deon. 384p. (FRE.). 1983. pap. 12.95 (*0-7859-1975-9*, 2070374718) Fr & Eur.

Carousel. (Vocal Score Ser.). 1987. pap. 35.00 (*0-7935-0809-6*, 01121001) H Leonard.

Carousel. 1992. pap. 4.95 (*1-56333-051-2*) Masquerade.

Carousel. Donald Crews. LC 82-3062. (Illus.). 32p. (J). (ps-1). 1982. lib. bdg. 15.93 (*0-688-00909-3*) Greenwillow.

Carousel. Linda Crockett. 512p. 1995. pap. 5.99 (*0-8125-0830-0*) Forge NYC.

Carousel. Pat Cummings. LC 93-8708. (Illus.). 32p. (J). (ps-3). 1994. text ed. 14.95 (*0-02-725512-3*, Bradbury S&S) S&S Childrens.

An Asterisk (*) at the beginning of an entry indicates that the title is appearing in BIP for the first time.

Carousel. J. Robert Janes. LC 92-54978. 1993. 20.00 (*1-55611-357-9*) D I Fine.

Carousel. Sonja Massie. 1990. mass mkt. 4.50 (*1-55817-363-3*, Pinnacle NY) Windsor NY.

Carousel. Judy Miller. (Illus.). 68p. (Orig.). 1990. pap. 7.16 (*0-912833-13-0*) J Miller Pubns.

Carousel. Rosamunde Pilcher. 1991. mass mkt. 4.99 (*0-312-92629-4*) St Martin.

***Carousel.** Belva Plain. 1995. 23.95 (*0-385-31107-9*) Delacorte.

Carousel. Liz Rosenberg. LC 94-7332. (J). 1995. 15.95 (*0-399-22704-0*, Philomel Bks) Putnam Pub Group.

***Carousel.** Liz Rosenberg. LC 94-47323. (Illus.). (J). 1995. 14.00 (*0-15-200853-5*) HarBrace.

Carousel. Daniel Vian. 1988. pap. 4.50 (*0-929654-00-5*) Blue Moon Bks.

Carousel. large type ed. Rosamunde Pilcher. LC 91-31107. 233p. 1992. reprint ed. lib. bdg. 19.95 (*1-56054-148-2*) Thorndike Pr.

***Carousel.** large type ed. Belva Plain. LC 95-2475. 436p. Date not set. pap. 19.95 (*0-7838-1117-9*, Large Print Bks) Hall.

***Carousel.** large type ed. Belva Plain. LC 95-2475. 436p. 1995. 25.95 (*0-7838-1116-0*, Large Print Bks) Hall.

Carousel: Vocal Selections from the Show. rev. ed. Rodgers & Hammerstein. (Illus.). 56p. 1989. pap. 8.95 (*0-88188-636-X*, 01121008) H Leonard.

Carousel Animal. Tobin Fraley. (Illus.). 128p. 1983. 24.95 (*0-913751-00-6*) Zephyr CA.

Carousel Animal. Tobin Fraley. (Illus.). 128p. 1987. reprint ed. 24.95 (*0-87701-460-4*); reprint ed. pap. 14.95 (*0-87701-454-X*) Chronicle Bks.

Carousel Animals Cut & Use Stencils: 44 Full-Size Stencils Printed on Durable Stencil Paper. Celeste Plowden. (Illus.). 64p. (Orig.). pap. 4.95 (*0-486-26889-6*) Dover.

Carousel Animals Iron-on Transfer Patterns. Celeste Plowden. (Transfer Patterns Ser.). (Illus.). 48p. (Orig.). 1991. pap. text ed. 2.95 (*0-486-26653-2*) Dover.

Carousel Coloring Book. Sue Hegarty & Judy Geoghegan. (Illus.). 32p. (Orig.). (J). (gr. k-8). 1989. pap. 4.50 (*0-9622526-1-1*) Freels Fndtn.

Carousel Elephant. Illus. by Frank Stinga. (Carousel Fantasy Ser.). 12p. (J). (ps). Date not set. 4.95 (*1-56828-066-1*) Red Jacket Pr.

Carousel Fantasy Gift Box & Mobile, 3 bks., Set. Illus. by Frank Stinga. 36p. (J). (ps). Date not set. bds. 13.95 (*1-56828-067-X*) Red Jacket Pr.

Carousel, for SATB recorders. Leonie Jenkins. (Contemporary Consort Ser.: No. 2). 15p. 1989. 9.00 (*1-56571-007-X*) PRB Prods.

Carousel Horse. Illus. by Frank Stinga. (Carousel Fantasy Ser.). 12p. (J). (ps). Date not set. 4.95 (*1-56828-065-3*) Red Jacket Pr.

Carousel Horses in Cross-Stitch: Beautiful Projects for Every Month of the Year. Donna Kooler. LC 92-38558. (Illus.). 128p. 1993. 24.95 (*0-8069-8836-3*) Sterling.

Carousel Horses in Cross-Stitch: Beautiful Projects for Every Month of the Year. Donna Kooler. LC 92-38558. (Illus.). 128p. 1994. pap. 14.95 (*0-8069-8837-1*, Chapelle) Sterling.

Carousel Lion. Illus. by Frank Stinga. (Carousel Fantasy Ser.). 12p. (J). (ps). Date not set. 4.95 (*1-56828-064-5*) Red Jacket Pr.

Carousel of Countries: Games, Songs, Recipes & Customs from Around the World. Mary K. Branson. (Illus.). 96p. (Orig.). (J). (gr. 1-6). 1986. pap. 5.95 (*0-936625-53-8*, New Hope AL) Womans Mission Union.

Carousel of Hearts. Mary J. Putney. (Regency Romance Ser.). 224p. 1989. pap. 3.99 (*0-451-16267-6*, Sig) NAL-Dutton.

Carousel of Limericks. Harvey N. Roehl. LC 85-22538. (Illus.). 60p. (Orig.). (J). (gr. 4-8). 1986. pap. 7.95 (*0-911572-47-3*) Vestal.

Carousel of Poetry. Alyce Lunsford. LC 85-50265. 94p. 1985. 7.95 (*0-938232-81-9*, Baker & Taylor) Winston-Derek.

Carousel of Stories. Priscilla L. McQueen. (Basic Readers Ser.). 1970. 10.98 (*0-917186-13-3*); student ed 7.53 (*0-917186-14-1*) McQueen.

Carousel Round & Round. Kay Chorao. LC 93-35520. (J). 1995. 14.95 (*0-395-63632-9*, Clarion Bks) HM.

Carousels: The Myth, the Magic, & the Memories. Tobin Fraley. 80p. 1991. write for info. (*0-9624693-2-7*) Willitts Designs.

Carovane du Caire Andre Gretry see Chefs-d'Oeuvres Classiques de l'Opera Francais

Carp. Konstantine Fedin. Ed. by G. A. Birkett. LC 66-25020. (RUS.). (C). 1966. pap. text ed. 2.75 (*0-89197-487-3*) Irvington.

***CARP: User's Guide & Introduction to Authoring Tutorials.** J. Scott Magruder. 119p. 1991. pap. text ed. 50.00 (*0-933179-07-3*) Bus Account Pubns.

Carp & Pond Fish Culture: Including Chinese Herbivorous Species, Pike, Tench, Zander, Wels Catfish, & Goldfish. Laszlo Horvath et al. LC 92-25308. 204p. 1992. text ed. 84.95 (*0-470-21969-6*) Halsted Pr.

Carp Are Gamefish. George Von Schrader. (Illus.). 119p. 1990. pap. 12.50 (*0-9618491-0-X*) Gil Finn Bks.

***Carp Challenge.** John Bailey. (Illus.). 160p. 1995. 39.95 (*1-85223-789-9*, Pub. by Crowood Pr UK) Trafalgar.

Carp Fishing: Expert Advice for Beginners. Tony Miles. (Fishing Facts Ser.). (Illus.). 96p. 1992. pap. 13.95 (*1-85223-474-1*, Pub. by Crowood Pr UK) Trafalgar.

Carp for Kimiko. Virginia L. Kroll. LC 93-6940. (Illus.). 32p. (J). 1993. 14.95 (*0-88106-412-2*); lib. bdg. 15.88 (*0-88106-413-0*) Charlesbridge Pub.

Carp in North America. Ed. by E. L. Cooper. LC 87-71550. 84p. 1987. pap. 10.50 (*0-913235-44-X*) Am Fisheries Soc.

Carp in the Bathtub. Barbara Cohen. LC 87-80446. 32p. (J). (gr. k-5). 1987. pap. 4.95 (*0-930494-67-9*) Kar Ben.

Carp in the Bathtub. Barbara Cohen. (Illus.). 48p. (J). (gr. 1-5). 1972. lib. bdg. 14.93 (*0-688-51627-0*) Lothrop.

CARP Recommended Practice for Pressurized Highway Tankers Made of Fiberglass Reinforced Plastic with Balsa Cores. (Illus.). 24p. 1993. pap. text ed. 35.00 (*0-931403-22-7*, 754) Am Soc Nondestructive.

***Carpaccio.** Vittorio Sgarbi. LC 94-39743. (Illus.). 272p. (ENG & ITA.). 1995. 95.00 (*0-7892-0000-7*) Abbeville Pr.

Carpaccio. Francesco Valcanover. Tr. by Lisa Pelleti. (Library of Great Masters). (Illus.). 80p. (Orig.). 1989. pap. 12.99 (*1-878351-06-0*) Riverside NY.

Carpal Bones. Margaret Aho. 40p. (Orig.). 1993. pap. text ed. 15.00 (*0-931659-13-2*) Limberlost Pr.

Carpal Injuries: Anatomy, Radiology, Current Treatment. P. Saffar. (Illus.). 208p. 1991. 161.00 (*0-387-59534-1*) Spr-Verlag.

***Carpal Tunnel Syndrome.** Montgomery. 1995. 10.95 (*1-880688-03-4*) New Life Opt.

Carpal Tunnel Syndrome: How to Relieve - Prevent Wrist "Burn Out" Rosemarie A. Atencio. LC 93-79066. 128p. 1994. pap. 13.95 (*0-9637360-1-9*) HWD Pub.

Carpal Tunnel Syndrome: Prevention & Treatment. Kate Montgomery. Ed. by Diane Gage. (Illus.). 80p. (Orig.). 1992. Wkbk. student ed 14.95 (*1-878069-03-9*) Sports Touch.

***Carpal Tunnel Syndrome: Prevention & Treatment. 3rd rev. ed. Kate Montgomery. Ed. by Diane Gage. (Illus.). 80p. (Orig.). 1994. pap. 16.95 (*1-878069-35-7*) Sports Touch. CARPAL TUNNEL SYNDROME/ PREVENTION & TREATMENT. Fully illustrated with graphics & photographs...easy to read & follow! This book introduces a series of quick & easy techniques to correct, strengthen & prevent Carpal Tunnel Syndrome. Using these simple steps, you can change the structural misalignment that causes the entrapment & compression of the median nerve in the elbow & wrist. The program consists of correct posture, acupressure, self-massage, stretching & strengthening exercises to restore over-worked, over- strained & sore muscles to their original pain-free state. Alleviating stress & tension on the elbow & wrist joints. The only self-help manual of its kind that teaches specific corrective exercises. This is a NON-SURGICAL, DRUG-FREE APPROACH! "I found her method safe, cost effective & eliminates the need for surgical intervention in most cases. The exercises are simple & easy-to-do, with minimal amount of instruction. The corrective techniques are designed to be done anywhere. It is an answer to decreasing the workers compensation problem & getting employees back to work with minimal or no work time lost. I highly recommend this program."-- Warren Jacobs, MD. Sports Touch (R) Publishing, P.O. Box 221074, San Diego, CA 92192-1074. FAX: (619) 455-5039.** *Publisher Provided Annotation.*

Carpal Tunnel Syndrome: Prevention, Treatment & Hand Exercises. 1992. lib. bdg. 250.95 (*0-8490-5610-1*) Gordon Pr.

***Carpal Tunnel Syndrome - Causes, Symptoms, Diagnosis, Treatments & Surgery: Index of New Information Including Complications.** American Health Research Institute Staff. (Illus.). 170p. 1995. 44.50 (*0-7883-0350-3*); pap. 37.50 (*0-7883-0351-1*) ABBE Pubs Assn.

Carpal Tunnel Syndrome & Its Cure. 1994. lib. bdg. 250.95 (*0-8490-5663-2*) Gordon Pr.

Carpal Tunnel Syndrome & Other Disorders of the Median Nerve. Richard B. Rosenbaum & Jose L. Ochoa. 1992. text ed. 95.00 (*0-7506-9229-4*) Buttrwrth-Heinemann.

Carpal Tunnel Syndrome & Overuse Injuries: Prevention, Treatment & Recovery. Tammy Crouch & Michael Madden. (Illus.). 90p. (Orig.). 1992. pap. 9.95 (*1-55643-135-X*) North Atlantic.

Carpal Tunnel Syndrome Book: Preventing & Treating CTS. Mark A. Pinsky. Orig. Title: Tendinitis & Related Cumulative Trauma Disorders. (Illus.). 224p. (Orig.). 1993. mass mkt. 5.99 (*0-446-36527-0*) Warner Bks.

Carpathians. Janet Frame. LC 92-35601. 1993. 11.95 (*0-8076-1298-7*) Braziller.

Carpatho-Rusyn Americans. Paul R. Magocsi. (Peoples of North America Ser.). (Illus.). 112p. (YA). (gr. 5 up). 1990. 17.95 (*0-87754-866-8*) Chelsea Hse.

***Carpe Diem.** Campolo. 1995. pap. text ed. (*0-8499-3680-2*) Word Inc.

Carpe Diem. Edward F. Madden. 204p. 1993. pap. text ed. 9.95 (*0-86720-782-5*) Jones & Bartlett.

***Carpe Diem: Odes I.** Horace. Tr. & Comment by David West. 224p. 1995. 45.00 (*0-19-872160-9*); pap. 15.95 (*0-19-872161-7*) OUP.

Carpe Diem: Seize the Day. Tony Campolo. 1994. 16.99 (*0-8499-1008-0*) Word Inc.

***Carpe Diem: Seize the Day: A Little Book of Latin Phrases.** Sean McMahon. (Illus.). 1995. text ed. 7.95 (*0-8118-0931-5*) Chronicle Bks.

Carpentaria Moon. large type ed. Kerry Allyne. 269p. 1993. 21.95 (*0-7505-0441-2*, Pub. by Magna Print Bks) Ulverscroft.

Carpenter. Douglas Florian. LC 90-30752. (Illus.). 24p. (J). (ps up). 1991. 13.95 (*0-688-09760-X*); lib. bdg. 13.88 (*0-688-09761-8*) Greenwillow.

Carpenter. Jack Rudman. (Career Examination Ser.: C-126). 1994. pap. 23.95 (*0-8373-0126-2*) Nat Learn.

Carpenter: A Personal Look at Jesus. Kenneth J. Holland & Ken McFarland. (Illus.). 54p. (Orig.). 1992. 3.95 (*0-945460-15-5*) Upward Way.

Carpenter Center, United Habitation, Firminy, & Other Buildings & Projects. Brooks. (Le Corbusier Archieve Ser.). 1984. lib. bdg. 260.00 (*0-8240-5080-0*) Garland.

Carpenter from Conway: George Washington Donaghey As Governor of Arkansas, 1909-1913. Calvin R. Ledbetter, Jr. LC 92-19853. (Illus.). 320p. 1993. pap. 12.00 (*1-55728-374-5*) U of Ark Pr.

Carpenter Handbook. 1991. lib. bdg. 250.00 (*0-8490-4119-8*) Gordon Pr.

Carpenter-Wier Family of Upper South Carolina & Other Ancestors, Including Benson, Beryy, Blassingame, Caldwell, Maxwell, Richey, Sloan, Stewart, Wilson. Henry B. McCoy. (Illus.). 326p. 1993. reprint ed. lib. bdg. 61.00 (*0-8328-3109-3*); reprint ed. pap. 51.00 (*0-8328-3110-7*) Higginson Bk Co.

Carpentered Hen. John Updike. LC 81-48133. 112p. 1982. 16.45 (*0-394-52394-6*) Knopf.

Carpenters. Steve Tesich. 1971. pap. 4.75 (*0-8222-0186-0*) Dramatists Play.

Carpenters: Karen & Richard's Untold Story. Ray Coleman. (Illus.). 352p. 1994. 22.00 (*0-06-018345-4*, HarpT) HarpC.

***Carpenters: The Untold Story.** Ray Coleman. 352p. 1995. pap. 12.00 (*0-06-092586-8*, PL) HarpC.

Carpenters & Builders Library. John E. Ball. 1986. 47.95 (*0-02-506450-9*) Macmillan.

Carpenters & Builders Library, 4 vols. rev. ed. John E. Ball & John Leeke. 1991. write for info. (*0-318-68344-X*, Audel) Macmillan.

Carpenters & Builders Library, Set: Vol. 1-4. 5th ed. John E. Ball. LC 82-133279. 1983. Set. 43.95 (*0-672-23369-X*) Macmillan.

Carpenters & Builders Library, Vol. 1. 5th ed. John E. Ball. 1984. 11.95 (*0-672-23365-7*, Audel) Macmillan.

Carpenters & Builders Library, 4 vols., Vol. 1: Tools, Steel Square, Joinery. 6th rev. ed. John E. Ball & John Leeke. 374p. 1991. text ed. 21.95 (*0-02-506451-7*, Audel) Macmillan.

Carpenters & Builders Library, Vol. 2. 5th ed. John E. Ball. 1984. 11.95 (*0-672-23366-5*, Audel) Macmillan.

Carpenters & Builders Library, 4 vols., Vol. 2: Builder's Math, Plans, Specifications. 6th rev. ed. John E. Ball & John Leeke. 292p. 1991. text ed. 21.95 (*0-02-506452-5*, Audel) Macmillan.

Carpenters & Builders Library, Vol. 3. 5th ed. John E. Ball. 1984. 11.95 (*0-672-23367-3*, Audel) Macmillan.

Carpenters & Builders Library, 4 vols., Vol. 3: Layouts, Foundations, Framing. 6th rev. ed. John E. Ball & John Leeke. 262p. 1991. text ed. 21.95 (*0-02-506453-3*, Audel) Macmillan.

Carpenters & Builders Library, Vol. 4. 5th ed. John E. Ball. 1984. 11.95 (*0-672-23368-1*, Audel) Macmillan.

Carpenters & Builders Library, 4 vols., Vol. 4: Millwork, Power Tools, Painting. 6th rev. ed. John E. Ball & John Leeke. 336p. 1991. text ed. 21.95 (*0-02-506454-1*, Audel) Macmillan.

Carpenters & Building Construction 1981. rev. ed. John L. Feirer. 1985. 34.64 (*0-02-662890-2*) Macmillan.

Carpenters & Building S G. Feiner. 1986. pap. 9.32 (*0-02-662900-3*) Macmillan.

Carpenter's Assistant. James Newland. 1990. 19.99 (*0-517-03303-8*) Random Hse Value.

Carpenter's Battery. C. A. Fonderon. 88p. 1911. reprint ed. 20.00 (*0-913419-02-8*, J M C & Co) Amereon Ltd.

***Carpenter's Child.** Betty L. Schwab. 1995. pap. write for info. (*0-7880-0570-7*) CSS OH.

Carpenters' Company Seventeen Eighty-Six Rule Book. Intro. by Charles E. Peterson. (Illus.). 158p. reprint ed. 14.95 (*1-879335-28-X*) Astragal Pr.

Carpenter's Gothic. William Gaddis. 262p. 1986. mass mkt. 12.95 (*0-14-008993-4*, Penguin Bks) Viking Penguin.

Carpenter's Lady. Barbara Delinsky. 1993. mass mkt. 4.99 (*0-06-104231-5*, Harp PBks) HarpC.

Carpenter's Manifesto. rev. ed. Jefferey Ehrlich & Marc Mannheimer. (Illus.). 320p. 1990. pap. 19.95 (*0-8050-1299-0*, Owl) H Holt & Co.

Carpenters of Light: Some Contemporary English Poets. Neil Powell. LC 79-54320. 154p. 1980. text ed. 38.00 (*0-06-495665-2*, N6785) B&N Imports.

Carpenters Rule to Measure Ordinarie Timber. Richard More. LC 74-26026. (English Experience Ser.: No. 252). 56p. 1970. reprint ed. 8.00 (*90-221-0252-1*) Walter J Johnson.

Carpenter's Shopping Center Management: Principles & Practices. 3rd ed. Intro. by Robert J. Flynn. 208p. 1984. 59.95 (*0-913598-23-2*, 553); 49.95 (*0-685-68037-1*) Intl Coun Shop.

Carpenter's Slide Rule: Its History & Use. Ed. by Kenneth D. Roberts. 32p. (Orig.). 1982. pap. text ed. 4.00 (*1-879335-16-6*) Astragal Pr.

***Carpenter's Son.** Brenton Yorgason. 1994. pap. 7.95 (*1-55503-765-8*) Covenant Comms.

Carpenter's Son: But Who Do You Say That I Am? (Sermons) Carlyle Marney. 96p. 1984. reprint ed. pap. 6.95 (*0-913029-02-5*) Stevens Bk Pr.

Carpenter's Toolbox Manual. Gary D. Meyers. (On-the-Job Reference Ser.). 352p. 1989. pap. 10.95 (*0-13-115296-3*) P-H.

Carpenter's Tools: 12 Contemporary Monologues on the Disciples. Jerry Cohagan. 1994. 8.50 (*0-8341-9059-1*, MP-700) Lillenas.

Carpentier-Edwards Pericardial Bioprosthesis Mini-Symposium. Ed. & Illus. by Silent Partners, Inc. Staff. 133p. (Orig.). 1989. pap. write for info. (*1-878353-00-4*) Silent Partners.

Carpentier's Proustian Fiction. Sally Harvey. (Series A: Monagrafias: No. 158). 144p. (C). 1994. text ed. 53.00 (*1-85566-034-2*, Pub. by Tamesis Bks Ltd UK) Boydell & Brewer.

Carpentry. Gaspar Lewis. LC 83-71049. 544p. 1984. teacher ed 10.00 (*0-8273-1801-4*); 10.95 (*0-8273-1808-1*); text ed. 38.95 (*0-8273-1800-6*) Delmar.

Carpentry. Gasper Lewis. LC 83-71049. (Illus.). 576p. 1988. 21.95 (*0-8069-6752-8*) Sterling.

Carpentry. Jack Rudman. (Occupational Competency Examination Ser.: OCE-10). 1994. pap. 23.95 (*0-8373-5710-1*) Nat Learn.

Carpentry. 2nd ed. L. Koel. (Illus.). 721p. 1991. 34.96 (*0-8269-0732-6*) Am Technical.

***Carpentry.** 2nd ed. Lewis. 48p. 1995. teacher ed, pap. text ed. 14.95 (*0-8273-7029-6*) Delmar.

Carpentry. 2nd ed. Gaspar Lewis. LC 94-8421. (Illus.). 800p. 1995. 38.95 (*0-8273-5979-9*) Delmar.

Carpentry. Gaspar Lewis. LC 83-71049. (Illus.). 566p. (C). 1991. reprint ed. lib. bdg. 47.00x (*0-8095-7600-7*) Borgo Pr.

Carpentry: Framing & Finishing. Byron W. Maguire. 352p. 1989. boxed 43.00 (*0-13-115494-X*) P-H.

Carpentry: Remodeling. Cy DeCosse Incorporated Staff. LC 92-16327. (Black & Decker Home Improvement Library). 128p. 1992. 14.95 (*0-86573-720-7*); pap. 12.95 (*0-86573-721-5*) Cy De Cosse.

Carpentry: Tools, Shelves, Walls, Doors. Cy De Cosse Incorporated Staff. LC 88-23718. (Black & Decker Home Improvement Library). (Illus.). 128p. 1989. 14.95 (*0-86573-704-5*); pap. 12.95 (*0-86573-705-3*) Cy De Cosse.

Carpentry & Building Construction. John L. Feirer. 1992. 43.96 (*0-02-668278-8*) Macmillan.

Carpentry & Building Construction. rev. ed. John L. Feirer & Gilbert R. Hutchings. (C). teacher ed 6.64 (*0-02-662930-5*); student ed 2.00 (*0-02-667820-9*); text ed. 30.60 (*0-02-667390-8*); student ed 7.92 (*0-02-667830-6*) Bennett IL.

Carpentry & Building Construction. rev. ed. John L. Feirer & Gilbert R. Hutchings. (Illus.). 1981. 44.50 (*0-684-16981-9*, Scribners) S&S Trade.

Carpentry & Building Construction. 3rd ed. John L. Feirer. 1986. text ed. 50.00 (*0-02-537360-9*) Macmillan.

Carpentry & Building Construction: Si Metric Edition. John L. Feirer et al. text ed. 31.80 (*0-02-662940-2*) Bennett IL.

Carpentry & Building in Late Imperial China: A Study of the Fifteenth-Century Carpenter's Manual Lu Ban Jing. K. Ruitenbeek. (Sinica Leidensia Ser.: No. 23). 500p. 1992. 120.00 (*90-04-09258-7*) E J Brill.

Carpentry & Construction. 2nd ed. Rex Miller & Glenn E. Baker. 1991. text ed. 42.95 (*0-07-157669-X*); pap. text ed. 34.95 (*0-07-157668-1*) McGraw.

Carpentry & Construction. 2nd ed. Rex Miller & Glenn E. Baker. (Illus.). 656p. 1991. 42.95 (*0-8306-8678-9*, 3678); pap. 29.95 (*0-8306-3678-1*) TAB Bks.

Carpentry & Exterior Finish: Some Tricks of the Trade. 3rd ed. Bob Syvanen. LC 93-2371. (Home Builder's Library). (Illus.). 112p. 1993. pap. 12.95 (*1-56440-078-6*) Globe Pequot.

Carpentry & Interior Finish: More Tricks of the Trade from an Old-Style Carpenter. 2nd ed. Bob Syvanen. LC 93-8771. (Home Builder's Library). (Illus.). 128p. (Orig.). 1995. pap. 12.95 (*1-56440-251-7*) Globe Pequot.

Carpentry & Joinery. Peter Brett. (Illus.). 128p. 1993. pap. 27.50 (*0-7487-1298-4*, Pub. by Stanley Thornes UK) Trans-Atl Phila.

Carpentry & Joinery. T. Goodard & S. Schoen. (Equipment Planning Guide for Vocational & Technical Training & Education Programmes Ser.: No. 8). v, 134p. 1982. 32.00 (*92-2-102930-1*) Intl Labour Office.

Carpentry & Joinery, Vol. 1. Ed. by B. Bayliss. (C). 1969. 80.00 (*0-7487-0292-X*, Pub. by S Thornes Pubs UK) St Mut.

Carpentry & Joinery, Vol. 1. Peter Brett. 196p. (C). 1981. 30.00x (*0-7487-0287-3*, Pub. by S Thornes Pubs UK) St Mut.

Carpentry & Joinery, Vol. 2. Stanley Thornes. (C). 1969. 100.00 (*0-7487-0296-2*, Pub. by S Thornes Pubs UK) St Mut.

Carpentry & Joinery, Vol. 2. Stanley Thornes. (C). 1981. 90.00 (*0-09-144191-9*, Pub. by S Thornes Pubs UK) St Mut.

Carpentry & Joinery, Vol. 3. Stanley Thornes. (C). 1989. 90.00 (*0-09-098671-7*, Pub. by S Thornes Pubs UK) St Mut.

Carpentry & Joinery, Vol. 4. Stanley Thornes. (C). 1989. 90.00 (*0-09-102291-6*, Pub. by S Thornes Pubs UK) St Mut.

Carpentry & Joinery: A Comprehensive Self-Teaching Text in the Fine Art of Carpentry, Complete Home Building Instructions. W. B. Douglas. 25.50 (*0-87559-109-4*) Shalom.

Carpentry & Joinery: A Multi-Questions Course. F. A. Inott. (Illus.). 112p. 1974. 14.95 (*0-8464-0235-1*) Beekman Pubs.

***Carpentry & Joinery for Advanced Craft Students: Purpose Made Joinery.** Peter Brett. 200p. (C). 1985. pap. 39.00x (*0-7487-0297-0*, Pub. by S Thornes Pubs UK) St Mut.

C

Carpentry & Joinery for Advanced Craft Students: Site Practice. 2nd ed. Peter Brett. (Illus.). 200p. (C). 1985. pap. 39.00x (*0-7487-0270-9*, Pub. by S Thornes Pubs UK) St Mut.

***Carpentry & Joinery for Building Craft Students 2.** Peter Brett. 196p. (C). 1981. 30.00x (*0-7487-0301-2*, Pub. by S Thornes Pubs UK) St Mut.

Carpentry & Light Construction. 5th ed. Ronald C. Smith & Ted L. Honkala. 384p. 1993. text ed. 52.00 (*0-13-096579-0*) P-H.

Carpentry & Woodworking. Dick Demske. Ed. by Roundtable Press Staff. LC 83-15094. (Illus.). 160p. (Orig.). 1984. pap. 9.95 (*0-932944-62-0*) Creative Homeowner.

Carpentry Estimating. W. P. Jackson. LC 94-7835. (Orig.). 1994. disk 35.50 (*0-934041-98-9*) Craftsman.

Carpentry for Building Construction. U. S. Department of the Army Staff. 1989. pap. 8.95 (*0-486-26071-2*) Dover.

Carpentry for Children. Lester Walker. LC 82-3469. (Illus.). 208p. 1985. pap. 12.95 (*0-87951-990-8*) Overlook Pr.

Carpentry for Children see Easy Carpentry Projects for Children

Carpentry for Residential Construction. Byron W. Maguire. 400p. (Orig.). 1987. pap. 19.75 (*0-934041-21-0*) Craftsman.

Carpentry Fundamentals. Glenn E. Baker & Rex Miller. (Contemporary Construction Ser.). (Illus.). 512p. (gr. 10-12). 1981. text ed. 35.96 (*0-07-003361-7*) McGraw.

Carpentry in Commercial Construction. Byron W. Maguire. 272p. 1988. reprint ed. pap. 19.00 (*0-934041-33-4*) Craftsman.

Carpentry in Residential Construction. 2nd ed. Stanley Badzinski, Jr. 1980. text ed. 63.00 (*0-13-115238-6*) P-H.

Carpentry Layout. Ken Todd. 240p. (Orig.). 1988. pap. 16.25 (*0-934041-32-6*) Craftsman.

Carpentry Toolmaking: An Instructor's Guide. Aaron Moore. 208p. (Orig.). 1994. pap. 28.50 (*1-85339-196-4*, Pub. by Intermed Tech UK) Women Ink.

***Carpentry Workbook.** Jack Rudman. (Workbook Ser.: No. 3020). 1994. pap. 23.95 (*0-8373-7904-0*) Nat Learn.

***Carpet & Floorcoverings for Your Home.** Stanely Lyons & Renate Beigel. 1995. 8.95 (*1-899163-09-3*) Cimino Pub Grp.

Carpet Cleaners Guide to Increased Sales & Profit. Roy Moore & F. T. Smith. Ed. by William R. Griffin. (Illus.). 38p. 1987. pap. text ed. 25.00 (*0-944352-01-4*) Cleaning Cons.

Carpet Installation. William Thomas. (Illus.). 71p. (C). 1988. lib. bdg. 45.00 (*0-943863-03-1*) Marsh-Wentworth.

Carpet of Blue: An Ex-Cop Takes a Tough Look at America's Drug Problem. Anthony V. Bouza. LC 91-72993. (Illus.). 176p. 1992. 19.95 (*0-925190-20-9*); pap. 12.95 (*0-925190-21-7*) Fairview Press.

Carpet of Dreams. large type ed. Susan Barrie. 310p. 1972. 15.95 (*0-85456-134-X*) Ulverscroft.

Carpet Sahib: A Life of Jim Corbett. Martin Booth. 288p. 1991. pap. 12.95 (*0-19-282859-2*) OUP.

Carpet Selection & Care. 60p. 1982. pap. 3.00 (*0-9609052-2-7*) Clean Mgmt Inst.

Carpet Specifier's Handbook. (Illus.). 91p. 1987. pap. 20.00 (*0-318-35130-7*) Carpet Rug Inst.

Carpet Substrates. Peter Ellis. 221p. (C). 1973. pap. 75.00 (*0-685-46412-1*, Pub. by Textile Institue UK) St Mut.

Carpet Surfaces. H. Pointon. 254p. (C). 1975. pap. 85.00 (*0-685-46411-3*, Pub. by Textile Institue UK) St Mut.

Carpet, Upholstery Cleaning, Carpet Repair. William Thomas. (Illus.). 141p. (C). 1988. lib. bdg. write for info. (*0-943863-02-3*) Marsh-Wentworth.

Carpetbagger: A Novel. Opie Read & Frank Pixley. LC 72-2070. (Black Heritage Library Collection). 1977. reprint ed. 27.95 (*0-8369-9056-0*) Ayer.

Carpetbagger from Vermont: The Autobiography of Marshall Harvey Twitchell. Ed. by Ted Tunnell. LC 88-8225. (Library of Southern Civilization). (Illus.). x, 216p. 1989. text ed. 32.50 (*0-8071-1415-4*) La State U Pr.

***Carpetbaggers.** Harold Robbins. 624p. 1995. 10.95 (*1-56865-130-9*, GuildAmerica) Dblday Bk Music.

***Carpetbaggers.** Harold Robbins. 1993. mass mkt. 5.99 (*0-671-87484-5*) PB.

Carpetbaggers. Harold Robbins. 1993. reprint ed. lib. bdg. 39.95x (*1-56849-141-7*) Buccaneer Bks.

Carpetbaggers: America's Secret War in Europe. rev. ed. Ben Parnell. Ed. by Melissa Roberts. (Illus.). 224p. 1993. 24.95 (*0-89015-592-5*) Sunbelt Media.

Carpetbagger's Crusade: The Life of Albion Winegar Tourgee. Otto H. Olsen. LC 65-13522. (Illus.). 413p. reprint ed. pap. 117.80 (*0-685-23485-1*, 2027900) Bks Demand.

Carpeting Simplified. Donald R. Brann. LC 72-91055. (Illus.). 1980. pap. 7.95 (*0-87733-683-0*) Easi-Bild.

Carpets: Back to Front, Vol. 19, No. 3. Textile Inst. Staff. 76p. (C). 1989. pap. text ed. 84.00 (*1-870812-14-X*, Pub. by Textile Institue UK) St Mut.

Carpets: The Comfort Factor & How Good Is a Carpet in Use? Ed. by Wira Staff. 1977. 30.00 (*0-686-87147-2*) St Mut.

Carpets & Floor Coverings of India. Kamaladevi Chattopadhyay. (Illus.). 71p. 1985. 34.95 (*0-318-36261-9*) Asia Bk Corp.

Carpets & Floor Coverings of India. 2nd rev. ed. Kamaladevi Chattopadhaya. (Illus.). viii, 71p. 1981. text ed. 35.00 (*0-86590-049-3*, Pub. by Taraporevala II) Apt Bks.

***Carpets & Rugs Market U. S. A.** (Orig.). 1995. pap. 995.00 (*0-7605-2085-2*) Rector Pr.

Carpets & Their Dating in Netherlandish Paintings, 1540-1700. Onno Ydema. 208p. 1991. 89.50 (*1-85149-151-1*) Antique Collect.

Carpets from China, Xinjiang & Tibet. Lennart Larsson, Jr. (Illus.). 141p. 1987. 60.00 (*0-87556-748-7*) Saifer.

Carpets from Eastern Turkestan: Known As Khotan, Samarkand & Kansu Carpets. Hans Bidder. Tr. by Grace M. Allen. LC 79-66596. (Illus.). 96p. 1979. reprint ed. 36.00 (*0-317-01331-9*) Wash Intl Assocs.

Carpets from Eastern Turkestan: Known As Khotan, Samarkand & Kansu Carpets. Hans Bidder. Tr. by Grace M. Allen & Gunther Wasmuth. LC 79-66596. (Illus.). 96p. 1979. reprint ed. 36.00 (*0-915036-02-9*) Wash Intl Assocs.

Carpets from Eastern Turkestan Known As Khotan, Samarkand & Kansu Carpets. Hans Bidder. Tr. by Grace M. Allen. LC 76-66596. Orig. Title: Teppiche aus Ost Turkestan Bekannt als Khotan, Samarkand, und KansuTeppiche. (Illus.). 96p. 1979. reprint ed. 36.00 (*0-318-21254-4*) Wash Intl Assocs.

***Carpets of Afghanistan.** R. D. Parsons. (Oriental Rugs Ser.: Vol. 3). 1992. 59.50 (*1-85149-144-9*) Antique Collect.

Carpets of Central Persia. May Beattie. (Illus.). 104p. 1988. pap. 14.95 (*0-905035-17-8*) Interlink Pub.

Carpets of China & Its Border Regions. William Hu & Virgina D. Hyman. LC 82-82969. (Illus.). 300p. 1982. 95.00 (*0-89344-030-2*) Ars Ceramica.

Carpets What's Afoot? Papers from the Textile Insitute's 1989 Floorcovering Group Conference (TIFCON) Textile Institute Staff. 139p. (C). 1989. 195.00 (*0-685-36112-8*, Pub. by Textile Institue UK) St Mut.

Carpinteria - Carpentry: Herramientas Anaqueles-Paredes-Pyertas - Tools, Shelves, Walls, Doors. Cy De Cosses Incorporated Staff. 1993. 14.95 (*0-86573-722-3*) Cy De Cosse.

Carpinteros & Cabinetmakers: Furniture Making in New Mexico, 1600-1900. 2nd ed. Lonn Taylor & Dessa Bokides. (Illus.). 18p. 1989. reprint ed. pap. text ed. 4.95 (*0-89013-146-5*) Museum NM Pr.

Carpool. Mary Cahill. 1993. pap. 3.99 (*0-517-11206-X*) Random Hse Value.

Carpool. Mary Cahill. 1992. reprint ed. mass mkt. 5.99 (*0-449-22198-9*, Crest) Fawcett.

***Carr Creek Legacy.** Don Miller. 1995. 14.95 (*0-533-11186-2*) Vantage.

Carr Family Records, Embracing the Records of the First Family Who Settled in America & Their Descendants, with Branches Who Came at a Later Date. Edson Carr. (Illus.). 540p. 1989. reprint ed. lib. bdg. 78.00 (*0-8328-0370-7*); reprint ed. pap. 68.00 (*0-8328-0371-5*) Higginson Bk Co.

Carrabassett, Sweet William, Was My River. John Judson. (Inland Seas Ser.: No. 2). 1981. 15.00 (*1-55780-082-0*); pap. 10.00 (*1-55780-131-2*) Juniper Pr WI.

Carradine Brand. Margaret Way. 1994. mass mkt. 2.99 (*0-373-03331-1*, 1-03331-5) Harlequin Bks.

Carranza & Mexico. Carlo De Fornaro. 1976. lib. bdg. 59.95 (*0-87968-814-9*) Gordon Pr.

Carrera Panamericana: The Mexican Road Race, 1950-54. Daryl Murphy. LC 92-33694. (Illus.). 160p. 1993. 49.95 (*0-87938-734-3*) Motorbooks Intl.

Carreta. Enrique Amorim. Ed. by Fernando Ainsa. (Latin American Series - Coleccion Archivos). 588p. (SPA.). (C). 1989. pap. 34.95 (*84-00-06882-3*) U of Pittsburgh Pr.

Carreta. B. Traven. LC 93-38262. 276p. 1994. reprint ed. pap. 11.95 (*1-56663-045-2*) I R Dee.

Carreta Made a U-Turn. 2nd ed. Tato Laviera. LC 92-38421. 74p. (Orig.). 1992. pap. 7.00 (*1-55885-064-3*) Arte Publico.

Carrett Collection: Japanese Art. Neil K. Davey & Susan G. Tripp. 326p. 1994. 190.00 (*1-872357-07-5*, Pub. by P Wilson Pubs) Sothebys Pubns.

Carriacou to Grenada. Wilson Ltd. Staff & Imray L. Norie. (C). 1989. 53.00 (*0-685-40384-X*, Pub. by Imray Laurie Norie & Wilson UK) St Mut.

Carriage & Other Traveling Clocks. Derek Roberts. (Illus.). 368p. 1993. 99.99 (*0-88740-454-5*) Schiffer.

Carriage & Wagon: Index of United States Patents, 1790-1910. Susan Green. (State & City Report Ser.). 820p. 1991. pap. text ed. 100.00 (*1-880499-00-2*) S Green PA.

***Carriage by Air.** Trevor Philipson. 1994. boxed 209.00 (*0-406-02136-8*, UK) Butterworth Legal Pubs.

Carriage Clocks: Their History & Development. Charles Allix. (Illus.). 496p. 1974. 89.50 (*0-902028-25-1*) Antique Collect.

Carriage Collection. Museums at Stony Brook Staff. LC 86-12594. (Illus.). 127p. (Orig.). 1986. pap. 8.00 (*0-943924-09-X*) Mus Stony Brook.

Carriage Driving: A Logical Approach Through Dressage Training. Heike Bean & Sarah Blanchard. (Illus.). 256p. 1992. 30.00 (*0-87605-898-5*) Howell Bk.

Carriage of Dangerous Goods by Sea: The Role of the International Maritime Organisation in International Legislation. Cleopatra E. Henry. LC 85-18380. 240p. 1985. text ed. 35.00 (*0-312-12258-6*) St Martin.

Carriage of Goods: Inland Waterways. 169p. 1992. pap. 25.00 (*92-825-9788-1*, CA-74-92-249-3A-C, Pub. by Europ Com) UNIPUB.

Carriage of Goods: Railways, 1989. 158p. 1919. pap. 30.00 (*92-826-2584-2*, CA-70-91-386-3A-C) UNIPUB.

Carriage of Goods: Railways, 1990. 158p. 1992. pap. 35.00 (*92-826-4605-X*, CA-75-92-550-3A-C, Pub. by Europ Com) UNIPUB.

Carriage of Goods: Road, 1988. 136p. 1990. pap. 25.00 (*92-826-1585-5*, CA-58-90-974-9A-C) UNIPUB.

Carriage of Goods: Road, 1989. 136p. 1991. pap. 20.00 (*92-826-2902-3*, CA-71-91-138-3A-C) UNIPUB.

Carriage of Goods: Road, 1990. 136p. 1992. pap. 25.00 (*92-826-4604-1*, CA-75-92-542-3A-C, Pub. by Europ Com) UNIPUB.

Carriage of Goods by Sea. Ed. by Peter K. Kwang. 216p. 1986. 89.00 (*0-409-99515-0*) Butterworth Legal Pubs.

Carriage of Goods by Sea. 2nd ed. John F. Wilson. 512p. (Orig.). 1993. pap. 87.50 (*0-273-60294-2*, Pub. by Pitman Pub Ltd UK) Trans-Atl Phila.

Carriage of Goods by Sea in the Practice of the U. S. S. R. Maritime Arbitration Commission. Wim A. Timmermans. (C). 1990. lib. bdg. 147.00 (*0-7923-0885-9*) Kluwer Ac.

Carriage of Goods by Sea, Payne & Ivamys. E. R. Ivamy. (C). 1989. 800.00 (*0-685-33784-7*, Pub. by Witherby & Co UK) St Mut.

***Carriage Stone.** Sigbjorn Holmebakk. Tr. by Frances Vardamis. 192p. 1995. 25.00 (*0-8023-1305-1*); pap. 13.95 (*0-8023-1309-4*) Dufour.

Carriage Terminology: An Historical Dictionary. Donald H. Berkebile. LC 77-118. (Smithsonian Institution Press Publication Ser.: No. 6028). 487p. reprint ed. pap. 138.80 (*0-685-20921-0*, 2056465) Bks Demand.

***Carriage Trade.** Stephen Briningham. 1995. mass mkt. 5.99 (*0-553-56878-7*) Bantam.

Carriage Trade. large type ed. Stephen Birmingham. 1993. 25.95 (*1-56895-027-6*) Wheeler Pub.

Carriages Without Horses: J. Frank Duryea & the Birth of the American Automobile Industry. Richard P. Scharchburg. LC 93-2370. 240p. 1993. 29.00 (*1-56091-380-0*, R-127) Soc Auto Engineers.

***Carribbean Diaspora in Toronto: Learning to Live with Rascism.** Frances Henry. 298p. 1994. 60.00 (*0-8020-2972-8*); pap. 60.00 (*0-8020-7742-0*) U of Toronto Pr.

Carrickmacross Lace. Nellie O'Cleirich. 1985. pap. 11.95 (*0-85105-436-6*, Pub. by Colin Smythe Ltd UK) Dufour.

***Carrie.** Frank E. Cooke. Ed. by Johnny Harris. LC 94-61941. 60p. (Orig.). (J). (gr. 6-10). 1995. pap. 24.95 (*0-940076-07-1*) Fiesta City.

Carrie. Stephen King. LC 73-9037. 216p. 1990. 25.00 (*0-385-08695-4*) Doubleday.

Carrie. Stephen King. 288p. (SPA.). 1992. pap. 3.95 (*1-56780-057-2*) La Costa Pr.

Carrie. Stephen King. (Stephen King Collectors Editions Ser.). 160p. 1991. pap. 12.95 (*0-452-26719-6*, Plume) NAL-Dutton.

Carrie. large type ed. Stephen King. LC 93-44171. 272p. 1994. 21.95 (*0-8161-5688-3*, Large Print Bks) Hall.

Carrie. Stephen King. 256p. 1975. reprint ed. pap. 6.99 (*0-451-15744-3*, Sig) NAL-Dutton.

Carrie: Springsong. Carole G. Page. (YA). 1994. pap. 3.99 (*1-55661-523-X*) Bethany Hse.

Carrie-Ambassador at Large. rev. ed. Elizabeth Dean. (Illus.). 269p. 1984. reprint ed. pap. 4.95 (*0-930033-00-0*) Christ Life Revivals.

Carrie Catt: Feminist Politician. Robert B. Fowler. (Illus.). 246p. 1988. pap. 14.95 (*1-55553-005-2*) NE U Pr.

Carrie Chapman Catt. Mary G. Peck. LC 75-23159. (Pioneers of the Woman's Movement: an International Perspective Ser.). (Illus.). 495p. 1976. reprint ed. 32.45 (*0-88355-279-5*) Hyperion Conn.

Carrie Chapman Catt: A Public Life. Jacqueline Van Voris. LC 87-8533. 320p. (C). 1987. text ed. 24.95 (*0-935312-63-3*) Feminist Pr.

***Carrie Chapman Catt: A Public Life.** Jacqueline Van Voris. (Women & Peace Ser.). (Illus.). 307p. 1996. reprint ed. pap. write for info. (*1-55861-139-8*) Feminist Pr.

***Carrie M. Willard among the Tlingits: The Letters of 1881-1883.** Carrie M. Willard. LC 95-75342. (Illus.). 240p. (Orig.). 1995. pap. 12.95 (*0-945519-20-6*) Mountn Meadw Pr.

***Carrie Mae Weems.** Bell Hooks. Ed. by Terry A. Neff. Tr. by Chantel Combes. (Illus.). 40p. (ENG & FRE.). 1994. pap. write for info. (*0-9619760-4-7*) Fabric Workshop Inc.

Carrie Mae Weems. Andrea Kirsh & Susan F. Sterling. LC 92-33000. (Illus.). 116p. 1993. pap. text ed. 29.95 (*0-940979-21-7*, NE U Pr) Natl Museum Women.

Carrie of Culver Road. large type ed. Dee Williams. 601p. 1993. 21.95 (*0-7505-0436-6*, Pub. by Magna Print Bks) Ulverscroft.

Carried Away: The Chronicles of a Feminist Cartoonist. Abbe Smith. LC 83-50553. 96p. (Orig.). 1984. pap. 4.25 (*0-9605210-1-1*) Sanguinaria.

Carrier. Keith Douglass. 1991. pap. 4.95 (*0-515-10593-7*) Jove Pubns.

Carrier. large type ed. John Wingate. 352p. 1984. 15.95 (*0-7089-1080-7*) Ulverscroft.

Carrier - Currier Families in Early Massachusetts: Vital Records from Printed Sources. Evelyn C. Lane. 117p. (Orig.). 1992. pap. 18.50 (*0-9626201-5-7*) E C Lane.

***Carrier & Bioreactor Red Blood Cells for Drug Delivery & Targeting.** DeLoach & Way. (Advances in the Biosciences Ser.: No. 92). 1994. 150.00 (*0-08-042496-1*, Pergamon Pr) Elsevier.

Carrier Battle in the Philippine Sea: The Marianas Turkey Shoot. Barrett Tillman. (Gold Wings Ser.). (Illus.). 48p. (C). 1994. pap. 12.95 (*1-883809-04-5*) Phalanx Pub.

Carrier Corps: Military Labor in the East African Campaign, 1914-1918. Geoffrey Hodges. LC 84-22557. (Contributions in Comparative Colonial Studies: No. 18). (Illus.). 248p. 1986. text ed. 59.95 (*0-313-24418-9*, HDG/, Greenwood Pr) Greenwood.

Carrier Dome, Syracuse, New York. (PCI Journal Reprints Ser.). 11p. 1981. pap. 6.00 (*0-686-40142-5*, JR238) P-PCI.

Carrier Down: The Story of the Sinking of the U. S. S. Princeton. Thomas I. Bradshaw & Marsha Clark. Ed. by Melissa Roberts. (Illus.). 220p. 1990. 24.95 (*0-89015-773-1*) Sunbelt Media.

Carrier, No. 2: Viper Strike. Keith Douglass. 1991. mass mkt. 4.99 (*0-515-10729-8*) Jove Pubns.

Carrier, No. 3: Armageddon Mode. Keith Douglass. 1992. mass mkt. 4.99 (*0-515-10864-2*) Jove Pubns.

Carrier, No. 4: Flame Out. Keith Douglass. 336p. (Orig.). 1992. mass mkt. 4.99 (*0-515-10994-0*) Jove Pubns.

Carrier, No. 5: Maelstrom. Keith Douglass. 336p. (Orig.). 1993. mass mkt. 4.99 (*0-515-11080-9*) Jove Pubns.

Carrier Scattering in Metals & Semiconductors. V. F. Gantmakher & Y. B. Levinson. (Modern Problems in Condensed Matter Sciences Ser.: Vol. 19). 451p. 1987. 154.00 (*0-444-87025-3*, North Holland) Elsevier.

Carrier State: An Original Anthology. Ed. by Barbara G. Rosenkrantz. LC 76-40660. (Public Health in America Ser.). (Illus.). 1977. reprint ed. 18.95 (*0-405-09870-7*) Ayer.

Carrier War. Edwin P. Hoyt. 176p. 1987. pap. 3.50 (*0-380-75360-X*) Avon.

Carrier Warfare. Time-Life Books Editors. (New Face of War Ser.). (Illus.). 160p. 1992. lib. bdg. write for info. (*0-8094-8626-1*) Time-Life.

Carrier Warfare in the Pacific: An Oral History Collection. Ed. by E. T. Wooldridge. LC 92-43343. (History of Aviation Ser.). (Illus.). 336p. 1993. 24.95 (*1-56098-264-0*) Smithsonian.

Carrier Wars. Hoyt. 1994. pap. 14.95 (*1-56924-874-5*) Marlowe & Co.

Carrier Wave: New Information Technology & the Geography of Innovation, 1846-2003. Peter Hall & Praschal Preston. (Illus.). 288p. 1988. 49.95 (*0-04-445081-8*) Routledge Chapman & Hall.

Carriere of Carpentras. Marianne Calmann. LC 82-48692. (Littman Library of Jewish Civilization). (Illus.). 288p. 1984. 15.00 (*0-19-710037-6*, Pub. by Littman Lib Jew UK) Bnai Brith Bk.

Carriers. Jerome McDonough. 34p. (Orig.). (YA). (gr. 7-12). 1992. pap. 3.00 (*0-88680-370-5*) I E Clark.

Carriers. Jean P. Montbayet. 1990. 12.99 (*0-517-01219-7*) Random Hse Value.

Carriers Cosmographie; or a Briefe Relation of the Innes in & Neere London. John Taylor. LC 74-80229. (English Experience Ser.: No. 698). 1974. reprint ed. 3.50 (*90-221-0698-5*) Walter J Johnson.

Carriers of Faith: Lessons from Congregational Studies. Ed. by Carl S. Dudley et al. 168p. (Orig.). 1991. pap. 13.99 (*0-664-25204-4*) Westminster John Knox.

Carrie's Games. Nancy J. Hopper. 128p. (YA). (gr. 7 up). 1989. pap. 2.50 (*0-380-70538-9*, Flare) Avon.

Carries Risk: A Practical Guide for Assessment & Control. Bo Krasse. (Illus.). 113p. 1985. pap. text ed. 24.00 (*0-86715-123-4*) Quint Pub Co.

Carrie's Story. Molly Weatherfield. (Orig.). 1995. pap. text ed. 4.95 (*1-56333-228-0*) Masquerade.

Carrie's War. Nina Bawden. LC 72-13253. (J). (gr. 4-7). 1973. lib. bdg. 14.89 (*0-397-31450-7*, Lipp Jr Bks) HarpC Child Bks.

***Carrie's World.** Scott Wheeler. 180p. 1995. pap. 7.95 (*1-56901-726-3*) NW Pub.

***Carrington.** Christopher Hampton. 124p. (Orig.). 1995. pap. 12.95 (*0-571-15336-4*) Faber & Faber.

Carrington: A Life. Gretchen H. Gerzina. 1989. 24.95 (*0-393-02698-1*) Norton.

Carrington: A Life. Gretchen H. Gerzina. 392p. 1992. pap. 14.95 (*0-393-30856-1*) Norton.

***Carrington: A Life.** Gretchen H. Gerzina. (Illus.). 384p. 1995. pap. 15.00 (*0-393-31328-X*, Norton Paperbks) Norton.

Carrion Comfort. Dan Simmons. 896p. 1990. mass mkt. 6.99 (*0-446-35920-3*) Warner Bks.

Carro De Bomberos Grande y Rojo. Rose Greydanus. (Illus.). 32p. (SPA.). (J). (gr. k-2). 1981. lib. bdg. 7.89 (*0-89375-555-9*); pap. 1.95 (*0-685-04944-2*) Troll Assocs.

Carrol Shelby's Racing Cobra. Dave Friedman & John Christy. (Illus.). 208p. 1990. 29.95 (*0-87938-481-6*) Motorbooks Intl.

***Carroll & Harrison County, Ohio: Eckley & Perry 1921 Ohio History Index.** Fay Maxwell. 24p. 1983. 10.00 (*1-885463-01-4*) Ohio Genealogy.

Carroll & OSBA Ohio Administrative Law. Administrative Law Committee Ohio, State Bar Association Staff. 348p. 1985. 35.00 (*0-8322-0069-7*) Banks-Baldwin.

Carroll College: The First Century, 1846-1946. Ellen Langill. LC 79-54879. (Illus.). 1980. text ed. 20.95 (*0-916120-06-6*) Carroll Coll.

Carroll County Indiana Rural Organizations 1828-1979: Vol. I History. John C. Peterson & Doris M. Peterson. LC 80-82231. (Illus.). 400p. 1980. 25.00 (*0-9604376-0-6*) J & D Peterson.

***Carroll County, Mississippi Cemetery Records.** Ethel Bibus & Louise Marshall. 310p. (Orig.). 1995. pap. 30.00 (*1-885480-04-0*) Pioneer Pubng.

Carroll County Physicians of the Nineteenth & Early Twentieth Century. Theodore E. Woodward. (Illus.). 1989. write for info. (*0-9614125-8-5*) Hist Soc Carroll.

Carroll County, Virginia: The Early Days to 1920. Owen Bowman. LC 92-41168. 1993. write for info. (*0-89865-855-1*) Donning Co.

Carroll Inheritance. Max Colwell. 174p. (C). 1989. 29.00 (*0-7270-1344-0*, Pub. by M Colwell Pubns AT) St Mut.

Carroll Smith's Nuts, Bolts, & Fasteners Handbook. Carroll Smith. (Illus.). 144p. (ENG & GER.). 1990. pap. 17.95 (*0-87938-406-9*) Motorbooks Intl.

Carroll Wright & Labor Reform: The Origin of Labor Statistics. James R. Leiby. LC 60-15240. (Historical Monographs: No. 46). 251p. 1960. 15.00 (*0-674-09800-5*) HUP.

Carroll's Heritage: Essays on the Architecture of a Piedmont Maryland County. Joe Getty. (Illus.). 128p. (Orig.). 1987. pap. 19.95 (*0-9614125-2-6*) Hist Soc Carroll.

Carros de Carrera. Norman S. Barrett. LC 90-70887. (Picture Library). (Illus.). 32p. (SPA.). (J). (gr. k-4). 1990. lib. bdg. 12.60 (*0-531-07905-8*) Watts.

An Asterisk (*) at the beginning of an entry indicates that the title is appearing in BIP for the first time.

C

Carteggio (Political Correspondence), 3 vols. Ed. by Pietro Pastorelli. Incl. Vol. Primo, 1891-1913. xvi, 592p. 1982. (*0-7006-0225-9*); Vol. Secondo, 1914-1916. xvi, 776p. 1975. (*0-7006-0139-2*); Vol. Terzo, 1916-1922. xvi, 788p. 1976. (*0-7006-0150-3*); (Opera Omnia di - The Complete Works of Sidney Sonnino Ser.). xvi, 592p. (ITA.). 1982. Set. 50.00 (*0-685-04295-2*) U Pr of KS.

Cartel. Paul-Loup Sulitzer. 1992. pap. 16.95 (*0-7859-3167-8*, 2253058904) Fr & Eur.

Cartel Problems: An Analysis of Collective Monopolies in Europe with American Application: The Institute of Economics of the Brookings Institution, No. 69. Karl Pribram. (Business Enterprises Reprint Ser.). x, 287p. 1986. reprint ed. lib. bdg. 40.00 (*0-89941-479-6*, 304060) W S Hein.

Carteles de Magia. Brett Kirkpatrick et al. (Orig.). 1983. pap. 5.00 (*0-940376-01-6*) White Horse.

Cartels & Trusts: Their Origin & Historical Development, from the Economic & Legal Aspects. Roman Piotrowski. LC 78-14461. 376p. 1979. reprint ed. lib. bdg. 45.00 (*0-87991-951-5*) Porcupine Pr.

Cartels, Concerns & Trusts. Robert Liefmann. Ed. by Mira Wilkins. LC 76-29997. (European Business Ser.). 1977. reprint ed. lib. bdg. 35.95 (*0-405-09755-7*) Ayer.

Cartels in Action, Case Studies in International Business Diplomacy. George W. Stocking & Myron W. Watkins. LC 91-71494. xii, 533p. reprint ed. 55.00 (*0-89941-759-0*, 306690) W S Hein.

Cartels or Competition? The Economics of International Controls by Business & Government. George W. Stocking & Myron W. Watkins. (Business Enterprises Reprint Ser.). xiv, 516p. 1986. reprint ed. lib. bdg. 48.50 (*0-89941-478-8*, 304070) W S Hein.

Carter: The Carter Tree, Tabulated & Indexed. R. R. Carter & R. I. Randolph. 241p. 1991. reprint ed. lib. bdg. 48.00 (*0-8328-2110-1*); reprint ed. pap. 38.00 (*0-8328-2111-X*) Higginson Bk Co.

Carter: The Will to Win. Jean H. Godden. (Illus.). 64p. 1980. ring bd. 24.00 (*0-88014-024-0*) Mosaic Pr OH.

Carter Administration & Palestinian Rights. Ed. by James J. Zogby. (Occasional Papers: No. 5). 28p. (Orig.). (C). 1977. pap. 1.00 (*0-937694-44-4*) Assn Arab-Amer U Grads.

Carter Administration, Human Rights & the Agony of Cambodia. Sheldon Neuringer. LC 93-23577. 108p. 1993. 59.95 (*0-7734-9367-0*) E Mellen.

C

Carter Administration's Quest for Global Community: Beliefs & Their Impact on Behavior. Jerel A. Rosati. 268p. 1987. text ed. 39.95 (*0-87249-508-6*) U of SC Pr.

Carter Administration's Quest for Global Community: Beliefs & Their Impact on Behavior. Jerel A. Rosati. LC 87-6006. (Illus.). 268p. 1991. reprint ed. pap. text ed. 21.95 (*0-87249-787-9*) U of SC Pr.

***Carter & Arms Sales: Implementing the Carter Administration's Arms Transfer Restraint Policy.** Joanna Spear. LC 95-4168. (Southampton Studies in International Policy). 1995. write for info. (*0-312-12681-6*) St Martin.

Carter, & Other People. Don Marquis. LC 75-142269. (Short Story Index Reprint Ser.). 1977. 20.95 (*0-8369-3753-8*) Ayer.

Carter & the Generals: Human Rights in the Southern Cone. (Report on the Americas: Vol. XIII, No. 2). 52p. 2.50 (*0-317-34959-7*) NA Cong Lat Am.

Carter Braxton, Virginia Signer: A Conservative in Revolt. Alonzo T. Dill. LC 83-6513. (Illus.). 306p. (Orig.). 1983. lib. bdg. 58.00 (*0-8191-3223-5*); pap. text ed. 26.00 (*0-8191-3224-1*) U Pr of Amer.

Carter Carbs. D. Emanuel. (Illus.). 112p. 1983. pap. 16.95 (*0-931472-11-3*, S-A Design Pub Co) Motorbooks Intl.

Carter Country: A Celebration of Rural Devon. Brian Carter. (Illus.). 120p. 1989. pap. 13.95 (*0-7126-2448-1*, Pub. by Century UK) Trafalgar.

Carter County, Tennessee Death Record Abstracts, 1926-1934. Eddie M. Nikazy. 335p. (Orig.). 1994. pap. text ed. 26.00 (*1-55613-953-5*) Heritage Bk.

Carter County, Tennessee, Marriages, 1796-1870. Goldene F. Burgner. 150p. 1987. pap. 25.00 (*0-89308-601-0*, TN 100) Southern Hist Pr.

Carter County, Tennessee, Marriages, 1871-1920. Eddie M. Nikazy. ix, 322p. (Orig.). 1993. pap. 24.50 (*1-55613-765-6*) Heritage Bk.

Carter G. Woodson: A Bio-Bibliography. Anthony Scally. LC 85-10051. (Bio-Bibliographies in Afro-American & African Studies: No. 1). (Illus.). xvii, 224p. 1985. text ed. 47.95 (*0-313-24185-6*, SWO/, Greenwood Pr) Greenwood.

Carter G. Woodson: A Life in Black History. Jacqueline Goggin. LC 92-35980. (Southern Biography Ser.). (Illus.). 288p. 1993. 24.95 (*0-8071-1793-5*) La State U Pr.

Carter G. Woodson: The Father of Black History. Patricia McKissack & Fredrick McKissack. LC 91-8813. (Great African Americans Ser.). (Illus.). 32p. (J). (gr. 1-4). 1991. lib. bdg. 12.95 (*0-89490-309-8*) Enslow Pubs.

Carter G. Woodson's Major Works, 26 vols., Set. Carter G. Woodson. 10000p. (C). Date not set. 895.00 (*0-87498-125-5*) Assoc Pubs DC.

Carter Glass: A Biography. Rixey Smith & Norman Beasley. LC 72-124258. (Select Bibliographies Reprint Ser.). 1977. 25.95 (*0-8369-5446-7*) Ayer.

Carter Glass: A Biography. R. Smith & N. Beasley. LC 72-172012. (FDR & the Era of the New Deal Ser.). (Illus.). 520p. 1972. reprint ed. lib. bdg. 55.00 (*0-306-70392-0*) Da Capo.

***Carter House Cookbook.** Mark Crater. 1995. pap. 8.95 (*0-89815-773-0*) Ten Speed Pr.

Carter Implosion: Jimmy Carter & the Amateur Style of Diplomacy. Donald S. Spencer. LC 88-12521. 176p. 1988. text ed. 49.95 (*0-275-93041-6*, C3041, Praeger Pubs) Greenwood.

Carter Presidency: Fourteen Intimate Perspectives of Jimmy Carter. Ed. by Kenneth W. Thompson. (Portraits of American Presidents Ser.: Vol. VIII). 266p. (C). 1990. lib. bdg. 44.50 (*0-8191-7812-8*); pap. text ed. 25.00 (*0-8191-7813-6*) U Pr of Amer.

Carter-Ruck on Libel & Slander. 4th ed. Peter F. Carter-Ruck et al. 1991. 160.00 (*0-406-12317-9*, U.K.) Butterworth Legal Pubs.

Carter Tree. Comp. by Robert R. Carter. 243p. 1973. reprint ed. 25.00 (*0-685-65064-2*) VA Bk.

Carter vs. Ford: The Counterfeit Debates of Nineteen Seventy-Six. Lloyd Bitzer & Theodore Rueter. LC 80-5110. 444p. 1980. 37.50 (*0-299-08280-6*); pap. 17.95 (*0-299-08284-9*) U of Wis Pr.

Carter Years: Toward a New Global Order. Richard C. Thornton. LC 91-29701. 568p. (C). 1992. 26.95 (*0-88702-062-3*) Washington Inst Pr.

Carter Years, 1977-80, 4 yearbooks, Set 6. (Facts on File Yearbooks). 285.00 (*0-8160-2750-1*) Facts on File.

***Carteret County, North Carolina Marriage Bonds & Certificates, 1755-1868.** Francis T. Ingmire. 120p. 1994. lib. bdg. 37.00 (*0-8095-8021-7*); pap. 15.00 (*0-8095-8531-6*) Borgo Pr.

Carteret Waterfowl Heritage. Jack Dudley. (Illus.). 152p. 1993. 40.00 (*0-9631815-2-1*) Decoy Mag.

Carters: First Families Ser. Cass A. Sandak. LC 93-3943. (Illus.). 48p. (J). (gr. 5). 1993. text ed. 4.95 (*0-89686-652-1*, Crstwood Hse) Silver Burdett Pr.

***Carters Criminal Law of Queensland.** 9th ed. R. F. Carter. 1994. pap. 161.00 (*0-409-30991-5*, Austral) Butterworth Legal Pubs.

***Carter's Grove: The Story of a Virginia Plantation.** Mark R. Wenger. LC 94-26980. (Illus.). 1994. 19.95 (*0-87935-129-2*) Colonial Williamsburg.

Carter's Lonesome Road to Peace: Perception, Bargaining, & the Limits of Multilateral Diplomacy in the Middle East. Edward Haley. (Research Note Ser.: No. 6). 28p. (Orig.). Date not set. pap. 5.00 (*0-86682-037-X*) Ctr Intl Relations.

Carters of Plains. Richard Hyatt. LC 76-58240. (Illus.). 1977. 10.95 (*0-87397-117-5*) Strode.

Carters of Virginia: Their English Ancestry. Noel Currer-Briggs. (C). 1979. 50.00 (*0-85033-307-5*) St Mut.

Carter's Pride. large type ed. Ailie Scullion. (Dales Romance Ser.). 245p. 1993. pap. 16.95 (*1-85389-366-8*, Dales) Ulverscroft.

Carter's Raid: An Episode of the Civil War in East Tennessee. William G. Piston. (Illus.). 92p. (Orig.). 1989. pap. 8.95 (*0-932807-42-9*) Overmountain Pr.

Cartes De Visite in Nineteenth Century Photography. William C. Darrah. (Illus.). 222p. 1981. 27.00 (*0-913116-05-X*) W C Darrah.

Cartes et Guides Vagnon de Navigation. Wilson Ltd. Staff & Imray L. Norie. (C). 1989. 67.00 (*0-685-40426-9*, Pub. by Imray Laurie Norie & Wilson UK) St Mut.

Cartesian & Argand Values. Philip H. Francis. (Mathematics Ser.: Vol. 3). (Illus.). 1978. pap. 9.95 (*0-900891-47-5*) Oleander Pr.

Cartesian Linguistics: A Chapter in the History of Rationalist Thought. Noam Chomsky. LC 83-6936. 132p. (C). 1983. reprint ed. pap. text ed. 14.00 (*0-8191-3092-3*) U Pr of Amer.

Cartesian Logic: An Essay on Descartes' Conception of Inference. Stephen Gaukroger. 160p. 1989. 42.00 (*0-19-824225-3*) OUP.

Cartesian Meditations, Vol. 1. Ed. by Edmund Husserl. Tr. by Dorion Cairns. 1988. pap. 14.50 (*0-317-67317-3*) Kluwer Ac.

Cartesian Method & the Problem of Reduction. Emily R. Grosholz. (Illus.). 176p. 1991. 42.50 (*0-19-824250-6*) OUP.

Cartesian Philosophers. Vere Chappell. LC 91-39378. (Essays on Early Modern Philosophers Ser.: Vol. 3). 368p. 1992. 60.00 (*0-8153-0577-X*) Garland.

***Cartesian Psychology & Physical Minds: Individualism & the Sciences of the Mind.** Robert A. Wilson. (Cambridge Studies in Philosophy). (Illus.). 288p. (C). 1995. 49.95 (*0-521-47402-7*) Cambridge U Pr.

Cartesian Tensors. Harold Jeffreys. (Orig.). 1931. pap. 15. 95 (*0-521-09191-8*) Cambridge U Pr.

Cartesian Women: Versions & Subversions of Rational Discourse in the Old Regime. Erica Harth. LC 91-55541. (Reading Women Writing Ser.). 288p. 1992. 44. 95 (*0-8014-2715-0*); pap. 15.95 (*0-8014-9998-4*) Cornell U Pr.

Cartesianische Meditationen und Pariser Vortrage: Photomechanischer Nachdruck. Edmund Husserl. (Husserliana Collected Work Ser.: No. 1). 1973. lib. bdg. 56.50 (*90-247-0214-3*) Kluwer Ac.

Carthage: A History. Serge Lancel. Tr. by Antonia Nevill. (Illus.). 420p. 1994. 34.95 (*1-55786-468-3*) Blackwell Pubs.

Carthage: Or, the Empire of Africa. Alfred J. Church & Arthur Gilman. LC 72-165620. (Select Bibliographies Reprint Ser.). 1977. reprint ed. 30.95 (*0-8369-5927-2*) Ayer.

Carthage & Her Remains. Nathan Davis. 680p. 1985. 300. 00 (*1-85077-033-6*, Darf Pubs Ltd) St Mut.

Carthage Conspiracy: The Trial of the Accused Assassins of Joseph Smith. Dallin H. Oaks & Marvin S. Hill. LC 78-1733. 262p. 1979. pap. 9.95 (*0-252-00762-X*) U of Ill Pr.

Carthaginian Peace or the Economic Consequences of Mr. Keynes. Etienne Mantoux. Ed. by Mira Wilkins. LC 78-3936. (International Finance Ser.). 1979. reprint ed. lib. bdg. 23.95 (*0-405-11237-8*) Ayer.

***Carthew Family Records, 1994: Sort by Date.** J. Robert Carthew. (Nineteen Ninety-Four Edition - Sort by Date Ser.). 461p. 1994. 59.95 (*1-885319-00-2*) Carthew Cnslt.

***Carthew Family Records, 1994: Sort by Name.** J. Robert Carthew. (Nineteen Ninety-Four Edition - Sort by Name Ser.). 461p. 1994. 59.95 (*1-885319-01-0*) Carthew Cnslt.

***Carthew Family Records, 1994: Sort by Place.** J. Robert Carthew. (Nineteen Ninety-Four Edition - Sort by Place Ser.). 461p. 1994. 59.95 (*1-885319-02-9*) Carthew Cnslt.

***Carthew Family Records, 1994: Sort by Relationship Number.** J. Robert Carthew. (Nineteen Ninety-Four Edition - Sort by Relationship Number Ser.). 461p. 1994. 59.95 (*1-885319-03-7*) Carthew Cnslt.

Carthusian Prayer & Hugh of Balma's Viae Sion Lugent. Patricia A. Guinan. 250p. 1994. 64.95 (*1-883255-51-1*); pap. 44.95 (*1-883255-50-3*) Intl Scholars.

Cartier: Jewelers Extraordinary. Hans Nadelhoffer. LC 83-26646. (Illus.). 312p. 1984. 60.00 (*0-8109-0770-4*) Abrams.

Cartier: Wrist & Pocket Watch, Clock & Misc. I. D. & PG. spiral bd. 25.00 (*0-913902-62-4*) Heart Am Pr.

Cartier: Wrist & Pocket Watch, Clocks & Misc. Ehrhardt & DeMesy. 100p. spiral bd. 200.00 (*0-913902-61-6*) Heart Am Pr.

***Cartier-Bresson, Henri Drawings & Paintings.** Text by David Elliot et al. (Illus.). 1984. pap. 22.00 (*0-905836-42-1*, Pub. by Museum Modern Art UK) St Mut.

Cartier's Hochelaga & the Dawson Site. James F. Pendergast & Bruce G. Trigger. LC 78-184767. (Illus.). 470p. 1972. 49.95 (*0-7735-0070-7*, Pub. by McGill CN) U of Toronto Pr.

Cartilage: Biomedical Aspects, Vol. 3. Ed. by Brian K. Hall. LC 82-20566. 1983. text ed. 132.00 (*0-12-319503-9*) Acad Pr.

Cartilage: Molecular Aspects. Brian K. Hall & Stuart A. Newman. (Illus.). 240p. 1991. 98.95 (*0-8493-8817-1*, QP88) CRC Pr.

Cartilage: Structure & Function & Biochemistry, Vol. 1. Ed. by Brian K. Hall. LC 82-11566. 420p. 1983. text ed. 132.00 (*0-12-319501-2*) Acad Pr.

Cartilaginous Tumors of the Skeleton: AFIP Atlas of Radiologic-Pathologic Correlation. Ed. by Alan J. Davidson. LC 90-82489. (AFIP Ser.). (Illus.). 208p. (Orig.). 1990. pap. text ed. 50.00 (*1-56053-004-9*) Hanley & Belfus.

Cartilla Espanola. Jose Robles. (Illus.). (Orig.). (SPA.). 1935. pap. text ed. 9.95 (*0-89197-064-9*) Irvington.

Carting Industry & Carrier's Trade in Capitalist Russia, 1897. Paul Shott. 1984. pap. 3.00 (*0-317-17710-9*) Intl Inst Adv Stud.

***Cartobibliography of Separately Published U. S. Geological Survey Special Maps & River Surveys.** Peter L. Stark. LC 89-14684. (Occasional Paper Ser.: No. 12). 1994. 40.00 (*0-939112-15-9*) Western Assn Map.

Cartographer. Jack Rudman. (Career Examination Ser.: C-127). 1994. pap. 27.95 (*0-8373-0127-0*) Nat Learn.

***Cartographer.** Robert Sargent. 80p. 1994. pap. 10.00 (*0-938572-09-1*) Bunny Crocodile.

Cartographer-Draftsman. Jack Rudman. (Career Examination Ser.: C-1160). 1994. pap. 29.95 (*0-8373-1160-8*) Nat Learn.

Cartographers of Hell: Essays on the Social History of England. Alok Bhalla. 188p. 1991. text ed. 25.00 (*81-207-1174-2*, Pub. by Sterling Pubs II) Apt Bks.

Cartographic Design & Production. 2nd ed. Keates. 400p. 1989. pap. text ed. 54.95 (*0-470-21071-0*) Wiley.

Cartographic Relief Presentation. Eduard Imhof. Ed. by Harry J. Steward. 389p. (C). 1982. 161.55 (*3-11-006711-0*) De Gruyter.

Cartographic Sources in the Rosenberg Library. Ed. by Jane A. Kenamore & Uli Haller, III. LC 83-45095. (Illus.). 248p. 1988. 32.50 (*0-89096-161-1*) Tex A&M Univ Pr.

Cartographic Technician. Jack Rudman. (Career Examination Ser.: C-3116). 1994. pap. 27.95 (*0-8373-3116-1*) Nat Learn.

Cartographies. Maya Sonenberg. LC 89-31841. (Drue Heinz Literature Prize Ser.). 176p. 1989. 22.50 (*0-8229-3627-5*) U of Pittsburgh Pr.

Cartographies. Maya Sonenberg. 170p. (C). 1990. reprint ed. pap. 9.95 (*0-88001-259-5*) Ecco Pr.

***Cartographies: Contemporary American Essays.** Diana Young. 368p. 1994. pap. text ed. 10.00 (*0-312-09495-7*) St Martin.

Cartographies: Poststructuralism & the Mapping of Bodies & Spaces. Ed. by Rosalyn Diprose & Robyn Ferrell. 176p. 1991. pap. 19.95 (*0-04-442291-1*, Pub. by Allen & Unwin Aust Pty AT) Paul & Co Pubs.

Cartography. Maria L. Carino. 120p. 1995. pap. 19.95 (*1-55921-117-2*) Moyer Bell.

Cartography. deluxe ed. Debora Greger. 1980. 75.00 (*0-686-28114-4*) Penumbra Press.

Cartography in France, Sixteen Sixty to Eighteen Forty-Eight: Science, Engineering, & Statecraft. Josef W. Konvitz. LC 86-11283. (Illus.). 214p. (C). 1987. 39.95 (*0-226-45094-5*) U Ch Pr.

Cartography of Iceland. Halldor Hermannsson. LC 32-4391. (Islandica Ser.: Vol. 21). 1931. 25.00 (*0-527-00351-4*) Periodicals Srv.

Cartography of North America. Pierluigi Portinara. 1990. 24.99 (*0-517-03079-9*) Random Hse Value.

Cartography Past, Present, & Future - a Festschrift for F. J. Ormeling: Published on Behalf of the International Cartographic Association. Ed. by David W. Rhind & D. R. Taylor. 196p. 1989. 110.00 (*1-85166-336-3*) Elsevier.

Cartons Cans & Orange Peels. Joanna Foster. (J). (gr. 4-7). 1993. pap. 7.95 (*0-395-66504-3*, Clarion Bks) HM.

Cartons, Cans, & Orange Peels: Where Does Our Garbage Go? Joanna Foster. (Illus.). 64p. (J). (gr. 3-6). 1991. 15. 95 (*0-395-56436-0*, Clarion Bks) HM.

Cartoon Aided Design: The Lighter Side of Computing. Roger Penwill. 100p. 1993. pap. 14.95 (*0-9639305-0-8*) A-E-C Systs.

Cartoon Animation. Preston Blair. (How to Draw & Paint Ser.). (Illus.). 40p. (Orig.). 1989. pap. 5.95 (*0-929261-51-8*, HT26) W Foster Pub.

Cartoon Animation. Preston Blair. (Collector's Ser.). (Illus.). 224p. (Orig.). 1994. pap. 24.95 (*1-56010-084-2*, CS03) W Foster Pub.

Cartoon Animation: Introduction to a Career. Milton Gray. LC 90-63934. (Illus.). 124p. (J). 1991. pap. 12.95 (*0-9628444-5-4*) Lions Den. An up-to-date guide to securing employment in the Hollywood animation industry at the entry & advanced levels where production is presently booming & the studios are actively seeking new qualified artists. The author is currently an animator/ producer who has worked at the Walt Disney Studio, Warner Bros. & other Hollywood studios for 25 years. This book is also a uniquely insightful how-to on animation, direction, writing & producing cartoon animation films, with special emphasis on high quality production. Illustrated, with bibliography & index. "A major step forward in learning how to animate & make cartoon films. I highly recommend it!"--Eddie Fitzgerald, Instructor, Animation Department, California Institute of the Arts, & Director, Warner Bros. Cartoons. Available through: Lion's Den Publications, Inc., P.O. Box 7368-W, Northridge, CA 91327-7368. Telephone (818) 772-7234.
Publisher Provided Annotation.

Cartoon Animation (Basic Skills) Walter Foster. (How to Draw & Paint Ser.). (Illus.). 32p. (Orig.). 1989. pap. 5.95 (*0-929261-50-X*, HT25) W Foster Pub.

Cartoon Art: An Adventure in Creativity. Beverly Page. Ed. by Linda H. Smith. 1980. pap. 5.95 (*0-936386-10-X*) Creative Learning.

***Cartoon Book 2.** Kemsley. 1995. pap. (*0-590-48511-3*) Scholastic Inc.

***Cartoon, Caricature, Animation.** Pointon. 1995. pap. (*0-631-19487-8*) Blackwell Pubs.

Cartoon Clip-Art for Youth Leaders. Ron Wheeler. (REPRObooks Ser.). (Illus.). 120p. (Orig.). 1987. pap. 14.99 (*0-8010-9682-0*) Baker Bk.

Cartoon Clip-Art for Youth Leaders, No. 2. Ron Wheeler. (REPRObooks Ser.). (Illus.). 208p. (Orig.). 1991. pap. 14.99 (*0-8010-9714-2*) Baker Bk.

Cartoon Confidential. Jim Korkis & John Cawley. 172p. (Orig.). 1992. 14.95 (*1-56398-005-3*) Malibu Graphics.

***Cartoon Drawing Kit.** Bruce Blitz. 1995. pap. 12.95 (*1-56010-188-1*) W Foster Pub.

Cartoon Friends of the Baby Boom Era: A Pictorial Price Guide. William R. Bruegman, III. Ed. by Joanne M. Bruegman. (Illus.). 180p. 1993. pap. 19.95 (*0-9632637-3-0*) Capn Penny.

Cartoon Fun. Hal Tollison. (Beginner's Art Ser.). (Illus.). 64p. (Orig.). (J). (gr. k up). 1989. pap. 3.95 (*1-56010-033-8*, BA07) W Foster Pub.

Cartoon Girl: The Best of Heather McAdams. Heather McAdams. LC 93-81142. (Illus.). 96p. 1994. pap. 8.95 (*1-56352-130-X*) Longstreet Pr Inc.

Cartoon Gospel. Richard L. Diesslin. (Illus.). 119p. (Orig.). 1990. pap. 9.95 (*0-940169-09-6*) Liturgical Pubns.

Cartoon Guide to Computers. Larry Gonick & Mark Wheelis. LC 82-48252. (Illus.). 224p. 1991. pap. 12.00 (*0-06-273097-5*, Harper Ref) HarpC.

Cartoon Guide to Genetics. rev. ed. Larry Gonick & Mark Wheelis. (J). 1991. pap. 12.00 (*0-06-273099-1*, Harper Ref) HarpC.

Cartoon Guide to (Non) Communication: The Use & Misuse of Information in the Modern World. Larry Gonick. (Illus.). 176p. (Orig.). 1993. pap. 13.00 (*0-06-273217-X*, Harper Ref) HarpC.

Cartoon Guide to Physics. Larry Gonick & Art Huffman. LC 90-55499. 256p. (Orig.). 1991. pap. 12.00 (*0-06-273100-9*, Harper Ref) HarpC.

Cartoon Guide to Statistics. Larry Gonick & Woolcott Smith. LC 92-54683. (Illus.). 208p. (Orig.). 1993. pap. 13.00 (*0-06-273102-5*, Harper Ref) HarpC.

Cartoon Guide to the Computer. Larry Gonick. LC 82-48251. (Illus.). 256p. 1991. pap. 9.95 (*0-685-48920-5*, Harper Ref) HarpC.

Cartoon History of California Politics. Ed Salzman & Ann L. Brown. LC 77-83965. 1978. pap. 3.95 (*0-930302-14-1*) Cal Journal.

Cartoon History of the United States. Larry Gonick. LC 91-55037. 416p. (Orig.). 1991. pap. 14.00 (*0-06-273098-3*, Harper Ref) HarpC.

***Cartoon History of the Universe II Vols. 8-13: From the Springtime of China to the Fall of Rome.** Larry Gonick. 1994. pap. 15.95 (*0-385-42093-5*) Doubleday.

Cartoon History of the Universe, Vol. 1: The Evolution of Everything. Larry Gonick. (Illus.). 52p. 1987. 2.50 (*0-89620-005-1*) Rip off.

Cartoon History of the Universe, Vol. 2: Sticks & Stones. Larry Gonick. (Illus.). 52p. 1987. 2.50 (*0-89620-006-X*) Rip off.

An Asterisk (*) at the beginning of an entry indicates that the title is appearing in BIP for the first time.

An Asterisk (*) at the beginning of an entry indicates that the title is appearing in BIP for the first time.

1065

C

Carving Jack-O-Lanterns. 2nd rev. ed. Sam Gendusa. Ed. & Intro. by Arnold Ruse. LC 89-92605. (Illus.). 80p. (Orig.). (YA). 1989. pap. 9.95 (0-9621071-1-5) SG Prodns.

Carving Miniature Wildfowl with Robert Guge. Roger Schroeder & Robert Guge. LC 87-18133. (Illus.). 272p. 1988. 39.95 (0-8117-0401-7) Stackpole.

*Carving Noah's Ark: Mrs. Noah & Friends. David Sabol. LC 94-37322. (Book for Wood Carvers Ser.). (Illus.). 64p. (Orig.). 1995. pap. 12.95 (0-88740-731-5) Schiffer.

Carving of Mount Rushmore. Rex A. Smith. (Illus.). 416p. 1994. pap. 19.95 (1-55859-665-8) Abbeville Pr.

*Carving on Turning. Chris Pye. (Illus.). 176p. 1995. pap. 14.95 (0-946819-88-2, Pub. by Guild Mstr Craftsman UK) Sterling.

Carving Ornamental Miniature Flying Birds. Anthony Hillman. 1991. pap. 6.95 (0-486-26726-1) Dover.

Carving Out the Wild West with Tom Wolfe: The Saloon. Tom Wolfe & Douglas Congdon-Martin. LC 91-61155. (Illus.). 64p. 1991. pap. 12.95 (0-88740-368-9) Schiffer.

Carving Realistic Animals with Power. Frank C. Russell. LC 94-66201. (Illus.). 64p. (Orig.). 1994. pap. 12.95 (0-88740-637-8) Schiffer.

Carving Realistic Birds: A Step-by-Step Manual with Full-Size Patterns. H. D. Green. LC 76-55216. (Illus.). (Orig.). 1978. pap. 3.95 (0-486-23484-3) Dover.

*Carving Realistic Faces with Power. Dale Power. (Illus.). 64p. (Orig.). 1993. pap. 12.95 (0-88740-486-3) Schiffer.

Carving Realistic Flowers. John Hagensick. Ed. by George Sheryka. (Illus.). 128p. (Orig.). 1989. pap. 14.95 (0-9626107-0-4) L-C Pub.

*Carving Santa Ornaments with Tom Wolfe. Tom Wolfe. (Illus.). 64p. 1994. pap. 12.95 (0-88740-617-3) Schiffer.

Carving Santas with Special Interests. Ron Ransom. LC 91-65655. (Illus.). 64p. 1991. pap. 12.95 (0-88740-328-X) Schiffer.

Carving Shorebirds: With Full-Size Patterns. Harry Shourds & Anthony Hillman. (Illus.). 72p. 1982. pap. 5.95 (0-486-24287-0) Dover.

Carving Stamps. Julie H. Bloch. (Illus.). 16p. 1992. 4.50 (1-882817-00-1) J Bloch.

Carving the Buddha. Jwing-Ming Yang. (YMAA Children's Book Ser.: Vol. 1). 32p. (Orig.). (J). (gr. 4 up). 1989. pap. 1.95 (0-940871-09-2, CB001) YMAA Pubn.

Carving the Cheetah. Dale Power & Jeff Snyder. (Illus.). 64p. (Orig.). 1994. pap. 12.95 (0-88740-696-3) Schiffer.

Carving the Civil War with Tom Wolfe. Tom Wolfe & Douglas Congdon-Martin. LC 91-61193. (Illus.). 64p. 1991. pap. 12.95 (0-88740-369-7) Schiffer.

*Carving the Coyote. Dale Power & Jeffrey B. Snyder. (Illus.). 64p. (Orig.). 1994. pap. 12.95 (0-88740-567-3) Schiffer.

*Carving the Elk. Dale Power & Jeffrey B. Snyder. (Illus.). 64p. (Orig.). 1994. pap. 12.95 (0-88740-566-5) Schiffer.

Carving the Historic Western Face. Robert E. Lundy. LC 87-73231. 112p. (Orig.). 1988. pap. 34.95 (0-9619094-0-4) BJ Enterprises.

Carving the Historic Western Face. Robert E. Lundy. LC 87-73231. (Illus.). 160p. (Orig.). 1991. pap. 14.95 (0-88740-321-2) Schiffer.

*Carving the Little Guys: An Introductory Text by Keith Randich. Keith Randich. LC 91-91341. (Illus.). 60p. (Orig.). 1991. pap. 9.00 (0-9642327-0-7) K Randich Pubng.

*Carving the Little Sailors: An Introductory Text by Keith Randich. Keith Randich. LC 93-92743. (Illus.). 80p. (Orig.). 1993. pap. 10.00 (0-9642327-1-5) K Randich Pubng.

*Carving the Native American Face. Terry Kramer. (Illus.). 64p. (Orig.). 1995. pap. 12.95 (0-88740-715-3) Schiffer.

Carving the Nativity with Helen Gibson. Helen Gibson & Douglas Congdon-Martin. LC 92-60640. (Illus.). 64p. 1992. pap. 12.95 (0-88740-438-3) Schiffer.

Carving the Old Woman's Shoe: With Larry Green. Larry Green & Mike Ahman. LC 94-65654. (Illus.). 64p. (Orig.). 1994. pap. 12.95 (0-88740-603-3) Schiffer.

Carving the Rose. John Hagensick. (Illus.). 84p. (Orig.). 1993. pap. 12.95 (0-9626107-1-2) L-C Pub.

*Carving the Wizards. Tom Wolfe. LC 94-23251. (Book for Woodcarvers Ser.). (Illus.). 64p. (Orig.). 1995. pap. 12.95 (0-88740-712-9) Schiffer.

Carving Totem Poles & Masks: Native American Folk Art. Alan Bridgewater & Gill Bridgewater. LC 91-726. (Illus.). 192p. 1991. pap. 14.95 (0-8069-8214-4) Sterling.

Carving Traditional Fish Decoys: With Patterns & Instructions for 16 Projects. Anthony Hillman. LC 92-41807. (Illus.). 56p. (Orig.). 1993. pap. 6.95 (0-486-27500-0) Dover.

Carving Traditional Woodspirits with Tom Wolfe. Tom Wolfe & Douglas Congdon-Martin. (Illus.). 48p. 1993. pap. 12.95 (0-88740-538-X) Schiffer.

*Carving Tropical Birds. Anthony Hillman. LC 95-2784. (Illus.). 56p. (Orig.). 1995. pap. text ed. 6.95 (0-486-28579-0) Dover.

Carving Tropical Fish: With Patterns & Instructions for 16 Projects. (Illus.). 40p. (Orig.). 1992. pap. 6.95 (0-486-27094-7) Dover.

Carving Twenty Realistic Game & Songbirds: Complete Patterns & Instructions. George Lehman & David Hunt. (Woodcarvers' Favorite Patterns Ser.: Bk. 1). 100p. 1991. spiral bd., pap. 19.95 (1-56523-004-3) Fox Chapel Pub.

Carving up California: A History of Redistricting, 1951-1984. T. Anthony Quinn. 334p. 1985. pap. text ed. 40.00 (1-883638-03-8) Rose Inst.

Carving Vermont Folk Figures, Bk. 1. Frank C. Russell. (Illus.). 80p. (Orig.). 1989. pap. 8.95 (0-685-29438-2) Stonegate Studios.

Carving Water Birds: Patterns & Instructions for 12 Models. Anothony Hillman. 1990. pap. 6.95 (0-486-26505-6) Dover.

Carving Weathered Wood: Tips & Techniques for Award-Winning Carvings. Gene Bass & Jack Portice. LC 91-37969. (Illus.). 72p. (Orig.). 1991. pap. 10.95 (1-879511-00-2) Vestal.

Carving Western Figures. Harold L. Enlow. LC 83-91429. 57p. 1984. pap. 6.00 (1-882475-05-4) Enlow Wood Carv.

Carving Wild Animals: Life-Size Wood Figures. Bill Dehos & Patrick Spielman. LC 88-12322. (Illus.). 240p. (Orig.). 1988. pap. 19.95 (0-8069-6732-3) Sterling.

Carving Wildlife in Wood: Complete Patterns & Instructions for 20 Exciting Projects. George Lehman & David Hunt. (Woodcarvers' Favorite Patterns Ser.: Bk. 4). 100p. 1991. spiral bd., pap. 19.95 (1-56523-007-8) Fox Chapel Pub.

Carving Wood Stone. Arnold Prince. 1994. pap. 15.95 (1-57101-004-1) MasterMedia Ltd.

Carving Wooden Critters: Includes Power Carving Techniques. Diane Ernst. (Illus.). 48p. 1994. pap. 6.95 (1-56523-038-8) Fox Chapel Pub.

Carving Your Own Carousel Animal. Gene Bass. LC 89-22683. (Illus.). 64p. (Orig.). 1989. pap. 9.95 (0-911572-84-8) Vestal.

Carvings. John Snellings. 400p. (Orig.). 1987. pap. 3.95 (0-8439-2455-1) Dorchester Pub Co.

Carvings, Casts & Replicas: Nineteenth-Century Sculpture from Europe & America in New England Collections. John M. Hunisak. LC 94-11142. (Illus.). 222p. (Orig.). 1994. pap. 39.95 (0-9625262-7-4) Middlebury Coll Mus.

*Carvings of the Moon: A Cycle of Poems. Tom O'Grady. 16p. (Orig.). 1992. pap. 9.95 (0-940475-00-6) Dolphin-Moon.

Cary Family in America. H. G. Cary & I. H. Cary. (Illus.). 120p. 1989. reprint ed. lib. bdg. 27.00 (0-8328-1318-4); reprint ed. pap. 17.00 (0-8328-1319-2) Higginson Bk Co.

Cary Family in England. H. G. Cary. (Illus.). 105p. 1989. reprint ed. lib. bdg. 26.00 (0-8328-1316-8); reprint ed. pap. 16.00 (0-8328-1317-6) Higginson Bk Co.

Cary Grant: A Bio-Bibliography. Beverly B. Buehrer. LC 90-31764. (Bibliographies & Indexes in the Performing Arts Ser.: No. 12). 224p. 1990. text ed. 35.00 (0-313-26443-0, BUG, Greenwood Pr) Greenwood.

Cary Grant: A Touch of Elegance. Warren G. Harris. 1988. mass mkt. 4.50 (0-8217-2539-4) Zebra.

Cary Grant: The Lonely Heart. Charles Higham & Roy Moseley. 436p. 1990. mass mkt. 5.99 (0-380-71009-9) Avon.

Cary Grant: The Lonely Heart. Charles Higham & Roy Moseley. 358p. 1989. 18.95 (0-15-115787-1) HarBrace.

Cary Memorials. S. F. Cary. 306p. 1989. reprint ed. lib. bdg. 59.00 (0-8328-0378-2); reprint ed. pap. 49.00 (0-8328-0379-0) Higginson Bk Co.

Cary-Yale Visconti Tarocchi. Stuart R. Kaplan. 40p. 1984. 35.00 (0-88079-038-5) US Games Syst.

Caryacarya, 3 vols. Anandanagar. pap. write for info. (0-686-95445-9) Ananda Marga.

Caryacarya, 3 vols., Vol. 1. Anandanagar. 37p. pap. 3.95 (0-88476-018-9) Ananda Marga.

Caryacarya, 3 vols., Vol. 2. Anandanagar. 49p. pap. 3.95 (0-88476-019-7) Ananda Marga.

Caryacarya, 3 vols., Vol. 3. Anandanagar. pap. 3.95 (0-88476-020-0) Ananda Marga.

Caryl Chessman: The Red Light Bandit. Frank J. Parker. LC 75-8760. (Illus.). 243p. 1975. 28.95 (0-88229-188-2) Nelson-Hall.

Caryl Churchill: Critical Essays. Ed. by Phyllis R. Randall. LC 88-24473. (Casebooks on Modern Dramatists Ser.: Vol. 3). 214p. 27.00 (0-8240-5841-0, H736) Garland.

Caryocaraceae. Ghillean T. Prance & Marlene F. Da Silva. LC 72-88119. (Flora Neotropica Monograph Ser.: No. 12). (Illus.). 75p. (Orig.). 1973. pap. 9.95 (0-89327-294-9) NY Botanical.

Caryophyllales: Evolution & Systematics. Ed. by H. D. Behnke & T. J. Mabry. LC 93-21309. 1994. 169.00 (0-387-56695-3) Spr-Verlag.

Caryopsis Morphology & Classification in the Triticeae (Pooideae : Poaceae) Edward E. Terrell & Paul M. Peterson. LC 92-47245. (Smithsonian Contributions to Botany Ser.: No. 83). (Illus.). 29p. reprint ed. pap. 25.00 (0-7837-5590-2, 2045383) Bks Demand.

Cas Wagner: Nietzsche Contre Wagner. Friedrich Nietzsche. (FRE.). 1991. pap. 9.95 (0-7859-3982-2) Fr & Eur.

Casa Adobe. 2nd rev. ed. William Lumpkins. LC 86-71415. (Illus.). 64p. 1987. reprint ed. pap. 11.95 (0-941270-34-3) Ancient City Pr.

Casa Braccio. Francis M. Crawford. (Works of Francis Marion Crawford Ser.). 1990. reprint ed. lib. bdg. 79.00 (0-7812-2544-2) Rprt Serv.

Casa Con Dos Puertas, Mala de Guardar. Pedro Calderon De La Barca. 296p. (SPA.). 1978. pap. write for info. (0-7859-5134-2) Fr & Eur.

Casa De Aizgorri. Pio Baroja. Ed. by Maitena Etxebarria. (Nueva Austral Ser.: No. 220). (SPA.). 1991. pap. text ed. 24.95x (84-239-7220-8) Elliots Bks.

Casa de Bernarda Alba. Federico Garcia Lorca. Ed. by Francisco Yndurain. (Nueva Austral Ser.: Vol. 77). (SPA.). 1991. pap. text ed. 13.95 (84-239-1877-7) Elliots Bks.

Casa de Bernarda Alba. Federico Garcia Lorca. Ed. by H. Ramsden. LC 83-19936. (Spanish Texts Ser.). 106p. (SPA.). 1988. text ed. 14.95 (0-7190-0950-2, Pub. by Manchester Univ Pr UK) St Martin.

Casa de Bernarda Alba. Federico Garcia Lorca. 126p. (SPA.). 1945. 6.95 (0-8288-7145-0) Fr & Eur.

Casa de Bernarda Alba. Federico Garcia Lorca. 194p. (SPA.). 1989. 11.95 (0-8288-7088-8, S30339) Fr & Eur.

Casa de Bernarda Alba. 15th ed. Federico G. Lorca. 194p. (SPA.). 1990. pap. 10.95 (0-318-65030-4, S30339) Fr & Eur.

Casa De Dona Constanza: The House of Mrs. Constanza. Emma Leslie. (SPA.). 3.25 (84-7228-322-4, 220140, Pub. by Edit Clie SP) TSELF.

Casa de la Nina Enferma. Angus & Hudson. (Pueblo Junto al Lago (Lakeside Town Ser.)). (SPA.). Date not set. 2.99 (1-56063-408-1, 493995) Editorial Unilit.

Casa De Las Comedias De Cordoba: 1601-1694: Reconstruccion Documental. Angel M. Gomez. (Series C: Fuentes Para La Historia Del Teatro En Espana: No. 15). (Illus.). 177p. (Orig.). (C). 1990. pap. 45.00 (1-85566-002-4, Pub. by Tamesis Bks Ltd UK) Boydell & Brewer.

*Casa de los Espiritus. Isabel Allende. (SPA.). 1995. pap. 9.95 (0-06-095130-3, Harp PBks) HarpC.

Casa de Pedro. Angus & Hudson. (Pueblo Junto al Lago (Lakeside Town Ser.)). (SPA.). Date not set. 2.99 (1-56063-410-3, 493997) Editorial Unilit.

Casa de Reunion. Angus & Hudson. (Pueblo Junto al Lago (Lakeside Town Ser.)). (SPA.). Date not set. 2.99 (1-56063-407-3, 493994) Editorial Unilit.

Casa del Hombre Rico. Angus & Hudson. (Pueblo Junto al Lago (Lakeside Town Ser.)). (SPA.). Date not set. 2.99 (1-56063-409-X, 493996) Editorial Unilit.

Casa di Marcus Lucretius Fronto e le Sue Pitture. W. J. Peters. (Scrinium (Monographs on History, Archaeology & Art History. Published under the Auspices of the Netherlands Institute & the Foundation of Friends of the Dutch Institute in Rome) Ser.: Vol. V). (Illus.). 400p. (ITA.). 1992. 177.00 (90-5170-163-2) IBD Ltd.

Casa Embrujada. Jan Pienkowski. (Illus.). 12p. (SPA.). (J). (ps-6). 1992. 14.95 (0-525-45002-5, DCB) Dutton Child Bks.

Casa en Mango Street. Sandra Cisneros. (SPA.). 1994. pap. 9.00 (0-679-75526-8, Vin) Random.

Casa Grace in Peru: Second Case Study in an NPA Series on United States Business Performance Abroad. Eugene W. Burgess & Frederick H. Harbison. Ed. by Stuart Bruchey. LC 80-557. (Multinational Corporations Ser.). (Illus.). 1981. reprint ed. lib. bdg. 19.95 (0-405-13353-7) Ayer.

Casa Grande: A Novel. Alvaro Cepeda Samudio. Tr. by Seymour Menton & Gabriel G. Marquez. (Texas Pan American Ser.). (Illus.). 112p. (Orig.). 1991. text ed. 17.95 (0-292-74667-9); pap. 9.95 (0-292-74673-3) U of Tex Pr.

Casa Grande Ruins National Monument. Rose Houk. Ed. by T. J. Priehs. LC 86-63416. (Illus.). 48p. (Orig.). 1988. pap. 4.95 (0-911408-71-1) SW Pks Mnmts.

Casa Llena de Gente. Angus & Hudson. (Pueblo Junto al Lago (Lakeside Town Ser.)). (SPA.). Date not set. 2.99 (1-56063-412-X, 493999) Editorial Unilit.

Casa Loma & the Man Who Made It. Ed. by John Denison. (Illus.). 48p. (Orig.). pap. 5.99 (0-317-05893-2, Pub. by Boston Mills Pr CN) Genl Dist Srvs.

Casa Malaparte. Marida Talamona et al. LC 91-44966. (Illus.). 168p. (Orig.). 1992. pap. 14.95 (1-878271-39-3) Princeton Arch.

Casa Mexicana: The Architecture, Design, & Style of Mexico. Tim Street-Porter. LC 89-11382. (Illus.). 272p. 1989. 50.00 (1-55670-097-0); pap. 27.50 (1-55670-367-8) Stewart Tabori & Chang.

Casa Sulla Collina. Nicolo D'Alessandro. (Illus.). 14p. 1988. pap. 75.00 (0-89304-650-7) Cross-Cultrl NY.

Casa Valledorres: Branded (Book II) Maggie R. Stone. 144p. (Orig.). 1991. pap. 5.95 (0-9627059-1-8) M R Stone Minst.

Casa Valledorres: Camden (Book III) Maggie R. Stone. 128p. (Orig.). 1991. pap. 5.95 (0-9627059-2-6) M R Stone Minst.

Casa Valledorres: The Portrait (Book I) Maggie R. Stone. 176p. (Orig.). 1990. pap. 5.95 (0-9627059-0-X) M R Stone Minst.

Casablanca: Fiftieth Anniversary Commemorative. Frank Miller. Ed. by Linda Sunshine. (Illus.). 224p. 1992. 29.95 (1-878685-14-7); pap. 19.95 (1-878685-17-1) Turner Pub GA.

Casablanca: Script & Legend - The 50th Anniversary Edition. Howard Koch. 255p. 1992. pap. 16.95 (0-87951-319-5) Overlook Pr.

Casablanca Companion. Jeff Siegel. LC 91-46776. 160p. 1992. pap. 10.95 (0-87833-796-2) Taylor Pub.

Casablanca Connection: French Colonial Policy, 1936-1943. William A. Hoisington, Jr. LC 83-5902. xiv, 320p. 1984. 37.50 (0-8078-1574-8) U of NC Pr.

Casablanca Cookbook: Wining & Dining at Rick's. Sarah Key et al. LC 92-26458. 1992. 7.95 (1-55859-474-4) Abbeville Pr.

Casablanca Man: The Career of Michael Curtiz. James C. Robertson. LC 92-33281. (Illus.). 224p. 1993. 25.00 (0-415-06804-5, B0722, Routledge NY) Routledge.

*Casablanca Man: The Cinema of Michael Curtiz. 1994. pap. 16.95 (0-415-11577-9, B4536) Routledge.

*Casablanca to VE Day: A Paratrooper's Memoir. Darrell G. Harris. 32p. 1995. pap. 7.00 (0-8059-3771-4) Dorrance.

Casado por Uida. Mike Phillipps & Marilyn Phillipps. 208p. 1986. pap. text ed. write for info. (1-884794-05-X) Eden Pubng.

Casado por Vida Manual de Liderato. Mike Phillipps & Marilyn Phillipps. 320p. 1986. pap. text ed. write for info. (1-884794-06-8) Eden Pubng.

Casados pero Felices (How to Be Happy Though Married) Tim LaHaye. (SPA.). 1986. 4.25 (0-8423-6252-5, 490210) Editorial Unilit.

Casals & the Art of Interpretation. David Blum. LC 77-1444. 1980. pap. 14.00 (0-520-04032-5) U CA Pr.

Casanova's Homecoming. Arthur Schnitzler. Tr. by Eden Paul & Cedar Paul. LC 74-175576. reprint ed. 37.50 (0-404-05619-9) AMS Pr.

Casanova's "Icosameron", or the Story of Edward & Elizabeth Who Spent 81 Years in the Land of the Megamicres, Original Inhabitants of Protocosmos in the Interior of Our Globe. abr. ed. Jacques Casanova De Seingalt. Tr. by Rachel Zurer. LC 83-82006. (Illus.). 260p. 1986. 17.95 (0-941752-02-X); pap. 10.95 (0-941752-00-3) Jenna Pr.

Casarett & Doull's Toxicology: The Basic Science of Poisons. 4th ed. Mary O. Amdur. 1056p. 1991. text ed. 69.00 (0-07-105239-9) Hlth Prof Div.

*Casarett & Doull's Toxicology: The Basic Science of Poisons. 5th rev. ed. Curtis D. Klaassen. 1056p. 1995. 70.00x (0-07-105476-6) Hlth Prof Div.

Casas: In Search of the Poor of Jesus Christ - En Busca de los Pobres de Jesucristo. Gustavo Gutierrez. Tr. by Robert R. Barr. 525p. 1992. reprint ed. 29.95 (0-88344-838-6) Orbis Bks.

Casas De Animales. Joy Evans & Jo E. Moore. Tr. by Liz Wolfe & Dora Ficklin. (Illus.). 20p. (SPA.). (J). (ps-1). 1990. pap. text ed. 4.95 (1-55799-189-8) Evan-Moor Corp.

Casava & Chica: Bread & Beer of the Amazonian Indians. Linda Mowat. 1989. pap. 25.00 (0-7478-0008-1, Pub. by Shire UK) St Mut.

Casca, No. 1: Eternal Mercenary. Barry Sadler. pap. 3.95 (0-515-09535-4) Jove Pubns.

Casca, No. 10: Conquistador. Barry Sadler. pap. 3.99 (0-515-09601-6) Jove Pubns.

Casca, No. 11: Legionaire. Barry Sadler. pap. 3.99 (0-515-09602-4) Jove Pubns.

Casca, No. 13: Assassin. Barry Sadler. 192p. 1988. pap. 3.99 (0-515-09911-2) Jove Pubns.

Casca, No. 14: The Phoenix. Barry Sadler. 192p. 1987. pap. 3.99 (0-515-09471-4) Jove Pubns.

Casca, No. 15: Pirate. Barry Sadler. 176p. 1987. pap. 3.99 (0-515-09599-0) Jove Pubns.

Casca, No. 16: Desert Mercenary. Barry Sadler. 192p. (Orig.). 1987. pap. 3.99 (0-515-09556-7) Jove Pubns.

Casca, No. 17: Warrior. Barry Sadler. 192p. 1987. pap. text ed. 3.99 (0-515-09603-2) Jove Pubns.

Casca, No. 18: Cursed. Barry Sadler. 192p. 1987. pap. text ed. 3.99 (0-515-09109-X) Jove Pubns.

Casca, No. 19: Samurai. Barry Sadler. 176p. 1988. pap. 3.99 (0-515-09516-8) Jove Pubns.

Casca, No. 2: God of Death. Barry Sadler. pap. 3.95 (0-515-09919-8) Jove Pubns.

Casca, No. 20: Soldier of Gideon. Barry Sadler. 1988. pap. 3.99 (0-515-09701-2) Jove Pubns.

Casca, No. 21: The Trench Soldier. Barry Sadler. 176p. 1989. pap. 3.99 (0-515-09931-7) Jove Pubns.

Casca, No. 22: The Mongol. Barry Sadler. 176p. 1990. pap. 3.99 (0-515-10240-7) Jove Pubns.

Casca, No. 3: The War Lord. Barry Sadler. (Orig.). 1991. pap. 3.99 (0-515-09996-1) Jove Pubns.

Casca, No. 4: Panzer Soldier. Barry Sadler. 1991. pap. 3.99 (0-515-09472-2) Jove Pubns.

Casca, No. 5: The Barbarian. Barry Sadler. (Orig.). 1991. pap. 3.99 (0-515-09147-2) Jove Pubns.

Casca, No. 6: The Persian. Barry Sadler. (Orig.). 1992. pap. 3.99 (0-515-10796-4) Jove Pubns.

Casca, No. 7: Damned. Barry Sadler. 1992. pap. 3.99 (0-515-09473-0) Jove Pubns.

Casca, No. 8: Soldier of Fortune. Barry Sadler. pap. 3.99 (0-515-09723-3) Jove Pubns.

Casca, No. 9: The Sentinel. Barry Sadler. pap. 3.99 (0-515-09997-X) Jove Pubns.

Cascade. John M. Bennett. 1987. 1.00 (0-318-41796-0) Luna Bisonte.

Cascade. Hannah Fisher. 32p. (Orig.). 1993. pap. 5.00 (1-882913-03-5) Thornton LA.

Cascade Air-Stripping System for Removal of Semi-Volatile Organic Contaminants: Feasibility Study. 68p. 1989. pap. 16.00 (0-89867-505-7, 90555) Am Water Wks Assn.

*Cascade Alpine Guide: Climbing & High Routes, Rainy Pass to Fraser River. 2nd ed. Fred Beckey. (Illus.). 322p. 1995. vinyl bd. 25.00 (0-89886-423-2) Mountaineers.

Cascade Alpine Guide: Columbia River to Stevens Pass. 2nd ed. Fred Beckey. LC 86-23899. (Climbing & High Routes Ser.: Vol. 1). (Illus.). 350p. 1987. vinyl bd. 25.00 (0-89886-127-6) Mountaineers.

Cascade Alpine Guide: Rainy Pass to Fraser River. Fred Beckey. LC 81-2335. (Climbing & High Routes Ser.: Vol. 3). (Illus.). 328p. (Orig.). 1981. pap. 25.00 (0-89886-002-4) Mountaineers.

Cascade Alpine Guide: Stevens Pass to Rainy Pass. 2nd ed. Fred Beckey. LC 86-23899. (Climbing & High Routes Ser.: Vol. 2). (Illus.). 360p. 1989. pap. 25.00 (0-89886-152-7) Mountaineers.

*Cascade Division. Martin Burwash. (Illus.). 128p. 1995. 39.95 (1-884831-00-1) Fox Pubns.

Cascade Emission Control Appl. Guide 1966-94. Ed. by Chilton Staff. 672p. 1994. pap. 35.00 (0-8019-8550-1) Chilton.

*Cascade Emission Control Application Guide, 1966-95. Ed. by Chilton Staff. 912p. 1995. pap. 45.00 (0-8019-8692-3) Chilton.

Cascade Emission Control Application Guide 1993. 256p. 1993. pap. 17.95 (0-8019-8516-1) Chilton.

Cascade Empire. Esther Smith. LC 81-10836. 1989. pap. 13.95 (0-87949-209-0) Ashley Bks.

Cascade of Arms: Controlling Conventional Weapons Proliferation in the 1990s. Ed. by Andrew J. Pierre. 385p. (C). Date not set. 42.95x (0-8157-7064-2); pap. 18.95 (0-8157-7063-4) Brookings.

Cascade-Olympic Natural History. Daniel Mathews. LC 88-61494. (Illus.). 640p. (Orig.). 1988. pap. 22.50 (0-9620782-0-4) Raven Edit.

An Asterisk (*) at the beginning of an entry indicates that the title is appearing in BIP for the first time.

Cascade Voices: Conversations with Washington Mountaineers. Malcolm S. Bates. (Illus.). 224p. (Orig.). 1992. pap. 19.95 (0-938567-34-9) Cloudcap.

Cascades & Courage: The History of the Town of Vernon & the City of Rockville (Connecticut) George S. Brookes. (Illus.). 529p. 1993. reprint ed. lib. bdg. 53.00 (0-8328-2902-1) Higginson Bk Co.

Cascadet Student Manual. Cascade Graphics Development Staff. 1985. pap. text ed. 16.95 (0-07-016392-8) McGraw.

Cascadia. McKee. (Illus.). 394p. (C). reprint ed. 45.00 (1-878907-51-4) TechBooks.

Cascadia Wild: Protecting an International Ecosystem. Ed. by Mitch Friedman & Paul Lindholdt. LC 93-78844. (Illus.). 192p. (Orig.). (C). 1994. pap. 19.95 (0-939116-35-9) Frontier OR.

Cascading Seasons: The Progression of Time in the Mountains. Michael P. Jones. (Illus.). 190p. (Orig.). 1988. 29.95 (0-89904-219-8); text ed. 18.95 (0-89904-217-1); pap. 13.95 (0-89904-218-X) Crumb Elbow Pub.

Cascading Seasons: 1988 Calendar. Michael P. Jones. (Illus.). 32p. (Orig.). 1987. text ed. 10.00 (0-89904-214-7); pap. text ed. 5.00 (0-89904-215-5) Crumb Elbow Pub.

Cascading Seasons: 1988 Calendar. limited ed. Michael P. Jones. (Illus.). 32p. (Orig.). 1987. 25.00 (0-89904-216-3) Crumb Elbow Pub.

Cascando see Comedies et Actes Divers

Cascanueces - Nutcracker. E. T. Hoffmann. (J). (ps-3). 1994. pap. 2.95 (0-486-28012-8) Dover.

Case. Barry J. Blake. (Textbooks in Linguistics Ser.). (Illus.). 226p. (C). 1994. 59.95 (0-521-44114-5); pap. 19.95 (0-521-44661-9) Cambridge U Pr.

CASE. Pieter R. Mimno. 250p. 1994. text ed. 40.00i (0-07-042326-1) McGraw.

Case: Computer-Aided Software Engineering. Theodore G. Lewis. 1991. text ed. 54.95 (0-442-00361-7) Van Nos Reinhold.

CASE: Current Practice, Future Prospects. Kathy Spurr & Paul Layzell. 250p. 1992. text ed. 54.95 (0-471-93304-X) Wiley.

***Case: I&T Shop Manual - Maxxum Models.** 1992. pap. 18.95 (0-87288-515-1, C-41) Intertec Pub.

CASE: The Potential & the Pitfalls. John A. Buckland. 1993. text ed. 49.95 (0-471-56048-0) Wiley.

CASE: Using Software Development Tools. 2nd ed. Alan S. Fisher. 352p. 1991. pap. text ed. 27.95 (0-471-53042-5) Wiley.

Case Against Abortion: A Logical Argument for Life. Lori Van Winden. LC 88-82302. 1988. pap. 4.95 (0-89243-295-0) Liguori Pubns.

Case Against Camoes: A Seldom Considered Chapter from Ezra Pound's Campaign to Discredit Rhetorical Poetry. Norwood Andrews, Jr. (Utah Studies in Literature & Linguistics: Vol. 27). 146p. 1988. text ed. 22.50 (0-8204-0524-8) P Lang Pubs.

Case Against Christianity. Michael Martin. 1991. 44.95 (0-87722-767-5) Temple U Pr.

Case Against Christianity. Michael Martin. 290p. 1993. pap. 22.95 (1-56639-081-8) Temple U Pr.

Case Against Direct Election of the President: A Defense of the Electoral College. Judith Best. LC 74-25366. 256p. 1975. 34.50 (0-8014-0916-0) Cornell U Pr.

Case Against Divorce. Diane Medved. 320p. 1989. 18.95 (1-55611-127-4) D I Fine.

Case Against Divorce. Diane Medved. 272p. 1990. mass mkt. 5.99 (0-8041-0633-9) Ivy Books.

Case Against "Free Trade" GATT, NAFTA, & the Globalization of Corporate Power. Ralph Nader et al. 230p. (Orig.). 1993. pap. 10.00 (1-55643-169-4) North Atlantic.

Case Against Hillman. Richard Darwick. 1980. pap. 2.25 (0-8439-0818-1) Dorchester Pub Co.

Case Against Jones: Study of Psychical Phenomena. John Vyvyan. 220p. 1966. 8.50 (0-227-67683-1) Attic Pr.

Case Against Old Habits. Janet L. Sadler. (Amherst Writers & Artists Chapbook Ser.). 32p. (Orig.). 1988. pap. 8.00 (0-941895-01-7) Amherst Wri Art.

Case Against Parliamentary Policing. Tony Jefferson. (Crime, Justice & Social Policy Ser.). 176p. 1990. 90.00 (0-335-09326-4, Open Univ Pr); pap. 32.00 (0-335-09325-6, Open Univ Pr) Taylor & Francis.

***Case Against Patents: Selected Reprints from Midnight Engineering & Nuts & volts Magazines.** Don Lancaster. 88p. (Orig.). 1994. pap. 12.50 (1-882193-70-9) Synergetics Pr.

Case Against Religion: A Psychotherapist's View & the Case Against Religiosity. Albert Ellis. 57p. 1985. 4.00 (0-910309-18-3, 5096) Am Atheist.

Case Against Satan. Ray Russell. 1962. 10.95 (0-8392-1008-6) Astor-Honor.

Case Against Satellites. 1974. 2.00 (0-686-09555-3) Network Project.

***Case Against School Choice.** Kevin B. Smith & Kenneth J. Meier. LC 94-33509. 184p. 1995. 55.00 (1-56324-519-1); pap. 19.95 (1-56324-520-5) M E Sharpe.

Case Against the Constitution: From the Antifederalists to the Present. Ed. by John F. Manley & Kenneth M. Dolbeare. LC 87-4640. 200p. 1987. pap. text ed. 22.95 (0-87332-433-1) M E Sharpe.

Case Against the General: Manuel Noriega & the Politics of American Justice. Steve Albert. (Illus.). 384p. 1994. text ed. 25.00 (0-684-19375-2, Scribners) S&S Trade.

Case Against the Reckless Congress. Marjorie Holt. LC 76-1806. (Republican Study Committee Papers Ser.: Vol. 1). 248p. 1976. pap. 1.95 (0-916054-08-X) Green Hill.

Case Against the SAT. James Crouse & Dale Trusheim. xvi, 224p. 1988. 22.50 (0-226-12142-9) U Ch Pr.

Case Aide. Jack Rudman. (Career Examination Ser.: C-187). 1994. pap. 19.95 (0-8373-0187-4) Nat Learn.

***Case Analysis & Fundamentals of Legal Writing.** William P. Statsky & R. John Wernet, Jr. LC 94-26223. 425p. 1994. pap. text ed. 53.25 (0-314-04018-8) West Pub.

Case Analysis & Fundamentals of Legal Writing. 3rd ed. William P. Statsky & R. John Wernet, Jr. (Illus.). 424p. 1988. reprint ed. text ed. 53.25 (0-314-43754-1) West Pub.

Case Analysis & Fundamentals of Legal Writing. William P. Statsky & R. John Wernet, Jr. (Illus.). 216p. 1992. reprint ed. teacher ed, pap. text ed. write for info. (0-314-46555-3) West Pub.

Case & Agreement in Inuit. Reineke Bok-Bennema. LC 91-34845. (Studies in Generative Grammar: No. 38). xx, 308p. (C). 1991. lib. bdg. 91.50 (3-11-013025-4) Mouton.

Case & Materials on EEC Law. Stephen Weatherill & Sharon Turner. 460p. (C). 1992. 51.00 (1-85431-122-0, Pub. by Blackstone Pr UK) W W Gaunt.

Case & Materials on Partnership Taxation, 1991 Supplement. Curtis J. Berger & Peter J. Wiedenbeck. (American Casebook Ser.). 118p. (C). 1991. pap. text ed. 12.00 (0-314-89930-8) West Pub.

***Case & Object Oriented Development.** Kathy Spurr et al. 233p. 1994. text ed. 44.95 (0-471-95187-0) Wiley.

Case & Other Functional Categories in Finnish Syntax. Ed. by Anders Homberg & Urpo Nikanne. LC 93-1774. (Studies in Generative Grammar: Vol. 38). ix, 248p. (C). 1993. 78.65 (3-11-013812-3) Mouton.

Case & Son: The Seventy-Five-Year Saga of Case, Pomeroy & Company, Inc. Brent Filson. Ed. by Ceila D. Robbins. (Illus.). 196p. 1992. write for info. (0-944641-03-2) Greenwich Pub Group.

***Case & the Issues for IS Management.** HMSO Staff. 148p. 1994. pap. 60.00 (0-11-330594-X, HM0594X) UNIPUB.

Case Approach to Counseling & Psychotherapy. 3rd ed. Gerald Corey. LC 90-36724. (Psychology-Counseling Ser.). 432p. (C). 1991. pap. 24.95 (0-534-13782-2) Brooks-Cole.

***Case Approach to Counseling & Psychotherapy.** 4th ed. Gerald Corey. LC 95-15146. 1996. pap. 25.95 (0-534-26580-4) Brooks-Cole.

Case Assessment & Evaluation. Don Howarth & Suzelle Smith. 1989. 98.00 (0-685-30635-6) Clark Boardman Callaghan.

Case Assessment & Evaluation. annuals suppl. ed. Don Howarth & Suzelle Smith. 1989. write for info. (0-318-66671-5) Clark Boardman Callaghan.

Case Atlas of Gastroenterology. Danzi & Landman. 335p. 1994. 129.00 (0-683-02366-7) Williams & Wilkins.

Case-Based Learning. Ed. by Janet L. Kolodner. LC 93-20470. 176p. (C). 1993. lib. bdg. 105.00 (0-7923-9343-0) Kluwer Ac.

Case-Based Planning: Viewing Planning As a Memory Task. Kristian J. Hammond. 277p. 1989. text ed. 53.00 (0-12-322060-2) Acad Pr.

Case-Based Reasoning. Janet Kolodner. LC 93-35703. 612p. 1993. 54.95 (1-55860-237-2) Morgan Kaufmann.

Case-Based Reasoning: Papers from the 1993 Workshop. Ed. by David Leake. (Technical Reports). (Illus.). 130p. (Orig.). 1993. spiral bd. 25.00 (0-929280-48-2) Amer Artificial.

Case Based Reasoning & Information Retrieval: Opportunities for Technology Sharing: Papers from the 1993 Spring Symposium. Ed. by Peter Anick & Evangelos Simoudis. (Technical Reports). (Illus.). 145p. (Orig.). (C). 1993. spiral bd. 25.00 (0-929280-45-8) Amer Artificial.

***Case-Based Reasoning in Design.** Mary L. Maher et al. 350p. 1995. text ed. 70.00 (0-8058-1831-6); pap. text ed. 35.00 (0-8058-1832-4) L Erlbaum Assocs.

***Case-Based Telematic Systems: Towards Equity in Health Care.** F. Roger-France et al. LC 94-77522. (Studies in Health Technology & Informatics: Vol. 14). 207p. 1994. 93.00 (90-5199-182-7) IOS Press.

CASE Benchmarks: Proceedings, 1988. 1988. 250.00 (0-318-41122-9) Digit Consult MA.

Case Book. Theodore Enslin. 105p. 1987. pap. 8.00 (0-937013-20-X) Potes Poets.

Case-Book of Astral Projection, 545-746. Robert Crookall. 160p. 1980. pap. 3.95 (0-8065-0730-6, Citadel Pr) Carol Pub Group.

Case-Book of Sherlock Holmes. Arthur Conan Doyle. Ed. by W. W. Robson. (Oxford Sherlock Holmes Ser.). 336p. (C). 1993. 11.00 (0-19-212311-4, 14608) OUP.

Case-Book of Sherlock Holmes. Arthur Conan Doyle. Ed. by W. W. Robson. (World's Classics Ser.). 336p. 1995. reprint ed. pap. 5.95 (0-19-282374-4) OUP.

Case Book on the Law of Delict - Vonnisbundel oor die Deliktereg. J. Neethling et al. 759p. 1991. pap. write for info. (0-7021-2593-8, Pub. by Juta SA) W W Gaunt.

***Case Book on the Law of Persons & Family Law.** D. S. Cronje. 544p. 1990. pap. 41.00 (0-409-02080-X, SA) Butterworth Legal Pubs.

Case Books of John Hunter, FRS. Ed. by Elizabeth Allen et al. (Illus.). 688p. 1993. 148.00 (1-85070-542-9) Prthnon Pub.

***CASE Campaign Standards: Management & Reporting Standards for Educational Fund-Raising Campaigns.** CASE Staff. 23p. 1994. 15.00 (0-89964-307-8) Coun Adv & Supp Ed.

Case Citation in the Babylonian Talmud. Eliezer Segal. 340p. 1990. 69.95 (1-55540-524-X, 14 02 10) Scholars Pr GA.

Case Citation Series, No. 9. Ed. by Stephen B. Thomas. 1991. 38.00 (1-56534-021-3) NOLPE.

Case Citation Series, No. 10. Ed. by Stephen B. Thomas. 1991. 38.00 (1-56534-022-1) NOLPE.

Case Citations, No. 8. 1989. 33.00 (1-56534-020-5) NOLPE.

***Case Citations No. 16: How Free Is Speech in the Schools?** Ed. by Perry Zirkel. (Nolpe Case Citations Ser.). 33p. (Orig.). Date not set. pap. 34.95 (1-56534-062-0) NOLPE.

***Case Citations No. 17: Violence & School Safety.** Ed. by Charles Russo. (Nolpe Case Citation Ser.). (Orig.). Date not set. pap. 40.00 (1-56534-065-5) NOLPE.

Case Citations, 1993. Joan Cursio et al. Ed. by Charles J. Russo. (Fifteenth Series - School Governance). 1993. pap. 40.00 (1-56534-054-X) NOLPE.

Case Closed: Lee Harvey Oswald & the Assassination of JFK. Gerald L. Posner. 1994. pap. 14.95 (0-385-47446-6, Anchor NY) Doubleday.

Case Closed: Lee Harvey Oswald & the Assassination of JFK. Gerald L. Posner. LC 93-12821. 1993. 25.00 (0-679-41825-3) Random.

Case Collection 1983: Bibliography Containing Detailed Case Abstracts of over 300 Cases. Case Publishing Staff. 300p. (Orig.). (C). 1983. pap. text ed. 10.00 (0-685-07831-0, Case Pub) Lord Pub.

Case Control Studies: Design, Conduct, Analysis. James J. Schlesselman & Paul D. Stolley. (Monographs in Epidemiology & Biostatistics: No. 2). (Illus.). (C). 1982. text ed. 35.00 (0-19-502933-X) OUP.

Case Counting in the Special Civil Part of the Essex County (NJ) Superior Court. National Center for State Courts Staff. 36p. 1985. 2.00 (0-685-16627-9, NERO-182) Natl Ctr St Courts.

Case de Bernarda Alba. Federico Garcia Lorca. 208p. (SPA.). 1988. 11.95 (0-8288-7012-8) Fr & Eur.

Case de Damballah. Petion Savain. (B. E. Ser.: No. 15). (FRE.). 1939. 29.00 (0-8115-2966-5) Periodicals Srv.

Case. Descendants of Stephen Case of Marlboro NY, Including Allied Families. Lynn M. Case. 82p. 1991. reprint ed. lib. bdg. 27.00 (0-8328-1985-9); reprint ed. pap. 17.00 (0-8328-1986-7) Higginson Bk Co.

Case Development Problems in Hematology: Ser. 1, the Red Cell. John W. Harris & Daniel L. Horrigan. LC 63-6774. (Commonwealth Fund Publications). (Illus.). 204p. 1963. pap. 7.95 (0-674-09850-1) HUP.

***Case Dragon in Distress.** E. W. Hildrick. 1994. pap. 2.99 (0-517-13316-4) Random.

CASE Environment Guide. Simon Holloway. 413p. 1993. 75.95 (0-291-39795-6) Ashgate Pub Co.

Case Exercises in Clinical Reasoning. P. Beck. 1981. 35.00 (0-8151-0597-5, Yr Bk Med Pubs) Mosby Yr Bk.

Case Exercises in Clinical Reasoning. Paul Beck. LC 81-10414. (Illus.). 333p. reprint ed. pap. 95.00 (0-8357-7587-9, 2056908) Bks Demand.

Case Exercises in Operations Research. Ed. by Michael J. Martin & Raymond A. Denison. LC 75-146548. (Illus.). 228p. reprint ed. pap. 65.00 (0-317-09630-3, 2020328) Bks Demand.

Case Filing & Disposition Reporting System for Circuit, Criminal, Chancery, & Law & Equity Courts of Tennessee, Vol. VI. National Center for State Courts. 107p. 1976. 6.42 (0-685-16628-7, MAB-125) Natl Ctr St Courts.

Case for a First-Dollar, Permanent Investment Tax Credit. write for info. (0-318-69877-3, PR-120) Manu All Prod & Innov.

Case for a Humanistic Poetics. Daniel R. Schwarz. LC 90-23546. 232p. (C). 1991. text ed. 34.95 (0-8122-3070-1); pap. text ed. 17.95 (0-8122-1353-X) U of Pa Pr.

***Case for a Long-Range State Telecommunications Policy for Texas.** 51p. (Orig.). (C). 1994. pap. text ed. 25.00x (0-7881-1437-9) Diane Pub.

Case for a Long-Range State Telecommunications Policy in Texas. Telecommunications Working Group. (Working Paper Ser.: No. 70). 43p. 1993. 5.00 (0-685-72210-4) LBJ Sch Pub Aff.

Case for a New ECU: Towards Another Monetary System. Jacques Riboud. Tr. by Stephen Harrison. LC 88-18641. 250p. 1989. text ed. 49.95 (0-312-02124-0) St Martin.

Case for Advertising Self-Regulation: An Essay. J. J. Boddewyn. 1991. 10.00 (0-685-64975-X) Intl Advertising Assn.

Case for an Auxiliary Priesthood. Raymond Hickey. LC 81-16950. 160p. (Orig.). reprint ed. pap. 45.60 (0-8357-8824-5, 2033559) Bks Demand.

Case for an Illinois Coal Severance Tax. Steve Pittman. (Illus.). (Orig.). 1984. pap. text ed. 2.00 (0-943724-08-2) Illinois South.

Case for & Against Psychical Belief. Carl Murchison. LC 75-7389. (Perspectives in Psychical Research Ser.). (Illus.). 1975. reprint ed. 33.95 (0-405-07037-3) Ayer.

Case for Animal Experimentation: An Evolutionary & Ethical Perspective. Michael A. Fox. 278p. 1985. pap. 11.00 (0-520-06023-7) U CA Pr.

Case for Animal Rights. Tom Regan. LC 83-1087. (C). 1983. pap. 14.00 (0-520-05460-1, CAL 741) U CA Pr.

Case for Bureaucracy: A Public Administration Polemic. 3rd ed. Charles T. Goodsell. LC 93-36367. 240p. (C). 1994. pap. text ed. 19.95x (1-56643-007-0) Chatham Hse Pubs.

Case for Case Studies: An Immigrant's Journal. Paul R. Abramson. 248p. (C). 1992. 49.95 (0-8039-3695-8); pap. 21.95 (0-8039-3696-6) Sage.

Case for Cases in Teacher Education. 1991. 14.00 (0-89333-071-X) AACTE.

Case for Change: Rethinking the Preparation of Educators. Seymour B. Sarason. LC 92-29937. (Education-Higher Education Ser.). 317p. 1993. 29.95 (1-55542-504-6) Jossey-Bass.

***Case for Christian Humanism.** fac. ed. R. William Franklin & Joseph M. Shaw. LC 91-26337. 288p. 1991. reprint ed. pap. 82.10 (0-7837-7954-2, 2047710) Bks Demand.

Case for Christianity. C. S. Lewis. 64p. 1989. pap. 5.95 (0-02-086750-6, Collier S&S) S&S Trade.

***Case for Clerical Celibacy: Its Historical Development & Theological Foundations.** Alfons Stickler. 106p. Date not set. pap. 10.95 (0-89870-533-9) Ignatius Pr.

Case for Commitment to Teacher Growth: Research on Teacher Evaluation. Richard J. Stiggins & Daniel L. Duke. LC 87-12470. (Educational Leadership Ser.). 164p. 1988. 59.50 (0-88706-669-0); pap. 19.95 (0-88706-670-4) State U NY Pr.

Case for Conservatism. Francis G. Wilson. 94p. 1990. 21.95 (0-88738-322-X) Transaction Pubs.

Case for Conservatism. Francis G. Wilson. LC 71-88996. 74p. 1969. reprint ed. text ed. 35.00 (0-8371-2113-2, WICC, Greenwood Pr) Greenwood.

Case for Creation. 3rd rev. ed. Wayne Frair & Percival Davis. (Illus.). 155p. 1983. reprint ed. pap. text ed. 7.95 (0-940384-11-6) Creation Research.

***Case for Dualism.** Ed. by John R. Smythies & John Beloff. LC 88-36540. 283p. 1989. pap. 80.70 (0-7837-8440-6, 2049244) Bks Demand.

Case for Early Reading. George L. Stevens. Ed. by William E. Amos. LC 67-26006. 180p. 1968. 7.20 (0-87527-076-X) Green.

Case for Earmarked Taxes: Government Spending & Public Choice. Ranjit S. Teja & Barry Bracewell-Milnes. 103p. (C). 1991. text ed. 59.95 (0-255-36241-2, Pub. by Inst Economic Affairs UK) St Mut.

Case for Federalism: Grace A. Tanner Lecture in Human Values. Rex E. Lee. 1985. 8.00 (0-685-60165-X) E T Woolf.

Case for God. William E. Kaufman. 120p. (Orig.). 1991. pap. 10.99 (0-8272-0458-2) Chalice Pr.

***Case for Heaven: Near-Death Experiences as Evidence of the Afterlife.** Mally Cox-Chapman. LC 94-46671. 1995. write for info. (0-399-14024-7) Putnam Pub Group.

Case for International Money. Norman R. Gibson. Ed. by Mira Wilkins. LC 78-3913. (International Finance Ser.). 1979. lib. bdg. 26.95 (0-405-11217-3) Ayer.

Case for IRAs. Aldona Robbins & Gary Robbins. 1991. pap. 10.00 (0-943802-66-0, 163) Natl Ctr Pol.

Case for Jenny Archer. Ellen Conford. LC 88-14169. (Springboard Bks.). (Illus.). (J). (gr. 2-4). 1988. 12.95 (0-316-15266-8) Little.

Case for Justice: Strengthening Decision Making & Policy in Public Administration. Gerald M. Pops & Thomas J. Pavlak. LC 91-12793. (Public Administration Ser.). 221p. 1991. 29.95 (1-55542-375-2) Jossey-Bass.

Case for Labour. Austin V. Mitchell. LC 82-17162. 228p. reprint ed. pap. 65.00 (0-317-30099-7, 2025267) Bks Demand.

Case for Latin see Foreign Language Teaching: Challenges to the Profession

Case for Legal Ethics: Legal Ethics As a Source for a Universal Ethic. Vincent Luizzi. (SUNY Series in Ethical Theory). 176p. (C). 1993. 59.50 (0-7914-1271-7); pap. 19.95 (0-7914-1272-5) State U NY Pr.

Case for Legalizing Drugs. Richard L. Miller. LC 90-7379. 264p. 1991. text ed. 21.95 (0-275-93459-4, C3459, Praeger Pubs) Greenwood.

Case for Legibility. John Ryder. (Illus.). 1979. 8.50 (0-89679-002-9) Moretus Pr.

Case for Liberty. Helen H. Miller. LC 65-16295. (Illus.). 270p. reprint ed. pap. 77.00 (0-8357-3051-4, 2039307) Bks Demand.

Case for Life After Death. Elizabeth McAdams & Raymond Bayless. LC 80-29289. 168p. 1981. 23.95 (0-88229-592-6) Nelson-Hall.

Case for Live Public Butterfly Habitats in the United States. W. Mark Cotham. (YES Special Publication Ser.: No. 7). 33p. 1992. pap. text ed. 5.95 (1-884256-08-2) Yng Entomol.

Case for Mars. Ed. by Penelope J. Boston. (Science & Technology Ser.: Vol. 57). 348p. 1984. lib. bdg. 45.00 (0-87703-197-5, Pub. by Am Astro Soc); pap. text ed. 25.00 (0-87703-198-3, Pub. by Am Astro Soc) Univelt Inc.

Case for Mars II. Christopher P. McKay. (Science & Technology Ser.: Vol. 62). (Illus.). 730p. (Orig.). 1985. lib. bdg. 30.00 (0-87703-219-X); pap. text ed. 20.00 (0-87703-220-3) Univelt Inc.

Case for Mars III: Strategies for Exploration - General Interest & Overview. Ed. by Carol Stoker. (Science & Technology Ser.: Vol. 74). (Illus.). 744p. 1989. lib. bdg. 37.50 (0-87703-303-X, Pub. by Am Astro Soc); pap. text ed. 27.50 (0-87703-304-8, Pub. by Am Astro Soc) Univelt Inc.

Case for Mars III: Strategies for Exploration - Technical. Ed. by Carol Stoker. (Science & Technology Ser.: Vol. 75). (Illus.). 646p. 1989. lib. bdg. 35.00 (0-87703-305-6, Pub. by Am Astro Soc); pap. text ed. 25.00 (0-87703-306-4, Pub. by Am Astro Soc) Univelt Inc.

Case for Mixed-Age Grouping in Early Education. Lilian G. Katz et al. LC 90-61182. 60p. 1990. pap. text ed. 6.00 (0-935989-31-5, NAEYC #333) Natl Assn Child Ed.

Case for Modern Man. Charles Frankel. LC 71-167342. (Essay Index Reprint Ser.). 1977. reprint ed. 24.95 (0-8369-2648-X) Ayer.

***Case for Multi-Family Housing.** ULI Staff. 1991. pap. text ed. 24.95 (0-87420-717-7, M36) Urban Land.

Case for NAFTA. Edward D. Hudgins. (Illus.). 15p. (Orig.). Date not set. pap. text ed. 5.00 (1-56808-014-X, BG130) Natl Ctr Pol.

Case for New Paradigms in Cell Biology & in Neurobiology. Harold Hillman. LC 91-29811. (Illus.). 356p. 1991. lib. bdg. 99.95 (0-7734-9690-4) E Mellen.

Case for Nuclear Arms Control. Barry M. Blechman. (CISA Working Paper Ser.: No. 47). 31p. (Orig.). Date not set. pap. 10.00 (0-86682-060-4) Ctr Intl Relations.

Case for Peace in Reason & Faith. Monika K. Hellwig. LC 92-13670. 112p. (Orig.). 1992. 6.95 (0-8146-5834-2, M Glazier) Liturgical Pr.

C

An Asterisk (*) at the beginning of an entry indicates that the title is appearing in BIP for the first time.

Case for Progressive Dispensationalism: The Interface Between Dispensational & Non-Dispensational Theology. Robert L. Saucy. 304p. 1993. pap. 21.99 (*0-310-30441-5*) Zondervan.

Case for Promoting Breastfeeding in Projects to Limit Fertility. Alan Berg & Susan Brems. (Technical Paper Ser.: No. 102). 60p. 1989. 6.95 (*0-8213-1247-2*, 11247) World Bank.

Case for Psycholinguistic Cases. Ed. by Gabriela Appel & Hans W. Dechert. LC 91-13230. viii, 195p. 1991. 35.00 (*1-55619-120-0*) Benjamins North Am.

Case for Punitive Damages: A New Audit. Thomas F. Lambert, Jr. (ATLA Monograph Ser.). 34p. (Orig.). 1988. pap. 6.00 (*0-941916-47-2*) ATLA Pr.

Case for Reincarnation. Joe Fisher. LC 92-15808. (Illus.). 208p. 1992. pap. 12.95 (*0-8065-1316-0*, Citadel Pr) Carol Pub Group.

Case for Reincarnation. James D. Freeman. LC 85-51938. 342p. 1986. 10.95 (*0-87159-021-2*) Unity Bks.

Case for School-Based Health Clinics. Dean F. Miller. LC 90-60219. (Fastback Ser.: No. 300). 40p. (Orig.). (C). 1990. pap. 1.25 (*0-87367-300-X*) Phi Delta Kappa.

Case for School Choice. David R. Henderson. LC 93-33331. (Essays in Public Policy Ser.: No. 44). 1993. 5.00 (*0-8179-5492-9*) Hoover Inst Pr.

Case for Sergeant Beef. large type ed. Leo Bruce. 320p. 1982. 15.95 (*0-7089-0842-X*) Ulverscroft.

Case for Socially Functional Art Culture & Education, 4 vols., Set. Harry Barba. Incl. Vol. 1. How to Teach Writing in the Time It Takes to Consume a Glass - a Quart - a Barrel of Wine. 1969. (*0-911906-02-9*); Vol. 2. Teaching in Your Own Write. 1970. (*0-911906-06-1*); Vol. 3. Two Connecticut Yankees Teaching in Appalachia. 1974. (*0-911906-10-X*); Vol. 4. Case for Socially Functional Education. 1973. (*0-911906-04-5*); (Barba-Cue Ser.). (Orig.). 1973. Set pap. 30.00 (*0-911906-17-7*) Harian Creative Bks.

Case for Socially Functional Education see Case for Socially Functional Art Culture & Education

***Case for Solar Energy Investments.** Dennis Anderson & Kulsum Ahmed. LC 95-1466. (World Bank Technical Paper: No. 279). 30p. 1995. pap. 6.95 (*0-8213-3196-5*, 13196) World Bank.

Case for Teaching Creation. A. J. Hoover. LC 81-66952. 84p. (Orig.). (C). 1980. pap. 4.99 (*0-89900-142-4*) College Pr Pub.

Case for the All-Day Kindergarden. Barry E. Herman. LC 83-83087. (Fastback Ser.: No. 205). 50p. (Orig.). 1984. pap. 1.25 (*0-87367-205-4*) Phi Delta Kappa.

Case for the Burial of Ancestors, Bk. 1. Paul Zelevansky. LC 80-54692. 1981. 27.00 (*0-9605610-3-X*); pap. 18.00 (*0-9605610-2-1*) P Zelevansky.

Case for the Burial of Ancestors, Bk. 1. Paul Zelevansky. LC 80-54692. (Illus.). 124p. 1981. write for info. (*0-89822-014-9*); pap. 30.00 (*0-89822-013-0*) Visual Studies.

Case for the Burial of Ancestors, Bk. 2. Paul Zelevansky. LC 80-54692. (Illus.). 144p. 1986. disk 30.00 (*0-9605610-4-8*) P Zelevansky.

Case for the Case Study. Joe R. Feagin et al. LC 90-27036. x, 290p. (C). 1991. 39.95 (*0-8078-1973-5*); pap. 13.95 (*0-8078-4321-0*) U of NC Pr.

Case for the Liberal Party & the Alliance. Alan Beith. LC 82-17168. 182p. reprint ed. pap. 51.90 (*0-317-08593-X*, 2022522) Bks Demand.

Case for the Multinational Corporation. Ed. by Carl H. Madden. LC 76-12863. (Special Studies). 234p. 1976. 45.00 (*0-275-90248-X*, C0248, Praeger Pubs) Greenwood.

Case for the Prosecution: Police Suspects & the Construction of Criminality. Mike McConville et al. 256p. 1991. 74.50 (*0-415-05577-6*, A5673) Routledge.

Case for the Prosecution: Police Suspects & the Construction of Criminality. Mike McConville et al. LC 93-14811. 240p. 1993. reprint ed. pap. 17.95 (*0-415-10103-4*, B0892) Routledge.

Case for Those Overlooked by the Baseball Hall of Fame. Brent P. Kelley. LC 91-38568. 336p. 1992. pap. 28.50x (*0-89950-715-8*) McFarland & Co.

Case for Three Detectives. Leo Bruce. 1985. pap. 5.95 (*0-89733-033-1*) Academy Chi Pubs.

Case for Trade: A Modern Reconsideration. J. David Richardson. 175p. (Orig.). (C). 1995. pap. text ed. 17.95 (*0-88132-210-5*) Inst Intl Eco.

Case for Transracial Adoption. Rita J. Simon et al. 150p. (Orig.). 1994. lib. bdg. 41.00 (*1-879383-19-5*); pap. 14.50 (*1-879383-20-9*) Am Univ Pr.

Case for Womens Suffrage. Brougham Villers. 1976. lib. bdg. 59.95 (*0-8490-1582-0*) Gordon Pr.

Case Grammar Theory. Walter A. Cook. LC 88-33553. 233p. (Orig.). (C). 1989. pap. 12.95 (*0-87840-276-4*) Georgetown U Pr.

***Case Grammar Theory.** Walter A. Cook. LC 88-33553. (Orig.). Date not set. reprint ed. pap. 66.70 (*0-7837-9389-8*, 2060134) Bks Demand.

Case Handbook for Information Managers: Selecting & Implementing CASE Tools. Simon Holloway & Tony Bidgood. 332p. 1991. text ed. 68.95 (*1-85628-189-2*, Pub. by Avebury Pub UK) Ashgate Pub Co.

Case Hardened Steels: Microstructural & Residual Stress Effects: Proceedings of the Symposium Held at the 112th AIME Annual Meeting, Atlanta, Georgia, March 9, 1983. Metallurgical Society of AIME Staff. Ed. by Daniel E. Diesburg. LC 83-63326. 247p. reprint ed. pap. 70.40 (*0-8357-2598-7*, 2052378) Bks Demand.

Case Histories. Dianne Hales. (Encyclopedia of Psychoactive Drugs Ser.: No. 2). (Illus.). 104p. 1988. lib. bdg. 19.95 (*1-55546-217-0*) Chelsea Hse.

Case Histories. Alexander Kluge. Tr. by Leila Vennewitz. LC 88-16259. (Modern German Voices Ser.). 200p. 1988. 19.95 (*0-8419-1044-8*); pap. 10.95 (*0-8419-1045-6*) Holmes & Meier.

Case Histories: Power Industries. Kevin R. Guy. 1993. pap. 49.95 (*0-9635450-0-0*) Vibration Inst.

Case Histories & Methods in Mineral Resource Evaluation. Ed. by A. E. Annels. (Geological Society Special Publications: No. 63). (Illus.). vi, 313p. (C). 1992. 107.00 (*0-903317-79-6*, Pub. by Geol Soc Pub Hse UK) AAPG.

***Case Histories in Chemical Engineering.** George E. Jacobs. (Illus.). 24p. 1995. pap. 8.00 (*0-8059-3725-0*) Dorrance.

Case Histories in Failure Analysis. American Society for Metals Staff. LC 79-9124. (Illus.). 439p. reprint ed. pap. 125.20 (*0-7837-1858-6*, 2042059) Bks Demand.

Case Histories in Human Physiology. Donna M. Van Wynsberghe & Gregory M. Cooley. 128p. (C). 1990. spiral bd. write for info. (*0-697-11606-9*) Wm C Brown Pubs.

Case Histories in International Logistics. 1987. 20.00 (*0-317-01531-1*) Coun Logistics Mgt.

Case Histories in International Politics. Kendall Stiles. LC 94-4750. (C). 1995. 20.00 (*0-06-501415-4*) HarpCollege.

Case Histories in Offshore Engineering. Ed. by G. Maier. (CISM International Centre for Mechanical Sciences Ser.: Vol. 283). (Illus.). ix, 365p. 1985. pap. 54.00 (*0-387-81817-0*) Spr-Verlag.

Case Histories Involving Fatigue & Fracture Mechanics: A Symposium Sponsored by ASTM Committe E-24 on Fracture Testing Charleston, SC, 21-22 March 1985. Ed. by C. Michael Hudson & Thomas P. Rich. (ASTM Special Technical Publication Ser.: No. 918). 66.00 (*0-8031-0485-5*, 04-91800030) ASTM.

Case Histories of Mineral Dicoveries, Vol. 2: Discoveries of Valuable Minerals & Precious Metal Deposits Related to Intrusions & Faults. Intro. by Victor F. Hollister. LC 88-61332. (Illus.). 436p. 1990. 75.00 (*0-87335-075-8*) SMM&E Inc.

Case Histories of Mineral Discoveries, Vol. 3: Porphyry Copper, Molybdenum, & Gold Deposits, Volcanogenic Deposits (Massive Sulfides), & Deposits in Layered Rock. Intro. by V. F. Hollister. LC 90-62295. (Illus.). 272p. 1991. 83.50 (*0-87335-094-4*) SMM&E Inc.

Case Histories of Psychopathology. 4th ed. Gloria R. Leon. 368p. 1989. pap. text ed. 25.00 (*0-205-12085-7*, H20852) Allyn.

Case History - Locos. Else Kooi. (Illus.). 1991. 19.95 (*0-7803-0302-4*, HL0450-7) Inst Electrical.

CASE I-S Software Automation. Carma L. McClure. 304p. 1988. text ed. 77.00 (*0-13-119330-9*) P-H.

Case-IMS School Improvement Process. Eugene R. Howard & James W. Keefe. 48p. (Orig.). (C). 1991. pap. text ed. 8.00 (*0-88210-253-2*) Natl Assn Principals.

Case in Camera. Oliver Onions. 320p. 1980. reprint ed. lib. bdg. 19.95 (*0-89968-205-7*, Lghtyr Pr) Buccaneer Bks.

Case in Point. Arthur Coleman. LC 78-68669. 1977. 8.95 (*0-88370-006-9*) Watermill Pubs.

Case in Point, Vol. 1. Ed. by Mark Gozonsky. (Illus.). 128p. (Orig.). 1991. pap. 14.95 (*1-877948-15-2*) Prof Train TX.

Case International Magnum 7110-7140. 1992. 18.95 (*0-87288-470-8*, C-40) Intertec Pub.

Case Is Closed. Patricia Wentworth. 20.95 (*0-8488-0326-4*) Amereon Ltd.

Case Law of the European Court of Human Rights (1960-1987), Vol. 1. Comp. by Vincent Berger. 478p. 1989. 85.00 (*0-89111-026-7*) UNIFO Pubs.

Case-Law of the World Bank Administrative Tribunal: An Analytical Digest. C. F. Amerasinghe. 304p. 1989. 98.00 (*0-19-825407-5*) OUP.

Case-Law of the World Bank Administrative Tribunal, Vol. II: An Analytical Digest. C. F. Amerasinghe. 274p. 1993. 79.00 (*0-19-825819-4*) OUP.

Case Law on Central Excise (Supreme Court & High Courts) S. P. Kampani. (C). 1988. 300.00 (*0-685-25679-0*) St Mut.

Case Law on Commodity Taxation in Sales Tax. K. Krishnamurty. (C). 1990. 85.00 (*0-89771-270-6*) St Mut.

***Case Law on Education.** W. Bray. 122p. 1989. pap. 44.00 (*0-409-01338-2*, SA) Butterworth Legal Pubs.

Case Law on the Central Sales Tax Act, 1956. Murty S. Krishna. (C). 1989. 160.00 (*0-685-27887-5*) St Mut.

Case Law System in America. Karl N. Llewellyn. Tr. by Michael Ansaldi. LC 89-32341. 160p. 1989. 24.95 (*0-226-48790-3*) U Ch Pr.

Case Load - Maximum. E. Richard Johnson. LC 90-84279. 204p. 1990. pap. 5.95 (*1-55882-083-3*) Intl Polygonics.

Case Management: Historical, Current & Future Perspectives. Ed. by Mary H. Linz et al. (Illus.). 140p. (Orig.). 1990. pap. text ed. 24.95 (*0-914797-65-4*) Brookline Bks.

Case Management & Rehabilitation Counseling: Procedures & Techniques. 2nd ed. Richard Roessler & Stanford E. Rubin. LC 91-26385. 227p. 1992. pap. text ed. 26.00 (*0-89079-519-3*, 3657) PRO-ED.

Case Management & Social Work Practice. Ed. by Stephen M. Rose. 320p. (Orig.). (C). 1992. pap. text ed. 27.50 (*0-8013-0332-X*, 78104) Longman.

Case Management & the Elderly: A Handbook for Planning & Administering Programs. Raymond M. Steinberg & Genevieve W. Carter. 224p. 1988. pap. 19.95 (*0-669-18909-X*) Free Pr.

Case Management by Nurses. Kathleen A. Bower. 52p. 1992. pap. 15.95 (*1-55810-073-3*, NS32) Am Nurses Pub.

Case Management for Healthcare Professionals. Ed. by Rufus S. Howe. LC 93-83247. 218p. 1994. pap. 39.95 (*0-944496-37-7*) Precept Pr.

Case Management for Mentally Ill Patients: Theory & Practice. Ed. by Maxine Harris & Helen Bergman. LC 92-42246. 1993. text ed. 35.00 (*3-7186-0565-1*) Gordon & Breach.

Case Management Handbook. Ed. by James J. Messina. (Professional Handbook Ser.). 84p. (Orig.). 1982. pap. text ed. 11.00 (*0-931975-18-2*) Advanced Dev Sys.

Case Management in Community Care. Devid Challis & Bleddyn Davies. 305p. 1989. pap. text ed. 24.95 (*0-566-05816-2*, Pub. by Avebury Pub UK) Ashgate Pub Co.

Case Management in Community Care: An Evaluated Experiment in the Care of the Elderly. David Challis & Bleddwyn Davis. 200p. 1987. text ed. 57.95 (*0-566-05287-3*, Pub. by Avebury Pub UK) Ashgate Pub Co.

Case Management in Mental Health Services. Ed. by Charlotte J. Sanborn. LC 82-15495. 198p. 1983. text ed. 49.95 (*0-86656-109-9*) Haworth Pr.

Case Management in Primary Care: A Manual. Cheryl Schraeder et al. 168p. (C). 1991. student ed 58.00 (*0-933948-29-8*, 2552) Ctr Res Ambulatory.

***Case Management in Service Integration: A Concept Paper.** Ellen L. Marks. 32p. 1994. pap. text ed. 8.00 (*0-926582-13-5*) NCCP.

***Case Management in the Human Services.** Julius R. Ballew & George Mink. 1986. pap. 34.95 (*0-398-06012-6*) C C Thomas.

Case Management in the Human Services. Julius R. Ballew & George Mink. (Illus.). 350p. (C). 1986. text ed. 56.95 (*0-398-05236-0*) C C Thomas.

***Case Management Mental Health.** Onyett. 1992. 44.95 (*1-56593-018-5*, 0261) Singular Publishing.

Case Management Model: Concept, Implementation & Training. rev. ed. Dan Boserup & Gerald Gouge. 178p. 1980. 6.00 (*0-318-16342-X*, B2) Regional Inst Social Welfare.

Case Management Resource Guide, 4 vols. Ed. by Diane S. Liebenson & Randi S. Rubenstein. 3000p. 1992. pap. 60.00 (*0-685-74384-5*) Ctr CHI.

Case Management Resource Guide, Set. 2nd ed. Ed. by Kevin F. O'Grady et al. 2500p. 1991. pap. 240.00 (*0-9624105-4-3*) Ctr CHI.

Case Management Resource Guide, 4 vols., Set. 3rd ed. Ed. by Diane S. Liebenson & Randi S. Rubenstein. 3000p. 1992. pap. 225.00 (*1-880874-00-8*) Ctr CHI.

Case Management Resource Guide, Set. 4th ed. Ed. by Kevin F. O'Grady et al. 3300p. 1993. pap. 225.00 (*1-880874-05-9*) Ctr CHI.

Case Management Resource Guide, 4 vols., Vol. 1: Eastern U. S. Ed. by Diane S. Liebenson & Randi S. Rubenstein. 3000p. 1992. Eastern U. S., Vol. 1. pap. 60.00 (*1-880874-01-6*) Ctr CHI.

Case Management Resource Guide, Vol. 1: Eastern U. S. 2nd ed. Ed. by Kevin F. O'Grady et al. 2500p. 1991. Vol. 1:Eastern U.S. pap. 75.00 (*0-9624105-5-1*) Ctr CHI.

Case Management Resource Guide, Vol. 1: Eastern U. S. 4th ed. Ed. by Kevin F. O'Grady et al. 3300p. 1993. Vol. 1: Eastern U.S. pap. 60.00 (*1-880874-06-7*) Ctr CHI.

Case Management Resource Guide, 4 vols., Vol. 2: Southern U. S. Ed. by Diane S. Liebenson & Randi S. Rubenstein. 3000p. 1992. Southern U. S., Vol. 2. pap. 60.00 (*1-880874-02-4*) Ctr CHI.

Case Management Resource Guide, Vol. 2: Southern U. S. 2nd ed. Ed. by Kevin F. O'Grady et al. 2500p. 1991. Vol. 2: Southern U.S. pap. 75.00 (*0-9624105-6-X*) Ctr CHI.

Case Management Resource Guide, Vol. 2: Southern U. S. 4th ed. Ed. by Kevin F. O'Grady et al. 3300p. 1993. Vol. 2: Southern U.S. pap. 60.00 (*1-880874-07-5*) Ctr CHI.

Case Management Resource Guide, 4 vols., Vol. 3: Midwestern U. S. Ed. by Diane S. Liebenson & Randi S. Rubenstein. 3000p. 1992. Midwestern U. S., Vol. 3. pap. 60.00 (*1-880874-03-2*) Ctr CHI.

Case Management Resource Guide, Vol. 3: Midwestern U. S. 2nd ed. Ed. by Kevin F. O'Grady et al. 2500p. 1991. Vol. 3: Midwestern U.S. pap. 75.00 (*0-9624105-7-8*) Ctr CHI.

Case Management Resource Guide, Vol. 3: Midwestern U. S. 4th ed. Ed. by Kevin F. O'Grady et al. 3300p. 1993. Vol. 3: Midwestern U.S. pap. 60.00 (*1-880874-08-3*) Ctr CHI.

Case Management Resource Guide, 4 vols., Vol. 4: Western U. S. Ed. by Diane S. Liebenson & Randi S. Rubenstein. 3000p. 1992. Western U. S., Vol. 4. pap. 60.00 (*1-880874-04-0*) Ctr CHI.

Case Management Resource Guide, Vol. 4: Western U. S. 2nd ed. Ed. by Kevin F. O'Grady et al. 2500p. 1991. Vol. 4: Western U.S. pap. 75.00 (*0-9624105-8-6*) Ctr CHI.

Case Management Resource Guide, Vol. 4: Western U. S. 4th ed. Ed. by Kevin F. O'Grady et al. 3300p. 1993. Vol. 4: Western U.S. pap. 60.00 (*1-880874-09-1*) Ctr CHI.

Case Management Resource Guide: A Directory of Homecare, Rehabilitation, Mental Health & Long Term Care Services, 1990 Edition, 3 vols., Set. LC 89-85982. (Illus.). 2059p. 1990. 225.00 (*0-9624105-0-0*) Ctr CHI.

Case Management Resource Guide: A Directory of Homecare, Rehabilitation, Mental Health & Long Term Care Services, 1990 Edition: Vol. 1: Eastern U. S. LC 89-85982. (Illus.). 645p. 1990. 95.00 (*0-9624105-1-9*) Ctr CHI.

Case Management Resource Guide: A Directory of Homecare, Rehabilitation, Mental Health & Long Term Care Services, 1990 Edition: Vol. 2: Central U. S. LC 89-85982. (Illus.). 800p. 1990. 95.00 (*0-685-35045-2*) Ctr CHI.

Case Management Resource Guide: A Directory of Homecare, Rehabilitation, Mental Health & Long Term Care Services, 1990 Edition: Vol. 3: Western U. S. Center for Consumer Healthcare Information. LC 89-85982. (Illus.). 589p. 1990. 95.00 (*0-9624105-3-5*) Ctr CHI.

Case Manager. Jack Rudman. (Career Examination Ser.: C-2744). 1994. pap. 34.95 (*0-8373-2744-X*) Nat Learn.

Case Manager's Handbook. Catherine M. Mullahy. 464p. 1994. 49.00 (*0-8342-0537-8*, 20537) Aspen Pub.

Case Marking & Grammatical Relations in Polynesian. Sandra Chung. LC 78-56993. 415p. reprint ed. pap. 118.30 (*0-8357-7732-4*, 2036089) Bks Demand.

***Case-Marking & Reanalysis: Grammatical Relations from Old to Early Modern English.** Cynthia L. Allen. 448p. 1995. 90.00 (*0-19-824096-1*) OUP.

***Case Material & Role Play in Counselling Training.** Janet Tolan & Susan Lendrum. LC 94-36747. (Illus.). 208p. 1995. 55.00x (*0-415-10214-6*, B4335); pap. 17.95 (*0-415-10215-4*, B4339) Routledge.

CASE Members' Directory, 1994. Comp. by Jeffrey Skillman. 156p. 1994. pap. 209.00 (*0-89964-304-3*) Coun Adv & Supp Ed.

Case Method Entity Relationship Modelling. Richard Barker. (C). 1990. pap. text ed. 50.50 (*0-201-41696-4*) Addison-Wesley.

Case Method in Management Development: Guide for Effective Use. John Reynolds. (Management Development Ser.: No. 17). vi, 264p. 1992. 24.00 (*92-2-102363-X*) Intl Labour Office.

Case Method Research & Application: An International Forum. Ed. by Hans E. Klein. 525p. (C). 1988. pap. 39.00 (*0-685-26584-6*) WACRA.

Case Method Research & Application: Forging New Partnerships with Cases, Simulations, Games & Other Interactive Methods. Hans E. Klein. (Illus.). 580p. (C). 1992. text ed. 49.00 (*1-877868-04-3*) WACRA.

Case Method Research & Application: Innovation Through Cooperation with Cases, Simulation, Games & Other Interactive Methods. Hans E. Klein. (Annual Ser.). 590p. 1993. text ed. 53.00 (*1-877868-05-1*) WACRA.

Case Method Research & Application: Managing Change with Cases, Simulations & Games & Other Interactive Methods. Ed. by Hans E. Klein. 610p. (C). 1991. 47.00 (*1-877868-03-5*) WACRA.

Case Method Research & Application: New Vistas, 1989. Ed. by Hans E. Klein. (Selected Papers). (Illus.). 544p. (C). 1989. text ed. 35.00 (*1-877868-01-9*) WACRA.

Case Method Research & Application: Problem Solving with Cases & Simulations, Games & Other Interactive Methods. Ed. by Hans E. Klein. (Illus.). 560p. (C). 1990. text ed. 35.00 (*1-877868-02-7*) WACRA.

CASE Method Tasks & Deliverables. Richard Barker. (C). 1990. pap. text ed. 50.50 (*0-201-41697-2*) Addison-Wesley.

Case Method Teaching in Community College: A Guide for Teaching & Faculty Development. Cynthia Lang. 106p. (C). 1986. write for info. (*0-89292-092-0*) Educ Dev Ctr.

Case Method Technique in Professional Training: A Survey of the Use of Case Studies As a Method of Instruction in Selected Fields, & a Study of Its Application in a Teachers College. Diana H. Sperle. LC 78-177748. (Columbia University. Teachers College. Contributions to Education Ser.: No. 571). reprint ed. 37.50 (*0-404-55571-3*) AMS Pr.

Case Methods in Teacher Education. Ed. by Judith Shulman. 272p. (C). 1991. text ed. 45.95 (*0-8077-3130-7*); pap. text ed. 19.95 (*0-8077-3129-3*) Tchrs Coll.

Case Methods Research & Application: An International Forum. Hans E. Klein. (Illus.). 545p. (C). 1988. text ed. 39.95 (*1-877868-00-0*) WACRA.

Case-Mix Payment Systems for Nursing Home Care. Paul L. Grimaldi & Thomas Jazwiecki. 181p. 1987. pap. text ed. 25.00 (*0-931028-85-X*, 0311, Pluribus) Health Admin Pr.

Case of: The Great Graffiti. Tim Jackson. (What Are Friends For? Ser.: No. 4). (Illus.). 19p. (Orig.). (J). (gr. 5-8). 1987. pap. 1.95 (*0-942675-04-5*) Creative License.

Case of Anna Kavan: A Biography. David Callard. (Illus.). 168p. 1994. 33.00 (*0-7206-0867-8*, Pub. by P Owen Ltd UK) Dufour.

***Case of Archbishop Lefebure: Trial by Canon Law.** Charles P. Nemeth. 173p. 1994. pap. text ed. 9.95 (*0-935952-50-0*) Angelus Pr.

***Case of Art Failure.** large type ed. Freda Bream. (Linford Mystery Large Pr. Ser.). 1994. pap. 14.95 (*0-7089-7636-0*) Ulverscroft.

Case of Authors by Profession or Trade, 1758, Champion 1739. James Ralph. LC 66-10008. 1966. 50.00 (*0-8201-1037-X*) Schol Facsimiles.

Case of Benedict Arnold. Cornel Lengyel. LC 79-56427. (New Poetic Drama Ser.: No. 2). 1982. pap. 3.50 (*0-934218-20-X*) Dragons Teeth.

Case of Betrayal? Women in Marguerite Yourcenar's Early Work. Ingeborg M. O'Sickey. LC 93-36531. (American University Studies: Vol. 36). 1994. write for info. (*0-8204-1311-9*) P Lang Pubs.

Case of Black & White: Northern Volunteers & the Southern Freedom Summers, 1964-1965. Mary A. Rothschild. LC 82-6175. (Contributions in Afro-American & African Studies: No. 69). xiv, 213p. 1982. text ed. 49.95 (*0-313-23430-2*, RBL/) Greenwood.

***Case of Black or White.** Blair Carr. 240p. 1995. pap. 11.95 (*0-9647013-0-8*) Kudzu Pubns.

Case of California. Laurence A. Rickels. LC 90-49952. (Parallax). 192p. 1991. text ed. 45.00 (*0-8018-4138-0*); pap. text ed. 14.95x (*0-8018-4139-9*) Johns Hopkins.

Case of Charles Dexter Ward. H. P. Lovecraft. 128p. (Orig.). 1987. mass mkt. 4.95 (*0-345-35490-7*) Ballantine.

An Asterisk (*) at the beginning of an entry indicates that the title is appearing in BIP for the first time.

An Asterisk (*) at the beginning of an entry indicates that the title is appearing in BIP for the first time.

C

Case of the Giggling Ghost. Linda L. Maifair. (Darcy J. Doyle, Daring Detective Ser.). 64p. (J). (gr. 2-5). 1993. pap. 3.99 (*0-310-57911-2*) Zondervan.

Case of the Gilded Fly. Edmund Crispin. 224p. pap. 8.95 (*1-55882-108-2*) Intl Polygonics.

Case of the Gilded Lily. Erle Stanley Gardner. LC 80-27291. 256p. 1981. reprint ed. lib. bdg. 18.00 (*0-8376-0396-X*) Bentley.

Case of the Glacier Park Swallow. Dina Anastasio. LC 94-65091. (Juliet Stone Mystery Ser.: No. 2). (Illus.). 96p. (Orig.). (J). (gr. 4 up). 1994. pap. 8.95 (*1-879373-85-8*) R Rinehart.

Case of the Gobbling Squash. Elizabeth Levy. (Illus.). (J). (gr. 2-4). 1988. pap. 13.00 (*0-671-63655-3*, S&S Bks Young Read) S&S Childrens.

Case of the Gobbling Squash. Elizabeth Levy. (Illus.). (J). (gr. 2-4). 1989. pap. 2.95 (*0-671-68873-1*, S&S Bks Young Read) S&S Childrens.

Case of the Good-for-Nothing Girlfriend: A Nancy Clue Mystery. Mabel Maney. LC 94-29820. (Illus.). 180p. (Orig.). 1994. lib. bdg. 24.95 (*0-939416-90-5*); pap. 10.95 (*0-939416-91-3*) Cleis Pr.

Case of the Goofy Game Show. Laura L. Hope. Ed. by Anne Greenberg. (New Bobbsey Twins Ser.: No. 24). (Illus.). 96p. (Orig.). (J). 1991. pap. 2.95 (*0-671-69296-8*, Minstrel Bks) PB.

Case of the Grand Canyon Eagle. Dina Anastasio. LC 94-65090. (Juliet Stone Mystery Ser.: No. 1). (Illus.). 96p. (Orig.). (J). (gr. 6 up). 1994. pap. 8.95 (*1-879373-84-X*) R Rinehart.

Case of the Great Train Robbery. Rae Bains. LC 81-7525. (Easy-to-Read Mystery Ser.). (Illus.). 48p. (J). (gr. 2-4). 1982. lib. bdg. 10.89 (*0-89375-588-5*); pap. text ed. 3.50 (*0-89375-589-3*) Troll Assocs.

Case of the Green-Eyed Sister. Erle Stanley Gardner. 1993. mass mkt. 4.50 (*0-345-37872-5*) Ballantine.

Case of the Gumball Bandits. William Alexander. LC 89-36558. (Clues Kids Ser.). (Illus.). 96p. (J). (gr. 4-7). 1990. lib. bdg. 9.89 (*0-8167-1696-X*); pap. text ed. 2.95 (*0-8167-1697-8*) Troll Assocs.

Case of the Half-Wakened Wife. Erle Stanley Gardner. 256p. 1991. pap. 4.99 (*0-345-37147-X*) Ballantine.

Case of the Haunted Camp. Francine Pascal. (Sweet Valley Kids Super Snooper Ser.: No. 3). (J). (gr. 4-7). 1992. pap. 3.50 (*0-553-15894-5*) Bantam.

Case of the Haunted Health Club. Carol Farley. 112p. (J). 1991. pap. 2.95 (*0-380-75918-7*, Camelot) Avon.

Case of the Haunted Husband. Erle Stanley Gardner. 281p. reprint ed. lib. bdg. 21.95 (*0-88411-418-X*, Aeonian Pr) Amereon Ltd.

Case of the Hesitant Hostess. Erle Stanley Gardner. 1993. mass mkt. 4.50 (*0-345-37871-7*) Ballantine.

Case of the Hesitant Hostess. large type ed. Erle Stanley Gardner. (Paperback Program Ser.). 377p. 1991. pap. 15.95 (*0-8161-5064-8*) G K Hall.

Case of the Hidden Treasure. Francine Pascal. (Sweet Valley Kids Super Snooper Ser.: No. 5). (J). (gr. 1-3). 1993. pap. 3.25 (*0-553-48064-2*) Bantam.

Case of the Hook-Billed Kites. J. S. Borthwick. 1991. mass mkt. 4.50 (*0-312-92604-9*) St Martin.

Case of the Howling Dog. Erle Stanley Gardner. (Perry Mason Books Ser.). 1976. reprint ed. lib. bdg. 22.95 (*0-88411-404-X*) Amereon Ltd.

Case of the Hungry Stranger. Crosby N. Bonsall. LC 91-13345. (I Can Read Bk.). (Illus.). 64p. (J). (gr. k-3). 1963. 13.00 (*0-06-020570-9*); lib. bdg. 12.89 (*0-06-020571-7*) HarpC Child Bks.

Case of the Hungry Stranger. Crosby N. Bonsall. LC 91-14365. (Trophy I Can Read Bk.). (Illus.). 64p. (J). (gr. k-3). 1980. pap. 3.50 (*0-06-444026-5*, Trophy) HarpC Child Bks.

*__Case of the Hungry Stranger.__ Duncan Searl. Ed. by J. Friedland & R. Kessler. (Novel-Ties Ser.). (J). (gr. k-2). 1994. student ed, pap. text ed. 15.95 (*1-56982-051-1*) Lrn Links.

Case of the Ice-Cold Hands. Erle Stanley Gardner. 1989. pap. 3.95 (*0-345-35939-9*) Ballantine.

Case of the Invisible Cat. A. E. Parker. (Clue Ser.: No. 3). (J). (gr. 4-7). 1992. pap. 2.95 (*0-590-45632-6*) Scholastic Inc.

Case of the Johannisberg Riesling. Gerry Maddren. Ed. by Nancy Chirich. LC 88-4326. 192p. 1988. 13.95 (*0-912761-15-6*) Cliffhanger Pr.

Case of the Lame Canary. Erle Stanley Gardner. (Perry Mason Books Ser.). 281p. reprint ed. lib. bdg. 21.95 (*0-88411-411-2*, Aeonian Pr) Amereon Ltd.

Case of the Late Pig. Margery Allingham. 160p. 1989. pap. 3.50 (*0-380-70577-X*) Avon.

Case of the Legless Veteran. 2nd rev. ed. James Kutcher. LC 73-77556. (Illus.). 309p. 1995. lib. bdg. 50.00 (*0-913460-16-8*); pap. 19.95 (*0-913460-17-6*) Pathfinder NY.

Case of the Lighthouse Ghost. Peggy Nicholson & John F. Warner. (Kerry Hill Casecrackers Ser.: No. 2). 120p. (J). (gr. 4-7). 1994. 14.95 (*0-8225-0710-2*, Lerner Publctns) Lerner Group.

Case of the Long-Legged Models. Erle Stanley Gardner. 1994. mass mkt. 4.99 (*0-345-37876-8*) Ballantine.

Case of the Lost Lookalike. Carol Farley. 112p. (J). 1988. pap. 2.50 (*0-380-75450-9*, Camelot) Avon.

Case of the Lucky Legs. Erle Stanley Gardner. (Perry Mason Books Ser.). 1976. reprint ed. lib. bdg. 21.95 (*0-88411-403-1*) Amereon Ltd.

Case of the Lucky Loser. Erle Stanley Gardner. 192p. 1990. pap. 3.95 (*0-345-36497-X*) Ballantine.

Case of the Ludicrous Letters. Anna Clarke. 208p. (Orig.). 1994. pap. 4.50 (*0-425-14048-2*) Berkley Pub.

Case of the Magic Christmas Bell. Francine Pascal. (Sweet Valley Kids Super Snooper Ser.: No. 2). (J). (ps-3). 1991. pap. 3.25 (*0-553-15964-X*) Bantam.

*__Case of the-Man-in-the-Moon.__ Grace M. Dyrek. 170p. (Orig.). 1995. pap. 7.95 (*0-7610-0063-1*) NW Pub.

*__Case of the Maybe Babies.__ Victoria Pade. (American Romance Ser.). 1995. mass mkt. 3.50 (*0-373-16590-0*, 1-16590-1) Harlequin Bks.

Case of the Million-Dollar Diamonds. Francine Pascal. (Sweet Valley Kids Super Snooper Ser.: No. 6). (J). (ps-3). 1993. pap. 3.25 (*0-553-48115-0*) Bantam.

Case of the Mind-Reading Mommies. Elizabeth Levy. (Illus.). (J). 1990. pap. 2.95 (*0-671-69435-9*) S&S Trade.

Case of the Missing Bike & Other Things. 2nd rev. ed. Peggy S. Moore. (Illus.). 40p. (Orig.). (J). (gr. 4-6). 1992. pap. 5.95 (*0-9613078-1-1*) Detroit Black.

Case of the Missing Blue Volkswagen. Gerald Locklin. LC 84-12442. 114p. (Orig.). 1984. pap. 6.95 (*0-930090-22-5*) Applezaba.

Case of the Missing Blue Volkswagen. deluxe limited ed. Gerald Locklin. LC 84-12442. 114p. (Orig.). 1984. 15.00 (*0-930090-21-7*) Applezaba.

Case of the Missing Bronte. Robert Barnard. 192p. 1994. reprint ed. mass mkt. 5.95 (*0-14-023785-2*, Penguin Bks) Viking Penguin.

Case of the Missing Calf. Paul Hutchens. (Sugar Creek Gang Ser.). (J). (gr. 2-7). 1988. pap. text ed. 3.99 (*0-8024-4837-2*) Moody.

Case of the Missing Canary. Robyn Supraner. LC 78-60122. (Easy-to-Read Mystery Ser.). (Illus.). 48p. (J). (gr. 2-4). 1979. lib. bdg. 10.89 (*0-89375-087-5*); pap. 3.50 (*0-89375-075-1*) Troll Assocs.

Case of the Missing Cat. Janet Palazzo-Craig. LC 81-7635. (Easy-to-Read Mystery Ser.). (Illus.). 48p. (J). (gr. 2-4). 1982. lib. bdg. 10.89 (*0-89375-594-X*); pap. text ed. 3.50 (*0-89375-595-8*) Troll Assocs.

Case of the Missing Cat: Discover the Land of Enchantment. John Erickson. (Hank the Cowdog Ser.: No. 15). (Illus.). 144p. (J). 1990. 11.95 (*0-87719-186-7*); pap. 6.95 (*0-87719-185-9*); audio 15.95 (*0-87719-187-5*) Gulf Pub.

Case of the Missing Chick. Erica Frost. LC 78-18036. (Easy-to-Read Mystery Ser.). (Illus.). 48p. (J). (gr. 2-4). 1979. lib. bdg. 10.89 (*0-89375-092-1*); pap. 3.50 (*0-89375-080-8*) Troll Assocs.

Case of the Missing Christmas. Nan Allen & Dennis Allen. (J). 1988. 4.95 (*0-685-68521-7*, MC-65); audio 10.98 (*0-685-68522-5*, TA-9095C) Lillenas.

Case of the Missing Dinosaur. Keith Brandt. LC 81-7620. (Easy-to-Read Mystery Ser.). (Illus.). 48p. (J). (gr. 2-4). 1982. lib. bdg. 10.89 (*0-89375-586-9*); pap. text ed. 3.50 (*0-89375-587-7*) Troll Assocs.

*__Case of the Missing Lynx.__ David LaRochelle. (Mad Mysteries Ser.). (Illus.). 48p. (Orig.). (J). (gr. 2 up). 1995. pap. 2.95 (*0-8431-3797-5*) Price Stern.

*__Case of the Missing Macon County Men.__ Joe Grimsley. 1995. 14.95 (*0-8062-5257-X*) Carlton.

Case of the Missing Max. Linda L. Maifair. (Darcy J. Doyle, Daring Detective Ser.: Bk. 8). 64p. (J). (gr. 2-5). 1994. pap. 3.99 (*0-310-43311-8*) Zondervan.

Case of the Missing Melody. Gayle Roper. LC 92-39317. (East Edge Mysteries Ser.: No. 4). (Illus.). (J). 1993. pap. 4.99 (*1-55513-702-4*, Chariot Bks) Chariot Family.

*__Case of the Missing Mother: The Pride Pack, No. 2.__ R. J. Hamilton. 144p. (Orig.). (YA). (gr. 6-12). 1995. pap. 5.95 (*1-55583-609-7*, Lace MA) Alyson Pubns.

*__Case of the Missing Movie.__ Hinter. (Clue, Jr. Ser.: No. 04). 1995. pap. (*0-590-26218-1*) Scholastic Inc.

Case of the Missing Phylactery. William N. Goetzmann. 11p. 1985. reprint ed. pap. 3.50 (*0-912296-78-X*, U Pr of Va) Am Antiquarian.

*__Case of the Missing Pitcher.__ Edwards. (Sports Mystery Ser.: No. 1). (J). 1995. pap. 2.99 (*0-590-48452-4*) Scholastic Inc.

Case of the Missing Rattles. Robyn Supraner. LC 81-10378. (Easy-to-Read Mystery Ser.). (Illus.). 48p. (J). (gr. 2-4). 1982. lib. bdg. 10.89 (*0-89375-590-7*); pap. text ed. 3.50 (*0-89375-591-5*) Troll Assocs.

Case of the Missing Shoes. Jane Norman & Frank Beazley. 24p. (J). (ps-3). 1993. pap. write for info. (*1-883585-07-4*) Pixanne Ent.

Case of the Missing Zebra Stripes: Zoo Math. Time Life Inc. Editors. Ed. by Jean B. Crawford et al. LC 92-16838. (I Love Math Ser.). (Illus.). 64p. (J). (gr. k-4). 1992. write for info. (*0-8094-9954-1*); lib. bdg. write for info. (*0-8094-9955-X*) Time-Life.

Case of the Mixed-up Monsters. Linda L. Maifair. (Darcy J. Doyle, Daring Detective Ser.). 64p. (J). 1993. pap. 3.99 (*0-310-57921-X*) Zondervan.

Case of the Moth-Eaten Mink. Erle Stanley Gardner. (Perry Mason Mystery Ser.: No. 57). 240p. 1990. pap. 3.95 (*0-345-36928-9*) Ballantine.

Case of the Moth-Eaten Mink: A Perry Mason Mystery. large type ed. Erle Stanley Gardner. (General Ser.). 365p. 1992. pap. 19.95 (*0-8161-5063-X*, Large Print Bks) Hall.

Case of the Muttering Mummy: A McGurk Mystery. E. W. Hildick. LC 85-23747. (Illus.). 144p. (J). (gr. 3-6). 1986. text ed. 13.95 (*0-02-743960-7*, Mac Bks Young Read) S&S Childrens.

Case of the Mysterious Codes. Peggy Nicholson & John F. Warner. (Kerry Hill Casecrackers Ser.: No. 4). 120p. (J). (gr. 4-7). 1994. 14.95 (*0-8225-0712-9*, Lerner Publctns) Lerner Group.

Case of the Mysterious Mermaid. Vivian Binnamin. Ed. by Bonnie Brook. (Field Trip Mysteries Ser.). (Illus.). 32p. (J). (gr. k-3). 1990. lib. bdg. 4.95 (*0-671-68817-0*); pap. 2.95 (*0-671-68821-9*) Silver Pr.

Case of the Mysterious Parables. Donna F. Crow. 1988. 8.50 (*0-685-68702-3*, MP-649) Lillenas.

Case of the Mystery Weekend. David D. Connell & Jim Thurman. (MatheNet Casebks.: No. 5). (Illus.). 64p. (J). (gr. 3-7). 1995. pap. text ed. 3.95 (*0-7167-6555-1*, Sci Am Yng Rdrs) W H Freeman.

Case of the Mystery Weekend. David D. Connell & Jim Thurman. (MatheNet Casebks.: No. 5). (Illus.). 64p. (J). (gr. 3-7). 1995. text ed. 10.95 (*0-7167-6554-3*, Sci Am Yng Rdrs) W H Freeman.

Case of the Mythical Monkeys. Erle Stanley Gardner. LC 80-27190. 288p. 1981. reprint ed. lib. bdg. 18.00 (*0-8376-0398-6*) Bentley.

Case of the Nazi Professor. David M. Oshinsky et al. LC 88-16895. 220p. (C). 1989. text ed. 35.00 (*0-8135-1363-4*); pap. text ed. 15.00 (*0-8135-1427-4*) Rutgers U Pr.

Case of the Nervous Accomplice. Erle Stanley Gardner. 1992. mass mkt. 3.99 (*0-345-37874-1*) Ballantine.

Case of the Nervous Newsboy. E. W. Hildick. (Illus.). 112p. (J). (gr. 4-6). 1991. reprint ed. pap. 3.50 (*0-88741-807-4*) Sundance Pub.

Case of the Not-So-Nice Nurse. Mabel Maney. 160p. (Orig.). 1993. 24.95 (*0-939416-75-1*); pap. 9.95 (*0-939416-76-X*) Cleis Pr.

*__Case of the One-Eyed Witness.__ Erle S. Gardner. 1995. mass mkt. 4.99 (*0-345-39225-6*) Ballantine.

Case of the One-Eyed Witness. large type ed. Erle Stanley Gardner. 1990. pap. 14.95 (*0-8161-5062-1*, Large Print Bks) Hall.

Case of the Pampered Poodler. Linda L. Maifair. (Darcy J. Doyle, Daring Detective Ser.). 64p. (J). (gr. 2-5). 1993. pap. 3.99 (*0-310-57891-4*) Zondervan.

Case of the Paranoid Patient. Anna Clarke. 192p. (Orig.). 1993. pap. 3.99 (*0-425-13858-5*) Berkley Pub.

Case of the Paranoid Patient. large type ed. Anna Clarke. LC 93-11537. (Nightingale Ser.). (Orig.). 1993. pap. 14.95 (*0-8161-5845-2*) Hall.

Case of the Pelican's Feather: An Ocean City, Maryland Novel. Wade B. Fleetwood. LC 91-77403. (Illus.). 296p. (YA). 1992. pap. 5.95 (*0-9631466-0-2*) W B Fleetwood.

Case of the Perjured Parrot. Erle Stanley Gardner. (Perry Mason Books Ser.). 288p. reprint ed. lib. bdg. 21.95 (*0-88411-414-7*, Aeonian Pr) Amereon Ltd.

Case of the Philippines. Amelia B. Alfonso et al. (Culture & Fertility Ser.). 67p. (Orig.). 1980. pap. text ed. 10.00 (*9971-902-14-1*, Pub. by Inst SE Asian Studies SI) Ashgate Pub Co.

Case of the Photo Finish. Carolyn Keene. Ed. by Ann Greenberg. (Nancy Drew Ser.: No. 96). 160p. (Orig.). (J). (gr. 3-6). 1990. pap. 3.99 (*0-671-69281-X*, Minstrel Bks) PB.

Case of the Pizza Pie Spy. William Alexander. LC 89-20156. (Clues Kids Ser.). (Illus.). 96p. (J). (gr. 4-7). 1990. lib. bdg. 9.89 (*0-8167-1698-6*); pap. text ed. 2.95 (*0-8167-1699-4*) Troll Assocs.

Case of the Planetarium Puzzle. Vivian Binnamin. Ed. by Bonnie Brook. (Field Trip Mysteries Ser.). (Illus.). 32p. (J). (gr. k-3). 1990. lib. bdg. 4.95 (*0-671-68819-7*); pap. 2.95 (*0-671-68823-5*) Silver Pr.

Case of the Purloined Parrot: A McGurk Mystery. E. W. Hildick. LC 89-37924. 144p. (J). (gr. 3-7). 1990. text ed. 13.95 (*0-02-743965-8*, Mac Bks Young Read) S&S Childrens.

Case of the Purloined Pork. Anita Gustafson. (Illus.). 32p. (J). (gr. 2-3). 1985. 7.95 (*0-88700-004-5*) Natl Live Stock.

Case of the Queenly Contestant. Erle Stanley Gardner. 1993. reprint ed. mass mkt. 4.50 (*0-345-37879-2*) Ballantine.

Case of the Reluctant Model. Erle Stanley Gardner. 208p. 1990. pap. 3.95 (*0-345-36689-1*) Ballantine.

Case of the Restless Redhead. Erle Stanley Gardner. 1985. pap. 3.95 (*0-345-33199-0*) Ballantine.

Case of the Revolutionist's Daughter: Sherlock Holmes Meets Karl Marx. Lewis S. Feuer. LC 83-61117. (Illus.). 159p. 1983. 23.95 (*0-87975-245-9*) Prometheus Bks.

Case of the Rising Stars. Carolyn Keene. Ed. by Anne Greenberg. (Nancy Drew Mystery Stories Ser.: No. 87). 160p. (J). (gr. 3-7). 1989. mass mkt. 3.99 (*0-671-66312-7*, Minstrel Bks) PB.

Case of the Rolling Bones. Erle Stanley Gardner. (Perry Mason Books Ser.). 288p. reprint ed. lib. bdg. 21.95 (*0-88411-415-5*, Aeonian Pr) Amereon Ltd.

Case of the Runaway Corpse. Erle Stanley Gardner. 224p. 1990. pap. 3.95 (*0-345-36498-8*) Ballantine.

Case of the Sabotaged School Play: A Sam & Dave Mystery. Marilyn Singer. LC 83-48437. (Trophy Bk.). (Illus.). 64p. (J). (gr. 3-7). 1987. pap. 3.95 (*0-06-440207-X*, Trophy) HarpC Child Bks.

Case of the Safecracker's Secret. Carolyn Keene. (Nancy Drew Ser.: No. 93). 160p. (J). 1990. mass mkt. 3.99 (*0-671-66318-6*, Minstrel Bks) PB.

Case of the Scaredy Cats. Crosby N. Bonsall. LC 75-159039. (Harper I Can Read Bk.). (Illus.). 64p. (J). (gr. k-3). 1971. lib. bdg. 14.89 (*0-06-020566-0*) HarpC Child Bks.

Case of the Scaredy Cats. Crosby N. Bonsall. LC 75-159039. (Trophy I Can Read Bk.). (Illus.). 64p. (J). (ps-3). 1984. pap. 3.50 (*0-06-444047-8*, Trophy) HarpC Child Bks.

*__Case of the Screaming Woman.__ Erle S. Gardner. 1994. mass mkt. 4.99 (*0-345-37875-X*) Ballantine.

*__Case of the Secret Code.__ Glen Robinson. LC 94-23914. (Shoebox Kids Ser.: Vol. 2). (J). 1995. 5.95 (*0-8163-1249-4*) Pacific Pr Pub Assn.

*__Case of the Secret Message.__ Parker C. Hinter. (Clue Jr. Ser.: No. 01). (J). (gr. 4-7). 1994. pap. 2.95 (*0-590-47907-5*) Scholastic Inc.

Case of the Secret Santa. Francine Pascal. (Sweet Valley Kids Super Snooper Ser.: No. 1). (J). (gr. k-3). 1990. pap. 3.50 (*0-553-15860-0*) Bantam.

Case of the Seneca Indians in the State of New York. (American Indians at Law Ser.). 1980. reprint ed. text ed. 32.50 (*0-930576-35-7*) E M Coleman Ent.

Case of the Severed Head. Larry Townsend. 239p. (Orig.). 1994. pap. 8.95 (*1-881684-04-0*) L T Pubns CA.

Case of the Shoplifter's Shoe. Erle Stanley Gardner. (Perry Mason Books Ser.). 312p. reprint ed. lib. bdg. 22.95 (*0-88411-413-9*, Aeonian Pr) Amereon Ltd.

Case of the Silent Partner. Erle Stanley Gardner. (Perry Mason Books Ser.). reprint ed. lib. bdg. 21.95 (*0-88411-417-1*, Aeonian Pr) Amereon Ltd.

Case of the Silk King. large type ed. Shannon Gilligan. (Choose Your Own Adventure Ser.). 114p. (J). (gr. 3-7). 1987. reprint ed. 8.95 (*0-942545-14-1*); reprint ed. lib. bdg. 9.95 (*0-942545-19-2*) Grey Castle.

Case of the Singing Skirt. Erle Stanley Gardner. 1992. mass mkt. 3.99 (*0-345-37149-6*) Ballantine.

Case of the Singing Skirt. Erle Stanley Gardner. LC 80-27263. 256p. 1981. reprint ed. 18.00 (*0-8376-0399-4*) Bentley.

Case of the Sleepwalker's Niece. Erle Stanley Gardner. (Perry Mason Books Ser.). 1976. reprint ed. lib. bdg. 19.95 (*0-88411-408-2*) Amereon Ltd.

Case of the Slippery Sharks. Stephen Mooser. LC 87-3490. (Treasure Hounds Ser.). (Illus.). 96p. (J). (gr. 3-6). 1988. lib. bdg. 9.89 (*0-8167-1177-1*); pap. text ed. 2.95 (*0-8167-1178-X*) Troll Assocs.

Case of the Smart Dummy. David D. Connell & Jim Thurman. (MathNet Casebks.: No. 6). (Illus.). 64p. (J). (gr. 3-7). 1995. text ed. 10.95 (*0-7167-6556-X*, Sci Am Yng Rdrs); pap. text ed. 3.95 (*0-7167-6557-8*, Sci Am Yng Rdrs) W H Freeman.

Case of the Sneaker Snatcher & Other Mysteries. L. E. Wolfe. (J). (gr. 4-7). 1991. pap. 3.50 (*0-316-95097-1*, Spts Illus Kids) Little.

Case of the Snoring Stegosaurus. Vivian Binnamin. Ed. by Bonnie Brook. (Field Trip Mysteries Ser.). (Illus.). 32p. (J). (gr. k-3). 1990. lib. bdg. 4.95 (*0-671-68818-9*); pap. 2.95 (*0-671-68822-7*) Silver Pr.

Case of the Socialist Witchdoctor & Other Stories. Hama Tuma. 192p. 1993. pap. 9.95 (*0-435-90590-2*) Heinemann.

Case of the Spurious Spinster. Erle Stanley Gardner. 1988. pap. 3.50 (*0-345-35203-3*) Ballantine.

Case of the Squeaky Thief. Peggy Nicholson & John F. Warner. (Kerry Hill Casecrackers Ser.: No. 3). 120p. (J). (gr. 4-7). 1994. 14.95 (*0-8225-0711-0*, Lerner Publctns) Lerner Group.

Case of the Stepdaughter's Secret. Erle Stanley Gardner. (Perry Mason Mystery Ser.). 192p. 1989. pap. 3.95 (*0-345-36221-7*) Ballantine.

Case of the Stolen Dinosaur: A Play in Two Versions: Stage & Radio. Courtaney Brooks. (Illus.). 26p. (Orig.). (J). (gr. 4 up). 1983. pap. text ed. 4.00 (*0-941274-02-0*) Belnice Bks.

*__Case of the Stolen Jewel.__ Parker C. Hinter. (Clue Jr. Ser.: No. 02). (J). (gr. 4-7). 1995. pap. 2.99 (*0-590-47908-3*) Scholastic Inc.

Case of the Stolen Jewels: Adventure Mystery for Kids Ages 8-12. Patricia Lakin. (Illus.). 24p. (J). (gr. 3-4). 1992. 14.00 (*0-922242-33-X*) Lombard Mktg.

Case of the Stuttering Bishop. Erle Stanley Gardner. 1988. mass mkt. 3.99 (*0-345-35680-2*) Ballantine.

Case of the Stuttering Bishop. large type ed. Erle Stanley Gardner. LC 93-39659. 1994. 21.95 (*0-7927-1907-7*, Curley Lrg Print); pap. 19.95 (*0-7927-1906-9*, Curley Lrg Print) Chivers N Amer.

Case of the Stuttering Bishop. Erle Stanley Gardner. (Perry Mason Books Ser.). 1976. reprint ed. lib. bdg. 21.95 (*0-88411-409-0*) Amereon Ltd.

Case of the Substitute Face. Erle Stanley Gardner. 224p. 1987. mass mkt. 3.99 (*0-345-34377-8*) Ballantine.

Case of the Substitute Face. large type ed. Erle Stanley Gardner. LC 92-46233. 1993. pap. 20.95 (*0-7927-1561-6*, Curley Lrg Print) Chivers N Amer.

Case of the Substitute Face. Erle Stanley Gardner. (Perry Mason Books Ser.). 310p. reprint ed. lib. bdg. 22.95 (*0-88411-412-0*, Aeonian Pr) Amereon Ltd.

Case of the Sulky Girl. Erle Stanley Gardner. 1992. mass mkt. 3.99 (*0-345-37145-3*) Ballantine.

Case of the Sulky Girl. large type ed. Erle Stanley Gardner. LC 92-8692. (All-Time Favorites Ser.). 394p. 1992. reprint ed. lib. bdg. 19.95 (*1-56054-389-2*) Thorndike Pr.

Case of the Sulky Girl. Erle Stanley Gardner. (Perry Mason Books Ser.). 1976. reprint ed. lib. bdg. 22.95 (*0-88411-402-3*, Aeonian Pr) Amereon Ltd.

Case of the Tattletale Heart. Elizabeth Levy. (Illus.). 64p. (J). (gr. 2-4). 1992. pap. 3.00 (*0-671-74064-4*, S&S Bks Young Read) S&S Childrens.

Case of the Toxic Spell Dump. Harry Turtledove. 432p. 1993. mass mkt. 5.99 (*0-671-72196-8*) Baen Bks.

*__Case of the Troubled Trustee.__ Erle S. Gardner. 1995. mass mkt. 4.99 (*0-345-39224-8*) Ballantine.

Case of the Twin Teddy Bears. Carolyn Keene. Ed. by Ellen Winkler. (Nancy Drew Ser.: No. 116). 160p. (Orig.). (J). 1993. pap. 3.99 (*0-671-79302-0*, Minstrel Bks) PB.

Case of the Two Masked Robbers. Lillian Hoban. LC 85-45819. (Harper I Can Read Bk.). (Illus.). 64p. (J). (gr. k-3). 1986. lib. bdg. 14.89 (*0-06-022299-9*) HarpC Child Bks.

Case of the Two Masked Robbers. Lillian Hoban. LC 85-45819. (Trophy I Can Read Bk.). (Illus.). 64p. (J). (gr. k-3). 1988. pap. 3.50 (*0-06-444121-0*, Trophy) HarpC Child Bks.

*__Case of the Two Spies.__ Donald J. Sobol. (Encyclopedia Brown Ser.: No. 19). (J). (gr. 4-7). 1995. pap. 3.50 (*0-553-48297-1*) Bantam.

Case of the U. S. to Be Laid Before the Tribunal of Arbitration to Be Convened at Geneva: Under the Provisions of the Treaty Between the U. S. of America & Her Majesty the Queen of Great Britain. LC 72-164595. (Select Bibliographies Reprint Ser.). 1977. reprint ed. 23.95 (*0-8369-5879-9*) Ayer.

An Asterisk (*) at the beginning of an entry indicates that the title is appearing in BIP for the first time.

C

An Asterisk (*) at the beginning of an entry indicates that the title is appearing in BIP for the first time.

1071

***Case Studies in Human Services Consultation.** 2nd ed. Michael A. Dougherty. 193p. 1995. text ed. 12.95 (*0-534-25130-7*) Brooks-Cole.

Case Studies in Immunology. Ivan M. Roitt et al. 77p. 1994. pap. 14.95 (*0-7234-2052-1*) Mosby Yr Bk.

Case Studies in Industrial Hygiene. Ed. by Jimmy L. Perkins & Vernon E. Rose. LC 86-15709. 188p. 1987. text ed. 79.95 (*0-471-84263-X*) Wiley.

Case Studies in Industrial Mathematics. Ed. by Heinz W. Engl et al. (C). 1988. lib. bdg. 100.50 (*90-277-2731-7*) Kluwer Ac.

Case Studies in Insomnia. Ed. by Peter J. Hauri. (Critical Issues in Psychiatry Ser.). (Illus.). 280p. 1991. 42.50 (*0-306-43791-0*, Plenum Med Bk) Plenum.

Case Studies in Instructional Design & Development. Alexander Romiszowski et al. 300p. 1994. text ed. 74.95 (*0-8464-1423-6*) Beekman Pubs.

Case Studies in Internal Auditing. Victor Z. Brink & Mortimer Dittenhofer. 300p. 1985. pap. text ed. 25.00 (*0-89413-139-7*) Inst Inter Aud.

Case Studies in International Business. Christine Grosse & Robert Grosse. (Illus.). 224p. (C). 1988. pap. text ed. 17.50 (*0-13-119314-7*) P-H.

Case Studies in International Management. Christopher Sawyer-Laucanno. (Illus.). 224p. (C). 1987. pap. text ed. 17.50 (*0-13-119298-1*) P-H.

Case Studies in Jewish School Management: Applying Educational Theory to School Practice. Burton I. Cohen. LC 92-27303. 1992. 15.95 (*0-87441-542-X*) Behrman.

***Case Studies in Law & Nursing: A Course Book for Project 2000 Training.** Young. 278p. 1992. pap. 47.75 (*1-56593-034-7*, 0675) Singular Publishing.

Case Studies in Library Computer Systems. Richard P. Palmer. LC 73-17008. (Bowker Series in Problem-Centered Approaches to Librianship). 230p. reprint ed. pap. 65.60 (*0-317-42309-6*, 2023052) Bks Demand.

Case Studies in Managing School Library Media Centers. Ed. by Daniel Callison & Jacqueline Morris. LC 89-3360. 208p. 1989. pap. 26.95 (*0-89774-441-1*) Oryx Pr.

Case Studies in Manufacturing with Advanced Materials, Vol. 1. Ed. by J. H. De Wit et al. LC 92-17042. 1992. write for info. (*0-444-88468-8*, North Holland) Elsevier.

***Case Studies in Manufacturing with Advanced Materials Vol. 2.** Ed. by A. Demaid & J. H. De Wit. 340p. 1995. 191.25 (*0-444-88934-5*, North Holland) Elsevier.

***Case Studies in Marine Science.** Andrea Huvard. 80p. (C). 1995. pap. write for info. (*0-697-29007-7*) Wm C Brown Pubs.

Case Studies in Matching Gift Administration: A Workbook. Joint Task Force on Matching Gifts Staff. 28p. 1988. 18.00 (*0-89964-260-8*) Coun Adv & Supp Ed.

Case Studies in Medical Ethics. Robert M. Veatch. 437p. 1980. pap. 17.95 (*0-674-09932-X*) HUP.

Case Studies in Medicine for the Elderly. S. C. Allen et al. 1987. pap. text ed. 43.50 (*0-85200-698-5*) Kluwer Ac.

Case Studies in Mental Health Treatment: A Cross Section of Journal Articles for Discussion & Evaluation. Intro. by Robert Kalina. (Illus.). 272p. (C). 1993. pap. text ed. 23.50 (*0-9623744-5-8*) Pyrczak Pub.

Case Studies in Missions. Frances F. Hiebert & G. Paul. LC 87-70401. 1987. pap. 11.99 (*0-8010-4308-5*) Baker Bk.

Case Studies in Music Therapy. Ed. by Kenneth E. Bruscia. 656p. (C). 1991. pap. text ed. 30.00 (*0-9624080-1-8*) Barcelona Pubs.

Case Studies in Neurosurgery for the House Officer. Ed. by Robert Solomon. (House Officer Ser.). 250p. 1989. pap. text ed. 20.00 (*0-683-07858-5*) Williams & Wilkins.

Case Studies in Nursing Management. Marriner & Tomey. (Illus.). 364p. 1990. pap. 26.95 (*0-8016-5848-9*) Mosby Yr Bk.

Case Studies in Nursing Theory. Patricia F. Winstead-Fry. 248p. (Orig.). (C). 1986. pap. 18.95 (*0-88737-253-8*) Natl League Nurse.

***Case Studies in Object-Oriented Analysis & Design.** Edward Yourdon. 1995. 39.00 (*0-13-305137-4*) P-H.

Case Studies in Object-Oriented Programming. Lewis S. Pinson & Richard S. Wiener. (Computer Science Ser.). (Illus.). (C). 1990. text ed. 40.95 (*0-201-50369-7*) Addison-Wesley.

Case Studies in Occupational Epidemiology. Ed. by Kyle Steenland. (Illus.). 224p. 1992. 35.00 (*0-19-506831-9*) OUP.

Case Studies in Ophthalmology for Medical Students. Mark J. Mannis & Morton E. Smith. 1989. student ed 10.00 (*0-317-94085-6*); teacher ed 15.00 (*0-317-94086-4*) Am Acad Ophthal.

Case Studies in Organizational Behaviour & Human Resource Management. 2nd ed. Ed. by Dan Gowler et al. LC 92-43837. 1993. 32.50 (*1-85396-177-9*, Pub. by Paul Chapman UK) Taylor & Francis.

Case Studies in Organizational Communication. Ed. by Beverly D. Sypher. LC 89-25917. (Guilford Communication Ser.). 326p. 1990. lib. bdg. 45.00 (*0-89862-309-X*); pap. text ed. 19.95 (*0-89862-287-5*) Guilford Pr.

Case Studies in Pediatric Intensive Care. Ed. by Mark C. Rogers & Mark A. Helfaer. LC 93-12263. (Illus.). 392p. 1993. 45.00 (*0-683-07323-0*) Williams & Wilkins.

Case Studies in Perinatal Nursing. Diane J. Angelini & Christine M. Knapp. LC 91-25953. (Illus.). 254p. 1992. 46.00 (*0-8342-0227-1*) Aspen Pub.

Case Studies in Personnel. Diana Winstanley & Jean Woodall. 268p. (C). 1992. pap. 95.00 (*0-685-60721-6*, Pub. by IPM Hse UK) St Mut.

Case Studies in Personnel. Ed. by Diana Winstanley & Jean Woodall. 300p. (C). 1992. 70.00 (*0-85292-475-5*, Pub. by IPM Hse UK) St Mut.

Case Studies in Personnel: Tutor's Manual. Diana Winstanley & Jean Woodall. 160p. (C). 1992. pap. 300.00 (*0-85292-492-5*, Pub. by IPM Hse UK) St Mut.

Case Studies in Pharmacy Practice. Roger Davis. 204p. 1979. text ed. 23.00 (*0-910769-00-1*) Am Coll Apothecaries.

Case Studies in Plant Taxonomy: Exercises in Applied Pattern Recognition. Tod F. Stuessy. LC 93-46062. 1994. pap. 25.00 (*0-231-07611-8*) Col U Pr.

Case Studies in Pollution Control in the Textile Dyeing & Finishing Industries: A Study in Non-Technical Language of Essential Information on the Economics of Control, the Problems & Their Solutions. M. H. Atkins & J. F. Lowe. 1979. 48.00 (*0-08-022457-1*, Pub. by Pergamon Repr UK) Franklin.

Case Studies in Population Policy: Argentina. 1991. 7.50 (*92-1-151205-0*, 90.XIII.19) UN.

Case Studies in Population Policy: Brazil. 42p. 1991. 7.50 (*92-1-151206-9*, 90.XIII.20) UN.

Case Studies in Population Policy: China. 74p. 1991. 7.50 (*92-1-151207-7*, 90.XIII.21) UN.

Case Studies in Population Policy: Cuba. 1990. 7.50 (*92-1-151208-5*, 90.XIII.22) UN.

Case Studies in Population Policy: France. 60p. 1991. 7.50 (*92-1-151209-3*, 90.XIII.23) UN.

Case Studies in Population Policy: Haiti. 72p. 1991. 7.50 (*92-1-151210-7*, 90.XIII.24) UN.

Case Studies in Population Policy: Hungary. 51p. 1991. 7.50 (*92-1-151211-5*, 90.XIII.25) UN.

Case Studies in Population Policy: Kuwait. 59p. 1991. 7.50 (*92-1-151217-4*, 90.XIII.30) UN.

Case Studies in Population Policy: Malaysia. 44p. 1991. 7.50 (*92-1-151212-3*, 90.XIII.26) UN.

Case Studies in Population Policy: Mexico. 52p. 1991. 7.50 (*92-1-151213-1*, 90.XIII.27) UN.

Case Studies in Population Policy: Nigeria. 38p. 1991. 7.50 (*92-1-151215-8*, 90.XIII.28) UN.

Case Studies in Population Policy: Tanzania. 42p. 1991. 7.50 (*92-1-151216-6*, 90.XIII.29) UN.

Case Studies in Pre-Hospital Care. Brady Jems. 128p. pap. text ed. 30.00 (*0-89303-838-5*) P-H.

Case Studies in Prehospital Care. Ed. by Diane Lofshult & Scott Bourn. (Illus.). 128p. (Orig.). (C). 1991. teacher ed 24.95 (*0-936174-09-9*); student ed 36.00 (*0-936174-08-0*); pap. text ed. 29.95 (*0-936174-07-2*) Jems Comm.

Case Studies in Psychology. Ed. by Robert M. Berne & Matthew N. Levy. 225p. 1994. pap. 14.95 (*0-8151-0544-4*) Mosby Yr Bk.

Case Studies in Psychotherapy. Ed. by Danny Wedding & Raymond J. Corsini. LC 88-61529. 241p. 1989. pap. 26.00 (*0-87581-338-0*) Peacock Pubs.

Case Studies in Psychotherapy. 2nd ed. Ed. by Danny Wedding & Raymond J. Corsini. 1995. pap. text ed. write for info. (*0-87581-393-3*) Peacock Pubs.

Case Studies in Public Budgeting & Financial Management. Aman Khan & W. B. Hildreth. 608p. (C). 1994. per., pap. text ed. 39.96 (*0-8403-9386-5*) Kendall-Hunt.

***Case Studies in Public Services Management.** Ed. by Alan Lawton & David McKevitt. (Illus.). 200p. (Orig.). (C). 1996. pap. write for info. (*0-631-19579-3*) Blackwell Pubs.

Case Studies in Purchasing & Supply. J. M. Stevens. 87p. (C). 1986. 50.00 (*0-685-39856-0*, Inst Pur & Supply) St Mut.

Case Studies in Purchasing & Supply. J. M. Stevens. 87p. 1988. 35.00 (*0-317-43789-5*, Inst Pur & Supply) St Mut.

Case Studies in Purchasing & Supply. J. M. Stevens. 87p. (C). 1989. 70.00 (*0-685-36129-2*, Inst Pur & Supply) St Mut.

Case Studies in Risk Management. 107p. (Orig.). 1988. pap. text ed. 37.95 (*0-937802-25-5*) RMSP.

Case Studies in Sample Design. Arlyn C. Rosander. LC 76-12283. (Statistics, Textbooks & Monographs: 21). 438p. reprint ed. pap. 124.90 (*0-685-17120-5*, 2027836) Bks Demand.

Case Studies in Science Education. Incl. Vol. 1. Case Reports. (*0-318-60113-3*, SE 78-741); Vol. 2. Design, Overview, & General Findings. (*0-318-60114-1*, SE78-7411); 11.00 (*0-318-18101-0*) USGPO.

***Case Studies in Sex Therapy.** Raymond C. Rosen & Sandra R. Leiblum. 1995. lib. bdg. 40.00 (*0-89862-848-2*, C2848) Guilford Pr.

Case Studies in Social Work Practice. Craig W. LeCroy. 296p. (C). 1992. pap. 31.95 (*0-534-15138-8*) Brooks-Cole.

***Case Studies in Superconducting Magnets: Design & Operational Issues.** Y. Iwasa. (Selected Topics in Superconductivity Series). (Illus.). 414p. (C). 1994. 59.50 (*0-306-44881-5*, Plenum Pr) Plenum.

Case Studies in Systematic Software Development. Cliff B. Jones & Roger Shaw. 350p. 1990. pap. text ed. 39.00 (*0-13-116088-5*) P-H.

Case Studies in Teaching Beginning Readers: The Howard Street Tutoring Manual. Darrell Morris. LC 92-71181. (Illus.). 258p. (Orig.). (C). 1992. pap. text ed. 23.00 (*0-9632376-0-8*) Fieldstream.

***Case Studies in the Achievement of Air Superiority.** (Military Science Ser.). 1995. lib. bdg. 625.95 (*0-8490-7507-6*) Gordon Pr.

Case Studies in the Achievement of Air Superiority. Ed. by Benjamin F. Cooling. 1989. pap. text ed. write for info. (*0-912799-63-3*) Off Air Force.

Case Studies in the Development of Close Air Support. Benjamin F. Cooling. 1989. text ed. write for info. (*0-912799-65-X*); pap. text ed. write for info. (*0-912799-64-1*) Off Air Force.

Case Studies in the Use of Algorithms. B. Lewis & I. Horabin. (Programmed Instruction in Industry Ser.). 18.00 (*0-08-014035-1*, Pub. by Pergamon Repr UK) Franklin.

Case Studies in Time Series Analysis. Xie Zhongjie. LC 93-2047. (Series on Probability & Statistics: No. 3). 300p. 1993. text ed. 61.00 (*981-02-1017-5*) World Scientific Pub.

Case Studies in Transfusion Medicine. Lucia Berte et al. 1992. 25.00 (*0-89189-311-3*, 35-6-001-00) Am Soc Clinical.

Case Studies in Twentieth-Century World History. 1988. pap. text ed. 18.66 (*0-582-34318-6*, 78042) Longman.

Case Studies in Waste Minimization. 290p. (Orig.). 1991. pap. text ed. 59.00 (*0-86587-267-8*) Gov Insts.

Case Studies in Whole Language. Richard T. Vacca & Timothy Rasinski. 250p. (C). 1992. pap. text ed. write for info. (*0-03-053227-2*) HB Coll Pubs.

Case Studies of Applied Advanced Data Collection & Management. Comp. by American Society of Civil Engineers Staff. LC 80-65303. 416p. 1980. pap. 32.00 (*0-87262-037-9*) Am Soc Civil Eng.

Case Studies of Child Play Areas & Child Support Facilities. Uriel Cohen et al. (Publications in Architecture & Urban Planning: No. R78-2). (Illus.). v, 405p. 1992. reprint ed. 18.00 (*0-938744-03-8*) U of Wis Ctr Arch-Urban.

Case Studies of Chinese Economic Reform. Ed. by Timothy King & Zhang Jiping. LC 92-31664. (EDI Development Policy Case Series: Teaching Cases: No. 2). 204p. 1992. 11.95 (*0-8213-2228-1*) World Bank.

Case Studies of Coastal Management: Experience from the United States. Ed. by Brian Needham. (Illus.). 117p. (Orig.). (C). 1993. pap. text ed. 30.00 (*1-56806-579-5*) Diane Pub.

Case Studies of Computer Aided Learning. Ed. by Robert L. Blomeyer, Jr. & C. Dianne Martin. 270p. 1991. pap. 30.00 (*1-85000-647-4*, Falmer Pr) Taylor & Francis.

Case Studies of Consumers' Cooperatives. H. Haines Turner. LC 68-58631. (Columbia University. Studies in the Social Sciences: No. 481). reprint ed. 24.50 (*0-404-51481-2*) AMS Pr.

***Case Studies of Exceptional Students: Handicapped & Gifted.** Carroll J. Jones. LC 93-6745. 272p. 1993. pap. 31.95 (*0-398-06188-2*) C C Thomas.

Case Studies of Exceptional Students: Handicapped & Gifted. Carroll J. Jones. LC 93-6745. 272p. (C). 1993. text ed. 53.95 (*0-398-05878-3*) C C Thomas.

Case Studies of Just-in-Time Implementation at Westinghouse & IBM. Spencer Duin et al. Ed. by American Production & Inventory Control Staff. LC 86-71914. 50p. 1986. pap. 15.00 (*0-935406-82-4*) Am Prod & Inventory.

***Case Studies of Mildly Handicapped Students: Learning Disabled, Mildly Mentally Retarded, & Behavior Disordered.** Carroll J. Jones. 236p. 1992. pap. 29.95 (*0-398-06189-0*) C C Thomas.

Case Studies of Mildly Handicapped Students: Learning Disabled, Mildly Mentally Retarded, & Behavior Disordered. Carroll J. Jones. 236p. (C). 1992. text ed. 49.95x (*0-398-05815-6*) C C Thomas.

Case Studies of Modified Disinfection Practices for Trihalomethane Control. 260p. 1990. pap. 25.00 (*0-89867-515-4*, 90574) Am Water Wks Assn.

Case Studies of Programs Serving Adults, Options: Expanding Educational Services for Adults. National Center for Research in Vocational Education Staff. 1987. 39.95 (*0-317-03858-3*, SP500G) Ctr Educ Trng Employ.

Case Studies of Project Sustainability: Implications for Policy & Operations from Asian Experience. Michael Bamberger & G. Shabbir Cheema. (EDI Seminar Ser.). 122p. 1990. 7.95 (*0-8213-1614-1*, 11614) World Bank.

Case Studies of Selected Leverage Buyouts. (Illus.). 131p. (Orig.). 1992. pap. text ed. 45.00 (*0-941375-47-1*) Diane Pub.

***Case Studies of Severely - Multihandicapped Students.** Carroll J. Jones. 174p. 1993. pap. 24.95 (*0-398-06190-4*) C C Thomas.

Case Studies of Severely - Multihandicapped Students. Carroll J. Jones. 174p. (C). 1993. text ed. 38.95x (*0-398-05832-6*) C C Thomas.

Case Studies of State-Level Dislocated Worker Program Coordination. Ed. by Gerry Feinstein & Karen Glass. 87p. (Orig.). 1991. pap. text ed. 15.00 (*1-55877-136-0*) Natl Governor.

Case Studies of Surface Mining: Proceedings of the International Surface Mining Conference, 2nd, Minneapolis, 1968. International Surface Mining Conference Staff. Ed. by Howard L. Hartman. LC 70-89678. 330p. reprint ed. pap. 94.10 (*0-317-10744-5*, 2004547) Bks Demand.

Case Studies of the Use of Drug Testing in Corporations: Deviance in Large Organizations. Darrell D. Irwin. LC 91-14161. 132p. 1991. lib. bdg. 69.95 (*0-7734-9844-3*) E Mellen.

Case Studies on Bayesian Statistics. Constantine Gatsonis et al. LC 93-17514. (Lecture Notes in Statistics Ser.: Vol. 83). 1993. 49.00 (*0-387-94043-X*) Spr-Verlag.

Case Studies on Documentary Credits: Problems, Queries, Answers. Jan Dekker. 144p. (Orig.). 1989. pap. 49.95 (*92-842-1079-8*, 459) ICC Pub.

Case Studies on Educational Administration. Theodore J. Kowalski. 208p. (Orig.). (C). 1991. pap. text ed. 25.95 (*0-8013-0387-7*, 78168) Longman.

Case Studies on Educational Administration. 2nd ed. Theodore Kowalski. LC 94-1359. 256p. (Orig.). (C). 1995. pap. text ed. 21.95 (*0-8013-1422-4*, 76486) Longman.

Case Studies on Educational Administration. 2nd ed. Theodore J. Kowalski. LC 94-1359. 224p. (Orig.). (C). 1995. teacher ed write for info. (*0-8013-1436-4*, 76722) Longman.

Case Studies on Human Rights & Fundamental Freedoms. Ed. by Veenhoven. 1987. write for info. (*0-685-01709-5*) Kluwer Ac.

Case Studies on Human Rights & Fundamental Freedoms, Set. Ed. by Veenhoven. Incl. Vol. 1. 1975. lib. bdg. 126.50 (*90-247-1780-9*); Vol. 2. 1975. lib. bdg. 86.00 (*0-685-02817-8*); Vol. 3. 1977. lib. bdg. 126.50 (*90-247-1955-0*); Vol. 4. 1976. lib. bdg. 86.00 (*0-685-02818-6*); Vol. 5. 1976. lib. bdg. 86.00 (*0-685-02819-4*); 1987. Set lib. bdg. 363.00 (*90-247-1779-5*) Kluwer Ac.

***Case Studies on Human Rights in Japan.** Ed. by Ian Neary & Roger Goodman. 192p. (C). 1995. text ed. 70.00 (*1-873410-35-2*, Pub. by Curzon Pr UK) Humanities.

Case Studies on Teaching in Higher Education. Peter Schwartz & Graham Webb. (Teaching & Learning in Higher Education Ser.). 1993. pap. 39.00 (*0-7494-0972-X*, Pub. by Kogan Page Educ UK) Taylor & Francis.

Case Studies on Women's Employment & Pay in Latin America. Ed. by George Psacharopoulos & P. Zafiris Tzannatos. LC 92-40880. 490p. 1992. 29.95 (*0-8213-2308-3*, 12308) World Bank.

CASE Study: Communication & Self-Esteem. M. Ann Marquis & Elaine Addy-Trout. LC 92-21826. (YA). (gr. 5-12). 1992. pap. 35.00 (*0-930599-75-6*) Thinking Pubns.

Case Study: How Twenty-One Koreans Perceive America. Byungchai C. Hahn. (TWEC World Education Monographs). 15p. 1978. 2.00 (*0-685-05135-8*) I N Thut World Educ Ctr.

Case Study Houses, 1945-1962. 2nd ed. Esther McCoy. LC 77-14499. (Illus.). 1977. reprint ed. pap. 24.50 (*0-912158-71-9*) Hennessey.

Case Study in Auditing. 4th ed. Donald H. Taylor & G. William Glenn. 1989. Net. pap. text ed. write for info. (*0-471-63480-8*) Wiley.

Case Study in the Development of Educational Training Programs. Floyd T. Waterman. 77p. (Orig.). 1981. pap. 6.50 (*1-55719-060-7*) U NE CPAR.

Case Study Methods. Jacques Hamel. (Qualitative Research Methods Ser.: Vol. 32). (Illus.). 96p. (C). 1993. text ed. 21.50 (*0-8039-5415-8*); pap. text ed. 9.50 (*0-8039-5416-6*) Sage.

Case Study of Latin American Unionization in Austin, Texas. Sam F. Parigi. Ed. by Carlos E. Cortes. LC 76-1265. (Chicano Heritage Ser.). 1977. 28.95 (*0-405-09518-X*) Ayer.

Case Study of Mainstream Protestantism. Ed. by D. Newell Williams. 574p. (Orig.). 1991. pap. 39.99 (*0-8272-0460-4*) Chalice Pr.

Case Study on Decision-Making in Selected Multinational Enterprises in India: Multinational Enterprises Programme, Working Paper, No. 38. P. N. Agarwala. ii, 44p. (Orig.). 1985. pap. 12.00 (*92-2-105121-8*) Intl Labour Office.

Case Study Research: Design & Methods. 2nd ed. Robert K. Yin. (Applied Social Research Methods Ser.: Vol. 5). 184p. (C). 1994. text ed. 37.00 (*0-8039-5662-2*); pap. text ed. 16.95 (*0-8039-5663-0*) Sage.

Case Study Research in Distance Education. Alistair Morgan. (C). 1991. pap. 24.00x (*0-7300-1349-9*, IDE806, Pub. by Deakin Univ AT) St Mut.

Case Study Research in Education: A Qualitative Approach. Sharan B. Merriam. LC 88-42795. (Education-Higher Education Ser.: No. HE). 248p. 1991. pap. 18.95 (*1-55542-359-0*) Jossey-Bass.

Case Study Research in Education: A Qualitative Approach. Sharan B. Merriam. LC 88-42795. (Illus.). 246p. reprint ed. pap. 70.20 (*0-7837-6523-1*, 2045635) Bks Demand.

Case Supervisor. Jack Rudman. (Career Examination Ser.: C-188). 1994. pap. 29.95 (*0-8373-0188-2*) Nat Learn.

Case Technology. Ed. by Raymond T. Yeh. (C). 1991. lib. bdg. 93.00 (*0-7923-9189-6*) Kluwer Ac.

Case That Shook India. P. Bhushan. 294p. 1978. 14.95 (*0-7069-0594-6*) Asia Bk Corp.

Case Tracking & Transcript Monitoring in Rhode Island: A Guide; Technical Assistance Report No. 6 in the Appellate Justice Improvement Project. National Center for State Courts Staff. 32p. 1980. 1.92 (*0-685-16296-6*, NERO, T/A-506) Natl Ctr St Courts.

Case Tractors: Steam to Diesel. Dave Arnold. (Illus.). 128p. 1990. pap. 19.95 (*0-87938-408-5*) Motorbooks Intl.

***Case Tractors: 1912-1959 Photo Archive.** Ed. by P. A. Letourneau. (Photo Archive Ser.). (Illus.). 144p. 1995. pap. 24.95 (*1-882256-28-X*) Iconografix.

***Case Tractors 1912-1959.** 1995. pap. text ed. 24.95 (*1-882256-32-8*) Iconografix.

Case User Survey, 1989. Robert V. Binder et al. (Illus.). 128p. (Orig.). 1989. pap. 3.00 (*0-9622513-0-5*) R Binder Systems.

Case with No Conclusion. Leo Bruce. (Sergeant Beef Mystery Ser.). 288p. 20.00 (*0-89733-117-6*); pap. 5.95 (*0-89733-118-4*) Academy Chi Pubs.

Case with Three Husbands. large type ed. Margaret Erskine. (Linford Mystery Library). 288p. 1988. pap. 11.95 (*0-7089-6505-9*, Linford) Ulverscroft.

Case Workbook in Personality. Robert W. White et al. 259p. (C). 1982. pap. text ed. 14.95 (*0-917974-80-8*) Waveland Pr.

Case Worker. Jack Rudman. (Career Examination Ser.: C-128). 1994. pap. 23.95 (*0-8373-0128-9*) Nat Learn.

Case Worker: Social Investigator, Eligibility Specialist. Ed. by Hy Hammer & Phyllis Cohen. LC 92-30786. 1992. 12.00 (*0-671-84713-9*, Arco Test) P-H Gen Ref & Trav.

***Casebeer: Incisional Keratotomy.** J. Charles Casebeer. LC 94-26528. 224p. 1995. 145.00 (*1-55642-236-9*, 62369) SLACK Inc.

Casebook: Applications of the Myers-Briggs Type Indicator in Counseling. 2nd ed. Ed. by Judith A. Provost. LC 93-41360. 124p. 1993. pap. 10.00 (*0-935652-17-5*) Ctr Applications Psych.

C

An Asterisk (*) at the beginning of an entry indicates that the title is appearing in BIP for the first time.

Cases & Materials on Criminal Procedure Code, with Supplement. 3rd ed. Ed. by N. Nath et al. (C). 1990. text ed. 275.00 (*0-89771-502-0*) St Mut.

Cases & Materials on Criminal Procedure Code, 1987: With Supplement 1989. 3rd ed. Bholeshwar Nath. (C). 1989. 275.00 (*0-685-36421-6*) St Mut.

Cases & Materials on Debtor & Creditor. 2nd ed. Vern Countryman. 1974. 29.00 (*0-316-15803-8*) Little.

Cases & Materials on Decedents' Estates & Trusts. 8th ed. John Ritchie, III et al. (University Casebook Ser.). 1424p. 1993. text ed. 46.95 (*1-56662-066-X*) Foundation Pr.

***Cases & Materials on EC Law.** 2nd ed. Stephen Weatherill. 590p. 1994. pap. 48.00 (*1-85431-329-0*, Pub. by Blackstone Pr UK) W W Gaunt.

Cases & Materials on Employment Law. Richard W. Painter et al. 672p. 1995. pap. 54.00 (*1-85431-197-2*, Pub. by Blackstone Pr UK) W W Gaunt.

Cases & Materials on Environmental Law. 2nd ed. Oscar S. Gray. LC 73-83169. 1442p. reprint ed. pap. 180.00 (*0-317-29772-4*, 2017240) Bks Demand.

***Cases & Materials on Environmental Law.** 4th ed. Roger W. Findley & Daniel A. Farber. LC 95-17815. (American Casebook Ser.). 1995. text ed. 47.00 (*0-314-05932-6*) West Pub.

Cases & Materials on Environmental Law: 1977 Supplement. 2nd ed. Oscar S. Gray. LC 73-83169. 619p. reprint ed. pap. 176.50 (*0-317-29770-8*, 2017241) Bks Demand.

***Cases & Materials on Equity & Trusts.** Paul Todd. 542p. 1994. pap. 50.00 (*1-85431-319-3*, Pub. by Blackstone Pr UK) W W Gaunt.

***Cases & Materials on Evidence.** 3rd ed. Simon Cooper et al. 586p. 1994. pap. 50.00 (*1-85431-279-0*, Pub. by Blackstone Pr UK) W W Gaunt.

Cases & Materials on Family Law. suppl. ed. Caleb Foote et al. (C). 1985. Statutory Supplement, 1985. 10.95 (*0-316-28855-1*) Little.

Cases & Materials on Family Law. 3rd ed. Caleb Foote et al. (C). 1985. 50.00 (*0-316-28847-0*) Little.

Cases & Materials on Federal Courts. 9th ed. Charles T. McCormick et al. LC 92-5649. (University Casebook Ser.). 1992. text ed. 42.95 (*0-88277-991-5*) Foundation Pr.

Cases & Materials on Federal Indian Law. 3rd ed. David H. Getches et al. (American Casebook Ser.). 1128p. (C). 1993. text ed. 53.00 (*0-314-02268-6*) West Pub.

Cases & Materials on Feminist Jurisprudence: Taking Women Seriously. Mary Becker et al. (American Casebook Ser.). 926p. 1993. text ed. 47.00 (*0-314-02807-2*) West Pub.

Cases & Materials on First Amendment: 1993 Supplement. Walter Van Alstyne. (University Casebook Ser.). 198p. 1993. pap. text ed. 7.95 (*1-56662-112-7*) Foundation Pr.

Cases & Materials on Florida Domestic Relations. Florida Bar Staff. 1008p. 1994. ring bd. 75.00 (*0-945979-14-2*, 275) FL Bar Legal Ed.

Cases & Materials on Fundamentals of Federal Income Taxation. 7th rev. ed. James J. Freeland et al. (University Casebook Ser.). 378p. (C). 1991. pap. text ed. write for info. (*0-88277-941-9*) Foundation Pr.

Cases & Materials on Fundamentals of Partnership Taxation: Teacher's Manual. 3rd ed. Stephen A. Lind et al. (University Casebook Ser.). 271p. 1991. pap. text ed. write for info. (*0-88277-978-8*) Foundation Pr.

Cases & Materials on Indian Penal Code. V. K. Dewan. (C). 1988. 110.00 (*0-685-25698-7*) St Mut.

Cases & Materials on International Law. Ed. by Martin Dixon & Robert McCorquodale. 582p. (C). 1991. 51.00 (*1-85431-123-9*, Pub. by Blackstone Pr UK) W W Gaunt.

Cases & Materials on International Law. 3rd ed. Louis Henkin et al. (American Casebook Ser.). 1596p. 1993. text ed. 59.00 (*0-314-02272-4*) West Pub.

Cases & Materials on Introduction to Law: Legal Process & Procedure. Cornelius F. Murphy. (American Casebook Ser.). 772p. 1977. text ed. 42.50 (*0-314-32845-9*) West Pub.

Cases & Materials on Labor Law: Process & Policy. 2nd ed. Douglas L. Leslie. 1247p. 1985. 42.00 (*0-316-52161-2*) Little.

Cases & Materials on Land Use. 2nd ed. David L. Callies et al. (American Casebook Ser.). 735p. 1994. text ed. 44.00 (*0-314-03253-3*) West Pub.

Cases & Materials on Law of Evidence. Bholeshwar Nath. 578p. 1983. 240.00 (*0-317-54684-8*) St Mut.

Cases & Materials on Law of Evidence. 2nd ed. Bholeshwar Nath. (C). 1991. 95.00 (*0-685-39713-0*) St Mut.

***Cases & Materials on Mass Media Law.** 5th ed. Marc A. Franklin & David A. Anderson. (University Casebook Ser.). 802p. (C). 1995. text ed. 45.95 (*1-56662-256-5*) Foundation Pr.

Cases & Materials on Mass Media Law, 1993 Supplement. 4th ed. Marc A. Franklin & David A. Anderson. (University Casebook Ser.). 100p. 1993. pap. text ed. 7.95 (*1-56662-073-2*) Foundation Pr.

Cases & Materials on Modern Property Law. 3rd ed. Jon W. Bruce & James W. Ely, Jr. (American Casebook Ser.). 945p. 1994. text ed. 46.00 (*0-314-03493-5*) West Pub.

***Cases & Materials on Nonprofit, Tax-Exempt Organizations, 1994.** Douglas Cook. 358p. Date not set. ring bd. 43.50 (*1-879581-18-3*) Lupus Pubns.

Cases & Materials on Oil & Gas Law: Teacher's Manual. 2nd ed. Eugene O. Kuntz et al. (American Casebook Ser.). 350p. 1993. pap. text ed. write for info. (*0-314-02915-X*) West Pub.

***Cases & Materials on Patent Law: Including Trade Secrets, Copyrights, Trademarks.** 4th ed. William H. Francis & Robert C. Collins. LC 95-17816. (American Casebook Ser.). 1995. text ed. write for info. (*0-314-05968-7*) West Pub.

Cases & Materials on Private International Law. J. H. Morris & P. M. North. 786p. 1984. U.K. pap. text ed. 68.00 (*0-406-25265-3*, UK) Butterworth Legal Pubs.

Cases & Materials on Products Liability. 2nd ed. David A. Fischer & William Powers, Jr. LC 94-7714. (American Casebook Ser.). 768p. 1994. text ed. 43.00 (*0-314-03511-7*) West Pub.

Cases & Materials on Review of Administrative Action. 2nd ed. S. D. Hotop. xxxiii, 1219p. 1983. 116.50 (*0-455-20377-6*, Pub. by Law Bk Co); pap. 89.00 (*0-455-20378-4*, Pub. by Law Bk Co) W W Gaunt.

Cases & Materials on Sales Transactions: Domestic & International Law. John O. Honnold & Curtis R. Reitz. LC 92-19841. (University Casebook Ser.). 1992. text ed. 38.00 (*1-56662-004-X*) Foundation Pr.

Cases & Materials on Secured Transactions. George E. Osborne. 559p. 1988. reprint ed. text ed. 37.00 (*0-314-28264-5*) West Pub.

Cases & Materials on Taxation. 2nd ed. R. Baxt et al. 1986. Australia. pap. 83.00 (*0-409-49172-1*) Butterworth Legal Pubs.

Cases & Materials on the Carriage of Goods by Sea. Martin Dockray. 1987. U.K. text ed. 68.00 (*0-86205-259-9*); U.K. pap. 68.00 (*0-86205-239-4*) Butterworth Legal Pubs.

***Cases & Materials on the English Legal System.** 6th rev. ed. Michael Zander. (Law in Context Ser.). 745p. (C). 1994. pap. text ed. 37.95 (*0-406-03148-7*, Trans) Northwestern U Pr.

Cases & Materials on the Income Taxation of Trusts, Estates, Grantors & Beneficiaries. Jeffrey L. Pennell. LC 87-10563. (American Casebook Ser.). 460p. 1987. text ed. 34.50 (*0-314-42565-9*) West Pub.

Cases & Materials on the Law of Employment Discrimination. 3rd ed. Joel W. Friedman & George M. Strickler, Jr. (University Casebook Ser.). 1992. text ed. 43.95 (*0-88277-974-5*) Foundation Pr.

Cases & Materials on the Law of Natural Resources. Clyde O. Martz. Ed. by Stuart Bruchey. LC 78-53553. (Development of Public Land Law in the U. S. Ser.). 1979. reprint ed. lib. bdg. 81.95 (*0-405-11379-X*) Ayer.

Cases & Materials on the Law of Oil & Gas. 6th ed. Richard C. Maxwell et al. LC 92-5650. (University Casebook Ser.). 1060p. 1992. text ed. 45.95 (*0-88277-983-4*) Foundation Pr.

Cases & Materials on the Law of Sales & Secured Financing. 6th ed. John O. Honnold et al. LC 93-9221. (University Casebook Ser.). 1000p. (C). 1993. text ed. 43.95 (*1-56662-061-9*) Foundation Pr.

Cases & Materials on the Law of the European Communities. 3rd ed. Richard Plender & Ushers. 1993. pap. write for info. (*0-406-01624-0*) Butterworth Legal Pubs.

***Cases & Materials on the Malaysian Law of Partnership.** E. R. Ivamy. 1993. 42.00 (*0-409-99650-5*, SI) Butterworth Legal Pubs.

Cases & Materials on the Regulation of International Business & Economic Relations. A. Swan & J. Murphy. 1991. write for info. (*0-8205-0056-9*) Bender.

Cases & Materials on the Regulation of International Business & Economic Relations, Documents Supplement. A. Swan & J. Murphy. 1991. write for info. (*0-8205-0057-7*) Bender.

Cases & Materials on the Theft Acts. Janet M. Dine. 224p. (C). 1985. 120.00 (*0-906322-80-4*, Pub. by Blackstone Pr UK) St Mut.

Cases & Materials on Torts. 2nd ed. Leon Green et al. 1360p. 1977. 27.95 (*0-685-07610-5*) West Pub.

Cases & Materials on Torts. 4th ed. Richard A. Epstein et al. LC 83-81566. 1456p. (C). 1984. 39.00 (*0-316-24571-2*) Little.

Cases & Materials on Transfer of Property Act, 1882: 1987 Edition. Bholeshwar Nath. (C). 1987. 175.00 (*0-685-36409-7*) St Mut.

Cases & Materials to Accompany Civil Procedure Cases. 6th ed. Jack M. Friedenthal et al. (American Casebook Ser.). 315p. 1993. teacher ed, pap. text ed. write for info. (*0-314-02883-8*) West Pub.

Cases & Problems in Contemporary Retailing. 3rd ed. J. Barry Mason et al. LC 91-73501. 459p. 1992. 19.95 (*0-87393-139-4*) Dame Pubns.

Cases & Problems in Criminal Law. Myron Moskovitz. 397p. 1989. 45.00 (*0-87084-592-6*) Anderson Pub Co.

***Cases & Problems in Criminal Procedure: The Police.** Myron Moskovitz. LC 95-5354. (Analysis & Skills Ser.). 1995. write for info. (*0-256-18479-8*) Bender.

Cases & Problems on Remedies. Shoben & Tabb. 1989. text ed. 41.95 (*0-88277-719-X*) Foundation Pr.

Cases & Readings in Management Science. 2nd ed. Barry Render et al. 350p. 1990. teacher ed write for info. (*0-318-66342-2*, H23039); pap. text ed. 33.00 (*0-205-12302-3*, H23021) Allyn.

Cases & Readings in Production & Operations Management. Ed. by Joseph C. Latona & Jay Nathan. LC 93-48384. 1994. pap. text ed. 34.80 (*0-205-13936-1*) Allyn.

Cases & Readings on Administrative Law. Ed. by James F. Davison & Nathan D. Grundstein. LC 72-108388. 777p. 1971. reprint ed. text ed. 145.00 (*0-8371-3811-6*, DAAL, Greenwood Pr) Greenwood.

Cases & Readings on Law & Society, 1948-1949, 3 vols., Set. Sidney P. Simpson & Julius Stone. LC 88-46175. 2389p. 1989. reprint ed. lib. bdg. 195.00 (*0-912004-70-3*) W W Gaunt.

Cases & Select Readings in Health Care Marketing. Ed. by Robert Sweeney et al. LC 88-16033. (Series in Marketing & Health Services Administration: No. 2). 351p. 1989. text ed. 59.95 (*0-86656-429-2*) Haworth Pr.

Cases & Text on Property. suppl. ed. A. James Casner & W. Barton Leach. LC 83-82695. 1427p. (C). 1984. 12.00 (*0-316-13205-5*) Little.

Cases & Text on Property. 3rd ed. A. James Casner & W. Barton Leach. LC 83-82695. 1427p. (C). 1984. 53.00 (*0-316-13183-0*) Little.

Cases for Analysis in Marketing. 3rd ed. W. Wayne Talarzyk. 408p. (C). 1984. text ed. 17.50 (*0-03-070767-6*) Dryden Pr.

Cases for Intervention Planning: A Sourcebook. Molly R. Hancock & Kenneth Millar. 150p. 1993. pap. text ed. 19.95 (*0-8304-1301-4*) Nelson-Hall.

Cases for Strategic Management. John H. Barnett & William D. Wilsted. 545p. (C). 1989. pap. 40.95 (*0-534-91742-9*) Intl Thomson.

Cases from Management Accounting Practice, 2 vols., Vol. 1. Ed. by Shane Moriarity. 35p. 4.95 (*0-86641-133-X*, 86198) Inst Mgmt Account.

Cases from Management Accounting Practice, 2 vols., Vol. 2. Ed. by Shane Moriarity. 42p. 4.95 (*0-86641-143-7*) Inst Mgmt Account.

Cases Illustrative of Oriental Life: The Application of English Law to India. Erskine Perry. (C). 1988. reprint ed. 36.00 (*81-206-0368-0*, Pub. by Asian Educ Servs II) S Asia.

Cases in Accounting Ethics & Professionalism. 2nd ed. Steven M. Mintz. 1992. text ed. write for info. (*0-07-042504-3*) McGraw.

Cases in Advertising & Promotion Management. 3rd ed. John A. Quelch & Paul W. Farris. 800p. (C). 1990. text ed. 61.95 (*0-256-09689-9*) Irwin.

Cases in Advertising & Promotion Management. 4th ed. John A. Quelch & Paul W. Farris. LC 93-5170. 768p. (C). 1993. text ed. 65.95 (*0-256-12272-5*) Irwin.

Cases in Advertising Communication Management. 3rd ed. Stephen A. Greyser. 784p. (C). 1991. text ed. write for info. (*0-13-116138-5*) P-H.

Cases in Advertising Management. Ed. by Terence Nevett. 320p. 1992. pap. 24.95 (*0-8442-3368-4*, NTC Busn Bks) NTC Pub Grp.

Cases in Agribusiness Management. James G. Beierlein et al. 224p. 1988. pap. text ed. 29.00 (*0-13-115445-1*) P-H.

***Cases in Agribusiness Management.** 2nd ed. Seperich et al. (Illus.). 225p. (C). 1995. pap. text ed. write for info. (*0-614-03565-1*) Gorsuch Scarisbrick.

Cases in Applied Corporate Finance. Sihler. (C). 1994. pap. text ed. 25.00 (*0-673-99223-3*) HarpCollege.

Cases in Applied Corporate Finance. Sihler. (C). 1994. Instr.'s Manual. teacher ed 10.00 (*0-673-55651-4*) HarpCollege.

Cases in Bioethics: Selections from the Hastings Center Report. 2nd ed. Ed. by Bette-Jane Crigger. LC 92-85011. 320p. (C). 1993. pap. text ed. 15.50 (*0-312-06746-1*) St Martin.

Cases in Business & Society. 2nd ed. Scott H. Partridge. 384p. (C). 1989. pap. text ed. write for info. (*0-13-115536-9*) P-H.

Cases in Business Policy. 2nd ed. Brian Kenny et al. 400p. (Orig.). 1992. pap. 34.95 (*0-631-18365-5*) Blackwell Pubs.

***Cases in Business to Business Relationship Selling.** 4th ed. Ernest Maier. LC 95-5112. 1995. pap. text ed. write for info. (*0-13-340290-8*) P-H.

Cases in Chemical Pathology: A Diagnostic Approach. R. N. Walmsley et al. 464p. 1992. pap. text ed. 28.00 (*981-02-1068-X*) World Scientific Pub.

Cases in Chemical Pathology: A Diagnostic Approach. 3rd ed. R. N. Walmsley et al. 464p. 1992. text ed. 78.00 (*981-02-1067-1*) World Scientific Pub.

Cases in Civil Liberties. 3rd ed. Robert F. Cushman. 1979. 18.95 (*0-685-03776-2*) P-H.

Cases in Civil Liberties. 6th ed. Robert F. Cushman & Susan P. Koniak. LC 93-1893. 1993. pap. text ed. write for info. (*0-13-146622-4*) P-H.

Cases in Collective Bargaining & Industrial Relations. 7th ed. Ray Hilgert & Sterling Schoen. 450p. (C). 1992. text ed. 32.95 (*0-256-08634-6*) Irwin.

Cases in Collective Bargaining & Industrial Relations: A Decisional Approach. 6th ed. Sterling H. Schoen & Raymond L. Hilgert. (C). 1988. pap. text ed. 28.50 (*0-256-06990-5*) Irwin.

***Cases in Collective Bargaining & Industrial Relations: A Decisional Approach.** 8th ed. Raymond L. Hilgert & Sterling H. Schoen. LC 95-806. 408p. (C). 1995. 32.95 (*0-256-16214-X*) Irwin.

***Cases in Collective Bargaining & Industrial Relations: Decisional Approach.** 3rd ed. Sterling Schoen & Raymond Hilgert. (C). 1977. 11.95 (*0-256-02002-7*) Irwin.

Cases in Commercial Bank Management. E. N. Roussaskis. LC 94-75194. 134p. 1994. pap. 20.00 (*1-878975-39-0*) Kolb Pub.

Cases in Communications Law. John D. Zelezny. 299p. 1993. pap. 15.95 (*0-534-13454-8*) Intl Thomson.

Cases in Company Financial Reporting. Brian Rutherford & Robert Wearing. (C). 1988. pap. 45.00 (*0-06-318371-4*, Pub. by P Chapman Pub UK); 36.00 (*0-317-93202-0*, Pub. by P Chapman Pub UK) St Mut.

***Cases in Company Financial Reporting.** 2nd ed. Jobert Jupe et al. 224p. 1995. pap. 24.95 (*1-85396-206-6*, Pub. by Paul Chapman UK) Taylor & Francis.

Cases in Compensation. 5th ed. George T. Milkovich et al. 100p. (C). 1994. pap. text ed. write for info. (*0-945601-02-6*) Compensation.

Cases in Competitive Strategy. Michael E. Porter. (Illus.). 400p. 1983. text ed. 35.00 (*0-02-925410-8*) Free Pr.

Cases in Constitutional Law. 5th ed. Robert F. Cushman. 1979. 29.95 (*0-685-03777-0*) P-H.

Cases in Constitutional Law. 7th ed. Robert F. Cushman & Susan P. Koniak. (C). 1989. text ed. write for info. (*0-13-118316-8*) P-H.

Cases in Constitutional Law. 8th ed. Robert F. Cushman & Susan P. Koniak. LC 93-1892. 1993. text ed. write for info. (*0-13-146630-5*) P-H.

Cases in Constitutional Law: Summaries & Critiques. James V. Calvi & Susan Coleman. LC 93-26954. 1993. pap. text ed. write for info. (*0-13-177346-1*) P-H.

Cases in Consumer Behavior. Hale N. Horngren. (Illus.). 224p. (C). 1987. pap. text ed. write for info. (*0-13-115346-3*) P-H.

Cases in Consumer Behavior. 2nd ed. F. Stewart DeBruicker et al. (Illus.). 336p. (C). 1986. pap. text ed. write for info. (*0-13-118332-X*) P-H.

Cases in Consumer Behavior. 2nd ed. Hale N. Tongren. 256p. (C). 1991. pap. text ed. write for info. (*0-13-116344-2*) P-H.

Cases in Corporate Finance. Elroy Dimson & Paul Marsh. LC 87-6299. 412p. 1988. text ed. 69.50 (*0-471-91764-8*) Wiley.

Cases in Corrections. Michael Braswell & Tyler Fletcher. LC 79-25043. (C). 1980. pap. text ed. write for info. (*0-394-33366-7*) Random.

***Cases in Cost Accounting.** Joseph Merrill. 224p. (C). 1994. pap. text ed., ring bd. 19.95 (*0-8403-9445-4*) Kendall-Hunt.

Cases in Developmental Psychology & Psychopathology. Robert G. Meyer. 410p. 1989. pap. text ed. 28.00 (*0-205-11907-7*, H19078) Allyn.

Cases in Early Education: Stories of Programs & Practices. Amy Driscoll. LC 93-1562. 1994. pap. text ed. 22.00 (*0-205-15021-7*) Allyn.

Cases in Engineering Economy. Theodore G. Eschenbach. LC 88-22764. 170p. 1989. Net. pap. text ed. write for info. (*0-471-62861-1*); 6.50 (*0-471-62022-X*) Wiley.

Cases in Environmental Management & Business Strategy. Richard Welford. 192p. (Orig.). 1994. pap. 53.50 (*0-273-60313-2*, Pub. by Pitman Pub Ltd UK) Trans-Atl Phila.

Cases in European Business. Jill Preston. 256p. (Orig.). 1992. pap. 47.50 (*0-273-03740-4*, Pub. by Pitman Pub Ltd UK) Trans-Atl Phila.

Cases in European Human Resource Management. 2nd ed. Ed. by Andrew Kakabadse & Shaun Tyson. LC 93-18903. 1993. write for info. (*0-415-07414-2*) Routledge.

Cases in European Marketing Management. John A. Quelch et al. LC 93-41069. (Series in Marketing). 544p. (C). 1994. pap. text ed. 48.95 (*0-256-15722-7*) Irwin.

***Cases in Finance.** Ed. by Ben Nunnally & Tony Plath. LC 94-27736. 400p. (C). 1994. 28.95 (*0-256-12338-1*) Irwin.

Cases in Finance. George C. Philippatos et al. (C). 1985. teacher ed write for info. (*0-8359-0718-X*, Reston); pap. text ed. write for info. (*0-8359-0717-1*, Reston) P-H.

Cases in Finance. 3rd ed. David F. Scott, Jr. et al. 336p. 1992. pap. text ed. write for info. (*0-13-117995-0*) P-H.

Cases in Financial Accounting. John S. Hughes. LC 94-9353. 1994. text ed. 20.95 (*0-538-83864-7*) S-W Pub.

Cases in Financial Accounting & Reporting. Ralph J. McQuade. LC 92-20563. 1992. pap. text ed. write for info. (*0-07-045655-0*) McGraw.

Cases in Financial Analysis. Pratt. 1994. text ed. 16.95 (*0-538-83676-8*) S-W Pub.

***Cases in Financial Engineering: Applied Studies of Financial Innovation.** Scott Mason et al. LC 94-32273. 1994. text ed. 59.00 (*0-13-079419-8*) P-H.

Cases in Financial Management. Martha A. Schary et al. LC 92-27357. 160p. (C). 1993. text ed. 19.95 (*0-256-14893-7*) Irwin.

Cases in Financial Management. Joseph M. Sulock & John S. Dunkelberg. 416p. (C). 1992. Net. text ed. write for info. (*0-471-52904-4*) Wiley.

Cases in Financial Management. 3rd ed. Vincent P. Apilado et al. LC 86-22470. (Illus.). 182p. (C). 1993. reprint ed. pap. text ed. 35.50 (*0-314-29526-7*) West Pub.

Cases in Financial Management, 3 Vols. 3rd ed. Jerry A. Viscione & George A. Aragon. LC 87-81509. (C). 1987. teacher ed, text ed. 4.36 (*0-395-35721-7*) HM.

Cases in Financial Management, 3 Vols. 3rd ed. Jerry A. Viscione & George A. Aragon. LC 87-81509. (C). 1987. text ed. 55.96 (*0-395-43404-1*) HM.

Cases in Financial Management: Directed, Non-Directed, & By-Request Versions. Eugene F. Brigham & Louis C. Gapenski. 520p. (C). 1993. teacher ed, pap. text ed. 6.00 (*0-03-097095-4*) Dryden Pr.

Cases in Financial Management: Directed Versions. Eugene F. Brigham & Louis C. Gapenski. 357p. (C). 1993. pap. text ed. 32.00 (*0-03-055024-6*) Dryden Pr.

Cases in Financial Management: Non-Directed Versions. Eugene F. Brigham & Louis C. Gapenski. 139p. (C). 1993. pap. text ed. 21.75 (*0-03-098329-0*) Dryden Pr.

Cases in Financial Management, Module C. Eugene F. Brigham & Louis C. Gapenski. 112p. (Orig.). (C). 1992. pap. text ed. 14.50 (*0-03-076743-1*) Dryden Pr.

Cases in Financial Statement Reporting & Analysis. Leopold A. Bernstein & Mostafa M. Maksy. (C). 1985. pap. text ed. 36.95 (*0-256-03316-1*) Irwin.

Cases in Financial Statement Reporting & Analysis. 2nd ed. Leopold A. Bernstein & Mostafa M. Maksy. LC 93-26316. 592p. (C). 1993. pap. text ed. 40.95 (*0-256-12584-8*) Irwin.

Cases in Health Care Financial Management. Ed. by James D. Suver et al. (Illus.). 398p. (C). 1984. teacher ed write for info. (*0-318-57711-9*); pap. text ed. 43.00 (*0-914904-95-7*, 0795) Health Admin Pr.

C

 An Asterisk (*) at the beginning of an entry indicates that the title is appearing in BIP for the first time.

An Asterisk (*) at the beginning of an entry indicates that the title is appearing in BIP for the first time.

Cash Box Black Contemporary Album Charts, 1975-1987. Frank Hoffmann & Albert George. LC 88-35663. 249p. 1989. 29.50 (*0-8108-2212-1*) Scarecrow.

Cash Box Black Contemporary Singles Charts, 1960-1984. Ed. by George Albert & Frank Hoffmann. LC 85-22078. (Cash Box Ser.: Vol. 3). 716p. 1986. 47.50 (*0-8108-1853-1*) Scarecrow.

Cash Box Charts for the Post-Modern Age: 1978-1988. Frank Hoffmann & George Albert. LC 93-51246. 601p. 1994. text ed. 62.50 (*0-8108-2850-2*) Scarecrow.

Cash Box Country Album Charts, 1964-1988. Ed. by George Albert. LC 89-27934. 300p. 1989. 29.50 (*0-8108-2273-3*) Scarecrow.

Cash Box Country Singles Charts, 1958-1982. George Albert & Frank Hoffmann. LC 84-1266. 605p. 1984. 37.50 (*0-8108-1685-7*) Scarecrow.

Cash Box Pop Singles 1950-1993. Pat Downey et al. LC 94-94367. 700p. (Orig.). 1994. pap. 29.95 (*0-9633718-4-3*) P Downey Ent.

Cash Box Pop Singles, 1950-1993. Pat Downey et al. 825p. 1994. lib. bdg. 55.00 (*1-56308-316-7*) Libs Unl.

Cash Boy. Horatio Alger, Jr. (Works of Horatio Alger Jr.). 1989. reprint ed. lib. bdg. 79.00 (*0-7812-3558-8*) Rprt Serv.

Cash Budgets & Other Financial Projections. 26p. 1975. 40.00 (*0-939050-42-0*); 5.00 (*0-685-43350-1*) Credit Res NYS.

Cash, Cash Who's Got the Cash? Practical Management Techniques for Mom & Pop Business Owners. Robert C. Link. 120p. (Orig.). 1988. student ed 13.95 (*0-9621819-0-0*); pap. 9.95 (*0-9621819-1-9*) Bobolink Busn Bks.

Cash Cleut: Political Money in Illinois Legislative Elections. Kent D. Redfield. 290p. 1994. pap. write for info. (*0-938943-05-7*) Sangamon Pub Affairs.

Cash Constituents of Congress. Larry Makinson. 300p. 1992. pap. 32.95 (*0-87187-690-6*) Congr Quarterly.

Cash Constituents of Congress, 1992 Elections. Larry Makinson & Joshua F. Goldstein. 362p. 1994. pap. 33.95 (*1-56802-010-4*) Congr Quarterly.

Cash Copy: How to Offer Your Products & Services so Your Prospects Buy Them ... Now! 3rd ed. Jeffrey Lant. 480p. 1992. pap. 35.00 (*0-940374-23-4*) JLA Pubns.

Cash, Credit & Crisis in Europe, 1300-1600. Harry A. Miskimin. (Collected Studies: No. CS289). 298p. (C). 1989. lib. bdg. 8,735.00 (*0-86078-237-9*, Pub. by Variorum UK) Ashgate Pub Co.

C

Cash-Credit Connection: The Way to Solve All Your Credit & Financial Problems Plus Make a Fortune. Conchita Rodriguez. 200p. (Orig.). 1990. 19.95 (*1-879497-02-6*) Natl Crdt Ctr.

Cash Credit Riches Success System. 4th ed. Tyler G. Hicks. 160p. 1990. pap. 100.00 (*0-934311-92-7*) Intl Wealth.

Cash Credit Riches Success System Kit. 5th ed. Tyler G. Hicks. 160p. 1992. pap. 100.00 (*1-56150-043-7*) Intl Wealth.

Cash Credit Riches Success System Kit. 6th ed. Tyler G. Hicks. 160p. 1993. pap. 100.00 (*1-56150-093-3*) Intl Wealth.

Cash Credit Riches Success System Kit. 7th ed. Tyler G. Hicks. 160p. 1994. pap. 100.00 (*1-56150-140-9*) Intl Wealth.

***Cash, Crisis & Corporate Governance: The Role of National Finance Systems in Industrial Restructuring.** Victoria Marklew. LC 95-8273. 1995. write for info. (*0-472-10504-3*) U of Mich Pr.

Cash Crop: An American Dream. Ray Raphael. LC 85-8376. (Illus.). 179p. (Orig.). (C). 1985. pap. 8.00 (*0-934203-03-2*) Ridge Times Pr.

Cash Crop--Growing Plants the Organic Way. Melvin L. Shaw. LC 85-90448. 263p. (Orig.). 1986. 24.00 (*0-9615773-0-4*) Shaw Pub.

Cash Flow. D. B. Gilles. 1989. pap. 4.75 (*0-8222-0187-9*) Dramatists Play.

Cash Flow: The First Step to Wealth Through Real Estate. Ken Otterman. 256p. 1986. 16.95 (*0-910019-32-0*) United Support.

Cash Flow Accounting: International Uses & Abuses. Gabriel D. Donleavy. LC 93-18904. (Series on International Accounting & Finance). 1993. write for info. (*0-415-08677-9*) Routledge.

Cash Flow & Security Analysis. Kenneth S. Hackel & Joshua Livnat. 288p. 1992. 65.00 (*1-55623-387-6*) Irwin Prof Pubng.

***Cash Flow & Security Analysis.** 2nd ed. Kenneth S. Hackel & Joshua Livnat. 368p. 1995. 70.00 (*0-7863-0407-3*) Irwin Prof Pubng.

Cash Flow Control Guide: Methods to Understand & Control Small Business's Number One Problem. David H. Bangs, Jr. 88p. (Orig.). 1989. pap. text ed. 14.95 (*0-936894-02-4*) Upstart Pub.

Cash-Flow Financial Statements: A Survey of the Application of FASB Statement, No. 95. AICPA Staff. (Financial Report Survey Ser.). 88p. (Orig.). 1989. pap. text ed. 26.50 (*0-87051-065-7*) Am Inst CPA.

Cash Flow Forecasting. William A. Loscalzo. (Illus.). 192p. 1982. text ed. 45.00 (*0-07-038746-X*) McGraw.

Cash Flow Letter Book for the Small Business. Thomas Morton. 194p. 1993. disk 75.00 (*0-471-58079-1*) Wiley.

Cash Flow Management with Framework. Wendy M. Greenfield & Dennis P. Curtin. (Illus.). 176p. 1986. 28.95 (*0-13-120106-9*) P-H.

Cash Flow Planning in Agriculture. Lowell B. Catlett et al. LC 93-45684. (Illus.). 232p. (C). 1994. pap. text ed. 29.95 (*0-8138-0642-9*) Iowa St U Pr.

Cash Flow Problem Solver: Common Problems & Practical Solutions. 3rd ed. Bryan E. Milling. LC 91-29705. (Illus.). 282p. 1991. reprint ed. 32.95 (*0-942061-28-4*, Sourcebooks Trade); reprint ed. pap. 19.95 (*0-942061-27-6*, Sourcebooks Trade) Sourcebks.

Cash Flow Reporting: A Recent History of an Accounting Practice. Ed. by Thomas A. Lee. LC 93-607. (New Works in Accounting History). 424p. 1993. reprint ed. 90.00 (*0-8153-1217-2*) Garland.

Cash for College. Cynthia R. McKee & Phillip C. McKee, Jr. LC 92-42410. 1993. 16.95 (*0-688-12179-9*) Hearst Bks.

***Cash for Your Business.** Adams. 1995. pap. text ed. 24.95 (*1-880539-32-2*) Garrett FL.

Cash In! Funding & Promoting the Arts. Alvin H. Reiss. LC 86-23040. (Illus.). 240p. (Orig.). 1986. 24.95 (*0-930452-62-3*); pap. 12.95 (*0-930452-59-3*) Theatre Comm.

Cash in a Flash!, Vol. 1: How to Make a Fortune in Photography. Dan Ledford. 150p. (Orig.). 1990. 19.95 (*1-879497-00-X*) Natl Crdt Ctr.

Cash in on Bank & Government Real Estate! Make & Save Big Dollars with the Most Complete Book on, HUD, VA, S&L's, FHA, RTC, IRS, FDIC, FmHA, Tax-Sheriff Sales & More. Investor Action Group Staff. Ed. by Laurence Leichman. 96p. (Orig.). 1993. pap. 14.95 (*0-9636867-3-9*) Leichman Assocs.

Cash in on Cash Flow: Fifty Tough-As-Nails Ideas for Revitalizing Your Business. A. David Silver. 224p. 1993. 24.95 (*0-8144-0210-0*) AMACOM.

Cash in on Today's Educational Market: Teachers-Make Real Money Outside the Classroom! Simone Bibeau. (Illus.). 256p. (Orig.). (C). pap. 14.95 (*0-940406-11-X*) Perception Pubns.

Cash in on Your Garage Sale: How to Clean Out & Clean Up. Florrie B. Kichler. 44p. 1992. pap. 3.95 (*1-882859-00-6*) Crnerstone Pr.

***Cash Incentives to Council Tenants.** 131p. 1994. pap. 35.00 (*0-11-753008-5*, HM30085, Pub. by HMSO UK) UNIPUB.

Cash Inflow Definitional Model. 12p. 1979. 40.00 (*0-939050-07-2*) Credit Res NYS.

Cash Is King: A Practical Guide to Strategic Cash Management. Keith Checkley. (Financial Times Management Ser.). 240p. 1994. 105.00x (*0-273-60465-1*, Pub. by Pitman Pubng UK) St Mut.

Cash Is King: How Hospitals Can Improve the Margin to Keep the Mission. David Zimmerman. 240p. 1993. text ed. 49.95 (*1-882987-00-4*) Eagle Pr WI.

Cash Management & the Payments System: Ground Rules, Costs & Risks. Globecon Group Staff. LC 86-82305. 105p. (Orig.). (C). 1986. "Electronic Data Interchange". pap. 10.00 (*0-910586-62-4*) Finan Exec.

Cash Management for the Design Firm. Frank A. Stasiowski. LC 93-14656. 288p. 1993. Alk. paper. text ed. 54.95 (*0-471-59711-2*) Wiley.

Cash Management Handbook. Christopher R. Malburg. 1992. disk 89.95 (*0-13-116989-0*, Busn) P-H.

Cash Management Templates: Basic Models in Banking, Forecasting, Investment & Currency Management. Kenneth L. Parkinson & Linda Stanley. 1993. disk 159.00 (*0-685-69583-2*, CMSM) Warren Gorham & Lamont.

***Cash Management Templats: Basic Models in Banking, Forecasting, Investment & Currency Management.** Kenneth L. Parkinson & Linda Stanley. 256p. 1992. 175.00 (*0-7913-1820-6*) Warren Gorham & Lamont.

Cash Markets: "Worthless" Items Worth Money to Collectors: A Guide to Old Toys, Old Cameras, Old Newspapers & Old Magazines, Etc. 1987. lib. bdg. 79.95 (*0-8490-3914-2*) Gordon Pr.

Cash McCall. Cameron Hawley. 1977. reprint ed. lib. bdg. 24.95 (*0-89244-038-4*) Queens Hse-Focus Serv.

Cash McCord. large type ed. Matt A. Chisholm. (Linford Western Library). 1990. pap. 15.99 (*0-7089-6936-4*, Linford) Ulverscroft.

Cash Operations Management: Profit from Within. Gerald R. Sinn. 1981. 20.00 (*0-89433-116-7*) Petrocelli.

Cash or Credit? A Nuts & Bolts Guide to Effective Credit Management. Paul D. Zuelke. 171p. 1989. 39.95 (*0-87814-338-6*, D4285) PennWell Bks.

Cash, Tokens, & Transfers: A History of Urban Mass Transit in North America. Brian J. Cudahy. LC 90-82348. (Illus.). 266p. 1990. 39.95 (*0-8232-1277-7*); pap. 24.95 (*0-8232-1278-5*) Fordham.

Cash Tracks: How to Make Money Scoring Soundtracks & Jingles. 3rd rev. ed. Jeffrey P. Fisher. LC 94-70518. Orig. Title: How to Make Big Money Scoring Soundtracks: Your Complete Guide to Writing & Selling Original Music. 208p. 1994. per., pap. 34.95 (*0-9636290-7-7*) Fisher Creat Grp.

Cash Traps: Small Business Secrets for Reducing Costs & Improving Cash Flow. Jeffrey P. Davidson & Charles W. Dean. 224p. 1991. text ed. 49.95 (*0-471-53625-3*); pap. text ed. 14.95 (*0-471-53624-5*) Wiley.

Cashbox. Richard S. Wheeler. 384p. 1994. 23.95 (*0-312-85382-3*) Forge NYC.

Cashbox. Richard S. Wheeler. 448p. 1995. pap. 5.99 (*0-8125-2143-9*) Forge NYC.

Cashel Byron's Profession. George Bernard Shaw. 1979. mass mkt. 4.95 (*0-14-004886-3*, Penguin Bks) Viking Penguin.

Cashelmara. Susan Howatch. 672p. 1984. mass mkt. 4.95 (*0-449-20623-8*, Crest) Fawcett.

Cashew & Its Relatives: Anacardium, Anacardiaceae. J. Mitchell & S. A. Mori. LC 87-11292. (Memoirs Ser.: Vol. 42). (Illus.). 76p. 1987. pap. 17.50 (*0-89327-313-9*) NY Botanical.

Cashews & Koumboloi: The Ninety-Year Odyssey of a Greek American. Arthur T. Androus. 1991. pap. 12.95 (*0-933905-18-1*) Claycomb Pr.

Cashflow Credit & Collection: Over 100 Proven Techniques for Protecting & Strengthening. Basil P. Mavrovitis. 1993. pap. 27.50 (*1-55738-522-X*) Probus Pub Co.

Cashier. Jack Rudman. (Career Examination Ser.: C-131). 1994. pap. 19.95 (*0-8373-0131-9*) Nat Learn.

Cashier - Cashier I. Jack Rudman. (Career Examination Ser.: C-1327). 1994. pap. 23.95 (*0-8373-1327-9*) Nat Learn.

Cashier II. Jack Rudman. (Career Examination Ser.: C-2899). 1994. pap. 27.95 (*0-8373-2899-3*) Nat Learn.

Cashier-Transit Authority. Jack Rudman. (Career Examination Ser.: C-1787). 1994. pap. 19.95 (*0-8373-1787-8*) Nat Learn.

Cashinahua of Eastern Peru, Vol. 1. Kenneth Kensinger et al. LC 75-6029. (Illus.). 238p. 1975. pap. 14.00 (*0-317-55205-8*) Haffenreffer Mus Anthro.

Cashing In: Getting the Most When You Sell Your Business. Lisa Berger et al. 224p. 1989. pap. 12.95 (*0-446-39056-9*) Warner Bks.

***Cashing In: Make More Money, Get a Promotion, Love Your Job.** Tschohl. 1994. pap. text ed. 14.95 (*0-9636268-2-5*) Best Sell Pub.

Cashing in on the Consulting Boom. Gregory F. Kishel & Patricia G. Kishel. 175p. 1985. pap. text ed. 12.95 (*0-471-81695-7*) Wiley.

Cashing Out: How to Value & Sell the Privately Held Company. A. David Silver. 1993. 39.95 (*0-7931-0469-6*, 561405) Dearborn Finan.

Cashin's Handbook for Auditors. 2nd ed. James A. Cashin et al. LC 85-14944. 1392p. 1986. text ed. 65.00 (*0-07-010264-3*) McGraw.

Cashless Pay & Deductions: Implications of the Wages Act 1986. IPM Information & Advisory Services Staff et al. 102p. (C). 1987. 50.00 (*0-85292-384-8*) St Mut.

***Cashmere Kid: A Tish McWhinny Mystery.** B. Comfort. (A Tish McWhinny Mystery Ser.). 224p. 1994. pap. 6.00 (*0-88150-321-5*, Foul Play) Countryman.

Cashmere Kid: A Tish McWhinny Mystery. Barbara Comfort. 224p. 1993. 18.00 (*0-88150-254-5*, Foul Play) Countryman.

CashPro. Steven R. Duffin. 131p. 1992. 329.00 (*0-685-71293-1*, D7215) PennWell Bks.

Cash's Textbook of Orthopaedics & Rheumatology for Physiotherapists. Patricia A. Downie. LC 65-73208. 1984. text ed. 19.75 (*0-397-58293-5*, Lippincott Medical) Lippincott.

Casi Doce Anos: Almost Twelve. Kenneth Taylor. (SPA.). 2.95 (*84-7228-265-1*, 220143, Pub. by Edit Clie SP) TSELF.

Casi Nada: A Study of Agrarian Reform in the Homeland of Cardenismo. John Gledhill. LC 91-7176. (Studies on Culture & Society: Vol. 4). (Illus.). 420p. (C). 1991. pap. 30.00 (*0-942041-13-5*) SUNYA Inst Mesoam.

Casimir Effect in Critical Systems. M. Krech. 268p. 1994. text ed. 61.00 (*981-02-1845-1*) World Scientific Pub.

***Casimir Pulaski: A Detailed Biography.** Rochelle A. Carman. 10p. (J). (gr. 5-9). 1995. pap. text ed. 0.90 (*1-886325-22-7*) DanNiall Pubng.

Casimir Pulaski: A Hero of the American Revolution. Leszek Szymanski. 300p. 1993. 24.95 (*0-7818-0157-5*) Hippocrene Bks.

***Casimir Pulaski: Soldier on Horseback.** David R. Collins. (Illus.). 96p. (J). (gr. 5-8). 1995. 13.95 (*1-56554-082-4*) Pelican.

Casina, Vol. II. Plautus. Bd. with Casket Comedy.; Curculio.; Epidicus.; Two Menaechmuses. (Loeb Classical Library: No. 61). 15.50 (*0-674-99068-4*) HUP.

Casing a Promised Land: The Autobiography of an Organizational Detective As Cultural Ethnographer. H. L. Goodall, Jr. LC 93-50654. (Illus.). 224p. (C). 1994. pap. 16.95x (*0-8093-1942-X*) S Ill U Pr.

Casing & Cementing. 2nd rev. ed. Ed. by Jeanette Paxson. (Rotary Drilling Ser.: Unit II, Lesson 4). (Illus.). 53p. (Orig.). 1982. pap. text ed. 14.00 (*0-88698-056-9*, 2.20420) PETEX.

***Casing Design: Theory & Practice.** S. S. Rahman & G. V. Chilingarian. LC 94-39740. (Developments in Petroleum Science Ser.: Vol. 42). 1994. write for info. (*0-444-81743-3*) Elsevier.

Casino. Robert Kirsch. 1979. 10.00 (*0-8184-0275-X*) Carol Pub Group.

***Casino: Love & Honor in Las Vegas.** Nicholas Pileggi. 1995. 24.00 (*0-684-80832-3*) S&S Trade.

Casino - Resort, Riverboat & Fun Book Guide: Summer 1993. Steve Bourie. 60p. 1993. 6.95 (*1-883768-02-0*) Casino Vac.

Casino - Resort, Riverboat & Fun Book Guide, 1994. Steve Bourie. 96p. 1994. pap. 6.95 (*1-883768-03-9*) Casino Vac.

Casino Accounting & Financial Management. Malcolm Greenlees. LC 87-25542. (Illus.). 392p. 1988. 39.95 (*0-87417-125-3*) U of Nev Pr.

Casino Almanac, Vol. 1. Lisa M. Hansen & Mariann L. Zyweic. (Illus.). 304p. (Orig.). 1994. pap. 24.95 (*0-9641871-0-8*) Limar Ent.

Casino Blackjack: A Guide. 1991. lib. bdg. 79.95 (*0-8490-4556-8*) Gordon Pr.

Casino Blackjack: Your Best Bet. Steve Aldrich. (Illus.). 1989. 6.00 (*0-9622229-1-7*) Zauberman Pr.

Casino Chip Collecting. Donald D. Spencer. LC 94-19172. (Illus.). 120p. (Orig.). 1994. pap. 16.95x (*0-89218-261-X*) Camelot Pub.

Casino Craps for the Winner. 3rd ed. Avery Cardoza. LC 91-93166. (Illus.). 80p. 1992. pap. 6.95 (*0-940685-21-3*) Cardoza Pub.

Casino Gambler's Winning Edge: How to Get in, Get the Money & Get Out. Jerry Patterson & Nancy Patterson. (Illus.). 144p. (Orig.). 1989. pap. text ed. 3.95 (*0-318-42764-8*) Echelon Gaming.

Casino Gambling. Virginia L. Graham. 1990. mass mkt. 5.50 (*0-671-70860-0*) PB.

Casino Gambling: Winning Techniques for Craps, Roulette, Baccarat & Blackjack. Jerry L. Patterson & Walter Jaye. 224p. 1983. pap. 10.00 (*0-399-50656-X*, Perigree Bks) Berkley Pub.

Casino Gambling for the Winner. Lyle Stuart. 1984. mass mkt. 5.99 (*0-345-32053-0*) Ballantine.

Casino Games. John Gollehon. LC 86-80200. 256p. 1989. pap. 6.99 (*0-914839-19-5*) Gollehon Pr.

Casino Guidepost, U. S. A. A Guide to Over Two-Hundred Casinos, Nevada & New Jersey. Ken Schroeder. 1991. pap. 25.95 (*0-9630931-0-X*) KWS Prods.

Casino Magazine's Play Smart & Win. Victor Royer. 1994. pap. 11.00 (*0-671-88024-1*, Fireside) S&S Trade.

Casino Management. 384p. 1982. 125.00 (*0-8184-0311-X*) Carol Pub Group.

***Casino Management.** Kathryn Hashimoto et al. 500p. 1995. pap. text ed. 38.95 (*0-7872-0483-8*) Kendall-Hunt.

***Casino Management Handbook: A Practical Guide for Increasing Casino Profits.** Mark Tracy. LC 95-92045. (Illus.). 125p. (C). 1995. pap. 29.95 (*0-9645148-7-7*) Preston Publ.

***Casino Marketing.** John S. Romero. Ed. by Robin M. Quiroga. LC 94-78077. 288p. 1994. 49.95 (*0-9642414-0-4*) J R Direct Mktg.

Casino Moon. Peter Blauner. 1994. 21.00 (*0-671-88177-9*) S&S Trade.

Casino of Pius IV. Graham Smith. LC 76-3017. (Illus.). 1976. 60.00 (*0-691-03915-1*) Princeton U Pr.

***Casino of Pius IV.** Graham Smith. LC 76-3017. (Illus.). Date not set. reprint ed. pap. 47.90 (*0-7837-9450-9*, 2060192) Bks Demand.

Casino Policy. Richard Lehne. 288p. 1986. lib. bdg. 40.00 (*0-8135-1153-4*) Rutgers U Pr.

Casino-Resort, Riverboat & Fun Book Guide, 1995. Steve Bourie. LC 94-94385. (Illus.). 144p. (Orig.). 1995. pap. 9.95 (*1-883768-04-7*) Casino Vac.

Casino Royale. Ian Fleming. (James Bond Ser.). 1994. 6.98 (*1-56731-056-7*, MJF Bks) Fine Comms.

Casino Supervision: A Basic Guide. Peter G. Demos, Jr. LC 83-72779. (Illus.). 160p. (Orig.). 1983. pap. 24.95 (*0-913421-00-6*) CSI Pr.

Casino Talk. S. S. Kuriscak. 96p. 1993. pap. 4.95 (*0-681-41825-7*) Longmeadow Pr.

Casino Talk: A Rapsheet for Dealers & Players. Stephen S. Kuriscak. (Illus.). 100p. (Orig.). 1990. pap. text ed. 9.95 (*0-9624865-6-6*) S Kuriscak.

Casino Tournament Strategy. Stanford Wong. (Illus.). 256p. (Orig.). 1992. pap. text ed. 19.95 (*0-935926-18-6*) Pi Yee Pr.

***Casinos: The International Casino Guide, 1995-1996.** 5th ed. Joseph H. Bain. (Illus.). 400p. 1995. pap. 16.95 (*0-9618612-8-2*) Bain Dror.

Casinos & Their Ashtrays: A Collector's Guide with Values & Casino Histories. Art Anderson. (Illus.). 208p. 1994. pap. 19.95 (*0-9640238-0-6*) A Anderson.

Casio SL-450: A Tool for Teaching Mathematics. David Glatzer & Joyce Glatzer. Ed. by Max Sobel. (Illus.). 72p. (J). (gr. k-6). 1993. student ed 9.95 (*1-878532-05-7*) Casio Inc.

Casiodora de Reina: Spanish Reformer of the Sixteenth Century. A. Gordon Kinder. (Serie A: Monagrafias, L). (Illus.). 142p. (Orig.). (C). 1975. pap. 45.00 (*0-7293-0010-2*, Pub. by Tamesis Bks Ltd UK) Boydell & Brewer.

Cask. Freeman W. Crofts. 1989. lib. bdg. 12.95 (*0-89966-245-5*) Buccaneer Bks.

Cask. Freeman W. Crofts. 1986. 3.50 (*0-88184-236-2*) Carroll & Graf.

Cask: A Classic Detective Novel. Freeman W. Crofts. 320p. 1977. reprint ed. pap. 6.95 (*0-486-23457-6*) Dover.

Cask of Amontillado. Edgar Allan Poe. LC 80-21466. (Creative's Classics Ser.). (Illus.). 32p. (YA). (gr. 9 up). 1980. lib. bdg. 13.95 (*0-87191-773-4*) Creative Ed.

Cask of Amontillado. Edgar Allan Poe. LC 81-15997. (Illus.). 32p. (J). (gr. 5-10). 1982. lib. bdg. 10.79 (*0-89375-622-9*); pap. text ed. 2.95 (*0-89375-623-7*) Troll Assocs.

***Cask of Amontillado.** rev. ed. Edgar Allan Poe. (Read-along Radio Dramas Ser.). (YA). (gr. 6-12). Date not set. 35.00 (*1-878298-03-8*) Balance Pub.

***Cask of Christopher Columbus.** Mary T. Bowermaster. 50p. (Orig.). 1995. pap. 9.95 (*0-7610-0161-1*) NW Pub.

Casket Comedy see **Casina**

Casket of Reminiscences. Henry S. Foote. LC 68-58057. 498p. 1969. reprint ed. text ed. 59.75 (*0-8371-0421-1*, FOR&, Negro U Pr) Greenwood.

Casket of Reminiscences. Henry S. Foote. (American Biography Ser.). 498p. 1991. reprint ed. lib. bdg. 89.00 (*0-7812-8135-0*) Rprt Serv.

Caso Lefevre: The Lefevre Case. Juan Quinteros. (SPA.). 3.00 (*84-7228-334-8*, 220147, Pub. by Edit Clie SP) TSELF.

CASOC - Computer Assisted Standard Occupational Coding Software Package. HMSO Staff. 127p. 1993. pap. 320.00 (*0-11-691359-2*, HM13592, Pub. by HMSO UK) UNIPUB.

Casos en Administracion de Servicios de Salud: Un Enfoque para la Solucion de Problemas. Ed. by Bernardo Ramirez & Santiago Lastiri. (Illus.). 180p. (Orig.). (SPA.). (C). 1989. pap. text ed. 14.55 (*0-910591-23-7*) AUPHA Pr.

Casos para el Estudio de la Doctrina General del Contrato. Pedro F. Silva-Ruiz. LC 86-19195. 1987. pap. 17.50 (*0-8477-3027-1*) U of PR Pr.

Casos y Cosas. 3rd ed. Maria C. Dominicis & Joseph A. Cussen. 1990. pap. text ed. write for info. (*0-07-017409-1*) McGraw.

Caspar & the Star. Francesca Bosca. (Illus.). 40p. (J). (gr. 1-8). 1991. 12.95 (*0-7459-2120-5*) Lion USA.

Caspar Branner of Virginia & His Descendants. John C. Branner. (Illus.). 477p. 1988. reprint ed. lib. bdg. 79.50 (*0-8328-0308-1*) Higginson Bk Co.

Caspar Collins: The Life & Exploits of an Indian Fighter of the Sixties. Agnes W. Spring. LC 27-11731. reprint ed. 32.50 (*0-404-06199-0*) AMS Pr.

An Asterisk (*) at the beginning of an entry indicates that the title is appearing in BIP for the first time.

Caspar David Friedrich. Comp. by Boris Avarisch. 36p. 1985. 95.00 (0-317-42804-7) St Mut.

Caspar David Friedrich. Jens Christian Jensen. LC 81-500. (Pocket Art Ser.). (Illus.). 265p. 1981. pap. 6.95 (0-8120-2102-9) Barron.

***Caspar David Friedrich.** Wieland Schmied. LC 94-30547. (Illus.). 1995. write for info. (0-8109-3327-6) Abrams.

Caspar David Friedrich & the Subject of Landscape. Joseph L. Koerner. 256p. (C). 1990. 55.00 (0-300-04926-9) Yale U Pr.

Caspar David Friedrich to Ferdinand Hodler: A Romantic Tradition Nineteenth-Century Paintings. Peter Wegmann. 1994. 65.00 (0-8109-6432-5) Abrams.

Caspar Hauser. Jacob Wassermann. 467p. 1985. pap. 9.95 (0-88184-194-3) Carroll & Graf.

Caspar Hauser. Jakob Wassermann. Tr. & Intro. by Michael Hulse. 416p. 1993. 11.95 (0-14-018195-4, Penguin Classics) Viking Penguin.

Caspar Hauser: Enigma of a Century. Jakob Wassermann. 468p. 1990. pap. 19.95 (0-86315-505-7, 293, Pub. by Floris Books UK) Anthroposophic.

Caspar Hauser: Enigma of a Century. 2nd aniversary ed. Jacob Wassermann. LC 91-91501. (Illus.). 480p. 1992. Anniv. Ed. pap. 16.00 (0-8334-0030-4, Spir Lit Lib) Garber Comm.

***Casper.** Lisa Rojany. LC 94-25837. (J). 1995. 3.95 (0-8431-3854-8) Price Stern.

***Casper.** Rossiter. (J). 1995. pap. text ed. 2.50 (0-307-12834-2, Golden Pr) Western Pub.

***Casper: The Movie Storybook.** Leslie McGuire. LC 94-24860. (J). (gr. 1-8). 1995. 8.95 (0-8431-3856-4) Price Stern.

***Casper Mad Libs.** Adapt. by Roger Price & Leonard Stern. (Mad Libs Ser.). 48p. (J). (gr. 1 up). 1995. pap. 2.95 (0-8431-3855-6) Price Stern.

Casper the Cantankerous Cougar see Involvement

***Casper, the Horse Who Hates Bands.** William O. Beazley. (Illus.). 50p. (Orig.). (J). (gr. k-5). 1994. pap. 7.95 (1-884758-08-8) W O Beazley.

***Casper, Wyoming.** Irving Garbutt & Edna Garbutt. (Illus.). 388p. 1990. 52.80 (0-88107-164-1) Curtis Media.

***Caspian Sea.** A. N. Kosarev & E. A. Yablonskaya. Tr. by A. K. Wistin. (Illus.). 1994. 85.00 (90-5103-088-6, Pub. by SPB Acad Pub NE) Koeltz Sci Bks.

Caspian Sea of Ink: The Meade-Sickles Controversy. Richard A. Sauers. (Illus.). 194p. (C). 1989. 30.00 (0-935523-20-0) Butternut & Blue.

Cass & Birnbaum's Guide to American Colleges. 16th ed. Ed. by Melissa Cass & Julia Cass-Liepmann. 928p. (Orig.). 1994. pap. 19.00 (0-06-273295-1, Harper Ref) HarpC.

Cass & the Stone Butch. Antoinette Azolakov. LC 87-24103. 168p. (Orig.). 1987. pap. 8.95 (0-934411-06-9, Banned Bks) Edward-William Austin.

***Cass County, Michigan: 1860 Census Index.** Ann Burton & Conrad Burton. (Illus.). 61p. 1995. fiche 5.00 (0-937505-08-0) Glyndwr Resc.

***Cass County, Michigan: 1870 Census Index.** Ann Burton & Conrad Burton. (Illus.). 80p. 1990. pap. 10.00 (0-937505-06-4) Glyndwr Resc.

***Cass County, Michigan: 1880 Federal Census Index.** Ann Burton. (Illus.). 120p. (Orig.). 1995. pap. 12.00 (0-937505-11-0) Glyndwr Resc.

Cass County, Michigan Eighteen Sixty Census Index. Ann Burton & Conrad Burton. 61p. (Orig.). 1986. pap. 7.50 (0-937505-01-3) Glyndwr Resc.

Cass County, Nebraska. Plattsmouth Journal Staff. (Illus.). 669p. 1989. 62.50 (0-88107-137-4) Curtis Media.

Cass Gilbert: Midwestern Architect in New York. Robert A. Jones. 1981. 15.95 (0-405-14090-8) Ayer.

Cass Scenic Railroad Fun Book. (Illus.). 24p. 1987. pap. 0.99 (0-938467-02-6) CR Pubns.

Cass Timberlane. Sinclair Lewis. 1976. 17.95 (0-8488-1411-8) Amereon Ltd.

Cass Timberlane. Sinclair Lewis. 1982. reprint ed. lib. bdg. 18.95 (0-89966-401-6) Buccaneer Bks.

Cassandra. Elizabeth Lodge. (Orig.). 1980. pap. 2.25 (0-8439-8009-5) Dorchester Pub Co.

Cassandra. Florence Nightingale. LC 79-15175. 64p. (Orig.). 1980. pap. 5.95 (0-912670-55-X) Feminist Pr.

Cassandra: A Novel & Four Essays. Christa Wolf. Tr. by Jan Van Heurck. 320p. 1984. 17.45 (0-374-11956-2) FS&G.

Cassandra: A Novel & Four Essays. Christa Wolf. Tr. by Jan Van Heurck. 320p. 1988. pap. 11.00 (0-374-51904-8) FS&G.

Cassandra & Suggestions for Thought. Florence Nightingale. Ed. by Mary Poovey. (Women's Classics Ser.). 250p. 1992. text ed. 55.00x (0-8147-5773-1); pap. 18.95 (0-8147-5775-8) NYU Pr.

***Cassandra Complex.** Schapira. 1995. pap. 16.00 (0-919123-35-X) Atrium Pubs.

Cassandra Files. 64p. 12.00 (0-87431-312-0, 20554) West End Games.

Cassandra in Red. Michael Collins. LC 91-55190. 256p. 1992. 19.95 (1-55611-316-1) D I Fine.

Cassandra Prophecy. Charles Wilson. LC 92-38238. 224p. 1993. 18.95 (0-88184-951-0) Carroll & Graf.

Cassandra Robbins, Esq. Pat C. Viglucci. 176p. (Orig.). (YA). (gr. 8-12). 1987. pap. 4.95 (0-938961-01-2, Stamp Out Sheep Pr) Sq One Pubs.

Cassandra Speaking. Judy Hogan. LC 77-3471. 60p. (Orig.). 1977. pap. 3.50 (0-914476-62-9) Thorp Springs.

Cassandra Who? Iris Hiskey. (J). (ps-3). 1992. pap. 14.00 (0-671-70574-1, S&S Bks Young Read) S&S Childrens.

***Cassandra's Conflict.** Fredrica Alleyn. (Black Lace Ser.). Date not set. pap. 5.95 (0-352-32859-2, London Bridge) Genl Dist Srvs.

Cassandra's Daughters: The Women in Hemingway. Roger Whitlow. LC 84-521. (Contributions in Women's Studies: No. 51). xii, 148p. 1984. text ed. 45.00 (0-313-24488-X, WCD/, Greenwood Pr) Greenwood.

Cassandra's Secret Manuscript. Frank R. Wallace. 176p. 1993. 99.95 (0-911752-71-4) Neo-Tech Pub.

Cassandra's Tale. Jean R. Jones. (Illus.). (J). (ps-5). 1994. pap. 5.00 (0-936204-69-9) Jelm Mtn.

Cassandre see Ronsard Poete de l'Amour

Cassatt. Adrian Biddell. (Masterworks Ser.). 144p. 1991. 19.99 (0-517-05377-2) Random Hse Value.

***Cassatt.** Rondebush. (Art Library). 1995. pap. 12.00 (0-517-88371-6, Crown) Crown Pub Group.

Cassatt & Her Circle: Selected Letters. Nancy M. Mathews. LC 83-21449. (Illus.). 256p. 1984. 19.95 (0-89659-421-1) Abbeville Pr.

Cassava Economy of Java. Walter P. Falcon et al. LC 82-42912. xxii, 212p. 1984. 42.50 (0-8047-1194-1) Stanford U Pr.

Cassava in Food, Feed, & Industry. C. Balagopalan et al. 224p. 1988. 191.00 (0-8493-4560-X, TP416) CRC Pr.

***Cassava Stew.** Barbara E. Alexander. (Nandi Bks.). 1992. 4.95 (0-938818-24-4) ECA Assoc.

Casse-Pipe. Louis-Ferdinand D. Celine. (Folio Ser.: No. 666). (FRE.). 1975. pap. 6.95 (2-07-036666-9) Schoenhof.

Casse-Pipe: Carnet de Cuirassier Destouches. Louis-Ferdinand D. Celine. (FRE.). 1975. pap. 10.95 (0-8288-3669-8, M3188) Fr & Eur.

Cassell Book of Proverbs. Patricia Houghton. 152p. 1994. pap. 6.95 (0-304-34419-2, Pub. by Cassell UK) Sterling.

Cassell Business Briefings: Japan. Michael Jenkins. LC 93-25809. (Asia Pacific Business Reference Ser.). (Illus.). 320p. 1994. boxed 29.95 (0-304-32637-2) Cassell.

***Cassell Business Briefings: Japan.** Michael Jenkins. 306p. 1994. 26.95 (0-304-43637-2, Pub. by Cassell UK) Sterling.

Cassell Business Briefings: Republic of Korea. Judith Cherry. (Asia Pacific Business Reference Ser.). 384p. 1994. 29.95 (0-304-32636-4, Pub. by Cassell UK) Sterling.

Cassell Business Companion: Spain. Karsta Neuhaus. 1993. 19.95 (0-304-34761-2, Pub. by Cassell UK) Sterling.

***Cassell Clue Finder: A Dictionary of Crossword Clues.** J. A. Coleman. 256p. 1995. 14.95 (0-304-34587-3, Pub. by Cassell UK) Sterling.

Cassell Complete Puzzler's Lists: The Ultimate Crossword Companion. Joan Burman. 320p. 1994. 19.95 (0-304-34285-8, Pub. by Cassell UK) Sterling.

Cassell Crossword Finisher. Comp. by John Griffiths. 496p. 1991. pap. 14.95 (0-304-34030-8, Pub. by Cassell UK) Sterling.

***Cassell Dictionary of Catchphrases.** Nigel Rees. 240p. 1995. 21.95 (0-304-34563-6, Pub. by Cassell UK) Sterling.

Cassell Dictionary of Cynical Quotations. Jonathon Green. 288p. 1994. 24.95 (0-304-34313-7, Pub. by Cassell UK) Sterling.

***Cassell Dictionary of First Names.** Adrian Room. 336p. 1995. 19.95 (0-304-34398-6, Pub. by Cassell UK) Sterling.

***Cassell Dictionary of Modern Politics.** 352p. 1995. 25.95 (0-304-34432-X, Pub. by Cassell UK) Sterling.

Cassell Dictionary of Proper Names. Adrian Room. 640p. 1994. 22.95 (0-304-34447-8, Pub. by Cassell UK) Sterling.

***Cassell Dictionary of Riddles.** Mark Bryant. 384p. 1995. pap. 12.95 (0-304-34439-7, Pub. by Cassell UK) Sterling.

Cassell Dictionary of Word & Phrase Origins. Nigel Rees. 224p. 1994. pap. 8.95 (0-304-34422-2, Pub. by Cassell UK) Sterling.

Cassell Directory of U. K. Visitor Attractions. Oxford Center for Tourism & Leisure Studies, Oxford Brooks University Staff. (Illus.). 256p. 1994. pap. text ed. 250.00 (0-304-32694-1) Cassell.

***Cassell Elementary Technical & Scientific Dictionary.** C. Vaughan James & William R. Lee. (Cassell A & P Reference Ser.). 196p. 1995. 19.95 (0-304-33143-0) Cassell.

Cassell English-Japanese Business Dictionary. Gene Ferber. 544p. 1993. text ed. 65.00 (0-304-32552-X, Pub. by Cassell UK) Sterling.

Cassell English-Japanese Legal Dictionary & Handbook. Samuel Jarman. 320p. 1995. text ed. 250.00 (0-304-32712-3) Cassell.

Cassell Everyday Phrases. Neil Ewart. 161p. 1994. pap. (0-304-34420-6, Pub. by Cassell UK) Sterling.

Cassell Handbook of Copyright in British Publishing Practice. 3rd rev. ed. Mavis Cavendish. 240p. 1993. text ed. 60.00 (0-304-32635-6) Cassell.

Cassell Language Guides: French. Valerie Worth-Stylianou. (Illus.). 384p. 1992. 19.95 (0-304-34033-2, Pub. by Cassell UK) Sterling.

Cassell Language Guides: German. Christine Eckhard-Black & Ruth Whittle. (Illus.). 384p. 1992. 19.95 (0-304-34049-9, Pub. by Cassell UK) Sterling.

Cassell Multilingual Dictionary of Local Government & Business. Leo McNeir. 288p. (ENG, FRE & GER.). 1993. text ed. 74.95 (0-304-32715-8) Cassell.

Cassell Paperback English Dictionary. 1550p. (Orig.). 1990. pap. 14.95 (0-304-34003-0, Pub. by Cassell UK) Sterling.

Cassell Sex & Sexuality: A Thematic Dictionary of Quotations. 304p. 1994. 24.95 (0-304-34247-5, Pub. by Cassell UK) Sterling.

Cassell, the Publishers Association & the Federation of European Publishers Directory of Publishing: Continental Europe 1994. (A & P Reference Ser.). 512p. 1993. pap. 125.00 (0-304-32819-7) Cassell.

Cassell's Colloquials, 4 bks. Cassell Staff. Incl. Learn in Your Car French. 160p. 1981. pap. 6.00 (0-02-079420-7); Learn in Your Car German. 176p. 1981. pap. 4.95 (0-02-079410-X); Learn in Your Car Spanish. 304p. 1981. pap. 7.00 (0-02-079430-4); Learn in Your Car Italian. 192p. 1981. pap. 4.95 (0-02-079440-1); 1981. Set pap. write for info. (0-318-54202-1) Macmillan.

Cassell's Contemporary French: A Handbook of Grammar, Current Usage, & Word Power. Valerie Worth-Stylianou. LC 92-32579. 420p. (FRE.). 1993. text ed. 25. 00 (0-02-631563-7) Macmillan.

Cassell's Contemporary German: A Handbook of Grammar, Current Usage, & Word Power. Christine Eckhard-Black. LC 92-32580. 502p. (GER.). 1993. text ed. 25.00 (0-02-534904-X) Macmillan.

Cassell's Contemporary Italian: A Handbook of Grammar, Current Usage, & Word Power. Noemi Messora. LC 93-18041. (Illus.). 528p. 1993. text ed. 25.00 (0-02-584375-3) Macmillan.

Cassell's Contemporary Spanish. Angeles Perez et al. (Illus.). 512p. 1994. text ed. 25.00 (0-02-595915-8) Macmillan.

Cassell's Cyclopaedia of Photography. Ed. by Bernard E. Jones. LC 72-9214. (Literature of Photography Ser.). 1979. reprint ed. 41.95 (0-405-04922-6) Ayer.

Cassell's Dictionary of Spanish Language: Diccionario de la Lengua Espanalo. Castell. 1036p. (SPA.). 1986. 34.95 (0-8288-2033-3, S15304) Fr & Eur.

Cassell's French & English Dictionary. Cassell Staff. 672p. 1986. pap. 5.00 (0-02-013680-3, Collier S&S) S&S Trade.

Cassell's French Dictionary. Ed. by Denis Girard et al. LC 77-7669. 1440p. (ENG & FRE.). 1977. text ed. 24.95 (0-02-522620-7); text ed. 22.95 (0-02-522610-X); text ed. 12.95 (0-02-522670-3) Macmillan.

Cassell's German & English Dictionary. Cassell Staff. 560p. 1986. pap. 6.00 (0-02-024850-4, Collier S&S) S&S Trade.

Cassell's German Dictionary: German-English, English-German. rev. ed. Harold T. Betteridge. LC 77-18452. 560p. (ENG & GER.). 1977. text ed. 13.95 (0-02-522650-9) Macmillan.

Cassell's German Dictionary: German-English, English-German. rev. ed. Harold T. Betteridge. LC 77-18452. 1600p. (ENG & GER.). 1978. text ed. 26.00 (0-02-522930-3); text ed. 25.00 (0-02-522920-6) Macmillan.

Cassell's Italian Dictionary: Italian-English, English-Italian. Comp. by Cassell Staff et al. LC 77-7405. 1152p. (ENG & ITA.). 1977. text ed. 23.95 (0-02-522540-5); text ed. 21.00 (0-02-522530-8) Macmillan.

Cassell's Latin & English Dictionary. Cassell Staff & D. P. Simpson. 416p. 1987. pap. 4.95 (0-02-013340-5, Collier S&S) S&S Trade.

Cassell's Latin Dictionary. Simpson. 1977. 16.95 (0-02-522570-7) Macmillan.

Cassell's Latin Dictionary: Latin-English, English-Latin. Ed. by D. P. Simpson. 912p. (ENG & LAT.). 1977. text ed. 24.95 (0-02-522580-4); text ed. 12.95 (0-02-522630-4) Macmillan.

Cassell's New Dutch Dictionary: English-Dutch, Dutch-English. 2nd ed. Cassells Editors. 729p. (DUT & ENG.). 1982. text ed. 55.00 (0-02-522940-0) Macmillan.

***Cassell's Queer Companion.** Ed. by William Stewart & Emily Hamer. Date not set. 65.00 (0-304-34303-X); pap. 18.95 (0-304-34301-3) InBook.

Cassell's Spanish & English Dictionary. Cassell Staff. 464p. 1986. pap. 3.95 (0-02-013690-0, Collier S&S) S&S Trade.

Cassell's Spanish Dictionary: Spanish-English, English-Spanish. Ed. by Edgar A. Peers. LC 77-7403. 464p. (ENG & SPA.). 1977. text ed. 13.00 (0-02-522660-6) Macmillan.

Cassell's Spanish Dictionary: Spanish-English, English-Spanish. Ed. by Edgar A. Peers. LC 77-7403. 1136p. (ENG & SPA.). 1978. text ed. 22.95 (0-02-522910-9); text ed. 19.95 (0-02-522900-1) Macmillan.

Casselwyk Book on Oil Painting see Basic Oil Painting the Van Wyk Way

Casserole Cookery. Ed. by Arthur Hettich & Marie T. Walsh. LC 75-42916. (Family Circle Bks.). (Illus.). 112p. 1977. 12.95 (0-405-06683-X) Ayer.

Casserole Sampler. Jan Siegrist. (Illus.). 48p. (Orig.). 1988. pap. 3.95 (0-933050-64-X) New Eng Pr VT.

Casseroles. P. Dutery. 36p. (Orig.). 1981. pap. 2.75 (0-940844-04-4) Wellspring.

Casseroles: Classic to Contemporary. Nina Graybill & Maxine Rapoport. LC 92-41354. 156p. 1993. pap. 11.95 (0-918535-15-8) Farragut Pub.

Casseroles: From Amish & Mennonite Kitchens. Ed. by Phyllis P. Good & Rachel T. Pellman. (Pennsylvania Dutch Cookbooks Ser.). (Illus.). 32p. (Orig.). 1983. pap. 2.95 (0-934672-11-3) Good Bks PA.

Casseroles: Meals in Minutes for Busy Women. 2nd ed. Sue Gregg & Emilie Barnes. (Illus.). 78p. 1989. pap. text ed. 5.00 (1-878272-02-0) Eating Better.

***Casseroles: The Salvation of Working Wives.** Ed. by G & R Publishing Staff. (Uni-Book Ser.). 160p. (Orig.). 1994. pap. text ed. 3.00 (1-56383-009-4, 1200) G & R Pub.

Casseroles & One-Dish Meals. Sophie Kay. (Illus.). 64p. 1985. pap. 3.95 (0-8249-3012-6) Ideals.

Casseroles from the Amish & Mennonite Kitchen. Phyllis P. Good. 1991. pap. 2.95 (1-56148-041-X) Good Bks PA.

Casseroles, Stews, Soups & More. (Favorite All Time Recipes Ser.). (Illus.). 96p. 1993. 7.98 (1-56173-969-3, 2013901) Pubns Intl Ltd.

Cassette Culture: Popular Music & Technology in North India. Peter Manuel. LC 92-27626. (Chicago Studies in Ethnomusicology). 365p. (C). 1993. pap. text ed. 22.00 (0-226-50401-8) U Ch Pr.

Cassette Culture: Popular Music & Technology in North India. Peter Manuel. LC 92-27626. (Chicago Studies in Ethnomusicology). 365p. (C). 1993. lib. bdg. 52.00 (0-226-50399-2) U Ch Pr.

Cassette Guide Culture Through Literature & Music. Alma F. Ada & Jan Mayer. (Spanish Elementary Ser.). (Illus.). 80p. 1989. pap. text ed. 17.25 (0-201-12947-7) Addison-Wesley.

Cassette Piece. Gerald Kaminski. LC 77-4995. 1977. pap. 3.00 (0-914974-14-9) Holmgangers.

Cassidy. Lee Leighton. 1980. pap. 1.75 (0-345-29120-4) Ballantine.

Cassidy's Girl. David Goodis. 1991. 8.00 (0-679-73851-7, Vin) Random.

Cassidy's Girl. rev. ed. David Goodis. 160p. 1988. reprint ed. pap. 3.95 (0-88739-027-7, Blk Lizard) Creat Arts Bk.

***Cassie.** Tom Brennan. 280p. Date not set. pap. 8.95 (0-7610-0206-5) NW Pub.

Cassie. Marilyn Kaye. LC 87-11944. (Sisters Ser.). 134p. (J). (gr. 3-7). 1987. 13.95 (0-15-200421-1, Gulliver Bks); pap. 4.95 (0-15-200422-X, Gulliver Bks) HarBrace.

Cassie. large type ed. E. V. Thompson. (Romance Ser.). 592p. 1992. 23.95 (0-7089-8653-6) Ulverscroft.

Cassie, No. 14. Vivian Schurfranz. 368p. (Orig.). (J). (gr. 7 up). 1985. pap. 2.95 (0-590-33688-6) Scholastic Inc.

Cassie Binegar. Patricia MacLachlan. LC 81-48641. (Charlotte Zolotow Bk.). 128p. (J). (gr. 3-7). 1982. lib. bdg. 13.89 (0-06-024034-2) HarpC Child Bks.

Cassie Binegar. Patricia MacLachlan. LC 81-48641. (Trophy Bk.). 128p. (J). (gr. 3-7). 1987. pap. 3.95 (0-06-440195-2, Trophy) HarpC Child Bks.

Cassie Jordan. large type ed. Elizabeth Jeffrey. 459p. 1993. 21.95 (0-7505-0417-X, Pub. by Magna Print Bks) Ulverscroft.

Cassie Perkins: A Dream to Cherish. Angela E. Hunt. 176p. (J). (gr. 4-8). 1992. pap. 4.99 (0-8423-1064-9) Tyndale.

Cassie Perkins: Love Burning Bright. Angela E. Hunt. 176p. (J). (gr. 4-8). 1992. pap. text ed. 4.99 (0-8423-1066-5) Tyndale.

Cassie Perkins: Much Adored Shore. Angela E. Hunt. 176p. (J). (gr. 4-8). 1992. pap. 4.99 (0-8423-1065-7) Tyndale.

Cassie Perkins, No. 1: No More Broken Promises. Angela E. Hunt. (J). 1991. lib. bdg. 4.99 (0-8423-0461-4) Tyndale.

Cassie Perkins, No. 2: A Forever Friend. Angela E. Hunt. (J). (gr. 4-7). 1991. pap. 4.99 (0-8423-0462-2) Tyndale.

Cassie Perkins, No. 3: A Basket of Roses. Angela E. Hunt. (J). 1991. lib. bdg. 4.99 (0-8423-0463-0) Tyndale.

Cassie Perkins, No. 7: Star Light, Star Bright. Angela E. Hunt. LC 92-18796. (YA). 1993. 4.99 (0-8423-1117-3) Tyndale.

Cassie's Journey: Going West in the 1860s. Brett Harvey. LC 87-23599. (Illus.). 40p. (J). (gr. 1-4). 1988. lib. bdg. 14.95 (0-8234-0684-9) Holiday.

***Cassie's Journey: Going West in the 1960s.** Brett Harvey. (Illus.). (J). (gr. 1-4). 1995. pap. 5.95 (0-8234-1172-9) Holiday.

Cassie's Last Goodbye. Shawna Delacorte. (Silhouette Desire Ser.). 1993. mass mkt. 2.99 (0-373-05814-4, 5-05814-4) Silhouette.

Cassie's Miracle. Michael Schnessel. 32p. 1982. pap. 3.50 (0-88680-020-X) I E Clark.

***Cassie's War.** Allan M. Winkler. (Orig.). (J). (gr. 5-7). 1994. lib. bdg. 15.00 (0-88092-107-2); pap. 5.00 (0-88092-106-4) Royal Fireworks.

Cassigneul's Graphic Work, Nineteen Sixty-Five to Eighty-Eight: Catalogue Raisonne. Roger Passeron & Jean-Francois Josselin. (Illus.). 196p. (ENG & FRE.). 1989. 475.00 (1-55660-091-7) A Wofsy Fine Arts.

Cassino: Anatomy of the Battle. Janusz Piekalkiewicz. (Illus.). 192p. 1988. 19.95 (0-918678-32-3) Natl Hist Soc.

Cassiodorus: Variae. Tr. & Intro. by S. J. Barnish. (Translated Texts for Historians Ser.). 254p. (Orig.). (C). 1992. pap. text ed. 17.95 (0-85323-436-1, Pub. by Liverpool Univ Pr UK) U of Pa Pr.

Cassiodorus, Explanation of the Psalms, Vol. I. annot. ed. Tr. & Anno. by P. G. Walsh. (Ancient Christian Writers Ser.: No. 51). 1990. 36.95 (0-8091-0441-5) Paulist Pr.

Cassiodorus, Vols 2-3: Explanation of the Psalms, 2. Ed. by P. G. Walsh. (Ancient Christian Writers Ser.: Nos. 52 & 53). 1991. 34.95 (0-8091-0444-X) Paulist Pr.

Cassiodorus, Vols 2-3: Explanation of the Psalms, 3. Ed. by P. G. Walsh. (Ancient Christian Writers Ser.: Nos. 52 & 53). 1991. 34.95 (0-8091-0445-8) Paulist Pr.

Cassique of Kiawah. William G. Simms. 650p. 1989. pap. 17.50 (0-916369-12-9) Magnolia Pr.

Cassirer's Conception of Causality. K. Sundaram. (American University Studies: Philosophy: Ser. V, Vol. 28). 151p. (C). 1987. text ed. 26.00 (0-8204-0405-5) P Lang Pubs.

Cassius Marcellus Clay: Firebrand of Freedom. H. Edward Richardson. LC 74-7882. (Illus.). 192p. 1987. 20.00 (0-8131-1418-7) U Pr of Ky.

Casson's Invariant for Oriented Homology Three- Spheres: An Exposition. Selman Akbulat & John McCarthy. 200p. (Orig.). 1990. pap. text ed. 19.50 (0-691-08563-3) Princeton U Pr.

Cassowary. Matthias Mander. Tr. by Michael Mitchell. (Studies in Austrian Literature, Culture, & Thought. Translation Ser.). 340p. 1994. pap. 23.95 (0-929497-73-2) Ariadne CA.

Cassubian Civilization. Friedrich Lorentz et al. LC 77-87520. 456p. 1983. reprint ed. 62.50 (0-404-16603-2) AMS Pr.

An Asterisk (*) at the beginning of an entry indicates that the title is appearing in BIP for the first time. 1077

Cassy. large type ed. Elizabeth Lyle. 512p. 1982. 15.95 (0-7089-0862-4) Ulverscroft.

Cast. Ed Jaworowski. LC 91-27360. (Illus.). 240p. 1992. 34.95 (0-8117-1917-0) Stackpole.

CAST: Cluster Analysis in Space & Time. Applied Biomathematics Staff. 278p. 1990. 950.00 (1-884977-06-5); teacher ed 1,900.00 (1-884977-07-3) Applied Biomath.

CAST: Methods in Modelling: Computer Aided Systems Theory for the Design of Intelligent Machines. Ed. by Franz R. Pichler & Heinz Schwartzel. LC 92-8524. (Illus.). 392p. 1992. 98.00 (0-387-55405-X) Spr-Verlag.

Cast a Cold Eye. Mary McCarthy. LC 50-9761. 212p. 1950. 12.95 (0-15-115941-6) HarBrace.

Cast a Cold Eye. Mary McCarthy. LC 92-21660. 1992. pap. 10.95 (0-15-615444-7, Harvest Bks) HarBrace.

Cast a Cold Eye: American Opinion Writing, 1990-91. Ed. by James Ridgeway. LC 91-10124. 200p. 1991. 25.00 (0-941423-55-7); pap. 12.95 (0-941423-54-9) FWEW.

Cast a Long Shadow. Linda J. Puckett. 228p. 1986. 25.00 (0-317-69301-8) Jay Banks.

***Cast a Long Shadow. Ruth C. Seamands. 458p. (Orig.). 1994. pap. 15.95 (0-9644387-0-4) R C Seamands. CAST A LONG SHADOW..is a saga of three generations of a Southern Illinois family, reaching from the coal mines of "Bloody" Williamson County to the dusty roads of India. Spanning a century, this story depicts the lives of three women, & the men & children they love. Amidst hardship & separation, in laughter & sorrow, these rugged people have a reverence of God, their faith enduring through the years. Julia-the beautiful young orphan forced to bear a child out of wedlock. Pearl-widowed with a small daughter at twenty. Ruth-faced with cobras & other crises across the sea. In CAST A LONG SHADOW, Ruth Seamands spreads a feast of love, better even than the cornbread & southern fried chicken her forebears made, for this feast continues to the present day in the lives of her family. Ruth left her Southern Illinois home to serve with her husband, J.T., in India for twenty years. In 1959, they settled in Wilmore, Kentucky, where he became a professor at Asbury Theological Seminary & Ruth pursued her writing. Among her books are MISSIONARY MAMA, HOUSE BY THE BO TREE, LAND OF THE SNAKE CHARMER, SANDY, PEARLS IN THE RAIN & ENGINEERED FOR GLORY. Order from Seamands Publishing, 407 Talbott Dr.,Wilmore, KY 40390. 606-858-3920.**

Publisher Provided Annotation.

Cast a Long Shadow. large type ed. Mary E. Pearce. 464p. 1988. 15.95 (0-7089-1790-9) Ulverscroft.

*Cast a Single Shadow. John C. Cooper. 360p. 1995. pap. 9.95 (0-7610-0309-6) NW Pub.

Cast a Spell. Bette Pesetsky. 1993. 21.95 (0-15-116072-4) HarBrace.

Cast a Yellow Shadow. Ross Thomas. 272p. 1987. reprint ed. mass mkt. 4.99 (0-445-40556-2, Mysterious Paperbk) Warner Bks.

Cast Adrift. Timothy S. Arthur. (Works of Timothy Shay Arthur). 1989. reprint ed. lib. bdg. 79.00 (0-7812-1805-5) Rprt Serv.

Cast Away at the Pole. William W. Cook. Ed. by R. Reginald & Douglas Melville. LC 77-84215. (Lost Race & Adult Fantasy Ser.). 1978. reprint ed. lib. bdg. 29.95 (0-405-10970-9) Ayer.

Cast by Means of Figures: Herman Melville's Rhetorical Development. Bryan C. Short. LC 92-8104. 216p. (C). 1992. 27.50x (0-87023-812-4) U of Mass Pr.

Cast Down but Not Destroyed. Bayless Conley. 31p. 1991. pap. text ed. write for info. (0-9638534-0-6) Cottonwood Chr.

Cast In a Racial Mould: Labour Process & Trade Unionism in the Foundries. Eddie Webster. 1986. text ed. 14.95 (0-86975-285-5, Pub. by Ravan Pr ZA) Ohio U Pr.

Cast in America. Justin Kramer. (Illus.). 11.95 (0-686-17157-8) J Kramer.

Cast in Doubt. Lynne Tillman. LC 92-17603. 1992. 20.00 (0-671-78814-0) S&S Trade.

Cast in Doubt. Lynne Tillman. (Masks Ser.). 244p. 1993. reprint ed. pap. 12.99 (1-85242-340-4) Serpents Tail.

Cast-in-Place Concrete in Tall Building Design & Construction. Council on Tall Buildings & Urban Habitat Staff. 448p. 1992. text ed. 54.00 (0-07-012536-8) McGraw.

Cast-in-Place-Walls. 74p. 13.95 (0-317-39819-9, CCS-2) ACI.

Cast in Stone: Selected Albany, Rensselaer & Saratoga County, New York Burials. Diane S. Ptak. (Illus.). 168p. 1990. 35.00 (1-56012-108-4) Kinship Rhinebeck.

Cast in the Fire. Greg Delanty. 1986. pap. 10.95 (0-85105-455-2, Pub. by Colin Smythe Ltd UK) Dufour.

Cast into the Fire. Carolyn C. Clark. Ed. by Mary Ann Liotta. (Illus.). 224p. (Orig.). 1994. pap. 12.95 (1-880254-19-0) Vista.

*Cast Iron. Jacqueline Fearn. (C). 1989. pap. 25.00x (0-7478-0083-9, Pub. by Shire UK) St Mut.

Cast Iron Architecture in New York. Margot Gayle & Edmund Gillon, Jr. (Illus.). (Orig.). 1974. pap. 14.95 (0-486-22980-7) Dover.

Cast Iron Cooking. A. D. Livingston. 1991. pap. 12.95 (1-55821-115-2) Lyons & Burford.

Cast Iron Decoration: A World Survey. E. Graeme & Joan Robertson. LC 93-61373. (Illus.). 336p. 1994. pap. 34.95 (0-500-27756-7) Thames Hudson.

Cast Iron Floor Trains: An Encyclopedia with Rarity & Price Guide. Rick Ralston. Ed. by George Engebretson. LC 93-92799. (Illus.). 336p. 1994. 89.95 (0-9638315-0-X) Ralston Pubng.

*Cast Iron from Central Europe 1800-1850. Derek E. Ostergard et al. 351p. 1994. pap. text ed. write for info. (1-887506-01-2) Bard Grad Ctr.

*Cast Iron from Central Europe, 1800-1850. Elisabeth Schmuttermeier & Derek E. Ostergard. (Illus.). 351p. Date not set. pap. 50.00 (0-614-07359-6) Bard Grad Ctr.

Cast Iron Man. large type ed. Michael Legat. 560p. 1988. 15.95 (0-7089-1881-6) Ulverscroft.

Cast Manual for Adults & Children. F. Freuler et al. Tr. by P. A. Casey. (Illus.). 1979. 35.00 (0-387-09590-X) Spr-Verlag.

Cast Metals Technology. J. Gerin Sylvia. LC 74-153067. (C). 1972. text ed. 27.96 (0-201-07395-1) Addison-Wesley.

Cast Metals Technology. J. Gerin Sylvia. 338p. 27.00 (0-317-32557-4, TE7208) Am Foundrymen.

Cast No Shadow: The Life of Betty Pack, the American Spy Who Changed the Course of World War II. Mary S. Lovell. LC 91-52625. (Illus.). 288p. 1992. 24.50 (0-394-57556-3) Pantheon.

Cast of Casts: A Biographical Dictionary of Shakespeare's Characters. large type ed. Ed. by Jedediah Clauss. 43.95 (0-88411-199-7, Aeonian Pr) Amereon Ltd.

Cast of Character: The Representation of Personality in Ancient & Medieval Literature. Warren Ginsberg. LC 83-205174. 208p. reprint ed. pap. 59.30 (0-7837-2664-3, 2043028) Bks Demand.

Cast of Characters. Sean C. Derek. (Illus.). 336p. (Orig.). 1982. pap. 3.50 (0-8439-1126-3) Dorchester Pub Co.

Cast of Consciousness: Concepts of the Mind in British & American Romanticism. Ed. by Beverly Taylor & Robert Bain. LC 87-17595. (Contributions to the Study of World Literature Ser.: No. 24). 256p. 1987. text ed. 49.95 (0-313-25891-0, TCC/) Greenwood.

Cast of Criminals. Franklin W. Dixon. (Hardy Boys Ser.: No. 97). (Orig.). (YA). (gr. 7 up). 1989. pap. 3.50 (0-671-66307-0, Minstrel Bks) PB.

Cast of Killers. Gallagher Gray. LC 92-53072. 256p. 1992. 20.95 (1-55611-328-5) D I Fine.

Cast of Killers. Gallagher Gray. 1994. mass mkt. 4.99 (0-8041-1146-4) Ivy Books.

Cast of Killers. Sidney D. Kirkpatrick. (Illus.). 336p. 1992. pap. 5.99 (0-451-17418-6, Onyx) NAL-Dutton.

Cast of Millions. Trevor M. Phillips. Ed. by Paul J. Young, Jr. 1985. write for info. (0-9622708-7-3) Zubra Pub.

Cast of One: One-Person Shows from the Chautauqua Platform to the Broadway Stage. John S. Gentile. LC 88-29553. (Illus.). 312p. 1989. 24.95 (0-252-01584-3) U of Ill Pr.

*Cast of Spaniards. Mark Jacobs. LC 94-37430. 208p. 1994. lib. bdg. 33.95 (1-883689-19-8); pap. 12.95 (1-883689-18-X) Talisman Hse.

Cast of Tens. David Bromige. Ed. by Cydney Chadwick. 96p. (Orig.). 1994. pap. text ed. 9.50 (1-880713-01-2) AVEC Bks.

Cast of Thousands. large type ed. Steve Shagan. 1993. 22.95 (1-56895-021-7) Wheeler Pub.

Cast of Thousands. Steve Shagan. Ed. by Bill Grose. 416p. 1994. reprint ed. mass mkt. 5.99 (0-671-74133-0, Pocket Star Bks) PB.

Cast of Thousands: A Compendium of Who Played What in Film, 3 vols., Set. Melinda Corey & George Ochoa. 1848p. 1992. lib. bdg. 245.00 (0-8160-2429-4) Facts on File.

Cast-off Youth: Policy & Training Methods from the Military Experience. Thomas G. Sticht et al. LC 87-11644. 224p. 1987. text ed. 55.00 (0-275-92621-4, C2621, Praeger Pubs) Greenwood.

*Cast Out the Fear. Mark A. Gattey. 140p. Date not set. pap. 7.95 (0-7610-0351-7) NW Pub.

Cast Out Your Nets: Sharing Your Faith with Others. Garth Lean. 144p. (Orig.). 1990. pap. 7.95 (1-85239-010-7, Pub. by Linden Hall UK) Grosvenor USA.

Cast Polyester Furniture. 1985. 39.00 (0-317-43777-1) St Mut.

CAST-Related Excerpts from U. S. House of Representatives Hearing on the Federal Insecticide, Fungicide & Rodenticide Act. (Special Publications Ser.: No. 9). 79p. 1982. 4.50 (0-318-13833-6) CAST.

*Cast the First Stone: Ethics in Analytical Practice. Lena B. Ross. Ed. by Adolf Guggenbuhl-Craig. 168p. (Orig.). 1995. pap. 19.95 (0-933029-89-6) Chiron Pubns.

Cast-to-Shape: A History of the Steel Castings Industry in the United States. 1977. 30.00 (0-686-44986-X) Steel Founders.

Cast with Style: Nineteenth Century Cast-Iron Stoves from the Albany Area. rev. ed. Tammis K. Groft. LC 84-72240. (Illus.). 120p. 1984. pap. 11.95 (0-939072-03-3) Albany Hist & Art.

Castafiore Emerald. Herge. (Illus.). 62p. (J). 19.95 (0-8288-5016-X) Fr & Eur.

Castanets. Carlos Reyles. Tr. by Jacques Le Clerq. 1977. lib. bdg. 59.95 (0-8490-1583-9) Gordon Pr.

Castanuelas, Ole! A Book about Castanets. rev. ed. Tabourot. (Illus.). 37p. 1993. pap. 12.00 (1-881428-03-6) Tactus Pr.

Castara: From the Third Edition, 1635. William Habington. Tr. by Edward Arber. 144p. 1984. pap. 15.00 (0-87556-118-7) Saifer.

Castaway. Laurel Ames. (Historical Ser.). 1993. mass mkt. 3.99 (0-373-28797-6, 1-28797-8) Harlequin Bks.

Castaway. James G. Cozzens. 120p. 1989. reprint ed. pap. 6.95 (0-929587-17-0, Elephant Paperbacks) I R Dee.

Castaway Angel. Kathleen Drymon. 1991. mass mkt. 4.50 (0-8217-3569-1) Zebra.

Castaway Cat, 3 bks. JoAnn Roe. (Illus.). 56p. (Orig.). (J). (gr. k-5). Castaway Cat. pap. 6.95 (0-931551-03-X) Montevista Pr.

Castaway Cat, 3 bks. JoAnn Roe. (Illus.). 56p. (Orig.). (J). (gr. k-5). 1988. Fisherman Cat, 1988. pap. 6.95 (0-931551-01-3) Montevista Pr.

Castaway Heart. Colleen Campbell. 384p. 1991. mass mkt. 4.25 (0-8217-3404-0) Zebra.

Castaway in Paradise: The Incredible Adventures of True-Life Robinson Crusoes. James C. Simmons. LC 93-13882. 264p. 1993. 22.95 (0-924486-44-9) Sheridan.

Castaways: Two Short Novels. Masuji Ibuse. LC 86-40435. (Illus.). 160p. 1987. 17.95 (0-87011-808-0) Kodansha.

Castaways: Two Short Novels. Masuji Ibuse. Ed. by Shaw & Tsuizaki. Tr. by Anthony Liman & David Aylward. 160p. 1993. pap. 8.00 (4-7700-1744-8) Kodansha.

Castaways - Alvar Nunez Cabeza de Vaca: The Narrative of Alvar Nunez Cabeza de Vaca. Ed. by Enrique Pupo-Walker. Tr. by Frances M. Lopez-Morillas. LC 92-25645. (C). 1993. 30.00 (0-520-07062-3); pap. 12.00 (0-520-07063-1) U CA Pr.

Castaways in Lilliput. Henry Winterfeld. 220p. (J). (gr. 3-7). 1990. pap. 4.95 (0-15-214822-1, Odyssey) HarBrace.

Caste: A Story of Republican Equality. Sydney A. Story. LC 73-152931. (Black Heritage Library Collection). 1977. 33.95 (0-8369-8776-4) Ayer.

Caste: At Home in Hindu India. Sophie Baker. (Illus.). 224p. 1990. 34.95 (0-224-02459-0, Pub. by Jonathan Cape UK) Trafalgar.

Caste: Identity & Continuity. V. C. Channa. 180p. 1979. 15.95 (0-318-36808-0) Asia Bk Corp.

Caste: The Emergence of the South Asian Social System. Morton Klass. (C). 1993. 24.00 (81-7304-054-0, Pub. by Manohar II) S Asia.

Caste Adaptation in Modernizing Indian Society. Harold Gould. 1988. 21.00 (0-685-37822-5, Pub. by Chanakya II) S Asia.

Caste & Adaptation in Modernizing Indian Society, Vol. 2. Harold A. Gould. (C). 1988. 21.00 (81-7001-045-4, Pub. by Chanakya II) S Asia.

Caste & Capitalism in Colonial India: The Nattukottai Chettiars. David W. Rudner. LC 92-38124. 1994. 50.00 (0-520-07236-7); pap. 18.00 (0-520-08350-4) U CA Pr.

Caste & Caste Conflict in Rural Society. R. B. Mishra. 1989. 31.00 (81-7169-013-0, Pub. by Commonwealth II) S Asia.

Caste & Class: Dynamics of Inequality in Indian Society. Raja Jayaraman. 168p. 1981. 19.95 (0-940500-22-1) Asia Bk Corp.

*Caste & Class: The Black Experience in Arkansas, 1880-1920. Fon Louise Gordon. LC 94-32652. (Illus.). 192p. 1995. 35.00 (0-8203-1711-X) U of Ga Pr.

Caste & Class Controversy on Race & Poverty: Round Two of the Willie-Wilson Debate. 2nd ed. Charles V. Willie. LC 89-84677. 192p. 1989. text ed. 34.95 (0-930390-97-0); pap. text ed. 18.95 (0-930390-96-2) Gen Hall.

Caste & Class in a Southern Town. John Dollard. LC 88-40430. 486p. (C). 1989. reprint ed. text ed. 39.75 (0-299-12130-5); reprint ed. pap. text ed. 17.50 (0-299-12134-8) U of Wis Pr.

*Caste & Class in India. Ed. by K. L. Sharma. (C). 1994. 44.00x (81-7033-205-2, Pub. by Rawat II) S Asia.

Caste & Class in Industrial Organisation. G. Karunanithi. (C). 1991. text ed. 17.50 (81-7169-142-0, Pub. by Commonwealth II) S Asia.

Caste & Communal Politics in South Asia. Ed. by Suranjan Das. (University of Calcutta Monograph: No. 8). (C). 1993. 20.00 (81-7074-137-8, Pub. by KP Bagchi IA) S Asia.

Caste & Ecology in the Social Insects. George F. Oster & Edward O. Wilson. LC 78-51185. (Monographs in Population Biology: Vol. 12). (Illus.). 1978. pap. 19.95 (0-691-02361-1) Princeton U Pr.

Caste & Family in the Politics of the Sinhalese, 1947-1976. Janice Jiggins. LC 78-54715. 203p. reprint ed. pap. 57.90 (0-685-16031-9, 2027232) Bks Demand.

Caste & Land Relations in India. S. M. Mandavdhare. 1989. 46.00 (81-85024-50-2, Pub. by Uppal Pub Hse II) S Asia.

Caste & Primary Occupations: A Geographical Analysis. Noor Mohammad. 1988. 32.00 (81-7022-038-6, Pub. by Concept II) S Asia.

Caste & Race in India. G. S. Ghurye. 493p. 1979. 24.95 (0-318-36803-X) Asia Bk Corp.

Caste & Race in India. G. S. Ghurye. 500p. 1986. reprint ed. pap. 11.50 (0-8364-1837-9, Pub. by Popular Prakashan II) S Asia.

Caste & Social Stratification among Muslim in India. Ed. by I. Ahmed. 314p. 1978. 24.95 (0-318-36798-X) Asia Bk Corp.

Caste & Social Stratification Among Muslims. 2nd ed. Ed. by Imtiaz Ahmad. 1978. 16.00 (0-8364-0050-X) S Asia.

Caste Challenge in India. Jagjivana Ram. 120p. 1980. 15.95 (0-318-36804-8) Asia Bk Corp.

Caste, Class & Democracy: Changes in a Stratification System. Vijai P. Singh. 158p. 1976. 32.95 (0-87073-576-4); pap. 18.95 (0-87073-577-2) Transaction Pubs.

Caste, Class, & Education: Politics of the Capitation Fee Phenomenon in Karnataka. Rekha Kaul. LC 92-43394. (Illus.). 264p. 1993. 36.00 (0-8039-9472-9) Sage.

Caste, Class, & Race. Oliver C. Cox. LC 59-8866. 1970. pap. 18.00 (0-85345-116-8) Monthly Rev.

Caste, Class & Social Movements. K. L. Sharma. 1986. 31.00 (81-7033-030-0, Pub. by Rawat II) S Asia.

Caste-Class Formation. V. M. Kurian. 1986. 19.95 (81-7018-298-0) Asia Bk Corp.

Caste, Community & Conflict in Social Change. Ed. by Virendra P. Singh. (C). 1992. 28.50 (81-7169-240-0, Commonwealth) S Asia.

Caste, Conflict & Ideology: Mahatma Jotirao Phule & Low Caste Protest in Nineteenth-Century Western India. Rosalind O'Hanlon. LC 84-9419. (Cambridge South Asian Studies: No. 30). (Illus.). 352p. 1985. 69.95 (0-521-26615-7) Cambridge U Pr.

Caste Differentiation in Social Insects: International Study Workshop on Termite Caste Differentiation, Nairobi, November 1982. Ed. by J. A. Watson & Kotber B. Okot. (Current Themes in Tropical Science Ser.: Vol. 3). (Illus.). 400p. 1985. 174.00 (0-08-030783-3, Pub. by Pergamon Repr UK) Franklin.

Caste Dimensions in Village. R. K. Mutatkar. 189p. 1978. 9.95 (0-318-36799-8) Asia Bk Corp.

Caste Dynamics Among the Bengali Hindus. Jyotimoyee Sarma. 1980. 11.50 (0-8364-0633-8, Pub. by Mukhopadhyaya II) S Asia.

Caste, Faction & Party in Indian Politics: Election Studies, Vol. 2. Paul Brass. 325p. 1986. 34.00 (81-7001-010-1, Pub. by Chanakya II) S Asia.

Caste, Faction & Party in Indian Politics, Vol. 1: Faction & Party. Paul Brass. 1985. 28.50 (0-8364-1299-0, Pub. by Chanakya II) S Asia.

Caste in a Peasant Society. Melvin M. Tumin. LC 75-29328. (Illus.). 300p. 1975. reprint ed. text ed. 59.75 (0-8371-8390-1, TUPS, Greenwood Pr) Greenwood.

Caste in Contemporary India: Beyond Organic Solidarity. Pauline Kolenda. (Illus.). 181p. (C). 1985. reprint ed. pap. text ed. 9.50 (0-88133-183-X) Waveland Pr.

Caste in India: Its Nature, Function & Origin. J. H. Hutton. 323p. 1980. 14.95 (0-318-36800-5) Asia Bk Corp.

Caste in India - The Facts & the System. E. Senart. 223p. 1978. 15.95 (0-318-36805-6) Asia Bk Corp.

Caste in Indian Politics. R. Kothari. 380p. 1973. 11.95 (0-86125-720-0) Asia Bk Corp.

Caste in Indian Politics. R. Kothari. 390p. 1970. text ed. 123.00 (0-677-61750-X) Gordon & Breach.

Caste in Modern Ceylon: The Sinhalese System in Transition. Bryce Ryan. (C). 1993. reprint ed. text ed. 32.00 (81-7013-106-5, Pub. by Navrang) S Asia.

Caste in Tamil Culture: The Religious Foundations of Sudra Domination in Tamil Sri Lanka. Bryan Pfaffenberger. LC 82-7321. (Foreign & Comparative Studies Program, South Asian Ser.: No. 7). (Illus.). (Orig.). (C). 1982. pap. 12.00 (0-915984-84-9) Syracuse U Foreign Comp.

Caste, Nationalism, & Communism in South India: Malabar, 1900-1948. Dilip M. Menon. LC 93-6609. (Cambridge South Asian Studies: No. 55). (Illus.). 200p. (C). 1994. 54.95 (0-521-41879-8) Cambridge U Pr.

Caste, Politics & the Raj: Bengal, 1872-1937. Sekhar Bandhopadhyay. 1990. 22.00 (81-7074-066-5, Pub. by KP Bagchi IA) S Asia.

Caste Politics in India. Kiran Shukla. 1987. 12.50 (81-7099-021-1, Pub. by Mittal II) S Asia.

Caste, Race, & Politics: A Comparative Study of India & the United States. Sidney Verba et al. LC 78-154207. (Illus.). 280p. reprint ed. pap. 79.80 (0-317-09729-6, 2021964) Bks Demand.

Caste Reservation in India: Law & the Constitution. G. P. Verma. 164p. 1980. 15.95 (0-940500-38-8) Asia Bk Corp.

Caste Status & Socialization among the Students. Aditi Pathak. (C). 1989. 20.00 (0-8364-2468-9) S Asia.

Caste System & Social Change. Ed. by Virendra P. Singh. (C). 1992. 34.00 (81-7169-238-9, Commonwealth) S Asia.

Caste System in India: Myth & Reality. Rajendra Pandey. 241p. 1986. 25.00 (0-8364-1861-1, Pub. by Minerva II) S Asia.

Caste, Tribes & Culture of India, 7 vols., Set. K. P. Bahadur. 1981. 149.95 (0-318-36807-2) Asia Bk Corp.

Caste War of Yucatan. Nelson Reed. (Illus.). xii, 308p. 1964. reprint ed. 42.50 (0-8047-0164-4); reprint ed. pap. 13.95 (0-8047-0165-2) Stanford U Pr.

Castel of Health. Thomas Elyot. LC 37-11679. 1979. reprint ed. 50.00 (0-8201-1176-7) Schol Facsimiles.

Castel of Memorie. Gulielmus Gratarolus. LC 72-38109. (English Experience Ser.: No. 382). 128p. 1971. reprint ed. 35.00 (90-221-0382-X) Walter J Johnson.

Castell of Pleasure. W. Nevill. (EETS, OS Ser.: No. 179). 1972. reprint ed. 26.00 (0-527-00176-7) Periodicals Srv.

Castellated & Domestic Architecture of Scotland. MacGibbon & Ross. (C). 1986. 500.00 (0-901824-18-6, Pub. by Mercat Pr Bks UK) St Mut.

Castello Branco: The Making of a Brazilian President. John W. Dulles. LC 77-99279. (Illus.). 544p. 1978. 34.50 (0-89096-043-7) Tex A&M Univ Pr.

Castellon: For Instructors with Utility Disk. Andrew M. Scott et al. 43p. (C). 1987. pap. text ed. 3.75 (0-15-505832-0) HB Coll Pubs.

Castellon: For Instructors with Utility Disk. Andrew M. Scott et al. 43p. (C). 1987. disk 28.50 (0-15-505831-2) HB Coll Pubs.

C

An Asterisk (*) at the beginning of an entry indicates that the title is appearing in BIP for the first time.

Castelvetro on the Art of Poetry: An Abridged Translation of Castelvetro's "Poetica d'Aristotele Vulgarizzata et Sposta" Andrew Bongiorno. LC 83-17386. (Medieval & Renaissance Texts & Studies: Vol. 29). 432p. 1984. 30.00 (*0-86698-063-6*) MRTS.

Castes & Races. Frithjof Schuon. Tr. by M. Pallis & M. Matheson. 88p. (Orig.). 1982. pap. 13.95 (*0-900588-22-5*) S Perennis.

Castes & Tribes of India Series 2: Socio-Cultural Study of Scheduled Tribes. S. R. Murkute. 1990. 29.00 (*0-317-99725-4*, Pub. by Ashish II) S Asia.

Castes & Tribes of Southern India, 7 vols., Set. Edgar Thurston & K. Rangachari. 3184p. reprint ed. text ed. 295.00 (*0-685-13653-1*) Coronet Bks.

Castes & Tribes of Southern India, 7 vols., Set: Vols. I-VII. Edgar Thurston & K. Rangachari. (C). 1987. reprint ed. Set. 188.00 (*0-8364-2403-4*, Pub. by Asian Educ Servs II) S Asia.

Castes & Tribes of the Nizam's Dominion, 2 vols., Set. Syed S. Hassan. 1990. reprint ed. 77.50 (*81-85326-32-0*, Pub. by Vintage II) S Asia.

Castes & Tribes on the Tea-Estates of NW India. (C). 1989. reprint ed. 42.50 (*0-8364-2469-7*, Pub. by Usha II) S Asia.

Castes, Customs, Manners & Literature of the Tamils. Simon C. Chitty. 1988. reprint ed. 15.00 (*81-206-0409-1*, Pub. by Asian Educ Servs II) S Asia.

Castiglione: The Ideal & the Real in Renaissance Culture. Robert W. Hanning & David Rosand. LC 82-6944. (Illus.). 240p. 1983. text ed. 37.00 (*0-300-02649-8*) Yale U Pr.

***Castigo Sin Venganza.** Lope De Vega. 264p. 1990. pap. 11.95 (*0-7859-5211-X*) Fr & Eur.

Castilian Crisis of the Seventeenth Century: New Perspectives on the Economic & Social History of Seventeenth-Century Spain. Ed. by I. A. Thompson & Bartolome Y. Casalilla. LC 93-27991. (Past & Present Publications). (Illus.). 336p. (C). 1994. 64.95 (*0-521-41624-8*) Cambridge U Pr.

Castilian Days. John Hay. 1977. text ed. 19.95 (*0-8369-7345-3*, 8138) Ayer.

Castilian Days. John Hay. LC 76-93537. reprint ed. 24.50 (*0-404-03157-9*) AMS Pr.

Castilian Days. John Hay. LC 79-108490. 1971. reprint ed. 8.00 (*0-403-00397-0*) Scholarly.

Castilian Days. John M. Hay. (Notable American Authors Ser.). 1992. reprint ed. lib. bdg. 75.00 (*0-7812-3057-8*) Rprt Serv.

Castilian Sculpture. Beatrice G. Proske. (Illus.). 525p. 1951. 15.00 (*0-317-00617-7*, Hispanic Soc) Interbk Inc.

Castilian Sculpture: Gothic to Renaissance. Beatrice G. Proske. (Illus.). 1988. reprint ed. 15.00 (*0-87535-069-0*) Hispanic Soc.

Castilla. J. Garcia Fernandez. 312p. (SPA.). 1985. 12.50 (*0-8288-7085-3*, S24966) Fr & Eur.

Castilla. Ed. by E. Inman Fox. (Nueva Austral Ser.: No. 254). (SPA.). 1991. pap. text ed. 24.95x (*84-239-7254-2*) Elliots Bks.

Castilla: A Cultural Reader. Ed. by P. Turnbull & G. Celaya. LC 71-92666. (Illus.). (Orig.). (SPA.). 1970. pap. text ed. 19.95 (*0-89197-067-3*) Irvington.

Castillo: The Politics of Tradition in an Andalusian Town. Richard Maddox. 1993. pap. 19.95 (*0-252-06339-2*) U of Ill Pr.

Castillo: The Politics of Tradition in an Andalusian Town. Richard Maddox. (Illus.). 368p. (C). 1993. 49.95 (*0-252-01946-6*) U of Ill Pr.

Castillo: Vision & Form. Ed. by Maria L. Borras. LC 91-52795. (Illus.). 346p. 1991. 85.00 (*0-8478-1416-5*) Rizzoli Intl.

Castillo de San Marcos: A Guide to Castillo de San Marcos National Monument. National Park Service Staff. LC 92-40413. (Illus.). 64p. (Orig.). 1994. pap. 2.75 (*0-912627-59-X*) Natl Park Serv.

Castillos (Castles) J. Cooper. (Maravillas de la Humanidad (Man-Made Wonders) Ser.: Set VI). (SPA.). (J). 1991. 8.95 (*0-86592-937-8*) Rourke Enter.

Castillos de Espana. 12th ed. Carlos Sarthou Carreres. (Illus.). 501p. 1989. 295.00x (*84-239-5250-9*) Elliots Bks.

Casting a Spell. rev. ed. Vaune Ainsworth-Land & Norma Fletcher. (Illus.). (Orig.). 1983. pap. text ed. 7.95 (*0-914634-65-8*, 7909) DOK Pubs.

Casting Aluminum. C. W. Ammen. (Illus.). 252p. (Orig.). 1985. pap. 14.95 (*0-8306-1910-0*) TAB Bks.

Casting & Fishing the Artificial Fly. John W. Ball. LC 79-140119. (Illus.). 1972. pap. 6.95 (*0-87004-217-3*) Caxton.

Casting Away of Mrs. Lecks & Mrs. Aleshine. Frank R. Stockton. 132p. 1992. reprint ed. lib. bdg. 13.95 (*0-89966-919-0*) Buccaneer Bks.

Casting Brass. C. W. Ammen. (Illus.). 252p. (Orig.). 1985. 18.95 (*0-8306-0810-9*, 1810H); pap. 14.95 (*0-8306-1810-4*, 1810P) TAB Bks.

Casting Copper-Base Alloys. 254p. 60.00 (*0-87433-022-X*, NF8500) Am Foundrymen.

Casting Copper-Base Alloys. 254p. 1987. 70.00 (*0-317-59824-4*, NF8500) Am Foundrymen.

Casting Couch & Other Front Row Seats: Women in Films of the 1970s & 1980s. Marsha McCreadie. LC 89-72131. 208p. 1990. text ed. 49.95 (*0-275-92912-4*, C2912, Praeger Pubs) Greenwood.

Casting Defects Handbook. 191p. 40.00 (*0-317-32558-2*, GM7204); 20.00 (*0-317-32559-0*); pap. 40.00 (*0-87433-008-4*, GM7204) Am Foundrymen.

Casting Design. Robert Johns. (Illus.). 200p. 1987. write for info. (*0-318-62101-0*) Am Foundrymen.

Casting Design Handbook: Prepared from the Contributions of 18 Committees (Sponsored by the United States Air Force & the American Society for Metals) American Society for Metals Staff. LC 62-53240. (Illus.). 344p. reprint ed. pap. 98.10 (*0-317-10976-6*, 2013216) Bks Demand.

***Casting down Imaginations.** Jonas B. Clark. 100p. (Orig.). Date not set. pap. 6.00 (*1-886885-03-6*) Spirit Life.

Casting down Imaginations - CDI: The CDI Process. Donald Shorter. Ed. by Kathy L. Shorter. 106p. (Orig.). 1991. pap. 5.95 (*1-879686-00-7*) Wrd Faith Min.

Casting for the Cutthroat & Other Poems. Charles Entrekin. 48p. (Orig.). 1980. pap. 5.95 (*0-917658-13-2*) BPW & P.

Casting Illusions: The World of Fly-Fishing. Text by Tom Rosenbauer. LC 88-4053. (Illus.). 144p. 1989. 19.98 (*0-934738-50-5*) Thomasson-Grant.

Casting into a Cloud: Southwest Haiku. Elizabeth S. Lamb. (Xtras Ser.: No. 11). (Illus.). 72p. (Orig.). 1985. pap. 3.95 (*0-89120-024-X*) From Here.

Casting Light on Writing. Fitzgerald. (C). 1991. text ed. 30.00 (*0-06-042037-5*) HarpCollege.

Casting Metal in Sand Made Easy. International Correspondence Schools Staff. (Illus.). 145p. 1991. reprint ed. 21.00 (*1-877767-29-8*); reprint ed. pap. 11.00 (*1-877767-23-9*) Univ Publng Hse.

Casting, Metals Handbook, Vol. 15. 9th ed. 960p. 1988. 147.00 (*0-87170-021-2*) ASM.

Casting Nets & Testing Specimens: Two Grand Methods of Psychology. Philip J. Runkel. LC 89-48665. 224p. 1990. text ed. 49.95 (*0-275-93533-7*, C3533, Greenwood Pr) Greenwood.

Casting of Bells. Jaroslav Seifert. Tr. by Paul Jagasich & Tom O'Grady. LC 83-10631. (Outstanding Author Ser.: No. 4). 64p. (Orig.). 1983. reprint ed. 15.00 (*0-930370-25-2*); reprint ed. per., pap. 7.00 (*0-930370-26-0*) Spirit That Moves.

Casting of Near Net Shape Products: Proceedings of an International Symposium on Casting of Near Net Shape Products. International Symposium on Casting of Near Net Shape Products (1988: Honolulu, Hawaii) Staff. Ed. by Y. Sahai et al. LC 88-62072. (Illus.). 752p. reprint ed. pap. 180.00 (*0-8357-4685-2*, 2052340) Bks Demand.

Casting of Steel. W. Newell. 1955. 252.00 (*0-08-009016-8*, Pub. by Pergamon Repr UK) Franklin.

Casting Out Anger: Religion among the Taita of Kenya. Grace G. Harris. LC 77-80837. (Cambridge Studies in Social Anthropology: No. 21). 213p. reprint ed. pap. 60.80 (*0-318-34804-7*, 2031667) Bks Demand.

Casting Out Anger: Religion among the Taita of Kenya. Grace G. Harris. (Illus.). 193p. (C). 1986. reprint ed. pap. text ed. 9.95 (*0-88133-233-X*) Waveland Pr.

Casting Properties of Metals & Alloys. Aleksei M. Korol'kov. LC 61-18757. 152p. reprint ed. pap. 43.40 (*0-317-10733-X*, 2003364) Bks Demand.

Casting Sequences: Poems. Marjorie Welish. LC 92-27609. (Contemporary Poetry Ser.). 88p. 1993. 20.00 (*0-8203-1511-7*); pap. 9.95 (*0-8203-1512-5*) U of Ga Pr.

Casting Shadows. Aba J. Opio. 24p. 1991. 3.00 (*1-877610-04-6*) Sea Island.

Casting Shakespeare's Plays: London Actors & Their Roles, 1590-1642. T. J. King. (Illus.). 320p. (C). 1992. 74.95 (*0-521-32785-7*) Cambridge U Pr.

Casting the Circle: A Women's Book of Ritual. Diane Stein. 300p. 1990. pap. 12.95 (*0-89594-411-1*) Crossing Pr.

Casting the First Stone. R. A. Gilbert. 192p. 1993. pap. 12.95 (*1-85230-367-0*) Element MA.

Casting the Horoscope. Alan Leo. (Astrologer's Library). 384p. 1989. pap. 12.95 (*0-89281-176-5*) Inner Tradit.

***Casting the Net: From ARPANET to Internet & Beyond.** Peter H. Salus. 240p. (C). 1995. pap. text ed. 24.95 (*0-201-87674-4*) Addison-Wesley.

Casting the Runes & Other Ghost Stories. M. R. James. (World's Classics Ser.). 400p. 1987. pap. 7.95 (*0-19-281719-1*) OUP.

Casting Your Cares. Carl E. Jacobsen. 96p. (Orig.). 1993. pap. 4.95 (*1-56794-042-0*, C2321) Star Bible.

Casting Your Cares Upon the Lord. Kenneth E. Hagin. 1981. pap. 1.95 (*0-89276-023-0*) Hagin Ministries.

Casting Your Vote in North Carolina. 2nd ed. William A. Campbell. 25p. (YA). (gr. 10-12). 1990. pap. text ed. 5.00 (*1-56011-171-2*) Institute Government.

Castings. J. Campbell. 368p. 1991. 100.00 (*0-7506-1072-7*) Buttrwrth-Heinemann.

Castings. 2nd ed. John Campbell. 288p. 1993. pap. 39.95 (*0-7506-1696-2*) Buttrwrth-Heinemann.

Castings. 2nd ed. Lola Haskins. 72p. (Orig.). 1992. pap. 9.95 (*0-9632782-0-7*, PS3358A7238C3) Betony Pr.

Castle. Gloria Evangelista. LC 93-87111. (Step into Storytelling Ser.). (Illus.). 24p. (Orig.). (J). (ps up). 1994. pap. 7.99 (*0-679-86195-5*) Random Bks Yng Read.

Castle. Christopher Gravett. LC 93-32594. (Eyewitness Bks.). (Illus.). (J). 1994. 16.00 (*0-679-86000-2*); lib. bdg. 16.99 (*0-679-96000-7*) Knopf Bks Yng Read.

Castle. Franz Kafka. Tr. by Willa Muir & Edwin Muir. LC 92-52904. 336p. 1992. 17.00 (*0-679-41735-4*, Everymans Lib) Knopf.

***Castle.** Franz Kafka. 504p. 1995. pap. 15.00 (*0-8052-1039-3*) Schocken.

Castle. David Macaulay. LC 77-7159. (Illus.). 80p. (J). (gr. 1 up). 1977. 16.95 (*0-395-25784-0*) HM.

Castle. David Macaulay. LC 77-7159. (Illus.). 80p. (J). (gr. 1 up). 1982. pap. 7.95 (*0-395-32920-5*) HM.

Castle. Jon Nichol. (Resource Units: Middle Ages, 1066-1485 Ser.). (Illus.). 24p. 1974. teacher ed, pap. text ed. 15.25 (*0-582-39379-5*) Longman.

Castle. Tom Partridge. (Illus.). (J). 1994. 19.95 (*0-312-11156-8*) St Martin.

Castle: Illustrated History of the Smithsonian Building. Cynthia R. Field et al. LC 92-45811. (Illus.). 192p. (Orig.). 1993. pap. 15.95 (*1-56098-287-X*) Smithsonian.

***Castle: The Story of a Kentucky Prison.** Bill Cunningham. LC 94-79333. (Illus.). 256p. 1994. 18.95 (*0-913383-32-5*) McClanahan Pub.

Castle & Kings. (Time Travel Activity Book Ser.). 48p. (J). (gr. 3 up). 1992. 1.95 (*0-88679-916-3*) Educ Insights.

Castle & Society in Medieval Hungary, 1000-1437. E. Fugedi. 162p. (C). 1986. 105.00 (*0-569-08893-3*) St Mut.

Castle & the Flaw. Felix Pollak. (J). 1963. pap. 4.00 (*0-685-01010-4*) Elizabeth Pr.

Castle at Glencarris. Jean Vicary. 1977. pap. 1.25 (*0-8439-0449-6*, LB449) Dorchester Pub Co.

Castle Builder. Dennis Nolan. LC 86-23784. (Illus.). 32p. (J). (gr. k-3). 1987. text ed. 13.95 (*0-02-768240-4*, Mac Bks Young Read) S&S Childrens.

Castle Builder. Dennis Nolan. LC 92-29563. (Illus.). 32p. (J). (gr. k-3). 1993. pap. 4.95 (*0-689-71703-2*, Aladdin Paperbacks) S&S Childrens.

Castle Builders: Georgia's Economy Under the Trustees, 1732-1754. Milton L. Ready. LC 77-14750. (Dissertations in American Economic History Ser.). 1978. 37.95 (*0-405-11053-7*) Ayer.

Castle Carnack. large type ed. Mary Williams. 434p. 1993. 21.95 (*0-7505-0529-X*) Ulverscroft.

Castle, Coast & Cottage: The National Trust in Northern Ireland. 2nd rev. ed. Lyn Gallagher & Dick Rogers. (Illus.). 194p. 1993. 29.00 (*0-85640-497-7*, Pub. by Blackstaff Pr IE) Dufour.

Castle Connolly Guide: How to Find the Best Doctors for You & Your Family: New York Metro Area. John J. Connolly. Ed. by Sue Berkman & Sandra Beach. LC 93-72954. 608p. 1993. pap. 21.95 (*1-883769-59-0*) Castle Connolly Med.

Castle Connolly Pocket Guide: How to Find the Best Doctors, Hospitals, & HMOs for You & Your Family. John J. Connolly. Ed. by Sue Berkman. LC 94-92449. 457p. (Orig.). 1994. pap. 9.95 (*1-883769-70-1*) Castle Connolly Med. The CASTLE CONNOLLY POCKET GUIDE: HOW TO FIND THE BEST DOCTORS, HOSPITALS, & HMOs FOR YOU & YOUR FAMILY offers a clearly written & concise guide to understanding the health care industry, as well as how to go about finding the best providers for you & your family. The guide contains vital information for anyone seeking a new doctor, hospital or HMO. The guide also contains the most extensive selection of sources for information ever available in this type of book, including how to obtain your medical records, how to get the best care in an emergency & over 250 help & information phone numbers. In addition, there are special chapters on health care for women, children & the elderly. To order, call 800-399-DOCS or FAX 212-980-1716, or write: Castle Connolly Medical Ltd., 150 E. 58th St., New York, NY 10155.** ***Publisher Provided Annotation.

Castle Craneycrow. George B. McCutcheon. 1976. lib. bdg. 17.25 (*0-89968-059-3*, Lghtyr Pr) Buccaneer Bks.

Castle Dismal. W. G. Simms. Ed. by Reid. (Masterworks of Literature Ser.). 1991. write for info. (*0-8084-0444-X*) NCUP.

Castle D'Or. Arthur Quiller-Couch & Daphne Du Maurier. reprint ed. lib. bdg. 21.95 (*0-88411-148-2*, Aeonian Pr) Amereon Ltd.

Castle Dreams. John DeChancie. 1992. mass mkt. 4.99 (*0-441-09414-7*) Ace Bks.

***Castle Falkenstein.** Michael Pondsmith. (Illus.). 224p. (Orig.). 1994. 32.00 (*0-937279-51-X*, CF6002); pap. 27.00 (*0-937279-43-9*, CF6001) R Talsorian.

Castle Fear. Franklin W. Dixon. Ed. by Ann Greenberg. (Hardy Boys Casefiles Ser.: No. 44). 160p. (Orig.). (YA). (gr. 7 up). 1991. pap. 3.75 (*0-671-74615-4*, Archway) PB.

Castle for Rent. John DeChancie. 1989. mass mkt. 4.99 (*0-441-09406-6*) Ace Bks.

Castle Gap & the Pecos Frontier. Patrick Dearen. LC 88-6067. (Chisholm Trail Ser.: No. 6). (Illus.). 240p. (Orig.). 1988. pap. 13.95 (*0-87565-030-9*) Tex Christian.

Castle Gay. John Buchan. LC 93-28809. 1993. pap. 7.00 (*0-7509-0483-6*) A Sutton Pub.

Castle Gripsholm. Kurt Tucholsky. LC 87-5766. 128p. 1989. Tusk. pap. 8.95 (*0-87951-337-3*) Overlook Pr.

Castle Gripsholm: A Summer Story. Kurt Tucholsky. LC 87-5766. 1988. 16.95 (*0-87951-293-8*) Overlook Pr.

Castle Hayne. Carole Marsh. (Carole Marsh Short Story Ser.). (Illus.). 60p. (J). (gr. 4-12). 1994. lib. bdg. 19.95 (*1-55609-159-1*); pap. 14.95 (*1-55609-241-5*) Gallopade Pub Group.

Castle Hopping in the U. K. with Elizabeth. Elizabeth Campbell. (Illus.). 60p. (Orig.). (YA). (gr. 9-12). 1988. pap. 12.95 (*0-9618324-0-1*) EFC Pub.

Castle in England & Wales: An Interpretative History. D. J. Cathcart-King. 196p. 1988. text ed. 36.95 (*0-918400-08-2*) Areopagitica.

Castle in England & Wales: An Interpretative History. D. J. King. (Studies in Archaeology). (Illus.). 224p. 1991. pap. 16.95 (*0-415-00350-4*, A5710) Routledge.

Castle in the Air. Diana W. Jones. LC 90-30266. (Illus.). 208p. (J). (gr. 6 up). 1991. 13.95 (*0-688-09686-7*) Greenwillow.

Castle in the Air. Donald E. Westlake, pseud. 288p. 1981. pap. 2.50 (*0-449-24382-6*, Crest) Fawcett.

***Castle in the Attic.** Myka-Lynne Sokoloff. Ed. by J. Friedland & R. Kessler. (Novel-Ties Ser.). (J). (gr. 4-6). 1993. student ed, pap. text ed. 15.95 (*0-88122-910-5*) Lrn Links.

Castle in the Attic. Elizabeth Winthrop. LC 85-5607. (Illus.). 192p. (J). (gr. 4-7). 1985. 15.95 (*0-8234-0579-6*) Holiday.

Castle in the Attic. Elizabeth Winthrop. 1986. mass mkt. 3.99 (*0-440-40941-1*) Dell.

Castle in the Sand. large type ed. Joanna Gale. (Linford Romance Library). 288p. 1992. pap. 14.95 (*0-7089-7193-8*, Linford) Ulverscroft.

Castle in the Sea. Scott O'Dell. 160p. (YA). (gr. 7 up). 1984. pap. 3.50 (*0-449-70123-9*, Juniper) Fawcett.

Castle in the Sea. Scott O'Dell. 192p. (J). (gr. 7-p). 1983. 13.95 (*0-395-34831-5*) HM.

Castle Keep. William Eastlake. 382p. 1989. pap. 4.95 (*0-88184-499-3*) Carroll & Graf.

Castle Kelpiesloch. large type ed. Theresa Charles. 309p. 1989. 17.95 (*0-7089-1925-1*) Ulverscroft.

Castle Kidnapped. John Dechancie. 1989. mass mkt. 4.99 (*0-441-09408-2*) Ace Bks.

Castle King-Four. Jim Reagan. LC 89-38938. 336p. (Orig.). 1990. pap. 10.95 (*0-931832-37-3*) Fithian Pr.

Castle Kintyle. large type ed. Mary Mackie. LC 94-3349. 263p. 1994. pap. 15.95 (*0-8161-7452-0*) Hall.

***Castle Kitchen: Recipes & Reminiscences from Brodick Castle to Bangalore.** Fiona Hannon. (Illus.). 317p. 1995. pap. 22.95 (*1-85158-655-5*, Pub. by Mnstream UK) Trafalgar.

***Castle Land Curriculum: "Especially for Four Year Olds"** Joyce Johnson & Wendy J. Horne. (Illus.). 720p. 1994. ring bd. 1,200.00 (*0-9641517-3-1*) Castle Land.

***Castle Land Curriculum: "Especially for Three Year Olds"** Joyce Johnson & Wendy J. Horne. (Illus.). 720p. 1994. ring bd. 1,200.00 (*0-9641517-2-3*) Castle Land.

***Castle Land Curriculum: "Especially for Two Year Olds"** Joyce Johnson & Wendy J. Horne. (Illus.). 720p. 1994. ring bd. 1,200.00 (*0-9641517-1-5*) Castle Land.

***Castle Land Curriculum: "Especially for Two Year Olds," "Especially for Three Year Olds", "Especially for Four Year Olds", 3 vols., Set.** Joce Johnson & Wendy J. Horne. (Illus.). 1994. ring bd. 3,600.00 (*0-9641517-0-7*) Castle Land.

Castle Mirage. large type ed. Alice Brennan. (Linford Mystery Library). 1991. pap. 13.95 (*0-7089-7029-X*) Ulverscroft.

Castle Murders. John DeChancie. 1991. mass mkt. 4.99 (*0-441-09273-X*) Ace Bks.

Castle Mystery. Gertrude C. Warner. (Boxcar Children Mysteries Ser.: No. 36). (J). (gr. 4-7). 1993. 10.95 (*0-8075-1078-5*); pap. 3.50 (*0-8075-1079-3*) A Whitman.

Castle Nowhere: Lake-Country Sketches. Constance F. Woolson. LC 79-137308. reprint ed. 29.50 (*0-404-07035-3*) AMS Pr.

Castle Nowhere: Lake-Country Sketches. Constance F. Woolson. (BCL1-PS American Literature Ser.). 386p. 1992. reprint ed. lib. bdg. 89.00 (*0-7812-6908-3*) Rprt Serv.

Castle Nowhere: Lake Country Sketches. Constance F. Woolson. 1972. reprint ed. lib. bdg. 14.50 (*0-8422-8129-0*) Irvington.

Castle of Argol. Julien Gracq. Tr. by Louise Varese. (Illus.). (C). 1991. 45.00 (*0-685-40904-X*) Lapis Pr.

Castle of Chuchurumbel: El Castillo de Churchurumbel. Anne Weissman. (Illus.). 19p. (ENG & SPA.). (J). (gr. k-2). 1987. 8.95 (*968-6217-00-2*) Hispanic Bk Dist.

Castle of Closing Doors. large type ed. Daoma Winston. 131p. 1993. reprint ed. lib. bdg. 17.95 (*1-56054-516-X*) Thorndike Pr.

Castle of Crossed Destinies. Italo Calvino. LC 78-23588. 129p. 1979. pap. 8.95 (*0-15-615455-2*, Harvest Bks) HarBrace.

Castle of Days. Gene Wolfe. 448p. 1995. pap. 14.95 (*0-312-89042-7*) Orb NYC.

Castle of Deception. Mercedes Lackey & Josepha Sherman. (Bard's Tale Ser.). 320p. (Orig.). 1992. mass mkt. 5.99 (*0-671-72125-9*) Baen Bks.

Castle of Dolls. Dorian Duncan. 1993. 13.95 (*0-8034-8992-7*) Bouregy.

***Castle of Doom.** Montgomery. (Choose Your Own Nightmare Ser.: No. 04). 1995. pap. (*0-553-48232-7*) Bantam.

Castle of Dreams. Donna F. Crow. LC 92-5352. 1992. pap. 8.99 (*0-8423-1068-1*) Tyndale.

Castle of Dreams. Flora M. Speer. 1990. mass mkt. 4.50 (*1-55817-334-X*, Pinnacle NY) Windsor NY.

Castle of Dreams. Flora M. Speer. 1990. pap. write for info. (*0-318-66669-3*) Zebra.

Castle of Eagles. large type ed. Constance Heaven. LC 92-37052. 1993. 21.95 (*0-7927-1480-6*, Curley Lrg Print); pap. 19.95 (*0-7927-1479-2*, Curley Lrg Print) Chivers N Amer.

***Castle of Eyes.** Penelope Love. (Fiction Bks.). 236p. (Orig.). (YA). 1993. pap. 14.95 (*1-56882-005-4*, 6000) Chaosium.

Castle of Fratta. Ippolito Nievo. Tr. by Lovett F. Edwards. LC 74-10017. 589p. 1974. reprint ed. text ed. 38.50 (*0-8371-7660-3*, NICA, Greenwood Pr) Greenwood.

Castle of Hearts see Candidate

***Castle of Horror.** Don Wulffson. LC 94-29371. (How Will It End? You Decide Ser.). (Illus.). 128p. (J). (gr. 3 up). 1995. pap. 3.50 (*0-8431-3862-9*) Price Stern.

C

An Asterisk (*) at the beginning of an entry indicates that the title is appearing in BIP for the first time.

***Castle of Intrigue.** P. Stewart. (Puzzle Adventure Ser.). (Illus.). 48p. (J). (gr. 2-7). 1994. lib. bdg. 11.96 (0-88110-719-0, Usborne); pap. 4.95 (0-7460-1705-7, Usborne) EDC.
Castle of Knowledge. Robert Record. LC 74-28882. (English Experience Ser.: No. 760). 1975. reprint ed. 44.00 (90-221-0760-4) Walter J Johnson.
Castle of Llyr. Lloyd Alexander. LC 66-13461. 208p. (J). (gr. 4-6). 1966. 16.95 (0-8050-1115-3, Bks Young Read) H Holt & Co.
Castle of Love. Diego De San Pedro. LC 51-634. 1979. reprint ed. 50.00 (0-8201-1217-8) Schol Facsimiles.
Castle of Otranto. Horace Walpole. Ed. by W. S. Lewis & Joseph W. Reed, Jr. (World's Classics Ser.). 1982. pap. 4.95 (0-19-281606-3) OUP.
Castle of Otranto. Horace Walpole. 128p. 1963. pap. 3.95 (0-02-055200-9, Collier S&S) S&S Trade.
Castle of Otranto. Horace Walpole. Bd. with Mysteries of Udolpho. Ann Radcliffe. LC 63-9181.; Northanger Abbey. Jane Austen. LC 63-9181. LC 63-9181. (Rinehart Editions Ser.). 543p. (C). 1963. Set pap. text ed. 20.50 (0-03-011950-2) HB Coll Pubs.
Castle of Otranto & Hieroglyphic Tales. Horace Walpole. 192p. 1993. pap. 5.95 (0-460-87198-6, Everyman's Classic Lib) C E Tuttle.
Castle of Otranto (Three Gothic Novels) 2nd ed. Horace Walpole. Ed. by E. F. Bleiler. Bd. with Vathek. William Beckford. Ed. by E. F. Bleiler. Tr. by Samuel Henley.; Vampyre. John Polidori. Ed. by E. F. Bleiler.; Fragment of a Novel. Byron. Set pap. 7.95 (0-486-21232-7) Dover.
Castle of Perseverance. LC 74-133644. (Tudor Facsimile Texts. Old English Plays Ser.: No. 1). reprint ed. 49.50 (0-404-53301-9) AMS Pr.
Castle of Pictures: A Grandmother's Tales, Vol. 1. George Sand. Ed. by Holly E. Hirko. (Illus.). 176p. (Orig.). (YA). (gr. 5 up). 1994. 19.95 (1-55861-091-X) Feminist Pr.
Castle of Pictures: A Grandmother's Tales, Vol. 2. George Sand. Ed. by Holly E. Hirko. (Illus.). 176p. (Orig.). (YA). (gr. 5 up). 1994. pap. 9.95 (1-55861-092-8) Feminist Pr.
Castle of the Crushed Shamrock. Lee Karr. 1989. pap. 3.95 (0-8217-2843-1) Zebra.
Castle of the Heart. Flora M. Speer. 1990. mass mkt. 4.50 (1-55817-411-7, Pinnacle NY) Windsor NY.
Castle of the Pearl. rev. ed. Christopher Biffle. LC 89-46073. (Illus.). 160p. 1990. reprint ed. pap. 14.00 (0-06-096506-1, PL) HarpC.
Castle of the Silver Wheel. Teresa Edgerton. 288p. (Orig.). 1993. mass mkt. 4.99 (0-441-09275-6) Ace Bks.
Castle of the Undead. Nick Baren. (Endless Quest, Ravenloft Ser.: No. 2). 192p. (Orig.). 1994. pap. 3.95 (1-56076-836-3) TSR Inc.
Castle of Wizardry. David Eddings. (Belgariad Ser.: Bk. 4). 416p. 1985. mass mkt. 5.99 (0-345-33570-8, Del Rey) Ballantine.
Castle on a Cliff: A History of Baylor School. John C. Longwith. (Illus.). 216p. 1994. 24.95 (0-944897-03-7) Magic Chef.
Castle on Hester Street. Linda Heller. (Illus.). 32p. (J). (gr. k-3). 1990. pap. 6.95 (0-8276-0323-1) JPS Phila.
Castle on the Hill. M. C. Campbell. 112p. 1993. pap. 6.00 (1-880365-50-2) Prof Pr NC.
Castle on the Hill. Elizabeth Goudge. 1976. 14.95 (0-8488-1338-3) Amereon Ltd.
Castle on the Hill. Elizabeth Goudge. 379p. 1983. reprint ed. lib. bdg. 25.95 (0-89966-101-7) Buccaneer Bks.
Castle or Picture of Policy. William Blandy. LC 71-38157. (English Experience Ser.: No. 436). 68p. 1972. reprint ed. 9.50 (90-221-0436-2) Walter J Johnson.
Castle Perilous. John DeChancie. mass mkt. 4.99 (0-441-09418-X) Ace Bks.
***Castle Rack.** 1994. write for info. (0-7869-0085-7) Random.
Castle Rackrent. Maria Edgeworth. Ed. by George Watson. (World's Classics Ser.). 1982. pap. 6.95 (0-19-281539-3) OUP.
***Castle Rackrent.** 2nd ed. Maria Edgeworth. Ed. & Intro. by Kathryn J. Kirkpatrick. (World's Classics Ser.). 160p. 1995. pap. 7.95 (0-19-282394-9) OUP.
Castle Rackrent & Ennui. Maria Edgeworth. 368p. 1993. 9.95 (0-14-043320-1, Penguin Classics) Viking Penguin.
***Castle Returns.** Harry Heuston. (Adventures of Hacker Ser.: Vol. 3). (Illus.). 160p. (Orig.). (J). (gr. 4-8). 1995. pap. 3.50 (1-57414-013-2) Value Network.
Castle Richmond. Anthony Trollope. Ed. by Mary Hamer. (World's Classics Ser.). (Illus.). 544p. 1989. pap. 10.95 (0-19-282173-3) OUP.
Castle Richmond, 3 vols. Anthony Trollope. Ed. by N. John Hall. LC 80-1878. (Selected Works of Anthony Trollope Ser.). 1981. reprint ed. lib. bdg. 115.95 (0-405-14134-3) Ayer.
Castle Richmond. Anthony Trollope. 440p. 1984. reprint ed. pap. 8.50 (0-486-24760-0) Dover.
Castle Richmond (1860) Anthony Trollope. 912p. 1993. 9.95 (0-14-043808-4, Penguin Classics) Viking Penguin.
Castle Roogna. Piers Anthony. 1987. mass mkt. 5.95 (0-345-35048-0, Del Rey) Ballantine.
Castle Skull. John D. Carr. 240p. 1987. pap. 3.50 (0-8217-1974-2) Zebra.
Castle Skye. Jesper Myrfors. (Pandevelopment Ser.). 128p. 1993. pap. 11.95 (1-880992-14-0) Wizards Coast.
Castle Spectre. Matthew G. Lewis. LC 90-40606. 122p. 1990. reprint ed. 43.00 (1-85477-049-7, Pub. by Woodstock Bks UK) Cassell.
Castle Spellbound. John DeChancie. 240p. (Orig.). 1992. mass mkt. 4.99 (0-441-09407-4) Ace Bks.
***Castle Terror.** Marion Z. Bradley. 1994. reprint ed. lib. bdg. 19.00 (0-7278-4660-4) Severn Hse.
Castle Times. Ed. by Robyn Gee. (Illus.). 24p. (J). (gr. 3-6). 1982. pap. 4.50 (0-86020-621-1) EDC.
Castle to Castle. Louis-Ferdinand D. Celine. 352p. 1987. pap. 8.95 (0-88184-360-1) Carroll & Graf.
Castle Tzingal: A Poem. Fred Chappell. LC 84-9716. 46p. 1984. text ed. 13.95 (0-8071-1190-2) La State U Pr.
Castle War! John DeChancie. 1990. mass mkt. 4.99 (0-441-09270-5) Ace Bks.
Castle Warlock. George MacDonald. (George MacDonald Original Works: Series I). 379p. 1992. reprint ed. 16.00 (1-881084-03-5) Johannesen.
Castles. Carolyn A. Aish. LC 90-86250. (Frencolian Chronicles Ser.: Bk. 2). 306p. 1991. pap. 6.99 (0-88965-090-X, Pub. by Horizon Books CN) Chr Pubns.
Castles. J. K. Anderson. (J). (gr. 1-9). 1992. pap. 3.95 (0-88388-088-1) Bellerophon Bks.
Castles. Francesca Baines. (Worldwise Ser.). (Illus.). 48p. (J). (gr. 4-6). 1994. lib. bdg. 14.98 (0-531-14334-1) Watts.
***Castles.** Francesca Baines. LC 94-24223. (Worldwise Ser.). (Illus.). 48p. (J). (gr. 4-7). 1995. pap. 14.99 (0-531-15267-7) Orchard Bks Watts.
Castles. R. Allen Brown. 1989. pap. 25.00 (0-85263-653-9, Pub. by Shire UK) St Mut.
Castles. J. Cooper. (Man-Made Wonders Ser.). (J). 1991. 8.95 (0-86592-629-8) Rourke Enter.
Castles. Julie Garwood. Ed. by Linda Marrow. 368p. (Orig.). 1993. mass mkt. 5.99 (0-671-74420-8) PB.
Castles. Longmeadow Press Editors. 128p. 1993. 14.98 (0-681-41807-9) Longmeadow Pr.
Castles. Christopher Maynard. LC 92-32844. 32p. (J). (gr. 1-4). 1993. 3.95 (1-85697-891-5, Kingfisher LKC) LKC.
Castles. Illus. by C. Millet & D. Millet. LC 92-15955. (First Discovery Bks.). (J). 1993. 11.95 (0-590-46377-2) Scholastic Inc.
***Castles.** David Mountfield. (Illus.). 144p. 1995. 15.98 (0-8317-1307-0) Smithmark.
Castles. Gillian Osband. LC 91-60082. (Illus.). 16p. (J). 1991. 17.95 (0-531-05949-9) Orchard Bks Watts.
***Castles.** Philip Steele. LC 94-29366. (J). (gr. 1-8). 1995. 14.95 (1-85697-547-9, Kingfisher LKC) LKC.
Castles. Rachel Wright. LC 91-32796. (Craft Topics Ser.). (Illus.). 32p. (J). (gr. 5-8). 1992. lib. bdg. 12.60 (0-531-14138-1) Watts.
Castles: An Enduring Fantasy. Ed. by Naomi R. Kline. 1985. write for info. (0-89241-374-3) PSC Art Gall.
Castles: Their Construction & History. Sidney Toy. LC 85-4598. 256p. 1985. reprint ed. pap. 6.95 (0-486-24898-4) Dover.
***Castles: Variations on An Original Theme.** Gomer Pr. Staff. 90p. 1993. pap. 20.00 (0-86383-956-8, Pub. by Gomer Pr UK) St Mut.
Castles & Cannon. Bryan H. O'Neil. LC 74-30843. (Illus.). 121p. 1975. reprint ed. text ed. 35.00 (0-8371-7933-5, ONCC, Greenwood Pr) Greenwood.
Castles & Cathedrals. John Robottom. (Longman Origin Ser.). 1991. pap. text ed. 10.64 (0-582-08250-1) Longman.
Castles & Cathedrals: The Architecture of Power. David Aldred. (Cambridge History Programme Ser.). (Illus.). 64p. (C). 1993. pap. 9.95 (0-521-42842-4) Cambridge U Pr.
Castles & Clouds. David A. Wilson. 44p. (Orig.). 1980. pap. 3.00 (0-934852-21-9) Lorien Hse.
Castles & Fortresses. Robin S. Oggins. LC 94-9454. 1994. write for info. (1-56799-095-9, MetroBooks) M Friedman Pub Grp Inc.
Castles & Mansions. Alan James. (Houses & Homes Ser.). (Illus.). 32p. (J). (gr. 2-5). 1989. 13.50 (0-8225-2128-8, Lerner Publctns) Lerner Group.
Castles & Other Dreams. Nelson A. Ossorio & Michele B. Salvadeo. (Life's Roadmap Ser.). (Illus.). 60p. (J). (gr. 4-6). 1994. pap. 6.95 (1-56721-065-1) Twnty-Fifth Cent Pr.
Castles & Other Interesting Places in Germany. C. E. Hockett. 1993. 16.95 (0-533-10514-5) Vantage.
***Castles & Palaces.** (Information Ser.). 32p. (J). Date not set. 3.50 (0-7214-1741-8) Ladybird Bks.
Castles Burning. Lyons. 1981. pap. 2.50 (0-671-41864-5) PB.
Castles, Codes, Calligraphy. Linda Spellman. (Enrichment & Gifted Ser.). 112p. (J). (gr. 4-6). 1984. 9.95 (0-88160-103-9, LW 904) Learning Wks.
Castles, Conquest & Charters: Collected Papers. R. Allen Brown. (Illus.). 352p. 1989. 99.00 (0-85115-524-3) Boydell & Brewer.
Castles Forlorn. TSR, Inc. Staff. (Illus.). 1993. 20.00 (1-56076-645-X) TSR Inc.
Castles in Cornwall & the Isles of Scilly. Ed. by L. D. Spreadbury. (C). 1989. 45.00 (0-907566-53-7, Pub. by Dyllansow Truran UK) St Mut.
Castles in Spain: A Traveller's Guide Featuring the National Parador Inns. Michael Busselle. (Illus.). 239p. 1991. pap. 24.95 (1-85145-546-9, Pub. by Pavilion UK) Trafalgar.
Castles in the Air. Christina Dodd. 1993. mass mkt. 4.99 (0-06-108034-9, Harp PBks) HarpC.
Castles in the Air. Leonard E. Read. 191p. 1975. 12.95 (0-910614-52-0) Foun Econ Ed.
Castles in Wales & the Marches: Essays in Honour of D. J. Cathcart King. Ed. by John R. Kenyon & Richard Avent. (Illus.). 248p. (C). 1987. text ed. 75.00 (0-7083-0948-8, Pub. by U of Wales UK) Bks Intl VA.
***Castles of Athlin & Dunbayne.** Ann Radcliffe. Ed. by Alison Milbank. (World's Classics Ser.). 152p. 1995. pap. 7.95 (0-19-282357-4) OUP.
Castles of Athlin & Dunbayne: A Highland Story. Ann Radcliffe. LC 78-131336. (Gothic Novels Ser.). 1974. reprint ed. 51.95 (0-405-00808-2) Ayer.
Castles of Dyfed. Paul Davis. 77p. (C). 1987. text ed. 35.00 (0-86383-382-9, Pub. by Gomer Pr UK) St Mut.
Castles of England, Scotland, & Wales. Paul Johnson. LC 89-45046. 1992. pap. 25.00 (0-06-092351-2, PL) HarpC.
Castles of Ireland. D. Newman Johnson. (Appletree Pocket Guide Ser.). (Illus.). 96p. (Orig.). 1995. pap. 7.95 (0-86281-449-9, Pub. by Appletree Pr IE) Irish Bks Media.
Castles of Our Conscience: Social Control & the American State, 1800-1985. William G. Staples. LC 90-37620. 206p. (C). 1991. text ed. 40.00 (0-8135-1626-9) Rutgers U Pr.
Castles of Scotland. J. K. Anderson. (J). (gr. 1-9). 1992. pap. 3.95 (0-88388-111-X) Bellerophon Bks.
Castles, Pirates, Knights & Other Learning Delights. Sally Weber & Paula Glasscock. 104p. (J). (gr. 5-8). 1980. 10.95 (0-916456-92-7, GA 158) Good Apple.
Castles, Pyramids & Palaces. C. Young. (Beginner's Knowledge Ser.). (Illus.). 48p. (J). (ps-8). 1990. lib. bdg. 13.96 (0-88110-411-6, Usborne); pap. 7.95 (0-7460-0463-X, Usborne) EDC.
Castle's Towers. Adam N. Gladefly. 1992. 15.95 (0-533-10153-0) Vantage.
***Castles Within Schools: Reflections of Youth, Facilities, Teachers & Administrators.** (Illus.). 75p. (Orig.). 1995. pap. 6.50 (0-9634399-1-X) Funmakers.
Castleview. Gene Wolfe. 1991. mass mkt. 4.95 (0-8125-0625-1) Tor Bks.
Castleweaver's Tales: A Dozen Glimpses of Medieval Madness, Vol. 1. Ann Wilmer-Lasky. (Illus.). 28p. (Orig.). 1987. pap. 4.95 (0-945152-00-0) Skye Isle Ent.
Castleweaver's Tales, Vol. 2: The Madness Continues. Ann Wilmer-Lasky. (Illus.). 28p. (Orig.). 1988. pap. 4.95 (0-945152-03-5) Skye Isle Ent.
Castner's Cutthroats: Saga of the Alaska Scouts. Jim Rearden. (Illus.). 380p. 1990. 28.95 (0-935632-93-X) Wolfe Pub Co.
Castor. Ed. by V. A. Moshkin. (C). 1986. 31.00 (0-685-22789-8, Pub. by Oxford IBH II) S Asia.
Castor. Ed. by V. A. Moskin. Tr. by R. K. Dhote. 329p. (C). 1986. text ed. 95.00 (90-6191-466-3, Pub. by A A Balkema NE) Ashgate Pub Co.
Castor et Pollux. Jean-Philippe Rameau. Ed. by Theodore De Lajarte. (Chefs-d'oeuvre classiques de l'opera francaise Ser.: Vol. 30). (Illus.). 318p. (FRE.). 1970. reprint ed. pap. 35.00 (0-8450-1130-8) Broude.
Castor et Pollux see Oeuvres Completes de Jean-Philippe Rameau
***Castor Family of Pennsylvania, & the Castor Family of New York.** George C. Martin et al. (Illus.). 161p. 1994. reprint ed. lib. bdg. 36.00 (0-8328-4305-9); reprint ed. pap. 26.00 (0-8328-4306-7) Higginson Bk Co.
***Castor Oil: Its Healing Properties.** Beth M. Ley. 42p. (Orig.). 1989. pap. 3.95 (0-614-02687-3) B L Pubns.
Castor Oil to Chlorosulfuric Acid see Encyclopedia of Chemical Technology
Castores (Beavers) L. Stone. (Spanish Language Books, Set 2: Animales Norteamericanos (North American Animals)). (J). 1991. 8.95 (0-86592-832-0) Rourke Enter.
Castorland: French Refugees in the Western Adirondacks 1793-1814. Edith Pilcher. LC 85-5456. (Illus.). 254p. 1985. 24.00 (0-916346-55-2) Harbor Hill Bks.
Castrati. Sven Delblanc. Tr. by C. W. Williams. LC 79-88924. 151p. 1979. 9.95 (0-89720-020-9) Karoma.
Castrati in Opera. Angus Heriot. LC 74-1332. (Music Ser.). 243p. 1974. reprint ed. lib. bdg. 32.50 (0-306-70650-4) Da Capo.
Castrati in Opera. Angus Heriot. LC 74-22310. (Music Reprint Ser.). (Illus.). 243p. 1975. reprint ed. pap. 5.95 (0-306-80003-9) Da Capo.
***Castration & Male Rage.** Monick. 1995. pap. 16.00 (0-919123-51-1) Atrium Pubs.
***Castration of Oedipus: Psychoanalysis, Postmodernism, & Feminism.** J. C. Smith & Carla J. Ferstman. 336p. 1996. 55.00 (0-8147-8018-0); pap. 18.95 (0-8147-8019-9) NYU Pr.
Castrato. Michael Collins. 288p. 1989. 17.95 (1-55611-113-4) D I Fine.
Castrato. Michael Collins. 416p. 1991. reprint ed. pap. 4.99 (0-8439-3131-0) Dorchester Pub Co.
Castro. Sebastian Balfour. (Profiles in Power Ser.). 184p. (C). 1990. pap. text ed. 19.50 (0-582-02972-4, 78607) Longman.
Castro! Don E. Beyer. LC 92-34534. (Impact Biographies Ser.). (Illus.). 176p. (YA). (gr. 7-12). 1993. lib. bdg. 15.47 (0-531-13027-4) Watts.
Castro. Rick Castro et al. (Illus.). 120p. (Orig.). 1991. 45.00 (1-879055-26-0, DPR Pr); pap. 25.00 (1-879055-27-9, DPR Pr) Tom Finland.
***Castro.** 2nd ed. Sebastian Balfour. (Profiles in Power Ser.). 224p. (C). 1995. pap. text ed. 17.95 (0-582-24558-3, 76983) Longman.
***Castro.** 2nd ed. Sebastian Balfour. LC 94-36634. (Profiles in Power Ser.). 1995. pap. write for info. (0-582-25992-4, Pub. by Longman UK) Longman.
***Castro & Cuba Trading Card Set.** 1995. boxed 12.95 (1-56060-216-3) InBook.
Castro & the Bankers: The Mortgaging of a Revolution - 1983 Update. Ernesto F. Betancourt & Wilson P. Dizard, III. 1982. 2.00 (0-317-90487-6) Cuban Amer Natl Fndtn.
Castro & the Narcotics Connection: Special Report. 88p. 1984. 5.00 (0-317-90490-6) Cuban Amer Natl Fndtn.
Castro Complex. Mel Arrighi. 1971. pap. 4.75 (0-8222-0188-7) Dramatists Play.
Castro Convicto: La Verdadera Historia Del Ataque Al Cuartel Moncada y Del Desembarco Del "Granma" Francisco J. Kindelan. LC 91-70023. (Coleccion Cuba y Sus Jueces Ser.). (Illus.). 96p. (Orig.). (SPA.). 1991. pap. 9.95 (0-89729-588-9) Ediciones.
Castro, Israel & the PLO. David J. Kopilow. 1984. 2.00 (0-317-90489-2) Cuban Amer Natl Fndtn.
Castro Revolution: Crime Without Punishment. Roberto M. Perez & Enrique G. Encinosa. Ed. by Robert Kvederas. 250p. 1992. 25.00 (0-944273-10-6) U S Cuba Inst.
Castro Street Memories. N. A. Diaman. LC 88-2503. 206p. (Orig.). 1988. pap. 14.95 (0-931906-05-9) Persona Pr.
Castro, the Blacks, & Africa. Carlos Moore. (Afro-American Culture & Society Monograph Ser.: Vol. 8). (Illus.). 472p. 1988. pap. 23.50 (0-934934-33-9) UCLA CAAS.
Castro, the Kremlin, & Communism in Latin America. D. Bruce Jackson. LC 68-9696. (Washington Center of Foreign Policy Research. Studies in International Affairs: No. 9). 173p. reprint ed. pap. 49.40 (0-317-42307-X, 2023103) Bks Demand.
Castroism & Communism in Latin America, 1959-1976: The Varieties of Marxist-Leninist Experience. William E. Ratliff. LC 76-28554. (AEI-Hoover Policy Studies: No. 19). 260p. reprint ed. pap. 74.10 (0-8357-4444-2, 2037279) Bks Demand.
Castro's America Department: Coordinating Cuba's Support for Marxist-Leninist Violence in the Americas. Rex Hudson. 1988. 5.00 (0-685-37918-3) Cuban Amer Natl Fndtn.
Castro's Colony: Empresario Development in Texas, 1842-1865. Bobby D. Weaver. LC 84-40139. (Illus.). 176p. 1985. 17.50 (0-89096-210-3) Tex A&M Univ Pr.
Castro's Cuba, Cuba's Fidel: Reprinted with a New Concluding Chapter. rev. ed. Lee Lockwood. 380p. (C). 1990. pap. text ed. 21.50 (0-8133-1086-5) Westview.
Castro's Cuba in the 1970s. Ed. by Lester A. Sobel. LC 77-87241. 250p. reprint ed. pap. 71.30 (0-317-20502-1, 2022902) Bks Demand.
Castro's Final Hour. Andres Oppenheimer. 1993. pap. 13.00 (0-671-87299-0, Touchstone Bks) S&S Trade.
Castro's Ploy, America's Dilemma: The 1980 Cuban Boatlift. Alex Larzelere. LC 88-28941. (Illus.). 581p. (Orig.). 1988. pap. 16.00 (0-318-42912-8, S/N 008-020-01144-4) USGPO.
Castro's Puerto Rico Obsession. 1987. 4.00 (0-317-90500-7) Cuban Amer Natl Fndtn.
Casts of Thought. George Otte & Linda J. Palumbo. 695p. (C). 1990. pap. write for info. (0-02-389961-1) Macmillan.
Casual Affairs. large type ed. Lillian O'Donnell. 377p. 1991. reprint ed. lib. bdg. 20.95 (1-56054-134-2) Thorndike Pr.
Casual Attribution: From Cognitive Processes to Collective Beliefs. Miles Hewstone. (Illus.). 288p. 1990. pap. text ed. 24.95 (0-631-17165-7) Blackwell Pubs.
***Casual Body.** Powell. 1995. 16.95 (971-616-002-X) Atrium Pubs.
***Casual Fare from Daybreak Cottage.** Patricia Schmidt. Tr. by Ingram. 280p. Date not set. pap. 8.95 (0-7610-0455-6) NW Pub.
Casual Laborer & Other Essays. Carleton H. Parker. LC 76-172904. (Americana Library Ser.: No. 25). 227p. 1972. reprint ed. 25.00 (0-295-95184-2) U of Wash Pr.
Casual Occasions Cookbook. Chuck Williams & Joyce Goldstein. LC 94-18474. (Williams-Sonoma Entertaining Ser.). (Illus.). 192p. 1995. 34.95 (1-875137-18-1) Weldon Owen.
Casual Reasoning: A Systems Approach. John Charles Francis. (Studies in Cybernetics: Vol. 23). 119p. 1992. pap. text ed. 40.00 (2-88124-854-3) Gordon & Breach.
Casual Slaughters. Robert A. Carter. 272p. 1992. 17.95 (0-89296-502-9) Mysterious Pr.
Casual Slaughters. Robert A. Carter. 272p. 1994. mass mkt. 5.50 (0-446-40302-4, Mysterious Paperbk) Warner Bks.
Casual Slaughters. large type ed. Robert A. Carter. (Cloak & Dagger Ser.). 445p. 1993. reprint ed. lib. bdg. 20.95 (1-56054-624-7) Thorndike Pr.
Casual View of America: The Home Letters of Salomon de Rothschild, 1859-1861. Salomon De Rothschild. Tr. by Sigmund Diamond. vi, 136p. 1961. 19.50 (0-8047-0053-2) Stanford U Pr.
Casual Witness: An Album of Photographs from the Hawkins Family Collection of the Museums at Stony Brook. Charles L. Sachs. LC 78-62367. (Illus.). 27p. (Orig.). 1978. pap. 4.50 (0-943924-01-4) Mus Stony Brook.
Casual You: Knitting Designs for the Family. Lee Andersen. (Unique Ser.). (Illus.). 112p. 1991. text ed. 23.95 (0-9629520-0-1) Eagle-Anderson.
Casualities, Public Opinion & U. S. Military Intervention: Implications for U. S. Regional Deterrence Strategies. Benjamin C. Schwarz. LC 94-7905. 1994. write for info. (0-8330-1526-5, MR-431-A/AF) Rand Corp.
***Casually Catered Affair, or, Who Forgot the Chocolate Cake?** Carole Curlee. (Illus.). 194p. 1980. spiral bd. 15.99 (0-9645657-0-6) Casually Catered.
Casualties. Katherine Carlson. LC 82-61652. (Minnesota Voices Project Ser.: No. 9). (Illus.). 124p. 1982. pap. 5.00 (0-89823-041-1) New Rivers Pr.
Casualties of Childhood: A Developmental Perspective on Sexual Abuse Using Projective Drawings. Bobbie Kaufman & Agnes Wohl. 224p. 1992. 29.95 (0-87630-652-0) Brunner-Mazel.
Casualties of Privilege: Essays on Prep Schools' Hidden Culture. Ed. by Louis M. Crosier. 170p. 1991. pap. 14.95 (0-9627671-0-7) Avocus Pub.
Casualties, Poems Nineteen Sixty-Six to Nineteen Sixty-Eight. John P. Clark. LC 73-113090. 63p. 1970. 14.50 (0-8419-0096-5, Africana); pap. 9.50 (0-8419-0041-8, Africana) Holmes & Meier.
Casualties Sustained by the British Army in the Korean War, 1950-1953. Ed. by Picton Publishing Staff. 85p. (C). 1987. 105.00 (0-317-90456-6, Pub. by Picton UK) St Mut.
Casualty. Heinrich Boll. Tr. by Leila Vennewitz. 192p. 1987. 16.95 (0-374-11967-8) FS&G.
Casualty. Heinrich Boll. 1989. pap. 7.95 (0-393-30599-6) Norton.

C

An Asterisk (*) at the beginning of an entry indicates that the title is appearing in BIP for the first time.

An Asterisk (*) at the beginning of an entry indicates that the title is appearing in BIP for the first time.

1081

Cat Horoscopes: For Each of Your Cat's Nine Lives. Genia Wennerstrom. (Illus.). 32p. 1992. 9.95 (0-8109-3185-0) Abrams.

***Cat in a Crimson Haze.** Carole N. Douglas. 384p. 1995. 22.95 (0-312-85901-5) Forge NYC.

***Cat in a Flap.** Shoo Rayner. (Illus.). 22p. (J). 1995. pap. 4.99 (0-14-054860-2) Puffin Bks.

Cat in Ancient Egypt. Jaromir Malek. (Illus.). 144p. (C). 1993. 29.95 (0-7141-0969-X) U of Pa Pr.

Cat in Magic, Mythology, & Religion. M. Oldfield Howey. 1989. 6.99 (0-517-68260-5) Random Hse Value.

Cat in Search of a Friend. Meshack Asare. LC 86-10583. (Illus.). 32p. (J). (ps-5). 1986. 10.95 (0-916291-07-3) Kane-Miller Bk.

Cat in Search of a Friend. Meshack Asare. LC 88-71622. (Illus.). 32p. (J). (ps-3). 1988. reprint ed. pap. 6.95 (0-86543-107-8) Africa World.

Cat in the Glass House. Lydia Adamson. 224p. 1993. pap. 3.99 (0-451-17706-1, Sig) NAL-Dutton.

Cat in the Hat. (J). 1993. 23.97 (0-679-86348-6) Random Bks Yng Read.

Cat in the Hat. Dr. Seuss. LC 56-5470. (Illus.). 72p. (J). (gr. 1-2). 1957. 7.99 (0-394-80001-X) Random Bks Yng Read.

Cat in the Hat. Dr. Seuss. LC 56-5470. (Illus.). 72p. (J). (gr. 1-2). 1966. lib. bdg. 9.99 (0-394-90001-4) Random Bks Yng Read.

Cat in the Hat. Dr. Seuss. (Beginner Book & Cassette Library). (Illus.). 64p. (J). (ps-1). 1987. audio 7.95 (0-394-89218-6) Random Bks Yng Read.

Cat in the Hat Beginner Book Dictionary. Philip D. Eastman. LC 64-1157. (Illus.). 144p. (J). (gr. k-6). 1964. 10.00 (0-394-81009-0) Random Bks Yng Read.

Cat in the Hat Beginner Book Dictionary. Philip D. Eastman. LC 64-1157. (Illus.). 144p. (J). (gr. k-6). 1984. lib. bdg. 9.99 (0-394-91009-5) Random Bks Yng Read.

Cat in the Hat Beginner Book Dictionary in French & English. Philip D. Eastman. LC 65-22650. (Illus.). 144p. (J). (gr. 2-3). 1965. 15.95 (0-394-81063-5) Beginner.

Cat in the Hat Beginner Book Dictionary in Spanish & English. Philip D. Eastman. LC 66-10688. (Illus.). 144p. (ENG & SPA.). (J). (gr. k-3). 1966. 16.00 (0-394-81542-4) Beginner.

Cat in the Hat Comes Back. Dr. Seuss. LC 58-9017. (Illus.). 72p. (J). (gr. k-3). 1958. 6.95 (0-394-80002-8); lib. bdg. 9.99 (0-394-90002-2) Random Bks Yng Read.

Cat in the Hat Comes Back. Dr. Seuss. (J). (ps-1). 1986. audio, pap. 6.95 (0-394-88327-6) Random Bks Yng Read.

Cat in the Hat Cuddly Doll & Collectible Book. Dr. Seuss. (Illus.). 70p. (J). (ps up). 1994. 15.00 (0-679-86011-8) Random Bks Yng Read.

Cat in the Hat in English & Spanish. Dr. Seuss. Tr. by Carlos Rivera. LC 67-5819. (Spanish Beginner Bks.: No. 1). (Illus.). 72p. (J). (gr. 1-2). 1967. 6.95 (0-394-81626-9) Beginner.

Cat in the Hat Songbook. Dr. Seuss. LC 67-21921. (Illus.). 72p. (J). (gr. k up). 1993. 12.00 (0-394-81695-1) Random Bks Yng Read.

Cat in the Manger. Lydia Adamson. (Alice Nestleton Mystery Ser.). 224p. 1990. pap. 3.99 (0-451-16787-2, Sig) NAL-Dutton.

***Cat in the Tree.** Roderick Hunt. (Oxford Reading Tree Ser.). (Illus.). 16p. (J). (gr. k-k). 1994. pap. 1.99 (0-19-916061-9) OUP.

Cat in the Tulips. David Evans. (Orig.). 1993. pap. 15.95 (1-873741-10-3, Pub. by Millvres Bks UK) InBook.

Cat in the Wings. Lydia Adamson. (Alice Nestleton Mystery Ser.: No. 5). 224p. (Orig.). 1992. pap. 4.50 (0-451-17336-8, Sig) NAL-Dutton.

Cat in Wolf's Clothing. Lydia Adamson. (Alice Nestleton Mystery Ser.). 224p. (Orig.). 1991. pap. 3.99 (0-451-17085-7, Sig) NAL-Dutton.

Cat in Wolf's Clothing: An Alice Nestleton Mystery. large type ed. Lydia Adamson. LC 92-36501. (General Ser.). 223p. 1993. 18.95 (0-8161-5400-7); pap. 15.95 (0-8161-5401-5) G K Hall.

Cat Inside. William S. Burroughs. LC 92-1126. (Illus.). 96p. 1992. 12.50 (0-670-84465-9, Viking) Viking Penguin.

Cat is Back at Bat. John Stadler. LC 90-24831. (Easy Reader Ser.). (Illus.). 32p. (J). (ps-2). 1991. 10.95 (0-525-44762-8, DCB) Dutton Child Bks.

Cat Is Watching. Roger A. Caras. 1990. pap. 10.00 (0-671-72443-6) S&S Trade.

Cat Is Watching: A Look at the Way Cats See Us. large type ed. Roger A. Caras. (General Ser.). 288p. 1990. 18. 95 (0-8161-5051-6, Large Print Bks); pap. 13.95 (0-8161-5052-4, Large Print Bks) G K Hall.

***Cat Journal.** (Janet Bolton Ser.). 112p. 1995. 6.95 (0-8069-3965-6) Sterling.

Cat Killer. Sandy Dengler. LC 93-1181. (Mirage Mysteries Ser.: No. 1). (Illus.). 276p. (Orig.). 1993. pap. 2.00 (1-56476-137-1, Victor Books) SP Pubns.

Cat, Kite, Bike, Cave: Four Stories, Level One, Progressive Phonics. Ernest H. Christman. LC 90-71307. (Illus.). 52p. (J). 1990. per., pap. text ed. 10.95 (0-912329-07-6) Tutorial Press.

Cat Legends, A New Beginning: Cat Nap Stories to Be Told to or among Friends of Cats. Rebecca Juul. LC 93-94281. (Illus.). 48p. (Orig.). 1994. pap. 9.95 (1-884653-45-6) Tellagain Pr.

***Cat Lips.** Mary Milton. (Illus.). 36p. (Orig.). 1994. pap. 5.00 (1-883348-05-6) Fresh Ink.

***Cat-Logo de Leyes del AOo.** 1992. 150.00 (0-614-05788-4) Michie Butterworth.

***Cat-Logo de Reglamentos de Puerto Rico.** 1992. 525.00 (0-614-05789-2) Michie Butterworth.

Cat Love: Understanding the Needs & Nature of Your Cat. Pam Johnson. Ed. by Constance Oxley. LC 89-46016. (Illus.). 256p. (Orig.). 1990. pap. 12.95 (0-88266-594-4, Garden Way Pub) Storey Comm Inc.

Cat Love Letters. Leigh W. Rutledge. LC 93-2528. 112p. 1994. 14.95 (0-525-93757-9, Dutton) NAL-Dutton.

Cat Lover & Other Stories. Wendy Owen. 128p. 1976. 24. 00 (0-7206-0104-5, Pub. by P Owen Ltd UK) Dufour.

Cat Lovers Against the Bomb: Nineteen Ninety-Five Wall Calendar. Betty Olson. (Illus.). 32p. 1994. 7.95 (0-86571-299-9) New Soc Pubs.

Cat Lovers' Book of Days. (Illus.). 128p. 1992. 10.95 (0-88363-092-3) H L Levin.

Cat-Lovers' Cookbook. Tony Lawson & Pate Lawson. LC 86-45042. (Illus.). 112p. (Orig.). 1986. pap. 7.95 (0-88266-426-3, Storey Pub) Storey Comm Inc.

Cat Lover's Cookbook. Franki B. Papai. 1993. pap. 6.95 (0-312-08904-X) St Martin.

Cat Lovers Cookbook: Recipes. Tony Lawson. LC 93-46033. 1994. 6.99 (0-517-10110-6, Pub. by Wings Bks) Random Hse Value.

Cat Lover's Diary. Shelley Tanaka. Ed. by Jenny Fanelli. (Illus.). 176p. (J). (gr. 5 up). 1984. pap. 8.95 (0-394-86613-4) Random Bks Yng Read.

Cat Lover's Dictionary: The Easy Reference Guide to Cats & Cat Care. Grace McHattie. (Illus.). 160p. (Orig.). 1994. pap. 12.95 (0-7867-0093-9) Carroll & Graf.

***Cat Lover's Notebook.** Juliette Clarke. Ed. by Helen Exley. (Illustrated Notebooks Ser.). (Illus.). 92p. 1994. 9.99 (1-85015-454-6) Exley Giftbooks.

Cat Lover's Yearbook: A Book of Cat Days & Cat Ways. Jean Moore. (Illus.). 160p. 1995. 9.98 (0-8317-5169-X) Smithmark.

Cat Made Me Buy It: A Collection of Cats Who Sold Yesterday's Products. Alice L. Muncaster & Ellen Yanow. (Illus.). 1984. pap. 12.00 (0-517-55338-4, Crown) Crown Pub Group.

Cat Man. Shereen Rutman. (Learn Today for Tomorrow, My Phonics Reader Ser.). (Illus.). 16p. (J). (ps). 1993. student ed 2.25 (1-56293-327-2) McClanahan Bk.

***Cat Mischief.** Teresa Knuckey. 1995. 8.95 (0-8062-5197-2) Carlton.

Cat Monsters & Head Pots: The Archaeology of Missouri's Pemiscot Bayou. Michael O'Brien. (Illus.). 472p. 1994. 39.95 (0-8262-0969-6) U of Mo Pr.

***Cat, Mouse & Moon.** Roxanne D. Powell. (Illus.). (J). 1994. 14.95 (0-395-59348-4) HM.

***Cat Mummies.** Kelly Trumble. LC 95-13093. (Illus.). (J). 1996. write for info. (0-395-68707-1, Clarion Bks) HM.

Cat Musculature: A Photographic Atlas. 2nd ed. Gordon M. Greenblatt. LC 80-25610. (Illus.). 32p. 1981. pap. text ed. 9.00 (0-226-30656-9) U Ch Pr.

Cat Names: The Best Book Ever. Eleanora Walker. LC 83-48941. (Illus.). 130p. (Orig.). 1984. pap. 6.95 (0-89366-244-5) Ultramarine Pub.

Cat Nap. Elizabeth Greenaway. (Cuddle Board Bks.). (Illus.). 14p. (J). (ps). 1994. bds. 2.99 (0-679-83958-5) Random Bks Yng Read.

Cat-Nappers. P. G. Wodehouse. LC 85-42604. 192p. 1990. reprint ed. pap. 10.00 (0-06-097250-5, PL) HarpC.

Cat Next Door. Elizabeth Koda-Callan. (Magic Charm Bks.). (Illus.). 40p. (J). (ps-3). 1993. 12.95 (1-56305-502-3, 3502) Workman Pub.

Cat Next Door. Betty R. Wright. LC 90-29080. (Illus.). 32p. (J). (ps-3). 1991. lib. bdg. 14.95 (0-8234-0896-5) Holiday.

Cat Notebook: Being an Illustrated Book with Quotes. 96p. pap. 5.95 (0-89471-133-4) Running Pr.

Cat of a Different Color. Lydia Adamson. 224p. 1991. pap. 3.99 (0-451-16955-7, Sig) NAL-Dutton.

Cat of a Different Color. large type ed. Lydia Adamson. (General Ser.). 200p. 1992. 18.95 (0-8161-5398-1, Large Print Bks); pap. 14.95 (0-8161-5399-X, Large Print Bks) Hall.

Cat of Many Tails. Ellery Queen. LC 88-82351. 247p. 1988. reprint ed. pap. 4.95 (0-930330-94-3, Lib Crime Classics) Intl Polygonics.

Cat on a Blue Monday. Carole N. Douglas. 384p. 1994. 21. 95 (0-312-85607-5) Forge NYC.

Cat on a Blue Monday. Carole N. Douglas. 384p. 1994. pap. 4.99 (0-8125-3441-7) Forge NYC.

Cat on a Blue Monday. Carole N. Douglas. LC 94-12830. 540p. 1994. lib. bdg. 17.95 (0-8161-7456-3) G K Hall.

Cat on a Hot Tin Roof. Tennessee Williams. 1958. pap. 8.95 (0-8222-0189-5) Dramatists Play.

Cat on a Hot Tin Roof. Tennessee Williams. 1958. pap. 4.50 (0-451-16523-3, Sig) NAL-Dutton.

Cat on a Hot Tin Roof. rev. ed. Tennessee Williams. LC 74-32032. 160p. 1975. pap. 9.95 (0-8112-0567-3, NDP398) New Directions.

***Cat on a Winning Streak.** Lydia Adamson. (Alice Nestleton Mystery Ser.). 240p. (Orig.). 1995. mass mkt. 4.50 (0-451-18082-8, Sig) NAL-Dutton.

Cat on My Shoulder. Lisa Rogak. LC 92-31333. 192p. 1993. 17.95 (0-681-41458-8) Longmeadow Pr.

***Cat on My Shoulder.** Ed. by Lisa A. Rogak. 192p. 1994. pap. 10.00 (0-380-72337-9) Avon.

Cat on the Cutting Edge: An Alice Nestleton Mystery. Lydia Adamson. 224p. (Orig.). 1994. pap. 4.50 (0-451-18080-1, Sig) NAL-Dutton.

***Cat on the Cutting Edge: An Alice Nestleton Mystery.** large type ed. Lydia Adamson. LC 94-45925. 1995. 20. 95 (0-7838-1243-4) Hall.

Cat on the Mat. Brian Wildsmith. (Illus.). 16p. (J). 1987. pap. 3.50 (0-19-272123-2) OUP.

Cat Owner's Home Veterinary Handbook. Delbert G. Carlson & James M. Giffin. LC 82-23383. (Illus.). 392p. 1983. 22.50 (0-87605-814-4) Howell Bk.

***Cat Owner's Home Veterinary Handbook.** Delbert G. Carlson et al. LC 95-6632. 1995. write for info. (0-87605-796-2) Howell Bk.

Cat Owner's Manual. Eric Allan. 1994. 9.99 (0-517-11821-1) Random Hse Value.

Cat Owners Shape up Manual: Learn Aerobics from Your Cat. Richard Porteus. 1993. pap. 5.95 (0-918259-51-7) CCC Pubns.

Cat Owner's Survival Guide. Al Brooks. (Illus.). 224p. 1994. pap. 4.95 (0-9633921-3-1) Humor Bks.

Cat Parade! Bethany Roberts. LC 93-26726. (J). 1995. write for info. (0-395-67893-5, Clarion Bks) HM.

Cat People. Gary Brandner. 1982. pap. 2.95 (0-449-14470-4) Fawcett.

Cat People Tarot. Karen Kuykendall. 64p. 1985. 14.00 (0-88079-078-4) US Games Syst.

Cat People Tarot Deck-Book Set. Karen Kuhkendall. (Illus.). 192p. 1991. 24.95 (0-88079-532-8) US Games Syst.

Cat Poems. Illus. by Trina S. Hyman. LC 86-14810. 32p. (ps-3). 1987. lib. bdg. 14.95 (0-8234-0631-8) Holiday.

Cat Poems. Joann Serger. (Illus.). 56p. (Orig.). 1993. pap. 7.95 (1-55618-119-1) Brunswick Pub.

Cat Postcard Book. Ed. by Running Press Staff. (Postcard Book Ser.). (Illus.). 64p. (Orig.). 1987. pap. 7.95 (0-89471-519-4) Running Pr.

Cat Quilts & Crafts. LaVera Langeman. LC 92-8556. (New Ser.). (Illus.). 96p. 1992. 12.95 (0-8019-8355-X) Chilton.

Cat Quotations. Ed. by Helen Exley. (Quotations Bks.). (Illus.). 60p. 1991. 6.99 (1-85015-082-6) Exley Giftbooks.

***Cat Repair Book: A Do-It-Yourself Guide for the Cat Owner.** Ruth B. James. (Illus.). 256p. (Orig.). 1995. pap. 16.95 (0-9615114-2-7) Alpine Pr.

Cat Running. Zilpha K. Snyder. LC 94-447. (J). 1994. 14.95 (0-385-31056-0) Delacorte.

***Cat Sat.** Kaitlin Rasburry. (Illus.). 32p. (J). (gr. k-3). 1995. pap. 8.95 (1-884825-15-X) Raspberry Pubns.

Cat Sat: A Study in Short & Long Vowels. Kaitlin Rasburry. (Illus.). 32p. (J). (gr. k-3). 1994. lib. bdg. 14.95 (1-884825-02-8) Raspberry Pubns.

Cat Sat on the Mat. Illus. by Carol Jones. LC 93-14341. (J). 1994. 13.95 (0-395-68392-0) HM.

Cat Scratch Fever. Tara K. Harper. 1994. mass mkt. 5.99 (0-345-38051-7) Ballantine.

Cat Scratch Fever. Robert Kelly. LC 90-46524. 150p. 1991. pap. 10.00 (0-929701-11-9) McPherson & Co.

***Cat Scratch Fever.** Bruce Richards. 224p. 1995. mass mkt. 3.99 (0-8217-4981-1) Windsor NY.

Cat Sitter Mystery. Carol Adorjan. 80p. 1976. pap. 2.95 (0-380-70094-8, Camelot) Avon.

Cat Sold It! The Feline Stars of the Advertising World. Alice L. Muncaster & Ellen Y. Sawyer. (Illus.). 96p. 1987. pap. 14.00 (0-517-56303-7, Crown) Crown Pub Group.

Cat Stevens Complete. (Illus.). 328p. 1988. pap. 24.95 (0-8256-1183-0, AM70624) Music Sales.

Cat Stevens Greatest Hits. (Illus.). 60p. 1988. pap. 11.95 (0-8256-1196-2, AM71208) Music Sales.

Cat Steven's Greatest Hits: Song Tab Edition. (Illus.). 96p. 1991. pap. 14.95 (0-8256-1328-0, AM87474) Music Sales.

Cat Story. R. C. Whatling. 16p. (J). (gr. 7-10). 1986. 35.00 (0-7223-2012-4, Pub. by A H S Ltd UK) St Mut.

***Cat Sweaters & Cushions: To Knit by Hand or Machine.** Val Love. (Illus.). 16p. (Orig.). 1994. pap. 12.00 (1-886828-01-6) Dovetail Desgn.

***Cat Tails: Book of Days.** RH Value Publishing Staff. 1995. pap. 12.99 (0-517-12138-7) Random.

Cat Tales. Ed. by Suzanne Beilenson. (Illus.). 48p. 1992. 7.99 (0-88088-074-0) Peter Pauper.

Cat Tales. Daisybelle Elkins & Denise Elkins. 45p. 1993. pap. 5.95 (0-9637261-0-2) Elkins Pr.

Cat Tales. Illus. by Robin Upward. LC 88-40394. 96p. 1989. pap. 12.95 (0-670-82692-8, Viking Studio) Studio Bks.

Cat Tales: Classic Stories from Favorite Writers. Photos by Robin Upward. (Illus.). 96p. 1993. pap. 8.95 (0-14-011949-3, Viking Studio) Studio Bks.

Cat Tales: Folktales Collected & Retold. Malachi McCormick. 1989. 14.00 (0-517-57256-7, C P Pubs) Crown Pub Group.

***Cat Tales: Lessons in Love from Guideposts.** Majorie Holmes et al. LC 94-33296. 96p. (Orig.). 1995. pap. 7.00 (0-687-01366-6) Dimen for Liv.

Cat Tales: The Life & Times of Cats of This Century. Grace McHattie. (Illus.). 128p. 1992. 9.95 (0-681-41570-3) Longmeadow Pr.

***Cat Talk.** Ariel Books Staff. (Illus.). 368p. 1995. pap. 4.95 (0-8362-0707-6) Andrews & McMeel.

Cat Talk: Over Three Hundred Questions about Cats Answered by Talk Radio's Favorite Veterinarian. Jim Humphries. 1993. pap. 14.95 (1-56530-101-3) Summit TX.

Cat Talk: What Your Cat Is Trying to Tell You. Carole C. Wilbourn. 168p. 1991. pap. 9.95 (1-879955-00-8) Ntl Syndictns.

Cat That Barked. rev. ed. Crystal Zapata. LC 88-36660. (J). (gr. 2-6). 1989. 4.00 (0-915541-71-8) Star Bks Inc.

Cat That Climbed the Christmas Tree. (Golden Story Book 'n' Tape Ser.). (Illus.). 24p. (J). (ps-3). Date not set. audio write for info. (0-307-14194-2, 14194-01) Western Pub.

***Cat That Climbed the Christmas Tree Little Golden Book.** Little Golden Book Staff. (J). 1994. pap. 1.59 (0-307-00150-4) Western Pub.

Cat That Could Spell Mississippi. Laura Hawkins. LC 92-8025. 160p. (J). (gr. 3-5). 1992. 13.95 (0-395-61627-1) HM.

***Cat That Sat: Level 1.** School Zone Staff. (J). (ps-3). 1994. pap. 3.95 (0-88743-432-0) Sch Zone Pub Co.

Cat That Walked by Himself. Rudyard Kipling. LC 90-34357. (J). 1989. 11.95 (0-85953-276-3) Childs Play.

Cat That Wasn't There. Stella Whitelaw. 240p. 1992. 3.99 (0-451-17255-8) NAL-Dutton.

Cat, the Crow, & the Banyan Tree. Penelope Lively. LC 93-22355. (Illus.). 32p. (J). (ps up). 1994. 14.95 (1-56402-325-7) Candlewick Pr.

Cat, Thy Name Is Edith. Roz Young. LC 91-62479. (Illus.). 200p. (Orig.). 1991. 22.95 (0-9619637-7-8) Orange Frazer.

***Cat Traps.** Molly Coxe. LC 94-34989. (Early Step into Reading Ser.). (J). 1995. write for info. (0-679-86441-5); 7.99 (0-679-96441-X) Random.

Cat Tricks: Pop-up Kittycats. Ruth Tilden. (J). (ps-3). 1994. pap. 7.95 (0-671-88305-4, Litl Simon S&S) S&S Childrens.

Cat Who Ate Danish Modern. Lilian J. Braun. 192p. 1986. mass mkt. 5.99 (0-515-08712-2) Jove Pubns.

Cat Who Blew the Whistle. Lilian J. Braun. 240p. 1995. 19. 95 (0-399-13981-8, Putnam) Putnam Pub Group.

***Cat Who Blew the Whistle.** large type ed. Lilian J. Braun. LC 95-2632. 352p. Date not set. pap. 17.95 (0-7838-1253-1, Large Print Bks) Hall.

***Cat Who Blew the Whistle.** large type ed. Lilian J. Braun. LC 95-2632. 352p. 1995. 22.95 (0-7838-1252-3, Large Print Bks) Hall.

***Cat Who Came for Christmas.** Cleveland Amory. (Illus.). 224p. 1995. pap. 8.95 (0-14-025273-8, Penguin Bks) Viking Penguin.

Cat Who Came for Christmas. large type ed. Cleveland Amory. (General Ser.). 336p. 1988. lib. bdg. 18.95 (0-8161-4644-6) G K Hall.

Cat Who Came for Christmas. Cleveland Amory. (Contemporary American Fiction Ser.). 224p. 1988. reprint ed. pap. 8.95 (0-14-099706-7, Penguin Bks) Viking Penguin.

***Cat Who Came to Breakfast.** Lilian J. Braun. 288p. (Orig.). 1995. mass mkt. 5.99 (0-515-11564-9) Jove Pubns.

Cat Who Came to Breakfast. Lilian J. Braun. 240p. (Orig.). 1994. 19.95 (0-399-13868-4, Putnam) Putnam Pub Group.

Cat Who Conducted with His Tail. Martha E. Radke. LC 81-90803. (Illus.). 28p. (Orig.). (J). (ps-3). 1982. pap. 1.95 (0-9607994-0-0) G E Radke.

Cat Who Could Read Backwards. Lilian J. Braun. 192p. 1986. mass mkt. 4.99 (0-515-09017-4) Jove Pubns.

Cat Who Couldn't Meow. Michele Spirn. (J). (ps-1). 1988. 8.49 (0-87386-054-3); audio 16.99 (0-685-25195-0); pap. 1.95 (0-87386-050-0); audio, pap. 9.95 (0-685-25196-9) Jan Prods.

Cat Who Drank Too Much. LeClair Bissell & Richard Watherwax. (Illus.). 48p. (ENG & SPA.). (J). (gr. 4 up). 1982. pap. 5.00 (0-911153-00-4) Bibulophile Pr.

Cat Who Drank Too Much. LeClair Bissell & Richard Watherwax. (Illus.). 48p. (ENG & SPA.). (J). (gr. 4 up). 1982. Spanish ed., 03/1984, pap. write for info. (0-911153-01-2) Bibulophile Pr.

Cat Who Escaped from Steerage. Evelyn W. Mayerson. LC 90-32890. 80p. (J). (gr. 4-6). 1990. text ed. 13.95 (0-684-19209-8, C Scribner Sons Young) S&S Childrens.

Cat Who Had Fourteen Tales. Lilian J. Braun. 1988. mass mkt. 4.99 (0-515-09497-8) Jove Pubns.

Cat Who Had Two Lives. Sally Huxley. LC 93-72579. (Illus.). 160p. 1994. 18.95 (1-55611-386-2) D I Fine.

***Cat Who Had Two Lives.** Sally Huxley. 1994. mass mkt. 4.99 (0-449-22320-5, Crest) Fawcett.

Cat Who Knew a Cardinal. Lilian J. Braun. 1992. mass mkt. 5.50 (0-515-10786-7) Jove Pubns.

Cat Who Knew a Cardinal. large type ed. Lilian J. Braun. (General Ser.). 316p. 1992. text ed. 19.95 (0-8161-5278-0, Large Print Bks); pap. 16.95 (0-8161-5279-9, Large Print Bks) Hall.

Cat Who Knew Shakespeare. Lilian J. Braun. 1988. mass mkt. 4.99 (0-515-09582-6) Jove Pubns.

Cat Who Learned to Sail. LC 89-64308. (Illus.). 32p. (J). (gr. 4-8). 1991. 13.95 (0-931595-07-X); pap. 7.95 (0-931595-04-5) Seascape Enters.

Cat Who Lived High. Lilian J. Braun. 1991. mass mkt. 4.99 (0-515-10566-X) Jove Pubns.

Cat Who Looked for a House. Bella Baram. Tr. by David Kriss. (Hippy Ser.). (Illus.). 24p. (Orig.). (J). (ps). 1992. pap. text ed. 3.00 (1-56134-140-1) Dushkin Pub.

Cat Who Loved Red. Lynn Salem & Josie Stewart. (Illus.). 8p. (J). (gr. 1). 1992. pap. 3.50 (1-880612-03-8) Seedling Pubns.

Cat Who Loved to Sing. Nonny Hogrogian. LC 86-27358. (Illus.). 40p. (J). (ps-2). 1988. lib. bdg. 13.99 (0-394-99004-8) Knopf Bks Yng Read.

Cat Who Moved a Mountain. Lilian J. Braun. 272p. 1992. mass mkt. 4.99 (0-515-10950-9) Jove Pubns.

Cat Who Moved a Mountain. large type ed. Lilian J. Braun. LC 92-31043. (General Ser.). 379p. 1993. 20.95 (0-8161-5550-X); pap. 16.95 (0-8161-5551-8) G K Hall.

***Cat Who Moved a Mountain.** large type ed. Lillian J. Braun. 384p. 1979. 6.99 (1-56865-064-7, GuildAmerica) Dblday Bk Music.

Cat Who Played Brahms. Lilian J. Braun. 192p. (Orig.). 1987. mass mkt. 5.99 (0-515-09050-6) Jove Pubns.

Cat Who Played Post Office. Lilian J. Braun. 1987. mass mkt. 5.99 (0-515-09320-3) Jove Pubns.

Cat Who Returned Nine Times. Joan P. Grubbs. Ed. & Illus. by Joan Abell. 50p. (Orig.). (J). (gr. 1-4). 1993. reprint ed. 25.00 (1-56611-060-2); reprint ed. pap. 15.00 (1-56611-061-0) Jonas.

Cat Who Saw Red. Lilian J. Braun. 192p. 1986. mass mkt. 4.99 (0-515-09016-6) Jove Pubns.

Cat Who Saw Red; The Cat Who Played Brahms; The Cat Who Played Post Office. Lilian J. Braun. LC 93-632. 608p. 1993. 11.98 (0-399-13885-4, Putnam) Putnam Pub Group.

Cat Who Sniffed Glue. Lilian J. Braun. (J). 1989. mass mkt. 5.99 (0-515-09954-6) Jove Pubns.

Cat Who Talked to Ghosts. Lilian J. Braun. 1990. mass mkt. 4.99 (0-515-10265-2) Jove Pubns.

C

An Asterisk (*) at the beginning of an entry indicates that the title is appearing in BIP for the first time.

An Asterisk (*) at the beginning of an entry indicates that the title is appearing in BIP for the first time.

1083

C

Catalog of Government Inventions Available for Licensing, 1990. Intro. by Edward J. Lehmann. (Orig.). 1991. pap. text ed. 54.00 (*0-934213-30-5*, PB91-100206) Natl Tech Info.

Catalog of Government Inventions Available for Licensing, 1991. Intro. & Pref. by Edward J. Lehmann. (Orig.). 1992. pap. text ed. 59.00 (*0-934213-35-6*, PB92-100171) Natl Tech Info.

Catalog of Government Inventions Available for Licensing, 1992. Ed. & Intro. by Edward J. Lehmann. (Orig.). 1993. pap. text ed. 59.00 (*0-934213-38-0*, PB93-128205) Natl Tech Info.

Catalog of Government Patents: Inventions Available for Licensing to U.S. Businesses, 1985. Ed. by Edward J. Lehmann. LC 86-116175. (Orig.). 1986. pap. 29.00 (*0-934213-01-1*) Natl Tech Info.

Catalog of Government Publications, Economics Division, 40 vols., Set. New York Public Library, Research Libraries Staff. 1972. lib. bdg. 4,350.00 (*0-8161-0781-5*, Hall Library) G K Hall.

Catalog of Government Publications, Supplement 1974, 2 vols., Set. New York Public Library, Research Libraries Staff. 1976. lib. bdg. 240.00 (*0-8161-0060-8*, Hall Library) G K Hall.

Catalog of Governments Patents: Inventions Available for Licensing to U. S. Businesses, 1986. Ed. by Edward J. Lehmann. LC 87-125670. 274p. (Orig.). 1987. pap. 33.00 (*0-934213-06-2*) Natl Tech Info.

Catalog of Greek Coins in the British Museum: Sicily see Coins of Ancient Sicily

Catalog of Greek Coins in the British Museum-Syria. P. Gardner. (Illus.). 1982. reprint ed. lib. bdg. 30.00 (*0-942666-21-6*) S J Durst.

Catalog of GTO I. D. Numbers, 1964-74. Cars & Parts Magazine Editors. (Illus.). 320p. 1993. pap. 19.95 (*1-880524-07-4*) Cars & Parts.

Catalog of Judea Capta Coinage. Howard B. Brin. (Illus.). 1986. pap. 16.95 (*0-934682-13-5*) Emmett.

Catalog of Lost Books: An Annotated & Seriously Addled Collection of Great Books That Should Have Been Written, But Never Were. Thaddeus F. Tuleja. 1989. pap. 7.95 (*0-449-90347-8*, Columbine) Fawcett.

Catalog of Manuscripts in the American Philosophical Society Library Including the Archival Shelflist, 10 vols. Whitfield J. Bell, Jr. LC 77-297105. 1970. text ed. 2,250.00 (*0-8371-4975-4*, AQE/, Greenwood Pr) Greenwood.

Catalog of Manuscripts of the Folger Shakespeare Library, 3 vols, Set. Folger Shakespeare Library Editors, Washington, D. C. (Library Catalogs). 1970. lib. bdg. 300.00 (*0-8161-0888-9*, Hall Library) G K Hall.

Catalog of Manuscripts of the Folger Shakespeare Library: First Supplement. Folger Shakespeare Library Staff. (Supplements Ser.). 524p. 1988. lib. bdg. 190.00 (*0-8161-0466-2*) G K Hall.

Catalog of Manuscripts of the Massachusetts Historical Society: First Supplement. Massachusetts Historical Society Staff. 1980. lib. bdg. 255.00 (*0-8161-0850-1*, Hall Library) G K Hall.

Catalog of Manuscripts of the Massachusetts Historical Society, Boston, 7 Vols, Set. Massachusetts Historical Society, Boston Staff. 1970. lib. bdg. 805.00 (*0-8161-0822-6*, Hall Library) G K Hall.

Catalog of Maps, Ships' Papers & Logbooks. Mariners Museum Library - Newport News - Virginia Staff. 1970. lib. bdg. 110.00 (*0-8161-0686-X*, Hall Library) G K Hall.

Catalog of Marine Photographs, 5 Vols, Set. Mariners Museum Library - Newport News - Virginia Staff. 1970. lib. bdg. 545.00 (*0-8161-0685-1*, Hall Library) G K Hall.

Catalog of Marine Prints & Paintings, 3 Vols, Set. Mariners Museum Library - Newport News - Virginia Staff. 1970. lib. bdg. 330.00 (*0-8161-0684-3*, Hall Library) G K Hall.

Catalog of Materials: Stockbridge-Munsee Historical Library Museum. Stockbridge-Munsee Historical Library Museum Committee Staff. (Illus.). 50p. (Orig.). (C). 1980. pap. text ed. 2.00 (*0-935790-00-4*) Muh-He-Con-Neew.

Catalog of Maya Hieroglyphs. J. Eric Thompson. (Civilization of the American Indian Ser.: Vol. 62). (Illus.). 1991. 39.95 (*0-8061-0520-8*); pap. 21.95 (*0-8061-2260-9*) U of Okla Pr.

***Catalog of Mean UBV Data on Stars.** Jean-Claude Mermilliod & Monique Mermilliod. 1994. write for info. (*0-387-94355-2*); write for info. (*3-540-94355-2*) Spr-Verlag.

Catalog of Meteorites from Victoria Land, Antarctica, 1978-1980. Ed. by Ursula B. Marvin & Brian Mason. LC 81-607125. (Smithsonian Contributions to the Earth Sciences Ser.: No. 24). 101p. reprint ed. pap. 28.80 (*0-317-08558-1*, 2017827) Bks Demand.

Catalog of Military Suppliers: A Complete Source Listing of over One Thousand Suppliers of Military Equipment. 1986. lib. bdg. 250.00 (*0-8490-3808-1*) Gordon Pr.

Catalog of Museum Publications & Media. 2nd ed. Ed. by Paul Wasserman. LC 79-22633. 1064p. 1979. 275.00 (*0-8103-0388-4*) Gale.

***Catalog of Music for the Cornett.** Michael Collver & Bruce Dickey. LC 94-44769. (Publications of the Early Music Institute). 1995. pap. write for info. (*0-253-20974-9*) Ind U Pr.

***Catalog of Musical Instruments Foreign & American of 1881.** J.C. Haynes & Co. Staff. (Illus.). 140p. 1995. pap. 25.00 (*0-87556-796-7*) Saifer.

Catalog of Mustang I. D. Numbers, 1964-5-1993. Cars & Parts Magazine Editors. (Matching Number Ser.). (Illus.). 245p. 1993. pap. text ed. 19.95 (*1-880524-10-4*) Cars & Parts.

Catalog of National ISDN Solutions for Selected NIUF Applications. 382p. (Orig.). (C). 1993. pap. text ed. 95.00 (*1-56806-517-5*) Diane Pub.

Catalog of Nonsmoking Hotel Rooms: A Consumer Service. rev. ed. Cindy Meek. 146p. (Orig.). 1986. pap. 43.50 (*0-938619-24-1*) Live Oak TX.

***Catalog of Oldsmobile I.D. Number 1964-1991.** (Illus.). 204p. 1995. pap. 19.95 (*1-880524-17-1*) Cars & Parts.

Catalog of Papal Medals. F. Lincoln. 1990. reprint ed. pap. 10.00 (*0-915262-83-5*) S J Durst.

Catalog of Periodical Literature in the Social & Behavioral Sciences Section, Library of the Institute for Sex Research, Including Supplement to Monographs, 1973-1975, 4 vols., Set. Indiana University, Institute for Sex Research Staff. 1976. lib. bdg. 435.00 (*0-8161-0041-1*, Hall Library) G K Hall.

Catalog of Pontiac GTO I.D. Numbers 1964-74. Cars & Parts Magazine Staff. (Matching Number Ser.). (Illus.). 101p. 1993. pap. 19.95 (*0-685-71991-X*) Cars & Parts.

Catalog of Pontiac I. D. Numbers 1964-74. Cars & Parts Magazine Staff. (Matching Number Ser.). (Illus.). 101p. 1993. pap. 19.95 (*0-685-72189-2*) Cars & Parts.

Catalog of Pre-1900 Vocal Manuscripts in the Music Library, University of California at Berkeley. John A. Emerson. (UC Publications in Catalogs & Bibliographies: Vol. 4). 372p. (Orig.). (C). 1988. 50.00 (*0-520-09703-3*) U CA Pr.

Catalog of Prenatally Diagnosed Conditions. 2nd ed. David D. Weaver. 416p. 1992. text ed. 75.00 (*0-8018-4415-0*) Johns Hopkins.

Catalog of Printed Books of the Folger Shakespeare Library, 28 vols, Set. Folger Shakespeare Library Editors, Washington, D. C. 1970. lib. bdg. 2,575.00 (*0-8161-0887-0*, Hall Library) G K Hall.

Catalog of Prints, Engravings, Photographs, & Original Art Materials in the Folger Shakespeare Library, 4 vols. (Illus.). 2185p. 1985. lib. bdg. 605.00 (*0-8161-0438-7*) G K Hall.

Catalog of Psychiatric Procedures. Frank T. Rafferty. 136p. 1988. 21.00 (*0-88048-314-8*) Am Psychiatric.

Catalog of Publications: Audio-Visuals & Computer Programs. 1995. write for info. (*0-318-64389-8*) Asphalt Inst.

Catalog of Publications, 1980-89: PHS 90-1301. write for info. (*0-318-69630-4*) Natl Ctr Health Stats.

Catalog of Published Works for String Orchestra & Piano by 20th Century American Women Composers. Ellen G. Schlegel. (Illus.). 64p. (Orig.). 1992. pap. 11.95 (*1-56883-002-5*) Colonial Pr AL.

***Catalog of Regulations, 2 vols., Set.** Date not set. ring bd. 525.00 (*0-614-05790-6*) Michie Butterworth.

Catalog of Research Issues for Understanding National Economic Planning. Kenneth W. Clarkson. LC 76-1551. 1976. pap. 15.00 (*0-916770-01-X*) Law & Econ U Miami.

Catalog of Roycrofters Furniture & Other Things see Roycroft Furniture Catalog, 1906

***Catalog of Russian Christian Serials, 1801-1917, 3 vols.** Comp. by Grigorii L. Andreev. 1995. lib. bdg. 250.00 (*0-614-01788-2*) N Ross.

***Catalog of Russian Christica Serials, 1801-1917 Vols. 1-3, Vol. 1.** Comp. by Grigorii L. Andreev. 1995. lib. bdg. write for info. (*0-88354-132-7*) N Ross.

***Catalog of Russian Christica Serials, 1801-1917 Vols. 1-3, Vol. 2.** Comp. by Grigorii L. Andreev. 1995. lib. bdg. write for info. (*0-88354-133-5*) N Ross.

***Catalog of Russian Christica Serials, 1801-1917 Vols. 1-3, Vol. 3.** Comp. by Grigorii L. Andreev. 1995. lib. bdg. write for info. (*0-88354-134-3*) N Ross.

Catalog of Silver, Copper, Pewter & Toleware. Ed. by Sandra S. Tinkham. (Index of American Design Ser.: Pt. 9). 32p. (Orig.). 1980. pap. text ed. 49.00 (*0-914146-79-3*) Chadwyck-Healey.

***Catalog of Small Business Research.** 1994. write for info. (*0-615-00243-9*) US SBA.

Catalog of Spanish Rare Books (1701-1974) in the Library of the University of Illinois & in Selected North American Libraries. Joseph L. Laurenti. LC 84-47693. (American University Studies: Romance Languages & Literature: Ser. II, Vol. 12). 215p. (Orig.). 1984. text ed. 23.40 (*0-8204-0129-3*) P Lang Pubs.

Catalog of Special & Private Presses in the Rare Book Division, the Research Libraries of the New York Public Library, 2 vols., Set. 1978. lib. bdg. 195.00 (*0-8161-0097-7*, Hall Library) G K Hall.

Catalog of Special Plane Curves. J. Dennis Lawrence. LC 72-80280. (Illus.). 218p. 1972. pap. text ed. 8.95 (*0-486-60288-5*) Dover.

Catalog of Statistics Publications in the NCSC Library. National Center for State Courts Staff. 143p. 1984. 9.00 (*0-685-16629-5*, NCSC-045) Natl Ctr St Courts.

Catalog of Teaching Aids & Resources. rev. ed. Ed. by Frank H. Stone. 271p. 1987. write for info. (*0-318-61705-6*) Soc Wine Educators.

Catalog of Teratogenic Agents. 7th ed. Thomas H. Shepard. 660p. 1992. text ed. 95.00 (*0-8018-4414-2*) Johns Hopkins.

***Catalog of Teratogenic Agents.** 8th ed. Thomas H. Shepard. LC 95-8539. 560p. 1995. text ed. 110.00x (*0-8018-5182-3*) Johns Hopkins.

Catalog of Textiles, Costume & Jewelry. Ed. by Sandra S. Tinkham. (Index of American Design Ser.: Pt. 1). 120p. (Orig.). 1979. pap. 25.00 (*0-914146-63-7*) Chadwyck-Healey.

Catalog of the Arabic Collection. Stanford University, Hoover Institution on War, Revolution & Peace Staff. 1970. lib. bdg. 110.00 (*0-8161-0170-1*, Hall Library) G K Hall.

Catalog of the Arabic Collection, Harvard University, 6 vols. (Illus.). 1983. lib. bdg. 1,660.00 (*0-8161-0398-4*) G K Hall.

Catalog of the Art & Design of Utopian & Religious Communities. Ed. by Sandra S. Tinkham. (Index of American Design Ser.: Pt. 2). 90p. (Orig.). 1979. pap. 49.00 (*0-914146-65-3*) Chadwyck-Healey.

Catalog of the Arthur & Elizabeth Schlesinger Library on the History of Women in America: The Manuscript Inventories & the Catalogs of Manuscripts, Books, & Periodicals, 10 vols. 2nd ed. Radcliffe College Editors. 7500p. 1983. lib. bdg. 2,290.00 (*0-8161-0425-5*, Hall Library) G K Hall.

Catalog of the Atmospheric Sciences Collection in the Library & Information Services Division, National Oceanic & Atmospheric Administration. 1978. lib. bdg. 2,405.00 (*0-8161-0240-6*, Hall Library) G K Hall.

Catalog of the Avery Memorial Architectural Library, 19 Vols, Set. 2nd enl. ed. Columbia University Editors. 1977. lib. bdg. 1,750.00 (*0-8161-0779-3*, Hall Library) G K Hall.

Catalog of the Ceramics Collection of the Nora Eccles Harrison Museum of Art. Intro. by Steven W. Rosen. (Illus.). 72p. (Orig.). 1993. pap. write for info. (*1-882710-00-2*) USU N E H Mus.

Catalog of the Charles L. Blockson Afro-American Collection. Charles L. Blockson. (Illus.). 900p. 1991. 69.95 (*0-87722-749-7*) Temple U Pr.

Catalog of the Chinese Collection, 13 Vols, Set. Stanford University, Hoover Institution on War, Revolution & Peace Staff. 1970. lib. bdg. 1,355.00 (*0-8161-0168-X*, Hall Library) G K Hall.

Catalog of the Chinese Collection: Second Supplement, 2 vols., Set. Stanford University, Hoover Institution on War, Revolution & Peace Staff. 1977. lib. bdg. 300.00 (*0-8161-0039-X*, Hall Library) G K Hall.

Catalog of the Chinese Collection First Supplement, 2 vols., Set. Stanford University, Hoover Institution on War, Revolution & Peace Staff. 1972. lib. bdg. 325.00 (*0-8161-1046-8*, Hall Library) G K Hall.

Catalog of the Clarence V. Mader Archive, Music Library, University of California at Los Angeles. University of California, Music Library Staff. (Illus.). 275p. (Orig.). 1980. pap. 35.00 (*0-934082-08-1*, Ruth & C Mader) Theodore Front.

Catalog of the Communications Library, 3 vols., Set. Ed. by University of Illinois, Communications Library Staff. 1975. lib. bdg. 365.00 (*0-8161-1174-X*, Hall Library) G K Hall.

Catalog of the Conservation Library, 6 vols, Set. Denver Public Library Staff. 1974. lib. bdg. 630.00 (*0-8161-1113-8*, Hall Library) G K Hall.

Catalog of the Cooper-Hewitt Museum of Design Library of the Smithsonian Institution Libraries, 6 vols., Set. Smithsonian Institution, Cooper-Hewitt Museum Library Staff. 3700p. 1993. lib. bdg. 1,150.00 (*0-8161-0525-1*, Hall Reference) Macmillan.

Catalog of the Defoe Collection in the Boston Public Library. Boston Public Library Staff. 1970. lib. bdg. 75.00 (*0-8161-0731-9*, Hall Library) G K Hall.

Catalog of the Dental School Library, 8 vols., Set. Ed. by Minnie Organos. 1978. lib. bdg. 825.00 (*0-8161-0239-2*, Hall Library) G K Hall.

Catalog of the Diptera of the Australasian & Oceanian Regions. Ed. by Neal L. Evenhuis. 1990. 100.00 (*0-930897-37-4*, SP86) Bishop Mus.

Catalog of the Diptera of the Oriental Region, Vol. 2: Suborder Brachycera, Suborder Cyclorrhapha Through Division Aschiza. Mercedes D. Delfinado & D. Elmo Hardy. LC 74-174544. 480p. 1975. text ed. 30.00 (*0-8248-0274-8*) UH Pr.

Catalog of the Documentation Center Interafrican Committee for Hydraulic Studies. Interafrican Committee for Hydraulic Studies. 1977. lib. bdg. 190.00 (*0-8161-0091-8*, Hall Library) G K Hall.

Catalog of the Drawings Collection of the Royal Institute of British Architects, 3 vols., C-F. 1968. reprint ed. write for info. (*0-576-15996-4*, Pub. by Gregg Intl Pubs UK) Gregg Intl.

Catalog of the Drawings Collection of the Royal Institute of British Architects, 3 vols., G-K. 1968. reprint ed. write for info. (*0-576-15554-3*, Pub. by Gregg Intl Pubs UK) Gregg Intl.

Catalog of the E. Azalia Hackley Memorial Collection of Negro Music, Dance & Drama. Detroit Public Library Staff. 1979. lib. bdg. 110.00 (*0-8161-0299-6*, Hall Library) G K Hall.

Catalog of the Edgar Fahs Smith Memorial Collection in the History of Chemistry. University of Pennsylvania Staff. 1970. lib. bdg. 100.00 (*0-8161-0522-7*, Hall Library) G K Hall.

Catalog of the Ephemeroptera of the Indian Subregion. M. D. Hubbard & W. L. Peters. (Oriental Insects Supplements Ser.: No. 9). 1978. 30.00 (*1-877711-19-5*) Assoc Pubs FL.

Catalog of the Flora of Colorado. Ronald C. Wittmann & William A. Weber. 272p. 1991. 34.95 (*0-87081-243-2*) Univ Pr Colo.

Catalog of the Foreign Relations Library, 9 Vols, Set. Council on Foreign Relations, Inc. Staff. 1970. lib. bdg. 960.00 (*0-8161-0840-4*, Hall Library) G K Hall.

Catalog of the Foreign Relations Library, First Supplement. Council on Foreign Relations, Inc. Staff. 1980. lib. bdg. 375.00 (*0-8161-0306-2*, Hall Library) G K Hall.

Catalog of the Friends Historical Library Book & Serial Collections, 6 vols., Set. Swarthmore College Staff. 1982. lib. bdg. 720.00 (*0-8161-0376-3*, Hall Library) G K Hall.

Catalog of the Genera of Recent Fishes. William N. Eschmeyer. Ed. by Tomio Iwamoto. 630p. 1990. 55.00 (*0-940228-23-8*) Calif Acad Sci.

Catalog of the Gerhard Mayer Collection of Rilkeiana. Ed. by Sara De Mundo Lo. 400p. 1988. lib. bdg. 95.00 (*0-8161-0468-9*, Hall Library) G K Hall.

Catalog of the German Americana Collection, University of Cincinnati, 2 vols., Set. Ed. by Don H. Tolzman. 749p. 1990. lib. bdg. 215.00 (*3-598-41241-X*) K G Saur.

Catalog of the Hampton L. Carson Collection Illustrative of the the Growth of the Common Law, 2 Vols, Set. Free Library of Philadelphia Staff. 1970. lib. bdg. 220.00 (*0-8161-0490-5*, Hall Library) G K Hall.

Catalog of the Harvard University Fine Arts Library, 15 vols. Harvard University Staff. 1971. Catalogue of Auction Sales Catalogues. lib. bdg. 115.00 (*0-8161-0105-1*, Hall Library) G K Hall.

Catalog of the Harvard University Fine Arts Library, 15 vols., Set. Harvard University Staff. 1971. lib. bdg. 1,925.00 (*0-8161-0919-2*, Hall Library) G K Hall.

Catalog of the Hebrew Collection, Harvard University Library, 11 vols. in 3 pts., Set. 5500p. 1993. lib. bdg. 2,755.00 (*3-598-22620-9*) U Pubns Amer.

Catalog of the Heteroptera, or True Bugs, of Canada & the Continental United States. Ed. by Thomas J. Henry & Richard C. Froeschner. LC 87-38212. (Illus.). 878p. 1988. text ed. 58.50 (*0-916846-44-X*) E J Brill.

Catalog of the Hoose Library of Philosophy, 6 Vols, Set. University of Southern California, Los Angeles Staff. 1970. lib. bdg. 655.00 (*0-8161-0816-1*, Hall Library) G K Hall.

Catalog of the Islamic Coins, Glass Weights, Dies & Medals in the Egyptian National Library, Cairo. N. D. Nicol et al. (American Research Center in Egypt, Catalogs Ser.: Vol. 3). (Illus.). xxviii, 314p. (ARA & ENG.). 1982. text ed. 52.50 (*0-89003-115-0*, Pub. by Amer Res Ctr Egypt UA) Eisenbrauns.

Catalog of the Japanese Collection, 7 Vols, Set. Stanford University, Hoover Institution on War, Revolution & Peace Staff. 1970. lib. bdg. 765.00 (*0-8161-0169-8*, Hall Library) G K Hall.

Catalog of the Japanese Collection: Second Supplement. Stanford University, Hoover Institution on War, Revolution & Peace Staff. 1977. lib. bdg. 155.00 (*0-8161-0040-3*, Hall Library) G K Hall.

Catalog of the Japanese Collection, First Supplement. Stanford University, Hoover Institution on War, Revolution & Peace Staff. 581p. 1972. lib. bdg. 140.00 (*0-8161-1051-4*, Hall Library) G K Hall.

Catalog of the Johannes Herbst Collection. Ed. by Marilyn Gombosi. (Illus.). 255p. 17.50 (*0-8078-1124-6*) Moravian Music.

Catalog of the Kristine Mann Library of the Analytical Psychology Club of New York, Inc. 1978. lib. bdg. 220.00 (*0-8161-0085-3*, Hall Library) G K Hall.

Catalog of the Latin American Collection of the University of Texas Library, 3 vols., Fourth Suppl. University of Texas at Austin Staff. 1977. lib. bdg. 365.00 (*0-8161-1156-1*, Hall Library) G K Hall.

Catalog of the Latin American Collection of the University of Texas Library, 31 Vols, Set. University of Texas Library, Austin Staff. 1970. lib. bdg. 3,255.00 (*0-8161-0815-3*, Hall Library) G K Hall.

Catalog of the Latin American Collection of the University of Texas Library: Second Supplement, 3 vols., Set. University of Texas at Austin Staff. 1973. lib. bdg. 375.00 (*0-8161-0979-6*, Hall Library) G K Hall.

Catalog of the Latin American Collection of the University of Texas Library, First Supplement, 5 vols. University of Texas Library, Austin Staff. 1971. lib. bdg. 475.00 (*0-8161-0889-7*, Hall Library) G K Hall.

Catalog of the Latin American Collection of the University of Texas Library, Third Supplement, 8 vols, Set. University of Texas at Austin Staff. 1975. lib. bdg. 1,025.00 (*0-8161-1107-3*, Hall Library) G K Hall.

Catalog of the Latin American Collection, University of Florida Libraries, First Supplement, 7 vols. 1980. lib. bdg. 1,090.00 (*0-8161-1090-5*, Hall Library) G K Hall.

Catalog of the Latin American Library of the Tulane University Library, 9 vols, Set. Tulane University, New Orleans Staff. 1970. lib. bdg. 980.00 (*0-8161-0894-3*, Hall Library) G K Hall.

Catalog of the Latin American Library of the Tulane University Library: Third Supplement, 2 vols., Set. Tulane University, New Orleans Staff. 1978. lib. bdg. 300.00 (*0-8161-0005-5*, Hall Library) G K Hall.

Catalog of the Latin American Library of the Tulane University Library, First Supplement, 2 vols., Set. Tulane University, New Orleans Staff. 1973. lib. bdg. 275.00 (*0-8161-0914-1*, Hall Library) G K Hall.

Catalog of the Latin American Library of the Tulane University Library, Second Supplement. Tulane University, New Orleans Staff. 1975. lib. bdg. 275.00 (*0-8161-1052-2*, Hall Library) G K Hall.

Catalog of the Library of the Academy of Natural Sciences of Philadelphia, 16 vols., Set. Ed. by Academy of Natural Sciences of Philadelphia Staff. 1972. lib. bdg. 1,755.00 (*0-8161-0946-X*, Hall Library) G K Hall.

Catalog of the Library of the American Hospital Association, Asa S. Bacon Memorial Library, Chicago, 5 vols, Set. American Hospital Association Staff. 1976. lib. bdg. 530.00 (*0-8161-1210-X*, Hall Library) G K Hall.

Catalog of the Library of the Graduate School of Design, Second Supplement, 5 vols., Set. Harvard University, Graduate School of Design Staff. 1974. lib. bdg. 660.00 (*0-8161-1173-1*, Hall Library) G K Hall.

Catalog of the Library of the Institute for Contemporary History, First Supplement. Institute for Contemporary History, Munich Staff. 1973. lib. bdg. 155.00 (*0-8161-0920-6*, Hall Library); Subject catalog, 2 vols. lib. bdg. 280.00 (*0-8161-0179-5*, Hall Library); Biographical & regional catalog. lib. bdg. 130.00 (*0-8161-1075-1*, Hall Library) G K Hall.

An Asterisk (*) at the beginning of an entry indicates that the title is appearing in BIP for the first time.

Catalog of the Library of the Institute for World Economics, 7 pts. Marine Biological Laboratory Staff & Woods Hole Oceanographic Institution, Woods Hole, Massachusetts Staff. Incl. Title Catalog, 12 vols. 1971. lib. bdg. 1,215.00 (*0-8161-0937-0*, Hall Library); write for info. (*0-318-52339-6*, Hall Library) G K Hall.

Catalog of the Library of the International Archives for the Women's Movement International Archief voor de Vrouwenbeweging, 4 vols. 2352p. 1980. lib. bdg. 400.00 (*0-8161-0287-2*, Hall Reference) G K Hall.

Catalog of the Library of the Law School of Harvard University, 2 vols., Set. reprint ed. lib. bdg. 160.00 (*0-89941-459-1*, 502190) W S Hein.

Catalog of the Library of the Museum of Modern Art, New York, 14 vols., Set. Ed. by Museum of Modern Art Library Staff. 1976. lib. bdg. 1,310.00 (*0-8161-0015-2*, Hall Library) G K Hall.

Catalog of the Library of the National Museum of African Art Branch of the Smithsonian Institution Libraries, 3 vols., Vol. 2. National Museum of African Art, Smithsonian Institution Libraries Staff. 1650p. 1991. Set. text ed. 595.00 (*0-8161-0521-9*) G K Hall.

Catalog of the Library of the Royal Entomological Society of London. Royal Entomological Society of London Staff. (Printed Book Catalogs). 1980. lib. bdg. 565.00 (*0-8161-0315-1*, Hall Library) G K Hall.

Catalog of the Library of the Whitney Museum of American Art, 2 vols. Whitney Museum of American Art Staff. 1979. lib. bdg. 220.00 (*0-8161-0288-0*, Hall Library) G K Hall.

Catalog of the Lichens of Ohio. John N. Wolfe. (Bulletin Ser.: No. 36). 1940. 3.00 (*0-86727-035-7*) Ohio Bio Survey.

Catalog of the Lititz Congregation Collection. Ed. by Robert Steelman. (Illus.). 488p. 35.00 (*0-8078-1477-6*) Moravian Music.

Catalog of the Marx Memorial Library, 3 vols., Set. Marx Memorial Library, London Staff. 1979. lib. bdg. 330.00 (*0-8161-0280-5*, Hall Library) G K Hall.

Catalog of the Melville J. Herskovits Library of African Studies, Northwestern University, & Africana in Selected Libraries, Evanston, 8 vols., Set. Northwestern University Staff. 1972. lib. bdg. 825.00 (*0-8161-0921-4*, Hall Library) G K Hall.

Catalog of the Menninger Clinic Library, 4 vols., Set. Menninger Foundation, Topeka, Kansas Staff. 1972. lib. bdg. 435.00 (*0-8161-0961-3*, Hall Library) G K Hall.

Catalog of the Metropolitan Museum of Art Publications. (Monograph Ser.). 200p. (C). 1989. lib. bdg. 150.00 (*0-8161-0485-9*) G K Hall.

Catalog of the Middle East Institute Library. George Camp Keiser Library Staff of the Middle East Institute. 2290p. 1984. lib. bdg. 715.00 (*0-8161-0430-1*, Hall Library) G K Hall.

Catalog of the Museum of Broadcasting, 2 vols. 1981. write for info. (*0-318-50798-6*) Ayer.

Catalog of the Musical Works of William Billings. Comp. by Karl Kroeger. LC 91-24002. (Music Reference Collection Ser.: No. 32). 184p. 1991. text ed. 49.95 (*0-313-27827-X*, KCA, Greenwood Pr) Greenwood.

Catalog of the Naval Observatory Library, Washington, D.C., 6 vols., Set. Naval Observatory Library Staff. 1977. lib. bdg. 655.00 (*0-8161-0031-4*, Hall Library) G K Hall.

Catalog of the Neotropical Collembola. Jose Mari-Mutt & Peter F. Bellinger. LC 89-70038. (Flora & Fauna Handbook Ser.: No. 5). 256p. (Orig.). 1990. pap. text ed. 39.95 (*1-877743-00-3*) Sandhill Crane.

***Catalog of the Official Gazeteers of China in the University of Washington (Seattle)** expanded rev. ed. Joseph D. Lowe. (Illus.). xiv, 121p. 1994. pap. 25.00 (*0-930325-31-1*) Lowe Pub.

Catalog of the Old Slave Mart Museum & Library. Old Slave Mart Museum & Library Staff. 1978. lib. bdg. 145.00 (*0-8161-0073-X*, Hall Library) G K Hall.

Catalog of the Oliveira Lima Library, 2 vols., Set. Catholic University of America, Washington, D. C. Staff. 1970. lib. bdg. 220.00 (*0-8161-0873-0*, Hall Library) G K Hall.

Catalog of the Oriental Institute Library, Supplement I., Vol. 1. University of Chicago Staff. 1977. lib. bdg. 120.00 (*0-8161-0067-5*, Hall Library) G K Hall.

Catalog of the Peace Collection. Swarthmore College Staff. 1982. lib. bdg. 345.00 (*0-8161-0377-1*, Hall Library) G K Hall.

Catalog of the Police Library of the Los Angeles Public Library, 2 vols., Set. Los Angeles Public Library Staff. 1972. lib. bdg. 220.00 (*0-8161-0964-8*, Hall Library) G K Hall.

Catalog of the Police Library of the Los Angeles Public Library, First Supplement. Los Angeles Public Library Staff. (Library Catalogs). 1980. lib. bdg. 255.00 (*0-8161-0328-3*, Hall Library) G K Hall.

Catalog of the Polish Room Collection: Lockwood Memorial Library, State University of New York at Buffalo, 2 vols., Set. Ed. by Manuel D. Lopez. LC 83-81936. 1983. lib. bdg. 195.00 (*0-89941-288-2*, 302970) W S Hein.

Catalog of the Predynastic Egyptian Collection. Joan C. Payne & Ashmolean Museum. LC 93-16134. 1994. 120.00 (*0-19-951355-4*) OUP.

Catalog of the Programmschriften Collection. University of Pennsylvania Staff. 1970. lib. bdg. 75.00 (*0-8161-0558-8*, Hall Library) G K Hall.

Catalog of the Rare Book Room, 11 vols., Set. Ed. by University of Illinois at Urbana, University Library, Champaign Staff. 1972. lib. bdg. 1,250.00 (*0-8161-0938-9*, Hall Library) G K Hall.

Catalog of the Robert Goldwater Library of Primitive Art, 4 vols., Set. Ed. by Metropolitan Museum of Art Staff. 1982. lib. bdg. 455.00 (*0-8161-0381-X*, Hall Library) G K Hall.

Catalog of the Roman Law Collection of the Columbia Law School Library. Columbia University Law Library Staff. (Library Catalogs Ser.). 450p. 1989. lib. bdg. 165.00 (*0-8161-0488-3*) G K Hall.

Catalog of the Roycrofters. Ed. by Stephen Gray. (Mission Furniture Catalogues Ser.: No. 10). 64p. (Orig.). 1989. pap. 11.95 (*0-940326-13-2*) Turn of Cent.

Catalog of the Russian War Loan Posters of 1916 & 1917. Neil J. Roult. (Illus.). 36p. (Orig.). 1993. pap. 12.50 (*0-9639726-0-X*) N J Roult.

Catalog of the Salem Congregation Music. Ed. by Frances Cumnock. (Illus.). 682p. 31.50 (*0-8078-1398-2*) Moravian Music.

Catalog of the Social & Behavioral Sciences Monograph Section of the Library of the Institute for Sex Research, 4 vols., Set. Indiana University, Institute for Sex Research Staff. 2572p. 1974. lib. bdg. 435.00 (*0-8161-1141-3*, Hall Library) G K Hall.

***Catalog of the Society des Beaux Arts, Paris.** (Illus.). 94p. Date not set. pap. 19.95 (*0-88740-706-4*) Schiffer.

Catalog of the Sophia F. Palmer Memorial Library, 2 vols., Set. American Journal of Nursing, New York Staff. 1973. lib. bdg. 210.00 (*0-8161-1066-2*, Hall Library) G K Hall.

Catalog of the Southeast Asia Collection, Cornell University: First Supplement. Cornell University Staff. 1887p. 1983. lib. bdg. 555.00 (*0-8161-0383-6*, Hall Library) G K Hall.

***Catalog of the Tabanidae (Diptera) of the Americas South of the United States.** Graham B. Fairchild & John F. Burger. Ed. by V. K. Gupta. (Memoirs of the American Entomological Institute Ser.: No. 55). (Illus.). 264p. 1994. 45.00 (*1-56665-055-0*) Assoc Pubs FL.

Catalog of the Texas Collection in the Barker Texas History Center, 14 vols. University of Texas, Austin Staff. (Library of Texas at Austin). 1979. lib. bdg. 1,375.00 (*0-8161-0273-2*, Hall Library) G K Hall.

Catalog of the Theatre & Drama Collections, 2 pts. New York Public Library, Research Libraries Staff. Incl. Set. Drama Collection: Listing by Cultural Origin, 6 vols. 1970. 640.00 (*0-685-01808-3*); Set. Drama Collection: Author Listing, 6 vols. 1970. lib. bdg. 985.00 (*0-8161-0106-X*); Set. Theatre Collection: Books on the Theatre, 9 vols. 1970. lib. bdg. 790.00 (*0-8161-0107-8*); 1970. write for info. (*0-318-52340-X*, Hall Library) G K Hall.

Catalog of the Theatre & Drama Collections, Pt. 3. 30 Vols. Non-book Collection. New York Public Library, Research Libraries Staff. 1976. lib. bdg. 3,990.00 (*0-8161-1195-2*, Hall Library) G K Hall.

Catalog of the Theatre & Drama Collections: First Supplement to Pt. 1, Drama Collection. New York Public Library, Research Libraries Staff. 1973. lib. bdg. 120.00 (*0-8161-0745-9*, Hall Library) G K Hall.

Catalog of the Theatre & Drama Collections: First Supplement to Pt. 2, Theatre Collection, 2 vols, Set. New York Public Library, Research Libraries Staff. 1973. lib. bdg. 310.00 (*0-8161-0747-5*, Hall Library) G K Hall.

Catalog of the Theatre & Drama Collections, Supplement 1974. New York Public Library, Research Libraries Staff. 1976. lib. bdg. 120.00 (*0-8161-0058-6*, Hall Library) G K Hall.

Catalog of the Transportation Center Library, Northwestern University. Northwestern University Staff. 1972. Subject Catalog 9 Vols. lib. bdg. 980.00 (*0-8161-0185-X*, Hall Library); Author-title Catalog. lib. bdg. 1,305.00 (*0-8161-0924-9*, Hall Library) G K Hall.

Catalog of the Transportation Center Library, Northwestern University, 12 vols., Set. Northwestern University Staff. 1972. lib. bdg. write for info. (*0-685-01569-6*, Hall Library) G K Hall.

Catalog of the Turkish & Persian Collections. Stanford University, Hoover Institution on War, Revolution & Peace Staff. 1970. lib. bdg. 110.00 (*0-8161-0171-X*, Hall Library) G K Hall.

Catalog of the United States Department of Labor Library (Washington, D. C.), 38 vols, Set. Ed. by U. S. Department of Labor, Washington D. C. Staff. 1975. lib. bdg. 4,350.00 (*0-8161-1165-0*, Hall Library) G K Hall.

Catalog of the United States Geological Survey Library, 25 vols., Set. Ed. by U. S. Department of the Interior, U. S. Geological Survey, Washington, D. C. Staff. 1970. lib. bdg. 2,720.00 (*0-8161-0712-2*, Hall Library) G K Hall.

Catalog of the United States Geological Survey Library: Supplement 1, 11 vols., Set. Ed. by U. S. Department of the Interior, U. S. Geological Survey, Washington, D. C. Staff. 1973. lib. bdg. 950.00 (*0-8161-0876-5*, Hall Library) G K Hall.

Catalog of the United States Geological Survey Library: 2nd Suppl, 4 vols., Set. Ed. by U. S. Department of the Interior, U. S. Geological Survey, Washington, D. C. Staff. 1973. lib. bdg. 475.00 (*0-8161-1031-X*, Hall Library) G K Hall.

Catalog of the United States Geological Survey 3rd Suppl., 6 vols. Ed. by U. S. Department of the Interior, U. S. Geological Survey, Washington, D. C. Staff. 1976. lib. bdg. 690.00 (*0-8161-0051-9*, Hall Library) G K Hall.

Catalog of the Warburg Institute Library, 12 Vols, Set. 2nd rev. ed. University of London - Warburg Institute Staff. 1970. lib. bdg. 1,135.00 (*0-8161-0744-0*, Hall Library) G K Hall.

Catalog of the Western History Department, Denver Public Library, 7 vols., Set. Denver Public Library Staff. 1970. lib. bdg. 765.00 (*0-8161-0864-1*, Hall Library) G K Hall.

Catalog of the Western History Department, Denver Public Library, 1st Suppl. Denver Public Library Staff. 1975. lib. bdg. 145.00 (*0-8161-0898-6*, Hall Library) G K Hall.

Catalog of the Western Language Collections, 63 Vols, Set. Stanford University, Hoover Institution on War, Revolution & Peace Staff. 1970. lib. bdg. 6,850.00 (*0-8161-0859-5*, Hall Library) G K Hall.

Catalog of the Western Language Collections, First Supplement, 5 vols., Set. Stanford University, Hoover Institution on War, Revolution & Peace Staff. 2627p. 1972. lib. bdg. 805.00 (*0-8161-1019-0*, Hall Library) G K Hall.

Catalog of the Western Language Collections, Second Supplement, 6 vols, Set. Stanford University, Hoover Institution on War, Revolution & Peace Staff. 1977. lib. bdg. 925.00 (*0-8161-0037-3*, Hall Library) G K Hall.

Catalog of the William Ransom Hogan Jazz Archive, 2 vols., Set. Howard-Tilton Memorial Library Staff. 900p. 1984. lib. bdg. 385.00 (*0-8161-0434-4*, Hall Reference) Macmillan.

Catalog of the Works of Arthur William Foote, Eighteen Fifty-Three to Nineteen Thirty-Seven. Wilma Cipolla. LC 79-92139. (Bibliographies in American Music Ser.: No. 6). 214p. 1980. 17.50 (*0-89990-000-3*) Info Coord.

Catalog of the Yale Collection of Western Americana, 4 Vols, Set. Yale University Staff. 1970. lib. bdg. 435.00 (*0-8161-0585-5*, Hall Library) G K Hall.

Catalog of the Yiddish Collection: Harvard College Library, 3 vols. Charles Berlin. 1265p. 1993. lib. bdg. 565.00 (*3-598-41242-8*) U Pubns Amer.

***Catalog of Thunderbird ID Numbers, 1955-93.** Cars & Parts Magazine Staff. (Matching Number Ser.). (Illus.). 229p. 1994. pap. text ed. 19.95 (*1-880524-14-7*) Cars & Parts.

Catalog of Tools, Hardware, Firearms & Vehicles. Ed. by Sandra S. Tinkham. (Index of American Design Ser.: Pt. 4). 80p. (Orig.). 1979. pap. 49.00 (*0-914146-69-6*) Chadwyck-Healey.

Catalog of Toys & Musical Instruments. Ed. by Sandra S. Tinkham. (Index of American Design Ser.: Pt. 10). 40p. (Orig.). 1980. pap. text ed. 49.00 (*0-914146-81-5*) Chadwyck-Healey.

Catalog of Travelers Rest Arabian Horses: Together with a Partial Account of Arabian Horses in the United States. Frwd. by Margaret D. Fleming. (Illus.). 295p. 1988. reprint ed. 20.00 (*0-938276-01-8*) Arabian Horse Trust.

Catalog of Type Specimens in the Ichthyological Collection of the Academy of Natural Sciences of Philadelphia. Eugenia B. Bohlke. (Special Publication: No. 14). 246p. 1984. pap. 10.00 (*0-910006-41-5*) Acad Nat Sci Phila.

Catalog of Type Specimens in the International Protozoan Type Collection. Linda Cole. No. 561. 1994. write for info. (*0-318-72690-4*) Smithsonian.

***Catalog of Type Specimens in the International Protozoan Type Collection.** fac. ed. Linda L. Cole. LC 94-9547. (Smithsonian Contributions to Zoology Ser.: No. 561). 34p. 1994. reprint ed. pap. 25.00 (*0-7837-8262-4*, 2049043) Bks Demand.

***Catalog of Types of Cleoptera in the Canadian National Collection of Insects Supplement No. III.** Jean McNamara. 65p. (Orig.). 1993. pap. 32.45x (*0-660-57939-1*, Pub. by Canada Commun Grp CN) Accents Pubns.

Catalog of United States Census Publications, 1790-1945. U. S. Library of Congress, Census Library Project Staff. LC 68-55126. (Illus.). 320p. 1969. reprint ed. text ed. 65.00 (*0-8371-0714-8*, USCP, Greenwood Pr) Greenwood.

Catalog of University Presentations, 1990-91: OMS 90-2011. write for info. (*0-318-69632-0*) Natl Ctr Health Stats.

***Catalog of University Presentations 1994-95.** National Center for Health Statistics Staff. 17p. Date not set. write for info. (*0-614-02956-2*) Natl Ctr Health Stats.

Catalog of Venetian Librettos at the University of California, Los Angeles. Irene Alm. LC 92-24457. (UC Publications in Catalogs & Bibliographies: Vol. 9). 1992. 120.00 (*0-520-09762-9*) U CA Pr.

Catalog of Wood Carvings & Weathervanes. Ed. by Sandra S. Tinkham. (Index of American Design Ser.: Pt. 7). 48p. (Orig.). 1980. pap. text ed. 49.00 (*0-914146-75-0*) Chadwyck-Healey.

Catalog of World Species of Proctotrupoidea, Exclusive of Platygastridae (Hymenoptera) Norman F. Johnson. (Memoirs of the American Entomological Institute Ser.: No. 51). 825p. 1992. 80.00 (*1-56665-051-8*) Assoc Pubs FL.

Catalog to Manuscripts at the National Anthropological Archives, 4 vols., Set. Smithsonian Institution, Washington, D. C. Staff. 1975. lib. bdg. 435.00 (*0-8161-1194-4*, Hall Library) G K Hall.

Cataloger's Guide to MARC Coding & Tagging for Audio Visual Materials. Nancy B. Olson. 29.50 (*0-933474-49-0*) Media Mktg Group.

Catalogi Bibliothecarum Antiqui, 2 vols. in 1. Gustav Becker. iv, 350p. 1973. reprint ed. write for info. (*3-487-04752-7*, Pub. by Georg Olms GW) Lubrecht & Cramer.

Cataloging, Vol. 7. Ed. by James E. Rush. LC 83-9584. (Library Systems Evaluation Guides Ser.). (Illus.). 262p. 1985. ring bd. 59.50 (*0-912803-07-X*) Rush Assoc.

Cataloging: The Professional Development Cycle. Ed. by Sheila S. Intner & Janet S. Hill. LC 90-19797. (New Directions in Information Management Ser.: No. 26). 176p. 1991. text ed. 45.00 (*0-313-27254-9*, ICC/, Greenwood Pr) Greenwood.

Cataloging & Catalogs: A Handbook for Library Management. David F. Kohl. LC 85-15835. 270p. 1985. lib. bdg. 49.00 (*0-87436-434-5*) ABC-CLIO.

Cataloging & Classification: An Introduction. 2nd ed. Lois M. Chan. LC 93-22606. 1993. text ed. write for info. (*0-07-010506-5*) McGraw.

***Cataloging & Classification for Library Technicians.** Mary L. Kao. LC 94-44815. (Illus.). 146p. 1995. lib. bdg. 24.95 (*1-56024-344-9*) Haworth Pr.

***Cataloging & Classification for Library Technicians.** Mary Liu Kao. LC 94-44815. 1995. pap. write for info. (*1-56024-970-6*) Haworth Pr.

Cataloging & Filing Rules for Maps & Atlases in the Society's Collection. Roman Drazniowsky. 92p. 1969. pap. 9.00 (*0-318-12729-6*) Am Geographical.

Cataloging & Indexing in Sci-Tech Libraries. Ed. by Ellis Mount. (Science & Technology Libraries: Vol. 2, No. 3). 86p. 1982. pap. text ed. 24.95 (*0-86656-204-4*) Haworth Pr.

Cataloging & the Small Special Library. Joseph W. Palmer. 49p. 1992. 28.00 (*0-87111-370-8*) SLA.

Cataloging Books: A Workbook of Examples. William E. Studwell & David V. Loertscher. 201p. 1989. student ed 17.50 (*0-87287-641-1*); IBM. disk 28.50 (*0-87287-696-9*); Apple. Apple II 28.00 (*0-87287-695-0*) Libs Unl.

Cataloging Computer Files. Nancy B. Olson. (Minnesota AACR 2 Trainers Ser.: No. 2). 1992. 30.00 (*0-936996-47-1*) Soldier Creek.

Cataloging Correctly for Kids: An Introduction to the Tools. rev. ed. Sharon Zuiderveld. LC 91-8675. (Illus.). 50p. (C). 1991. pap. text ed. 16.00 (*0-8389-3395-5*) ALA.

Cataloging for School Libraries Guide to Simplified Form. 2nd ed. M. Scott & D. Fennell. LC 73-12507. 1970. 78.00 (*0-08-016509-5*, Pub. by Pergamon Repr UK) Franklin.

Cataloging Government Documents: A Manual of Interpretation for AACR2. Ed. by Bernadine Hoduski. LC 84-6499. 260p. 1984. 20.00 (*0-8389-3304-1*) ALA.

Cataloging Government Publications Online. Ed. by Carolyn C. Sherayko. LC 94-14320. (Cataloging & Classification Quarterly Ser.). (Illus.). 170p. 1994. text ed. 39.95 (*1-56024-689-8*) Haworth Pr.

Cataloging Heresy: Challenging the Standard Bibliographic Product. Ed. by Bella H. Weinberg. 1992. 35.00 (*0-938734-60-1*) Learned Info.

Cataloging in Publication Program Survey Findings. SKP Associates Staff. LC 93-20551. 1993. write for info. (*0-8444-0789-5*) Lib Congress.

Cataloging Legal Literature: A Manual on AACR2 & Library of Congress Subject Headings for Legal Material with Illustrations. 2nd ed. Peter Envingi et al. (American Association of Law Libraries Publications Ser.: No. 22). 1988. ring bd. 65.00 (*0-8377-0129-5*) Rothman.

Cataloging Made Easy. rev. ed. Ruth S. Smith. LC 86-30974. (Guide Ser.: No. 5). (Illus.). 40p. 1987. pap. 8.25 (*0-915324-25-3*); pap. 6.50 (*0-685-18762-4*) CSLA.

Cataloging Microcomputer Software. Nancy B. Olson. 263p. 1989. lib. bdg. 33.00 (*0-87287-513-X*) Libs Unl.

Cataloging Motion Pictures & Videorecordings. Nancy B. Olson. (Minnesota AACR 2 Trainers Ser.: No. 1). 1991. pap. 30.00 (*0-936996-38-2*) Soldier Creek.

Cataloging Nonbook Resources: A How-to-Do-It Manual for Librarians. Mary B. Fecko. LC 93-4213. (How-to-Do-It Manuals for Libraries Ser.: No. 31). 204p. 1993. pap. 39.95 (*1-55570-124-8*) Neal-Schuman.

Cataloging of Audiovisual Materials: A Manual Using AACR 2. 3rd ed. Nancy B. Olson. 300p. 1991. lib. bdg. 55.00 (*0-933474-48-2*) Media Mktg Group.

Cataloging Phonorecordings: Problems & Possibilities. Jay E. Daily. LC 73-90723. (Practical Library & Information Science Ser.: No. 1). 192p. reprint ed. pap. 54.80 (*0-7837-0927-7*, 2041232) Bks Demand.

Cataloging Service Bulletin Index: Index to Bulletins 1-62 (Summer 1978-Winter 1993) annuals Comp. by Nancy B. Olson. 1994. 30.00 (*0-936996-65-X*) Soldier Creek.

Cataloging Unpublished Nonprint Materials: A Manual of Suggestions, Comments, & Examples. Verna Urbanski et al. 144p. 1992. 30.00 (*0-936996-61-7*) Soldier Creek.

Catalogo Bibliografico Y Biografico del Teatro Antiguo Espanol, Desde Sus Origenes hasta Mediados del Siglo XVIII. Cayetano A. De la Barrera Y Leirado. (Serie D: Reproducciones en Facsimil, I). 727p. (Orig.). (SPA.). (C). 1968. pap. 48.00 (*0-900411-02-3*, Pub. by Tamesis Bks Ltd UK) Boydell & Brewer.

***Catalogo Bibliografico y Biografico Del Teatro Antiguo Espanol Desde Sus Origenes Hasta Mediados Del Siglo XVIII.** Cayetano A. De la Barrera Y Leirado. (SPA.). 1968. 100.00 (*84-249-1914-9*) Elliots Bks.

Catalogo de Informes y Documentos Tecnicos de la OEA: Suplemento 1978. OAS, General Secretariat, Department of Material Resources Staff. (SG Ser. A: No. III.1). 81p. 1981. pap. text ed. 4.00 (*0-8270-1300-0*) OAS.

Catalogo de la Biblioteca Nacional de Antropologia y Historia - Catalogs of the National Library of Anthropology & History, 10 vols., Set. National Library of Anthropology & History Staff, Mexico City. 1972. lib. bdg. 960.00 (*0-8161-0918-4*, Hall Library) G K Hall.

Catalogo de la Familia Poaceae en la Republica Argentina. Ed. by Marshall R. Crosby. (Monographs in Systematic Botany from the Missouri Botanical Garden: No. 47). 178p. (SPA.). 1994. 18.00 (*0-915279-21-5*) Miss Botan.

Catalogo de las Algas de Agua Dulce de la Republica Argentina. G. Tell. (Bibliotheca Phycologica Ser.: No. 70). 284p. 1985. lib. bdg. 60.00 (*3-7682-1409-5*) Lubrecht & Cramer.

***Catalogo de las Lenguas de America del Sur Con Clasificaciones, Indicaciones Tipologicas, Bibliografia y Mapas.** rev. ed. A. Tovar & C. Larrucea De Tovar. 632p. (SPA.). 1993. 150.00 (*84-249-0958-5*) Elliots Bks.

Catalogo de las Lenguas de las Naciones, 6 vols. Lorenzo Hervas y Pandura. reprint ed. write for info. (*0-318-71799-9*, Pub. by Georg Olms GW) Lubrecht & Cramer.

C

An Asterisk (*) at the beginning of an entry indicates that the title is appearing in BIP for the first time.

Catalogo de Leyes del Ano. Butterworth Staff. (SPA.). 1992. 150.00 (0-685-75307-7) Butterworth Legal Pubs.

Catalogo de los Manuscritos Existentes en la Coleccion Latino Americana de la Biblioteca de la Universidad de Texas Relativos a la History de Centro America. J. Joaquin Pardo. 45p. 1988. reprint ed. pap. 6.50 (0-913129-19-4) La Tienda.

Catalogo de los Manuscritos Poeticos Castellanos de la Sociedad Hispana de America, 3 vols. Ed. by Antonio Rodriguez-Monino & Maria B. Marino. (Illus.). 1966. 50.00 (0-87535-103-4); lib. bdg. 60.00 (0-87535-129-8) Hispanic Soc.

Catalogo de Reglamentos de Puerto Rico, 2 vols., Set. Butterworth Staff. 1992. 525.00 (0-685-75308-5) Butterworth Legal Pubs.

Catalogo della Raccolta Colombiana (Catalog of the Columbus Collection) Civica Biblioteca Berio (Berio Civic Library). Genoa Staff. 1970. lib. bdg. 85.00 (0-8161-0637-1, Hall Library) G K Hall.

***Catalogo Generale dei Periodici Italiani, 5 vols.** 1995. text ed. write for info. (3-598-11197-5) K G Saur.

Catalogo Metodico de la Biblioteca de la Facultad de Derecho y Ciencias Sociales de Buenos Aires Seguido de una Tabla Alfabetica de Autores. Buenos Aires, Universidad Nacional, Facultad de Derecho y Ciencias Sociales Biblioteca Staff. 1976. lib. bdg. 134.95 (0-8490-1584-7) Gordon Pr.

Catalogs of the Asia Library, the University of Michigan, 25 vols, Set. University of Michigan Staff. 1978. lib. bdg. 2,690.00 (0-8161-0096-9, Hall Library) G K Hall.

Catalogs of the Bureau of the Census Library, 20 vols, Set. U. S. Bureau of the Census, Washington, D. C. Staff. 1976. lib. bdg. 2,060.00 (0-8161-0050-0, Hall Library) G K Hall.

Catalogs of the Bureau of the Census Library: First Supplement, 5 vols., Set. U. S. Bureau of the Census, Washington, D. C. Staff. (Library Catalogs-Bib. Guides). 1979. lib. bdg. 680.00 (0-8161-0296-1, Hall Library) G K Hall.

Catalogs of the F. B. Power Pharmaceutical Library, 4 vols., Set. University of Wisconsin, Madison, School of Pharmacy Staff. 1976. lib. bdg. 435.00 (0-8161-0021-7, Hall Library) G K Hall.

Catalogs of the Far Eastern Library, 6 vols, Set. University of Chicago Staff. 1972. lib. bdg. 910.00 (0-8161-1119-7, Hall Library) G K Hall.

Catalogs of the Home Economics Library, Ohio State University. 1977. lib. bdg. 330.00 (0-8161-0054-3, Hall Library) G K Hall.

Catalogs of the Opera Collections in the Music Libraries: University of California, Berkeley & University of California, Los Angeles. 1983. lib. bdg. 145.00 (0-8161-0392-5, Hall Library) G K Hall.

Catalogs of the Scripps Institution of Oceanography Library, 4 pts. University of California - San Diego Staff. Incl. Set. Author-Title Catalog, 7 vols. 1970. lib. bdg. 730.00 (0-8161-0860-9); Set. Subject Catalog, 2 vols. 1970. lib. bdg. 220.00 (0-8161-0112-4); Set. Shelf List, 2 vols. 1970. lib. bdg. 205.00 (0-8161-0113-2); Pt. 4. Shelf List of Documents, Reports & Translations Collection. 1970. lib. bdg. 105.00 (0-8161-0114-0); write for info. (0-318-52341-8, Hall Library) G K Hall.

Catalogs of the Scripps Institution of Oceanography Library, First Supplement to Pt. 1: Author-Title Catalog, 3 vols. Ed. by University of California, San Diego Staff. 1973. lib. bdg. 270.00 (0-8161-0897-8, Hall Library) G K Hall.

Catalogs of the Scripps Institution of Oceanography Library, First Supplement to Pts. 2-4, Subject Catalog, Shelf List, Shelf List of Documents & Reports. University of California, San Diego Staff. 1973. lib. bdg. 120.00 (0-8161-1144-8, Hall Library) G K Hall.

Catalogs of the Venice Biennale, 1895-1920, 12 Vols, Set. LC 74-86642. (Contemporary Art Ser.). (Illus.). (ITA.). 1971. reprint ed. 198.95 (0-405-00743-4) Ayer.

Catalogs of the Western Language Serials & Newspaper Collection, 3 Vols. Stanford University, Hoover Institution on War, Revolution & Peace Staff. 1970. lib. bdg. 330.00 (0-8161-0167-1, Hall Library) G K Hall.

Catalogue. George Milburn. LC 87-5432. 312p. 1987. reprint ed. lib. bdg. 18.95 (0-940827-00-X) Davenport NYC.

Catalogue: Special Exhibition of the Saltonstall Family Portraits. Ernest S. Dodge. 1962. pap. 1.00 (0-87577-022-3, Peabody Museum) Peabody Essex Mus.

Catalogue: Winter 1984-85. 96p. write for info. (0-318-60100-1) Art Students.

Catalogue & Buyers Guide Summer & Spring 1895: No. 57. Montgomery Ward Staff. 1969. reprint ed. pap. 19.95 (0-486-22377-9) Dover.

Catalogue & Index of Contributions to North American Geology: 1732-1891. Nelson H. Darton. Ed. by I. Bernard Cohen. LC 79-7958. (Three Centuries of Science in America Ser.). 1980. reprint ed. lib. bdg. 94.95 (0-405-12539-9) Ayer.

Catalogue & Index of Publications of the Hayden, King, Powell & Wheeler Surveys. Schmeckebier. LC 71-167945. 206p. 1971. reprint ed. lib. bdg. 32.50 (0-306-70403-X) Da Capo.

Catalogue & Reclassification of the Ethiopian Ichneumonidae. Henry Townes et al. (Memoir Ser.: No. 19). 416p. 1973. 45.00 (1-56665-017-8) Assoc Pubs FL.

Catalogue & Reclassification of the Indo-Australian Ichneumonidae. Henry Townes et al. (Memoir Ser.: No. 1). 522p. 1961. 50.00 (1-56665-000-3) Assoc Pubs FL.

Catalogue & Reclassification of the Neotropic Ichneumonidae. Henry Townes & Marjorie Townes. (Memoir Ser.: No. 8). 1966. 45.00 (1-56665-006-2) Assoc Pubs FL.

Catalogue Checklist of English Prose Fiction: 1750-1800. Leonard Orr. LC 79-64848. 204p. 1979. 13.50 (0-87875-171-8) Whitston Pub.

Catalogue-Checklist of the Butterflies of North America of Mexico (Memoir No. 2) 280p. 1981. 17.00 (0-930282-02-7); 10.00 (0-318-14747-5); pap. 8.50 (0-930282-03-5); pap. 5.00 (0-318-14748-3) Lepidopterists.

Catalogue Critique Des Manuscrits De Leibniz, Vol. Two: Mars 1672-Novembre 1676. Gottfried W. Leibniz. xiv, 257p. 1986. reprint ed. write for info. (3-487-07797-3, Pub. by Georg Olms GW) Lubrecht & Cramer.

Catalogue de Fonds Speciaux de la Bibliotheque Litteraire Jacques Doucet, (Paris, France) Jacques Doucet. (Fonds Valery Ser.). 1972. lib. bdg. 110.00 (0-8161-0952-4, Hall Library); lib. bdg. 110.00 (0-8161-0954-0, Hall Library); lib. bdg. 110.00 (0-8161-0951-6, Hall Library) G K Hall.

Catalogue de la Bibliotheque de l'ecole Biblique et Archeologique Francaise (Catalog of the Library of the French Biblical & Archaeological School), 13 vols. Ecole Biblique et Archeologique Francaise. Jerusalem. 1975. lib. bdg. 1,545.00 (0-8161-1154-5, Hall Library) G K Hall.

Catalogue de Manuscrits de la Bibliotheque Litteraire Jacques Doucet, (Paris, France) Jacques Doucet. 1972. lib. bdg. 115.00 (0-8161-0950-8, Hall Library) G K Hall.

Catalogue Demotic Papyri in the Ashmolean Museum, Vol. 1: Embalmers Archives from Hawara. Reymond. 1973. 85.00 (0-900416-08-4, Pub. by Aris & Phillips UK) David Brown.

Catalogue des Incunables et des Livres Imprimes de MD a MDXX. M. Pellechet. viii, 302p. reprint ed. write for info. (0-318-71854-5, Pub. by Georg Olms GW) Lubrecht & Cramer.

Catalogue des Mammifers du Quercy. Bernard Sigel. (Fossilium Catalogus, Animalia Pars Ser.: No. 126). 1979. pap. 35.00 (90-6193-385-4) Kluwer Ac.

Catalogue Des Manuscrits de la Collection Prosper-Marchand. Christiane Berkvens-Stevelinck & Adele Nieuweboer. (Codices Manuscripti Ser.: No. XXVI). (Illus.). x, 214p. (FRE.). 1988. pap. 68.75 (90-04-08618-8) E J Brill.

Catalogue Des Manuscrits Egyptiens. Theodule Deveria. iv, 272p. 1980. reprint ed. write for info. (3-487-06908-3, Pub. by Georg Olms GW) Lubrecht & Cramer.

***Catalogue Des Manuscrits Francais De la Bibliotheque Parker.** Ed. by Nigel Wilkins. 192p. (C). 1995. text ed. 35.00 (1-897852-00-2) Boydell & Brewer.

Catalogue D'Expressions Techniques Pour Appareils de Levage et Elevateurs. 104p. 1985. write for info. (0-8288-2162-3) Fr & Eur.

Catalogue d'Ouvrages sur l'Histoire de l'Amerique, et en Particulier sur Celle du Canada, da la Louisiane, de l'Acadie et Autres Lieux. G. B. Faribault. (Canadiana Avant 1867 Ser.: No. 13). 1966. 24.75 (90-279-6330-4) Mouton.

Catalogue du Fonds de Musique Ancienne de la Bibliotheque Nationale, 8 vols. in 4, Set. Ed. by Jules A. Ecorcheville. LC 79-166103. (Music Ser.). (Illus.). 1973. reprint ed. lib. bdg. 225.00 (0-306-70280-0) Da Capo.

Catalogue for the Mary Columbro Rodgers Literary Trust. 1992. write for info. (0-89848-271-2) Open Univ Am.

Catalogue General Des Monuments D'Abydos Decouverts Pendant les Fouilles De Cette Ville. Auguste E. Mariette. viii, 596p. reprint ed. write for info. (0-318-71377-2, Pub. by Georg Olms GW) Lubrecht & Cramer.

Catalogue General des Ouvrages en Langue Francaise 1926-1929, 9 vols., Set. Ed. by Bernard Dermineur. 7250p. (FRE.). 1986. lib. bdg. 1,835.00 (3-598-30990-2) K G Saur.

Catalogue General des Ouvrages en Langue Francaise 1926-1929: Auteurs, 3 vols. Ed. by Bernard Dermineur. 7250p. (FRE.). 1986. Author Index, Vols. 1-3. lib. bdg. write for info. (3-598-30991-0) K G Saur.

Catalogue General des Ouvrages en Langue Francaise 1926-1929: Matieres, 4 vols. Ed. by Bernard Dermineur. 7250p. (FRE.). 1986. Subject Index, Vols. 6-9. lib. bdg. write for info. (3-598-30995-3) K G Saur.

Catalogue General des Ouvrages en Langue Francaise 1926-1929: Titres, 2 vols. Ed. by Bernard Dermineur. 7250p. (FRE.). 1986. Title Index, Vols. 4-5. lib. bdg. write for info. (3-598-30992-9) K G Saur.

Catalogue General des Ouvrages en Langue Francaise 1930-1933, 15 vols., Set. Ed. by Bernard Dermineur. 7500p. (FRE.). 1992. lib. bdg. 3,770.00 (3-598-32860-5) U Pubns Amer.

Catalogue Generale des Livres Imprimes: Auteurs, Collectivites-Auteurs, Anonymes, 1960-1969, 15 vols. Bibliotheque Nationale Staff. (Serie I). 2,995.00 (0-685-11067-2) Fr & Eur.

Catalogue Listing of Works of Art Stolen by the Third Reich. 34p. (Orig.). 1986. pap. 24.95 (0-934393-00-1) Rector Pr.

Catalogue of a Collection of Ancient Rings Formed by the Late E. Guilhou. 2nd rev. ed. Intro. by DeRicci. (Illus.). 194p. 1980. 100.00 (0-930088-01-8) Antique Classic.

Catalogue of a Collection of Objects Illustrating the Folk-Lore of Mexico. Frederick Starr. (Folk-Lore Society, London, Monographs: Vol. 43). 1972. reprint ed. pap. 15.00 (0-8115-0519-7) Periodicals Srv.

Catalogue of a Special Exhibition of Bronze Mirrors in the National Palace Museum Taipei. (Illus.). 268p. 1986. pap. 69.50 (0-89346-805-3) Heian Intl.

Catalogue of a Special Exhibition of Hindustan Jade in the National Palace Museum Taipe. (Illus.). 290p. 1983. pap. 39.50 (0-89346-806-1) Heian Intl.

***Catalogue of Additions to MSS: 1986-1990, 3 Vol. Set.** (Catalogues of the British Library Collections). 1993. 250.00 (0-7123-0305-7, Pub. by Brit Library UK) U of Toronto Pr.

Catalogue of American Silver: The Cleveland Museum of Art Collection. Phillip M. Johnston. LC 93-42125. (Illus.). 176p. 1994. text ed. 65.00 (0-940717-22-0) Cleveland Mus Art.

Catalogue of an Exhibition of Silver Used in New York, New Jersey & the South: With a Note on Early New York Silversmiths. R. T. Halsey. LC 72-168421. (Metropolitan Museum of Art Publications in Reprint). 184p. 1974. reprint ed. 15.95 (0-405-02259-X) Ayer.

Catalogue of Arabic Manuscripts in the Library of the University of Leiden & Other Collections in the Netherlands, Fasc. 3. J. J. Witkam. (Codices Manuscripti Ser.: No. 21-3). (Illus.). 14p. 1985. pap. 36.00 (90-04-07157-1) E J Brill.

Catalogue of Arabic Manuscripts in the Oriental Institute of Chicago. Miroslav Krek. (Essays Ser.: No. 3). 1961. pap. 3.00 (0-940490-93-5) Am Orient Soc.

Catalogue of Arabic Manuscripts (Yahuda Section) in the Garrett Collection, Princeton University Library. Rudolph Mach. LC 75-2999. (Illus.). 1976. 350.00x (0-691-03908-9) Princeton U Pr.

Catalogue of Artifacts in the Babylonian Collection of the Lowie Museum of Anthropology. Yoko Tomabechi. LC 81-71739. (Bibliotheca Mesopotamica Ser.: Vol. 15). (Illus.). viii, 95p. (Orig.). 1984. pap. 33.75 (0-89003-106-1) Undena Pubns.

Catalogue of Artificial Intelligence Techniques. 3rd ed. Ed. by Alan Bundy et al. (Symbolic Computation - Artificial Intelligence Ser.). 190p. 1990. 35.00 (0-387-52959-4) Spr-Verlag.

Catalogue of Artificial Intelligence Tools. 2nd rev. ed. Ed. by Alan Bundy. (Symbolic Computation Ser.). iv, 168p. 1986. pap. 29.70 (0-387-16893-1) Spr-Verlag.

Catalogue of Audio & Video Collections of Holocaust Testimony. 2nd ed. Comp. by Joan Ringelheim. LC 91-43368. (Bibliographies & Indexes in World History Ser.: No. 23). 209p. 1992. text ed. 72.50 (0-313-28221-8, RAV/, Greenwood Pr) Greenwood.

Catalogue of Balinese Manuscripts in the Library of the University of Leiden & Other Collections in the Netherlands, 2 vols., Pts. 1 & 2. H. I. Hinzler. Vols. 22 & 23. (Illus.). Pt. 1, 1987, vii, 432pp. pap. write for info. (0-318-62167-5); Pt. 2, 1986, vi, 518pp. pap. write for info. (0-318-62168-1) E J Brill.

Catalogue of Balinese Manuscripts in the Library of the University of Leiden & Other Collections in the Netherlands, 2 vols., Set. H. I. Hinzler. (Codices Manuscripti Ser.: Vols. 22 & 23). (Illus.). pap. 171.50 (90-04-07234-9) E J Brill.

Catalogue of Books: The Famous "Guinea Catalogue" Henry G. Bohn. LC 74-8717. reprint ed. 137.50 (0-404-11610-8) AMS Pr.

Catalogue of Books & Journals, 1891-1965. University of Chicago Press Staff. 1967. lib. bdg. 7.50 (0-226-83611-8) U Ch Pr.

Catalogue of Books & Literary Material Relating to the Flute & Other Musical Instruments. Dayton C. Miller. 1988. reprint ed. lib. bdg. 59.00 (0-7812-0679-0) Rprt Serv.

Catalogue of Books & Literary Material Relating to the Flute & Other Musical Instruments, with Annotations. Dayton C. Miller. LC 72-181210. 29.00 (0-403-01621-5) Scholarly.

Catalogue of Books on Hermetic Philosophy: The E. A. Hitchcock Collection. Ed. by Bangs, Merwin, & Co. Staff. reprint ed. pap. 6.95 (0-916411-33-8) Holmes Pub.

***Catalogue of Books Printed in the German-Speaking Countries & of German Books Printed in Other Countries from 1601 to 1700 Now in the British Library, 5 vols., Set.** Comp. by David Paisey. (Catalogues of the British Library Collections). 3024p. 1994. 590.00 (0-7123-0351-0, Pub. by Brit Library UK) U of Toronto Pr.

Catalogue of Books Printed on the Continent of Europe, 2 Vols, Set. H. M. Adams. 1968. 500.00 (0-521-06951-3) Cambridge U Pr.

Catalogue of Books Relating to the Literature of the Law. John V. L. Pruyn. 300p. 1982. reprint ed. lib. bdg. 32.50 (0-8377-1015-4) Rothman.

Catalogue of British Drawings for Architecture, Decoration, Sculpture & Landscape Gardening: 1550-1900, in American Collections. John Harris. LC 75-93124. (Illus.). 1971. lib. bdg. 185.00 (0-8398-0766-X) Irvington.

***Catalogue of British Historical Medals.** R. P. Puddester. 245p. 1987. 150.00 (0-9511308-2-X, Pub. by R C Senior UK) St Mut.

Catalogue of British Official Publications Not Published by HMSO, 1980. Intro. by Charles Chadwyck-Healey. 256p. 1981. lib. bdg. 290.00 (0-85964-101-5) Chadwyck-Healey.

Catalogue of British Official Publications Not Published by HMSO, 1981. Pref. by Charles Chadwyck-Healey. 303p. 1983. lib. bdg. 290.00 (0-85964-102-3) Chadwyck-Healey.

Catalogue of British Official Publications Not Published by HMSO, 1982. Pref. by Charles Chadwyck-Healey. xxiii, 437p. 1983. lib. bdg. 290.00 (0-85964-114-7) Chadwyck-Healey.

Catalogue of British Official Publications Not Published by HMSO, 1983. Ed. by Alison Moss. 500p. 1984. lib. bdg. 290.00 (0-85964-132-5) Chadwyck-Healey.

Catalogue of British Official Publications Not Published by HMSO, 1984. 500p. 1985. lib. bdg. 290.00 (0-85964-154-6) Chadwyck-Healey.

Catalogue of British Official Publications Not Published by HMSO, 1985. lib. bdg. 290.00 (0-85964-167-8) Chadwyck-Healey.

Catalogue of British Official Publications Not Published by HMSO, 1986. lib. bdg. 290.00 (0-85964-179-1) Chadwyck-Healey.

***Catalogue of Byzantine Seals at Dumbarton Oaks & in the Fogg Museum of Art Vol. 2: South of the Balkans, the Islands, South of Asia Minor.** Ed. by John Nesbitt & Nicolas Oikonomides. LC 91-12861. (Illus.). 248p. 1994. 35.00x (0-88402-226-9, BYS2, Dumbarton Rsch Lib) Dumbarton Oaks.

Catalogue of Byzantine Seals at Dumbarton Oaks & in the Fogg Museum of Art, Vol. 1: Italy, North of the Balkans, North of the Black Sea. Ed. by John Nesbitt & Nicolas Oikonomides. LC 91-12861. (Illus.). 276p. 1991. 30.00 (0-88402-194-7, BYS1, Dumbarton Oaks) Dumbarton Oaks.

Catalogue of Canadian Composers. Helmut Kallmann. 1988. reprint ed. lib. bdg. 59.00 (0-7812-0530-1) Rprt Serv.

Catalogue of Canadian Composers. Ed. by Helmut Kallmann. LC 75-166240. 1972. reprint ed. 29.00 (0-403-01375-5) Scholarly.

Catalogue of Catalogues Raisonnes of Twentieth Century Artists, 1945-83, 2 vols. Wilhelm F. Arntz. (Illus.). (GER.). 1984. Set, 128p., 164p. pap. 150.00 (1-55660-206-5) A Wofsy Fine Arts.

Catalogue of Chamber Music for Woodwind Instruments. Roy Houser. LC 76-166093. (Music Ser.). 1973. reprint ed. lib. bdg. 25.00 (0-306-70257-6) Da Capo.

***Catalogue of Chaucer Manuscripts.** M. C. Seymour. LC 95-1273. 1995. write for info. (1-85928-056-0, Pub. by Scolar Pr UK) Ashgate Pub Co.

Catalogue of Chinese Earthquakes. Gu Gongxu et al. (Science Press Ser.). 888p. 1991. 204.95 (7-03-001592-4, C1592HR) CRC Pr.

Catalogue of Choral Music Arranged in Biblical Order. Comp. by James Laster. LC 82-16745. 269p. 1983. 39.50 (0-8108-1592-3) Scarecrow.

Catalogue of Chromosome Aberrations in Cancer. F. Mitelman. (Journal: Cytogenetics & Cell Genetics: Vol. 36, No. 1-2). (Illus.). 516p. 1983. pap. 105.75 (3-8055-3813-8) S Karger.

Catalogue of Clandestine Tools, Weapons & Gadgets: Guns, Saws, Knives, Daggers & Biological Weapons. 1991. lib. bdg. 75.00 (0-8490-4234-8) Gordon Pr.

Catalogue of Coins Illustrative of the History of the Rulers of Dehli up to 1858 AD. R. B. Whitehead. 1990. 19.00 (81-85425-24-8, Pub. by Manohar II) S Asia.

***Catalogue of Coins in the Provincial Museum Lucknow: Coins of the Mughal Emperors.** C. J. Brown. 560p. 1986. 150.00 (0-9511308-1-1, Pub. by R C Senior UK) St Mut.

Catalogue of Conodonts, Vol. 1. Ed. by W. Ziegler et al. (Illus.). 504p. 1973. ring bd. 68.60 (3-510-65049-2) Lubrecht & Cramer.

Catalogue of Conodonts, Vol. 2. Ed. by W. Ziegler et al. (Illus.). 404p. 1975. ring bd. 64.40 (3-510-65050-6) Lubrecht & Cramer.

Catalogue of Conodonts, Vol. 3. Ed. by W. Ziegler et al. (Illus.). 574p. 1977. ring bd. 86.80 (3-510-65051-4) Lubrecht & Cramer.

Catalogue of Conodonts, Vol. 4. Ed. by W. Ziegler et al. (Illus.). 445p. 1981. ring bd. 85.40 (3-510-65052-2) Lubrecht & Cramer.

Catalogue of Conodonts, Vol. 5. Willi Ziegler et al. (Illus.). 212p. 1991. ring bd. 60.00 (3-510-65053-0, Pub. by E Schweizerbartsche GW) Lubrecht & Cramer.

Catalogue of Crime: A Reader's Guide to the Literature of Mystery, Detection, & Related Genres. Jacques Barzun & Wendell H. Taylor. LC 88-45884. 864p. (YA). (gr. 7 up). 1989. 50.00 (0-06-010263-2, HarpT) HarpC.

Catalogue of Cuneiform Sources Pertaining to Specific Monarchs of the Kassite Dynasty. J. A. Brinkman. LC 76-44965. (Materials & Studies for Kassite History (MSKH): Vol. 1). (Illus.). 1976. pap. 30.00 (0-918986-00-1) Orientl Inst Pr IT.

Catalogue of Cuneiform Tablets in Birmingham City Museum, Vol. 1: Neo-Sumerian Texts from Drehem. Watson. 1986. pap. 35.00 (0-85668-356-6, Pub. by Aris & Phillips UK) David Brown.

Catalogue of Cuneiform Texts, Vol. II. Watson. 1992. pap. write for info. (0-85668-387-6, Pub. by Aris & Phillips UK) David Brown.

Catalogue of Cuneiform Texts, Vol. III. Watson. Date not set. pap. write for info. (0-85668-388-4, Pub. by Aris & Phillips UK) David Brown.

Catalogue of Cycles, Pt. 1: Economics. Louise L. Wilson. 422p. 1964. pap. 15.00 (1-879192-02-0) Fndtn Study Cycles.

Catalogue of Cyrenaican Portrait Sculpture. Elizabeth Rosenbaum. 160p. 1979. 26.00 (0-686-26936-5) St Mut.

Catalogue of Dated & Datable Manuscripts c. 737-1600 in Cambridge Libraries, 2 vols., Set. P. R. Robinson. (Illus.). 144p. 1988. text ed. 390.00 (0-85991-249-3) Boydell & Brewer.

Catalogue of Demotic Papyri in the John Rylands Library, Manchester, 3 vols. in 2, Set. Francis L. Griffith. 1972. reprint ed. 369.20 (3-487-04399-8, Pub. by Georg Olms GW) Lubrecht & Cramer.

Catalogue of Distributed File-Operating Systems. U. M. Borghoff. xi, 214p. 1991. pap. 40.00 (0-387-54450-X) Spr-Verlag.

Catalogue of Drawing Defects: Defects in Wire, Tube & Bar. I. Stander. (Illus.). 120p. 1986. pap. text ed. 32.00 (3-88355-069-8, Pub. by DGM Metallurgy Info GW) IR Pubns.

***Catalogue of Drawings & Watercolors in the Allen Memorial Art Museum, Oberlin College.** Wolfgang Stechow. LC 79-23495. (Illus.). 295p. 1979. 12.50 (0-614-04824-9) Ober Coll Allen.

An Asterisk (*) at the beginning of an entry indicates that the title is appearing in BIP for the first time.

Catalogue of Early Books on Music (Before 1800) Hazel Bartlett & Julia Gregory. LC 69-12684. (Music Ser.). 1969. reprint ed. lib. bdg. 45.00 (*0-306-71223-7*) Da Capo.

Catalogue of Eighteenth Century Symphonies: Vol. I, Thematic Identifier. Jan LaRue. LC 86-46404. 368p. 1988. 29.95 (*0-253-31363-5*) Ind U Pr.

Catalogue of Embroideries: Lady Lever Art Gallery. Xanthe Brooke. LC 92-18401. 1992. 50.00 (*0-7509-0149-7*) A Sutton Pub.

Catalogue of English Bible Translations: A Classified Bibliography of Versions & Editions Including Books, Parts, & Old & New Testament Apocrypha & Acpocryphal Books. William J. Chamberlin. LC 91-27497. (Bibliographies & Indexes in Religious Studies: No. 21). 960p. 1991. text ed. 175.00 (*0-313-28041-X*, CTJ/, Greenwood Pr) Greenwood.

Catalogue of English Books Printed Before 1801 Held by the University Library at Gottingen, 2 vols., Pt. 1: Books Printed Before 1701. Ed. by Karen Kloth. 1987. 180.70 (*0-685-74556-2*, Pub. by Georg Olms GW) Lubrecht & Cramer.

Catalogue of English Books Printed Before 1801 Held by the University Library at Gottingen, 4 vols., Pt. 2: Books Printed Between 1701 & 1800. Ed. by Karen Kloth. 1988. 180.70 (*0-685-74557-0*, Pub. by Georg Olms GW) Lubrecht & Cramer.

Catalogue of English Books Printed Before 1801 Held by the University Library at Gottingen, 4 pts., Pt. 3. Ed. by Karen Kloth. 180.70 (*0-685-74558-9*, Pub. by Georg Olms GW) Lubrecht & Cramer.

Catalogue of English Books Printed Before 1801 Held by the University Library at Gottingen, 4 pts., Pt. 4. Ed. by Karen Kloth. 180.70 (*0-685-74559-7*, Pub. by Georg Olms GW) Lubrecht & Cramer.

Catalogue of English Books Printed Before 1801 Held by the University Library at Gottingen, 4 pts., Set. Ed. by Karen Kloth. write for info. (*3-487-07886-4*, Pub. by Georg Olms GW) Lubrecht & Cramer.

***Catalogue of English Legal Manuscripts in Cambridge University Library: With Codicological Descriptions of the Early Manuscripts by J. S. Ringrose.** Ed. by J. H. Baker. 544p. 1996. text ed. 135.00 (*0-85115-376-3*) Boydell & Brewer.

Catalogue of English Post-Conquest Vernacular Documents. David A. Pelteret. 152p. 1990. 63.00 (*0-85115-259-7*) Boydell & Brewer.

Catalogue of European Industrial Capabilities in Remote Sensing. 320p. (C). 1982. text ed. 105.00 (*90-6191-263-6*, Pub. by A A Balkema NE) Ashgate Pub Co.

Catalogue of European Paintings in the Worcester Art Museum, 2 vols., Set. Ed. by Louisa Dresser. LC 73-90538. (Illus.). 696p. 1974. 45.00 (*0-87023-169-3*) U of Mass Pr.

Catalogue of European Printed Books, India Office Library, 10 Vols, Set. Commonwealth Relations Office, Great Britain Staff. 1970. lib. bdg. 920.00 (*0-8161-0671-1*, Hall Library) G K Hall.

Catalogue of European Sculpture in the Ashmolean Museum, 1540 to the Present Day. Nicholas Penny. LC 92-21820. (C). 1992. write for info. (*0-19-951329-5*, Clarendon Pr) OUP.

Catalogue of Exhibition Catalogues. Victoria & Albert Museum National Art Library, London Staff. 1972. lib. bdg. 140.00 (*0-8161-1022-0*, Hall Library) G K Hall.

Catalogue of Fancy Goods...Alfred, ME. (Hands to Work Ser.: No. 1). (Illus.). 10p. 1971. reprint ed. pap. 0.75 (*0-915836-05-X*) United Soc Shakers.

Catalogue of Fifteenth-Century Books in the Library of Trinity-College, Dublin, & in Marsh's Library, Dublin. Thomas K. Abbott. (Illus.). vi, 225p. 1977. reprint ed. 50.70 (*3-487-06319-0*, Pub. by Georg Olms GW) Lubrecht & Cramer.

Catalogue of Films & Television Programmes on Architecture, Town Planning & the Environment. Jane MacFarlane. (C). 1988. 95.00 (*0-685-30243-1*, Pub. by Oxford Polytechnic UK) St Mut.

Catalogue of Films & Videos in the British Medical Association Library. LAP Staff. 347p. 1993. 60.00 (*1-85604-082-8*, LAP0828, Pub. by Lib Assn Pub UK) UNIPUB.

Catalogue of First Editions of Edward MacDowell. Oscar G. Sonneck. LC 72-155232. (Music Reprint Ser.). 1971. reprint ed. lib. bdg. 21.50 (*0-306-70161-8*) Da Capo.

Catalogue of First Editions of Edward MacDowell, 1861-1908. Oscar G. Sonneck. LC 70-151053. (Library of Congress Publications in Reprint). 1971. reprint ed. 8.00 (*0-405-03422-9*) Ayer.

Catalogue of First Editions of Stephen C. Foster. W. R. Whittlesey & O. G. Sonneck. LC 76-155233. (Music Ser.). 1971. reprint ed. lib. bdg. 21.50 (*0-306-70162-6*) Da Capo.

Catalogue of French Harpsichord Music, 1699-1780. Bruce Gustafson & David Fuller. 472p. 1990. 125.00 (*0-19-315256-8*) OUP.

Catalogue of Gaelic Manuscripts in Selected Libraries in Great Britain & Ireland, 2 vols, Set. Comp. by John Mackechnie. 1973. lib. bdg. 265.00 (*0-8161-0832-3*, Hall Library) G K Hall.

Catalogue of Greek Coins in the British Museum, 29 vols., Set. 1,800.00 (*0-318-19609-3*) Numismatic Fine Arts.

Catalogue of Handel's Musical Autographs. Donald Burrows & Martha J. Ronish. 568p. (C). 1994. 150.00 (*0-19-315250-9*) OUP.

Catalogue of Hebrew Books, 6 Vols, Set. Harvard University Library Staff. LC 68-22146. 3621p. 1968. text ed. 225.00 (*0-674-10150-2*) HUP.

Catalogue of Hebrew Books: Supplement I, 3 vols., Set. Harvard University Library Staff. LC 68-22416. 2161p. 1972. text ed. 185.00 (*0-674-10173-1*) HUP.

Catalogue of Hebrew Books in the British Museum: Acquired During the Years 1868-1892. S. Van Straalen. vii, 532p. 1977. reprint ed. write for info. (*3-487-06345-X*, Pub. by Georg Olms GW) Lubrecht & Cramer.

Catalogue of Herbs, Roots, Barks, Powdered Articles, &c., Prepared in the United Society, New Gloucester, Maine. (Hands to Work Ser.: No. 2). 14p. 1981. reprint ed. pap. 0.75 (*0-915836-06-8*) United Soc Shakers.

Catalogue of Horace Walpole's Library, 3 vols. Allen T. Hazen. Bd. with Horace Walpole's Library. (Illus.). 1969. Set. 200.00 (*0-300-01122-9*) Yale U Pr.

Catalogue of Imaginary Creatures from the Orient. Ed. by Michael P. Jones. (Illus.). 20p. (Orig.). 1983. pap. 4.00 (*0-89904-055-1*) Crumb Elbow Pub.

Catalogue of Incipits of Mediaeval Scientific Writings in Latin. enl. rev. ed. Ed. by Lynn Thorndike & Pearl Kibre. (Medieval Academy Bks.: No. 29). 1963. 50.00 (*0-910956-11-1*) Medieval Acad.

Catalogue of Index Foraminifera, 3 vols., Set. (Illus.). 1967. 75.00 (*0-686-84240-5*) Am Mus Natl Hist.

Catalogue of Index Smaller Foraminifera, 3 vols., Set. (Illus.). 1969. 75.00 (*0-686-84241-3*) Am Mus Natl Hist.

Catalogue of Indian Folk & Tribal Art in the Collection of Home of Folk Art, Museum of Folk, Tribal & Neglected Art. S. Aryan. (Illus.). 12p. 1990. 18.00 (*81-85304-28-9*, Rekha Prakashan) Nataraj Bks.

Catalogue of Indian Synonyms of the Medicinal Plants, Inorganic Substances Propes to be Included in the Pharmacopeia of India. M. Sheriff. 676p. (C). 1978. reprint ed. 275.00 (*0-317-91391-3*, Pub. by Intl Bk Distr II) St Mut.

Catalogue of International Law, 4 vols., Set. University of Cambridge, Squire Law Library Staff et al. LC 71-147816. 1972. 200.00 (*0-379-20030-9*) Oceana.

Catalogue of Invalid Genus Group & Species Group Names in Siphonaptera (Insecta) R. E. Lewis & J. H. Lewis. (Theses Zoologicae Ser.: Vol. 11). 263p. 1989. lib. bdg. 135.00 (*3-87429-302-5*) Koeltz Sci Bks.

Catalogue of Invertebrate Fossil Types at the Academy of Natural Sciences of Philadelphia. Comp. by Horace G. Richards. (Special Publication: No. 8). 222p. (Orig.). 1968. pap. 7.00 (*0-910006-36-9*) Acad Nat Sci Phila.

Catalogue of Investor-Owned Electric Utility Companies Operating in the United States. annuals 33p. 2.50 (*0-317-34086-7*, 04048003) Edison Electric.

Catalogue of Italian Drawings in the Art Museum, Princeton University, 2 vols., Set. Felton Gibbons. LC 76-3252. (Illus.). 1977. text ed. 175.00 (*0-691-03888-0*) Princeton U Pr.

Catalogue of Ivories from Hasanlu, Iran. Oscar W. Muscarella. Ed. by Robert H. Dyson, Jr. (University Museum Monographs: Hasanlu Special Studies: Nos. 40 & 2). (Illus.). xi, 231p. (Orig.). (C). 1980. pap. 30.00 (*0-934718-33-4*) U PA Mus Pubns.

Catalogue of Japanese Illustrated Books & Manuscripts in the Spencer Collection of the New York Public Library. Ed. by Shigeo Sorimachi. (Illus.). 152p. 1978. pap. 35.00 (*0-87104-306-8*) NY Pub Lib.

***Catalogue of Jewish Ossuaries: In the Collections of the State of Israel.** L. Y. Rahmani. (Illus.). 466p. 1994. text ed. 60.00x (*0-614-03629-1*, Ctr Judaic Studies) Eisenbrauns.

Catalogue of Kanagawa Prefecture Magazines: 1945-1949. Ed. by Hisayo Murakami. LC 91-34018. 133p. 1991. 35.00 (*1-880223-00-7*) G W Prange Collect.

Catalogue of Kumaon Plants. S. R. Strachey. 269p. (C). 1974. text ed. 100.00 (*0-89771-661-2*, Pub. by Intl Bk Distr II) St Mut.

Catalogue of Laces & Embroideries in the Collection. F. L. May. (Illus.). 1936. 10.00 (*0-87535-038-0*) Hispanic Soc.

Catalogue of Late Roman Coins in the Dumbarton Oaks Collection & in the Whittemore Collection: From Arcadius & Honorius to the Accession of Anastasius. Philip Grierson & Melinda Mays. LC 91-12862. (Illus.). 500p. 1992. 95.00 (*0-88402-193-9*) Dumbarton Oaks.

Catalogue of Latin American Flat Maps, 1926-1964, Vols. 1 & 2, 1. Palmyra V. Monteiro. LC 67-64686. (Guides & Bibliographies Ser.: No. 2). reprint ed. pap. 102.80 (*0-685-17114-0*, 2027325) Bks Demand.

Catalogue of Latin American Flat Maps, 1926-1964, Vols. 1 & 2, 2. Palmyra V. Monteiro. LC 67-64686. (Guides & Bibliographies Ser.: No. 2). reprint ed. pap. 110.50 (*0-685-17115-9*) Bks Demand.

Catalogue of Lichens of Australia: Exclusive of Tasmania. W. A. Weber & C. M. Wetmore. 1972. 28.00 (*3-7682-5441-0*) Lubrecht & Cramer.

***Catalogue of Manuscripts & Drawings in the General Library of the Natural History Museum.** Natural History Museum (London), General Library Staff. LC 95-6190. (Historical Studies in the Life & Earth Sciences: No. 4). 1995. write for info. (*0-7201-2291-0*, Mansell Pub) Cassell.

Catalogue of Manuscripts in the Houghton Library, Harvard University, 8 vols. 4000p. 1987. lib. bdg. 2,649.00 (*0-89887-040-2*) Chadwyck-Healey.

Catalogue of Manuscripts in the Institute of Cistercian Studies Collection & the University Collection, Western Michigan University. Anna Kirkwood. LC 93-45567. (Cistercian Studies: No. 154). 1994. write for info. (*0-87907-354-3*) Cistercian Pubns.

Catalogue of Manuscripts in the University of Oregon Library. Martin Schmitt. LC 72-30080. 1971. pap. text ed. 7.50 (*0-87114-054-3*) U of Oreg Bks.

Catalogue of Martin Fierro Materials in the University of Texas Library. University of Texas at Austin, Library. LC 72-97224. (Guides & Bibliographies Ser.: 6). 147p. reprint ed. pap. 41.90 (*0-685-16454-3*, 2027319) Bks Demand.

Catalogue of Medicinal Plant Exhibits. S. N. Bal. 121p. (C). 1984. 35.00 (*0-685-22364-7*, Scientific) St Mut.

Catalogue of Medieval & Renaissance Manuscripts in the Beinecke Rare Book & Manuscript Library, Yale University: Vol. I, MSS 1-250. Barbara Shailor. LC 84-667. (Medieval & Renaissance Texts & Studies: Vol. 34). (Illus.). 480p. 1984. 45.00 (*0-86698-065-2*) MRTS.

Catalogue of Medieval & Renaissance Manuscripts in the Beinecke Rare Book & Manuscript Library, Yale University: Vol. II, MSS 251-500. Barbara Shailor. (Medieval & Renaissance Texts & Studies: Vol. 48). (Illus.). 656p. 1987. 50.00 (*0-86698-030-X*) MRTS.

Catalogue of Medieval & Renaissance Manuscripts in the Beinecke Rare Book & Manuscript Library, Yale University, Vol. III: In the Beinecke Rare Book & Manuscript Library, Yale, Vol. III. Barbara Shailor. (Medieval & Renaissance Texts & Studies: Vol. 100). 750p. 1992. 55.00 (*0-86698-115-2*, MR100) MRTS.

Catalogue of Medieval Lead-Glazed Earthenware Tiles in the Department of Medieval & Later Antiquities, British Museum. Elizabeth S. Eames. 794p. 1981. 410.00 (*0-685-04757-1*, Pub. by Brit Mus UK) Parkwest Pubns.

Catalogue of Memoirs. Intro. by Millton E. Krents. LC 87-70786. (William E. Wiener Oral History Library: Vol. 2). xii, 224p. (Orig.). 1987. pap. 10.00 (*0-87495-086-4*) Am Jewish Comm.

Catalogue of Meteorites. 4th ed. A. L. Graham et al. LC 84-48681. 460p. 1985. 75.00 (*0-8165-0912-3*) U of Ariz Pr.

Catalogue of Music by American Moravians, 1742-1842. Albert G. Rau & Hans T. David. LC 76-134283. reprint ed. 29.50 (*0-404-07206-2*) AMS Pr.

Catalogue of Music for Small Orchestra. Cecilia D. Saltonstall. 267p. 1993. reprint ed. lib. bdg. 79.00 (*0-7812-9692-7*) Rprt Serv.

Catalogue of Nevada Checks, 1860-1933. Douglas McDonald. (Illus.). 128p. 1993. 19.50 (*1-879767-02-3*) Castenholz Sons.

Catalogue of Nineteenth Century Bindery Equipment. Harold E. Sterne. LC 78-63315. 1978. 14.95 (*0-932606-01-6*) Ye Olde Print.

Catalogue of Nineteenth Century Printing Presses. Harold E. Sterne. LC 78-63314. (Illus.). 384p. 1978. 19.95 (*0-932606-00-8*) Ye Olde Print.

Catalogue of Non-Herbaceous Phanerogams. A. T. Gage. 367p. (C). 1977. text ed. 260.00 (*0-89771-621-3*, Pub. by Intl Bk Distr II) St Mut.

Catalogue of Numbers, Vol. 4: Sexuality, Courtship, Marriage. Pref. by Arden Rizer, Jr. (Orig.). pap. 20.00 (*0-939795-38-8*) Amer Spirit.

Catalogue of Paintings, Vol. 3: British School by J. W. Goodison. Cambridge University, Fitzwilliam Museum Staff. LC 61-19559. 385p. reprint ed. pap. 109.80 (*0-317-26398-6*, 2024455) Bks Demand.

Catalogue of Paintings at the Theatre Museum, London. Geoffrey Ashton. (Illus.). 128p. 1992. 85.00 (*1-85177-102-6*, Pub. by Victoria & Albert Mus UK) Trafalgar.

Catalogue of Paintings in Public Collections, Vol. 1. (C). 1989. 210.00 (*0-9514166-0-X*, Pub. by Visual Arts UK) St Mut.

Catalogue of Paintings in Public Collections, Vol. 2. (C). 1990. 210.00 (*0-9514166-1-8*, Pub. by Visual Arts UK) St Mut.

Catalogue of Paintings in the Folger Shakespeare Library: "As Imagination Bodies Forth" William L. Pressly. (Illus.). 416p. (C). 1993. text ed. 50.00 (*0-300-05214-6*) Yale U Pr.

Catalogue of Paintings (14th & 15th Centuries) in the Collection. Elizabeth D. Trapier. (Illus.). 1930. 10.00 (*0-87535-028-3*) Hispanic Soc.

***Catalogue of Palaearctic Diptera.** Arpad Soos & Laszlo Papp. 435p. (C). 1989. 150.00x (*963-05-4822-4*, Pub. by Akad Kiado HU) St Mut.

Catalogue of Palaearctic Diptera, 2 vols., Vol. 10: Clusiidae-Chloropidae. Ed. by A. Soos & L. Papp. LC 84-13534. 1984. Vol. 10, Clusiidae-Chloropidae. 156.50 (*0-444-99601-X*) Elsevier.

Catalogue of Palaearctic Diptera, 2 vols., Vol. 11: Scathophagidae-Hypodermatidae. Ed. by A. Soos & L. Papp. 576p. 1986. 148.75 (*0-444-99579-X*) Elsevier.

Catalogue of Palaearctic Diptera, 2 vols., Vol. 12: Calliphoridae-Sarcophagidae. Ed. by A. Soos & L. Papp. 576p. 1986. 148.75 (*0-444-99578-1*) Elsevier.

Catalogue of Palaearctic Diptera: Sciaridae-Anisopodidae, Vol. 4. A. Soos & L. Papp. 444p. 1987. 197.50 (*0-444-99529-3*) Elsevier.

Catalogue of Palaearctic Diptera: Volume Three - Ceratopogonidae. Ed. by A. Soos. 220p. 1988. 202.75 (*0-444-98995-1*) Elsevier.

Catalogue of Palaearctic Diptera - Volume Six: Therevidae - Empididae. Ed. by A. Soos & L. Papp. 436p. 1989. 202.75 (*0-444-98886-6*) Elsevier.

Catalogue of Palaearctic Diptera, Vol. 5: Athericadae & Asilidae. Ed. by A. Soos & L. Papp. 448p. 1988. 197.50 (*0-444-98968-4*) Elsevier.

Catalogue of Pamphlets on Economic Subjects 1750-1900 & Now Housed in Irish Libraries. R. Collison Black. LC 79-81989. 1969. 75.00 (*0-678-08002-X*) Kelley.

Catalogue of Parasites & Predators of Terrestrial Arthropods, Vol. 1: Arachnida to Heteroptera. B. Herting. (Orig.). 1979. pap. text ed. 23.00 (*0-85198-031-7*) CAB Intl.

Catalogue of Parasites & Predators of Terrestrial Arthropods, Vol. 2: Homoptera. B. Herting. (Orig.). 1972. pap. text ed. 23.00 (*0-85198-285-9*) CAB Intl.

Catalogue of Parasites & Predators of Terrestrial Arthropods, Vol. 3: Coleoptera. B. Herting. (Orig.). 1973. pap. text ed. 23.00 (*0-85198-286-7*) CAB Intl.

Catalogue of Parasites & Predators of Terrestrial Arthropods, Vol. 4: Hymenoptera. B. Herting. (Orig.). 1977. pap. text ed. 23.00 (*0-85198-394-4*) CAB Intl.

Catalogue of Parasites & Predators of Terrestrial Arthropods, Vol. 6: Lepidoptera 1 (Microlepidoptera) B. Herting. (Orig.). 1978. pap. text ed. 23.00 (*0-85198-357-X*) CAB Intl.

Catalogue of Parasites & Predators of Terrestrial Arthropods, Vol. 7: Lepidoptera 2 (Macrolepidoptera) B. Herting. (Orig.). 1976. pap. text ed. 23.00 (*0-85198-376-6*) CAB Intl.

Catalogue of Pashto Manuscripts in the Libraries of the British Isles. J. F. Blumhardt & D. N. MacKenzie. 160p. 1965. 210.00 (*0-685-05733-X*, Pub. by Brit Library UK) U of Toronto Pr.

Catalogue of Pepys Library: 3.1 Prints & Drawings. Ed. by A. W. Aspital. 1970. 216.00 (*0-85991-045-8*) Boydell & Brewer.

Catalogue of Pepys Library: 5.2 Modern Manuscripts. Ed. by C. S. Knighton. 1970. 216.00 (*0-85991-078-4*) Boydell & Brewer.

Catalogue of Pepys Library: 6 Bindings. Ed. by Howard M. Nixon. (Illus.). 1970. 171.00 (*0-85991-145-4*) Boydell & Brewer.

Catalogue of Permanent Collections. Addison Gallery of American Art Staff. (Illus.). 66p. 1931. write for info. (*1-879886-00-6*) Addison Gallery.

Catalogue of Planktonic Foraminifera, 7 vols., Set. 1987. 700.00 (*0-686-84238-3*) Am Mus Natl Hist.

Catalogue of Polycystine Radiolaria, 1834-1862, 2 vols., Set. 1972. 50.00 (*0-686-84244-8*) Am Mus Natl Hist.

Catalogue of Portrait Miniatures in the Fitzwilliam Museum. Robert L. Bayne-Powell. (Illus.). 256p. 1985. 105.00 (*0-521-26777-3*) Cambridge U Pr.

Catalogue of Portraits of Naturalists, Mostly Botanists in the Collections of the Hunt Institute, The Linnean Society of London & the Conservatoire et Jardin Botaniques de la Ville de Geneve, Pt. 1: Group Portraits. Comp. by M. T. Stieber et al. 93p. (Orig.). 1987. 6.00 (*0-913196-50-9*) Hunt Inst Botanical.

Catalogue of Portraits of Naturalists, Mostly Botanists in the Collections of the Hunt Institute, The Linnean Society of London & the Conservatoire et Jardin Botaniques de la Ville de Geneve, Pt. 2: Portraits of Individuals, A-D. Comp. by M. T. Stieber et al. 294p. (Orig.). 1988. 15.00 (*0-685-58916-1*) Hunt Inst Botanical.

***Catalogue of Portraits, Paintings & Sculpture at the Natural History Museum.** John C. Thackray. LC 95-9822. (Historical Studies in the Life & Earth Sciences: Vol. 3). 1995. write for info. (*0-7201-2289-9*, Mansell Pub) Cassell.

Catalogue of Pre-Revival Appalachian Dulcimers. L. Allen Smith. LC 82-2697. (Illus.). 144p. 1983. text ed. 25.00 (*0-8262-0376-0*) U of Mo Pr.

***Catalogue of Prehistoric Works East of the Rocky Mountains.** Cyrus Thomas. (Bureau of American Ethnology Bulletins Ser.). 246p. 1995. lib. bdg. 89.00 (*0-7812-4012-3*) Rprt Serv.

Catalogue of Prehistoric Works East of the Rocky Mountains. Cyrus Thomas. reprint ed. 19.00 (*0-403-03547-3*) Scholarly.

Catalogue of Prince William Sound Killer Whales, 1976-1991. Kathy Heise et al. (Illus.). (C). 1992. pap. write for info. (*0-9633467-3-3*) N Gulf Oceanic.

Catalogue of Printed Music in the British Library to 1980, 62 vols., Set. Ed. by Laureen Baillie. (Illus.). 1987. text ed. write for info. (*0-86291-300-4*) U Pubns Amer.

Catalogue of Printed Music in the British Museum. Trustees of the British Museum Staff. 438p. 1991. reprint ed. 119.00 (*0-7812-9301-4*) Rprt Serv.

Catalogue of Published Mean Sea Level Data: 1807-1958. (Publications Scientifique Ser.). 64p. 1961. (*0-318-14512-X*) Intl Assoc Phys Sci Ocean.

Catalogue of Radial Velocities of Galaxies. Giorgio G. Palumbo. 596p. 1983. text ed. 207.00 (*0-677-06090-4*) Gordon & Breach.

Catalogue of Rembrandt's Etchings 2 Vols. in 1. 2nd ed. Arthur M. Hind. LC 67-27456. (Graphic Art Ser.). 1967. reprint ed. lib. bdg. 65.00 (*0-306-70977-5*) Da Capo.

Catalogue of Renaissance Philosophers. John O. Reidl. 192p. 10.00 (*0-87462-433-9*) Marquette.

Catalogue of Rolling Defects: Defects on Hot & Cold Rolled Non-Ferrous Metal Strip. Ed. by W. V. Asten et al. (Illus.). 76p. 1986. Lab manual. student ed 21.00 (*3-88355-106-6*, Pub. by DGM Metallurgy Info GW) IR Pubns.

Catalogue of Royal & Noble Authors, 5 vols., Set. Horace Walpole. LC 76-149672. reprint ed. 345.00 (*0-404-06820-0*) AMS Pr.

Catalogue of Salmonella First Isolations 1965-1984. E. Kelterborn. 1987. lib. bdg. 133.00 (*0-89838-832-5*) Kluwer Ac.

Catalogue of Sanborn Atlases at California State University, Northridge. Gary W. Rees & Mary Hoeber. LC 73-5773. (Occasional Papers: No. 1). (Illus.). 143p. (Orig.). 1973. pap. 4.00 (*0-939112-01-9*) Western Assn Map.

Catalogue of Sculpture (13th to 15th Centuries) in the Collection. Beatrice G. Proske. (Illus.). 360p. 1932. 10.00 (*0-87535-030-5*) Hispanic Soc.

Catalogue of Sculpture (16th to 18th Centuries) in the Collection. Beatrice G. Proske. (Illus.). 1930. 10.00 (*0-87535-027-5*) Hispanic Soc.

Catalogue of Seventeenth Century Printed Books in the National Library of Medicine. National Institutes of Health, Health & Human Services Dept. Staff. 1329p. 1989. text ed. 45.00 (*0-16-002651-2*) USGPO.

Catalogue of Solar Particle Events, 1955-1969. Ed. by Z. Svestka & P. Simon. LC 74-81944. (Astrophysics & Space Science Library: No. 49). 1975. lib. bdg. 196.00 (*90-277-0490-2*) Kluwer Ac.

C

An Asterisk (*) at the beginning of an entry indicates that the title is appearing in BIP for the first time.

1087

Catalogue of Sources for a Linguistic Atlas of Early Medieval English. Margaret Laing. LC 93-18969. 1993. 53.00 (*0-85991-384-8*, DS Brewer) Boydell & Brewer.

Catalogue of Southern Peculiar Galaxies & Associations, 2 Vols., Set. Ed. by C. Arp Halton & Barry F. Madore. 400p. 1987. 150.00 (*0-521-34336-4*) Cambridge U Pr.

Catalogue of Southern Peculiar Galaxies & Associations, Vol. 1: Positions & Descriptions. Halton C. Arp & Barry F Madore. (Illus.). 200p. 1987. 79.95 (*0-521-33086-6*) Cambridge U Pr.

Catalogue of Southern Peculiar Galaxies & Associations, Vol. 2: Selected Photographs. Halton C. Arp & Barry F. Madore. (Illus.). 200p. 1987. 94.95 (*0-521-33087-4*) Cambridge U Pr.

Catalogue of Spanish Rugs: Twelfth-Nineteenth Centuries. Ernest Kuhnel. LC 53-9533. (Illus.). 128p. 1953. pap. 250.00 (*0-685-24464-4*) Textile Mus.

Catalogue of Standard Specifications & Load Tables. 40th ed. 20.00 (*0-318-04020-4*) Steel Joist Inst.

Catalogue of Star Clusters & Associations. G. Alter et al. 76p. 1970. 45.00 (*0-569-08810-0*) St Mut.

***Catalogue of Star Clusters & Associations.** G. Alter et al. 76p. (C). 1970. 171.00x (*963-05-5555-7*, Pub. by Akad Kiado HU) St Mut.

Catalogue of Star Clusters & Associations: Supplement 1. J. Ruprecht et al. 440p. 1981. 308.00 (*0-569-08698-1*) St Mut.

Catalogue of Such English Books As Lately Have Been, or Now Are, in Printing for Publication. William Jaggard. LC 78-26323. (English Experience Ser.: No. 196). 1969. reprint ed. 25.00 (*90-221-0196-7*) Walter J Johnson.

Catalogue of Systems for the Monitoring of Working Conditions Relating to Health. European Communities Staff. 200p. 1992. pap. 25.00 (*92-826-4312-3*, SY-74-92-960-EN-C, Pub. by Europ Com) UNIPUB.

Catalogue of Technical Reports & Documents of the OAS, 1974-1976. (ENG & SPA.). 1977. 4.00 (*0-8270-0200-9*) OAS.

Catalogue of the American Collection: Hunter Museum of Art. William T. Henning, Jr. LC 83-82809. (Illus.). 290p. (Orig.). 1985. 75.00 (*0-9615080-0-0*); pap. text ed. 29.95 (*0-9615080-1-9*) Hunter Art.

Catalogue of the American Library of George Brinley, 5 Pts. in 2 Vols, Set. George Brinley. Ed. by J. Hammond Trumbull. LC 68-54529. reprint ed. lib. bdg. 125.00 (*0-404-01081-4*) AMS Pr.

Catalogue of the American Oriental Society. Elizabeth Strout. (Supplements Ser.). 1930. pap. 7.50 (*0-940490-00-5*) Am Orient Soc.

Catalogue of the Amon Carter Museum Photography Collection. Carol E. Roark et al. LC 92-36173. (Illus.). 720p. 1993. 95.00 (*0-88360-063-3*) Amon Carter.

Catalogue of the Avery Memorial Architectural Library, First Supplement, 4 vols., Set. Columbia University Editors. 3166p. 1978. lib. bdg. 485.00 (*0-8161-0780-7*, Hall Library) G K Hall.

Catalogue of the Avery Memorial Architectural Library, Second Edition, Fourth Supplement. Columbia University Editors. 1980. lib. bdg. 375.00 (*0-8161-0283-X*, Hall Library) G K Hall.

***Catalogue of the Barakat Collection, Vol. 1.** (Illus.). 320p. 300.00 (*0-685-37760-1*) Barakat.

Catalogue of the Batrachia Gradienta S. Caudata & Batrachia Apoda: Collection of the British Museum. 2nd ed. G. A. Boulenger. (Illus.). 1966. 24.00 (*3-7682-0289-5*) Lubrecht & Cramer.

Catalogue of the Batrachia Salienta S. Ecaudata: Collection of the British Museum. G. A. Boulenger. (Illus.). 1966. 81.60 (*3-7682-0291-7*) Lubrecht & Cramer.

Catalogue of the Book Library of the British Film Institute, 3 vols., Set. British Film Institute, London Staff. 1975. lib. bdg. 325.00 (*0-8161-0004-7*, Hall Library) G K Hall.

Catalogue of the Botanical Art Collection at the Hunt Institute: Plant Portraits, Pt. 1: Artists A-D. Ed. by J. J. White & E. R. Smith. 164p. (Orig.). 1985. 9.00 (*0-913196-42-8*) Hunt Inst Botanical.

Catalogue of the Botanical Art Collection at the Hunt Institute: Plant Portraits, Pt. 2: Artists E-G. Comp. by J. J. White & E. R. Smith. (Illus.). 99p. (Orig.). 1987. 6.00 (*0-685-11888-6*) Hunt Inst Botanical.

Catalogue of the Botanical Art Collection at the Hunt Institute: Plant Portraits, Pt. 3: Artists H. Comp. by J. J. White & E. R. Smith. (Illus.). 300p. (Orig.). 1988. 15.00 (*0-685-11889-4*) Hunt Inst Botanical.

Catalogue of the Botanical Art Collection at the Hunt Institute: Plant Portraits, Pt. 4: Artists I-O. Comp. by J. J. White & E. R. Smith. 146p. (Orig.). 1991. 9.00 (*0-685-58001-6*) Hunt Inst Botanical.

***Catalogue of the Botanical Art Collection at the Hunt Institute: Plant Portraits, Pt. 5: Artists P-S.** Ed. by J. J. White & E. R. Smith. 248p. (Orig.). 1994. pap. 16.00 (*0-614-01925-7*) Hunt Inst Botanical.

Catalogue of the Burrell Collection of Wagner Documents, Letters, & Other Biographical Material. Mary W. Burrell. LC 74-26032. reprint ed. 17.50 (*0-404-12876-9*) AMS Pr.

Catalogue of the Byzantine & Early Mediaeval Antiquities in the Dumbarton Oaks Collection, 2 vols. Incl. Vol. I. Metalwork, Ceramics, Glass, Glyptics, Paintings. Marvin C. Ross. LC 68-250. 115p. 1962. 20.00 (*0-88402-006-0*); Vol. III. Ivories & Steatites. Kurt Weitzmann. LC 68-250. 126p. 1972. 25.00 (*0-88402-038-X*); LC 68-250. (Illus.). write for info. (*0-318-51782-5*) Dumbarton Oaks.

Catalogue of the Byzantine Coins in the Dumbarton Oaks Collection & in the Whittemore Collection, Vol. 1: Anastasius the First to Maurice, 491-602. Alfred R. Bellinger. Ed. by Philip Grierson. LC 92-9036. (Illus.). 490p. 1992. reprint ed. 130.00 (*0-88402-012-6*) Dumbarton Oaks.

Catalogue of the Byzantine Coins in the Dumbarton Oaks Collection & in the Whittemore Collection, Vol. 2: Phocas to Theodosius III, 602-717. Philip Grierson. LC 56-10351. (Illus.). 800p. 1993. reprint ed. 165.00 (*0-88402-024-X*) Dumbarton Oaks.

Catalogue of the Byzantine Coins in the Dumbarton Oaks Collection & in the Whittemore Collection, Vol. 3: Leo III to Nicephorus III, 717 - 1801. Philip Grierson. (Illus.). 1993. reprint ed. 215.00 (*0-88402-045-2*) Dumbarton Oaks.

Catalogue of the Cashel Diocesan Library. Cashel Diocesan Library, County Tipperary, Republic of Ireland Staff. 1973. lib. bdg. 110.00 (*0-8161-1065-4*, Hall Library) G K Hall.

Catalogue of the Chelonians, Rhynchocephalians, & Crocodiles in the British Museum. G. A. Boulenger. (Illus.). 1966. 45.00 (*3-7682-0443-X*) Lubrecht & Cramer.

Catalogue of the Chess Collection, Including Checkers, 2 Vols, Set. Cleveland Public Library Editors - John G. White Department. (Series Seventy). 1970. lib. bdg. 145.00 (*0-8161-0681-9*, Hall Library) G K Hall.

Catalogue of the Chiroptera in the Collection of the British Museum. G. E. Dobson. (Illus.). 1966. 65.00 (*3-7682-0300-X*) Lubrecht & Cramer.

Catalogue of the Cicadoidea (Homoptera, Auchenorhyncha) 1956-1980. J. P. Duffels & P. A. Van der Laan. 1985. lib. bdg. 145.50 (*90-6193-522-9*) Kluwer Ac.

Catalogue of the Classical Collection: Vases. Ann H. Ashmead & Kyle M. Phillips, Jr. LC 76-45537. (Illus.). 1976. 10.00 (*0-911517-11-1*) Mus of Art RI.

Catalogue of the Coins Found at Corinth, Nineteen Twenty-Five, with a Note on the Cleaning of the Coins. Alfred R. Bellinger & Charlotte B. Bellinger. (Illus.). 1930. pap. 100.00 (*0-686-51349-5*) Elliots Bks.

Catalogue of the Coins in the Prince of Wales Museum of Western India, Bombay. Ed. by G. V. Acharya. (C). 1988. reprint ed. 27.50 (*0-317-93931-9*, Pub. by Munshiram Manoharial II) S Asia.

Catalogue of the Coins in the Prince of Wales Museum of Western India, Bombay: The Sultans of Gujarat. Comp. by C. R. Singhal. (Illus.). 1979. 40.00 (*0-916710-55-6*) Obol Intl.

Catalogue of the Coins in the Prince of Wales Museum of Western India Bombay (The Sultans of Gujarat. Ed. by V. Acharay. (Illus.). 186p. 1988. reprint ed. 30.00 (*0-317-99946-X*, Pub. by M Manoharial II) Coronet Bks.

Catalogue of the Coins of Dalmatia et Albania, 1410-1797. S. Gardiakos. (Illus.). 32p. 1970. pap. 5.00 (*0-916710-67-X*) Obol Intl.

Catalogue of the Collection. Columbus Museum of Art Staff. LC 78-74705. (Illus.). 249p. (Orig.). 1978. pap. 7.50 (*0-918881-02-1*) Columbus Mus Art.

Catalogue of the Collection Museum of Fine Arts, St. Petersburg, Florida. Ed. by Diane Lesko et al. LC 93-78274. (Illus.). 367p. (Orig.). (C). 1993. pap. 35.00 (*1-878390-02-3*) Mus St Pete.

Catalogue of the Collection of American Art at Randolph-Macon Woman's College: A Selection of Paintings, Drawings, & Prints. 2nd ed. Mary F. Williams. LC 76-51281. (Illus.). 211p. 1977. 20.00 (*0-8139-0591-5*) U Pr of Va.

Catalogue of the Collection of Drawings in the Ashmolean Museum Vol. VI: French Ornament Drawings of the Sixteenth Century. Jon Whiteley. (Illus.). 256p. 1995. 98.00 (*0-19-951328-7*) OUP.

Catalogue of the Collection of Mazatlan Shells in the British Museum. Philip P. Carpenter. (Illus.). 576p. reprint ed. 8.00 (*0-87710-371-2*); reprint ed. 8.00 (*0-87710-372-0*) Paleo Res.

Catalogue of the Collection of Persian Manuscripts in the Metropolitan Museum of Art. Ed. by Abraham V. Jackson & Abraham Yohannan. LC 14-4238. (Columbia University. Indo-Iranian Ser.: No. 1). reprint ed. 19.50 (*0-404-50471-X*) AMS Pr.

Catalogue of the Colonial Office Library: Third Supplement, 1971-1977, 4 vols., Set. Foreign & Commonwealth Office Editors, London. 1979. lib. bdg. 600.00 (*0-8161-0010-1*, Hall Library) G K Hall.

Catalogue of the Colonial Office Library, London, 15 vols. Foreign & Commonwealth Office Editors, London. 1972. First Suppl. 1963-67. lib. bdg. 155.00 (*0-8161-0729-7*, Hall Library); Second Suppl. 1972. 2 Vols. lib. bdg. 240.00 (*0-8161-0843-9*, Hall Library) G K Hall.

Catalogue of the Colonial Office Library, London, 15 vols., Set. Foreign & Commonwealth Office Editors, London. 1972. lib. bdg. 1,640.00 (*0-8161-0688-6*, Hall Library) G K Hall.

Catalogue of the Comparative Education Library. University of London, Institute of Education Staff. (Library Catalogs-Bib. Guides). 1971. lib. bdg. 630.00 (*0-8161-0923-0*, Hall Library) G K Hall.

Catalogue of the Comparative Education Library, 1st Suppl., 3 vols., Set. University of London, Institute of Education Staff. 1974. lib. bdg. 365.00 (*0-8161-0988-5*, Hall Library) G K Hall.

Catalogue of the Compositions of S. Rachmaninoff. Robert Threltall & Geoffrey Norris. 1982. 93.95 (*0-85967-617-X*, Pub. by Scolar Pr UK) Ashgate Pub Co.

Catalogue of the Connecticut Historical Society Loan Collection. Connecticut Historical Society Staff. viii, 97p. 1987. pap. 5.00 (*0-940748-92-4*) Conn Hist Soc.

Catalogue of the Constable Collection. Graham Reynolds. (Illus.). 264p. 1991. 55.00 (*1-85177-042-9*, Pub. by Victoria & Albert Mus UK) Trafalgar.

Catalogue of the Crawford Library of Philatelic Literature: At the British Museum. rev. ed. Edward D. Bacon. 550p. 1991. reprint ed. 225.00 (*0-941480-10-0*, Postilion Pubns) Subway Stamp.

Catalogue of the Culture Collection. 9th ed. International Mycological Institute Staff. 271p. (Orig.). 1988. pap. text ed. 52.00 (*0-85198-585-8*) CAB Intl.

Catalogue of the Edward E. Ayer Ornithological Library. John T. Zimmer. LC 73-17850. (Natural Sciences in America Ser.). 726p. 1974. reprint ed. 47.95 (*0-405-05773-3*) Ayer.

Catalogue of the Edward E. Ayer Ornithologival Library, 2 vols. in one. John T. Zimmer. 706p. 1990. reprint ed. lib. bdg. 55.00 (*0-685-39119-1*) Lubrecht & Cramer.

Catalogue of the Egyptian Collection in the National Museum: Rio de Janeiro, 2 vols. Kitchen. 1991. 199.00 (*0-85668-551-8*, Pub. by Aris & Phillips UK) David Brown.

Catalogue of the Egyptian Hieroglyphic Printing Type. Alan H. Gardiner. 1977. pap. 12.50 (*0-89005-098-8*) Ares.

Catalogue of the Engraved Gems in the Royal Coin Cabinet, The Hague: The Greek, Etruscan & Roman Collections. Marianne Maaskant-Kleibrink. (Illus.). 576p. 1978. text ed. 175.00 (*3-515-02919-2*) Coronet Bks.

Catalogue of the Entire & Valuable Library of the Books of the Late Henry Fielding Esq. Henry Fielding. reprint ed. lib. bdg. 19.50 (*0-404-52315-3*) AMS Pr.

Catalogue of the Erasmus Collection in the City Library of Rotterdam. LC 90-45107. (Bibliographies & Indexes in Philosophy Ser.: No. 2). 704p. 1990. text ed. 215.00 (*0-313-27698-6*, MRO, Greenwood Pr) Greenwood.

Catalogue of the Evelyn Waugh Collection at the Humanities Research Center: The University of Texas at Austin. Robert M. Davis. LC 80-50840. 376p. 1981. 25.00 (*0-87875-194-7*) Whitston Pub.

Catalogue of the Everett D. Graff Collection of Western Americana. Ed. by Colton Storm. LC 66-20577. (Illus.). 1968. lib. bdg. 50.00 (*0-226-77579-8*) U Ch Pr.

Catalogue of the Exhibition of Ch'ing Dynasty Costume Accessories Taipei. (Illus.). 352p. 1986. pap. 95.00 (*957-562-021-6*) Heian Intl.

Catalogue of the Farlow Reference Library of Cryptogamic Botany. Harvard University Staff. 1979. lib. bdg. 760.00 (*0-8161-0279-1*, Hall Library) G K Hall.

Catalogue of the Fifteenth-Century Printed Books in the Harvard University Library, Vol. 1: Books Printed in Germany, German-Speaking Switzerland, & Austria-Hungary. James E. Walsh. (Medieval & Renaissance Texts & Studies: Vol. 84). 672p. 1991. 50.00 (*0-86698-096-2*, MR84) MRTS.

Catalogue of the Fifteenth-Century Printed Books in the Harvard University Library, Vol. 2: Books Printed in Rome & Venice. James E. Walsh. (Medieval & Renaissance Texts & Studies: Vol. 97). 720p. 1993. 60.00 (*0-86698-111-X*) MRTS.

Catalogue of the Fifteenth-Century Printed Books in the Harvard University Library, Vol. 3: Books Printed in Italy with the Exception of Rome & Venice. James E. Walsh. (Medieval & Renaissance Texts & Studies: Vol. 119). 700p. 1994. 50.00 (*0-86698-174-8*) MRTS.

Catalogue of the Fishes in the British Museum (Natural History), 8 vols. Albert Guenther. 4368p. 1981. lib. bdg. 295.00 (*3-7682-7109-9*) Lubrecht & Cramer.

Catalogue of the Flora of Arizona. J. Harry Lehr. 1978. 4.75 (*0-9605656-0-4*) Desert Botanical.

Catalogue of the Flowering Plants & Ferns of Connecticut Growing Without Cultivation. C. B. Graves et al. (Illus.). 1974. 36.00 (*3-7682-0952-0*) Lubrecht & Cramer.

Catalogue of the Flowering Plants & Gymnosperms of Peru - Catalogo De las Angiospermas y Gimnospermas Del Peru. Ed. by Marshall Crosby. (Monographs in Systematic Botany from the Missouri Botanical Garden: No. 45). 1286p. 1993. 60.00 (*0-915279-19-3*) Miss Botan.

Catalogue of the Foreign Office Library, 1926-1968, 8 vols. Foreign & Commonwealth Office Editors, London. 6208p. 1973. lib. bdg. 870.00 (*0-8161-0998-2*, Hall Library) G K Hall.

Catalogue of the Fossil & Recent Genera & Species of Diatoms & Their Syhonyms: Navicula, Pt. 5. S. L. Van Landingham. 2963p. 1975. text ed. 75.00 (*3-7682-0475-8*) Lubrecht & Cramer.

Catalogue of the Fossil & Recent Genera & Species of Diatoms & Their Synonyms, Pt. 1. S. L. Van Landingham. Incl. Pt. 1. Acanthoceras - Bacillaria. 1967. 75.00 (*3-7682-0471-5*); Pt. 2. Bacteriastrum - Coscinodiscus. 1968. 75.00 (*3-7682-0472-3*); Pt. 3. Coscinophaena - Fibula. 1969. 75.00 (*3-7682-0473-1*); Pt. 4. Fragilaria - Maunema. 1971. 75.00 (*3-7682-0474-X*); Set pap. 125.00 (*0-685-55590-9*) Lubrecht & Cramer.

Catalogue of the Fossil & Recent Genera & Species of Diatoms & Their Synonyms: Suppl. Taxa, Additions & Corrections, Pt. 8. S. L. Van Landingham. 1979. lib. bdg. 75.00 (*3-7682-0478-2*) Lubrecht & Cramer.

Catalogue of the Fossil & Recent Genera & Species of Diatoms & Their Synonyms-Part 7: Rhoicosphenia Through Zygoceros. S. L. Van Landingham. 1979. lib. bdg. 75.00 (*3-7682-0477-4*) Lubrecht & Cramer.

Catalogue of the Francis Trigge Chained Library: St. Wulfram's Church, Grantham. John Glenn & David Walsh. 1988. 63.00 (*0-85991-258-2*) Boydell & Brewer.

Catalogue of the Gennadius Library. American School of Classical Studies at Athens, 7 Vols. American School of Classical Studies at Athens Staff. 1970. lib. bdg. 765.00 (*0-8161-0707-6*, Hall Library) G K Hall.

Catalogue of the Gennadius Library. American School of Classical Studies at Athens, First Supplement. American School of Classical Studies at Athens Staff. 1973. lib. bdg. 140.00 (*0-8161-0835-8*, Hall Library) G K Hall.

Catalogue of the Gennadius Library. American School of Classical Studies at Athens, Second Supplement. American School of Classical Studies at Athens Staff. 1981. lib. bdg. 190.00 (*0-8161-0011-X*, Hall Library) G K Hall.

Catalogue of the Glenbow Historical Library, 4 vols., Set. Glenbow Historical Library Staff, Glenbow-Alberta Institute. 1973. lib. bdg. 440.00 (*0-8161-0994-X*, Hall Library) G K Hall.

Catalogue of the Goldsmith's Library of Economic Literature, 4 vols., Set. Ed. by Margaret Canney et al. (C). 1983. text ed. 550.00 (*0-485-15016-6*, Pub. by Athlone Pr UK) Humanities.

Catalogue of the Goldsmith's Library of Economic Literature, Vol. 1. Ed. by Margaret Canney et al. 838p. (C). 1970. text ed. 130.00 (*0-485-15014-X*) Humanities.

***Catalogue of the Goldsmiths Library of Economic Literature, 5 vols., Vol. I-V.** Angela Whitelegge & Ruth Vyse. 1995. text ed. 790.00 (*0-485-15021-2*, Pub. by Athlone Pr UK) Humanities.

Catalogue of the Goldsmith's Library of Economic Literature, Vol. 2. Ed. by Margaret Canney et al. 772p. (C). 1975. text ed. 130.00 (*0-485-15015-8*) Humanities.

Catalogue of the Goldsmith's Library of Economic Literature, Vol. 4. Ed. by Margaret Canney et al. 449p. (C). 1983. text ed. 160.00 (*0-485-15013-1*) Humanities.

Catalogue of the Goldsmith's Library of Economic Literature Vol. 3: Additions to Printed Books 1840 Periodicals & Manuscripts. Ed. by Margaret Canney et al. (C). 1982. text ed. 130.00 (*0-485-15012-3*, Pub. by Athlone Pr UK) Humanities.

***Catalogue of the Goldsmiths' Library of Economic Literature Vol. 5: Additions to the Printed Books, Periodicals & Manuscripts to 1850.** Comp. by Angela Whitelegge & Ruth Vyse. 120p. (C). 1995. text ed. 120.00 (*0-485-15020-4*, Pub. by Athlone Pr UK) Humanities.

Catalogue of the Greek & Roman Antiquities in the Dumbarton Oaks Collection. Gisela M. Richter. LC 56-10351. (Illus.). 77p. 1956. 20.00 (*0-88402-002-9*) Dumbarton Oaks.

Catalogue of the Greek Manuscripts in the Library of the Laura on Mt. Athos, with Notices from Other Libraries. Athos Monasteries Staff. (Harvard Theological Studies: Vol. 12). 1925. 56.00 (*0-527-01012-X*) Periodicals Srv.

Catalogue of the Greek Manuscripts in the Library of the Monastery of Vatopedi on Mt. Athos. Athos Monasteries Staff. (Harvard Theological Studies: Vol. 11). 1924. 26.00 (*0-527-01011-1*) Periodicals Srv.

Catalogue of the Greenlee Collection, 2 vols, Set. Newberry Library, Chicago Staff. 1970. lib. bdg. 220.00 (*0-8161-0903-6*, Hall Library) G K Hall.

Catalogue of the Hans Syz Collection, Vol. 1: Meissen Porcelain & Hausmalerei. Hans Syz et al. LC 76-608122. (Illus.). 608p. 1980. 85.00 (*0-87474-168-8*, SYCH) Smithsonian.

Catalogue of the Harleian Manuscripts in the British Museum: With Indexes of Persons, Places, & Matters, 4 vols., Set. (Anglistica & Americana Ser.: No. 88). 1973. reprint ed. 702.00 (*3-487-05036-6*, Pub. by Georg Olms GW) Lubrecht & Cramer.

Catalogue of the Harvard University Fine Arts Library, First Supplement, 3 vols., Set. Harvard University, Fogg Art Museum Staff. 1975. lib. bdg. 440.00 (*0-8161-1224-X*, Hall Library) G K Hall.

Catalogue of the Hebrew Manuscripts in the Bodleian Library & in the College Libraries of Oxford, Vol. I. A. D. Neubauer. 624p. 1995. 130.00 (*0-19-951357-0*) OUP.

Catalogue of the Hebrew Manuscripts in the Bodleian Library & in the College Libraries of Oxford: Supplement of Addenda & Corrigenda to Volume I. Malachi Beit-Arie. Ed. by R. A. May. 300p. (C). 1995. 98.00 (*0-19-817386-5*) OUP.

Catalogue of the Icelandic Collection: Additions 1913-1926. Comp. by Halldor Hermannsson. (University Library Publications). 293p. 1960. pap. 47.50 (*0-8014-9817-1*) Cornell U Pr.

Catalogue of the Icelandic Collection: Additions 1927-1942. Comp. by Halldor Hermannsson. (University Library Publications). 312p. 1960. pap. 47.50 (*0-8014-9818-X*) Cornell U Pr.

Catalogue of the Imagist Poets. LC 78-64008. (Des Imagistes: Literature of the Imagist Movement Ser.). 72p. reprint ed. 27.50 (*0-404-17079-X*) AMS Pr.

Catalogue of the IMMRC Communication Research Library Vol. I. 200p. 1995. 25.00 (*0-88477-036-2*) Intl General.

Catalogue of the Imperial College of Tropical Agriculture, 8 vols, Set. University of the West Indies, Imperial College of Tropical Agriculture, Trinidad Staff. 1975. lib. bdg. 825.00 (*0-8161-1190-1*, Hall Library) G K Hall.

Catalogue of the Joanna Southcott Collection at the University of Texas. Ed. by Eugene P. Wright. LC 68-65505. (Tower Bibliographical Ser.: No. 7). (Illus.). 1968. 15.00 (*0-87959-045-9*) U of Tex H Ransom Ctr.

Catalogue of the Joseph Hergesheimer Collection at the University of Texas. Comp. by Herb Stappenbeck. LC 78-169267. (Tower Bibliographical Ser.: No. 10). (Illus.). 1974. 15.00 (*0-87959-043-2*) U of Tex H Ransom Ctr.

Catalogue of the Lansdowne Manuscripts in the British Museum: With Indexes of Persons, Places, & Matters, 2 vols. in 1. (Anglistica & Americana Ser.: No. 91). xii, 677p. 1974. reprint ed. 193.70 (*3-487-05184-2*, Pub. by Georg Olms GW) Lubrecht & Cramer.

Catalogue of the Libraries of Sir Thomas Browne & Dr. Edward Browne, His Son: A Facsimile Reproduction with an Introduction, Notes, & Index. Jeremiah S. Finch. (Publications of the Sir Thomas Browne Institute, Leiden, New Ser.: No. 7). xiv, 178p. 1986. 29.75 (*90-04-07920-3*) E J Brill.

An Asterisk (*) at the beginning of an entry indicates that the title is appearing in BIP for the first time.

Catalogue of the Library at Abbotsford. Walter Scott. Ed. by J. G. Cochrane. LC 79-144430. (Bannatyne Club, Edinburgh. Publications: No. 60). reprint ed. 39.50 (*0-404-52770-1*) AMS Pr.

Catalogue of the Library of Adam Smith: Prepared for the Royal Economic Society. 2nd ed. Ed. by James Bonar. LC 66-15561. (Reprints of Economic Classics Ser.). 1966. reprint ed. 35.00 (*0-678-00188-X*) Kelley.

Catalogue of the Library of Sir Richard Burton, K. C. M. G. B. J. Kirkpatrick. 182p. pap. 5.95 (*0-900632-13-5*) Huntington Lib.

Catalogue of the Library of Sir Richard Burton, K. C. M. G., Held by the Royal Anthropological Institute. Royal Anthropological Institute of Great Britain & Ireland Staff. Ed. by B. J. Kirkpatrick. LC 80-473753. 182p. reprint ed. pap. 51.90 (*0-7837-6667-X*, 2046279) Bks Demand.

Catalogue of the Library of the Arctic Institute of North America, 4 Vols, Set. Arctic Institute of North America, Montreal Editors. 1970. lib. bdg. 410.00 (*0-8161-0823-4*, Hall Library) G K Hall.

Catalogue of the Library of the Arctic Institute of North America, First Supplement, 1. Arctic Institute of North America, Montreal Editors. 1971. lib. bdg. 130.00 (*0-8161-0830-7*, Hall Library) G K Hall.

Catalogue of the Library of the Arctic Institute of North America, Second Supplement, 2 vols, Set. Arctic Institute of North America, Montreal Editor. 1974. lib. bdg. 265.00 (*0-8161-1030-1*, Hall Library) G K Hall.

Catalogue of the Library of the Arctic Institute of North America, Third Supplement. Arctic Institute of North America, Montreal Editor. 1980. lib. bdg. 455.00 (*0-8161-1162-6*, Hall Library) G K Hall.

Catalogue of the Library of the Boston Athenaeum: 1807-1871, 5 vols. 3402p. 1969. reprint ed. 25.00 (*0-934552-05-3*) Boston Athenaeum.

Catalogue of the Library of the Freshwater Biological Association, 6 vols., Set. Freshwater Biological Association Editors, Cumbria England. 1979. lib. bdg. 725.00 (*0-8161-0289-9*, Hall Library) G K Hall.

Catalogue of the Library of the Graduate School of Design, 44 Vols, Set. Harvard University - Graduate School of Design Staff. 1970. lib. bdg. 4,100.00 (*0-8161-0812-9*, Hall Library) G K Hall.

Catalogue of the Library of the Graduate School of Design: Third Supplement. Harvard University Staff. (Library Catalogs). 1979. lib. bdg. 490.00 (*0-8161-0284-8*, Hall Library) G K Hall.

Catalogue of the Library of the Graduate School of Design, First Supplement, 2 vols., Set. Harvard University - Graduate School of Design Staff. 1970. lib. bdg. 265.00 (*0-8161-0831-5*, Hall Library) G K Hall.

Catalogue of the Library of the Hispanic Society of America, 10 Vols, Set. Hispanic Society of America, New York. 1970. lib. bdg. 1,090.00 (*0-8161-0624-X*, Hall Library) G K Hall.

Catalogue of the Library of the Hispanic Society of America, First Supplement, 4 vols. Hispanic Society of America, New York. 1970. lib. bdg. 485.00 (*0-8161-0910-9*, Hall Library) G K Hall.

Catalogue of the Library of the Institute of Advanced Legal Studies, 6 vols. Institute of Advanced Legal Studies, University of London Staff. 1978. lib. bdg. 655.00 (*0-8161-0099-3*, Hall Library) G K Hall.

Catalogue of the Library of the Museum of Comparative Zoology, 8 Vols. Harvard University Museum of Comparative Zoology Staff. 1970. lib. bdg. 835.00 (*0-8161-0767-X*, Hall Library) G K Hall.

Catalogue of the Library of the Museum of Comparative Zoology, First Supplement. Harvard University Museum of Comparative Zoology Staff. 1977. lib. bdg. 140.00 (*0-8161-0811-0*, Hall Library) G K Hall.

Catalogue of the Library of the National Gallery of Canada, 8 vols., Set. National Gallery of Canada Staff. 1973. Eight Vols. lib. bdg. 870.00 (*0-8161-1043-3*, Hall Library) G K Hall.

Catalogue of the Library of the National Gallery of Canada, First Supplement, 6 vols., Set. National Gallery of Canada, Ottawa Staff. (Library Catalogs & Supplements). 1981. lib. bdg. 800.00 (*0-8161-0291-0*, Hall Library) G K Hall.

Catalogue of the Library of the Society for Psychical Research, London, England. Society for Psychical Research, London, England Staff. 1977. lib. bdg. 80.00 (*0-8161-0008-X*, Hall Library) G K Hall.

Catalogue of the Library of Thomas Baker. Frans Korsten. 480p. (C). 1990. 94.95 (*0-521-37394-8*) Cambridge U Pr.

Catalogue of the Library of Thomas Jefferson, 5 Vols., 2. Comp. by Millicent E. Sowerby. LC 83-1265. 1983. reprint ed. 50.00 (*0-685-73550-8*) U Pr of Va.

Catalogue of the Library of Thomas Jefferson, 5 Vols., 3. Comp. by Millicent E. Sowerby. LC 83-1265. 1983. reprint ed. 50.00 (*0-685-73551-6*) U Pr of Va.

Catalogue of the Library of Thomas Jefferson, 5 Vols., 4. Comp. by Millicent E. Sowerby. LC 83-1265. 1983. reprint ed. 50.00 (*0-685-73552-4*) U Pr of Va.

Catalogue of the Library of Thomas Jefferson, 5 Vols., 5. Comp. by Millicent E. Sowerby. LC 83-1265. 1983. reprint ed. 50.00 (*0-685-73553-2*) U Pr of Va.

Catalogue of the Lichens of Papua New Guinea & Irian Jaya. Heinar Streimann. (Bibliotheca Lichenologica Monograph: No. 22). (Illus.). 146p. 1986. text ed. 45.00 (*3-443-58001-7*) Lubrecht & Cramer.

Catalogue of the Living Marine Bivalve Molluscs of China. F. R. Bernard et al. 160p. (Orig.). 1993. pap. 39.50 (*962-209-324-8*, Pub. by Hong Kong Univ Pr HK) Coronet Bks.

Catalogue of the Lizards in the British Museum, 3 vols. in 2. G. A. Boulenger. (Illus.). 1964. 280.00 (*3-7682-0239-9*) Lubrecht & Cramer.

Catalogue of the Louis Zukofsky Manuscript Collection. Ed. by Marcella Booth. LC 70-38572. (Tower Bibliographical Ser.: No. 11). (Illus.). 1975. 22.50 (*0-87959-038-6*) U of Tex H Ransom Ctr.

Catalogue of the Manchu-Mongol Section of Toyo Bunko. Nicholas N. Poppe et al. LC 65-63112. (Publications on Asia of the School of International Studies: No. 12). 391p. 1964. 35.00 (*0-295-73732-8*) U of Wash Pr.

Catalogue of the Manuscript Collections of the American Antiquarian Society, 40 Vols. American Antiquarian Society Staff. 1979. lib. bdg. 430.00 (*0-8161-0258-9*, Hall Library) G K Hall.

Catalogue of the Manuscripts in the Collection of Western Americana Founded by William Robertson Coe, Yale University Library. Comp. by Mary C. Withington. 1952. 200.00 (*0-685-30614-3*) Elliots Bks.

Catalogue of the Manuscripts in the Cottonian Library Deposited in the British Museum. (Anglistica & Americana Ser.: No. 92). xv, 618p. 1974. reprint ed. 167.70 (*3-487-05018-8*, Pub. by Georg Olms GW) Lubrecht & Cramer.

Catalogue of the Manuscripts in the Cottonian Library, 1696. Thomas Smith. Ed. by Colin G. Tite. 400p. 1985. 190.00 (*0-85991-159-4*) Boydell & Brewer.

Catalogue of the Manuscripts in the Library of the Royal Geographical Society of Australasia (South Australian Branch) Inc. Phyllis Mander-Jones. (C). 1981. 75.00 (*0-7855-0333-1*, Pub. by Royal Geograp Soc AT) St Mut.

Catalogue of the Manuscripts of Hereford Cathedral Library. Ed. by R. M. Thomson. (Illus.). 344p. (C). 1993. text ed. 195.00 (*0-85991-390-2*) Boydell & Brewer.

Catalogue of the Manuscripts of Lincoln Cathedral Chapter Library. R. M. Thompson. (Illus.). 360p. (C). 1990. 190.00 (*0-85991-278-7*) Boydell & Brewer.

Catalogue of the McClean Collection of Greek Coins (in the Fitzwilliam Museum, Cambridge), 3 vols. S. W. Grose. (Illus.). 1476p. 1979. text ed. 295.00 (*0-916710-50-5*) Obol Intl.

Catalogue of the Mesozoic Mammalia in the Geological Department of the British Museum & American Mesozoic Mammalia: Memoirs of the Peabody Museum of Yale University, Vol. Iii, Pt. 1, 2vols. In 1. George G. Simpson. Ed. by Stephen J. Gould. LC 79-8350. (History of Paleontology Ser.). (Illus.). 1980. reprint ed. lib. bdg. 73.95 (*0-405-12743-X*) Ayer.

Catalogue of the Morse Collection of Japanese Pottery. Edward S. Morse. LC 77-83037. (Illus.). 544p. 1979. reprint ed. boxed 60.00 (*0-8048-1299-3*) C E Tuttle.

Catalogue of the Names of the Early Puritan Settlers of Connecticut. Royal R. Hinman. 884p. 1993. reprint ed. lib. bdg. 89.00 (*0-685-65230-0*) Higginson Bk Co.

Catalogue of the National Gallery of Canada: Canadian Art, Vol. I- A-F. Charles C. Hill & Pierre B. Landry. (Illus.). 500p. 1988. 74.95 (*0-226-56456-8*, Pub. by Natl Gallery CN) U Ch Pr.

Catalogue of the National Map Collection, 16 vols., Set. Public Archives Staff of Canada Ottawa. 1976. lib. bdg. 1,640.00 (*0-8161-1215-0*, Hall Library) G K Hall.

Catalogue of the Nevill Collection of Sinhalese Manuscripts in the British Library, Vol. 1. Somadasa. (C). 1987. write for info. (*0-86013-273-0*, Pub. by Pali Text) Wisdom MA.

Catalogue of the Nevill Collection of Sinhalese Manuscripts in the British Library, Vol. II. Somadasa. 1989. write for info. (*0-86013-286-2*) Wisdom MA.

Catalogue of the Nevill Collection of Sinhalese Manuscripts in the British Library, Vol. III. Somadasa. 1990. write for info. (*0-86013-300-1*) Wisdom MA.

Catalogue of the Nevill Collection of Sinhalese Manuscripts in the British Library, Vol. IV. Somadasa. 1990. write for info. (*0-86013-301-X*) Wisdom MA.

Catalogue of the Newark Tibetan Collection: Introduction, 5 vols., Set. 2nd ed. Valrae Reynolds & Amy Heller. Tr. by Mary S. Sweeney. (Illus.). 84p. (Orig.). 1983. pap. (*0-932828-12-4*) Newark Mus.

Catalogue of the Newark Tibetan Collection: Introduction, Vol. I. 2nd ed. Valrae Reynolds & Amy Heller. Tr. by Mary S. Sweeney. (Illus.). 84p. (Orig.). 1983. pap. 12.50 (*0-932828-13-2*) Newark Mus.

Catalogue of the Oriental Collection. Ed. by Stephen Addiss & Chu-tsing Li. LC 80-82048. (Illus.). 145p. 1980. pap. 8.50 (*0-685-57442-3*) Spencer Muse Art.

Catalogue of the Orthoptera of Spain. L. Herrera. 1982. lib. bdg. 80.00 (*90-6193-131-2*) Kluwer Ac.

Catalogue of the Papers of James Boswell at Yale University, 3 vols., Set. Ed. by Marion S. Pottle et al. 1400p. (C). 1993. text ed. 275.00 (*0-300-05410-6*) Yale U Pr.

Catalogue of the Pedro Traversari Collection of Musical Instruments. Ricahrd T. Rephann. Tr. by Lola Odiaga. (Illus.). 146p. (Orig.). (ENG & SPA.). 1978. pap. 10.00 (*0-929530-01-2*) Yale U Coll Musical Instruments.

Catalogue of the Pepys Library, Vol. 1. Ed. by Robert Latham & N. A. Smith. (Printed Bks.). 201p. 1978. 125.00 (*0-87471-819-8*) Rowman.

Catalogue of the Pepys Library at Magdalene College, Cambridge, 2 vols., Set. Ed. by Robert Latham. (Illus.). 840p. (C). 1991. 315.00 (*0-85991-304-X*) Boydell & Brewer.

Catalogue of the Pepys Library at Magdalene College, Cambridge, IV: Music, Maps & Calligraphy. Ed. by Robert Latham. (Illus.). 192p. 1989. 216.00 (*0-85991-246-9*) Boydell & Brewer.

Catalogue of the Pepys Library at Magdalene College, Cambridge, Vol. II: Ballads, 2 pts., Pt. 1: Catalogue. Ed. by Robert Latham & Helen Weinstein. (Illus.). 256p. (C). 1993. text ed. 234.00 (*0-85991-315-5*) Boydell & Brewer.

Catalogue of the Pepys Library at Magdalene College, Cambridge, Vol. II: Ballads, 2 pts., Pt. 2. Ed. by Robert Latham & Helen Weinstein. (Illus.). 240p. (C). 1993. Pt 2 240p. text ed. 216.00 (*0-85991-333-3*) Boydell & Brewer.

Catalogue of the Pepys Library at Magdalene College, Cambridge, Vol. 3: Pt. 1 - Prints & Drawings (General) Robert Latham. Ed. by A. Aspital. (Illus.). 396p. 1980. 188.25 (*0-8476-3637-2*) Rowman.

Catalogue of the Pepys Library at Magdalene College, Cambridge, Vol. 3, No. 2: Prints & Drawings: Portraits. Comp. by Eric Chamberlain. 284p. (C). 1994. text ed. 216.00 (*0-85991-332-5*, DS Brewer) Boydell & Brewer.

Catalogue of the Pepys Library at Magdalene College, Cambridge, Vol. 5: V.i. Medieval Manuscripts. Ed. by Robert Latham & Richard Beadle. 160p. (C). 1993. text ed. 171.00 (*0-85991-341-4*) Boydell & Brewer.

Catalogue of the Permanent Collection. Intro. by Kenneth H. Lindquist. (Illus.). 175p. 1973. 7.95 (*1-877885-00-2*) Arnot Art.

Catalogue of the Personal Library of Stephen Girard (1750-1831) William F. Zeil. LC 81-85267. (American Philosophical Society, Memoirs Ser.: No. 190). 245p. reprint ed. pap. 69.90 (*0-8357-6981-X*, 2039042) Bks Demand.

Catalogue of the Plants of Kumaon. S. R. Strachey. 269p. (C). 1974. reprint ed. 75.00 (*0-685-21822-8*, Pub. by Intl Bk Distr II) St Mut.

Catalogue of the Population Council Library. Population Council Editors. 1979. lib. bdg. 325.00 (*0-8161-0278-3*, Hall Library) G K Hall.

Catalogue of the Pre-1500 Western Manuscript Books at the Newberry Library. Paul Saenger. (Illus.). 332p. 1989. lib. bdg. 125.00 (*0-226-73350-5*) U Ch Pr.

Catalogue of the Printed Books in the Library of the Honourable Society of the Middle Temple, 4 vols. incl. suppl., Set. C. E. Bedwell. 1961. reprint ed. lib. bdg. 150.00 (*0-89941-352-8*, 500070) W S Hein.

Catalogue of the Public Archives Library of Canada: Collection of Published Material with a Chronological List of Pamphlets. Public Archives Staff of Canada Ottawa. 1979. lib. bdg. 1,375.00 (*0-8161-0316-X*, Hall Library) G K Hall.

Catalogue of the Rebecca Darlington Stoddard Collection of Greek & Roman Vases. P. V. Baur. LC 78-63552. (Yale Oriental Series: Researches: No. 8). reprint ed. 74.50 (*0-404-60278-9*) AMS Pr.

Catalogue of the Regional Oral History Office: 1954-1979. Ed. by Suzanne B. Riess & Willa K. Baum. (Illus.). 119p. (Orig.). (C). 1980. pap. text ed. 6.50 (*0-9604164-0-4*) U CA Region Oral Hist.

Catalogue of the Rischel & Birket-Smith Collection of Guitar Music in the Royal Library of Copenhagen. Jytte T. Larsson. Ed. by Peter Danner. LC 89-80417. 272p. 1989. 45.00 (*0-936186-20-8*); pap. 29.00 (*0-936186-33-X*) Edit Orphee.

Catalogue of the Roland P. Murdock Collection of the Wichita Art Museum. George P. Tomko. Ed. by Jan Von Adlmann & Ruth Lawner. LC 72-82939. (Illus.). 237p. 1972. 20.00 (*0-939324-00-8*); pap. 10.00 (*0-939324-01-6*) Wichita Art Mus.

Catalogue of the Scarabs Belonging to George Fraser. George Fraser. LC 79-83551. (Illus.). 1979. reprint ed. 12.50 (*0-915018-19-5*) Attic Bks.

Catalogue of the Sculpture Collection. Ed. by Douglas Hyland & Marilyn Stokstad. LC 81-51939. (Illus.). 143p. 1981. pap. 8.50 (*0-685-57443-1*) Spencer Muse Art.

Catalogue of the Sculpture in the Dumbarton Oaks Collection from the Ptolemaic Period to the Renaissance. Gary Vikan. LC 93-22567. 1994. write for info. (*0-88402-212-9*) Dumbarton Oaks.

Catalogue of the Severence & Greta Millikin Collection. Cleveland Museum of Art Staff. LC 90-38882. (Illus.). 112p. reprint ed. pap. 32.00 (*0-7837-7084-7*, 2046897) Bks Demand.

Catalogue of the Singapore-Malaysia Collection. University of Singapore Library Staff. 1970. lib. bdg. 145.00 (*0-8161-0818-8*, Hall Library) G K Hall.

Catalogue of the Spanish Library, & of the Portuguese Books Bequeathed by George Ticknor to the Boston Public Library. Boston Public Library Staff. 1970. lib. bdg. 85.00 (*0-8161-0865-X*, Hall Library) G K Hall.

Catalogue of the Special Exhibition of Emperors' Porcelain Taipei. (Illus.). 180p. 1986. pap. 69.50 (*957-562-073-9*) Heian Intl.

Catalogue of the Special Exhibition of Kuan Ware Porcelain Taipei. (Illus.). 198p. 1989. pap. 49.50 (*957-562-019-4*) Heian Intl.

Catalogue of the Special Exhibition of Ting Ware White Porcelain. 2nd ed. Hsieh Ming-liang. (Collections of the National Palace Museum, Taipei). 231p. 1987. reprint ed. boxed 54.50 (*957-562-123-9*) Heian Intl.

Catalogue of the Stowe Manuscripts in the British Museum, 2 vols., Set. (Anglistica & Americana Ser.: No. 9). 1973. reprint ed. 193.70 (*3-487-04782-9*, Pub. by Georg Olms GW) Lubrecht & Cramer.

Catalogue of the Tavistock Joint Library, 2 vols, Set. Tavistock Joint Library, London Staff. 1975. lib. bdg. 160.00 (*0-8161-1167-7*, Hall Library) G K Hall.

Catalogue of the Translator's Library of the Department of Trade & Industry: Dictionaries, Glossaries, Encyclopedias, Books about Languages, 3 vols., Set. Great Britain, Her Britannic Majesty's Stationery Office Staff & G. E. Hamilton. LC 74-31406. 1600p. 1976. 270.00 (*0-379-00375-9*) Oceana.

Catalogue of the Universe. Margaret Mahy. 192p. (YA). (gr. 7 up). 1994. pap. 3.99 (*0-14-036600-8*) Puffin Bks.

Catalogue of the Universe. Margaret Mahy. LC 85-72262. 192p. (YA). (gr. 9 up). 1986. text ed. 15.95 (*0-689-50391-1*, McElderry) S&S Childrens.

Catalogue of the Vanderpoel Dickens Collection at the University of Texas. Illus. by Kim Taylor. LC 68-65506. (Tower Bibliographical Ser.: No. 1). 1968. 25.00 (*0-87959-077-7*) U of Tex H Ransom Ctr.

Catalogue of the Works of Charles Ricketts R.A. Michael R. Barclay. 69p. 1985. pap. 15.00 (*0-904995-07-0*, Pub. by Catalpa Pr Ltd UK) Oak Knoll.

Catalogue of the Works Printed for the Maitland Club. Maitland Club Staff. LC 72-1043. (Maitland Club, Glasgow. Publications: No. 38). reprint ed. 10.00 (*0-404-53011-7*) AMS Pr.

Catalogue of the 2nd International Exhibition of Botanical Art & Illustration. Comp. by G. H. Lawrence. (Illus.). 267p. 1968. 7.00 (*0-913196-11-8*) Hunt Inst Botanical.

Catalogue of the 3rd International Exhibition of Botanical Art & Illustration. Comp. by K. A. Korach. (Illus.). ii, 187p. 1972. pap. 10.00 (*0-913196-14-2*) Hunt Inst Botanical.

Catalogue of the 4th International Exhibition of Botanical Art & Illustration. Comp. by S. W. Secrist & N. A. Howard. (Illus.). viii, 138p. 1977. 12.00 (*0-913196-19-3*) Hunt Inst Botanical.

Catalogue of the 5th International Exhibition of Botanical Art & Illustration. Comp. by J. J. White & D. E. Wendel. (Illus.). 115p. 1983. pap. 15.00 (*0-913196-41-X*) Hunt Inst Botanical.

Catalogue of the 6th International Exhibition of Botanical Art & Illustration. J. J. White & D. E. Wendel. (Illus.). 142p. (Orig.). 1988. pap. 15.00 (*0-913196-52-5*) Hunt Inst Botanical.

Catalogue of the 7th International Exhibition of Botanical Art & Illustration. J. J. White & A. M. Farole. (Illus.). 142p. (Orig.). 1992. pap. 18.00 (*0-913196-55-X*) Hunt Inst Botanical.

Catalogue of Thomists, 1270-1900. Comp. by Leonard A. Kennedy. LC 86-72913. (Center for Thomistic Studies). 240p. 1987. 29.95 (*0-268-00763-2*) Ctr Thomistic.

Catalogue of Tools. 1994. lib. bdg. 275.95 (*0-8490-5679-9*) Gordon Pr.

Catalogue of Tools for Watch & Clock Makers. John Wyke. LC 77-12219. (Illus.). 153p. 1978. 27.50 (*0-8139-0751-9*, Winterthur Museum) U Pr of Va.

Catalogue of Translations from the Chinese Dynastic Histories for the Period 220-960. Comp. by Hans H. Frankel. LC 74-9395. (Chinese Dynastic Studies. Translations. U of Cal Pr). 295p. 1974. reprint ed. text ed. 59.75 (*0-8371-7661-1*, FRDH) Greenwood.

Catalogue of Treaties: Eighteen Hundred Fourteen to Nineteen Hundred Eighteen. U. S. Department of State Staff. LC 20-13106. xxv, 3716p. 1965. reprint ed. lib. bdg. 52.50 (*0-89941-450-8*, 500230) W S Hein.

Catalogue of Turkish Manuscripts in the Bodleian Library. Gunay Kut & Michael Daly. (Illus.). 400p. 1995. 90.00 (*0-19-951351-1*) OUP.

Catalogue of Two Hundred Type-I UFO Events in Spain & Portugal. Vicente-Juan B. Olmos. (Illus.). 91p. (C). 1976. pap. 6.00 (*0-929343-50-6*) J A Hynek Ctr UFO.

***Catalogue of Type Specimens (Cormophyta) in the Herbaria of China.** Ed. by Jin Shuyin. Date not set. 86.00 (*7-03-003476-7*) Intl Spec Bk.

Catalogue of Type Specimens of Neotropical Bats in Selected European Museums. Dilford C. Carter & Patricia G. Dolan. (Special Publications: No. 15). 136p. 1978. pap. 8.00 (*0-89672-063-2*) Tex Tech Univ Pr.

Catalogue of Unbalanced Chromosome Aberrations in Man. Albert Schinzel. LC 83-7645. (Illus.). xviii, 913p. 1983. 229.25 (*0-89925-450-0*) De Gruyter.

***Catalogue of Unbalanced Chromosome Aberrations in Man.** Albert Schinzel. LC 83-7645. (Illus.). xviii, 913p. 1983. 229.25 (*3-11-008370-1*) De Gruyter.

Catalogue of Visual & Infrared Photometry of Galaxies from 0.5 um to 10 um (1961-1985) Antoinette De Vaucouleurs & Giuseppe Longo. Ed. by Marshall Joy. (Monographs in Astronomy: No. 5). 210p. (Orig.). 1988. pap. 10.00 (*0-9603796-5-7*) U of Tex Dept Astron.

Catalogue of Vocal Recordings from the 1898-1926 German Catalogues of the Gramophone Company Limited, Duetsche Grammophon. John R. Bennett & Wilhelm Wimmer. LC 77-28980. (Voices of the Past Ser.: Vol. 7). 404p. 1978. reprint ed. text ed. 79.50 (*0-313-20236-2*, BECVG) Greenwood.

Catalogue of Vocal Solos & Duets Arranged in Biblical Order. Comp. by James H. Laster. LC 84-14187. 212p. 1984. 25.00 (*0-8108-1748-9*) Scarecrow.

Catalogue of Works by Artists Born Between 1816 & 1845. Natalie Spassky et al. (American Paintings in the Metropolitan Museum of Art Ser.: Vol, 2). 728p. 1985. 75.00 (*0-87099-439-5*) Metro Mus Art.

Catalogue of Works by Artists Born Between 1845-1864. Doreen B Burke. (American Paintings in the Metropolitan Museum of Art Ser.: Vol. 3). 524p. 1980. 75.00 (*0-87099-244-9*) Metro Mus Art.

***Catalogue of Works by Artists Born by 1815.** John Caldwell & Oswaldo R. Roque. Ed. by Kathleen Luhrs. (American Paintings in the Metropolitan Museum of Art Ser.: Vol. 1). (Illus.). 672p. 1994. 110.00 (*0-614-01783-1*); pap. 75.00 (*0-614-01784-X*) Metro Mus Art.

Catalogue of Yiddish & Hebrew Sheet Music. 1987. lib. bdg. 79.95 (*0-8490-3927-4*) Gordon Pr.

Catalogue Raisonne of the Etchings of Charles Meryon. rev. ed. Loys Delteil & Harold J. Wright. 224p. 1989. 95.00 (*1-55660-021-6*) A Wofsy Fine Arts.

Catalogue Raisonne of the Graphic Work of Richard Florsheim. Ed. by Domenic J. Iacono. LC 88-21015. (Illus.). 112p. 1989. text ed. 34.95 (*0-8156-8113-5*) Syracuse U Pr.

Catalogue Raisonne of the Painting of Sir Lawrence Alma-Tadema. Vern G. Swanson. (Illus.). 96p. 1990. text ed. 535.00 (*0-906030-22-6*, Pub. by Scolar Pr UK) Ashgate Pub Co.

C

An Asterisk (*) at the beginning of an entry indicates that the title is appearing in BIP for the first time. 1089

Catalogue Raisonne of the Prints of Charles Meryon. Richard Schneiderman. (Illus.). 200p. 1990. text ed. 250.00 (*0-906030-23-4*, Pub. by Scolar Pr UK) Ashgate Pub Co.

Catalogue Raisonne of the Works of Samuel Palmer. Raymond Lister. (Illus.). 300p. 1988. 170.00 (*0-521-34455-7*) Cambridge U Pr.

Catalogue Raisonne of the Works of the Most Eminent Dutch Painters of the Seventeenth Century, 2 vols. C. Hofstede De Groot. Ed. by E. G. Hawke. 6128p. 1976. reprint ed. Vol.1. write for info. (*0-85964-023-X*) Chadwyck-Healey.

Catalogue Raisonne of the Works of the Most Eminent Dutch Painters of the Seventeenth Century, 2 vols., 2. C. Hofstede De Groot. Ed. by E. G. Hawke. 6128p. 1976. reprint ed. write for info. (*0-85964-024-8*) Chadwyck-Healey.

Catalogue Raisonne of the Works of the Most Eminent Dutch Painters of the Seventeenth Century, 2 vols., Set. C. Hofstede De Groot. Ed. by E. G. Hawke. 6128p. 1976. reprint ed. 400.00 (*0-685-04684-2*) Chadwyck-Healey.

Catalogue Raisonnee. Wolf Breitling & Morgan Mickles. 1985. 5.00 (*0-318-18268-8*) Brandon-Lane-Pr.

Catalogue Roses. Sallie Chesham. 150p. 1987. 7.95 (*0-86544-042-5*) Salv Army Suppl South.

Catalogue Sourcebook: Sources for Everything in 70,000 Catalogues. 1992. lib. bdg. 299.89 (*0-8490-8899-2*) Gordon Pr.

Catalogue Systematique de la Section Afrique (Classified Catalog of the Africa Section), 2 Vols, Set. Bibliotheque du Musee de l'Homme, Paris Staff. 1970. lib. bdg. 165.00 (*0-8161-0827-7*, Hall Library) G K Hall.

Catalogue Thematique Des Oeuvres De Chr. W. von Gluck. Alfred Wotquenne. xi, 246p. 1983. reprint ed. write for info. (*3-487-01610-9*, Pub. by Georg Olms GW) Lubrecht & Cramer.

Catalogue with Abstracts of Studies in the Field of Transport. 65p. 1989. 7.50 (*92-1-104326-3*, E.89.II.A.19) UN.

Catalogue Yvert & Tellier de Timbres-Poste: A Collection of 8 Postage Stamp Catalogs. Yvert & Tellier. (FRE.). 1991. 75.00 (*0-8288-7233-3*) Fr & Eur.

Catalogues & Counters: A History of Sears, Roebuck & Company. Boris Emmet & John E. Jeuck. LC 50-7387. 1965. lib. bdg. 45.00 (*0-226-20710-2*) U Ch Pr.

C

Catalogues of Indian Synonyms of the Medicinal Plants, Inorganic Substances Proposed to Be Included in the Pharmacopeia of India. M. Sheriff. 675p. (C). 1978. text ed. 375.00 (*0-89771-650-7*, Pub. by Intl Bk Distr II) St Mut.

Catalogues of Japanese Crests. Ed. by Michael P. Jones. (Illus.). 26p. (Orig.). 1983. pap. 4.00 (*0-89904-029-2*) Crumb Elbow Pub.

Catalogues of Non-Herbaceous Phanergomas. A. T. Gage. 367p. 1977. reprint ed. 250.00 (*0-685-21756-6*, Pub. by Intl Bk Distr II) St Mut.

Catalogues of the Berenson Library, 4 vols. Harvard University Center for Italian Renaissance Studies at Villa I Tatti (Florence, Italy) Staff. 1973. lib. bdg. 480.00 (*0-8161-0973-7*, Hall Library) G K Hall.

Catalogues of the Canning House Library: Author & Subject Catalogues, 2 pts. Canning House Library Editors. Incl. First Supplement, 4 vols. 1973. lib. bdg. 120.00 (*0-8161-1100-6*); First Supplement, 4 vols. suppl. ed. 1973. First Supplement, 1973. lib. bdg. 125.00 (*0-8161-1125-1*); Pt. 2. Luso-Brazilian Catalogues. 1967. lib. bdg. 110.00 (*0-8161-0126-4*); Pt. 2. Luso-Brazilian Catalogues. suppl. ed. 1973. First Supplement, 1973. lib. bdg. 120.00 (*0-685-57728-7*); write for info. (*0-318-52342-6*, Hall Library) G K Hall.

Catalogues of the Collection of American Paintings, 2 vols., 1. (Illus.). 10.00 (*0-686-20534-0*); pap. 7.50 (*0-686-20535-9*) Corcoran.

Catalogues of the Collection of American Paintings, 2 vols., 2. (Illus.). 14.50 (*0-686-20536-7*); pap. 10.00 (*0-686-20537-5*) Corcoran.

Cataloguing: Theory & Practice. 4th rev. ed. C. G. Viswanathan. 415p. 1970. 7.50 (*0-88065-207-1*, Messers Today & Tomorrow) Scholarly Pubns.

Cataloguing Audiovisual Materials: A Manual Based on the AACR II. Eugene Fleischer & Helen Goodman. LC 80-18782. (Illus.). 387p. 1981. pap. 39.50 (*0-918212-39-1*) Neal-Schuman.

Cataloguing in Context: The African Studies Program Slide Archives. Steven G. Ohrn. 49p. 1975. pap. 2.00 (*0-941934-16-0*) Indiana Africa.

Cataloguing Practice. 2nd ed. S. R. Ranganathan. 517p. reprint ed. text ed. 50.00 (*81-85273-14-6*, Pub. by Sarada Ranganathan Endowment for Library Science II) Advent Bks Div.

Catalogus Bibliothecae Historico-Naturalis Josephi Banks, 5 vols., Set. Jonas Dryander. 1966. 240.00 (*90-6123-003-9*) Lubrecht & Cramer.

Catalogus Bibliothecae quam J. Ch. Gottschedius...Collegit atque Reliquit. Johann C. Gottsched. (Deutsche Dichter - und Gelehrtenbibliotheken Ser.). 1990. reprint ed. 45.00 (*0-8115-3759-5*) Periodicals Srv.

Catalogus Bibliothecae Selectae Duabus Partibus Consignatae Quam...Collegit...B. Ioann Ioachim Schwabe, 2 vols., Set. Johann J. Schwabe. (Deutsche Dichter - und Gelehrtenbibliotheken Ser.). 1990. reprint ed. 100.00 (*0-8115-3822-2*) Periodicals Srv.

Catalogus Codicum Bernensium. Ed. by Hermann Hagen. lxvii, 662p. 1974. reprint ed. write for info. (*3-487-05055-2*, Pub. by Georg Olms GW) Lubrecht & Cramer.

Catalogus Codicum Copticorum Manuscriptorum. Georg Zoega. xliii, 663p. 1973. reprint ed. write for info. (*3-487-04241-X*, Pub. by Georg Olms GW) Lubrecht & Cramer.

Catalogus Codicum Graecorum Bibliothecae Ambrosianae, 2 vols. in 1. Aemidius Martini & Domenicus Bassi. li, 1297p. 1978. reprint ed. write for info. (*3-487-06499-5*, Pub. by Georg Olms GW) Lubrecht & Cramer.

Catalogus Codicum Latinorum Classicorum. Konrat Ziegler. viii, 289p. 1975. reprint ed. write for info. (*3-487-05612-7*, Pub. by Georg Olms GW) Lubrecht & Cramer.

Catalogus Codicum Manuscriptorum Bibliothecae Regiae Et Universitatis Regimontanae. xiv, 201p. 1978. reprint ed. write for info. (*3-487-05901-0*, Pub. by Georg Olms GW) Lubrecht & Cramer.

Catalogus Codicum Manuscriptorum Graecorum, 2 vols., Set. V. Benesevic. xxxii, 1008p. 1965. reprint ed. write for info. (*0-318-70716-0*, Pub. by Georg Olms GW) Lubrecht & Cramer.

Catalogus Codicum Manuscriptorum Orientalium Qui in Murso Britannico Asservantur: Supplement to the Catalogue of the Arabic Manuscripts in the British Museum. Charles Rieu. xv, 935p. reprint ed. write for info. (*0-318-71497-3*, Pub. by Georg Olms GW) Lubrecht & Cramer.

Catalogus Codicum Manuscriptorum Orientalium Qui in Murso Britannico Asservantur, Pt. 2: Codices Arabicos Complectens. Ed. by W. Cureton & C. Rieu. xiv, 882p. reprint ed. write for info. (*0-318-71496-5*, Pub. by Georg Olms GW) Lubrecht & Cramer.

Catalogus Librorum Hebraeorum in Bibliotheca Bodleiana, 3 vols. in 1. Moritz Steinschneider. 1964. reprint ed. write for info. (*0-318-71865-0*, Pub. by Georg Olms GW) Lubrecht & Cramer.

Catalogus Librorum Manscriptorum Orientalium in Bibliotheca Academica Bonnensi Servatorum. Joannis Gildmeister. vi, 154p. reprint ed. write for info. (*0-318-71498-1*, Pub. by Georg Olms GW) Lubrecht & Cramer.

Catalogus Translations & Commentariorum: Medieval & Renaissance Latin Translations & Commentaries, Vol. 5. Ed. by F. Edward Cranz & Paul O. Kristeller. 448p. 1984. pap. 54.95 (*0-8132-0580-8*) Cath U Pr.

Catalogus Translationum et Commentariorum: Mediaeval & Renaissance Latin Translation & Commentaries, Vol. 3. Ed. by F. Edward Cranz. 481p. 1976. pap. 41.95 (*0-8132-0540-9*) Cath U Pr.

Catalogus Translationum et Commentariorum: Mediaeval & Renaissance Latin Translations & Commentaries, Annotated Lists & Guides, Vol. 2. Ed. by Paul O. Kristeller. LC 60-4006. 454p. 1971. reprint ed. pap. 122.60 (*0-7837-0026-1*, 2029818) Bks Demand.

***Catalogus Translationum et Commentariorum: Mediaeval & Renaissance Latin Translations & Commentaries; Annotated Lists & Guides, Vol. 3, 1976.** Ed. by Paul O. Kristeller. LC 60-4006. reprint ed. pap. 142.50 (*0-7837-9012-0*, 2029818) Bks Demand.

Catalogus Translationum et Commentariorum: Mediaeval & Renaissance Latin Translations & Commentaries, Annotated Lists & Guides, Vol. 4. Ed. by F. Edward Cranz. LC 60-4006. 524p. 1980. pap. 66.95 (*0-8132-0547-6*) Cath U Pr.

***Catalogus Translationum et Commentariorum: Mediaeval & Renaissance Latin Translations & Commentaries; Annotated Lists & Guides, Vol. 4, 1980.** Ed. by Paul O. Kristeller. LC 60-4006. reprint ed. pap. 130.00 (*0-7837-9013-9*, 2029818) Bks Demand.

Catalogus Translationum et Commentariorum: Mediaeval & Renaissance Latin Translations & Commentaries, Annotated Lists & Guides, Vol. 5. Ed. by Paul O. Kristeller. LC 60-4006. 449p. reprint ed. pap. 128.00 (*0-7837-0027-X*) Bks Demand.

Catalogus Translationum et Commentariorum: Mediaeval & Renaissance Latin Translations & Commentaries, Annotated Lists & Guides, Vol. 6. Ed. by F. Edward Cranz & Virginia Brown. 204p. 1986. 54.95 (*0-8132-0618-9*) Cath U Pr.

Catalogus Translationum et Commentariorum, Vol. VII: Medieval & Renaissance Latin Translations & Commentaries. Ed. by Virginia Brown et al. LC 60-4006. 356p. 1992. text ed. 59.95 (*0-8132-0713-4*) Cath U Pr.

Catalogus van Eenige der Merkwaardigste Zoo in- Als Witheemsche Gewassen: Te Winden in's Land Plantentium te Buitenzorg. K. L. Blume. 1946. pap. 10.00 (*0-934454-20-5*) Lubrecht & Cramer.

Catalonia. (Insight Guides Ser.). 1993. pap. 21.95 (*0-395-66284-2*) HM.

Catalonia: A Complete Guide. Jane Holliday & Peter Holliday. 213p. 1992. pap. 29.95 (*0-9518767-0-8*, Pub. by Iberia Pr UK) St Mut.

Catalonia, a Self Portrait. Ed. & Tr. by Josep M. Sobrer. LC 91-4050. (Illus.). 256p. 1992. text ed. 35.00 (*0-253-35290-8*); pap. text ed. 12.95 (*0-253-28883-5*) Ind U Pr.

Catalonia Infelix. Edgar A. Peers. LC 77-109819. 326p. 1970. reprint ed. text ed. 35.00 (*0-8371-4310-1*, PECI, Greenwood Pr) Greenwood.

***Catalonia, Traditions, Places, Wind & Food.** Jan Read & Maite Manjon. (Illus.). 324p. 1992. pap. 19.95 (*1-871569-42-7*, Herbert Pr UK) New Amsterdam Bks.

Catalonian Ambassadors. Gerald Kaminski. LC 93-28772. (Circumstantial Evidence Ser.: Vol. 7). 48p. 1993. pap. 50.00 (*0-931896-14-2*) Cove View.

Cataloque Des Incunables et Des Livres Imprimes De MD A MDXX. M. Pellechet. viii, 302p. reprint ed. write for info. (*0-318-71386-1*, Pub. by Georg Olms GW) Lubrecht & Cramer.

Cataloue of the Avery Memorial Architectural Library, Columbia University, Second Supplement, 4 vols., Set. Columbia University Editors. 1975. lib. bdg. 485.00 (*0-8161-1070-0*, Hall Library) G K Hall.

***Catalpa: Poems by George Ella Lyon.** George E. Lyon. 62p. (Orig.). 1993. pap. 9.95 (*0-9636545-2-7*) Wind Pubns.

***Catalpa Blossoms.** James Magorian. 42p. 1994. 15.00 (*0-930674-39-1*) Black Oak.

Catalpa Rescue. Sean O'Luing. 184p. 1965. 13.95 (*0-900068-89-2*, Pub. by Anvil Bks Ltd IE); pap. 4.95 (*0-900068-84-1*) Irish Bks Media.

Catalyses Catacoustical. Spiros Pantos. 1979. 9.95 (*0-87881-074-9*) Mojave Bks.

Catalysis. Ed. by J. R. Anderson & M. Boudart. (Science & Technology Ser.: Vol. 7). (Illus.). 230p. 1985. 101.00 (*0-387-15035-8*) Spr-Verlag.

Catalysis, Vol. 5. Ed. by J. R. Anderson & M. Boudart. (Science & Technology Ser.). (Illus.). 280p. 1984. 102.00 (*0-387-12665-1*) Spr-Verlag.

Catalysis, Vol. 10. Ed. by J. J. Spivey & S. K. Agarwal. 180p. 1993. 170.00 (*0-85186-614-X*, R6614) CRC Pr.

***Catalysis, Vol. 11.** Ed. by James J. Spivey & Sanjay K. Agarwal. (Specialist Periodicals Reports Ser.). 480p. 1994. 250.00 (*0-85186-654-9*, R6654) CRC Pr.

Catalysis: An Integrated Approach to Homogeneous, Heterogeneous & Industrial Catalysis. Ed. by J. A. Moulijn et al. (Studies in Surface Science & Catalysis: Vol. 79). 500p. 1993. 168.50 (*0-444-89229-X*) Elsevier.

Catalysis: Science & Technology, Vol. 3. Ed. by J. R. Anderson & M. Boudart. (Illus.). 290p. 1983. 102.00 (*0-387-11634-6*) Spr-Verlag.

Catalysis: Science & Technology, Vol. 4. (Illus.). 280p. 1983. 102.00 (*0-387-11855-1*) Spr-Verlag.

Catalysis: Science & Technology, Vol. 6. Ed. by J. R. Anderson & M. Boudart. (Illus.). 320p. 1984. 109.00 (*0-387-12815-8*) Spr-Verlag.

Catalysis: Science & Technology, Vol. 8. Ed. by J. R. Anderson & M. Boudart. (Illus.). 280p. 1987. 99.00 (*0-387-15034-X*) Spr-Verlag.

Catalysis: Science & Technology, Vol. 9. Ed. by J. R. Anderson & M. Boudart. (Illus.). 192p. 1991. 89.00 (*0-387-52972-1*) Spr-Verlag.

Catalysis & Adsorption by Zeolites: Proceedings of the ZEOCAT 90, Leipzig, FRG, Aug. 20-23, 1990. Ed. by G. Ohlmann et al. (Studies in Surface Science & Catalysis: No. 65). 718p. 1991. 225.75 (*0-444-89088-2*) Elsevier.

Catalysis & Automotive Pollution Control. Ed. by A. Crucq & A. Frennet. (Studies in Surface Science & Catalysis: No. 30). 520p. 1987. 138.50 (*0-444-42778-3*) Elsevier.

Catalysis & Automotive Pollution Control II: Proc. of the 2nd Internat. Symp., Brussels, 10-13 Sept., 1990. Ed. by A. Crucq. (Studies in Surface Science & Catalysis: Vol. 71). 684p. 1991. 197.50 (*0-444-88787-3*) Elsevier.

Catalysis & Surface Properties of Liquid Metals & Liquid Alloys. Ogino. (Chemical Industries Ser.: Vol. 29). 224p. 1987. 125.00 (*0-8247-7699-2*) Dekker.

Catalysis at Surfaces. Ian M. Campbell. (Illus.). 200p. 1988. text ed. 65.00 (*0-412-31880-6*); pap. text ed. 25.50 (*0-412-28970-9*) Chapman & Hall.

Catalysis by Acids & Bases. B. Imelik. (Studies in Surface Science & Catalysis: Vol. 20). 1985. 141.00 (*0-444-42449-0*) Elsevier.

***Catalysis by Microporous Materials: Proceedings of ZEOCAT '95, Szombathely, Hungary, July 9-13, 1995.** ZEOCAT '95 Staff. Ed. by H. K. Beyer et al. LC 95-16762. (Studies in Surface Science & Catalysis: Vol. 94). 812p. 1995. 291.25 (*0-444-82049-3*) Elsevier.

Catalysis by Supported Complexes. Y. I. Yermakov et al. (Studies in Surface Science & Catalysis: Vol. 8). 522p. 1981. 146.25 (*0-444-42014-2*) Elsevier.

Catalysis 'Eighty-Seven: Proceedings of the 10th North American Catalysis Society Meeting, San Diego, CA, May 17-22, 1987. Ed. by J. W. Ward. (Studies in Surface Science & Catalysis: Vol. 38). 952p. 1988. 164.00 (*0-444-42955-7*) Elsevier.

Catalysis in C-Chemistry. Keim. 1983. lib. bdg. 126.50 (*90-277-1527-0*) Kluwer Ac.

Catalysis in Chemistry & Biochemistry: Theory & Experiment. Ed. by Bernard Pullman. (Jerusalem Symposia on Quantum Chemistry & Biochemistry Ser.: No. 12). 1979. lib. bdg. 94.00 (*90-277-1039-2*) Kluwer Ac.

Catalysis in Chemistry & Enzymology. William P. Jencks. (Illus.). 864p. 1987. reprint ed. pap. text ed. 18.95 (*0-486-65460-5*) Dover.

Catalysis in Petrochemical Processes. Ed. by Sami Matar et al. (C). 1988. lib. bdg. 114.50 (*90-277-2721-X*) Kluwer Ac.

Catalysis in Polymer Synthesis. Ed. by Edwin J. Vandenberg & Joseph C. Salamone. LC 92-15608. (ACS Symposium Ser.: No. 496). (Illus.). 292p. (C). 1992. 74.95 (*0-8412-2456-0*) Am Chemical.

Catalysis Looks to the Future. National Research Council Staff. 96p. 1991. pap. 19.00 (*0-309-04584-3*) Natl Acad Pr.

Catalysis of Organic Reactions. Robert Augustine. LC 85-10242. (Chemical Industries Ser.: Vol. 22). 416p. (C). 1985. 175.00 (*0-8247-7263-6*) Dekker.

Catalysis of Organic Reactions. Blackburn. (Chemical Industries Ser.: Vol. 40). 376p. 1990. 150.00 (*0-8247-8286-0*) Dekker.

Catalysis of Organic Reactions. Ed. by Kosak & Johnson. (Chemical Industries Ser.: Vol. 53). 608p. 1994. 199.00 (*0-8247-9140-1*) Dekker.

Catalysis of Organic Reactions. Ed. by William R. Moser. LC 81-15172. (Chemical Industries Ser.: Vol. 5). (Illus.). 496p. 1981. 175.00 (*0-8247-1341-9*) Dekker.

Catalysis of Organic Reactions. Pascoe. (Chemical Industries Ser.: Vol. 47). 408p. 1991. 190.00 (*0-8247-8573-8*) Dekker.

Catalysis of Organic Reactions. Rylander. (Chemical Industries Ser.: Vol. 33). 456p. 1988. 160.00 (*0-8247-7927-4*) Dekker.

***Catalysis of Organic Reactions.** Ed. by Michael Scaros & Michael L. Prunier. LC 94-32718. (Chemical Industries Ser.: 62). 1994. 195.00 (*0-8247-9364-1*) Dekker.

Catalysis of Organic Reactions by Supported Inorganic Reagents. James H. Clark et al. 1992. 49.50 (*1-56081-010-6*) VCH Pubs.

Catalysis of Organic Reactions (TBC) Kosak. (Chemical Industries Ser.: Vol. 18). 504p. 1984. 190.00 (*0-8247-7153-2*) Dekker.

Catalysis on the Energy Scene: Proceedings of the Canadian Symposium on Catalysis, 9th, Quebec, P. Q., Sept. 30-Oct. 3, 1984. Ed. by S. Kaliaguine & A. Mahay. (Studies in Surface Science & Catalysis: Vol. 19). 602p. 1984. 164.00 (*0-444-42402-4*) Elsevier.

Catalysis-Science & Technology, Vol. 1. M. Boudart. Ed. by J. R. Anderson. (Illus.). 320p. 1981. 102.00 (*0-387-10353-8*) Spr-Verlag.

Catalysis-Science & Technology, Vol. 2. Ed. by J. R. Anderson & M. Boudart. (Illus.). 280p. 1982. 94.00 (*0-387-10593-X*) Spr-Verlag.

Catalysis under Transient Conditions. Ed. by Alexis T. Bell & L. Louis Hegedus. LC 82-20639. (ACS Symposium Ser.: No. 178). 1982. 38.95 (*0-8412-0688-0*) Am Chemical.

Catalyst. Sara Adamson. (Orig.). 1992. pap. 4.95 (*1-56333-015-6*) Masquerade.

Catalyst. large type ed. Rowena Lee. 1975. 15.95 (*0-85456-335-0*) Ulverscroft.

***Catalyst.** 2nd ed. Sara Adamson. 1995. pap. text ed. 5.95 (*1-56333-328-7*) Masquerade.

Catalyst: A Life Devoted to Others. Arthur Weider. 184p. 1994. text ed. 20.00 (*0-8059-3500-2*) Dorrance.

Catalyst & Emission Technology: Twenty-four Papers. 1993. 75.00 (*1-56091-353-3*, SP-968) Soc Auto Engineers.

Catalyst Characterization: Physical Techniques for Solid Materials. Ed. by B. Imelik & J. C. Vedrine. (Fundamental & Applied Catalysis Ser.). (Illus.). 916p. 1994. 125.00 (*0-306-43950-6*, Plenum Pr) Plenum.

Catalyst Deactivation. Petersen & Bell. (Chemical Industries Ser.: Vol. 30). 376p. 1987. 175.00 (*0-8247-7741-7*) Dekker.

Catalyst Deactivation: Proceedings. Ed. by B. Delmon & G. F. Fremont. (Studies in Surface Science & Catalysis: Vol. 6). 602p. 1980. 169.25 (*0-444-41920-9*) Elsevier.

Catalyst Deactivation Nineteen Ninety-One: Proceedings of the 5th International Symposium, Evanston, IL, June 24-26, 1991. Ed. by C. H. Bartholomew & John B. Butt. (Studies in Surface Science & Catalysis: No. 68). 826p. 1991. 254.50 (*0-444-88832-2*) Elsevier.

***Catalyst Deactivation 1994: Proceedings of the Sixth International Symposium, Ostend, Belgium, October 3-5, 1994.** Ed. by B. Delmon & G. F. Froment. (Studies in Surface Science & Catalysis: Vol. 88). 698p. 1994. 290.75 (*0-444-81682-8*) Elsevier.

Catalyst Design: Progress & Perspectives. Ed. by L. Louis Hegedus. LC 86-28133. 288p. 1987. text ed. 94.95 (*0-471-85138-8*) Wiley.

***Catalyst Design for Tailor-Made Polyolefins: Proceedings of the International Symposium on Catalyst Design for Tailor-Made Polyolefins, Kanazawa, Japan, March 10-12, 1994.** Ed. by K. Soga & M. Terano. (Studies in Surface Science & Catalysis: Vol. 89). 429p. 1994. 278.50 (*0-444-98656-1*) Elsevier.

Catalyst for Change: A History of the Joint Center for Political & Economic Studies, 1970-1990. Darlene C. Hine. 160p. (C). 1991. pap. text ed. 29.95 (*0-941410-91-9*) Jt Ctr Pol Studies.

Catalyst for Controversy: Paul Carus of Open Court. Harold Henderson. LC 92-17303. 216p. (C). 1993. 24.95 (*0-8093-1797-4*) S Ill U Pr.

***Catalyst Manufacture.** 2nd expanded rev. ed. Ed. by Stiles & Koch. (Chemical Industries Ser.). 186p. 1995. write for info. (*0-8247-9430-3*) Dekker.

Catalyst Poisoning. L. Hegedus & R. McCabe. (Chemical Industries Ser.: Vol. 17). (Illus.). 128p. 1984. 95.00 (*0-8247-7173-7*) Dekker.

Catalyst Supports & Supported Catalysts. Ed. by Alvin B. Stiles. (Illus.). 327p. 1987. text ed. 79.95 (*0-409-95148-X*) Buttrwrth-Heinemann.

Catalyst Surface: Physical Methods of Studying. Kh. M. Minachev & E. S. Shapiro. 375p. 1990. 76.95 (*0-8493-7532-0*, T) CRC Pr.

Catalysts. Rene Dionne & Michael Fitzgerald. 308p. 1980. 5.95 (*0-318-14910-9*) Missionaries Africa.

***Catalysts.** Stanley Middleton. 266p. 1995. 26.00 (*0-09-178494-8*, Pub. by Hutchnson UK) Trafalgar.

***Catalyst's Adventure in Science: Simple Machines.** Ann P. McMahon & Kimberly A. Brake. (Illus.). 32p. (J). (gr. k-4). 1995. pap. 9.95 (*0-9642550-1-4*) Curiosity Unltd.

***Catalyst's Adventures in Science: Bubble Rainbows.** rev. ed. Ann P. McMahon & Kimberly A. Brake. LC 94-67847. (Illus.). 32p. (J). (gr. k-4). 1994. pap. 9.95 (*0-9642550-0-6*) Curiosity Unltd.

Catalysts for Change: Concepts & Principles for Enabling Innovation. William B. Rouse. (Series in Systems Engineering). 272p. 1993. text ed. 69.95 (*0-471-59196-3*, Wiley-Interscience) Wiley.

Catalysts for Change: Managing Libraries in the 1990s. Ed. by Jennifer Cargill. LC 93-37279. (Journal of Library Administration: Vol. 18, Nos. 3-4). (Illus.). 200p. 1994. lib. bdg. 39.95 (*1-56024-516-6*) Haworth Pr.

Catalysts for Environmental Management, No. C-166. 202p. 1993. 2,650.00 (*1-56965-004-7*) BCC.

Catalysts for Organic Synthesis. 197p. 1992. 2,950.00 (*0-89336-900-4*, C-151) BCC.

Catalysts for the Control of Automotive Pollutants. Ed. by James E. McEvoy. LC 75-20298. (Advances in Chemistry Ser.: No. 143). 199p. 1975. 27.95 (*0-8412-0219-2*) Am Chemical.

An Asterisk (*) at the beginning of an entry indicates that the title is appearing in BIP for the first time.

Catalysts in Petroleum Refining, 1989: Proceedings of the 1st International Conference, Kuwait, March 5-8, 1989. Ed. by D. L. Trimm et al. (Studies in Surface Science & Catalysis: No. 53). 594p. 1990. 197.50 (0-444-88211-1) Elsevier.

*Catalysts of Development: Voluntary Agencies in India. fac. ed. Terry Alliband. LC 82-83155. (Kumarian Press Library of Management for Development). 128p. (Orig.). 7194. pap. 36.50 (0-7837-7572-5, 2047325) Bks Demand.

Catalytic Activation of Carbon Dioxide. Ed. by William M. Ayers. LC 87-30832. (Symposium Ser.: No. 363). (Illus.). 214p. 1988. 54.95 (0-8412-1447-6) Am Chemical.

Catalytic Activation of Carbon Monoxide. Ed. by Peter Ford. LC 81-1885. (ACS Symposium Ser.: No. 152). 358p. 1981. 43.95 (0-8412-0620-1) Am Chemical.

Catalytic Activation of Dioxygen by Metal Complexes. Laszlo I. Simandi. LC 92-22107. (Catalysis by Metal Complexes Ser.: Vol. 13). 408p. (C). 1992. lib. bdg. 137.50 (0-7923-1896-X) Kluwer Ac.

Catalytic Air Pollution Control: Commercial Technology. Robert J. Farrauto & Ronald M. Heck. LC 94-21465. (Illus.). 224p. 1994. text ed. 59.95 (0-442-01782-0) Van Nos Reinhold.

Catalytic Ammonia Synthesis: Fundamentals & Practice. Ed. by J. R. Jennings. (Fundamental & Applied Catalysis Ser.). (Illus.). 420p. 1991. 69.50 (0-306-43628-0, Plenum Pr) Plenum.

Catalytic Antibodies: Symposium, No. 159. CIBA Foundation Symposium Staff. (CIBA Foundation Symposia Ser.). 259p. 1991. text ed. 76.00 (0-471-92962-X, Wiley-Liss) Wiley.

Catalytic Aspects of Metal Phosphine Complexes. Ed. by Elmer C. Alyea & Devon W. Meek. LC 81-12903. (Advances in Chemistry Ser.: No. 196). 1982. 76.95 (0-8412-0601-5) Am Chemical.

Catalytic Asymmetric Synthesis. Ed. by Iwao Ojima. LC 93-19389. 476p. 1993. 110.00 (1-56081-532-9) VCH Pubs.

Catalytic Chemistry: An Introductory Text. Bruce C. Gates. 480p. (C). 1991. Net. text ed. write for info. (0-471-51761-5) Wiley.

Catalytic Chemistry of Solid-State Inorganics, Vol. 272. Ed. by William R. Moser & John R. Happel. (Annals Ser.). 1976. 10.00 (0-89072-051-7) NY Acad Sci.

Catalytic Control of Air Pollution: Mobile & Stationary Sources. Ed. by Ronald G. Silver et al. LC 92-15615. (Symposium Ser.: Vol. 495). (Illus.). 175p. 1992. 49.95 (0-8412-2455-2) Am Chemical.

Catalytic Cracking: Catalysts, Chemistry & Kinetics. Wojciechowski & Corma. (Chemical Industries Ser.: Vol. 25). 248p. 1986. 115.00 (0-8247-7603-8) Dekker.

*Catalytic Cracking of Heavy Petroleum Fractions. Daniel Decroocq. (Illus.). 140p. (C). 1984. text ed. 54.00 (2-7108-0455-7) Technip.

Catalytic Hydrogenation. L. Cerveny. 677p. 1986. 161.75 (0-444-42682-5) Elsevier.

Catalytic Hydrogenation: Techniques & Applications in Organic Synthesis. Robert L. Augustine. LC 65-27430. 200p. reprint ed. pap. 57.00 (0-685-15939-6, 2026312) Bks Demand.

Catalytic Hydrogenation in Organic Synthesis: Procedures & Commentary. Morris Freifelder. LC 78-9458. 205p. reprint ed. pap. 58.50 (0-685-15199-9, 2056154) Bks Demand.

Catalytic Hydroprocessing of Petroleum & Distillates: Proceedings of the AIChE Spring National Meeting, Houston, Texas, 1993. Ed. by Michael C. Oballa & Stuart S. Shih. LC 94-12079. (Chemical Industries Ser.: Vol. 58). 480p. 1994. 165.00 (0-8247-9255-6) Dekker.

Catalytic Isomerization of Hydrocarbons. A. A. Petrov. 168p. 1963. text ed. 44.25 (0-7065-0250-7, Pub. by Keter Pub IS) Coronet Bks.

Catalytic Materials: Relationship Between Structure & Reactivity. Ed. by Thaddeus E. Whyte, Jr. et al. LC 84-2776. (ACS Symposium Ser.: No. 248). 480p. 1984. lib. bdg. 82.95 (0-8412-0831-X) Am Chemical.

Catalytic Naphtha Reforming: Science & Technology. Ed. by George J. Antos et al. (Chemical Industries Ser.: Vol. 61). 528p. 1995. 165.00 (0-8247-9236-X) Dekker.

Catalytic Olefin Polymerization: Proceedings of the International Symposium on Recent Developments, Tokyo, Japan, Oct. 23-25, 1989. Ed. by T. Keii & K. Soga. (Studies in Surface Science & Catalysis: No. 56). 596p. 1990. 179.50 (0-444-98747-9) Elsevier.

Catalytic Oxidations with Hydrogen Peroxide As Oxidant. Ed. by Giorgio Strukul. LC 92-13459. (Catalysis by Metal Complexes Ser.: Vol. 9). 304p. (C). 1993. lib. bdg. 131.50 (0-7923-1771-8) Kluwer Ac.

Catalytic Polymerization of Olefins: Proceedings of the International Symposium on Future Aspects of Olefins Polymerization, Tokyo, Japan, 4-6 July 1985. Ed. by T. Keii & K. Soga. (Studies in Surface Science & Catalysis: Vol. 25). 500p. 1986. 187.25 (0-444-99518-8) Elsevier.

Catalytic Processes under Unsteady-State Conditions. Yu S. Matros. (Studies in Surface Science & Catalysis: No. 43). 404p. 1989. 192.50 (0-444-87116-0) Elsevier.

Catalytic Reforming. Donald M. Little. 256p. 1985. 79.95 (0-87814-281-9, P4348) PennWell Bks.

Catalytic Science & Technology, Vol. 1: Proceedings of the First Tokyo Conference on Advanced Catalytic Science & Technology Tokyo, July 1-5, 1990. Ed. by Satohiro Yoshida et al. 529p. 1991. lib. bdg. 162.00 (1-56081-132-3) VCH Pubs.

Catalytic Selective Oxidation: Developed from a Symposium. Ed. by S. Ted Oyama & Joe W. Hightower. LC 92-45894. (ACS Symposium Ser.: No. 523). (Illus.). 466p. 1993. 109.95 (0-8412-2637-7) Am Chemical.

Catalytic Transition Metal Hydrides, Vol. 415. Ed. by D. W. Slocum & William R. Moser. 65.00 (0-89766-224-5); pap. 65.00 (0-89766-225-3) NY Acad Sci.

Catalytical & Radical Polymerization. (Advances in Polymer Science Ser.: Vol. 81). (Illus.). 200p. 1986. 96.00 (0-387-16754-4) Spr-Verlag.

Catalyzed Direct Reactions of Silicon. Ed. by Kenrich M. Lewis & David G. Rethwisch. LC 93-34294. (Studies in Organic Chemistry: No. 49). 1993. write for info. (0-444-81715-8) Elsevier.

Catamaran Book. 2nd ed. Brian Phipps. (C). 1993. text ed. 59.00 (0-906754-86-0, Pub. by Fernhurst Bks UK) St Mut.

Catamaran Racing. Kim Furniss & Sarah Powell. 96p. (C). 1993. text ed. 59.00 (0-906754-90-9, Pub. by Fernhurst Bks UK) St Mut.

Catamaran Racing: For the 90's. Rick White & Mary Wells. (Illus.). 352p. (Orig.). 1992. pap. 29.95 (1-880871-00-9) Ram Pr.

Catamaran Racing from Start to Finish. Phil Berman. (Illus.). 1989. pap. 19.95 (0-393-30602-X) Norton.

Catamaran Sailing. Derek Kelsall. (Helmsman Guide Ser.). (Illus.). 128p. 1993. pap. 19.95 (1-85223-708-2, Pub. by Crowood Pr UK) Trafalgar.

Catamaran Sailing: From Start to Finish. Phil Berman. (Illus.). 1982. pap. 14.95 (0-393-00084-2) Norton.

Catapult. Vladimir Paral. LC 88-34053. 240p. 1989. 15.95 (0-945774-04-4, PG 5039.26.A7K313) Catbird Pr.

Catapult. Vladimir Paral. Tr. by William Harkins. LC 88-34053. 224p. 1993. reprint ed. pap. 10.95 (0-945774-17-6, PG5039-26-A7K313) Catbird Pr.

Catapult: Harry & I Build a Siege Weapon. Jim Paul. 1991. 17.50 (0-394-58507-0, Villard Bks) Random.

Catapult: Harry & I Build a Siege Weapon. Jim Paul. 272p. 1992. pap. 9.00 (0-380-71840-5) Avon.

Catapult: The Biography of Robert A. Monroe. Bayard Stockton. 400p. 1989. 19.95 (0-89865-756-3) Donning Co.

*Cataract. Tara K. Harper. 1995. pap. 5.99 (0-345-38052-5, Del Rey) Ballantine.

Cataract: A Study in Diderot. Jeffrey Mehlman. LC 76-65332. 121p. reprint ed. pap. 34.50 (0-7837-0217-5, 2040525) Bks Demand.

Cataract: Biochemistry, Epidemiology & Pharmacology. John Harding. 382p. 1991. 139.95 (0-412-36050-0, A5562) Chapman & Hall.

Cataract: Detection, Measurement & Management in Optometric Practice. William A. Douthwaite & Mark A. Hurst. (Illus.). 168p. 1994. 39.95 (0-7506-0369-0) Buttrwrth-Heinemann.

Cataract Canyon & Approaches: A River Runner's Guide. Don Baars. LC 87-70045. (Waterproof River Runner's Guides Ser.). (Illus.). 80p. (Orig.). 1987. pap. 12.95 (0-9616591-1-4) Canon Pubs.

Cataract Epidemiology. Ed. by K. Sasaki et al. (Developments in Ophthalmology Ser.: Vol. 15). (Illus.). vi, 106p. 1987. 70.50 (3-8055-4597-5) S Karger.

Cataract in Adults: Management of Functional Impairment. (Illus.). 226p. (Orig.). (C). 1994. pap. text ed. 60.00 (0-7881-0294-X) Diane Pub.

*Cataract in Adults: Management of Functional Impairment. 1995. lib. bdg. 255.75 (0-8490-6804-5) Gordon Pr.

Cataract Pathogenesis: Results of Epidemiological Studies & Experimental Models. Ed. by O. Hockwin & K. Sasaki. (Developments in Ophthalmology Ser.: Vol. 26). (Illus.). viii, 100p. 1994. 94.50 (3-8055-5987-9) S Karger.

Cataract Surgery. Ed. by Arthur Steele & Robert C. Drews. (Butterworth International Medical Reviews Rheumatology Ser.: Vol. 2). 1984. text ed. 140.00 (0-407-02341-0) Buttrwrth-Heinemann.

Cataract Surgery: A Literature Review & Ratings of Appropriateness & Cruciality. Paul P. Lee et al. LC 93-25076. 1993. write for info. (0-8330-1405-6, JRA-06) Rand Corp.

Cataract Surgery: Alternative Small-Incision Techniques. Ed. by George Rozakis. LC 89-43622. 196p. 1990. vhs 99.00 (1-55642-166-4) SLACK Inc.

*Cataract Surgery: Technique, Complications & Management. Roger F. Steinert. (Illus.). 448p. 1995. text ed. 185.00 (0-7216-5044-9) Saunders.

Cataract Surgery & Its Complications. 5th ed. Jaffee. 712p. 1989. text ed. 139.00 (0-8016-2885-7) Mosby Yr Bk.

Cataract Surgery & Lens Implantation. R. L. Lindstrom. (Current Opinion in Ophthalmology 1993 Ser.). (Illus.). 112p. (Orig.). 1993. pap. 59.95 (1-870485-67-X) Current Science.

Cataract Surgery & Lens Implantation. Richard L. Lindstrom. (Current Opinion in Ophthalmology 1994 Ser.). (Illus.). 110p. (Orig.). 1994. pap. text ed. 59.95 (1-85922-624-8) Current Science.

*Cataract Surgery & Lens Implantation. Richard L. Lindstrom. (Current Opinion in Ophthalmology Ser.). (Illus.). 65p. (Orig.). 1995. pap. text ed. 59.95 (1-85922-730-9) Current Science.

Cataract 1993. Ed. by O. Hockwin & K. Sasaki. (Journal: Ophthalmic Research Ser.: Vol. 26, Suppl. 1, 1994). (Illus.). iv, 90p. 1994. pap. 26.50 (3-8055-5986-0) S Karger.

Cataracts. Ed. by Delmar R. Caldwell. (Transactions of the New Orleans Academy of Ophthalmology Ser.). (Illus.). 380p. 1988. text ed. 142.50 (0-88167-380-3) Raven.

Cataracts. Kratz & Shammas. (Illus.). 226p. 1991. text ed. 99.50 (0-397-51071-3) Lippincott.

Cataracts. rev. ed. Ed. by Julius Schulman. LC 92-44032. 1993. 18.95 (0-312-08732-2) St Martin.

Cataracts: What You Must Know about Them. Charles D. Kelman. 96p. 1982. 14.00 (0-517-54850-X, Crown) Crown Pub Group.

Catasterismorum Reliquiae. Eratosthenes. Ed. by Carl Robert. vii, 254p. 1963. write for info. (3-296-12610-4, Pub. by Georg Olms GW) Lubrecht & Cramer.

Catastrofe de Corinto. George E. Gardiner. Orig. Title: The Corinthian Catastrophe. 64p. (SPA.). 1976. pap. 2.75 (0-8254-1254-4) Kregel.

Catastrope According to Hans Burkhardt. Donald Kuspit. (Illus.). 52p. 1990. pap. 20.00 (0-9625911-0-6) Muhlenberg College.

*Catastrophe! Great Engineering Failure--& Success. Fred Bortz. (Illus.). (J). (gr. 4-9). 1995. text ed. 19.95 (0-7167-6538-1, Sci Am Yng Rdrs); pap. text ed. 13.95 (0-7167-6539-X, Sci Am Yng Rdrs) W H Freeman.

Catastrophe Ahead: AIDS & the Case for a New Public Policy. William B. Johnston & Kevin R. Hopkins. LC 89-72139. 256p. 1990. text ed. 55.00 (0-275-93589-2, C3589, Praeger Pubs) Greenwood.

Catastrophe in the Making: With Letters to the Pope. Keith C. Barrons. 320p. 1992. 18.95 (0-931541-21-2) Mancorp Pub.

Catastrophe in the Opening. Ed. by Yakov Nieshtadt. (Chess Ser.). (Illus.). 271p. 1980. 25.95 (0-08-023121-7, Pergamon Pr); pap. 14.95 (0-08-024097-6, Pergamon Pr) Elsevier.

Catastrophe of Coma: A Way Back. E. A. Freeman. (Illus.). 272p. (Orig.). 1989. pap. text ed. 14.95 (0-911378-93-6) Sheridan Med Bks.

Catastrophe of Rainbows. Martha Collins. (CSU Poetry Ser.: No. XVII). 67p. (Orig.). 1985. pap. 6.00 (0-914946-48-X) Cleveland St Univ Poetry Ctr.

Catastrophe Practice. rev. ed. Nicholas Mosley. LC 88-30391. 342p. 1989. 19.95 (0-916583-35-X) Dalkey Arch.

Catastrophe Theoretical Semantics: An Elaboration & Application of Rene Thom's Theory. Wolfgang Wildgen. (Pragmatics & Beyond Ser.: Vol. III, No. 5). iv, 124p. (Orig.). 1982. pap. 41.00x (90-272-2525-7) Benjamins North Am.

Catastrophe Theory. Sandra Hayes & Domenico Castrigiano. 208p. (C). 1993. 44.95 (0-201-55590-5, Adv Bk Prog) Addison-Wesley.

Catastrophe Theory. 2nd rev. ed. V. I. Arnold. (Illus.). 120p. 1987. pap. 17.00 (0-387-16199-6) Spr-Verlag.

Catastrophe Theory. 3rd rev. ed. V. I. Arnold. Tr. by G. S. Wassermann & R. K. Thomas. LC 92-9633. (Illus.). 144p. 1994. pap. 24.00 (0-387-54811-4) Spr-Verlag.

Catastrophe Theory & Phase Transitions: Topological Aspects of Phase Transtions & Critical Phenomena. Kenchiki Okada. (Solid State Phenomena Ser.: Vol. 34). (Illus.). 232p. (C). 1993. text ed. 92.00 (3-908450-01-2, Pub. by Trans Tech SZ) LPS Dist Ctr.

Catastrophe Theory for Scientists & Engineers. Robert Gilmore. LC 92-43547. (Illus.). 688p. 1993. reprint ed. pap. 16.95 (0-486-67539-4) Dover.

Catastrophes. Ed. by Isaac Asimov et al. 416p. (Orig.). 1981. pap. 2.50 (0-449-24425-3, Crest) Fawcett.

Catastrophes & Evolution: Astronomical Foundations. Ed. by Victor Clube. (C). 1990. 54.95 (0-521-37420-0) Cambridge U Pr.

Catastrophes in Earth History. Steven A. Austin. LC 83-80181. (ICR Technical Monograph). 1984. pap. 13.95 (0-932766-08-0, Inst Creation) Master Bks.

Catastrophes in the Earth's History. I. A. Rezanov. 168p. 1984. pap. 30.00 (0-317-89619-9) St Mut.

Catastrophe's Spell. Mayer A. Brenner. (Dance of Gods Ser.: No. 1). 320p. 1989. mass mkt. 4.99 (0-88677-357-1) DAW Bks.

*Catastrophic Brain Injury. Ed. by Harvey S. Levin et al. (Illus.). 288p. 1995. 39.95 (0-19-508533-7) OUP.

Catastrophic Coastal Storms: Hazard Mitigation & Development Management. David R. Godschalk et al. LC 88-9572. (Duke Press Policy Studies). (Illus.). 344p. (C). 1988. lib. bdg. 52.95 (0-8223-0855-X) Duke.

Catastrophic Diseases: Who Decides What? Jay Katz & Alexander M. Capron. LC 80-21899. 275p. 1982. reprint ed. pap. text ed. 19.95x (0-87855-686-9) Transaction Pubs.

Catastrophic Diseases: Who Decides What? A Psychosocial & Legal Analysis of the Problems Posed by Hemodialysis & Organ Transplantation. Jay Katz & Alexander M. Capron. LC 75-7175. 280p. 1975. 34.95 (0-87154-439-3) Russell Sage.

Catastrophic Flooding: The Origin of the Channeled Scabland. Ed. by Victor R. Baker. LC 79-22901. (Benchmark Papers in Geology: Vol. 55). 384p. 1981. 54.95 (0-87933-360-X) Van Nos Reinhold.

Catastrophic Illness & the Family. Bert E. Park. LC 91-70967. 1992. 19.95 (0-8158-0471-7) Chris Mass.

*Catastrophic Politics: The Rise & Fall of the Medicare Catastrophic Coverage Act of 1988. Richard Himelfarb. LC 95-4251. 144p. 1995. 28.50 (0-271-01465-2); pap. 13.95 (0-271-01466-0) Pa St U Pr.

*Catastrophic Rights: Experimental Drugs & AIDS. John Dixon. 132p. (Orig.). Date not set. pap. 10.95 (0-921586-07-8, Pub. by New Star Bks CN) InBook.

Catastrophic Universe: An Essay in the Philosophy of Cosmology. A. G. Pacholczyk. LC 83-62523. (Philosophy in Science Library: Vol. 2). (Illus.). 128p. 1984. pap. 9.95 (0-88126-702-3) Pachart Pub Hse.

Catastrophism: Systems of Earth History. Richard J. Huggett. 224p. 1990. 49.95 (0-340-51757-3, A4530, Pub. by E Arnold UK) Routledge Chapman & Hall.

Catatonia. K. L. Kahlbaum. LC 72-9960. 120p. reprint ed. pap. 34.20 (0-317-28791-5, 2020539) Bks Demand.

Catawba Assembly. Charles A. Miller. LC 73-84983. (Illus.). 250p. 1973. pap. 7.00 (0-9606522-0-5) Trackaday.

Catawba Texts. Frank G. Speck. LC 77-82345. (Columbia Univ. Contributions to Anthropology Ser.: Vol. 24). reprint ed. 18.00 (0-404-50574-0) AMS Pr.

Catawbas. James H. Merrell. (Indians of North America Ser.). (Illus.). 112p. (YA). (gr. 5 up). 1989. 17.95 (1-55546-694-X) Chelsea Hse.

Catawbe County, North Carolina, Marriages, 1842 (50) - 1880, Vol. 1. Elizabeth B. Sherrill. 135p. (Orig.). 1994. pap. 22.00 (1-55613-897-0) Heritage Bk.

Catbirds & Dogfish. Bernard Most. LC 94-17839. (J). 1995. 13.00 (0-15-292844-8) HarBrace.

*Catbirds & Dogfish. Bernard Most. LC 94-17839. (J). (ps-3). 1995. pap. 5.00 (0-15-200779-2) HarBrace.

Catboat Book. Ed. by John M. Leavens. 1992. pap. text ed. 17.95 (0-07-010442-5) McGraw.

Catboat Book. John M. Leavens. 160p. 1991. pap. 17.95 (0-87742-314-8) Intl Marine.

Catboats. Stan Grayson. LC 83-49415. (Illus.). 176p. 1984. 27.00 (0-87742-162-5, C233) Intl Marine.

Catch. Iefke Goldberger & Felix Pollak. 1982. pap. 4.95 (0-913370-15-0, Sol Press) Wisconsin Bks.

Catch a Comet by the Tail. Mark J. Rauzon. (Illus.). 48p. (J). (gr. 5-10). 1985. pap. 6.95 (0-935181-00-8) Marine Endeavors.

Catch a Falling Spy. L. Deighton. 1991. mass mkt. 5.50 (0-06-100207-0) HarpC.

Catch a Falling Star: (Showcase) Tracy Hughes. (Superromance Ser.). 1994. mass mkt. 3.50 (0-373-70623-5, 1-70623-3) Harlequin Bks.

*Catch a Falling Star: Living with Alzheimer's Disease. Betty B. Spohr & Jean V. Bullard. Ed. by Jean V. Bullard. (Illus.). 214p. (Orig.). 1995. pap. 9.95 (0-9641357-1-X) Storm Peak.

Catch a Fire: The Life of Bob Marley. rev. ed. Timothy White. LC 82-25850. (Illus.). 496p. 1989. pap. 13.95 (0-8050-1152-8, Owl) H Holt & Co.

Catch a Rising Star. Laura Phillips. 224p. (Orig.). 1991. pap. 2.75 (1-878702-39-4, Kismet) Meteor Pub.

Catch a Whiffle-Poofle! Claire Ottenstein. (Illus.). 64p. (Orig.). (J). 1991. lib. bdg. 8.95 (1-878149-03-2) Counterpoint Pub.

Catch a Winner. Pat Eytcheson. Ed. by Edwin M. Eakin. 48p. (J). (gr. 2-3). 1989. 10.95 (0-89015-704-9) Sunbelt Media.

*Catch a Winner & the Mystery Horse. Pat Eytcheson. LC 95-10305. (Illus.). (J). 1995. write for info. (0-89015-995-5, Eakin Pr) Sunbelt Media.

Catch a Winner Leaves the Ranch. Pat Eytcheson. (Illus.). 48p. (J). (gr. 1-3). 1991. 10.95 (0-89015-828-2) Sunbelt Media.

Catch & Other War Stories. Kenzaburo Oe et al. LC 80-84420. 156p. 1981. pap. 9.00 (0-87011-457-3, L46) Kodansha.

Catch As Catch Can. Charlotte Armstrong. 1990. pap. 3.50 (0-8217-3126-2) Zebra.

Catch As Catch Can. Frances Lockridge & Richard Lockridge. 1976. 18.95 (0-89190-913-3) Amereon Ltd.

Catch Bass! Doug Hannon & Don Wirth. LC 84-73347. (Illus.). 1984. pap. 6.95 (0-8200-0123-6) Great Outdoors.

*Catch Colt. Sidner J. Larson. LC 94-32267. (American Indian Lives Ser.). x, 164p. 1995. 21.00 (0-8032-2908-9) U of Nebr Pr.

Catch Colt. Mary O'Hara. 1964. pap. 4.75 (0-8222-0190-9) Dramatists Play.

Catch Effort Sampling Strategies: Their Application in Freshwater Fisheries Management. Ian G. Cowx. (Illus.). 432p. 1992. 115.00 (0-85238-177-8) Blackwell Sci.

*Catch Every Eddy...Surf Every Wave: A Contemporary Guide to Whitewater Playboating. Thomas S. Foster & Kel Kelly. (Illus.). 260p. (Orig.). 1995. pap. 16.95 (0-9645221-4-4) Outdoor Centre.

CATCH Guide to Planning Services with Families: Coordinated Transitions from the Hospital to the Community & Home. Yvonne Gillette. 261p. (Orig.). 1992. pap. text ed. 39.00 (0-88450-531-6, 7818) Commun Skill.

Catch Kid Curry! William R. Garwood. LC 81-71394. 250p. 1982. 13.95 (0-937618-02-0) Bath St Pr.

Catch Me a Colobus. large type ed. Gerald Durrell. 1978. 15.95 (0-7089-0094-1) Ulverscroft.

Catch Me a Nightingale. large type ed. Joan Ash. (General Ser.). (Illus.). 416p. 1993. 21.95 (0-7089-2853-6) Ulverscroft.

Catch Me a Rainbow. rev. ed. Lester Bach. (Illus.). 412p. 1991. pap. 10.00 (0-944996-08-6) Carlsons.

Catch Me, Catch Me! A Thomas the Tank Engine Story. W. Awdry. LC 89-37547. (Pictureback Ser.). (Illus.). 24p. (Orig.). (J). (ps-2). 1990. pap. 2.25 (0-679-80485-4) Random Bks Yng Read.

Catch Me If You Can. Frank W. Abagnale. 1990. mass mkt. 5.99 (0-671-73140-8) PB.

Catch Me If You Can! Densey Clyne. (J). (gr. 4-7). 1993. pap. 6.95 (1-86373-205-5, Pub. by Allen & Unwin Aust Pty AT) IPG Chicago.

Catch Me If You Can! Densey Clyne. (J). 1993. pap. 6.95 (0-685-63824-3) Routledge Chapman & Hall.

Catch Me If You Can. Casey McAllister. 288p. (Orig.). 1993. mass mkt. 4.50 (0-380-76571-3) Avon.

Catch Me If You Can. D. M. Souza. (J). (gr. 1-4). 1992. 18.95 (0-87614-713-9, Carolrhoda) Lerner Group.

Catch of Anti-Letters. Thomas Merton & Robert Lax. LC 94-1262. (Illus.). 136p. (Orig.). 1994. pap. 9.95 (1-55612-712-X, LL1712) Sheed & Ward MO.

Catch of Hands: An Autobiography. Benedicta Leigh. 144p. 1992. pap. 13.95 (1-85381-191-2, Pub. by Virago Pr UK) Trafalgar.

Catch of the Day. Kristine V. Smith. (Illus.). 112p. (Orig.). 1991. pap. write for info. (0-9627294-1-8) Hawaiian Resources.

Catch Phrases, Cliches & Idioms: A Dictionary of Familiar Expressions. Comp. by Doris Craig. LC 89-43644. 238p. 1990. lib. bdg. 27.50x (0-89950-467-1) McFarland & Co.

C

An Asterisk (*) at the beginning of an entry indicates that the title is appearing in BIP for the first time.

Catch Rope: The Long Arm of the Cowboy. John R. Erickson. LC 93-35820. (Western Life Ser.). (Illus.). 200p. 1994. 26.50 (*0-929398-66-1*) UNTX Pr.

Catch That Cat! A Picture Book of Rhymes & Puzzles. Monika Beisner. (Illus.). 32p. (J). 1990. 15.00 (*0-374-31226-5*) FS&G.

Catch That Catch Can. John Hilton. LC 75-87492. (Music Ser.). 1970. reprint ed. lib. bdg. 25.00 (*0-306-71498-1*) Da Capo.

Catch That Hat! Emma C. Clark. LC 89-34881. (Illus.). (J). (ps-2). 1990. 12.95 (*0-316-14496-7*) Little.

Catch That Pass!, Vol. 1. Matt Christopher. LC 77-77442. (Illus.). (J). (gr. 4-6). 1972. lib. bdg. 15.95 (*0-316-13932-7*) Little.

Catch That Pass!, Vol. 1. Matt Christopher. LC 77-77442. (Illus.). (J). (gr. 4-6). 1989. mass mkt. 3.95 (*0-316-13924-6*) Little.

Catch the Age Wave: A Handbook for Effective Ministry with Senior Adults. Win Arn & Charles Arn. LC 92-38316. 176p. (Orig.). 1993. pap. 9.99 (*0-8010-0231-1*) Baker Bk.

Catch the Baby! Lee Kingman. LC 92-26588. (Illus.). (J). 1993. pap. 4.99 (*0-14-050762-0*) Puffin Bks.

***Catch the Christmas Spirit.** 96p. (Orig.). 1994. pap. 10.95 (*0-89724-379-X*) Warner Brothers.

***Catch the Spirit: Riding the Waves of Life.** Christian C. Sorensen. Ed. by Marcia J. Hootman. 160p. (Orig.). 1995. pap. 9.95 (*0-943172-95-0*) New Wave.

***Catch the Spirit of Creativity: Based on Creative Writing, Art, Science, & Heritage.** Amy A. Garza. (Illus.). 32p. (J). 1994. pap. 3.50 (*0-914875-25-6*) Bright Mtn Bks.

Catch the Vision on Prayer in the Last Days. George A. McCabe. (Illus.). 152p. 1988. pap. 6.95 (*0-317-90967-3*) Vision Ministry Pr.

Catch the Vision Two Thousand. Bill Stearns. 192p. (Orig.). 1991. pap. 7.99 (*1-55661-184-6*) Bethany Hse.

Catch the Vision 2000: The Study Guide. Bill Stearns & Amy Stearns. 96p. 1992. student ed 8.95 (*0-9635051-0-6*) Wrldview CO.

***Catch the Whisper of the Wind.** rev. ed. Cheewa James. 128p. 1995. audio, pap. 21.95 (*0-614-05117-7*) Horzn Two Thou.

Catch the Whisper of the Wind. 2nd rev. ed. Illus. by David Villasenor & Jean Villasenor. 128p. 1995. pap. 11.95 (*0-9632665-2-7*) Horzn Two Thou.

***Catch the Whisper of the Wind: Collected Stories & Proverbs from Native Americans.** Cheewa James. 180p. 1995. pap. 9.95 (*1-55874-369-3*, 3693) Health Comm.

Catch the Wind! All about Kites. Gail Gibbons. LC 88-28820. (Illus.). (J). (gr. k-3). 1989. 15.95 (*0-316-30955-9*) Little.

***Catch Them Learning: A Handbook of Classroom Strategies - Grades K-12.** Mary Prentice. LC 94-78534. 120p. 1994. pap. 17.95 (*0-932935-79-6*) IRI-Skylght.

Catch Them Thinking: A Handbook of Classroom Strategies. James Bellanca & Robin Fogarty. (Illus.). 293p. (Orig.). (J). (gr. 4-12). 1986. pap. text ed. 25.95 (*0-932935-02-8*) IRI-Skylght.

Catch Them Thinking in Science: A Handbook of Classroom Strategies. Sally Berman. LC 93-78421. (Illus.). 112p. (Orig.). (YA). (gr. 5-12). 1993. pap. 19.95 (*0-932935-55-9*) IRI-Skylght.

Catch Them Young: Vocationalisation for Higher Employability. K. Sudha Rao & N. K. Chowdhary. viii, 120p. (C). 1992. 22.50 (*81-207-1398-2*, Pub. by Sterling Pubs II) Apt Bks.

Catch Trap. Marion Zimmer Bradley. 688p. 1984. mass mkt. 5.95 (*0-345-31564-2*) Ballantine.

Catch Twenty-Two. (Book Notes Ser.). 1985. pap. 2.95 (*0-8120-3506-2*) Barron.

Catch-22. Joseph Heller. 1989. mass mkt. 6.99 (*0-440-20439-9*, LE) Dell.

Catch 22. Joseph Keller. LC 94-13984. 1994. 25.00 (*0-671-50233-6*); 125.00 (*0-671-89854-X*) S&S Trade.

Catch-Twenty-Two: Antiheroic Antinovel. Stephen W. Potts. (Masterwork Studies). 160p. 1989. text ed. 21.95 (*0-8057-7992-2*, Twayne); pap. 12.95 (*0-8057-8041-6*, Twayne) Macmillan.

Catch Twenty-Two Notes. C. A. Peek. 48p. 1975. pap. 3.75 (*0-8220-0296-5*) Cliffs.

Catch You on the Flip Side. Pete Johnson. 135p. (YA). (gr. 7-9). 1989. pap. 9.95 (*0-233-98074-1*, Pub. by A Deutsch UK) Trafalgar.

Catcher. Mia Wolff. LC 93-33802. (J). 1994. 16.00 (*0-374-31227-3*) FS&G.

***Catcher in the Rye.** R. Holzman & G. Perkins. (Max Notes Ser.). (Illus.). 128p. 1995. pap. text ed. 3.95 (*0-87891-752-7*) Res & Educ.

***Catcher in the Rye.** Pinsker. 128p. 1993. 22.95 (*0-8057-7978-7*, Twayne) Macmillan.

Catcher in the Rye. J. D. Salinger. 302p. (YA). 1951. 22.95 (*0-316-76953-3*) Little.

Catcher in the Rye. J. D. Salinger. 224p. (J). 1991. mass mkt. 4.99 (*0-316-76948-7*) Warner Bks.

Catcher in the Rye. large type ed. J. D. Salinger. LC 92-46198. 1993. 21.95 (*0-7927-1517-9*, Curley Lrg Print); pap. 19.95 (*0-7927-1516-0*, Curley Lrg Print) Chivers N Amer.

Catcher in the Rye. J. D. Salinger. 300p. 1991. reprint ed. lib. bdg. 23.95 (*0-89966-782-1*) Buccaneer Bks.

Catcher in the Rye: A Study Guide. Joy Leavitt. (Novel-Ties Ser.). (gr. 7-12). 1985. student ed, teacher ed 15.95 (*0-88122-107-4*) Lrn Links.

Catcher in the Rye: Innocence under Pressure. Sanford Pinsker. LC 92-31048. (Masterwork Studies Ser.: No. 114). 107p. 1993. lib. bdg. 21.95 (*0-8057-8365-2*, Twayne); pap. 12.95 (*0-8057-8028-9*, Twayne) Macmillan.

Catcher in the Rye Notes. Robert B. Kaplan. 1965. pap. 3.75 (*0-8220-0301-5*) Cliffs.

Catcher in the Rye (Salinger) Claro. (Book Notes Ser.). (C). 1984. pap. 2.95 (*0-8120-3407-4*) Barron.

***Catcher in the Sky.** Rick McKinney. Tr. by Ingram. 250p. 1996. pap. 8.95 (*0-7610-0445-9*) NW Pub.

Catcher in the Wry. Bob Uecker & Micky Herskowitz. (Illus.). 240p. 1987. mass mkt. 4.99 (*0-515-09029-8*) Jove Pubns.

***Catcher Was a Spy.** Dawidoff. 1995. pap. 13.00 (*0-679-76289-2*) Random.

***Catcher Was A Spy.** Dawidoff. Date not set. pap. write for info. (*0-679-76279-5*) Random Hse Value.

Catcher Was a Spy: The Mysterious Life of Moe Berg. Nicholas Dawidoff. LC 93-41324. 480p. 1994. 24.00 (*0-679-41566-1*) Pantheon.

Catcher with a Glass Arm. Matt Christopher. (Illus.). (J). (gr. 4-6). 1985. mass mkt. 3.95 (*0-316-13985-8*) Little.

***Catchers of Heaven - A Trilogy.** Michael Wolf. Ed. by Molly Sanford & Joan S. Koole. 248p. 1995. 20.00 (*1-882188-10-1*) Magnolia Mktg.

Catching a Cold: How You Get Ill, Suffer & Recover. Steve Parker. (Body in Action Ser.). (Illus.). 32p. (J). (gr. k-4). 1992. lib. bdg. 12.25 (*0-531-14146-2*) Watts.

Catching a Feather on a Fan: A Zen Retreat with Master Sheng Yen. Ed. by John Crook. 144p. 1990. pap. 12.95 (*1-85230-194-5*) Element MA.

Catching a Glimpse of Heaven. E. M. Bounds. 150p. 1985. pap. text ed. 4.99 (*0-88368-167-6*) Whitaker Hse.

Catching a Meal. Paul Bennett. (Nature's Secrets Ser.). (Illus.). 32p. (J). (gr. 2-4). 1994. 14.95 (*1-56847-207-2*) Thomson Lrning.

***Catching Babies: The Professionalization of Childbirth, 1870-1920.** Charlotte G. Borst. LC 95-5261. (Illus.). 288p. (C). 1995. text ed. 39.95 (*0-674-10262-2*) HUP.

Catching Bodies. Phillip Mahony. 80p. 1984. text ed. 20.00 (*0-938190-56-3*); pap. 7.95 (*0-938190-55-5*) North Atlantic.

Catching Good Health with Homeopathic Medicine: A Concise, Self-Help Introduction to Homeopathy. Raymond J. Garrett & TeRessa Stone. 152p. (Orig.). 1991. pap. 8.95 (*0-916360-45-8*) CRCS Pubns CA.

Catching Ideas: Activity Book for Creative Writing. Kathleen C. Phillips & Barbara Steiner. (Illus.). 164p. 1988. student ed 20.00 (*0-87287-712-4*) Libs Unl.

Catching Lake Trout. John Gale. (Illus.). 144p. 1990. 29.00 (*0-85115-267-8*) Boydell & Brewer.

Catching Lobsters for Food, Fun & Profit. P. M. Pekar. (Illus.). 1985. 3.95 (*0-318-19500-3*); lib. bdg. 4.95 (*0-318-19499-6*) Comtech Pubns.

Catching More Flounder - Fluke. Barney Rowe. (Illus.). 36p. (Orig.). 1982. pap. 2.75 (*0-940844-74-5*) Wellspring.

***Catching My Breath.** Brookes. 1995. pap. 12.00 (*0-679-76206-X*) Random.

Catching My Breath: An Asthmatic Explores His Illness. Tim Brookes. 1994. 22.00 (*0-8129-2182-8*, Times Bks) Random.

Catching on to American Idioms. Esther Ellins-Elmakiss. LC 84-50703. (Illus.). 144p. 1984. pap. text ed. 11.95 (*0-472-08049-0*) U of Mich Pr.

Catching on to American Idioms. rev. ed. Esther Ellin-Elmakiss. LC 92-63377. 200p. 1993. pap. text ed. 12.95 (*0-472-08208-6*) U of Mich Pr.

Catching Our Breath: Next Steps for Reducing Urban Ozone. (Illus.). 248p. 1989. pap. 10.00 (*0-16-005565-2*, S/N 052-003-01158-1) USGPO.

Catching Our Breath: Next Steps to Reducing Urban Ozone. 1994. lib. bdg. 259.95 (*0-8490-9067-9*) Gordon Pr.

***Catching Rainbows: Stories to Support Children During Life Crises.** K. Hemery et al. Ed. by Joy Johnson. (Illus.). 25p. (J). (gr. k-4). 1995. pap. 4.95 (*1-56123-079-0*) Centering Corp.

***Catching Sense: African American Communities on a South Carolina Sea Island.** Patricia Guthrie. LC 94-36623. 160p. 1995. text ed. 49.95 (*0-89789-425-1*, Bergin & Garvey) Greenwood.

Catching Serial Killers: Learning from Past Serial Murder Investigations. Earl James. Ed. by Virginia McPhail & Lisa Waddell. LC 91-72098. 369p. (C). 1991. text ed. 19.95 (*0-9629714-0-5*); pap. text ed. 14.95 (*0-9629714-1-3*) Intl Forensic Serv.

CATCHING SERIAL KILLERS examines twenty-eight serial murderers to determine how the killers were finally apprehended. The purpose was to determine the most effective means of investigation in future cases. The book also delves into other areas, such as: The difference between a serial murder & other homicide investigations. Common errors made by the police during a serial murder investigation. Why it is very important for the police to have good community relations. Myths about serial killers. Why serial killers are frequently questioned by the police & released--only to kill again. How the attitude of a serial killer can be used to the investigator's advantage. The types of trace evidence laboratory scientists are most likely to find at the body recovery site. Where the police are most apt to find evidence linking the murderers to the victims. Why an ad hoc task force is usually necessary in serial murder cases. Where materials can be found to help establish a task force. What kind of personnel should make up the task force. How an investigator can help avoid inconclusive or inaccurate polygraph tests. How to conduct a fair lineup. And other related areas. About the Author: Earl James spent more than 27 years on active duty in the law enforcement profession. He has served as a peace officer with the U.S. Marines, on the Sturgis Michigan Police Department, Washington's Metropolitan Police Department, & the Michigan State Police. He has participated in hundreds of homicide investigations, including serial murder investigations, during his life. He has lectured extensively on effective investigative techniques to apprehend serial killers both in the United States & in Europe. Dr. James has been elected a Fellow in the American Academy of Forensic Sciences. ***Publisher Provided Annotation.***

Catching Shadows: A Directory of Nineteenth-Century Texas Photographers. David Haynes. 1993. pap. 19.95 (*0-87611-130-4*) Tex St Hist Assn.

Catching Striped Bass. Keith Walters. (Illus.). 48p. (Orig.). 1993. pap. 3.95 (*0-9627039-2-3*) Aerie Hse.

Catching the Drift: Authority, Gender, & Narrative Strategy in Fiction. Laura Tracy. 240p. (C). 1988. text ed. 40.00 (*0-8135-1319-7*) Rutgers U Pr.

Catching the Light. Lynn Kozma. LC 89-38954. 100p. (Orig.). 1989. pap. 5.95 (*0-936015-21-7*) Pocahontas Pr.

***Catching the Light: The Entwined History of Light & Mind.** Arthur Zajonc. (Illus.). 400p. 1995. pap. 12.95 (*0-19-509575-8*) OUP.

Catching the Spirit: Songs of Light & Shadow. Maureen McCarthy. LC 94-12991. 67p. 1994. 6.95 (*1-879007-12-6*) St Bedes Pubns.

Catching the Tune. Pike et al. Ed. by Armstrong. LC 84-4845. (Illus.). 68p. (Orig.). 1984. pap. 5.00 (*0-943924-08-1*) Mus Stony Brook.

Catching the Vision. William G. Dyer. 1993. 11.95 (*0-88494-908-7*) Bookcraft Inc.

***Catching the Water under Fish.** Leslie L. Fields. (Dog River Review Poetry Ser.). 56p. (Orig.). 1994. pap. 4.95 (*0-916155-28-5*) Trout Creek.

***Catching the Wave: Workplace Reform in Australia.** John A. Mathews. LC 94-25504. (Cornell International Industrial & Labor Relations Reports: No. 26). 359p. 1994. pap. 21.95 (*0-87546-706-7*) ILR Pr.

***Catching the Wave: Workplace Reform in Australia.** John A. Mathews. LC 94-25504. (Cornell International Industrial & Labor Relations Reports: No. 36). 376p. 1994. 45.00 (*0-87546-707-5*) ILR Pr.

Catching the Wind. Joanne Ryder. LC 88-23446. (Just for a Day Book Ser.). (Illus.). 32p. (J). (gr. k up). 1989. 13.95 (*0-688-07170-8*); lib. bdg. 13.88 (*0-688-07171-6*) Morrow Jr Bks.

Catching the Wind. Diane Stanley et al. LC 88-23446. (Illus.). 48p. (J). (gr. 2 up). 1993. pap. 4.95 (*0-688-13333-9*) Morrow Jr Bks.

Catching the Writing Express. Iris Tiedt. (J). (gr. 2-4). 1987. pap. 10.99 (*0-8224-1307-8*) Fearon Teach Aids.

Catching Their Talk in a Box. Betty M. Hockett. LC 87-81296. 1987. pap. 4.95 (*0-943701-13-9*) George Fox Pr.

Catching Up? Organizational & Management Change in the Ex-Socialist Block. Andrzej K. Kozminski. LC 92-40891. (SUNY Series in International Management). 236p. (C). 1993. 59.50 (*0-7914-1597-X*); pap. 19.95 (*0-7914-1598-8*) State U NY Pr.

Catching Up: Remedial Education. John E. Roueche & R. Wade Kirk. LC 73-1851. (Jossey-Bass Higher Education Ser.). 122p. reprint ed. 34.80 (*0-8357-9299-4*, 2013746) Bks Demand.

Catching 100 Australian Fish. Steve Starling. (Lothian Australian Fishing Guides Ser.). (Illus.). 96p. (Orig.). 1995. pap. 5.95 (*0-85091-603-8*, Pub. by Lothian Pub AT) Seven Hills Bk.

Catchment Runoff & Rational Formula. Ed. by Ben C. Yen. 169p. 1992. 28.00 (*0-918334-71-3*) WRP.

Catchpenny Prints: One Hundred Sixty-Three Popular Engravings from the 18th Century. Bowles & Carver. LC 79-103068. (Pictorial Archive Ser.). (Illus.). 163p. (Orig.). 1970. pap. 8.95 (*0-486-22569-0*) Dover.

***Catchwords: A Book of Cats & Words.** Ann Katzenbach. (Illus.). 52p. (Orig.). Date not set. pap. write for info. (*0-9644116-0-1*) Catapult Port Townsend.

***Cate Ate My Gymsuit.** Michael Golden. Ed. by J. Friedland & R. Kessler. (Novel-Ties Ser.). (J). (gr. 4-6). 1992. student ed, pap. text ed. 15.95 (*0-88122-715-3*) Lrn Links.

Catechesis: The Mission of the World Apostolate of Fatima. John A. Hardon. 1991. 0.50 (*1-56036-012-7*) AMI Pr.

Catechesis for Liturgy. Gilbert Ostdiek. 1986. 10.95 (*0-912405-23-6*) Pastoral Pr.

Catechesis in Our Time. Pope John Paul Second. (C). 1988. 30.00 (*0-85439-169-X*, Pub. by St Paul Pubns UK) St Mut.

Catechesis of the Orthodox Church. rev. ed. Apostolos Makrakis. Ed. by Orthodox Christian Educational Society Staff. 239p. 1969. reprint ed. pap. text ed. 9.95 (*0-938366-14-9*) Orthodox Chr.

***Catechesis on the Mystery of Crowning: Leader's Guide.** 18p. 1985. teacher ed 3.00 (*1-56125-001-5*) Educ Services.

Catechesis-The Maturation of the Body. Daniel Sahas. 79p. 1984. pap. 5.00 (*0-917651-04-9*) Holy Cross Orthodox.

Catechetical Exposition of the Constitution of the State of Tennessee. Willie Blount. LC 74-583. (Tennessee Beginnings Ser.). 1974. 17.50 (*0-685-04320-7*) Reprint.

Catechetical Helps. Edwin W. Kurth. (gr. 4-12). 1981. pap. text ed. 6.00 (*0-570-03507-4*, 14-1261) Concordia.

Catechetical Review. A. H. Lange. 1968. pap. 0.75 (*0-570-03520-1*, 14-1102) Concordia.

***Catechetical Sunday 1995 Kit: Imagine God's Mercy.** Tr. by Marina Herrera. (Illus.). 78p. (Orig.). 1995. pap. text ed. 8.95 (*1-55586-036-2*) US Catholic.

Catechetics in the Catholic School. James F. Hawker. 61p. 1986. 6.60 (*0-318-20569-6*) Natl Cath Educ.

Catechism. C. H. Spurgeon. 32p. 1985. pap. 1.50 (*1-56186-346-7*) Pilgrim Pubns.

Catechism: Highlights & Commentary. Brennan Hill & William Madges. LC 93-61482. 160p. (Orig.). 1994. pap. 9.95 (*0-89622-589-5*) Twenty-Third.

Catechism & Guide: Navaho-English. Berard Haile. (Orig.). 1937. pap. 3.00 (*0-686-32657-1*) St Michaels.

Catechism Explained: An Enhaustive Exposition of the Christian Religion - a Practical Manual for the Use of the Preacher, the Catechist, the Teacher & the Family. Francis Spirago. Ed. by Richard F. Clarke. LC 93-61206. 752p. 1993. 37.50 (*0-89555-497-6*) TAN Bks Pubs.

Catechism for Inquirers. 4th ed. Ed. by Joseph L. Malloy. 1984. pap. 4.95 (*0-8091-5012-3*) Paulist Pr.

Catechism for Young Children with Cartoons, Bk. 1. Vic Lockman. (Illus.). 45p. (Orig.). (J). (ps-6). 1984. pap. 1.50 (*0-936175-01-X*); pap. text ed. 1.00 (*0-936175-03-6*) V Lockman.

Catechism for Young Children with Cartoons, Bk II. Vic Lockman. (Illus.). 45p. (Orig.). 1985. pap. 1.50 (*0-936175-02-8*) V Lockman.

Catechism Handbook. David P. Kuske. 228p. 1982. ring bd. 19.95 (*0-938272-12-8*) WELS Board.

Catechism Lessons: Pupil's Book. Adolph Fehlauer. Ed. by Richard Grunze. (Illus.). 336p. (J). (gr. 5-6). 1981. 6.95 (*0-938272-09-8*) WELS Board.

Catechism Lessons-Teacher's Book. Adolph Fehlauer. Ed. by R. Grunze. 392p. (J). (gr. 5-6). 1978. ring bd. 9.95 (*0-938272-08-X*) WELS Board.

Catechism of Catholic Social Teaching. Gerald Darring. LC 87-62380. 126p. (Orig.). (C). 1987. pap. 4.95 (*1-55612-084-2*) Sheed & Ward MO.

Catechism of Christian Doctrine. Catholic Bishops of England & Wales Staff. LC 82-50599. 72p. 1982. reprint ed. pap. 2.50 (*0-89555-176-4*) TAN Bks Pubs.

Catechism of Eastern Greek Orthodox Church. M. Polyzoides. 96p. 5.00 (*0-686-79625-X*) Divry.

Catechism of Family Values Based on the Bible. Arthur F. Ide. LC 92-27360. (Illus.). 337p. (Orig.). 1993. pap. 25.00 (*0-935175-26-1*) Monument Pr.

Catechism of Health. Bernhard C. Faust. Tr. by J. H. Basse. LC 74-180574. (Medicine & Society in America Ser.). 116p. 1972. reprint ed. 17.95 (*0-405-03951-4*) Ayer.

Catechism of Hindu Dharma. 2nd ed. rev. ed. Srisa Chandra Vasu. Tr. by Srisa Chandra Vidyarnava. LC 73-3829. (Sacred Books of the Hindus: No. 3). reprint ed. 18.00 (*0-404-57847-0*) AMS Pr.

Catechism of Mental Prayer. Joseph Simler. LC 84-51901. 69p. 1985. reprint ed. pap. 1.50 (*0-89555-256-6*) TAN Bks Pubs.

Catechism of Modernism. J. B. Lemius. LC 81-52536. 160p. 1981. reprint ed. pap. 4.00 (*0-89555-167-5*) TAN Bks Pubs.

Catechism of Musical History & Biography. Frederick J. Crowest. 187p. 1991. reprint ed. 69.00 (*0-7812-9312-X*) Rprt Serv.

Catechism of the Catholic Church. 600p. 1993. 29.95 (*0-89870-481-2*); pap. 19.95 (*0-89870-482-0*) Ignatius Pr.

Catechism of the Catholic Church. 816p. 1993. text ed. 19.95 (*0-89243-565-8*); pap. text ed. 19.95 (*0-89243-566-6*) Liguori Pubns.

Catechism of the Catholic Church. (Liberia Editrice Vaticana Ser.). 600p. 1994. pap. 19.95 (*0-8091-3434-9*) Paulist Pr.

Catechism of the Catholic Church. (Illus.). 816p. 1994. 29.95 (*0-915245-01-9*); pap. 19.95 (*0-915245-02-7*) Wanderer Pr.

***Catechism of the Catholic Church.** 860p. 1995. mass mkt. 7.99 (*0-385-47967-0*) Doubleday.

***Catechism of the Catholic Church.** 860p. (SPA.). 1995. mass mkt. 7.99 (*0-385-47984-0*) Doubleday.

***Catechism of the Catholic Church.** Doubleday. 1995. pap. (*0-385-47985-9*) Doubleday.

***Catechism of the Catholic Church.** David Konstant. 1994. 29.95 (*1-884660-00-2*) Urbi Et Orbi.

***Catechism of the Catholic Church.** David Konstant. 1994. pap. 19.95 (*1-884660-01-0*) Urbi Et Orbi.

***Catechism of the Catholic Church.** United States Catholic Conference Staff. (Illus.). 804p. 1994. text ed. 29.95 (*0-88347-277-5*) Thomas More.

***Catechism of the Catholic Church: A Family Perspective Bulletin Course.** David M. Thomas & Mary J. Calnan. 26p. 1994. pap. 39.95 (*0-88347-280-5*) Thomas More.

***Catechism of the Catholic Church: Familystyle, 4 vols., Set.** David M. Thomas & Mary J. Calnan. (Orig.). 1994. boxed, pap. 39.95 (*0-88347-281-3*, 7281) Thomas More.

***Catechism of the Catholic Church Spanish - Gift Edition.** Doubleday. (SPA.). 1995. pap. (*0-385-47986-7*) Doubleday.

Catechism of the Council of Trent. Council of Trent Staff. LC 82-50588. 603p. 1983. reprint ed. pap. 20.00 (*0-89555-185-3*) TAN Bks Pubs.

C

An Asterisk (*) at the beginning of an entry indicates that the title is appearing in BIP for the first time.

Catechism of the Orthodox Church. Metropolitan Philaret of Moscow Staff. 1901. pap. 2.95 (*0-89981-009-8*) Eastern Orthodox.

Catechism of the Orthodox Church. Ed. by St. Tikhon's Religious Center Staff. 110p. (Orig.). 1989. pap. 4.50 (*1-878997-33-5*) St Tikhons Pr.

Catechism of the Summa Theologica of Saint Thomas Aquinas. R. P. Pegues. Tr. by Aelred Whitacre. 315p. 1993. reprint ed. text ed. 15.95 (*0-912141-03-4*) Roman Cath Bks.

Catechism on the Christian Religion. Helen F. Rothwell & Mel-Thomas Rothwell. 1989. pap. 3.99 (*0-88019-000-0*) Schmul Pub Co.

***Catechism Resource Library, 3 vols., Set.** Date not set. 59.95 (*0-88347-319-4*, 7319) Thomas More.

Catechism Yesterday & Today: A Short Story. Bernard Marthaler. 200p. (Orig.). 1995. pap. text ed. write for info. (*0-8146-2151-1*) Liturgical Pr.

Catechisme de l'Eglise Catholique. Mame & Plon. (FRE.). 1992. pap. 59.95 (*0-7859-1006-9*, 2728905495) Fr & Eur.

Catechisme, or First Instruction & Learning of Christian Religion. Alexander Nowell. LC 74-23570. 185p. 1975. reprint ed. lib. bdg. 50.00 (*0-8201-1143-0*) Schol Facsimiles.

Catechisme Politique Ou Elemens Du Droit Public et Constitutionnel Du Canada, Mis a la Portee Du Peuple (Montreal 1851) Antoine Gerin-Lajoie. (Canadiana Avant 1867 Ser.: No. 15). 1967. 17.50 (*90-279-6337-1*) Mouton.

Catechisms & Controversies: Religious Education in the Postconciliar Years. Michael J. Wrenn. LC 91-71630. 256p. (Orig.). 1991. pap. 15.95 (*0-89870-371-9*) Ignatius Pr.

Catechist as a Minister. Carmen L. Caltagirone. LC 82-1605. 116p. (Orig.). 1982. pap. 4.95 (*0-8189-0430-5*) Alba.

Catechist Guide. (J). (gr. 1). 1992. 15.95 (*0-7829-0012-7*, 88012); 15.95 (*0-7829-0013-5*, 88013) Tabor Pub.

Catechist Guide. (J). (gr. 2). 1992. 15.95 (*0-7829-0017-8*, 88022); 15.95 (*0-7829-0018-6*, 88023) Tabor Pub.

Catechist Guide. (J). (gr. 3). 1992. 15.95 (*0-7829-0022-4*, 88032); 15.95 (*0-7829-0023-2*, 88033) Tabor Pub.

Catechist Guide. (J). (gr. 4). 1992. 15.95 (*0-7829-0027-5*, 88042); 15.95 (*0-7829-0028-3*, 88043) Tabor Pub.

Catechist Guide. (J). (gr. 5). 1992. 15.95 (*0-7829-0032-1*, 88052); 15.95 (*0-7829-0033-X*, 88053) Tabor Pub.

Catechist Guide. (J). (gr. 6). 1992. 15.95 (*0-7829-0037-2*, 88062); 15.95 (*0-7829-0038-0*, 88063) Tabor Pub.

Catechist Guide. (J). (gr. 7). 1993. 15.95 (*0-7829-0340-1*, 88175); 15.95 (*0-7829-0341-X*, 88176) Tabor Pub.

Catechist Guide. (J). (gr. 8). 1993. 15.95 (*0-7829-0345-2*, 88185); 15.95 (*0-7829-0346-0*, 88186) Tabor Pub.

***Catechist's Guide.** Thomas Zanzig. Ed. by Robert Stamschror. (Confirmed in a Faithful Community Ser.). (Illus.). 323p. (Orig.). 1995. teacher ed, spiral bd. 19.90 (*0-88489-314-6*) St Marys.

***Catechist's Theology Handbook.** Thomas Zanzig. Ed. by Robert Stamschror. (Confirmed in a Faithful Community Ser.). (Illus.). 175p. (Orig.). 1995. teacher ed, pap. 12.90 (*0-88489-343-X*) St Marys.

Catechol Estrogens. Ed. by George R. Merriam & Mortimer B. Lipsett. 300p. 1983. text ed. 98.00 (*0-89004-892-4*) Raven.

Catecholamine Function in Posttraumatic Stress Disorder: Emerging Concepts. Ed. by Michele Murburg. LC 93-5677. (Progress in Psychiatry Ser.: Vol. 42). 352p. 1994. text ed. 35.00 (*0-88048-473-X*) Am Psychiatric.

Catecholamines & Behaviour. Stephen T. Mason. LC 83-7722. 400p. 1984. 84.95 (*0-521-24930-9*); pap. 34.95 (*0-521-27082-0*) Cambridge U Pr.

Catecholamines & Heart Disease. Pallab K. Ganguly. 312p. 1991. 190.00 (*0-8493-5810-8*, RC682) CRC Pr.

Catecholamines & Stress. Ed. by Earl Usdin et al. 644p. 1976. 265.00 (*0-08-020588-7*, Pub. by Pergamon Repr UK) Franklin.

Catecholamines & Their Enzymes in the Neuropathology of Schizophrenia. Steven Matthysse & Seymour S. Kety. LC 75-4093. (Illus.). 382p. 1975. 163.00 (*0-08-018242-9*, Pub. by Pergamon Repr UK) Franklin.

Catecholamines II. Ed. by U. Trendelenburg & N. Weiner. (Handbook of Experimental Pharmacology Ser.: Vol. 90). (Illus.). 590p. 1988. 317.00 (*0-387-19117-8*) Spr-Verlag.

Catecholamines in Normal & Abnormal Cardiac Function. W. M. Manger. (Advances in Cardiology Ser.: Vol. 30). (Illus.). xxiv, 152p. 1982. 78.50 (*3-8055-3516-3*) S Karger.

Catecholamines in the Non-Ischaemic & Ischaemic Myocardium: Proceedings of the Sixth Argenteuil Symposiym, Waterloo, Belgium, 1981. Ed. by R. A. Riemersma & M. F. Oliver. (Argenteuil Symposia Ser.: Vol. 6). 260p. 1982. 134.00 (*0-444-80439-0*) Elsevier.

Catecholamines One. Ed. by U. Trendelenburg & N. Weiner. (Handbook of Experimental Pharmacology Ser.: Vol. 90-I). (Illus.). 610p. 1988. 317.00 (*0-387-18904-1*) Spr-Verlag.

***Catechumenate & the Law: A Pastoral & Canonical Commentary for the Church in the United States.** John M. Huels. LC 94-24026. (Font & Table Ser.). 104p. (Orig.). 1995. pap. 6.95 (*1-56854-082-5*) Liturgy Tr Pubns.

Catechumenate Needs Everybody: Study Guides for Parish Ministers. Ed. by James A. Wilde. (Font & Table Ser.). (Illus.). 58p. 1988. pap. 6.95 (*0-930467-75-2*) Liturgy Tr Pubns.

Catechumen's Lectionary. Ed. by Robert Hamma. 1988. pap. 16.95 (*0-8091-2998-1*) Paulist Pr.

Catecismo Basico. LC 85-13103. (SPA.). 1992. reprint ed. 2.00 (*0-8198-1445-8*) Pauline Bks.

Catecismo Basico de la Doctrina Cristiana: Spanish Basic Catechism (Pocket) Catholic Truth Society London Staff. 1992. 0.25 (*1-56036-028-3*) AMI Pr.

Catecismo Biblico y Doctrinal Para el Nuevo Creyente. Adolfo Robleto. 164p. 1987. reprint ed. pap. 2.25 (*0-311-09088-5*) Casa Bautista.

Catecismo de la Iglesia Catolica. Santa Sede. (Illus.). 662p. (Orig.). (SPA.). (C). Date not set. pap. text ed. 18.90 (*0-9637823-2-0*) Span Speak Bkstore.

***Catecismo de la Iglesia Catolica.** Santa Sede. Tr. by Jose M. Llaurens et al. (Illus.). 662p. (Orig.). (C). 1994. pap. text ed. 18.90 (*0-06-378232-4*) Span Speak Bkstore.

Catecismo De la Inglesia Catolica: Catechism of the Catholic Church. Liberia Editrice Vaticana. 662p. (Orig.). (SPA.). 1993. pap. 9.95 (*0-89243-583-6*) Liguori Pubns.

Catedrales de Espana. 10th ed. Carlos Sarthou Carreres et al. (Illus.). 374p. 1989. 295.00x (*84-239-5270-3*) Elliots Bks.

Categoriae Et Liber De Interpretatione. Aristotle. Ed. by L. Minio-Paluello. (Oxford Classical Texts Ser.). 1936. 19.95 (*0-19-814507-1*) OUP.

Categorial Grammar. Ed. by W. Buszkowski et al. LC 88-338. viii, 365p. (C). 1988. 133.00x (*90-272-1530-8*) Benjamins North Am.

Categorial Grammars. Mary M. Wood. LC 92-21083. (Linguistic Theory Guides Ser.). 184p. 1993. 49.95 (*0-415-04954-7*, B0316); pap. 17.95 (*0-415-04955-5*, B0320) Routledge.

Categorial Investigations: Logical & Linguistic Aspects of the Lambek Calculus. Michael Moortgat. (Groningen-Amsterdam Studies in Semantics: No. 9). xiv, 278p. 1988. pap. 34.95 (*90-6765-387-X*) Mouton.

Categorial Structure of the World. Reinhardt Grossmann. LC 81-48615. 447p. reprint ed. pap. 127.40 (*0-7837-3709-2*, 2057887) Bks Demand.

Categorias. Jo E. Moore & Joy Evans. Tr. by Liz Wolfe & Dora Ficklin. (Illus.). 32p. (SPA.). (J). (gr. 1-2). 1990. pap. text ed. 4.95 (*1-55799-180-4*) Evan-Moor Corp.

Categorical Algebra & Its Applications. Ed. by F. Borceux. (Lecture Notes in Mathematics Ser.: Vol. 1348). viii, 375p. 1988. pap. 47.90 (*0-387-50362-5*) Spr-Verlag.

Categorical Combinators, Sequential Algorithms, & Functional Programming. 2nd ed. Pierre-Louis Curien. LC 93-281. (Progress in Theoretical Computer Science Ser.). xx, 403p. 1993. 64.50 (*0-8176-3654-4*) Birkhauser.

Categorical Data Analysis. Alan Agresti. (Probability & Mathematical Statistics: Applied Probability & Statistics Section Ser.). 1990. text ed. 69.95 (*0-471-85301-1*) Wiley.

Categorical Data Analysis by AIC. Y. Sakamoto. (Mathematics & Its Applications Japanese Ser.). 276p. 1992. lib. bdg. 115.50 (*0-7923-1429-8*) Kluwer Ac.

Categorical Framework for the Study of Singular Spaces. William Fulton & Robert MacPherson. LC 81-2246. (Memoirs Ser.: No. 31/243). 165p. 1984. reprint ed. pap. 22.00 (*0-8218-2243-8*, MEMO 31/243) Am Math.

Categorical Longitudinal Data: Log-Linear Panel, Trend, & Cohort Analysis. Jacques A. Hagenaars. (Illus.). 400p. (C). 1990. text ed. 48.00 (*0-8039-2957-9*); pap. text ed. 29.95 (*0-8039-5898-6*) Sage.

Categorical Methods in Computer Science. Ed. by H. Ehrig et al. (Lecture Notes in Computer Science Ser.: Vol. 393). vi, 350p. 1989. pap. 43.00 (*0-387-51722-7*, 3575) Spr-Verlag.

Categorical Perception. Ed. by Stevan Harnad. (Illus.). 616p. (C). 1990. pap. 29.95 (*0-521-38594-6*) Cambridge U Pr.

Categorical Perceptions. Ed. by Stevan Harnad. (Illus.). 670p. 1987. 99.95 (*0-521-26758-7*) Cambridge U Pr.

***Categorical Variables in Developmental Research: Methods of Analysis.** Ed. by Alexander Von Eye & Clifford C. Clogg. (Illus.). 275p. 1995. boxed write for info. (*0-12-724965-6*) Acad Pr.

Categories. Aristotle. Bd. with On Interpretation. (ENG & GRE.). (C).; Prior Analytics: Bks. 1 & 2. (ENG & GRE.). (C).; Prior Analytics: Bks. 1 & 2. (ENG & GRE.). (C). (Loeb Classical Library: No. 325). (ENG & GRE.). (C). 15.50 (*0-674-99359-4*) HUP.

Categories. T. S. Blyth. 152p. 1986. text ed. 62.95 (*0-470-20676-4*) Halsted Pr.

Categories. Carlos Navarro. (Start Smart Ser.). (J). (gr. k-2). 1990. student ed 4.50 (*1-878396-02-1*) Start Smart Bks.

Categories. H. Schubert. Tr. by J. Gray. LC 72-83016. 390p. 1973. 69.00 (*0-387-05783-8*) Spr-Verlag.

Categories, Allegories. P. J. Freyd. (North-Holland Mathematical Library: No. 39). 294p. 1990. 82.00 (*0-444-70368-3*, North Holland); pap. 30.75 (*0-444-70367-5*, North Holland) Elsevier.

Categories & Case: The Sentence Structure of Korean. William O'Grady. LC 90-42137. (Current Issues in Linguistic Theory Ser.: Vol. 71). vii, 294p. 1990. 65.00x (*1-55619-127-8*) Benjamins North Am.

Categories & Computer Science. R. F. Walters. (Computer Science Texts Ser.: No. 29). (Illus.). 200p. (C). 1992. 54.95 (*0-521-41997-2*); pap. 21.95 (*0-521-42226-4*) Cambridge U Pr.

Categories & Concepts. Edward E. Smith & Douglas L. Medin. LC 81-4629. (Cognitive Science Ser.: No. 4). 215p. reprint ed. pap. 61.30 (*0-7837-1529-3*, 2041806) Bks Demand.

Categories & Concepts: Theoretical Views & Inductive Data Analysis. Ed. by Iven Van Mechelen et al. (Cognitive Science Ser.). (Illus.). 374p. 1992. pap. text ed. 64.50 (*0-12-714175-8*) Acad Pr.

Categories & de Interpretatione. Aristotle. Tr. by J. L. Ackrill. (Clarendon Aristotle Ser.). 1975. pap. 22.00 (*0-19-872086-6*) OUP.

Categories & Processes in Language Acquisition. Ed. by Y. Levy et al. 296p. 1988. text ed. 59.95 (*0-8058-0151-0*) L Erlbaum Assocs.

Categories & Variables in Special Education. Maynard C. Reynolds. (Augustana College Library Occasional Papers, Wallin Lecture: No. 9). 16p. 1968. pap. 0.50 (*0-910182-39-6*) Augustana Coll.

Categories, Constituents & Constituent Order in Pitjantjatjara. Heather Bowe. (Theoretical Linguistics Ser.). 192p. (C). 1991. text ed. 82.00 (*0-415-05694-2*, A5136) Routledge.

Categories du Materialisme Dialectique: L'Ontologie Sovietique Contemporaine. G. Planty-Bonjour. (Sovietica Ser.: No. 21). 206p. (FRE.). 1965. lib. bdg. 45.50 (*90-277-0063-X*) Kluwer Ac.

Categories for the Working Mathematician. S. MacLane. LC 78-166080. (Graduate Texts in Mathematics Ser.: Vol. 5). 272p. 1994. 39.95 (*0-387-90035-7*) Spr-Verlag.

Categories for Types. Roy L. Crole. (Illus.). 320p. (C). 1994. 64.95 (*0-521-45092-6*); pap. 29.95 (*0-521-45701-7*) Cambridge U Pr.

Categories in Computer Science & Logic. Ed. by J. Gray & A. Scedrov. LC 89-32893. 382p. 1991. pap. 50.00 (*0-8218-5100-4*, CONM-92) Am Math.

Categories in Continuum Physics. Ed. by F. W. Lawvere & S. H. Schanuel. (Lecture Notes in Mathematics Ser.: Vol. 1174). v, 126p. 1986. pap. 23.00 (*0-387-16096-5*) Spr-Verlag.

Categories of a Racial Mind (Underlayments of Bias) Richard S. Hoehler. LC 80-83380. 304p. 1980. pap. 10.00 (*0-930590-02-3*) R Hoehler Pub.

Categories of Boolean Sheaves of Simple Algebras. Yves Diers. (Lecture Notes in Mathematics Ser.: Vol. 1187). vi, 168p. 1986. pap. 35.30 (*0-387-16459-6*) Spr-Verlag.

Categories of Commutative Algebra. Yves Diers. 288p. 1992. 79.00 (*0-19-853586-4*) OUP.

Categories of Dialectical Materialism: Contemporary Soviet Ontology. G. Planty-Bonjour. (Sovietica Ser.: No. 24). 182p. 1967. lib. bdg. 42.50 (*90-277-0064-8*) Kluwer Ac.

Categories of Highest Weight Modules: Applications to Classical Hermitian Symmetric Pairs. T. J. Enright & B. Shelton. LC 87-1446. (Memoirs of the American Mathematical Society Ser.: Vol. 67/367). 94p. 1987. 18.00 (*0-8218-2429-5*, MEMO 67/367) Am Math.

Categories of Medieval Culture. A. J. Gurevich. LC 84-9906. 224p. 1985. 45.00 (*0-7100-9578-3*, 95783, RKP) Routledge.

Categories of Modules over Endomorphism Rings. Theodore G. Faticoni. LC 93-465. (Memoirs of the American Mathematical Society Ser.: No. 492). 140p. 1993. 32.00 (*0-8218-2554-2*) Am Math.

Categories, Types, & Structures: An Introduction to Category Theory for the Working Computer Scientist. Andrea Asperti & Giuseppe Longo. 1990. 37.50 (*0-262-12145-X*) MIT Pr.

Categorization & Differentiation. L. L. Martin. (Recent Research in Psychology Ser.). vii, 87p. 1985. pap. 30.00 (*0-387-96150-X*) Spr-Verlag.

Categorization & Naming in Children: Problems of Induction. Ellen M. Markman. (Learning, Development & Conceptual Change Ser.). (Illus.). 264p. 1991. reprint ed. pap. 13.95 (*0-262-63136-9*, Bradford Bks) MIT Pr.

Category. Illus. by Edward Gorey. LC 86-10938. (J). (ps up). 1986. reprint ed. 8.95 (*0-685-13444-X*) Modan-Adama Bks.

Category Formation & the History of Religions. 2nd ed. Robert D. Baird. 192p. 1991. pap. text ed. 22.95 (*3-11-012821-7*) Mouton.

***Category Killers Markets to the Year 2000 International.** (Illus.). 500p. (Orig.). 1994. pap. 9,950.00 (*0-7605-0945-X*) Rector Pr.

Category Management: Positioning Your Organization to Win. Nielsen Marketing Research Staff. 1993. 27.95 (*0-8442-3489-3*) NTC Pub Grp.

Category of H-Modules over a Spectrum. Jack P. Sanders. LC 73-22409. (Memoirs Ser.: No. 1/141). 136p. 1974. pap. 18.00 (*0-8218-1841-4*, MEMO 1/141) Am Math.

Category of the Aesthetic in the Philosophy of Saint Bonaventure. Emma J. Spargo. (Philosophy Ser.). 1953. 8.00 (*0-686-11541-4*) Franciscan Inst.

Category of the Person. Ed. by Michael Carrithers et al. 304p. 1985. 74.95 (*0-521-25909-6*); pap. 19.95 (*0-521-27757-4*) Cambridge U Pr.

Category Theory & Computer Science. D. H. Pitt et al. (Lecture Notes in Computer Science Ser.: Vol. 283). v, 300p. 1987. pap. 39.00 (*0-387-18508-9*) Spr-Verlag.

Category Theory & Computer Science. Ed. by D. H. Pitt et al. (Lecture Notes in Computer Science Ser.: Vol. 389). vi, 365p. 1989. pap. 43.00 (*0-387-51662-X*, 3506) Spr-Verlag.

Category Theory & Computer Science: Paris, France, September 3-6, 1991 Proceedings. Ed. by D. H. Pitt et al. (Lecture Notes in Computer Science Ser.: Vol. 530). vii, 301p. 1991. pap. 34.00 (*0-387-54495-X*) Spr-Verlag.

Category Theory, 1991: Proceedings of an International Summer Category Theory Meeting, Held June 23-30, 1991. Ed. by R. A. Seely. LC 92-24186. (CMSAMS Ser.: No. 13). 447p. 1992. 76.00 (*0-8218-6018-6*, CMSAMS-13) Am Math.

Catena of Buddhist Scriptures from the Chinese. 2nd ed. Samuel Beal. (Bibliotheca Indo-Buddhica Ser.: No. 62). 436p. (C). 1989. reprint ed. 35.00 (*81-7030-183-1*) S Asia.

Catenae Graecorum Patrum in Novum Testamentum, 8 vols. Ed. by John A. Cramer. lxxviii, 4039p. 1967. reprint ed. Bd. I: Catenae in Evangelia S. Matthaei et S. Marci ad Fidem Codd. mss. write for info. (*0-318-70891-4*, Pub. by Georg Olms GW); reprint ed. Bd. II: Catenae in Evangelia S. Lucae et S. Joannis ad Fidem Codd. mss. write for info. (*0-318-70892-2*, Pub. by Georg Olms GW); reprint ed. Bd. III: Catenae in Acta SS. Apostolorum e Cod. Nov. Coll. write for info. (*0-318-70893-0*, Pub. by Georg Olms GW); reprint ed. Bd. IV: Catenae in Sancti Pauli Epistolam ad Romanos ad Fidem Codd. mss. write for info. (*0-318-70894-9*, Pub. by Georg Olms GW); reprint ed. Bd. V: Catenae in Sancti Pauli Epistolas ad Corinthios ad Fidem Codd. mss. write for info. (*0-318-70895-7*, Pub. by Georg Olms GW); reprint ed. Bd. VI: Catenae in Saancti Pauli Epistolas ad Galatas, Ephesios, Philippenses, Colossenses Thessalon. write for info. (*0-318-70896-5*, Pub. by Georg Olms GW); reprint ed. Bd. VII: Catenae in Sancti Pauli Epistolas ad Timotheum, Titum, Philomena et ad Hebraeos ad Fidem Co. write for info. (*0-318-70897-3*, Pub. by Georg Olms GW); reprint ed. Bd. VIII: Catenae in Epistolas Catholicas Accesserunt Oecumenii et Arethae Commentarii in Apocalypsi. write for info. (*0-318-70898-1*, Pub. by Georg Olms GW) Lubrecht & Cramer.

Catenae Graecorum Patrum in Novum Testamentum, 8 vols., Set. Ed. by John A. Cramer. lxxviii, 4039p. 1967. reprint ed. write for info. (*0-318-70890-6*, Pub. by Georg Olms GW) Lubrecht & Cramer.

Catenary Odes. Ted Pearson. LC 87-91337. 48p. 1987. 6.00 (*0-917588-17-7*) O Bks.

Catequesis de Adultos en la Communidad Cristiana. United States Catholic Conference Staff. Ed. by Jack McBride. 60p. (SPA.). 1992. pap. 3.95 (*1-55586-526-7*) US Catholic.

Cater from Your Kitchen. Marjorie P. Blanchard. 1981. pap. write for info. (*0-672-52688-3*) Macmillan.

Cater Street Hangman. Anne Perry. 1985. mass mkt. 4.95 (*0-449-20867-2*, Crest) Fawcett.

Caterfly. Don DePaul. LC 76-39691. (Illus.). (YA). (gr. 7 up). 1977. pap. 4.25 (*0-8356-0490-X*, Quest) Theos Pub Hse.

***Caterfly: Mac's Back Struggling to Stay Drug-Free.** Debra L. Wert. (Illus.). (J). (gr. 4-6). Date not set. pap. text ed. write for info. (*0-944576-11-7*) Rocky River Pubs.

Caterina di Guisa. Coccia. (Italian Opera Ser., 1810-1840: Vol. 4). 1986. text ed. 108.00 (*0-8240-6553-0*) Garland.

Caterina the Clever Farm Girl: A Tuscan Tale. Illus. by Enzo Giannini. LC 93-15161. (J). 1996. 14.99 (*0-8037-1181-6*); lib. bdg. 14.89 (*0-8037-1182-4*) Dial Bks Young.

Catering: Start & Run a Money-Making Business. Judy Richards. 1994. pap. text ed. 17.95 (*0-07-052272-3*) McGraw.

Catering Equipment & Supplies Survey. Euromonitor Staff. (C). 1989. 3,980.00 (*0-685-37359-2*, Pub. by Euromonitor Pubns UK) Gale.

Catering Equipment & Systems Design. Ed. by G. Glew. (Illus.). 480p. 1977. 124.25 (*0-85334-730-1*, Pub. by Elsevier Applied Sci UK) Elsevier.

Catering Equipment in the UK. Euromonitor Staff. 90p. (C). 1987. 705.00 (*0-86338-204-5*, Pub. by Euromonitor Pubns UK) Gale.

Catering Equipment Management. P. Pine. (C). 1989. 130.00 (*0-09-182413-3*, Pub. by S Thornes Pubs UK) St Mut.

***Catering for Consumers Market International Handbook.** (Illus.). (Orig.). 1994. pap. 8,900.00 (*0-7605-0942-5*) Rector Pr.

Catering for Health. 292p. 1988. pap. 11.95 (*0-11-321129-5*, HM3582, Pub. by HMSO UK) UNIPUB.

Catering for Health. S. Stevenson & S. Scobi. (C). 1989. 100.00 (*0-09-164981-1*, Pub. by S Thornes Pubs UK) St Mut.

Catering for Large Numbers. Stephen Ashley & Sean Anderson. (Illus.). 304p. 1993. pap. 35.00 (*0-409-30642-8*) Buttrwrth-Heinemann.

Catering for Profit: How to Make Money on Your Favorite Recipes. William Hartonczyk & Christina G. Hartonczyk. LC 93-1048. (Illus.). 144p. (Orig.). 1994. text ed. 39.95 (*0-685-63819-7*); pap. 29.95 (*1-883262-98-4*) Progeny Pub.

Catering Hall: Seven Vignettes. Norman Filzman. (Orig.). 1991. pap. 2.00 (*0-9605626-4-8*) Low-Tech.

Catering Handbook. Edith Weiss & Hal Weiss. (Illus.). 300p. 1991. text ed. 34.95 (*0-442-00728-0*) Van Nos Reinhold.

Catering in Pubs. Euromonitor Staff. (C). 1989. 4,790.00 (*0-685-37360-6*, Pub. by Euromonitor Pubns UK) Gale.

Catering Like a Pro: From Planning to Profit. Francine Halvorsen. LC 93-29809. 288p. 1994. text ed. 39.95 (*0-471-00688-2*); pap. text ed. 17.95 (*0-471-59522-5*) Wiley.

Catering Menu Management. Nancy Scanlon. 256p. 1992. text ed. 49.95 (*0-471-54615-1*) Wiley.

Catering Service Business Possibility Encyclopedia. rev. ed. 1991. ring bd. 59.95 (*0-317-04116-9*) Prosperity & Profits.

Catering Service Reference on Breads. rev. ed. Carrol, Frieda, Research Division Staff. 1992. pap. text ed. 15.95 (*0-317-04790-6*, Pub. by Frieda Carrol) Prosperity & Profits.

Catering Services: Creative Suggestion Pages. rev. ed. Alpha Pyramis Research Division Staff. 1992. ring bd. 29.95 (*0-913597-89-9*) Prosperity & Profits.

Catering Supplies in the UK. Euromonitor Staff. 130p. (C). 1988. 975.00 (*0-86338-340-8*, Pub. by Euromonitor Pubns UK) Gale.

C

An Asterisk (*) at the beginning of an entry indicates that the title is appearing in BIP for the first time.

Catering to Every Whim: A Complete Guide to Catering Sales, Administration & Operations. G. Eugene Wigger. 304p. 1990. pap. 30.00 (*0-13-120494-7*) P-H.

Catering to Every Whim: A Complete Guide to Catering Sales, Administration & Operations. G. Eugene Wigger. 352p. 1990. text ed. 71.00 (*0-13-120502-1*) P-H.

Catering to Nobody. Diane M. Davidson. 1992. reprint ed. mass mkt. 5.99 (*0-449-22046-X*) Fawcett.

Caterpillar. Aunt Peggy. (Illus.). 24p. (J). 1992. Coloring bk. 2.95 (*0-9636185-3-9*); pap. 6.95 (*0-9636185-0-4*) Aunt Peggys Pub.

Caterpillar. Randy Leffingwell. (Illus.). 192p. 1994. 29.95 (*0-87938-921-4*) Motorbooks Intl.

Caterpillar. 2nd ed. Aunt Peggy. (Illus.). 24p. (J). (ps). 1994. 13.95 (*0-9636185-2-0*) Aunt Peggys Pub.

Caterpillar: Fun Pack. Aunt Peggy. (Illus.). 24p. (J). (ps-00). 1994. Set, Story bk. & color bk. 8.95 (*0-9636185-4-7*) Aunt Peggys Pub.

Caterpillar & the Polliwog. Jack Kent. LC 82-7533. (Illus.). 32p. (J). (gr. k-4). 1982. pap. 14.00 (*0-671-66280-5*, S&S Bks Young Read) S&S Childrens.

Caterpillar & the Polliwog. Jack Kent. LC 82-7533. (Illus.). 32p. (J). (gr. k-4). 1985. pap. 5.95 (*0-671-66281-3*, S&S Bks Young Read) S&S Childrens.

Caterpillar Association of the United States. Turner Publishing Co. Staff. LC 91-75220. 112p. 1991. 48.00 (*1-56311-031-8*) Turner Pub KY.

Caterpillar Books. Laura C. Busch. (Little Readers Ser.). 180p. (J). (ps-1). 1990. 13.95 (*1-880642-02-6*) Little Read.

Caterpillar, Caterpillar. Vivian French. LC 92-544006. (Read & Wonder Ser.). (Illus.). 32p. (J). (ps up). 1993. 14.95 (*1-56402-206-4*) Candlewick Pr.

***Caterpillar, Caterpillar.** Vivian French. LC 92-544006. (J). (ps-3). 1995. pap. 5.99 (*1-56402-493-8*) Candlewick Pr.

Caterpillar Green. Marla Martin. 1977. 6.10 (*0-686-23330-1*) Rod & Staff.

Caterpillar Had a Dream: A Poetic Story about Dreams Coming True. Jaye Bartlett. (Illus.). (J). 1991. 8.95 (*1-878064-02-9*) TLC Books.

Caterpillar Had a Dream: A Story about Dreams Coming True. Jaye Bartlett. (Illus.). 38p. (Orig.). (J). (ps up). 1990. audio, lib. bdg. 11.95 (*1-878064-00-2*) New Age CT.

Caterpillar Military Tractors: The Vital Edge of Victory. Ed. by P. A. Letourneau. LC 94-76266. (Photo Archive Ser.: Vol. 1). (Illus.). 144p. 1994. pap. 24.95 (*1-882256-16-6*) Iconografix.

Caterpillar Military Tractors: Workpower on the Side of Victory. Ed. by P. A. Letourneau. LC 94-76266. (Photo Archive Ser.). (Illus.). 144p. 1994. pap. 24.95 (*1-882256-17-4*) Iconografix.

Caterpillar Sixty Photo Archive. Ed. by P. A. Letourneau. (Photo Archive Ser.). (Illus.). 144p. 1993. pap. 24.95 (*1-882256-05-0*) Iconografix.

Caterpillar Stew: A Feast of Animal Poems. Gavin Ewart. (Illus.). 80p. (J). (gr. 3-5). 1992. 15.95 (*0-09-174097-5*, Pub. by Hutchinson UK) Trafalgar.

Caterpillar That Came to Church - la Oruga Que Fue a Misa: A Story of the Eucharist - Un Cuento de la Eucaristia. Irene H. Hooker & Susan A. Brindle. Ed. by Miriam A. Lademan. Tr. by Jane F. Houtman & Luz M. De Martinez. LC 92-63219. (Illus.). 64p. (Orig.). (ENG & SPA.). (J). 1993. 9.95 (*0-87973-874-X*, 874); pap. 7.95 (*0-87973-875-8*, 875) Our Sunday Visitor.

Caterpillar Thirty Photo Archive. Ed. by P. A. Letourneau. (Photo Archive Ser.). (Illus.). 144p. 1993. pap. 24.95 (*1-882256-04-2*) Iconografix.

Caterpillar to Butterfly. Oliver S. Owen. LC 94-14306. (Lifewatch Ser.). (J). 1994. lib. bdg. 14.96 (*1-56239-290-5*) Abdo & Dghtrs.

Caterpillar Who Turned into a Butterfly. (Chubby Board Bks.). 16p. (J). (ps-00). 1980. pap. 3.95 (*0-671-41347-3*, Litl Simon S&S) S&S Childrens.

Caterpillars: Ecological & Evolutionary Constraints on Foraging. Ed. by Nancy E. Stamp & Timothy M. Casey. (Illus.). 432p. 1992. 75.00 (*0-412-02681-3*, A4645, Chapman & Hall) Chapman & Hall.

***Caterpillars, Bugs, & Butterflies.** Mel Boring. (Take-Along Guide Ser.). (Illus.). 48p. (J). (gr. 3-7). 1996. write for info. (*1-55971-479-4*) NorthWord.

Caterpillars, Cocoons & Butterflies. James Bloom. (Orig.). 1988. pap. 1.85 (*1-55673-052-7*, 8823) CSS OH.

Caterpillars or Butterflies. Jane McWhorter. (Illus.). 1977. pap. 6.50 (*0-89137-410-8*) Quality Pubns.

Caterpillar's Question. Piers Anthony. 1992. 18.95 (*0-441-09488-0*) Ace Bks.

***Caterpillar's Question.** Piers Anthony. Ed. by Philip J. Farmer. 272p. 1995. pap. text ed. 5.99 (*0-441-00213-7*) Ace Bks.

Caterpillar's Wish. First Graders of A. R. Shepherd Washington, D. C. (Kids Are Authors Ser.). (Illus.). 24p. (Orig.). (J). (ps-2). 1988. pap. 3.50 (*0-87406-307-8*) Willowisp Pr.

Catesby's Birds of Colonial America. Alan Feduccia. LC 85-1176. (Fred W. Morrison Series in Southern Studies). (Illus.). xv, 192p. 1985. 39.95 (*0-8078-1661-2*) U of NC Pr.

Catfantastic III. Ed. by Andre Norton & Martin H. Greenberg. 320p. (Orig.). 1994. mass mkt. 4.99 (*0-88677-591-4*) DAW Bks.

Catfish: "How to Fish" rev. ed. Dan D. Gapen, Sr. (Illus.). 126p. 1987. reprint ed. pap. text ed. 7.95 (*0-932985-06-8*) Whitewater Pubns.

Catfish & the Delta. Richard Schweid. (Illus.). 196p. 1992. pap. 9.95 (*0-89815-454-5*) Ten Speed Pr.

Catfish at the Pump: Humor & the Frontier. Roger L. Welsch & Linda K. Welsch. LC 86-4295. x, 152p. 1986. reprint ed. 15.95 (*0-8032-4740-0*); reprint ed. pap. 8.00 (*0-8032-9712-2*) U of Nebr Pr.

Catfish Book. Linda Crawford. LC 90-28686. (Muscadine Book Ser.). 1991. pap. 10.95 (*0-87805-502-9*) U Pr of Miss.

Catfish Cookbook. rev. ed. Ed. by Barry Fast. LC 82-11253. 128p. 1983. pap. 8.95 (*0-87106-603-3*) Globe Pequot.

Catfish in the Aquarium. Carl Ferraris. (Illus.). 200p. 1991. 21.95 (*3-89356-043-2*, 16015) Tetra Pr.

Catfish in the Bodoni: The Golden Age of Tramp Printers. Otto J. Boutin. LC 70-141186. (Illus.). 1971. 9.95 (*0-87839-004-9*) North Star.

Catfish Palace. lib. bdg. 15.95 (*1-55037-316-1*, Pub. by Annick CN); pap. 5.95 (*1-55037-317-X*, Pub. by Annick CN) Firefly Bks Ltd.

***Catfishing.** Chris Altman. LC 91-91473. (Complete Angler's Library). 247p. 1992. write for info. (*0-914697-44-7*) N Amer Outdoor Grp.

Catfishing: How "YOU" Can Be Successful. Niles R. Shiflet. (Illus.). 90p. (Orig.). 1992. 9.95 (*0-9633189-0-X*) Am Catfish Ent.

Catfood Factory. Jack Evans. 64p. 1993. pap. 8.00 (*0-944550-33-9*) Pygmy Forest Pr.

Cath Finntraga. Ed. by Kuno Meyer. (Anecdota Oxoniensia Ser.: No. 4). 1988. reprint ed. 47.50 (*0-404-63954-2*) AMS Pr.

Cath Lab: An Introduction. 2nd ed. David L. Lubell. LC 92-48998. (Illus.). 143p. 1993. pap. text ed. 29.95 (*0-8121-1675-5*) Williams & Wilkins.

Cath ruis na Rig for Boinn. Ed. by Edmund Hogan. LC 78-72678. (Royal Irish Academy. Todd Lecture Ser.: Vol. 4). reprint ed. 27.50 (*0-404-60564-8*) AMS Pr.

***Cathal the Giant Killer: And the Dun Shaggy Filly.** Downie & Gilliland. Date not set. per. 7.95 (*1-55082-009-5*, Pub. by Quarry Pr CN) InBook.

Catharine & Other Writings. Jane Austen. Ed. by Margaret A. Doody & Douglas Murray. LC 92-12787. (World's Classics Ser.). 424p. 1993. pap. 9.95 (*0-19-282823-1*) OUP.

Catharine Beecher: A Study in American Domesticity. Kathryn K. Sklar. LC 73-77166. (Illus.). 352p. 1973. 40.00 (*0-300-01580-1*) Yale U Pr.

Catharine Maria Sedgwick. Edward H. Foster. Ed. by Sylvia E. Bowman. LC 73-14674. (Twayne's United States Authors Ser.). 167p. 1974. text ed. 17.95 (*0-8057-0658-5*) Irvington.

Catharine Parr Traill & Her Works. Carl P. Ballstadt. 46p. (C). 1990. pap. text ed. 9.95 (*0-920763-39-1*, Pub. by ECW Press CN) Genl Dist Srvs.

***Cathars & Reincarnation.** Guirdham. (Guirdham Trilogy Ser.). 1995. pap. 10.95 (*0-85207-224-4*) Atrium Pubs.

Catharsis. Gregory O. Ucheagwu. 18p. 1992. pap. write for info. (*0-9636682-1-8*) Ojemba Musings.

Catharsis: Poems by Laurier. Laurier. 65p. (Orig.). Date not set. pap. 9.95 (*1-55605-231-6*) Wyndhall Pr.

Catharsis & Cognition in Psychotherapy. B. J. Guinagh. (Illus.). 135p. 1987. pap. 42.00 (*0-387-96530-0*) Spr-Verlag.

Catharsis & the Healing: South Africa in the 1990s. Zeki Ergas. 336p. 1994. 25.00 (*1-85756-079-5*, Pub. by Janus Pubng UK) Paul & Co Pubs.

Catharsis in Healing, Ritual & Drama. Thomas J. Scheff. LC 78-57314. 1979. pap. 12.00 (*0-520-04125-9*) U CA Pr.

Catharsis of Comedy. Dana F. Sutton. (Greek Studies: Interdisciplinary Approaches). 120p. (C). 1994. lib. bdg. 39.50 (*0-8476-7905-5*); pap. text ed. 18.95 (*0-8476-7906-3*) Rowman.

Cathay & the Way Thither, 4 vols., Set. rev. ed. Ed. by Henri Cordier. (Hakluyt Society Works Ser.: No. 2, Vols. 33, 37, 38 & 41). (Illus.). 1972. reprint ed. 200.00 (*0-8115-0349-6*) Periodicals Srv.

Cathay by the Bay: San Francisco Chinatown in 1950. George Kao. 160p. 1989. pap. 23.50 (*962-201-423-2*, Pub. by Chinese Univ HK) Coronet Bks.

Cathay Stories & Other Fictions. MacDonald Harris. 189p. (Orig.). 1988. 16.00 (*0-934257-14-0*); pap. 9.00 (*0-934257-13-2*) Story Line.

Cathederal Singer. James L. Allen. (Principle Works of James Lane Allen). 1989. reprint ed. lib. bdg. 79.00 (*0-7812-1741-5*) Rprt Serv.

Cathedral. Raymond Carver. LC 84-40009. 1989. pap. 10.00 (*0-679-72369-2*) Random.

Cathedral. Nelson DeMille. 576p. 1990. mass mkt. 6.99 (*0-446-35857-6*) Warner Bks.

Cathedral. Joris K. Huysmans. (Dedalus European Classics Ser.). 357p. 1990. pap. 11.95 (*0-87052-615-4*) Hippocrene Bks.

Cathedral. Jouis K. Huysmans. 1972. 59.95 (*0-87968-815-7*) Gordon Pr.

Cathedral. David Macaulay. (Illus.). (J). (gr. k up). 1981. pap. 7.95 (*0-395-31668-5*) HM.

Cathedral. large type ed. Nelson De Mille. 720p. 1982. 23.95 (*0-7089-8079-1*, Charnwood) Ulverscroft.

Cathedral. Joris K. Huysmans. Ed. by C. Kegan Paul. Tr. by Clara Bell. LC 77-10270. reprint ed. 32.50 (*0-404-16322-X*) AMS Pr.

Cathedral: Seventy-Five Years. B. Shover & Obergfell. 410p. 1994. 39.95 (*1-878208-35-7*); pap. 29.95 (*1-878208-36-5*) Guild Pr IN.

Cathedral: The Social & Architectural Dynamics of Construction. Alain Erlande-Brandenburg. LC 93-29216. (Cambridge Studies in the History of Architecture). (Illus.). 388p. (ENG & FRE.). (C). 1994. 89.95 (*0-521-41118-1*) Cambridge U Pr.

Cathedral: The Story of Its Construction. David Macaulay. LC 73-6634. (Illus.). 80p. (J). (gr. 1-5). 1973. 16.95 (*0-395-17513-5*) HM.

Cathedral Builders. Marie-Pierre Perdrizet. Tr. by Mary B. Raycraft. LC 91-24233. (Peoples of the Past Ser.). (Illus.). 64p. (J). (gr. 4-6). 1992. lib. bdg. 15.90 (*1-56294-162-3*) Millbrook Pr.

Cathedral Builders. Jean Gimpel. Tr. by Teresa Waugh. LC 84-47572. (Illus.). 176p. 1984. reprint ed. pap. 12.00 (*0-06-091158-1*, CN 1158, PL) HarpC.

Cathedral Cats. Richard Surman & Giles Semper. 1993. 16.00 (*0-00-627658-X*) Harper SF.

Cathedral Cities of Spain. W. Collins. 1976. lib. bdg. 59.95 (*0-8490-1585-5*) Gordon Pr.

Cathedral Cooking School Cookbook. Ed. by Lucy Core & Clara Lyman. (Illus.). 208p. (Orig.). 1974. spiral bd. 12.95 (*0-88289-033-6*) Pelican.

Cathedral Folk. Nikolai S. Leskov. Tr. by I. Hapgood. LC 76-23885. (Classics of Russian Literature Ser.). 439p. 1986. reprint ed. pap. 22.00 (*0-88355-488-7*) Hyperion Conn.

Cathedral, Forge, & Waterwheel: Technology & Invention in the Middle Ages. Frances Geis & Joseph Geis. LC 93-14293. (Illus.). 368p. 1994. 25.00 (*0-06-016590-1*, HarpT) HarpC.

***Cathedral, Forge, & Waterwheel: Technology & Invention in the Middle Ages.** Joseph Gies & Frances Gies. 368p. 1995. pap. 13.00 (*0-06-092581-7*, PL) HarpC.

Cathedral Mouse. Kay Chorao. LC 87-33398. (Illus.). 32p. (J). (ps-2). 1988. 12.95 (*0-525-44400-9*, DCB) Dutton Child Bks.

Cathedral of Healing. Vernon K. Brown. (Illus.). 264p. 1981. 12.50 (*0-9605996-1-4*) Northwest Memorial.

Cathedral of Ice. James Schevill. Ed. by Peter Kaplan. LC 75-33465. 1975. 3.00 (*0-915176-10-6*) Pourboire.

Cathedral of Palma de Mallorca, Vol. 14. R. A. Cram. 1932. 40.00 (*0-527-01687-X*) Periodicals Srv.

Cathedral of St. Paul: An Architectural Biography. Eric C. Hansen. LC 90-80194. (Illus.). 144p. 1990. 25.00 (*0-9625765-0-6*) Cathedral St Paul.

Cathedral of St. Peter & St. Paul. Photos by Robert Llewellyn. LC 88-80088. (Illus.). 120p. 1988. 19.95 (*0-943231-07-8*) Howell Pr VA.

Cathedral of the August Heat. Pierre Clitandre. Tr. by Bridget Jones. (Readers International Ser.). (Illus.). 161p. (C). 1987. pap. 8.95 (*0-930523-31-8*) Readers Intl.

***Cathedral of Thorns.** Steven Frankos. 336p. 1995. pap. text ed. 5.50 (*0-441-00221-8*) Ace Bks.

Cathedral on the Nile: The History of All Saints Cathedral, Cairo. Arthur Burrell. 120p. 1985. 35.00 (*0-317-43629-5*, Pub. by Amate Pr Ltd UK) St Mut.

Cathedral Option. Ron Montana. (Orig.). 1978. pap. 2.25 (*0-89083-404-0*) Zebra.

Cathedral Organist. Roy Brunner. 1992. 8.95 (*0-685-68264-1*, MB-642) Lillenas.

Cathedral-Tree-Train. Richard Elman. 72p. (Orig.). 1992. pap. 9.00 (*1-881523-03-9*) Junction CA.

Cathedral Window: A Fresh Look. Nancy J. Martin. Ed. by Liz McGehee & Shellie Tucker. LC 90-50783. (Illus.). 36p. 1991. pap. 8.95 (*0-943574-81-1*) That Patchwork.

Cathedrale de Chartre. Marcel Aubert. (Illus.). 84p. (FRE.). 1961. lib. bdg. 14.95 (*0-8288-3983-2*) Fr & Eur.

Cathedrale de Haine. Guy Des Cars. 280p. (FRE.). 1969. pap. 6.95 (*0-8288-9553-8*, M5717); pap. 3.95 (*0-686-55613-5*) Fr & Eur.

Cathedrales Abbatiales, Collegiales et Prieures Romans en France. Marcel Aubert & Goubet. 153.25 (*0-685-34010-4*) Fr & Eur.

Cathedrales et Tresors Gothiques en France. Marcel Aubert & Goubet. 153.25 (*0-7859-0344-5*, F22241) Fr & Eur.

Cathedrals. Tom Stainer & Harry Sutton. (Illus.). 32p. (J). (gr. 4-6). 1992. pap. 4.95 (*0-563-34161-0*, BBC-Parkwest) Parkwest Pubns.

Cathedrals: Stone upon Stone. Brigitte Gandiol-Coppin. Tr. by Vicki Bogard. LC 89-5361. (Young Discovery Library). (Illus.). 38p. (J). (gr. k-5). 1989. 5.95 (*0-944589-24-3*, 024) Young Discovery Lib.

***Cathedrals & Castles: Building in the Middle Ages.** Alain Erlande-Brandenburg. Tr. by Rosemary Stonehewer. (Discoveries Ser.). (Illus.). 176p. 1995. pap. 12.95 (*0-8109-2812-4*) Abrams.

Cathedrals of Britain. David L. Edwards. LC 89-12740. (Illus.). 160p. 1989. 29.95 (*0-8192-1503-1*) Morehouse Pub.

Cathedrals of England. rev. ed. Alec Clifton-Taylor. LC 79-66135. (World of Art Ser.). (Illus.). 1989. reprint ed. pap. 11.95 (*0-500-20062-9*) Thames Hudson.

Cathedrals of France. rev. ed. Auguste Rodin. Tr. by Elisabeth C. Geissbuhler. (Art of the Middle Ages Ser.). (Illus.). 278p. 1981. 30.00 (*0-933806-07-8*) Black Swan CT.

Cathedrals of Science: The Development of Colonial Natural History Museums During the Late Nineteenth Century. Susan Sheets-Pyenson. (Illus.). 128p. (C). 1988. text ed. 44.95 (*0-7735-0655-1*, Pub. by McGill CN) U of Toronto Pr.

Cathedrals of the Episcopal Church in the U. S. A. David A. Kalvelage. (Illus.). (Orig.). 1993. pap. 14.95 (*0-88028-143-X*, 1219) Forward Movement.

***Cathedrals under Siege: Cathedrals in English Society, 1600-1700.** Stanford E. Lehmberg. LC 95-7502. 1996. write for info. (*0-271-01494-6*) Pa St U Pr.

Cathelin Lithographs, 1957-89, 2 vols. Roger Passeron. (Illus.). Set, 218p., 214p. 400.00 (*1-55660-212-X*) A Wofsy Fine Arts.

Cather, Canon, & the Politics of Reading. Deborah Carlin. LC 92-12670. 208p. 1992. 27.50x (*0-87023-822-1*) U of Mass Pr.

Cather Studies, Vol. 1. Ed. by Susan J. Rosowski. (Illus.). xii, 189p. 1990. 30.00x (*0-8032-3895-9*) U of Nebr Pr.

Catherine. Mark Dunster. (Borgia Ser.: Pt. 2). 49p. (Orig.). 1980. pap. 4.00 (*0-89642-067-1*) Linden Pubs.

Catherine. Mark Dunster. (Henry the 8th Ser.: Pt. 2). 22p. (Orig.). 1984. pap. 4.00 (*0-89642-111-2*) Linden Pubs.

Catherine. Robert S. Macdonald. 356p. 1982. 12.95 (*0-89433-181-7*) Petrocelli.

Catherine: The Portrait of an Empress. Gina Kaus. Tr. by June Head. LC 75-37351. (Select Bibliographies Reprint Ser.). 1977. reprint ed. 26.95 (*0-8369-6698-8*) Ayer.

Catherine, Called Birdy. Karen Cushman. 224p. (J). (gr. 7 up). 1994. 13.95 (*0-395-68186-3*, Clarion Bks) HM.

***Catherine Called Birdy.** Karen Cushman. (YA). (gr. 7 up). 1995. pap. 3.95 (*0-06-440584-2*, Trophy) HarpC Child Bks.

Catherine Carmier. Ernest J. Gaines. LC 92-50589. 1993. pap. 10.00 (*0-679-73891-6*, Vin) Random.

Catherine Certitude. Patrick Modiano. Tr. by William Rodarmor. (Illus.). 64p. (J). (gr. 4-9). 1995. 17.95 (*0-87923-959-X*) Godine.

Catherine Certitude. Patrick Modiano & J. J. Sempe. (Folio - Junior Ser.: No. 600). 95p. (FRE.). (J). (gr. 5-10). 1988. pap. 9.95 (*2-07-033600-X*) Schoenhof.

Catherine De Medicis. Louisa S. Costello. LC 70-162911. (Bentley's Standard Novels Ser.: No. 112). reprint ed. 17.00 (*0-404-54512-2*) AMS Pr.

Catherine Duval: Sketches of Paris Life. Ludovic Halevy. Tr. by Mary K. Ford. LC 70-125214. (Short Story Index Reprint Ser.). 1977. 17.95 (*0-8369-3581-0*) Ayer.

Catherine Esther Beecher: Pioneer Educator. Mae E. Harveson. LC 70-89189. (American Education: Its Men, Institutions & Ideas, Ser.). 1975. reprint ed. 20.95 (*0-405-01427-9*) Ayer.

Catherine Furze, 1893. William H. White. Ed. by Robert L. Wolff. Bd. with Clara Hopgood, 1896. LC 75-1516. LC 75-1516. (Victorian Fiction Ser.). 1976. Set lib. bdg. 73.00 (*0-8240-1589-4*) Garland.

Catherine Helen Spence. Catherine H. Spence. Ed. by Helen Thomson. LC 86-16063. (UQP Australian Authors Ser.). 578p. (Orig.). (C). 1987. pap. text ed. 20.95 (*0-7022-2004-3*, Pub. by Univ Queensland Pr AT) Intl Spec Bk.

Catherine, Her Book. John Wheatcroft. LC 81-66295. 1983. 13.95 (*0-8453-4742-X*, Cornwall Bks) Assoc Univ Prs.

Catherine II's Charters of 1785 to the Nobility & the Towns. Ed. by David Griffiths & George E. Munro. Tr. by George E. Munro. LC 90-42835. (Laws of Russia Ser.: Series II, Vol. 289). 338p. (C). 1993. 150.00 (*1-884445-06-3*) C Schlacks Pub.

Catherine II's Greek Prelate: Eugenios Voulgaris in Russia, 1771-1806. Stephen K. Batalden. (East European Monographs: No. 115). 197p. 1983. text ed. 48.00 (*0-88033-006-6*) East Eur Quarterly.

Catherine Lucille Moore & Henry Kuttner: A Marriage of Souls & Talent, a Working Bibliography. Ed. by Virgil Utter & Gordon Benson, Jr. 45p. (Orig.). 1986. pap. 2.50 (*0-912613-04-1*) Galactic Central.

Catherine Lucille Moore & Henry Kuttner: A Marriage of Souls & Talent: A Working Bibliography. 3rd ed. Gordon Benson, Jr. & Phil Stephensen-Payne. (Galactic Central Bibliographies Ser.: No. 21). ix, 92p. (C). 1990. lib. bdg. 23.00x (*0-8095-4720-1*) Borgo Pr.

***Catherine Marshall: Inspiration Writings.** Marshall. 1995. 12.98 (*0-88486-118-X*) Arrowood Pr.

Catherine Marshall's Story Bible. Catherine Marshall. 200p. (J). (ps-5). 1985. pap. 10.95 (*0-380-69961-3*) Avon.

***Catherine McAuley & the Tradition of Mercy.** Mary C. Sullivan. LC 95-12283. (C). 1995. text ed. 32.95 (*0-268-00811-6*) U of Notre Dame Pr.

Catherine Murphy. Judith Hoos. (Illus.). 1976. pap. 2.50 (*0-910663-10-6*) ICA Inc.

Catherine of Aragon. Garrett Mattingly. LC 83-45808. reprint ed. 32.50 (*0-404-20169-5*) AMS Pr.

Catherine of Aragon & Her Friends. John E. Paul. LC 66-15774. 285p. reprint ed. pap. 81.30 (*0-7837-0461-5*, 2040784) Bks Demand.

Catherine of Genoa: Purgation & Purgatory, the Spiritual Dialogue. Ed. by Serge Hughes. LC 79-88123. (Classics of Western Spirituality Ser.). 190p. 1979. pap. 12.95 (*0-8091-2207-3*) Paulist Pr.

Catherine of Siena: A Biography. Anne B. Baldwin. LC 86-63595. 192p. (Orig.). 1987. pap. 7.95 (*0-87973-510-4*, 510) Our Sunday Visitor.

Catherine of Siena: The Dialogue. Ed. by Suzanne Noffke. LC 79-56755. (Classics of Western Spirituality Ser.). 416p. 1980. 22.95 (*0-8091-0295-1*); pap. 18.95 (*0-8091-2233-2*) Paulist Pr.

Catherine of Siena's Way. Mary Ann Fatula. LC 86-45350. (Way of the Christian Mystics Ser.: Vol. 4). 219p. (Orig.). 1987. pap. 14.95 (*0-8146-5589-0*) Liturgical Pr.

Catherine Schuyler. Mary G. Humphreys. LC 67-30160. 1968. reprint ed. 20.00 (*0-87152-040-0*) Reprint.

Catherine the Great. Leslie McGuire. (World Leaders - Past & Present Ser.). (Illus.). 112p. (YA). (gr. 5 up). 1986. lib. bdg. 17.95 (*0-87754-577-4*) Chelsea Hse.

Catherine the Great. Henri Troyat. Tr. by Joan Pinkham. 464p. 1984. mass mkt. 5.99 (*0-425-07981-3*) Berkley Pub.

Catherine the Great. Henri Troyat. Tr. by Joan Pinkham. LC 93-23521. 1994. 12.95 (*0-452-01120-5*, Mer) NAL-Dutton.

Catherine the Great: A Short History. Isabel De Madariaga. 244p. (C). 1991. text ed. 32.50 (*0-300-04845-9*) Yale U Pr.

Catherine the Great: A Short History. Isabel De Madariaga. (Illus.). 244p. (C). 1993. reprint ed. pap. text ed. 14.00 (*0-300-05427-0*) Yale U Pr.

Catherine the Great: Autocrat & Empress of All Russia. Ian Grey. LC 75-14598. (Illus.). 254p. 1975. reprint ed. text ed. 59.75 (*0-8371-8219-0*, GRCTG, Greenwood Pr) Greenwood.

Catherine the Great: Life & Legend. John T. Alexander. (Illus.). 432p. 1988. 30.00 (*0-19-505236-6*) OUP.

Catherine the Great: Life & Legend. John T. Alexander. (Illus.). 432p. 1989. reprint ed. pap. 13.95 (*0-19-506162-4*) OUP.

An Asterisk (*) at the beginning of an entry indicates that the title is appearing in BIP for the first time.

An Asterisk (*) at the beginning of an entry indicates that the title is appearing in BIP for the first time.

C

Catholic Church's Message to United States Citizens of the Twenty-First Century: The 10th Convention of the Fellowship of Catholic Scholars. Ed. by Paul L. Williams. 256p. (Orig.). 1988. pap. 10.95 (*0-937374-04-0*) NE Bks.

Catholic Citizens in the Third Reich: Psyco-Social Principles & Moral Reasoning. Donald J. Dietrich. 385p. 1988. 39.95 (*0-88738-131-6*) Transaction Pubs.

Catholic Classics. Dinesh D'Souza. LC 86-61500. (Orig.). 1993. 19.95 (*0-87973-525-2*, 525) Our Sunday Visitor.

Catholic Classics, No. I. Dinesh D'Souza. LC 86-61500. 168p. (Orig.). 1986. pap. 6.95 (*0-87973-545-7*, 545) Our Sunday Visitor.

Catholic Clergy in Indiana: A Necrology of Those Who Served in the Archdiocese of Indianapolis, Formerly the Diocese of Vincennes. William F. Stineman & Jack W. Porter. (Illus.). 206p. (Orig.). 1992. pap. 19.95 (*0-9616134-1-6*) St John Evang.

***Catholic College & University Directory, 1995: Catholic College Admission Association.** Ed. by Elizabeth Hunt. 104p. (YA). (gr. 10-12). 1995. 8.95 (*0-9645495-0-6*) R H Bailey.

Catholic College Students & the Draft. Paul Frazier. 58p. 1981. 2.50 (*0-685-43344-7*) Cath Peace Fell.

Catholic Colonialism: A Parish History of Guatemala, 1524-1821. Adriaan C. Van Oss. (Cambridge Latin American Studies: No. 57). (Illus.). 320p. 1986. 74.95 (*0-521-32072-0*) Cambridge U Pr.

Catholic Colonization on the Western Frontier. James Shannon. LC 76-6365. (Irish Americans Ser.). (Illus.). 1976. reprint ed. 29.95 (*0-405-09357-8*) Ayer.

Catholic Communicators. D. P. Noonan. LC 89-62495. 144p. (Orig.). 1990. pap. 5.95 (*0-87973-503-1*, 503) Our Sunday Visitor.

Catholic-Communist Collaboration in Italy. Ed. by Leonard Swidler & Edward J. Grace. 180p. (Orig.). (C). 1988. pap. text ed. 20.00 (*0-8191-7045-3*) U Pr of Amer.

Catholic-Communist Dialogue in Italy: 1944 to the Present. Rosanna M. Giammanco. LC 88-37000. 184p. 1989. text ed. 49.95 (*0-275-93205-2*, C3205, Praeger Pubs) Greenwood.

Catholic Concept of Genuine & Just Peace As a Basic Collective Human Right. Frank Przetacznik. LC 90-44321. (Roman Catholic Studies: Vol. 2). 352p. 1990. lib. bdg. 99.95 (*0-88946-239-9*) E Mellen.

Catholic Concordance. Nicolaus of Cusa. Ed. by Paul E. Sigmund. (Texts in the History of Political Thought Ser.). 376p. 1992. 19.95 (*0-521-40207-7*) Cambridge U Pr.

Catholic Conscience: Foundation & Formation. Ed. by Russell E. Smith. (Proceedings of the Tenth Bishop's Workshop Ser.). 289p. 1991. pap. text ed. 17.95 (*0-935372-32-6*) Pope John Ctr.

Catholic Controversy: St. Francis de Sales' Defense of the Faith. Francis De Sales. Tr. by Henry B. Mackey. LC 89-52138. 413p. 1989. reprint ed. pap. 13.00 (*0-89555-387-2*) TAN Bks Pubs.

Catholic Counterculture in America, 1933-1962. James T. Fisher. LC 88-35971. (Studies in Religion). (Illus.). xviii, 306p. (C). 1989. 34.95 (*0-8078-1863-1*) U of NC Pr.

Catholic Cults & Devotions: A Psychological Inquiry. Michael P. Carroll. (Illus.). 256p. 1989. 47.95 (*0-7735-0693-4*, Pub. by McGill CN) U of Toronto Pr.

Catholic Customs & Traditions: A Popular Guide. rev. ed. Greg Dues. LC 92-80801. 224p. 1992. pap. 9.95 (*0-89622-515-1*) Twenty-Third.

***Catholic Devotion in Victorian England.** Mary Heimann. (Oxford Historical Monographs). (Illus.). 316p. 1995. 55.00 (*0-19-820597-X*) OUP.

***Catholic Diary 1995.** (Illus.). 160p. Date not set. write for info. (*0-9643146-0-6*) Dais Grp.

Catholic Dictionary. Ed. by Peter M. Stravinskas. LC 93-83237. 500p. 1993. 29.95 (*0-87973-507-4*, 507) Our Sunday Visitor.

Catholic Doctrine of Non-Christian Religions According to the Second Vatican Council. Miikka Ruokanen. LC 91-46332. (Studies in Christian Mission: Vol. 7). 169p. 1992. 51.50 (*90-04-09517-9*) E J Brill.

Catholic Education: New Partnerships in the Service of the Church. Intro. by Benito M. Lopez, Jr. (Current Issues in Catholic Higher Education Ser.: Vol. 14, No. 1). 46p. (Orig.). 1993. pap. text ed. 6.00 (*1-55833-127-1*) Natl Cath Educ.

Catholic Elementary & Secondary Schools, 1991-92. Frederick H. Brigham, Jr. (Data Bank Ser.). (Illus.). 40p. (Orig.). 1992. pap. 7.00 (*1-55833-120-4*) Natl Cath Educ.

Catholic Elementary School Extension Program. Arlene F. McElligott & Joseph P. McElligott. 33p. 1986. 5.30 (*0-318-20576-9*) Natl Cath Educ.

Catholic Elementary Schools & Their Finances, 1991. 1991. 7.50 (*1-55833-118-2*) Natl Cath Educ.

Catholic Emancipation: An Anglo-Irish Episode. Wendy Hinde. (Illus.). 256p. 1992. 39.95 (*0-631-16783-8*) Blackwell Pubs.

Catholic Emancipation Crisis in Ireland, 1823-1829. James A. Reynolds. LC 74-95134. 204p. 1970. reprint ed. text ed. 55.00 (*0-8371-3141-3*, RECE, Greenwood Pr) Greenwood.

Catholic Emancipation Eighteen Twenty-Nine to Nineteen Twenty-Nine: Essays by Various Writers. LC 67-22084. (Essay Index Reprint Ser.). 1977. 23.95 (*0-8369-0284-X*) Ayer.

Catholic Encyclopedia. Ed. by Peter M. Stravinskas. LC 90-62920. 1008p. 1991. 34.95 (*0-87973-457-4*, 457); kivar 29.95 (*0-87973-475-2*) Our Sunday Visitor.

***Catholic Encyclopedia & Dictionary.** (Illus.). 1200p. (Orig.). 1995. pap. 195.00 (*0-7605-1669-3*) Rector Pr.

Catholic England: Faith, Religion, & Observance Before Reformation. R. N. Swanson. LC 92-29427. (Medieval Sources Ser.). 1993. text ed. 69.95 (*0-7190-3464-7*, Pub. by Manchester Univ Pr UK) St Martin.

Catholic Epistles & Hebrews. Rea McDonnell. (Message of Biblical Spirituality Ser.: Vol. 14). 150p. 1986. 12.95 (*0-8146-5564-5*); pap. 7.95 (*0-8146-5580-7*) Liturgical Pr.

Catholic Essays. Stanley L. Jaki. 200p. 1990. pap. 9.95 (*0-931888-39-5*) Christendom Pr.

Catholic Ethic & the Spirit of Capitalism. Michael Novak. 200p. 1993. text ed. 24.95 (*0-02-923235-X*) Free Pr.

***Catholic Ethic in American Society: An Exploration of Values.** John E. Tropman. LC 95-12644. (Nonprofit Sector Ser.). 1995. 22.95 (*0-7879-0123-7*) Jossey-Bass.

Catholic Evidence: A Classic Guide to Understanding & Explaining the Truths of the Catholic Church. Frank Sheed & Maisie Ward. 362p. (C). 1992. 9.95 (*0-940535-55-6*, UP155) Franciscan U Pr.

Catholic Fact Book. John Deedy. 1986. pap. 15.95 (*0-88347-252-X*) Thomas More.

Catholic Faith. Robert J. Fox. LC 83-61889. 360p. (Orig.). 1983. pap. 8.95 (*0-87973-614-3*, 614) Our Sunday Visitor.

Catholic Faith. Roderick Strange. 192p. 1986. pap. 15.95 (*0-19-283051-1*) OUP.

Catholic Faith: A Reader. Ed. by Lawrence S. Cunningham. 1988. pap. 9.95 (*0-8091-3020-3*) Paulist Pr.

Catholic Faith: An Introduction. Lawrence S. Cunningham. 192p. (Orig.). 1987. pap. 6.95 (*0-8091-2859-4*) Paulist Pr.

Catholic Faith & the Industrial Order. Ruth Kenyon. 1980. lib. bdg. 59.95 (*0-8490-3129-X*) Gordon Pr.

Catholic Faith in a Process Perspective. William N. Pittenger. LC 81-9615. 160p. (Orig.). reprint ed. pap. 45.60 (*0-8357-8825-3*, 2033560) Bks Demand.

Catholic Faith Inventory. Kenneth Boyack et al. 1986. pap. 9.95 (*0-8091-5196-0*); pap. 4.95 (*0-8091-2866-7*) Paulist Pr.

***Catholic Faith Inventory.** Kenneth Boyack et al. 1986. pap. 24.95 (*0-8091-5197-9*) Paulist Pr.

Catholic Faith Today. Bennet Kelley. 1975. 3.00 (*0-89942-243-8*, 243-04) Catholic Bk Pub.

***Catholic Family.** William Sander. (C). 1995. text ed. 49.95 (*0-8133-2264-2*) Westview.

Catholic Family Bible. 1992. 95.00 (*0-911156-43-7*) Bern Porter.

***Catholic Family Book of Novenas.** (Illus.). x, 371p. 1995. reprint ed. pap. text ed. 14.95 (*0-912141-20-4*) Roman Cath Bks.

Catholic Family-Time Bible Stories in Pictures. Kenneth N. Taylor. (Illus.). 307p. (J). (gr. 3-6). 1993. 14.95 (*0-87973-882-0*, 882) Our Sunday Visitor.

Catholic Girls. Kit Reed. LC 87-81418. 240p. 1987. 17.95 (*1-55611-063-4*) D I Fine.

Catholic Girls: Stories, Poems, & Memoirs by Louise Erdich, Mary Gordon, Audre Lorde, Mary McCarthy, Francine Prose, & 47 Others. Ed. by Amber C. Sumrall & Patrice Vecchione. LC 92-53561. 304p. (Orig.). 1992. pap. 11.00 (*0-452-26842-7*, Plume) NAL-Dutton.

Catholic Guide to the Bible. Oscar Lukefahr. LC 92-82795. 208p. (Orig.). 1992. pap. text ed. 5.95 (*0-89243-477-5*) Liguori Pubns.

Catholic Guide to the Bible Workbook. Oscar Lukefahr. 62p. (Orig.). 1992. pap. text ed. 2.95 (*0-89243-478-3*) Liguori Pubns.

***Catholic Handbook for Engaged & Newly Married Couples.** Frederick W. Marks. LC 94-72069. 126p. (Orig.). 1994. pap. 5.00 (*1-880033-14-3*) Faith Pub OH.

Catholic Health Association Members, 1994. 470p. 1993. pap. 200.00 (*0-87125-222-8*, 140) Cath Health.

***Catholic Health Care System & National Health Care Reform: An Overview.** Cynthia Gibson. 43p. (Orig.). 1994. pap. 10.00 (*0-915365-24-3*) Cath Free Choice.

Catholic Heritage: Martyrs, Ascetics, Pilgrims, Warriors, Mystics, Theologians, Artists, Humanists, Activists, Outsiders & Saints. Lawrence S. Cunningham. 256p. 1983. pap. 14.95 (*0-8245-0685-5*) Crossroad NY.

Catholic Heros & Heroines of America. John O. Murray. 1972. 35.00 (*0-87968-818-1*) Gordon Pr.

Catholic Hierarchy of the United States, 1790-1922. John H. O'Donnell. LC 73-3558. (Catholic University of America. Studies in Romance Languages & Literatures: No. 4). reprint ed. 39.50 (*0-404-57754-7*) AMS Pr.

Catholic High School: A National Portrait. 254p. 1985. 12.00 (*0-318-04383-1*) Natl Cath Educ.

Catholic High School Entrance Examination. Jack Rudman. (Admission Test Ser.: ATS-81). 1994. pap. 23.95 (*0-8373-5081-6*) Nat Learn.

Catholic High School Entrance Examinations. 6th ed. Eve P. Steinberg. 320p. 1991. pap. 12.00 (*0-13-121013-0*, Arco Test) P-H Gen Ref & Trav.

Catholic High School Entrance Exams. 7th ed. Eve P. Steinberg. LC 93-48701. (YA). 1994. 13.00 (*0-671-88149-3*, Arco Test) P-H Gen Ref & Trav.

Catholic High School Teacher: Building on Research. 80p. 1987. 5.30 (*0-317-66623-1*) Natl Cath Educ.

Catholic High Schools: Their Impact on Low-Income Students. 254p. 1985. 12.00 (*0-685-11853-3*) Natl Cath Educ.

Catholic High Schools & Minority Students. Andrew M. Greeley. LC 81-23131. (Illus.). 125p. 1982. 24.95 (*0-87855-452-1*) Transaction Pubs.

Catholic High Schools & Their Finances 1988. Michael J. Guerra & Michael Donahue. (Data Bank Ser.). 46p. (Orig.). 1988. pap. 10.00 (*1-55833-017-8*) Natl Cath Educ.

Catholic High Schools & Their Finances 1990. Michael J. Guerra & Michael J. Donahue. (Data Bank Ser.). (Illus.). 60p. (Orig.). 1990. pap. 8.50 (*1-55833-056-9*) Natl Cath Educ.

Catholic Higher Education, Theology, & Academic Freedom. Charles E. Curran. LC 89-40742. 272p. (C). 1990. text ed. 27.95 (*0-268-00625-3*) U of Notre Dame Pr.

Catholic History of Alabama & the Floridas. Mary A. Carroll. LC 70-124228. (Select Bibliographies Reprint Ser.). 1977. 20.95 (*0-8369-5417-3*) Ayer.

Catholic Home & School Association Guidebook. David F. Menicucci. 108p. (Orig.). 1990. pap. 6.00 (*1-55833-058-5*) Natl Cath Educ.

Catholic Home Schooling: A Handbook for Parents. Mary K. Clark. LC 93-60757. 448p. (Orig.). 1993. pap. 15.00 (*0-89555-494-1*, 1227) TAN Bks Pubs.

Catholic Household Blessings & Prayers. Bishops' Committee on the Liturgy Staff & National Conference of Catholic Bishops Staff. (Illus.). 434p. 1988. 19.95 (*1-55586-220-9*) US Catholic.

Catholic Household Blessings & Prayers. National Conference of Catholic Bishops Staff & United States Catholic Conference Staff. 444p. (Orig.). 1989. pap. 8.95 (*1-55586-292-6*) US Catholic.

Catholic Identity. Ed. by James Provost & Knut Walf. (Concilium Ser.). 125p. (Orig.). 1994. pap. 15.00 (*0-88344-880-7*) Orbis Bks.

Catholic Identity after Vatican II. Frans J. Van Beeck. 113p. 1985. 9.95 (*0-8294-0498-8*) Loyola Univ Pr.

Catholic Identity in Health Care: Principles & Practice. Orville N. Griese. 537p. (Orig.). 1987. pap. 17.95 (*0-935372-19-9*) Pope John Ctr.

Catholic Identity of Catholic Schools. James Heft & Carleen Reck. (National Congress Catholic Schools for the 21st Century Ser.). 43p. (Orig.). 1991. pap. 2.50 (*1-55833-066-6*) Natl Cath Educ.

Catholic Immigrant Colonization Projects in the United States, 1815-1860. Mary G. Kelly. LC 74-145485. (American Immigration Library). x, 290p. 1971. reprint ed. lib. bdg. 32.95 (*0-89198-016-4*) Ozer.

Catholic Immigrants in America. James S. Olson. 260p. 1986. 31.95 (*0-8304-1037-6*) Nelson-Hall.

Catholic Imperialism & World Freedom. Avro Manhattan. LC 73-161336. (Atheist Viewpoint Ser.). 528p. 1972. reprint ed. 31.95 (*0-405-03810-0*) Ayer.

Catholic Indian Missions in Maine (1611-1820) Mary C. Leger. LC 73-3563. (Catholic University of America. Studies in Romance Languages & Literatures: No. 8). reprint ed. 39.50 (*0-404-57758-X*) AMS Pr.

Catholic Intellectuals & Conservative Politics in America, 1950-1985. Patrick Allitt. (Illus.). 328p. 1993. 29.95 (*0-8014-2295-7*) Cornell U Pr.

***Catholic Intellectuals & Conservative Politics in America, 1950-1985.** Patrick Allitt. 336p. 1995. pap. 15.95 (*0-8014-8300-X*) Cornell U Pr.

Catholic Is Wonderful! How to Make the Most of It. Mitch Finley. (Spirit Life Ser.). 64p. (Orig.). 1994. pap. 4.95 (*1-878718-24-X*) Resurrection.

***Catholic-Jewish Encounter.** Peter M. Stravinskas & Leon Klenicki. LC 94-66023. 160p. 1994. 14.95 (*0-87973-619-4*, 619) Our Sunday Visitor.

Catholic Journalism. Apollinaris W. Baumgartner. LC 75-159997. (BCL Ser. I). reprint ed. 21.50 (*0-404-00693-0*) AMS Pr.

Catholic Laity in Elizabethan England, 1558-1603. William R. Trimble. LC 63-20773. 298p. reprint ed. pap. 85.00 (*0-7837-4131-6*, 2057954) Bks Demand.

Catholic Lawyer: 1955-1991, 35 vols. 962.50 (*0-8377-9037-9*); mic. film write for info. (*0-318-57421-7*) Rothman.

Catholic Literary France. Mary J. Keeler. (Essay Index Reprint Ser.). 290p. 1982. reprint ed. lib. bdg. 18.00 (*0-8290-0785-7*) Irvington.

Catholic Literary France from Verlaine to the Present Time. Mary J. Keeler. LC 76-90649. (Essay Index Reprint Ser.). 1977. 21.95 (*0-8369-1219-5*) Ayer.

Catholic Lives - Contemporary America. Ed. by Thomas J. Ferraro. 204p. 1994. pap. 10.00 (*0-8223-6420-4*) Duke.

Catholic Living Bible. deluxe ed. 1982. Personal Gift Burgundy Imitation Leather. 16.99 (*0-8423-2364-3*, 2364) Tyndale.

Catholic Living Childrens Bible. 16.99 (*0-8423-2334-1*) Tyndale.

Catholic Loyalism in Elizabethan England. Arnold Pritchard. LC 78-10208. 255p. reprint ed. pap. 72.70 (*0-7837-6851-6*, 2046680) Bks Demand.

Catholic Makers of America: Biographical Sketches of Catholic Statesmen & Political Thinkers in America's First Century, 1776-1876. Ed. by Stephen M. Krason. 262p. (Orig.). 1993. pap. 11.95 (*0-931888-49-2*) Christendom Pr.

Catholic Marriage Poems 1962-1979. Mary C. Rodgers. LC 94-15579. (Illus.). 72p. 1994. pap. 14.95 (*0-7734-0013-3*) E Mellen.

Catholic Martyrs of the Spanish Civil War, 1936-1939. Fray J. De Urbel. Tr. by Michael F. Ingrams. (Illus.). 242p. (Orig.). 1993. pap. 10.00 (*0-939952-96-3*) Angelus Pr.

Catholic Marxist Ideological Dialogue in Poland: 1945-1980. Norbert A. Zimjewski. 160p. 1991. text ed. 59.95 (*1-85521-200-5*, Pub. by Dartmth Pub UK) Ashgate Pub Co.

Catholic Milieu. Thomas Storck. 80p. (Orig.). 1987. pap. 5.95 (*0-931888-25-5*) Christendom Pr.

Catholic Ministry to the Addicted. Roy Barkley. LC 91-67224. 144p. (Orig.). 1992. pap. 5.95 (*0-87973-441-8*, 441) Our Sunday Visitor.

Catholic Missions in China During the Middle Ages: 1294-1368, No. 37. Paul Stanislaus Hsiang. (Studies in Sacred Theology, Second Series). 57p. 1983. reprint ed. 12.00 (*0-939738-32-5*) Zubal Inc.

Catholic Moral Tradition: In Christ, A New Creation. David Bohr. LC 89-62497. 425p. 1990. 19.95 (*0-87973-439-6*, 439) Our Sunday Visitor.

Catholic Morality: Sin, Virtue, Conscience, Duties to God, Neighbor, Etc. John Laux. LC 90-70439. (Course in Religion for Catholic High Schools & Academies Ser.: Bk. III). (Illus.). 164p. 1990. reprint ed. pap. text ed. 8.00 (*0-89555-393-7*) TAN Bks Pubs.

Catholic Morality Revisited: Origins & Contemporary Challenges. Gerard S. Sloyan. LC 89-51580. 160p. 1990. pap. 9.95 (*0-89622-418-X*) Twenty-Third.

Catholic Myth: The Behavior & Beliefs of American Catholics. Andrew M. Greeley. 240p. 1991. pap. 10.95 (*0-02-085201-0*, Collier S&S) S&S Trade.

Catholic Myth: The Behavior & Beliefs of American Catholics. Andrew M. Greeley. 352p. reprint ed. pap. 12.95 (*0-685-40606-7*, Collier S&S) S&S Trade.

Catholic Novel: An Annotated Bibliography. Ed. by J. Alberb Menendez. LC 88-1718. (Reference Library of the Humanities). 344p. 1988. lib. bdg. 48.00 (*0-8240-8534-5*) Garland.

Catholic Novelists in Defense of Their Faith, 1829-1865. Willard Thorp. 1978. 17.95 (*0-405-10862-1*, 11860) Ayer.

Catholic One-Year Bible. 1376p. 1987. kivar 16.95 (*0-87973-215-6*) Our Sunday Visitor.

Catholic One Year Bible Journal. 35p. 1987. pap. 1.95 (*0-87973-216-4*) Our Sunday Visitor.

Catholic Parish: Shifting Membership in a Changing Church. Thomas P. Sweetser. LC 74-84543. (Studies in Religion & Society). 134p. 1974. pap. 12.95 (*0-913348-13-9*) Ctr Sci Study.

Catholic Parish as a Way-Station of Ethnicity & Americanization: Chicago's Germans & Italians, 1903-1939. Stephen J. Shaw. LC 91-26847. (Chicago Studies in the History of American Religion Ser.: Vol. 19). 255p. 1991. 50.00 (*0-926019-55-4*) Carlson Pub.

Catholic Parochial Elementary School in the United States - Where Is It Headed. Kenneth J. Becker. LC 91-66855. 162p. 1992. pap. 7.95 (*1-55523-480-1*) Winston-Derek.

Catholic Peacemakers: A Collection of Readings, 2 vols. Ed. by Ronald G. Musto. LC 92-42658. (Illus.). 864p. 1993. Vol. 2, From the Renaissance to the Twentieth Century, 450p. 95.00 (*0-8153-0605-9*, H1372) Garland.

Catholic Peacemakers: A Collection of Readings, 2 vols., Set. Ed. by Ronald G. Musto. LC 92-42658. (Illus.). 864p. 1993. 170.00 (*0-8240-7388-6*) Garland.

Catholic Peacemakers: A Collection of Readings, 2 vols., Vol. 1: From the Bible to the Crusades. Ed. by Ronald G. Musto. LC 92-42658. (Illus.). 350p. 1993. Vol. 1, From the Bible to the Crusades, 350p. 95.00 (*0-8153-0604-0*, H1346) Garland.

Catholic Pentecostals Today. rev. ed. Kevin Ranaghan & Dorothy Ranaghan. LC 83-70963. 196p. 1983. pap. 4.95 (*0-943780-03-9*, 8039) Charismatic Ren Servs.

Catholic Periodical Index. Incl. 1934-1938LC 70-649588. 50.00 (*0-87507-010-8*); Vol. 4. 1943-1948. LC 70-649588. 50.00 (*0-87507-011-6*); Vol. 10. 1959-1960. LC 70-649588. 30.00 (*0-87507-012-4*); Vol. 12. 1963-1964. LC 70-649588. 40.00 (*0-87507-014-0*); Vol. 14. Catholic Periodical & Literature Index, 1967-68. LC 70-649588. 40.00 (*0-87507-015-9*); Vol. 15. 1969-1970. LC 70-649588. 45.00 (*0-87507-016-7*); Vol. 16. 1971-1972. LC 70-649588. 60.00 (*0-87507-017-5*); Vol. 17. 1973-1974. LC 70-649588. 55.00 (*0-87507-018-3*); Vol. 18. 1975-1976. LC 70-649588. 60.00 (*0-87507-019-1*); Vol. 19. 1977-1978. LC 70-649588. 70.00 (*0-87507-020-5*); Vol. 20. 1979-1980. LC 70-649588. 90.00 (*0-87507-021-3*, 1979-1980); 1981-1982LC 70-649588. 90.00 (*0-87507-025-6*, 1981-1982); 1983-1984LC 70-649588. 100.00 (*0-87507-036-1*, 1983-1984); Vol. 22. 1983-1984. LC 70-649588. 100.00 (*0-685-42050-7*); Vol. 23. 1985-1986. LC 70-649588. 120.00 (*0-685-42051-5*); Vol. 24. 1987-1988. LC 70-649588. 175.00 (*0-685-42052-3*); 1934-1938LC 70-649588. 50.00 (*0-87507-010-8*); Vol. 4. 1943-1948. LC 70-649588. 50.00 (*0-87507-011-6*); Vol. 15. 1969-1970. LC 70-649588. 45.00 (*0-87507-016-7*); Vol. 16. 1971-1972. LC 70-649588. 60.00 (*0-87507-017-5*); Vol. 18. 1975-1976. LC 70-649588. 60.00 (*0-87507-019-1*); Vol. 20. 1979-1980. LC 70-649588. 90.00 (*0-87507-021-3*, 1979-1980); Vol. 23. 1985-1986. LC 70-649588. 120.00 (*0-685-42051-5*); Vol. 24. 1987-1988. LC 70-649588. 175.00 (*0-685-42052-3*); LC 70-649588. Orig. Title: The Catholic Periodical Index & The Guide to Catholic Literature. write for info. (*0-318-51304-8*) Cath Lib Assn.

Catholic Periodical Index & The Guide to Catholic Literature see Catholic Periodical Index

***Catholic Perspective: Physical Exercise & Sports.** Robert Feeney. LC 94-94623. 134p. (Orig.). 1995. pap. 7.95 (*0-9622347-3-7*) Aquinas Pr.

Catholic Perspectives on Baptism, Eucharist & Ministry: A Study Commissioned by the Catholic Theological Society of America. Ed. by Michael A. Fahey. 240p. (Orig.). (C). 1986. lib. bdg. 49.00 (*0-8191-5431-8*, Catholic Theological Soc of Amer); pap. text ed. 23.00 (*0-8191-5432-6*, Catholic Theological Soc of Amer) U Pr of Amer.

Catholic Perspectives on Medical Morals: Foundational Issues. Ed. by Edmund D. Pellegrino et al. (C). 1989. lib. bdg. 84.50 (*1-55608-083-2*) Kluwer Ac.

Catholic Pharmacist: 1985, Vol. 18. Ed. by John P. Winkelmann. 1985. 10.00 (*0-317-00367-4*) Natl Cath Pharm.

Catholic Philanthropic Tradition in America. Mary J. Oates. LC 94-13027. (Philanthropic Studies). 1995. 27.95 (*0-253-34159-0*) Ind U Pr.

Catholic Philosophy of History, Vol. 3. American Catholic Historic Association Staff. LC 67-23190. (Essay Index Reprint Ser.). 1977. 18.95 (*0-8369-0285-8*) Ayer.

Catholic Pioneers of America. John O. Murray. 1972. 35.00 (*0-87968-819-X*) Gordon Pr.

An Asterisk (*) at the beginning of an entry indicates that the title is appearing in BIP for the first time.

C

An Asterisk (*) at the beginning of an entry indicates that the title is appearing in BIP for the first time.

Catholicism, Protestantism, & Capitalism. Amintore Fanfani. LC 84-40363. 272p. (C). 1984. reprint ed. pap. text ed. 11.95 (0-268-00752-7) U of Notre Dame Pr.

Catholicism Today. Jerome A. Welch. LC 76-29584. (Illus.). 1977. 7.95 (0-917728-01-7); pap. 6.95 (0-917728-02-5) Jewel Pubns.

Catholicism Today: A Survey of Catholic Belief & Practice. rev. ed. Matthew F. Kohmescher. LC 80-82085. 216p. (Orig.). 1980. pap. 7.95 (0-8091-3146-3) Paulist Pr.

Catholicity & Secession: A Study of Ecumenicity in the Christian Reformed Church. Henry Zwaanstra. 136p. (Orig.). 1991. pap. 14.99 (0-8028-0604-X) Eerdmans.

Catholicity & the Church. John Meyendorff. LC 83-20218. (Illus.). 160p. (Orig.). 1983. pap. 8.95 (0-88141-006-3) St Vladimirs.

Catholicity of Protestantism: Being a Report Presented to His Grace the Archbishop of Canterbury by a Group of Free Churchmen. Ed. by Robert N. Flew & Rupert E. Davies. LC 80-29108. 159p. 1981. reprint ed. text ed. 49.75 (0-313-22825-6, FLCAT) Greenwood.

Catholicity of the Church. Avery Dulles. 208p. 1987. pap. 14.95 (0-19-826695-2) OUP.

Catholics Against the Church: Anti-Abortion Protest in Toronto, 1969-1985. Michael W. Cuneo. 40.00 (0-8020-2726-1); pap. 18.95 (0-8020-6758-1) U of Toronto Pr.

Catholics & American Politics. Mary Hanna. LC 79-11035. 271p. 1979. 29.95 (0-674-10325-4) HUP.

Catholics & Fundamentalists: What's the Difference? Martin Pable. LC 91-70460. 64p. (Orig.). 1991. pap. 4.95 (0-937997-18-8) Hi-Time Pub.

Catholics & German Unity, 1866-1871. George G. Windell. LC 54-13011. 324p. reprint ed. pap. 92.40 (0-685-15894-2, 2056196) Bks Demand.

Catholics & Radicals: The Association of Catholic Trade Unionists & the American Labor Movement, from Depression to Cold War. Douglas P. Seaton. 272p. 1981. 36.50 (0-8387-2193-1) Bucknell U Pr.

Catholics & the New Age: How Good People Are Being Drawn into Jungian Psychology, the Enneagram, & the Age of Aquarius. Mitch Pacwa. 235p. (Orig.). 1992. pap. 8.99 (0-89283-756-X) Servant.

Catholics & the Welfare State. Peter Coman. LC 76-49523. 128p. reprint ed. pap. 36.50 (0-317-08456-9, 2011288) Bks Demand.

C

Catholics, Anglicans, & Puritans: Seventeenth-Century Essays. Hugh Trevor-Roper. 317p. 1988. 27.50 (0-226-81228-6) U Ch Pr.

***Catholics at the "Gathering Place" Historical Essays on the Archidiocese of Toronto 1841-1991.** Ed. by Mark G. McGowan & Brian P. Clarke. (Illus.). 352p. Date not set. pap. 18.99 (0-614-06787-1) Dun.

Catholics Coming Home: A Journey of Reconciliation. Carrie Kemp & Donald Pologruto. LC 89-46458. 256p. 1991. pap. 14.95 (0-06-066657-9) Harper SF.

Catholics, Divorce & Remarriage. John Hosie. 1994. pap. 5.95 (0-85574-349-2, Pub. by E J Dwyer AT) Morehouse Pub.

Catholics Experiencing Divorce: Grieving, Healing, & Learning to Live Again. William Rabior & Vicki W. Bedard. LC 91-60945. 80p. (Orig.). 1991. pap. text ed. 3.95 (0-89243-347-7) Liguori Pubns.

***Catholics in Bombay: A Historical Demographic Study of the Roman Catholic Population in the Archdiocese of Bombay.** S. Irudaya Rajan. (C). 1993. 44.00x (81-85408-08-4, Pub. by Firma KLM) S Asia.

Catholics in Caroline England. Martin J. Havran. ix, 208p. 1962. 29.50 (0-8047-0112-1) Stanford U Pr.

Catholics in Colonial Law. Francis X. Curran. LC 63-24861. 139p. reprint ed. pap. 39.70 (0-8357-8567-X, 2034933) Bks Demand.

Catholics in South Carolina: A Record. Richard C. Madden. 428p. (Orig.). 1985. lib. bdg. 54.00 (0-8191-4457-6); pap. text ed. 29.00 (0-8191-4458-4) U Pr of Amer.

Catholics in Soviet-Occupied Lithuania: Faith Under Persecution. (Illus.). 120p. 1981. pap. 2.00 (0-318-14777-7) Lith Info Ctr.

Catholics in the Old South: Essays on Church & Culture. Jon L. Wakelyn & Randall M. Miller. LC 83-7893. x, 262p. 1983. 15.95 (0-86554-080-2, H74) Mercer Univ Pr.

Catholics in the Promised Land of the Saints. James Hennessey. LC 81-80935. (Pere Marquette Lectures). 100p. (C). 1981. 10.00 (0-87462-536-X) Marquette.

Catholics, Jews, & Protestants: A Study of Relationships in the United States & Canada. Claris E. Silcox. LC 78-21101. 1979. reprint ed. text ed. 75.00 (0-313-20882-4, SICJ, Greenwood Pr) Greenwood.

Catholics, Jews, & the State of Israel. Anthony J. Kenny. LC 93-17833. (Studies in Judaism & Christianity). 192p. 1993. pap. 9.95 (0-8091-3406-3) Paulist Pr.

Catholics of Harvard Square. Jeffery Wills. (Illus.). (Orig.). 1993. 22.95 (1-879007-01-0); pap. 15.95 (1-879007-00-2) St Bedes Pubns.

***Catholics on the Edge.** Tim Unsworth. 192p. 1995. 19.95 (0-8245-1463-7) Crossroad NY.

Catholics, the State, & European Radicals. Wolf & Hoensch. 1987. text ed. 40.50 (0-88033-126-7, SC50) Col U Pr.

Catholics, the State & the European Radical Right, 1919-1945. Ed. by Richard Wolff. (Atlantic Studies: No. 50). write for info. (0-88033-101-1) Brooklyn Coll Pr.

Catholikes Supplication Unto the King's Majestie, for Toleration of Catholike Religion in England. Gabriel Powell. LC 76-57406. (English Experience Ser.: No. 822). 1977. lib. bdg. 6.00 (90-221-0822-8) Walter J Johnson.

Catholocism's Developing Social Teaching. Robert A. Sirico. 32p. (Orig.). 1992. pap. text ed. 3.00 (1-880595-01-X) Acton Inst Stu Rel.

Cathouse Canyon. Buck Gentry. (Scout Ser.: No. 14). 1984. pap. 2.50 (0-8217-1345-0) Zebra.

Cathouse Kitten. Dirk Fletcher. (Spur Ser.). 224p. 1984. pap. 2.50 (0-8439-2078-5) Dorchester Pub Co.

Cathy. Don Lawrence. (Illus.). 45p. 1991. pap. 9.95 (1-56398-020-7) Malibu Graphics.

Cathy IV. Frances Lucas. LC 91-43339. (Orig.). 1992. pap. 8.95 (0-934678-41-3) New Victoria Pubs.

Catilinarian Conspiracy. Charles M. Odahl. 1972. 14.95 (0-8084-0032-0); pap. write for info. (0-8084-0033-9) NCUP.

Catilinarian Conspiracy in Its Context: A Re-Study of the Evidence. Ernest G. Hardy. LC 75-41128. reprint ed. 27.50 (0-404-14549-3) AMS Pr.

Catilina's Riddle. Steven W. Saylor. 448p. 1993. 22.95 (0-312-09763-8) St Martin.

Catiline. Ben Jonson. Ed. by W. F. Bolton & Jane F. Gardner. LC 75-128681. (Regents Renaissance Drama Ser.). 229p. reprint ed. pap. 65.30 (0-8357-4128-1, 2057063) Bks Demand.

Catiline & the Burial Mound. Henrik Ibsen. Ed. by James J. Wilhelm. Tr. by Thomas Van Laan. LC 90-3257. (Library of World Literature in Translation: Vol. 11). 516p. 1992. 80.00 (0-8240-2997-6) Garland.

Catiline's Dream: An Essay on Ibsen's Plays. James Hurt. LC 79-186346. 214p. reprint ed. pap. 61.00 (0-317-29048-7, 2020230) Bks Demand.

Cation Binding by Macrocycles: Complexation of Cationic Species by Crown Ethers. Inoue & Gokel. 768p. 1990. 199.00 (0-8247-8187-2) Dekker.

Cation Ordering & Electron Transfer. Ed. by J. B. Goodenough & C. K. Jorgensen. (Structure & Bonding Ser.: Vol. 61). (Illus.). 170p. 1985. 64.00 (0-387-15446-9) Spr-Verlag.

Cationic Isomerization: Polymerization of Three-Methyl-One-Butene & Four-Methyl-One-Penene see Polymerization Reactions

Cationic Ring-Opening Polymerization. S. Penczek et al. (Advances in Polymer Science Ser.: Vols. 68 & 69). (Illus.). 300p. 1985. 131.00 (0-387-13781-5) Spr-Verlag.

Cationic Surfactants. Ed. by Eric Jungermann. LC 77-84776. (Surfactant Science Ser.: Vol. 4). 672p. 1970. pap. 235.00 (0-8247-7199-0) Dekker.

Cationic Surfactants: Analytical & Biological Evaluation. John Cross & Edward J. Singer. LC 93-48585. (Surfactant Science Ser.: Vol. 53). 392p. (Orig.). 1994. 150.00 (0-8247-9177-0) Dekker.

Cationic Surfactants: Organic Chemistry. Richmond. (Surfactant Science Ser.: Vol. 34). 320p. 1990. 165.00 (0-8247-8381-6) Dekker.

Cationic Surfactants: Physical Chemistry. Ed. by Donn N. Rubingh & Paul M. Holland. (Surfactant Science Ser.: Vol. 37). 544p. 1991. 165.00 (0-8247-8357-3) Dekker.

Catitudes: How to Listen for & Really See Your Loves. 2nd ed. Marianna Thomas. (Illus.). 111p. (Orig.). (C). 1988. 12.95 (0-9620969-0-3); pap. 12.95 (0-317-91282-8) Jubilee Pub Hse.

***Catkin.** Antonia Barber & Errol Le Cain. LC 94-10565. 48p. (J). 1994. lib. bdg. write for info. (1-56402-485-7) Candlewick Pr.

Catkin. Alexis Lykiard. 60p. 1985. 21.00 (0-947612-08-4, Pub. by Rivelin Grapheme Pr) St Mut.

***Catkin Willow Flats.** Liu Shaotang. 120p. 1995. lib. bdg. 27.00 (0-8095-4505-5) Borgo Pr.

***Catland Companion: Classic Cats by Louis Wain & Many Others.** John Silvester & Anne Mobbs. LC 94-28108. 1994. 12.99 (0-517-12025-9) Random Hse Value.

***Catlin.** Jamilah Ritchey. 160p. 1995. pap. 7.95 (1-56901-874-X) NW Pub.

Catlin & His Contemporaries: The Politics of Patronage. Brian W. Dippie. LC 89-4963. (Illus.). xx, 569p. 1990. 60.00 (0-8032-1683-1) U of Nebr Pr.

Catline & the Roman Conspiracy: Two Accounts. Ed. by Phyllis O. Flug & Michael J. Miller. LC 77-39300. (Conspiracy: Historical Perspectives Ser.). 1972. 23.95 (0-405-04151-9) Ayer.

Catlin's Indians: The Kemper Portfolio. 1990. write for info. (0-9615372-1-3) Albrecht Art Mus.

Catlin's North American Indian Portfolio. (Illus.). 1989. 2,000.00 (0-89659-762-8) Abbeville Pr.

Catlin's North American Indian Portfolio. deluxe ed. (Illus.). 1989. ring bd. write for info. (0-318-63476-7) Abbeville Pr.

Catlin's North American Indian Portfolio. George Catlin. (Works of George Catlin Ser.). 1990. reprint ed. lib. bdg. 198.00 (0-7812-2248-6) Rprt Serv.

Catlin's Notes on Eight Years Travels & Residence in Europe. George Catlin. (Works of George Catlin Ser.). 1990. reprint ed. lib. bdg. 79.00 (0-7812-2249-4) Rprt Serv.

Catlives: Sarah Kirsch's Katzenleben. Ed. by Marina Roscher & Charles Fishman. Tr. by Charles Fishman. 177p. 1990. 24.95 (0-89672-232-5); pap. 12.95 (0-89672-231-7) Tex Tech Univ Pr.

Catlore. Desmond Morris. (Illus.). 192p. 1988. 12.95 (0-517-56903-5, Crown) Crown Pub Group.

Catlore. Desmond Morris. 1993. pap. 8.00 (0-517-88057-1, Crown) Crown Pub Group.

***CatLove: Two Hundred Ten Wonderful Things You Can Do for Your Cat.** Jill Kramer. LC 94-29059. (Illus.). 208p. (Orig.). 1994. pap. 6.95 (1-56170-105-X, 107) Hay House.

Catlow. Louis L'Amour. 160p. (Orig.). 1984. pap. 3.99 (0-553-24767-0) Bantam.

Catlyst Deactivation 1987: Proceedings of the Fourth International Symposium, Antwerp, Belgium, September October, 1987. B. Delmon & G. F. Froment. (SSS Ser.: Vol. 34). 1987. 174.50 (0-444-42855-0) Elsevier.

Catmagic. Whitley Strieber. 448p. 1987. reprint ed. mass mkt. 4.95 (0-8125-1550-1) Tor Bks.

Catmas Carols. Laurie Loughlin. LC 92-34649. (Illus.). 48p. 1993. 6.95 (0-8118-0237-X) Chronicle Bks.

CatMinder. Monique Maniet. 100p. 1991. 19.95 (0-914783-52-1) Charles.

Catnap: A Midnight Louie Mystery. Carole N. Douglas. 256p. 1993. mass mkt. 4.99 (0-8125-1682-6) Tor Bks.

Catnap: A Midnight Louie Mystery. large type ed. Carole N. Douglas. LC 93-19764. 1993. pap. 21.95 (0-7927-1643-4, Curley Lrg Print) Chivers N Amer.

Catnapper. Mel Cebulash. (Author's Signature Collection). (J). (gr. 3-8). 1992. lib. bdg. 12.79 (0-89565-878-X) Childs World.

Catnips: A Book of Haiku on Cats. Joseph Gustafson. (Illus.). 37p. (Orig.). 1984. pap. 5.95 (0-9620313-1-3) Leicester Hill Bks.

Cato - Concordantia in Catonis Librum De Agri Cultura. Ed. by Ward W. Briggs. (Alpha-Omega, Reihe A Ser.: Bd. LXX). viii, 166p. (GER.). 1983. write for info. (3-487-06696-3, Pub. by Georg Olms GW) Lubrecht & Cramer.

***Cato Design.** LC 94-61692. (Illus.). 160p. 1995. 29.95 (0-500-09928-6) Thames Hudson.

***Cato Design.** Date not set. 34.99 (1-56496-085-4) Rockport Pubs.

Cato Evaluation Report. Dinah Tennent. (C). 1989. 40.00 (0-685-52507-4, Pub. by Jordanhill College UK) St Mut.

Cato Maior de Senectute. Marcus T. Cicero. Ed. by J. G. Powell. (Cambridge Classical Texts & Commentaries Ser.: No. 28). (Illus.). 336p. 1988. 74.95 (0-521-33501-9) Cambridge U Pr.

Cato Major. Marcus T. Cicero. Ed. by Robert Kastenbaum. LC 78-22193. (Aging & Old Age Ser.). 1979. reprint ed. lib. bdg. 17.95 (0-405-11810-4) Ayer.

Cato Report, Final. Patricia Watterson. (C). 1989. 40.00 (1-85098-184-1, Pub. by Jordanhill College UK) St Mut.

Cato Report, Interim. Patricia Watterson. (C). 1989. 40.00 (1-85098-095-0, Pub. by Jordanhill College UK) St Mut.

Catolicismo Romano: Roman Catholicism. Francisco Lacueva. (SPA.). 6.95 (84-7228-001-2, 220146, Pub. by Edit Clie SP) TSELF.

Catone in Utica. Ernest Warburton. (Johann Christian Bach Ser.). 800p. 1988. lib. bdg. 164.00 (0-8240-6051-2) Garland.

Catone in Utica (Piccinni) see Italian Opera Librettos, Vol. III, 1640-1770

Caton's History of Jason. Ed. by John Munro. (EETS, ES Ser.: No. 111). 1972. reprint ed. 32.00 (0-527-00314-X) Periodicals Srv.

Catoons: The Ultimate Cat Dictionary. Trish Collins & Anthony Prince. 128p. 1992. pap. 6.95 (1-56755-012-6) Silverlake.

***Catorce Reglas Para el Conflicto Matrimonial.** Victor Ricardo. 1992. pap. 1.00 (1-885630-14-X) HLM Producciones.

Catore Reglas-Conflictos-Matrimonio (Fourteen Rules to Handle Conflict-Marriage) V. Ricardo. (SPA.). Date not set. 1.79 (0-945792-68-9, 498106) Editorial Unilit.

Cato's Letters, 4 Vols. in 2, Set. John Trenchard & Thomas Gordon. LC 74-121105. (Civil Liberties in American History Ser.). 1971. reprint ed. lib. bdg. 125.00 (0-306-71965-7) Da Capo.

Catquotes & Anecdotes, Etc., Etc. Photos & Comp. by Richard Gordon. (Illus.). 130p. (Orig.). 1994. pap. 12.95 (0-9622873-1-8) R O Gordon. CATQUOTES is a compilation of humorous cat-related quotations, proverbs, anecdotes, poems, limericks, nursery rhymes, & 22 photos. The quotes section features the wit of Mark Twain, Henry David Thoreau, Ben Franklin, Alexander Pope, Winston Churchill, Abraham Lincoln, Albert Einstein, Edgar Allen Poe & William Shakespeare. CATQUOTES includes anecdotes about Sir Issac Newton, Adlai Stevenson, & Calvin Coolidge & their cats as well as poems by Margaret Sherwood, William Wordsworth, Sir Alexander Gray, Carl Sandburg, dozens of limericks, & a host of nursery rhymes. "I got it, & I love it," says Ginny O'Reilly. "From cover to cover, CATQUOTES is a delight," echoes Mary MacDonald. "For cat lovers like me, this book is purr-fect," boasts Joe Swan. "CATQUOTES & ANECDOTES would be a wonderful addition to the cat library & with all the quotes in one place could even become a collector's piece someday,"-- Natural Pet Magazine. Order direct from Gordon Publishing, 91B Jane Ann Way, Campbell, CA 95008-2712; 408/378-2791. $12.95 p/h & CA tax incl.

Publisher Provided Annotation.

Catriona. large type ed. Robert Louis Stevenson. (Classics Ser.). 416p. 1982. 23.95 (0-7089-8089-9, Charnwood) Ulverscroft.

Catriona see Kidnapped & Catriona

Cats. David Alderton. LC 92-7611. (Eyewitness Handbks.). (Illus.). 256p. 1992. 29.95 (1-56458-073-3); 17.95 (1-56458-070-9) Dorling Kindersley.

***Cats.** David Alderton. LC 94-24739. (DK Pocket Ser.). (Illus.). 160p. (YA). (gr. 7 up). 1995. pap. 5.95 (1-56458-886-6) Dorling Kindersley.

Cats. Pascale De Bourgoing. (First Discovery Bks.). (Illus.). (J). 1992. bds. 10.95 (0-590-45269-X, 039, Cartwheel) Scholastic Inc.

Cats. Walter Foster. (How to Draw & Paint Ser.). (Illus.). 32p. (Orig.). 1989. pap. 5.95 (0-929261-74-7, HT13) W Foster Pub.

Cats. P. Jameson. (Responsible Pet Care Ser.). (Illus.). 32p. (J). (gr. 2-5). 1989. lib. bdg. 15.94 (0-86625-183-9) Rourke Corp.

Cats. H. Kavet. 64p. 1993. 8.95 (0-88032-352-3) Ivory Tower Pub.

Cats. Virginia L. Lang. 1994. 7.50 (0-934536-56-2) Rose Shell Pr.

***Cats.** H. Loxton. (Spotter's Guide Ser.). (Illus.). 64p. (YA). (gr. 4 up). 1995. pap. 4.95 (0-7460-2151-8, Usborne) EDC.

Cats. Peter Mchoy. 1988. 6.98 (1-55521-218-2) Bk Sales Inc.

Cats. Cynthia Overbeck. LC 83-17530. (Lerner Natural Science Bks.). (Illus.). 48p. (J). (gr. 4 up). 1983. lib. bdg. 19.95 (0-8225-1480-X, Lerner Publctns) Lerner Group.

Cats. Kate Petty. (First Pets Ser.). (Illus.). 24p. (J). (ps-3). 1993. pap. 3.95 (0-8120-1485-5) Barron.

Cats. Elsa Posell. LC 82-23484. (New True Bks.). (Illus.). 48p. (J). (gr. k-4). 1983. lib. bdg. 12.90 (0-516-01671-7) Childrens.

Cats. Yvonne Rees. (Nature Library). (Illus.). 64p. (J). 1991. 4.99 (0-517-05153-2) Random Hse Value.

Cats. Peggy Roalf. LC 91-73829. (Looking at Paintings Ser.). (Illus.). 48p. (J). (gr. 3-7). 1992. lib. bdg. 14.89 (1-56282-092-3); pap. 6.95 (1-56282-091-5) Hyprn Child.

Cats. Eileen Spinelli. (Childrens' Nature Library). (Illus.). 64p. (J). (gr. k-4). 1992. lib. bdg. 12.95 (1-878363-82-4, HTS Bks) Forest Hse.

Cats. Britt Strader. 192p. 1994. 19.95 (0-934429-72-3) Thunder Bay CA.

Cats. Laura Tayne. (Illus.). 10p. 1991. pap. 3.95 (0-935133-43-7) CKE Pubns.

Cats. T.F.H. Editors. (Illus.). 82p. 1989. 5.95 (0-86622-229-4, PB-103) TFH Pubns.

Cats. rev. ed. Dean Morris. LC 87-16699. (Read about Animals Ser.). (Illus.). 48p. (J). (gr. 2-6). 1987. lib. bdg. 10.95 (0-8172-3205-2) Raintree Steck-V.

Cats: A Book of Days. (Illus.). 96p. 1992. 7.00 (1-56657-024-7) NDM Pubns.

Cats: A Celebration in Words & Paintings. Helen Exley. (Words & Paintings Ser.). (Illus.). 60p. 1992. 6.99 (1-85015-328-0) Exley Giftbooks.

Cats: A Complete Pet Owner's Manual. Katrin Behrend. 64p. 1990. pap. 5.95 (0-8120-4442-8) Barron.

***Cats: A Cross Stitch Alphabet.** Julie Hasler. 1994. 18.95 (1-870586-12-3, Pub. by D Porteous Edits UK) Seven Hills Bk.

Cats: A Feline Potpourri. Ariel Books Staff. (Illus.). 80p. 1992. 4.95 (0-8362-3002-7) Andrews & McMeel.

Cats: An Educational Coloring Book. Spizzirri Publishing Co. Staff & Linda Spizzirri. (Illus.). 32p. (J). (gr. k-5). 1985. pap. 1.75 (0-86545-069-2) Spizzirri.

Cats: Anything Book. 1993. 7.99 (0-517-10003-7) Random Hse Value.

Cats: Art, Legend, History. Fabio Amodeo. LC 92-30653. (Bulfinch Library of Collectibles). 1993. 14.95 (0-8212-2008-X) Little.

***Cats: Drawing & Painting in Watercolor.** Lesley Fotherby. (Illus.). 1994. 10.98 (0-7858-0170-7) Bk Sales Inc.

***Cats: Homoeopathic Remedies.** MacLeod. 1995. pap. 11.95 (0-85207-190-6) Atrium Pubs.

Cats: Homoeopathic Remedies. George Macleod. 156p. (Orig.). 1990. pap. 19.95 (0-8464-1335-3) Beekman Pubs.

Cats: In from the Wild. Caroline Arnold. LC 92-32986. (Illus.). (J). (gr. 4-6). 1993. 19.95 (0-87614-692-2, Carolrhoda) Lerner Group.

Cats: Look & Learn. Doris De Prisco. (Illus.). 64p. 1993. 7.95 (0-7938-0092-7, KD001) TFH Pubns.

Cats: The Book of the Musical, Based on Old Possum's Book of Practical Cats. T. S. Eliot. LC 82-48026. (Illus.). 112p. 1983. pap. 14.95 (0-15-615582-6, Harvest Bks) HarBrace.

Cats: The Most Comprehensive Guide to All the World's Breeds. Paddy Cutts. 1994. 14.98 (0-681-45334-6) Longmeadow Pr.

Cats: Their Health & Care. 2nd ed. Eddie Straiton. (Illus.). 124p. 1991. 27.95 (0-85236-218-8, Pub. by Farming Pr UK) Diamond Farm Bk.

Cats: Those Wonderful Creatures. Ariel Books Staff. 1994. 4.95 (0-8362-3052-3) Andrews & McMeel.

Cats see Books for Young Explorers

Cats - Directory of Covers & Cards. Marilyn Johnson. (Illus.). 85p. 1992. pap. text ed. 10.95 (1-879390-09-4) Am First Day.

Cats' ABC. Josie Firmin. (Illus.). 32p. (J). 1994. 8.95 (0-307-17514-6, Artsts Writrs) Western Pub.

Cat's Adventure in Alphabet Town. L. Alden. LC 91-3605. (Read Around Alphabet Town Ser.). (Illus.). 32p. (J). (ps-2). 1992. lib. bdg. 12.23 (0-516-05403-1) Childrens.

Cats, Ancient & Modern. Juliet Clutton-Brock. LC 93-19128. 96p. 1993. text ed. 16.95 (0-674-10407-2) HUP.

Cats & Cat Lovers. Ann Hornaday. (Matters of Fact Ser.). (Illus.). 64p. 1988. pap. 3.50 (0-681-40696-8) Longmeadow Pr.

Cats & Dogs. (I Want to Draw Ser.). (Illus.). 64p. (Orig.). (J). (gr. 3-8). 1993. pap. 3.95 (1-56144-310-7, Honey Bear Bks) Modern Pub NYC.

Cats & Kittens Charted Designs. Julie Hasler. 48p. (Orig.). 1986. pap. 2.95 (0-486-25071-7) Dover.

An Asterisk (*) at the beginning of an entry indicates that the title is appearing in BIP for the first time.

C

Cattle Barons of Early Oregon. David Braly. LC 78-105220. (Illus.). 44p. (J). (gr. 7-12). 1982. reprint ed. pap. 4.50 (0-942206-00-2) Mediaor Co.

***Cattle Behavior.** Clive Phillips. (Illus.). 224p. 1993. text ed. 34.95 (0-85236-251-X, Pub. by Farming Pr UK) Diamond Farm Bk.

Cattle Brands: A Collection of Western Campfire Stories. Andy Adams. LC 70-150534. (Short Story Index Reprint Ser.). 1977. reprint ed. 18.95 (0-8369-3831-3) Ayer.

Cattle Brands of Baja California Sur: 1809-1885. W. Michael Mathes. LC 75-43217. (Baja California Travels Ser.: No. 40). 78p. 1978. 18.00 (0-87093-240-3) Dawsons.

Cattle Buyers & Cattle Poop by the Pound or by the Scoop. Jerry Nine. (Illus.). 64p. 1989. pap. write for info. (0-318-65802-X) Rocking Nine.

***Cattle Camp: Murrie Drovers & Their Stories.** Herb Wharton. Date not set. pap. 14.95 (0-7022-2638-6) Intl Spec Bk.

Cattle Camp Cookie: A Treasury of Western Ranches & Recipes. Kathy Weber. 390p. (Orig.). 1992. pap. 19.95 (1-878438-02-6) Ranch House Pr.

Cattle, Capitalism & Class: Ilparakuyo Maasai Transformations. Peter Rigby. (Illus.). 272p. (C). 1992. 39.95 (0-87722-954-6); pap. 18.95 (1-56639-204-7) Temple U Pr.

Cattle Country. Lorna McDonald. 250p. (C). 1990. 90.00 (0-685-67404-5, Pub. by Boolarong Pubns AT) St Mut.

Cattle Country of Peter French. 2nd ed. Giles French. LC 64-23094. (Illus.). 170p. 1982. reprint ed. pap. 9.95 (0-8323-0280-5) Binford Mort.

Cattle Drive. Ed. by Fred Rendell. (C). 1989. 35.00 (1-85098-110-8, Pub. by Jordanhill College UK) St Mut.

Cattle, Economics & Development. R. Crotty. 253p. 1980. 42.00 (0-85198-452-5) CAB Intl.

Cattle Egret: A Texas Focus & World View. Ray C. Telfair, II. (Kleberg Studies in Natural Resources). (Illus.). 144p. 1984. 16.95 (0-89096-198-0); pap. 10.95 (0-89096-200-6) Tex A&M Univ Pr.

Cattle Embryo Transfer Procedure. John L. Curtis. (Illus.). 131p. (Orig.). 1991. spiral bd. 29.95 (0-12-200240-7) Acad Pr.

Cattle Embryo Transfer Procedure. John L. Curtis. (Orig.). (C). 1990. pap. text ed. 39.50 (0-9627130-0-7) J Curtis KS.

Cattle Empire: The Fabulous Story of the 3,000,000 Acre XIT. Lewis Nordyke. Ed. by Mira Wilkins. LC 76-29745. (European Business Ser.). (Illus.). 1977. reprint ed. lib. bdg. 26.95 (0-405-09762-X) Ayer.

Cattle Feeding. John Owen. (Illus.). 182p. 24.95 (0-85236-134-3, Pub. by Farming Pr UK) Diamond Farm Bk.

Cattle Feeding: A Guide to Management. Ed. by G. B. Thompson & R. C. Albin. (Illus.). (C). 1990. pap. text ed. 19.95 (0-9627761-0-6) Trafton Printing.

Cattle Feeding: A Guide to Management. rev. ed. Ed. by G. B. Thompson & R. C. Albin. (Illus.). (C). 1991. reprint ed. pap. text ed. write for info. (0-9627761-1-4) Trafton Printing.

Cattle Footcare & Claw Trimming. E. Toussaint Raven. (Illus.). 128p. (Orig.). 1985. pap. 27.95 (0-85236-149-1, Pub. by Farming Pr UK) Diamond Farm Bk.

Cattle Genetic Resources. Ed. by C. G. Hickman. (World Animal Science Ser.: No. 7B). 328p. 1991. 177.25 (0-444-88638-9) Elsevier.

Cattle, Horses & Men of the Western Range. John H. Culley. LC 84-2769. (Illus.). 337p. 1984. reprint ed. 40.00 (0-8165-0891-7); reprint ed. pap. 16.95 (0-8165-0865-8) U of Ariz Pr.

Cattle, Horses, Sky, & Grass: Cowboy Poetry of the Late Twentieth Century. Ed. by Warren E. Miller. LC 94-6724. (Illus.). 224p. 1994. 21.95 (0-87358-570-4); pap. 14.95 (0-87358-578-X) Northland AZ.

Cattle, Horses, Sky, & Grass: Cowboy Poetry of the Late Twentieth Century. limited ed. Ed. by Warren E. Miller. LC 94-6724. (Illus.). 224p. 1994. 40.00 (0-87358-579-8) Northland AZ.

Cattle Housing Systems, Lameness & Behaviour. Ed. by H. K. Wierenga & O. J. Peterse. (Current Topics in Veterinary Medicine & Animal Science Ser.). 1987. lib. bdg. 92.00 (0-89838-862-7) Kluwer Ac.

Cattle in the Cold Desert. 2nd ed. James A. Young & Abbott B. Sparks. (Illus.). 255p. 1988. reprint ed. pap. 6.00 (0-87421-137-9) Utah St U Pr.

Cattle Industry in Northern Nigeria, 1900-1939. Florence A. Okediji. (African Humanities Ser.). (Illus.). (Orig.). 1973. pap. text ed. 2.00 (0-941934-07-1) Indiana Africa.

Cattle Inspection. Ed. by Institute of Medicine Staff. 114p. 1990. pap. 19.00 (0-309-04345-X) Natl Acad Pr.

Cattle King. Edward F. Treadwell. LC 81-50165. (Illus.). xii, 375p. 1981. reprint ed. pap. 9.95 (0-934136-10-6) Western Tanager.

Cattle Kings. Lewis Atherton. LC 61-13722. (Illus.). xii, 342p. 1972. reprint ed. pap. 9.95 (0-8032-5759-7, Bison Books) U of Nebr Pr.

Cattle Kings of Texas. C. L. Douglas. LC 89-21772. (Illus.). 400p. 1989. pap. 14.95 (0-938349-45-7) State House Pr.

Cattle Kings of Texas. Dian L. Malouf. LC 91-73402. (Illus.). 176p. 1991. 39.95 (0-941831-69-8) Beyond Words Pub.

***Cattle Lameness & Hoofcare.** Roger Blowey. (Illus.). 96p. 1993. text ed. 36.95 (0-85236-252-8, Pub. by Farming Pr UK) Diamond Farm Bk.

Cattle Lords & Clansmen: The Social Structure of Early Ireland. 2nd ed. Nerys Patterson. (C). 1994. reprint ed. pap. text ed. 21.95 (0-268-00800-0) U of Notre Dame Pr.

Cattle Management. Cheryl May. 350p. (C). 1981. teacher ed write for info. (0-8359-0722-8, Reston) P-H.

Cattle Nutrition Primer. D. Porter Price. 1986. write for info. (0-9606246-4-3) SWI.

Cattle on a Thousand Hills Southern California, 1850-1880. Robert G. Cleland. (Illus.). 392p. 1990. reprint ed. 24.95 (0-87328-006-7); reprint ed. pap. 12.95 (0-87328-097-0) Huntington Lib.

Cattle Raid of Cualnge. Tain Bo Cuailnge. LC 77-177729. (Grimm Library: No. 16). reprint ed. 29.50 (0-404-53559-3) AMS Pr.

Cattle-Raids & Courtships: Medieval Narrative Genres in a Traditional Context. Vincent A. Dunn. LC 88-37675. (Garland Monographs in Medieval Literature: Vol. 2). 288p. 1989. 20.00 (0-8240-4428-2, 866) Garland.

Cattle Raising on the Plains, 1900-1961. John T. Schlebecker. LC 63-14691. 249p. reprint ed. pap. 71.00 (0-317-27115-6, 2024692) Bks Demand.

Cattle Ranchers. H. Upton. (Wild West in American History Ser.). (Illus.). 32p. (J). (gr. 3-8). 1990. lib. bdg. 18.00 (0-86625-372-6) Rourke Corp.

Cattle Reproduction Primer. D. Porter Price. 1986. write for info. (0-9606246-5-1) SWI.

Cattle Towns. Robert R. Dykstra. LC 83-6485. (Illus.). xii, 412p. 1983. reprint ed. pap. 12.95 (0-8032-6561-1, Bison Books) U of Nebr Pr.

Cattle-Trailing Industry: Between Supply & Demand, 1866-1890. Jimmy M. Skaggs. LC 91-50312. (Illus.). 186p. 1991. pap. 14.95 (0-8061-2391-5) U of Okla Pr.

Cattle Trespass Act, 1871. J. N. Jaiswal. 132p. 1982. 65.00 (0-317-54650-3) St Mut.

Cattle Trespass Act, 1871. 2nd rev. ed. N. Jaiswal. (C). 1982. 40.00 (0-685-39790-4) St Mut.

Cattle, Women, & Wells: Managing Household Survival in the Sahel. Camilla Toulmin. (Illus.). 320p. 1993. 69.00 (0-19-829006-3) OUP.

***Cattleboat to Oxford: The Education of R.I.W. Westgate.** Ed. by Sheila M. Westgate. (Illus.). 208p. 1994. 21.95 (0-8027-1300-9) Walker & Co.

Cattleman. large type ed. R. S. Porteous. 368p. 1982. 23.95 (0-7089-8070-8, Charnwood) Ulverscroft.

Cattleman vs. Sheepherders: Violence in the West, 1880-1920. Bill O'Neal. 1989. 16.95 (0-89015-665-4) Sunbelt Media.

Cattleman's Backcountry Florida. Alto Adams, Jr. LC 84-20890. (Illus.). 54p. 1985. pap. 15.95 (0-8130-0809-3) U Press Fla.

***Cattleman's Choice.** Palmer. 1995. mass mkt. 4.99 (1-55166-056-3, Mira Bks) Harlequin Bks.

Cattlemen. W. R. McAfee. 228p. 1989. 29.95 (0-9623394-0-7) Davis Mntn Pr.

Cattlemen. Bill Pronzini. 1987. pap. 2.50 (0-449-13145-9) Fawcett.

Cattlemen. W. R. McAfee. 270p. 1991. reprint ed. 27.95 (0-9623394-1-5) Davis Mntn Pr.

Cattlemen: From the Rio Grande Across the Far Marias. Mari Sandoz. LC 77-14078. xii, 527p. 1978. reprint ed. pap. 16.95 (0-8032-5882-8, Bison Books) U of Nebr Pr.

Cattleyas & Their Relatives: The Cattleyas, Vol. I. Carl L. Withner. LC 88-8560. (Illus.). 147p. 1988. 29.95 (0-88192-099-1) Timber.

Cattleyas & Their Relatives Vol. II: The Laelias. Carl L. Withner. LC 88-8560. (Illus.). 160p. 1990. 31.95 (0-88192-161-0) Timber.

Cattleyas & Their Relatives Vol. III: Schomburgkia, Sophronitis, & Other South American Genera. Carl L. Withner. LC 88-8560. (Illus.). 1993. 39.95 (0-88192-269-2) Timber.

Catullan Games. Sandor Rakos. Tr. by Maria Korosy. LC 89-60942. 80p. (Orig.). 1989. pap. 9.00 (0-910395-53-5) Marlboro Pr.

***Catullan Provocations: Lyric Poetry & the Drama of Position.** William Fitzgerald. (Classics & Contemporary Thought Ser.: Vol. 1). 1996. 45.00 (0-520-20062-4) U CA Pr.

Catullan Self-Revelation. Eve Adler. Ed. by W. R. Connor. LC 80-2638. (Monographs in Classical Studies). (Illus.). 1981. lib. bdg. 34.95 (0-405-14026-6) Ayer.

Catullus. John Ferguson. viii, 363p. 1985. 25.00 (0-87291-158-6) Coronado Pr.

Catullus. Charles Martin. (Hermes Bks.). 192p. (Orig.). (C). 1992. text ed. 32.00 (0-300-05199-9); pap. text ed. 13.00 (0-300-05200-6) Yale U Pr.

Catullus. Gaius V. Catullus. Ed. by Elmer T. Merrill. 273p. 1965. reprint ed. 29.95 (0-674-10350-5) HUP.

Catullus. C. J. Fordyce. 456p. 1990. reprint ed. pap. 29.95 (0-19-872147-1) OUP.

Catullus. Ed. by Elmer T. Merrill. (College Classical Ser.). (LAT.). 1988. reprint ed. text ed. 32.50 (0-89241-023-X); reprint ed. pap. text ed. 16.00 (0-89241-381-6) Caratzas.

Catullus: Love & Hate: Selected Short Poems Series. Ed. & Tr. by Leo M. Kaiser. 42p. (Orig.). (ENG & LAT.). 1986. pap. 8.00 (0-86516-180-1) Bolchazy-Carducci.

Catullus & His Renaissance Readers. Julia H. Gaisser. LC 92-14489. (Illus.). 464p. 1993. 75.00 (0-19-814882-8, Clarendon Pr) OUP.

Catullus & His World: A Reappraisal. T. P. Wiseman. (Illus.). 305p. 1985. 59.95 (0-521-26606-8) Cambridge U Pr.

Catullus & His World: A Reappraisal. T. P. Wiseman. (Illus.). 305p. 1986. pap. 21.95 (0-521-31968-4) Cambridge U Pr.

Catullus & Horace. Andrew C. Aronson & Robert Boughner. 1988. pap. text ed. 14.88 (0-582-36750-6, 72526) Longman.

Catullus & Horace: Selections from Latin Readings. Robert P. Sonkowsky. (Living Voice of Greek & Latin Literature Ser.). 102p. 1988. audio 29.95 (0-88432-262-9, S23800) Audio-Forum.

Catullus' Carmen 61. Paolo Fedeli. (London Studies in Classical Philology: Vol. 8). viii, 180p. (C). 1983. 46.00 (90-70265-62-1, Pub. by Gieben NE) Benjamins North Am.

Catullus' Indictment of Rome: The Meaning of Catullus 64. David Konstan. vii, 149p. 1977. pap. 34.00 (90-256-0742-X, Pub. by A M Hakkert NE) Benjamins North Am.

Catullus of William Hull. Catullus. Tr. by William Hull. 8.00 (0-89253-791-4) Ind-US Inc.

Catullus, Poems: A Commentary. Kenneth Quinn. LC 76-94751. (C). 1971. pap. text ed. 23.00 (0-312-12495-3) St Martin.

Catullus Redivivus. Sam Hamill. 96p. (Orig.). 1986. pap. 23.00 (0-911287-10-8) Blue Begonia.

Catullus, Tibullus & Pervigilium Veneris. Ed. by E. H. Warmington. (Loeb Classical Library: No. 6). 394p. (ENG & LAT.). 1950. 18.95 (0-674-99007-2) HUP.

Catundra. Stephen Cosgrove. (Serendipity Bks). (Illus.). 32p. (Orig.). (J). (gr. 1-4). 1978. pap. 2.95 (0-8431-0571-2) Price Stern.

Catuvellauni. K. Branigan. (Peoples of Roman Britain Ser.). (Illus.). 236p. (C). 1991. text ed. 28.00 (0-86299-255-9) A Sutton Pub.

CATV: End of a Dream. 1974. 2.00 (0-686-09556-1) Network Project.

CATV & Fiber Optics: The Impact of Strategic Alliances, Teko Competition & Technological Development. IGIC, Inc. Staff. 250p. 1993. pap. 1,995.00 (1-56851-103-5) Info Gatekeepers.

CATV & Video Application of Fiber Otics. rev. ed. IGIC, Inc. Staff. (Fiber Optic Reprint Ser.: Vol. 12). (Illus.). 200p. 1994. pap. 75.00 (1-56851-061-6) Info Gatekeepers.

***CATV Cable & RF Distribution Products - U. S. Markets, Competitors, & Opportunities: 1995-2000 Analysis & Forecasts.** Amadee Bender et al. 170p. 1995. pap. text ed. 3,490.00 (1-878218-56-5) World Info Tech.

CATV, Class A USoA. 120p. 1977. ring bd. 5.50 (0-317-01624-5) NARUC.

CATV, Class B USoA. 72p. 1978. ring bd. 4.00 (0-318-14975-3) NARUC.

***Catv Measurements Handbook.** Jeff Thomas. 1995. text ed. 40.00 (0-13-306382-8) P-H.

CatWalk. Mary Stolz. LC 82-47576. (Trophy Bk.). (Illus.). 128p. (J). (gr. 3-7). 1985. reprint ed. pap. 3.95 (0-06-440155-3, Trophy) HarpC Child Bks.

Catwalk: Fashion Models of Japan. Illus. by Curtis Knapp. (Studio Editions Ser.). 88p. 1993. 49.95 (0-8048-1908-4) C E Tuttle.

Catwatching. Desmond Morris. 1987. 13.00 (0-517-56518-8, Crown) Crown Pub Group.

Catwatching. Desmond Morris. 1993. pap. 8.00 (0-517-88053-9, Crown) Crown Pub Group.

***Catwatching.** Desmond Morris. 1994. 17.99 (0-517-12065-8) Random Hse Value.

Catwings. Ursula K. Le Guin. LC 87-33104. (Illus.). 48p. (J). (gr. 2-5). 1988. 11.95 (0-531-05759-3); lib. bdg. 11.99 (0-531-08359-4) Orchard Bks Watts.

Catwings. Ursula K. Le Guin. 1990. pap. 2.95 (0-590-42833-0) Scholastic Inc.

Catwings. Ursula K. LeGuin. (Illus.). 64p. (J). (gr. 2-5). 1992. pap. 2.95 (0-590-46072-2) Scholastic Inc.

Catwings Return. Ursula K. Le Guin. LC 88-17902. (Illus.). 56p. (J). (gr. 2-5). 1989. 11.95 (0-531-05803-4); lib. bdg. 11.99 (0-531-08403-5) Orchard Bks Watts.

Catwing's Return. Ursula K. Le Guin. (J). (ps-3). 1991. pap. 2.95 (0-590-42832-2) Scholastic Inc.

Catwise. Wilbur Pippin & Marian Winters. LC 78-27344. (Illus.). 1979. pap. 5.95 (0-394-73786-5) Knopf.

Catwise. Wilbur Pippin & Marion Winters. (Illus.). 96p. 1991. reprint ed. 8.99 (0-517-06506-1) Random Hse Value.

Catwoman. Lynn Abbey & Robert Asprin. 208p. 1992. mass mkt. 4.99 (0-446-36043-0) Warner Bks.

Catwoman: Her Sister's Keeper. Mindy Newell. Ed. by Dennis O'Neil. (Illus.). 104p. 1991. pap. 9.95 (0-930289-97-8) DC Comics.

Catwoman: Her Sister's Keeper. Mindy Newell et al. (Illus.). 1992. reprint ed. pap. 9.99 (0-446-39366-5) Warner Bks.

Catwoman Defiant. Peter Milligan. Ed. by Dennis O'Neil. 48p. 1992. pap. 4.95 (1-56389-071-2) DC Comics.

Caty: A Biography of Catharine Littlefield Greene. John F. Stegeman & Janet A. Stegeman. LC 77-76317. (Brown Thrasher Bks.). 272p. 1985. reprint ed. pap. 11.95 (0-8203-0792-0) U of Ga Pr.

Catzilla. Mike Thaler. (J). (gr. 4-7). 1991. pap. 2.95 (0-671-73297-8) S&S Trade.

Caucasian & the Negro in the United States: They Must Separate, If Not, Then Extermination. a Proposed Solution : Colonization. William P. Calhoun. Ed. by Gerald Grob. LC 76-46070. (Anti-Movements in America Ser.). 1977. reprint ed. lib. bdg. 19.95 (0-405-09944-4) Ayer.

Caucasian Book of Longevity & Well-Being. Murat Yagan. LC 88-40222. 67p. (Orig.). 1988. pap. 8.00 (0-939660-28-8) Threshold VT.

Caucasian Chalk Circle. Bertolt Brecht. Ed. by John Willett & Ralph Manheim. Tr. by James Stern et al. 144p. (C). 1994. pap. 8.95 (1-55970-253-2) Arcade Pub Inc.

***Caucasian Knot: The History & Geopolitics of Nagorno-Karabagh.** Levon Chorbajian et al. (Politics in Contemporary Asia Ser.). 224p. (C). 1994. text ed. 55.00 (1-85649-287-7, Pub. by Zed Books UK); pap. 22.50 (1-85649-288-5, Pub. by Zed Books UK) Humanities.

Caucasian Rugs. Ulrich Schurmann. LC 90-60466. (Illus.). 359p. 1990. reprint ed. 160.00 (0-9625857-0-X) Old Ninetynine Assocs.

Caucasians Only: The Supreme Court, the NAACP, & the Restrictive Covenant Cases. Clement E. Vose. LC 59-8758. (Illus.). 310p. reprint ed. pap. 88.40 (0-7837-4695-4, 2044442) Bks Demand.

Cauchemar. David Goodis. 278p. (FRE.). 1991. pap. 10.95 (0-7859-2615-1, 2070383814) Fr & Eur.

Cauchy-Goursat Problem. Paul DuChateau. LC 52-42839. (Memoirs Ser.: No. 1/118). 60p. 1972. pap. 16.00 (0-8218-1818-X, MEMO 1/118) Am Math.

Cauchy Method of Residues. Jovan D. Keckic & Dragoslav S. Mitrinovic. 1984. lib. bdg. 67.00 (0-318-00441-0) Kluwer Ac.

Cauchy Method of Residues, Vol. 2: Theory & Applications. Dragoslav S. Mitrinovic. (Mathematics & Its Applications Ser.). 208p. (C). 1993. lib. bdg. 86.50 (0-7923-2311-4) Kluwer Ac.

Cauchy Problem. H. O. Fattorini. (Encyclopedia of Mathematics & Its Applications Ser.: No. 18). 1984. 115.00 (0-521-30238-2) Cambridge U Pr.

***Cauchy Problem for Solutions of Elliptic Equations.** Nikolai N. Tarkhanov. LC 95-12878. (Mathematical Topics Ser.: Vol. 7). 1995. write for info. (3-05-501663-7) VCH Pubs.

Cauchy Transform, Potential Theory & Conformal Mapping. Bell. 1992. 49.95 (0-8493-8270-X, QA360) CRC Pr.

Caucus System in American Politics. Ed. by Leon Stein. LC 73-19189. (Politics & People Ser.). 186p. 1974. reprint ed. 17.95 (0-405-05861-6) Ayer.

Caudill: Misioneros Audaces. Tom McMinn. (Meet the Missionary-Conoce al Misionero Ser.). Orig. Title: Caudills: Courageous Missionaries. 64p. 1987. pap. 2.75 (0-311-01072-5) Casa Bautista.

Caudillo, a Portrait of Antonio Guzman Blanco. George S. Wise. LC 72-104232. 190p. 1971. reprint ed. text ed. 35.00 (0-8371-3349-1, WICA, Greenwood Pr) Greenwood.

Caudillo, Estado, Nacion: Literatura, Historia e Ideologia en el Uruguay. Abril Trigo. LC 90-80200. 280p. 1990. 18.00 (0-935318-17-8) Edins Hispamerica.

Caudillos: Dictators in Spanish America. Intro. by Hugh Hamill. LC 91-50863. (Illus.). 384p. (C). 1992. 26.95 (0-8061-2412-1) U of Okla Pr.

***Caudillos: Dictators in Spanish America.** Ed. & Intro. by Hugh Hamill. LC 91-50863. (Illus.). 384p. 1995. pap. 14.95 (0-8061-2428-8) U of Okla Pr.

Caudillos in Spanish America, 1800-1850. John Lynch. (Illus.). 420p. 1992. 76.00 (0-19-821135-X) OUP.

Caudills: Courageous Missionaries see Caudill: Misioneros Audaces

Caudine Country: The Old World & an American Childhood. Anthony M. Gisolfi. LC 85-61281. (Senda Biografica Ser.). (Illus.). 223p. (Orig.). 1985. 18.95 (0-918454-55-7); pap. 12.95 (0-918454-50-6) Senda Nueva.

Caught. Gregg Lewis. 1987. pap. 6.95 (0-89066-091-3) World Wide Pubs.

Caught! Willo D. Roberts. LC 93-14422. 160p. (J). (gr. 3-7). 1994. text ed. 14.95 (0-689-31903-7, Atheneum Bks Young) S&S Childrens.

Caught by One Wing. Linda Hasselstrom. 59p. 1990. reprint ed. pap. 4.95 (0-944024-20-3) Spoon Riv Poetry.

***Caught Dead.** Bridget McKenna. 240p. (Orig.). 1995. pap. text ed. 4.99 (0-425-14493-3, Prime Crime) Berkley Pub.

Caught Dead in Philadelphia. Gillian Roberts. 1988. mass mkt. 4.95 (0-345-35340-4) Ballantine.

Caught in a Still Place. Jonathan Lerner. 128p. (Orig.). 1990. pap. 9.95 (1-85242-146-0) Serpents Tail.

Caught in a Tornado: A Chinese American Woman Survives the Cultural Revolution. James R. Ross. 192p. 1994. text ed. 21.95 (1-55553-192-X) NE U Pr.

Caught in a Trap. Rick Stanley. 256p. 1992. 17.99 (0-8499-0979-1) Word Inc.

Caught in a Willow Net. Louis Oliver. LC 83-80757. (American Indian Poetry Ser.). 88p. 1983. 5.00 (0-912678-57-7, Greenfld Rev Pr) Greenfld Rev Lit.

Caught in Kuwait. Fern G. Babcock. (Destiny Ser.). 122p. 1992. pap. 4.99 (0-8163-1087-4) Pacific Pr Pub Assn.

Caught in the Act. Jane Archer. LC 90-53079. (Orig.). (C). 1991. pap. 6.00 (0-88734-222-1) Players Pr.

***Caught in the Act.** Janis R. Hudson. (Loveswept Ser.: No. 731). 1995. pap. 3.50 (0-553-44462-X, Loveswept) Bantam.

Caught in the Act. Betina Krahn. 384p. 1990. mass mkt. 4.50 (0-380-75778-8) Avon.

Caught in the Act. Joan L. Nixon. (YA). (gr. 7 up). 1989. mass mkt. 3.99 (0-553-27912-2, Starfire) Bantam.

Caught in the Act. Patricia Sealey. (Junior African Writers Ser.). (Illus.). (J). (gr. 3-4). 1992. pap. 2.95 (0-7910-2901-8) Chelsea Hse.

Caught in the Act: A Guide to Assessment, Provision & Law Relating to Children with Special Needs. Harry Chasty & John Friel. 200p. 1991. pap. 24.95 (1-85302-096-6, Pub. by J Kingsley Pubs UK) Taylor & Francis.

Caught in the Act: The Decisive Reading of Some Notable Men & Women & Its Influence on Their Actions & Attitudes. Edwin Castagna. LC 82-10276. 228p. 1982. 17.50 (0-8108-1566-4) Scarecrow.

***Caught in the Act: The Feldberg Investigation.** MacDonald & Acig. 1994. pap. 9.95 (1-897766-05-X, Pub. by Jon Pubng UK) InBook.

Caught in the Act: Theatricality in the Nineteenth-Century English Novel. Joseph Litvak. LC 91-10222. (C). 1992. 42.00 (0-520-07452-1); pap. 15.00 (0-520-07454-8) U CA Pr.

***Caught in the Acts.** Edward Whetstone. 1995. pap. write for info. (0-7880-0443-3) CSS OH.

Caught in the Butterfly Net. Ed. by Ferill J. Rice & LaVeria McMichael. 140p. 1992. pap. 19.95 (0-9632974-0-6) Fenton Art Glass.

Caught in the Conflict: My Life with James Watt. 2nd ed. Leilani Watt. LC 92-93028. 191p. 1992. reprint ed. pap. 7.99 (0-9632018-0-8) Wrds Encourage.

An Asterisk (*) at the beginning of an entry indicates that the title is appearing in BIP for the first time.

Caught in the Crisis: Women & the U. S. Economy Today. Teresa Amott. LC 93-7326. (Cornerstone Bks.). (Illus.). 144p. (J). (ps-12). 1993. text ed. 22.00 (0-85345-845-6); pap. text ed. 10.00 (0-85345-846-4) Monthly Rev.

***Caught in the Crossfire.** Georgia L. Barnes-Payne. 200p. (Orig.). 1995. pap. 7.95 (0-7610-0065-8) NW Pub.

Caught in the Crossfire: Children & the Northern Ireland Conflict. Ed Cairns. (Irish Studies). 192p. 1987. text ed. 29.95x (0-8156-2421-2) Syracuse U Pr.

Caught in the Crossfire: Helping Christians Discuss Homosexuality. Sally B. Geis & Donald E. Messer. LC 93-33341. 192p. (Orig.). 1994. pap. 12.95 (0-687-09524-7) Abingdon.

***Caught in the Crossfire: The Baptism That Demonstrates the Faith That Justifies.** Boyd Lammiman. 1994. pap. 5.95 (1-56794-074-9) Star Bible.

Caught in the Crossfire: The Impact of Divorce on Young People. Lorraine Henricks. 128p. (Orig.). 1991. pap. 8.95 (0-929162-29-3) PIA Pr.

Caught in the Crossfire: The R. E. "Gus" Payne Story. R. E. Payne. Ed. by Sidney L. Arroyo. (Illus.). 217p. (Orig.). 1995. pap. 14.95 (1-885308-01-9) Sr Polit Action.

***Caught in the Crossfire: Young Victims of War Speak Out.** Maria Oussiemi & Lamia Abuhaidar. (YA). 1995. 19.95 (0-8027-8363-5); lib. bdg. 20.85 (0-8027-8364-3) Walker & Co.

Caught in the Crossfire see Children of Divorce

Caught in the Loop: How Eastern Money Won the West . . . Or Did It? L. S. Anderson. 224p. (Orig.). 1992. pap. 12.95 (0-9633672-1-8) Hot Iron Pr.

Caught in the Middle. Kelly A. Murray. 1993. 10.95 (0-8062-4730-4) Carlton.

Caught in the Middle. Francine Pascal. (Sweet Valley High Ser.: No. 42). 160p. 1988. pap. 2.99 (0-553-26951-8) Bantam.

Caught in the Middle. Beverly B. Smith & Pat DeVorss. 240p. 1988. pap. 8.99 (0-8423-0355-3) Tyndale.

Caught in the Middle: A Dichotomy of an African American Man (They Called Him Troublemaker) Thomas H. McPhatter. (Illus.). (Orig.). (C). 1993. write for info. (0-9634658-0-5); pap. 24.95 (0-9634658-1-3) Audacity Pubns.

Caught in the Middle: A Leadership Guide for Partnership in the Workplace. Rick Maurer. LC 91-23238. 258p. 1992. 30.00 (1-56327-004-8) Prod Press.

Caught in the Middle: Education Reform for Young Adolescents in California Public Schools. California Department of Education Staff. 162p. 1987. pap. 7.50 (0-8011-0488-2) Calif Education.

Caught in the Middle: How to Survive & Thrive in Today's Management Squeeze. Lynda C. McDermott. LC 92-20791. 1992. text ed. 21.95 (0-13-121229-X) P-H.

Caught in the Middle: How to Survive & Thrive in Today's Management Squeeze. Lynda C. McDermott. 1994. pap. 12.95 (0-13-311424-4) P-H.

Caught in the Middle: How to Unleash the Potential of Average Students. Peggy O. Gonder. 28p. (Orig.). 1991. pap. 1.50 (0-87652-167-7, 021-00340) Am Assn Sch Admin.

Caught in the Middle: Meeting God in the Midst of Problems. Henry Liebersath. 176p. (Orig.). 1987. 8.95 (0-8245-0822-X) Crossroad NY.

Caught in the Middle: Protecting the Children of High-Conflict Divorce. Carla Garrity & Mitchell Baris. 256p. 1994. text ed. 19.95 (0-02-911330-X) Free Pr.

Caught in the Mix: An Oral Portrait of Homelessness. Philip M. Bulman. LC 92-43385. 224p. 1993. text ed. 52.95 (0-86569-229-7, T229, Auburn Hse) Greenwood.

Caught in the Moment. Linda U. Foley. (Illus.). 62p. (Orig.). 1991. pap. write for info. (0-9629147-0-3) LUF Enterp.

Caught in the Moving Mountains. Gloria Skurzynski. (Illus.). 144p. (J). (gr. 7 up). 1994. reprint ed. pap. 4.95 (0-688-12945-5, Pub. by Beech Tree Bks) Morrow.

Caught in the Net. Tates Locke & Bob Ibach. LC 81-86382. (Illus.). 176p. (Orig.). 1982. text ed. 17.95 (0-88011-044-9, PLOC0044) Human Kinetics.

***Caught in the Net: The Global Tuna Industry, Environmentalists, & the State.** Alessandro Bonanno & Douglas Constance. (Illus.). 346p. (C). 1996. 40.00 (0-7006-0738-2); pap. 19.95 (0-7006-0739-0) U Pr of KS.

Caught in the Shadows. C. A. Haddad. (Worldwide Library Mystery). 1994. mass mkt. 3.99 (0-373-26138-1, 1-26138-7) Harlequin Bks.

***Caught in the Sluice: Tales from Alaska's Gold Camps.** Neil Davis. (Illus.). 169p. 1994. 19.95 (0-9632596-2-8); pap. 13.95 (0-9632596-1-X) McRoy & Blackburn.

***Caught in the Storm.** Seydou Badian. Tr. by Marie-Therese Noiset. 208p. 1995. 24.00 (0-89410-793-3); pap. 14.00 (0-89410-794-1) Three Continents.

***Caught in the Web of Words: James A. H. Murray & the "Oxford English Dictionary"** Murray. 1995. pap. text ed. 16.00 (0-300-06310-5) Yale U Pr.

Caught in the Web of Words: James A. H. Murray & the "Oxford English Dictionary" K. M. Murray. LC 77-76309. (Illus.). 1977. 45.00 (0-300-02131-3) Yale U Pr.

Caught Looking: Feminism, Pornography & Censorship. Hannah Alderfer et al. (Illus.). 96p. (Orig.). 1987. pap. 10.00 (0-9617884-0-2) Caught Looking.

Caught Looking: Feminism, Pornography & Censorship. 3rd rev. ed. Ed. by Ellis et al. (Illus.). 96p. reprint ed. 15.95 (0-942986-12-1) LongRiver Bks.

Caught on the Fly. Arthur S. Newberry. (Illus.). 306p. 1989. reprint ed. 30.00 (0-9620609-1-7) Meadow Run Pr.

Caught Short! Eddie Cantor. 13.95 (0-89190-984-2, Am Repr) Amereon Ltd.

Caught Short! A Saga of Wailing Wall Street. Eddie Cantor. (Illus.). 48p. 1992. reprint ed. pap. text ed. 7.00 (0-87034-108-1) Fraser Pub Co.

Caught up in Time: Arduous Treks of Pioneers Who Migrated to the Untamed West. Mary R. Dees. 200p. (Orig.). 1991. pap. 9.95 (0-9630600-0-7) Marmor.

Caught up in Time: Oral History Narratives of Appalachian Vietnam Veterans. John Hennen. LC 88-71124. 144p. (Orig.). (C). 1989. pap. 8.00 (0-916383-60-1) Aegina Pr.

Caught up into Paradise. Richard E. Eby. 1984. reprint ed. pap. 4.99 (0-8007-8489-8) Revell.

Caught 'Ya! Grammar with a Giggle. Jane B. Kiester. (Illus.). 253p. (Orig.). 1990. pap. 14.95 (0-929895-04-5) Maupin Hse.

Caughtya Again! Jane B. Kiester. 320p. (Orig.). 1992. pap. 14.95 (0-929895-09-6) Maupin Hse.

Cauldron. Larry Bond. 768p. 1994. mass mkt. 6.50 (0-446-60026-1, Warner Vision) Warner Bks.

Cauldron: Celtic Mythology & Witchcraft. Rhuddlwm Gawr. LC 85-73764. (Illus.). 224p. (Orig.). 1989. 18.95 (0-931760-43-7, CP 10121); pap. 15.95 (0-931760-21-6) Camelot GA.

Cauldron & the Grail: Ritual Astronomy & the Stones of Ancient Europe. Hank Harrison. Ed. by Eckhard Gerdes. (Grail Trilogy Ser.: Vol. I). (Illus.). 288p. (C). 1993. 22.50 (0-918501-22-9); pap. 18.50 (0-918501-23-7) Archives Pr.

Cauldron of Blood. Jim Schutze. 1989. mass mkt. 4.95 (0-380-75997-7) Avon.

Cauldron of Change: Myths, Mysteries & Magick of the Goddess. De-Anna Alba. 256p. (Orig.). 1994. pap. 13.95 (1-878980-08-4) Delphi IL.

Cauldron of Ethnicity in the Modern World. Manning Nash. LC 88-29522. 152p. 1989. lib. bdg. 24.95 (0-226-56866-0); pap. text ed. 9.95 (0-226-56867-9) U Ch Pr.

***Cauldron of Halloween Ideas: Literature-Based & Cross Curricular.** Lorrie Birchall. 1993. pap. 7.95 (0-590-49342-6) Scholastic Inc.

Cauldrons in the Cosmos: Nuclear Astrophysics. Claus E. Rolfs & William S. Rodney. (Theoretical Astrophysics Ser.). (Illus.). xviii, 562p. 1988. pap. text ed. 34.95 (0-226-72457-3) U Ch Pr.

Caulkers & Carpenters in a New World: The Shipyards of Colonial Guayaquil. Lawrence A. Clayton. LC 80-11547. (Papers in International Studies: Latin America Ser.: No. 8). 199p. (Orig.). reprint ed. pap. 56.80 (0-7837-1331-2, 2041479) Bks Demand.

Caurasi Pad of Sri Hit Harivams: Introduction, Translation, Notes, & Edited Hindi Text. Ed. by Charles S. White. LC 76-54207. (Asian Studies at Hawaii: No. 16). 212p. 1977. pap. text ed. 10.50 (0-8248-0359-0) UH Pr.

Causa. Eulalia Donoso. LC 91-73416. 156p. 1991. 15.00 (0-89729-615-X) Ediciones.

Causa: The Migrant Farmworkers' Story. Dana C. De Ruiz & Richard Larios. LC 92-12806. (Stories of America Ser.). (Illus.). 92p. (J). (gr. 2-5). 1992. lib. bdg. 21.34 (0-8114-7231-0) Raintree Steck-V.

Causa Chicana: The Movement for Justice. Ed. by Margaret M. Mangold. LC 72-92083. 236p. reprint ed. pap. 67.30 (0-685-24010-X, 2031597) Bks Demand.

CAUSA Lecture Manual. CAUSA Institute Staff. (Illus.). (Orig.). (C). 1985. pap. text ed. 5.00 (0-933901-00-3) Causa Intl.

Causal AI Models: Steps Toward Applications. Ed. by Werner Horn. 322p. 1989. 70.00 (1-56032-048-6) Hemisp Pub.

Causal Analysis of the Relationship Between Learning Disabilities & Juvenile Delinquency. National Center for State Courts Staff. 103p. 1984. 6.18 (0-685-16955-3, LDJD-016) Natl Ctr St Courts.

***Causal Analysis with Panel Data.** Steven E. Finkel. (Quantitative Applications in the Social Science Ser.). 96p. 1995. pap. text ed. 9.95 (0-8039-3896-9) Sage.

***Causal Cognition: A Multidisciplinary Approach.** Ed. by D. Sperber et al. (Illus.). 710p. 1995. text ed. 110.00 (0-19-852314-9) OUP.

Causal Explanation & Model Building in History, Economics, & the New Economic History. Peter D. McClelland. LC 74-25372. (Illus.). 296p. 1975. 38.95 (0-8014-0929-2) Cornell U Pr.

Causal Inference. Ed. & Intro. by Kenneth J. Rothman. LC 87-22227. 207p. (Orig.). 1988. pap. text ed. 25.00 (0-917227-03-4) Epidemiology.

Causal Mechanisms of Behavioural Development. Ed. by Jerry A. Hogan & Johan J. Bolhuis. (Illus.). 480p. (C). 1994. 54.95 (0-521-43241-3) Cambridge U Pr.

Causal Modeling. Herbert B. Asher. LC 76-25696. (Quantitative Applications in the Social Sciences Ser.: Vol. 3). 1976. 9.95 (0-8039-0654-4) Sage.

Causal Models in Panel & Experimental Designs. Ed. by H. M. Blalock, Jr. LC 84-24276. (Illus.). 297p. (C). 1985. lib. bdg. 54.95 (0-202-30315-2); pap. text ed. 32.95 (0-202-30316-0) Aldine de Gruyter.

Causal Models in the Social Sciences. 2nd ed. Ed. by H. M. Blalock, Jr. LC 84-24258. (Illus.). 458p. (C). 1985. lib. bdg. 54.95 (0-202-30313-6); pap. text ed. 34.95 (0-202-30314-4) Aldine de Gruyter.

Causal Nets of Operator Algebras. (Mathematische Monographien Ser.: Bd. 80). 460p. 1993. 125.00 (0-685-67328-6, Pub. by Akademie GW) VCH Pubs.

Causal Realism: An Essay on Philosophical Method & the Foundations of Knowledge. John C. Cahalan. Ed. by John Deely & Brooke Williams. LC 85-3309. (Sources in Semiotics Ser.: Vol. II). 516p. (Orig.). 1985. lib. bdg. 75.50 (0-8191-4621-8); pap. 41.00 (0-8191-4622-6) U Pr of Amer.

Causal Theories of Mind: Action, Knowledge, Memory, Perception & Reference. Ed. by Steven Davis. LC 83-15082. (Foundations of Communication & Cognition Ser.). x, 421p. 1983. 173.10x (3-11-007730-2) De Gruyter.

Causal Theory of Justice. Karol E. Soltan. LC 86-30915. (California Series on Social Choice & Political Economy: Vol. 10). 240p. 1987. 40.00 (0-520-05955-7) U CA Pr.

Causal Thinking in the Child. Monique Laurendeau & Adrien Pinard. LC 62-21895. 293p. 1963. text ed. 35.00 (0-8236-0680-5) Intl Univs Pr.

Causality & Chance in Modern Physics. David Bohm. LC 57-28894. 128p. 1971. reprint ed. pap. 16.95 (0-8122-1002-6) U of Pa Pr.

Causality & Determinism. Georg H. Wright. LC 74-11030. (Woodbridge Lectures Columbia University Ser.: No. 10). 165p. reprint ed. pap. 47.10 (0-317-10177-3, 2017576) Bks Demand.

Causality & Modern Science. Mario Bunge. LC 78-74117. (Illus.). (C). 1979. reprint ed. pap. 9.95 (0-486-23728-1) Dover.

***Causality & Narrative in French Fiction from Zola to Robbe-Grillet.** Roy J. Nelson. 245p. 1990. 49.50 (0-8142-0504-6) Ohio St U Pr.

Causality & Physical Theories: Proceedings of Conference, No. 16. American Institute of Physics. Ed. by William B. Rolnick. LC 73-93420. 177p. 1974. 12.00 (0-88318-115-0) Am Inst Physics.

Causality, Electromagnetic Induction, & Gravitation: A Different Approach to the Theory of Electromagnetic & Gravitational Fields. Oleg D. Jefimenko. LC 92-71127. (Illus.). 192p. (C). 1992. lib. bdg. 29.50 (0-917406-09-5); pap. 19.75 (0-917406-12-5) Electret Sci.

Causality in Sociological Research. Jakub Karpinski. (C). 1990. lib. bdg. 85.50 (0-7923-0546-9) Kluwer Ac.

Causality, Interpretation, & the Mind. William Child. LC 93-36597. (Oxford Philosophical Monographs). 232p. (C). 1994. 39.95 (0-19-823978-5, Clarendon Pr) OUP.

Causality, Method, & Modality: Essays in Honor of Jules Vuillemin. Ed. by Gordon G. Brittan, Jr. (University of Western Ontario Series in Philosophy of Science). 248p. 1990. lib. bdg. 85.50 (0-7923-1045-4) Kluwer Ac.

Causation. Ed. by Ernest Sosa & Michael Tooley. LC 92-28442. (Oxford Readings in Philosophy Ser.). 264p. 1993. 15.95 (0-19-875094-3) OUP.

Causation. Ed. by Ernest Sosa & Michael Tooley. LC 92-28442. (Oxford Readings in Philosophy Ser.). 264p. 1993. 39.95 (0-19-875093-5) OUP.

Causation: A Realist Approach. Michael Tooley. (Illus.). 376p. 1988. 72.00 (0-19-824962-4) OUP.

Causation & Causal Theories. Ed. by Peter A. French et al. LC 84-234. (Midwest Studies in Philosophy: Vol. 9). 633p. 1984. text ed. 49.95 (0-8166-1349-4); pap. text ed. 21.95 (0-8166-1352-4) U of Minn Pr.

Causation & Clinical Management of Pelvic Radiation Disease. Ed. by Philip F. Schofield & E. Lupton. (Illus.). xviii, 153p. 1989. 105.00 (0-387-19561-0, 3098) Spr-Verlag.

Causation & Conditionals. Ed. by Ernest Sosa. LC 75-310580. (Oxford Readings in Philosophy Ser.). (Illus.). 208p. reprint ed. pap. 59.30 (0-685-20328-X, 2056398) Bks Demand.

Causation & Disease: A Chronological Journal. A. S. Evans. (Illus.). 235p. (C). 1993. 35.00 (0-306-44283-3, Plenum Pr) Plenum.

Causation & Prevention of Colorectal Cancer. J. Faivre & M. J. Hill. (International Congress Ser.: Vol. 774). 1987. 98.00 (0-444-80935-X) Elsevier.

Causation & Prevention of Human Cancer. Ed. by M. J. Hill & A. Giacosa. (Developments in Oncology Ser.). (C). 1991. lib. bdg. 59.00 (0-7923-1084-5) Kluwer Ac.

Causation & Universals. Evan Fales. 384p. 1990. 65.00 (0-415-04438-3, A4251) Routledge.

Causation, Chance & Credence. Brian Skyrms & William L. Harper. (C). 1988. lib. bdg. 100.50 (90-277-2633-7) Kluwer Ac.

Causation, Course & Treatment of Reflex Insanity in Women. Horatio R. Storer. LC 71-180592. (Medicine & Society in America Ser.). 240p. 1979. reprint ed. 23.95 (0-405-03974-3) Ayer.

Causation in Decision, Belief Change & Statistics. William L. Harper & Brian Skyrms. (C). 1988. lib. bdg. 100.50 (90-277-2634-5) Kluwer Ac.

Causation in Early Modern Philosophy: Cartesianism, Occasionalism, & Preestablished Harmony. Ed. by Steven Nadler. 232p. (C). 1993. 32.50 (0-271-00863-6) Pa St U Pr.

Causation in the Law. Herbert L. Hart & Tony Honore. LC 83-26836. 1985. pap. 32.00 (0-19-825474-1) OUP.

Causation of Cardiovascular Risk Factors in Children: Perspectives on Cardiovascular Risk in Early Life. Ed. by Gerald S. Berenson. (Illus.). 428p. 1986. text ed. 121.50 (0-88167-138-X) Raven.

Causation of Rheumatoid Disease & Many Human Cancers: A Precis & Addenda Including the Nature of Multiple Sclerosis. Roger Wyburn-Mason. LC 83-71522. 32p. 1983. 7.50 (0-931150-13-2) Rheumatoid.

Causation, Prediction & Legal Analysis. Stuart S. Nagel. LC 86-8142. 298p. 1986. text ed. 55.00 (0-89930-180-0, NCP/, Quorum Bks) Greenwood.

Causation, Prediction, & Search. Peter Spirtes et al. LC 92-40263. (Lecture Notes in Statistics Ser.: Vol. 81). 1994. 49.00 (0-387-97979-4) Spr-Verlag.

Causatives & Transitivity. Ed. by Bernard Comrie & Maria Polinsky. LC 93-11698. (Studies in Language Companion: Vol. 23). ix, 399p. 1993. 124.00x (1-55619-375-0) Benjamins North Am.

Causatives of Malagasy. Charles Randriamasimanana. (Oceanic Linguistics Special Publications: No. 21). 704p. 1986. pap. text ed. 30.00 (0-8248-1079-1) UH Pr.

Cause & Control of the Business Cycle. E. C. Harwood. 82p. 1974. 6.00 (0-318-12795-4) Am Inst Econ Res.

Cause & Cure of All Disease. Rasmus Alsaker. 8p. 1972. reprint ed. spiral bd. 3.30 (0-7873-1278-9) Mokelumne.

Cause & Effect. Patricia Ackert. 264p. 1986. pap. 19.95 (0-8384-2809-6, Newbury); teacher ed. pap. 7.95 (0-8384-2810-X, Newbury) Heinle & Heinle.

Cause-&-Effect. Paul E. Johnson. (Why Ser.: Sect. 1, Vol. 1; Pubn. 26, Vol. 1). 49p. 1985. pap. text ed. 5.00 (0-685-28934-6) P E Johnson.

Cause & Effect: Intermediate Reading Practice. 2nd ed. Patricia Ackert & Nikki S. Giroux De Navarro. LC 93-42859. 1994. pap. 19.95 (0-8384-3814-8) Heinle & Heinle.

Cause & Management of Aneurysms. Greenhalgh & Mannick. (Illus.). 504p. 1990. text ed. 142.00 (0-7020-1499-0, Bailliere-Tindall) Saunders.

Cause & Management of Hirsutism. Ed. by R. B. Greenblatt et al. (Illus.). 225p. 1987. 48.00 (1-85070-174-1) Prthnon Pub.

***Cause & Prevention of War.** 2nd ed. Seyom Brown. 272p. 1994. pap. text ed. 14.00 (0-312-04906-4) St Martin.

Cause, Experiment, & Science: A Galilean Dialogue Incorporating a New English Translation of Galileo's "Bodies That Stay Atop Water, Or Move in It" Stillman Drake. LC 81-2974. (Illus.). 288p. (C). 1985. pap. 9.95 (0-226-16230-3) U Ch Pr.

Cause for Alarm. Eric Ambler. 264p. 1990. pap. 3.95 (0-88184-664-3) Carroll & Graf.

Cause for Alarm. Eric Ambler. 246p. reprint ed. lib. bdg. 20.95 (0-89190-466-2, Rivercity Pr) Amereon Ltd.

Cause for Alarm. Eric Ambler. 1990. reprint ed. lib. bdg. 22.95 (0-89968-470-X) Buccaneer Bks.

Cause for Alarm: Issues That Threaten Our Nation. George H. Harris. Ed. by Valerie Bailey et al. 117p. (Orig.). 1988. pap. 4.95 (0-945641-00-1) Castle Hills.

Cause for Dying. Brian Morrison. 1992. mass mkt. 5.50 (0-06-104124-6, Harp PBks) HarpC.

Cause for Our Time: Oxfam: The First Fifty Years. Maggie Black. LC 92-29021. (Illus.). 366p. 1993. 19.95 (0-19-285283-3) OUP.

Cause for Our Times Oxfam: The First Fifty Years. Maggie Black. 336p. (C). 1992. text ed. 80.00 (0-85598-172-5, Pub. by Oxfam Pubns UK); pap. text ed. 40.00 (0-85598-173-3, Pub. by Oxfam Pubns UK) St Mut.

Cause for Wonder. Wright Morris. LC 77-14594. vi, 272p. 1978. 22.50 (0-8032-0966-5); pap. 5.95 (0-8032-5885-2) U of Nebr Pr.

***Cause Lawyering in South Africa: The Process of Empowering a Rights Based Legal Culture & Its Socio-Political Impact.** Andrew Caiger. 287p. 1995. text ed. 64.95 (1-57292-015-7); pap. text ed. 39.95 (1-57292-014-9) Austin & Winfield.

Cause, Mind, & Reality. Ed. by John Heil. (C). 1989. lib. bdg. 91.50 (0-7923-0462-4) Kluwer Ac.

Cause of Anti-Jewism in the United States. Irving Potter. 1982. lib. bdg. 59.95 (0-87700-394-7) Revisionist Pr.

Cause of Blindness in Childhood: A Study of 776 Children with Severe Visual Handicaps. George R. Fraser & A. T. Friedmann. LC 67-22893. 265p. reprint ed. pap. 75.60 (0-317-42303-7, 2023097) Bks Demand.

Cause of Business Depressions. Hugo Bilgram & L. Levy. 1973. 250.00 (0-87968-095-4) Gordon Pr.

Cause of Christian Education. Richard I. Edlin. (Illus.). 180p. (Orig.). 1994. pap. 13.95 (0-9630700-7-X) Vision AL.

Cause of Death. Cyril Wecht et al. 352p. 1994. pap. 5.99 (0-451-18141-7, Onyx) NAL-Dutton.

Cause of Death. large type ed. Michael Underwood. (Scarlet Dagger Ser.). 1993. 18.95 (0-7451-6445-5, Scarlet Dagger Lrg Print) Chivers N Amer.

Cause of Death: A Writer's Guide to Death, Murder & Forensic Medicine. Keith D. Wilson. (Howdunit Ser.). 240p. 1992. pap. 15.99 (0-89879-524-9) Writers Digest.

***Cause of Death Contributing to Changes in Life Expectancy: United States, 1984-89.** National Center for Health Statistics Staff. LC 94-1851. (Series Reports: Series 20, No. 23). 35p. Date not set. 3.00 (0-614-02920-1, 017-022-01256-1) Natl Ctr Health Stats.

Cause of Diabetes: Genetic & Environmental Factors. Ed. by R. D. Leslie. LC 93-11222. 1993. text ed. 159.95 (0-471-94040-2) Wiley.

Cause of Liberation in U. S. S. R. Rene Laurentin. Tr. by Leslie S. Turner. LC 93-83222. 208p. 1993. pap. 9.95 (1-882972-07-4) Queenship Pub.

***Cause of Man's Dysfunctional Behavior.** Mildred L. Buchanan. (Orig.). 1995. pap. text ed. 9.95 (1-883866-07-3) Clarion Pub.

***Cause of Suppression.** L. Ron Hubbard. 10p. 1994. pap. 4.00 (0-88404-918-3) Bridge Pubns Inc.

Cause of the South: Selections from De Bow's Review, 1846-1867. Ed. by Paul F. Paskoff & Daniel J. Wilson. LC 81-23680. (Library of Southern Civilization). xii, 306p. (C). 1982. pap. text ed. 12.95 (0-8071-1039-6) La State U Pr.

Cause of World Unrest. Intro. by H. A. Gwynne. 264p. 1978. pap. 6.00 (0-911038-40-X) Noontide.

Cause, Principle & Unity: Five Dialogues. Giordano Bruno. Tr. by Jack Lindsay. LC 76-28448. 177p. 1976. reprint ed. text ed. 59.75 (0-8371-9040-1, BRCP, Greenwood Pr) Greenwood.

Cause That Failed: Communism in American Political Life. Guenter Lewy. 384p. 1990. 24.95 (0-19-505748-1) OUP.

Causes & Coincidences. David Owens. (Studies in Philosophy). (Illus.). 200p. (C). 1992. 47.95 (0-521-41650-7) Cambridge U Pr.

Causes & Consequences. John J. Chapman. 1972. 59.95 (0-87968-821-1) Gordon Pr.

C

An Asterisk (*) at the beginning of an entry indicates that the title is appearing in BIP for the first time.

*__Causes & Consequences in International Relations: A Conceptual Analysis.__ Michael Nicholson. 256p. 1995. text ed. 59.95 (*1-85567-242-1*, Pub. by Pinter Pubs UK) St Martin.

Causes & Consequences of Antitrust: The Public-Choice Perspective. Ed. by Fred S. McChesney & William F. Shughart, II. (Illus.). 392p. 1994. pap. text ed. 32.95 (*0-226-55635-2*) U Ch Pr.

Causes & Consequences of Antitrust: The Public-Choice Perspective. Ed. by Fred S. McChesney & William F. Shughart, II. (Illus.). 392p. 1995. lib. bdg. 66.00 (*0-226-55634-4*) U Ch Pr.

Causes & Consequences of Chromosomal Aberrations. Kirsch. 1992. 167.95 (*0-8493-8893-7*, RB155) CRC Pr.

Causes & Consequences of Variation in Growth Rate & Productivity of Higher Plants. Ed. by Hans Lanbers et al. (Illus.). x, 364p. 1989. 115.00 (*90-5103-033-9*, Pub. by SPB Acad Pub NE) Koeltz Sci Bks.

Causes & Cures of Criminality. Ed. by Hans J. Eysenck & Gisli H. Gudjonsson. (Perspectives on Individual Differences Ser.). (Illus.). 326p. 1989. 42.50 (*0-306-42968-3*, Plenum Pr) Plenum.

Causes & Cures of Unemployment. William H. Beveridge. LC 75-41030. (BCL Ser. II). 1976. reprint ed. 9.00 (*0-685-70886-1*) AMS Pr.

Causes & Cures of Welfare: New Evidence on the Social Psychology of the Poor. Leonard Goodwin. LC 82-48634. 224p. 1983. pap. 14.00 (*0-685-06322-4*) Free Pr.

Causes & Deterrents of Transportation Accidents: An Analysis by Mode. Peter D. Loeb et al. LC 94-8541. 240p. 1994. text ed. 59.95 (*0-89930-806-6*, Quorum Bks) Greenwood.

Causes & Effects in Communication & Language Intervention, Vol. 1. Ed. by Steven F. Warren & Joe Reichle. LC 91-15659. (Communication & Language Intervention Ser.: Vol. 1). 432p. (C). 1992. text ed. 42.00 (*1-55766-075-1*) P H Brookes.

Causes & Effects of Agricultural Labor Migration from the Mixteca of Oaxaca to California. James Stuart & Michael Kearney. (Research Report Ser.: No. 28). 39p. (Orig.). (C). 1981. pap. 5.00 (*0-935391-27-4*, RR-28) UCSD Ctr US-Mex.

Causes & Effects of Stratospheric Ozone Reduction: An Update. National Research Council Staff. 339p. (C). 1982. pap. text ed. 29.95 (*0-309-03248-2*) Natl Acad Pr.

Causes & Effects of Stratospheric Ozone Reduction, an Update: A Report. National Research Council (U. S.) Staff. LC 82-81229. 351p. reprint ed. pap. 100.10 (*0-8357-3446-3*, 2039706) Bks Demand.

Causes & Prevention of War. 2nd ed. Seyom Brown. 288p. 1994. text ed. 45.00 (*0-312-10269-0*) St Martin.

Causes, Controls & Organization of Behavior in the Neonate. Peter H. Wolff. LC 66-22207. (Psychological Issues Monograph: No. 17, Vol. 5, No. 1). 105p. (Orig.). 1966. text ed. 26.00x (*0-8236-0700-3*) Intl Univs Pr.

Causes, Coping & Consequences of Stress at Work. Ed. by Cary L. Cooper & Roy Payne. LC 87-35399. (Studies in Occupational Stress). 418p. 1988. text ed. 109.00 (*0-471-91879-2*) Wiley.

*__Causes, Coping & Consequences of Stress at Work.__ Ed. by Cary L. Cooper & Roy E. Payne. (Studies in Occupational Stress). 1994. pap. text ed. 36.95 (*0-471-94453-X*) Wiley.

Causes, Cures, Sense & Nonsense. Roland Dickison & Carolyn Gruner. LC 87-71853. (Illus.). 300p. (Orig.). 1987. pap. 10.00 (*0-9618946-1-X*) Bishop Publishing.

Causes Du Suicide: The Causes of Suicide. Maurice Halbwachs. LC 74-25757. (European Sociology Ser.). 530p. 1975. reprint ed. 42.95 (*0-405-06511-6*) Ayer.

Causes of Action, 36 vols., Set. Shepard's Citation, Inc. Staff. 1989. text ed. 2,250.00 (*0-07-056763-8*) Shepards-McGraw.

Causes of Climatic Change: A Collection of Papers Derived from the INQUA-NCAR Symposium on Causes of Climate Change, August 30-31, 1968. Ed. by J. Murray Mitchell, Jr. (Meteorological Monograph Ser.: Vol. 8, No. 30). (Illus.). 159p. 1968. 25.00 (*0-933876-28-9*) Am Meteorological.

Causes of Contemporary Stagnation. Ed. by Herbert Frisch & B. Gahlen. (Studies in Contemporary Economics). ix, 216p. 1986. pap. 36.00 (*0-387-16465-0*) Spr-Verlag.

*__Causes of Continuing Conflict in Nicaragua: A View from the Radical Middle.__ Timothy C. Brown. LC 95-11396. (Essays in Public Policy: No. 59). 1995. write for info. (*0-8179-5642-5*) Hoover Inst Pr.

Causes of Crime. Arthur E. Fink. LC 84-22493. xii, 309p. 1985. reprint ed. text ed. 65.00 (*0-313-24746-3*, FICA, Greenwood Pr) Greenwood.

Causes of Crime: Distinguishing Between Fact & Opinion. Stacey Tipp. LC 91-22123. (Opposing Viewpoints Juniors Ser.). (Illus.). 32p. (J). (gr. 4-7). 1991. lib. bdg. 11.95 (*0-89908-615-2*) Greenhaven.

Causes of Death Contributing to Changes in Life Expectancy: United States, 1984-1989. Kenneth D. Kochanek et al. LC 94-671. (Vital & Health Statistics Ser. 20: Data from the National Vital Statistics System: No. 23). 1994. write for info. (*0-8406-0488-2*) Natl Ctr Health Stats.

*__Causes of Death in the Workplace.__ J. Paul Leigh. LC 94-36796. 328p. 1995. text ed. 59.95 (*0-89930-951-8*, Quorum Bks) Greenwood.

Causes of Demographic Change: Experimental Research in South India. John C. Caldwell et al. LC 88-40189. (Orig.). 1988. text ed. 37.50 (*0-299-11610-7*); pap. text ed. 19.95 (*0-299-11614-X*) U of Wis Pr.

Causes of Depopulation in the Western Islands of the Territory of New Guinea. Raphael W. Cilento. LC 75-32809. reprint ed. 16.00 (*0-404-14113-7*) AMS Pr.

Causes of Development: Interdisciplinary Perspectives. Ed. by George Butterworth & Peter Bryant. 288p. 1990. 49.95 (*0-8058-0796-9*) L Erlbaum Assocs.

Causes of Evolution. J. B. Haldane. 310p. (Orig.). 1990. pap. 10.95 (*0-691-02442-1*) Princeton U Pr.

Causes of Evolution: A Paleontological Perspective. Ed. by Robert M. Ross & Warren D. Allmon. (Illus.). 368p. 1990. pap. text ed. 24.95 (*0-226-72824-2*) U Ch Pr.

Causes of Evolution: A Paleontological Perspective. Ed. by Robert M. Ross & Warren D. Allmon. (Illus.). 368p. 1991. lib. bdg. 65.00 (*0-226-72823-4*) U Ch Pr.

Causes of Failure in Performance Appraisal & Supervision: A Guide to Analysis & Evaluation for Human Resources Professionals. Joe Baker, Jr. LC 87-37571. 172p. 1988. text ed. 45.00 (*0-89930-348-X*, BKA/, Quorum Bks) Greenwood.

Causes of International War. G. Lowes Dickinson. LC 84-12797. 110p. 1984. reprint ed. text ed. 35.00 (*0-313-24565-7*, DICI, Greenwood Pr) Greenwood.

*__Causes of Litigation in Workers' Compensation Programs.__ Evangelos M. Falaris et al. 170p. 1995. 24.00 (*0-88099-162-3*); pap. 14.00 (*0-88099-161-5*) W E Upjohn.

Causes of Molecular Evolution. John H. Gillespie. (Ecology & Evolution Ser.). (Illus.). 352p. 1994. reprint ed. pap. 19.95 (*0-19-509271-6*) OUP.

Causes of Photooxidative Stress in Plants & Amelioration of Defense Systems. Ed. by Christine H. Foyer & Philip M. Mullineaux. LC 93-25101. 195.00 (*0-8493-5443-9*, QK757) CRC Pr.

Causes of Profound Deafness in Childhood: A Study of 3, 535 Individuals with Severe Hearing Loss Present at Birth or of Childhood Onset. George R. Fraser. LC 75-36954. 428p. reprint ed. pap. 122.00 (*0-685-15511-0*, 2026326) Bks Demand.

Causes of Spatial & Temporal Patterns Rocky Intertidal Communities of CEntral & Northern California. Michael S. Foster et al. (Memoirs of the California Academy of Sciences Ser.: No. 9). (Illus.). 1988. pap. 13.00 (*0-940228-18-1*) Calif Acad Sci.

Causes of the American Civil War. 2nd ed. Ed. by Edwin C. Rozwenc. (Problems in American Civilization Ser.). (C). 1972. pap. text ed. 8.50 (*0-669-82727-4*) Heath.

Causes of the American Civil War: Eyewitness Accounts. Intro. by Albert B. Hart. (American History As Told By Contemporaries Ser.). 128p. (Orig.). (C). 1992. pap. text ed. 2.25 (*1-877891-28-2*) Paperbook Pr Inc.

Causes of the American Revolution. Thomas Ladenburg. (SSEC American History Ser.). (Illus.). 132p. (Orig.). 1989. pap. 21.95 (*0-89994-326-8*) Soc Sci Ed.

Causes of the American Revolution. 3rd ed. Ed. by John C. Wahlke. (Problems in American Civilization Ser.). 256p. (C). 1973. pap. text ed. 8.50 (*0-669-82685-5*) Heath.

Causes of the American Revolution. James A. Woodburn. LC 78-63815. (Johns Hopkins University. Studies in the Social Sciences. Thirtieth Ser. 1912: 12). reprint ed. 11.50 (*0-404-61078-1*) AMS Pr.

Causes of the American Revolution: Eyewitness Accounts. Intro. by Albert B. Hart. (American History As Told By Contemporaries Ser.). (Illus.). 128p. (Orig.). (C). 1992. pap. text ed. 2.00 (*1-877891-27-4*) Paperbook Pr Inc.

Causes of the Civil War. rev. ed. Ed. by Kenneth M. Stampp. LC 74-892. (Eyewitness Accounts of American History Ser.). 192p. 1974. pap. 4.95 (*0-13-121194-3*, Spectrum Bks) P-H.

Causes of the Civil War. rev. ed. Ed. by Kenneth M. Stampp. 18.00 (*0-8446-2993-6*) Peter Smith.

Causes of the Civil War. 3rd rev. ed. Ed. by Kenneth M. Stampp. 224p. 1992. pap. 10.00 (*0-671-75155-7*, Touchstone Bks) S&S Trade.

Causes of the Civil War: A Note on Historical Sentimentalism. Arthur M. Schlesinger, Jr. (Irvington Reprint Series in American History). (C). 1991. reprint ed. pap. text ed. 2.30 (*0-8290-2609-6*, H-187) Irvington.

Causes of the Civil War: Institutional Failure or Human Blunder? rev. ed. Hans L. Trefousse. LC 81-23696. (American Problem Studies). 134p. 1982. reprint ed. pap. 9.50 (*0-89874-472-5*) Krieger.

Causes of the Elimination of Students in Public Secondary Schools of New York City. Joseph K. Van Denburg. LC 74-177684. (Columbia University. Teachers College. Contributions to Education Ser.: No. 47). reprint ed. 37.50 (*0-404-55047-9*) AMS Pr.

Causes of the English Civil War. Ann Hughes. LC 90-47353. (British History in Perspective Ser.). 180p. 1991. text ed. 45.00 (*0-312-05226-X*) St Martin.

Causes of the English Civil War. Conrad Russell. 256p. 1990. pap. 17.95 (*0-19-822141-X*) OUP.

Causes of the War of Eighteen Twelve: National Honor or National Interest? Ed. by Bradford Perkins. LC 76-3657. (American Problem Studies). 126p. 1976. reprint ed. pap. 9.50 (*0-88275-408-4*) Krieger.

Causes of the War of Independence. Claude H. Van Tyne. (BCL1 - U. S. History Ser.). 499p. 1991. reprint ed. lib. bdg. 99.00 (*0-7812-6114-7*) Rprt Serv.

Causes of War. 3rd ed. Geoffrey Blainey. 312p. 1988. text ed. 29.95 (*0-02-903592-9*); pap. 13.95 (*0-02-903591-0*) Free Pr.

Causes of War: Economic, Industrial, Racial, Religious, Scientific & Political. Ed. by Arthur Porritt. LC 70-99719. (Essay Index Reprint Ser.). 1977. 21.95 (*0-8369-1372-8*) Ayer.

Causes of Wars. Michael C. Howard. 256p. 1983. pap. 14.95 (*0-674-10417-X*) HUP.

Causes of Wealth. Jean Fourastie. LC 74-25748. (European Sociology Ser.). 250p. 1975. reprint ed. 25.95 (*0-405-06503-5*) Ayer.

Causes of World War Three. Charles W. Mills. LC 75-31436. 172p. 1976. reprint ed. text ed. 49.75 (*0-8371-8513-0*, MICW, Greenwood Pr) Greenwood.

Causes of World War Three. Wright C. Mills. LC 85-14381. 188p. 1985. reprint ed. pap. 25.95 (*0-87332-357-2*) M E Sharpe.

Causes, Preventive Measures, & Methods of Controlling Riots & Disturbances in Correctional Institutions. 3rd rev. ed. (Illus.). 85p. 1990. pap. 23.25 (*0-929310-23-3*, 132) Am Correctional.

Causewayed Enclosures. R. J. Mercer. 1989. pap. 25.00 (*0-7478-0064-2*, Pub. by Shire UK) St Mut.

Causing Death & Saving Lives. Jonathan Glover. 1977. mass mkt. 6.95 (*0-14-022003-8*, Penguin Bks) Viking Penguin.

Causing Harm: A Logico - Legal Study. Aqvist & Philip Mullock. (Foundations of Communication & Cognition Ser.). xx, 353p. (C). 1989. lib. bdg. 134.65x (*0-89925-424-1*) De Gruyter.

Causing Others to Want Your Leadership. Robert L. DeBruyn. LC 76-29223. 184p. (C). 1976. 15.95 (*0-914607-06-5*) Master Tchr.

Causing, Perceiving & Believing: An Examination of the Philosophy of C. J. Ducasse. Peter H. Hare & Edward H. Madden. LC 74-4899. (Philosophical Studies: No. 6). vii, 212p. 1975. lib. bdg. 80.00 (*90-277-0563-1*) Kluwer Ac.

Caustics, Catastrophes, & Wave Fields. Yu A. Kravtsov & Yu I. Orlov. LC 93-31099. (Wave Phenomena Ser.: Vol. 15). 1993. 98.00 (*0-387-56587-6*) Spr-Verlag.

Cautantowwit's House: An Indian Burial Ground on the Island of Conanicut in Narragansett Bay. William S. Simmons. LC 77-111456. (Illus.). 198p. reprint ed. pap. 56.50 (*0-317-41779-7*, 2025642) Bks Demand.

Cauterizing the Soul: A Book of Poems. Dan Skelton. LC 89-62643. 64p. 1990. pap. 5.00 (*0-938991-45-0*) Colonial Pr AL.

*__Caute's Confrontations: A Study of the Novels of David Caute.__ Nicolas Tredell. 122p. 1995. lib. bdg. 30.00 (*0-8095-6778-4*); pap. 20.00 (*0-946650-51-9*) Borgo Pr.

Caution: Baby Ahead. Marie Ferrarella. (Silhouette Romance Ser.). 1994. pap. 2.75 (*0-373-19007-7*, 5-19007-9) Harlequin Bks.

Caution: Baby Ahead. Marie Ferrarella. 1994. 2.75 (*0-373-91007-X*) Silhouette.

Caution: Charm at Work. Raye Morgan. (Silhouette Desire Ser.). 1993. mass mkt. 2.99 (*0-373-05807-1*, 5-05807-8) Silhouette.

Caution: Christians under Construction. Bill Hybels. LC 77-93854. 144p. 1986. pap. 1.20 (*0-88207-759-7*, Victor Books) SP Pubns.

*__Caution: Thin Ice.__ Lawrence Schug. 70p. 1993. pap. 6.95 (*0-87839-083-9*) North Star.

Caution! Computer at Work. Hal Schuster. 1990. pap. 14.95 (*1-55698-248-8*) Movie Pubs Servs.

Caution: Contents under Pressure. Fran Sciacca & Jill Sciacca. (Lifelines Ser.). (YA). 1990. pap. 3.95 (*0-89066-199-5*) World Wide Pubs.

Caution: Faulty Thinking Can Be Harmful to Your Happiness: Everyday Logic for Stress Reduction, Assertiveness, Effective Decision Making & Improved Interpersonal Relations, Self Help Edition. Elliot D. Cohen. 160p. (C). 1992. pap. 9.95 (*1-880454-01-7*); disk 58.95 (*1-880454-06-8*); disk 49.95 (*1-880454-03-3*) Trace-Wilco.

Caution: I Brake for Plastic Bags: Real-Life Encouragement for Parents & Families. Anna C. Willis. LC 94-90075. 208p. 1994. 19.95 (*0-9641087-0-4*) Upper Rm Educ.

Caution: Soul Mate Ahead! Spiritual Love in the Physical Dimension. Janet Cunningham & Michael Ranucci. LC 94-90007. (Illus.). 115p. (Orig.). 1994. pap. 9.95 (*0-9640026-9-8*) Two Suns Pr.

Caution: This May Be an Advertisement: A Teen Guide to Advertising. Kathlyn Gay. LC 91-38159. (Illus.). 160p. (YA). (gr. 9-12). 1992. lib. bdg. 15.82 (*0-531-11039-7*) Watts.

Caution: Working Waterfront: The Impact of Change on Marine Enterprises. (Illus.). 88p. 1985. 24.95 (*0-935957-07-3*) Waterfront DC.

Cautionary Tales. Barbara Goldberg. 1990. pap. 8.95 (*0-931848-78-4*) Dryad Pr.

Cautionary Tales. John Murtagh. 220p. 1992. pap. 39.00 (*0-07-452806-8*) Hlth Prof Div.

Cautionary Tales: Young People, Crime & Policing in Edinburgh. Simon Anderson et al. LC 94-18854. 1994. 51.95 (*1-85628-851-X*, Pub. by Avebury Pub UK) Ashgate Pub Co.

Cautionary Tales & Other Verses. Picton Publishing (Chippenham) Ltd. Staff. (C). 1987. 50.00 (*0-948251-20-4*, Pub. by Picton UK) St Mut.

Cautious Diplomat: Charles E. Bohlen & the Soviet Union, 1929-1969. T. Michael Ruddy. LC 86-4705. 234p. 1986. 27.00 (*0-87338-331-1*) Kent St U Pr.

Cautious Expert. John C. Quicke. 192p. 1982. 91.00 (*0-335-10110-0*, Open Univ Pr) Taylor & Francis.

Cautious Heart. large type ed. Stella Kent. (Linford Romance Library). 304p. 1986. pap. 11.95 (*0-7089-6240-8*) Ulverscroft.

Cautious Revolution: The European Community Arrives. Clifford Hackett. LC 90-34318. 256p. 1990. text ed. 55.00 (*0-313-27416-9*, B3605, Greenwood Pr); pap. text ed. 17.95 (*0-275-93605-8*, B3605, Praeger Pubs) Greenwood.

Cautious Welcome: The Legalization Programs of the Immigration Reform & Control Act. Susan G. Baker. LC 90-43203. (Urban Institute Report Ser.: No. 90-9). 205p. (Orig.). (C). 1990. lib. bdg. 52.00 (*0-87766-493-5*); pap. text ed. 21.50 (*0-87766-494-3*) Urban Inst.

*__Cav-Ox Cavitation Oxidation Process Magnum Water Technology, Inc. Applications Analysis Report.__ (Illus.). 72p. (Orig.). (C). 1995. pap. text ed. 40.00x (*0-7881-1542-1*) Diane Pub.

Cavalcade of American Ballroom Dancing. L. Dorfman. (Ballroom Dance Ser.). 1986. lib. bdg. 79.95 (*0-8490-3328-4*) Gordon Pr.

Cavalcade of American Ballroom Dancing. L. Dorfman. (Ballroom Dance Ser.). 1985. lib. bdg. 250.00 (*0-87700-764-0*) Revisionist Pr.

Cavalcade of Carbonates. Ed. by John D. Cooper. (Illus.). 144p. (Orig.). 1989. pap. 11.00 (*1-878861-08-5*) Pac Section SEPM.

Cavalcade of Clowns. Laurence Selenick. (J). (gr. 1-9). 1992. pap. 3.95 (*0-88388-042-3*) Bellerophon Bks.

Cavalcade of Dolls: A Basic Sourcebook for Collectors. Ruth Freeman. LC 75-30167. (Illus.). 363p. 1978. lib. bdg. 35.00 (*0-87282-001-7*, 78282) Am Life Foun.

Cavalcade of the American Negro. Writers' Program, Illinois Staff. LC 73-3614. (American Guide Ser.). reprint ed. 21.50 (*0-404-57917-5*) AMS Pr.

Cavalerie Rouge. Isaac Babel. (FRE.). 1983. pap. 10.95 (*0-7859-1968-6*, 2070374408) Fr & Eur.

Cavalier. George W. Cable. (Works of George Washington Cable). 1990. reprint ed. lib. bdg. 79.00 (*0-7812-1143-3*) Rprt Serv.

Cavalier see Collected Works of George W. Cable

Cavalier - Skyhawk - Cimarron - Frenza - Sunbird 82-92. Chilton Automotives Editorial Staff. 384p. 1992. pap. 16.95 (*0-8019-8366-5*) Chilton.

Cavalier Case. Antonia Fraser. 1992. mass mkt. 4.99 (*0-553-29544-6*) Bantam.

Cavalier Case: A Jemima Shore Mystery. large type ed. Antonia Fraser. 1992. 18.95 (*0-7927-0817-2*, E0014, Eagle Lrg Print) Chivers N Amer.

Cavalier Case: A Jemima Shore Mystery. large type ed. Antonia Fraser. 1992. pap. 14.95 (*0-7927-0818-0*, Paragon Lrg Print) Chivers N Amer.

Cavalier Courtship. large type ed. Marina Oliver. (Romance Ser.). 1991. 21.95 (*0-7089-2466-2*) Ulverscroft.

Cavalier in Buckskin: George Armstrong Custer & the Western Military Frontier. Robert M. Utley. LC 88-5426. (Oklahoma Western Biographies Ser.: Vol. 1). (Illus.). 248p. 1988. 24.95 (*0-8061-2150-5*) U of Okla Pr.

Cavalier in Buckskin: George Armstrong Custer & the Western Military Frontier. Robert M. Utley. LC 88-5426. (Oklahoma Western Biographies Ser.: Vol. 1). (Illus.). 248p. 1991. pap. 12.95 (*0-8061-2292-7*) U of Okla Pr.

Cavalier in the Wilderness. Ross Phares. LC 76-1409. (Illus.). 290p. (J). (gr. 6-12). 1976. reprint ed. 18.95 (*0-88289-128-6*); reprint ed. pap. 13.95 (*0-88289-127-8*) Pelican.

*__Cavalier in Virginia Fiction.__ fac. ed. Ritchie D. Watson. LC 84-21306. (Southern Literary Studies). (Illus.). 312p. 1985. reprint ed. pap. 89.00 (*0-7837-7926-7*, 2047682) Bks Demand.

Cavalier in White. Marcia Muller. 1993. mass mkt. 3.99 (*0-373-83304-0*, 1-83304-5) Harlequin Bks.

Cavalier King Charles Spaniels. Beverley Cuddy. (Illus.). 190p. 1991. text ed. 11.95 (*0-86622-780-6*, KW-193) TFH Pubns.

Cavalier King Charles Spaniels: An Owner's Companion. John Evans. (Illus.). 224p. 1990. text ed. 24.00 (*0-87605-098-4*) Macmillan.

*__Cavalier King Charles Spaniels: An Owner's Companion.__ John Evans. (Illus.). 176p. 1995. 39.95 (*1-85223-253-6*, Pub. by Crowood Pr UK) Trafalgar.

*__Cavalier King Charles Spaniels Today.__ Sheila Smith. LC 95-7585. (Illus.). 160p. 1997. 25.95 (*0-87605-093-3*) Howell Bk.

Cavalier of Malaga. David Raphael. 190p. 1989. 15.00 (*0-9620772-1-6*) Carmi Hse Pr.

Cavalier Parliament & the Reconstruction of the Old Regime, 1661-1667. Paul Seaward. (Cambridge Studies in Early Modern British History). 367p. (C). 1989. 69.95 (*0-521-34030-6*) Cambridge U Pr.

Cavalier Pietro Tempesta & His Time. Marcel Roethlisberger-Bianco. LC 78-101052. (Illus.). 313p. 75.00 (*0-87413-105-7*) U Delaware Pr.

*__Cavalier Poets.__ Ed. by Crofts. (Thrift Editions Ser.). 1995. pap. 1.00 (*0-486-28766-1*) Dover.

Cavalier Poets: Their Lives, Their Day, & Their Poetry. Carl Holliday. (Essay Index Reprint Ser.). 1977. reprint ed. 21.95 (*0-518-10147-9*) Ayer.

Cavalier Saints & Sinners. George H. Tucker. 1991. pap. 9.95 (*1-878901-07-9*) Hampton Roads Pub Co.

Cavalier Seul. Jacques Audiberti. 256p. (FRE.). 1974. pap. 11.95 (*0-7859-1147-2*, 2070321304) Fr & Eur.

Cavalier Spirit. Cyril H. Hartmann. LC 72-3666. (English Literature Ser.: No. 33). 1972. reprint ed. lib. bdg. 75.00 (*0-8383-1560-7*) M S G Haskell Hse.

Cavaliere Elsa. Pierre M. Orlan. (FRE.). 1980. pap. 10.95 (*0-7859-4136-3*) Fr & Eur.

Cavaliers. Joseph Kessel. (Folio Ser.: No. 1373). (FRE.). pap. 14.95 (*2-07-037373-8*) Schoenhof.

Cavaliers. Joseph Kessel. 608p. (FRE.). 1982. pap. 16.95 (*0-7859-2459-0*, 2070373738) Fr & Eur.

Cavaliers & Cardinals: Nineteenth-Century French Anecdotal Paintings. Eric M. Zafran. LC 92-81383. (Illus.). 156p. (Orig.). 1992. pap. text ed. 27.95 (*0-915577-23-2*, U of Pa Pr) Taft Museum.

Cavaliers & Pioneers: Abstracts of Virginia Land Patents & Grants 1623-1666, Vol. 1. Nell M Nugent. LC 63-23761. (Illus.). 767p. 1991. reprint ed. 40.00 (*0-8063-0264-X*) Genealog Pub.

Cavaliers & Pioneers: Abstracts of Virginia Land Patents & Grants, 1695-1732, No. 1. Nell M. Nugent. LC 80-141230. iii, 18p. 1980. 4.95 (*0-88490-088-6*) VA State Lib.

Cavaliers & Pioneers: Abstracts of Virginia Land Patents & Grants, 1695-1732, Vol. 2. Nell M. Nugent. LC 34-42407. xi, 609p. 1992. reprint ed. text ed. 30.00 (*0-88490-009-6*, F225 N842) VA State Lib.

Cavaliers & Pioneers: Abstracts of Virginia Land Patents & Grants, 1695-1732, Vol. 3. Nell M. Nugent. LC 34-42407. ix, 578p. 1979. 30.00 (*0-88490-083-5*) VA State Lib.

An Asterisk (*) at the beginning of an entry indicates that the title is appearing in BIP for the first time.

C

*Cavitation & Gas-Liquid Flow in Fluid Machinery & Devices. Ed. by T. J. O'Hern. LC 94-71579. (Fluid Engineering Division Conference Ser.: Vol. 190). 343p. 1994. pap. text ed. 55.00 (0-7918-1373-8) ASME.

Cavitation & Inhomogeneities in Underwater Acoustics: Proceedings. Ed. by W. Lauterborn. (Electrophysics Ser.: Vol. 4). (Illus.). 319p. 1980. 46.00 (0-387-09939-5) Spr-Verlag.

Cavitation & Multiphase Flow - 1993. Ed. by O. Furuya. (FED Ser.: Vol. 153). 236p. 1993. 45.00 (0-7918-0961-7, H00793) ASME.

*Cavitation & Multiphase Flow 1994. Ed. by J. Katz. LC 86-71951. (Fluid Engineering Division Conference Ser.: Vol. 194). 157p. 1994. pap. 55.00 (0-7918-1377-0) ASME.

Cavitation & Polyphase Flow Forum, 1977. Ed. by Robert L. Waid. 53p. reprint ed. pap. 25.00 (0-317-08529-8, 2005689) Bks Demand.

Cavitation & Polyphase Flow Forum, 1980: Proceedings of the Cavitation & Polyphase Flow Forum, New Orleans, 1980. Cavitation & Polyphase Flow Forum Staff. Ed. by J. W. Hoyt. 52p. reprint ed. pap. 25.00 (0-317-42301-0, 2023148) Bks Demand.

Cavitation Erosion in Fluid Systems: Presented by the Fluids Engineering Conference, Boulder, Colorado, June 22-24, 1981. Ed. by Walter L. Swift & Roger E. Arndt. LC 80-71111. 179p. reprint ed. pap. 51.10 (0-317-58244-5, 2056390) Bks Demand.

Cavitation Inception 1993. Ed. by M. L. Billet & W. B. Morgan. LC 79-54430. 159p. Date not set. pap. 50.00 (0-7918-1048-8) ASME.

Cavitation State of Knowledge: Discussions Presented at the ASME Fluids Engineering & Applied Mechanics Conference, Northwestern University, Evanston, Illinois, June 16-18, 1969. American Society of Mechanical Engineers Staff. Ed. by J. M. Robertson & G. F. Wislicenus. LC 73-173121. 50p. reprint ed. pap. 25.00 (0-317-29797-X, 2016853) Bks Demand.

Cavitation State of Knowledge: Presented at the ASME Fluids Engineering & Applied Mechanics Conference, Northwestern University, Evanston, Ill., June 16-18, 1969. Ed. by J. M. Robertson & G. F. Wislicenus. LC 73-173121. 247p. reprint ed. pap. 70.40 (0-317-29952-2, 2051713) Bks Demand.

Cavities & Cracks in Creep & Fatigue. John H. Gittus. 1981. 93.75 (0-85334-965-7, Pub. by Elsevier Applied Sci UK) Elsevier.

Cavity Flows: Presented at the Fluids Engineering Conference, Minneapolis, Minnesota, May 5-7, 1975. Fluids Engineering Conference Symposium on Cavity Flows Staff. Ed. by Blaine R. Parkin & W. B. Morgan. LC 75-8089. (Illus.). 145p. reprint ed. pap. 41.40 (0-317-08133-0, 2016869) Bks Demand.

Cavity Quantum Electrodynamics. Ed. by Paul R. Berman. (Advances in Atomic, Molecular & Optical Physics Ser.: Supplement 2). (Illus.). 368p. 1993. text ed. 99.95 (0-12-092245-2) Acad Pr.

Cavour. Evelyn M. Cesaresco. LC 76-150174. (Select Bibliographies Reprint Ser.). 1977. 18.95 (0-8369-5687-7) Ayer.

Cavour. Harry Hearder. LC 93-38424. (Profiles in Power Ser.). (C). 1994. text ed. 52.50 (0-582-01899-4) Longman.

Cavour. Harry Hearder. LC 93-38424. (Profiles in Power Ser.). (C). 1995. pap. text ed. 17.95 (0-582-10903-5) Longman.

Cavour. Maurice Paleoloque. Tr. by Ian F. Morrow & Muriel M. Morrow. LC 77-130561. (Select Bibliographies Reprint Ser.). 1977. reprint ed. 23.95 (0-8369-5534-X) Ayer.

Cavour & Garibaldi Eighteen Sixty: A Study in Political Conflict. Denis Mack-Smith. 480p. 1985. pap. 27.95 (0-521-31637-5) Cambridge U Pr.

Cavour & the Economic Modernization of the Kingdom of Sardinia. Frank M. Murtaugh. LC 91-28338. (Modern European History Ser.: No. 2). 368p. 1991. 76.00 (0-8153-0671-7) Garland.

Cavour & the Making of Modern Italy. Pietro Orsi. LC 73-14461. (Heroes of the Nations Ser.). reprint ed. 30.00 (0-404-58279-6) AMS Pr.

*CAVS: From Fitch to Fratello. Joe Menzer & Burt Graeff. (Illus.). 250p. 1994. 23.95 (1-57167-006-8) Sagamore Pub.

Cawdor & Medea. Robinson Jeffers. LC 76-103374. 1970. reprint ed. pap. 11.95 (0-8112-0073-6, NDP293) New Directions.

Cawthorn: Residential Estate Conveyancing. 2nd ed. John Cawthorn. 1992. write for info. (0-406-14822-8) Butterworth Legal Pubs.

*Caxton Club, 1895-1995: Celebrating a Century of the Book in Chicago. Frank J. Piehl. LC 94-45203. 1995. write for info. (0-615-00566-7) Caxton Club.

*Caxton Club 1895-1995: Celebrating a Century of the Book in Chicago. Frank J. Piehl. (Illus.). 224p. 1995. 75.00 (0-940550-09-1) Caxton Club.

Caxtons, a Family Picture, 3 vols., Set. Edward B. Lytton. (BCL1-PR English Literature Ser.). 1992. reprint ed. lib. bdg. 225.00 (0-7812-7590-3) Rprt Serv.

Caxton's Book. William H. Rhodes. LC 73-13263. (Classics of Science Fiction Ser.). 308p. 1974. reprint ed. 15.00 (0-88355-117-9); reprint ed. pap. 10.00 (0-88355-146-2) Hyperion Conn.

Caxton's Malory: A New Edition of Sir Thomas Malory's Le Mort d'Arthur, Based on the Pierpont Morgan Copy of William Caxton's Edition of 1485, 2 vols., Set. Ed. by James W. Spisak & William Matthews. LC 81-7434. (Illus.). (C). 1983. 150.00 (0-520-03825-8) U CA Pr.

Caxton's Mirrour of the World: With All the Woodcuts. Ed. by O. H. Prior. (EETS, ES Ser.: Vol. 110). 1972. reprint ed. 25.00 (0-8115-3410-3) Periodicals Srv.

Cay. Theodore Taylor. 144p. (J). (gr. 6). 1977. pap. 3.99 (0-380-00142-X, Camelot) Avon.

Cay. Theodore Taylor. LC 69-15161. 160p. (J). (gr. 6-9). 1987. pap. 14.95 (0-385-07906-0) Doubleday.

Cay. Theodore Taylor. 144p. 1976. reprint ed. mass mkt. 3.99 (0-380-01003-8, Flare) Avon.

Cay: A Study Guide. Marcia Tretler. (Novel-Ties Ser.). (J). (gr. 4-7). 1986. student ed, teacher ed 15.95 (0-88122-081-7) Lrn Links.

Cayapa Indians of Ecuador, 2 vols, Set. S. A. Barrett. 1977. lib. bdg. 250.00 (0-8490-1588-X) Gordon Pr.

Cayman: Underwater Paradise. Feodor U. Pitcairn & Paul Humann. Ed. by Kirstin Pitcairn. LC 79-84293. (Illus.). (Orig.). 1979. 21.95 (0-9602530-0-9); pap. 14.95 (0-685-04291-X) Reef Dwellers.

Cayman Duppy. William Hezlep. (J). (gr. 5 up). 1984. pap. 5.00 (0-88734-403-8) Players Pr.

*Cayman Islands: Commercial Law. 300p. (Orig.). 1994. pap. 295.00 (0-7605-1237-X) Rector Pr.

Cayman Islands: Consolidated Index of Statutes & Subsidiary Legislation. Ed. by C. J. Hammett. (West Indian Legislation Indexing Project Ser.). x, 74p. (Orig.). 1991. pap. text ed. 25.00 (0-317-60537-2, Pub. by UWI Fac Law BB) W W Gaunt.

Cayman Islands: Natural History & Biogeography. Ed. by M. A. Brunt. LC 93-27017. (Monographiae Biologicae Ser.: Vol. 71). 576p. (C). 1995. lib. bdg. 320.00 (0-7923-2462-5) Kluwer Ac.

*Cayman Islands - The Beach & Beyond. Martha Smith. (Illus.). 224p. (Orig.). 1995. pap. 12.95 (1-55650-678-3) Hunter NJ.

*Cayman Islands Commercial Law. 150p. (C). 1994. pap. 295.00 (0-7605-0094-0) Rector Pr.

*Cayman Islands Seashore Vegetation: A Study in Comparative Biogeography. Jonathan D. Sauer. LC 82-2608. (University of California Publications in Entomology: No. 25). 177p. 1982. pap. 50.50 (0-7837-8423-6, 2049225) Bks Demand.

Cayman Seascapes Paul Humann's Portfolio of Marine Life. Paul Hummann. Ed. by Patricia R. Collins. (Illus.). 96p. 1986. 26.00 (0-936655-00-3); pap. 20.00 (0-936655-01-1) Underwater Spec Ltd.

Cayo Santiago Macaques: History, Behavior, & Biology. Ed. by Richard G. Rawlins & Matt J. Kessler. LC 86-19616. (Primatology Ser.). 306p. (Orig.). (C). 1986. 74.50 (0-88706-135-4); pap. 24.95 (0-88706-136-2) State U NY Pr.

Cayuga. Jill D. Duvall. LC 91-3038. (New True Bks.). 48p. (J). (gr. k-4). 1991. pap. 5.50 (0-516-41123-3) Childrens.

Cayuga Lake: Past, Present, Future. Carol U. Sisler. (Illus.). 160p. (Orig.). 1989. write for info. (0-9623904-1-0) Enterprise NY.

Cayuse Indians: Imperial Tribesmen of Old Oregon. Robert H. Ruby & John A. Brown. (Illus.). 345p. (Orig.). 1989. reprint ed. pap. text ed. 10.95 (0-914019-21-X) NW Interpretive.

Caz & His Cat: Now We Like the Night. Jean A. Wilson. (Illus.). 32p. (J). 1995. 14.95 (1-884739-00-8) Wahr.

*Cazadero Poems. Susan Kennedy & Mike Tuggle. 48p. (Orig.). 1994. pap. 8.00 (0-912449-43-8) Floating Island.

Cazenove & Company: A History. David Kynaston. (Illus.). 352p. 1992. 65.00 (0-7134-6059-8, Pub. by Batsford UK) Trafalgar.

Cazenove Journal, 1794: A Journey Through New Jersey & Pennsylvania. Theophile Cazenove. Ed. by Rayner W. Kelsey. (Haverford Coll. Studies: No. 13). 1922. 20.00 (0-686-17388-0) R S Barnes.

CA90s: Computing Architecture for the 90s. Computer Associates International Inc. Staff. LC 91-147374. (Illus.). 166p. (C). 1990. 54.95 (0-923108-06-8) Comp Assocs NY.

CA90s: Computing Architecture for the 90s. 2nd ed. Computer Associates International, Inc. Staff. (Illus.). (C). 1991. 54.95 (0-923108-07-6) Comp Assocs NY.

CB: A Book about Time. Time Life Inc. Editors. Ed. by Elizabeth Ward & Neil Kagan. (Early Learning Program Ser.). (Illus.). 30p. (J). (ps-2). 1992. write for info. (0-8094-9303-9); lib. bdg. write for info. (0-8094-9304-7) Time-Life.

CB: Custer & Battle of Washita. Carroll. 1995. 39.95 (0-8488-0207-1, J M C & Co) Amereon Ltd.

C.B. Greenfield: A Little Madness. Lucille Kallen. 1987. pap. 3.50 (0-345-31119-1) Ballantine.

CB PLL Data Book. Louis M. Franklin. (Illus.). 130p. (Orig.). 1982. pap. 20.00 (0-943132-05-3) CB City Intl.

*CB&Q Color Guide to Freight & Passenger Equipment. M. Spoor. (Illus.). 128p. 1995. 49.95 (1-878887-40-8) Morning NJ.

CBE: MultiMedia Sequencer. Steve Holden & Ron Doering. Ed. by Richard A. Pollak. (Illus.). 48p. 1992. disk, ring bd. 69.95 (0-922649-13-8) ETC MN.

CBE Style Manual. 5th rev. ed. CBE Style Manual Committee. LC 83-7172. (Council of Biology Editors Style Manual). (Illus.). 324p. 1983. text ed. 27.95 (0-914340-04-2) Coun Biology Eds.

CBEST: Basic Educational Skills Test. Elna M. Dimock. 256p. 1989. pap. 13.00 (0-13-111949-4, Arco Test) P-H Gen Ref & Trav.

CBEST: California Basic Educational Skills Test Preparation Guide. Jerry Bobrow et al. (Cliffs Test Preparation Ser.). (Illus.). 244p. (Orig.). (C). 1992. pap. text ed. 8.95 (0-8220-2069-6) Cliffs.

CBEST - California Basic Educational Skills Test. rev. ed. Stanley L. Swartz et al. 336p. 1993. 16.95 (0-87891-894-9) Res & Educ.

*CBI European Business Handbook: The Essential Guide to Trading & Investment in the New Europe. 2nd ed. Ed. by Jonathan Reuvid. 680p. 1995. pap. 55.00 (0-7494-1376-X, Pub. by Kogan Pg UK) Cassell.

CBIOS for IBM PS-2 Computers & Compatibles: The Complete Guide to ROM-Based System Software for DOS. Phoenix Technologies Staff. 1989. pap. 26.95 (0-201-51804-X) Addison-Wesley.

*CBL Explorations in Calculus for the TI-82: Calculator-Based Laboratory. Larson Texts, Inc. (Meridian Creative Group) Staff. 112p. (Orig.). (C). 1995. pap. text ed. write for info. (0-9639121-1-9) Meridian Creative.

*CBMS Issues in Mathematics Education: Research in Collegiate Mathematics Education, I, Vol. 4. Ed. by Ed Dubinsky et al. 229p. 1994. pap. text ed. 42.00 (0-8218-3504-1) Am Math.

CBreeze Plus Plus: BASIC to C Plus Plus Tutorial-Translator. Robert J. Traister. 80p. 1994. disk 59.95 (0-12-697422-5, AP Prof) Acad Pr.

CBS Course of Mycology. 3rd ed. W. Gams et al. (Illus.). 136p. 1987. text ed. 37.50 (90-70351-12-9, Pub. by Ctrl Bur voor Schimmel NE) Lubrecht & Cramer.

CBS News- New York Times National Surveys, 1981. CBS News & New York Times. LC 84-219135. 1983. write for info. (0-89138-919-9) ICPSR.

CBS News Index, 1986: Key to the Television News Broadcasts. 983p. 1989. 125.00 (0-685-46003-7) Univ Microfilms.

CBS News-New York Times Election Day Surveys, 1982. 2nd ed. CBS News Staff & New York Times Staff The. LC 84-81926. 1984. write for info. (0-89138-895-8) ICPSR.

CBS News-New York Times National Surveys, 1982. 2nd ed. CBS News Staff & New York Times Staff The. LC 84-81221. 1984. write for info. (0-89138-897-4) ICPSR.

CBS News-New York Times National Surveys, 1983. 2nd ed. CBS News Staff & New York Times Staff The. LC 85-60276. 1985. write for info. (0-89138-891-5) ICPSR.

CBS News-The New York Times Election Surveys 1980, 2 vols., I. CBS News Staff & New York Times Staff The. LC 82-81160. 1982. write for info. (0-89138-933-4) ICPSR.

CBS News-The New York Times Election Surveys 1980, 2 vols., II. CBS News Staff & New York Times Staff The. LC 82-81160. 1982. write for info. (0-89138-932-6) ICPSR.

CBS News-The New York Times Election Surveys 1980, 2 vols., Set. CBS News Staff & New York Times Staff The. LC 82-81160. 1982. write for info. (0-89138-931-8, ICPSR 7812) ICPSR.

CBT Course Administrator's Guide. Center for Occupational Research & Development Staff. (EUTEC Power Plant Operator Curriculum Ser.). 76p. 1987. pap. text ed. write for info. (1-55502-343-6) CORD Commns.

CBT Documentation for ALT Authoring System. Center for Occupational Research & Development Staff. (EUTEC Power Plant Operator Curriculum Ser.). 82p. 1986. pap. text ed. write for info. (1-55502-288-X) CORD Commns.

CBT Documentation for the Test Development System. Center for Occupational Research & Development Staff. (EUTEC Power Plant Operator Curriculum Ser.). 51p. 1987. pap. text ed. write for info. (1-55502-344-4) CORD Commns.

CBW: the Poor Man's Atomic Bomb. Neil C. Livingstone & Joseph D. Douglass. Tr. by John Tower. LC 84-47502. (National Security Papers). 36p. 1984. 7.50 (0-89549-057-9) Inst Foreign Policy Anal.

*CC: Mail Administrator's Guide. Cindy Rennie. 1995. 34.99 (0-7821-1743-0) Sybex.

CC: Mail for Windows Version 2.0 Quick Reference Guide. Don Gosselin. Ed. by Kathy Berkemeyer. (DDC Quick Reference Guides Ser.). (Illus.). 238p. (Orig.). 1993. pap. text ed., spiral bd. 8.95 (1-56243-135-8, CC-18) DDC Pub.

*CC: Mail Release X Plain & Simple. Penni Rosen. 1995. write for info. (0-7821-1797-X) Sybex.

CC: Mail: The Pocket Reference. Christopher Germann. 1992. pap. text ed. 9.95 (0-07-881830-3) Osborne-McGraw.

CC: Mail Plain & Simple. Cindy Rennie. LC 94-66853. 278p. 1994. pap. 16.99 (0-7821-1553-5) Sybex.

CC, NT, Vol. 10: First & Second Chronicles. Leslie Allen. 445p. 1987. write for info. (0-8499-0415-3) Word Inc.

CC, NT, Vol. 10: Hebrews. Louis Evans. 259p. 1985. write for info. (0-8499-0163-4) Word Inc.

CC, NT, Vol. 11: James, First & Second Peter, Jude. Paul A. Cedar. 262p. 1984. write for info. (0-8499-0164-2) Word Inc.

CC, NT, Vol. 12: First, Second, Third John & Revelation. Earl Palmer. 259p. 1982. write for info. (0-8499-0165-0) Word Inc.

CC, NT, Vol. 2: Mark. David L. McKenna. 332p. 1982. write for info. (0-8499-0155-3) Word Inc.

CC, NT, Vol. 3: Luke. Bruce Larson. 347p. 1983. write for info. (0-8499-0156-1) Word Inc.

CC, NT, Vol. 4: John. Roger L. Fredrikson. 299p. 1985. write for info. (0-8499-0157-X) Word Inc.

CC, NT, Vol. 5: Acts. Lloyd J. Ogilvie. 369p. 1983. write for info. (0-8499-0158-8) Word Inc.

CC, NT, Vol. 6: Romans. D. Stuart Briscoe. 264p. 1982. write for info. (0-8499-0159-6) Word Inc.

CC, NT, Vol. 7: First & Second Corinthians. Kenneth L. Chafin & Lloyd J. Ogilvie. 298p. 1985. write for info. (0-8499-0347-5) Word Inc.

CC, NT, Vol. 8: First & Second Samuel. Kenneth Chafin. 404p. 1990. write for info. (0-8499-0413-7) Word Inc.

CC, NT, Vol. 8: Galatians, Ephesians, Philippians, Colossians, Philemon. Maxie Dunnam. 420p. 1982. write for info. (0-8499-0161-8) Word Inc.

CC, NT, Vol. 9: I.II Thessalonians, I.II Timothy - Titus. Gary Demarest. 333p. 1984. write for info. (0-8499-0162-6) Word Inc.

CC, OT, Vol. 1: Genesis. D. Stuart Briscoe. 414p. 1987. write for info. (0-8499-0406-4) Word Inc.

CC, OT, Vol. 11: Ezra-Nehemiah. Mark Roberts. 1993. 21.99 (0-8499-0416-1) Word Inc.

CC, OT, Vol. 12: Job. David L. McKenna. 331p. 1986. write for info. (0-8499-0418-8) Word Inc.

CC, OT, Vol. 13: Psalms 1-72. Donald Williams. 493p. 1986. write for info. (0-8499-0419-6) Word Inc.

CC, OT, Vol. 14: Psalms 73-150. Donald Williams. 543p. 1989. write for info. (0-8499-0420-X) Word Inc.

CC, OT, Vol. 15A: Proverbs. David Hubbard. 496p. 1989. write for info. (0-8499-0421-8) Word Inc.

CC, OT, Vol. 17: Jeremiah - Lamentations. John Guest. 390p. 1988. write for info. (0-8499-0423-4) Word Inc.

CC, OT, Vol. 18: Ezekiel. Douglas Stuart. 426p. 1989. write for info. (0-8499-0424-2) Word Inc.

CC, OT, Vol. 19: Daniel. Sinclair B. Ferguson. 252p. 1988. write for info. (0-8499-0425-0) Word Inc.

CC, OT, Vol. 2: Exodus. Maxie Dunnam. 295p. 1987. write for info. (0-8499-0407-2) Word Inc.

CC, OT, Vol. 20: Hosea, Joel, Amos, Obadiah, Jonah. Lloyd J. Ogilvie. 1991. 19.99 (0-8499-0426-9) Word Inc.

CC, OT, Vol. 21: Micah-Malachi. Walter Kaiser. 1992. 19.99 (0-8499-0427-7) Word Inc.

CC, OT, Vol. 3: Leviticus. Gary Demarest. 286p. 1990. write for info. (0-8499-0408-0) Word Inc.

CC, OT, Vol. 4: Numbers. James Philip. 364p. 1987. write for info. (0-8499-0409-9) Word Inc.

CC, OT, Vol. 5: Deuteronomy. John Maxwell. 351p. 1987. write for info. (0-8499-0410-2) Word Inc.

CC, OT, Vol. 6: Joshua. John Huffman. 282p. 1986. write for info. (0-8499-0411-0) Word Inc.

CC, OT, Vol. 7: Judges & Ruth. David Jackman. 1991. 19.99 (0-8499-0412-9) Word Inc.

CC, OT, Vol. 9: First & Second Kings. Russell Dilday. 512p. 1987. write for info. (0-8499-0414-5) Word Inc.

*CC-ROM Bibliothek. Langenscheidt Staff. 695p. (ENG & GER.). 1994. write for info. (0-614-00359-8, 3468909012) Fr & Eur.

CCAR Yearbook. Incl. Vol. 86. 1977. 1978. 15.00 (0-916694-36-4); Vol. 89. 1980. 1981. 20.00 (0-685-42060-4); write for info. (0-318-51321-8) Central Conf.

*CCAR Yearbook, Vol. CII. annuals 323p. 1994. 20.00 (0-88123-062-6) Central Conf.

CCAR Yearbook, 1889-1891, 3 vols., Vols. I-III. (Illus.). 1951. 15.00 (0-916694-59-3) Central Conf.

CCC: Short Term Counseling, Vol. 3. David Dillon. 1992. 15.99 (0-8499-0775-6) Word Inc.

CCC, Vol. 1: Baby Boomer Blues. Gary Collins. 1992. 13.99 (0-8499-3375-7); pap. 10.99 (0-8499-3373-0) Word Inc.

CCC, Vol. 2: Broken Promises, Understanding, Healing & Preventing Affairs in Christian Marriages. Henry Virkler. 1992. 13.99 (0-8499-0838-8) Word Inc.

CCC, Women, Vol. 4: Women: The Misunderstood Majority. Gay Hubbard. 1992. 15.99 (0-8499-0834-5); pap. 10.99 (0-8499-3380-3) Word Inc.

CCCC Bibliography of Composition & Rhetoric 1987. Ed. by Erika Lindemann et al. 216p. (C). 1990. 29.95 (0-8093-1647-1); pap. 19.95 (0-8093-1648-X) S Ill U Pr.

CCCC Bibliography of Composition & Rhetoric, 1988. Ed. by Erika Lindemann & Mary B. Harding. 224p. (C). 1990. 29.95 (0-8093-1669-2); pap. 19.95 (0-8093-1670-6) S Ill U Pr.

CCCC Bibliography of Composition & Rhetoric, 1989. annot. ed. Ed. by Erika Lindemann & Sandra M. Fleming. 224p. (C). 1991. 29.95 (0-8093-1712-5) S Ill U Pr.

CCCC Bibliography of Composition & Rhetoric 1991. Ed. by Gail E. Hawisher & Cynthia L. Selfe. 213p. (C). 1993. pap. 19.95 (0-8093-1892-X) S Ill U Pr.

CCCC Bibliography of Composition & Rhetoric 1992. Ed. by Gail E. Hawisher & Cynthia L. Selfe. 224p. (C). 1994. 29.95 (0-8093-1959-4); pap. 19.95 (0-8093-1960-8) S Ill U Pr.

*CCCC Bibliography of Composition & Rhetoric 1993. Ed. by Gail E. Hawisher & Cynghia L. Selfe. 272p. (C). 1995. lib. bdg. 49.95x (0-8093-1993-4); pap. 19.95x (0-8093-1994-2) S Ill U Pr.

CCD Astronomy. Buil. 1991. 24.95 (0-943396-29-8) Willmann-Bell.

CCD Camera Cookbook. Richard Berry et al. LC 93-6378. 1993. write for info. (0-943396-41-7) Willmann-Bell.

CCDs in Astronomy. Ed. by G. H. Jacoby. (ASP Conference Series Publications: Vol. 8). 407p. 1990. 25.00 (0-937707-25-2) Astron Soc Pacific.

CCDs in Astronomy, No. II. Ed. by A. G. Davis Philip et al. 302p. 1990. 27.00 (0-933485-12-3) L Davis Pr.

*CCE: An Integration Platform for Distributed Manufacturing Applications. Ed. by Consortium CCE/CNMA, ESPRIT Editors. (Research Reports ESPRIT: Vol. 1). 207p. 1995. pap. 43.00 (3-540-59060-9) Spr-Verlag.

CCH Guide to Nineteen Ninety-Three: Changes in EEC Law. 2nd ed. Chance. 168p. 1990. pap. 33.00 (0-685-67172-0, 5620) Commerce.

CCL: Cajun & Creole Cookbook. Jack Robertson. 96p. 1994. 10.98 (0-8317-1306-2) Smithmark.

CCL: Cl Pasta Sauces. Elizabeth Martin. 96p. 1994. 10.98 (0-8317-1305-4) Smithmark.

*CCL: Classic Main Courses. Linda Fraser. (Illus.). 96p. 1995. 10.98 (0-8317-1491-3) Smithmark.

*CCL: Essential Vegetarian. Linda Fraser. (Illus.). 96p. 1995. 10.98 (0-8317-1184-1) Smithmark.

*CCL: Finger Foods & Party Snacks. Linda Fraser. (Illus.). 1995. 10.98 (0-8317-1190-6) Smithmark.

CCL: Indian Curry Cookbook. Shehzad Husain. 96p. 1994. 10.98 (0-8317-1304-6) Smithmark.

CCL: Low-Fat Indian Cookbook. Shehzad Husain. 96p. 1994. 10.98 (0-8317-1303-8) Smithmark.

*CCL: New Chicken Cookbook. Linda Fraser. (Illus.). 96p. 1995. 10.98 (0-8317-1873-0) Smithmark.

An Asterisk (*) at the beginning of an entry indicates that the title is appearing in BIP for the first time.

C

An Asterisk (*) at the beginning of an entry indicates that the title is appearing in BIP for the first time.

1105

Ceausecu's Romania: An Annotated Bibliography. Ed. by Opritsa D. Popa. LC 94-13055. (Bibliographies & Indexes in World History Ser.: Vol. 36). 168p. 1994. text ed. 59.95 (*0-313-28939-5*, Greenwood Pr) Greenwood.
*__Ceausescu & the Securitate: Coercion & Dissent in Romania, 1965-1989.__ Dennis Deletant. (Illus.). 256p. 1995. 65.00 (*1-56324-633-3*); pap. write for info. (*1-56324-634-1*) M E Sharpe.
CEB-FIP Model Code for Concrete Structures. 348p. 1978. 135.25 (*0-317-32075-0*, CEB-FIP) ACI.
CEB Style Manual. California Continuing Education of the Bar Staff. LC 80-67155. 1982. 55.00 (*0-88124-076-1*, MI-34510) Cont Ed Bar-CA.
CEB Style Manual. suppl. ed. California Continuing Education of the Bar Staff. LC 80-67155. 1987. Dec. '87 suppl. 18.00 (*0-685-08731-X*, MI-34517) Cont Ed Bar-CA.
CEBAF Publications Title. (Orig.). 1988. pap. text ed. 35.00 (*0-317-92310-2*) CEBAF.
CEBAF Publications Title Pages Attached. (Orig.). 1988. pap. text ed. 35.00 (*0-685-22985-8*) CEBAF.
CEBAF Summer Workshop, 1992: Proceedings of the Workshop Held in Newport News, VA 1992. Ed. by F. Gross & R. Holt. (AIP Conference Proceedings Ser.: No. 269). (Illus.). 624p. 1993. text ed. 150.00 (*1-56396-067-2*, AIP Pr) Am Inst Physics.
Cebes' Tablet. Cebes. Ed. & Intro. by Sandra Sider. (Renaissance Text Ser.: No. 6). (Illus.). iv, 230p. 1979. 9.95 (*0-9602696-2-2*) Renaiss Society Am.
Ceb's Amazing Tail. David R. Collins. (Illus.). (J). (ps-2). 1987. lib. bdg. 8.99 (*0-8136-5185-9*); pap. 4.79 (*0-8136-5685-0*) Modern Curr.
Cebu. Peter Bacho. LC 91-323. 212p. (Orig.). 1991. text ed. 25.00 (*0-295-97113-4*); pap. 14.95 (*0-295-97132-0*) U of Wash Pr.
Cebu under the Spanish Flag, 1521-1896: An Economic & Social History. Bruce L. Fenner. (San Carlos Humanities Ser.: No. 14). (Illus.). 201p. 1986. 16.75 (*971-10-0044-X*, Pub. by San Carlos Univ PH); pap. 12.50 (*0-318-60375-6*, Pub. by San Carlos Univ PH) Cellar.
Cebuano Folk Tales, 1 & 2, 2 vols. Ed. by Erlinda K. Alburo. 4.00 (*0-686-09462-X*) Cellar.
Cebuano Folksongs One. Ed. by Erlinda K. Alburo. (Illus.). 1978. pap. 3.75 (*0-686-24098-7*) Cellar.
Cebuano Harvest One. Ed. by Lina Espina-Moore. (Illus.). 110p. (Orig.). 1992. pap. 6.50 (*0-317-04958-5*, Pub. by New Day Pub PH) Cellar.
Cebuano Newspaper Reader. R. David Zorc. LC 86-51670. 121p. 1987. text ed. 37.00 (*0-931745-34-9*); audio 15.00 (*0-931745-42-X*) Dunwoody Pr.
Cebuano-Visayan Dictionary. Elsa P. Yap & Maria V. Bunye. LC 74-152461. (Pacific & Asian Linguistics Institute. PALI Language Texts: Philippines Ser.). 534p. reprint ed. pap. 152.20 (*0-685-17863-3*, 2029587) Bks Demand.
CEC Project Mirage: Second Phase on Migration of Radionuclides in the Geosphere. Ed. by B. Come. 223p. 1989. pap. 25.00 (*92-826-0941-3*, CD-NA-12229-EN-) UNIPUB.
CEC Project Mirage Second Phase on Migration of Radionuclides in the Geosphere, No. EUR 12858. CEC Staff. (Illus.). 258p. 1990. pap. 30.00 (*92-826-1710-6*, CD-NA-12858-EN-C) UNIPUB.
CEC Thermal Hydraulic Benchmark Exercise on Fiploc Verification Experiment F2, No. EUR 13588. K. Fischer et al. 96p. 1991. pap. 11.00 (*92-826-2777-2*, CD-NA-13588-EN-C) UNIPUB.
CEC Thermal Hydraulic Benchmark Exercise on Fiploc Verification Experiment F2, No. EUR 14454. K. Fishcher et al. 208p. 1993. pap. 35.00 (*92-826-6454-6*, CD-NA-14454-EN-C, Pub. by Europ Com) UNIPUB.
CECAF Report of the () Session of the Working Party on Resource Evaluation. 9th ed. Food & Agriculture Organization Staff. (Fisheries Reports: No. 454). 86p. (ENG & FRE.). 1991. pap. 12.00 (*92-5-003091-6*, F0916) UNIPUB.
Cecco, As I Am & Was: The Poems of Cecco Angiolieri. Cecco Angiolieri. Ed. by Adolfo Caso. Tr. & Contrib by Tracy Barrett. 140p. (Orig.). 1994. pap. 12.95 (*0-8283-2000-4*, Intl Pocket Lib) Branden Pub Co.
Cech & Steenrod Homotopy Theories with Applications to Geometric Topology. D. A. Edwards & H. M. Hastings. (Lecture Notes in Mathematics Ser.: Vol. 542). 1976. pap. 19.00 (*3-540-07863-0*) Spr-Verlag.
*__Cech Centennial: A Conference on Homotopy Theory, June 22-26, 1993, Northeastern University.__ Ed. by Mila Cenkl et al. LC 94-43164. (Contemporary Mathematics Ser.: Vol. 181). 1995. write for info. (*0-8218-0296-8*) Am Math.
Cecil. John R. Lease. Ed. by Graham Core. LC 92-61877. (Illus.). 47p. 1992. 16.95 (*1-880439-01-8*) PERQ Pubns.
Cecil, a Peer, 3 vols. in 2, 1. Catherine G. Gore. LC 79-8274. reprint ed. write for info. (*0-404-61880-4*) AMS Pr.
Cecil, a Peer, 3 vols. in 2, 2. Catherine G. Gore. LC 79-8274. reprint ed. write for info. (*0-404-61881-2*) AMS Pr.
Cecil, a Peer, 3 vols. in 2, Set. Catherine G. Gore. LC 79-8274. reprint ed. 84.50 (*0-404-61879-0*) AMS Pr.
Cecil & Ida Green, Philanthropists Extraordinary. Robert R. Shrock. 300p. 1989. 27.50x (*0-262-19276-4*) MIT Pr.
Cecil B. DeMille. Charles Higham. (Quality Paperbacks Ser.). (Illus.). 335p. 1980. reprint ed. pap. 7.95 (*0-306-80131-0*) Da Capo.
Cecil B. DeMille: In Pursuit of the Grand Award. Robert S. Birchard. (Illus.). Date not set. write for info. (*1-879511-05-3*) Vestal.
Cecil B. DeMille & American Culture: The Silent Era. Sumiko Higashi. LC 94-6580. 1994. 40.00 (*0-520-08556-6*); pap. 18.00 (*0-520-08557-4*) U CA Pr.
Cecil Beaton: A Biography. Hugo Vickers. LC 86-46384. 1987. pap. 12.95 (*1-55611-021-9*, Primus Lib Contemp) D I Fine.
*__Cecil Beaton: Photographs 1920-1970.__ David Mellor & Philippe Garner. (Illus.). 320p. Date not set. 75.00 (*0-8212-2180-9*) Bulfinch Pr.
*__Cecil Beaton Photographs 1920-1970.__ Cecil Beaton. (Illus.). 320p. 1995. 85.00 (*1-55670-433-X*) Stewart Tabori & Chang.
Cecil Castlemaine's Gage, Lady Marabout's Troubles & Other Stories. Louise De La Ramee. LC 75-121534. (Short Story Index Reprint Ser.). 1977. 23.95 (*0-8369-3490-3*) Ayer.
Cecil Collins: A Retrospective Exhibition. Judith Collins. (Illus.). 136p. (Orig.). 1990. pap. 24.95 (*0-295-96924-5*) U of Wash Pr.
Cecil Essentials of Medicine. 3rd ed. Thomas E. Andreoli et al. LC 92-22928. (Illus.). 928p. 1993. pap. text ed. 41.95 (*0-7216-3272-6*) Saunders.
Cecil Kimber Centenary Book. Ed. by Richard L. Knudson. (Illus.). 208p. (Orig.). 1988. pap. 30.00 (*0-938253-01-8*) NEMGTRL.
Cecil Kunkle. Charles A. Wagner. (Illus.). 100p. (Orig.). 1994. pap. 5.00 (*0-9640245-0-0*) C Minus Comics.
Cecil; or the Adventures of a Coxcomb, 3 vols. in 2, 1. Catherine G. Gore. LC 79-8273. reprint ed. write for info. (*0-404-61876-6*) AMS Pr.
Cecil; or the Adventures of a Coxcomb, 3 vols. in 2, 2. Catherine G. Gore. LC 79-8273. reprint ed. write for info. (*0-404-61877-4*) AMS Pr.
Cecil; or the Adventures of a Coxcomb, 3 vols. in 2, Set. Catherine G. Gore. LC 79-8273. reprint ed. 84.50 (*0-404-61875-8*) AMS Pr.
Cecil Rhodes. Herbert Baker. LC 77-102223. (Select Bibliographies Reprint Ser.). 1977. 26.95 (*0-8369-5108-5*) Ayer.
Cecil Roth, Historian Without Tears: A Memoir. Irene Roth. (Illus.). 288p. 1982. 17.50 (*0-87203-103-9*) Hermon.
Cecil Sharp. Arthur H. Fox Stangways. LC 79-24412. (Music Reprint Ser.). 1980. reprint ed. lib. bdg. 29.50 (*0-306-76019-3*) Da Capo.
Cecil Spring Rice: A Diplomat's Life. David H. Burton. LC 89-46135. (Illus.). 232p. 1990. 35.00 (*0-8386-3395-1*) Fairleigh Dickinson.
Cecil Textbook of Medicine. 19th ed. James Wyngaarden. 1991. text ed. 99.00 (*0-7216-2928-8*) Saunders.
*__Cecil Textbook of Medicine.__ 20th ed. Ed. by Russell L. Cecil et al. LC 94-43773. 1996. text ed. write for info. (*0-7216-3561-X*) Saunders.
Cecil Textbook of Medicine, 2 vols., Set. 19th ed. James Wyngaarden. 1991. text ed. 129.00 (*0-7216-2931-8*) Saunders.
*__Cecil Textbook of Medicine, 2 vols., Set.__ 20th ed. Ed. by Russell L. Cecil et al. LC 94-43773. 1996. text ed. write for info. (*0-7216-3573-3*) Saunders.
*__Cecil Textbook of Medicine, 2 vols., Vol. 1.__ 20th ed. Ed. by Russell L. Cecil et al. LC 94-43773. 1996. write for info. (*0-7216-3574-1*) Saunders.
*__Cecil Textbook of Medicine, 2 vols., Vol. 2.__ 20th ed. Ed. by Russell L. Cecil et al. LC 94-43773. 1996. write for info. (*0-7216-3575-X*) Saunders.
CECIL Tutorial. Ivor Green. (Illus.). 111p. (Orig.). 1990. pap. text ed. 8.00 (*1-878606-00-X*) JAARS Inc.
Cecile. Janine Boissard. Tr. by Mary Feeny. 250p. 1988. 17.95 (*0-316-10103-6*) Little.
Cecile. Theodor Fontane. Tr. by Stanley Radcliffe. 200p. 1993. 35.00 (*0-946162-42-5*, Pub. by Angel Bks UK); pap. 16.95 (*0-946162-43-3*, Pub. by Angel Bks UK) Dufour.
Cecile. Ruthann Robson. LC 91-29775. 168p. (Orig.). 1991. lib. bdg. 18.95 (*1-56341-002-8*); pap. 8.95 (*1-56341-001-X*) Firebrand Bks.
Cecile see One Act: Eleven Short Plays of the Modern Theater
Cecile Chaminade: A Bio-Bibliography. Marcia J. Citron. LC 88-21315. (Bio-Bibliographies in Music Ser.: No. 15). 257p. 1988. text ed. 59.95 (*0-313-25319-6*, CCA/, Greenwood Pr) Greenwood.
Cecile ou, l'Ecole des Peres. Jean Anouilh. 1954. pap. 7.95 (*0-7859-0349-6*, F81840) Fr & Eur.
Cecile ou L'ecole des Peres see Pieces Brillantes
Cecile Parmi Nous. Georges Duhamel. (Chronique Des Pasquier Ser.: Vol. VII). (FRE.). 1976. pap. 10.95 (*0-7859-1778-0*, 2070365530) Fr & Eur.
Cecile Parmi Nous see Chronique des Pasquier
Cecile Parminous see Chronique des Pasquier
Cecilia. Francis M. Crawford. (Works of Francis Marion Crawford Ser.). 1990. reprint ed. lib. bdg. 79.00 (*0-7812-2553-1*) Rprt Serv.
Cecilia: Or, Memoirs of an Heiress. Fanny Burney. Ed. by Peter Sabor & Margaret A. Doody. (World's Classics Ser.). 1056p. 1988. pap. 8.95 (*0-19-281742-6*) OUP.
Cecilia of Rome. Lawrence J. Babin. 1977. 4.00 (*0-912492-09-0*) Pyquag.
Cecilia Reclaimed: Feminist Perspectives on Gender & Music. Ed. by Susan C. Cook & Judy S. Tsou. LC 93-18463. (Illus.). 296p. 1994. 34.95 (*0-252-02036-7*); pap. 12.95 (*0-252-06341-4*) U of Ill Pr.
Cecils Montana Adventure Activity Book. Sheri Amsel. (Illus.). 32p. (Orig.). (J). (gr. 4-7). 1992. pap. 3.95 (*1-56044-138-0*) Falcon Pr MT.
*__Cecil's Story.__ George E. Lyon. LC 90-7775. (Illus.). 32p. (J). (gr. k-2). 1995. pap. text ed. 5.95 (*0-531-07063-8*) Orchard Bks Watts.
Cecil's Story. George-Ella Lyon. LC 90-7775. (Illus.). 32p. (J). (gr. k-2). 1991. 15.95 (*0-531-05912-X*); lib. bdg. 15.99 (*0-531-08512-0*) Orchard Bks Watts.
Cecily. Clare Darcy. 1990. pap. 2.95 (*1-55817-350-1*, Pinnacle NY) Windsor NY.
Cecily. Gillian Plowman. 1992. pap. 2.75 (*0-87129-132-0*, C83) Dramatic Pub.
Cecily G. & the Nine Monkeys. H. A. Rey. (Illus.). 32p. (J). (gr. 1-3). 1974. 14.95 (*0-395-18430-4*) HM.
Cecily G. & the Nine Monkeys. H. A. Rey. (Illus.). (J). (ps-3). 1989. pap. 3.95 (*0-395-50651-4*, Sandpiper) HM.
Cecily Parsley's Nursery Rhymes. Beatrix Potter. (Original Peter Rabbit Books: No. 23). (J). 1987. 5.95 (*0-7232-3482-5*); pap. 2.25 (*0-7232-3507-4*) Warne.
*__Cecily Small & the Rainy Day Adventure.__ Cecily Mitchell. (Illus.). 48p. 1995. 14.95 (*0-8362-0747-5*) Andrews & McMeel.
Cecily's Christmas. Iris VanRynbach. LC 87-34083. (Illus.). 32p. (J). (ps-1). 1988. 11.95 (*0-688-07832-X*); lib. bdg. 11.88 (*0-688-07833-8*) Greenwillow.
Cecropiaceae: Coussapoa & Pourouma, with an Introduction to the Family. C. C. Berg et al. (Flora Neotropica Monographs.: No. 51). (Illus.). 208p. 1990. pap. text ed. 41.50 (*0-89327-352-X*) NY Botanical.
Cecyl Allen Johnson: Pioneer History of Life in Churchill County Nevada: The Allen Family & Their Descendants. Intro. by Mary E. Glass. 203p. 1970. lib. bdg. 34.00 (*1-56475-086-8*); fiche write for info. (*1-56475-087-6*) U NV Oral Hist.
CED & Education: National Impact & Next Steps. 44p. 1988. pap. 7.50 (*0-87186-342-1*) Comm Econ Dev.
CEDA Yearbook, 1991. CEDA Staff. 128p. 1991. per. 6.50 (*0-8403-7176-4*) Kendall-Hunt.
CEDA Yearbook, 1992. CEDA Staff. 100p. 1992. per. 7.00 (*0-8403-8039-9*) Kendall-Hunt.
CEDA Yearbook, 1993. CEDA Staff. 100p. 1993. per. 7.00 (*0-8403-8876-4*) Kendall-Hunt.
CEDAC: A Tool for Continuous Systematic Improvement. Ryuji Fukuda. LC 89-43210. 144p. 1990. 55.00 (*0-915299-26-7*) Prod Press.
*__Cedar: Tree of Life to the Northwest Coast Indians.__ Hilary Stewart. (Illus.). 192p. 1995. pap. 22.95 (*0-295-97448-6*) U of Wash Pr.
Cedar Bay: The Alternative. Kenneth R. Potier. 1986. 23.00 (*0-7223-2047-7*, Pub. by A H S Ltd UK) St Mut.
Cedar Bog. Walter B. Evans, Jr. & Mary A. Skardon. (Annual Monograph Ser.). Orig. Title: Journal-Walter B. Evans. (Illus.). 54p. 1974. reprint ed. pap. 4.00 (*0-686-28231-0*) Clark County Hist Soc.
Cedar Breaks for Kids. Pat Kittelson & Brooke Connor. (Illus.). (J). (gr. k-4). 1979. pap. 1.00 (*0-915630-14-1*) Zion.
Cedar Canoe. Karen A. Fish. LC 87-13755. (Contemporary Poetry Ser.). 64p. 1987. pap. 7.95 (*0-8203-0969-9*) U of Ga Pr.
Cedar City Reflections. 2nd rev. ed. Alva Matheson. LC 87-51370. (Illus.). 227p. Date not set. text ed. 24.95 (*0-935615-03-2*) S Utah St Coll.
Cedar City Rendezvous. Douglas Savage. 1994. 18.95 (*0-87131-762-1*) M Evans.
Cedar Fever: Story of a German-Texan Girl During World War I. Marian L. Martinello. LC 92-73295. (Multicultural Texas Ser.). (Illus.). 212p. (YA). (gr. 7-9). 1992. 15.95 (*0-931722-90-X*); pap. 7.95 (*0-931722-95-0*) Corona Pub.
Cedar Glen Secret. Sandra M. Maitland. (Illus.). 24p. (J). (ps-8). 1983. 6.95 (*0-920806-44-9*, Pub. by Penumbra Pr CN) U of Toronto Pr.
Cedar Grove Cemetery Inscriptions--South Bend, St. Joseph Co., Indiana. Genevieve Szymarck. ix, 93p. (Orig.). 1987. pap. text ed. 8.00 (*1-55613-038-4*) Heritage Bk.
Cedar Hill. Katie West. LC 82-81126. 180p. (Orig.). 1982. 12.95 (*0-88100-002-7*); pap. 6.95 (*0-88100-001-9*) Ranch House Pr.
Cedar Mountain - Ashdown Gorge, UT. rev. ed. Ed. by Trails Illustrated Staff. (Illus.). 1989. 8.99 (*0-925873-66-7*) Trails Illustrated.
Cedar Plank Mask. Nan McNutt. (Illus.). 34p. (J). (gr. 3-6). 1991. pap. 9.95 (*0-9614534-2-7*) N McNutt Assocs.

***Cedar Point: The Queen of American Watering Places. aniversary enl. rev. ed. David W. Francis & Diane D. Francis. LC 94-73676. (Illus.). 222p. 1995. reprint ed. 29.95 (*0-935408-03-7*) Amusement Pk Bks.**
On May 13, 1995, Cedar Point Amusement Park of Sandusky, Ohio, celebrates its 125th anniversary. CEDAR POINT: THE QUEEN OF AMERICAN WATERING PLACES, a completely revised & enlarged anniversary edition, tells the story of the birth, development & ascendancy of this significant resort - also known as the "Amazement Park". Now one of the nation's premier summer fun spots, Cedar Point on Lake Erie has become America's "roller coast". With eleven roller coasters, this flourishing facility takes the crown in the number of up & down thrill rides. Started as a lakeside bathing spot, Cedar Point, under the direction of George A. Boeckling, was established as one of Ohio's most visited places. It weathered the Depression, narrowly eluded demise in the 1950s & emerged triumphant in the 1960s. QUEEN OF AMERICAN WATERING PLACES presents that story in 222 pages with words & over 300 pictures. David & Diane Francis have meticulously researched & presented the rich & varied history of this resort in CEDAR POINT; THE QUEEN OF AMERICAN WATERING PLACES. This 8 1/2 x 11 hardcover volume, with index, is available through Amusement Park Books, Inc., 20925 Mastick Rd., Fairview Park, OH 44126. (216) 331-6429. ***Publisher Provided Annotation.***

*__Cedar Rapids: Tall Corn & High Te.__ Ernie Danek. 19.95 (*0-89781-021-X*) Preferred Mktg.
Cedar Rapids: The Magnificent Century. Harold F. Ewoldt. 128p. 1988. 29.95 (*0-89781-286-7*, 5242) Preferred Mktg.
Cedar River Daydreams, Bks. 1-5. Judy Baer. (Orig.). (J). 1991. Giftset. 19.99 (*1-55661-763-1*) Bethany Hse.
Cedar River Daydreams, Bks. 6-10. Judy Baer. (Orig.). (J). 1991. Giftset. 19.99 (*1-55661-764-X*) Bethany Hse.
Cedar River Daydreams, Bks. 11-15. Judy Baer. (Orig.). (J). (gr. 7-10). 1992. Giftset. pap. 19.99 (*1-55661-765-8*) Bethany Hse.
Cedar River Daydreams 16-20 Giftset. Judy Baer. (Cedar River Daydreams Ser.). (J). 1993. 19.99 (*1-55661-772-0*) Bethany Hse.
Cedar Tree in the Morning Sun. Morris Earle. LC 93-1976. 1994. 20.00 (*0-87233-111-3*) Bauhan.
*__Cedars.__ Ray L. Saunders. 220p. (Orig.). Date not set. pap. 8.95 (*0-7610-0248-0*) NW Pub.
Cedulario Puertorriqueno, 2 bks. Vicente Murga-Sanz. Incl. Bk. 1. 1505-1517. 3.50 (*0-8477-0813-6*); Bk. 2. 1518-1525. 3.50 (*0-8477-0814-4*); (C). write for info. (*0-318-56124-7*); Incl. Bk. 1. 3.50 (*0-8477-0813-6*); Bk. 2. 3.50 (*0-8477-0814-4*); Set. write for info. (*0-8477-0812-8*) U of PR Pr.
*__Cee Vee, Our Home on the Range.__ Marion W. McClendon & June R. Grelle. 500p. 1991. text ed. 58.50 (*0-9629112-0-8*) Cee Vee Hist.
CEGB: Modern Power Station-System Practice - MPSP, 11 vols. Incl. Vol. L. System Operation. 1986. (*0-318-60742-5*); 1986. Set. (*0-318-60741-7*) Inst Elect Eng.
Cegos Dictionary: Definition of Micro - Computer & Electronic Vocabulary: Dictionnaire Cegos: Definition Du Vocabulaire Micro-Informatique - Electronique. P. Morvan. 322p. (ENG & FRE.). 1986. 65.00 (*0-8288-1375-2*, M8340) Fr & Eur.
Cei & the Arthurian Legend. Linda Gowans. (Arthurian Studies). 224p. 1988. 71.00 (*0-85991-261-2*) Boydell & Brewer.
Ceiling Framing. Charley G. Chatwick et al. Ed. by Louis Harrington. (Basic Carpentry Skills Ser.). (Illus.). 12p. 1990. teacher ed 3.00 (*0-89606-319-4*, 702TK); pap. text ed. 6.00 (*0-89606-272-4*, 702) Am Assn Voc Materials.
Ceiling of Amber. Elizabeth Ogilvie. reprint ed. text ed. 17.95 (*0-88411-329-9*, Aeonian Pr) Amereon Ltd.
Cel Magic: Collecting Animation Art. R. Scott Edwards & Bob Stobener. (Illus.). 104p. (C). 1991. 19.95 (*0-9624792-2-5*) Laughs Unltd.
Cel Magic: The Book on Collecting Animation Art. R. Scott Edwards & Bob Stobener. (Illus.). 104p. 1990. pap. 19.95 (*0-9624792-1-7*) Laughs Unltd.
Celebrant. Greenberg. 1976. 27.95 (*0-8488-1577-7*) Amereon Ltd.
Celebrant: A Novel. Eric R. Greenberg. LC 92-25509. 272p. 1993. pap. 9.95 (*0-8032-7037-2*, Bison Books) U of Nebr Pr.
Celebrate. Ed. by Pat Rost et al. (Illus.). 1989. 15.00 (*0-9622333-0-7*) Missouri Bankers.
Celebrate!, Vol. VI. Ed. by Eugene T. Sullivan & Marilynn C. Sullivan. LC 75-24148. 1980. pap. 11.99 (*0-912696-28-1*) Wilton.
Celebrate: A Book of Jewish Holidays. Judith Gross. (All Aboard Bks.). (Illus.). 32p. (J). (gr. k-3). 1992. lib. bdg. 7.99 (*0-448-40303-X*, Platt & Munk Pubs); pap. 2.25 (*0-448-40302-1*, Platt & Munk Pubs) Putnam Pub Group.
*__Celebrate! A Sourcebook of Children's Parties & Family Traditions.__ 2nd ed. First United Nursery School Parents & Teachers. Ed. by Laurie Bunkers & Mary Ziegler. (Illus.). 200p. (J). 1995. pap. 14.95 (*0-9616693-0-6*) Rainbow Nursery.
Celebrate! A Toast to Fine Food & Good Friends from the Junior League of Sacramento. Junior League of Sacramento, Inc. 272p. 1991. 26.95 (*0-9630857-0-0*) JL of Sacramento.
Celebrate: Holidays, Puppets & Creative Drama. Tamara Hunt & Nancy Renfro. Ed. by Ann W. Schwalb. (Puppetry in Education Ser.). (Illus.). 208p. (J). (ps-4). 1987. 24.95 (*0-931044-09-X*); pap. 18.95 (*0-317-58474-X*) Renfro Studios.
Celebrate! III. Ed. by Eugene T. Sullivan & Marilynn C. Sullivan. LC 75-24148. 1976. pap. 11.99 (*0-912696-20-6*) Wilton.
Celebrate! IV. Ed. by Eugene T. Sullivan & Marilynn C. Sullivan. LC 75-24148. 1977. pap. 11.99 (*0-912696-10-9*) Wilton.
Celebrate! No. V. Ed. by Eugene T. Sullivan & Marilynn C. Sullivan. LC 75-24148. 1978. pap. 11.99 (*0-912696-22-2*) Wilton.
Celebrate! The Complete Jewish Holidays Handbook. Lesli K. Ross. LC 94-1940. 376p. 1994. pap. 35.00 (*1-56821-154-6*) Aronson.
Celebrate: Traditional Ethnic Entertaining in America. Hillary Davis. 1992. 17.99 (*0-517-05179-6*) Random Hse Value.

An Asterisk (*) at the beginning of an entry indicates that the title is appearing in BIP for the first time.

C

Celebrating Life. Robert R. Leichtman & Carl Japikse. 90p. 1993. pap. 7.95 (*0-89804-806-0*, Enthea Pr) Ariel GA.
Celebrating Life. Luci Swindoll. 112p. 1989. pap. 6.00 (*0-89109-547-0*) NavPress.
Celebrating Life: Rites of Passage for All Ages. Tzipora Klein. 228p. (Orig.). 1992. pap. 14.95 (*1-878980-05-X*) Delphi IL.
Celebrating Love. Mary Hathaway. (Celebrating Ser.). (Illus.). 48p. 1993. 13.95 (*0-7459-2397-6*) Lion USA.
Celebrating Marriage. Mary Hathaway. LC 92-38553. (Celebrating Ser.). (Illus.). 48p. 1993. 13.95 (*0-7459-2398-4*) Lion USA.
Celebrating Marriage: Preparing the Wedding Liturgy - A Workbook for the Engaged Couple. Ed. by Paul Covino. 1987. pap. 5.95 (*0-912405-34-1*) Pastoral Pr.
***Celebrating Me & My World: A Unitarian Universalist Preschool Curriculum.** Debora C. Pratt. Ed. by Patricia Hoertdoerfer. 1995. pap. 30.00 (*1-55896-328-6*) Unitarian Univ.
Celebrating Motherhood. Mary Hathaway. LC 92-38993. (Celebrating Ser.). (Illus.). 48p. 1993. 13.95 (*0-7459-2395-X*) Lion USA.
Celebrating Motherhood. Anne Williams & Haden H. Pickel. (Illus.). 144p. 1994. 14.99 (*0-8007-7212-1*) Revell.
***Celebrating Muhammad: Images of the Prophet in Popular Muslim Poetry.** Ali S. Asani & Kamal Abdel-Malek. LC 95-10341. 1995. write for info. (*1-57003-050-2*) U of SC Pr.
***Celebrating Multiple Intelligences: Teaching for Success.** Faculty of the New City School Staff. 1994. pap. 29.95 (*0-9643514-0-4*) New City Schl.
Celebrating New Year - Miss Yuan-Shiau: Festivals: English - Cambodian Version. Wonder Kids Publications Group Staff. Ed. by Emily Ching et al. Tr. by Wonder Kids Publications Staff. (Chinese Children's Stories Ser.). (Illus.). 28p. (J). (gr. 3-6). 1992. reprint ed. 12.95 (*1-56162-133-1*) Wonder Kids.
Celebrating New Year - Miss Yuan-Shiau: Festivals: English - Spanish Version. Wonder Kids Publications Group Staff. Ed. by Emily Ching et al. Tr. by Wonder Kids Publications Staff. (Chinese Children's Stories Ser.). (Illus.). 28p. (J). (gr. 3-6). 1992. reprint ed. 12.95 (*1-56162-131-5*) Wonder Kids.
Celebrating New Year - Miss Yuan-Shiau: Festivals: English - Vietnamese Version. Wonder Kids Publications Group Staff. Ed. by Emily Ching et al. Tr. by Wonder Kids Publications Staff. (Chinese Children's Stories Ser.). (Illus.). 28p. (J). (gr. 3-6). 1992. reprint ed. 12.95 (*1-56162-132-3*) Wonder Kids.
Celebrating Oregon. Mellisa Mathie. Ed. by Janice Bishop. (Illus.). 40p. 1993. pap. 30.00 (*0-9636258-0-2*) Will Creek W.
Celebrating Our Differences: Living Two Faiths in One Marriage. Mary H. Rosenbaum & Stanley N. Rosenbaum. LC 94-8447. 240p. (C). 1994. 19.95 (*0-942597-69-9*, Ragged Edge) White Mane Pub.
Celebrating Our Diversity. Marti Abbott & Betty J. Polk. 1992. pap. 21.99 (*0-86653-989-1*) Fearon Teach Aids.
Celebrating Our Heritage. 1991. pap. 3.95 (*1-55673-378-X*, 9223) CSS OH.
Celebrating Our Heritage: Kendall, Wisconsin 1894-1994. Donnaphee Murray & Carol Kunz. (Illus.). 152p. 1994. pap. 25.00 (*0-938627-21-X*) New Past Pr.
Celebrating Our Mothers' Kitchens: Words of Wisdom & Treasured Recipes. National Council of Negro Women Staff. Ed. by Glen Wimmer. (Illus.). 224p. 1994. 15.95 (*1-879958-23-6*) Tradery Hse.
***Celebrating Our Past, Building for the Future: Ladue Chapel, 1943-1993.** Ladue Chapel, Missouri Staff. (Illus.). 128p. (Orig.). 1993. pap. text ed. 9.95 (*1-881576-18-3*) Providence Hse.
Celebrating Our Seasons & Saints. 1993. text ed. 2.19 (*0-8215-1511-X*); text ed. 1.98 (*0-8215-1512-8*); text ed. 1.98 (*0-8215-1513-6*); text ed. 1.98 (*0-8215-1514-4*); text ed. 1.98 (*0-8215-1515-2*); text ed. 1.98 (*0-8215-1516-0*); audio 9.95 (*0-8215-1531-4*); audio write for info. (*0-318-72658-0*); audio 9.95 (*0-8215-1532-2*); audio write for info. (*0-318-72659-9*) Sadlier.
Celebrating Our Seasons & Saints. annot. ed. 1993. teacher ed 3.27 (*0-8215-1521-7*); teacher ed 3.27 (*0-8215-1522-5*); teacher ed 3.27 (*0-8215-1523-3*); teacher ed 3.27 (*0-8215-1524-1*); teacher ed 3.27 (*0-8215-1525-X*); teacher ed 3.27 (*0-8215-1526-8*) Sadlier.
***Celebrating Our United Methodist Heritage: A Resource Packet for the Local Church.** Susan E. Warrick. 70p. 1994. pap. 9.50 (*1-880927-17-9*) Gen Comm Arch.
Celebrating Ourselves: A Crone Ritual. Ed. by Edna M. Ward. (Illus.). 40p. 1991. pap. 6.00 (*0-9624626-3-2*) Astarte Shell Pr.
***Celebrating Peace.** Kelly Guinan. LC 94-40966. 1994. spiral bd. 9.95 (*0-8309-0681-9*) Herald Hse.
Celebrating Peace. Ed. by Leroy S. Rouner. LC 90-36381. (Boston University Studies in Philosophy & Religion: Vol. 11). 256p. (C). 1990. text ed. 31.95 (*0-268-00779-9*) U of Notre Dame Pr.
Celebrating Pentecost Through Dance. Joan Huff. Ed. by Doug Adams. (Orig.). 1986. pap. 3.00 (*0-941500-41-1*) Sharing Co.
Celebrating Retirement. Mary Hathaway. (Celebrating Ser.). (Illus.). 48p. 1993. 13.95 (*0-7459-2396-8*) Lion USA.
Celebrating Sacraments. Joseph Stoutzenberger. Ed. by Stephan Nagel. (Illus.). 199p. (Orig.). 1984. pap. text ed. 8.50 (*0-88489-159-3*); teacher ed, spiral bd. 12.00 (*0-88489-160-7*) St Marys.
Celebrating Sacraments. Joseph Stoutzenberger. Ed. by Barbara Allaire. (Illus.). 257p. (Orig.). (YA). (gr. 10). 1993. teacher ed, spiral bd. 24.95 (*0-88489-280-8*) St Marys.
Celebrating Sacraments. rev. ed. Joseph Stoutzenberger. Ed. by Barbara Allaire. (Illus.). 304p. (Orig.). (YA). (gr. 10). 1993. pap. text ed. 14.25 (*0-88489-279-4*) St Marys.
Celebrating School Liturgies: Guidelines for Planning. Timothy Joseph & Joan P. Vos. 64p. (Orig.). 1991. pap. 7.95 (*0-8146-1906-1*) Liturgical Pr.
Celebrating Sixty Years: San Francisco Museum of Modern Art, 1935-1995. Ed. by Kara Kirk. LC 94-17616. 1995. write for info. (*0-918471-32-X*); pap. write for info. (*0-918471-31-1*) San Fran MOMA.
Celebrating Special Days in the Church School Year. Judy G. Smith. Ed. by Arthur L. Zapel. LC 81-83441. (Illus.). 125p. (Orig.). 1981. pap. text ed. 9.95 (*0-916260-14-3*, B-146) Meriwether Pub.
***Celebrating Summer.** Rita Kohn. LC 94-37048. (Woodland Adventures Ser.). (Illus.). 32p. (J). (ps-2). 1995. lib. bdg. 13.95 (*0-516-05201-2*) Childrens.
Celebrating the Advent-Christmas Season. Anne N. Rupp. 60p. (Orig.). 1989. pap. 9.25 (*0-940754-79-7*) Ed Ministries.
Celebrating the Birth of Christ. Robert Shannon & Michael Shannon. 112p. 1985. pap. 4.99 (*0-87239-916-8*, 18-3022) Standard Pub.
Celebrating the Birth of the Savior. C. Welton Gaddy. (Orig.). 1993. pap. 8.99 (*0-8054-6063-2*) Broadman.
Celebrating the Centennial 1892-1992. Huntington Memorial Hospital Volunteers Staff. 156p. 1991. 17.50 (*0-9630378-0-3*) Hunt Mem Hosp.
Celebrating the Christian Year: Building Family Traditions Around All the Major Christian Holidays. Martha Zimmerman. 1993. pap. 8.99 (*1-55661-349-0*) Bethany Hse.
Celebrating the Church Year with Young Children. Joan Halmo. (Illus.). 159p. 1989. pap. 12.95 (*0-8146-1580-5*) Liturgical Pr.
***Celebrating the Circle: Recognizing Women & Children.** Ed. by B. Cutland & W. George. (Theytus Gatherings Ser.). 292p. (Orig.). 1995. pap. 10.95 (*0-919441-61-0*, Pub. by Theytus Bks Ltd CN) Orca Bk Pubs.
Celebrating the Disciplines: A Journal Workbook to Accompany Celebration of Discipline. Richard J. Foster. 160p. 1992. student ed, pap. 14.00 (*0-06-069867-5*) Harper SF.
Celebrating the Dream. 31p. 1990. pap. 5.00 (*0-87104-706-3*, Branch Libraries) NY Pub Lib.
***Celebrating the Duke, & Louis, Bessie, Billie, Bird, Carmen, Miles, Dizzy & Other Heroes.** Ralph J. Gleason. (Illus.). 302p. 1995. reprint ed. pap. 13.95 (*0-306-80645-2*) Da Capo.
Celebrating the Earth: An Earth-Centered Theology of Worship with Blessings, Prayers, & Rituals. enl. rev. ed. Scott McCarthy. Orig. Title: Creation Liturgy. (Illus.). 360p. 1991. pap. text ed. 19.95 (*0-89390-199-7*) Resource Pubns.
Celebrating the Easter Vigil. Ed. by Rupert Berger & Hans Hollerweger. Tr. by Matthew J. O'Connell. 157p. 1992. pap. 12.95 (*0-8146-6056-8*, Pueblo Bks) Liturgical Pr.
Celebrating the Eucharist. Luis Alonso-Schoekel. 160p. 1989. 14.95 (*0-8245-0938-2*) Crossroad NY.
Celebrating the Eucharist. Yvette Nelson. (Discovering Program Ser.). (Illus.). 73p. (Orig.). (YA). (gr. 7-8). 1992. teacher ed 6.00 (*0-88489-270-0*); pap. text ed. 2.80 (*0-88489-269-7*) St Marys.
Celebrating the Eucharist. Luis A. Schokel. 160p. (C). 1990. 39.00 (*0-85439-277-7*, Pub. by St Paul Pubns UK) St Mut.
Celebrating the Family: Steps to Planning a Family Reunion. Vandella Brown. (Illus.). 64p. (Orig.). 1991. pap. 9.95 (*0-916489-46-9*) Ancestry.
Celebrating the Fifty Days of Easter. Daniel Connors. LC 90-71559. 80p. (Orig.). 1991. pap. 3.95 (*0-89622-463-5*) Twenty-Third.
***Celebrating the Great Mother: A Handbook of Earth-Honoring Activities for Parents & Children.** Cait Johnson & Maura D. Shaw. LC 94-43712. 240p. 1995. pap. 14.95 (*0-89281-550-7*, Destiny Bks) Inner Tradit.
Celebrating the Hero. Lyll Becerra de Jenkins. (Illus.). 160p. (YA). (gr. 7 up). 1993. 15.99 (*0-525-67399-7*, Lodestar Bks) Dutton Child Bks.
***Celebrating the Hero.** Lyll B. De Jenkins. 192p. (YA). (gr. 7 up). 1995. pap. 3.99 (*0-14-037605-4*) Puffin Bks.
Celebrating the Land: Women's Nature Writings, 1850-1991. Ed. by Karen Knowles. LC 92-18071. 144p. (Orig.). 1992. pap. 12.95 (*0-87358-545-3*) Northland AZ.
***Celebrating the Liturgy with Children Cycle A.** Bridget M. Meehan & Regina M. Oliver. 1995. pap. text ed. write for info. (*0-8146-2359-X*, Liturg Pr Bks) Liturgical Pr.
Celebrating the Lives of Students. Ed. by Robert Atkinson & Kelly Nelson. 1990. write for info. (*0-939561-08-5*) Univ South ME.
Celebrating the Medieval Heritage: A Colloquy on the Thought of Aquinas & Bonaventura. Ed. by David Tracy. LC 78-113803. (Journal of Religion Ser.: Vol. 58, Supplement, 1978). 248p. reprint ed. pap. 71.60 (*0-685-23842-3*, 2056626) Bks Demand.
Celebrating the National Reading Initiative. California Department of Education Staff. (Illus.). 96p. 1989. pap. 6.75 (*0-8011-0760-1*) Calif Education.
***Celebrating the New Moon: A Rosh Chodesh Sourcebook.** Susan Berrin. 1995. write for info. (*1-56821-459-6*) Aronson.
Celebrating the New Woman: In the Family. Donald Joy. 116p. (Orig.). (J). (gr. 6-8). 1993. pap. 9.95 (*0-917851-77-3*) Bristol Hse.
Celebrating the New World: Chicago's Columbian Exposition of 1893. Robert Muccigrosso. (American Ways Ser.). (Illus.). 224p. 1993. 24.95 (*1-56663-013-4*); pap. text ed. 11.95 (*1-56663-014-2*) I R Dee.
Celebrating the Other. Edward E. Sampson. (Psychology, Gender, & Theory Ser.). 1993. text ed. 58.00 (*0-8133-1941-2*) Westview.
Celebrating the Other: A Dialogic Account of Human Nature. Edward E. Sampson. 207p. (C). 1993. pap. text ed. 21.50 (*0-8133-1942-0*) Westview.
Celebrating the Rites of Adult Initiation: Pastoral Reflections. Ed. by Victoria Tufano. LC 91-40485. (Font & Table Ser.). 124p. (Orig.). 1992. pap. 7.95 (*0-929650-45-X*) Liturgy Tr Pubns.
***Celebrating the Sabbath the Messianic Jewish Way.** Richard Berkowitz & Michele Berkowitz. (Illus.). 48p. 1988. pap. 4.95 (*1-880226-00-6*) Lederer Pubns.
Celebrating the Seasons of Life. Mary Batchelor. 1990. 14.95 (*0-7459-1434-9*) Lion USA.
Celebrating the Seasons with Children (Year B) Philip E. Johnson. LC 84-14791. 112p. (Orig.). (J). (ps-3). 1984. pap. 9.95 (*0-8298-0723-3*) Pilgrim OH.
Celebrating the Second Year of Life: A Parent's Guide for a Happy Child. Lucie W. Barber. LC 78-21484. 148p. (Orig.). 1979. pap. 8.95 (*0-89135-015-2*) Religious Educ.
Celebrating the Single Life. Susan A. Muto. 192p. 1989. pap. 11.95 (*0-8245-0954-4*) Crossroad NY.
Celebrating the Stitch. Barbara Smith. 240p. 1991. 34.95 (*0-942391-39-X*) Taunton.
Celebrating the Wild Mushroom: A Passionate Quest. Sara A. Friedman. (Illus.). 265p. 1986. lib. bdg. 15.00 (*0-396-08845-7*) Lubrecht & Cramer.
***Celebrating the Woman You Are.** S. Suzanne Mayer. LC 94-49164. (Illumination Bks.). (Illus.). 80p. (Orig.). 1995. pap. 3.95 (*0-8091-3559-0*) Paulist Pr.
***Celebrating Times of Change: A Wiccan Book of Shadows for Family & Coven Growth.** Stanley J. Modrzyk. (Illus.). 176p. (Orig.). 1995. pap. 12.95 (*0-87728-820-8*) Weiser.
Celebrating Vermont: Myths & Realities. William Hosley et al. Ed. by Nancy P. Graff. LC 91-9299. (Illus.). 192p. 1991. pap. 24.95 (*0-9625262-2-3*) Middlebury Coll Mus.
Celebrating with Books. Nancy Polette & Marjorie Hamlin. LC 77-3862. (Illus.). 184p. 1977. 20.00 (*0-8108-1032-8*) Scarecrow.
Celebrating with Mary: Reflections for Personal Prayer & Parish Devotions. Gerard McGinnity. 92p. (Orig.). 1987. pap. 7.95 (*0-86217-289-6*, Pub. by Veritas Publns IE) Ignatius Pr.
Celebrating Women: International Women's Day in the Soviet Union, 1917-1939. Choitali Chatterjee. Ed. by Victoria Cuffel. (MacArthur Scholar Ser.). 54p. (Orig.). 1991. pap. 1.85 (*1-881157-02-4*) In Ctr Global.
***Celebrating Women's Spirituality: Engagement Calendar, 1996.** Ed. by Claudia L'Amoreaux. (Illus.). 128p. 1995. spiral bd. 12.95 (*0-89594-728-5*) Crossing Pr.
***Celebrating Women's Spirituality: Wall Calendar, 1996.** Claudia L'Amoreaux. (Illus.). 1995. 11.95 (*0-89594-729-3*) Crossing Pr.
Celebrating Your Church's Anniversary. Fred Anderson. Ed. by Charles W. Deweese. (Resource Kit for Your Church's History Ser.). 8p. 1984. pap. 0.60 (*0-939804-23-9*) Hist Comm S Baptist.

Celebrating 50 Whaling Walls. Wyland & Mark Doyle. LC 94-60365. 198p. 1995. 39.95 (*1-884840-00-0*) Wyland Galleries. Sold over 50,000 copies so far! Wyland, the world's finest ocean artist...this name to millions of people around the world has become synonymous with whales & man's efforts to save these magnificent creatures from extinction. This beautifully designed coffee table book features color plates chosen from over 300,000 slides, & the genesis of Wyland's stunning murals, paintings & sculpture. "CELEBRATING 50 WYLAND WHALING WALLS takes you with Wyland around the world as he competes 66 magnificent Whaling Walls From his first wall in Laguna Beach, California, to Whaling Wall 33, "Planet Ocean" in Long Beach, California. Acknowledged by the Guinness Book of World Records (May 4, 1992) as the largest mural in the world. Then topping that feat by barnstorming down the Eastern Seaboard of the United States, completing 17 walls, in 17 cities, in 17 weeks. Then the following year 13 walls, in 8 cities, in 8 weeks down the West Coast, from Alaska to Mexico City. This book is a must for marine art enthusiasts & anyone who appreciates the ocean & life within it.** ***Publisher Provided Annotation.

Celebration. (Illus.). 1981. 7.95 (*0-88188-066-3*, 00312070); pap. 35.00 (*0-88188-010-8*, 00312071) H Leonard.
***Celebration.** Alonzo Lopez. (J). (gr. k-2). 1993. audio 8.95 (*0-7608-0484-2*) Sundance Pub.
***Celebration.** Alonzo Lopez. (J). (gr. k-2). 1993. pap. 4.95 (*0-88741-878-3*) Sundance Pub.
***Celebration.** Alonzo Lopez. (J). (gr. k-2). 1993. 21.95 (*0-88741-897-X*) Sundance Pub.
Celebration. Kay Moser. LC 93-1662. 1993. 9.95 (*1-56233-044-6*) Star Song TN.
***Celebration.** Kay Moser. 1994. pap. 7.99 (*1-56233-300-3*, Star Song Contemp) Star Song TN.
Celebration. Sherwin T. Wine. 439p. 1988. 25.95 (*0-87975-442-7*) Prometheus Bks.
***Celebration.** Ludwig Zeller. 118p. 1995. lib. bdg. 37.00 (*0-8095-4912-3*) Borgo Pr.
Celebration! large type ed. Dana F. Ross. (General Ser.). 384p. 1991. lib. bdg. 18.95 (*0-8161-4978-X*) G K Hall.
Celebration: A Taste of Arkansas. Ed. by Ida M. Stone & Suzanne A. Wray. (Illus.). 368p. 1985. 13.95 (*0-9614182-0-6*) Sevier County Cookbk.
Celebration: Banners, Dance & Holiness in Worship. Lora Allison & Rob Kerby. (Illus.). 160p. 1988. pap. 16.95 (*0-936369-10-8*) Son-Rise Pubns.
***Celebration: Banners, Dance, & Holiness in Worship.** rev. ed. Lora Allison. LC 87-83390. (Illus.). 148p. (C). 1995. pap. 16.95 (*0-9631284-2-6*) Celebrat Minist.
Celebration: Collected Poems. Henry Chapin. 1974. 10.00 (*0-87233-030-3*) Bauhan.
Celebration! Festivities for Reading. Wayne W. Haverson & Susan Haverson. Ed. by Helen Munch. (Illus.). 340p. (YA). (gr. 3-12). 1987. pap. text ed. 9.00 (*0-88084-241-5*); 79.95 (*0-13-122086-1*); 102.60 (*0-88084-240-7*) Alemany Pr.
Celebration: Hanukkah. Women's League for Conservative Judaism Staff. Ed. by Maureen Wise. (Illus.). 96p. (Orig.). 1990. pap. 8.00 (*0-936293-02-0*) WLCJ.
Celebration: Manuscript Edition. Nat Perrin. 1964. pap. 13.00 (*0-8222-0194-1*) Dramatists Play.
Celebration: Purim. Women's League for Conservative Judaism Staff. Ed. by Shelley Buxbaum. (Celebration Ser.). (Illus.). 96p. (Orig.). 1992. pap. 8.00 (*0-932293-05-0*) WLCJ.
Celebration: Rosh HaShanah & Yom Kippur. Women's League for Conservative Judaism Staff. Ed. by Rhonda Kahn. (Celebration Ser.). (Illus.). 1992. pap. 8.00 (*0-936293-04-7*) WLCJ.
Celebration: Saint Andrew's School Thirtieth Anniversary. Saint Andrew's School Parents' Association Staff. (Book of Celebrated Recipes Ser.). (Illus.). 1992. 14.95 (*0-9632099-0-6*) St Andrews Schl.
Celebration: The Book of Jewish Festivals. Ed. by Naomi Black. 160p. 1989. 26.95 (*0-8246-0340-0*) Jonathan David.
Celebration: The Story of American Holidays. Lucille R. Penner. LC 92-25871. (Illus.). 80p. (J). (gr. 1 up). 1993. text ed. 15.95 (*0-02-770903-5*, Mac Bks Young Read) S&S Childrens.
Celebration: Theology, Ministry & Practice. Eugene A. Walsh. (Illus.). 96p. (Orig.). 1994. pap. 4.95 (*0-915531-20-8*) OR Catholic.
Celebration: Visions & Voices of the African Diaspora. Ed. by Roger Rosen & Patra Sevastiades. LC 93-47413. (Icarus World Issues Ser.). 1994. 16.95 (*0-8239-1808-4*); pap. 8.95 (*0-8239-1809-2*) Rosen Group.
Celebration, a Cerebration: Constitutional Essays for the Bicentennial. Ed. by Theodore L. Zawistowski. (Illus.). 60p. (Orig.). (C). 1987. pap. text ed. 2.00 (*0-9619136-0-6*) LCCBC.
Celebration & Experience in Preaching. Henry H. Mitchell. LC 90-35024. 1990. pap. 11.95 (*0-687-04744-7*) Abingdon.
Celebration & Remembrance: Commemorative Textiles in America, 1790-1990. Diane L. Affleck & Paul Hudon. 87p. (Orig.). 1990. pap. 18.95 (*0-937474-13-4*) Mus Am Textile Hist.
Celebration & Renewal: Rites of Passage in Judaism. Ed. by Rela M. Geffen. LC 93-12493. 288p. 1993. 34.95 (*0-8276-0422-X*); pap. 19.95 (*0-8276-0510-2*) JPS Phila.
Celebration at Green Thrush. Miss Read. LC 93-22983. 1993. 19.95 (*0-395-65030-5*) HM.
Celebration Cakes: Their Production & Decorating. 2nd rev. ed. Morris Howkins. (Illus.). xix, 223p. 1984. reprint ed. 39.75 (*0-85334-316-0*, Pub. by Elsevier Applied Sci UK) Elsevier.
Celebration Flowers: Designing & Arranging. Ming Veevers-Carter. LC 89-27997. (Illus.). 144p. 1990. 19.95 (*0-8069-7300-5*) Sterling.
Celebration for May Sarton. Ed. by Constance Hunting. 1994. pap. 24.95 (*0-913006-53-X*) Puckerbrush.
Celebration for Stanley Kunitz. Illus. by Philip Guston et al. 159p. (Orig.). 1986. pap. 10.00 (*0-935296-59-X*) Sheep Meadow.
Celebration II: Cleveland in Color. Jennie Jones. (Illus.). 92p. 1991. 29.95 (*0-9617637-2-8*) CL Stock Images.
Celebration in Darkness. Yoshioka Minoru. Tr. by Onuma Tadayoshi. Bd. with Strangers' Sky. LC 84-23423. LC 84-23423. (Asian Poetry in Translation Ser: Japan: No. 6). 206p. (Orig.). 1985. Set pap. 10.95 (*0-295-96360-3*) U of Wash Pr.
Celebration in Darkness & Strangers' Sky. Minoru Yoshioka & Koichi Iijima. Ed. by Thomas Fitzsimmons. Tr. by Tadayoshi Onuma. LC 84-23423. (Asian Poetry in Translation: Japan Ser.: No. 6). (Illus.). 200p. (Orig.). (ENG & JPN.). 1985. pap. 10.95 (*0-942668-07-3*) Katydid Bks.
Celebration in Poetry: Wyndham Hall Press Inaugural Edition. Ed. by John H. Morgan. 180p. (Orig.). 1988. pap. 14.95 (*0-932269-38-9*) Wyndhall Pr.
Celebration in Postwar American Fiction. Richard H. Rupp. LC 77-102187. 1970. 11.95 (*0-87024-145-1*) U of Miami Pr.
Celebration in Times of War. Arny Reichler. Ed. by Carol Layne. 30p. (Orig.). 1987. pap. 6.95 (*0-933865-13-9*) Doris Pubns.
Celebration Legal Essays by Various Authors to Mark the Twenty-Fifth Year of Service of John H. Wigmore As Professor of Law in Northwestern University. xi, 602p. 1981. reprint ed. lib. bdg. 42.50 (*0-8377-0432-4*) Rothman.

C

An Asterisk (*) at the beginning of an entry indicates that the title is appearing in BIP for the first time.

An Asterisk (*) at the beginning of an entry indicates that the title is appearing in BIP for the first time.

1109

Celeste: A Fable for All Ages. Ruth Shigezawa. LC 93-72194. (Illus.). 28p. (J). (gr. 2 up). 1993. 16.95 (0-9637101-0-9); pap. 7.95 (0-9637101-1-7) Cndlelght Pr.

Celeste & Crabapple Sam. Jennifer Brutschy. LC 92-1587. (Illus.). (J). (gr. k-3). 1994. 14.99 (0-525-67416-0, Lodestar Bks) Dutton Child Bks.

***Celestial Bar: A Spiritual Journey.** Tom Youngholm. LC 94-94545. 204p. (Orig.). 1995. pap. 12.95 (0-9642488-6-7) Creat Info Concepts.

***Celestial Bar: A Spiritual Journey.** Tom Youngholm. LC 95-11706. (J). 1995. write for info. (0-385-31548-1) Delacorte.

Celestial Brides: A Study in Mythology & Archaeology. Octavio Alvarez. LC 77-91208. (Illus.). 1978. 30.00 (0-9601520-0-8) H Reichner.

Celestial Charts. Carol Stott. 1991. 19.99 (0-517-05025-0) Random Hse Value.

Celestial Chess. Thomas Bontly. 1980. pap. 3.95 (0-345-28678-2) Ballantine.

***Celestial Chorus.** (Mage). Date not set. 10.00 (1-56504-411-8) White Wolf.

***Celestial Cuisine: Cloud 9 Cooking.** Dorothy F. Weber. (Illus.). 62p. (Orig.). 1995. spiral bd., pap. 6.95 (0-9620905-2-2) D F Weber.

Celestial Cycles: The Theme of Paradise Lost in World Literature with Translations of the Major Analogues. Watson Kirkconnell. LC 67-30308. 701p. 1967. reprint ed. 75.00 (0-87752-058-5) Gordian.

Celestial Delights: The Best Astronomical Events Through 2001. Francis Reddy & Greg Walz-Chojnacki. (Illus.). 192p. 1992. pap. 16.95 (0-89087-675-4) Celestial Arts.

Celestial Democracy. Voss E. Wysinger. LC 66-24014. 149p. (C). 1966. text ed. 16.95 (0-914002-02-3); lib. bdg. 16.95 (0-914002-01-5); pap. text ed. 14.00 (0-686-36904-1) Wysinger Pub.

Celestial Dynamics: A Course of Astro-Metaphysical Study. 107p. 1966. reprint ed. spiral bd. 4.95 (0-7873-0034-9) Mokelumne.

Celestial for the Cruising Navigator. Merle B. Turner. LC 85-47837. (Illus.). 232p. (Orig.). 1986. pap. 14.95 (0-87033-341-0) Cornell Maritime.

Celestial Gems Books, 1. Gypsy A. Coolidge. (Illus.). 48p. 1972. 10.00 (0-318-51319-6) Celestial Gems.

Celestial Gems Books, 2. Gypsy A. Coolidge. LC 73-88209. (Illus.). 48p. 1972. 10.00 (0-914154-01-X) Celestial Gems.

Celestial Gems Books, 5. Gypsy A. Coolidge. LC 73-88209. (Illus.). 150p. 1975. write for info. (0-914154-05-2) Celestial Gems.

Celestial Gems Books, Vol. 1. rev. ed. Gypsy A. Coolidge. LC 73-88209. 150p. 1971. 10.00 (0-914154-00-1) Celestial Gems.

Celestial Gems Books, Vol. 4. Gypsy A. Coolidge. LC 73-88209. 65p. 1974. spiral bd. 10.00 (0-914154-03-6) Celestial Gems.

Celestial Gems Books, Vols. 5-6. Gypsy A. Coolidge. (Illus.). 150p. 1975. 10.00 (0-318-51320-X) Celestial Gems.

Celestial Hit List. Charles Ingrid. (Sand Wars Ser.: Bk. 3). 1988. pap. 3.95 (0-88677-394-6) DAW Bks.

Celestial Inspirations: Channeled Affirmations & Prayers by the "Nameless Ones", St. Therese, Archangel Michael, St. Germain, & Thalius. Susan E. Rose, pseud. 48p. 1995. pap. write for info. (0-9644840-0-5) Celestial Insp.

Celestial Inventory. Steve R. Tem. (Booklet Ser.: No. 36). 54p. (Orig.). 1991. pap. text ed. 4.00 (0-936055-47-2) C Drumm Bks.

Celestial Inventory. deluxe ed. Steve R. Tem. (Booklet Ser.: No. 36). 54p. (Orig.). 1991. pap. 7.00 (0-936055-48-0) C Drumm Bks.

Celestial Journey: Far Eastern Ways of Thinking: Comparative Studies in Buddhist, Taoist, & Confucian Philosophy. Toshihiko Izutsu. (Illus.). 200p. (Orig.). 1994. pap. 16.00 (1-883991-04-8) Whte Cloud Pr.

***Celestial Journey: Far Eastern Ways of Thinking: Comparative Studies in Buddhist, Taoist, & Confucian Philosophy.** Toshihiko Izutsu. 240p. (Orig.). 1995. pap. 16.00 (1-883991-08-0) Whte Cloud Pr.

***Celestial Liaisons.** Astara V. Antara-An. 96p. Date not set. pap. 11.11 (1-885226-25-X) Star Lineage.

***Celestial Matters.** Richard Garfinkle. 1996. write for info. (0-614-05504-0) Tor Bks.

Celestial Mechanics, Set. Pierre S. Laplace. LC 69-11316. text ed. 250.00 (0-8284-0194-2) Chelsea Pub.

Celestial Mechanics, Vol. 5. Pierre S. Laplace. LC 63-11316. 1969. reprint ed. text ed. 39.50 (0-8284-0214-0) Chelsea Pub.

Celestial Mechanics: A Computational Guide for the Practitioner. Laurence G. Taff. LC 84-20989. 520p. 1985. text ed. 125.00 (0-471-89316-1, Wiley-Interscience) Wiley.

Celestial Mechanics, Vol. 2: Perturbation Theory, 2 pts., Pt. 1. Yusuke Hagihara. 512p. 1972. 70.00x (0-262-08048-6) MIT Pr.

Celestial Navigation. Tom Cunliffe. 64p. (C). 1990. text ed. 59.00 (0-906754-39-9, Pub. by Fernhurst Bks UK) St Mut.

Celestial Navigation. Arthur Davies. (Practical Guide Ser.). (Illus.). 128p. 1993. pap. 29.95 (1-85223-679-5, Pub. by Crowood Pr UK) Trafalgar.

Celestial Navigation. Jeff Toghill. 1988. pap. 12.00 (0-393-30294-6) Norton.

Celestial Navigation. Anne Tyler. 1993. mass mkt. 5.99 (0-8041-0888-9) Ivy Books.

Celestial Navigation. large type ed. Anne Tyler. LC 94-649. 1994. 24.95 (0-7927-1977-8, Curley Lrg Print); pap. 22.95 (0-7927-1976-X, Curley Lrg Print) Chivers N Amer.

Celestial Navigation. 2nd ed. Frances W. Wright. LC 82-4964. (Illus.). 144p. 1982. pap. 12.00 (0-87033-291-0) Cornell Maritime.

Celestial Navigation. 3rd ed. Jonah Slocum. 120p. 1985. pap. 16.95 (0-317-19561-1) Basic Sci Pr.

***Celestial Navigation - Step by Step.** 2nd ed. Warren Norville. (Illus.). 251p. (C). 1994. pap. text ed. 30.00 (1-879778-20-3, BK-203) Marine Educ.

Celestial Navigation by H. O. 249. John E. Milligan. LC 74-1464. (Illus.). 111p. 1974. pap. 7.50 (0-87033-191-4) Cornell Maritime.

Celestial Navigation for Lower Level Licenses. (USCG Examination Questions & Answers Ser.). 163p. (Orig.). 1990. pap. text ed. 49.95 (0-932889-15-8) Examco Inc.

Celestial Navigation for Upper Level Licenses. (USCG Examination Questions & Answers Ser.). 204p. (Orig.). 1990. pap. text ed. 99.95 (0-932889-13-1) Examco Inc.

***Celestial Navigation for Yachtsmen.** 2nd ed. Mary Blewitt. 1994. pap. 12.95 (0-07-005928-4) McGraw.

Celestial Navigation Step by Step. 2nd ed. Warren Norville. LC 83-47888. (Illus.). 272p. 1987. pap. text ed. 22.95 (0-87742-177-3, C250) Intl Marine.

***Celestial Navigation with the S Table: A Complete Sight Reduction Method for All Bodies in Nine Pages.** Mike Pepperday. (Illus.). 32p. (Orig.). Date not set. reprint ed. pap. 9.95 (0-939837-09-9) Paradise Cay Pubns.

Celestial Navigation with the 2102-D Star Finder. David Burch. (Illus.). 80p. (Orig.). 1984. pap. 8.95 (0-914025-00-7) Starpath.

Celestial Objects for Common Telescopes, 2 Vol, 1. Thomas W. Webb. Ed. by Margaret W. Mayall. (Illus.). 1962. pap. 6.00 (0-486-20917-2) Dover.

Celestial Objects for Common Telescopes, 2 Vol, 2. Thomas W. Webb. Ed. by Margaret W. Mayall. (Illus.). 1962. pap. 6.00 (0-486-20918-0) Dover.

Celestial Omnibus & Other Stories. E. M. Forster. LC 76-10586. (YA). 1976. pap. 8.00 (0-394-72176-4) Random Bks Yng Read.

Celestial Pantomime: Poetic Structures of Transcendence. rev. ed. Justus G. Lawler. 320p. (C). 1994. pap. text ed. 19.95 (0-8264-0679-3) Continuum.

Celestial Psychology. Doris Hebel. 136p. 1985. pap. text ed. 9.95 (0-943358-18-3) Aurora Press.

Celestial Railroad & Other Stories. Nathaniel Hawthorne. 1963. pap. 5.95 (0-451-52213-3, CE1784, Sig Classics) NAL-Dutton.

Celestial Railroad & Other Stories. Nathaniel Hawthorne. 300p. 1990. reprint ed. lib. bdg. 21.95 (0-89966-716-3) Buccaneer Bks.

Celestial Raise. Marcus. 230p. (Orig.). 1987. 24.95 (0-9618316-0-X); pap. 21.95 (0-941131-01-7) ASSK Pub.

Celestial Ship of the North: With Symbolical Illustrations & a Glossary. E. Valentia Straiton. 557p. 1992. pap. 33.00 (1-56459-265-0) Kessinger Pub.

Celestial Song - Gobind Geet. Swami Rama. LC 86-33664. 140p. (Orig.). 1986. pap. 12.95 (0-89389-103-7) Himalayan Pubs.

Celestial Splendor Shining Forth from Geometric Thought & on the Motion of the Apparently Fixed Stars. Britton Wilkie. LC 77-9899. (Illus.). 1977. pap. 1.50 (0-916382-13-3) Telephone Bks.

Celestial Stems: Five Element Diet & Exercise Program. William N. Clearfield. LC 92-19423. (Illus.). 100p. (Orig.). 1992. pap. 19.95 (0-912975-15-6) Upshur Pr.

Celestial Symbols: Symbolism in Doctrine, Religous Traditions & Temple Architecture. Allen H. Barber. LC 89-83436. 176p. 1989. 13.98 (0-88290-344-6) Horizon Utah.

Celestial Symphonies: A History of Chinese Music. Robert W. Clack. 1975. lib. bdg. 250.00 (0-87968-447-X) Gordon Pr.

Celestial Teachings: The Emergence of the True Testament of Jmmanuel (Jesus) James Deardorff. 336p. (Orig.). 1990. pap. 12.95 (0-926524-11-9, Wild Flower Pr) Blue Wtr Pubng.

Celestial Telegraph: Or, Secrets of the Life to Come Revealed Through Magnetism... Louis A. Cahagnet. LC 75-36832. (Occult Ser.). 1976. reprint ed. 36.95 (0-405-07944-3) Ayer.

Celestial Tradition: A Study of Pound's "The Cantos" Demetres Tryphonopoulous. 200p. (C). 1992. text ed. 35.00 (0-88920-202-8, Pub. by Wilfrid Laurier CN) Humanities.

Celestial Verses: The Lost Tale of the Arabian Nights. Joseph Covino, Jr. LC 91-72214. 300p. (Orig.). Date not set. pap. 14.95 (0-943283-01-9) New Human Pr.

***Celestial Wisdom Cards: Guidance from the Angels.** Juliet J. Hubbs & Nora Monaco. LC 95-1865. 1995. write for info. (0-517-70211-8, Harmony) Crown Pub Group.

Celestina. Intro. by Bruno M. Damiani. 302p. 1990. 45.00 (0-916379-86-8) Scripta.

Celestina. De Rojas. Tr. by James Mabbe. (Hispanic Classics Ser.). 1987. 49.95 (0-85668-344-2, Pub. by Aris & Phillips UK); pap. 25.00 (0-85668-345-0, Pub. by Aris & Phillips UK) David Brown.

Celestina. Fernando De Rojas. Tr. by James Mabbe. 112p. 1986. pap. 6.95 (0-936839-01-5) Applause Theatre Bk Pubs.

Celestina. (Illus.). 661p. 1984. reprint ed. write for info. (3-487-07312-9, Pub. by Georg Olms GW) Lubrecht & Cramer.

Celestina: A Feminist Reading of the "Carpe Diem" Theme. Diane Hartunian. 1990. 45.50 (0-916379-81-7) Scripta.

Celestina: A Fifteenth-Century Spanish Novel in Dialogue. Tr. by Lesley B. Simpson. LC 55-7961. 1955. pap. 10.00 (0-520-01177-5) U CA Pr.

Celestina: A Play in Twenty-One Acts, Attributed to Fernando de Rojas. Fernando De Rojas. Tr. by Mack H. Singleton. LC 58-13446. 318p. reprint ed. pap. 90.70 (0-7837-4385-8, 2044125) Bks Demand.

Celestina: Genre & Rhetoric. Charles A. Fraker. (Series A: Monagrafias: No. CXXXVIII). 256p. (Orig.). (C). 1990. pap. 35.00 (0-7293-0296-2, Pub. by Tamesis Bks Ltd UK) Boydell & Brewer.

***Celestina: Two Facsimiles (1499? & 1528)** fac. ed. (Illus.). 318p. (SPA.). Date not set. 20.00 (0-87535-150-6) Hispanic Soc.

***Celestina & Castilian Humanism at the End of the Fifteenth Century.** Ciriaco M. Arroyo. LC 94-40654. (Medieval & Renaissance Texts & Studies; Professional Papers: No. 3). 44p. 1994. pap. 6.00 (0-86698-144-6, CM3) MRTS.

Celestina or the Tragicke-Comedy of Calisto & Melibea. Fernando De Rojas. Tr. by James Mabbe. LC 01-19039. (Tudor Translations, First Ser.: No. 6). reprint ed. 57.50 (0-404-51853-2) AMS Pr.

Celestina's Brood: Continuities of the Baroque in Spanish & Latin American Literature. Roberto Gonzalez Echevarria. LC 93-16488. (Illus.). 272p. (C). 1993. lib. bdg. 45.00 (0-8223-1353-7); pap. text ed. 17.95 (0-8223-1371-5) Duke.

Celestine: In the French Translation of 1578 by Jacques De Lavardin. Ed. by Denis L. Drysdall. (Serie B: Textos, XVIII). 266p. (Orig.). (C). 1974. pap. 45.00 (0-900411-83-X, Pub. by Tamesis Bks Ltd UK) Boydell & Brewer.

Celestine Prophecy. James Redfield. 256p. 1994. 17.95 (0-446-51862-X) Warner Bks.

Celestine Prophecy. large type ed. James Redfield. LC 94-19119. 1994. 26.95 (1-56895-113-2) Wheeler Pub.

Celestine Prophecy: An Adventure. James F. Redfield. 256p. (Orig.). 1993. pap. 13.95 (0-944353-00-2) Satori.

Celestine Prophecy: An Experiential Guide. James Redfield & Carol Adrienne. 304p. 1995. pap. 8.99 (0-446-67122-3) Warner Bks.

Celia. Ruby J. Jensen. 352p. 1991. mass mkt. 4.50 (0-8217-3446-6) Zebra.

***Celia.** Lois Menzel. 1995. pap. 4.50 (0-449-22342-6) Fawcett.

Celia. E. H. Young. 273p. 1992. pap. 10.95 (0-86068-856-9, Pub. by Virago Pr UK) Trafalgar.

Celia, A Slave. Melton A. McLaurin. LC 90-23045. 160p. 1991. 19.95 (0-8203-1352-1) U of Ga Pr.

Celia, a Slave. Melton A. McLaurin. 192p. 1993. reprint ed. pap. 10.00 (0-380-71935-5) Avon.

Celia Thaxter: An Anthology in Memoriam (1835-1894) Ed. by M. Myers. LC 93-74631. (Orig.). 1994. pap. 24.95 (1-879183-23-4) Bristol Banner.

Celia's House. large type ed. D. E. Stevenson. 1973. 12.00 (0-85456-163-3) Ulverscroft.

Celia's Island Journal. Celia Thaxter. (J). (ps-3). 1992. 15.95 (0-316-83921-3) Little.

Celibacy: Gift or Law? Heinz-Jurgen Vogels. LC 93-19235. 144p. (Orig.). 1993. pap. 12.95 (1-55612-653-0) Sheed & Ward MO.

Celibacy: Renewing the Gift, Releasing the Power. Raymond J. Gunzel. LC 88-61680. 132p. (Orig.). 1988. pap. 8.95 (1-55612-197-0) Sheed & Ward MO.

Celibacy - a Fullness of Life. Anselm Gruen. Ed. by Alphonse Lauer. Tr. by Gregory J. Roettger & Luise R. Pugh. (Schuyler Spiritual Ser.: No. 8). 94p. 1993. pap. 5.00 (1-56788-007-X, 10-008) BMH Pubns.

Celibacy Is Better Than Really Bad Sex: And Other Classic Rules for Single Women. Patti Putnicki. (Illus.). 176p. 1994. pap. 9.95 (0-944042-35-X) CorkScrew Pr.

***Celibacy Is Hard, Right?** Mary Mortalsin. 1994. pap. 4.99 (0-671-52422-4) PB.

Celibacy Myth. Board of St. Paul Editorial Staff. (C). 1989. 55.00 (0-85439-295-5, Pub. by St Paul Pubns UK) St Mut.

Celibacy Myth: Loving for Life. Charles A. Gallagher & Thomas Vandenberg. 160p. 1989. pap. 8.95 (0-8245-0942-0) Crossroad NY.

Celibacy of Felix Greenspan. Lionel Abrahams. 181p. 1993. reprint ed. 19.00 (0-89733-396-9) Academy Chi Pubs.

Celibacy, Prayer & Friendship: A Making-Sense-Out-of-Life Approach. Christopher Kiesling. LC 77-25084. 1978. pap. 7.95 (0-8189-0365-1) Alba.

Celibataires. Henry De Montherlant. 256p. 1972. write for info. (0-318-63445-7) Fr & Eur.

Celibataires. Henry de Montherlant. (FRE.). 1972. pap. 10.95 (0-8288-3716-3, F115690) Fr & Eur.

***Celibate Season.** Shields & Howard. Date not set. per. 14.95 (1-55050-024-4, Pub. by Coteau Bks CN) InBook.

Celibate Wives: Breaking the Silence. Joan Avna & Diana Waltz. 1992. 21.95 (0-929923-99-5) Lowell Hse.

Celibate Wives: Breaking the Silence. Joan Avna & Diana Waltz. 252p. 1994. reprint ed. pap. 12.95 (1-56565-122-7) Lowell Hse.

Celibates. Padraig Standun. 148p. 1994. pap. 7.95 (1-85371-236-1, Pub. by Poolbeg Pr IE) Dufour.

Celibato Forzoso Del Clero: The Forced Celibacy of the Clero. Juan B. Cabrera. (SPA.). 4.95 (84-7645-398-1, 223433, Pub. by Edit Clie SP) TSELF.

***Celie & the Harvest Fiddler.** Valerie Flournoy & Vanessa Flournoy. LC 94-47322. (Illus.). (J). 1995. write for info. (0-688-11457-1, Tambourine Bks); lib. bdg. write for info. (0-688-11458-X, Tambourine Bks) Morrow.

Celimare le Bien Aime. Eugene Labiche. (FRE.). 1978. pap. 14.95 (0-7859-5350-7) Fr & Eur.

***Celina or the Cats.** Julieta Campos. Ed. by Yvette E. Miller. Tr. by Leland Chambers & Kathleen Ross. (Discoveries Ser.). 130p. Date not set. pap. 15.95 (0-935480-72-2) Lat Am Lit Rev Pr.

Celine. Brock Cole. (YA). (gr. 7 up). 1989. 15.00 (0-374-31234-6) FS&G.

Celine. Brock Cole. 224p. (YA). (gr. 7 up). 1991. pap. 3.95 (0-374-41082-8, Sunburst Bks) FS&G.

Celine. Brock Cole. (YA). 1993. pap. 3.95 (0-374-41083-6) FS&G.

Celine. Brock Cole. Tr. by Pedro Barbadillo. 172p. (SPA.). (YA). (gr. 9-12). 1992. pap. write for info. (84-204-4711-0) Santillana.

Celine: "Journey to the End of the Night" John Sturrock. (Landmarks of World Literature Ser.). 128p. (C). 1990. pap. 10.95 (0-521-37854-0) Cambridge U Pr.

***Celine: A Biography.** Frederic Vitoux. (Illus.). 601p. (C). 1994. pap. 15.00 (1-56924-888-5) Marlowe & Co.

Celine: Remembering Louisiana, 1850-1871. Celine F. Garcia. Ed. by Patrick J. Geary. LC 87-5939. (Illus.). 316p. 1991. pap. 14.95 (0-8203-1384-X) U of Ga Pr.

Celine & His Critics: Scandals & Paradox. Stanford L. Luce. (Stanford French & Italian Studies: Vol. 44). 224p. 1986. pap. 46.50 (0-915838-59-1) Anma Libri.

Celine & the Politics of Difference. Ed. by Rosemarie Scullion et al. LC 94-2945. (Illus.). 304p. 1994. 39.95 (0-87451-697-8) U Pr of New Eng.

Celinian Trove: Elizabeth Craig's Jewelry Box. Alphonse Juilland. (Illus.). 82p. (Orig.). (C). 1991. pap. 24.00 (1-884868-05-3) Montparnasse.

Celioscopy & Ancillary Techniques in the Study of Gynecological Pathology. E. Cittadini & T. Rossi. 96p. 1974. text ed. 32.00 (1-57235-058-X) Piccin NY.

Cell. Horst Bienek. Tr. by Mahlendorf. LC 74-134739. 1973. 17.50 (0-87775-024-6); pap. 9.95 (0-87775-070-X) Unicorn Pr.

Cell. Lyn Hejinian. (Sun & Moon Classics Ser.: No. 21). 154p. 1992. pap. 11.95 (1-55713-021-3) Sun & Moon CA.

Cell: Biochemistry, Physiology, Morphology, 6 vols. Ed. by Jean Brachet & A. E. Mirsky. Incl. Vol. 1. Methods: Problems of Cell Biology. 1959. 97.50 (0-12-123301-4); write for info. (0-318-50240-2) Acad Pr.

Cell see Anatomy & Physiology: A Programmed Approach

Cell - A Door: Growing up Southern. Gladys O. Hughes. (Poetry Ser.: No. 3). 1989. pap. 10.00 (0-9624737-6-6) S P-Persephone Pr.

Cell Activation: Genetic Approaches. James J. Mond et al. (Advances in Regulation of Cell Growth Ser.: Vol. 2). 352p. 1991. 116.50 (0-88167-819-8) Raven.

***Cell Activation & Apoptosis in HIV Infection: Implications for Pathogenesis & Therapy.** Ed. by Jean-Marie Andrieu & Wei Lu. (Advances in Experimental Medicine & Biology Ser.: Vol. 374). 240p. 1995. 79.50 (0-306-45063-1) Plenum.

***Cell Adhesion & Cancer.** Ed. by I. Hart & N. Hogg. (Cancer Surveys Ser.: Vol. 24). (Illus.). 250p. (C). 1995. text ed. 75.00 (0-87969-468-8) Cold Spring Harbor.

***Cell Adhesion & Human Disease.** Ed. by Joan Marsh & Jamie A. Goode. (CIBA Foundation Symposium Ser.: Vol. 189). 1995. text ed. 79.95 (0-471-95279-6) Wiley.

***Cell Adhesion in Bioprocessing & Biotechnology.** Ed. by Martin A. Hjortso & J. W. Roos. LC 94-22882. (Bioprocess Technology Ser.: Vol. 20). 288p. 1995. 135.00 (0-8247-8945-8) Dekker.

Cell Adhesion Molecules. Ed. by Martin E. Hemler & Enrico Mihich. LC 93-18554. (Pezcoller Foundation Symposia Ser.: Vol. 4). 1993. 89.50 (0-306-44496-8, Plenum Pr) Plenum.

Cell Adhesion Molecules in Human Organ Transplants. Gustaf Steinhoff. LC 93-40843. (Medical Intelligence Unit Ser.). 122p. 1994. 89.95 (1-57059-015-X) R G Landes.

Cell Aging & Cell Death. Ed. by I. Davies & David C. Sigee. (Illus.). 350p. 1985. 69.95 (0-521-26172-4) Cambridge U Pr.

Cell Analysis, Vol. 1. Ed. by Nicholas Catsimpoolas. LC 82-5289. 350p. 1982. 75.00 (0-306-40864-3, Plenum Pr) Plenum.

Cell & Animal Models in Aging & Dementia Research. Ed. by S. Hoyer et al. 1995. pap. 96.00 (0-387-82549-5) Spr-Verlag.

Cell & Animal Physiology Laboratory Textbook. Barbara Grimes. (Illus.). 200p. (C). 1990. pap. text ed. 22.95 (0-89892-084-1) Contemp Pub Co of Raleigh.

Cell & Environmental Temperature. A. Troshin & C. Prosser. LC 66-20411. (International Series of Monographs on Pure & Applied Mathematics: Vol. 34). 1967. 194.00 (0-08-011830-5, Pub. by Pergamon Repr UK) Franklin.

Cell & Model Membrane Interactions. Ed. by S. Ohki. (Illus.). 284p. 1992. 89.50 (0-306-44097-0, Plenum Pr) Plenum.

Cell & Molecular Biology. 3rd ed. Phillip Sheeler & Don Bianchi. LC 86-28113. 704p. 1987. Net. text ed. write for info. (0-471-81758-9) Wiley.

Cell & Molecular Biology. 8th ed. E. D. De Robertis & E. M. De Robertis, Jr. LC 86-123. (Illus.). 734p. 1987. text ed. 48.00 (0-8121-1012-9) Williams & Wilkins.

Cell & Molecular Biology of Artemia Development. Ed. by A. H. Warner et al. (NATO ASI Series A, Life Sciences: Vol. 174). (Illus.). 464p. 1989. 120.00 (0-306-43248-X, Plenum Pr) Plenum.

Cell & Molecular Biology of Colon Cancer. Ed. by Leonard H. Augenlicht. 224p. 1989. 242.00 (0-8493-4710-6, RC280) CRC Pr.

Cell & Molecular Biology of Fish Oogenesis. S. S. Guraya. (Monographs in Developmental Biology: Vol. 18). (Illus.). vii, 232p. 1986. 140.00 (3-8055-4253-4) S Karger.

Cell & Molecular Biology of the Cytoskeleton. Ed. by Jerry W. Shay. LC 86-4912. 356p. 1986. 85.00 (0-306-42175-5, Plenum Pr) Plenum.

Cell & Molecular Biology of the Testis. Ed. by Claude Desjardins & Larry L. Ewing. (Illus.). 512p. 1993. 125.00 (0-19-506269-8) OUP.

Cell & Molecular Biology of the Uterus. Ed. by W. W. Leavitt. LC 88-5793. (Advances in Experimental Medicine & Biology Ser.: Vol. 230). (Illus.). 254p. 1988. 75.00 (0-306-42836-9, Plenum Pr) Plenum.

An Asterisk (*) at the beginning of an entry indicates that the title is appearing in BIP for the first time.

C

An Asterisk (*) at the beginning of an entry indicates that the title is appearing in BIP for the first time.

1111

Cell Mediated Reactions, Miscellaneous Topics: PAR, Vol. 3 Pseudo-Allergic Reactions. Involvement of Drugs & Chemicals. Ed. by P. Dukor et al. (Illus.). viii, 160p. 1982. 63.25 (3-8055-0960-X) S Karger.

Cell Membrane: A Key to Disease Processes. 1992. 74.95 (0-8493-8091-X, RB152) CRC Pr.

Cell Membrane in Function & Dysfunction of Vascular Tissue, 1981. Ed. by K. Godfraind & P. Meyer. (Argenteuil Symposia Ser.: Vol. 5). 278p. 1981. 117.50 (0-444-80316-5) Elsevier.

Cell Membrane Transport: Experimental Approaches & Methodologies. Ed. by D. L. Yudilevich et al. (Illus.). 470p. 1991. 110.00 (0-306-43831-3, Plenum Pr) Plenum.

Cell Membranes: Biochemistry, Cell Biology & Pathology. Ed. by Gerald Weissmann & Robert Claiborne. (Illus.). 296p. (C). 1975. text ed. 17.95 (0-913800-06-6) HP Pub Co.

Cell Membranes: Methods & Reviews, Vol. 1. Ed. by Elliot Elson et al. 212p. 1983. 65.00 (0-306-41298-5, Plenum Pr) Plenum.

Cell Membranes: Methods & Reviews, Vol. 2. Ed. by Elliot Elson et al. 396p. 1984. 89.50 (0-306-41761-8, Plenum Pr) Plenum.

Cell Membranes: Methods & Reviews, Vol. 3. Ed. by Elliot Elson et al. LC 83-646233. 432p. 1987. 95.00 (0-306-42620-X, Plenum Pr) Plenum.

Cell Membranes & Cancer. Ed. by T. Galeotti et al. 446p. 1986. 141.75 (0-444-80723-3) Elsevier.

Cell Membranes & Ion Transport. John L. Hall & D. A. Baker. LC 77-3142. (Integrated Themes in Biology Ser.). (Illus.). 135p. reprint ed. pap. 38.50 (0-685-20313-1, 2030353) Bks Demand.

Cell Metabolism: Growth & Environment, 2 vols., Vol. I. Ed. by T. A. Subramanian. 168p. 1986. 124.95 (0-8493-5750-0, QR88, CRC Reprint) Franklin.

Cell Metabolism: Growth & Environment, 2 vols., Vol. II. Ed. by T. A. Subramanian. 208p. 1986. 124.95 (0-8493-5751-9, QR88, CRC Reprint) Franklin.

Cell Motility. Howard Stebbings & Jeremy S. Hyams. LC 78-40543. (Integrated Themes in Biology Ser.). (Illus.). 200p. reprint ed. pap. 57.00 (0-8357-6051-0, 2034504) Bks Demand.

Cell Motility, 3 vols., Set. Ed. by R. D. Goldman et al. LC 76-17144. (Cold Spring Harbor Conferences on Cell Proliferation Ser.: Vol. 3). (Illus.). 1404p. 1976. 133.00 (0-87969-117-4) Cold Spring Harbor.

Cell Motility Factors. Ed. by Irving D. Goldberg. (Experientia Supplementa Ser.: Vol. 59). xii, 224p. 1991. 124.00 (0-8176-2569-0) Birkhauser.

Cell Movement & Cell Behaviour. J. M. Lackie. (Illus.). 224p. 1986. pap. text ed. 34.95 (0-04-574035-6) Routledge Chapman & Hall.

Cell Movements. Dennis Bray. LC 91-24911. (Illus.). 424p. 1992. text ed. 44.95 (0-8153-0404-8, 3-0404-8); pap. text ed. 27.95 (0-8153-0717-9) Garland.

Cell Neoplastic Transformations: Index of Modern Medical Reviews Compiling 20,000 References. Jennie M. Kahndike. LC 88-47547. 150p. 1988. 49.50 (0-88164-770-5); pap. 39.50 (0-88164-771-3) ABBE Pubs Assn.

Cell of Self-Knowledge. Richard of St. Victor et al. Ed. by E. G. Gardner. LC 66-25702. (Medieval Library). reprint ed. 42.00 (0-8154-0188-4) Cooper Sq.

Cell Organelles. Ed. by R. Herrmann et al. (Plant Gene Research Ser.). 270p. 1994. 169.00 (0-387-82264-X) Spr-Verlag.

Cell Pathology. 2nd ed. Norman F. Cheville. LC 83-134. (Illus.). 682p. 1983. text ed. 69.95 (0-8138-0310-1) Iowa St U Pr.

Cell Patterning. Ciba Foundation Staff. LC 78-304197. (Ciba Foundation Symposium: New Ser.: No. 29). 364p. reprint ed. pap. 103.80 (0-317-29180-7, 2022157) Bks Demand.

Cell Physiology: Molecular Dynamics. 2nd ed. Henry Tedeschi. 560p. (C). 1992. text ed. write for info. (0-697-16949-9) Wm C Brown Pubs.

Cell Physiology & Genetics of Higher Plant, 2 vols. A. Rashid. 1988. Vol. I, Cell Multiplication Cell Differentiation, Cell Totipotency, 208 pgs. 106.00 (0-8493-6062-5, QK725, CRC Reprint); Vol. II, Protoplast--Isolation & Cell Regeneration, 224 pgs. 117.00 (0-8493-6063-3, QK725, CRC Reprint) Franklin.

Cell Physiology of Blood. Ed. by Robert Gunn & John L. Parker. 450p. 1988. 50.00 (0-87470-044-2) Rockefeller.

***Cell Physiology Source Book.** Nicholas Sperelakis. (Illus.). 738p. 1995. boxed 99.00 (0-12-656970-3) Acad Pr.

Cell Proliferation & Cytogenesis in the Mouse Hippocampus. K. Y. Reznikov. Ed. by F. Beck et al. (Advances in Anatomy, Embryology & Cell Biology Ser.: Vol. 122). (Illus.). 96p. 1991. pap. 72.00 (0-387-53689-2) Spr-Verlag.

Cell Proliferation, Cancer, & Cancer Therapy, Vol. 397. Conference in Honor of Anna Goldfeder, Feb 17-19, 1982. Ed. by Renato Baserga. 328p. 1982. 65.00 (0-89766-184-2); pap. 65.00 (0-89766-185-0) NY Acad Sci.

***Cell Proliferation in Cancer: Regulatory Mechanisms of Neoplastic Cell Growth.** Ed. by Lajos Pusztai et al. (Illus.). 360p. 1995. 90.00 (0-19-854791-9) OUP.

Cell Proliferation in Lymphomas. J. Crocker. (Illus.). 224p. 1993. 140.00 (0-632-02925-0) Blackwell Sci.

Cell Relay: Market & Technology Assessment Study. IGIC, Inc. Staff. 1991. 2,995.00 (0-918435-52-8) Info Gatekeepers.

Cell Separation: Methods & Selected Applications, Vol. 1. Thomas G. Pretlow, II & Theresa P. Pretlow. 1982. text ed. 90.00 (0-12-564501-5) Acad Pr.

Cell Separation: Methods & Selected Applications, Vol. 2. Ed. by Thomas G. Pretlow, II & Theresa P. Pretlow. 1983. text ed. 93.00 (0-12-564502-3) Acad Pr.

Cell Separation: Methods & Selected Applications, Vol. 3. Ed. by Thomas G. Pretlow, II & Theresa P. Pretlow. 1984. text ed. 103.00 (0-12-564503-1) Acad Pr.

Cell Separation: Methods & Selected Applications, Vol. 4. Ed. by Thomas G. Pretlow, II & Theresa P. Pretlow. 1987. text ed. 97.00 (0-12-564504-X) Acad Pr.

Cell Separation: Methods & Selected Applications, Vol. 5. Ed. by Thomas G. Pretlow, II & Theresa P. Pretlow. 374p. 1987. text ed. 115.00 (0-12-564505-8) Acad Pr.

Cell Separation Science & Technology. Ed. by Dhinakar S. Kompala & Paul Todd. LC 91-17033. (ACS Symposium Ser.: No. 464). (Illus.). 301p. 1991. 69.95 (0-8412-2090-5) Am Chemical.

Cell Shape: Determinants, Regulation, & Regulatory Role. Ed. by Wilfred D. Stein & Felix Bronner. 450p. 1989. text ed. 128.00 (0-12-664655-4) Acad Pr.

***Cell Signal Transduction, Second Messengers, & Protein Phosphorylation in Health & Disease.** Ed. by A. M. Municio & M. T. Miras-Portugal. (Illus.). 258p. 1994. 79.50 (0-306-44814-9, Plenum Pr) Plenum.

Cell Signalling. Noel G. Morgan. LC 89-11931. (Guilford Molecular Cell Biology Ser.). i, 203p. 1990. pap. text ed. 22.95 (0-89862-518-1) Guilford Pr.

Cell Signalling: Biology & Medicine of Signal Transduction. Ed. by Barry L. Brown & Pauline R. Dobson. (Advances in Second Messenger & Phosphoprotein Research Ser.: Vol. 28). 368p. 1993. 93.50 (0-7817-0076-0) Raven.

Cell Structure & Cell Function: A Symposium in Honor of Bjorn Afzelius on His Sixtieth Birthday Stockholdm, Dec. 1985. Ed. by G. M. Roomans & Bo Forslind. (Illus.). vi, 138p. 1988. pap. text ed. 23.00 (0-931288-38-X) Scanning Microscopy.

Cell Structure & Function. 3rd ed. Ariel G. Loewy et al. 896p. (C). 1991. text ed. 67.00 (0-03-047439-6) SCP.

Cell Structure & Function by Microspectrofluorometry. Ed. by Elli Kohen. (Analytical Cytology Ser.). 450p. 1989. text ed. 213.00 (0-12-417760-3) Acad Pr.

***Cell Study Sampler.** Handt Hanson. 1992. pap. 5.00 (0-933173-45-8) Prince Peace Pub.

Cell Surface. (Symposia on Quantitative Biology Ser.: Vol. LVII). (Illus.). 752p. (C). 1993. text ed. 210.00 (0-87969-063-1); pap. 95.00 (0-87969-064-X) Cold Spring Harbor.

Cell Surface & Differentiation. T. Muramatsu. (Illus.). 160p. 1990. text ed. 69.95 (0-412-30850-9, A4750) Chapman & Hall.

Cell Surface & Extracellular Glycoconjugates: Structure & Function. Ed. by David D. Roberts & Robert P. Mecham. (Biology of Extracellular Matrix Ser.). (Illus.). 314p. 1993. text ed. 79.95 (0-12-589630-1) Acad Pr.

Cell Surface & Neuron & Neuronal Function. Ed. by Carl W. Cotman et al. (Cell Surface Reviews Ser.: Vol. 6). 546p. 1981. 202.75 (0-444-80202-9) Elsevier.

Cell Surface Antigen Thy-1: Immunology, Neurology & Therapeutic Applications. Reif & Schlesinger. (Immunology Ser.: Vol. 45). 640p. 1989. 55.00 (0-8247-7925-8) Dekker.

Cell Surface Carbohydrates & Cell Development. Minoru Fukuda. 1991. 179.00 (0-8493-6435-3, QH545) CRC Pr.

Cell Surface Dynamics: Concepts & Models. Perelson et al. (Receptors & Ligands in Intercellular Communication Ser.: Vol. 3). 584p. 1984. 195.00 (0-8247-7115-X) Dekker.

Cell Surface Factors, Immune Deficiencies, Twin Studies. Ed. by Robert Summitt & Daniel Bergsma. (Alan R. Liss, Inc. Ser.: Vol. 14, No 6A). 1978. 34.00 (0-686-23949-0) March of Dimes.

Cell Surface Factors,Immune Deficiencies, Twin Studies see Annual Review of Birth Defects, 1977: Proceedings of the Birth Defects Annual Conference, 10th, Memphis, Tenn., June, 1977

Cell Surface in Animal Embryogenesis & Development. Ed. by George Poste & G. Nicholson. (Cell Surface Reviews Ser.: Vol. 1). 766p. 1977. 236.50 (0-7204-0597-1) Elsevier.

Cell Surface in Development. Ed. by Aron Moscona. LC 74-7308. 348p. reprint ed. 99.20 (0-685-07768-3, 2015197) Bks Demand.

Cell Surface in Embryogenesis & Carcinogenesis: Common Mechanisms. Esmond J. Sanders. 450p. 1989. 59.50 (0-936923-27-X); pap. 32.50 (0-936923-26-1) Telford Pr.

Cell Surface Labeling. Robert P. Becker & Om Johari. (Illus.). 100p. 1979. pap. text ed. 10.00 (0-931288-07-X) Scanning Microscopy.

Cell Surface Proteases & Metastasis. W. T. Chen. (Molecular Biology Intelligence Unit Ser.). (Illus.). 123p. 1995. 89.95 (1-57059-083-4) R G Landes.

Cell, the Human Organism & Cancer. A. Leroi. 1973. lib. bdg. 79.95 (0-87968-538-7) Krishna Pr.

Cell Theory: A Restatement, History, & Critique. John R. Baker. LC 88-23428. (Genes Cells & Organisms Ser.). (Illus.). 386p. 1988. 15.00 (0-8240-1388-3) Garland.

Cell-to-Cell Communication. Ed. by W. C. DeMello. LC 87-18573. (Illus.). 388p. 1987. 85.00 (0-306-42623-4, Plenum Pr) Plenum.

Cell to Cell Interaction. Ed. by M. M. Burger et al. (Illus.). xx, 252p. 1990. 158.50 (3-8055-5322-6) S Karger.

Cell-to-Cell Mapping. C. S. Hsu. (Applied Mathematical Sciences Ser.: Vol. 64). (Illus.). 345p. 1987. 54.00 (0-387-96520-3) Spr-Verlag.

Cell to Cell Signalling: From Experiments to Theoretical Models. Ed. by Albert Goldbeter. 647p. 1989. text ed. 170.00 (0-12-287960-0) Acad Pr.

Cell to Cell Signals in Plant, Animal & Microbial Symbiosis. Ed. by S. Scannerini et al. (NATO ASI Series H: Vol. 17). (Illus.). xx, 414p. 1988. 181.00 (0-387-18555-0) Spr-Verlag.

Cell to Cell Signals in Plants & Animals Progress Report. Ed. by V. Neuhoff & J. Friend. (NATO ASI Series H: Cell Biology: Vol. 51). (Illus.). 386p. 1991. 139.00 (0-387-53739-2) Spr-Verlag.

Cell Transformation Systems Relevant to Radiation-Induced Cancer in Man: Proceedings of a Workshop Jointly Organized by the Nuclear Energy Board of Ireland, the United States Department of Energy & the Commission of the European Communities, Held in Dublin, Ireland on 4-7 April 1989. Ed. by K. H. Chadwick et al. (Illus.). 428p. 1989. 105.00 (0-85274-084-0) IOP Pub.

Cell Transplantation for Huntington's Disease. Ed. by Paul R. Sanberg et al. (Medical Intelligence Unit Ser.). 125p. 1994. 89.95 (1-57059-079-6, LN9079) R G Landes.

Cell Types in the Adenohypophysis of the Primitive Actinopterygians: With Special Reference to Immunocytochemical Identification of Pituitary Hormone Producing Cells in the Distal Lobe. G. N. Hansen. (Illus.). 88p. 1983. pap. 29.00 (0-08-029827-3, Pergamon Pr) Elsevier.

Cell Ultrastructure. Stephen L. Wolfe. 114p. (C). 1985. pap. 18.95 (0-534-05058-1) Intl Thomson.

Cell Volume Regulation. Ed. by K. W. Beyenbach. (Comparative Physiology Ser.: Vol. 4). (Illus.). 166p. 1990. text ed. 119.25 (3-8055-5148-7) S Karger.

Cell Volume Regulation. Ed. by F. Lang. (Journal: Renal Physiology & Biochemistry: Vol. 11, No. 3-5, 1988). (Illus.). 180p. 1989. pap. 109.75 (3-8055-4986-5) S Karger.

Cell Wall Deficient Forms. 2nd ed. Mattman. 1992. 49.95 (0-8493-4405-0, QR77) CRC Pr.

Cell Wall Mechanics of Tracheids. Richard E. Mark. 1967. 100.00 (0-685-45682-X) Elliots Bks.

Cell Wars. Fran Balkwill. LC 92-6377. (Illus.). (J). (gr. 3-6). 1992. 17.50 (0-87614-761-9, Carolrhoda) Lerner Group.

Cell Wars. Fran Balkwill. (J). (gr. 3-6). 1994. pap. 8.95 (0-87614-637-X, Carolrhoda) Lerner Group.

Cellar. Ellen Howard. LC 90-23190. (Illus.). 64p. (J). (gr. 2-4). 1992. text ed. 12.95 (0-689-31724-7, Atheneum Bks Young) S&S Childrens.

Cellar at No. Five. Shelley Smith. 160p. 1985. pap. 5.95 (0-89733-131-1) Academy Chi Pubs.

Cellar Doors & Hollyhocks: Writing by Older Minnesotans. Illus. by Rochelle Woldorsky. 184p. (Orig.). 1988. pap. 7.00 (0-927663-02-3) COMPAS.

Cellar of Horror. Ken Englade. 1992. mass mkt. 4.99 (0-312-92929-3) St Martin.

Cellars & Attics. Michele Brailow. 48p. 1981. 6.95 (0-87881-099-4) Mojave Bks.

Celles qu'on Prend dans ses Bras. Henry De Montherlant. pap. 10.95 (0-8288-9634-8, F115690) Fr & Eur.

Celles Qu'on Prend dans Ses Bras. Henry de Montherlant. (FRE.). 1983. pap. 10.95 (0-8288-3717-1, F115290) Fr & Eur.

Cellini. John Pope-Hennessy. LC 85-6111. (Illus.). 320p. 1985. 125.00 (0-89659-453-X) Abbeville Pr.

Cellist. Gregor Piatagorsky. LC 76-3697. (Music Reprint Ser.). 1976. reprint ed. lib. bdg. 37.50 (0-306-70822-1) Da Capo.

Cellist's Guide to the Core Technique. 2nd ed. G. Jean Smith. Ed. by Carl Simpson. LC 93-14833. 1993. 13.00 (1-883026-00-8) Am String Tchrs.

Cello Book One. Tortelier. Date not set. pap. 9.50 (0-685-68989-1, Chester Music) Music Sales.

Cello Book Two. Paul Tortelier. Date not set. pap. 9.95 (0-685-68990-5, Chester Music) Music Sales.

Cello Ensembles. Ed. by Rick Mooney. 87p. 1987. 6.50 (0-87487-296-0) Summy-Birchard.

Cello Music Since 1960: A Bibliography of Solo, Chamber & Orchestral Works for the Solo Cellist. Donald Homuth. LC 94-15453. (Reference Books in Music: No. 26). x, 452p. 1994. 69.50 (0-914913-27-1) Fallen Leaf.

Cello Solos, EFS40. (Illus.). 160p. 1940. pap. 11.95 (0-8256-2040-6, AM40205) Music Sales.

Cello Story. Dimitry Markevitch. Tr. by Florence Seder. (Illus.). 192p. (Orig.). 1984. pap. 13.95 (0-87487-406-8) Summy-Birchard.

Cello Suites. J. S. Bach. Ed. by Jacqueline Du Pre. Date not set. pap. 17.95 (0-685-68993-X, Pub. by Wilhelm Hansen DK) Music Sales.

Cello Suites: Arranged for Viola. J. S. Bach. Date not set. pap. 10.95 (0-685-68992-1, Pub. by Wilhelm Hansen DK) Music Sales.

Cells. Michael George. (Images Ser.). (J). (gr. 5 up). 1992. lib. bdg. 16.95 (0-88682-437-0) Creative Ed.

Cells. Michael George. (J). (gr. 4-7). 1993. 15.95 (1-56846-057-0) Creative Ed.

Cells. 2nd ed. Michael W. Berns. 256p. (C). 1983. pap. text ed. 20.50 (0-03-061578-X) SCP.

Cells: Principles of Molecular Structure & Function. David Prescott. 640p. (C). 1988. teacher ed 435.00 (0-86720-102-9); Intl student ed. pap. 5.65 (0-534-98266-2); student ed 13.75 (0-86720-098-7); trans. 195.00 (0-86720-100-2); boxed 46.25 (0-86720-092-8); sl. 195.00 (0-86720-099-5); 45.00 (0-86720-101-0) Jones & Bartlett.

Cells & Cytokines in Lung Inflammation. Ed. by Michel Chignard et al. LC 94-18939. (Annals Ser.: Vol. 725). 1994. write for info. (0-89766-855-3); pap. write for info. (0-89766-856-1) NY Acad Sci.

Cells & Societies. John T. Bonner. LC 55-5002. 1955. 39.50x (0-691-07919-6) Princeton U Pr.

Cells & Tissues. Robert B. Jubenville & Salvatore Drogo. 250p. 1993. spiral bd. 19.95 (0-8403-8968-X) Kendall-Hunt.

Cells & Tissues. Leslie J. LeMaster. LC 85-6695. (New True Bks.). (Illus.). 45p. (J). (gr. k-3). 1985. lib. bdg. 12.90 (0-516-01266-5) Childrens.

Cells & Tissues. Ed. by Andy W. Rogers. 1983. pap. text ed. 43.00 (0-12-593120-4) Acad Pr.

Cells Are Us. Fran Balkwill. (Cells & Things Ser.). (Illus.). 32p. (J). (gr. 3-6). 1993. 17.50 (0-87614-762-7, Carolrhoda) Lerner Group.

Cells Are Us. Fran Balkwill. (J). (gr. 3-6). 1994. pap. 8.95 (0-87614-636-1, Carolrhoda) Lerner Group.

Cells, Development, & the Biology of Cancer. Harold E. Varmus & Robert A. Weinberg. LC 92-20554. 1995. text ed. write for info. (0-7167-5037-6) W H Freeman.

***Cells, Genes, & Chromosomes.** (Invisible World Ser.). (Illus.). 32p. (YA). (gr. 4 up). 1995. lib. bdg. 14.95 (0-7910-3154-3) Chelsea Hse.

***Cells, Genes, Genetics.** Wright State University (Biological Science) Staff. 112p. (C). 1994. pap. text ed., spiral bd. 13.56 (0-7872-0027-1) Kendall-Hunt.

Cells in Industry: Managing Teams for Profit. Jim Kirton & Ellen Brooks. LC 94-20471. 1994. 24.95 (0-07-707850-0) McGraw.

Cells, Membranes, & Disease: Including Renal. Ed. by E. Reid et al. LC 87-22060. (Methodological Surveys in Biochemistry & Analysis Ser.: Vol. 17). (Illus.). 506p. 1987. 125.00 (0-306-42678-1, Plenum Pr) Plenum.

Cells of Knowledge. Sian Hayton. 202p. 1990. 16.95 (1-56131-000-X) New Amsterdam Bks.

Cells of Knowledge. Sian Hayton. 202p. 1992. pap. 9.95 (1-56131-031-X) New Amsterdam Bks.

***Cells of the Body: A History of Somatic Cell Genetics.** Henry Harris. (Illus.). 300p. (C). 1995. 55.00 (0-87969-460-2) Cold Spring Harbor.

Cells, Products, Safety. Ed. by J. C. Petricciani & W. Hennessen. (Developments in Biological Standardization Ser.: Vol. 68). (Illus.). vi, 90p. 1987. pap. 44.00 (3-8055-4676-9) S Karger.

Cells, Tissues, & Disease. Guido Majno & Isabelle Joris. (Illus.). 832p. 1994. 75.00 (0-86542-372-5) Blackwell Sci.

Cellular - Molecular Physiology of Cell Volume Regulation. Kevin Strange. 1993. 95.00 (0-8493-4448-4, QP90) CRC Pr.

Cellular Adhesion: Molecular Definition to Therapeutic Potential. Ed. by B. W. Metcalf et al. (New Horizons in Therapeutics Ser.). (Illus.). 312p. (C). 1994. 79.50 (0-306-44685-5, Plenum Pr) Plenum.

Cellular Ageing. Ed. by H. W. Sauer. (Monographs in Developmental Biology: Vol. 17). (Illus.). x, 278p. 1984. 118.50 (3-8055-3860-X) S Karger.

Cellular Ageing: Concepts & Mechanisms: Part I: General Concepts. Mechanisms I: Fidelity of Information Flow, 2 pts. Ed. by R. G. Cutler. (Interdisciplinary Topics in Gerontology Ser.: Vol. 9). (Illus.). 150p. 1976. pap. 91.25 (3-8055-2283-5) S Karger.

Cellular Ageing: Concepts & Mechanisms: Part II: Mechanisms II: Translation, Transcription & Structural Properties, 2 pts. Ed. by R. G. Cutler. (Interdisciplinary Topics in Gerontology Ser.: Vol. 10). (Illus.). 150p. 1976. pap. 60.00 (3-8055-2284-3) S Karger.

Cellular Analogues of Conditioning & Neural Plasticity: Proceedings of a Satellite Symposium of the 28th International Congress of Physiological Sciences, Szeged, Hungary, 1980. Ed. by O. Feher & F. Joo. LC 80-41992. (Advances in Physiological Sciences Ser.: Vol. 36). (Illus.). 300p. 1981. 147.00 (0-08-027372-6, Pub. by Pergamon Repr UK) Franklin.

Cellular & Cordless Phone Phreaking. John J. Williams. 89p. 1993. pap. 64.00 (0-934274-45-2) Consumertronics.

Cellular & Humoral Components of Cerebrospinal Fluid in Multiple Sclerosis. Ed. by A. Lowenthal & J. Raus. (NATO ASI Series A, Life Sciences: Vol. 129). (Illus.). 538p. 1987. 135.00 (0-306-42578-5, Plenum Pr) Plenum.

Cellular & Humoral Defense against Disease. Ed. by M. E. Rafelson. (Journal: Clinical Physiology & Biochemistry: Vol. 1, No. 2-5, 1983). (Illus.). 228p. 1983. pap. 104.00 (3-8055-3693-3) S Karger.

Cellular & Humoral Immunotherapy & Apheresis. Daniel B. Brubaker et al. LC 91-32912. (Illus.). (C). 1991. text ed. 45.00 (1-56395-001-4) Am Assn Blood.

***Cellular & Microcellular Materials: 1994 International Mechanical Engineering Congress & Exposition, Chicago, Illinois - November 6-11, 1994.** (MD Ser.: Vol. 53). 292p. 1994. 90.00 (0-7918-1428-9, G00923) ASME.

Cellular & Molecular Alterations in the Failing Human Heart. Ed. by G. Hasenfuss et al. 368p. 1992. 87.00 (0-387-91419-6) Spr-Verlag.

***Cellular & Molecular Approaches to Fish Ionic Regulation Vol. 14.** Ed. by Chris M. Wood et al. (Fish Physiology Ser.: Vol. 14). (Illus.). 388p. 1995. text ed. 85.00 (0-12-350438-4) Acad Pr.

Cellular & Molecular Aspects of Developmental Biology. Ed. by M. Fougereau & R. Stora. 312p. 1986. 95.00 (0-444-86981-6, North Holland) Elsevier.

Cellular & Molecular Aspects of Endotoxin Reactions: Proceedings of the 1st Congress of the International Endotoxin Society, San Diego, CA, 9-12 May, 1990. Ed. by A. Nowotny et al. (International Congress Series, No. 923: Endotoxin Research Ser.: Vol. 1). 566p. 1990. 231.25 (0-444-81365-9, Excerpta Medica) Elsevier.

Cellular & Molecular Aspects of Fiber Carcinogenesis. Ed. by B. R. Brinkley et al. (Current Communications in Cell & Molecular Biology Ser.: No. 2). (Illus.). 260p. (C). 1991. text ed. 36.00 (0-87969-361-4) Cold Spring Harbor.

Cellular & Molecular Aspects of Implantation. Ed. by Stanley R. Glasser & David W. Bullock. LC 80-20471. 518p. 1981. 115.00 (0-306-40581-4, Plenum Pr) Plenum.

Cellular & Molecular Aspects of Inflammation. Ed. by George Poste & Stanley T. Crooke. LC 87-37400. (New Horizons in Therapeutics Ser.). (Illus.). 460p. 1988. 110.00 (0-306-42852-0, Plenum Pr) Plenum.

An Asterisk (*) at the beginning of an entry indicates that the title is appearing in BIP for the first time.

An Asterisk (*) at the beginning of an entry indicates that the title is appearing in BIP for the first time.

1113

C

Cellular Radio: Analog & Digital Systems. Asha Mehrotra. LC 94-5944. 1994. 89.00 (0-89006-731-7) Artech Hse.

***Cellular Radio & Personal Communications: Selected Readings.** Ed. by Theodore S. Rappaport. LC 94-40139. 522p. 1995. pap. 39.95 (0-7803-2283-5) IEEE Comp Soc.

Cellular Radio Handbook: A Reference for Cellular System Operation. enl. rev. ed. Neil J. Boucher. LC 92-20093. 1992. write for info. (0-930633-15-6) Quantum Pub.

***Cellular Radio Handbook: A Reference for Cellular System Operation.** 3rd ed. Neil Boucher. LC 94-41196. 1995. write for info. (0-930633-16-4) Quantum Pub.

Cellular Radio Performance Engineering. Asha Mehrotra. LC 94-7673. 1994. 89.00 (0-89006-748-1) Artech Hse.

Cellular Radio Principles & Design. Raymond Macario. 1993. text ed. 40.00 (0-07-044301-7) McGraw.

Cellular Radio Systems. Ed. by D. M. Balston & Raymond C. V. Macario. LC 93-31141. 373p. 1993. text ed. 75.00 (0-89006-646-9) Artech Hse.

***Cellular Receptors for Animal Viruses.** Ed. by Eckard Wimmer. (Monographs: No. 28). (Illus.). 600p. (C). 1994. 97.00 (0-87969-429-7) Cold Spring Harbor.

Cellular Receptors for Hormones & Neurotransmitters. Dennis Schulster & Alexander Levitzki. LC 79-41216. 412p. 1980. text ed. 225.00 (0-471-27682-0, Wiley-Interscience) Wiley.

Cellular Receptors for Hormones & Neurotransmitters. Ed. by Dennis Schulster & Alexander Levitzki. LC 79-41216. (Illus.). 432p. reprint ed. pap. 123.20 (0-685-20743-9, 2030381) Bks Demand.

Cellular Recognition. M. F. Greaves. 1975. pap. 6.95 (0-412-13110-2, NO.6129) Chapman & Hall.

Cellular Regulation by Protein Phosphorylation. Ed. by Ludwig M. Heilmeyer, Jr. (NATO ASI Series H: Cell Biology: Vol. 56). xiii, 501p. 1991. 191.00 (0-387-51776-6) Spr-Verlag.

Cellular Regulatory Mechanisms. Cold Spring Harbor Symposia on Quantitative Biology Staff. LC 34-8174. (Cold Spring Harbor Symposia on Quantitative Biology Ser.: No. 26). 424p. reprint ed. pap. 120.90 (0-7837-2014-9, 2042289) Bks Demand.

Cellular Robotics & Micro Robotics Systems. T. Fukuda & T. Ueyama. 284p. 1994. text ed. 48.00 (981-02-1457-X) World Scientific Pub.

Cellular Signals Controlling Uterine Function. Ed. by L. A. Lavia. (Illus.). 184p. 1991. 75.00 (0-306-43822-4, Plenum Pr) Plenum.

Cellular Structure of the Mammalian Nervous System. H. Hillman. 1986. lib. bdg. 191.00 (0-85200-916-X) Kluwer Ac.

Cellular Structures in Instabilites. Ed. by J. E. Wesfreid & S. Zaleski. (Lecture Notes in Physics Ser.: Vol. 210). vi, 389p. 1984. 39.00 (0-387-13879-X) Spr-Verlag.

Cellular Structures in Topology. Rudolf Fritsch & Renzo Piccinini. (Cambridge Studies in Advanced Mathematics: No.19). (Illus.). 300p. (C). 1990. 79.95 (0-521-32784-9) Cambridge U Pr.

Cellular Systems for Toxicity Testing. Ed. by G. M. Williams et al. 1983. 95.00 (0-89766-206-7); pap. 95.00 (0-89766-207-5, VOL. 407) NY Acad Sci.

Cellular Telephone Installation Handbook. Michael Losee. Ed. by Paul Mandelstein & Cornelia Mandelstein. (Illus.). 352p. (C). 1988. text ed. 49.95 (0-930633-05-9) Quantum Pub.

Cellular Telephone Product Operation Handbook. Dennis Bishop. (Illus.). 982p. 1995. ring bd. 149.00 (0-945592-04-3) Comns Pub.

Cellular Telephone Program Handbook. Dennis Bishop. 396p. 1995. ring bd. 149.00 (0-945592-05-1) Comns Pub.

***Cellular Telephone Travel Handbook.** (Illus.). 1200p. (Orig.). 1995. pap. 195.00 (0-7605-1890-4) Rector Pr.

Cellular Telephones. Richard K. Miller & Terri C. Walker. LC 88-81674. (Survey on Technology & Markets Ser.: No. 83). 50p. 1989. pap. text ed. 200.00 (1-55865-082-2) Future Tech Surveys.

Cellular Thalamic Mechanisms: Based on Contributions to the Symposium Held in Verona, Italy, 22-25 Aug., 1987. Ed. by M. Bentivoglio & R. Spreafico. (International Congress Ser.: No. 765). 596p. 1988. 205.25 (0-444-80989-9, Excerpta Medica) Elsevier.

Cellular Toxicology & Marine Pollution. Ed. by Brian L. Bayne. 44p. 1985. pap. 8.25 (0-08-032621-8, Pub. by PPL UK) Elsevier.

***Cellular Travel Guide: How to Use Your Cellular Telephone Wherever You Travel in North America.** 5th ed. Steven Brown. (Illus.). 700p. 1995. pap. text ed. 19.95 (0-945592-11-6) Comns Pub.

Cellular Ultrastructure of Woody Plants. Advanced Science Seminar (1964: Pinebrook Conference Center). Ed. by Wilfred A. Cote, Jr. LC 65-15857. 617p. reprint ed. pap. 175.90 (0-317-52000-8, 2027395) Bks Demand.

Cellular Variation & Adaptation in Cancer: Biological Basis & Therapeutic Consequences. Michael Woodruff. (Illus.). 152p. 1990. 32.50 (0-19-854254-2) OUP.

Cellulite Solution: A Breakthrough Program That Really Works. Laura Simms. LC 91-67052. (Illus.). 288p. (Orig.). Date not set. pap. 14.95 (0-9625499-1-6) Natural CA.

Cellulite Solution: A Wholistic Guide for a Beautiful Body. Laura Simms. Ed. by Wilhelmine Hartnack. (Illus.). 192p. (Orig.). 1990. pap. 12.95 (0-9625499-0-8) Natural CA.

Celluloid Closet: Homosexuality in the Movies. rev. ed. Vito Russo. (Illus.). 320p. 1991. lib. bdg. 35.00x (0-8095-9107-3) Borgo Pr.

Celluloid Closet: Homosexuality in the Movies. rev. ed. Vito Russo. LC 86-45684. (Illus.). 320p. 1987. pap. 14.00 (0-06-096132-5, PL 6132, PL) HarpC.

Celluloid Gangs. Tom Tolnay. 192p. 1990. 17.95 (0-8027-5753-7) Walker & Co.

Celluloid Ivy: Higher Education in the Movies 1960-1990. David B. Hinton. LC 94-13869. 1994. 25.00 (0-8108-2891-X) Scarecrow.

Celluloid Persuasion: Movies & the Liberal Arts. Lawrence Murray. LC 79-16764. 181p. reprint ed. 51.60 (0-685-07746-2, 2019346) Bks Demand.

Celluloid Power: Social Film Criticism from the Birth of a Nation to Judgement at Nuremberg. David Platt. LC 91-35568. (Illus.). 700p. 1992. 72.50 (0-8108-2442-6) Scarecrow.

Celluloid Wars: A Guide to Film & the American Experience of War. Frank J. Wetta & Stephen J. Curley. LC 92-8210. (Research Guides in Military Studies: No. 5). 320p. 1992. text ed. 47.95 (0-313-26099-0, WCG, Greenwood Pr) Greenwood.

Cellulose: Biosynthesis & Structure. I. A. Tarchevsky & G. N. Marchenko. Tr. by L. V. Backinowski & M. A. Chlenov. 335p. 1991. 173.00 (0-387-52247-6) Spr-Verlag.

Cellulose: Sources & Exploitation. John F. Kennedy et al. 1991. 75.00 (0-13-121955-3, 310102) P-H.

Cellulose & Fiber Science Developments: A World View. Ed. by Jett C. Arthur. LC 77-22540. (American Chemical Society Symposium Ser.: No. 50). 296p. reprint ed. pap. 84.40 (0-317-08900-5, 2019941) Bks Demand.

Cellulose & Other Natural Polymer Systems: Biogenesis, Structure, & Degradation. Ed. by R. Malcolm Brown, Jr. LC 82-3796. 540p. 1982. 110.00 (0-306-40856-2, Plenum Pr) Plenum.

Cellulose & Wood: Chemistry & Technology. Ed. by Contrad E. Schuerch. LC 08-931461. 1989. pap. text ed. 135.00 (0-471-51256-7) Wiley.

Cellulose Chemistry & Technology: A Symposium Sponsored by the Cellulose, Paper, & Textile Division at the Meeting of American Chemical Society, 171st, New York, N. Y., April 5-9, 1976. American Chemical Society, International Developments in Cellulose, Papers & Textiles Symposium Staff. Ed. by Jett C. Arthur, Jr. LC 77-6649. (American Chemical Society Symposium Ser.: No. 48). (Illus.). 406p. reprint ed. pap. 115.80 (0-317-11051-9, 2015235) Bks Demand.

***Cellulose Decomposition & Soil Fertility.** J. Szegi. 186p. (C). 1988. 75.00x (963-05-4575-6, Pub. by Akad Kiado HU) St Mut.

Cellulose Hydrolysis. L. T. Fan et al. (Biotechnology Monographs: Vol. 3). (Illus.). 210p. 1987. 128.00 (0-387-17671-3) Spr-Verlag.

Cellulose; Leather; Flexible Barrier Materials (91 Standards) see ASTM Annual Book of Standards, 1986

Cellulose Nitrate in Conservation: Research in Conservation, No. 2. Charles Selwitz. LC 88-8803. 72p. 1988. pap. 20.00 (0-89236-098-4) J P Getty Trust.

Cellulose Nitrate Motion Picture Film. National Fire Protection Association Staff. 18p. 1988. 16.75 (0-317-63072-5, 40-94) Natl Fire Prot.

Cellulose Technology Research: A Symposium Sponsored by the Cellulose, Paper, & Textile Division at the 168th Meeting of the American Chemical Society, Atlantic City, NJ, September 11-12, 1974. Ed. by Albin F. Turbak. LC 75-2021. (ACS Symposium Ser.: No. 10). (Illus.). 208p. reprint ed. pap. 59.30 (0-685-33215-2, 2052319) Bks Demand.

Cellulosic Ion Exchangers. E. A. Peterson. (Laboratory Techniques in Biochemistry & Molecular Biology Ser.: Vol. 2, Pt. 2). 1970. pap. 18.50 (0-444-10057-1, North Holland) Elsevier.

Cellulosic Polymers Blends & Composites. Gilbert. (C). Date not set. text ed. write for info. (1-56990-166-X) Hanser-Gardner.

Cellulosics: Chemical, Biochemical, & Material Aspects. Ed. by John F. Kennedy et al. LC 93-25363. (Ellis Horwood Series in Polymer Science & Technology). 1993. write for info. (0-13-053042-5, Tavistock-E Horwood) Routledge Chapman & Hall.

Cellulosics: Pulp, Fibre, & Environmental Aspects. Ed. by John F. Kennedy et al. LC 93-25162. (Ellis Horwood Series in Polymer Science & Technology). 1993. write for info. (0-13-053059-X, Tavistock-E Horwood) Routledge Chapman & Hall.

Cellulosics Utilization: Research & Rewards. Ed. by H. Inagaki & G. O. Phillips. 274p. 1989. 57.75 (1-85166-406-8) Elsevier.

Celluoid Sisters: Women & Popular Cinema. Janet Thumin. LC 91-30215. 224p. 1992. text ed. 39.95 (0-312-07254-6) St Martin.

Celni Qui Ne M'Accompagnait Pas see One Who Was Standing Apart from Me

Celos Aun Del Aire Matan. Pedro Calderon De La Barca. Tr. & Intro. by Matthew D. Stroud. 219p. 25.00 (0-911536-90-6); pap. 15.00 (0-685-54676-4) Trinity U Pr.

Celos Del Aire. J. Lopez Rubio. 125p. (SPA.). 1982. 9.50 (0-8288-7159-0) Fr & Eur.

Celos Hacen Estrellas. Juan V. De Guevara. Ed. by J. E. Varey et al. (Serie B: Textos, IV). (Illus.). 277p. (Orig.). (SPA.). (C). 1970. pap. 45.00 (0-900411-06-6, Pub. by Tamesis Bks Ltd UK) Boydell & Brewer.

Celsa's World: Conversations with a Mexican Peasant Woman. Thomas C. Tirado. (Special Studies: No. 27). 120p. (Orig.). (C). 1991. pap. text ed. 11.00 (0-87918-073-0) ASU Lat Am St.

Celso. Leo Romero. LC 84-72302. 80p. (Orig.). (C). 1984. pap. 7.00 (0-934770-36-0) Arte Publico.

Celt & the World: A Study of the Relation of Celt & Teuton in History. S. Leslie. 1972. 59.95 (0-87968-822-X) Gordon Pr.

Celt, Druid & Culdee. Isabel H. Elder. LC 89-84444. 168p. (Orig.). 1990. reprint ed. pap. 7.00 (0-934666-36-9) Artisan Sales.

Celtic: A Comparative Study. Douglas B. Gregor. (Language & Literature Ser.). 1980. 35.00 (0-900891-41-6); pap. 25.00 (0-900891-56-4) Oleander Pr.

Celtic: Design & Style in Homes of Scotland, Ireland & Wales. Deborah Krasner. LC 89-40780. 272p. 1990. 35.00 (0-670-81849-6, Viking Studio) Studio Bks.

Celtic Airs, Jigs, Hornpipes, & Reels. Comp. by Stefan Grossman. (Guitar Workshop Ser.). 1993. 7.95 (1-56222-070-5, 94504); audio 9.98 (1-56222-083-7, 94504) Mel Bay.

Celtic & Early Medieval Designs from Britain for Artists & Craftspeople. Eva Wilson. (Pictorial Archive Ser.). 128p. 1987. reprint ed. pap. 5.95 (0-486-25340-6) Dover.

Celtic & Germanic Themes in European Literature: Proceedings of a Conference Held in Grey College, University of Durham, April 3-5, 1992. Ed. by Neil Thomas. LC 93-33607. 144p. 1993. text ed. 69.95 (0-7734-9420-0) E Mellen.

Celtic & Scandinavian Religions. John A. MacCulloch. LC 72-11739. 180p. 1973. reprint ed. text ed. 38.50 (0-8371-6705-1, MCSR, Greenwood Pr) Greenwood.

Celtic Art. George Bain. 168p. 1982. 45.00 (0-85335-196-1, Pub. by Stuart Titles Ltd UK) St Mut.

Celtic Art. Barry Raftery. (Illus.). 172p. 1991. 50.00 (2-08-013509-0, Pub. by Flammarion) Abbeville Pr.

Celtic Art: From Its Beginnings to the Book of Kells. Ruth Megaw & Vincent Megaw. LC 88-50245. (Illus.). 288p. 1990. pap. 24.95 (0-500-27585-8) Thames Hudson.

Celtic Art: The Methods of Construction. George Bain. (Illus.). 160p. 1973. reprint ed. pap. 8.95 (0-486-22923-8) Dover.

***Celtic Art & Design.** Iain Zaczek. Ed. by Stephen Calloway. (Illus.). 64p. 1995. pap. 9.95 (1-55921-153-9) Moyer Bell.

Celtic Art in Pagan & Christian Times. J. Romilly Allen. 1977. lib. bdg. 69.95 (0-8490-1589-8) Gordon Pr.

Celtic Art Source Book. Courtney Davis. (Illus.). 128p. 1994. pap. 16.95 (0-7137-2144-8, Pub. by Blandford Pr UK) Sterling.

Celtic Astrology: The Twelve Mysteries of the Ancient Druids. Rhuddlwm Gawr. LC 85-73747. (Illus.). 156p. 1989. 15.95 (0-931760-26-7, CP 10112); pap. 12.95 (0-931760-12-7) Camelot GA.

***Celtic Blood: Selected Poems 1968-1994.** Philip Daughtry LC 94-69076. 104p. (Orig.). 1995. pap. 9.95 (1-883197-05-8) New Native Pr.

***Celtic Book of Days: A Guide to Celtic Spirituality & Wisdom.** Caitlin Matthews. LC 95-11996. (Illus.). 128p. 1996. 19.95 (0-89281-565-5, Destiny Bks) Inner Tradit.

Celtic Book of the Dead. Caitlin Matthews. 1992. 27.95 (0-312-07241-4) St Martin.

Celtic Borders, Alphabets, & Motifs. Amy L. Lusebrink. LC 93-10729. (Pictorial Archive Ser.). 1993. pap. write for info. (0-486-27688-0) Dover.

Celtic Borders & Decoration. Courtney Davis. (Illus.). 96p. 1994. pap. 9.95 (0-7137-2330-0, Pub. by Blandford Pr UK) Sterling.

***Celtic Britain.** (Weidenfeld Country Miniature Ser.). (Illus.). 64p. 1995. 8.95 (0-297-83488-6, Pub. by Orion) Trafalgar.

Celtic Britain. Charles Thomas. LC 86-50220. (Ancient Peoples & Places Ser.). (Illus.). 200p. 1986. 22.50 (0-500-02107-4) Thames Hudson.

***Celtic Britain & Ireland: Art & Society.** Lloyd Laing & Jennifer Laing. LC 95-16925. 1995. write for info. (0-312-12613-1) St Martin.

Celtic Britain & the Pilgrim Movement. Griffith H. Jones. LC 78-63466. reprint ed. 92.50 (0-404-16378-5) AMS Pr.

Celtic Charted Designs. Co Spinhoven. 64p. (Orig.). 1987. pap. 3.50 (0-486-25411-9) Dover.

***Celtic Chiefdom, Celtic State.** Ed. by Bettina Arnold & Blair Gibson. (New Directions in Archaeology Ser.). (Illus.). 160p. (C). 1995. write for info. (0-521-46469-2) Cambridge U Pr.

Celtic, Christian, Socialist: The Novels of Anthony C. West. Audrey S. Eyler. LC 92-54185. 160p. 1993. 29.50 (0-8386-3515-6) Fairleigh Dickinson.

***Celtic Christian Spirituality: An Anthology of Mythology & Modern Sources.** Ed. by Davies & Bowie. 224p. 1995. pap. text ed. 17.95 (0-8264-0835-4) Continuum.

Celtic Christianity: Ecology & Holiness. Christopher Bamford & William P. Marsh. 144p. (Orig.). 1987. pap. text ed. 8.95 (0-940262-07-X) Lindisfarne Pr.

Celtic Civilization & Its Heritage. J. Filip. 232p. (C). 1977. pap. 20.00 (0-685-31512-6, Pub. by Collets UK) Pro-Am Music.

Celtic Civilization & Its Heritage. J. Filip. 232p. (C). 1977. 66.00 (0-569-08324-9) St Mut.

Celtic Collection: Knitwear Designs for Men & Women. Alice Starmore. (Illus.). 144p. 1994. pap. 19.95 (1-57076-005-5, Trafalgar Sq Pub) Trafalgar.

***Celtic Connection.** Ed. by Glanville Price. 361p. (C). 1994. lib. bdg. 76.50 (0-86140-248-0, Pub. by C Smythe Ltd UK) B&N Imports.

Celtic Consciousness. Ed. by Robert O'Driscoll. LC 82-1269. (Illus.). 642p. 1982. 40.00 (0-8076-1041-0) Braziller.

Celtic Consciousness. Ed. by Robert O'Driscoll. LC 82-1269. (Illus.). 642p. 1985. reprint ed. pap. 27.95 (0-8076-1136-0) Braziller.

Celtic Contraries. Robin Skelton. (Irish Studies). 260p. 1989. text ed. 34.95 (0-8156-2479-4) Syracuse U Pr.

Celtic Cookbook. Helen Smith-Twiddy. pap. 12.50 (0-89979-003-8) British Am Bks.

Celtic Cross. Ed. by Ray B. Browne et al. LC 78-121453. (Essay Index Reprint Ser.). 1980. 23.95 (0-8369-1744-8) Ayer.

***Celtic Cross Stitch Samplers.** Angela Wainwright. (Illus.). 96p. 1995. 19.95 (0-304-34443-5, Pub. by Cassell UK) Sterling.

Celtic Crystal Magick, Vol. 1. Rhuddlwm Gawr. LC 85-73766. (Illus.). 114p. (Orig.). 1987. pap. 10.95 (0-931760-51-8, CP 10129); pap. 8.95 (0-931760-29-1) Camelot GA.

Celtic Crystal Magick, Vol. II. Rhuddlwm Gawr. LC 85-73766. (Illus.). 140p. (Orig.). 1989. text ed. 12.95 (0-931760-91-7); pap. 10.95 (0-931760-92-5) Camelot GA.

Celtic Daily Prayer: A Northumbrian Office. John Skinner & Andy Raine. 224p. 1994. pap. 12.00 (0-551-02845-9, Pub. by Marshall Pickering) Harper SF.

Celtic Design: A Beginner's Manual. Aidan Meehan. LC 90-71434. (Illus.). 160p. (Orig.). 1991. pap. 14.95 (0-500-27629-3) Thames Hudson.

Celtic Design: Animal Patterns. Aidan Meehan. LC 91-67307. (Illus.). 160p. 1992. pap. 14.95 (0-500-27662-5) Thames Hudson.

Celtic Design: Illuminated Letters. Aidan Meehan. LC 92-80339. (Illus.). 160p. 1992. pap. 15.95 (0-500-27685-4) Thames Hudson.

Celtic Design: Knotwork. Aidan Meehan. LC 90-71465. (Illus.). 160p. (Orig.). 1991. pap. 15.95 (0-500-27630-7) Thames Hudson.

Celtic Design: Maze Patterns. Aidan Meehan. LC 93-61000. (Illus.). 160p. 1994. pap. 15.95 (0-500-27747-8) Thames Hudson.

Celtic Design: Spirals. Aidan Meehan. LC 92-62132. (Illus.). 160p. 1993. pap. 14.95 (0-500-27705-2) Thames Hudson.

Celtic Design: The Dragon & the Griffin. Aidan Meehan. LC 94-60346. (Illus.). 160p. (Orig.). 1995. pap. 15.95 (0-500-27792-3) Thames Hudson.

***Celtic Design: The Tree of Life.** Aidan Meehan. LC 94-61399. (Celtic Design Ser.). (Illus.). 160p. (Orig.). 1995. pap. 15.95 (0-500-27827-X) Thames Hudson.

***Celtic Design - Pattern Motif.** 17.99 (0-517-12178-6) Random Hse Value.

Celtic Design Book. Rebecca McKillip. (International Design Library). (Illus.). 48p. (Orig.). 1981. pap. 5.95 (0-916144-75-5) Stemmer Hse.

Celtic Designs & Motifs. Courtney Davis. 1991. pap. 3.95 (0-486-26718-0) Dover.

Celtic Designs Coloring Book. Ed Sibbett, Jr. Date not set. 2.95 (0-486-23796-6) Dover.

Celtic Designs Stained Glass Coloring Book. Courtney Davis. Date not set. 3.95 (0-486-27456-X) Dover.

Celtic Divination: Witchcraft, Dowsing & Ley Lines. Rhuddlwm Gawr. LC 85-73765. (Illus.). 160p. (Orig.). 12.95 (0-931760-46-1, CP 10124); pap. 10.95 (0-931760-24-0) Camelot GA.

Celtic Druids. Godfrey Higgins. 420p. 1993. pap. 45.00 (1-56459-346-0) Kessinger Pub.

Celtic Druids Year: Seasonal Cycles of the Ancient Celts. John King. (Illus.). 256p. 1994. 24.95 (0-7137-2461-7, Pub. by Blandford Pr UK) Sterling.

Celtic Empire: The First Millennium of Celtic History c. 1000 BC to 51 AD. Peter Berresford-Ellis. LC 91-70474. (Illus.). 256p. 1991. 29.95 (0-89089-457-4) Carolina Acad Pr.

Celtic Fairy Tales. Ed. by Joseph Jacobs. 21.95 (0-89190-078-0, Am Repr) Amereon Ltd.

Celtic Fairy Tales. Joseph Jacobs. 1972. 59.95 (0-87968-823-8) Gordon Pr.

Celtic Fairy Tales. Joseph Jacobs. (Illus.). (J). 19.25 (0-8446-2302-4) Peter Smith.

Celtic Fairy Tales. Joseph Jacobs. 1990. 8.99 (0-517-02724-0) Random Hse Value.

Celtic Fairy Tales. Ed. by Joseph Jacobs. LC 67-24223. (Illus.). xvi, 267p. (J). (ps-6). 1968. reprint ed. pap. 5.95 (0-486-21826-0) Dover.

Celtic Fire: The Passionate Religious Vision of Ancient Britain & Ireland. 1991. pap. 17.50 (0-385-41958-9) Doubleday.

Celtic Folklore, 2 vols., Set. John Rhys. 1973. lib. bdg. 500.00 (0-87968-099-7) Gordon Pr.

Celtic Folklore: Welsh & Manx, 2 vols. in 1. John L. Rhys. LC 72-80504. 1980. reprint ed. 53.95 (0-405-08885-X, Pub. by Blom Pubns UK) Ayer.

***Celtic Garden.** Philomena Durcan. (Illus.). 68p. 1995. 16.95 (0-9631982-2-X) Celtic Design.

Celtic Gauls: Gods, Rites & Sanctuaries. Jean-Louis Brunaux. Tr. by Daphne Nash. (Illus.). 154p. 1988. 39.95 (1-85264-009-X, Pub. by Seaby UK) Trafalgar.

Celtic Gods, Celtic Goddesses. R. J. Stewart. (Illus.). 160p. 1994. pap. 14.95 (0-7137-2113-8, Pub. by Blandford Pr UK) Sterling.

Celtic Hand Stroke by Stroke (Irish Half-Uncial from "The Book of Kells") Arthur Baker. (Arthur Baker Calligraphy Manual: Lettering, Calligraphy, Typography Ser.). (Illus.). 48p. (Orig.). 1983. pap. 2.95 (0-486-24336-2) Dover.

***Celtic Harp at Stonehenge: The Structure of Ancient British & Celtic Learning.** C. W. Bayer. LC 94-92038. 100p. 1994. pap. 20.00 (0-9628890-1-6) Purple Mntn.

***Celtic Harp Music of Carolan & Others for Solo Guitar.** Glenn Weiser. (Illus.). 112p. (YA). (gr. 9 up). 1995. pap. text ed. 14.95 (0-931759-95-1) Centerstream Pub.

Celtic Healing: The Healing Arts of Ancient Britain, Wales & Ireland. C. J. Thompson. 1994. pap. 8.95 (1-55818-278-0, Sure Fire) Holmes Pub.

Celtic Heart. Kathryn M. Cocquyt. LC 94-13189. (Psi-Fi Ser.). (Illus.). 592p. 1994. pap. 14.95 (1-56718-156-2) Llewellyn Pubns.

An Asterisk (*) at the beginning of an entry indicates that the title is appearing in BIP for the first time.

C

An Asterisk (*) at the beginning of an entry indicates that the title is appearing in BIP for the first time.

1115

Cemeteries of Lawrence County, Pa, Bk. 2. Ed. by Dwight E. Copper et al. 36p. 1989. pap. text ed. 8.00 (*1-55856-024-6*) Closson Pr.

Cemeteries of Lawrence County, Pa, Bk. 3. Ed. by Dwight E. Copper et al. 33p. 1989. pap. text ed. 8.00 (*1-55856-025-4*) Closson Pr.

Cemeteries of Lawrence County, Pa, Bk. 4. Comp. by Dwight E. Copper. 31p. 1989. pap. text ed. 8.00 (*1-55856-026-2*) Closson Pr.

Cemeteries of Lawrence County, Pa, Bk. 5. Comp. by Dwight E. Copper. 39p. 1989. pap. text ed. 8.00 (*1-55856-027-0*) Closson Pr.

Cemeteries of Lawrence County, Pa, Bk. 6. Comp. by Dwight E. Copper. 41p. 1989. pap. text ed. 8.00 (*1-55856-028-9*) Closson Pr.

Cemeteries of Lawrence County, PA, Bk. 7. Comp. by Dwight E. Copper. 77p. 1990. pap. 8.00 (*1-55856-072-6*) Closson Pr.

Cemeteries of Lawrence County, PA, Bk. 9. Comp. by Dwight E. Copper. 49p. 1990. pap. 8.00 (*1-55856-074-2*) Closson Pr.

Cemeteries of Lawrence County, PA, Bk. 11: Mahoning Township. Dwight E. Copper. 45p. 1994. pap. text ed. 8.00 (*1-55856-159-5*) Closson Pr.

Cemeteries of Montgomery, Orange County, New York. Orange County Genealogical Society Staff. (Orange County, New York Cemeteries Ser.). (Orig.). 1986. pap. write for info. (*0-9604116-5-8*) Orange County Genealog.

Cemeteries of Scott Country, Arakansas, Pt. I. rev. ed. 220p. 1993. pap. 40.00 (*1-884683-02-9*) Historian AR.

Cemeteries of Scott Country, Arakansas, Pt. II. rev. ed. 242p. 1993. pap. 40.00 (*1-884683-03-7*) Historian AR.

Cemeteries of Scott County, Arkansas, 2 pts., Set. rev. ed. Wanda M. Gray. 462p. 1993. pap. 40.00 (*1-884683-04-5*) Historian AR.

***Cemeteries of the Early Middle Ages: 6th-9th Centuries AD at Pokaszepetk.** A. Cs Sos & A. Salamon. 430p. 1994. 190.00 (*963-05-6759-8*, Pub. by Akad Kiado HU) St Mut.

Cemeteries of the Northeast Section of Dearborn County, Indiana. Dianne Fox & Lois Harper. 250p. 1993. pap. 24.95 (*1-55856-136-6*) Closson Pr.

Cemeteries of the Town of Hamptonburgh, Orange County, New York. Presbyterian Church Historical Society of Campbell Hall, N.Y. Staff. LC 80-81240. (Orange County, New York Cemeteries Ser.: No. 2). 88p. (Orig.). 1980. pap. 5.00 (*0-9604116-2-3*) Orange County Genealog.

Cemeteries of Town of Minisink: Names & Dates. Orange County Genealogical Society Staff. (Orange County, New York Cemeteries Ser.: No. 3). 1988. 10.00 (*0-937135-00-3*) Orange County Genealog.

Cemeteries of Unicoi County. Unicoi County Historical Society Staff. 464p. 1992. reprint ed. 32.50 (*0-932807-70-4*) Overmountain Pr.

Cemeteries, 1995. American Business Directories Staff. 1995. spiral bd., pap. 465.00 (*1-56105-601-4*) Am Busn Direct.

Cemetery at Tell es-Sa'idiyeh, Jordan. James B. Pritchard. (University Museum Monographs: No. 41). (Illus.). xii, 103p. (Orig.). (C). 1980. pap. 25.00 (*0-934718-32-6*) U PA Mus Pubns.

Cemetery Inscriptions: Atchison County, Kansas. Don Ford. viii, 362p. (Orig.). 1987. pap. 25.00 (*1-55613-062-7*) Heritage Bk.

Cemetery Inscriptions: Holy Cross R. C. Cemetery Parish of Przytuly, Province of Lomza, Poland. Jonathan D. Shea & Constance M. Ochnio. (Illus.). 50p. 1986. pap. 5.00 (*0-318-22287-6*) Pol Geneal CT.

Cemetery Inscriptions, & Revolutionary War of 1812, & Civil War Veterans of Bowdoin, Maine. Charlene Bartlett & Jayne E. Bickford. x, 182p. (Orig.). 1993. pap. text ed. 18.50 (*1-55613-771-0*) Heritage Bk.

Cemetery Inscriptions from Green County, Wisconsin, Vol. 1&2. 2nd rev. ed. John M. Irvin. (Illus.). 72p. 1986. pap. 8.00 (*0-910255-47-4*) Wisconsin Gen.

Cemetery Inscriptions in Windsor, Connecticut. (Illus.). 178p. 1992. reprint ed. lib. bdg. 18.00 (*0-8328-2518-2*) Higginson Bk Co.

***Cemetery Inscriptions of Barnstable, Massachusetts, and Its Villages, 1600-1900, with Corrections & Additions.** 434p. (Orig.). 1995. pap. text ed. 32.00 (*0-7884-0176-9*) Heritage Bk.

***Cemetery Inscriptions of Claiborne Parish, Louisiana, Vol. I.** John P. Frazier & Wanda V. Head. 218p. (Orig.). 1985. pap. 16.50 (*1-57088-016-6*) J&W Ent.

***Cemetery Inscriptions of Claiborne Parish, Louisiana, Vol. II.** Wanda V. Head & Elinor M. Seward. 217p. (Orig.). 1985. pap. 16.50 (*1-57088-017-4*) J&W Ent.

***Cemetery Inscriptions of Claiborne Parish, Louisiana, Vol. III.** Wanda V. Head & Elinor M. Seward. 164p. (Orig.). 1986. pap. 16.50 (*1-57088-018-2*) J&W Ent.

***Cemetery Inscriptions of Claiborne Parish, Louisiana, Vol. IV.** Wanda V. Head & Elinor M. Seward. 154p. (Orig.). 1986. pap. 16.50 (*1-57088-019-0*) J&W Ent.

Cemetery Inscriptions of Dennis, Massachusetts. Burton N. Derick. 567p. (Orig.). 1994. pap. 37.00 (*1-55613-901-2*) Heritage Bk.

Cemetery Inscriptions of the Town of Barnstable, Massachusetts, & Its Villages, 1600-1900. Paul J. Bunnell. 430p. 1992. pap. 30.00 (*1-55613-652-8*) Heritage Bk.

***Cemetery Inscriptions of Union Parish, Louisiana, Vol. I.** W. C. Nolan. 190p. (Orig.). 1988. pap. 16.00 (*1-57088-020-4*) J&W Ent.

***Cemetery Inscriptions of Union Parish, Louisiana, Vol. II.** W. C. Nolan. 192p. (Orig.). 1988. pap. 16.00 (*1-57088-021-2*) J&W Ent.

***Cemetery Inscriptions of Union Parish, Louisiana, Vol. III.** W. C. Nolan. 200p. (Orig.). 1988. pap. 16.00 (*1-57088-022-0*) J&W Ent.

***Cemetery Inscriptions of Union Parish, Louisiana, Vol. IV.** W. C. Nolan. 188p. (Orig.). 1988. pap. 16.00 (*1-57088-023-9*) J&W Ent.

***Cemetery Inscriptions of York County, ME, 2 vols., Set.** (Maine Old Cemeteries Association Ser.: No. 1). 1800p. Date not set. write for info. (*0-89725-228-4*, 1568) Picton Pr.

Cemetery Inscriptions, St. Stanislaus Kostka Cemetery, Dabrowa Bialostocka, Poland. Constance M. Ochnio et al. LC 89-61487. (Illus.). 130p. 1989. write for info. (*0-945440-02-2*) Pol Geneal CT.

Cemetery Inscriptions, Wolfeboro, New Hampshire. John S. Fipphen. vi, 298p. (Orig.). 1993. pap. text ed. 23.50 (*1-55613-759-1*) Heritage Bk.

Cemetery Jones. large type ed. William R. Cox. (Linford Western Library). 1989. pap. 11.95 (*0-7089-6758-2*, Linford) Ulverscroft.

Cemetery Jones: Dancing Guns. large type ed. William R. Cox. 1990. pap. 12.95 (*0-7089-6857-0*, Linford) Ulverscroft.

Cemetery Jones: Gunslingers. large type ed. William R. Cox. 1990. pap. 12.95 (*0-7089-6944-5*, Linford) Ulverscroft.

Cemetery Jones - Maverick Kid. large type ed. William R. Cox. (Linford Western Library). 1990. pap. 12.95 (*0-7089-6805-8*, Linford) Ulverscroft.

Cemetery Listings of Acadia Parish, Louisiana: Tombstone Inscriptions from Rayne, La. & the Surrounding Area. Pointe de l'Eglise Genealogical & Historical Society Staff. Ed. by Irma H. Gremillion. 260p. 1994. pap. 18.00 (*0-926764-91-8*) LAcadie Pubng.

Cemetery Listings of Acadia Parish, Louisiana, Vol. 1: Tombstone Inscriptions from Church Point, La. & the Surrounding Area. Pointe de l'Eglise Genealogical & Historical Society Staff. Ed. by Irma H. Gremillion. 210p. 1991. pap. 15.00 (*0-926764-90-X*) LAcadie Pubng.

Cemetery Nights. Stephen Dobyns. 128p. 1987. pap. 11.00 (*0-14-058584-2*, Penguin Bks) Viking Penguin.

***Cemetery of Angels.** Noel Hynd. 416p. 1995. 19.95 (*0-8217-5029-1*) Zebra.

Cemetery of Europe: Including the German Connection, the Spanish Play & the Murphy Girls. Seamus Finnegan. 256p. (Orig.). 1994. reprint ed. pap. 11.95 (*0-7145-2895-1*) M Boyars Pubs.

Cemetery Plots. Kathleen Williams & Joe Williams. (Lost Souls Ser.). 128p. 1994. pap. 14.95 (*0-9625166-5-1*) Marquee Pr.

Cemetery Quilt. Kent Rose & Alice Rose. LC 94-17617. (Illus.). (J). 1995. 14.95 (*0-395-70948-2*) HM.

Cemetery Records - Benson Vermont. Glenn Griswold. 27p. (Orig.). 1994. pap. 7.00 (*1-878545-04-3*) ACETO Bookmen.

Cemetery Records of Bainbridge Township in Berrien County, Michigan. Genealogical Association of Southwestern Michigan Staff. 44p. 1983. 9.60 (*0-686-40546-3*) Genealog Assn SW.

Cemetery Records of Baroda Township in Berrien County, Michigan. Genealogical Association of Southwestern Michigan Staff. 30p. 1983. 7.60 (*0-686-40547-1*) Genealog Assn SW.

Cemetery Records of Bedford County, Tennessee. rev. ed. Helen C. Marsh & Timothy R. Marsh. (Illus.). 352p. 1986. pap. 25.00 (*0-89308-569-3*, TN 91) Southern Hist Pr.

Cemetery Records of Bertrand Township in Berrien County, Michigan. Genealogical Association of Southwestern Michigan Staff. 32p. (Orig.). 1978. pap. 7.60 (*0-686-37855-5*) Genealog Assn SW.

Cemetery Records of Blair Township. Comp. by Evelyn Buckingham. 66p. 1988. pap. 8.00 (*0-9622372-0-5*) Grand Traverse.

Cemetery Records of Chikaming Township in Berrien County, Michigan. Genealogical Association of Southwestern Michigan Staff. 50p. (Orig.). 1982. pap. 9.60 (*0-686-37856-3*) Genealog Assn SW.

Cemetery Records of Coloma Township in Berrien County, Michigan. Genealogical Association of Southwestern Michigan Staff. 57p. (Orig.). 1983. pap. 9.60 (*0-686-37858-X*) Genealog Assn SW.

Cemetery Records of Fife Lake & Union Townships. Comp. by Evelyn Buckingham. 110p. 1989. pap. 11.00 (*0-9622372-1-3*) Grand Traverse.

Cemetery Records of Galien Township in Berrien County, Michigan. Genealogical Association of Southwestern Michigan Staff. 75p. 1984. 9.60 (*0-318-11904-8*) Genealog Assn SW.

Cemetery Records of Green Co., AL & Related Areas: The Journal of Mrs. Mary Marshall. O'Levia N. Wiese. 142p. (Orig.). 1994. pap. text ed. 24.00 (*1-55613-943-8*) Heritage Bk.

Cemetery Records of Lake Township in Berrien County, Michigan. Genealogical Association of Southwestern Michigan Staff. 48p. 1983. pap. 9.60 (*0-318-03118-3*) Genealog Assn SW.

Cemetery Records of Long Lake & Green Lake Townships. Comp. by Evelyn Buckingham. 60p. 1990. pap. 6.00 (*0-9622372-2-1*) Grand Traverse.

Cemetery Records of New Buffalo Township in Berrien County, Michigan. Genealogical Association of Southwestern Michigan Staff. 60p. (Orig.). 1978. pap. 9.60 (*0-686-37857-1*) Genealog Assn SW.

Cemetery Records, Pleasant Hill Township, Cass County, Missouri. LC 82-188689. vi, 221p. 1980. pap. 8.00 (*0-913233-00-5*) AFRA.

Cemetery World. Clifford D. Simak. 160p. 1993. pap. 3.50 (*0-88184-985-5*) Carroll & Graf.

Cemetries Are a Grave Matter. Peg Kehret. 1975. 2.50 (*0-87129-259-9*, C14) Dramatic Pub.

Cemit. David B. Hopes. 54p. (Orig.). 1991. pap. 6.19 (*0-685-48259-6*) Dayspring Pr.

Cemochechobee: Archaeology of a Mississippian Ceremonial Center on the Chattahoochee River. Frank T. Schnell et al. LC 81-16080. (Ripley P. Bullen Monographs in Anthropology & History: No. 3). (Illus.). xiii, 290p. 1982. 32.95 (*0-8130-0710-0*) U Press Fla.

Cen Pictures of St. Paul, Minnesota & Biographical Sketches of Old Settlers, Vol. I. T. M. Newson. 746p. 1993. reprint ed. lib. bdg. 75.00 (*0-8328-3473-4*) Higginson Bk Co.

Cena Trimalchionis. Petronius. Ed. by Martin S. Smith. 1983. 24.95 (*0-19-814459-8*) OUP.

Cenacle Sessions: A Modern Mystagogy. William R. Bruns. 1991. pap. 6.95 (*0-8091-3249-4*) Paulist Pr.

Cenci. Percy Bysshe Shelley. Ed. by Roland A. Duerksen. (Library of Liberal Arts). (C). 1970. write for info. (*0-672-51322-6*, LLA170, Bobbs); pap. write for info. (*0-672-60398-5*, Bobbs) Macmillan.

Cenci. Percy Bysshe Shelley. LC 91-29564. 130p. 1991. reprint ed. pap. 55.00 (*1-85477-078-0*, Pub. by Woodstock Bks UK) Cassell.

Cenci: A Tragedy in Five Acts. Percy Bysshe Shelley. LC 79-93255. 122p. 1970. reprint ed. pap. 7.95 (*0-87753-035-1*) Phaeton.

Cenci: A Tragedy in Five Acts, Given from the Poets Own Editions. Percy Bysshe Shelley. LC 74-30298. (Shelley Society, Fourth Ser.: No. 3). reprint ed. 24.00 (*0-404-11515-2*) AMS Pr.

Cendres Aux Pieds de Mon Guru. Gurumayi Chidvilasananda. Ed. by Swami Kripananda. 80p. 1990. 19.95 (*0-911307-17-6*) SYDA Found.

Cendres et Diamant. Jerzy Andrzejewski. 405p. (FRE.). 1986. pap. 17.95 (*0-7859-2047-1*, 2070377679) Fr & Eur.

***Cendrillon - Le Conif de Fees.** Tr. by DigiPro Staff. (Comes to Life Bks.). 16p. (FRE.). (J). (ps-2). 1994. write for info. (*1-883366-69-0*) YES Ent.

Cenelles: Choix de Poesies Indigenes. Ed. by Armand Lanusse. (B. E. Ser.: No. 53). (FRE.). 1845. 30.00 (*0-8115-3004-3*) Periodicals Srv.

***Cenerentola.** Tr. by DigiPro Staff. (Comes to Life Bks.). 16p. (ITA.). (J). (ps-2). 1994. write for info. (*1-883366-99-2*) YES Ent.

Cenerentola. Gioachino Rossini. Ed. by Nicholas John. Tr. by Arthur Jacobs. (English National Opera Guide Series: Bilingual Libretto, Articles: No. 1). (Illus.). (Orig.). 1980. pap. 9.95 (*0-7145-3819-1*) Riverrun NY.

Cenicienta. (Spanish Well Loved Tales Ser.: No. 700-3). (SPA.). (J). (gr. 3). 1990. boxed 3.50 (*0-7214-1405-2*) Ladybird Bks.

***Cenicienta.** Yani Cannetti. (Illus.). 24p. (J). (gr. 3-5). Date not set. pap. 4.50 (*1-56492-240-5*) Laredo.

***Cenicienta.** Zoe Lewis. Tr. by Susana Leuci. LC 94-79552. (Libros Buena Vista Ser.). (Illus.). 64p. (SPA.). (J). (gr. 2-6). 1995. pap. 3.50 (*0-7868-4045-5*) Disney Pr.

Cenicienta: Cinderella. LC 86-21526. (Spanish Start-Off Stories Ser.). 32p. (J). (ps-2). 1986. pap. 3.95 (*0-516-52361-9*) Childrens.

Cenicienta: Cinderella. LC 86-21526. (Spanish Start-Off Stories Ser.). 32p. (J). (ps-2). 1986. lib. bdg. 10.65 (*0-516-32361-X*) Childrens.

Cenicienta (Cinderella) Sarah Hayes. Tr. by Maria Puncel. (Cuentame un Cuento Ser.). (Illus.). 32p. (SPA.). (J). (gr. 2-4). 1990. Incl. cass. audio 11.95 (*84-372-8055-9*) Santillana.

***Cenicienta el Cuento de Hadas.** Tr. by DigiPro Staff. (Comes to Life Bks.). 16p. (SPA.). (J). (ps-2). 1994. write for info. (*1-57234-011-8*) YES Ent.

Cenote of Sacrifice: Maya Treasures from the Sacred Well at Chichen Itza. Clemency C. Coggins & Orrin C. Shane, III. (Illus.). 176p. 1984. 40.00 (*0-292-71097-6*); pap. 27.50 (*0-292-71098-4*) U of Tex Pr.

Cenozoic Basin Development of Coastal California. Ed. by Raymond V. Ingersoll & W. G. Ernst. (Illus.). 544p. (C). 1987. text ed. 105.00 (*0-13-122243-0*) P-H.

Cenozoic Evolution of the Alticostate Venericards in Gulf & East Coastal North America see Palaeontographica Americana: No. 2

Cenozoic Geology of Southwestern High Plateaus of Utah. John J. Anderson et al. LC 75-10395. (Geological Society of America, Special Paper Ser.: No. 160). 134p. reprint ed. pap. 38.20 (*0-317-28376-6*, 2025457) Bks Demand.

Cenozoic Geology of the Trans-Pecos Volcanic Field of Texas. Ed. by A. W. Walton & C. D. Henry. (Guidebook Ser.: GB 19). 202p. 1980. reprint ed. 4.00 (*0-686-31763-7*) Bur Econ Geology.

Cenozoic History & Paleoceanography of the Central Equatorial Pacific Ocean: A Regional Synthesis Deep Sea Drilling Project Data. Tjeerd H. Andel et al. LC 75-20815. (Geological Society of America, Memoir Ser.: No. 143). 231p. reprint ed. pap. 65.90 (*0-317-29104-1*, 2023732) Bks Demand.

Cenozoic Marine Sedimentation, Pacific Margin U. S. A. Ed. by D. K. Larue & R. J. Steel. (Illus.). 247p. (Orig.). 1983. pap. 8.00 (*1-878861-44-1*) Pac Section SEPM.

***Cenozoic Plants & Climates of the Arctic.** Michael C. Boulter & Helen C. Fisher. (NATO ASI Ser.: Vol. 27). 1994. 185.00 (*3-540-58616-4*) Spr-Verlag.

Cenozoic Reef Biofacies: Tertiary Larger Foraminifera & Scleractinian Corals from Chiapas, Mexico. Stanley H. Frost & Ralph L. Langenheim, Jr. LC 72-7513. (Illus.). 388p. 1974. 50.00 (*0-87580-027-0*) N Ill U Pr.

Cenozoic Stratigraphy of the Transverse Ranges & Adjacent Areas, Southern California. LC 75-2953. (Geological Society of America, Special Paper Ser.: No. 162). 137p. reprint ed. pap. 39.10 (*0-317-28374-X*, 2025455) Bks Demand.

***Cenozoic Tectonics & Regional Geophysics of the Western Cordillera.** fac. ed. Ed. by Robert B. Smith & Gordon P. Eaton. LC 78-55296. (Geological Society of America Memoir Ser.: No. 152). (Illus.). 596p. 1978. reprint ed. pap. 169.90 (*0-7837-8043-5*, 2047796) Bks Demand.

Cenozoic Volcanism in the Cascade Range & Columbia Plateau, Southern Washington & Northernmost Oregon. Ed. by Swanson. (IGC Field Trip Guidebooks Ser.). 64p. 1989. 21.00 (*0-87590-604-4*, T106) Am Geophysical.

Cenozoic Volcanism in the Western United States. Ed. by P. W. Lipman et al. 1989. 42.00 (*0-87590-242-1*) Am Geophysical.

Censo Neotropical De Aves Aquaticas, 1991. D. Blanco & P. Canevari. 62p. 1992. pap. text ed. 10.00 (*1-883861-00-4*) Wetlnds Amer.

Censo Neotropical De Aves Aquaticas, 1992. D. Blanco & P. Canevari. 75p. 1993. pap. text ed. 10.00 (*1-883861-03-9*) Wetlnds Amer.

Censor Cometh. Ray C. Kasper. 62p. (Orig.). 1989. pap. 3.95 (*0-317-93605-0*) Eastfield Pub.

Censored: Suppressed Stories Your Newspapers Won't Print - A Guide to the Blackout Conspiracy. 1992. lib. bdg. 254.95 (*0-8490-9901-3*) Gordon Pr.

Censored: The News You Need to Know, 1994 Edition, the Project Censored Yearbook. Carl Jensen. 1994. pap. 12. 95 (*1-56858-012-6*) FWEW.

Censored Books: Critical Viewpoints. Ed. by Nicholas J. Karolides et al. LC 93-349. 524p. 1993. 49.50 (*0-8108-2667-4*) Scarecrow.

Censored Hollywood: Sex, Sin & Violence on Screen. Frank Miller. LC 94-19982. 1994. 24.95 (*1-57036-116-9*); pap. 14.95 (*1-878685-55-4*) Turner Pub GA.

Censored Japanese Serials of the Pre-1946 Period: A Checklist of the Microfilm Collection - Ken'etsu Wazasshi (1945-nen Izen): Maikurofirumu Chekkurisuto. Comp. by Yoshiko Yoshimura. LC 93-20511. 1994. 29.00 (*0-8444-0787-9*) Lib Congress.

***Censored Letters.** Betsy Struthers. 48p. 1995. lib. bdg. 20. 00 (*0-8095-4530-6*) Borgo Pr.

***Censored: The News That Didn't Make the News-& Why: The 1995 Project Censored Yearbook.** Carl Jensen & Project Censored Staff. (1995 Project Censored Yearbook Ser.). 320p. (Orig.). 1995. pap. 14.95 (*1-56858-030-4*) FWEW.

***Censored War: American Visual Experience During World War II.** Roeder. 1995. pap. text ed. 16.00 (*0-300-06291-5*) Yale U Pr.

Censored War: American Visual Experience During World War II. George H. Roeder, Jr. LC 92-31859. (C). 1993. 32.50x (*0-300-05723-7*) Yale U Pr.

Censorial System of Ming China. Charles O. Hucker. LC 66-10916. (Stanford Studies in the Civilizations of Eastern Asia). 416p. reprint ed. pap. 30.00 (*0-685-23812-1*, 2032920) Bks Demand.

Censoring of Diderot's Encyclopedia & the Re-Established Text. Douglas H. Gordon & Norman L. Torrey. LC 78-168156. reprint ed. 15.00 (*0-404-02865-9*) AMS Pr.

Censorini De die Natali Liber. Censorinus. xxiv, 109p. 1965. reprint ed. write for info. (*0-318-71088-9*, Pub. by Georg Olms GW) Lubrecht & Cramer.

Censors: A Bilingual Selection of Stories. Luisa Valenzuela. LC 91-58995. 288p. (Orig.). 1992. pap. 12.95 (*0-915306-12-3*) Curbstone.

Censors & the Schools. Jack Nelson & Gene Roberts, Jr. LC 77-23390. 208p. 1977. reprint ed. text ed. 55.00 (*0-8371-9687-6*, NECE, Greenwood Pr) Greenwood.

Censorship. Susan S. Lang & Paul Lang. (Illus.). 96p. (YA). (gr. 9-12). 1993. lib. bdg. 14.21 (*0-531-10999-2*) Watts.

Censorship. Judy Monroe. LC 89-25407. (Facts About Ser.). (Illus.). 48p. (J). (gr. 5-6). 1990. text ed. 4.95 (*0-89686-490-1*, Crstwood Hse) Silver Burdett Pr.

Censorship. Philip Steele. LC 91-40235. (Past & Present Ser.). (Illus.). 48p. (J). (gr. 6 up). 1992. text ed. 12.95 (*0-02-735404-0*, Mac Bks Young Read) S&S Childrens.

Censorship. Bradley Steffens. (Lucent Overview Ser.). (Illus.). (J). (gr. 5-8). 1994. 16.95 (*1-56006-166-9*) Lucent Bks.

Censorship. David K. Wright. LC 92-19664. (Pro - Con Ser.). (J). 1993. 17.50 (*0-8225-2604-2*, Lerner Publctns) Lerner Group.

Censorship: A Guide for Successful Workshop Planning. Linda Schexnaydre et al. LC 83-43209. (Illus.). 120p. 1984. pap. 30.00 (*0-89774-093-9*) Oryx Pr.

Censorship: A Threat to Critical Reading. Ed. by John S. Simmons. 296p. 1994. pap. 16.00 (*0-87207-123-5*) Intl Reading.

Censorship: Five Hundred Years of Conflict. Ed. by William Zeisel. (Illus.). 144p. 1984. pap. 19.95 (*0-87104-284-3*) NY Pub Lib.

***Censorship: How Does It Conflict with Freedom?** Richard Steins. (Issues of Our Time Ser.). (Illus.). 64p. (J). (gr. 5-8). 1995. lib. bdg. 15.98 (*0-8050-3879-5*) TFC Bks NY.

Censorship: Opposing Viewpoints. Ed. by Lisa Orr. LC 90-42854. (Opposing Viewpoints Ser.). (Illus.). 240p. (YA). (gr. 10 up). 1990. lib. bdg. 19.95 (*0-89908-479-6*); pap. text ed. 11.55 (*0-89908-454-0*) Greenhaven.

Censorship: The Knot That Binds Power & Knowledge. Sue C. Jansen. (Communication & Society Ser.). 288p. (C). 1991. reprint ed. pap. text ed. 14.95 (*0-19-506906-4*) OUP.

Censorship: The Problem That Won't Go Away. Edna N. Boardman. (Professional Growth Ser.). 80p. 1993. pap. text ed. 16.95 (*0-938865-18-8*) Linworth Pub.

Censorship & Art in Pre-enlightenment Lima: Pedro de Peralta Barnuevo's Dialogo De las Muertos: la Causa Academica. Tr. by Jerry M. Williams. LC 93-48189. (Scripta Humanistica Ser.: No. 110). 1994. 59.50 (*1-882528-06-9*) Scripta.

1116 An Asterisk (*) at the beginning of an entry indicates that the title is appearing in BIP for the first time.

C

An Asterisk (*) at the beginning of an entry indicates that the title is appearing in BIP for the first time.

1117

Census of Medieval & Renaissance Manuscripts in the United States & Canada, 2 vols. & index, Set. W. H. Bond & C. U. Faye. Incl. Supplement. 1962. (*0-685-23298-0*); 1972. reprint ed. 460.00 (*0-527-75200-2*) Periodicals Srv.

Census of Modern Greek Literature: Check-List of English-Language Sources Useful in the Study of Modern Greek Literature (1824-1987) Dia M. Philippides. (Series of Occasional Papers). 300p. (Orig.). (C). 1990. pap. text ed. 3.00 (*0-912105-01-1*) Modern Greek Studies Assn.

Census of Montgomery County, NY, 1855: An Index. David P. Davenport. LC 89-84656. 314p. 1989. lib. bdg. 38.00 (*1-56012-102-5*) Kinship Rhinebeck.

***Census of Motor Traffic on Main International Traffic Arteries.** Economic Commission of Europe Staff. 143p. 1993. pap. text ed. 80.00 (*92-1-016285-4*) UN.

Census of Nova Scotia: Index Heads of Households, 1860-1861: Consolidated Listing for Guysborough County. Mary E. Koen. 47p. (Orig.). 1985. pap. 7.50 (*0-9621164-3-2*) Mary E Koen.

Census of Ohio County, KY, 1850. 138p. 1988. 12.00 (*0-318-32461-X*) West Cent KY Family Re Assoc.

Census of Pontotoc County, Ms., 1840. Comp. by Berniece Douglas Coyle. 27p. 1988. pap. text ed. 10.00 (*1-882111-44-3*) Coyle Data Co.

Census of Population & Housing, 2 vols., Set. 1994. lib. bdg. 395.00 (*0-8490-8577-2*) Gordon Pr.

***Census of Population & Housing. Metropolitan Area Housing of the U. S. Subject Report, 2 vols., Set.** 1995. lib. bdg. 500.00 (*0-8490-5852-X*) Gordon Pr.

***Census of Population & Housing Population & Housing Characteristics, Census Tracts & Block Numbering Areas, 2 vols., Set.** 1995. lib. bdg. 699.00 (*0-8490-5853-8*) Gordon Pr.

Census of Population & Housing, 1990: Guide. (Illus.). 205p. (Orig.). (C). 1994. pap. text ed. 39.95 (*1-56806-075-0*) Diane Pub.

***Census of Population: Social & Economic Characteristics: American Indian & Alaska Native Areas, 10 vols., Set.** 1995. lib. bdg. 2,100.00 (*0-8490-5854-6*) Gordon Pr.

***Census of Population: Social & Economic Characteristics: Metropolitan Areas, 10 vols., Set.** 1995. lib. bdg. 3,600. 00 (*0-8490-5855-4*) Gordon Pr.

Census of Population, 1950, Vol. 2. U. S. Bureau of the Census Staff. LC 75-22862. (America in Two Centuries Ser.). 1976. reprint ed. 46.95 (*0-405-07728-9*) Ayer.

Census of Pre-Nineteenth-Century Italian Paintings in North American Public Collections. Burton B. Fredericksen & Federico Zeri. LC 73-182813. 702p. 1972. text ed. 35.95 (*0-674-10491-9*) J P Getty Trust.

Census of Rowan County, North Carolina, 1850: A Genealogical Compilation of the Schedules. Jo W. Linn. LC 91-77702. (Illus.). 158p. 1992. lib. bdg. 28.00 (*0-918470-20-X*); pap. 26.00 (*0-918470-21-8*) J W Linn.

***Census of Sc. 367-9 FDC's: The Lincoln Memorial Issue of 1909.** Robert Colby & Robert Drummond. (Illus.). 42p. (Orig.). 1994. pap. 8.95 (*1-879390-19-1*) Am First Day.

Census of Schenectady, NY, 1855: An Index. David P. Davenport. LC 89-80272. 228p. 1989. lib. bdg. 41.00 (*1-56012-101-7*) Kinship Rhinebeck.

Census of Schoharie County, NY, 1855: An Index. David P. Davenport. 350p. 1988. lib. bdg. 47.00 (*1-56012-089-4*) Kinship Rhinebeck.

Census of Shakespeare's Plays in Quarto, 1594-1709. Henrietta Bartlett & Alfred Pollard. LC 70-135724. reprint ed. 24.50 (*0-404-00669-8*) AMS Pr.

Census of the Cumberland Settlements, 1770-1790: Davidson, Sumner & Tennessee Counties. Richard C. Fulcher. 253p. 1990. 22.50 (*0-8063-1174-6*, 2085) Genealog Pub.

Census of the Exact Sciences in Sanskrit, Ser. A, Vol. 1. David Pingree. LC 70-115882. (Memoirs Ser.: Vols. 81, 86, & 146). 1970. pap. 10.00 (*0-87169-081-0*, M081-PID) Am Philos.

Census of the Exact Sciences in Sanskrit, Ser. A, Vol. 2. David Pingree. LC 70-115882. (Memoirs Ser.: Vols. 81, 86, & 146). 1970. pap. 12.00 (*0-87169-086-1*, M086-PID) Am Philos.

***Census of the Exact Sciences in Sanskrit Ser. A, Vol. 5.** David Pingree. LC 94-72374. (Memoirs Ser.: Vol. 213). 756p. (C). 1994. pap. 45.00 (*0-87169-213-9*, M213pid) Am Philos.

Census of the Exact Sciences in Sanskrit Series A, Vol. 3. David E. Pingree. LC 70-115882. (Memoirs of the American Philosophical Society Ser.: Vol. 111). 214p. reprint ed. pap. 61.00 (*0-7837-0541-7*, 2040869) Bks Demand.

Census of the Indian Polygonums. A. T. Gage. 452p. 1977. 95.00 (*0-685-21757-4*, Pub. by Intl Bk Distr II) St Mut.

Census of the Indian Polygonums. A. T. Gage. (C). 1977. text ed. 95.00 (*0-89771-620-5*, Pub. by Intl Bk Distr II) St Mut.

Census of the Inhabitants of the Colony of Rhode Island & Providence Plantations: 1774. John R. Bartlett. 246p. 1984. reprint ed. pap. 12.50 (*0-912606-20-7*) Hunterdon Hse.

Census of the Inhabitants of the Colony of Rhode Island & Providence Plantations, 1774. John R. Bartlett. 359p. 1990. reprint ed. 22.00 (*0-685-60438-1*, 380) Clearfield Co.

Census of the Swedes on the Delaware, 1693: Family Histories of the Swedish Lutheran Church Members Residing in Pennsylvania, Delaware, West New Jersey & Cecil County, Md., 1638-1693. Peter S. Craig. LC 92-82858. (Studies in Swedish American Genealogy: Vol. 3). (Illus.). 224p. 1993. lib. bdg. 37.50 (*0-9616105-1-4*) SAG Pubns.

Census of the Territory of Arkansas, 1820 (Reconstructed) James L. Morgan. 108p. 1992. reprint ed. pap. 16.00 (*0-941765-77-6*) Arkansas Res.

***Census of the United States: Eleventh Decennial Census, 1890, Vol. 46, No. 177, Pt. 1.** ccxii, 968p. 1994. lib. bdg. write for info. (*0-88354-446-6*) N Ross.

***Census of the United States: Eleventh Decennial Census, 1890, Vol. 47, No. 178, Pt. 2.** clxxv, 824p. 1994. lib. bdg. write for info. (*0-88354-447-4*) N Ross.

***Census of the United States: Eleventh Decennial Census, 1890, Vol. 48, No. 179.** xi, 755p. 1994. lib. bdg. 350.00 (*0-88354-448-2*) N Ross.

***Census of the United States: Eleventh Decennial Census, 1890, Vol. 49, No. 181, Pt. 1.** vii, 411p. 1994. lib. bdg. 350.00 (*0-88354-449-0*) N Ross.

***Census of the United States: Eleventh Decennial Census, 1890, Vol. 50, No. 182, Pt. 2.** xi, 1035p. 1994. lib. bdg. 350.00 (*0-88354-450-4*) N Ross.

***Census of the United States: Eleventh Decennial Census, 1890, Vol. 51, No. 184, Pt. 1.** xvii, 1059p. 1994. lib. bdg. write for info. (*0-88354-451-2*) N Ross.

***Census of the United States: Eleventh Decennial Census, 1890, Vol. 52, No. 185, Pt. 2.** ix, 1181p. 1994. lib. bdg. write for info. (*0-88354-452-0*) N Ross.

***Census of the United States: Eleventh Decennial Census, 1890, Vol. 53, No. 186, Pt. 3.** v, 1050p. 1994. lib. bdg. 350.00 (*0-88354-453-9*) N Ross.

***Census of the United States: Eleventh Decennial Census, 1890, Vol. 54, No. 187, Pt. 4.** v, 1033p. 1994. lib. bdg. 350.00 (*0-88354-454-7*) N Ross.

***Census of the United States: Eleventh Decennial Census, 1890, Vol. 55, No. 188.** 1994. lib. bdg. write for info. (*0-88354-455-5*) N Ross.

***Census of the United States: Eleventh Decennial Census, 1890, Vol. 56, No. 193, Pt. 1.** v, 1002p. 1994. lib. bdg. 350.00 (*0-88354-456-3*) N Ross.

***Census of the United States: Eleventh Decennial Census, 1890, Vol. 57, No. 194, Pt. 2.** xliv, 287p. 1994. lib. bdg. write for info. (*0-88354-457-1*) N Ross.

***Census of the United States: Eleventh Decennial Census, 1890, Vol. 58, No. 195, Pt. 3.** vii, 725p. 1994. lib. bdg. write for info. (*0-88354-458-X*) N Ross.

***Census of the United States: Eleventh Decennial Census, 1890, Vol. 59, No. 199.** xvi, 857p. 1994. lib. bdg. write for info. (*0-88354-459-8*) N Ross.

***Census of the United States: Eleventh Decennial Census, 1890, Vol. 60, No. 200.** xi, 282p. 1994. lib. bdg. write for info. (*0-88354-460-1*) N Ross.

***Census of the United States: Eleventh Decennial Census, 1890, Vol. 61, No. 201.** xxvii, 812p. 1994. lib. bdg. write for info. (*0-88354-461-X*) N Ross.

***Census of the United States: Eleventh Decennial Census, 1890, Vol. 62, No. 202.** vii, 683p. 1994. lib. bdg. write for info. (*0-88354-462-8*) N Ross.

***Census of the United States: Eleventh Decennial Census, 1890, Vol. 63, No. 204, Pt. 1.** x, 1127p. 1994. lib. bdg. write for info. (*0-88354-463-6*) N Ross.

***Census of the United States: Eleventh Decennial Census, 1890, Vol. 65, No. 206.** xi, 943p. 1994. lib. bdg. write for info. (*0-88354-465-2*) N Ross.

***Census of the United States: Eleventh Decennial Census, 1890, Vol. 66, No. 207.** xi, 646p. 1994. lib. bdg. write for info. (*0-88354-466-0*) N Ross.

***Census of the United States: Eleventh Decennial Census, 1890, Vol. 67, No. 209, Pt. 1.** viii, 867p. 1994. lib. bdg. write for info. (*0-88354-467-9*) N Ross.

***Census of the United States: Eleventh Decennial Census, 1890, Vol. 68, No. 211, Pt. 2.** xii, 532p. 1994. lib. bdg. write for info. (*0-88354-468-7*) N Ross.

***Census of the United States: Eleventh Decennial Census, 1890, Vol. 69, No. 216, Pt. 1.** xi, 890p. 1994. lib. bdg. write for info. (*0-88354-469-5*) N Ross.

***Census of the United States: Eleventh Decennial Census, 1890, Vol. 70, No. 217, Pt. 2.** vii, 654p. 1994. lib. bdg. write for info. (*0-88354-470-9*) N Ross.

Census of the United States: Third Decennial Census: 1810. United States Census Office Staff. (Aggregate Amount of Each Description of Persons Within the United States of America...Ser.). (Illus.). 176p. 1990. reprint ed. lib. bdg. 200.00 (*0-88354-403-2*, 08021063) N Ross.

Census of the United States Vol. 4: Third Decennial Census: 1810. United States Census Office Staff. (Statement of the Arts & Manufactures of the United States of America Ser.). (Illus.). 256p. 1990. reprint ed. lib. bdg. 200.00 (*0-88354-404-0*, 0815916) N Ross.

***Census of the United States; Eleventh Decennial Census, 1890: Report on Insurance Business Pt. II Life Insurance, 25 vols., Vol. 19, Ser. 64.** xxi, 478p. 1994. reprint ed. lib. bdg. 350.00 (*0-88354-464-4*) N Ross.

Census of the United States; Tenth Decennial Census: 1880: Statistics of the Population of the Unitedx States... Embracing Extended Tables of the Population of States, Counties, & Minor Civil Divisions, with Distinction of Race, Sex, Age, Nativity, & Occupations, 22 vols., Vol. 1, Series 24. LC 07-18862. (Illus.). xc, 961p. 1991. reprint ed. fiche, lib. bdg. 500.00x (*0-88354-424-5*) N Ross.

Census of the United States: U. S. Decennial Census Reports, Tenth Census: 1880, Vol. 25, No. 63: Report on the Manufactures of the United States, Embracing General Statistics & Monographs. Ed. by Peter Allison. LC 07-18862. (Illus.). 1248p. reprint ed. fiche, lib. bdg. 500.00 (*0-88354-425-3*) N Ross.

Census of the United States: U. S. Decennial Census Reports, Tenth Census: 1880, Vol. 26, No. 75: Report on the Production of Agriculture, Embracing General Statistics & Monographs. Ed. by Peter Allison. LC 07-18862. (Illus.) 1192p. reprint ed. fiche, lib. bdg. 500.00 (*0-88354-426-1*) N Ross.

Census of the United States: U. S. Decennial Census Reports, Tenth Census: 1880, Vol. 27, No. 82: Report on the Agencies of Transportation in the United States, Including the Statistics of Railroads, Steam Navigation, Canals, Telegraphs, & Telephones. Ed. by Peter Allison. LC 07-18862. (Illus.). 872p. reprint ed. lib. bdg. 300.00 (*0-88354-427-X*) N Ross.

Census of the United States: U. S. Decennial Census Reports, Tenth Census: 1880, Vol. 28, No. 89: Report on Cotton Production in the United States; Also Embracing Agricultural & Physico-geographical Descriptions of the Several Cotton States & of California, Mississippi Valley & Southwestern States, Pt. I. Ed. by Peter Allison. LC 07-18862. (Illus.). 928p. reprint ed. fiche, lib. bdg. 500.00 (*0-88354-428-8*) N Ross.

Census of the United States: U. S. Decennial Census Reports, Tenth Census: 1880, Vol. 29, No. 98: Report on Cotton Production in the United States; Also Embracing Agricultural & Physico-geographical Descriptions of the Several Cotton States & of California, Eastern Gulf, Atlantic & Pacific States, Pt. II. Ed. by Peter Allison. LC 07-18862. (Illus.). 848p. reprint ed. fiche, lib. bdg. 500.00 (*0-88354-429-6*) N Ross.

Census of the United States: U. S. Decennial Census Reports, Tenth Census: 1880, Vol. 30, No. 105: Report on Valuation, Taxation, & Public Indebtedness in the United States. Ed. by Peter Allison. LC 07-18862. (Illus.). 920p. reprint ed. lib. bdg. 300.00 (*0-88354-430-X*) N Ross.

Census of the United States: U. S. Decennial Census Reports, Tenth Census: 1880, Vol. 31, No. 107: The Newspaper & Periodical Press, S. N. D. North Alaska: Its Population, Industries, & Resources; the Seal Islands of Alaska; Ship-building Industry in the United States. Ivan Petroff et al. Ed. by Peter Allison. LC 07-18862. (Illus.). 1120p. reprint ed. fiche, lib. bdg. 500.00 (*0-88354-431-8*) N Ross.

Census of the United States: U. S. Decennial Census Reports, Tenth Census: 1880, Vol. 32, No. 112: Report on the Forests of North America (Exclusive of Mexico) Charles S. Sargent. Ed. by Peter Allison. LC 07-18862. (Illus.). 624p. reprint ed. fiche, lib. bdg. 500.00 (*0-88354-432-6*) N Ross.

Census of the United States: U. S. Decennial Census Reports, Tenth Census: 1880, Vol. 33, No. 113: Production Technology, & Uses of Petroleum & Its Products; the Manufacture of Coke; Building Stones of the United States & Statistics of Quarry Industry for 1880. S. F. Peckham & Joseph D. Weeks. Ed. by Peter Allison. LC 07-18862. (Illus.). 448p. reprint ed. fiche, lib. bdg. 500.00 (*0-88354-433-4*) N Ross.

Census of the United States: U. S. Decennial Census Reports, Tenth Census: 1880, Vol. 34, No. 117, Pt I: Report on the Mortality & Vital Statistics of the United States, Statistics of Deaths by States, Principal Cities, Etc. Ed. by Peter Allison. LC 07-18862. (Illus.). 832p. reprint ed. fiche, lib. bdg. 500.00 (*0-88354-434-2*) N Ross.

Census of the United States: U. S. Decennial Census Reports, Tenth Census: 1880, Vol. 35, No. 118, Pt. II: Report on the Mortality & Vital Statistics of the United States, Statistics of Deaths by Locality, Cause, Etc. Ed. by Peter Allison. LC 07-18862. (Illus.). 968p. reprint ed. fiche, lib. bdg. 500.00 (*0-88354-435-0*) N Ross.

Census of the United States: U. S. Decennial Census Reports, Tenth Census: 1880, Vol. 36, No. 119: Statistics & Technology of the Precious Metals. S. F. Emmons & G. F. Becker. Ed. by Peter Allison. LC 07-18862. (Illus.). 560p. reprint ed. lib. bdg. 300.00 (*0-88354-436-9*) N Ross.

Census of the United States: U. S. Decennial Census Reports, Tenth Census: 1880, Vol. 37, No. 122: The United States Mining Laws & Regulations Thereunder, & State & Territorial Mining Laws, to Which are Appended Local Mining Rules & Regulation. Ed. by Peter Allison. LC 07-18862. (Illus.). 712p. reprint ed. lib. bdg. 300.00 (*0-88354-437-7*) N Ross.

Census of the United States: U. S. Decennial Census Reports, Tenth Census: 1880, Vol. 38, No. 123: Report on the Mining Industries of the United States (Exclusive of Precious Metals), with Special Investigation into the Iron Resources of the Republic & into the Cretaceous Coals of the Northwest. Raphael Pumpelly. Ed. by Peter Allison. LC 07-18862. (Illus.). 1064p. reprint ed. lib. bdg. 300.00 (*0-88354-438-5*) N Ross.

Census of the United States: U. S. Decennial Census Reports, Tenth Census: 1880, Vol. 39, No. 125, Pt. I: Reports on Water-Power of the United States, 1885-1887. Ed. by Peter Allison. LC 07-18862. (Illus.). 1904p. reprint ed. lib. bdg. 300.00 (*0-88354-439-3*) N Ross.

Census of the United States: U. S. Decennial Census Reports, Tenth Census: 1880, Vol. 40, No. 134, Pt. II: Water-power of the Northwest, 1885-1887. Ed. by Peter Allison. LC 07-18862. (Illus.). 1560p. reprint ed. lib. bdg. 300.00 (*0-88354-440-7*) N Ross.

Census of the United States: U. S. Decennial Census Reports, Tenth Census: 1880, Vol. 41, No. 141, Pt. I: Report on the Social Statistics of Cities; the New England & the Middle States. Ed. by Peter Allison. LC 07-18862. (Illus.). 936p. reprint ed. lib. bdg. 300.00 (*0-88354-441-5*) N Ross.

Census of the United States: U. S. Decennial Census Reports, Tenth Census: 1880, Vol. 42, No. 142, Pt. II: The Southern & the Western States. Ed. by Peter Allison. LC 07-18862. (Illus.). 640p. reprint ed. lib. bdg. 300.00 (*0-88354-442-3*) N Ross.

Census of the United States: U. S. Decennial Census Reports, Tenth Census: 1880, Vol. 43, No. 144: Report on the Statistics of Wages in Manufacturing Industries; with Supplementary Reports on the Average Retail Prices of Necessaries of Life, & on Trades Societies, & Strikes & Lockouts. Joseph D. Weeks. Ed. by Peter Allison. LC 07-18862. (Illus.). 640p. reprint ed. lib. bdg. 300.00 (*0-88354-443-1*) N Ross.

Census of the United States: U. S. Decennial Census Reports, Tenth Census: 1880, Vol. 44, No. 145: Report on the Defective, Dependent, & Delinquent Classes of the Population of the United States. Ed. by Peter Allison. LC 07-18862. (Illus.). 640p. reprint ed. lib. bdg. 300.00 (*0-88354-444-X*) N Ross.

Census of the United States: U. S. Decennial Census Reports, Tenth Census: 1880, Vol. 45, No. 146: Report on Power & Machinery Employed in Manufactures, Embracing. Ed. by Peter Allison. LC 07-18862. (Illus.). 912p. reprint ed. lib. bdg. 300.00 (*0-88354-445-8*) N Ross.

Census of the United States, Vol. 1: First Decennial Census: 1790. United States Census Office Staff. (Return of the Whole Number of Persons Within the Several Districts of the United States Ser.). (Illus.). 64p. 1990. reprint ed. lib. bdg. 200.00 (*0-88354-401-6*, 09019547) N Ross.

Census of the United States, Vol. 10: Sixth Decennial Census: 1840. United States Census Office Staff. (Compendium of the Enumeration of the Inhabitants of the United States...Ser.). (Illus.). 384p. 1990. reprint ed. lib. bdg. 200.00 (*0-88354-410-5*, 06029060) N Ross.

Census of the United States, Vol. 11: Sixth Decennial Census: 1840. United States Census Office Staff. (Census of Pensioners for Revolutionary or Military Services; with Their Names, Ages, Etc....Ser.). (Illus.). 200p. 1990. reprint ed. lib. bdg. 200.00 (*0-88354-411-3*, 035267) N Ross.

Census of the United States, Vol. 12: Seventh Decennial Census: 1850. United States Census Office Staff. (Embracing a Statistical View of Each of the United States & Territories...Ser.). (Illus.). 1160p. 1990. reprint ed. lib. bdg. 200.00 (*0-88354-412-1*, 0719238) N Ross.

Census of the United States, Vol. 13: Seventh Decennial Census: 1850. United States Census Office Staff. (Message of the President of the United States Communicating a Digest of the Statistics...Ser.). (Illus.). 144p. 1990. reprint ed. lib. bdg. 200.00 (*0-88354-413-X*, 0719240) N Ross.

Census of the United States, Vol. 14: Seventh Decennial Census: 1850. United States Census Office Staff. (Mortality Statistics of the Seventh Census of the United States, 1850 Ser.). (Illus.). 304p. 1990. reprint ed. lib. bdg. 200.00 (*0-88354-414-8*, 0719239) N Ross.

Census of the United States, Vol. 15: Seventh Decennial Census: 1850. United States Census Office Staff. (Compendium, Statistical View of the United States Embracing Its Territory, Population-White,...Ser.). (Illus.). 400p. 1990. reprint ed. lib. bdg. 200.00 (*0-88354-415-6*, 06036734) N Ross.

Census of the United States, Vol. 16: Eighth Decennial Census: 1860. United States Census Office Staff. (Population of the United States in 1860 Compiled from the Original Returns of the Eighth Census Ser.). (Illus.). 800p. 1990. reprint ed. lib. bdg. 200.00 (*0-88354-416-4*, 06044891) N Ross.

Census of the United States, Vol. 17: Eighth Decennial Census: 1860. United States Census Office Staff. (Agriculture of the United States in 1860, Compiled from the Original Returns of the Eighth Census Ser.). (Illus.). 464p. 1990. reprint ed. lib. bdg. 200.00 (*0-88354-417-2*, 06044894) N Ross.

Census of the United States, Vol. 18: Eighth Decennial Census: 1860. United States Census Office Staff. (Manufactures of the United States in 1860, Compiled from the Original Returns...Ser.). (Illus.). 976p. 1990. reprint ed. lib. bdg. 200.00 (*0-88354-418-0*, 0719246) N Ross.

Census of the United States, Vol. 19: Eighth Decennial Census: 1860. United States Census Office Staff. (Statistics of the United States (Including Mortality, Property, Etc.)...Ser.). (Illus.). 656p. 1990. reprint ed. lib. bdg. 200.00 (*0-88354-419-9*, 06008716) N Ross.

Census of the United States, Vol. 2: Second Decennial Census: 1800. United States Census Office Staff. (Return of the Whole Number of Persons Within the Several Districts of the United States Ser.). (Illus.). 80p. 1990. reprint ed. lib. bdg. 200.00 (*0-88354-402-4*, 0820293) N Ross.

Census of the United States, Vol. 20: Ninth Decennial Census: 1870. United States Census Office Staff. (Statistics of the Population of the United States - Tables of Race, Nationality, Sex, Select Ages...Ser.). (Illus.). 816p. 1990. reprint ed. lib. bdg. 200.00 (*0-88354-420-2*, 0519328) N Ross.

Census of the United States, Vol. 21: Ninth Decennial Census. United States Census Office Staff. (Statistics of the United States, Embracing the Tables of Deaths, Births, Sex & Age...Ser.). (Illus.). 704p. 1990. reprint ed. lib. bdg. 200.00 (*0-88354-421-0*, 0519328) N Ross.

Census of the United States, Vol. 22: Ninth Decennial Census: 1870. United States Census Office Staff. (Statistics of the Wealth & Industry of the United States, Embracing the Tables of Wealth...Ser.). (Illus.). 848p. 1990. reprint ed. lib. bdg. 200.00 (*0-88354-422-9*, 0519328) N Ross.

Census of the United States, Vol. 5: Fourth Decennial Census: 1820. United States Census Office Staff. (Census for 1820 Ser.). (Illus.). 160p. 1990. reprint ed. lib. bdg. 175.00 (*0-88354-405-9*, 04011778) N Ross.

C

1118

An Asterisk (*) at the beginning of an entry indicates that the title is appearing in BIP for the first time.

Census of the United States, Vol. 6: Fourth Decennial Census: 1820. United States Census Office Staff. (Digest of the Accounts of Manufacturing Establishments in the United States...Ser.). (Illus.). 128p. 1990. reprint ed. lib. bdg. 200.00 (0-88354-406-7, 0919033) N Ross.

Census of the United States, Vol. 7: Fifth Decennial Census: 1830. United States Census Office Staff. (Fifth Census; or Enumeration of the Inhabitants of the United States, 1830 Ser.). (Illus.). 176p. 1990. reprint ed. lib. bdg. 200.00 (0-88354-407-5, 0420566) N Ross.

Census of the United States, Vol. 8: Sixth Decennial Census: 1840. United States Census Office Staff. (Sixth Census; or Enumeration of the Inhabitants of the United States...Ser.). (Illus.). 480p. 1990. reprint ed. lib. bdg. 200.00 (0-88354-408-3, 0411779) N Ross.

Census of the United States, Vol. 9: Sixth Decennial Census: 1840. United States Census Office Staff. (Statistics of the United States of America...Ser.). (Illus.). 416p. 1990. reprint ed. lib. bdg. 200.00 (0-88354-409-1, 0646445) N Ross.

Census of United States Plate Blocks 1851-1882. John C. Chapin. (Illus.). 116p. 19.50 (0-912574-35-6) Collectors.

Census of United States Plate Blocks 1851-1882. John C. Chapin. (Illus.). 116p. 1986. pap. 12.50 (0-912574-36-4) Collectors.

Census of Yazoo County, Mississippi, 1840. Comp. by Berniece D. Coyle. 1990. pap. text ed. 10.00 (1-56088-001-5) Coyle Data Co.

Census Reconstruction Garland & Montgomery Counties, Arkansas, 1890. Bobbie J. McLane et al. 175p. (Orig.). 1985. pap. 18.00 (0-929604-34-2) Arkansas Ancestors.

Census Records of Elbert Co., 1820 to 1860, & the Eighteen Fifty Census of Wilkes Co., Georgia. Irene S. Wilcox. 142p. 1979. 20.00 (0-89308-155-8) Southern Hist Pr.

Census Registration Districts (Index to) (C). 1987. 35.00 (0-317-89880-9, Pub. by Birmingham Midland Soc UK) St Mut.

Census Regulations, 1990. (Statutory Instruments, 1990 Ser.: No. 307). 44p. 1990. pap. 12.00 (0-11-003307-8, HM7038) UNIPUB.

Census Returns on Microfilm, 1841-81. 4th ed. (C). 1987. 35.00 (0-317-89805-1, Pub. by Birmingham Midland Soc UK) St Mut.

Census Returns, 1841-1881. 5th ed. Jeremy S. Gibson. 50p. 1989. mic. film 7.00 (0-8063-1243-2, 2181) Genealog Pub.

Census Taker. Marilyn Stablein. 92p. 1992. reprint ed. pap. 8.95 (0-930223-23-3) Black Heron Pr.

Census Taker: Stories of a Traveler in India & Nepal. Marilyn Stablein. LC 85-10641. 96p. (Orig.). 1985. pap. 8.95 (0-88089-009-6) Madrona Pubs.

Census That Mirrors America: Interim Report. National Research Council, Commission on Behavioral & Social Sciences & Education Staff. 108p. (Orig.). (C). 1993. pap. text ed. 29.00 (0-309-04979-2) Natl Acad Pr.

***Census User's Handbook.** Ed. by Stanley Openshaw. 1995. pap. text ed. 47.95 (0-470-23481-4) Halsted Pr.

Census with Index, 1810: Dutchess County, New York. Dutchess County Genealogical Society Staff. 181p. 1990. reprint ed. lib. bdg. 20.00 (1-56012-107-6) Kinship Rhinebeck.

Census, 1841-1881: Use & Interpretation. (C). 1987. 35.00 (0-317-89816-7, Pub. by Birmingham Midland Soc UK) St Mut.

Censuses of Asia & the Pacific: 1980 Round. Ed. by Lee-Jay Cho & Robert L. Hearn. LC 84-28662. xxiv, 380p. 1985. 8.00 (0-86638-052-3) EW Ctr HI.

Cent a Story: The Best from Ten Detective Aces. Garyn G. Roberts. LC 86-70384. 179p. 1986. 22.95 (0-87972-353-X); pap. 10.95 (0-87972-354-8) Bowling Green Univ.

Cent Jours. Jacques Audiberti. 288p. (FRE.). 1950. pap. 14.95 (0-8288-9052-8) Fr & Eur.

Cent Mille Milliards de Poemes. Raymond Queneau. (Gallimard Ser.). 38p. (FRE.). 1965. 59.95 (2-07-010467-2) Schoenhof.

Cent Motets du XIIIe Siecle, 3 vols. Pierre Aubry. (Illus.). 540p. (FRE.). 1964. reprint ed. pap. 150.00 (0-8450-0001-2) Broude.

Cent Nouvelles Nouvelles. Conteurs Francais du XVI Siecle Staff. 1520p. 89.95 (0-7859-0699-1, F27560) Fr & Eur.

Cent Phrases pour Eventails. Paul Claudel. (FRE.). 1942. pap. 10.95 (0-7859-1139-1, 2070269094) Fr & Eur.

Cent Vingt Journees de Sodome. Donatien A. Sade. 530p. (FRE.). 1992. pap. 29.95 (0-7859-1555-9, 2867442222) Fr & Eur.

Cent Vingt Jours de Sodome, 2 vols., 1. Donatien A. Sade. 320p. (FRE.). 1993. pap. 18.95 (0-7859-3206-2, 2264018798) Fr & Eur.

Cent Vingt Jours de Sodome, 2 vols., 2. Donatien A. Sade. 320p. (FRE.). 1993. pap. 18.95 (0-7859-3207-0, 2264018801) Fr & Eur.

Centaur. May Swenson. LC 92-14897. (Illus.). 32p. (J). (gr. k-3). 1995. text ed. 14.95 (0-02-788726-X, Mac Bks Young Read) S&S Childrens.

Centaur. John Updike. 1963. 24.95 (0-394-41881-6) Knopf.

Centaur. John Updike. 1987. mass mkt. 5.95 (0-449-21522-9) Fawcett.

Centaur. Algernon Blackwood. Ed. by R. Reginald & Douglas Menville. LC 75-46254. (Supernatural & Occult Fiction Ser.). 1976. reprint ed. lib. bdg. 29.95 (0-405-08113-8) Ayer.

Centaur Aisle. Piers Anthony. (Magic of Xanth Ser.). 1987. mass mkt. 5.95 (0-345-35246-7, Del Rey) Ballantine.

Centaur Letters. D. H. Lawrence. Ed. by F. W. Roberts. LC 75-110977. 1970. 25.00 (0-87959-060-2) U of Tex H Ransom Ctr.

Centaur of the North: Francisco Villa, the Mexican Revolutions, & Northern Mexico. Manuel A. Machado, Jr. Ed. by Melissa Roberts. (Illus.). 288p. 1988. 17.95 (0-89015-641-7) Sunbelt Media.

Centaur Types. Bruce Rogers. (Illus.). 90p. 1948. 50.00 (1-55753-052-1) Purdue U Pr.

***Centauren-Geburten: Wissenschaft, Kunst und Philosophie Beim Jungen Nietzsche.** Ed. by Tilman Borsche et al. (Monographien und Texte Zur Nietzsche-Forschung Ser.: Bd. 27). 558p. (GER.). (C). 1994. lib. bdg. 215.40 (3-11-013796-8) De Gruyter.

Centauro: Persona y Pensamiento De Ortega y Gasset. Domingo Marrero. (UPREX, Ensayo Ser.: No. 30). 319p. (C). 1974. pap. 1.50 (0-8477-0030-5) U of PR Pr.

Centaurs & Amazons: Women & the Pre-History of the Great Chain of Being. Page DuBois. (Women & Culture Ser.). (Illus.). 192p. 1991. pap. 14.95 (0-472-08153-5) U of Mich Pr.

Centaurs of Many Lands. Edward L. Tinker. (Illus.). 1964. 12.50 (0-87959-065-3) U of Tex H Ransom Ctr.

Centenarian. Rene De Obaldia. Tr. by Alexander Trocchi. 192p. 1997. 12.95 (0-7145-0159-X); pap. 9.95 (0-7145-0160-3) Riverrun NY.

Centenarian: Or, the Two Beringhelds. Ed. by R. Reginald & Douglas Menville. Tr. by George E. Slusser. LC 75-46250. (Supernatural & Occult Fiction Ser.). (Illus.). 1976. lib. bdg. 34.95 (0-405-08110-3) Ayer.

***Centenarian Women.** Milich. 1995. 26.95 (0-8057-9131-0, Twayne); pap. 14.95 (0-8057-9132-9, Twayne) Macmillan.

Centenarians: The New Generation. Ed. by Belle B. Beard et al. LC 90-40899. (Contributions to the Study of Aging Ser.: No. 20). 304p. 1990. text ed. 59.95 (0-313-27479-7, WID, Greenwood Pr) Greenwood.

Centenarians in Hungary. Ed. by Edit Beregi. (Interdisciplinary Topics in Gerontology Ser.: Vol. 27). (Illus.). xii, 210p. 1990. 134.50 (3-8055-5204-1) S Karger.

Centenarians: People over One Hundred - a Triumph of Will & Spirit. Lynn Adler. LC 89-26895. (Illus.). 348p. 1995. 24.95 (0-929173-02-3) Health Press.

Centenary Biographical Edition of the Works of Thackeray, 26 Vols, Set. William Makepeace Thackeray. Ed. by Anne T. Richie & Leslie Stephens. LC 79-22239. reprint ed. 2,340.00 (0-404-18310-7) AMS Pr.

Centenary Charter Lectures in Modern Political History, 1945-1946. Oscar Halecki et al. Ed. by William J. Schlaerth. LC 47-4025. (Burke Society Ser.: No. 2). 45p. reprint ed. pap. 25.00 (0-7837-5572-4, 2045351) Bks Demand.

Centenary Corbiere. Corbiere. Tr. by Val Warner. LC 74-18607. 171p. 1975. 19.95 (0-8023-1256-X) Dufour.

Centenary Essays on Alfred Marshall. Ed. by John K. Whitaker. (Illus.). 240p. (C). 1990. 69.95 (0-521-38133-9) Cambridge U Pr.

Centenary History As Related to the Baptist General Conference of America. Adolf Olson. Ed. by Edwin S. Ganstad. LC 79-52602. (Baptist Tradition Ser.). (Illus.). 1980. reprint ed. lib. bdg. 61.95 (0-405-12467-8) Ayer.

Centenary History of Indian National Congress. B. N. Pande. (Illus.). 1986. Vol. I: 1885-1919; 645p. write for info. (0-7069-3012-6, Pub. by Vikas II); Vol. II: 1919-1935; 672 pgs. write for info. (0-7069-3013-4, Pub. by Vikas II); Vol. III: 1935-1947; 886 pgs. write for info. (0-7069-3014-2, Pub. by Vikas II) S Asia.

Centenary History of Indian National Congress, Set. B. N. Pande. (Illus.). 1986. text ed. 150.00 (0-317-46164-8, Pub. by Vikas II) S Asia.

Centenary History of Indian National Congress, Vol. IV. Ed. by B. N. Pande. 1990. text ed. 60.00 (0-7069-4986-2, Pub. by Vikas II) S Asia.

Centenary History of South Place Chapel. Moncure D. Conway. (Works of Moncure Daniel Conway Ser.). 1990. reprint ed. lib. bdg. 79.00 (0-7812-2344-X) Rprt Serv.

Centenary Issues of the Pendleton Act of 1883: The Problematic Legacy of Civil Service Reform. Ed. by David H. Rosenbloom et al. LC 82-10041. (Annals of Public Administration Ser.: No. 3). 149p. reprint ed. pap. 42.50 (0-7837-3357-7, 2043315) Bks Demand.

Centenary of John Masefield's Birth: An Exhibition of First Editions, Letters, Manuscripts, Photographs, Drawings & Portraits. (Illus.). 1978. 7.50 (0-9607862-0-1) Columbia U Libs.

Centenary of the Torrens System in Malaysia. Ibrahim & Sihombing. 1989. 103.00 (9971-70-067-0) Butterworth Legal Pubs.

Centenary Selection from Robert Browning's Poetry. Intro. by Michael Meredith. LC 89-34659. (Illus.). xvi, 196p. 1989. 24.00 (0-930252-25-X); pap. 12.75 (0-930252-26-8) Browning Inst.

Centenary Tribute to J. M. Synge. Suhbil B. Bushrui. 1979. pap. 12.95 (0-901072-78-8, Pub. by Colin Smythe Ltd UK) Dufour.

Centennial. James A. Michener. 1987. mass mkt. 6.99 (0-449-21419-2, Crest) Fawcett.

Centennial. James A. Michener. 1994. mass mkt. 6.99 (0-449-45269-7, Crest) Fawcett.

Centennial. James A. Michener. 1974. 40.50 (0-394-47970-X) Random.

Centennial. Michael Rosenthal. 1986. pap. 9.95 (0-918223-86-5) Pindar Pr.

Centennial Address with Historical Sketches of Cromwell, Portland, Chatham, Middle-Haddam, & Middletown in the State of Connecticut. David D. Field. 318p. 1987. reprint ed. pap. 17.50 (1-55613-064-3) Heritage Bk.

Centennial Album: An Illustrated History of Eastern Washington University. Edmund V. Haag. 88p. (Orig.). 1982. pap. 6.00 (0-910055-01-7) East Wash Univ.

Centennial Bibliography of Huntington's Chorea: 1872-1972. George W. Bruyn. 1974. pap. text ed. 62.00 (90-6186-011-3) Kluwer Ac.

Centennial Biographical History of Ruhland & Ashland Co., Ohio. Ed. by A. J. Baughman. (Illus.). 831p. 1993. reprint ed. lib. bdg. 83.00 (0-8328-3004-6) Higginson Bk Co.

***Centennial Biographical History of Seneca County.** (Illus.). 757p. 1995. reprint ed. lib. bdg. 77.50 (0-8328-4728-3) Higginson Bk Co.

Centennial Campaign: The Sioux War of 1876. John S. Gray. LC 88-4836. (Illus.). 408p. 1988. pap. 17.95 (0-8061-2152-1) U of Okla Pr.

Centennial Celebration: Proceedings of the Actuarial Profession in North America, 1989. Ed. by M. Stanley Hughey. LC 90-9942. 1990. text ed. 60.00 (0-938959-14-X) Soc Actuaries.

Centennial Celebration: Recipes from Solo. LC 88-70392. 1988. write for info. (0-87502-229-4) Benjamin Co.

Centennial Celebration & Centennial History of the Town of Lee, MA. C. M. Hyde & Alexander Hyde. (Illus.). 352p. 1992. reprint ed. lib. bdg. 38.50 (0-8328-2496-8) Higginson Bk Co.

Centennial Celebration Cookbook. Ed. by Michael Janger & Mary Neznek. (Centennial Celebration Ser.). (Illus.). 250p. 1990. pap. text ed. 9.95 (0-88200-168-X) Alexander Graham.

Centennial Churches of Washington's 'Fourth Corner' (Occasional Papers: No. 20). 1986. pap. 8.95 (0-318-23338-X) WWU CPNS.

Centennial Clairette Eighteen Eighty to Nineteen Eighty. Becky Farrar. 333p. 1980. 20.00 (0-9609406-0-X) Greens Creek.

Centennial Cookbook, 1889-1989: Second Printing with Historical Vignettes. Orange County Pioneer Council Staff. (Illus.). 134p. 1989. 12.00 (0-943480-69-8) Friis-Pioneer Pr.

Centennial Cookbook, 1889-1989: With Historical Vignettes. Orange County Pioneer Council Staff. (Illus.). 134p. 1988. 12.00 (0-943480-68-X) Friis-Pioneer Pr.

***Centennial Directory of the American Academy in Rome.** Ed. by Benjamin G. Kohl et al. 408p. 1995. 50.00 (1-879549-02-6) Am Acad Rome.

Centennial Edition of the Works of Sidney Lanier, 10 vols., Set. Incl. Poems & Poem Outlines. Ed. by Charles R. Anderson. 396p. 1945. 50.00 (0-8018-0029-3); Science of English Verse & Essays on Music. Ed. by Paull F. Baum & Charles R. Anderson. 389p. 1945. 50.00 (0-8018-0030-7); Shakespeare & His Forerunners. Ed. by Kemp Malone & Charles R. Anderson. 443p. 1945. 50.00 (0-8018-0031-5); English Novel & Essays on Literature. Ed. by Clarence Gohdes et al. 411p. 1945. 50.00 (0-8018-0032-3); Tiger Lilies & Southern Prose. Ed. by Garland Greever et al. 407p. 1945. 50.00 (0-8018-0033-1); Florida & Miscellaneous Prose. Ed. by Philip Graham & Charles R. Anderson. 437p. 1945. 50.00 (0-8018-0034-X); Vol. 7. Letters. Ed. by Charles R. Anderson & Aubrey H. Starke. 401p. 1945. 50.00 (0-8018-0035-8); Letters. Ed. by Charles R. Anderson & Aubrey H. Starke. 450p. 1945. Vol. 8, 450p. 50.00 (0-8018-0036-6); Letters. Ed. by Charles R. Anderson & Aubrey H. Starke. 575p. 1945. Vol. 9, 575p. 50.00 (0-8018-0037-4); Letters. Ed. by Charles R. Anderson & Aubrey H. Starke. 542p. 1945. Vol. 10, 542p. 50.00 (0-8018-0038-2); 4241p. 1945. 385.00 (0-685-73362-9) Johns Hopkins.

Centennial Edition of the Works of Sidney Lanier, Vol. 10: Letters 1878-1881. Sidney Lanier. Ed. by C. R. Anderson & A. H. Starke. LC 46-2793. (Illus.). 558p. reprint ed. pap. 159.10 (0-7837-3396-8, 2043354) Bks Demand.

Centennial Essays for Robinson Jeffers. Ed. by Robert Zaller. LC 90-50542. 288p. 1991. 42.50 (0-87413-414-5) U Delaware Pr.

Centennial Exposition, Described & Illustrated. J. S. Ingram. LC 75-22824. (America in Two Centuries Ser.). (Illus.). 1976. reprint ed. 60.95 (0-405-07695-9) Ayer.

Centennial History of Arkansas, 3 vols. Dallas Herndon. Incl. Vol. 1. General History. 1040p. 1977. 37.50 (0-89308-068-3); Vol. 2. Biographical Sketches. 1176p. 1977. 37.50 (0-89308-069-1); Vol. 3. Biographical Sketches. 1160p. 1977. (0-89308-070-5); 3366p. 1977. reprint ed. 37.50 (0-685-73577-X) Southern Hist Pr.

Centennial History of Chautauqua County, New York, Vol. I. Chautauqua History Company Staff. (Illus.). 698p. 1993. reprint ed. lib. bdg. 69.00 (0-8328-2913-7) Higginson Bk Co.

Centennial History of Chautauqua County, New York, Vol. II. Chautauqua History Company Staff. (Illus.). 1173p. 1993. reprint ed. lib. bdg. 109.00 (0-8328-2914-5) Higginson Bk Co.

Centennial History of Columbus & Franklin County, Ohio, Vol. I. William A. Taylor. (Illus.). 832p. 1993. reprint ed. lib. bdg. 81.00 (0-8328-2829-7) Higginson Bk Co.

Centennial History of Columbus & Franklin County, Ohio, Vol. II. William A. Taylor. (Illus.). 820p. reprint ed. lib. bdg. 81.00 (0-8328-2830-0) Higginson Bk Co.

Centennial History of Coshocton Co., Ohio, Vol. 1: History. William J. Bahmer. (Illus.). 531p. 1993. reprint ed. lib. bdg. 52.00 (0-8328-3002-X) Higginson Bk Co.

Centennial History of Coshocton, Co. Ohio, Vol. 2: Biography. William J. Bahmer. (Illus.). 488p. 1993. reprint ed. lib. bdg. 52.00 (0-8328-3003-8) Higginson Bk Co.

Centennial History of Cottonwood County, Minnesota. (Illus.). 701p. 1994. reprint ed. lib. bdg. 72.00 (0-8328-3832-2) Higginson Bk Co.

Centennial History of Harden County, Ohio. Herbert T. Blue. (Illus.). 180p. 1993. reprint ed. lib. bdg. 25.00 (0-8328-3447-5) Higginson Bk Co.

Centennial History of Hardin County, Ohio. Herbert T. Blue. (Illus.). 180p. 1993. reprint ed. lib. bdg. 28.00 (0-8328-3227-8) Higginson Bk Co.

***Centennial History of Harrison, Containing the Celebration of 1905 & Historical & Biographical Matter.** Ed. by A. Moulton et al. (Illus.). 727p. 1995. reprint ed. lib. bdg. 75.00 (0-8328-4595-7) Higginson Bk Co.

Centennial History of Mason County, Illinois (1876) Joseph Cochrane. 427p. 1987. reprint ed. lib. bdg. 19.95 (1-877869-09-0) Mason Cnty Hist Proj.

Centennial History of New Brighton, Minnesota. Gene F. Skiba. LC 87-61680. (Illus.). 300p. 1987. 15.00 (0-9618704-0-0) New Brighton.

Centennial History of New York City from the Discovery to the Present Day. William L. Stone. 1977. lib. bdg. 75.00 (0-8490-1591-X) Gordon Pr.

Centennial History of Norway, Oxford County, Maine. William B. Lapham. (Illus.). 822p. 1986. reprint ed. 55.00 (0-89725-061-3) Picton Pr.

Centennial History of Nunda, New York. Ed. by H. Wells Hand. (Illus.). 637p. 1993. reprint ed. lib. bdg. 65.00 (0-8328-2835-1) Higginson Bk Co.

Centennial History of Sheltering Arms Hospital. Anne R. Lower. (Illus.). 96p. 1989. lib. bdg. 20.00 (0-9623370-0-5); pap. write for info. (0-9623370-1-3) Sheltering Arms.

Centennial History of Susquehanna County, Pa. Rhamanthus M. Stocker. (Illus.). 851p. 1993. reprint ed. lib. bdg. 86.00 (0-8328-2875-0) Higginson Bk Co.

Centennial History of Texas A&M University: 1876-1976, 2 vols. Henry C. Dethloff. LC 75-18687. (Centennial Series of the Association of Former Students: No. 1). 744p. 1975. boxed 25.00 (0-89096-007-0) Tex A&M Univ Pr.

Centennial History of the American Administrative State. Ed. by Ralph C. Chandler. 1987. text ed. 55.00 (0-02-905301-3) Free Pr.

Centennial History of the American Administrative State. Ralph C. Chandler. 917p. 1987. write for info. (0-318-61270-4) Macmillan.

Centennial History of the American Society of Mechanical Engineers: 1880-1980. Bruce Sinclair. 256p. 1980. text ed. 15.00 (0-686-69842-8, H0175H); pap. text ed. 10.00 (0-686-69843-6, H0175P) ASME.

Centennial History of the American Society of Mechanical Engineers, 1880-1980. Bruce Sinclair. LC 80-501784. (Illus.). 268p. reprint ed. pap. 76.40 (0-7837-4283-5, 2043975) Bks Demand.

Centennial History of the Boston Medical Library, 1875-1975. Joseph E. Garland. (Illus.). 223p. 1975. 9.95 (0-686-15546-7) F A Countway.

Centennial History of the Indiana General Assembly, 1816-1978, 3 vols. Justin Walsh. 605p. 1980. A Biographical Directory of the Indiana General Assembly, Vol. 1, 1816-1899. 20.00 (1-885323-35-2) IN Hist Bureau.

Centennial History of the Indiana General Assembly, 1816-1978, 3 vols. Justin Walsh. 610p. 1984. A Biographical Directory of the Indiana General Assembly, Vol. 2, 1901-1984. 20.00 (1-885323-36-0) IN Hist Bureau.

Centennial History of the Indiana General Assembly, 1816-1978, 3 vols. Justin E. Walsh. 832p. 1987. 20.00 (1-885323-37-9) IN Hist Bureau.

Centennial History of the Indiana General Assembly, 1816-1978, 3 vols., Set. Justin Walsh. xxvii, 832p. 1984. 50.00 (1-885323-38-7) IN Hist Bureau.

Centennial History of the Music Teachers National Association. Homer Ulrich. 306p. 1976. 10.50 (0-318-14929-X); 9.45 (0-318-14930-3) Music Tchrs.

Centennial History of the National Society of the Sons of the American Revolution. Sons of the American Revolution Staff. LC 90-72152. 112p. 1991. 29.95 (1-56311-028-8) Turner Pub KY.

Centennial History of the Pennsylvania Railroad Company, 1846-1946. George H. Burgess et al. LC 75-41750. (Companies & Men: Business Enterprises in America Ser.). (Illus.). 1976. reprint ed. 67.95 (0-405-08067-0) Ayer.

Centennial History of the Society of Naval Architects & Marine Engineers: 1893-1993. William D. Thomas. (Illus.). 205p. 1993. pap. 30.00 (0-939773-13-9, SOS) Soc Naval Arch.

Centennial History of the Town of Dryden (New York) Ed. by George E. Goodrich. (Illus.). 272p. 1993. reprint ed. lib. bdg. 32.50 (0-8328-3539-0) Higginson Bk Co.

***Centennial History of the Town of Millbury, Massachusetts.** (Illus.). 814p. 1994. reprint ed. lib. bdg. 82.50 (0-8328-4357-1) Higginson Bk Co.

Centennial History of the Town of Nunda 1808-1908. H. Wells Hand. 704p. 1993. reprint ed. lib. bdg. 50.00 (1-55787-108-6, NY26027) Hrt of the Lakes.

***Centennial History of the Village of Ballston Spa, Including the Towns of Ballston & Milton.** Edward F. Grose & J. C. Booth. (Illus.). 258p. 1995. reprint ed. lib. bdg. 34.50 (0-8328-4708-9) Higginson Bk Co.

***Centennial History of the Woodstock Country Club.** Bob Labbance. 26p. 1995. 40.00 (0-9622354-2-3); pap. text ed. 12.00 (0-9622354-3-1) NEGS.

Centennial History of Waterville, Kennebec Co, Maine, 1802-1902. Ed. by Edwin C. Whittemore et al. (Illus.). 592p. 1988. reprint ed. lib. bdg. 61.00 (0-8328-0036-8, ME0013) Higginson Bk Co.

Centennial Index - Generalregister, Vol. 29, Pt. 10: C19 - C20 H24. Comp. by Beilstein-Institut fur Literatur der Organischen Chemie Staff. 1280p. 1992. 707.00 (0-387-55682-6) Spr-Verlag.

Centennial Index - Generalregister, Vol. 29, Pt. 11: C20 H26 - C22 H28. Comp. by Beilstein-Institut fur Literatur der Organischen Chemie Staff. 1280p. 1992. 707.00 (0-387-55683-4) Spr-Verlag.

An Asterisk (*) at the beginning of an entry indicates that the title is appearing in BIP for the first time. 1119

Centennial Index - Generalregister, Vol. 29, Pt. 12: C22 H29 - C25. Comp. by Beilstein-Institut fur Literatur der Organischen Chemie Staff. 1280p. 1992. 707.00 (*0-387-55684-2*) Spr-Verlag.

Centennial Index - Generalregister, Vol. 29, Pt. 13: C26 - C372. Comp. by Beilstein-Institut fur Literatur der Organischen Chemie Staff. 1280p. 1992. 707.00 (*0-387-55685-0*) Spr-Verlag.

Centennial of Entomology in Canada, 1863-1963: A Tribute to Edmund M. Walker. Glenn B. Wiggins. LC 67-3350. (Royal Ontario Museum. Life Sciences. Contribution Ser.: No. 69). (Illus.). 116p. reprint ed. pap. 33.10 (*0-8357-8060-0*, 2034027) Bks Demand.

***Centennial of Incorporation-Charleston, S. C.** 259p. 1994. lib. bdg. 29.50 (*0-8328-4366-0*) Higginson Bk Co.

Centennial of the Settlement of Upper Canada by the United Empire Loyalists, 1784-1884. United Empire Loyalists Centennial Committee. Ed. by George Billias. LC 72-8670. (American Revolutionary Ser.). reprint ed. lib. bdg. 49.50 (*0-8398-2000-3*) Irvington.

Centennial of the Sheffield Scientific School. Ernest O. Lawrence. Ed. by George A. Baitsell. LC 70-107681. (Essay Index Reprint Ser.). 1977. 23.95 (*0-8369-1544-5*) Ayer.

Centennial of the United States Military Academy at West Point, New York, 1802-1902, 2 Vols, Set. U. S. Military Academy Staff. LC 68-54808. 1970. reprint ed. text ed. 75.00 (*0-8371-2665-7*, MACE, Greenwood Pr) Greenwood.

Centennial Park: A History. Paul Ashton & Kate Blackmore. 1988. 29.95 (*0-86840-346-6*, Pub. by New South Wales Univ Pr AT) Intl Spec Bk.

Centennial Proceedings & Historical Incidents of the Early Settlers of Northfield, VT. John Gregory. (Illus.). 319p. 1993. reprint ed. lib. bdg. 37.50 (*0-8328-3201-4*) Higginson Bk Co.

***Centennial Register: Sons of the Revolution in the State of California.** Richard H. Breithaupt, Jr. 1325p. 1994. 49.95 (*1-886085-00-5*) Walika.

Centennial Review. S. Richard Silverman & Patricia B. Kricos. (Centennial Celebration Ser.). (Orig.). (C). 1990. 16.95 (*0-685-36396-1*); pap. text ed. 9.95 (*0-685-36397-X*) Alexander Graham.

Centennial Sampler of Edmonds Writing. Ed. by Ann Saling. (Illus.). 208p. (Orig.). 1990. pap. 5.95 (*0-9618530-1-8*) Edmonds Arts.

Centennial Selections: A Heritage of Recipes from Stillwater, Okla. Joanna Gardiner & Peggy McCormick. LC 89-85638. (Illus.). 157p. 1989. pap. 14.95 (*0-934188-30-0*) Evans Pubns.

Centennial Snapshots: Historic Places Around King County from the First Twenty-Five Years of Statehood. Florence K. Lentz. (Illus.). 119p. (Orig.). 1991. pap. text ed. 8.95 (*0-914019-28-7*) NW Interpretive.

***Centennial Usage Studies: Publication of the American Dialect Society 78.** Michael B. Montgomery. Ed. by Greta D. Little. LC 94-31291. (Publication of the American Dialect Society: Vol. 78). 1994. pap. 16.00 (*0-8173-0739-7*) U of Ala Pr.

***Centennial Utah: The Beehive State on the Eve of the Twenty-First Century.** G. Wesley Johnson & Marian A. Johnson. (Illus.). 216p. 1995. 34.95 (*1-882933-07-9*) Cherbo Pub Grp.

Centennial West: Essays on the Northern Tier States. Ed. by William L. Lang. LC 90-6167. 300p. 1991. 30.00 (*0-295-96965-2*); pap. 17.50 (*0-295-96966-0*) U of Wash Pr.

Centennial 1986 Cookbook: Waggoner, Illinois. Ed. by Ellen A. Waggoner & Barbara M. Pope. (Illus.). 310p. 1986. spiral bd. 10.00 (*0-9616552-2-4*) Waggoner Cent.

Centennials in Action. George R. Cockle. LC 78-51541. (Overland Railbook Ser.). (Illus.). 1980. pap. 11.95 (*0-916160-05-X*) G R Cockle.

Center: Ideas & Institutions. Ed. by Liah Greenfeld & Michel Martin. (Illus.). 328p. 1988. 39.95 (*0-226-30686-0*) U Ch Pr.

Center, Bulge, & Disk of the Milky Way. Ed. by Leo Blitz. LC 92-24067. (Astrophysics & Space Science Library: Vol. 180). 176p. (C). 1992. lib. bdg. 59.50 (*0-7923-1913-3*) Kluwer Ac.

Center City Churches: The New Urban Frontier. Lyle E. Schaller. LC 92-40681. 176p. (Orig.). 1993. pap. 11.95 (*0-687-04802-8*) Abingdon.

Center Counter. John Grefe & Jeremy Silman. (Illus.). 96p. (Orig.). 1983. pap. 6.50 (*0-931462-22-3*) Chess Ent Inc.

Center Counter! Paul Hodges & Alex Fishbein. (ChessBase University Power Play! Ser.). (Illus.). 72p. (Orig.). 1994. pap. 10.95 (*1-883358-07-8*) R&D Pub NJ.

Center Field Grasses: Poems from Baseball. Gene Fehler. LC 90-53604. 192p. 1991. lib. bdg. 20.95x (*0-89950-604-6*) McFarland & Co.

Center for Cold Weather. Cleopatra Mathis. LC 89-10838. 81p. 1990. 14.95 (*0-935296-84-0*); pap. 10.95 (*0-935296-85-9*) Sheep Meadow.

***Center for Medical Consumers Ultimate Medical Answerbook.** Ed. by Maryann Napoli. LC 95-60. 1995. 23.00 (*0-688-12753-3*) Hearst Bks.

Center for Research Libraries Handbook. 161p. 1987. pap. 10.00 (*0-932486-23-1*) Ctr Res Lib.

***Center Holds: The Power Struggle Insider the Rehnquist Court.** James F. Simon. 384p. 1995. 25.00 (*0-684-80293-7*) S&S Trade.

***Center Ice.** Melissa Lowell. (Silver Blades Ser.: No. 10). (J). (gr. 4-7). 1995. mass mkt. 3.50 (*0-553-48313-7*) Bantam.

Center Lane... Turn Only. Penny J. Mann. No. 2. 64p. Date not set. pap. write for info. (*0-318-72210-0*) Good News Express.

Center of Attention. Francine Pascal. 1988. pap. 3.25 (*0-553-15668-3*) Bantam.

Center of Distance. Melody Davis. Ed. by Roy Zarucchi. (Poetry Book Ser.). 72p. (Orig.). 1992. pap. 7.95 (*1-879205-30-0*) Nightshade Pr.

Center of Nature Concentrated: Or, The Regenerated Salt of Nature. Ali Puli. 1988. pap. 4.95 (*1-55818-110-5*) Holmes Pub.

Center of the Circle of Commerce: Or A Refutation of a Treatise Intituled "The Circle of Commerce" Gerard De Malynes. LC 66-21687. (Reprints of Economic Classics Ser.). 1973. reprint ed. 27.50 (*0-678-00296-7*) Kelley.

Center of the Galaxy. Ed. by Mark Morris. (C). 1989. lib. bdg. 186.50 (*0-7923-0221-4*); pap. text ed. 80.50 (*0-7923-0222-2*) Kluwer Ac.

Center of the Universe: The Geopolitics of Iran. Graham E. Fuller. 301p. (C). 1991. pap. text ed. 21.50 (*0-8133-1159-4*) Westview.

Center of the Universe: The Geopolitics of Iran. Graham E. Fuller. 301p. (C). 1991. text ed. 48.00 (*0-8133-1158-6*) Westview.

Center of the Web. Time-Life Books Editors. (Third Reich Ser.). 1990. write for info. (*0-8094-6987-1*); lib. bdg. write for info. (*0-8094-6988-X*) Time-Life.

Center of the Web: Women & Solitude. Ed. by Delese Wear. 279p. (C). 1993. 59.50 (*0-7914-1545-7*); pap. 19.95 (*0-7914-1546-5*) State U NY Pr.

Center of the World: Native American Spirituality. Rita Robinson. 1992. pap. 12.95 (*0-87877-172-7*) Newcastle Pub.

Center on the Periphery: Historical Aspects of 20th-Century Swedish Physics. Ed. by Svante Lindqvist. LC 93-32830. (Uppsala Studies in the History of Science: No. 17). (Illus.). 576p. (C). 1993. 50.00 (*0-88135-157-1*, Sci Hist) Watson Pub Intl.

Center Ring. Barner & Vermillion-Witt. 1992. pap. 10.95 (*1-878901-31-1*) Hampton Roads Pub Co.

Center Scriptures. Robley E. Whitson. LC 87-50797. 225p. (Orig.). 1987. pap. text ed. 14.95 (*1-55605-009-7*) Wyndhall Pr.

Center Solution. Linda Schwartz. (Teacher Time-Savers Ser.). 74p. (J). (gr. 4-6). 1977. 7.95 (*0-88160-025-3*, LW 210) Learning Wks.

Center Stage. Elizabeth Bernard. (Satin Slippers Ser.: No. 02). (YA). 1987. pap. 2.95 (*0-449-13300-1*, Girls Only) Fawcett.

Center Stage. L. E. Blair. (Girl Talk Ser.: No. 28). 128p. (J). (gr. 3-7). 1992. pap. 2.95 (*0-307-22028-1*, 22028, Golden Pr) Western Pub.

Center Stage: An Anthology of Twenty-One Contemporary Black-American Plays. Ed. by Eileen J. Ostrow. LC 80-53143. (Illus.). 328p. (Orig.). 1981. pap. 29.95 (*0-9605208-0-5*) Sea Urchin.

Center Stage: An Anthology of Twenty-One Contemporary Black-American Plays. Ed. by Eileen J. Ostrow. (Illus.). 328p. (Orig.). 1991. pap. 19.95 (*0-252-06178-0*) U of Ill Pr.

***Center Stage: Helen Gahagan, a Life.** Ingrid W. Scobie. (Illus.). 389p. 1995. pap. 17.95 (*0-8135-2195-5*) Rutgers U Pr.

Center Stage: Helen Gahagan Douglas - A Life, 1900-1980. Ingrid W. Scobie. (Illus.). 368p. 1992. 24.95 (*0-19-506896-3*) OUP.

Center Stage: One-Act Plays for Teenage Readers & Actors. Ed. by Donald R. Gallo. LC 90-4050. (Trophy Keypoint Bk.). 384p. (YA). (gr. 7 up). 1991. pap. 4.95 (*0-06-447078-4*, Trophy) HarpC Child Bks.

Center Stage Summer. Cynthia K. Lukas. 157p. (Orig.). (YA). (gr. 8-12). 1988. pap. 4.95 (*0-938961-02-0*, Stamp Out Sheep Pr) Sq One Pubs.

Center Stuff for Nooks Crannie. Forte. 1986. pap. 10.95 (*0-913916-07-2*) Incentive Pubns.

Center, the Group under Observation, Sources of Information & Studies in Progress. Harold C. Stuart. (SRCD M: Vol. 4, No. 1). 1939. 23.00 (*0-527-01508-3*) Periodicals Srv.

***Center Time: A Complete Guide to Learning Centers.** Dana McMillan. 144p. 1994. teacher ed, pap. 11.95 (*1-57310-007-2*) Teachng & Lrning Co.

***Center Tree: Dreams & the Search for Self & Love.** Alice C. Beck. 1995. 24.95 (*0-533-11346-6*) Vantage.

Center Within. Gyomay M. Kubose. 144p. (Orig.). 1986. pap. 7.95 (*0-89346-271-3*) Heian Intl.

Centerbeam. Ed. by Otto Piene & Elizabeth Goldring. (Illus.). 144p. (Orig.). 1981. pap. 17.50 (*0-262-66047-4*) MIT Pr.

Centerbrook: Reinventing American Architecture. 1993. 39.95 (*1-55835-092-6*) AIA Press.

Centerbrook: Reinventing American Architecture. 192p. 1993. 39.99 (*1-56496-053-6*) Rockport Pubs.

Centerburg Tales. Robert McCloskey. (Illus.). (J). (gr. 1-3). 1977. pap. 4.99 (*0-14-031072-X*, Puffin) Puffin Bks.

Centerburg Tales. Robert McCloskey. LC 51-10675. (Illus.). 192p. (J). (gr. 4-6). 1951. pap. 15.99 (*0-670-20977-5*) Viking Child Bks.

Centered in the Soul: Psycho-Spiritual Development of Black Children. John Bolling. (Illus.). 250p. (Orig.). 1989. pap. text ed. 15.95 (*0-317-93364-7*) Mandala Rising Pr.

Centered Living: The Way of Centering Living. M. Basil Pennington. LC 85-27474. 1988. mass mkt. 9.95 (*0-385-24291-3*, Image Bks) Doubleday.

Centered on Christ: An Introduction to Monastic Profession. rev. ed. Augustine Roberts. LC 93-7100. 1993. pap. 12.95 (*0-932506-99-2*) St Bedes Pubns.

Centered Riding. Sally Swift. (Illus.). 224p. 1985. 17.95 (*0-312-12734-0*) Trafalgar.

Centered Skier. Denise McCluggage. (Illus.). 230p. 1992. reprint ed. pap. 14.95 (*0-9632484-0-5*) Tempest Bk.

Centerfield Ballhawk. Matt Christopher. (Illus.). 64p. (J). (gr. 2-4). 1992. 13.95 (*0-316-14079-1*) Little.

Centerfield Ballhawk. Matt Christopher. (J). (ps-3). 1994. 3.95 (*0-316-14272-7*) Little.

***Centerfold Syndrome: Overcoming Voyeurism & the Objectification of Women's Bodies.** Gary R. Brooks. LC 95-8838. (Social & Behavioral Studies). 1995. 21.50 (*0-7879-0104-0*) Jossey-Bass.

Centering: A Guide to Inner Growth. 2nd ed. Sanders G. Laurie & Melvin J. Tucker. LC 92-44726. 224p. 1993. pap. 9.95 (*0-89281-420-9*, Destiny Bks) Inner Tradit.

Centering: Finding the Place of Inner Power. Jessica Macbeth. 63p. 1995. audio 10.95 (*0-946551-38-3*, Pub. by Gateway Bks UK) Atrium Pubs.

Centering: Six Steps Toward Inner Liberation. Gerald Kushel. 288p. 1990. mass mkt. 4.95 (*1-55817-470-2*, Pinnacle NY) Windsor NY.

Centering & the Art of Intimacy Handbook: A New Psychology of Close Relationships. Gay Hendricks & Kathlyn T. Hendricks. 176p. (Orig.). 1993. pap. 9.00 (*0-671-76719-4*, Fireside) S&S Trade.

Centering in Poetry, Pottery, & the Person. 2nd ed. Mary C. Richards. LC 88-38316. 187p. 1989. pap. 12.95 (*0-8195-6200-9*, Wesleyan Univ Pr) U Pr of New Eng.

Centering Moment. Howard Thurman. LC 80-67469. 1980. reprint ed. pap. 9.50 (*0-913408-64-6*) Friends United.

Centering on God: Method & Message in Luke-Acts. Robert L. Brawley. (Literary Currents in Biblical Interpretation Ser.). 256p. (Orig.). 1990. pap. 16.99 (*0-664-25133-1*) Westminster John Knox.

Centering Prayer: Renewing an Ancient Christian Prayer Form. M. Basil Pennington. LC 82-45077. 256p. 1982. mass mkt. 6.50 (*0-385-18179-5*, Image Bks) Doubleday.

***Centering the Self: Subjectivity, Society & Reading from Thomas Gray to Thomas Hardy.** Ed. by Vincent Newey. 300p. 1995. 59.95 (*1-85928-151-6*, Pub. by Scolar Pr UK) Ashgate Pub Co.

Centerport. Harvey Weber. Ed. by James Stear. (Illus.). 144p. (Orig.). 1990. pap. 18.95 (*0-9627346-0-8*) Harmad Enterprises.

Centers. Jonathan Bliss. LC 93-42533. (Hockey Greats Ser.). (J). 1994. write for info. (*1-55916-014-4*) Rourke Bk Co.

Centers: Upscale Specialty & Festival 1989. Ed. by Tama J. Shor. (Illus.). 114p. 1989. pap. 195.00 (*0-932599-05-2*) JOMURPA Pub.

Centers: Upscale Specialty, Urban Mixed-Use & Festival 1991. 2nd ed. Ed. by Murray Shor. (Illus.). 224p. 1991. pap. 195.00 (*0-932599-08-7*) JOMURPA Pub.

Centers for Early Learners Throughout the Year. Jeri A. Carroll. 144p. 1991. 11.95 (*0-86653-615-9*, GA1334) Good Apple.

Centers of Influence & U. S. Forest Policy. Ed. by Frank J. Convery & Jean E. Davis. 168p. reprint ed. pap. 47.90 (*0-7837-6041-8*, 2045854) Bks Demand.

Centers of Interest see Total Teaching for Today's Church

Centers of Learning: Britain, France, Germany, United States. Joseph Ben-David & Philip G. Altbach. 240p. (C). 1992. pap. 19.95 (*1-56000-604-8*) Transaction Pubs.

Centers of the Self: Best Short Stories by Black American Women, 1859-1994. Ed. by Martin J. Hamer. LC 94-14724. 1994. pap. 10.95 (*0-8090-1576-5*) Hill & Wang.

Centers, Symbols, & Hierarchies: Essays on the Classical States of Southeast Asia. Ed. by Lorraine Gesick. LC 83-50993. (Monograph Ser. - Yale University Southeast Asia Studies: No. 26). 241p. 1983. pap. 14.00 (*0-938692-04-6*) Yale U SE Asia.

Centerstage: American Diplomacy since World War II. Ed. by L. Carl Brown. LC 89-24676. (Illus.). 483p. 1989. 49.95 (*0-8419-1265-3*); pap. 24.95 (*0-8419-1270-X*) Holmes & Meier.

Centerville, U. S. A. Charles Merz. LC 78-160943. (Short Story Index Reprint Ser.). 1977. reprint ed. 20.95 (*0-8369-3922-0*) Ayer.

Centinel: Warnings of a Revolution. Ed. by Elizabeth I. Nybakken. LC 77-92570. 240p. 1980. 25.00 (*0-87413-141-3*) U Delaware Pr.

Centinela Site (CA-LAN-60) Data Recovery at a Middle Period, Creek-Edge Site in the Ballona Wetlands, Los Angeles, California. Donn R. Grenda et al. (Statistical Research Technical Ser.: No. 45). (Illus.). 209p. (Orig.). (C). 1994. pap. text ed. 22.50 (*1-879442-05-1*) Stats Res.

Centipedes & Millipedes of Southern Africa: A Guide. R. F. Lawrence. 168p. (C). 1984. text ed. 70.00 (*0-86961-142-9*, Pub. by A A Balkema NE) Ashgate Pub Co.

Cento Citta. Paul Hofmann. LC 87-28512. 1991. pap. 12.95 (*0-8050-1465-9*, Owl) H Holt & Co.

Central Actions of Angiotensin & Related Hormones: Proceedings of Symposium Sponsored U Houston 1-76. J. Buckley & C. Ferrario. LC 77-520. 252.00 (*0-08-020933-5*, Pub. by Pergamon Repr UK) Franklin.

Central Activity in Galaxies: From Observational Data to Astrophysical Diagnostics, Proceedings of the Predoctoral Astrophysics School III, Dublin, Ireland, 10-22 September 1990. Ed. by Aage Sandqvist & Thomas P. Ray. LC 92-42743. (Lecture Notes in Physics Ser.: Vol. 413). 1993. 55.00 (*0-387-56371-7*); write for info. (*3-540-56371-7*) Spr-Verlag.

Central Acts & Ordinances, Nineteen Seventy-Five. P. L. Malik. 518p. 1976. 180.00 (*0-317-54867-0*) St Mut.

Central Adrenaline Neurons: Basic Aspects & Their Role in Cardiovascular Disease: Proceedings of an International Symposium 27-28 August 1979, Wenner-Gren Center, Stockholm. Ed. by Kjell Fuxe et al. (Wenner-Gren Center International Symposium Ser.: Vol. 33). (Illus.). 356p. 1980. 151.00 (*0-08-025927-8*, Pub. by Pergamon Repr UK) Franklin.

Central Africa: A Travel Survival Kit. 2nd ed. Alex Newton. (Illus.). 576p. (Orig.). 1994. pap. 16.95 (*0-86442-138-9*) Lonely Planet.

Central African Republic. (Let's Visit Places & Peoples of the World Ser.). (Illus.). (J). (gr. 5 up). 1989. 14.95 (*0-7910-0146-6*) Chelsea Hse.

***Central African Republic.** Dona Bretherick. Ed. by Dale E. Gough. (OIES Country Guide Ser.). 20p. (C). 1995. write for info. (*0-929851-27-7*) Am Assn Coll Registrars.

Central African Republic. Pierre Kalck. (World Bibliographical Ser.). 1993. lib. bdg. 76.50 (*1-85109-172-6*) ABC-CLIO.

Central African Republic in Pictures. Ed. by Lerner Publications, Department of Geography Staff. (Visual Geography Ser.). (Illus.). 64p. (YA). (gr. 5 up). 1989. 18.95 (*0-8225-1858-9*, Lerner Publctns) Lerner Group.

Central America. (Great Contemporary Issues Ser.). 1979. lib. bdg. 35.00 (*0-686-59847-4*) Ayer.

Central America. Ed. by Jan L. Flora & Edelberto T. Rivas. (Sociology of "Developing Societies" Ser.). 288p. (C). 1989. 27.00 (*0-85345-766-2*); pap. 11.00 (*0-85345-765-4*) Monthly Rev.

Central America. Marion Morrison. LC 92-14537. (World in View Ser.). 96p. (J). 1992. lib. bdg. 24.26 (*0-8114-2458-8*) Raintree Steck-V.

Central America. Marion Morrison. (People & Places Ser.). (Illus.). 48p. (J). (gr. 4-8). 1989. lib. bdg. 12.95 (*0-382-09824-2*) Silver Burdett Pr.

Central America: A Nation Divided. 2nd ed. Ralph L. Woodward, Jr. LC 75-25467. (Latin American Histories Ser.). 1985. pap. 16.95 (*0-19-503593-3*) OUP.

Central America: Anatomy of Conflict. Carnegie Endowment for International Peace Staff & Robert S. Leiken. LC 83-27440. 1984. 40.00 (*0-08-030950-X*, Pergamon Pr) Elsevier.

***Central America: Business Financing Handbook.** (Illus.). 70p. (Orig.). 1994. pap. 295.00 (*0-7605-1183-7*) Rector Pr.

Central America: Can Europe Play a Part? Hugh Thomas. (C). 1990. 35.00 (*0-907967-84-1*, Pub. by Inst Euro Def & Strat UK) St Mut.

Central America: Covering Political Unrest in the States of Nicaragua, El Salvador, Guatemala, Honduras & Costa Rica. Deakin University Press Staff. 66p. (C). 1988. 23.00 (*0-7300-0597-6*, Pub. by Deakin Univ AT) St Mut.

Central America: Democracy, Development, & Change. Ed. by John M. Kirk & George W. Schuyler. LC 88-6922. 211p. 1988. text ed. 55.00 (*0-275-93049-1*, C3049, Praeger Pubs) Greenwood.

Central America: Guatemala, Costa Rica, Honduras, Belize, Panama, El Salvador, Nicaragua. Natascha Norton & Mark Whitmore. (Cadogan Guides Ser.). (Illus.). 400p. (Orig.). 1994. pap. 17.95 (*1-56440-070-0*) Globe Pequot.

Central America: Historical Perspectives on the Contemporary Crises. Ed. by Ralph L. Woodward, Jr. LC 88-208. (Contributions to the Study of World History Ser.: No. 10). 310p. 1988. text ed. 59.95 (*0-313-25938-0*, WDA/, Greenwood Pr) Greenwood.

Central America: International Dimensions of the Crisis. Ed. by Richard E. Feinberg. LC 81-13232. 300p. 1982. 34.50 (*0-8419-0737-4*) Holmes & Meier.

Central America: On a Shoestring. 2nd ed. Brosnahan et al. (Illus.). 636p. 1994. pap. 16.95 (*0-86442-218-0*) Lonely Planet.

Central America: Opposing Viewpoints. Ed. by Carol Wekesser et al. LC 90-13922. (Opposing Viewpoints Ser.). (Illus.). 240p. (YA). (gr. 10 up). 1990. lib. bdg. 19.95 (*0-89908-484-2*); pap. text ed. 11.55 (*0-89908-459-1*) Greenhaven.

Central America: Options for the Poor. Neil MacDonald. 78p. (C). 1988. pap. text ed. 35.00 (*0-85598-113-X*, Pub. by Oxfam Pubns UK) St Mut.

Central America: Postal History & a Listing of Pre-Philatelic Postmarks. Leo J. Harris. (Illus.). 142p. 1985. 40.00 (*0-912574-42-9*) Collectors.

Central America & Its Problems. Frederick Palmer. (Central America Ser.). 1979. lib. bdg. 69.95 (*0-8490-2882-5*) Gordon Pr.

Central America & the Caribbean. Graham Hovey & Gene Brown. LC 79-26120. (Great Contemporary Issues Ser.). 1980. 27.95 (*0-405-12937-8*) Ayer.

Central America & the Law: The Constitution, Civil Liberties, & the Courts. Mark Tushnet. LC 88-6693. 72p. (Orig.). 1988. pap. 5.00 (*0-89608-340-3*) South End Pr.

Central America & the Middle East: The Internationalization of the Crises. Ed. by Damian J. Fernandez. 239p. (C). 1990. lib. bdg. 32.95 (*0-8130-1001-2*); pap. text ed. 19.95 (*0-8130-1018-7*) U Press Fla.

Central America & the Polls. Washington Office on Latin America Staff & William M. LeoGrande. 50p. (Orig.). 1987. pap. 6.50 (*0-9613249-7-X*) WOLA.

Central America & the United States: The Clients & the Colossus. John H. Coatsworth. LC 93-29998. (Twayne's International History Ser.: No. 12). 296p. 1994. text ed. 28.95 (*0-8057-7901-9*, Twayne); pap. 15.95 (*0-8057-9210-4*, Twayne) Macmillan.

Central America & the United States: The Search for Stability. Thomas M. Leonard. LC 90-24818. (United States & the Americas Ser.). 256p. 1991. 35.00 (*0-8203-1320-3*); pap. 15.00 (*0-8203-1321-1*) U of Ga Pr.

Central America & the Western Alliance. Ed. by Joseph Cirincione. LC 84-19770. 225p. 1985. 32.95 (*0-8419-1003-0*) Holmes & Meier.

***Central America Guide.** Paul Glassman. Ed. by J. Stein. LC 94-69848. 480p. (Orig.). 1995. pap. 16.95 (*1-883323-17-7*) Open Rd Pub.

Central America in the Nineteenth & Twentieth Centuries: An Annotated Bibliography. Kenneth J. Grieb. 1988. text ed. 100.00 (*0-8161-8130-6*, Hall Reference) Macmillan.

C

An Asterisk (*) at the beginning of an entry indicates that the title is appearing in BIP for the first time.

C

An Asterisk (*) at the beginning of an entry indicates that the title is appearing in BIP for the first time.

Central Government & the Localities: Hampshire 1649-1689. Andrew M. Coleby. (Cambridge Studies in Early Modern British History). (Illus.). 270p. 1987. 59.95 (*0-521-32979-5*) Cambridge U Pr.

Central Grants to Local Governments: The Political & Economic Impact of the Rate Support Grant in England & Wales. Robert J. Bennett. LC 82-4378. (Cambridge Geographical Studies: No. 17). 365p. reprint ed. pap. 104.10 (*0-685-20626-2*, 2030581) Bks Demand.

Central Greece Earthquakes of February-March 1981: A Reconaissance & Engineering Report. P. G. Carydis et al. 160p. 1982. 12.00 (*0-685-14392-9*) Earthquake Eng.

Central Ideas in the Development of American Journalism: A Narrative History. Marvin Olasky. 208p. 1990. text ed. 36.00 (*0-8058-0893-0*) L Erlbaum Assocs.

Central Illinois Expressway Archeology: Floodplain Archaic Occupations of the Illinois Valley Crossing. Barbara D. Stafford. LC 89-938. (Kampsville Archeological Center Technical Reports: No. 4). (Illus.). 132p. (Orig.). 1989. pap. 8.95 (*0-942118-28-6*) Ctr Amer Arche.

Central Illinois Expressway Archeology: Upland Occupations of the Illinois Valley Crossing. Ed. by Barbara D. Stafford. LC 94-8805. (Kampsville Archeological Center Technical Reports: No. 5). (Illus.). 219p. (Orig.). 1994. pap. 10.00 (*0-942118-35-9*) Ctr Amer Arche.

Central Information File: Conversion & Implementation. Charles F. Bates. LC 76-55780. (Bank Study Ser.). 191p. reprint ed. pap. 54.50 (*0-685-15976-0*, 2052182) Bks Demand.

Central Intelligence Agency. Rafaela Ellis. (Know Your Government Ser.). (Illus.). 96p. 1988. lib. bdg. 14.95 (*0-87754-831-5*) Chelsea Hse.

Central Intelligence Agency: An Instrument of Government, to 1950. Arthur P. Darling. Ed. by Bruce D. Berkowitz & Allan E. Goodman. 672p. 1990. 60.00 (*0-271-00715-X*); pap. 17.50 (*0-271-00717-6*) Pa St U Pr.

Central Intelligence Agency: History & Documents. Ed. by William M. Leary. LC 83-17896. 200p. 1984. pap. 12.95 (*0-8173-0219-0*) U of Ala Pr.

Central Issues in Moral & Ethical Education. John B. Wilson & Samuel M. Natale. (Ethical Conflict Ser.). 172p. (C). 1991. lib. bdg. 35.50 (*0-8191-8136-6*); pap. text ed. 19.00 (*0-8191-8137-4*) U Pr of Amer.

Central Italian Painting, Fourteen Hundred - Fourteen Sixty-Five: An Annotated Bibliography. Martha L. Dunkleman. (Reference Books - Art History). 358p. (C). 1986. lib. bdg. 70.00 (*0-8161-8546-8*, Hall Reference) Macmillan.

***Central Latin America (CLA) Transportation Yearbooks.** (Airport & Handling Agents 95-96 Ser.). 1995. pap. text ed. 325.00 (*0-7106-1279-6*) Janes Info Group.

Central Life Interests: Creative Individualism in a Complex World. Robert Dubin. 256p. (C). 1992. 34.95 (*1-56000-051-1*) Transaction Pubs.

Central Lithuania: Specialized Stamp Catalogue. A. G. Pacholczyk. LC 90-70422. (Illus.). 208p. 1990. pap. 67.50 (*1-878543-01-6*) Stochastic Pr.

***Central Local Government Relations in the 1980's.** Paul Carmichael. 368p. 1995. boxed, pap. 59.95 (*1-85972-033-1*, Pub. by Avebury Pub UK) Ashgate Pub Co.

Central Market Cookbook. Phyllis P. Good & Louise Stoltzfus. LC 89-23321. 224p. 1989. 19.95 (*0-934672-81-4*); pap. 11.95 (*0-934672-82-2*) Good Bks PA.

Central Materials Research Institute (TSNIIM) of the Soviet Ministry of the Defense Industry. Karl Greenberg. Ed. by Andrew Michta. 105p. (Orig.). 1986. pap. text ed. 75.00 (*1-55831-014-2*) Delphic Associates.

***Central Mechanisms of Anorectic Drugs.** fac. ed. Ed. by Silvio Garattini & Rosario Samanin. LC 77-17749. (Monographs of the Mario Negri Institute for Pharmacological Research). (Illus.). 501p. Date not set. pap. 142.80 (*0-7837-7169-X*, 2047128) Bks Demand.

Central Message of the New Testament. Joachim Jeremias. LC 81-66890. 95p. reprint ed. pap. 27.10 (*0-685-17067-5*, 2027865) Bks Demand.

Central Mexico Handbook: Mexico City & Other Colonial Cities within the Highland States. Chicki Mallan. LC 94-9364. 350p. 1994. pap. 15.95 (*1-56691-023-4*) Moon Pubns CA.

Central Middle East: A Handbook of Anthropology & Published Research on the Nile Valley, the Arab Levant, Southern Mesopotamia, the Arabian Peninsula & Israel. Ed. by Louise E. Sweet. LC 70-148003. (Area & Country Surveys Ser.). 336p. 1971. 20.00x (*0-87536-107-2*); pap. 10.00x (*0-87536-108-0*) HRAFP.

***Central Mine - A Ghost Town, Vol. I.** (Copper Country Local History Ser.: Vol. 50). (Illus.). 128p. 1995. 4.00 (*0-942363-49-3*) C J Monette.

Central Missouri Hopewell Subsistence Settlement System. Marvin Kay. Ed. by W. Raymond Wood. LC 80-80373. (Research Ser.: No. 15). (Illus.). 58p. (Orig.). 1980. pap. 4.00 (*0-943414-16-4*) MO Arch Soc.

Central Mountain & Plains States. Harold W. Rickett. LC 66-17920. (Wild Flowers of the United States Ser.: Vol. 6, 3 Pts.). (Illus.). 784p. 1973. text ed. 92.00 (*0-89327-287-6*) NY Botanical.

Central Nervous System: Structure & Function. Per Brodal. (Illus.). 480p. 1992. 39.95 (*0-19-505518-7*) OUP.

Central Nervous System: The Structural Basis of Human Neurobiology. O. Eugene Millhouse. 1991. pap. text ed. write for info. (*0-07-042314-8*) McGraw.

***Central Nervous System & Eye Infections.** Ed. by Gerald L. Mandell & Thomas P. Bleck. LC 94-41262. (Atlas of Infectious Diseases Ser.: Vol. 3). 1995. write for info. (*0-443-07700-2*) Current Med.

Central Nervous System Control of the Heart. Ed. by T. Stober et al. (Topics in the Neurosciences Ser.). 1986. lib. bdg. 93.50 (*0-89838-820-1*) Kluwer Ac.

Central Nervous System Diseases. Ed. by H. S. Rosenberg & J. Bernstein. (Perspectives in Pediatric Pathology Ser.: Vol. 10). viii, 264p. 1987. 211.25 (*3-8055-4403-0*) S Karger.

Central Nervous System Disorders of Aging: Clinical Intervention & Research. Ed. by Randy Strong et al. (Aging Ser.: Vol. 33). 254p. 1988. text ed. 54.50 (*0-88167-354-4*) Raven.

***Central Nervous System Effects of Hypothalamic Hormones & Other Peptides.** fac. ed. Ed. by Robert Collu et al. LC 77-94310. (Illus.). 453p. Date not set. pap. 129.20 (*0-7837-7515-6*, 2046990) Bks Demand.

Central Nervous System in AIDS. Ed. by J. Artigas et al. (Illus.). 250p. 1993. write for info. (*3-540-55839-X*) Spr-Verlag.

Central Nervous System in AIDS: Neurology, Radiology, Pathology, Ophthalmology. Ed. by Artigas G. Grosses et al. LC 93-22713. 1993. 198.00 (*0-387-55839-X*) Spr-Verlag.

Central Nervous System Leukemia Prevention & Treatment. Ed. by R. Mastrangelo. (Developments in Oncology Ser.). 1983. lib. bdg. 84.00 (*0-89838-570-9*) Kluwer Ac.

Central Nervous System Mechanisms in Hypertension. Ed. by Joseph P. Buckley & Carlos Ferrario. (Perspectives in Cardiovascular Research Ser.: Vol. 6). 434p. 1981. 101.50 (*0-89004-545-3*) Raven.

Central Nervous System Monitoring in Anesthesia & Intensive Care. Ed. by J. Schulte Am Esch & E. Kochs. LC 94-2610. 1993. 88.00 (*0-387-57134-5*) Spr-Verlag.

Central Nervous System of Vertebrates: A General Survey of Its Comparative Anatomy with an Introduction to Pertinent Fundamental Biologic & Logical Concepts, 5 vols., Set. H. Kuhlenbeck. Incl. Vol. 1. Propaedeutics to Comparative Neurology. 1967. 72.00 (*3-8055-0897-2*); Vol. 2. Invertebrates & Origin of Vertebrates. 1967. 72.00 (*3-8055-0896-4*); Vol. 3, Pt. 1. Structural Elements: Biology of Nervous Tissue. 1970. 173.00 (*3-8055-0900-6*); Vol. 3, Pt. 2. Overall Morphology Pattern. 1973. 272.00 (*3-8055-1393-3*); Vol. 4. Spinal Cord & Deuterencephalon. 1975. 318.50 (*3-8055-1732-7*); Vol. 5, Pt. 1. Derivatives of the Proencephalon: Diencephalon & Telencephalon. 1977. 318.50 (*3-8055-2638-5*); Vol. 5, Pt. 2. Mammalian Telencephalon: Surface Morphology & Cerebral Cortex. The Vertebrate Neuraxis As a Whole. Subject & Authors Index to Vols. 1-5. 1978. 256.00 (*3-8055-2645-8*); (Illus.). 1966. 1,037.00 (*3-8055-1725-4*) S Karger.

Central Nervous System Pathology: A New Approach. G. N. Kryzhanovsky. Tr. by Nicholas Bobrov. 444p. 1986. 110.00 (*0-306-10982-4*, Consultants) Plenum.

Central Nervous System Peptide Mechanisms in Stress & Depression. Ed. by S. Craig Risch. LC 90-14503. (Progress in Psychiatry Ser.: No. 30). 190p. 1991. text ed. 27.00 (*0-88048-249-4*) Am Psychiatric.

Central Nervous System Pharmaceuticals. (Market Research Reports: No. 343). 160p. 1993. 795.00 (*0-317-05019-2*) Theta Corp.

***Central Nervous System Plasticity & Repair.** fac. ed. Ed. by A. Bignami et al. LC 84-24180. (Illus.). 198p. Date not set. pap. 56.50 (*0-7837-7517-2*) Bks Demand.

Central Nervous System Trauma Research Techniques, Vol. 4. Ed. by S. Tsuyoshi Ohnishi & Tomoko Ohnishi. (Membrane-Linked Diseases Ser.). 560p. 1995. 149.95 (*0-8493-8094-4*, 8094) CRC Pr.

Central Neural Mechanisms of Cardiovascular Regulation. Ed. by George Kunos & John Ciriello. (Illus.). xv, 282p. 1991. 105.00 (*0-8176-3545-9*) Spr-Verlag.

Central Neural Organization of Cardiovascular Control. John Ciriello et al. (Progress in Brain Research Ser.: Vol. 81). 1990. 217.50 (*0-444-81224-5*, PBR 81) Elsevier.

Central New York Mountain Biking: The 30 Best Back Road & Trail Rides in Upstate New York. Dick Mansfield. LC 94-2715. 176p. 1994. pap. 12.95 (*0-937921-50-5*) Acorn Pub.

Central Nilo-Hamites. Pamela Gulliver & P. H. Gulliver. LC 71-408455. (Ethnographic Survey of Africa: East Central Africa Ser.: No. 7). 117p. reprint ed. pap. 33.40 (*0-8357-6957-7*, 2039016) Bks Demand.

Central of Georgia Railway Album. William F. Beckunn, Jr. & Albert M. Langley, Jr. LC 86-50539. (Illus.). 144p. (Orig.). 1986. pap. 19.95 (*0-9615257-1-1*) Union Sta.

Central Office Plant. 2nd ed. Frank E. Lee. LC 73-85629. (ABC of the Telephone Ser.: Vol. 3). (Illus.). 68p. (C). 1985. pap. text ed. 13.95 (*1-56016-002-0*) ABC TeleTraining.

Central Oregon Wilderness Areas: (Cascades to the Coast) Donna I. Aitkenhead. Ed. by Oral Bullard. (Illus.). 112p. (Orig.). 1991. pap. 12.95 (*0-911518-83-5*) Touchstone Oregon.

Central Pacific Campaign, 1943-1944: A Bibliography. James T. Controvich. LC 90-5508. (Bibliographies of Battles & Leaders Ser.: No. 2). 160p. 1990. text ed. 49.95 (*0-313-28074-6*, CCY, Greenwood Pr) Greenwood.

Central Pain: A Neurosurgical Survey. Valentino Cassinari & Carlo A. Pagni. LC 68-54017. (Illus.). 102p. 1969. 18.00 (*0-674-10540-0*) HUP.

Central Panel System for Administrative Law Judges: A Survey of Seven States. Malcolm C. Rich & Wayne E. Brucar. LC 82-74139. 99p. 1983. text ed. 42.95 (*0-313-27084-8*, U7084, Greenwood Pr) Greenwood.

***Central Park.** Bruce Davidson. 88p. Date not set. 40.00 (*0-89381-625-6*) FS&G.

Central Park: A Visit to One of the World's Most Treasured Landscapes. L. C. Burnham. 1993. 14.99 (*0-517-07343-9*) Random Hse Value.

Central Pennsylvania Marriages, 1700-1896. Charles A. Fisher. LC 74-16925. 90p. 1993. reprint ed. pap. 8.00 (*0-8063-0646-7*) Genealog Pub.

Central Peruvian Prehistoric Interaction Sphere, Vol. 7. R. Macneish et al. 1975. 10.00 (*0-939312-08-5*) Peabody Found.

Central Philosophy of the Rig-Veda. A. Ramamurty. (C). 1991. 32.00 (*81-202-0306-2*, Pub. by Ajanta II) S Asia.

Central Philosophy of Tibet. Robert A. Thurman. (Illus.). 460p. 1991. pap. text ed. 19.95 (*0-691-02067-1*) Princeton U Pr.

Central Plains Prehistory: Holocene Environments & Culture Change in the Republican River Basin. Waldo R. Wedel. LC 85-1151. (Illus.). xxiv, 352p. 1986. 40.00x (*0-8032-4729-X*) U of Nebr Pr.

Central Planning Evaluation of Variants. K. Porwit & J. Stadler. LC 66-17808. 1967. 83.00 (*0-08-011773-2*, Pub. by Pergamon Repr UK) Franklin.

Central Planning in Poland. John M. Montias. LC 74-6785. (Yale Studies in Economics: No. 13). (Illus.). 410p. 1974. reprint ed. text ed. 75.00 (*0-8371-7560-7*, MOCP, Greenwood Pr) Greenwood.

Central Power in the Australian Commonwealth: An Examination of the Growth of Commonwealth Power in the Australian Federation. Robert G. Menzies. LC 67-28061. (Virginia Legal Studies). 208p. reprint ed. pap. 59.30 (*0-8357-8061-9*, 2033973) Bks Demand.

Central Problem of Paradise Lost: The Fall of Man. E. L. Marilla. (Essays & Studies on English Language & Literature: Vol. 15). 1972. reprint ed. pap. 15.00 (*0-8115-0213-9*) Periodicals Srv.

Central Problems in Social Theory: Action, Structure & Contradiction in Social Analysis. Anthony Giddens. LC 79-64667. 1979. pap. 15.00 (*0-520-03975-0*) U CA Pr.

Central Railroad of New Jersey's First Hundred Years: 1849-1949. Elaine Anderson. Ed. by James Lee & Lance Metz. LC 84-21449. (Illus.). 238p. (Orig.). 1984. pap. 14.00 (*0-930973-00-3*, TF25, C43A 53) Canal Hist Tech.

Central Readings in the History of Modern Philosophy: Descartes to Kant. Robert Cummins & David Owen. 483p. (C). 1992. text ed. 39.95 (*0-534-16272-X*) Intl Thomson.

Central Registries for Child Abuse & Neglect: A National Review of Records Management, Due Process Safeguards, & Data Utilization. 377p. 1988. 23.00 (*0-685-24111-4*, NCSC-062) Natl Ctr St Courts.

Central Regulation of Autonomic Functions. Ed. by Arthur D. Loewy & K. Michael Spyer. (Illus.). 416p. 1990. 85.00 (*0-19-505106-8*) OUP.

Central Regulation of Energy Metabolism. Nagai. 1992. 110.00 (*0-8493-6657-7*, QP356) CRC Pr.

Central Regulation of the Pituitary-Adrenal Complex. Evgenii V. Naumenko. LC 73-17250. (Studies in Soviet Science). 205p. reprint ed. pap. 58.50 (*0-317-28730-3*, 2020686) Bks Demand.

Central Republic in Mexico, 1835-1846: Hombres de Bien in the Age of Santa Anna. Michael P. Costeloe. LC 92-33950. (Cambridge Latin American Studies: No. 73). 336p. (C). 1993. 59.95 (*0-521-44121-8*) Cambridge U Pr.

Central Reservations: New & Selected Poems. Connie Bensley. 126p. (Orig.). 1990. pap. 18.95 (*1-85224-128-4*, Pub. by Bloodaxe Bks UK) Dufour.

Central Route to the Pacific. Gwinn H. Heap. Ed. by Stuart Bruchey. LC 80-1315. (Railroads Ser.). (Illus.). 1981. reprint ed. lib. bdg. 18.95 (*0-405-13787-7*) Ayer.

Central Science: Essays on the Uses of Chemistry. Ed. by George B. Kauffman & H. Harry Szmant. LC 83-18054. 182p. 1984. 15.00 (*0-912646-84-5*) Tex Christian.

Central Serotonin Receptors & Psychotropic Drugs. C. A. Marsden & D. J. Heal. (Frontiers in Pharmacology & Therapeutics Ser.). (Illus.). 334p. 1992. 135.00 (*0-632-02883-1*) Blackwell Sci.

Central Services Policy & Procedure Guideline Manual. Diane Howery. 1991. 70.00 (*1-879575-09-4*) Acad Med Sys.

Central Standard Time. Harlan Hatcher. 1993. reprint ed. lib. bdg. 89.00 (*0-7812-5370-5*) Rprt Serv.

Central State University. Ed. by William Strode & William Butler. (Illus.). 112p. 1991. 39.00 (*0-916509-66-4*) Harmony Hse Pub LO.

***Central Station Signaling Systems.** (Seventy Ser.). 1993. pap. 32.25 (*0-614-03112-5*, 72-93) Natl Fire Prot.

Central Still: Circle & Sphere in Thoreau's Prose. Pref. by Richard Tuerk. (De Proprietatibus Litterarum, Ser. Practica: No. 98). 104p. 1975. pap. text ed. 23.10 (*90-279-3317-0*) Mouton.

Central Tendency & Variability. Herbert F. Weisberg. (Quantitative Applications in the Social Sciences Ser.: Vol. 83). (Illus.). 96p. (C). 1992. pap. text ed. 9.95 (*0-8039-4007-6*) Sage.

Central Texas Gardener. Cheryl Hazeltine & Joan Filvaroff. LC 79-7409. (Illus.). 242p. 1980. 18.95 (*0-89096-078-X*); pap. 11.95 (*0-89096-086-0*) Tex A&M Univ Pr.

Central Themes & Principles of Ericksonian Therapy. Ed. by Stephen R. Lankton. LC 87-13831. (Ericksonian Monographs: No. 2). 152p. 1987. 26.95 (*0-87630-470-6*) Brunner-Mazel.

Central Themes in Early Modern Philosophy: Essays Presented to Jonathan Bennett. Ed. by Jan Cover & Mark Kolstad. LC 90-44730. 350p. (C). 1990. lib. bdg. 34.95 (*0-87220-110-4*); pap. text ed. 16.95 (*0-87220-109-0*) Hackett Pub.

Central Thought. Karlyn Kamm & Gerald Chastain, Jr. (Solar Reading - Flight One Ser.). (J). (gr. 3). Date not set. disk 70.00 (*0-912899-10-7*) Lrning Multi-Systs.

Central Thought. Karlyn Kamm & Gerald Chastain, Jr. (Solar Reading - Flight Two Ser.). (J). (gr. 5). Date not set. disk 95.00 (*0-912899-14-X*) Lrning Multi-Systs.

***Central Tire Inflation Systems - Managing the Vehicle to Surface.** 1994. pap. 45.00 (*1-56091-580-3*, SP1061) Soc Auto Engineers.

Central Tribes of the North-Eastern Bantu. John Middleton. LC 76-44758. reprint ed. 27.50 (*0-404-15952-4*) AMS Pr.

Central Tribes of the North-Eastern Bantu: The Kikuyu Including Embu, Meru, Mere, Chuka, Mwimbi, Tharaka, & the Kamba of Kenya. John Middleton & Greet Kershaw. LC 76-351844. (Ethnographic Survey of Africa: East Central Africa Ser.: Pt. 5). 108p. pap. 30.80 (*0-8357-6962-3*, 2039022) Bks Demand.

***Central Valley Cities Street Guide & Directory: Zip Code Edition, 1995.** Thomas Bros. Maps Staff. (Illus.). 168p. 1994. pap. 23.95 (*0-88130-748-3*) Thomas Bros Maps.

Central Valley Cities Street Guide & Directory: 1993 Edition. (Illus.). 168p. pap. 17.95 (*0-88130-529-4*) Thomas Bros Maps.

Central Valley Cities Street Guide & Directory, 1990. Thomas Bros. Maps Staff. (Illus.). 168p. 1990. 17.95 (*0-88130-424-7*) Thomas Bros Maps.

Central Valley Counties. David W. Kean. (Wide Places in the California Roads: The Encyclopedia of California's Small Towns Ser.: Vol. 4). (Illus.). 336p. (Orig.). Date not set. pap. write for info. (*1-884261-03-5*) Concord Pr CA.

Central Valley Gate. 64p. 1992. per., pap. 12.00 (*0-87431-335-X*, 20573) West End Games.

***Central Vermont: The South End: Remembering the Banana Belt.** Robert P. Brittin. (Illus.). 84p. 1995. pap. 20.95 (*0-942035-32-1*) South Platte.

Central Workers' Circle of St. Petersburg, 1889-94: A Case Study of the Workers' Intelligentsia. Michael Share. Ed. by William H. McNeill & Barbara Jelavich. (Modern European History Ser.). 349p. 1987. lib. bdg. 15.00 (*0-8240-8063-7*) Garland.

Central Zionist Archives, 1933-1945: Jerusalem. Ed. by Francis R. Nicosia. LC 89-16915. (Archives of the Holocaust Ser.: Vol. 3). 450p. 1990. 115.00 (*0-8240-5485-7*) Garland.

Central Zionist Archives 1939-1945, Jerusalem. Ed. by Francis R. Nicosia. LC 89-16915. (Archives of the Holocaust Ser.: Vol. 4). 470p. 1990. reprint ed. 125.00 (*0-8240-5486-5*) Garland.

***Centralia: A Pictorial History.** George E. Ross. (Illinois Pictorial History Ser.). (Illus.). 1992. write for info. (*0-943963-31-1*) G Bradley.

Centralia Case: Three Views of the Armistice Day Tragedy at Centralia, Washington, November 11, 1919. Ralph Chaplin et al. LC 77-160845. (Civil Liberties in American History Ser.). 1971. reprint ed. lib. bdg. 35.00 (*0-306-70211-8*) Da Capo.

Centralia Dead March. Thomas Churchill. LC 79-9146. 214p. 1980. pap. 9.95 (*0-915306-17-4*) Curbstone.

Centralia Mine Fire. Leonard Kress. LC 87-27351. 1987. pap. 4.00 (*0-9613984-3-4*) Flume Pr.

Centralia Tragedy of Nineteen Nineteen: Elmer Smith & the Wobblies. Tom Copeland. LC 93-13453. (Illus.). 256p. (C). 1993. 35.00 (*0-295-97211-4*); pap. 17.50 (*0-295-97274-2*) U of Wash Pr.

Centrality & Commonality: An Essay on Confucian Religiousness: A Revised & Enlarged Edition of Centrality & Commonality: An Essay on Chung-yung. Wei-ming Tu. LC 88-33718. (Chinese Philosophy & Culture Ser.). 165p. (C). 1989. 57.50 (*0-88706-927-4*); pap. 18.95 (*0-88706-928-2*) State U NY Pr.

Centrality of Central Asia. Andre G. Frank. 64p. 1993. pap. text ed. 15.00 (*90-5383-079-0*, Pub. by VU Univ Pr NE) Paul & Co Pubs.

Centrality of Metaphors to Biblical Thought: A Method for Interpreting the Bible. Peter W. Macky. LC 89-49023. (Studies in the Bible & Early Christianity: Vol. 19). 312p. 1990. lib. bdg. 99.95 (*0-88946-619-X*) E Mellen.

Centrality of the Cross. Jessie Penn-Lewis. 1993. pap. 4.95 (*0-87508-939-9*) Chr Lit.

Centralization & Decentralization in Economic Policy. Jan Tinbergen. LC 81-2723. (Contributions to Economic Analysis Ser.: No. 6). 80p. 1981. reprint ed. text ed. 59.75 (*0-313-23077-3*, TICD, Greenwood Pr) Greenwood.

Centralization & Power in Social Service in Delivery Systems. J. Rogers Hollingsworth & Robert Hanneman. 1983. lib. bdg. 56.00 (*0-89838-142-8*) Kluwer Ac.

Centralization & the Law: Scientific Legal Education, an Illustration. Intro. by Melville M. Bigelow. LC 72-181856. xx, 296p. 1972. reprint ed. text ed. 16.50 (*0-8377-2004-4*) Rothman.

Centralization of Administration in New York State. John A. Fairlie. LC 77-77990. (Columbia University. Studies in the Social Sciences: Vol. 25). reprint ed. 34.50 (*0-404-51025-6*) AMS Pr.

Centralization of Administration in Ohio. Samuel P. Orth. LC 68-56679. (Columbia University Studies in the Social Sciences Ser.: No. 43). reprint ed. 27.50 (*0-404-51043-4*) AMS Pr.

Centralization vs. Decentralization in Organizing the Controller's Department. Herbert A. Simon et al. LC 77-90343. 1978. reprint ed. text ed. 20.00 (*0-914348-24-8*) Scholars Bk.

Centralized Administration of Liquor Laws in the American Commonwealths. Clement M. Sites. LC 68-56687. (Columbia University. Studies in the Social Sciences: No. 28). reprint ed. 29.50 (*0-404-51028-0*) AMS Pr.

Centralized Administration of Public Buildings. 78p. 1984. 20.00 (*0-917084-46-2*) Am Public Works.

Centralized & Automatic Controls in Ships. D. Gray. LC 66-28418. 1966. 104.00 (*0-08-012084-9*, Pub. by Pergamon Repr UK) Franklin.

Centralized & Distributed Operating Systems. Gary J. Nutt. 384p. 1991. text ed. 62.00 (*0-13-122326-7*, 270610) P-H.

An Asterisk (*) at the beginning of an entry indicates that the title is appearing in BIP for the first time.

An Asterisk (*) at the beginning of an entry indicates that the title is appearing in BIP for the first time.

1123

C

Century of Biblical Archaeology. P. R. Moorey. LC 92-19808. 208p. (Orig.). 1992. pap. 14.99 (*0-664-25392-X*) Westminster John Knox.

Century of Biological Research. Harlow B. Mills et al. Ed. by Frank N. Egerton, 3rd. LC 77-74240. (History of Ecology Ser.). (Illus.). 1978. reprint ed. lib. bdg. 17.95 (*0-405-10409-X*) Ayer.

Century of Black Surgeons: The U. S. A. Experience. Ed. by Margaret M. Kosiba. 973p. 1991. reprint ed. 75.00 (*0-9617380-0-6*); reprint ed. text ed. 75.00 (*0-685-48806-3*); reprint ed. lib. bdg. 75.00 (*0-685-48805-5*) C H Organ.

Century of British Painters. Richard Redgrave & Samuel Redgrave. Ed. by Ruthven Todd. (Landmarks in Art History Ser.). (Illus.). 622p. 1981. pap. 19.95 (*0-8014-9217-3*) Cornell U Pr.

Century of Calculus, Set. Ed. by T. M. Apostol et al. 500p. 1992. pap. 70.00 (*0-88385-207-1*) Math Assn.

Century of Calculus, 1894-1968, Pt. I. Ed. by T. M. Apostol et al. (Raymond W. Brink Selected Mathematical Papers). 500p. 1992. pap. 39.00 (*0-88385-205-5*) Math Assn.

Century of Calculus, 1969-1991, Pt. II. Ed. by T. M. Apostol et al. (Raymond W. Brink Selected Mathematical Papers). 500p. 1992. pap. 39.00 (*0-88385-206-3*) Math Assn.

Century of Cameras. rev. ed. Eaton S. Lothrop, Jr. LC 73-88444. (Illus.). 196p. 1982. pap. 24.00 (*0-87100-163-2*, 2163) Morgan.

Century of Caring. Ohio Veterinary Medical Association Staff. Ed. by Flournoy & Gibbs, Inc. Staff. (Illus.). 132p. 1984. 30.00 (*0-9613273-0-8*) Ohio Vet.

Century of Caring: A History of the Guelph Humane Society. Bob Rutter. (Illus.). 96p. (Orig.). 1993. pap. 11.95 (*1-879260-13-1*) Evanston Pub.

Century of Caring: One Hundred Years of American Realism. (Illus.). 64p. 1986. pap. 12.00 (*0-933742-09-6*) Kalamazoo Inst Arts.

Century of Caring: The Upjohn Story. Robert D. Carlisle. LC 86-70731. 1987. write for info. (*0-87502-191-3*) Benjamin Co.

Century of Catholic Social Thought: Essays on 'Rerum Novarum' & Nine other Key Documents. Ed. by George Weigel & Robert Royal. 195p. 1991. lib. bdg. 49.50 (*0-89633-155-5*); pap. 14.95 (*0-89633-156-3*) Ethics & Public Policy.

C

Century of Ceramics in the United States: 1878-1978 see American Ceramics: Eighteen Seventy-Six to the Present

Century of Challenge: The New Jersey State Federation of Women's Clubs First 100 Years. First Centuryans Committee Staff. Ed. by Grace M. Williams. LC 93-86926. (Illus.). 500p. 1994. 25.00 (*0-9638106-0-X*) NJSFWC.

Century of Challenge: The Story of Southern College. Dennis Pettibone. 356p. (C). 1992. 44.95 (*0-9634258-0-3*) So Coll Seventh-day.

Century of Champions: The Centennial History of Alabama Football. Wayne Hester. (Illus.). 240p. (Orig.). 1991. pap. 15.00 (*1-878561-05-7*) Seacoast AL.

Century of Change in Eastern Africa. Ed. by W. Arens. (World Anthropology Ser.). xii, 310p. 1976. 44.65 (*90-279-7879-4*) Mouton.

Century of Change in Gutemalan Textiles. Ann Row. (Illus.). 150p. 1981. pap. 18.95 (*0-89192-328-4*, Ctr Inter-Am Rel) Interbk Inc.

Century of Chemistry: The Role of Chemists & the American Chemical Society. Ed. by Kenneth M. Reese. LC 76-6126. 468p. 1976. 17.95 (*0-8412-0307-5*) Am Chemical.

Century of Childhood, Eighteen Twenty to Nineteen Twenty. Marylynn S. Heininger et al. (Illus.). 1984. pap. 9.95 (*0-940365-02-2*) Strong Mus.

Century of Childhood, 1820-1920. Mary L. Heininger et al. (Illus.). 142p. (Orig.). 1984. pap. 9.95 (*0-318-23127-1*) Strong Mus.

Century of Children's Baseball Stories. Debra Dagavarian. (J). (gr. 4-7). 1990. pap. 7.95 (*0-9625132-0-2*) Cyberbooks.

Century of Children's Baseball Stories. Ed. by Debra A. Dagavarian. 200p. (Orig.). (J). 1992. lib. bdg. 16.95 (*0-88736-832-8*) Mecklermedia.

Century of Children's Baseball Stories, No. 2. Ed. by Debra A. Dagavarian. 200p. (Orig.). (J). (gr. 5 up). 1993. 16.95 (*0-9625132-2-9*) Mecklermedia.

Century of Children's Books. Florence V. Barry. 1972. 59.95 (*0-87968-828-9*) Gordon Pr.

Century of Children's Sports Stories. Ed. by Debra A. Dagavarian. 200p. (J). (gr. 5-8). 1993. lib. bdg. 16.95 (*0-88736-852-2*) Mecklermedia.

Century of Christian Science Healing. Intro. by Christian Science Board of Directors Staff. LC 66-15060. 256p. 1966. pap. 9.95 (*0-87510-067-8*) Christian Sci.

Century of Church History: The Legacy of Philip Schaff. Ed. by Henry W. Bowden. LC 87-15630. 398p. 1988. text ed. 37.50 (*0-8093-1439-8*) S Ill U Pr.

Century of Civil Rights: With a Study of State Law Against Discrimination by Theodore Leskes. Milton R. Konvitz. LC 61-8988. 303p. reprint ed. pap. 86.40 (*0-317-09422-X*, 2015388) Bks Demand.

Century of Civil Rights: With a Study of State Law Against Discrimination by Theodore Leskes. Milton R. Konvitz. LC 83-12762. viii, 293p. 1983. reprint ed. text ed. 59.75 (*0-313-24123-6*, K0CE, Greenwood Pr) Greenwood.

Century of Color: Ogunquit, Maine's Art Colony, 1886-1986. (Illus.). 1988. 24.95 (*0-317-93352-3*) Barn Gallery.

Century of Concern: A History of the American Association on Mental Deficiency 1876-1976. W. Sloan. 1976. pap. 10.00 (*0-940898-01-2*) Am Assn Mental.

Century of Conflict, 1821-1913: Incidents in the Lives of William Neale & William A. Neale, Early Settlers in South Texas. Ed. by John C. Rayburn et al. LC 76-1556. (Chicano Heritage Ser.). (Illus.). 1977. reprint ed. 16.95 (*0-405-09520-1*) Ayer.

Century of Controversy. Elman R. Service. (Studies in Anthropology). (C). 1985. text ed. 65.00 (*0-12-637380-9*); pap. text ed. 36.00 (*0-12-637382-5*) Acad Pr.

Century of Creepy Stories. LC 74-37261. (Short Story Index Reprint Ser.). 1977. reprint ed. 56.95 (*0-8369-4072-5*) Ayer.

Century of Darwin. Ed. by Samuel A. Barnett. LC 71-76891. (Essay Index Reprint Ser.). 1977. 23.95 (*0-8369-1019-2*) Ayer.

Century of Debt Crises in Latin America: From Independence to the Great Depression, 1820-1930. Carlos Marichal. 352p. 1989. text ed. 55.00 (*0-691-07792-4*); pap. text ed. 19.95 (*0-691-02299-2*) Princeton U Pr.

Century of Developmental Psychology. Ed. by Ross D. Parke et al. 695p. 1994. text ed. 49.95 (*1-55798-233-3*); pap. text ed. 29.95 (*1-55798-238-4*, 431-6411) Am Psychol.

Century of Diplomatic Blue Books, 1814-1914. H. W. Temperley & L. M. Penson. 600p. 1966. reprint ed. 45.00 (*0-7146-1519-6*, Pub. by F Cass Pubs UK) Intl Spec Bk.

Century of Dishonor: A Sketch of the United States Government's Dealing with Some of the Indian Tribes. Helen Jackson. LC 71-108499. x, 514p. 1972. reprint ed. 49.00 (*0-403-00382-2*) Scholarly.

Century of Dishonor: A Sketch of the United States Government's Dealings. Helen Jackson. 1988. reprint ed. lib. bdg. 79.00 (*0-7812-0363-5*) Rprt Serv.

***Century of Dishonor: A Sketch of the United States Government's Dealings with Some of the Indian Tribes.** Helen H. Jackson. LC 94-24389. 552p. 1995. pap. 14.95 (*0-8061-2726-0*) U of Okla Pr.

Century of Dutch Manuscript Illumination. L. M. Delaisse. (California Studies in the History of Art: No. VI). (Illus.). 1968. 100.00 (*0-520-00315-2*) U CA Pr.

Century of Economics: One Hundred Years of the Royal Economic Society & the Economic Journal. Ed. by John D. Hey & Donald Winch. (Illus.). 288p. (C). 1990. text ed. 54.95 (*0-631-16745-5*) Blackwell Pubs.

Century of Electrical Engineering & Computer Science at MIT, 1882-1982. Karl Wildes & Nilo Lindgren. (Illus.). 480p. 1985. 27.50 (*0-262-23119-0*) MIT Pr.

Century of Emblems: Curiously Culled & Delightfully Displayed. An Introductory Anthology. Charles Moseley. (Illus.). 250p. 1989. text ed. 54.95 (*0-85967-750-8*, Pub. by Scolar Pr UK) Ashgate Pub Co.

Century of English Farce. Leo Hughes. LC 79-13278. 307p. 1980. reprint ed. text ed. 59.75 (*0-313-21993-1*, HUCEF, Greenwood Pr) Greenwood.

Century of Enterprise: St. Louis, 1894-1994. Gray Rockwell. Ed. by Candace O'Connor & Lee A. Schreiner. (Illus.). 135p. (Orig.). 1993. pap. 14.95 (*1-883982-02-2*) MO Hist Soc.

Century of Ethnomusicological Thought. Ed. by Kaye Shelemay. LC 90-3567. (Ethnomusicology Ser.: Vol. 7). 392p. 1990. reprint ed. 86.00 (*0-8240-6499-2*) Garland.

Century of European Migrations, 1830-1930. Ed. by Rudolph J. Vecoli & Suzanne M. Sinke. (Statue of Liberty-Ellis Island Centennial Ser.). (Illus.). 408p. 1991. 44.95 (*0-252-01796-X*) U of Ill Pr.

Century of Excavation in Palestine. Robert A. Macalister. Ed. by Moshe Davis. LC 77-70720. (America & the Holy Land Ser.). (Illus.). 1977. reprint ed. lib. bdg. 35.95 (*0-405-10265-8*) Ayer.

***Century of Faith: One Hundred Years in the Life of the Las Placitas Presbyterian Church.** Suzanne S. Forrest. (Illus.). 200p. 1995. lib. bdg. 18.00 (*0-9644349-0-3*); pap. 12.00 (*0-9644349-1-1*) Las Placitas.

Century of Fine Carriage Clocks. Joseph Fanelli & Charles Terwilliger. (Illus.). 224p. 1987. 59.95 (*0-916316-04-1*) Arlington Bk.

Century of Fisheries in North America. Ed. by N. G. Benson. LC 73-129249. (AFS Special Publication Ser.: No. 7). 330p. 1970. text ed. 8.50 (*0-913235-05-9*) Am Fisheries Soc.

Century of French Painting: Fourteen Hundred to Fifteen Hundred. Grete Ring. LC 79-83857. (Illus.). 1979. reprint ed. lib. bdg. 50.00 (*0-87817-249-1*) Hacker.

Century of French Verse: Brief Biographical & Critical Notices of Thirty-Three French Poets of the Nineteenth Century. William J. Robertson. LC 77-11481. (Symbolists Ser.). 392p. reprint ed. 52.50 (*0-404-16342-4*) AMS Pr.

***Century of Fun: A Pictorial History of New England Amusement Parks.** Bob Goldsack. (Illus.). 144p. 1993. pap. 27.95 (*1-880545-01-2*) Midway Mus.

***Century of Gold: (Yukon Gold: High Hopes & Dashed Dreams)** James Preyde & Susan Preyde. 1995. pap. 15.95 (*0-88839-362-8*) Hancock House.

Century of Great Actors Seventeen Fifty to Nineteen Fifty. Cecil F. Armstrong. 1972. 24.95 (*0-405-09134-6*, 116) Ayer.

Century of Greco-Roman Philology: Featuring the American Philological Association & the Society of Biblical Literature. Frederick W. Danker. LC 85-30412. (Society of Biblical Literature Ser.). 320p. 1988. 28.95 (*0-89130-985-3*, 06 11 12); pap. 20.95 (*0-89130-986-1*, 06 11 12) Scholars Pr GA.

Century of Growth: The Kachin Baptist Church of Burma. Herman Tegenfeldt. LC 74-4415. 540p. 1974. 11.95 (*0-87808-416-9*) William Carey Lib.

Century of Guns: A Sketch of the Leading Types of Sporting & Military Small Arms. H. J. Blanch. (Illus.). 1977. reprint ed. 25.00 (*0-7158-1156-8*) Charles River Bks.

Century of Handbags. Kate Dooner. (Illus.). 160p. 1993. pap. 29.95 (*0-88740-465-0*) Schiffer.

Century of Hero Worship see Cult of the Superman

Century of Heroes: One Hundred Years of Ole Miss Football. Longstreet Press Staff. LC 92-84005. (Illus.). 192p. 1993. 29.95 (*1-56352-072-9*) Longstreet Pr Inc.

Century of Higher Education for American Women. Mabel Newcomer. LC 75-40214. 1976. reprint ed. 19.95 (*0-89201-002-9*) Zenger Pub.

Century of Honors. LC 84-6712. 456p. 1984. 29.95 (*0-87942-176-2*, PC01719) Inst Electrical.

Century of Horror Stories. Ed. by Dennis Wheatley. LC 71-160952. (Short Story Index Reprint Ser.). 1977. reprint ed. 44.95 (*0-8369-3931-X*) Ayer.

Century of Human Capital by Education & Training. August C. Bolino. 350p. 1989. 30.00 (*0-939133-02-4*) Kensington Hist.

Century of Indian Orchids. J. D. Hooker. (Calutta Royal Bot. Gard. Ser.). (Illus.). 1967. 120.00 (*3-7682-0464-2*) Lubrecht & Cramer.

Century of Indian Orchids, Vol. V, Pt. 1. J. D. Hooker. (C). 1978. text ed. 750.00 (*0-89771-641-8*, Pub. by Intl Bk Distr II) St Mut.

Century of Indian Orchids, Vol. V, Pt. 1. J. D. Hooker. 68p. 1978. reprint ed. 525.00 (*0-685-54026-X*, Pub. by Intl Bk Distr II) St Mut.

Century of Industrial Progress. Ed. by Frederick W. Wile. LC 73-2540. (Big Business; Economic Power in a Free Society Ser.). 1973. reprint ed. 40.95 (*0-405-05119-0*) Ayer.

Century of Innovation: A History of European & American Theatre & Drama, 1870-1970. 2nd ed. Oscar G. Brockett & Robert R. Findlay. 480p. 1990. text ed. 60.00 (*0-205-12878-5*, H28780) Allyn.

Century of International Dermatological Congresses: An Illustrated History, 1889-1992. Walter B. Shelley & E. Dorinda Shelley. (Illus.). 96p. (C). 1992. 36.00 (*1-85070-432-5*) Prthnon Pub.

Century of Judging: A Political History of the Washington Supreme Court. Charles H. Sheldon. LC 87-16081. (Illus.). 392p. 1988. 35.00 (*0-295-96524-X*) U of Wash Pr.

Century of Law Reform: Twelve Lectures on the Changes in the Law of England During the Nineteenth Century. LC 93-78458. 448p. 1993. reprint ed. 80.00 (*1-56169-046-5*) W W Gaunt.

Century of Light, Set. James A. Cox. LC 78-19204. (Illus.). 1979. 17.50 (*0-87502-062-3*) Benjamin Co.

Century of Marketing Series, 33 bks. Ed. by Henry Assael. (Illus.). 1978. lib. bdg. 1,157.50 (*0-405-11156-8*) Ayer.

Century of Mathematics in America, Pt. I. Ed. by Peter Duren. (History of Mathematics Ser.: Vol. 1). 477p. 1992. reprint ed. 75.00 (*0-8218-0124-4*, HMATH/1C) Am Math.

Century of Mathematics in America, Pt. II. P. Duren et al. LC 88-22155. (HMATH Ser.: Vol. 2). 585p. 1992. 87.00 (*0-8218-0130-9*, HMATH-2) Am Math.

Century of Mathematics in America, 3 vols., Set. (History of Mathematics Ser.). 1737p. 232.00 (*0-8218-0138-4*, HMATHSETC); 162.00 (*0-8218-0152-X*) Am Math.

Century of Mathematics in America, Pt. III. Ed. by P. Duren et al. (HMATH Ser.: Vol. 3). 675p. 1991. 93.00 (*0-8218-0136-8*, HMATH-3) Am Math.

Century of Mathematics Through the Eyes of the Monthly. Ed. by John Ewing. 323p. 1994. 39.50 (*0-88385-457-0*) Math Assn.

Century of Ministry: The History of Trinity Lutheran Church. Ruth A. Peck. 140p. 1992. pap. 10.00 (*0-9632829-0-5*) Trinity Evang Luth.

Century of Model Trains. 2nd ed. A. Levy. (Illus.). 208p. (ENG & GER.). 1974. 45.00 (*0-911868-02-X*, C02) Carstens Pubns.

Century of Modern Hebrew Literary Criticism, 1784-1884. Morris Neiman. 1983. 25.00 (*0-88125-011-2*) Ktav.

Century of Mormon Cookery. Hermine B. Horman & Connie Fairbanks. (Illus.). 495p. (Orig.). 1984. reprint ed. pap. text ed. 15.95 (*1-880328-23-2*) Distinctive UT.

Century of Moses Montefiore. Ed. by V. D. Lipman & Sonia Lipman. LC 84-27225. (Littman Library of Jewish Civilization). (Illus.). 396p. 1985. 17.50 (*0-19-710041-4*, Pub. by Littman Lib Jew UK) Bnai Brith Bk.

Century of Municipal Progress, 1835-1935. Harold J. Laski et al. Ed. by H. J. Laski et al. LC 75-41171. reprint ed. 29.50 (*0-685-14561-1*) AMS Pr.

Century of Municipal Progress, 1835-1935. Ed. by Harold J. Laski et al. LC 77-27362. 511p. 1978. reprint ed. text ed. 75.00 (*0-313-20192-7*, LACE, Greenwood Pr) Greenwood.

Century of Municipal Progress, 1835-1935: From Self-Government to National Sovereignty. Harold J. Laski et al. Ed. by H. J. Laski & W. Ivor Jennings. LC 75-41171. reprint ed. 45.00 (*0-404-14561-2*) AMS Pr.

Century of Music-Making: The Lives of Josef & Rosina Lhevinne. Robert K. Wallace. LC 75-28908. (Illus.). 361p. reprint ed. 102.90 (*0-8357-9199-8*, 2055193) Bks Demand.

Century of Musical Humor & Show Business Wit. Walter K. Bauer. Ed. by Norman Levine. LC 88-90883. (Illus.). iv, 52p. (Orig.). 1988. pap. text ed. 5.95 (*0-9614120-9-7*) Plucked.

Century of Musicals in Black & White: An Encyclopedia of Musical Stage Works by, about, or Involving Black Americans. Bernard L. Peterson. LC 92-41976. 529p. 1993. text ed. 85.00 (*0-313-26657-3*, PEG, Greenwood Pr) Greenwood.

Century of Natural History. Ed. by J. C. Daniel. (Illus.). 958p. 1988. 35.00 (*0-19-562166-2*) OUP.

Century of Nature Stories, Vol. 1. Intro. by J. Robertson Scott. LC 72-5951. (Short Story Index Reprint Ser.). 1977. reprint ed. 52.95 (*0-8369-4197-7*) Ayer.

Century of Negro Migration. Carter G. Woodson. (BCL1 - U. S. History Ser.). 221p. 1991. reprint ed. lib. bdg. 79.00 (*0-7812-6090-6*) Rprt Serv.

Century of New & Rare Indian Plants. P. A. Bruhi. (C). 1988. 80.00 (*0-685-22290-X*, Scientific) St Mut.

Century of New & Rare Indian Plants, Vol. V, Pt. II. Royal Botanic Garden, Calcutta Staff et al. (Illus.). 1971. reprint ed. 50.00 (*0-88065-011-7*, Messers Today & Tomorrow) Scholarly Pubns.

Century of New Testament Study. John Riches. LC 93-23575. 1993. pap. 17.00 (*1-56338-064-1*) TPI PA.

Century of Nitrogen Fixation Research. Ed. by F. J. Bergersen & J. R. Postgate. (Illus.). 240p. 1987. text ed. 110.00 (*0-85403-327-0*) Scholium Intl.

Century of Parody & Imitation. Walter C. Jerrold. 1972. 59.95 (*0-87968-829-7*) Gordon Pr.

Century of Philadelphia Artists. Frank S. Schwarz. LC 88-90651. (Illus.). 72p. 1988. pap. text ed. 15.00 (*0-944067-01-8*) F S Schwarz.

Century of Philanthropy: A History of the Samuel N. & Mary Castle Foundation. (Illus.). 384p. 1992. pap. text ed. 24.95 (*0-8248-1470-3*) HI Hist Soc.

Century of Photographs, 1846-1946: Selected from the Collections of the Library of Congress. Renata V. Shaw. LC 79-21624. 211p. 1980. 20.00 (*0-8444-0295-8*, 030-000-00117-6) Lib Congress.

Century of Pioneering: A History of the Ursulines in New Orleans (1727-1827) Jane F. Heaney. 360p. 1993. 25.00 (*0-9635044-0-1*) Ursuline Sis.

Century of Planting: A History of the American Friends Mission in India. E. Anna Nixon. LC 85-72070. (Illus.). 493p. (Orig.). 1985. 16.95 (*0-913342-55-6*); pap. 11.95 (*0-913342-54-8*) Barclay Pr.

Century of Pointers - Field & Show. Jan Linzy. (Illus.). 450p. 1996. text ed. 59.95 (*1-55893-024-8*) Camino E E & Bk.

Century of Political Cartoons: Caricature in the United States from 1800 to 1900. Allan Nevins. (BCL1 - U. S. History Ser.). 190p. 1991. reprint ed. lib. bdg. 69.00 (*0-7812-6038-8*) Rprt Serv.

Century of Portuguese Fertility. Massimo Livi Bacci. LC 70-120758. (Office of Population Research Ser.). 1970. 37.50 (*0-691-09307-5*) Princeton U Pr.

Century of Progress. Ed. by Charles A. Beard. LC 79-128205. (Essay Index Reprint Ser.). 1977. 30.95 (*0-8369-1903-3*) Ayer.

Century of Progress. Fred Saberhagen. 1989. pap. 3.95 (*0-8125-5341-1*) Tor Bks.

Century of Progress: History of the New Mexico School for the Deaf. Marian Meyer. (Illus.). 1989. text ed. write for info. (*0-318-64812-1*) NM School Deaf.

Century of Progress in the Natural Sciences, 1853-1953. Ed. by Edward L. Kessel. LC 73-17827. (Natural Sciences in America Ser.). (Illus.). 824p. 1974. reprint ed. 59.95 (*0-405-05745-8*) Ayer.

Century of Protestant Theology. Alasdair I. Heron. LC 80-17409. 240p. 1980. pap. 14.99 (*0-664-24346-0*, Westminster) Westminster John Knox.

Century of Psychical Research: The Continuing Doubts & Affirmations; Proceedings of the International Conference, September 2-4, 1970. International Conference, France Staff. LC 73-153407. 1971. 16.00 (*0-912328-19-3*) Parapsych Foun.

Century of Psychology As Science. Ed. by Sigmund Koch & David E. Leary. 1022p. 1992. text ed. 49.95 (*1-55798-171-X*) Am Psychol.

Century of Pullman Cars, Vol II: The Palace Cars. Ralph L. Barger. Ed. by Terri Glaser & Wendy Burgio. (Illus.). 440p. 1990. 75.00 (*0-89778-140-6*, 10-6810) Greenberg Bks.

Century of Recollections: A Personal Account of Pioneer Life Written to Commerate Her 100 Years. Esther S. Gilliland. 132p. 1990. pap. 8.95 (*0-89992-122-1*) Coun India Ed.

Century of Research: Centennial History of the Arkansas Agricultural Experiment Station. Stephen F. Strausberg. (Illus.). (C). 1990. write for info. (*0-9622858-0-3*) UAAAES.

Century of Revivals, Vol. 31, Nos. 2-3. Ulysses G. Dietz & Newark Museum Quarterly. (Illus.). 64p. 1983. 4.00 (*0-686-39826-2*) Newark Mus.

***Century of Revolution: Social Movements Is Iran.** Ed. by John Foran. (Social Movements, Protest, & Contention Ser.: Vol. 2). 320p. 1994. text ed. 44.95x (*0-8166-2487-9*); pap. text ed. 19.95x (*0-8166-2488-7*) U of Minn Pr.

Century of Revolution, 1603-1714. Christopher Hill. (Illus.). 304p. 1982. pap. 9.95 (*0-393-30016-1*) Norton.

Century of Russian Agriculture: From Alexander Second to Khrushchev. Lazar Volin. LC 72-119075. (Russian Research Center Studies: No. 63). 654p. 1970. 48.50 (*0-674-10621-0*) HUP.

Century of Russian Ballet: Documents & Accounts, 1810-1910. Roland J. Wiley. (Illus.). 464p. 1991. 65.00 (*0-19-316416-7*) OUP.

Century of Science & Other Essays. John Fiske. (Notable American Authors Ser.). 1992. reprint ed. lib. bdg. 75.00 (*0-7812-2858-1*) Rprt Serv.

Century of Science Fiction. Damon Knight. 1976. 24.95 (*0-8488-0554-2*) Amereon Ltd.

Century of Science in America. Ed. by Edward S. Dana et al. LC 72-94344. (American Scientific Community, 1790-1920 Ser.). 1973. reprint ed. lib. bdg. 37.00 (*0-8420-1654-6*) Scholarly Res Inc.

Century of Sculpture in Texas, 1889-1989. Patricia D. Hendricks & Becky D. Reese. (Illus.). 200p. 1989. pap. 24.95 (*0-935213-18-X*) A M Huntington Art.

An Asterisk (*) at the beginning of an entry indicates that the title is appearing in BIP for the first time.

C

An Asterisk (*) at the beginning of an entry indicates that the title is appearing in BIP for the first time.

1125

Ceramic Materials for Electronics, Processing, Properties & Applications: Processing, Properties & Applications. 2nd expanded rev. ed. Ed. by Relva Buchanan. (Electrical Engineering & Electronics Ser.: Vol. 72). 560p. 1991. 175.00 (*0-8247-8194-5*) Dekker.

Ceramic Materials Research: Proceedings of Symposium A, European-Materials Research Society Conference, Strasbourg, France, 31 May-2 June, 1988. Ed. by R. Brook. 420p. 1989. 113.00 (*0-444-87318-X*) Elsevier.

Ceramic-Matrix Composites. Ed. by R. Warren. (Illus.). 256p. 1991. 133.95 (*0-412-02021-1*, A3601, Blackie & Son-Chapman NY) Routledge Chapman & Hall.

Ceramic Matrix Composites, No. GB-110R. Business Communications Co., Inc. Staff. 240p. 1990. 2,850.00 (*0-89336-791-5*) BCC.

Ceramic Matrix Composites: Components, Preparation, Microstructure & Properties. Ed. by R. Naslain & B. Harris. 346p. 1990. reprint ed. 171.00 (*1-85166-460-2*) Elsevier.

***Ceramic Matrix Composites - Advanced High-Temperature Structural Materials: 1994 MRS Fall Meeting, Boston, MA, Vol. 365.** Ed. by R. A. Lowden et al. (MRS Symposium Proceedings Ser.). 1995. 67.00 (*1-55899-266-9*, 365K4) Materials Res.

Ceramic Microstructures: Their Analysis, Significance & Production. Ed. by Richard M. Fulrath & Joseph A. Pask. LC 74-32351. 1028p. 1976. reprint ed. 89.50 (*0-88275-262-6*) Krieger.

Ceramic Microstructures '86: Role of Interfaces. Ed. by Joseph A. Pask & A. G. Evans. LC 87-22758. (Materials Science Research Ser.: Vol. 21). 1002p. 1987. 150.00 (*0-306-42681-1*, Plenum Pr) Plenum.

Ceramic Packaging of Electronic Circuits. G. Phillips. 1992. text ed. write for info. (*0-442-00665-9*) Van Nos Reinhold.

***Ceramic Precursor Technology & Its Applications.** Narula. 308p. 1995. write for info. (*0-8247-9310-2*) Dekker.

Ceramic Processing Before Firing. Ed. by George Y. Onoda, Jr. & Larry L. Hench. LC 77-10553. 490p. 1978. text ed. 144.00 (*0-471-65410-8*, Wiley-Interscience) Wiley.

***Ceramic Processing Science & Technology.** Ed. by Hans Hausner et al. LC 95-12137. (Ceramic Transactions Ser.: Vol. 51). (Illus.). 820p. 1995. 83.00 (*0-944904-89-0*) Am Ceramic.

Ceramic Production & Distribution: An Integrated Approach. Ed. by George J. Bey, III & Christopher A. Pool. (Special Studies in Archaeological Research). 342p. (C). 1992. text ed. 79.00 (*0-8133-7920-2*) Westview.

***Ceramic Production in the America Southwest.** Ed. by Barbara J. Mills & Patricia L. Crown. LC 95-8771. 1995. write for info. (*0-8165-1508-5*) U of Ariz Pr.

Ceramic Projects. Ed. by Thomas Sellers. 1963. 2.95 (*0-934706-08-5*) Prof Pubns Ohio.

Ceramic Raw Materials. Ed. by D. J. Renzo. LC 87-22002. (Illus.). 890p. 1988. 96.00 (*0-8155-1143-4*) Noyes.

Ceramic Raw Materials. 2nd rev. ed. W. E. Worrall. (Institute of Ceramics Texbook Ser.). (Illus.). 120p. 1982. 48.00 (*0-08-028710-7*, Pub. by Pergamon Repr UK) Franklin.

Ceramic Raw Materials. Worall. (Illus.). 111p. (C). reprint ed. 25.00 (*1-878907-30-1*) TechBooks.

Ceramic Sequence at Uaxactun, Guatemala, 2 vols., Set. Robert E. Smith. (Publication Ser.: No. 20). (Illus.). 388p. 1955. 25.00 (*0-939238-22-5*) Tulane MARI.

Ceramic Sequence in Colima: Capacha, an Early Phase. Isabel Kelly. LC 80-21301. (Anthropological Papers: No. 37). 110p. 1980. pap. 9.95 (*0-8165-0565-9*) U of Ariz Pr.

Ceramic Sequence in the Chaco Canyon, New Mexico, & Its Relation to the Cultures of the San Juan Basin. Frank H. Roberts. LC 91-20404. (Evolution of North American Indians Ser.). 350p. 1991. 30.00 (*0-8240-2513-X*) Garland.

***Ceramic Sequences at Tres Zapotes, Veracruz, Mexico.** Philip Drucker. (Bureau of American Ethnology Bulletins Ser.). 148p. 1995. lib. bdg. 79.00 (*0-7812-4140-5*) Rprt Serv.

Ceramic Spectrum: A Simplified Approach to Glaze & Color Development. Robin Hopper. LC 83-70777. (Illus.). 224p. 1984. 48.00 (*0-8019-7275-2*) Chilton.

***Ceramic Stratigraphy at Cerro De las Mesas, Veracruz, Mexico.** Philip Drucker. (Bureau of American Ethnology Bulletins Ser.). 95p. 1995. lib. bdg. 79.00 (*0-7812-4141-3*) Rprt Serv.

Ceramic Studies of the Historic Periods in Ancient Nubia. Florence C. Lister. (Nubian Ser.: No. 2). reprint ed. 30.00 (*0-404-60686-5*) AMS Pr.

***Ceramic Study of Virginia Archeology.** Clifford Evans. (Bureau of American Ethnology Bulletins Ser.). 195p. 1995. lib. bdg. 79.00 (*0-7812-4160-X*) Rprt Serv.

***Ceramic Style: Making & Decorating Patterned Ceramic Ware.** John Hinchcliffe & Wendy Barber. (Illus.). 160p. 1995. 29.95 (*0-304-34392-7*, Pub. by Cassell UK) Sterling.

Ceramic Superconductors. Ed. by J. A. Cogordan et al. (Progress in High Temperature Super Conductivity Ser.: Vol. 26). 208p. (C). 1991. text ed. 74.00 (*981-02-0212-1*) World Scientific Pub.

Ceramic Technology for Potters & Sculptors. Yvonne H. Cuff. (Illus.). 368p. (Orig.). (C). 1995. text ed. 39.95 (*0-8122-3071-X*) U of Pa Pr.

Ceramic Technology for Potters & Sculptors. Yvonne H. Cuff. (Illus.). 368p. (Orig.). (C). 1995. pap. 21.95 (*0-8122-1377-7*) U of Pa Pr.

Ceramic Test Procedures. Investment Casting Institute Staff. (Illus.). 350p. 1979. 105.00 (*0-317-94091-0*, ICI-B6) ICI Dallas.

Ceramic Theory & Cultural Process. Dean E. Arnold. (New Studies in Archaeology). (Illus.). 279p. 1988. pap. 22.95 (*0-521-27259-9*) Cambridge U Pr.

Ceramic Tile Manual. 3rd ed. George N. Lavenberg. Ed. by Sam Jaffe. (Illus.). 416p. 1988. text ed. 49.95 (*0-07-036651-9*) McGraw.

Ceramic Tile Setting. John P. Bridge. 1992. text ed. 24.95 (*0-07-007737-1*); pap. text ed. 14.95 (*0-07-007738-X*) McGraw.

Ceramic Tile Setting. John P. Bridge. (Illus.). 240p. 1992. 24.95 (*0-8306-2573-9*, 2803); pap. 14.95 (*0-8306-2572-0*, 2803) TAB Bks.

Ceramic Traditions of South-East Asia. John S. Guy. (Asia Collection). (Illus.). 80p. 1990. 38.00 (*0-19-588934-7*) OUP.

Ceramic Uncles & Celluloid Mammies. Patricia A. Turner. LC 93-38542. 1994. 12.95 (*0-385-46784-2*, Anchor NY) Doubleday.

Ceramic Windchimes. John W. Conrad. (Illus.). 80p. (Orig.). 1985. 6.95 (*0-935921-00-1*); pap. 10.70 (*0-935921-01-X*) Falcon Co.

Ceramics. Philip Rawson. LC 83-12480. (Illus.). 203p. 1983. reprint ed. pap. 17.95 (*0-8122-1156-1*) U of Pa Pr.

Ceramics: A Potter's Handbook. Glenn C. Nelson. LC 83-12633. (Illus.). (C). 1984. pap. text ed. 34.75 (*0-03-063227-7*) HB Coll Pubs.

Ceramics: A Potter's Handbook. 5th ed. Glenn C. Nelson. LC 83-12633. (Illus.). (C). 1984. 34.50 (*0-03-064163-2*) HB Coll Pubs.

Ceramics: Industrial Processing & Testing. 2nd ed. John T. Jones & Michael F. Berard. LC 93-7316. (Illus.). 336p. (C). 1993. pap. text ed. 34.95 (*0-8138-0291-1*) Iowa St U Pr.

Ceramics: Mastering the Craft. Richard Zakin. LC 89-45966. (Illus.). 304p. 1990. pap. 22.95 (*0-8019-7991-9*) Chilton.

Ceramics: Physical & Chemical Fundamentals. Hermann Salmang. LC 62-52610. 390p. reprint ed. pap. 111.20 (*0-317-42299-5*, 2055832) Bks Demand.

Ceramics & Glass at the Essex Institute. Tanya Barter et al. LC 85-71260. (E.I. Museum Booklet Ser.). (Illus.). 64p. 1985. pap. 5.95 (*0-88389-088-7*, Essx Institute) Peabody Essex Mus.

Ceramics & Glasses. (Engineered Materials Handbook Ser.: Vol. 4). 1217p. 1991. 147.00 (*0-87170-282-7*, 6912U) ASM Intl.

Ceramics & Ideology: Salado Polychrome Pottery. Patricia L. Crown. LC 93-35700. (Illus.). 262p. 1994. 45.00x (*0-8263-1477-5*) U of NM Pr.

Ceramics & Inorganic Crystals for Optics, Electro-Optics & Nonlinear Conversion, Vol. 968. Ed. by R. W. Schwartz. 1988. 38.00 (*0-8194-0003-3*) SPIE.

Ceramics & Pottery. Photos by Mark Seelen. LC 93-47526. 64p. 1994. 16.95 (*0-8118-0763-0*) Chronicle Bks.

***Ceramics & Print.** Paul Scott. (Illus.). 127p. 1995. pap. text ed. 24.95 (*0-8122-1575-3*) U of Pa Pr.

Ceramics Applications in Manufacturing. Ed. by D. Richerson. LC 88-63021. 250p. 1989. 42.00 (*0-87263-339-X*) SME.

Ceramics Arts Studio: Identification & Price Guide. Michael Schneider. LC 94-65427. (Illus.). 112p. (Orig.). 1994. pap. 24.95 (*0-88740-608-4*) Schiffer.

Ceramics, Chronology & Community Patterns: An Archaeological Study at Moundville. Vincas Steponaitis. LC 81-17672. (Studies in Archaeology). 1982. text ed. 63.00 (*0-12-666280-0*) Acad Pr.

Ceramics Databook. H. Yanagida. 768p. 1987. text ed. 411.00 (*2-88124-247-2*) Gordon & Breach.

Ceramics for the Archaeologist. Anna O. Shepard. LC 56-4818. (Illus.). (C). 1985. reprint ed. 15.00 (*0-87279-620-5*, 609) Carnegie Inst.

Ceramics Handbook: A Guide to Glaze Calculation, Materials & Processes. Charles McKee. (Illus.). 176p. (C). 1984. pap. text ed. 24.95 (*0-89863-072-X*) Star Pub CA.

Ceramics in Advanced Energy Technologies. Ed. by H. Krockel et al. 568p. 1984. lib. bdg. 167.00 (*90-277-1787-7*) Kluwer Ac.

Ceramics in America: Winterthur Conference Report 1972. Ed. by Ian M. Quimby. LC 72-96715. (Winterthur Conference Report). 374p. 1980. reprint ed. pap. 16.95 (*0-8139-0476-5*) U Pr of Va.

Ceramics in Clinical Applications. Ed. by P. Vencenzini. 476p. 1987. 187.25 (*0-444-42777-5*) Elsevier.

***Ceramics in Energy Applications.** Institute of Energy. 1994. pap. 145.00 (*0-08-042133-4*, Pergamon Pr) Elsevier.

***Ceramics in Energy Applications: New Opportunities: Proceedings of the Institute of Energy Conference Held in Sheffield, U. K., 9-11 April, 1990.** fac. ed. Institute of Energy Staff. LC 90-4228. (Illus.). 295p. 1990. reprint ed. pap. 84.10 (*0-7837-7994-1*, 2047750) Bks Demand.

***Ceramics in Scholarly Taste.** Maura Rinaldi & Eng-Lee Seok Chee. (Illus.). 152p. (C). Date not set. pap. 34.95 (*981-00-4395-3*) Heian Intl.

Ceramics in Severe Environments. Ed. by W. W. Kriegel, III & Hayne Palmour, III. LC 63-17645. (Materials Science Research Ser.: Vol. 5). 628p. 1971. 125.00 (*0-306-38505-8*, Plenum Pr) Plenum.

Ceramics in Surgery. Ed. by P. Vincenzini. (Materials Science Monographs: Vol. 17). 408p. 1983. 172.00 (*0-444-42172-6*) Elsevier.

Ceramics in the Pacific Northwest: A History. LaMar Harrington. LC 78-4369. (Index of Art in the Pacific Northwest Ser.: No. 10). (Illus.). 128p. 1979. 25.00 (*0-295-95623-2*) U of Wash Pr.

***Ceramics (Industrial) Market.** 400p. (Orig.). 1994. pap. 1,900.00 (*1-57205-985-0*) Rector Pr.

Ceramics of Ancient Peru. Christopher B. Donnan. LC 92-72522. (Illus.). 128p. (C). 1992. 35.00 (*0-930741-21-8*); pap. 19.00 (*0-930741-22-6*) UCLA Fowler Mus.

Ceramics of Betty Woodman. Ed. by Judith E. Tannenbaum. LC 85-82266. (Illus.). (Orig.). 1985. pap. text ed. 5.00 (*0-941972-03-8*) Freedman.

Ceramics of South-East Asia, Their Dating & Identification. 2nd ed. Roxanna M. Brown. (Oxford in Asia Studies in Ceramics). (Illus.). 268p. 1989. 95.00 (*0-19-588889-8*) OUP.

Ceramics of William H. Grueby: The Spirit of New Idea in Artistic Handicraft. Susan J. Montgomery. Ed. by David Rago & Michelle S. Schoen. (Illus.). 165p. 1993. 55.00 (*0-9637896-0-0*); pap. 40.00 (*0-9637896-3-5*) Arts & Crafts.

***Ceramics, Powders, Corrosion & Advanced Processing: Proceedings of the Symposia C: Powder Preparation; G: Corrosion-Coating of Advanced Materials; J: Structural Ceramics; P: Advanced Processing; W: Fabrication of Silicon Based Ceramics of the 3rd IUMRS International Conference on Advanced Materials.** IUMRS International Conference on Advanced Materials Staff. Ed. by N. Mizutani et al. LC 94-24590. (Transactions of the Materials Research Society of Japan Ser., Vol. 14A, Advanced Materials '93 Ser.: Vol. 1). 1994. write for info. (*0-444-81991-6*) Elsevier.

Ceramics Prints. (Illus.). 1992. 29.95 (*1-56290-089-7*, 6027) Crystal.

Ceramics Testing Guidebook. Investment Casting Institute Staff. Ed. by R. Russell Stratton. (Illus.). 1989. lib. bdg. 165.00 (*1-56061-001-8*) ICI Dallas.

Ceramics Today - Tomorrow Ceramics, 4 vols., Set. P. Vincenzini. (Materials Science Monographs: Vol. 66). 1991. 914.50 (*0-444-88365-7*, MSM 66) Elsevier.

Ceramo-Metal Fixed Partial Dentures. George Isaacson. Ed. by D. Walter Cohen. (Continuing Dental Education Ser.). 122p. 1981. pap. text ed. 22.00 (*0-931386-27-6*) Quint Pub Co.

Ceran St. Vrain. 2nd ed. Edward Broadhead. 56p. (Orig.). 1986. pap. 4.00 (*0-915617-13-7*) Pueblo Co Hist Soc.

Ceratocystis & Ophiostoma: Taxonomy, Ecology, & Pathogenicity. Ed. by Michael J. Wingfield et al. LC 93-79368. (Illus.). 304p. 1993. pap. 39.00 (*0-89054-156-6*) Am Phytopathol Soc.

Ceratophyllidae. Ed. by R. Traub et al. 1984. text ed. 190.00 (*0-12-697680-5*) Acad Pr.

Ceratophyllidae: Currently Accepted Valid Taxa (Insecta: Siphonaptera) Robert E. Lewis. (Theses Zoologicae Ser.: Vol. 13). (Illus.). 267p. 1990. text ed. 143.00 (*3-87429-304-1*) Koeltz Sci Bks.

***Ceratopsia: A Natural History of the Horned Dinosaurs.** Peter Dodson. (C). 1995. 21.00 (*0-201-40699-3*) Addison-Wesley.

Ceratopsia: Based on Preliminary Studies by Othniel C. Marsh. John B. Hatcher. Ed. by Stephen J. Gould. LC 79-8332. (Monographs of the U. S. Geological Survey: Vol. XLIX). (Illus.). 1980. reprint ed. lib. bdg. 73.95 (*0-405-12713-8*) Ayer.

Cerberus. Bernard Evslin. (Monsters of Mythology Ser.). (Illus.). 92p. 1987. lib. bdg. 19.95 (*1-55546-243-X*) Chelsea Hse.

Cerca De Dios: Near to God. Abraham Kuyper. (SPA.). 3.95 (*84-7228-006-3*, 220150, Pub. by Edit Clie SP) TSELF.

Cerceau. Viktor Slavkin. Tr. by Fritze Brun & Laurence Maslon. 1992. pap. 4.95 (*0-87129-145-2*, C82) Dramatic Pub.

CERCLA Enforcement Policy Manual. Mark H. Mays. LC 93-8578. (Environmental Law Ser.). 1993. text ed. 95.00 (*0-07-172506-7*) Shepards-McGraw.

CERCLA Law & Procedure. Fred R. Light. LC 91-26413. 416p. 1991. text ed. 150.00 (*0-87179-707-0*, 0707) BNA.

***CERCLA Law & Procedure.** suppl. ed. Fred R. Light. 122p. 1993. pap. text ed. 38.00 (*0-614-04035-3*) BNA.

CERCLA Law & Procedure Compendium. Fred R. Light. 1284p. 1992. text ed. 88.00 (*0-87179-742-9*, 0742) BNA.

CERCLA Litigation. Richard H. Mays. LC 93-4325. (Environmental Law Ser.). 1993. text ed. 190.00 (*0-07-172443-5*) Shepards-McGraw.

Cercle De Famille. Andre Maurois. (Coll. Diamant). 1959. 23.25 (*0-685-11071-0*) Fr & Eur.

Cercle de Famille. Andre Maurois. 437p. (FRE.). 1977. 10.95 (*0-8288-9882-0*, F114050) Fr & Eur.

Cercle des Mahe. Georges Simenon. (FRE.). 1981. pap. 10.95 (*0-7859-4161-4*) Fr & Eur.

***Cerco de Dios.** Francisco M. Paoli. (Illus.). 157p. (SPA.). 1995. lib. bdg. 10.00 (*1-881708-09-8*) Edcnes Mairena.

***Cerdos en el Cielo.** Barbara Kingsolver. (SPA.). 1995. pap. 10.00 (*0-06-095122-2*, HarpT) HarpC.

Cerdos en la Sala: Pigs in the Parlor. Frank Hammond & Ida M. Hammond. 176p. (SPA.). 1989. pap. 5.95 (*958-95462-3-4*) Impact Christian.

Cerdos en la Sala (Pigs in the Parlor) Frank Hammonds. (SPA.). Date not set. 4.99 (*1-56063-323-9*, 497717) Editorial Unilit.

Cerdos (Pigs) L. Stone. (Spanish Language Books, Set 1: Animales de Granja (Farm Animals)). (J). 1991. 8.95 (*0-86592-989-0*) Rourke Enter.

Cereal Banks - at Your Service. Abdou Fall. (C). 1991. pap. text ed. 28.00 (*0-85598-157-1*, Pub. by Oxfam Pubns UK) St Mut.

***Cereal Box Bonanza - The Nineteen Fifties: Identification & Value Guide.** Scott Bruce. 144p. 1995. pap. 16.95 (*0-89145-634-1*, 3959) Collector Bks.

Cereal Grain: Mycotoxins, Fungi & Quality in Drying & Storage. Ed. by J. Chelkowski. (Developments in Food Science Ser.: Vol. 26). 610p. 1991. 202.50 (*0-444-88554-4*) Elsevier.

Cereal Grain Crops. Neal C. Stoskopf. (C). 1985. teacher ed write for info. (*0-8359-0734-1*, Reston); text ed. 52.00 (*0-8359-0733-3*, Reston) P-H.

Cereal Grass: Nature's Greatest Health Gift. Ronald Seibold. 1994. pap. 9.95 (*0-87983-631-8*) Keats.

Cereal Husbandry. E. John Wibberley. (Illus.). 272p. 1989. 37.95 (*0-85236-124-6*, Pub. by Farming Pr UK) Diamond Farm Bk.

***Cereal Industry Report: Pain & Reform.** 108p. (Orig.). 1995. pap. 1,195.00 (*0-7605-2202-2*) Rector Pr.

Cereal Miller's Handbook. Association of Operative Millers. 1963. 25.00 (*0-686-00364-0*) AG Pr.

Cereal Murders. Diane M. Davidson. 1994. mass mkt. 4.99 (*0-553-56773-X*) Bantam.

Cereal Pests & Diseases. 4th ed. R. Gair et al. (Illus.). 268p. 1987. 27.95 (*0-85236-164-5*, Pub. by Farming Pr UK) Diamond Farm Bk.

Cereal Processing. UNIFEM Staff. (Illus.). 72p. (Orig.). 1993. pap. 13.50 (*1-85339-136-0*, Pub. by Intermed Tech UK) Women Ink.

Cereal Production: Proceedings of the International Meeting on Production of Temperate Cereal Crops. Royal Dublin Society Staff. Ed. by E. Gallagher. 304p. 1984. text ed. 125.00 (*0-407-00303-7*) Buttrwrth-Heinemann.

***Cereal (RTE) Market.** 150p. (Orig.). 1995. pap. 2,195.00 (*0-7605-2200-6*) Rector Pr.

Cereal Rusts: Vol. 1: Origins, Specificity, Structure & Physiology. William R. Bushnell & Alan P. Roelfs. LC 83-15035. 1984. text ed. 148.00 (*0-12-148401-7*) Acad Pr.

Cereal Rusts: Vol. 2, Diseases, Distribution, Epidemiology, & Control. Ed. by Alan P. Roelfe & William R. Bushnell. 1985. text ed. 157.00 (*0-12-148402-5*) Acad Pr.

Cereal Seed Industry in Asia & the Pacific. 422p. 1987. pap. 30.00 (*0-317-59547-4*, Pub. by APO JA) Qual Resc.

Cerealizing America: The Unsweetened Story of American Breakfast Cereal. Scott Bruce & Bill Crawford. (Illus.). 312p. 1995. 24.95 (*0-571-19851-1*) Faber & Faber.

Cereals: A Renewable Resource, Theory & Practice. Ed. by Y. Pomeranz & Lars Munck. LC 81-71369. 728p. 1981. 69.00x (*0-913250-22-8*) Am Assn Cereal Chem.

Cereals, Grain, Malt & Millet: Index of New Information with Authors & Subjects. Harrison B. Younge. LC 92-54189. 180p. 1992. 49.50 (*1-55914-746-6*); pap. 39.50 (*1-55914-747-4*) ABBE Pubs Assn.

Cereals in a European Context: First European Conference on Food Science & Technology. I. D. Morton. (Ellis Horwood Series in Food Science & Technology). 523p. 1987. lib. bdg. 220.00 (*0-89573-523-7*) VCH Pubs.

Cereals in Breadmaking: A Molecular Colloidal Approach. Eliasson & Larsson. (Food Science & Technology Ser.: Vol. 55). 392p. 1993. 150.00 (*0-8247-8816-8*) Dekker.

Cereals in the United Kingdom. Denis K. Britton. 1969. 346.00 (*0-08-013896-9*, Pub. by Pergamon Repr UK) Franklin.

Cerebellar Degenerations: Clinical Neurobiology. Ed. by Andreas Plaitakis. (Foundations of Neurology Ser.). 528p. (C). 1992. lib. bdg. 218.50 (*0-7923-1490-5*) Kluwer Ac.

Cerebellar Functions. Ed. by J. Dichgans et al. (Proceedings in Life Sciences Ser.). (Illus.). 350p. 1984. 105.00 (*0-387-13728-9*) Spr-Verlag.

Cerebellar Infarct: Minimal Invásive Endoscopy Neurosurgery - Midline Tumors. Ed. by B. L. Bauer et al. 1994. pap. 79.00 (*0-387-57668-1*) Spr-Verlag.

Cerebellar Stimulation for Spasticity & Seizures. Ed. by Ross Davis & James Bloedel. 360p. 1984. 180.00 (*0-8493-6067-6*, RC350, CRC Reprint) Franklin.

***Cerebellar Stimulation in Man.** fac. ed. Irving S. Cooper. LC 77-76925. (Illus.). 232p. Date not set. pap. 66.20 (*0-7837-7536-9*, 2046968) Bks Demand.

Cerebellar Tumors: Clinical Analysis & Physiopathologic Correlations. R. Amici et al. (Monographs in Neural Sciences: Vol. 4). 1976. pap. 51.25 (*3-8055-2358-0*) S Karger.

Cerebellum & Neural Control. Masao Ito. (Illus.). 598p. 1984. 133.00 (*0-89004-106-7*) Raven.

Cerebellum & Neuronal Plasticity. Ed. by M. Glickstein et al. LC 88-2409. (NATO ASI Series A, Life Sciences: Vol. 148). (Illus.). 368p. 1988. 95.00 (*0-306-42822-9*, Plenum Pr) Plenum.

Cerebellum in Health & Disease. William S. Fields et al. LC 78-78016. (Illus.). 588p. 1970. 31.80 (*0-87527-009-3*) Green.

Cerebellum Revisited. Ed. by R. Llinas & C. Sotelo. (Illus.). 320p. 1992. 89.00 (*0-387-97693-0*) Spr-Verlag.

Cerebral Aneurysms: Microvascular & Endovascular Management. R. R. Smith et al. LC 93-23192. 256p. 1994. 150.00 (*0-387-94132-0*) Spr-Verlag.

Cerebral Aneurysms: Perioperative Management, Vol. 6. Fremont P. Wirth & Robert A. Ratcheson. (Illus.). 600p. 1994. 75.00 (*0-683-09199-9*) Williams & Wilkins.

***Cerebral Angio-CT.** fac. ed. Kazuhiko Sadamoto & Keiji Fukui. LC 87-43182. (Illus.). 110p. Date not set. pap. 31.40 (*0-7837-7180-0*, 2047119) Bks Demand.

Cerebral Blood Flow: Mathematical Models, Instrumentation, & Imaging Techniques. Ed. by A. Rescigno & A. Boicelli. LC 88-25519. (NATO ASI Series A, Life Sciences: Vol. 153). (Illus.). 272p. 1988. 85.00 (*0-306-43019-3*, Plenum Pr) Plenum.

Cerebral Blood Flow & Intracranial Pressure: Proceedings of the International Symposium on Cerebral Blood Flow Regulation, Acid-Base & Engergy Metabolism Acute Brain Injuries, 5th, Roma Siena, 1971, 2 pts. International Symposium on Cerebral Blood Flow Regulation, Acid-Base & Energy Metabolism Acute Brain Injuries Staff. Ed. by C. Fieschi. 1972. 128.00 (*3-8055-1440-9*) S Karger.

Cerebral Blood Flow & Metabolism. Lars Edvinsson et al. 688p. 1993. 136.50 (*0-88167-918-6*) Raven.

Cerebral Blood Flow in Acute Head Injury: The Regulation of Cerebral Blood Flow & Metabolism During the Acute Phase of Head Injury, & Its Significance for Therapy. G. E. Cold. (Acta Neurochirugica - Supplementum Ser.: Supplementum No. 49). (Illus.). 100p. 1990. 64.00 (*0-387-82224-0*) Spr-Verlag.

An Asterisk (*) at the beginning of an entry indicates that the title is appearing in BIP for the first time.

Cerebral Blood Flow Measurement with Stable Xenon-Enhanced Computed Tomography. Ed. by Howard Yonas. 352p. 1992. 84.00 (*0-88167-853-8*) Raven.

Cerebral Circulation. Luyendijk. (Progress in Brain Research Ser.: Vol. 30). 1968. 56.50 (*0-444-40691-3*) Elsevier.

Cerebral Computer. Robert Baron. 552p. 1987. text ed. 110.00 (*0-89859-824-9*); pap. 49.95 (*0-8058-0037-9*) L Erlbaum Assocs.

Cerebral Control of Speech & Limb Movements. Ed. by G. R. Hammond. (Advances in Psychology Ser.: No. 70). 712p. 1991. 154.50 (*0-444-88477-7*, North Holland) Elsevier.

Cerebral Contusions, Lacerations & Hematomas. Ed. by R. A. Frowein. (Advances in Neurotraumatology Ser.: Vol. 3). (Illus.). xiii, 259p. 1991. 104.00 (*0-387-81982-7*) Spr-Verlag.

Cerebral Cortex, No. 10. Ed. by A. Peters & K. S. Rockland. (Illus.). 440p. 1993. 115.00 (*0-306-44605-7*, Plenum Pr) Plenum.

***Cerebral Cortex, Vol. 11.** Ed. by E. G. Jones & I. T. Diamond. (Illus.). 434p. (C). 1995. 110.00 (*0-306-44847-5*, Plenum Pr) Plenum.

Cerebral Cortex of the Rat. Ed. by Bryan Kolb & Richard C. Tees. 570p. 1990. 70.00 (*0-262-11150-0*); pap. 39.95x (*0-262-61064-7*) MIT Pr.

Cerebral Cortex, Vol. 1: Cellular Components of the Cerebral Cortex. Ed. by Alan A. Peters & Edward G. Jones. LC 84-1982. 580p. 1984. 110.00 (*0-306-41544-5*, Plenum Pr) Plenum.

Cerebral Cortex, Vol. 2: Functional Properties of Cortical Cells. Ed. by Edward G. Jones & Alan A. Peters. LC 84-1982. 354p. 1984. 85.00 (*0-306-41755-3*, Plenum Pr) Plenum.

Cerebral Cortex, Vol. 3: Visual Cortex. Ed. by Alan A. Peters & Edward G. Jones. LC 84-1982. 438p. 1985. 95.00 (*0-306-42025-2*, Plenum Pr) Plenum.

Cerebral Cortex, Vol. 4: Association & Auditory Cortices. Ed. by Alan A. Peters & Edward G. Jones. LC 84-1982. 376p. 1985. 89.50 (*0-306-42040-6*, Plenum Pr) Plenum.

Cerebral Cortex, Vol. 5: Sensory-Motor Areas & Aspects of Cortical Connectivity. Ed. by Edward G. Jones & Alan A. Peters. LC 84-1982. 528p. 1986. 110.00 (*0-306-42174-7*, Plenum Pr) Plenum.

Cerebral Cortex, Vol. 6: Further Aspects of Cortical Function, Including Hippocampus. Ed. by Alan A. Peters & Edward G. Jones. LC 84-1982. 478p. 1987. 110.00 (*0-306-42503-3*, Plenum Pr) Plenum.

Cerebral Cortex, Vol. 7: Development & Maturation of Cerebral Cortex. Ed. by Alan A. Peters & Edward G. Jones. LC 84-1982. (Illus.). 536p. 1988. 110.00 (*0-306-42881-4*, Plenum Pr) Plenum.

Cerebral Cortex, Vol. 8: Comparative Structure & Evolution of Cerebral Cortex, 2 pts., Pt. A. Ed. by Edward G. Jones & Alan A. Peters. LC 84-1982. (Illus.). 360p. 1990. 95.00 (*0-306-43477-6*, Plenum Pr) Plenum.

Cerebral Cortex, Vol. 8: Comparative Structure & Evolution of Cerebral Cortex, 2 pts., Pt. B. Ed. by Edward G. Jones & Alan A. Peters. LC 84-1982. (Illus.). 480p. 1990. 110.00 (*0-306-43635-3*, Plenum Pr) Plenum.

Cerebral Cortex, Vol. 8: Comparative Structure & Evolution of Cerebral Cortex, 2 pts., Set. Ed. by Edward G. Jones & Alan A. Peters. LC 84-1982. (Illus.). 1990. 175.00 (*0-685-45067-8*, Plenum Pr) Plenum.

Cerebral Cortex, Vol. 9: Normal & Altered States of Function. Ed. by Alan A. Peters & Edward G. Jones. LC 84-1982. (Illus.). 530p. 1991. 110.00 (*0-306-43648-5*, Plenum Pr) Plenum.

Cerebral Damage Before & after Cardiac Surgery. Ed. by Allen Willner. (Developments in Critical Care, Medicine, & Anesthesiology Ser.). 280p. (C). 1993. lib. bdg. 150.50 (*0-7923-1928-1*) Kluwer Ac.

Cerebral Dominance: The Biological Foundations. Ed. by Norman Geschwind & Albert M. Galaburda. (Illus.). 240p. 1984. 44.00 (*0-674-10658-X*) HUP.

Cerebral Dominance: The Biological Foundations. Ed. by Norman Geschwind & Albert M. Galaburda. (Illus.). 248p. 1988. reprint ed. pap. 17.95 (*0-674-10659-8*) HUP.

Cerebral Dominance & Its Relation to Psychological Function. Oliver L. Zangwill. LC 78-72831. (Brainedness, Handedness, & Mental Abilities Ser.). reprint ed. 28.00 (*0-404-60899-X*) AMS Pr.

Cerebral Dynamics, Laterality & Psychopathology. Ed. by R. Takahashi et al. (Developments in Psychiatry Ser.: Vol. 8). 588p. 1987. 196.00 (*0-444-80882-5*) Elsevier.

Cerebral Dysfunction: Pathophysiology & Management of Mental Decline. Kewal K. Jain et al. (Illus.). 600p. 1990. 94.95 (*0-88416-608-2*, Yr Bk Med Pubs) Mosby Yr Bk.

Cerebral Dysgenesis: Embryology & Clinical Expression. Harvey B. Sarnat. (Illus.). 496p. 1992. 75.00 (*0-19-506442-9*) OUP.

***Cerebral Embolism.** Ed. by Michael Hennerici. (Journal: Vol. 5, No. 2, 1995). (Illus.). 94p. (Orig.). 1995. pap. 31.50 (*3-8055-6153-9*) S Karger.

Cerebral Energy Metabolism & Metabolic Encephalopathy. Ed. by D. W. McCandless. 478p. 1985. 125.00 (*0-306-41797-9*, Plenum Pr) Plenum.

Cerebral Gliomas: Proceedings of the International Workshop on Brain Tumors, Santa Margherita, 20-22 June, 1988. Ed. by G. Broggi & M. A. Gerosa. (International Congress Ser.: No.828). 270p. 1989. 92.50 (*0-444-81081-1*, Excerpta Medica) Elsevier.

Cerebral Hemisphere Function in Depression. Marcel Kinsbourne. LC 87-19304. (Progress in Psychiatry Ser.). 240p. 1988. text ed. 26.50 (*0-88048-143-9*) Am Psychiatric.

Cerebral Hyperemia & Ischemia: From the Standpoint of Cerebral Blood Flow. Ed. by M. Tomita et al. (International Congress Ser.: No. 764). 282p. 1988. 113.00 (*0-444-80973-2*) Elsevier.

Cerebral Insufficiency: A Review of the Pathophysiology & Management of Mental Decline. K. K. Jain. (Illus.). 600p. 1990. 95.00 (*0-8151-4878-X*, Yr Bk Med Pubs) Mosby Yr Bk.

Cerebral Ischemia. A. Bes et al. (International Congress Ser.: Vol. 654). 1984. 132.00 (*0-444-80586-9*) Elsevier.

Cerebral Ischemia. Werner Hacke et al. (Illus.). 240p. 1991. 83.00 (*0-387-52341-3*) Spr-Verlag.

Cerebral Ischemia: Clinical Implications & Therapeutics. Ed. by Robert H. Rosenwasser et al. (Illus.). 179p. (C). 1994. lib. bdg. 62.00 (*1-56072-137-5*) Nova Sci Pubs.

Cerebral Ischemia: From Pathophysiology to Treatment - Journal: Cerebrovascular Diseases, Vol. 1, Suppl. 1, 1991. Ed. by J. Biller et al. (Illus.). iv, 140p. 1991. pap. 57.75 (*3-8055-5448-6*) S Karger.

Cerebral Ischemia & Basic Mechanisms. Ed. by A. Hartman et al. LC 93-24247. 1994. 198.00 (*0-387-56573-6*) Spr-Verlag.

Cerebral Ischemia & Dementia. Ed. by A. Hartmann et al. (Illus.). xv, 472p. 1991. 198.00 (*0-387-53331-1*) Spr-Verlag.

Cerebral Ischemia Resuscitation. Ed. by Schurr. 1990. 121.00 (*0-8493-6715-8*, RC171) CRC Pr.

Cerebral Laterality: Theory & Research. Ed. by F. L. Kitterle. 248p. (C). 1991. text ed. 49.95 (*0-8058-0471-4*) L Erlbaum Assocs.

Cerebral Localization & Organization: Proceedings of a Symposium Sponsored by the World Federation of Neurology & Held at Lisbon, Portugal, October, 1960. Ed. by Georges Schaltenbrand & Clinton N. Woolsey. LC 64-22236. 184p. reprint ed. pap. 52.50 (*0-317-30076-8*, 2021146) Bks Demand.

Cerebral Microcirculation. Ed. by F. Hammersen & K. Messmer. (Progress in Applied Microcirculation Ser.: Vol. 16). (Illus.). x, 102p. 1990. 70.50 (*3-8055-5054-5*) S Karger.

***Cerebral Microcirculation & Metabolism.** fac. ed. Ed. by J. Cervos-Navarro & Emmanuel Fritschka. LC 80-5444. (Illus.). 499p. Date not set. pap. 142.30 (*0-7837-7511-3*, 2046994) Bks Demand.

Cerebral Monitoring in the Operating Room & the Intensive Care Unit: Development in Critical Care Medicine & Anaesthesiology. Enno Freye. 196p. (C). 1990. lib. bdg. 109.50 (*0-7923-0439-X*) Kluwer Ac.

Cerebral Motor Control in Man: Cerebral Event-Related Potentials. Ed. by J. E. Desmedt. (Progress in Clinical Neurophysiology Ser.: Vol. 4). (Illus.). 1977. 94.50 (*3-8055-2712-8*) S Karger.

Cerebral Palsies of Children: A Clinical Study from the Infirmary for Nervous Diseases, Philadelphia. William Osler. (Classics in Developmental Medicine Ser.: No. 1). (Illus.). 92p. (C). 1991. 15.95 (*0-521-41326-5*, Pub. by Mc Keith Pr UK) Cambridge U Pr.

Cerebral Palsy. Nathan Aaseng. (Venture Bks.). (Illus.). 112p. (YA). (gr. 9-12). 1991. lib. bdg. 14.28 (*0-531-12529-7*) Watts.

Cerebral Palsy. Daniel Boone. LC 76-190708. (Studies in Communicative Disorders). (C). 1972. pap. text ed. write for info. (*0-672-61290-9*, Bobbs) Macmillan.

Cerebral Palsy. James C. Hardy. (Illus.). 288p. 1983. text ed. write for info. (*0-13-122820-X*) P-H.

Cerebral Palsy. Eugene T. McDonald & B. Chance, Jr. 1964. pap. text ed. 25.67 (*0-13-122812-9*) P-H.

Cerebral Palsy. Merlin J. Mecham. Ed. by Harvey Halpern. LC 86-3271. (PRO-ED Studies in Communicative Disorders). (Illus.). 64p. (Orig.). 1986. pap. text ed. 9.00 (*0-89079-087-6*, 1376) PRO-ED.

***Cerebral Palsy: A Complete Guide for Caregiving.** Freeman Miller et al. LC 95-8826. (Health Book Ser.). (Illus.). 488p. 1995. 35.95 (*0-8018-5091-6*) Johns Hopkins.

Cerebral Palsy: A Developmental Disability. 3rd rev. ed. Ed. by William M. Cruickshank. LC 75-34275. 644p. reprint ed. pap. 180.00 (*0-685-20509-6*, 2029967) Bks Demand.

Cerebral Palsy: The Child & Young Person. L. Cogher. 1992. 69.95 (*0-442-31641-0*) Chapman & Hall.

Cerebral Palsy Not Necessary: No Cause for Life Long Handicap. Hildegard Winky-Lotz. (Illus.). 85p. 1989. spiral bd. 30.00 (*0-936112-04-2*) Willyshe Pub.

Cerebral Pathophysiology: An Integral Approach with Some Emphasis on Clinical Implications. K. G. Go. 432p. 1991. 275.75 (*0-444-81386-1*) Elsevier.

Cerebral Psychophysiology: Studies in Event-Related Potentials. Ed. by W. Cheyne McCallum et al. 592p. 1987. 244.00 (*0-444-80741-1*) Elsevier.

Cerebral Revascularization by Microneurosurgical Bypass. P. Conforti et al. 240p. 1984. text ed. 64.00 (*1-57235-042-3*) Piccin NY.

Cerebral Sinus Thrombosis: Experimental & Clinical Aspects. Ed. by K. Einhupl et al. LC 91-2456. (Illus.). 242p. 1990. 79.50 (*0-306-43832-1*, Plenum Pr) Plenum.

Cerebral Small Artery Disease. Ed. by Patrick M. Pullicino et al. LC 92-48462. (Advances in Neurology Ser.: Vol. 62). 256p. 1993. 103.00 (*0-7817-0051-5*) Raven.

Cerebral SPECT Imaging. Ed. by Ronald S. Tikofsky. LC 94-7879. 240p. 1995. 140.00 (*0-7817-0188-0*) Raven.

Cerebral Torment: The Game of Mental Madness. Vince Tucker. Ed. by Cole Wilder. 256p. (Orig.). 1992. pap. 14.95 (*0-9614914-3-4*) Pax Pub.

Cerebral Vascular Disease, Vol. 3. J. S. Meyer et al. (International Congress Ser.: No. 532). 352p. 1981. 98.50 (*0-444-90197-3*, Excerpta Medica) Elsevier.

Cerebral Vascular Disease: Proceedings of the World Federation of Neurology 13th International Salzburg Conference, Sept. 25-27, 1986, Vol. 6. Ed. by J. S. Meyer et al. (International Congress Ser.: No. 736). 254p. 1988. 108.75 (*0-444-80875-2*, Excerpta Medica) Elsevier.

Cerebral Vascular Disease 5: Proceedings of the World Federation of Neurology 12th International Salzburg Conference, Sept. 26-29, 1984. Ed. by J. S. Meyer et al. (International Congress Ser.: No. 687). 392p. 1986. 122.75 (*0-444-80706-3*, Excerpta Medica) Elsevier.

Cerebral Vascular Smooth Muscle & Its Control. Ciba Foundation Staff. LC 77-28855. (Ciba Foundation Symposium: New Ser.: 56). 408p. reprint ed. pap. 116.30 (*0-317-29773-2*, 2022181) Bks Demand.

Cerebral Vascular Spasm: A New Diagnostic & Neurosurgical Approach Based on Advances in Neuropharmacology & Neurosciences. Ed. by D. Voth & P. Glees. LC 84-22983. (Illus.). xii, 515p. 1985. 113.85 (*3-11-010029-0*) De Gruyter.

Cerebral Vasospasm. Ed. by K. Sano et al. 1991. text ed. 160.00 (*0-86008-471-X*, Pub. by U of Tokyo JA) Col U Pr.

Cerebral Vasospasm. Ed. by Robert H. Wilkins. (Illus.). 544p. 1988. text ed. 133.00 (*0-88167-462-1*) Raven.

Cerebral Vasospasm. David J. Boullin. LC 79-40735. (Wiley-Interscience Publication Ser.). 347p. reprint ed. pap. 98.90 (*0-317-26198-3*, 2052068) Bks Demand.

Cerebral Vasospasm: Proceedings of the 5th International Conference on Cerebral Vasospasm, Edmonton & Jasper, Alberta, Canada, May 17-21, 1993. Ed. by J. Max Findlay. LC 93-21009. (Developments in Neurology Ser.: Vol. 8). 1993. write for info. (*0-444-81535-X*) Elsevier.

Cerebral Veins. Ed. by L. M. Auer & F. Loew. (Illus.). 380p. 1984. 124.00 (*0-387-81767-0*) Spr-Verlag.

***Cerebral Vessel Wall.** fac. ed. Erwin Riesch Symposium on the Cerebral Vessel Wall Staff. Ed. by J. Cervos-Navarro et al. LC 75-25110. (Illus.). 287p. Date not set. pap. 81.80 (*0-7837-7540-7*, 2046964) Bks Demand.

Cerebral Visual Disturbance in Infantile Encephalogathy. O. Van Nieuwenhuizen. (Monographs in Ophthalmology). 1987. lib. bdg. 107.00 (*0-89838-860-0*) Kluwer Ac.

Cerebrale Metabolism in Aging & Neurological Disorders, Second Joint Meeting. A. Agnoli et al. Ed. by H. Lechner et al. (Journal: Gerontology: Vol. 33, No. 3-4, 1987). (Illus.). 164p. 1987. pap. 88.00 (*3-8055-4640-8*) S Karger.

Cerebralism: Creating a New Millenium of Minds, Bodies & Civilizations. Todd Siler. (Illus.). 42p. (Orig.). 1993. pap. text ed. 20.00 (*0-914661-07-8*) Feldman Fine Arts.

Cerebro-Cerebellar Interactions. Ed. by J. Massion & K. Sasaki. LC 79-18156. (Developments in Neuroscience Ser.: Vol. 6). 1979. 78.50 (*0-444-80147-2*) Elsevier.

Cerebrospinal Fluid. Ed. by Robert M. Herndon & Roger A. Brumback. (C). 1989. lib. bdg. 133.50 (*0-7923-0121-8*) Kluwer Ac.

Cerebrospinal Fluid & the Brain Edemas. Thomas H. Milhorat. (Illus.). 172p. (C). 1987. 45.00 (*0-944809-00-6*) NeuroSci Soc NY.

Cerebrospinal Fluid (CSF) & Peptide Hormones. Ed. by E. M. Rodriguez & T. B. Van Wimersma Greidanus. (Frontiers of Hormone Research Ser.: Vol. 9). (Illus.). viii, 220p. 1982. 105.75 (*3-8055-2823-X*) S Karger.

Cerebrospinal Fluid in Diseases of the Nervous System. 2nd ed. Robert A. Fishman. (Illus.). 416p. 1992. text ed. 66.50 (*0-7216-3557-1*) Saunders.

Cerebrospinal Meningitis Control: Report. WHO Staff. (Technical Report Ser.: No. 588). 1976. pap. 2.40 (*92-4-120588-1*) World Health.

Cerebrospinal Meningitis in West Africa & the Sudan in the Twentieth Century. K. David Patterson & Gerald Hartwig. 1984. pap. 15.00 (*0-918456-55-X*) African Studies Assn.

Cerebrovascular Disease. Masakuni Kameyama & Masanori Tomonaga. LC 87-22670. 186p. 1988. 92.00 (*0-89640-133-2*) Igaku-Shoin.

Cerebrovascular Disease: Imaging & International Treatment Options. Rumbaugh et al. LC 94-27327. 544p. 1995. 225.00 (*0-89640-259-2*) Igaku-Shoin.

Cerebrovascular Disease: Neuro-Ophthalmology & Neuro-Otology. Vladimir Hachinski & John W. Norris. Ed. by Renato Boeri & Andrea Salmaggi. (Current Opinion in Neurology 1994 Ser.). (Illus.). 92p. (Orig.). 1994. pap. text ed. 49.95 (*1-85922-674-4*) Current Science.

Cerebrovascular Disease: Research & Clinical Management, Vol. 1. Ed. by H. Lechner et al. 350p. 1986. 153.00 (*0-444-80782-9*) Elsevier.

Cerebrovascular Disease in Childhood & Adolescence. Michael Edwards & Harold Hoffman. (Illus.). 512p. 1988. 115.00 (*0-683-02747-6*) Williams & Wilkins.

Cerebrovascular Diseases. Myron D. Ginsberg & W. Dalton Dietrich. (Research (Princeton) Conferences on Cerebrovascular Diseases Ser.: No. 16). 496p. 1989. 165.50 (*0-88167-485-0*) Raven.

***Cerebrovascular Diseases: Eleventh Princeton Conference.** fac. ed. Ed. by Thomas R. Price & Erland Nelson. LC 75-25125. (Illus.). 424p. Date not set. pap. 120.90 (*0-7837-7191-6*, 2047108) Bks Demand.

Cerebrovascular Diseases: Fifteenth Research (Princeton) Conference on Cerebrovascular Diseases. Ed. by William J. Powers & Marcus E. Raichle. (Illus.). 396p. 1987. text ed. 142.50 (*0-88167-289-0*) Raven.

***Cerebrovascular Diseases: Fourteenth Research (Princeton-Williamsburg) Conference.** Research (Princeton-Williamsburg) Conference on Cerebrovascular Disease Staff. Ed. by Fred Plum & William A. Pulsinelli. LC 75-25125. (Illus.). Date not set. reprint ed. pap. 80.10 (*0-7837-9527-0*, 2060276) Bks Demand.

Cerebrovascular Diseases: Proceedings of the WHO Expert Committee, Monaco, 1970. WHO Staff. (Technical Report Ser.: No. 469). 57p. 1971. pap. 2.00 (*92-4-120469-9*, 243) World Health.

Cerebrovascular Diseases in Children. Ed. by Anthony J. Raimondi et al. (Principles of Pediatric Neurosurgery Ser.). (Illus.). xi, 256p. 1992. 138.00 (*0-387-97626-4*) Spr-Verlag.

***Cerebrovascular Disorders.** 3rd fac. ed. James F. Toole. LC 84-3254. 446p. Date not set. pap. 127.20 (*0-7837-7279-3*, 2047027) Bks Demand.

Cerebrovascular Disorders. 4th ed. James F. Toole. 576p. 1990. 109.50 (*0-88167-673-X*) Raven.

Cerebrovascular Occlusive Disease & Brain Ischemia. Ed. by Issam Awad. (Neurosurgical Topics Ser.). 306p. 1992. 90.00 (*1-879284-01-4*) Am Assn Neuro.

Cerebrovascular Surgery, Vol. 1. Ed. by J. M. Fein & E. S. Flamm. 300p. 1985. 187.00 (*0-387-90995-8*) Spr-Verlag.

Cerebrovascular Surgery, Vol. 2. Ed. by J. M. Fein & E. S. Flamm. 300p. 1985. 187.00 (*0-387-90996-6*) Spr-Verlag.

Cerebrovascular Surgery, Vol. 3. Ed. by J. M. Fein & E. S. Flamm. 350p. 1985. 187.00 (*0-387-96041-4*) Spr-Verlag.

Cerebrovascular Surgery, Vol. 4. Ed. by J. M. Fein & E. S. Flamm. 350p. 1985. 187.00 (*0-387-96026-0*) Spr-Verlag.

Cerebrum, 2 vols., Set. Emanuel Swedenborg. Tr. & Intro. by Alfred Acton. 1976. reprint ed. 50.00 (*0-915221-18-7*) Swedenborg Sci Assn.

Cerebrum, 2 vols., Vol. I. Emanuel Swedenborg. Tr. & Intro. by Alfred Acton. 1203p. 1976. reprint ed. 34.95 (*0-915221-35-7*) Swedenborg Sci Assn.

Cerebrum, 2 vols., Vol. II. Emanuel Swedenborg. Tr. & Intro. by Alfred Acton. 258p. 1976. reprint ed. 16.95 (*0-915221-36-5*) Swedenborg Sci Assn.

***Ceremonial & Commemorative Chairs in Great Britain.** Clare Graham. (Illus.). 112p. 1995. 75.00 (*1-85177-136-0*, Pub. by Victoria & Albert Mus UK) Trafalgar.

Ceremonial Centers of the Maya. Roy C. Craven. LC 74-2016. 160p. reprint ed. pap. 45.60 (*0-8357-6918-6*, 2037977) Bks Demand.

Ceremonial Chemistry: The Ritual Persecution of Drugs, Addicts, & Pushers. Thomas S. Szasz. 272p. 1987. pap. 19.95 (*1-55691-019-3*) Learning Pubns.

Ceremonial Circle: Practice, Ritual, & Renewal for Personal & Community Healing. Sedonia Cahill & Joshua Halpern. LC 91-55321. (Illus.). 240p. 1992. pap. 14.00 (*0-06-250154-2*) Harper SF.

***Ceremonial City: Toulouse Observed.** Robert A. Schneider. LC 94-26081. 1994. 24.95 (*0-691-03465-6*) Princeton U Pr.

Ceremonial Costumes of the Pueblo Indians: Their Evolution, Fabrication, & Significance in the Prayer Drama. Virginia M. Roediger. (Illus.). 268p. 1991. 50.00 (*0-520-07630-3*); pap. 25.00 (*0-520-07631-1*) U CA Pr.

Ceremonial de Guerra. Jose Triana. (Teatro Ser.). 64p. (Orig.). (SPA.). 1989. pap. text ed. 15.00 (*0-945791-07-0*) Editorial Persona.

Ceremonial of Bishops. rev. ed. 340p. 39.95 (*1-55586-376-0*) US Catholic.

Ceremonial Ox of India: The Mithan in Nature, Culture, & History. Frederick J. Simoons & Elizabeth S. Simoons. LC 68-9023. (Illus.). 340p. 1968. 40.00 (*0-299-04980-9*) U of Wis Pr.

Ceremonial Patterns in the Greater Southwest: Bound with Factionalism in Isleta Pueblo. Ruth M. Underhill & David H. French. LC 84-45518. (American Ethnological Society Monographs: Nos. 13-14). 1988. reprint ed. 20.00 (*0-404-62913-X*) AMS Pr.

Ceremonial, Stories 1936-1940: The Collected Stories of Paul Goodman, Vol. 2. Paul Goodman. Ed. by Taylor Stoehr. LC 78-16977. 273p. (Orig.). 1978. 20.00 (*0-87685-354-8*); 25.00 (*0-87685-355-6*); pap. 10.00 (*0-87685-353-X*) Black Sparrow.

Ceremonie des Adieux. Simone De Beauvoir. (Folio Ser.: No. 1805). (FRE.). pap. 13.95 (*2-07-037805-5*) Schoenhof.

Ceremonie des Adieux: Entretiens avec Sartre. Simone De Beauvoir. (FRE.). 1987. pap. 16.95 (*0-8288-3623-X*) Fr & Eur.

Ceremonies. Essex Hemphill. 192p. (Orig.). 1992. pap. 10.00 (*0-452-26817-6*, Plume) NAL-Dutton.

Ceremonies. John High. LC 84-70284. (Literature-Poetry Ser.). (Illus.). 86p. (Orig.). 1984. pap. 5.95 (*0-911323-07-4*) Concourse Pr.

Ceremonies see Florentine Codex, General History of the Things of New Spain

Ceremonies, Heroines of Jericho. 6.00 (*0-685-19468-X*) Powner.

Ceremonies in Girl Scouting. (Illus.). 72p. 1990. pap. 6.95 (*0-88441-469-8*, 26-801) Girl Scouts USA.

Ceremonies of Charles I: The Note Books of John Finet, 1628-1641. John Finet. Ed. by Albert J. Loomie. LC 87-80118. (Illus.). 340p. reprint ed. pap. 96.90 (*0-7837-5611-9*, 2045517) Bks Demand.

***Ceremonies of Escape: A Zen Romance.** Deborah Boehm. 288p. Date not set. 25.00 (*4-7700-1979-3*) FS&G.

Ceremonies of Innocence: Pastoralism in the Poetry of Edmund Spenser. John D. Bernard. 220p. (C). 1989. 64.95 (*0-521-36252-0*) Cambridge U Pr.

***Ceremonies of Possession in Europe's Conquest of the New World, 1492-1640.** Patricia Seed. 208p. (C). 1995. write for info. (*0-521-49748-5*); pap. write for info. (*0-521-49757-4*) Cambridge U Pr.

Ceremonies of the Eucharist: A Guide to Celebration. Howard Galley. LC 89-22145. 240p. 1989. pap. 19.95 (*0-936384-83-2*) Cowley Pubns.

Ceremonies of the Heart: Celebrating Lesbian Unions. Ed. by Becky Butler. LC 90-8721. (Illus.). 328p. (Orig.). 1990. pap. 14.95 (*0-931188-92-X*) Seal Pr Feminist.

Ceremonies of the Lhasa Year. Hugh Richardson. Ed. by Michael Aris. (Illus.). 136p. (Orig.). 1994. pap. 24.95 (*0-906026-29-6*) Weatherhill.

C

An Asterisk (*) at the beginning of an entry indicates that the title is appearing in BIP for the first time.

Ceremonies of the Liberal Catholic Rite. 2nd ed. Irving S. Cooper. (Illus.). 225p. 1981. reprint ed. 16.50 (0-935461-07-8) St Alban Pr CA.

***Ceremonies of the Modern Roman Rite.** Peter Elliott. 375p. Date not set. pap. 24.95 (0-89870-526-6) Ignatius Pr.

Ceremonies of the Pawnee. James R. Murie. Ed. by Douglas R. Parks. LC 88-28290. (Studies in the Anthropology of North American Indians). (Illus.). xiv, 497p. 1989. reprint ed. 46.00 (0-8032-3138-5); reprint ed. pap. 19.95 (0-8032-8162-5) U of Nebr Pr.

Ceremonies Sampler. Elizabeth R. Levine. LC 90-70834. 127p. (Orig.). 1991. pap. 9.95 (0-9608054-9-4) Womans Inst-Cont Jewish Ed.

Ceremony. Robert B. Parker, Jr. 1992. mass mkt. 4.99 (0-440-10993-0) Dell.

Ceremony. Leslie M. Silko. (Contemporary American Fiction Ser.). 272p. 1986. pap. 9.95 (0-14-008683-8, Penguin Bks) Viking Penguin.

Ceremony & Art: Robert Herrick's Poetry. Robert H. Deming. (De Proprietatibus Litterarum, Series Practica: No. 64). 1974. pap. text ed. 64.65 (90-279-2621-2) Mouton.

Ceremony & Civility in English Renaissance Prose. Anne D. Hall. 213p. 1992. 32.50 (0-271-00770-2) Pa St U Pr.

Ceremony & Other Stories. Weldon Kees. LC 83-83186. 147p. (C). 1984. pap. 6.00 (0-915308-53-3) Graywolf.

***Ceremony & Ritual in Japan: Religious Practices in an Industrialized Society.** Ed. by Jan van Bremen & D. P. Martinez. LC 94-26158. (Nissan Institute - Routledge Japanese Studies). 288p. 1995. 69.95x (0-415-11663-5, B4537) Routledge.

Ceremony & Symbolism in the Japanese Home. Michael Jeremy & M. E. Robinson. (Illus.). 212p. 1989. text ed. 35.00 (0-8248-1226-3) UH Pr.

Ceremony in Lone Tree. Wright Morris. LC 60-7775. viii, 304p. 1973. reprint ed. pap. 9.95 (0-8032-5782-1, Bison Books) U of Nebr Pr.

Ceremony in Scarlet. Francis J. Thornton. 448p. (Orig.). 1991. pap. 4.50 (0-8439-3010-1) Dorchester Pub Co.

Ceremony in the Circle of Life. White Deer of Autumn. (Illus.). 32p. (J). (gr. 2-6). 1991. reprint ed. pap. 6.95 (0-941831-68-X) Beyond Words Pub.

Ceremony of Innocence. Ronald Ribman. 1968. pap. 4.75 (0-8222-0195-X) Dramatists Play.

Ceremony of Innocence: Tears, Power & Protest. Kay Carmichael. 216p. 1991. text ed. 45.00 (0-312-05699-0) St Martin.

Ceremony of Memory: Contemporary Hispanic Spiritual & Ceremonial Art. Amalia Mesa-Bains et al. (Illus.). 48p. (Orig.). 1988. pap. text ed. 15.00 (0-685-21899-6) CCA Santa Fe.

Ceremony of Names. Sue Scalf. 64p. (Orig.). 1990. pap. 8.95 (0-945301-04-9) Druid Pr.

Ceremony of Passing. W. L. Wilmshurst. 54p. 1993. pap. 9.95 (1-56459-317-7) Kessinger Pub.

Ceremony of Spirit: Nature & Memory in Contemporary Latino Art. LC 93-34619. 1993. write for info. (1-880508-02-8) Mexican Museum.

Ceremony of the Innocent. Taylor Caldwell. 1984. mass mkt. 5.95 (0-449-20626-2, Crest) Fawcett.

Ceremony of Things. limited ed. Enzo Cucchi. Tr. by Franco Martinelli. (Illus.). 88p. (ENG & ITA.). 1985. pap. 27.50 (0-935875-02-6) P Blum Edit.

Ceren Site: A Prehistoric Village Buried by Volcanic Ash. Payson D. Sheets. Ed. by Jeffrey Quilter. (Case Studies in Archaeology Ser.). 120p. (C). 1992. pap. text ed. 13.50 (0-03-078856-0) HB Coll Pubs.

***Cerenex Family Health Counselor.** Hippocrates Magazine Editors. 256p. 1994. student ed write for info. (0-9644119-0-3) Health Pubng.

Cerenkov Radiation & Its Applications. United Kingdom Atomic Energy Staff & J. Jelley. LC 58-9691. 1958. 127.00 (0-08-013127-1, Pub. by Pergamon Repr UK) Franklin.

CERES-Maize: A Simulation Model of Maize Growth & Development. Ed. by C. A. Jones & J. R. Kiniry. LC 86-5745. (Illus.). 208p. 1986. disk 33.50 (0-89096-269-3) Tex A&M Univ Pr.

Ceres' Runaway & Other Essays. Alice C. Meynell. LC 67-30223. (Essay Index Reprint Ser.). 1977. 17.95 (0-8369-0704-3) Ayer.

***Cerf-Volant Precision: Votre Guide Complet Pour le Pilotage de Cerfs-Volants Acrobatiques.** Ron Reich. Tr. & Intro. by Raoul Fosset. (Illus.). 184p. (Orig.). (FRE.). 1994. pap. 14.95 (0-9639010-3-6) Tutor Text.

Cerfs-volant. Romain Gary, pseud. (Folio Ser.: No. 1467). (FRE.). pap. 10.95 (2-07-037467-X) Schoenhof.

Cerfs-Volants. Romain Gary. 372p. (FRE.). 1980. pap. 11.95 (0-7859-2645-3, 207037467X) Fr & Eur.

Cerise. Alphonse Boudard. (FRE.). 1973. pap. 10.95 (0-7859-1748-9, 2070364038) Fr & Eur.

Cerissa. Jessica St. Claire. 352p. 1985. reprint ed. pap. 3.50 (0-8439-2198-6) Dorchester Pub Co.

***Cermony of Innocence.** Maud Nerman. 240p. Date not set. pap. 8.95 (0-7610-0298-7) NW Pub.

Cernuda y el Poema en Prosa. James Valender. (Serie A: Monagrafias, CI). 137p. (SPA.). (C). 1984. 45.00 (0-7293-0191-5, Pub. by Tamesis Bks Ltd UK) Boydell & Brewer.

Ceroid Lipofuscinosis: Batten's Disease. D. Armstrong et al. 422p. 1982. 132.00 (0-444-80329-7) Elsevier.

Ceroli Pistoletto. Robert M. Murdock. (Illus.). (Orig.). 1969. pap. 1.50 (0-685-07680-6) Buffalo Acad.

Cerrillos: Yesterday, Today & Tomorrow. Jacqueline Lawson. LC 88-34578. (Illus.). 96p. (Orig.). 1989. pap. 8.95 (0-86534-130-3) Sunstone Pr.

Cerrillos Adventure at the Bar TH Ranch. Maggie D. Trigg. LC 85-9789. (Illus.). 148p. (Orig.). 1985. pap. 9.95 (0-86534-057-9) Sunstone Pr.

Cerritos. Gertrude F. Atherton. LC 68-23711. (Americans in Fiction Ser.). 1977. reprint ed. lib. bdg. 17.50 (0-8398-0065-7); reprint ed. pap. text ed. 5.50 (0-89197-695-7) Irvington.

***Cerro Gordo, Illinois.** Sandy Miller. (Illus.). 140p. 1989. 52.50 (0-88107-145-5) Curtis Media.

Cerro Palenque: Power & Identity on the Maya Periphery. Rosemary A. Joyce. (Illus.). 200p. (C). 1991. text ed. 32.50 (0-292-71140-9) U of Tex Pr.

Cerro Prieto Geothermal Field: Proceedings of the First Symposium Held at San Diego, California, Sept. 1978. Ed. by E. Barbier. (Illus.). 300p. 1981. pap. 94.00 (0-08-026241-4, Pergamon Pr) Elsevier.

Cerro Prieto Geothermal Field: Proceedings of the Second Symposium, 17-19 October 1979, Mexicali, Mexico-Selected Papers. Ed. by E. Barbier. 144p. 1982. pap. 46.00 (0-08-028746-8, Pergamon Pr) Elsevier.

Certain Accepted Heroes. Henry C. Lodge. LC 79-37119. (Essay Index Reprint Ser.). 1977. reprint ed. 23.95 (0-8369-2514-9) Ayer.

***Certain Age: Reflections on Menopause.** Ed. by Joanna Goldsworthy. (Gender & Culture Ser.). 236p. 1994. pap. 12.95 (0-231-10151-1) Col U Pr.

Certain As the Dawn. Peter G. Van Breemen. 1981. pap. 11.95 (0-87193-150-8) Dimension Bks.

Certain Blind Man: And Other Essays on the American Mood. Robert E. Fitch. LC 75-142628. (Essay Index Reprint Ser.). 1977. reprint ed. 21.95 (0-8369-2549-1) Ayer.

Certain Blindness. Paul L. Brady. (Illus.). 325p. 1990. write for info. (0-9623720-0-5) ALP Pub.

Certain Change. David Macarov. LC 90-27568. 185p. 1991. 21.95 (0-87101-191-3) Natl Assn Soc Wkrs.

Certain Climate: Essays in History, Arts, & Letters. Paul Horgan. LC 88-137. 271p. 1988. 22.95 (0-8195-5202-X, Wesleyan Univ Pr) U Pr of New Eng.

Certain Club: One Hundred Years of the Players. John Tebbel. 1989. 75.00 (0-914373-17-X) Wieser & Wieser.

Certain Considerations upon the Government of England. Roger B. Twysden. Ed. by John M. Kemble. (Camden Society, London. Publications, First Ser.: No. 45). reprint ed. 65.00 (0-404-50145-1) AMS Pr.

Certain Crossroad. Emilie Loring. reprint ed. lib. bdg. 20.95 (0-88411-375-2, Aeonian Pr) Amereon Ltd.

Certain Days: Zionist Memoirs & Selected Papers. Julius Simon. Ed. by Evyatar Friesel. 388p. 1971. 39.95x (0-87855-183-2) Transaction Pubs.

Certain Difficulty of Being: Essays on the Quebec Novel. Anthony Purdy. 200p. (C). 1990. text ed. 44.95 (0-7735-0770-1, Pub. by McGill CN) U of Toronto Pr.

Certain Discourses Military. John Smythe. Ed. by J. R. Hale. (Documents Ser.). 1978. 24.50 (0-918016-39-8) Folger Bks.

Certain Distance. Robert Francis. Ed. by Peter Kaplan. LC 76-28159. 1976. 3.00 (0-915176-15-7) Pourboire.

Certain Dr. French. Elizabeth Seifert. 1973. reprint ed. lib. bdg. 22.95 (0-88411-008-7, Aeonian Pr) Amereon Ltd.

Certain Factors in the Development of a New Spatial Co-Ordination see Memory Defects in Organic Psychoses

Certain Faith. Norman Warren. (Pocketbooks Ser.). (Illus.). 48p. 1989. pap. 2.99 (0-7459-1449-7) Lion USA.

***Certain Finkelmeyer.** Felix Roziner. Tr. by Michael H. Heim. 362p. Date not set. pap. 16.95 (0-8101-1263-9) Northwestern U Pr.

Certain Hunger. large type ed. Stella Whitelaw. 1994. 17.95 (0-263-13850-X, Pub. by Mills & Boon Ltd UK) Chivers N Amer.

Certain Idea of France: French Security Policy & the Gaullist Legacy. Philip H. Gordon. LC 92-23532. (Studies in International History & Politics). 264p. (C). 1993. text ed. 37.50 (0-691-08647-8) Princeton U Pr.

***Certain Justice: A Novel.** John T. Lescroart. 448p. 1995. 22.95 (1-55611-445-1) D I Fine.

Certain Language Skills in Children, Vol. 26. Ed. by Mildred C. Templin. LC 75-14338. (University of Minnesota Institute of Child Welfare Monographs: No. 26). (Illus.). 183p. 1970. reprint ed. text ed. 45.00 (0-8371-8082-1, CWTL, Greenwood Pr) Greenwood.

Certain Language Skills in Children: Their Development & Interrelationships. Mildred C. Templin. LC 57-8922. (University of Minnesota Institute of Child Welfare Monographs: No. 26). 201p. reprint ed. pap. 57.30 (0-317-28163-1, 2055964) Bks Demand.

***Certain Level of Denial.** Karen Finley. LC 94-78835. (Illus.). 52p. Date not set. pap. 15.98 (0-9627014-0-8, RCD 40317) Rykodisc.

Certain Life: Contemporary Meditations on the Way of Christ. large type ed. Herbert O'Driscoll. 192p. (Orig.). 1985. reprint ed. pap. 8.95 (0-8027-2491-4) Walker & Co.

Certain, Lively Episodes: The Articulation of Passion in Eighteenth-Century Prose. Alan T. McKenzie. LC 89-4826. (Illus.). 280p. 1990. 35.00 (0-8203-1167-7) U of Ga Pr.

Certain Longing: The Photography of Bob Nandell. Bob Nandell. LC 94-72899. (Illus.). 96p. (Orig.). 1994. pap. 10.00 (1-883477-01-8) Lone Oak MN.

Certain Lucas. Julio Cortazar. Tr. by Gregory Rabassa. LC 83-48850. 139p. 1984. 12.95 (0-394-50723-1) Knopf.

***Certain Magic.** Morgan. 1995. mass mkt. 5.50 (0-312-95423-9) St Martin.

Certain Magnificence: Lyman Beecher & the Transformation of American Protestantism, 1775-1863. Vincent Harding. LC 91-27976. (Chicago Studies in the History of American Religion Ser.: Vol. 6). (Illus.). 570p. 1995. 75.00 (0-926019-43-0) Carlson Pub.

Certain Marvellous Thing. John P. Ward. 66p. 1993. pap. 13.95 (1-85411-086-1, Pub. by Seren Bks UK) Dufour.

Certain Monsieur Blot. Pierre Daninos. (FRE.). 1964. pap. 10.95 (0-8288-9181-8, F97970) Fr & Eur.

Certain Necessary Directions As well for the Cure of the Plague As for Preventing the Infection: Also Certaine Select Statutes. London College of Physicians Staff. LC 79-84120. (English Experience Ser.: No. 939). 148p. 1979. reprint ed. lib. bdg. 14.00 (90-221-0939-9) Walter J Johnson.

***Certain Paper Clips from the People's Republic of China: An International Trade Investigation.** Frederick W. Ruggles. (Illus.). 81p. (Orig.). (C). 1994. pap. text ed. 60.00x (0-7881-1505-7) Diane Pub.

Certain Patterns. Hastings Wyman, Jr. LC 81-86641. (Series Seven). 50p. (Orig.). 1980. pap. 7.00 (0-931846-22-6) Wash Writers Pub.

Certain Phases of County Educational Organization with Special Reference to Florida. Edmund L. Tink. LC 79-177708. (Columbia University. Teachers College. Contributions to Education Ser.: No. 363). reprint ed. 37.50 (0-404-55363-X) AMS Pr.

Certain Phases of the Administration of High School Chemistry. William W. Carpenter. LC 70-176627. (Columbia University. Teachers College. Contributions to Education Ser.: No. 191). reprint ed. 37.50 (0-404-55191-2) AMS Pr.

Certain Philosophical Questions: Newton's Trinity Notebook. J. E. McGuire & Martin Tamny. LC 82-22200. 512p. 1983. 125.00 (0-521-23164-7) Cambridge U Pr.

Certain Places: Photographs by William Clift. William Clift. (Illus.). 1987. 75.00 (0-9618165-0-3) Wm Clift Editions.

Certain Poets of Importance: Victorian Verse Chosen for Comparison. Comp. by Hattie H. Sloss. LC 72-11918. (Granger Index Reprint Ser.). 1977. reprint ed. 30.95 (0-8369-6411-X) Ayer.

Certain Polycyclic Aromatic Hydrocarbons & Heterocyclic Compounds. IARC Working Group on the Evaluation of the Carcinogenic Risk of Chemicals to Man (1972: Lyon, France) Staff. (IARC Monographs on the Evaluation of Carcinogenic Risk of Chemicals to Man: No. 3). 273p. reprint ed. pap. 77.90 (0-8357-6456-7, 2035827) Bks Demand.

Certain Realism: Toward a Use of Passolini's Film Theory & Practice. Maurizio Viano. LC 92-28189. 1993. 38.00 (0-520-07854-3); pap. 18.00 (0-520-07855-1) U CA Pr.

***Certain Reputation.** Emma Lange. (Signet Regency Romance Ser.). 224p. (Orig.). 1995. mass mkt., pap. 3.99 (0-451-18398-3) NAL-Dutton.

Certain Rich Men. Meade Minnigerode. LC 71-121489. (Essay Index Reprint Ser.). 1977. 20.95 (0-8369-1714-6) Ayer.

***Certain Seamless Carbon & Alloy Standard, Line, & Pressure Steel Pipe from Argentina, Brazil, Germany & Italy: An International Trade Investigation.** Debra Baker. (Illus.). 106p. (Orig.). (C). 1994. pap. text ed. 75.00x (0-7881-1438-7) Diane Pub.

***Certain Slant of Light.** Terese Ramin. (Intimate Moments Ser.). 1995. mass mkt. 3.75 (0-373-07634-7, 1-07634-8) Silhouette.

Certain Slant of Light: Regionalism & the Form of Southern & Midwestern Fiction. David M. Holman. (Southern Literary Ser.). 160p. 1995. text ed. 25.00 (0-8071-1870-2) La State U Pr.

Certain Slant of Light: The Contemporary American Landscape. Naomi Vine & Peter B. Hales. LC 88-72150. (Illus.). 72p. 1989. pap. write for info. (0-937809-04-7) Dayton Art.

Certain Slant of Sunlight. Ted Berrigan. LC 88-90556. 112p. 1988. pap. 9.00 (0-929022-00-9) O Bks.

Certain Small Shepherd. Rebecca Caudill. LC 65-17604. (Illus.). 48p. (J). (gr. 2-4). 1965. 14.95 (0-8050-1323-7, Bks Young Read) H Holt & Co.

Certain Small Works. Robert H. Taylor. LC 79-3891. (Illus.). 164p. 1980. 25.00 (0-87811-023-2) Princeton Lib.

Certain Smiles. Dorothy Tell. 256p. 1994. pap. 9.95 (1-56280-066-3) Naiad Pr.

Certain Sound: The Struggle for Liberation in South Africa. Cedric Mayson. LC 85-13678. 160p. (Orig.). reprint ed. pap. 45.60 (0-8357-8546-7, 2034884) Bks Demand.

Certain Sound of the Trumpet: Crafting a Sermon of Authority. Samuel D. Proctor. 152p. 1994. pap. 12.00 (0-8170-1202-8) Judson.

Certain Sourire. Francoise Sagan. 124p. (FRE.). 1992. pap. 10.95 (0-7859-1488-9, 2266049461) Fr & Eur.

Certain Style: The Art of the Plastic Handbag, 1949-1959. Robert Gottlieb. LC 88-45340. (Illus.). 128p. 1988. 35.00 (0-394-56893-1) Knopf.

Certain Techniques Used in Developing a Course of Study in Science for the Horace Mann Elementary School. Gerald S. Craig. LC 77-176677. (Columbia University. Teachers College. Contributions to Education Ser.: No. 276). reprint ed. 37.50 (0-404-55276-5) AMS Pr.

Certain Tendency of the American Cinema: 1930-1980. Robert B. Ray. LC 84-42901. (Illus.). 405p. 1985. pap. 19.95 (0-691-10174-4) Princeton U Pr.

Certain Terror: Heterosexism, Militarism, Violence & Change. Ed. by Richard Cleaver et al. (Illus.). 400p. 1993. pap. 14.95 (0-9635516-0-4) Grt Lks Reg AFSC.

Certain Things Last: The Selected Stories of Sherwood Anderson. Sherwood Anderson. 360p. 1992. 24.95 (0-941423-85-9) FWEW.

***Certain Things Last: The Selected Stories of Sherwood Anderson.** Sherwood Anderson. 388p. 1992. pap. 14.95 (1-56858-022-3) FWEW.

Certain Tract of Land. Jean A. Seder. 112p. 1988. 8.95 (0-87426-057-4) Whitmore.

Certain Tragical Discourses of Bandello, 2 Vols, 1. Matteo Bandello. Tr. by Geffraie Fenton. LC 73-160008. (Tudor Translations, First Ser.: Nos. 19-20). reprint ed. 45.00 (0-404-51901-6) AMS Pr.

Certain Tragical Discourses of Bandello, 2 Vols, 2. Matteo Bandello. Tr. by Geffraie Fenton. LC 73-160008. (Tudor Translations, First Ser.: Nos. 19-20). reprint ed. 45.00 (0-404-51902-4) AMS Pr.

Certain Tragical Discourses of Bandello, 2 Vols, Set. Matteo Bandello. Tr. by Geffraie Fenton. LC 73-160008. (Tudor Translations, First Ser.: Nos. 19-20). reprint ed. 115.00 (0-404-51900-8) AMS Pr.

Certain Trumpets. Gary Will. 1994. 23.00 (0-671-65702-X) S&S Trade.

***Certain Trumpets: The Nature of Leadership.** Garry Wills. 1995. pap. 14.00 (0-684-80138-8, Litl Simon S&S) S&S Childrens.

Certain Uncertainties: New Literacy & the Evaluation of Student Writing. Joanne K. Peters. (Concept Paper Ser.: No. 5). 53p. 1992. pap. 6.95 (0-8141-0526-2) NCTE.

Certain Victory: The American Army in the Gulf, 2 vols., Set. 1994. lib. bdg. 595.00 (0-8490-8538-1) Gordon Pr.

Certain Victory: The U. S. Army in the Gulf War. Robert H. Scales et al. (Association of the U. S. Army Book Ser.). (Illus.). 435p. 1994. 30.00 (0-02-881111-9) Brasseys Inc.

Certain Victory: The United States Army in the Gulf War. (Illus.). 451p. (Orig.). (C). 1994. pap. text ed. 150.00 (0-7881-0476-4) Diane Pub.

Certain Voices: Short Stories about Gay Men. Ed. by Darryl Pilcher. 224p. (Orig.). 1991. pap. 8.95 (1-55583-194-X) Alyson Pubns.

Certain Women. Madeleine L'Engle. 1992. 21.00 (0-374-12025-0) FS&G.

Certain Women. Madeleine L'Engle. LC 92-56136. 368p. 1993. Alk. paper. pap. 12.00 (0-06-065207-1) Harper SF.

Certaine Brief & Necessarie Rules of Geographie. LC 76-57402. (English Experience Ser.: No. 818). 1977. reprint ed. lib. bdg. 3.50 (90-221-0818-X) Walter J Johnson.

Certaine Dame. Guy Des Cars. 392p. 1971. 17.95 (0-686-55614-3) Fr & Eur.

Certaine Dame. Guy Des Cars. (FRE.). 1978. pap. 9.95 (0-8288-9573-2, M5718) Fr & Eur.

Certaine Errors in Navigation (the Voyage of George Earl of Cumberland to the Azores) Edward Wright. LC 74-80224. (English Experience Ser.: No. 703). 1974. reprint ed. 35.00 (90-221-0703-5) Walter J Johnson.

Certaine Experiments Concerning the Fish & the Fruite. John Taverner. LC 76-6030. (English Experience Ser.: No. 75). 38p. 1968. reprint ed. 25.00 (90-221-0075-8) Walter J Johnson.

Certaine Learned & Elegant Works. Fulke Greville. LC 90-8952. 392p. 1990. reprint ed. 50.00 (0-8201-1448-0) Schol Facsimiles.

Certaine Miscellany Works. Francis Bacon. LC 79-25440. (English Experience Ser.: No. 222). 166p. 1970. reprint ed. 35.00 (90-221-0222-X) Walter J Johnson.

Certaine Parente. Carlos Fuentes. 320p. (FRE.). 1988. pap. 11.95 (0-7859-2559-7, 2070380653) Fr & Eur.

Certaine Schoole: A History of Cowbridge Grammar School. Iolo Davies. 392p. (C). 1989. 59.00 (0-685-61450-6, Pub. by D Brown & Sons Ltd UK) St Mut.

Certaine Sermons or Homilies Appointed to Be Read in the Churches in the Time of Elizabeth 1st, 1547-1571, 2 vols. in 1. Church of England. LC 68-17016. 1968. reprint ed. 75.00 (0-8201-1008-6) Schol Facsimiles.

Certaine Workes of Chirurgerie. Thomas Gale. LC 79-38108. (English Experience Ser.: No. 420). (Illus.). 200p. 1971. reprint ed. 74.00 (90-221-0420-6) Walter J Johnson.

Certainly, Future: Selected Writing by Dimitrije Mitrinovic. Ed. by H. C. Rutherford. 450p. 1987. text ed. 62.50 (0-88033-118-6, 222) East Eur Quarterly.

Certainties & Doubts: Collected Papers, 1962-1985. George C. Homans. 420p. 1988. 34.95 (0-88738-139-1) Transaction Pubs.

***Certainty.** Ed. by Jonathan Westphal. LC 94-44149. (Readings in Philosophy Ser.). 192p. (C). 1995. lib. bdg. 24.95x (0-87220-319-0); pap. text ed. 5.95x (0-87220-318-2) Hackett Pub.

Certainty, a Refutation of Scepticism. Peter D. Klein. LC 81-13040. 256p. reprint ed. pap. 73.00 (0-7837-2940-5, 2057514) Bks Demand.

Certainty & Surface in Epistemology & Philosophical Method: Essays in Honor of Avrum Stroll. Ed. by A. P. Martinich & Michael White. LC 91-27368. (Problems in Contemporary Philosophy Ser.: Vol. 32). 228p. 1991. lib. bdg. 89.95 (0-7734-9711-0) E Mellen.

Certainty for a Doubt see Four Plays of Lope de Vega

Certainty of Bible Prophecy. Robert Lindsted. 72p. (Orig.). 1991. pap. 5.95 (1-879366-07-X) Hearthstone OK.

***Certainty of Justice: Reform in the Crime Victim Movement.** Frank J. Weed. (Social Problems & Social Issues Ser.). 168p. 1995. lib. bdg. 41.95 (0-202-30517-1); pap. 20.95 (0-202-30518-X) Aldine de Gruyter.

Certainty of Literature: Essays in Polemic. George Watson. LC 89-24123. 240p. 1989. text ed. 39.95 (0-312-04043-1) St Martin.

Certainty of Spring: Poems by a Guatemalan in Exile. Julia Esquivel. Tr. by Anne Woehrle. LC 92-35394. 188p. (Orig.). (ENG & SPA.). 1992. pap. 11.95 (0-918346-11-8) EPICA.

Certane Tractatis for Reformatioun of Doctryne & Maneris in Scotland. Ninian Winzet. LC 79-178311. (Maitland Club, Glasgow. Publications: No. 33). reprint ed. 20.00 (0-404-53001-X) AMS Pr.

Certayne News of Christian Princes. LC 74-38155. (English Experience Ser.: No. 442). 16p. 1972. reprint ed. 7.00 (90-221-0442-7) Walter J Johnson.

Certeza (Assurance) large type ed. J. C. Ryle. (SPA.). Date not set. 3.50 (1-56063-340-9, 494022) Editorial Unilit.

An Asterisk (*) at the beginning of an entry indicates that the title is appearing in BIP for the first time.

C

An Asterisk (*) at the beginning of an entry indicates that the title is appearing in BIP for the first time.

Cervical Spine. 2nd ed. Ed. by Cervical Spine Research Society Staff. 1989. text ed. 140.00 (*0-397-50827-1*, Lippincott Medical) Lippincott.

Cervical Spine. Robert W. Bailey. LC 79-152020. 271p. reprint ed. pap. 77.30 (*0-317-07772-4*, 2055676) Bks Demand.

Cervical Spine, No. II. Ed. by R. Louis & A. Weidner. (Illus.). 304p. 1990. 91.00 (*0-387-82151-1*, 3624) Spr-Verlag.

Cervical Spine: A Surgical Atlas. 3rd ed. Henry H. Sherk. 1993. text ed. 135.00 (*0-397-51203-1*) Lippincott.

Cervical Spine I. Ed. by P. Kehr & A. Weidner. (Illus.). 330p. 1987. 106.00 (*0-387-81953-3*) Spr-Verlag.

***Cervical Spondylosis - Sponsored by the Subcommittee on Continuing Education II (Expanded Program), American Association of Neurological Surgeons, & Congress of Neurological Surgeons.** fac. ed. Ed. by Stewart B. Dunsker. LC 79-5395. (Seminars in Neurological Surgery Ser.). (Illus.). 229p. Date not set. pap. 65.30 (*0-7837-7229-7*, 2047069) Bks Demand.

Cervical Spondylotic Myelopathy. R. L. Saunders & P. M. Bernini. (Contemporary Issues in Neurological Surgery Ser.). (Illus.). 1992. 85.00 (*0-86542-193-5*) Blackwell Sci.

Cervical Syndrome. 4th ed. Ruth Jackson. (Illus.). 416p. 1978. 49.95x (*0-398-03696-9*) C C Thomas.

***Cervical Syndrome.** 4th ed. Ruth Jackson. (Illus.). 416p. 1978. pap. 29.95 (*0-398-06178-5*) C C Thomas.

Cervicothoracic Trauma. 2nd ed. F. William Blaisdell & D. Trunkey. LC 93-4002. (Trauma Management Ser.). (Illus.). 424p. 1993. text ed. 99.00 (*0-86577-492-7*) Thieme Med Pubs.

Cervin Robinson - Cleveland, Ohio. Cervin Robinson. LC 89-22050. (Published in Association with the Cleveland Museum of Art Ser.). 124p. 1989. 44.95 (*0-910386-98-6*); pap. 21.95 (*0-910386-99-4*) Cleveland Mus Art.

Cervix Cancer. Ed. by Earl A. Surwit & David S. Alberts. (Cancer Treatment & Research Ser.). 1987. lib. bdg. 100.00 (*0-89838-822-8*) Kluwer Ac.

Ces Jours Lointains: Avec: Alphonse Sechee et Romain Rolland, Lettres et autres Ecrits. Romain Rolland & Alphonse Seche. 176p. (FRE.). 1962. pap. 8.95 (*0-7859-5441-4*) Fr & Eur.

Cesar. Marcel Pagnol. 1956. 11.50 (*0-685-23892-X*) Fr & Eur.

C

Cesar. Marcel Pagnol. 292p. (FRE.). 1976. 13.95 (*0-8288-9890-1*, F117430) Fr & Eur.

Cesar see Oeuvres Completes

Cesar Birotteau. Honore De Balzac. 10.95 (*0-8288-9362-4*, 2070367037) Fr & Eur.

Cesar Birotteau. Honore De Balzac. (Folio Ser.: No. 703). (FRE.). pap. 9.95 (*2-07-036703-7*) Schoenhof.

Cesar Birotteau. Honore De Balzac. 1987. pap. write for info. (*0-14-044347-9*, Penguin Bks) Viking Penguin.

Cesar Birotteau. Honore De Balzac. (Illus.). 320p. 1994. 9.95 (*0-14-044600-1*, Penguin Classics) Viking Penguin.

***Cesar Chavez.** (Hispanos Notables Ser.). (Illus.). 128p. (SPA.). (YA). (gr. 5 up). Date not set. 18.95 (*0-7910-3102-0*) Chelsea Hse.

***Cesar Chavez.** (Hispanos Notables Ser.). (Illus.). 128p. (SPA.). (YA). (gr. 5 up). Date not set. pap. 7.95 (*0-7910-3112-8*) Chelsea Hse.

Cesar Chavez. Ruth Franchere. LC 78-101927. (Crowell Biogrpahy Ser.). (Illus.). 40p. (J). (gr. 2-5). 1970. lib. bdg. 14.89 (*0-690-18384-4*, Crowell Jr Bks) HarpC Child Bks.

Cesar Chavez. Burnham Holmes. LC 92-18225. (American Troublemakers Ser.). (Illus.). 128p. (J). (gr. 7-10). 1992. lib. bdg. 24.26 (*0-8114-2326-3*) Raintree Steck-V.

Cesar Chavez. Consuelo Rodriguez. (Hispanics of Achievement Ser.). (Illus.). 112p. (YA). (gr. 5 up). 1991. lib. bdg. 17.95 (*0-7910-1232-8*) Chelsea Hse.

***Cesar Chavez: A Triumph of Spirit.** Richard Griswold del Castillo & Richard A. Garcia. LC 95-15230. (Oklahoma Western Biographies Ser.: Vol. 11). 1995. write for info. (*0-8061-2758-9*) U of Okla Pr.

Cesar Chavez: Hope for the People. David Goodwin. (Great Lives Biography Ser.). (Illus.). 144p. (Orig.). (ENG & SPA.). 1991. mass mkt. 4.00 (*0-449-90626-4*, Columbine) Fawcett.

Cesar Chavez: Labor Leader. Maria E. Cedeno. LC 92-22620. (Hispanic Heritage Ser.). (Illus.). 32p. (J). (gr. 2-4). 1993. lib. bdg. 13.40 (*1-56294-280-8*); pap. 4.95 (*1-56294-808-3*) Millbrook Pr.

***Cesar Chavez: Mexican-American Labor Leader.** C. Rodriguez. Ed. by Rodolfo Cardona & James Cockcroft. (Hispanics of Achievement Ser.). (Illus.). 128p. (YA). (gr. 5 up). 1995. pap. 7.95 (*0-7910-1259-X*) Chelsea Hse.

Cesar Chavez: Mini Play. (Mexican-American Ser.). (J). (gr. 5 up). 1978. 5.00 (*0-89550-305-0*) Stevens & Shea.

Cesar Chavez: Union Leader. Bruce W. Conord. (Junior Hispanics of Achievement Ser.). (Illus.). 80p. (J). (gr. 3-6). 1993. lib. bdg. 14.95 (*0-7910-1757-5*, Am Art Analog); pap. 4.95 (*0-7910-1999-3*, Am Art Analog) Chelsea Hse.

Cesar Chavez & La Causa. Naurice Roberts. LC 85-27980. (Picture Story Biographies Ser.). (Illus.). 32p. (J). (gr. 2-4). 1986. lib. bdg. 11.85 (*0-516-03484-7*); pap. 3.95 (*0-516-43484-5*) Childrens.

Cesar Chavez & the United Farm Workers: A Selective Bibliography. Beverly Fodell. LC 73-6365. 116p. 1974. pap. text ed. 13.95 (*0-8143-1502-X*) Wayne St U Pr.

***Cesar Chavez, Labor Leader.** Clara S. De Morris. (Illus.). (J). (gr. 1-4). 1994. lib. bdg. 9.95 (*0-8136-5266-9*); pap. 4.95 (*0-8136-5272-3*) Modern Curr.

***Cesar Chavez, Lider Laboral.** Clara S. De Morris. (Illus.). (SPA.). (J). (gr. 1-4). 1994. lib. bdg. 9.95 (*0-8136-5294-4*); pap. 4.95 (*0-8136-5300-2*) Modern Curr.

Cesar Chavez y la Causa. Naurice Roberts. (Spanish Picture-Story Biographies Ser.). 32p. (J). (gr. 2-5). 1986. pap. 3.95 (*0-516-53484-X*) Childrens.

Cesar Franck. Vincent D'Indy. 286p. 1990. reprint ed. lib. bdg. 69.00 (*0-7812-9062-7*) Rprt Serv.

Cesar Franck. Leon Vallas. LC 73-5210. (Illus.). 283p. 1973. reprint ed. text ed. 55.00 (*0-8371-6873-2*, VACF, Greenwood Pr) Greenwood.

Cesar Franck: Music Book Index. Norman Demuth. 228p. 1993. reprint ed. lib. bdg. 79.00 (*0-7812-9598-X*) Rprt Serv.

Cesar Franck & His Circle. Laurence Davies. LC 77-4231. (Music Reprint Ser.). (Illus.). 1977. reprint ed. lib. bdg. 45.00 (*0-306-77410-0*) Da Capo.

Cesar Paternosto. Ricardo Martin-Crosa & Lucy R. Lippard. (Illus.). (ENG & SPA.). 1981. pap. 5.00 (*0-89192-338-1*, Ctr Inter-Am Rel) Interbk Inc.

Cesar Pelli. (Architecture & Urbanism Extra Edition Ser.). (Illus.). 232p. (Orig.). (ENG & JPN.). (C). pap. text ed. 68.00 (*4-900211-11-7*, Pub. by Japan Architect JA) Gingko Press.

Cesar Pelli. Ed. by Toshio Nakamura. (Illus.). 232p. (ENG & JPN.). 1985. 150.00 (*0-685-63203-2*); pap. 100.00 (*0-685-63204-0*) Elliots Bks.

Cesar Pelli. John Pastier. (Illus.). 120p. 1980. 89.50 (*0-8230-7414-5*) Elliots Bks.

Cesar Pelli: Buildings & Projects 1965-1990. Mario Gandelsonas & John Pastier. LC 90-34572. (Illus.). 288p. 1990. 60.00 (*0-8478-1261-8*); pap. 35.00 (*0-8478-1262-6*) Rizzoli Intl.

Cesar Vallejo: An Anthology of Poetry. Ed. by J. Higgins. 1970. 90.00 (*0-08-015762-9*, Pub. by Pergamon Repr UK) Franklin.

Cesar Vallejo en Su Fase Trilcica. Eduardo Neale-Silva. 664p. 1976. pap. 10.00x (*0-299-06774-2*) U of Wis Pr.

Cesar Vallejo en Trilce. Jose L. Vega. LC 79-26380. (UPREX, Estudios Literarios Ser.: No. 60). ix, 132p. 1983. pap. 3.00 (*0-8477-0060-7*) U of PR Pr.

Cesare Borgia. John Haney. (World Leaders - Past & Present Ser.). (Illus.). 112p. (YA). (gr. 5 up). 1986. lib. bdg. 17.95 (*0-87754-595-2*) Chelsea Hse.

Cesare e la Retorica dell'Assedio. Giovanni Cipriani. (London Studies in Classical Philology: Vol. 16). 81p. (Orig.). (ITA.). (C). 1987. pap. 21.00 (*90-70265-59-1*, Pub. by Gieben NE) Benjamins North Am.

Cesare Pavese. Anne-Marie O'Healy. (Twayne World Authors Ser.: No. 785). 192p. (C). 1988. text ed. 26.95 (*0-8057-8242-7*, 398, Twayne) Macmillan.

Cesare Pavese: Selected Letters 1924 to 1950. Cesare Pavese. Ed. by A. E. Murch. 270p. 1969. 17.95 (*0-8464-1192-X*) Beekman Pubs.

Cesarean Birth Experience: A Practical, Comprehensive & Reassuring Guide for Parents & Professionals. Bonnie Donovan. LC 85-47520. 283p. reprint ed. pap. 80.70 (*0-7837-1383-5*, 2041559) Bks Demand.

Cesarean Delivery. Ed. by J. P. Phelan & S. L. Clark. 610p. 1988. 63.25 (*0-444-01304-0*) Elsevier.

***Cesarean Delivery in the United States, 1990.** National Center for Health Statistics Staff. LC 95-1929. (Series Reports: Series 21, No. 51). 24p. Date not set. 2.25 (*0-614-02923-6*, PB94-168234) Natl Ctr Health Stats.

Cesarean Delivery in the United States, 1990. S. M. Tafel. LC 94-10794. (Vital & Health Statistics. Series 21, Data on Natality, Marriage, & Divorce: No. 51). 1994. write for info. (*0-8406-0490-4*) Natl Ctr Health Stats.

***Cesarean Section: Guidelines for Appropriate Utilization.** Ed. by Bruce L. Flamm & Edward J. Quilligan. LC 94-29533. (Clinical Perspectives in Obstetrics & Gynecology Ser.). 1995. write for info. (*0-387-94238-6*); write for info. (*3-540-94238-6*) Spr-Verlag.

Cesarian Delivery in Current Obstetric Practice. Jack W. Pearson. 1991. 39.95 (*0-8151-6663-X*, Yr Bk Med Pubs) Mosby Yr Bk.

Cesario Gussago: Sonate a Quattro, sei, et Otto, con Alcuni Concerti a Otto, Venice, 1608. Ed. by Andrew Dell'Antonio. LC 93-41237. (Italian Instrumental Music of the Sixteenth & Early Seventeenth Centuries Ser.: Vol. 20). 440p. 1994. 120.00 (*0-8240-4519-X*) Garland.

Cesium-137 from the Environment to Man: Metabolism & Dose. LC 77-77789. (Report Ser.: No. 52). 1977. 15.00 (*0-913392-34-0*) NCRP Pubns.

Cesko-Francouzsky-Cesky Slovnik na Cesty. V. Capkova. 431p. (CZE & FRE.). 1981. 8.95 (*0-8288-1696-4*, M14021) Fr & Eur.

CESSNA: A Master's Expression. Edward H. Phillips. LC 85-81741. (Illus.). 152p. 1985. 24.95 (*0-911139-04-4*) Flying Bks.

Cessna: The House of Cessna. 2nd ed. H. Cessna. (Second Ser.). (Illus.). 199p. 1992. reprint ed. lib. bdg. 41.00 (*0-8328-2366-X*); reprint ed. pap. 31.00 (*0-8328-2367-8*) Higginson Bk Co.

Cessna Citations. Donald J. Porter. 1993. pap. 14.95 (*0-07-050619-1*) McGraw.

Cessna Citations. Donald J. Porter. LC 93-18321. 1993. pap. 14.60 (*0-8306-4147-5*) TAB Bks.

Cessna One Hundred & Seventy-Two. 2nd ed. Bill Clarke. 1993. pap. 15.95 (*0-8306-4293-5*) TAB Bks.

Cessna One Hundred Fifty & One Hundred Fifty-Two. Bill Clark. (Illus.). 272p. (Orig.). 1987. 19.95 (*0-8306-9022-0*, 2422); pap. 13.95 (*0-8306-0222-4*) TAB Bks.

Cessna One Hundred Seventy Two. Bill Clarke. (Illus.). 320p. (Orig.). 1987. 19.95 (*0-8306-0912-1*, 2412) TAB Bks.

***Cessna 150.** Jeremy M. Pratt. LC 95-16303. (Pilot's Guide Ser.). 1995. write for info. (*1-56027-213-9*) Av Suppl & Acad.

Cessna 150 & 152. Bill Clarke. 1987. pap. text ed. 13.95 (*0-07-155256-1*) McGraw.

Cessna 150 & 152. 2nd ed. Bill Clarke. 1993. pap. text ed. 14.95 (*0-07-011269-X*) McGraw.

Cessna 150 & 152. 2nd ed. Bill Clarke. LC 92-35194. 1993. pap. 14.95 (*0-8306-4293-5*) TAB Bks.

***Cessna 152.** Jeremy M. Pratt. LC 95-16302. (Pilot's Guide Ser.). 1995. write for info. (*1-56027-212-0*) Av Suppl & Acad.

***Cessna 172.** Jeremy M. Pratt. LC 95-16301. (Pilot's Guide Ser.). 1995. write for info. (*1-56027-211-2*) Av Suppl & Acad.

Cessna 172. 2nd ed. Bill Clarke. 1993. pap. text ed. 14.95 (*0-07-011270-3*) McGraw.

C'est-a-Dire. Edward C. Knox & Carol D. Rifelj. 317p. (C). 1980. pap. text ed. 20.00 (*0-15-505860-6*) HB Coll Pubs.

C'est a Vous. Boston. 1988. pap. text ed. 12.13 (*0-582-35526-5*, 78047); audio 23.00 (*0-582-35570-2*, 78046) Longman.

C'est Beau une Village la Nuit. Richard Bohringer. 316p. (FRE.). 1989. pap. 10.95 (*0-7859-2112-5*, 2070381161) Fr & Eur.

C'est Bizarre l'Ecriture. Christiane Rochefort. 160p. (FRE.). 1970. pap. 27.95 (*0-7859-5436-8*) Fr & Eur.

C'est Comme Ca. 2nd ed. Jean-Paul Valette & Rebecca M. Valette. LC 85-60974. (Manual de Lecture et de Communication). 336p. (FRE.). (C). 1987. pap. text ed. 17.00 (*0-669-05202-7*) Heath.

C'est Comme Ca: Manuel De Lecture et De Communication. Jean-Paul Valette & Rebecca M. Valette. (FRE.). (C). 1978. pap. text ed. write for info. (*0-669-01162-2*) Heath.

C'est la Vie. 4th ed. Paul Pimsleur & Beverly Pimsleur. 225p. (C). 1987. pap. text ed. 18.00 (*0-15-505893-2*) HB Coll Pubs.

C'est la Vie. 5th ed. Paul Pimsleur & Beverly Pimsleur. 225p. (FRE.). (C). 1992. pap. text ed. 20.00 (*0-03-055813-1*) HB Coll Pubs.

Cest Oaucasi & De Nicolete. Ed. by F. W. Bourdillon. LC 80-2241. (Illus.). reprint ed. 32.50 (*0-404-19036-7*) AMS Pr.

C'est Si Bon: It's So Good. Illus. by Nancy Harris. LC 72-95549. 354p. 1969. pap. 9.95 (*0-9608282-1-4*) YWCO.

C'est Simple. Susan C. Hall. (Illus.). 192p. (Orig.). 1985. 10.95 (*0-912243-01-5*) Hennepin Hall.

C'est Ton Tour. Rosemary Haigh & Carol Pulver. (Aiming for Proficiency Ser.). (Illus.). 160p. (Orig.). (FRE.). 1990. student ed 14.94 (*1-879279-02-9*, TX 3-018-187) Proficiency Pr.

Cestas De Mimbre. (Productos Latinoamericanos Incluidos en el Sistema Genearlizado de Preferencias de los Estados Unidos Ser.). 21p. 1977. pap. text ed. 3.00 (*0-8270-3475-X*) OAS.

Cestoda, Vol. 1. T. Southwell. (Fauna of British India Ser.). xxxii, 391p. 1983. 50.00 (*1-55528-021-8*, Pub. by Today & Tomorrows P & P II) Scholarly Pubns.

Cestoda, Vol. 2. T. Southwell. (Fauna of British India Ser.). x, 262p. 1983. 50.00 (*1-55528-022-6*, Pub. by Today & Tomorrows P & P II) Scholarly Pubns.

Cestods, Parasites of Indian Animals. H. S. Nama. (C). 1990. text ed. 150.00 (*81-85046-97-2*, Pub. by Scientific Pubs II) St Mut.

CET Communications Exam Book. Dick Glass & Ron Crow. (Illus.). 252p. 1988. 24.95 (*0-8306-7910-3*, 2910H); pap. 15.95 (*0-8306-2910-6*, 2910P) TAB Bks.

Cet Ete La. Marie Cardinal. (FRE.). 1980. pap. 10.95 (*0-7859-3103-1*) Fr & Eur.

CET Exam Book. 3rd ed. Dick Glass & Ron Crow. (Illus.). 304p. 1992. 27.95 (*0-8306-4069-X*, 4199); pap. 17.95 (*0-8306-4068-1*, 4199) TAB Bks.

Cet Exam Book. 3rd ed. Dick Glass & Ron Crow. 1992. text ed. 29.95 (*0-07-023555-4*); pap. text ed. 17.95 (*0-07-023556-2*) McGraw.

CET Study Guide. Sam Wilson. LC 84-8517. (Illus.). 308p. (Orig.). 1984. 17.95 (*0-8306-0791-9*) TAB Bks.

CET Study Guide. 2nd ed. Sam Wilson. (Illus.). 336p. (Orig.). 1987. 21.95 (*0-8306-0941-5*, 2941) TAB Bks.

CET Study Guide. 3rd ed. Sam Wilson. LC 92-7499. (Illus.). 280p. 1992. 27.95 (*0-8306-3600-5*, 4076); pap. 17.95 (*0-8306-3556-4*, 4076) TAB Bks.

Cet Study Guide. 3rd ed. Sam Wilson. 1992. text ed. 27.95 (*0-07-070818-5*); pap. text ed. 17.95 (*0-07-070819-3*) McGraw.

CETA: Accomplishments, Problems, Solutions. William Mirengoff et al. LC 82-2856. 321p. 1982. pap. 7.00 (*0-911558-96-9*) W E Upjohn.

CETA: Politics & Policy, 1973-1982. Grace A. Franklin & Randall B. Ripley. LC 84-5145. 268p. 1984. text ed. 31.00x (*0-87049-437-6*) U of Tenn Pr.

CETA & the Arts in Santa Barbara. Kirk Robertson. (Illus.). 1978. pap. 3.00 (*0-916918-10-6*) Duck Down.

CETA at the Crossroads: Employment Policy & Politics. Paul Bullock. (Monograph & Research Ser.: No. 29). 280p. 1981. 8.50 (*0-89215-113-7*) U Cal LA Indus Rel.

Cetace-Composition see Grande Encyclopedie

Cetacean Behavior: Mechanisms & Functions. Ed. by Louis M. Herman. LC 87-31065. 480p. (C). 1988. reprint ed. lib. bdg. 53.50 (*0-89464-272-3*) Krieger.

Cetaceen, Vergleichend-Anatomisch und Systematisch. E. J. Slijper. (Illus.). 1973. reprint ed. lib. bdg. 108.00 (*90-6123-226-0*) Lubrecht & Cramer.

***Ceto's New Friends.** Leah A. Haley. LC 94-77255. (Illus.). 28p. (J). (ps-2). 1994. 18.95 (*1-883729-01-7*) Greenleaf AL.

Cetro de Ottokar. Herge. (Illus.). 62p. (SPA.). (J). 19.95 (*0-8288-5017-8*) Fr & Eur.

Cette Ame Ardente: Avec: Choix de Lettres d'Andre Suares a Romain Rolland (1887-1891) Romain Rolland & Andre Suares. 408p. (FRE.). 1954. pap. 8.95 (*0-7859-5442-2*) Fr & Eur.

Cette Emotion Appelee Poesie: Ecrits sur la Poesie. Pierre Reverdy. 288p. (FRE.). 1989. pap. 29.95 (*0-7859-1599-0*, 208060659X) Fr & Eur.

Cette Etrange Tendresse. Guy Des Cars. 336p. 1960. 9.95 (*0-686-55616-X*) Fr & Eur.

Cette Etrange Tendresse. Guy Des Cars. 320p. (FRE.). 1968. pap. 6.95 (*0-8288-9547-3*, M5719) Fr & Eur.

***Cette Ombre Familiere - Dark Companion.** Elisabeth Manuel. Tr. by Judith Suther. 230p. (Orig.). (FRE.). 1995. pap. 18.00 (*0-9645677-0-9*) Starbks.

Cette Voix. Robert Pinget. 232p. (FRE.). 1991. pap. 24.95 (*0-7859-1503-6*, 2707300470) Fr & Eur.

Cetywayo & His White Neighbours. H. Rider Haggard. LC 74-15045. 320p. 1983. reprint ed. 34.50 (*0-404-12075-X*) AMS Pr.

Ceux de la Soif. Georges Simenon. (FRE.). 1978. pap. 10.95 (*0-7859-4098-7*) Fr & Eur.

Cev'armiut Qanemciit Qulirait-llu: Eskimo Narratives & Tales from Chevak, Alaska. Ed. by Jacob Nash et al. (Illus.). 88p. (C). 1984. pap. 9.00 (*0-933769-09-1*); audio 4.00 (*0-933769-10-5*) Alaska Native.

Cev'armiut Qanemciit Qulirait-luu Eskimo Narratives & Tales from Chevak, Alaska. Ed. by Anthony C. Woodbury. (Illus.). 88p. 1989. pap. 9.00 (*0-912006-35-8*) U of Alaska Pr.

Ceylon. P. E. Mele. (Illus.). 90p. lib. bdg. 9.95 (*0-8288-3932-8*) Fr & Eur.

Ceylon Gazetteer. Simon C. Chitty. (C). 1989. 48.50 (*81-7013-053-0*, Pub. by Navarang II) S Asia.

Ceylon Lucius & Elmira (Klinetob) Brown Family Genealogy. Arthur Fry. LC 87-73149. (Illus.). 68p. (C). 1987. pap. 10.00 (*0-938041-02-9*) Arc Pr AR.

Ceylon under British Rule, 1795-1932. Lenox A. Mills. 311p. 1964. 30.00 (*0-7146-2019-X*, Pub. by F Cass Pubs UK) Intl Spec Bk.

Cezanne. (Phidal Art Ser.). (Illus.). 60p. 1990. 9.95 (*2-89393-042-5*) Firefly Bks Ltd.

Cezanne. (Artists & Their Work Ser.). (Illus.). 168p. 1991. 12.99 (*0-517-69482-4*) Random Hse Value.

Cezanne. Catherine Barry. (Pocket Painters Ser.). (Illus.). (J). 1994. 6.50 (*0-517-59967-8*, Clarkson Potter) Crown Bks Yng Read.

Cezanne. Mariel Brion. (Classic Art Ser.). 1988. 9.98 (*0-671-09414-9*) S&S Trade.

Cezanne. Eleanor Marrack. 1993. 5.98 (*1-55521-823-7*) Bk Sales Inc.

Cezanne. Antony Mason. (Famous Artists Ser.). (Illus.). 32p. (J). (gr. 5 up). 1994. 10.95 (*0-8120-6459-3*); pap. 5.95 (*0-8120-1293-3*) Barron.

Cezanne. Meyer Schapiro. (Library of Great Painters). (Illus.). 1962. 49.50 (*0-8109-0052-1*) Abrams.

Cezanne. Meyer Schapiro. (Library of Great Painters). (Illus.). 128p. 1988. 22.95 (*0-8109-1043-8*) Abrams.

Cezanne. Yvon Taillandier. (CAL Art Ser.). (Illus.). 1988. 14.95 (*0-517-03717-3*, Crown) Crown Pub Group.

***Cezanne.** Yvon Taillandier. 1995. 12.00 (*0-517-88417-8*) Random.

Cezanne. Richard Verdi. LC 92-80596. (World of Art Ser.). (Illus.). 216p. 1992. pap. 12.95 (*0-500-20258-3*) Thames Hudson.

Cezanne. Ambroise Vollard. 160p. 1984. pap. 3.95 (*0-486-24729-5*) Dover.

Cezanne. Catherine Dean. (Color Library Ser.). (Illus.). 128p. (C). 1994. reprint ed. pap. 14.99 (*0-7148-2682-0*, Pub. by Phaidon Press UK) Chronicle Bks.

***Cezanne.** Catherine Dean. (Color Library). (Illus.). 128p. (C). 1994. reprint ed. 19.95 (*0-7148-3208-1*, Pub. by Phaidon Press UK) Chronicle Bks.

Cezanne: A Biography. John Rewald. (Illus.). 288p. 1986. 75.00 (*0-8109-0775-5*) Abrams.

Cezanne: A Study of His Development. Roger Fry. LC 88-29645. (Illus.). 176p. 1989. lib. bdg. 32.50 (*0-226-26644-3*) U Ch Pr.

Cezanne: Father of Twentieth-Century Art. Michel Hoog. 1994. pap. 12.95 (*0-8109-2879-5*) Abrams.

Cezanne: Form. C. F. Ramuz. (Rhythm & Color Two Ser.). 1970. 9.95 (*0-8288-9515-5*) Fr & Eur.

Cezanne: Masterworks. Naubert. 1992. 15.99 (*0-517-06629-7*) Random Hse Value.

Cezanne: The Late Work. William Rubin. 1990. 55.00 (*0-8109-6019-2*) Abrams.

Cezanne: The Late Work. Ed. by William Rubin. (Illus.). 416p. 1977. 55.00 (*0-87070-278-5*, 0-8109-6019-0) Mus of Modern Art.

Cezanne & America: Dealers, Collectors, Artists, & Critics 1891-1921. John Rewald. (Bollingen Ser.). 352p. 1989. text ed. 65.00 (*0-691-09960-X*) Princeton U Pr.

Cezanne & Formalism in Bloomsbury. Beverly H. Twitchell. LC 86-16164. (Studies in the Fine Arts: Criticism: No. 20). (Illus.). 325p. reprint ed. pap. 92.70 (*0-8357-1737-2*, 2070581) Bks Demand.

Cezanne & Modernism: The Poetics of Painting. Joyce Medina. (SUNY Series, The Margins of Literature). (Illus.). 320p. (C). 1995. text ed. 59.50 (*0-7914-2231-3*); pap. 19.95 (*0-7914-2232-1*) State U NY Pr.

***Cezanne & Post Impressionism.** Diana Vowels. 64p. 1994. write for info. (*0-9640034-8-1*) World Pubns.

Cezanne & the End of Impressionism: A Study of the Theory, Technique, & Critical Evaluation of Modern Art. Richard Shiff. LC 83-18142. (Illus.). xviii, 318p. (C). 1986. pap. text ed. 25.00 (*0-226-75306-9*) U Ch Pr.

***Cezanne by Himself.** Richard Kendall. 1994. 32.98 (*0-7858-0167-7*) Bk Sales Inc.

Cezanne, Gauguin, Seurat, Van Gogh: First Loan Exhibition. Alfred H. Barr, Jr. LC 72-169295. (Museum of Modern Art Publications in Reprint). (Illus.). 152p. 1972. reprint ed. 26.95 (*0-405-01555-0*) Ayer.

Cezanne in Provence. Jacqueline Guillaud. 1989. 65.00 (*0-517-57372-5*, C P Pubs) Crown Pub Group.

***Cezanne in Provence.** Evmarie Schmitt. (Pegasus Library). (Illus.). 128p. 1995. 25.00 (*3-7913-1451-3*, Pub. by Prestel) TeNeues.

Cezanne in the Hedge & Other Memories of Charleston & Bloomsbury. Ed. by Hugh Lee. LC 92-7268. (Illus.). 1992. 24.95 (*0-226-47003-2*) U Ch Pr.

An Asterisk (*) at the beginning of an entry indicates that the title is appearing in BIP for the first time.

Cezanne in the Hedge & Other Memories of Charleston & Bloomsbury. Ed. by Hugh Lee. LC 92-7268. 192p. 1993. pap. 11.95 (*0-226-47004-0*) U Ch Pr.

Cezanne Letters. 5th rev. ed. Ed. by John Rewald. LC 81-81716. (Illus.). 400p. 1985. lib. bdg. 60.00 (*0-87817-276-9*) Hacker.

Cezanne Paintings. Gotz Adriani. LC 94-20396. (Illus.). Date not set. write for info. (*0-8109-4026-4*) Abrams.

Cezanne (Paul) the Watercolors: A Catalogue Raisonne. John Rewald. (Illus.). 486p. 1984. boxed 200.00 (*1-55660-167-0*) A Wofsy Fine Arts.

Cezanne Pinto. Mary Stolz. LC 92-46765. 256p. (YA). (gr. 7 up). 1994. 15.00 (*0-679-84917-3*) Knopf Bks Yng Read.

Cezanne Sketchbook: Figures, Portraits, Landscapes & Still Lives. Paul Cezanne. (Fine Art Ser.). 144p. 1985. reprint ed. pap. 5.95 (*0-486-24790-2*) Dover.

***Cezanne's & The Provencal Table.** Jacqueline Sauliner & Jean B. Nauden. 1995. 40.00 (*0-517-70185-5*) Random Hse Value.

Cezanne's Art & Oeuvre: A Catalogue Raisonne, 2 vols. Lionello Venturi. (Illus.). (FRE.). 1989. reprint ed. Set, Vol. 1, 408p, Vol. 2, 406p. 295.00 (*1-55660-026-7*) A Wofsy Fine Arts.

Cezanne's Composition: Analysis of His Form with Diagrams & Photographs of His Motifs. 3rd ed. Erle Loran. (Illus.). 1963. pap. 17.00 (*0-520-05459-8*) U CA Pr.

Cezanne's Early Imagery. Mary T. Lewis. 300p. (C). 1989. 48.00 (*0-520-06561-1*) U CA Pr.

Cezanne's Early Imagery. Mary T. Lewis. 1992. pap. 20.00 (*0-520-06563-8*) U CA Pr.

Cezanne's Graphic Work. Jean Cherpin. (Illus.). 128p. (Orig.). (FRE.). 1972. pap. 60.00 (*0-915346-87-7*) A Wofsy Fine Arts.

CF-252 Neutron Brachytherapy. Yosh Maruyama. (Nuclear Science Applications Ser.: Section B, Vol. 1, No. 8). 72p. 1984. pap. text ed. 39.00 (*3-7186-0208-3*) Gordon & Breach.

CF-252 Neutron Brachytherapy & Fast Neutron Beam Therapy. Y. Maruyama et al. 658p. 1986. text ed. 290.00 (*3-7186-0324-1*) Gordon & Breach.

CFA Candidate Study & Examination Program Review, 1991. (Orig.). 1990. pap. text ed. 30.00 (*1-879087-01-4*) Assn I M&R.

CFA Candidate Study & Examination Program Review, 1993. (Orig.). 1992. pap. text ed. 30.00 (*1-879087-18-9*) Assn I M&R.

***CFA Candidate Study & Examination Program Review, 1994.** 1994. write for info. (*1-879087-34-0*) Assn I M&R.

CFA Readings in Financial Analysis. 6th ed. 348p. 1981. 12.00 (*0-318-14391-7*) Inst Charter Finan Analysts.

CFA Readings in Financial Statement Analysis. 2nd ed. Ed. by Gerald I. White & Ashwinpaul C. Sandhi. (Orig.). (C). 1990. pap. text ed. 30.00 (*1-879087-00-6*) Assn I M&R.

C.F.A. Readings in Portfolio Management. Institute of Chartered Financial Analysts Staff. 262p. 1980. 7.00 (*0-318-14392-5*) Inst Charter Finan Analysts.

CFAR. Gary Minkler & Jing Minkler. 300p. (Orig.). (C). 1988. pap. text ed. 65.00 (*0-685-24050-9*) Magellan Bk.

CFAR: The Principles of Automatic Radar Detection in Clutter. Gary Minkler & Jing Minkler. (Illus.). 374p. (C). 1990. 68.00 (*0-9621618-1-0*) Magellan Bk.

CFC Alternatives. Richard K. Miller & Marcia E. Rupnow. LC 90-83916. (Survey on Technology & Markets Ser.: No. 110). 50p. 1991. pap. text ed. 200.00 (*1-55865-133-0*) Future Tech Surveys.

CFC Handbook. Carl E. Salas & Fairmont Press Staff. 1992. 85.33 (*0-13-117953-5*, 340802) P-H.

CFC Recovery & Recycling Equipment. Richard K. Miller & Marcia E. Rupnow. LC 90-83934. (Survey on Technology & Markets Ser.: No. 140). 50p. 1991. pap. text ed. 200.00 (*1-55865-165-9*) Future Tech Surveys.

***CFC Story: How America's Rural Electric Cooperatives Introduced Wall Street to Main Street. Patricia L. Williams. Ed. by Christine Welch. (Illus.). xii, 340p. 1995. pap. 17.00 (*0-9645302-0-1*) NRUCFC.**
THE CFC STORY dramatizes the initiative, persistence & dedication of rural Americans to provide for themselves when all other means fall short. When federal funds for rural electrification began to wane in the mid 1960s, rural leaders took charge of their destiny. Aided by leading financial consultants, they devised an innovative plan for using Wall Street capital to finance Main Street's most important technological advance--electricity. In the process, they created an enduring non-profit financing cooperative--CFC--that is responsible for bringing billions of dollars of private capital into what had previously been solely a government funded enterprise. THE CFC STORY tracks the history of this unique organization, from conceptualization through its first 25 years of operation, & details its ever growing challenges & successes. This thoughtful & revealing profile is a must read for anyone embarking on a public/private partnership. *Publisher Provided Annotation.*

***CFC Story: How America's Rural Electric Cooperatives Introduced Wall Street to Main Street. Patricia L. Williams. Ed. by Christine Welch. (Illus.). xii, 340p. 1995. 30.00 (*0-9645302-1-X*) NRUCFC.**
THE CFC STORY dramatizes the initiative, persistence & dedication of rural Americans to provide for themselves when all other means fall short. When federal funds for rural electrification began to wane in the mid 1960's, rural leaders took charge of their destiny. Aided by leading financial consultants, they devised an innovative plan for using Wall Street capital to finance Main Street's most important technological advance--electricity. In the process, they created an enduring non-profit financing cooperative--CFC--that is responsible for bringing billions of dollars of private capital into what had previously been solely a government funded enterprise. THE CFC STORY tracks the history of this unique organization, from conceptualization through its first 25 years of operation, & details its ever growing challenges & successes. This thoughtful & revealing profile is a must read for anyone embarking on a public/private partnership. *Publisher Provided Annotation.*

CFC Strategies & Alternatives. (Illus.). 9p. 1993. pap. 25.00 (*0-913359-74-2*) APPA VA.

CFCs: Time of Transition. Ed. by Mildred Geshwiler. (Illus.). 262p. (Orig.). (C). 1989. pap. 68.00 (*0-910110-58-1*) Am Heat Ref & Air Eng.

CFCs & the Polyurethane Industry: A Compilation of Technical Publications, 1986-1988. Ed. by Fran W. Lichtenberg. LC 88-51497. 178p. 1988. pap. 35.00 (*0-87762-653-7*) Technomic.

CFCs & the Polyurethane Industry, Vol. 2: A Compilation of Technical Publications, 1988-1989. Ed. by Fran W. Lichtenberg. LC 88-51497. 360p. 1989. pap. 55.00 (*0-87762-729-0*) Technomic.

CFCs & the Polyurethane Industry, Vol. 3: A Compilation of Technical Publications, 1990. Ed. by Fran W. Lichtenberg. LC 88-51497. 328p. 1990. 55.00 (*0-87762-811-4*) Technomic.

CFCs & the Polyurethane Industry, Vol. 4: A Compilation of Technical Publications, 1991. Ed. by Fran W. Lichtenberg. 425p. 1992. pap. 55.00 (*0-87762-928-5*) Technomic.

CFCs & the Polyurethane Industry, Vol. 5: A Compilation of Technical Publications, 1992. Ed. by Fran W. Lichtenberg. (Illus.). 312p. 1993. pap. 65.00 (*1-56676-009-7*, 760097) Technomic.

CFD Algorithms & Applications for Parallel Processors. Ed. by O. Baysal & V. Saxena. LC 93-71640. (FED Ser.: Vol. 156). 83p. 1993. pap. 30.00 (*0-7918-0964-1*, H00796) ASME.

CFD & CAD in Ship Design: Proceedings of the International Symposium, Wageningen, The Netherlands, 25-26 Sept., 1990. Ed. by G. Van Oortmerssen. (Developments in Marine Technology Ser.: No. 6). 246p. 1990. 97.50 (*0-444-88765-2*) Elsevier.

CFD Triathlon: Three Laminar Flow Simulations by Commercial CFD Codes. Ed. by C. J. Freitas. LC 93-71643. (FED Ser.: Vol. 160). 69p. 1993. pap. 25.00 (*0-7918-0968-4*, H00800) ASME.

CFE Treaty: An Overview & an Assessment. Ivo H. Daalder. 49p. 1991. pap. 9.95 (*0-941700-71-2*) JH FPI SAIS.

CFI Test Prep. rev. ed. ASA Staff. (Illus.). 328p. 1993. pap. 19.95 (*1-56027-175-2*, ASA-CFI-18A) Av Suppl & Acad.

CFJ Directory, 1991-92: A Register of Education, Training, Fellowship Programs & Awards for Journalists Worldwide. rev. ed. Ed. by David F. Hume. 150p. 1991. lib. bdg. (*0-9626584-5-6*) Ctr Foreign Journalists.

CFO's Expectations for Patient Financial Services. Vicki L. Romero & Judith B. Henry. 50p. 1992. 20.00 (*0-930228-87-1*) Hlthcare Fin Mgmt.

CFO's Handbook. Ed. by Richard F. Vancil & Benjamin R. Makela. 1985. 85.00 (*0-87094-591-2*) Irwin Prof Pubng.

CFS: Conquering the Crippler: Nature & Management of Chronic Fatigue Syndrome. 1993. pap. write for info. (*0-9636487-0-5*) C&C Communs.

***CG-FFT Method: Application of Signal Processing Techniques to Electromagnetics.** Manuel F. Catedra et al. LC 94-5746. 361p. 1994. 95.00 (*0-89006-634-5*) Artech Hse.

CG International '90: Computer Graphics Around the World. Ed. by T. S. Chua & Toshiyasu L. Kunii. (Illus.). x, 606p. 1990. 154.00 (*0-387-70062-5*) Spr-Verlag.

C.G. Jung & the Problem of Evil: Confronting the Power of the Human Shadow As Witnessed in the Strange Trial of Mr. Hyde. John Sanford. 1991. 27.50 (*0-938434-94-2*); pap. 14.95 (*0-938434-93-4*) Sigo Pr.

***CGAP Five-Year Assessment Project.** Comp. by Victoria I. Walch. 250p. 1990. pap. 25.00 (*0-614-01637-1*) Soc Am Archivists.

CGFNS Qualifying Exam: Practice English Test, No. 1. 20p. 1992. 15.00 (*0-9630592-1-1*) Grads of For Nursing.

CGI 1. Hironori Yasuda. (Super Special Background Patterns (SPATS) Ser.: No. 14). (Illus.). 208p. 1993. pap. 32.95 (*4-87708-105-4*, Pub. by KDC Co Ltd JA) Bks Nippan.

CGL Insurance Coverage for Clean up of Hazardous Substances: A Research Guide. Emily M. De Falla. LC 89-2095. 83p. 1989. lib. bdg. 32.50 (*0-89941-684-5*, 305820) W S Hein.

***CGL Reporter.** Date not set. 180.00 (*1-886813-18-3*) Intl Risk Mgt.

CGM & CGI. D. B. Arnold & P. R. Bono. (Symbolic Computation Ser.). (Illus.). xxiii, 279p. 1988. 52.00 (*0-387-18950-5*) Spr-Verlag.

CGM Handbook. Anne Mumford & Loften Henderson. (Illus.). 480p. 1993. text ed. 59.95 (*0-12-510560-6*) Acad Pr.

CGnet Story: A Case Study in International Computer Networking. G. Lindsey et al. 140p. 1994. pap. 16.95 (*0-88936-678-0*, IDRC6780, Pub. by IDRC CN) UNIPUB.

***CGS Design Handbook.** 200p. (Orig.). 1995. pap. 125.00 (*0-7605-1822-X*) Rector Pr.

CH-Acids. O. A. Reutov et al. LC 77-30618. (Illus.). 1978. 104.00 (*0-08-021610-2*, Pub. by Pergamon Repr UK) Franklin.

***CH Classics: Little Women/Little Men.** (Illus.). 816p. (Orig.). (J). 1995. 12.98 (*0-8317-1212-0*) Smithmark.

***CH Classics: Secret Garden/Little Princess.** (Illus.). 448p. (Orig.). (J). 1995. 12.98 (*0-8317-1213-9*) Smithmark.

***CH Classics: Tom Sawyer/Huck Finn.** (Illus.). 560p. (J). 1995. 12.98 (*0-8317-1211-2*) Smithmark.

***CH Classics: Water Babies/Peter Pan.** (Illus.). 384p. (J). 1995. 12.98 (*0-8317-1214-7*) Smithmark.

Cha Cha Cha. (Ballroom Dance Ser.). 1986. lib. bdg. 79.95 (*0-8490-3448-5*) Gordon Pr.

Cha Cha Cha. (Ballroom Dance Ser.). 1985. lib. bdg. 68.00 (*0-87700-738-1*) Revisionist Pr.

Cha Cha Cha. Earl Atkinson. (Ballroom Dance Ser.). 1986. lib. bdg. 250.00 (*0-8490-3622-4*) Gordon Pr.

Cha Cha Cha. Earl Atkinson. (Ballroom Dance Ser.). 1983. lib. bdg. 250.00 (*0-87700-478-1*) Revisionist Pr.

Cha-Cha-Cha. Jane Heller. 1994. 18.95 (*0-8217-4615-4*) Zebra.

***Cha Cha Cha.** Jane Heller. 400p. 1995. mass mkt. 4.99 (*0-8217-4996-X*) Windsor NY.

Cha Cha Champagne. (Ballroom Dance Ser.). 1986. lib. bdg. 79.95 (*0-8490-3444-2*) Gordon Pr.

Cha Cha Champagne. (Ballroom Dance Ser.). 1985. lib. bdg. 68.00 (*0-87700-737-3*) Revisionist Pr.

Cha Cha Cuties. (Ballroom Dance Ser.). 1985. lib. bdg. 74.50 (*0-87700-736-5*) Revisionist Pr.

Cha Cha-Lypso. (Ballroom Dance Ser.). 1986. lib. bdg. 79.95 (*0-8490-3446-9*) Gordon Pr.

Cha Cha-Lypso. (Ballroom Dance Ser.). 1985. lib. bdg. 74.25 (*0-87700-735-7*) Revisionist Pr.

Cha Cha Syllabus. (Ballroom Dance Ser.). 1986. lib. bdg. 79.95 (*0-8490-3341-1*) Gordon Pr.

Cha Cha Syllabus. (Ballroom Dance Ser.). 1985. lib. bdg. 79.00 (*0-87700-732-2*) Revisionist Pr.

Cha-No-Yu: The Japanese Tea Ceremony. A. L. Sadler. LC 62-19787. 296p. 1977. pap. 12.95 (*0-8048-1224-1*) C E Tuttle.

Chacal. Frederick Forsyth. 512p. (FRE.). 1990. pap. 11.95 (*0-7859-2341-1*, 2070365697) Fr & Eur.

Chacho: Reading Level 4. 1993. 3.95 (*0-88336-763-7*); 18.95 (*0-88336-739-4*) New Readers.

Chaco. Mark A. Tayler. LC 93-5158. 288p. (Orig.). 1993. pap. 14.95 (*0-86534-203-2*) Sunstone Pr.

***Chaco: A Cultural Legacy.** Michele Strutin. Ed. by Sandra Scott & Ron Foreman. LC 94-68875. 68p. 1994. pap. 9.95 (*1-877856-45-2*) SW Pks Mnmts.

Chaco Anasazi: Sociopolitical Evolution in the Prehistoric Southwest. Lynne Sebastian. (New Studies in Archaeology). (Illus.). 220p. (C). 1992. 59.95 (*0-521-40367-7*) Cambridge U Pr.

Chaco & Hohokam: Prehistoric Regional Systems in the American Southwest. Ed. by Patricia L. Crown & W. James Judge. LC 90-26559. (Advanced Seminar Ser.). (Illus.). 325p. (Orig.). 1991. text ed. 35.00x (*0-933452-75-6*) Schol Am Res.

Chaco & Hohokam: Prehistoric Regional Systems in the American Southwest. Ed. by Patricia L. Crown & W. James Judge. LC 90-26559. (Advanced Seminar Ser.). (Illus.). 325p. (Orig.). 1991. pap. 15.95 (*0-933452-76-4*) U of Wash Pr.

Chaco Banyon: Sheriff of Lordsburg. Fred Schmidt. 308p. 1994. pap. text ed. 9.95 (*0-9639574-0-6*) Book Hse Pub.

Chaco Body. V. B. Price. (Illus.). 88p. 1990. 40.00 (*0-8263-1277-2*); pap. 19.95 (*0-8263-1278-0*) U of NM Pr.

Chaco Canyon. deluxe limited ed. Edgar Bowers. 4p. (Orig.). 1988. pap. 15.00 (*0-936576-14-6*) Symposium Pr.

Chaco Canyon: A Center & Its World. Stephen Lekson et al. (Illus.). 124p. 1994. 35.00 (*0-89013-260-7*) Museum NM Pr.

Chaco Canyon: Archaeology & Archaeologists. Robert H. Lister & Florence C. Lister. LC 80-54566. (Illus.). 296p. 1984. reprint ed. pap. 18.95 (*0-8263-0756-6*) U of NM Pr.

Chaco Canyon: Sunrise to Sunset. Lee Dubois. 76p. (Orig.). 1993. pap. 19.95 (*0-9622932-0-2*) San Miguel Pr.

Chaco Coal Scandal. Jeff Radford. (Illus.). 257p. (Orig.). (C). 1986. pap. 8.00 (*0-936455-01-2*) Rhombus Pub.

Chaco Phenomenon. J. J. Brody. (Illus.). 32p. 1983. pap. 6.25 (*0-912535-01-6*) Max Mus.

Chaco Roads Project Phase One: A Reappraisal of Prehistoric Roads in the San Juan Basin. Ed. by Chris Kincaid. (Illus.). 371p. (Orig.). 1983. pap. write for info. (*0-318-68061-0*) Bureau of Land Mgmt NM.

Chacoan Prehistory of the San Juan Basin. R. Gwinn Vivian. (New World Archaeological Record Ser.). 523p. 1990. text ed. 109.00 (*0-12-722440-8*) Acad Pr.

Chacoan Roads in the Southern Periphery: Results of Phase II of the BLM Chaco Roads Project. Fred Nials et al. No. 1. (Illus.). 214p. (Orig.). 1987. pap. write for info. (*0-318-68062-9*) Bureau of Land Mgmt NM.

Chaconne in D Minor for Six Viols. Christine Hodgkinson. (Charney Manor Ser.: No. 4). i, 21p. 1991. 10.00 (*1-56571-039-8*) PRB Prods.

Chacs & Chiefs: The Iconography of Mosaic Stone Sculpture in Pre-Conquest Yucatan, Mexico. Rosemary Sharp. LC 80-26269. (Studies in Pre-Columbian Art & Archaeology: No. 24). (Illus.). 48p. 1981. pap. 10.00 (*0-88402-099-1*) Dumbarton Oaks.

Chad. (Let's Visit Places & Peoples of the World Ser.). (Illus.). (J). (gr. 5 up). 1989. 14.95 (*0-7910-0147-4*) Chelsea Hse.

Chad. Lewis B. Sckolnick. (Civil Rights Reporter Ser.). (Illus.). 60p. (Orig.). (C). 1994. pap. 45.00 (*1-57205-087-X*) Rector Pr.

***Chad.** Joseph Sevigny. Ed. by Dale E. Gough. (OIES Country Guide Ser.). (C). 1995. write for info. (*0-929851-32-3*) Am Assn Coll Registrars.

Chad: A Country Study. 2nd ed. Ed. by Thomas Collelo. LC 89-600373. (Area Handbook Ser.). (Illus.). 278p. 1990. boxed 15.00 (*0-16-024770-5*, S/N 008-020-01220-3) USGPO.

Chad & Brad, a Home for Spot: Blend Book, 2 bks., Set, Nos. 1 & 2. Debbie Strayer. (Bridge Story Bks.). (Illus.). 14p. (J). (gr. 1). 1992. Set. pap. 8.00 (*1-880892-11-1*) Fam Lrng Ctr.

Chadbourne: Chadbourne Genealogy. W. M. Emery. (Illus.). 66p. 1991. reprint ed. pap. 13.00 (*0-8328-1746-5*) Higginson Bk Co.

Chadeayne Family in America. Leander Chadeayne. 65p. 1984. 15.00 (*0-318-17306-9*) Huguenot Hist.

Chadha: The Story of an Epic Constitutional Struggle. Barbara H. Craig. 1990. pap. 13.00 (*0-520-06955-2*) U CA Pr.

Chadian & Sudanese Arabic in the Light of Comparative Arabic Dialectology. Alan S. Kaye. (Janua Linguarum, Ser. Practica: No. 236). 1976. pap. text ed. 70.80 (*90-279-3324-3*) Mouton.

Chado: The Japanese Way of Tea. Soshitsu Sen. LC 78-26503. (Illus.). 188p. 1979. 25.00 (*0-8348-1518-4*) Weatherhill.

Chadur-ha-ye Siah see Black Tents

Chadwick: Notes on Descendants of John & Joan Chadwick & Related Families. A. D. Kilham. (Illus.). 120p. 1991. reprint ed. lib. bdg. 29.50 (*0-8328-1713-9*); reprint ed. pap. 19.50 (*0-8328-1714-7*) Higginson Bk Co.

CHADWICK: Smoking Cessation Education Program. George W. Trewitt. 1994. pap. 1.95 (*1-56794-060-9*) Star Bible.

Chadwick: Yankee Composer. Victor F. Yellin. LC 89-39869. (Studies of American Musicians). 208p. (C). 1990. 36.00 (*0-87474-988-3*) Smithsonian.

Chadwick: Yankee Composer. braille ed. Victor F. Yellin. 588p. 1993. vinyl bd. 47.04 (*1-56956-434-5*, BR8900) W A T Braille.

Chadwick & the Garplegrungen. Priscilla Cummings. LC 87-71087. (Illus.). 32p. (J). (gr. k-4). 1987. 8.95 (*0-87033-377-1*, Tidewtr Pubs) Cornell Maritime.

Chadwick Coloring Book. Priscilla Cummings. (Illus.). 32p. (Orig.). (J). (gr. k-4). 1988. pap. 3.95 (*0-87033-389-5*, Tidewtr Pubs) Cornell Maritime.

Chadwick Forever. Priscilla Cummings. (Illus.). 30p. (J). (gr. 4-8). 1993. bds. 8.95 (*0-87033-450-6*, Tidewtr Pubs) Cornell Maritime.

Chadwick on Subjective Landscaping. James M. Chadwick. Ed. by Hinda R. Minor. (Illus.). (Orig.). 1989. pap. text ed. 29.95 (*0-685-27002-5*) J Chadwick.

Chadwick the Crab. Priscilla Cummings. LC 85-41005. (Illus.). 32p. (J). (gr. k-4). 1986. 8.95 (*0-87033-347-X*, Tidewtr Pubs) Cornell Maritime.

Chadwick's Wedding. Priscilla Cummings. LC 88-51677. (Illus.). 30p. (J). (gr. k-4). 1989. 8.95 (*0-87033-390-9*, Tidewtr Pubs) Cornell Maritime.

Chaetoceros Ehrenberg (Bacillariophyceae) Flora of Narragansett Bay, Rhode Island, U. S. A. J. E. Rines & P. E. Hargraves. (Bibliotheca Phycologica Ser.: Vol. 79). (Illus.). 196p. 1988. pap. text ed. 78.00 (*3-443-60006-9*) Lubrecht & Cramer.

Chafetz Graphics: Satire & Homage. Sidney Chafetz. (Illus.). 184p. (Orig.). 1988. pap. 46.50 (*0-8142-0473-2*) Ohio St U Pr.

Chaff & Wheat: Poems: Nineteen Twenty-Nine, to Seventy-Nine. Gregory J. Palma. LC 79-56716. 203p. (Orig.). 1979. 14.00 (*0-933402-08-2*); pap. 9.00 (*0-933402-01-5*) Charisma Pr.

Chaff Before the Wind. Sigurd Christiansen. Tr. by Isaac Anderson. LC 73-22750. 319p. 1974. reprint ed. text ed. 59.75 (*0-8371-7349-3*, CHCB, Greenwood Pr) Greenwood.

Chaffee Genealogy: Descendants of Thomas Chaffee of Hingham, Hull, Rehoboth & Swansea, Mass, 1635-1909. W. H. Chaffee. (Illus.). 663p. 1989. reprint ed. lib. bdg. 93.00 (*0-8328-0380-4*); reprint ed. pap. 83.00 (*0-8328-0381-2*) Higginson Bk Co.

Chaffee of Roaring Horse. large type ed. Ernest Haycox. LC 93-22209. 1994. 19.95 (*0-7929-1859-2*, Roundup Lrg Print Westerns); pap. 17.95 (*0-7929-1858-4*, Roundup Lrg Print Westerns) Chivers N Amer.

C

An Asterisk (*) at the beginning of an entry indicates that the title is appearing in BIP for the first time.

Chaffee of Roaring Horse. large type ed. Ernest Haycox. 1994. 19.95 (*0-7927-1859-3*, Roundup Lrg Print Westerns); pap. 17.95 (*0-7927-1858-5*, Roundup Lrg Print Westerns) Chivers N Amer.

Chag Sameach! A Jewish Holiday Book for Children. Patricia Schaffer. (Illus.). 28p. (Orig.). (J). (ps-4). 1985. pap. 5.95 (*0-935079-16-5*) Tabor Sarah Bks.

***Chaga Childhood: A Description.** O. F. Raum. (Classics in African Anthropology Ser.). (C). 1996. text ed. 64.50 (*3-89473-690-9*); pap. text ed. 25.50 (*3-89473-874-X*) Westview.

Chaga Childhood: A Description of Indigenous Education in an East African Tribe. Otto F. Raum. LC 76-44782. reprint ed. 30.00 (*0-404-15966-4*) AMS Pr.

Chaga Childhood: A Description of Indigenous Education in an East African Tribe. Otto F. Raum. LC 41-12399. 435p. reprint ed. pap. 124.00 (*0-8357-6966-6*, 2039026) Bks Demand.

Chagall. Werner Haftmann. (Masters of Art Ser.). 1984. 22.95 (*0-8109-0794-1*) Abrams.

Chagall. Artemis Herald. 1993. 5.98 (*1-55521-824-5*) Bk Sales Inc.

Chagall. Francois Le Targat. LC 85-42875. (Illus.). 128p. 1985. 24.95 (*0-8478-0624-3*) Rizzoli Intl.

Chagall. Ed. by P. Le Targat. (C). 1990. 100.00 (*0-685-34373-1*, Pub. by Collets) St Mut.

Chagall. Michel Makario. (Masterworks Ser.). (Illus.). 144p. 1991. 19.99 (*0-517-64646-3*) Random Hse Value.

Chagall: A Postcard Book. (Postcard Book Ser.). (Illus.). 64p. (Orig.). 1990. pap. 7.95 (*0-89471-806-1*) Running Pr.

***Chagall: A Retrospective.** Jacob Baal-Teshuva. (Illus.). 384p. 1995. 75.00 (*0-88363-495-3*) H L Levin.

Chagall: My Sad & Joyous Village. Jacqueline Loumaye. Tr. by John Goodman. LC 93-39109. (Art for Children Ser.). (Illus.). 64p. (J). (gr. 3 up). 1994. lib. bdg. 14.95 (*0-7910-2807-0*) Chelsea Hse.

Chagall in Chicago. Illus. by Marc Chagall. LC 79-64519. 26p. (Orig.). (C). 1979. pap. 3.00 (*0-935982-15-9*, SMJ-06) Spertus Coll.

Chagall l'Admirable. Louis Aragon. (D. L. M. Ser.: No. 198). (Illus.). 32p. (FRE.). 1972. 450.00 (*1-55660-090-9*) A Wofsy Fine Arts.

Chagall Lithographs, Nineteen Eighty to Nineteen Eighty-Five. Charles Sorlier. (Illus.). 224p. 1986. 125.00 (*1-55660-095-X*) A Wofsy Fine Arts.

C

Chagall to Kitaj: Jewish Experience in Twentieth Century Art. Avram Kampf. 208p. 1991. text ed. 79.50 (*0-275-93900-6*, C3900, Praeger Pubs) Greenwood.

Chagall's Complete Lithographs, 1922-1985, 6 vols. in 3. Fernand Mourlot & Charles Sorlier. (Illus.). 900p. 1987. boxed 2,200.00 (*1-55660-081-X*) A Wofsy Fine Arts.

Chagall's Etchings for the Bible, Dead Souls & Fables of Ambroise Vollard. Charles Sorlier & Marc Chagall. (Illus.). (FRE.). 1981. 125.00 (*1-55660-069-0*) A Wofsy Fine Arts.

Chagall's Illustrated Books: Catalogue Raisonne. Patrick Cramer. (Illus.). 310p. 1995. 275.00 (*1-55660-144-1*) A Wofsy Fine Arts.

***Chagall's Illustrated Books: Catalogue Raisonne.** Charles Sorlier. (Illus.). 240p. 1993. 125.00 (*1-55660-245-6*) A Wofsy Fine Arts.

Chagall's Monotypes, 1966-1975. Gerald Cramer. 104p. (FRE.). 1976. 175.00 (*1-55660-114-X*) A Wofsy Fine Arts.

Chagas Disease Vectors: Anatomic & Physiological Aspects. R. Brenner & Stoka A. Merced. LC 87-13209. 1987. reprint ed. 83.00 (*0-8493-4348-8*, CRC Reprint) Franklin.

Chagas' Disease Vectors: Biochemical Aspects & Control, 3 vols., Set. Ed. by Rodolfo R. Brenner & Angel de la Merced Stoka. 512p. 1987. 99.00 (*0-8493-4346-1*, RA644, CRC Reprint) Franklin.

Chagas Disease Vectors: Taxonomic Ecological & Epidemiological Aspects. R. Brenner & Stoka A. Merced. LC 87-13209. 1987. reprint ed. 93.00 (*0-8493-4347-X*, CRC Reprint) Franklin.

Chagga & Meru of Tanzania. Sally F. Moore & Paul Puritt. LC 78-309993. (Ethnographic Survey of Africa: East Central Africa Ser.: No. 18). 156p. reprint ed. pap. 44.50 (*0-8357-6963-1*, 2039023) Bks Demand.

Chagrin d'Amour et d'Ailleurs. Francoise Mallet-Joris. (FRE.). 1983. pap. 6.95 (*0-7859-3111-2*) Fr & Eur.

Chahar Maqala: The Four Discourses of Nidhami-I-Arudi-I-Samarqandi. Al-Samarqandi. (Gibb Memorial Old Ser.: Vols. 11-12). pap. 9.95 (*0-906094-06-2*, Pub. by Aris & Phillips UK) David Brown.

Chahta-Ima & St. Tammany's Choctaws. Blaise C. D'Antoni. (St. Tammany Historical Society Gazette Ser.: Vol. 7). (Illus.). 1987. pap. 7.00 (*0-9617771-7-6*) St Tammany Hist Soc.

***Chai & Friends.** Francis. Date not set. per. 14.95 (*0-85449-108-2*, Pub. by Gay Mens Pr UK) InBook.

Chai Kheun. E. M. Pemberton. Ed. by James B. Van Treese. 260p. 1994. pap. 8.95 (*1-56901-131-1*) NW Pub.

Chaim: The Story of a Russian Emigre Boy. Tricia Brown. LC 93-44853. (J). 1994. 15.95 (*0-8050-2354-2*) H Holt & Co.

Chaim Potok. Edward A. Abramson. (United States Authors Ser.: No. 503). 176p. (C). 1986. text ed. 20.95 (*0-8057-7463-7*, Twayne) Macmillan.

Chaim Weizmann. Richard Amdur. (World Leaders - Past & Present Ser.). (Illus.). 112p. (YA). (gr. 5 up). 1988. lib. bdg. 17.95 (*0-87754-446-8*) Chelsea Hse.

Chaim Weizmann: The Making of a Statesman, Vol. 2. Jehuda Reinharz. (Illus.). 560p. 1993. 39.95 (*0-19-507215-4*) OUP.

Chaim Weizmann: The Making of a Zionist Leader. Jehuda Reinharz. LC 84-7898. (Illus.). 1987. pap. 15.95 (*0-19-505069-X*) OUP.

Chaimkel the Dreamer. Meir U. Gottesman. (Illus.). 157p. (J). (gr. 3-5). 1987. 9.95 (*0-935063-26-9*); pap. 7.95 (*0-935063-27-7*) CIS Comm.

***Chain Chain Change: For Black Women in Abusive Relationships.** 2nd expanded ed. Evelyn C. White. (New Leaf Ser.). 120p. (Orig.). 1995. pap. 8.95 (*1-878067-60-5*) Seal Pr Feminist.

Chain Dance: Selected Poems. Lars Hulden. Tr. & Intro. by George C. Schoolfield. (Studies in Scandinavian Literature & Culture: Vol. 2). (Illus.). 150p. 1991. 56.00 (*0-938100-84-X*) Camden Hse.

Chain Dogs: The German Army Military Police of World War II. Robert E. Witter. LC 93-87778. (Illus.). 128p. 1994. pap. text ed. 9.95 (*0-929521-86-2*) Pictorial Hist.

Chain Her by One Foot: The Subjugation of Native Women in Seventeeth-Century New France. Karen L. Anderson. LC 93-19097. 1993. pap. 16.95 (*0-415-90827-2*, B2291, Routledge NY) Routledge.

Chain Her by One Foot: The Subjugation of Women in 17th Century New France. Karen L. Anderson. 240p. 1991. 35.00 (*0-415-04758-7*, A4936) Routledge.

Chain Letter. Ruby J. Jensen. 1987. pap. 3.95 (*0-8217-2162-3*) Zebra.

Chain Letter. Ann M. Martin. LC 92-44587. (J). 1993. 14.95 (*0-590-47151-1*) Scholastic Inc.

Chain Letter. Christopher Pike. 192p. 1986. mass mkt. 3.99 (*0-380-89968-X*, Flare) Avon.

Chain Lightning. Elizabeth Lowell. 1993. mass mkt. 4.50 (*0-373-48278-7*) Harlequin Bks.

***Chain Mail: The History of the Duke of Lancaster's Own Yeomanary 1798-1991.** John Brereton. 1990. 129.00 (*0-948251-67-0*, Pub. by Picton UK) St Mut.

Chain of Attack. Gene DeWeese. (Star Trek Ser.: No. 32). 1988. mass mkt. 5.50 (*0-671-66658-4*) PB.

Chain of Becoming: The Philosophical Tale, the Novel & a Neglected Realism of the Enlightenment: Swift, Montesquieu, Voltaire, Johnson & Austen. Frederick M. Keener. LC 82-12878. 376p. 1983. text ed. 52.00 (*0-231-04001-6*); pap. text ed. 20.00 (*0-231-05573-0*) Col U Pr.

Chain of Chance. Stanislaw Lem. LC 83-22620. 182p. 1984. pap. 7.95 (*0-15-616500-7*, Harvest Bks) HarBrace.

Chain of Change: A Study of Aristotle's Physics VII. Robert Wardy. (Classical Studies). (Illus.). 300p. (C). 1990. 69.95 (*0-521-37327-1*) Cambridge U Pr.

Chain of Change: Struggles for Black Community Development. Mel King. LC 80-52135. 304p. 1981. pap. 15.00 (*0-89608-105-2*) South End Pr.

Chain of Circumstances. Conrad S. Smith. 1962. pap. 4.75 (*0-8222-0196-8*) Dramatists Play.

***Chain of Command.** Date not set. (*0-8317-5328-5*) Smithmark.

Chain of Days. James Berry. 96p. 1985. pap. 8.95 (*0-19-211964-8*) OUP.

Chain of Evidence: A True Story of Law Enforcement & One Woman's Bravery. Michael Detroit. (Illus.). 320p. 1994. 21.95 (*0-525-93671-8*, Dutton) NAL-Dutton.

***Chain of Evidence: A True Story of Law Enforcement & One Woman's Bravery.** Michael Detroit. 352p. 1995. mass mkt. 5.99 (*0-451-40462-9*, Onyx) NAL-Dutton.

Chain of Fire. Beverley Naidoo. LC 89-27551. (Illus.). 256p. (J). (gr. 6 up). 1990. lib. bdg. 14.89 (*0-397-32427-8*, Lipp Jr Bks) HarpC Child Bks.

Chain of Fire. Beverley Naidoo. LC 89-27551. (Trophy Bk.). 256p. (J). (gr. 6 up). 1993. pap. 3.95 (*0-06-440468-4*, Trophy) HarpC Child Bks.

Chain of Friendship: Selected Letters of Dr. John Fothergill of London, 1735-1780. John Fothergill. Ed. by Betsy C. Corner & Christopher C. Booth. LC 75-127877. (Illus.). 566p. 1971. 47.50 (*0-674-10660-1*) Belknap Pr.

Chain of Gold. Judith H. Wall. pap. 3.95 (*0-317-56981-3*) PB.

Chain of Hands. Carol R. Brink. LC 93-6908. 200p. 1993. pap. 15.95 (*0-87422-098-X*) Wash St U Pr.

Chain of Kindness. Paul T. Jones. 240p. 1992. 21.95 (*0-87483-197-0*); pap. 12.95 (*0-87483-196-2*) August Hse.

Chain of Life. 3rd ed. Guyon Richards. 232p. pap. 17.95 (*0-8464-4202-7*) Beekman Pubs.

Chain of Love. Martha McClymonds. 288p. (Orig.). 1981. pap. 2.75 (*0-8439-1002-X*) Dorchester Pub Co.

Chain of Quality: Market Dominance Through Product Superiority. John B. Groocock. LC 85-32291. 390p. 1986. text ed. 22.95 (*0-471-82847-5*) Wiley.

Chain of Tradition Series, 4 vols. Louis Jacobs. Incl. Vol. 5. Hasidic Thought. LC 78-1487. 1974. pap. text ed. 8.95 (*0-87441-242-0*); LC 78-1487. (Illus.). (J). (gr. 8 up). 1974. Set pap. write for info. (*0-318-51046-4*) Behrman.

Chain of Voices. Andre Brink. 528p. 1983. pap. 12.95 (*0-14-006538-5*, Penguin Bks) Viking Penguin.

Chain Reaction. Lee Jordan. 207p. 1993. 19.95 (*0-8027-1249-5*) Walker & Co.

Chain Reaction: Children & Divorce. Ofra Ayalon & Adina Flasher. 200p. 1993. pap. 29.00 (*1-85302-136-9*, Pub. by J Kingsley Pubs UK) Taylor & Francis.

Chain Reaction: Expert Debate & Public Participation in American Commercial Nuclear Power, 1945-1975. Brian Balogh. 420p. (C). 1991. 42.95 (*0-521-37296-8*) Cambridge U Pr.

Chain Reaction: Expert Debate & Public Participation in American Commercial Nuclear Power, 1945-1975. Brian Balogh. 352p. (C). 1993. pap. 17.95 (*0-521-45736-X*) Cambridge U Pr.

Chain Reaction: The Impact of Race, Rights & Taxes on American Politics. Thomas B. Edsall. 416p. 1991. 22.95 (*0-393-02983-2*) Norton.

Chain Reaction: The Impact of Race, Rights & Taxes on American Politics. Thomas B. Edsall & Mary D. Edsall. 352p. 1992. pap. 10.95 (*0-393-30903-7*) Norton.

Chain Restaurants. W. Whitehall. (C). 1989. 90.00 (*0-09-175690-1*, Pub. by S Thornes Pubs UK) St Mut.

Chain Saw Flat Rate Pricing Guide. Intertec Staff. 1993. 24.95 (*0-87288-526-7*, CF-11) Intertec Pub.

Chain Saw Manual. 2nd ed. America Pulpwood Association Staff. 92p. 1988. pap. 13.25 (*0-685-02535-7*); pap. text ed. 9.95 (*0-8134-2776-2*) Interstate.

Chain Saw Safety. Don Brooks. 1983. student ed 6.00 (*0-8064-0035-8*, 268); audio 99.00 (*0-8064-0036-6*) Bergwall.

Chain Saw Savvy. Neil Soderstrom. (Illus.). 144p. 1984. pap. 12.00 (*0-87100-187-X*, 2187) Morgan.

Chain Saw Service Manual. Intertec Staff. 568p. 1993. 24.95 (*0-87288-521-6*, CSS-9) Intertec Pub.

Chain Store Inquiry Reports: Nineteen Hundred Thirty-One to Nineteen Hundred Thirty-Four, 4 vols., Set. Federal Trade Commission. 1985. reprint ed. lib. bdg. 395.00 (*0-89941-427-3*, 201690) W S Hein.

Chain Store Problem: A Critical Analysis. Theodore N. Beckman & Herman C. Nolen. LC 75-39231. (Illus.). 1976. reprint ed. 29.95 (*0-405-08008-5*) Ayer.

Chain Stores: Letters from the Chairman of the Federal Trade Commission Transmitting in Response to Senate Resolution No. 224, 3 pts. in 1. U. S. Federal Trade Commission Staff. LC 75-39243. (Getting & Spending The Consumer's Dilemma Ser.). (Illus.). 1976. reprint ed. 23.95 (*0-405-08051-4*) Ayer.

Chain Structure & Conformation of Macromolecules. Ed. by Frank A. Bovey & Lynn W. Jelinski. LC 82-20779. (Monograph). 1982. text ed. 59.00 (*0-12-119780-8*) Acad Pr.

Chainbearer. James Fenimore Cooper. (Works of James Fenimore Cooper Ser.). 1990. reprint ed. lib. bdg. 79.00 (*0-7812-2394-6*) Rprt Serv.

Chainbearer: Or, the Littlepage Manuscripts, 2 vols. in 1. James Fenimore Cooper. LC 70-37651. reprint ed. 39.50 (*0-404-01704-5*) AMS Pr.

Chainbearer or the Littlepage Manuscripts, 2 vols. in 1. James Fenimore Cooper. LC 06-32149. 1981. reprint ed. 19.00 (*0-403-00135-8*) Scholarly.

Chainbreaker: The Revolutionary War Memoirs of Governor Blacksnake. Chainbreaker. Ed. by Thomas S. Abler. LC 88-28085. (American Indian Lives Ser.). (Illus.). xviii, 306p. 1989. 35.00 (*0-8032-1446-4*) U of Nebr Pr.

Chainbreakers: A True Story of Healing from Abuse. Michele R. Sorensen. LC 93-21678. 230p. 1993. 14.95 (*0-87579-744-X*) Deseret Bk.

Chained Eagle. Everett Alvarez, Jr. & Anthony S. Pitch. LC 89-45547. (Illus.). 308p. (YA). (gr. 8-12). 1989. 18.95 (*1-55611-167-3*) D I Fine.

Chained Together: Mandela, De Klerk, & the Struggle to Remake South Africa. David B. Ottaway. 1993. 25.00 (*0-8129-2014-7*, Times Bks) Random.

Chaingang. Rex Miller. Ed. by Doug Grad. 320p. (Orig.). 1992. mass mkt. 4.99 (*0-671-74847-5*) PB.

Chaining the Hudson: The Fight for the River in the American Revolution. Lincoln Diamant. 1989. 21.95 (*0-8184-0502-3*) Carol Pub Group.

Chaining the Hudson: The Fight for the River in the American Revolution. Linocln Diamont. LC 94-20044. 1994. pap. 16.95 (*0-8065-1535-X*, Citadel Pr) Carol Pub Group.

Chaining the Lady. Piers Anthony. (Cluster Ser.: No. 2). 1978. pap. 3.50 (*0-380-01779-2*) Avon.

Chaining the Land. Francois D. Uzes. (Illus.). 315p. 1977. 35.00 (*0-910845-01-8*, 914) Landmark Ent.

Chainlink. large type ed. Owen Evens. (Linford Western Library). 272p. 1988. pap. 11.95 (*0-7089-6597-0*, Linford) Ulverscroft.

Chains. Larry Townsend. 1994. pap. text ed. 4.95 (*1-56333-158-6*) Masquerade.

Chains. Theodore Dreiser. LC 86-27113. 425p. 1987. reprint ed. lib. bdg. 45.00 (*0-86527-354-5*) Fertig.

Chains & Images of Psychological Slavery. Na'im Akbar. 76p. (Orig.). (C). reprint ed. pap. 3.50 (*0-933821-00-X*) New Mind Prod.

Chains, Clusters, Inclusion Compounds, Paramagnetic Labels, & Organic Rings. Ed. by Piero Zanello. LC 93-42633. (Stereochemistry of Organometallic & Inorganic Compounds Ser.: Vol. 5). 1994. 305.75 (*0-444-81581-3*) Elsevier.

Chains for Power Transmission & Material Handling: Design & Applications Handbook. American Chain Association Staff. LC 82-17971. (Mechanical Engineering Ser.: No. 18). (Illus.). 371p. reprint ed. pap. 105.80 (*0-7837-0803-3*, 2041118) Bks Demand.

Chains for Power Transmission & Materials Handling: Design & Applications Handbook. American Chain Association Staff. (Mechanical Engineering Ser.: Vol. 18). (Illus.). 376p. 1982. 110.00 (*0-8247-1701-5*) Dekker.

Chains of Command. Dale Brown. 480p. 1993. 22.95 (*0-399-13822-6*, Putnam) Putnam Pub Group.

Chains of Command. W. A. McCay & E. L. Flood. Ed. by David Stern. (Star Trek: The Next Generation Ser.: No. 21). 288p. (Orig.). 1992. mass mkt. 5.50 (*0-671-74264-7*) PB.

Chains of Command. Dale Brown. 528p. 1994. reprint ed. mass mkt. 6.99 (*0-425-14207-8*) Berkley Pub.

Chains of Darkness. Michelle M. Sagara. (Orig.). 1994. mass mkt. 4.99 (*0-345-37949-7*) Ballantine.

Chains of Fear: American Race Relations since Reconstruction. Michael J. Cassity. LC 82-21092. (Grass Roots Perspectives on American History Ser.: No. 3). xxx, 253p. 1984. text ed. 59.95 (*0-313-21324-0*, CRR/, Greenwood Pr) Greenwood.

Chains of Gold: Marketing the Ratings & Rating the Markets. Karen S. Buzzard. LC 90-19487. 226p. 1990. 29.50 (*0-8108-2356-X*) Scarecrow.

Chains of Opportunity: System Models of Mobility in Organizations. Harrison C. White. LC 78-105374. 434p. 1970. 37.00 (*0-674-10674-1*) HUP.

Chains of Protection: The Judicial Response to Women's Labor Legislation. Judith A. Baer. LC 77-82695. (Contributions in Women's Studies: No. 1). x, 238p. 1978. text ed. 49.95 (*0-8371-9785-6*, BCP/, Greenwood Pr) Greenwood.

Chains of Servitude: Bondage & Slavery in India. Ed. by Utes Patnaik & Manjari Dingwaney. 392p. 1985. text ed. 40.00 (*0-86131-491-3*, Pub. by Sangam Bks II) Apt Bks.

Chains to Be Broken: Dr. Robin Eames, Archbishop of Armagh & Primate of All Ireland. (Illus.). 224p. 1993. 39.95 (*0-297-81150-9*) Trafalgar.

Chains to Roses: The Joseph Cicippio Five-Year Hostage Ordeal. Joseph Cicippio & Richard Hope. (Illus.). 224p. 1993. 21.95 (*1-56796-025-1*) WRS Group.

Chainsaw Massacre Suite & Other Poems of Psychotic Bliss. John Grey. Ed. by Brian T. Gallagher. (Illus.). 36p. 1991. 3.00 (*1-879484-00-5*) Radio Void.

Chainsaw Sculptor: The Art of J. Chester "Skip" Armstrong. Sharon R. Sherman. (Folk Art & Artists Ser.). (Illus.). 72p. 1995. lib. bdg. 29.50 (*0-87805-740-4*); pap. 15.95 (*0-87805-741-2*) U Pr of Miss.

Chair. Elizabeth S. Hermoso. (Illus.). 15p. (Orig.). (J). (gr. k-2). 1991. pap. 3.00 (*971-10-0442-9*, Pub. by New Day Pub PH) Cellar.

Chair: From Artifact to Object. Trevor Richardson. Ed. by Ruth K. Beesch. (Illus.). 40p. 1991. pap. text ed. 10.00 (*0-9627541-2-9*) Weatherspoon.

Chair et Cuir. Felicien Marceau. (FRE.). 1974. pap. 10.95 (*0-7859-4028-6*) Fr & Eur.

Chair for Elijah. Menke Katz. LC 85-61563. (Illus.). 96p. 1985. 9.95 (*0-912292-78-4*); pap. 6.95 (*0-912292-77-6*) The Smith.

***Chair for My Mother.** Garrett Christopher. Ed. by J. Friedland & R. Kessler. (Novel-Ties Ser.). (J). (gr. k-1). 1993. student ed, pap. text ed. 14.95 (*0-88122-950-4*) Lrn Links.

Chair for My Mother. Vera B. Williams. LC 81-7010. (Illus.). 32p. (J). (gr. k-3). 1982. 15.00 (*0-688-00914-X*); lib. bdg. 15.93 (*0-688-00915-8*) Greenwillow.

Chair for My Mother. Vera B. Williams. LC 81-7010. (Read with Me Ser.). (Illus.). 32p. (J). (ps up). 1988. pap. 4.95 (*0-688-04074-8*, Mulberry) Morrow.

Chair for My Mother. Vera Williams. Tr. by Aida Marcuse. (Books in Spanish). (Illus.). 32p. (SPA.). (J). (ps up). 1994. reprint ed. pap. 4.95 (*0-688-13200-6*, Mulberry) Morrow.

Chair for My Mother: Big Book Edition. Vera B. Williams. (Illus.). 32p. (J). (ps up). 1993. reprint ed. pap. 18.95 (*0-688-12612-X*, Mulberry) Morrow.

Chair of Babel. Peter Porter. 80p. 1992. pap. 11.95 (*0-19-282920-3*) OUP.

Chair Seating: Techniques on Cane, Rush, Willow & Cords. Kay Johnson et al. (Illus.). 192p. 1989. 50.00 (*0-85219-736-5*, Pub. by Batsford UK) Trafalgar.

Chair to Sit On. large type ed. Eva Burfield. 368p. 1986. 15.95 (*0-7089-1414-4*) Ulverscroft.

Chairing a Meeting with Confidence: An Easy Guide to Rules & Procedure. 2nd ed. Kevin Paul. (Reference Ser.). 96p. 1992. 7.95 (*0-88908-992-2*) Self-Counsel Pr.

Chairing Child Protection Conferences: An Exploration of Role & Attitude. Ann Lewis. 135p. 1994. 51.95 (*1-85628-691-6*, Pub. by Avebury Pub UK) Ashgate Pub Co.

Chairing Meetings in French As Well As in English. Benedicte Lapeyre & Pamela Sheppard. 87p. (ENG & FRE.). 1992. 39.95 (*0-7859-1001-8*, 2708114557) Fr & Eur.

Chairing the Academic Department: Leadership among Peers. Ed. by Allan Tucker. 1992. lib. bdg. 29.95 (*0-02-897425-5*) Macmillan.

Chairing the Academic Department: Leadership among Peers. Allan Tucker. LC 93-4915. 576p. 1992. 29.95 (*0-89774-826-3*) Oryx Pr.

Chairing the Foreign Language & Literature Department. Ed. by Ann Bugliani. 130p. (Orig.). 1994. pap. 15.00 (*0-87352-564-7*, W405P) Modern Lang.

Chairman: John J. McCloy - The Making of the American Establishment. Kai Bird. 608p. 1992. 30.00 (*0-671-45415-3*) S&S Trade.

Chairman, Academic Subjects (English & Social Studies) Jack Rudman. (Teachers License Examination Ser.: CH-1). 1994. pap. 29.95 (*0-8373-8151-7*) Nat Learn.

Chairman, Accounting & Business Practices. Jack Rudman. (Teachers License Examination Ser.: CH-2). 1994. pap. 29.95 (*0-8373-8152-5*) Nat Learn.

Chairman & Speaker's Role Made Easy. David Belson & Ruth Belson. 1968. pap. 1.95 (*0-8065-0187-1*, C269, Citadel Pr) Carol Pub Group.

Chairman Cazort's Little Red Book of Writing: A Revolutionary Guide for Getting Better Grades. Douglas Cazort. (Illus.). 132p. 1993. pap. 12.95 (*1-56565-074-3*) Lowell Hse.

Chairman, Civil Service Commission. Jack Rudman. (Career Examination Ser.: C-1164). 1994. pap. 49.95 (*0-8373-1164-0*) Nat Learn.

Chairman, Distributive Education (Merchandising & Salesmanship), Sr. H. S. Jack Rudman. (Teachers License Examination Ser.: CH-3). 1994. pap. 29.95 (*0-8373-8153-3*) Nat Learn.

Chairman, English, Jr. H. S. Jack Rudman. (Teachers License Examination Ser.: CH-4). 1994. pap. 29.95 (*0-8373-8154-1*) Nat Learn.

Chairman, English, Sr. H. S. Jack Rudman. (Teachers License Examination Ser.: CH-5). 1994. pap. 29.95 (*0-8373-8155-X*) Nat Learn.

Chairman, Fine Arts, Sr. H. S. Jack Rudman. (Teachers License Examination Ser.: CH-7). 1994. pap. 29.95 (*0-8373-8157-6*) Nat Learn.

Chairman, Foreign Languages, Jr. H. S. Jack Rudman. (Teachers License Examination Ser.: CH-8). 1994. pap. 29.95 (*0-8373-8158-4*) Nat Learn.

An Asterisk (*) at the beginning of an entry indicates that the title is appearing in BIP for the first time.

C

An Asterisk (*) at the beginning of an entry indicates that the title is appearing in BIP for the first time.

1133

Challenge for Excellence in Foreign Language Education. Ed. by Gilbert A. Jarvis. (Reports of the Northeast Conference on the Teaching of Foreign Languages). 159p. 1984. pap. 10.95 (*0-915432-84-6*) NE Conf Teach Foreign.

Challenge for Geography: A Changing World, a Changing Discipline. Ed. by R. J. Johnston. LC 92-25239. 272p. 1993. 49.95 (*0-631-18713-8*); pap. 19.95 (*0-631-18714-6*) Blackwell Pubs.

***Challenge for Living: Dying, Death, & Bereavement.** Ed. by Inge B. Corless & Barbara B. Germino. 1994. write for info. (*0-615-00079-7*) Jones & Bartlett.

Challenge for Living: Dying Death Bereavement. Inge Corless. (Death & Dying Ser.). 760p. 1995. 33.75 (*0-86720-817-1*) Jones & Bartlett.

Challenge for Research in Higher Education: Harmonizing Excellence & Utility. Alan Lindsay & Ruth Neumann. Ed. & Frwd. by Jonathan D. Fife. LC 89-83630. (ASHE-ERIC Higher Education Report Ser.: No. 8, 1988). 150p. (Orig.). (C). 1989. pap. 15.00 (*0-913317-52-7*) GWU Schl E&HD.

Challenge for Survival: Land, Air, & Water for Man in Megalopolis. Ed. by Pierre Dansereau. LC 78-98397. 235p. 1970. text ed. 47.50 (*0-231-03267-6*) Col U Pr.

Challenge for Tanzania's Economy. C. George Kahama et al. 392p. 1986. text ed. 40.00 (*0-435-08014-8*) Heinemann.

Challenge for Teachers. John Eggleston. Ed. by Jonathan Solity. (Introduction to Education Ser.). 160p. 1992. 65.00 (*0-304-32368-3*) Cassell.

Challenge for Teachers. John Eggleston. Ed. by Jonathan Solity. (Introduction to Education Ser.). 160p. 1992. pap. 25.00 (*0-304-32369-1*) Weidner & Sons.

Challenge for the Actor. Uta Hagen. 352p. 1991. text ed. 22.50 (*0-684-19040-0*, Scribners) S&S Trade.

Challenge in Mathematics & Science Education: Psychology's Response. Ed. by Louis A. Penner et al. 395p. 1993. text ed. 40.00 (*1-55798-207-4*) Am Psychol.

Challenge in South Asia: Development, Democracy, & Regional Cooperation. Ed. by Poona Wignaraja & Akmal Hussain. 360p. (C). 1989. text ed. 29.95 (*0-8039-9603-9*) Sage.

Challenge Met. Charles Ingrid. (Sand Wars Ser.: Bk. 6). 1990. pap. 3.95 (*0-88677-436-5*) DAW Bks.

Challenge of a Generation: Beyond the Crash of 87. E. S. Gayed. 240p. 1988. 21.95 (*0-13-124397-7*, Busn) P-H.

Challenge of a Generation: Beyond the Crash of '87. Michael E. Gayed. 1988. 21.95 (*0-317-04621-7*) NY Inst Finance.

Challenge of a Liberal Faith. 3rd ed. George N. Marshall. 224p. (Orig.). 1993. pap. 14.00 (*0-933840-31-4*, Skinner Hse Bks) Unitarian Univ.

Challenge of African Economic Recovery & Development. Ed. by Adebayo Adedeji et al. 796p. 1991. text ed. 55.00 (*0-7146-3388-7*, Pub. by F Cass Pubs UK); pap. text ed. 37.00 (*0-7146-4074-3*, Pub. by F Cass Pubs UK) Intl Spec Bk.

Challenge of Age: A Guide to Growing Older in Health & Happiness. E. Fritz Schmerl & Sally P. Tubach. 192p. 1991. pap. 14.95 (*0-8245-1296-0*) Crossroad NY.

Challenge of Ageing: A Multidisciplinary Approach to Extended Care. 2nd ed. Ed. by Marion W. Shaw. (Illus.). 192p. (Orig.). 1991. pap. text ed. 27.00 (*0-443-04357-4*) Churchill.

Challenge of America: Can Judaism Survive in Freedom? Ed. by Jacob Neusner. LC 92-33631. (Judaism in Cold War America, 1945-1990 Ser.: Vol. 1). 320p. 1993. 53.00 (*0-8153-0074-3*) Garland.

Challenge of Anthropology: Old Encounters & New Excursions. Robin Fox. LC 93-15532. 524p. (C). 1994. text ed. 49.95 (*1-56000-119-4*) Transaction Pubs.

Challenge of Arctic Shipping: Science, Environmental Assessment & Human Values. Ed. by David L. VanderZwaag & Cynthia Lamson. (McGill-Queen's Native & Northern Ser.). 288p. (C). 1990. text ed. 49.95 (*0-7735-0700-0*, Pub. by McGill CN) U of Toronto Pr.

Challenge of Art to Psychology. Seymour B. Sarason. 224p. (C). 1990. 30.00 (*0-300-04754-1*) Yale U Pr.

Challenge of Asian Developing Countries: Issues & Analyses. Ed. by Shinichi Ichimura. (Illus.). 691p. 1988. 63.25 (*92-833-1095-0*, Pub. by APO JA); pap. 58.00 (*92-833-1096-9*, Pub. by APO JA) Qual Resc.

Challenge of Baha'u'llah. Gary L. Matthews. 284p. (Orig.). 1993. pap. 9.95 (*0-85398-360-7*) G Ronald Pub.

Challenge of Belatedness: Goethe, Kleist, & Hofmannsthal. Jean Wilson. 254p. (C). 1991. lib. bdg. 50.00 (*0-8191-8093-9*, Pub. by McMaster Colloquium) U Pr of Amer.

Challenge of Bewilderment: Understanding & Representation in James, Conrad, & Ford. Paul B. Armstrong. LC 87-6683. 320p. (C). 1987. 38.95 (*0-8014-1949-2*) Cornell U Pr.

Challenge of Bilingualism see **Foreign Language Teaching: Challenges to the Profession**

***Challenge of Catholic Youth: Called to Be Witnesses & Storytellers.** NFCYM Staff. 28p. 1993. 8.50 (*0-89944-273-0*) Don Bosco Multimedia.

Challenge of Change. Laurence G. Thompson. LC 73-9267. 127p. 1973. reprint ed. text ed. 55.00 (*0-8371-6998-4*, THCH, Greenwood Pr) Greenwood.

Challenge of Change: Perspectives on Family, Work, & Education. Ed. by Matina S. Horner et al. LC 83-8994. (Women in Context Ser.). 346p. 1983. 65.00 (*0-306-41237-3*, Plenum Pr) Plenum.

Challenge of Change: Questions & Resources for Computer-Using Educators. Gail Marshall. 129p. 1993. pap. text ed. 23.95 (*1-56484-030-1*) Intl Society Tech Educ.

Challenge of Change: The Sun Oil Company, 1945-1977. Arthur M Johnson. LC 82-14395. (Illus.). 500p. 1983. 49.50 (*0-8142-0340-X*) Ohio St U Pr.

Challenge of Change: Three Centuries of Enfield, Connecticut History. Ruth E. Bridge. LC 77-7148. (Illus.). 1977. 6.50 (*0-914016-43-1*) Phoenix Pub.

***Challenge of Change in Organizations: Helping Employees Thrive in the New Frontier.** Nancy J. Barger & Linda K. Kirby. LC 95-8817. 232p. 1995. 24.95 (*0-89106-079-0*, 7113) Davies-Black.

Challenge of Chemical Weapons: An American Perspective. Victor A. Utgoff. LC 90-43363. 224p. 1991. text ed. 49.95 (*0-312-05337-1*) St Martin.

Challenge of China & Japan: Politics & Development in East Asia. Ed. by Susan L. Shirk. LC 84-24862. 560p. 1985. text ed. 75.00 (*0-275-90163-7*, C0163, Praeger Pubs) Greenwood.

Challenge of Christian Marriage: Marriage in Scripture, History & Contemporary Life. Thomas M. Martin. 1990. 9.95 (*0-8091-3190-0*) Paulist Pr.

Challenge of Church Growth: A Symposium. Ed. by Wilbert R. Shenk et al. (Institute of Mennonite Studies: Missionary Studies: No. 1). 112p. reprint ed. pap. 32.00 (*0-7837-5113-3*, 2044812) Bks Demand.

Challenge of Clean Air. Martin J. Gutnik. LC 89-39422. (Environmental Issues Ser.). (Illus.). 64p. (J). (gr. 6 up). 1990. lib. bdg. 15.95 (*0-89490-272-5*) Enslow Pubs.

Challenge of Cognitive Therapy: Applications to Nontraditional Populations. Ed. by T. Michael Vallis et al. LC 90-14306. (Applied Clinical Psychology Ser.). (Illus.). 180p. 1991. 42.50 (*0-306-43629-9*, Plenum Pr) Plenum.

Challenge of Command: Reading for Military Excellence. Roger H. Nye. LC 85-30614. (West Point Military History Ser.). 200p. (Orig.). 1986. pap. 9.95 (*0-89529-280-7*) Avery Pub.

***Challenge of Communist Education: A Look at the German Democratic Republic.** Margrete S. Klein. (East European Monographs: No. 70). 174p. 1980. 45.00 (*0-914710-64-8*) East Eur Quarterly.

Challenge of Community Education. Colin Fletcher. (C). 1982. 29.00 (*0-685-50348-8*, Pub. by Univ Nottingham UK) St Mut.

Challenge of Community Policing: Testing the Promises. David H. Bayley et al. Ed. by Dennis P. Rosenbaum. LC 94-811. 1994. 48.00 (*0-8039-5443-3*); pap. 22.95 (*0-8039-5444-1*) Sage.

Challenge of Comparative Literature. Claudio Guillen. Tr. by Cola Franzen. (Studies in Comparative Literature: No. 42). 462p. (C). 1993. 52.00 (*0-674-10687-3*); pap. 21.50 (*0-674-10688-1*) HUP.

Challenge of Complex School Problems. Jim Norby et al. LC 90-33191. 120p. (Orig.) (C). 1990. pap. text ed. 14.00 (*0-89079-242-9*, 1436) PRO-ED.

Challenge of Connecting Learning. (Liberal Learning & the Arts & Sciences Major Ser.: Vol. 1). xiii, 33p. 1991. 10.00 (*0-911696-51-2*) Assn Am Coll.

Challenge of Counseling in Middle Schools. Ed. by Edwin R. Gerler, Jr. et al. 1990. pap. write for info. (*1-56109-030-1*) ERIC Clearinghouse.

Challenge of Crime in a Free Society. H. Ruth et al. LC 79-152126. (Symposia on Law & Society Ser.). 1971. reprint ed. lib. bdg. 22.50 (*0-306-70124-3*) Da Capo.

Challenge of Cross-Border Environmentalism: The U. S.-Mexico Case. Tom Barry. 121p. 1994. pap. 9.95 (*0-911213-45-7*) Interhemisp Res Ctr.

Challenge of Curriculum Innovation: A Study of Curriculum Ideologies & Practices in two Secondary Schools, Vol. 6. Thomas Dalton. (Education Policy Perspectives Ser). 225p. 1988. 70.00 (*1-85000-214-2*, Falmer Pr); pap. 35.00 (*1-85000-215-0*, Falmer Pr) Taylor & Francis.

Challenge of D & F Electrons: Theory & Computation. Michael C. Zerner. Ed. by Dennis R. Salahub. LC 89-6926. (Symposium Ser.: No. 394). (Illus.). 392p. 1989. text ed. 89.95 (*0-8412-1628-2*) Am Chemical.

Challenge of D. H. Lawrence. Ed. by Michael Squires & Keith Cushman. LC 89-40537. 240p. (C). 1990. pap. text ed. 14.95 (*0-299-12424-X*) U of Wis Pr.

Challenge of Daycare. Sally Provence et al. LC 75-43331. 313p. 1977. reprint ed. pap. 89.20 (*0-7837-3307-0*, 2057709) Bks Demand.

Challenge of Democracy, 3 Vols. 2nd ed. Kenneth Janda et al. (C). 1991. text ed. 52.76 (*0-395-47287-3*) HM.

Challenge of Democracy: Government in America. Kenneth Janda et al. 702p. (C). 1987. trans. 26.76 (*0-685-17243-0*) HM.

Challenge of Democracy: Government in America. 2nd ed. Kenneth Janda et al. LC 88-81336. 1988. Incl. test item bank. teacher ed 3.16 (*0-318-36894-3*); student ed 12.36 (*0-318-36893-5*); Incl. videotape. trans., vhs write for info. (*0-318-63308-6*) HM.

Challenge of Democracy: Government in America, Brief Edition. Kenneth Janda et al. (C). 1990. teacher ed write for info. (*0-318-66709-6*); pap. write for info. (*0-318-66708-8*) HM.

Challenge of Detracking: A Collection. Ed. by James Bellanca & Elizabeth Swartz. LC 93-79951. (Illus.). 240p. (J). (gr. k-12). 1993. pap. text ed. 19.95 (*0-932935-50-8*) IRI-Skylght.

Challenge of Diversity. Richard E. Engler, Jr. LC 72-167337. (Essay Index Reprint Ser.). 1977. reprint ed. 23.95 (*0-8369-2687-0*) Ayer.

Challenge of Diversity: EDRA Proceedings: 1984. Ed. by Donna Duerk & David Campbell. 344p. 1984. 35.00 (*0-939922-05-3*) EDRA.

Challenge of Diversity: Equal Employment Opportunity & Managing Differences in the 1990's. 36p. 1991. write for info. (*0-318-68949-9*) BNA.

Challenge of Diversity: Involvement or Alienation in the Academy? Daryl G. Smith. Ed. by Jonathan D. Fife. LC 89-63437. (ASHE-ERIC Higher Education Report Ser.: No. 5, 1989). 115p. (Orig.). (C). 1989. pap. text ed. 15.00 (*0-9623882-5-4*) GWU Schl E&HD.

Challenge of Economics: Readings from Challenge, the Magazine of Economic Affairs. Richard D. Bartel. LC 83-27108. 352p. reprint ed. pap. 100.40 (*0-8357-2585-5*, 2040290) Bks Demand.

Challenge of Education Change: The Content & Organization of Schooling. M. Bloomer & K. E. Shaw. 1979. 104.00 (*0-08-022994-8*, Pub. by Pergamon Repr UK) Franklin.

Challenge of Educational Innovation & National Development in Southern Africa. Dickson A. Mungazi. LC 91-38677. (American University Studies: Education: Ser. XIV, Vol. 36). 200p. (C). 1992. text ed. 41.95 (*0-8204-1713-0*) P Lang Pubs.

Challenge of Effective Speaking. 8th ed. Rudolph F. Verderber. 410p. (C). 1991. pap. 28.95 (*0-534-13968-X*) Intl Thomson.

Challenge of Effective Speaking. 9th ed. Rudolph F. Verderber. 436p. (C). 1994. pap. 31.95 (*0-534-16332-7*) Intl Thomson.

***Challenge of English in the National Curriculum.** Ed. by Robert Protherough & Peter King. LC 94-45380. 1995. write for info. (*0-415-09061-X*) Routledge.

Challenge of Epilepsy. rev. ed. Sally Fletcher. LC 85-90992. (Illus.). 128p. 1986. pap. 9.95 (*0-9615513-9-9*) Aura Pub Co.

Challenge of Ethics in Pharmacy Practice: A Symposium. David A. Knapp. 68p. 1985. 6.00 (*0-931292-15-8*) Am Inst Hist Pharm.

Challenge of European Integration: Internal & External Problems of Trade & Money. Abegaz. LC 94-8109. (Political Economy of Global Interdependence Ser.). (C). 1994. text ed. 59.95 (*0-8133-2355-X*) Westview.

Challenge of Excellence: Learning the Ropes of Change. rev. ed. Scout Lee et al. (Skill Builder Ser.). (Illus.). 192p. 1990. pap. 16.95 (*1-55552-004-9*) Metamorphous Pr.

Challenge of Existentialism. John D. Wild. LC 78-12402. 297p. 1979. reprint ed. text ed. 59.75 (*0-313-21127-2*, WICE, Greenwood Pr) Greenwood.

Challenge of Extinction. Dorothy H. Patent. LC 90-3288. (Environmental Issues Ser.). (Illus.). 64p. (J). (gr. 6 up). 1991. lib. bdg. 15.95 (*0-89490-268-7*) Enslow Pubs.

Challenge of Facework: Cross-Cultural & Interpersonal Issues. Ed. by Stella Ting-Toomey. (SUNY Series, Human Communication Processes). 346p. 1994. 59.50 (*0-7914-1633-X*); pap. 19.95 (*0-7914-1634-8*) State U NY Pr.

Challenge of Facts & Other Essays. William G. Sumner. LC 72-128963. reprint ed. 45.00 (*0-404-06303-9*) AMS Pr.

Challenge of Famine: Recent Experience, Lessons Learned. Ed. by John O. Field. LC 93-975. (Library of Management for Development). (Illus.). xiv, 281p. 1993. 38.00 (*1-56549-019-3*); pap. 24.95 (*1-56549-018-5*) Kumarian Pr.

Challenge of Fate. 1991. pap. 12.95 (*0-904575-35-7*) Sigo Pr.

Challenge of Feminist Biography: Writing the Lives of Modern American Women. Ed. by Sara Alpern et al. (Women in American History Ser.). (Illus.). 224p. (C). 1992. 44.95 (*0-252-01926-1*); pap. 14.95 (*0-252-06292-2*) U of Ill Pr.

Challenge of Free Economic Zones in Central & Eastern Europe: International Perspectives. 1990. 75.00 (*92-1-104358-1*, E 90.II.A.27) UN.

Challenge of Free Trade: Report to the Eminent Persons Group on World Trade. Alan Oxley. LC 90-9109. 262p. 1990. text ed. 39.95 (*0-312-05675-3*) St Martin.

Challenge of Geriatric Medicine. Bernard Isaacs. (Illus.). 280p. 1992. 75.00 (*0-19-262022-3*); pap. 31.95 (*0-19-262021-5*) OUP.

Challenge of German Literature. Ed. by Horst S. Daemmrich & Diether H. Haenicke. LC 75-131425. 434p. (C). 1971. 34.95 (*0-8143-1435-X*) Wayne St U Pr.

Challenge of Global Warming. Ed. by Dean E. Abrahamson. LC 89-1830. (Illus.). 356p. (Orig.). 1989. 34.95 (*0-933280-87-4*); pap. 19.95 (*0-933280-86-6*) Island Pr.

***Challenge of Grassroots Development: Society, Economy, & Change in Southern Mexico.** Jeffrey H. Cohen. Ed. by Victoria Cuffel. (Occasional Papers). 67p. (Orig.). 1994. pap. 4.00 (*1-881157-28-8*) In Ctr Global.

Challenge of Hospital Governance: How to Become an Exemplary Board. Michael E. Rindler. 183p. 1992. 34.95 (*1-55648-086-5*, 196627) AHPI.

Challenge of Human Rights Education. Ed. by Hugh Starkey. (Council of Europe Ser.). 300p. 1992. pap. text ed. 24.95 (*0-304-31943-0*) Cassell.

Challenge of Human Rights Education. Hugh Starkey et al. 272p. (C). 1991. pap. 39.95 (*0-89397-412-9*) Nichols Pub.

Challenge of Hunger in Africa: A Call to Action: Le defi de la faim en Afrique: Pour une Action Commune. 20p. English. 6.95 (*0-685-28286-4*, 31099) World Bank.

***Challenge of Illiteracy: From Reflection to Action.** Ed. by Zaghloul Morsy. LC 94-32885. (IBE Studies on Education: Vol. 1). 352p. 1994. 40.00 (*0-8153-1854-5*, SS995) Garland.

***Challenge of Immigration.** Vic Cox. LC 94-34645. (Multicultural Issues Ser.). (Illus.). 128p. (YA). (gr. 6 up). 1995. lib. bdg. 17.95 (*0-89490-628-3*) Enslow Pubs.

Challenge of Information Technology: Proceedings of the 41st FID Congress, Hong-Kong, September 13-16, 1982. Ed. by K. R. Brown. xii, 356p. 1983. 66.75 (*0-444-86646-9*, North Holland) Elsevier.

***Challenge of Institutional Reform in Mexico.** Riordan Roett. LC 95-3465. 216p. 1995. lib. bdg. 36.50 (*1-55587-545-9*) Lynne Rienner.

Challenge of Integration: Europe & the Americas. Ed. by Peter H. Smith. (University of Miami North-South Center Ser.). 272p. (C). 1993. pap. text ed. 21.95 (*1-56000-687-0*) Transaction Pubs.

Challenge of Interdependence: Mexico & the United States. Bilateral Commission on the Future of United States-Mexican Relations Staff. 260p. (Orig.). (C). 1988. lib. bdg. 48.00 (*0-8191-7273-1*); pap. text ed. 25.00 (*0-8191-7274-X*) U Pr of Amer.

Challenge of Japan Before World War Two & After: A Study of National Growth & Expansion. Nazli Choucri et al. (Studies in International Conflict). (Illus.). 320p. 1992. 49.95 (*0-415-07589-0*, A7986) Routledge.

Challenge of Jesus. John Shea. (Rev. John Shea Library). 192p. 1984. pap. 11.95 (*0-88347-169-8*, 7169) Thomas More.

Challenge of Labour: Shaping British Society, 1850-1930. Keith Burgess. LC 80-5100. 224p. 1980. text ed. 29.95 (*0-312-12805-3*) St Martin.

Challenge of l'Arche. Jean Vanier. (Illus.). 286p. 1982. reprint ed. pap. 9.95 (*0-89088-072-7*) Harper SF.

Challenge of Law Reform. Arthur T. Vanderbilt. LC 76-3784. 194p. 1976. reprint ed. text ed. 52.50 (*0-8371-8809-1*, VALR, Greenwood Pr) Greenwood.

Challenge of Liberation Theology: A First-World Response. Ed. by Brian Mahan & L. Dale Richesin. LC 81-9527. 160p. reprint ed. pap. 45.60 (*0-8357-2683-5*, 2040219) Bks Demand.

Challenge of Life: Three Lectures. Lawrence P. Jacks. LC 77-27147. (Hibbert Lectures). reprint ed. 35.00 (*0-404-60423-4*) AMS Pr.

Challenge of Loving: Building Healthy Relationships. Ed. by Casey Peterson. 34p. 1986. pap. 2.50 (*0-936098-47-3*) Intl Marriage.

Challenge of Management. William G. Dyer et al. 640p. (C). 1989. text ed. 51.25 (*0-15-505910-6*); disk, vhs write for info. (*0-318-67017-8*) Dryden Pr.

Challenge of Marriage. Rudolf Dreikurs. 1978. pap. 8.95 (*0-8015-1177-1*, Dutton) NAL-Dutton.

Challenge of Married Life. William E. Drake. Ed. by Helen Graves. LC 86-51345. 124p. 1987. 8.95 (*1-55523-063-6*) Winston-Derek.

Challenge of Marxism. 190p. (C). reprint ed. pap. 12.95 (*0-939443-00-7*) Helmers Howard Pub.

Challenge of Maturity: A Comprehensive Guide to Understand & Achieve Psychological & Social Self-Actualization As We Grow Older. William D. Eldridge. 342p. (Orig.). (C). 1991. lib. bdg. 51.00 (*0-8191-8177-3*); pap. text ed. 27.00 (*0-8191-8178-1*) U Pr of Amer.

Challenge of Midlife. Anselm Gruen. Ed. by Alphonse Lauer. Tr. by Quentin Kathol & Bill D. Bell. (Schuyler Spiritual Ser.: No. 10). 1993. pap. 4.50 (*1-56788-004-5*, 10-010) BMH Pubns.

Challenge of Mineral Resources. Robert L. Bates. LC 90-35948. (Environmental Issues Ser.). (Illus.). 64p. (J). (gr. 6 up). 1991. lib. bdg. 15.95 (*0-89490-245-8*) Enslow Pubs.

Challenge of Missions. Oswald J. Smith. 128p. (Orig.). reprint ed. pap. text ed. 4.99 (*1-884543-02-2*) O M Lit.

Challenge of Modern Church-Public Relations. Ed. by Michael V. Reagen & Doris S. Chertow. LC 72-5637. (Occasional Papers: No. 33). 68p. (Orig.). 1972. pap. 3.00 (*0-87060-056-7*, OCP 33) Syracuse U Cont Ed.

Challenge of Modernity: A Reader on Post-Confederation Canada. Ian McKay. 1991. pap. text ed. write for info. (*0-07-551150-9*) McGraw.

Challenge of Modernity: The Quest for Authenticity in the Arab World. Louay M. Safi. 232p. (Orig.). (C). Date not set. lib. bdg. 49.50 (*0-8191-9375-5*); pap. text ed. 28.50 (*0-8191-9376-3*) U Pr of Amer.

Challenge of Motorcycling: A Guide for the New Street Rider. LC 80-81526. 57p. pap. 2.00 (*0-686-37012-0*) Motorcycle Safety.

Challenge of Nationhood. Tom Mboya. (African Writers Ser.). 1970. pap. 9.95 (*0-435-90081-1*) Heinemann.

Challenge of New Technology: Innovation in British Business Since 1850. Jonathan Liebenau. 200p. 1988. text ed. 58.95 (*0-566-05147-8*, Pub. by Avebury Pub UK) Ashgate Pub Co.

Challenge of New Technology & Macro Political Change. Ed. by William M. Lafferty & Eliezer Rosenstein. LC 93-9607. (International Handbook of Participation in Organizations Ser.: Vol. 3). 1993. 89.00 (*0-19-828382-2*) OUP.

Challenge of Nuclear Armaments: Essays Dedicated to Niels Bohr & His Appeal for an Open World. Ed. by A. Boserup et al. (Illus.). 346p. (Orig.). 1986. pap. 78.00x (*87-7245-142-4*) Coronet Bks.

Challenge of Numbers: People in the Mathematical Sciences. Commission on Physical Sciences, Mathematics & Resources Staff. 136p. 1990. text ed. 9.95 (*0-309-04190-2*) Natl Acad Pr.

***Challenge of Old Chemical Munitions & Toxic Armament Wastes.** Ed. by Thomas Stock & Karlheinz Lohs. (SIPRI Chemical & Biological Warfare Studies: No. 16). (Illus.). 280p. 1995. pap. text ed. 35.00 (*0-19-829190-6*) OUP.

Challenge of Open Housing: Good Neighborhood. Morris Milgram. 248p. 1977. 8.00 (*0-318-15820-5*, O-2) Natl Neighbors.

Challenge of Organizational Change: How People Experience & Manage It. Rosabeth M. Kanter et al. 400p. 1992. text ed. 35.00 (*0-02-916991-7*) Free Pr.

Challenge of Our Culture. Ed. by Clarence T. Craig. LC 70-167331. (Essay Index Reprints - Interseminary Ser.: Vol. 1). 1977. reprint ed. 20.95 (*0-8369-2765-6*) Ayer.

Challenge of Our Past: Studies in Orthodox Canon Law & Church History. John H. Erickson. 164p. 1990. pap. 10.95 (*0-88141-086-1*) St Vladimirs.

Challenge of Overpopulation, 1955 edition see **Standing Room Only: The World's Exploding Population**

C

An Asterisk (*) at the beginning of an entry indicates that the title is appearing in BIP for the first time.

An Asterisk (*) at the beginning of an entry indicates that the title is appearing in BIP for the first time.

C

Challenger. Sandra D. Bricker. Ed. by Liz Parker. (Take Ten Bks.). 47p. (Orig.). (YA). (gr. 6-12). 1993. pap. text ed. 2.95 (*1-56254-096-3*) Saddleback Pubns.

Challenger at Sea: A Ship That Revolutionized Earth Science. Kenneth J. Hsu. (Illus.). 400p. 1992. text ed. 39.50 (*0-691-08735-0*) Princeton U Pr.

Challenger Countdown. Rose B. Green. LC 87-47859. 64p. 1988. 14.95 (*0-8453-4816-7*, Cornwall Bks) Assoc Univ Prs.

Challenger Crossword Puzzles, No 1. Ed. by Louis Sabin. 64p. 1981. pap. 4.95 (*0-686-46719-1*) PB.

Challenger Foraminifera. Robert W. Jones. (Illus.). 280p. 1994. 275.00 (*0-19-854096-5*) OUP.

Challenger Placement Tool, Set 1. 1993. Incl. student bklt. & tchr's. scoring bklt. student ed, teacher ed 2.00 (*0-88336-872-2*) New Readers.

Challenger Placement Tool, Set 2. 1993. Incl. student bklt. & 5 tchr's. scoring bklts. student ed, teacher ed 3.25 (*0-88336-873-0*) New Readers.

Challenger Set, 8 bks., Set. 1993. teacher ed 79.95 (*0-88336-800-5*) New Readers.

Challenger Sketchbook: B. Shephard's Sketchbook of the H.M.S. Challenger Expedition 1872-1874. Ed. by Harris B. Stewart, Jr. & J. Welles Henderson. (Illus.). 34p. 1972. 7.50 (*0-913346-01-2*) Phila Maritime Mus.

Challenger 1. 1993. 5.50 (*0-88336-781-5*); 1.60 (*0-88336-863-3*); 0.20 (*0-88336-581-2*) New Readers.

Challenger 1-4 Teacher's Manual. 1993. 6.50 (*0-88336-874-9*); 3.15 (*0-88336-789-0*) New Readers.

Challenger 2. 1993. 5.50 (*0-88336-782-3*); 1.60 (*0-88336-864-1*); 0.20 (*0-88336-582-0*) New Readers.

Challenger 3. 1993. 5.50 (*0-88336-783-1*); 1.60 (*0-88336-865-X*); 0.20 (*0-88336-583-9*) New Readers.

Challenger 4. 1993. 5.50 (*0-88336-784-X*); 1.60 (*0-88336-866-8*); 0.20 (*0-88336-584-7*) New Readers.

Challenger 5. 1993. 6.80 (*0-88336-785-8*); 1.60 (*0-88336-867-6*); teacher ed 5.25 (*0-88336-875-7*); 0.20 (*0-88336-585-5*) New Readers.

Challenger 5-8 Answer Key. 1993. 4.20 (*0-88336-790-4*) New Readers.

Challenger 6. 1993. 7.90 (*0-88336-786-6*); 1.60 (*0-88336-868-4*); teacher ed 5.75 (*0-88336-793-9*); 0.20 (*0-88336-586-3*) New Readers.

Challenger 7. 1993. 7.90 (*0-88336-787-4*); 1.60 (*0-88336-869-2*); teacher ed 5.75 (*0-88336-794-7*); 0.20 (*0-88336-587-1*) New Readers.

Challenger 8. 1993. 7.90 (*0-88336-788-2*); 1.60 (*0-88336-870-6*); teacher ed 5.75 (*0-88336-795-5*); 0.20 (*0-88336-588-X*) New Readers.

Challengers. 1978. 4.00 (*0-939418-14-2*) Ferguson-Florissant.

Challengers, No. 80. Grace L. Hill. 240p. 1989. pap. 4.99 (*0-8423-0362-6*) Tyndale.

Challengers: A Century of Ballooning. Diane T. Darnall. (Illus.). 224p. (Orig.). 1990. pap. write for info. (*0-318-66930-7*) Hunter Ariz.

Challengers, Competition, & Reelection: Comparing Senate & House Elections. Jonathan S. Krasno. LC 94-15900. 200p. 1994. 26.00 (*0-300-05844-6*) Yale U Pr.

Challenger's Hope. David Feintuch. 416p. (Orig.). 1995. mass mkt. 5.50 (*0-446-60097-0*, Aspect) Warner Bks.

Challenges. Ben Bova. LC 93-18413. 352p. 1993. 21.95 (*0-312-85550-8*) Tor Bks.

Challenges. Ben Bova. 352p. 1994. mass mkt. 4.99 (*0-8125-1408-4*) Tor Bks.

Challenges: A Process Writing Course in English. Douglas H. Brown et al. 256p. (C). 1990. pap. text ed. 18.00 (*0-13-009085-9*) P-H.

Challenges: A Young Man's Journal for Self-Awareness & Personal Planning. Mindy Bingham et al. Ed. by Barbara Greene et al. LC 84-70108. (Illus.). 240p. (YA). (gr. 8 up). 1993. student ed 5.95 (*0-911655-25-5*) Advocacy Pr.

Challenges: A Young Man's Journal for Self-Awareness & Personal Planning. Mindy Bingham et al. Ed. by Barbara Greene et al. LC 84-70108. (Illus.). 240p. (YA). (gr. 8 up). 1993. pap. 18.95 (*0-911655-24-7*) Advocacy Pr.

Challenges Ahead: Flood Loss Reduction Strategies for the '90s: Proceedings of the Fourteenth Annual Conference of the Association of State Floodplain Managers, June 11-15, 1990, Asheville, North Carolina. (Special Publications: No. 23). 300p. (Orig.). 1991. pap. 10.00 (*0-685-49321-0*) Natural Hazards.

***Challenges & Choices: Using Creative Stories to Identify & Resolve Middle Grades Issues.** Nancy Ullinskey & Lorri Hibbert. Ed. by Leslie Britt & Marta Drayton. LC 94-77093. (Illus.). 144p. (Orig.). (J). (gr. 5-8). 1994. pap. text ed. 12.95 (*0-86530-297-9*) Incentive Pubns.

Challenges & Choices Facing the American Labor. Ed. by Thomas A. Kochan. (Illus.). 290p. 1985. pap. 17.50 (*0-262-61039-6*) MIT Pr.

Challenges & Choices in Corporate Aviation Safety: 35th Annual Corporate Aviation Safety Seminar: Proceedings, April 18-20, 1990, Four Seasons Hotel, Montreal, Quebec, Canada. Corporate Aviation Safety Seminar Staff. 178p. reprint ed. pap. 50.80 (*0-8357-2647-9*, 2040135) Bks Demand.

Challenges & Innovations in Homecare. Ed. by Joanne Handy & Charlotte K. Scheurman. (Critical Debates in an Aging Society Ser.). 101p. (Orig.). 1994. pap. 19.95 (*0-9640387-1-4*) Am Soc Aging.

Challenges & Opportunities: From Now to 2001. Howard F. Didsbury, Jr. 310p. 1986. pap. 16.95 (*0-930242-31-9*) World Future.

Challenges & Opportunities for Business in Post-Apartheid South Africa. Ed. by Meg Voorhes. 120p. (Orig.). 1994. write for info. (*1-879775-18-2*) IRRC Inc DC.

Challenges & Priorities in the Nineteen Nineties: An Alternative U. S. International Affairs Budget, FY1993. John W. Sewell et al. 80p. (C). 1992. pap. 9.95 (*1-56517-008-3*) Overseas Dev Council.

Challenges & Responses in European Security: TAPRI Yearbook 1986. Vilho Harle. (Tapri Yearbook Ser.). 256p. 1987. text ed. 55.95 (*0-566-05363-2*, Pub. by Dartmth Pub UK) Ashgate Pub Co.

Challenges & Responsibilities of a Law School Board of Visitors. ABA, Legal Education & Admissions to the Bar Section Staff. 19p. 1985. pap. 2.00 (*0-685-21545-8*, 529-0034) Amer Bar Assn.

***Challenges Facing Distributors.** Don A. Rice. 180p. 1994. pap. 31.00 (*1-881154-11-4*) Darco Pr.

Challenges Facing Dwarf Parents: Preparing for a New Baby. Ellen H. Fernandez. LC 90-80575. 64p. 1990. pap. 7.95 (*0-942963-03-2*) Distinctive Pub.

Challenges Facing Environmental Laboratories: Methods, Quality, Media & Liability. 1993. pap. 150.00 (*1-881369-25-0*) Water Environ.

Challenges Facing Special Education. Ed. by Edward L. Meyen et al. LC 92-74810. 404p. 1993. pap. 29.95 (*0-89108-229-8*, 9305) Love Pub Co.

***Challenges Facing the United Nations: Building A Safer World.** Ed. by Erskine Childers. 224p. 1995. 45.00 (*0-312-12566-6*); pap. 17.95 (*0-312-12575-5*) St Martin.

Challenges for a Changing America: Perspectives on Immigration & Multiculturalism in the United States. Ed. by Ernest R. Myers. LC 93-42350. 1994. 54.95 (*1-880921-71-5*); pap. 34.95 (*1-880921-70-7*) Austin & Winfield.

Challenges for a Service System in Transition: Ensuring Quality Community Experiences for Persons with Developmental Disabilities. Ed. by Mary Hayden & Brian Abery. 416p. (Orig.). 1993. pap. 35.00 (*1-55766-125-1*) P H Brookes.

Challenges for Champions. Andrew Robinson. Ed. by Rob Bell. (Champions Ser.). (Illus.). 64p. (Orig.). (C). 1989. pap. 9.00 (*1-55806-046-4*, 404) Hero Games.

***Challenges for International Broadcasting Vol. III: Identity, Economics, Integration.** Ed. by Elzbieta Olechowska & Howard Aster. (Illus.). 300p. 1995. lib. bdg. 48.00 (*0-8095-4886-0*) Borgo Pr.

Challenges for Macroeconomic Modelling. Ed. by W. Driehuis et al. (Contributions to Economic Analysis Ser.: No. 178). 484p. 1989. 95.00 (*0-444-70529-5*) Elsevier.

Challenges for Public Utility Regulation in the 1980s: Proceedings of the Institute of Public Utilities Annual Conference, 12th, Williamsburg, VA., 1980. Ed. by Harry M. Trebing. LC 81-83389. (MSU Public Utilities Papers). 696p. reprint ed. pap. 180.00 (*0-317-55818-8*, 2029404) Bks Demand.

***Challenges for Russian Economic Reform.** Ed. by Alan Smith. 300p. (C). 1995. pap. text ed. 19.95x (*0-8157-8025-7*, Pub. by Royal Inst Intl Affairs UK) Brookings.

Challenges for School Leaders. Kristen Amundson. 120p. (Orig.). 1988. pap. text ed. 12.95 (*0-87652-125-1*, 021-00215) Am Assn Sch Admin.

Challenges for the College Bound: Advice & Encouragement from a College President. Jay L. Kesler. LC 93-36779. 160p. (YA). (gr. 12). 1994. 8.99 (*0-8010-5262-9*) Baker Bk.

***Challenges for the Eighties.** CRM Staff. 77p. (CHI.). 1985. pap. 3.00 (*1-56582-088-6*) Christ Renew Min.

***Challenges for the New Peacekeepers.** Ed. by Trevor Findlay. (SIPRI Research Reports: No. 12). 160p. 1995. 39.95 (*0-19-829198-1*); pap. 21.00 (*0-19-829199-X*) OUP.

Challenges for the 1990s. Ed. by Richard A. Victor. 64p. 1990. 25.00 (*0-935149-24-4*, WC-90-3) Workers Comp Res Inst.

Challenges for the 1990's for Arms Control & International Security. International Affairs Office Staff. 86p. 1989. pap. text ed. 15.00 (*0-309-04084-1*) Natl Acad Pr.

Challenges in Aging. Ed. by M. Bergener et al. (Sandoz Lectures in Gerontology). (Illus.). 285p. 1991. text ed. 83.00 (*0-12-090163-3*) Acad Pr.

Challenges in Arms Control for the 1990's. Ed. by James Brown. 250p. 1993. pap. text ed. 49.50 (*90-5383-154-1*, Pub. by VU Univ Pr NE) Paul & Co Pubs.

Challenges in Cardiology I. Ed. by Charles E. Rackley. (Bakken Research Center Ser.). (Illus.). 226p. 1991. pap. 39.00 (*0-87993-515-4*) Futura Pub.

***Challenges in College Admissions.** (C). 1995. write for info. (*0-614-03625-9*) Am Assn Coll Registrars.

***Challenges in College Admissions: Report of a Survey of Undergraduate Admissions Policies, Practices & Procedures.** American Association of Collegiate Registrars & Admissions Officers Staff. LC 95-7713. 1995. write for info. (*0-929851-37-4*) Am Assn Coll Registrars.

Challenges in Education. Victoria Sherrow. (Issues for the Nineteen Ninety's Ser.). (YA). 1990. lib. bdg. 13.98 (*0-671-70556-3*, Julian Messner) Silver Burdett Pr.

Challenges in Educational Management: Principles into Practice. W. F. Dennison & Ken Shenton. (Educational Management Ser.). 256p. 1987. 42.50 (*0-7099-0892-X*, Pub. by Croom Helm UK); lib. bdg. 42.50 (*0-685-19162-1*, Pub. by Croom Helm UK) Routledge Chapman & Hall.

Challenges in Gifted Education: Developing Potential & Investing in Knowledge for the 21st Century. (Illus.). 122p. (Orig.). (C). 1993. pap. text ed. 45.00 (*0-7881-0074-2*) Diane Pub.

Challenges in Health Care Management: Strategic Perspectives for Managing Key Stakeholders. John D. Blair & Myron D. Fottler. LC 90-41826. (Health-Management Ser.). 396p. 1990. 40.95 (*1-55542-288-8*) Jossey-Bass.

Challenges in Indian Education. rev. ed. S. Lakshmi. 200p. 1992. text ed. 27.50 (*81-207-1143-2*, Pub. by Sterling Pubs II) Apt Bks.

Challenges in Medical Care. Ed. by Andrew Grubb. 196p. 1992. text ed. 79.95 (*0-471-93102-0*, Wiley-Liss) Wiley.

Challenges in Mental Retardation. Gunnar Dybwad. LC 64-14238. 299p. reprint ed. 85.30 (*0-8357-9059-2*, 2011001) Bks Demand.

Challenges in Military Health Care: Perspectives on Health Status & the Provision of Care. Jay Stanley & John D. Blair. 192p. (C). 1992. 29.95 (*1-56000-650-1*) Transaction Pubs.

***Challenges in Mineral Processing: Proceedings of a Symposium Honoring Douglas W. Fuerstenau on his 60th Birthday, Berkeley, California, December 7-9, 1988.** fac. ed. Ed. by K. V. Sastry & M. C. Fuerstenau. LC 88-63497. (Illus.). 798p. 1989. reprint ed. pap. 180.00 (*0-7837-7865-1*, 2047623) Bks Demand.

Challenges in Natural Language Processing. Ed. by Madeleine Bates & Ralph M. Weischedel. (Studies in Natural Language Processing). (Illus.). 272p. (C). 1993. 54.95 (*0-521-41015-0*) Cambridge U Pr.

Challenges in Neurology. Ed. by Vladimir Hachinski. LC 91-42517. (Illus.). 294p. 1992. text ed. 80.00 (*0-8036-4504-X*) Davis Co.

Challenges in Pediatric Surgery. Thomas C. Moore. (Medical Intelligence Unit Ser.). 130p. 1994. 89.95 (*1-57059-048-6*, LN9048) R G Landes.

Challenges in Predicting New Firm Performance. Arnold C. Cooper. 25p. (Orig.). (C). 1993. pap. text ed. 30.00 (*1-56806-662-7*) Diane Pub.

Challenges in Public Sector Labor Relations. Ed. by Paul A. Weinstein. LC 75-21268. (Public Sector Labor Relations Conference Board Ser.: No. 2). 1975. pap. 7.50 (*0-913400-01-7*) Pub Sect Lab Rel.

***Challenges in Studying the Socio-Economic Dimensions in Cancer Therapy.** Ed. by Maureen O'Reilly. 88p. (Orig.). 1995. write for info. (*1-57130-013-9*) Medicine Grp USA.

Challenges in Synthetic Organic Chemistry. Teruaki Mukaiyama. Ed. by J. E. Baldwin. (International Series of Monographs on Chemistry: No. 20). (Illus.). 240p. 1994. reprint ed. pap. 29.95 (*0-19-855855-4*) OUP.

***Challenges in the Binational Management of Water Resources in the Rio Grande - Rio Bravo.** David Eaton & David Hurlburt. (U. S. - Mexican Occasional Paper Ser.). 154p. 1992. 15.00 (*0-89940-315-8*) LBJ Sch Pub Aff.

Challenges in the Treatment of Congenital Cardiac Anomalies. Matoso Takahashi et al. (Illus.). 272p. 1986. 39.50 (*0-87993-220-1*) Futura Pub.

Challenges of a Generalized System Theory: Proceedings of the Colloquium, Amsterdam, the Netherlands, June 1992. Ed. by P. Dewilde et al. 252p. 1993. pap. 45.75 (*0-444-85769-9*, North Holland) Elsevier.

Challenges of Adolescence: Sexuality. Mary E. Gryczka. 128p. (C). 1990. pap. text ed. 8.90 (*0-8403-5801-6*) Kendall-Hunt.

Challenges of Adolescence: Sexuality Teacher's Guide. Mary E. Gryczka. 80p. (C). 1991. teacher ed 16.90 (*0-8403-5802-4*) Kendall-Hunt.

Challenges of Agricultural Production & Food Security in Africa. Ed. by Olusegun Obasanjo. 250p. 1992. 42.00 (*0-8448-1724-4*, Crane Russak) Taylor & Francis.

***Challenges of Astronomy: Hands-on Experiments for the Sky & Laboratory.** Schlosser. 1994. 39.00 (*3-540-97408-3*) Spr-Verlag.

Challenges of Astronomy: Hands-on Experiments for the Sky & Laboratory. W. Schlosser et al. (Illus.). 380p. 1994. 39.00 (*0-387-97408-3*) Spr-Verlag.

***Challenges of Change: The Helsinki Summit of the CSCE & Its Aftermath.** Ed. by Arie Bloed. LC 94-30591. 1994. lib. bdg. 144.00 (*0-7923-3089-7*) Kluwer Ac.

Challenges of Community Education. Colin Fletcher. 317p. (C). 1983. text ed. 60.00 (*0-685-22145-8*, Pub. by Univ Nottingham UK) St Mut.

Challenges of Community Education. F. Fletcher. (C). 1982. 45.00 (*0-902031-93-7*, Pub. by Univ Nottingham UK) St Mut.

Challenges of Economic Reform & Industrial Growth: China's Wool War. Ed. by Christopher Findlay. 256p. 1992. 45.00 (*1-86373-203-9*, Pub. by Allen Unwin AT); pap. text ed. 29.95 (*1-86373-204-7*, Pub. by Allen Unwin AT) Paul & Co Pubs.

Challenges of Emerging Leadership: Community Based Independent Living Programs & the Disability Rights Movement. Robert Funk. Ed. by Lisa J. Walker. viii, 62p. pap. 4.95 (*0-937846-94-5*) Inst Educ Lead.

Challenges of Famine Relief: Emergency Operations in the Sudan. Francis M. Deng & Larry Minear. 165p. (C). 1992. 26.95 (*0-8157-1792-X*); pap. 9.95 (*0-8157-1791-1*) Brookings.

***Challenges of High Temperature Heat Transfer Equipment: 1994 International Mechanical Engineering Congress & Exposition, Chicago, Illinois - November 6-11, 1994.** (HTD Ser.: Vol. 282). 60p. 1994. 40.00 (*0-7918-1389-4*, G00884) ASME.

Challenges of Holistic Teaching: Answering the Tough Questions. Linda Crafton. (Illus.). 232p. (Orig.). (J). (gr. k-8). 1994. pap. text ed. 21.95 (*0-926842-34-X*) CG Pubs Inc.

Challenges of Israel. Ora Shem-Or. LC 80-52915. 80p. 1980. 18.00 (*0-88400-071-0*) Shengold.

Challenges of Labour: Central & Western Europe, 1917-1920. Ed. by Chris Wrigley. LC 92-9966. 312p. 1993. 59.95 (*0-415-07686-2*, A7835) Routledge.

Challenges of Leadership in African Government. Ed. by Olusegun Obasanjo & Hans D'Orville. 200p. 1990. 63.00 (*0-8448-1669-8*, Crane Russak); pap. 35.00 (*0-8448-1670-1*, Crane Russak) Taylor & Francis.

Challenges of Measuring an Ethnic World: Science, Politics & Reality, 2 vols., Set. 1994. lib. bdg. 595.00 (*0-8490-8416-4*) Gordon Pr.

Challenges of Our Time: Disarmament & Social Progress Includes the Political Report of the CPSU Central Committee, Delivered by Mikhail Gorbachev to the 27th Congress of the CPSU. Mikhail S. Gorbachev. LC 86-10473. 226p. reprint ed. pap. 64.50 (*0-7837-0581-6*, 2040925) Bks Demand.

Challenges of Power: American Diplomacy, 1900-1921. abr. ed. Samuel F. Wells, Jr. (Illus.). 148p. (C). 1990. reprint ed. pap. text ed. 17.50 (*0-8191-7636-2*) U Pr of Amer.

Challenges of Racial & Cultural Diversity to Counseling, Vol. 2: Mexico City Conference Proceedings. Ed. by Gerardo M. Gonzalez et al. 110p. 1992. 8.95 (*1-55620-102-8*, 72105) Am Coun Assn.

Challenges of Retrenchment: Strategies in Consolidating Programs, Cutting Costs, & Reallocating Resources. James R. Mingle et al. LC 81-47770. (Jossey-Bass Series in Higher Education). 416p. reprint ed. pap. 118.60 (*0-8357-4865-0*, 2037797) Bks Demand.

Challenges of South-South Cooperation, Set. Ed. by H. W. Singer et al. (C). 1988. 90.00 (*81-7024-185-5*, Pub. by Ashish II) S Asia.

Challenges of Testing Space Systems: Symposium Proceedings, 1986. 1986. 30.00 (*0-318-22330-9*) Int Test Eval.

Challenges of the Heart. Cynthia P. Miller. LC 90-21432. (Illus.). 144p. (Orig.). (YA). 1991. pap. 6.99 (*0-932581-79-X*) Word Aflame.

Challenges of the Twenty-First Century: Conference Held in the Memory of Indira Gandhi, 1991. Ed. by Indira Gandhi Memorial Trust Staff. (C). 1993. 28.00 (*81-224-0488-X*, Pub. by Wiley Eastern II) S Asia.

Challenges of Tomorrow: Profile of Future Teacher Education. R. P. Singh. 160p. 1992. 25.00 (*81-207-1423-7*, Pub. by Sterling Pubs II) Apt Bks.

Challenges of Verification: Smaller States & Arms Control. Heinz Gaertner. 96p. 1989. pap. text ed. 12.85 (*0-8133-7798-6*) Westview.

Challenges of Wealth: Mastering the Personal & Financial Conflicts. Amy L. Domini et al. 420p. 1988. text ed. 24.95 (*0-87094-960-8*) Irwin Prof Pubng.

Challenges Past, Challenges Present: An Analysis of American Higher Education Since 1930. David D. Henry. LC 75-24013. (Carnegie Council Ser.). 191p. reprint ed. pap. 54.50 (*0-8357-4946-0*, 2037877) Bks Demand.

Challenges, Projects, Texts: Canadian Editing: Papers Given at the Conference on Editorial Problems, University of Toronto, 17-18, November, 1989. Ed. by John Lennox & Janet M. Paterson. LC 91-12400. (Conference on Editorial Problems Ser.: No. 25). Orig. Title: Defis, Projets et Textes dans l'Edition Critique au Canada. 120p. 1993. 37.50 (*0-404-63675-6*) AMS Pr.

Challenges to a Liberal International Economic Order. Ed. by Ryan C. Amacher et al. LC 79-11687. 504p. reprint ed. pap. 143.70 (*0-8357-4445-0*, 2037282) Bks Demand.

Challenges to American National Security in the 1990s. Ed. by J. J. Weltman et al. (Issues in International Security Ser.). (Illus.). 256p. 1991. 37.50 (*0-306-43858-5*, Plenum Pr) Plenum.

Challenges to American Values: Society, Business & Religion. Thomas C. Cochran. LC 84-19102. 1987. pap. text ed. 13.95 (*0-19-503535-6*) OUP.

Challenges to Astronomy & Astrophysics: Working Documents of the Astronomy Survey Committee. National Research Council (U. S.), Astronomy Survey Committee Staff. LC 83-60509. (Illus.). 296p. reprint ed. pap. 84.40 (*0-8357-6810-4*, 2035493) Bks Demand.

Challenges to Civil Engineering Educators & Practitioners - Where Should We Be Going? 564p. 1985. 50.00 (*0-317-65756-9*, 436-5) Am Soc Civil Eng.

Challenges to Collective Bargaining. Ed. by Lloyd Ulman. LC 67-14836. 1967. pap. 1.95 (*0-317-02947-9*, 12436) Am Assembly.

Challenges to Democracy: The Next Ten Years. Center for the Study of Democratic Institutions Staff. Ed. by Edward Reed. LC 78-156709. (Essay Index Reprint Ser.). 1977. reprint ed. 20.95 (*0-8369-2293-X*) Ayer.

Challenges to Deterrence: Resources, Technology & Policy. Stephen J. Cimbala. LC 87-2227. 327p. 1987. text ed. 59.95 (*0-275-92350-9*, C2350, Praeger Pubs) Greenwood.

Challenges to Developmental Paradigms: Implications for Theory, Assessment & Treatment. Ed. by Philip Zelazo & Ronald Barr. 312p. (C). 1989. text ed. 59.95 (*0-8058-0045-X*) L Erlbaum Assocs.

Challenges to Empiricism. Harold Morick. LC 72-10731. 339p. (C). 1980. reprint ed. 34.95 (*0-915144-89-1*); reprint ed. pap. text ed. 12.95 (*0-915144-90-5*) Hackett Pub.

Challenges to Graduate Schools. Ann M. Heiss. LC 73-129770. (Jossey-Bass Higher Education Ser.). 348p. reprint ed. pap. 99.20 (*0-8357-9300-1*, 2013955) Bks Demand.

Challenges to Local Government. Ed. by Desmond S. King & Jon Pierre. (Modern Politics Ser.: Vol. 28). 272p. 1991. 59.95 (*0-8039-8405-7*) Sage.

Challenges to Morality. Jonathan Harrison. LC 92-26225. (Philosophical Topics Ser.). (Illus.). 320p. (Orig.). (C). 1993. pap. write for info. (*0-02-350591-5*) Macmillan.

Challenges to Party Government. Ed. by John K. White & Jerome M. Mileur. LC 91-41855. 280p. (Orig.). (C). 1992. 32.50 (*0-8093-1799-0*); pap. 19.95 (*0-8093-1834-2*) S Ill U Pr.

Challenges to Social Policy. Richard Berthoud. LC 85-14699. 230p. 1985. text ed. 63.95 (*0-566-05011-0*) Ashgate Pub Co.

C

An Asterisk (*) at the beginning of an entry indicates that the title is appearing in BIP for the first time.

An Asterisk (*) at the beginning of an entry indicates that the title is appearing in BIP for the first time.

Chamber Music Primer: Four Piano Trio Pieces. Ann Taylor. (Illus.). (Orig.). (J). (gr. 1-6). 1983. pap. 6.75 (*0-943644-01-1*); audio 5.98 (*0-685-06794-7*) Ivory Pal.

Chamber Music Sampler, 3 bks., Bk. 1. Joanne Haroutounian. 31p. 1992. 9.95 (*0-8497-9461-7*, WP324) Kjos.

Chamber Music Sampler, 3 bks., Bk. 2. Joanne Haroutounian. 38p. 1992. 13.95 (*0-8497-9462-5*, WP325) Kjos.

Chamber Music Sampler, 3 bks., Bk. 3. Joanne Haroutounian. 40p. 1992. 13.95 (*0-8497-9463-3*, WP326) Kjos.

Chamber Music; The Growth & Practice of an Intimate Art: Music Book Index. Homer Ulrich. 430p. 1993. reprint ed. lib. bdg. 99.00 (*0-7812-9642-0*) Rprt Serv.

Chamber Music Two Trio-Sonatas, Pt. I. Ed. by Kenneth Cooper. LC 89-755809. (Three Centuries of Music in Score Ser.: Vol. 8). 288p. 1990. 30.00 (*0-8240-0935-5*) Garland.

Chamber Music with Piano. Ed. by Clive Brown. LC 87-754279. (Selected Works of Louis Spohr, 1784-1859: Vol. 10). 254p. 1988. 25.00 (*0-8240-1509-6*) Garland.

Chamber of Maiden Thought: Literary Origins of the Psychoanalytic Model of the Mind. Meg H. Williams & Margot Waddell. 192p. 1991. 64.50 (*0-415-04364-6*, A5922, Tavistock); pap. 16.95 (*0-415-04365-4*, A5926, Tavistock) Routledge.

Chamber of Princes. S. M. Verma. 1990. 36.00 (*81-85135-44-4*, Pub. by Natl Bk Org II) S Asia.

Chamber Plays. August Strindberg. Tr. by Evert Sprinchorn. LC 62-20431. 228p. 1962. 14.95 (*0-910278-49-0*) Boulevard.

Chamber Theatre. Robert S. Breen. LC 86-72771. xi, 129p. (C). 1986. reprint ed. pap. 16.95 (*0-940473-00-3*) Wm Caxton.

Chamber World Reports: Germany Restructures: Opportunities in a Changing Market. Peter Johnson. Ed. by Jonathan Schmidt. 524p. (Orig.). 1994. pap. 95.00 (*0-9634914-2-3*) Chamber Wrld.

Chamber World Reports: Russia, 1994: Political & Economic Analysis & Business Directory. Ed. by Jonathan Schmidt. (Illus.). 360p. (Orig.). 1993. pap. 65.00 (*0-9634914-1-5*) Chamber Wrld.

Chambered Cairns of Caithness. James L. Davidson & Audrey S. Henshall. 1990. text ed. 50.00 (*0-7486-0256-9*, Pub. by Edinburgh U Pr UK) Col U Pr.

Chambered Cairns of Orkney: An Inventory of the Structures & Their Contents. Audrey S. Henshall & James L. Davidson. (Illus.). 350p. 1987. 50.00 (*0-85224-547-5*, Pub. by Edinburgh U Pr UK) Col U Pr.

Chambered Tombs of South-West Wales. Christopher T. Barker. (Oxbow Monographs in Archaeology). (Illus.). 96p. 1992. pap. 21.00 (*0-946897-33-6*, Pub. by Oxbow Bks UK) David Brown.

Chamberet: Recollections from an Ordinary Childhood. Claude Morhange-Begue. Tr. by Austryn Wainhouse. LC 87-81087. 130p. 1987. 14.95 (*0-910395-25-X*); pap. 9.00 (*0-910395-26-8*) Marlboro Pr.

Chamberlain: Annual Report of the Chamberlain Association of America, 1906-7, with Four Generations of the Descendants of Henry Chamberlin of Hingham, England, & Hingham, MA, & Other Papers. (Illus.). 90p. 1993. reprint ed. lib. bdg. 28.00 (*0-8328-3653-2*); reprint ed. lib. bdg. 36.00 (*0-8328-3655-9*); reprint ed. pap. 18.00 (*0-8328-3654-0*); reprint ed. pap. 26.00 (*0-8328-3656-7*) Higginson Bk Co.

***Chamberlain & Appeasement: British Policy & the Coming of the Second World War.** R. A. C. Parker. 384p. 1993. pap. text ed. 14.50 (*0-312-09969-X*) St Martin.

Chamberlain & the Lost Peace. John Charmley. (Illus.). 272p. 1990. 27.95 (*0-929587-33-2*) I R Dee.

Chamberlain Area, South Dakota. Barbara Speck. (Illus.). 406p. 1989. 64.50 (*0-88107-133-1*) Curtis Media.

Chamberlain's Symptoms & Signs in Clinical Medicine. 11th ed. Colin Ogilvie. (Illus.). 608p. 1987. 60.00 (*0-7236-0864-4*) Buttrwrth-Heinemann.

Chamberlens & the Midwifery Forceps. James H. Aveling. LC 75-23677. reprint ed. 41.50 (*0-404-13230-8*) AMS Pr.

***Chambers: nterviews with the Composer by Douglas Simon.** fac. ed. Alvin Lucier. LC 79-24870. 187p. 1980. reprint ed. pap. 53.30 (*0-7837-8197-0*, 2047902) Bks Demand.

Chambers Dictionary. Catherine Schwarz. 2080p. 1994. 35.00 (*0-550-10255-8*, Chambers LKC); 40.00 (*0-550-10256-6*, Chambers LKC) LKC.

Chambers Earth Sciences Dictionary. Ed. by Peter Walker. (Illus.). 256p. 1992. 40.00 (*0-550-13244-9*, Chambers LKC) LKC.

Chambers English-Hindi Dictionary. Ed. by Suresh Awasthi. 1985. 18.00 (*0-8364-1474-8*, Pub. by Allied II) S Asia.

Chambers Film Quotes. Ed. by Tony Crawley. 304p. (Orig.). 1992. pap. 9.95 (*0-550-21024-5*, Chambers LKC) LKC.

Chambers for a Memory Palace. Donlyn Lyndon & Charles W. Moore. (Illus.). 182p. 1994. 29.95x (*0-262-12182-4*, October Bk) MIT Pr.

Chambers Murray Latin-English Dictionary. Ed. by William Smith & John Lockwood. 832p. 1995. pap. 25.00 (*0-550-19003-1*, Chambers LKC) LKC.

Chambers Nuclear Energy & Radiation Dictionary. Ed. by Peter Walker. 352p. 1992. 40.00 (*0-550-13246-5*, Chambers LKC) LKC.

Chambers of the Heart. Helen C. Chetin. (Illus.). 80p. (Orig.). 1990. pap. write for info. (*0-9618699-3-3*) Stone Circle.

Chambers of the Palace: Teachings of Rabbi Nachman of Bratslav. Y. David Shulman. LC 92-35707. 320p. 1993. 30.00 (*0-87668-180-1*) Aronson.

Chambersburg. George Chambers. (Juniper Bk. Ser.: No. 9). 1972. pap. 5.00 (*1-55780-008-1*) Juniper Pr WI.

***Chambre Close.** Serge Bramly. (Illus.). 144p. 1995. pap. 29.95 (*3-929078-14-7*) Dist Art Pubs.

Chambre d'Hotel. Sidonie-Gabrielle Colette. (FRE.). 1964. pap. 11.95 (*0-8288-9153-2*, F85830) Fr & Eur.

Chambre Rouge. Francoise Mallet-Joris. 284p. (FRE.). 1955. 9.95 (*0-8288-9836-7*, F110720) Fr & Eur.

Chambres de Bois. A. Hebert. (FRE.). 1985. 14.95 (*0-7859-2703-4*) Fr & Eur.

Chambres Des Poetes. Jonathan Greene. (Illus.). 40p. (Orig.). 1990. pap. 9.00 (*0-9622572-6-5*); 65.00 (*0-9622572-7-3*); write for info. (*0-9622572-8-1*) French Broad.

Chameleon. William Diehl. 490p. 1982. mass mkt. 5.95 (*0-345-29445-9*) Ballantine.

Chameleon. Marie F. Gillespie. 124p. 1991. 17.50 (*0-9622815-4-9*) Black Belt Pr.

Chameleon. Shelley Kaplan. LC 92-70212. (Illus.). 24p. (J). 1992. 15.00 (*0-9631833-0-3*) Kaplan IL.

Chameleon. William X. Kienzle. 1992. mass mkt. 5.99 (*0-345-36621-2*) Ballantine.

Chameleon. large type ed. William X. Kienzle. LC 91-18666. 495p. 1991. reprint ed. lib. bdg. 19.95 (*1-56054-194-6*) Thorndike Pr.

Chameleon. large type ed. William X. Kienzle. LC 91-18666. 495p. 1992. pap. 13.95 (*1-56054-976-9*) Thorndike Pr.

***Chameleon: The Lives of Dorothy Proctor from Street Criminal to International Special Agent.** Dorothy Proctor & Fred Rosen. LC 94-66762. 304p. 1994. 22.95 (*0-88282-099-0*) New Horizon NJ.

Chameleon: The Unauthorized Biography of George Bush. Jonathan Slevin & Steven Wilmsen. 256p. 1992. 21.95 (*0-915765-97-7*) Krantz Co.

Chameleon & the Dream: The Image of Reality in Cexov's Stories. Karl D. Kramer. LC 76-106463. (Slavistic Printings & Reprintings Ser.: No. 78). 1970. text ed. 63.10 (*90-279-0519-3*) Mouton.

Chameleon Lady. Dan Hamilton. LC 94-16541. (Tales of the Forgotten God Ser.). 168p. (Orig.). 1994. pap. 7.99 (*0-8308-1672-0*, 1672) InterVarsity.

Chameleon Strategy: Change & Grow Rich Trading Using Artificial Intelligence & the Mathematical Edge. Harry L. Edwards. LC 89-92428. (Illus.). 116p. (Orig.). 1989. 79.95 (*0-9624965-0-2*) Cybernetic Trading.

Chameleon with Camera: A Unique Primer on Travel Photography & How to Survive the Trip. Dennis C. Darling. (Illus.). 96p. 1989. pap. 8.95 (*0-945618-02-6*) Dorsoduro Pr.

Chameleons. John Broderick. 1961. 10.95 (*0-8392-1010-8*) Astor-Honor.

Chameleons. L. Martin. (Reptile Discovery Library). (Illus.). 24p. (J). (gr. k-5). 1989. lib. bdg. 11.94 (*0-86592-576-3*) Rourke Corp.

Chameleons. Peter Murray. LC 92-41543. (Naturebook Ser.). (J). (gr. 2-6). 1993. lib. bdg. 22.79 (*1-56766-016-9*) Childs World.

Chameleons. Claudia Schnieper. (Nature Watch Bks.). (Illus.). 48p. (J). (gr. 2-5). 1989. 19.95 (*0-87614-341-9*, Carolrhoda); pap. 6.95 (*0-87614-520-9*, Carolrhoda) Lerner Group.

***Chameleons, Vol. 1.** Schmidt. 1995. pap. text ed. (*0-7938-0264-4*) TFH Pubns.

***Chameleons, Vol. 2.** Schmidt. 1995. pap. text ed. (*0-7938-0285-7*) TFH Pubns.

Chameleons: Dragons in the Trees. James Martin. LC 91-8736. (Illus.). 36p. (J). (gr. 1-5). 1991. 13.00 (*0-517-58388-7*); lib. bdg. 13.99 (*0-517-58389-5*) Crown Bks Yng Read.

***Chameleons: Their Care & Breeding.** Linda J. Davison. 1995. pap. 24.95 (*0-88839-353-9*) Hancock House.

Chameleon's Rainbow. Marilyn J. Walton. LC 84-17760. (Clippers Ser.). (Illus.). 32p. (J). (gr. 3-6). 1985. lib. bdg. 14.65 (*0-940742-45-4*); audio 27.99 (*0-8172-2285-5*) Raintree Steck-V.

Chameleons' Rainbow. Marilyn J. Walton. (Use Your Imagination Ser.). (J). (ps-3). 1993. pap. 4.95 (*0-8114-8402-5*) Raintree Steck-V.

Chamfort: A Biography. Claude Arnaud. Tr. by Deke Dusinberre. LC 91-31913. (Illus.). 288p. 1992. 27.50 (*0-226-02697-3*) U Ch Pr.

Chaminuka: Prophet of Zimbabwe. Solomon T. Mutswairo. Tr. by Donald Herdeck. LC 77-71232. (Illus.). 120p. 1983. 15.00 (*0-89410-002-5*); pap. 8.00 (*0-89410-003-3*) Three Continents.

Chamisa Dreams. Robert B. Salter. LC 94-6780. 160p. (Orig.). 1994. pap. 12.95 (*0-86534-220-2*) Sunstone Pr.

Chamizal National Memorial. Luis Torres. Ed. by Sandra Scott & T. J. Priehs. LC 93-86937. (Illus.). 16p. (Orig.). (YA). 1994. pap. 2.95 (*1-877856-40-1*) SW Pks Mnmts.

Chamomile Farm. Lyle Williams. (Illus.). 128p. 1987. pap. 19.95 (*0-947062-08-4*, Pub. by Hyland Hse AT) Intl Spec Bk.

Chamorro. Kent J. Olsen. Ed. by James B. Van Treese. Tr. by Ingram. 212p. 1994. pap. 8.95 (*1-56901-126-5*) NW Pub.

Chamorro-English Dictionary. Donald M. Topping et al. LC 74-16907. (PALI Language Texts, Micronesia Ser.). 365p. (Orig.). 1975. pap. text ed. 12.00 (*0-8248-0353-1*) UH Pr.

Chamorro Reference Grammar. Donald M. Topping. LC 72-98012. (PALI Language Texts, Micronesia Ser.). 313p. 1973. pap. text ed. 11.95 (*0-8248-0269-1*) UH Pr.

Champ. Kenward Elmslie & Joe Brainard. 1994. per. 12.00 (*0-935724-66-4*) Figures.

Champ: The Virgil Hill Story. Stacy Herron. Ed. by Abe Winter. LC 91-70155. (Illus.). 84p. (Orig.). 1991. pap. 19.95 (*0-9628857-0-3*) Bismarck Trib.

Champ - Beyond the Legend. Joseph W. Zarzynski. LC 88-60702. (Illus.). 240p. (J). (gr. 7-12). 1988. reprint ed. pap. 12.95 (*0-937559-01-6*) M-Z Info.

Champ Ferguson: Confederate Guerilla. Thurman Sensing. LC 42-18672. 256p. (C). 1994. reprint ed. pap. 14.95 (*0-8265-1253-4*) Vanderbilt U Pr.

Champ Fleury. Geofroy Tory. Tr. by George B. Ives. 10.00 (*0-8446-3082-9*) Peter Smith.

Champ Hobarth. Judith B. Strommen. 192p. (J). (gr. 4-6). 1993. 14.95 (*0-8050-2414-X*, Bks Young Read) H Holt & Co.

Champ on Ice. Sharon Peters. LC 87-10908. (Giant First Start Reader Ser.). (Illus.). 32p. (J). (gr. k-2). 1988. lib. bdg. 11.59 (*0-8167-1093-7*); pap. text ed. 2.95 (*0-8167-1094-5*) Troll Assocs.

Champa: History & Culture of an Indian Colonial Kingdom in the Far East 2nd Century A.D. R. C. Majumdar. (C). 1985. 36.00 (*0-8364-2802-1*, Pub. by Gian Publng Hse II) S Asia.

***Champagne.** Sara Slavin & Karl Petzke. LC 94-41852. 1995. 22.95 (*0-8118-0928-5*); pap. 14.95 (*0-8118-0903-X*) Chronicle Bks.

Champagne. Tom Stevenson. LC 86-50037. (Illus.). 416p. 1986. lib. bdg. 39.95 (*0-85667-318-8*, Pub. by P Wilson Pubs) Sothebys Pubns.

Champagne. Nicola Thorne. 1990. mass mkt. 4.95 (*0-06-100023-X*) HarpC.

Champagne & Caviar: A Connoisseur's Guide to Survival. Arthur Von Wiesenberger. LC 92-15090. (Illus.). 240p. 1992. 39.95 (*0-88496-356-X*) Capra Pr.

Champagne & Roses. Nancy Bacon. 1982. pap. 1.75 (*0-345-29758-X*) Ballantine.

***Champagne-Ardennes Green Guide French Edition.** Michelin Staff. (FRE.). Date not set. pap. 17.95 (*0-614-00370-9*, 206700316X) Fr & Eur.

Champagne Blues. Nan Lyons & Ivan Lyons. 1980. pap. 2.25 (*0-449-24317-6*, Crest) Fawcett.

Champagne Charlie Stakes. Bruce Graham. 1993. 4.75 (*0-8222-1362-1*) Dramatists Play.

Champagne Companion. Michael Edwards. (Illus.). 224p. 1994. 24.95 (*1-56138-440-2*) Running Pr.

Champagne Cookbook. Malcolm P. Herbert. (Wine Cookbook Ser.). (Illus.). 144p. 1988. pap. 8.95 (*0-932664-07-5*) Wine Appreciation.

Champagne Diet Book. Lynn Carlisle & Marsha Cornwell. (Illus.). 64p. 1988. pap. 4.95 (*0-943678-07-2*) Wellton Enter.

Champagne Girls. large type ed. Tessa Barclay. 1993. 39.95 (*0-7066-1016-4*, Pub. by Remploy Pr CN) St Mut.

Champagne Gold. Nicola Thorne. 1992. mass mkt. 5.50 (*0-06-100398-0*, Harp PBks) HarpC.

Champagne Green Guide. 2nd ed. (FRE.). Date not set. pap. 18.00 (*2-06-700316-X*, 316) Michelin.

Champagne Mist. Marla S. Hess. Ed. by Helen Graves. LC 88-50118. 80p. 1988. 6.95 (*1-55523-147-0*) Winston-Derek.

Champagne Nights. large type ed. Nancy John. (Romance Ser.). 448p. 1993. 21.95 (*0-7089-2912-5*) Ulverscroft.

Champagne of Concrete. Kit Robinson. 104p. (Orig.). 1990. pap. 9.00 (*0-937013-32-3*) Potes Poets.

Champagne on a Budget. D. Delaforce. (C). 1989. text ed. 29.95 (*0-948032-87-1*, Pub. by Rosters Ltd) St Mut.

***Champaign: A Pictorial History.** Raymond Bial. (Illinois Pictorial History Ser.). (Illus.). 1994. write for info. (*0-943963-35-4*) G Bradley.

Champerty: The Ambulance-Chasers. Jorgen U. Schlegel. 205p. (Orig.). 1990. pap. 15.00 (*0-9611114-7-X*) Bryn Ffyliaid.

Champfleury, the Realist Writer As Art Critic. David A. Flanary. LC 80-17475. (Studies in the Fine Arts: Criticism: No. 1). 107p. reprint ed. pap. 30.50 (*0-685-20871-0*, 2070182) Bks Demand.

Champignon Kochbuch: Ueber 100 Gerichte und Zubereitungstips fuer Frische Kulturchampignons. Nora Richter. (Illus.). 72p. (GER.). 1984. pap. text ed. 7.50 (*3-923090-00-5*) Lubrecht & Cramer.

Champignons: De la Cueillette a la Table. Y. Girel & R. Girel. (Illus.). 264p. (FRE.). 1986. lib. bdg. 32.50 (*2-7234-0452-8*) Lubrecht & Cramer.

Champignons d'Europe: Generalities-Ascomycetes-Basidiomycetes. 2nd ed. Roger Heim. (Illus.). 680p. (FRE.). 1984. lib. bdg. 90.00 (*2-85004-042-8*) Lubrecht & Cramer.

Champignons "Opportunistes" Ed. by D. Grigoriu. (Dermatologica Ser.: Vol. 159, Suppl. 1, 1979). (Illus.). 1979. pap. 61.75 (*3-8055-0084-X*) S Karger.

Champignons Toxiques et Hallucinogenes. Roger Heim. (Collection "Faunes et Flore Actuelles"). (Illus.). 270p. (FRE.). 1978. lib. bdg. 50.00 (*2-85004-013-4*) Lubrecht & Cramer.

Champion. Roch Carrier. LC 90-70134. (Illus.). 24p. (FRE.). (J). (gr. 3 up). 1991. 14.95 (*0-88776-250-6*) Tundra Bks.

Champion. Maurice Gee. LC 92-37670. (J). 1993. pap. 14.00 (*0-671-86561-7*, S&S Bks Young Read) S&S Childrens.

Champion. Annie Kubler. LC 90-24246. (Pride Ser.). (J). (gr. 4 up). 1991. 3.95 (*0-85953-531-2*) Childs Play.

Champion: Bicycle Racing in the Age of Miguel Indurain. Samuel Abt. LC 92-83826. (Illus.). 160p. pap. 12.95 (*0-933201-59-1*) Bicycle Books.

***Champion & Jewboy.** Bruce Siegel. LC 94-44172. (Illus.). (J). 1995. 6.95 (*1-881283-11-9*) Alef Design.

Champion Batsmen of the Twentieth Century. John Thom. (Illus.). 96p. (Orig.). 1983. pap. 5.95 (*0-9611242-0-2*) Bat & Ball.

Champion for Children's Health: A Story about Dr. S. Josephine Baker. Greg Ptacek & Lydia M. Anderson. LC 93-10482. (Illus.). (J). (gr. 3-6). 1994. 15.95 (*0-87614-806-2*, Carolrhoda) Lerner Group.

Champion Genealogy: A History of the Descendants of Henry Champion of Saybrook & Lyme, Conn., Together with Some Account of Other Families of That Name. F. Trowbridge. (Illus.). 575p. 1989. reprint ed. lib. bdg. 81.50 (*0-8328-0384-7*); reprint ed. pap. 71.50 (*0-8328-0385-5*) Higginson Bk Co.

***Champion International Corp. A Report on the Company's Environmental Policies & Practices.** (Illus.). 63p. (C). 1994. reprint ed. pap. text ed. 200.00x (*0-7881-0953-7*, Coun on Econ) Diane Pub.

***Champion Joe Louis: A Biography.** Chris Mead. (Illus.). 330p. 1995. pap. 12.95 (*0-86051-848-5*, Robson-Parkwest) Parkwest Pubns.

Champion Lives Within. Boyd C. Matheson. Date not set. text ed. 16.95 (*1-882441-24-9*); pap. text ed. 10.95 (*1-882441-25-7*) InANutshell Bks.

Champion of a Cause: Essays & Addresses on Librarianship. Archibald MacLeish. LC 70-150577. 262p. reprint ed. pap. 74.70 (*0-317-26595-4*, 2024191) Bks Demand.

Champion of Faith: David Gomez see Cuando Triunfa la Fe

Champion of Faith (The Sermons of John Alexander Dowie) John A. Alexander. 1961. per. 3.95 (*0-89985-193-2*) Christ for the Nations.

***Champion of Justice.** Frederic James. 430p. 1995. pap. 12.95 (*1-56901-612-7*) NW Pub.

Champion of Kingdom. Philip Mauro. pap. 2.99 (*0-87377-047-1*) GAM Pubns.

Champion of Liberty. Charles Bradlaugh. 1974. 59.95 (*0-87968-833-5*) Gordon Pr.

Champion of Liberty: Charles Bradlaugh. Centenary Committee. LC 75-161323. (Atheist Viewpoint Ser.). (Illus.). 384p. 1972. reprint ed. 28.95 (*0-405-03626-4*) Ayer.

Champion of the Cross. Charles F. Sweet. LC 76-144692. reprint ed. 49.50 (*0-404-07202-X*) AMS Pr.

Champion of the Great American Family: A Personal & Political Book. Patricia S. Schroeder et al. LC 88-42682. (Illus.). 288p. 1989. 17.95 (*0-394-56574-6*) Random.

Champion of the Last Battle. Robert Adams. (Horseclans Ser.: No. 11). 201p. 1983. pap. 2.95 (*0-451-13304-8*, Sig) NAL-Dutton.

***Champion Quotes.** Great Quotations Publishing Staff. 366p. (Orig.). 1995. spiral bd., pap. 5.95 (*1-56245-177-4*) Great Quotations.

Championing the Faith. Steven Collins. 310p. 1991. teacher ed 16.99 (*1-56322-038-5*); pap. text ed. 16.99 (*1-56322-030-X*) V Hensley.

Champions. Patricia King. 623p. (Orig.). 1992. pap. text ed. 19.95 (*1-883224-00-4*) Presump Pr.

Champions: A View of the Mastiff in America. Joan Hahn & Judy Powers. LC 82-21714. (Illus.). 269p. 1984. 45.00 (*0-910468-9-9*) Mastiff Club Am.

Champions! Hawthorne, Hill, Clark, Surteas, Stewart, Hunt, Mansell. Christopher Hilton. 320p. 1994. text ed. 39.95 (*0-947981-76-4*, Pub. by Motor Racing UK) Motorbooks Intl.

Champions: Lou Holtz's Fighting Irish. Bill Bilinski. LC 89-1333. 208p. 1989. 16.95 (*0-912083-34-4*) Diamond Communications.

Champions: Lou Holtz's Fighting Irish. rev. ed. Bill Bilinski. LC 89-1333. (Illus.). 286p. 1990. reprint ed. pap. 10.95 (*0-912083-43-3*) Diamond Communications.

Champions: The Super Hero Role Playing Game. rev. ed. George MacDonald et al. (Illus.). 352p. (C). 1989. 32.00 (*1-55806-043-X*, 400) Hero Games.

Champions: Their Glory & Beyond. Bill Littlefield. LC 92-31390. (J). 1993. 22.95 (*0-316-52805-6*) Little.

Champion's Choice. John R. Tunis. 206p. (J). (gr. 3-7). 1990. pap. 3.95 (*0-15-216074-4*, Odyssey) HarBrace.

Champion's Choice. John R. Tunis. 1992. 16.50 (*0-8446-6509-6*) Peter Smith.

Champions in the Library: A Positive Approach to Discipline for Librarians. J. Zink. 28p. 1982. pap. 3.95 (*0-686-94909-9*) J Zink.

Champions in the Library: A School & Public Librarian's Guide for a Positive Approach to Discipline in the Library. J. Zink. 28p. (Orig.). 1982. pap. 3.95 (*0-942490-04-5*) J Zink.

Champions in the Sun. Ed. by Frances Ring. (Illus.). 112p. 1984. lib. bdg. 6.95 (*0-910312-47-8*) Calif Hist.

Champions in 3-D. Nonie Quinlan. Ed. by Rob Bell. (Champions Ser.). (Illus.). 160p. (Orig.). (C). 1990. pap. 16.00 (*1-55806-109-6*, 411) Iron Crown Ent Inc.

Champions of Appledore. Romayne Dawnay. (Illus.). 160p. (J). (gr. 3-7). 1994. text ed. 14.95 (*0-02-789355-3*, Four Winds Pr) S&S Childrens.

Champions of Democracy. Joseph Cottler. LC 78-128229. (Essay Index Reprint Ser.). 1977. 21.95 (*0-8369-1826-6*) Ayer.

Champions of Freedom: Austrian Economics: A Reader, Vol. 18. Ed. by Richard M. Ebeling. LC 90-84344. 500p. 1991. boxed 19.95 (*0-916308-82-0*) Hillsdale Coll Pr.

Champions of Freedom, Austrian Economics: Perspectives on the Past & Prospects for the Future, Vol. 17. Ed. by Richard M. Ebeling. LC 90-84343. 516p. 1991. boxed 19.95 (*0-916308-83-9*) Hillsdale Coll Pr.

***Champions of Freedom Vol. 22: Economic Education: What Should We Learn about the Free Market?** Ed. by Richard M. Ebeling. 187p. 1994. pap. 9.95 (*0-916308-69-3*) Hillsdale Coll Pr.

Champions of Freedom, Vol. 14: The Privatization Revolution. Dick Armey et al. (Ludwig von Mises Lecture Ser.: Vol. 14). 135p. 1989. pap. 5.00 (*0-916308-88-X*) Hillsdale Coll Pr.

Champions of Freedom, Vol. 15: The Politics of Hunger. Frank Vorhies et al. (Ludwig von Mises Lecture Ser.: Vol. 15). 1989. pap. 5.00 (*0-916308-86-3*) Hillsdale Coll Pr.

An Asterisk (*) at the beginning of an entry indicates that the title is appearing in BIP for the first time.

An Asterisk (*) at the beginning of an entry indicates that the title is appearing in BIP for the first time.

1139

Chandigarh Capitole, Vol. II. Brooks. (Le Corbusier Archieve Ser.). 1983. text ed. 260.00 (*0-8240-5072-X*) Garland.

Chandler: Descendants of Roger Chandler. C. H. Chandler. 152p. 1991. reprint ed. pap. 24.50 (*0-8328-2112-8*) Higginson Bk Co.

Chandler Family, Descendants of William & Annis Chandler Who Settled in Roxbury, Mass., 1637. G. Chandler. (Illus.). 1323p. 1989. reprint ed. lib. bdg. 167.00 (*0-8328-0386-3*); reprint ed. pap. 157.00 (*0-8328-0387-1*) Higginson Bk Co.

Chandlers of Kansas: A Banking Family. Billy M. Jones. (Illus.). 220p. 10.00 (*0-86546-048-5*) Wichita Ctr Entrep SBM.

Chandogya Upanisad. Tr. by Swami Gambhirananda. 623p. 1987. pap. 8.95 (*0-87481-227-5*, Pub. by Advaita Ashrama II) Vedanta Pr.

Chandogya Upanisad (Swaha) Upanishads. 1956. pap. 7.95 (*0-87481-416-2*) Vedanta Pr.

Chandra. Catherine Coulter. (Scarlet Ribbons Ser.). 352p. 1985. pap. 4.99 (*0-451-15881-4*, Onyx) NAL-Dutton.

Chandra: A Biography of S. Chandrasekhar. Kameshwar C. Wali. LC 90-10845. (Illus.). 360p. 1990. lib. bdg. 29.95 (*0-226-87054-5*) U Ch Pr.

Chandra: A Biography of S. Chandrasekhar. Kameshwar C. Wali. LC 90-10845. (Centennial Publication Ser.). (Illus.). x, 342p. 1992. pap. 16.95 (*0-226-87055-3*) U Ch Pr.

Chandra Shekhar: A Political Biography. Yogendra Bali. (C). 1991. 27.95 (*0-7069-5798-9*, Pub. by Vikas II) S Asia.

Chandragupta Maurya & His Times. Radha K. Mookerji. (C). 1988. reprint ed. 18.00 (*81-208-0405-8*, Pub. by Motilal Banarsidass II) S Asia.

Chandranath. Saratchandra Chattopadhyaya. 101p. 1969. pap. 2.50 (*0-88253-027-5*) Ind-US Inc.

Chandris Liners. William H. Miller. (Illus.). 80p. (Orig.). 1993. pap. text ed. 19.95 (*0-9518656-2-5*, Waterfront Pubns) Hallenbook.

Chanel: A Woman of Her Own. Axel Madsen. (Illus.). 400p. 1991. pap. 15.95 (*0-8050-1639-2*, Owl) H Holt & Co.

***Chanel: The Couturiere at Work.** Amy De La Hey. LC 94-27235. 1994. 35.00 (*0-87951-570-8*) Overlook Pr.

Chanel Fashions: Review Paper Dolls in Full Color. Tom Tierney. (J). 1986. pap. 3.95 (*0-486-25105-5*) Dover.

Chaney Edge. T. J. Jack. Ed. by Doug Grad. 192p. (Orig.). 1992. pap. 3.50 (*0-671-75403-3*) PB.

Chaneysville Incident. David Bradley. 464p. 1982. mass mkt. 4.95 (*0-380-58586-3*) Avon.

Chaneysville Incident. David Bradley. 442p. 1991. reprint ed. lib. bdg. 31.00x (*0-8095-9096-4*) Borgo Pr.

Chaneysville Incident: A Novel. David Bradley. LC 80-8225. 432p. 1990. reprint ed. pap. 13.00 (*0-06-091681-8*, PL) HarpC.

***Chang.** Reginald Dickenson. (Illus.). 256p. 1995. pap. 12.50 (*0-8059-3719-6*) Dorrance.

Chang Chih-Tung & Educational Reform in China. William Ayers. LC 71-129121. (Harvard East Asian Ser.: No. 54). 300p. reprint ed. pap. 86.70 (*0-7837-2219-2*, 2057309) Bks Demand.

Chang Tso-lin in Northeast China, 1911-1928: China, Japan, & the Manchurian Idea. Gavan McCormack. LC 76-48028. (Illus.). x, 334p. 1977. 42.50 (*0-8047-0945-9*) Stanford U Pr.

***Changchau: The Tiger of Burma.** Marv Lewis. 270p. Date not set. pap. 8.95 (*0-7610-0421-1*) NW Pub.

Change. Barry B. Longyear. Ed. by Kevin Ryan. (Alien Nation Ser.: No. 4). 320p. (Orig.). 1994. mass mkt. 5.50 (*0-671-73602-7*) PB.

Change. Willie. 196p. 1991. 25.00 (*0-9629204-3-6*); pap. 45.00 (*0-9629204-4-4*) Constance Ent.

Change: Eight Lectures on the I Ching. Hellmut Wilhelm. Tr. by C. F. Baynes. (Bollingen Ser.: Vol. 62). 115p. 1960. pap. 9.95x (*0-691-01787-5*) Princeton U Pr.

Change: Getting to Know about Ebb & Flow. Laura Greene. LC 80-81081. (Illus.). 32p. (J). (gr. k-3). 1981. 16.95 (*0-87705-401-0*) Human Sci Pr.

Change: How to Live with, Manage, Create & Enjoy It. Dorri Jacobs. LC 81-81369. (Illus.). 212p. (Orig.). (C). 1981. 33.00 (*0-685-73418-8*); lib. bdg. 33.00 (*0-916471-05-5*); audio, pap. 39.00 (*0-9606012-0-1*) Progs on Change.

Change: Meet It & Greet It! Sue Waechter & Trudy Seita. 1991. pap. 11.95 (*0-911029-35-4*) Heritage Arts.

Change: Principles of Problem Formation & Problem Resolution. Paul Watzlawick et al. LC 73-17485. (Illus.). 172p. 1974. 19.95 (*0-393-01104-6*) Norton.

Change: The Overhauling of the United States, As Seen by a Taxpayer. Juan G. Rios, I. 1994. 15.95 (*0-533-10755-5*) Vantage.

Change: Threat or Opportunity?, 5 Vols., Set. Ed. by Uner Kirdar. 1992. pap. 75.00 (*92-1-126029-9*) UN.

Change: Women, Aging & the Menopause. Germaine Greer. LC 92-52949. 448p. 1992. 23.50 (*0-394-58269-1*) Knopf.

Change: Women, Aging, & the Menopause. Germaine Greer. 432p. 1993. pap. 12.50 (*0-449-90853-4*, Columbine) Fawcett.

Change - Education: Issues in Perspective. Ed. by Glenn Smith et al. LC 93-26523. 410p. 1993. pap. 39.95 (*1-879528-08-8*) LEPS Pr.

Change Agent: Pay's New Role. Ed. by Steve Palmer & Ken Birkett. 150p. (C). 1989. 65.00 (*0-85292-416-X*) St Mut.

Change-Agent Skills A: Assessing & Designing Excellence. Gerard Egan. LC 88-10653. (Illus.). 224p. (Orig.). 1988. text ed. 29.95 (*0-88390-219-2*) Pfeiffer & Co.

Change-Agent Skills B: Managing Innovation & Change. Gerard Egan. LC 88-10652. (Illus.). 176p. (Orig.). 1988. text ed. 29.95 (*0-88390-220-6*) Pfeiffer & Co.

Change Agents: New Roles & Innovation Strategies for Human Resource Professionals. Manuel London. LC 88-42793. (Management Ser.). 311p. 1988. 33.95 (*1-55542-107-5*) Jossey-Bass.

Change Agents at Work. Richard N. Ottaway. LC 79-24. (Contributions in Economics & Economic History Ser.: No. 27). 169p. 1979. text ed. 49.95 (*0-313-21252-X*, OCA/, Greenwood Pr) Greenwood.

Change Agent's Guide. 2nd ed. Ronald G. Havelock & Steve Zlotolow. LC 95-1103. 250p. 1995. pap. 37.95 (*0-87778-279-2*) Educ Tech Pubns.

Change Agent's Handbook: A Survival Guide to Quality Improvement Champions. David W. Hutton. LC 94-10361. 1994. write for info. (*0-87389-287-9*) ASQC Qual Pr.

Change & a Parting: My Story of Amana. Barbara S. Yambura & Eunice Bodine. LC 86-18598. (Iowa Heritage Collection Ser.). (Illus.). 362p. 1986. reprint ed. pap. 8.95 (*0-8138-0261-X*) Iowa St U Pr.

Change & Challenge in Library & Information Science Education. Margaret F. Stieg. LC 91-18081. 250p. (C). 1991. pap. text ed. 30.00 (*0-8389-0576-5*) ALA.

Change & Choice. Ed. by Beatrice Musgrave & Zoe Menell. 1980. text ed. 29.95 (*0-7206-0539-3*) Dufour.

Change & Choice: Women & Middle Age. Beatrice Musgrave. Ed. by Zoe Menell. 186p. 1980. 19.95 (*0-685-18790-X*, Pub. by P Owen Ltd UK) Dufour.

Change & Compensation: Parallel Weakening of (s) in Italian, French & Spanish. Diana R. Seklaoui. (Currents in Comparative Romance Languages & Literatures Ser.: Vol. 4). 258p. (C). 1989. text ed. 41.20 (*0-8204-0760-7*) P Lang Pubs.

Change & Conflict: A Study of Community Work in Glasgow. B. Bryant & R. Bryant. 250p. 1983. text ed. 26.00 (*0-08-028475-2*, Pergamon Pr); pap. text ed. 14.95 (*0-08-028480-9*, Pergamon Pr) Elsevier.

***Change & Conflict: Britain, Ireland & Europe from the Late 16th to the Early 18th Centuries.** Patricia Rice. (Irish History in Perspective Ser.). (Illus.). 80p. 1994. pap. 10.95 (*0-521-46603-2*) Cambridge U Pr.

***Change & Conflict: Teachers Resource Book: Britain, Ireland & Europe from the Late 16th to the Early 18th Centuries.** Patricia Rice. (Irish History in Perspective Ser.). (Illus.). 32p. 1995. teacher ed, pap. 10.95 (*0-521-46604-0*) Cambridge U Pr.

Change & Continuity: A Pictorial History of the Boston Athenaeum. 2nd ed. Jane S. Knowles. LC 85-71587. (Illus.). 31p. 1985. 7.50 (*0-934552-32-0*) Boston Athenaeum.

Change & Continuity: A Reader on Pre-Confederation Canada. Carol Wilton. 1993. pap. text ed. write for info. (*0-07-551151-7*) McGraw.

Change & Continuity: Tennessee Politics since the Civil War. William R. Majors. LC 86-12523. 144p. (Orig.). (C). 1986. pap. 12.95 (*0-86554-209-0*, P25) Mercer Univ Pr.

Change & Continuity in Adult Life. Marjorie Fiske & David A. Chiriboga. LC 90-4966. (Social & Behavioral Sciences Ser.). 364p. 1990. 34.95 (*1-55542-249-7*) Jossey-Bass.

Change & Continuity in Eastern Europe. Ed. by Timo Piirainen. 256p. 1994. 59.95 (*1-85521-499-7*, Pub. by Dartmth Pub UK) Ashgate Pub Co.

Change & Continuity in Europe's Northern Region: A Conference Report. Ed. by Paul J. Cook. (Significant Issues Ser.). 53p. 1991. pap. text ed. 1.00 (*0-89206-170-7*) CSI Studies.

Change & Continuity in Indian Religion. J. Gonda. 1984. text ed. 32.50 (*0-685-13642-6*) Coronet Bks.

Change & Continuity in Minangkabau: Local, Regional & Historical Perspectives on West Sumatra. Ed. by Lynn L. Thomas & Franz Von Benda-Beckmann. LC 85-5026. (Monographs in International Studies, Southeast Asia Ser.: No. 71). 360p. 1985. pap. text ed. 16.00 (*0-89680-127-6*, Ohio U Ctr Intl) Ohio U Pr.

Change & Continuity in Seventeenth-Century England. Christopher Hill. LC 74-12878. 370p. 1975. 37.50 (*0-674-10765-9*) HUP.

Change & Continuity in Seventeenth-Century England. Christopher Hill. 392p. (C). 1991. pap. 22.00 (*0-300-05044-5*) Yale U Pr.

Change & Continuity in the French Episcopate: The Bishops & the Wars of Religion, 1547-1610. Frederic J. Baumgartner. LC 86-13495. (Duke Monographs in Medieval & Renaissance Studies: No. 7). (Illus.). xv, 340p. 1986. text ed. 37.00 (*0-8223-0675-1*) Duke.

Change & Continuity in the 1992 Elections. Paul R. Abramson et al. LC 94-837. 395p. 1994. pap. text ed. 25.95 (*0-87187-821-6*) Congr Quarterly.

***Change & Continuity in the 1992 Elections.** rev. ed. Paul R. Abramson et al. 376p. 1995. pap. 23.95 (*0-87187-839-9*) Congr Quarterly.

Change & Effectiveness in Schools: A Cultural Perspective. Gretchen B. Rossman et al. LC 87-33539. (Frontiers in Education Ser.). 173p. 1988. 64.50 (*0-88706-725-5*); pap. 21.95 (*0-88706-726-3*) State U NY Pr.

Change & Habit: The Challenge of Our Time. Arnold J. Toynbee. LC 66-25824. 240p. reprint ed. pap. 68.40 (*0-317-29814-3*, 2051999) Bks Demand.

Change & Harmonization in European Education. Robert H. Beck. LC 75-167299. 222p. reprint ed. pap. 63.30 (*0-317-29401-6*, 2055841) Bks Demand.

Change & Intervention: Vocational Education & Training. Ed. by Peter Raggatt & Lorna Unwin. 224p. 1991. 65.00 (*1-85000-694-6*, Falmer Pr); pap. 27.00 (*1-85000-695-4*, Falmer Pr) Taylor & Francis.

Change & Permanence. Ann C. Fehn. (Stanford German Studies: Vol. 12). 200p. 1978. pap. 31.40 (*3-261-02921-8*) P Lang Pubs.

Change & Persistence in Thai Society: Essays in Honor of Lauriston Sharp. Ed. by G. William Skinner & A. Thomas Kirsch. LC 74-25374. (Illus.). 392p. 1975. 43.50 (*0-8014-0860-1*) Cornell U Pr.

***Change & Policy in Wales in the Era of Privatism.** Richard Prentice. 305p. 1993. pap. 39.00 (*0-86383-978-9*, Pub. by Gomer Pr UK) St Mut.

Change & Stability in Foreign Policy: The Problems & Possibilities of Detente. Kjell Goldmann. (Illus.). 248p. 1988. 39.50 (*0-691-07778-9*) Princeton U Pr.

Change & Stability in International Law-Making. Ed. by Antonio Casses & Joseph H. Weiler. (European University Institute, Series A (Law): No. 9). 214p. (C). 1988. lib. bdg. 73.10 (*0-89925-420-9*) De Gruyter.

***Change & Stability in International Law-Making.** Ed. by Antonio Casses & Joseph H. Weller. (European University Institute, Series A (Law): No. 9). 214p. (C). 1988. lib. bdg. 73.10 (*3-11-011494-1*) De Gruyter.

Change & Stability in Schooling. Thomas S. Popkewitz. 112p. (C). 1983. 45.00 (*0-7300-0002-8*, Pub. by Deakin Univ AT) St Mut.

***Change & the Bottom Line.** Alan Warner. 200p. 1995. 33.95 (*0-566-07560-1*, Pub. by Gower UK) Ashgate Pub Co.

Change & the Curriculum. Geva M. Blenkin et al. 160p. 1992. pap. 27.00 (*1-85396-154-X*, Pub. by Paul Chapman UK) Taylor & Francis.

Change & the New International Economic Order. Ed. by Jan A. Van Lith. (Tilburg Studies in Economics: Vol. 20). 1980. lib. bdg. 40.50 (*0-89838-028-6*) Kluwer Ac.

Change & the Study on International Relations. Ed. by Barry G. Buzan & R. J. Jones. LC 81-1203. 1981. text ed. 32.50 (*0-312-12858-4*) St Martin.

Change & Tradition: A Portrait of the University of Melbourne. University of Melbourne Staff. 169p. 1993. 49.95 (*0-7325-0510-0*) Intl Spec Bk.

Change & Tradition in the American Small Town. Ed. by Robert Craycroft & Michael Fazio. LC 83-14638. (Small Town Ser.). 122p. 1984. pap. text ed. 11.95 (*0-87805-194-5*) U Pr of Miss.

Change & Uncertainty in a Peasant Economy: The Maya Corn Farmers of Zinacantan. Frank Cancian. LC 72-153814. (Illus.). xvi, 208p. 1972. 29.95 (*0-8047-0787-1*) Stanford U Pr.

Change As the Status Quo: Implications for HR Professionals, No. 2. J. Bardwick et al. 80p. 1993. pap. 24.95 (*1-881115-01-1*) Human Res Plan.

Change at the Top: The Effects of Corporate Mergers, Takeovers, & Management Changes. Ed. by Fritz A. Henn et al. (Problems of Industrial Psychiatric Medicine Ser.: Vol. XIII). 190p. 1989. 19.95 (*0-930545-07-9*) Maple Hill Pr.

Change at Work: A Comprehensive Management Process for Transforming Organizations. Oscar Mink. (Management Ser.). 288p. 1993. 29.95 (*1-55542-587-9*) Jossey-Bass.

Change Begins with Me. 7th ed. Katherine Cain. (Illus.). (Orig.). 1976. pap. 2.95 (*0-9603188-0-1*) K Anzinger-Cain.

Change Bulletin: Information That Helps You Make the Most of Your Human Capital. Dorri Jacobs. 36p. (Orig.). 1993. 17.40 (*0-685-71439-X*); lib. bdg. 19.00 (*0-916471-07-1*); spiral bd., pap. 22.00 (*0-685-59564-1*) Progs on Change.

Change by Design. Robert R. Blake et al. (Organization Development Ser.). (Illus.). 200p. (C). 1989. pap. text ed. 26.95 (*0-201-50748-X*) Addison-Wesley.

Change, Cause & Contradiction: A Defence of the Tenseless Theory of Time. Robin Le Poidevin. LC 90-19925. 186p. 1991. text ed. 55.00 (*0-312-05786-5*) St Martin.

Change, Challenge, & Choices: Women's Role in Modern Corrections. Ed. by Joann B. Morton. (Illus.). 117p. 1991. 16.80 (*0-929310-54-3*, 322) Am Correctional.

Change Control: Whilst Developing Computer Systems. E. Ferraby. 250p. 1991. pap. text ed. 54.00 (*0-13-126350-1*, 270201) P-H.

Change Cycle: Managing Life Means Managing Changes. Lillie Brock & Mary Ann Salerno. (Successful Changes Ser.). (Illus.). 256p. 1994. 24.00 (*0-9638959-0-7*) Bridge Builder.

Change Detection. Basseville & Nikirov. 450p. 1993. text ed. 67.00 (*0-13-126780-9*) P-H.

Change Detection & Input Design in Dynamical Systems. Feza Kerestecioglu. LC 93-2374. (UMIST Control Systems Centre Ser.: Vol. 1). 152p. 1993. text ed. 75.00 (*0-471-94173-5*) Wiley.

Change Direction. Shmuel B. Yizhak. 1994. 12.95 (*0-533-10837-3*) Vantage.

Change for a Penny. Samuel Epstein. 21.95 (*0-8488-0078-8*, Amereon Hse) Amereon Ltd.

Change for Children: Grades 3 - 6. 2nd rev. ed. Sandra Kaplan et al. (Illus.). 225p. (Orig.). 1980. pap. 14.95 (*0-673-16348-2*) GdYrBks.

Change for Continuity: The People of a Thousand Lakes. Vivian J. Rohrl. LC 80-6077. 269p. 1981. pap. text ed. 24.00 (*0-8191-1539-8*) U Pr of Amer.

***Change for the Better.** Davis. 1995. pap. 21.95 (*0-85207-265-1*) Atrium Pubs.

Change for the Better. Patricia Davis. 256p. (Orig.). 1993. pap. 26.95 (*0-8464-4174-8*) Beekman Pubs.

Change for the Better: Building New Dimensions in Public Interest Leadership. Advocacy Institute Staff. ix, 58p. 1991. pap. text ed. 7.50 (*1-882215-02-8*) Advocacy Inst.

Change from Within: Humanizing Social Welfare Organizations. Ed. by Herman Resnick & J. Patti Rino. LC 80-13344. 344p. 1980. 29.95 (*0-87722-173-1*); pap. 19.95 (*0-87722-200-2*) Temple U Pr.

Change from Within: Nurse Intrapreneurs As Health Care Innovators. Jo Manion. 171p. (Orig.). (C). 1990. pap. 26.75 (*0-685-39092-6*, G-178) Am Nurses Pub.

Change from Within: People Make the Difference. Robert Reid & Howard Scott. (Illus.). 224p. 1995. 23.95 (*0-941893-04-9*) CEEPress Bks.

Change, Grief & Renewal in the Church: A Spirituality for a New Era. Gerald A. Arbuckle. LC 90-85926. 176p. (Orig.). 1991. pap. 14.95 (*0-87061-181-X*) Chr Classics.

Change, Growth & Profit in the Nineties. Edward D. Curry. (Illus.). 125p. (Orig.). 1992. pap. 59.95 (*0-9633590-0-2*) Target Mktg-Mgmt.

Change, Hope & the Bomb. David E. Lilienthal. LC 63-16236. 178p. reprint ed. pap. 50.80 (*0-8357-8827-X*, 2033384) Bks Demand.

Change in Agriculture: The Northern United States, 1820-1870. Clarence H. Danhof. LC 70-75430. 336p. 1969. 27.50 (*0-674-10770-5*) HUP.

Change in Alaska. Ed. by George Rogers. LC 75-11734. 213p. 1970. 7.95 (*0-912006-40-4*) U of Alaska Pr.

Change in an African Village: Kefa Speaks. Else Skjonsberg. LC 88-26685. (Library of Management for Development). (Illus.). viii, 271p. (C). 1989. pap. text ed. 18.95 (*0-931816-57-2*) Kumarian Pr.

Change in Bengal Agrarian Society, Seventeen Sixty to Eighteen Fifty. Ratnalakha Ray. 1980. 20.00 (*0-8364-0646-X*, Pub. by Manohar II) S Asia.

Change in British Politics. Ed. by Hugh Berrington. (Illus.). 248p. 1984. 32.50 (*0-7146-3243-0*, BHA-03243, Pub. by F Cass Pubs UK) Intl Spec Bk.

***Change in British Society.** 4th ed. A. H. Halsey. (Illus.). 288p. 1995. pap. 14.95 (*0-19-289236-3*) OUP.

Change in Byzantine Culture in the Eleventh & Twelfth Centuries. Alexander P. Kazhdan & Ann W. Epstein. 1985. pap. 16.00 (*0-520-06962-5*) U CA Pr.

Change in Classroom Practice. Ed. by Hilary Constable et al. LC 93-37807. 168p. 1994. 79.00 (*0-7507-0198-6*, Falmer Pr); pap. 31.00 (*0-7507-0199-4*, Falmer Pr) Taylor & Francis.

Change in Contemporary South Africa. Ed. by Leonard L. Thompson & Jeffrey Butler. (Perspectives on Southern Africa Ser.: No. 17). 400p. 1975. reprint ed. pap. 12.00 (*0-520-03052-4*) U CA Pr.

Change in Delinquent Behavior As a Function of Learning Disabilities: A Two-Year Longitudinal Study. National Center for State Courts Staff. 41p. 1981. 2.46 (*0-685-16958-8*, LDJD-009) Natl Ctr St Courts.

Change in Dynasties: Loyalty in Thirteenth-Century China. Jennifer W. Jay. (Studies on East Asia: Vol. 18). (Illus.). 309p. 1991. 35.00 (*0-914584-18-9*) WWUCEAS.

Change in Eastern Europe. Robert Weiner. LC 93-50061. 192p. 1994. text ed. 55.00 (*0-275-94539-1*, Praeger Pubs) Greenwood.

Change in Habit. Arnold Toynbee. 256p. 1992. pap. 15.95 (*1-85168-044-6*) Onewrld Pubns.

Change in Industrial Relations: The Organization & Environment. Phil Beaumont. 352p. 1990. 75.00 (*0-415-04344-1*, A4009) Routledge.

Change in Language: Whitney, Breal & Wegener. Brigitte Nerlich. 224p. 1990. 47.50 (*0-415-00991-X*, A4081) Routledge.

Change in Mame Fadden. John B. Keane. 1973. pap. 9.95 (*0-85342-332-6*) Dufour.

Change in Medieval Society: Europe North of the Alps 1050-1500. Ed. by Sylvia Thrupp. 338p. 1988. pap. text ed. 12.95 (*0-8020-6699-2*) U of Toronto Pr.

Change in Organizations: New Perspectives on Theory, Research, & Practice. Paul S. Goodman et al. LC 82-48069. (Jossey-Bass Social & Behavioral Science Ser.). 466p. reprint ed. pap. 132.90 (*0-7837-0171-3*, 2040468) Bks Demand.

Change in Piero Della Francesca. Creighton Gilbert. LC 62-19124. (Illus.). 5.00 (*0-685-71754-2*) J J Augustin.

Change in Public Bureaucracies. M. W. Meyer. LC 76-47193. (Illus.). 1979. 59.95 (*0-521-22670-8*) Cambridge U Pr.

Change in Public Education: A Technological Perspective. Thomas V. Gillman. (Trends & Issues Ser.). vi, 26p. (Orig.). 1989. 7.00 (*0-86552-097-6*) U of Oreg ERIC.

***Change in Rural Appalachia: Implications for Action Programs.** Ed. by John D. Photiadis & Harry K. Schwarzweller. 284p. 1971. text ed. 39.95 (*0-8122-7618-3*) U of Pa Pr.

Change in Schools: Facilitating the Process. Gene E. Hall & Shirley M. Hord. LC 86-5714. (Educational Leadership Ser.). 393p. 1987. 64.50 (*0-88706-346-2*); pap. 21.95 (*0-88706-347-0*) State U NY Pr.

Change in Social Welfare from Deregulation: The Case of the Natural Gas Industry. Alice G. Breed. LC 78-22683. (Energy in the American Economy Ser.). (Illus.). 1979. lib. bdg. 18.95 (*0-405-11986-0*) Ayer.

Change in Societal Institutions. Ed. by Maureen T. Hallinan et al. (Illus.). 292p. 1990. 42.50 (*0-306-43541-1*, Plenum Pr) Plenum.

***Change in South Africa.** Jakes Gerwel et al. Ed. by J. E. Spence. LC 94-20476. 114p. 1994. pap. 16.95 (*0-87609-169-9*) Coun Foreign.

Change in South Africa: Blind Alleys or New Directions? Christopher R. Hill. LC 83-2837. 234p. (C). 1983. text ed. 56.00 (*0-389-20386-6*, N7263) B&N Imports.

***Change in Taiwan & Potential Adversity in the Strait.** Evan A. Feigenbaum. LC 95-8390. (MR-558-OSD Ser.). 59p. (Orig.). 1995. pap. text ed. 7.50 (*0-8330-1635-0*) Rand Corp.

Change in the Amazon Basin, 2 vols. Ed. by John H. Hemming. Incl. Vol. 1. Man's Impact on Forests & Rivers. LC 84-873. 222p. 1985. 46.00 (*0-7190-0967-7*); Vol. 2. Frontier after a Decade of Colonisation. LC 84-873. 295p. 1985. 46.00 (*0-7190-0968-5*); LC 84-873. 1985. write for info. (*0-318-58171-X*, Pub. by Manchester Univ Pr UK) St Martin.

Change in the Contemporary South. Ed. by Allan P. Sindler. LC 63-21317. 257p. reprint ed. pap. 73.30 (*0-317-26850-3*, 2023451) Bks Demand.

1140

An Asterisk (*) at the beginning of an entry indicates that the title is appearing in BIP for the first time.

An Asterisk (*) at the beginning of an entry indicates that the title is appearing in BIP for the first time.

1141

Changes. Travis Williams. Ed. by Nancy R. Thatch. LC 93-13420. (Books for Students by Students Ser.). (Illus.). 29p. (J). (gr. 6-9). 1993. lib. bdg. 14.95 (*0-933849-44-3*) Landmark Edns.

Changes. Matt Howarth. (Illus.). 96p. 1992. reprint ed. pap. 7.95 (*1-879450-22-4*) Tundra MA.

Changes: A Companion to Nutrition Nuggets. Ronda Gates. 96p. (Orig.). 1989. pap. 5.95 (*0-685-29326-2*) Lifestyles Four.

Changes: A Love Story. Ama A. Aidoo. 188p. (Orig.). 1992. pap. 12.95 (*1-55861-065-0*) Feminist Pr.

Changes: A Love Story. Ama A. Aidoo. 208p. (Orig.). 1993. 35.00 (*1-55861-064-2*) Feminist Pr.

***Changes: A Spiritual Journal.** John M. Talbot. 138p. (Orig.). 1993. reprint ed. pap. 10.00 (*1-883803-00-4*) Element MA.

Changes: A Woman's Journal for Self-Awareness & Personal Planning. Mindy Bingham et al. Ed. by Barbara Greene & Kathy Araujo. LC 87-14383. (Illus.). 104p. (Orig.). 1993. student ed. pap. 5.95 (*0-911655-41-7*) Advocacy Pr.

Changes: A Woman's Journal for Self-Awareness & Personal Planning. Mindy Bingham et al. Ed. by Barbara Greene & Kathy Araujo. LC 87-14383. (Illus.). 240p. (Orig.). 1993. 18.95 (*0-911655-39-5*) Advocacy Pr.

***Changes: A Woman's Journal for Self-Awareness & Personal Planning.** Mindy Bingham et al. Ed. by Barbara Greene & Kathy Araujo. LC 87-14383. (Illus.). 240p. (Orig.). 1993. pap. 18.95 (*0-911655-40-9*) Advocacy Pr.

Changes: Adapting to Earth's Renewal. Jonathon D. Miller. (Orig.). pap. 4.95 (*0-935815-07-4*) Lifecircle.

Changes: An Anthology by New Writers. Ed. by Readers House Staff. (New Writers' Voices Ser.). 64p. (Orig.). 1993. pap. text ed. 3.50 (*1-56853-006-4*, Signal Hill) New Readers.

Changes: Becoming the Best You Can Be. rev. ed. Bill Cosby et al. Ed. by Linda Barr & Marba Wojcicki. (Skills for Adolescence Ser.). (Illus.). 196p. (YA). (gr. 6-8). 1988. pap. text ed. 6.85 (*0-933419-24-4*) Quest Intl.

Changes: Readings for ESL Writers. Jean Withrow et al. LC 88-63055. 225p. (Orig.). (C). 1990. pap. text ed. 17.00 (*0-312-01994-7*) St Martin.

Changes: Readings for ESL Writers. Jean Withrow et al. LC 88-63055. 225p. (Orig.). (C). 1990. pap. text ed. 0.76 (*0-312-01993-9*) St Martin.

Changes: You & Your Body. 1988. 3.00 (*0-930659-01-5*) Choice.

Changes & Challenges: City Schools in America. Journalism Research Fellows Staff. Ed. by Susan C. Farkas. 96p. (Orig.). 1983. pap. 7.95 (*0-937846-95-3*) Inst Educ Lead.

***Changes & Challenges: Economic Transformation in East-Central Europe.** Ed. by Pal Gaspar. 190p. 1995. 29.00 (*963-05-6874-8*, Pub. by A K HU) Intl Spec Bk.

Changes & Challenges for the Human Resource Professional. Ronald R. Sims & Serbrenia J. Sims. LC 09-415876. 272p. 1994. text ed. 59.95 (*0-89930-885-6*, Quorum Bks) Greenwood.

Changes & Chances. Mary Elmblad. 1992. mass mkt. 4.99 (*0-8041-0824-2*) Ivy Books.

Changes & Chances. Stanley Middleton. 215p. 1991. 18.95 (*1-56131-004-2*) New Amsterdam Bks.

Changes & Chances. Henry W. Nevinson. 1972. 69.95 (*0-87968-834-3*) Gordon Pr.

Changes & Choices, Personal Development & Relationships. Ruth E. Bragg. LC 85-27155. 431p. 1993. 34.64 (*0-87006-982-9*) Goodheart.

Changes & Socio-Religious Conflict in an Ethnic Minority Group: The Serbian Orthodox Church in America. Djuro J. Vrga & Frank J. Fahey. LC 74-31771. 1975. pap. 8.00 (*0-88247-335-2*) Ragusan Pr.

Changes at Fairacre. large type ed. Miss Read. LC 92-47256. 1993. 20.95 (*0-7927-1593-4*, Eagle Lrg Print) Chivers N Amer.

Changes at Fairacre. large type ed. Miss Read. 1994. pap. 18.95 (*0-7927-1592-6*, Paragon Lrg Print) Chivers N Amer.

Changes, Changes. Pat Hutchins. LC 70-123133. (Illus.). 32p. (J). (ps-k). 1971. text ed. 14.95 (*0-02-745870-9*, Mac Bks Young Read) S&S Childrens.

Changes, Changes. Pat Hutchins. LC 86-22331. (Illus.). 32p. (J). (ps-1). 1987. reprint ed. pap. 4.95 (*0-689-71137-9*, Aladdin Paperbacks) S&S Childrens.

Changes Facing the Men's Tailored Clothing Industry in the 21st Century & Other Presentations at the April 1989 Production-Management Seminar. 46p. 1989. 60.00 (*0-317-01807-8*) Clothing Mfrs.

Changes for Addy. Connie Porter. (American Girls Collection Ser.). (Illus.). 80p. (Orig.). (J). (gr. 2-5). 1994. lib. bdg. 12.95 (*1-56247-086-8*); pap. 5.95 (*1-56247-085-X*) Pleasant Co.

Changes for Felicity: A Winter Story. Valerie Tripp. (American Girls Collection Ser.). (Illus.). (J). (gr. 2-5). 1992. lib. bdg. 12.95 (*1-56247-038-8*); pap. 5.95 (*1-56247-037-X*) Pleasant Co.

Changes for Kirsten: A Winter Story. Janet Shaw. Ed. by Jeanne Thieme. (American Girls Collection Ser.). (Illus.). 72p. (Orig.). (J). (gr. 2-5). 1988. lib. bdg. 12.95 (*0-937295-94-9*) Pleasant Co.

Changes for Kirsten: A Winter Story. Janet Shaw. (American Girls Collection Ser.). (Illus.). 65p. (Orig.). (J). (gr. 2-5). 1988. pap. 5.95 (*0-937295-45-0*) Pleasant Co.

Changes for Molly: A Winter Story. Valerie Tripp. (American Girls Collection Ser.). (Illus.). 67p. (Orig.). (J). (gr. 2-5). 1988. 12.95 (*0-937295-96-5*); pap. 5.95 (*0-937295-49-3*) Pleasant Co.

Changes for Samantha: A Winter Story. Valerie Tripp. Ed. by Jeanne Thieme. (American Girls Collection Ser.). (Illus.). 72p. (Orig.). (J). (gr. 2-5). 1988. pap. 5.95 (*0-937295-47-7*) Pleasant Co.

Changes for Samantha: A Winter Story. Valerie Tripp. Ed. by Jeanne Thieme. (American Girls Collection Ser.). (Illus.). 72p. (Orig.). (J). (gr. 2-5). 1988. lib. bdg. 12.95 (*0-937295-95-7*) Pleasant Co.

Changes in Agrarian Structure in India. H. Lakshminarayana & S. S. Tyagi. 163p. 1982. 21.95 (*0-318-36789-0*) Asia Bk Corp.

Changes in American Society, Nineteen Sixty to Nineteen Seventy-Eight: An Annotated Bibliography of Official Government Publications. David W. Parish. LC 80-12561. 478p. 1980. 35.00 (*0-8108-1309-2*) Scarecrow.

Changes in Attitude. Jeffrey Solomon. (City Kids Novelizations Ser.). 128p. (Orig.). (J). (gr. 3-9). 1994. pap. 3.99 (*0-679-86858-5*, Bullseye Bks) Random Bks Yng Read.

Changes in Breeding Bird Populations Between 1930 & 1985 in the Quarter Run Valley of Allegany State Park, New York. Timothy L. Baird. (Bulletin Ser.: No. 477). (Illus.). 41p. (Orig.). (C). 1991. pap. text ed. 6.00 (*1-55557-189-1*) NYS Museum.

Changes in Cereals & Dairy Policies in OECD Countries: A Model-Based Analysis. OECD Staff. 170p. (Orig.). 1991. pap. text ed. 33.00 (*92-64-13582-0*, 51-91-6-1) OECD.

Changes in China: Party, State, & Society, Vol. 1. Ed. by Shao-Chuan Leng. LC 88-36681. (Miller Center Series on Asian Political Leadership). (Illus.). 386p. (Orig.). (C). 1989. lib. bdg. 56.00 (*0-8191-7365-7*, Pub. by White Miller Center); pap. text ed. 31.00 (*0-8191-7366-5*, Pub. by White Miller Center) U Pr of Amer.

***Changes in Energy Intensity in the Manufacturing Sector.** 1995. lib. bdg. 250.00 (*0-8490-6460-0*) Gordon Pr.

Changes in Federal Diversity Jurisdiction: Effects on State Court Caseloads. Victor Flango & Craig Boersema. 66p. 1990. 4.00 (*0-685-38117-X*, NCSC-122) Natl Ctr St Courts.

Changes in Gene Expression in Response to Environmental Stress. Ed. by B. G. Atkinson & S. B. Walden. 1985. text ed. 81.00 (*0-12-066290-6*) Acad Pr.

Changes in Income Distribution During the Great Depression. Horst Mendershausen. LC 75-19726. (National Bureau of Economic Research Ser.). (Illus.). 1975. reprint ed. 20.95 (*0-405-07604-5*) Ayer.

Changes in Income Distribution During the Great Depression. Horst Mendershausen. (Studies in Income & Wealth: No. 7). 191p. 1946. reprint ed. 49.70 (*0-87014-162-7*); reprint ed. mic. film 24.90 (*0-685-61265-1*) Natl Bur Econ Res.

Changes in Labor Cost During Cycles in Production & Business. Thor Hultgren. (Occasional Papers: No. 74). 105p. 1960. reprint ed. 27.30 (*0-87014-388-3*) Natl Bur Econ Res.

Changes in Land Use & Land Cover: A Global Perspective. Ed. by William B. Meyer & B. L. Turner, II. (Illus.). 380p. (C). 1994. 49.95 (*0-521-47085-4*) Cambridge U Pr.

Changes in Latitudes. Will Hobbs. 176p. (YA). 1993. mass mkt. 3.99 (*0-380-71619-4*, Flare) Avon.

Changes in Latitudes. Will Hobbs. LC 87-17462. 176p. (YA). (gr. 7 up). 1988. text ed. 14.95 (*0-689-31385-3*, Atheneum Bks Young) S&S Childrens.

Changes in Nutritional Components of Stored Seeds Due to Fungal Association. K. S. Bilgrami et al. (International Bioscience Monographs: No. 9). 90p. 1979. 8.00 (*0-88065-061-3*, Messers Today & Tomorrow) Scholarly Pubns.

Changes in Physical Production, Industrial Productivity, & Manufacturing Costs, 1927-1932. Frederick C. Mills. (NBER Bulletin Ser.: No. 45). 1993. reprint ed. 20.00 (*0-685-61155-8*) Natl Bur Econ Res.

Changes in Position. Catherine Rutan. 1983. pap. 3.50 (*0-911623-00-0*) I Klang.

Changes in Prices, Manufacturing Costs, & Industrial Productivity, 1929-1934. Frederick C. Mills. (NBER Bulletin Ser.: No. 53). 1934. reprint ed. 20.00 (*0-685-61166-3*) Natl Bur Econ Res.

Changes in Revenue Structures: Proceedings of the 42nd Congress of the IIPF, Athens, 1986. Ed. by Aldo Chiancone & Kenneth Messere. 350p. 1989. 45.00 (*0-8143-2032-5*) Wayne St U Pr.

Changes in Student Participation in Adult Education. Daines et al. (C). 1982. 35.00 (*0-902031-73-2*, Pub. by Univ Nottingham UK) St Mut.

Changes in Student Participation in Adult Education. J. Daines et al. 62p. (C). 1982. text ed. 45.00 (*0-685-22150-4*, Pub. by Univ Nottingham UK) St Mut.

Changes in the Cyclical Behavior of Interest Rates. Phillip Cagan. (Occasional Papers: No. 100). 40p. 1966. reprint ed. 20.00 (*0-87014-414-6*) Natl Bur Econ Res.

Changes in the Dutch Bryophyte Flora & Air Pollution. - Significance of Mosses for Nature Conservation. - Recommendations for Management. H. C. Greven. (Dissertationes Botanicae Ser.: Vol. 194). (Illus.). 237p. 1992. pap. 55.00 (*3-443-64106-7*, Pub. by Cramer-Borntraeger GW) Lubrecht & Cramer.

Changes in the Field of Transport Studies. Ed. by Jacob B. Polak & Jan B. Van Der Kamp. (Developments in Transportation Studies: No. 1). 1979. lib. bdg. 87.50 (*90-247-2147-4*) Kluwer Ac.

Changes in the Japanese University: A Comparative Perspective. William K. Cummings et al. LC 78-19787. 288p. 1979. text ed. 42.95 (*0-275-90344-3*, C0344, Praeger Pubs) Greenwood.

Changes in the Land: Indians, Colonists, & the Ecology of New England. William Cronon. (American Century Ser.). (Illus.). 252p. (C). 1983. pap. 9.95 (*0-8090-0158-6*) Hill & Wang.

Changes in the Market Structure of Grocery Retailing. Willard F. Mueller & Leon Garoian. LC 86-18317. 240p. 1986. reprint ed. 65.00 (*0-313-25222-X*, MUCM, Greenwood Pr) Greenwood.

Changes in the Material Culture of Two Indian Tribes Under the Influence of New Surroundings. Erland Nordenskiold. LC 75-46055. (Comparative Ethnographical Studies: Vol 2). reprint ed. 39.50 (*0-404-15142-6*) AMS Pr.

Changes in the Nineteen Eighty-One National Electrical Code. George W. Flach. 145p. 1981. 18.95 (*0-13-127860-6*, Reward); pap. 9.95 (*0-13-127852-5*, Reward) P-H.

Changes in the Recession Behavior of Wholesale Prices in the 1920s & Post-World War II. Phillip Cagan. (Explorations in Economic Research Two Ser.: No. 2). 51p. 1975. reprint ed. 35.00 (*0-685-61380-1*) Natl Bur Econ Res.

Changes in the Roman Empire: Essays in the Ordinary. Ramsay MacMullen. (Illus.). 444p. 1990. text ed. 44.50 (*0-691-03601-2*) Princeton U Pr.

Changes in the Share of Wealth Held by Top Wealth-Holders, 1922-1956. Robert J. Lampman. (Occasional Papers: No. 71). 38p. 1960. reprint ed. 20.00 (*0-87014-385-9*) Natl Bur Econ Res.

Changes in the State: Causes & Consequences. Ed. by Edward S. Greenberg. (Focus Editions Ser.: Vol. 122). 320p. (C). 1990. text ed. 49.95 (*0-8039-3877-2*); pap. text ed. 24.95 (*0-8039-3878-0*) Sage.

Changes in the Theory & Tactics of the German Social Democracy. Paul Kampffmeyer. LC 74-22748. (Labor Movement in Fiction & Non-Fiction Ser.). reprint ed. 34.50 (*0-404-58500-0*) AMS Pr.

Changes in the Wind: The Earth's Shifting Climate. Margery Facklam & Howard Facklam. LC 85-5475. (Illus.). 128p. (YA). (gr. 7 up). 1986. 14.95 (*0-15-216115-5*, HB Juv Bks) HarBrace.

Changes in the Workweek of Fixed Capital: U. S. Manufacturing, 1929 to 1976. Murray F. Foss. LC 80-28063. (AEI Studies: No. 309). 114p. reprint ed. pap. 32.50 (*0-8357-4446-9*, 2037283) Bks Demand.

Changes in Washoe Land Use Patterns: A Study of Three Archaeological Sites in Diamond Valley, Alpine County, California. Ed. by Charles D. Zeier & Robert G. Elston. LC 91-45854. (Monographs in World Archaeology: No. 5). 248p. (C). 1992. pap. text ed. 20.00 (*0-9629110-5-4*) Prehistory Pr.

Changes in Western European Banking: An International Banker's Guide. Edward P. Gardener & Philip Molyneux. 336p. 1993. pap. 35.00 (*0-415-08320-6*, B0180) Routledge.

Changes in Western European Banking: An International Banker's Guide. Edward P. Gardner & Philip Molyneux. (European Financial Institutions & Markets Staff Ser.: No. 1). 288p. (C). 1990. text ed. 85.00 (*0-04-445220-9*) Routledge Chapman & Hall.

Changes in You & Me: A Book about Puberty, Mostly for Boys. Bourgeois & Wolfish. LC 94-1162. (YA). (gr. 7-12). 1994. 14.95 (*0-8362-2814-6*) Andrews & McMeel.

Changes in You & Me: A Book about Puberty, Mostly for Girls. Paulette Bourgeois & Martin Wolfish. LC 94-1161. (YA). (gr. 7-12). 1994. 14.95 (*0-8362-2815-4*) Andrews & McMeel.

Changes in You for Boys: A Clearly Illustrated, Simply Worded Explanation of the Changes of Puberty for Boys. Peggy C. Siegel. LC 90-86238. (Illus.). 44p. (Orig.). (J). (gr. 4-8). 1991. pap. 8.95 (*0-9628687-1-X*) Fam Life Ed.

Changes in You for Girls: A Beautifully Illustrated, Simply Worded Explanation of the Changes of Puberty for Girls. Peggy C. Siegel. LC 90-86237. (Illus.). 52p. (Orig.). (J). (gr. 4-8). 1991. pap. 8.95 (*0-9628687-0-1*) Fam Life Ed.

Changes in Youth Morality: What Caused Them?, No. 1. rev. ed. Charles D. Barton. (Illus.). 40p. (YA). 1988. pap. 3.00 (*0-317-93057-5*) Wallbuilders.

Changes of Cain: Violence & the Lost Brother in Cain & Abel Literature. Ricardo J. Quinones. 304p. 1991. text ed. 29.95 (*0-691-06883-6*) Princeton U Pr.

***Changes of Mind: A Holonomic Theory of the Evolution of Consciousness.** Jenny Wade. (SUNY Series in the Philosophy of Psychology). 320p. 1996. text ed. 59.50x (*0-7914-2849-4*); pap. 19.95x (*0-7914-2850-8*) State U NY Pr.

Changes-Orders-Becomings. Peyton Houston. (Illus.). 1990. 20.00 (*0-912330-70-8*) Jargon Soc.

Changes That Heal. Henry Cloud. 272p. 1993. pap. 10.99 (*0-310-60631-4*) Zondervan.

***Changes That Heal.** 2nd ed. Henry Cloud. 496p. 1995. pap. 5.99 (*0-06-104345-1*) Zondervan.

Changes That Heal Workbook: How to Understand Your Past to Ensure a Healthier Future. Henry Cloud. 128p. 1994. pap. 8.99 (*0-310-60633-0*) Zondervan.

Changeweaver. Margaret Ball. (Fantasy Ser.). 304p. (Orig.). 1993. mass mkt. 4.99 (*0-671-72173-9*) Baen Bks.

Changing. Maggi H. Meyer. LC 84-62316. 90p. 1984. pap. 6.00 (*0-915727-10-2*) im-Press.

Changing Administration: The 1961 & 1964 Transitions in Six Departments. LC 65-28725. 160p. reprint ed. pap. 45.60 (*0-317-26366-8*, 2025408) Bks Demand.

Changing Adolescent Attitudes Toward Police. Robert Portune. LC 77-358331. (Criminal Justice Ser.: Vol. 4). 285p. reprint ed. pap. 81.30 (*0-8357-9036-3*, 2015227) Bks Demand.

Changing Aesthetic Views of Instrumental Music in 18th Century Germany. Bellamy Hosler. LC 81-4754. (Studies in Musicology: No. 42). 319p. reprint ed. pap. 91.00 (*0-8357-1172-2*, 2070255) Bks Demand.

Changing Africa: The First Literary Generation of Independent Cape Verde. Gerald M. Moser. LC 92-72961. (Transactions Ser.: Vol. 82, Pt. 4). (Illus.). 102p. (C). 1992. pap. 15.00 (*0-87169-824-2*, T824-MOG) Am Philos.

Changing Agenda: World Politics since 1945. 2nd ed. Sylvia Woodby & Martha Cottam. 242p. (C). 1991. pap. text ed. 19.95 (*0-8133-1209-4*) Westview.

Changing Agenda of Israeli Sociology: Theory, Ideology, & Identity. Uri Ram. (SUNY Series in Israeli Studies). 264p. (C). 1995. text ed. 59.50x (*0-7914-2301-8*); pap. text ed. 19.95x (*0-7914-2302-6*) State U NY Pr.

Changing Agenda of West German Public Policy. Simon Bulmer. (Association for the Study of German Politics Ser.). 218p. 1989. text ed. 55.95 (*1-85521-041-X*, Pub. by Dartmth Pub UK) Ashgate Pub Co.

Changing Agrarian Structure & Labour Relations. G. Satyanarayana. (C). 1992. 18.00 (*81-7033-146-3*, Pub. by Rawat II) S Asia.

***Changing Agricultural Production Systems & the Fate of Agricultural Chemicals: Proceedings of a Conference Sponsored by ARI, February 21-23, 1984.** Ed. by G. W. Irving, Jr. 160p. Date not set. pap. 25.00 (*0-614-04328-X*) Agri Research Inst.

Changing Agriculture. 2nd ed. Jim Wilson. (Illus.). 80p. 1993. 12.95 (*0-86417-489-6*, Pub. by Kangaroo Pr AT) Seven Hills Bk.

Changing All Those Changes. James P. Girard. Ed. by Al Young. LC 76-11428. 1976. pap. 3.95 (*0-918412-01-3*) Yardbird Wing.

Changing America: Blueprints for the New Admininstration. Ed. by Mark Green et al. LC 92-43972. 1993. pap. 19.95 (*1-55704-161-X*) Newmarket.

Changing American Assessments of the Soviet Threat in Sub-Saharan Africa 1975-1985. Donald Jordan. LC 87-22756. 106p. (Orig.). (C). 1988. pap. text ed. 14.50 (*0-8191-6665-0*) U Pr of Amer.

Changing American Education: Recapturing the Past or Inventing the Future? Ed. by Kathryn Borman & Nancy P. Greenman. LC 92-42842. (SUNY Series, Teacher Preparation & Development). 416p. (C). 1994. 74.50 (*0-7914-1659-3*); pap. 24.95 (*0-7914-1660-7*) State U NY Pr.

Changing American Family: Sociological & Demographic Perspectives. Ed. by Scott J. South & Stewart E. Tolnay. 304p. 1992. text ed. 67.00 (*0-8133-1100-4*) Westview.

Changing American Family & Public Policy. Ed. by Andrew J. Cherlin. 263p. 1988. pap. text ed. 25.00 (*0-87766-421-8*) U Pr of Amer.

Changing American Family & Public Policy. Ed. by Andrew J. Cherlin. 263p. 1988. lib. bdg. 57.00 (*0-87766-422-6*) U Pr of Amer.

Changing American Legal System: Some Selected Phases. Francis R. Aumann. LC 79-92625. (Law, Politics & History Ser.). 1969. reprint ed. 39.50 (*0-306-71762-X*) Da Capo.

Changing American Mind: How & Why American Public Opinion Changed Between 1960 & 1988. William G. Mayer. LC 92-26578. 400p. (C). 1992. text ed. 52.50 (*0-472-09498-X*); pap. 18.95 (*0-472-06498-3*) U of Mich Pr.

Changing American People: Are We Deteriorating or Improving? Ed. by James C. Charlesworth. LC 68-27641. (Annals of the American Academy of Political & Social Science Ser.: No. 378). 1968. 27.00 (*0-87761-109-2*); pap. 18.00 (*0-87761-108-4*) Am Acad Pol Soc Sci.

Changing American Voter. Norman H. Nie et al. LC 75-42429. 450p. 1980. 37.50 (*0-674-10830-2*); pap. 16.95 (*0-674-10835-3*) HUP.

Changing American Workplace: Work Alternatives in the '80s. Goodmeasure, Inc. LC 85-11187. (AMA Survey Report Ser.). 48p. reprint ed. pap. 25.00 (*0-685-15240-5*, 2027146) Bks Demand.

Changing an Army: An Oral History of General William E. DePuy, U. S. A. Retired. Romie L. Brownlee & William J. Mullen, III. (Center for Military History Publication German Report Series, DA Pam: No. 70-23). (Illus.). 221p. 1989. per., pap. 14.00 (*0-16-001975-3*, S/N 008-029-001) USGPO.

Changing & Learning in the Lives of Physicians. Robert D. Fox & Paul E. Maxmanian. LC 89-3886. 201p. 1989. text ed. 49.95 (*0-275-93338-5*, C3338, Praeger Pubs) Greenwood.

Changing Appearance. Toby Olson. 1975. pap. 10.00 (*0-87924-021-0*) Membrane Pr.

Changing Approaches to Studying Adult Education. Huey B. Long et al. LC 78-62579. (Jossey-Bass Series in Higher Education). 174p. reprint ed. pap. 49.60 (*0-7837-2520-5*, 2042679) Bks Demand.

Changing Architecture of Politics: Structure, Agency, & the Future of the State. Philip G. Cerny. 288p. (C). 1990. text ed. 47.50 (*0-8039-8255-0*); pap. text ed. 18.95 (*0-8039-8256-9*) Sage.

Changing Aspects of Rural Relief. A. L. Mangus. LC 74-165685. (Research Monograph Ser.: Vol. 14). 1971. reprint ed. lib. bdg. 29.50 (*0-306-70346-7*) Da Capo.

Changing Aspects of Urban Relief. Fitzhugh L. Carmichael & Raymond Nassimbene. LC 72-173446. (FDR & the Era of the New Deal Ser.). 94p. 1971. reprint ed. lib. bdg. 19.50 (*0-306-70370-X*) Da Capo.

Changing Atmosphere: A Global Challenge. John Firor. (Illus.). 160p. (C). 1990. 22.00 (*0-300-03381-8*) Yale U Pr.

Changing Atmosphere: A Global Challenge. John Firor. (Illus.). 160p. (C). 1992. reprint ed. pap. 9.00 (*0-300-05664-8*) Yale U Pr.

An Asterisk (*) at the beginning of an entry indicates that the title is appearing in BIP for the first time.

An Asterisk (*) at the beginning of an entry indicates that the title is appearing in BIP for the first time.

1143

C

Changing Education: Women As Radicals & Conservators. Ed. by Joyce Antler & Sari K. Biklen. LC 89-35030. (Feminist Theory in Education Ser.). 388p. 1990. 74.50 (*0-7914-0233-9*); pap. 24.95 (*0-7914-0234-7*) State U NY Pr.

Changing Emphasis in Environmental Education: Proceedings of the Natural Science Centers Conference 1972-Jacksonville Florida. Ed. by Natural Science for Youth Foundation Staff. (Illus.). (Orig.). 1973. 5.00 (*0-916544-02-8*) Natural Sci Youth.

***Changing Employment Relations: Behavioral & Social Perspectives.** Ed. by Lois Tetrick & Julian Barling. 200p. 1995. text ed. 40.00 (*1-55798-315-1*) Am Psychol.

Changing Energy Prices & Colorado Industry: Summary of an International Research Center for Energy & Economic Development Study. 24p. 1988. pap. 10.00 (*0-918714-15-X*) Intl Res Ctr Energy.

Changing English Countryside. Leonard Cantor. 1987. 47.50 (*0-7102-0501-5*, 05015, RKP) Routledge.

Changing English Primary Schools: The Impact of the Education Reform Act at Key Stage One. Andrew Pollard et al. LC 93-40675. (Cassell Education Ser.). (Illus.). 224p. 1994. 60.00 (*0-304-32921-5*); pap. 17.95 (*0-304-32923-1*) Cassell.

Changing Environment. J. W. Moore. (Environmental Management Ser.). (Illus.). x, 240p. 1986. 79.00 (*0-387-96314-6*) Spr-Verlag.

Changing Environment of Business: A Managerial Approach. 3rd ed. Grover Starling. 648p. (C). 1988. text ed. 53.95 (*0-534-07662-9*) Intl Thomson.

Changing Environment of International Financial Markets: Issues & Analysis. Ed. by Dilip K. Ghosh & Edgar Ortiz. LC 93-17783. 1994. text ed. 79.95 (*0-312-10189-9*) St Martin.

Changing Esoteric Values. 2nd ed. Foster Bailey. 1970. pap. 3.00 (*0-85330-125-5*) Lucis.

***Changing European Defence Industry: The Trend Towards Internationalisation in the Defence Industry of Western Europe.** Madelene Sandstrom & Christina Wilen. (Illus.). 76p. (Orig.). (C). 1994. pap. text ed. 45.00 (*0-7881-1380-1*) Diane Pub.

***Changing European Economy: From Community to Union.** Ed. by Nigel M. Healey. LC 94-39620. 280p. 1995. 59.95x (*0-415-10874-8*, C0391); pap. 22.95 (*0-415-10875-6*, C0392) Routledge.

***Changing European Firm: Limits to Convergence.** Ed. by Richard Whitley & Peer H. Kristensen. LC 95-6364. 1995. write for info. (*0-415-12999-0*); pap. write for info. (*0-415-13000-X*) Routledge.

***Changing European Identities.** Ed. by Glynis M. Breakwell & Evanthia Lyons. (International Series in Experimental Social Psychology: Vol. 29). 360p. 1995. write for info. (*0-08-042412-0*, Pergamon Pr) Elsevier.

Changing Exchange Rate Systems, Vol. 3: Lloyds Bank Annual Review. Ed. by Christopher Johnson. 224p. 1990. text ed. 47.50 (*0-86187-810-8*, Pub. by Pinter Pubs UK) St Martin.

Changing Expectations: A Key to Effective Psychotherapy. Irving Kirsch. 304p. (C). 1990. text ed. 44.95 (*0-534-12648-0*) Brooks-Cole.

***Changing Experience of Women.** Ed. by Elizabeth Whitelegg. 416p. 1982. pap. write for info. (*0-631-14836-1*) Blackwell Pubs.

***Changing Face of Aids: Implications for Social Work Practice.** Ed. by Vincent J. Lynch et al. LC 92-42902. 288p. 1995. pap. text ed. 18.95 (*0-86569-260-2*, Auburn Hse) Greenwood.

Changing Face of Arthurian Romance: From Chretian de Troyes to the End of the Middle Ages. Ed. by Alison Adams & Kenneth Varty. (Arthurian Studies: Vol. XVI). 208p. 1986. 70.00 (*0-85991-227-2*) Boydell & Brewer.

Changing Face of Beauty. Romm. 346p. 1991. 99.00 (*0-8016-5505-6*) Mosby Yr Bk.

***Changing Face of Boston over Three Hundred Fifty Years.** (Picture Books Ser.). 1980. pap. 4.00 (*0-934909-63-6*) Mass Hist Soc.

Changing Face of Brazil. Kempton Webb. LC 74-1029. 1974. text ed. 50.00 (*0-231-03767-8*) Col U Pr.

Changing Face of Britain. Edward Hyams. 1977. pap. 12.95 (*0-8464-0237-8*) Beekman Pubs.

Changing Face of College Teaching. Ed. by Marilla D. Svinicki. LC 85-644763. (New Directions for Teaching & Learning Ser.: No. TL 42). 1990. 16.95 (*1-55542-839-8*) Jossey-Bass.

Changing Face of Educational Assessment. Roger Murphy & Harry Torrance. 128p. 1988. 80.00 (*0-335-15827-7*, Open Univ Pr); pap. 27.00 (*0-335-15826-9*, Open Univ Pr) Taylor & Francis.

Changing Face of European Banks & Securities Markets. Ed. by Jack Revell. LC 93-29483. 1994. text ed. 75.00 (*0-312-10645-9*) St Martin.

Changing Face of Fiscal Federalism. Ed. by Thomas R. Swartz & John E. Peck. LC 89-49027. 192p. 1990. 46.95 (*0-87332-664-4*); pap. text ed. 20.95 (*0-87332-665-2*) M E Sharpe.

Changing Face of Friendship. Ed. by Leroy S. Rouner. LC 94-15462. (Boston University Studies in Philosophy & Religion: Vol. 15). (C). 1994. text ed. 29.95 (*0-268-00804-3*) U of Notre Dame Pr.

Changing Face of Horror in the Nineteenth Century French Fantastic Short Story. Gary R. Cummiskey. LC 91-40091. (Age of Revolution & Romanticism: Interdisciplinary Studies: Vol. 3). 170p. (C). 1992. text ed. 39.95 (*0-8204-1775-0*) P Lang Pubs.

Changing Face of Jewish & Christian Worship in North America. Ed. by Paul F. Bradshaw & Lawrence A. Hoffman. LC 90-50967. (Two Liturgical Traditions Ser.: Vol. 2). (C). 1991. text ed. 32.95 (*0-268-00784-5*) U of Notre Dame Pr.

Changing Face of Jewish & Christian Worship in North America. Ed. by Paul F. Bradshaw & Lawrence A. Hoffman. LC 90-50967. (Two Liturgical Traditions Ser.: Vol. 2). (C). 1992. pap. text ed. 11.95 (*0-268-00785-3*) U of Notre Dame Pr.

Changing Face of National Security. Robert Mandel. LC 94-17982. (Contributions in Military Studies Ser.: No. 156). 176p. 1994. text ed. 49.95 (*0-313-28519-5*, Greenwood Pr) Greenwood.

***Changing Face of Peacekeeping: Proceedings of Peacekeeping '93.** Ed. by Alex Morrison. 243p. (Orig.). (C). 1994. pap. 45.00x (*0-7881-1286-4*) Diane Pub.

Changing Face of Poverty: Trends in New York City's Population in Poverty, 1960-1990. Emanuel Tobier. LC 85-125680. 130p. (Orig.). 1984. pap. 10.00 (*0-88156-024-3*) Comm Serv Soc NY.

Changing Face of Religion. Ed. by James A. Beckford & Thomas Luckmann. (International Sociology Ser.: Vol. 37). 192p. (C). 1989. 39.95 (*0-8039-8211-9*); pap. text ed. 18.95 (*0-8039-8592-4*) Sage.

Changing Face of Testing & Assessment: Problems & Solutions. Donald Hymes & Ann Chafin. Ed. by Peggy Gonder. LC 91-61874. (Critical Issues Report Ser.). 102p. 1991. pap. 14.95 (*0-87652-164-2*, 321-00338) Am Assn Sch Admin.

Changing Face of the Hero. Rodney Standen. LC 86-40404. 179p. (Orig.). 1987. pap. 6.95 (*0-8356-0616-3*, Quest) Theos Pub Hse.

Changing Face of the Newsroom. Linda G. Cunningham et al. Ed. by Lee Stinnett. (Illus.). 120p. (Orig.). 1989. pap. 9.50 (*0-943086-05-1*) Nwspaper Assn Amer.

Changing Face of the Suburbs. Ed. by Barry Schwartz. LC 75-7221. (Illus.). 364p. reprint ed. pap. 104.10 (*0-685-23866-0*, 2056650) Bks Demand.

Changing Face of Tibet: The Impact of Chinese Communist Ideology on the Landscape. Pradyumna P. Karan. LC 74-18935. 138p. reprint ed. pap. 39.40 (*0-7837-5797-2*, 2045463) Bks Demand.

Changing Face of U. S. Politics: Working-Class Politics & the Trade Unions. 2nd ed. Jack Barnes. LC 81-80718. 346p. (C). 1994. reprint ed. lib. bdg. 55.00 (*0-87348-791-5*); reprint ed. pap. 22.95 (*0-87348-785-0*) Pathfinder NY.

Changing Face of Welfare. Adalbert Evers et al. (Studies in Social Policy & Welfare). 300p. 1987. text ed. 68.95 (*0-566-05145-1*, Pub. by Avebury Pub UK) Ashgate Pub Co.

Changing Face of Western Communism. Ed. by David Childs. LC 79-25754. 286p. 1980. text ed. 35.00 (*0-312-12951-3*) St Martin.

Changing Faces: The Best of 10cc & Godley & Creme. (Illus.). 104p. 1988. pap. 12.95 (*0-7119-1477-X*, AM71036) Music Sales.

Changing Faces: The Challenge of Facial Disfigurement. James Partridge. 1990. 11.95 (*0-14-011597-8*) Phoenix Soc.

Changing Faces of Madness: Early American Attitudes & Treatment of the Insane. Mary Ann Jimenez. LC 86-40112. 231p. 1987. text ed. 30.00 (*0-87451-375-8*) U Pr of New Eng.

Changing Families. Judy R. Aulette. 506p. 1994. text ed. 43.95 (*0-534-21306-5*) Intl Thomson.

Changing Families. Ed. by Irving E. Sigel & Luis M. Laosa. LC 83-11192. 352p. 1983. 60.00 (*0-306-41288-8*, Plenum Pr) Plenum.

Changing Families: A Group Activities Manual for Middle & High School Students from Separated, Divorced, or Single-Parent Families or Stepfamilies. Teresa M. Schmidt. LC 93-45455. 208p. 1994. pap. 59.95 (*1-56246-087-0*, P317) Johnsn Inst.

Changing Families: A Guide for Kids & Grown-Ups. David Fassler et al. LC 87-40470. (Illus.). 192p. (Orig.). 1988. pap. 14.95 (*0-914525-08-5*); 16.95 (*0-914525-09-3*) Waterfront Bks.

Changing Family. Paul J. Ciborowski. (Focus on Behavior Ser.: No. 2). (Illus.). (Orig.). 1986. teacher ed 11.75 (*0-935465-03-0*); pap. 7.25 (*0-935465-02-2*) Stratmar Ed Sys.

Changing Family: Comparative Perspectives. 2nd ed. Mark Hutter. (Illus.). 550p. (C). 1988. write for info. (*0-02-359241-9*) Macmillan.

Changing Family: Group Manual. Paul J. Ciborowski. (Focus on Behavior Ser.: No. 1). (Illus.). 52p. (Orig.). 1984. student ed 7.25 (*0-935465-00-6*) Stratmar Ed Sys.

Changing Family: Leader's Guide. Paul J. Ciborowski. (Focus on Behavior Ser.: No. 1). (Illus.). 68p. (Orig.). 1984. student ed 11.75 (*0-935465-01-4*) Stratmar Ed Sys.

Changing Family Life Cycle. 2nd ed. Carter & Monica McGoldrick. 1989. text ed. 56.00 (*0-205-12063-6*, H2063-9) Allyn.

Changing Family Life in East Africa: Women & Children at Risk. Philip L. Kilbride & Janet C. Kilbride. LC 89-2961. 272p. 1990. lib. bdg. 35.00 (*0-271-00676-5*) Pa St U Pr.

Changing Family Lifestyles: Their Effect on Children. Ed. & Intro. by James D. Quisenberry. LC 82-20628. (Illus.). 64p. (C). 1982. reprint ed. pap. 7.50 (*0-87173-100-2*) ACEI.

Changing Family Patterns in the Arab East. Edwin T. Prothro & Lutfy N. Diab. 1974. 29.95 (*0-8156-6039-1*, Am U Beirut) Syracuse U Pr.

Changing Fate. Elisabeth Waters. 240p. (Orig.). 1994. mass mkt. 4.99 (*0-88677-608-2*) DAW Bks.

***Changing Federal Laboratories: Is There a Role for the States.** Dave Furneaux. (State Legislative Report Ser.: Vol. 19, No. 7). 8p. 1994. 5.00 (*1-55516-094-8*, 7302-1907) Natl Conf State Legis.

Changing Fictions of Masculinity. David Rosen. LC 92-35300. (Illus.). 216p. 1993. 29.95 (*0-252-02004-9*); pap. 14.95 (*0-252-06309-0*) U of Ill Pr.

Changing Folkways of Parenthood: A Content Analysis. Herbert L. Costner. Ed. by Harriet Zuckerman & Robert K. Merton. LC 79-8987. (Dissertations on Sociology Ser.). 1980. lib. bdg. 39.95 (*0-405-12960-2*) Ayer.

Changing Food Technology: Products & Processes. Ed. by Manfred Kroger & Ralph Shapiro. LC 87-71936. 178p. 1987. pap. 24.00 (*0-87762-534-4*) Technomic.

Changing Food Technology, No. 2: Food Technology for a Dynamic Marketplace. Ed. by Manfred Kroger & Allen Freed. LC 89-50811. (Selected Papers from the 5th Eastern Food Science & Technology Conference). 215p. 1989. pap. 24.00 (*0-87762-644-8*) Technomic.

Changing Food Technology, No. 3: A View of the Future. Ed. by Allen J. Freed. LC 90-71253. 110p. 1990. 29.00 (*0-87762-800-9*) Technomic.

Changing for Good. James Prochaska et al. LC 93-44897. 1994. 22.00 (*0-688-11263-3*) Morrow.

***Changing for Good.** James O. Prochaska et al. 304p. 1995. reprint ed. pap. 11.00 (*0-380-72572-X*) Avon.

***Changing Forever: The Well-Kept Secret of America's Leading Companies.** Carl Frost. 160p. 1996. 24.95 (*0-87013-404-3*) Mich St U Pr.

Changing Forms in Modern Music. 2nd ed. Karl Eschman. LC 67-26898. (Illus.). 213p. 1967. 7.50 (*0-911318-01-1*) E C Schirmer.

Changing Fortunes: The Industrial Sector & Workers' Earnings. Leann M. Tigges. LC 87-2357. 192p. 1987. text ed. 55.00 (*0-275-92580-3*, C2580, Praeger Pubs) Greenwood.

Changing Fortunes: The Shaping of the International Monetary Order. Paul A. Volcker. 1992. 24.50 (*0-8129-2018-X*, Times Bks) Random.

Changing Fortunes: The World's Money & the Threat to American Leadership. Paul A. Volcker & Toyoo Gyohten. LC 91-51035. 416p. 1993. pap. 14.00 (*0-8129-2218-2*, Times Bks) Random.

Changing Franco-American Security Relationship: New Directions for NATO & European Defense Cooperation. Robert P. Grant. viii, 88p. (Orig.). 1993. pap. 12.00 (*0-9629930-3-4*) US Crest.

Changing Frontiers of Flow & Particle Diagnostics, ICALEO 1986: Proceedings, Vol. 58. 202p. 1987. 55.00 (*0-912035-33-1*) Laser Inst.

Changing Frontiers of Optical Techniques for Industrial Measurement & Control Symposium, No. 557. 258p. 1986. 80.00 (*0-948507-64-0*) Laser Inst.

Changing Functions of Lower & Middle Management in France. Serge Alecian & Pierre Girard. (Illus.). 108p. (Orig.). (C). 1993. pap. text ed. 40.00 (*0-7881-0139-0*) Diane Pub.

Changing Functions of Lower & Middle Management in the Netherlands. J. M. Baaijens et al. (Illus.). 56p. (Orig.). (C). 1993. pap. text ed. 30.00 (*0-7881-0140-4*) Diane Pub.

***Changing Functions of the Western European Union (WEU) Introduction & Basic Documents.** Arie Bloed. LC 94-24130. 260p. (C). 1994. lib. bdg. 115.50 (*0-7923-3221-0*, Pub. by M Nijhoff) Kluwer Ac.

Changing Gears: Bicycling America's Perimeter. Jane Schnell. (Illus.). 400p. 1990. 19.95 (*0-9626112-0-4*) Milner Pr.

Changing Gears: The Development of the Automotive Transmission. Philip G. Gott. 437p. 1991. 29.00 (*1-56091-099-2*, R-108) Soc Auto Engineers.

Changing Geographic Perspectives: Proceedings of the Centennial Symposium. (Illus.). 392p. 1989. 39.95 (*0-8109-3156-7*) Abrams.

Changing Geography of Advanced Producer Services: Theoretical & Empirical Perspectives. Ed. by Peter W. Daniels & Frank Moulaert. (Illus.). 216p. 1992. text ed. 64.95 (*0-470-21891-6*) Halsted Pr.

***Changing Geography of Advanced Producer Services: Theoretical & Empirical Perspectives.** Ed. by Peter W. Daniels & Frank Moulaert. 1993. text ed. 74.95 (*0-471-94519-6*) Wiley.

Changing Geography of Africa. 2nd ed. A. T. Grove. (Illus.). 256p. (C). 1993. pap. text ed. 16.95 (*0-19-913386-7*) OUP.

Changing Geography of Africa & the Middle East. Ed. by Graham P. Chapman & Kathleen M. Baker. LC 92-44795. (Illus.). 224p. 1992. 55.00 (*0-415-05709-4*, A7313); pap. 16.95 (*0-415-05710-8*, A7317) Routledge.

Changing Geography of Asia. Ed. by Graham P. Chapman & Kathleen M. Baker. LC 91-44801. (Illus.). 224p. 1992. 55.00 (*0-415-05707-8*, A7306); pap. 16.95 (*0-415-05708-6*, A7310) Routledge.

Changing Geography of China. Frank Leeming. LC 92-14969. (IBG Studies in Geography). 208p. 1993. 44.95 (*0-631-17675-6*); pap. 19.95 (*0-631-18137-7*) Blackwell Pubs.

Changing Geography of the U. K. 2nd ed. R. J. Johnston & Vince Gardiner. (Illus.). 448p. (C). 1991. text ed. 85.00 (*0-415-03241-5*, A5252) Routledge.

Changing Geography of the U. S. Automobile Industry. James M. Rubenstein. (Illus.). 288p. 1992. 63.50 (*0-415-05544-X*, A6907) Routledge.

Changing Global Environment. Neil Roberts. LC 92-35490. 1993. 64.95 (*1-55786-271-0*); pap. 34.95 (*1-55786-272-9*) Blackwell Pubs.

Changing Global Environment. Ed. by S. F. Singer. LC 73-86096. viii, 423p. (C). 1975. lib. bdg. 107.50 (*90-277-0385-X*); pap. text ed. 64.00 (*90-277-0402-3*) Kluwer Ac.

Changing Gods in Medieval China, 1127-1276. Valerie Hansen. 231p. (C). 1990. text ed. 45.00 (*0-691-05559-9*) Princeton U Pr.

Changing Habits. rev. ed. Dana Britton. 18p. 1989. ring bd. 2.00 (*0-944478-09-3*) Dock Pub Co.

***Changing Hands.** Nancy Esposito. (QRL Poetry Book Ser.: Vol. XXV). 20.00 (*0-614-06410-4*) Quarterly Rev.

Changing Hats: From Social Work Practice to Administration. Felice D. Perlmutter. LC 90-6436. 161p. 1990. 21.95 (*0-87101-184-0*) Natl Assn Soc Wkrs.

Changing Health & Changing Culture: The Yemenite Jews in Israel. Michael A. Weingarten. LC 91-38329. 208p. 1992. text ed. 49.95 (*0-275-94230-9*, C4230, Praeger Pubs) Greenwood.

Changing Health Care for an Aging Society: Planning for the Social Health Maintenance Organization. Walter N. Leutz et al. LC 84-40811. (University Health Policy Consortium Ser.). (Illus.). 272p. 1985. text ed. 37.95 (*0-669-10139-7*) Free Pr.

Changing Health Care Market. Employee Benefit Research Institute Staff. LC 87-619. (Orig.). 1987. 39.95 (*0-86643-055-5*); pap. 19.95 (*0-86643-053-9*) Empl Benefit Res Inst.

Changing Health Care Market. Ed. by Frank B. McArdle. LC 87-619. (EBRI-ERF Policy Forum Ser.). 292p. (Orig.). (C). 1987. text ed. 61.00 (*0-8191-6510-7*, Pub. by Employee Benefit Rsch Inst); pap. text ed. 31.00 (*0-8191-6511-5*, Empl Benefit Res Inst) U Pr of Amer.

Changing Health Care Team-Improving Effectiveness: Proceedings of the Hawaii Conference on Advances in Patient Care, 3rd Annual. Hawaii Conference on Advances in Patient Care. Ed. by S. R. Yarnall & Spring Zoog. 1976. 19.00 (*0-917054-11-3*) Med Communications.

Changing Hearts: Making Good Decisions about Relationships & Separating. Jill Burrett. 1993. pap. 7.95 (*1-86373-314-0*, Pub. by Allen & Unwin Aust Pty AT) IPG Chicago.

Changing Heaven. Jane Urquhart. 260p. 1993. 22.95 (*0-87923-895-X*) Godine.

Changing Hemispheric Trade Environment: Opportunities & Obstacles. Ed. by Mark B. Rosenberg. LC 91-32431. (Orig.). (C). 1991. pap. text ed. 11.95 (*1-879862-01-8*) FL Intl U Latin.

Changing History: Women, Power, & Politics. Geraldine Ferraro. LC 92-17797. 184p. 1993. 16.95 (*1-55921-077-X*); pap. 4.95 (*1-55921-078-8*) Moyer Bell.

Changing Horizon. B. N. Puri. 249p. (C). 1986. 125.00 (*81-85009-19-8*, Pub. by Print Hse II) St Mut.

Changing Horizons: Britain, 1914-1980. Stanley Thornes. (C). 1986. 90.00 (*0-85950-226-0*, Pub. by S Thornes Pubs UK) St Mut.

***Changing Horses in Midstream Without Drowning: 25 Stories about Men & Women Who Changed Setbacks into Comebacks.** Sandy Hogan. 220p. (Orig.). 1995. pap. 14.95 (*1-885221-04-5*) BookPartners.

Changing Hospital Environments for Children. Roslyn Lindheim et al. LC 75-188969. (Illus.). 218p. reprint ed. pap. 62.20 (*0-7837-1715-6*, 2057244) Bks Demand.

Changing Human Reproduction: Social Science Perspectives. Meg Stacey. (Illus.). 192p. (C). 1992. 55.00 (*0-8039-8653-X*); pap. 19.95 (*0-8039-8654-8*) Sage.

Changing Human Service Organizations: Politics & Practice. George A. Brager & Stephen M. Holloway. LC 77-87572. 1978. text ed. 24.95 (*0-02-904620-3*) Free Pr.

Changing Humanities. David H. Stevens. LC 70-90682. (Essay Index Reprint Ser.). 1977. 23.95 (*0-8369-1482-1*) Ayer.

Changing Humors of Portsmouth. J. Worth Estes & David M. Goodman. 1986. 22.95 (*0-88135-029-X*) Watson Pub Intl.

Changing Humors of Portsmouth: The Medical Biograpy of an American Town, 1623-1983. J. Worth Estes & David M. Goodman. (Illus.). 363p. 1987. 22.95 (*0-318-23486-6*) F A Countway.

Changing Idea of a Teachers' Union. Charles T. Kerchner & Douglas Mitchell. (Stanford Series on Education & Public Policy: Vol. 7). 280p. 1988. 70.00 (*1-85000-333-5*, Falmer Pr); pap. 34.00 (*1-85000-334-3*, Falmer Pr) Taylor & Francis.

Changing Ideals in Modern Architecture. Peter Collins. (Illus.). 1965. pap. 19.95 (*0-7735-0048-0*, Pub. by McGill CN) U of Toronto Pr.

Changing Ideas in Health Care. Ed. by David Seedhouse & Alan Cribb. 1990. pap. text ed. 39.95 (*0-471-92068-1*) Wiley.

Changing Ideas on Architecture in the Encyclopedia, 1750-1776. Kevin Harrington. LC 84-16165. (Architecture & Urban Change Ser.: No. 11). 279p. reprint ed. pap. 79.60 (*0-8357-1591-4*, 2070498) Bks Demand.

Changing Identities in Modern Southeast Asia. Ed. by David J. Banks. (World Anthropology Ser.). (Illus.). x, 358p. 1976. 35.40 (*90-279-7949-9*) Mouton.

***Changing Identities of Chinese Women: Rhetoric, Experience & Self-Perception in Twentieth-Century China.** Elisabeth Croll. LC 95-13687. 240p. (C). 1995. text ed. 59.95 (*1-85649-341-5*, Pub. by Zed Books UK); pap. 22.50 (*1-85649-342-3*, Pub. by Zed Books UK) Humanities.

Changing Identities of the Southeast Asian Chinese since World War II. Ed. by Jennifer Cushman & Wang Gungwu. 354p. (Orig.). 1988. pap. 43.50 (*962-209-207-1*, Pub. by Hong Kong Univ Pr HK) Coronet Bks.

Changing Image: American Perceptions of the Arab-Israeli Dilemma. 2nd ed. Richard Curtiss. 1986. 14.95 (*0-937165-00-X*) Am Educ Trust.

Changing Image of George Washington. Barbara J. Mitnick. (Illus.). 51p. (Orig.). 1989. pap. 5.00 (*0-9616415-7-6*) Fraunces Tavern.

Changing Image of the City: Planning for Downtown Omaha, 1945-1973. Janet R. Daly-Bednarek. LC 91-42758. (Illus.). xii, 304p. 1992. 40.00 (*0-8032-1692-0*) U of Nebr Pr.

Changing Images: Nineteenth-Century British Book Illustration. Stephen H. Cape. (Illus.). 62p. 1991. pap. 6.00 (*1-879598-00-0*) IN Univ Lilly Library.

An Asterisk (*) at the beginning of an entry indicates that the title is appearing in BIP for the first time.

An Asterisk (*) at the beginning of an entry indicates that the title is appearing in BIP for the first time.

1145

C

Changing Patterns of Finance in Higher Education. Gareth Williams. 192p. 1992. 95.00 (*0-335-15664-9*, Open Univ Pr); pap. 39.00 (*0-335-15663-0*, Open Univ Pr) Taylor & Francis.

Changing Patterns of Higher Education in Canada. Ed. by Robin S. Harris. LC 66-7877. 106p. reprint ed. pap. 30.30 (*0-685-15370-3*, 2026525) Bks Demand.

***Changing Patterns of Human Existence: Assumptions, Beliefs & Coping with the Stress of Change.** Louis E. LaGrand. 216p. 1988. pap. 25.95 (*0-398-06220-X*) C C Thomas.

Changing Patterns of Human Existence: Assumptions, Beliefs & Coping with the Stress of Change. Louis E. LaGrand. 216p. (C). 1988. 42.95x (*0-398-05464-9*) C C Thomas.

***Changing Patterns of Illiteracy in Morocco: Assessment Methods Compared.** Victor Lavy et al. LC 95-12294. (LSMS Working Paper Ser.: No. 115). 1995. write for info. (*0-8213-3192-2*) World Bank.

Changing Patterns of Infectious Disease. Lois M. Bergquist. LC 84-3957. 295p. reprint ed. pap. 84.10 (*0-7837-2692-9*, 2043070) Bks Demand.

Changing Patterns of International Cooperation in Space. Joan Johnson-Freese. 134p. 1990. 52.50 (*0-89464-022-4*); pap. 28.50 (*0-89464-042-9*) Krieger.

Changing Patterns of International Rivalry. Ed. by Etsuo Abe & Yoshitaka Suzuki. 1991. text ed. 54.50 (*0-86008-475-2*, Pub. by U of Tokyo JA) Col U Pr.

Changing Patterns of Law: The Courts & the Handicapped: An Original Anthology. Ed. by William R. Phillips & Janet Rosenberg. LC 79-6009. (Physically Handicapped in Society Ser.). 1980. lib. bdg. 44.95 (*0-405-13101-1*) Ayer.

Changing Patterns of Mental Health Care: A Case Study in the Development of Local Services. Jacie Powell & Robin Lovelock. 190p. 1992. 59.95 (*1-85628-333-X*, Pub. by Avebury Pub UK) Ashgate Pub Co.

Changing Patterns of Power: Social Regulation & Teacher Education Reform. Ed. by Thomas S. Popkewitz. (SUNY Series, Teacher Preparation & Development). 382p. (C). 1993. 59.50 (*0-7914-1447-7*); pap. 19.95 (*0-7914-1448-5*) State U NY Pr.

Changing Patterns of Scholarship & the Future of Research Libraries. Pennsylvania University Library Staff. LC 68-14910. (Essay Index Reprint Ser.). 1977. 19.95 (*0-8369-0782-5*) Ayer.

Changing Patterns of U. S. Industrial Activity & Comparative Advantage. John Mutti & Peter Morici. LC 83-62893. (Committee on Changing International Realities Ser.). 72p. 1983. pap. 8.00 (*0-89068-069-8*, NPA 201) Natl Planning.

Changing Pay Practices: New Developments in Employee Compensation. 323p. 1988. 55.00 (*1-55871-004-3*, BSP81) BNA.

Changing Peasantry of Eastern Europe. Joseph Obrebski. (Illus.). 100p. 1976. pap. 18.95x (*0-87073-741-4*) Transaction Pubs.

Changing Perceptions: The Evolution of Twentieth Century American Art. Ruth K. Beesch et al. (Illus.). 112p. (C). 1990. per. 15.00 (*0-9627541-0-2*) Weatherspoon.

Changing Perceptions: Writings on Gender with Development. Ed. by Tina Wallace & Candida March. 336p. (C). 1991. 115.00 (*0-85598-136-9*, Pub. by Oxfam Pubns UK); pap. 36.00 (*0-85598-137-7*, Pub. by Oxfam Pubns UK) St Mut.

Changing Perceptions of Aging & the Aged. Ed. by Dena Shenk & W. Andrew Achenbaum. LC 94-1071. 200p. 1994. 26.95 (*0-8261-8420-0*) Springer Pub.

Changing Perceptions of International Relations. Indian Council of Social Science Research Staff. 1988. 32.50 (*81-7062-039-2*, Pub. by Lancer II) S Asia.

***Changing Perceptions of Mann's Dr. Faustus: Criticism 1947-1992.** John Fetzer. (LCGER Ser.). 1995. 54.95 (*1-57113-070-5*) Camden Hse.

Changing Perceptions of Wealth among the Bambara (Lower Zaire) Norm Schrag. Ed. by D. Martin. 1990. pap. 6.00 (*0-941934-56-X*) Indiana Africa.

Changing Perspective: Attitudes Toward Creole Society in New Spain (1521-1610) Marvyn H. Bacigalupo. (Serie A: Monagrafias, LXXVI). 159p. (C). 1981. 45.00 (*0-7293-0072-2*, Pub. by Tamesis Bks Ltd UK) Boydell & Brewer.

***Changing Perspectives.** Gyeorgos C. Hatonn. (Phoenix Journals). 208p. 1994. pap. 6.00 (*1-56935-031-0*) Phoenix Source.

Changing Perspectives: Multi-Viewing Model. Frances K. Wiggins. (Illus.). 18p. (Orig.). 1986. pap. 4.00 (*0-942937-00-7*) Rivijon Pr.

Changing Perspectives in British Foreign Policy. Kenneth G. Younger. LC 76-15296. (Chatham House Essays: No. 7). 139p. 1976. reprint ed. text ed. 35.00 (*0-8371-8962-4*, YOCP, Greenwood Pr) Greenwood.

Changing Perspectives in Latin American Studies: Insights from Six Disciplines. Ed. by Christopher Mitchell. 256p. 1988. 32.50 (*0-8047-1493-2*) Stanford U Pr.

Changing Perspectives in Literature & the Visual Arts, 1650-1820. Murray Roston. (Illus.). 469p. 1993. text ed. 70.00 (*0-691-06795-3*); pap. text ed. 26.95 (*0-691-01539-2*) Princeton U Pr.

Changing Perspectives in Marketing Management: Sixth Annual Conference on Marketing Management, March 30, 1962. Conference on Marketing Management (6th: 1962: University of Michigan). Ed. by Martin R. Warshaw. (Michigan Business Papers: No. 37). 112p. reprint ed. pap. 32.00 (*0-317-28859-8*, 2022082) Bks Demand.

Changing Perspectives in Nutrition & Caries Research. 1979. 10.00 (*0-318-19099-0*) Am Dental Hygienists.

Changing Perspectives of Anthropology in India. Intro. by S. C. Tiwari. (Illus.). 361p. 1989. 59.00 (*1-55528-168-0*, Pub. by Today & Tomorrows P & P II) Scholarly Pubns.

Changing Perspectives of the Archaic on the Northwestern Plains & Rocky Mountains. Ed. by Julie E. Francis & Mary Lou Larson. LC 94-10585. 1994. pap. 28.95 (*0-929925-27-0*) Univ SD Pr.

Changing Perspectives on Menopause. Ed. by Ann M. Voda et al. (Illus.). 424p. 1982. text ed. 45.00 (*0-292-71069-0*) U of Tex Pr.

Changing Phases of Buddhist Thought: A Study in the Background of East-West Philosophy. Anil K. Sarkar. 1983. 16.00 (*0-8364-2544-8*, Pub. by S Asia Pubs II) S Asia.

Changing Physical Environment of the Hopi Indians of Arizona. John T. Hack. (Harvard University Peabody Museum of Archaeology & Ethnology Papers). 1972. reprint ed. 26.00 (*0-527-01288-2*) Periodicals Srv.

***Changing Physician Practice Patterns: Strategies for Success in a Capitated Health Care System.** Elaine Zablocki. 224p. 1995. ring bd. 175.00 (*0-8342-0688-9*) Aspen Pub.

Changing Pitches. Steve Kluger. LC 88-83330. 272p. 1989. pap. 7.95 (*1-55583-155-9*) Alyson Pubns.

Changing Places. David Lodge. 256p. (Orig.). 1979. pap. 10.00 (*0-14-017098-7*, Penguin Bks); mass mkt. 5.95 (*0-14-004656-9*, Penguin Bks) Viking Penguin.

Changing Places. Sheryl Prenzlau. (Kid Sisters Ser.: No. 8). (Illus.). 112p. (J). (gr. 3-5). 1994. pap. 6.95 (*1-56871-044-5*) Targum Pr.

Changing Places: A Kid's View of Shelter Living. Margie Chalofsky. 1992. pap. 4.95 (*0-87659-161-6*) Gryphon Hse.

***Changing Places: Australian Writers in Europe.** Ed. by Laurie Hergenhan & Irmtraud Petersson. 1994. pap. 16.95 (*0-7022-2615-7*, Pub. by Univ Queensland Pr AT) Intl Spec Bk.

Changing Places - Remaking Institutional Buildings. Schneeckloth et al. 1992. 30.00 (*1-877727-04-0*) White Pine.

***Changing Plastics.** 1995. 26.50 (*0-614-03492-2*, P157) BCC.

Changing Plastics Film Business. Business Communications Co., Inc. Staff. 168p. 1990. 2,450.00 (*0-89336-756-7*, P063U) BCC.

Changing Policies, Changing Teachers: New Directions for Schooling. Stephen Walker & Len Barton. 308p. 1987. 85.00 (*0-335-10292-1*, Open Univ Pr); pap. 32.00 (*0-335-10291-3*, Open Univ Pr) Taylor & Francis.

Changing Political Economies: Privatization in Post-Communist & Reforming Communist States. Ed. by Vedat Milor. LC 93-34548. (Emerging Global Issues Ser.). 238p. 1994. lib. bdg. 42.00 (*1-55587-405-3*) Lynne Rienner.

***Changing Political Economy of the Third World.** Ed. by Manochehr Dorraj. LC 94-31378. 490p. 1995. lib. bdg. 47.00 (*1-55587-554-8*); pap. text ed. 19.95 (*1-55587-577-7*) Lynne Rienner.

Changing Political Structure of Europe: Aspects of International Law. Ed. by Rene Lefeber. 298p. (C). 1991. lib. bdg. 100.00 (*0-7923-1379-8*) Kluwer Ac.

Changing Political Thought of John Adams. John R. Howe. LC 66-10272. 275p. reprint ed. pap. 78.40 (*0-8357-6550-4*, 2035914) Bks Demand.

Changing Politics of Federal Grants. Lawrence D. Brown et al. LC 84-45275. 169p. 1984. 31.95 (*0-8157-1168-9*); pap. 11.95 (*0-8157-1167-0*) Brookings.

Changing Politics of German Security. Stephen F. Szabo. LC 90-37864. 180p. 1990. text ed. 49.95 (*0-312-05228-6*) St Martin.

Changing Politics of Non-Governmental Organizations & African States. Ed. by Eve Sandberg. LC 93-30987. 216p. 1994. text ed. 55.00 (*0-275-93930-8*, Praeger Pubs) Greenwood.

Changing Politics of Sport. Ed. by Lincoln Allison. LC 92-26931. 1993. text ed. 69.95 (*0-7190-3670-4*, Pub. by Manchester Univ Pr UK); text ed. 24.95 (*0-7190-3671-2*, Pub. by Manchester Univ Pr UK) St Martin.

Changing Politics of the South. Ed. by William C. Havard. LC 75-181357. 781p. reprint ed. pap. 180.00 (*0-317-29874-7*, 2051880) Bks Demand.

Changing Population of Britain. Ed. by Heather Joshi. (Illus.). 256p. 1989. pap. text ed. 21.95 (*0-631-16515-0*) Blackwell Pubs.

Changing Population of Europe. Ed. by Daniel Noin & Robert Woods. LC 92-430003. 288p. 1993. 49.95 (*0-631-17635-7*); pap. 19.95 (*0-631-18972-6*) Blackwell Pubs.

Changing Population of States & Regions: Analysis & Projections, 1970-2000. George Masnick & John Pitkin. (Illus.). 250p. (Orig.). (C). 1982. pap. 12.00 (*0-943142-01-6*) St Local Inter.

Changing Position of Philanthropy in the American Economy. Frank G. Dickinson. (Occasional Papers: No. 110). 236p. 1970. reprint ed. 61.40 (*0-87014-209-7*) Natl Bur Econ Res.

Changing Positions. Ed. by Paul Needham & Jan Oldelsted. (Philosophical Studies, University of Uppsala: No.38). x, 278p. (Orig.). 1986. pap. 45.00x (*0-317-65665-1*) Coronet Bks.

Changing Practices in Faculty Evaluation: A Critical Assessment & Recommendations for Improvement. Peter Seldin. LC 83-49268. (Higher & Adult Education Ser.). 221p. 1984. 32.95x (*0-87589-601-4*) Jossey-Bass.

Changing Prairie: North American Grasslands. Anthony Joern & Kathleen Keeler. (Illus.). 304p. 1995. 65.00 (*0-19-507410-6*) OUP.

Changing Primary Practice. Ed. by Roben Alexander et al. 200p. 1989. 75.00 (*1-85000-632-6*, Falmer Pr); pap. 35.00 (*1-85000-633-4*, Falmer Pr) Taylor & Francis.

Changing Primary School, Vol. 16. Ed. by Roy Lowe. (Contemporary Analysis in Education Ser.). 200p. 1987. 65.00 (*1-85000-188-X*, Falmer Pr); pap. 33.00 (*1-85000-189-8*, Falmer Pr) Taylor & Francis.

***Changing Priorities of Codes & Standards: Failure, Fatigue & Creep; Proceedings of the Pressure Vessels & Piping Conference, Minneapolis, MN, 1994.** Ed. by K. R. Rao & J. A. Todd. LC 94-71665. (PVP Ser.: Vol. 286). 175p. 1994. pap. 50.00 (*0-7918-1359-2*) ASME.

Changing Problem Behavior in Schools. Alex Molnar & Barbara Lindquist. LC 88-31388. (Social & Behavioral Science - Education Ser.). 224p. 1989. 24.95 (*1-55542-134-2*) Jossey-Bass.

Changing Production Patterns with Social Equity. (Libros de la CEPAL Ser.: No. 25). 177p. 1990. 8.00 (*92-1-121155-7*, 90.II.G.6) UN.

Changing Professoriate, Educational Administration. Gmelch et al. (Orig.). (C). 1992. pap. text ed. 7.00 (*1-55996-155-4*) Univ Council Educ Admin.

Changing Profile of Pensions in America. Emily S. Andrews. LC 85-25296. 234p. 1985. 39.95 (*0-86643-043-1*); pap. 24.95 (*0-86643-038-5*) Empl Benefit Res Inst.

Changing Public Policies in Information Technology: Canada, the Netherlands, & Sweden. OECD Staff. 156p. 1992. pap. 19.00 (*92-64-03694-6*) OECD.

***Changing Public Role in a Rice Economy Approaching Self-Sufficiency: The Case of Bangladesh.** Francesco Goletti. LC 94-29466. (Research Report, International Food Policy Research Institute Ser.: No. 98). 1994. write for info. (*0-89629-101-4*) Intl Food Policy.

Changing Realities in Southern Africa: Implications for American Policy. Ed. by Michael Clough. LC 82-12124. (Research Ser.: No. 47). x, 320p. 1982. pap. 12.50 (*0-87725-147-9*) U of Cal IAS.

Changing Reality: Recent Soviet Photography. Leah Bendavid-Val. (Illus.). 132p. 1991. 34.95 (*0-912347-76-7*) Fulcrum Pub.

Changing Refrigeration Industry, No. GB-166: Implications for CFC's Insulation, Other Materials, Systems. 182p. 1993. 2,450.00 (*0-89336-982-9*) BCC.

Changing Rehabilitation World: Into the Twenty-First Century. Ed. by Dorothy Warms & Leslie D. Park. (Orig.). 1986. pap. 10.00 (*0-318-19619-0*) United CP.

Changing Relations: Newcomers & Established Residents in U. S. Communities : A Report to the ford Foundation by the National Board of the Changing Relations Project. National Board of the Changing Relations Project Staff & Robert L. Bach. LC 92-46770. 1993. (*0-916584-48-8*) Ford Found.

Changing Resource Problems of the Fourth World. Ed. by Ronald G. Ridker. LC 75-42978. (Resources for the Future Working Paper Ser.: Pd-1). (Illus.). 162p. 1976. pap. 8.00 (*0-8018-1847-8*) Johns Hopkins.

Changing Resource Problems of the Fourth World. Ed. by Ronald G. Ridker. LC 75-42978. (RFF Working Paper Ser.: No. PD-1). 161p. reprint ed. pap. 45.90 (*0-685-20406-5*, 2030213) Bks Demand.

***Changing River Channels.** Ed. by Angela Gurnell & Geoff Petts. LC 95-3062. 1995. 45.00 (*0-471-95727-5*) Wiley.

***Changing Role of Career Services.** Ed. by Jack R. Rayman. LC 85-644751. (New Directions for Student Services Ser.: No. 62). 114p. (Orig.). 1993. pap. 16.95 (*1-55542-699-9*) Jossey-Bass.

Changing Role of Environmental Stress Screening: Seminar Notes. LC 62-38584. (Illus.). 135p. (Orig.). 1980. pap. text ed. 10.00 (*0-915414-61-9*) Inst Environ Sci.

Changing Role of Government Research Laboratories. OECD Staff. 74p. (Orig.). 1989. pap. 15.00 (*92-64-13181-7*) OECD.

Changing Role of Mexican Labor in the U. S. Economy: Sectoral Perspectives. Ed. by Wayne A. Cornelius. Date not set. pap. write for info. (*0-685-21986-0*) UCSD Ctr US-Mex.

Changing Role of Professional Women in Research & Development. Herbert R. Northrup. LC 88-81113. (Manpower & Human Resources Studies: No. 11A). 78p. 1988. pap. 15.00 (*0-89546-072-6*) U PA Wharton Ctr Human Resc.

Changing Role of Public Libraries: Background Papers from the White House Conference. Comp. by Whitney N. Seymour, Jr. LC 80-17338. 298p. 1980. 29.50 (*0-8108-1333-5*) Scarecrow.

Changing Role of the Common Agricultural Policy: The Future of Farming in Europe. Ed. by John Marsh et al. 164p. 1992. text ed. 64.95 (*0-470-21882-7*) Halsted Pr.

***Changing Role of the Common Agricultural Policy: The Future of Farming in Europe.** Ed. by John Marsh. 1993. text ed. 74.95 (*0-471-94712-1*) Wiley.

Changing Role of the Educator: The Instructioneer. Don Stewart. LC 75-13470. (Instruction As a Humanizing Science Ser.: Vol. 1). 370p. 1975. 14.75 (*0-913448-05-2*); pap. 10.95 (*0-913448-06-0*) SLATE Servs.

Changing Role of the Market in National Economies. William U. Chandler. LC 86-50992. (Worldwatch Paper Ser.). 60p. (Orig.). 1986. pap. 5.00 (*0-916468-73-9*) Worldwatch Inst.

Changing Role of Volunteerism. Ed. by Susan Wyant & Phyllis Brooks. LC 93-9491. (Paper Ser.). 32p. 1993. pap. 10.00 (*1-881277-05-4*) United Hosp Fund.

Changing Role of Women in Bengal, 1849-1905. Meredith Borthwick. LC 83-43061. (Illus.). 450p. 1984. 65.00 (*0-691-05409-6*) Princeton U Pr.

Changing Roles for Local & Regional Government in Environmental Management: Extra Burdens or New Opportunities? xiv, 315p. 1984. lib. bdg. 90.00 (*90-6764-036-0*, Pub. by VSP NE) Coronet Bks.

Changing Roles in Information Distribution. Ed. by Ann M. Cunningham & Wendy Wicks. (Report Series, 1994: No. 1). 160p. (Orig.). (C). 1993. pap. 60.00 (*0-942308-43-3*) NFAIS.

Changing Roles in Social Work Practice. Ed. by Francine Sobey. LC 77-70327. 305p. 1977. pap. 12.95 (*0-87722-096-4*) Temple U Pr.

Changing Roles in Water Resources Management & Policy: Water Resources Education: A Lifetime of Learning. Ed. by Donald F. Potts & N. Earl Spangenberg. LC 93-71755. (Technical Publication Ser.: No. 93-2). (Illus.). 716p. (Orig.). 1993. pap. 55.00 (*1-882132-25-4*) Am Water Resources.

Changing Roles of Debt & Equity in Financing U. S. Capital Formation. Ed. by Benjamin M. Friedman. LC 81-16353. (National Bureau of Economic Research Project Report Ser.). viii, 116p. (C). 1987. reprint ed. pap. text ed. 12.00 (*0-226-26342-8*) U Ch Pr.

Changing Roles of Financial Management. Patrick J. Keating & Stephen F. Jablonsky. LC 90-81172. 214p. (Orig.). 1990. pap. 15.00 (*0-910586-78-0*, 082-90) Finan Exec.

Changing Roles of Occupational Therapists in the 1980s. Ed. by Florence S. Cromwell. LC 83-22818. (Occupational Therapy in Health Care Ser.: Vol. 1, No. 1). 99p. 1984. text ed. 29.95 (*0-86656-294-X*) Haworth Pr.

Changing Roles of Women in the Criminal Justice System: Offenders, Victims, & Professionals. 2nd rev. ed. Imogene Moyer. (Illus.). 367p. (C). 1992. pap. text ed. 19.95 (*0-88133-654-8*) Waveland Pr.

***Changing Roles of Women Within the Christian Church in Canada.** Ed. by Elizabeth G. Muir & Marilyn F. Whiteley. (Illus.). 376p. 1995. 60.00 (*0-8020-0669-8*) U of Toronto Pr.

***Changing Roles of Women Within the Christian Church in Canada.** Ed. by Elizabeth G. Muir & Marilyn F. Whiteley. (Illus.). 376p. 1995. pap. 24.95 (*0-8020-7623-8*) U of Toronto Pr.

Changing Room & Mother's Day Room see Home-Changing Room-Mother

Changing Rural Landscapes. Ed. by Ervin H. Zube & Margaret J. Zube. LC 76-46599. 160p. (C). 1977. 22.50 (*0-87023-228-2*); pap. 12.95x (*0-87023-235-5*) U of Mass Pr.

Changing Same: Studies in Fiction by Black Women. Deborah E. McDowell. LC 94-10663. Date not set. 29.95 (*0-253-33629-5*); pap. 12.95 (*0-253-20926-9*) Ind U Pr.

Changing Samoans: Behavior & Health in Transition. Ed. by Paul T. Baker et al. (Research Monographs on Human Population Biology). (Illus.). 494p. 1986. 55.00 (*0-19-504093-7*) OUP.

Changing Scene. Lucette R. Kenan. 253p. (C). 1982. pap. text ed. 14.75 (*0-15-505900-9*) HB Coll Pubs.

Changing Scene: Memoirs of a Civil Servant. Chandra B. Ias. (C). 1992. 18.00 (*81-7169-221-4*, Commonwealth) S Asia.

Changing Scene of Health Care & Technology. Ed. by R. G. Kensett. 220p. 1990. pap. 78.95 (*0-442-31287-3*) Chapman & Hall.

Changing Scenes in Natural Sciences, 1776-1976. Ed. by Clyde E. Goulden. (Special Publication: No. 12). 362p. 1977. lib. bdg. 9.00 (*0-910006-38-5*); pap. 7.00 (*0-910006-39-3*) Acad Nat Sci Phila.

Changing Scenes of the United States Defense: Essays on National Security. Joseph D. Lowe. LC 90-91734. (Illus.). xiv, 186p. 1982. reprint ed. pap. 36.00 (*0-9605506-5-8*) Lowe Pub.

Changing School Culture Through Staff Development: Yearbook of the Association for Supervision & Curriculum Development, 1990. Michael G. Fullan et al. LC 44-6213. (Illus.). 256p. (Orig.). 1990. pap. 19.95 (*0-87120-167-4*, 610-90009) Assn Supervision.

Changing School Reading Programs: Principles & Case Studies. Ed. by S. Jay Samuels & P. David Pearson. LC 87-22532. 238p. reprint ed. pap. 67.90 (*0-7837-4592-3*, 2044311) Bks Demand.

***Changing Schools.** Ed. by Erwin Flaxman & A. Harry Passow. 280p. 1995. 29.00 (*0-226-60167-6*) U Ch Pr.

Changing Schools: Open Corridors & Teaching Centers. Ed. by Ruth Dropkin. 1978. pap. 3.50 (*0-918374-02-2*) City Coll Wk.

Changing Schools: Progressive Education Theory & Practice, 1930-1960. Arthur Zilversmit. LC 92-21402. (Illus.). 272p. (C). 1993. pap. text ed. 14.95 (*0-226-98330-7*) U Ch Pr.

Changing Schools: Progressive Education Theory & Practice, 1930-1960. Arthur Zilversmit. LC 92-21402. (Illus.). 272p. (C). 1993. lib. bdg. 38.95 (*0-226-98329-3*) U Ch Pr.

Changing Schools: Pupil Perspectives on Transferring to a Comprehensive. Peter Woods & Lynda Measor. 192p. 1984. pap. 32.00 (*0-335-10599-8*, Open Univ Pr) Taylor & Francis.

Changing Schools: The Language Minority Student in the Eighties. Herbert Teitelbaum et al. LC 82-14602. 59p. reprint ed. pap. 25.00 (*0-8357-2746-7*, 2039858) Bks Demand.

Changing Schools from the Inside Out. Robert Larson. LC 91-68578. 170p. 1992. pap. text ed. 35.00 (*0-87762-901-3*) Technomic.

Changing Schools from Within: Creating Communities of Inquiry. Gordon Wells et al. LC 93-33327. 286p. (C). 1994. pap. text ed. 22.00 (*0-435-08811-4*) Heinemann.

Changing Schools Through the Arts: How to Build on the Power of an Idea. Jane Remer. LC 90-1293. 250p. 1990. pap. 14.95 (*0-915400-86-3*, 2150, ACA Bks) Am Council Arts.

Changing Scottish Landscape, 1500-1800. Ian D. Whyte & Kathleen Whyte. (Illus.). 288p. 1991. 110.00 (*0-415-02992-9*, A5757) Routledge.

Changing Seasons. Rose Greydanus. LC 82-19959. (Now I Know Ser.). (Illus.). 32p. (J). (gr. k-2). 1983. lib. bdg. 11.59 (*0-89375-902-3*); pap. 2.95 (*0-8167-1478-9*) Troll Assocs.

C

An Asterisk (*) at the beginning of an entry indicates that the title is appearing in BIP for the first time.

***Changing Seasons.** Henry Pluckrose. LC 93-44700. (Walkabout Ser.). 32p. (J). (ps-3). 1994. lib. bdg. 12.00 (*0-614-04457-X*) Childrens.

***Changing Seasons.** Henry Pluckrose. LC 93-44700. (Walkabout Ser.). 32p. (J). (ps-3). 1994. pap. 4.95 (*0-516-40116-5*) Childrens.

Changing Seasons: Quilt Patterns from Japan. Patchwork Quilt Tsushin Staff & Jill Liddell. LC 92-52873. (Illus.). 160p. 1992. 35.00 (*0-525-93438-3*, Dutton Studio); pap. 25.00 (*0-525-48601-1*, Dutton Studio) Studio Bks.

***Changing Seasons-Humor in Literature.** Ingrid Daemmrich. 236p. 1995. per., pap. text ed. 36.95 (*0-7872-0604-0*) Kendall-Hunt.

Changing Seasons Macrobiotic Cookbook. Aveline Kushi & Wendy Esko. LC 84-21713. 228p. (Orig.). 1985. pap. 12. 95 (*0-89529-232-7*) Avery Pub.

Changing Seasons of Humor in Literature. Ingrid G. Daemmrich. 212p. 1992. per. 34.95 (*0-8403-7423-2*) Kendall-Hunt.

Changing Seasons Text & Prints. (Illus.). 16p. 1992. pap. text ed. 52.50 (*0-935493-65-4*) Modern Learn Pr.

Changing Seattle's Middle Schools. 36p. 1990. 5.00 (*0-317-05353-1*) NASBE.

Changing Secondary School. Ed. by Roy Lowe. 240p. 1989. 65.00 (*1-85000-555-9*, Falmer Pr); pap. 33.00 (*1-85000-556-7*, Falmer Pr) Taylor & Francis.

Changing Services for Changing Clients. National Association of Social Workers Staff. LC 69-18878. 139p. reprint ed. pap. 39.70 (*0-317-55467-0*, 2052205) Bks Demand.

Changing Services for People with Learning Disabilities. R. Farmer et al. LC 92-37599. 1992. 97.50 (*1-56593-059-2*) Singular Publishing.

Changing Sex Differential in Mortality. Robert D. Retherford. LC 74-19808. (Studies in Demography & Urban Population). (Illus.). 139p. 1975. text ed. 45.00 (*0-8371-7848-7*, RSX/, Greenwood Pr) Greenwood.

Changing Shape. Paul Bennett. LC 93-49798. (Nature's Secrets Ser.). 32p. (J). (gr. 1-5). 1994. 14.95 (*1-56847-205-6*) Thomson Lrning.

Changing Shape of Government in the Asia-Pacific Region. Ed. by John W. Langford & K. Lorne Brownsey. 326p. 1988. pap. text ed. 22.00 (*0-88645-060-8*, Pub. by Inst SE Asian Studies SI) Ashgate Pub Co.

Changing Shape of Retail Banking: Responding to Customer Needs. (Illus.). 60p. (Orig.). (C). 1993. pap. text ed. 40. 00 (*1-56806-295-8*) Diane Pub.

Changing Shape of World Mission. Bryant L. Myers. 52p. 1993. pap. write for info. (*0-912552-83-2*) MARC.

***Changing Shapes with Matrices.** Donald Cohen. (Illus.). (Orig.). 1995. student ed. pap. 9.95 (*0-9621674-3-6*) D Cohen Mathman.

Changing Sky. Steven Forrest. (Illus.). 328p. (Orig.). 1989. reprint ed. pap. 12.95 (*0-935127-05-4*) ACS Pubns.

Changing Social Geography of Canadian Cities. Ed. by Larry S. Bourne & David F. Ley. (Canadian Association of Geographers Series in Canadian Geography). 496p. 1993. 65.00 (*0-7735-0926-7*, Pub. by McGill CN); pap. 29.95 (*0-7735-0972-0*, Pub. by McGill CN) U of Toronto Pr.

Changing Social Science: Critical Theory & Other Critical Perspectives. Ed. by Daniel R. Sabia & Jerald Wallulis. LC 82-10454. 220p. (C). 1983. 64.50 (*0-87395-679-6*); pap. 21.95 (*0-87395-680-X*) State U NY Pr.

Changing Social Security in Latin America: Toward Alleviating the Social Costs of Economic Reform. Carmelo Mesa-Lago. LC 93-38662. 220p. 1994. lib. bdg. 42.00 (*1-55587-486-X*) Lynne Rienner.

***Changing Social Stratification in Rural Bangladesh.** A. F. Ali. (C). 1993. 22.00x (*81-7169-267-2*, Commonwealth) S Asia.

Changing Social Structure. Ed. by Chris Hamnett et al. (Restructuring Britain Ser.). 290p. (C). 1989. text ed. 45. 00 (*0-8039-8199-6*); pap. text ed. 16.95 (*0-8039-8200-3*) Sage.

Changing Social Work & Welfare. Ed. by Pam Carter et al. 240p. 1992. 95.00 (*0-335-15757-2*, Open Univ Pr); pap. 36.00 (*0-335-15756-4*, Open Univ Pr) Taylor & Francis.

Changing Song: The Marxist Manifestos of Nakano Shigeharu. Miriam Silverberg. 265p. 1990. pap. text ed. 35.00 (*0-691-06816-X*) Princeton U Pr.

Changing South. Ed. by Raymond W. Mack. LC 72-91467. 115p. 1970. 29.95x (*0-87855-060-7*); pap. 16.95x (*0-87855-557-9*) Transaction Pubs.

Changing South Africa: Political Considerations. Sam C. Nolutshungu. 219p. 1982. 19.50 (*0-8419-0807-9*, Africana) Holmes & Meier.

Changing Soviet Navy. Barry M. Blechman. LC 73-2881. (Studies in Defense Policy). 51p. 1973. pap. 7.95 (*0-8157-0995-1*) Brookings.

Changing Soviet System: Mono-Organisational Socialism from Its Origins to Gorbachev's Restructuring. T. H. Rigby. 288p. 1990. 63.95 (*1-85278-304-4*, Pub. by E Elgar Pub UK) Ashgate Pub Co.

Changing Soviet Union in the New Europe: Towards a New Europe. Jyrki Livonen. 256p. 1991. text ed. 63.95 (*1-85278-532-2*, Pub. by E Elgar Pub UK) Ashgate Pub Co.

Changing Special Education Now. rev. ed. Wilfred K. Brennan. 192p. 1987. reprint ed. pap. 27.00 (*0-335-10277-8*, Open Univ Pr) Taylor & Francis.

Changing States: Transformation in Modern Irish Writing. Robert Welch. LC 92-24801. 288p. 1993. 59.95 (*0-415-08666-3*, B0136, Routledge NY) Routledge.

Changing Status & Adjustment of Women. Rita Sood. ix, 159p. 1991. 13.00 (*0-685-62653-9*, Pub. by Manak Pubns Pvt Ltd) Nataraj Bks.

***Changing Status & Role of Women in Indian Society.** Ed. by C. Chakrapani & S. Vijaya Kumar. 361p. (C). 1994. 120.00x (*81-85880-27-1*, Pub. by Print Hse II) St Mut.

Changing Status of Depressed Castes in Contemporary India. S. N. Chaudhary. (C). 1988. 23.50 (*81-7035-042-5*) S Asia.

Changing Status of German Reunification in Western Diplomacy, 1955-1966. Charles R. Planck. LC 67-22894. (Washington Center of Foreign Policy Research. Studies in International Affairs: No. 4). 73p. reprint ed. pap. 25.00 (*0-317-28471-1*, 2020742) Bks Demand.

Changing Sterilization Picture. Business Communications Co., Inc. Staff. 245p. 1988. pap. 2,450.00 (*0-89336-595-5*, GA-056) BCC.

Changing Structure of American Banking: Competition, Concentration, & Performance. Peter S. Rose. LC 86-18843. (Columbia Studies in Business, Government & Society). 392p. 1987. text ed. 64.00 (*0-231-05980-9*) Col U Pr.

Changing Structure of American Industry & Energy Use Patterns: Issues, Scenarios, & Forecasting Models. John Broehl & Ahmad Faruqui. LC 86-17488. 512p. 1987. 44.50 (*0-935470-33-6*) Battelle.

Changing Structure of Comparative Advantage in American Manufacturing. Keith E. Maskus. Ed. by Fred Bateman. LC 83-9209. (Research in Business Economics & Public Policy Ser.: No. 4). 110p. reprint ed. 31.40 (*0-8357-1443-8*, 2070405) Bks Demand.

Changing Structure of Europe: Economic, Social, & Political Trends. Robert H. Beck et al. LC 73-110659. 296p. reprint ed. pap. 84.40 (*0-317-29403-2*, 2055840) Bks Demand.

Changing Structure of Infrastructure Finance. Ed. by James C. Nicholas. 98p. 1985. 15.00 (*0-317-01542-7*) Fla Atlantic.

Changing Structure of Infrastructure Finance. Ed. by James C. Nicholas. (Monograph: No. 85-5). (Illus.). 98p. 1985. pap. text ed. 5.25 (*1-55844-092-5*) Lincoln Inst Land.

***Changing Structure of Mexico: Political, Social & Economic Prospects.** Ed. by Laura Randall. (Columbia University Seminars Ser.). 350p. 1995. 69.95 (*1-56324-641-4*); pap. 24.95 (*1-56324-642-2*) M E Sharpe.

Changing Structure of the American Economy: Lessons from the Steel Industry. Zoltan J. Acs. LC 84-15930. 268p. 1984. text ed. 49.95 (*0-275-91112-8*, C1112, Praeger Pubs) Greenwood.

Changing Structure of the City: What Happened to the Urban Crisis. Ed. by Gary A. Tobin. LC 78-27602. (Urban Affairs Annual Reviews Ser.: No. 16). (Illus.). 320p. reprint ed. pap. 91.20 (*0-8357-8401-0*, 2034675) Bks Demand.

***Changing Structure of the Electric Power Industry: 1970-1991.** 1995. lib. bdg. 251.75 (*0-8490-7413-4*) Gordon Pr.

Changing Structure of the U. S. Coal Industry: An Update. (Illus.). 56p. (Orig.). (C). 1994. pap. text ed. 45.00 (*0-7881-0284-2*) Diane Pub.

Changing Structure of the Western Economy. Douglas B. Copland. LC 65-9230. (Beatty Memorial Lectures). 96p. reprint ed. pap. 27.40 (*0-317-20720-2*, 2023827) Bks Demand.

***Changing Structures of World Oil Markets & OPEC's Financial Needs.** Cyrus H. Tahmassebi. 20p. 1995. pap. 10.00 (*0-918714-46-X*) Intl Res Ctr Energy.

Changing Styles In Fashion: Who, What, Why. Maggie P. Murray. (Illus.). 280p. (C). 1988. text ed. 25.00 (*0-87005-585-2*) Fairchild.

Changing Subjects: The Making of Feminist Literary Criticism. Ed. by Coppelia Kahn & Gayle Greene. LC 92-12699. 304p. 1993. 49.95 (*0-415-08685-X*, A9532, Routledge NY); pap. 15.95 (*0-415-08686-8*, A9536, Routledge NY) Routledge.

Changing Supervisor Behavior. Goldstein. (C). 1974. pap. 25.95 (*0-205-14341-5*, H4341) Allyn.

Changing Supervisor Behavior. Arnold P. Goldstein & Melvin Sorcher. LC 73-10059. 1975. text ed. 37.00 (*0-08-017742-5*, Pergamon Pr); pap. text ed. 22.95 (*0-08-017769-7*, Pergamon Pr) Elsevier.

***Changing Supreme Court.** Edmund Lindop. LC 95-13842. (Democracy in Action Ser.). (Illus.). (YA). (gr. 7-12). 1995. lib. bdg. 15.33 (*0-531-11224-1*) Watts.

Changing System of Scholarly Communication. Association of Research Libraries Staff. 7p. 1986. pap. 1.00 (*0-918006-12-0*) ARL.

***Changing Systems for Children & Families.** Linda McCart. Ed. by Karen Glass. 60p. (Orig.). 1994. pap. text ed. 15.00 (*1-55877-224-3*) Natl Governor.

Changing Teachers, Changing Times. Andy Hargreaves. (Teacher Development Ser.). (Illus.). 206p. 1993. 65.00 (*0-304-32257-1*) Cassell.

Changing Teachers, Changing Times: Teachers' Work & Culture in the Post-Modern Age. Andy Hargreaves. LC 93-38007. (Professional Development & Practice Ser.). 256p. (C). 1993. pap. text ed. 19.95 (*0-8077-3340-7*) Tchrs Coll.

Changing Teaching, Changing Schools: Bringing Early Childhood Practice into Public Education: Case Studies from Kindergarten. Frances O. Rust. LC 93-17378. (Early Childhood Education Ser.). 144p. (C). 1993. text ed. 32.00 (*0-8077-3286-9*); pap. text ed. 15.95 (*0-8077-3285-0*) Tchrs Coll.

Changing Teaching for Better Learning. Welko Tomic & Peter Van der Sijde. 124p. 1989. pap. 23.95 (*90-265-1019-5*, Pub. by Swets Pub Serv NE) Taylor & Francis.

Changing Technology: Opportunity & Challenge. Ed. by Alphonse F. Trezza. (Professional Librarian Ser.). 136p. 1988. pap. 22.50 (*0-8161-1900-7*, Hall Reference) Macmillan.

Changing Technology & Education for Librarianship & Information Science. B. Stuart-Stubbs. LC 84-21330. (Foundations in Library & Information Science: Vol. 20). 188p. 1985. 73.25 (*0-89232-515-1*) Jai Pr.

Changing Technology & Employment in Agriculture. John A. Hopkins. LC 73-174470. (FDR & the Era of the New Deal Ser.). 242p. 1973. reprint ed. lib. bdg. 29.50 (*0-306-70380-7*) Da Capo.

Changing Television Audience in America. Robert T. Bower. LC 85-6674. 160p. 1985. text ed. 35.00 (*0-231-06114-5*) Col U Pr.

Changing the Blue: IBM's Emerging S-390, Communication, & Software Strategies. 1990. 97.00 (*0-929286-13-8*) DataTrends Pubns.

Changing the Boundaries: Women-Centered Perspectives on Population & the Environment. Janice Jiggins. LC 94-21949. 350p. 1994. text ed. 45.00 (*1-55963-259-3*); pap. text ed. 22.00 (*1-55963-260-7*) Island Pr.

***Changing the Business: A Practical Guide to Performance Improvement.** Roger N. Swaris. (C). 1994. 150.00x (*0-7478-1822-3*, Pub. by S Thornes Pubs UK) St Mut.

Changing the Code: Police Detention under the Revised Codes of Practice. D. Bown et al. (Home Office Research Study Ser.: No. 129). 123p. 1993. pap. 25.00 (*0-11-341052-2*, HM10522, Pub. by HMSO UK) UNIPUB.

Changing the Colonial Climate. Rexford G. Tugwell. LC 70-111734. (American Imperialism: Viewpoints of United States Foreign Policy, 1898-1941 Ser.). 1977. reprint ed. 25.95 (*0-405-02052-X*) Ayer.

Changing the Corporate Culture to Support Work & Family Programs. Katharine Esty & Jane Bermont. (Special Report Series on Work & Family: No. 42). 32p. 1991. 35.00 (*1-55871-223-2*, BSP217) BNA.

Changing the Course of Marketing: Alternative Paradigms for Widening Marketing Theory. Ed. by Nikhilesh Dholakia & Johnan Arndt. (Research in Marketing Ser.: Suppl. 2). 331p. 1985. 73.25 (*0-89232-627-1*) Jai Pr.

Changing the Curriculum. Lewis B. Mayhew & Patrick J. Ford. LC 79-159265. (Jossey-Bass Higher Education Ser.). 206p. reprint ed. pap. 58.80 (*0-8357-9302-8*, 2017237) Bks Demand.

Changing the Economic System in Russia. Ed. by Anders Aslund & Richard Layard. LC 92-43673. 300p. 1993. text ed. 39.95 (*0-312-09581-3*) St Martin.

Changing the Educational Landscape: Philosophy, Women, & Curriculum. Jane R. Martin. 256p. 1994. 49.95 (*0-415-90794-2*, B0660, Routledge NY); pap. 15.95 (*0-415-90795-0*, B0664, Routledge NY) Routledge.

Changing the Essence: The Art of Creating & Leading Fundamental Change in Organizations. Richard Beckhard & Wendy Pritchard. LC 91-37204. (Management Ser.). 125p. 1992. 24.00 (*1-55542-412-0*) Jossey-Bass.

***Changing the Face of Nationalism: The Case of Bangladesh.** Muhammad Ghulamkabir. (C). 1994. 22.50 (*81-7003-187-7*, Pub. by S Asia Pubs II) S Asia.

Changing the Face of the Earth: The Human Impact. I. G. Simmons. (Illus.). 350p. 1989. text ed. 69.95 (*0-631-14049-2*); pap. text ed. 24.95 (*0-631-16351-4*) Blackwell Pubs.

Changing the Game: The New Way to Sell. Larry Wilson & Hersch Wilson. 286p. 1988. pap. 11.00 (*0-671-67135-9*, Fireside) S&S Trade.

Changing the Global Environment: Perspectives on Human Involvement. Ed. by Daniel B. Botkin et al. 459p. 1989. text ed. 85.00 (*0-12-118730-6*); pap. text ed. 49.00 (*0-12-118731-4*) Acad Pr.

Changing the Guard: Canada's Defense in Transition. Peter Langille. 224p. 1990. 32.50 (*0-8020-5870-1*) U of Toronto Pr.

Changing the Guard: How Bill Clinton Beat an Unbeatable President & a Billionaire Populist to Capture the White House. Peter Goldman. 1993. 25.00 (*0-8129-2191-7*, Times Bks) Random.

Changing the Guard in Brussels: An Insider's View of the EC Presidency. Guy De Bassompierre. LC 88-23580. (Washington Papers: No. 135). 179p. 1988. text ed. 49. 95 (*0-275-93186-2*, C3186, Praeger Pubs); pap. text ed. 13.95 (*0-275-93187-0*, B3187, Praeger Pubs) Greenwood.

***Changing the History of Africa: Angola & Namibia.** Ed. by David Deutschmann. (Illus.). 177p. 1993. pap. 12.95 (*1-875284-00-1*, Pub. by Ocean Pr AT) Talman.

Changing the Landscape: Ending the Violence, Achieving Equality. Canadian Panel on Violence Against Women Staff. 452p. (Orig.). 1993. pap. 41.60x (*0-660-15144-8*, Pub. by Canada Commun Grp CN) Accents Pubns.

Changing the Lawbreaker: The Treatment of Delinquents & Criminals. Don C. Gibbons. LC 81-65008. 330p. 1981. reprint ed. pap. text ed. 16.00 (*0-86598-017-9*, Allanheld Osmun) Rowman.

Changing the Name to Ochester. Ed Ochester. LC 87-71455. (Poetry Ser.). 1988. 16.95 (*0-88748-068-3*); pap. 9.95 (*0-88748-069-1*) Carnegie-Mellon.

***Changing the Odds: Cancer Prevention Through Personal Choice & Public Policy.** R. Grant Sheen. LC 94-25291. 1995. 35.00 (*0-8160-3167-3*) Facts on File.

Changing the Past. Laurie Taylor. LC 81-83881. (Minnesota Voices Project Ser.: No. 6). (Illus.). 72p. 1981. pap. 3.00 (*0-89823-029-2*) New Rivers Pr.

***Changing the Patterns Vol. II: Participants Manual - From the "A Path to Responsibility" Treatment Program.** G. Richard Kishur. 168p. (Orig.). 1994. student ed, pap. text ed. 14.95 (*1-885473-02-8*) Wood NBarnes.

Changing the Practice of Teacher Education. 1991. 30.00 (*0-89333-080-9*) AACTE.

Changing the River. Alex Kuo. 96p. (Orig.). 1986. pap. 8.95 (*0-918408-24-5*) Reed & Cannon.

Changing the Rules. Frank Bowe. 1986. 10.95 (*0-932666-31-0*) T J Pubs.

Changing the Rules. Gina Wilkins. (Temptation Ser.: No. 299). 1990. pap. 2.65 (*0-373-25399-0*) Harlequin Bks.

Changing the Rules: A Client-Directed Approach to Therapy. Barry L. Duncan et al. LC 92-1550. (Guilford Family Therapy Ser.). 284p. 1992. lib. bdg. 32.00 (*0-89862-108-9*) Guilford Pr.

Changing the Rules: President Ronald Reagan's Strategic Defense Initiative Decision. Frederick Donovan & James E. Goodby. (Pew Case Studies in International Affairs). 50p. (C). 1991. pap. text ed. 2.50 (*1-56927-320-0*) Geo U Inst Dplmcy.

***Changing the Rules: Psychology in the Netherlands, 1900-1985.** Trudy Dehue. (Cambridge Studies in the History of Psychology). (Illus.). 228p. (C). 1995. 49.95 (*0-521-47522-8*) Cambridge U Pr.

Changing the Rules: Technological Change, International Competition, & Regulation in Communications. Ed. by Robert W. Crandall & Kenneth Flamm. 450p. 1989. 39. 95 (*0-8157-1596-X*); pap. 18.95 (*0-8157-1595-1*) Brookings.

Changing the School Culture. Per Dalin. Ed. by David Hopkins & David Reynolds. (School Development Ser.). (Illus.). 208p. 1993. text ed. 65.00 (*0-304-32745-X*); pap. text ed. 24.95 (*0-304-32737-9*) Cassell.

Changing the Seen & Shaping the Unseen. Charles Capps. 1981. pap. 2.95 (*0-89274-220-8*, HH-220) Harrison Hse.

Changing the Self: Philosophies, Techniques, & Experiences. Ed. by Thomas M. Brinthaupt & Richard P. Lipka. (SUNY Series, Studying the Self). 373p. 1994. 64.50 (*0-7914-1867-7*); pap. 21.95 (*0-7914-1868-5*) State U NY Pr.

Changing the Signs: The Fifteenth-Century Breakthrough. Albert S. Cook. LC 84-17280. 189p. reprint ed. pap. 53. 90 (*0-7837-1833-0*, 2042033) Bks Demand.

Changing the Situs of a Trust. Robert A. Hendrickson & Neal R. Silverman. 400p. 1986. reprint ed. ring bd. 85. 00 (*0-318-21429-6*, 00573) NY Law Pub.

***Changing the Status of Women in India.** 3rd ed. Kiran Devendra. (C). 1994. text ed. 28.50 (*0-7069-7618-5*, Pub. by Vikas II) S Asia.

Changing the Story: Feminist Fiction & the Tradition. Gayle Greene. LC 91-6849. 320p. 1992. 45.00 (*0-253-32606-0*); pap. 17.50 (*0-253-20672-3*, MB-672) Ind U Pr.

Changing the Subject. Carole Satyamurti. 72p. 1991. pap. 9.95 (*0-19-282738-3*) OUP.

Changing the Subject: Paintings & Prints 1992-94. Bell Hooks. (Illus.). 16p. 1994. pap. 10.00 (*1-883967-01-5*) Art in General.

***Changing the Subject: Women in Higher Education.** Ed. by Jocey Quinn et al. 240p. 1994. 75.00x (*0-7484-0281-0*); pap. 27.00x (*0-7484-0282-9*) Taylor & Francis.

Changing the Subject: Women's Discourses & Feminist Theology. Mary M. Fulkerson. LC 93-31062. 1994. 18. 00 (*0-8006-2747-4*, 1-2747) Augsburg Fortress.

Changing the System. Lawrence D. Longley. (New Directions in Comparative Politics Ser.). 192p. 1929. text ed. 38.50 (*0-8133-1506-9*) Westview.

Changing the System. Lawrence D. Longley. (New Directions in Comparative Politics Ser.). 192p. (C). 1929. pap. text ed. 16.95 (*0-8133-1507-7*) Westview.

Changing the System: The Twenty-Five Year Crusade of the Institute of Judicial Administration for Equal Justice in American Courts, an Historical Perspective. Fannie J. Klein. 128p. 1977. 1.00 (*0-318-14431-X*) IJA NYU.

Changing the View: Student - Parent Conferences. Austin. LC 94-21497. 122p. 1994. pap. text ed. 14.50 (*0-435-08818-1*) Heinemann.

Changing the Way America Thinks. Bob Slosser. 1989. write for info. (*0-8499-0657-1*) Word Inc.

***Changing the Way We Change: Gaining Control of Major Manufacturing Operational Change.** Jeannenne LaMarsh. (Engineering Process Improvement). 224p. 1995. 26.95 (*0-201-63364-7*) Addison-Wesley.

Changing the Way We Prepare Educational Leaders: The Danforth Experience. Mike M. Milstein. 264p. 1993. 43.95 (*0-8039-6077-8*); pap. 21.95 (*0-8039-6078-6*) Corwin Pr.

Changing the World. Deena Borchers. (Active Bible Curriculum Ser.). (Illus.). 48p. 1993. pap. 9.99 (*1-55945-236-6*) Group Pub.

Changing the World: A Framework for the Study of Creativity. David H. Feldman et al. LC 93-11868. 200p. 1994. text ed. 55.00 (*0-275-94769-6*, Praeger Pubs); pap. text ed. 16.95 (*0-275-94775-0*, Praeger Pubs) Greenwood.

Changing the World: An Agenda for the Churches. Vincent Cosmao. LC 84-5153. 127p. (Orig.). reprint ed. pap. 36. 20 (*0-8357-8548-3*, 2034862) Bks Demand.

Changing the World - Amy's Way. Sandra M. Gerhardt. 128p. 1994. 12.95 (*0-9637647-6-4*) Ardara Hse.

Changing the World Within: The Dynamics of Personal & Spiritual Growth. Joseph A. Grassi. 128p. (Orig.). 1986. pap. 5.95 (*0-8091-2755-5*) Paulist Pr.

***Changing Theories & Practices of Discipline.** Roger Slee. LC 94-36903. 190p. 1994. 75.00 (*0-7507-0296-6*, Falmer Pr); pap. 24.95 (*0-7507-0297-4*, Falmer Pr) Taylor & Francis.

Changing Threat Perceptions & Military Doctrines. Ed. by Laszlo Valki. LC 91-25355. 256p. 1992. text ed. 69.95 (*0-312-06837-9*) St Martin.

Changing Thymes: New Traditions in Texas Cooking. LC 93-74405. 1995. spiral bd. 17.95 (*0-9607152-2-3*) Austin Junior.

Changing Tide. Sylvia Thorpe. 1977. pap. 1.75 (*0-449-23418-5*, Crest) Fawcett.

Changing Tide. large type ed. Iris Bromige. 304p. 1988. 15. 95 (*0-7089-1828-X*) Ulverscroft.

C

An Asterisk (*) at the beginning of an entry indicates that the title is appearing in BIP for the first time.

***Changing Tides: Twilight & Dawn in the Spanish Sea, 1763-1803.** Robert S. Weddle. LC 95-11476. (Centennial Series of the Association of Former Students: No. 58). (Illus.). 384p. (C). 1995. 49.50x (*0-89096-661-3*) Tex A&M Univ Pr.

Changing Times. Paul Fridlund. (Illus.). 219p. 19.95 (*0-87770-404-X*) Ye Galleon.

Changing Times: A View from Cache Valley, 1890-1915. Charles S. Peterson. LC 93-80099. (Faculty Honor Lecture Ser.: No. 60). 32p. reprint ed. pap. 25.00 (*0-7837-6210-0*, 2045934) Bks Demand.

Changing Times: Toward an Integrated Approach to Reading. Lewis Levine & Lucinda S. Hughey. (Illus.). 300p. (C). 1985. pap. text ed. 20.50 (*0-13-128182-8*) P-H.

Changing Times - Changing Styles: The Ruth Stoever Fleming Collection of Southern California Art. Ed. by John McGinnis. LC 85-5011. (Illus.). 80p. 1985. pap. 10.00 (*0-9614891-1-1*) Newport Mesa Sch.

Changing Times in Teacher Education: Restructuring or Reconceptualising? Ed. by Marvin F. Wideen & Peter P. Grimmett. 176p. 1994. 75.00 (*0-7507-0182-X*, Falmer Pr); pap. 27.50 (*0-7507-0183-8*, Falmer Pr) Taylor & Francis.

Changing Times in Trial Courts: Caseflow Management & Delay Reduction in Urban Trial Courts. 245p. 1989. pap. 8.95 (*0-89656-087-2*, R-105) Natl Ctr St Courts.

Changing to a Developmentally Appropriate Curriculum - Successfully: 4 Case Studies. Ed. by James K. Uphoff. (Illus.). 80p. (Orig.). 1989. teacher ed, pap. 16.95 (*0-935493-19-0*, RRB 444) Programs Educ.

Changing to National Health Care: Ethical & Policy Issues. Ed. by Robert P. Huefner & Margaret P. Battin. LC 91-40041. (Ethics in a Changing World Ser.: Vol. 4). 384p. (C). 1992. 24.95 (*0-87480-389-6*) U of Utah Pr.

Changing Tools. M. Feher. 256p. Date not set. 35.00 (*963-05-6728-8*, Pub. by A K HU) Intl Spec Bk.

Changing Trade Patterns Manufactured Goods: An Econometric Investigation. Bela A. Balassa & L. Bauwens. (Contributions to Economic Analysis Ser.: No. 176). 176p. 1988. 77.00 (*0-444-70492-2*, North Holland) Elsevier.

Changing Trends: Content & Style. Text by Francis Colpitt et al. LC 82-82924. (Illus.). 84p. (Orig.). 1982. pap. 10.00 (*0-911291-00-8*) Fellows Cont Art.

Changing Trends in Antarctic Research. Ed. by Aant Elzinga. LC 93-10277. (Environment & Assessment Ser.: Vol. 3). 1993. lib. bdg. 55.50 (*0-7923-2267-3*) Kluwer Ac.

Changing Trends in Coronary Heart Disease: Journal: Cardiology, Vol. 72, Nos. 1 & 2. Ed. by K. Pyorala et al. (Illus.). 104p. 1985. pap. 56.00 (*3-8055-4015-9*) S Karger.

***Changing Trends in Structural Natural Products Chemistry: Selected Papers of Koji Nakanishi.** Koji Nakanishi. (Series on 20th Century Chemistry). 600p. 1995. text ed. 109.00 (*981-02-1827-3*) World Scientific Pub.

Changing Tropical Forests: Historical Perspectives on Today's Challenges in Central & South America. Ed. by Harold K. Steen & Richard P. Tucker. 311p. 1992. lib. bdg. 31.95 (*0-8223-1236-0*); pap. text ed. 16.95 (*0-8223-1247-6*) Duke.

Changing Trucking to Match a Changing Work Force. 1993. 23.00 (*1-56091-387-8*, SP-979) Soc Auto Engineers.

Changing U. S. Health Care: A Study of Four Metropolitan Areas. Eli Ginzberg et al. 221p. (C). 1993. text ed. 55.50 (*0-8133-8544-X*) Westview.

Changing U. S. Labor Market. Ed. by Eli Ginzberg. LC 94-3994. (Eisenhower Center for the Conservation of Human Resources Studies in the New Economy). (C). 1994. text ed. 48.50 (*0-8133-2163-8*) Westview.

Changing Uganda: The Dilemmas of Structural Adjustment & Revolutionary Change. Ed. by Holger B. Hansen & Michael Twaddle. (Eastern African Studies). 400p. (C). 1991. text ed. 39.95 (*0-8214-1004-0*); pap. text ed. 19.95 (*0-8214-1005-9*) Ohio U Pr.

Changing University: How Increased Demand for Scientists & Technology Is Transforming Academic Institutions Internationally. Ed. by Dorothy S. Zinberg. (C). 1991. lib. bdg. 77.50 (*0-7923-1281-3*) Kluwer Ac.

Changing Utilization of Fixed Capital: An Element in Long-Term Growth. Murray F. Foss. LC 84-9206. (AEI Studies: No. 407). (Illus.). 144p. reprint ed. pap. 41.10 (*0-8357-4447-7*, 2037284) Bks Demand.

Changing Values & Social Trends: How Do Organizations React? Presented Jointly by the Market Research Society & the American Marketing Association, June 1974, Oxford, England. American Marketing Association Staff. 224p. reprint ed. pap. 63.90 (*0-317-26627-6*, 2011593) Bks Demand.

Changing Values & Tribal Societies. A. R. Srivastava. (C). 1992. 33.00 (*81-210-0279-6*, Pub. by Inter-India Pubns) S Asia.

Changing Values in American Industrial Relations, 1933-1985. Milton Derber. (Occasional Publication: No. 156). 54p. 1983. 6.00 (*0-318-21794-5*) U Hawaii.

Changing Values in College: An Exploratory Study of the Impact of College Teaching. Philip E. Jacob. LC 76-48178. 174p. 1977. reprint ed. text ed. 52.50 (*0-8371-9343-5*, JACV, Greenwood Pr) Greenwood.

Changing Values in Medical & Healthcare Decision-Making. Ed. by Uffe J. Jensen & Gavin Mooney. 1990. text ed. 85.00 (*0-471-92634-5*) Wiley.

Changing Values in Medicine. Ed. by Eric J. Cassell & Mark Siegler. LC 85-10033. 275p. 1979. text ed. 55.00 (*0-313-27050-3*, U7050, Greenwood Pr); pap. text ed. 19.95 (*0-313-27060-0*, P7060, Greenwood Pr) Greenwood.

***Changing Values in Medieval Scotland: A Study of Prices, Money, & Weights & Measures.** Elizabeth Gemmill & Nicholas Mayhew. (Illus.). 416p. (C). 1995. 79.95 (*0-521-47385-3*) Cambridge U Pr.

Changing Values of the Japanese Family. Chie Sano. LC 73-8257. 142p. 1973. reprint ed. text ed. 49.75 (*0-8371-6974-7*, SACV, Greenwood Pr) Greenwood.

Changing Views - The Impressionist Photographs of Caren Nederlander, Ph.D. Caren Nederlander. (Illus.). 30p. (Orig.). 1988. pap. 10.00 (*0-9622466-0-3*) C Nederlander.

Changing Views about the Principles of Scientific Theory Evaluation. Ed. by G. Buchdahl. 90p. 1981. pap. 20.00 (*0-08-027408-0*, Pergamon Pr) Elsevier.

Changing Views of Poverty. Ed. by Elinor M. Bowles. 43p. 1985. 6.50 (*0-88156-042-1*) Comm Serv Soc NY.

Changing Views of the Human Condition. Ed. by Paul W. Pruyser. LC 86-31067. 256p. 1987. pap. 13.95 (*0-86554-230-9*, P32) Mercer Univ Pr.

Changing Visual System: From Early to Late Stages of Life. Ed. by P. Bagnoli & W. Hodos. (NATO ASI Series A, Life Sciences: Vol. 222). (Illus.). 382p. 1992. 115.00 (*0-306-44090-3*, Plenum Pr) Plenum.

Changing Voices: The Modern Quoting Poem. Leonard Diepeveen. 220p. (C). 1993. text ed. 39.50x (*0-472-10369-5*) U of Mich Pr.

***Changing Wales Vol. I: Cymru or Wales?** R. S. Thomas. 1992. pap. 21.00 (*0-86383-896-0*, Pub. by Gomer Pr UK) St Mut.

***Changing Wales Vol. II: The Aesthetics of Relevance.** Peter Lord. 1992. pap. 21.00 (*0-86383-897-9*, Pub. by Gomer Pr UK) St Mut.

***Changing Wales Vol. III: The Democratic Challenge.** John Osmond. 1993. pap. 21.00 (*0-86383-927-4*, Pub. by Gomer Pr UK) St Mut.

***Changing Wales Vol. IV: Language Regained.** Bobi Jones. 1993. pap. 21.00 (*1-85902-056-9*, Pub. by Gomer Pr UK) St Mut.

***Changing Wales Vol. V: The Political Conundrum.** Ed. by Clive Betts. 1993. pap. 21.00 (*1-85902-011-9*, Pub. by Gomer Pr UK) St Mut.

Changing Ways: A Practical Tool for Implementing Change Within an Organization. Murray Dalziel & Stephen C. Schoonover. 176p. 1988. 21.95 (*0-8144-5924-2*) AMACOM.

Changing West. Laurence M. Larson. 180p. 1937. 10.00 (*0-87732-018-7*) Norwegian-Am Hist Assn.

Changing West, & Other Essays. Laurence M. Larson. LC 68-16946. (Essay Index Reprint Ser.). (Illus.). 1977. reprint ed. 19.95 (*0-8369-0606-3*) Ayer.

Changing Western Analysis of the Soviet Threat. Ed. by Carl-Christophe Schweitzer. 250p. 1990. text ed. 45.00 (*0-312-04184-5*) St Martin.

Changing Wilderness Values, 1930-1990: An Annotated Bibliography. Comp. by Joan S. Elbers. LC 91-7716. (Bibliographies & Indexes in American History Ser.: No. 18). 160p. 1991. text ed. 45.00 (*0-313-27377-4*, ECW/, Greenwood Pr) Greenwood.

Changing Wind. Don Coldsmith. (Spanish Bit Saga Super Ser.: No. 1). 1990. pap. 4.99 (*0-553-28334-0*) Bantam.

Changing with Families. Virginia Satir et al. LC 76-15450. 1976. 13.95 (*0-8314-0051-X*) Sci & Behavior.

Changing with the Seasons of Our Life. Geoffrey A. Wells & Susan Huss. LC 84-73215. (Illus.). 1985. 14.95 (*0-932667-01-5*); pap. 9.95 (*0-317-18275-7*) Griefworks Pub Co.

***Changing Witness: Catholic Bishops & Public Policy, 1917-1994.** Michael Warner. 224p. 1995. pap. 19.99 (*0-8028-4071-X*) Eerdmans.

Changing Woman. Lindy Hough. (Illus.). 90p. 1971. pap. 20.00 (*0-913028-01-0*) North Atlantic.

Changing Woman. Sue Ann Martinson. 60p. 1985. 8.95 (*0-911051-15-5*) Plain View.

Changing Woman: The Life & Art of Helen Hardin. Jay Scott. LC 89-42662. (Illus.). 176p. 1993. reprint ed. pap. 19.95 (*0-87358-567-4*) Northland AZ.

Changing Woman & Her Sisters. Sheila Moon. LC 84-27901. 233p. (Orig.). 1985. 14.00 (*0-917479-02-5*); pap. 11.50 (*0-917479-03-3*) Guild Psy.

Changing Woman Changing Work. Nina B. Krebs. LC 93-77399. 400p. 1993. 22.95 (*1-878448-56-0*) MacMurray & Beck.

Changing Woman's Workbook: Approaching Menopause As Journey of Spiritual Transformation. Magdalen Daniels. (Illus.). 152p. (Orig.). 1993. pap. 12.95 (*1-883230-08-X*) Purple Iris Pr.

Changing Women, Changing Church. Marie L. Uhr. Date not set. pap. 8.95 (*0-85574-909-1*, Pub. by E J Dwyer AT) Morehouse Pub.

Changing Work & Retirement: Social Policy & the Older Worker. Frank Laczko & Chris Phillipson. 192p. 1991. 90.00 (*0-335-09931-9*, Open Univ Pr); pap. 32.00 (*0-335-09930-0*, Open Univ Pr) Taylor & Francis.

Changing Workforce: Comparison of Federal & Nonfederal Work - Family Programs & Approaches. (Illus.). 127p. (Orig.). (C). 1993. pap. text ed. 25.00 (*1-56806-211-7*) Diane Pub.

Changing Workplace: Career Counseling Strategies for the 1990s & Beyond. Carl McDaniels. LC 88-46081. (Management Ser.). 280p. 1989. 28.95 (*1-55542-146-6*) Jossey-Bass.

Changing Workplace: Implications of Quality of Work Life for Vocational Education. Frank C. Pratzner & Jill F. Russell. 89p. 1984. 7.25 (*0-318-22062-8*, RD249) Ctr Educ Trng Employ.

Changing Workplace: New Directions in Staffing & Scheduling. (Special Report Ser.). 144p. 1986. 35.00 (*0-87179-910-3*) BNA.

Changing World: Proceedings of the North American Serials Interest Group, Inc. Ed. by Suzanne McMahon et al. LC 91-39991. (Serials Librarian Ser.). 218p. 1992. lib. bdg. 24.95 (*1-56024-263-9*); pap. text ed. 19.95 (*1-56024-298-1*) Haworth Pr.

Changing World Energy Economy. Ed. by David O. Wood. 545p. 1987. write for info. (*0-318-62685-3*) Intl Assn Energy Econ.

Changing World Food Prospect: The Nineties & Beyond. Lester R. Brown. 60p. (Orig.). (C). 1988. pap. 5.00 (*0-916468-86-0*) Worldwatch Inst.

Changing World in Plays & Theatre. Anita Block. LC 73-77721. (Theatre, Film & Literature Ser.). 448p. 1971. reprint ed. lib. bdg. 55.00 (*0-306-71359-4*) Da Capo.

Changing World Market for Iron Ore, 1950-1980: An Economic Geography. Gerald Manners. LC 70-146734. 400p. reprint ed. pap. 114.00 (*0-317-26471-0*, 2023806) Bks Demand.

Changing World Metals Industries: A Special Issue of the Journal Processing & Extractive Metallurgy Review. Ed. by David A. Gulley & Paul Duby. 378p. 1988. 45.00 (*0-685-22968-8*) Gordon & Breach.

Changing World Metals Industries: Proceedings of the Arden House Conference, Harriman Campus, Columbia University. D. A. Gulley & P. Duby. 378p. 1988. pap. text ed. 78.00 (*2-88124-262-6*) Gordon & Breach.

***Changing World of Finance & Its Problems.** Harold Rose. 57p. (Orig.). 1993. pap. text ed. 9.00 (*0-89068-116-3*, NPA 264) Natl Planning.

Changing World of Geography: A Critical Guide to Concepts & Methods. 2nd ed. James Bird. LC 92-29463. 1993. pap. 24.95 (*0-19-874182-0*, Clarendon Pr) OUP.

Changing World of Mongolia's Nomads. Melvyn C. Goldstein & Cynthia M. Beall. LC 93-24004. 1994. pap. 20.00 (*0-520-08551-5*) U CA Pr.

Changing World of Mormonism. Jerald Tanner & Sandra Tanner. LC 79-18311. (C). 1979. 19.99 (*0-8024-1234-3*) Moody.

Changing World of the U. S. Senate. Ed. by John Hibbing & John G. Peters. LC 90-34826. 408p. (Orig.). (C). 1990. pap. 19.95 (*0-87772-325-7*) UCB IGS.

Changing World of Weather. Clive Carpenter. 192p. 1991. 22.95 (*0-8160-2521-5*) Facts on File.

Changing Worlds of Older Women in Japan. Anne O. Freed et al. LC 92-14990. 250p. (C). 1993. 27.95 (*1-879198-10-X*); pap. 17.95 (*1-879198-09-6*) Knwldg Ideas & Trnds.

Changing Years. Martin Morrissey. 158p. 1993. pap. 13.95 (*0-86278-279-1*, Pub. by OBrien Pr IE) Dufour.

Changing Your Life: A New Psychology for Turning Your Life Around. Strephon Kaplan-Williams. Ed. by Judith Bess. (Practice of Personal Transformation Ser.). (Illus.). 230p. 1987. pap. 11.95 (*0-918572-30-4*) Journey Pr.

Changing Your Life Style. Frieda Porat & Karen Myers. LC 73-76821. 1973. 6.95 (*0-8184-0020-X*) Carol Pub Group.

Changing Your Life Through the Power of Prayer. Evelyn Christenson. 1993. write for info. (*0-88486-081-7*) Arrowood Pr.

***Changing Your Lifestyle.** Frieda Porat et al. 1973. write for info. (*0-614-01666-5*) NewLife Bks.

***Changing Your Management Style.** Benfari. 1995. 23.00 (*0-02-902635-0*) Free Pr.

Changing Your Name Legally in Massachusetts. 1989. write for info. (*1-877784-01-X*) T Scott Pub.

Changing Your Story. Patricia C. Smith. 61p. (Orig.). 1990. pap. 8.95 (*0-931122-61-9*) West End.

Changing Youth: Starting a Youth Credit Union & Learning Center. DEWFCU Staff. 128p. 1993. pap. text ed. 15.95 (*0-8403-8395-9*) Kendall-Hunt.

Changing Youth in a Changing Society: Patterns of Adolescent Development & Disorder. Michael Rutter. LC 82-242973. (Illus.). 333p. 1980. 32.00 (*0-674-10875-2*) HUP.

Chang's Paper Pony. Eleanor Coerr. LC 87-45679. (Harper I Can Read Bk.). (Illus.). 64p. (J). (gr. k-3). 1988. lib. bdg. 14.89 (*0-06-021329-9*) HarpC Child Bks.

Chang's Paper Pony. Eleanor Coerr. LC 87-45679. (Trophy I Can Read Bk.). (Illus.). 64p. (J). (gr. k-3). 1993. pap. 3.50 (*0-06-444163-6*, Trophy) HarpC Child Bks.

***Chang's Paper Pony.** Laurie Diamond. Ed. by J. Friedland & R. Kessler. (Novel-Ties Ser.). (J). (gr. 1-3). 1995. student ed, pap. text ed. 15.95 (*1-56982-263-8*) Lrn Links.

Chanhu-Daro Excavations, 1935-1936. E. J. Mackay. (American Folklore Society Memoirs Ser.: Vol. 20). 1972. reprint ed. 45.00 (*0-527-02694-8*) Periodicals Srv.

Channel. Annemarie Eversmeyer. LC 93-93786. 192p. (Orig.). 1994. pap. 10.00 (*1-56002-321-X*, Univ Edtns) Aegina Pr.

Channel. Barbara Jordan. LC 89-43074. (Barnard New Women Poets Ser.). 80p. 1990. 21.95 (*0-8070-6808-X*); pap. 9.95 (*0-8070-6809-8*) Beacon Pr.

Channel Analysis & Design. Ed. by Silent Partners, Inc. Staff. 130p. (Orig.). 1991. pap. write for info. (*1-878353-13-6*) Silent Partners.

Channel Assault. large type ed. Kenneth Royce. 480p. 1984. 15.95 (*0-7089-1131-5*) Ulverscroft.

Channel Catfish Culture. Ed. by C. S. Tucker. (Developments in Aquaculture & Fisheries Science Ser.: 15). 647p. 1985. 143.75 (*0-444-42527-6*) Elsevier.

Channel Catfish Farming Handbook. C. S. Tucker. 1990. text ed. 57.95 (*0-442-31836-7*) Chapman & Hall.

Channel Catfish Farming Set. Meade Tucker. 1992. text ed. 168.85 (*0-442-01381-7*) Van Nos Reinhold.

Channel Catfish Fever. Doug Stange. 1989. pap. 11.95 (*0-929384-04-0*) In-Fisherman.

***Channel Change on the Santa Cruz River, Pima County, Arizona, 1936-1986.** Contrib by Pima County Department of Transportation & Flood Control District Staff. LC 94-41169. (Water-Supply Papers: Vol. 2429). 1995. write for info. (*0-614-03357-8*) US Geol Survey.

Channel Coding Theory: Proceedings of CISM, Department of Automation & Information, 1970. CISM (International Center for Mechanical Sciences), Department of Automation & Information Staff. Ed. by I. Csiszar. (CISM Publications: No. 29). 79p. 1974. pap. 16.00 (*0-387-81089-7*) Spr-Verlag.

Channel Crossing. Hereward Davies. 115p. 1986. 25.00 (*0-7223-1990-8*, Pub. by A H S Ltd UK) St Mut.

Channel Fever see NEA Series

Channel Flow Resistance: Centennial of Manning's Formula. Ed. by Ben C. Yen. 453p. 1992. 57.00 (*0-918334-72-1*) WRP.

***Channel Island Handbook.** 240p. 1994. 225.00 (*0-7605-0886-0*) Rector Pr.

Channel Islands. (Insight Guides Ser.). 1993. pap. 21.95 (*0-395-66303-2*) HM.

Channel Islands. 2nd ed. Peter M. Eadie. (Blue Guides Ser.). (Illus.). 1987. pap. 16.95 (*0-393-30371-3*) Norton.

Channel Islands: Larchipel de la Manche. Hugo. (Jersey Heritage Editions Ser.). 1991. write for info. (*0-86120-012-8*, Pub. by Aris & Phillips UK) David Brown.

***Channel Islands: Occupation & Liberation 1940-1945.** Asa Briggs. (Illus.). 96p. 1995. pap. 17.95 (*0-7134-7822-5*, Pub. by Batsford UK) Trafalgar.

Channel Islands: The Story Behind the Scenery. Peter C. Howorth. LC 81-84964. 48p. 1982. pap. 6.95 (*0-916122-75-1*) KC Pubns.

Channel Islands - Tax Haven. Bob Hall & Jami Hall. Ed. by Gary Scott & Merri Scott. 219p. 1985. lib. bdg. 99.00 (*1-884875-10-6*) Adams Carter.

Channel Islands Banking: Private & Safe Banking. Bob Hall & Jami Hall. Ed. by Gary Scott & Merri Scott. 209p. 1985. lib. bdg. 99.00 (*1-884875-09-2*) Adams Carter.

Channel Islands Collection. Bob Evans. Ed. by Susanne Chess & Chris Swann. LC 87-81414. (Illus.). 24p. (Orig.). 1987. pap. 4.95 (*0-943881-00-5*) La Mer Bleu Prodns.

Channel Islands (North) Imray Laurie Norie & Wilson Ltd. Staff. (Illus.). (C). 1988. text ed. 60.00 (*0-685-40224-X*, Pub. by Imray Laurie Norie & Wilson UK) St Mut.

Channel Islands (South) Imray Laurie Norie & Wilson Ltd. Staff. (Illus.). (C). 1989. text ed. 65.00 (*0-685-40223-1*, Pub. by Imray Laurie Norie & Wilson UK) St Mut.

Channel Markers. A. E. Stringer. LC 85-29602. (Wesleyan New Poets Ser.). 64p. 1987. 22.50 (*0-8195-2129-9*, Wesleyan Univ Pr); pap. 10.95 (*0-8195-1129-3*, Wesleyan Univ Pr) U Pr of New Eng.

Channel Networks Hydrology. Keith J. Beven. 319p. 1993. text ed. 152.95 (*0-471-93534-4*) Wiley.

***Channel of Deceit.** Robin Harfouche. 152p. (Orig.). 1995. reprint ed. pap. text ed. 9.00 (*0-9634451-6-2*) Christian FL.

Channel Setting Diamonds with Illustrated Procedures. Robert R. Wooding. LC 87-91115. (Illus.). 136p. 1987. 29.95 (*0-9613545-3-4*) Dry Ridge.

Channel Sweep. Maritime Books Staff. (C). 1986. text ed. 60.00 (*0-907771-40-8*, Pub. by Maritime Bks UK) St Mut.

Channel Three Networking Arrangements: RPT on Whether Arrangements Satisfy Competition Test Contained in the Broadcasting Act, 1990. 95p. 1993. pap. 40.00 (*0-11-515330-6*, HM53306, Pub. by HMSO UK) UNIPUB.

Channel Tunnel: A Geographic Perspective. Ed. by Richard Gibb. LC 94-7964. 1994. text ed. 59.95 (*0-471-94908-6*) Wiley.

Channel Tunnel Safety Authority Annual Report, 1988-89. 72p. 1990. pap. 21.00 (*0-11-550948-8*, HM9488) UNIPUB.

***Channel Tunnel Story.** Anderson. 1994. pap. 26.00 (*0-419-19620-X*, E & FN Spon) Routledge Chapman & Hall.

***Channel Tunnel Visions: 1850-1945: Dreams & Nightmares.** Keith Wilson. LC 95-5972. 1995. write for info. (*1-85285-132-5*) Hambledon Press.

Channel X Short-Short Stories, Vol. 1, No. 1. Ed. by Lachlan P. MacDonald. (Illus.). 64p. 1990. pap. 6.95 (*1-877947-06-7*) Pr MacDonald & Reinecke.

Channeling: A Bibliographic Exploration. Joel Bjorling. LC 91-13554. (Sects & Cults in America Ser.: Vol. 15). 350p. 1992. 57.00 (*0-8240-5691-4*, 589) Garland.

Channeling: How to Reach Out to Your Spirit Guides. Kathryn Ridall. 1988. mass mkt. 5.99 (*0-553-27181-4*) Bantam.

***Channeling & How to Be a Medium.** Beverly Jaegers & W. Evans. Ed. by Thor Templar. 320p. (Orig.). Date not set. 25.00 (*1-57179-046-2*) Intern Guild ASRS.

Channeling & Other Penetration Phenomena. Ed. by E. Uggerhoj & A. Zucker. (Nuclear Science Applications Ser.: Vol. 3, No. 3). 182p. 1989. pap. text ed. 296.00 (*3-7186-4945-4*) Gordon & Breach.

Channeling Children: Sex Stereotyping in Prime Time TV. LC 75-568. 1975. pap. 2.50 (*0-9600724-2-X*) Women on Words.

Channeling: Communicating with the Unseen. K. W. Rinkieviczus. (Illus.). 48p. (Orig.). 1987. pap. 3.95 (*0-940137-00-3*) Prism Pubns ME.

Channeling Grace. Carl L. Jech. (Orig.). 1988. pap. 9.20 (*1-55673-054-3*, 8851) CSS OH.

Channeling Handbook. Carla L. Rueckert. 118p. 1987. pap. 6.95 (*0-945007-07-8*) L-L Resrch.

Channeling in the New Age. David Spangler. 64p. (Orig.). (C). 1988. pap. text ed. 6.95 (*0-929660-00-5*) Morningtown.

An Asterisk (*) at the beginning of an entry indicates that the title is appearing in BIP for the first time.

CHANSON DE BEL-AMI, a compelling chronicle of Haiti's saga & the poet's nostalgia, the romantic LES CHEVEUX DE MELINDA & POUR L'AMOUR D'ALEXIS, beautiful poems to please all audiences. Based in Salt Lake City, Utah, this poet draws his inspiration from Haiti's soul, the ancestral folklore, & his American experiences. "From Bel-Ami's poems, I must cite two whose beauty reminds me of Appolinaire & Supervielle. They are L'ADJECTIF & EN ECOLE PRIMAIRE, beautiful & spiritual chef-d'oeuvres that merit inclusion in any anthology of French poetry," wrote University of California Professor Emeritus Mark Temmer. Copies may be ordered by sending a check or money order for $17.50 per copy to: Saint-Arromand, c/o Montreaux Media, 310 South Main, Suite 1200, Salt Lake City, UT 84101. 801-322-3021. *Publisher Provided Annotation.*

C

An Asterisk (*) at the beginning of an entry indicates that the title is appearing in BIP for the first time.

1149

Chanukkah Guest. Eric A. Kimmel. LC 89-20073. (Illus.). 32p. (J). (ps-3). 1990. lib. bdg. 15.95 (*0-8234-0788-8*); pap. 5.95 (*0-8234-0978-3*) Holiday.

Chanukkah Tree. Eric A. Kimmel. LC 88-4510. (Illus.). 32p. (J). (ps-3). 1988. lib. bdg. 15.95 (*0-8234-0705-5*) Holiday.

Chanur's Homecoming. C. J. Cherryh. (Chanur Novels Ser.: Bk. 4). 400p. 1991. mass mkt. 4.99 (*0-88677-177-3*) DAW Bks.

Chanur's Homecoming. C. J. Cherryh. (Chanur Ser.). 320p. 1986. 18.00 (*0-932096-42-5*) Phantasia Pr.

Chanur's Legacy. C. J. Cherryh. (Chanur Novels Ser.: Bk. 5). 320p. 1992. 15.00 (*0-88677-519-1*) DAW Bks.

Chanur's Legacy. C. J. Cherryh. 1993. mass mkt. 4.99 (*0-88677-559-0*) DAW Bks.

Chanur's Venture. C. J. Cherryh. (Chanur Ser.). 1984. 17.00 (*0-932096-31-X*) Phantasia Pr.

Chanur's Venture: The Chanur Novels, Bk. 2. C. J. Cherryh. (Alliance-Union Universe Ser.). 320p. 1987. pap. 3.95 (*0-88677-293-1*) DAW Bks.

Chanzeaux, a Village in Anjou. Laurence W. Wylie. LC 66-18258. 413p. reprint ed. pap. 117.80 (*0-317-09350-9*, 2005803) Bks Demand.

***Chao Chun: The Most Virtuous.** rev. ed. Shu-Chiung. (Beauties of Ancient China Ser.). 166p. 1981. reprint ed. pap. 8.95 (*9971-947-05-6*) Heian Intl.

Chaonian Dove: Studies in the Eclogues, Georgics, & Aeneid of Virgil. A. J. Boyle. (Mnemosyne Ser.: Supplement 94). xi, 196p. 1986. pap. 41.25 (*90-04-07672-7*) E J Brill.

Chaos. Hao Bai-Lin. 592p. 1984. text ed. 89.00 (*9971-966-50-6*); pap. text ed. 41.00 (*9971-966-51-4*) World Scientific Pub.

Chaos. Ed. by Arun V. Holden. 332p. (Orig.). 1986. pap. text ed. 25.00x (*0-691-08424-6*) Princeton U Pr.

Chaos: A Program Collection for the PC. H. J. Korsch. 1994. disk 59.00 (*0-387-57457-3*) Spr-Verlag.

Chaos: From Theory to Applications. A. A. Tsonis. (Illus.). 255p. (C). 1992. 65.00 (*0-306-44171-3*, Plenum Pr) Plenum.

Chaos: Making a New Science. James Gleick. 368p. 1988. pap. 16.95 (*0-14-009250-1*, Penguin Bks) Viking Penguin.

Chaos: Proceedings of the International Conference. G. Brown & A. Opie. 212p. 1993. text ed. 81.00 (*981-02-1375-1*) World Scientific Pub.

Chaos: The New Science. Ilya Prigogine et al. Ed. by John Holte. LC 92-34498. (Nobel Conference Ser.). (Illus.). 144p. (Orig.). 1993. lib. bdg. 44.00 (*0-8191-8933-2*); pap. 17.50 (*0-8191-8934-0*) U Pr of Amer.

Chaos - XAOC. Ed. by D. K. Campbell. 512p. 1990. 65.00 (*0-88318-777-9*); pap. 29.00 (*0-88318-778-7*) Am Inst Physics.

Chaos & All That: An Irreverent Novel by Liu Sola. Liu Sola. Tr. by Richard King. LC 94-9228. (Fiction from Modern China Ser.). 144p. (C). 1994. reprint ed. text ed. 19.95 (*0-8248-1617-X*, Kolowalu Bk); reprint ed. pap. 11.95 (*0-8248-1651-X*, Kolowalu Bk) UH Pr.

***Chaos & Beyond: The Best of Trajectories.** Robert A. Wilson. LC 94-68465. 275p. (Orig.). (YA). 1994. pap. text ed. 14.95 (*1-886404-00-3*) Permanent San Jose.

***Chaos & Catastrophe Theories: Nonlinear Modeling in the Social Sciences.** Courtney Brown. (Quantitative Applications in the Social Science Ser.: Vol. 107). 96p. (C). 1995. pap. 9.95 (*0-8039-5847-1*) Sage.

Chaos & Complexity: Proceedings of the Workshop on Chaos & Complexity. Ed. by R. Livi et al. 452p. (C). 1988. pap. 46.00 (*9971-5-0568-1*) World Scientific Pub.

Chaos & Cosmos: Ritual in Early & Medieval Japanese Literature. H. E. Plutschow. LC 89-9761. (Japanese Studies Library: Vol. 1). xii, 284p. 1990. 71.50 (*90-04-08628-5*) E J Brill.

Chaos & Creation: An Introduction to Quantavolution in Human & Natural History. Alfred De Grazia. (Quantavolution Ser.). (Illus.). xiii, 336p. 1981. 22.00 (*0-940268-00-0*) Metron Pubns.

***Chaos & Cyber Culture.** Timothy Leary. 1994. pap. 19.95 (*0-614-00335-0*) Ronin Pub.

Chaos & Determinism: Turbulence As a Paradigm for Complex Systems Converging Toward Final States. Alexandre Favre et al. Tr. by Bertram E. Schwarzbach. LC 94-12691. (Illus.). 192p. 1994. text ed. 45.00x (*0-8018-4911-X*) Johns Hopkins.

Chaos & Determinism: Turbulence As a Paradigm for Complex Systems Converging Toward Final States. Alexandre Favre et al. LC 94-12691. 1995. pap. text ed. 19.95x (*0-8018-4912-8*) Johns Hopkins.

***Chaos & Forecasting.** Howell Tong. (Nonlinear Time Series & Chaos: Vol. 2). 356p. 1995. text ed. 55.00 (*981-02-2126-6*) World Scientific Pub.

Chaos & Fractals: New Frontiers of Science. Heinz-Otto Peitgen et al. LC 92-23277. 1992. write for info. (*0-387-97345-1*) Spr-Verlag.

Chaos & Fractals: New Frontiers of Science. Heinz-Otto Peitgen et al. (Illus.). 1016p. 1993. 49.00 (*0-387-97903-4*) Spr-Verlag.

Chaos & Fractals: The Mathematics Behind the Computer Graphics. R. Devaney & L. Keen. (PSAPM Ser.: Vol. 39). 208p. 1989. 36.00 (*0-8218-0137-6*, PSAPM-39) Am Math.

***Chaos & Fractals in Chemical Engineering: Proceedings of the 1st Italian Conference.** G. Biavdi et al. 300p. 1995. text ed. 86.00 (*981-02-1904-0*) World Scientific Pub.

***Chaos & Gauge Field Theory.** T. S. Biro et al. (Lecture Notes in Physics: Vol. 56). 300p. 1995. text ed. 61.00 (*981-02-2079-0*) World Scientific Pub.

Chaos & Information Processing. J. S. Nicolis. 304p. 1991. text ed. 48.00 (*981-02-0076-5*) World Scientific Pub.

Chaos & Insect Ecology: Does Chaos Exist in Ecological Systems? Ed. by Jesse A. Logan & Fred P. Hain. (Illus.). 109p. (Orig.). (C). 1993. pap. text ed. 40.00 (*0-7881-0092-0*) Diane Pub.

Chaos & Networks: Statistical & Probabilistic Aspects. O. B. Nielsen. LC 93-3333. 1993. write for info. (*0-412-46530-2*) Chapman & Hall.

Chaos & Non-Linear Models in Economics: Theory & Applications. Ed. by John Creedy & Vance Martin. (Illus.). 224p. 1994. 69.95 (*1-85278-722-8*, Pub. by E Elgar Pub UK) Ashgate Pub Co.

Chaos & Nonlinear Dynamics: An Introduction for Scientists & Engineers. Robert C. Hilborn. LC 92-40059. 672p. (C). 1994. 55.00 (*0-19-505760-0*) OUP.

***Chaos & Nonlinear Mechanics: Proceedings of Euromechanical Colloquim 308 Chaos & Noise in Dynamical System.** T. Kapitaniak & J. Brindley. 320p. 1994. text ed. 109.00 (*981-02-2009-X*) World Scientific Pub.

Chaos & Order: Complex Dynamics in Literature & Science. Ed. by N. Katherine Hayles. LC 90-20264. (New Practices of Inquiry Ser.). 312p. 1991. pap. text ed. 14.95 (*0-226-32144-4*) U Ch Pr.

Chaos & Order: Complex Dynamics in Literature & Science. Ed. by N. Katherine Hayles. LC 90-20264. (New Practices of Inquiry Ser.). 312p. 1991. lib. bdg. 39.95 (*0-226-32143-6*) U Ch Pr.

Chaos & Order: The Complex Structure of Living Systems. F. Cramer. Tr. by D. I. Loewus. LC 93-32939. 1993. 31.00 (*1-56081-812-3*) VCH Pubs.

Chaos & Order in the Capital Markets. Edgar E. Peters. 256p. 1991. text ed. 55.00 (*0-471-53372-6*) Wiley.

Chaos & Order in the World of the Psyche. Joanne Wieland-Burston. LC 91-40117. (Illus.). 176p. 1992. 59.95 (*0-415-07212-3*, A7772); pap. 15.95 (*0-415-07213-1*, A7776) Routledge.

Chaos & Order, Miniconference on - Proceedings of the Center for Mathematical Analysis. N. Joshi & R. L. Dewar. 128p. 1991. text ed. 74.00 (*981-02-0400-0*) World Scientific Pub.

Chaos & Quantum Chaos: Proceedings of the Eighth Chris Engelbrecht Summer School on Theoretical Physics, Held at Blydepoort, Eastern Transvaal, South Africa, 13-24 January 1992. Ed. by W. Dieter Heiss. LC 92-37387. (Lecture Notes in Physics Ser.: Vol. 411). 1992. 64.00 (*0-387-56253-2*) Spr-Verlag.

***Chaos & Society.** P. Lemieux. LC 94-74250. 1995. 75.00 (*90-5199-214-9*) IOS Press.

Chaos & Socio-Spatial Dynamics. D. S. Dendrinos & M. Sonis. Ed. by F. John et al. (Applied Mathematical Sciences Ser.: Vol. 86). (Illus.). xvii, 184p. 1990. 44.00 (*0-387-97283-8*) Spr-Verlag.

Chaos & Stability in Defect Processes in Semiconductors. I. V. Verner et al. 212p. 1992. text ed. 92.00 (*0-87849-650-5*, Pub. by Trans Tech SZ) LPS Dist Ctr.

Chaos & the Evolving Ecological Universe. Sally J. Goerner. (World Futures General Evolution Studies: Vol. 7). 255p. 1994. text ed. 43.00 (*2-88124-635-4*) Gordon & Breach.

***Chaos Applied to Fluid Mixing.** AREF Staff. 1995. text ed. 99.00 (*0-08-042028-1*, Pergamon Pr) Elsevier.

Chaos Bound: Orderly Disorder in Contemporary Literature & Science. N. Katherine Hayles. LC 89-23893. (Illus.). 328p. 1990. 39.95 (*0-8014-2262-0*); pap. 15.95 (*0-8014-9701-9*) Cornell U Pr.

***Chaos Burning on My Brow: Don Juan Valera in His Novels.** Robert G. Trimble. LC 95-2050. (Milford Ser.: Popular Writers of Today: Vol. 61). 160p. 1995. lib. bdg. 29.00 (*0-89370-987-5*); pap. 19.00 (*0-89370-989-1*) Borgo Pr.

***Chaos, Catastrophe, & Human Affairs: Applications of Nonlinear Dynamics to Work, Organizations, & Social Evolution.** Stephen J. Guastello. 360p. 1995. text ed. 55.00 (*0-8058-1634-8*) L Erlbaum Assocs.

Chaos Comics. Jack Marshall. 32p. (Orig.). 1994. pap. 6.00 (*0-938631-25-X*) Pennywhistle Pr.

***Chaos Cookbook.** 2nd ed. Pritchard. 1995. pap. write for info. (*0-7506-1777-2*, Focal) Buttrwrth-Heinemann.

Chaos Cookbook: A Practical Programming Guide. Joe Pritchard. (Illus.). 240p. 1992. 39.95 (*0-7506-0304-6*) Buttrwrth-Heinemann.

Chaos Curse. R. A. Salvatore. (Forgotten Realms Cleric Quintet Ser.: No. 5). 320p. 1994. pap. 4.95 (*1-56076-860-6*) TSR Inc.

Chaos, Dynamics, & Fractals: An Algorithmic Approach to Deterministic Chaos. Joseph L. McCauley. (Nonlinear Science Ser.: No. 2). (Illus.). 320p. (C). 1993. 94.95 (*0-521-41658-2*) Cambridge U Pr.

Chaos, Dynamics, & Fractals: An Algorithmic Approach to Deterministic Chaos. Joseph L. McCauley. (Nonlinear Science Ser.: No. 2). (Illus.). 320p. (C). 1994. pap. 27.95 (*0-521-46747-0*) Cambridge U Pr.

Chaos et la Nuit. Henry De Montherlant. (Folio Ser.: No. 422). (Illus.). (FRE.). 8.95 (*2-07-036422-4*) Schoenhof.

Chaos et la Nuit. Henry de Montherlant. (FRE.). 1973. pap. 10.95 (*0-8288-3718-X*, M3786) Fr & Eur.

Chaos Expansions, Multiple Wiener-Ito Integrals & Their Applications. Ed. by Christian Houdre & Victor Perez-Abreu. LC 93-47073. (Probability & Stochastics Ser.). 400p. 1994. 79.95 (*0-8493-8072-3*, 8072) CRC Pr.

Chaos Factor. James A. Moore. (Mage). 160p. 1994. per., pap. 15.00 (*1-56504-125-9*, 4101) White Wolf.

Chaos, Fractals & Dynamics. Robert L. Devaney. 1990. pap. text ed. 34.50 (*0-201-23288-X*) Addison-Wesley.

Chaos, Fractals & Dynamics. P. Fischer & W. Smith. (Lecture Notes in Pure & Applied Mathematics Ser.: Vol. 98). 280p. 1985. 110.00 (*0-8247-7325-X*) Dekker.

***Chaos, Fractals & Dynamics: Computer Experiments in Mathematics, incl. 2 videocassettes, Set.** Robert L. Devaney. 181p. (Orig.). 1989. pap., vhs 99.00 (*1-878310-34-8*) Science TV.

Chaos, Fractals, & Noise: Stochastic Aspects of Dynamics. Andrzej Lasota & Michael C. Mackey. LC 93-10432. (Applied Mathematical Sciences Ser.: Vol. 97). 1993. 49.00 (*0-387-94049-9*) Spr-Verlag.

Chaos Fractals & Non-Linear Dynamic Systems. Richard K. Miller & Terri C. Walker. LC 88-80491. (Survey on Technology & Markets Ser.: No. 12). 50p. 1989. pap. text ed. 200.00 (*1-55865-011-3*) Future Tech Surveys.

Chaos Frontier. Ralph D. Stacey. 409p. 1993. pap. 39.95 (*0-7506-0950-8*) Buttrwrth-Heinemann.

Chaos Frontier: Creative Strategic Control for Business. Ralph D. Stacey. 300p. 1991. 67.95 (*0-7506-0139-6*) Buttrwrth-Heinemann.

Chaos, Gaia, Eros: A Chaos Pioneer Uncovers the Three Great Streams of History. Ralph H. Abraham. LC 94-2820. 256p. 1994. pap. 16.00 (*0-06-250013-9*) Harper SF.

Chaos Gate. Josepha Sherman. (Bard's Tale Ser.: Vol. 4). 320p. (Orig.). 1994. mass mkt. 5.99 (*0-671-87597-3*) Baen Bks.

Chaos II. Hao Bailin. 752p. (C). 1990. text ed. 97.00 (*981-02-0095-1*); pap. text ed. 43.00 (*981-02-0096-X*) World Scientific Pub.

Chaos in America. John L. King. (Illus.). 112p. (Orig.). (C). 1990. pap. 11.95 (*0-922356-24-6*) Amer West Pubs.

Chaos in Biological Systems. Ed. by H. Degn et al. LC 87-7203. (NATO ASI Series A, Life Sciences: Vol. 138). (Illus.). 336p. 1987. 85.00 (*0-306-42685-4*, Plenum Pr) Plenum.

Chaos in Chemistry & Biochemistry. R. J. Field & L. Gyorgyi. 200p. 1993. text ed. 81.00 (*981-02-1024-8*) World Scientific Pub.

Chaos in Classical & Quantum Mechanics. M. C. Gutzwiller. (Interdisciplinary Applied Mathematics Ser.). (Illus.). xiii, 432p. 1993. 39.95 (*0-387-97173-4*) Spr-Verlag.

Chaos in Dynamic Systems. G. M. Zaslavsky. 388p. 1985. 235.00 (*0-685-24190-4*); text ed. 249.00 (*3-7186-0225-3*) Gordon & Breach.

Chaos in Dynamical Systems. Edward Ott. LC 93-9344. (Illus.). 425p. (C). 1993. 74.95 (*0-521-43215-4*); pap. 32.95 (*0-521-43799-7*) Cambridge U Pr.

Chaos in Experiment: Self-Organized Hierachical Complexity in Semiconductor Experiments. J. Peinke et al. LC 92-25600. (Illus.). 320p. 1993. write for info. (*3-540-55647-8*); 59.00 (*0-387-55647-8*) Spr-Verlag.

***Chaos in Heat Transfer & Fluid Dynamics: 1994 International Mechanical Engineering Congress & Exposition, Chicago, Illinois - November 6-11, 1994.** (HTD Ser.: Vol. 298). 124p. 1994. 54.00 (*0-7918-1420-3*, G00915) ASME.

Chaos in Laser-Matter Interactions. P. Milonni et al. 384p. 1987. text ed. 70.00 (*9971-5-0179-1*); pap. text ed. 37.00 (*9971-5-0180-5*) World Scientific Pub.

Chaos in Systems with Noise. Tomasz Kapitaniak. 140p. (C). 1988. text ed. 33.00 (*9971-5-0542-8*) World Scientific Pub.

Chaos in Systems with Noise. 2nd ed. Tomasz Kapitaniak. 244p. (C). 1990. text ed. 59.00 (*981-02-0409-4*); pap. text ed. 36.00 (*981-02-0410-8*) World Scientific Pub.

Chaos in the Courthouse: The Inner Workings of the Urban Criminal Courts. Paul B. Wice. LC 84-15976. 208p. 1985. text ed. 49.95 (*0-275-90185-8*, C0185, Praeger Pubs) Greenwood.

***Chaos in the Humanities.** Ed. & Intro. by Patrick Brady. 200p. (Orig.). 1994. pap. 19.95 (*1-886935-06-8*) New Prdigm Pr.

Chaos in the Laboratory & Thirteen Other Science Projects Using the Apple II. Ed. by David L. Vernier. LC 91-90900. (Illus.). 288p. (Orig.). (YA). (gr. 9 up). 1991. pap. 25.95 (*0-918731-46-1*) Vernier Soft.

Chaos in Wonderland: Visual Adventures in a Fractal World. Clifford A. Pickover. 256p. 1994. 29.95 (*0-312-10743-9*) St Martin.

***Chaos Marketing: How to Win in a Turbulent World.** Torsten H. Nilson. LC 95-1442. (Marketing for Professionals Ser.). 1995. pap. 19.95 (*0-07-707991-4*) McGraw.

***Chaos Mode.** Piers Anthony. 368p. (Orig.). 1995. pap. text ed. 5.99 (*0-441-00132-7*) Ace Bks.

Chaos Mode. Piers Anthony. 304p. (Orig.). 1994. 19.95 (*0-399-13893-5*) Putnam Pub Group.

Chaos (Moebius Artbook) Moebius. 96p. 1991. 18.95 (*0-87135-833-6*) Marvel Entmnt.

Chaos, Noise & Fractals. Ed. by E. R. Pike & L. A. Lugiato. (Malvern Physics Ser.). (Illus.). 614p. 1987. 75.00 (*0-85274-364-5*) IOP Pub.

Chaos of the Psychics, Vol. 4 of 4. Gordon Lindsay. (Sorcery in America Ser.: Vol. 4). 2.95 (*0-89985-094-4*) Christ for the Nations.

Chaos on the Shop Floor: A Worker's View of Quality, Productivity, & Management. Tom Juravich. 160p. (C). 1988. pap. 16.95 (*0-87722-561-3*) Temple U Pr.

***Chaos or Community? Seeking Solutions, not Scapegoats to Bad Economics.** Holly Sklar. (Illus.). 250p. 1995. 35.00 (*0-89608-512-0*); pap. 15.00 (*0-89608-511-2*) South End Pr.

Chaos or Creation: Spirituality in Mid-Life. L. Patrick Carroll & Katherine M. Dyckman. 176p. 1986. pap. 9.95 (*0-8091-2832-2*) Paulist Pr.

Chaos, Order, & Patterns. Ed. by R. Artuso et al. (NATO ASI Series B, Physics: Vol. 280). (Illus.). 326p. (C). 1992. 95.00 (*0-306-44080-6*, Plenum Pr) Plenum.

***Chaos Paradigm: Developments & Applications in Engineering & Science.** Ed. by Richard A. Katz. (AIP Conference Proceedings Ser.: No. 296). 500p. 1994. text ed. 320.00x (*1-56396-254-3*) Am Inst Physics.

Chaos, Resonance & Collective Dynamical Phenomena in the Solar System: Proceedings of the 152nd Symposium of the International Astronomical Union Held in Angra dos Reis, Brazil, 15-19 July, 1991. Ed. by S. Ferraz-Mello. LC 92-10238. (International Astronomical Union Highlights Ser.). 432p. (C). 1992. lib. bdg. 119.00 (*0-7923-1781-5*) Kluwer Ac.

Chaos, Solitude, Desire. Zezeu Vieira. (Illus.). 65p. 1993. write for info. (*0-9635638-0-7*) Midland Hghts.

***Chaos Theory & Nonlinear Dynamics in the Financial Markets: Theory, Evidence & Applications.** Ed. by Robert R. Trippi. 300p. 1995. 75.00 (*1-55738-857-1*) Probus Pub Co.

***Chaos Theory in Psychology.** Fred D. Abraham & Albert R. Gilgen. LC 94-29848. (Contributions in Psychology Ser.). 400p. 1995. text ed. 75.00 (*0-313-28961-1*, Greenwood Pr) Greenwood.

***Chaos Theory in Psychology.** Frederick D. Abraham & Albert R. Gilgen. 400p. 1995. pap. text ed. 29.95 (*0-275-95140-5*, Praeger Pubs) Greenwood.

***Chaos Theory in Psychology & the Life Sciences.** Ed. by Robin Robertson & Allan Combs. 424p. 1995. text ed. 79.95 (*0-8058-1736-0*) L Erlbaum Assocs.

***Chaos Theory in Psychology & the Life Sciences.** Ed. by Robin Robertson & Allan Combs. 424p. 1995. pap. text ed. 39.95 (*0-8058-1737-9*) L Erlbaum Assocs.

Chaos Theory in the Financial Markets: Applying Fractals, Fuzzy Logic, Genetic Algorithms. Ditmitris N. Chorafas. 1994. 75.00 (*1-55738-555-6*) Probus Pub Co.

Chaos to Cosmos: Studies in Biblical Patterns of Creation. Susan Niditch. (Studies in Humanities: No. 6). (C). 1985. pap. 14.95 (*0-89130-763-X*, 00 01 06) Scholars Pr GA.

Chaos under Control: The Art & Science of Complexity. David Peak & Michael Frame. LC 94-3092. (C). 1995. pap. text ed. 24.95 (*0-7167-2429-4*) W H Freeman.

Chaos under Heaven: The Untold Story of China's Search for Democracy. Gordon Thomas. (Illus.). 352p. 1991. 21.95 (*1-55972-059-X*, Birch Ln Pr) Carol Pub Group.

Chaosmos: Literature, Science, & Theory after Modernism. LC 93-44752. (SUNY Series, The Margins of Literature). 211p. (C). 1994. 49.50x (*0-7914-1913-4*); pap. 16.95x (*0-7914-1914-2*) State U NY Pr.

Chaotic & Fractal Dynamics: An Introduction for Applied Scientists & Engineers. Francis C. Moon. 528p. 1992. text ed. 64.95 (*0-471-54571-6*) Wiley.

Chaotic & Stochastic Behavior in Automatic Production Lines. Max-Olivier Hongler. LC 94-20329. (Lecture Notes in Physics, New Series M, Monographs: Vol. M22). 1994. 39.00 (*0-387-58121-9*) Spr-Verlag.

Chaotic Behavior in Quantum Systems: Theory & Applications. Ed. by G. Casati. (NATO ASI Series B, Physics: Vol. 120). 380p. 1985. 89.50 (*0-306-41898-3*, Plenum Pr) Plenum.

Chaotic Behavior of Deterministic Systems. Ed. by Gerard Iooss et al. (Houches Summer School Proceedings Ser.: Vol. 36). 1984. 213.00 (*0-444-86542-X*, I-440-83) Elsevier.

Chaotic Behaviour of Deterministic Dissipative Systems. Milos Marek & Igor Schreiber. (Illus.). 378p. (C). 1992. pap. 39.95 (*0-521-43830-6*) Cambridge U Pr.

Chaotic Cognition: Principles & Application. Ronald A. Finke & Jonathan Bettle. 275p. 1995. 55.00 (*0-8058-1739-5*); pap. 30.00 (*0-8058-1740-9*) L Erlbaum Assocs.

Chaotic Dynamical Systems. S. Ushiki. (Advanced Series in Dynamical Systems). 192p. 1993. text ed. 81.00 (*981-02-1276-3*) World Scientific Pub.

Chaotic Dynamics: An Introduction. Gregory L. Baker & Jerry P. Gollub. (Illus.). 180p. (C). 1990. pap. 19.95 (*0-521-38897-X*) Cambridge U Pr.

Chaotic Dynamics: An Introduction. Gregory L. Baker & Jerry P. Gollub. (Illus.). 180p. (C). 1990. 59.95 (*0-521-38258-0*) Cambridge U Pr.

Chaotic Dynamics: From the One-Dimensional Endomorphism to the Two-Dimensional Diffeomorphism. C. Mira. 472p. (C). 1987. text ed. 87.00 (*9971-5-0324-7*) World Scientific Pub.

Chaotic Dynamics: Theory & Applications to Economics. Alfredo Medio & Giampaolo Gallo. (Illus.). 250p. (C). 1993. 64.95 (*0-521-39488-0*) Cambridge U Pr.

Chaotic Dynamics: Theory & Applications to Economics. Alfredo Medio & Giampaolo Gallo. (Illus.). 250p. (C). 1993. pap. 49.95 (*0-521-42107-1*) Cambridge U Pr.

***Chaotic Dynamics: Theory & Applications to Economics.** Alfredo Medio. (Illus.). 362p. (C). 1995. pap. 19.95 (*0-521-48461-8*) Cambridge U Pr.

Chaotic Dynamics: Theory & Practice. Ed. by T. Bountis. LC 92-21986. (NATO ASI Series B, Physics: Vol. 298). 1992. 120.00 (*0-306-44247-7*, Plenum Pr) Plenum.

Chaotic Dynamics: Two-Dimensional Endomorphism Problems. L. Gardini & C. Mira. 500p. 1995. text ed. 86.00 (*981-02-1647-5*) World Scientific Pub.

Chaotic Dynamics & Fractals. Michael F. Barnsley & Stephen G. Demko. (Notes & Reports in Mathematics in Science & Engineering). 1986. text ed. 64.00 (*0-12-079060-2*) Acad Pr.

Chaotic Dynamics & Transport in Fluids & Plasmas. I. Prigogine et al. (Research Trends in Physics Ser.). 256p. 1992. 120.00 (*0-88318-923-2*) Am Inst Physics.

Chaotic Dynamics of Nonlinear Systems. S. Neil Rasband. 230p. 1990. text ed. 64.95 (*0-471-63418-2*) Wiley.

Chaotic Economic Dynamics. Richard M. Goodwin. (Illus.). 152p. 1990. 45.00 (*0-19-828335-0*) OUP.

Chaotic Evolution & Strange Attractors. David Ruelle. (Lezioni Lincee Ser.). (Illus.). 120p. 1989. pap. 17.95 (*0-521-36830-8*) Cambridge U Pr.

Chaotic Hierarchy. Ed. by G. Baier & M. Klein. 412p. (C). 1991. text ed. 104.00 (*981-02-0023-4*) World Scientific Pub.

Chaotic Logic: Language, Thought & Reality from the Perspective of Complex Systems Analysis. B. Goertzel. (IFSR International Series on Systems Science: Vol. 9). (Illus.). 288p. 1994. 75.00 (*0-306-44690-1*, Plenum Pr) Plenum.

Chaotic Miss Crispino. Kasey Michaels. 192p. (Orig.). 1991. mass mkt. 3.99 (*0-380-76300-1*) Avon.

1150

An Asterisk (*) at the beginning of an entry indicates that the title is appearing in BIP for the first time.

An Asterisk (*) at the beginning of an entry indicates that the title is appearing in BIP for the first time.

1151

Chapters on the Principles of International Law. John Westlake. xix, 275p. 1982. reprint ed. lib. bdg. 27.50 (*0-8377-1328-5*) Rothman.

Chapters on the Theory & History of Banking. Charles F. Dunbar. Ed. by Stuart Bruchey. LC 80-1145. (Rise of Commercial Banking Ser.). 1981. reprint ed. lib. bdg. 20. 95 (*0-405-13648-X*) Ayer.

Chapwoman's Alwomanac: Pilot Handling Throughout the Year. Anne L. Sirna. (Illus.). 96p. 1989. pap. text ed. 7.95 (*0-915160-98-6*) Seven Seas.

Chapwoman's Alwomanac: Pilot Handling throughout the Year. Anne L. Sirna. 1989. pap. text ed. 7.95 (*0-07-155535-8*) McGraw.

Chapwoman's Boating: Wit & Wisdom. Anne L. Sirna. LC 93-90811. (Illus.). 208p. (Orig.). 1993. pap. 9.95 (*0-940073-02-1*) Anagram Group.

ChapWoman's Galley Guide. Anne L. Sirna & Antonia F. Ritchie. LC 91-71600. (Illus.). 155p. (Orig.). 1991. pap. 12.95 (*0-940073-01-3*) Anagram Group.

Chapwoman's Guide to Shemanship & Pilot Handling. Anne L. Sirna & Antonia F. Ritchie. 1988. pap. 8.95 (*0-07-156826-3*) McGraw.

Chapwoman's Guide to Shemanship & Pilot Handling. Anne L. Sirna & Antonia F. Ritchie. LC 82-16933. (Illus.). 96p. 1988. pap. text ed. 8.95 (*0-915160-93-5*) Seven Seas.

Chaque Homme dans sa Nuit. Julien Green. (FRE.). 1992. pap. 17.95 (*0-7859-2732-8*) Fr & Eur.

Chaqueta En la Piel. Marie-Francine Hebert. (Primeros Lectores Ser.). (Illus.). 60p. (SPA.). (J). (gr. 5 up). 1994. pap. 5.95 (*958-07-0074-5*) Firefly Bks Ltd.

Char Siu Bao Boy. Sandra S. Yamate. (Illus.). 32p. (J). (gr. k-4). 1991. 12.95 (*1-879965-00-3*) Polychrome Pub.

Char Voki see Evil Spirit

***Characeae of Tasmania.** J. C. Van Raam. (Nova Hedwigia Ser.: Vo. 110). (Illus.). 50p. 1995. pap. 40.00 (*3-443-51032-9*, Pub. by Cramer-Borntraeger GW) Lubrecht & Cramer.

Character. F. Bordewijk. Tr. by E. M. Prince. 286p. (C). 1990. 17.95 (*0-941533-96-4*) New Amsterdam Bks.

Character. Bill Hybels. (Christian Basics Bible Studies). 64p. (Orig.). 1994. pap. 4.99 (*0-8308-2003-5*, 2003) InterVarsity.

Character. Joel J. Kupperman. 208p. 1991. 39.95 (*0-19-506870-X*) OUP.

C

***Character.** Joel J. Kupperman. 208p. 1995. pap. 14.95 (*0-19-509654-1*) OUP.

Character. Lao Russell. Ed. by Emilia L. Lombardi. 20p. (Orig.). 1991. pap. text ed. 5.00 (*1-879605-35-X*) U Sci & Philos.

Character, No. 2. pap. 0.15 (*0-87377-134-6*) GAM Pubns.

***Character: The Grandest Thing in the World.** Orison S. Marden. (Illus.). 55p. 1995. pap. 5.00 (*0-89540-297-1*) Sun Pub.

Character Analysis. rev. ed. Wilhelm Reich. Tr. by Vincent R. Carfagno. 576p. 1980. pap. 18.00 (*0-374-50980-8*) FS&G.

Character & Characterization in Shakespeare. Leo Kirschbaum. LC 61-12265. (Wayne Bks.: No. WB4). 179p. (Orig.). reprint ed. pap. 51.10 (*0-7837-3657-6*, 2043528) Bks Demand.

Character & Conflict: An Introduction to Drama. 2nd ed. Ed. by Alvin B. Kernan. 721p. (Orig.). (C). 1969. pap. text ed. 21.50 (*0-15-506271-9*) HB Coll Pubs.

Character & Consciousness in Eighteenth-Century Comic Fiction. Elizabeth Kraft. LC 91-7715. 216p. 1992. 35.00 (*0-8203-1365-3*) U of Ga Pr.

Character & Context: Studies in the Fiction of Abramovitsh, Brenner & Agnon. Jeffrey Fleck. LC 83-9068. (Brown Judaic Studies). 136p. 1984. pap. 15.00 (*0-89130-643-9*, 14 00 45) Scholars Pr GA.

Character & Cops: Ethics in Policing. 2nd ed. Edwin J. Delattre. LC 94-18150. 331p. 1994. 21.95 (*0-8447-3868-9*, AEI Pr) Am Enterprise.

Character & Crime: An Inquiry into the Causes of the Virtue of Nations. Michael Novak. 152p. (C). 1986. pap. text ed. 18.50 (*0-8191-6661-8*) U Pr of Amer.

Character & Culture. Sigmund Freud. 320p. 1963. pap. 8.00 (*0-02-076200-3*, Collier S&S) S&S Trade.

Character & Destiny: A Nation in Search of Its Soul. James Kennedy & James N. Black. 256p. 1994. pap. 18. 99 (*0-310-44380-6*) Zondervan.

Character & Environment in the Novels of Thomas Hardy. Herbert Grimsditch. LC 68-788. (Studies in Thomas Hardy: No. 14). 1969. reprint ed. lib. bdg. 75.00 (*0-8383-0662-4*) M S G Haskell Hse.

Character & Handwriting Recognition: Expanding Frontiers. Ed. by P. S. Wang. 300p. (C). 1991. text ed. 89.00 (*981-02-0710-7*) World Scientific Pub.

Character & Health. Yves Requena. Ed. by Robert L. Felt. Tr. by Carol Bell. (Illus.). 224p. (Orig.). 1989. pap. 16.95 (*0-912111-23-2*) Paradigm Publns.

Character & Ideology in the Book of Esther. Michael V. Fox. Ed. by James L. Crenshaw. (Studies on Personalities of the Old Testament). 332p. 1991. text ed. 34.95 (*0-87249-757-7*) U of SC Pr.

Character & Influence of the Indian Trade in Wisconsin. Frederick J. Turner. LC 78-63807. (Johns Hopkins University. Studies in the Social Sciences. Thirtieth Ser. 1912: 11-12). reprint ed. 11.50 (*0-404-61070-6*) AMS Pr.

Character & Influence of the Roman Civil Law. Peter Stein. 480p. 1988. text ed. 60.00 (*1-85285-005-1*) Hambledon Press.

Character & Motive in Shakespeare. John I. Stewart. LC 76-51261. (Studies in Shakespeare: No. 24). 1977. lib. bdg. 75.00 (*0-8383-2134-8*) M S G Haskell Hse.

Character & Narration in the Short Fiction of Saul Bellow. Marianne M. Friedrich. LC 93-46249. (Twentieth-Century American Jewish Writers Ser.: Vol. 5). 208p. (C). 1995. text ed. 47.95 (*0-8204-2436-6*) P Lang Pubs.

Character & Neurosis: An Integrative View. Claudio Naranjo. LC 94-21263. 352p. (Orig.). 1994. pap. 18.95 (*0-89556-066-6*) Gateways Bks & Tapes.

Character & Opinion in the United States. George Santayana. 296p. (C). 1991. pap. 21.95 (*0-88738-890-6*) Transaction Pubs.

Character & Origins of Smog Aerosols: A Digest of Results from the California Aerosol Characterization Experiment (ACHEX) Ed. by George M. Hidy et al. LC 79-4585. (Advances in Environmental Science & Technology Ser.: No. 9). (Illus.). 798p. reprint ed. pap. 180.00 (*0-7837-3448-4*, 2057773) Bks Demand.

***Character & Personality in the Novels of William Faulkner: A Study in Psychostylistics.** Ineke Bockting. 312p. (C). 1995. lib. bdg. 44.00 (*0-8191-9849-8*) U Pr of Amer.

Character & Personality of Children from Broken Homes. Nehemiah Wallenstein. LC 70-177664. (Columbia University. Teachers College. Contributions to Education Ser.: No. 721). reprint ed. 22.50 (*0-404-55721-X*) AMS Pr.

***Character & Self-Experience: Working with Obsessive-Compulsive, Depressive-Masochistic, Narcissistic, & Other Character Styles.** Lawrence Josephs. 344p. 1995. pap. 30.00 (*1-56821-580-0*) Aronson.

Character & Social Structure: The Psychology of Social Institutions. Hans Gerth & C. Wright Mills. LC 53-12721. 514p. 1964. pap. 7.95 (*0-15-616759-X*, Harvest Bks) HarBrace.

Character & Style in English Politics. J. H. Grainger. LC 69-10428. 299p. reprint ed. pap. 85.30 (*0-317-09563-3*, 2013252) Bks Demand.

Character & the Christian Life. Stanley Hauerwas. 1990. pap. 5.95 (*0-02-680077-2*) Macmillan.

Character & the Christian Life: A Study in Theological Ethics. Stanley Hauerwas. LC 85-5873. 272p. (C). 1989. pap. text ed. 11.95 (*0-268-00772-1*) U of Notre Dame Pr.

Character & the Novel. William J. Harvey. 217p. 1966. pap. 11.95 (*0-8014-9067-7*) Cornell U Pr.

Character & Timing of Rapid Environmental & Climatic Changes: Abstracts. American Quaternary Association. Biennial Meeting, 7th, 1982. 188p. 1982. 10.00 (*0-318-16892-8*) Am Quaternary Assn.

Character As a Subversive Force in Shakespeare: The History & Roman Plays. Bernard J. Paris. LC 90-55839. 224p. 1991. 39.50 (*0-8386-3429-X*) Fairleigh Dickinson.

Character Book: A Workbook to Accompany "Read Chinese", Bk. 1. Timothy Light & Tao-Chung Yao. (Mirror Ser.). 316p. (Orig.). (CHI.). 1985. pap. text ed. 12.95 (*0-88710-137-2*) Yale Far Eastern Pubns.

Character Building. Booker T. Washington. LC 75-38848. (Studies in Black History & Culture: No. 54). 291p. 1972. reprint ed. lib. bdg. 75.00 (*0-8383-1394-9*) M S G Haskell Hse.

Character Building: A Guide for Parents & Teachers. David Isaacs. 268p. (Orig.). 1984. reprint ed. pap. 11.95 (*0-906127-67-X*, Pub. by Four Courts Pr EIRE) Scepter Pubs.

Character Building Thought Power. Ralph W. Trine. 51p. 1993. pap. 4.50 (*0-89540-251-3*, SB-251) Sun Pub.

Character-Building Through Power. Ralph W. Trine. 51p. 1994. reprint ed. spiral bd. 3.85 (*0-7873-1138-3*) Mokelumne.

Character Connection. E. W. Price. 196p. (Orig.). 1992. pap. 7.99 (*1-56043-066-4*) Destiny Image.

***Character Counts--Who's Counting Yours?** Rod Handley. 176p. (Orig.). (YA). 1995. pap. 8.95 (*1-887002-00-6*) Cross Trng.

Character Dance. Jurgen Pagels. LC 82-49013. (Illus.). 208p. 1984. 25.00 (*0-253-31337-6*) Ind U Pr.

Character Development: Encouraging Self-Esteem & Self-Discipline, 3 vols., Set. Polly Greenberg. LC 91-60826. (Illus.). 1991. pap. text ed. write for info. (*0-935989-46-3*) Natl Assn Child Ed.

Character Development: Encouraging Self-Esteem & Self-Discipline in Infants, Toddlers & Two-Year-Olds. Polly Greenberg. LC 91-60826. (Character Development: Encouraging Self-Esteem & Self-Discipline Ser.: Vol. 1). (Illus.). 197p. (Orig.). 1991. pap. text ed. 8.00 (*0-935989-43-9*, NAEYC #175) Natl Assn Child Ed.

Character Development & Physical Activity. David L. Shields & Brenda J. Bredemeier. LC 94-7514. 288p. 1995. 35.00x (*0-87322-711-5*, BSHI0711) Human Kinetics.

Character Development in Schools & Beyond. enl. ed. Ed. by Kevin Ryan & Thomas Lickona. LC 92-10115. (Cultural Heritage & Contemporary Change Series VI: Foundations of Moral Education,: Vol. 3). 350p. 1992. pap. 17.50 (*1-56518-059-3*) Coun Res Values.

Character Development in Schools & Beyond. 2nd enl. ed. Ed. by Kevin Ryan & Thomas Lickona. LC 92-10115. (Cultural Heritage & Contemporary Change Series VI: Foundations of Moral Education,: Vol. 3). 350p. 1992. 45.00 (*1-56518-058-5*) Coun Res Values.

Character Dictionary Accompanying "Japanese: A Manual of Reading & Writing" Samuel E. Martin et al. LC 86-50705. 378p. 1986. pap. 19.95 (*0-8048-1511-9*) C E Tuttle.

Character Disorders & Adaptive Mechanisms. rev. ed. Peter L. Giovacchini. LC 83-11957. 552p. 1984. 60.00 (*0-87668-641-2*) Aronson.

Character Disorders in Parents of Delinquents. Beatrice S. Reiner & Irving Kaufman. LC 59-15631. 183p. reprint ed. pap. 52.20 (*0-317-07996-4*, 2019945) Bks Demand.

Character Dressed Kewpies. Ada Fitzsimmons. (Illus.). 44p. 1982. pap. 4.00 (*0-915195-02-X*) Paper Pile.

Character Education Curriculum: Kindergarten, K-9. Character Education Institute Staff. Ed. by Young J. Mulkey. (Illus.). 1990. Kindergarten kit: The Happy Life Series. 130.00 (*0-913413-00-3*) Char Ed Inst.

Character Education Curriculum: Kindergarten, K-9, Level C: Character for Citizenship. Character Education Institute Staff. Ed. by Young J. Mulkey. (Illus.). 1990. Level C - 3rd. gr., Character for Citizenship. 95.00 (*0-913413-11-9*) Char Ed Inst.

Character Education Curriculum: Kindergarten, K-9, Level D: Character for Citizenship. Character Education Institute Staff. Ed. by Young J. Mulkey. (Illus.). 1990. Level D - 4th. gr., Character for Citizenship. 95.00 (*0-913413-12-7*) Char Ed Inst.

Character Education Curriculum: Kindergarten, K-9, Level A: Character for Citizenship. Character Education Institute Staff. Ed. by Young J. Mulkey. (Illus.). 1990. Level A - 1st gr., Character for Citizenship. 95.00 (*0-913413-09-7*) Char Ed Inst.

Character Education Curriculum: Kindergarten, K-9, Level B: Character for Citizenship. Character Education Institute Staff. Ed. by Young J. Mulkey. (Illus.). 1990. Level B - 2nd. gr., Character for Citizenship. 95.00 (*0-913413-10-0*) Char Ed Inst.

Character Education Curriculum: Kindergarten, K-9, Level E: Character for Citizenship. Character Education Institute Staff. Ed. by Young J. Mulkey. (Illus.). 1990. Level E - 5th. gr., Character for Citizenship. 95.00 (*0-913413-13-5*) Char Ed Inst.

Character Education Curriculum: Kindergarten, K-9, Level F: Living with Me & Others. Character Education Institute Staff. Ed. by Young J. Mulkey. (Illus.). 1990. Level F - 6th gr., Living with Me & Others. 95.00 (*0-913413-06-2*) Char Ed Inst.

Character Education Curriculum: Kindergarten, K-9, Level G: Decisions about Me. Character Education Institute Staff. Ed. by Young J. Mulkey. (Illus.). (J). (gr. 7-9). 1990. Level G - 7th-9th gr. Decisions about Me. 95.00 (*0-913413-07-0*) Char Ed Inst.

Character Education Curriculum: Kindergarten, K-9, Set. Character Education Institute Staff. Ed. by Young J. Mulkey. (Illus.). 1990. 795.00 (*0-913413-08-9*) Char Ed Inst.

Character Education Curriculum: The Happy Life Series Plus Living with Me & Others Including Our Rights & Responsibilities, Level C. American Institute for Character Education Staff. (Illus.). 148p. (J). (gr. 1-7). 1984. 95.00 (*0-913413-03-8*) Char Ed Inst.

Character Education Curriculum: The Happy Life Series Plus Living with Me & Others Including Our Rights & Responsibilities, Level D. American Institute for Character Education Staff. (Illus.). 152p. (J). (gr. 1-7). 1984. 95.00 (*0-913413-04-6*) Char Ed Inst.

Character Education Curriculum: The Happy Life Series Plus Living with Me & Others Including Our Rights & Responsibilities, Level A. American Institute for Character Education Staff. (Illus.). 124p. (J). (gr. 1-7). 1984. 95.00 (*0-913413-01-1*) Char Ed Inst.

Character Education Curriculum: The Happy Life Series Plus Living with Me & Others Including Our Rights & Responsibilities, Level B. American Institute for Character Education Staff. (Illus.). 127p. (J). (gr. 1-7). 1984. 95.00 (*0-913413-02-X*) Char Ed Inst.

Character Education Curriculum: The Happy Life Series Plus Living with Me & Others Including Our Rights & Responsibilities, Level E. American Institute for Character Education Staff. (Illus.). 160p. (J). (gr. 1-7). 1984. 95.00 (*0-913413-05-4*) Char Ed Inst.

Character Education Curriculum: The Happy Life Series Plus Living with Me & Others Including Our Rights & Responsibilities, Level F. American Institute for Character Education Staff. (Illus.). (J). (gr. 1-6). 1984. 95.00 (*0-685-09647-5*) Char Ed Inst.

Character Education Curriculum: The Happy Life Series Plus Living with Me & Others Including Our Rights & Responsibilities, Level G: Middle School; Level K: Kindergarten. American Institute for Character Education Staff. (Illus.). (J). (gr. 1-7). 1984. Level G, Middle School#Level K, Kindergarten with film strips. flmstrp 125.00 (*0-685-09648-3*) Char Ed Inst.

Character Education Curriculum: The Happy Life Series Plus Living with Me & Others Including Our Rights & Responsibilities, Set, Levels A-F. American Institute for Character Education Staff. (Illus.). (J). (gr. 1-7). 1984. Set. 820.00 (*0-685-09646-7*) Char Ed Inst.

***Character Education in America's Schools.** Terri Akin et al. 170p. (Orig.). (J). (gr. 1-6). Date not set. pap. text ed. 18.95 (*1-56499-026-5*) Innerchoice Pub.

Character First: The Hyde School Difference. Joseph W. Gauld. LC 93-16884. 1993. 18.95 (*1-55815-262-8*) ICS Pr.

Character Graphics: For the Commodore C-64 & C-128, Vol. I. James L. Farvour. (Commodore Information Ser.). (Illus.). 96p. (Orig.). 1985. pap. 9.95 (*0-932679-02-1*) Blue Cat.

Character in Literature. Baruch Hochman. LC 84-45809. 208p. (C). 1985. 27.95 (*0-8014-1787-2*) Cornell U Pr.

Character in the Book. Zemach-Bers. (J). Date not set. 15. 00 (*0-06-205060-5*, HarpT); lib. bdg. 14.89 (*0-06-205061-3*) HarpC.

Character Indicated by Handwriting. Rosa Baughan. 140p. 1972. reprint ed. spiral bd. 6.05 (*0-7873-1143-X*) Mokelumne.

***Character Jug Collectors Handbook.** 6th ed. Francis Salmon & Peter Miller. 1995. pap. 22.95 (*1-870703-26-X*) Chilton.

Character Law & Campaign Law. 2nd ed. Peter C. Fenlon, Jr. & S. C. Charlton. (Illus.). 144p. 1989. 14.00 (*1-55806-093-6*, 1300) Iron Crown Ent Inc.

Character Lines. Larry Ketron. 1980. pap. 4.75 (*0-8222-0197-6*) Dramatists Play.

Character, Object & Effects of Trades' Unions: With Some Remarks on the Law Concerning Them. Edward C. Tufnell. LC 72-2551. (British Labour Struggles Before 1850 Ser.). 1974. reprint ed. 20.95 (*0-405-04442-9*) Ayer.

Character of a Quaker. Henry J. Cadbury. LC 59-10262. (C). 1959. pap. 3.00 (*0-87574-103-7*) Pendle Hill.

Character of American Higher Education & Intercollegiate Sport. Donald Chu. LC 87-34015. (Frontiers in Education Ser.). 252p. (C). 1989. 59.50 (*0-88706-791-3*); pap. 19.95 (*0-88706-793-X*) State U NY Pr.

Character of Caring People. Phyllis J. Le Peau. (Caring People Bible Studies). 96p. (Orig.). 1991. pap. 4.99 (*0-8308-1197-4*, 1197) InterVarsity.

***Character of God.** Jackie Banas. 73p. (Orig.). 1994. pap. 10.00 (*0-9614014-7-8*) Know Him Pr.

***Character of God: Discovering the God Who Is.** R. C. Sproul. 190p. 1995. 8.99 (*0-89283-908-2*, Vine Bks) Servant.

Character of God's Workman. Watchman Nee. Ed. by Herbert L. Fader. Tr. by Stephen Kaung. 229p. (Orig.). 1988. pap. 5.50 (*0-935008-69-1*) Christian Fellow Pubs.

Character of Hamlet. John E. Hankins. LC 76-14884. (Select Bibliographies Reprint Ser.). 1977. reprint ed. 24. 95 (*0-8369-5676-1*) Ayer.

Character of Hugh Legare. Michael O'Brien. LC 85-3207. 372p. 1985. text ed. 40.00x (*0-87049-471-6*) U of Tenn Pr.

Character of John Adams. Peter Shaw. LC 75-14306. 342p. reprint ed. pap. 97.50 (*0-8357-4399-3*, 2037219) Bks Demand.

Character of King Arthur in Medieval Literature. Rosemary Morris. (Arthurian Studies: No. IV). 175p. 1985. 70.00 (*0-85991-088-1*) Boydell & Brewer.

Character of Melodrama. William P. Steele. 1968. pap. 5.95 (*0-89101-017-3*) U Maine Pr.

Character of Mind. Colin McGinn. 1982. pap. 15.95 (*0-19-289159-6*) OUP.

Character of Organizations: Using Jungian Type in Organizational Development. William Bridges. 152p. 1992. pap. 12.95 (*0-89106-052-9*) Consulting Psychol.

***Character of Our Communities: Toward an Ethic of Liberation for the Church.** Gloria Albrecht. 192p. (Orig.). 1995. pap. 16.95 (*0-687-00283-4*) Abingdon.

Character of Physical Law. Richard Feynman. 1994. 14.50 (*0-679-60127-9*, Modern Lib) Random.

Character of Physical Law. Richard P. Feynman. (Illus.). 1967. pap. 10.95x (*0-262-56003-8*) MIT Pr.

Character of Races: Influenced by Physical Environment, Natural Selection & Historical Development. Ellsworth Huntington. Ed. by Gerald Grob. LC 76-46082. (Anti-Movements in America Ser.). 1977. lib. bdg. 34.95 (*0-405-09955-X*) Ayer.

Character of Swift's Satire: A Revised Focus. Ed. by Claude Rawson. LC 81-72062. 344p. 1983. 45.00 (*0-87413-209-6*) U Delaware Pr.

Character of the Christian. rev. ed. Navigators Staff. (Design for Discipleship Ser.: Bk. 4). 48p. 1980. pap. 3.00 (*0-89109-039-8*) NavPress.

Character of the Euripidean Hippolytos: An Ethno-Psychoanalytical Study. George Devereux. (Studies in Humanities). 1985. pap. 21.95 (*0-89130-789-3*, 00-01-08) Scholars Pr GA.

Character of the Indian State: A Non-Marxist View. J. D. Sethi. (C). 1992. pap. 6.00 (*81-7304-029-X*, Pub. by Manohar II) S Asia.

***Character of the King.** Kathy C. Miller. (Bible Study Series for Daughters of the King). 1994. pap. text ed. 4.95 (*0-89636-310-4*) Accent CO.

Character of the King: Studies in the Parables. Ward B. Schaap. (Challenge Bible Study Guides Ser.). 128p. (Orig.). 1994. pap. 4.99 (*0-8010-8369-9*) Baker Bk.

Character of the Kingdom: Studies in the Parables. Ward B. Schaap. (Challenge Bible Study Guides Ser.). 128p. (Orig.). 1994. pap. 4.99 (*0-8010-8370-2*) Baker Bk.

Character of the One Who Says Go: A Pamphlet Dealing with God's Character & Missions. Joy Dawson. 16p. 1986. pap. 2.99 (*0-927545-08-X*) YWAM Pub.

Character of the Poet. Louis Simpson. (Poets on Poetry Ser.). 224p. 1986. 39.50 (*0-472-09369-X*); pap. 13.95 (*0-472-06369-3*) U of Mich Pr.

Character of the Poet: Wordsworth in The Prelude. Richard J. Onorato. LC 74-131126. 1971. 65.00 (*0-691-06049-5*) Princeton U Pr.

***Character of the Poet: Wordsworth in the Prelude.** Richard J. Onorato. LC 74-131126. Date not set. reprint ed. pap. 127.40 (*0-7837-9409-6*, 2060154) Bks Demand.

Character of the Province of Maryland. George Alsop & Newton D. Mereness. LC 74-39491. (Select Bibliographies Reprint Ser.). 1977. reprint ed. 12.95 (*0-8369-9900-2*) Ayer.

Character of the Word: The Texts of Zora Neale Hurston. Karla F. Holloway. LC 86-19457. (Contributions in Afro-American & African Studies: No. 102). 144p. 1987. text ed. 55.00 (*0-313-25264-5*, HUT/, Greenwood Pr) Greenwood.

Character of the Year Project: A Catalog. (Bologna Children's Book Fair Ser.). pap. 5.00 (*0-686-70269-7*) Boston Public Lib.

Character of Truth: Historical Figures in Contemporary Fiction. Naomi Jacobs. LC 89-39329. (Crosscurrents-Modern Critiques, Third Ser.). 256p. (C). 1990. 26.95 (*0-8093-1607-2*) S Ill U Pr.

Character of Xenophon's Hellenica. Vivienne Gray. LC 88-13744. 224p. 1989. text ed. 32.50 (*0-8018-3809-6*) Johns Hopkins.

Character Parts. John Mortimer. write for info. (*0-670-81124-6*) Viking Penguin.

Character People. (Illus.). 1979. pap. 8.95 (*0-8065-0701-2*, Citadel Pr) Carol Pub Group.

An Asterisk (*) at the beginning of an entry indicates that the title is appearing in BIP for the first time.

Character Portraits from Dickens. Charles Dickens. Ed. by Charles Welsh. LC 72-3628. (Studies in Dickens: No. 52). 1972. reprint ed. lib. bdg. 75.00 (*0-8383-1552-6*) M S G Haskell Hse.

Character Problems in Shakespeare's Plays. Levin L. Schucking. 11.50 (*0-8446-1397-5*) Peter Smith.

Character Reading Through Analysis of the Features. G. E. Fosbroke. 1977. lib. bdg. 59.95 (*0-8490-1594-4*) Gordon Pr.

Character Recognition. Ed. by A. Holt. 1976. pap. 28.00 (*0-08-020715-4*, Pergamon Pr) Elsevier.

Character Shifts: The Challenge of Improving Executive Performance Through Personal Growth. Robert E. Kaplan. (Technical Report Ser.: No. 143). 1990. pap. 25. 00 (*0-912879-41-6*) Ctr Creat Leader.

Character Sketches: From the Pages of Scripture, Illustrated in the World of Nature, 3 vols., 1. LC 76-3050. (Illus.). 382p. 1976. 25.00 (*0-916888-01-0*) Inst Basic Youth.

Character Sketches: From the Pages of Scripture, Illustrated in the World of Nature, 3 vols., 2. LC 76-3050. (Illus.). 382p. 1976. 25.00 (*0-916888-02-9*) Inst Basic Youth.

Character Sketches: From the Pages of Scripture, Illustrated in the World of Nature, 3 vols., Vol. 3. LC 76-3050. (Illus.). 382p. 1985. 30.00 (*0-916888-10-X*) Inst Basic Youth.

Character Sketches from the Life of Daniel. Ellen White. Ed. by Steve Wallace. 124p. (Orig.). 1992. pap. 7.95 (*0-945460-13-9*) Upward Way.

Character Sketches in Pope's Poems. Benjamin Boyce. LC 62-10050. 153p. reprint ed. pap. 43.70 (*0-317-42240-5*, 2026190) Bks Demand.

Character Steins: A Collector's Guide. Eugene Manusov & Mike Wald. LC 84-45009. (Illus.). 272p. 1987. 45.00 (*0-8453-4784-5*, Cornwall Bks) Assoc Univ Prs.

Character Structure & the Organization of Self. Lawrence Josephs. (Illus.). 288p. 1992. text ed. 50.00 (*0-231-07312-7*) Col U Pr.

Character Styles. Stephen M. Johnson. LC 93-42540. 320p. (C). 1994. 32.00 (*0-393-70171-9*) Norton.

Character Tables & Compatibility Relations of the Eighty Layer Groups & Seventeen Plane Groups. D. B. Litvin & T. R. Wike. (Illus.). 250p. 1991. 85.00 (*0-306-43917-4*, Plenum Pr) Plenum.

Character Text for Advanced Chinese. John DeFrancis. LC 66-21516. (Yale Language Ser.). (Illus.). 716p. (CHI & ENG.). reprint ed. pap. 180.00 (*0-7837-2499-3*, 2080279) Bks Demand.

Character Text for Beginning Chinese. 2nd ed. John Defrancis. LC 76-5105. 1976. text ed. 55.00 (*0-300-02055-4*); pap. 27.50 (*0-300-02059-7*) Yale U Pr.

Character Text for Speak Cantonese Bk. 1. Huang Po-Fei & Gerard P. Kok. 1961. 12.95 (*0-88710-008-2*) Yale Far Eastern Pubns.

Character Text for Speak Chinese. Loretta Pan. 1964. 9.95 (*0-88710-009-0*) Yale Far Eastern Pubns.

Character Theory of Finite Groups. I. Martin Isaacs. LC 94-6305. 320p. 1994. reprint ed. pap. 8.95 (*0-486-68014-2*) Dover.

Character Toys & Collectibles. David Longest. (Illus.). 160p. 1990. 19.95 (*0-89145-266-4*) Collector Bks.

Character Trademarks. John Mendenhall. (Illus.). 132p. (Orig.). 1990. pap. 14.95 (*0-87701-752-2*) Chronicle Bks.

Character Transition in the Writings of Hans Erich Nossack. Peter J. Schroeck. LC 91-16977. (Studies in Modern German Literature: Vol. 42). 184p. (C). 1992. text ed. 38.95 (*0-8204-1394-1*) P Lang Pubs.

Character User Interface Programming. Unix System Lab Staff. 1993. pap. text ed. 44.00 (*0-13-042581-8*) P-H.

***Character User Interface Programming (UNIX SVR 4.2)** UNIX Staff. (Illus.). 448p. (C). 1994. pap. text ed. 69.00 (*0-13-157959-2*) P-H.

***Character Variation & Evolution of Sibling Species in the Empidonax Difficilis-Flavescens Complex (Aves: Tyrannidae)** Ned K. Johnson. LC 78-59456. (University of California Publications in Entomology: No. 112). 170p. 1980. pap. 48.50 (*0-7837-7487-7*, 2049209) Bks Demand.

Character Witnesses. Mike Gillespie. 96p. 1991. student ed, pap. 0.60 (*0-89693-838-7*, Victor Books); teacher ed, pap. text ed. 2.80 (*0-89693-837-9*, Victor Books) SP Pubns.

Character Witnesses: Dramatic Monologues for Christmas & Easter. Raymond Kostulias. LC 92-40733. 120p. (Orig.). 1993. pap. 8.95 (*0-8298-0954-6*) Pilgrim OH.

Characterising Complex Systems. Ed. by Henrik Bohr. 210p. (C). 1990. pap. 23.00 (*981-02-0182-6*) World Scientific Pub.

Characteristacts of Volcanoes. James D. Dana. (Notable American Authors Ser.). 1992. reprint ed. lib. bdg. 75.00 (*0-7812-2608-2*) Rprt Serv.

Characteristic Classes. John W. Milnor & James D. Stasheff. LC 72-4050. (Annals of Mathematics Studies: No. 76). 250p. 1973. 47.00 (*0-691-08122-0*) Princeton U Pr.

Characteristic Classes & the Cohomology of Finite Groups. C. B. Thomas. (Cambridge Studies in Advanced Mathematics: No. 7). 160p. 1987. 47.95 (*0-521-25661-5*) Cambridge U Pr.

Characteristic Studies of the Cornet. Herbert Clark. (Illus.). 64p. 1915. pap. 8.95 (*0-8258-0250-4*, 0-2281) Fischer Inc NY.

Characteristically American. Ralph B. Perry. LC 73-134125. (Essay Index Reprint Ser.). 1977. 20.95 (*0-8369-2013-9*) Ayer.

Characteristics see Reaching for the Stars: A Minicourse for Education of Gifted Students

Characteristics & Capabilities of Dutch Freight Transportation Systems Models. Lorant A. Tavasszy. LC 94-20801. 1994. write for info. (*0-8330-1549-4*, MR382EACVW) Rand Corp.

Characteristics & Identification of Gifted & Talented Students. 3rd ed. Frederick B. Tuttle, Jr. & Laurence A. Becker. 160p. 1988. 14.95 (*0-8106-0729-8*) NEA.

Characteristics & Peculiarities of the Arabic Language. Emir Nasiruddin. (ARA.). 1971. 25.00 (*0-86685-056-2*) Intl Bk Ctr.

***Characteristics & Petrogenesis of Alaskan-Type Ultramafic-Mafic Intrusions, Southeastern Alaska.** Glen R. Himmelberg & Robert A. Loney. LC 95-2236. (U. S. Geological Survey Professional Papers: Vol. 1564). 1995. write for info. (*0-615-00488-1*) USGPO.

Characteristics & Recognizability of Vocal Expressions of Emotion. R. Van Bezooyen. (Netherlands Phonetic Archives Ser.). x, 158p. 1984. 52.35 (*90-6765-085-4*); pap. 38.50 (*90-6765-084-6*) Mouton.

Characteristics & Strategies for Teaching Students with Mild Disabilities. Martin Henley et al. LC 92-28682. 1992. write for info. (*0-205-13901-9*) Allyn.

Characteristics of a Successful Exchange Rate System. Jacob A. Frenkel et al. (Occasional Paper Ser.: No. 82). v, 40p. 1991. pap. 10.00 (*1-55775-215-X*) Intl Monetary.

Characteristics of & Strategies for Students with Mild Disabilities. Martin Henley et al. 450p. (C). 1992. text ed. write for info. (*0-205-14575-2*, H45750) Allyn.

Characteristics of & Strategies for Students with Mild Disabilities. Martin Henley et al. 450p. (C). 1993. teacher ed (*0-318-70135-9*) Allyn.

Characteristics of Aphasia. Ed. by Chris Code. 224p. 1989. text ed. 49.95 (*0-86377-185-8*); pap. 29.95 (*0-86377-186-6*) L Erlbaum Assocs.

Characteristics of Behavior Disorders of Children & Youth see Characteristics of Emotional & Behavioral Disorders of Children & Youth

***Characteristics of Business Owners.** 1995. lib. bdg. 250.00 (*0-8490-6523-2*) Gordon Pr.

Characteristics of Children in New York City's Foster Care System. Synia Yam-Wong. 30p. 1987. pap. text ed. 5.00 (*0-88156-064-2*) Comm Serv Soc NY.

Characteristics of Distributed-Parameter Systems: Handbook of Equations of Mathematical Physics & Distributed-Parameter Systems. A. G. Butkovskiy. LC 93-30135. (Mathematics & Its Applications Ser.). 408p. (C). 1993. lib. bdg. 162.00 (*0-7923-2499-4*) Kluwer Ac.

***Characteristics of Elderly Home Health Patients: Preliminary Data from the 1992 National Home & Hospice Care Survey.** National Center for Health Statistics Staff. (Advance Data Ser.: No. 247). 12p. Date not set. write for info. (*0-614-02934-1*) Natl Ctr Health Stats.

Characteristics of Emotional & Behavioral Disorders of Children & Youth. 5th rev. ed. James M. Kauffman. LC 92-13408. Orig. Title: Characteristics of Behavior Disorders of Children & Youth. 592p. (C). 1992. write for info. (*0-02-362141-9*, Merrill Pub Co) Macmillan.

Characteristics of Excellence. Stefan Neilson. 81p. 1986. student ed, audio 69.95 (*0-9606110-1-0*) AEON-Hierophant.

Characteristics of Facilitators: The Ecuador Project & Beyond. Arlen W. Etling. 283p. (Orig.). (C). 1975. pap. 6.00 (*0-932288-32-4*) Ctr Intl Ed U of MA.

Characteristics of Initial Effluent Quality & Its Implications for the Filter to Waste Procedure. 166p. 1988. pap. 21.00 (*0-89867-439-5*, 90538) Am Water Wks Assn.

Characteristics of Legal Malpractice. 615p. 1989. 80.00 (*0-685-44881-9*, 414-0009) Amer Bar Assn.

Characteristics of Literature: Illustrated by the Genius of Distinguished Men, 2 vols. Henry T. Tuckerman. LC 72-1309. (Essay Index Reprint Ser.). (Illus.). 1977. reprint ed. 38.95 (*0-8369-2869-5*) Ayer.

Characteristics of Men, Manners, Opinions, 3 vols., Set. A. A. Shaftesbury. (Anglistica & Americana Ser.: Vol. 123). 1152p. 1978. reprint ed. lib. bdg. 210.00 (*3-487-06680-7*, Pub. by Georg Olms GW) Lubrecht & Cramer.

Characteristics of Parallel Algorithms. Ed. by Leah H. Jamieson et al. (Scientific Computation Ser.). 275p. 1987. 44.00x (*0-262-10036-3*) MIT Pr.

Characteristics of Persons Dying from Cerebrovascular Diseases: PHS 90-1250. No. 180. write for info. (*0-318-69629-0*) Natl Ctr Health Stats.

Characteristics of Persons with & Without Health Care Coverage: United States, 1989 PHS 91-1250. No. 201. 1991. write for info. (*0-318-69605-3*) Natl Ctr Health Stats.

Characteristics of South Dakota County Officers. Alan L. Clem. 1962. 1.00 (*1-55614-025-8*) U of SD Gov Res Bur.

Characteristics of the Mid-Carboniferous Boundary & Associated Coal-Bearing Rocks in the Appalachian Basin. Ed. by Englund. (IGC Field Trip Guidebooks Ser.). 120p. 1989. 28.00 (*0-87590-661-3*, T352) Am Geophysical.

Characteristics of the Present Age, Vol. 2. Johann G. Fichte. Tr. by W. Smith. Bd. with Way Towards the Blessed Life. LC 77-72191. (Contributions to the History of Psychology Ser.: Pt. A, Orientations). 495p. 1977. reprint ed. Set text ed. 75.00 (*0-313-26926-2*, U6926, Greenwood Pr) Greenwood.

Characteristics of the Present Political State of Great Britain. 2nd ed. Robert Wallace. LC 69-19551. (Reprints of Economic Classics Ser.). 1969. reprint ed. 35.00 (*0-678-00496-X*) Kelley.

Characteristics of Wastepaper Markets & Trends in Scrap Paper Recycling, Prices, Demand & Availability: A National & Regional Overview. Thomas Plaut & Gene Steiker. (Discussion Paper Ser.: No. 103). 1978. pap. 10. 00 (*1-55869-012-3*) Regional Sci Res Inst.

Characteristics of Women: Moral, Poetical & Historical. Anna B. Jameson. LC 71-155221. reprint ed. 45.00 (*0-404-03554-X*) AMS Pr.

Characteristics of Work-Related Injuries & Illnesses in Maine. Janet A. Callahan. (Illus.). 67p. (Orig.). (C). 1993. pap. text ed. 20.00 (*1-56806-343-1*) Diane Pub.

Characteristics, Practices & Productivity: A Data Based Analysis of the Consumer Energy Council of America's Survey of Energy Service Companies. 157p. 1985. 90. 00 (*0-318-23868-3*) Consumer Energy Coun.

Characterization & Analysis of Polymers by Gas Chromatography. Malcolm P. Stevens. LC 74-84778. (Techniques & Methods of Polymer Education Ser.: Vol. 3). (Illus.). 210p. reprint ed. pap. 59.90 (*0-317-07829-1*, 2055033) Bks Demand.

Characterization & Catalyst Development: An Interactive Approach. Ed. by Ralph J. Bertolacini et al. LC 89-17777. (Symposium Ser.: No. 411). (Illus.). 488p. 1989. 99.95 (*0-8412-1684-3*) Am Chemical.

***Characterization & Chemical Modification of the Silica Surface.** Ed. by E. F. Vansant et al. LC 95-10628. (Studies in Surface Science & Catalysis: Vol. 93). 1995. write for info. (*0-444-81928-2*) Elsevier.

Characterization & Complexation of Humic Acids, No. EUR 13181. J. Kim et al. 111p. 1991. pap. 14.00 (*92-826-2221-5*, CD-NA-13181-EN-C, Pub. by Europ Com) UNIPUB.

***Characterization & Control of Odours & VOC in the Process Industries: Proceedings of the Second International Symposium on Characterization & Control of Odours & VOC in the Process Industries, Louvain-la Neuve, Belgium, 3-5 November 1993.** International Symposium on Characterization & Control of Odours & VOC in the Process Industries. Ed. by S. Vigneron et al. LC 94-29193. (Studies in Environmental Science: Vol. 61). 1994. 248.50 (*0-444-81789-1*) Elsevier.

Characterization & Determination of Erosion Resistance - STP474. 440p. 1970. 28.75 (*0-8031-0029-9*, 04-474000-29) ASTM.

Characterization & Interpretation of Rock Mass Joint Patterns. P. R. La Pointe & J. A. Hudson. (Special Paper Ser.: No. 199). (Illus.). 45p. 1985. pap. 2.00 (*0-8137-2199-7*) Geol Soc.

Characterization & Performance of Calcium Phosphate Coatings for Implants, No. 1196. Ed. by Emanual Horowitz & Jack E. Parr. LC 94-4736. (Special Technical Publication: No. 1196). (Illus.). 220p. 1994. pap. 59.00 (*0-8031-1854-6*, 0401196054) ASTM.

Characterization & Performance Prediction of Cement & Concrete. Ed. by J. Francis Young. LC 83-83068. 219p. 1982. pap. 45.00 (*0-939204-22-3*, 82-15) Eng Found.

Characterization & Toxicity of Smoke, STP 1082. Ed. by Harry K. Hasegawa. LC 90-30759. (Special Technical Publication (STP) Ser.). (Illus.). 175p. 1990. text ed. 51. 00 (*0-8031-1386-2*, 04-010820-31) ASTM.

Characterization & Washability Studies of Raw Coal from the Little Tonzona Field, Alaska. P. Dharma Rao et al. (MIRL Report Ser.: No. 88). 120p. (Orig.). 1991. pap. 7.00 (*0-911043-11-X*) UAKF Min Ind Res Lab.

Characterization in Dickens. James A. Davies. 1988. 52.50 (*0-389-20588-5*, N8146) B&N Imports.

Characterization in Semiconductor Compound Processing. Yale Strausser. (Materials Characterization Ser.). 250p. 1995. 64.95 (*0-7506-9266-9*) Buttrwrth-Heinemann.

Characterization in Silicon Processing. Yale Strausser. (Materials Characterization Ser.). 240p. 1993. 59.95 (*0-7506-9172-7*) Buttrwrth-Heinemann.

Characterization in the Conflict of Laws. Arthur H. Robertson. LC 40-10604. (Harvard Studies in the Conflict of Laws: Vol. 4). xxix, 301p. 1978. reprint ed. lib. bdg. 45.00 (*0-89941-129-0*, 301350) W S Hein.

Characterization of a Karsted, High-Energy, Ramp-Margin Carbonate Reservoir: Taylor-Link West San Andres Unit, Pecos County, Texas. F. J. Lucia et al. (Illus.). 46p. 1992. pap. 3.50 (*0-317-05175-X*, RI 208) Bur Econ Geology.

Characterization of a Karsted, High-Energy Ramp-Margin Carbonate Reservoir: Taylor-Lynd West San Andres Unit, Pecos County, Texas. F. J. Lucia et al. (Report of Investigations Ser.: RI 208). (Illus.). 46p. 1992. 3.50 (*0-317-05186-5*) Bur Econ Geology.

Characterization of Advanced Materials. Ed. by W. Altergott & E. Henneke. (Illus.). 180p. 1991. 69.50 (*0-306-43837-2*, Plenum Pr) Plenum.

Characterization of Arc Welding Fumes (CAWF) 56p. 1983. pap. 32.00 (*0-87171-229-6*) Am Welding.

Characterization of Carbon Dioxide Absorbing Agents for Life Support Equipment: Presented at the Winter Annual Meeting of the American Society of Mechanical Engineers, Phoenix, Arizona, November 14-19, 1982. American Society of Mechanical Engineers Staff. Ed. by Marshall L. Nuckols & Karen A. Smith. LC 82-73176. (OED Ser.: Vol. 10). (Illus.). 214p. reprint ed. pap. 61.00 (*0-8357-2835-8*, 2039071) Bks Demand.

Characterization of Catalysts. Ed. by J. M. Thomas & R. M. Lambert. LC 80-40961. (Illus.). 295p. reprint ed. pap. 84.10 (*0-8357-3086-7*, 2039343) Bks Demand.

Characterization of Catalytic Materials. Israel E. Wachs. 1992. 59.95 (*0-7506-9241-3*) Buttrwrth-Heinemann.

Characterization of Ceramics. Ronald E. Loehman. LC 92-21549. (Materials Characterization Ser.). 312p. 1993. 59. 95 (*0-7506-9253-7*) Buttrwrth-Heinemann.

Characterization of Ceramics. Ed. by L. L. Hench et al. LC 74-160516. (Ceramics & Glass: Science & Technology Ser.: Vol. 3). (Illus.). 666p. reprint ed. pap. 180.00 (*0-317-08003-2*, 2021508) Bks Demand.

Characterization of Chemical Purity: Organic Compounds. IUPAC Staff & L. Staveley. (IUPAC, Physical Chemistry Division Ser.). 1971. 82.00 (*0-08-020823-1*, Pub. by Pergamon Repr UK) Franklin.

Characterization of Clay (Bentonite) - Crushed Granite Mixtures to Build. E. Mingarro et al. 142p. 1991. pap. 15.00 (*92-826-3066-8*, CD-NA-13666-EN-C) UNIPUB.

Characterization of Coatings, Pt. 1: Physical Techniques. Ed. by Raymond R. Myers & J. S. Long. (Treatise on Coatings Ser.: No. 2). 680p. reprint ed. pap. 180.00 (*0-317-08360-0*, 2055321) Bks Demand.

Characterization of Coatings, Pt. 2: Physical Techniques. Ed. by Raymond R. Myers & J. S. Long. LC 67-21701. (Treatise on Coatings Ser.: No. 2). (Illus.). 677p. reprint ed. pap. 180.00 (*0-7837-4303-3*, 2043994) Bks Demand.

Characterization of Composite Materials. Ed. by Hatsuo Ishida. LC 93-27083. (Materials Data Ser.). 250p. 1993. 59.95 (*0-7506-9386-X*) Buttrwrth-Heinemann.

Characterization of Copper-Binding Agents Released by Daphnia Magna. Massachusetts Institute of Technology Staff. 31p. 1982. write for info. (*0-318-60400-0*) Intl Copper.

Characterization of C(X) Among Its Subalgebras. R. B. Burckel. (Lecture Notes in Pure & Applied Mathematics Ser.: Vol. 6). 176p. 1972. 99.75 (*0-8247-6038-7*) Dekker.

Characterization of Defects in Materials. Ed. by R. W. Siegel et al. (MRS Symposium Proceedings Ser.: Vol. 82). 1987. text ed. 42.00 (*0-931837-47-2*) Materials Res.

Characterization of Distributions by the Method of Intensively Monotone Operators. A. V. Kakosyan et al. LC 84-26796. (Lecture Notes in Mathematics Ser.: Vol. 1088). x, 175p. 1984. pap. 31.10 (*0-387-13857-9*) Spr-Verlag.

Characterization of Fluvial & Aeolian Reservoirs. Ed. by C. P. North & D. J. Prosser. (Geological Society Special Publications: No. 73). (Illus.). 450p. 1993. 108.00 (*0-903317-90-7*, Pub. by Geol Soc Pub Hse UK) AAPG.

Characterization of Hazardous Household Wastes in Marin County, California. 53p. 1987. 5.00 (*0-317-05714-6*, P87004HAZ) Assn Bay Area.

Characterization of Heterogenous Catalysts. Delannay. (Chemical Industries Ser.: Vol. 15). 424p. 1984. 155.00 (*0-8247-7100-1*) Dekker.

Characterization of Highly Cross-Linked Polymers. Ed. by S. S. Labana & R. A. Dickie. LC 83-25733. (ACS Symposium Ser.: No. 243). 321p. 1984. lib. bdg. 54.95 (*0-8412-0824-7*) Am Chemical.

Characterization of Integrated Circuit Packaging Materials. Ed. by Thomas M. Moore & Robert G. McKenna. LC 93-7685. (Materials Characterization Ser.). 274p. 1993. 59.95 (*0-7506-9267-7*) Buttrwrth-Heinemann.

Characterization of Materials. John B. Wachtman. 480p. 1992. 74.95 (*0-7506-9215-4*) Buttrwrth-Heinemann.

Characterization of Materials for Service at Elevated Temperatures: Presented at 1978 ASME-CSME Montreal Pressure Vessel & Piping Conference, Montreal, Quebec, Canada, June 25-29, 1978. CSME Montreal Pressure Vessel & Piping Conference Staff ASME. Ed. by George V. Smith. LC 78-57284. (MPC Ser.: Vol. 7). 542p. reprint ed. pap. 154.50 (*0-685-23446-0*, 2032700) Bks Demand.

Characterization of Metals & Alloys. Paul H. Holloway. (Surface Characterization Ser.). 309p. 1993. 59.95 (*0-7506-9246-4*) Buttrwrth-Heinemann.

Characterization of Metamorphism Through Mineral Equilibria. Ed. by J. M. Ferry. (Reviews in Mineralogy Ser.: Vol. 10). 397p. 1982. per. 17.00 (*0-939950-12-X*) Mineralogical Soc.

Characterization of Optical Materials. Gregory J. Exarhos. (Materials Characterization Ser.). 220p. 1993. 59.95 (*0-7506-9298-7*) Buttrwrth-Heinemann.

Characterization of Organic Compounds by Chemical Methods: An Introductory Laboratory Textbook. T. C. Owen. 256p. 1969. 50.00 (*0-8247-1510-1*) Dekker.

Characterization of Organic Thin Films. Abraham Ulman. (Materials Characterization Ser.). 220p. 1994. 59.95 (*0-7506-9467-X*) Buttrwrth-Heinemann.

Characterization of Plasma-Enhanced CVD Processes: Materials Research Society Symposium Proceedings, Vol. 165. Ed. by G. Lucovsky et al. 1990. text ed. 36.00 (*1-55899-053-4*) Materials Res.

Characterization of Plastics by Physical Methods: Experimental Techniques & Practical Application. Gunther Kampf. 351p. (C). 1986. text ed. 54.50 (*1-56990-045-0*) Hanser-Gardner.

Characterization of Polymers: Surfaces, Interfaces, Thin Films. Ho-Ming Tong et al. (Materials Characterization Ser.). 250p. 1994. 59.95 (*0-7506-9287-1*) Buttrwrth-Heinemann.

Characterization of Porous Solids: Proceedings of the IUPAC Symposium, Bad Soden, FRG, April 26-29, 1987. Ed. by K. K. Unger et al. (Studies in Surface Science & Catalysis: Vol. 39). 646p. 1988. 166.75 (*0-444-42953-0*) Elsevier.

***Characterization of Porous Solids III: Proceedings of the IUPAC Symposium (COPS III), Marseille, France, May 9-12, 1993.** Ed. by J. Rouquerol et al. LC 94-27695. 1994. write for info. (*0-444-81491-4*) Elsevier.

Characterization of Porous Solids, No. Two: Proceedings of the IUPAC Symposium (COPS II), Alicante, Spain, May 6-9, 1990. Ed. by F. Rodriguez-Reinoso et al. (Studies in Surface Science & Catalysis: No. 62). 782p. 1991. 243.00 (*0-444-88569-2*) Elsevier.

Characterization of Powder & Compacts: Preprint of a Seminar Held at the 1992 Powder Metallurgy World Congress, San Francisco, California, June 22-23, 1992. Powder Metallurgy World Congress Staff. 212p. reprint ed. pap. 60.50 (*0-7837-6977-6*, 2046788) Bks Demand.

Characterization of Proteins. Felix Franks. LC 87-29874. (Biological Methods Ser.). (Illus.). 576p. 1988. 89.50 (*0-89603-109-8*) Humana.

Characterization of Semiconductor Materials: Principles & Methods, Vol. 1. Ed. by Gary E. McGuire. LC 89-30273. (Illus.). 330p. 1989. 64.00 (*0-8155-1200-7*) Noyes.

C

An Asterisk (*) at the beginning of an entry indicates that the title is appearing in BIP for the first time. 1153

Characterization of Solid Surfaces. Ed. by Philip F. Kane & Graydon B. Larrabee. LC 73-84000. (Illus.). 670p. 1974. 115.00 (*0-306-30752-9*, Plenum Pr) Plenum.

***Characterization of Spilled Oil Samples: Purpose, Sampling, Analysis & Interpretation.** fac. ed. Ed. by J. A. Butt et al. LC 85-17955. (Illus.). 105p. 1994. pap. 30.00 (*0-7837-7662-4*, 2047415) Bks Demand.

***Characterization of the Boom Clay & Its Multilayered Hydrogeological Environment.** R. Beaufays et al. 355p. 1994. pap. 60.00 (*92-826-7697-8*, CDNA14961ENC, Pub. by Europ Com) UNIPUB.

Characterization of the Bovine Immune System & the Genes Regulating Expression of Immunity with Particular Reference to Their Role in Disease Resistance. Ed. by W. C. Davis et al. LC 86-7750. xi, 217p. pap. 18.00 (*0-936375-00-0*) WA State U Vet.

***Characterization of the Cottonwood Grove & Ridgely Faults Near Reelfoot Lake, Tennessee, from High-Resolution Seismic Reflection Data.** William J. Stephenson et al. LC 95-2235. (Investigations of the New Madrid Seismic Zone Ser.: Vol. I). 1995. write for info. (*0-615-00515-2*) US Geol Survey.

Characterization of the Electrical Environment. David W. Bodle et al. LC 76-22886. 335p. reprint ed. pap. 95.50 (*0-317-55655-X*, 2029325) Bks Demand.

Characterization of the Grayburg Reservoir. University Lands Dune Field, Crane County, Texas. D. G. Bebout et al. (Report of Investigations Ser.: RI 168). (Illus.). 98p. 1987. 6.50 (*0-318-23677-X*) Bur Econ Geology.

Characterization of the Structure & Chemistry of Defects in Materials: Materials Research Society Symposium Proceedings, Vol. 138. Ed. by B. C. Larson et al. 1989. text ed. 54.00 (*1-55899-011-9*) Materials Res.

Characterization of Tribological Materials. Ed. by William A. Glaeser. (Materials Characterization Ser.). 174p. 1993. 59.95 (*0-7506-9297-9*) Buttrwrth-Heinemann.

Characterization of Very High Speed Semiconductor Devices & Integrated Circuits: Critical Reviews. Ed. by Jain. 369p. 1987. 84.00 (*0-89252-830-3*, 795) SPIE.

Characterization Problems Associated with the Exponential Distribution. R. A. Azlarov & N. A. Volodin. Tr. by M. Stein. 140p. 1986. 43.00 (*0-387-96316-2*) Spr-Verlag.

Characterization, Propagation, & Simulation of Sources & Backgrounds, Vol. 1486. D. Clement & W. R. Watkins. 1991. 70.00 (*0-8194-0595-7*) SPIE.

Characterization, Propogation, & Simulation of Infrared Scenes. Ed. by M. J. Triplett et al. 446p. 1990. 70.00 (*0-8194-0362-8*, VOL. 1311) SPIE.

Characterization, Treatment & Use of Sewage Sludge. Ed. by P. L. L'Hermite & H. Ott. xviii, 803p. 1981. lib. bdg. 154.50 (*90-277-1294-8*) Kluwer Ac.

Characterizing & Measuring Mechanical Design Productivity. William S. Gatley. LC 92-35647. (Six Sigma Research Institute Ser.). 1993. write for info. (*0-201-63416-3*) Addison-Wesley.

Characterizing Heterogeneous Wastes: Methods & Recommendations. Ed. by Gretchen L. Rupp & Roy R. Jones, Sr. LC 92-35493. 1992. 54.95 (*0-8493-8720-5*, TD793) CRC Pr.

Characterizing k-Dimensional Universal Menger Compacta. Mladen Bestvina. LC 87-28829. (Memoirs of the American Mathematical Society Ser.: Vol. 380). 110p. 1988. 21.00 (*0-8218-2443-0*, MEMO/71/380C) Am Math.

Characterological Transformation: The Hard Work Miracle. Stephen M. Johnson. 1985. 34.95 (*0-393-70001-1*) Norton.

Characterology. Carl Wagner. (Illus.). 240p. 1986. pap. 12.95 (*0-87728-626-4*) Weiser.

Characters. Theophrastus. Ed. by E. H. Warmington. Bd. with Herodes, Cercidas, & the Greek Choliambic Poets (Loeb Classical Library: No. 225). (ENG & GRE.). 15.50 (*0-674-99248-2*) HUP.

Characters. Jean De La Bruyere. Tr. by Henri Van Laun. LC 89-23836. 494p. 1992. reprint ed. lib. bdg. 47.50 (*0-86527-394-4*) Fertig.

Characters: Comedies, Dramas, & Raps Featuring Bible Characters. James Watkins & Lois Watkins. 1993. 8.50 (*0-685-72869-2*, MP-677) Lillenas.

Characters & Character of a Mountain Town: Spruce Pine, North Carolina. Martin L. Sanders & James J. Hite. LC 93-91805. (Illus.). 150p. 1993. 15.95 (*0-9638730-0-8*) Hite Effects.

Characters & Commentaries. Giles L. Strachey. LC 78-23722. 1979. reprint ed. text ed. 69.50 (*0-313-20763-1*, STCCO, Greenwood Pr) Greenwood.

Characters & Computers. Ed. by Victor H. Mair & Yongquan Liu. 200p. 1991. 65.00 (*90-5199-061-8*, Pub. by IOS Pr NE) IOS Press.

Characters & Passages from Note-Books. Samuel Butler. (BCL1-PR English Literature Ser.). 489p. 1992. reprint ed. lib. bdg. 99.00 (*0-7812-7328-5*) Rprt Serv.

Characters & Passages from Notebooks. Samuel Butler. 489p. reprint ed. 69.00 (*0-403-08911-5*) Somerset Pub.

Characters & Probable History of the Hawaiian Rat. G. S. Miller, Jr. Bd. with Ectoparasites of Some Polynesian and Malaysian Rats of the Genus Rattus. (BMB Ser.). 1972. reprint ed. Set pap. 15.00 (*0-527-02117-2*) Periodicals Srv.

Characters & Their Landscapes. Ronald Blythe. LC 83-7890. (Helen & Kurt Wolff Bk.). Orig. Title: From the Headlands. 224p. 1983. 14.95 (*0-15-116792-3*) HarBrace.

Characters & Viewpoint. Orson S. Card. (Elements of Fiction Writing Ser.). 192p. 1988. 14.99 (*0-89879-307-6*) Writers Digest.

Characters by Lord Chesterfield Contrasted with Characters of the Same Great Personages by Other Respectable Writers: And Four Additional Characters from the Letters of Philip Dormer Stanhope, Earl of Chesterfield, Ed. Lord Mahon, Vol. 2. Philip D. Chesterfield. Ed. by Lord Mahon. LC 92-22685. (Augustan Reprints Ser.: Nos. 259-260 (1990)). reprint ed. 18.50 (*0-404-70259-7*) AMS Pr.

Characters from Proust: Poems. Wallace Fowlie. LC 82-18641. 50p. 1983. pap. 6.95 (*0-8071-1071-X*) La State U Pr.

***Characters from Proust: Poems.** fac. ed. Wallace Fowlie. LC 82-18641. 62p. 1983. reprint ed. pap. 25.00 (*0-7837-7733-7*, 2047489) Bks Demand.

Characters from the Mahabharata, 22 vols., Set. Chander K. Suri. (C). 1992. pap. 30.00 (*0-8364-2775-0*, Pub. by BR Pub II) S Asia.

Characters from the Old Testament: From Adam to Moses. Sung Ku Kang. 254p. (Orig.). (KOR.). 1993. pap. 8.60 (*0-9635536-2-3*) Korei Pr.

Characters from Young Adult Literature. Mary E. Snodgrass. 230p. 1991. lib. bdg. 27.00 (*0-87287-883-X*) Libs Unl.

***Characters in Action: Playwriting the Easy Way.** Marsh Cassady. Ed. by Theodore O. Zapel. 216p. (Orig.). (YA). (gr. 9 up). 1995. pap. 14.95 (*1-56608-010-X*, B106) Meriwether Pub.

***Characters in Action: Playwriting the Easy Way.** Marsh Cassady. LC 95-7721. 1995. pap. write for info. (*1-56608-01X-0*) Meriwether Pub.

Characters in Mythology. William R. Farrell. (Illus.). 60p. (J). (gr. k-10). 1992. spiral bd. 9.25 (*0-939507-38-2*, B423) Amer Classical.

Characters in Tales of a Wayside Inn. John Van Schaick, Jr. LC 74-1159. (Henry W. Longfellow Ser.: No. 58). 1974. lib. bdg. 75.00 (*0-8383-2028-7*) M S G Haskell Hse.

Characters in the Novels of Thomas Love Peacock (1785-1866) Claude A. Prance. LC 92-5982. 312p. 1992. 99.95 (*0-7734-9510-X*) E Mellen.

Characters in the Twilight: Hardy, Zola, & Chekhov. Anthony Winner. LC 81-10355. 1981. 25.00 (*0-8139-0894-9*) U Pr of Va.

Characters in Twentieth Century Literature: A Guide to Major Characters in World Fiction. Harris. 850p. 1989. 54.00 (*0-8103-1847-4*) Gale.

Characters in 19th Century Literature. 1992. 54.00 (*0-8103-8398-5*) Gale.

Characters in 20th Century Literature II. Kelly K. Howes. LC 94-2687. 1995. 54.00 (*0-8103-9203-8*) Gale.

***Characters, Legends & Three Dollar Bills.** Donald Gwaltney. 1995. 17.95 (*0-8062-5360-6*) Carlton.

Characters Make Your Story. Maren Elwood. 1987. pap. 14.95 (*0-87116-019-6*) Writer.

Characters of Reductive Groups Over a Finite Field. George Lusztig. LC 83-43083. (Annals of Mathematics Studies: Vol. 107). 495p. 1984. 69.50 (*0-691-08350-9*); pap. 29.95 (*0-691-08351-7*) Princeton U Pr.

Characters of Shakespeare's Plays. William Hazlitt. (BCL1-PR English Literature Ser.). 275p. 1992. reprint ed. lib. bdg. 79.00 (*0-7812-7301-3*) Rprt Serv.

Characters of the Inquisition. William T. Walsh. LC 87-50977. 301p. 1987. reprint ed. pap. 12.50 (*0-89555-326-0*) TAN Bks Pubs.

Characters of the Reformation. Hilaire Belloc. LC 72-121449. (Essay Index Reprint Ser.). 1977. 26.95 (*0-8369-1696-4*) Ayer.

Characters of the Reformation: Historical Portraits of the 23 Men & Women & their Place in the Great Religious Revolution of the 16th Century. Hilaire Belloc. LC 92-60961. 208p. 1992. reprint ed. pap. 10.00 (*0-89555-466-6*) TAN Bks Pubs.

Characters of Theophrastus. Theophrastus. Ed. by W. R. Connor. LC 78-18600. (Greek Texts & Commentaries Ser.). (ENG & GRE.). 1979. reprint ed. lib. bdg. 29.95 (*0-405-11441-9*) Ayer.

Characters, Plots & Settings of Calderon's Comedies. Richard W. Tyler & Sergio D. Elizondo. LC 80-538325. 495p. reprint ed. pap. 141.10 (*0-317-41824-6*, 2025616) Bks Demand.

Characters We Know: A to Z. Robert Perine. (Illus.). 16p. 1978. ring bd. 15.00 (*0-932300-00-6*, AP00) Artra Pub.

Charade. Sandra Brown. 416p. 1994. 21.95 (*0-446-51656-2*) Warner Bks.

Charade. Sandra Brown. 496p. 1995. mass mkt. 6.99 (*0-446-60185-3*, Warner Vision) Warner Bks.

Charade. Christina Hamlett. 1993. mass mkt. 4.50 (*0-06-108163-9*, Harp PBks) HarpC.

Charade. John Mortimer. 1976. 18.95 (*0-8488-0595-X*) Amereon Ltd.

Charade. John Mortimer. 192p. 1988. mass mkt. 5.95 (*0-14-009267-6*, Penguin Bks) Viking Penguin.

Charade. Friedrich C. Zauner. Tr. by Michael Roloff. LC 93-51100. (Studies in Austrian Literature, Culture, & Thought). 131p. 1994. pap. 12.50 (*0-929497-83-X*) Ariadne CA.

Charade. large type ed. Sandra Brown. LC 94-9233. 672p. 1994. 22.95 (*0-7862-0228-9*) Thorndike Pr.

Charade. large type ed. Sandra Brown. LC 94-9233. 1995. pap. 17.95 (*0-7862-0229-7*) Thorndike Pr.

Charade: A Film Adaptation of "The Unsuspecting Wife" Directed by Stanley Donan. Peter Stone et al. Ed. by George P. Garrett et al. LC 71-135273. (Film Scripts Ser.). 1989. pap. 19.95 (*0-89197-696-5*) Irvington.

Charade of Hearts. Carol Michaels. 1992. pap. 3.99 (*1-55773-688-X*) Diamond.

Charades. Janine T. Hospital. 1995. pap. write for info. (*0-8050-3297-5*) H Holt & Co.

Charades Pour Ecroules. Raymond Chandler. 253p. (FRE.). 1991. pap. 10.95 (*0-7859-2170-2*, 2070384098) Fr & Eur.

Charaka Samhita, 2 vols., Set. Charaka. Tr. by Ram K. Sharma & Vaidya B. Dash. 619p. 1983. text ed. 85.00 (*0-89744-050-1*) Auromere.

Charakterisierung und Identifizierung von Ektomykorrhizen aus dem Nationalpark Bertesgaden. Roland Treu. (Bibliotheca Mycologica Ser.: Vol. 134). (Illus.). 196p. 1990. pap. 77.95 (*3-443-59035-7*, Pub. by Cramer-Borntraeger GW) Lubrecht & Cramer.

Charakterisierung und Identifizierung von Ektomykorrizen in einem Fichtenbestand mit Untersuchungen zur Merkmalsvariabilitaet in Sauer Beregneten Flaechen. Eva Gronbach. (Bibliotheca Mycologica Ser.: Vol. 125). (Illus.). 292p. (GER.). 1988. pap. 82.00 (*3-443-59026-8*) Lubrecht & Cramer.

Charater of Townsville: A Community Photography Book. Boolarong Publications Staff. (C). 1990. pap. 48.00 (*0-86439-141-2*, Pub. by Boolarong Pubns AT) St Mut.

Charbonneau. Winfred Blevins. 20.95 (*0-8488-0110-5*, Amereon Hse) Amereon Ltd.

Charbonneau. Winfred Blevins. LC 85-14761. (Frontier Library). 280p. 1985. pap. 7.95 (*0-915463-16-4*) Green Hill.

Charca. Manuel Zeno-Gandia. Tr. by Kal Wagenheim. 216p. (C). 1994. reprint ed. pap. text ed. 14.95 (*1-55876-092-X*) Wiener Pubs Inc.

Charca de Manuel Zeno Gandia: Temas y Estilo. Olga Casanova. 160p. (Orig.). (SPA.). 1992. pap. text ed. write for info. (*1-56328-022-1*) Edit Plaza Mayor.

Charcoal: Small Scale Production & Use. M. Boutette & G. E. Karch. (GATE Ser.). 60p. 1984. pap. 12.00 (*3-528-02009-1*, Pub. by Vieweg & Sohn GW) Ballen Bkslr.

Charcoal & Cadmium Red: Special Gifts Remembered & Nineteen Thirty-Eight. Donald S. Vogel. Ed. by Billie Anastasi. LC 89-50647. (Illus.). 50p. (Orig.). 1989. pap. 20.00 (*1-879154-02-1*) Vlly Hse Gllry.

Charcoal & Charcoal Burners. aniversary ed. Fritz A. Toepperwein & Emilie Toepperwein. 1987. reprint ed. pap. 6.95 (*0-910722-15-3*) Highland Pr.

***Charcoal & Charcoal Burning.** D. W. Kelley. (C). 1989. pap. 25.00x (*0-85263-731-4*, Pub. by Shire UK) St Mut.

Charcoal Foundry. David J. Gingery. LC 80-66142. (Build Your Own Metalworking Shop from Scrap Ser.). (Illus.). (Orig.). 1980. pap. 6.95 (*1-878087-00-2*) D J Gingery.

***Charcoal Grilling: For Outdoor Fun.** Ed. by G & R Publishing Staff. (Uni-Book Ser.). 160p. (Orig.). 1994. pap. text ed. 3.00 (*1-56383-016-7*, 2000) G & R Pub.

Charcoal Sketches. Katherine S. Ayres. LC 72-6512. (Black Heritage Library Collection). 1977. reprint ed. 16.95 (*0-8369-9156-7*) Ayer.

Charcoal Sketches & Other Tales. Henryk Sienkiewicz. Tr. by Adam Zamoyski. 240p. 1990. 33.00 (*0-946162-31-X*, Pub. by Angel Bks UK); pap. 17.95 (*0-946162-32-8*, Pub. by Angel Bks UK) Dufour.

Charcoal's World. Hugh A. Dempsey. LC 79-14920. (Illus.). x, 178p. 1979. pap. 3.95 (*0-8032-6552-2*) U of Nebr Pr.

***Charcot.** Christopher G. Goetz et al. (Illus.). 448p. 1995. 55.00 (*0-19-507643-5*) OUP.

Charcot-Marie-Tooth (CMTA) Handbook. (Illus.). 52p. (Orig.). (C). 1993. pap. text ed. 20.00 (*1-56806-416-0*) Diane Pub.

Charcot, the Clinician: The Tuesday Lessons. Jean-Martin Charcot. Tr. by Christopher G. Goetz. (Illus.). 224p. 1987. text ed. 75.00 (*0-88167-315-3*) Raven.

Chardin. Philip Conisbee. LC 84-23259. (Illus.). 240p. 1986. 75.00 (*0-8387-5091-5*) Bucknell U Pr.

***Chardin.** Gabriel Naughton. (Color Library). (Illus.). (C). 1995. pap. 14.95 (*0-7148-3336-3*, Pub. by Phaidon Press UK) Chronicle Bks.

***Chardin.** Gabriel Naughton. (Color Library). (Illus.). 128p. (C). 1995. 19.95 (*0-7148-3337-1*, Pub. by Phaidon Press UK) Chronicle Bks.

Chardin. Pierre Rosenberg. LC 90-50883. (Illus.). 1991. pap. 25.00 (*0-8478-1350-9*) Rizzoli Intl.

Chardin: New Thoughts. Pierre Rosenburg. LC 83-50337. (Franklin D. Murphy Lectures: No. 1). (Illus.). 1983. 12.00 (*0-913689-11-4*) Spencer Muse Art.

Chardonnay. Tim Atkin. (Illus.). 336p. 1993. 20.00 (*0-670-82515-8*, Viking) Viking Penguin.

Chardon's Journal at Fort Clark 1834-39. Ed. by Annie H. Abel. LC 77-140349. (Select Bibliographies Reprint Ser.). 1977. 24.95 (*0-8369-5592-7*) Ayer.

Charette Bleue. Rene Barjavel. 256p. (FRE.). 1982. pap. 10.95 (*0-7859-1963-5*, 2070374068) Fr & Eur.

Charge! Weapons & Warfare in Ancient Times. Rivka Gonen. LC 92-36772. (Buried Worlds Ser.). (YA). 1993. lib. bdg. 22.95 (*0-8225-3201-8*, Lerner Publctns) Lerner Group.

Charge & Field Effects in Biosystems, Vol. 2. Ed. by M. J. Allen et al. LC 89-26551. (Illus.). 400p. 1989. 120.00 (*0-306-43401-6*, Plenum Pr) Plenum.

Charge & Field Effects in Biosystems - 3. Ed. by M. J. Allen et al. x, 502p. 1991. 79.50 (*0-8176-3564-5*) Birkhauser.

***Charge & Field Effects in Biosystems-Four Proceedings of the 1994 International Symposium.** S.F. Cleary et al. 500p. 1994. text ed. 106.00 (*981-02-1909-1*) World Scientific Pub.

***Charge Composition of Ultra Heavy Nuclei.** Ed. by D. O'Sullivan & S. Ramadurai. 88p. 1995. pap. 94.00 (*0-08-042556-9*, Pergamon Pr) Elsevier.

Charge-Coupled Devices. Ed. by D. F. Barbe. (Topics in Applied Physics Ser.: Vol. 38). (Illus.). 1980. 61.00 (*0-387-09832-1*) Spr-Verlag.

Charge-Coupled Devices: Technology & Applications. Ed. by Roger Melen & Dennis Buss. LC 76-20887. 424p. 1977. 49.95 (*0-87942-083-9*, PC00802) Inst Electrical.

Charge-Coupled Devices & Solid-State Optical Devices. Ed. by M. M. Blouke. 1990. 62.00 (*0-8194-0289-3*, VOL. 1242) SPIE.

Charge-Coupled Devices & Solid State Optical Sensors II, Vol. 1447. M. M. Blouke. 1991. 62.00 (*0-8194-0546-9*) SPIE.

Charge d'Ame: Roman. Romain Gary. 310p. (FRE.). 1977. 24.95 (*0-7859-0125-6*, M5974) Fr & Eur.

Charge Density Waves in Solids. Ed. by L. P. Gor'kov & G. Gruner. (Modern Problems in Condensed Matter Sciences Ser.: Vol. 25). 1990. 146.25 (*0-444-87370-8*, North Holland); 124.00 (*0-685-34640-4*, North Holland) Elsevier.

Charge Distributions & Chemical Effects. S. Fliszar. (Illus.). 225p. 1983. 84.00 (*0-387-90854-4*) Spr-Verlag.

Charge Exchange & the Theory of Ion-Atom Collisions. Brian H. Bransden & Martin R. McDowell. (International Series of Monographs on Physics: No. 82). (Illus.). 416p. 1992. 125.00 (*0-19-852020-4*) OUP.

Charge Nurse. Patricia Rae. (Orig.). 1982. pap. 2.95 (*0-8217-1044-3*) Zebra.

Charge of Angels. L. D. Clark. LC 86-72561. 200p. 1987. 14.95 (*0-917652-49-5*) Confluence Pr.

Charge of Sir F. Bacon Touching Duells. Francis Bacon. LC 68-27475. (English Experience Ser.: No. 7). 62p. 1968. reprint ed. 15.00 (*90-221-0007-3*) Walter J Johnson.

***Charge of the Dwarf Brigade.** Gray McCoy. 1994. 15.95 (*0-533-11034-3*) Vantage.

Charge of the Light Cavalry: The Plow of the Ox's Amble. Richard Clough. 1991. 7.95 (*0-533-09161-6*) Vantage.

***Charge of the Parasols: Women's Entry to the Medical Profession.** Catriona Blake. 1994. pap. 16.99 (*0-7043-4239-1*) Interlink Pub.

Charge-Transfer Devices in Spectroscopy. Ed. by Jonathan V. Sweedler et al. LC 93-42138. 1994. pap. 95.00 (*1-56081-060-2*) VCH Pubs.

Charge Transfer Photochemistry of Coordination Compounds. Otto Horvath & Kenneth L. Stevenson. LC 92-36578. 380p. 1993. 145.00 (*1-56081-564-7*) VCH Pubs.

Charge Transfer Reactions in Electrochemical & Chemical Processes. L. I. Krishtalik. Tr. by R. S. Wadhwa & N. V. Deineko. LC 86-8866. 344p. 1986. 95.00 (*0-306-10986-7*, Consultants) Plenum.

Chargeback Combat Kit. Larry Schwartz & Pearl Sax. 200p. 1993. disk 199.95 (*0-914801-21-X*) Nat Assn Credit.

Charged! Places & Things. Howard D. Spencer. (Illus.). 8p. 1988. pap. 1.00 (*0-939324-37-7*) Wichita Art Mus.

Charged & Reactive Polymers. Incl. Vol. 3. Charged Gels & Membranes, Pt. 1. LC 76-6086. 1976. lib. bdg. 131.50 (*90-277-0665-4*); Vol. 4. Charged Gels & Membranes, Pt. 2. LC 76-6086. 1976. lib. bdg. 94.00 (*90-277-0666-2*); LC 76-6086. 1976. write for info. (*0-318-53998-5*) Kluwer Ac.

Charged & Reactive Polymers, No. 1, Polyelectrolytes: Proceedings of the NATO Advanced Study Institute, Forges-les-Eaux, June 18-28, 1972. NATO Advanced Study Institute Staff. Ed. by Eric Selegny et al. LC 73-91435. 300p. 1974. lib. bdg. 172.50 (*90-277-0434-1*) Kluwer Ac.

Charged & Reactive Polymers, Vol. 2: Polyelectrolytes & Their Applications. Ed. by Alan Rembaum & Eric Selegny. LC 74-34151. 350p. 1975. lib. bdg. 121.50 (*90-277-0561-5*) Kluwer Ac.

Charged Beam Interaction with Solids. Ed. by Y. H. Ohtsuki. 260p. (C). 1983. 90.00 (*0-8002-3083-3*) Taylor & Francis.

Charged Gels & Membranes, Pt. 2 see Charged & Reactive Polymers

Charged Image: French Lithographic Caricature, 1816-1848. Beatrice Farwell. LC 89-10427. (Illus.). 188p. 1990. pap. 24.95 (*0-295-96954-7*) U of Wash Pr.

Charged Particle Beams. Stanley Humphries. 1990. text ed. 225.00 (*0-471-60014-8*) Wiley.

Charged Particles. Karl Kempton. 47p. (Orig.). 1991. pap. 5.00 (*0-926935-52-6*) Runaway Spoon.

***Charged with Guilt.** White. 1995. mass mkt. (*0-440-22049-1*) Dell.

Charged with the Spirit: Mission Is for Everyone? Joseph G. Donders. LC 93-1613. 133p. (Orig.). 1993. pap. 12.95 (*0-88344-915-3*) Orbis Bks.

Charged with Treason: Jury Verdict - Not Guilty. John C. Elliott & Ellen G. Hammett. LC 85-90938. 358p. 1986. pap. 12.00 (*0-9615630-0-1*) McClain.

Charged with Treason: Mill Workers in Roswell, GA, 1864. Michael D. Hitt. LC 91-36379. (Illus.). 187p. 1992. 32.50 (*0-912526-55-6*) Lib Res.

***Charger Muscle Portfolio 1966-1974.** R. M. Clarke. (Brooklands Muscle Portfolio Ser.). (Illus.). 140p. 1994. pap. 18.95 (*1-85520-261-1*) Motorbooks Intl.

Charger, Road Runner & Super Bee. Paul A. Herd & Mike Mueller. LC 93-34444. (Muscle Car Color History Ser.). (Illus.). 128p. 1994. pap. text ed. 19.95 (*0-87938-844-7*) Motorbooks Intl.

Charger, Road Runner & Super Bee Restoration Guide. Paul A. Herd. (Illus.). 1994. pap. 26.95 (*0-87938-889-7*) Motorbooks Intl.

Charges to the Grand Jury in the Eighteenth Century, 1689-1803. Ed. by Georges Lamoine. (Royal Historical Society: Camden Fourth Ser.: No. 43). (C). 1992. text ed. 50.00 (*0-86193-130-0*, Royal Historical Soc) Boydell & Brewer.

***Charges to the Grand Jury, 1689-1803.** Ed. by Georgees Lamoine. (Camden Fourth Ser.: No. 43). 648p. (C). 1995. 54.95 (*0-521-55163-3*) Cambridge U Pr.

***Charging Charlie.** Charles Wise. Ed. by Debbie Bowen. (Illus.). (J). (gr. k-6). Date not set. lib. bdg. 11.95 (*1-56763-145-2*); pap. text ed. 5.95 (*1-56763-146-0*) Ozark Pub.

Charging for Government: User Charges & Earmarked Taxes in Principle & Practice. Ed. by Richard E. Wagner. 160p. 1991. 69.95 (*0-415-06463-5*, A5777) Routledge.

An Asterisk (*) at the beginning of an entry indicates that the title is appearing in BIP for the first time.

C

An Asterisk (*) at the beginning of an entry indicates that the title is appearing in BIP for the first time.

1155

Charles A. Lindbergh: A Bio-Bibliography. Perry D. Luckett. LC 86-3165. (Popular Culture Bio-Bibliographies Ser.). 159p. 1986. text ed. 42.95 (*0-313-23098-6*, LCL/, Greenwood Pr) Greenwood.

Charles A. Lindbergh: A Photographic Album. Joshua Stoff. (Illus.). 160p. (Orig.). 1994. pap. text ed. 14.95 (*0-486-27878-6*) Dover.

Charles A. Lindbergh & the American Dilemma: The Conflict of Technology & Human Values. Susan M. Gray. LC 88-70505. 140p. (C). 1988. text ed. 26.95 (*0-87972-422-6*); pap. text ed. 13.95 (*0-87972-423-4*) Bowling Green Univ.

Charles A. Lindbergh House. Donald H. Westfall. LC 93-21917. (Minnesota Historic Sites Pamphlet Ser.: No. 22). 32p. 1994. pap. 7.50 (*0-87351-292-8*) Minn Hist.

***Charles A. Lindbergh, Lone Eagle.** Walter L. Hixson. Ed. by Oscar Handlin. LC 95-5844. (Library of American Biography). 1995. pap. write for info. (*0-673-99265-9*) HarpC.

Charles Albert Fechter. Kate Field. LC 70-82827. 1972. 20.95 (*0-405-08502-8*, Pub. by Blom Pubns UK) Ayer.

Charles Alexander Eastman (Ohiyesa) Marion W. Copeland. LC 78-52562. (Western Writers Ser.: No. 33). 43p. 1978. pap. 3.95 (*0-88430-057-9*) Boise St U W Writ Ser.

Charles & Diana: The Tenth Anniversary. Brian Hoey. LC 90-50750. (Illus.). 160p. 1991. 18.95 (*0-670-83948-5*, Viking Studio) Studio Bks.

Charles & Elsa Chauvel - Movie Pioneers: Thirty Years of Australian Film Making. Susanne C. Carlsson. 1989. 49.95 (*0-7022-2213-5*, Pub. by Univ Queensland Pr AT); pap. 29.95 (*0-7022-2251-8*) Intl Spec Bk.

***Charles & Ray Eames: Designers of the Twentieth Century.** Pat Kirkham. (Illus.). 400p. 1995. 55.00 (*0-262-11199-3*) MIT Pr.

Charles Arnoldi. Nicholas Wilder. Ed. & Intro. by Craig A. Subler. (Illus.). 14p. (Orig.). 1986. pap. text ed. 4.00 (*0-914489-04-6*) Univ Miss-KS Art.

Charles Arnoldi & Laddie John Dill. California State University, Fullerton Staff. (Orig.). 1983. pap. write for info. (*0-935314-24-5*) CSU Art Gallery.

Charles August Lindberg Sr. A Case Study of Congressional Insurgency, 1906-1912. Richard B. Lucas. (Studia Historica Upsaliensia: No. 61). (Illus.). 194p. (Orig.). 1974. pap. 25.00x (*91-554-0214-3*, Pub. by Uppsala Univ Acta Univ Uppsaliensis SW) Coronet Bks.

Charles-Augustin Sainte-Beuve. George M. Harper. LC 74-124237. (Select Bibliographies Reprint Ser.). 1977. 23.95 (*0-8369-5425-4*) Ayer.

Charles Augustus Briggs & Tensions in Late-Nineteenth Century American Theology. M. James Sawyer. LC 93-35754. 212p. 1993. 89.95 (*0-7734-9961-X*) E Mellen.

Charles Augustus Briggs & the Crisis of Historical Criticism. Mark S. Massa. (Harvard Dissertations in Religion Ser.). 232p. (Orig.). 1990. pap. 17.00 (*0-8006-7079-5*, 1-7079) Augsburg Fortress.

Charles B. Hoyt Collection in the Museum of Fine Arts, Boston, Vol. 1. Hsien-Chi Teng. 1964. 32.50 (*0-87846-022-5*) Mus Fine Arts Boston.

Charles B. Hoyt Collection in the Museum of Fine Arts, Boston, Vol. 2. Hsien-Chi Teng. 1972. 38.50 (*0-87846-059-4*) Mus Fine Arts Boston.

Charles Babbage: On the Principle & Development of the Calculator & Other Seminal Writings. Charles Babbage et al. 400p. 1984. reprint ed. pap. 9.95 (*0-486-24691-4*) Dover.

Charles Baber Cemetery at Pottsville. Comp. by Schuylkill Roots Staff. 218p. 1990. pap. 23.50 (*1-55856-050-5*) Closson Pr.

Charles Baillairge: Architect & Engineer. Christina Cameron. (Illus.). 232p. (C). 1989. 49.95 (*0-7735-0638-1*, Pub. by McGill CN) U of Toronto Pr.

Charles Baudelaire. Theophile Gautier. Tr. by Guy Thorne. LC 77-10264. (Illus.). 1977. reprint ed. 27.50 (*0-685-00373-6*) AMS Pr.

Charles Baudelaire: Une Micro-Histoire. Raymond P. Poggenburg. LC 87-6194. 739p. (Orig.). 1987. pap. 47.50 (*0-8265-1224-0*) Vanderbilt U Pr.

Charles Baudelaire Revisited. Lois B. Hyslop. (Twayne's World Authors Ser.: No. 827). 180p. (C). 1992. text ed. 22.95 (*0-8057-8265-6*, Twayne) Macmillan.

Charles Baudelaire, un poete maudit: Choix de poemes traduits en vers anglais avec une biographie et des notes. Charles P. Baudelaire. LC 77-10245. reprint ed. 18.50 (*0-404-16301-7*) AMS Pr.

Charles Beard & the Constitution: A Critical Analysis of "An Economic Interpretation of the Constitution" Robert E. Brown. LC 78-14426. 219p. 1979. reprint ed. text ed. 55.00 (*0-313-21048-9*, BRBC, Greenwood Pr) Greenwood.

Charles Beckendorf--Texas. Charles Beckendorf. LC 86-71956. (Illus.). 160p. 1986. 75.00 (*0-939929-05-8*, GB/T-1) C Beckendorf Gallery.

Charles Bell: The Complete Works, 1970-1990. Henry Geldzahler. 1991. 45.00 (*0-8109-3114-1*) Abrams.

Charles Berlitz's World of Strange Phenomena. Charles Berlitz. 368p. 1989. mass mkt. 5.99 (*0-449-21825-2*, Crest) Fawcett.

Charles Berlitz's World of the Odd & the Awesome. Charles Berlitz. (Illus.). 288p. 1991. mass mkt. 4.99 (*0-449-22013-3*, Crest) Fawcett.

Charles Bonnet & the Order of the Known. Lorin Anderson. 1982. lib. bdg. 80.00 (*90-277-1389-8*) Kluwer Ac.

Charles Booth on the City: Physical Pattern & Social Structure: Selected Writings. Charles Booth. Ed. by Harold W. Pfautz. LC 67-28466. (Heritage of Sociology Ser.). 320p. reprint ed. pap. 91.20 (*0-685-15672-9*, 2026766) Bks Demand.

Charles Booth, Social Scientist. Thomas S. Simey & Margaret B. Simey. LC 80-18810. (Illus.). x, 282p. 1980. reprint ed. text ed. 35.00 (*0-313-22610-5*, SICB, Greenwood Pr) Greenwood.

Charles Bragg on Medicine. Charles Bragg. (Illus.). 80p. (Orig.). 1984. mass mkt. 7.95 (*0-446-38059-8*) Warner Bks.

Charles Bragg on the Law. Charles Bragg. (Illus.). 80p. (Orig.). 1984. mass mkt. 7.95 (*0-446-38057-1*) Warner Bks.

Charles Brenton Fisk: Organ Builder, 2 vols., Set. Ed. by Fenner Douglass et al. 1986. 100.00 (*0-9616755-0-0*) Westfield Ctr.

Charles Brenton Fisk: Organ Builder, Vol. I: Essays in His Honor. Ed. by Fenner Douglass et al. 291p. 1986. write for info. (*0-9616755-1-9*) Westfield Ctr.

Charles Brenton Fisk: Organ Builder, Vol. II: His Work. Comp. by Barbara Owen. 198p. 1986. write for info. (*0-9616755-2-7*) Westfield Ctr.

Charles Bridges & William Dering: Two Virginia Painters, 1735-1750. Graham Hood. LC 77-13772. (Illus.). 125p. 1978. 19.95 (*0-87935-047-4*) Colonial Williamsburg.

Charles Brockden Brown. Donald A. Ringe. (Twayne's United States Authors Ser.). 1966. pap. 13.95x (*0-8084-0071-1*, T98) NCUP.

Charles Brockden Brown. rev. ed. Donald A. Ringe. (Twayne's United States Authors Ser.). 226p. 1991. text ed. 22.95 (*0-8057-7606-0*, TUSAS 98, Twayne) Macmillan.

Charles Brockden Brown: An American Tale. Alan Axelrod. 223p. 1983. text ed. 27.50 (*0-292-71076-3*) U of Tex Pr.

Charles Brockden Brown: Pioneer Voice of America. David L. Clark. LC 75-181909. (BCL Ser.). reprint ed. 34.50 (*0-404-01548-4*) AMS Pr.

Charles Brockden Brown, American Gothic Novelist. Harry Warfel. (BCL1-PS American Literature Ser.). 255p. 1993. reprint ed. lib. bdg. 79.00 (*0-7812-6947-4*) Rprt Serv.

Charles Brown Poetry Transcripts at Harvard: Facsimiles Including the Fair Copy of Otho the Great. Intro. & Notes by Jack Stillinger. (Manuscripts of the Younger Romantics: Vol. VII). 290p. 1988. 81.00 (*0-8240-7023-2*) Garland.

Charles Buckmaster Collected Poems. Charles Buckmaster. Ed. by Simon MacDonald. 150p. (Orig.). 1989. pap. text ed. 16.95 (*0-7022-2242-9*, Pub. by Univ Queensland Pr AT) Intl Spec Bk.

Charles Bukowski: A Critical & Biographical Study. Hugh Fox. LC 72-129088. 1968. pap. 3.75 (*0-911856-01-3*) Abyss.

Charles Bukowski Sampler. 3rd ed. Ed. by Douglas Blazek. 1979. reprint ed. pap. 3.00 (*0-685-04197-2*) Quixote.

Charles Bulfinch: Architect & Citizen. Charles A. Place. LC 68-27717. (Architecture & Decorative Art Ser.). (Illus.). 1968. reprint ed. lib. bdg. 45.00 (*0-306-71150-8*) Da Capo.

Charles Burchfield's Journals: The Poetry of Place. Charles Burchfield. Ed. by J. Benjamin Townsend. LC 91-17389. (Illus.). 768p. 1992. 74.50 (*0-7914-0991-0*) State U NY Pr.

Charles Burchfield's Seasons. Guy Davenport. LC 93-46654. (Essential Paintings Ser.). (Illus.). 88p. 1994. 21.95 (*1-56640-979-9*) Pomegranate Calif.

Charles Burns Sketchbook. Charles Burns. Ed. by Jim Vance. (Illus.). 64p. (J). (gr. 4 up). 1993. pap. 6.95 (*0-87816-250-X*) Kitchen Sink.

***Charles, Burrows & Charles: TV's Top Producers.** Keith Greenberg. (Partners II Ser.). 112p. (J). (gr. 5 up). 1995. lib. bdg. 14.95 (*1-56711-136-X*) Blackbirch.

Charles C. DeRudio. Charles K. Mills. 1976. 14.95 (*0-8488-0582-8*, J M C & Co) Amereon Ltd.

***Charles Carpenter Fries: His Oral Approach for Teaching & Learning Foreign Languages.** fac. ed. Ed. by William E. Norris & Jeris E. Strain. LC 88-33465. (Illus.). 77p. 1989. reprint ed. pap. 25.00 (*0-7837-7783-3*, 2047538) Bks Demand.

Charles Caterpillar. James Haas. Ed. by Mary C. Kendzia. (Illus.). 32p. (Orig.). (J). 1992. pap. 4.95 (*0-89622-530-5*) Twenty-Third.

Charles Chesnutt. Cliff Thompson. (Black Americans of Achievement Ser.). (Illus.). 112p. (J). (gr. 5 up). 1993. lib. bdg. 17.95 (*1-55546-578-1*) Chelsea Hse.

Charles Churchill. Raymond J. Smith. LC 76-42988. (Twayne's English Authors Ser.). 156p. (C). 1977. lib. bdg. 17.95 (*0-8057-6669-3*) Irvington.

***Charles City County: Virginia Publick Claims.** Janice L. Abercrombie & Richard Slatten. (Virginia Publick Claims Ser.). ix, 30p. 1991. pap. 5.00x (*0-8095-8534-0*) Borgo Pr.

Charles City County: Virginia Publick Claims. Janice L. Abercrombie & Richard Slatten. (Virginia Publick Claims Ser.). ix, 30p. (C). 1991. reprint ed. lib. bdg. 20.00 (*0-8095-8312-7*) Borgo Pr.

Charles City County Inventory: Circuit Court Clerk. Comp. by B. Kirke White, Jr. xii, 61p. 1976. pap. text ed. 7.95 (*0-88490-033-9*) VA State Lib.

***Charles City County, Virginia Court Orders, 1687-1695: With a Fragment of a Court Order Book for the Year 1680.** Benjamin B. Weisiger, III. 249p. 1980. pap. 23.00x (*0-935931-77-5*) Borgo Pr.

Charles City County, Virginia Court Orders, 1687-1695: With a Fragment of a Court Order Book for the Year 1680. Benjamin B. Weisiger, III. 249p. (C). 1980. reprint ed. lib. bdg. 49.00x (*0-8095-8156-6*) Borgo Pr.

***Charles City County, Virginia Records, 1737-1774.** Benjamin B. Weisiger, 3rd. 201p. 1986. lib. bdg. 47.00 (*0-8095-8192-2*); pap. 20.00 (*0-8095-8535-9*) Borgo Pr.

***Charles City County, Virginia, 1725-1731.** Benjamin B. Weisiger, 3rd. 63p. 1984. lib. bdg. 27.00 (*0-8095-8191-4*); pap. 10.00 (*0-8095-8533-2*) Borgo Pr.

***Charles Clark in Memoriam: European & American Prints since 1960.** Contrib by Jonathan Bober. (Illus.). 40p. 1991. pap. 12.00 (*0-935213-20-1*) A M Huntington Art.

Charles Colson. W. Terry Whalin. (Today's Heroes Ser.). 112p. 1994. pap. 4.99 (*0-310-41261-7*) Zondervan.

***Charles Colson.** Stella Wiseman. (Men of Faith Ser.). 192p. 1995. mass mkt. 4.99 (*1-55661-629-5*) Bethany Hse.

Charles Correa. Hassan-Uddin Khan. (Illus.). 176p. 1987. 49.95 (*0-408-50043-3*, Butterwrth Archit) Buttrwrth-Heinemann.

Charles Cotesworth Pinckney, Founding Father. Marvin R. Zahniser. LC 67-28010. 307p. reprint ed. pap. 87.50 (*0-8357-4415-9*, 2037235) Bks Demand.

Charles Cotton's Works, 1663-1665: Critical Editions of "The Valiant Knight" & "Scarronides" A. I. Dust. LC 91-41637. (Renaissance Imagination Ser.). 488p. 1992. 105.00 (*0-8153-0452-8*) Garland.

Charles County Gentry. Harry W. Newman. (Illus.). 321p. 1990. reprint ed. 25.00 (*0-685-60386-5*, 4095) Clearfield Co.

***Charles County, Maryland, Court Records, 1774-1778.** T. L.C. Genealogy. (Orig.). Date not set. spiral bd., pap. 20.00 (*1-886633-23-1*) TLC Genealogy.

***Charles County, Maryland, Land Records, 1722-1733.** T. L.C. Genealogy Staff. 206p. (Orig.). 1994. spiral bd., pap. 20.00 (*1-886633-19-3*) TLC Genealogy.

***Charles County, Maryland, Land Records, 1733-1743.** T. L.C. Genealogy Staff. 169p. (Orig.). 1993. spiral bd., pap. 20.00 (*1-886633-20-7*) TLC Genealogy.

***Charles County, Maryland, Land Records, 1743-1752.** T. L.C. Genealogy. 222p. (Orig.). 1993. spiral bd., pap. 20.00 (*1-886633-21-5*) TLC Genealogy.

***Charles County, Maryland, Land Records, 1765-1775.** T. L.C. Genealogy. (Orig.). Date not set. spiral bd., pap. 20.00 (*1-886633-22-3*) TLC Genealogy.

***Charles County, Maryland, Land Records, 1790-1796.** T. L.C. Genealogy Staff. (Orig.). 1994. spiral bd., pap. 20.00 (*1-886633-24-X*) TLC Genealogy.

Charles Crawford Pettett: A Plucky Fellow, Vol. 1. George Pettett. LC 89-92192. (Illus.). 300p. 1989. 14.95 (*0-9624353-0-9*) Lochaber Bks.

Charles Cresson on the American Flower Garden. LC 92-16748. (Burpee Expert Gardner Ser.). 1993. 18.00 (*0-13-091026-0*) P-H.

Charles Cresson on the American Flower Garden. Charles O. Cresson. (Burpee Expert Gardener Ser.). (Illus.). 320p. 1993. bds. 20.00 (*0-671-84720-1*, P-H Gardening) P-H Gen Ref & Trav.

Charles Crodel: The Graphic Work, 1919-1960. Cornelius Steckner. 198p. (GER.). 1974. 110.00 (*1-55660-108-5*) A Wofsy Fine Arts.

Charles Cruft's Dog Book: Popular Breeds & Their Care. Charles Cruft. (Illus.). 96p. (Orig.). 1983. pap. 13.95 (*0-572-01208-X*) Trans-Atl Phila.

Charles D. Gallagher: Memoir & Autobiography. Intro. by Mary E. Glass. 165p. 1965. lib. bdg. 33.00 (*1-56475-009-4*); fiche write for info. (*1-56475-010-8*) U NV Oral Hist.

***Charles Darwin.** (Great Explorers Ser.). (Illus.). 32p. (YA). (gr. 4 up). 1995. lib. bdg. 14.95 (*0-7910-2831-3*) Chelsea Hse.

Charles Darwin. Brenda Clarke. (Children of History Ser.). (Illus.). 32p. (J). (gr. 3-8). 1988. lib. bdg. 9.95 (*0-86307-923-7*) Marshall Cavendish.

Charles Darwin. Richard Milner. (Makers of Modern Science Ser.). 128p. (J). (gr. 5 up). 1993. lib. bdg. 16.95 (*0-8160-2557-6*) Facts on File.

Charles Darwin. Don Nardo. (Library of Biography). (Illus.). 112p. (J). (gr. 5 up). 1993. 18.95 (*0-7910-1729-X*, Am Art Analog); pap. write for info. (*0-7910-1730-3*, Am Art Analog) Chelsea Hse.

Charles Darwin. Renee Skelton. LC 87-19564. (Barron's Solutions Ser.). (Illus.). 144p. (J). (gr. 3-6). 1987. pap. 5.95 (*0-8120-3923-8*) Barron.

Charles Darwin: A Biography. James Bunting. 126p. 1974. 18.00 (*0-8464-1459-7*) Beekman Pubs.

Charles Darwin: A Biography, Vol. 1. Janet Browne. LC 94-6598. 1995. 35.00 (*0-394-57942-9*) Knopf.

Charles Darwin: A New Life. John Bowlby. 528p. 1992. pap. 14.95 (*0-393-30930-4*) Norton.

Charles Darwin: Evolution by Natural Selection. Gavin R. De Beer. LC 74-1779. (British Men of Science Ser.). 290p. 1976. reprint ed. text ed. 69.50 (*0-8371-7378-7*, DECD, Greenwood Pr) Greenwood.

Charles Darwin: Naturalist. Margaret J. Anderson. LC 93-29839. (Great Minds of Science Ser.). (Illus.). 128p. (J). (gr. 4-10). 1994. lib. bdg. 17.95 (*0-89490-476-0*) Enslow Pubs.

Charles Darwin: Revolutionary Biologist. Nathan Aaseng. LC 92-45281. (YA). (gr. 5 up). 1993. 21.50 (*0-8225-4914-X*, Lerner Publctns) Lerner Group.

Charles Darwin: The Man & His Influence. Peter J. Bowler. Ed. by David Knight. (Scientific Biographies Ser.). (Illus.). 1990. 26.95 (*0-631-16818-4*) Blackwell Pubs.

***Charles Darwin & Evolution.** Steve Parker. LC 94-20656. (Science Discoveries Ser.). (Illus.). 32p. (YA). (gr. 3 up). 1995. lib. bdg. 13.95 (*0-7910-3007-5*) Chelsea Hse.

Charles Darwin & Other English Thinkers. Samuel P. Cadman. LC 76-142612. (Essay Index Reprint Ser.). 1977. 20.95 (*0-8369-2040-6*) Ayer.

Charles Darwin As Geologist. Archibald Geikie. 1977. lib. bdg. 59.95 (*0-8490-1596-0*) Gordon Pr.

Charles Darwin in Western Australia. Patrick Armstrong. 88p. 1986. pap. 12.95 (*0-85564-237-8*, Pub. by Univ of West Aust Pr AT) Intl Spec Bk.

Charles Darwin, the Adventurer. Vargie Johnson. (J). 1992. 10.00 (*0-533-10092-5*) Vantage.

***Charles Darwin, the Origin of Species: New Interdisciplinary Essays.** Ed. by David Amigoni & Jeff Wallace. LC 94-26485. 1995. text ed. write for info. (*0-7190-4024-8*); text ed. write for info. (*0-7190-4025-6*) St Martin.

Charles Darwin's Beagle Diary. Ed. by R. D. Keynes. (Illus.). 512p. 1988. 74.95 (*0-521-23503-0*) Cambridge U Pr.

Charles Darwin's Marginalia, Vol. 1. Mario A. Di Gregorio. LC 90-2970. 792p. 1990. 102.00 (*0-8240-6639-1*, 783) Garland.

Charles Darwin's Natural Selection: Being the Second Part of His Big Species Book Written from 1856 to 1858. Ed. by R. C. Stauffer. 712p. 1987. pap. 44.95 (*0-521-34807-2*) Cambridge U Pr.

Charles Darwin's Notebooks, 1836-1844: Geology, Transmutation of Species, Metaphysical Enquiries. Charles Darwin. Ed. by Paul H. Barrett et al. LC 87-47953. 800p. (C). 1989. 78.50 (*0-8014-1660-4*); pap. 37.50 (*0-8014-9580-6*); mic. film 79.50 (*0-8014-1659-0*) Cornell U Pr.

Charles de Foucauld. Philip Hillyer. (Way of the Christian Mystics Ser.: Vol. 9). 207p. (C). 1991. pap. 14.95 (*0-8146-5629-3*) Liturgical Pr.

Charles de Gaulle. Susan Banfield. (World Leaders - Past & Present Ser.). (Illus.). 112p. (YA). (gr. 5 up). 1985. lib. bdg. 17.95 (*0-87754-551-0*) Chelsea Hse.

Charles de Gaulle: I Am France. Nancy Whitelaw. LC 91-13095. (People in Focus Ser.). (Illus.). 112p. (J). (gr. 4-6). 1991. text ed. 13.95 (*0-87518-486-3*, Dillon Silver Burdett) Silver Burdett Pr.

Charles de Gaulle, Existentialist of the Nation. Regis Debray. LC 93-46232. 1994. 64.95 (*0-86091-622-7*, Pub. by Verso UK); pap. 18.95 (*0-86091-452-6*, Pub. by Verso UK) Routledge Chapman & Hall.

Charles de Lannoy: Victor of Pavia. Lucile Delano. 144p. 1983. 9.75 (*0-8158-0417-2*) Chris Mass.

Charles DeGarmo: Professor of Education. Carl Gross. (DeGarmo Lecture Ser.: No. 1). 1975. 3.00 (*0-933669-26-7*) Soc Profs Ed.

Charles DeMorse: Pioneer Statesman & Father of Texas Journalism. Ernest Wallace. Ed. & Illus. by Skipper Steely. 275p. 1985. reprint ed. 17.95 (*0-915263-07-6*); reprint ed. pap. 12.95 (*0-915263-06-8*) Wright Pr.

Charles Demuth. Barbara Haskell. (Illus.). 240p. 1987. 49.50 (*0-8109-1135-3*) Abrams.

Charles Demuth: Behind a Laughing Mask. Emily Farnham. LC 70-108804. (Illus.). 290p. reprint ed. 82.70 (*0-8357-9721-X*, 2016212) Bks Demand.

***Charles Demuth Poster Portraits, 1923-1929.** Robin J. Frank. LC 94-3441. 1994. write for info. (*0-89467-065-4*) Yale U Pr.

Charles Desmarais: Proof: Los Angeles Art & the Photograph, 1960-1980. Charles Desmarais. LC 92-72754. 144p. 1992. pap. 30.00 (*0-911291-20-2*) Fellows Cont Art.

***Charles Dickens.** (Great Writers Ser.). (Illus.). 64p. Date not set. 9.95 (*1-85410-261-3*, London Bridge) Genl Dist Srvs.

Charles Dickens. Intro. by Harold Bloom. (Modern Critical Views Ser.). 367p. 1987. 34.95 (*0-87754-690-8*) Chelsea Hse.

Charles Dickens. Philip Collins. (Critical Heritage Ser.). 602p. 1987. 69.50 (*0-7100-2942-X*, 69073, RKP) Routledge.

Charles Dickens. Sidney Dark. LC 75-38650. (Studies in Dickens: No. 52). 1976. lib. bdg. 75.00 (*0-8383-2113-5*) M S G Haskell Hse.

Charles Dickens. Charles Dickens. 1989. 12.98 (*0-8300-0210-3*) Aurora News Reg.

Charles Dickens. Charles Dickens. 1993. 12.99 (*0-517-09339-1*) Random Hse Value.

Charles Dickens. Mary Dickens. LC 76-52967. (Studies in Dickens: No. 52). 1977. lib. bdg. 75.00 (*0-8383-2174-7*) M S G Haskell Hse.

Charles Dickens. George Gissing. LC 73-21711. (Studies in Dickens: No. 52). 1974. lib. bdg. 75.00 (*0-8383-1774-X*) M S G Haskell Hse.

Charles Dickens. Nancy Goodman. (Great Authors Ser.). 1988. 7.95 (*0-943718-04-X*) Kipling Pr.

Charles Dickens. Michael Harrison. LC 74-34403. (Studies in Dickens: No. 52). 1974. lib. bdg. 54.95 (*0-8383-2064-3*) M S G Haskell Hse.

Charles Dickens. Brian Murray. (Literature & Life Ser.). 192p. (C). 1994. 19.95 (*0-8264-0565-7*) Continuum.

Charles Dickens. Harland S. Nelson. (English Authors Ser.: No. 314). 264p. (C). 1981. text ed. 21.95 (*0-8057-6805-X*, Twayne) Macmillan.

Charles Dickens. Julian Symons. LC 74-6373. (Studies in Dickens: No. 52). 1979. lib. bdg. 75.00 (*0-8383-1979-3*) M S G Haskell Hse.

Charles Dickens: A Critical Study. George Gissing. reprint ed. lib. bdg. 79.00 (*0-7812-0309-0*) Rprt Serv.

Charles Dickens: Apostle of the People. Edwin W. Pugh. LC 75-176497. (Studies in Dickens: No. 52). 1971. reprint ed. lib. bdg. 52.95 (*0-8383-1364-7*) M S G Haskell Hse.

***Charles Dickens: Critical Assessments, 4 vols., Set.** Ed. by Graham Clarke. (Critical Assessments of Writers in English Ser.). 2500p. 1995. 635.00 (*1-873403-13-5*, C0540, Routledge NY) Routledge.

Charles Dickens: Great Expectations. Ed. by Louis Crompton. 567p. (C). 1964. pap. write for info. (*0-02-325710-5*) Macmillan.

Charles Dickens: How to Know Him. R. Burton. 1972. 59.95 (*0-87968-838-6*) Gordon Pr.

Charles Dickens: Linguistics Innovator. Knud Sorensen. (Acta Jutlandica LX. Humanistic Ser.: No. 58). 176p. (Orig.). 1985. pap. 42.00x (*87-7244-009-0*) Coronet Bks.

Charles Dickens: Master Storyteller. Nan Goodman. 1989. 8.95 (*0-943718-34-1*) Kipling Pr.

C

An Asterisk (*) at the beginning of an entry indicates that the title is appearing in BIP for the first time.

An Asterisk (*) at the beginning of an entry indicates that the title is appearing in BIP for the first time.

1157

Charles J. Kickham: A Biography. R. V. Comerford. 256p. 1979. pap. 12.95 (*0-86327-024-7*, Pub. by Wolfhound Pr IE) Dufour.

Charles James Fox. L. G. Mitchell. (Illus.). 356p. 1992. 49.95 (*0-19-820104-4*) OUP.

Charles James Fox, 1749-1806: A Bibliography. David Schweitzer. LC 91-8424. (Bibliographies of British Statesmen Ser.: No. 4). 248p. 1991. text ed. 69.50 (*0-313-28118-1*, SZX, Greenwood Pr) Greenwood.

Charles Jencks. (Architecture & Urbanism Extra Edition Ser.). (Illus.). 240p. (Orig.). (ENG & JPN.). (C). pap. text ed. 75.00 (*4-900211-13-3*, Pub. by Japan Architect JA) Gingko Press.

Charles Jordan's Best Card Tricks. Karl Fulves. 256p. (Orig.). 1992. pap. 5.95 (*0-486-26931-0*) Dover.

Charles Joseph La Trobe. Alan Gross. 167p. 1980. 19.95 (*0-522-84210-0*) Intl Spec Bk.

Charles Keeping an Illustrator's Life. Douglas Martin. (Illus.). 224p. 1993. 65.00 (*1-85681-062-3*, Pub. by J MacRae UK) Trafalgar.

Charles Kemble, Man of the Theatre. Jane Williamson. LC 69-19105. 281p. reprint ed. pap. 80.10 (*0-7837-1830-6*, 2042030) Bks Demand.

Charles Kenneth Leith, Scientific Adviser. Sylvia W. McGrath. 278p. 1971. 10.00 (*0-299-05970-7*) U of Wis Pr.

Charles King, American Army Novelist: A Bibliography. Charles E. Dornbusch. 1963. pap. 5.00 (*0-910746-05-2*, CKA01) Hope Farm.

Charles, King of England, Sixteen Hundred to Sixteen Thirty-Seven. Esme C. Wingfield-Stratford. LC 74-31871. (Illus.). 361p. 1975. reprint ed. text ed. 59.75 (*0-8371-7949-1*, WICK, Greenwood Pr) Greenwood.

Charles Kingsley: His Letters & Memories of His Life, 2 Vols. Charles Kingsley. LC 74-148803. (Illus.). reprint ed. 19.00 (*0-685-73112-X*) AMS Pr.

Charles Kingsley: His Letters & Memories of His Life, 2 Vols, 1. Charles Kingsley. LC 74-148803. (Illus.). reprint ed. 19.00 (*0-404-08870-8*) AMS Pr.

Charles Kingsley: His Letters & Memories of His Life, 2 Vols, 2. Charles Kingsley. LC 74-148803. (Illus.). reprint ed. 19.00 (*0-404-08871-6*) AMS Pr.

Charles Kingsley: His Letters & Memories of His Life, 2 Vols, Set. Charles Kingsley. LC 74-148803. (Illus.). reprint ed. 95.00 (*0-404-08869-4*) AMS Pr.

Charles Kingsley & His Ideas. Guy Kendall. LC 72-6679. (English Biography Ser.: No. 31). 195p. 1972. reprint ed. lib. bdg. 49.95 (*0-8383-1639-5*) M S G Haskell Hse.

Charles Kingsley & the Christian Social Movement. Charles W. Stubbs. LC 70-148310. reprint ed. 37.50 (*0-404-08914-3*) AMS Pr.

Charles Koechlin (Eighteen Sixty-Seven to Nineteen Fifty) His Life & Works. R. Orledge. (Contemporary Music Studies: Vol. 1). xxvi, 458p. 1989. pap. text ed. 128.00 (*3-7186-4898-9*) Gordon & Breach.

***Charles L. Peterson: Of Time & Place.** Charles Peterson & Norbert Blei. Ed. by Mark E. Quale & Susan Peterson. (Illus.). 96p. 1994. 135.00 (*0-9643438-0-0*) White Door.

***Charles L. Peterson: Of Time & Place.** 2nd ed. Charles Peterson & Norbert Blei. Ed. by Mark E. Quale & Susan Peterson. (Illus.). 96p. 1994. pap. text ed. 45.00 (*0-9643438-1-9*) White Door.

Charles L. Wood Agricultural History Lecture: Recent Trends in United States Agricultural History. Gilbert C. File. 15p. 1985. pap. 5.00 (*0-318-18994-1*, 85-2) Intl Ctr Arid & Semi-Arid.

Charles Lamb. George L. Barnett. (Twayne's English Authors Ser.). (C). 1976. 17.95 (*0-8057-6668-5*) Irvington.

Charles Lamb. Alfred Ainger. Ed. by John Morley. LC 68-58369. (English Men of Letters Ser.). reprint ed. lib. bdg. 34.50 (*0-404-51701-3*) AMS Pr.

Charles Lamb. Alfred Ainger. (BCL1-PR English Literature Ser.). 191p. 1992. reprint ed. lib. bdg. 69.00 (*0-7812-7585-7*) Rprt Serv.

Charles Lamb: Prose & Poetry. Charles Lamb. LC 77-28850. 216p. 1978. reprint ed. text ed. 35.00 (*0-313-20274-5*, LAPP0, Greenwood Pr) Greenwood.

Charles Lamb: The Evolution of Elia. George L. Barnett. LC 72-6858. (English Literature Ser.: No. 33). 1972. reprint ed. lib. bdg. 75.00 (*0-8383-1652-2*) M S G Haskell Hse.

Charles Lamb & His Life: Recorded by His Contemporaries. E. Blunden. 1972. 59.95 (*0-87968-841-6*) Gordon Pr.

Charles Lanman: Landscapes & Nature Studies. Harry F. Orchard. (Illus.). 28p. 1983. pap. 4.00 (*0-9613046-0-X*) Morris Mus.

Charles Lathrop Pack. Alexandra Eyle. 376p. 1993. 34.95 (*0-8156-8117-8*) Syracuse U Pr.

Charles Le Brun: First Painter to King Louis XIV. Michel Gareau. (Illus.). 260p. 1992. 85.00 (*0-8109-3567-8*) Abrams.

Charles Lecorgne: The Deaf Mute of Normandy. W. Sleight. 1972. lib. bdg. 59.95 (*0-87968-842-4*) Gordon Pr.

***Charles Leonhard: American Music Educator.** George N. Heller. LC 94-30742. 1995. 35.00 (*0-8108-2942-8*) Scarecrow.

Charles Lever: New Evaluations. Ed. by Tony Bareham. 128p. (C). 1991. text ed. 49.50 (*0-389-20964-3*) B&N Imports.

Charles Lindbergh: Hero Pilot. David R. Collins. (Discovery Biographies Ser.). (Illus.). 80p. (J). (gr. 2-6). 1991. reprint ed. lib. bdg. 12.95 (*0-7910-1417-7*) Chelsea Hse.

Charles Loewner: Collected Works. Ed. by Lipman Bers. (Contemporary Mathematicians Ser.). 272p. 1988. 100.00 (*0-8176-3377-4*) Birkhauser.

Charles Loewner: Theory of Continuous Groups. Ed. by Charles Loewner et al. (Mathematicians of Our Time Ser.). 1971. text ed. 30.00 (*0-262-06041-8*) MIT Pr.

Charles-Louis Clerisseau & the Genesis of Neoclassicism: The Birth of Neoclassicism. Thomas McCormick. (Illus.). 272p. 1990. 40.00 (*0-262-13262-1*) MIT Pr.

Charles Lyell on North American Geology: An Original Anthology. Ed. by Claude C. Albritton. LC 77-6524. (History of Geology Ser.). (Illus.). 1978. lib. bdg. 56.95 (*0-405-10446-4*) Ayer.

Charles M. Russell. Peter H. Hassrick. (Library of American Art). (Illus.). 160p. 1989. 39.95 (*0-8109-1571-5*) Abrams.

Charles M. Russell: Masterpieces from the Amon Carter Museum. Rick Stewart. LC 92-54539. (Illus.). 60p. 1992. pap. 17.95 (*0-88360-071-4*) Amon Carter.

Charles M. Russell: The Frederic G. Renner Collection. Ginger Renner. 80p. (Orig.). 1981. pap. 10.00 (*0-910407-09-6*) Phoenix Art.

Charles M. Russell, Sculptor. Rick Stewart. LC 94-4369. 1994. write for info. (*0-8109-3772-7*) Abrams.

Charles M. Russell, Word Painter: Letters 1887-1926. Ed. by Brian W. Dippie. LC 92-46329. (Illus.). 435p. 1993. pap. 49.95 (*0-88360-073-0*) Amon Carter.

Charles M. Russell, Word Painter: Letters 1887-1926. Comp. by Brian W. Dippie. LC 92-46329. 1993. 95.00 (*0-8109-3764-6*) Abrams.

Charles M. Russell: 1864-1926: Paintings & Sculpture in the R. W. Norton Art Gallery Collection. Norton, R. W., Art Gallery Staff. LC 78-7115. (Illus.). 1980. pap. 8.50 (*0-913060-15-1*) Norton Art.

Charles Mair & His Works. Fred Cogswell. 42p. (C). 1988. pap. text ed. 9.95 (*0-920763-70-7*, Pub. by ECW Press CN) Genl Dist Srvs.

Charles Marsteller Alexander: An Alexander Family History. Guy B. Alexander. Ed. by L. Glen Pew. (Illus.). 1990. 50.00 (*0-9623915-4-9*) Jackson Pub.

Charles Martin Loeffler: A Life Apart in Music. Ellen Knight. (Music in American Life Ser.). (Illus.). 392p. (C). 1993. 42.50 (*0-252-01908-3*) U of Ill Pr.

Charles Masson of Afghanistan: Explorer, Archaeologist, Numismatist. Whitteridge. (Central Asian Studies). 1986. pap. 39.95 (*0-85668-318-3*, Pub. by Aris & Phillips UK) David Brown.

Charles McLean Andrews: A Study in American Historical Writing. Abraham S. Eisenstadt. LC 68-54261. (Columbia University. Studies in the Social Sciences: No. 588). reprint ed. 20.00 (*0-404-51588-6*) AMS Pr.

Charles Men, 2 Vols, Set. Verner Von Heidenstam. Tr. by Charles W. Stork. LC 72-122718. (Short Story Index Reprint Ser.). 1977. 39.95 (*0-8369-3551-9*) Ayer.

Charles Meryon & Jean-Francois Millet: Etchings of Urban & Rural 19th-Century France. Patricia Phagan. LC 92-39756. 1992. 25.00 (*0-915977-10-9*) Georgia Museum of Art.

Charles Mills Gayley Anniversary Papers. Charles Gayley. LC 67-30814. (Studies in Poetry: No. 38). 1969. reprint ed. lib. bdg. 64.95 (*0-8383-0715-9*) M S G Haskell Hse.

Charles Mingus: More Than a Fake Book. Charles Mingus. 160p. 1991. pap. 19.95 (*0-7935-0900-9*, 00673220) H Leonard.

Charles Moore: Buildings & Projects, Nineteen Forty-Nine to Nineteen Eighty-Six. Ed. by Eugene J. Johnson. (Illus.). 307p. 1986. pap. 35.00 (*0-8478-0759-2*) Rizzoli Intl.

Charles Morgan & the Development of Southern Transportation. James P. Baughman. LC 68-17281. (Illus.). 342p. reprint ed. pap. 97.50 (*0-8357-3201-0*, 2039472) Bks Demand.

Charles Morgan on Retrievers. Ed. by Ann Fowler & D. K. Walters. (Illus.). 1968. 22.50 (*0-8079-0026-5*) October.

Charles Morris & the Criticism of Discourse. Richard A. Fiordo. LC 75-39426. (Studies in Semiotics: Vol. IV). viii, 197p. (Orig.). 1977. pap. 24.00 (*0-87750-193-9*, Pub. by Peter de Ridder NE) Benjamins North Am.

Charles Morton's Compendium Physicae. Charles Morton. Ed. by Theodore Hornberger. (Publications - Colonial Society of Massachusetts: Vol. 33). 277p. reprint ed. pap. 79.00 (*0-7837-0267-1*, 2040576) Bks Demand.

Charles N. Hunter & Race Relations in North Carolina. John H. Haley. LC 86-11369. (James Sprunt Studies in History & Political Science: Vol. 60). xiv, 352p. (Orig.). 1987. pap. 22.50 (*0-8078-5061-6*) U of NC Pr.

Charles Nodier, Pilot of Romanticism. A. Richard Oliver. LC 64-8670. (Illus.). 1964. 39.95x (*0-8156-2073-X*) Syracuse U Pr.

Charles Olson. Eniko Bollobas. (Twayne's United States Authors Ser.: No. 590). 190p. (C). 1992. text ed. 22.95 (*0-8057-7629-X*, Twayne) Macmillan.

Charles Olson: The Scholar's Art. Robert Von Hallberg. LC 78-4464. 264p. 1978. 28.50 (*0-674-11130-3*) HUP.

Charles Olson & Cid Corman Complete Correspondence, 1956-1964, Vol. 1. Ed. by George Evans. LC 85-61154. 332p. (Orig.). 1988. 30.00 (*0-915032-13-9*); pap. 16.95 (*0-915032-14-7*) Natl Poet Foun.

Charles Olson & Cid Corman Complete Correspondence, 1956-1964, Vol. 2. Ed. by George Evans. 186p. (Orig.). 1991. 30.00 (*0-943373-16-6*); pap. 16.95 (*0-943373-17-4*) Natl Poet Foun.

Charles Olson & Robert Creeley: The Complete Correspondence, Vol. 1. Charles Olson & Robert Creeley. Ed. by George F. Butterick. LC 80-12222. (Illus.). 184p. (Orig.). 1980. 20.00 (*0-87685-400-5*); pap. 10.00 (*0-87685-399-8*) Black Sparrow.

Charles Olson & Robert Creeley: The Complete Correspondence, Vol. 2. Charles Olson & Robert Creeley. Ed. by George F. Butterick. LC 80-12222. (Illus.). 184p. (Orig.). 1980. 20.00 (*0-87685-441-2*); pap. 10.00 (*0-87685-440-4*) Black Sparrow.

Charles Olson & Robert Creeley: The Complete Correspondence, Vol. 3. Charles Olson & Robert Creeley. Ed. by George F. Butterick. LC 80-12222. (Illus.). 175p. (Orig.). (C). 1981. 20.00 (*0-87685-483-8*); pap. 10.00 (*0-87685-482-X*) Black Sparrow.

Charles Olson & Robert Creeley: The Complete Correspondence, Vol. 3, signed ed. deluxe ed. Charles Olson & Robert Creeley. Ed. by George F. Butterick. LC 80-12222. (Illus.). 175p. (Orig.). (C). 1981. 30.00 (*0-87685-484-6*) Black Sparrow.

Charles Olson & Robert Creeley: The Complete Correspondence, Vol. 4. Charles Olson & Robert Creeley. Ed. by George F. Butterick. LC 80-12222. (Illus.). 158p. (Orig.). (C). 1982. 20.00 (*0-87685-486-2*); pap. 10.00 (*0-87685-485-4*) Black Sparrow.

Charles Olson & Robert Creeley: The Complete Correspondence, Vol. 4, signed ed. deluxe ed. Charles Olson & Robert Creeley. Ed. by George F. Butterick. LC 80-12222. (Illus.). 158p. (Orig.). (C). 1982. 30.00 (*0-87685-487-0*) Black Sparrow.

Charles Olson & Robert Creeley: The Complete Correspondence, Vol. 5. Charles Olson et al. Ed. by George F. Butterick. LC 80-12222. (Illus.). 222p. (Orig.). (C). 1983. 20.00 (*0-87685-561-3*); pap. 10.00 (*0-87685-560-5*) Black Sparrow.

Charles Olson & Robert Creeley: The Complete Correspondence, Vol. 5, signed ed. deluxe ed. Charles Olson et al. Ed. by George F. Butterick. LC 80-12222. (Illus.). 222p. (Orig.). (C). 1983. 30.00 (*0-87685-562-1*) Black Sparrow.

Charles Olson & Robert Creeley: The Complete Correspondence, Vol. 6. Charles Olson & Robert Creeley. LC 80-12222. (Illus.). 247p. (Orig.). 1985. 20.00 (*0-87685-586-9*); pap. 12.50 (*0-87685-585-0*) Black Sparrow.

Charles Olson & Robert Creeley: The Complete Correspondence, Vol. 6, signed ed. deluxe ed. Charles Olson & Robert Creeley. LC 80-12222. (Illus.). 247p. (Orig.). 1985. 30.00 (*0-87685-587-7*) Black Sparrow.

Charles Olson & Robert Creeley: The Complete Correspondence, Vol. 7. Charles Olson & Robert Creeley. Ed. by George F. Butterick. LC 80-12222. (Illus.). 286p. (Orig.). 1987. 20.00 (*0-87685-690-3*); pap. 12.50 (*0-87685-689-X*) Black Sparrow.

Charles Olson & Robert Creeley: The Complete Correspondence, Vol. 7, signed ed. deluxe ed. Charles Olson & Robert Creeley. Ed. by George F. Butterick. LC 80-12222. (Illus.). 286p. (Orig.). 1987. 30.00 (*0-87685-691-1*) Black Sparrow.

Charles Olson & Robert Creeley: The Complete Correspondence, Vol. 8. Charles Olson & Robert Creeley. LC 80-12222. (Illus.). 284p. (Orig.). (C). 1987. 20.00 (*0-87685-705-5*); pap. 12.50 (*0-87685-704-7*) Black Sparrow.

Charles Olson & Robert Creeley: The Complete Correspondence, Vol. 8, signed ed. deluxe ed. Charles Olson & Robert Creeley. LC 80-12222. (Illus.). 284p. (Orig.). (C). 1987. 30.00 (*0-87685-706-3*) Black Sparrow.

Charles Olson & Robert Creeley: The Complete Correspondence, Vol. 9. Charles Olson & Robert Creeley. Ed. by Richard Blevins. LC 80-12222. (Illus.). 346p. (Orig.). (C). 1990. 25.00 (*0-87685-782-9*); pap. 15.00 (*0-87685-781-0*) Black Sparrow.

Charles Olson & Robert Creeley: The Complete Correspondence, Vol. 9, signed ed. deluxe ed. Charles Olson & Robert Creeley. Ed. by Richard Blevins. LC 80-12222. (Illus.). 346p. (Orig.). (C). 1990. 35.00 (*0-87685-783-7*) Black Sparrow.

Charles Olson in Connecticut. Charles Boer. LC 91-62199. 1991. pap. 12.95 (*0-933598-28-9*) NC Wesleyan Pr.

***Charles Olson's Reading: A Biography.** Ralph Maud. LC 94-44403. 1995. write for info. (*0-8093-1995-0*) S Ill U Pr.

***Charles Olson's Reading: A Biography.** Ralph Maud. LC 94-44403. 448p. (C). 1995. 44.95x (*0-614-07244-1*) S Ill U Pr.

Charles P. Lazarus: The Titan of Toys R Us. Anne Koopman. Ed. by Richard G. Young. LC 91-32054. (Wizards of Business Ser.). (Illus.). 64p. (J). (gr. 4-8). 1992. lib. bdg. 17.26 (*1-56074-022-1*) Garrett Ed Corp.

Charles Parsons Collection of Paintings. Graham W. Beal. LC 77-3962. (Illus.). 80p. 1977. pap. 5.00 (*0-936316-08-X*) Wash U Gallery.

Charles Peguy. F. C. St. Aubyn. LC 77-5948. (Twayne's World Authors Ser.). 175p. (C). 1977. lib. bdg. 17.95 (*0-8057-6304-X*) Irvington.

Charles Peguy: de Jean Coste: Edition Critique avec le Roman d'Antonin Lavergne. Charles Peguy & Anne Roche. 670p. (FRE.). 1976. pap. 69.95 (*0-7859-1463-3*, 2252017406) Fr & Eur.

Charles Peirce's Guess at the Riddle: Grounds for Human Significance. John K. Sheriff. LC 93-33835. 1994. 20.00 (*0-253-35204-5*); pap. 9.95 (*0-253-20880-7*) Ind U Pr.

Charles Peirce's Pragmatic Pluralism. Sandra B. Rosenthal. LC 93-46977. (SUNY Series in Philosophy). 177p. (C). 1994. text ed. 51.50x (*0-7914-2157-0*); pap. text ed. 18.95x (*0-7914-2158-9*) State U NY Pr.

Charles Peirce's Theory of Scientific Method. Francis E. Reilly. LC 79-105527. (Orestes Brownson Series on Contemporary Thought & Affairs: No. 7). 208p. reprint ed. pap. 59.30 (*0-7837-0465-8*, 2040788) Bks Demand.

Charles Perrault: Memoirs of My Life. Ed. by Jeanne M. Zarucchi. LC 88-39865. (Illus.). 152p. 1989. text ed. 22.00 (*0-8262-0667-0*) U of Mo Pr.

Charles Platt: The Artist As Architect. Keith Morgan. (American Monographs). (Illus.). 265p. 1985. 37.50 (*0-262-13188-9*) MIT Pr.

Charles Porterfield Krauth. Adolph Spaeth. LC 78-83440. (Religion in America, Ser. 1). 1970. reprint ed. 49.95 (*0-405-00265-3*) Ayer.

***Charles Press Handbook of Current Medical Abbreviations.** 4th ed. Charles Press Staff. LC 94-27658. 240p. 1995. pap. 11.95 (*0-914783-76-9*) Charles.

***Charles Preston's Giant Crossword Puzzle Treasury No. 11.** Charles Preston. 128p. (Orig.). 1994. pap. 8.95 (*0-399-52147-X*) Berkley Pub.

Charles Preston's Giant Crossword Treasury, No. 10. Charles Preston. 1993. pap. 8.95 (*0-399-52114-3*) Putnam Pub Group.

Charles R. Drew. Robyn Mahone-Lonesome. (Black Americans of Achievement Ser.). (Illus.). (YA). (gr. 5 up). 1990. 17.95 (*1-55546-581-1*) Chelsea Hse.

Charles R. Harrison's Life & Adventures. Charles R. Harrison. 1993. 12.95 (*0-533-10491-2*) Vantage.

Charles R. Kleeman Festschrift. Ed. by S. G. Massry. (Journal: Mineral & Electrolyte Metabolism: Vol. 12, Nos. 5-6, 1986). (Illus.). lv, 124p. 1987. pap. 56.00 (*3-8055-4454-5*) S Karger.

Charles R. Wood Sermon Outline Series, 14 titles, Set. Charles R. Wood. pap. 62.50 (*0-8254-4050-5*) Kregel.

Charles Ray. Lucinda Barnes & Dennis Cooper. LC 90-6359. (Illus.). 44p. (Orig.). 1990. pap. 22.50 (*0-917493-16-8*) Newport Harbor.

Charles Reade. Elton E. Smith. 179p. 1976. 49.50 (*0-685-63208-3*) Elliots Bks.

Charles Reade: A Study in Victorian Authorship. Wayne Burns. LC 61-7182. 360p. 1961. text ed. 34.50 (*0-8290-0161-1*) Irvington.

***Charles Rennie Mackintosh.** Alan Crawford. LC 94-62072. (World of Art Ser.). (Illus.). 216p. (Orig.). 1995. pap. 14.95 (*0-500-20283-4*) Thames Hudson.

Charles Rennie Mackintosh: Textile Designs. rev. ed. Roger Billcliffe. LC 93-20632. (Illus.). 112p. 1993. 30.00 (*1-56640-314-6*) Pomegranate Calif.

Charles Rennie Mackintosh: The Architectural Papers. Ed. by Pamela Robertson. (Illus.). 240p. 1991. 35.00x (*0-262-18142-8*) MIT Pr.

Charles Rennie Mackintosh & the Modern Movement. Thomas Howarth. (Illus.). 388p. 1990. pap. 45.00 (*0-415-05307-2*, A4966) Routledge.

Charles Renouvier, Philosopher of Liberty. William Logue. LC 92-15585. 224p. (C). 1992. text ed. 35.00x (*0-8071-1788-9*) La State U Pr.

Charles Reznikoff: A Critical Essay. Milton Hindus. 75p. (Orig.). 1977. pap. 3.00 (*0-87685-365-3*) Black Sparrow.

Charles Reznikoff: Man & Poet. Ed. by Milton Hindus. LC 84-61195. (Man & Poet Ser.). (Illus.). 450p. 1984. 35.00 (*0-915032-59-7*) Natl Poet Foun.

Charles Reznikoff: Man & Poet. Ed. by Milton Hindus. LC 84-61195. (Man & Poet Ser.). (Illus.). 450p. 1984. pap. 15.95 (*0-915032-60-0*) Natl Poet Foun.

Charles Richard Drew: A Navigator on the River of Life. AESOP Enterprises, Inc. Staff & Gwendolyn J. Crenshaw. (Heroes & Sheroes Ser.). 16p. (J). (gr. 3-12). 1991. audio, pap. write for info. (*1-880771-06-3*) AESOP Enter.

Charles Richard Drew: The Man & the Myth. Charles E. Wynes. LC 88-4738. (Blacks in the New World Ser.). 167p. reprint ed. pap. 47.60 (*0-7837-5746-8*, 2045407) Bks Demand.

Charles Richard Drew, M. D. Rinna E. Wolfe. (First Bks.). (Illus.). 64p. (J). (gr. 3-6). 1991. lib. bdg. 13.93 (*0-531-20021-3*) Watts.

Charles Ricketts: A Biography. J. G. Delaney. (Illus.). 456p. 1990. text ed. 105.00 (*0-19-817212-5*) OUP.

Charles Ricketts' Stage Designs. Richard Cave. (Theatre in Focus Ser.). 1987. sl., pap. 105.00 (*0-85964-195-3*) Chadwyck-Healey.

Charles River: Exploring Nature & History on Foot & by Canoe. Ron McAdow. LC 91-21450. (Illus.). 224p. (Orig.). 1992. pap. 13.95 (*0-9625144-1-1*) Bliss Pub Co.

Charles Robert Maturin. Robert E. Lougy. 89p. 1975. 8.50 (*0-8387-7941-7*); pap. 1.95 (*0-8387-7986-7*) Bucknell U Pr.

Charles Robert Maturin: The Forgotten Imitator. John B. Harris. Ed. by Devendra P. Varma. LC 79-8456. (Gothic Studies & Dissertations). 1980. lib. bdg. 41.95 (*0-405-12646-8*) Ayer.

Charles Russell. (American Art Ser.). 1989. 15.99 (*0-517-67598-6*) Random Hse Value.

Charles Ryder's Schooldays & Other Stories. Evelyn Waugh. 1982. pap. 10.95 (*0-316-92639-6*) Little.

***Charles S. Peirce: From Pragmatism to Pragmaticism.** Karl-Otto Apel. Tr. by John M. Krois. 286p. (C). 1995. pap. 17.50 (*0-391-03895-8*) Humanities.

Charles S. Peirce: Selected Writings. Charles S. Peirce. Ed. by Philip P. Wiener. pap. text ed. 9.95 (*0-486-21634-9*) Dover.

Charles S. Peirce & the Linguistic Sign. David A. Pharies. LC 85-11053. (Foundations of Semiotics Ser.: No. 9). vi, 118p. 1985. 39.00x (*90-272-3279-2*) Benjamins North Am.

Charles S. Peirce, Phenomenologue et Semioticien. Gerard Deledalle. LC 86-3333. (Foundations of Semiotics Ser.: Vol. 14). ix, 114p. 1986. 35.00x (*90-272-3285-7*) Benjamins North Am.

Charles S. Peirce, 1839-1914: An Intellectual Biography. Gerard Deledalle. Tr. by S. Petrilli. LC 89-35843. xxxii, 92p. 1990. 41.00x (*1-55619-082-4*) Benjamins North Am.

Charles S. Pierce & the Philosophy of Science: Papers from the Harvard Sesquicentennial Congress. Ed. by Edward C. Moore. 512p. (C). 1993. 49.95 (*0-8173-0665-X*) U of Ala Pr.

Charles S. Pierce's Evolutionary Philosophy. Carl R. Hausman. LC 92-10648. 288p. (C). 1993. 54.95 (*0-521-41559-4*) Cambridge U Pr.

Charles S. Pierce's Method of Methods. Roberta Kevelson. LC 87-19698. (Foundations of Semiotics Ser.: No. 17). xiii, 180p. 1987. 55.00 (*90-272-3289-X*) Benjamins North Am.

An Asterisk (*) at the beginning of an entry indicates that the title is appearing in BIP for the first time.

An Asterisk (*) at the beginning of an entry indicates that the title is appearing in BIP for the first time.

1159

C

Charlie & the Great Glass Elevator: The Further Adventures of Charlie Bucket & Willie Wonka, the Chocolate-Maker Extraordinaire. Roald Dahl. (Illus.). (J). (gr. k-7). 1972. 15.00 (*0-394-82472-5*); lib. bdg. 15.99 (*0-394-92472-X*) Knopf Bks Yng Read.

Charlie & the Sir. large type ed. Frank Roderus. LC 93-6616. (Nightingale Ser.). 1993. 14.95 (*0-8161-5774-X*) G K Hall.

Charlie & the Stinking Ragbags. John Wood. (Illus.). (Orig.). (J). (gr. 4-6). 1991. pap. 8.95 (*0-86327-298-3*, Pub. by Wolfhound Pr IE) Dufour.

***Charlie & Tyler at the Seashore.** Helen Craig. LC 94-24620. 1995. write for info. (*1-56402-573-X*) Candlewick Pr.

***Charlie Anderson.** Abercrombie. (J). 1995. pap. 4.95 (*0-689-80114-9*, Aladdin Paperbacks) S&S Childrens.

Charlie Anderson. Barbara Abercrombie. LC 89-2449. (Illus.). 32p. (J). (ps-4). 1990. text ed. 13.95 (*0-689-50486-1*, McElderry) S&S Childrens.

Charlie Best. Ruth Corrin. LC 93-9229. (J). 1994. write for info. (*0-383-03681-X*) SRA Schl Grp.

Charlie Brown: A Book of Good Griefs. Ed. by Virgil Burns. 1985. 10.95 (*0-685-60163-3*) Entheo Bks.

Charlie Brown Christmas. Charles M. Schulz. LC 87-83488. (Illus.). 40p. (J). (gr. 1 up). 1988. write for info. (*0-307-13723-6*) Western Pub.

Charlie Brown Dictionary. Charles M. Schulz. (Illus.). (J). (ps-3). 1973. text ed. 17.32 (*0-13-084269-9*) P-H.

Charlie Brown's All-Stars. (Peanuts Storybook & Dramatized Tape Ser.). 24p. 1993. pap. 5.98 (*1-57007-001-6*, XU1001) Astor Bks.

Charlie Brown's Favorite Sunday School Songs. Fred Bock. (Peanuts Piano Course Ser.). (Illus.). 24p. (Orig.). (J). (gr. 1-6). 1992. pap. 7.95 (*1-56516-012-6*) Houston IN.

Charlie Brown's Greatest Hits. Charles Schulz. 1987. 9.95 (*0-7935-0820-7*, 0240155) H Leonard.

Charlie Brown's Piano Album. John Welch. (Peanuts Piano Course Ser.). (Illus.). 38p. (Orig.). (J). (gr. 1-6). 1989. pap. 5.50 (*1-56516-054-1*) Houston IN.

Charlie Carrillo: Tradition & Soul - Tradicion y Alma. Barbe Awalt & Paul Rhetts. LC 94-77890. (Illus.). 128p. (Orig.). 1995. 39.95 (*0-9641542-0-X*) LPD Enterprises.

Charlie Chan: House Without a Key. Earl D. Biggers. 19.95 (*0-8488-0917-3*) Amereon Ltd.

Charlie Chan at the Movies: History, Filmography, & Criticism. Ken Hanke. LC 89-42718. 286p. 1989. lib. bdg. 38.50 (*0-89950-427-2*) McFarland & Co.

Charlie Chan Carries on. Earl D. Biggers. (Charlie Chan Mysteries Ser.). 1976. reprint ed. lib. bdg. 23.95 (*0-89966-073-8*) Buccaneer Bks.

Charlie Chan is Dead: An Anthology of Contemporary Asian-American Fiction. Ed. by Jessica Hagedorn. LC 93-10703. 640p. (Orig.). 1993. pap. 14.00 (*0-14-023111-0*, Penguin Bks) Viking Penguin.

***Charlie Chaplin.** Intro. by Leeza Gibbons. (Pop Culture Legends Ser.). (Illus.). 128p. (YA). (gr. 5 up). 1995. 18.95 (*0-7910-2334-6*) Chelsea Hse.

Charlie Chaplin. Gloria Kamen. LC 82-1674. (Illus.). 96p. (J). (gr. 2-6). 1982. text ed. 13.95 (*0-689-30925-2*, Atheneum Bks Young) S&S Childrens.

Charlie Chaplin. John McCabe. (Illus.). 298p. (Orig.). 1993. pap. 13.95 (*0-86051-791-8*, Robson-Parkwest) Parkwest Pubns.

Charlie Chaplin. Theodore Huff. LC 72-169358. (Arno Press Cinema Program Ser.). (Illus.). 452p. 1979. reprint ed. 29.95 (*0-405-03920-4*) Ayer.

Charlie Chaplin: A Bio-Bibliography. Wes D. Gehring. LC 82-20964. (Popular Culture Bio-Bibliographies Ser.). (Illus.). 256p. 1983. text ed. 49.95 (*0-313-23288-1*, GEC/, Greenwood Pr) Greenwood.

Charlie Chaplin: A Centenary Celebration. Peter Haining. (Illus.). 144p. 1995. 21.95 (*0-572-01318-3*, Pub. by Foulsham UK) Atrium Pubs.

Charlie Chaplin: Comic Genius Who Brought Laughter & Hope to Millions. Pam Brown. LC 88-27568. (People Who Have Helped the World Ser.). (Illus.). 64p. (J). (gr. 5-6). 1991. lib. bdg. 21.26 (*1-55532-838-5*) Gareth Stevens Inc.

Charlie Chaplin: Famous Silent Movie Actor & Comic. Blythe F. Finke. Ed. by D. Steve Rahmas. LC 07-12. (Outstanding Personalities Ser.: No. 43). 32p. (YA). 1973. lib. bdg. 4.95 (*0-87157-539-6*) SamHar Pr.

Charlie Chaplin: His Life & Art. W. Dodgson Bowman. LC 74-1090. (American Biography Ser.: No. 32). 1974. lib. bdg. 75.00 (*0-8383-1841-X*) M S G Haskell Hse.

Charlie Chaplin: His Reflection in Modern Times. Ed. by Adolphe Nysenholc. LC 91-25247. (Approaches to Semiotics Ser.: No. 101). xvi, 412p. (C). 1991. lib. bdg. 121.55 (*3-11-012600-1*) Mouton.

***Charlie Chaplin: Intimate Close-Ups.** Georgia Hale. Ed. & Intro. by Heather Kiernan. LC 95-5002. (Filmmakers Ser.: No. 44). (Illus.). 271p. 1995. 32.50 (*0-8108-3003-5*) Scarecrow.

Charlie Chaplin's One-Man Show. Dan Kamin. LC 83-20396. 196p. 1984. 37.50 (*0-8108-1675-X*) Scarecrow.

Charlie Chaplin's One-Man Show. Dan Kamin. LC 90-44732. (Illus.). 176p. (C). 1991. pap. 19.95 (*0-8093-1711-7*) S Ill U Pr.

Charlie Chaplin's Own Story. Ed. by Harry M. Geduld. LC 84-43173. 224p. 1985. 20.00 (*0-253-11179-X*) Ind U Pr.

Charlie Christian. Stan Ayeroff. 72p. Date not set. pap. 10.95 (*0-8256-4084-9*) Music Sales.

Charlie Claus: Santa's Best Friend. Nina Pellegrini. LC 93-1495. (Illus.). (J). (ps-6). 1993. 4.99 (*0-517-09309-X*, Derrydale Bks) Random Hse Value.

Charlie Company: What Vietnam Did to Us. Peter Goldman. 1992. pap. 12.00 (*0-688-11610-8*, Quill) Morrow.

Charlie Drives the Stage. Eric A. Kimmel. LC 88-24558. (Illus.). 32p. (J). (ps-3). 1989. lib. bdg. 13.95 (*0-8234-0738-1*) Holiday.

Charlie Dye. Paul Weaver. (Illus.). 135p. 1981. 47.50 (*0-940143-39-9*) Safari Pr.

Charlie et la Chocolaterie. Roald Dahl. (Folio - Junior Ser.: No. 446). (Illus.). 190p. (FRE.). (J). (gr. 5-10). 1987. pap. 9.95 (*2-07-033446-5*) Schoenhof.

Charlie et le Grand Ascenseur de Verre. Roald Dahl. (Folio - Junior Ser.: No. 65). (Illus.). 151p. (FRE.). (J). (gr. 5-10). 1978. pap. 7.95 (*2-07-033065-6*) Schoenhof.

***Charlie Frye & His Times.** Helen E. Vogt. LC 94-66192. (Illus.). 352p. 1994. 29.95 (*1-877882-15-1*); pap. 19.95 (*1-877882-11-9*) SCW Pubns.

***Charlie Kiot.** Charles Potts. 1976. per. 10.00 (*0-914656-01-5*) Current.

Charlie Malarkey & the Belly Button Machine. William P. Kennedy. (J). (ps-3). 1990. pap. 4.95 (*0-14-054239-6*, Puffin) Puffin Bks.

Charlie Malarkey & the Singing Moose. William Kennedy & Brendan Kennedy. LC 93-41483. (Illus.). 32p. (J). 1994. 14.99 (*0-670-84605-8*) Viking Child Bks.

Charlie McTwiddle & the Wobbly-Wheeled Sputter Putter Popper. Jerry S. Warner. Ed. by Judy Telfer. LC 90-70308. (Charlie McTwiddle Bks.: Vol. 1). (Illus.). 128p. (J). (gr. 3-7). 1990. lib. bdg. 12.95 (*0-9626293-0-8*) Windsor Medallion.

Charlie Mike. Leonard B. Scott. 1988. mass mkt. 5.99 (*0-345-34402-2*) Ballantine.

Charlie Mosher's Civil War: From Fair Oaks to Andersonville with the Plymouth Pilgrims (85th N. Y. Inf.) Ed. by Wayne Mahood. (Illus.). 378p. 1994. 30.00 (*0-944413-20-X*) Longstreet Hse.

Charlie Needs a Cloak. Tomie De Paola. LC 73-16365. (Illus.). 32p. (J). (gr. k-4). 1982. pap. 14.00 (*0-671-66466-2*, S&S Bks Young Read); pap. 5.95 (*0-671-66467-0*, S&S Bks Young Read) S&S Childrens.

Charlie of Nob Hill. Gene Arceri. pap. 3.95 (*0-932298-46-X*) Tri-State Pr Corp.

Charlie Parker. Ron Frankl. (Black Americans of Achievement Ser.). (Illus.). 112p. (YA). (gr. 5 up). 1992. lib. bdg. 17.95 (*0-7910-1134-8*); pap. write for info. (*0-7910-1159-3*) Chelsea Hse.

Charlie Parker Discography. Robert M. Bregman et al. 94p. (Orig.). 1993. pap. 14.00 (*1-881993-25-6*) Cadence Jazz.

Charlie Parker for E Flat Sax. Stuart Isacoff. 48p. pap. 10.95 (*0-8256-4090-3*) Music Sales.

Charlie Parker for Piano: Fifteen Piano Solos Arranged from His Recorded Solos, Bk. 1. 1987. 7.95 (*0-317-61702-8*) Criterion Mus.

Charlie Parker for Piano: Fifteen Piano Solos Arranged from His Recorded Solos, Bk. 2. Paul Smith. 1988. pap. 7.95 (*0-685-22446-5*) Criterion Mus.

Charlie Parker for Piano: 15 Piano Solos Arranged from His Recordings, Bk. 3. Paul Smith. 1989. pap. 7.95 (*0-685-27017-3*) Criterion Mus.

Charlie Parker Omnibook: Recorded Solos for B Flat Instruments. 1981. 12.95 (*0-910468-11-7*) Criterion Mus.

Charlie Parker Omnibook: Recorded Solos for Bass Clef Intruments. 1987. 12.95 (*0-317-61706-0*) Criterion Mus.

Charlie Parker Omnibook: Recorded Solos for "C" Instruments. 12.95 (*0-910468-10-9*) Criterion Mus.

Charlie Parker Omnibook for E Flat Instruments: Recorded Solos. 1978. 12.95 (*0-910468-00-1*) Criterion Mus.

Charlie Parker Played Be Bop. Chris Raschka. LC 91-38420. (Illus.). 32p. (J). (ps-1). 1992. 14.95 (*0-531-05999-5*); lib. bdg. 14.99 (*0-531-08599-6*) Orchard Bks Watts.

Charlie Peace. Paul Pickering. 1991. 19.50 (*0-394-58544-5*) Random.

Charlie Pippin. Candy D. Boyd. 192p. (J). (gr. 3-7). 1988. pap. 3.99 (*0-14-032587-5*, Puffin) Puffin Bks.

Charlie Pippin. Candy D. Boyd. LC 86-23780. 192p. (J). (gr. 3-7). 1987. text ed. 14.95 (*0-02-726350-9*, Mac Bks Young Read) S&S Childrens.

Charlie Rangers. Don Ericson & John L. Rotundo. 320p. 1995. mass mkt. 5.99 (*0-8041-0288-0*) Ivy Books.

***Charlie Russell & the Ladies in His Life.** Ginger K. Renner. 32p. Date not set. pap. 3.25 (*0-614-06138-5*) Falcon Pr MT.

***Charlie Sheen, Emilio Estevez & Martin Sheen.** Skip Press. LC 95-11619. (Star Families Ser.). (J). 1995. write for info. (*0-89686-884-2*, Crstwood Hse); pap. write for info. (*0-382-39180-2*, Crstwood Hse) Silver Burdett Pr.

Charlie the Bunny. Charles B. McLaughlin. LC 82-73040. 169p. 1982. pap. 4.25 (*0-686-40531-5*) Dnomro Pubns.

Charlie the Caterpillar. Dom DeLuise. LC 90-31557. (Illus.). 40p. (J). (ps-1). 1990. pap. 13.95 (*0-671-69358-1*, S&S Bks Young Read) S&S Childrens.

Charlie the Caterpillar. Dom DeLuise. LC 90-31557. (Illus.). 40p. (J). (ps-1). 1993. pap. 5.95 (*0-671-79607-0*, S&S Bks Young Read) S&S Childrens.

Charlie the Champ. Clare Mishica. (Really Reading! Bks.). (Illus.). 48p. (J). (gr. k-3). 1994. pap. 4.49 (*0-7847-0138-5*, 24-03958) Standard Pub.

Charlie the Chicken & Other Plays. Jonathan Levy. 86p. (Orig.). 1990. 10.00 (*0-685-32638-1*) Playsmith.

Charlie the Mole & Other Droll Souls. Howard Jacobs. LC 73-12219. (Illus.). 288p. 1973. 10.00 (*0-88289-001-8*) Pelican.

Charlie the Shy Cowboy. Richard A. Payne. (Illus.). 36p. (J). (gr. 1-9). 1993. pap. 4.95 (*0-9636186-2-8*) Blue Sky Grap.

Charlie Trotter's Cookbook. Charlie Trotter. 1994. pap. 39.95 (*0-89815-628-9*) Ten Speed Pr.

Charlie Young Bear. Katherine Van Ahnan & Joan A. Young Bear. Ed. by Hap Gilliland. (Illus.). 32p. (Orig.). (J). (gr. 3-6). 1990. pap. 4.95 (*0-89992-128-0*) Coun India Ed.

Charlie Young Bear. Katherine Von Ahnen. LC 94-66100. (Council for Indian Education Ser.). (Illus.). 48p. (J). (gr. k-4). 1994. pap. 4.95 (*1-57098-001-2*) R Rinehart.

Charlie's ABC. Nona Hatay. LC 92-72030. (Illus.). 32p. (J). (ps-00). 1993. 10.95 (*1-56282-352-3*); lib. bdg. 10.89 (*1-56282-353-1*) Hyprn Child.

***Charlie's Apprentice.** large type ed. Brian Freemantle. LC 94-5394. 577p. 1994. 21.95 (*0-8161-7489-X*) Hall.

Charlie's Apprentice: A Charlie Muffin Mystery. Brian Freemantle. 320p. 1994. 21.95 (*0-312-10951-2*, Pub. by Thomas Dunne Bks) St Martin.

***Charlie's Challenge.** Linda Gladden & Ann Root. (Illus.). 36p. (Orig.). (J). (gr. 2-4). 1995. per., pap. 9.95 (*0-9647186-0-X*) L Gladden & A Root.

Charlie's Charts: Hawaiian Islands. Ed. by Charles E. Wood. 80p. (C). 1986. 109.00 (*0-9691412-3-8*, Pub. by Imray Laurie Norie & Wilson UK) St Mut.

Charlie's Charts: North to Alaska. Ed. by Charles E. Wood. 208p. (C). 1989. 179.00 (*0-9691412-2-X*, Pub. by Imray Laurie Norie & Wilson UK) St Mut.

Charlie's Charts: Polynesia. Wilson Ltd. Staff & Imray L. Norie. (C). 1989. 180.00 (*0-9691412-6-2*, Pub. by Imray Laurie Norie & Wilson UK) St Mut.

Charlie's Charts: U. S. Pacific Coast. Charles E. Wood. (C). 1988. 165.00 (*0-685-40361-0*, Pub. by Imray Laurie Norie & Wilson UK) St Mut.

Charlie's Charts: Western Coast of Mexico, Including Baja & Incorporating Cruising Mexico A-Z. Janet Steele. (C). 1990. 185.00 (*0-9691412-4-6*, Pub. by Imray Laurie Norie & Wilson UK) St Mut.

Charlie's Fourteenth Giant Book of Crossword Puzzles. 1985. pap. 5.95 (*0-671-55676-2*) PB.

***Charlie's Great Escape.** Jane L. Wilson. Ed. by Debbie Bowen. (Illus.). (J). (gr. k-8). Date not set. lib. bdg. 11.95 (*1-56763-139-8*); pap. text ed. 5.95 (*1-56763-140-1*) Ozark Pub.

Charlie's House. Clyde R. Bulla. LC 92-23998. (Illus.). 96p. (J). (gr. 3-6). 1993. 14.00 (*0-679-83841-4*) Knopf Bks Yng Read.

Charlie's House. Reviva Schermbrucker. (J). (ps-3). 1991. 13.95 (*0-670-84024-6*) Viking Child Bks.

Charlie's Little Moon Trip. Ellen C. Perlwitz. (Illus.). 32p. (J). (gr. k-3). 1992. 7.95 (*1-880851-01-6*) Greene Bark Pr.

Charlie's Monument. Blaine M. Yorgason. 5.95 (*0-88494-324-0*) Bookcraft Inc.

Charlie's Oasis. Jane Boyd & Gregg Opelka. 80p. 1992. pap. 5.95 (*1-56850-003-3*) Chicago Plays.

Charlie's Seventeenth Giant Book of Crossword Puzzles. 1987. pap. 5.95 (*0-671-62194-7*) S&S Trade.

Charlotte. Archibald C. Edwards. LC 90-63680. (Illus.). 112p. (Orig.). (J). (gr. 7 up). 1990. pap. 11.95 (*0-9626413-0-8*) Rosedale Pr.

Charlotte: Spirit of the New South. 2nd rev. ed. Mary N. Kratt. LC 92-25020. (Illus.). 1992. reprint ed. 34.95 (*0-89587-095-9*) Blair.

***Charlotte & Emily Bronte Vol. 1.** Winnifrith. Date not set. 16.95 (*0-312-12227-6*) St Martin.

Charlotte & Emily Bronte, 1846-1915: A Reference Guide. R. W. Crump. xvii, 194p. (C). 1982. text ed. 40.00 (*0-8161-7953-0*, Hall Reference) Macmillan.

Charlotte & Emily Bronte, 1955-1983: A Reference Guide. R. W. Crump. (Reference Guides to Literature Ser.). 350p. 1986. text ed. 40.00 (*0-8161-8797-5*, Hall Reference) Macmillan.

Charlotte & Leo. Anne-Marie Vesco. (Child's World Library). (Illus.). 32p. (J). (gr. 3-5). 1991. lib. bdg. 18.50 (*0-89565-818-6*) Childs World.

Charlotte & the White Horse. Ruth Krauss. LC 55-8819. (Illus.). 24p. (J). (gr. k-3). 1969. lib. bdg. 11.89 (*0-06-023361-3*) HarpC Child Bks.

***Charlotte & Vicinity, NC.** (Streetfinder Ser.). (Illus.). 1994. pap. 14.95 (*0-528-91320-4*) Rand McNally.

Charlotte Armstrong Treasury. C. Armstrong. 28.95 (*0-88411-576-3*, Aeonian Pr) Amereon Ltd.

***Charlotte Avery on Isle Royale.** Rebecca S. Curtis. LC 95-75504. 160p. (YA). (gr. 5 up). 1995. 14.95 (*1-883953-09-X*) Midwest Trad.

Charlotte Bronte. Margaret Blom. (English Authors Ser.: No. 203). 176p. 1977. text ed. 21.95 (*0-8057-6673-1*, Twayne) Macmillan.

Charlotte Bronte. Penny Boumelha. (Key Women Writers Ser.). 166p. 1990. pap. 12.95 (*0-253-25455-8*) Ind U Pr.

***Charlotte Bronte.** Hoeveler. 1996. text ed. 22.95 (*0-8057-4513-0*) Macmillan.

Charlotte Bronte. E. F. Benson. LC 70-173101. (Illus.). 1977. reprint ed. 25.95 (*0-405-08262-2*) Ayer.

Charlotte Bronte. T. W. Reid. LC 75-130243. (English Biography Ser.: No. 31). 1970. reprint ed. lib. bdg. 75.00 (*0-8383-1133-4*) M S G Haskell Hse.

Charlotte Bronte: A Passionate Life. Lyndall Gordon. 416p. 1994. 27.50 (*0-393-03722-3*) Norton.

Charlotte Bronte: A Psychological Study. R. Langbridge. LC 72-3280. (English Literature Ser.: No. 33). 1972. reprint ed. lib. bdg. 75.00 (*0-8383-1529-1*) M S G Haskell Hse.

Charlotte Bronte: A Thematic Study of Her Novels. S. N. Singh. (C). 1987. 17.50 (*0-8364-2226-0*, Pub. by Mittal II) S Asia.

Charlotte Bronte: The Self Conceived. Helene Moglen. LC 76-16010. 256p. 1984. reprint ed. text ed. 27.50 (*0-299-10140-1*); reprint ed. pap. 13.95 (*0-299-10144-4*) U of Wis Pr.

Charlotte Bronte & Defensive Conduct: The Author & the Body at Risk. Janet Gezari. LC 92-22716. 216p. (C). 1992. text ed. 29.95 (*0-8122-3162-7*) U of Pa Pr.

Charlotte Bronte & Her Circle. Clement K. Shorter. LC 73-98874. 512p. 1970. reprint ed. text ed. 65.00 (*0-8371-2811-0*, SHCB, Greenwood Pr) Greenwood.

Charlotte Bronte & Her Circle. Clement K. Shorter. (BCL1-PR English Literature Ser.). 512p. 1992. reprint ed. lib. bdg. 99.00 (*0-7812-7454-0*) Rprt Serv.

Charlotte Bronte & Her Sisters. Clement K. Shorter. LC 73-148303. reprint ed. 32.50 (*0-404-08911-9*) AMS Pr.

Charlotte Bronte & the Mysteries of Love: Myth & Allegory in Jane Eyre. Elizabeth Imlay. LC 89-10621. 192p. 1989. text ed. 39.95 (*0-312-03734-1*) St Martin.

Charlotte Bronte & the Storyteller's Audience. Carol Bock. LC 92-13446. (Illus.). 204p. 1992. 34.95 (*0-87745-363-2*) U of Iowa Pr.

Charlotte Bronte at the Seaside. Kevin Berry. (C). 1989. text ed. 35.00 (*0-948929-39-1*) St Mut.

Charlotte Bronte's "Jane Eyre" Intro. by Harold Bloom. (Modern Critical Interpretations Ser.). 151p. 1987. 34.95 (*0-87754-731-9*) Chelsea Hse.

Charlotte Bronte's "Jane Eyre" Pauline Nestor. LC 92-17623. (Critical Studies of Key Texts). 1992. text ed. 35.00 (*0-312-08423-4*); pap. 12.95 (*0-312-08601-6*) St Martin.

Charlotte Bronte's World of Death. Robert Keefe. LC 78-9853. 246p. 1979. text ed. 15.00 (*0-292-75043-9*) U of Tex Pr.

Charlotte Corday & Certain Men of the Revolutionary Torment. Marie Scherr. LC 79-100512. reprint ed. 30.00 (*0-404-05588-5*) AMS Pr.

***Charlotte County: Virginia Publick Claims.** Janice L. Abercrombie & Richard Slatten. (Virginia Publick Claims Ser.). ix, 33p. 1991. pap. 5.00x (*0-8095-8536-7*) Borgo Pr.

Charlotte County: Virginia Publick Claims. Janice L. Abercrombie & Richard Slatten. (Virginia Publick Claims Ser.). ix, 33p. (C). 1991. reprint ed. lib. bdg. 20.00 (*0-8095-8313-5*) Borgo Pr.

Charlotte County Marriages, Seventeen Sixty-Four to Eighteen Fifteen. Catherine L. Knorr. 128p. 1982. reprint ed. 17.50 (*0-89308-262-7*, VA 25) Southern Hist Pr.

***Charlotte County, Virginia Deeds, 1771-1777.** T. L. C. Genealogy Staff. LC 90-71807. 120p. (Orig.). 1990. spiral bd., pap. 12.00 (*1-886633-55-X*) TLC Genealogy.

***Charlotte County, Virginia Wills, 1765-1791.** T. L. C. Genealogy Staff. LC 91-66026. 218p. (Orig.). 1991. spiral bd., pap. 19.00 (*1-886633-56-8*) TLC Genealogy.

Charlotte County, Virginia, 1765-1771, Deed Bks. 1 & 2. Comp. by Joanne L. Nance. LC 90-6208. (Illus.). viii, 102p. 1990. per. 18.00 (*0-944334-01-6*) N W Lapin.

Charlotte County, Virginia, 1816-1850: Marriage Bonds & Ministers' Returns (with Additions to Marriages, 1764-1815) Joanne L. Nance. LC 87-81976. 176p. 1987. per. 22.00 (*0-944334-00-8*) N W Lapin.

Charlotte Cushman. Clara E. Waters. 1977. 16.95 (*0-8369-7143-4*, 7976) Ayer.

Charlotte Cushman: Her Letters & Memories of Her Life. Charlotte Cushman. Ed. by Emma Stebbins. LC 76-82823. (Illus.). 1972. reprint ed. lib. bdg. 20.95 (*0-405-08417-X*, Pub. by Blom Pubns UK) Ayer.

***Charlotte Dine-a-Mate.** 272p. 1994. pap. 30.00 (*1-57393-011-3*) Dine-A-Mate.

Charlotte Forten: A Black Teacher in the Civil War. Peter Burchard. LC 94-18305. (Illus.). 96p. (J). (gr. 4-7). 1995. 16.00 (*0-517-59242-8*) Crown Bks Yng Read.

***Charlotte Hawkins Brown: One Woman's Dream.** Diane Silcox-Jarrett. (Illus.). (Orig.). 1995. pap. 11.95 (*1-878177-07-9*) Bandit Bks.

Charlotte Hornets. Richard Rambeck. (NBA Today Ser.). (YA). (gr. 5 up). 1993. lib. bdg. 14.95 (*0-88682-559-8*) Creative Ed.

Charlotte Hornets: Sharpening the Stinger. Rick Bonnell. LC 93-84955. (Illus.). 268p. 1993. 19.95 (*0-915611-82-1*) Sagamore Pub.

Charlotte Hughes Herbert's Cookery for Special Occasions. Charlotte H. Herbert. (Illus.). 1980. pap. 7.85 (*0-9604928-0-1*) Sullivan Prod.

Charlotte Jobs. (Career Search System Ser.). 200p. 1990. pap. 11.95 (*0-929255-04-6*) CareerSource.

Charlotte Jobs. 2nd ed. Steve Hines. 200p. 1994. pap. 15.95 (*0-929255-09-7*) CareerSource.

Charlotte News Hollywood & Me. Emery Wister. (Illus.). 138p. 1991. write for info. (*0-912081-16-3*) Delmar Co.

Charlotte Observer: Its Time & Place, 1869-1986. Jack Claiborne. LC 86-40026. xv, 391p. 1986. 27.50 (*0-8078-1712-0*) U of NC Pr.

Charlotte of South Manitou Island. Donna Winters. Ed. by Anne Severance. LC 92-70331. (Great Lakes Romances Ser.). (Illus.). 256p. (Orig.). 1992. pap. 8.95 (*0-923048-79-0*) Bigwater Pub.

***Charlotte Perkins Gilman.** Knight. 1997. text ed. 23.95 (*0-8057-0866-9*) Macmillan.

Charlotte Perkins Gilman: A Bibliography. Gary Scharnhorst. LC 84-27625. (Author Bibliographies Ser.: No. 71). 233p. 1985. 20.00 (*0-8108-1780-2*) Scarecrow.

Charlotte Perkins Gilman: A Nonfiction Reader. Larry Ceplair. 320p. 1991. text ed. 65.00 (*0-231-07616-9*); pap. text ed. 17.50 (*0-231-07617-7*) Col U Pr.

Charlotte Perkins Gilman: Great American Short Stories II. Ed. by Emily Hutchinson. LC 94-75027. (Classic Short Stories Ser.). (Illus.). 80p. 1994. pap. 4.50 (*1-56103-019-8*) Lake Pub Co.

Charlotte Perkins Gilman: Her Progress Towards Utopia with Selected Writings. Carol F. Kessler. LC 94-18591. (Utopianism & Communitarianism Ser.). 288p. 1994. text ed. 34.95 (*0-8156-2644-4*); pap. 16.95 (*0-8156-0304-5*) Syracuse U Pr.

Charlotte Perkins Gilman: The Woman & Her Work. Ed. by Sheryl L. Meyering. LC 88-27771. (Challenging the Literary Canon Ser.). 224p. 1991. 50.00 (*0-8357-1931-6*) Univ Rochester Pr.

Charlotte Perkins Gilman Reader. Charlotte P. Gilman. 1992. 23.00 (*0-8446-6618-1*) Peter Smith.

Charlotte Perkins Gilman Reader: "The Yellow Wallpaper" & Other Fiction. Ed. by Ann J. Lane. 1980. pap. 14.00 (*0-394-73933-7*) Pantheon.

***Charlotte Pug (The Walnut War) (The Walnut War)** Catherine S. Cardinal. (Illus.). 16p. (J). (gr. k-5). 1994. pap. 3.40 (*0-9630655-2-1*) Garden Gate.

An Asterisk (*) at the beginning of an entry indicates that the title is appearing in BIP for the first time.

Charlotte Shakespeare & Annie the Great. Barbara W. Holmes. LC 89-2037. (Illus.). 160p. (J). (gr. 4-6). 1989. lib. bdg. 14.89 (*0-06-022615-3*) HarpC Child Bks.

***Charlotte Smith.** Fry. 1996. 21.95 (*0-8057-7046-1*, Twayne) Macmillan.

Charlotte Smith, Popular Novelist. Carroll L. Fry. Ed. by Devendra P. Varma. LC 79-8453. (Gothic Studies & Dissertations). 1980. lib. bdg. 30.95 (*0-405-12667-0*) Ayer.

Charlotte Sometimes. Penelope Farmer. (Orig.). (J). (gr. 5-9). 1993. 17.00 (*0-8446-6673-4*) Peter Smith.

Charlotte Stephens: Little Rock's First Black Teacher. Adolphine F. Terry. (Illus.). 129p. 1973. 14.95 (*0-686-47043-5*) J W Bell.

Charlotte Temple. Susanna Rowson. 160p. 1987. pap. 7.95 (*0-19-504238-7*) OUP.

Charlotte Temple: A Tale of Truth. Susanna Rowson. Ed. by Clara M. Kirk & Rudolf Kirk. (Masterworks of Literature Ser.). 1964. pap. 9.95 (*0-8084-0073-8*) NCUP.

Charlotte Temple: A Tale of Truth, 2 vols. in 1, Set. Susanna H. Rowson. (BCL1-PS American Literature Ser.). 1992. reprint ed. lib. bdg. 99.00 (*0-7812-6846-X*) Rprt Serv.

Charlotte Temple & Lucy Temple. Susanna Rowson. Ed. & Intro. by Ann Douglas. 336p. 1991. pap. 10.95 (*0-14-039080-4*, Penguin Classics) Viking Penguin.

Charlotte Yonge, Novelist of the Oxford Movement, 1823-1901: A Literature of Victorian Culture & Society. Barbara Dennis. LC 92-12773. (Illus.). 188p. 1992. lib. bdg. 79.95 (*0-7734-9544-4*) E Mellen.

***Charlotte's Cowboy.** Jeanne Allan. 1995. mass mkt. 2.99 (*0-373-03384-2*) Harlequin Bks.

Charlotte's Daughter: Or the Three Orphans. Susanna Rowson. LC 72-78812. 1828. reprint ed. 39.00 (*0-403-01983-4*) Somerset Pub.

Charlotte's Temple, a Tale of Truth. Susanna Rowson. LC 72-78814. 1794. reprint ed. 39.00 (*0-403-01984-2*) Somerset Pub.

Charlotte's Web. E. B. White. 1983. 4.95 (*0-87129-243-2*, C58) Dramatic Pub.

Charlotte's Web. E. B. White. LC 52-9760. (Illus.). (J). (gr. 2-6). 1952. lib. bdg. 12.89 (*0-06-026386-5*) HarpC Child Bks.

Charlotte's Web. E. B. White. LC 52-9760. (Illus.). (J). (gr. 2-6). 1952. 13.00 (*0-06-026385-7*) HarpC Child Bks.

Charlotte's Web. E. B. White. LC 52-9760. (Trophy Bk.). (Illus.). (J). 1974. pap. 3.95 (*0-06-440055-7*, Trophy) HarpC Child Bks.

Charlotte's Web. E. B. White. (J). 1990. mass mkt. 3.50 (*0-06-107010-6*, Harp PBks) HarpC.

Charlotte's Web. E. B. White. (Illus.). 192p. (J). (ps-8). 1990. reprint ed. lib. bdg. 21.95 (*0-89966-696-5*) Buccaneer Bks.

Charlotte's Web: A Literature Unit. Patsy Carey & Susan Kilpatrick. (Literature Units Ser.). (Illus.). 48p. (Orig.). (J). (gr. k-3). 1993. pap. 6.95 (*1-55734-435-3*) Tchr Create Mat.

Charlotte's Web: A Pig's Salvation. John Griffith. (Twayne's Masterworks Ser.). 136p. 1993. text ed. 20.95 (*0-8057-8812-3*, Twayne); pap. 12.95 (*0-8057-8813-1*, Twayne) Macmillan.

Charlotte's Web: A Study Guide. Joyce Friedland & Rikki Kessler. (Novel-Ties Ser.). (J). (gr. 2-5). 1983. student ed, teacher ed 15.95 (*0-88122-015-9*) Lrn Links.

Charlotte's Web: Musical. E. B. White & Joseph Robinette. 1990. 4.95 (*0-87129-258-0*, C06) Dramatic Pub.

Charlotte's Web see E. B. White Boxed Set

***Charlotte's Web - Touring-1-Act.** E. B. White. 1989. 5.00 (*0-87129-389-7*, C63) Dramatic Pub.

Charlottesville & the University of Virginia in the Civil War. Ervin L. Jordan, Jr. (Virginia Civil War Battles & Leaders Ser.). (Illus.). 225p. 1988. 19.95 (*0-930919-61-0*) H E Howard.

Charlottesville Collection: Traditional Recipes for Today's Lifestyles. Ed. by June P. Oakley. (Illus.). 221p. 1994. write for info. (*0-9641731-0-7*) Feathrstne & Brown.

Charlottesville, Lee, Lynchburg & Johnson's Bedford Artillery. Robert H. Moore, II. (Virginia Regimental Histories Ser.). (Illus.). 142p. 1990. 19.95 (*1-56190-008-7*) H E Howard.

***Charlottesville, VA.** Historical Briefs, Inc. Ed. by Thomas Antonucci & Michael Antonucci. 176p. 1993. pap. 14.95 (*0-89677-031-1*) Hist Briefs.

Charlottetown Accord: The Referendum, & the Future of Canada. Ed. by Kenneth McRoberts & Patrick Monahan. LC 93-94681. 361p. 1993. 55.00 (*0-8020-2989-2*) U of Toronto Pr.

Charlou's Five-Finger Puppets & Stuffed Toys. Charlou B. Dolan. (Illus.). 168p. 1987. write for info. (*0-02-496820-X*) Macmillan.

Charlsie's Chuckle. Clara W. Berkus. LC 91-46655. (Illus.). 32p. (J). (gr. k-6). 1992. 14.95 (*0-933149-50-6*) Woodbine House.

Charlston Stories: L4. Jerry Messec. Ed. by Jean McConochie. (Regents Readers Ser.). (gr. 7-12). 1987. pap. text ed. 3.50 (*0-13-128257-3*, 20951) Prentice ESL.

***Charlton Collector's Guide to Ontario.** 1995. pap. 9.95 (*0-88968-133-3*) IPG Chicago.

***Charlton Price Guide to Royal Doulton Beswick.** Jean Dale. 1995. pap. 19.95 (*0-88968-174-0*) IPG Chicago.

***Charlton Standard Catalogue of Canadian Baseball & Football Cards.** 1995. pap. 24.95 (*0-88968-172-4*) IPG Chicago.

***Charlton Standard Catalogue of Canadian Clocks.** J. E. Connell. 1995. pap. 17.50 (*0-88968-170-8*) IPG Chicago.

Charly. Daniel Keyes. 18.95 (*0-89190-875-7*, Am Repr) Amereon Ltd.

Charly. Jack Weyland. LC 80-11216. 98p. 1980. reprint ed. pap. 4.95 (*0-87579-121-2*) Deseret Bk.

Charly's Game. Bren Flemming. (Orig.). 1994. pap. text ed. 4.95 (*1-56333-221-3*) Masquerade.

***Charm.** Sextus Propertius. Tr. & Intro. by Vincent Katz. (Sun & Moon Classics Ser.: No. 89). 61p. (Orig.). 1995. pap. 11.95 (*1-55713-224-0*) Sun & Moon CA.

Charm: A Southwestern Supernatural Thriller. Adam Niswander. LC 93-26241. 288p. 1993. lib. bdg. 21.95 (*0-9626148-1-5*) Integra Pr.

Charm & Disorder of Democracy: Decentralization, Ownership Restructuring & Regulatory Reform in Poland. Martha P. Farrell & James D. Farrell. Ed. by A. Jesse Norman. (Sabre Foundation Studies in Polish Market Reform: No. 1). 64p. (Orig.). 1991. pap. 5.95 (*0-938864-15-7*) Ipswich Pr.

Charm Countryview Favorites: Famous Recipes from the Inn. Abe Mast. (Illus.). 160p. Date not set. 14.95 (*0-9637560-0-1*) Charm Cntryview Inn.

Charm of Dolphins. rev. ed. Howard Hall. Ed. by Vicki Leon. LC 93-9752. (Marine Life Ser.). (Illus.). 48p. (Orig.). (J). (gr. 5 up). 1993. per. 9.95 (*0-918303-33-8*) Blake Pub.

***Charm of Dolphins.** rev. ed. Howard Hall. Ed. by Vicki Leon. LC 94-31820. (Close up: A Focus on Nature Ser.). (Illus.). 48p. (YA). (gr. 5 up). 1994. lib. bdg. 14.95 (*0-382-24880-5*) Silver Burdett Pr.

***Charm of Dolphins.** rev. ed. Howard Hall. Ed. by Vicki Leon. LC 94-31820. (Close up: A Focus on Nature Ser.). (Illus.). 48p. (YA). (gr. 5 up). 1994. pap. 7.95 (*0-382-24881-3*) Silver Burdett Pr.

Charm of Evil: The Life & Films of Terence Fisher. Wheeler W. Dixon. LC 91-7687. (Filmmakers Ser.: No. 26). (Illus.). 591p. 1991. 59.50 (*0-8108-2375-6*) Scarecrow.

Charm of London. Alfred H. Hyatt. 1976. lib. bdg. 59.95 (*0-8490-1597-9*) Gordon Pr.

Charm of Paris. Alfred H. Hyatt. 1976. lib. bdg. 59.95 (*0-8490-1598-7*) Gordon Pr.

Charm of Physics. Sheldon L. Glashow. 1991. 24.95 (*0-88318-708-6*) Am Inst Physics.

Charm of Physics. Sheldon L. Glashow. 1991. pap. 12.95 (*0-671-74013-X*, Touchstone Bks) S&S Trade.

***Charm of Silver.** Cameron Ferguson. 189p. (Orig.). (YA). (gr. 9-12). 1994. lib. bdg. 15.00 (*0-88092-165-X*); pap. 5.00 (*0-88092-164-1*) Royal Fireworks.

Charm of the Bear Claw Necklace. Margaret Z. Searcy. LC 89-78044. (Illus.). 80p. (J). (gr. 3-7). 1990. reprint ed. 13.95 (*0-88289-821-3*); reprint ed. pap. 6.95 (*0-88289-777-2*) Pelican.

***Charm of the Central Coast.** Eizabeth Spurr. (Illus.). 72p. Date not set. pap. 12.95 (*0-9645311-1-9*) Pilothse Pub.

***Charm of the Trolley Car.** Frank Sullivan & Fred Winkowski. (Illus.). 128p. 1995. pap. 19.95 (*0-87938-972-9*) Motorbooks Intl.

Charm of Words: Essays & Papers on Language. Eric Partridge. LC 73-167400. (Essay Index Reprint Ser.). 1977. reprint ed. 18.95 (*0-8369-2707-9*) Ayer.

Charm Physics. Ming-han Ye & Tao Huang. xii, 562p. 1988. text ed. 117.00 (*2-88124-233-2*) Gordon & Breach.

Charm School. Nelson DeMille. 640p. 1989. mass mkt. 6.99 (*0-446-35320-5*) Warner Bks.

Charm School. Toni Goffe. LC 91-32061. (J). 1992. 7.95 (*0-85953-367-0*); pap. 3.95 (*0-85953-357-3*) Childs Play.

Charm School Mystery. Francine Pascal. (Sweet Valley Twins & Friends Ser.: No. 64). (J). (gr. 4-7). 1992. pap. 3.25 (*0-553-48050-2*) Bantam.

Charmaine Solomon's Complete Asian Cookbook. rev. ed. Charmaine Solomon. LC 91-67463. (Illus.). 512p. 1992. 34.95 (*0-8048-1791-X*) C E Tuttle.

***Charmaine Solomon's Complete Vegetarian Cookbook.** Charmaine Solomon. 1994. pap. 22.00 (*0-207-18436-4*, Pub. by Angus & Robertson AT) HarpC.

Charmaine Solomon's Thai Cookbook. Charmaine Solomon. (Illus.). 228p. 1991. 34.95 (*0-8048-1710-3*) C E Tuttle.

***Charmaine Solomon's Thai Cookbook.** Charmaine Solomon. 1994. pap. 19.95 (*0-8048-3039-8*) C E Tuttle.

Charme Noir. Yann Queffelec. (Folio Ser.: No. 1665). (FRE.). pap. 9.95 (*2-07-037665-6*) Schoenhof.

Charme Noir. Yann Queffelec. (FRE.). 1985. pap. 11.95 (*0-7859-4225-4*) Fr & Eur.

***Charmed.** Stella Cameron. 384p. (Orig.). 1995. mass mkt. 5.99 (*0-380-77075-X*) Avon.

Charmed. Marilyn Singer. LC 90-518. 224p. (J). (gr. 5-9). 1990. text ed. 14.95 (*0-689-31619-4*, Atheneum Bks Young) S&S Childrens.

Charmed. large type ed. Nora Roberts. LC 93-613. 1993. pap. 16.95 (*1-56054-716-2*) Thorndike Pr.

Charmed Betrothal. Irene L. Black. 352p. 1991. pap. 3.95 (*0-8217-3378-8*) Zebra.

Charmed Circle. Catherine Gaskin. 1990. mass mkt. 4.95 (*0-380-70778-0*) Avon.

***Charmed Circle.** Anna Kavan. (Illus.). 168p. 1994. 30.00 (*0-614-00583-3*, Pub. by P Owen Ltd UK) Dufour.

Charmed Circle. Barbara Whitnell. 352p. 1993. 21.95 (*0-312-10438-3*, Pub. by Thomas Dunne Bks) St Martin.

Charmed Circle. large type ed. Barbara Whitnell. LC 94-14265. 701p. 1994. 21.95 (*0-7862-0222-X*) Thorndike Pr.

Charmed Circle, No. I. large type ed. Catherine Gaskin. 1989. 23.95 (*0-7089-8523-8*, Trail West Pubs) Ulverscroft.

Charmed Circle, No. II. large type ed. Catherine Gaskin. 1989. 23.95 (*0-7089-8524-6*, Trail West Pubs) Ulverscroft.

Charmed Circle: Theology for the Head, Heart, Hands & Feet. Robert Masson. LC 86-61358. 260p. (Orig.). 1987. pap. 10.95 (*0-934134-40-5*) Sheed & Ward MO.

***Charmed Circle-Indianapolis, 1895: A Mystery.** Nancy N. Baxter. 350p. 1994. pap. 15.95 (*1-878208-52-7*) Guild Pr IN.

***Charmed Kitchen: Cooking with Herbs & Spices.** Judi Strauss. (Illus.). (Orig.). Date not set. pap. write for info. (*1-879863-67-7*) Goosefoot Acres.

Charmed Life. Diana W. Jones. (J). (gr. 4-7). 1993. 16.25 (*0-8446-6668-8*) Peter Smith.

Charmed Life. McCarthy. 1992. pap. 10.95 (*0-15-616774-3*, Harvest Bks) HarBrace.

Charmed Life. Mary McCarthy. LC 55-10153. 318p. 1955. 15.95 (*0-15-116907-1*) HarBrace.

Charmed Life. Bernard Taylor. 368p. 1994. reprint ed. pap. 4.50 (*0-8439-3561-8*) Dorchester Pub Co.

Charmed Lives. Bruce Beaver. LC 88-17306. (Poetry Ser.). 131p. (Orig.). 1989. pap. text ed. 14.95 (*0-7022-2141-4*, Pub. by Univ Queensland Pr AT) Intl Spec Bk.

Charmed Lives. Michael Korda. 560p. 1981. pap. 3.95 (*0-380-53017-1*, 53017-1) Avon.

Charmed Places: Hudson River Artists & Their Houses, Studios, & Vistas. Ed. by Sandra S. Phillips & Linda Weintraub. (Illus.). 1988. 45.00 (*0-8109-1041-1*) Abrams.

Charmed World: Colette, Her Life & Times. Claude Francis & Fernande Gontier. 576p. 1993. 29.95 (*0-312-09258-X*) St Martin.

Charmer. Jack Olsen. LC 94-3320. 1994. write for info. (*0-688-10903-9*) Morrow.

Charmers. Shirley Moody. LC 87-61416. 65p. (Orig.). 1991. pap. 9.95 (*0-932662-69-2*) St Andrews NC.

Charmes. Paul Valery. Tr. by James L. Brown. LC 83-81792. 128p. (ENG & FRE.). (C). 1983. pap. 8.75 (*0-9612298-0-2*) Forsan Bks.

Charmes see Poesies

Charmides. Plato. Ed. by Thomas G. West & Grace S. West. Tr. by Grace S. West. LC 85-24934. (HPC Classics Ser.). 60p. (Orig.). (C). 1986. lib. bdg. 19.50 (*0-87220-011-6*); pap. 3.95 (*0-87220-010-8*) Hackett Pub.

Charmides, Alcibiades First & Second, Hipparchus, the Lovers, Theages, Minos, Epinomis, Vol. XII. Plato. (Loeb Classical Library: No. 201). 512p. 1927. text ed. 18.95 (*0-674-99221-0*) HUP.

Charmides of Plato: Problems & Interpretations. N. Van Der Ben. iv, 107p. 1985. pap. 21.00 (*90-6032-274-6*, Pub. by B R Gruener NE) Benjamins North Am.

Charming Ghost of Charleston Set. Carole Marsh. (Carole Marsh Mysteries Ser.). 1994. teacher ed 125.00 (*0-7933-6958-4*) Gallopade Pub Group.

***Charming Small Hotel Guide: Spain.** Chris Gill. (Charming Small Hotels Ser.). (Illus.). 224p. (Orig.). 1994. pap. 12.95 (*1-55650-674-0*) Hunter NJ.

***Charming Small Hotels in France: Charming Small Hotels, 1995.** Chris Gill. (Charming Small Hotels Ser.). (Illus.). 224p. (Orig.). 1995. pap. 12.95 (*1-55650-675-9*) Hunter NJ.

Charming Small Hotels in Italy. Chris Gill. (Charming Small Hotels Ser.). (Illus.). 224p. 1994. pap. 12.95 (*1-55650-635-X*) Hunter NJ.

Charming Small Hotels in Switzerland. Chris Gill. (Charming Small Hotels Ser.). (Illus.). 224p. (Orig.). 1994. pap. 14.95 (*1-55650-636-8*) Hunter NJ.

Charming Train. T. K. Teas. Ed. & Illus. by Abell. 1994. 25.00 (*1-56611-093-9*); pap. 15.00 (*1-56611-094-7*) Jonas.

Charmion Von Wiegand: Her Art & Life. Nancy J. Troy. (Illus.). 48p. (Orig.). 1991. pap. 5.00 (*1-880511-05-3*) Bass Museum.

Charms. Jonathan Cott. LC 80-28181. 19p. (Orig.). 1981. pap. 4.00 (*0-915124-48-3*, Toothpaste) Coffee Hse.

***Charms.** Kathleen Kane. 304p. (Orig.). 1995. pap. 4.99 (*0-7865-0068-9*) Diamond.

Charms. Tom Koontz. 32p. (Orig.). 1983. pap. 2.00 (*0-935306-28-5*) Barnwood Pr.

Charms for the Easy Life. Kaye Gibbons. 256p. 1994. mass mkt. 5.99 (*0-380-72270-4*) Avon.

Charms for the Easy Life. Kaye Gibbons. 256p. 1993. 19.95 (*0-399-13791-2*, Putnam) Putnam Pub Group.

***Charms for the Easy Life.** Kaye Gibbons. 256p. 1995. pap. 10.00 (*0-380-72557-6*) Avon.

Charms for the Easy Life. large type ed. Kaye Gibbons. LC 93-8596. 1993. 23.95 (*1-56895-030-6*) Wheeler Pub.

Charms, Spells & Formulas for the Making & Use of Gris-Gris Bags, Herb Candles, Doll Magick, Incenses, Oils & Powders...to Gain Love, Protection, Prosperity, Luck & Prophetic Dreams. Ray T. Malbrough. LC 85-45286. (Practical Magick Ser.). (Illus.). 192p. (Orig.). 1986. pap. 6.95 (*0-87542-501-1*) Llewellyn Pubns.

Charms to Collect. Marjorie Congram. (Illus.). 115p. (Orig.). 1988. pap. 9.95 (*0-9617801-2-6*) Dockwra Pr.

Charnel House. Eamonn McGrath. 240p. 1990. pap. 14.95 (*0-85640-447-0*, Pub. by Blackstaff Pr IE) Dufour.

Charnel Imp. Alan Singer. LC 87-11859. 1988. 15.95 (*0-932511-11-2*); pap. 8.95 (*0-932511-12-0*) Fiction Coll.

Charnel Rose, Senlin: A Biography & Other Poems. Conrad Aiken. LC 79-156910. (Studies in Poetry: No. 38). 1972. reprint ed. lib. bdg. 75.00 (*0-8383-1247-0*) M S G Haskell Hse.

Charney Quadrille, for Six Viols. Tricia Warhurst. (Charney Manor Ser.: No. 1). i, 49p. 1991. 12.00 (*1-56571-036-3*) PRB Prods.

Charon: A Dragon at the Gate, Bk. 3. Jack L. Chalker. (Orig.). 1982. pap. 3.95 (*0-345-29370-3*, Del Rey) Ballantine.

Charon & the Crossing: Ancient Medieval, & Renaissance Transformations of a Myth. Ronnie H. Terpening. LC 82-74492. (Illus.). 296p. 1985. 45.00 (*0-8387-5061-3*) Bucknell U Pr.

Charon's Daughter. Nancy C. De Foret. (Illus.). 1977. 12.50 (*0-87140-628-4*); pap. 5.95 (*0-87140-116-9*) Liveright.

Charophycees de France et de l'Europe Occidentale. Robert Corillion. (Illus.). 499p. 1972. 157.00 (*3-87429-014-X*) Koeltz Sci Bks.

Charophytes of North America. R. D. Wood. 1967. 2.25 (*0-9603898-0-6*) R D Wood.

Charousek's Games of Chess. Philip W. Sergeant. 242p. 1989. pap. 5.95 (*0-486-25832-7*) Dover.

Charpente Modale du Sens Pour une Semio-Linguistique Morphogenetique et Dynamique. Per A. Brandt. (Nouveaux Actes Semiotiques Ser.: No. 2). 368p. (FRE.). 1992. pap. 47.00 (*90-272-2268-1*) Benjamins North Am.

Charpy Impact Test: Factors & Variables. Ed. by John M. Holt. LC 90-85687. (Special Technical Publication Ser.: STP 1072). (Illus.). 220p. 1990. text ed. 44.00 (*0-8031-1295-5*, 04-010720-23) ASTM.

Charreria Mexicana: An Equestrian Folk Tradition. Kathleen M. Sands. LC 92-40197. (Illus.). 375p. (Orig.). 1993. lib. bdg. 45.00 (*0-8165-1406-2*); pap. 24.95 (*0-8165-1346-5*) U of Ariz Pr.

Charrette at York, Pennsylvania: April 1970. George Shumway & Charles E. Trotter, Jr. LC 78-142598. (Illus.). 240p. 1973. pap. 7.50 (*0-87387-040-9*) Shumway.

Charrette Pleine D'Etoiles. Frederic H. Fajardie. 155p. (FRE.). 1991. pap. 10.95 (*0-7859-2605-4*, 2070383369) Fr & Eur.

Charrette Processes: A Tool in Urban Planning. William Riddick. LC 74-14257. (Illus.). 110p. 1971. pap. 7.50 (*0-87387-041-7*) Shumway.

Charro! Harry Whittington. 160p. 1989. pap. 2.75 (*0-380-70732-2*) Avon.

Charro! Harry Whittington. 1981. pap. 1.75 (*0-449-14189-6*, GM) Fawcett.

Charrs: Salmonid Fishes of the Genus Salvelinus. Ed. by Eugene K. Balon. (Perspectives in Vertebrate Science Ser.: No. 1). (Illus.). 919p. 1980. lib. bdg. 373.50 (*90-6193-701-9*) Kluwer Ac.

Chart & Graph Puzzles. K. Bryant-Mole. (Math Skills Ser.). (Illus.). 32p. (J). (gr. 1-5). 1994. pap. 4.95 (*0-7460-1724-3*, Usborne) EDC.

***Chart Forms.** Ed. by Susan Lampe. 260p. (Orig.). 1991. pap. 50.00 (*0-9621520-8-0*) Creative Nursing.

***Chart Kit Region 10: Virgin Islands.** 5th ed. BBA, Inc. Staff. 1994. ring bd. 44.95 (*1-885595-01-8*) Better Boating.

***Chart Kit Region 4: Chesapeake & Delaware Bays.** 7th ed. BBA, Inc. Staff. 78p. 1994. ring bd. 99.95 (*1-885595-00-X*) Better Boating.

***Chart of Accounts for Hospitals: An Accounting & Reporting Reference Guide.** Vann L. Seawell. 1994. pap. 65.00 (*1-55738-619-6*) Probus Pub Co.

Chart of Education. Lawrence H. Hufendick. 1973. 3.00 (*0-910268-05-3*) Books.

Chart on the Course of Time. A. E. Booth. 3.99 (*0-87213-072-X*) Loizeaux.

Chart Rectification. Doris V. Thompson. LC 78-56417. 144p. 1978. 9.00 (*0-86690-163-9*, T1481-014) Am Fed Astrologers.

Chart Set: Green Set. Alma F. Ada. (Dias y Dias de Poesia Ser.). (Illus.). (Orig.). (SPA.). (J). (gr. 1-3). 1992. Set incl. anthology, tapes, charts. pap. 179.95 (*1-56334-122-0*) Hampton-Brown.

Chartbook of Trends Affecting Higher Education Finance, 1960-1990, 3 vols., Set, Vol. 1. Common Fund Staff. Ed. by Dan Wingerd. 73p. 1992. Set. pap. write for info. (*1-882778-03-0*) Common Fund.

Chartbook of Trends Affecting Higher Education Finance, 1960-1990, 3 vols., Vol. 1. Common Fund Staff. Ed. by Dan Wingerd. 73p. 1992. pap. write for info. (*1-882778-00-6*) Common Fund.

Chartbook on Health Data on Older Americans: United States. 1994. lib. bdg. 250.00 (*0-8490-8547-0*) Gordon Pr.

Chartbook on Health Data on Older Americans: United States, 1992, No. 29. Ed. by Robin A. Cohen et al. LC 92-48231. (Vital & Health Statistics Ser. 3: Analytical & Epidemiological Studies). (Illus.). 1992. write for info. (*0-8406-0475-0*) Natl Ctr Health Stats.

Chartbreaker. Gillian Cross. LC 86-46199. 184p. (YA). (gr. 7 up). 1987. 14.95 (*0-8234-0647-4*) Holiday.

Charted Bird Designs. Lindberg Press Staff. 1989. pap. 2.95 (*0-486-26138-7*) Dover.

Charted Borders, Bands & Corners. Sandra Urban. 1981. pap. 2.95 (*0-486-24147-5*) Dover.

Charted Christmas Designs for Counted Cross-Stitch & Other Needlecrafts: From the Archives of the Lindberg Press. Lindberg Press Staff. (Illus.). 42p. (Orig.). 1982. pap. 2.95 (*0-486-24356-7*) Dover.

Charted Decorative Initials. Illus. by Misse Moeller. (Embroidery, Needlepoint, Charted Designs Ser.: 3). 32p. 1984. pap. 2.50 (*0-486-24646-9*) Dover.

Charted Designs for Holidays & Special Occasions: Over 224 Motifs for Counted Cross-Stitch & Other Needlecrafts. Georgia Gorham & Jeanne Warth. (Illus.). 48p. (Orig.). 1981. pap. 3.50 (*0-486-24192-0*) Dover.

Charted Designs for Needlemade Rugs. Sibyl I. Mathews. LC 75-21350. (Illus.). 160p. 1976. reprint ed. pap. 6.95 (*0-486-23264-6*) Dover.

Charted Designs for the Kitchen. Ed. by Lindberg Press Staff. 48p. (Orig.). 1987. pap. 2.95 (*0-486-25496-8*) Dover.

Charted Folk Designs for Cross-Stitch Embroidery. Maria Foris & Andreas Foris. LC 75-9175. Orig. Title: Susann Folk Cross-Stitch Charts. (Illus.). 1975. reprint ed. pap. 5.95 (*0-486-23191-7*) Dover.

Charted Knitting Designs. Barbara G. Walker. (Illus.). 1986. pap. 14.95 (*0-684-12566-8*, Scribners) S&S Trade.

Charted Knitting Designs: A Treasury of Knitting Patterns. Barbara G. Walker. (Illus.). 304p. 1982. pap. 21.00 (*0-684-17462-6*, Scribners) S&S Trade.

Charted Monograms for Needlepoint & Cross-Stitch. Rita Weiss. LC 77-77047. 1978. pap. 3.50 (*0-486-23555-6*) Dover.

Charted Peasant Designs from Saxon Transylvania. Hienz Kiewe. LC 76-24564. (Illus.). 1977. pap. 3.50 (*0-486-23425-8*) Dover.

C

Charted Seashell Designs. Barbara Christopher. 1990. pap. 3.50 (*0-486-26286-3*) Dover.

Charted Swiss Folk Designs. Elvira Parolini-Ruffini. LC 77-87356. (Illus.). 1978. reprint ed. pap. 2.50 (*0-486-23574-2*) Dover.

Charter: Ten Years after Essays on the Charter's Place in Canada's Political, Legal, & Intellectual Life. Ed. by Philip Bryden et al. 272p. 1993. 45.00 (*0-8020-2902-7*); pap. 18.95 (*0-8020-7410-3*) U of Toronto Pr.

Charter & Criminal Procedure: The Application of Sections 7 & 11. Atrens. 376p. 1989. 120.00 (*0-409-80659-5*) Butterworth Legal Pubs.

***Charter 88: A Successful Challenge to the British Political Tradition?** Mark Evans. LC 94-44047. (Illus.). 300p. 1995. text ed. 57.95 (*1-85521-524-1*, Pub. by Dartmth Pub UK) Ashgate Pub Co.

Charter for the Arts in Scotland. Joyce McMillian. 128p. 1993. pap. 25.00 (*0-11-494231-5*, HM42315, Pub. by HMSO UK) UNIPUB.

Charter for the Church: Sharing a Vision for the 21st Century. George Carey. LC 93-26327. 200p. 1993. pap. 14.95 (*0-8192-1612-7*) Morehouse Pub.

Charter for World Trade. Clair Wilcox. LC 72-4309. (World Affairs Ser.: National & International Viewpoints). 352p. 1972. reprint ed. 25.95 (*0-405-04598-0*) Ayer.

Charter Litigation. Sharpe. 456p. 1987. 114.00 (*0-409-80527-0*) Butterworth Legal Pubs.

Charter of Maryland, June 20, 1632. (Illus.). 31p. 1982. write for info. (*0-318-59090-5*) MD St Archives.

Charter of the Heart Mountain Relocation Center, Wyoming. limited ed. Illus. by Irving Block. (Santa Susana Press California Masters Ser.: No. 4). 56p. 1983. 36.00 (*0-937048-32-1*) CSUN.

Charter of the OAS & Inter-American Treaty of Reciprocal Assistance. Inter-American Juridical Committee. (Treaty Ser.: No. 25). (ENG & SPA.). 1972. pap. 1.00 (*0-8270-0395-1*) OAS.

Charter of the Organization of American States As Amended by the Protocol of Buenos Aires in 1967. (Treaty Ser.: No. 1-C). (ENG, FRE, POR & SPA.). pap. 1.00 (*0-8270-0270-X*) OAS.

Charter of the Organization of American States, Bogota, 1948. Organization of American States Staff. (Treaty Ser.: No. 1). (ENG, FRE, POR & SPA.). 1948. pap. 1.00 (*0-8270-0245-9*) OAS.

C

Charter of the Rights of the Family. Veritas Publications Staff. 1989. pap. 22.00 (*0-86217-156-3*, Pub. by Veritas IE) St Mut.

Charter of the United Nations. U. N. Conference on International Organization, U. S. Delegation Staff. LC 73-94623. 266p. 1969. reprint ed. text ed. 49.75 (*0-8371-2467-0*, CHUN, Greenwood Pr) Greenwood.

Charter of the United Nations: A Commentary. Ed. by Bruno Simma. 1000p. 1995. 220.00 (*0-19-825703-1*) OUP.

Charter on Ground-Water Management. 21p. 1990. 4.00 (*92-1-116456-7*, 89.II.E.21) UN.

Charter Reform in Chicago. Maureen A. Flanagan. LC 86-29696. 222p. 1987. text ed. 24.95x (*0-8093-1391-X*) S Ill U Pr.

Charter Revision Activity in Michigan. Susan B. Hannah. Ed. by Michigan Municipal League Staff et al. 1993. (*0-318-72314-X*) MI Municipal.

Charter Versus Federalism: The Dilemmas of Constitutional Reform. Alan C. Cairns. 160p. 1992. 39.95 (*0-7735-0891-0*, Pub. by McGill CN); pap. 17.95 (*0-7735-0892-9*, Pub. by McGill CN) U of Toronto Pr.

Charter Your Boat for Profit. Fred Edwards. LC 89-43019. 240p. (Orig.). 1989. pap. 17.50 (*0-87033-401-8*) Cornell Maritime.

Chartered Accounting in England & Wales: A Guide to Historical Records. Ed. by Wendy Habgood. LC 93-27913. (Studies in British Business Archives). 1994. text ed. 69.95 (*0-7190-4229-1*, Pub. by Manchester Univ Pr UK) St Martin.

Charterers Liability Insurance. D. Schwampe. 1988. 90.00 (*1-85044-184-7*) Lloyds London Pr.

Charterers Liability Insurance: Dr. Dieter Schwampe. Witherby's Editorial Staff. (C). 1988. 380.00 (*0-685-33735-9*, Pub. by Witherby & Co UK) St Mut.

Charterhouse of Parma. Stendhal. Tr. by Margaret R. Shaw. (Classics Ser.). (Orig.). 1958. mass mkt. 8.95 (*0-14-044061-5*, Penguin Classics) Viking Penguin.

Charterhouse of Parma. Stendhal. LC 92-52908. 1992. 20.00 (*0-679-41743-5*, Everymans Lib) Knopf.

Chartering & Charter Parties. Henry B. Cooley. LC 47-27564. 166p. reprint ed. pap. 47.40 (*0-685-10876-7*, 2022552) Bks Demand.

Chartering Urban School Reform: Reflections on Public High Schools in the Midst of Change. Michelle Fine. LC 93-41347. (Series on School Reform). 240p. (C). 1994. text ed. 39.00 (*0-8077-3318-0*); pap. 18.95 (*0-8077-3317-2*) Tchrs Coll.

Charters & Basic Laws of Selected American Universities & Colleges. Ed. by Edward C. Elliott & Merritt M. Chambers. LC 70-108773. reprint ed. 21.00 (*0-404-00605-1*) AMS Pr.

Charters & Basic Laws of Selected American Universities & Colleges. Ed. by Edward C. Elliott & M. M. Chambers. LC 70-104261. vii, 640p. reprint ed. lib. bdg. 24.00 (*0-8371-3920-1*, ELCL, Greenwood Pr) Greenwood.

Charters & Custumals of the Abbey of Holy Trinity, Caen, Part II: The French Estates. Ed. by John Walmsley. (Records of Social & Economic History, New Series British Academy: Vol. XXII). (Illus.). 160p. 1994. 69.00 (*0-19-726137-X*) OUP.

Charters & Documents Illustrating the History of the Cathedral: City & Diocese of Salisbury in the 12th & 13th Centuries. Ed. by W. D. Macray. (Rolls Ser.: No. 97). 1972. reprint ed. 80.00 (*0-8115-1176-6*) Periodicals Srv.

Charters of St-Fursy of Peronne. William M. Newman. LC 75-36479. (Medieval Academy Bks.: No. 85). 1977. 25.00 (*0-910956-59-6*) Medieval Acad.

***Charters of the Medieval Hospitals of Bury St. Edmunds.** Ed. by Christopher Harper-Bill. (Suffolk Charters Ser.: Vol. XIV). 288p. (C). 1994. text ed. 35.00 (*0-85115-558-8*, Boydell Pr) Boydell & Brewer.

ChartGuide Mexico West. 3rd rev. ed. Ed Winlund et al. LC 82-73303. (Illus.). 76p. 1988. pap. 58.00 (*0-938206-14-1*) ChartGuide Ltd.

ChartGuide Southern California. 7th rev. ed. Ed Winlund. LC 74-29812. (Illus.). 68p. 1987. pap. 44.00 (*0-938206-12-5*) ChartGuide Ltd.

Charting. AgriData Staff. 32p. 1982. pap. 9.95 (*0-685-16470-5*) AgriData.

Charting: The Systematic Approach to Achieving Control. Janice L. Roth. 38p. 1991. pap. 3.95 (*0-9631701-0-4*) R A Rapaport.

Charting a Course: A Guide to the Excellence Movement in Education. Ian McNett. 55p. (C). 1984. pap. 8.95 (*0-931989-06-X*) Coun Basic Educ.

Charting a Future for the Civil Jury System: Report of a Brookings Symposium. 50p. (C). 1992. pap. 5.95 (*0-8157-1265-0*) Brookings.

Charting Approach to Wall Street Profits. Carroll D. Aby & Donald E. Vaugn. LC 89-80222. 312p. 1989. write for info. (*0-936176-16-4*) Chartcraft Inc.

Charting by Exception: Cost Effective in Nursing Documentation. Ed. by Laura Burke & Judy Murphy. (Orig.). 1988. pap. text ed. 39.95 (*0-8273-4216-0*) Delmar.

Charting by Exception Applications. Laura J. Burke & Judith A. Murphy. LC 94-10957. 512p. 1995. spiral bd. 99.50 (*0-8273-6048-7*) Delmar.

Charting Democracy in America: Landmarks from History & Political Thought. rev. ed. Alfred Fernbach & Julian Bishko. 425p. (C). 1995. lib. bdg. 68.50 (*1-879383-37-3*); pap. text ed. 34.00 (*1-879383-38-1*) Am Univ Pr.

Charting Global Responsibilities: Legal Philosophy & Human Rights. Kevin T. Jackson. LC 94-5988. 258p. (Orig.). 1994. pap. text ed. 29.50 (*0-8191-9478-6*) U Pr of Amer.

Charting Intellectual Development: A Practical Guide to Piagetian Tasks. 2nd ed. Ruth Formanek & Anita Gurian. (Illus.). 136p. 1981. 25.95x (*0-398-04476-7*) C C Thomas.

***Charting My Life.** Henry Howard. (American Autobiography Ser.). 398p. 1995. reprint ed. lib. bdg. 89.00 (*0-7812-8560-7*) Rprt Serv.

Charting New Waters. Chocolate Waters. (Illus.). 96p. 1980. pap. 8.00 (*0-935060-06-5*) Eggplant Pr.

Charting Nursing's Future: Agenda for the 1990's. Linda H. Aiken & Claire Fagin. (Illus.). 560p. 1991. pap. 29.50 (*0-397-54800-1*) Lippincott.

Charting Presidential Elections. Sylvia DeLong. LC 82-70713. 160p. 1982. 14.00 (*0-86690-030-6*, D2456-0114) Am Fed Astrologers.

Charting the Agenda: Educational Activity after Vygotsky. Ed. by Harry Daniels. LC 92-12223. 256p. 1993. 69.95 (*0-415-05510-5*, A5923) Routledge.

Charting the Agenda: Educational Activity after Vygotsky. Ed. by Harry Daniels. LC 94-9765. 1994. pap. 17.95 (*0-415-11757-7*, B4716) Routledge.

Charting the Corporate Mind. Charles T. Hampden-Turner. 1990. text ed. 29.95 (*0-02-913706-5*) Free Pr.

Charting the Course for Business Growth Through the 1990s. Fowler-McCracken Commission Staff. LC 89-29798. (Illus.). 310p. (C). 1990. text ed. 49.50 (*0-8191-7685-0*) U Pr of Amer.

Charting the Future. Reader's Digest Editors. LC 92-8818. (Quest for the Unknown Ser.). (Illus.). 144p. 1992. 16.98 (*0-89577-441-0*) RD Assn.

Charting the Future: The Supreme Court Responds to a Changing Society, 1890-1920. John E. Semonche. LC 77-94745. (Contributions in Legal Studies: No. 5). xiii, 470p. 1978. text ed. 38.50 (*0-313-20314-8*, SCF/, Greenwood Pr) Greenwood.

Charting the Inland Seas: A History of the U. S. Lake Survey. Arthur M. Woodford. (Illus.). 286p. 1994. text ed. 27.50 (*0-8143-2499-1*, Great Lks Bks) Wayne St U Pr.

***Charting the Mexican Labyrinth: A Practical Guide to Success in Mexico.** Keith P. McGuinness. (Illus.). (Orig.). 1995. pap. 48.00 (*0-9623014-9-3*) HPH Partners.

Charting the Operator Terrain. John Ernest. LC 76-3583. (Memoirs Ser.: No. 6/171). 207p. 1976. pap. 24.00 (*0-8218-1871-6*, MEMO 6/171) Am Math.

Charting the Post-Cold War Order. Ed. by James L. Richardson & Richard L. Leaver. LC 93-32736. (C). 1993. text ed. 52.50 (*0-8133-8753-1*); pap. text ed. 20.95 (*0-8133-2150-6*) Westview.

Charting the Russian Northern Sea Route: The Arctic Ocean Hydrographic Expedition, 1910-1915. Leonid M. Starokadomskiy. Ed. by William Barr. LC 77-469460. 398p. reprint ed. pap. 113.50 (*0-317-27199-7*, 2023861) Bks Demand.

Charting the Sea of Darkness: The Four Voyages of Henry Hudson. Donald S. Johnson. (Illus.). 256p. 1992. 22.95 (*0-87742-321-0*, 60302) Intl Marine.

***Charting the Sea of Darkness: The Four Voyages of Henry Hudson.** Donald S. Johnson. Ed. by Philip Turner. (Kodansha Globe Ser.). (Illus.). 256p. 1995. pap. 13.00 (*1-56836-105-X*, Kodansha Globe) Kodansha.

Charting the Stock Market: The Wyckoff Method. Jack K. Hutson et al. LC 91-66714. 216p. (Orig.). 1991. pap. 14.95 (*0-938773-06-2*) Tech Analysis.

Charting the Uncharted Course: Proletarian Revolution in the U. S. see Strategic Outlook & Alliances

Charting the Uncharted Course: Questions of Revolutionary Strategy for the 1980s: Leadership, No. 2. Bob Avakian. 306p. 1983. 5.00 (*0-685-06713-0*) RCP Pubns.

Charting the Uncharted Course: Questions of Revolutionary Strategy for the 1980s: Strategic Outlook & Alliances, No. 1. Bob Avakian. 279p. 1983. 5.00 (*0-685-06712-2*) RCP Pubns.

Charting Your Course: How to Prepare to Teach More Effectively. Richard Pregent. 1994. 21.50 (*0-912150-30-0*) Magna Pubns.

Charting Your Course by the Dream in Your Heart. Robert Tilton. 178p. (Orig.). 1983. pap. text ed. 5.95 (*0-914307-11-8*, Harrison Hse) R Tilton Ministries.

Chartism. E. H. Haraszti. 276p. 1978. 67.50 (*0-317-53842-X*) St Mut.

***Chartism.** E. H. Haraszti. 276p. (C). 1978. 72.00x (*963-05-1477-X*, Pub. by Akad Kiado HU) St Mut.

***Chartism & Chartists in Manchester & Salford.** Paul A. Pickering. LC 95-8228. 1995. write for info. (*0-312-12727-8*) St Martin.

Chartism & Paisley. (C). 1989. 30.00 (*0-903915-22-7*, Pub. by Jordanhill College UK) St Mut.

Chartism & Society. Ed. by F. C. Mather. LC 80-15587. 488p. 1980. 54.50 (*0-8419-0625-4*) Holmes & Meier.

Chartism & the Churches. Harold U. Faulkner. LC 79-76712. (Columbia University. Studies in the Social Sciences: No. 173). reprint ed. 30.00 (*0-404-51173-2*) AMS Pr.

Chartism & the Churches: A Study in Democracy. Harold U. Faulkner. 152p. 1970. reprint ed. 35.00 (*0-7146-1308-8*, Pub. by F Cass Pubs UK) Intl Spec Bk.

Chartism in Scotland. Bill Groves. (C). 1989. 50.00 (*1-85098-222-8*, Pub. by Jordanhill College UK) St Mut.

Chartist Lives: The Anatomy of a Working Class Movement. Christopher Godfrey. Ed. by William H. McNeill & Peter Stansky. (Modern European History Ser.). 600p. 1987. lib. bdg. 15.00 (*0-8240-7807-1*) Garland.

Chartist Movement. Mark Hovell. (Modern Revivals in Economic & Social History Ser.). 368p. (C). 1993. text ed. 59.95 (*0-7512-0241-X*, Pub. by Gregg Revivals UK) Ashgate Pub Co.

***Chartist Movement: A New Annotated Bibliography.** annot. ed. Owen Ashton et al. LC 94-37219. 192p. 1995. pap. 85.00 (*0-7201-2177-9*, Mansell Pub) Cassell.

Chartist Movement in Its Social & Economic Aspects. Frank F. Rosenblatt. 248p. 1967. reprint ed. 32.50 (*0-7146-1103-4*, BHA-01103, Pub. by F Cass Pubs UK) Intl Spec Bk.

Chartist Movement in Its Social & Economic Aspects, 2 vols., Set. F. F. Rosenblatt. LC 74-120203. (Columbia University. Studies in the Social Sciences: No. 171-172). reprint ed. 74.50 (*0-404-51696-3*) AMS Pr.

Chartist Portraits. George D. Cole. LC 74-22738. reprint ed. 29.00 (*0-404-58490-X*) AMS Pr.

ChartMaker. Stella Systems Staff. 1988. 69.95 (*0-87280-288-4*, Asher-Gallant) Caddylak Systs.

Chartmakers: History of Nautical Surveying in Canada. Stanley Filmore & R. W. Sandilands. (Illus.). 264p. Date not set. text ed. 19.95 (*0-919601-92-8*, Pub. by NC Press CN) U of Toronto Pr.

Chartres & Prose Poems. Jean Garrigue. LC 71-152053. (Illus.). 1970. 20.00 (*0-87130-007-9*); pap. 14.00 (*0-87130-008-7*) Eakins.

***Chartres & the Birth of the Cathedral.** Titus Burckhardt. Tr. by William Stoddart. (Illus.). 160p. (Orig.). 1996. pap. 37.50 (*0-941532-21-6*) Wrld Wisdom Bks.

Chartres Cathedral. Ed. by Robert Branner. (Critical Studies in Art History Ser.). (Illus.). (C). 1969. pap. text ed. 8.95 (*0-393-09851-6*) Norton.

Chartres Cathedral. Malcolm Miller. (Illus.). 96p. (Orig.). 1991. pap. 14.95 (*1-878351-13-3*) Riverside NY.

Chartres Cathedral: Sources & Literary Interpretation, a Critical Bibliography. Jan Van Der Meulen et al. 1080p. 1989. lib. bdg. 80.00 (*0-8161-8346-5*, Hall Reference) Macmillan.

Chartreuse Clue. William F. Love. 1990. 18.95 (*1-55611-211-4*) D I Fine.

Chartreuse Clue. William F. Love. 352p. 1991. reprint ed. pap. 5.50 (*0-451-40273-1*, Onyx) NAL-Dutton.

Chartreuse de Parme. Stendhal, pseud. Ed. by Henri Martineau. (Coll. Prestige). 49.95 (*0-685-35009-6*) Fr & Eur.

Chartreuse de Parme. Stendhal, pseud. (Coll. Grand Ecran Litteraire). 538p. (FRE.). 1990. pap. 10.95 (*0-7859-1491-9*, 2277227552) Fr & Eur.

Chartreuse de Parme. Stendhal. Ed. by Henri Martineau. 512p. (FRE.). 1973. pap. 13.95 (*0-7859-1368-8*, 2070361551) Fr & Eur.

Chartreuse de Parme. Stendhal. (Folio Ser.: No. 155). (FRE.). pap. 10.95 (*2-07-036155-1*) Schoenhof.

Chartreuse Leotard in a Magenta Limousine: And Other Words Named after People & Places. large type ed. Lynda Graham-Barber. LC 94-8597. (Illus.). 80p. (J). (gr. 3-7). 1995. 14.95 (*0-7868-0003-8*) Hyprn Child.

***Chartreuse Leotard in a Magenta Limousine: And Other Words Named after People & Places.** large type ed. Lynda Graham-Barber. LC 94-8597. (Illus.). 80p. (J). (gr. 3-7). 1995. lib. bdg. 14.89 (*0-7868-2002-0*) Hyprn Child.

Chartreux Cat. Jean Simonnet. Tr. & Intro. by Jerome M. Auerbach. LC 91-196563. (Illus.). 191p. (Orig.). 1990. pap. 17.95 (*2-9506009-0-5*, Pub. by J Simonnet FR) J M Auerbach.

Charts & Fundamentals in the Foreign Exchange Market. H. L. Allen & M. P. Taylor. (Bank of England. Discussion Papers: No. 40). 58p. reprint ed. pap. 25.00 (*0-7837-6658-0*, 2046269) Bks Demand.

Charts & Sermons for Overhead Projectors. Benny B. Bristow. 1989. pap. 8.95 (*0-89137-622-4*) Quality Pubns.

Charts & Tables for Beginning Reading. B. Robert Ross. (Illus.). 48p. 1971. 5.00 (*0-87916-003-9*) Upstat.

***Charts for Children: Print Awareness Activities for Young Children.** Judy Nyberg. 176p. (Orig.). (J). (ps-k). 1995. pap. 12.95 (*0-673-36176-4*) GdYrBks.

Charts, Graphs & Stats Index, 1988-1991. Ed. by Robert Skapura. 250p. 1992. 32.00 (*0-917846-09-5*, 95509) Highsmith Pr.

Charts of Christian Theology & Doctrine. H. Wayne House. 128p. 1992. pap. 17.99 (*0-310-41661-2*) Zondervan.

Charts of the Kennet & Avon Waterway: Eastern Chart. Devizes to Reading. Nicholas Hammond. (C). 1989. 40.00 (*0-85288-120-7*, Pub. by Imray Laurie Norie & Wilson UK) St Mut.

Charts of the Kennet & Avon Waterway: Western Chart. Avonmouth to Devizes. Nicholas Hammond. (C). 1989. 35.00 (*0-85288-119-3*, Pub. by Imray Laurie Norie & Wilson UK) St Mut.

Charts on File. Diagram Group Staff. (On File Ser.). (Illus.). 300p. 1988. ring bd. 155.00 (*0-8160-1727-1*) Facts on File.

Charts on Prophecy. Salem Kirban. 1982. pap. 14.92 (*0-912582-39-1*) Kirban.

Chartularies of St. Mary's Abbey, Dublin, Preserved in the Bodleian Library: Annals of Ireland, 2 vols., Set. Ed. by John T. Gilbert. (Rolls Ser.: No. 80). 1972. reprint ed. 160.00 (*0-8115-1150-2*) Periodicals Srv.

***Chartwell Bulletins: January-June 1935.** Winston S. Churchill. Ed. by Martin Gilbert. (Churchill Ser.: No. 2). (Illus.). 68p. 1989. per., pap. 15.00 (*0-943879-03-5*) Intl Churchill Soc.

Chartwell Kent. Mary Soames. (Illus.). 96p. 1992. pap. 10.95 (*0-7078-0147-8*, Pub. by Natl Trust UK) Trafalgar.

Chartwork & Marine Nagivation: For Fishermen & Boat Operators. Geoff A. Motte & Thomas M. Stout. LC 83-46037. (Illus.). 187p. reprint ed. pap. 53.30 (*0-7837-6296-8*, 2046011) Bks Demand.

Charybdis Complex: The Redemption of Rejected Marriage & Family Journal Articles. Marvin B. Sussman. LC 86-7686. (Marriage & Family Review Ser.: Vol. 10, No. 1). 183p. 1986. text ed. 39.95 (*0-86656-503-5*) Haworth Pr.

Chas & the Summer of '26. Charles B. Garrigus. 322p. 1994. 12.50 (*0-9638964-0-7*) Cypress Pr.

Chas. F. Lummis: The Centennial Exhibition Commemorating His Tramp Across the Continent. Ed. by Daniela P. Moneta. LC 84-27589. (Illus.). 80p. (Orig.). 1985. 24.95 (*0-916561-67-4*); pap. 14.95 (*0-916561-01-1*) Southwest Mus.

Chas H. Reinike. Dode Platou. Ed. by Rosanne McCaffrey. (Illus.). 16p. 1981. pap. 5.50 (*0-917860-07-1*) Historic New Orleans.

Chasam Sofer. Yaakov D. Shulman. LC 92-70692. 225p. 1992. 14.95 (*1-56062-117-6*); pap. 11.95 (*1-56062-118-4*) CIS Comm.

***Chasdei Aurahom: Hacoloh B'Halacha.** Abraham Friedlander. 620p. 1994. 17.50 (*0-9643008-1-8*) A Friedlander.

Chase. Alejo Carpentier. Tr. by Alfred MacAdam. 1990. pap. 7.95 (*0-374-52239-1*, Noonday) FS&G.

Chase. Horton Foote. 1952. pap. 4.75 (*0-8222-0198-4*) Dramatists Play.

Chase. Gerald Locklin. LC 76-5706. (Illus.). 1976. pap. 3.00 (*0-916918-00-9*) Duck Down.

Chase. L. T. Smith. Ed. by Pat MacDonald. (Forbidden Game Ser.: Vol. II). 240p. (Orig.). (J). 1994. pap. 3.50 (*0-671-87452-7*, Archway) PB.

Chase. Robert Stein. LC 88-20647. 207p. 1988. 12.95 (*0-87414-065-X*) U IA Pubns Dept.

Chase. Beatrice Tamaka. Date not set. pap. 4.99 (*0-517-11129-2*) Random Hse Value.

Chase: A Computer Companion for Mastering the One Hundred Sixty Scriptures of the Standard Works Used in Scripture Chases. Victor K. Broderick. 1987. 5.25 hd, pap. 19.95 (*0-934153-03-5*) Marietta Pub.

Chase: The Compulsive Gambler. Henry Lesieur. 352p. 1984. 29.95 (*0-87073-642-6*); pap. 15.95 (*0-87073-643-4*) Schenkman Bks Inc.

Chase a Tall Shadow. John Ell. 240p. (Orig.). 1995. reprint ed. pap. 2.25 (*0-8439-2264-8*) Dorchester Pub Co.

***Chase Across the Globe: Intern.** Dick Bryan. (C). 1995. text ed. 49.95 (*0-8133-2356-8*) Westview.

Chase & Civil War Politics. Donnal V. Smith. LC 72-34. (Select Bibliographies Reprint Ser.). 1977. reprint ed. 25.95 (*0-8369-9971-1*) Ayer.

Chase & William & Helen. Gottfried A. Burger. Tr. by Walter Scott. LC 90-119099. 56p. 1989. reprint ed. 40.00 (*1-85477-008-X*, Pub. by Woodstock Bks UK) Cassell.

Chase, Chance, & Creativity. James H. Austin. LC 77-23011. 236p. 1985. pap. text ed. 17.50 (*0-231-04295-7*) Col U Pr.

Chase for Labour. Austin Mitchell. LC 82-17162. reprint ed. pap. 57.00 (*0-317-20766-0*, 2025267) Bks Demand.

***Chase Investment Performance Digest, 1995.** C. David Chase. 1995. pap. 22.95 (*0-944822-07-X*) Chase Global.

Chase of Saint-Castin, & Other Stories of the French in the New World. Mary Catherwood. LC 77-128723. (Short Story Index Reprint Ser.). 1977. 19.95 (*0-8369-3614-0*) Ayer.

***Chase of the Blue Tiger: Spider Man.** Rick Geary. (Come to Life Bks.). 16p. (J). 1995. write for info. (*1-57234-062-2*) YES Ent.

Chase of the Meteor, & Other Stories. Edwin L. Bynner. LC 79-81264. (Short Story Index Reprint Ser.). (Illus.). 1977. 19.95 (*0-8369-3016-9*) Ayer.

Chase of the Sorceress. Philip R. Johnson. LC 89-50958. 152p. (YA). (gr. 7-12). 1989. pap. 8.25 (*0-943864-58-5*) Davenport.

An Asterisk (*) at the beginning of an entry indicates that the title is appearing in BIP for the first time.

An Asterisk (*) at the beginning of an entry indicates that the title is appearing in BIP for the first time.

1163

C

***Chattanooga: An Illustrated Histo.** James W. Livingood. 1981. 19.95 (0-89781-027-9) Preferred Mktg.

Chattanooga: Delivering the Dream. Libby Wann. LC 90-71486. (Urban Tapestry Ser.). (Illus.). 224p. 1990. 33.95 (0-9628128-0-3) Towery Pub.

Chattanooga Country 1540-1976: From Tomahawks to TVA. 3rd rev. ed. Gilbert E. Govan & James W. Livingood. LC 77-21751. (Illus.). 552p. reprint ed. pap. 157.40 (0-7837-5389-6, 2045153) Bks Demand.

***Chattanooga Great Places Plus a Hundred Miles. Linda L. Burton. (Illus.). 256p. (Orig.). 1995. pap. 11.95 (0-9644760-0-2) Phase II Publ. After you've seen the Choo Choo, then what? CHATTANOOGA GREAT PLACES PLUS A HUNDRED MILES has the answers for visitors & residents alike. With over 700 reviews & maps, it's easy to find the Great Places to Eat, Go, Shop, Stay & Use in Chattanooga, Tennessee, & the four-state area within 100 miles. Written & illustrated by well-traveled locals who live in & love this beautiful place of rivers & ridges, the book guides you to popular attractions as well as great places not on the tourist trail. From Buck's BBQ to the classy cuisine at Cirrus, from Olympic-class Ocoee whitewaters to downtown's world-class Aquarium, from Civil War-cannoned battlefields to glass & brassy shopping malls, from high-bluffed campgrounds to bubble-elevatored hotels, in fact, from Arts to Zoos, this book tells it like it is, with all the who, what, when, where & how you need. Useful, honest, & fun to read, it covers SE Tennessee, SW North Carolina, Northern Georgia, & NE Alabama; includes Atlanta, Birmingham, Huntsville, Knoxville, Nashville. Coming to visit? A life-long resident? Either way, you'll want this book! To order, contact Phase II: Publications, 5600 Lake Resort Terr., Suites 404-I, Chattanooga, TN 37415; 615-875-4795; FAX 615-877-4089.** *Publisher Provided Annotation.*

Chattanooga Wild & Scenic River: A Guide to Boating, Hiking & Camping in the Chattanooga National Wild & Scenic River Corridor. Brian A. Boyd. Ed. by K. W. Boyd & D. A. Todd. (Illus.). 96p. (Orig.). 1990. pap. 7.95 (0-9625737-0-1) Ferncreek Pub.

Chatte. Sidonie-Gabrielle Colette. 212p. (FRE.). 1950. 24.95 (0-8288-9146-X, F97030) Fr & Eur.

Chatte. Sidonie-Gabrielle Colette. (FRE.). 1955. pap. 10.95 (0-8288-9155-9, F97031) Fr & Eur.

Chatte Rouge. Jean-Pierre Chabrol. (FRE.). 1976. pap. 10.95 (0-7859-1828-0, 2070367967) Fr & Eur.

Chattel or Person? The Status of Women in the Mishnah. Judith R. Wegner. 286p. 1988. 39.95 (0-19-505169-6) OUP.

Chattel or Person? The Status of Women in the Mishnah. Judith R. Wegner. 288p. 1992. reprint ed. pap. 16.95 (0-19-508003-3) OUP.

Chatter: Language & History in Kierkegaard. Peter D. Fenves. LC 93-16347. (Meridian: Crossing Aesthetics Ser.). 328p. (C). 1993. 42.50 (0-8047-2207-2); pap. 15.95 (0-8047-2208-0) Stanford U Pr.

Chatter with the Angels: Folk Songs from the American Black Tradition for Voices & Orff Instruments. Shirley W. McRae. 44p. 1980. pap. 8.95 (0-918812-09-7, SE 0239) MMB Music.

Chatterbox. Voller & Widdows. 1989. pap. 16.95 (0-8384-3331-6) Heinle & Heinle.

Chatterbox - Teachers Annotated Edition. Voller & Widdows. 1989. pap. 18.95 (0-8384-3332-4) Heinle & Heinle.

Chatterbox Jamie. Nancy E. Cooney. LC 92-11001. (Illus.). 32p. (J). (ps-1). 1993. lib. bdg. 14.95 (0-399-22208-1, Putnam) Putnam Pub Group.

Chattering Man. Merrill J. Gerber. LC 91-61930. 208p. 1991. 18.95 (1-56352-011-7) Longstreet Pr Inc.

Chattering Wagtails of Mikuyu Prison. Jack Mapanje. (African Writers Ser.). 1993. pap. 9.95 (0-435-91198-8) Heinemann.

Chatterton. Alfred De Vigny. Ed. by Sylvie Germain. Bd. with Quitte pour la Peur. (Coll. GF). (FRE.). 1964. Set pap. 7.95 (0-8288-9666-6, F75878) Fr & Eur.

Chatterton. Starling. 1983. 12.00 (0-317-02725-5) Byzantine Pr.

Chatterton & His Poetry. John H. Ingram. LC 77-120985. (Poetry & Life Ser.). reprint ed. 27.50 (0-404-52521-0) AMS Pr.

Chatting. Shirley Hughes. LC 93-22747. 24p. (J). (ps up). 1994. 13.95 (1-56402-340-0) Candlewick Pr.

***Chatting in Idiomatic English: Challenging for Advancing ESL Learners.** Anne Simeon. 52p. (Orig.). (C). 1995. pap. text ed. 6.95 (0-9696985-1-8) Bendall Bks.

Chatto Book of Love Stories. Helen Byatt. 288p. 1994. 19.95 (0-7011-6101-9, Pub. by Chatto & Windus UK) Trafalgar.

Chatto Book of Modern Poetry: Nineteen Fifteen to Nineteen Fifty-Five. Ed. by Cecil Day-Lewis & John Lehman. LC 77-25967. 287p. 1978. reprint ed. text ed. 35.00 (0-313-20099-8, DLCB, Greenwood Pr) Greenwood.

Chatto Book of Modern Poetry: Nineteen Fifteen to Nineteen Fifty-Five. Ed. by Cecil Day-Lewis & John Lehmann. reprint ed. 29.00 (0-403-03067-6) Somerset Pub.

Chattooga River Section Four Flip Map. Ron Rathnow. LC 86-28475. (Great American Rivers Flip Map Ser.). (Illus.). 36p. 1986. pap. text ed. 5.95 (0-89732-047-6) Menasha Ridge.

Chattooga Wild & Scenic River: A Guide to Boating, Hiking, & Camping in the Chattooga National Wild & Scenic River Corridor. 2nd ed. Brian A. Boyd. (Illus.). 112p. 1993. pap. 7.95 (0-9625737-4-4) Ferncreek Pub.

Chatty Cathy Dolls. Kathy Lewis. 1994. pap. 15.95 (0-89145-579-5) Collector Bks.

Chatty Chipmunk's Nutty Day. Suzanne Gruber. LC 84-8665. (Giant First Start Reader Ser.). (Illus.). 32p. (J). (gr. k-2). 1985. lib. bdg. 11.59 (0-8167-0360-4); pap. text ed. 2.95 (0-8167-0440-6) Troll Assocs.

Chatty Hats & Other Props. Denise Mantione. (Illus.). 148p. 1990. teacher ed 22.95 (0-937857-17-3, 1581) Speech Bin.

***Chaturanga.** Arthur Bove. 230p. Date not set. pap. 8.95 (0-7610-0391-6) NW Pub.

Chaturanga. Rabindranath Tagore. Tr. by Ashok Mitra. 101p. 1974. reprint ed. bds. 4.95 (0-88253-279-0) Ind-US Inc.

Chaucer. (Little Brown Notebook Ser.). (Illus.). 256p. 6.95 (1-897954-22-0) Sterling.

Chaucer. Geoffrey Chaucer. (J). (gr. 1-9). 1992. pap. 3.95 (0-88388-017-2) Bellerophon Bks.

Chaucer. Alfred W. Pollard. LC 73-114911. (Select Bibliographies Reprint Ser.). 1977. 19.95 (0-8369-5316-9) Ayer.

Chaucer. Gilbert K. Chesterton. LC 69-13856. 285p. 1970. reprint ed. text ed. 59.75 (0-8371-2237-6, CHCH, Greenwood Pr) Greenwood.

Chaucer. George H. Cowling. LC 74-150179. (Select Bibliographies Reprint Ser.). 1977. reprint ed. 18.95 (0-8369-5692-3) Ayer.

Chaucer. Alfred W. Pollard. LC 76-174278. reprint ed. 21.50 (0-404-05069-7) AMS Pr.

Chaucer. Alfred W. Pollard. LC 69-14038. 136p. 1969. reprint ed. text ed. 45.00 (0-8371-1856-5, POCH, Greenwood Pr) Greenwood.

Chaucer. Adolphus W. Ward. (BCL1-PR English Literature Ser.). 207p. 1992. reprint ed. lib. bdg. 79.00 (0-7812-7180-0) Rprt Serv.

Chaucer: "The Canterbury Tales" Winthrop Wetherbee. (Landmarks of World Literature Ser.). (Illus.). (C). 1989. 29.95 (0-521-32331-2); pap. 10.95 (0-521-31159-4) Cambridge U Pr.

Chaucer: A Bibliographical Manual. Eleanor P. Hammond. 579p. reprint ed. lib. bdg. 65.00 (0-8328-3129-8) Higginson Bk Co.

Chaucer: A Critical Appreciation. Paul F. Baum. LC 58-12587. 244p. reprint ed. pap. 69.60 (0-317-41836-X, 2026185) Bks Demand.

Chaucer: A Selected Bibliography. Ed. by John Leyerle & Anne Quick. (Medieval Bibliographies Ser.). 352p. 1986. pap. 10.95 (0-8020-6408-6) U of Toronto Pr.

Chaucer: Complaint & Narrative. W. A. Davenport. (Chaucer Studies: No. XIV). 224p. (C). 1988. 79.00 (0-85991-277-9) Boydell & Brewer.

Chaucer: Essays & Studies. Oliver F. Emerson. (BCL1-PR English Literature Ser.). 455p. 1992. reprint ed. lib. bdg. 99.00 (0-7812-7173-8) Rprt Serv.

Chaucer: Essays & Studies - a Selection from the Writings of Oliver Farrar Emerson, 1860-1927. Oliver F. Emerson. LC 78-114907. (Select Bibliographies Reprint Ser.). 1977. 30.95 (0-8369-5311-8) Ayer.

Chaucer: Sources & Backgrounds. Ed. by Robert P. Miller. (Illus.). (C). 1977. pap. text ed. 18.95 (0-19-502167-3) OUP.

Chaucer: The Critical Heritage, 2 vols. Ed. by Derek Brewer. 1978. write for info. (0-685-00609-3) Routledge.

Chaucer: The Critical Heritage, 2 vols. Ed. by Derek Brewer. Incl. Vol. 1. 1385-1837. 1978. 42.50 (0-7100-0223-8, 02238); Vol. 2. 1837-1933. 1978. 42.50 (0-7100-0224-6); (Critical Heritage Ser.). 1978. Set. 50.00 (0-7100-8497-8, RKP) Routledge.

Chaucer - the Consolation of Philosophy of Boethius. Bernard L. Jefferson. LC 65-21091. (Studies in Comparative Literature: No. 35). 1969. reprint ed. lib. bdg. 75.00 (0-8383-0574-1) M S G Haskell Hse.

Chaucer - The Early Poetry: A Study in Poetic Development. Derek Traversi. LC 85-41047. 160p. 1987. 29.50 (0-87413-306-8) U Delaware Pr.

Chaucer & Dante. Howard Schless. LC 84-483. 268p. 1984. 44.95 (0-937664-59-6) Pilgrim Bks OK.

Chaucer & Fifteenth-Century Verse & Prose. H. S. Bennett. (Oxford History of English Literature Ser.: Vol. 2). 364p. 1990. 49.95 (0-19-812229-2) OUP.

Chaucer & His French Contemporaries: Natural Music in the Fourteenth Century. James I. Wimsatt. 393p. 1993. pap. 19.95 (0-8020-7189-9) U of Toronto Pr.

Chaucer & His Poetry. Edward W. Edmunds. LC 79-120972. (Poetry & Life Ser.). reprint ed. 27.50 (0-404-52509-1) AMS Pr.

Chaucer & His Readers: Imagining the Author in Late Medieval England. Seth Lerer. LC 92-33454. (Illus.). 320p. (C). 1993. text ed. 39.50 (0-691-06811-9) Princeton U Pr.

Chaucer & His Times. Grace E. Hadow. LC 75-114909. (Select Bibliographies Reprint Ser.). 1977. 19.95 (0-8369-5314-2) Ayer.

Chaucer & His World. Derek Brewer. 256p. (C). 1992. pap. text ed. 25.00 (0-85991-366-X, DS Brewer) Boydell & Brewer.

Chaucer & His World. Derek Brewer. 256p. (C). 1994. text ed. 63.00 (0-85991-365-1, DS Brewer) Boydell & Brewer.

Chaucer & Menippean Satire. F. Anne Payne. LC 79-5412. 304p. 1981. 29.50 (0-299-08170-2) U of Wis Pr.

Chaucer & Pagan Antiquity. Alastair Minnis. (Chaucer Studies: No. VIII). 168p. 1982. 79.00 (0-85991-098-9) Boydell & Brewer.

Chaucer & Some of His Friends. George L. Kittredge. 1973. 59.95 (0-87968-844-0) Gordon Pr.

Chaucer & the Common People. Howard R. Patch. (Studies in Chaucer: No. 6). (C). 1970. reprint ed. pap. 12.95 (0-8383-0060-X) M S G Haskell Hse.

Chaucer & the Consolation of Philosophy of Boethius. Bernard L. Jefferson. LC 67-30878. 168p. 1967. reprint ed. 40.00 (0-87752-055-0) Gordian.

Chaucer & the Country of Stars: Poetic Uses of Astrological Imagery. Chauncey Wood. LC 68-56324. 371p. reprint ed. 105.80 (0-8357-9496-2, 2010396) Bks Demand.

Chaucer & the Craft of Fiction. John Fleming et al. Ed. by Leigh A. Arrathoon. (Illus.). 430p. (C). 1986. pap. 20.00 (0-933760-05-1) Solaris Pr.

Chaucer & the Cult of Saint Valentine. Henry A. Kelly. (Davis Medieval Texts & Studies: No. 5). xii, 188p. 1986. pap. 33.25 (90-04-07849-5) E J Brill.

Chaucer & the Early Writings of Boccaccio. David Wallace. LC 84-24366. (Chaucer Studies: Vol. XII). 209p. (C). 1985. 79.00 (0-85991-186-1) Boydell & Brewer.

Chaucer & the English Tradition. Ian Robinson. (C). 1986. 125.00 (0-907839-29-0, Pub. by Brynmill Pr Ltd UK) St Mut.

Chaucer & the English Tradition. Ian Robinson. LC 79-163179. 308p. reprint ed. pap. 87.80 (0-317-26392-7, 2024530) Bks Demand.

Chaucer & the Fictions of Gender. Elaine T. Hansen. 385p. 1992. 42.50 (0-520-07133-6); pap. 16.00 (0-520-07499-8) U CA Pr.

Chaucer & the French Tradition: A Study in Style & Meaning. Charles Muscatine. (C). 1957. pap. 14.00 (0-520-00908-8) U CA Pr.

Chaucer & the Imagery of Narrative: The First Five Canterbury Tales. V. A. Kolve. LC 80-50907. (Illus.). xvi, 551p. 1984. 52.50 (0-8047-1161-5); pap. 19.95 (0-8047-1349-9) Stanford U Pr.

Chaucer & the Law. Ed. by Joseph A. Hornsby, IV. 180p. 1988. 33.95 (0-937664-79-0) Pilgrim Bks OK.

Chaucer & the Legend of Good Women. Robert W. Frank, Jr. LC 72-81271. 233p. 1972. 25.00 (0-674-11190-7) HUP.

Chaucer & the Making of English Poetry, 2 vols. P. M. Kean. Incl. Vol. 2. Art of Narrative. 1972. 19.95 (0-7100-7250-3); (Illus.). 1972. Set. 38.00 (0-7100-7345-3) Routledge Chapman & Hall.

Chaucer & the Medieval Book. Beverly Boyd. LC 73-77021. (Illus.). 177p. reprint ed. pap. 50.50 (0-7837-6675-0, 2046291) Bks Demand.

***Chaucer & the Mystics: The Canterbury Tales & the Genre of Devotional Prose.** Robert Boeing. LC 94-33130. 1995. write for info. (0-8387-5288-8) Bucknell U Pr.

Chaucer & the Poems of "CH"in University of Pennsylvania MS French 15. James I. Wimsatt. (Chaucer Studies: No. IX). 136p. 1982. 79.00 (0-85991-130-6) Boydell & Brewer.

Chaucer & the Poets: An Essay on Troilus & Criseyde. Winthrop Wetherbee. LC 84-7080. 248p. 1984. 31.50 (0-8014-1684-1) Cornell U Pr.

Chaucer & the Rival Poet in Shakespeare's Sonnets, a New Theory. Hubert W. Ord. LC 71-173810. reprint ed. 21.50 (0-404-07829-X) AMS Pr.

Chaucer & the Roman Poets. Edgar F. Shannon. (BCL1-PR English Literature Ser.). 401p. 1992. reprint ed. lib. bdg. 99.00 (0-7812-7177-0) Rprt Serv.

Chaucer & the Social Contest. Peggy Knapp. 192p. 1990. 35.00 (0-415-90150-2, A3421, Routledge NY); pap. 13.95 (0-415-90151-0, A3425, Routledge NY) Routledge.

Chaucer & the Subject of History. Lee Patterson. LC 90-50651. 504p. (Orig.). (C). 1991. pap. 16.95 (0-299-12834-2) U of Wis Pr.

Chaucer & the Tradition of the "Roman Antique" Barbara Nolan. (Studies in Medieval Literature: No. 15). 350p. (C). 1992. 69.95 (0-521-39169-5) Cambridge U Pr.

Chaucer at Oxford & at Cambridge. Jack A. Bennett. LC 74-81706. (Illus.). 141p. reprint ed. pap. 40.20 (0-7837-0533-6, 2040861) Bks Demand.

Chaucer at Work: Making of Canterbury Tales. Peter Brown. LC 93-39019. 224p. (C). 1994. pap. text ed. 24.75 (0-685-72601-0, 76440) Longman.

Chaucer Bibliography, 1925-1933. Willard E. Martin, Jr. LC 72-1042. reprint ed. 31.50 (0-404-04195-7) AMS Pr.

Chaucer Canon. W. W. Skeat. 1973. 49.95 (0-87968-845-9) Gordon Pr.

Chaucer Canon. Walter Skeat. LC 68-817. (Studies in Chaucer: No. 6). 1969. reprint ed. lib. bdg. 59.95 (0-8383-0623-3) M S G Haskell Hse.

Chaucer Canon, with a Discussion of the Works Associated with the Name of Geoffrey Chaucer. Walter W. Skeat. (BCL1-PR English Literature Ser.). 167p. 1992. reprint ed. lib. bdg. 69.00 (0-7812-7178-9) Rprt Serv.

Chaucer Criticism: The Canterbury Tales. Ed. by Richard Schoeck & Jerome Taylor. LC 60-10279. 1960. pap. 8.95 (0-268-00036-0) U of Notre Dame Pr.

Chaucer Criticism: Troilus & Criseyde & the Minor Poems. Ed. by Richard Schoeck & Jerome Taylor. LC 60-10279. 1961. pap. 8.95 (0-268-00037-9) U of Notre Dame Pr.

Chaucer Gazetteer. Francis P. Magoun. LC 61-11293. 173p. reprint ed. pap. 49.40 (0-685-10700-0, 2024058) Bks Demand.

Chaucer Glossary. Norman Davis et al. 1979. pap. 17.95 (0-19-811171-1) OUP.

Chaucer Handbook. 2nd ed. Robert D. French. LC 83-45763. reprint ed. 35.00 (0-404-20100-8) AMS Pr.

Chaucer in His Time. Derek Brewer. LC 77-77517. 243p. 1977. reprint ed. text ed. 65.00 (0-8371-9649-3, BRCI, Greenwood Pr) Greenwood.

Chaucer in the Eighties. Ed. by Julian Wasserman & Robert Blanch. 300p. 1986. pap. text ed. 18.50 (0-8156-2364-X) Syracuse U Pr.

Chaucer Name Dictionary: Guide to Astrological, Biblical, Historical, Literary, & Mythological Names in the Works of Geoffrey Chaucer. Jacqueline De Weever. LC 87-21236. 429p. 1988. 65.00 (0-8240-8306-7, H709) Garland.

***Chaucer on Love, Knowledge & Sight.** Norman Klassen. (Chaucer Studies: No. 21). 256p. (C). 1995. text ed. 53.00 (0-85991-464-X) Boydell & Brewer.

Chaucer Reads 'The Divine Comedy' Karla Taylor. LC 89-4424. 289p. 1989. 32.50 (0-8047-1544-0) Stanford U Pr.

Chaucer, Spenser, Milton: Mythopoeic Continuities & Transformations. A. Kent Hieatt. (Illus.). 336p. 1975. 32.50 (0-7735-0228-9, Pub. by McGill CN) U of Toronto Pr.

Chaucer, Spenser, Milton: Mythopoeic Continuities & Transformations. A. Kent Hieatt. LC 76-363422. (Illus.). 310p. reprint ed. pap. 88.40 (0-7837-6924-5, 2046753) Bks Demand.

Chaucer Story Book. Eva M. Tappan. 1908. 20.00 (0-8196-1360-6) Biblo.

Chaucer to Shakespeare: Essays in Honour of Shinsuke Ando. Ed. by Toshiyuki Takamiya & Richard Beadle. 288p. (C). 1992. text ed. 99.00 (0-85991-351-1, DS Brewer) Boydell & Brewer.

Chaucer Tradition. Aage Brusendorff. (BCL1-PR English Literature Ser.). 510p. 1992. reprint ed. lib. bdg. 99.00 (0-7812-7171-1) Rprt Serv.

Chaucer Traditions: Studies in Honour of Derek Brewer. Ed. by Ruth Morse & Barry Windeatt. (Illus.). 292p. (C). 1990. 69.95 (0-521-35247-9) Cambridge U Pr.

Chaucer Yearbook: A Journal of Late Medieval Studies (1992), Vol. 1. Ed. by Jean E. Jost & Michael N. Salda. 296p. 1992. text ed. 49.95 (0-7734-9238-0); 19.95 (0-685-62544-3) E Mellen.

***Chaucer Yearbook II.** Ed. by Michael N. Salda & Jean E. Jost. (Chaucer Yearbook Ser.). 256p. (C). 1995. text ed. 53.00 (0-85991-465-8) Boydell & Brewer.

Chaucerian Belief: The Poetics of Reverence & Delight. John M. Hill. 228p. (C). 1991. text ed. 32.50x (0-300-04782-7) Yale U Pr.

Chaucerian Papers. Albert S. Cook. (Connecticut Academy of Arts & Sciences Ser., Trans.: Vol. 23, No. 1). 1919. pap. 49.50 (0-685-22836-3) Elliots Bks.

Chaucerian Papers. Albert S. Cook. LC 72-1040. reprint ed. 29.50 (0-404-01697-9) AMS Pr.

Chaucerian Play: Comedy & Control in the Canterbury Tales. Laura Kendrick. (C). 1988. 37.50 (0-520-06194-2) U CA Pr.

Chaucerian Problems. Russell Krauss. LC 71-171631. reprint ed. 22.50 (0-404-03781-X) AMS Pr.

Chaucerian Realism. Robert Myles. LC 94-5852. (Chaucer Studies: Vol. XX). 224p. (C). 1994. text ed. 53.00 (0-85991-409-7, DS Brewer) Boydell & Brewer.

Chaucerian Theatricality. John M. Ganim. 184p. (C). 1991. text ed. 29.50 (0-691-06779-1) Princeton U Pr.

Chaucer's Boccaccio: Sources for Troilus & the Knight's & Franklin's Tales. rev. ed. N. R. Havely. (Chaucer Studies: Vol. 5). 231p. (C). 1992. reprint ed. text ed. 79.00 (0-85991-036-9); reprint ed. pap. text ed. 29.00 (0-85991-349-X) Boydell & Brewer.

Chaucer's "Boece" & the Medieval Tradition of Boethius. Boethius. Ed. by A. J. Minnis. Tr. by Geoffrey Chaucer. (Chaucer Studies: Vol. XVIII). (Illus.). 256p. (C). 1993. text ed. 70.00 (0-85991-368-6) Boydell & Brewer.

Chaucer's Canterbury Art. J. W. Cook. 176p. 1976. 16.00 (0-86578-103-6); 10.00 (0-86578-102-8) Ind-US Inc.

Chaucer's Canterbury Tales: A Reading. Derek Traversi. LC 83-1121. 224p. 1983. 25.00 (0-686-89525-8) U Delaware Pr.

Chaucer's Canterbury Tales Complete in Presentday English. Geoffrey Chauser & James J. Donohoe. LC 79-90384. 626p. 1979. write for info. (0-936875-03-8) Loras Coll Pr.

Chaucer's Checklist. Michael Jeneid. (Birds in Great Literature Ser.). (Illus.). 140p. 1993. write for info. (0-9636169-0-0) Pandion Pr.

Chaucer's Clerk's Tale: The Griselda Story Received, Rewritten, Illustrated. Judith Bronfman. LC 94-10195. (Reference Library of the Humanities; Studies in Medieval Literature: Vol. 1831; Vol. 11). (Illus.). 184p. 1994. 28.00 (0-8153-1640-2, H1831) Garland.

Chaucer's Constance & Accused Queens. Margaret Schlauch. LC 71-93253. 150p. 1970. reprint ed. 40.00 (0-87752-097-6) Gordian.

Chaucer's Constance (in "The Man of Law's Tale") & Accused Queens. Margaret Schlauch. LC 77-17536. reprint ed. 20.00 (0-404-05604-0) AMS Pr.

Chaucer's Dante: Allegory & Epic Theater in "The Canterbury Tales" Richard Neuse. 332p. 1991. 45.00 (0-520-07241-3) U CA Pr.

Chaucer's Drama of Style: Poetic Variety & Contrast in the Canterbury Tales. C. David Benson. LC 85-20849. x, 183p. (C). 1988. reprint ed. 27.50 (0-8078-1679-5); reprint ed. pap. 12.95 (0-8078-4238-9) U of NC Pr.

Chaucer's England, 2 Vols, Set. Matthew Browne, pseud. LC 74-113566. reprint ed. 84.50 (0-404-01139-X) AMS Pr.

Chaucer's England: Literature in Historical Context. Ed. by Barbara A. Hanawalt. (Medieval Studies at Minnesota: Vol. 4). 256p. (C). 1992. pap. text ed. 16.95 (0-8166-2020-2) U of Minn Pr.

C

1164 An Asterisk (*) at the beginning of an entry indicates that the title is appearing in BIP for the first time.

An Asterisk (*) at the beginning of an entry indicates that the title is appearing in BIP for the first time.

1165

Cheating the Government: The Economics of Evasion. Frank A. Cowell. 180p. 1990. 32.50 (*0-262-03153-1*) MIT Pr.

Cheating to Win. Francine Pascal. (Sweet Valley High Ser.: No. 77). (YA). 1991. pap. 2.99 (*0-553-29145-9*) Bantam.

Cheatnotes on Life. Donna Blaurock. 168p. (Orig.). 1994. pap. 5.95 (*1-56245-028-X*) Great Quotations.

Cheats at Work: An Anthology of Workplace Crime. Gerald Mars. 260p. 1994. 62.95 (*1-85521-379-6*, Pub. by Dartmoth Pub UK); pap. 26.95 (*1-85521-528-4*, Pub. by Dartmth Pub UK) Ashgate Pub Co.

Chebyshev Polynomials: From Approximation Theory to Algebra & Number Theory. 2nd ed. Theodore J. Rivlin. 249p. 1990. text ed. 91.95 (*0-471-62896-4*) Wiley.

***Cheche yon Mo! Search-a-Word, No. 2.** Oreste Joseph. Ed. by Maryse Joseph & Rita Parisse. 32p. (CRP.). 1995. pap. 3.00 (*1-885566-00-X*) Oresjozef.

***Chechnya CIS Atlas.** (Illus.). 70p. (Orig.). 1995. pap. 75. 00 (*0-7605-1493-3*) Rector Pr.

***Chechnya Human Rights Report: U. S. State Department 1995.** 70p. (Orig.). 1995. pap. 45.00 (*0-7605-1656-1*) Rector Pr.

Check Exchanging: The Bankers' Ticket to Free Lunches. 1992. lib. bdg. 75.00 (*0-8490-8737-6*) Gordon Pr.

Check Fraud Investigation. Burt Rapp. LC 91-60413. (Illus.). 176p. (Orig.). 1991. pap. 16.95 (*1-55950-065-4*, 40072) Loompanics.

***Check in to Danger.** Joan L. Nixon. LC 94-71794. (Disney Adventures Casebusters Ser.: Bk. 4). (Illus.). 96p. (J). (gr. 2-6). 1995. 13.95 (*0-7868-3049-2*); pap. 3.95 (*0-7868-4026-9*) Disney Pr.

Check Is Not in the Mail: How to Get Paid More in Full, On Time, at Less Cost & Without Losing Valued Customers. Leonard Sklar. LC 89-82041. 300p. 1990. 19.95 (*0-9624833-5-4*) Baroque Pub.

Check It Out: A Top Investigator Tells You How to Use Publicly Available Sources. Edmund J. Pankau. 1992. pap. 10.95 (*0-8092-3945-0*) Contemp Bks.

Check It Out: Everyone's Guide to Investigation. Edmund J. Pankau. 146p. (Orig.). 1991. pap. 19.95 (*0-89896-444-X*) Larksdale.

Check It Out: The Book about Libraries. Gail Gibbons. LC 85-5414. (Illus.). 32p. (J). (ps-3). 1985. 13.95 (*0-15-216400-6*, HB Juv Bks) HarBrace.

Check It Out! The Book about Libraries. Gail Gibbons. (Illus.). 32p. (J). (ps-3). 1988. pap. 4.95 (*0-15-216401-4*, Voyager Bks) HarBrace.

***Check It Out - & Die.** M. T. Coffin. (Spinetingler Ser.: No. 5). 160p. (Orig.). (J). (gr. 6-8). 1995. pap. 3.50 (*0-380-78116-6*) Avon.

Check List for Marriage. G. Frank Leedy. LC 72-181367. 1971. 10.00 (*0-87212-023-6*) Libra.

Check List Materials for Public School Building Specifications, Covering the General Specifications. Lee Byrne. LC 71-178797. (Columbia University. Teachers College. Contributions to Education Ser.: No. 492). reprint ed. 37.50 (*0-404-55492-X*) AMS Pr.

Check List of Chicago Ante-Fire Imprints, 1851-1871. Works Progress Administration Staff. (American Imprints Inventory Ser.: No. 4). 362p. 1989. reprint ed. pap. 35.00 (*0-924772-04-2*) CH Bookworks.

Check List of Crosses in the Gramineae. Irving W. Knobloch. 1968. pap. 10.00 (*0-934454-22-1*) Lubrecht & Cramer.

Check List of English Prose Fiction: 1700-1739. William H. McBurney. LC 60-13292. 164p. reprint ed. pap. 46.80 (*0-317-10464-0*, 2001585) Bks Demand.

Check-List of Hawaiian Land & Freshwater Mollusca. E. L. Caum. (BMB Ser.: No. 56). 1972. reprint ed. 15.00 (*0-527-02162-8*) Periodicals Srv.

Check List of Historical Records Survey Publications. Sargent B. Child & Dorothy P. Holmes. 110p. 1989. reprint ed. 12.95 (*0-685-60310-5*, 980) Clearfield Co.

Check List of Imprints of the German Press of Northampton County, Pennsylvania. Alfred L. Shoemaker. 162p. 1943. text ed. 35.00 (*1-877701-11-4*) NCH&GS.

Check-List of Instrumental Ensemble Music Before Haydn. Manfred F. Bukofzer. 1993. reprint ed. lib. bdg. 89.00 (*0-7812-9694-3*) Rprt Serv.

Check List of Kentucky Imprints, 1811-1820, with Notes in Supplement to the Check List of 1787-1810. D. C. McMurtrie. Ed. by A. H. Allen. (Historical Records Survey Monographs). 1972. reprint ed. 20.00 (*0-527-01903-8*) Periodicals Srv.

Check-List of Legislative Journals of States of the United States of America. Comp. by Grace E. MacDonald. LC 79-92126. (Legal Bibliographic & Research Reprint Ser.: Vol. 3). 274p. 1980. reprint ed. lib. bdg. 42.00 (*0-89941-034-0*, 300900) W S Hein.

Check List of Plant & Soil Nematodes: A Nomenclatorial Compilation. Armen C. Tarjan. LC 60-10226. 214p. reprint ed. pap. 61.00 (*0-7837-5831-6*, 2045550) Bks Demand.

Check-List of Recent Latin American Music Periodicals. Lee Fairley. 1993. reprint ed. lib. bdg. 89.00 (*0-7812-9558-0*) Rprt Serv.

Check-List of Recorded Songs in the English Language in the Archive of American Folk Song to July, 1940, Set. U. S. Library of Congress, Music Division Staff. LC 74-26091. reprint ed. 72.50 (*0-404-13121-2*) AMS Pr.

Check List of Texas Imprints, 1846-1860. Ed. by Ernest W. Winkler. 1949. 19.95 (*0-87611-021-9*) Tex St Hist Assn.

Check List of Texas Imprints, 1861-1876. Ed. by Ernest W. Winkler & Llerena B. Friend. 1963. 24.95 (*0-87611-022-7*) Tex St Hist Assn.

Check List of the Lepidoptera of America North of Mexico. Ed. by Ronald W. Hodges et al. xxiv, 284p. (Orig.). (C). 1983. pap. text ed. 20.00 (*0-86096-016-1*) Wedge Entomological.

Check List of the Paintings, Drawings & Prints at the Kendall Whaling Museum. M. V. Brewington. (Illus.). 74p. 1957. pap. 2.00 (*0-937854-02-6*) Kendall Whaling.

Check-Mate: A Pocket-Size Guide to Everyday Spellings for Dyslexics. Alan O'Brien. 64p. 1993. pap. 12.50 (*1-85302-165-2*, Pub. by J Kingsley Pubs UK) Taylor & Francis.

Check on Democracy: New Military Power in Latin America. Ed. by Augusto Varas. LC 88-25105. (Contributions in Military Studies: No. 84). 230p. 1989. text ed. 55.00 (*0-313-26034-6*, VDY/, Greenwood Pr) Greenwood.

Check out a Librarian. Johanna E. Tallman. LC 85-10845. (Illus.). 190p. 1985. text ed. 20.00 (*0-8108-1823-X*) Scarecrow.

***Check-Out Time.** Kate Kingsbury. 224p. (Orig.). 1995. pap. text ed. 4.99 (*0-425-14640-5*, Prime Crime) Berkley Pub.

Check Points on How to Buy Oriental Rugs. Charles W. Jacobsen. (Illus.). 208p. 1979. pap. 24.95 (*0-8048-1627-1*) C E Tuttle.

***Check Processing Operations: A Hands-on-Guide to Developing & Managing a State-of-the-Art Check Processing Operation.** Louis L. Barton. 250p. 1994. 60. 00 (*1-55738-735-4*) Probus Pub Co.

Check Sample Stack: Cytopathology. Ed. by James Linder. 1992. disk 200.00 (*0-89189-323-7*, D69-3-002-33) Am Soc Clinical.

Check Six. Frederick C. Blesse. 178p. 1987. 17.95 (*0-912173-15-7*) Champlin Museum.

Check the Oil: Gas Station Collectibles with Prices. Scott Anderson. LC 84-52521. 200p. (Orig.). 1986. pap. 18.95 (*0-87069-446-4*, Wallace-Hmestead) Chilton.

Check This Out: Library Program Models. (Library Science Ser.). 1991. lib. bdg. 75.00 (*0-8490-4332-8*) Gordon Pr.

Check Up: A Guide to Quality Control. Don Aslett. (Illus.). 33p. (Orig.). 1985. pap. 10.00 (*0-318-19117-2*) Article One.

***Check Your Christian Knowledge.** Abingdon Staff. 1994. pap. 5.95 (*0-687-85122-X*) Abingdon.

Check Your IQ. Ken Russell & Philip Carter. (Illus.). 175p. (Orig.). 1992. pap. 11.95x (*0-572-01807-X*, Pub. by W Foulsham UK) Trans-Atl Phila.

Check Your Morality. Knofel Staton. 144p. (Orig.). (C). 1989. reprint ed. pap. 5.99 (*0-89900-346-X*) College Pr Pub.

Check Your Neck: More of "You Might Be a Redneck If..." Jeff Foxworthy. LC 92-71790. (Illus.). 80p. 1992. pap. 5.95 (*1-56352-048-6*) Longstreet Pr Inc.

Check Your Own IQ. Hans J. Eysenck. (Illus.). (Orig.). 1962. pap. 3.95 (*0-14-020656-6*, Penguin Bks) Viking Penguin.

Check Your Panoply. Herman H. Rocke. 240p. 1977. pap. text ed. 6.00 (*0-910424-71-3*) Concordant.

Checkbook Management: A Guide to Saving Money. Eric Gelb. LC 93-74331. 96p. 1995. pap. 6.50 (*0-9631289-3-0*) Career Advan.

Checkbooks: Comprehension. Ed. by B. Deller & M. Taylor. (C). 1989. 25.00 (*0-09-149291-2*, Pub. by S Thornes Pubs UK) St Mut.

Checkbooks: Oral Work. R. Blatchford & M. Elphee. (C). 1989. 25.00 (*0-09-159521-5*, Pub. by S Thornes Pubs UK) St Mut.

Checkbooks: Writing. L. Cookson. (C). 1989. 35.00 (*0-09-154701-6*, Pub. by S Thornes Pubs UK) St Mut.

Checker Playing Hound Dog Tall Tales from a Southwestern Storyteller. Illus. by Lucy Jelinek. 80p. (Orig.). 1986. pap. 9.95 (*0-933553-04-8*) Mariposa Print Pub.

***"Checkerboard Method" A New Way to Estimate the Numbers of Undiscovered Hydrocarbon Accumulations in Sparsely Drilled Areas.** Richard G. Stanley. LC 95-2317. (Bulletins Ser.: Vol. 2120). 1995. write for info. (*0-615-00631-0*) US Geol Survey.

Checkerboard Press Kids' Science Dictionary. Q. L. Pearce. LC 88-71150. (Illus.). 124p. (J). (gr. 4-6). 1991. reprint ed. 12.95 (*1-56288-003-9*) Checkerboard.

Checkerboard Press Nature Encyclopedia. Donald M. Silver. LC 89-48801. (Illus.). 128p. (J). (gr. 3-7). 1990. 12.95 (*1-56288-001-2*) Checkerboard.

Checkerboard Square: Culture & Resistance in a Homeless Community. David Wagner. LC 93-3744. 200p. 1993. text ed. 58.00 (*0-8133-1585-9*) Westview.

Checkerboard Square: Culture & Resistance in a Homeless Community. David Wagner. LC 93-3744. 200p. (C). 1993. pap. text ed. 17.95 (*0-8133-1586-7*) Westview.

Checkered Beetles of Ohio (Coleoptera: Cleridae) Josef N. Knull. (Bulletin Ser.: No. 42). 1972. reprint ed. 5.00 (*0-86727-041-1*) Ohio Bio Survey.

Checkered Career of Tobias Lear. Ray Brighton. LC 84-18105. (Portsmouth Marine Society Ser.: No. 4). (Illus.). 320p. 1984. 20.00 (*0-915819-03-1*) Portsmouth Marine Soc.

Checkered Demon Anthology. S. Clay Wilson. 1995. 16.95 (*0-86719-384-0*) Last Gasp.

Checkered Flag: Hundred Years of Auto Racing. Ivan Rendall. 1993. 34.98 (*1-55521-961-6*) Bk Sales Inc.

Checkered Flag! The History of the Racing Car. David Jefferis & Peter Lafferty. LC 90-32128. (Wheels Ser.). (Illus.). 32p. (J). (gr. 5-8). 1991. lib. bdg. 13.23 (*0-531-14122-5*) Watts.

Checkered Past: My Twenty Years As Indy 500 Chief Steward. Tom Binford & Florrie B. Kichler. LC 93-90170. (Illus.). 144p. (Orig.). 1993. pap. 14.95 (*1-882859-01-4*) Crnerstone Pr.

Checkered Years: A Bonanza Farm Diary, 1884-88. Mary D. Woodward. Ed. by Mary B. Cowdry. LC 89-30974. xxxvii, 265p. 1989. reprint ed. pap. 8.95 (*0-87351-237-5*, Borealis Book) Minn Hist.

Checkering & Carving of Gunstocks. rev. ed. Monty Kennedy. (Illus.). 352p. 1952. 37.95 (*0-8117-0630-3*) Stackpole.

***Checkertails: The 325th Fighter Group in WW II.** Ernest R. McDowell. (Groups - Squadrons Ser.). (Illus.). 80p. 1994. pap. 10.95 (*0-89747-316-7*) Squad Sig Pubns.

Checkfire! William P. Mack. LC 92-50363. 1992. 22.95 (*1-877853-17-8*) Nautical & Aviation.

Checking Accounts see Getting Ready for Pay Day

Checking & Coordinating Architectural & Engineering Working Drawings. F. Duggar, III. 1984. text ed. 44.00 (*0-07-018023-7*) McGraw.

Checking C Programs with Lint. Ian F. Darwin. (Nutshell Handbook Ser.). 84p. (Orig.). 1988. pap. 12.95 (*0-937175-30-7*) OReilly & Assocs.

Checking Guide for the I. D. 1991. lib. bdg. 76.95 (*0-8490-4776-5*) Gordon Pr.

Checking In. Suzanne Weyn. LC 89-49703. (Sitting Pretty Ser.). 128p. (J). (gr. 4-8). 1991. lib. bdg. 9.89 (*0-8167-2003-7*); pap. text ed. 2.95 (*0-8167-2004-5*) Troll Assocs.

Checking on the Moon. Jenny Davis. (YA). 1993. pap. 3.50 (*0-440-21491-2*) Dell.

Checking on the Moon. Jenny Davis. LC 91-8284. 224p. (YA). (gr. 6 up). 1991. 15.95 (*0-531-05960-X*); 15.99 (*0-531-08560-0*) Orchard Bks Watts.

Checking Out. Marilyn Kaye. (Video High Ser.: No. 6). 224p. 1994. mass mkt. 3.50 (*0-8217-4790-8*) Zebra.

***Checking Your Church's Pulse.** Ed. by Joani Schultz. (Projects with a Purpose for Youth Ministry Ser.). 47p. 1994. pap. 9.99 (*1-55945-408-3*) Group Pub.

Checking Your Grammar. Marvin Terban. (YA). 1994. pap. 4.95 (*0-590-49455-4*) Scholastic Inc.

Checklist, Vol. 1, Pt. 2. Ed. by J. B. Heppner & H. Inoue. (Lepidoptera of Taiwan Ser.). 276p. (Orig.). 1992. pap. text ed. 29.95 (*0-945417-77-2*) Sci Pubs.

Checklist Pt. 2: Pyraloidea-Tortricoidea, Pt. 2. Ed. by J. B. Heppner. (Atlas of Neotropical Lepidoptera: No. 3). 236p. (Orig.). 1995. pap. text ed. 27.95x (*0-945417-26-8*) Sci Pubs.

Checklist for a Perfect Wedding. 5th ed. Barbara L. Follett. LC 92-16502. 1986. 4.95 (*0-385-46815-6*) Doubleday.

***Checklist for Change: A Pragmatic Approach to Creating & Controlling Change.** Thomas R. Hardy. LC 95-60681. 190p. 1995. text ed. 29.00 (*1-56676-281-2*) Technomic.

***Checklist for Leaders.** Gabriel Hevesi. (Management Master Ser.). (Illus.). 50p. 1995. 15.95 (*1-56327-100-1*) Prod Press.

Checklist for Technical Skills & Other Training. Ed. by William Garry et al. (Illus.). 94p. 7.75 (*0-318-13266-4*); pap. 10.00 (*0-318-13265-6*, GACTP) Am Soc Train & Devel.

***Checklist for the Future of Intelligence.** John H. Hedley. (ISD Occasional Papers). 50p. (Orig.). (C). 1995. pap. text ed. 5.00 (*0-934742-79-0*) Geo U Inst Dplmcy.

Checklist for the Structural Survey of Period Timber Framed Buildings. David Swindells & Malcolm Hutchins. 86p. 1993. 80.00 (*0-85406-543-1*, Pub. by R-I-C-S Bks UK) St Mut.

Checklist for Use in Juvenile Delinquency Proceedings. LC 85-72728. 52p. 1986. pap. 6.50 (*0-89707-197-2*, 509-0021-01) Amer Bar Assn.

Checklist for Your New Baby. Dylan Landis. 112p. (Orig.). 1993. pap. 3.99 (*0-425-13679-5*) Berkley Pub.

Checklist for Your New Baby: The Indispensable Guide to What to Buy Before Your Baby Arrives. Dylan Landis. 96p. 1991. pap. 5.95 (*0-399-51657-3*, Perigee Bks) Berkley Pub.

Checklist-Guide for Assessing Data Processing Safeguards. Phillip G. Elam. LC 82-22320. 64p. 1983. pap. 5.00 (*0-87576-101-1*) Pilot Bks.

Checklist-Guide to Selecting a Small Computer. Wilma E. Bennett. LC 80-13996. 32p. 1980. pap. 5.00 (*0-87576-091-0*) Pilot Bks.

Checklist-Guide to Successful Acquisitions. rev. ed. Victor Harold. LC 77-180209. 45p. 1987. pap. 5.00 (*0-87576-039-2*) Pilot Bks.

Checklist Management: The Eight-Hour Manager. Jeff Davidson. (Illus.). 150p. (Orig.). 1986. 19.95 (*0-915765-26-8*) Natl Pr Bks.

Checklist of American Coverlet Weavers. Ed. by John Heisey et al. LC 77-15968. (Illus.). 149p. 1980. reprint ed. 25.00 (*0-87935-048-2*) U Pr of Va.

Checklist of American Imprints, Eighteen Twenty to Eighteen Twenty-Nine: Title Index. M. Frances Cooper. (Checklist of American Imprints Ser.). 1972. 42. 50 (*0-8108-0513-8*) Scarecrow.

Checklist of American Imprints for 1833: Items 17208-22795. Comp. by Scott Bruntjen & Carol R. Bruntjen. LC 64-11784. (Checklist of American Imprints Ser.: Vol. 1833). 482p. 1979. lib. bdg. 45.00 (*0-8108-1191-X*) Scarecrow.

Checklist of American Imprints for 1834: Items 22796-29893. Carol Rinderknecht & Scott Bruntjen. LC 64-11784. 646p. 1982. reprint ed. 45.00 (*0-8108-1487-0*) Scarecrow.

Checklist of American Imprints for 1835: Items 29894-35601. Comp. by Carol Rinderknecht. LC 64-11784. 547p. 1985. 47.50 (*0-8108-1828-0*) Scarecrow.

Checklist of American Imprints for 1836: Items 35602-42652. Comp. by Carol Rinderknecht. LC 64-11784. 617p. 1986. 55.00 (*0-8108-1839-6*) Scarecrow.

Checklist of American Imprints for 1837: Items 42653-48672. Comp. by Carol Rinderknecht. LC 64-11784. 514p. 1986. 45.00 (*0-8108-1841-8*) Scarecrow.

Checklist of American Imprints for 1838: Items 48673-53805. Comp. by Carol Rinderknecht. LC 64-11784. 261p. 1988. 39.50 (*0-8108-2123-0*) Scarecrow.

Checklist of American Imprints for 1839: Items 53806-59415. Carol Rinderknecht. LC 64-11784. 291p. 1988. 42.50 (*0-8108-2124-9*) Scarecrow.

Checklist of American Imprints for 1840: Items 40-1 - 40-7198. Ed. by Scott Bruntjen. LC 64-11784. 566p. 1990. 65.00 (*0-8108-2376-4*) Scarecrow.

Checklist of American Imprints for 1841: Items 41-1 to 41-5692. Ed. by Scott Bruntjen. LC 64-11784. 471p. 1990. 55.00 (*0-8108-2377-2*) Scarecrow.

Checklist of American Imprints for 1842: Items 42-1 - 42-5379. Ed. by Carol Rinderknecht & Scott Bruntjev. LC 64-11784. 428p. 1992. 52.50 (*0-8108-2533-3*) Scarecrow.

Checklist of American Imprints for 1844: Items 44-1 - 44-6827. Carol Rinderknecht & Scott Bruntjen. LC 64-11784. 524p. 1993. 62.50 (*0-8108-2654-2*) Scarecrow.

Checklist of American Imprints, 1830-1839: Author Index. Comp. by Carol Rinderknecht. LC 64-11784. 177p. 1989. 29.50 (*0-8108-2252-0*) Scarecrow.

Checklist of American Imprints, 1830-1839, Title Index, 2 vols. Carol Rinderknecht. LC 64-11784. 830p. 1989. Vol. I, A-L, Vol. II, M-Z. 87.50 (*0-8108-2208-3*) Scarecrow.

Checklist of American Imprints 1843: Items 43-1 - 43-5454. Ed. by Carol Rinderknecht & Scott Bruntjeu. LC 64-11784. 500p. 1992. 52.50 (*0-8108-2653-4*) Scarecrow.

Checklist of American Newspaper Carriers' Addresses, 1720-1820. Gerald D. McDonald et al. (Illus.). 248p. 1990. 30.00 (*0-944026-16-8*) Am Antiquarian.

Checklist of American Paintings at Yale University. Theodore Stebbins, Jr. & Galina Gorokhoff. LC 82-60116. (Illus.). 213p. (Orig.). 1982. pap. 20.00 (*0-89467-019-0*) Yale Art Gallery.

Checklist of American Sculpture at Yale University. Ed. by Robin J. Frank. LC 92-19928. (Illus.). 220p. 1992. pap. 35.00 (*0-89467-058-1*) Yale Art Gallery.

Checklist of Anne Rice. C. P. Stephens. 1992. pap. 3.95 (*0-89366-216-X*) Ultramarine Pub.

Checklist of Anne Rice. Christopher P. Stephens. (Ultramarine Checklists Ser.). 11p. (C). 1991. reprint ed. lib. bdg. 17.00x (*0-8095-5707-X*) Borgo Pr.

Checklist of Arthur Upfield. C. P. Stephens. 1992. pap. 3.95 (*0-89366-135-X*) Ultramarine Pub.

Checklist of Arthur Upfield. Christopher P. Stephens. (Ultramarine Checklists Ser.). 18p. (C). 1991. reprint ed. lib. bdg. 17.00x (*0-8095-5711-8*) Borgo Pr.

Checklist of Bibliographies Appearing in the Bulletin of Bibliography, 1897-1987. Naomi Caldwell-Wood & Patrick W. Wood. 200p. 1989. text ed. 79.50 (*0-313-27668-4*) Greenwood.

Checklist of Birds of the World: Sylviidae, Muscicapidae (sensu stricto), Maluridae, Acanthizidae, Monarchidae, Eopsaltriidae, Platysteiridae, Vol. 11. xii, 638p. 1986. 75.00 (*0-910999-11-2*) Mus Comp Zoo.

Checklist of Birds of the World, Vol. 1: Struthioniformes, Tinamiformes, Procellariiformes, Sphenisciformes, Gaviiformes, Podicipediformes, Pelecaniformes, Ciconiiformes, Phoenicopteriformes, Falconiformes, Anseriformes. xviii, 547p. 1979. 50.00 (*0-910999-01-5*) Mus Comp Zoo.

Checklist of Birds of the World, Vol. 10: Prunellidae, Turdinae, Orthonychinae, Timaliinae, Panurinae, Picathartinae, Polioptilinae. xii, 502p. 1964. 35.00 (*0-910999-10-4*) Mus Comp Zoo.

Checklist of Birds of the World, Vol. 12: Pachycephalinae, Aegithalidae, Remizidae, Paridae, Sittidae, Certhiidae, Rhabdornithidae, Climacteridae, Dicaeidae, Nectariniidae, Zosteropidae, Meliphagidae. xii, 495p. 1967. 40.00 (*0-910999-12-0*) Mus Comp Zoo.

Checklist of Birds of the World, Vol. 13: Emberizinae, Catablyrhynchinae, Cardinalinae, Thraupinae, Tersininae. xvi, 443p. 1970. 40.00 (*0-910999-13-9*) Mus Comp Zoo.

Checklist of Birds of the World, Vol. 14: Parulidae, Drepanididae, Vireonidae, Icteridae, Fringillinae, Carduelinae, Estrildidae, Viduinae. xii, 443p. 1968. 40. 00 (*0-910999-14-7*) Mus Comp Zoo.

Checklist of Birds of the World, Vol. 15: Bubalornithinae, Passerinae, Ploceinae, Sturnidae, Oriolidae, Dicruridae, Callaeidae, Grallinidae, Artamidae, Cracticidae, Ptilonorhychidae, Paradisaeidae, Corvidae. xii, 315p. 1962. 35.00 (*0-910999-15-5*) Mus Comp Zoo.

CheckList of Birds of the World, Vol. 2: Galliformes, Gruiformes, Charadriiformes. x, 401p. 1934. 35.00 (*0-910999-02-3*) Mus Comp Zoo.

Checklist of Birds of the World, Vol. 4: Cuculiformes, Strigiformes, Caprimulgiformes, Apodes. xiv, 291p. 1940. 35.00 (*0-910999-04-X*) Mus Comp Zoo.

Checklist of Birds of the World, Vol. 5: Trochili, Coliiformes, Trogoniformes, Coraciiformes. xiv, 306p. 1945. 35.00 (*0-910999-05-8*) Mus Comp Zoo.

Checklist of Birds of the World, Vol 6: Piciformes. xiii, 259p. 1948. 35.00 (*0-910999-06-6*) Mus Comp Zoo.

Checklist of Birds of the World, Vol. 7: Eurylaimidae, Dendrocolaptidae, Furnariidae, Formicariidae, Conopophagidae, Rhinocryptidae. xii, 318p. 1951. 35.00 (*0-910999-07-4*) Mus Comp Zoo.

Checklist of Birds of the World, Vol. 8: Tyrannidae, Pipridae, Cotingidae, Oxyruncidae, Phytotomidae, Pittidae, Philepittidae, Acanthisittidae, Menuridae, & Atrichornithidae. xv, 365p. 1979. 45.00 (*0-910999-08-2*) Mus Comp Zoo.

Checklist of Birds of the World, Vol. 9: Alaudidae, Hirundinidae, Motacillidae, Campephagidae, Pycnonotidae Irenidae, Laniidae, Vangidae, Bombycillidae, Dulidae, Cinclidae, Troglodytidae, Mimdae. xii, 506p. 1960. 35.00 (*0-910999-09-0*) Mus Comp Zoo.

Checklist of Canadian Literature & Background Materials, 1628-1960, in Two Parts. 2nd enl. rev. ed. Reginald E. Watters. LC 72-80713. 1109p. reprint ed. pap. 180.00 (*0-8357-8065-1*, 2034029) Bks Demand.

An Asterisk (*) at the beginning of an entry indicates that the title is appearing in BIP for the first time.

Checklist of Corporate Operations & Management Performance: For Managers, Consultants, Lenders, Investors, Corporate Buyers-Sellers, Acquisition Specialists. Allan J. Siposs. 150p. (Orig.). (C). pap. 60.00 (*0-935402-21-7*) IBMI Tustin.

Checklist of David Goodis. C. P. Stephens. 1992. pap. 3.95 (*0-89366-233-X*) Ultramarine Pub.

Checklist of Dean Koontz. C. P. Stephens. 1992. pap. 3.95 (*0-89366-133-3*) Ultramarine Pub.

Checklist of Dean Koontz. Christopher P. Stephens. (Ultramarine Checklists Ser.). 22p. (C). 1991. reprint ed. lib. bdg. 17.00x (*0-8095-5719-3*) Borgo Pr.

Checklist of Donald Westlake. Christopher P. Stephens. (Ultramarine Checklists Ser.). 25p. (C). 1992. reprint ed. lib. bdg. 18.00x (*0-8095-5732-0*) Borgo Pr.

Checklist of E. A. Reproductions. W. Nutting. LC 73-96940. 1969. 4.95 (*0-87282-087-4*) Am Life Foun.

Checklist of Editions of Greek & Latin Papyri, Ostraca & Tablets. 4th ed. John F. Oates et al. LC 92-33810. (Bulletin of the American Society of Papyrologists Supplements Ser.: No. 7). 94p. 1992. 29.95 (*1-55540-782-X*, 31 11 07) Scholars Pr GA.

Checklist of Editions of Greek Papyri & Ostraca. John F. Oates et al. LC 85-2027. (Bulletin of the American Society of Papyrologists Supplements Ser.: No. 4). 74p. reprint ed. pap. 25.00 (*0-7837-5420-5*, 2045184) Bks Demand.

Checklist of Elmore Leonard. C. P. Stephens. 1992. pap. 3.95 (*0-89366-215-1*) Ultramarine Pub.

Checklist of Elmore Leonard. Christopher P. Stephens. (Ultramarine Checklists Ser.). 15p. (C). 1991. reprint ed. lib. bdg. 17.00x (*0-8095-5703-7*) Borgo Pr.

Checklist of Fantastic Literature in Paperbound Books. Ed. by Bradford M. Day. LC 74-15961. (Science Fiction Ser.). 128p. 1977. reprint ed. 15.95 (*0-405-06326-1*) Ayer.

Checklist of Federal Revised Laws: A Bibliography of Current Editions. Comp. by Carol J. Gray. (Washington University Law Library Bibliography Ser.: No. 5). iii, 54p. (Orig.). 1984. pap. text ed. 8.00 (*0-318-11694-4*) Wash U Law Lib.

Checklist of First Days & Earliest Documented Covers (1847-1931) Edward J. Siskin. 50p. (Orig.). 1991. pap. 12.95 (*1-879390-03-5*) Am First Day.

Checklist of Four-Shape Shape-Note Tunebooks. Intro. by Richard J. Stanislaw. LC 78-61291. (I.S.A.M. Monographs: No. 10). 61p. 1978. pap. 8.00 (*0-914678-10-8*) Inst Am Music.

Checklist of Fredric Brown. C. P. Stephens. 82p. 1992. pap. 12.95 (*0-89366-225-9*) Ultramarine Pub.

Checklist of Fredric Brown. Christopher P. Stephens. (Ultramarine Checklists Ser.). 32p. (C). 1992. reprint ed. lib. bdg. 18.00x (*0-8095-5733-9*) Borgo Pr.

Checklist of French Political Pamphlets, 1560-1644. Ed. by Doris V. Welsh. 204p. 1950. pap. 5.00 (*0-911028-04-8*) Newberry.

Checklist of Fuchsias Registered 1973-1983. Ed. by American Fuchsia Society Staff. (Illus.). 91p. 1983. 1.00 (*0-9613167-0-5*) Am Fuchsia.

Checklist of Gene Wolfe. C. P. Stephens. 1992. pap. 7.95 (*0-89366-181-3*) Ultramarine Pub.

Checklist of Gene Wolfe. Christopher P. Stephens. (Ultramarine Checklists Ser.). 40p. (C). 1991. reprint ed. lib. bdg. 20.00 (*0-8095-5728-2*) Borgo Pr.

Checklist of Harry Whittington. C. P. Stephens. 1992. pap. 6.95 (*0-89366-235-6*) Ultramarine Pub.

Checklist of Hemiptera (Excepting the Aphididae, Aleurodidae & Coccidae) of America, North of Mexico. E. P. Van Duzee. 1916. pap. 12.50 (*0-934454-23-X*) Lubrecht & Cramer.

Checklist of Holdings on Borneo in the Cornell University Libraries. Michael Leigh. LC 67-63728. (Cornell University, Southeast Asia Program, Data Paper Ser.: No. 62). 78p. reprint ed. pap. 25.00 (*0-317-29895-X*, 2021840) Bks Demand.

Checklist of Indonesian Serials in the Cornell University Library (1945-1970) Yvonne Thung & John M. Echols. LC 73-160795. (Cornell University, Southeast Asia Program, Data Paper Ser.: No. 89). 231p. reprint ed. pap. 65.90 (*0-8357-3678-4*, 2036402) Bks Demand.

Checklist of James P. Blaylock. C. P. Stephens. 1992. pap. 3.95 (*0-89366-199-6*) Ultramarine Pub.

Checklist of James P. Blaylock. Christopher P. Stephens. (Ultramarine Checklists Ser.). 17p. (C). 1991. reprint ed. lib. bdg. 17.00x (*0-8095-5714-2*) Borgo Pr.

Checklist of Jim Thompson. C. P. Stephens. 1992. pap. 3.95 (*0-89366-197-X*) Ultramarine Pub.

Checklist of Jim Thompson. Christopher P. Stephens. (Ultramarine Checklists Ser.). 14p. (C). 1991. reprint ed. lib. bdg. 17.00x (*0-8095-5709-6*) Borgo Pr.

Checklist of Joe Lansdale. Steve Hankow. 1992. pap. 3.95 (*0-89366-208-9*) Ultramarine Pub.

Checklist of John Sladek. C. P. Stephens. 1992. pap. 6.95 (*0-89366-219-4*) Ultramarine Pub.

Checklist of John Sladek. Christopher P. Stephens. (Ultramarine Checklists Ser.). 31p. (C). 1992. reprint ed. lib. bdg. 20.00 (*0-8095-5734-7*) Borgo Pr.

Checklist of K. W. Jeter. Christopher P. Stephens. (Ultramarine Checklists Ser.). 13p. (C). 1991. reprint ed. lib. bdg. 17.00x (*0-8095-5718-5*) Borgo Pr.

Checklist of Kim Stanley Robinson. C. P. Stephens & Tom Joyce. 1992. pap. 4.95 (*0-89366-204-6*) Ultramarine Pub.

Checklist of Kim Stanley Robinson. Christopher P. Stephens & Tom Joyce. (Ultramarine Checklists Ser.). 28p. (C). 1991. reprint ed. lib. bdg. 18.00x (*0-8095-5723-1*) Borgo Pr.

Checklist of Loren D. Estleman. C. P. Stephens. 1992. pap. 3.95 (*0-89366-176-7*) Ultramarine Pub.

Checklist of Loren D. Estleman. Christopher P. Stephens. (Ultramarine Checklists Ser.). 15p. (C). 1993. reprint ed. lib. bdg. 17.00x (*0-8095-5702-9*) Borgo Pr.

Checklist of Louis L'Amour. C. P. Stephens. 1992. pap. 7.95 (*0-89366-223-2*) Ultramarine Pub.

Checklist of Lucius Shepard. C. P. Stephens & Tom Joyce. 1992. pap. 3.95 (*0-89366-203-8*) Ultramarine Pub.

Checklist of Lucius Shepard. Christopher P. Stephens & Tom Joyce. (Ultramarine Checklists Ser.). 18p. (C). 1991. reprint ed. lib. bdg. 17.00x (*0-8095-5725-8*) Borgo Pr.

Checklist of Melville Reviews. Ed. by Hershel Parker & Kevin Hayes. 157p. 1992. 34.95 (*0-8101-1028-8*) Northwestern U Pr.

Checklist of Monographs & Periodicals on the Japanese Colonial Empire. Michiko Kiyohara. LC 80-84459. (Special Project Ser.: No. 28). 352p. 1981. pap. 11.95 (*0-8179-4284-X*) Hoover Inst Pr.

Checklist of Morrigan Press & Kerosina Press. Christopher P. Stephens. (Ultramarine Checklists Ser.). 19p. (C). 1991. reprint ed. lib. bdg. 17.00x (*0-8095-5720-7*) Borgo Pr.

Checklist of New Jersey Imprints. 1972. reprint ed. pap. 16.00 (*0-685-02851-8*) Periodicals Srv.

Checklist of New London, Connecticut, Imprints, 1709-1800. Hazel A. Johnson. 492p. 1978. 25.00 (*0-914930-06-0*) Biblio Soc Am.

Checklist of New Plays & Entertainments on the London Stage, 1700-1737. William J. Burling. LC 90-56230. 240p. 1993. 35.00 (*0-8386-3451-6*) Fairleigh Dickinson.

Checklist of New York State Plants. Richard S. Mitchell. (Bulletin Ser.: No. 458). 272p. 1986. 12.50 (*1-55557-004-6*) NYS Museum.

Checklist of North American Birds. 5th ed. 691p. 15.00 (*0-318-12914-0*) Am Ornithologists.

Checklist of North American Butterflies. T. C. Emmel & J. B. Heppner. (Atlas of North American Lepidoptera Ser.). 1995. 18.95 (*0-945417-24-1*) Sci Pubs.

Checklist of North American Plants for Wildlife Biologists. Clinton H. Wasser. Ed. by Thomas G. Scott. LC 79-89208. 58p. (Orig.). (C). 1980. pap. 6.00 (*0-933564-07-4*) Wildlife Soc.

Checklist of Ontario Freshwater Fishes: Annotated with Distribution Maps. Nicholas E. Mandrak & E. J. Crossman. (Illus.). 1994. pap. 15.95 (*0-88854-402-2*, Pub. by Royal Ont Mus CN) U of Toronto Pr.

Checklist of Ostracoda from Japan & Its Adjacent Seas. Ed. by Tetsuro Hanai et al. 119p. 1977. 34.50 (*0-86008-180-X*, Pub. by U of Tokyo JA) Col U Pr.

Checklist of Ostracoda from Southeast Asia. Ed. by Tetsuro Hanai et al. 236p. 1981. 49.50 (*0-86008-267-9*, Pub. by U of Tokyo JA) Col U Pr.

Checklist of P. C. Wren. C. P. Stephens. 1992. pap. 3.95 (*0-89366-178-3*) Ultramarine Pub.

***Checklist of Painters c. 1200-1994 Represented in the Witt Library, Courtauld Institute of Art, London.** 2nd ed. LC 95-9819. 1995. write for info. (*1-884964-37-0*) Fitzroy Dearborn.

Checklist of Painters from c.1200. Witt Library, Courtauld Institute of Art Staff. 512p. 1995. 120.00 (*0-7201-2178-7*) Cassell.

***Checklist of Painters from 1200 to the Present.** 2nd ed. Witt Library of the Courtauld Institute Staff. 600p. 1995. lib. bdg. 95.00 (*0-614-06189-X*) Fitzroy Dearborn.

Checklist of Paul West. C. P. Stephens. 1992. pap. 3.95 (*0-89366-238-0*) Ultramarine Pub.

Checklist of Percival Charles Wren. Christopher P. Stephens. (Ultramarine Checklists Ser.). 18p. (C). 1991. reprint ed. lib. bdg. 17.00x (*0-8095-5713-4*) Borgo Pr.

Checklist of Phantasia Press. C. P. Stephens. 1992. pap. 3.95 (*0-89366-201-1*) Ultramarine Pub.

Checklist of Phantasia Press. Christopher P. Stephens. (Ultramarine Checklists Ser.). 19p. (C). 1991. reprint ed. lib. bdg. 17.00x (*0-8095-5721-5*) Borgo Pr.

Checklist of Philip K. Dick. C. P. Stephens. 48p. 1992. pap. 7.95 (*0-89366-174-0*) Ultramarine Pub.

Checklist of Philip K. Dick. Christopher P. Stephens. (Ultramarine Checklists Ser.). 47p. (C). 1991. reprint ed. lib. bdg. 20.00 (*0-8095-5716-9*) Borgo Pr.

Checklist of Philippine Linguistics in the Newberry Library. Ed. by Doris V. Welsh. 176p. 1950. pap. 5.00 (*0-911028-05-6*) Newberry.

Checklist of Popular Islamic Coins. Stephen Album. 1993. pap. 8.00 (*0-9636024-0-3*) S Album.

Checklist of Printed Maps of the Middle West to 1900: Subject, Author & Title Index, Vol. 14. Ed. by R. W. Karrow. 303p. 1983. 45.00 (*0-318-37704-7*) Newberry.

Checklist of Professional Schools in Canada. Catherine Purcell. 300p. (C). 1993. pap. text ed. 28.00 (*1-55022-194-9*, Pub. by ECW Press CN) Genl Dist Srvs.

Checklist of Publications of Harrison of Paris & Monroe Wheeler. Christopher P. Stephens. (Ultramarine Checklists Ser.). 16p. (C). 1991. reprint ed. lib. bdg. 17.00 (*0-685-67892-X*) Borgo Pr.

Checklist of Robertson Davies. C. P. Stephens. 1992. pap. 3.95 (*0-89366-179-1*) Ultramarine Pub.

Checklist of Robertson Davies. Christopher P. Stephens. (Ultramarine Checklists Ser.). 16p. (C). 1991. reprint ed. lib. bdg. 17.00x (*0-8095-5700-2*) Borgo Pr.

Checklist of Roger Zelazny. C. P. Stephens. 1992. pap. 3.95 (*0-89366-166-X*) Ultramarine Pub.

Checklist of Roger Zelazny. Christopher P. Stephens. (Ultramarine Checklists Ser.). 44p. (C). 1991. reprint ed. lib. bdg. 20.00 (*0-8095-5729-0*) Borgo Pr.

Checklist of Ross Thomas. C. P. Stephens. 1992. pap. 3.95 (*0-89366-228-3*) Ultramarine Pub.

Checklist of Samuel R. Delany. C. P. Stephens. 1992. pap. 3.95 (*0-89366-184-8*) Ultramarine Pub.

Checklist of Samuel R. Delany. Christopher P. Stephens. (Ultramarine Checklists Ser.). 18p. (C). 1991. reprint ed. lib. bdg. 17.00x (*0-8095-5715-0*) Borgo Pr.

Checklist of Science-Fiction Anthologies. W. R. Cole. LC 74-15956. (Science Fiction Ser.). (Illus.). 390p. 1977. reprint ed. 30.95 (*0-405-06323-7*) Ayer.

Checklist of Standard Sets. C. P. Stephens. 48p. 1992. pap. 6.95 (*0-89366-209-7*) Ultramarine Pub.

Checklist of Standard Sets. Christopher P. Stephens. (Ultramarine Checklists Ser.). 56p. (C). 1991. reprint ed. lib. bdg. 20.00 (*0-8095-5708-8*) Borgo Pr.

Checklist of State Bar Publications. Eleanor DeLashmitt. (Legal Bibliography Ser.: No. 28). 82p. (Orig.). 1985. pap. 30.00 (*0-935630-11-2*) U of Tex Tarlton Law Lib.

Checklist of Stone House Press Books & Ephemera: 1978-1988. limited ed. Ed. by Catherine T. Brody. (Illus.). 96p. (C). 1989. 75.00 (*0-937035-13-0*) Stone Hse NY.

Checklist of the Amphibians & Reptiles of Connecticut: With Notes on Uncommon Species. Michael W. Klemens. (Bulletin Ser.: No. 14). (Illus.). 24p. (Orig.). 1991. pap. 6.00 (*0-942085-01-9*) DEP Nat Resc Ctr.

Checklist of the Birds of Belize. D. Scott Wood et al. (Special Publication CMNH Ser.: No. 12). 24p. (Orig.). 1986. pap. 3.00 (*0-911239-31-6*) Carnegie Mus.

Checklist of the Birds of Brooks County, Texas. A. W. O'Neil & Paul C. Palmer. 6p. (Orig.). 1988. pap. 0.50 (*0-9611604-4-6*) C Del Grullo.

Checklist of the Birds of South America. 2nd rev. ed. Allen Altman & Byron Swift. LC 89-90962. 85p. 1989. pap. 6.50 (*0-9622559-1-2*) A Altman & B Swift.

Checklist of the Birds of South America. 3rd rev. ed. Allen Altman & Byron Swift. LC 89-90962. 84p. 1993. pap. 6.50 (*0-9622559-2-0*) A Altman & B Swift.

Checklist of the Boni Books. C. P. Stephens. 1992. pap. 3.95 (*0-89366-240-2*) Ultramarine Pub.

***Checklist of the Cerambycidae & Disteniidae (Coleoptera) of the Western Hemisphere.** Miguel A. Monne & Edmund F. Giesbert. (C). 1994. write for info. (*0-614-01928-1*); lib. bdg. 74.60 (*1-885850-00-X*) Wolfsgarden.

Checklist of the Coleopterous Insects of Mexico, Central America, the West Indies, & South America, Pts. 1-6. Richard E. Blackwelder. LC 81-607585. 1492p. 1982. text ed. 49.00 (*0-87474-244-7*, BLCI) Smithsonian.

Checklist of the Hogarth Press, Nineteen Seventeen to Nineteen Forty-Six. rev. ed. J. Howard Woolmer. LC 86-50251. (Illus.). 288p. 1986. 45.00 (*0-913506-17-6*) Woolmer-Brotherson.

Checklist of the Issues of the Press of New Jersey, 1723-1800. W. Nelson. 1969. 5.00 (*0-87556-223-X*) Saifer.

Checklist of the Lepiotaceous Fungi with Information on Its Synonymy, Distribution, Edibility, & Bibliography. Gaston Guzman & Laura Guzman-Davalos. (Illus.). 220p. 1992. 49.95 (*1-878762-05-2*, 047489) Koeltz Sci Bks.

Checklist of the Letters of Richard Aldington. Norman Gates. LC 76-21638. 186p. 1977. 9.85 (*0-8093-0781-2*) S Ill U Pr.

Checklist of the Newberry Library's Printed Books in Science, Medicine, Technology, & the Pseudosciences. Jean S. Gottlieb. LC 92-17941. (Illus.). 328p. 1992. 67.00 (*0-8240-5171-8*, H01195) Garland.

Checklist of the Non-Italian Humanists, 1300-1800. Comp. by Mario E. Cosenza. 1970. lib. bdg. 85.00 (*0-8161-0839-0*, Hall Library) G K Hall.

Checklist of the Publications of Dennis McMillan. C. P. Stephens. 1992. pap. 3.95 (*0-89366-202-X*) Ultramarine Pub.

Checklist of the Publications of Dennis McMillan. Christopher P. Stephens. (Ultramarine Checklists Ser.). 19p. (C). 1991. reprint ed. lib. bdg. 17.00x (*0-8095-5705-3*) Borgo Pr.

Checklist of the Publications of Harrison of Paris & Monroe Wheeler. C. P. Stephens. 1992. pap. 3.95 (*0-89366-175-9*) Ultramarine Pub.

Checklist of the Robert A Feer Collection of World Fairs of North America. Comp. by Earl R. Taylor. pap. 3.00 (*0-89073-045-8*) Boston Public Lib.

Checklist of the Tor Doubles. Christopher P. Stephens. (Ultramarine Checklists Ser.). 18p. (C). 1991. reprint ed. lib. bdg. 17.00x (*0-8095-5726-6*) Borgo Pr.

Checklist of the World, Vol. 16: Comprehensive Index. xii, 550p. 1987. 75.00 (*0-910999-16-3*) Mus Comp Zoo.

Checklist of Thomas M. Disch. C. P. Stephens. 1992. pap. 3.95 (*0-89366-136-8*) Ultramarine Pub.

Checklist of Thomas M. Disch. Christopher P. Stephens. (Ultramarine Checklists Ser.). 22p. (C). 1991. reprint ed. lib. bdg. 17.00x (*0-8095-5717-7*) Borgo Pr.

Checklist of Tim Powers. C. P. Stephens & Tom Joyce. 1992. pap. 3.95 (*0-89366-198-8*) Ultramarine Pub.

Checklist of Tim Powers. Christopher P. Stephens & Tom Joyce. (Ultramarine Checklists Ser.). 15p. (C). 1991. reprint ed. lib. bdg. 17.00x (*0-8095-5722-3*) Borgo Pr.

Checklist of Ultramarine Press. C. P. Stephens. 1992. pap. 3.95 (*0-89366-180-5*) Ultramarine Pub.

Checklist of Ultramarine Press. Christopher P. Stephens. (Ultramarine Checklists Ser.). 18p. (C). 1991. reprint ed. lib. bdg. 17.00x (*0-8095-5710-X*) Borgo Pr.

Checklist of Vietnam War Literature. C. P. Stephens. 150p. 1992. pap. 19.95 (*0-89366-177-5*) Ultramarine Pub.

Checklist of Vietnam War Literature. Christopher P. Stephens. (Ultramarine Checklists Ser.). 158p. (C). 1991. reprint ed. lib. bdg. 41.00x (*0-8095-5712-6*) Borgo Pr.

Checklist of West Indian Amphibians & Reptiles. Albert Schwartz et al. LC 75-326719. (Special Publication CMNH Ser.: No. 1, 5). (Illus.). 216p. 1975. pap. 10.50 (*0-911239-06-5*) Carnegie Mus.

Checklist of Wilson Tucker. Christopher P. Stephens. (Ultramarine Checklists Ser.). 18p. (C). 1991. reprint ed. lib. bdg. 17.00x (*0-8095-5706-1*) Borgo Pr.

Checklist of Women Writers, 1801-1900: Fiction, Verse, Drama. R. C. Alston. 530p. 1991. text ed. 65.00 (*0-8161-7295-1*, Hall Reference) Macmillan.

Checklist of Works of British Authors Printed Abroad in Languages Other than English to 1641. M. A. Shaaber. 168p. 1975. 15.00 (*0-914930-05-2*) Biblio Soc Am.

Checklist of Writings About Edwin Muir. Peter C. Hoy & Elgin W. Mellown. LC 70-150336. 1971. 7.50 (*0-87875-012-6*) Whitston Pub.

Checklist of Writings about John Dewey, 1887-1977. 2nd enl. ed. Ed. by Jo Ann Boydston & Kathleen Poulos. LC 77-17136. 488p. 1978. 19.95 (*0-8093-0842-8*) S Ill U Pr.

Checklist Supplement & Illustrative Financial Statements for Construction Contractors: August 1992 Edition. American Institute of Certified Public Accountants Staff. Ed. by Martin S. Safran. LC 91-656163. (Financial Accounting & Reporting Practice Aid Ser.). 40p. reprint ed. pap. 25.00 (*0-7837-6792-7*, 2046624) Bks Demand.

Checklist to ACC Clinical Nursing Skills. 3rd ed. Sandra S. Smith & Donna D. Duell. 240p. (C). 1992. pap. text ed. 13.00 (*0-8385-1364-6*, A1364-7) Appleton & Lange.

Checklist with Distribution Maps of the Turtles of the World. John B. Iverson. (Illus.). 287p. (Orig.). 1986. pap. 20.00 (*0-9617431-0-7*) J P Iverson.

Checklists & Guidelines for Reviewing Computer Security & Installations (Map-4) Updated & Complete Edition 1976. Ed. by J. F. Kuong. (Illus.). 1976. ring bd. 45.00 (*0-940706-02-4*, MAP-4) Management Advisory Pubns.

Checklists & Illustrative Financial Statements for Agricultural Cooperatives: March 1993 Edition. American Institute of Certified Public Accountants Staff. Ed. by Richard Rikert. LC 93-42103. (Financial Accounting & Reporting Practice Aid Ser.). 115p. reprint ed. pap. 32.80 (*0-7837-6793-5*, 2046625) Bks Demand.

Checklists & Illustrative Financial Statements for Banks. American Institute of Certified Public Accountants Staff. Ed. by Neil Selden. LC 91-660138. (Financial Accounting & Reporting Practice Aid Ser.). 102p. reprint ed. pap. 29.10 (*0-7837-5353-5*, 2045114) Bks Demand.

Checklists & Illustrative Financial Statements for Banks: October 1992 Edition. American Institute of Certified Public Accountants Staff. Ed. by Neil Selden. LC 91-660138. (Financial Accounting & Reporting Practice Aid Ser.). 116p. reprint ed. pap. 33.10 (*0-7837-6789-7*, 2046621) Bks Demand.

Checklists & Illustrative Financial Statements for Colleges & Universities: July 1991 Edition. American Institute of Certified Public Accountants Staff. LC 90-35497. (Financial Accounting & Reporting Practice Aid Ser.). 90p. reprint ed. pap. 25.70 (*0-7837-6640-8*, 2046247) Bks Demand.

Checklists & Illustrative Financial Statements for Common Interest Realty Associations: June 1992 Edition. American Institute of Certified Public Accountants Staff. Ed. by Gail K. Polin. LC 92-37455. (Financial Accounting & Reporting Practice Aid Ser.). 76p. reprint ed. pap. 25.00 (*0-7837-6794-3*, 2046626) Bks Demand.

Checklists & Illustrative Financial Statements for Corporations. 68p. 1993. pap. 25.00 (*0-685-34578-5*) Am Inst CPA.

Checklists & Illustrative Financial Statements for Corporations: Oct. 1991 Edition. American Institute of Certified Public Accountants Staff & Michael A. Tursi. LC 91-660069. (Financial Accounting & Reporting Practice Aid Ser.). 115p. reprint ed. pap. 32.80 (*0-7837-5496-5*, 2045161) Bks Demand.

Checklists & Illustrative Financial Statements for Corporations: October 1992 Edition. American Institute of Certified Public Accountants Staff. LC 91-660069. (Financial Accounting & Reporting Practice Aid Ser.). 121p. reprint ed. pap. 34.50 (*0-7837-6791-9*, 2046623) Bks Demand.

Checklists & Illustrative Financial Statements for Credit Unions: November 1992 Edition. American Institute of Certified Public Accountants Staff. Ed. by Arthur R. Kappel. LC 91-656164. (Financial Accounting & Reporting Practice Aid Ser.). 83p. reprint ed. pap. 25.00 (*0-7837-6790-0*, 2046622) Bks Demand.

Checklists & Illustrative Financial Statements for Credit Unions: September 1991 Edition. American Institute of Certified Public Accountants Staff. Ed. by Arthur R. Kappel. LC 91-656164. (Financial Accounting & Reporting Practice Aid Ser.). 63p. reprint ed. pap. 25.00 (*0-7837-5499-X*, 2045264) Bks Demand.

***Checklists & Illustrative Financial Statements for Defined Benefit Pension Plans, April 1992 Edition.** fac. ed. American Inst. of Certified Public Accountants Staff. Ed. by Arthur Kappel. (Financial Accounting & Reporting Practice Aid Ser.). 53p. 1992. reprint ed. pap. 25.00 (*0-7837-8218-7*, 2047977) Bks Demand.

***Checklists & Illustrative Financial Statements for Employee Health & Welfare Benefit Plans, May 1992 Edition.** American Institute of Certified Public Accountants Staff. LC 92-19067. (Financial Accounting & Reporting Practice Aid Ser.). 60p. 1993. pap. 25.00 (*0-7837-8537-2*, 2049351) Bks Demand.

Checklists & Illustrative Financial Statements for Finance Companies: November 1992 Edition. American Institute of Certified Public Accountants Staff. Ed. by Michael A. Tursi. LC 91-656162. (Financial Accounting & Reporting Practice Aid Ser.). 88p. reprint ed. pap. 25.10 (*0-7837-6787-0*, 2046619) Bks Demand.

Checklists & Illustrative Financial Statements for Finance Companies, January 1992. American Institute of Certified Public Accountants Staff. Ed. by Michael A. Tursi. LC 91-656162. (Financial Accounting & Reporting Practice Aid Ser.). 86p. reprint ed. pap. 25.00 (*0-7837-5351-9*, 2045112) Bks Demand.

C

An Asterisk (*) at the beginning of an entry indicates that the title is appearing in BIP for the first time. 1167

Checklists & Illustrative Financial Statements for Health Care Providers. American Institute of Certified Public Accountants Staff et al. LC 91-19501. (Financial Accounting & Reporting Practice Aid Ser.). 118p. reprint ed. pap. 33.70 (0-7837-6630-0, 2046218) Bks Demand.

Checklists & Illustrative Financial Statements for Health Care Providers: May 1993 Edition. American Institute of Certified Public Accountants Staff. Ed. by Martin S. Safran. LC 91-19501. (Financial Accounting & Reporting Practice Aid Ser.). 140p. reprint ed. pap. 39.90 (0-7837-6788-9, 2046620) Bks Demand.

***Checklists & Illustrative Financial Statements for Life Insurance Companies.** fac. ed. American Institute of Certified Public Accountants Staff. Ed. by Rosemary M. Reilly. LC 92-37178. (Financial Accounting & Reporting Practice Aid Ser.). 99p. 1992. pap. 28.30 (0-7837-8248-9, 2049011) Bks Demand.

Checklists & Illustrative Financial Statements for Life Insurance Companies: December 1992 Edition. American Institute of Certified Public Accountants Staff. Ed. by Steven Molitero. LC 92-37178. (Financial Accounting & Reporting Practice Aid Ser.). 113p. reprint ed. pap. 32.30 (0-7837-6786-2, 2046618) Bks Demand.

Checklists & Illustrative Financial Statements for Nonprofit Organizations: November 1990. American Institute of Certified Public Accountants Staff. LC 91-649899. (Financial Accounting & Reporting Practice Aid Ser.). (Illus.). 131p. reprint ed. pap. 37.40 (0-7837-4639-3, 2044363) Bks Demand.

***Checklists & Illustrative Financial Statements for Not-for-Profit Organizations, May 1993 Edition.** American Institute of Certified Public Accountants Staff. Ed. by Moshe S. Levitin. LC 91-649899. (Financial Accounting & Reporting Practice Aid Ser.). 126p. 1993. pap. 36.00 (0-7837-8479-1, 2049284) Bks Demand.

Checklists & Illustrative Financial Statements for Property & Liability Insurance Companies: April 1992 Edition. American Institute of Certified Public Accountants Staff. Ed. by Rosemary M. Reilly. LC 92-37374. (Financial Accounting & Reporting Practice Aid Ser.). 102p. reprint ed. pap. 29.10 (0-7837-5497-3, 2045262) Bks Demand.

Checklists & Illustrative Financial Statements for Savings Institutions: January 1993 Edition. American Institute of Certified Public Accountants Staff. Ed. by Neil Selden. LC 92-37422. (Financial Accounting & Reporting Practice Aid Ser.). 121p. reprint ed. pap. 34.50 (0-7837-6795-1, 2046627) Bks Demand.

Checklists & Illustrative Financial Statements for Savings Institutions: May 1992 Edition. American Institute of Certified Public Accountants Staff. Ed. by Neil Selden. LC 92-37422. (Financial Accounting & Reporting Practice Aid Ser.). 125p. reprint ed. pap. 35.70 (0-7837-5498-1, 2045263) Bks Demand.

Checklists & Illustrative Financial Statements for State & Local Governmental Units: April, 1992 Edition. American Institute of Certified Public Accountants Staff. Ed. by Susan Cornwall. LC 91-94264. (Financial Accounting & Reporting Practice Aid Ser.). 208p. reprint ed. pap. 59.30 (0-7837-6639-4, 2046246) Bks Demand.

***Checklists & Illustrative Financial Statements for State & Local Governmental Units, June 1993 Edition.** American Institute of Certified Public Accountants Staff. Ed. by Moshe Levitin. (Financial Accounting & Reporting Practice Aid Ser.). 165p. 1993. pap. 47.10 (0-7837-8478-3, 2049283) Bks Demand.

Checklists & Illustrative Financial Statements for Stock Life Insurance Companies: November 1990. American Institute of Certified Public Accountants Staff. (Financial Accounting & Reporting Practice Aid Ser.). (Illus.). 102p. reprint ed. pap. 29.10 (0-7837-4638-5, 2044362) Bks Demand.

***Checklists & Operating Forms for Small Businesses, 1995.** 19th ed. John C. Wisdom. 1995. pap. text ed. 95.00 (0-471-11558-4); pap. text ed. 95.00 (0-471-11562-2) Wiley.

Checklists for Corporate Counsel, No. 103. 500p. 1992. ring bd. 145.00 (0-929576-82-9) Busn Laws Inc.

***Checklists for Environmental Compliance.** 60p. 1994. 29.95 (0-934165-22-X) Gulf Pub.

Checklists for Preparing National Environmental Policy Act Documents. LC 87-81829. 68p. 1987. pap. 29.95 (0-89707-814-4, 535-0013) Amer Bar Assn.

Checklists for Print Media Advertising Planning & Buying. R. L. Ehler. LC 90-63638. (Print Media Advertising Ser.: Bk. 4). 57p. 1992. pap. text ed. 19.95 (1-879299-14-3) Richler.

Checklists for Public Library Managers. Jay Wozny. LC 89-33769. 236p. 1989. 19.50 (0-8108-2235-0) Scarecrow.

Checklists for Searches & Seizures in Public Schools: 1992 Edition. Jon M. Van Dyke & Melvin M. Sakurai. LC 91-40247. 1992. pap. 49.50 (0-87632-929-6) Clark Boardman Callaghan.

Checklists for Vocabulary Study. Richard C. Yorkey. (English As a Second Language Bk.). (Illus.). 1981. pap. text ed. 14.24 (0-582-79767-5, 75021) Longman.

Checklists T-A Clinical Nursing Skills & Techniques. Perry. 304p. 1993. 12.95 (0-8016-7747-5) Mosby Yr Bk.

Checkmate. Dorothy Dunnett. 1976. 20.95 (0-8488-1292-1) Amereon Ltd.

Checkmate. Dorothy Dunnett. 425p. 1983. lib. bdg. 39.95 (0-89966-319-2) Buccaneer Bks.

Checkmate. James R. Lynch. Ed. by Hazel Choppin & Anne Frost. 150p. 1991. text ed. write for info. (0-318-68542-6) Frost Pub.

Checkmate. Svend Novrup. 160p. 1990. pap. write for info. (0-08-037790-4, Pub. by CHES UK) Macmillan.

Checkmate, 3 vols., 1. Joseph S. Le Fanu. Ed. by Devendra P. Varma. LC 76-4184. (Collected Works). 1977. reprint ed. 30.95 (0-405-09195-8) Ayer.

Checkmate, 3 vols., 2. Joseph S. Le Fanu. Ed. by Devendra P. Varma. LC 76-4184. (Collected Works). 1977. reprint ed. 30.95 (0-405-09196-6) Ayer.

Checkmate, 3 vols., 3. Joseph S. Le Fanu. Ed. by Devendra P. Varma. LC 76-4184. (Collected Works). 1977. reprint ed. 30.95 (0-405-09197-4) Ayer.

Checkmate, 3 vols., Set. Joseph S. Le Fanu. Ed. by Devendra P. Varma. LC 76-4184. (Collected Works). 1977. reprint ed. 90.95 (0-405-09194-X) Ayer.

Checkmate: Fighting Tradition in Central Persia. F. A. Forbes-Leith. LC 73-6279. (Middle East Ser.). 1973. reprint ed. 20.95 (0-405-05335-5) Ayer.

Checkmate Artistry. rev. ed. Eugene A. Furst. (Artistry Series of Chess Encyclopedias: Vol. 2). (Illus.). 320p. 1991. pap. 19.95 (1-879394-02-2, 626-346) Caissas Pr.

Checkmate at Ruweisat: Auchinleck's Finest Hour. Donald G. Brownlow. (Illus.). 1977. 12.95 (0-8158-0356-7) Chris Mass.

Checkpoint: A Science Project Survival Guide...for Kids & Adults. Edward P. Short. (Illus.). 48p. (Orig.). (J). (gr. 3-8). 1992. pap. 9.95 (0-963675-1-7) Quest Dists.

Checkpoints. 2nd ed. Page. (C). 1993. text ed. 32.50 (0-06-501366-2); teacher ed, pap. text ed. 10.00 (0-06-501367-0) HarpCollege.

***Checkpoints: Daily Meditations.** Bill Hybels. 208p. 1996. 15.99 (1-56476-561-X, 6-3561) SP Pubns.

Checks, Drafts & Notes. Jeffrey B. Reitman & Harold Weisblatt. 1983. write for info. (0-8205-1074-2) Bender.

Checkup. Helen Oxenbury. (Out & about Bks.). (Illus.). 24p. (J). (ps-1). 1994. pap. 3.99 (0-14-055275-8, Puff Pied Piper) Puffin Bks.

***Checua: Una Secuencia Cultural Entre 8500 y 3000 Anos Antes del Presente.** Ana M. Groot de Mahecha. (Illus.). 100p. (SPA.). 1992. pap. 10.00 (1-877812-20-X) UPLAAP.

Cheech Wizard. Vaughn Bode. (Illus.). 64p. 1990. pap. 9.95 (1-56097-042-1) Fantagraph Bks.

Cheech Wizard, Vol. 2. Vaughn Bode. (Illus.). 64p. 1991. pap. 9.95 (1-56097-054-5) Fantagraph Bks.

Cheechakoes. Wayne Short. 254p. 1990. reprint ed. lib. bdg. 21.95 (0-89966-656-6) Buccaneer Bks.

Cheek, Chin, Knuckle or Knee. Rick Veitch. Ed. by Marc Arsenault. (Maximortal Ser.: No. 6). (Illus.). 32p. 1993. pap. 2.95 (1-56862-027-6) Tundra MA.

Cheek To Cheek: Poems & Excerpts From Interviews. Jo Harvey Allen. Ed. by Kirk Robertson. (Windriver Ser.). (Illus.). 64p. (Orig.). (C). 1983. pap. 6.00 (0-916918-22-X); pap. text ed. 25.00 (0-916918-23-8) Duck Down.

Cheeks on Fire. Raymond Radiguet. Tr. by Alan Stone. 112p. (ENG & FRE.). 1986. 13.95 (0-7145-3513-3) Riverrun NY.

Cheekwood National Contemporary Painting Competition, 1991. Ed. by Christine Kreyling. (Illus.). 36p. (Orig.). 1991. pap. 16.00 (0-9631349-0-6) TBG & FAC Cheekwd.

Cheekwood National Contemporary Painting Competition, 1992. Intro. by Christine Kreyling. (Illus.). 44p. (Orig.). 1992. pap. 16.00 (0-9631349-1-4) TBG & FAC Cheekwd.

Cheekwood National Contemporary Painting Competition, 1993. Intro. by Christine Kreyling. (Illus.). 36p. (Orig.). 1993. pap. write for info. (0-9631349-2-2) TBG & FAC Cheekwd.

***Cheeky & the Grapevine.** S. Bernadine Riske. (Illus.). 20p. (Orig.). (J). (gr. 1-9). 1995. pap. 7.95 (1-885981-06-6, Brisk Pubns) Brisk Pubng.

Cheeky Rubs. Barbara J. Stiles. LC 89-164732. (Illus.). 20p. (J). (ps-5). 1989. text ed. 12.95 (0-9622057-1-0); pap. text ed. 7.95 (0-9622057-0-2) Manzanita Canyon.

***Cheep! Cheep!** (Sound Board Bks.). 16p. (J). Date not set. bds. 4.98 (0-86112-966-0) Brimax Bks.

Cheep Thrills. Bruce Cochran. (Illus.). 96p. 1994. pap. write for info. (1-55971-437-9) NorthWord.

Cheer Leader. Jill McCorkle. 288p. 1984. 15.95 (0-912697-11-3) Algonquin Bks.

Cheer Leader. Jill McCorkle. 288p. 1992. pap. 8.95 (1-56512-001-9, 72001, Frnt Porch PB) Algonquin Bks.

Cheer Up You Could Have Been a Tax Collector. Donald F. Smith. 120p. (Orig.). 1984. pap. 10.00 (0-9613357-0-X) D F Smith.

Cheerful Americans. Charles B. Loomis. LC 73-86150. (Short Story Index Reprint Ser.). 1977. 21.95 (0-8369-3054-1) Ayer.

Cheerful Ascetic, & Other Essays. James J. Daly. LC 68-24847. (Essay Index Reprint Ser.). 1977. 17.95 (0-8369-0359-5) Ayer.

Cheerful, by Request. Edna Ferber. LC 78-169547. (Short Story Index Reprint Ser.). 1977. reprint ed. 23.95 (0-8369-4009-1) Ayer.

Cheerful Charmers. Joan Zeigler. (Illus.). (Orig.). 1985. pap. 5.95 (0-933491-04-2) Hot off Pr.

Cheerful Devotions to Give. Amy Bolding. (Amy Bolding Library). 96p. 1984. pap. 5.99 (0-8010-0868-9) Baker Bk.

Cheerful Giver. Margaret Sinclair & Felicity O'Brien. 96p. (C). 1990. text ed. 29.00 (0-85439-310-2, Pub. by St Paul Pubns UK) St Mut.

Cheerful Giver: Essays. Samuel M. Crothers. LC 73-156634. (Essay Index Reprint Ser.). 1977. reprint ed. 20.95 (0-8369-2389-8) Ayer.

Cheerful Heart: A Collection of Thoughts, Poems, Sentiments, & Recipes to Share with Those You Love. Barbara M. Ohrbach. (Illus.). 64p. 1991. 3.50 (0-517-58181-7, C P Pubs) Crown Pub Group.

Cheerful Hearts - Are Better Than Medicine. Leroy Brownlow. 1967. 8.99 (0-915720-07-8) Brownlow Pub Co.

Cheerful Pessimist. Peter Tarnov. 204p. 1983. pap. 8.00 (0-911109-01-3) Oxymora Bk Pr.

Cheerful Yesterdays. Thomas W. Higginson. LC 68-29000. (American Negro: His History & Literature, Ser. No. 1). 1969. reprint ed. 17.95 (0-405-01819-3) Ayer.

Cheerful Yesterdays. Thomas W. Higginson. (American Biography Ser.). 374p. 1991. reprint ed. lib. bdg. 79.00 (0-7812-8184-9) Rprt Serv.

Cheerfulness, No. 5. pap. 0.15 (0-87377-137-0) GAM Pubns.

Cheerfulness Breaks In. Angela Thirkell. (Barsetshire Novels Ser.). 342p. 1990. pap. 4.95 (0-88184-601-5) Carroll & Graf.

Cheerleader. Caroline B. Cooney. (YA). 1991. pap. 3.25 (0-590-44316-X, Point) Scholastic Inc.

Cheerleader. Norma Klein. LC 85-224. (Illus.). 144p. (YA). (gr. 7-12). 1985. lib. bdg. 11.99 (0-394-97577-4) Knopf Bks Yng Read.

Cheerleader for a Funeral: Poems. Nina Cassian. Tr. by Brenda Walker. LC 92-72463. (Illus.). 67p. 1993. pap. 15.95 (1-85610-013-8, Pub. by Forest Bks UK) Dufour.

Cheerleader U. S. A. - Tryouts to Triumph. Lynda Haller. 68p. (J). (gr. 1-12). 1989. spiral bd., pap. 10.00 (0-317-93086-9) Cheertime USA.

Cheerleaders. Maggi Brocher. 352p. 1984. pap. 3.50 (0-8439-2132-3) Dorchester Pub Co.

***Cheerleaders.** John Hall. (YA). 1994. pap. 3.99 (0-06-106259-6, HarpT) HarpC.

Cheerleaders Boxed Set, 4 vols. Incl. Trying Out. Caroline B. Cooney. 1985. (0-318-59402-1); Getting Even. Christopher Pike. 1985. (0-318-59403-X); Rumors. Caroline B. Cooney. 1985. (0-318-59404-8); Feuding. Lisa Norby. 1985. (0-318-59405-6); (Cheerleaders Ser.: Nos. 1-4). (J). (gr. 7 up). 1985. Set. Set pap. 9.00 (0-590-37816-3) Scholastic Inc.

Cheerleaders Can't Afford to Be Nice. Susan S. Saiter. 1991. 19.95 (1-55611-181-9) D I Fine.

Cheerleaders from Gomorrah: Tales from the Lycra Archipelago. John Rember. 125p. 1994. 20.00 (1-881090-03-5); pap. 12.00 (1-881090-06-X) Confluence Pr.

***Cheerleader's Guide to Life.** Cindy Villarreal. LC 94-27910. 1994. pap. 13.00 (0-06-273291-9, PL) HarpC.

Cheerleading. Cindy Danielson. (You Can Do It! Ser.). (Illus.). 128p. (Orig.). (J). (ps up). 1992. pap. 12.95 (1-56530-005-X) Summit TX.

***Cheerleading Book.** Stephanie French. 96p. 1995. pap. 12.95 (0-8092-3411-4) Contemp Bks.

Cheerleading Conditioning for Peak Performance. Elaine Hart & Chris Kirby. 176p. (C). 1989. per., pap. text ed. 19.95 (0-8403-5279-4) Kendall-Hunt.

Cheers: Lovable, Livable, Laughable Lines. Marcia Kaplan & David Kaplan. (Illus.). 96p. (Orig.). 1981. reprint ed. 6.95 (0-9617744-0-1) Cheers.

Cheers! The Best of British Pubs. Neil Saunders. 88p. 1988. 9.95 (0-945332-22-X) Agora Inc MD.

***Cheers! The World of a "Wine-Osaur"** Phillip Silverstone. LC 95-8612. 1995. pap. write for info. (0-940159-32-5) Camino Bks.

Cheers: Where Everybody Knows Your Name. Edward Gross. 1991. pap. 14.95 (1-55698-291-7) Movie Pubs Servs.

Cheers Bartending Guide. Marcia Rosen & Gerry Hunt. 192p. 1986. pap. 3.95 (0-380-70189-8) Avon.

Cheers, Smiles, Friends: Lovable, Livable, Laughable, Lines, 3 bks., Set. Marcia Kaplan & David Kaplan. (Illus.). 96p. (Orig.). 1991. pap. text ed. 21.00 (0-9617744-5-2) Cheers.

***Cheers! The World of a "Wine-Osaur"** Phillip Silverstone. LC 95-8612. (Illus.). 150p. (Orig.). 1995. pap. 12.00 (0-940159-29-5) Camino Bks.

Cheers Trivia Book. Mark Wenger. LC 93-45402. 1994. 9.95 (0-8065-1482-5, Citadel Pr) Carol Pub Group.

Cheery Bim Band, No. 3. Chaim Finkelstein. LC 93-73854. 176p. (J). (gr. 5-6). Date not set. 10.95 (1-56062-218-0) CIS Comm.

***Cheery Bim Band No. 4: Color War!** M. C. Millman. LC 94-70754. 150p. (YA). Date not set. write for info. (1-56062-260-1) CIS Comm.

***Cheery Bim Band No. 5: In the Spotlight!** M. C. Millman. LC 94-60672. 141p. (J). (gr. 5-8). Date not set. 10.95 (1-56062-265-2) CIS Comm.

***Cheery Bim Band No. 6: Trumpet Trouble.** M. C. Millman. LC 94-72546. 176p. (J). (gr. 5-8). 1994. 10.95 (1-56062-271-7) CIS Comm.

Cheery Bim Band 1. Chaim Finkelstein. 204p. (J). 1993. 9.95 (1-56062-189-3) CIS Comm.

Cheery Bim Band 2: Let's Do It Again. Chaim Finkelstein. LC 93-72269. 204p. (J). (gr. 5-6). 1993. write for info. (1-56062-209-1) CIS Comm.

***Cheery Hello.** Date not set. 8.99 (0-310-96493-8) Zondervan.

***Cheescakes Galore.** Linda Fuentes. 250p. (Orig.). Date not set. 12.95 (0-9645668-0-X) Grapevne Pubns.

Cheese. Linda Illsley. (Foods We Eat Ser.). (Illus.). 32p. (J). (gr. 1-4). 1991. lib. bdg. 14.96 (0-87614-654-X, Carolrhoda) Lerner Group.

Cheese. L. L. Van Slyke & W. V. Price. (Illus.). 522p. (C). 1980. reprint ed. pap. text ed. 35.00 (0-917930-11-8) Ridgeview.

Cheese. L. L. Van Slyke & W.V. Price. (Illus.). 522p. (C). 1980. reprint ed. lib. bdg. 45.00 (0-917930-31-2) Ridgeview.

Cheese: Chemistry, Physics, & Microbiology, 2 vols., Set. 2nd ed. Ed. by P. F. Fox. LC 92-42748. xxviii, 1164p. 1993. 408.00 (1-85861-010-9, Pub. by Elsevier Applied Sci UK) Elsevier.

Cheese: Chemistry, Physics, & Microbiology, 2 vols., Vol. 1: General Aspects. 2nd ed. Ed. by P. F. Fox. LC 92-42748. xiv, 594p. 1993. 208.00 (1-85861-008-7, Pub. by Elsevier Applied Sci UK) Elsevier.

Cheese: Chemistry, Physics, & Microbiology, 2 vols., Vol. 2: Major Cheese Groups. 2nd ed. Ed. by P. F. Fox. LC 92-42748. xiv, 570p. 1993. 200.00 (1-85861-009-5, Pub. by Elsevier Applied Sci UK) Elsevier.

Cheese: General Aspects. Ed. by P. F. Fox. 402p. 1987. 117.00 (1-85166-052-6, Pub. by Elsevier Applied Sci UK) Elsevier.

Cheese: Major Cheese Group. Ed. by P. F. Fox. 394p. 1987. 117.00 (1-85166-053-4, Pub. by Elsevier Applied Sci UK) Elsevier.

Cheese & Cream Cheese Alternatives (with or Without Soy) - Bibliography & Sourcebook, 1896 to 1994: Detailed Information on 334 Published Documents (Extensively Annotated Bibliography), 159 Commercial Cheese Alternatives Products, 119 Original Interviews (Many Full Text) & Overviews, 44 Unpublished Archival Documents. Ed. by Akiko Aoyagi. 225p. (Orig.). 1994. spiral bd. 69.00 (0-933332-92-0) Soyfoods Center.

Cheese & Dairy Sampler. Jan Siegrist. (Illus.). 48p. (Orig.). 1988. pap. 3.95 (0-933050-59-3) New Eng Pr VT.

Cheese & Fermented Milk Foods. 2nd ed. Frank V. Kosikowski. LC 65-65128. (Illus.). 1982. 58.00 (0-9602322-6-5) F V Kosikowski.

Cheese & the Worms: Cosmos of a Sixteenth Century Miller. Carlo Ginzburg. Tr. by John Tedeschi & Anne Tedeschi. (Reprints Ser.). (Illus.). 177p. 1990. 17.95 (0-88029-448-5) Dorset Pr.

Cheese & the Worms: The Cosmos of a Seventeenth-Century Miller. Carlo Ginzburg. Tr. by Anne Tedeschi & John Tedeschi. 208p. 1992. reprint ed. pap. 11.95 (0-8018-4387-1) Johns Hopkins.

Cheese & the Worms: The Cosmos of a Sixteenth-Century Miller. Carlo Ginzburg. LC 79-3654. 207p. reprint ed. pap. 59.00 (0-685-15552-8, 2026706) Bks Demand.

Cheese Chronicles. Tommy Womack. Ed. by Richard Courtney & Emily Hines. 245p. 1995. 18.95 (0-9635026-5-4) Eggman Pub.

***Cheese Chronicles: The True Story of a Rock 'n' Roll Band You Never Heard Of.** Tommy Womack. Ed. by Richard Courtney & Maryglenn McCombs. 320p. (Orig.). 1995. pap. 14.95 (1-886371-02-4) Eggman Pub.

Cheese Doll. Rabindranath Tagore. Tr. by Meenakshi Mukherjee. (Illus.). (J). (gr. 3-11). 1979. 6.25 (0-89744-143-5) Auromere.

Cheese Effects & Selective Mao-a Inhibitors. M. B. Youdim et al. (Journal of Neural Transmission Ser.: Suppl. 26). (Illus.). 160p. 1988. pap. 47.00 (0-387-82031-0) Spr-Verlag.

Cheese Favorites. Bobbe Wooldridge. 36p. (Orig.). 1981. pap. 2.75 (0-940844-06-0) Wellspring.

Cheese Handbook: A Guide to the World's Best Cheeses. rev. ed. T. A. Layton. 160p. 1973. reprint ed. pap. 4.50 (0-486-22955-6) Dover.

***Cheese Market.** 300p. (Orig.). 1994. pap. 1,495.00 (1-57205-888-9) Rector Pr.

***Cheese Market.** 200p. (Orig.). 1995. pap. 2,195.00 (0-7605-2220-0) Rector Pr.

Cheese Market. Ed. by Peter Allen. 245p. 1985. pap. text ed. 295.00 (0-931634-55-5) FIND-SVP.

Cheese Market. Ed. by Peter Allen. 246p. 1988. pap. 1,295.00 (0-941285-36-7) FIND-SVP.

Cheese Please! Recipes for Cheese Lovers. Ed. by Judith Bosley. (Illus.). 100p. (Orig.). 1986. pap. 5.95 (0-930809-02-5) Grand Bks Inc.

Cheese Stands Alone. Joyce Wells. (Illus.). pap. 4.95 (0-88839-004-1) Hancock House.

Cheese Starters: Development & Application of the Lewis System. J. E. Lewis. 226p. 1987. 66.75 (1-85166-024-0, Pub. by Elsevier Applied Sci UK) Elsevier.

Cheesecake Extraordinaire. Mary Crownover. LC 90-34639. 128p. 1990. 24.95 (0-87833-721-0) Taylor Pub.

Cheesecake Extraordinaire: More than 100 Sumptuous Recipes for the Ultimate Dessert. Mary Crownover. (Illus.). 128p. 1994. pap. 12.95 (0-8092-3544-7) Contemp Bks.

Cheesecake Only. Ann B. Hutchinson. (Illus.). 82p. (Orig.). 1985. pap. text ed. 7.95 (0-9615825-0-2) A B Hutchinson.

Cheesecake Only Two. Ann B. Hutchinson. (Illus.). 104p. 1991. 11.00 (0-9615825-1-0) A B Hutchinson.

Cheesecakes. Lou S. Pappas. LC 92-47463. 1993. 9.95 (0-8118-0322-8) Chronicle Bks.

Cheesemaking Made Easy: Sixty Delicious Varieties. Robert Carroll & Ricki Carroll. LC 82-9300. (Illus.). 144p. 1982. pap. 9.95 (0-88266-267-8, Garden Way Pub) Storey Comm Inc.

Cheesemaking Practice. 2nd ed. R. Scott. 552p. 1986. 95.50 (0-85334-392-6, Pub. by Elsevier Applied Sci UK) Elsevier.

Cheeses of the World. U. S. Department of Agriculture Staff. 1972. reprint ed. pap. 4.95 (0-486-22831-2) Dover.

Cheetah. Caroline Arnold. LC 88-39940. (Illus.). 48p. (J). (gr. 2 up). 1989. 16.00 (0-688-08143-6); lib. bdg. 15.93 (0-688-08144-4) Morrow Jr Bks.

Cheetah. Caroline Arnold. Ed. by ALC Staff. LC 88-39940. (Illus.). 48p. (J). (gr. 3 up). 1992. pap. 5.95 (0-688-11696-5, Mulberry) Morrow.

Cheetah. large type ed. Katharine Gordon. 533p. 1987. 23.95 (0-7089-8388-X, Charnwood) Ulverscroft.

Cheetah: Animal Close-Ups. Philippe Dupont & Valerie Tracqui. (Illus.). 28p. (J). (ps-3). 1992. pap. 6.95 (0-88106-425-4) Charlesbridge Pub.

Cheetah: The Biology, Ecology, & Behavior of an Endangered Species. Randall L. Eaton. LC 81-18556. 192p. (C). 1982. reprint ed. lib. bdg. 22.50 (0-89874-451-2) Krieger.

***Cheetah Chase.** Karin McQuillan. 1995. pap. 5.99 (0-345-39780-0) Ballantine.

1168

An Asterisk (*) at the beginning of an entry indicates that the title is appearing in BIP for the first time.

Cheetah Named Angel. Cathryn Hosea Hilker. LC 92-14623. (Cincinnati Zoo Book Ser.). (Illus.). 32p. (J). (gr. k-4). 1992. 15.95 (0-531-15252-9); lib. bdg. 15.47 (0-531-11055-9) Watts.

Cheetahs. (Zoobooks Ser.). (J). 1991. lib. bdg. 14.95 (0-88682-417-6) Creative Ed.

Cheetahs. Jenny Markert. (Nature Books Ser.). 32p. (J). (gr. 2-6). 1991. lib. bdg. 22.79 (0-89565-716-3) Childs World.

Cheetahs. L. Stone. (Big Cat Discovery Library). (Illus.). 24p. (J). (gr. k-5). 1989. lib. bdg. 11.94 (0-86592-503-8) Rourke Corp.

Cheetahs. Wildlife Education, Ltd. Staff. (Zoobooks Ser.). (Illus.). 24p. (J). 1992. 13.95 (0-937934-77-1); pap. 2.75 (0-937934-67-4) Wildlife Educ.

Cheetahs of the Serengeti Plains: Groups Living in an Asocial Species. T. M. Caro. LC 93-35466. (Wildlife Behavior & Ecology Ser.). (C). 1994. lib. bdg. 70.00 (0-226-09433-2); pap. text ed. 26.95 (0-226-09434-0) U Ch Pr.

***Cheever Evening.** A. R. Gurney. (Illus.). 128p. 1995. 8.99 (1-56865-135-X, GuildAmerica) Dblday Bk Music.

***Cheever Evening.** A. R. Gurney. 1995. pap. 4.75 (0-8222-1458-X) Dramatists Play.

Cheez! Uncle Sam. Ed Nagel. 1978. 8.95 (0-9603096-0-8) Santa Fe Comm Sch.

Chef. Douglas Florian. LC 91-29545. (Illus.). 32p. (J). (ps-3). 1992. 14.00 (0-688-11108-4); lib. bdg. 13.93 (0-688-11109-2) Greenwillow.

Chef des Briquets. Charles M. Schulz. (Peanuts Ser.). (FRE.). (J). 1985. 4.95 (0-8288-4518-2) Fr & Eur.

Chef d'Oeuvre Inconnu. large type ed. Honore De Balzac. (FRE.). 29.95 (0-7859-6520-3) Fr & Eur.

Chef-d'Oeuvre Inconnu. Honore De Balzac. 443p. (FRE.). 1991. reprint ed. pap. 10.95 (0-7859-3397-2) Fr & Eur.

Chef John Folse's Plantation Celebrations: Recipes from Our Louisiana Mansions. John D. Folse. 1993. 24.95 (0-9625152-2-1) Chef John Folse.

***Chef Neil's International Vegetarian Cookbook: Healthy Food That Tastes Great.** 64p. 1995. 5.00 (1-57067-008-0) Book Pub Co.

Chef Paul Prudhomme's Fork in the Road. Paul Prudhomme. 1993. 23.00 (0-688-12165-9) Morrow.

Chef Paul Prudhomme's Louisiana Cajun Magic Cookbook. (Favorite All Time Recipes Ser.). (Illus.). 96p. 1993. spiral bd. 3.50 (1-56173-377-6, 2001000) Pubns Intl Ltd.

Chef Paul Prudhomme's Louisiana Cajun Magic Cookbook. Paul Prudhomme. 96p. 1989. 6.99 (0-517-68642-2) Random Hse Value.

Chef Paul Prudhomme's Louisiana Kitchen. Paul Prudhomme. LC 83-63236. (Cookbook Library). (Illus.). 344p. 1984. 23.00 (0-688-02847-0) Morrow.

***Chef Paul Prudhomme's Pure Magic: Great Recipes Featuring Chef Paul's Magic Seasoning Blends.** Paul Prudhomme. LC 94-46213. (Illus.). 1995. write for info. (0-688-14202-8) Morrow.

Chef Paul Prudhomme's Seasoned America. Paul Prudhomme. (Illus.). 384p. 1991. 23.00 (0-688-05282-7) Morrow.

Chef Prefers: Favorite Recipes by the Chef of Preferred Hotels. Preferred Hotels Worldwide Staff. 1989. 19.98 (0-8241-4010-9) Allan Pubs.

Chef Tell Tells All: A Gourmet Guide from the Market to the Table. Tell Erhardt & Hermie Kranzdorf. LC 79-52440. (Illus.). 272p. pap. 9.95 (0-916838-48-X) Schiffer.

***Chef Tells' Be My Guest: Traditional & Caribbean Cuisine.** Charles Knight. Ed. by Dave Geralds. (Illus.). 136p. (Orig.). 1994. pap. text ed. 13.95 (1-884784-00-3) Health Craft.

Chef Wolfe's New American Turkey Cookery. Ken Wolfe & Olga Bier. LC 84-14526. (Illus.). 156p. 1984. pap. 8.95 (0-943186-17-X) Aris Bks.

***Cheffy Baby's Low Fat Gourmet Secrets: Cut the Fat, Not the Flavor.** Miles Norris. Ed. by Linda Chaney. 120p. (Orig.). 1995. pap. text ed. write for info. (0-9644597-0-1); pap. text ed., vhs write for info. (0-9645697-2-8) Madison Direct.

Chef's Art: Secrets of Four-Star Cooking at Home. Wayne Gisslen. LC 92-13393. 680p. 1992. text ed. 35.00 (0-471-83684-2) Wiley.

***Chef's Companion: A Concise Dictionary of Culinary Terms.** Elizabeth Riely. (Hospitality, Travel & Tourism Ser.). 224p. 1995. pap. 19.95 (0-442-02002-3) Van Nos Reinhold.

Chef's Companion: A Dictionary of Culinary Terms. Elizabeth Riely. (Professional Bks.). (Illus.). 160p. (C). 1986. text ed. 29.95 (0-442-27846-2) Van Nos Reinhold.

Chef's Compendium of Professional Recipes. 3rd ed. John Fuller et al. Ed. by David Foskett. 340p. 1992. 27.95 (0-7506-0490-5) Buttrwrth-Heinemann.

***Chefs Creating Lean: A Nutrition Course for Food Professionals.** Carolyn Leontos & Jeanne Palmer. LC 94-38126. 1994. ring bd. 95.00 (0-88091-136-0) Am Dietetic Assn.

Chefs-d'Oeuvre, 3 tomes. Incl. Tome I. Cyrano De Bergerac. Illus. by Barrere. (0-318-51946-1); Tome II. Aiglon. Illus. by Thevenet. (0-318-51947-X); Tome III. Chantecler. Illus. by Boucher. (0-318-51948-8); Set. 250.00 (0-685-34970-5) Fr & Eur.

Chefs-d'Oeuvres Classiques de l'Opera Francais, 40 vols. Incl. Vol. 1. Ballet-Comique de la Reine Balthazar de Beau Joyeux. Ed. by J. -B. Weckerlin. 1970. pap. 30.00 (0-8450-1101-4); Vol. 2. Peines et les Plaisirs de l'Amour Robert Cambert. Ed. by J. -B. Weckerlin. 1970. pap. 30.00 (0-8450-1102-2); Vol. 4. Europe Galante Andre Campra. Ed. by Theodore De Lajarte. 1970. pap. 32.50 (0-8450-1104-9); Vol. 5. Festes Venitiennes Andre Campra. Ed. by Alexandre Guilmant. 1970. pap. 35.00 (0-8450-1105-7); Vol. 6. Tancreds Andre Campra. Ed. by Alexandre Guilmant. 1970. pap. 40.00 (0-8450-1106-5); Vol. 7. Bayaderes 'Charles -Simon Catel. Ed. by Vincent D'Indy. 1970. pap. 40.00 (0-8450-1107-3); Vol. 8. Saisons Pascal Collasse. Ed. by Louis Soumis. 1970. pap. 40.00 (0-8450-1108-1); Vol. 9. Thetis et Pelee Pascal Collasse. Ed. by Pascal Collasse. 1970. pap. 40.00 (0-8450-1109-X); Vol. 10. Isse. Andre -Cardinale Destouches. Ed. by Hector Salomon. 1970. pap. 35.00 (0-8450-1110-3); Vol. 11. Omphale Andre -Cardinal Destouches. Ed. by Hector Salomon. 1970. pap. 35.00 (0-8450-1111-1); Vol. 12. Carovane du Caire Andre Gretry. Ed. by F. A. Gevaert. 1970. pap. 32.50 (0-8450-1112-X); 12586p. (FRE.). 1970. reprint ed. Set pap. 1,250.00 (0-8450-1100-6) Broude.

Chef's Escort. Ed. by Betty Sarlin. (Illus.). 300p. 1990. 15.00 (0-9624696-1-0) Womens Am ORT.

Chefs' Healthy Collection. Peggy Barnes. LC 92-30692. 208p. 1993. 17.95 (0-88289-929-5) Pelican.

Chef's Helper. Bob Altshuler. LC 84-730283. 1984. student ed 7.00 (0-8064-0403-5, 926); audio 189.00 (0-8064-0404-3) Bergwall.

Chefs of the Southwest Cookbook. rev. ed. Frank L. Bouquet. (Illus.). 115p. 1989. 25.00x (0-937041-64-5); pap. 18.00x (0-937041-65-3) Systems Co.

Chef's Secrets. Chef Cosmo Appleduck Staff. 8.95 (0-911505-05-9) Lifecraft.

Chef's Secrets from Great Restaurants in Louisiana. Louisiana Restaurant Association Staff. 1989. 16.95 (0-88289-639-3) Pelican.

Chef's Table. Barbara Ross. 208p. 1991. pap. 19.95 (0-04-442221-0, Pub. by Allen Unwin AT) Paul & Co Pubs.

Chef's Tale: A Memoir of Food, France, & America. Pierre Franey. LC 93-24991. 1994. 25.00 (0-394-58600-X) Knopf.

Chehalis River Treaty Council & the Treaty of Olympia. Robert B. Lane & Barbara Lane. (Treaty Manuscripts Ser.: No. 1). 77p. 15.00 (0-944253-23-7) Inst Dev Indian Law.

Cheikh Anta Diop: An African Scientist. E. Curtis Alexander. LC 84-81324. (Pan African Internationalist Handbook Ser.). 84p. (Orig.). 1984. pap. 6.95 (0-938818-07-4) ECA Assoc.

Cheikh Anta Diop: On Science, History & Technology. Ed. by E. Curtis Alexander. 85p. 1987. pap. 7.95 (0-938818-10-4) ECA Assoc.

Cheiro Returns. Robert R. Leichtman. (From Heaven to Earth Ser.). (Illus.). 80p. (Orig.). 1979. pap. 3.50 (0-89804-053-1) Ariel GA.

Cheirolumbar Dysostosis. A. Wackenheim. (Illus.). 102p. 1980. pap. 49.00 (0-387-10371-6) Spr-Verlag.

Cheiro's Language of the Hand. Cheiro. 202p. 1963. reprint ed. spiral bd. 9.90 (0-7873-0167-1) Mokelumne.

Cheiro's Language of the Hand: A Complete Practical Work on the Sciences of Cheirognomy & Cheiromancy, Containing the System, Rules & Experience of Cheiro the Palmist. Louis Hamon. (Illus.). 162p. reprint ed. write for info. (0-8094-8100-6); reprint ed. lib. bdg. write for info. (0-8094-8101-4) Time-Life.

Cheiro's World Predictions. Cheiro. 240p. 1981. pap. 22.00 (0-89540-088-X, SB-088) Sun Pub.

Cheirosophy (the Hand) A Scientific Treatise on Palmistry. A. Raphael. reprint ed. spiral bd. 7.70 (0-7873-0707-6) Mokelumne.

Chejudo: A Pictorial Guidebook. Suzanne C. Han. 72p. 1989. pap. 9.95 (0-930878-64-7) Hollym Intl.

***Chekhov.** Edward Sanders. LC 95-11802. 240p. (Orig.). (C). 1995. pap. 13.50 (0-87685-965-1) Black Sparrow.

***Chekhov.** Edward Sanders. LC 95-11802. 240p. (Orig.). (C). 1995. 25.00 (0-87685-966-X) Black Sparrow.

Chekhov. Henri Troyat. Tr. by Michael H. Heim. 1988. pap. 10.95 (0-449-90281-1, Columbine) Fawcett.

***Chekhov, signed ed.** deluxe ed. Edward Sanders. LC 95-11802. 240p. (Orig.). (C). 1995. 35.00 (0-87685-967-8) Black Sparrow.

Chekhov: A Spirit Set Free. Victor S. Pritchett. LC 87-43213. 224p. 1988. 17.95 (0-394-54650-4) Random.

Chekhov: A Spirit Set Free. Victor S. Pritchett. 1989. pap. 8.95 (0-679-72546-6, Vin) Random.

Chekhov: Plays. Anton Chekhov. Tr. by Michael Frayn. (Methuen World Dramatists Ser.). 377p. 1988. pap. 11.95 (0-413-18160-X, A0332, Pub. by Methuen UK) Heinemann.

Chekhov: Selected Stories. Anton P. Chekhov. Tr. by Ann Dunnigan. 1960. pap. 4.95 (0-451-52085-8, CE1847, Sig Classics) NAL-Dutton.

Chekhov: The Major Plays. annot. ed. Chekhov. Ed. by Vitaly Voulf. Tr. by Jean C. Van Italie. 368p. 1995. pap. 7.95 (1-55783-162-9) Applause Theatre Bk Pubs.

Chekhov, a Life. David Magarshack. LC 69-13983. 431p. 1970. reprint ed. text ed. 79.50 (0-8371-4095-1, MACH, Greenwood Pr) Greenwood.

Chekhov & Other Essays. Lev Shestov. LC 66-3055. (Ann Arbor Paperbacks Ser.: No. AA-113). 233p. reprint ed. pap. 66.50 (0-317-09970-1, 2055647) Bks Demand.

Chekhov & Our Age. Ed. by James McConkey. 237p. 1985. 24.95 (0-86731-078-2); pap. 8.95 (0-86731-081-2) Cornell CIS RDC.

Chekhov & Tagore: A Comparative Study of Their Short Stories. Sankar Basu. 1985. text ed. 18.95 (0-86590-619-X, Pub. by Sterling Pubs II) Apt Bks.

Chekhov & Women: Women in the Life & Work of Chekhov. Carolina De Maegd-Soep. 373p. (Orig.). 1987. pap. 19.95 (0-89357-175-X) Slavica.

Chekhov Companion. Ed. by Toby W. Clyman. LC 84-29024. (Illus.). ix, 347p. 1985. text ed. 69.50 (0-313-23423-X, CHC/, Greenwood Pr) Greenwood.

Chekhov Criticism, 1880 Through 1986. Charles W. Meister. LC 88-42508. 360p. 1988. lib. bdg. 52.50x (0-89950-355-1) McFarland & Co.

Chekhov for the Stage: The Sea Gull; Uncle Vanya; The Three Sisters; The Cherry Orchard. Anton Chekhov. Tr. & Intro. by Milton Ehre. 225p. (Orig.). 1992. 43.95 (0-8101-1023-7); pap. 14.95 (0-8101-1048-2) Northwestern U Pr.

Chekhov I Nizhegorodtsy. N. M. Fortunatov. 160p. 1982. 29.00 (0-317-40699-X, Pub. by Collets UK) St Mut.

Chekhov in My Life. Lydia Avilov. Tr. & Intro. by David Magarshack. (Methuen Drama Ser.). (Illus.). 152p. (C). 1989. reprint ed. 21.95 (0-413-62120-0, A0393, Pub. by Methuen UK) Heinemann.

Chekhov in Performance in Russia & Soviet Russia. Vera Gottlieb. (Theatre in Focus Ser.). (Illus.). 90p. 1984. sl., pap. 105.00 (0-85964-119-8) Chadwyck-Healey.

Chekhov on the British Stage. Ed. & Tr. by Patrick Miles. LC 92-26037. (Illus.). 270p. (C). 1993. 59.95 (0-521-38467-2) Cambridge U Pr.

Chekhov Play: A New Interpretation. Harvey Pitcher. 224p. 1984. pap. 12.00 (0-520-05311-7) U CA Pr.

Chekhov, the Major Plays: Ivanov, Sea Gull, Uncle Vanya, Three Sisters, Cherry Orchard. Anton P. Chekhov. Tr. by Ann Dunnigan. 1968. pap. 4.95 (0-451-52270-2, Sig Classics) NAL-Dutton.

Chekhov, the Man. Kornei Chukovsky. LC 74-6384. (Studies in Russian Literature & Life: No. 100). 1974. lib. bdg. 75.00 (0-8383-1867-3) M S G Haskell Hse.

Chekhov's Journey. Ian Watson. 181p. 1991. pap. 3.95 (0-88184-675-9) Carroll & Graf.

Chekhov's Sister. W. D. Wetherell. 1990. 18.95 (0-316-93162-4) Little.

Chekisty: The KGB in Soviet History. John J. Dziak. LC 84-43178. 256p. 1987. text ed. 22.95 (0-669-10258-X) Free Pr.

Chekov's Enterprise: A Personal Journal of the Making of Star Trek: The Motion Picture. Walter Koenig. 222p. 1991. reprint ed. pap. 9.95 (0-9629432-0-7) Inter Trading.

Chela & the Path. El Morya. Ed. by Elizabeth C. Prophet. LC 76-7634. (Illus.). 172p. (Orig.). 1976. pap. 4.95 (0-916766-12-8) Summit Univ.

***Chelan.** Thomas Hickey. 300p. 1995. pap. 8.95 (1-56901-627-5) NW Pub.

Chela's Song: The Beginning of This Journey. Joyce Carbone. LC 91-93084. (Illus.). 124p. (Orig.). 1991. pap. 8.95 (1-878116-10-X) JVC Bks.

Chelates & Clathrates: Markets & Opportunities. 2,450.00 (0-89336-979-9, C-173) BCC.

Chelates in Analytical Chemistry, Vol. 1. Ed. by Hermenegild A. Flaschka et al. LC 67-17003. (Illus.). 432p. reprint ed. pap. 123.20 (0-317-07987-5, 2055074) Bks Demand.

Chelates in Analytical Chemistry, Vol. 2. Ed. by Hermenegild A. Flaschka et al. LC 67-17003. (Illus.). 412p. reprint ed. pap. 117.50 (0-317-07986-7, 2055075) Bks Demand.

Chelates in Analytical Chemistry, Vol. 5. Ed. by H. A. Flaschka & A. J. Barnard, Jr. LC 67-17003. (Illus.). 344p. reprint ed. pap. 98.10 (0-7837-0645-6, 2040986) Bks Demand.

Chelates in Nutrition. Frank H. Kratzer & Pran N. Vohra. 184p. 1986. 124.95 (0-8493-6544-9, QP141, CRC Reprint) Franklin.

Chelating Extractants, Pt. 4. J. Stary & H. Freiser. 1978. 104.00 (0-08-022343-5, Pub. by Pergamon Repr UK) Franklin.

Chelation Answer: How to Prevent Hardening of the Arteries & Rejuvenate Your Cardiovascular System. Morton Walker. Ed. by Steven E. Kroening. LC 93-86538. 300p. reprint ed. pap. 14.95 (0-9626646-7-7) Second Opinion.

Chelation Can Cure: How to Reverse Heart Disease, Diabetes, Stroke, High Blood Pressure & Poor Circulation Without Drugs or Surgery. Edward W. McDonagh. 225p. (Orig.). 1983. pap. 9.95 (0-912815-00-0) Platinum Pen Pubs.

Chelation of Heavy Metals. Ed. by W. G. Levine. LC 77-30495. 1979. 108.00 (0-08-017719-0, Pub. by Pergamon Repr UK) Franklin.

Chelation Therapy: Patient Handbook. Bruce W. Halsted. 1981. 2.00 (0-933904-00-2) Gold Quill Pubs CA.

Chelation Therapy: The Key to Unclogging Your Arteries, Improving Oxygenation, Treating Vision Problems, Etc. 3rd rev. ed. John P. Trowbridge & Morton Walker. (Dr. Morton Walker Better Health Booklets Ser.). 64p. 1990. pap. 4.95 (0-8159-5228-7) Devin.

Chelation Therapy, Vol. 2, No. 1 - 2: Special Issue of Journal of Advancement in Medicine. Ed. by E. Cranton. (Illus.). 280p. 1989. pap. 21.95 (0-89885-480-6) Human Sci Pr.

Chelation Way: The Complete Book of Chelation Therapy. Morton Walker. LC 89-17511. 320p. 1990. pap. 12.95 (0-89529-415-X) Avery Pub.

***Chelewa, Chelewa: The Dilemma of Teenage Girls in Tanzania.** Ed. by Z. Tumbo-Masabo & Rita Liljestrom. (Scandinavian Institute of African Studies). 218p. (Orig.). 1994. pap. 55.00x (91-7106-354-4, Pub. by Almqv & Wiksell SW) Coronet Bks.

Chelkeinu. Abraham Atkin. 200p. (J). 1984. text ed. 7.00 (0-914131-09-5, A120) Torah Umesorah.

Chelovek: Ego Rabota see Man & His Work

Chelovek, Sobytiia Vremiia. V. V. Maiakovskii. 184p. 1984. 75.00 (0-685-12134-8, Pub. by Collets UK) St Mut.

Chelovek V. Literature. N. G. Zhulinskii. 304p. 1983. 50.00 (0-317-40865-8) St Mut.

Chelsea: The Story of a Signal Dog. Paul Ogden. 1993. mass mkt. 4.99 (0-449-22200-4) Fawcett.

Chelsea: The Story of Signal Dog. Paul Ogden. 1992. 18.95 (0-316-63375-5) Little.

Chelsea & the Alien Invasion. Hilda Stahl. LC 93-8294. (Best Friends Ser.: Vol. 14). 160p. (Orig.). (J). (gr. 4-7). 1993. pap. 3.99 (0-89107-749-9) Crossway Bks.

Chelsea & the Green-Haired Kid. Carol Gorman. Ed. by Ruth Ashby. 128p. (YA). (gr. 7 up). 1992. reprint ed. pap. 2.99 (0-671-78713-6, Archway) PB.

Chelsea & the Outrageous Phone Bill. Hilda Stahl. LC 91-33078. (Best Friends Ser.: No. 1). 160p. (J). (gr. 4-7). 1992. pap. 3.99 (0-89107-657-3) Crossway Bks.

Chelsea Gardener: Philip Miller, 1691-1771. 2nd ed. Hazel LeRougetel. (Illus.). 228p. 1990. 29.95 (0-88192-176-9) Timber.

Chelsea Girl. large type ed. Barbara Hanrahan. 1990. 21.95 (0-7089-2137-X) Ulverscroft.

Chelsea Girls. Eileen Myles. LC 94-9895. 276p. (Orig.). 1994. 25.00 (0-87685-933-3); pap. 14.00 (0-87685-932-5) Black Sparrow.

Chelsea Martin Turns Green. Becky T. Lindberg. Ed. by Kathy Tucker. LC 92-31613. (Illus.). 144p. (J). (gr. 2-4). 1993. lib. bdg. 11.95 (0-8075-1134-X) A Whitman.

Chelsea on the Edge: The Adventures of an American Theater. Davi R. Napoleon. (Illus.). 318p. 1991. text ed. 29.95 (0-8138-1713-7) Iowa St U Pr.

Chelsea Porcelain at Williamsburg. John C. Austin. LC 76-49537. (Williamsburg Decorative Arts Ser.). (Illus.). 227p. 1977. 30.00 (0-87935-023-7) U Pr of Va.

Chelsea Reach. large type ed. Claire Rayner. (General Fiction Ser.). 576p. 1992. 21.95 (0-7089-2700-9) Ulverscroft.

Chelsea Year 1988-1989. Ed. by David Joyce. 1989. pap. 16.45 (0-7011-3387-2) Random.

Chelsea's Special Touch. Hilda Stahl. LC 92-37203. (Best Friends Ser.: Vol. 10). 160p. (YA). (gr. 4-7). 1993. 3.99 (0-89107-712-X) Crossway Bks.

Chelsea's Story. Amy Kristoff. 1993. 16.95 (0-533-10607-9) Vantage.

Chelsey & the Green-Haired Kid. Carol Gorman. (J). (gr. 5 up). 1987. 13.95 (0-395-41854-2) HM.

Chem Byl Bolen V. I. Lenin? Mikhail Volin. LC 91-68042. 80p. (Orig.). (RUS.). 1992. pap. 8.00 (0-911971-76-9) Effect Pub.

Chem-Facts: Belgium (1990) Ed. by Chemical Intelligence Services Staff. (C). 1990. 525.00 (1-871798-03-5, Pub. by Chem Intell Srvs UK) St Mut.

Chem-Facts: Ethylene & Propylene. Ed. by Chemical Intelligence Services Staff. (C). 1990. 525.00 (1-871798-05-1, Pub. by Chem Intell Srvs UK) St Mut.

Chem-Facts: European Review. Chemical Intelligence Services Staff. (C). 1990. 525.00 (1-871798-08-6, Pub. by Chem Intell Srvs UK) St Mut.

Chem-Facts: France. Ed. by Chemical Intelligence Services Staff. (C). 1990. 525.00 (1-871798-04-3, Pub. by Chem Intell Srvs UK) St Mut.

Chem-Facts: Netherlands. Ed. by Chemical Intelligence Services Staff. (C). 1990. 525.00 (1-871798-02-7, Pub. by Chem Intell Srvs UK) St Mut.

Chem-Facts: PVC. Chem-Intell Staff. (C). 1992. 920.00 (0-7855-0063-4, Pub. by Chem Intell Srvs UK) St Mut.

Chem-Facts: Styrenics. Chemical Intelligence Services Staff. (C). 1990. 525.00 (1-871798-07-8, Pub. by Chem Intell Srvs UK) St Mut.

Chem-Facts: United Kingdom. Chemical Intelligence Services Staff. (C). 1990. 525.00 (1-871798-06-X, Pub. by Chem Intell Srvs UK) St Mut.

Chem Lab Notebook, No. 50. (Chemistry Ser.). 50p. (C). 1994. pap. text ed. 6.50 (0-86720-877-5) Jones & Bartlett.

Chem Lab Notebook, No. 100. (Chemistry Ser.). 100p. (C). 1994. pap. text ed. 8.50 (0-86720-876-7) Jones & Bartlett.

***Chem Labs: Experiments in General, Organic & BioChemistry.** Charles Henrickson et al. 368p. (C). 1994. pap. text ed., spiral bd. 29.95 (0-8403-9317-2) Kendall-Hunt.

Chem Sources - International, 1992. 4th ed. 1992. 250.00 (0-937020-17-6) Chem Srcs Intl.

Chem Sources - U. S. A., 1992. 33th ed. 1992. 250.00 (0-937020-16-8) Chem Srcs Intl.

Chem Sources International 1994 Edition. Ed. by Mike Desing & Kurt Gandenberger. 1336p. 1994. 285.00 (0-937020-21-4) Chem Srcs Intl.

***Chem Sources U. S. A. 1995.** Ed. by Mike Desing & Kurt Gandenberger. 1300p. 1995. 295.00 (0-937020-22-2) Chem Srcs Intl.

***Chem TV: Organic Chem IBM Version 2.0.** Betty A. Lucfigh. (Chemistry Ser.). Date not set. disk 495.00 (0-86720-904-6) Jones & Bartlett.

Chema Cobo. Kyoichi Tsuzuki. (Art Random Ser.: No. 84). (Illus.). 48p. 1991. 32.95 (4-7636-8585-6, Pub. by Kyoto Shoin JA) Bks Nippan.

CHEMCALC (TM) 4: Version 2.0--Applied Fluid Flow Calculations. Mahesh Talwar. LC 85-843. (CHEMCALC (TM) Software for Chemical Engineers Ser.). 1985. 495.00 (0-87201-088-0) Gulf Pub.

CHEMCALC (TM) 5: Heat Exchanger Network Optimization. Jim C. Otar. LC 85-16856. (CHEMCALC (TM) Software for Chemical Engineers Ser.). 80p. 1986. disk 295.00 (0-87201-089-9) Gulf Pub.

CHEMCALC (TM) 8: Centrifugal Pump Selection & Rating. Gordon S. Buck. LC 85-21919. (CHEMCALC (TM) Software for Chemical Engineers Ser.). 50p. 1986. 395.00 (0-87201-112-7) Gulf Pub.

Chemcom: Chemistry in the Community. 2nd ed. American Chemical Society (ACS) Staff. 464p. (C). 1992. teacher ed, pap. text ed. 49.90 (0-8403-5506-8) Kendall-Hunt.

C

An Asterisk (*) at the beginning of an entry indicates that the title is appearing in BIP for the first time. 1169

Chemeca, 89: Technology for Our Third Century. (Illus.). 1047p. (Orig.). 1989. pap. 78.00 (0-318-68311-3, Pub. by Inst Engrs Aust-EA Bks AT) Accents Pubns.

Chemehuevi, a Grammar & Lexicon. Margaret L. Press. LC 78-62874. (University of California Publications in Social Welfare: No. 92). 211p. reprint ed. pap. 60.20 (0-685-44444-9, 2032901) Bks Demand.

Chememetrics in Instrumental Analysis, Vol. 1: Solved Problems by IBM PC. Milan Meloun et al. 500p. 1992. write for info. (0-13-126376-5) P-H.

Chemfate. Howard. 1992. 1,500.00 (0-87371-785-6, T) Lewis Pubs.

Chemi-& Bioluminescence. Burr. LC 85-10423. (Clinical & Biochemical Analysis Ser.: Vol. 16). 632p. (C). 1985. 190.00 (0-8247-7277-6) Dekker.

Chemical Abuse Assessment Workbook for Adolescents. rev. ed. Ed. by Audrey De la Martre. 34p. (YA). (gr. 6-12). 1989. reprint ed. student ed 7.00 (0-317-92294-7) New Connect Pub.

Chemical Accident. Christopher Lampton. (Disaster! Ser.). (Illus.). 48p. (J). (gr. 4-6). 1994. 13.90 (1-56294-316-2) Millbrook Pr.

Chemical Accident Contamination Control. 1991. lib. bdg. 250.00 (0-8490-4187-2) Gordon Pr.

Chemical Activities. Christie L. Borgford & Lee R. Summerlin. LC 86-20673. (Illus.). xii, 244p. 1988. student ed, spiral bd. 12.95 (0-8412-1417-4); teacher ed, spiral bd. 19.95 (0-8412-1416-6) Am Chemical.

Chemical Additives for the Plastics Industry: Properties, Applications, Toxcologies. Radian Corporation Staff. LC 86-31155. (Illus.). 884p. 1987. 64.00 (0-8155-1114-0) Noyes.

Chemical Additives in Booze. Center for Science in the Public Interest Staff & Michael Lipske. Ed. by Michael Jacobson. 133p. (Orig.). 1983. pap. 4.95 (0-89329-098-X) Ctr Sci Public.

Chemical Admixtures. 72p. 1993. 31.25 (0-685-72301-1, C-23) ACI.

Chemical Admixtures for Concrete. M. R. Rixom & N. P. Mailvaganam. 275p. 1986. text ed. 47.50 (0-419-12630-9, 9571, E & FN Spon) Routledge Chapman & Hall.

Chemical Alert! A Community Action Handbook. rev. ed. Ed. by Marvin S. Legator & Sabrina F. Strawn. LC 92-25304. Orig. Title: The Health Detective's Handbook. 254p. (C). 1993. text ed. 35.00 (0-292-74675-X); pap. text ed. 14.95 (0-292-74676-8) U of Tex Pr.

C

Chemical Analysis. Kenneth A. Rubinson. (C). 1987. text ed. 41.75 (0-673-39552-9) HarpCollege.

Chemical Analysis by Flame Photometry. 2nd rev. ed. Roland Herrmann. LC 63-17446. (Chemical Analysis Ser.: Vol. 14). 658p. reprint ed. pap. 180.00 (0-317-08956-0, 2006352) Bks Demand.

Chemical Analysis by Nuclear Methods. Ed. by Z. B. Alfassi. LC 93-33546. 1994. text ed. 150.00 (0-471-93834-3) Wiley.

Chemical Analysis in Complex Matrices. Malcolm R. Smyth. 400p. 1992. text ed. 88.00 (0-13-127671-9) P-H.

Chemical Analysis of Additives in Plastics. 2nd ed. T. R. Crompton. 1977. 152.00 (0-08-020497-X, Pub. by Pergamon Repr UK) Franklin.

Chemical Analysis of Ecological Materials. 2nd ed. Ed. by Stewart E. Allen. (Illus.). 384p. (C). 1989. text ed. 124.95 (0-632-01742-2) Blackwell Sci.

Chemical Analysis of Electroplating Solutions. T. H. Irvine. (Illus.). 1970. 41.50 (0-8206-0206-X) Chem Pub.

Chemical Analysis of Industrial Water. James W. McCoy. (Illus.). 1969. 65.00 (0-8206-0017-2) Chem Pub.

Chemical Analysis of Inorganic Constituents of Water, Vol. I. Ed. by Jon C. Van Loon. 264p. 1982. 139.00 (0-8493-5209-6, QD142, CRC Reprint) Franklin.

Chemical Analysis of Metals, Sampling & Analysis of Metal Bearing Ores (87 Standards) see ASTM Annual Book of Standards, 1986

Chemical Analysis of Metals, STP 944. Ed. by F. T. Coyle. LC 86-32130. (Special Technical Publication Ser.). (Illus.). 140p. 1986. text ed. 27.00 (0-8031-0942-3, 04-944000-01) ASTM.

Chemical Analysis of Polycyclic Aromatic Compounds. Tuan Vo-Dinh. (Analytical Chemistry & Its Applications Ser.). 1989. text ed. 170.00 (0-471-62889-1) Wiley.

Chemical Analysis of the Environment & Other Modern Techniques. Eastern Analytical Symposium Staff, 1971. LC 73-82575. (Progress in Analytical Chemistry Ser.: No. 5). 394p. reprint ed. pap. 112.30 (0-317-27112-1, 2024703) Bks Demand.

Chemical Anatomy, Physiology & Pathology of Extracellular Fluid: A Lecture Syllabus. 6th ed. James L. Gamble. 172p. reprint ed. pap. 49.10 (0-317-29767-8, 2017261) Bks Demand.

Chemical & Biochemical Methodology for the Assessment of Hazards of Pesticides for Man: Proceedings of the WHO Scientific Group, Geneva, 1974. WHO Staff. (Technical Report Ser.: No. 560). 1975. pap. 2.40 (92-4-120560-1) World Health.

Chemical & Biochemical Reactivity, April, 1973. Ed. by E. D. Bergmann & B. Pullmann. (Jerusalem Symposia on Quantum Chemistry & Biochemistry Ser.: No. 6). 1975. lib. bdg. 117.00 (90-277-0554-2) Kluwer Ac.

Chemical & Biochemical Sensors, Pt. II, Vol. 3. Ed. by W. Gopel et al. 514p. 1992. lib. bdg. 285.00 (0-89573-675-6) VCH Pubs.

Chemical & Biological Aspects of Drug Dependence. S. J. Mule & Henry Brill. LC 72-191695. (Drug Dependence Ser.). 576p. 1972. 55.00 (0-87819-011-2, CRC Reprint) Franklin.

Chemical & Biological Aspects of Pyridoxal Catalysis. Ed. by E. E. Snell et al. 1963. 252.00 (0-08-010423-1, Pub. by Pergamon Repr UK) Franklin.

Chemical & Biological Characterization of Municipal Sludges, Sediments, Dredge Spoils, & Drilling Muds. Ed. by James Lichtenberg et al. LC 88-3295. (Special Technical Publication Ser.: No. 976). (Illus.). 510p. 1988. text ed. 69.00 (0-8031-0987-3, 04-976000-16) ASTM.

Chemical & Biological Controls in Forestry. Ed. by Willa Y. Garner & John Harvey, Jr. LC 83-22440. (ACS Symposium Ser.: No. 238). 406p. 1984. text ed. 76.95 (0-8412-0818-2) Am Chemical.

Chemical & Biological Regulation of Aquatic Systems. Jacques Buffle. 1993. 59.95 (0-87371-448-2, TD139) Lewis Pubs.

Chemical & Biological Warfare. Elaine Landau. 128p. (J). (gr. 5-9). 1991. 14.95 (0-525-67364-4, Lodestar Bks) Dutton Child Bks.

Chemical & Biological Warfare. rev. ed. L. B. Taylor, Jr. & C. L. Taylor. LC 92-17083. (Impact Bks). (Illus.). (YA). (gr. 9-12). 1992. lib. bdg. 14.98 (0-531-13029-0) Watts.

Chemical & Biological Warfare: A Source Guide. 1991. lib. bdg. 250.00 (0-8490-4810-9) Gordon Pr.

Chemical & Biological Warfare: The Cruelest Weapons. Laurence Pringle. LC 92-16641. (Issues in Focus Ser.). (Illus.). 104p. (J). 1993. lib. bdg. 17.95 (0-89490-280-6) Enslow Pubs.

Chemical & Biological Warfare Development, 1985. Ed. by Julian P. Robinson. (SIPRI Chemical & Biological Warfare Studies). 1986. pap. 29.95 (0-19-829110-8) OUP.

Chemical & Biological Warfare Developments, 1986-87. Julian P. Robinson. (SIPRI Chemical & Biological Warfare Studies: No. 11). 160p. Date not set. pap. 29.95 (0-19-829140-X) OUP.

Chemical & Biological Weapons. Edward M. Spiers. LC 93-48525. 1994. text ed. 49.95 (0-312-12121-0) St Martin.

Chemical & Botanical Guide to Lichen Products. Chicita F. Culberson. 672p. 1979. reprint ed. pap. text ed. 84.00 (3-87429-165-0) Koeltz Sci Bks.

Chemical & Catalytic Reactor Modeling. Ed. by Milorad P. Dudukovic & Patrick L. Mills. LC 83-22378. (ACS Symposium Ser.: No. 237). 426p. 1984. lib. bdg. 65.95 (0-8412-0815-8) Am Chemical.

Chemical & Engineering Thermodynamics. 2nd ed. Stanley I. Sandler. LC 88-10141. 622p. 1989. Net. text ed., disk write for info. (0-471-83050-X) Wiley.

Chemical & Medical Sensors, Vol. 1510. O. S. Wolfbeis. 1991. 58.00 (0-8194-0619-8) SPIE.

Chemical & Physical Behavior of Human Hair. C. R. Robbins. (Illus.). 330p. 1988. 79.00 (0-387-96660-9) Spr-Verlag.

Chemical & Physical Behavior of Human Hair. Clarence R. Robbins. LC 93-38111. 1994. 69.00 (0-387-94191-6) Spr-Verlag.

Chemical & Physical Data. Arthur M. James & M. P. Lord. LC 92-25365. 1992. text ed. 59.95 (0-442-30895-7) Van Nos Reinhold.

Chemical & Process Thermodynamics. 2nd ed. Benjamin G. Kyle. 576p. 1991. text ed. 74.00 (0-13-130030-X) P-H.

Chemical & Radionuclide Food Contamination. M. E. Alpert et al. (Illus.). 220p. (C). 1973. text ed. 29.50 (0-8422-7091-4) Irvington.

Chemical & Structural Approaches to Rational Drug Design. David B. Weiner & William V. Williams. 288p. 1994. 115.00 (0-8493-7818-4, 7818) CRC Pr.

Chemical & Structural Aspects of High Temperature Superconductors. C. N. Rao. 248p. (C). 1988. pap. 39.00 (9971-5-0608-4) World Scientific Pub.

Chemical & Technical Stenography: Anniv. Gregg. James Kanegis. 1950. 10.00 (0-9600226-1-9) Kanegis.

Chemical & Technological Dictionary of Biological Sciences: Dictionnaire Chimique & Technologique des Sciences Biologiques. 2nd ed. Jacques Dupayrat. 138p. (ENG & FRE.). 1993. reprint ed. pap. 85.00 (0-8288-0781-7, F63490) Fr & Eur.

***Chemical Applications Management. 2nd ed. Ed. by Deere & Company Staff. (Farm Business & Management Ser.). (Illus.). 108p. 1994. pap. text ed. 33.20 (0-86691-062-X, FMO13502T) Deere & Co.**
A practical guide to the selection & application of agricultural chemicals. Explains the two major functions: to increase plant growth & to protect against pests. Covers types of fertilizers & their uses, identifies common weeds, insects & diseases which threaten farm & ranch crops. Details various types of herbicides, fungicides, insecticides & fumigants & their uses. Shows the proper use of sprayers & applicators for maximum efficiency & safety. CONTENTS: Purpose of crop chemicals, ecology & safety factors, alternatives to chemicals, goal of chemical use, uses of crop nutrients, fertilizers, limes, use of weed controls, herbicides, uses of plant disease controls, fungicides, uses of insect controls, insecticides, fumigants, applying liquid chemicals, applying dry chemicals, safety, glossary & tables, weed identification, insect identification & crop disease photos. *Publisher Provided Annotation.*

***Chemical Applications Management. 2nd rev. ed. Ed. by Deere & Company Staff. (Farm Business & Management Ser.). (Illus.). 76p. 1994. student ed, pap. text ed. 13.25 (0-86691-071-9, FMO13602W); sl. 226.95 (0-614-03188-5, FMO13202S) Deere & Co.**
A practical guide to the selection & application of agricultural chemicals. Explains the two major functions: to increase plant growth & to protect against pests. Covers types of fertilizers & their uses, identifies common weeds, insects & diseases which threaten farm & ranch crops. Details various types of herbicides, fungicides, insecticides & fumigants & their uses. Shows the proper use of sprayers & applicators for maximum efficiency & safety. CONTENTS: Purpose of crop chemicals, ecology & safety factors, alternatives to chemicals, goal of chemical use, uses of crop nutrients, fertilizers, limes, use of weed controls, herbicides, uses of plant disease controls, fungicides, uses of insect controls, insecticides, fumigants, applying liquid chemicals, applying dry chemicals, safety, glossary & tables, weed identification, insect identification & crop disease photos. *Publisher Provided Annotation.*

Chemical Applications Management. 3rd rev. ed. Ed. by Deere & Company Staff. (Farm Business & Management Ser.). (Illus.). 282p. 1994. pap. text ed. 32.95 (0-86691-206-1, FBM19103B) Deere & Co.
A practical guide to the selection & application of agricultural chemicals. Explains the two major functions: to increase plant growth & to protect against pests. Covers types of fertilizers & their uses, identifies common weeds, insects & diseases which threaten farm & ranch crops. Details various types of herbicides, fungicides, insecticides & fumigants & their uses. Shows the proper use of sprayers & applicators for maximum efficiency & safety. CONTENTS: Purpose of crop chemicals, ecology & safety factors, alternatives to chemicals, goal of chemical use, uses of crop nutrients, fertilizers, limes, use of weed controls, herbicides, uses of plant disease controls, fungicides, uses of insect controls, insecticides, fumigants, applying liquid chemicals, applying dry chemicals, safety, glossary & tables, weed identification, insect identification & crop disease photos. *Publisher Provided Annotation.*

Chemical Applications of Group Theory. 3rd ed. F. Albert Cotton. LC 08-916434. 461p. 1990. text ed. 64.95 (0-471-51094-7) Wiley.

Chemical Applications of Nuclear Probes. Ed. by K. Yoshihara. (Topics in Current Chemistry Ser.: Vol. 157). 192p. 1990. 109.00 (0-387-52423-1) Spr-Verlag.

Chemical Approach to Glass. M. B. Volf. (Glass Science & Technology Ser.: Vol. 7). 1984. 172.00 (0-444-99635-4, I-036-84) Elsevier.

Chemical Approaches to the Synthesis of Inorganic Materials. C. N. Rao. LC 94-21800. 1995. text ed. 27.95 (0-470-23431-8) Wiley.

Chemical Arts of Old China. Li Ch'iao-P'ing. LC 75-36234. reprint ed. 24.50 (0-404-14482-9) AMS Pr.

Chemical Aspects of Biosynthesis. John Mann. (Chemistry Primers Ser.: No. 20). (Illus.). 96p. (C). 1995. text ed. 29.95 (0-19-855677-2); pap. text ed. 9.95 (0-19-855676-4) OUP.

Chemical Aspects of Enzyme Biotechnology: Fundamentals. Ed. by T. O. Baldwin et al. LC 91-10371. (Industry-University Cooperative Chemistry Program Symposia Ser.). (Illus.). 356p. 1991. 79.50 (0-306-43815-1, Plenum Pr) Plenum.

Chemical Aspects of the Structure of Small Peptides: An Introduction. Dorothy M. Wrinch. LC 62-160. 201p. reprint ed. pap. 57.30 (0-317-09409-2, 2020699) Bks Demand.

Chemical Atomism in the Nineteenth Century: From Dalton to Cannizzaro. Alan J. Rocke. LC 83-25082. 404p. 1984. 57.50 (0-8142-0360-4) Ohio St U Pr.

Chemical Basis of Radiation Biology. C. Von Sonntag. 400p. 1987. 150.00 (0-85066-353-9) Taylor & Francis.

Chemical, Biochemical & Environmental Applications of Fibers, Vol. 990. Ed. by R. A. Lieberman & M. T. Wlodarczyk. 1988. 45.00 (0-8194-0025-4) SPIE.

Chemical, Biochemical, & Environmental Fiber Sensors. Ed. by R. A. Lieberman & M. T. Wlodarczyk. 310p. 1990. 70.00 (0-8194-0208-7, VOL. 1172) SPIE.

Chemical, Biochemical, & Environmental Fiber Sensors II, Vol. 1368. R. A. Lieberman & M. T. Wlodarczyk. 1991. 62.00 (0-8194-0429-2) SPIE.

Chemical, Biochemical, & Environmental Fiber Sensors Three. M. T. Wlodarczyk. 1992. 70.00 (0-8194-0718-6, 1587) SPIE.

Chemical, Biological & Industrial Applications of Infrared Spectroscopy. James R. Durig. LC 85-16719. 399p. 1985. text ed. 130.00 (0-471-90834-7) Wiley.

Chemical Biology of Fishes: Vol. 2, Advances 1968-1977. R. M. Love. 1980. text ed. 248.00 (0-12-455852-6) Acad Pr.

Chemical Bond. 2nd ed. John N. Murrell et al. LC 85-6383. (Illus.). 345p. reprint ed. pap. 98.40 (0-7837-1875-6, 2042076) Bks Demand.

Chemical Bond. 2nd ed. John N. Murrell et al. LC 85-6383. 333p. 1985. pap. text ed. 34.95 (0-471-90760-X) Wiley.

Chemical Bond: Structure & Dynamics. Ed. by Ahmed Zewail. (Illus.). 313p. 1992. text ed. 54.95 (0-12-779620-7) Acad Pr.

Chemical Bonding. Mark J. Winter. LC 93-28866. (Oxford Chemistry Primers Ser.: No. 15). (Illus.). 96p. (C). 1994. text ed. 29.95 (0-19-855695-0); pap. text ed. 9.95 (0-19-855694-2) OUP.

Chemical Bonding & the Geometry of Molecules. George E. Ryschkewitsch. LC 62-20784. (Selected Topics in Modern Chemistry Ser.). 129p. reprint ed. pap. 36.80 (0-317-09188-3, 2005794) Bks Demand.

Chemical Bonding Clarified Through Quantum Mechanics. George C. Pimentel & Richard D. Sprately. LC 71-75914. 1969. 22.95 (0-8162-6781-2) Holden-Day.

***Chemical Bonding in Solids.** Jeremy K. Burdett. (Topics in Inorganic Chemistry Ser.). (Illus.). 336p. (C). 1995. text ed. 65.00 (0-19-508991-X) OUP.

***Chemical Bonding in Solids.** Jeremy K. Burdett. (Topics in Inorganic Chemistry Ser.). (Illus.). 336p. (C). 1995. pap. text ed. 35.00 (0-19-508992-8) OUP.

Chemical Bonding in Solids & Fluids. Mark Ladd. 1995. text ed. 55.00 (0-13-474933-2) P-H.

Chemical Bonding in Solids & Fluids. Mark Ladd. LC 93-26821. (Ellis Horwood Series in Physical Chemistry). 1994. pap. text ed. write for info. (0-13-474925-1, Tavistock-E Horwood) Routledge Chapman & Hall.

Chemical Bonding Models. Ed. by J. F. Liebman & A. Greenberg. (Molecular Structure & Energetics Ser.). 360p. 1986. lib. bdg. 95.00 (0-89573-139-8, VOL. 1) VCH Pubs.

***Chemical Bonds: An Introduction to Atomic & Molecular Structure.** Harry B. Gray. LC 94-61186. (Illus.). 232p. (C). 1994. pap. text ed. 28.00 (0-935702-35-0) Univ Sci Bks.

Chemical Bonds Outside Metal Surfaces. Norman H. March. LC 86-5022. (Physics of Solids & Liquids Ser.). 294p. 1986. 75.00 (0-306-42059-7, Plenum Pr) Plenum.

Chemical Calculations. 14th rev. ed. George I. Sackheim. (Series A). 168p. 1994. pap. text ed. 11.20 (0-87563-448-6) Stipes.

Chemical Calculations. 15th rev. ed. George I. Sackheim. (Series B). 241p. (C). 1993. pap. text ed. 11.20 (0-87563-447-8) Stipes.

Chemical Carcinogenesis: Models & Mechanisms. Ed. by F. Feo et al. LC 88-29013. (Illus.). 696p. 1988. 135.00 (0-306-43085-1, Plenum Pr) Plenum.

Chemical Carcinogenesis: Selected Papers, 2 pts. World Symposium on Model Studies in Chemical Carcinogenesis Staff. Ed. by Paul O. Ts'O & Joseph A. DiPaolo. LC 73-84816. (Biochemistry of Disease Ser.: No. 4). (Illus.). reprint ed. Pt. A, 464p. pap. 125.30 (0-7837-0665-0, 2041001); reprint ed. Pt. B, 375p. pap. 106.90 (0-7837-0666-9) Bks Demand.

Chemical Carcinogenesis & Mutagenesis I. Ed. by C. S. Cooper & P. L. Grover. (Handbook of Experimental Pharmacology Ser.: Vol. 94-I). (Illus.). 656p. 1989. 375.00 (0-387-51182-2, 3138) Spr-Verlag.

Chemical Carcinogenesis & Mutagenesis II. Ed. by C. S. Cooper & P. L. Grover. (Handbook of Experimental Pharmacology Ser.: Vol. 94, Pt. 2). (Illus.). 510p. 1990. 310.00 (0-387-51183-0, 3316) Spr-Verlag.

Chemical Carcinogenesis Essays: Proceedings of a Workshop on Approaches to Assess the Significance of Experimental Chemical Carcinogenesis Data for Man, Organized by IARC & the Catholic University of Louvain, Brussels, Belgium, 10-12 December 1973. International Agency for Research on Cancer Staff. Ed. by R. Montesano & L. Tomatis. LC 76-356996. (IARC Scientific Publications: No. 10). 241p. reprint ed. pap. 68.70 (0-7837-3993-1, 2043824) Bks Demand

Chemical Carcinogenesis Essays - Workshop on Approaches to Assess the Significance of Experimental Chemical Carcinogenesis Data for Man: Proceedings of the International Agency for Research on Cancer Workshop, Brussels, Belgium, December 10-12, 1973. International Agency for Research on Cancer Staff & Catholic University of Louvain Staff. Ed. by R. Montesano et al. (IARC Scientific Pub.: No. 10). 1974. 20.00 (0-686-16779-1) World Health.

Chemical Carcinogenesis II: Modulating Factors. Ed. by A. Columbano et al. (Illus.). 666p. 1991. 135.00 (0-306-43896-8, Plenum Pr) Plenum.

Chemical Carcinogens. M. Castegnaro & Eric B. Sansone. 130p. 1986. pap. 23.00 (0-387-16719-6) Spr-Verlag.

Chemical Carcinogens: Activation Mechanisms, Structural & Elctronic Factors, & Reactivity. Ed. by P. Politzer & F. J. Martin, Jr. (Bioactive Molecules Ser.: No. 5). 366p. 1988. 143.75 (0-444-43008-3) Elsevier.

An Asterisk (*) at the beginning of an entry indicates that the title is appearing in BIP for the first time.

Chemical Equilibrium of Gaseous Systems. Robert Holub & Petr Vonka. LC 75-34393. 1975. lib. bdg. 103.00 (*90-277-0556-9*) Kluwer Ac.

Chemical Events in the Atmosphere & Their Impact on the Environment: Proceedings of a Study at the Pontifical Academy of Sciences, Nov., 7-11, 1983. Ed. by G. B. Marini-Bettolo. 702p. 1986. 248.75 (*0-444-99513-7*) Elsevier.

Chemical Evolution: Origin of Life. Ed. by Cyril Ponnamperuma & Julian Chela-Flores. (Illus.). 336p. 1993. 50.00 (*0-937194-31-X*) A Deepak Pub.

***Chemical Evolution: Self-Organization of the Macromolecules of Life.** Ed. by Julian Chela-Flores et al. (Illus.). 352p. 1995. 62.00 (*0-937194-32-8*) A Deepak Pub.

Chemical Evolution of the Atmosphere & Oceans. Heinrich D. Holland. LC 83-43077. (Geochemistry Ser.). (Illus.). 656p. 1984. 99.50 (*0-691-08348-7*); pap. 35.00x (*0-691-02381-6*) Princeton U Pr.

***Chemical Evolution: Structure & Model of the First Cell: Conference on the Structure & Model of the First Cell (ICTP) Held in Trieste, Italy on 29 August-2 September 1994.** Ed. by Cyril Ponnamperuma. 392p. (C). 1995. lib. bdg. 230.00 (*0-7923-3562-7*) Kluwer Ac.

Chemical Explorations: A Laboratory Manual for Introductory Chemistry. Jerry Bell. 400p. (C). 1993. write for info. (*0-669-26916-6*); Instr.'s resource guide. teacher ed write for info. (*0-669-26917-4*) Heath.

Chemical Exposure: What Are We Doing to Our Children? Dawn S. Davis. LC 91-75006. (Illus.). 52p. (Orig.). 1991. pap. 7.95 (*1-879318-04-0*) Magnolia South Pub.

***Chemical Exposure & Disease.** Janette D. Sherman. (Illus.). 293p. 1994. 35.00 (*0-911131-31-0*) Princeton Sci Pubs.

Chemical Exposure & Human Health: A Reference to 314 Chemicals, with a Guide to Symptoms & a Directory of Organizations. Cynthia Wilson. LC 92-51010. 351p. 1993. lib. bdg. 45.00 (*0-89950-810-3*) McFarland & Co.

Chemical Exposure Predictions. Ed. by Davide Calamari. 1992. 69.95 (*0-87371-852-6*, RA566) Lewis Pubs.

Chemical Exposures: Low Levels & High Stakes. Nicholas A. Ashford & Claudia S. Miller. 1991. text ed. 24.95 (*0-442-00499-0*) Van Nos Reinhold.

Chemical Fate & Transport in the Environment. Harold F. Hemond & Elizabeth Fechner. (Illus.). 338p. 1994. text ed. 49.95 (*0-12-340270-0*) Acad Pr.

***Chemical Feast.** William H. Le Riche. LC 82-2442. 216p. 1982. reprint ed. pap. 61.60 (*0-7837-8155-5*, 2047860) Bks Demand.

Chemical Feed Systems Pocket Guide. Langworthy. 1995. write for info. (*0-87371-543-8*) Lewis Pubs.

Chemical Fire Engines. W. Fred Conway. (Fire Service History Ser.). (Illus.). 127p. 1987. 24.95 (*0-685-25255-8*) Fire Buff Hse.

Chemical Fixation & Solidification. Jesse R. Conner. 1989. text ed. 99.95 (*0-442-20511-2*) Chapman & Hall.

Chemical Fixation of Carbon Dioxide: Methods of Recycling CO b2 s into Useful products. Martin Halmann. 1993. 69.95 (*0-8493-4428-X*, TP244) CRC Pr.

Chemical Formulae from Mass Determinations see Tables for Use in High Resolution Mass Spectrometry

Chemical Formulary, Vol. 23. Ed. by H. Bennett. 1981. 60.00 (*0-8206-0282-5*) Chem Pub.

Chemical Formulary, Vol. 24. Ed. by H. Bennett. 1982. 60.00 (*0-8206-0291-4*) Chem Pub.

Chemical Formulary, Vol. 25. Ed. by H. Bennett. 1983. 60.00 (*0-8206-0304-X*) Chem Pub.

Chemical Formulary, Vol. 26. H. Bennett. 1985. 60.00 (*0-8206-0313-9*) Chem Pub.

Chemical Formulary, Vol. 27. H. Bennett. 1986. 60.00 (*0-8206-0318-X*) Chem Pub.

Chemical Formulary, Vol. 29. H. Bennett. 1990. 60.00 (*0-8206-0338-4*) Chem Pub.

Chemical Formulary, Vol. 30. H. Bennett. 1992. 60.00 (*0-8206-0341-4*) Chem Pub.

Chemical Formulary, Vols. 1-30. Ed. by H. Bennett. Incl. Vol. 1. 1933. 60.00 (*0-8206-0259-0*); Vol. 2. 1935. 60.00 (*0-8206-0260-4*); Vol. 3. 1936. 60.00 (*0-8206-0261-2*); Vol. 4. 1939. 60.00 (*0-8206-0262-0*); Vol. 5. 1941. 60.00 (*0-8206-0263-9*); Vol. 6. 1943. 60.00 (*0-8206-0264-7*); Vol. 7. 1945. 60.00 (*0-8206-0265-5*); Vol. 8. 1948. 60.00 (*0-8206-0266-3*); Vol. 9. 1950. 60.00 (*0-8206-0267-1*); Vol. 10. 1957. 60.00 (*0-8206-0268-X*); Vol. 11. 1961. 60.00 (*0-8206-0269-8*); Vol. 12. 1965. 60.00 (*0-8206-0270-1*); Vol. 13. 1967. 60.00 (*0-8206-0271-X*); Vol. 14. 1968. 60.00 (*0-8206-0272-8*); Vol. 15. 1970. 60.00 (*0-8206-0273-6*); Vol. 16. 1971. 60.00 (*0-8206-0274-4*); Vol. 17. 1973. 60.00 (*0-8206-0275-2*); Vol. 18. 1975. 60.00 (*0-8206-0276-0*); Vol. 19. 1976. 60.00 (*0-8206-0277-9*); Vol. 20. 1977. 60.00 (*0-8206-0278-7*); Vol. 21. 1979. 60.00 (*0-8206-0279-5*); Vol. 22. 1979. 60.00 (*0-8206-0280-9*); write for info. (*0-318-51346-3*) Chem Pub.

Chemical Formulary Series, Vol. XXVIII. Ed. by H. Bennett. 450p. 1989. 60.00 (*0-8206-0328-7*) Chem Pub.

Chemical Formulary Series: Cumulative Index, Vols. 1-25. Ed. by H. Bennett. 473p. 1986. text ed. 85.00 (*0-8206-0319-8*) Chem Pub.

Chemical Formulas for Profit. 1991. lib. bdg. 88.00 (*0-8490-5037-5*) Gordon Pr.

Chemical-Free Lawn: The Newest Varities Techniques to Grow Lush, Hardy Grass. Warren Schultz. LC 88-26352. (Illus.). 208p. 1989. pap. 14.95 (*0-87857-801-3*, 01-261-1) Rodale Pr Inc.

Chemical Fundamentals of Geology. R. Gill. (Illus.). 256p. 1988. 65.00 (*0-04-551123-3*); pap. 27.95 (*0-00-302091-6*) Routledge Chapman & Hall.

Chemical Generation & Reception of Radio & Microwaves. Anatoly L. Buchachenko & Eugene L. Frankevich. LC 93-28335. 1993. 65.00 (*1-56081-630-9*) VCH Pubs.

Chemical Graph Theory. 2nd ed. Nenad Trinajstic. 1992. 98.95 (*0-8493-4256-2*, QD39) CRC Pr.

Chemical Graph Theory, 2 Vols., Vol. I. Nenad Trinajstic. 160p. 1983. 132.00 (*0-8493-5273-8*, QD39, CRC Reprint) Franklin.

Chemical Graph Theory, 2 Vols., Vol. II. Nenad Trinajstic. 184p. 1983. 132.00 (*0-8493-5274-6*, CRC Reprint) Franklin.

Chemical Ground Water Quality: Anthology. 77p. 6.25 (*1-56034-002-9*, K062) Natl Water Well.

Chemical Group Theory: Introduction & Fundamentals. Ed. by Danail Bonchev & Dennis H. Rouvray. LC 93-38653. (Mathematical Chemistry Ser.: Vol. 3). 1994. text ed. 120.00 (*2-88124-959-0*) Gordon & Breach.

Chemical Grouting. 2nd rev. ed. Karol. (Civil Engineering Ser.: Vol. 8). 384p. 1990. 125.00 (*0-8247-7888-X*) Dekker.

Chemical Hardness. Ed. by D. M. P. Mingos et al. LC 93-16082. (Structure & Bonding Ser.). 1993. write for info. (*3-540-56091-2*); 167.00 (*0-387-56091-2*) Spr-Verlag.

***Chemical Hazard Communication Guidebook: OSHA, EPA & DOT Requirements.** 2nd ed. Waldo & Hinds. 1994. text ed. 75.00 (*0-471-12592-X*); pap. text ed. 49.95 (*0-471-12591-1*) Wiley.

Chemical Hazard Communication Guidebook: OSHA, EPA, & DOT Requirements. 2nd ed. Andrew B. Waldo & Richard D. Hinds. 350p. 1991. 75.00 (*1-55840-758-8*, P7437) Exec Ent Pubns.

Chemical Hazard Communication Guidebook: OSHA, EPA, & DOT Requirements. 2nd ed. Andrew B. Waldo. 1993. text ed. 70.00 (*0-07-067755-7*) McGraw.

Chemical Hazards & Waste Disposal Safety & Health. Center for Occupational Research & Development Staff. (Job Safety & Health Instructional Materials Ser.). (Illus.). 38p. (C). 1981. pap. text ed. 3.25 (*1-55502-145-X*) CORD Commns.

Chemical Hazards at Water & Wastewater Treatment Plants. Buzz. 1992. 65.00 (*0-87371-491-1*, TD434) Lewis Pubs.

Chemical Hazards in the Workplace. Ronald M. Scott. (Industrial Toxicology Ser.). (Illus.). 380p. 1989. 64.95 (*0-87371-134-3*, RA1229) Lewis Pubs.

Chemical Hazards in the Workplace: Measurement & Control. Ed. by G. Choudhary. LC 81-130. (ACS Symposium Ser.: No. 149). 1981. 60.95 (*0-8412-0608-2*) Am Chemical.

Chemical History of a Candle. Michael Faraday. LC 78-12458. (Illus.). 192p. 1978. reprint ed. pap. 12.95 (*0-87797-209-5*) Cherokee.

***Chemical Imbalance.** Martin Jensen. 190p. 1995. 23.00 (*0-7872-0591-5*) Kendall-Hunt.

Chemical Induction of Cancer, Vol. 3B. Joseph C. Arcos. (Structural Basis & Biological Mechanisms Ser.). 1985. text ed. 172.00 (*0-12-059323-8*) Acad Pr.

Chemical Induction of Cancer, Vols. 1 & 2. Joseph C. Arcos et al. Incl. Vol. 1. LC 66-30118. 1968. 100.00 (*0-12-059301-7*); Vol. 2A. LC 66-30118. 1974. 100.00 (*0-12-059302-5*); LC 66-30118. write for info. (*0-318-50243-7*) Acad Pr.

***Chemical Induction of Cancer: Modulation & Combination Effects: An Inventory of the Many Factors Which Influence Carcinogenesis.** Ed. by Joseph C. Arcos et al. LC 94-29782. 1994. write for info. (*0-8176-3766-4*); write for info. (*3-7643-3766-4*) Birkhauser.

Chemical Induction of Cancer, Vol. 3C - Natural, Metal, Fiber & Macromolecular Carcinogens: Structural Bases & Biological Mechanisms. Ed. by Yin-Tak Woo et al. 869p. 1988. text ed. 189.00 (*0-12-059353-X*) Acad Pr.

***Chemical Induction of New Tumors & Cancers: Index of New Information Including Human Risks & Results.** John C. Bartone, Sr. (Illus.). 190p. 1995. 44.50 (*0-7883-0482-8*); pap. 37.50 (*0-7883-0483-6*) ABBE Pubs Assn.

Chemical Industries: An Information Sourcebook. Phae H. Dorman. LC 87-23180. (Sourcebook Series in Business & Management). 112p. 1988. 32.50 (*0-89774-257-5*) Oryx Pr.

Chemical Industries Information Sources. Ed. by Theodore P. Peck. LC 76-6891. (Management Information Guide Ser.: No. 29). 624p. 1979. 68.00 (*0-8103-0829-0*) Gale.

Chemical Industry. 2nd ed. Ed. by Alan Heaton. LC 93-28656. 383p. 1994. pap. 37.50 (*0-7514-0018-1*, Pub. by Blackie Acad & Prof UK) Routledge Chapman & Hall.

Chemical Industry & the Projected Chemical Weapons Convention: Proceedings of a SIPRI-Pugwash Conference, 2 vols., 1. Stockholm International Peace Research Institute Staff. Ed. by Julian P. Robinson. (SIPRI Chemical & Biological Warfare Studies: Nos. 5 & 6). 1986. 29.95 (*0-19-829107-8*) OUP.

Chemical Industry & the Projected Chemical Weapons Convention: Proceedings of a SIPRI-Pugwash Conference, 2 vols., 2. Stockholm International Peace Research Institute Staff. Ed. by Julian P. Robinson. (SIPRI Chemical & Biological Warfare Studies: Nos. 5 & 6). 1986. 29.95 (*0-19-829109-4*) OUP.

Chemical Industry Applications of Industrial Minerals & Metals. Bureau of Mines Staff. 1993. write for info. (*0-318-71683-6*) US Interior.

Chemical Industry in the U. S. S. R. Matthew J. Sagers. (C). 1990. text ed. 121.50 (*0-685-68133-5*); text ed. 134.00 (*0-8133-1068-7*) Westview.

Chemical Industry in the U. S. S. R. Matthew J. Sagers & Theodore Shabad. 590p. (C). 1990. text ed. 127.50 (*0-8133-1748-7*) Westview.

Chemical Industry in the U. S. S. R. An Economic Geography. Matthew J. Sagers & Theodore Shabad. LC 90-34540. (ACS Professional Reference Bk.). 420p. 1990. 89.95 (*0-8412-1760-2*) Am Chemical.

Chemical Information. Ed. by H. R. Collier. (Illus.). 320p. 1990. pap. 91.00 (*0-387-51804-5*, 3720) Spr-Verlag.

Chemical Information Management. Wendy Warr & Claus Suhr. LC 92-8826. 261p. 1992. 90.00 (*1-56081-180-3*) VCH Pubs.

Chemical Information Manual. 2nd ed. EPA Staff. 332p. 1991. pap. text ed. 69.00 (*0-86587-265-1*) Gov Insts.

Chemical Information, No. 2: Information in Chemistry, Pharmacology & Patents: 2nd Proceedings of the International Conference Montreux, Switzerland, September 1990. Ed. by H. R. Collier. (Illus.). viii, 232p. 1991. pap. 89.00 (*0-387-53199-8*) Spr-Verlag.

Chemical Information Sources. Gary D. Wiggins. Ed. by Kirk Emry. (McGraw-Hill Series in Advanced Chemistry). 256p. (C). 1991. text ed. write for info. (*0-07-909939-4*) McGraw.

Chemical Instabilities: Applications in Chemistry, Engineering, Geology, & Materials Science. Ed. by G. Nicolis & F. Baras. 1983. lib. bdg. 145.50 (*90-277-1705-2*) Kluwer Ac.

***Chemical Instrumentation.** Richard P. Wayne. (Oxford Chemistry Primers Ser.: No. 24). (Illus.). 96p. (C). 1994. pap. text ed. 9.95 (*0-19-855796-5*) OUP.

***Chemical Instrumentation.** Richard P. Wayne. (Oxford Chemistry Primers Ser.: No. 24). (Illus.). 96p. (C). 1994. text ed. 29.95 (*0-19-855797-3*) OUP.

Chemical Instrumentation. 2nd ed. Howard A. Strobel. 1973. write for info. (*0-201-07301-3*) Addison-Wesley.

Chemical Instrumentation: Systematic Approach to Instrumental Analysis. 3rd ed. Howard A. Strobel. LC 88-11687. 1989. text ed. 74.95 (*0-471-61223-5*) Wiley.

Chemical Investigation for Changing Times. 4th rev. ed. Laurence W. Scott. 175p. 1984. pap. text ed. write for info. (*0-317-03497-9*) Macmillan.

Chemical Investigations. Nancy Konigsberg-Kerner. (Illus.). 343p. (C). 1986. teacher ed 10.75 (*0-8053-5415-8*); pap. text ed. 29.25 (*0-8053-5410-7*) Benjamin-Cummings.

Chemical Investigations for the Nonscientist. John Tonnis & Gerald Rausch. 1988. spiral bd. 15.50 (*0-88252-139-X*) Paladin Hse.

Chemical Ionization Mass Spectrometry. Ed. by Alex G. Harrison. 168p. 1983. 144.00 (*0-8493-5616-4*, QD96) CRC Pr.

Chemical Ionization Mass Spectrometry. 2nd ed. Ed. by Alex G. Harrison. 168p. 1992. 99.95 (*0-8493-4254-6*, QD496) CRC Pr.

Chemical Kinetics. Houston et al. (Physical Chemistry Ser.). 256p. 1996. pap. 13.45 (*0-8016-6759-3*) Mosby Yr Bk.

Chemical Kinetics. 3rd ed. Keith J. Laidler & J. Keith. 531p. (C). 1990. text ed. 80.00 (*0-06-043862-2*) HarpCollege.

Chemical Kinetics: Homogeneous Reactions. N. M. Emanuel & D. G. Knorre. 456p. 1974. text ed. 107.50 (*0-7065-1318-5*, Pub. by Keter Pub IS) Coronet Bks.

Chemical Kinetics: The Study of Reaction Rates in Solution. Kenneth A. Connors. 480p. 1990. lib. bdg. 95.00 (*1-56081-006-8*); pap. text ed. 49.50 (*1-56081-053-X*) VCH Pubs.

Chemical Kinetics & Chain Reactions: Historical Aspects. V. A. Kritsman & G. E. Zaikov. (Illus.). 543p. (C). 1994. lib. bdg. 89.00 (*1-56072-166-9*) Nova Sci Pubs.

Chemical Kinetics & Dynamics. Jeffrey I. Steinfeld et al. 592p. 1989. text ed. 84.00 (*0-13-129479-2*) P-H.

Chemical Kinetics & Process Dynamics in Aquatic Systems. Brezonik. 1993. 69.95 (*0-87371-431-8*, GB855) Lewis Pubs.

Chemical Kinetics & Reaction Mechanisms. James H. Espenson. (Advanced Chemistry Ser.). (Illus.). 240p. 1981. text ed. write for info. (*0-07-019667-2*) McGraw.

***Chemical Kinetics & Reaction Mechanisms.** James H. Espenson. LC 94-49445. (Advanced Chemistry Ser.). 1995. write for info. (*0-07-020260-5*) McGraw.

Chemical Kinetics & Surface & Colloid Chemistry. A. F. Trotman-Dickenson & Geoffrey D. Parfitt. (Illus.). 1966. 80.00 (*0-08-011257-9*, Pub. by Pergamon Repr UK) Franklin.

Chemical Kinetics of Gas Reactions. V. N. Kondratiev. 1964. 295.00 (*0-08-010108-9*, Pub. by Pergamon Repr UK) Franklin.

Chemical Kinetics of Homogeneous Systems. Ed. by R. Schaal. Tr. by John T. Edward. LC 73-94455. Orig. Title: La Cinetique Chimique Homogene. 200p. 1974. lib. bdg. 56.50 (*90-277-0446-5*) Kluwer Ac.

Chemical Kinetics of Small Organic Radicals. Ed. by Zeev B. Alfassi. 1988. write for info. (*0-318-62926-7*, QD471) CRC Pr.

Chemical Kinetics of Small Organic Radicals, Vol. I: General. Ed. by Zeev B. Alfassi. 192p. 1988. 96.00 (*0-8493-4362-3*, QD471, CRC Reprint) Franklin.

Chemical Kinetics of Small Organic Radicals, Vol. II: Reactions of Special Radicals. Ed. by Zeev B. Alfassi. 256p. 1988. 121.00 (*0-8493-4363-1*, QD471, CRC Reprint) Franklin.

Chemical Kinetics of Small Organic Radicals, Vol. III: Correlation & Calculation Methods. Ed. by Zeev B. Alfassi. 240p. 1988. 125.00 (*0-8493-4364-X*, QD471, CRC Reprint) Franklin.

Chemical Kinetics of Small Organic Radicals, Vol. IV: Reactions in Special Systems. Ed. by Zeev B. Alfassi. 240p. 1988. 134.00 (*0-8493-4365-8*, QD471, CRC Reprint) Franklin.

***Chemical Kinetics of Solids.** Hermann Schmalzried. LC 94-45510. 1995. 214.00 (*3-527-29094-X*) VCH Pubs.

Chemical Labeling: The Inter-Agency Guide. Keller, J. J. & Assoc., Inc. Staff. LC 91-60801. 1992. 145.00 (*0-934674-92-2*, 36G) J J Keller.

Chemical Laboratory - It's Design & Operation: A Practical Guide for Planners of Industrial, Medical, or Educational Facilities. Sigurd J. Rosenlund. LC 86-31183. (Illus.). 158p. 1987. 36.00 (*0-8155-1110-8*) Noyes.

***Chemical Laboratory Safety & Chemical Hygiene Compliance Handbook.** (Illus.). 300p. (Orig.). 1995. pap. 295.00 (*0-7605-1509-3*) Rector Pr.

Chemical Lectures of H. T. Scheffer. Ed. by T. O. Bergman. Tr. by J. A. Schufle. LC 92-8726. (Chemists & Chemistry Ser.: Vol. 14). 560p. (C). 1992. lib. bdg. 212.50 (*0-7923-1760-2*) Kluwer Ac.

Chemical Literature, 1700-1860: A Bibliography with Annotations, Detailed Descriptions, Comparisons & Locations. W. A. Cole. 606p. 1988. text ed. 280.00 (*0-7201-1967-7*, Mansell Pub) Cassell.

Chemical Machining. 2nd ed. Guy Bellows. (Machining Process Ser.: MDC 82-102). (Illus.). 96p. 1982. pap. 12.50 (*0-936974-08-7*) Metcut Res Assocs.

Chemical Magic. John Lippy. 164p. pap. 4.00 (*0-913022-32-2*) Angriff Pr.

Chemical Magic. 2nd rev. ed. Leonard A. Ford. LC 92-42557. (Illus.). 128p. 1993. reprint ed. pap. 5.95 (*0-486-67628-5*) Dover.

***Chemical Magic from the Grocery Store.** Andy Sae. 149p. (C). 1995. 10.00 (*1-881604-20-9*) Scopcraeft.

Chemical Manipulation of Crop Growth. J. S. McLaren. 1982. text ed. 125.00 (*0-408-10767-7*) Buttrwrth-Heinemann.

***Chemical Manufacturers Directory International.** 80p. (Orig.). 1994. pap. 295.00 (*1-57205-875-7*) Rector Pr.

Chemical Mechanisms in Bioenergetics. Ed. by D. Rao Sanadi. LC 76-26707. (ACS Monograph: No. 172). 272p. 1976. 37.95 (*0-8412-0274-5*) Am Chemical.

Chemical Mediation of Coevolution. Ed. by Kevin C. Spencer. 1000p. 1988. text ed. 140.00 (*0-12-656855-3*); pap. text ed. 66.00 (*0-12-656856-1*) Acad Pr.

Chemical Mediators & Cellular Interactions in Clinical Immunology. Ed. by G. Marone. (Journal: International Archives of Allergy & Applied Immunology: Vol. 99 Nos. 2-4). (Illus.). 348p. 1993. 289.00 (*3-8055-5723-X*) S Karger.

Chemical Mediators & Cellular Interactions in Clinical Immunology. Ed. by G. Marone. (International Archives of Allergy & Applied Immunology Ser.: Vol. 99, Nos. 2-4, 1992). (Illus.). 346p. 1993. reprint ed. 196.00 (*3-8055-5757-4*) S Karger.

Chemical Mediators in the Acute Inflammatory Reaction. M. Rocha E Silva & J. Garcia Leme. 374p. 1972. 118.00 (*0-08-017040-4*, Pub. by Pergamon Repr UK) Franklin.

Chemical Mediators of Inflammation & Immunity. Ed. by Stanley Cohen et al. 344p. 1986. text ed. 79.00 (*0-12-179065-7*) Acad Pr.

Chemical, Medical, & Pharmaceutical Books Printed Before 1800: In the Collections of the University of Wisconsin Libraries. Ed. by John Neu et al. 288p. 1965. 27.50 (*0-299-03680-4*) U of Wis Pr.

Chemical Metal Wood, Tobacco & Printing Industries: Present Trends & Future Development, Vol. 1a. (Metropolitan America Ser.). 284p. 1974. 32.95 (*0-405-05415-7*) Ayer.

Chemical Metallurgy. 2nd ed. J. J. Moore. (Illus.). 456p. 1993. pap. 39.95 (*0-7506-1646-6*) Buttrwrth-Heinemann.

Chemical Metallurgy. 2nd ed. John J. Moore. 408p. 1990. text ed. 70.00 (*0-408-05369-0*) Buttrwrth-Heinemann.

Chemical Metallurgy: A Tribute to Carl Wagner: Proceedings of a Symposium. Metallurgical Society of AIME Staff. Ed. by Nev A. Gokoen. LC 81-83779. (Conference Proceedings Ser.). 516p. reprint ed. pap. 147.10 (*0-685-23486-X*, 2029123) Bks Demand.

Chemical Methods for Assessing Bio-Available Metals in Sludges & Soils: Proceedings of a CEC Seminar Held at the Josef-Konig Institute, Munster, West Germany, 11-13 April 1984. Ed. by R. Leschber et al. 104p. 1985. 47.00 (*0-85334-359-4*, Pub. by Elsevier Applied Sci UK) Elsevier.

Chemical Methods in Bacterial Systematics. Ed. by Michael Goodfellow & David E. Minnikin. LC 84-11032. (Society for Applied Bacteriology Technical Ser.). 1985. text ed. 134.00 (*0-12-289675-0*) Acad Pr.

Chemical Methods in Gas Chromatography. V. G. Berezkin. (Journal of Chromatography Library: No. 24). 314p. 1983. 147.00 (*0-444-41951-9*, I-383-83) Elsevier.

Chemical Methods in Prokaryotic Systematics. Ed. by Michael Goodfellow & Anthony G. O'Donnell. LC 93-42033. (Modern Microbiological Methods Ser.). 1994. text ed. 129.95 (*0-471-94191-3*) Wiley.

Chemical Methods of Rock Analysis. 3rd ed. P. G. Jeffery & D. Hutchison. (Series in Analytical Chemistry: Vol. 4). (Illus.). xv, 385p. 1981. 115.00 (*0-08-023806-8*, Pergamon Pr) Elsevier.

Chemical Microanalysis of Solids Using Electron Beams. I. P. Jones. 241p. 1992. 70.00 (*0-901716-06-5*, Pub. by Inst Materials UK) Ashgate Pub Co.

Chemical, Microbiological, Health & Comfort Aspects of Indoor Air Quality - State of the Art in SBS: Based on the Lectures Given During the Eurocourse on Chemical, Microbiological, Health & Comfort Aspects of Indoor Air Quality - State of the Art in SBS Held at the Joint Research Centre, Ispra, Italy, March 23-27, 1992. Ed. by Kelmut Knoppel. 388p. (C). 1992. lib. bdg. 122.00 (*0-7923-1703-3*) Kluwer Ac.

Chemical Microbiology. 2nd ed. Anthony H. Rose. LC 68-28664. 324p. reprint ed. pap. 92.40 (*0-685-15664-8*, 2026288) Bks Demand.

Chemical Microstructure of Polymer Chains. Jack L. Koenig. LC 89-31764. 432p. 1990. reprint ed. 69.50 (*0-89464-392-4*) Krieger.

Chemical Mobility & Reactivity in Soil Systems. Ed. by D. W. Nelson et al. (Special Publication Ser.). 262p. 1983. pap. 12.00 (*0-89118-771-5*) Soil Sci Soc Am.

Chemical Modeling in Aqueous Systems. Ed. by Everett A. Jenne. LC 79-242. (ACS Symposium Ser.: No. 93). 1979. 76.95 (*0-8412-0479-9*) Am Chemical.

An Asterisk (*) at the beginning of an entry indicates that the title is appearing in BIP for the first time.

°C

An Asterisk (*) at the beginning of an entry indicates that the title is appearing in BIP for the first time.

1173

Chemical Reactor Theory: An Introduction. Kenneth G. Denbigh & J. C. Turner. LC 76-123661. 236p. reprint ed. pap. 67.30 (*0-317-10504-3*, 2013219) Bks Demand.

Chemical Reactors. Ed. by H. Scott Fogler. LC 81-12672. (ACS Symposium Ser.: No. 168). 1981. 43.95 (*0-8412-0658-9*) Am Chemical.

***Chemical Reactors: Design, Engineering, Operation.** Pierre Trambouze et al. (Illus.). 640p. (C). 1988. text ed. 192.00 (*2-7108-0542-1*) Technip.

Chemical Reactors for Gas-Liquid Systems. F. Kastenek et al. 250p. 1993. text ed. write for info. (*0-13-127390-6*) P-H.

Chemical Reagents for Protein Modification. 2nd ed. Roger L. Lundblad. (Illus.). 376p. 1991. 167.00 (*0-8493-5097-2*, QP551) CRC Pr.

Chemical Reagents for Protein Modification, Vol. I. Roger L. Lundblad & Claudia M. Noyes. 192p. 1984. 144.00 (*0-8493-5086-7*, TP453) CRC Pr.

Chemical Reagents for Protein Modification, Vol. II. Roger L. Lundblad & Claudia M. Noyes. 184p. 1984. 144.00 (*0-8493-5087-5*) CRC Pr.

Chemical Reagents in the Mineral Processing Industry. Ed. by Deepak Malhotra & William F. Riggs. LC 86-63354. 320p. reprint ed. pap. 91.20 (*0-8357-3484-6*, 2039743) Bks Demand.

Chemical Recognition in Biology. Ed. by F. Chapeville & A. O. Haenni. (Molecular Biology, Biochemistry & Biophysics Ser.: Vol. 32). (Illus.). 430p. 1980. 82.00 (*0-387-10205-1*) Spr-Verlag.

***Chemical Recovery in the Alkaline Pulping Processes.** Gerald Hough. LC 85-50956. 308p. 1985. 120.00 (*0-89852-255-2*, 0102B046) TAPPI.

Chemical Recovery in the Alkaline Pulping Processes. 3rd rev. ed. Technical Association of the Pulp & Paper Industry Staff. Ed. by Robert P. Green & Gerald Hough. LC 85-50956. reprint ed. pap. 56.20 (*0-7837-3033-0*, 2042906) Bks Demand.

Chemical Reference Handbook. 1991. lib. bdg. 79.95 (*0-8490-4083-3*) Gordon Pr.

***Chemical Reference Handbook.** 1995. lib. bdg. 260.75 (*0-8490-6562-3*) Gordon Pr.

Chemical Regulation Reporter. BNA's Environment & Safety Services Staff. 1977. ring bd. 1,605.00 (*0-685-07301-7*) BNA.

Chemical Regulatory Cross-Reference. 240p. 1991. ring bd. 75.00 (*0-934674-93-0*, 271009) J J Keller.

Chemical Rejuvenation of the Face. Kotler. (Illus.). 230p. 1991. 129.00 (*0-8016-2615-3*) Mosby Yr Bk.

Chemical Relaxation: An Introduction to Theory & Application of Stepwise Perturbation. George H. Czerlinski. LC 66-16501. 328p. reprint ed. pap. 93.50 (*0-685-15964-7*, 2027077) Bks Demand.

Chemical Research Faculties: An International Directory, 1988 Edition. LC 87-37420. 750p. 1988. 159.95 (*0-8412-1017-9*) Am Chemical.

Chemical Resistance Vol. 1: Thermoplastics. 2nd ed. Plastics Design Library Staff. (PDL Handbook Ser.). 1100p. 1994. lib. bdg. 285.00 (*1-884207-12-X*, 6531U) William Andrew.

Chemical Resistance Vol. 2: Thermoplastic Elastomers, Thermosets & Rubbers. 2nd ed. Plastics Design Library Staff. (PDL Handbook Ser.). 977p. 1994. lib. bdg. 285.00 (*1-884207-13-8*, 6533U) William Andrew.

Chemical Resistance of Polymers in Aggressive Media. Yu V. Moiseev & G. E. Zaikov. Tr. by R. J. Mosley. LC 87-9075. (Illus.). 384p. 1987. 110.00 (*0-306-10997-2*, Consultants) Plenum.

Chemical Resistant Materials. EEMUA Staff. 1965. Pt. II (1968). write for info. (*0-318-61901-6*, Pub. by EEMUA UK) St Mut.

Chemical Resistant Materials, Pt. I. EEMUA Staff. 1965. 125.00 (*0-85931-047-7*, Pub. by EEMUA UK) St Mut.

Chemical-Resistant Non Metallic Materials; Vitrified Clay & Concrete Pipe & Tile; Masonry Mortars & Units; Asbestos-Cement Products (125 Standards) see ASTM Annual Book of Standards, 1986

Chemical Revolution. Archibald Clow & Nan L. Clow. (Essay Index Reprint Ser.). 1977. 46.95 (*0-8369-1909-2*) Ayer.

Chemical Revolution: A Contribution to Social Technology. Archibald Clow & Nan L. Clow. LC 92-7259. 680p. 1992. pap. text ed. 58.00 (*2-88124-549-8*) Gordon & Breach.

Chemical Risk Assessment & Occupational Health: Current Applications, Limitations, & Future Prospects. Ed. by C. Mark Smith et al. LC 93-40165. 304p. 1994. text ed. 59.95 (*0-86569-219-X*, Auburn Hse) Greenwood.

Chemical Rocket Propulsion & Combustion Research. S. S. Penner. (Illus.). 170p. 1962. text ed. 136.00 (*0-677-00710-8*) Gordon & Breach.

Chemical Rockets, & Flame & Explosives Technology. Richard T. Holzmann. LC 69-18125. 461p. reprint ed. pap. 131.40 (*0-685-15572-2*, 2026755) Bks Demand.

Chemical Safety: International Reference Manual. Ed. by Mervyn Richardson. LC 94-7950. 1994. 145.00 (*1-56081-815-8*) VCH Pubs.

Chemical Safety Handbook for the Semiconductor - Electronics Industry. David G. Baldwin et al. 432p. 1991. pap. 16.95 (*0-9623864-2-1*) OEM Health.

Chemical Safety in the Laboratory. Steven K. Hall. 1993. 59.95 (*0-87371-896-8*) Lewis Pubs.

Chemical Safety Matters: Safe Use & Disposal of Chemicals in Laboratories. World Health Organization Staff & International Union of Pure & Applied Chemistry Staff. (Illus.). 200p. (C). 1992. 42.95 (*0-521-41375-3*) Cambridge U Pr.

Chemical Safety (Reference Card) Tel-A-Train, Inc. Staff. 1985. student ed 0.15 (*1-56355-187-X*) Tel-A-Train.

Chemical Safety Regulation & Compliance. Ed. by F. Homburger & Judith K. Marquis. (Illus.). x, 130p. 1985. 92.00 (*3-8055-3941-X*) S Karger.

Chemical Safety Sheets: Working Safely with Hazardous Chemicals. Ed. by Dutch Institute for the Working Environment Staff & Dutch Chemical Industry Association Staff. (C). 1991. lib. bdg. 124.00 (*0-7923-1258-9*) Kluwer Ac.

Chemical Sampling Methods Handbook. S. Ness. 1994. text ed. write for info. (*0-442-01463-5*) Van Nos Reinhold.

Chemical Sciences Graduate School Finder, 1992-1993. 600p. 1992. pap. 44.95 (*0-8412-2522-2*) Am Chemical.

Chemical Sciences Graduate School Finder, 1993-1994. 3rd ed. 702p. 49.95 (*0-8412-2739-X*) Am Chemical.

Chemical Sciences in the Modern World. Ed. by Seymour H. Mauskopf. (Chemical Sciences in Society Ser.). (Illus.). 448p. (C). 1994. text ed. 39.95 (*0-8122-3156-2*) U of Pa Pr.

Chemical Scythe: The Lessons of 2, 4, 5-T & Dioxin. Alastair Hay. LC 82-12249. (Disaster Research in Practice Ser.). 278p. 1982. 59.50 (*0-306-40973-9*, Plenum Pr) Plenum.

Chemical Searching on an Array Processor. Terence Wilson. LC 92-19978. (Computers & Chemical Structure Information Ser.: Vol. 2). 197p. 1993. text ed. 69.95 (*0-471-93436-4*) Wiley.

Chemical Sediments & Geomorphology. Ed. by Andrew S. Goudie & Kenneth Pye. 1983. text ed. 134.00 (*0-12-293480-6*) Acad Pr.

Chemical Sense see Handbook of Sensory Physiology

Chemical Senses, Vol. 2: Irritation. Green et al. 384p. 1990. 125.00 (*0-8247-8323-9*) Dekker.

Chemical Senses, Vol. 3: Genetics of Perception & Communication. Ed. by Charles J. Wysocki & Morely R. Kare. 400p. 1991. 140.00 (*0-8247-8370-0*) Dekker.

Chemical Senses, Vol. 4: Appetite & Nutrition. Ed. by Mark I. Friedman & Michael G. Tordoff. 504p. 1991. 185.00 (*0-8247-8371-9*) Dekker.

Chemical Sensing with Solid State Devices. Marc J. Madou & S. Roy Morrison. 556p. 1989. text ed. 142.00 (*0-12-464965-3*) Acad Pr.

Chemical Sensitivities: Physiological Effects & Treatment. Robert W. Gardner. 1993. 59.95 (*0-8493-8926-7*) CRC Pr.

Chemical Sensitivity. Sherry Rogers. Ed. by Don R. Bensen. 1995. 3.95 (*0-87983-634-2*) Keats.

Chemical Sensitivity, 4 vols., I. William J. Rea. 1992. 75.00 (*0-87371-541-1*, RB152) Lewis Pubs.

Chemical Sensitivity, 4 vols., II. William J. Rea. 1992. 75.00 (*0-87371-963-8*) Lewis Pubs.

Chemical Sensitivity, 4 vols., III. William J. Rea. 848p. 1995. 89.95 (*0-87371-964-6*, L964) Lewis Pubs.

Chemical Sensitivity, 4 vols., IV. William J. Rea. 1992. write for info. (*0-87371-965-4*) Lewis Pubs.

Chemical Sensitivity: A Guide to Coping with Hypersensitivity Syndrome, Sick Building Syndrome & Other Environmental Illnesses. Bonnye L. Matthews. LC 92-54089. 292p. 1992. lib. bdg. 29.95 (*0-89950-731-X*) McFarland & Co.

Chemical Sensor Technology, Vol. 1. Ed. by T. Seiyama. 250p. 1988. 146.25 (*0-444-98901-3*) Elsevier.

Chemical Sensor Technology, Vol. 2. Ed. by T. Seiyama. 304p. 1990. 174.50 (*0-444-98784-3*) Elsevier.

Chemical Sensor Technology, Vol. 3. Ed. by N. Yamazoe. 292p. 1991. 194.50 (*0-444-98701-0*) Elsevier.

Chemical Sensors & Microinstrumentation. Ed. by Raymond E. Dessy et al. LC 89-15149. (Symposium Ser.: No. 403). (Illus.). 395p. 1989. 89.95 (*0-8412-1661-4*) Am Chemical.

Chemical Sensors for IN Vivo Monitoring. Palleschi. 1992. write for info. (*0-8493-6139-7*) CRC Pr.

Chemical Separation of the Uranium Isotopes. Clyde A. Hutchison & AEC Technical Information Center Staff. (National Nuclear Energy Ser.: Div. III, Vol. 3). 178p. 1952. mic. film 9.00 (*0-87079-160-5*, TID-5224) DOE.

Chemical Separations & Measurements: Theory & Practice of Analytical Chemistry. Dennis G. Peters et al. LC 73-87385. (Illus.). 749p. (C). 1974. text ed. 53.25 (*0-7216-7203-5*) SCP.

Chemical Separations, Vol. I: Principles. Ed. by C. Judson King & James D. Navratil. LC 86-81868. 462p. 1986. lib. bdg. 77.00 (*0-937557-02-1*) Litarvan Lit.

Chemical Separations, Vol. II: Applications. Ed. by C. Judson King & James D. Navratil. 469p. 1986. lib. bdg. 77.00 (*0-937557-03-X*) Litarvan Lit.

Chemical Shift Ranges in Carbon-13 NMR Spectroscopy. W. Bremser et al. Ed. by H. Wagner. 891p. 1982. 200.00 (*0-89573-053-7*) VCH Pubs.

Chemical Signaling in the Basal Ganglia. Ed. by G. W. Arbuthnott & P. C. Emson. LC 93-1791. (Progress in Brain Research Ser.). 1993. write for info. (*0-444-81562-7*) Elsevier.

Chemical Signals in Vertebrates. Ed. by D. W. Macdonald et al. (Illus.). 688p. 1991. 95.00 (*0-19-857731-1*) OUP.

Chemical Signals in Vertebrates, Vol. 3. Ed. by Robert M. Silverstein & Dietland Muller-Schwarze. LC 83-2151. 378p. 1983. 79.50 (*0-306-41254-3*, Plenum Pr) Plenum.

Chemical Signals in Vertebrates, Vol. 6. Ed. by Richard L. Doty & Dietland Muller-Schwarze. LC 92-22006. 1992. 135.00 (*0-306-44250-7*, Plenum Pr) Plenum.

Chemical Signals in Vertebrates, Vol. 4: Ecology, Evolution, & Comparative Biology. Ed. by David Duvall et al. LC 86-17013. 754p. 1986. 125.00 (*0-306-42382-0*, Plenum Pr) Plenum.

Chemical Signals System, Vol. 2: Chemical Signalling in Living Organisms. Alfred T. Kornfield. LC 90-61295. (C). 1990. 60.00 (*0-9626494-0-6*) Biosearch Pr.

Chemical Skills. 4th ed. Edward I. Peters & William T. Scroggins. 1992. pap. text ed. write for info. (*0-07-049562-9*) McGraw.

Chemical Soldiers: British Gas Warfare in World War I. Donald Richter. LC 92-12329. (Modern War Studies). (Illus.). xii, 284p. 1992. 35.00 (*0-7006-0544-4*) U Pr of KS.

Chemical Soldiers: British Gas Warfare in World War One. Donald Richter. (Illus.). 286p. 1994. 43.50 (*0-85052-388-5*, Pub. by L Cooper Bks UK) Trans-Atl Phila.

Chemical Solutions: Reagent Useful to the Chemist, Biologist & Bacteriologist. Frank Welcher. 412p. 1966. pap. 10.50 (*0-442-09280-6*) Van Nos Reinhold.

***Chemical Speciation in the Environment.** A. M. Ure. 1994. 129.00 (*0-7514-0021-1*, Pub. by Blackie Acad & Prof UK) Routledge Chapman & Hall.

Chemical Spectroscopy & Photochemistry in the Vacuum: Proceedings of the NATO Advanced Study Institute, 1973. NATO Advanced Study Institute Staff. Ed. by Camille Sandorfy et al. LC 73-91209. (NATO Advanced Studies Institute Ser.: No. C-8). 1974. lib. bdg. 149.50 (*90-277-0418-X*) Kluwer Ac.

Chemical Spills & Emergency Management at Sea. Ed. by P. Bockholts & I. Heidebrink. (C). 1989. lib. bdg. 193.50 (*0-7923-0052-1*) Kluwer Ac.

Chemical Stability of Pharmaceuticals: A Handbook for Pharmacists. 2nd ed. Kenneth A. Connors et al. LC 85-31455. 847p. 1986. text ed. 115.00 (*0-471-87955-X*) Wiley.

Chemical Sterilants & Sterilization Methods: A Guide to Selection & Use. 45p. 1990. 59.00 (*0-910275-98-X*, TIR7-113) Assn Adv Med Instrn.

Chemical Storage Buildings. Richard K. Miller & Marcia E. Rupnow. LC 90-83882. (Survey on Technology & Markets Ser.: No. 178). 50p. 1991. pap. text ed. 200.00 (*1-55865-202-7*) Future Tech Surveys.

Chemical Storage Drums. Richard K. Miller & Marcia E. Rupnow. (Survey on Technology & Markets Ser.: No. 156). 50p. 1991. 200.00 (*1-55865-226-4*) Future Tech Surveys.

Chemical Structure - Biological Activity Relationships, Quantitative Approaches: Proceedings of the Third Congress of the Hungarian Pharmacological Society, Budapest, 1979. Ed. by F. Darvas & J. Knoll. LC 80-41281. (Advances in Pharmacological Research & Practice Ser.: Vol. III). 355p. 1980. 168.00 (*0-08-026388-7*, Pub. by Pergamon Repr UK) Franklin.

Chemical Structure & Bonding. 2nd ed. Roger L. Dekock & Harry B. Gray. (Illus.). 490p. (C). 1989. reprint ed. text ed. 36.50 (*0-935702-61-X*) Univ Sci Bks.

Chemical Structure Information Systems: Interfaces, Communication, & Standards. Ed. by Wendy A. Warr. LC 89-14988. (Symposium Ser.: No. 400). (Illus.). 146p. 1989. 34.95 (*0-8412-1664-9*) Am Chemical.

Chemical Structure Software for Personal Computers. Ed. by Daniel E. Meyer et al. LC 88-8153. (ACS Professional Reference Bk.). (Illus.). xiv, 107p. 1988. 39.95 (*0-8412-1538-3*); pap. 24.95 (*0-8412-1539-1*) Am Chemical.

Chemical Structures. Ed. by Wendy A. Warr. (Illus.). 488p. 1988. 128.00 (*0-387-50143-6*) Spr-Verlag.

Chemical Structures 2: The International Language of Chemistry - Proceedings of the Second International Conference, Leeuewenhorst Congress Center, Noordwijkerhout, the Netherlands, 3rd June 1990. Ed. by Wendy A Warr. LC 92-45010. 1993. 159.00 (*0-387-56369-5*) Spr-Verlag.

Chemical Substances Control. BNA's Environment & Safety Services Staff. (Policy & Practice Ser.). 660.00 (*0-685-42618-1*) BNA.

Chemical Surface Preparation, Passivation & Cleaning for Semiconductor Growth & Processing. Ed. by R. J. Nemanich et al. (Materials Research Society Symposium Proceedings Ser.: Vol. 259). 1992. text ed. 57.00 (*1-55899-154-9*) Materials Res.

Chemical Synthesis in Molecular Biology: Biological Macromolecules. Ed. by H. Blocker et al. LC 87-8131. (GBF Monographs: Vol. 8). (Illus.). 222p. 1987. pap. text ed. 105.00 (*0-89573-618-7*) VCH Pubs.

Chemical Synthesis in the Laboratory: An Advanced Course. J. M. Burlitch. 280p. (C). 1993. text ed. 42.00 (*981-02-0449-3*); pap. text ed. 28.00 (*981-02-0450-7*) World Scientific Pub.

Chemical Synthesis of Advanced Ceramics. Daniel L. Segal. (Chemistry of Solid State Materials Ser.: No. 1). (Illus.). (C). 1989. 74.95 (*0-521-35436-6*) Cambridge U Pr.

Chemical Synthesis of Advanced Ceramics. Daniel L. Segal. (Chemistry of Solid State Materials Ser.: No. 1). (Illus.). 200p. (C). 1991. pap. 24.95 (*0-521-42418-6*) Cambridge U Pr.

Chemical Synthesis of Ether Lipids, Vol. 12. G. A. Serebrennikova & R. P. Evstigneeva. (Soviet Scientific Reviews Ser.: Vol. 12, Pt. 4). 70p. 1989. pap. text ed. 42.00 (*3-7186-4900-4*) Gordon & Breach.

Chemical Synthesis of Peptides. John Jones. (International Series of Monographs on Chemistry: Vol. 23). (Illus.). 240p. 1994. reprint ed. pap. 29.95 (*0-19-855839-2*) OUP.

Chemical Tankers. Lorne & MacLean Marine & Offshore Publications Staff. (C). 1987. 75.00 (*0-685-33869-X*, Pub. by Lorne & MacLean Marine) St Mut.

Chemical Technician's Ready Reference Handbook. 3rd ed. Gershon J. Shugar. 912p. 1990. text ed. 74.50 (*0-07-057183-X*) McGraw.

Chemical Technology. F. A. Henglein. (C). 1969. 376.00 (*0-08-011848-8*, Pub. by Pergamon Repr UK) Franklin.

Chemical Technology: An Encyclopedic Treatment, 8 vols. Intro. by John J. McKetta, Jr. Incl. Vol. 4. Petroleum & Organic Chemicals. (Illus.). 792p. 1972. Pgs. 792. 68.50 (*0-06-491105-5*, 06298); Vol. 5. Natural Organic Materials & Related Synthetic Products. (Illus.). 898p. 1972. Pgs. 898. 68.50 (*0-06-491106-3*, 06299); Vol. 6. Wood, Paper, Textiles, Plastics & Photographic Materials. (Illus.). 686p. 1973. 68.50 (*0-06-491107-1*, 06300); Vol. 8. Edible Oils & Fats & Animal Food Products: Material Resources. (Illus.). 600p. 1975. Pgs. 600. 68.50 (*0-06-491109-8*, 06302); (Illus.). write for info. (*0-318-51000-6*) B&N Imports.

Chemical Technology Dictionary: English, French-German-Arabic. A. M. Abd-El-Wahed. 383p. (ARA, ENG, FRE & GER.). 1974. 75.00 (*0-8288-5975-2*, M9759) Fr & Eur.

Chemical Technology for Appropriate Development. J. Van Brakel. 242p. (Orig.). 1978. pap. text ed. 29.50x (*90-6275-010-9*, Pub. by Delft U Pr NE) Coronet Bks.

Chemical Technology Handbook. Ed. by Robert L. Pecsok et al. LC 75-22497. 1975. 24.95 (*0-8412-0242-7*); pap. 14.95 (*0-8412-0578-7*) Am Chemical.

Chemical Technology in Printing & Imaging Systems. Ed. by J. A. Drake. 188p. 1994. 79.95 (*0-85186-655-7*, Pub. by Royal Soc Chem UK) CRC Pr.

Chemical Testing & Analysis. E. B. Jones. 1978. 70.00 (*0-686-63754-2*) St Mut.

Chemical Testing & Analysis, Vol. 6, No. 3. A. G. De Boos. (C). 1974. pap. text ed. 75.00 (*0-685-46409-1*, Pub. by Textile Institue UK) St Mut.

Chemical Testing & Analysis, Vol. 10, No. 4. E. B. Jones. 101p. (C). 1983. pap. text ed. 110.00 (*0-900739-33-9*, Pub. by Textile Institue UK) St Mut.

Chemical Thermodynamics. A. N. Krestovnikov & V. N. Vigdorovich. 224p. 1964. text ed. 56.75 (*0-7065-0571-9*, Pub. by Keter Pub IS) Coronet Bks.

Chemical Thermodynamics. Lindenberg et al. 352p. 1996. pap. 20.00 (*0-8016-6750-X*) Mosby Yr Bk.

Chemical Thermodynamics. M. L. McGlashan. LC 79-40919. 1980. text ed. 88.00 (*0-12-482650-4*) Acad Pr.

Chemical Thermodynamics. C. E. Reid. 1990. text ed. write for info. (*0-07-051769-X*); write for info. (*0-318-67328-2*) McGraw.

Chemical Thermodynamics. Peter A. Rock. Ed. by Donald A. McQuarrie. LC 82-51233. (Physical Chemistry Ser.). (Illus.). 553p. (C). 1983. 54.00 (*0-935702-12-1*) Univ Sci Bks.

Chemical Thermodynamics: Basic Theories & Methods. 4th ed. Irving M. Klotz & Robert M. Rosenberg. LC 85-17475. (Illus.). 470p. (C). 1986. text ed. 44.25 (*0-8053-5501-4*) Benjamin-Cummings.

Chemical Thermodynamics: Basic Theory & Methods. 4th ed. Irving M. Klotz & Robert M. Rosenberg. LC 90-26664. 528p. (C). 1991. reprint ed. 52.50 (*0-89464-572-2*) Krieger.

Chemical Thermodynamics: Basic Theory Methods. 5th ed. Irving M. Klotz & Robert M. Rosenberg. LC 93-38711. 1994. text ed: 64.95 (*0-471-53439-0*) Wiley.

Chemical Thermodynamics: Proceedings of an International Conference, Baden Bei Wein, Austria, 1973, Vol. 3. International Union of Pure & Applied Chemistry. 110p. 1974. 55.00 (*0-08-020735-9*, Pub. by Pergamon Repr UK) Franklin.

Chemical Thermodynamics for Earth Scientists. Philip Fletcher. 464p. (C). 1993. pap. text ed. 49.95 (*0-470-22072-4*) Halsted Pr.

Chemical Thermodynamics of Materials. C. P. Lupis. LC 93-9743. 1983. pap. text ed. 79.00 (*0-13-050238-3*) P-H.

Chemical Thermodynamics of Materials. Claude H. Lupis. 608p. 1983. pap. 60.00 (*0-444-00779-2*) P-H.

Chemical Thermodynamics of Organic Compounds. Daniel R. Stull et al. LC 83-19972. 888p. 1987. reprint ed. 98.50 (*0-89874-706-6*) Krieger.

Chemical Thermodynamics of Uranium. Ingmar Grenthe et al. (Chemical Thermodynamics Ser.). 714p. 1992. 228.50 (*0-444-89381-4*, QD504) CRC Pr.

Chemical Toxicology & Clinical Chemistry of Metals. Ed. by Stanley S. Brown & John Savory. 1984. text ed. 93.00 (*0-12-137520-X*) Acad Pr.

Chemical Tradename Dictionary. Ed. by Irene Ash. LC 92-35154. 530p. 1992. 85.00 (*1-56081-625-2*) VCH Pubs.

Chemical Transmission in the Brain: The Role of Amines, Amino Acids & Peptides: Proceedings of the 12th International Summer School of Brain Research, held at the Royal Netherlands Academy of Arts & Sciences, Amsterdam, The Netherlands, Aug. 31-Sept. 4, 1981. Ed. by R. M. Buijs et al. (Progress in Brain Research Ser.: Vol. 55). 490p. 1982. 142.00 (*0-444-80411-0*) Elsevier.

Chemical Transmission of Nerve Impulses: A Historical Sketch. Z. M. Bacq. 1975. 55.00 (*0-08-020512-7*, Pub. by Pergamon Repr UK) Franklin.

Chemical Treatment of Boiler Water. James W. McCoy. (Illus.). 1981. 58.50 (*0-8206-0284-1*) Chem Pub.

Chemical Treatment of Cooling Water. 2nd ed. James W. McCoy. (Illus.). 1983. 58.50 (*0-8206-0298-1*) Chem Pub.

Chemical Triggering: Reactions of Potential Utility in Industrial Processes. C. J. Sabongi. LC 87-25742. (Topics in Applied Chemistry Ser.). (Illus.). 296p. 1987. 85.00 (*0-306-42643-9*, Plenum Pr) Plenum.

***Chemical Use among Older Adults: Risks, Reactions, & Concerns.** Phillip J. Levine. 40p. 1993. pap. 3.95 (*1-56246-071-4*, P267) Johnsn Inst.

Chemical Vapor Deposited Materials. Francis S. Galasso. 120p. 1991. 79.95 (*0-8493-4219-8*, TS695) CRC Pr.

Chemical Vapor Deposition. BCC Staff. 144p. 1990. 2,450.00 (*0-89336-693-5*, GB-130) BCC.

An Asterisk (*) at the beginning of an entry indicates that the title is appearing in BIP for the first time.

An Asterisk (*) at the beginning of an entry indicates that the title is appearing in BIP for the first time.

1175

Chemistry: A First Course. 3rd ed. Jackueline Kroschwitz et al. 256p. 1995. student ed, spiral bd. write for info. (0-697-23665-X) Wm C Brown Pubs.

Chemistry: A First Course. 3rd ed. Jackueline Kroschwitz et al. 640p. (C). 1995. student ed, text ed. write for info. (0-697-23660-9) Wm C Brown Pubs.

Chemistry: A First Course. 3rd ed. Jackueline Kroschwitz et al. 160p. 1995. student ed, spiral bd. write for info. (0-697-23663-3) Wm C Brown Pubs.

Chemistry: A Quantitative Approach. Robert N. Smith. LC 71-75642. 655p. reprint ed. pap. 180.00 (0-317-08672-3, 2012507) Bks Demand.

Chemistry: A Science for Today. H. Stephen Stoker. (C). 1988. write for info. (0-02-417740-7) Macmillan.

Chemistry: A Science for Today. H. Stephen Stoker. (C). 1989. student ed, pap. write for info. (0-02-417850-0) Macmillan.

Chemistry: A Search to Understand. Anna J. Harrison & Edwin S. Weaver. 640p. (C). 1988. text ed. 45.25 (0-15-506476-2) SCP.

Chemistry: A Systematic Approach. Harry H. Sisler et al. (Illus.). 1980. text ed. 32.50 (0-19-502630-6) OUP.

Chemistry: An Experimental Science. George M. Bodner & Harry L. Pardue. 1989. Net. student ed write for info. (0-471-63286-4); trans. 180.00 (0-471-62133-1) Wiley.

Chemistry: An Experimental Science. George M. Bodner & Harry L. Pardue. 1989. Net. text ed. write for info. (0-471-87053-6) Wiley.

Chemistry: An Experimental Science. George M. Bodner & Harry L. Pardue. 1993. Net. 19.95 (0-471-62137-4) Wiley.

Chemistry: An Experimental Science. Ed. by George C. Pimentel. LC 63-18323. (Chemical Education Material Study Ser.). (Illus.). 466p. (C). 1995. pap. text ed. 5.95 (0-7167-0002-6) W H Freeman.

*Chemistry: An Experimental Science. 2nd ed. George M. Bodner & Harry L. Pardue. LC 94-22161. 983p. 1994. text ed. 54.50 (0-471-59386-9) Wiley.

*Chemistry: An Introduction to General, Organic, & Biological Chemistry. 6th ed. Karen C. Timberlake. LC 95-17. (C). 1995. write for info. (0-673-99054-0) HarpCollege.

Chemistry: An Investigative Approach. rev. ed. F. A. Cotton et al. (Illus.). 298p. 1980. text ed. 56.92 (0-395-27839-2) HM.

C

Chemistry: Concepts & Calculations. Arnold B. Loebel. LC 77-26720. 576p. reprint ed. pap. 164.20 (0-317-09888-8, 2022508) Bks Demand.

Chemistry: Concepts & Connections. Charles H. Corwin. 816p. 1993. text ed. write for info. (0-13-481946-2) P-H.

Chemistry: Concepts & Models. William R. Robinson et al. 753p. (C). 1992. text ed. write for info. (0-669-32800-6); Study guide. student ed write for info. (0-669-28948-5); Instr.'s guide. teacher ed write for info. (0-669-28949-3); Transparencies. trans. write for info. (0-318-70089-1); Solutions guide. write for info. (0-669-28950-7) Heath.

Chemistry: Concepts & Problems. Clifford C. Houk & Richard Post. 370p. 1977. pap. text ed. 14.95 (0-471-41500-6, Wiley) Wiley.

Chemistry: Experiment & Theory. 2nd ed. Bernice G. Segal. LC 88-20896. 960p. 1989. Net. text ed. write for info. (0-471-84929-4); Net. student ed write for info. (0-471-85116-7); Net. write for info. (0-471-85115-9) Wiley.

Chemistry: General, Organic, Biological. 2nd ed. Jacqueline I. Kroschwitz & Melvin Winokur. 944p. (C). 1990. text ed. write for info. (0-07-035546-0) McGraw.

Chemistry: General, Organic, Biological. 2nd ed. Jacqueline I. Kroschwitz & Melvin Winokur. 944p. (C). 1990. Study guide. student ed, pap. text ed. write for info. (0-07-035573-8) McGraw.

*Chemistry: Hands on Elementary School Science. Linda Poore. 40p. 1994. teacher ed 35.00 (1-883410-15-0); teacher ed 35.00 (0-614-02583-4) L Poore.

Chemistry: Impact on Society. Melvin D. Joesten et al. 487p. (C). 1988. pap. text ed. 36.00 (0-03-008897-6) SCP.

Chemistry: In a Flash. Elizabeth Burchard. (Exambusters Ser.). 464p. (J). (gr. 7-12). 1994. pap. 9.95 (1-881374-01-7) Flash Blasters.

Chemistry: Objective Type Questions with Answers for Civil Services & Other Competitive. M. Yadav & G. Raj. 182p. (C). 1986. text ed. 17.95 (0-685-13520-9, Pub. by Sterling Pubs II) Apt Bks.

Chemistry: Principles & Reactions. William L. Masterton & Cecile N. Hurley. 960p. (C). 1989. text ed. 61.25 (0-03-013643-1) SCP.

Chemistry: Science of Change. David W. Oxtoby et al. 848p. (C). 1990. text ed. 69.25 (0-03-004814-1) SCP.

Chemistry: Structure & Dynamics. F. M. Miller. 1984. Instr's. manual. teacher ed write for info. (0-07-041986-8); Solutions supplement. write for info. (0-07-041988-4) McGraw.

Chemistry: The Central Science. 5th ed. Theodore L. Brown et al. 1124p. 1990. text ed. 77.00 (0-13-126202-5) P-H.

Chemistry: The Central Science. 6th ed. Theodore L. Brown et al. LC 93-35988. 1993. text ed. 77.00 (0-13-336397-X) P-H.

Chemistry: The Experience. Ann Ratcliffe. LC 92-27306. 324p. 1993. Net. pap. text ed. write for info. (0-471-57707-3) Wiley.

Chemistry: The Molecular Science. Olmsted & Williams. 992p. 1993. 52.00 (0-8016-7485-9) Mosby Yr Bk.

Chemistry: The Study of Matter & Its Changes. James E. Brady & John R. Holum. 1024p. (C). 1993. text ed. write for info. (0-471-53008-5) Wiley.

*Chemistry: The Study of Matter & Its Changes & Qualitative & Instrumental Analysis of Environmentally Significant Elements. James E. Brady et al. 1993. text ed. write for info. (0-471-31054-9) Wiley.

Chemistry Answers to Selected Problems. 3rd ed. James V. Quagliano & Lidia M. Vallarino. (C). 1969. 11.95 (0-685-03783-5) P-H.

Chemistry Exam Copy. 2nd ed. Ronald J. Gillespie et al. 1216p. 1989. write for info. (0-318-63892-4, H18666) P-H.

Chemistry Lab Manual. 2nd ed. Ronald J. Gillespie et al. 1216p. 1989. 15.75 (0-685-44216-0) P-H.

Chemistry see Comprehensive Dissertation Index: Ten Year Cumulation, 1973-1982

Chemistry see Bilirubin

Chemistry - Advanced Materials. 1993. 129.95 (0-632-03385-1) CRC Pr.

*Chemistry - for All Practical Purposes: A Programmed Approach 2. William E. Cheer. (Illus.). 273p. (C). 1995. student ed 7.50 (1-886855-04-8) Tavenner Pub.

Chemistry: A Structural View: Practical Manual. G. R. Withers & D. R. Stranks. 112p. reprint ed. pap. 32.00 (0-317-08971-4, 2051417) Bks Demand.

Chemistry, Air, & Climate: A ChemCom Module. American Chemical Society Staff. 76p. (C). 1988. per. 5.90 (0-8403-5102-X) Kendall-Hunt.

Chemistry, Alchemy & the New Philosophy, 1550-1700: Studies in the History of Science & Medicine. Allen G. Debus. (Collected Studies: No. CS249). (Illus.). 332p. (C). 1987. reprint ed. text ed. 95.00 (0-86078-197-6, Pub. by Variorum UK) Ashgate Pub Co.

Chemistry, an Environmental Perspective. Phyllis E. Buell & James E. Girard. LC 93-33454. 1993. text ed. write for info. (0-13-644659-0) P-H.

Chemistry & Analysis of Hydrocarbons in the Environment. Ed. by J. Albaiges et al. LC 83-1603. (Current Topics In Environmental & Toxicological Chemistry Ser.: Vol. 5). 326p. 1983. text ed. 121.00 (0-677-06140-4) Gordon & Breach.

Chemistry & Analysis of Volatile Organic Compounds in the Environment. Ed. by H. J. Bloemen & J. Burn. LC 93-9751. 1993. write for info. (0-7514-0000-9, Pub. by Blackie Acad & Prof UK) Routledge Chapman & Hall.

Chemistry & Application of Dyes. Ed. by D. R. Waring & G. Hallas. LC 89-27837. (Topics in Applied Chemistry Ser.). (Illus.). 430p. 1990. 105.00 (0-306-43278-1, Plenum Pr) Plenum.

*Chemistry & Artists' Colors. Mary V. Orna & Madeline Goodstein. (Illus.). 426p. (C). 1993. pap. text ed. 22.00 (0-9637747-0-0) Chemsource.

Chemistry & Biochemistry of Amino Acids, Peptides, & Proteins, Vol. 1. B. Weinstein. LC 75-142896. 190p. reprint ed. pap. 54.20 (0-317-08528-X, 2055061) Bks Demand.

Chemistry & Biochemistry of Amino Acids, Peptides, & Proteins, Vol. 2. Ed. by Boris Weinstein. LC 75-142896. 392p. reprint ed. pap. 111.80 (0-7837-0011-3, 2021511) Bks Demand.

Chemistry & Biochemistry of Amino Acids, Peptides, & Proteins, Vol. 3. Ed. by Boris Weinstein. LC 75-142896. 336p. reprint ed. pap. 95.80 (0-7837-0012-1) Bks Demand.

Chemistry & Biochemistry of Amino Acids, Peptides, & Proteins, Vol. 5. Ed. by Boris Weinstein. LC 75-142896. 367p. reprint ed. pap. 104.60 (0-685-15967-1, 2027078) Bks Demand.

Chemistry & Biochemistry of Amino Acids, Peptides, & Proteins: A Survey of Recent Developments, Vol. 4. Ed. by Boris Weinstein. LC 75-142896. 352p. reprint ed. pap. 100.40 (0-317-29935-2, 2021511) Bks Demand.

*Chemistry & Biochemistry of Amino Acids, Peptides & Proteins Vol. 6 - 1982. fac. ed. Ed. by Boris Weinstein. LC 75-142896. 343p. 1982. pap. 97.80 (0-7837-8636-0, 2021511) Bks Demand.

*Chemistry & Biochemistry of Amino Acids, Peptides & Proteins Vol. 7 - 1983. fac. ed. Ed. by Boris Weinstein. LC 75-142896. 407p. Date not set. pap. 116.00 (0-7837-8637-9, 2021511) Bks Demand.

Chemistry & Biochemistry of Flavoenzymes, II. Franz Muller. (Illus.). 512p. 1991. 225.00 (0-8493-4394-1, QP552) CRC Pr.

Chemistry & Biochemistry of Flavoenzymes, Vol. I. Franz Muller. (Illus.). 528p. 1991. 251.00 (0-8493-4393-3, QP552) CRC Pr.

Chemistry & Biochemistry of Flavoenzymes, Vol. III. Franz Muller. (Illus.). 512p. 1991. 230.00 (0-8493-4395-X, QP552) CRC Pr.

Chemistry & Biochemistry of N-Substituted Porphyrins. David K. Lavallee. LC 87-23206. 313p. 1988. lib. bdg. 55.00 (0-89573-147-9) VCH Pubs.

Chemistry & Biochemistry of Natural Waxes. Ed. by P. E. Kolattukudy. 460p. 1976. 131.00 (0-444-41470-3) Elsevier.

Chemistry & Biochemistry of Plant Nutrition. John Manthey. 1994. 99.95 (0-87371-942-5, S592) Lewis Pubs.

Chemistry & Biochemistry of the Sulfhydryl Group in Amino Acids, Peptides & Proteins. Mendel Friedman. 1973. 241.00 (0-08-016845-0, Pub. by Pergamon Repr UK) Franklin.

Chemistry & Biogeochemistry of Estuaries. Ed. by Eric Olausson & Ingemar Cato. LC 79-41211. (Illus.). 462p. reprint ed. pap. 131.70 (0-685-20648-3, 2030434) Bks Demand.

Chemistry & Biology in Pteridines & Folates. Ed. by June E. Ayling et al. (Advances in Experimental Medicine & Biology Ser.: Vol. 338). (Illus.). 806p. (C). 1993. 159.50 (0-306-44581-6, Plenum Pr) Plenum.

Chemistry & Biology Laboratories: Design Construction Equipment. W. Schramm & J. Leytham. LC 63-10066. 1960. 115.00 (0-08-013612-5, Pub. by Pergamon Repr UK) Franklin.

Chemistry & Biology of Antibiotics. V. Betina. (Pharmacochemistry Library: No. 5). 590p. 1983. 172.00 (0-444-99678-8) Elsevier.

Chemistry & Biology of A2-Macroglobulin, Vol. 421. Ed. by Richard D. Feinman. 95.00 (0-89766-236-9); pap. 95.00 (0-89766-237-7) NY Acad Sci.

Chemistry & Biology of B-Lactam Antibiotics, 1. Ed. by Robert B. Morin & Marvin Gorman. 402p. 1982. text ed. 156.00 (0-12-506301-6) Acad Pr.

Chemistry & Biology of B-Lactam Antibiotics, 2. Ed. by Robert B. Morin & Marvin Gorman. 402p. 1982. text ed. 146.00 (0-12-506302-4) Acad Pr.

Chemistry & Biology of B-Lactam Antibiotics, 3. Ed. by Robert B. Morin & Marvin Gorman. 402p. 1982. text ed. 146.00 (0-12-506303-2) Acad Pr.

Chemistry & Biology of Hydroxamic Acids. H. Kehl. xii, 192p. 1982. 190.50 (3-8055-3453-1) S Karger.

Chemistry & Biology of Mineralized Connective Tissue. Veis. (Developments in Biochemistry Ser.: Vol. 22). 630p. 1981. 179.00 (0-444-00678-8) Elsevier.

Chemistry & Biology of Mineralized Tissue: Proceedings of the Third International Conference on the Chemistry & Biology of Mineralized Tissues, Massachusetts, October 1988: A Special Issue of the Journal Connective Tissue Research. Ed. by M. J. Glimcher & J. B. Lian. lxii, 968p. 1989. pap. text ed. 129.00 (0-677-22320-X) Gordon & Breach.

Chemistry & Biology of Mineralized Tissues: Proceedings of the Fourth International Conference on the Chemistry & Biology of Mineralized Tissues Held in Coronado, California on February 5-9, 1992. Ed. by Harold Slavkin & Paul Price. LC 92-49899. (International Congress Ser.: No. 1002). 1992. write for info. (0-444-89494-2, Excerpta Medica) Elsevier.

Chemistry & Biology of N-Nitroso Compounds. William Lijinsky. (Monographs on Cancer Research). 400p. (C). 1992. 175.00 (0-521-34629-0) Cambridge U Pr.

Chemistry & Biology of Naturally Occurring Acetylenes & Related Compounds: Proceedings of a Conference. Ed. by J. Lam et al. (Bioactive Molecules Ser.: No. 7). 384p. 1989. 100.00 (0-444-87115-2) Elsevier.

Chemistry & Biology of One-Three - B - Glucans. Bruce A. Stone & Adrienne E. Clarke. (C). 175.00 (1-86324-409-3, Pub. by LaTrobe Univ AT) Intl Spec Bk.

Chemistry & Biology of Pteridines: Pteridines & Folic Acid Derivatives. Ed. by J. A. Blair. LC 83-7666. xxxvi, 1070p. 1983. 265.40 (3-11-008560-7) De Gruyter.

Chemistry & Biology of Pteridines, 1986 - Pteridines & Folic Acid Derivatives: Proceedings of the 8th International Symposium. Ed. by B. A. Cooper & V. M. Whitehead. xxviii, 1048p. (C). 1986. lib. bdg. 292.35 (0-89925-271-0) De Gruyter.

*Chemistry & Biology of Pteridines, 1986 - Pteridines & Folic Acid Derivatives: Proceedings of the 8th International Symposium. Ed. by B. A. Cooper & V. M. Whitehead. xxviii, 1048p. (C). 1986. lib. bdg. 292.35 (3-11-010771-6) De Gruyter.

Chemistry & Biology of Pteridines, 1989: Pteridines & Folic Acid Derivatives: Proceedings of the Ninth International Symposium. Chemical, Biological & Clinical Aspects. Zurich, Switzerland, Sept. 3-8, 1989. Ed. by H. C. Curtius et al. (Illus.). xxxvi, 1340p. (C). 1990. lib. bdg. 290.00 (0-89925-609-0) De Gruyter.

Chemistry & Biology of Pteridines, 1989: Pteridines & Folic Acid Derivatives Proceedings of the Ninth Int'l Symposium on Pteridines & Folic Acid Derivatives. Chemical, Biological & Clinical Aspects. Zurich, Switzerland, Sept. 3-8, 1989. Ed. by H. Curtius et al. (Illus.). xxxvi, 1340p. (C). 1990. lib. bdg. 346.15 (3-11-012199-9) De Gruyter.

Chemistry & Biology of Sialic Acids & Related Substances. Alfred Gottschalk. LC 60-50363. 133p. reprint ed. pap. 38.00 (0-317-08958-7, 2050783) Bks Demand.

Chemistry & Biology of Solid Waste. Ed. by W. Salomons & U. Forstner. (Illus.). 320p. 1988. 108.00 (0-387-18231-4) Spr-Verlag.

Chemistry & Biology of Synthetic Retinoids. Ed. by Marcia I. Dawson & William H. Okamura. 560p. 1990. 344.00 (0-8493-4797-1, QP801) CRC Pr.

Chemistry & Biology of Water, Air, & Soil: Environmental Aspects (Chemia, Biologia a Toxikologia Vody a Ovzdusia) Ed. by J. Tolgyessy. LC 92-30190. (Studies in Environmental Science: Vol. 53). (ENG & SLO.). 1993. write for info. (0-444-98798-3) Elsevier.

*Chemistry & Biotechnology of Biologically Active Natural Produces: Proceedings of the 4th Intl. Conf. Budapest, 10-14, August 1987. C. S. Szantay et al. 402p. (C). 1988. 117.00x (963-05-4950-6, Pub. by Akad Kiado HU) St Mut.

Chemistry & Biotechnology of Biologically Active Natural Products. C. S. Szantay. 402p. (C). 1988. 235.00 (0-569-09122-5, Pub. by Collets) St Mut.

Chemistry & Biotechnology of Biologically Active Natural Products: Proceedings of the International Conference, 2nd, Budapest, 15-19 Aug., 1983. Ed. by C. Szantay et al. (Studies in Organic Chemistry: No. 17). 378p. 1984. 115.50 (0-444-99608-7, I-232-84) Elsevier.

Chemistry & Catalytic Reaction Engineering. James J. Carberry. (Chemical Engineering Ser.). (Illus.). (C). 1976. text ed. write for info. (0-07-009790-9) McGraw.

Chemistry & Characterization of Coal Macerals. Randall E. Winans & John C. Crelling. LC 84-6260. (ACS Symposium Ser.: No. 252). 192p. 1984. lib. bdg. 40.95 (0-8412-0838-7) Am Chemical.

Chemistry & Chemical Engineering in the People's Republic of China. Ed. by John D. Baldeschwieler. LC 79-11217. 266p. 1979. pap. 14.95 (0-8412-0502-7) Am Chemical.

Chemistry & Chemical Reactivity. John C. Kotz & Keith F. Purcell. 1088p. (C). 1986. Incl. study guide. student ed, pap. text ed. 46.00 (0-03-012848-X) SCP.

Chemistry & Chemical Reactivity. 2nd ed. John C. Kotz & Keith F. Purcell. 1184p. (C). 1991. text ed. 69.25 (0-03-047562-7) SCP.

Chemistry & Chemical Taxonomy of the Rutales. Ed. by Peter G. Waterman & Michael F. Grundon. (Phytochemical Society of Europe Symposia Ser.). 1984. text ed. 176.00 (0-12-737680-1) Acad Pr.

Chemistry & Chemistry with Inorganic Qualitative Analysis. 3rd ed. John C. Bailar, Jr. et al. 102p. (C). 1989. 173.75 (0-15-506463-0) HB Coll Pubs.

Chemistry & Crime: From Sherlock Holmes to Today's Courtroom. Ed. by Samuel M. Gerber. LC 83-11907. (Other Technical Bks.). 135p. 1983. lib. bdg. 19.95 (0-8412-0784-4); pap. 16.95 (0-8412-0785-2) Am Chemical.

Chemistry & Defects in Semiconductor Heterostructures: Materials Research Society Symposium Proceedings, Vol. 148. Ed. by E. Weber et al. 1989. text ed. 53.00 (1-55899-021-6) Materials Res.

Chemistry & Energy, Vol. 1: Proceedings of the European East-West Workshop, 1st, Sintra, Portugal, 25-29 March, 1990. Cesar A. Sequeira. (Materials Science Monographs: No. 65). 384p. 1991. 137.25 (0-444-88725-3) Elsevier.

*Chemistry & Environment: Legislation, Methodologies & Applications: Based on the Lectures Given During the Eurocourse on 'Chemistry & Environment: Legislation, Methodologies & Applications' Held at the Joint Research Centre Ispra, Italy, June 1-5 & 22-26, 1992. Ed. by S. Facchetti. LC 94-39130. (Eurocourses: Vol. 4). 548p. (C). 1995. lib. bdg. 205.00 (0-7923-3240-7) Kluwer Ac.

Chemistry & Exotoxicology of Pollution: Environmental Science & Technology. Des W. Connell & Gregory Miller. LC 83-16794. (Wiley-Interscience Series of Text & Monographs: No. 1121). 444p. 1984. text ed. 115.00 (0-471-86249-5, Wiley-Interscience) Wiley.

Chemistry & Fate of Organophosphorus Compounds: Selected Papers from the Workshop, The Free University, Amsterdam, June 18-19, 1986. Ed. by E. Merian et al. (Current Topics In Environmental & Toxicological Chemistry Ser.: Vol. 12). xviii, 210p. 1987. text ed. 74.00 (2-88124-215-4) Gordon & Breach.

Chemistry & Function of Pectins. Ed. by Marshall L. Fishman & Joseph J. Jen. LC 86-7983. (ACS Symposium Ser.: No. 310). (Illus.). ix, 288p. 1986. 60.95 (0-8412-0974-X) Am Chemical.

Chemistry & General Science. Jack Rudman. (National Teachers Examination Ser.: NT-7A). 1994. pap. 23.95 (0-8373-8409-5) Nat Learn.

Chemistry & General Science, Senior High School. Jack Rudman. (Teachers License Examination Ser.: T-6). 1994. pap. 23.95 (0-8373-8006-5) Nat Learn.

Chemistry & Geochemistry of Oil Shales: Preprints of Papers Presented at Seattle, Washington, March 20-25, 1983. American Chemical Society, Division of Fuel Chemistry Staff. (American Chemical Society Division of Fuel Chemistry, Preprints of Papers Ser.: Vol. 28, No. 3). 251p. reprint ed. pap. 71.60 (0-317-28800-8, 2020320) Bks Demand.

Chemistry & Geochemistry of Solutions at High Temperatures & Pressures: Proceedings of the Royal Swedish Academy of Sciences, Nobel Symposium, Bjorkborns Herrgard, Karlskoga, Sweden, Sept., 1979. Royal Swedish Academy of Sciences Staff. Ed. by David Rickard & Frans E. Wickman. (Physics & Chemistry of the Earth Series; International Series in Earth Sciences: Vols. 13 & 37). (Illus.). 600p. 1982. 205.00 (0-08-026285-6, Pergamon Pr) Elsevier.

Chemistry & Life: An Introduction to General Organic & Biological Chemistry. 4th ed. John W. Hill et al. LC 92-11254. (Illus.). 848p. (C). 1993. text ed. write for info. (0-02-354541-0) Macmillan.

Chemistry & Light. Paul Suppan. 320p. 1994. pap. 45.00 (0-85186-814-2, R6814) CRC Pr.

Chemistry & Medicine: Papers Presented at the Fiftieth Anniversary of the Founding of the Medical School of the University of Minnesota. Ed. by Maurice B. Visscher. LC 67-30234. (Essay Index Reprint Ser.). 1977. 23.95 (0-8369-0962-3) Ayer.

Chemistry & Metabolism of the Vitamin B6 Antagonist, 4' Deoxypyridoxine. Stephen P. Coburn. 224p. 1981. 79.00 (0-8493-5783-7, QP772, CRC Reprint) Franklin.

Chemistry & Metallurgy of Miscellaneous Materials. AEC Technical Information Center Staff. Ed. by Lawrence L. Quill. (National Nuclear Energy Ser.: Div. IV, Vol. 19c). 172p. 1955. mic. film 9.00 (0-87079-162-1, TID-5212); pap. 27.00 (0-87079-161-3, TID-5212) DOE.

Chemistry & Microstructure of Solidified Waste Forms. Ed. by Roger D. Spence. 1992. 95.00 (0-87371-748-1, TD1030) Lewis Pubs.

Chemistry & Modern Society. Ed. by John Parascandola & James C. Whorton. LC 83-11740. (ACS Symposium Ser.: No. 228). 203p. 1983. lib. bdg. 27.95 (0-8412-0795-X); pap. 16.95 (0-8412-0803-4) Am Chemical.

Chemistry & Our Changing World. 2nd ed. Sharon J. Sherman & Alan Sherman. 592p. (C). 1989. pap. text ed. write for info. (0-13-130071-7) P-H.

Chemistry & Our Changing World. 3rd ed. Alan Sherman & Sharon J. Sherman. 608p. (C). 1991. pap. text ed. write for info. (0-13-131541-2) P-H.

1176 An Asterisk (*) at the beginning of an entry indicates that the title is appearing in BIP for the first time.

*__Chemistry & Physics of Aqueous Gas Solutions: Proceedings.__ Electrochemical Society Staff. Ed. by W. A. Adams et al. LC 74-21451. (Illus.). 533p. 1975. pap. 152.00 (*0-7837-8990-4*, 2059255) Bks Demand.

Chemistry & Physics of Carbon. Thrower. 336p. 1994. 175.00 (*0-8247-9091-X*) Dekker.

Chemistry & Physics of Carbon, Vol. 2. Ed. by Philip L. Walker. LC 66-58302. 400p. reprint ed. pap. 114.00 (*0-317-08352-X*, 2055058) Bks Demand.

Chemistry & Physics of Carbon, Vol. 4. Philip L. Walker. LC 66-58302. 411p. reprint ed. pap. 117.20 (*0-317-08348-1*, 2017695) Bks Demand.

Chemistry & Physics of Carbon, Vol. 10. Ed. by Philip L. Walker, Jr. & Peter A. Thrower. LC 65-27434. 286p. reprint ed. pap. 81.60 (*0-7837-0025-3*, 2029018) Bks Demand.

Chemistry & Physics of Carbon, Vol. 13. Ed. by Philip L. Walker, Jr. & Peter A. Thrower. LC 66-58302. 303p. reprint ed. pap. 86.40 (*0-685-23487-8*, 2029018) Bks Demand.

Chemistry & Physics of Carbon, Vol. 18. Thrower. (Illus.). 208p. 1982. 170.00 (*0-8247-1740-6*) Dekker.

Chemistry & Physics of Carbon, Vol. 19. Thrower. 336p. 1984. 170.00 (*0-8247-7245-8*) Dekker.

Chemistry & Physics of Carbon, Vol. 20. Thrower. 296p. 1987. 170.00 (*0-8247-7740-9*) Dekker.

Chemistry & Physics of Carbon, Vol. 22. Thrower. 264p. 1989. 170.00 (*0-8247-8113-9*) Dekker.

Chemistry & Physics of Carbon: A Series of Advances, 2 vols., 6. Ed. by Philip L. Walker. LC 65-27434. (Illus.). 368p. reprint ed. pap. 104.90 (*0-8357-6278-5*, 2027079) Bks Demand.

Chemistry & Physics of Carbon: A Series of Advances, Vol. 1. Ed. by Philip L. Walker. LC 65-27434. 398p. reprint ed. pap. 113.50 (*0-685-15971-X*, 2027079) Bks Demand.

Chemistry & Physics of Carbon: A Series of Advances, 2 vols., Vol. 3. Ed. by Philip L. Walker. LC 65-27434. (Illus.). 461p. reprint ed. pap. 131.40 (*0-8357-6277-7*, 2027079) Bks Demand.

Chemistry & Physics of Carbon: A Series of Advances, Vol. 7. Walker. 424p. 1971. 170.00 (*0-8247-1762-7*) Dekker.

Chemistry & Physics of Carbon: A Series of Advances, Vol. 8. Walker & Thrower. 334p. 1973. 170.00 (*0-8247-1755-4*) Dekker.

Chemistry & Physics of Carbon: A Series of Advances, Vol. 12. Walker & Thrower. 232p. 1975. 170.00 (*0-8247-6304-1*) Dekker.

Chemistry & Physics of Carbon: A Series of Advances, Vol. 15. Walker & Thrower. 320p. 1979. 170.00 (*0-8247-6816-7*) Dekker.

Chemistry & Physics of Carbon: A Series of Advances, Vol. 16. Walker & Thrower. 336p. 1981. 170.00 (*0-8247-6991-0*) Dekker.

Chemistry & Physics of Carbon: A Series of Advances, Vol. 17. Walker & Thrower. 320p. 1981. 170.00 (*0-8247-1209-9*) Dekker.

Chemistry & Physics of Carbon: A Series of Advances, Vol. 23. Thrower. 384p. 1991. 199.00 (*0-8247-8482-0*) Dekker.

Chemistry & Physics of Carbon, Vol. 14: A Series of Advances. Ed. by Philip L. Walker. LC 66-58302. 319p. reprint ed. pap. 91.00 (*0-318-35003-3*, 2030863) Bks Demand.

Chemistry & Physics of Carbon, Vol. 21: A Series of Advances. Thrower. 400p. 1989. 170.00 (*0-8247-7939-8*) Dekker.

Chemistry & Physics of Clays. Rex W. Grimshaw. (Illus.). 1024p. (C). reprint ed. 81.00 (*1-878907-44-1*) TechBooks.

Chemistry & Physics of Coal Utilization - 1980 (APS, Morgantown) Ed. by B. R. Cooper & L. Petrakis. LC 81-65106. (AIP Conference Proceedings Ser.: No. 70). 472p. 1981. lib. bdg. 34.50 (*0-88318-169-X*) Am Inst Physics.

Chemistry & Physics of Coatings. Ed. by Alastair R. Marrion. 186p. 1994. 39.95 (*0-85186-994-7*, R6994) CRC Pr.

Chemistry & Physics of Crystalline Solids. D. McKie & C. McKie. 1994. pap. write for info. (*0-632-01661-2*) Blackwell Sci.

Chemistry & Physics of DNA-Ligand Interactions. Ed. by N. R. Kallenback. (Illus.). 250p. 1989. lib. bdg. 65.00 (*0-940030-25-X*) Adenine Pr.

Chemistry & Physics of Electrocatalysis: Proceedings of the Symposium. Symposium on the Chemistry & Physics of Electrocatalysis Staff. Ed. by J. D. McIntyre et al. LC 84-73015. (Electrochemical Society Proceedings Ser.: No. 84-12). 692p. reprint ed. pap. 180.00 (*0-8357-2591-X*, 2052371) Bks Demand.

Chemistry & Physics of Energetic Materials. Ed. by Surya N. Bulusu. (C). 1990. lib. bdg. 239.00 (*0-7923-0745-3*) Kluwer Ac.

Chemistry & Physics of Fracture. Ed. by R. M. Latanision & R. H. Jones. (C). 1987. lib. bdg. 216.50 (*90-247-3580-7*) Kluwer Ac.

Chemistry & Physics of High Energy Reactions. Ernest J. Henley & Everett R. Johnson. LC 69-19832. 481p. reprint ed. pap. 137.10 (*0-685-15676-1*, 2026289) Bks Demand.

Chemistry & Physics of Macromolecules: Final Report of the SonderfChemie und Physik Chemistry & Physics of Macromolecules. Ed. by Erhard W. Fischer et al. 558p. 1991. lib. bdg. 110.00 (*0-89573-982-8*) VCH Pubs.

Chemistry & Physics of Matrix-Isolated Species. Ed. by L. Andrews & M. Moskovits. 400p. 1989. 100.00 (*0-444-70549-X*) Elsevier.

Chemistry & Physics of Minerals. Ed. by J. R. Clark & G. E. Brown. (Transactions of the American Crystallographic Association Ser.: Vol. 15). 120p. 1979. pap. 25.00 (*0-686-60385-0*) Polycrystal Bk Serv.

Chemistry & Physics of Rapidly Solidified Materials: Proceedings of a Symposium Sponsored by the Chemistry & Physics of Metals Committee of the Metallurgical Society of AIME, St. Louis MO, October 26-27, 1982. Metallurgical Society of AIME Staff. Ed. by B. J. Berkowitz & R. O. Scattergood. LC 83-61484. (Illus.). 323p. reprint ed. pap. 92.10 (*0-8357-5537-1*, 2035151) Bks Demand.

Chemistry & Physics of Solid Surfaces. Ed. by Ralf Vanselow & S. Y. Tong. LC 76-49020. (Monotopic Reprint Ser.). 1977. reprint ed. 28.95 (*0-8493-0125-4*, CRC Reprint) Franklin.

Chemistry & Physics of Solid Surfaces, Vol. III. Ed. by Vanselow & England. 352p. 1982. 89.95 (*0-8493-0128-9*, QD508, CRC Reprint) Franklin.

Chemistry & Physics of Solid Surfaces, Vol. VIII. Ed. by R. Vanselow et al. (Surface Sciences Ser.: Vol. 22). (Illus.). 480p. 1990. 90.00 (*0-387-52679-X*) Spr-Verlag.

Chemistry & Physics of Solid Surfaces V. Ed. by R. Vanselow & Russel F. Howe. (Chemical Physics Ser.: Vol. 35). (Illus.). 570p. 1984. 84.00 (*0-387-13315-1*) Spr-Verlag.

Chemistry & Physics of Solid Surfaces VI. Ed. by R. Vanselow & Russel F. Howe. (Surface Sciences Ser.: Vol. 5). (Illus.). 690p. 1986. 100.00 (*0-387-16264-X*) Spr-Verlag.

Chemistry & Physics of Solid Surfaces VII. Ed. by R. Vanselow & Russel F. Howe. (Surface Sciences Ser.: Vol. 10). (Illus.). 630p. 1988. 111.00 (*0-387-50044-8*) Spr-Verlag.

Chemistry & Physics of Terrestrial Planets. Ed. by Surendra K. Saxena. (Advances in Physical Geochemistry Ser.: Vol. 6). (Illus.). 370p. 1986. 109.00 (*0-387-96287-5*) Spr-Verlag.

Chemistry & Physics of the Stratosphere. Ed. by Joseph Chamberlain. 171p. 1976. pap. 3.00 (*0-87590-221-9*) Am Geophysical.

Chemistry & Physics with Related Applications: Chemie und Physik mit Anwendungsgebieten. 2nd ed. F. L. Boschke. 200p. (ENG & GER.). 1981. 49.95 (*0-8288-0860-0*, M15298) Fr & Eur.

Chemistry & Physiology in Their Historical & Philosophical Relations. E. Glas. 217p. (Orig.). 1979. pap. text ed. 28.50 (*90-6275-035-4*, Pub. by Delft U Pr NE) Coronet Bks.

Chemistry & Physiology of Bile Acids & Their Influence on Atherosclerosis. W. T. Beher. (Monographs on Atherosclerosis: Vol. 6). (Illus.). 1976. 78.50 (*3-8055-2242-8*) S Karger.

Chemistry & Processing of Sugarbeet & Sugarcane: Proc. of the Symp. on the Chemistry & Processing of Sugarbeet, Denver, CO, April, 1987, & the Symp. of the Chemistry & Processing of Sugarcane, New Orleans, LA, Sept. 3-4 1987. Ed. by M. A. Clarke & M. A. Godshall. (Sugar Ser.: No. 9). 406p. 1988. 133.50 (*0-444-43020-2*) Elsevier.

Chemistry & Properties of Biomolecular Systems. Ed. by E. Rizzarelli & Theophile M. Theophanides. 248p. (C). 1991. lib. bdg. 97.00 (*0-7923-1393-3*) Kluwer Ac.

Chemistry & Properties of Biomolecular Systems Vol. II: Proceedings of the Second Joint Greek-Italian Meeting on Chemistry & Biological Systems & Molecular Chemical Engineering, Cetraro, Italy, October 1992. Ed. by N. Russo et al. LC 93-44247. (Topics in Molecular Organization & Engineering Ser.: Vol. 11). 432p. (C). 1994. lib. bdg. 137.00 (*0-7923-2666-0*) Kluwer Ac.

*__Chemistry & Qualitative Analysis of Anions.__ James G. Boyles et al. Ed. by H. A. Neidig. (Modular Laboratory Program in Chemistry Ser.). 12p. (C). 1989. pap. text ed. 1.25x (*0-87540-367-0*) Chem Educ Res.

*__Chemistry & Qualitative Analysis of Cations: Group II.__ James G. Boyles et al. Ed. by H. A. Neidig. (Modular Laboratory Program in Chemistry Ser.). 16p. (C). 1989. pap. text ed. 1.25x (*0-87540-365-4*) Chem Educ Res.

*__Chemistry & Qualitative Analysis of Cations: Group Separations & Separation of Group 1 Cations.__ James G. Boyles et al. Ed. by H. A. Neidig. (Modular Laboratory Program in Chemistry Ser.). 16p. (C). 1989. pap. text ed. 1.25x (*0-87540-364-6*) Chem Educ Res.

*__Chemistry & Qualitative Analysis of Cations: Groups III & IV.__ James G. Boyles et al. Ed. by H. A. Neidig. (Modular Laboratory Program in Chemistry Ser.). 16p. (C). 1989. pap. text ed. 1.25x (*0-87540-366-2*) Chem Educ Res.

Chemistry & Significance of Condensed Tannins. Ed. by R. W. Hemingway & J. J. Karchesy. (Illus.). 566p. 1989. 135.00 (*0-306-43326-5*, Plenum Pr) Plenum.

Chemistry & Society. 5th ed. Mark M. Jones et al. 718p. (C). 1987. text ed. 46.00 (*0-03-008139-4*) SCP.

Chemistry & Spectroscopy of Interstellar Molecules. Ed. by Norio Kaifu et al. (Illus.). 310p. 1990. 100.00 (*0-86008-465-5*, Pub. by U of Tokyo JA) Col U Pr.

Chemistry & Structure at Interfaces: New Laser & Optical Techniques. Ed. by R. B. Hall & A. B. Ellis. LC 86-4055. 351p. 1986. text ed. 85.00 (*0-89573-311-0*) VCH Pubs.

Chemistry & Technology: Fabric Preparation & Refinishing. Tomasino. 1993. write for info. (*0-8493-8932-1*) CRC Pr.

Chemistry & Technology of Biodegradable Polymers. Ed. by G. J. Griffin. LC 93-33974. 1994. 99.95 (*0-7514-0003-3*, Pub. by Blackie Acad & Prof UK) Routledge Chapman & Hall.

Chemistry & Technology of Cereals As Food & Feed. 2nd ed. Samuel A. Matz. (Illus.). 650p. 1991. text ed. 98.00 (*0-942849-06-X*) Pan Tech Intl.

Chemistry & Technology of Cereals As Food & Feed. 2nd rev. ed. Samuel A. Matz. (Illus.). 700p. 1991. text ed. 105.00 (*0-442-30830-2*) Chapman & Hall.

Chemistry & Technology of Coal. 2nd expanded rev. ed. Speight. (Chemical Industries Ser.: Vol. 59). 680p. 1994. 195.00 (*0-8247-9200-9*) Dekker.

Chemistry & Technology of Combustible Shales & Their Products. 288p. 1962. text ed. 71.00 (*0-7065-0171-3*, Pub. by Keter Pub IS) Coronet Bks.

Chemistry & Technology of Edible Oils & Fats: Proceedings of the Conference, Port Sunlight, March, 1959. J. Devine & P. Williams. LC 60-7401. 1961. 74.00 (*0-08-009349-3*, Pub. by Pergamon Repr UK) Franklin.

Chemistry & Technology of Edible Oils & Fats & Their High Fat Products. G. Hoffman. (Food Science & Technology Ser.). 384p. 1989. text ed. 128.00 (*0-12-352055-X*) Acad Pr.

Chemistry & Technology of Explosives, 4 vols., Set. T. Urbanski. 1984. 1,040.00 (*0-08-030252-1*, Pergamon Pr) Elsevier.

Chemistry & Technology of Gypsum - STP 861. ASTM Committee C-11 on Gypsum. Ed. by Richard A. Kuntze. LC 84-70880. 208p. 1984. text ed. 29.00 (*0-8031-0219-4*, 04-861000-07) ASTM.

Chemistry & Technology of Jojoba Oil. Jaime Wisniak. 272p. 1987. 40.00 (*0-935315-17-9*) AOCS Pr.

Chemistry & Technology of Katha (Catechin) & Cutch (Catechu) Tannic Acid Manufacturing. O. P. Sharma. 303p. (C). 1984. text ed. 185.00 (*0-685-52008-0*, Pub. by Intl Bk Distr II) St Mut.

Chemistry & Technology of Katha (Catechin) & Cutch (Catechu) Tannic Acid Manufacturing. Ed. by O. P. Sharma. 303p. 1984. 100.00 (*0-685-49622-8*, Pub. by Intl Bk Distr II) St Mut.

Chemistry & Technology of Katha (Catechin) & Cutch (Catechul) Tannic Acid Manufacturing. O. P. Sharma. 303p. (C). 1989. 185.00 (*81-7089-004-7*, Pub. by Intl Bk Distr II) St Mut.

Chemistry & Technology of Katha (Cathechin) & Cutch (Catechu) Tannic Acid Manufacturing. O. P. Sharma. 303p. (C). 1984. 185.00 (*0-685-61459-X*, Pub. by Intl Bk Distr II) St Mut.

Chemistry & Technology of Lime & Limestone. 2nd ed. Robert S. Boynton. LC 79-16140. (Information & Resources Ser.). 578p. 1980. text ed. 199.00 (*0-471-02771-5*) Wiley.

Chemistry & Technology of Lubricants. Ed. by K. M. Mortier & S. T. Orszulik. LC 91-44485. 302p. 1993. 110.00 (*1-56081-594-9*) VCH Pubs.

Chemistry & Technology of Pacific Fish. I. V. Kizevetter. 304p. 1972. text ed. 58.00x (*0-7065-1271-5*, Pub. by Keter Pub IS) Coronet Bks.

Chemistry & Technology of Pectin. Ed. by Reginald H. Walter. (Food Science & Technology Ser.). (Illus.). 276p. 1991. text ed. 110.00 (*0-12-733870-5*) Acad Pr.

Chemistry & Technology of Petroleum. 2nd rev. ed. James G. Speight. (Chemical Industries Ser.: Vol. 44). 784p. 1991. 225.00 (*0-8247-8481-2*) Dekker.

Chemistry & Technology of Silicon & Tin: Proceedings of the First Asian Network for Analytical & Inorganic Chemical International Chemistry Conference on Silicon & Tin. Ed. by Kumar Das et al. (Illus.). 600p. 1992. 165.00 (*0-19-855580-6*) OUP.

Chemistry & Technology of Tellurium & Selenium. A. Kudrynvtsev. 300p. 1974. 55.00 (*0-569-08009-6*, Pub. by Collets) St Mut.

Chemistry & Technology of the Cosmetics & Toiletries. Ed. by D. F. Williams & W. M. Schmitt. 320p. (C). 1992. text ed. 99.95 (*0-412-03311-9*, A6874, Blackie & Son-Chapman NY) Chapman & Hall.

Chemistry & Technology of UV & EB Formulation for Coatings, Inks & Paints. FMJ International Staff. (C). 1989. 1,650.00 (*0-685-60822-0*, Pub. by Fuel Metallurgical Jrnl UK) St Mut.

*__Chemistry & Technology of UV & EB Formulation for Coatings, Inks & Paints, Vol. 5.__ J. P. Dowling. (Illus.). 185p. 1994. text ed. 95.00 (*0-947798-37-4*) Scholium Intl.

Chemistry & Technology of UV & EB Formulation for Coatings, Inks & Paints, Vol. 1: Markets & Curing Equipment. P. Dufour & R. E. Knight. Ed. by Peter Oldring. (Illus.). 306p. 1991. text ed. 99.00x (*0-947798-11-0*, Pub. by SITA Tech UK) Scholium Intl.

Chemistry & Technology of UV & EB Formulation for Coatings, Inks & Paints, Vol. 2: Prepolymers & Reactive Diluents for UV & EB Curable Formulations. N. S. Allen et al. (Illus.). 349p. 1991. text ed. 99.00x (*0-947798-10-2*, Pub. by SITA Tech UK) Scholium Intl.

Chemistry & Technology of UV & EB Formulation for Coatings, Inks & Paints, Vol. 3: Photoinitiators for Free Radical & Cationic Polymerisation. K. K. Dietliker. Ed. by Peter Oldring. (Illus.). 300p. 1991. text ed. 119.00x (*0-947798-16-1*, Pub. by SITA Tech UK) Scholium Intl.

Chemistry & Technology of UV & EB Formulation for Coatings, Inks & Paints, Vol. 4: Formulation. M. Braithwaite et al. Ed. by Peter Oldring. (Illus.). 250p. 1991. text ed. 119.00x (*0-947798-21-8*, Pub. by SITA Tech UK) Scholium Intl.

Chemistry & Technology of Water-Soluble Polymers. Ed. by C. A. Finch. 372p. 1983. 110.00 (*0-306-41251-9*, Plenum Pr) Plenum.

Chemistry & the Environment. Ed. by B. N. Noller & M. Chadha. 334p. 1990. pap. 65.00 (*0-85092-350-6*, Pub. by CSIRO AT) Intl Spec Bk.

Chemistry & the Environment: Laboratory Manual. Walter Scharf & Charles Malerich. 160p. (C). 1993. pap. text ed., spiral bd. 16.95 (*0-8403-8904-3*) Kendall-Hunt.

Chemistry & the Food System. ACS Committee on Chemistry & Public Affairs. LC 80-11194. 138p. 1980. 14.95 (*0-8412-0557-4*); pap. 14.95 (*0-8412-0563-9*) Am Chemical.

Chemistry & the Living Organism. 5th ed. Molly M. Bloomfield. 784p. (C). 1991. Net. text ed. write for info. (*0-471-51292-3*); Net. write for info. (*0-471-51804-2*); write for info. (*0-471-51807-7*) Wiley.

Chemistry & Theology in Mid-Victorian London: The Diary of Herbert McLeod, 1860-1870. F. James. 1987. fiche 260.00 (*0-7201-1752-6*, Mansell Pub) Cassell.

Chemistry & Toxicology of Pyrrolizidine Alkloids. A. R. Mattocks. 1986. text ed. 129.00 (*0-12-480570-1*) Acad Pr.

Chemistry & Unit Operations in Sewage Treatment. D. Barnes & F. Wilson. (Illus.). 339p. 1978. 90.00 (*0-85334-783-2*, Pub. by Elsevier Applied Sci UK) Elsevier.

Chemistry & Unit Operations in Water Treatment. D. Barnes & F. Wilson. (Illus.). 325p. 1983. 90.00 (*0-85334-169-9*, I-463-82, Pub. by Elsevier Applied Sci UK) Elsevier.

Chemistry & Uses of Fire Retardants. John W. Lyons. LC 84-11213. 478p. (C). 1987. reprint ed. lib. bdg. 64.00 (*0-89874-767-8*) Krieger.

Chemistry & Wonders of the Human Body. George W. Carey. 156p. 1921. reprint ed. spiral bd. 6.60 (*0-7873-0142-6*) Mokelumne.

Chemistry & World Food Supplies: The New Frontiers (Chemrawn II), Proceedings of the International Conference, Manila, Philippines, December 6-10, 1982. L. W. Shemilt. LC 83-8218. (IUPAC Symposium Ser.). 680p. 1983. 278.00 (*0-08-029243-7*, Pub. by Pergamon Repr UK) Franklin.

Chemistry at Interfaces. Finlay MacRitchie. 283p. 1990. text ed. 69.00 (*0-12-464785-5*) Acad Pr.

Chemistry at Work in the Northern States. Charles Kline. 1992. pap. text ed. write for info. (*0-07-010992-3*) McGraw.

Chemistry at Work in the Southern State. Charles Kline. 1991. pap. text ed. write for info. (*0-07-010990-7*) McGraw.

Chemistry at Work in the United States. Charles Kline. 1992. pap. text ed. write for info. (*0-07-010993-1*) McGraw.

Chemistry at Work in the Western States. Charles Kline. 1992. pap. text ed. write for info. (*0-07-010991-5*) McGraw.

Chemistry, Biochemistry & Pharmacology of Prostanoids. Ed. by S. M. Roberts & F. Scheinmann. 1979. 175.00 (*0-08-023799-1*, Pub. by Pergamon Repr UK) Franklin.

Chemistry, Biology, & Clinical Uses of Nucleoside Analogs, Vol. 255. Ed. by Alexander Bloch. (Annals Ser.). 610p. 1975. 71.00 (*0-89072-009-6*) NY Acad Sci.

Chemistry Builder for Standardized Tests. Research & Education Association Staff. 544p. 1994. pap. text ed. 14.95 (*0-87891-939-2*) Res & Educ.

Chemistry by Computer: An Overview of the Applications of Computers in Chemistry. Stephen Wilson. LC 86-18746. 246p. 1986. 69.50 (*0-306-42152-6*, Plenum Pr) Plenum.

Chemistry Computations & Reactions. George S. Sasin et al. pap. 4.95 (*0-914770-06-3*) Littoral Develop.

Chemistry Concepts. Lorraine Conway. (Illus.). 64p. (J). (gr. 5 up). 1983. student ed 7.95 (*0-86653-100-9*, GA 460) Good Apple.

Chemistry Cornerstones. D. Barlex. (C). 1984. text ed. 50.00 (*0-7175-1197-9*, Pub. by S Thornes Pubs UK) St Mut.

*__Chemistry, Ecology & Health.__ Ione. 452p. 1995. lib. bdg. 98.00 (*1-56072-236-3*) Nova Sci Pubs.

*__Chemistry Experiment & Theory: With Solutions Manual.__ Bernice G. Segal. 1993. text ed. write for info. (*0-471-31149-9*) Wiley.

Chemistry Experiments. May Johnson. (Pocket Scientist Ser.). (Illus.). 64p. (J). (gr. 3-6). 1983. lib. bdg. 11.96 (*0-88110-161-3*); pap. 4.95 (*0-86020-527-4*) EDC.

Chemistry Experiments for Children. Virginia L. Mullin. LC 68-9306. (Illus.). (J). (gr. 3-10). 1968. reprint ed. pap. 3.50 (*0-486-22031-1*) Dover.

Chemistry Experiments for Instrumental Methods. Donald T. Sawyer et al. LC 83-23297. 427p. (C). 1984. Net. pap. text ed. write for info. (*0-471-89303-X*) Wiley.

Chemistry Flipper. Leona B. Bronstein & Eleanore McGrain. 49p. (J). (gr. 7 up). 1989. reprint ed. 6.25 (*1-878383-06-X*) C Lee Pubns.

Chemistry for Biologists. R. S. Boikess. Ed. by J. J. Head. LC 86-72195. (Carolina Biology Readers Ser.: No. 172). (Illus.). 16p. (Orig.). (gr. 10 up). 1987. pap. text ed. 2.75 (*0-89278-172-6*, 45-9772) Carolina Biological.

Chemistry for Changing Times. 6th rev. ed. John W. Hill & Diane M. Bunce. (Illus.). 848p. (C). 1992. Addtl. materials avail. text ed. write for info. (*0-02-355070-8*); student ed, pap. write for info. (*0-02-351695-X*); student ed, pap. write for info. (*0-02-317125-1*) Macmillan.

Chemistry for Changing Times. 7th ed. John W. Hill & Doris K. Kolb. LC 94-16250. 848p. (C). 1994. text ed. write for info. (*0-02-355100-3*) Macmillan.

*__Chemistry for Electronic Materials: Proceedings of Symposium C, 1992 E-MRS Spring Conference, Strasbourg, France, 2-5 June 1992.__ Ed. by Y. Pauleau et al. (European Materials Research Society Symposia Proceedings Ser.: 33). viii, 206p. 1993. 197.25 (*0-444-89907-3*) Elsevier.

Chemistry for Energy. Ed. by M. Tomlinson. LC 79-26175. (ACS Symposium Ser.: No. 90). 1979. 38.95 (*0-8412-0469-1*) Am Chemical.

Chemistry for Engineers & Scientists. Leonard W. Fine & Herbert Beall. 800p. (C). 1990. text ed. 68.00 (*0-03-021537-4*) SCP.

Chemistry for Environmental Engineering. 3rd ed. Clair Sawyer & Perry L. McCarty. (Water Resources & Environmental Engineering Ser.). (Illus.). 1978. text ed. write for info. (*0-07-054971-0*) McGraw.

C

An Asterisk (*) at the beginning of an entry indicates that the title is appearing in BIP for the first time. 1177

Chemistry for Environmental Engineering. 4th ed. Clair N. Sawyer et al. LC 94-261. (Series in Water Resources & Environmental Engineering, Chemical Engineering Ser.). 1994. text ed. write for info. (*0-07-054978-8*) McGraw.

Chemistry for Every Kid: One Hundred & One Easy Experiments That Really Work. Janice P. Vancleave. 1989. text ed. 24.95 (*0-471-50974-4*); pap. text ed. 10.95 (*0-471-62085-8*) Wiley.

Chemistry for Nonscientists. Kelter & Carr. 672p. 1994. 47.00 (*0-8016-2728-1*) Mosby Yr Bk.

Chemistry for Nuclear Medicine. Mervyn W. Billinghurst & Alan R. Fritzberg. (Illus.). 328p. 1981. 43.50 (*0-8151-3295-6*, BKR-1, Yr Bk Med Pubs) Mosby Yr Bk.

Chemistry for Nuclear Medicine. Mervyn W. Billinghurst & Alan R. Fritzberg. LC 81-2957. (Illus.). 339p. reprint ed. pap. 96.70 (*0-8357-7588-7*, 2056909) Bks Demand.

Chemistry for Power Plant Technicians. Center for Occupational Research & Development Staff. (EUTEC Instrumentation & Control Curriculum Ser.). (Illus.). 368p. (C). 1985. pap. text ed. write for info. (*1-55502-185-9*) CORD Commns.

Chemistry for Protection of the Environment: Proceedings of an International Conference, Toulouse, France, 19-25, Sept., 1983. Ed. by L. Pawlowski et al. (Studies in Environmental Science: No. 23). 626p. 1984. 200.00 (*0-444-42347-8*, I-227-84) Elsevier.

Chemistry for Protection of the Environment: Proceedings of the 6th International Conference, Torino, Italy, 15-18 September, 1987. Ed. by L. Pawloski et al. (Studies in Environmental Science: No. 34). 412p. 1989. 164.00 (*0-444-87130-6*) Elsevier.

Chemistry for Science & Engineering. Breck et al. 450p. 1982. text ed. 29.95 (*0-07-092372-8*) McGraw.

Chemistry for Technicians I. Center for Occupational Research & Development Staff. (High Technology Ser.). (Illus.). 252p. (C). 1986. pap. text ed. 28.00 (*1-55502-173-5*) CORD Commns.

Chemistry for Technicians II. Center for Occupational Research & Development Staff. (High Technology Ser.). (Illus.). 262p. 1981. pap. text ed. 30.00 (*1-55502-174-3*) CORD Commns.

Chemistry for the Allied Health Sciences. Raymond A. Bauer & R. Loeschen. 1980. 28.95 (*0-685-03784-3*); 16.95 (*0-685-03785-1*); student ed 10.95 (*0-685-03786-X*) P-H.

Chemistry for the Applied Scientist. 2nd ed. W. Steedman et al. 1980. text ed. 160.00 (*0-08-022851-8*, Pergamon Pr); pap. text ed. 32.00 (*0-08-022852-6*, Pergamon Pr) Elsevier.

Chemistry for the Future: Proceedings of the 29th IUPAC Congress, Cologne, Federal Republic of Germany, 5-10 June 1983. Ed. by H. Grunewald. LC 83-23825. (IUPAC Symposium Ser.). 268p. 1984. 196.00 (*0-08-029249-6*, Pub. by Pergamon Repr UK) Franklin.

Chemistry for the Graphic Arts. 2nd ed. Nelson R. Eldred. Ed. by Thomas M. Destree. LC 91-75157. (Illus.). 250p. (C). 1990. pap. text ed. 45.00 (*0-88362-149-5*, 1401) Graphic Arts Tech Found.

Chemistry for the Health Sciences. 7th ed. George I. Sackheim & Dennis D. Lehman. LC 92-36078. (Illus.). 704p. (C). 1993. write for info. (*0-02-405161-6*) Macmillan.

Chemistry for the Health Sciences. 7th ed. George I. Sackheim & Dennis D. Lehman. LC 92-36078. (Illus.). 704p. (C). 1994. student ed, pap. write for info. (*0-02-405166-7*) Macmillan.

Chemistry for the Health Sciences. 7th suppl. ed. George I. Sackheim & Dennis D. Lehman. (Illus.). 704p. (C). 1994. write for info. (*0-318-69795-5*) Macmillan.

Chemistry for the Life Sciences. William Hendrickson & Juanita Healy. Incl. 1981. (*0-318-55399-6*); 631p. (C). 1981. Set text ed. 24.00 (*0-394-32215-0*) Random.

Chemistry for the Protection of the Environment. Ed. by L. Pawlowski et al. (Environmental Science Research Ser.). (Illus.). 824p. 1991. 159.50 (*0-306-43904-2*, Plenum Pr) Plenum.

Chemistry for the Protection of the Environment 1985: Proceedings of the 5th International Conference, Leuven, Belgium, September 9-13, 1985. Ed. by L. Pawlowski et al. (Studies in Environmental Science: No. 29). 796p. 1986. 251.50 (*0-444-42715-5*) Elsevier.

Chemistry for Today: General, Organic & Biochemistry. Spencer L. Seager & Michael R. Slabaugh. LC 86-24623. (Illus.). 848p. (C). 1987. text ed. 61.00 (*0-314-25881-7*); student ed, pap. text ed. 20.00 (*0-314-35391-7*) West Pub.

Chemistry for Today: General, Organic, & Biochemistry. 2nd ed. Spencer L. Seager & Michael R. Slabaugh. Ed. by Westby. LC 93-33036. 750p. (C). 1994. text ed. 63.75 (*0-314-02652-5*) West Pub.

Chemistry Fundamentals. (Illus.). 545p. 1981. ring bd. 195.00 (*0-87683-331-8*); trans. 95.00 (*0-87683-333-4*); 995.00 (*0-87683-332-6*); 185.00 (*0-87683-334-2*); 1,295.00 (*0-87683-330-X*) GP Pub.

Chemistry, Health Physics, & Nuclear Instrumentation. Ed. by R. W. Deutsch & J. W. Whitney. (Academic Program for Nuclear Power Plant Personnel Ser., BWR Version: Vol. IV). (Illus.). 454p. 1972. ring bd. 39.50 (*0-87683-150-1*, A 373977); 195.00 (*0-87683-157-9*); 25.00 (*0-87683-164-1*); 35.00 (*0-87683-171-4*) GP Pub.

***Chemistry Imagined: Reflections on Science.** Ronald Hoffman & Vivian Torrence. (Illus.). 168p. 1995. pap. 19.95 (*1-56098-539-9*) Smithsonian.

Chemistry Imagined: Reflections on Science. Roald Hoffmann & Vivian Torrence. LC 92-31996. (Illus.). 168p. 1993. 19.95 (*1-56098-214-4*) Smithsonian.

Chemistry in Action: A Laboratory Manual. 2nd ed. Boschmann & Wells. 464p. 1990. pap. text ed. write for info. (*0-07-006531-4*) McGraw.

***Chemistry in Action: The Molecules of Everyday Life.** Nina Morgan. (The New Encyclopedia of Science Ser.). (Illus.). 160p. 1995. text ed. 35.00 (*0-19-521086-7*) OUP.

Chemistry in America: Chapters from the History of the Science in the United States. Edgar F. Smith. LC 72-5073. (Technology & Society Ser.). 1972. reprint ed. 25.95 (*0-405-04723-1*) Ayer.

Chemistry in America, Eighteen Seventy-Six to Nineteen Seventy-Six. Robert F. Bud et al. 1985. lib. bdg. 164.50 (*90-277-1720-6*) Kluwer Ac.

Chemistry in America, Eighteen Seventy-Six to Nineteen Seventy-Six: Historical Indicators. Arnold Thackray et al. (C). 1988. pap. text ed. 57.50 (*90-277-2662-0*) Kluwer Ac.

Chemistry in Anhydrous Liquid Ammonia, Pt. 2: Organic Reactions in Liquid Ammonia. Harold Smith & G. Jander. (Chemistry in Nonaqueous Ionizing Solvents Ser.: Vol. 4, Pt. 2). 160.00 (*0-08-013115-8*, Pub. by Pergamon Repr UK) Franklin.

Chemistry in Anhydrous Prototropic Inorganic Solvents: Inorganic Chemistry in Liquid Hydrogen Cyanide & Liquid Hydrogen Flouride. G. Jander & B. Gruttner. LC 65-2550. (Chemistry in Nonaqueous Ionizing Solvents Ser.: Vol. 2, Pt. 1). 1971. 136.00 (*0-08-017570-8*, Pub. by Pergamon Repr UK) Franklin.

Chemistry in Civilization. I. Dwaine Eubanks & Otis C. Derner. LC 74-80913. 358p. reprint ed. pap. 102.10 (*0-317-08908-0*, 2055101) Bks Demand.

Chemistry in Context: Applying Chemistry to Society. American Chemical Society Staff. 432p. (C). 1993. write for info. (*0-697-21951-8*) Wm C Brown Pubs.

Chemistry in Context: Applying Chemistry to Society. American Chemical Society Staff. 432p. (C). 1993. pap. write for info. (*0-697-21948-8*) Wm C Brown Pubs.

***Chemistry in Context: Applying Chemistry to Society.** American Chemical Society Staff. 1994. student ed, pap. text ed. write for info. (*0-697-27732-1*) Wm C Brown Pubs.

Chemistry in Microscale. David Ehrenkranz & Mauch. 208p. (C). 1990. spiral bd. 19.95 (*0-8403-7071-7*) Kendall-Hunt.

Chemistry in Microscale, Bk. 1: Student Edition. David Ehrenkranz & John J. Mauch. 112p. 1993. pap. text ed., spiral bd. 11.95 (*0-8403-8879-9*) Kendall-Hunt.

Chemistry in Non-Aoueous Solvents. B. Tremillon. Tr. by N. Corcoran. LC 73-86094. 1974. lib. bdg. 84.00 (*90-277-0389-2*) Kluwer Ac.

Chemistry in Perspective. Mohrig & Child. 560p. 1987. teacher ed write for info. (*0-318-61504-5*, H05648); text ed. write for info. (*0-205-10270-0*) P-H.

Chemistry in Premixed Flames. C. Fenimore & A. Dickenson. LC 63-19532. (International Encyclopedia of Physical Chemistry & Chemical Physics Ser.: Vol. 5, No. TP19). 1964. 52.00 (*0-08-010460-6*, Pub. by Pergamon Repr UK) Franklin.

Chemistry in Space. Ed. by J. M. Greenberg & V. Pirronello. (NATO Advanced Science Institutes Series C: Mathematical & Physical Sciences). 448p. 1990. lib. bdg. 147.00 (*0-7923-0987-1*) Kluwer Ac.

Chemistry in the Laboratory. Lidia M. Vallarino et al. 1976. pap. text ed. 5.72 (*0-07-051027-X*) McGraw.

Chemistry in the Laboratory, No. 161. Paul W. Hunter. Ed. by Robert N. Hammer. (Illus.). 176p. (Orig.). (C). 1992. 12.50 (*0-9630471-0-8*) Okemos Pr.

Chemistry in the Laboratory, No. 162. Paul W. Hunter. (Illus.). 136p. (Orig.). (C). 1992. 12.50 (*0-9630471-1-6*) Okemos Pr.

Chemistry in the Soil Environment. Ed. by R. H. Dowdy et al. (Illus.). 259p. 1981. pap. 10.00 (*0-89118-065-6*) Am Soc Agron.

Chemistry in the Utilization of Wood. R. Farmer & K. Kape. LC 66-29789. (Pergamon Series of Monographs on Furniture & Timber: Vol. 9). 1967. 82.00 (*0-08-012137-3*, Pub. by Pergamon Repr UK) Franklin.

Chemistry, Industry & the Environment. James N. Lowe. 352p. (C). 1993. pap. 40.23 (*0-697-17087-X*) Wm C Brown Pubs.

Chemistry Lab Manual. Gene Peck. (C). 1993. student ed 10.00 (*1-881592-02-2*) Hayden-McNeil.

***Chemistry Labs for Distance Learning: A Microscale Laboratory Manual.** David P. Licata. (Illus.). 64p. (C). 1994. student ed 16.65 (*0-9636095-2-1*) Licatas Edutype.

Chemistry Liquid Dinitrogen Tetroxide & Sulphur Dioxide. G. Jander & C. Addison. LC 65-2550. (Chemistry in Nonaqueous Ionizing Solvents Ser.: Vol. 3). 1967. 93.00 (*0-08-012680-4*, Pub. by Pergamon Repr UK) Franklin.

Chemistry Made Easy, 2 vols., Set, Pts. I & II. Joachim Nentwig et al. 750p. (C). 1992. Set. pap. text ed. 59.95 (*1-56081-549-3*) VCH Pubs.

Chemistry Made Simple. Fred C. Hess. LC 82-46054. (Made Simple Ser.). (Illus.). 224p. 1984. pap. 12.00 (*0-385-18850-1*) Doubleday.

Chemistry, Matter, & Life. Stephen Miall & Laurence M. Miall. LC 70-39099. (Essay Index Reprint Ser.). 1977. reprint ed. 23.95 (*0-8369-2703-6*) Ayer.

Chemistry of Acetylenes. Ed. by Heinz G. Viehe. LC 69-10275. 1312p. reprint ed. pap. 180.00 (*0-7837-0932-3*, 2041237) Bks Demand.

Chemistry of Acid Derivatives, Pts. 1 & 2. Ed. by Saul Patai. Suppl. B. (Illus.). 767p. reprint ed. pap. write for info. (*0-318-65330-3*); reprint ed. Pt. 1. pap. 180.00 (*0-8357-8829-6*, 2033325); reprint ed. Pt. 2. pap. 180.00 (*0-8357-8835-0*, 2033325) Bks Demand.

Chemistry of Acid Derivatives, Vol. 2: Supplement B, Pts. 1 & 2. Ed. by Saul E. Patai. (Chemistry of Functional Groups Ser.). 2723p. 1992. text ed. 1,460.00 (*0-471-93111-X*) Wiley.

Chemistry of Acid Rain: Sources & Atmospheric Processes. Ed. by Russell W. Johnson & Glen E. Gordon. LC 87-19404. (ACS Symposium Ser.: No. 349). (Illus.). xi, 337p. 1987. 59.95 (*0-8412-1414-X*) Am Chemical.

Chemistry of Acyl Halides. Ed. by Saul Patai. LC 70-37114. (Chemistry of Functional Groups Ser.). 561p. reprint ed. pap. 159.90 (*0-8357-8830-X*, 2033324) Bks Demand.

Chemistry of Air Pollution. Karl Westberg et al. LC 73-11037. (Air Pollution Ser.: Vol. 1). 199p. 1974. text ed. 25.50 (*0-8422-7152-X*) Irvington.

Chemistry of Alicyclic Compounds: Structure & Chemical Transformations. G. Haufe & G. Mann. (Studies in Organic Chemistry: No. 38). 468p. 1990. 179.50 (*0-444-98878-5*) Elsevier.

Chemistry of Alkanes & Cycloalkanes. Saul E. Patai. (Chemistry of Functional Groups Ser.: No. 1078). 1092p. 1992. text ed. 795.00 (*0-471-92498-9*) Wiley.

Chemistry of Alkenes, 2 vols., Vol. 1. Ed. by Saul Patai & Jacob Zabicky. LC 64-25218. (Chemistry of Functional Groups Ser.: Vol. 1). (Illus.). 616p. reprint ed. pap. 160.00 (*0-685-23859-8*, 2056645) Bks Demand.

Chemistry of Alkenes, 2 vols., Vol. 2. Ed. by Saul Patai & Jacob Zabicky. LC 64-25218. (Chemistry of Functional Groups Ser.: Vol. 1). (Illus.). 616p. reprint ed. pap. 160.00 (*0-685-23860-1*) Bks Demand.

Chemistry of Allelopathy: Biochemical Interactions Among Plants. Ed. by Alonzo C. Thompson. LC 84-24626. (ACS Symposium Ser.: No. 268). 470p. 1985. lib. bdg. 87.95 (*0-8412-0886-7*) Am Chemical.

Chemistry of Aluminium, Gallium, Indium, & Thallium. Ed. by A. J. Downs. LC 92-47139. 1993. write for info. (*0-7514-0103-X*, Pub. by Blackie Acad & Prof UK) Routledge Chapman & Hall.

Chemistry of Americium. Wallace W. Schulz. LC 76-25824. (ERDA Critical Review Ser.). 302p. 1976. pap. 15.50 (*0-87079-040-4*, TID-26971); fiche 9.00 (*0-87079-163-X*, TID-26971) DOE.

Chemistry of Amides. Ed. by Jacob Z. Zabicky. LC 76-116520. (Chemistry of Functional Groups Ser.). 943p. reprint ed. pap. 180.00 (*0-317-30332-5*, 2024809) Bks Demand.

Chemistry of Amidines & Imidates. Ed. by Saul Patai. LC 75-6913. (Chemistry of Functional Groups Ser.). (Illus.). 691p. reprint ed. pap. 180.00 (*0-8357-8831-8*, 2033320) Bks Demand.

Chemistry of Amidines & Imidates, Vol. 2. Ed. by Saul E. Patai & Zvi Rappoport. (Chemistry of Functional Groups Ser.: No. 1078). 918p. 1991. text ed. 915.00 (*0-471-92457-1*) Wiley.

Chemistry of Amino, Nitroso, & Nitro Compounds & Their Derivatives, Pts. 1 & 2. Ed. by Saul Patai. LC 81-16153. (Chemistry of Functional Groups Ser.: Supplement F). (Illus.). reprint ed. pap. 160.00 (*0-685-73964-3*, 2030491); reprint ed. pap. 160.00 (*0-685-73965-1*) Bks Demand.

Chemistry of Antitumor Antibiotics, Vol. 1. William A. Remers. LC 78-12436. 299p. reprint ed. pap. 85.30 (*0-317-09762-8*, 2017401) Bks Demand.

Chemistry of Antitumor Antibiotics, Vol. 2. William A. Remers. 290p. 1988. text ed. 79.95 (*0-471-08180-9*) Wiley.

Chemistry of Antitumour Agents. Ed. by D. E. Wilman. 352p. 1990. 160.00 (*0-412-02031-9*, A3602, Chap & Hall NY) Chapman & Hall.

Chemistry of Aquatic Systems: Local & Global Perspectives - Based on the Lectures Given During the Eurocourse Held at the Joint Research Centre, Ispra, Italy, September 27-October 1, 1993. Ed. by Giovanni Bidoglio & Werner Stumm. LC 94-15441. (Eurocourses: Chemical & Environmental Science Ser.: Vol. 5). 544p. (C). 1994. lib. bdg. 185.50 (*0-7923-2867-1*) Kluwer Ac.

Chemistry of Arsenic. C. A. McAuliffe & A. Mackie. 350p. 1994. text ed. 57.00 (*0-13-126368-4*) P-H.

Chemistry of Art. 1980. 6.50 (*0-910362-13-0*) Chem Educ.

Chemistry of Art: A Sequel. 1981. pap. 9.00 (*0-910362-16-5*) Chem Educ.

Chemistry of Artificial Lighting Devices: Lamps, Phosphors, & Cathode Ray Tubes. R. C. Ropp. LC 93-33113. (Studies in Inorganic Chemistry: No. 17). 1993. write for info. (*0-444-81709-3*) Elsevier.

Chemistry of Atmospheres: An Introduction to the Chemistry of the Atmospheres of Earth, the Planets, & Their Satellites. 2nd ed. Richard P. Wayne. (Illus.). 464p. (C). 1991. pap. text ed. 39.95 (*0-19-855571-7*) OUP.

Chemistry of Atopic Allergens. L. Berrens. (Monographs in Allergy: Vol. 7). 1971. 74.50 (*3-8055-1150-7*) S Karger.

Chemistry of B-Lactams. Ed. by M. I. Page. 320p. 1992. 159.95 (*0-7514-0061-0*, A6875, Pub. by Blackie Acad & Prof UK) Routledge Chapman & Hall.

Chemistry of Behavior: A Molecular Approach to Neuronal Plasticity. Stanislav Reinis & Jerome M. Goldman. LC 82-13294. 622p. 1982. 110.00 (*0-306-41161-X*, Plenum Pr) Plenum.

Chemistry of Beverages. Torkko. (Illus.). (Orig.). 1989. pap. text ed. 16.95 (*1-877991-11-2*, AP4282) Flinn Scientific.

Chemistry of Biosurfaces, 2 vols., Vol. 1. Ed. by Michael L. Hair. LC 70-142892. 392p. reprint ed. pap. 105.90 (*0-7837-0751-7*, 2041068) Bks Demand.

Chemistry of Biosurfaces, 2 vols., Vol. 2. Ed. by Michael L. Hair. LC 70-142892. 493p. reprint ed. pap. 140.60 (*0-7837-0752-5*) Bks Demand.

Chemistry of Carboxylic Acids & Esters. Saul Patai. LC 70-82547. (Chemistry of Functional Groups Ser.). (Illus.). 1169p. reprint ed. pap. 180.00 (*0-685-23488-6*, 2027888) Bks Demand.

Chemistry of Catalytic Hydrocarbon Conversions. Herman Pines. 1981. text ed. 80.00 (*0-12-557160-7*) Acad Pr.

Chemistry of Catalytic Processes. Bruce C. Gates et al. (McGraw Hill Series in Chemical Engineering). (Illus.). 1979. text ed. write for info. (*0-07-022987-2*) McGraw.

Chemistry of Cationic Polymerization. P. Plesch. LC 63-10034. 1963. 298.00 (*0-08-010289-1*, Pub. by Pergamon Repr UK) Franklin.

Chemistry of Cellulose & Wood. N. I. Nikitin. 704p. 1966. text ed. 149.50 (*0-7065-0583-2*, Pub. by Keter Pub IS) Coronet Bks.

Chemistry of Cement & Concrete. F. M. Lea. 1971. 80.00 (*0-8206-0212-4*) Chem Pub.

***Chemistry of Cements for Nuclear Applications: Proceedings of Symposium D, E-MRS Fall Conference, Strasbourg, France, 5-7 November 1991.** Ed. by P. Barret & F. P. Glasser. (European Materials Research Society Symposia Proceedings Ser.: 27). viii, 314p. 1992. 185.75 (*0-444-89575-2*) Elsevier.

Chemistry of Cereal Proteins. Radomir Lasztity. 216p. 1984. 139.95 (*0-8493-5140-5*, TP453, CRC Reprint) Franklin.

***Chemistry of Cereal Proteins.** 2nd ed. Radomir Lasztity. 300p. 1995. write for info. (*0-8493-2763-6*, 2763) CRC Pr.

Chemistry of Clay-Organic Reactions. B. K. Theng. LC 74-12524. 355p. reprint ed. pap. 101.20 (*0-317-37282-3*, 2020262) Bks Demand.

Chemistry of Clays & Clay Minerals. Ed. by A. C. Newman. 480p. 1987. text ed. 156.95 (*0-471-01141-X*) Wiley.

Chemistry of Coal: Coal Science & Technology, 7. N. Berkowitz. LC 85-20280. 504p. 1985. 151.50 (*0-444-42509-8*) Elsevier.

Chemistry of Coal Conversion. Ed. by Richard H. Schlosberg. LC 85-16977. 348p. 1985. 82.50 (*0-306-41974-2*, Plenum Pr) Plenum.

Chemistry of Coal Weathering. Ed. by C. R. Nelson. (Coal Science & Technology Ser.: Vol. 14). 1989. 141.00 (*0-444-88088-7*, CST 14) Elsevier.

Chemistry of Color. Eby. (Illus.). (Orig.). 1989. pap. text ed. 14.95 (*1-877991-10-4*, AP4281) Flinn Scientific.

Chemistry of Combustion Processes. Ed. by Thompson M. Sloane. LC 84-2816. (ACS Symposium Ser.: No. 249). 296p. 1984. lib. bdg. 54.95 (*0-8412-0834-4*) Am Chemical.

Chemistry of Conjugated Cyclic Compounds: To Be or Not to Be Like Benzene? Douglas Lloyd. 1990. text ed. 115.00 (*0-471-91721-4*) Wiley.

Chemistry of Conscious States: How the Brain Changed Its Mind. J. Allan Hobson. LC 94-15538. 1994. 24.95 (*0-316-36754-0*) Little.

Chemistry of Corrosion Inhibitors in Potable Water. 230p. 1989. pap. 24.00 (*0-89867-506-5*, 90561) Am Water Wks Assn.

Chemistry of Cyanates & Their Thio Derivatives, Pt. 1. Saul Patai. (Interscience Publication, Chemistry of Functional Groups Ser.). reprint ed. Part 1. pap. 158.00 (*0-317-26341-2*, 2025197) Bks Demand.

Chemistry of Cyanates & Their Thio Derivatives, Pt. 2. Saul Patai. (Interscience Publication, Chemistry of Functional Groups Ser.). reprint ed. Part 2. pap. 160.00 (*0-317-26342-0*) Bks Demand.

***Chemistry of Cyclopropyl Groups Part 2.** Zvi Rappoport. LC 87-10440. (The Chemistry of Functional Groups Ser.). 944p. reprint ed. pap. 180.00 (*0-7837-8274-8*, 2049054) Bks Demand.

Chemistry of Defeat: Asymmetries in U. S. & Soviet Chemical Warfare Postures. Amoretta M. Hoeber. LC 81-84989. (Special Report Ser.). 91p. 1981. 11.95 (*0-89549-037-4*) Inst Foreign Policy Anal.

Chemistry of Delignification with Oxygen, Ozone & Peroxides: Symposium Held at Raleigh, North Carolina, May 27-29, 1975, under the Auspices of the School of Forest Resources of North Carolina State University. International Symposium on Delignification with Oxygen, Ozone & Peroxides (1st, 1975, Raleigh, NC). 280p. reprint ed. pap. 79.80 (*0-685-15298-7*, 2052173) Bks Demand.

Chemistry of Diacetylenes. M. F. Shostakovskii & A. V. Bogdanova. 512p. 1974. text ed. 110.00 (*0-7065-1381-9*, Pub. by Keter Pub IS) Coronet Bks.

Chemistry of Diazirines, 2 vols., Set. Ed. by Michael T. Liu. 352p. 1987. 189.00 (*0-8493-5047-6*, QD341, CRC Reprint) Franklin.

Chemistry of Diazonium & Diazo Groups, 2 pts., Pt. 1. Ed. by Saul Patai. LC 75-6913. (Chemistry of Functional Groups Ser.). reprint ed. pap. 131.00 (*0-317-10696-1*, 2022404) Bks Demand.

Chemistry of Diazonium & Diazo Groups, 2 pts., Pt. 2. Ed. by Saul Patai. LC 75-6913. (Chemistry of Functional Groups Ser.). reprint ed. pap. 143.00 (*0-317-10697-X*) Bks Demand.

Chemistry of Double-Bonded Functional Groups: Supplement A, Vol. 2. Ed. by Saul E. Patai. (Chemistry of Functional Groups Ser.). 891p. 1989. text ed. 795.00 (*0-471-92493-8*) Wiley.

Chemistry of Doubled-Bonded Functional Groups, Pts. 1 & 2. Ed. by Saul Patai. Suppl. A. (Illus.). 667p. reprint ed. pap. write for info. (*0-318-65329-X*); reprint ed. Pt. 1. pap. 180.00 (*0-8357-8832-6*, 2033319); reprint ed. Pt. 2. pap. 180.00 (*0-8357-8836-9*, 2033319) Bks Demand.

Chemistry of Effluent Treatment. George Kakabadse. (Illus.). 148p. 1979. 48.75 (*0-85334-840-5*, Pub. by Elsevier Applied Sci UK) Elsevier.

Chemistry of Electronic Ceramic Materials: International Conference, Aug. 17-22, 1990, Jackson WY. Ed. by Peter K. Davies & Robert S. Roth. 532p. 1991. pap. 49.00 (*0-87762-860-2*) Technomic.

Chemistry of Enamines. Ed. by Zvi Rappoport. (Chemistry of Functional Groups Ser.). 800p. 1994. text ed. 875.00 (*0-471-93339-2*) Wiley.

An Asterisk (*) at the beginning of an entry indicates that the title is appearing in BIP for the first time.

C

An Asterisk (*) at the beginning of an entry indicates that the title is appearing in BIP for the first time.

Chemistry of Soil Organic Matter. K. Kumada. (Developments in Soil Science Ser.: Vol. 17). 1988. 89.75 (*0-444-98936-6*) Elsevier.

Chemistry of Soil Solutions. Ed. by Adel M. Elprince. 432p. (C). 1990. reprint ed. 57.95 (*0-89464-470-X*) Krieger.

Chemistry of Soils. Garrison Sposito. (Illus.). 304p. (C). 1989. text ed. 42.50 (*0-19-504615-3*) OUP.

Chemistry of Solid Wood. R. M. Rowell. 614p. (C). 1986. 475.00 (*0-685-61460-3*, Pub. by Intl Bk Distr II) St Mut.

Chemistry of Solid Wood. Ed. by Roger Rowell. LC 83-22451. (Advances in Chemistry Ser.: No. 207). 614p. 1984. lib. bdg. 89.95 (*0-8412-0796-8*) Am Chemical.

Chemistry of Solid Wood. R. M. Rowell. 614p. (C). 1986. reprint ed. 210.00 (*81-7089-040-3*, Pub. by Intl Bk Distr II) St Mut.

***Chemistry of Structure-Function Relationships in Cheese: Proceedings of ACS Symposium Held in Chicago, Illinois, August 23-25, 1993.** Ed. by Edyth L. Malin & Michael H. Tunick. (Advances in Experimental Medicine & Biology Ser.: Vol. 367). 385p. 1995. 95.00 (*0-306-44982-X*) Plenum.

Chemistry of Sulfides. Ed. by Arthur V. Tobolsky. LC 67-29545. 291p. reprint ed. pap. 83.00 (*0-317-09194-8*, 2006362) Bks Demand.

Chemistry of Sulphenic Acids & Their Derivatives. Ed. by Saul E. Patai. 819p. 1990. text ed. 795.00 (*0-471-92373-7*) Wiley.

Chemistry of Sulphinic Acids, Esters & Derivatives. Ed. by Saul E. Patai. (Chemistry of Functional Groups). 728p. 1990. text ed. 695.00 (*0-471-91918-7*) Wiley.

Chemistry of Sulphonic Acids, Esters & Their Derivatives. Ed. by Saul E. Patai & Zvi Rappoport. (Chemistry of Functional Groups Ser.). 1121p. 1991. text ed. 1,150.00 (*0-471-92201-3*) Wiley.

Chemistry of Sulphur Dioxide in Foods. Ed. by B. L. Wedzicha. (Illus.). 384p. 1984. 97.25 (*0-85334-267-9*, I-264-84, Pub. by Elsevier Applied Sci UK) Elsevier.

Chemistry of Superconductor Materials: Preparation, Chemistry, Characterization & Theory. Terrell A. Vanderah. LC 90-27624. (Illus.). 818p. 1992. 125.00 (*0-8155-1279-1*) Noyes.

Chemistry of Synthethic Dyes, 8 vols. Ed. by Krishnasami Venkataraman. Incl. Vol. 4. 1971. 98.50 (*0-12-717004-9*); Vol. 6. 1972. 98.50 (*0-12-717006-5*); (Organic & Biological Chemistry Ser.). write for info. (*0-318-50246-1*) Acad Pr.

Chemistry of Synthetic Dyes & Pigments. Ed. by H. A. Lubs. LC 64-7905. (A C S Ser.: No. 127). 750p. 1971. reprint ed. 69.50 (*0-88275-039-9*) Krieger.

Chemistry of Textiles. Eby. (Illus.). (Orig.). 1989. pap. text ed. 16.95 (*1-877991-09-0*, AP4280) Flinn Scientific.

Chemistry of the Actinide Elements, 2 vols. 2nd ed. Ed. by J. J. Katz et al. 1986. write for info. (*0-318-60999-1*) Chapman & Hall.

Chemistry of the Actinide Elements, 2 vols., Vol. I. 2nd ed. Ed. by J. J. Katz et al. 998p. 1986. text ed. 210.00 (*0-412-10550-0*, 9641) Chapman & Hall.

Chemistry of the Actinide Elements, 2 vols., Vol. II. 2nd ed. Ed. by J. J. Katz et al. 912p. 1986. text ed. 210.00 (*0-412-27370-5*, 9642) Chapman & Hall.

***Chemistry of the Amazon: Biodiversity, Natural Products, & Environmental Issues.** Ed. by Peter R. Seidl et al. LC 95-5473. (ACS Symposium Ser.: No. 588). (Illus.). 328p. 1995. 89.95 (*0-8412-3159-1*) Am Chemical.

Chemistry of the Amino Acids, 3 vols., Vol. 3. Jessie P. Greenstein & Milton Winitz. LC 83-13616. 1070p. 1983. reprint ed. 120.00 (*0-89874-484-9*) Krieger.

Chemistry of the Amino Group. Ed. by Saul Patai. LC 67-31072. (Chemistry of Functional Groups Ser.). (Illus.). 827p. reprint ed. pap. 180.00 (*0-8357-8833-4*, 2033321) Bks Demand.

Chemistry of the Atmosphere: Its Impact on Global Change, a Chemistry for the 21st Century Monograph. Ed. by Jack G. Calvert. LC 93-20857. 1994. write for info. (*0-632-03779-2*) Blackwell Sci.

Chemistry of the Atmosphere: Its Impact on Global Change, Perspectives & Recommendations. Ed. by John W. Birks et al. LC 92-41499. (Illus.). 180p. 1993. 34.95 (*0-8412-2532-X*); pap. 24.95 (*0-8412-2533-8*) Am Chemical.

Chemistry of the Azido Group. Ed. by Saul Patai. LC 73-149579. (Chemistry of Functional Groups Ser.). (Illus.). 640p. reprint ed. pap. 180.00 (*0-8357-8834-2*, 2033322) Bks Demand.

Chemistry of the Blood. Martin R. DeHaan. 160p. 1983. reprint ed. pap. 8.99 (*0-310-23291-0*, 9582P) Zondervan.

Chemistry of the Carbon-Carbon Triple Bond, 2 pts., Pt. 1. Ed. by Saul Patai. LC 75-6913. (Chemistry of Functional Groups Ser.). (Illus.). 536p. reprint ed. pap. 152.80 (*0-8357-8837-7*, 2033323) Bks Demand.

Chemistry of the Carbon-Carbon Triple Bond, 2 pts., Pt. 2. Ed. by Saul Patai. LC 75-6913. (Chemistry of Functional Groups Ser.). (Illus.). 536p. reprint ed. pap. 159.10 (*0-8357-8838-5*, 2033323) Bks Demand.

Chemistry of the Carbon-Nitrogen Double Bond. Ed. by Saul Patai. (Illus.). 808p. reprint ed. Pt. 2. write for info. (*0-318-65331-1*) Bks Demand.

Chemistry of the Carbon-Nitrogen Double Bond, Pt. 1. Ed. by Saul Patai. LC 70-104166. (Chemistry of Functional Groups Ser.). (Illus.). 808p. reprint ed. pap. 180.00 (*0-8357-8839-3*, 2033327) Bks Demand.

Chemistry of the Carbonyl Group, 2 vols., 1. Ed. by Saul Patai & J. Zabicky. LC 66-18177. (Chemistry of Functional Groups Ser.: Vol. 2). (Illus.). 1027p. reprint ed. pap. 160.00 (*0-685-23861-X*, 2056646) Bks Demand.

Chemistry of the Carbonyl Group, 2 vols., 2. Ed. by Saul Patai & J. Zabicky. LC 66-18177. (Chemistry of Functional Groups Ser.: Vol. 2). (Illus.). 1027p. reprint ed. pap. 120.70 (*0-685-23862-8*) Bks Demand.

Chemistry of the Copper & Zinc Triads. Ed. by Alan J. Welch & Stephen K. Chapman. 259p. 1993. 95.00 (*0-85186-715-4*, Pub. by Royal Soc Chem UK) CRC Pr.

Chemistry of the Cosmos. George W. Carey. 144p. 1963. reprint ed. spiral bd. 5.50 (*0-7873-0140-X*) Mokelumne.

Chemistry of the Cosmos: Armageddon, Astrology, Wonders & Possibilities of the Human Body, Paradoxes of Civilization & the Coming Man. G. W. Carey. 1991. lib. bdg. 79.95 (*0-8490-4249-6*) Gordon Pr.

Chemistry of the Cyano Group. Ed. by Zvi Rappoport. LC 70-116165. (Chemistry of Functional Groups Ser.: Vol. 8). (Illus.). 1059p. reprint ed. pap. 180.00 (*0-685-23865-2*, 2056648) Bks Demand.

***Chemistry of the Cyclopropyl Group Part 1.** Zvi Rappoport. LC 87-10440. (The Chemistry of Functional Groups Ser.). 822p. 1987. reprint ed. pap. 180.00 (*0-7837-8273-X*, 2049054) Bks Demand.

Chemistry of the Elements. N. N. Greenwood & A. Earnshaw. LC 83-13346. (Illus.). 1542p. 1984. pap. text ed. 46.00 (*0-08-022057-6*, Pergamon Pr) Elsevier.

Chemistry of the Farm & the Sea. James R. Nichols. LC 73-125755. (American Environmental Studies). 1974. reprint ed. 15.95 (*0-405-02681-1*) Ayer.

Chemistry of the Food Cycle. 1984. 13.00 (*0-910362-24-6*) Chem Educ.

Chemistry of the Hydrazo, Azo, & Azoxy Groups, 2 pts., Pt. 1. Ed. by Saul Patai. LC 75-2194. (Chemistry of Functional Groups Ser.). (Illus.). 611p. reprint ed. pap. 174.20 (*0-8357-8840-7*, 2033326) Bks Demand.

Chemistry of the Hydrazo, Azo, & Azoxy Groups, 2 pts., Pt. 2. Ed. by Saul Patai. LC 75-2194. (Chemistry of Functional Groups Ser.). (Illus.). 611p. reprint ed. pap. 173.00 (*0-8357-8841-5*, 2033326) Bks Demand.

Chemistry of the Hydroxyl Group, 2 vols., 1. Ed. by Saul Patai. LC 77-116164. (Chemistry of Functional Groups Ser.: Vol. 10). (Illus.). 632p. reprint ed. pap. 160.00 (*0-685-23863-6*, 2056647) Bks Demand.

Chemistry of the Hydroxyl Group, 2 vols., 2. Ed. by Saul Patai. LC 77-116164. (Chemistry of Functional Groups Ser.: Vol. 10). (Illus.). 632p. reprint ed. pap. 157.10 (*0-685-23864-4*) Bks Demand.

Chemistry of the Metal Carbon: The Structure Preparation, Thermochemistry & Characterization of Organometallic Compounds, 4 vols., Vol. 5. Ed. by Frank R. Hartley & Saul E. Patai. (Chemistry of Functional Groups Ser.). 1007p. 1990. text ed. 460.00 (*0-471-91556-4*) Wiley.

Chemistry of the Metal Carbon Bond, Vol. 4: The Use of Organometallic Compounds in Organic Synthesis, Vol. 4. Ed. by Frank R. Hartley. (Chemistry of Functional Groups Ser.). 1987. text ed. 975.00 (*0-471-90888-6*) Wiley.

Chemistry of the Monoterpenes: An Encyclopedia Handbook, Set, Pt. A. Erman. (Studies in Organic Chemistry: Vol. 11). 832p. 1985. 480.00 (*0-8247-1573-X*) Dekker.

Chemistry of the Monoterpenes: An Encyclopedia Handbook, Set, Pt. B. Erman. (Studies in Organic Chemistry: Vol. 11.1). 536p. 1985. 480.00 (*0-8247-7312-8*) Dekker.

Chemistry of the Nitro & Nitroso Groups, Pt. 1. Ed. by Henry Feuer. LC 80-21491. 780p. 1980. reprint ed. text ed. write for info. (*0-89874-271-4*) Krieger.

Chemistry of the Nitro & Nitroso Groups, Pt. 2. Ed. by Henry Feuer. LC 80-21491. 458p. 1980. reprint ed. text ed. write for info. (*0-89874-272-2*) Krieger.

Chemistry of the Nitro & Nitroso Groups, Pts. 1 & 2. Ed. by Henry Feuer. LC 80-21491. 1238p. 1980. reprint ed. text ed. 19.50 (*0-89874-320-6*) Krieger.

Chemistry of the Non-Metallic Elements. E. Sherwin & G. J. Weston. 1966. 82.00 (*0-08-011296-X*, Pub. by Pergamon Repr UK) Franklin.

Chemistry of the Non-Metals: With an Introduction to Atomic Structure & Chemical Bonding. Ralf Steudel. Tr. by E. C. Nachod & J. J. Zuckerman. (Illus.). (C). 1977. 36.95 (*3-11-004882-5*) De Gruyter.

Chemistry of the O-Glycosidic Bond: Formation & Cleavage. A. E. Bochkov & G. E. Zaikov. 1979. 88.00 (*0-08-022949-2*, Pub. by Pergamon Repr UK) Franklin.

Chemistry of the Platinum Group Metals: Recent Developments. Ed. by F. R. Hartley. (Studies in Inorganic Chemistry: Vol. 11). 624p. 1991. 246.25 (*0-444-88189-1*) Elsevier.

***Chemistry of the Prostaglandins & Leukotrienes.** Ed. by John E. Pike & Douglas R. Morton, Jr. LC 84-42772. (Advances in Prostaglandin, Thromboxane & Leukotriene Research Ser.: No. 14). (Illus.). reprint ed. pap. 130.00 (*0-7837-9636-6*, 2060389) Bks Demand.

Chemistry of the Quinonoid Compounds, 2 pts., Pt. 1. Ed. by Saul Patai. LC 73-17765. 630p. reprint ed. pap. 179.60 (*0-685-20919-9*, 2052254) Bks Demand.

Chemistry of the Quinonoid Compounds, 2 pts., Pt. 2. Ed. by Saul Patai. LC 73-17765. 673p. reprint ed. pap. 180.00 (*0-685-20920-2*, 2052254) Bks Demand.

Chemistry of the Quinonoid Compounds, Vol. 2. Ed. by Zvi Rappoport. LC 86-32494. (Chemistry of Functional Groups Ser.). 1740p. 1988. Set. text ed. 1,950.00 (*0-471-91916-0*) Wiley.

***Chemistry of the Quinonoid Compounds, Vol. 2, Pt. 1.** Ed. by Saul Patai & Zvi Rappoport. LC 86-32494. (The Chemistry of Functional Groups Ser.). 892p. 1988. pap. 180.00 (*0-7837-8489-9*, 2049296) Bks Demand.

Chemistry of the Radio-Elements. Frederick Soddy. 1991. lib. bdg. 79.95 (*0-8490-4502-9*) Gordon Pr.

Chemistry of the Semiconductor Industry. Ed. by S. J. Moss & A. Ledwith. (Illus.). 352p. 1986. pap. text ed. 125.00 (*0-412-01321-5*, 9953, Chap & Hall NY) Chapman & Hall.

Chemistry of the Solar System: An Elementary Introduction to Cosmochemistry. Hans E. Suess. 156p. (C). 1987. lib. bdg. 27.95 (*0-471-83107-7*) Krieger.

Chemistry of the Solid-Water Interface: Processes at the Mineral-Water & Particle-Water Interface in Natural Systems. Werner Stumm. 448p. (Orig.). 1992. pap. text ed. 49.95 (*0-471-57672-7*) Wiley.

Chemistry of the Sulphonium Group, 2 pts., Pt. 1. Ed. by Charles J. Stirling. LC 80-40122. (Chemistry of Functional Groups Ser.). (Illus.). 399p. reprint ed. pap. 113.80 (*0-685-20677-7*, 2030466) Bks Demand.

Chemistry of the Sulphonium Group, 2 pts., Pt. 2. Ed. by Charles J. Stirling. LC 80-40122. (Chemistry of Functional Groups Ser.). (Illus.). 399p. reprint ed. pap. 135.70 (*0-685-20678-5*, 2030466) Bks Demand.

Chemistry of the Tetracycline Antibiotics. L. A. Mitscher. (Medicinal Research Ser.: Vol. 9). 352p. 1978. 170.00 (*0-8247-6716-0*) Dekker.

Chemistry of the Unpolluted & Polluted Troposphere. Ed. by H. W. Georgii & W. Jaeschke. 1982. lib. bdg. 136.50 (*90-277-1487-8*) Kluwer Ac.

Chemistry of Thione S-Imides. S. Motoki & T. Saito. 24p. 1984. pap. text ed. 23.00 (*3-7186-0271-7*) Gordon & Breach.

Chemistry of Thiophosgene. Sharma. 102p. 1986. pap. text ed. 66.00 (*3-7186-0346-2*) Gordon & Breach.

Chemistry of Tin. Ed. by P. G. Harrison. 352p. 1989. 120.00 (*0-412-01751-2*, A1998, Chap & Hall NY) Chapman & Hall.

Chemistry of Triple-Bonded Functional Groups, Pts. 1 & 2. Ed. by Saul Patai & Zvi Rappoport. LC 82-17355. (Chemistry of Functional Groups Ser.: Supplement C). (Illus.). reprint ed. pap. 160.00 (*0-685-73962-7*, 2030489); reprint ed. pap. 160.00 (*0-685-73963-5*) Bks Demand.

Chemistry of Triple-Bonded Functional Groups, Vol. 2. Ed. by Saul E. Patai. LC 93-21238. (Chemistry of Functional Groups, Supplementary Ser.: Vol. C2). 1200p. 1994. text ed. 600.00 (*0-471-93559-X*) Wiley.

***Chemistry of Vat Dyes.** Dianne N. Epp. (Palette of Color Ser.). (Illus.). 55p. 1995. pap. 12.95 (*1-883822-05-X*) Terrific Sci.

Chemistry of Water. Eby. (Illus.). (Orig.). 1989. pap. text ed. 16.95 (*1-877991-12-0*, AP4283) Flinn Scientific.

Chemistry of Water & Water Pollution. Jan Dojlido & Gerald Best. 500p. 1994. text ed. 73.00 (*0-13-878919-3*) P-H.

Chemistry of Weathering. Ed. by James I. Drever. 1985. lib. bdg. 105.50 (*90-277-1962-4*) Kluwer Ac.

Chemistry of Winemaking. Ed. by A. Dinsmore Webb. LC 74-19186. (Advances in Chemistry Ser.: No. 137). 1974. 29.95 (*0-8412-0208-7*); pap. 14.95 (*0-8412-0435-7*) Am Chemical.

Chemistry of Wood. Ed. by B. L. Browning. LC 74-23593. 700p. 1975. reprint ed. 66.00 (*0-88275-245-6*) Krieger.

Chemistry of Youth. Edmond B. Szekely. (Search for the Ageless Ser.: Vol. 3). (Illus.). 184p. 1977. pap. 7.50 (*0-89564-024-4*) IBS Intl.

Chemistry of 2-Alkoxy-1,3-Benzodithioles & 1,3-Benzodithiolium Salts, Reactions & Synthetic Applications. J. Nakayama. 35p. 1985. pap. text ed. 26.00 (*3-7186-0288-1*) Gordon & Breach.

Chemistry One Hundred Eleven Laboratory Manual. Jeanne Domoleczny. 112p. (C). 1992. pap. text ed. 15.95 (*0-8403-7986-2*) Kendall-Hunt.

Chemistry, Physics & Application of Surface Active Substances, 3 vols., Set. F. Asinger et al. 3004p. 1970. text ed. 1,476.00 (*0-677-10510-X*) Gordon & Breach.

Chemistry, Physics & General Science. Jack Rudman. (National Teachers Examination Ser.: NT-7). 1994. pap. 23.95 (*0-8373-8417-6*) Nat Learn.

Chemistry, Physics & Technology of Macromolecular Inorganic Compounds & Materials, Pt. 1. F. Gimblett & K. Hood. 1969. 27.00 (*0-686-92699-4*) Elsevier.

Chemistry, Physics & Technology of Macromolecular Inorganic Compounds & Materials, Pt. 2. F. Gimblett & K. Hood. 1970. 27.00 (*0-686-92697-8*) Elsevier.

Chemistry, Physiology, Pathology, Methods. Ed. by W. H. Sebrell, Jr. & Robert S. Harris. Incl. Vol. 1. 2nd ed. 1967. 81.00 (*0-12-633761-6*); Vol. 2. 1968. 78.00 (*0-12-633762-4*); write for info. (*0-318-50387-5*) Acad Pr.

Chemistry Problem Solver. rev. ed. Research & Education Association Staff. LC 77-70335. (Illus.). 960p. 1994. pap. text ed. 23.95 (*0-87891-509-5*) Res & Educ.

Chemistry Problem Solving: Student Guide. James W. Wheeler. 144p. (C). 1979. pap. text ed. 8.95 (*0-89420-061-5*, 237050); audio 342.20 (*0-89420-133-6*, 237000) Natl Book.

***Chemistry Quick Review.** Harold D. Nathan. 1993. pap. 7.95 (*0-614-07038-4*) Cliffs.

Chemistry Quick Review. Harold D. Nathan. (Cliffs Quick Reviews Ser.). (Illus.). 174p. (C). 1993. pap. text ed. 6.95 (*0-8220-5318-7*) Cliffs.

Chemistry Quizzes & Puzzles: Spiritmasters. G. Curtis. (C). 1985. text ed. 210.00 (*0-7175-1355-6*, Pub. by S Thornes Pubs UK) St Mut.

Chemistry Research Activities: Student Lab Manual. David Williams. Ed. by Eugene Kutscher. (Illus.). 1988. write for info. (*0-318-64019-8*) Alpha Pub MD.

Chemistry Research Activities: Teacher's Edition (with Answers) David Williams. Ed. by Eugene Kutscher. (Illus.). 1988. write for info. (*0-318-64018-X*) Alpha Pub MD.

Chemistry Review: Synthesis Using Alkali Metal Vapors; Silaalkenes & Related Intermediates, Vol. 13. L. E. Gusel'nikov et al. Ed. by M. E. Vol'pin. (Soviet Scientific Reviews Ser.: Vol. 13, Pt. 4). ii, 150p. 1989. pap. text ed. 75.00 (*3-7186-4951-9*) Gordon & Breach.

Chemistry Reviews, Vol. 1, Section B. Ed. by M . E. Vol'pin. 288p. 1979. text ed. 372.00 (*3-7186-0008-0*) Gordon & Breach.

Chemistry Reviews, Vol. 2. Ed. by E. Vol'pin. (Soviet Scientific Reviews Ser.: Section B). 480p. 1980. text ed. 372.00 (*3-7186-0018-8*) Gordon & Breach.

Chemistry Reviews, Vol. 3. Ed. by M. E. Vol'pin. (Soviet Scientific Reviews Ser.: Section B). 307p. 1981. text ed. 372.00 (*3-7186-0057-9*) Gordon & Breach.

Chemistry Reviews, Vol. 4. Ed. by M. E. Vol'pin. Tr. by Kurt Gingold. (Soviet Scientific Reviews Ser.: Section B, Vol. 4). 382p. 1982. text ed. 372.00 (*3-7186-0114-1*) Gordon & Breach.

Chemistry Reviews, Vol. 5. Ed. by M. E. Vol'pin. 408p. 1984. text ed. 372.00 (*3-7186-0137-0*) Gordon & Breach.

Chemistry Reviews, Vol. 6. M. E. Vol'pin. (Soviet Scientific Reviews Ser.: Section B, Vol. 6). 452p. 1984. text ed. 339.00 (*3-7186-0139-7*) Gordon & Breach.

Chemistry Reviews, Vol. 7. M. E. Vol'pin. (Soviet Scientific Reviews Ser.: Section B, Vol. 7). x, 340p. 1985. text ed. 339.00 (*3-7186-0154-0*) Gordon & Breach.

Chemistry Reviews, Vol. 8. Ed. by M. E. Vol'pin. (Soviet Scientific Reviews Ser.: Section B, Vol. 8). xii, 294p. 1987. text ed. 436.00 (*3-7186-0176-1*) Gordon & Breach.

Chemistry Reviews, Vol. 10. Ed. by M. E. Vol'pin. 512p. 1987. text ed. 510.00 (*3-7186-0409-4*) Gordon & Breach.

Chemistry Reviews: Active States in Mechanochemical Reactions, Vol. 14. P. Y. Butyagin. Ed. by M. E. Vol'pin. (Soviet Scientific Reviews Ser.: Vol. 14, Pt. 1). ii, 146p. 1989. pap. text ed. 76.00 (*3-7186-4987-X*) Gordon & Breach.

Chemistry Reviews: Electronic Excitation During the Plastic Deformation & Fracture of Crystals, Vol. 13. M. I. Molotskii. Ed. by M. E. Vol'pin. (Soviet Scientific Reviews Ser.: Vol. 13, Pt. 3). ii, 94p. 1989. pap. text ed. 44.00 (*3-7186-4949-7*) Gordon & Breach.

Chemistry Reviews: Heterolytic Cleavage Reactions of the Siloxane Bond, Vol. 15. M. G. Voronkov & S. V. Basenko. Ed. by M. E. Vol'pin. (Soviet Scientific Reviews Ser.: Vol. 15, Pt. 1). 100p. 1990. pap. text ed. 53.00 (*3-7186-4995-0*) Gordon & Breach.

Chemistry Reviews: Mechanochemistry, Vol. 14. T. M. Khrenkova et al. Ed. by M. E. Vol'pin. (Soviet Scientific Reviews Ser.: Vol. 14, Pt. 3). 160p. 1989. pap. text ed. 89.00 (*3-7186-4989-6*) Gordon & Breach.

Chemistry Reviews: New 13C NMR Approaches to the Structural Analysis of Carbohydrates, Vol. 13. N. K. Kochetov et al. Ed. by M. E. Vol'pin. (Soviet Scientific Reviews Ser.: Vol. 13, Pt. 2). ii, 82p. 1989. pap. text ed. 54.00 (*3-7186-4938-1*) Gordon & Breach.

Chemistry Reviews: Pulsed NMR Study of Molecular Motion in Solids, Vol. 14. G. B. Manelis et al. Ed. by M. E. Vol'pin. (Soviet Scientific Reviews Ser.: Vol. 14, Pt. 2). ii, 92p. 1989. pap. text ed. 46.00 (*3-7186-4959-4*) Gordon & Breach.

Chemistry Reviews: Synthetic Studies in the Field of Organic Germanium Compounds, Vol. 12. V. F. Mironov. Ed. by M. E. Vol'pin. (Soviet Scientific Reviews Ser.: Vol. 12, Pt. 6). ii, 78p. 1989. pap. text ed. 46.00 (*3-7186-4855-5*) Gordon & Breach.

Chemistry Reviews: The Structures of O-Specific Polysaccharides of Bacterium "Pseudomonas Aeruginosa", Vol. 13. N. K. Kochetov & Y. A. Knirel. Ed. by M. E. Vol'pin. (Soviet Scientific Reviews Ser.: Vol. 13, Pt. 1). ii, 110p. 1989. pap. text ed. 72.00 (*3-7186-4940-3*) Gordon & Breach.

Chemistry Survival Skills. Margaret A. Brault & Margaret L. MacDevitt. 128p. (C). 1988. pap. text ed. 5.00 (*0-669-17143-3*) Heath.

Chemistry Tests for First Examinations. A. Porter & T. Wood. (C). 1987. text ed. 35.00 (*0-85950-754-8*, Pub. by S Thornes Pubs UK) St Mut.

***Chemistry That Matters.** Andy Sae. (Illus.). 35p. (C). 1995. 4.00 (*1-881604-21-7*) Scopcraeft.

Chemistry the Easy Way. 2nd ed. Joseph A. Mascetta. (Easy Way Ser.). 350p. 1989. pap. 9.95 (*0-8120-4198-4*) Barron.

Chemistry, the Environment, & Life Quality. Jack Barrett. 320p. 1994. 39.95 (*0-685-72607-X*); pap. 18.95 (*0-685-72608-8*) Albion Pub.

Chemistry Through the Language Barrier: How to Scan Chemical Articles in Foreign Languages with Emphasis on Russian & Japanese. Ebenezer E. Reid. LC 75-112360. 150p. reprint ed. pap. 42.80 (*0-317-09870-5*, 2003893) Bks Demand.

Chemistry Today. R. Whitman & E. Zinck. 1976. text ed. 19.90 (*0-13-129486-5*); 8.72 (*0-13-129502-0*); 13.12 (*0-13-129494-6*) P-H.

Chemistry Transformed: The Paradigmatic Shift from Phlogiston to Oxygen. H. Gilman McCann. LC 78-19173. (Modern Sociology Ser.). 1978. 37.50 (*0-89391-004-X*) Ablex Pub.

Chemistry Trivia. Sylvia Tascher. Ed. by James D. Navratil. 126p. 1986. 12.50 (*0-937557-00-5*) Litarvan Lit.

***Chemistry with Computation: An Introduction to Spartan.** Warren J. Hehre & Wayne W. Huang. 108p. 1995. student ed 15.00 (*0-9643495-2-3*) Wavefunction.

Chemistry with Inorganic Qualitative Analysis. 3rd ed. Clyde Metz et al. 263p. (C). 1989. Instr's manual by Clyde Metz & John Williams, 263 pgs. teacher ed, pap. text ed. 12.00 (*0-15-506457-6*) HB Coll Pubs.

Chemistry with Inorganic Qualitative Analysis. 3rd ed. Therald Moeller et al. 964p. (C). 1989. text ed. 64.00 (*0-15-506492-4*) HB Coll Pubs.

Chemistry with Ultrasound, Vol. 28: Critical Reports on Applied Chemistry. Ed. by T. J. Mason. 196p. 1990. 83.00 (*1-85166-422-X*) Elsevier.

Chemistry Wonders of the Human Body. G. W. Carey. 1991. lib. bdg. 74.50 (*0-8490-4133-3*) Gordon Pr.

An Asterisk (*) at the beginning of an entry indicates that the title is appearing in BIP for the first time.

C

An Asterisk (*) at the beginning of an entry indicates that the title is appearing in BIP for the first time.

1181

Cheques. Derek Roebuck. 120p. (C). 1991. pap. text ed. 22.00 (962-209-288-8, Pub. by Hong Kong U Pr HK) St Mut.

Cheques Sent in Settlement. D. W. Andrews. (Waterlow Publications). 152p. 1991. pap. 33.90 (0-08-040874-5, Waterlow) Macmillan.

Cher. J. Randy Taraborrelli. 1992. mass mkt. 4.99 (0-312-92909-9) St Martin.

Cher, Reading Level 2. Petrucelli. (Reaching Your Goal Bks.: Set II). (Illus.). 24p. (J). (gr. 1-4). 1989. lib. bdg. 14.60 (0-86592-432-5) Rourke Corp.

Cher: In Her Own Words. Nigel Goodall. (Illus.). 96p. 1992. pap. 15.95 (0-7119-3030-9, OP46960) Omnibus NY.

Cher Antoine see Rendez-Vous de Senlis Suivi de Leocadia

Cher Antoine Ou l'Amour Rate. Jean Anouilh. (FRE.). 1975. pap. 10.95 (0-7859-1810-8, 2070366979) Fr & Eur.

Cher Antoine ou l'amour Rote. Jean Anouilh. (Folio Ser.: No. 697). (FRE.). 6.95 (2-07-036697-9) Schoenhof.

Cheran: A Sierra Tarascan Village. Ralph L. Beals. LC 69-13812. (Illus.). 225p. 1971. reprint ed. text ed. 59.75 (0-8371-3166-9, BECH, Greenwood Pr) Greenwood.

Chercheir D'or. J. M. Le Clezio. (Folio Ser.: No. 2000). (FRE.). pap. 10.95 (2-07-038082-3) Schoenhof.

Chercheur d'Or. J. M. Le Clezio. (FRE.). 1988. pap. 13.95 (0-8288-3706-6) Fr & Eur.

Cherchez la Femme: The Ancient Art of Putting Your Yin-Yang Back Together. Joyce V. Spoerke. 80p. 1991. pap. text ed. 8.95 (0-9630851-0-7) Maijoy Pubns.

Chere Annette: Letters from Russia 1820-1828. Ed. by S. W. Jackman. (Illus.). 192p. 1994. 36.00 (0-7509-0552-2) A Sutton Pub.

Chere Francoise: Revision de la Grammaire Francaise. 2nd ed. Jeannette D. Bragger & Robert Ariew. LC 83-81324. 368p. (FRE.). (C). 1984. audio 17.50 (0-685-08250-4) HM.

Chere Lambert! Ann Swarbrick & Mary Swarbrick. (Serie Rouge). 64p. (C). 1994. pap. 5.50 (0-521-44978-2) Cambridge U Pr.

Chere Sofia: Choix de Lettres de Romain Rolland a Sofia Bertolini Guerrieri-Gonzaga (1901-1908), 2 vols. Romain Rolland & Bertolini Guerrieri-Gonzaga. (Illus.). 387p. 1959. 6.95 (0-685-73254-1) Fr & Eur.

Cheremis-Chuvash Lexical Relationships. Ed. by John R. Krueger. LC 67-66161. (Uralic & Altaic Ser.: Vol. 94). 113p. 1968. pap. text ed. 12.00 (0-87750-039-8) Res Inst Inner Asian Studies.

Cheremis Literary Reader: With Glossary. Thomas A. Sebeok. LC 81-622860. (Uralic & Altaic Ser.: Vol. 132). 120p. 1978. 17.00 (2-8017-0096-7) Res Inst Inner Asian Studies.

Cheremis Musical Styles. Bruno Nettl. LC 60-64259. (Indiana University Folklore Institute Monograph Ser.: Vol. 14). 126p. reprint ed. pap. 36.00 (0-317-09424-6, 2050045) Bks Demand.

Cherenkov Radiation in High-Energy Physics, 2 vols., Set. V. P. Zrelov. 550p. 1970. text ed. 155.00 (0-317-46419-1, Pub. by Keter Pub IS) Coronet Bks.

Cheri. Sidonie-Gabrielle Colette. (FRE.). 1958. pap. 10.95 (0-8288-9154-0, F97041) Fr & Eur.

***Cheri: And, The Last of Cheri.** Colette. LC 94-30318. 1994. 7.99 (0-517-12260-X) Random Hse Value.

***Cheri & the Last of Cheri.** Colette. (Twentieth Century Classics Ser.). 1995. pap. 9.95 (0-14-018317-5, Penguin Bks) Viking Penguin.

Cheri & the Last of Cheri. Sidonie-Gabrielle Colette. 240p. 1986. mass mkt. 4.95 (0-345-34017-5) Ballantine.

Cheri Govertsen Greer's Coloring Southeast Alaska. Teri J. Christensen. (Illus.). 36p. (Orig.). 1988. pap. 6.95 (0-945816-00-6) Inkwell AK.

Cherish Me, Embrace Me. Sylvie F. Sommerfield. 1983. pap. 3.75 (0-8217-1199-7) Zebra.

Cherish the Cat. Jane P. Resnick. 96p. 1993. 5.99 (0-681-41737-4) Longmeadow Pr.

Cherish the Children: Parenting Skills for Indian Mothers with Young Children. Priscilla Buffalohead. 154p. 1988. 85.00 (1-881949-03-6) MN Ind Wom Res.

Cherish the Dream. Kathleen Harrington. 400p. 1990. pap. 3.95 (0-380-76123-8) Avon.

Cherish the Dream. Jodi Thomas. 352p. (Orig.). 1993. mass mkt. 4.99 (1-55773-881-5) Diamond.

Cherish the Earth: The Environment & Scripture. Janice E. Kirk & Donald R. Kirk. 184p. (Orig.). 1993. pap. 9.95 (0-8361-3635-7) Herald Pr.

Cherish the Memories. Glenna Oldham. (Illus.). 1990. 9.95 (0-685-51754-3, D1028) Warner Pr.

Cherish the Night. Penelope Neri. 1992. mass mkt. 5.99 (0-8217-3654-X) Zebra.

***Cherishable: Love & Marriage.** fac. ed. David W. Augsburger. LC 71-171536. 175p. 1994. pap. 49.90 (0-7837-7330-7, 2047259) Bks Demand.

Cherished. Jill Gregory. 1992. mass mkt. 4.99 (0-440-20620-0) Dell.

Cherished. Elizabeth Thornton. 448p. 1993. mass mkt. 4.50 (1-55817-748-5, Pinnacle NY) Windsor NY.

Cherished Bible Stories. Brownlow Publishing Company Editors. 1993. 4.99 (1-57051-010-5) Brownlow Pub Co.

Cherished Czech Recipes. Pat Martin. 160p. 1988. spiral bd. 5.50 (0-941016-46-3) Penfield.

Cherished Enemy. Patricia Veryan. 304p. 1989. pap. 3.50 (0-449-21751-5, Crest) Fawcett.

Cherished Events of Sri Guru Gobind Singh, the Tenth Sikh Guru. Vir Singh & Ujagar S. Bawa. (Books on Sikhism Ser.). 130p. (Orig.). (YA). (gr. 8-12). 1988. pap. 5.00 (0-942245-01-6) Wash Sikh Ctr.

Cherished Events of the Life of Sri Guru Nanak Dev Ji, Founder of the Sikh Religion. Vir Singh & Ujagar S. Bawa. (Books on Sikhism Ser.). 129p. (Orig.). (YA). (gr. 8-12). 1989. pap. 5.00 (0-942245-04-0) Wash Sikh Ctr.

Cherished Love. Evelyn Kennedy. 208p. 1988. pap. 9.95 (0-941483-08-8) Naiad Pr.

***Cherished Memories.** C. R. Gibson. (Illus.). 68p. 1994. 20.00 (0-8378-4792-3) Gibson.

Cherished Moments. Anita Mills et al. LC 93-47563. 1994. 17.95 (0-681-45413-X) Longmeadow Pr.

Cherished Objects: Living with & Collecting Victoriana. Allison K. Leopold. 1991. 35.00 (0-517-57435-7, C P Pubs) Crown Pub Group.

Cherishing & Challenging Your Children. Jody Capehart. 180p. 1991. pap. 8.99 (0-89693-899-9) SP Pubns.

Cherishing Life, Vol. I. Buddhist Text Translation Society Staff. (Illus.). 150p. (Orig.). (J). (gr. 3 up). 1983. pap. 7.00 (0-88139-004-6) Buddhist Text.

Cherishing Life, Vol. II. Buddhist Text Translation Society Staff. (Illus.). 160p. (Orig.). (J). (gr. 3 up). 1983. pap. 7.00 (0-88139-015-1) Buddhist Text.

***Cherishing Men from Afar: Qing Guest Ritual & the Macartney Embassy of 1793.** James L. Hevia. LC 94-43610. 1995. write for info. (0-8223-1625-0); pap. write for info. (0-8223-1637-4) Duke.

Chern, a Great Geometer. Ed. by S. T. Yau. (Monographs in Geometry & Topology). 319p. 1993. 22.00 (0-685-72218-X) Intl Pr Boston.

Chern Symposium Nineteen Seventy Nine. Ed. by W. Y. Hsiang et al. (Illus.). 259p. 1980. 79.00 (0-387-90537-5) Spr-Verlag.

Chernenko: The Last Bolshevik: The Soviet Union on the Eve of Perestroika. Ilya Zemtsov. 325p. 1989. 49.95 (0-88738-260-6) Transaction Pubs.

Chernevog. C. J. Cherryh. 320p. 1991. mass mkt. 5.99 (0-345-37351-0, Del Rey) Ballantine.

Chernikov: Fantasy & Construction: Chernikov's Approach to Architectural Design. R. Cooke. (C). 1990. pap. 150.00 (0-685-34372-3, Pub. by Collets) St Mut.

Chernobyl. 96p. 1987. 21.00 (0-7277-0394-3, Pub. by T Telford UK) Am Soc Civil Eng.

Chernobyl. Don Nardo. LC 90-33567. (World Disasters Ser.). (Illus.). 64p. (J). (gr. 5-8). 1990. lib. bdg. 14.95 (1-56006-008-5) Lucent Bks.

Chernobyl: A Policy Response Study. B. Segerstahl. (Environmental Management Ser.). (Illus.). 180p. 1991. 59.00 (0-387-53465-2) Spr-Verlag.

Chernobyl: Insight from the Inside. V. M. Chernousenko. (Illus.). 390p. 1991. 34.00 (0-387-53698-1) Spr-Verlag.

Chernobyl: Law & Communication. Philippe J. Sands. 346p. (C). 1988. 174.00 (0-949009-22-9, Pub. by Grotius Pubns UK) St Mut.

Chernobyl: Nuclear Power Plant Explosion. Sue L. Hamilton. Ed. by John C. Hamilton. LC 91-73040. (Day of the Disaster Ser.). (J). 1991. lib. bdg. 11.96 (1-56239-060-0) Abdo & Dghtrs.

Chernobyl: The End of the Nuclear Dream. Observer Staff. LC 86-22462. 256p. 1986. pap. 4.95 (0-394-75107-8, Vin) Random.

***Chernobyl: The Forbidden Truth.** Yaroshinskaya. 1994. 17.95 (1-897766-03-3, Pub. by Jon Pubng UK) InBook.

***Chernobyl: The Forbidden Truth.** Alla Yaroshinskaya. Tr. by David MacRae. 412p. 1995. text ed. 25.00 (0-8032-4912-8) U of Nebr Pr.

***Chernobyl: The Forbidden Truth.** Alla Yaroshinskaya. 1995. pap. 10.00 (0-8032-9910-9) U of Nebr Pr.

Chernobyl: The Long Shadow. Chris C. Park. 192p. 1989. 39.95 (0-415-03553-8, A3394) Routledge.

Chernobyl: The Ongoing Story of the World's Deadliest Nuclear Disaster. Glenn A. Cheney. LC 93-17508. (Illus.). 128p. (J). (gr. 6). 1994. text ed. 13.95 (0-02-718305-X, Mac Bks Young Read) S&S Childrens.

Chernobyl: The Real Story. R. F. Mould. 256p. 1988. text ed. write for info. (0-08-035718-0, Pub. by Pergamon Repr UK) Franklin.

Chernobyl Accident & Its Implications for the United Kingdom. Ed. by N. Worley & Jeffery D. Lewins. 148p. 1988. pap. 72.00 (1-85166-219-7) Elsevier.

***Chernobyl & Its Aftermath: A Chronology of Events.** Robert E. Ebel. LC 94-23253. (CSIS Report Ser.). 43p. (C). 1994. pap. text ed. 9.95 (0-89206-302-5) CSI Studies.

Chernobyl & Nuclear Power in the U. S. S. R. David R. Marples. LC 86-42967. 192p. 1986. pap. 15.95 (0-312-00457-5) St Martin.

Chernobyl Insight from the Inside. V. M. Chernousenko. 1993. pap. 34.00 (0-387-53638-8) Spr-Verlag.

Chernobyl Papers: Doses to the Soviet Population & Early Health Effects Studies. Ed. by S. Morwin et al. 500p. 1993. 75.00 (1-883021-02-2) Research Ent.

***Chernobyl Update & in the Future.** Ed. by Shigenobu Nagataki. LC 94-35040. (International Congress Ser.: No. 1074). 1994. write for info. (0-444-81953-3) Elsevier.

***Chernobyl Victims at Polesskoe.** William M. Mandel. (Illus.). 60p. (Orig.). 1994. pap. 19.95 (1-57205-747-5) Rector Pr.

Chernowitz. Fran Arrick. 192p. 1983. pap. 2.95 (0-451-15350-2, Sig Vista) NAL-Dutton.

Chernowitz? Fran Arrick. 1983. pap. 3.99 (0-451-16253-6) NAL-Dutton.

Chernyshevskii: The Man & the Journalist. William F. Woehrlin. LC 73-156137. (Russian Research Center Studies: No. 67). 416p. 1971. 39.95 (0-674-11385-3) HUP.

Chernyshevsky & the Age of Realism: A Study in the Semiotics of Behavior. Irina Paperno. LC 88-2311. (Illus.). 320p. 1988. 37.50 (0-8047-1453-3) Stanford U Pr.

Cherokee. Jean Echenoz. LC 86-46529. 160p. 1987. 16.95 (0-87923-665-5) Godine.

Cherokee. Jean Echenoz. Tr. by Mark Polizzotti. LC 94-19003. 218p. 1994. pap. 10.00 (0-8032-6724-X, Bison Books) U of Nebr Pr.

Cherokee. Emilie U. Lepthien. LC 84-27476. (New True Bks.). (Illus.). 48p. (J). (gr. k-4). 1985. lib. bdg. 12.90 (0-516-01938-4); pap. 4.95 (0-516-41938-2) Childrens.

Cherokee. B. McCall. (Native American People Ser.). (Illus.). 32p. (J). (gr. 5-8). 1989. lib. bdg. 15.94 (0-86625-376-9); lib. bdg. 11.95 (0-685-58583-2) Rourke Corp.

Cherokee. Thea Perdue. (Indians of North America Ser.). (Illus.). 111p. (Orig.). (YA). (gr. 5 up). 1989. 17.95 (1-55546-695-8); pap. 9.95 (0-7910-0357-4) Chelsea Hse.

Cherokee. Giles Tippette. 240p. (Orig.). 1993. pap. 4.50 (0-515-11118-X) Jove Pubns.

Cherokee Americans: The Eastern Band of Cherokees in the Twentieth Century. John R. Finger. LC 90-43227. (Indians of the Southeast Ser.). xviii, 247p. 1991. pap. 9.95 (0-8032-6879-3) U of Nebr Pr.

Cherokee Animal Tales. rev. ed. Illus. by Robert Frankenberg. LC 91-73537. 80p. (J). (gr. 3-6). 1991. pap. 7.95 (0-933031-60-2) Coun Oak Bks.

Cherokee Archaeology: A Study of the Appalachian Summit. Bennie C. Keel. LC 75-41444. (Illus.). 312p. 1976. 36.00x (0-87049-189-X); pap. 18.00x (0-87049-546-1) U of Tenn Pr.

Cherokee Bat & the Goat Guys. Francesca L. Block. LC 91-30706. (Charlotte Zolotow Bk.). 112p. (YA). (gr. 7 up). 1992. lib. bdg. 14.89 (0-06-020270-X) HarpC Child Bks.

Cherokee Bat & the Goat Guys. Francesca L. Block. LC 91-20706. (Trophy Keypoint Bk.). 128p. (YA). (gr. 7 up). 1993. pap. 3.95 (0-06-447095-4, Trophy) HarpC Child Bks.

Cherokee Bows & Arrows: How to Make & Shoot Primitive Bows & Arrows. Al Herrin. LC 89-51184. (Illus.). 160p. (Orig.). 1989. pap. text ed. 14.95 (0-9623601-3-9) White Bear Pub.

Cherokee Bride. Teresa Warfield. 336p. (Orig.). 1994. mass mkt. 4.99 (0-515-11390-5) Jove Pubns.

Cherokee Bride. Patricia Werner. 1992. mass mkt. 4.25 (0-8217-3761-9) Zebra.

Cherokee by Blood: Records of Eastern Cherokee Ancestry in the U.S. Court of Claims 1906-1910. Jerry W. Jordan. 501p. (Orig.). 1989. pap. 25.00 (1-55613-160-7) Heritage Bk.

Cherokee by Blood: Records of Eastern Cherokee Ancestry in the U.S. Court of Claims 1906-1910. Jerry W. Jordan. (Cherokee by Blood Ser.). 490p. (Orig.). 1991. pap. 25.00 (1-55613-294-8); pap. 25.00 (1-55613-446-0) Heritage Bk.

Cherokee by Blood: Records of Eastern Cherokee Ancestry in the U.S. Court of Claims 1906-1910, Vol. 1. Jerry W. Jordan. xv, 482p. (Orig.). 1987. pap. text ed. 25.00 (1-55613-048-1) Heritage Bk.

Cherokee by Blood: Records of Eastern Cherokee Ancestry in the U.S. Court of Claims 1906-1910, Vol. 2. Jerry W. Jordan. 501p. (Orig.). 1988. pap. 25.00 (1-55613-111-9) Heritage Bk.

***Cherokee by Blood No. 4.** Jerry W. Jordan. 490p. (Orig.). 1989. pap. text ed. 25.00 (1-55613-239-5) Heritage Bk.

***Cherokee by Blood No. 6.** Jerry W. Jordan. 505p. (Orig.). 1990. pap. text ed. 25.00 (1-55613-338-3) Heritage Bk.

Cherokee by Blood, Vol. 8: Records of Eastern Cherokee Ancestry in the U. S. Court of Claims, 1906-1910. Jerry W. Jordan. 489p. (Orig.). 1992. pap. 25.00 (1-55613-573-4) Heritage Bk.

***Cherokee Cases: The Confrontation of Law & Politics.** Jill Norgren. LC 95-13761. 1995. write for info. (0-07-047191-6) McGraw.

***Cherokee Cavaliers: Forty Years of Cherokee History As Told in the Correspondence of the Ridge-Watie-Boudinot Family.** Edward E. Dale & Gaston Litton. LC 94-24337. (Civilization of the American Indian Ser.: Vol. 19). (Illus.). 319p. 1995. pap. 15.95 (0-8061-2721-X) U of Okla Pr.

***Cherokee Connections.** Myra V. Gormley. (Illus.). 64p. (Orig.). 1995. pap. 9.95 (1-886962-55-3) Fam Hist Bks.

Cherokee Country. Elizabeth Baker. (Illus.). 326p. (C). 1968. pap. 9.95 (0-937766-24-0) Drelwood Comns.

Cherokee County Georgia Land Records, 4 vols., Set. Wyndell O. Taylor & Bernice O. Taylor. write for info. (1-885052-00-6) Bots Bks.

***Cherokee County Georgia Land Records Vol. 5: Deed Book "E"** Wyndell O. Taylor & Bernice O. Taylor. LC 93-147433. 1994. 25.00 (1-885052-05-7) Bots Bks.

***Cherokee County Georgia Land Records Vol. 6: Deed Book "E"** Wyndell O. Taylor & Bernice O. Taylor. LC 93-147433. 1995. 25.00 (1-885052-06-5, CHER06) Bots Bks.

Cherokee County Georgia Land Records, Vol. 1: Deed Book "A" Wyndell O. Taylor. LC 93-147433. 200p. 1992. 25.00 (1-885052-01-4, CHERO1) Bots Bks.

Cherokee County Georgia Land Records, Vol. 2: Deed Book "B" Wyndell O. Taylor & Bernice O. Taylor. LC 93-147433. 203p. 1993. 25.00 (1-885052-02-2, CHERO2) Bots Bks.

Cherokee County Georgia Land Records, Vol. 3: Deed Book "C" Wyndell O. Taylor & Bernice O. Taylor. LC 93-147433. 276p. 1993. 25.00 (1-885052-03-0, CHERO3) Bots Bks.

Cherokee County Georgia Land Records, Vol. 4: Deed Book "D" Wyndell O. Taylor & Bernice O. Taylor. LC 93-147433. 224p. 1994. 25.00 (1-885052-04-9, CHERO4) Bots Bks.

Cherokee County Summer. Eleanor B. Murray. (Illus.). 48p. (Orig.). (YA). (gr. 9-12). 1981. pap. 3.98 (1-879313-01-4) Murrays Leprechaun Bks.

Cherokee Dance & Drama. Frank G. Speck. LC 83-47839. (C). 1993. pap. 9.95 (0-8061-2580-2) U of Okla Pr.

Cherokee Dawn. Genell Dellin. 368p. 1990. mass mkt. 4.50 (0-380-76013-4) Avon.

Cherokee Editor: The Writings of Elias Boudinot. Ed. by Theda Perdue. LC 82-11110. 254p. 1983. text ed. 30.00x (0-87049-366-3) U of Tenn Pr.

Cherokee Embrace. Teresa Howard. 1992. mass mkt. 4.25 (0-8217-3650-7) Zebra.

Cherokee Feast of Days: Native American Daily Meditations. Joyce S. Hifler. LC 91-77973. 405p. 1992. 14.95 (0-933031-65-3); pap. 10.95 (0-933031-68-8) Coun Oak Bks.

Cherokee Folk Zoology: The Animal World of a Native American People, 1700-1838. Arlene Fradkin. LC 90-14064. (Evolution of North American Indians Ser.: Vol. 10). 583p. 1990. reprint ed. 35.00 (0-8240-2504-0) Garland.

Cherokee Freedmen: From Emancipation to American Citizenship. Daniel F. Littlefield, Jr. LC 78-53659. (Contributions in Afro-American & African Studies: No. 40). 281p. 1978. text ed. 59.95 (0-313-20413-6, LCH/, Greenwood Pr) Greenwood.

Cherokee Fun & Learn Book. J. Ed Sharpe. 20p. 1970. 3.50 (0-935741-03-8) Cherokee Pubns.

Cherokee Indian Nation: A Troubled History. Ed. by Duane H. King. LC 78-13222. (Illus.). 276p. 1979. 22.95 (0-87049-227-6) U of Tenn Pr.

Cherokee Indians. Nicole Claro. (Junior Library of American Indians). (Illus.). 80p. (J). (gr. 3-7). 1991. lib. bdg. 14.95 (0-7910-1652-8) Chelsea Hse.

Cherokee Indians. Nicole Claro. (Junior Library of American Indians). (Illus.). 80p. (J). (gr. 3-7). 1994. pap. 6.95 (0-7910-2030-4) Chelsea Hse.

Cherokee Joe. large type ed. Cameron Judd. LC 92-16522. 250p. 1992. reprint ed. lib. bdg. 17.95 (1-56054-481-3) Thorndike Pr.

***Cherokee Land Lottery: Containing a Numerical List of the Names of the Fortunate Drawers in Said Lottery, with an Engraved Map of Each District, with an Added Index of Names & a Map.** James F. Smith. (Illus.). 579p. 1994. pap. 45.00 (0-614-00916-2, 5470) Clearfield Co.

Cherokee Legends & the Trail of Tears. Tom Underwood. (Illus.). 32p. (J). (gr. 4-12). 1956. 3.50 (0-935741-00-3) Cherokee Pubns.

Cherokee Lighthorse. Gary McCarthy. (Horsemen Ser.: Bk. 2). 192p. (Orig.). 1992. pap. 3.99 (1-55773-797-5) Diamond.

Cherokee Mist: The Lost Writings of Jimi Hendrix. Bill Nitopi. 1994. pap. 10.00 (0-06-092562-0, PL) HarpC.

Cherokee Nation: Life Before the Tears. Intro. by Madeleine Meyers. LC 93-70437. (Perspectives on History Ser.). (Illus.). 64p. (Orig.). (YA). (gr. 5-12). 1993. pap. 4.95 (1-878668-26-9) Disc Enter Ltd.

Cherokee Nation Code Annotated. 300p. 1986. 55.00 (0-88063-454-5, Equity Pub NH) Butterworth Legal Pubs.

Cherokee Nights. Genell Dellin. 352p. 1991. mass mkt. 4.50 (0-380-76014-2) Avon.

***Cherokee Outlet Cowboy: Recollections of Laban S. Records.** Laban S. Records. Ed. by Ellen J. Wheeler. LC 94-37534. (Illus.). 370p. 1995. 24.95 (0-8061-2694-9) U of Okla Pr.

Cherokee Passage. Karen Weinberg. 160p. (Orig.). (J). (gr. 6-8). 1995. pap. 12.95 (0-942597-47-8) White Mane Pub.

Cherokee People. Thomas E. Mails. LC 91-73541. (Illus.). 368p. 1992. 49.95 (0-933031-45-9) Coun Oak Bks.

Cherokee People. deluxe ed. Thomas E. Mails. LC 91-73541. (Illus.). 368p. 1992. ring bd. 250.00 (0-933031-46-7) Coun Oak Bks.

Cherokee Prehistory: The Pisgah Phase in the Appalachian Summit Region. Roy S. Dickens, Jr. LC 76-1972. 260p. 1976. 30.00x (0-87049-193-8) U of Tenn Pr.

***Cherokee Princess.** Rena B. Will. 120p. 1995. pap. 7.95 (1-56901-723-9) NW Pub.

Cherokee Psalms. Tr. by Dan Scott. (Illus.). 32p. 1991. pap. 3.50 (0-935741-16-X) Cherokee Pubns.

***Cherokee Removal.** Theda Perdue & Michael Green. 144p. 1995. pap. text ed. 8.65 (0-312-08658-X) St Martin.

***Cherokee Removal: A Brief History with Documents.** Ed. by Theda Perdue. (Bedford Series in History & Culture). 160p. 1995. 35.00 (0-312-12254-3) St Martin.

Cherokee Removal: Before & After. Ed. by William L. Anderson. LC 90-36731. (Brown Thrasher Bks.). (Illus.). 176p. 1992. pap. 12.95 (0-8203-1482-X) U of Ga Pr.

Cherokee Removal: Mini-Play. (U. S. History Ser.). (J). (gr. 5 up). 1982. 6.50 (0-89550-377-8) Stevens & Shea.

Cherokee Removal: The "William Penn" Essays & Other Writings. Jeremiah Evarts. LC 80-28449. 324p. reprint ed. pap. 92.40 (0-8357-8842-3, 2033368) Bks Demand.

Cherokee Renascence in the New Republic. William G. McLoughlin. (Illus.). 494p. 1992. text ed. 69.50 (0-691-04741-3); pap. text ed. 18.95 (0-691-00627-X) Princeton U Pr.

Cherokee Roots, 2 vols., Set. 2nd ed. Bob Blankenship. 163p. 1992. pap. text ed. 27.00 (0-9633774-0-X) Cherokee Roots.

Cherokee Roots, 2 vols., Vol. I: Eastern Version. 2nd ed. Bob Blankenship. 200p. 1992. pap. text ed. 12.00 (0-9633774-1-8) Cherokee Roots.

Cherokee Roots, 2 vols., Vol. II: Western Version. 2nd ed. Bob Blankenship. 400p. 1992. pap. text ed. 18.00 (0-9633774-2-6) Cherokee Roots.

Cherokee Rose. Teresa Warfield. 1993. mass mkt. 4.99 (0-515-11210-0) Jove Pubns.

Cherokee Strip: A Tale of an Oklahoma Boyhood. Marquis James. (C). 1993. pap. 14.95 (0-8061-2537-3) U of Okla Pr.

Cherokee Strip: Its History & Grand Opening. Earl D. Newsom. (Oklahoma Legacies Ser.). (Illus.). (Orig.). 1992. pap. 10.95 (0-913507-27-X) New Forums.

Cherokee Strip Fever. 2nd ed. Zola Sample. 160p. 1984. reprint ed. 14.95 (0-934188-13-0) Evans Pubns.

An Asterisk (*) at the beginning of an entry indicates that the title is appearing in BIP for the first time.

C

An Asterisk (*) at the beginning of an entry indicates that the title is appearing in BIP for the first time.

1183

Chesapeake Colors: National Life, History, Recipes, & Local Color. Amelia Amoriell & Susan Lindbeck. LC 82-60329. (Illus.). 48p. 1982. pap. 3.25 (*0-87033-298-8*, Tidewtr Pubs) Cornell Maritime.

Chesapeake Cookbook. Susan Belsinger. 1990. 35.00 (*0-517-57328-8*, C P Pubs) Crown Pub Group.

Chesapeake Country. Lucian Niemeyer & Eugene L. Meyer. (Illus.). 224p. 1990. 35.00 (*1-55859-063-3*) Abbeville Pr.

Chesapeake Country Postcard Book. 1993. pap. 7.95 (*1-55859-624-0*) Abbeville Pr.

Chesapeake Family & Their Slaves: A Study in Historical Archaeology. Anne E. Yentsch. (New Studies in Archaeology). (Illus.). 300p. (C). 1994. 89.95 (*0-521-43293-6*); pap. 24.95 (*0-521-46730-6*) Cambridge U Pr.

Chesapeake Gold: Man & Oyster on the Bay. Susan Brait. LC 90-12664. 160p. 1990. 20.00 (*0-8131-1716-X*) U Pr of Ky.

Chesapeake in the Seventeenth Century: Essays on Anglo-American Society. Ed. by Thad W. Tate & David L. Ammerman. LC 78-31720. (Illus.). 318p. reprint ed. pap. 90.70 (*0-8357-3892-2*, 2036624) Bks Demand.

Chesapeake in the Seventeenth Century: Essays on Anglo-American Society & Politics. Ed. by Thad W. Tate & David L. Ammerman. 1980. pap. 10.95 (*0-393-00956-4*) Norton.

Chesapeake Legacy: Tools & Traditions. Larry S. Chowning. (Illus.). 304p. 1995. 37.50 (*0-87033-462-X*, Tidewtr Pubs) Cornell Maritime.

Chesapeake Odysseys: An Nineteen Thousand Eight Hundred Eighty-Three Cruise Revisited. Joseph T. Rothrock & Jane C. Rothrock. LC 84-40343. (Illus.). 138p. 1984. 15.95 (*0-87033-323-2*, Tidewtr Pubs) Cornell Maritime.

Chesapeake Politics, Seventeen Eighty One to Eighteen Hundred. Norman K. Risjord. LC 78-7996. 1978. text ed. 74.00 (*0-231-04328-7*) Col U Pr.

***Chesapeake Prehistory: Old Traditions, New Directions.** Richard J. Dent, Jr. (Interdisciplinary Contributions to Archaeology Ser.). 320p. 1995. 45.00 (*0-306-45028-3*) Plenum.

Chesapeake Reflections: A Journey on a Boat & a Bike. Ken Carter. (Illus.). 316p. (Orig.). 1991. pap. 19.95 (*0-9628793-4-7*) Amantha Pub.

Chesapeake Song. Brenda L. Richardson. LC 93-26412. 371p. 1993. 19.95 (*1-56743-040-6*) Amistad Pr.

***Chesapeake Song.** Brenda L. Richardson. LC 93-26412. 371p. 1994. pap. 10.95 (*1-56743-063-5*) Amistad Pr.

Chesapeake Steamboats: Vanished Fleet. David C. Holly. (Illus.). 320p. 1994. 29.95 (*0-87033-455-7*, Tidewtr Pubs) Cornell Maritime.

Chesapeake Stripers. Keith Walters. LC 90-90280. (Illus.). 350p. (Orig.). 1990. pap. 19.95 (*0-9627039-0-7*) Aerie Hse.

Chesapeake, the Eastern Shore: Gardens & Houses. Photos by Taylor Lewis. LC 92-35045. 1993. 45.00 (*0-671-75857-8*) S&S Trade.

Chesapeake Waters: Pollution, Public Health, & Public Opinion, 1607-1972. John Capper et al. LC 83-40102. (Illus.). 217p. reprint ed. pap. 61.90 (*0-8357-8066-X*, 2033966) Bks Demand.

Cheshire & Burn: Modern Law of Real Property. 14th ed. E. H. Burn. 1988. U.K. pap. 56.00 (*0-406-56548-1*) Butterworth Legal Pubs.

***Cheshire & Fifoot's Law of Contract.** 6th ed. J. G. Starke. 953p. 1992. boxed 152.00 (*0-409-30880-3*, Austral) Butterworth Legal Pubs.

***Cheshire & Fifoot's Law of Contract.** 6th ed. J. G. Starke. 953p. 1992. pap. 102.00 (*0-409-30890-0*, Austral) Butterworth Legal Pubs.

***Cheshire & Fifoot's Law of Contract.** 8th ed. J. F. Burrows. 671p. 1992. pap. 126.00 (*0-409-78981-X*, NZ); boxed 117.00 (*0-409-78968-2*, NZ) Butterworth Legal Pubs.

Cheshire & Hillsboro Counties, New Hampshire. Biographical Review Staff. (Illus.). 521p. 1993. reprint ed. pap. 31.00 (*1-55613-723-0*) Heritage Bk.

Cheshire & North: Private International Law. 12th ed. Ed. by P. M. North & J. J. Fawcett. 1040p. 1992. U.K. pap. 66.00 (*0-406-53081-5*) Butterworth Legal Pubs.

***Cheshire Beagle.** Charles Schulz. 1995. pap. 6.95 (*0-8050-3571-0*) H Holt & Co.

***Cheshire Cat & Other Interactive Experiments in Perception.** Paul Doherty & Don Rathjan. Ed. by Exploratorium Teacher Institute Staff. LC 94-47034. (Exploratorium Science Snackbook Ser.). (J). 1995. pap. text ed. 10.95 (*0-471-11516-9*) Wiley.

Cheshire Cat's Eye. Marcia Muller. 224p. 1990. reprint ed. mass mkt. 5.50 (*0-445-40850-2*, Mysterious Paperbk) Warner Bks.

Cheshire, Fifoot & Furmston's Law of Contract. 12th ed. M. P. Furmston. 1991. pap. 48.00 (*0-406-51491-7*, U.K.) Butterworth Legal Pubs.

***Cheshire, Fifoot & Furmston's Law of Contract: Singapore & Malaysian Edition.** Andrew P. Leong & Chin Yoong Kheong. 1006p. 1994. pap. 186.00 (*0-409-99682-3*, SI) Butterworth Legal Pubs.

Cheshire Moon. Robert Ferrigno. 352p. 1994. mass mkt. 5.99 (*0-380-71397-0*) Avon.

Cheshire Moon. Robert Ferrigno. LC 92-22573. 1993. 20.00 (*0-688-10314-6*) Morrow.

***Chesney's Care of the Patient in Diagnostic Radiography.** 7th ed. Pauline J. Chesney & D. Noreen Chesney. LC 94-30883. (Illus.). 1995. write for info. (*0-632-03762-8*) Blackwell Sci.

Chesney's Equipment for Student Radiographers. 4th ed. P. R. Carter. (Illus.). 416p. 1994. pap. write for info. (*0-632-02724-X*, Pub. by Blckwell Sci Pubns UK) Blackwell Sci.

Chesney's Radiographic Imaging. 5th ed. Ed. by J. Ball & A. Price. (Illus.). 392p. 1990. pap. 42.95 (*0-632-01943-3*, Yr Bk Med Pubs) Mosby Yr Bk.

Chesrow: A Paleoindian Complex in the Southern Lake Michigan Basin. David F. Overstreet. (Case Studies in Great Lakes Archaeology). (Illus.). 183p. (C). 1993. pap. 15.00 (*1-881354-02-4*) Gt Lks Archaeol.

Chess. 104p. (Orig.). 1986. pap. 12.95 (*0-88188-918-0*, 00123037) H Leonard.

Chess. R. R. McCready. LC 81-83687. 64p. 1981. 24.00 (*0-88014-035-6*) Mosaic Pr OH.

Chess: An Annotated Bibliography, 1969-1988. A. S. Lusis. 350p. 1991. text ed. 100.00 (*0-7201-2079-9*, Mansell Pub) Cassell.

Chess - Trick & Treat. E. M. Reubens. (Illus.). (Orig.). 1962. pap. 3.95 (*0-8283-1431-4*, 37, Intl Pocket Lib) Branden Pub Co.

Chess & Machine Intuition. George W. Atkinson. LC 93-28529. (Series in Artificial Intelligence). 184p. 1993. 39.50 (*0-89391-901-2*); pap. 22.50 (*1-56750-026-9*) Ablex Pub.

Chess & Playing-Cards. Stewart Culin. LC 75-35065. (Studies in Play & Games). (Illus.). 1976. reprint ed. 34.95 (*0-405-07916-8*) Ayer.

Chess Artists. H. Golombek. 1989. write for info. (*0-08-024108-5*, Pergamon Pr); pap. write for info. (*0-08-024107-7*, Pergamon Pr) Elsevier.

Chess As Metaphor in the Art of Samuel Bak. Samuel Bak. Tr. by David Melody. (Illus.). 80p. (ENG & FRE.). 1991. 35.00 (*1-879985-02-0*) Pucker Safrai.

Chess at the Top: Nineteen Seventy-Nine to Nineteen Eighty-Four. Anatoly Karpov. Tr. by Kenneth P. Neat. (Russian Chess Ser.). (Illus.). 196p. 1984. 27.90 (*0-08-029771-4*, Pergamon Pr); pap. 15.95 (*0-08-029770-6*, Pergamon Pr) Elsevier.

Chess Basics. Nigel Short. LC 94-21479. (Illus.). 96p. 1994. pap. 10.95 (*0-8069-0798-3*) Sterling.

Chess Beat. L. Evans. (Chess Ser.). 105p. 1982. 25.95 (*0-08-026926-5*, P115, Pergamon Pr); pap. 15.95 (*0-08-026925-7*, Pergamon Pr) Elsevier.

Chess Coaching. John Littlewood. (Illus.). 153p. 1991. pap. 19.95 (*1-85223-239-0*, Pub. by Crowood Pr UK) Trafalgar.

Chess Combination from Philidor to Karpov. R. D. Keene. LC 77-4379. 176p. 1977. 15.95 (*0-08-019758-2*, Pergamon Pr) Elsevier.

Chess Combinations As a Fine Art: One Hundred Twenty Unusual Puzzles. Ed. by Werner Golz & Paul Keres. (Illus.). 256p. 1990. pap. 13.95 (*1-85223-285-4*) Trafalgar.

Chess Computer Book. T. D. Harding. (Chess Ser.). (Illus.). 215p. 1981. 19.95 (*0-08-026885-4*, Pergamon Pr); pap. 10.95 (*0-08-026884-6*, Pergamon Pr) Elsevier.

***Chess Detective: Kriegspiel Strategies, Endgames, & Problems.** David H. Li. 191p. 1995. pap. 12.95 (*0-9637852-4-9*) Premier MD.

Chess-Dream in a Garden. Rosemary Sutcliff. LC 92-54595. 48p. (J). (ps up). 1993. 16.95 (*1-56402-192-0*) Candlewick Pr.

Chess Endings: Essential Knowledge. 2nd ed. Y. Averbakh. Tr. by P. H. Clarke. (Chess Ser.: No. 5). (Illus.). 150p. 1987. 19.95 (*0-08-032050-3*, Pergamon Pr); pap. 13.90 (*0-08-032045-7*, Pergamon Pr) Elsevier.

Chess Exchanges. S. Taulbut & S. Jones. (Chess Ser.). (Illus.). 261p. 1986. 27.95 (*0-08-029752-8*, Pub. by PPL UK); pap. 17.90 (*0-08-029751-X*, Pub. by PPL UK) Elsevier.

***Chess Explorations: The Best of the Journal Chess Notes.** Winter. 1995. pap. 24.95 (*1-85744-171-0*, Scribners) S&S Trade.

Chess for Absolute Beginners. Raymond Keene. (Batsford Chess Library Ser.). (Illus.). 80p. 1993. pap. 14.95 (*0-8050-2945-1*) H Holt & Co.

Chess for Beginners. Israel A. Horowitz & Alexandra Mark. 1971. pap. 8.00 (*0-671-21184-6*, Fireside) S&S Trade.

Chess for Beginners: A Picture Guide. Al Horowitz. LC 91-58522. (Illus.). 144p. 1992. reprint ed. pap. 10.00 (*0-06-092294-X*, PL) HarpC.

Chess for Children. Ted Nottingham et al. LC 93-24832. (Illus.). 128p. (J). (gr. 3 up). 1993. 14.95 (*0-8069-0452-6*) Sterling.

Chess for Children. Martin J. Richardson. (J). (gr. 4-7). 1991. 13.00 (*0-08-041109-6*, Pub. by CHES UK) Macmillan.

Chess for Children Pack. (Illus.). 128p. (J). 19.95 (*0-8069-0906-4*) Sterling.

Chess for Children Step by Step: A New, Easy Way to Learn the Game. William Lombardy & Bette Marshall. (Illus.). (J). 1977. 18.95i (*0-316-53091-3*); pap. 18.95i (*0-316-53090-5*) Little.

Chess for Fun & Chess for Blood. 2nd ed. Edward Lasker. (Illus.). 1942. pap. 5.95 (*0-486-20146-5*) Dover.

Chess for Juniors: A Complete Guide for the Beginner. Robert M. Snyder. 1991. pap. 14.00 (*0-8129-1867-3*) Random.

Chess for Tigers. 2nd ed. S. Webb. (Chess Library). 120p. 1990. pap. 9.95 (*0-08-037788-2*, Pub. by CHES UK) Macmillan.

***Chess for Tomorrow's Champions.** John Walker. 1995. 14.95 (*1-85744-195-8*) Macmillan.

***Chess Fundamentals.** Jose Capablanca. 144p. 1994. pap. 15.95 (*1-85744-073-0*, Pub. by Cadogan Books UK) Macmillan.

Chess Fundamentals. Jose R. Capablanca. (Illus.). 1979. pap. 13.00 (*0-679-14004-2*, 27, Tarten) McKay.

Chess Garden. Brooks Hansen. LC 94-10873. (Illus.). 400p. 1995. 22.00 (*0-374-16015-5*) FS&G.

Chess in Ten Easy Lessons. Larry Evans. 1978. pap. 10.00 (*0-87980-015-1*) Wilshire.

Chess in the Classroom: A Complete Guide. Rosalyn B. Katz. 217p. 1992. 24.95 (*0-9633866-0-3*) Exec Trng Concepts.

Chess in the Eighties. David Bronstein & Georgy Smolyan. Tr. by Kenneth P. Neat. (Russian Chess Ser.). 120p. 1982. 19.90 (*0-08-024126-3*, Pergamon Pr) Elsevier.

Chess Kaleidoscope. Anatoly Karpov & Y. Gik. (Russian Chess Ser.). (Illus.). 176p. 1981. 27.90 (*0-08-026897-8*, Pergamon Pr); pap. 15.90 (*0-08-026896-X*, Pergamon Pr) Elsevier.

Chess Labels: A Discography, 2 vols. Comp. by Michel Ruppli. LC 82-25148. (Discographies Ser.: No. 7). xviii, 743p. 1983. text ed. 125.00 (*0-313-23471-X*, RCL/) Greenwood.

Chess Labels: A Discography, 2 vols., 1. Comp. by Michel Ruppli. LC 82-25148. (Discographies Ser.: No. 7). xviii, 743p. 1983. text ed. 75.00 (*0-313-23980-0*, RCL/01) Greenwood.

Chess Labels: A Discography, 2 vols., Vol. 2. Comp. by Michel Ruppli. LC 82-25148. (Discographies Ser.: No. 7). xviii, 743p. 1983. text ed. 75.00 (*0-313-23981-9*, RCL/02) Greenwood.

Chess Made Easy. Milton L. Hanauer. 1979. pap. 5.00 (*0-87980-016-X*) Wilshire.

Chess Master vs. Chess Amateur. Max Euwe & Walter Meiden. LC 93-50842. (Illus.). 314p. reprint ed. pap. 8.95 (*0-486-27947-2*) Dover.

***Chess Master...at Any Age.** Rolf Wetzell. Ed. by Robert B. Long. (Illus.). 300p. 1994. pap. 23.95 (*0-938650-58-0*) Thinkers Pr.

***Chess Middlegames : Essential Knowledge.** Yuri Averbakh. 128p. 1995. 14.95 (*1-85744-125-7*, Pub. by Cadogan Books UK) Macmillan.

Chess Mysteries of Sherlock Holmes: Fifty Tantalizing Problems of Chess Detection. Raymond Smullyan. 1994. pap. 11.00 (*0-8129-2389-8*, Times Bks) Random.

***Chess of Bobby Fischer.** rev. ed. Robert E. Burger. (Great Chess Ser.). 350p. 1994. pap. 24.95 (*1-886040-12-5*) Hypermodern Pr.

Chess Olympiads. Arpad Foldeak. (Illus.). 1966. 25.95 (*0-8283-1175-7*) Branden Pub Co.

Chess Openings. Mike Basman. (Crowood Chess Library). 256p. 1989. pap. 19.95 (*0-946284-74-1*, Pub. by Crowood Pr UK) Trafalgar.

Chess Openings: Theory & Practice. Israel A. Horowitz. 1970. pap. 18.00 (*0-671-20553-6*, Fireside) S&S Trade.

Chess Openings: Traps & Zaps. Bruce Pandolfini. 1989. pap. 11.00 (*0-671-65690-2*, Fireside) S&S Trade.

Chess Openings: Your Choice. S. Reuben. (Chess Ser.). (Illus.). 150p. 1985. 23.95 (*0-08-026895-1*, Pub. by PPL UK); pap. 17.90 (*0-08-026894-3*, Pub. by PPL UK) Elsevier.

***Chess Openings for Juniors.** John Walker. 1995. 14.95 (*1-85744-180-X*) Macmillan.

Chess Openings Simplified. Arthur A. Merrill. 1974. pap. 3.75 (*0-911894-24-1*) Analysis.

Chess Personalia: A Biobibliography. Comp. by Jeremy Gaige. LC 86-43123. 528p. 1987. lib. bdg. 49.95x (*0-89950-293-8*) McFarland & Co.

Chess Players. Anjana Basu. 42p. 1976. 8.00 (*0-86578-257-1*); 4.00 (*0-317-42436-X*) Ind-US Inc.

***Chess Players' Thinking: A Cognition Approach.** Pertti Saariluoma. LC 94-45422. 1995. write for info. (*0-415-12079-9*) Routledge.

Chess Points: How You Can Win Chess Games. George M. Lapoint. (Illus.). 226p. (Orig.). (C). 1989. pap. 9.95 (*0-9623240-0-0*) Gemla Pub.

Chess Praxis. Aron Nimzovich. Orig. Title: Praxis of My System. (Illus.). 1936. pap. 6.95 (*0-486-20296-8*) Dover.

Chess Praxis: Twenty First Century Edition. Aron Nimzowitsch. Ed. by Ken Artz. Tr. by J. Du Mont. 296p. 1993. pap. 17.95 (*1-880673-91-6*) Hays Pub.

***Chess Problems.** Jeremy Morse. (Orig.). 1995. pap. 29.95 (*0-571-15363-1*) Faber & Faber.

Chess Problems for Beginners. Fred Reinfeld. 1979. pap. 7.00 (*0-87980-017-8*) Wilshire.

Chess Puzzles. D. Norwood. (Usborne Guides Ser.). (Illus.). 64p. (J). (gr. 5 up). 1992. lib. bdg. 12.96 (*0-88110-464-7*); pap. text ed. 6.95 (*0-7460-0950-X*) EDC.

***Chess Puzzles for Children.** David H. Levin. (Illus.). 124p. (Orig.). (J). (gr. 2-6). 1994. pap. 11.95 (*0-9638001-1-6*) Syllogism Pr.

Chess Reading Treasure. Wilf Holloway. 1992. 20.00 (*1-85744-000-5*, Maxwell Macmillan) Macmillan.

***Chess Rules for Students.** John A. Bain. Ed. by Robert P. Mitchell. (Illus.). 43p. 1994. pap. text ed. 2.50 (*0-9639614-2-X*) Lrning Plus.

Chess Scandals: The Nineteen Seventy-Eight World Championship Match. E. B. Edmondson. (Chess Ser.). (Illus.). 234p. 1981. 21.90 (*0-08-024145-X*, Pergamon Pr) Elsevier.

Chess Self-Teacher: Eight Lessons with Quizzes & Reviews. Al Horowitz. LC 61-11378. (Illus.). 208p. 1992. reprint ed. pap. 11.00 (*0-06-092295-8*, PL) HarpC.

Chess Set & Other Stories. J. M. Baggiani & V. M. Tewell. (Illus.). 21p. (J). (gr. 2-3). 1966. pap. 3.50 (*0-934329-07-9*) Baggiani-Tewell.

Chess Skill in Man & Machine. 2nd ed. Ed. by P. W. Frey. (Illus.). 335p. 1984. pap. 39.00 (*0-387-90815-3*) Spr-Verlag.

Chess Strategy. Edward Lasker. Tr. by J. Du Mont. (Illus.). 1959. pap. 5.95 (*0-486-20528-2*) Dover.

Chess Struggle & Practice. David Bronstein. 1980. pap. 9.95 (*0-679-14152-9*) McKay.

Chess Studies & Endgames. 2nd rev. ed. B. Horwitz & J. Kling. (Illus.). 370p. 1989. reprint ed. lib. bdg. 60.00 (*3-283-00172-3*, Pub. by Georg Olms GW) Lubrecht & Cramer.

Chess Tactics. Paul Littlewood. (Crowood Chess Library). 136p. 1989. pap. 16.95 (*0-946284-95-4*, Pub. by Crowood Pr UK) Trafalgar.

Chess Tactics for Beginners. Ed. by Fred Reinfeld. 1975. pap. 7.00 (*0-87980-019-4*) Wilshire.

Chess Tactics for Students. John A. Bain. Ed. by Robert P. Mitchell. (Illus.). 228p. (Orig.). (J). (gr. 2-12). 1994. teacher ed 14.95 (*0-9639614-1-1*); pap. 14.95 (*0-9639614-0-3*) Lrning Plus.

Chess Target Practice. Bruce Pandolfini. 1994. pap. 12.00 (*0-671-79500-7*, Fireside) S&S Trade.

***Chess Teacher.** Phillips. 1995. pap. 14.95 (*1-85744-161-3*, Scribners) S&S Trade.

***Chess the Adventurous Way: Best Games & Analyses 1983-1993.** Jan Timman. 256p. 1995. 32.00x (*90-71689-85-9*) Chess Combi.

Chess, the History of a Game. R. G. Eales. LC 84-24685. 256p. reprint ed. pap. 73.00 (*0-8357-3479-X*, 2039738) Bks Demand.

***Chess Thinking.** Bruce Pandolfini. 1995. pap. 15.00 (*0-671-79502-3*, Fireside) S&S Trade.

***Chess Training.** Nigel Povah. 1995. 17.95 (*1-85744-170-2*) Macmillan.

Chess Traps. Israel A. Horowitz & Fred Reinfeld. 1971. pap. 10.00 (*0-671-21041-6*, Fireside) S&S Trade.

Chess Travellers Quiz Book. Julian Hodgson. (Illus.). 128p. 1991. pap. write for info. (*0-08-037804-8*, Pub. by CHES UK) Macmillan.

Chess with a Dragon. David Gerrold. 1988. pap. 3.50 (*0-380-70662-8*) Avon.

Chess with a Dragon. David Gerrold. LC 87-8202. 208p. 1987. 15.95 (*0-8027-6688-9*) Walker & Co.

Chess World Championships: All the Games, 1834-1984. James H. Gelo. LC 88-42519. (Illus.). 718p. 1988. lib. bdg. 49.95x (*0-89950-305-5*) McFarland & Co.

ChessBase University Blue Book Guide to Winning with the King's Indian Attack! Ron Henley & Don Maddox. (ChessBase University Opening Ser.). 192p. (Orig.). 1993. pap. 15.95 (*1-883358-00-0*) R&D Pub NJ.

ChessBase University Power Play! Series, Set. Paul H. Hodges et al. (Illus.). 80p. (Orig.). 1993. pap. write for info. (*1-883358-19-1*) R&D Pub NJ.

Chessboards: Planes of Possibility. David Howell. (Primal Order Ser.). 128p. 1993. pap. 12.95 (*1-880992-12-4*) Wizards Coast.

Chessed As an Expression of Emunah: A Schmuess. Nosson Finkel. Ed. by Joseph Kaminetsky. 1.00 (*0-914131-10-9*, B100) Torah Umesorah.

Chessercizes: New Winning Techniques for Players of All Levels. Bruce Pandolfini. (Illus.). 224p. (Orig.). 1991. pap. 10.00 (*0-671-70184-3*, Fireside) S&S Trade.

Chessie, the Long Island Squirrel. Sachiko Komoto. LC 90-46860. (Quality Time Bks.). (Illus.). 64p. (J). (gr. 1-3). 1993. lib. bdg. 19.93 (*0-8368-0198-9*) Gareth Stevens Inc.

Chessie, the Railroad Kitten. Thomas W. Dixon, Jr. (Illus.). 64p. (Orig.). 1988. pap. text ed. 10.95 (*0-317-93275-6*) TLC VA.

Chessie, the Sea Monster That Ate Annapolis. Jeffrey Holland. (Illus.). 32p. (J). (gr. k-4). 1990. 8.95 (*0-9618461-0-0*) BaySailor Bks.

Chessie's Road. Charles W. Turner et al. 310p. 1986. 29.95 (*0-939487-00-4*) Ches & OH Hist.

***Chessman.** Photos by Erwin Olaf. (Illus.). 72p. 1995. pap. 29.95 (*90-72216-40-7*) Dist Art Pubs.

Chessman of Doom. John Bellairs. (J). (gr. 4-7). 1991. 3.50 (*0-553-15884-8*) Bantam.

Chessman of Mars. Edgar Rice Burroughs. 1987. pap. 3.95 (*0-345-35038-3*, Del Rey) Ballantine.

Chessmaster & His Moves. Raja Rao. (C). 1988. 45.00 (*0-8364-2365-8*, Pub. by Vision) S Asia.

Chessmen of Doom. John Bellairs. (J). (gr. 4-8). 1992. 16.50 (*0-8446-6579-7*) Peter Smith.

Chessmen of Mars see Three Martian Novels

Chessplayer's Laboratory, Vol. 1: Polugayevsky-Nyezhmetdinor, Sochi, 1958. Eric Schiller. 1993. pap. 8.95 (*1-880673-88-6*) Hays Pub.

Chest. Mohammed Mrabet. Tr. by Paul Bowles. 120p. (ARA.). 1983. pap. 7.50 (*0-939180-18-9*) Tombouctou.

Chest. deluxe limited ed. Mohammed Mrabet. Tr. by Paul Bowles. 120p. (ARA.). 1983. 35.00 (*0-939180-21-9*) Tombouctou.

Chest & Cardiac Imaging: An Atlas of Differential Diagnosis. Ronald L. Eisenberg. LC 92-49460. 288p. 1993. 104.00 (*0-7817-0046-9*) Raven.

Chest & Cardiac Radiology. Ed. by Charles Higgins & Holger Pettersson. (Nicer Series on Diagnostic Imaging). (Illus.). 436p. (C). 1991. text ed. 52.00 (*1-873413-25-4*) Merit Pub Intl.

Chest Atlas: Correlated Thin-Section Anatomy in Five Planes. J. T. Littleton & M. L. Durizch. LC 92-49474. 336p. 1993. 250.00 (*0-387-97928-X*); write for info. (*3-540-97928-X*) Spr-Verlag.

Chest Disease (Fourth Series) Test & Syllabus. Anthony V. Proto et al. (Professional Self-Evaluation & Continuing Education Program Ser.: Vol. 27). (Illus.). 814p. 1989. 150.00 (*1-55903-027-5*) Am Coll Radiology.

Chest Drainage. Springhouse Publishing Company. (Procedures Video Ser.). 1992. 34.95 (*0-87434-372-0*) Springhouse Pub.

Chest, Heart & Lungs, Vols. 11 & 11a. Jules R. Kalisch & Harold Williams. (Courtroom Medicine Ser.). 1975. Updates. ring bd. write for info. (*0-8205-1254-0*, 254) Bender.

Chest Medicine. P. S. Shankar. 1990. 24.00 (*81-204-0502-1*, Pub. by Oxford IBH II) S Asia.

Chest Medicine: Essentials of Pulmonary & Critical Care Medicine. 2nd ed. Ronald George. (Illus.). 512p. 1990. pap. 69.00 (*0-683-03453-7*) Williams & Wilkins.

An Asterisk (*) at the beginning of an entry indicates that the title is appearing in BIP for the first time.

C

Chevrolet Full Size 1968-91 RTUG. rev. ed. Chilton Automotives Editorial Staff. (Illus.). 464p. 1992. pap. 16.95 (0-8019-8250-2) Chilton.

Chevrolet-GMC Pick-ups & Suburb 70-86 Spanish, 1970-86. LC 88-98017. 349p. 1989. 16.95 (0-8019-7879-3) Chilton.

Chevrolet High Performance Tips & Techniques. R. M. Clarke. (Brooklands Bks.). (Illus.). 196p. 1991. pap. 17.95 (1-85520-077-5, Pub. by Brooklands Bks UK) Motorbooks Intl.

Chevrolet Impala & SS, 1958-71. R. M. Clarke. (Brooklands Bks.). (Illus.). 100p. 1989. pap. 16.95 (1-870642-28-7, Pub. by Brooklands Bks UK) Motorbooks Intl.

Chevrolet Lumina - Pontiac Transport - Olds Silhouette 1990-91. (Total Car Care Ser.). 576p. 1991. pap. 21.95 (0-8019-8134-4) Chilton.

Chevrolet Muscle Cars, 1966-1971. R. M. Clarke. (Brooklands Bks.). (Illus.). 100p. 1983. pap. 16.95 (0-907073-61-1, Pub. by Brooklands Bks UK) Motorbooks Intl.

Chevrolet Pace Car Book from 1948-1990. D. M. Crispino & John R. Hooper. (Illus.). 224p. 1992. pap. text ed. 21.95 (0-9633802-1-4) J&D Pubns.

Chevrolet Passenger Car Shop Manual, 1955-1957. GMC, Chevrolet Division Staff. Ed. by Dan R. Post. (Illus.). 1464p. 1988. 32.95 (0-911160-38-8) Post Group.

Chevrolet Pickup Color History. Tom Brownell & Mike Mueller. (Illus.). 128p. 1994. pap. 19.95 (0-87938-876-5) Motorbooks Intl.

Chevrolet Pickup Red Book: 1946-1972. Peter Sessler. 1993. pap. 9.95 (0-87938-771-8) Motorbooks Intl.

Chevrolet Pickups, 1946-1972: How to Identify, Select & Restore These Collector Light Trucks. John Gunnell. (Illus.). 192p. 1988. pap. 21.95 (0-87938-282-1) Motorbooks Intl.

Chevrolet Power. Ed. by Rich Voegelin. (Illus.). 192p. (Orig.). 1993. pap. 19.95 (1-55788-087-5, HP Books) Berkley Pub.

Chevrolet Restoration Directory. Bruce M. Kneifl. 96p. 1989. pap. 6.98 (0-87938-369-0) Motorbooks Intl.

Chevrolet S-10 Blazer, GMC S-15 Jimmy & Olds Bravada 1982-91. (Total Car Care Ser.). 800p. 1991. pap. 21.95 (0-8019-8139-5) Chilton.

Chevrolet S-10 Blazer, GMC S-15 Jimmy & Olds Bravada 1982-91: Update. (Total Car Care Ser.). 320p. 1991. pap. 16.95 (0-8019-8140-9) Chilton.

Chevrolet S-10, GMC S-15 Pick-Ups 1982-91: Update. (Repair & Tune-up Guides Ser.). 320p. 1991. pap. 16.95 (0-8019-8142-5) Chilton.

Chevrolet Saturdays. Candy D. Boyd. LC 92-32119. 176p. (J). (gr. 3-7). 1993. text ed. 14.95 (0-02-711765-0, Mac Bks Young Read) S&S Childrens.

***Chevrolet Saturdays.** Candy D. Boyd. LC 94-30185. 192p. (J). 1995. pap. 3.99 (0-14-036859-0) Puffin Bks.

Chevrolet Small-Block V-8 Interchange Manual. David Lewis. (Illus.). 160p. 1989. pap. 17.95 (0-87938-357-7) Motorbooks Intl.

Chevrolet Small Block V-8 Speed Equipment. Michael Lamm. (Illus.). 282p. 1989. pap. 6.98 (0-932128-05-X, Pub. by Lamm-Morada) Motorbooks Intl.

Chevrolet SS Red Book. Peter C. Sessler. 1991. pap. 9.95 (0-87938-501-4) Motorbooks Intl.

Chevrolet, 1955. Michael Lamm. 1991. 14.95 (0-932128-06-8) Lamm-Morada Pub.

Chevrolet, 1955-1957. Ed. by R. M. Clarke. (Brooklands Bks.). (Illus.). 100p. (Orig.). 1988. pap. 16.95 (1-869826-78-7, Pub. by Brooklands Bks UK) Motorbooks Intl.

Chevrolet 1955-1957. Consumer Guide Staff. 1991. 9.98 (1-56173-311-3) Pubns Intl Ltd.

Chevrolet 55-56 Restoration Guide. Aregood Oakley. (Illus.). 352p. 1992. pap. text ed. 26.95 (0-87938-581-2) Motorbooks Intl.

***Chevrolet's Hot Ones 1955, 1956, 1957.** Anthony Young & Mike Mueller. (Illus.). 160p. 1995. 29.95 (0-87938-994-X) Motorbooks Intl.

Chevron. David Gordon. (Illus.). 224p. 1991. 39.95 (1-85260-318-6, Pub. by J H Haynes & Co UK) Motorbooks Intl.

Chevron & Nueva Cadiz Beads. John Picard & Ruth Picard. (Beads from the West African Trade Ser.: Vol. VII). (Illus.). 128p. 1993. 35.00 (0-9622884-2-X) Picard African.

***Chevron Corp. A Report on the Company's Environmental Policies & Practices.** (Illus.). 40p. (C). 1994. reprint ed. pap. text ed. 200.00x (0-7881-0977-4, Coun on Econ) Diane Pub.

Chevron-Notch Fracture Test Experience - Metals & Non-Metals. Ed. by Kevin R. Brown & Francis I. Baratta. LC 92-24966. (Special Technical Publication Ser.: No. 1172). (Illus.). 210p. 1992. text ed. 68.00 (0-8031-1480-X, 04-011720-30) ASTM.

Chevron Notched Specimens: Testing & Stress Analysis - STP 855. Ed. by Underwood et al. 360p. 1984. 44.00 (0-8031-0401-4, 04-855000-30) ASTM.

Chevy - GM Full Size Trucks 1988-93. (Update Ser.). 920p. 1994. pap. 21.95 (0-8019-8490-4) Chilton.

Chevy - GMC Vans 1987-90. Chilton Staff. 368p. 1991. pap. 16.95 (0-8019-8216-2) Chilton.

Chevy Astro - GMC Safari 1985-90. Chilton Staff. 448p. 1991. pap. 16.95 (0-8019-8217-0) Chilton.

Chevy Camaro 1982-92. rev. ed. Chilton Automotives Editorial Staff. 408p. 1992. pap. 16.95 (0-8019-8306-1) Chilton.

Chevy Camaro 1982-92: Total Car Care. 784p. 1992. pap. 21.95 (0-8019-8260-X) Chilton.

Chevy Cavalier, Buick Skyhawk, Cadillac Cimarron, Pontiac 2000, Olds Firenza 1982-92. 960p. 1992. pap. 21.95 (0-8019-8269-3) Chilton.

Chevy Celebrity, Buick Century, Olds Ciera, Pontiac 6000 1982-92: Total Car Care. 736p. 1992. pap. 21.95 (0-8019-8252-9) Chilton.

Chevy El Camino & SS Nineteen Fifty-Nine to Eighty Seven. R. M. Clarke. (Book Ser.). (Illus.). 100p. 1990. pap. 16.95 (1-85520-018-X, Pub. by Brooklands Bks UK) Motorbooks Intl.

Chevy Engine Swapping Tips & Technology. R. M. Clarke. (Illus.). 140p. 1992. pap. 17.95 (1-85520-160-7, Pub. by Brooklands Bks UK) Motorbooks Intl.

Chevy GMC Full Size Trucks 1988-93. (Update Ser.). 450p. 1994. pap. 16.95 (0-8019-8491-2) Chilton.

Chevy-GMC Vans, 1987-90. Chilton Staff. (Illus.). 640p. 1990. pap. text ed. 21.95 (0-8019-8040-2) Chilton.

Chevy High Performance. Robert Ackerson. (Illus.). 304p. 1994. pap. 24.95 (0-87341-326-1) Krause Pubns.

***Chevy II Nova & SS 1986-1994.** R. M. Clarke. (Brooklands Muscle Portfolio Ser.). (Illus.). 140p. 1994. pap. 18.95 (1-85520-258-1) Motorbooks Intl.

Chevy Krohn Model Camper. D. Shreiber. 140p. 1992. pap. 7.95 (0-944070-78-7) Targum Pr.

Chevy Lumina, Pontiac Grand Prix, Olds Cutlass Supreme, Buick Regal 1988-92. rev. ed. Chilton Automotives Editorial Staff. 320p. 1992. pap. 16.95 (0-8019-8304-5) Chilton.

Chevy Lumina, Pontiac Grand Prix, Olds Cutlass Supreme, Buick Regal 1988-92: Total Car Care. 736p. 1992. pap. 21.95 (0-8019-8258-8) Chilton.

Chevy Muscle Cars. Mike Mueller. (Enthusiast Color Ser.). (Illus.). 96p. 1994. pap. 12.95 (0-87938-864-1) Motorbooks Intl.

***Chevy Odyssey & Other Plays.** Young Playwrights Festival Staff. 62p. 1993. pap. 5.95 (1-56850-029-7) Chicago Plays.

Chevy Performance. John Michelsen. 1981. 16.95 (0-931472-07-5) Motorbooks Intl.

***Chevy S-10 Blazer - S-15 Jimmy, 1982-95.** Ed. by Chilton Staff. 704p. 1995. pap. 21.95 (0-8019-8661-3) Chilton.

Chevy Six, the Early Years: Construction, Operation, Service for the Restorer. Victor W. Page. LC 76-26324. (Illus.). 912p. 1979. reprint ed. 28.95 (0-911160-40-X) Post Group.

Chevy Small-Block V-8: History of the Engine & the Cars. Anthony Young. (Illus.). 128p. 1992. pap. 4.98 (0-87938-575-8) Motorbooks Intl.

Chevy Super Sports: 1961-1976. Terry V. Boyce. LC 80-22034. (Illus.). 1982. pap. 17.95 (0-87938-096-9) Motorbooks Intl.

Chevy Two & Nova, 1962 to 1979. Chilton Automotives Editorial Staff. LC 78-20253. (Chilton's Repair & Tune-up Guides Ser.). (Illus.). 296p. 1979. pap. 16.95 (0-8019-6841-0, 6841) Chilton.

Chevy 396 & 427. R. M. Clarke. (Muscle Car & High Powered Engines Ser.). (Illus.). 100p. 1991. pap. 16.95 (1-85520-098-8, Pub. by Brooklands Bks UK) Motorbooks Intl.

Chevy 55-56-57. Mike Mueller. LC 93-17024. (Enthusiast Color Ser.). 1993. 12.95 (0-87938-816-1) Motorbooks Intl.

Chewata: Tobia B'Yerusalem. Tesfa Workneh. 425p. (AMH.). 1989. pap. write for info. (0-318-65866-6) Shinfa Pr.

Chewbone: Readings from the Paris Cafe, 1993. Ed. by Willard Gellis & Nicholas Bono. 38p. 1993. pap. write for info. (0-917455-17-7) Big Foot NY.

Chewing Gum, Baling Wire & Guts: Story of the Gates Flying Circus. William Rhode. (Illus.). 194p. 1994. reprint ed. pap. write for info. (0-9632295-1-6) H V Pubs.

Chewing Gum Book. Robert Young. LC 88-31015. (Illus.). 72p. (J). (gr. 3 up). 1989. text ed. 12.95 (0-87518-401-4, Dillon Silver Burdett) Silver Burdett Pr.

Chewing-Gum Rescue & Other Stories. Margaret Mahy. (Illus.). 142p. (J). (gr. 3-7). 1991. 12.95 (0-87951-424-8) Overlook Pr.

Chewing Gum Rescue & Other Stories. Margaret Mahy. LC 93-35963. 192p. (J). (gr. 5 up). 1994. reprint ed. pap. 4.95 (0-688-12798-3, Pub. by Beech Tree Bks) Morrow.

Chewing the Cud. Henry Brewis. (Illus.). 256p. 1988. pap. 8.95 (0-85236-187-4, Pub. by Farming Pr UK) Diamond Farm Bk.

***Chewing Tobacco Tin Tags, 1870-1930.** Louis Storino. (Illus.). 128p. (Orig.). 1995. pap. 19.95 (0-88740-857-5) Schiffer.

***Chewy Cookies: Over 125 Fabulous Recipes.** Eileen Talanian. LC 95-1516. 1995. pap. text ed. write for info. (0-7615-0004-9) Prima Pub.

Cheyene Captives see Hunt the Man Down

Cheyenne. George A. Dorsey. 72p. 1975. 12.00 (0-87770-157-1) Ye Galleon.

Cheyenne. Dennis B. Fradin. LC 87-33792. (New True Bks.). (Illus.). 48p. (J). (gr. k-4). 1988. lib. bdg. 12.90 (0-516-01211-8); pap. 4.95 (0-516-41211-6) Childrens.

Cheyenne. Stan Hoig. (Indians of North America Ser.). (Illus.). 112p. (YA). (gr. 5 up). 1989. 17.95 (1-55546-696-6); pap. 9.95 (0-7910-0358-2) Chelsea Hse.

Cheyenne. Sally Lodge. (Native American People Ser.). (Illus.). 32p. (J). (gr. 5-8). 1990. lib. bdg. 15.94 (0-86625-387-4); lib. bdg. 11.95 (0-685-36388-0) Rourke Corp.

Cheyenne. Arthur Meyers. (First Bks.). (Illus.). 64p. (J). (gr. 5-8). 1992. pap. 5.95 (0-531-15636-2) Watts.

Cheyenne: City of Blue Sky. Judith Adams. 128p. 1988. 27.95 (0-89781-229-8, 5154) Preferred Mktg.

***Cheyenne Again.** Eve Bunting. LC 94-43287. (Illus.). 1995. 14.95 (0-395-70364-6, Clarion Bks) HM.

Cheyenne Amber. C. Anderson. 1994. mass mkt. 5.50 (0-06-108061-6, Harp PBks) HarpC.

Cheyenne & Arapaho Music. Frances Densmore. 111p. 1964. reprint ed. pap. 5.00 (0-916561-12-7) Southwest Mus.

Cheyenne & Arapaho Ordeal: Reservation & Agency Life in the Indian Territory, 1875-1907. Donald J. Berthrong. LC 75-17795. (Civilization of the American Indian Ser.: Vol. 136). (Illus.). 424p. (Orig.). (C). 1992. pap. 15.95 (0-8061-2416-4) U of Okla Pr.

Cheyenne Autumn. Mari Sandoz. (J). 1976. mass mkt. 4.95 (0-380-01094-1) Avon.

Cheyenne Autumn. Mari Sandoz. LC 91-40930. (Illus.). xx, 282p. 1992. reprint ed. 25.00 (0-8032-4223-9); reprint ed. pap. 9.95 (0-8032-9212-0) U of Nebr Pr.

Cheyenne Bottoms: Wetland in Jeopardy. John L. Zimmerman. LC 90-12907. (Illus.). 216p. 1990. 19.95 (0-7006-0443-X) U Pr of KS.

***Cheyenne Bottoms: Wetland in Jeopardy.** John L. Zimmerman. LC 90-12907. (Illus.). 216p. 1995. pap. 12.95 (0-7006-0712-9) U Pr of KS.

Cheyenne Captive. G. Gentry. 1994. mass mkt. 4.50 (0-8217-3880-1) Zebra.

Cheyenne Caress. Cheyenne Gentry. 1990. mass mkt. 4.50 (0-8217-2864-4) Zebra.

***Cheyenne Challenge.** William W. Johnstone. 352p. 1995. pap. 4.50 (0-8217-5048-8) Zebra.

Cheyenne, Cheyenne, Our Blue Collar Heritage. Gladys P. Jones. (Illus.). 235p. 1983. 11.50 (0-685-40788-8) G P Jones.

Cheyenne, Cheyenne,..."Our Blue Collar Heritage" Gladys P. Jones. LC 83-82304. (Illus.). 220p. (Orig.). 1983. pap. 11.55 (0-9612628-0-X) G P Jones.

Cheyenne Community, Wyoming. Sharon Field. (Illus.). 553p. 1989. 62.50 (0-88107-127-7) Curtis Media.

Cheyenne County Kansas. Cheyenne County Historical Society Staff. (Illus.). 747p. 1987. 60.00 (0-88107-095-5) Curtis Media.

Cheyenne Crossfire. Jon Sharpe. (Trailsman Ser.: No. 145). 176p. 1994. 3.50 (0-451-17757-6, Sig) NAL-Dutton.

***Cheyenne Desire.** Robin Gideon. 448p. 1995. mass mkt. 4.99 (0-8217-4808-4) Windsor NY.

Cheyenne Dreams. Paul J. Lederer. (Indian Heritage Ser.: No. 4). 1989. pap. 3.50 (0-451-13651-9) NAL-Dutton.

Cheyenne Gauntlet & Indian Territory, 2 vols. in 1. David Everitt. 384p. 1991. pap. 4.50 (0-8439-3194-9) Dorchester Pub Co.

Cheyenne in Plains Indian Trade Relations. Joseph Jablow. LC 84-45520. (American Ethnological Society Monographs: No. 19). 1988. reprint ed. 20.00 (0-404-62918-0) AMS Pr.

Cheyenne in Plains Indian Trade Relations, 1795-1840. Joseph Jablow. (Illus.). xxii, 100p. 1994. pap. 6.95 (0-8032-7581-1, Bison Books) U of Nebr Pr.

Cheyenne Indians. Liz Sonneboen. (Junior Library of American Indians). (Illus.). 80p. (J). (gr. 3-7). 1994. pap. 6.95 (0-7910-2031-2) Chelsea Hse.

Cheyenne Indians. Liz Sonneborn. (Junior Library of American Indians). (Illus.). 80p. (J). (gr. 3-7). 1992. lib. bdg. 14.95 (0-7910-1654-4) Chelsea Hse.

Cheyenne Indians: Their History & Ways of Life. Incl. Vol. 1. LC 23-17688. x, 358p. pap. 12.95 (0-8032-5771-6); LC 23-17688. viii, 478p. pap. 14.95 (0-8032-5772-4); LC 23-17688. (Illus.). 1972. reprint ed. Set pap. write for info. (0-318-56105-0, Bison Books) U of Nebr Pr.

Cheyenne Lance - Medicine Wagon, 2 vols. in 1. John P. Legg. 464p. 1990. pap. 3.95 (0-8439-2994-4) Dorchester Pub Co.

Cheyenne Legends of Creation. Henry Tall Bull & Tom Weist. (Indian Culture Ser.). (J). (gr. 4-9). 1972. 1.25 (0-89992-025-X) Coun India Ed.

Cheyenne Manhunt. Lester Merha. (Orig.). 1980. pap. 1.75 (0-8439-0742-8) Dorchester Pub Co.

Cheyenne Memories. John Stands In Timber & Margot Liberty. LC 67-24515. (Illus.). xvi, 348p. 1972. reprint ed. pap. 11.95 (0-8032-5751-1, Bison Books) U of Nebr Pr.

Cheyenne Moon. large type ed. John Murphy. (Western Ser.). 208p. 1994. pap. 14.95 (0-7089-7583-6, Trailtree Bookshop) Ulverscroft.

Cheyenne Nation: A Social & Demographic History. John H. Moore. LC 87-5856. (Illus.). xxvi, 390p. 1987. 40.00 (0-8032-3107-5) U of Nebr Pr.

Cheyenne Pool. Lewis B. Patten. Bd. with Tired Gun. 272p. 1983. Set pap. 2.95 (0-451-12492-8, Sig) NAL-Dutton.

Cheyenne Princess. G. Gentry. 1994. mass mkt. 4.50 (0-8217-3876-3) Zebra.

Cheyenne Princess. Georgina Gentry. 1987. pap. 3.75 (0-8217-2176-3) Zebra.

Cheyenne Short Stories: A Collection of Ten Traditional Stores of the Cheyenne. (Indian Culture Ser.). (CHY & ENG.). (J). (gr. 2 up). 1977. 3.95 (0-89992-057-8) Coun India Ed.

Cheyenne Splendor. Georgina Gentry. 432p. 1994. mass mkt. 5.99 (0-8217-4741-X) Zebra.

Cheyenne Sunrise. Constance O'Banyon. 1990. mass mkt. 4.95 (0-8217-3088-6) Zebra.

Cheyenne Surrender. Madeline Baker. 448p. (Orig.). 1994. pap. 4.99 (0-8439-3581-2) Dorchester Pub Co.

Cheyenne Surrender. Karen A. Bale. (Sweet Medicine's Prophecy Ser.: No. 6). 1990. pap. 3.95 (0-8217-2789-3) Zebra.

Cheyenne Temptress. Veronica Blake. 320p. 1991. mass mkt. 4.25 (0-8217-3281-1) Zebra.

Cheyenne Warriors. Henry Tall Bull & Tom Weist. (Indian Culture Ser.). (J). (gr. 4-12). 1976. pap. 4.95 (0-89992-015-2) Coun India Ed.

Cheyenne Way: Conflict & Case Law in Primitive Jurisprudence. Karl N. Llewellyn & E. Adamson Hoebel. LC 41-23735. (Civilization of the American Indian Ser.: Vol. 21). (Illus.). 374p. 1983. reprint ed. 34.95 (0-8061-0099-0); reprint ed. pap. 16.95 (0-8061-1855-5) U of Okla Pr.

Cheyennes: Indians of the Great Plains. 2nd ed. E. A. Hoebel. LC 77-25471. 224p. (C). 1978. pap. text ed. 13.50 (0-03-022686-4) HB Coll Pubs.

Cheyennes & Horse Soldiers: The 1857 Expedition & the Battle of Solomon's Fork. William Y. Chalfant. LC 89-32203. (Illus.). 432p. 1989. 29.95 (0-8061-2194-7) U of Okla Pr.

Cheyennes of Montana. Thomas B. Marquis. Ed. by Thomas D. Weist. LC 78-59715. 1978. 19.95 (0-917256-04-2) Ref Pubns.

Cheyenne's Shadow. Deborah Camp. 400p. (Orig.). 1994. mass mkt. 4.99 (0-380-76739-2) Avon.

Cheyenne's Woman - the Kansan's Lady. Robert E. Mills. (Kansan Double Edition Ser.). 416p. 1993. pap. 4.99 (0-8439-3450-6) Dorchester Pub Co.

Cheyne Mystery. Freeman W. Crofts. 20.95 (0-88411-070-2, Aeonian Pr) Amereon Ltd.

***Chez Chance: A Novel.** Jay Gummerman. LC 95-1731. 224p. 1995. 21.00 (0-679-43991-9) Pantheon.

Chez Charlotte & Emily. Jonathan Baumbach. LC 79-52033. 1979. 15.95 (0-914590-56-1); pap. 7.95 (0-914590-57-X) Fiction Coll.

Chez Francois Cookbook: Featuring the Cuisine of Alsace. Jacques E. Haeringer. LC 91-29630. 240p. 1991. 19.95 (0-910155-19-4) Bartleby Pr.

Chez Game. Lexigraph Company Staff. (Illus.). 76p. (Orig.). 1985. pap. 10.00 (0-934365-00-8) Leco Pub.

Chez les Canses. Charles E. Hoffhaus. LC 84-72933. (Illus.). 224p. 1984. pap. 9.95 (0-913504-91-2) Lowell Pr.

***Chez Nous: Home Cooking from the South of France.** Lydie Marshall. (Illus.). 320p. 1995. 25.00 (0-06-017203-7) HarpC.

Chez Panisse Cooking. Paul Bertolli. 1994. pap. 18.00 (0-679-75535-7) Random.

Chez Panisse Cooking: New Tastes & Techniques. Paul Bertolli & Alice L. Waters. LC 87-28546. (Illus.). 320p. 1988. 28.00 (0-394-56970-9) Random.

Chez Panisse Desserts. Lindsey R. Shere. (Illus.). 1985. 27.00 (0-394-53860-9) Random.

Chez Panisse Desserts. Lindsey R. Shere. 1994. pap. 17.00 (0-679-75571-3) Random.

***Chez Panisse Menu Cookbook.** Alice Waters. 1995. pap. 16.00 (0-679-75818-6) Random.

Chez Panisse Menu Cookbook. Alice L. Waters. (Illus.). 1982. 25.00 (0-394-51787-3) Random.

***Chez Panisse Pasta, Pizza & Calzone.** Alice Waters. 1995. 14.00 (0-679-75536-5) Random.

Chez Panisse Pasta, Pizza & Calzone. Alice L. Waters et al. (Illus.). 196p. 1984. 25.00 (0-394-53094-2) Random.

Chez Vous, Chez Nous: Language in Action: First Year. June K. Phillips et al. 608p. (C). 1988. student ed 12.95 (0-685-18204-5); 12.95 (0-685-18205-3); text ed. write for info. (0-07-554123-8) McGraw.

Chhandogya Upanisad. Tr. by Srisa Chandra Vasu. LC 73-3788. (Sacred Books of the Hindus: No. 3). reprint ed. 57.50 (0-404-57803-9) AMS Pr.

CHI 'Eighty-Five Human Factors in Computing Systems. LC 60-8850. (Illus.). 231p. 1985. pap. text ed. 22.00 (0-89791-149-0) Assn Compu Machinery.

CHI Eighty-Five Pediatric Hospice Conference Report. Ed. by Mary M. Hunter. 98p. 1985. pap. 30.00 (0-317-61841-5) Child Hospice VA.

CHI 'Eighty-Six Human Factors in Computing Systems. LC 60-8860. (Illus.). 361p. 1986. pap. text ed. 30.00 (0-89791-180-6) Assn Compu Machinery.

***Chi Gong: The Ancient Chinese Way to Health.** Paul Dong & Aristide Esser. (Illus.). 212p. (C). 1995. pap. 13.00 (1-56924-856-7) Marlowe & Co.

Chi-Hoon: A Korean Girl. Patricia McMahon. LC 92-81331. (Illus.). 48p. (J). (gr. 4-7). 1993. 16.95 (1-56397-026-0) Boyds Mills Pr.

Chi Kung. Lily Siou. 1976. 21.95 (0-685-83521-9) Wehman.

Chi Kung: Health & Martial Arts. 4th ed. Jwing-Ming Yang. LC 87-50144. (Illus.). 121p. 1985. pap. 12.95 (0-940871-00-9, B005) YMAA Pubn.

Ch'i-Kung: The Art of Mastering the Unseen Life Force. Lily Siou. LC 75-32212. 174p. 1975. 18.95 (0-8048-1169-5) C E Tuttle.

Chi-la-pe & the White Buffalo. John Necholson. (Indian Culture Ser.). 44p. (J). (gr. 2-10). 1981. pap. 5.95 (0-89992-064-0) Coun India Ed.

***Chi-lin-Purse: A Collection of Ancient Chinese Stories.** Linda Fang. (Illus.). 160p. (J). (gr. 3 up). 1995. 16.00 (0-374-31241-9) FS&G.

Chi Nei Tsang: Internal Organ Chi Message. Mantak Chia & Maneewan Chia. (Illus.). 448p. 1991. pap. 16.95 (0-935621-35-0) Heal Tao Bks.

Ch'i Pai-shih. T. C. Lai. LC 73-76338. (Illus.). 208p. 1973. 20.00 (0-295-95315-2) U of Wash Pr.

Chi Self-Massage: The Tao of Rejuvenation. Mantak Chia. LC 85-82051. (Illus.). 176p. (Orig.). 1986. pap. 9.95 (0-935621-01-6) Heal Tao Bks.

Chi Square, Pie Square & Me. Susan Baum et al. 120p. (Orig.). 1987. pap. 12.99 (0-89824-171-5) Trillium Pr.

Chi Town. Norbert Blei. 384p. 1990. 19.95 (0-944024-10-6) Ellis Pr.

Chia-Ting Loyalists: Confucian Leadership & Social Change in Seventeenth-Century China. Jerry Dennerline. LC 80-21417. (Historical Publications, Miscellany Ser.: No. 126). (Illus.). 416p. 1981. text ed. 52.00 (0-300-02548-3) Yale U Pr.

Chiang Ching-kuo Remembered: The Man & His Political Legacy. Ray S. Cline. Ed. by Marjorie W. Cline. (Illus.). 205p. (C). 1989. pap. text ed. 21.50 (0-943057-01-9) US Global Strat.

Chiang Ching-Kuo's Leadership in the Development of the Republic of China on Taiwan, Vol. III. Ed. by Shao-Chuan Leng. LC 92-31103. (Miller Center Series on Asian Political Leadership). 230p. (Orig.). (C). 1993. lib. bdg. 52.00 (0-8191-8903-0, Pub. by White Miller Center); pap. text ed. 21.50 (0-8191-8904-9, Pub. by White Miller Center) U Pr of Amer.

An Asterisk (*) at the beginning of an entry indicates that the title is appearing in BIP for the first time.

C

An Asterisk (*) at the beginning of an entry indicates that the title is appearing in BIP for the first time.

1187

Chicago Families: A Study of Unpublished Census Data. Day Monroe. LC 70-169395. (Family in America Ser.). 370p. 1972. reprint ed. 20.95 (0-405-03872-0) Ayer.

Chicago Fire. Lois Warburton. LC 89-33554. (World Disasters Ser.). (Illus.). 64p. (J). (gr. 5-8). 1989. lib. bdg. 14.95 (1-56006-002-6) Lucent Bks.

Chicago for Kids: Of All Ages. rev. ed. Gary Grimm & Associates Staff. (Illus.). 32p. (J). (gr. k-8). reprint ed. student ed 4.00 (1-56490-001-0) G Grimm Assocs.

***Chicago from the River.** Joan V. Lindsay. (Illus.). 48p. (Orig.). 1995. pap. 14.95 (0-9647350-0-8) J V & D Lindsay.

Chicago Fun-ics: You Can Talk Like the Windy City. Michael L. Ellis, III. LC 88-50184. (Illus.). (Orig.). 1993. pap. text ed. 3.50 (0-929178-20-3) Valley Forge Pub.

Chicago Gangster Theory of Life: Ecology, Culture & Society. Andrew Ross. LC 94-18514. 1994. 24.95 (0-86091-429-1, B4529, Pub. by Verso UK) Routledge Chapman & Hall.

Chicago Golf the First Hundred Years. Thomas Govedarica. 300p. 1991. pap. 14.95 (0-9630761-0-8) Eagle Comms.

Chicago Graphic Design. 224p. 1994. 49.99 (1-56496-071-4) Rockport Pubs.

Chicago Great Western in Minnesota. Roger Bee & Gary F. Browne. (Illus.). 115p. 1984. write for info. (0-930431-00-6) Blue River Pubns.

Chicago Guide to Preparing Electronic Manuscripts. Chicago Editorial Staff. 120p. 1987. 25.00 (0-226-10392-7); pap. 9.95 (0-226-10393-5) U Ch Pr.

Chicago Heist. John O'Brien & Edward W. Baumann. LC 81-68394. (Illus.). 280p. (Orig.). 1981. pap. 6.95 (0-89708-053-X) And Bks.

Chicago Historical Geographic Laboratory Guide. James Piety. (Illus.). 140p. (Orig.). (C). 1990. student ed, pap. text ed. 11.80 (0-87563-290-4) Stipes.

Chicago Home. Linnea Johnson. LC 86-80006. 72p. 1986. 14.95 (0-914086-62-6); pap. 9.95 (0-914086-63-4) Alicejamesbooks.

Chicago Home Book. 600p. 1995. 19.95 (0-9642057-0-X) IdeaCorp.

Chicago Hustle. Odie Hawkins. (Orig.). 1983. pap. 3.50 (0-87067-366-1, BH366) Holloway.

Chicago, Illinois: 1870 Census Index. Ed. by Bradley W. Steuart. 1216p. 1990. lib. bdg. 175.00 (1-877677-06-X) Precision Indexing.

Chicago Imagist Print: Ten Artists' Works, 1958-1987 - A Catalogue Raisonne. Dennis Adrian & Richard Born. Ed. by Sue Taylor. LC 87-72605. (Illus.). 216p. (Orig.). 1987. pap. 25.00 (0-935573-01-1) D & A Smart Museum.

Chicago in Story: A Literary History. Clarence A. Andrews. (Illus.). 414p. 1983. lib. bdg. 19.95 (0-934582-03-3) Midwest Heritage.

Chicago Jack's All Right, All Night & After Hours Fun Finder...a Cabbie's Guide to Chicago at Night: 1992. Jack A. Smith. Ed. by Jan E. Jaben & Andrea Rock. (Illus.). 200p. (Orig.). 1992. pap. 6.95 (0-9633021-4-0) Fun Guide Comms.

Chicago Jazz: A Cultural History, 1904-1930. William H. Kenney. LC 92-27397. (Illus.). 256p. 1993. 25.00 (0-19-506453-4) OUP.

Chicago Jazz: A Cultural History, 1904-1930. William H. Kenney. 256p. 1994. reprint ed. pap. 10.95 (0-19-509260-0) OUP.

***Chicago Jobbank, 1995.** Adams Staff. 1994. pap. 15.95 (1-55850-449-4) Adams Pubng.

Chicago-Kezys: Sixty-four Photographs of Chicago. Algimantas Kezys. LC 82-17175. (Illus.). 78p. 1983. 14.95 (0-8294-0408-2) Loyola Univ Pr.

***Chicago Labor & the Quest for a Democratic Diplomacy, 1914-1924.** Elizabeth McKillen. 256p. 1995. 35.00x (0-8014-2905-6) Cornell U Pr.

Chicago Lawyers: The Social Structure of the Bar. John P. Heinz & Edward O. Laumann. LC 82-50355. xxvi, 575p. 1982. 45.00 (0-87154-378-8) Russell Sage.

Chicago Lawyers: The Social Structure of the Bar. rev. ed. John P. Heinz & Edward O. Laumann. 260p. 1994. pap. 19.95 (0-8101-1189-6) Northwestern U Pr.

Chicago Loop. Paul Theroux. 1994. mass mkt. 5.99 (0-8041-1161-8) Ivy Books.

Chicago Loop. Paul Theroux. 1991. 18.95 (0-685-39016-0); 19.50 (0-679-40188-1) Random.

Chicago Magazine's Guide to Chicago. rev. ed. Carla Kelson et al. 224p. 1988. write for info. (0-318-63766-9) Chicago Magazine.

Chicago Magazine's One-Hundred Menus. Carla Kelson & Allen Kelson. 208p. (Orig.). 1984. pap. 4.95 (0-9613952-0-6) W F M T Inc.

Chicago Manual of Style: The Essential Guide for Authors, Editors, & Publishers. 14th ed. Chicago Editorial Staff. LC 92-37475. 800p. 1993. 40.00 (0-226-10389-7) U Ch Pr.

Chicago Mapmakers: Essays on the Rise of the City's Map Trade. Ed. by Michael P. Conzen. LC 84-5853. (Illus.). 76p. 1984. 12.00 (0-916789-01-2) Chicago Map.

Chicago May. Aleister Crowley. 1993. reprint ed. 27.50 (1-55818-213-6, First Impress) Holmes Pub.

Chicago Memorial Day Incident, June 30, July 1 & 28, 1937 & La Follette Committee Report. U. S. Committee on Education & Labor. LC 70-154595. (Police in America Ser.). 1971. reprint ed. 28.95 (0-405-03402-4) Ayer.

Chicago Municipal Code Handbook: Annual Edition. Gould Editorial Staff. 610p. ring bd. 19.95 (0-87526-264-3) Gould.

Chicago Northwestern in Minnesota. John C. Luecke. (Illus.). 250p. (C). 1990. 39.95 (0-9621020-2-4) Grenadier Pubns.

Chicago on Foot: Walking Tours of Chicago's Architecture. 5th rev. ed. Ira J. Bach & Susan Wolfson. LC 93-39802. (Illus.). 304p. 1994. pap. 14.95 (1-55652-209-6) Chicago Review.

***Chicago Originals.** Kenan Heise & Ed Baumann. (Illus.). 310p. 1995. pap. text ed. 11.95 (1-56625-033-1) Bonus Books.

Chicago Originals: A Cast of the City's Colorful Characters. Kenan Heise & Ed Baumann. (Illus.). 291p. (Orig.). 1990. pap. 9.95 (0-933893-94-9) Bonus Books.

Chicago Pinkas. Ed. by Simon Rawidowicz. 319p. (ENG & HEB.). (C). 1952. 7.95 (0-935982-05-1, SR-01) Spertus Coll.

Chicago Plan & the New Deal Banking Reform. Ronnie J. Phillips. 240p. 1994. text ed. 55.00 (1-56324-469-1); pap. text ed. 21.95 (1-56324-470-5) M E Sharpe.

Chicago Poems. Carl Sandburg. 19.95 (0-8488-1138-0) Amereon Ltd.

Chicago Poems. Carl Sandburg. (Prairie State Bks.). 216p. 1992. pap. 10.95 (0-252-06234-5) U of Ill Pr.

Chicago Poems. Carl Sandburg. 1986. reprint ed. lib. bdg. 16.95 (0-89966-545-4) Buccaneer Bks.

Chicago Poems. Carl Sandburg. 80p. 1994. reprint ed. pap. 1.00 (0-486-28057-8) Dover.

Chicago Police Investigations: Three Reports. Chicago Civil Service Commission. LC 76-154567. (Police in America Ser.). 1971. reprint ed. 13.95 (0-405-03365-6) Ayer.

Chicago Police Problems. Citizens' Police Committee. LC 69-16230. (Criminology, Law Enforcement, & Social Problems Ser.: No. 89). 1969. reprint ed. 25.00 (0-87585-089-8) Patterson Smith.

Chicago Politics Ward by Ward. David K. Fremon. LC 87-46094. (Illus.). 384p. (Orig.). 1988. 29.95 (0-253-31344-9); pap. 14.95 (0-253-20490-9) Ind U Pr.

Chicago Portraits: Two Hundred Fifty Biographies of Famous Chicagoans. June S. Sawyers. LC 91-24741. (Illus.). 368p. (Orig.). 1991. pap. 22.95 (0-8294-0700-6) Loyola Univ Pr.

Chicago Portraits: Two Hundred Fifty Biographies of Famous Chicagoans. June S. Sawyers. LC 91-24741. (Illus.). 368p. (Orig.). 1991. 22.35 (0-8294-0701-4) Loyola Univ Pr.

Chicago Postal History. Harvey M. Karlen. LC 79-135669. (Illus.). 191p. 1970. 35.00 (0-318-41051-6) Collectors Club IL.

Chicago Pragmatists & American Progressivism. Andrew Feffer. LC 92-54974. 304p. 1993. 32.95 (0-8014-2502-6) Cornell U Pr.

Chicago Primary of 1926: A Study in Election Methods. Carroll H. Wooddy. LC 73-19188. (Politics & People Ser.). (Illus.). 308p. 1974. reprint ed. 23.95 (0-405-05908-6) Ayer.

Chicago Prop Finders Handbook. Ed. by Christian Maniates. 596p. 1990. write for info. (0-9625639-0-0) Print Grp.

Chicago Prop Finders Handbook: 1991. 3rd ed. Ed. by Chris Maniates. 600p. 1991. write for info. (0-9625639-1-9) Print Grp.

***Chicago Quick Reference.** Nick Pandher. 1994. pap. 9.99 (1-56529-931-0) Que.

Chicago Real Estate Board: The Growth of an Institution. Everett C. Hughes. Ed. by Lewis A. Coser & Walter W. Powell. LC 79-6999. (Perennial Works in Sociology Ser.). 1980. reprint ed. lib. bdg. 18.95 (0-405-12098-2) Ayer.

Chicago Red. R. M. Meluch. 1990. pap. 4.95 (0-451-45034-5, ROC) NAL-Dutton.

Chicago Renaissance in American Letters: A Critical History. Bernard I. Duffey. LC 72-6193. 285p. 1973. reprint ed. text ed. 55.00 (0-8371-6461-3, DUCR, Greenwood Pr) Greenwood.

***Chicago Review Press NCLEX-PN Practice Test & Review.** Ed. by Linda Waide & Berta Roland. 200p. 1995. pap. 15.95 (1-55652-256-8) Chicago Review.

***Chicago Review Press NCLEX-RN Practice Test & Review.** Ed. by Linda Waide & Berta Roland. 240p. 1995. pap. 17.95 (1-55652-255-X) Chicago Review.

Chicago Revival, Eighteen Seventy-Six: Society & Revivalism in a Nineteenth-Century City. Darrel M. Robertson. LC 88-34865. (Studies in Evangelicalism: No. 9). 239p. 1989. 25.00 (0-8108-2181-8) Scarecrow.

Chicago Run. David Robbins. (Endworld Ser.: No. 27). 192p. (Orig.). 1991. pap. 3.50 (0-8439-3145-0) Dorchester Pub Co.

Chicago School: A Liberal Critique of Capitalism. Dennis Smith. LC 87-16680. (Theoretical Traditions in the Social Sciences Ser.). 288p. 1988. text ed. 49.95 (0-312-00384-6); pap. 14.95 (0-312-00386-2) St Martin.

Chicago School: Voices in Liberal Religious Thought. Creighton Peden. LC 87-51605. 220p. (C). 1987. text ed. 29.95 (1-55605-031-3); pap. text ed. 19.95 (1-55605-032-1) Wyndhall Pr.

Chicago School Architects & Their Critics. Wichit Charernbhak. Ed. by Stephen Foster. LC 83-24299. (Architecture & Urban Design Ser.: No. 1). 228p. reprint ed. 65.00 (0-8357-1537-X, 2070330) Bks Demand.

Chicago School Law Survey. Brian A. Braun. 422p. 1992. pap. text ed. 18.00 (1-880331-02-0) IL Assn Sch Bds.

Chicago School of Architecture. Carl W. Condit. LC 64-13287. (Illus.). xvii, 238p. 1973. pap. 24.95 (0-226-11455-4, P540) U Ch Pr.

Chicago School of Political Economy. Ed. by Warren J. Samuels. LC 92-15711. 542p. (C). 1992. pap. 24.95 (1-56000-633-1) Transaction Pubs.

Chicago School of Sociology: Institutionalization, Diversity, & the Rise of Sociological Research. Martin Bulmer. LC 84-8494. (Illus.). xx, 286p. 1986. pap. text ed. 12.95 (0-226-08005-6) U Ch Pr.

Chicago Securities Market: An Original Arno Press Anthology. Ed. by Vincent P. Carosso. LC 75-2627. (Wall Street & the Security Market Ser.). 1975. 18.95 (0-405-06953-7) Ayer.

Chicago Show. Ed. by Robert V. Sharp & Amy Linenthal. (Catalogue Ser.). (Illus.). 48p. 1990. pap. 10.00 (0-938903-09-8) Chi Ofc Fine Arts.

Chicago Six-Guns. Jon Sharpe. (Canyon O'Grady Ser.: No. 24). 176p. (Orig.). 1993. pap. 3.50 (0-451-17529-8, Sig) NAL-Dutton.

Chicago '68. David Farber. (Illus.). xxii, 304p. 1988. 19.95 (0-226-23800-8) U Ch Pr.

Chicago '68. David Farber. (Illus.). xxii, 304p. 1994. pap. 14.95 (0-226-23801-6) U Ch Pr.

Chicago Sketchbook. Robert Tolf. (Great Places Ser.). (Illus.). 144p. 1988. 30.00 (0-923078-00-2) Olendorf Graph.

***Chicago Sketches: Urban Tales, Stories, & Legends from Chicago History.** June S. Sawyers. LC 94-40991. 1995. pap. write for info. (0-8294-0819-3) Loyola.

***Chicago Sketches: Urban Tales, Stories, & Legends from Chicago History.** June S. Sawyers. LC 94-40991. (Illus.). 250p. 1995. 21.95 (0-8294-0820-7, Campion Bks) Loyola Univ Pr.

Chicago Soul. Robert Pruter. (Music in American Life Ser.). (Illus.). 464p. 1992. pap. 21.95 (0-252-06259-0) U of Ill Pr.

Chicago Sourcebook, No. 12: 1992 Edition. (Illus.). 600p. 1991. spiral bd., pap. 50.00 (0-942454-24-3) Black Bk.

Chicago Sourcebook, 1993, No. 13. 374p. Date not set. 50.00 (0-942454-41-3) Black Bk.

Chicago South Shore & South Bend Railroad: How the Medal Was Won. Ed. by Norman Carlson. LC 85-72308. 160p. 1985. 20.00 (0-915348-24-1, B-124) Central Electric.

Chicago Special Occasion Sourcebook. Ed. by Catherine Cox. (Illus.). 160p. (Orig.). 1990. pap. 12.95 (0-9625177-0-4) Reader Bks.

Chicago Special Occasion Sourcebook. 2nd enl. rev. ed. Catherine Cox. (Illus.). 224p. (Orig.). 1992. pap. 15.95 (0-9625177-1-2) Reader Bks.

***Chicago Special Occasion Sourcebook.** 3rd expanded ed. Judith L. Eftekhar. 1994. pap. 19.95 (0-9625177-2-0) Reader Bks.

Chicago Sports Quiz. Brenda Alesii & Daniel Locche. LC 92-19305. (Illus.). 208p. 1992. pap. 9.95 (0-8065-1372-1, Citadel Pr) Carol Pub Group.

Chicago Stained Glass. Erne Frueh & Florence Frueh. (Illus.). 160p. 1983. 19.95 (0-8294-0435-X) Loyola Univ Pr.

***Chicago State Business Handbook.** 400p. (C). 1995. text ed. 495.00 (0-7605-1931-5) Rector Pr.

Chicago Stories: Great Writers on the City. Ed. by John Miller & Genevieve Anderson. LC 92-20490. 256p. 1993. pap. 10.95 (0-8118-0164-0) Chronicle Bks.

Chicago Studies in Political Economy. Ed. by George J. Stigler. (Illus.). 664p. 1988. pap. text ed. 22.50 (0-226-77438-4) U Ch Pr.

Chicago Sun-Times Metro Chicago Almanac - New Edition. Don Hayner. 433p. 1993. pap. 13.00 (0-929387-95-3) Bonus Books.

Chicago Symphony Orchestra. Philo A. Otis. LC 79-37904. (Select Bibliographies Reprint Ser.). 1977. reprint ed. 35.95 (0-8369-6742-9) Ayer.

Chicago Symphony Orchestra: A Critical History. Tom Willis. 288p. Date not set. 35.00 (0-8101-1128-4) Northwestern U Pr.

Chicago Talent Handbook. Julia C. Westrich & Ronda P. Farrell. 124p. 1985. reprint ed. pap. 8.95 (0-914091-82-4) Chicago Review.

Chicago Talent Sourcebook, No. 10. Alexander Communications, Inc. Staff. (Illus.). 600p. 1989. write for info. (0-318-64727-3) Macmillan.

Chicago Taxi Drivers Guide, 1994. Bruce Wolff et al. 1994. pap. write for info. (0-9631365-2-6) Chi Taxi Dr.

Chicago Tenants' Handbook: The Tenants' Rights Bible. 2nd rev. ed. Ed Sacks. 420p. 1992. pap. 16.95 (0-9631224-0-1) Pro Se Pr.

Chicago, the Coloring Book. Lois C. Beh. 16p. (J). (gr. 3). 1990. pap. 3.95 (0-9641328-0-X) Passport Coloring.

Chicago, the Rising City. Thomas Knudtson. LC 75-27770. (Illus.). 1975. pap. 4.95 (0-9603264-0-5) Chicago Publishing.

Chicago To-Day: Or, the Labour War in America. William T. Stead. LC 76-90192. (Mass Violence in America Ser.). (Illus.). 1969. reprint ed. 27.95 (0-405-01337-X) Ayer.

Chicago Tribune Chicagoland Map, 1983-1984. Chicago Tribune Staff. 1983. reprint ed. 195.00 (0-686-40853-5) Chicago Trib.

Chicago Tribune Cookbook: Contemporary & Classic Favorites. Ed. by Jean M. Brownson. LC 89-15899. (Illus.). 752p. 1989. 24.95 (1-55652-069-7) Chicago Review.

Chicago Used Car Seller's Guide, Vol. 1. Kirk Martensen. (Orig.). 1989. pap. 6.95 (0-685-30130-3) Green Light Pr.

***Chicago Visual Reference.** Michael Watson. 1994. pap. 12.99 (1-56529-930-2) Que.

Chicago Ward Maps, Eighteen Thirty-Seven to Nineteen Seventy: Cook County, Chicago Maps. Sherrie A. Styx. (Illus.). 55p. (C). 1989. pap. text ed. 3.00 (1-882121-54-6) Styx Enter.

Chicago White Sox. Richard Rambeck. (Baseball: The Great American Game Ser.). 48p. (J). (gr. 4-10). 1992. lib. bdg. 14.95 (0-88682-448-6) Creative Ed.

Chicago Wipeout. Don Pendleton. (Executioner Ser.: No. 8). 1989. pap. 3.50 (1-55817-067-7, Pinnacle NY) Windsor NY.

Chicago Worker. Vernon M. Briggs et al. LC 76-28237. 143p. reprint ed. pap. 40.80 (0-8357-7729-4, 2036086) Bks Demand.

Chicago Works: A Collection of Chicago Author's Best Stories. Morton Press Staff. Ed. by Laurie Levy. 270p. (Orig.). 1990. 18.95 (0-9625446-0-4); pap. 10.00 (0-9625446-1-2) Morton Pr.

***Chicago Works: Art from the Windy City.** Joyce Fernandes. (Illus.). 52p. 1989. 4.95 (0-9616623-1-X) Erie Art Mus.

Chicago World's Fair of Eighteen Ninety-Three: A Photographic Record. Stanley Appelbaum. (Illus.). 116p. (Orig.). 1980. pap. 9.95 (0-486-23990-X) Dover.

Chicago 1992. Mary A. Mattoon. 550p. 1995. 35.00 (3-85630-538-6, Pub. by Daimon Verlag SZ); pap. 25.00 (3-85630-537-8, Pub. by Daimon Verlag SZ) Atrium Pubs.

***Chicago 1995.** Frommer Staff. 1995. pap. 12.95 (0-614-00677-5) Macmillan.

Chicagoization of America: 1893-1917. Kenan Heise. (Illus.). 256p. (Orig.). 1989. pap. 12.95 (0-924772-01-8) CH Bookworks.

Chicagoland: A World Class Metropolis, English-German. limited ed. Bert Lachner & Associates Staff. LC 94-96081. (Illus.). 246p. (ENG & GER.). 1994. write for info. (0-9640659-0-8) Lachner & Assocs.

Chicagoland & Beyond: Nature & History within 200 Miles. Gerald Gutek & Patricia Gutek. (U. S. A. Guides Ser.). (Illus.). 200p. (Orig.). 1991. pap. 14.95 (0-87052-036-9) Hippocrene Bks.

***Chicagoland Atlas.** 1995. spiral bd. 39.95 (0-933162-83-9) Creative Sales.

***Chicagoland Employment Law Manual.** Ed. by Keith A. Reed & Robert J. Mignin. 456p. 1994. pap. 75.00 (0-614-06735-9) Amer CC Pubs.

Chicagoland Trail Guide. Eileen Kelley. (Orig.). 1993. pap. 10.95 (0-9639686-0-2) Amateur Athlete.

Chicago's Best-Kept Secrets. Mike Michaelson. LC 90-63162. (Illus.). 300p. (Orig.). 1991. pap. 9.95 (0-8442-9636-8, Passport Bks) NTC Pub Grp.

Chicago's Best Restaurants. 7th ed. Sherman Kaplan. (Illus.). 250p. 1994. pap. 9.95 (0-685-73034-4) Surrey Bks.

***Chicago's Best Restaurants.** 7th ed. Sherman Kaplan. 1995. pap. 10.95 (0-940625-94-6) Surrey Bks.

Chicago's Crabgrass Communities: A History of the Independent Suburbs & Their Post Offices That Became Part of Chicago. Harvey M. Karlen. 400p. 1992. write for info. (0-318-69213-9) Collectors Club IL.

***Chicago's Crabgrass Communities: A History of the Independent Suburbs & Their Post Offices That Became Part of Chicago.** Harvey M. Karlen. 400p. 1992. write for info. (0-916675-04-1) Collectors Club IL.

Chicago's Dream, a World's Treasure: The Art Institute of Chicago, 1893-1993. Neil Harris. Ed. by Teri J. Edelstein. (Illus.). 64p. 1993. pap. 9.95 (0-86559-121-0) Art Inst Chi.

Chicago's Famous Buildings: A Photographic Guide to the City's Architectural Landmarks & Other Notable Buildings. enl. rev. ed. Ed. by Franz Schulze & Kevin P. Harrington. LC 92-26334. (Illus.). 300p. (C). 1993. pap. 9.95 (0-226-74062-5) U Ch Pr.

Chicago's Famous Buildings: A Photographic Guide to the City's Architectural Landmarks & Other Notable Buildings. 4th enl. rev. ed. Ed. by Franz Schulze & Kevin P. Harrington. LC 92-26334. (Illus.). 300p. (C). 1993. 19.95 (0-226-74061-7) U Ch Pr.

Chicago's Future in a Time of Change. Ed. by Richard Simpson. 1993. pap. text ed. 24.80 (0-87563-441-9) Stipes.

Chicago's Irish Nationalists, 1881-1890. Michael F. Funchion. LC 76-6342. (Irish Americans Ser.). 1976. 18.95 (0-405-09337-3) Ayer.

Chicago's Museums: A Complete Guide to the City's Cultural Attractions. rev. ed. Victor J. Danilov. LC 90-27049. (Illus.). 304p. 1991. pap. 11.95 (1-55652-135-9) Chicago Review.

Chicago's North Michigan Avenue: Planning & Development, 1900-1930. John W. Stamper. LC 90-43226. (Illus.). 272p. 1991. 45.00 (0-226-77085-0) U Ch Pr.

Chicago's North Shore Shipwrecks. Mark S. Braun. LC 92-25129. (Illus.). 88p. 1992. pap. 17.00 (0-933449-18-6) Transport Trails.

Chicago's One Hundred Menus for 1986. Carla Kelson & Allen Kelson. 208p. (Orig.). 1986. pap. 5.95 (0-9613952-1-4) W F M T Inc.

Chicago's One Hundred Menus for 1987. Carla Kelson & Allen Kelson. 208p. pap. 4.95 (0-9613952-2-2) W F M T Inc.

Chicago's Pride: The Stockyards, Packingtown, & Environs in the Nineteenth Century. Louise C. Wade. LC 85-16525. (Illus.). 440p. 1986. 34.95 (0-252-01266-6) U of Ill Pr.

Chicago's Riverfront: Where the Present Meets the Past. 1991. write for info. (1-880005-00-X) Perspectvs Intl.

Chicago's Schools: 'Worst in America' Chicago Tribune Staff. (Illus.). 208p. (Orig.). 1988. pap. write for info. (0-9621267-0-5) Chicago Trib.

***Chicago's Streetguide to the Supernatural.** Richard Crowe. (Illus.). 1995. spiral bd., pap. 17.50 (0-940542-06-4) Carolando.

Chicago's Trick or Treats: A Chiller Story. J. Abell. 50p. (Orig.). 1993. lib. bdg. 25.00 (1-56611-019-X); pap. 15.00 (1-56611-249-4) Jonas.

Chicago's War on Syphilis, 1937-40: The Times, The Trib & the Clap Doctor. Suzanne Poirier. LC 94-19357. 1995. write for info. (0-252-02147-9) U of Ill Pr.

Chicago's White City of Eighteen Ninety-Three. David F. Burg. LC 75-3542. (Illus.). 400p. 1976. pap. 15.00 (0-8131-0140-9) U Pr of Ky.

1188

An Asterisk (*) at the beginning of an entry indicates that the title is appearing in BIP for the first time.

An Asterisk (*) at the beginning of an entry indicates that the title is appearing in BIP for the first time.

1189

Chicken Little. Illus. by Karen L. Schmidt. (Pudgy Pal Board Bks.). 18p. (J). (ps). 1986. 3.95 (*0-448-10223-4*, G&D) Putnam Pub Group.

Chicken Little & Little Half Chick. Illus. by Berta Hader & Elmer Hader. LC 93-38611. (Little Activity Bks.). (J). 1994. pap. write for info. (*0-486-27979-0*) Dover.

Chicken Little & Little Half Chick. Berta Hader & Elmer Hader. (Little Activity Bks.). (J). (ps-3). 1994. pap. 1.00 (*0-486-27987-1*) Dover.

Chicken Little, Tomato Sauce & Agriculture: Who Will Product Tomorrow's Food. Joan D. Gussow. LC 91-8899. (TOES Bks.). 150p. (Orig.). 1991. pap. 13.50 (*0-942850-32-7*) Intermediate Tech.

***Chicken Little, Tomato Sauce & Agriculture: Who Will Product Tomorrow's Food.** Joan D. Gussow. 150p. (Orig.). 1991. 33.95 (*0-942850-34-3*) Intermediate Tech.

Chicken Little Was Right. Jean Ruryk. 208p. 1994. 18.95 (*0-312-10952-0*, Pub. by Thomas Dunne Bks) St Martin.

Chicken Man. Michelle Edwards. LC 90-32625. (Illus.). (J). (gr. k-3). 1991. 13.95 (*0-688-09708-1*) Lothrop.

Chicken Man. Michelle Edwards. LC 90-32625. (J). (ps-3). 1991. lib. bdg. 13.88 (*0-688-09709-X*) Lothrop.

Chicken Man. Michelle Edwards. LC 93-11728. (Illus.). 32p. (J). (ps up). 1994. reprint ed. pap. 4.95 (*0-688-13106-9*, Mulberry) Morrow.

Chicken on the Farm. Jennifer Coldrey. LC 86-5716. (Animal Habitats Ser.). (Illus.). 32p. (J). (gr. 4-6). 1986. lib. bdg. 17.27 (*1-55532-067-8*) Gareth Stevens Inc.

Chicken on the Grill. (Illus.). 1992. pap. 17.00 (*0-06-096890-7*, PL) HarpC.

Chicken on the Run. Leslie Bloom. Ed. by Marian Levine. 64p. 1988. pap. 3.49 (*0-942320-31-X*) Am Cooking.

Chicken: One Hundred One Ways to Cook Your Bird. Janice M. Fukuhara. (Illus.). 230p. 1987. ring bd. 8.50 (*0-9619287-0-0*) Kelcis.

Chicken or the Egg? Allan Fowler. LC 92-35054. (Rookie Read-about Science Ser.). (Illus.). 32p. (J). (ps-2). 1993. 23.48 (*0-516-49639-5*); lib. bdg. 11.93 (*0-516-06008-2*); pap. 3.95 (*0-516-46008-0*) Childrens.

***Chicken Parts.** Pierce. write for info. (*0-517-70135-9*) Random Hse Value.

Chicken Pox. Shen Roddie. LC 92-53851. (Illus.). (J). 1993. 14.95 (*0-316-75347-5*, Joy St Bks) Little.

***Chicken Pox Christmas.** Bobbi McPeak-Bailey. (Illus.). 64p. (Orig.). (J). (gr. k-4). 1994. pap. 9.95 (*0-9625005-2-6*) Wee Pr.

***Chicken Pox Panic.** Beverly Lewis. (Cul-De-Sac Kids Ser.). 80p. 1995. mass mkt. 2.99 (*1-55661-626-0*) Bethany Hse.

Chicken Pox Panic. Squeaky Sneaker Books Staff. (J). (ps-3). 1993. pap. 3.95 (*1-56233-176-0*, Squeaky Sneaker) Star Song TN.

Chicken Salad Soup. (Illus.). (J). (ps-2). 1991. lib. bdg. 8.99 (*0-8136-5146-8*) Modern Curr.

Chicken Salads: More Than Fifty Scrumptious Recipes for an American Classic. Carole Lalli. 128p. (Orig.). 1994. pap. 10.00 (*0-06-095062-5*, PL) HarpC.

Chicken Sampler. Jan Siegrist. (Illus.). 48p. (Orig.). 1993. pap. 3.95 (*0-933050-96-8*) New Eng Pr VT.

Chicken Scratch. Barbara Gregorich. Ed. by Joan Hoffman. (Fast Forward Enrichment Ser.). 32p. (Orig.). (J). (ps-1). 1986. student ed 1.99 (*0-88743-127-5*) Sch Zone Pub Co.

Chicken Smells Good. William P. Pickett. LC 83-3420. (Illus.). 224p. (C). 1983. pap. text ed. 12.75 (*0-13-130260-4*) P-H.

Chicken Socks: And Other Contagious Poems. Brod Bagert. (Illus.). 32p. (J). (gr. 3-7). 1994. 15.95 (*1-56397-292-1*, Wordsong) Boyds Mills Pr.

Chicken Soup. Joan Wilen & Lydia Wilen. 1985. pap. 11.00 (*0-449-90190-4*) Fawcett.

Chicken Soup: Thirty-Eight Easy Recipes from Classic to New. Linda Zimmerman. LC 93-19280. (Illus.). 1993. 11.00 (*0-517-58622-3*, C P Pubs) Crown Pub Group.

Chicken Soup & Other Folk Remedies. Lydia Wilen & Joan Wilen. 192p. (Orig.). 1984. mass mkt. 4.95 (*0-449-90109-2*, Columbine) Fawcett.

Chicken Soup & Other Yiddish Sayings. Peggy Schaffer. 168p. (Orig.). 1993. pap. 5.95 (*1-56245-069-7*) Great Quotations.

Chicken Soup Book. Janet Hazen. LC 93-39580. (Illus.). 1994. 14.95 (*0-8118-0461-5*) Chronicle Bks.

Chicken Soup, Boots. Maira Kalman. (Illus.). 40p. (J). 1993. 15.00 (*0-670-85201-5*) Viking Child Bks.

Chicken Soup for the Soul. Jack Canfield. 1993. 24.00 (*1-55874-291-3*) Health Comm.

Chicken Soup for the Soul: One-Hundred One Stories to Open the Heart & Rekindle the Spirit. Jack Canfield & Mark Hansen. 320p. (Orig.). 1993. pap. 12.95 (*1-55874-262-X*, 262X) Health Comm.

***Chicken Soup for the Soul Cookbook: Recipes & Stories from the Hearth.** Jack Canfield et al. 480p. 1995. 29.95 (*1-55874-363-4*); pap. 16.95 (*1-55874-354-5*) Health Comm.

Chicken Soup with Rice. Maurice Sendak. (Illus.). 48p. (J). (ps-3). 1962. lib. bdg. 13.89 (*0-06-025535-8*) HarpC Child Bks.

Chicken Soup with Rice. Maurice Sendak. (Illus.). 32p. (J). (gr. k-3). 1986. Big book. 19.95 (*0-590-64645-1*); pap. 2.50 (*0-590-41033-4*) Scholastic Inc.

Chicken Soup with Rice. Maurice Sendak. (Big Book Ser.). (J). (ps-3). 1992. pap. 19.95 (*0-590-71789-8*) Scholastic Inc.

Chicken Soup with Rice: A Book of Months. Maurice Sendak. LC 62-13315. (Trophy Picture Bk.). (Illus.). 32p. (J). (ps-3). 1991. pap. 3.95 (*0-06-443253-X*, Trophy) HarpC Child Bks.

Chicken Soup with Rice see Nutshell Library

Chicken Sunday. Patricia Polacco. (Illus.). 32p. (J). (ps-3). 1992. lib. bdg. 14.95 (*0-399-22133-6*, Philomel Bks) Putnam Pub Group.

Chicken That Could Swim. Paul Adshead. LC 90-34358. (J). (ps-3). 1990. 11.95 (*0-85953-294-1*); pap. 5.95 (*0-85953-346-8*) Childs Play.

Chicken That Won a Dogfight: The Humor & Hope of an Arkansas Boyhood. Ben Burton. LC 92-35636. 159p. 1993. 17.95 (*0-87483-259-4*); pap. 8.95 (*0-87483-258-6*) August Hse.

Chicken Today, Feathers Tomorrow. Belle T. Hinther. 329p. (Orig.). 1985. pap. 12.95 (*0-9619970-0-1*) Blue Sky Bks.

Chicken Tommy & Other Stories. Richard L. Thomas. (Illus.). 286p. (Orig.). 1994. pap. 14.95 (*1-878044-16-8*) Mayhaven Pub.

Chicken Toons. Branko E. Romano. LC 82-83844. 1982. pap. 2.00 (*0-89229-010-2*) TQS Pubns.

Chicken Tractor: The Gardener's Guide to Happy Hens & Healthy Soil. Andy Lee. LC 92-76194. (Illus.). 232p. 1995. pap. 15.95 (*0-9624648-2-1*) Good Earth Pubns.

***Chicken War & Other Wild Stories about Texas: The Era of the Missions.** Patrick M. Reynolds. (Texas Lore Ser.). (Illus.). 104p. (Orig.). 1995. pap. 6.95 (*0-932514-30-8*) Red Rose Studio.

Chicken Without a Head: A New Version. Charles Simic. (Poetry Ser.). (Illus.). 20p. (Orig.). 1983. pap. 7.50 (*0-317-39880-6*) Seluzicki Fine Bks.

Chicken Without a Head: A New Version. deluxe ed. Charles Simic. (Poetry Ser.). (Illus.). 20p. (Orig.). 1983. 15.00 (*0-317-39881-4*) Seluzicki Fine Bks.

Chickencoop Chinaman & The Year of the Dragon: Two Plays. Frank Chin. LC 81-985. (Illus.). 172p. 1981. pap. 14.95 (*0-295-95833-2*) U of Wash Pr.

Chickenhawk. Robert C. Mason. 476p. 1984. pap. 10.00 (*0-14-007218-7*, Penguin Bks) Viking Penguin.

Chickenhawk: Back in the World: Life after Vietnam. Robert Mason. (Illus.). 400p. 1994. pap. 10.95 (*0-14-015876-6*, Penguin Bks) Viking Penguin.

Chickenhouse House. Ellen Howard. LC 90-38007. (Illus.). 64p. (J). (gr. 2-5). 1991. text ed. 12.95 (*0-689-31695-X*, Atheneum Bks Young) S&S Childrens.

Chickens. Lynn Stone. (Farm Animals Discovery Library). (Illus.). 24p. (J). (gr. k-5). 1990. lib. bdg. 11.94 (*0-86593-034-1*); lib. bdg. 8.95 (*0-685-36308-2*) Rourke Corp.

Chickens Are Restless. Gary Larson. (Illus.). 96p. (Orig.). 1993. pap. 8.95 (*0-8362-1717-9*) Andrews & McMeel.

Chickens Aren't the Only Ones. Ruth Heller. LC 80-85257. (Illus.). 48p. (J). (ps-1). 1981. 10.95 (*0-448-01872-1*, G&D) Putnam Pub Group.

Chickens Aren't the Only Ones. Ruth Heller. (Sandcastle Ser.). (Illus.). 48p. (J). (ps-3). 1993. pap. 6.95 (*0-448-40454-0*, G&D) Putnam Pub Group.

***Chickens! Chickens!** Barbara A. Porte. LC 94-19552. (J). (ps-3). 1995. lib. bdg. 14.99 (*0-531-08727-1*) Orchard Bks Watts.

***Chickens! Chickens!** Barbara A. Porte. LC 94-19552. (Illus.). 32p. (J). (ps-2). 1995. 14.95 (*0-531-06877-3*) Orchard Bks Watts.

Chickens in the Greenhouse: And Other Wyoming Escapades. Sandra Guzzo. LC 85-31719. 96p. (Orig.). 1986. pap. 9.95 (*0-931271-03-7*) Hi Plains Pr.

Chickens in Your Backyard. Rick Luttmann & Gail Luttmann. LC 76-14357. 168p. 1976. pap. 9.95 (*0-87857-125-6*, 13-488-1) Rodale Pr Inc.

Chickens of the Interventionist Liberals Have Come to Roost. Harry E. Barnes. 1971. 250.00 (*0-87700-194-4*) Revisionist Pr.

Chicken...with Love. Jeannine B. Browning. 1994. pap. write for info. (*0-9627729-8-4*) J B Browning.

***Chickie Riddles.** Katy Hall & Lisa Eisenberg. LC 94-33170. (Illus.). (J). 1997. write for info. (*0-8037-1778-4*); lib. bdg. write for info. (*0-8037-1779-2*) Dial Bks Young.

Chickie Stop & Go. Gorbaty. (Pet Parade Bks.). (J). 1995. 4.50 (*0-671-89836-1*, Litl Simon S&S) S&S Childrens.

***Chicks: A Man's Guide to Gettin' Some.** Jim Florentine. 118p. Date not set. pap. 7.95 (*0-9645555-0-6*) Florentine Pub.

Chicks & Ducks...As Pets. Jack C. Harris. (TS Ser.). (Illus.). 64p. 1992. pap. 3.95 (*0-86622-431-9*, TS-215) TFH Pubns.

***Chicks in Chainmail.** Ed. by Esther Friesner. 1995. mass mkt. 5.99 (*0-671-87682-1*) Baen Bks.

Chicks' Trick. Photos & Text by Jeni Bassett. LC 93-18471. (J). 1995. 13.99 (*0-525-65152-7*, Cobblehill Bks) Dutton Child Bks.

Chicksands: A Millennium of History. William C. Grayson. 350p. 1992. pap. 21.95 (*0-9633208-0-7*) Shefford Pr.

Chico Mendes: Defender of the Rain Forest. Joann Burch. (Gateway Greens Ser.). (Illus.). 48p. (J). (gr. 2-4). 1994. lib. bdg. 13.40 (*1-56294-413-4*) Millbrook Pr.

Chico Mendes: Fight for the Forest. Susan DeStefano. (Earth Keepers Ser.). (Illus.). 76p. (J). (gr. 4-7). 1992. lib. bdg. 14.98 (*0-8050-2887-0*) TFC Bks NY.

Chico the Street Boy. Evelyn Puig. (Illus.). 85p. (J). (gr. 4-8). 1991. 3.95 (*0-901269-79-4*) Grosvenor USA.

Chicorel Abstracts to Reading & Learning Disabilities. 1, 983th ed. Ed. by Robert E. Lynn. (Chicorel Index Ser.: Vol. 19). 325p. 1984. text ed. 125.00 (*0-934598-85-1*) Am Lib Pub Co.

Chicorel Abstracts to Reading & Learning Disabilities: Periodicals, 1978 Annual. (Chicorel Index Ser.: Vol. 19). 584p. 1979. 125.00 (*0-934598-16-9*) Am Lib Pub Co.

Chicorel Abstracts to Reading & Learning Disabilities: Periodicals, 1979 Annual. (Chicorel Index Ser.: Vol. 19). 414p. 1980. 125.00 (*0-934598-10-X*) Am Lib Pub Co.

Chicorel Abstracts to Reading & Learning Disabilities: 1977 Annual. Ed. by Marietta Chicorel. (Chicorel Index Ser.: Vol. 19). 1977. text ed. 125.00 (*0-934598-17-7*) Am Lib Pub Co.

Chicorel Abstracts to Reading & Learning Disabilities, Periodicals, 1980 Annual. Ed. by Marietta Chicorel. (Chicorel Index Ser.: Vol. 19). (Illus.). 380p. 1982. 125.00 (*0-934598-80-0*) Am Lib Pub Co.

Chicorel Abstracts to Reading & Learning Disabilities, 1976 Annual. Marietta Chicorel. (Chicorel Index Ser.: Vol. 19). 384p. 1976. text ed. 125.00 (*0-934598-15-0*) Am Lib Pub Co.

Chicorel Abstracts to Reading & Learning Disabilities, 1981. Ed. by Robert E. Lynn. (Chicorel Index Ser.: Vol. 19). 490p. 1983. 125.00 (*0-934598-83-5*) Am Lib Pub Co.

Chicorel Abstracts to Reading & Learning Disabilities, 1982. Ed. by Robert E. Lynn. (Chicorel Index Ser.: Vol. 19). 424p. 1984. 125.00 (*0-934598-84-3*) Am Lib Pub Co.

Chicorel Bibliography to Books on Music & Musicians. Ed. by Marietta Chicorel. LC 74-161012. (Chicorel Index Ser.: Vol. 10). 500p. 1974. 125.00 (*0-934598-18-5*) Am Lib Pub Co.

Chicorel Bibliography to the Performing Arts. Ed. by Marietta Chicorel. LC 73-155102. (Chicorel Index Ser.: Vol. 3A). 498p. reprint ed. pap. 142.00 (*0-7837-3086-1*, 2057605) Bks Demand.

Chicorel Index to Abstracting & Indexing, 2 vols., Set. 2nd ed. Marietta Chicorel. (Chicorel Index Ser.: Vols. 11 & 11A). 1978. text ed. 250.00 (*0-934598-20-7*) Am Lib Pub Co.

Chicorel Index to Biographies, Vol. 15. Ed. by Marietta Chicorel. LC 74-175082. (Chicorel Index Ser.: Vol. 15 & 15a). 475p. reprint ed. pap. 135.40 (*0-7837-3105-1*, 2057613) Bks Demand.

Chicorel Index to Biographies, Vol. 15A. Ed. by Marietta Chicorel. LC 74-175082. (Chicorel Index Ser.: Vol. 15 & 15a). 426p. reprint ed. pap. 121.50 (*0-7837-3106-X*, 2057613) Bks Demand.

Chicorel Index to Environment & Ecology, Vol. 16. Ed. by Marietta Chicorel. LC 75-306805. (Chicorel Index Ser.: Vol. 16 & 16A). 392p. reprint ed. pap. 111.80 (*0-7837-3107-8*, 2057614) Bks Demand.

Chicorel Index to Environment & Ecology, Vol. 16A. Ed. by Marietta Chicorel. LC 75-306805. (Chicorel Index Ser.: Vol. 16 & 16A). 355p. reprint ed. pap. 101.20 (*0-7837-3108-6*, 2057614) Bks Demand.

Chicorel Index to Film Literature, Vol. 22. Ed. by Marietta Chicorel. LC 75-22340. (Chicorel Index Ser.: Vol. 22 & 22A). 454p. reprint ed. pap. 129.40 (*0-7837-3114-0*, 2057618) Bks Demand.

Chicorel Index to Film Literature, Vol. 22A. Ed. by Marietta Chicorel. LC 75-22340. (Chicorel Index Ser.: Vol. 22 & 22A). 467p. reprint ed. pap. 133.10 (*0-7837-3115-9*, 2057618) Bks Demand.

Chicorel Index to Learning Disorders, 2 vols., 18. Ed. by Marietta Chicorel. LC 75-9713. (Chicorel Index Ser.: Vols. 18 & 18A). 1000p. 1975. write for info. (*0-934598-30-4*) Am Lib Pub Co.

Chicorel Index to Learning Disorders, 2 vols., 18A. Ed. by Marietta Chicorel. LC 75-9713. (Chicorel Index Ser.: Vols. 18 & 18A). 1000p. 1975. write for info. (*0-934598-31-2*) Am Lib Pub Co.

Chicorel Index to Learning Disorders, 2 vols., Set. Ed. by Marietta Chicorel. LC 75-9713. (Chicorel Index Ser.: Vols. 18 & 18A). 1000p. 1975. 250.00 (*0-934598-32-0*) Am Lib Pub Co.

Chicorel Index to Literary Criticism in Books: U. S. A., Canada. Ed. by Marietta Chicorel. LC 79-116354. (Chicorel Index Ser.: Vol. 23). 350p. reprint ed. pap. 99.80 (*0-7837-3116-7*, 2057619) Bks Demand.

Chicorel Index to Mental Health Book Reviews: 1977 Annual. (Chicorel Index Ser.: Vol. 26). 400p. 1978. 125.00 (*0-934598-77-0*) Am Lib Pub Co.

Chicorel Index to Mental Health Book Reviews: 1978 Annual. (Chicorel Index Ser.: Vol. 26). 400p. 1980. 125.00 (*0-934598-08-8*) Am Lib Pub Co.

Chicorel Index to Mental Health Book Reviews: 1979 Annual. (Chicorel Index Ser.: Vol. 26). 400p. 1980. 125.00 (*0-934598-79-7*) Am Lib Pub Co.

Chicorel Index to Mental Health Book Reviews, 1974 Annual. Ed. by Marietta Chicorel. (Chicorel Index Ser.: Vol. 26). 322p. 1982. 125.00 (*0-934598-81-9*) Am Lib Pub Co.

Chicorel Index to Mental Health Book Reviews, 1975 Annual. Ed. by Marietta Chicorel. (Chicorel Index Ser.: Vol. 26). 287p. 1982. 125.00 (*0-934598-82-7*) Am Lib Pub Co.

Chicorel Index to Mental Health Book Reviews, 1980-84, 3 vols. Ed. by Marietta S. Chicorel. (Chicorel Index Ser.: Vol. 26). 1986. 375.00 (*0-934598-93-2*) Am Lib Pub Co.

Chicorel Index to Parapsychology & Occult. Ed. by Marietta Chicorel. (Chicorel Index Ser.: Vol. 24). 1978. text ed. 125.00 (*0-934598-33-9*) Am Lib Pub Co.

Chicorel Index to Poetry & Poets: Literature, Vol. 20. Ed. by Marietta Chicorel. LC 75-40039. (Chicorel Index Ser.: Vol. 20 & 20A). 472p. reprint ed. pap. 134.60 (*0-7837-3111-6*, 2057616) Bks Demand.

Chicorel Index to Poetry & Poets: Literature, Vol. 20A. Ed. by Marietta Chicorel. LC 75-40039. (Chicorel Index Ser.: Vol. 20 & 20A). 555p. reprint ed. pap. 158.20 (*0-7837-3112-4*, 2057616) Bks Demand.

Chicorel Index to Poetry in Anthologies & Collections: Retrospective, Vol. 6. Ed. by Marietta Chicorel. LC 75-9587. (Chicorel Index Ser.: Vols. 6, 6A, 6B & 6C). 461p. reprint ed. pap. 131.40 (*0-7837-3091-8*, 2057607) Bks Demand.

Chicorel Index to Poetry in Anthologies & Collections: Retrospective, Vol. 6A. Ed. by Marietta Chicorel. LC 75-9587. (Chicorel Index Ser.: Vols. 6, 6A, 6B & 6C). 465p. reprint ed. pap. 132.60 (*0-7837-3092-6*, 2057607) Bks Demand.

Chicorel Index to Poetry in Anthologies & Collections: Retrospective, Vol. 6B. Ed. by Marietta Chicorel. LC 75-9587. (Chicorel Index Ser.: Vols. 6, 6A, 6B & 6C). 456p. reprint ed. pap. 130.00 (*0-7837-3093-4*, 2057607) Bks Demand.

Chicorel Index to Poetry in Anthologies & Collections: Retrospective, Vol. 6C. Ed. by Marietta Chicorel. LC 75-9587. (Chicorel Index Ser.: Vols. 6, 6A, 6B & 6C). 483p. reprint ed. pap. 137.70 (*0-7837-3094-2*, 2057607) Bks Demand.

Chicorel Index to Poetry in Anthologies & Collections in Print, Vol. 5. Ed. by Marietta Chicorel. LC 74-195254. (Chicorel Index Ser.: Vols. 5, 5A, 5B & 5C). 450p. reprint ed. pap. 128.30 (*0-7837-3087-X*, 2057606) Bks Demand.

Chicorel Index to Poetry in Anthologies & Collections in Print, Vol. 5A. Ed. by Marietta Chicorel. LC 74-195254. (Chicorel Index Ser.: Vols. 5, 5A, 5B & 5C). 455p. reprint ed. pap. 129.70 (*0-7837-3088-8*, 2057606) Bks Demand.

Chicorel Index to Poetry in Anthologies & Collections in Print, Vol. 5B. Ed. by Marietta Chicorel. LC 74-195254. (Chicorel Index Ser.: Vols. 5, 5A, 5B & 5C). 355p. reprint ed. pap. 101.20 (*0-7837-3089-6*, 2057606) Bks Demand.

Chicorel Index to Poetry in Anthologies & Collections in Print, Vol. 5C. Ed. by Marietta Chicorel. LC 74-195254. (Chicorel Index Ser.: Vols. 5, 5A, 5B & 5C). 452p. reprint ed. pap. 128.90 (*0-7837-3090-X*, 2057606) Bks Demand.

Chicorel Index to Poetry in Anthologies, 1975-1977, 2 vols., 5. Ed. by Marietta Chicorel. (Chicorel Index Ser.: Vols. 5 & 5A). 1979. write for info. (*0-934598-11-8*) Am Lib Pub Co.

Chicorel Index to Poetry in Anthologies, 1975-1977, 2 vols., 5A. Ed. by Marietta Chicorel. (Chicorel Index Ser.: Vols. 5 & 5A). 1979. write for info. (*0-934598-12-6*) Am Lib Pub Co.

Chicorel Index to Poetry in Anthologies, 1975-1977, 2 vols., Set. 2nd ed. Ed. by Marietta Chicorel. (Chicorel Index Ser.: Vols. 5 & 5A). 1979. text ed. 250.00 (*0-934598-13-4*) Am Lib Pub Co.

Chicorel Index to Poetry in Collections on Discs & Tapes. Ed. by Marietta Chicorel. LC 71-106198. (Chicorel Index Ser.: Vol. 4). 443p. 1972. 125.00 (*0-934598-48-7*) Am Lib Pub Co.

Chicorel Index to Reading & Learning Disabilities: An Annotated Guide, 1976. Ed. by Marietta Chicorel. (Chicorel Index Ser.: Vol. 14A). 1976. 125.00 (*0-934598-49-5*) Am Lib Pub Co.

Chicorel Index to Reading & Learning Disabilities: Books, 1977 Annual. Ed. by Marietta Chicorel. LC 76-14381. (Chicorel Index Ser.: Vol. 14A). 1977. text ed. 125.00 (*0-934598-50-9*) Am Lib Pub Co.

Chicorel Index to Reading & Learning Disabilities: Books, 1978 Annual. (Chicorel Index Ser.: Vol. 14A). 400p. 1980. 125.00 (*0-934598-09-6*) Am Lib Pub Co.

Chicorel Index to Reading Disabilities: An Annotated Guide. Ed. by Marietta Chicorel. (Chicorel Index Ser.: Vol. 14). 500p. 1974. 125.00 (*0-934598-51-7*) Am Lib Pub Co.

Chicorel Index to Short Stories: 1977 Edition, 2 vols., 12. Ed. by Marietta Chicorel. (Chicorel Index Ser.: Vols. 12 & 12A). 1977. write for info. (*0-934598-06-1*) Am Lib Pub Co.

Chicorel Index to Short Stories: 1977 Edition, 2 vols., 12A. Ed. by Marietta Chicorel. (Chicorel Index Ser.: Vols. 12 & 12A). 1977. write for info. (*0-934598-07-X*) Am Lib Pub Co.

Chicorel Index to Short Stories: 1977 Edition, 2 vols., Set. 2nd ed. Ed. by Marietta Chicorel. (Chicorel Index Ser.: Vols. 12 & 12A). 1977. text ed. 250.00 (*0-934598-05-3*) Am Lib Pub Co.

Chicorel Index to Short Stories in Anthologies & Collections, Vol. 12. Ed. by Marietta Chicorel. LC 75-330087. (Chicorel Index Ser.: Vol. 12, 12A, 12B, & 12C). 391p. reprint ed. pap. 111.50 (*0-7837-3098-5*, 2057611) Bks Demand.

Chicorel Index to Short Stories in Anthologies & Collections, Vol. 12A. Ed. by Marietta Chicorel. LC 75-330087. (Chicorel Index Ser.: Vol. 12, 12A, 12B, & 12C). 428p. reprint ed. pap. 122.00 (*0-7837-3099-3*, 2057611) Bks Demand.

Chicorel Index to Short Stories in Anthologies & Collections, Vol. 12B. Ed. by Marietta Chicorel. LC 75-330087. (Chicorel Index Ser.: Vol. 12, 12A, 12B, & 12C). 566p. reprint ed. pap. 161.40 (*0-7837-3100-0*, 2057611) Bks Demand.

Chicorel Index to Short Stories in Anthologies & Collections, Vol. 12C. Ed. by Marietta Chicorel. LC 75-330087. (Chicorel Index Ser.: Vol. 12, 12A, 12B, & 12C). 539p. reprint ed. pap. 153.70 (*0-7837-3101-9*, 2057611) Bks Demand.

Chicorel Index to the Crafts, Vol. 13: Needlework: Crocheting to Tie-Dyeing. Ed. by Marietta Chicorel. LC 74-195924. (Chicorel Index Ser.: Vol. 13, 13A & 13C). 428p. reprint ed. Vol. 13, Needlework: Crocheting to Tie-Dyeing, 428p. pap. 122.00 (*0-7837-3102-7*, 2057612) Bks Demand.

Chicorel Index to the Crafts, Vol. 13A: Glass, Enamel, Metal. Ed. by Marietta Chicorel. LC 74-195924. (Chicorel Index Ser.: Vol. 13, 13A & 13C). 507p. reprint ed. Vol. 13A, Glass, Enamel, Metal, 507p. pap. 144.50 (*0-7837-3103-5*, 2057612) Bks Demand.

Chicorel Index to the Crafts, Vol. 13C: Education, Recreation, Therapy. Ed. by Marietta Chicorel. LC 74-195924. (Chicorel Index Ser.: Vol. 13, 13A & 13C). 500p. reprint ed. Vol. 13C, Education, Recreation, Therapy, 500p. pap. 142.50 (*0-7837-3104-3*, 2057612) Bks Demand.

C

An Asterisk (*) at the beginning of an entry indicates that the title is appearing in BIP for the first time.

C

An Asterisk (*) at the beginning of an entry indicates that the title is appearing in BIP for the first time.

Chief Rabbi, the Pope, & the Holocaust: An Era in Vatican-Jewish Relations. Robert G. Weisbord & Wallace P. Sillanpoa. 224p. (C). 1991. 34.95 (0-88738-416-1) Transaction Pubs.

Chief Recreation Therapist. Jack Rudman. (Career Examination Ser.: C-3279). 1994. pap. 39.95 (0-8373-3279-6) Nat Learn.

Chief Registrar. Jack Rudman. (Career Examination Ser.: C-1183). 1994. pap. 34.95 (0-8373-1183-7) Nat Learn.

Chief Resident As Manager. Neal A. Whitman et al. 143p. (Orig.). 1988. pap. text ed. 20.00 (0-940193-05-1) Univ UT Sch Med.

Chief Rivals of Corneille & Racine. Tr. by Lacy Lockert. LC 56-14366. 1956. 29.95 (0-8265-1047-7) Vanderbilt U Pr.

Chief S. Ladoke Akintola: His Life & Times. Akinjide Osuntokun. (Illus.). 212p. 1984. text ed. 29.50 (0-7146-3219-8, BHA-00169, Pub. by F Cass Pubs UK) Intl Spec Bk.

***Chief Safety & Security Officer.** (Career Examination Ser.: Series 1). Date not set. pap. 39.95 (0-8373-3629-5) Nat Learn.

Chief Sarah: Sarah Winnemucca's Fight for Indian Rights. Dorothy N. Morrison. (Eager Beaver Bks.). (Illus.). 192p. (J). (gr. 4 up). 1990. reprint ed. pap. 7.95 (0-87595-204-6) Oregon Hist.

Chief Schedule Maker. Jack Rudman. (Career Examination Ser.: C-1729). 1994. pap. 39.95 (0-8373-1729-0) Nat Learn.

Chief Seattle. (Northwest Mythic Landscape Ser.). (Illus.). 28p. (Orig.). 1992. text ed. 5.95 (0-912365-57-9) Sasquatch Bks.

***Chief Seattle & the Indian in the Moon: The Legend of Star Child & Mud Child.** LC 94-34477. (Illus.). (J). (gr. 3 up). 1996. lib. bdg. write for info. (0-8037-1614-1) Dial Bks Young.

***Chief Seattle & the Indian in the Moon: The Legend of Star Child & Mud Child.** Illus. by Jewell P. W. James & Darby A. James. LC 94-34477. (J). (gr. 3 up). 1996. write for info. (0-8037-1613-3) Dial Bks Young.

Chief Seattle's Unanswered Challenge. John M. Rich. 61p. 1977. reprint ed. pap. 7.50 (0-87770-072-9) Ye Galleon.

Chief Security Officer. Jack Rudman. (Career Examination Ser.: C-1185). 1994. pap. 34.95 (0-8373-1185-3) Nat Learn.

Chief Sewage Treatment Plant Operator. (Career Examination Ser.: C-2434). 1994. pap. 39.95 (0-8373-2434-3) Nat Learn.

Chief Shabbona's Path of Peace. Alice F. Zeman. (Illus.). 1986. 3.00 (0-9633266-1-9) A Zeman.

Chief Sitting Bull. Alan Grey. (American Indian Chiefs & Leaders Ser.). (Illus.). 64p. (J). 1993. pap. 5.00 (1-56883-031-9) Colonial Pr AL.

Chief Sitting Bull. abr. ed. Alan Grey. 40p. (J). 1994. pap. 6.95 (1-56901-427-2) NW Pub.

Chief Special Investigator. Jack Rudman. (Career Examination Ser.: C-1591). 1994. pap. 39.95 (0-8373-1591-3) Nat Learn.

Chief Stationary Engineer. Jack Rudman. (Career Examination Ser.: C-1184). 1994. pap. 39.95 (0-8373-1184-5) Nat Learn.

Chief Stephen's Parky: One Year in the Life of an Athapascan Girl. Ann Chandonnet. Ed. by Hap Gilliland. (Indian Culture Ser.). (Illus.). 72p. (Orig.). (J). (gr. 4-12). 1989. pap. 7.95 (0-89992-119-1) Coun India Ed.

Chief Stephen's Parky: One Year in the Life of An Athapascan Girl. 2nd ed. Ann Chandonnet. LC 92-61910. (Council for Indian Education Ser.). (Illus.). 80p. (J). (gr. 4-6). 1993. reprint ed. pap. 7.95 (1-879373-39-4) R Rinehart.

Chief Student Affairs Officer: Leader, Manager, Mediator, Educator. Arthur Sandeen. LC 90-28987. (Higher & Adult Education Ser.). 255p. 1991. 29.95 (1-55542-351-5) Jossey-Bass.

Chief Supervisor of Mechanical Installations. Jack Rudman. (Career Examination Ser.: C-2482). 1994. pap. 39.95 (0-8373-2482-3) Nat Learn.

Chief Support Investigator. Jack Rudman. (Career Examination Ser.: C-2767). 1994. pap. 39.95 (0-8373-2767-9) Nat Learn.

Chief Surface Line Dispatcher. Jack Rudman. (Career Examination Ser.: C-944). 1994. pap. 29.95 (0-8373-0944-1) Nat Learn.

Chief Technology Officer. Thomas B. Cross. 300p. 1990. 24.95 (0-685-34871-7) Smith Micro.

***Chief, the Reporters Are Here! The Police Executive's Personal Guide to Press Relations.** Gerald W. Garner. 194p. 1987. pap. 29.95 (0-398-06144-0) C C Thomas.

Chief, the Reporters Are Here! The Police Executive's Personal Guide to Press Relations. Gerald W. Garner. 194p. 1987. 45.95x (0-398-05321-9) C C Thomas.

Chief Truths of the Faith: Creation, Original Sin, Christ, Faith, Grace, Eternal Life, Etc. John Laux. LC 90-70439. (Course in Religion for Catholic High Schools & Academies Ser.: Bk. I). (Illus.). 179p. 1990. reprint ed. pap. text ed. 8.00 (0-89555-391-0) TAN Bks Pubs.

Chief Water Pollution Control Inspector. Jack Rudman. (Career Examination Ser.: C-1187). 1994. pap. 39.95 (0-8373-1187-X) Nat Learn.

Chief Water Treatment Plant Operator. Jack Rudman. (Career Examination Ser.: C-2149). 1994. pap. 39.95 (0-8373-2149-2) Nat Learn.

Chief William McIntosh: A Man of Two Worlds. George Chapman. LC 88-11872. (Illus.). 160p. 1987. 13.95 (0-87797-133-1) Cherokee.

Chiefdoms: Power, Economy & Ideology. Ed. by Timothy K. Earle. (School of American Research Advanced Seminar Ser.). (Illus.). 336p. (C). 1991. 74.95 (0-521-40190-9) Cambridge U Pr.

Chiefdoms: Power, Economy & Ideology. Ed. by Timothy K. Earle. (School of American Research Advanced Seminar Ser.). (Illus.). 336p. (C). 1993. pap. write for info. (0-521-44801-8) Cambridge U Pr.

Chiefdoms & Early States in the Near East: The Organizational Dynamics of Complexity. Ed. by Mitchell S. Rothman. LC 94-10284. (Monographs in World Archaeology: No. 18). (Illus.). 248p. 1994. pap. 35.00 (1-881094-07-3) Prehistory Pr.

Chiefly Feasts: The Enduring Kwakiutl Potlatch. Ed. by Aldona Jonaitis. LC 91-16778. (Illus.). 300p. 1991. 60.00 (0-295-97114-2) U of Wash Pr.

Chiefs. Edwin Bramall & William Jackson. (Illus.). 272p. 1992. text ed. 39.95 (0-08-040370-0, Pub. by Brasseys UK) Brasseys Inc.

Chiefs. Rotary Club of Chester, South Carolina Staff. Ed. by Tommy Grant & Sandy Wilson. LC 83-73060. 128p. 1983. 16.95 (0-912081-01-5) Delmar Co.

Chiefs. Stuart Woods. 432p. 1987. mass mkt. 5.99 (0-380-70347-5) Avon.

Chiefs. Stuart Woods. 1981. 14.95 (0-393-01461-4) Norton.

Chiefs, Agents & Soldiers: Conflict on the Navajo Frontier, 1868-1882. William H. Moore. LC 93-35896. 380p. 1994. 45.00x (0-8263-1475-9) U of NM Pr.

Chiefs & Chief Traders: Indian Relations at Fort Nez Perces, 1818-1855. Theodore Stern. LC 92-31671. (Illus.). 288p. 1993. text ed. 35.95x (0-87071-368-X) Oreg St U Pr.

Chiefs & Cities of Central Africa: Across Lake Chad by Way of British, French, & German Territories. Olive MacLeod. LC 78-161269. (Illus.). 408p. 1977. reprint ed. 36.95 (0-8369-8828-0) Ayer.

Chiefs & Leading Families in Rajputana. C. S. Bayley. (C). 1992. 16.00 (81-85326-58-4, Pub. by Vintage II) S Asia.

Chiefs & Politicians: The Politics of Regionalism in Northern Ghana. Paul A. Ladouceur. LC 79-670408. (Legon History Ser.). 318p. reprint ed. pap. 90.70 (0-317-27751-0, 2025230) Bks Demand.

Chiefs Hole-in-the-Day of the Mississippi Chippewa. Mark Diedrich. LC 86-70921. (Illus.). 58p. (Orig.). 1986. pap. 10.95 (0-9616901-0-0) Coyote Bks MN.

***Chiefs of the Sea & Sky: Haida Heritage Sites of the Queen Charlotte Islands.** George F. MacDonald. (Illus.). 96p. 1989. pap. 19.95 (0-7748-0331-2) U of Wash Pr.

Chief's Son. Leoda Buckwalter. Ed. by Glen A. Pierce. LC 89-84625. 160p. (Orig.). 1989. pap. 7.95 (0-916035-32-8) Evangel Indiana.

Chiefs Without Indians: Asquith, Lloyd George, & the Liberal Remnant, 1916-1935. Don M. Cregier. LC 82-17546. (Illus.). 330p. (Orig.). 1983. pap. text ed. 25.00 (0-8191-2807-4) U Pr of Amer.

Chiefship & Cosmology: An Historical Study of Political Competition. Randall M. Packard. LC 81-47013. (African Systems of Thought Ser.). (Illus.). 256p. 1981. 25.00 (0-253-30831-3) Ind U Pr.

Chieftain. Arnette Lamb. 1994. mass mkt. 5.50 (0-671-77937-0) PB.

***Chieftain.** large type ed. Arnette Lamb. LC 95-2474. 419p. 1995. 18.95 (0-7838-1279-5) Hall.

Chieftain of Chaucer. Oetting. LC 73-87806. (Sound Ser.). (Illus.). 32p. (J). (gr. 2-5). 1974. lib. bdg. 9.95 (0-87783-137-8) Oddo.

Chieftain of Chaucer. deluxe ed. Oetting. LC 73-87806. (Sound Ser.). (Illus.). 32p. (J). (gr. 2-5). 1974. pap. 3.94 (0-87783-138-6) Oddo.

Chieftains in the Mughal Empire During the Reign of Akbar. Ahsan R. Khan. 271p. 1986. 12.00 (0-8364-1842-5, Pub. by Minerva II) S Asia.

CHI'Eighty-Eight Factors in Computing Systems. 292p. 1988. pap. text ed. 26.95 (0-89791-265-9, 608880) Assn Compu Machinery.

Chiem Van Houweninge Double Trouble: Writing & Filming. Thomas Elsaesser et al. (Film Culture in Transition Ser.). 204p. 1994. pap. 29.50 (90-5356-025-4) IBD Ltd.

Chien. Marcel Ayme. (Folio - Cadet Bleu Ser.: No. 201). (Illus.). 72p. (FRE.). (J). (gr. 1-5). 1990. pap. 10.95 (2-07-031201-1) Schoenhof.

Chien Andalou. Luis Bunuel & Salvador Dali. 64p. 1994. pap. 9.95 (0-571-17372-1) Faber & Faber.

Chien Blanc. Romain Gary. (FRE.). 1972. pap. 10.95 (0-7859-2262-8, 2070360504) Fr & Eur.

Chien Blanc. Romain Gary. (Folio Ser.: No. 50). (FRE.). 1972. 8.95 (2-07-036050-4) Schoenhof.

Chien Dans l'Arbre. Germaine Beaumont. 306p. (FRE.). 1978. pap. 10.95 (0-7859-1869-8, 2070370097) Fr & Eur.

Chien Negre: A Tale of the Vaudoux. Nemours H. Nunez. LC 72-4645. (Black Heritage Library Collection). 1977. reprint ed. 29.95 (0-8369-9116-8) Ayer.

Chiendent. R. Queneau. (FRE.). 1974. pap. 13.95 (0-8288-3767-8, M3944) Fr & Eur.

Chiendent. Raymond Queneau. (Folio Ser.: No. 588). 431p. (FRE.). 1933. pap. 10.95 (2-07-036588-3) Schoenhof.

Chiens de Guerre. Frederick Forsyth. (FRE.). 1979. pap. 13.95 (0-7859-2419-1, 2070371247) Fr & Eur.

***Chiens de Paris.** Barnaby Conrad, III. LC 94-19721. 1995. 12.95 (0-8118-0743-6) Chronicle Bks.

Chiens Perdue s.c.-La Cle'sur la Porte, Cesbron-Cardinal: Critical Monographs in English. Colin Roberts. 64p. 1993. pap. 32.00 (0-85261-249-4, Pub. by Univ of Glasgow UK) St Mut.

Chiese Di Roma Nel Medio Evo, Cataloghi Ed Appunti. Christian Hulsen. cxiii, 640p. 1975. reprint ed. write for info. (3-487-05610-0, Pub. by Georg Olms GW) Lubrecht & Cramer.

Chiffon Scarf. Mignon G. Eberhart. 301p. 1975. reprint ed. lib. bdg. 22.95 (0-88411-752-9, Aeonian Pr) Amereon Ltd.

Chiffon Stranger. Pete Smith. LC 92-91107. 136p. (Orig.). Date not set. pap. 9.95 (1-56002-274-4, Univ Edtns) Aegina Pr.

Chiffre De Nos Jours. Andre Chamson. (FRE.). 1973. pap. 10.95 (0-7859-2204-0, 207036433X) Fr & Eur.

Chiga of Western Uganda. May M. Edel. LC 76-442670. 208p. reprint ed. pap. 59.30 (0-317-29888-7, 2019413) Bks Demand.

Chihuahua That Roared. Charles Holley. 32p. (J). 1993. pap. 8.95 (0-9636754-0-0) Sequitur Systs.

Chihuahuas. Beverly Pisano. (Illus.). 160p. 1989. 11.95 (0-86622-506-4, KW-087) TFH Pubns.

***Chihuahuas: Everything about Purchase, Care, Nutrition, Diseases, Behavior & Breeding.** D. Caroline Coile. LC 95-15009. (Complete Pet Owner's Manual Ser.). (Illus.). 1995. write for info. (0-8120-9345-3) Barron.

Chihuly Alla Macchia. Robert Hobbs. 152p. 1993. 25.00 (0-9608382-2-8) Portland Pr.

***Chihuly Baskets.** Linda Norden & Murray Morgan. Ed. by Diana Johnson. (Illus.). 162p. (C). 1994. 60.00 (0-9608382-0-1) Portland Pr.

Chihuly in Australia: Glass & Works on Paper. Geoffrey Edwards. (Illus.). 32p. 1993. pap. 15.00 (0-9608382-1-X) Portland Pr.

***Chihuly Installations, 1964-1992.** Patterson Sims. 72p. 1992. pap. 20.00 (0-614-04704-8) Portland Pr.

Chikan Embroidery: The Floral Whitework of India. Sheila Paine. (Shire Ethnography Ser.). (Illus.). 60p. 1989. pap. 10.50 (0-7478-0009-X, Pub. by Shire Pubns UK) Lubrecht & Cramer.

Chike & the River. Chinua Achebe. 1966. pap. 3.95 (0-521-04003-5) Cambridge U Pr.

Chikitsa Nyaya Shastra: (Medical Jurisprudence) B. L. Babel. (HIN.). (C). 1988. 40.00 (0-685-37426-2) St Mut.

Chikuma River Sketches. Toson Shimazaki. Tr. by William E. Naff. LC 90-26474. (SHAPS Library of Translations). (Illus.). 280p. 1991. text ed. 25.00 (0-8248-1314-6) UH Pr.

Chilandar. Dimitrijc Bogdanovic. 220p. 1978. 35.00 (0-918660-28-9) Ragusan Pr.

Chilandarians: Serbian Monks on the Green Mountain. Slavko Todorovich. (East European Monographs: No. 264). 160p. 1990. text ed. 20.00 (0-88033-161-5) East Eur Quarterly.

Child. Eli Siegel. 1970. pap. write for info. (0-911492-16-X) Aesthetic Realism.

Child: A Contemporary View of Development. 3rd ed. Judith R. Harris & Robert M. Liebert. 640p. (C). 1991. text ed. 33.00 (0-13-131046-1, 670108) P-H.

Child: A Literary Companion. rev. ed. Ed. by Helen Handley & Andra Samelson. (Illus.). 120p. 1993. 14.95 (0-916366-76-6) Pushcart Pr.

***Child: An Archetypal Symbol in Literature for Children & Adults.** Alice Byrnes. LC 94-34710. (American University Studies: Vol. 53). 128p. (C). 1995. text ed. 31.95 (0-8204-2416-1) P Lang Pubs.

Child: Development in a Social Context. Claire B. Kopp & Joanne B. Krakow. (Illus.). 640p. 1982. teacher ed write for info. (0-201-10591-8); student ed write for info. (0-201-10592-6) Addison-Wesley.

Child: His Nature & His Needs. Ed. by M. V. O'Shea. LC 74-21424. (Classics in Child Development Ser.). (Illus.). 576p. 1975. reprint ed. 56.95 (0-405-06473-X) Ayer.

Child: His Thinking, Feeling, & Doing. enl. rev. ed. Amy E. Tanner. LC 78-72826. (Brainedness, Handedness, & Mental Abilities Ser.). reprint ed. 40.00 (0-404-60894-9) AMS Pr.

Child Abuse. Jonathan Bliss. (Family Ser.). (Illus.). 64p. (YA). (gr. 7 up). 1990. lib. bdg. 17.27 (0-86593-081-3); lib. bdg. 12.95 (0-685-46438-5) Rourke Corp.

Child Abuse. William A. Check. Ed. by Dale C. Garell et al. (Encyclopedia of Health Ser.). (Illus.). 104p. (YA). (gr. 7 up). 1990. lib. bdg. 18.95 (0-7910-0043-5) Chelsea Hse.

Child Abuse. William A. Check. Ed. by Dale C. Garell et al. (Encyclopedia of Health Ser.). (Illus.). 128p. (YA). (gr. 7 up). 1995. pap. 7.95 (0-7910-0509-7) Chelsea Hse.

Child Abuse. Tom Ito. (Lucent Overview Ser.). (Illus.). (J). (gr. 5-8). 1994. 16.95 (1-56006-115-4) Lucent Bks.

Child Abuse. E. Clay Jorgensen. 144p. 1990. 16.95 (0-8245-1297-9) Crossroad NY.

Child Abuse. Ruth S. Kempe & C. Henry Kempe. (Developing Child Ser.). 144p. 1978. pap. text ed. 8.95 (0-674-11426-4) HUP.

Child Abuse. G. S. Kewalramani. (C). 1992. text ed. 19.00 (81-7033-151-X, Pub. by Rawat II) S Asia.

Child Abuse. Eli H. Newberger. (Clinical Pediatrics Ser.). 1982. 52.95 (0-316-60410-0) Little.

Child Abuse. Kim Oates. (Illus.). 320p. 1986. pap. 9.95 (0-8065-0962-7, Citadel Pr) Carol Pub Group.

Child Abuse. Gail Stewart. LC 89-1386. (Facts About Ser.). (Illus.). 48p. (J). (gr. 5-6). 1989. text ed. 12.95 (0-89686-442-1, Crstwood Hse) Silver Burdett Pr.

Child Abuse. Barbara C. Thompson. (Orig.). 1981. pap. 6.50 (0-8309-0328-3) Herald Hse.

Child Abuse. rev. ed. Edward F. Dolan. LC 92-11355. 128p. (YA). (gr. 9-12). 1992. lib. bdg. 14.77 (0-531-11042-7) Watts.

Child Abuse. 3rd ed. Peggy Murray. LC 94-60264. (Illus.). 272p. (C). 1993. pap. 49.95 (1-878025-59-7) Western Schls.

Child Abuse. Angela Carl. 128p. 1993. reprint ed. What You Can Do about It. teacher ed, pap. 6.99 (0-89900-462-8); reprint ed. Good Hugs & Bad Hugs. student ed, pap. 3.99 (0-89900-463-6) College Pr Pub.

Child Abuse: A Crying Shame. Shirley O'Brien. LC 80-23708. 184p. 1980. 9.95 (0-8425-1829-0) BYU Scholarly.

***Child Abuse: A Handbook for Health Care Practitioners.** Ivan Blumenthal. (Illus.). 160p. 1994. pap. text ed. 39.95 (1-56593-505-5, 1168) Singular Publishing.

Child Abuse: A Medical Reference. 2nd ed. Ed. by Stephen Ludwig & Allan E. Kornberg. (Illus.). 563p. 1992. text ed. 64.95 (0-443-08722-9) Churchill.

***Child Abuse: A Multidisciplinary Survey, 6 vols.** Ed. by Byrgen P. Finkelman. Incl. Vol. 1. Physical & Emotional Abuse & Neglect. LC 95-753. 418p. 1995. 75.00 (0-8153-1813-8); Vol. 2. Sexual Abuse. LC 95-753. 434p. 1995. 65.00 (0-8153-1814-6); Vol. 3. Causes, Prevention & Remedies. LC 95-753. 400p. 1995. 66.00 (0-8153-1815-4); Vol. 4. Short & Long Term Effects. LC 95-753. 270p. 1995. 55.00 (0-8153-1816-2); Vol. 5. Treatment of Child & Adult Survivors. LC 95-753. 245p. 1995. 55.00 (0-8153-1817-0); Vol. 6. Treatment of Offenders & Families. LC 95-753. 280p. 1995. 55.00 (0-8153-1818-9); LC 95-753. write for info. (0-614-03885-5) Garland.

Child Abuse: A Police Guide. 37p. 1987. pap. 3.00 (0-89707-324-X, 549-0068-01) Amer Bar Assn.

Child Abuse: A Reader & Source-Book. Ed. by C. M. Lee. 312p. 1978. pap. 32.00 (0-335-00230-7, Open Univ Pr) Taylor & Francis.

Child Abuse: A Study Text. Ed. by Vida Carver. 312p. 1978. pap. 32.00 (0-335-00231-5, Open Univ Pr) Taylor & Francis.

Child Abuse: Abstracts of the Psychological & Behavioral Literature, Vol. 1, 1967-1985. Ed. by Diane J. Willis et al. LC 91-18149. (Bibliographies in Psychology Ser.: No. 9). 236p. 1991. pap. 27.50 (1-55798-163-9) Am Psychol.

Child Abuse: Abstracts of the Psychological & Behavioral Literature, Vol. 2, 1986-1990. Ed. by Diane J. Willis et al. LC 91-18149. (Bibliographies in Psychology Ser.: No. 9). 280p. 1991. pap. 27.50 (1-55798-147-7) Am Psychol.

Child Abuse: An American Epidemic. Elaine Landau. LC 84-996. (Illus.). 128p. (J). (gr. 7 up). 1984. lib. bdg. 11.29 (0-671-47988-1, Julian Messner) Silver Burdett Pr.

Child Abuse: An American Epidemic. rev. ed. Elaine Landau. 128p. (J). (gr. 7 up). 1990. lib. bdg. 12.98 (0-671-68874-X, Julian Messner); lib. bdg. 5.95 (0-671-68875-8, Julian Messner) Silver Burdett Pr.

Child Abuse: An Annotated Bibliography. Susheela Bhan. (C). 1991. 97.50 (81-7211-002-2, Pub. by Northern Bk Ctr II) S Asia.

Child Abuse: An Interactional Event. Alfred Kadushin & Judith A. Martin. LC 80-39654. (Illus.). 360p. 1981. text ed. 45.00 (0-231-04774-6) Col U Pr.

Child Abuse: Aspects of Interprofessional Co-operation. Christine Hallett & Olive Stevenson. LC 80-504216. (Studies in the Personal Social Services: No. 2). 128p. reprint ed. pap. 36.50 (0-317-20043-7, 2023266) Bks Demand.

***Child Abuse: Betraying a Trust.** Ed. by Alison Landes. (Information Plus Reference Ser.). (Illus.). 124p. (YA). (gr. 9-12). 1995. pap. 22.95 (1-878623-95-8) Info Plus TX.

Child Abuse: Detecting Bias. Stacey Tipp. LC 91-22101. (Opposing Viewpoints Juniors Ser.). (Illus.). 32p. (J). (gr. 4-7). 1991. lib. bdg. 11.95 (0-89908-611-X) Greenhaven.

***Child Abuse: Fear in the Home.** Ed. by Nancy Jacobs et al. (Compact Reference Ser.). 44p. (YA). 1994. pap. text ed. 11.95 (1-878623-75-3) Info Plus TX.

Child Abuse: Implications for Child Development & Psychopathology. David Wolfe. (Developmental Clinical Psychology & Psychiatry Ser.: Vol. 10). 160p. 1987. text ed. 37.00 (0-8039-2832-7); pap. text ed. 16.95 (0-8039-2833-5) Sage.

Child Abuse: Is It Happening to You? Bridget Wakcher. (Illus.). 32p. (Orig.). (J). (gr. 1 up). 1984. pap. 3.50 (0-930363-00-0) Teknek.

Child Abuse: Legal Issues for Schools. NSBA Council of School Attorneys Staff. 125p. (Orig.). 1994. pap. 25.00 (0-88364-184-4) Natl Sch Boards.

Child Abuse: Medical & Scientific Guide for Reference & Research. Lottie F. Lydeen. LC 83-46098. 150p. 1987. 39.50 (0-88164-128-6); pap. 34.50 (0-88164-129-4) ABBE Pubs Assn.

Child Abuse: Medical Diagnosis & Management. Robert M. Reece. (Illus.). 450p. 1993. text ed. 69.50 (0-8121-1498-1) Williams & Wilkins.

Child Abuse: Opposing Viewpoints. Ed. by Katie DeKoster & Karin L. Swisher. LC 93-9240. (YA). 1994. lib. bdg. 19.95 (1-56510-056-5); pap. 11.55 (1-56510-055-7) Greenhaven.

Child Abuse: Prevention & Treatment Through Social Group Work. Julianne Wayne. (Orig.). 1979. text ed. 20.00 (0-89182-012-4); pap. text ed. 10.00 (0-89182-013-2) Charles River Bks.

Child Abuse: The Scottish Experience. F. Stone. (C). 1989. 39.00 (0-903534-83-5, Pub. by Brit Ag for Adopt & Fost UK) St Mut.

Child Abuse: Towards a Knowledge Base. Brian Corby. LC 92-34683. 192p. 1993. 88.00 (0-335-15747-5, Open Univ Pr); pap. 32.50 (0-335-15746-7, Open Univ Pr) Taylor & Francis.

Child Abuse see Breaking the Deadly Embrace of Child Abuse

Child Abuse - The Parent's Guide to Protective Investigation & Foster Care. Janet V. Ward. (Illus.). 39p. (Orig.). 1992. pap. 10.00 (0-9633916-0-7, TXU503304) Family Systs.

Child Abuse & Child Abusers: Protection & Prevention. Ed. by Lorraine Waterhouse. (Research Highlights in Social Work Ser.: No. 24). 200p. 1993. 45.00 (1-85302-133-4, Pub. by J Kingsley Pubs UK) Taylor & Francis.

Child Abuse & Child Protection: Policy & Practice. Ed. by Stephen Antler. LC 82-80767. (Readings in Social Work Ser.). 182p. (Orig.). reprint ed. pap. 51.90 (0-7837-5369-1, 2045133) Bks Demand.

Child Abuse & Moral Reform in England: 1870-1908. George K. Behlmer. LC 81-51331. (Illus.). xii, 320p. 1982. 42.50 (0-8047-1127-5) Stanford U Pr.

An Asterisk (*) at the beginning of an entry indicates that the title is appearing in BIP for the first time.

An Asterisk (*) at the beginning of an entry indicates that the title is appearing in BIP for the first time.

C

***Child Care: Selected Bibliography.** 156p. (Orig.). (C). 1995. reprint ed. pap. text ed. 25.00x (*0-7881-0538-8*) Diane Pub.

Child Care Administration. Judith W. Seaver & Carol A. Cartwright. 438p. (C). 1986. text ed. 18.95 (*0-534-03681-3*) Intl Thomson.

Child Care Aide Skills. Flora S. Conger & Irene B. Rose. (Careers in Home Economics Ser.). (Illus.). 1978. text ed. 25.84 (*0-07-012420-5*) McGraw.

Child Care Alternatives & Emotional Well-Being. Judith D. Schiller. LC 80-409. 204p. 1980. 38.50 (*0-275-90546-2*, C0546, Praeger Pubs) Greenwood.

Child Care & ABC's Too. Sar A. Levitan & Karen Cleary Alderman. LC 75-11355. (Illus.). 136p. 1976. 20.00 (*0-8018-1733-1*) Johns Hopkins.

Child Care & Adult Crime. Brian Minty & Colin Ashcroft. 224p. 1988. text ed. 75.00 (*0-7190-2469-2*) St Martin.

Child Care & Corporate Productivity. John P. Fernandez. 1985. text ed. 24.95 (*0-669-10335-7*) Free Pr.

Child Care & Culture: Lessons from Africa. Robert A. LeVine et al. LC 93-33584. (Illus.). 304p. (C). 1994. 49.95 (*0-521-33171-4*) Cambridge U Pr.

Child Care & Health for Nursery Nurses. Stanley Thornes. (C). 1989. pap. 27.00 (*1-871402-13-1*, Pub. by S Thornes UK) Dufour.

Child Care & Health for Nursery Nurses. 3rd ed. Jean Brain & Molly D. Martin. pap. 21.00 (*0-7175-1196-0*) Dufour.

Child Care & Maternal Employment: A Social Ecology Approach. Ed. by Kathleen McCartney. LC 85-644581. (New Directions for Child Development Ser.: No. CD 49). 1990. 17.95 (*1-55542-805-3*) Jossey-Bass.

Child Care & Mediating Structures: A Conference. Brigette Berger. Ed. by Sidney Callahan. LC 79-17710. (AEI Symposia Ser.: No. 796). 96p. reprint ed. pap. 27.40 (*0-8357-4448-5*, 2037285) Bks Demand.

***Child Care & the ADA: A Handbook for Inclusive Programs.** Rab & Wood. 208p. 1995. pap. 25.00 (*1-55766-185-5*) P H Brookes.

Child Care & the Psychology of Development. Elly Singer. (Critical Psychology Ser.). 176p. 1992. 49.95 (*0-415-05591-1*, A6622); pap. 14.95 (*0-415-05592-X*, A6626) Routledge.

Child Care Arrangements - Health of Our Nation's Children, United States, 1988: PHS 90-1250. No. 187. write for info. (*0-318-69622-3*) Natl Ctr Health Stats.

Child Care Assistance Programs. 16p. 1987. 30.00 (*0-87179-978-2*) BNA.

Child Care Centers: Quality Indicators. 31p. 1993. 25.00 (*0-89584-159-2*) Catalyst.

Child Care Challenge: Creating Solutions Through Employer-Supported Programs & Public-Private Initiatives. 61p. 1990. 15.00 (*0-89788-108-7*, 6118) Natl Conf State Legis.

Child Care Challenges for Employers: Proceedings from the Governor's Conference on Employer Sponsored Child Care. Ed. by Ellen E. Kossek. LC 91-23804. 358p. (Orig.). 1991. pap. 35.00 (*0-934753-50-4*) LRP Pubns.

Child Care Choices, Consumer Education, & Low-Income Families. Anne Mitchell et al. 64p. (Orig.). 1992. pap. text ed. 11.00 (*0-926582-07-0*) NCCP.

Child Care Consumer Education: A Curriculum for Working Parents. Melissa L. Thomas & Barbara L. Makris. 20p. 1983. pap. text ed. 15.00 (*0-934966-13-3*) Wider Oppor Women.

Child Care Crisis: Balancing the Needs of Children, Families, & Society. Edward F. Zigler. 288p. 1990. text ed. 24.95 (*0-02-935821-3*) Macmillan.

Child Care, Family Benefits & Working Parents. Sheila B. Kamerman & Alfred J. Kahn. LC 80-39690. (Illus.). 352p. 1981. text ed. 47.50 (*0-231-05170-0*) Col U Pr.

Child Care for the 'Nineties: An Owner's Manual. Alfredo O. Santesteban. (Illus.). 240p. (Orig.). 1993. 12.95 (*0-9634035-0-8*) ABC & F Pr.

Child Care Guarantee in Welfare Reform. Lorraine A. Dixon-Jones. 52p. 1990. pap. 15.00 (*1-55516-629-6*, 6117) Natl Conf State Legis.

Child Care Handbook. G. Morgan et al. (Illus.). 32p. 1988. reprint ed. write for info. (*0-9618201-1-X*) Work Family Direct.

Child Care, Higher Education, & Pension System in Japan & the United States. Ed. by Laura Lein. (Special Project Report Ser.). 84p. 1983. 9.00 (*0-89940-901-6*) LBJ Sch Pub Aff.

Child Care in a Family Setting: A Comprehensive Guide To Family Day Care. Vijay T. Jaisinghani & Vivian G. Morris. LC 85-81032. (Illus.). 200p. 1986. pap. 17.95 (*0-935467-01-7*) Family Care Assocs.

Child Care in Context: Cross-Cultural Perspectives. Ed. by Michael E. Lamb et al. 560p. 1991. text ed. 89.95 (*0-8058-0797-7*); pap. 39.95 (*0-8058-0798-5*) L Erlbaum Assocs.

Child Care in Corporate America: Quality Indicators & Model Programs. 102p. 1993. 85.00 (*0-89584-158-4*) Catalyst.

Child Care in General Practice. 3rd ed. Cyril Hart & John Bain. (Illus.). 486p. 1989. pap. text ed. 66.00 (*0-443-03943-7*) Churchill.

Child Care in Omaha, Pt. 1: Facilities. C. J. Lunbeck. (Illus.). 33p. (Orig.). 1971. pap. 3.00 (*1-55719-073-9*) U NE CPAR.

Child Care in Rural America. LC 70-169360. (Family in America Ser.). (Illus.). 462p. 1977. 33.95 (*0-405-03884-4*) Ayer.

Child Care in Russia: In Transition. Jean Ispa. LC 94-18561. 240p. 1994. text ed. 55.00 (*0-89789-390-5*, Bergin & Garvey) Greenwood.

Child Care in Spanish & English: La Guia-the Guide. Anita M. Sostek. 350p. (Orig.). (ENG & SPA.). 1986. pap. 12.95 (*0-912101-05-9*) Katanya Pubns.

Child Care in the EC: A Country-Specific Guide to Foster & Residential Care. M. J. Colton & W. Hellinckx. 267p. 1993. 54.95 (*1-85742-178-7*, Pub. by Arena UK); pap. 24.95 (*1-85742-179-5*, Pub. by Arena UK) Ashgate Pub Co.

Child Care in the One Hundredth Congress: Legislation & Policy Issues. (National Report on Work & Family Special Report Ser.: No. 10). 32p. 1988. 35.00 (*1-55871-016-7*, BSP121) BNA.

Child Care in the 1990s: Trends & Consequences. Ed. by Alan Booth. 264p. 1992. text ed. 49.95 (*0-8058-1060-9*); pap. 17.95 (*0-8058-1061-7*) L Erlbaum Assocs.

***Child Care Inventory.** Martha S. Abbott-Shim & Annette M. Sibley. LC 85-81658. 48p. (Orig.). 1986. student ed, pap. text ed. 19.95 (*0-89334-090-1*) Humanics Ltd.

Child Care Inventory: Administration Manual. Martha S. Abbott-Shim & Annette M. Sibley. LC 85-81658. 32p. (Orig.). 1986. pap. text ed. 10.95 (*0-89334-088-X*) Humanics Ltd.

Child Care Law: A Summary of the Law in England & Wales. D. Rawstron & D. Cullen. (C). 1989. 60.00 (*0-903534-64-9*, Pub. by Brit Ag for Adopt & Fost UK) St Mut.

Child Care Law: A Summary of the Law in Scotland. S. Macleod & D. Giltinan. (C). 1989. 50.00 (*0-903534-70-3*, Pub. by Brit Ag for Adopt & Fost UK) St Mut.

Child Care Manual. 6th ed. Henry F. Greenberg et al. Ed. by Joseph W. St. Geme, Jr. LC 75-21904. (Illus.). (Orig.). 1986. pap. text ed. 9.50 (*0-89119-000-7*) Sutherland Learn Assocs.

Child Care Now: A Survey of Placement Patterns. J. Rowe et al. (C). 1989. 50.00 (*0-903534-85-1*, Pub. by Brit Ag for Adopt & Fost UK) St Mut.

Child Care Options: A Workplace Initiative for the 21st Century. Margery L. Sher & Madeline Fried. LC 94-2547. 192p. 1994. pap. 27.50 (*0-89774-858-1*) Oryx Pr.

Child Care, Parental Leave, & the Under Three's: Policy Innovation in Europe. Ed. by Sheila B. Kamerman & Alfred J. Kahn. LC 91-14263. 248p. 1991. text ed. 49.95 (*0-86569-037-5*, T037, Auburn Hse) Greenwood.

Child Care Programs. (YMCA Program Discovery Ser.: Vol. 2, No. 2). 96p. (Orig.). 1991. pap. 18.00 (*0-87322-337-3*, 5117, YMCA USA) Human Kinetics.

Child Care Programs for Health Care Organizations: Decision Making & Implementation. Jane M. Allis. LC 89-1842. 312p. (Orig.). 1989. pap. 31.00 (*0-910701-44-X*, 0894) Health Admin Pr.

Child Care Resource & Referral Counselors & Trainers Manual. Nancy Mullin-Rindler & Susan Twombly. LC 89-5233. 112p. (Orig.). 1989. pap. 14.95 (*0-934140-54-5*) Redleaf Pr.

***Child Care Runner.** Dora C. Fowler. 136p. 1988. pap. 9.95 (*1-57323-001-4*) Woodhaven Pbg.

Child Care Safety. Ted S. Ferry. (Illus.). 268p. (Orig.). 1993. pap. 19.95 (*0-939874-96-2*, 4347) ASSE.

Child Care Services: A Guide for Colleges & Universities. June S. Sale. LC 93-34139. 1993. 50.00 (*0-915164-90-6*) NACUBO.

Child Care That Works: How Families Can Share Their Lives with Child Care & Thrive. braille ed. Ann Muscari & Wenda W. Marrone. 433p. 1991. vinyl bd. 34.64 (*1-56956-209-1*, BR8441) W A T Braille.

Child Care Work with Emotionally Disturbed Children. Genevieve W. Foster et al. LC 74-158185. (Contemporary Community Health Ser.). (C). 1971. 49.95 (*0-8229-3231-8*) U of Pittsburgh Pr.

Child Care Work with Emotionally Disturbed Children. Genevieve W. Foster et al. LC 74-158185. (Contemporary Community Health Ser.). 296p. 1982. reprint ed. pap. 19.95 (*0-8229-5335-8*) U of Pittsburgh Pr.

Child-Care Worker Manual. Carol A. Nimmons. Ed. by Jim Wren & Suzanne Bowman. (Illus.). 24p. 1989. teacher ed 3.00 (*0-89606-320-8*, 805TK); pap. 9.00 (*0-89606-267-8*, 805) Am Assn Voc Materials.

Child Care Workers' Salaries. Diana M. Pearce. 13p. 1988. pap. 5.00 (*0-685-29947-3*) Inst Womens Policy Rsch.

***Child-Centered Counseling & Psychotherapy.** Angelo V. Boy & Gerald J. Pine. LC 95-13348. 1995. write for info. (*0-398-06521-7*); pap. write for info. (*0-398-06522-5*) C C Thomas.

***Child-Centered, Family Sensitive Schools: An Educator's Guide to Family Dynamics.** Michael J. Garanzini. (Orig.). 1995. pap. 14.60 (*1-55833-144-1*) Natl Cath Educ.

Child-Centered Group Guidance of Parents. S. R. Slavson. LC 58-11380. 1958. pap. text ed. 24.95 (*0-8236-8016-9*, 20760) Intl Univs Pr.

Child-Centered Kindergarten. Joan Moyer et al. 1987. pap. 2.50 (*0-87173-115-0*) ACEI.

Child-Centered School: An Appraisal of the New Education. Harold Rugg & Ann Shumaker. LC 75-89227. (American Education: Its Men, Institutions & Ideas, Ser.). 1974. reprint ed. 24.95 (*0-405-01466-X*) Ayer.

Child-Centered Skiing: The American Teaching System for Children. Rosemary Peterson et al. (Illus.). 543p. (Orig.). (C). 1988. pap. 39.95 (*0-318-39838-9*) Prof Ski Instructors.

***Child Clinician's Handbook.** William G. Kronenberger & Robert G. Meyer. 1995. 55.95 (*0-205-14752-6*) Allyn.

Child Custody. James C. Black & Donald Cantor. 288p. 1989. text ed. 39.00 (*0-231-06248-6*) Col U Pr.

***Child Custody: Building Agreements That Work.** Mimi E. Lyster. (Illus.). 275p. 1995. pap. 24.95 (*0-87337-283-2*) Nolo Pr.

Child Custody: How & Where to Find Facts & Get Help. Robert D. Reed & Danek S. Kaus. Ed. by Diane Parker. LC 92-53757. (Abuse Ser.). 48p. 1993. pap. 4.50 (*0-88247-947-4*) R & E Pubs.

Child Custody & Support. (Litigation & Administrative Practice Course Handbook, 1983-84 Ser.: Vol. 167). 136p. 1993. 35.00 (*0-685-69743-6*, C4-4206) PLI.

Child Custody & the Politics of Gender. Carol Smart & Selma Sevenhuijsen. 224p. 1989. 45.00 (*0-415-02669-5*, A3482); pap. 18.95 (*0-415-02670-9*, A3486) Routledge.

Child Custody & Visitation Law & Practice, 4 vols. Bender's Editorial Staff. LC 82-84733. (Illus.). 1983. Updates. ring bd. write for info. (*0-8205-1213-3*) Bender.

Child Custody Disputes: Searching for Solomon. 336p. 1989. pap. 25.00 (*0-89707-481-5*, 513-0029) Amer Bar Assn.

Child Custody Evaluations: A Practical Manual. Dianne Skafte. LC 84-27637. 1985. pap. 18.95 (*0-8039-2437-2*) Sage.

Child Custody, Foster Care, & Adoptions. Joseph R. Carrieri. 352p. 1991. text ed. 35.00 (*0-669-27638-3*) Free Pr.

Child Custody Investigation. Richard L. Lappan. 35p. 1990. pap. text ed. 19.95 (*0-918487-36-6*) Thomas Pubns TX.

Child Custody Litigation: A Guide for Parents & Mental Health Professionals. Richard A. Gardner. LC 85-28029. 365p. 1986. 35.00 (*0-933812-12-4*) Creative Therapeutics.

Child Custody Practice and Procedure, 1 vol. Linda Elrod. (Arab Translation Ser.). 1993. 135.00 (*0-685-68848-8*) Clark Boardman Callaghan.

***Child Day Care Center Market.** 190p. (Orig.). 1995. pap. 1,295.00 (*0-7605-2115-8*) Rector Pr.

Child Day Care in the One Hundred First Congress: Early Initiatives. (Special Report Series on Work & Family: No. 17). 1989. 35.00 (*1-55871-126-0*, BSP 157) BNA.

Child Death Review Teams: A Manual for Design & Implementation. American Academy of Pediatrics Staff & American Bar Association Staff. 147p. 1992. pap. 17.95 (*0-89707-715-6*) Am Acad Pediat.

Child Development. Karen C. Barrett et al. LC 93-27325. 1993. write for info. (*0-02-801359-X*) Glencoe.

Child Development. Thomas Berndt. LC 91-32073. (Illus.). 672p. (C). 1992. text ed. 46.75 (*0-03-022712-7*) HB Coll Pubs.

***Child Development.** Thomas J. Berndt. 800p. (C). 1994. boxed write for info. (*0-697-27399-7*) Brown & Benchmark.

***Child Development.** Thomas J. Berndt. 416p. (C). 1994. student ed, pap. write for info. (*0-697-27400-4*) Brown & Benchmark.

Child Development. Bill Cunningham. LC 92-53288. (College Outline Ser.). 256p. (C). 1993. pap. 12.00 (*0-06-467149-6*, Harper Ref) HarpC.

Child Development. V. Fahlberg. (C). 1989. 39.00 (*0-903534-40-1*, Pub. by Brit Ag for Adopt & Fost UK) St Mut.

Child Development. Fantino. 1989. disk write for info. (*0-318-68148-X*) W H Freeman.

Child Development. Greta Fein. (Illus.). 1978. student ed 8.95 (*0-13-132555-8*) P-H.

Child Development. Fergus P. Hughes et al. 533p. (C). 1988. pap. text ed. 54.75 (*0-314-64017-7*) West Pub.

Child Development. Neil J. Salkind. (Illus.). 864p. (C). Date not set. pap. text ed. 23.95 (*0-15-501031-X*) HB Coll Pubs.

Child Development. Mary J. Tudor. 544p. 1981. text ed. 35.95 (*0-07-065412-3*) McGraw.

Child Development. 2nd ed. A. Christine Harris. Ed. by Clyde Perlee. LC 92-28570. 670p. (C). 1993. text ed. 52.75 (*0-314-00961-2*) West Pub.

Child Development. 3rd ed. Laura E. Berk. LC 93-39062. 1993. text ed. 28.00 (*0-205-15027-6*) Allyn.

Child Development. 6th ed. Neil J. Salkind. 608p. (C). 1990. text ed. write for info. (*0-318-69129-9*) HB Coll Pubs.

Child Development: A Study in Health Culture of a Low Income Urban Settlement. M. A. Muttalib. 1989. text ed. 30.00 (*81-207-0448-7*, Pub. by Sterling Pubs II) Apt Bks.

***Child Development: An Introduction.** John W. Santrock. 720p. (C). 1995. boxed write for info. (*0-697-23554-8*) Brown & Benchmark.

***Child Development: An Introduction.** John W. Santrock. 720p. (C). 1995. pap. write for info. (*0-697-23555-6*) Brown & Benchmark.

***Child Development: An Introduction.** John W. Santrock. 720p. (C). 1995. student ed write for info. (*0-697-23557-2*) Brown & Benchmark.

Child Development: An Introduction. 6th ed. John W. Santrock. 640p. 1994. boxed 58.00 (*0-697-14511-5*) Brown & Benchmark.

Child Development: An Observation Manual. Patty Earle et al. 256p. (C). 1982. pap. text ed. write for info. (*0-13-130427-5*) P-H.

Child Development: Diagnosis & Assessment. K. S. Holt. 232p. 1991. pap. text ed. 60.00 (*0-7506-1035-2*) Buttrwrth-Heinemann.

Child Development: Its Natural Course. 2nd ed. L. Alan Sroufe et al. 1992. text ed. write for info. (*0-07-060565-3*) McGraw.

***Child Development: Its Nature & Course.** 3rd ed. L. Alan Sroufe et al. Ed. by Mary E. Marshall & Urie Bronfenbrenner. LC 95-12636. 1995. write for info. (*0-07-060570-X*) McGraw.

***Child Development: Readings for Teachers.** Ed. by Claudio Violato & Anthony Marini. 391p. (Orig.). (C). 1989. pap. text ed. 21.95x (*1-55059-001-4*) Temeron Bks.

Child Development: Reproducible Masters. (YA). (gr. 7-12). 1989. Package of 10. 15.95 (*1-877844-04-7*, 2321M) Meridian Educ.

Child Development: Risk & Opportunity. Murray Krantz. 605p. 1994. text ed. 47.95 (*0-534-13170-0*) Intl Thomson.

Child Development & Child Health. Ed. by Martin Bax et al. (Illus.). 432p. 1990. pap. 54.95 (*0-632-02048-2*) Blackwell Sci.

Child Development & Early Education: Infancy Through Preschool. Pauline H. Turner & Tommie J. Hamner. 332p. 1993. text ed. 39.00 (*0-205-14260-5*) Allyn.

Child Development & Education: A Piagetian Perspective. David Elkind. (C). 1976. pap. text ed. 19.95 (*0-19-502069-3*) OUP.

Child Development & Learning. Ed. by William C. Johnson. LC 73-655. 193p. 1973. pap. text ed. 9.95 (*0-8422-0294-3*) Irvington.

Child Development & Learning Through Dance. James H. Humphrey. LC 86-47832. (AMS Studies in Education: No. 7). 1987. 32.50 (*0-404-12668-5*) AMS Pr.

Child Development & Personality. 7th ed. Paul Mussen et al. 688p. (C). 1989. text ed. 57.50 (*0-06-044695-1*) HarpCollege.

Child Development & Psychopathology. Donna M. Gelfand & Lizette Peterson. LC 85-1962. (Developmental Clinical Psychology & Psychiatry Ser.: Vol. 1). 1985. 37.00 (*0-8039-2282-5*); pap. 16.95 (*0-8039-2283-3*) Sage.

Child Development & Relationships. Carol Flake-Hobson et al. 1983. text ed. write for info. (*0-07-554843-7*); pap. text ed. write for info. (*0-07-554844-5*) McGraw.

Child Development & Socialisation. B. G. Benerjee. 156p. 1987. 29.95 (*81-7100-031-2*) Asia Bk Corp.

Child Development at Primary School: A Report of the Educational Research Workshop Held in Madrid, 24-27 September 1985. E. A. Lunzer. 162p. 1987. pap. 15.00 (*0-317-91053-1*, Pub. by Swets Pub Serv NE) Taylor & Francis.

***Child Development, Design Implications & Accident Prevention: Making Products Safe for Children.** L. P. Steenbekkers. (Physical Ergonomics, Faculty of Industrial Design Engineering Ser.: No. 1). (Illus.). 315p. (Orig.). 1993. pap. 67.50x (*90-6275-895-9*) Coronet Bks.

Child Development in Cultural Context. Ed. by J. Valsiner. LC 87-8799. (Illus.). 320p. (C). 1989. 38.00 (*0-88937-015-X*) Hogrefe & Huber Pubs.

Child Development in India: Health, Welfare & Management, 2 vols., Set. R. Kumar. (C). 1988. 67.50 (*81-7024-189-8*, Pub. by Ashish II) S Asia.

Child Development in Life-Span Perspective. Ed. by E. Mavis Hetherington et al. 336p. 1988. text ed. 59.95 (*0-8058-0189-8*); pap. text ed. 32.50 (*0-8058-0190-1*) L Erlbaum Assocs.

***Child Development Point of View: A Teacher's Guide to Action.** James L. Hymes, Jr. 96p. 1995. reprint ed. pap. text ed. 14.95 (*0-940139-35-9*) Consortium RI.

Child Development Policy. Contrib by Jurgen Schmandt. (Policy Research Project Report Ser.: No. 2). 91p. 1973. 3.00 (*0-318-00184-5*) LBJ Sch Pub Aff.

***Child Development Psychology International Annals of Adolescent Psychiatry, 3.** Ed. by Allan Z. Schwartzberg. 400p. 1995. lib. bdg. 39.95 (*0-226-74220-2*) U Ch Pr.

Child Development Research & Social Policy, Vol. I. Ed. by Harold W. Stevenson & Alberta E. Siegel. LC 84-50197. (Child Development Research & Social Policy Ser.). 520p. 1985. pap. text ed. 15.00 (*0-226-77397-3*) U Ch Pr.

Child Development Research & Social Policy, Vol. I. Ed. by Harold W. Stevenson & Alberta E. Siegel. LC 84-50197. (Child Development Research & Social Policy Ser.). 520p. 1985. lib. bdg. 30.00 (*0-226-77396-5*) U Ch Pr.

Child Development Through Literature. Elliott Landau et al. 1972. pap. text ed. write for info. (*0-13-130674-X*) P-H.

Child Development Today & Tomorrow. Ed. by William Damon. LC 88-42785. (Social & Behavioral Science Ser.). 484p. 1988. 42.95x (*1-55542-103-2*) Jossey-Bass.

***Child Development Within Culturally Structured Environments Vol. 3: Comparative-Cultural & Constructivist Perspectives.** Ed. by Jaan Valsiner. (Illus.). 304p. 1995. 59.50 (*0-89391-833-4*) Ablex Pub.

Child Development within Culturally Structured Environments, Vol. 1: Parental Cognition & Adult Child Interaction. Jaan Valsiner. LC 88-6361. 272p. 1989. text ed. 49.50 (*0-89391-487-8*) Ablex Pub.

Child Development Within Culturally Structured Environments, Vol. 2: Social Co-Construction & Environmental Guidance in Development. Jaan Valsiner. LC 88-6364. 312p. 1989. text ed. 57.50 (*0-89391-488-6*) Ablex Pub.

Child Dianetics. L. Ron Hubbard. 288p. Date not set. pap. 4.99 (*0-88404-790-3*) Bridge Pubns Inc.

***Child Dianetics.** L. Ron Hubbard. 308p. 1989. 28.00 (*0-88404-421-1*) Bridge Pubns Inc.

Child Dianetics. L. Ron Hubbard. 20.00 (*0-686-30781-X*) Church Scient NY.

Child Dies: A Portrait of Family Grief. 2nd ed. Penelope B. Gemma & Joan H. Arnold. LC 94-204. (Illus.). 136p. (Orig.). 1994. pap. 16.95 (*0-914783-72-6*) Charles.

Child Disabilities in Developing Countries. Ed. by Kofi Marfo et al. LC 85-20871. 1985. text ed. 49.95 (*0-275-90217-X*, C0217, Praeger Pubs) Greenwood.

Child Discipline Made Simple see Lay Counseling Series

Child Discourse. Ed. by S. Ervin-Tripp & C. Mitchell-Kernan. 1977. text ed. 54.00 (*0-12-241950-2*) Acad Pr.

Child Drama: A Selected & Annotated Bibliography, 1974-1979. Carol J. Kennedy. 56p. (C). 1983. reprint ed. pap. text ed. 15.00 (*0-8191-3524-0*) U Pr of Amer.

Child Education. 1990. write for info. (*81-900106-8-9*, Pub. by Kalakshetra Pubns II) N Montessori.

Child Education in India. S. P. Agarwal & Naresh Kanta. 1990. 16.00 (*81-7022-274-5*, Pub. by Concept II) S Asia.

Child Effects on Adults. Richard Q. Bell & Lawrence V. Harper. LC 80-16565. xiv, 253p. 1980. reprint ed. pap. 5.95 (*0-8032-6058-X*, Bison Books) U of Nebr Pr.

An Asterisk (*) at the beginning of an entry indicates that the title is appearing in BIP for the first time.

Child Employment in the Capitalist Labour Market. Michael Lavalette. 318p. 1994. 54.95 (1-85628-600-2, Pub. by Avebury Pub UK) Ashgate Pub Co.

Child Evangelism Handbook. CEF Staff. 218p. 1987. text ed. 35.99 (1-55976-200-4) CEF Press.

***Child Eyewitness Testimony: Ecological Sexual Abuse Investigations.** Bruce E. Mapes. LC 94-41029. 1995. write for info. (0-88422-154-7) Clinical Psych.

***Child, Family & Community: ECE 110 Course.** Collins & Broughton. 212p. (C). 1992. ring bd. write for info. (0-933195-42-7) Allied Hlth Pubns.

Child, Family & State: Cases & Materials on Children & the Law. Robert H. Mnookin. 857p. 1978. 32.00 (0-316-57650-6) Little.

Child, Family, Community. Roberta M. Berns. (Illus.). 560p. (C). 1993. text ed. 38.75 (0-03-072382-5) HB Coll Pubs.

Child, Family, Community: Socialization & Support. 2nd ed. Robert M. Berns. (Illus.). 592p. (C). 1989. teacher ed write for info. (0-03-028588-7); text ed. 42.75 (0-03-022848-4) HB Coll Pubs.

Child Fatality Investigative Procedures. American Academy of Pediatrics Staff & American Bar Association Staff. 202p. 1992. pap. 17.95 (0-89707-713-X) Am Acad Pediat.

***Child from the Sea.** Taylor Caldwell. 1994. lib. bdg. 39.95x (1-56849-488-2) Buccaneer Bks.

Child Garden. Geoff Ryman. 400p. 1994. pap. 13.95 (0-312-89023-0) Orb NYC.

Child Goes Forth: A Curriculum Guide for Preschool Children. 8th ed. Barbara J. Taylor. 464p. (C). 1995. pap. write for info. (0-02-419282-1, Merrill Pub Co) Macmillan.

Child Group Psychotherapy: Future Tense. Ed. by Albert E. Riester & Irvin A. Kraft. LC 86-10486. 1986. 37.50 (0-8236-0765-8, BN#00765) Intl Univs Pr.

Child Growth & Behavior. Joan Wyde & Stanley Fitch. 1992. pap. 49.35 (1-56226-107-X) CT Pub.

Child Growth & Development. 5th ed. Elizabeth B. Hurlock. (Illus.). 1977. text ed. 30.56 (0-07-031437-3) McGraw.

Child Growth & Nutrition in Developing Countries: Priorities for Action. Ed. by Per Pinstrup-Andersen et al. (Food Systems & Agrarian Change Ser.). (Illus.). 496p. 1994. 57.00 (0-8014-3001-1); pap. 25.00 (0-8014-8189-9) Cornell U Pr.

Child Guidance & Education: Collected Papers. Rudolf Dreikurs. pap. 6.50 (0-918560-11-X) Adler Sch Prof Psy.

Child Guidance Centres. D. Buckle & Serge Lebovici. (Monograph Ser.: No. 40). 133p. (ENG, FRE & SPA.). 1960. 5.60 (92-4-140040-4) World Health.

Child Health. 2nd ed. Ed. by David Harvey & Ilya Kovar. (Illus.). 460p. 1991. text ed. 78.00 (0-443-04026-5) Churchill.

Child Health: The Screening Tests. Aidan Macfarlane et al. (Practical Guides for General Practice Ser.: No. 11). (Illus.). 64p. 1989. pap. 12.95 (0-19-261768-0) OUP.

Child Health & Disease. B. K. Chakraborty. (C). 1989. 60. 00 (0-89771-378-8, Current Dist) St Mut.

Child Health & the Community. 2nd enl. ed. Robert J. Haggerty et al. 486p. (C). 1992. 49.95 (1-56000-036-8) Transaction Pubs.

Child Health & Welfare - UNICEF. (Terminology Bulletin Ser.: No. 341). 750p. 1991. 55.00 (92-1-002054-5, 90.I. 24) UN.

Child Health Care: Process & Practice. Patricia Castiglia & Richard E. Harbin. (Illus.). 1072p. 1992. text ed. 56.95 (0-397-54728-5) Lippincott.

Child Health Care & the Working Mother: The Juggling Act. Jenny Hewison & Therese Dowswell. LC 93-36300. 192p. 1993. pap. 41.50 (1-56593-235-8, 0555) Singular Publishing.

Child Health Care Communication. Ed. by William K. Frankenburg & Susan M. Thornton. LC 84-13270. 400p. 1984. text ed. 75.00 (0-275-91430-5, C1430, Praeger Pubs) Greenwood.

Child Health Care Communications. Ed. by Susan M. Thornton. (Pediatric Round Table Ser.: No. 8). 217p. 1983. 10.00 (0-931562-08-2) J & J Consumer Prods.

***Child Health Care in Ayurveda.** Abhimanya Kuman. (C). 1994. 28.00x (81-7030-389-3, Pub. by Sri Satguru Pubns II) S Asia.

***Child Health for All.** 2nd ed. Ed. by M. A. Kibel & L. A. Wagstaff. (Illus.). 544p. 1995. pap. 39.95 (0-19-571253-6) OUP.

Child Health in a Changing Society. Ed. by John O. Forfar. (Illus.). 320p. 1988. pap. 24.95 (0-19-261687-0) OUP.

Child Health in Nigeria: The Impact of a Depressed Economy. Tola Pearce & Toyin Falola. 168p. 1994. 54. 95 (1-85628-607-X, Pub. by Avebury Pub UK) Ashgate Pub Co.

Child Health in the Tropics. Ed. by R. E. Eeckels. 1985. lib. bdg. 149.50 (0-89838-719-1) Kluwer Ac.

Child Health Matters: Caring for Children in the Community. Ed. by Sally Wyke & Jenny Hewison. 160p. 1991. 85.00 (0-335-09394-9, Open Univ Pr); pap. 29.00 (0-335-09393-0, Open Univ Pr) Taylor & Francis.

Child Health Nursing. Fields. 1984. pap. 17.75 (0-8385-1090-6, A1090-8, Medical Exam) Appleton & Lange.

Child Health Nursing. Jackson. (Illus.). 1993. text ed. 59.95 (0-397-54725-0) Lippincott.

Child Health Nursing: Essential Care of Children & Families. James & Sandra R. Mott. Ed. by Debra Hunter. 1315p. (C). 1988. text ed. 55.95 (0-201-14178-7); Workbook. student ed 12.76 (0-201-14056-X); sl. write for info. (0-201-14057-8); disk write for info. (0-318-67272-3); write for info. (0-201-14197-3) Addison-Wesley.

Child Health Nursing Review. 2nd ed. Luz Porter. LC 79-14390. (Arco Nursing Review Ser.). 192p. pap. text ed. 10.95 (0-668-04825-5, Arco Test) P-H Gen Ref & Trav.

***Child Health, Nutrition, & Physical Activity.** Ed. by Lilian W. Cheung & Julius B. Richmond. (Illus.). 368p. 1995. text ed. write for info. (0-87322-774-3, BCHE0774) Human Kinetics.

Child Health Policy in an Age of Fiscal Austerity: Critiques of the Select Panel Report. Ed. by Ron Haskins & James J. Gallagher. LC 82-22820. (Child & Family Policy Ser.: Vol. 2). 256p. 1983. 49.50 (0-89391-118-6) Ablex Pub.

Child Health Psychology. Karoly. (C). 1982. 55.95 (0-205-14384-9, H4384) Allyn.

Child Health Psychology. Ed. by Barbara Melamed et al. 360p. 1987. pap. text ed. 24.95 (0-8058-0085-9) L Erlbaum Assocs.

Child Health Psychology: Concepts & Issues. Ed. by Paul Karoly et al. (General Psychology Ser.: No. 113). (Illus.). 288p. 1982. 55.00 (0-08-029368-9, J115, Pergamon Pr) Elsevier.

Child Health Services & Pediatric Education: Report of the Committee for the Study of Child Health Services. American Academy of Pediatrics Staff. LC 74-1661. (Children & Youth Ser.). 304p. 1974. reprint ed. 26.95 (0-405-05943-4) Ayer.

***Child Health Supervision: Analytical Studies in the Financing, Delivery, & Cost-Effectiveness of Preventive.** Ed. by M. R. Solloway & P. P. Budetti. 420p. 1995. pap. write for info. (1-57285-014-0) Nat Ctr Educ.

Child Health U. S. A. '92. (Illus.). 56p. (Orig.). (C). 1993. pap. text ed. 20.00 (0-7881-0122-6) Diane Pub.

Child Heart. rev. ed. Louis Gordon et al. (Illus.). 132p. 1990. pap. 7.95 (0-9627609-0-0) Heart Menders.

Child Hero in the Canadian Novel. Theresia M. Quigley. 192p. (Orig.). Date not set. pap. 17.95 (1-55021-069-6, Pub. by NC Press CN) U of Toronto Pr.

Child, His "Illness," & the Others. Maud Mannoni. 292p. 1970. reprint ed. pap. 32.95 (0-946439-39-7, Pub. by Karnac Bks UK) Brunner-Mazel.

Child Horizons, 10 vols, Set. Incl. Bible Story Hour. Louisa M. Johnson. (J). (gr. k-4). 1967. 18.96 (0-87392-002-3); Guideposts for Growing Up. Barbara K. Polland. (J). 1991. 18.96 (0-87392-208-5); Parade of Stories. Ed. by Anne Neigoff. (J). (gr. k-4). 1973. 18.96 (0-87392-005-8); Questions Children Ask. Edith Bonhivert & Ernest Bonhivert. (J). (gr. 2-4). 1989. 18.96 (0-87392-010-4); Story Hour. Esther M. Bjoland. (J). (gr. k-4). 1969. 18.96 (0-87392-003-1); Things to Make & Do. Douglas W. Downey & Karin Wisiol. (J). (gr. k-5). 1974. 18.96 (0-87392-107-0); Words to Know. Harry Bricker & Yvonne Beckwith. (J). (gr. k-3). 1989. 18.96 (0-87392-011-2); World & Its Wonders. Paul E. Blackwood. (J). (gr. 4-6). 1978. 18.96 (0-87392-109-7); Plant & Animal Ways. Margaret Murphy. (J). (gr. 4-6). 1990. 18.96 (0-87392-114-3); World of the Arts. Frederick M. Logan. (J). (gr. 4-6). 1974. 18.96 (0-87392-306-5); (J). (gr. 1 up). 190.00 (0-87392-500-9) Standard Ed.

Child in Amber. Stephen McNally. LC 92-33398. 80p. 1993. lib. bdg. 20.00 (0-87023-839-6); pap. 9.95 (0-87023-840-X) U of Mass Pr.

Child in Art. Ed. by Stephen Longstreet. (Master Draughtsman Ser.). (Illus.). (Orig.). 1966. 10.95 (0-87505-041-7); pap. 4.95 (0-87505-194-4) Borden.

Child in Children: A Child's Message to Parents, Teachers & Adults Everywhere. Carol C. Sabol. (Illus.). 60p. (Orig.). 1991. pap. 9.95 (0-9630432-0-X) SELF.

Child in Each of Us. Richard W. Dickinson & Carol G. Page. 64p. 1991. teacher ed, pap. 5.99 (0-89693-944-8) SP Pubns.

Child in Each of Us. Richards W. Dickinson & Carol G. Page. 180p. 1991. pap. 7.99 (0-89693-937-5) SP Pubns.

Child in Each of Us Workbook. Beth Funk. (Orig.). 1992. pap. 14.99 (1-56476-026-X, Victor Books) SP Pubns.

Child in His Family, Vol. 4. Ed. by Elwyn J. Anthony et al. 685p. reprint ed. pap. 180.00 (0-317-28589-0, 2055181) Bks Demand.

Child in India. S. D. Gokhale & N. K. Sohnoi. 320p. 1979. 24.95 (0-318-36931-1) Asia Bk Corp.

Child in Our Times: Studies in the Development of Resiliency. Ed. by Timothy F. Dugan & Robert Coles. LC 89-515. 240p. 1989. 35.95 (0-87630-528-1) Brunner-Mazel.

Child in Placement: Common Behavioural Problems. F. Fahlberg. (C). 1989. 39.00 (0-903534-80-0, Pub. by Brit Ag for Adopt & Fost UK) St Mut.

Child in Prison Camp. Shizuye Takashima. (Illus.). 100p. (J). (gr. 4 up). 1991. pap. 7.95 (0-88776-241-7) Tundra Bks.

Child in Seventeenth-Century Dutch Painting. Mary F. Durantini. LC 81-21852. (Studies in the Fine Arts: Iconography: No. 7). (Illus.). 406p. reprint ed. pap. 115. 80 (0-8357-1292-3, 2070481) Bks Demand.

Child in the Bamboo Grove. Rosemary Harris. LC 72-4064. (Illus.). (J). (gr. 1-3). 1972. 22.95 (0-87599-194-7) S G Phillips.

Child in the City: A Series of Papers Presented at the Conference Held During the Chicago Child Welfare Exhibit. Ed. by Sophonisba P. Breckinridge. LC 70-112541. (Rise of Urban America Ser.). (Illus.). 1974. reprint ed. 29.95 (0-405-02437-1) Ayer.

Child in the City: Vol. 2: Changes & Challenges. William Michelson et al. 1979. pap. 15.95 (0-8020-6338-1) U of Toronto Pr.

Child in the Family. Ed. by Jay Belsky et al. 288p. 1985. pap. text ed. 14.95 (0-89859-717-X) L Erlbaum Assocs.

Child in the Family. Jay Belsky et al. LC 83-12255. (Illus.). 288p. 1984. pap. text ed. write for info. (0-07-554803-8) McGraw.

Child in the Family & the Community. Janet Gonzalez-Mena. (Illus.). 320p. (Orig.). (C). 1993. pap. write for info. (0-02-344561-0, Merrill Pub Co) Macmillan.

***Child in the House.** Edward Butscher. 87p. (Orig.). 1994. pap. 10.00 (0-9630164-9-0) Canios Edit.

Child in the Physical Environment: The Development of Spatial Knowledge & Cognitive. Christopher Spencer et al. 302p. 1989. text ed. 116.95 (0-471-91235-2) Wiley.

Child in the Wilderness. Harold Klemp. 280p. 1989. pap. 11.00 (1-57043-020-9) ECKANKAR.

Child in the Wilderness. Harold Klemp. LC 89-80105. (Illus.). 280p. 1989. 11.00 (0-88155-080-9) Illum Way Pub.

Child in the World of Tomorrow ; A Window into the Future: Proceedings of the Institute of Child Health International Symposium 2-8, July, 1978 Athens, Greece. Institute of Child Health Staff. Ed. by Spyros Doxiadis et al. (Illus.). 1979. 231.00 (0-08-023685-5, Pub. by Pergamon Repr UK) Franklin.

Child in Time. Ian McEwan. 272p. 1988. pap. 10.95 (0-14-011246-4, Penguin Bks) Viking Penguin.

***Child in Time: The Life Story of the Singer from Deep Purple.** 2nd ed. Ian Gillan & David Cohen. (Illus.). 211p. 1995. pap. 16.99 (1-886894-00-0, MBS Paperbk) Mus Bk Servs.

Child Incest. O'Neil & Brown. (Changing Behavior Through Understanding Ser.). 20p. (Orig.). 1991. pap. text ed. 2.95 (1-56456-052-X) W Gladden Found.

Child Influencers: Restoring the Lost Art of Parenting. Dan Adams. (Illus.). 246p. (Orig.). 1990. pap. 9.95 (0-9626349-0-5) Home Team Pr.

Child Influences on Marital & Family Interaction: A Life-Span Perspectives. Ed. by Richard M. Lerner & Graham B. Spanier. 1978. text ed. 59.00 (0-12-444450-4) Acad Pr.

Child Is a Child, You Know: The Inversion of Father & Daughter in Dickens's Novels. Catarina Ericsson. 94p. (Orig.). 1986. pap. text ed. 28.50x (91-22-00814-4, Pub. by Almqv & Wiksell SW) Coronet Bks.

Child Is Born. Jindra Capek. (Illus.). (J). (gr. 5 up). 1987. 12.95 (1-55774-007-0) Modan-Adama Bks.

***Child Is Born.** Mary Cassatt. (Miniature Editions Ser.). (Illus.). 160p. (Orig.). (C). 1994. pap. 8.99 (0-7148-3253-7, Pub. by Phaidon Press UK) Chronicle Bks.

***Child Is Born.** Gary Moore. (J). 1994. 3.99 (0-517-10273-0) Random Hse Value.

Child Is Born: Meditations for Advent & Christmas. J. Barrie Shepherd. LC 87-30978. 130p. 1988. 13.00 (0-664-21410-X, Westminster) Westminster John Knox.

Child Is Born: The Christmas Story. Elizabeth Winthrop. LC 82-11728. (Illus.). 32p. (J). (ps-3). 1983. lib. bdg. 15. 95 (0-8234-0472-2) Holiday.

Child Is Born: The Completely New Edition. Lennart Nilsson. (Illus.). 1990. 27.50 (0-385-30237-1, Sey Lawr) Delacorte.

Child Is Not a Knife: Selected Poems of Goran Sonnevi. Goran Sonnevi. Ed. & Tr. by Rika Lesser. LC 92-19959. (Lockert Library of Poetry in Translation). 136p. (ENG & SWE.). (C). 1993. text ed. 24.95 (0-691-06983-2); pap. text ed. 9.95 (0-691-01543-0) Princeton U Pr.

Child Is Not a Little Adult: Modified Approaches to Sport for Australian Children. 2nd ed. Gillian Winter. 156p. 1983. 10.95 (0-7246-1124-X) No Amer Youth.

Child Is Waiting. Christine D'Angelo. (Silhouette Intimate Moments Ser.). 1993. mass mkt. 3.50 (0-373-07509-X, 5-07509-8) Silhouette.

Child Is Waiting. Abby Mann. 16.95 (0-89190-629-0, Am Repr) Amereon Ltd.

Child Jesus: A Christmas Cantata for Mixed Voices. Joseph W. Clokey & Hazel J. Kirk. 23p. reprint ed. pap. 25.00 (0-317-09646-X, 2017838) Bks Demand.

Child King James Version. 1990. Light Blue New Testament. 5.99 (1-55819-043-0, 463376) Holman Bible Pub.

Child King James Version Bible. deluxe ed. 1990. Pink Gift Imitation Leather. 5.95 (1-55819-042-2, 463375) Holman Bible Pub.

Child Labor: Mini-Play. (Black Americans Ser.). (J). (gr. 5 up). 1978. 6.50 (0-89550-334-4) Stevens & Shea.

Child Labor: Then & Now. Laura O. Greene. LC 92-17721. (Impact Bks.). (J). 1992. 14.42 (0-531-13008-8) Watts.

Child Labor & the Constitution. Raymond G. Fuller. LC 74-1684. (Children & Youth Ser.: Vol. 26). (Illus.). 344p. 1974. reprint ed. 28.95 (0-405-05961-2) Ayer.

Child Labor & the Industrial Revolution. Clark Nardinelli. LC 89-46001. (Illus.). 208p. 1990. 25.00 (0-253-33971-5) Ind U Pr.

Child Labor Bulletin, 1912, 1913. Ed. by Robert H. Bremner. LC 74-1673. (Children & Youth Ser.: Vol. 5). 314p. 1974. 29.95 (0-405-05953-1) Ayer.

Child Labor in City Streets. Edward N. Clopper. LC 74-22737. (Labor Movement in Fiction & Non-Fiction Ser.). reprint ed. 34.50 (0-404-58489-6) AMS Pr.

Child Labor in City Streets. Edward N. Clopper. LC 74-1677. (Children & Youth Ser.: Vol. 2). 294p. 1974. reprint ed. 28.95 (0-405-05956-6) Ayer.

Child Labor Reform in Nineteenth-Century France: Assuring the Future Harvest. Lee S. Weissbach. LC 88-30349. xvi, 296p. 1989. text ed. 42.50 (0-8071-1483-9) La State U Pr.

Child Labour. Alec Fyfe. 220p. 1989. text ed. 44.95 (0-7456-0399-8); pap. 24.95 (0-7456-0400-5) Blackwell Pubs.

Child Labour: A Briefing Manual. 82p. (Orig.). 1986. pap. 12.00 (92-2-105639-2) Intl Labour Office.

Child Labour: A Guide to Project Design. Alec Fyfe. (Child Labour Collection Ser.). v, 99p. 1993. pap. 14.00 (92-2-108005-6) Intl Labour Office.

Child Labour: Law & Practice. (Conditions of Work Digest 1991 Ser.: Vol. 10, No. 1). ix, 224p. (Orig.). 1991. pap. 36.00 (92-2-107751-9) Intl Labour Office.

Child Labour & Child Work. George Ivy. (C). 1990. 29.50 (81-7024-357-2, Pub. by Ashish II) S Asia.

***Child Labour & Women Workers.** Gursharan Varandani. (Illus.). xvi, 327p. 1994. 32.00x (81-7024-627-X, Pub. by Ashish Pub Hse II) Nataraj Bks.

***Child Labour in Agrarian Society.** U. C. Sahoo. (C). 1995. 22.50x (81-7033-272-9, Pub. by Rawat II) S Asia.

Child Labour in Agriculture. Surendra Singh. 241p. (C). 1987. 150.00 (81-85009-27-9, Pub. by Print Hse II) St Mut.

Child Labour in Sri Lanka: Learning from the Past. S. W. Goonesekere. v, 77p. (Orig.). 1993. pap. 12.00 (92-2-106473-5) Intl Labour Office.

Child Labour in the Indian Subcontinent: Dimensions & Implications. Ramesh Kanbargi. 188p. 1991. text ed. 28.00 (0-8039-9693-4) Sage.

***Child Language.** Jean S. Peccei. (Language Workbooks Ser.). (Illus.). 128p. 1994. pap. 12.95 (0-415-08567-5, B4016) Routledge.

Child Language: A Language Which Does Not Exist. Willem Kaper. 126p. 1985. pap. 34.65 (90-6765-096-X) Mouton.

Child Language: A Reader. Ed. by Margery B. Franklin & Sybil S. Barten. 416p. 1987. pap. 21.95 (0-19-504333-2) OUP.

Child Language & Developmental Dysphasia. Linguistic Studies of the Acquisition of German. Harald Clahsen. Tr. by Karin Richman. LC 91-22437. (Studies in Speech Pathology & Clinical Linguistics: Vol. 2). x, 350p. 1991. 100.00 (1-55619-388-2) Benjamins North Am.

Child Language Aphasia & Phonological Universals. Roman Jakobson. (Janua Linguarum, Ser. Minor: No. 72). (Orig.). 1968. pap. text ed. 20.00 (90-279-2103-2) Mouton.

Child Language Disability: Implications in an Educational Setting. Ed. by Kay Mogford & Jane Sadler. 104p. 1989. 49.00 (1-85359-052-5, Pub. by Multilingual Matters UK); pap. 17.00 (1-85359-051-7, Pub. by Multilingual Matters UK) Taylor & Francis.

Child Language Disability, Vol. 2: Semantic & Pragmatic Difficulties. Ed. by Kay Mogford-Bevan & Jane Sadler. 114p. 1991. 59.00 (1-85359-128-9, Pub. by Multilingual Matters UK); pap. 19.50 (1-85359-127-0, Pub. by Multilingual Matters UK) Taylor & Francis.

Child Language Disability, Vol. 3: Hearing Impairment. Ed. by Kay Mogford-Bevan & Jane Sadler. 120p. 1992. 59.00 (1-85359-169-6, Pub. by Multilingual Matters UK); pap. 19.50 (1-85359-168-8, Pub. by Multilingual Matters UK) Taylor & Francis.

***Child Law.** 2nd ed. 750p. 1995. boxed write for info. (0-406-00265-7, UK) Butterworth Legal Pubs.

Child Law: Parent, Child, & State. Ed. by Harry D. Krause. LC 92-33417. (International Library of Essays in Law & Legal Theory: Vol. 13). (C). 1992. 150.00 (0-8147-4631-4) NYU Pr.

***Child Letters: Public & Private Life in a Canadian Merchant-Politician's Family, 1841-1845.** Ed. by J. I. Little. (Illus.). 200p. 1995. 39.95 (0-7735-1260-8) U of Toronto Pr.

Child Life. Ed. by John Greenleaf Whittier. LC 73-128162. (Granger Index Reprint Ser.). 1977. 19.95 (0-8369-6191-9) Ayer.

Child Life: A Safety Course Designed for Child Care. Clark County Fire District 11 Staff. 39p. Date not set. pap. text ed. 8.00 (0-9637692-0-0) Clark Cnty Fire.

Child Life in Colonial Days. Alice M. Earle. 418p. 1993. pap. 14.95 (0-936399-52-X) Berkshire Hse.

Child Life in Colonial Days. Alice M. Earle. 418p. 1975. reprint ed. 24.00 (0-87928-062-X) Corner Hse.

Child Life in Colonial Days. Alice M. Earle. LC 89-61540. (Illus.). xxii, 418p. 1989. reprint ed. lib. bdg. 48.00 (1-55888-822-5) Omnigraphics Inc.

Child Life in Hospitals: Theory & Practice. Richard H. Thompson & Gene Stanford. 286p. 1981. spiral bd., pap. 38.95 (0-398-04456-2) C C Thomas.

Child Life in Town & Country see Merrie Tales of Jacques Tournebroche: Short Story Reprint Ser.

Child-Lore: A Study in Folklore & Psychology. S. Herbert. 1976. lib. bdg. 59.95 (0-8490-1599-5) Gordon Pr.

Child-Lovers. Wilson. 1983. 29.95 (0-685-45643-9, Pub. by Peter Owen Ltd UK) Dufour.

Child-Lovers: A Study of Paedophiles in Society. Glenn D. Wilson & David N. Cox. 132p. 1983. 35.00 (0-7206-0603-9, Pub. by P Owen Ltd UK) Dufour.

Child-Loving: The Erotic Child & Victorian Culture. James Kincaid. 416p. 1992. 35.00 (0-415-90595-8, A7307, Routledge NY) Routledge.

***Child-Loving: The Erotic Child & Victorian Literature.** 2nd ed. James Kincaid. 1994. pap. 16.95 (0-415-91003-X, B4017) Routledge.

***Child Lures: A Family Guide to Prevention of Sexual Assault & Abduction.** Kenneth Wooden. (Illus.). 1995. 13.95 (1-56530-175-7) Summit TX.

Child Maintenance: A Guide to the Child Support Act 1991. Chris Bazell et al. 111p. (C). 1993. 110.00 (1-85190-193-0, Pub. by Tolley Pubng UK) St Mut.

Child Maintenance Made Simple! How Grown-ups & Children Can Work Creatively & Lovingly Together. Larry Pastor & Michael Pastore. LC 92-82025. 128p. (Orig.). 1993. pap. 14.95 (0-927379-48-1, ZP 64) Zorba Pr.

***Child Maltreatment, 2 Vols. Incl. Vol. 1. Child Maltreatment: A Clinical Guide & Reference. James A. Monteleone & Armand E. Brodeur. (C). 1994. text ed. 100.00 (1-878060-10-4); Vol. 2. Child**

An Asterisk (*) at the beginning of an entry indicates that the title is appearing in BIP for the first time. 1195

Maltreatment: A Comprehensive Photographic Reference Identifying Potential Child Abuse. James A. Monteleone. (Illus.). (C). 1994. text ed. 115.00 (*1-878060-13-9*); 185.00 (*1-878060-20-1*) GW Medical. THE CLINICAL GUIDE & REFERENCE BOOK (ISBN 1-878060-10-4) is the first publication on child abuse without gaps, an encyclopedia of child abuse. GENERAL PRACTITIONERS, EMERGENCY MEDICINE PHYSICIANS, PEDIATRICIANS, EMTs, RADIOLOGISTS, LAWYERS, JUDGES, PSYCHIATRISTS, POLICE & SAFETY PERSONNEL & STATE HUMAN SOCIAL SERVICE AGENCIES cannot afford to be without it. While addressing the physical finds in sexual abuse, the reference emphasizes the most important components of the process - disclosure & interview of the suspected victim. In-depth information is provided on medical, psychological, social & legal aspects of child abuse. Readers will learn how to testify in court & how the legal & social systems process a child abuse case. A COMPREHENSIVE PHOTOGRAPHIC REFERENCE IDENTIFYING POTENTIAL CHILD ABUSE (ISBN 1-878060-13-9) The atlas, a valuable reference & teaching tool, presents 625 full color quality photos of the various aspects of child abuse, principally physical & X-ray. Emotional aspects are represented by abused children's drawings. A brief descriptive history of the case accompanies most of the photos with an explanation of the salient features demonstrated. In addition to the professions listed above, this text would benefit psychologist & forensic specialists. A two-volume case bound set with a free slipcase. *Publisher Provided Annotation.*

Child Maltreatment: A Handbook for Mental Health Professionals & Child Care Workers. Arthur Green. LC 80-66923. 328p. 1980. 40.00 (*0-87668-420-7*) Aronson.

Child Maltreatment: Emerging Perspectives. Dean D. Knudsen. LC 91-75939. 228p. 1992. lib. bdg. 36.95 (*0-930390-22-9*); pap. text ed. 18.95 (*0-930390-21-0*) Gen Hall.

Child Maltreatment: Expanded Concepts of Helping. Ed. by M. Rothery & G. Cameron. 336p. 1990. text ed. 69.95 (*0-8058-0455-2*) L Erlbaum Assocs.

Child Maltreatment: Theory & Research on the Causes & Consequences of Child Abuse & Neglect. Ed. by Dante Cicchetti & Vicki K. Carlson. (Illus.). 800p. (C). 1989. 84.95 (*0-521-36455-8*); pap. 34.95 (*0-521-37969-5*) Cambridge U Pr.

***Child Maltreatment & the Family: Background Briefing Report with Seminar Presentations.** M. Anne Powell. 94p. 1994. pap. 10.00 (*0-929722-80-9*) CA State Library Fndtn.

Child Maltreatment in the United States: A Challenge to Social Institutions. Saad Z. Nagi. LC 77-22121. 1977. text ed. 36.50 (*0-231-04394-5*) Col U Pr.

Child Management: A Program for Parents & Teachers. Judith M. Smith & Donald E. Smith. LC 76-22829. 140p. (C). 1976. pap. text ed. 9.95 (*0-87822-125-5*, 1255) Res Press.

Child Management in Dentistry. 2nd ed. Wright et al. (Dental Practitioners' Handbook Ser.: No. 28). 241p. 1987. pap. 37.50 (*0-7236-0717-6*, Pub. by John Wright UK) Buttrwrth-Heinemann.

Child Manuela: The Novel of Maedchen in Uniform. Christa Winsloe. LC 75-12360. (Homosexuality Ser.). 1975. reprint ed. 28.95 (*0-405-07377-1*) Ayer.

Child Manuela: The Novel of Maedchen in Uniform. Christa Winsloe. LC 75-12360. (Homosexuality Ser.). 1989. reprint ed. pap. 22.95 (*0-88143-104-4*) Ayer.

Child-Marriages, Divorces, & Ratifications Etc. 1561-66. Chester, England Diocese Staff. Ed. by F. J. Furnivall. (EETS, OS Ser.: No. 108). 1972. reprint ed. 45.00 (*0-527-00112-0*) Periodicals Srv.

Child-Menders. George H. Weber. LC 79-4244. 224p. reprint ed. pap. 63.90 (*0-317-09474-2*, 2021967) Bks Demand.

Child Mental Health & the Law. Barry Nurcombe & David F. Partlett. LC 93-50557. 1994. text ed. 39.95 (*0-02-923245-7*) Free Pr.

Child Mental Health in the 1990s: Curricula for Graduate & Undergraduate Professional Education. 1994. lib. bdg. 250.00 (*0-8490-5751-5*) Gordon Pr.

Child Mental Health Practice from the Ecological Perspective. Richard L. Munger. 426p. (Orig.). (C). 1991. lib. bdg. 60.50 (*0-8191-8318-0*); pap. 38.00 (*0-8191-8319-9*) U Pr of Amer.

Child Mental Status Examination. Jerome D. Goodman & John Sours. LC 93-74193. 148p. 1994. pap. 22.50 (*1-56821-187-2*) Aronson.

Child Molestation: An Annotated Bibliography. Mary De Young. LC 86-27418. 190p. 1987. pap. 32.50x (*0-89950-243-1*) McFarland & Co.

Child Molester: An Integrated Approach to Evaluation & Treatment. George W. Barnard et al. LC 88-19466. (Clinical Psychiatry Monograph Ser.: No. 1). 272p. 1989. 33.95 (*0-87630-526-5*) Brunner-Mazel.

Child Multimodal Therapy. Donald B. Keat, II. Ed. by Glenn Caddy. LC 89-6835. (Developments in Clinical Psychology Ser.: Vol. 12). 184p. (C). 1990. text ed. 35.00 (*0-89391-420-7*) Ablex Pub.

***Child Neglect: A Guide for Intervention.** James M. Gaudin, Jr. 84p. (Orig.). (C). 1995. pap. text ed. 35.00x (*0-7881-1666-5*) Diane Pub.

Child Neglect: Understanding & Reaching the Parent. Norman A. Polansky et al. LC 72-83496. 94p. (C). 1972. pap. 5.00 (*0-87868-097-7*) Child Welfare.

Child Neurology: A Clinical Manual. Bruce O. Berg. (Illus.). 450p. 1994. 50.00 (*0-397-51328-3*) Lippincott.

Child Neurology: A Clinical Manual. Bruce O. Berg. LC 84-80920. (Illus.). 316p. 1984. pap. text ed. 17.95 (*0-930010-05-1*) Jones Med.

Child Neurology: Proceedings of the Tokyo Meeting, 1981. Ed. by Y. Fukuyama et al. (International Congress Ser.: Vol. 579). 420p. 1983. 130.25 (*0-444-90257-0*, Excerpta Medica) Elsevier.

Child Neuropsychology, Vol. 1. John E. Obrzut & George W. Hynd. (Perspectives in Neurolinguistics, Neuropsychology & Psycholinguistics Ser.). 1986. text ed. 75.00 (*0-12-524041-4*); pap. text ed. 49.00 (*0-12-524043-0*) Acad Pr.

Child Neuropsychology, Vol. 2. John E. Obrzut & George W. Hynd. (Perspectives in Neurolinguistics, Neuropsychology & Psycholinguistics Ser.). 1986. text ed. 75.00 (*0-12-524042-2*); pap. text ed. 49.00 (*0-12-524044-9*) Acad Pr.

Child Neuropsychology: An Introduction to Theory, Research, & Clinical Practice. Byron P. Rourke et al. LC 83-1657. 389p. 1983. lib. bdg. 50.00 (*0-89862-620-X*) Guilford Pr.

Child Neuropsychology: An Introduction to Theory, Research, & Clinical Practice. Byron P. Rourke et al. LC 83-1657. 389p. 1991. reprint ed. pap. text ed. 25.00 (*0-89862-468-1*) Guilford Pr.

Child New American Bible. (J). 1990. Catholic Hardback 4 Colors. 4.99 (*0-529-06809-5*, 2301) World Bible.

Child Nurturance, Vol 1: Philosophy, Children, & the Family. Ed. by Albert C. Cafagna et al. LC 82-3701. 392p. 1982. 75.00 (*0-306-41003-6*, Plenum Pr) Plenum.

Child Nurturance, Vol. 2: Patterns of Supplementary Parenting. Ed. by Marjorie J. Kostelnik et al. LC 82-16530. 332p. 1982. 75.00 (*0-306-41175-X*, Plenum Pr) Plenum.

Child Nurturance, Vol. 3: Studies of Development in Nonhuman Primates. Ed. by Hiram E. Fitzgerald et al. LC 82-16670. 284p. 1982. 75.00 (*0-306-41176-8*, Plenum Pr) Plenum.

Child Nurturance, Vol. 4: Child Nurturing in the 1980s. Ed. by Robert P. Boger et al. LC 83-20373. 204p. 1984. 69.50 (*0-306-41505-4*, Plenum Pr) Plenum.

Child Nutrition & Health. Bobbie Hutchins. (Careers in Home Economics Ser.). (Illus.). 1979. text ed. 18.12 (*0-07-031527-2*) McGraw.

Child Nutrition & Poverty in South India. Barbara Harriss. (C). 1989. 17.50 (*81-7022-280-X*, Pub. by Concept II) S Asia.

Child Nutrition & WIC Reauthorization Act of 1989. (State-Federal Issue Brief Ser.: Vol. 3, No. 1). 9p. 1990. 6.50 (*1-55516-883-3*, 8500-0301) Natl Conf State Legis.

Child Nutrition in South East Asia: Eighth Nutricia - Cow & Gate Symposium. Ed. by H. K. Viser & J. G. Bindels. (Nutricia Symposium Ser.). (C). 1990. lib. bdg. 126.50 (*0-7923-0690-2*) Kluwer Ac.

Child Observation Skills. Phillip Slee. 192p. 1987. lib. bdg. 49.50 (*0-7099-5408-5*, Pub. by Croom Helm UK) Routledge Chapman & Hall.

Child Occupant Protection. 100p. pap. 69.00 (*1-56091-422-X*, SP-986) Soc Auto Engineers.

Child of All Nations. Pramoedya A. Toer. Tr. by Max Lane. LC 93-3516. 1993. 22.00 (*0-688-12726-6*) Morrow.

Child of an Ancient City. Tad Williams & Nina K. Hoffman. LC 92-16802. (Dragonflight Ser.). (Illus.). 144p. (YA). (gr. 7 up). 1992. text ed. 14.95 (*0-689-31577-5*, Atheneum Bks Young) S&S Childrens.

Child of an Ancient City. Tad Williams & Nina K. Hoffman. 288p. 1994. reprint ed. mass mkt. 6.99 (*0-8125-3391-7*) Tor Bks.

Child of Awe. Kathryn L. Davis. Ed. by Linda Marrow. 480p. 1990. reprint ed. pap. 6.50 (*0-671-72550-5*) PB.

Child of Dark. C. M. DeJesus. 1963. pap. 4.99 (*0-451-62731-8*) NAL-Dutton.

Child of Demons. Mason Burgess. 352p. (Orig.). 1985. pap. 3.95 (*0-8439-2687-2*) Dorchester Pub Co.

Child of Dreams. Celeste Hamilton. (Silhouette Special Edition Ser.). 1993. mass mkt. 3.50 (*0-373-09827-8*, 5-09827-2) Silhouette.

Child of Faerie, Child of Earth. Josepha Sherman. 144p. (YA). (gr. 7 up). 1992. 15.95 (*0-8027-8112-8*) Walker & Co.

Child of Fire. large type ed. Elizabeth Webster. 448p. 1985. 21.95 (*0-7089-1303-2*) Ulverscroft.

Child of Fortune. Jeffrey St. John. 300p. 1990. 24.95 (*0-915463-56-3*, Jameson Bks) Green Hill.

Child of Fortune. Yuko Tsushima. Tr. by Geraldine Harcourt. 186p. 1992. reprint ed. pap. 7.00 (*4-7700-1524-0*) Kodansha.

Child of God. Cormac McCarthy. 1994. 21.00 (*0-8446-6750-1*) Peter Smith.

Child of God. Cormac McCarthy. LC 92-50587. 1993. pap. 10.00 (*0-679-72874-0*, Vin) Random.

Child of Her Dreams. Sandra Steffen. (Silhouette Romance Ser.). 1994. pap. 2.75 (*0-373-19005-0*, 5-19005-3) Harlequin Bks.

Child of Her Dreams. Sandra Steffen. (Silhouette Romance Ser.). 1994. pap. 2.75 (*0-373-91005-3*, 5-91005-4) Silhouette.

***Child of Her Heart.** Arlene James. (Special Edition Ser.). 1995. mass mkt. 3.75 (*0-373-09964-9*, 1-09964-7) Silhouette.

Child of Her People. Anne Cameron. LC 87-62315. 250p. (Orig.). 1987. pap. 8.95 (*0-933216-28-9*) Spinsters Ink.

Child of Hitler: Germany in the Days When God Wore a Swastika. Alfons Heck. LC 84-24805. (Illus.). 225p. 1985. pap. 11.95 (*0-939650-44-4*) R H Pub.

Child of Icaria. Marie Ross. LC 75-343. (Radical Tradition in America Ser.). 147p. 1975. reprint ed. 17.60 (*0-88355-246-9*) Hyperion Conn.

Child of Love. Lela Burger. 288p. 1976. 9.95 (*0-87881-045-5*); pap. 3.95 (*0-87881-046-3*) Mojave Bks.

***Child of Mine.** Jennifer Mikels. 1995. mass mkt. 3.75 (*0-373-09993-2*, 1-09993-6) Silhouette.

Child of Mine: Feeding with Love & Good Sense. Ellyn Satter. (Orig.). 1991. pap. 16.95 (*0-923521-14-3*) Bull Pub.

***Child of Montmartre.** Paul Leautaud. 1995. 13.50 (*0-679-60158-9*) Random.

Child of Paradise: Marcel Carne & the Golden Age of French Cinema. Edward B. Turk. LC 88-17558. (Harvard Film Studies). (Illus.). 495p. 1989. 47.50x (*0-674-11460-4*) HUP.

Child of Paradise: Marcel Carne & the Golden Age of French Cinema. Edward B. Turk. (Harvard Film Studies). (Illus.). 512p. 1992. pap. 21.50x (*0-674-11461-2*) HUP.

Child of Pleasure. Gabrielle D'Annunzio. (Dedalus European Classics Ser.). 326p. 1991. pap. 11.95 (*0-946626-60-X*) Hippocrene Bks.

Child of Pleasure. Gabriele D'Annunzio. Tr. by G. Harding. LC 89-26950. 311p. 1990. reprint ed. lib. bdg. 35.00 (*0-86527-396-0*) Fertig.

Child of Promise. Tom Fettke. 1981. 4.75 (*0-685-68496-2*, MC-44); audio 10.98 (*0-685-68497-0*, TA-9036C) Lillenas.

Child of Rage. Jim Thompson. (Fiction Ser.). 239p. 1991. 45.00 (*0-940941-08-2*) Blood & Guts Pr.

Child of Shadows. John Coyne. 1990. 19.95 (*0-446-51555-8*) Warner Bks.

Child of Silence. Abigail Padgett. 208p. 1993. 17.95 (*0-89296-488-X*) Mysterious Pr.

Child of Silence. Abigail Padgett. 208p. 1994. mass mkt. 4.99 (*0-446-40184-6*, Mysterious Paperbk) Warner Bks.

Child of Storm. H. Rider Haggard. reprint ed. lib. bdg. 23.95 (*0-89190-707-6*, Rivercity Pr) Amereon Ltd.

Child of the Bay. Ann Nock. 1993. 37.50 (*1-878901-51-6*) Hampton Roads Pub Co.

Child of the Century. Ben Hecht. LC 85-70637. (Illus.). 608p. 1985. pap. 11.95 (*0-917657-41-1*, Primus Lib Contemp) D I Fine.

Child of the City. Tito Matias & Randy Petersen. 304p. pap. 4.99 (*0-8423-7224-5*) Tyndale.

Child of the Dark: The Diary of Carolina Maria De Jesus. Carolina M. De Jesus. (Illus.). 1963. pap. 2.95 (*0-451-62452-1*, Ment) NAL-Dutton.

Child of the Dawn. Clare Coleman. 336p. (Orig.). 1994. mass mkt. 4.99 (*0-515-11334-4*) Jove Pubns.

Child of the Dawn: A Journey from Death to Rebirth. Arthur C. Benson. 1994. reprint ed. 16.95 (*1-885018-02-9*); reprint ed. pap. 9.95 (*1-885018-03-7*) Logo Press.

***Child of the Dead.** Don Coldsmith. LC 94-25680. 1995. 21.95 (*0-385-47029-0*) Doubleday.

Child of the Earth: Tarjei Vesaas & Scandinavian Primitivism. Frode Hermundsgard. LC 88-7721. (Contributions to the Study of World Literature Ser.). 159p. 1989. text ed. 45.00 (*0-313-25944-5*, HTJ, Greenwood Pr) Greenwood.

Child of the Grove, Bk. 1. Tanya Huff. (Novels of Crystal Ser.). 1988. mass mkt. 3.95 (*0-88677-432-2*) DAW Bks.

Child of the Holocaust. Jack Kuper. 288p. 1993. mass mkt. 5.99 (*0-425-13582-9*) Berkley Pub.

Child of the Holy Ghost. Robert Laxalt. LC 92-7216. (Basque Ser.). 168p. (C). 1992. 20.00 (*0-87417-196-2*) U of Nev Pr.

***Child of the Homesteads.** Eloise E. McIvor. Date not set. 21.95 (*0-943099-10-2*) M&M Pr.

Child of the Jago. Arthur Morrison. (Victorian Classics Ser.). 208p. 1994. pap. 10.00 (*0-89733-392-6*) Academy Chi Pubs.

Child of the Lily Bed. 42p. 5.00 (*0-930061-04-7*) Interspace Bks.

Child of the Mist. Kathleen Morgan. 400p. (Orig.). 1993. pap. 4.50 (*0-8439-3379-8*) Dorchester Pub Co.

Child of the Morning. Pauline Gedge. 1976. 28.95 (*0-8488-1335-9*) Amereon Ltd.

Child of the Morning. Pauline Gedge. LC 77-4385. 403p. 1993. 12.00 (*0-939149-85-0*) Soho Press.

Child of the Morning. Pauline Gedge. 300p. 1986. reprint ed. lib. bdg. 32.95 (*0-89966-567-5*) Buccaneer Bks.

Child of the Night: Becoming a Woman, Becoming a Mother. Silvia Vegetti-Finzi. Tr. by Kathrine Jason. (Feminism & Psychoanalysis Ser.). 200p. 1995. lib. bdg. 27.95 (*0-89862-334-0*, C2334) Guilford Pr.

Child of the Northern Spring. Persia Woolley. 480p. 1988. mass mkt. 5.99 (*0-671-62199-8*) PB.

Child of the Owl. Laurence Yep. LC 76-24314. 224p. (YA). (gr. 7 up). 1977. lib. bdg. 13.89 (*0-06-026743-7*) HarpC Child Bks.

Child of the Owl. Laurence Yep. LC 76-24314. (Trophy Bk.). 224p. (YA). (gr. 7 up). 1990. pap. 3.95 (*0-06-440336-X*, Trophy) HarpC Child Bks.

Child of the Sea. Elizabeth W. Williams. (Illus.). 229p. 1983. reprint ed. pap. 8.00 (*0-944216-04-8*) Beaver Island.

Child of the Sea: A Chronicle of Puerto Rico. Janie P. Duggan. 1976. lib. bdg. 69.95 (*0-8490-1600-2*) Gordon Pr.

***Child of the Silent Night.** Edith F. Hunter. LC 94-26217. (Illus.). (J). Date not set. pap. write for info. (*0-688-13794-6*) Morrow.

Child of the Silent Night: The Story of Laura Bridgman. Edith F. Hunter. (Illus.). 128p. (J). (gr. 2-5). 1963. 14.95 (*0-395-06835-5*) HM.

Child of the Sun. Frank Cheavens. 200p. 1985. pap. 10.00 (*0-89540-161-4*, SB-161) Sun Pub.

***Child of the Sun: A Cuban Legend.** Illus. by Philip Kuznicki & Dave Albers. LC 95-13230. (Legends of the World Ser.). 32p. (J). (gr. 1-4). 1995. lib. bdg. 11.89 (*0-8167-3747-9*); pap. 3.95 (*0-8167-3748-7*) Troll Assocs.

***Child of the Warsaw Ghetto.** David A. Adler. LC 94-27779. (Illus.). (J). (gr. 3-8). 1995. lib. bdg. 15.95 (*0-8234-1160-5*) Holiday.

Child of the Winds: "My Mission with Radul Wallenberg" Agnes Adachi. LC 88-83367. (Illus.). 192p. 1989. lib. bdg. write for info. (*0-9621930-0-3*) A Adachi.

***Child of the Wing.** Glenda S. Smithers. (Petite Ser.). 54p. 1995. pap. 4.00 (*1-884754-16-3*) Potpourri Pubns.

Child of Thunder. Mickey Z. Reichert. (Last of the Renshai Trilogy Ser.: Bk. 3). 592p. (Orig.). 1993. mass mkt. 5.99 (*0-88677-549-3*) DAW Bks.

Child of Two Mothers. Malcolm Rosholt & Margaret Rosholt. LC 83-63177. (Illus.). 108p. (J). (gr. 4 up). 1983. lib. bdg. 9.95 (*0-910417-03-2*) Rosholt Hse.

Child of Two Worlds. Norman Reyes. (Illus.). 196p. 1995. 26.00x (*0-89410-777-1*); pap. 16.00x (*0-89410-778-X*) Three Continents.

Child of Two Worlds. Hannie Wolf. (Illus.). 156p. 1979. 13.00 (*0-931068-02-9*) Purcells.

Child of War & Revolution: The Memoirs of Abe Koosis. Abe Koosis. (Illus.). 96p. (Orig.). 1984. pap. 7.00 (*0-9605208-4-8*) Sea Urchin.

Child of War, Woman of Peace. James Hayslip & Jenny Wurts. 1994. pap. 12.95 (*0-385-47147-5*, Anchor NY) Doubleday.

Child of Your Dreams: Approaching Conception & Pregnancy with Inner Peace & Reverence for Life. Laura A. Huxley & Piero Ferrucci. (Illus.). 112p. (Orig.). 1992. pap. 12.95 (*0-89281-365-2*) Inner Tradit.

Child Offenders: A Study in Diagnosis & Treatment. Harriet L. Goldberg. LC 69-14928. (Criminology, Law Enforcement, & Social Problems Ser.: No. 75). 1969. reprint ed. 22.00 (*0-87585-075-8*) Patterson Smith.

Child, Parent, & State: Law & Policy Reader. Ed. by S. Randall Humm et al. LC 93-8223. 672p. 1994. 59.95 (*1-56639-133-4*); pap. 29.95 (*1-56639-134-2*) Temple U Pr.

Child Patient & the Therapeutic Process: A Psychoanalytic, Developmental, Object Relations Approach. Diana Siskind. LC 91-47068. 328p. 1992. 35.00 (*0-87668-494-0*) Aronson.

Child Pedestrian Accidents. James Thomson. (Facts About Ser.). 112p. 1991. text ed. 45.00 (*0-304-32261-X*); pap. text ed. 13.95 (*0-304-32273-3*) Cassell.

Child Personality Structure & Development: Multivariate Theory & Research. Ted Dielman & Keith Barton. LC 82-16583. 224p. 1983. text ed. 49.95 (*0-275-90970-0*, C0970, Praeger Pubs) Greenwood.

Child Phonology: A Book of Exercises for Students. Ken M. Bleile. (Illus.). 150p. (C). 1991. pap. text ed. 27.50x (*1-879105-31-4*, 0216) Singular Publishing.

***Child Phonology: Characteristics, Assessment & Intervention with Special Populations.** Ed. by John E. Bernthal et al. LC 94-31616. (Current Therapy of Communication Disorders). (Illus.). 256p. 1994. 39.00 (*0-86577-502-8*) Thieme Med Pubs.

Child Phonology: Vol. I Production. Ed. by Grace H. Yeni-Komshian et al. LC 80-981. (Perspectives in Neurolinguistics & Psycholinguistics Ser.). 1980. text ed. 55.00 (*0-12-770601-1*) Acad Pr.

Child Phonology: Vol. II, Perception. Ed. by Grace H. Yeni-Komshian et al. LC 80-981. (Perspectives in Neurolinguistics & Psycholinguistics Ser.). 1980. text ed. 55.00 (*0-12-770602-X*) Acad Pr.

Child Physical Abuse-Neglect: A Categorized Bibliography & Reference List. R. Geffner et al. 101p. 1992. 16.95 (*1-882948-07-6*) Family Violence.

***Child Physical Abuse-Neglect: A Categorized Bibliography & Reference List, Update 1994.** R. Geffner & C. Lloyd. 1995. 16.95 (*0-614-04195-3*) Family Violence.

Child Placement: Principles & Practice. June Thoburn. (Community Care Practice Handbook Ser.). 1988. text ed. 16.50 (*0-7045-0583-5*, Pub. by Gower UK) Ashgate Pub Co.

Child Placement: Principles & Practice. 2nd ed. June Thoburn. 187p. 1994. pap. 14.95 (*1-85742-119-1*, Pub. by Arena UK) Ashgate Pub Co.

Child Placement Through Clinically Oriented Casework. Esther Glickman. LC 56-10783. 448p. 1957. text ed. 48.00 (*0-231-02127-5*) Col U Pr.

Child-Placing in Families: Manual for Students & Social Workers. W. H. Slingerland. LC 74-1705. (Children & Youth Ser.: Vol. 22). (Illus.). 267p. 1974. reprint ed. 26.95 (*0-405-05982-5*) Ayer.

***Child Play.** Peter Slade. 300p. 1995. pap. 24.95x (*1-85302-246-2*, Pub. by J Kingsley Pubs UK) Taylor & Francis.

1196 An Asterisk (*) at the beginning of an entry indicates that the title is appearing in BIP for the first time.

An Asterisk (*) at the beginning of an entry indicates that the title is appearing in BIP for the first time.

1197

C

Child Support Guidelines Summary. Janice Munsterman & Thomas Henderson. 139p. 1988. 9.00 (*0-685-33611-5*, WPO-003) Natl Ctr St Courts.

Child Support Guidelines Summary. Janice Munsterman & Claire Grimm. 139p. 1990. 9.00 (*0-685-38116-1*, WPO-015) Natl Ctr St Courts.

***Child Support Handbook for Paralegals.** Gila Brownstein. text ed. write for info. (*0-471-05363-5*) Wiley.

Child Support in America: Practical Advice for Negotiating & Collecting - a Fair Settlement. Joseph I. Lieberman. LC 86-5501. 128p. (C). 1988. reprint ed. 10.00 (*0-300-04210-8*) Yale U Pr.

Child Support Payment Procedures: Judicial Administration & Procedures Manual. National Center for State Courts Staff. 55p. 1976. 3.30 (*0-685-15100-X*, NCSC-027) Natl Ctr St Courts.

Child Support Specialist. (Career Examination Ser.: C-3433). 1994. pap. 29.95 (*0-8373-3433-0*) Nat Learn.

Child Support Training Package. 25p. 1987. pap. 2.50 (*0-317-03754-4*, 42,508) NCLS Inc.

***Child Surveillance Handbook.** David Hall et al. 1995. pap. 29.95 (*1-870905-24-5*) Scovill Paterson.

Child Survival. Ed. by Nancy Scheper-Hughes. (C). 1987. lib. bdg. 126.50 (*1-55608-028-X*); pap. text ed. 50.00 (*1-55608-029-8*) Kluwer Ac.

Child Survival: Strategies for Research - Supplement to Population & Development Review, Vol. 10. Ed. by W. Henry Mosley & Lincoln C. Chen. LC 84-15985. 401p. 1992. reprint ed. pap. text ed. 12.00 (*0-685-66120-2*) Population Coun.

***Child Survival under Threat.** Dominic E. Azuh. (C). 1994. 21.00 (*81-7018-821-0*, Pub. by BR Pub II) S Asia.

***Child Survivors & Perpetrators of Sexual Abuse: Treatment Innovations.** Mic Hunter. LC 94-42211. 152p. 1995. text ed. 38.95 (*0-8039-7194-X*); pap. text ed. 17.95 (*0-8039-7195-8*) Sage.

Child Talk: Process in Language Acquisition. Chapman. 305p. 1992. 39.95 (*0-8151-1617-9*, Yr Bk Med Pubs) Mosby Yr Bk.

Child, the Family, & the Outside World. Donald W. Winnicott. (Illus.). 256p. 1992. pap. 10.53 (*0-201-63268-3*) Addison-Wesley.

Child Therapist: Markers of Effectiveness. Christiane Brems. LC 93-25949. 1993. pap. text ed. 12.00 (*0-205-15521-9*) Allyn.

***Child Therapy Today.** Ed. by Laura Slap-Shelton. (Child Therapy News Ser.: Vol. 1). 279p. (C). 1994. text ed. 36.95 (*1-882732-12-X*) Ctr Applied Psy.

Child Training & Personality: A Cross-Cultural Study. John W. Whiting & Irvin L. Child. LC 84-10794. vi, 353p. 1984. reprint ed. text ed. 41.50 (*0-313-24387-5*, WHCT, Greenwood Pr) Greenwood.

Child Training & the Home School: A Legacy of Grace. Jeff Barth & Marge Barth. 172p. (Orig.). 1991. pap. write for info. (*0-9624067-2-4*) Parable Pub.

Child Trauma I: Issues & Research. Ann W. Burgess. LC 92-7875. 504p. 1992. 55.00 (*0-8153-0036-0*, SS739) Garland.

Child under Sail. Elizabeth Linklater. (C). 1987. 60.00 (*0-85174-302-1*, Pub. by Brwn Son Ferg) St Mut.

Child under Six. 2nd ed. James L. Hymes, Jr. 332p. 1994. reprint ed. pap. text ed. 18.95 (*0-940139-27-8*) Consortium RI.

Child under Stress - Dyslexia? Zita M. Albes. 106p. (C). 1986. 50.00 (*0-86236-007-2*, Pub. by Granary UK) St Mut.

Child Victims, Child Witnesses: Understanding & Improving Testimony. Ed. by Gail S. Goodman & Bette L. Bottoms. LC 92-30072. 328p. 1992. lib. bdg. 33.95 (*0-89862-789-3*) Guilford Pr.

***Child Visitation Datebook & Journal.** Jerry K. Thomas. (Market & Main Ser.). 140p. 1994. student ed, audio 34.95 (*0-9643428-0-4*) Buenerkemper & Howe.

Child Watch: New York City - Looking Out for America's Children. Eleanor Marshall & Anjean Carter. LC 85-105275. 30p. 1983. 5.00 (*0-88156-012-X*) Comm Serv Soc NY.

Child Welfare: A Multicultural Focus. Ed. by Neil A. Cohen. 304p. (C). 1991. pap. text ed. 29.00 (*0-205-13098-4*) Allyn.

Child Welfare: A Source Book of Knowledge & Practice. Ed. by Frank Maidman. 454p. 1984. 32.95 (*0-87868-236-8*) Child Welfare.

Child Welfare: An Africentric Perspective. Joyce E. Everett et al. Ed. by Bogart R. Leashore. LC 90-28752. 300p. (C). 1991. text ed. 40.00 (*0-8135-1712-5*); pap. text ed. 16.00 (*0-8135-1713-3*) Rutgers U Pr.

Child Welfare: Policies & Practice. 4th ed. Lela B. Costin et al. 608p. (C). 1991. text ed. 50.95 (*0-8013-0398-2*, 78177) Longman.

Child Welfare & Foster Home Care: Index of Modern Information. Greta T. Lithmond. LC 88-47999. 150p. 1990. 39.50 (*1-55914-078-X*); pap. 34.50 (*1-55914-079-8*) ABBE Pubs Assn.

Child Welfare & the Law. Theodore J. Stein. 224p. (Orig.). (C). 1991. pap. text ed. 22.95 (*0-8013-0315-X*, 78083) Longman.

Child Welfare Around the World. Ed. by Emily J. McFadden. 303p. 1991. pap. 7.50 (*0-87868-424-7*) Child Welfare.

Child Welfare Challenge: Policy, Practice, & Research. Peter J. Pecora et al. (Modern Applications of Social Work Ser.). 543p. 1992. lib. bdg. 49.95 (*0-202-36081-4*); pap. text ed. 27.95 (*0-202-36082-2*) Aldine de Gruyter.

Child Welfare in Israel. Eliezer D. Jaffe. Ed. by Neil Gilbert & Harry Specht. LC 81-15422. (Studies in Social Welfare). 336p. 1982. text ed. 59.95 (*0-275-90825-9*, C0825, Praeger Pubs) Greenwood.

Child Welfare Practice. Thelma F. Baily & Walter H. Baily. LC 82-49034. (Jossey-Bass Social & Behavioral Science Ser.). 263p. reprint ed. pap. 75.00 (*0-8357-4804-9*, 2037741) Bks Demand.

Child Welfare Problems: Prevention, Early Identification, & Intervention. Greta L. Singer et al. LC 82-20263. 180p. (Orig.). 1983. lib. bdg. 48.50 (*0-8191-2874-0*) U Pr of Amer.

Child Welfare Reform. National Center for Children in Poverty Staff. 62p. (Orig.). 1991. pap. text ed. 8.00 (*0-926582-06-2*) NCCP.

Child Welfare Research Review. Ed. by Richard Barth et al. LC 94-1252. 392p. 1994. 55.00 (*0-231-08074-3*); pap. write for info. (*0-231-08075-1*) Col U Pr.

Child Welfare Services. 4th ed. Alfred Kadushin & Judith A. Martin. 1275p. (C). 1988. write for info. (*0-02-362710-7*) Macmillan.

***Child Welfare Services along the U. S.-Mexico Border.** Lesley Daigle. (Working Paper Ser.: No. 74). 74p. 1994. 5.00 (*0-614-01225-2*) LBJ Sch Pub Aff.

Child Welfare Stat Book 1993. Lisa A. Merkel-Holguin & Audrey J. Sobel. 1993. 32.95 (*0-87868-531-6*) Child Welfare.

Child Welfare Training & Practice: An Annotated Bibliography. Rebecca L. Hegar et al. LC 82-11686. 143p. 1982. text ed. 49.95 (*0-313-23383-7*, PCH/, Greenwood Pr) Greenwood.

Child Well-Being Scales & Rating Form. 1987. 10.00 (*0-87868-306-2*) Child Welfare.

Child Who Never Grew. Pearl S. Buck. 22.95 (*0-8488-1250-6*) Amereon Ltd.

Child Who Never Grew. 2nd ed. Pearl S. Buck. LC 92-34844. 128p. (C). 1992. text ed. 14.95 (*0-933149-49-2*) Woodbine House.

Child Who Stutters: To the Family Physician, No. 24. Barry Guitar & Edward G. Conture. 16p. 1992. pap. 1.00 (*0-933388-31-4*) Stuttering Fnd Am.

Child Who Stutters: To the Pediatrician, No. 23. Barry Guitar & Edward G. Conture. 16p. 1991. pap. 1.00 (*0-933388-29-2*) Stuttering Fnd Am.

Child Who Walks Alone: Case Studies of Rejection in the Schools. Anne Stilwell & Hart Stilwell. LC 79-38569. 207p. reprint ed. pap. 59.00 (*0-8357-7764-2*, 2036122) Bks Demand.

Child Windows. Richard P. Braden. LC 94-17676. (Hands-On Windows Programming Ser.: Bk. 2). 160p. 1994. disk, pap. 15.95 (*1-55622-433-8*) Wordware Pub.

Child-Wise. Cathy R. Templesman. 1994. 23.00 (*0-688-11740-6*) Hearst Bks.

***Child with a Disability.** 2nd rev. ed. David M. Hall & Peter D. Hill. LC 95-14060. Orig. Title: The Child with a Handicap. 1995. write for info. (*0-86542-850-6*) Blackwell Sci.

Child with Cancer. Jennifer Thompson. (Illus.). 189p. 1990. pap. 29.50 (*1-871364-36-1*) Ishiyaku Euro.

***Child with Cochlear Impairment.** Nevins. 1995. 45.00 (*1-56593-160-2*, 1140) Singular Publishing.

Child with Disabling Illness: Principles of Rehabilitation. 2nd ed. Ed. by John A. Downey & Niels L. Low. 700p. 1982. text ed. 114.00 (*0-89004-664-6*) Raven.

Child Within. Mari Hanes. 1983. pap. 3.99 (*0-8423-0219-0*) Tyndale.

Child Within: A Powerful Therapeutic Ally. S. F. Monaghan. (Illus.). 245p. 1989. 35.50 (*0-89885-471-7*) Human Sci Pr.

***Child Within Has Been Awakened but the Old Lady on the Outside Just Collapsed.** Cathy Guisewite. 1994. pap. 8.95 (*0-8362-1761-6*) Andrews & McMeel.

Child Within Us Lives! A Synthesis of Science, Religion & Metaphysics. William Samuel. LC 89-90674. 413p. 1989. reprint ed. pap. 12.95 (*1-877999-09-1*) W Samuel Fndtn.

Child Without Tomorrow. A. Graziano. LC 73-3394. (Pergamon General Psychology Ser.: Vol. 36). 1974. 125.00 (*0-08-017722-0*, Pub. by Pergamon Repr UK) Franklin.

***Child Witness.** large type ed. Howard C. Davis. (Linford Mystery Large Pr. Ser.). 1994. pap. 14.95 (*0-7089-7632-8*) Ulverscroft.

Child Witness: Legal Issues & Dilemmas. Nancy W. Perry & Lawrence S. Wrightsman. (Illus.). 280p. 1991. text ed. 49.95 (*0-8039-3771-7*); pap. text ed. 24.00 (*0-8039-3772-5*) Sage.

Child Witness Bibliography. Ed. by Beecher Threatt. (Tarlton Law Library Legal Bibliography Ser.: No. 38). 38p. (C). 1994. 18.00 (*0-935630-45-7*) U of Tex Tarlton Law Lib.

Child Witnesses. James S. Baxter. Ed. by Bill Gillham. (Facts About Ser.). 128p. 1994. text ed. 55.00 (*0-685-63586-4*) Cassell.

Child Witnesses. James S. Baxter. Ed. by Bill Gillham. (Facts About Ser.). 128p. 1995. pap. text ed. 17.95 (*0-304-32660-7*) Cassell.

Child Witnesses: Fragile Voices in the American Legal System. Lucy S. McGough. LC 93-49769. 1994. 30.00 (*0-300-05748-2*) Yale U Pr.

Child Work, Poverty & Underdevelopment: Issues for Research in Low-Income Countries. Ed. by Gerry Rodgers & Guy Standing. (WEP Study Ser.). xii, 310p. (Orig.). 1981. 28.00 (*92-2-102812-7*); pap. 20.00 (*92-2-102813-5*) Intl Labour Office.

Child-World. James W. Riley. LC 76-39403. (Granger Index Reprint Ser.). 1977. reprint ed. 22.95 (*0-8369-6350-4*) Ayer.

Childbearing: A Book of Choices. Ruth W. Lubic & Giene R. Hawes. (Illus.). 326p. 1987. 18.95 (*0-318-37618-0*) Maternity Ctr.

Childbearing: A Book of Choices see Environmental Hazards During Pregnancy

Childbearing after Thirty-Five: The Risks & the Rewards. Francesca C. Fay & Kathy S. Smith. 192p. 1985. 24.95 (*0-917439-08-2*); pap. 12.95 (*0-917439-05-8*) Balsam Pr.

Childbearing among Hispanics in the United States: An Annotated Bibliography. Comp. by Katherine F. Darabi et al. LC 86-33716. (Bibliographies & Indexes in Women's Studies Ser.: No. 6). 179p. 1987. text ed. 55.00 (*0-313-25617-9*, DCH/) Greenwood.

Childbearing Decision: Fertility Attitudes & Behavior. Ed. by Greer L. Fox. LC 82-3354. (New Perspectives on Family Ser.). (Illus.). 271p. reprint ed. pap. 77.30 (*0-8357-8461-4*, 2034727) Bks Demand.

Childbearing Family, No. 2. Miller. 1983. 30.50 (*0-316-57338-8*) Little.

Childbearing Family, Vol. 1: Pregnancy & Family Health. 2nd ed. Betty A. Anderson et al. (Illus.). 1979. pap. text ed. 25.95 (*0-07-001683-6*) McGraw.

Childbearing Family, Vol. 2: Interruptions in Family Health During Pregnancy. 2nd ed. Betty A. Anderson et al. (Illus.). 1979. pap. text ed. 25.95 (*0-07-001684-4*) McGraw.

Childbearing Year: Reading Level 4. 1993. 7.75 (*0-88336-567-7*) New Readers.

***Childbed Fever: A Documentary History.** Irvine Loudon. LC 94-33390. (Diseases, Epidemics, & Medicine Ser.: Vol. 2). (Illus.). 288p. 1995. 43.00 (*0-8153-1079-X*, SS868) Garland.

Childbed Fever: A Scientific Biography of Ignaz Semmelweis. K. Codell Carter & Barbara R. Carter. LC 93-32618. (Contributions in Medical Studies: No. 39). 144p. 1994. text ed. 45.00 (*0-313-29146-2*, Greenwood Pr) Greenwood.

Childbirth. Jacques Guillemeau. LC 77-38196. (English Experience Ser.: No. 464). 396p. 1972. reprint ed. 75.00 (*90-221-0464-8*) Walter J Johnson.

Childbirth: A Consumer's Perspective. Betsy Quitko et al. Ed. by Kathy Leth. (Illus.). 144p. (Orig.). 1988. pap. 6.95 (*0-936320-20-6*) LIFETIME.

Childbirth: A Unique Experience. Margaret Brisco & Gloria Bencivenne. LC 87-80846. (Illus.). 120p. 1988. 14.00 (*0-940670-08-9*) Kingston Pr.

***Childbirth: Your Choices for Managing the Pain.** Gillian Van Hasselt. 176p. 1995. pap. 12.95 (*0-87833-902-7*) Taylor Pub.

Childbirth Activists' Handbook: or, How to Get the Childbirth Options You Want... in Less Than Nine Months. David Stewart & Lee Stewart. LC 81-85423. 489p. (Orig.). 1983. pap. text ed. 12.95 (*0-934426-03-1*) NAPSAC Reprods.

Childbirth & Marriage: The Transition to Parenthood. Tracy Hotchner. 576p. (Orig.). 1988. pap. 10.95 (*0-380-75201-8*) Avon.

***Childbirth Choices Today: Everything You Need to Know to Plan a Safe & Rewarding Birth.** Carl Jones. LC 94-44434. 256p. 1995. pap. 12.95 (*0-8065-1640-2*, Citadel Pr) Carol Pub Group.

Childbirth Education: Practice, Research & Theory. Francine H. Nichols & Sharron S. Humenick. (Illus.). 544p. 1988. text ed. 52.50 (*0-7216-2052-3*) Saunders.

Childbirth for Men. Herbert A. Brant. (Illus.). 1985. pap. 12.95 (*0-19-261450-9*) OUP.

Childbirth God's Way. 1982. 1.95 (*0-89858-027-7*) Fill the Gap.

Childbirth in America: Anthropological Perspectives. Karen L. Michaelson et al. LC 87-37490. 320p. 1988. text ed. 49.95 (*0-89789-136-8*, Bergin & Garvey) Greenwood.

Childbirth in Toledo. Cheaney Engel et al. Ed. by TAPSAC Staff. 97p. (Orig.). 1990. pap. 7.95 (*0-9626125-0-2*) TAPSAC Titles.

***Childbirth Kit: Ideas & Images to Help You Through Labor.** M. Fellenstein Hale & Liz Chalmers. LC 94-92447. (Illus.). 96p. (Orig.). 1995. pap. 22.95 (*0-9643530-0-8*) Swanstone Pr.

Childbirth Picture Book. Fran P. Hosken. 60p. (Orig.). 1981. 7.00 (*0-942096-00-2*); Flip Chart. 25.00 (*0-685-57806-2*) WINNEWS.

Childbirth Wisdom: From the World's Oldest Societies. Judith Goldsmith. 291p. 1990. pap. 10.95 (*0-936184-10-8*) E W-Nat Hlth Bks.

Childbirth with Confidence. Helen Wood. 160p. (C). 1989. 59.00 (*1-85183-035-9*, Silent Bks) St Mut.

Childbirth with Hypnosis. William S. Kroger. (Illus.). 1975. pap. 5.00 (*0-87980-021-6*) Wilshire.

Childbirth with Love. Niels H. Lauersen. 1985. pap. 9.95 (*0-425-07390-4*, Berkley Trade) Berkley Pub.

Childbirth Without Fear. 1994. mass mkt. 5.99 (*0-06-109248-7*, Harp PBks) HarpC.

Childbirth Without Fear. Grantly Dick-Read. 1979. mass mkt. 3.95 (*0-06-080490-4*, PL) HarpC.

Childcare: Chula Vista. Susan Garfin & Katherine DeGenaro. (Illus.). 44p. (Orig.). 1989. pap. text ed. 4.95 (*0-9625870-0-1*) Suka Pubns.

Childcare: San Diego. Susan Garfin & Katherine DeGenaro. (Illus.). (Orig.). 1990. pap. text ed. write for info. (*0-9625870-1-X*) Suka Pubns.

***Childcare Cookbook.** Derek Van Loan. (Illus.). 26p. (Orig.). 1995. pap. 4.95 (*0-9614068-3-6*) Epoch Pr.

Childcare Guide: A Directory to Childcare Facilities in Metropolitan Atlanta. Clinton-Williams Corporation Staff. (Illus.). 400p. (Orig.). 1989. pap. write for info. (*0-318-65308-7*) Clinton-Williams.

Childcare in Rural Communities - Scotland in Europe. HMSO Staff. 136p. 1991. pap. 17.00 (*0-11-494157-2*, HM7251) UNIPUB.

Childcare Solutions: A Guide for Parents. Aphra R. Katzev & Nancy H. Bragdon. 224p. 1990. pap. 7.95 (*0-380-75834-2*) Avon.

***Childcraft - The How & Why Library, 1995, 15 vols., Set.** World Book Editors. LC 94-60730. (Illus.). (J). (ps-6). 1994. write for info. (*0-7166-0195-8*) World Bk.

Childcraft Dictionary (1993) rev. ed. Ed. by World Book Staff. LC 92-64303. (Illus.). 900p. (J). (gr. 3-6). 1993. lib. bdg. write for info. (*0-7166-1493-6*) World Bk.

Childcraft Supplement, 5 vols., Set. Ed. by World Book Staff. LC 91-65174. (Illus.). (J). (gr. 2-6). 1991. write for info. (*0-7166-0666-6*) World Bk.

Childcraft Supplement: About Dogs, 5 vols. Ed. by World Book Staff. (Illus.). 304p. (J). (gr. 2-6). 1991. write for info. (*0-318-68630-9*) World Bk.

Childcraft Supplement: Prehistoric Animals, 5 vols. Ed. by World Book Staff. (Illus.). 304p. (J). (gr. 2-6). 1991. write for info. (*0-318-68629-5*) World Bk.

Childcraft Supplement: Prehistoric Animals, About Dogs, The Magic of Words, The Indian Book, The Puzzle Book, 5 vols. Ed. by World Book Staff. (Illus.). 1520p. (J). (gr. 2-6). 1989. lib. bdg. write for info. (*0-7166-0669-0*) World Bk.

Childcraft Supplement: The Indian Book, 5 vols. Ed. by World Book Staff. LC 91-65174. (Illus.). 304p. (J). (gr. 2-6). 1991. write for info. (*0-318-68632-X*) World Bk.

Childcraft Supplement: The Magic of Words, 5 vols. Ed. by World Book Staff. (Illus.). 304p. (J). (gr. 2-6). 1991. write for info. (*0-318-68631-7*) World Bk.

Childcraft Supplement: The Puzzle Book, 5 vols. Ed. by World Book Staff. (Illus.). 304p. (J). (gr. 2-6). 1991. write for info. (*0-318-68633-3*) World Bk.

Childcraft's Whole Wide World. rev. ed. Ed. by World Book Editors. LC 93-60197. (Illus.). 288p. (J). (gr. 5-8). 1993. lib. bdg. write for info. (*0-7166-3250-0*) World Bk.

Childe Byron. Romulus Linney. 1981. pap. 4.75 (*0-8222-0201-8*) Dramatists Play.

Childe Harold's Pilgrimage, Canto 3: A Facsimile of the Autograph Fair Copy Found in the "Scrope Davies" Notebook. Intro. & Notes by T. A. Burnett. LC 87-29120. (Manuscripts of the Younger Romantics: Vol. VII). 236p. 1988. 83.00 (*0-8240-7026-7*) Garland.

Childe Hassam. Donelson F. Hoopes. (Great Artists Ser.). (Illus.). 88p. (Orig.). 1988. pap. 16.95 (*0-8230-0621-2*, Watsn-Guptill) Watsn-Guptill.

Childe Hassam: An Island Garden Revisited. David P. Curry. 1990. 45.00 (*0-393-02869-0*) Norton.

Childe Hassam in Indiana. Alain G. Joyaux et al. 72p. (Orig.). 1985. pap. 6.50 (*0-915511-03-7*) Ball State Art.

Childe Hassam, 1859-1935. (Illus.). 8p. 1988. pap. 15.00 (*0-945936-02-8*) Spanierman Gallery.

Childe Hassam, 1859-1935: American Impressionist. Ed. by Ulrich W. Hiesinger. (Illus.). 192p. 1994. 65.00 (*3-7913-1364-9*, Pub. by Prestel) TeNeues.

Childe Hassam's Etchings & Drypoints: A Catalogue Raisonne. rev. ed. Royal Cortissoz & Leonard Clayton Gallery Staff. 450p. 1989. 95.00 (*1-55660-029-1*) A Wofsy Fine Arts.

Childe Hassam's New York. Ilene S. Fort. LC 93-15920. (Essential Paintings Ser.). (Illus.). 82p. 1993. 21.95 (*1-56640-317-0*) Pomegranate Calif.

Childerley: The Moral Landscape of a Country Village. Michael M. Bell. LC 93-24209. (Morality & Society Ser.). (Illus.). 1994. 32.50 (*0-226-04197-2*) U Ch Pr.

Childerley: The Moral Landscape of a Country Village. Michael M. Bell. LC 93-24209. (Morality & Society Ser.). (Illus.). 1995. pap. text ed. 17.95 (*0-226-04198-0*) U Ch Pr.

Childermass. Wyndham Lewis. LC 76-145141. (Literature Ser.). 328p. 1972. reprint ed. 49.00 (*0-403-01072-1*) Scholarly.

Childers' Diet to Stop Arthritis: Nightshades, Aging & Ill Health. 4th rev. ed. Ed. by Norman F. Childers. (Illus.). 220p. 1993. pap. 17.00 (*0-938378-05-8*) Horticult Pubns.

Childes - Bib: An Annotated Bibliography of Child Language & Language Disorders. Roy Higginson & Brian MacWhinney. 1176p. (C). 1991. 200.00 (*0-8058-0859-0*) L Erlbaum Assocs.

***Childes - Bib: An Annotated Bibliography of Child Language & Language Disorders, 2 vols., Set.** Roy Higginson & Brian MacWhinney. 275.00 (*0-8058-1601-1*) L Erlbaum Assocs.

Childes - Bib: An Annotated Bibliography of Child Language & Language Disorders, 1994 Supplement. Roy Higginson & Brian MacWhinney. 700p. 1994. text ed. 125.00 (*0-8058-1478-7*) L Erlbaum Assocs.

***Childes Project: Tools for Analyzing Talk.** 2nd ed. Brian MacWhinney. 460p. 1995. text ed. 35.00 (*0-8058-2027-2*) L Erlbaum Assocs.

Childhood. Bill Cosby. 192p. 1992. pap. 7.95 (*0-425-13476-8*) Berkley Pub.

Childhood. Bruce Friedland. (Life Cycle Ser.). (Illus.). 112p. (YA). (gr. 7-12). 1993. 18.95 (*0-7910-0036-2*) Chelsea Hse.

Childhood. Melvin Konner. 1991. 27.95 (*0-316-50184-0*) Little.

Childhood. Roberta Meyer. LC 94-9418. 1994. write for info. (*0-07-061234-X*) McGraw.

Childhood. Jan Myrdal. Tr. by Christine Swanson. LC 91-26744. 192p. (SWE.). 1991. 18.95 (*0-941702-29-4*) Lake View Pr.

Childhood. Teo Savory. LC 78-8912. 1978. 17.50 (*0-87775-123-4*); pap. 7.95 (*0-87775-124-2*) Unicorn Pr.

Childhood. Leo Tolstoy. Ed. by B. Faden. (Library of Russian Classics). (Illus.). 120p. pap. text ed. 15.95x (*0-631-14396-3*) Blackwell Pubs.

Childhood. Nicholas Tucker. LC 90-21867. (Human Development Ser.). (Illus.). 64p. (J). (gr. 5-9). 1991. lib. bdg. 11.95 (*0-8114-7804-1*) Raintree Steck-V.

Childhood. large type ed. Bill Cosby. 197p. 1992. lib. bdg. 17.95 (*1-56054-371-X*) Thorndike Pr.

Childhood. large type ed. Bill Cosby. 197p. 1993. pap. 10.95 (*1-56054-934-3*) Thorndike Pr.

Childhood. Nathalie Sarraute. Tr. by Barbara Wright. LC 83-20864. 246p. 1985. reprint ed. pap. 10.95 (*0-8076-1116-6*) Braziller.

C

An Asterisk (*) at the beginning of an entry indicates that the title is appearing in BIP for the first time.

C

An Asterisk (*) at the beginning of an entry indicates that the title is appearing in BIP for the first time.

Childhood, 1892-1992. Sue C. Wortham. LC 92-27561. 1992. 15.00 (*0-87173-126-6*) ACEI.

Childhood's End. Arthur C. Clarke. 19.95 (*0-8488-0157-1*, Amereon Hse) Amereon Ltd.

Childhood's End. Arthur C. Clarke. LC 53-10419. 1987. mass mkt. 5.95 (*0-345-34795-1*, Del Rey) Ballantine.

***Childhood's End.** Arthur C. Clarke. 1994. lib. bdg. 24.95x (*1-56849-415-7*) Buccaneer Bks.

Childhood's End. Arthur C. Clarke. LC 53-10419. 216p. 1963. 14.95 (*0-15-117205-6*) HarBrace.

Childhood's Future. Richard Louv. 1992. pap. 11.00 (*0-385-42390-X*, Anchor NY) Doubleday.

Childhood's Thief: One Woman's Journey of Healing from Sexual Abuse. Rose M. Evans. 336p. 1994. text ed. 22.00 (*0-02-536610-6*, L Drew Bks) S&S Trade.

***Childhood's Thief: One Woman's Journey of Healing from Sexual Abuse.** Rose M. Evans. LC 95-1654. 1995. write for info. (*0-553-37546-6*) Bantam.

Childhoood in Germany During World War II: The Story of a Little Girl. Karla O. Poewe. LC 88-8956. (Studies in German Thought & History: Vol. 4). 230p. 1989. lib. bdg. 89.95 (*0-88946-354-9*) E Mellen.

Childish Questions? O. A. Battista & H. K. Battista. LC 73-85069. (Illus.). 1973. 8.95 (*0-915074-05-2*) Knowledge Bk Pubs.

Childish Things. Valery Larbaud. Tr. by Catherine Wald. (Sun & Moon Classics Ser.: No. 19). 200p. (Orig.). 1990. pap. 13.95 (*1-55713-119-8*) Sun & Moon CA.

Childishness & Brutality of the Time. Hargrave Jennings. 340p. 1992. pap. text ed. 35.00 (*1-56459-209-X*) Kessinger Pub.

Childless: The Hurt & the Hope. Beth Spring. (Pocketbooks Ser.). (Illus.). 48p. (Orig.). 1989. pap. text ed. 2.99 (*0-7459-1607-4*) Lion USA.

Childless by Choice: An Anthology. Ed. by Irene Reti. 96p. 1992. pap. 9.95 (*0-939821-03-6*) HerBooks.

Childless Is Not Less. Vicky Love. LC 84-20464. 144p. (Orig.). 1984. pap. 8.99 (*0-87123-449-1*) Bethany Hse.

Childless Marriage: An Exploratory Study of Couples Who Do Not Want Children. Elaine Campbell. 200p. 1986. text ed. 33.00 (*0-422-60060-1*, 9777, Pub. by Tavistock UK); pap. text ed. 14.95 (*0-422-60070-9*, 9780, Pub. by Tavistock UK) Routledge Chapman & Hall.

Childless, No Choice: The Experience of Involuntary Childlessness. James H. Monach. LC 92-26075. (Illus.). 272p. 1993. 65.00 (*0-415-04090-6*, A9946, Routledge NY) Routledge.

Childlessness Transformed: Stories of Alternative Parenting. 168p. 1989. pap. 9.50 (*0-934747-20-2*) Earth Heart.

Childlike Achilles: Ontogeny & Phylogeny in the Iliad. W. T. MacCary. LC 82-4458. 304p. 1982. text ed. 50.00 (*0-231-05504-8*) Col U Pr.

Childlike Achilles: Ontogeny & Phylogeny in the Iliad. W. Thomas MacCary. LC 82-4458. 294p. reprint ed. pap. 83.80 (*0-7837-0422-4*, 2040745) Bks Demand.

Childmade: Awakening Children to Creative Writing. Cynde Gregory. 256p. 1990. 19.95 (*0-88268-093-5*); pap. 10.95 (*0-88268-088-9*) Station Hill Pr.

Childproofing Your Dog: A Complete Guide to Preparing Your Dog for the Children in Your Life. Brian Kilcommons & Sarah Wilson. 96p. (Orig.). 1994. pap. 8.99 (*0-446-67016-2*) Warner Bks.

Childrearing. Leigh Wood. LC 94-5878. (Native American Culture Ser.). (J). 1994. write for info. (*0-86625-537-0*) Rourke Bk Co.

Children. (Illus.). 1991. text ed. write for info. (*1-56290-069-2*, 6000) Crystal.

***Children.** (Postcard Bks.). (Illus.). 18p. 1994. 8.95 (*3-7913-1407-6*) TeNeues.

Children. Mary Calvert. LC 88-70829. (Illus.). 160p. 1990. 23.50 (*0-9609914-5-X*) M Calvert.

Children. A. R. Gurney. 1977. pap. 4.75 (*0-8222-0202-6*) Dramatists Play.

***Children.** Concept by L. Ron Hubbard. 40p. 1994. pap. 4.00 (*0-88404-921-3*) Bridge Pubns Inc.

Children. Daryl Lucas. (Famous Bible People Ser.). (Illus.). 18p. (J). (gr. 2). 1992. 7.99 (*0-8423-1013-4*) Tyndale.

Children. J. M. Parramon et al. (Barron's Family Ser.). 32p. (J). (gr. 3-5). 1987. pap. 6.95 (*0-685-73872-8*); Eng. ed. pap. 6.95 (*0-8120-3850-9*); Span. ed.: Los Ninos. pap. 6.95 (*0-8120-3854-1*) Barron.

Children. Illus. by Priscilla Rattazzi. LC 91-50744. 128p. 1992. 30.00 (*0-8478-1498-X*) Rizzoli Intl.

Children. Peggy Roalf. LC 92-52982. (Looking at Paintings Ser.). (Illus.). 48p. (Orig.). (J). (gr. 3-7). 1993. lib. bdg. 14.89 (*1-56282-308-6*); pap. 6.95 (*1-56282-309-4*) Hyprn Child.

Children. Edith Wharton. (Hudson River Editions Ser.). 1985. text ed. 25.00 (*0-684-18453-2*, Scribners) S&S Trade.

Children. Edith Wharton. 352p. 1992. pap. 10.00 (*0-02-026477-1*, Collier S&S) S&S Trade.

Children. 2nd ed. Cole & June Havlena. (C). 1995. Study Guide. student ed, pap. text ed. write for info. (*0-7167-2345-X*); Instr.'s Manual. teacher ed, pap. text ed. write for info. (*0-7167-2346-8*) W H Freeman.

Children. 4th ed. John W. Santrock. 688p. (C). 1995. pap. text ed. write for info. (*0-697-15042-9*) Brown & Benchmark.

Children. 4th ed. John W. Santrock. 496p. (C). 1995. student ed, pap. write for info. (*0-697-15043-7*) Brown & Benchmark.

Children: A Pictorial Archive from Nineteenth Century Sources; 242 Copyright-Free Illustrations for Artists & Designers. Ed. by Carol B. Grafton. (Pictorial Archive Ser.). (Illus.). 1978. pap. 5.95 (*0-486-23694-3*) Dover.

Children: Behavior & Development. 3rd ed. Boyd R. McCandless & Robert J. Trotter. LC 76-54683. 512p. (C). 1977. text ed. 34.75 (*0-03-089750-5*) HB Coll Pubs.

Children: Blessing or Burden? rev. ed. Max Heine. 257p. 1994. pap. 8.95 (*0-923463-94-1*) Noble Pub Assocs.

Children: Development & Social Issues. Edward F. Zigler & Matia Finn-Stevenson. LC 86-82189. 799p. (C). 1987. text ed. 30.00 (*0-669-07754-2*); Study guide. student ed 11.00 (*0-669-07753-4*); Instr.'s guide. teacher ed 2.00 (*0-669-07752-6*); Archive test program, IBM pc. 150.00 (*0-669-15681-7*); Archive test program, Apple. 150.00 (*0-669-15684-1*) Heath.

Children: Early Childhood. 3rd ed. John W. Santrock. (C). 1993. student ed write for info. (*0-697-17119-1*) Brown & Benchmark.

Children: Needs & Rights. Ed. by Vincent Greaney. 200p. 1986. text ed. 26.50 (*0-8290-1553-1*) Irvington.

Children: New Perspectives: Child Welfare in England, 1872-1969. Harry Hendrick. LC 93-22964. 1993. write for info. (*0-415-00773-9*) Routledge.

Children: Rights & Childhood. David Archard. LC 92-2464. (Ideas Ser.). 177p. 1993. 49.95 (*0-415-08251-X*, B0290); pap. 14.95 (*0-415-08252-8*, B0294) Routledge.

Children: The Adventures of Rex & Zendah in the Zodiac. Esme Swainson. Ed. by Rosicrucian Fellowship Staff. (Illus.). 112p. (J). (ps-8). 1981. reprint ed. pap. text ed. 4.95 (*0-911274-61-8*) Rosicrucian.

Children: The Challenge. Rudolf Dreikurs & Vicki Soltz. 1964. pap. 7.95 (*0-8015-9010-8*, Dutton) NAL-Dutton.

Children: The Challenge. Rudolf Dreikurs & Vicki Soltz. 336p. 1987. pap. 7.95 (*0-525-48308-X*, 0772-230, Dutton) NAL-Dutton.

Children: The Challenge. Rudolf Dreikurs et al. 1991. pap. 11.00 (*0-452-26655-6*, Plume) NAL-Dutton.

***Children: The Early Years.** 3rd ed. Celia A. Decker. LC 94-30247. (Illus.). 544p. 1995. 42.60 (*1-56637-107-4*) Goodheart.

Children: The Rosicrucian Principles of Child Training. 5th ed. Max Heindel. Ed. by Rosicrucian Fellowship Staff. 52p. (C). 1987. reprint ed. pap. 3.25 (*0-911274-62-6*) Rosicrucian.

Children: Their Growth & Development. Sheila G. Terry et al. (Careers in Home Economics Ser.). (Illus.). 1979. text ed. 19.96 (*0-07-063731-8*) McGraw.

Children - Development & Relationships. 4th ed. Mollie S. Smart et al. 550p. (C). 1982. text ed. write for info. (*0-02-411910-5*) Macmillan.

Children Above One Hundred Eighty IQ Stanford-Binet: Origins & Development. Leta S. Hollingworth. LC 74-21417. (Classics in Child Development Ser.). (Illus.). 356p. 1977. reprint ed. 33.95 (*0-405-06467-5*) Ayer.

Children Achieving Potential: An Introduction to Elementary School Counseling & State-Level Policies. 38p. 1990. 10.00 (*1-55516-322-X*, 3112) Natl Conf State Legis.

Children Act & Family Support. Jane Gibbons. 204p. 1993. pap. 40.00 (*0-11-321549-5*, HM15495, Pub. by HMSO UK) UNIPUB.

***Children Act in Practice.** Richard White et al. Date not set. pap. write for info. (*0-406-03259-9*, U.K.) Butterworth Legal Pubs.

Children Act Report, 1992. (Command Paper Ser.: No. 2144). 106p. 1993. pap. 30.00 (*0-10-121442-1*, HM14421, Pub. by HMSO UK) UNIPUB.

Children Act, 1989: Putting It into Practice. Mary Ryan. 240p. 1994. 51.95 (*1-85742-192-2*, Pub. by Ashgate UK) Ashgate Pub Co.

Children Act 1989: The Private Law. Anne Barlow. 78p. 1991. 33.00 (*1-85190-146-9*, Pub. by Tolley Pubng UK) St Mut.

Children Act 1989: The Public Law. John Williams. 94p. 1991. 33.00 (*1-85190-145-0*, Pub. by Tolley Pubng UK) St Mut.

Children Act 1989 - A Procedural Handbook. P. M. Harris. 1991. pap. 42.00 (*0-406-00140-5*, U.K.) Butterworth Legal Pubs.

Children Adapt: A Theory of Sensorimotor-Sensory Development. 2nd ed. Elnora M. Gilfoyle et al. LC 86-43125. 312p. 1990. pap. 36.00 (*1-55642-187-7*) SLACK Inc.

Children, Adolescents, & AIDS. Ed. by Jeffrey M. Seibert & Roberta A. Olson. LC 89-4866. (Children & the Law Ser.). viii, 243p. 1989. 25.00 (*0-8032-4186-0*) U of Nebr Pr.

***Children Aflame.** David Walters. 48p. 1995. pap. write for info. (*0-9629559-7-3*) Good News Min.

Children Afloat. Pippa Driscoll. 1989. pap. text ed. 12.60 (*0-07-155720-2*) McGraw.

Children Afloat. Pippa Driscoll. (Illus.). 96p. 1989. pap. 12.95 (*0-906754-42-9*) TAB Bks.

Children & Adolescents. 3rd ed. David Elkind. (C). 1981. text ed. 23.95 (*0-19-502820-1*); pap. text ed. 14.95 (*0-19-502821-X*) OUP.

***Children & Adolescents in Need: A Legal Primer for Professionals Serving Children.** Virginia G. Weisz. 280p. 1994. 45.00 (*0-8039-4659-7*); pap. 19.95 (*0-8039-4660-0*) Sage.

Children & AIDS: Clinical Issues for Psychiatrists. Ed. by Margaret L. Stuber. LC 91-4581. (Clinical Practice Ser.: No. 19). 250p. 1991. text ed. 30.00 (*0-88048-199-4*) Am Psychiatric.

Children & Anthropological Research. Ed. by Barbara Butler & Diane M. Turner. LC 86-30517. 174p. 1987. 59.50 (*0-306-42499-1*, Plenum Pr) Plenum.

Children & Arson: America's Middle Class Nightmare. Wayne S. Wooden & Martha L. Berkey. LC 84-11731. 276p. 1984. 19.95 (*0-306-41773-1*, Plenum Pr) Plenum.

Children & Art Teaching. Keith Gentle. LC 84-17615. 216p. 1985. pap. 22.50 (*0-7099-1123-8*, Pub. by Croom Helm UK) Routledge Chapman & Hall.

***Children & Asthma: The New Epidemic & How to Treat It.** Bob Lanier. 1992. 23.95 (*1-56530-027-0*) Summit TX.

Children & Books. 8th ed. Zena Sutherland. (C). 1990. text ed. 57.00 (*0-673-46357-5*) HarpCollege.

***Children & Books I: African American Story Books & Activities for All Children.** Patricia B. Moll. (Children &... Ser.). (Illus.). 250p. 1994. spiral bd. 14.95 (*0-9616511-5-6*) Hampton Mae.

***Children & Books I: African American Story Books & Activities for All Children.** 2nd ed. Patricia B. Moll. (Children &... Ser.). (Illus.). 250p. 1994. pap. 14.95 (*0-9616511-4-8*) Hampton Mae.

Children & Books I: African American Storybooks & Activities for all Children. Patricia B. Moll. 218p. (J). (ps-3). 1991. pap. 14.95 (*0-9616511-2-1*); spiral bd. 14.95 (*0-9616511-3-X*) Hampton Mae.

Children & Childhood in Classical Athens. Mark Golden. LC 89-24748. (Ancient Society & History Ser.). (Illus.). 288p. 1990. text ed. 42.50x (*0-8018-3980-7*) Johns Hopkins.

Children & Childhood in Classical Athens. Mark Golden. (Ancient Society & History Ser.). (Illus.). 288p. 1993. reprint ed. pap. text ed. 14.95 (*0-8018-4600-5*) Johns Hopkins.

***Children & Childhood in Western Society since 1500.** Hugh Cunningham. LC 94-49402. (Studies in Modern History). (C). 1995. text ed. 43.95 (*0-582-23853-6*, Pub. by Longman UK); pap. text ed. 13.95 (*0-582-23854-4*, Pub. by Longman UK) Longman.

Children & Communication: Verbal & Nonverbal Language Development. 2nd ed. Barbara S. Wood. (Illus.). 320p. 1981. text ed. write for info. (*0-13-131920-5*) P-H.

***Children & Communities.** Ed. by Paul Henderson. LC 94-42411. (Pluto Studies in Community Development). (C). 1995. text ed. 59.95 (*0-7453-0798-1*, Pub. by Pluto Pr UK) Westview.

***Children & Communities.** Ed. by Paul Henderson. (Pluto Studies in Community Development). (C). 1995. pap. text ed. 16.95 (*0-7453-0799-X*, Pub. by Pluto Pr UK) Westview.

Children & Computers Together in the Early Childhood Classroom. Jane I. Davidson. Ed. by Jay Whitney. 256p. 1988. teacher ed 12.00 (*0-8273-3342-0*) Delmar.

Children & Controversial Issues: Strategies for the Early & Middle Years. Barry Troyna & Bruce Carrington. 240p. 1988. 65.00 (*1-85000-416-1*, Falmer Pr); pap. 34.00 (*1-85000-417-X*, Falmer Pr) Taylor & Francis.

Children & Conversion. Ed. by Clifford Ingle. LC 79-113212. 160p. 1991. pap. 6.99 (*0-8054-2514-4*) Broadman.

***Children & Counseling.** Crompton. 1992. 35.95 (*1-56593-563-2*, 0532) Singular Publishing.

Children & Criminality: The Child As Victim & Perpetrator. Ronald B. Flowers. LC 86-12027. (Contributions in Criminology & Penology Ser.: No. 13). (Illus.). 237p. 1986. text ed. 55.00 (*0-313-25124-X*, FCH/, Greenwood Pr) Greenwood.

Children & Day Nurseries. Caroline Garland & Stephanie White. LC 80-24264. (Oxford Preschool Research Project Ser.: Vol. 4). 128p. 1980. pap. 10.00 (*0-931114-12-8*) High-Scope.

Children & Daycare: Lessons from Research. Eilis Hennessey et al. 112p. 1992. pap. 23.00 (*1-85396-184-1*, Pub. by Paul Chapman UK) Taylor & Francis.

Children & Death. Ed. by Costa Papadatos & Danai Papadatou. (Death Education, Aging & Health Care Ser.). 280p. 1991. 63.00 (*1-56032-043-5*) Hemisp Pub.

Children & Death: Perspectives from Birth Through Adolescence. Ed. by John E. Showalter et al. LC 87-15866. (Foundation of Thanatology Ser.: Vol. 9). 224p. 1987. text ed. 62.50 (*0-275-92558-7*, C2558, Praeger Pubs) Greenwood.

Children & Development in the 1990s: A UNICEF Sourcebook on the Occasion of the World Summit for Children. 256p. 1990. 35.00 (*92-806-0056-7*, 90.XX. USA.8) UN.

Children & Disasters. Ed. by C. F. Saylor. (Issues in Clinical Child Psychology Ser.). (Illus.). 260p. (C). 1993. 39.50 (*0-306-44431-3*, Plenum Pr) Plenum.

Children & Discipline: A Teacher's Guide. John Wilson & Barbara Cowell. Ed. by Cedric Cullingford. (Children, Teachers & Learning Ser.). 160p. 1990. text ed. 60.00 (*0-304-32282-2*); pap. text ed. 18.95 (*0-304-32266-0*) Cassell.

***Children & Divorce.** 250p. (Orig.). 1995. pap. 65.00 (*0-7605-1469-0*) Rector Pr.

Children & Divorce. Archibald Hart. 157p. 1985. write for info. (*0-8499-3041-3*) Word Inc.

Children & Divorce. Ed. by Lawrence A. Kurdek. LC 82-82180. (New Directions for Child Development Ser.: No. CD 19). 1983. 17.95 (*0-87589-931-5*) Jossey-Bass.

Children & Divorce: The Role of Statutory Supervision. Stephen Goode. 140p. 1992. 55.95 (*1-85628-278-3*, Pub. by Avebury Pub UK) Ashgate Pub Co.

Children & Dying, an Exploration & Selective Bibliographies. Sarah S. Cook. LC 73-383. 106p. 1974. pap. 5.95 (*0-930194-87-X*) Ctr Thanatology.

Children & Emotion: The Development of Psychological Understanding. Paul Harris. (Dunn: Understanding Childrens' Worlds Ser.). 224p. 1989. pap. text ed. 21.95 (*0-631-16753-6*) Blackwell Pubs.

Children & ESL: Integrating Perspectives. Ed. by Pat Rigg & D. S. Enright. 171p. 1986. 12.50 (*0-939791-24-2*) Tchrs Eng Spkrs.

Children & Exercise, Vol. XII. Ed. by Joseph Rutenfranz et al. LC 86-10556. 432p. 1986. text ed. 47.00 (*0-87322-062-5*, BRUT0062) Human Kinetics.

Children & Exercise XI. Ed. by Rob A. Binkhorst et al. (International Series on Sport Sciences: Vol. 15). 372p. (C). 1985. text ed. 42.00 (*0-87322-019-6*, BBIN0019) Human Kinetics.

Children & Exercise XIII. Ed. by Svein C. Oseid & Carlsen Kai-Hakon. LC 88-26665. (International Series on Sport Sciences: Vol. 19). 464p. 1989. text ed. 52.00x (*0-87322-188-5*, BOSE0188) Human Kinetics.

***Children & Families: Australian Perspectives.** Ed. by Freda Briggs. 224p. 1995. pap. 22.95 (*1-86373-626-3*, Pub. by Allen Unwin AT) Paul & Co Pubs.

Children & Families: Studies in Prevention & Intervention. Ed. by Euthymia D. Hibbs. 570p. (C). 1988. text ed. 67.50 (*0-8236-0790-9*) Intl Univs Pr.

Children & Families "at Promise" Reconstructing the Discource of Risk. Ed. by Beth B. Swadener & Sally Lubeck. LC 94-7750. 320p. (C). 1995. text ed. 64.50x (*0-7914-2291-7*); pap. text ed. 21.95x (*0-7914-2292-5*) State U NY Pr.

Children & Families in the Social Environment. 2nd ed. James Garbarino et al. (Modern Applications of Social Work Ser.). 406p. 1992. lib. bdg. 45.95 (*0-202-36080-6*); pap. text ed. 24.95 (*0-202-36079-2*) Aldine de Gruyter.

Children & Family Breakdown. (EURO Reports & Studies: No. 101). 56p. 1986. pap. 4.20 (*92-890-1267-6*) World Health.

***Children & Fools.** Erich Fried. 1995. pap. 14.99 (*1-85242-211-4*) Serpents Tail.

Children & Fools. Thomas Mann. Tr. by Herman G. Scheffauer. LC 71-142268. (Short Story Index Reprint Ser.). 1977. 18.95 (*0-8369-3752-X*) Ayer.

Children & Gardens. Gertrude Jekyll. (Illus.). 200p. 1982. 29.50 (*0-907462-27-8*) Antique Collect.

Children & Gardens: An Annotated Bibliography of Children's Garden Books, 1829-1988. Heather S. Miller. Ed. by Meryl A. Miasek. (CBHL Plant Bibliography Ser.). 60p. (Orig.). (J). pap. write for info. (*0-9621791-1-6*) CBHL Inc.

Children & Grief, Vol. 5: Big Issues for Little Hearts. Johnette Hartnett. LC 93-90778. (Good Mourning Ser.). 64p. 1993. pap. 6.95 (*1-883171-87-3*) Good Mourning.

Children & Hazardous Work in the Philippines. Victoria Rialp. (Child Labour Collection Ser.). v, 72p. 1993. pap. 12.00 (*92-2-106474-3*) Intl Labour Office.

Children & Health Care: Moral & Social Issues. Ed. by Loretta M. Kopelman & John C. Moskop. (C). 1989. lib. bdg. 123.00 (*1-55608-078-6*) Kluwer Ac.

Children & Hope: A History of the Children's Home Society of Florida. Lawrence Mahoney. (Illus.). 112p. (Orig.). 1987. 22.95 (*0-940495-02-3*) Pickering Pr.

Children & Justice. Stewart Asquith. 258p. 1983. 26.00 (*0-85224-429-0*, Pub. by Edinburgh U Pr UK); pap. 17.50 (*0-85224-466-5*, Pub. by Edinburgh U Pr UK) Col U Pr.

***Children & Languages: Research, Practice & Rationale for the Early Grades.** Rosemarie Benya & Kurt E. Muller. 241p. 1987. 15.00 (*0-614-03011-0*); pap. 10.00 (*0-614-03012-9*) Amer Forum.

Children & Learning. Ed. by Walter McVitty. (Illus.). 120p. (Orig.). (C). 1985. pap. text ed. 14.00 (*0-909955-53-0*, 00586, Pub. by PETA AT) Heinemann.

Children & Literature, 2 Vols. 2nd ed. John W. Stewig. LC 87-80337. 576p. (C). 1987. text ed. 50.76 (*0-395-42950-1*) HM.

Children & Lovers: Fifteen Stories. Helga Sandburg. LC 75-42207. 204p. 1976. 8.95 (*0-15-117250-1*) HarBrace.

Children & Marital Conflict: The Impact of Family Dispute & Resolution. E. Mark Cummings & Patrick Davies. LC 93-43572. (Series on Social & Emotional Development). 216p. 1994. lib. bdg. 40.00 (*0-89862-304-9*); pap. 16.95 (*0-89862-303-0*) Guilford Pubns.

Children & Media. A. Simatos & K. Spencer. 1993. 75.00 (*1-873534-01-9*, Pub. by Manutius Pr UK) St Mut.

Children & Mental Health: Group Rejection & Self-Rejection. Ed. by Morris Rosenberg. (Research in Community & Mental Health Ser.: Vol. 1). 1979. lib. bdg. 73.25 (*0-89232-063-X*) Jai Pr.

Children & Microcomputers: Research on the Newest Medium. Ed. by Milton Chen & William Paisley. LC 85-1789. (Sage Focus Editions Ser.: No. 70). (Illus.). 320p. reprint ed. pap. 91.20 (*0-8357-8485-1*, 2034753) Bks Demand.

Children & Minders. Bridget Bryant et al. LC 80-24692. (Oxford Preschool Research Project Ser.: Vol. 3). 244p. 1980. pap. 10.00 (*0-931114-11-X*) High-Scope.

Children & Movement: Physical Education in the Elementary School. 2nd ed. Jennifer A. Wall & Nancy R. Murray. 480p. 1994. pap. write for info. (*0-697-12666-8*) Brown & Benchmark.

Children & Movement: Physical Education in the Elementary School. Jennifer A. Wall & Nancy R. Murray. 464p. (C). 1990. boxed write for info. (*0-697-00068-0*); write for info. (*0-697-10825-2*) Brown & Benchmark.

Children & Movies. Alice M. Mitchell. LC 70-160240. (Moving Pictures Ser.). xxiv, 181p. 1971. reprint ed. lib. bdg. 24.95 (*0-89198-041-5*) Ozer.

Children & Nonviolence. Bob Aldridge & Janet Aldridge. LC 87-4126. 136p. (Orig.). 1987. text ed. 16.95 (*0-932727-18-2*); pap. 10.95 (*0-932727-17-4*) Hope Pub Hse.

Children & Number: Difficulties in Learning Mathematics. Martin Hughes. 208p. 1986. pap. text ed. 21.95 (*0-631-13581-2*) Blackwell Pubs.

Children & other Strangers. Ruth S. Ginzberg. (C). 1991. text ed. 24.95 (*0-88738-445-5*) Transaction Pubs.

Children & Painting. Cathy W. Topal. LC 91-73902. (Illus.). 160p. 1992. 31.50 (*0-87192-241-X*) Davis Mass.

Children & Parents in Hospitals. Ed. by J. Lind et al. (Journal: Pediatrician: Vol. 9, No. 3-4). (Illus.). 120p. 1980. pap. 16.00 (*3-8055-1476-X*) S Karger.

***Children & Personal Injury Litigation.** Roderick L. Denyer. 250p. 1993. pap. text ed. 30.00 (*0-406-01313-6*, UK) Butterworth Legal Pubs.

C

An Asterisk (*) at the beginning of an entry indicates that the title is appearing in BIP for the first time.

C

An Asterisk (*) at the beginning of an entry indicates that the title is appearing in BIP for the first time.

1201

Children, Dying, & Grief. Ed. by Margot Tallmer et al. (Thanatology Service Ser.). 200p. 1991. pap. text ed. 16.95 (*0-930194-26-8*) Ctr Thanatology.

Children, Education, & the First Amendment: A Psycholegal Analysis. David Moshman. LC 88-29094. (Children & the Law Ser.). xviii, 218p. 1989. 30.00 (*0-8032-3110-5*) U of Nebr Pr.

Children, Ethics, & the Law: Professional Issues & Cases. Gerald P. Koocher. LC 89-78514. (Children & the Law Ser.). xii, 230p. 1990. pap. 12.00 (*0-8032-7776-8*) U of Nebr Pr.

Children Everywhere. Jack Larkin. LC 87-22685. (Illus.). 47p. 1987. 6.95 (*0-913387-02-9*) Old Sturbridge.

Children Experience Literature. Bernard J. Lonsdale & Helen K. Mackintosh. 1973. text ed. 11.25 (*0-394-30368-7*) Random.

Children Exploring Their World: Theme Teaching in Elementary School. Ed. by Sean A. Walmsley. LC 93-31221. (Illus.). 317p. (YA). 1994. pap. text ed. 21.50 (*0-435-08804-1*, Pub. by Heinemann Educ Bks UK) Heinemann.

Children Facing Grief. Janis Romond. LC 88-83363. 40p. (Orig.). 1989. pap. 2.95 (*0-87029-221-8*, 20211-9) Abbey.

Children, Families, & Government: Perspectives on American Social Policy. Ed. by Edward F. Zigler et al. LC 82-234444. 460p. 1983. 74.95 (*0-521-24219-3*) Cambridge U Pr.

Children, Families, & HIV - AIDS: Psychosocial & Psychotherapeutic Issues. Ed. by Nancy Boyd-Franklin et al. LC 93-34761. 380p. 1995. lib. bdg. 40.00 (*0-89862-147-X*); pap. text ed. 19.95 (*0-89862-502-5*) Guilford Pr.

***Children, Families, & Substance Abuse: Challenges for Changing Educational & Social Outcomes.** Smith et al. 304p. 1995. pap. 25.00 (*1-55766-175-8*) P H Brookes.

Children Figurines of Bisque & Chinawares, 1850-1950. Elyse Z. Karlin. LC 90-63499. (Illus.). 176p. 1991. pap. 19.95 (*0-88740-297-6*) Schiffer.

***Children First.** Penelope Leach. 1995. pap. 12.00 (*0-679-75466-0*) Random.

***Children First: A Complete Guide for Parenting Through the Elementary School Years.** Len Brass. LC 94-32877. 144p. (Orig.). 1994. pap. 14.95 (*0-942963-58-X*) Distinctive Pub.

***Children First: Planning an Early Childhood Program.** Marie Keenan. (Illus.). 116p. 1993. teacher ed 14.95 (*1-895411-51-3*) Peguis Pubs Ltd.

Children First: What Our Society Must Do--& Is Doing--for Our Children Today. Penelope Leach. 1994. 22.00 (*0-679-42133-5*) Random.

Children First - a Study of Hospital Services. HMSO Staff. 72p. 1993. pap. 17.00 (*0-11-886096-8*, HM60968, Pub. by HMSO UK) UNIPUB.

Children from Alcoholic Families. Waln K. Brown et al. 20p. 1989. 2.95 (*1-56456-018-X*, 212) W Gladden Found.

***Children from the Golden Age.** Day. (J). Date not set. pap. 14.95 (*0-671-75200-6*, S&S Bks Young Read) S&S Childrens.

Children from the Golden Age. Welleran Poltarnees. (Illus.). 128p. (J). 1991. pap. 14.95 (*0-88138-094-6*, Green Tiger S&S) S&S Childrens.

Children Going to the Hospital. Harold Geist & Morse P. Manson. LC 65-28467. (Illus.). 28p. 1965. pap. 4.10 (*0-87424-202-9*, W-202) Western Psych.

***Children Grieve, Too: Developing, Understanding & Interventions for the Grief & Loss Process.** Melba F. Coleman et al. (Illus.). 75p. (Orig.). 1994. pap. 79.95 (*0-9642578-0-7*) Caring About.

Children Growing up. Ed. by Alan Branthwaite & Don Rogers. LC 85-4838. 270p. 1985. pap. 32.00 (*0-335-15067-5*, Open Univ Pr) Taylor & Francis.

Children Having Children: Global Perspectives on Teenage Pregnancy. Ed. by Gary McCuen. LC 87-91954. (Ideas in Conflict Ser.). (Illus.). 210p. 1988. lib. bdg. 12.95 (*0-86596-064-X*) G E M.

Children Held Hostage. Phillip C. Snyder & Earl E. Hogan. LC 81-68766. 300p. (Orig.). 1981. pap. 5.95 (*0-940560-01-1*) Custom Hse.

Children Helping Children. Ed. by Hugh C. Foot et al. (Series in Developmental Psychology). 392p. 1990. text ed. 136.95 (*0-471-92292-7*) Wiley.

Children Helping Children: Teaching Students to Become Friendly Helpers. Robert D. Myrick & Robert P. Bowman. Ed. by Don L. Sorenson. LC 81-82900. (Illus.). 280p. 1991. pap. text ed. 10.95 (*0-932796-09-5*) Ed Media Corp.

Children: How to Evaluate Their Symptoms. American Medical Association Staff. LC 85-25681. (Illus.). 128p. 1986. pap. 11.95 (*0-394-74046-7*) Random.

Children, Imagination & Prayer: Creative Techniques for Middle Grade Students. pat E. Dexter. LC 93-60437. 80p. (Orig.). 1993. pap. 7.95 (*0-89622-565-8*) Twenty-Third.

Children in a Changing Health System: Assessments & Proposals for Reform. Mark J. Schlesinger & Leon Eisenberg. LC 89-24406. (Series in Contemporary Medicine & Public Health). 416p. 1990. text ed. 55.00 (*0-685-34280-8*) Johns Hopkins.

Children in a Changing World: Development & Social Issues. 2nd ed. Edward Zigler & Matia F. Stevenson. 768p. (C). 1993. text ed. 53.95 (*0-534-14238-9*) Brooks-Cole.

Children in a Depression Decade. James H. Bossard. LC 74-1667. (Children & Youth Ser.). 302p. 1974. reprint ed. 26.95 (*0-405-05948-5*) Ayer.

Children in Action. Carmen Argardizzo. 144p. 1992. pap. 12.95 (*0-13-131467-X*) P-H.

Children in Africa: A Review of Psychological Research. Judith L. Evans. LC 71-113095. (Publications of the Center for Education in Africa). 123p. reprint ed. pap. 35.10 (*0-685-20809-5*, 2030151) Bks Demand.

Children in an Information Age: Tomorrow's Problems Today: Selected Papers from the International Conference, Varna, Bulgaria, 6-9 May 1985. Ed. by B. Sendov & I. Stanchev. LC 85-28528. 216p. 1986. 88.00 (*0-08-033890-9*, M110, L110, D135, Pub. by PPL UK) Franklin.

Children in Art. Robin Richmond. LC 92-7184. (Story in a Picture Ser.). (Illus.). 48p. (J). (gr. 2-5). 1992. 15.95 (*0-8249-8552-4*, Ideals Child); lib. bdg. 16.00 (*0-8249-8588-5*, Ideals Child) Hambleton-Hill.

Children in Art Text & Prints. (Illus.). 18p. 1992. pap. text ed. 52.50 (*0-935493-71-9*) Modern Learn Pr.

Children in Bondage. Edwin Markham et al. LC 76-89753. (American Labor, from Conspiracy to Collective Bargaining Ser., No. 1). 411p. 1974. reprint ed. 25.95 (*0-405-02140-2*) Ayer.

Children in Care: The Medical Contribution. Ed. by M. Oxtoby. (C). 1989. 50.00 (*0-903534-81-9*, Pub. by Brit Ag for Adopt & Fost UK) St Mut.

Children in Care Revisited. Pamela Mann. LC 84-9915. 192p. 1984. text ed. 29.95 (*0-312-13234-4*) St Martin.

Children in Chaos: A Philosophy for Children Experience. D. C. Government Staff & Leonard Harris. 128p. 1991. pap. 14.95 (*0-8403-6644-2*) Kendall-Hunt.

Children in Chaos: How Israel & the United States Attempt to Integrate At-Risk Youth. Ivan C. Frank. LC 92-7484. 164p. 1992. text ed. 39.95 (*0-275-94291-0*, C4291, Praeger Pubs) Greenwood.

Children in Classrooms: An Investigation of Person-Environment Interaction. Daniel Solomon & Arthur J. Kendall. LC 79-62899. (Praeger Special Studies). 336p. 1979. text ed. 49.95 (*0-275-90427-X*, C0427, Praeger Pubs) Greenwood.

Children in Community: A Photographic Essay. rev. ed. Ed. by Society of Brothers Staff. LC 74-4383. (Illus.). 184p. 1975. 16.00 (*0-87486-015-6*) Plough.

Children in Confinement. Ed. by Robert H. Bremner. LC 74-1675. (Children & Youth Ser.: Vol. 4). 458p. 1977. 21.95 (*0-405-05954-X*) Ayer.

Children in Conflict: Educational Strategies for the Emotionally Disturbed & Behaviorally Disordered. 3rd ed. H. Robert Reinert & Allen Huang. 320p. (C). 1987. pap. write for info. (*0-675-20740-1*, Merrill Pub Co) Macmillan.

Children in Crisis. Ed. by Robin Brown. LC 94-2779. (Reference Shelf Ser.: Vol. 66, No. 1). 1994. 15.00 (*0-8242-0853-6*) Wilson.

Children in Crisis: A Team Approach in the Schools. Sharon R. Morgan. LC 90-20860. 253p. (Orig.). (C). 1985. pap. text ed. 28.00 (*0-89079-289-5*, 1747) PRO-ED.

Children in Custody. Gillian Stewart & Norman Tutt. 250p. 1987. text ed. 59.95 (*0-566-05075-7*) Ashgate Pub Co.

Children in Danger: Coping with the Consequences of Community Violence. James Garbarino et al. LC 91-42319. (Social & Behavioral Sciences Ser.). 280p. 1992. 28.95 (*1-55542-416-3*) Jossey-Bass.

Children in English-Canadian Society: Framing the Twentieth-Century Consensus. Neil Sutherland. LC 76-44228. (Canadian University Paperbooks Ser.: No. 210). (Illus.). 360p. reprint ed. pap. 102.60 (*0-8357-4170-2*, 2036944) Bks Demand.

Children in Exile: Poems, 1968-1984. James Fenton. LC 93-40177. 1994. pap. 12.00 (*0-374-52406-8*) FS&G.

***Children in Families at Risk: Maintaining the Connections.** Lee Combrinck-Graham. 1995. lib. bdg. 42.00 (*0-89862-852-0*) Guilford Pr.

Children in Families under Stress. Ed. by Anna-Beth Doyle et al. LC 83-82717. (New Directions for Child Development Ser.: No. CD 24). 1984. 17.95 (*0-87589-984-6*) Jossey-Bass.

Children in Family Contexts: Perspectives on Treatment. Ed. by Lee Combrinck-Graham. LC 88-5108. 537p. 1988. lib. bdg. 44.95 (*0-89862-732-X*) Guilford Pr.

Children in Foster Care: A Longitudinal Investigation. David Fanshel & Eugene B. Shinn. LC 77-2872. 538p. reprint ed. pap. 153.40 (*0-7837-0426-7*, 2040749) Bks Demand.

Children in Foster Care: Destitute, Neglected...Betrayed. Alan R. Gruber. LC 77-521. 226p. 1978. 35.95 (*0-87705-265-4*) Human Sci Pr.

Children in Front of the Small Screen. Grant Noble. LC 75-15432. (Communication & Society Ser.: No. 5). 256p. reprint ed. pap. 73.00 (*0-7837-1116-6*, 2041646) Bks Demand.

Children in Halachah. S. B. Cohen. 1993. 17.95 (*0-89906-611-9*); 14.95 (*0-89906-612-7*) Mesorah Pubns.

Children in Historical & Comparative Perspective: An International Handbook & Research Guide. Ed. by Joseph M. Hawes & N. Ray Hiner. LC 90-38416. 584p. 1991. text ed. 79.50 (*0-313-25760-4*, HCH, Greenwood Pr) Greenwood.

Children in History, Vol 1: Middle Ages. Molly Harrison. (Illus.). 1978. Vol. 1, Middle Ages. pap. 9.95 (*0-7175-0754-8*) Dufour.

Children in History, Vol. 2: 16th-17th Century. Molly Harrison. (Illus.). 1978. Vol. 2, 16th-17th Century. pap. 8.95 (*0-7175-0773-4*) Dufour.

Children in History, Vol. 3: 18th Century. Molly Harrison. (Illus.). 1978. Vol. 3, 18th Century. pap. 8.95 (*0-7175-0766-1*) Dufour.

Children in History, Vol. 4: 19th Century. Molly Harrison. (Illus.). 1978. Vol. 4, 19th Century. pap. 8.95 (*0-7175-0794-7*) Dufour.

Children in India: Critical Issues in Human Development. Ed. by Alfred De Souza. 1980. 17.50 (*0-8364-0601-X*, Pub. by Manohar II) S Asia.

Children in India: Critical Issues in Human Development. Ed. by A. Desouza. 262p. 1979. 24.95 (*0-318-36938-9*) Asia Bk Corp.

Children in Jeopardy: A Study of Abused Minors & Their Families. Elizabeth Elmer. LC 67-22278. (Contemporary Community Health Ser.). 144p. (C). 1967. pap. 9.95 (*0-8229-5130-4*) U of Pittsburgh Pr.

Children in Libraries: Patterns of Access to Materials & Services in Schools & Public Libraries. Ed. by Zena Sutherland. LC 80-53135. (Studies in Library Science Ser.). 128p. (C). 1981. lib. bdg. 12.95 (*0-226-78063-5*) U Ch Pr.

***Children in Need: Family Support under the Children Act 1989.** Matthew Colton et al. 259p. 1995. boxed, pap. 59.95 (*1-85628-932-X*, Pub. by Avebury Pub UK) Ashgate Pub Co.

Children in Need: Investment Strategies for the Educationally Disadvantaged. (CED Statement on National Policy Ser.). 112p. 1987. pap. 10.50 (*0-87186-086-4*) Comm Econ Dev.

Children in Northern Ireland: Abused by Security Forces & Paramilitaries. Ed. by Human Rights Watch Staff. 112p. (Orig.). 1992. pap. 10.00 (*1-56432-080-4*) Hum Rts Watch.

Children in Our Lives: Knowing & Teaching Them. Jane Adan. LC 90-22958. (Feminist Theory in Education Ser.). 313p. (C). 1991. 71.50 (*0-7914-0811-6*); pap. 23.95 (*0-7914-0812-4*) State U NY Pr.

Children in Pain: Clinical & Research Issues from a Developmental Perspective. Ed. by J. P. Bush & S. W. Harkins. xvii, 476p. 1991. 65.00 (*0-387-97501-2*) Spr-Verlag.

Children in Pain: Helping Chronically Addicted Adolescents. C. C. Nuckols. 224p. 1992. pap. 12.95 (*0-8306-3768-0*, 4096, TAB-Human Servs Inst) TAB Bks.

Children in Photography: One Hundred Fifty Years. Text by Gary M. Dault. (Illus.). 320p. (Orig.). 1990. 50.00 (*0-920668-75-5*); pap. 29.95 (*0-920668-68-2*) Firefly Bks Ltd.

Children in Poverty: Child Development & Public Policy. Ed. by Aletha C. Huston. (Illus.). 330p. (C). 1992. 47.95 (*0-521-39162-8*) Cambridge U Pr.

Children in Poverty: Child Development & Public Policy. Ed. by Aletha C. Huston. (Illus.). 350p. (C). 1994. pap. 19.95 (*0-521-47756-5*) Cambridge U Pr.

Children in Recovery. Rosalie C. Jesse. (C). 1989. 24.95 (*0-393-70074-7*) Norton.

Children in Residential Care: Critical Issues in Treatment. Ed. by Charles E. Schaefer & Arthur J. Swanson. LC 93-7955. 312p. 1993. pap. 35.00 (*1-56821-000-0*) Aronson.

Children in Society: A Libertarian Critique. Stephen Cullen. (Anarchist Discussion Ser.). 43p. (Orig.). 1991. pap. 3.00 (*0-900384-62-X*) Left Bank.

***Children in Sport.** Andrew Hills & Tony Parker. (Illus.). 400p. 1994. pap. 34.95 (*0-86793-313-5*) Blackwell Sci.

Children in Sport. 3rd ed. Ed. by Frank L. Small et al. LC 88-1877. (Illus.). 368p. (C). 1988. 32.00x (*0-87322-183-4*, BSMO0183) Human Kinetics.

Children in Sport. Ed. by Richard A. Magill et al. LC 82-82668. 327p. reprint ed. pap. 93.20 (*0-318-34932-9*, 2031470) Bks Demand.

Children in the Age of Info: Opportunities for Creativity Innovation & New Activities. B. Sendov & I. Stanchev. LC 85-28528. 1988. 105.00 (*0-08-036464-0*, Pub. by Pergamon Repr UK) Franklin.

Children in the Assembly of the Church. Ed. by Eleanor Bernstein & John Brooks-Leonard. LC 92-36339. 101p. 1993. pap. 8.95 (*0-929650-66-2*) Liturgy Tr Pubns.

Children in the Church Today: An Orthodox Perspective. Magdalen. (Illus.). 104p. (Orig.). 1990. pap. 7.95 (*0-88141-104-3*) St Vladimirs.

Children in the Cinema. Richard Ford. LC 70-160232. (Moving Pictures Ser.). viii, 232p. 1971. reprint ed. lib. bdg. 25.95 (*0-89198-033-4*) Ozer.

Children in the Field: Anthropological Experiences. Ed. by Joan Cassell. LC 86-23160. 288p. 1994. pap. 16.95 (*1-56639-206-3*) Temple U Pr.

Children in the Field: Anthropological Experiences. Ed. by Joan Cassell. LC 86-23160. (Illus.). 288p. 1994. 39.95 (*0-87722-477-3*) Temple U Pr.

Children in the Fields: An Original Anthology. Ed. by Dan C. McCurry & Richard E. Rubenstein. LC 74-30624. (American Farmers & the Rise of Agribusiness Ser.). (Illus.). 1975. 29.95 (*0-405-06775-5*) Ayer.

***Children in the Holocaust & World War II: Their Secret Diaries.** Laurel Holliday. 1995. 20.00 (*0-671-52054-7*) PB.

Children in the Hospital. Thesi Bergmann & Anna Freud. LC 65-28803. 162p. 1966. text ed. 27.50 (*0-8236-0800-X*); pap. 24.95 (*0-8236-8017-7*, 020800) Intl Univs Pr.

Children in the House: The Material Culture of Early Childhood, 1600-1900. Karin Calvert. 200p. 1992. text ed. 35.00 (*1-55553-138-5*) NE U Pr.

Children in the House: The Material Culture of Early Childhood 1600-1900. Karin Calvert. 208p. 1994. reprint ed. pap. text ed. 14.95 (*1-55553-189-X*) NE U Pr.

***Children in the Industrial Age.** Clement. 1995. text ed. 26.95 (*0-8057-4109-7*) Macmillan.

Children in the Legal System, Cases & Materials On. Walter J. Wadlington et al. LC 82-21114. (University Casebook Ser.). 972p. 1991. reprint ed. text ed. 35.50 (*0-88277-101-9*); reprint ed. pap. text ed. write for info. (*0-88277-125-6*) Foundation Pr.

Children in the Legal System, 1990 Supplement to Cases & Materials On. Walter J. Wadlington et al. (University Casebook Ser.). 324p. 1991. reprint ed. pap. text ed. 12.95 (*0-88277-822-6*) Foundation Pr.

Children in the Martial Arts: What Every Parent Should Know Before Their Child Takes Karate Lessons. William Gregory. (Orig.). 1991. pap. 7.95 (*0-9627702-1-3*) K & L Pub Co.

Children in the Middle: Living Through Divorce. Ann Mitchell. 224p. (Orig.). 1985. 32.00 (*0-422-79260-8*, 9377, Pub. by Tavistock UK); pap. 13.95 (*0-422-79270-5*, 9378, Pub. by Tavistock UK) Routledge Chapman & Hall.

***Children in the Muslim Middle East.** Elizabeth W. Fernea. LC 94-46181. 1996. write for info. (*0-292-71133-6*) U of Tex Pr.

Children in the Night. Harold Myra. 350p. 1991. pap. 9.99 (*0-310-57251-7*) Zondervan.

Children in the Picture. Stephanie Tebbutt. (C). 1993. pap. text ed. 21.00 (*1-85172-050-2*, Pub. by Pluto Pr UK) Westview.

Children in the Public Care. W. Utting. 78p. 1991. pap. 25.00 (*0-11-321455-3*, HM7177) UNIPUB.

Children in the Wind. Joji Tsubota. Tr. by Robert Epp. 180p. 1991. 22.50 (*0-7103-0393-9*, A5365, Pub. by Kegan Paul Intl UK) Routledge Chapman & Hall.

***Children in the Woods.** Frederick Busch. 352p. 1995. pap. 12.00 (*0-449-90979-4*) Fawcett.

Children in the Woods: New & Selected Stories. Frederick Busch. LC 93-5008. 1994. 21.95 (*0-395-64724-X*) HM.

Children in the World. Magda C. McHale et al. LC 78-24731. (Illus.). 1979. pap. 3.00 (*0-917136-03-9*) Population Ref.

Children in the Worshipping Community. David Ng & Virginia Thomas. LC 80-84655. (Illus.). 128p. (Orig.). (C). 1981. pap. 9.99 (*0-8042-1688-6*, John Knox) Westminster John Knox.

Children in Time & Place: Developmental & Historical Insights. Ed. by Glen H. Elder, Jr. et al. (Cambridge Studies in Social & Emotional Development). (Illus.). 375p. (C). 1993. 49.95 (*0-521-41784-8*) Cambridge U Pr.

Children in Time & Place: Developmental & Historical Insights. Ed. by Glen H. Elder, Jr. et al. (Cambridge Studies in Social & Emotional Development). (Illus.). 302p. (C). 1994. pap. 16.95 (*0-521-47801-4*) Cambridge U Pr.

Children in Treatment: A Primer for Beginning Therapists. M. S. Cooper & L. Wanerman. LC 77-7637. 191p. 1977. pap. 18.50 (*0-87630-333-5*) Brunner-Mazel.

Children in Tudor England. Tony Kelly. 52p. (J). (gr. 6-9). 1987. pap. 7.95 (*0-85950-545-6*, Pub. by S Thornes UK) Dufour.

Children in Watercolor. Lori Quarton. (How to Draw & Paint Ser.). (Illus.). 32p. (Orig.). 1990. pap. 5.95 (*1-56010-053-2*, HT224) W Foster Pub.

***Children Just Like Me.** Susan E. Copsey. 72p. (J). 1995. 16.95 (*0-7894-0201-7*, 5-70614) Dorling Kindersley.

Children Learn to Communicate: Language Arts Through Creative Problem Solving. Sara Lundsteen. LC 75-19324. (Illus.). 1976. Ideas into practice companion guide. write for info. (*0-13-449231-5*) P-H.

Children Learn to Measure: Foundation Activities in the Classroom. J. A. Glenn. 144p. (C). 1980. pap. 40.00 (*0-06-318156-8*, Pub. by P Chapman Pub UK) St Mut.

Children Learning: A Teacher's Classroom Diary. Paula P. Lillard. LC 80-16151. 256p. 1987. write for info. (*0-8052-3745-3*) Schocken.

Children Learning at Home. Julie Webb. 208p. 1990. 70.00 (*1-85000-811-6*, Falmer Pr); pap. 30.00 (*1-85000-812-4*, Falmer Pr) Taylor & Francis.

Children Learning Geometry: Foundation Activities in Shape. Ed. by J. A. Glenn. 128p. (C). 1979. pap. 29.00 (*0-06-318119-3*, Pub. by P Chapman Pub UK) St Mut.

Children Learning Language. Robert Hopper. (C). 1990. text ed. 45.50 (*0-06-042898-8*) HarpCollege.

Children Learning Mathematics: A Cognitive Approach to Teaching. Emma E. Holmes. (Illus.). 416p. (C). 1985. pap. text ed. write for info. (*0-13-132481-0*) P-H.

Children Learning Through Literature: A Teacher Researcher Study. June McConaghy. LC 89-71089. (Illus.). 80p. (Orig.). 1990. pap. text ed. 13.50 (*0-435-08515-8*) Heinemann.

***Children Learning to Read - International Concerns: Curriculum & Assesment Issues, 2 Vols., Vol. 2.** Ed. by Pamela Owen & Peter Pumfrey. LC 49-37967. 210p. 1995. pap. 24.95 (*0-7507-0366-0*, Falmer Pr) Taylor & Francis.

***Children Learning to Read - International Concerns: Curriculum & Assesment Issues, 2 Vol., Vol. 2.** Ed. by Pamela Owen & Peter Pumfrey. LC 49-37967. 210p. 1995. 75.00 (*0-7507-0365-2*, Falmer Pr) Taylor & Francis.

***Children Learning to Read - International Concerns: Emergent & Developing Reading, 2 Vols., Vol. 1.** Ed. by Pamela Owen & Peter Pumfrey. LC 94-37967. 210p. 1995. pap. 24.95 (*0-7507-0364-4*, Falmer Pr) Taylor & Francis.

***Children Learning to Read - International Concerns: Emergent & Developing Reading, 2 Vols., Vol. 1.** Ed. by Pamela Owen & Peter Pumfrey. LC 94-37967. 210p. 1995. 75.00 (*0-7507-0363-6*, Falmer Pr) Taylor & Francis.

Children, Literature & Social Studies: Activities for the Intermediate Grades. Tom McGowan & Meredith McGowan. (Illus.). 218p. (J). (gr. 4-6). 1986. spiral bd. 18.95 (*0-938594-06-0*) Spec Lit Pr.

Children, Liturgy, & Music. Ed. by Virgil C. Funk. (Pastoral Music in Practice Ser.: No. 2). 144p. (Orig.). 1990. pap. 9.95 (*0-912405-73-2*) Pastoral Pr.

Children Living Apart from Their Mothers: A Bibliography of Fiction for Children & Young People. Harriet Edwards. 30p. (Orig.). 1989. pap. text ed. 6.50 (*0-9622462-0-4*) Mayflower Assocs.

An Asterisk (*) at the beginning of an entry indicates that the title is appearing in BIP for the first time.

An Asterisk (*) at the beginning of an entry indicates that the title is appearing in BIP for the first time.

1203

C

***Children of Los Alamos: An Oral History of the Town Where the Atomic Age Began.** Katrina R. Mason. LC 95-13825. (Twayne's Oral History Ser.). 1995. write for info. (*0-8057-9138-8*, Twayne); pap. write for info. (*0-8057-9139-6*, Twayne) Macmillan.

Children of Lylr: The Second Branch of the Mabinogion. Evangeline Walton. 240p. 1992. pap. 9.00 (*0-02-026474-7*, Collier S&S) S&S Trade.

Children of Mao: Personality Development & Political Activism in the Red Guard Generation. Anita Chan. LC 84-21944. 262p. 1985. pap. 25.00 (*0-295-96212-7*) U of Wash Pr.

Children of Maria: Adolescent Substance Abusers, Their Families & Schooling. Christina Andersson. (Uppsala Studies in Education: No. 46). 136p. (Orig.). 1993. pap. 41.50x (*91-554-3086-4*, Pub. by Uppsala Universitet SW) Coronet Bks.

Children of Mariel from Shock to Integration: Cuban Refugee Children in South Florida Schools. Helga Silva. 1985. 3.00 (*0-317-90492-2*) Cuban Amer Natl Fndtn.

Children of Mariplata. Miguel Benavides. LC 91-72159. 1992. pap. 17.95 (*1-85610-019-7*) Dufour.

Children of Mauritania: Days in the Desert & by the River Shore. Lauren Goodsmith. LC 92-46145. (World's Children Ser.). 56p. (J). (gr. 3-6). 1994. lib. bdg. 19.95 (*0-87614-782-1*, First Ave Edns) Lerner Group.

***Children of Mauritania: Days in the Desert & by the River Shore.** Lauren Goodsmith. (World's Children Ser.). 56p. (J). (gr. 3-6). 1994. pap. 7.95 (*0-87614-849-6*, First Ave Edns) Lerner Group.

Children of Men. Rudolph E. Block. LC 76-103496. (Short Story Index Reprint Ser.). 1977. 21.95 (*0-8369-3238-2*) Ayer.

Children of Men. P. D. James. LC 92-54280. 1993. 22.00 (*0-679-41873-3*) Knopf.

Children of Men. P. D. James. 368p. 1994. mass mkt. 6.50 (*0-446-36462-2*, Warner Vision) Warner Bks.

Children of Men. P. D. James. 1993. 24.00 (*0-679-42210-2*) Random.

***Children of Men.** P. D. James. 1994. pap. 5.98 (*0-517-13068-8*) Random Hse Value.

Children of Men: A Novel. Jeanne Schinto. LC 90-45495. 240p. 1991. 19.95 (*0-89255-156-9*) Persea Bks.

Children of Mercury: The Education of Artists in the Sixteenth & Seventeenth Centuries. Brown University, Department of Art Staff. LC 84-70128. (Illus.). 143p. (Orig.). 1984. pap. text ed. 14.00 (*0-933519-03-6*) D W Bell Gallery.

Children of Mexico. Connie Bickman. LC 94-12497. (Through the Eyes of Children Ser.). (J). 1994. lib. bdg. 14.96 (*1-56239-328-6*) Abdo & Dghtrs.

Children of Micronesia. Jules Hermes. LC 93-31268. (World's Children Ser.). (J). (gr. 3-6). 1994. 19.95 (*0-87614-819-4*, Carolrhoda) Lerner Group.

***Children of Morocco.** Jules Hermes. 48p. (J). (gr. 3-6). 1995. pap. 7.95 (*0-87614-899-2*, Carolrhoda) Lerner Group.

Children of Morocco. Jules Hermes. LC 94-12709. (Worlds Children Ser.). 48p. (J). (gr. 3-6). 1995. lib. bdg. 19.95 (*0-87614-857-7*, Carolrhoda) Lerner Group.

Children of Mount Vernon: A Guide to George Washington's Home. Miriam A. Bourne. (Illus.). 56p. pap. 4.95 (*0-931917-11-5*) Mt Vernon Ladies.

Children of Mu. James Churchward. 272p. Date not set. pap. 21.95 (*0-8464-4199-3*) Beekman Pubs.

Children of Mu. James Churchward. 1991. lib. bdg. 300.00 (*0-8490-4803-6*) Gordon Pr.

Children of Mu. James Churchward. (Illus.). 267p. 1988. reprint ed. pap. 15.95 (*0-914732-22-6*) Bro Life Inc.

Children of Nepal. Reijo Harkonen. (World's Children Ser.). (Illus.). 48p. (J). (gr. 3-6). 1990. lib. bdg. 19.95 (*0-87614-395-8*, Carolrhoda) Lerner Group.

Children of Nigh. Naomi S. Nye et al. 1993. pap. text ed. 5.95 (*1-885405-00-6*) IOC Pr.

Children of Noisy Village. Astrid Lindgren. (J). (gr. 3-7). 1988. pap. 5.99 (*0-14-032609-X*, Puffin) Puffin Bks.

Children of Nowhere. Inez Exton. (Illus.). 220p. 1991. pap. 17.50 (*0-929497-41-4*) Ariadne CA.

Children of Nuggets: The Definitive Guide to "Psychedelic Sixties" Punk Rock on Compilation Albums. David Walters. LC 89-92331. (Rock & Roll Reference Ser.: No. 30). (Illus.). 300p. 1990. 50.00 (*1-56075-001-4*) Popular Culture.

Children of Nya. Maryse Conde. LC 88-40486. 512p. 1989. 18.95 (*0-685-28276-7*) Viking Penguin.

Children of Odin: The Book of Northern Myths. Padraic Colum. LC 83-20368. (Illus.). 280p. (YA). (gr. 5 up). 1984. text ed. 15.95 (*0-02-722890-8*, Mac Bks Young Read); pap. 8.95 (*0-02-042100-1*, Mac Bks Young Read) S&S Childrens.

Children of Oedipus: Brother & Sister Incest in Psychiatry, Literature, History & Mythology. Luciano P. Santiago. LC 73-79773. 1973. 12.95 (*0-87212-028-7*) Libra.

Children of Oedipus & Other Essays on the Imitation of Greek Tragedy, 1550-1800. Martin Mueller. LC 79-26018. 296p. reprint ed. pap. 84.40 (*0-8357-8068-6*, 2034070) Bks Demand.

Children of One God: A History of the Council of Christians & Jews. Marcus Braybrooke. 1991. text ed. 25.00 (*0-85303-242-4*, Pub. by Vallentine Mitchell UK); pap. text ed. 15.00 (*0-85303-250-5*, Pub. by Vallentine Mitchell UK) Intl Spec Bk.

Children of Open Adoption. Kathleen Silber & Patricia M. Dorner. LC 89-85840. 193p. (Orig.). 1990. pap. 9.95 (*0-931722-78-0*) Corona Pub.

Children of Our Children. Augusta Feller et al. LC 87-40262. 82p. 1987. 14.95 (*1-55523-102-0*) Winston-Derek.

Children of Our Time: The Children of the Fourth World-International Movement-A.T.D. Ed. by International Movement A.T.D.-Fourth World Staff. (Symposium Ser.: Vol. 7). (Illus.). 127p. 1981. lib. bdg. 59.95 (*0-88946-911-3*) E Mellen.

Children of Paradise. Liz Rosenberg. LC 92-62426. (Poetry Ser.). 80p. (C). 1993. text ed. 19.95 (*0-8229-3750-6*); pap. text ed. 10.95 (*0-8229-5502-4*) U of Pittsburgh Pr.

Children of Paradise: A Northampton Memoir. Allison M. Lockwood. (Illus.). 166p. (Orig.). 1986. pap. 9.95 (*0-9618052-0-X*) Daily Hampshire.

Children of Parting Parents. 2nd ed. Lora H. Tessman. Date not set. write for info. (*1-56821-055-8*) Aronson.

Children of Paul's: The Story of a Theatre Company, 1553-1608. Reavley Gair. LC 82-4185. (Illus.). 232p. 1982. 47.95 (*0-521-24360-2*) Cambridge U Pr.

***Children of Peace.** W. John McIntyre. (McGill-Queen's Studies in the History of Religion: No. 14). 260p. 1994. 39.95 (*0-7735-1195-4*, Pub. by McGill CN) U of Toronto Pr.

Children of Perestroika: Moscow Teenagers Talk about Their Lives & the Future. Deborah Adelman. LC 90-25104. (Illus.). 280p. 1992. text ed. 36.95 (*1-56324-000-9*); pap. 20.95 (*1-56324-001-7*) M E Sharpe.

Children of Perestroika Come of Age: Young People of Moscow Talk about Life in the New Russia. Deborah Adelman. LC 90-10936. 200p. (J). 1994. text ed. 35.95 (*1-56324-286-9*); pap. 19.95 (*1-56324-287-7*) M E Sharpe.

Children of Peru. Connie Bickman. LC 94-9905. (Through the Eyes of Children Ser.). (J). 1994. lib. bdg. 14.96 (*1-56239-325-1*) Abdo & Dghtrs.

***Children of Pornography.** B. D. Wallace & M. J. Philippus. 94p. (YA). (gr. 7-12). 1990. pap. write for info. (*1-57515-003-4*) PPI Pubng.

***Children of Poverty: Research, Health, & Policy Issues.** Ed. by Hiram E. Fitzgerald et al. LC 94-11694. (Reference Books on Family Issues Ser.: Vol. 23). (Illus.). 392p. 1995. 54.00 (*0-8153-1738-7*, SS968) Garland.

Children of Prejudiced Parents. Jayshree Biswass. 1990. text ed. 27.50 (*0-7069-5323-1*, Pub. by Vikas II) S Asia.

Children of Prenatal Substance Abuse. Shirley N. Sparks. LC 92-28621. (School-Age Children Ser.). (Illus.). 219p. (Orig.). (C). 1992. pap. text ed. 39.95 (*1-56593-071-1*, 0375) Singular Publishing.

Children of Pride. Robert M. Myers. LC 83-10377. 688p. 1987. reprint ed. pap. 20.00 (*0-300-04053-9*, Y-675) Yale U Pr.

Children of Privilege: Student Revolt in the Sixties. Cyril Levitt. 288p. 1984. 40.00 (*0-8020-5636-9*) U of Toronto Pr.

Children of Privilege: Student Revolt in the Sixties: a Study of Student Movements in Canada, the United States & West Germany. Cyril Levitt. LC 84-211030. (Illus.). 280p. reprint ed. pap. 79.80 (*0-7837-0526-3*, 2040852) Bks Demand.

Children of Promise: African-American Literature & Art for Young People. Ed. by Charles Sullivan. (Illus.). 128p. (J). 1991. 24.95 (*0-8109-3170-2*) Abrams.

Children of Promise: Literate Activity in Linguistically & Culturally Diverse Classrooms. Shirley B. Heath & Leslie Mangiola. 62p. 1991. 8.95 (*0-8106-1844-3*) NEA.

Children of Renaissance Florence. Richard C. Trexler. LC 92-44785. (Power & Dependence in Renaissance Florence Ser.: Vol. 1). 144p. 1993. pap. 8.00 (*0-86698-156-X*) MRTS.

Children of Russia. Connie Bickman. LC 94-19299. (Through the Eyes of Children Ser.). (J). (gr. 4 up). 1994. lib. bdg. 14.96 (*1-56239-329-4*) Abdo & Dghtrs.

Children of Sanchez. Oscar Lewis. 1979. pap. 16.00 (*0-394-70280-8*, Vin) Random.

Children of Separation: An Annotated Bibliography for Professionals. Greta W. Stanton. LC 93-43575. 369p. 1994. 42.50 (*0-8108-2695-X*) Scarecrow.

Children of Silence: Or, the Story of the Deaf. Joseph Seiss. 1972. 69.95 (*0-87968-849-1*) Gordon Pr.

Children of Social Worlds. Ed. by Martin Richards & Paul C. Light. 336p. 1986. 38.00 (*0-674-11622-4*) HUP.

Children of Strangers. Anthony Bukoski. LC 93-24483. 200p. (Orig.). 1993. 22.50 (*0-87074-350-3*); pap. 10.95 (*0-87074-364-3*) SMU Press.

Children of Strangers. Lyle Saxon. LC 89-3842. 304p. 1989. reprint ed. pap. 10.95 (*0-88289-397-1*) Pelican.

Children of Strangers: The Stories of a Black Family. Kathryn L. Morgan. LC 80-21144. 122p. 1981. pap. 14.95 (*0-87722-240-1*) Temple U Pr.

Children of the Air. Theodore Deppe. LC 89-24409. 72p. 1990. pap. 9.95 (*0-914086-91-X*) Alicejamesbooks.

Children of the Albatross. Anais Nin. LC 66-6826. 111p. 1959. pap. 6.95 (*0-8040-0039-5*) Swallow.

Children of the Albatross see Cities of the Interior

***Children of the Alley.** Naguib Mahfouz. Tr. by Peter Theroux. LC 95-15510. 1996. write for info. (*0-385-42094-3*) Doubleday.

Children of the Arbat. Anatoli Rybakov. 1989. mass mkt. 5.99 (*0-440-20353-8*) Dell.

Children of the Atom. Wilmar H. Shiras. 1993. reprint ed. lib. bdg. 18.95 (*0-89968-364-9*, Lghtyr Pr) Buccaneer Bks.

***Children of the Atomic Bomb: An American Physician's Memoir: Nagasaki, Hiroshima, & the Marshall Islands.** James N. Yamazaki & Louis B. Fleming. LC 95-6683. (Asian & Pacific Studies). 1995. write for info. (*0-8223-1658-7*); pap. write for info. (*0-8223-1670-6*) Duke.

Children of the Bible. Doris Seger. (Illus.). 64p. (J). (gr. k-6). 1967. pap. text ed. 8.99 (*1-55976-028-1*) CEF Press.

Children of the Bible - Kit., 2 bks. (Illus.). (J). (gr. k-6). 1975. 19.99 (*1-55976-106-7*) CEF Press.

Children of the Bible Activity Book. Anita R. Stohs. (Illus.). 32p. (Orig.). (J). 1993. pap. 3.49 (*0-570-04750-1*) Concordia.

Children of the Black Triangle. Armet Francis. LC 88-83755. (Illus.). 96p. 1989. 19.95 (*0-86543-129-9*) Africa World.

Children of the Blitz. large type ed. Robert Westall. 248p. 1989. reprint ed. lib. bdg. 19.95 (*1-85089-340-3*, Pub. by ISIS UK) Transaction Pubs.

Children of the Blood. Michelle M. Sagara. 1992. mass mkt. 4.99 (*0-345-37621-8*, Del Rey) Ballantine.

Children of the Boat People: A Study of Educational Success. Nathan Caplan et al. 176p. (C). 1991. text ed. 42.50 (*0-472-10285-0*); pap. text ed. 16.95 (*0-472-08162-4*) U of Mich Pr.

Children of the Cave. Joshua Stevens. LC 90-70911. 106p. 1991. 7.95 (*1-55523-358-9*) Winston-Derek.

Children of the Chapel at Blackfriars, 1597-1603. Charles W. Wallace. LC 75-115007. reprint ed. 29.50 (*0-404-06808-1*) AMS Pr.

Children of the Children of Aquarius. Dennis Hiatt. 107p. (Orig.). 1991. pap. 12.26 (*0-685-48256-1*) Dayspring Pr.

Children of the Circle. Adolf Hungrywolf & Star Hungrywolf. LC 92-268. (Illus.). 160p. 1992. pap. 9.95 (*0-913990-89-2*) Book Pub Co.

Children of the Cities. Jo Boyden & Pat Holden. LC 90-20999. 192p. (C). 1991. text ed. 49.95 (*0-86232-956-6*, Pub. by Zed Books UK); pap. 17.50 (*0-86232-957-4*, Pub. by Zed Books UK) Humanities.

Children of the City: At Work & at Play. David Nasaw. (Illus.). 256p. 1986. pap. 10.95 (*0-19-504015-5*) OUP.

Children of the Cold. Frederick Schwatka. LC 75-5875. reprint ed. 20.00 (*0-404-11683-3*) AMS Pr.

Children of the Colossus: The Rhodian Greek Immigrants in the United States. James W. Kiriazis. LC 89-45375. (Immigrant Communities & Ethnic Minorities in the U. S. & Canada Ser.: No. 67). 1989. 64.50 (*0-404-19477-X*) AMS Pr.

***Children of the Dawn.** Patricia Rowe. (Orig.). 1996. mass mkt. write for info. (*0-446-60205-1*) Warner Bks.

Children of the Dawn: Visions of the New Family. Joshua Halpern. 200p. 1986. pap. 5.00 (*0-9613143-7-0*) Owl Pub Co.

Children of the Drake. Richard A. Knaak. 1991. mass mkt. 4.99 (*0-446-36153-4*, Aspect) Warner Bks.

Children of the Dream: The Psychology of Black Success. Audrey Edwards & Craig K. Polite. LC 92-36101. 1993. pap. 10.95 (*0-385-24269-7*, Anchor NY) Doubleday.

***Children of the Dust.** Bill Bauer. 64p. 1995. pap. 10.00 (*1-886157-01-4*) BkMk.

***Children of the Dust.** Clancy Carlile. 1995. 20.00 (*0-679-44132-8*) Random.

Children of the Dust Bowl: The True Story of the School at Weedpatch Camp. Jerry Stanley. LC 92-323. (Illus.). 96p. (J). (gr. 4 up). 1993. pap. 6.99 (*0-517-88094-6*) Crown Bks Yng Read.

Children of the Dustbowl: The True Story of the School at Weedpatch Camp. Jerry Stanley. LC 92-393. (Illus.). 96p. (J). (gr. 4 up). 1992. 15.00 (*0-517-58781-5*); lib. bdg. 15.99 (*0-517-58782-3*) Crown Bks Yng Read.

Children of the Earth: Literature, Politics, & Nationhood. Marc Shell. (Illus.). 368p. 1993. 35.00 (*0-19-506864-5*) OUP.

Children of the Earth & Sky: Five Stories about Native American Children. Stephen Krensky. (J). (ps-3). 1992. pap. 3.95 (*0-590-42853-5*) Scholastic Inc.

Children of the East: Childcare Policy & Practice in South East Asia. Leonard Davis. (Illus.). 72p. 1994. pap. 19.95 (*1-85756-171-6*, Pub. by Janus Pubng UK) Paul & Co Pubs.

Children of the End. Mark Clements. 1994. pap. 4.50 (*0-8439-3594-4*) Dorchester Pub Co.

Children of the End. Mark A. Clements. LC 92-54467. 1993. 20.00 (*1-55611-342-0*) D I Fine.

Children of the Enemy: Oral Histories of Vietnamese Amerasians & Their Mothers. Steven DeBonis. (Illus.). 304p. 1994. lib. bdg. 36.50x (*0-89950-975-4*) McFarland & Co.

Children of the Fire. Harriette G. Robinet. LC 91-9484. 144p. (J). (gr. 3-7). 1991. text ed. 13.95 (*0-689-31655-0*, Atheneum Bks Young) S&S Childrens.

Children of the First People: A Photographic Essay. Dorothy Haegart. (Illus.). 132p. (Orig.). 1984. pap. 21.95 (*0-88978-145-1*) Left Bank.

Children of the Flames: Dr. Josef Mengele & the Untold Story of the Twins of Auschwitz. Lucette M. Lagnado & Sheila C. Dekel. (Illus.). 320p. 1992. pap. 12.95 (*0-14-016931-8*, Penguin Bks) Viking Penguin.

***Children of the Flesh, Children of the Promise: A Rabbi Talks with Paul.** Jacob Neusner. 168p. (Orig.). 1995. pap. 14.95 (*0-8298-1026-9*) Pilgrim OH.

Children of the Frost see Nam Bok

Children of the Gilded Ghetto: Conflict Resolutions of Three Generations of American Jews. Judith P. Kramer. 1961. 59.50 (*0-685-26679-6*) Elliots Bks.

***Children of the Gods.** A. B. Curtiss. (Illus.). 88p. (YA). 1995. 18.95 (*0-932529-57-7*) Oldcastle.

Children of the Gods. Charles V. Shelton. 168p. 1985. pap. 8.00 (*1-877712-01-9*) Forbes Nichols.

Children of the Great Lake. Percy Trezise. (J). (ps-3). 1993. 10.00 (*0-207-17677-9*, Pub. by Angus & Robertson AT) HarpC.

Children of the Great Muskeg. Sean Ferris. (Illus.). 84p. (J). (gr. 3-5). 1991. pap. 12.95 (*0-88753-128-8*, Pub. by Black Moss Pr CN) Firefly Bks Ltd.

Children of the Healer: The Story of Dr. Bob's Kids. Bob Smith & Sue S. Windows. LC 92-64114. (Illus.). 176p. (Orig.). 1992. pap. 12.95 (*0-942421-48-5*) Hazelden.

Children of the Holocaust. Helen Epstein. 320p. 1988. pap. 11.95 (*0-14-011284-7*, Penguin Bks) Viking Penguin.

***Children of the Holocaust.** Lustig. 1995. pap. text ed. (*0-8101-1279-5*) Northwestern U Pr.

Children of the Ice. Charlotte Prentiss. 496p. (Orig.). 1993. pap. 5.50 (*0-451-17792-4*, Onyx) NAL-Dutton.

Children of the Isles. Colwell. (British Island Heritage Editions Ser.). 1991. pap. write for info. (*0-86120-024-1*, Pub. by Aris & Phillips UK) David Brown.

***Children of the Jedi.** Barbara Hambly. 1995. 21.95 (*0-615-00728-7*, Spectra) Bantam.

Children of the Kibbutz: A Study in Child Training & Personality. Melford E. Spiro & Audrey G. Spiro. LC 74-21689. 534p. 1975. pap. 17.95 (*0-674-11606-2*) HUP.

Children of the King. Max Lucado. LC 94-15160. (Illus.). 32p. (J). (gr. 3-6). 1994. 12.99 (*0-89107-823-1*) Crossway Bks.

Children of the Legend. R. A. Dicke. 375p. (Orig.). 1991. pap. 10.95 (*0-929827-09-0*) New Saga Pubs.

Children of the Light: The Rise & Fall of New Bedford Whaling & the Death of the Arctic Fleet. Everett S. Allen. 320p. 1983. reprint ed. pap. 9.95 (*0-940160-23-4*) Parnassus Imprints.

***Children of the Light: True Stories of Children's Near-Death Experiences.** Brad Steiger & Sherry H. Steiger. 304p. 1995. pap. 4.99 (*0-451-18533-1*, Sig) NAL-Dutton.

Children of the Light & Children of the Dark. Reinhold Neibuhr. 1985. pap. 13.50 (*0-684-15027-1*, Scribners) S&S Trade.

Children of the Lion. Peter Danielson. 480p. (Orig.). 1984. 4.99 (*0-553-26912-7*) Bantam.

Children of the Lion, No. 17. Peter Danielson. (Orig.). 1994. mass mkt. 4.99 (*0-553-56146-4*, Bantam Domain) Bantam.

Children of the Living God. Sinclair B. Ferguson. 127p. (Orig.). 1989. pap. 6.95 (*0-85151-536-3*) Banner of Truth.

Children of the Maker. Lucy C. Babbitt. LC 88-45482. 208p. (YA). (gr. 6 up). 1988. 15.00 (*0-374-31245-1*) FS&G.

Children of the Mill: Schooling & Society in Gary, Indiana, 1906-1960. Ronald D. Cohen. LC 89-45477. (Midwestern History & Culture Ser.). 296p. 1990. 35.00 (*0-253-31377-5*) Ind U Pr.

Children of the Mire: Modern Poetry from Romanticism to the Avant-Garde. Octavio Paz. LC 73-88498. (Charles Eliot Norton Lectures: 1970-1971). 192p. 1974. pap. text ed. 5.95 (*0-674-11626-7*) HUP.

Children of the Mist. Edwin Parrish. 328p. (Orig.). 1992. pap. 13.95 (*1-56672-008-7*) Seabar Pub.

Children of the Mist. Nigel Tranter. 224p. 1993. 24.95 (*0-340-55898-9*, Pub. by H & S UK) Trafalgar.

Children of the Morning Light: Wampanoag Tales As Told by Manitonquat. Story Medicine. LC 92-32328. (Illus.). 72p. (J). (gr. 1 up). 1994. text ed. 16.95 (*0-02-765905-4*, Mac Bks Young Read) S&S Childrens.

Children of the Mountains: Short Stories by the Elementary School Children of Pagosa Springs, Colorado. Intro. by Pamela Camille. LC 88-81602. (Illus.). 150p. (Orig.). (J). (gr. 4-8). 1988. pap. 7.95 (*0-945985-01-0*) Freedom Lights Pr.

***Children of the New Amazon.** Veronica McClearin. 40p. (J). Date not set. pap. 9.95 (*0-7610-0389-4*) NW Pub.

Children of the New Forest. Captain Marryat. Ed. by Dennis Butts. (World's Classics Ser.). 352p. 1992. pap. 7.95 (*0-19-282725-1*) OUP.

Children of the New Forest. Captain Marryat. 1990. reprint ed. lib. bdg. 21.95 (*0-89966-700-7*) Buccaneer Bks.

Children of the Night. Jess Mowry. (Orig.). 1989. pap. 3.95 (*0-87067-575-3*) Holloway.

Children of the Night. Edwin A. Robinson. 1974. 200.00 (*0-87968-186-1*) Gordon Pr.

Children of the Night. Dan Simmons. 464p. 1993. mass mkt. 5.99 (*0-446-36475-4*) Warner Bks.

Children of the Night. deluxe ed. Dan Simmons. 450p. 1992. 125.00 (*0-935716-63-7*) Lord John.

Children of the Night: A Diana Tregarde Investigation. Mercedes Lackey. 320p. 1992. mass mkt. 4.99 (*0-8125-2272-9*) Tor Bks.

Children of the Night: A Study of Adolescent Prostitution. D. Kelly Weisberg. LC 82-48957. 320p. 1984. text ed. 39.95 (*0-669-06389-4*) Free Pr.

Children of the Paper Crane: The Story of Sadako Sasaki & Her Struggle with the A-Bomb Disease. Masamoto Nasu. Tr. by Elizabeth W. Baldwin et al. 232p. 1991. 45.00 (*0-87332-715-2*) M E Sharpe.

Children of the Paper Crane: The Story of Sadako Sasaki & Her Struggle with the A-Bomb Disease. Masamoto Nasu. Tr. by Elizabeth W. Baldwin & Steven L. Leeper. 232p. 1994. pap. 18.95 (*0-87332-716-0*) M E Sharpe.

Children of the Past in Photographic Portraits: An Album with 165 Prints. Ed. by Alison Mager. (Illus.). 1978. pap. 7.95 (*0-486-23697-8*) Dover.

Children of the Pearl. Ching Y. Bezine. 400p. (Orig.). 1991. pap. 4.99 (*0-451-17056-3*, Sig) NAL-Dutton.

Children of the Pool & Other Stories. Arthur Machen. Ed. by R. Reginald & Douglas Menville. LC 76-1366. (Supernatural & Occult Fiction Ser.). 1976. reprint ed. lib. bdg. 24.95 (*0-405-08424-2*) Ayer.

Children of the Poor. Jacob A. Riis. LC 73-137186. (Poverty U. S. A.). 1971. reprint ed. 25.95 (*0-405-03124-6*) Ayer.

Children of the Poor in England: Representations of Childhood Since the Seventeenth Century. Hugh Cunningham. (Family, Sexuality & Social Relations in Past Times Ser.). 240p. (C). 1991. text ed. 48.95 (*0-631-17162-2*) Blackwell Pubs.

An Asterisk (*) at the beginning of an entry indicates that the title is appearing in BIP for the first time.

An Asterisk (*) at the beginning of an entry indicates that the title is appearing in BIP for the first time.

1205

Children Who Hate: The Disorganization & Breakdown of Behavior Controls. Fritz Redl & David Wineman. LC 51-13784. 1965. pap. 14.95 (*0-02-925960-6*) Free Pr.

Children Who Hit the Mark. Marilyn Hickey. 52p. (Orig.). pap. write for info. (*1-56441-124-9*) M Hickey Min.

Children Who Lived in a Tree. Carolyn White. LC 92-46428. (J). 1994. pap. 15.00 (*0-671-79818-9*, S&S Bks Young Read) S&S Childrens.

Children Who Molest: A Guide for Parents of Young Sex Offenders. 26p. (Orig.). 1987. pap. 3.00 (*0-9613205-5-9*) Launch Pr.

Children Who Read Early. Dolores Durkin. LC 66-25980. 1966. text ed. 12.95 (*0-8077-1260-4*) Tchrs Coll.

Children Who Remember Previous Lives. Ian Stevenson. LC 87-8262. 1987. pap. 14.95 (*0-8139-1154-0*) U Pr of Va.

Children Who Sleep by the River. Debbie Taylor. LC 92-8008. (Emerging Voices: New International Fiction Ser.). 256p. 1992. 24.95 (*1-56656-102-7*); pap. 9.95 (*0-940793-96-2*) Interlink Pub.

Children Who Soil: Assessment & Treatment. Ann Buchanan & Graham Clayden. LC 92-15864. 268p. (Orig.). 1992. pap. text ed. 34.95 (*0-471-93479-8*) Wiley.

Children Who Tell Lies. Warren A. Rhodes. 20p. 1990. 2.95 (*1-56456-027-9*, 238) W Gladden Found.

Children Who Wait (Extracts) J. Rowe & L. Lambert. (C). 1989. 50.00 (*0-903534-31-2*, Pub. by Brit Ag for Adopt & Fost UK) St Mut.

Children Who Wet the Bed. Waln K. Brown & Thomas A. Newnam. 20p. 1989. 2.95 (*1-56456-025-2*, 222) W Gladden Found.

Children with a Star: Jewish Youth in Nazi Europe. Deborah Dwork. (Illus.). 384p. (C). 1991. 32.50 (*0-300-05054-2*) Yale U Pr.

Children with a Star: Jewish Youth in Nazi Europe. Deborah Dwork. (Illus.). 384p. (C). 1993. reprint ed. pap. text ed. 17.00 (*0-300-05447-5*) Yale U Pr.

***Children with Acquired Aphasia.** Lees. 1993. 36.50 (*1-56593-252-8*, 0545) Singular Publishing.

Children with ADD: A Shared Responsibility. Created by Council for Exceptional Children's Task Force on Children with Attention Deficit Disorder Staff. 32p. 1992. 8.90 (*0-86586-233-8*, P385) Coun Exc Child.

Children with Asthma: A Manual for Parents. 2nd ed. Thomas F. Plaut. LC 87-34311. (Illus.). 291p. 1989. pap. 14.95 (*0-914625-03-9*); Pocket-size ed. pap. 7.95 (*0-914625-05-5*) Pedipress.

Children with Autism: A Parents' Guide. Ed. by Michael Powers. LC 87-51322. (Illus.). 368p. (Orig.). 1989. pap. 14.95 (*0-933149-16-6*) Woodbine House.

***Children with Autism: Diagnosis & Interventions to Meet Their Needs.** Colwyn Trevarthen et al. 256p. 1995. pap. 24.95x (*1-85302-314-0*, Pub. by J Kingsley Pubs UK) Taylor & Francis.

Children with Brain Dysfunction: Neurology, Cognition, Language, & Behavior. Isabelle Rapin. (International Review of Child Neurology Ser.). 300p. 1982. text ed. 83.00 (*0-89004-844-4*) Raven.

Children with Cancer. B. F. Last & VanVeldhuizn. 1991. 43.00 (*90-265-1038-1*, Pub. by Swets Pub Serv NE) Taylor & Francis.

Children with Cancer: A Comprehensive Reference Guide for Parents. Jeanne M. Bracken. (Illus.). 288p. 1986. 35.00 (*0-19-503482-1*) OUP.

Children with Cancer: A Comprehensive Reference Guide for Parents. Jeanne M. Bracken. (Illus.). 432p. 1988. pap. 10.95 (*0-19-505659-0*) OUP.

Children with Cerebral Palsy: A Parents' Guide. Ed. by Elaine Geralis. LC 88-40660. 434p. 1991. 14.95 (*0-933149-15-8*) Woodbine House.

Children with Conduct Disorders: A Psychotherapy Manual. Paulina F. Kernberg & Saralea Chazen. LC 90-55665. 320p. 1991. text ed. 40.00 (*0-465-01055-5*) Basic.

***Children with Diabetes.** Date not set. 19.95 (*0-945448-41-1*) Am Diabetes.

Children with Diabetes. Linda M. Siminerio & Jean Betschart. (Illus.). 76p. 1986. pap. 9.95 (*0-945448-08-2*, CCHCWD) Am Diabetes.

Children with Disabilities: A Medical Primer. 3rd ed. Mark L. Batshaw & Yvonne M. Perret. (Illus.). 688p. (C). 1992. pap. text ed. 29.00 (*1-55766-102-2*) P H Brookes.

Children with Downs Syndrome: A Developmental Perspective. Ed. by Dante Cicchetti & Marjorie Beeghly. (Illus.). 499p. (C). 1990. 74.95 (*0-521-37458-8*); pap. 27.95 (*0-521-38667-5*) Cambridge U Pr.

Children with Dyslexia. Aimy J. Vigilante & Waln K. Brown. 20p. 1990. 2.95 (*1-56456-043-0*, 229) W Gladden Found.

***Children with Emotional & Behavioural Difficulties: Strategies for Assessment & Intervention.** Ed. by Peter Farrell. LC 94-24339. 156p. 1994. 75.00 (*0-7507-0361-X*, Falmer Pr); pap. 21.95 (*0-7507-0362-8*, Falmer Pr) Taylor & Francis.

Children with Epilepsy: A Parents' Guide. Ed. by Helen Reisner. LC 87-51319. 314p. (Orig.). 1987. pap. 14.95 (*0-933149-19-0*) Woodbine House.

Children with Exceptional Needs in Regular Classrooms. Libby G. Cohen. 208p. 1992. 11.95 (*0-8106-3009-5*) NEA.

***Children with Facial Difference: A Parents Guide.** Hope Charkins. 1995. pap. 16.95 (*0-933149-61-1*) Woodbine House.

Children with Glue. Shannon Wheeler. (Illus.). 96p. (Orig.). 1991. pap. 4.95 (*1-883611-03-2*) Blckbird Comics.

Children with Handicaps: A Review of Behavioral Research. Gershon Berkson. 464p. 1992. text ed. 99.95 (*0-89859-987-3*) L Erlbaum Assocs.

Children with Hearing Difficulties. Webster & Wood. 192p. 1989. pap. text ed. 22.50 (*0-304-31724-1*) Cassell.

Children with Language Disabilities. Michael Beveridge & Gina Conti-Ramsden. 178p. 1987. 80.00 (*0-335-10280-8*, Open Univ Pr); pap. 27.00 (*0-335-10279-4*, Open Univ Pr) Taylor & Francis.

***Children with Language Disorders.** Lees. 254p. 1990. pap. 62.25 (*1-56593-540-3*, 0043) Singular Publishing.

Children with Language Disorders. Janet Lees & Shelagh Urwin. 208p. 1990. 56.00 (*0-85066-496-9*); pap. 28.00 (*0-85066-497-7*) Singular Publishing.

Children with Language Disorders: An Introduction. Vicki Reed. LC 85-26409. 368p. 1986. write for info. (*0-02-399140-2*) Macmillan.

***Children with Language Impairments: An Introduction.** Morag L. Donaldson. 144p. 1995. pap. 19.95 (*1-85302-313-2*, Pub. by J Kingsley Pubs UK) Taylor & Francis.

Children with Learning Difficulties. D. Montgomery. Ed. by Peter Mittler. (Special Needs in Ordinary Schools Ser.). 304p. 1990. pap. text ed. 22.50 (*0-304-31472-2*) Cassell.

Children with Learning Difficulties. Diana Montgomery. 224p. 1990. pap. 29.95 (*0-89397-351-3*) Nichols Pub.

Children with Limited English: Teaching Strategies for the Regular Classroom. Ellen Kottler. (New Survival Skills for Teachers Ser.). 72p. 1994. pap. 11.95 (*0-8039-6083-2*) Corwin Pr.

Children with Limited Vision. Jack Rudman. (Teachers License Examination Ser.: T-7). 1994. pap. 23.95 (*0-8373-8007-3*) Nat Learn.

Children with Mental Handicaps: A Guide for Parents & Carers. Fred Heddell. 256p. 1989. pap. 24.95 (*1-85223-069-X*, Pub. by Crowood Pr UK) Trafalgar.

Children with Mental Retardation: A Parents' Guide. Ed. by Romayne Smith. LC 90-50258. (Illus.). 437p. (Orig.). (C). 1993. pap. text ed. 14.95 (*0-933149-39-5*) Woodbine House.

Children with Obsessive-Compulsive Disorder. Siegel & Brown. (Changing Behavior Through Understanding Ser.). 20p. (Orig.). 1991. pap. text ed. 2.95 (*1-56456-047-3*) W Gladden Found.

Children with Physical Handicaps: A Guide for Parents & Carers. Fred Heddell. 320p. 1989. pap. 24.95 (*1-85223-074-6*, Pub. by Crowood Pr UK) Trafalgar.

Children with Profound Handicaps: Parents' Views & Integration. Philip Seed. 180p. 1988. 55.00 (*1-85000-383-1*, Falmer Pr); pap. 30.00 (*1-85000-384-X*, Falmer Pr) Taylor & Francis.

Children with School Phobia. Cyma J. Siegel & Waln K. Brown. 20p. 1991. 2.95 (*1-56456-036-8*, 244) W Gladden Found.

Children with Special Needs. Ed. by Katharine T. Bartlett & Judith W. Wegner. 512p. 1987. 39.95 (*0-88738-690-3*) Transaction Pubs.

Children with Special Needs. Michael Luxford. (Rudolf Steiner's Ideas in Practice Ser.). (Illus.). 128p. (Orig.). 1994. pap. 9.95 (*0-88010-381-7*) Anthroposophic.

Children with Special Needs. 2nd ed. Lauren Bradway & Lawrence Block. 1989. pap. 7.95 (*0-929240-08-1*) Essential Med Info Syst Inc.

***Children with Special Needs: Assessment, Law & Practice - Caught in the Act.** John Friel. 240p. 1995. pap. 24.95 (*1-85302-280-2*, Pub. by J Kingsley Pubs UK) Taylor & Francis.

Children with Special Needs: Assessment, Law & Practice - Caught in the Act. 2nd ed. Harry Chasty & John Friel. 240p. 1993. pap. 34.00 (*1-85302-155-5*, Pub. by J Kingsley Pubs UK) Taylor & Francis.

Children with Special Needs: Family, Culture, & Society. 2nd ed. Ed. by James L. Paul & Rune J. Simeonsson. (Illus.). 352p. (C). 1993. text ed. 29.50 (*0-03-055743-7*) HB Coll Pubs.

Children with Special Needs in Early Childhood Settings: Identification, Intervention. Carol L. Paasche. 1990. text ed. 22.00 (*0-201-23139-5*) Addison-Wesley.

Children with Specific Reading Disabilities. Che K. Leong. 360p. 1988. pap. 86.00 (*90-265-0291-5*, Pub. by Swets Pub Serv NE) Taylor & Francis.

Children with Specific Speech & Language Impairment. Corinne Haynes & Sandhya Naidoo. (Clinics in Developmental Medicine Ser.: No. 119). (Illus.). 290p. (C). 1991. 54.95 (*0-521-41275-7*) Cambridge U Pr.

***Children with Speech, Language, & Listening Problems: What Every Parent Needs to Know.** Patricia M. Hamaguchi. LC 94-27556. 1995. pap. text ed. 12.95 (*0-471-03413-4*) Wiley.

Children with Tourette Syndrome: A Parents' Guide. Ed. by Tracy Haerle. LC 90-50766. (Illus.). 340p. (Orig.). (C). 1992. pap. 14.95 (*0-933149-44-1*) Woodbine House.

Children with Visual Impairments: A Parents' Guide. Ed. by Cay Holbrook. (Illus.). 350p. (C). 1995. pap. 16.95 (*0-933149-36-0*) Woodbine House.

Children Without Justice. 1975. pap. 2.25 (*0-686-81722-2*) NCJW.

Children Won't Wait: Sharing the Precious Moments of Your Baby's Childhood. Helen Young. 1985. 8.99 (*0-915720-83-3*) Brownlow Pub Co.

Children, Work & Ideology: A Cross-Cultural Comparison of Children's Understanding of Work & the Social Division of Labour. Gunilla Dahlberg et al. (Stockholm Studies in Education & Psychology: No. 24). 116p. (Orig.). 1987. pap. 33.00x (*91-22-01178-1*, Pub. by Almqv & Wiksell SW) Coronet Bks.

Children, Youth & Church, No. 1453. (Illus.). 48p. 1988. reprint ed. 5.95 (*1-878259-08-3*) Neibauer Pr.

Children, Youth, & Families: The Action Research Relationship. Ed. by Robert N. Rapoport. (Illus.). 320p. 1985. 49.95 (*0-521-30143-2*) Cambridge U Pr.

***Children, Youth, & Suicide: Developmental Perspectives.** Ed. by Gil G. Noam & Sophie Borst. LC 85-644581. (New Directions for Child Development Ser.: no. 64). 121p. (Orig.). 1994. pap. 17.95 (*0-7879-9960-1*) Jossey-Bass.

Children-Youth Physical Fitness Program Management System. 1986. 13.95 (*0-88314-318-6*) AAHPERD.

***Children...Like a Garden.** John Kest. 32p. (Orig.). (J). 1995. pap. 9.95 (*1-886094-09-8*) Chicago Spectrum.

Children's ABC Christmas. Patricia McKissack & Frederick McKissack. LC 87-73525. (Illus.). 32p. (J). (ps-6). 1988. pap. 5.99 (*0-8066-2356-X*, 10-1046, Augsburg) Augsburg Fortress.

Children's Act 1989. Jane Bridge et al. 384p. 1990. pap. 39.00 (*1-85431-058-5*, Pub. by Blackstone Pr UK) W W Gaunt.

Children's Adaptive Behavior Report. Bert O. Richmond & Richard H. Kicklighter. 16p. (Orig.). 1982. pap. 1.00 (*0-89334-030-8*) Humanics Ltd.

Children's Adaptive Behavior Scale. Bert O. Richmond & Richard Kicklighter. 32p. (Orig.). 1980. pap. 29.95 (*0-89334-054-5*); 24.95 (*0-89334-055-3*) Humanics Ltd.

Children's Adaptive Behavior Scale: Administrator's Manual. rev. ed. Bert O. Richmond & Richard H. Kicklighter. 42p. (Orig.). (C). 1983. pap. 14.95 (*0-89334-040-5*) Humanics Ltd.

Children's Aesop: Selected Fables. Illus. by Robert Byrd. LC 91-73884. 64p. (J). (ps-3). 1992. 14.95 (*1-56397-041-4*) Boyds Mills Pr.

Children's Aid Society Annual Reports, Nos. 1-10, February, 1854-February, 1863. Children's Aid Society Staff. LC 72-137191. (Poverty U. S. A. Historical Record Ser.). 1975. reprint ed. 51.95 (*0-405-03135-1*) Ayer.

Children's Allowance & the Economic Welfare of Children: Proccedings of the Children's Allowance Conference, 1967. Children's Allowance Conference Staff. Ed. by Eveline M. Burns. LC 74-1695. (Children & Youth Ser.). 208p. 1974. reprint ed. 23.95 (*0-405-05971-X*) Ayer.

Children's Animal Atlas. David Lambert. LC 91-30147. (Children's Atlases Ser.). (Illus.). 96p. (J). (gr. 2-6). 1992. 16.95 (*1-56294-101-1*); lib. bdg. 18.90 (*1-56294-167-4*) Millbrook Pr.

Children's Animal Atlas. David Lambert. (Children's Atlases Ser.). (J). (gr. 4-7). 1993. pap. 12.95 (*1-56294-720-6*) Millbrook Pr.

Children's Arithmetic: How They Learn It & How You Teach It. 2nd ed. Herbert P. Ginsburg. LC 88-23845. (Illus.). 266p. 1989. pap. text ed. 27.00 (*0-89079-181-3*, 1466) PRO-ED.

Children's Arkansas Puzzle Book. Donna L. Pape. (Illus.). 28p. (J). (gr. k up). 1984. pap. 2.00 (*0-914546-55-4*) Rose Pub.

Children's Art: A Study of Normal Development in Children's Modes of Visualization. Miriam Lindstrom. LC 57-10499. (Illus.). 1957. reprint ed. pap. 11.00 (*0-520-00752-2*) U CA Pr.

Children's Art Hazards. L. Jacobson. 16p. 1984. 3.95 (*0-318-20469-X*) Natl Resources Defense Coun.

Children's Association Frequency Tables see Voluntary Isolation of Control in a Natural Muscle Group

Children's Atlas of Civilizations. Antony Mason. LC 93-23564. (Children's Atlases Ser.). (Illus.). 96p. (J). (gr. 2-6). 1994. lib. bdg. 18.90 (*1-56294-494-0*); pap. 12.95 (*1-56294-733-8*) Millbrook Pr.

Children's Atlas of Earth Through Time. Rand McNally Staff. Ed. by Elizabeth Fagan. (Illus.). 80p. (J). 1990. 14.95 (*0-528-83415-0*) Rand McNally.

Children's Atlas of Exploration. Antony Mason & Keith Lye. LC 92-28856. (Children's Atlases Ser.). (Illus.). 96p. (J). (gr. 2-6). 1993. pap. 12.95 (*1-56294-711-7*) Millbrook Pr.

Children's Atlas of Exploration. Antony Mason & Keith Lye. LC 92-28856. (Children's Atlases Ser.). (Illus.). 96p. (J). (gr. 2-6). 1993. lib. bdg. 18.90 (*1-56294-256-5*) Millbrook Pr.

Children's Atlas of Native Americans. (J). 1992. 14.95 (*0-528-83494-0*) Rand McNally.

Children's Atlas of Native Americans Rand McNally: Native Cultures of North & South America. Rand McNally Staff & Francis Reddy. Ed. by Elizabeth Adelman. (United States & Its Flag Ser.). (Illus.). 78p. (J). (gr. 3-12). Date not set. 14.95 (*0-685-66563-1*); lib. bdg. 18.95 (*1-878363-99-9*) Forest Hse.

***Children's Atlas of Natural Wonders.** Joyce Pope. LC 95-11778. (Illus.). 96p. (J). (gr. 3-6). 1995. 18.90 (*1-56294-564-5*) Millbrook Pr.

***Children's Atlas of Natural Wonders.** Joyce Pope. (Illus.). 96p. (J). (gr. 2-6). 1995. pap. 12.95 (*1-56294-886-5*) Millbrook Pr.

Children's Atlas of People & Places. Jenny Wood & David Munro. LC 92-28857. (Children's Atlases Ser.). (Illus.). 96p. (J). (gr. 2-6). 1993. pap. 10.95 (*1-56294-712-5*) Millbrook Pr.

Children's Atlas of People & Places. Jenny Wood & David Munro. LC 92-28857. (Children's Atlases Ser.). (Illus.). 96p. (J). (gr. 2-6). 1993. lib. bdg. 18.90 (*1-56294-257-3*) Millbrook Pr.

Children's Atlas of the Environment. Rand McNally Staff. (J). (gr. 4-7). 1991. 14.95 (*0-528-83438-X*) Rand McNally.

Children's Atlas of the Human Body. Richard Walker. LC 93-41527. (Children's Atlases Ser.). (Illus.). 64p. (J). (gr. 2-6). 1994. lib. bdg. 18.90 (*1-56294-503-3*); pap. 10.95 (*1-56294-732-X*) Millbrook Pr.

Children's Atlas of the Human Body. Richard Walker. (Children's Atlases Ser.). (Illus.). 64p. (J). (gr. 2-6). 1994. 18.90 (*1-56294-496-7*) Millbrook Pr.

***Children's Atlas of the Twentieth Century.** Sarah Howarth. (Children's Atlases Ser.). (Illus.). 96p. (J). (gr. 3-6). 1995. 18.90 (*1-56294-563-7*) Millbrook Pr.

***Children's Atlas of the Twentieth Century.** Sarah Howarth. (Illus.). 96p. (J). (gr. 2-6). 1995. pap. 12.95 (*1-56294-885-7*) Millbrook Pr.

Children's Atlas of the United States. (J). (gr. 5-9). 1989. 14.95 (*0-528-83362-6*); pap. 7.95 (*0-528-83540-8*) Rand McNally.

Children's Atlas of the Universe. Rand McNally Staff. (Illus.). (J). (gr. 3-7). 1990. 14.95 (*0-528-83408-8*) Rand McNally.

Children's Atlas of the World. rev. ed. Stephen Attmore. (Illus.). 32p. (J). (gr. 1-3). 1994. reprint ed. pap. 5.95 (*0-8249-8662-8*, Ideals Child) Hambleton-Hill.

Children's Atlas of World History. (Illus.). (J). (gr. 4-8). 1991. 14.95 (*0-528-83444-4*) Rand McNally.

Children's Attendance at Motion Pictures. Edgar Dale. Bd. with Emotional Responses of Children to the Motion Picture Situation. LC 75-125462. LC 75-125462. (Literature of Cinema: Payne Fund Studies of Motion Pictures & Social Values). 1970. reprint ed. 18.95 (*0-405-01643-3*) Ayer.

Children's Authors & Illustrators. 5th ed. 1994. 156.00 (*0-8103-2899-2*) Gale.

Children's Authors & Illustrators. 6th ed. Date not set. 156.00 (*0-8103-5507-8*) Gale.

Children's Authors & Illustrators: An Index to Biographical Dictionaries. 4th ed. Ed. by Joyce Nakamura. 1000p. 1986. 156.00 (*0-8103-2525-X*) Gale.

Children's Authors Speak. Ed. by Jeannine L. Laughlin & Sherry Laughlin. (Illus.). 250p. 1993. lib. bdg. 25.00 (*0-87287-921-6*) Libs Unl.

Children's Behavior. Sophie Ritholz. 1966. 16.95 (*0-317-18406-7*) NCUP.

Children's Bible. (Prestige Editions Ser.). (Illus.). (J). (gr. k-12). 1965. write for info. (*0-307-16520-5*, Golden Bks) Western Pub.

***Children's Bible.** (DK Family Library). (J). Date not set. write for info. (*0-7894-0343-9*, 5-70681) Dorling Kindersley.

Children's Bible. W. Hillmann. 95p. (J). (ps-8). 1959. pap. 4.95 (*0-8146-0120-0*) Liturgical Pr.

Children's Bible Basics Ser., 11 bks., Set. Carolyn Nystrom. (Illus.). (J). (ps-2). pap. 54.89 (*0-8024-5988-9*) Moody.

***Children's Bible in Three Hundred & Sixty-Five Stories.** Mary Batchlor. 1995. 16.99 (*0-7459-3068-9*) Lion USA.

Children's Bible Stories: From Genesis to Daniel. Illus. by Yvonne Gilbert. LC 90-42588. 96p. (J). (gr. 1-5). 1993. 17.99 (*0-8037-0956-0*); lib. bdg. 17.89 (*0-8037-0990-0*) Dial Bks Young.

Children's Bible Stories to Read & Color: New Testament. (Illus.). 144p. (J). 1991. pap. 2.49 (*0-517-68993-6*) Random Hse Value.

Children's Bible Stories with Questions. Graham P. Matthews, Jr. LC 93-19623. (Illus.). (J). (gr. 3 up). 1993. write for info. (*0-910683-18-2*) Townsnd-Pr.

Children's Bible Treasury, 12 bks., Set. (Illus.). (J). 1993. 19.98 (*0-7853-0275-1*) Pubns Intl Ltd.

Children's Big Airplane. Alex N. Holland. (Illus.). 12p. (J). (gr. 1-4). 1992. pap. 10.95 (*1-56606-000-1*) Bradley Mann.

Children's Book. annot. ed. (J). (gr. 1). 1992. 11.95 (*0-7829-0011-9*, 88011) Tabor Pub.

Children's Book. annot. ed. (J). (gr. 2). 1992. 11.95 (*0-7829-0016-X*, 88021) Tabor Pub.

Children's Book. annot. ed. (J). (gr. 3). 1992. 11.95 (*0-7829-0021-6*, 88031) Tabor Pub.

Children's Book. annot. ed. (J). (gr. 4). 1992. 11.95 (*0-7829-0026-7*, 88041) Tabor Pub.

Children's Book. annot. ed. (J). (gr. 5). 1992. 11.95 (*0-7829-0031-3*, 88051) Tabor Pub.

Children's Book. annot. ed. (J). (gr. 6). 1992. 11.95 (*0-7829-0036-4*, 88061) Tabor Pub.

Children's Book: A Communication Workbook for Separate Parenting after Divorce. Marilyn S. Erickson & Stephen K. Erickson. 122p. (Orig.). 1992. pap. 7.95 (*1-881111-02-4*) CPI Pub MN.

Children's Book Awards International: A Directory of Awards & Winners, from Inception Through 1990. Laura Smith. LC 91-50940. 671p. 1992. lib. bdg. 82.00x (*0-89950-686-0*) McFarland & Co.

Children's Book Collecting. Carolyn Michaels. LC 92-35088. (Illus.). xii, 202p. (C). 1993. lib. bdg. 35.00 (*0-208-02267-8*, Lib Prof Pubns) Shoe String.

Children's Book Illustration & Design. Julie Cummins. (Illus.). 240p. 1992. 60.00 (*0-86636-147-2*) PBC Intl Inc.

Children's Book Illustration Annual 1987: Bologna International Children's Book Fair. (Illus.). 296p. 1991. pap. 24.95 (*0-88708-047-2*, Picture Book Studio) S&S Childrens.

Children's Book Illustration III. (Illus.). 140p. 1975. 21.50 (*0-89192-352-7*, Graphis Pr) Interbk Inc.

Children's Book Illustration IV. (Illus.). 152p. 1980. 24.00 (*0-89192-339-X*, Graphis Pr) Interbk Inc.

Children's Book of Embroidery. Tess Marsh. (Illus.). 64p. 1986. 22.95 (*0-7134-5142-4*, Pub. by Batsford UK) Trafalgar.

Children's Book of Irish Fairy Tales. Patricia Dunn. (J). 1988. pap. 9.95 (*0-85342-843-3*) Dufour.

Children's Book of Irish Folktales. Kevin Danaher. (Illus.). 108p. (J). 1987. pap. 11.95 (*0-85342-718-6*, Pub. by Mercier Pr IE) Dufour.

Children's Book of Jewish Holidays. David A. Adler. (ArtScroll Youth Ser.). (Illus.). 48p. (J). (gr. k-6). 1987. 12.95 (*0-89906-810-3*); pap. 8.95 (*0-89906-811-1*) Mesorah Pubns.

Children's Book of Poetry. Ed. by Henry T. Coates. LC 70-149101. (Granger Index Reprint Ser.). 1977. 40.95 (*0-8369-6226-5*) Ayer.

Children's Book of Saints. (J). (gr. 1-4). 1989. 5.95 (*0-88271-130-X*) Regina Pr.

An Asterisk (*) at the beginning of an entry indicates that the title is appearing in BIP for the first time.

An Asterisk (*) at the beginning of an entry indicates that the title is appearing in BIP for the first time.

1207

Children's Directory. Riviera Publications Staff. Ed. by Elizabeth Nelson. 1989. 4.95 (*0-317-93658-1*) Riviera Pubns.
Children's Divorce Center Reading Guide: 1992 Edition. Ed. by Marcia Lebowitz. 1991. 24.95 (*0-935769-08-0*) CDC Pr.
Children's Drawings. Maureen Cox. (Illus.). 240p. (Orig.). 1992. pap. 11.00 (*0-14-013910-9*, Penguin Bks) Viking Penguin.
Children's Drawings: Iconic Coding of the Environment. M. Krampen. LC 90-25210. (Topics in Contemporary Semiotics Ser.). (Illus.). 200p. 1991. 49.50 (*0-306-43647-7*, Plenum Pr) Plenum.
Children's Drawings As Diagnostic Aids. Joseph H. DiLeo. LC 73-79882. (Illus.). 240p. 1970. reprint ed. pap. 22.95 (*0-87630-249-5*) Brunner-Mazel.
Children's Dreams in Clinical Practice. S. Catalano. LC 89-28470. (Illus.). 240p. 1990. 35.00 (*0-306-43308-7*, Plenum Pr) Plenum.
Children's Dulcimer Method, 1. Mara Wasburn. 1993. 4.95 (*0-87166-279-5*, 93995) Mel Bay.
Children's Dulcimer Method, 2. Mara Wasburn. 1993. 4.95 (*0-87166-280-9*, 94104) Mel Bay.
***Children's Early Text Construction.** Ed. by Clotilde Pontecorvo & Margherita Orsolini. 360p. 1995. text ed. 60.00 (*0-8058-1504-X*) L Erlbaum Assocs.
Children's Education in Community: The Basis of Bruderhof Education. Eberhard Arnold. Ed. by Merrill Mow. LC 76-27728. 68p. 1976. pap. 5.00 (*0-87486-164-0*) Plough.
Children's Emergent Literacy: From Research to Practice. David F. Lancy. LC 93-23475. 416p. 1994. text ed. 65.00 (*0-275-94589-8*, Praeger Pubs) Greenwood.
Children's Emotions & Moods: Developmental Theory & Measurement. Ed. by Michael Lewis & Linda Michalson. LC 83-2456. 488p. 1983. 59.50 (*0-306-41209-8*, Plenum Pr) Plenum.
***Children's Encyclopedia.** (J). Date not set. write for info. (*0-7894-0344-7*, 5-70682) Dorling Kindersley.
Children's Encyclopedia. J. Elliot. (Encyclopedias Ser.). (Illus.). 128p. (J). (gr. 3-6). 1987. lib. bdg. 17.96 (*0-88110-265-2*); pap. 14.95 (*0-7460-0000-6*) EDC.
Children's Ethnic Socialization. Jean S. Phinney & Mary Rotheram. Ed. by Society for Research in Child Development Staff. (Focus Editions Ser.: Vol. 81). 400p. (Orig.). 1986. text ed. 49.95 (*0-8039-2815-7*); pap. text ed. 24.95 (*0-8039-2816-5*) Sage.
Children's Experiences Prior to First Grade & Success in Beginning Reading. Millie C. Almy. LC 71-176516. (Columbia University. Teachers College. Contributions to Education Ser.: No. 954). reprint ed. 37.50 (*0-404-55954-9*) AMS Pr.
Children's Explanations: A Psycholinguistic Study. Morag L. Donaldson. (Illus.). 200p. 1986. 59.95 (*0-521-32006-2*) Cambridge U Pr.
Children's Exposure to Environmental Cigarette Smoke Before & after Birth: PHS 91-1250. No. 202. 1991. write for info. (*0-318-69606-1*) Natl Ctr Health Stats.
Children's Eyewitness Memory. Ed. by Stephen J. Ceci et al. LC 86-24852. 1987. 46.00 (*0-387-96429-0*) Spr-Verlag.
Children's Fashions, 1860-1912: One Thousand Sixty-Five Costume Designs from "La Mode Illustree" Intro. by JoAnne Olian. (Illus.). 1993. pap. write for info. (*0-486-27615-5*) Dover.
Children's Favorite Story of Santa Claus. Robert T. Stout. (Illus.). 32p. (J). (ps-6). 1982. 5.95 (*0-911049-08-8*); pap. 3.95 (*0-911049-04-5*) Yuletide Intl.
Children's Favorites: Inspirational Songs Arranged for the Piano. Carolyn S. Stevens. 40p. 1986. pap. 8.98 (*0-88290-275-X*) Horizon Utah.
Children's Fiction Sourcebook. Jennifer Madden et al. 200p. 1992. 43.95 (*1-85742-022-5*, Pub. by Ashgate UK) Ashgate Pub Co.
***Children's Fiction Sourcebook: A Survey of Children's Books for 6-13 Year Olds.** Margaret Hobson et al. LC 94-31292. 300p. 1995. 68.95 (*1-85928-083-8*, Pub. by Scolar Pr UK) Ashgate Pub Co.
Children's Fiddling Method. Carol A. Wheeler. 1993. 7.95 (*1-56222-452-2*, 94817); audio 9.98 (*1-56222-453-0*, 94817) Mel Bay.
Children's Film Programming: A Handbook. Gallery Association of New York State Staff. LC 91-44824. (Illus.). 106p. 1992. pap. text ed. 15.00 (*0-917846-06-0*, 95508) Highsmith Pr.
Children's First Atlas. (Illus.). (J). (gr. 2-6). 1985. 2.98 (*0-517-47997-4*) Random Hse Value.
Children's First Dictionary. (Illus.). 192p. (J). 1991. 7.99 (*0-517-64469-X*) Random Hse Value.
Children's First Encyclopedia. Walter Dempsey. (J). 1985. 6.98 (*0-671-07744-9*) S&S Trade.
Children's First Geography Encyclopedia. Michael W. Dempsey. (J). 1985. 6.98 (*0-671-07746-5*) S&S Trade.
Childrens First Nature Encyclopedia. (J). 1991. pap. 19.95 (*0-671-08189-6*) S&S Trade.
Children's First School Books: Introductions to the Culture of Literacy. Carolyn D. Baker & Peter Freebody. (Language Library). (Illus.). 240p. 1989. pap. text ed. 25.95 (*0-631-15927-4*) Blackwell Pubs.
Children's First Science Encyclopedia. Michael W. Dempsey. (J). 1987. 6.98 (*0-671-07745-7*) S&S Trade.
Children's Folklore: A Sourcebook. Ed. by Brian Sutton-Smith et al. LC 95-5152. (Illus.). 392p. 1995. 50.00 (*0-8240-5418-0*, SS647) Garland.
***Childrens Food (Prepared) Market.** 208p. (Orig.). 1995. pap. 2,295.00 (*0-7605-2222-7*) Rector Pr.
Children's Fractures. 2nd ed. Ed. by Mercer Rang. (Illus.). 300p. 1983. text ed. 79.50 (*0-397-50476-4*, 65-06182, Lippincott Medical) Lippincott.
Children's Friendship. Zick Rubin. (Developing Child Ser.). 165p. 1980. pap. text ed. 10.95 (*0-674-11619-4*) HUP.
Children's Furniture. Sunset Magazine & Book Editors. LC 84-82286. (Illus.). 96p. (Orig.). 1985. pap. 8.99 (*0-376-01268-4*) Sunset Menlo Pk.
Children's Furniture & Toy Projects You Can Build. Jonathan Press Staff. Ed. by Al Gutierrez. (Illus.). 100p. (Orig.). 1988. pap. 10.95 (*0-317-90852-9*) Jonathan Pr.
Children's Furniture You Can Make: Complete Plans & Instructions for Bunks & Bureaus, Chests & Chairs, Cradles & Computer Tables. Paul Gerhards. LC 92-42008. (Illus.). 128p. 1993. pap. 14.95 (*0-8117-2534-0*) Stackpole.
Children's Game Anthology: Studies in Folklore & Anthropology. Photos by Brian Sutton-Smith. LC 75-35080. (Studies in Play & Games). (Illus.). 1978. reprint ed. 41.95 (*0-405-07928-1*) Ayer.
Children's Games & Rhymes. Ed. by Paul G. Brewster. LC 75-35063. (Studies in Play & Games: Vol. 1). 1980. reprint ed. 18.95 (*0-405-07914-1*) Ayer.
Childrens Games & Songs in Puerto Rico. Maria C. De Martinez. (Puerto Rico Ser.). 1979. lib. bdg. 59.95 (*0-8490-2883-3*) Gordon Pr.
Children's Games from Many Lands. Nina Millen. LC 65-24039. (Illus.). 194p. reprint ed. pap. 55.30 (*0-7837-1952-3*, 2042169) Bks Demand.
Children's Games in Street & Playground. Iona Opie & Peter Opie. (Illus.). (C). 1985. reprint ed. pap. 10.95 (*0-19-281489-3*) OUP.
Children's Games Throughout the Year. Leslie Daiken. LC 75-35067. (Studies in Play & Games). (Illus.). 1976. reprint ed. 25.95 (*0-405-07918-4*) Ayer.
***Children's Garden of Verses.** Date not set. 12.99 (*0-517-12397-5*) Random.
Children's Garland: From the Best Poets. Ed. by Coventry K. Patmore. LC 73-167478. (Granger Index Reprint Ser.). 1977. reprint ed. 19.95 (*0-8369-6283-4*) Ayer.
Children's Glass Dishes, China & Furniture. 2nd ed. Doris A. Lechler. 208p. 1990. 19.95 (*0-89145-303-2*, 1627) Collector Bks.
Children's God. David Heller. LC 85-24581. (Illus.). 176p. 1986. lib. bdg. 15.95 (*0-226-32635-7*) U Ch Pr.
Children's God. David Heller. LC 85-24581. (Illus.). 176p. 1988. pap. 9.95 (*0-226-32636-5*) U Ch Pr.
Children's Group Therapy: Methods & Case Histories. Mortimer Schiffer. LC 84-47659. 416p. (C). 1984. text ed. 45.00 (*0-02-928090-7*) Free Pr.
Children's Guide to Islam. rev. ed. Allama M. Asifi. 145p. (J). 1983. reprint ed. pap. 7.00 (*0-941724-11-5*) Islamic Seminary.
Children's Guide to Parents & Other Matters: Little Essays for Children & Others. Eli Siegel. LC 78-171393. (Illus.). 77p. (J). (gr. 1-6). 1971. text ed. 7.50 (*0-910492-16-6*) Definition.
Children's Guide to Santa Fe. Anne Hillerman. LC 84-8782. (Illus.). 48p. (Orig.). (J). (gr. 3 up). 1984. pap. 4.95 (*0-86534-030-7*) Sunstone Pr.
Children's Guitar Hymnal. Steve Griffin. 32p. (J). (gr. 4-10). 1978. student ed, pap. 2.95 (*0-89228-052-2*) Impact Christian.
Children's Guitar Hymnal. Steve Griffin. 1993. 3.95 (*0-87166-725-8*, 93481) Mel Bay.
Children's Guitar Method, Vol. 1. William Bay. (Illus.). (J). 1993. 5.95 (*0-87166-386-4*, 93833); audio 14.95 (*0-87166-388-0*, 93833); audio 9.98 (*0-87166-387-2*, 93833) Mel Bay.
Children's Guitar Method, Vol. 2. William Bay. (Illus.). (J). 1993. 5.95 (*0-87166-389-9*, 93834) Mel Bay.
Children's Guitar Method, Vol. 3. William Bay. (J). 1993. 5.95 (*0-87166-392-9*, 93835) Mel Bay.
Children's Haggadah. Howard Bogot & Robert Orkand. LC 93-21340. (Illus.). 72p. (J). (gr. 4 up). 1994. 17.95 (*0-88123-060-X*) Central Conf.
Children's Haggadah. Howard Bogot & Robert Orkand. LC 93-21340. (Illus.). 72p. (J). (ps-4). 1994. pap. 12.95 (*0-88123-059-6*) Central Conf.
Children's Handbook of Real Magic. Linda Waldron & LeRoy Montana. 32p. (J). (gr. 3-4). 1993. pap. 10.00 (*1-883783-00-3*) Crystal Oracle.
Children's Harmonica Method. William Bay. 1993. 3.95 (*0-87166-917-X*, 94068) Mel Bay.
Children's Head Injury: Who Cares? David Johnson et al. 254p. 1989. text ed. 49.95 (*0-86377-187-4*); pap. 27.50 (*0-86377-188-2*) L Erlbaum Assocs.
Children's Health & Achievement in School. Jere R. Behrman & Victor Lavy. LC 94-12591. (LSMS Working Papers: No. 104). 1994. write for info. (*0-8213-2853-0*) World Bank.
***Children's Health & Beauty Aids Market.** 130p. (Orig.). 1995. pap. 2,195.00 (*0-7605-2036-4*) Rector Pr.
Children's Health & Well-Being in the Nordic Countries. Lennart Kohler & Gunborg Jakobsson. LC 65-80567. (Clinics in Developmental Medicine Ser.: No. 98). (Illus.). 140p. (C). 1991. 49.95 (*0-521-41217-X*, Pub. by Mc Keith Pr UK) Cambridge U Pr.
***Children's Health Food Book.** Ron Seaborn. 40p. (J). Date not set. 14.95 (*0-9647089-0-6*) Life Line NY.
Children's Health in America: A History. Charles King. LC 93-6756. 240p. 1993. text ed. 26.95 (*0-8057-4101-1*, Twayne); pap. 14.95 (*0-8057-4111-9*, Twayne) Macmillan.
Children's Homer. Padraic Colum. pap. 20.00 (*0-8196-1278-2*) Biblo.
Children's Homer: The Adventures of Odysseus & the Tale of Troy. Padraic Colum. LC 82-12643. (Illus.). 256p. (J). (gr. 5 up). 1982. pap. 8.95 (*0-02-042520-1*, Collier Bks Young) S&S Childrens.
***Children's Hospital: The Book of the BBC-TV Series.** Richard Bradley et al. (Illus.). 128p. (Orig.). (J). (gr. 3-5). 1995. pap. 11.95 (*0-563-36972-8*, Pub. by BBC UK) Parkwest Pubns.
Children's Hospital Killer. Steven A. Chevalier. 1991. pap. 14.95 (*0-87949-298-8*) Ashley Bks.
Children's Hospital of Boston. Clement Smith. 284p. 1983. 22.50 (*0-316-80170-4*) Little.
***Children's Hospital of Philadelphia 1974-1994: An Informal Report.** Shirley Bonnem. (Illus.). 1995. write for info. (*0-9617370-3-4*); text ed. write for info. (*0-9617370-1-8*); pap. write for info. (*0-9617370-2-6*) Childrens Hospital of Philadelphia.
Children's Hour. Lillian Hellman. 1953. pap. 4.75 (*0-8222-0205-0*) Dramatists Play.
Children's Hour. William W. Longfellow. 1993. 17.95 (*0-87923-971-9*) Godine.
Children's Hour. Jerry Pournelle & S. M. Stirling. 1991. mass mkt. 4.99 (*0-671-72089-9*) Baen Bks.
Children's Hour: Radio Programs for Children, 1929-1956. Marilyn L. Boemer. LC 89-24133. 230p. 1989. 25.00 (*0-8108-2270-9*) Scarecrow.
Children's Humour. Ed. by Paul E. McGhee & Antony J. Chapman. LC 79-40648. 336p. reprint ed. pap. 95.80 (*0-318-35027-0*, 2030927) Bks Demand.
Children's Hymnary. Ed. by Arlene Hartzler & John Gaeddert. LC 67-24327. (J). (gr. k-7). 1967. 5.95 (*0-87303-095-8*) Faith & Life.
Children's Ideas in Science. Ed. by Rosalind Driver et al. LC 85-7104. 256p. 1985. pap. 32.00 (*0-335-15040-3*, Open Univ Pr) Taylor & Francis.
Children's Illustrated Bible. Selina Hastings. (Illus.). 320p. (J). (gr. k-3). 1994. 19.99 (*1-56233-106-X*) Star Song TN.
Children's Illustrated Bible. Illus. by Eric Thomas. LC 93-30814. (J). (gr. 3 up). 1994. 19.95 (*1-56458-472-0*) Dorling Kindersley.
***Children's Illustrated Bible.** Illus. by Eric Thomas. LC 93-30814. 320p. (J). (gr. 3 up). 1994. 19.95 (*1-56458-574-3*) Dorling Kindersley.
Children's Illustrated Old Testament. (Illus.). (J). (gr. 4-7). 1993. 14.95 (*0-15-238220-8*, HB Juv Bks) HarBrace.
Children's Illustrated World Atlas: A Young Person's Guide to the World. Molly Perham & Philip Steele. LC 93-70591. (Illus.). 56p. (J). (gr. 1 up). 1993. 9.98 (*1-56138-331-7*) Courage Bks.
Children's Informal Ideas about Science. Ed. by Paul Black & Arthur Lucas. LC 92-41878. 256p. 1993. 59.95 (*0-415-00539-6*, A1783) Routledge.
Children's Interests in Library Books of Fiction. Marie Rankin. LC 70-177178. (Columbia University. Teachers College. Contributions to Education Ser.: No. 906). reprint ed. 37.50 (*0-404-55906-9*) AMS Pr.
Children's Interests in Reading. Arthur M. Jordan. LC 73-176921. (Columbia University. Teachers College. Contributions to Education Ser.: No. 107). reprint ed. 37.50 (*0-404-55107-6*) AMS Pr.
Children's Interpersonal Trust: Sensitivity to Lying, Deception & Promise Violations. Ed. by K. J. Rotenberg. (Illus.). viii, 172p. 1991. 49.00 (*0-387-97511-X*) Spr-Verlag.
Children's Island. P. C. Jersild. Tr. by Joan Tate. LC 86-1396. (Modern Scandinavian Literature in Translation Ser.). vi, 288p. 1986. 30.00 (*0-8032-2569-5*); pap. 11.50 (*0-8032-7567-6*) U of Nebr Pr.
Children's Jewish Holiday Kitchen. Joan Nathan. LC 86-22016. (Illus.). 144p. 1987. spiral bd. 14.00 (*0-8052-0827-5*) Schocken.
Children's Jubilee: A Bibliographical Survey of Hymnals for Infants, Youth & Sunday Schools Published in Britain & America, 1655-1900. Comp. by Samuel J. Rogal. LC 83-1661. (Illus.). xliv, 91p. 1983. text ed. 42.95 (*0-313-23880-4*, RCJ/) Greenwood.
***Children's Jutebox: A Subject Guide to Musical Recordings & Programming Ideas for Songsters.** Rob Reid. LC 95-6163. 195p. (Orig.). 1995. pap. text ed. 25.00x (*0-8389-0650-8*) ALA.
Children's Language, Vol. 3. Ed. by Keith E. Nelson. 522p. (C). 1982. text ed. 89.95 (*0-89859-264-X*) L Erlbaum Assocs.
Children's Language, Vol. 4. Ed. by Keith E. Nelson. 496p. 1983. text ed. 89.95 (*0-89859-272-0*) L Erlbaum Assocs.
Children's Language, Vol. 5. Ed. by Keith E. Nelson. 472p. (C). 1985. text ed. 89.95 (*0-89859-346-8*) L Erlbaum Assocs.
Children's Language, Vol. 6. Ed. by Keith Nelson & Anne E. Van Kleeck. 366p. 1987. text ed. 89.95 (*0-89859-760-9*) L Erlbaum Assocs.
Children's Language, Vol. 7. Gina Conti-Ramsden & Catherine E. Snow. 352p. (C). 1990. text ed. 69.95 (*0-8058-0523-0*) L Erlbaum Assocs.
Children's Language, Vol. 8. Ed. by Keith E. Nelson & Zita Reger. 304p. 1994. text ed. 59.95 (*0-8058-1367-5*) L Erlbaum Assocs.
***Children's Language, Vol. 9.** Ed. by Carolyn E. Johnson & John H. Gilbert. 400p. 1996. text ed. 60.00 (*0-8058-2054-X*) L Erlbaum Assocs.
Children's Language & Communication Vol. 12: The Minnesota Symposium on Child Psychology. Ed. by W. Andrew Collins. LC 79-364. (Minnesota Symposium on Child Psychology Ser.). (Illus.). 256p. 1979. text ed. 49.95 (*0-89859-000-0*) L Erlbaum Assocs.
Children's Language & Learning. 2nd ed. Judith W. Lindfors. (Illus.). 512p. (C). 1987. text ed. 53.00 (*0-13-131962-0*) P-H.
Children's Language & the Language Arts: A Literature-Based Approach. 3rd ed. Carol J. Fisher & C. Ann Terry. 512p. 1990. teacher ed write for info. (*0-318-66358-9*, H22981); text ed. 45.00 (*0-205-11431-8*, H14319) Allyn.
Children's Learning Difficulties: A Cognitive Approach. Julie Dockrell & John McShane. LC 92-19116. 1993. pap. 19.95 (*0-631-17017-0*) Blackwell Pubs.
Children's Letters to God: The New Collection. Ed. by Eric Marshall & Julie Hansen. LC 90-21211. (Illus.). 96p. (Orig.). 1991. pap. 6.95 (*0-89480-999-7*, 1999) Workman Pub.
Children's Letters to Santa Claus. Comp. by Bill Adler. LC 93-25377. (Illus.). (J). (ps-3). 1993. 9.95 (*1-55972-196-0*, Birch Ln Pr) Carol Pub Group.
Children's Letters to Socks: Kids Write to America's "First Cat" Ed. by Bill Adler. LC 93-46694. (YA). 1994. 9.95 (*1-55972-221-5*, Birch Ln Pr) Carol Pub Group.
Children's Liberation: A Biblical Perspective. Joseph A. Grassi. 128p. (Orig.). 1991. pap. 5.95 (*0-8146-1964-9*) Liturgical Pr.
Children's Library Services Handbook. Jane Gardner Connor. LC 89-8568. (Illus.). 144p. 1990. pap. 29.95 (*0-89774-489-6*) Oryx Pr.
Children's Lifeworlds: Gender, Welfare & Labour in the Developing World. Olga Nieuwenhuys. LC 93-17607. 1994. 69.95 (*0-415-09750-9*); pap. 19.95 (*0-415-09751-7*) Routledge.
Children's Literature, 6 vols. Bennett Brockman & William E. Sheidley. Ed. by Francelia Butler et al. Incl. Vol. 1. LC 75-21550. 1972. 17.95 (*0-87722-082-4*); Vol. 1. LC 75-21550. 1972. pap. 10.95 (*0-87722-081-6*); Vol. 2. LC 75-21550. 1973. 17.95 (*0-87722-080-8*); Vol. 2. LC 75-21550. 1973. pap. 10.95 (*0-87722-079-4*); Vol. 3. LC 75-21550. 1974. 17.95 (*0-87722-078-6*); Vol. 3. LC 75-21550. 1974. pap. 10.95 (*0-87722-077-8*); Vol. 4. LC 75-21550. 1975. 17.95 (*0-87722-042-5*); Vol. 4. LC 75-21550. 1975. pap. 10.95 (*0-87722-076-X*); Vol. 5. LC 75-21550. 1976. 17.95 (*0-87722-069-7*); Vol. 5. LC 75-21550. 1976. pap. 10.95 (*0-87722-070-0*); Vol. 6. LC 75-21550. 1978. 17.95 (*0-87722-104-9*); Vol. 6. LC 75-21550. 1978. pap. 10.95 (*0-87722-105-7*); LC 75-21550. write for info. (*0-318-55917-X*) Temple U Pr.
Children's Literature. Harriet Campbell. (Illus.). 64p. 1981. 24.00 (*0-88014-032-1*) Mosaic Pr OH.
***Childrens Literature.** Hendricks. 1996. text ed. 65.00 (*0-8161-1638-5*) G K Hall.
Children's Literature. Kim Reynolds. 1990. 39.00 (*0-7463-0723-3*, Pub. by Northcote House UK) St Mut.
Children's Literature. Kimberly Reynolds. (Writers & Their Work Ser.). 96p. 1994. pap. text ed. 11.50 (*0-7463-0728-4*, Pub. by Northcote House UK) Trans-Atl Phila.
Children's Literature, No. 18. Francelia Butler et al. 240p. (C). 1990. text ed. 45.00 (*0-300-04644-8*); pap. 16.00 (*0-300-04645-6*) Yale U Pr.
Children's Literature, Vol. 10. Ed. by Francelia Butler et al. LC 79-66588. 272p. (C). 1982. text ed. 45.00 (*0-300-02805-9*) Yale U Pr.
Children's Literature, Vol. 12. Francelia Butler & Compton Rees. LC 79-66588. (Illus.). 264p. 1984. pap. text ed. 45.00 (*0-300-03144-0*) Yale U Pr.
Children's Literature, Vol. 15. Francelia Butler. LC 79-66588. 256p. 1987. text ed. 45.00 (*0-300-03812-7*); pap. 16.00 (*0-300-03813-5*) Yale U Pr.
Children's Literature, Vol. 16. Ed. by Francelia Butler. LC 79-66588. 256p. (C). 1988. pap. 16.00 (*0-300-04193-4*) Yale U Pr.
Children's Literature, Vol. 17. Francelia Butler. LC 79-66588. 256p. (C). 1989. text ed. 45.00 (*0-300-04421-6*); pap. 16.00 (*0-300-04422-4*) Yale U Pr.
Children's Literature: A Guide to the Criticism. Linnea Hendrickson. (Reference Bks.). 696p. 1987. text ed. 38.50 (*0-8161-8670-7*, Hall Reference) Macmillan.
***Children's Literature: An Illustrated History.** Peter Hunt. (Oxford Illustrated Histories Ser.). (Illus.). 480p. 1995. text ed. 39.95 (*0-19-212320-3*) OUP.
Children's Literature: An Issues Approach. 2nd ed. Masha K. Rudman. LC 83-22217. 448p. (C). 1984. text ed. 34.95 (*0-582-28398-1*, 71430) Longman.
Children's Literature: An Issues Approach. 3rd rev. ed. Masha K. Rudman. LC 94-6627. 512p. (C). 1995. pap. text ed. 34.95 (*0-8013-0537-3*, 78414) Longman.
Children's Literature: Annual of the Modern Language Association Division on Children's Literature & the Children's Literature Association, No. 11. Francelia Butler et al. LC 79-66588. (Illus.). 224p. 1983. text ed. 45.00 (*0-300-02991-8*) Yale U Pr.
Children's Literature: Annual of the Modern Language Association Division on Children's Literature & the Children's Literature Association, No. 13. Ed. by Francelia Butler & Margaret R. Higonnet. LC 79-66588. 240p. 1985. text ed. 45.00 (*0-300-03319-2*) Yale U Pr.
Children's Literature: Criticism & the Fictional Child. Karin Lesnik-Oberstein. LC 93-35484. 264p. 1994. 39.95 (*0-19-811998-4*) OUP.
Children's Literature: Promotion, Use, & Teaching in the School Media Center. LMS Staff. (School Library Media Ser.). 1991. lib. bdg. 24.95 (*0-87436-666-6*) ABC-CLIO.
Children's Literature: Resource for the Classroom. 2nd ed. Ed. by Masha K. Rudman. 252p. (J). (gr. k-8). 1993. pap. text ed. 27.95 (*0-926842-31-5*) CG Pubs Inc.
Children's Literature: Selected Essays & Bibliographies. Ed. by Anne S. MacLeod & Jerry S. Kidd. LC 77-620023. (Student Contribution Ser.: No. 9). 1977. pap. 9.75 (*0-911808-13-2*) U of Md Lib Serv.
Children's Literature: Strategies of Teaching. Robert Whitehead. (Orig.). 1968. pap. text ed. 20.95 (*0-685-03788-6*) P-H.
Children's Literature: The Development of Criticism. Peter Hunt. 224p. 1990. 57.50 (*0-415-02993-7*, A4695); pap. 14.95 (*0-415-02994-5*, A4942) Routledge.
Children's Literature: Theory, Research, & Teaching. Kay E. Vandergrift. 277p. 1990. lib. bdg. 32.50 (*0-87287-749-3*) Libs Unl.
***Children's Literature & Critical Theory: Reading & Writing for Understanding.** Jill P. May. 288p. (C). 1995. text ed. 30.00 (*0-19-509584-7*); pap. text ed. 16.95 (*0-19-509585-5*) OUP.
Children's Literature & Social Studies: Selecting & Using Notable Books in the Classroom. NCSS Staff. 96p. 1993. per. 13.95 (*0-8403-8951-5*) Kendall-Hunt.

An Asterisk (*) at the beginning of an entry indicates that the title is appearing in BIP for the first time.

Children's Literature Awards & Winners. 3rd ed. Schuman. 1994. 94.00 (*0-8103-6900-1*) Gale.

***Children's Literature, Briefly.** James S. Jacobs & Michael O. Tunnell. LC 95-10379. 1995. write for info. (*0-675-21401-7*, Merrill Pub Co) Macmillan.

Children's Literature for All God's Children. Virginia Thomas & Betty Miller. LC 85-17169. 120p. 1986. pap. 11.99 (*0-8042-1690-8*, John Knox) Westminster John Knox.

Children's Literature for Health Awareness. Anthony L. Manna & Cynthia W. Symons. LC 92-29737. (Illus.). 629p. 1992. 49.50 (*0-8108-2582-1*) Scarecrow.

Children's Literature From A to Z: A Guide for Parents & Teachers. Jon Stott. 318p. 1984. pap. text ed. 16.95 (*0-07-061791-0*) McGraw.

Children's Literature Handbook. Johnny J. Wheelbarger. LC 74-9989. 94p. 1974. pap. text ed. 6.95 (*0-8422-0442-3*) Irvington.

***Children's Literature in an Integrated Curriculum: The Authentic Voice.** Ed. by Bette Bosma & Nancy Guth. 144p. (C). 1995. pap. text ed. 16.95x (*0-8077-3437-3*) Tchrs Coll.

Children's Literature in Canada. Elizabeth Waterston. (Twayne's World Authors Ser.: No. 823). 200p. (C). 1992. text ed. 22.95 (*0-8057-8264-8*, Twayne) Macmillan.

Children's Literature in the Classroom: Extending Charlotte's Web. Ed. by Janet Hickman et al. 232p. (J). (gr. k-8). 1994. pap. text ed. 26.95 (*0-926842-32-3*) CG Pubs Inc.

Children's Literature in the Classroom: Weaving Charlotte's Web. Ed. by Janet Hickman & Bernice E. Cullinan. (Illus.). 296p. (J). (gr. k-8). 1989. text ed. 33.95 (*0-926842-00-5*) CG Pubs Inc.

***Children's Literature in the Elementary School.** 5th ed. Charlotte S. Huck. 924p. (C). 1994. boxed write for info. (*0-697-27397-0*) Brown & Benchmark.

Children's Literature in the Elementary School. 5th ed. Charlotte S. Huck et al. 775p. (C). 1993. text ed. 46.00 (*0-03-047528-7*) HB Coll Pubs.

Children's Literature in the Reading Program. Ed. by Bernice E. Cullinan. LC 86-27786. (Illus.). 181p. reprint ed. pap. 51.60 (*0-7837-4585-0*, 2044304) Bks Demand.

Children's Literature, No. 19: Annual of the Modern Language Association Division on Children's Literature & the Children's Literature. Ed. by Francelia Butler et al. (Illus.). 240p. (Orig.). (C). 1991. text ed. 45.00 (*0-300-04972-2*); pap. text ed. 16.00 (*0-300-04973-0*) Yale U Pr.

Children's Literature, No. 22: Annual of the Modern Language Association Division on Children's Literature & the Children's Literature Association. Ed. by Francelia Butler et al. (Illus.). 212p. 1994. 45.00 (*0-300-05874-8*); pap. 16.00 (*0-300-05875-6*) Yale U Pr.

Children's Literature of Peter Hacks. Thomas DiNapoli. (DDR-Studien - East German Studies: Vol. 2). 321p. (C). 1987. text ed. 52.50 (*0-8204-0377-6*) P Lang Pubs.

Children's Literature of the English Renaissance. Warren W. Wooden. Ed. by Jeanie Watson. LC 86-15651. 208p. 1986. 23.00 (*0-8131-1587-6*) U Pr of Ky.

Children's Literature Review, Vol. 11. Ed. by Gerald J. Senick. 300p. 1986. 114.00 (*0-8103-0343-4*) Gale.

Children's Literature Review, Vol. 12. Ed. by Gerald J. Senick. 299p. 1987. 114.00 (*0-8103-0344-2*) Gale.

Children's Literature Review, Vol. 13. Ed. by Gerald J. Senick. 315p. 1987. 114.00 (*0-8103-0348-5*) Gale.

Children's Literature Review, Vol. 14. Ed. by Gerald J. Senick. LC 75-34953. 300p. 1987. 114.00 (*0-8103-0349-3*) Gale.

Children's Literature Review, Vol. 15. Ed. by Gerald J. Senick. 1988. 114.00 (*0-8103-0319-1*) Gale.

Children's Literature Review, Vol. 16. Ed. by Gerald J. Senick. 250p. 1988. 114.00 (*0-8103-2776-7*) Gale.

Children's Literature Review, Vol. 17. Ed. by Gerald J. Senick. 1989. 114.00 (*0-8103-2777-5*) Gale.

Children's Literature Review, Vol. 18. Gale Research Inc. Staff. Ed. by Gerald J. Senick. 1989. 114.00 (*0-8103-2778-3*) Gale.

Children's Literature Review, Vol. 19. Gerald J. Senick. 300p. 1989. 114.00 (*0-8103-2779-1*) Gale.

Children's Literature Review, Vol. 20. Ed. by Gerald J. Senick. 300p. 1990. 114.00 (*0-8103-2780-5*) Gale.

Children's Literature Review, Vol. 21. Ed. by Gerald J. Senick. 300p. 1990. 114.00 (*0-8103-4645-1*) Gale.

Children's Literature Review, Vol. 22. 1990. 114.00 (*0-8103-4646-X*) Gale.

Children's Literature Review, Vol. 23. Gerald J. Senick. 1991. 114.00 (*0-8103-4647-8*) Gale.

Children's Literature Review, Vol. 24. Gerald J. Senick. 1991. 114.00 (*0-8103-4648-6*) Gale.

Children's Literature Review, Vol. 25. Gerald J. Senick. 1991. 114.00 (*0-8103-4649-4*) Gale.

Children's Literature Review, Vol. 26. Gerald J. Senick. 1992. 114.00 (*0-8103-4863-2*) Gale.

Children's Literature Review, Vol. 27. Gerald J. Senick. 1992. 114.00 (*0-8103-5700-3*) Gale.

Children's Literature Review, Vol. 28. Gerald J. Senick. 1992. 114.00 (*0-8103-5701-1*) Gale.

Children's Literature Review, Vol. 29. Gerald J. Senick. 1993. 114.00 (*0-8103-5702-X*) Gale.

Children's Literature Review, Vol. 30. Gerald J. Senick. 1993. 114.00 (*0-8103-5703-8*) Gale.

Children's Literature Review, Vol. 31. Gerald J. Senick. 1993. 114.00 (*0-8103-5704-6*) Gale.

Children's Literature Review, Vol. 32. Gerald J. Senick. 1994. 114.00 (*0-8103-8471-X*) Gale.

Children's Literature Review, Vol. 33. Gerald J. Senick. 1994. 114.00 (*0-8103-8472-8*) Gale.

Children's Literature Review, Vol. 34. Gerald J. Senick. 1994. 114.00 (*0-8103-8473-6*) Gale.

***Children's Literature Review, Vol. 35.** Ed. by Gerard J. Senick & Alan Hedblad. 1995. 114.00 (*0-8103-8949-5*) Gale.

Children's Literature Review: Excerpts from Critical Commentaries on Juvenile & Young People's Authors & Their Books. Ed. by Gerald J. Senick. Incl. Vol. 1. LC 77-1665. 224p. 1976. 110.00 (*0-8103-0077-X*); Vol. 2. LC 77-1665. 272p. 1976. 110.00 (*0-8103-0078-8*); Vol. 3. LC 77-1665. 296p. 1978. 110.00 (*0-8103-0079-6*); Vol. 4. LC 58-1212. 380p. 1982. 114.00 (*0-8103-0080-X*); Vol. 5. LC 75-17091. 304p. 1983. 110.00 (*0-8103-0330-2*); Vol. 6. LC 77-84583. 272p. 1984. 114.00 (*0-8103-0331-0*); Vol. 7. Vol. 7. LC 75-34953. 276p. 1984. 114.00 (*0-8103-0332-9*); Vol. 8. Vol. 8. LC 75-34953. 292p. 1985. 114.00 (*0-8103-0333-7*); Vol. 9. Vol. 9. LC 75-34953. 284p. 1985. 114.00 (*0-8103-0334-5*); LC 75-34953. write for info. (*0-318-52354-X*) Gale.

Children's Literature, Twenty: Annual of the Modern Language Association Division on Children's Literature & the Children's Literature Association. Ed. by Francelia Butler et al. (Illus.). 265p. (Orig.). (C). 1992. text ed. 45.00 (*0-300-05173-5*); pap. text ed. 16.00 (*0-300-05172-7*) Yale U Pr.

Children's Literature, vol. 14: Annual of the Modern Language Association Division on Children's Literature & the Children's Literature Association. rev. ed. Ed. by Francelia Butler et al. LC 79-66588. 224p. 1986. text ed. 45.00 (*0-300-03564-0*) Yale U Pr.

Children's Literature, Vol. 21: Annual of the Modern Language Association Division on Children's Literature & the Children's Literature Association. Ed. by Francelia Butler. (Illus.). 264p. (C). 1993. text ed. 45.00 (*0-300-05423-8*); pap. text ed. 16.00 (*0-300-05424-6*) Yale U Pr.

Children's Live-Action Musical Films: A Critical Survey & Filmography. Thomas J. Harris. LC 89-42719. 207p. 1989. lib. bdg. 27.50x (*0-89950-375-6*) McFarland & Co.

Children's Living French. Ed. by Suzanne Jacob. (Complete Living Language Course Ser.). (Illus.). (J). 1987. 4.95 (*0-517-56331-2*, Crown); pap. 4.95 (*0-517-56332-0*, Crown) Crown Pub Group.

Children's Living French. Ed. by Suzanne Jacob. (Complete Living Language Course Ser.). (Illus.). (J). 1988. audio 18.95 (*0-517-56329-0*, Crown) Crown Pub Group.

Children's Living Spanish. Ed. by Mary Finocchiaro. (Complete Living Language Course Ser.). (Illus.). (J). 1987. 5.00 (*0-517-56336-3*, Crown); 5.00 (*0-517-56335-5*, Crown) Crown Pub Group.

Children's Living Spanish. Ed. by Mary Finocchiaro. (Complete Living Language Course Ser.). (Illus.). (J). 1988. 20.00 (*0-517-56333-9*, Crown) Crown Pub Group.

Children's Lore in "Finnegans Wake" Grace Eckley. (Irish Studies). (Illus.). 304p. 1985. text ed. 29.95 (*0-8156-2317-8*) Syracuse U Pr.

Children's Lunch Boxes & Party Snack. Rosetta Schuman. 85p. 1987. 12.50 (*0-318-23878-0*) Beechwold Pr.

Children's Macbeth. Illus. by Meredith Johnson. (J). (gr. 5-9). Date not set. pap. 3.95 (*0-88388-186-1*) Bellerophon Bks.

Children's Machine: Rethinking School in the Age of the Computer. Seymour Papert. 256p. 1994. reprint ed. pap. 12.00 (*0-465-01063-6*) Basic.

Children's Magic Kit: Sixteen Easy-to-Do Tricks Complete with Cardboard Cutouts. Karl Fulves. (Illus.). 32p. (Orig.). (J). (gr. 3-6). 1981. pap. 3.95 (*0-486-24019-3*) Dover.

Children's Market: Infants', Toddlers', Girls', Boys' (Apparel, Playthings & Related Products) Fairchild Market Research Staff. (Fact File Ser.). 50p. 1989. pap. 37.50 (*0-685-55982-3*) Fairchild.

***Children's Market U. S. A. Handbook.** 175p. (Orig.). 1995. pap. 2,195.00 (*0-7605-1975-7*) Rector Pr.

Children's Market, 1991. Fairfield Market Research Staff. (Fact File Ser.). 50p. 1992. pap. 37.50 (*0-87005-750-2*) Fairchild.

Children's Material. Bette Martin. (Illus.). 100p. (J). (gr. k-4). 1980. pap. write for info. (*1-880436-02-7*) Miracle Exper.

Children's Mathematical Concepts: Six Piagetian Studies in Mathematics Education. Myron F. Rosskopf. LC 75-12872. (Illus.). 224p. reprint ed. pap. 63.90 (*0-317-09439-4*, 2017767) Bks Demand.

***Children's Mathematical Development: Research & Practical Applications.** 2nd ed. David C. Geary. 327p. 1994. text ed. 40.00 (*1-55798-258-9*) Am Psychol.

Children's Mathematical Thinking: A Developmental Framework for Pre-School, Primary, & Special Education Teachers. Arthur J. Baroody. 320p. (C). 1987. pap. text ed. 20.95 (*0-8077-2837-3*) Tchrs Coll.

Children's Media Market Place. 3rd ed. Ed. by Delores B. Jones. 397p. 1988. pap. text ed. 45.00 (*1-55570-007-1*) Neal-Schuman.

Children's Medications Guide Book. Jackie Webber. LC 92-30291. 1992. 22.95 (*0-13-151887-9*); pap. 9.95 (*0-13-151895-X*) P-H.

Children's Medicine Chest. John Coppola. LC 93-16237. 1993. 11.95 (*0-385-46818-0*) Doubleday.

Children's Mental Health: Problems & Services. Ed. by Technology Assessment Office Staff & Leonard M. Saxe. LC 86-600539. (Illus.). viii, 184p. (C). 1987. lib. bdg. 36.95 (*0-8223-0796-0*); pap. text ed. 14.95 (*0-8223-0815-0*) Duke.

Children's Minds. Margaret Donaldson. (Illus.). (C). 1979. pap. text ed. 8.95 (*0-393-95101-4*) Norton.

Children's Ministry: Nursing Faith Within the Family of God. Lawrence O. Richards. 448p. 1988. pap. 24.99 (*0-310-52071-1*, 18215P) Zondervan.

Children's Ministry Clip Art. Mary L. Ulrich. (Illus.). 128p. (Orig.). 1990. pap. 15.99 (*1-55945-018-5*, Group Bks) Group Pub.

***Children's Ministry Guide for Smaller Churches.** Rick Chromey. Ed. by Beth Wolf. (Illus.). 156p. 1995. pap. 12.99 (*1-55945-600-0*) Group Pub.

Children's Ministry That Works! Ed. by Jolene L. Roehlkepartain. (Illus.). 228p. (Orig.). 1991. pap. 15.99 (*0-931529-69-7*, Group Bks) Group Pub.

Childrens Money Making Jobs. Jodi Jill. 32p. (J). 1993. pap. 6.95 (*1-883438-04-7*) J J Features.

Children's Museum Activity Book: Bubbles. Bernie Zubrowski. LC 78-27497. (Children's Museum Bks.). (Illus.). (J). (gr. 5-7). 1979. mass mkt. 8.95 (*0-316-98881-2*) Little.

Children's Museums, Zoos, & Discovery Rooms: An International Reference Guide. Barbara F. Zucker. LC 86-22793. 278p. 1987. text ed. 59.95 (*0-313-24538-X*, ZUM/) Greenwood.

Children's National Medical Center A to Z Guide to Your Child's Behavior. Children's National Medical Center Staff. 384p. (Orig.). 1993. pap. 14.95 (*0-399-51796-0*, Perigree Bks) Berkley Pub.

Children's Needs: Psychological Perspectives. Alex Thomas & Jeff Grimes. 750p. 1987. pap. text ed. 35.00 (*0-932955-05-3*) Natl Assn Psych.

Children's New International Holy Bible. (Illus.). (J). (gr. 2 up). 1984. 14.99 (*0-310-90272-X*, 80659) Zondervan.

Children's Night. Alex Holland. (Illus.). 13p. (J). (gr. k-3). 1994. pap. 9.95 (*1-56606-030-3*) Bradley Mann.

Children's Numbers. Catherine Sophian. 148p. (C). 1995. pap. text ed. write for info. (*0-697-13135-1*) Brown & Benchmark.

***Children's Nursing in Practice: The Nottingham Model.** Fiona Smith. LC 94-23687. 1995. write for info. (*0-632-03909-4*) Blackwell Sci.

Children's Nutrition. Lifshitz. (Health Science Ser.). 1991. boxed 50.00 (*0-86720-186-X*) Jones & Bartlett.

Children's Object Sermons for the Seasons. C. W. Bess. (Object Lesson Ser.). 144p. (Orig.). 1993. pap. 6.99 (*0-8010-1026-8*) Baker Bk.

***Children's Omnibus Study, Waves III & IV.** 140p. (Orig.). 1995. pap. 795.00 (*0-7605-1980-3*) Rector Pr.

Children's Oral Communication Skills. Ed. by W. Patrick Dickson. (Developmental Psychology Ser.). 1981. text ed. 85.00 (*0-12-215450-9*) Acad Pr.

Children's Organizer: A Calendar System of Daily Tasks for Children. Toni Pighetti. (Illus.). 32p. (Orig.). (J). (gr. k-8). 1983. pap. 7.95 (*0-913005-03-7*) TAM Assoc.

Children's Orthopaedics & Fractures. Michael K. Benson. 1994. 110.00 (*0-443-04372-8*) Churchill.

Children's Own Longfellow. Henry Wadsworth Longfellow. (Illus.). 109p. (J). (gr. 4-6). 1908. 19.95 (*0-395-06889-4*) HM.

Children's Own Stories: A Literature-Based Language Arts Program. Lynn Landor. (Illus.). 118p. 1990. pap. 20.00 (*0-936434-25-2*, Pub. by Zellerbach Fam Fund) SF Study Ctr.

Children's Pages: A Parent Source Book for North Central Texas. Joylyn Niebes. 320p. (Orig.). 1986. pap. 8.95 (*0-933547-02-1*) Lauren Pubns.

Children's Pages: A Parent Source Book for the Dallas Area. Joylyn Niebes. 128p. (Orig.). 1985. pap. 8.95 (*0-933547-00-5*) Lauren Pubns.

Children's Pages of Metro Denver - Fall Edition, 1988: A Directory of Products & Services for Children of All Ages & Their Parents. Ed. by Frances Hawley. (YA). (gr. 7 up). 1988. pap. write for info. (*0-932439-08-X*) Denver Busn Media.

Children's Pages of Metro Denver 1988. Ed. by Frances Hawley. 96p. 1987. pap. write for info. (*0-932439-07-1*) Denver Busn Media.

Children's Parties Made Easy. Penny Fulk. (Illus.). 142p. (Orig.). (YA). pap. 6.00 (*0-941951-00-6*) JJJ Pubs.

***Children's Party Food.** Murfitt. 1995. pap. text ed. 8.95 (*0-316-54807-3*) Little.

Children's Party Handbook. Alison Boteler. 188p. 1986. 16.95 (*0-8120-5636-1*) Barron.

Children's Party Handbook. Alison Boteler. 160p. 1991. pap. 13.95 (*0-8120-4747-8*) Barron.

Children's Party Ideas. Margaret Dunne. 272p. (Orig.). 1994. mass mkt. 4.99 (*0-425-14344-9*) Berkley Pub.

Children's Patterns for Cake Decorating. Roland A. Winbeckler. (Illus.). 24p. (Orig.). 1990. pap. 4.95 (*0-930113-11-X*) Winbeckler.

Children's Peer Relations: Issues in Assessment & Intervention. Ed. by Barry H. Schneider et al. LC 85-12660. (Illus.). 290p. 1985. 73.00 (*0-387-96163-1*) Spr-Verlag.

Children's Perceptions of Gender & Work Roles. Gloria M. Nemerowicz. LC 79-11783. 201p. 1979. text ed. 49.95 (*0-275-90399-0*, C0399, Praeger Pubs) Greenwood.

Children's Periodicals of the United States. Ed. by R. Gordon Kelly. LC 83-8574. (Historical Guides to the World's Periodicals & Newspapers Ser.). xxiv, 591p. 1984. text ed. 79.50 (*0-313-22117-0*, KCP/, Greenwood Pr) Greenwood.

Children's Perspectives on the Family. Ed. by Inge Bretherton & Malcolm W. Watson. LC 85-644581. (New Directions for Child Development Ser.: No. 48). 1990. 17.95 (*1-55542-825-8*) Jossey-Bass.

Children's Phantasies: The Shaping of Relationships. Otto Weininger. 344p. 1989. pap. 34.95 (*0-946439-54-0*, Pub. by Karnac Bks UK) Brunner-Mazel.

***Children's Phobias: A Behavioral Perspective.** Neville J. King et al. 1994. pap. text ed. 29.95 (*0-471-95139-0*) Wiley.

Children's Phobias: A Behavioural Perspective. Neville J. King et al. 1988. text ed. 100.00 (*0-471-10276-8*) Wiley.

Children's Phonetic Disorders: Theory & Treatment. Paul R. Hoffman et al. LC 90-9198. 330p. (C). 1989. pap. text ed. 34.00 (*0-89079-334-4*, 1686) PRO-ED.

***Children's Phonology Disorders: Pathways & Patterns.** 2nd ed. Ed. by Evelyn J. Williams. 91p. 1994. pap. text ed. 25.00 (*0-614-06521-6*, 0111907) Am Speech Lang Hearing.

Children's Physical Education: Teaching for the Vitality of Movement. Judith B. Carlson. 152p. 1993. per. 22.95 (*0-8403-8982-5*) Kendall-Hunt.

Children's Piano Method. John Brimhall. (Illus.). 64p. (Orig.). (J). (gr. 1-6). 1984. pap. text ed. 5.95 (*0-8494-2887-4*, T430) Hansen Ed Mus.

Children's Piano Pieces the Whole World Plays. (Whole World Ser.: Vol. 16). pap. 12.95 (*0-8256-1002-8*) Music Sales.

***Children's Picture Bibles.** pap. text ed. 9.99 (*0-517-12038-0*) Random Hse Value.

Children's Picture Book of African American History. Julia A. Davis. (Illus.). 150p. (J). (ps-5). 1992. 20.00 (*0-9631110-3-5*) Epps-Alford.

Children's Picture Books. R. S. Freeman. LC 66-29514. (Victorian Culture Ser.). (*0-87282-063-7*); pap. 7.50 (*0-87282-107-2*) Am Life Foun.

Children's Picture Dictionary: English-Chinese, Illus. by Dennis Sheheen. (Children's Picture Dictionary Ser.). (J). (gr. k up). 9.95 (*0-685-18873-6*) Modan-Adama Bks.

Children's Pilgrims Progress. Jean Gray. 1990. pap. 4.95 (*0-85244-170-3*, Pub. by Gracewing UK) Morehouse Pub.

Children's Play: Research Developments & Practical Applications. Ed. by Peter K. Smith. (Special Aspects of Education Ser.: Vol. 6). 162p. 1986. text ed. 62.00 (*0-677-21390-5*); pap. text ed. 27.00 (*0-677-20000-5*) Gordon & Breach.

Children's Play & Learning: Perspectives & Policy Implications. Ed. by Edgar Klugman & Sara Smilansky. (Early Childhood Education Ser.: No. 28). 320p. (C). 1990. text ed. 44.95 (*0-8077-3033-5*); pap. text ed. 21.95 (*0-8077-3032-7*) Tchrs Coll.

Children's Play in Child Care Settings. Ed. by Hillel Goelman & Ellen V. Jacobs. LC 93-18083. (SUNY Series, Children's Play in Society). 234p. (C). 1994. Alk. paper. 64.50 (*0-7914-1697-6*); pap. 21.95 (*0-7914-1698-4*) State U NY Pr.

Children's Play in Diverse Cultures. Ed. by Jaipaul L. Roopnarine et al. LC 93-12177. (SUNY Series, Children's Play in Society). 234p. (C). 1994. 59.50 (*0-7914-1753-0*); pap. 19.95 (*0-7914-1754-9*) State U NY Pr.

C

Children's Play Spaces. Jacques Simon & Marguerite Rouard. LC 76-57882. (Illus.). 160p. 1983. 37.95 (*0-87951-056-0*); pap. 17.95 (*0-87951-166-4*) Overlook Pr.

Children's Play Yards. Ed. by Southern Living Staff. (Southern Living Home Improvement Ser.). 64p. 1992. pap. 7.99 (*0-376-09040-5*) Oxmoor Hse.

Children's Play Yards: Ideas, Plans, Projects. Sunset Editors. LC 88-51146. (Illus.). 64p. 1989. pap. 8.99 (*0-376-01790-2*) Sunset Menlo Pk.

Children's Plays for Creative Actors. Claire Boiko. 384p. (J). (gr. 3-7). 1985. reprint ed. pap. 15.00 (*0-8238-0267-1*) Plays.

Children's Plays from Favorite Stories. Ed. by Sylvia E. Kamerman. 583p. (J). (gr. 1-6). 1990. pap. 16.95 (*0-8238-0270-1*) Plays.

Children's Poems. H. Amery. (Poetry Bks.). (Illus.). 96p. (J). (gr. 2-6). 1992. pap. 12.95 (*0-7460-0482-6*) EDC.

Children's Poets. Walter Barnes. 1972. 59.95 (*0-87968-851-3*) Gordon Pr.

***Children's Prayers from Around the World.** Comp. by Mary Batchelor. LC 95-8518. (J). 1995. write for info. (*0-8066-2830-8*, Augsburg) Augsburg Fortress.

Children's Priest. (Illus.). 64p. 1985. pap. 1.50 (*0-89944-133-5*) Don Bosco Multimedia.

Children's Problems in Text Comprehension: An Experimental Investigation. Nicola Yuill & Jane Oakhill. (Monographs & Texts in Applied Psycholinguistics). (Illus.). 256p. (C). 1991. 59.95 (*0-521-35324-6*) Cambridge U Pr.

Children's Prose Comprehension: Research & Practice. Ed. by Carol M. Santa & Bernard L. Hayes. LC 80-21883. (Illus.). 192p. (Orig.). reprint ed. pap. 54.80 (*0-8357-8656-0*, 2035102) Bks Demand.

***Children's Publishing, Media & Entertainment.** James Moses. 252p. Date not set. 265.00 (*0-9626749-7-4*) Primary Research.

***Children's Puzzle Packet.** rev. ed. Ralph McCoy. Ed. by Sandra Sladkey. (H. I. S. Songs for Children Ser.). (Illus.). 18p. (J). (gr. 1-5). 1994. pap. 1.95 (*1-885819-06-4*) His Songs.

Children's Question Book: A Parent Teacher Guide. William M. Willis. LC 81-83727. 115p. (Orig.). (J). (gr. 1 up). 1981. pap. text ed. 7.95 (*0-9607028-1-4*) Ocean East.

Children's Questions. Miriam S. Dorn. (Occasional Paper Ser.). 22p. 1987. pap. 3.00 (*0-918374-24-3*) City Coll Wk.

Children's Quiz Book. Robert Duffy. 132p. (J). 1988. pap. 5.95 (*1-85371-020-2*, Pub. by Poolbeg Pr IE) Dufour.

Children's Radiographic Technic. Forrest E. Shurtleff. LC 62-17821. (Illus.). 92p. reprint ed. 26.30 (*0-8357-9399-0*, 2014580) Bks Demand.

Children's Reading in America, 1776. 1992. lib. bdg. 75.00 (*0-8490-8776-7*) Gordon Pr.

Children's Reading Problems. Peter Bryant & Lynette Bradley. 256p. 1985. pap. 19.95 (*0-631-17799-X*) Blackwell Pubs.

Children's Reference PLUS, CD-ROM. 1994. 595.00 (*0-8352-2839-8*) Bowker.

Children's Rhymes, Children's Games, Children's Songs & Stories. Robert Ford. 1972. 59.95 (*0-87968-852-1*) Gordon Pr.

An Asterisk (*) at the beginning of an entry indicates that the title is appearing in BIP for the first time.

Children's Rights. Beverly C. Edmonds. (Contemporary World Issues Ser.). 225p. 1995. lib. bdg. 39.50 (*0-87436-764-6*) ABC-CLIO.

Children's Rights. Lewis B. Sckolnick. (Civil Rights Reporter Ser.). (Illus.). 60p. (Orig.). (C). 1994. pap. 45.00 (*1-57205-154-X*) Rector Pr.

Children's Rights: Contemporary Perspectives. Ed. by Patricia Vardin & Ilene Brody. LC 78-12584. (Orig.). 1978. pap. 14.95 (*0-8077-2550-1*) Tchrs Coll.

Children's Rights: Legal & Educational Issues. Ed. by Heather Berkeley et al. LC 80-454939. (Ontario Institute for Studies in Education, Symposium Ser.: No. 9). 181p. pap. 51.60 (*0-317-41913-7*, 2026146) Bks Demand.

***Children's Rights & Representation Vol. 1.** Judith Timms. 1994. pap. text ed. 32.00 (*0-421-49720-3*, Pub. by Sweet & Maxwll) W W Gaunt.

Children's Rights & the Mental Health Profession. Ed. by Gerald P. Koocher. LC 76-16062. (Wiley Series on Personality Processes). 270p. reprint ed. pap. 77.00 (*0-317-08436-4*, 2055526) Bks Demand.

Children's Rights & the Wheel of Life. Elise Boulding. LC 78-62890. 179p. 1979. 32.95 (*0-87855-295-2*) Transaction Pubs.

Children's Rights: Crisis & Challenge: A Global Report on the Situation of Children in View of the U. N. Convention on the Rights of the Child. Ed. by Dennis Nurkse & Kay Castelle. 384p. (Orig.). 1990. pap. 25.00 (*0-943965-13-6*) DCI USA.

Children's Rights in Haiti. Minnesota Lawyers International Human Rights Committee Staff. 27p. (Orig.). 1989. pap. 5.00 (*0-929293-04-5*) MN Advocates.

Children's Rights Movement in the United States: A History of Advocacy & Protection. Joseph M. Hawes. (Social Movements Past & Present Ser.). 184p. (C). 1991. text ed. 26.95 (*0-8057-9747-5*, Twayne); pap. 13.95 (*0-8057-9748-3*, Twayne) Macmillan.

***Children's Rights Revisioned: Philosophical Readings.** Rosalind E. Ladd. LC 95-3845. 1996. pap. 18.95 (*0-534-23532-8*) Intl Thomson.

Children's Room. Louis R. Des Forets. Tr. by Jean Stewart. 240p. (Orig.). 1987. pap. 11.95 (*0-7145-0165-4*) Riverrun NY.

Children's Rooms & Play Yards. LC 87-82525. (Illus.). 96p. 1988. 8.99 (*0-376-01057-6*) Sunset Menlo Pk.

***Children's Running: An After-School Program for Elementary School Children.** Joyce Rankin. Ed. by Warren H. Ohlrich. LC 94-61609. (Illus.). 88p. 1995. pap. 15.00 (*1-882426-02-9*) W H O Pr.

***Children's Science, Constructivism & Learning in Science.** Beverley Bell. 109p. 1993. pap. 60.00 (*0-7300-1607-2*, ECS 810, Pub. by Deakin Univ AT) St Mut.

Children's Scripture Puzzles: Reproducible Activities & Family Discussion for Sundays Through the Year. Kathleen O. Chesto & Elizabeth Chesto. (Cycle C Ser.). (Illus.). 64p. (Orig.). 1991. pap. 39.95 (*1-55612-471-6*) Sheed & Ward MO.

Children's Scripture Puzzles: Reproducible Activities & Family Discussion for Sundays Through the Year. Kathleen O. Chesto & Elizabeth E. Chesto. (Illus.). 64p. (Orig.). 1992. pap. 39.95 (*1-55612-571-2*, LL1571) Sheed & Ward MO.

Children's Scripture Puzzles: Reproducible Activities & Family Discussion for Sundays Through the Year. Kathleen O. Chesto & Elizabeth Chesto. (Illus.). 116p. (Orig.). (J). (gr. k-8). 1993. pap. 39.95 (*1-55612-619-0*) Sheed & Ward MO.

Children's Searching: The Development of Search Skill & Spatial Representation. Ed. by Henry M. Wellman. 344p. (C). 1985. text ed. 69.95 (*0-89859-567-3*) L Erlbaum Assocs.

Childrens Self Scoring I. Q. Test. Dan Pape. (Illus.). 40p. (Orig.). (C). Date not set. pap. text ed. write for info. (*1-882330-14-5*) Magni Co.

Children's Sermons for Special Occasions. Roy E. De Brand. LC 82-72228. (Orig.). 1983. pap. 5.99 (*0-8054-4927-2*) Broadman.

Children's Sermons Made Easy. Ann S. Wright. (Illus.). 69p. (Orig.). 1992. spiral bd. 9.98 (*0-9636030-0-0*) Annco.

Children's Services in the American Public Library: A Selected Bibliography. Ed. by Fannette H. Thomas. LC 90-40197. (Bibliographies & Indexes in Library & Information Science: No. 4). 192p. 1990. text ed. 45.00 (*0-313-24721-8*, TCS, Greenwood Pr) Greenwood.

Children's Sexual Encounters with Adults: A Scientific Study. C. K. Li et al. LC 92-43601. 343p. (C). 1993. 39.95 (*0-87975-820-1*) Prometheus Bks.

Children's Sibling Relationships: Developmental & Clinical Issues. Ed. by Fritz Boer & Judith F. Dunn. 184p. 1992. text ed. 36.00 (*0-8058-1107-9*) L Erlbaum Assocs.

Children's Singing Games in Five Sets. Ed. by Alice B. Gomme & Cecil J. Sharp. LC 75-35071. (Studies in Play & Games). 1976. reprint ed. 17.95 (*0-405-07921-4*) Ayer.

***Children's Single-Word Speech.** Ed. by Martyn D. Barrett. LC 84-29101. (Wiley Series in Developmental Psychology & Its Applications). 339p. 1985. pap. 96.70 (*0-7837-8491-0*, 2049298) Bks Demand.

Children's Sleep: A Series of Studies on the Influence of Motion Pictures. Samuel Renshaw et al. LC 76-124031. (Literature of Cinema Ser.). 1970. reprint ed. 21.95 (*0-405-01631-X*) Ayer.

Children's Social Behavior: Development, Assessment, & Modification. Phillip S. Strain et al. 1986. text ed. 91.00 (*0-12-673455-0*) Acad Pr.

Children's Social Competence in Context: The Contributions of Family, School & Culture. Barry H. Schneider. LC 92-31195. (International Series in Experimental Social Psychology). 1992. 67.00 (*0-08-037763-7*, Pergamon Pr) Elsevier.

Children's Social Networks & Social Supports. Belle. (Personality Processes Ser.). 1989. text ed. 55.00 (*0-471-62879-4*) Wiley.

Children's Song Index: An Index to More Than Twenty-Two Thousand Songs. Helen G. Cushing. 1988. reprint ed. lib. bdg. 199.00 (*0-7812-9714-1*) Rprt Serv.

Children's Song Index: An Index to More Than Twenty-Two Thousand Songs. Helen G. Cushing. 798p. 1936. reprint ed. 195.00 (*0-403-01530-8*) Scholarly.

***Children's Song Index, 1978-1993.** Kay Laughlin et al. 200p. 1995. lib. bdg. 37.50 (*1-56308-332-9*) Libs Unl.

Children's Songbook. H. Amery. 1989. pap. 9.95 (*0-7460-0264-5*, Usborne) EDC.

Children's Songbook Companion. Patricia Graham et al. (Illus.). 304p. 1994. pap. 16.95 (*1-56236-100-7*) Aspen Bks.

Children's Songs. Jerry Silverman. (Traditional Black Music Ser.). (Illus.). 80p. (YA). (gr. 5 up). 1992. pap. 9.95 (*0-7910-1847-4*) Chelsea Hse.

Children's Songs. Comp. by Jerry Silverman. (Traditional Black Music Ser.). (Illus.). 80p. (YA). (gr. 5 up). 1992. lib. bdg. 15.95 (*0-7910-1831-8*) Chelsea Hse.

Children's Songs: Hide 'n' Seek. Katy K. Arnsteen. (J). 1990. 3.99 (*0-517-02569-8*) Random Hse Value.

Children's Songs for Harmonica. Ed. by Pat Conway. (Illus.). 48p. 1992. pap. 7.95 (*0-7119-2831-2*, AM87060) Music Sales.

Children's Songs for Piano. John Brimhall. 96p. (Orig.). (J). (gr. 1-6). 1985. pap. text ed. 7.95 (*0-8494-2264-7*, 0496) Hansen Ed Mus.

Children's Space Atlas. Robin Kerrod. LC 91-30148. (Children's Atlases Ser.). (Illus.). 96p. (J). (gr. 2-6). 1992. 16.95 (*1-56294-721-4*); 6.95 (*1-56294-100-3*); lib. bdg. 18.90 (*1-56294-164-X*) Millbrook Pr.

Children's Special Places: Exploring the Role of Forts, Dens, & Bush Houses in Middle Childhood. David Sobel. LC 92-24058. 168p. (J). (gr. 1-6). 1993. pap. text ed. 17.95 (*0-913705-81-0*) Zephyr Pr AZ.

Children's Step-by-Step Cookbook. Angela Wilkes. LC 93-28860. (Illus.). (J). (gr. 1-7). 1994. 18.95 (*1-56458-474-7*) Dorling Kindersley.

Children's Stories. Rick Steber. (Tales of the Wild West Ser.: Vol. 6). (Illus.). 60p. (Orig.). (J). 1989. pap. 4.95 (*0-945134-06-1*); audio 9.95 (*0-945134-56-8*) Bonanza Pub.

Children's Stories & How to Tell Them. Woutrina A. Bone. (Illus.). 1975. reprint ed. 42.00 (*1-55888-939-6*) Omnigraphics Inc.

Children's Stories for Teenage Adults. rev. ed. Robert F. Brooks. (Illus.). 32p. (Orig.). (J). (gr. 5-9). pap. 3.00 (*0-936868-05-8*) Freeland Pubns.

Children's Stories from Dickens. Harold Copping. LC 92-37666. (Illus.). (J). 1993. 8.99 (*0-517-08485-6*, Derrydale Bks) Random Hse Value.

Children's Stories Two: Coloring Nature's Harmony. Ralph E. Johnson. Ed. by Paul T. Johnson. (Children's Stories Ser.). (Illus.). 100p. (Orig.) (J). (gr. k-12). 1989. pap. write for info. (*0-9621929-0-2*) J-p Press.

Children's Story. James Clavell. 1989. pap. 4.50 (*0-440-20468-2*) Dell.

Children's Story. adapted ed. Adapt. by James Clavell & George Selden. 1966. pap. 2.75 (*0-8222-0206-9*) Dramatists Play.

Children's Story: Sexually Molested Children in Criminal Court. rev. ed. Sandra B. Smith. LC 87-82077. 110p. 1987. pap. 8.00 (*0-9613205-2-4*) Launch Pr.

Children's Story Rhyme Guide to Locating Museums, Entertainment, Amusement, Etc. A Story Search Reference. Update Publicare Research Staff. 25p. 1985. pap. text ed. 8.95 (*0-318-01242-1*, Update Pub Co) Prosperity & Profits.

Children's Strategies: Contemporary Views of Child Development. Ed. by D. F. Bjorklund. 348p. 1990. text ed. 69.95 (*0-8058-0315-7*) L Erlbaum Assocs.

Children's Stress & Coping: A Family Perspective. Elaine S. Sorenson. (Perspectives on Marriage & the Family Ser.). 192p. 1993. lib. bdg. 19.95 (*0-89862-084-8*) Guilford Pr.

Children's Talk. Catherine Garvey. (Developing Child Ser.). 256p. 1984. 24.00 (*0-674-11634-8*); pap. text ed. 7.95 (*0-674-11635-6*) HUP.

Children's Tarot: The Road Is a River. Mary K. Rose. (Illus.). 52p. (Orig.) (J). (gr. k-6). 1993. pap. 18.95 (*0-9636234-0-0*) Wild Rose CO.

Children's Television: The Art, the Business & How It Works. Cy Schneider. LC 87-60440. (Illus.). 256p. 1987. 29.95 (*0-8442-3146-0*, Crain Bks) NTC Pub Grp.

Children's Television: The Economics of Exploitation. William H. Melody. LC 73-80079. 176p. reprint ed. pap. 50.20 (*0-8357-8069-4*, 2033825) Bks Demand.

Children's Television: The First Thirty-Five Years, 1946-1981. George W. Woolery. LC 82-5841. (Live, Film, & Tape Ser.: Pt. II). 820p. 1985. 59.50 (*0-8108-1651-2*) Scarecrow.

Children's Television: The First Thirty-Five Years, 1946-1981: Animated Cartoon Series, Pt. I. George W. Woolery. LC 82-5841. 404p. 1983. 32.50 (*0-8108-1557-5*) Scarecrow.

Children's Television, 1947-1990: Over Two Hundred Series, Game & Variety Shows, Cartoons, Educational Programs & Specials. Jeffery Davis. (Illus.). 256p. 1995. lib. bdg. 42.50 (*0-89950-911-8*) McFarland & Co.

Children's Texas Cool Cat Cookbook. large type ed. Maxine S. Sommers. (Texas Cool Cat Children's Bks.). (Illus.). 10p. (Orig.). (J). (gr. 1-9). 1991. pap. 3.25 (*0-943991-22-6*) Pound Sterling Pub.

Children's Theories of Mind: The Development of the Social Understanding of Self & Others. D. Frye & C. Moore. 224p. (C). 1990. text ed. 49.95 (*0-8058-0417-X*); pap. 27.50 (*0-8058-0418-8*) L Erlbaum Assocs.

Children's Thinking. 2nd ed. Robert S. Siegler. 448p. (C). 1990. pap. text ed. write for info. (*0-13-131210-3*) P-H.

Children's Thinking: Developmental Function & Individual Differences. David F. Bjorklund. LC 88-22241. 357p. (C). 1988. text ed. 44.95 (*0-534-09384-1*) Brooks-Cole.

***Children's Thinking: Developmental Function & Individual Differences.** 2nd ed. David F. Bjorklund. LC 94-34020. 384p. 1995. text ed. 33.95 (*0-534-21000-7*) Brooks-Cole.

Children's Thinking: Promoting Understanding in the Primary School. Michael Bonnett. LC 93-44086. (Children, Teachers & Learning Ser.). (Illus.). 192p. 1995. 60.00 (*0-304-32937-1*); pap. 17.95 (*0-304-32939-8*) Cassell.

Children's Thinking: What Develops? Ed. by Robert S. Siegler. 384p. 1990. reprint ed. pap. 39.95 (*0-8058-0884-1*) L Erlbaum Assocs.

Children's Thinking & Learning in the Elementary School. Peter Langford. LC 88-51818. 176p. 1989. 24.50 (*0-87762-604-9*) Technomic.

Children's Time in Worship. Arline J. Ban. 128p. 1981. pap. 7.00 (*0-8170-0902-7*) Judson.

***Children's Topical Bible.** Mary Hollingsworth. (J). (ps-3). 1994. 9.95 (*1-56292-067-7*) Honor Bks OK.

***Childrens Topical Bible with Activity Package.** Hollingsworth. 1994. 14.95 (*1-56292-154-1*) Honor Bks OK.

Children's Tour of Red Stick City. Illus. by David Norwood et al. 32p. (J). (gr. 1-6). 1980. pap. text ed. 2.00 (*0-9608282-2-2*) YWCO.

Children's Toys & Furniture. U Bild Editors & Monte Burch. Ed. by Roundtable Press Staff. LC 81-71606. (Illus.). 160p. (Orig.). 1983. pap. 9.95 (*0-932944-57-4*) Creative Homeowner.

***Children's Traditional Games: Games from 130 Countries & Cultures.** Robert Kaminski & Judy Sierra. Ed. by Natalie Lang. (Illus.). 328p. 1995. pap. 25.95 (*0-89774-967-7*, 2346) Oryx Pr.

Children's Treasure House of Poetry. Mildred Sproxton. (YA). (gr. 7-10). 1986. 30.00 (*0-7223-2073-6*, Pub. by A H S Ltd UK) St Mut.

Children's Treasure Hunt Travel Guide to Britain. Frances Goldstein. LC 78-71424. (Illus.). (J). (gr. 1-12). 1979. pap. 6.95 (*0-933334-00-1*) Paper Tiger Pap.

Children's Treasure Hunt Travel Guide to Italy. Frances Goldstein. LC 79-67280. (Illus.). (Orig.). (J). (gr. k-12). 1980. pap. 6.95 (*0-933334-01-X*) Paper Tiger Pap.

Children's Treasure Hunt Travel to Belgium & France. Frances Goldstein. LC 80-85012. (Children's Treasure Hunt Travel Guide Ser.). (Illus.). 230p. (Orig.). (J). (gr. k-12). 1981. pap. 6.95 (*0-933334-02-8*) Paper Tiger Pap.

Children's Treasure of Sephardic Tales. Tzvia Klein-Ehlich. (ArtScroll Youth Ser.). (Illus.). 64p. (YA). (gr. 4-10). 1985. 11.95 (*0-89906-787-5*); pap. 8.95 (*0-89906-788-3*) Mesorah Pubns.

Children's Treasury of Animal Stories. Ed. by Ann Roberts. (Illus.). 192p. (J). (ps-5). 1993. 18.95 (*1-55013-504-X*, Pub. by Key Porter Bks CN) Natl Bk Netwk.

Children's Treasury of Graces, Hymns & Prayers, 3 vols. Elizabeth Laird. (Illus.). (J). 1991. 7.99 (*0-517-05384-5*) Random Hse Value.

Children's Treasury of Holiday Tales. E. Van Hansel. 7p. (J). 1992. 11.95 (*0-89906-416-7*); pap. 8.95 (*0-89906-417-5*) Mesorah Pubns.

Children's Trilogy: Ali's Flying Rug, the Shadow Workers, & the Magic Cricket. Ernie L. Guderjahn. (Orig.). (J). (gr. 3 up). 1984. pap. 6.00 (*0-88734-504-2*) Players Pr.

Children's Understanding: The Development of Mental Models. Graeme Halford. 528p. 1992. text ed. 99.95 (*0-89859-970-9*); pap. 39.95 (*0-8058-1233-4*) L Erlbaum Assocs.

***Children's Understanding of Disability.** Ann Lewis. LC 94-34162. 224p. 1995. 55.00x (*0-415-10131-X*, 0338); pap. 17.95 (*0-415-10132-8*, B4018) Routledge.

Children's Understanding of Emotion. Ed. by Carolyn Saarni & Paul L. Harris. (Cambridge Studies in Social & Emotional Development). (Illus.). 400p. (C). 1989. 69.95 (*0-521-33394-6*) Cambridge U Pr.

Children's Understanding of Emotion. Ed. by Carolyn Saarni & Paul L. Harris. (Cambridge Studies in Social & Emotional Development). (Illus.). 400p. (C). 1991. pap. 24.95 (*0-521-40777-X*) Cambridge U Pr.

Children's Vaccine Initiative: Achieving the Vision. Institute of Medicine Staff. 250p. (Orig.). (C). 1993. pap. text ed. 24.95 (*0-309-04940-7*) Natl Acad Pr.

Children's Views about Television. Barrie Gunter et al. 198p. 1991. text ed. 63.95 (*1-85628-069-1*, Pub. by Avebury Pub UK) Ashgate Pub Co.

Children's Views of Foreign People: A Cross-National Study. Wallace E. Lambert & Otto Klineberg. LC 66-24057. (Century Psychology Ser.). (Illus.). 1967. 28.00 (*0-89197-076-2*) Irvington.

***Children's Visual Botany Dictionary: English-Arabic.** 1993. 19.95 (*0-86685-605-6*) Intl Bk Ctr.

***Children's Visual Dictionary.** Illus. by Dave Hopkins. LC 94-29950. 64p. (J). (gr. k-8). 1995. 14.95 (*1-56458-881-5*) Dorling Kindersley.

Children's Voices: Children Talk about Literacy. Ed. by Sally Hudson-Ross et al. LC 92-33307. 265p. 1992. pap. 20.00 (*0-435-08737-1*, 08737) Heinemann.

Children's Voices: Talk in the Classroom. Ed. by Bernice E. Cullinan. LC 93-13319. 104p. 1993. pap. 12.00 (*0-87207-381-5*) Intl Reading.

Children's War. David Bellin. LC 79-54050. 1980. 10.95 (*0-935210-00-8*); pap. 4.95 (*0-935210-01-6*) Dundee Pub.

Children's Ward. Patricia Wallace. 1985. pap. 3.50 (*0-8217-1585-2*) Zebra.

Children's Way of the Cross. Anne J. Flanagan. (Illus.). 39p. (Orig.). (J). (gr. 2-6). 1992. pap. 1.50 (*0-8198-6954-6*) Pauline Bks.

Children's Wear Design. Hilde Jaffe. LC 77-180154. 284p. reprint ed. pap. 81.00 (*0-318-35018-1*, 2030881) Bks Demand.

Children's Wear Merchandiser. 19.00 (*0-87102-012-2*, 45-9481) Natl Ret Merch.

Children's Welfare & the Law: The Limits of Legal Intervention. Michael King & Judith Trowell. (Illus.). 192p. (C). 1992. 55.00 (*0-8039-8730-7*); pap. 19.95 (*0-8039-8731-5*) Sage.

Children's Word Games & Crossword Puzzles, Vol. 1. Ed. by Eugene T. Maleska. LC 86-888. 80p. 1986. pap. 7.00 (*0-8129-1243-8*, Times Bks) Random.

Children's Word Games & Crossword Puzzles, Vol. 2. Eugene T. Maleska. (J). (gr. 2-4). 1988. pap. 7.50 (*0-8129-1692-1*) Random.

Children's Word Games & Crossword Puzzles, Vol. 3. Eugene T. Maleska. (J). (gr. 2-4). 1992. pap. 7.00 (*0-8129-1980-7*, Times Bks) Random.

Children's Word Games & Puzzles. 2nd ed. Ed. by Eugene T. Maleska. LC 86-886. 80p. (J). (gr. 3 up). 1986. pap. 7.00 (*0-8129-1308-6*) Random.

Children's Word Liturgies, Vol. 1. Marjorie Moffatt. 120p. 1986. pap. 9.95 (*0-8146-1537-6*) Liturgical Pr.

Children's World Atlas. (Illus.). (J). (gr. 5-9). 1991. 14.95 (*0-528-83455-X*) Rand McNally.

Children's Worlds & Children's Language. Ed. by Jenny Cook-Gumperz et al. (New Babylon Studies in the Social Sciences: No. 47). (Illus.). 487p. 1986. lib. bdg. 161.55 (*0-89925-089-0*) Mouton.

Children's Writer's & Illustrator's Market 1995. Ed. by Christine Martin. 384p. 1995. pap. 19.95 (*0-89879-679-2*) Writers Digest.

Children's Writer's Word Book. Alijandra Mogliner. 352p. 1992. 19.99 (*0-89879-511-7*) Writers Digest.

Children's Writing: An Approach for the Primary Grades - Written for the Learning Research & Development Center, University of Pittsburgh. Leonard Sealey et al. LC 78-19195. (Illus.). 83p. reprint ed. pap. 25.00 (*0-8357-4304-7*, 2037101) Bks Demand.

Children's Writing & Reading: Analyzing Classroom Language. Katharine Perera. Ed. by David Crystal. (Language Library). 352p. 1984. pap. 22.95 (*0-631-13654-1*) Blackwell Pubs.

Children's Year. Stephanie Cooper et al. (Illus.). 220p. 1990. pap. 18.95 (*1-869890-00-0*, 1187, Pub. by Hawthorn Press UK) Anthroposophic.

Children's Yellow Pages: A Resource Book for Parents & Children, 1987 Boston Edition. Comp. by Boston Parents' Paper Staff. pap. 7.95 (*0-201-11165-9*) Addison-Wesley.

Children's Zoo. Tana Hoban. LC 84-25318. (Illus.). 24p. (J). (ps-1). 1985. 15.00 (*0-688-05202-9*); lib. bdg. 14.93 (*0-688-05204-5*) Greenwillow.

Children's Zoo. Tana Hoban. LC 84-25318. (Illus.). 24p. (J). (ps up). 1987. reprint ed. pap. text ed. 4.95 (*0-688-07044-2*, Mulberry) Morrow.

Childrenswear Design. 2nd ed. Hilda Jaffe & Rosa Rosa. (Illus.). 300p. (C). 1990. pap. text ed. 25.00 (*0-87005-706-5*) Fairchild.

Child's Alaska. Claire R. Murphy. LC 93-48164. (Illus.). 48p. (J). (gr. 4-10). 1994. 14.95 (*0-88240-457-1*) Alaska Northwest.

Child's Annual Video Interview Kit. Louis R. Woodhill. (Illus.). 130p. 1989. pap. text ed. 29.95 (*0-9623920-1-4*) Living Family Albums.

***Child's Anthology of Poetry.** Ed. by Elizabeth H. Sword & Victoria McCarthy. LC 95-15742. (Illus.). 1995. write for info. (*0-88001-378-8*) Ecco Pr.

Child's Anti-Slavery Book. LC 72-83925. (Black Heritage Library Collection). 1977. 22.95 (*0-8369-8541-9*) Ayer.

Child's Bible: Lessons from the Writings & Prophets, Vol. 2. Seymour Rossel. (J). (gr. 4-5). 1989. teacher ed, pap. 14.95 (*0-87441-485-7*); pap. text ed. 8.95 (*0-87441-487-3*) Behrman.

Child's Bible: Old Testament & New Testament. Shirley Steen & Anne Edwards. (J). (gr. 1-8). 1986. pap. 13.95 (*0-8091-2867-5*) Paulist Pr.

Child's Bible: The Torah & Its Lessons. Seymour Rossel. (J). (gr. 3 up). 1988. pap. 8.95 (*0-87441-466-0*); teacher ed, pap. 14.95 (*0-87441-467-9*) Behrman.

Child's Bible History. F. J. Knecht. Tr. by Philip Schumacher. (Illus.). (J). (gr. 5). 1973. reprint ed. pap. 4.00 (*0-89555-005-9*) TAN Bks Pubs.

Child's Bible: Old Testament: Rewritten for Children by Anne Edwards. LC 78-51444. 384p. (J). (gr. 1-8). 1978. pap. 4.95 (*0-8091-2117-4*) Paulist Pr.

Child's Book of Angels: Stories from the Bible about God's Special Messengers. Marilyn J. Woody. LC 92-12862. (J). 1992. 10.99 (*1-55513-756-3*, Chariot Bks) Chariot Family.

Child's Book of Art: Great Pictures, First Words. Sel. by Lucy Micklethwait. LC 93-54320. (Illus.). 64p. (J). (gr. k up). 1993. 16.95 (*1-56458-203-5*) Dorling Kindersley.

***Child's Book of Character Building Bk. 1: Growing up in God's World - at Home, at School, at Play.** Ron Coriell & Rebekah Coriell. (Illus.). 128p. (Orig.). (J). 1995. pap. 14.99 (*0-8007-5494-8*) Revell.

***Child's Book of Character Building Bk. 2: Growing up in God's World - at Home, at School, at Play.** Ron Coriell & Rebekah Coriell. (Illus.). 128p. (J). 1995. pap. 14.99 (*0-8007-5495-6*) Revell.

Child's Book of Country Stories. Ada M. Skinner & Eleanor L. Skinner. (Children's Classics Ser.). (Illus.). 224p. (J). (gr. 1-7). 1992. 12.99 (*0-517-69333-X*, Child Classics) Random Hse Value.

Child's Book of Flowers. Janet Marsh. (Illus.). 60p. (J). (ps-1). 1994. 19.95 (*0-09-176231-6*, Pub. by Hutchinson UK) Trafalgar.

Child's Book of Flowers see Book of Flowers

An Asterisk (*) at the beginning of an entry indicates that the title is appearing in BIP for the first time.

Child's Book of Manners. Ruth S. Odor. Ed. by Shirley Beegle. (Happy Day Bks.). (Illus.). 24p. (J). (ps-3). 1994. reprint ed. pap. 1.89 (0-7847-0252-7) Standard Pub.

Child's Book of Midrash: Fifty-Two Jewish Stories from the Sages. Barbara Goldin. LC 90-39598. 124p. (J). 1990. 25.00 (0-87668-837-7) Aronson.

Child's Book of Miracles. Mary K. Glavich. LC 94-2378. (J). (gr. 3 up). 1994. 2.50 (0-8294-0802-9) Loyola Univ Pr.

Child's Book of Mormon Activity, No. 3. Molgard Burgess. pap. 3.95 (0-88494-828-5) Bookcraft Inc.

Child's Book of Mormon Activity Book, 2 bks., Bk. 1. Burgess & Molgard. (J). pap. 3.95 (0-88494-625-8) Bookcraft Inc.

Child's Book of Mormon Activity Book, 2 bks., Bk. 2. Burgess & Molgard. (J). pap. 3.95 (0-88494-661-4) Bookcraft Inc.

Child's Book of Myths & Enchantments. LC 89-15905. (J). (gr. 4-7). 12.95 (1-56288-395-X) Checkerboard.

Child's Book of Parables. Mary K. Glavich. LC 94-2383. (J). 1994. 2.50 (0-8294-0801-0) Loyola Univ Pr.

*Child's Book of Prayer in Art. Wendy Beckett. LC 94-40362. (Illus.). 32p. (J). (ps-4). 1995. 12.95 (1-56458-875-0) Dorling Kindersley.

Child's Book of Prayers. Michael Hague. LC 85-8380. (Illus.). 32p. (J). (ps-2). 1985. 14.95 (0-8050-0211-1, Bks Young Read) H Holt & Co.

Child's Book of Prayers. Christine H. Tangvald. Ed. by Julie Smith. LC 86-32971. 32p. (J). (gr. 1-3). Date not set. 5.99 (0-7814-1519-5, Chariot Bks) Chariot Family.

Child's Book of Prayers. Ed. by Linda Yeatman. LC 91-37706. (Illus.). 96p. (J). 1992. 19.95 (1-55670-251-5) Stewart Tabori & Chang.

Child's Book of Stories. Jessie W. Smith. (Children's Classics Ser.). 1988. 12.99 (0-517-61886-9) Random Hse Value.

Child's Book of Stories. Jessie Willcox Smith. (J). (gr. k-6). 1986. 8.98 (0-685-16856-5, 618869) Random Hse Value.

Child's Book of Wildflowers. M. A. Kelly. LC 91-30368. (Illus.). 32p. (J). (gr. k-4). 1992. text ed. 15.95 (0-02-750142-6, Four Winds Pr) S&S Childrens.

Child's Brain: The Impact of Advanced Research on Cognitive & Social Behavior. Ed. by Mary Frank. LC 84-678. (Journal of Children in Contemporary Society Ser.: Vol. 16, Nos. 1-2). 243p. 1984. text ed. 49.95 (0-86656-269-9) Haworth Pr.

Child's Calendar. John Updike. LC 61-21555. (Illus.). 32p. (J). (gr. k-3). 1965. 11.95 (0-394-81059-7) Knopf Bks Yng Read.

Child's Carrousel of Verse. Shirley Jentzen. (J). 1994. 7.95 (0-533-11011-4) Vantage.

Child's Christmas. (Illus.). 32p. (J). 1989. pap. text ed. 10.95 (0-929648-62-5) Galison.

Child's Christmas. Evelyn Sharp. (Children's Classics Ser.). (J). 1991. 12.99 (0-517-03369-0) Random Hse Value.

Child's Christmas Cookbook. Betty Chancellor. (Illus.). 40p. (Orig.). (J). (gr. 1-8). 1969. pap. 4.00 (0-914510-00-2) Evergreen.

Child's Christmas in Wales. Dylan Thomas. LC 80-66216. (Illus.). 48p. (J). 1980. 14.95 (0-87923-339-7); pap. 9.95 (0-87923-529-2) Godine.

Child's Christmas in Wales. Dylan Thomas. LC 85-766. (Illus.). 48p. (J). (gr. 4-6). 1985. lib. bdg. 15.95 (0-8234-0565-6) Holiday.

*Child's Christmas in Wales. Dylan Thomas. LC 77-88732. (Illus.). 64p. 1995. 10.95 (0-8112-1308-0); pap. 6.00 (0-8112-1309-9) New Directions.

Child's Christmas in Wales. Dylan Thomas. LC 93-83460. (Miniature Editions Ser.). (Illus.). 96p. 1993. 4.95 (1-56138-306-6) Running Pr.

Child's Christmas in Wales: Christmas Musical. Dylan Thomas. Ed. by Adrian Mitchell. 1984. 4.95 (0-87129-375-7, C62) Dramatic Pub.

Child's Christmas Treasury. Comp. by Mark Daniel. LC 87-36527. (Illus.). 112p. (J). (ps up). 1988. 15.95 (0-8037-0484-4) Dial Bks Young.

*Child's Coloring Book of Angels. Mr. George. (J). 1995. pap. 7.95 (0-533-11437-3) Vantage.

Child's Communicative Competence: Language Capacity in Three Groups of Children from Different Social Classes. Ton Van Der Geest et al. (Janua Linguarum, Series Minor: No. 202). 1973. pap. text ed. (3-10-800147-7) Mouton.

Child's Concept of Story. Arthur N. Applebee. 224p. 1989. pap. text ed. 13.95 (0-226-02120-3, Midway Reprint) U Ch Pr.

Child's Conception of Geometry. Jean Piaget et al. 432p. 1981. reprint ed. pap. 8.95 (0-393-00057-5) Norton.

Child's Conception of Language. Ed. by A. Sinclair et al. (Language & Communication Ser.: Vol. 2). (Illus.). 1980. 31.00 (0-387-09153-X) Spr-Verlag.

Child's Conception of the World. Jean Piaget. (Quality Paperback Ser.: No. 213). 397p. 1975. reprint ed. pap. 14.95 (0-8226-0213-X) Littlefield.

Child's Construction of Economics. Anna E. Berti & Anna S. Bombi. Tr. by Gerard Duveen. (European Monographs in Social Psychology). (Illus.). 256p. 1988. 59.95 (0-521-33299-0) Cambridge U Pr.

Child's Construction of Knowledge: Piaget for Teaching Children. George E. Forman & David S. Kuschner. LC 77-8676. 244p. 1983. reprint ed. pap. text ed. 6.00 (0-912674-92-X, NAEYC #116) Natl Assn Child Ed.

Child's Construction of Language Behavioral Development: Monographs. Ed. by W. Deutsch. 408p. 1982. text ed. 128.00 (0-12-213580-6) Acad Pr.

Child's Construction of Politics. R. W. Connell. 251p. 1975. pap. 19.95 (0-522-84006-X) Intl Spec Bk.

Child's Construction of Social Inequality. Ed. by Robert L. Leahy. LC 82-24287. (Developmental Psychology Ser.). 1983. text ed. 84.00 (0-12-439880-4) Acad Pr.

Child's Creation of a Pictorial World. Claire Golomb. LC 90-11171. (Illus.). 480p. 1991. 85.00 (0-520-06845-9); pap. 30.00 (0-520-07084-4) U CA Pr.

*Child's Cry: There's No Safe Place. Dimitri Gat. 320p. 1995. mass mkt. 4.50 (0-8217-4906-4) Zebra.

Child's Day. Bobbie Kalman & Tammy Everts. (Historic Communities Ser.). (Illus.). 32p. (Orig.). (J). (gr. k-9). 1994. lib. bdg. 15.95 (0-86505-494-0); pap. 7.95 (0-86505-514-9) Crabtree Pub Co.

Child's Developing Sense of Theme: A Response to Literature. Susan S. Lehr. (Language & Literacy Ser.: No. 3). 208p. (C). 1991. text ed. 38.95 (0-8077-3106-4); pap. text ed. 17.95 (0-8077-3105-6) Tchrs Coll.

Child's Diary - the 1930's. Hilda S. Johnson. LC 88-51304. (Illus.). 64p. (Orig.). (J). (gr. 3-8). 1988. pap. 3.95 (0-931563-02-X) Wishing Rm.

Child's Discovery of the Mind. Janet W. Astington. LC 93-4784. (Developing Child Ser.). 236p. 1994. 27.50 (0-674-11641-0); pap. text ed. 9.95 (0-674-11642-9) HUP.

*Child's Environment. C. Spencer. (Readings in Environmental Psychology Ser.). (Illus.). 320p. 1995. boxed 24.95 (0-12-656640-2) Acad Pr.

Child's Eye. Baljean Dhillon & Geoffrey T. Millar. LC 92-48410. (Oxford Medical Publications). 144p. 1995. 79.00 (0-19-262303-6); pap. 43.95 (0-19-262302-8) OUP.

Child's Eye View: A Collection of Poetry by the Children of Washington State, Vol. 1. Elementary School Children of Washington State. Ed. by Lillian E. Gillman. 143p. (J). (ps-6). 1987. 7.95 (0-317-93371-X) Other Eye.

Child's Eye View: A Collection of Poetry by the Children of Washington State, Vol. 2. Elementary School Children of Washington State. Ed. by Lillian E. Gillman. 200p. (J). (ps-6). 1988. 7.95 (0-317-93372-8) Other Eye.

Child's Fairy Tale Book. Kay Chorao. LC 89-49480. (Illus.). 64p. (J). (ps-3). 1990. 14.95 (0-525-44630-3, DCB) Dutton Child Bks.

Childs Family. Martha Childs & Virginia Westfall. 79p. 1992. pap. 10.00 (1-883166-01-2) Frst Edition.

Child's Fear: Vision of Hope. Marsha A. Meyers. (J). 1993. pap. 12.95 (0-9637083-9-2) Myi-Way Prod.

Child's First Bible. Sandol Stoddard. (Illus.). 96p. (J). (ps-3). 1991. 16.99 (0-8037-0941-2) Dial Bks Young.

Child's First Book about Hawaii. Cassandra L. Nellist. (Illus.). 24p. (J). (ps). 1987. 8.95 (0-916630-58-7) Pr Pacifica.

Child's First Book about Play Therapy. Marc A. Nemiroff & Jane Annunziata. LC 90-49954. (Illus.). 60p. (Orig.). (J). 1990. 19.95 (1-55798-112-4); pap. text ed. write for info. (1-55798-089-6) Am Psychol.

Child's First Catholic Dictionary. Richard Dyches & Thomas Mustachio. LC 94-71885. (Illus.). 112p. (J). (gr. k-3). 1994. 14.95 (0-87793-525-4) Ave Maria.

Child's First Library of Learning, 17 bks., Set. (Illus.). (J). (ps-3). 1990. 270.81 (0-8094-4825-4); lib. bdg. 361.59 (0-8094-4826-2) Time-Life.

Child's First Picture Book. rev. ed. Ruth Freeman. 1946. 6.50 (0-87282-064-5) Am Life Foun.

Child's Foot & Ankle. James C. Drennan. 576p. 1992. 136.50 (0-88167-879-1) Raven.

Childs Gallery, Boston: Exhibition Chronology & Publications, 1937-1980. Comp. by Gladys I. Dratch. 1985. pap. 5.00 (0-317-13415-9) Boston Public Lib.

*Child's Garden. James Haining. LC 86-20330. (Lucky Heart Book Ser.). (Illus.). reprint ed. pap. 25.00 (0-7837-9157-7, 2049857) Bks Demand.

Child's Garden Diary: Coloring & Activity Book. Ruth K. Lopez. (Illus.). 56p. (Orig.). (J). (gr. k-6). 1992. pap. 5.95 (0-9627463-4-7) Gardens Growing People.

Child's Garden of Bible Stories. Arthur W. Gross. (Concordia Primary Religion Ser.). (gr. 1-3). 1981. 9.99 (0-570-03414-0, 56-1001); pap. 6.95 (0-570-03402-7, 56-1012) Concordia.

Child's Garden of Bible Stories. large type ed. (J). write for info. (0-318-68641-4, 9301) LBW.

Child's Garden of Prayer. Ed. by Herman W. Gockel & Edward J. Saleska. (Illus.). (J). (gr. k-2). 1981. pap. 2.99 (0-570-03412-4, 56-1016) Concordia.

*Child's Garden of Quilts. Christal Carter. Ed. by Janet White. (Illus.). 88p. (Orig.). 1994. pap. 19.95 (1-56477-077-X) That Patchwork.

Child's Garden of Verses. Henriette LeMair. (Illus.). 112p. (J). (gr. k up). 1991. 15.95 (0-399-21818-1, Philomel Bks) Putnam Pub Group.

Child's Garden of Verses. Robert Louis Stevenson. LC 85-12766. (Airmont Classics Ser.). (Illus.). (J). (gr. 3 up). 1969. pap. 2.25 (0-8049-0195-3, CL-195) Airmont.

Child's Garden of Verses. Robert Louis Stevenson. LC 92-53175. (Everyman's Library of Children's Classics). (Illus.). 128p. (J). 1992. 12.95 (0-679-41799-0, Evrymans Lib Childs) Knopf.

Child's Garden of Verses. Robert Louis Stevenson. LC 85-12766. (J). (gr. 5-6). 15.95 (0-89190-739-4, Am Repr) Amereon Ltd.

Child's Garden of Verses. Robert Louis Stevenson. LC 93-41101. (Little Barefoot Bks.). (Illus.). (J). 1994. pap. 6.00 (1-56957-926-1) Barefoot Bks.

*Child's Garden of Verses. Robert Louis Stevenson. 128p. (J). 1994. 9.98 (1-85854-095-X) Brimax Bks.

Child's Garden of Verses. Robert Louis Stevenson. (Illus.). 128p. (J). 1989. 16.95 (0-87701-608-9) Chronicle Bks.

Child's Garden of Verses. Robert Louis Stevenson. (Storytime Bks.). (Illus.). 24p. (J). (ps-2). 1993. pap. text ed. 0.99 (1-56293-351-5) McClanahan Bk.

Child's Garden of Verses. Robert Louis Stevenson. (Illus.). 96p. (J). (gr. 1-4). 1987. pap. 10.95 (0-19-276065-3) OUP.

Child's Garden of Verses. Robert Louis Stevenson. LC 85-12766. (Illus.). (J). (gr. 3-5). 1950. pap. 2.95 (0-14-030022-8, Puffin) Puffin Bks.

*Child's Garden of Verses. Robert Louis Stevenson. (Puffin Classics Ser.). 144p. (J). 1995. pap. 2.99 (0-14-036692-X) Puffin Bks.

Child's Garden of Verses. Robert Louis Stevenson. LC 88-43564. (Miniature Editions Ser.). 144p. (J). 1989. 4.95 (0-89471-715-4) Running Pr.

Child's Garden of Verses. Robert Louis Stevenson. LC 85-12766. (Illus.). 120p. (J). (ps-4). 1905. text ed. 18.95 (0-684-20949-7, C Scribner Sons Young) S&S Childrens.

Child's Garden of Verses. Robert Louis Stevenson. (Illus.). 140p. 1992. 16.95 (1-85158-391-2, Pub. by Mnstream UK) Trafalgar.

Child's Garden of Verses. Robert Louis Stevenson. (Illus.). 12p. (J). (ps-6). 1992. 13.95 (0-525-44997-3, DCB) Dutton Child Bks.

*Child's Garden of Verses. Robert Louis Stevenson. 1994. 14.95 (0-8109-3196-6) Abrams.

Child's Garden of Verses. Robert Louis Stevenson. (J). 1984. 4.98 (0-671-06537-8) S&S Trade.

*Child's Garden of Verses. Robert Louis Stevenson. LC 94-33717. (Illus.). (J). 1994. write for info. (0-681-00771-0) Longmeadow Pr.

Child's Garden of Verses. unabridged ed. Robert Louis Stevenson. LC 92-25818. (Illus.). 96p. (J). 1992. reprint ed. pap. 1.00 (0-486-27301-6) Dover.

Child's Garden of Verses. 2nd ed. Robert Louis Stevenson. LC 85-12766. (Illus.). 72p. (J). (ps up). 1992. text ed. 13.95 (0-02-788365-5, Mac Bks Young Read) S&S Childrens.

Child's Garden of Verses. Robert Louis Stevenson. (Illus.). 90p. 1988. reprint ed. lib. bdg. 18.95 (0-89966-594-2) Buccaneer Bks.

Child's Garden of Verses-Coloring Book. Robert Louis Stevenson. (J). 1950. pap. 2.75 (0-486-23481-9) Dover.

Child's Garden of Weirdness: Illustrations, Verse, & Worse. Dick Gautier. LC 92-43033. (J). 1993. 14.95 (0-8048-1825-8) C E Tuttle.

Child's Garden of Yoga. Baba Hari Dass. Ed. by Karuna Ault. LC 80-80299. (Illus.). 108p. (J). (ps-7). 1980. pap. 9.95 (0-918100-02-X) Sri Rama.

Child's Gift of Bedtime Stories, Vol. 1. Linda Burnsed & Garry Chaffin. Ed. by J. Aaron Brown. (Illus.). 28p. (J). (gr. 1-4). 1993. audio 12.95 (0-927945-07-X) Someday Baby.

Child's Gift of Bedtime Stories, Vol. 1. Gary Chaffin & Linda Burnsed. LC 93-17766. (Illus.). 44p. (J). (ps-6). 1993. 6.98 (1-56566-044-7) Thomasson-Grant.

Child's Gift of Lullabyes. Ed. by J. Aaron Brown. (Illus.). 14p. (J). (ps). 1987. Book packaged with cassette. audio 12.95 (0-927945-01-0) Someday Baby.

*Child's Good Morning Book. Margaret W. Brown. (Illus.). (J). (ps-2). 1995. lib. bdg. 9.89 (0-06-024539-5, Trophy) HarpC Child Bks.

Child's Good Morning Book. Margaret W. Brown. LC 94-719. (J). 1995. 10.00 (0-06-024538-7) HarpC.

Child's Good Night Book. Margaret W. Brown. LC 91-45340. (Illus.). 32p. (J). (ps-3). 1989. lib. bdg. 10.89 (0-06-020752-3) HarpC Child Bks.

Child's Good Night Book. Margaret W. Brown. LC 91-45340. (Illus.). 32p. (J). (ps-3). 1992. 10.95 (0-06-021028-1) HarpC Child Bks.

Child's Good Night Book. Margaret W. Brown. LC 84-43123. (Trophy Picture Bk.). (Illus.). 32p. (J). (ps-2). 1986. reprint ed. pap. 4.95 (0-06-443114-2, Trophy) HarpC Child Bks.

Child's Growth & Society. Ed. by Noboru Kobayashi & T. Berry Brazelton. (Illus.). 202p. 1984. 32.50 (0-86008-336-5, Pub. by U of Tokyo JA) Col U Pr.

Child's Guide to Computers, 4 vols., Bk. 1. Mimi Stankowich. (Illus.). 32p. (J). (ps-3). 1984. 3.95 (0-916881-00-8, ALP701) Advan Learning.

Child's Guide to Computers, 4 vols., Bk. 2. Mimi Stankowich. (Illus.). 32p. (J). (ps-3). 1984. 3.95 (0-916881-01-6, ALP702) Advan Learning.

Child's Guide to Computers, 4 vols., Bk. 3. Mimi Stankowich. (Illus.). 32p. (J). (ps-3). 1984. 3.95 (0-916881-02-4, ALP703) Advan Learning.

Child's Guide to Computers, 4 vols., Bk. 4. Mimi Stankowich. (Illus.). 32p. (J). (ps-3). 1984. 3.95 (0-916881-03-2, ALP704) Advan Learning.

Child's Guide to Historical Places. Deena Cole. (Illus.). 64p. (J). (ps-6). 1993. teacher ed 6.95 (1-878893-31-9) Telcraft Bks.

Child's Guide to Natural Wonders. Deena Cole. (Illus.). 64p. (J). (ps-6). 1993. teacher ed 6.95 (1-878893-33-5) Telcraft Bks.

Child's Guide to Parent Rearing. Harold H. Mosak. LC 80-66084. (Illus.). 79p. (Orig.). (C). 1980. pap. text ed. 3.50 (0-918560-27-6) Adler Sch Prof Psy.

Child's Guide to the BBC Micro - Scl Unicorn. John Dewhirst. 94p. (C). 1986. 24.00 (0-685-57268-4, Pub. by Interprint II) St Mut.

Child's Guide to ZX-Spectrum. Ed. by John Dwhirst. 95p. (C). 1988. 45.00 (81-85017-34-4, Pub. by Interprint II) St Mut.

Child's Health Log: Personal Health History from Birth to Age 18. Charles R. Stark. LC 92-8666. 112p. 1992. pap. 9.95 (1-56164-018-2) Pineapple Pr.

*Child's Health Record: Two Years & Up. Sandy Abrams. 120p. 1995. pap. 8.95 (0-9641332-5-3) Jormax Pubng.

Child's Heart & a Child's Dreams: Growing up with Spiritual Wisdom, a Guide for Parents & Children. Sri Chinmoy. 123p. 1986. pap. text ed. 5.95 (0-88497-862-1) Aum Pubns.

Child's History of America: Some Ribs & Riffs for the Sixties. Charles Newman. LC 82-73500. 307p. 1973. 13.95 (0-89366-245-3) Ultramarine Pub.

Child's History of Ireland. P. W. Joyce. Ed. by Hank Harrison. (Illus.). 225p. (J). (gr. 8-12). 14.95 (0-918501-24-5); pap. write for info. (0-918501-26-1) Archives Pr.

Child's History of Placentia. rev. ed. Virginia L. Carpenter. LC 84-81997. (Illus.). 80p. 1984. 6.50 (0-943480-57-4) Friis-Pioneer Pr.

Child's History of Texas. Sarah Jackson & Mary Ann Patterson. (Illus.). (J). (gr. 1-6). 1972. 5.95 (0-89015-056-7) Sunbelt Media.

Child's History of the United States. Charles A. Goodrich. (Notable American Authors Ser.). (J). 1992. reprint ed. lib. bdg. 75.00 (0-7812-2935-9) Rprt Serv.

Child's History of the World. V. M. Hillyer. (Illus.). 508p. 1992. reprint ed. lib. bdg. 33.95 (0-89966-938-7) Buccaneer Bks.

Child's Introduction to a Garden. Grace Schnatz. (Illus.). 33p. (J). (gr. 4-8). 1984. lib. bdg. 4.75 (0-9614145-0-2) G Schnatz Pubns.

Child's Introduction to General Semantics: First Ten Word Games. B. Robert Ross. 60p. pap. 15.00 (0-87916-013-6) Upstat.

Child's Introduction to the Early Prophets. Shirley Newman. LC 75-14052. (Illus.). 128p. (J). (gr. 3-4). 1975. pap. 7.50x (0-87441-244-7); teacher ed, pap. 14.95x (0-87441-227-7) Behrman.

Child's Introduction to the Early Prophets, No. 1. Amye Rosenberg & Shirley Newman. LC 75-14052. (Illus.). 128p. (J). (gr. 3-4). 1975. student ed, pap. 2.95 (0-87441-268-4) Behrman.

Child's Introduction to the Early Prophets, No. 2. Shirley Newman. LC 75-14052. (Illus.). 128p. (J). (gr. 3-4). 1975. student ed, pap. 2.95x (0-87441-269-2) Behrman.

Child's Introduction to Torah. Shirley Newman. Ed. by Louis Newman. (Illus.). 128p. (Orig.). (J). (gr. 2-3). 1972. pap. text ed. 7.50 (0-87441-067-3) Behrman.

Child's Journey Through Placement. Vera Fahlberg. LC 91-32036. 432p. 1991. 27.95 (0-944934-04-8) Perspect Indiana.

*Child's Journey Through Placement. Vera Fahllberg. 432p. 1995. pap. 20.00 (0-944934-11-0) Perspect Indiana.

Child's Life of Christ. Esther A. Peterson. (Illus.). 44p. (J). (gr. 3-8). 1987. 6.95 (1-55523-045-8) Winston-Derek.

*Child's Longing for Home: A Psychological Childhood Memoir. Zellig Bach. 1995. 11.95 (0-614-00691-0) Carlton.

Child's Look at the Twenty-Third Psalm. W. Phillip Keller. LC 84-13718. (Illus.). 96p. (J). (gr. 3 up). 1985. mass mkt. 7.95 (0-385-15457-7, Galilee) Doubleday.

Child's Odyssey: Child & Adolescent Development. 2nd ed. Paul S. Kaplan. Ed. by Marshall. 643p. (C). 1993. reprint ed. text ed. 53.75 (0-314-80198-7) West Pub.

Child's Old Testament Activity Book. Burgess & Molgard. (J). pap. 3.95 (0-88494-720-3) Bookcraft Inc.

Child's Organic Garden. Lee Fryer & Leigh Bradford. 88p. (C). 1990. pap. 39.00 (0-86439-097-1, Pub. by Boolarong Pubns AT) St Mut.

Child's Own Speaker. Comp. by E. C. Rook & Lizzie J. Rook. LC 71-116413. (Granger Index Reprint Ser.). 1977. 16.95 (0-8369-6154-4) Ayer.

Child's Parent Dies: Studies in Childhood Bereavement. Erna Furman. LC 73-86894. 1981. pap. 15.00 (0-300-02645-5) Yale U Pr.

Child's Passover Haggadah. Ed. by Saul Meyzlisch. (Illus.). 76p. (J). (gr. 1-6). 1987. 9.95 (0-915361-70-1) Modan-Adama Bks.

Child's Path to Spoken Language. John L. Locke. LC 92-34661. (Illus.). 530p. (Orig.). 1993. text ed. 42.50 (0-674-11640-2) HUP.

*Child's Path to Spoken Language. John L. Locke. (Illus.). 536p. (Orig.). (C). 1995. pap. text ed. 19.95 (0-674-11639-9) HUP.

Child's Picture English-Arabic Dictionary. Illus. by Dennis Sheheen. LC 85-15658. (Children's Picture Dictionary Ser.). (J). (gr. k-2). 1985. 9.95 (0-915361-30-2) Modan-Adama Bks.

Child's Picture English-Chinese Dictionary. Illus. by Dennis Sheheen. (J). (gr. k-6). 1987. reprint ed. 9.95 (1-55774-001-1) Modan-Adama Bks.

Child's Picture English-French Dictionary. LC 84-71800. (Children's Picture Dictionary Ser.). (Illus.). 48p. (J). (gr. k-6). 1984. 9.95 (0-915361-12-4) Modan-Adama Bks.

Child's Picture English-German Dictionary. Illus. by Dennis Sheheen. LC 86-13987. (Children's Picture Dictionary Ser.). (J). (gr. k-2). 1986. 9.95 (0-915361-41-8) Modan-Adama Bks.

Child's Picture English-Hebrew Dictionary. Ed. by Dennis Sheheen. (Children's Picture Dictionaries Ser.). (Illus.). (J). (gr. 1-3). 1987. 9.95 (0-915361-75-2) Modan-Adama Bks.

Child's Picture English-Italian Dictionary. Illus. by Dennis Sheheen. LC 86-14052. (Children's Picture Dictionaries Ser.). (J). (gr. k-2). 1986. 9.95 (0-915361-57-4) Modan-Adama Bks.

Child's Picture English-Japanese Dictionary. Illus. by Dennis Sheheen. (Children's Picture Dictionary Ser.). (J). (gr. k-6). 1987. 9.95 (1-55774-000-3) Modan-Adama Bks.

Child's Picture English-Spanish Dictionary. Illus. by Dennis Sheheen. LC 84-71801. (Children's Picture Dictionary Ser.). (J). (gr. k-2). 1984. 9.95 (0-915361-11-6, 09407-3) Modan-Adama Bks.

Child's Picture English-Yiddish Dictionary. Illus. by Dennis Sheheen. LC 85-15659. (Children's Picture Dictionary Ser.). (J). (gr. k-2). 1985. 9.95 (0-915361-29-9) Modan-Adama Bks.

Child's Picture Hebrew Dictionary. (J). 1984. 9.95 (0-915361-07-8) Modan-Adama Bks.

Child's Play. Leslie Hamilton. 1989. pap. 10.00 (0-517-57171-4, Crown) Crown Pub Group.

Child's Play. Warren Murphy. (Destroyer Ser.: No. 23). 1989. pap. 3.50 (1-55817-258-0, Pinnacle NY) Windsor NY.

Child's Play. large type ed. Reginald Hill. 560p. 1988. 21.95 (0-7089-1912-X) Ulverscroft.

Child's Play. Sal Conte. 400p. (Orig.). 1990. reprint ed. pap. 3.95 (*0-8439-2894-8*) Dorchester Pub Co.

Child's Play. R. E. Herron & Brian Sutton-Smith. LC 81-18560. 400p. (C). 1982. reprint ed. text ed. 39.00 (*0-89874-406-7*) Krieger.

Child's Play: A Self-Teaching Guide to the Commodore 64. Susan E. Sutphin. 160p. 1986. 16.95 (*0-13-130949-8*) P-H.

Child's Play: An Activities & Materials Handbook. Barbara Trencher. LC 76-46501. (Illus.). 160p. (C). 1976. lib. bdg. 26.95 (*0-89334-168-1*, 168-1) Humanics Ltd.

Child's Play: An Activities & Materials Handbook. Barbara R. Trencher. LC 76-46501. (Illus.). 160p. 1976. pap. text ed. 16.95 (*0-89334-003-0*) Humanics Ltd.

Child's Play: Developmental & Applied. Ed. by Thomas D. Yawkey & Anthony D. Pellegrini. 408p. 1984. text ed. 69.95 (*0-89859-300-X*) L Erlbaum Assocs.

Child's Play: The Bread of Time To Come. David Malouf. 282p. 1994. pap. 7.95 (*0-8076-1351-7*) Braziller.

Child's Play & Play Therapy. Ed. by Thomas D. Yawkey et al. LC 83-51730. 175p. 1984. 22.50 (*0-87762-339-2*) Technomic.

Child's Play for Quilters. Betty Boyink. 60p. (Orig.). 1984. pap. 10.00 (*0-9612608-3-1*) B Boyink.

Child's Play Life: An Ethnographic Study. Diana Kelly-Byrne. (Early Childhood Education Ser.: No. 20). 304p. (C). 1989. text ed. 37.95 (*0-8077-2942-6*); pap. text ed. 18.95 (*0-8077-2941-8*) Tchrs Coll.

Child's Play Museum. Illus. by P. Adams. LC 90-46592. (J). (ps-2). 1976. 9.95 (*0-85953-094-9*, Pub. by Childs Play UK) Childs Play.

Child's Play Six-Twelve: One Hundred Sixty Instant Activities, Crafts & Science Projects. Leslie Hamilton. (J). 1992. 10.00 (*0-517-58354-2*, Crown) Crown Pub Group.

Child's Play Weather. Sue Baker. (J). (ps-3). 1993. 12.95 (*0-85953-929-6*) Childs Play.

Child's Ploy. Bill Pronzini. 1984. 16.95 (*0-02-599250-3*) Macmillan.

Child's Point of View. 2nd ed. Maureen Cox. LC 91-6691. 256p. 1991. reprint ed. lib. bdg. 49.95 (*0-89862-761-3*); reprint ed. pap. text ed. 19.95 (*0-89862-471-1*) Guilford Pr.

Child's Political World: A Longitudinal Perspective. Stanley W. Moore et al. LC 84-15975. 304p. 1985. text ed. 59.95 (*0-275-90167-X*, C0167, Praeger Pubs) Greenwood.

Child's Prayer. Jeanne Titherington. LC 88-16566. (Illus.). 24p. (J). (ps up). 1989. 13.95 (*0-688-08317-X*); lib. bdg. 13.88 (*0-688-08318-8*) Greenwillow.

Child's Prayer: Miniature Edition. Jeanne Titherington. (Illus.). 32p. (J). (ps up). 1993. 4.95 (*0-688-12751-7*, Tupelo Bks) Morrow.

***Child's Promise.** Deborah Bedford. 1994. pap. 4.50 (*0-06-108323-2*, Harp PBks) HarpC.

Child's Psychosocial Development: From Birth to Early Adolescence. Margot B. Nadien. 164p. (Orig.). 1980. pap. 11.95 (*0-89529-115-0*) Avery Pub.

Child's Reality: Three Developmental Themes. D. Elkind. 180p. 1978. 36.00 (*0-89859-224-0*) L Erlbaum Assocs.

***Child's Seasonal Treasury.** Illus. & Comp. by Betty M. Jones. LC 95-13190. 1995. write for info. (*1-883672-30-9*) Tricycle Pr.

Child's Shining Pathway. Louise Eavey. (Illus.). (J). (ps-1). 1976. pap. 1.95 (*0-915374-08-0*, 08-0) Rapids Christian.

***Child's Song: The Religious Abuse of Children.** Donald Capps. LC 94-27462. 208p. (Orig.). 1995. pap. 15.99 (*0-664-25554-X*) Westminster John Knox.

Child's Story: Recovering Through Creativity. Pat Harris & Jeannette Batz. LC 93-3089. (Illus.). 154p. 1993. 29.95 (*0-9633555-2-X*) Cracom.

Child's Story Bible. Catherine F. Vos. (Illus.). 432p. (J). (gr. 3 up). 1983. reprint ed. lib. bdg. 19.99 (*0-8028-5011-1*) Eerdmans.

Child's Story Book. Kay Chorao. LC 87-8899. (Illus.). 64p. (J). (ps-3). 1987. 12.95 (*0-525-44328-2*, 01258-370, DCB) Dutton Child Bks.

Child's Story of Canada. Karin Moorhouse. 72p. (J). (ps-8). 1987. 6.95 (*0-920806-50-3*, Pub. by Penumbra Pr CN) U of Toronto Pr.

Child's Story of the Book of Mormon. Deta P. Neeley. LC 87-19903. 382p. (J). (gr. 1-6). 1987. 13.95 (*0-87579-101-8*) Deseret Bk.

Child's Talk: Learning to Use Language. Jerome S. Bruner. LC 83-42676. (Illus.). (C). 1985. pap. text ed. 7.95 (*0-393-95345-9*) Norton.

Child's Theory of Mind. Ed. by George E. Butterworth et al. 352p. 1991. 59.95 (*0-19-852252-5*) OUP.

***Child's Theory of Mind.** Henry M. Wellman. 1990. 42.00 (*0-262-23153-0*) MIT Pr.

Child's Theory of Mind. Henry M. Wellman. (Illus.). 376p. 1992. reprint ed. pap. 19.00x (*0-262-73099-5*) MIT Pr.

Child's Therapy: Hour by Hour. Mary R. Haworth. LC 89-15374. 240p. 1990. 32.50x (*0-8236-0838-7*) Intl Univs Pr.

Child's Treasure for a Lifetime. Gwendolyn Ross. 24p. (J). (gr. 2-6). 1988. pap. 2.95 (*0-88144-134-1*) Christian Pub.

Child's Treasury of Beatrix Potter. Beatrix Potter. (Illus.). 80p. (J). (gr. k-3). 1987. 6.98 (*0-681-40281-4*) Longmeadow Pr.

Child's Treasury of Poems. Ed. by Mark Daniel. LC 86-2194. (Illus.). 160p. (J). (ps up). 1986. 17.99 (*0-8037-0330-9*) Dial Bks Young.

Child's Treasury of Seaside Verse. Comp. by Mark Daniel. LC 90-2819. (Illus.). 144p. (J). (ps up). 1991. 16.95 (*0-8037-0889-0*) Dial Bks Young.

Child's Treasury of the Worthwhile. (Little Remembrance Gift Editions Ser.). (J). (gr. 3-11). 6.95 (*0-87741-007-0*) Makepeace Colony.

Child's Trip to Christmas in Santa Fe: A Photographic Documentary. Don Patterson. LC 91-62868. (Illus.). 120p. (J). (gr. k-3). 1991. 29.95 (*0-9629093-2-7*) MyndSeye.

Child's Understanding of Number. Rochel Gelman & Charles R. Gallistel. LC 78-5124. (Illus.). 280p. 1978. 34.00 (*0-674-11636-4*) HUP.

Child's Understanding of Number. Rochel Gelman & Charles R. Gallistel. 280p. 1986. pap. 10.50 (*0-674-11637-2*) HUP.

***Child's View of Grief.** Alan D. Wolfelt. 45p. (Orig.). 1991. pap. 5.95 (*1-879651-00-9*) Ctr Loss Life.

Child's View of Inflation. Philip Gompertz. (Illus.). 40p. 1974. pap. 1.15 (*0-918248-01-9*) Word Doctor.

Child's View of Reading: Understandings for Teachers & Parents. Pamela A. Michel. LC 93-24104. 156p. 1994. pap. 25.95 (*0-205-13784-9*, Longwood Div) Allyn.

Child's Walk Through Africa. Bobbie Levine & Carolyn Lichter. (Illus.). 38p. (J). (gr. 3-6). 1987. spiral bd. 1.50 (*0-912303-38-7*) Michigan Mus.

Child's Walk Through Asia. Bobbie Levine & Carolyn Lichter. (Illus.). 25p. (J). (gr. 2-6). 1984. spiral bd. 1.50 (*0-912303-31-X*) Michigan Mus.

Child's Walk Through Twentieth Century American Painting & Sculpture. Bobbie Levine et al. (Illus.). 29p. (J). (gr. 2-6). 1986. spiral bd. 1.50 (*0-912303-37-9*) Michigan Mus.

Child's War: World War II Through the Eyes of Children. Kati David. 224p. 1990. pap. 7.95 (*0-380-71109-5*) Avon.

Child's War: World War II Through the Eyes of Children. Kati David. LC 88-34463. 210p. 1989. 17.95 (*0-941423-24-7*) FWEW.

***Child's Way Home.** Rob Wilkins. 224p. 1995. pap. 10.99 (*0-310-20019-9*) Zondervan.

Child's Work: Taking Children's Choices Seriously. Nancy Wallace. (Illus.). 170p. (Orig.). 1990. pap. 12.95 (*0-913677-06-X*) Holt Assocs.

***Child's World: Infancy Through Adolescence.** Diane E. Papalia & Sally W. Olds. LC 95-10671. 1996. write for info. (*0-07-048765-0*) McGraw.

Child's World: Infancy Through Adolescence. 6th ed. Diane E. Papalia & Sally W. Olds. LC 92-11246. 1993. text ed. write for info. (*0-07-048749-9*) McGraw.

***Child's World: Children's: A Bibliography of 275 Oregon Authors & 50 Illustrators of Children's Book in the 20th Century.** 4th ed. Comp. by Juanita B. Price. 60p. 1995. pap. 19.95 (*0-9621683-3-5*) Price Prodns.

Child's World: Children's Books: A Bibliography of 220 Oregon Authors & 30 Illustrators of Children's Books in the 20th Century. 3rd ed. Comp. by Juanita B. Price. 45p. 1991. pap. 19.95 (*0-9621683-2-7*) Price Prodns.

***Child's World Encyclopedia, 10 vols., Set.** rev. ed. LC 94-48591. (J). 1995. write for info. (*0-8114-8171-9*) Raintree Steck-V.

Child's World of Illness: The Development of Health & Illness Behaviour. Simon Wilkinson. (Illus.). 275p. 1988. 74.95 (*0-521-32873-X*) Cambridge U Pr.

Child's Year. Joan W. Anglund. (Little Golden Bks.). (Illus.). 24p. (J). (ps-00). 1992. write for info. (*0-307-00141-5*, 312-06, Golden Pr) Western Pub.

Childsong. Barbara Wood. 288p. 1982. pap. 2.95 (*0-449-24528-4*, Crest) Fawcett.

***Childsplay: A Collection of Scenes & Monologues for Children.** Ed. by Kerry Muir. (Illus.). 200p. (Orig.). (J). 1995. pap. 10.00 (*0-87910-188-1*) Limelight Edns.

Childtimes: A Three-Generation Memoir. Eloise Greenfield & Lessie J. Little. LC 77-26581. (Illus.). 160p. (J). (gr. 5 up). 1979. lib. bdg. 14.89 (*0-690-03875-5*, Crowell Jr Bks) HarpC Child Bks.

Childtimes: A Three-Generation Memoir. Eloise Greenfield. LC 77-26581. (Trophy Nonfiction Bk.). (Illus.). 192p. (J). (gr. 4-6). 1993. pap. 5.95 (*0-06-446134-3*, Trophy) HarpC Child Bks.

Childwatching at Playgroup & Nursery School. Kathy Sylva et al. LC 80-24146. (Oxford Preschool Research Project Ser.: Vol. 2). 270p. 1980. pap. 10.95 (*0-931114-10-1*) High-Scope.

Childwise Catalog: A Consumer Guide to Buying the Safest & Best Products & Services for Your Children - Newborns Through Age 5. 3rd ed. Jack Gillis & Mary E. Fise. LC 92-54682. (Illus.). 448p. 1993. pap. 14.00 (*0-06-273182-3*, Harper Ref) HarpC.

Childwold. Joyce Carol Oates. 288p. 1981. pap. 2.95 (*0-449-23450-9*, Crest) Fawcett.

Chile. Chris Dwyer. (Let's Visit Places & Peoples of the World Ser.). (Illus.). 128p. (J). (gr. 5 up). 1990. 14.95 (*0-7910-1102-X*) Chelsea Hse.

Chile. Martin Hintz. LC 84-23104. (Enchantment of the World Ser.). (Illus.). 128p. (J). (gr. 5-9). 1985. lib. bdg. 20.55 (*0-516-02755-7*) Childrens.

Chile. Karen Jacobsen. LC 90-20818. (New True Bks.). (Illus.). 48p. (J). (gr. k-4). 1991. lib. bdg. 12.90 (*0-516-01111-1*); pap. 4.95 (*0-516-41111-X*) Childrens.

Chile. Jane K. Winter. LC 90-22472. (Cultures of the World Ser.: Group 2: Latin America). (Illus.). 128p. (YA). (gr. 5-9). 1991. lib. bdg. 21.95 (*1-85435-383-7*) Marshall Cavendish.

Chile. Jere H. Behrman. (Special Conference Series on Foreign Trade Regimes & Economic Development: No. 8). 434p. 1976. reprint ed. 112.90 (*0-87014-508-8*) Natl Bur Econ Res.

Chile. Jere R. Behrman. LC 74-82376. (Foreign Trade Regimes & Economic Development Ser.: No. 8). (Illus.). 434p. reprint ed. pap. 123.70 (*0-8357-7566-6*, 2056887) Bks Demand.

Chile. Rosa Q. Mesa. LC 73-180800. (Latin American Serial Documents Ser.: Vol. 7). 359p. reprint ed. pap. 102.40 (*0-317-10752-6*, 2013549) Bks Demand.

Chile: A Handbook. Ed. by International Bureau of American Republics Staff. 1976. lib. bdg. 69.95 (*0-8490-1603-7*) Gordon Pr.

Chile: An Anthology of New Writing. Ed. by Miller Williams. LC 68-18781. (Illus.). 168p. reprint ed. 47.90 (*0-8357-9361-3*, 2017297) Bks Demand.

Chile: An Outline of Its Geography, Economics & Politics. Gilbert J. Butland. LC 81-13237. vii, 128p. 1981. reprint ed. text ed. 49.75 (*0-313-23193-1*, BUCL, Greenwood Pr) Greenwood.

***Chile: Business Financing Handbook.** (Illus.). 70p. (Orig.). 1994. pap. 295.00 (*0-7605-1185-3*) Rector Pr.

Chile: Business Risk Overview. Ed. by Lewis B. Sckolnick. 125p. (Orig.). (C). 1994. pap. text ed. 495.00 (*1-57205-568-5*) Rector Pr.

***Chile: Commercial Law.** 300p. (Orig.). 1994. pap. 295.00 (*0-7605-1238-8*) Rector Pr.

Chile: Country Reporter. Lewis B. Sckolnick. (Illus.). 60p. 1994. pap. 895.00 (*1-57205-175-2*) Rector Pr.

Chile: Death in the South. Jacobo Timerman. 1988. pap. 6.95 (*0-679-72012-X*, Vin) Random.

Chile: Dictatorship & the Struggle for Democracy. Grinor Rojo & John J. Hassett. LC 88-82164. 112p. 1988. 12.00 (*0-935318-14-3*) Edins Hispamerica.

***Chile: Finanzas De los Gobiernos Subnacionales - Chile: Subnational Government Finance.** (Country Study Ser.). 156p. (SPA.). 1994. 9.95 (*0-8213-2778-X*, 12778) World Bank.

Chile: Foreign Financing Reporter. Ed. by Lewis B. Sckolnick. (Illus.). 60p. (Orig.). 1994. pap. 225.00 (*1-57205-244-9*) Rector Pr.

Chile: From Within. Ed. by Susan Meiselas. 1990. 39.95 (*0-393-02817-8*) Norton.

Chile: Human Rights & U. S. Policy. Jan Shinpoch et al. Ed. by Gail Lehman. Tr. by Maureen Dunn. 52p. (Orig.). 1985. pap. text ed. 5.00 (*0-9613249-1-0*) WOLA.

Chile: Its Land & People. Francis Maitland. 1976. lib. bdg. 59.95 (*0-8490-1604-5*) Gordon Pr.

Chile: Land of Poets & Patriots. Irene F. Galvin. LC 89-28747. (Discovering Our Heritage Ser.). (Illus.). 128p. (J). (gr. 5 up). 1990. text ed. 14.95 (*0-87518-421-9*, Dillon Silver Burdett) Silver Burdett Pr.

Chile: Politics & Society. Ed. by Arturo Valenzuela & J. Samuel Valenzuela. LC 73-92814. 415p. reprint ed. pap. 118.30 (*0-317-20611-7*, 2024153) Bks Demand.

Chile: Prospects for Democracy. Mark Falcoff et al. 96p. 1988. pap. 8.95 (*0-87609-045-5*) Coun Foreign.

Chile: Reality & Prospects of Popular Unity. Kate Clark. 142p. 1972. pap. 14.00 (*0-8464-0245-9*) Beekman Pubs.

Chile: Subnational Government Finance. LC 93-27904. (Country Study Ser.). 122p. 1993. 7.95 (*0-8213-2524-8*, 12524) World Bank.

***Chile: The Adult Health Policy Challange.** LC 95-8630. (Country Study). 1995. write for info. (*0-8213-3224-4*) World Bank.

Chile: The Legacy of Hispanic Capitalism. 2nd ed. Brian Loveman. (Latin American Histories Ser.). (Illus.). 464p. 1988. pap. 19.95 (*0-19-505219-6*) OUP.

Chile: The Multilateral Development Banks & U. S. Human Rights Law. Washington Office on Latin America Staff. 45p. (Orig.). 1986. pap. 6.00 (*0-9613249-5-3*) WOLA.

Chile: The Political Economy of Development & Democracy in the 1990s. David E. Hojman. LC 92-50200. (Latin American Ser.). (C). 1993. text ed. 49.95 (*0-8229-1169-8*) U of Pittsburgh Pr.

Chile: Third Report. (Country Reports on the Situation on Human Rights). 92p. 1979. 2.00 (*0-8270-2550-5*) OAS.

Chile: Trade & Investment Guide. Lewis B. Sckolnick. (Illus.). 149p. (Orig.). (C). Date not set. pap. 125.00 (*1-57205-629-0*) Rector Pr.

Chile: Trade, Licensing & Investing Rules & Regulations. Ed. by Lewis B. Sckolnick. (Illus.). 80p. (Orig.). (C). 1994. pap. 225.00 (*1-57205-057-8*) Rector Pr.

Chile see American Nations Past & Present

Chile see Statements of the Laws of the OAS Member States in Matters Affecting Business

Chile & Allende. Ed. by Lester A. Sobel. LC 74-81148. 196p. reprint ed. pap. 55.90 (*0-317-20501-3*, 2022903) Bks Demand.

Chile & Easter Island: A Travel Survival Kit. 3rd ed. Wayne Bernhardson. (Illus.). 436p. 1993. pap. 15.95 (*0-86442-181-8*) Lonely Planet.

Chile & the United States: Empires in Conflict. William F. Sater. LC 90-35055. (United States & the Americas Ser.). 256p. 1991. 35.00 (*0-8203-1249-5*); pap. 15.00 (*0-8203-1250-9*) U of Ga Pr.

Chile & the War of the Pacific. William F. Sater. LC 85-24584. 343p. reprint ed. pap. 101.20 (*0-7837-4205-3*, 2059055) Bks Demand.

Chile Briefing: "Disappearances" 1988. Spanish ed. 5.00 (*0-86210-146-8*) Amnesty Intl USA.

Chile Business Forecaster. Ed. by Lewis B. Sckolnick. 70p. (Orig.). (C). 1994. pap. 675.00 (*1-57205-368-2*) Rector Pr.

***Chile Business Intelligence Handbook.** (Illus.). 70p. (Orig.). 1994. pap. 295.00 (*0-7605-1073-3*) Rector Pr.

***Chile Business Risk Outlook.** 70p. (Orig.). 1994. pap. 495.00 (*0-7605-1394-5*) Rector Pr.

***Chile Commercial Law.** 150p. (C). 1994. pap. 295.00 (*0-7605-0097-5*) Rector Pr.

Chile, Corn & Croissants: Recipes from New Mexico Country Inns. Joan Stromquist. Ed. by Carl Stromquist. (Illus.). 368p. (Orig.). 1994. pap. 18.95 (*0-9622807-6-3*) Tierra Pubns.

***Chile Country Studies: Area Handbook.** 3rd ed. Library of Congress, Federal Research Division Staff & Rex A. Hudson. LC 94-21663. (Area Handbook DA Pam Ser.: Vol. 550-77). 1994. 25.00 (*0-8444-0828-X*) Lib Congress.

***Chile Fever: A Celebration of Peppers.** Elizabeth King. (Illus.). 32p. (J). (gr. 2-6). 1995. 14.99 (*0-525-45255-9*) Dutton Child Bks.

Chile in Pictures. Ed. by Lerner Publications, Department of Geography Staff. (Visual Geography Ser.). (Illus.). 64p. (YA). (gr. 5 up). 1988. lib. bdg. 18.95 (*0-8225-1809-0*, Lerner Publctns) Lerner Group.

Chile in the Nitrate Era: The Evolution of Economic Dependence, 1880-1930. Michael Monteon. LC 81-70009. 284p. 1982. 35.00 (*0-299-08820-0*) U of Wis Pr.

Chile in Transition: Human Rights since the Plebiscite. Americas Watch Staff. 98p. 1989. 7.00 (*0-929692-36-5*, Am Watch) Hum Rts Watch.

Chile Nineteen Hundred Seventy to Nineteen Hundred Seventy-Three: Economic Development & Its International Setting. Ed. by Sandro Sideri. (Institute of School Studies on the Development of Societies: No. 4). 1979. lib. bdg. 60.50 (*90-247-2198-9*) Kluwer Ac.

Chile of Today: Its Commerce Production & Resources. Adolfo Ortuzar. 1976. lib. bdg. 69.95 (*0-8490-1605-3*) Gordon Pr.

Chile Pepper Book: A Fiesta of Flavorful Recipes. Carolyn Dille & Susan Belsinger. Ed. by Linda Ligon. 96p. 1994. pap. 9.95 (*0-934026-93-9*) Interweave.

***Chile Pepper Fever: Mine's Hotter Than Yours.** Hazen & Hammond. 1995. pap. text ed. 19.95 (*0-89658-228-0*) Voyageur Pr.

Chile Pepper Fever: Mine's Hotter than Yours. Susan Hazen-Hammond. LC 93-13590. (Illus.). 128p. 1993. 29.95 (*0-89658-195-0*) Voyageur Pr.

***Chile Pepper Passion Poster Book.** Eduardo Fuss. (Illus.). 1994. pap. 20.00 (*0-06-258538-X*) HarpC.

Chile Pot. Frederick Hayes & Jean Hayes. (J). 1988. 6.95 (*0-925605-00-X*) Pinto Pub.

Chile since Independence. Ed. by Leslie Bethell. LC 92-17160. (Illus.). 240p. (C). 1993. 64.95 (*0-521-43375-4*); pap. 21.95 (*0-521-43987-6*) Cambridge U Pr.

Chile Since the Coup: Ten Years of Repression. Americas Watch Staff. 137p. 1983. 7.00 (*0-938579-00-2*, Fund Free Exp) Hum Rts Watch.

***Chile Tax Law.** 150p. (C). 1994. pap. 295.00 (*0-7605-0096-7*) Rector Pr.

Chile Through Embassy Windows, Nineteen Thirty-Nine to Nineteen Fifty-Three. Claude G. Bowers. LC 76-56739. 375p. 1977. reprint ed. text ed. 65.00 (*0-8371-9435-0*, BOCH, Greenwood Pr) Greenwood.

Chile Today & Tomorrow. Ed. by L. E. Elliott. 1976. lib. bdg. 59.95 (*0-8490-1606-1*) Gordon Pr.

Chilean Agriculture under Military Rule: From Reform to Reaction, 1973-1980. Lovell S. Jarvis. LC 84-27833. (Research Ser.: No. 59). (Illus.). 220p. 1985. pap. 11.50 (*0-87725-159-2*) U of Cal IAS.

Chilean Development Corporation - A Study in National Planning to Raise Living see Nutrition in Industry, Nineteen Forty-Six

Chilean Economy: Policy Lessons & Challenges. Barry P. Bosworth et al. LC 93-43252. 441p. (C). 1994. 44.95 (*0-8157-1046-1*); pap. 19.95 (*0-8157-1045-3*) Brookings.

Chilean Folktales Retold. Marjorie Agosin et al. Tr. by Celeste Kostopulos-Cooperman. 106p. (Orig.). 1992. pap. 9.95 (*0-88795-093-0*) Distributors.

Chilean Novel: A Critical Study of Its Secondary Sources & a Bibliography. Jorge Roman-Lagunas. LC 94-4566. 1994. write for info. (*0-8108-2868-5*) Scarecrow.

Chilean Political Process. Manuel A. Garreton. (Thematic Studies in Latin America Ser.). 1989. text ed. 45.00 (*0-685-68132-7*) Westview.

Chilean Press During the Allende Years, 1970-1973. Jerry W. Knudson. (Council on International Studies & Programs Special Studies: No. 152). 80p. 1986. pap. text ed. 10.00 (*0-924197-03-X*, 152) SUNYB Coun Intl Studies.

Chilean Rural Society from the Spanish Conquest to 1930. Arnold J. Bauer. LC 75-2724. (Cambridge Latin American Studies: No. 21). 287p. reprint ed. pap. 81.80 (*0-317-26054-5*, 2024421) Bks Demand.

Chilean Senate: Internal Distribution of Influence. Weston H. Agor. LC 79-165918. (Latin American Monographs: No. 23). 228p. reprint ed. pap. 65.00 (*0-8357-7720-0*, 2036077) Bks Demand.

Chilean Short Story: Writers from the Generation of 1950. Kenneth Fleak. (American University Studies: Ser. XXII, Vol. 4). 250p. (C). 1989. text ed. 39.10 (*0-8204-0828-X*) P Lang Pubs.

Chilean Theater, 1973-1985: Marginality, Power, Selfhood. Catherine M. Boyle. LC 88-46172. 224p. 1992. 36.50 (*0-685-50340-2*) Fairleigh Dickinson.

Chilean Wine. Jan Read. LC 87-60746. (Illus.). 176p. 1988. 39.95 (*0-85667-343-9*, Pub. by P Wilson Pubs) Sothebys Pubns.

Chileans in Exile: Private Struggles, Public Lives. Diana Kay. LC 86-2920. 242p. 1987. 24.95 (*0-89341-537-5*, Longwood Academic) Hollowbrook.

Chilenas. Manuel Matias. LC 91-73140. 128p. 1991. 13.00 (*0-89729-611-7*) Ediciones.

***Chiles & Other Peppers.** Sunset Books Staff. (Gourmet Kitchen Ser.). 1994. 9.95 (*0-376-02761-4*) Sunset Menlo Pk.

***Chile's Free-Market Miracle: A Second Look.** Joseph Collins & John Lear. 345p. (Orig.). 1994. pap. 15.95x (*0-935028-63-3*) Inst Food & Develop.

Chile's Middle Class: A Struggle for Survival in the Face of Neoliberalism. Larissa Lomnitz & Ana Meinick. LC 91-19118. (LACC Studies on Latin America & the Caribbean). 180p. 1991. lib. bdg. 34.00 (*1-55587-258-1*) Lynne Rienner.

***Chile's Native Forest: A Conservation Legacy.** Ken Wilcox. (Illus.). 156p. 1995. pap. 16.95 (*0-9617879-2-9*) NW Wild Bks.

C

An Asterisk (*) at the beginning of an entry indicates that the title is appearing in BIP for the first time.

An Asterisk (*) at the beginning of an entry indicates that the title is appearing in BIP for the first time.

1213

Chilton's Auto Repair Manual, 1972-79. Chilton Automotives Editorial Staff. LC 76-48878. (Collector's Edition Manual Ser.). (Illus.). 1152p. 1979. 28.95 (*0-8019-6914-X*) Chilton.

Chilton's Auto Repair Manual 1988-92. 1584p. 1991. 28.95 (*0-8019-7906-4*) Chilton.

Chilton's Auto Repair Manual 87-91. Chilton Book Co. Staff. 1344p. (SPA.). 1992. 26.95 (*0-8019-8138-7*) Chilton.

Chilton's Auto Service Manual: 1987-1991 Domestic Cars, Motor-Age Professional Mechanic's Edition. Chilton Staff. 2112p. 1990. text ed. 95.00 (*0-8019-8074-7*) Chilton.

Chilton's Auto Service Manual, 1983-87. Chilton Automotives Editorial Staff. LC 82-72944. 1856p. 1987. pap. 95.00 (*0-8019-7690-1*) Chilton.

Chilton's Auto Service Manual, 1985-1989: Motor Age Professional Mechanic's Edition. Chilton Automotives Editorial Staff. LC 82-72944. (Illus.). 1856p. 1988. text ed. 95.00 (*0-8019-7854-8*) Chilton.

Chilton's Auto Service Manual, 1986-90: Motor-Age Professional Mechanic's Edition. Chilton Automotives Editorial Staff. LC 82-72944. (Illus.). 1920p. 1989. text ed. 95.00 (*0-8019-7955-2*) Chilton.

Chilton's Auto Service Manual 1988-92: Motor Age Professional Mechanic's Edition. 2112p. 1991. 95.00 (*0-8019-8178-6*) Chilton.

Chilton's Automatic Transmission Repair Manual, 1984-88: Import Cars & Trucks: Motor-Age Professional Mechanic's Edition. Chilton Automotives Editorial Staff. LC 88-43196. (Illus.). 1920p. 1989. text ed. 95.00 (*0-8019-7960-9*) Chilton.

Chilton's Automatic Transmission Service Manual, 1980-84. Chilton Automotives Editorial Staff. LC 83-45327. 1472p. 1984. pap. 95.00 (*0-8019-7390-2*) Chilton.

Chilton's Automatic Transmission Service Manual, 1984-88: Domestic Cars & Trucks. Chilton Automotives Editorial Staff. LC 88-43180. (Motor Age Professional Mechanics Edition Ser.), (Illus.). 1920p. 1989. pap. text ed. 95.00 (*0-8019-7959-5*) Chilton.

Chilton's Buick Century & Regal, 1975-87. Chilton Automotives Editorial Staff. LC 87-47943. 368p. (Orig.). 1988. pap. 16.95 (*0-8019-7823-8*) Chilton.

Chilton's Chassis Electronic & Power Accessory Service Manual 1982-86: Motor-Age Professional Mechanic's Edition. Chilton Automotives Editorial Staff. LC 85-43611. 1536p. 1986. 95.00 (*0-8019-7726-6*) Chilton.

Chilton's Chassis Electronics & Power Accessories Service Manual 1987-89: Motor-Age Professional Mechanic's Edition. Chilton Automotives Editorial Staff. LC 87-47920. (Illus.). 1536p. 1988. text ed. 95.00 (*0-8019-7857-2*) Chilton.

Chilton's Chevette & Pontiac T1000 1976-88. Chilton Automotives Editorial Staff. LC 87-47930. (Illus.). 304p. (Orig.). 1989. pap. text ed. 16.95 (*0-8019-7845-9*) Chilton.

Chilton's Chevrolet-GMC Pick-ups & Suburban 1970-87. Chilton Automotives Editorial Staff. LC 87-47947. 496p. (Orig.). 1988. pap. 16.95 (*0-8019-7828-9*) Chilton.

Chilton's Chevrolet Mid-Size 1964-88. Chilton Automotives Editorial Staff. LC 87-47938. 488p. (Orig.). 1988. pap. 16.95 (*0-8019-7824-6*) Chilton.

Chilton's Chevrolet Repair Manual 1980-1987. Chilton Automotives Editorial Staff. LC 86-47792. (Update Ser.). (Illus.). 640p. 1987. pap. 19.95 (*0-8019-7772-X*) Chilton.

Chilton's Component Locator Manual, 1982-89: Motor-Age Professional Mechanic's Edition. Chilton Book Company Staff. (Illus.). 640p. 1990. pap. text ed. 60.00 (*0-8019-8045-3*) Chilton.

Chilton's Corvette 1963-83. Chilton Automotives Editorial Staff. LC 85-47981. 320p. (Orig.). 1986. pap. 16.95 (*0-8019-7681-2*) Chilton.

Chilton's Cutlass, 1970-87. Chilton Staff. LC 86-47775. 304p. 1987. 16.95 (*0-8019-7753-3*) Chilton.

Chilton's Datsun-Nissan, Maxima-Datsun 200SX 510, 610, 710, 810 1973-1989. Chilton Automotives Editorial Staff. LC 87-47922. (Illus.). 488p. (Orig.). 1989. pap. 16.95 (*0-8019-7852-1*) Chilton.

Chilton's Datsun-Nissan Z & ZX 1970-88. Chilton Automotives Editorial Staff. LC 87-47924. (Illus.). 384p. (Orig.). 1989. pap. 16.95 (*0-8019-7851-3*) Chilton.

Chilton's Dodge-Plymouth Trucks 1967-1988. Chilton Automotives Editorial Staff. LC 87-47931. (Illus.). 672p. (Orig.). 1989. pap. 16.95 (*0-8019-7844-0*) Chilton.

Chilton's Dodge-Plymouth Vans 1967-88. Chilton Automotives Editorial Staff. LC 87-47933. (Illus.). 528p. (Orig.). 1989. pap. text ed. 16.95 (*0-8019-7842-4*) Chilton.

Chilton's Dodge, 1968-1977. Chilton Automotives Editorial Staff. LC 77-71635. (Chilton's Repair & Tune-up Guides Ser.). (Illus.). 280p. 1977. pap. 16.95 (*0-8019-6554-3*) Chilton.

Chilton's Electronic Chassis Controls Manual Import Cars & Trucks (A-M) 1989-91: Motor Age Professional Mechanics Edition. 1920p. 1991. 95.00 (*0-8019-8152-2*) Chilton.

Chilton's Electronic Controls Code Manual, 80-90: Motor-Age Professional Mechanic's Edition. Chilton Book Company Staff. (Illus.). 1632p. 1990. pap. text ed. 95.00 (*0-8019-8051-8*) Chilton.

Chilton's Electronic Engine Controls Manual 1984-88--Import Cars & Trucks: Motor-Age Professional Mechanic's Edition. Chilton Automotives Editorial Staff. LC 87-51237. 1584p. 1988. text ed. 90.00 (*0-8019-7800-9*) Chilton.

Chilton's Electronic Engine Controls Manual, 1988-90: European Cars & Light Trucks - Motor Age Professional. Chilton Staff. 960p. 1990. text ed. 95.00 (*0-8019-8112-3*) Chilton.

Chilton's Electronic Engine Controls Manual, 1988-90 - Domestic Cars & Trucks: Motor-Age Professional Mechanic's Edition. Chilton Automotives Editorial Staff. LC 88-43195. (Illus.). 1920p. 1989. text ed. 95.00 (*0-8019-7957-9*) Chilton.

Chilton's Electronic Engine Controls Manual, 1988-90 European Cars & Light Trucks: M-A Professional Mechanic's Edition. Chilton Book Company Staff. (Illus.). 1920p. 1990. text ed. 95.00 (*0-8019-8046-1*) Chilton.

Chilton's Electronic Engine Controls Manual, 1988-90 Japanese & Asian Cars & Light Trucks: M-A Professional Mechanic's Edition. Chilton Book Company Staff. 1920p. 1990. text ed. 95.00 (*0-8019-8047-X*) Chilton.

Chilton's Electronic Instrumentation Service Manual 1980-1987: Motor Age Professional Mechanic's Edition. Chilton Automotives Editorial Staff. LC 87-47952. 1988. text ed. 90.00 (*0-8019-7864-5*) Chilton.

Chilton's Emission Component Application Guide 1966-1990: Motor-Age Professional Mechanics Edition. Chilton Staff. 192p. 1990. pap. 25.00 (*0-8019-8082-8*) Chilton.

Chilton's Emission Control Manual 1991: Motor Age Professional Mechanics Edition. 2112p. 1991. 85.00 (*0-8019-8154-9*) Chilton.

Chilton's Emission Diagnosis, Tune-up & Service Manual, 1989 Import Cars & Light Trucks: M-A Professional Mechanic's Edition. Chilton Book Company Staff. (Illus.). 768p. 1990. pap. text ed. 60.00 (*0-8019-8049-6*) Chilton.

Chilton's Emission Diagnostic Manual: Import Cars 1983-84. Chilton Automotives Editorial Staff. LC 83-45334. (Motor Age Professional Mechanics Edition Ser.). 480p. 1984. pap. 30.00 (*0-8019-7491-7*) Chilton.

Chilton's Firebird, 1982-90 Repair & Tuneup Guide. rev. ed. Chilton Staff. 400p. 1990. pap. 16.95 (*0-8019-8060-7*) Chilton.

Chilton's for Barracuda & Challenger 1965-1972. Chilton Automotives Editorial Staff. LC 72-7036. (Illus.). 232p. 1972. pap. 16.95 (*0-8019-5807-5*) Chilton.

Chilton's Ford Courier, 1972-1982. Chilton Automotives Editorial Staff. LC 82-72923. 232p. 1983. pap. 16.95 (*0-8019-7341-4*) Chilton.

Chilton's Ford Pickups, 1965-1986. Chilton Automotives Editorial Staff. LC 85-47964. 416p. (Orig.). 1986. pap. 16.95 (*0-8019-7662-6*) Chilton.

Chilton's Ford Vans, 1961-88. Chilton Automotives Editorial Staff. LC 87-47934. 672p. 1988. pap. 16.95 (*0-8019-7841-6*) Chilton.

Chilton's GM Sub-Compacts, 1971-1980. LC 79-8303. (New Automotive Ser.). 280p. 1980. pap. 16.95 (*0-8019-6935-2*) Chilton.

Chilton's Granada-Monarch, 1975-1982. Chilton Automotives Editorial Staff. LC 82-72933. 264p. 1983. pap. 16.95 (*0-8019-7311-2*) Chilton.

Chilton's Guide to Air Conditioning Repair & Service 1989-91. (Total Car Care Ser.). 960p. 1991. pap. 19.95 (*0-8019-8147-6*) Chilton.

Chilton's Guide to Air Conditioning Service & Repair 1982-85. Chilton Automotives Editorial Staff. LC 84-45472. (Illus.). 566p. (Orig.). 1985. pap. 19.95 (*0-8019-7580-8*) Chilton.

Chilton's Guide to Automatic Transmission Repair Manual, 1984-89 Domestic Cars & Trucks. Chilton Staff. 896p. 1990. pap. 24.95 (*0-8019-8054-2*) Chilton.

Chilton's Guide to Automatic Transmission Repair 1974-80. (Illus.). 352p. 1985. pap. 19.95 (*0-8019-7645-6*) Chilton.

Chilton's Guide to Automatic Transmission Repair, 1980-84: Domestic Cars & Trucks. LC 88-48013. (Illus.). 592p. 1988. 24.95 (*0-8019-7890-4*) Chilton.

Chilton's Guide to Automatic Transmission Repair, 1980-84: Import Cars & Trucks. LC 88-48012. (Illus.). 672p. 1988. 24.95 (*0-8019-7891-2*) Chilton.

Chilton's Guide to Brakes, Steering & Suspension 1980-87: Domestic & Import Cars & Trucks. Chilton Automotives Editorial Staff. LC 87-47939. (Illus.). 592p. (Orig.). 1988. pap. 19.95 (*0-8019-7819-X*) Chilton.

Chilton's Guide to Electronic Engine Controls & Fuel Injection 1984-88: Import Cars & Trucks. Chilton Automotives Editorial Staff. (Illus.). 704p. (Orig.). 1988. pap. 19.95 (*0-8019-7818-1*) Chilton.

Chilton's Guide to Electronic Engine Controls 1984-88. Chilton Automotives Editorial Staff. 704p. 1987. pap. 19.95 (*0-8019-7768-1*) Chilton.

Chilton's Guide to Emission Diagnosis & Vacuum Diagrams 1979-80. (Illus.). 544p. 1985. pap. 19.95 (*0-8019-7649-9*) Chilton.

Chilton's Guide to Emission Diagnosis, Tune-up & Vacuum Diagrams 1984-86 (Domestic Cars) 512p. 1987. pap. 19.95 (*0-8019-7756-8*) Chilton.

Chilton's Guide to Engine Rebuilding & Repair. LC 85-47925. (Illus.). 240p. 1985. pap. 19.95 (*0-8019-7643-X*) Chilton.

Chilton's Guide to Fuel Injection & Carburetors 1978-85. Chilton Automotives Editorial Staff. LC 83-45323. 416p. 1985. pap. 19.95 (*0-8019-7488-7*) Chilton.

Chilton's Guide to Fuel Injection & Electronic Engine Controls 88-90 European Cars And Trucks. 768p. 1990. pap. 19.95 (*0-8019-8120-4*) Chilton.

Chilton's Honda, 1973-88. Chilton Automotives Editorial Staff. LC 87-47936. 464p. (Orig.). 1989. pap. 16.95 (*0-8019-7840-8*) Chilton.

Chilton's IMP Emission Diagnostic & Service Manual, Vacuum Circuit 1984-87 Import Cars & Truck: Motor-Age Professional Mechanic's Edition. Chilton Automotives Editorial Staff. LC 83-45334. 1200p. 1987. 85.00 (*0-8019-7775-4*) Chilton.

Chilton's Import Car Parts & Labor Guide 1987-91: Motor Age Professional Mechanics Edition. 1824p. 1991. 95.00 (*0-8019-8132-8*) Chilton.

Chilton's Import Car Repair Manual: 1980-87. Chilton Automotives Editorial Staff. LC 80-68280. 1488p. 1987. 28.95 (*0-8019-7672-3*) Chilton.

Chilton's Import Car Repair Manual 1980-87: Motor Age Professional Mechanics Edition. 1872p. 1991. reprint ed. 95.00 (*0-8019-8149-2*) Chilton.

Chilton's Import Car Repair Manual 1987-91: Motor Age Professional Mechanics Edition. 2016p. 1991. 95.00 (*0-8019-8133-6*) Chilton.

Chilton's Import Car Repair Manual 1988-92. 1632p. 1991. 28.95 (*0-8019-7907-2*) Chilton.

Chilton's Import Car Wiring Diagrams Manual 1987-88: Motor-Age Professional Mechanic's Edition. Chilton Automotives Editorial Staff. LC 83-70545. 1216p. 1988. text ed. 95.00 (*0-8019-7858-0*) Chilton.

Chilton's Import Car Wiring Diagrams Manual 1989. Chilton Automotives Editorial Staff. LC 88-43181. (Motor Age Professional Mechanics Edition Ser.). (Illus.). 1344p. 1989. pap. text ed. 95.00 (*0-8019-7938-2*) Chilton.

Chilton's Jeep CJ 1945 - 1987. Chilton Automotives Editorial Staff. LC 85-47977. 544p. (Orig.). 1987. pap. 16.95 (*0-8019-7675-8*) Chilton.

Chilton's Labor Guide & Manual 1988-92: Motor-Age ProfessionalMechanic's Edition. 1920p. 1991. 95.00 (*0-8019-8179-4*) Chilton.

Chilton's Labor Guide & Parts Manual, 1987-91: Motor-Age Professional Mechanic's Edition. Chilton Staff. 1536p. 1990. 95.00 (*0-8019-8076-3*) Chilton.

Chilton's M-A Truck & Van Service Manual, 1986-90: Motor-Age Professional Mechanic's Edition. Chilton Book Company Staff. 1920p. 1990. text ed. 95.00 (*0-8019-8048-8*) Chilton.

Chilton's Mercedes-Benz, 1959-1970. Chilton Automotives Editorial Staff. LC 70-131236. (Illus.). 288p. 1970. pap. 16.95 (*0-8019-6065-7*) Chilton.

Chilton's Mercedes Benz 2, 1968-1973. Chilton Automotives Editorial Staff. LC 74-1487. (Illus.). 264p. 1974. pap. 16.95 (*0-8019-5907-1*) Chilton.

Chilton's Minor Auto Body Repair Manual. Chilton Automotives Editorial Staff. LC 88-43167. (Illus.). 368p. 1989. pap. 19.95 (*0-8019-7898-X*) Chilton.

Chilton's Mustang & Cougar, 1965-1973. Chilton Automotives Editorial Staff. LC 83-70992. 240p. (Orig.). 1983. pap. 16.95 (*0-8019-7405-4*) Chilton.

Chilton's Mustang-Capri-Merkur 1979-88. Chilton Automotives Editorial Staff. LC 87-47944. 416p. (Orig.). 1989. pap. 16.95 (*0-8019-7825-4*) Chilton.

Chilton's Mustang II: 1974-1978, Repair & Tune-up Guide. Chilton Automotives Editorial Staff. LC 78-22143. (Repair & Tune-up Guides Ser.). (Illus.). 292p. 1979. pap. 16.95 (*0-8019-6812-7*) Chilton.

Chilton's Nissan Sentra, Datsun 1200 & B210, 1973-88. Chilton Automotives Editorial Staff. LC 87-47925. (Illus.). 320p. (Orig.). 1989. pap. text ed. 16.95 (*0-8019-7850-5*) Chilton.

Chilton's Nissan Stanza-Datsun F-10, 310, 1976-88. Chilton Automotives Editorial Staff. LC 87-47921. (Illus.). 360p. (Orig.). 1989. pap. 16.95 (*0-8019-7853-X*) Chilton.

Chilton's Pinto & Bobcat, 1971-1980. LC 80-70340. (Illus.). 304p. 1981. pap. 16.95 (*0-8019-7027-X*) Chilton.

Chilton's Pontiac Mid-Size 1974-83. Chilton Automotives Editorial Staff. LC 82-72928. 336p. 1983. pap. 16.95 (*0-8019-7346-5*) Chilton.

Chilton's Porsche 924 & 928, 1977-1981. Chilton Automotives Editorial Staff. LC 87-70328. (Illus.). 232p. 1981. pap. 16.95 (*0-8019-7048-2*) Chilton.

Chilton's Prof. Chassis Electronic Service Manual: 1989-1991 Domestic Cars & Light Trucks. Chilton Staff. 1920p. 1990. 95.00 (*0-8019-8077-1*) Chilton.

Chilton's Professional Electronics Diagnostic Manual Ford Cars & Trucks 1984-88: Motor-Age Professional Mechanic's Edition. Chilton Automotives Editorial Staff. LC 87-47918. (New Ser.). (Illus.). 768p. 1988. pap. 95.00 (*0-8019-7861-0*) Chilton.

Chilton's Professional Import Automotive Service Manual, 1975-81. Chilton Staff. 1920p. 1981. 95.00 (*0-8019-7061-X*) Chilton.

Chilton's Professional Truck & Van Repair Manual 1982-88. Chilton Automotives Editorial Staff. LC 81-70221. 1856p. 1988. text ed. 95.00 (*0-8019-7832-7*) Chilton.

Chilton's Professional Wiring Diagrams Manual: 1988 Domestic Cars. Chilton Automotives Editorial Staff. LC 83-45329. 1344p. 1988. text ed. 95.00 (*0-8019-7833-5*) Chilton.

***Chilton's Repair & Tune-up Guide - Chevrolet, 1968 60 1983: Bel Air, Biscayne, Brookwood, Caprice.** Chilton Staff. 1983. pap. text ed. (*0-8019-7313-9*) Chilton.

Chilton's Repair & Tune-up, Saab 99: All Models, 1969-75. Chilton Book Company. LC 75-40448. 232p. reprint ed. pap. 66.20 (*0-685-17108-6*, 2027020) Bks Demand.

Chilton's Road Report 1994, Trade Edition. Daniel Heraud. 400p. 1993. pap. 17.95 (*0-8019-8574-9*) Chilton.

***Chilton's Road Report, 1995.** Daniel Heraud. 400p. 1994. pap. 17.95 (*0-8019-8634-6*) Chilton.

Chilton's Road Runner, Satellite, Belvedere, GTX, 1968-1973. Chilton Automotives Editorial Staff. LC 73-4347. (Illus.). 192p. 1973. pap. 16.95 (*0-8019-5821-0*) Chilton.

Chilton's Saab 900, 1979-1985. Chilton Automotives Editorial Staff. LC 84-45477. 176p. (Orig.). 1985. pap. 16.95 (*0-8019-7572-7*) Chilton.

Chilton's Service Bay Handbook 1992: Motor Age Professional Mechanic's Edition. 256p. 1991. pap. 20.00 (*0-8019-8180-8*) Chilton.

Chilton's Spanish Auto Repair Manual 1976-83. Chilton Automotives Editorial Staff. LC 76-648878. 1336p. (SPA.). 1984. 26.95 (*0-8019-7476-3*) Chilton.

Chilton's Spanish Auto Repair Manual, 1980-87. LC 88-47802. (Illus.). 1320p. (SPA.). 1987. 26.95 (*0-8019-7795-9*) Chilton.

Chilton's Subaru 1970-88. Chilton Automotives Editorial Staff. LC 87-47945. 416p. (Orig.). 1988. pap. 16.95 (*0-8019-7826-2*) Chilton.

Chilton's Toyota Celica-Supra 1971-87. Chilton Automotives Editorial Staff. LC 86-47784. 384p. 1987. pap. 16.95 (*0-8019-7763-0*) Chilton.

Chilton's Toyota Celica Supra, 1986-90. rev. ed. Chilton Staff. 416p. 1991. pap. 16.95 (*0-8019-8058-5*) Chilton.

Chilton's Toyota Corolla - Tercel - Mr2, 1984-90 Rtug. Chilton Staff. 592p. 1991. pap. 16.95 (*0-8019-8061-5*) Chilton.

Chilton's Toyota Corolla, Carina, Tercel, Starlet, 1970-87. Chilton Automotives Editorial Staff. LC 86-47788. 320p. 1987. pap. 16.95 (*0-8019-7767-3*) Chilton.

Chilton's Toyota Corona, Crown Cressida, Mark II, Camry 1970-86. Chilton Automotives Editorial Staff. LC 88-70268. 224p. 1987. pap. 16.95 (*0-8019-7674-X*) Chilton.

Chilton's Toyota Cressida, Van 1983-1990 Rtug. Chilton Staff. 480p. 1991. pap. 16.95 (*0-8019-8068-2*) Chilton.

Chilton's Toyota Trucks 1970-88. Chilton Automotives Editorial Staff. LC 87-47950. 560p. (Orig.). 1988. pap. 16.95 (*0-8019-7831-9*) Chilton.

Chilton's Truck & Van Repair Manual: 1979-86. Chilton Automotives Editorial Staff. LC 78-52225. (Illus.). 1440p. 1986. 28.95 (*0-8019-7655-3*) Chilton.

Chilton's Truck & Van Repair Manual: 1980-86 Motor-Age Professional Mechanics Edition. Chilton Automotives Editorial Staff. LC 82-71518. 1920p. 1986. 95.00 (*0-8019-7688-X*) Chilton.

Chilton's Truck & Van Repair Manual 1971-1978. LC 78-52225. (Illus.). 1360p. 1980. 28.95 (*0-8019-7012-1*) Chilton.

Chilton's Truck Repair Manual 1961-1971. LC 70-153137. (Illus.). 1200p. 1974. 28.95 (*0-8019-6198-X*) Chilton.

Chilton's U.S. Emission Diagnostic & Service Manual, Vacuum Circuit 1984-87 Domestic Car: Motor-Age Professional Mechanic's Edition. Chilton Automotives Editorial Staff. LC 85-47954. 1200p. 1987. 85.00 (*0-8019-7774-6*) Chilton.

Chilton's Vacuum Diagram Manual 1980-86: Domestic Cars & Trucks. Chilton Automotives Editorial Staff. LC 87-47941. (Illus.). 480p. (Orig.). 1988. pap. text ed. 19.95 (*0-8019-7821-1*) Chilton.

Chilton's Volkswagon, 1949-1971. Chilton Automotives Editorial Staff. LC 74-154691. (Illus.). 232p. 1972. reprint ed. pap. 16.95 (*0-8019-5796-6*) Chilton.

Chilton's Wiring Diagram Manual: Domestic Cars 1982-84. Chilton Automotives Editorial Staff. LC 83-45329. (Motor Age Professional Mechanics Edition Ser.). 1408p. 1984. text ed. 95.00 (*0-8019-7493-3*) Chilton.

Chilton's Wiring Diagram Manual: 1985 Domestic Cars, Motor-Age Professional Mechanics Edition. Chilton Automotives Editorial Staff. LC 85-47956. 1408p. 1986. pap. 95.00 (*0-8019-7641-3*) Chilton.

Chilton's Wiring Diagram Manual 1984-86 Import Cars: Motor-Age Professional Mechanic's Edition. Chilton Automotives Editorial Staff. LC 85-47955. 1216p. 1986. pap. 95.00 (*0-8019-7642-1*) Chilton.

Chilton's Wiring Diagrams Manual: 1990 Import Cars Motor-Age Professional Mechanic's Edition. Chilton Staff. 1344p. 1992. pap. 95.00 (*0-8019-8072-0*) Chilton.

Chilton's Wiring Diagrams Manual, 1989: Domestic Cars. Chilton Automotives Editorial Staff. LC 88-43179. (Motor Age Professional Mechanics Edition Ser.). (Illus.). 1216p. 1989. pap. text ed. 85.00 (*0-8019-7937-4*) Chilton.

Chilula. Elaine Landau. LC 93-31423. (First Book Ser.). (Illus.). 64p. (J). (gr. 5-8). 1994. lib. bdg. 13.93 (*0-531-20132-5*) Watts.

Chilula. Elaine Landau. LC 93-31423. (First Bks.). (Illus.). 64p. (J). (gr. 4-6). 1994. pap. 5.95 (*0-531-15685-0*) Watts.

Chimaera. Bernard Evslin. (Monsters of Mythology Ser.). (Illus.). 93p. 1988. lib. bdg. 19.95 (*1-55546-244-8*) Chelsea Hse.

Chimaera of His Age. 146p. pap. 8.95 (*0-87907-863-4*) Cistercian Pubns.

Chimaera's Copper. Piers Anthony & Robert E. Margroff. 1991. mass mkt. 4.95 (*0-8125-0915-3*) Tor Bks.

Chimaeras in Development Biology. Ed. by Nicole Le Douarin & Anne McLaren. 1984. text ed. 176.00 (*0-12-440580-0*) Acad Pr.

Chimalpahin & the Kingdoms of Chalco. Susan Schroeder. LC 90-11170. (Illus.). 264p. 1991. 45.00 (*0-8165-1182-9*) U of Ariz Pr.

Chimayo Valley Traditions. Intro. by Elizabeth Kay. LC 86-71418. (Illus.). 104p. (Orig.). 1987. pap. 10.95 (*0-941270-35-1*) Ancient City Pr.

Chimbu: A Study of Change in the New Guinea Highlands. Paula Brown. (Illus.). 192p. 1972. pap. 13.95 (*0-87073-757-0*) Schenkman Bks Inc.

Chime Clock Repair. Steven G. Conover. LC 89-91577. (Illus.). 210p. 1990. 28.50 (*0-9624766-0-9*) Clockmakers.

Chime of Windbells: A Year of Japanese Haiku in English Verse. Harold Stewart. LC 69-12084. (Illus.). 238p. 1969. 24.95 (*0-8048-0092-8*) C E Tuttle.

Chimene: Ou, Le Cid. Antonio Sacchini. Ed. by Eugene Gigout. (Chefs-d'oeuvre classiques de l'opera francaise Ser.: Vol. 37). (Illus.). 282p. (FRE.). 1970. reprint ed. pap. 35.00 (*0-8450-1137-5*) Broude.

***Chimera.** Candace Alhric & Angus Lachlan. LC 94-90277. 160p. (Orig.). 1995. pap. 12.95 (*1-56002-480-1*, Univ Edtns) Aegina Pr.

Chimera. John Barth. 320p. 1985. mass mkt. 4.95 (*0-449-21113-4*, Crest) Fawcett.

Chimera. Mary Rosenblum. 1993. mass mkt. 4.99 (*0-345-38528-4*) Ballantine.

Chimera. Sebastiano Vassalli. Tr. by Patrick Creagh. 320p. 1994. text ed. 21.00 (*0-689-12202-0*, Atheneum S&S) S&S Trade.

1214

An Asterisk (*) at the beginning of an entry indicates that the title is appearing in BIP for the first time.

C

C

An Asterisk (*) at the beginning of an entry indicates that the title is appearing in BIP for the first time.

1215

China: Railways & Agricultural Development, 1875 to 1935. Ernest P. Liang. LC 82-4749. (Research Papers Ser.: No. 203). 186p. (C). 1982. pap. 10.00 (*0-89065-109-4*) U Chicago Comm Geo.

China: Reform & Development in 1992-93. Peter Harrold & Rajiv Lall. LC 93-31850. (Discussion Paper, East Asia & Pacific Region Ser.: No. 215). 70p. 1993. 6.95 (*0-8213-2651-1*, 12651) World Bank.

China: Reforming Intergovernmental Fiscal Relations. Ramgopal Agarwala. LC 92-23554. (Discussion Paper Ser.: Vol. 178). 96p. 1992. 7.95 (*0-8213-2223-0*, 12223) World Bank.

China: Regional Study. 2nd ed. Hyman Kublin. Ed. by Howard R. Anderson. (World Regional Studies). (gr. 7-12). 1976. pap. 24.52 (*0-395-21685-0*) HM.

China: Revenue Mobilization & Tax Policy. 388p. 1990. 23.95 (*0-8213-1593-5*, 11593) World Bank.

China: Revolution to Revolution. K. R. Sharma. 1989. 29.00 (*81-7099-101-3*, Pub. by Mittal II) S Asia.

China: Second Liberation. Rama Sharma. xiii, 299p. 1985. 19.00 (*0-318-18471-0*, Pub. by Lancers Books II) Nataraj Bks.

China: Strategies for Reducing Poverty in the 1990s. LC 92-34227. (Country Study Ser.). 174p. 1992. 10.95 (*0-8213-2248-6*, 12248) World Bank.

China: Stratigraphy, Paleogeography & Tectonics. Arthur A. Meyerhoff et al. (C). 1991. lib. bdg. 142.00 (*0-7923-0972-3*) Kluwer Ac.

China: Teacher's Guide. (J). (gr. 4-7). 1991. 18.00 (*0-8172-3479-9*) Raintree Steck-V.

China: The Achievement & Challenge of Price Reform. World Bank Staff. LC 93-21836. (Country Study Ser.). 48p. 1993. 6.95 (*0-8213-2340-7*, 12340) World Bank.

China: The Church's Long March. David Adency. 1985. pap. 4.95 (*0-8307-1096-5*) OMF Bks.

China: The Criminal Code of the People's Republic of China. Tr. by Chin Kim. (American Series of Foreign Penal Codes: Vol. 25). xv, 74p. 1982. text ed. 18.50 (*0-8377-0045-0*) Rothman.

China: The Dragon Awakes. Tony Zurlo. LC 94-8015. (Discovering Our Heritage Ser.). (J). 1994. text ed. 14.95 (*0-87518-596-7*, Mac Bks Young Read) S&S Childrens.

China: The Land & Its People. rev. ed. D. Merton & Shio Yun-Kan. LC 85-72107. (Countries Ser.). (Illus.). 48p. (J). (gr. 5 up). 1991. lib. bdg. 14.95 (*0-382-24242-4*) Silver Burdett Pr.

China: The Land & the People. D. C. Money. (Illus.). 192p. 1992. 34.95 (*0-237-51164-9*, Pub. by Evans Bros Ltd UK); pap. 17.95 (*0-237-51118-5*, Pub. by Evans Bros Ltd UK) Trafalgar.

China: The March Toward Unity. Mao Tse-Tung et al. LC 75-36225. reprint ed. 37.50 (*0-404-14475-6*) AMS Pr.

***China: The Next Decades.** Denis E. Dwyer. 1993. pap. text ed. 35.95 (*0-470-22172-0*) Wiley.

China: The Opening Door. ICHCA Staff. 74p. (C). 1985. 250.00 (*0-685-37352-5*, Pub. by ICHCA UK) St Mut.

China: The Opening Door. ICHCA Staff. (C). 1988. 150.00 (*0-685-46528-4*, Pub. by ICHCA UK) St Mut.

China: The People's Middle Kingdom & the U. S. A. John K. Fairbank. LC 67-17307. 156p. 1967. 18.50 (*0-674-11651-8*) Belknap Pr.

China: The Sick Dragon. Doug Ward. LC 78-65281. 1979. 6.00 (*0-932410-06-5*) Sundowner Serv.

China: The Suppression of the Left. 111p. 4.00 (*0-89567-024-0*) World View Forum.

China: Then & Now. Susan Finney & Patricia Kindle. (Gifted Learning Ser.). 64p. (J). (gr. 4-8). 1988. student ed 8.95 (*0-86653-458-X*, GA1062) Good Apple.

China: Trade, Licensing & Investing Rules & Regulations. Ed. by Lewis B. Sckolnick. (Illus.). 80p. (Orig.). (C). 1994. pap. 225.00 (*1-57205-058-6*) Rector Pr.

China: Tradition & Transformation, 2 Vols. rev. ed. John K. Fairbank et al. (C). 1989. pap. 34.76 (*0-395-49692-6*) HM.

China: Travels & Investigation in the "Middle Kingdom" James H. Wilson. LC 72-79843. (China Library Ser.). 1972. reprint ed. lib. bdg. 36.00 (*0-8420-1364-4*) Scholarly Res Inc.

China: Treaties, Conventions, Etc. Between China & Foreign States, 2 vols. LC 70-38056. (China Classic & Contemporary Works in Reprint Ser.). reprint ed. 225.00 (*0-404-56910-2*) AMS Pr.

China: Urban Land Management in an Emerging Market Economy. LC 93-543. (Country Study Ser.). 1993. write for info. (*0-8213-2395-4*) World Bank.

China: Urbanization & National Development. Ed. by C. K. Leung & Norton Ginsburg. LC 80-29142. (Research Papers Ser.: No. 196). 283p. 1980. pap. 12.00 (*0-89065-103-5*) U Chicago Comm Geo.

China - the Culture. Bobbie Kalman. (Lands, Peoples, & Cultures Ser.). (Illus.). 32p. (J). (gr. 4-5). 1989. lib. bdg. 15.95 (*0-86505-209-3*); pap. 7.95 (*0-86505-289-1*) Crabtree Pub Co.

China - The Land. Bobbie Kalman. (Lands, Peoples, & Cultures Ser.). (Illus.). 32p. (J). (gr. 4-5). 1989. lib. bdg. 15.95 (*0-86505-207-7*); pap. 7.95 (*0-86505-287-5*) Crabtree Pub Co.

China - The Lion & the Dragon: A Personal Interpretation of Chinese Life. Pearl Evans. LC 87-13110. (Illus.). 304p. 1988. pap. 14.95 (*0-938453-01-7*, 100) Small Helm Pr.

China - the Opening Door. ICHCA Staff. (C). 1988. 150.00 (*0-685-46504-7*, Pub. by ICHCA UK) St Mut.

China - The People. Bobbie Kalman. (Lands, Peoples, & Cultures Ser.). (Illus.). 32p. (J). (gr. 4-5). 1989. lib. bdg. 15.95 (*0-86505-208-5*); pap. 7.95 (*0-86505-288-3*) Crabtree Pub Co.

***China a Historical & Cultural Dictionary.** Ed. by Dillon. (Durham East Asia Ser.). 1996. text ed. 90.00 (*1-873410-55-7*, Pub. by Curzon Pr UK); pap. 29.95 (*1-873410-50-6*, Pub. by Curzon Pr UK) Humanities.

***China, a Macrohistory.** Ray Huang. LC 87-28898. 1988. pap. 12.95 (*0-87332-453-6*) M E Sharpe.

China after Deng. Guo-Guang Wu & Zhao-Jun Wang. 300p. (CHI.). 1994. pap. 20.00 (*0-9640904-0-6*) Transpacific Info.

***China after Deng Xiaoping.** Willy Wo-Lap Lam. LC 95-12275. xviii,497p. 1995. write for info. (*0-471-13114-8*) Wiley.

China after Mao: With Selected Documents. A. Doak Barnett. 1967. 49.50 (*0-691-03008-1*); pap. 14.95 (*0-691-00000-X*) Princeton U Pr.

***China after Mao: With Selected Documents.** A. Doak Barnett. LC 67-14406. (Walter E. Edge Lectures). reprint ed. pap. 84.70 (*0-7837-9295-6*, 2060034) Bks Demand.

***China after Socialism: In the Footsteps of Eastern Europe or East Asia?** Ed. by Barrett McCormick & Jonathan Unger. (Socialism & Social Movements Ser.). (Illus.). 262p. 1995. 55.00 (*1-56324-666-X*); pap. 25.00 (*1-56324-667-8*) M E Sharpe.

China Airlift - The Hump, Vol. III. Turner Publishing Co. Staff. LC 79-66379. (Illus.). 304p. 1991. 48.00 (*1-56311-029-6*) Turner Pub KY.

China Almanac of Foreign Economic Relations & Trade 1993-1994. Ed. by Lewis B. Sckolnick. 450p. (Orig.). (C). 1994. pap. 325.00 (*1-57205-327-5*) Rector Pr.

***China Almanac of Foreign Economic Relations & Trade, 1994-1995.** 450p. (Orig.). 1995. pap. 345.00 (*0-7605-1644-8*) Rector Pr.

China among Equals: The Middle Kingdom & Its Neighbors, 10th-14th Centuries. Ed. by Morris Rossabi. LC 81-11486. 400p. (C). 1983. pap. 16.00 (*0-520-04562-9*) U CA Pr.

China among the Nations of the Pacific. Ed. by Harrison Brown. LC 81-14828. (Westview Special Studies on China & East Asia). 148p. (Orig.). reprint ed. pap. 42.20 (*0-7837-3977-X*, 2043807) Bks Demand.

China, an Analysis. Frank J. Goodnow. 1979. 28.95 (*0-405-10603-3*) Ayer.

China & America: A Bibliography of Interactions, Foreign & Domestic. James M. McCutcheon. LC 74-190449. 85p. (Orig.). reprint ed. pap. 25.00 (*0-8357-8678-1*, 2056835) Bks Demand.

China & Charles Darwin. James R. Pusey. (East Asian Monographs: No. 100). 556p. 1983. 28.00 (*0-674-11735-2*) HUP.

China & Christianity: The Missionary Movement & the Growth of Chinese Anti-Foreignism, 1860-1870. Paul A. Cohen. LC 63-19135. (Harvard East Asian Ser.: No. 11). (Illus.). 406p. reprint ed. pap. 115.80 (*0-7837-6070-1*, 2059116) Bks Demand.

China & die Osteurasische Kavallierie-Revolution. Karl A. Wittfogel. (Bibliotheca Nostratica Ser.: Vol. 3). 69p. 1978. 20.00 (*0-685-08658-5*) Eurolingua.

China & Eastern Europe. Hemen Ray. 150p. 1988. text ed. 25.00 (*81-7027-115-0*, Pub. by Radiant Pubs II) S Asia.

China & Europe. A. Reichwein. 1972. 59.95 (*0-87968-853-X*) Gordon Pr.

China & Europe: Images & Influences in 16th-18th Centuries. Ed. by Thomas H. Lee. (Illus.). 356p. 1991. 87.50x (*962-201-465-8*, Pub. by Chinese Univ HK) Coronet Bks.

China & Gardens of Europe of the Eighteenth Century. Osvald Siren. LC 90-40872. (Reprints & Facsimiles in Landscape Architecture Ser.: No. 1). (Illus.). 464p. 1990. reprint ed. 120.00 (*0-88402-190-4*, SICH) Dumbarton Oaks.

China & Glassware Merchandiser. 161p. pap. 9.00 (*0-87102-018-1*, 45-3436) Natl Ret Merch.

China & Global Change: Opportunities for Collaboration. Global Climate Change Sciences in China Panel & Scholarly Communication with People's Republic of China Committee. LC 92-62952. (Illus.). 240p. (Orig.). (C). 1992. pap. text ed. 27.00 (*0-309-04841-9*) Natl Acad Pr.

China & Great Britain: The Diplomacy of Commercial Relations, 1860-1864. Britten Dean. LC 73-75059. (East Asian Monographs: No. 50). 223p. 1974. pap. 14.00 (*0-674-11725-5*) HUP.

China & Her Unfinished Revolution. Helen G. Pratt. LC 75-32327. (Studies in Chinese History & Civilization). 173p. 1977. reprint ed. text ed. 55.00 (*0-313-26970-X*, U6970, Greenwood Pr) Greenwood.

***China & Hong Kong Law Firm Directory 1994.** 300p. (Orig.). 1994. pap. 295.00 (*0-7605-0664-7*) Rector Pr.

China & Human Rights. Ann Kent. LC 92-19756. 1994. 59.00 (*0-19-585519-1*) OUP.

China & Human Rights. Ann Kent. LC 92-19756. 312p. 1995. reprint ed. pap. 23.00 (*0-19-585521-3*) OUP.

China & International Law: The Boundary Disputes. Byron N. Tzou. LC 89-23098. 169p. 1990. text ed. 49.95 (*0-275-93462-4*, C3462, Praeger Pubs) Greenwood.

China & International Organizations: Participation in Non-Governmental Organizations since 1971. Gerald Chan. (Illus.). 240p. 1989. 35.00 (*0-19-582738-4*) OUP.

China & Its National Minorities: Autonomy or Assimilation? Thomas Heberer. Tr. by Michel Vale. LC 88-38363. 180p. (C). 1990. 57.95 (*0-87332-549-4*) M E Sharpe.

China & Its People in Early Photographs. John Thomson. (Photography Ser.). (Illus.). 320p. 1983. reprint ed. pap. 13.95 (*0-486-24393-1*) Dover.

China & Its Religious Inheritance. John H. Chamberlayne. 175p. (Orig.). 1993. pap. 17.95 (*1-85756-052-3*, Pub. by Janus Pubng UK) Paul & Co Pubs.

China & Japan: A Search for Balance since World War I. Ed. by Alvin D. Coox & Hilary Conroy. LC 77-10006. (Topics in Diplomatic History Ser.). 468p. 1978. 10.95 (*0-87436-275-X*) Regina Bks.

China & Japan: History, Trends & Prospects. Ed. by Christopher Howe & Brian Hook. (Studies on Contemporary China). (Illus.). 150p. 1995. pap. 23.00 (*0-19-828932-4*) OUP.

China & Japan: New Economic Diplomacy. Chae-Jin Lee. LC 84-6602. (Publication Ser.: No. 297). (Illus.). xviii, 174p. (C). 1984. lib. bdg. 19.95 (*0-8179-7971-9*); pap. 9.95 (*0-8179-7972-7*) Hoover Inst Pr.

China & Japan at War, 1937-1945: The Politics of Collaboration. John H. Boyle. LC 76-183886. (Illus.). 456p. 1972. 52.50 (*0-8047-0800-2*) Stanford U Pr.

China & Japan in the Global Setting. Akira Iriye. (Edwin O. Reischauer Lectures). 156p. 1993. 25.00 (*0-674-11838-3*) HUP.

***China & Japan in the Global Setting.** Akira Iriye. (Edwin O. Reischauer Lectures). 156p. 1994. pap. text ed. 12.95 (*0-674-11839-1*, IRICHX) HUP.

China & Malaysia: Social & Economic Effects of Petroleum Development. Peter Hills & Paddy Bowie. xi, 148p. (Orig.). 1987. pap. 18.00 (*92-2-105508-6*) Intl Labour Office.

China & Northeast Asia: The Political Dimension. Harry Harding. (Asian Agenda Report Ser.: No. 12). (Illus.). 100p. (Orig.). 1988. lib. bdg. 27.00 (*0-8191-6591-3*); pap. text ed. 10.50 (*0-8191-6592-1*) U Pr of Amer.

China & Pakistan: Diplomacy of an Entente Cordiale. Anwar H. Syed. LC 73-93177. 272p. 1974. 30.00 (*0-87023-159-6*); pap. 16.95 (*0-87023-160-X*) U of Mass Pr.

China & People's War in Thailand, 1964-1969. Daniel D. Lovelace. LC 72-184630. (China Research Monographs: No. 8). 101p. reprint ed. pap. 28.80 (*0-317-08371-6*, 2004586) Bks Demand.

China & Russia: The "Great Game" Oliver E. Clubb. LC 72-155362. (Studies of the East Asian Institute, Columbia University). (Illus.). 614p. reprint ed. pap. 175.00 (*0-8357-4584-8*, 2037515) Bks Demand.

China & South Asia. M. A. Ramakant & D. Phil. 1988. 17.50 (*81-7003-092-7*) South Asia Pubns.

China & Southeast Asia: Into the 21st-Century. Ed. by Richard L. Grant. (Significant Issues Ser.). 88p. (Orig.). (C). 1993. pap. text ed. 10.50 (*0-89206-213-4*) CSI Studies.

China & Southeast Asia, the Politics of Survival: A Study of Foreign Policy Interaction. Melvin Gurtov. LC 74-24792. 256p. reprint ed. pap. 73.00 (*0-8357-6749-3*, 2035404) Bks Demand.

China & Tanzania: A Study in Cooperative Interaction. George T. Yu. LC 75-632290. (China Research Monographs: No. 5). 100p. reprint ed. pap. 28.50 (*0-317-08376-7*, 2004585) Bks Demand.

China & the American Dream: A Moral Inquiry. Richard Madsen. LC 93-45003. (C). 1995. 27.50 (*0-520-08613-9*) U CA Pr.

China & the Arms Trade. Anne Gilks & Gerald Segal. LC 85-2113. 240p. 1985. text ed. 39.95 (*0-312-13269-7*) St Martin.

China & the Bomb. Ken Coates. 1986. 21.00 (*0-85124-444-0*) Dufour.

China & the Chinese, 2 vols., Set. Henry Charles. 1977. reprint ed. 40.00 (*0-89986-378-7*) Oriental Bk Store.

China & the Christian Impact: A Conflict of Cultures. Jacques Gernet. Tr. by Janet Lloyd. 280p. 1985. pap. 29.95 (*0-521-31319-8*) Cambridge U Pr.

China & the Cold War: A Study in International Politics. Michael Lindsay. LC 79-2834. 286p. 1984. reprint ed. 25.75 (*0-8305-0011-1*) Hyperion Conn.

China & the Ethnic Chinese in Malaysia & Indonesia 1949-1992. Indira Ramanathan. (C). 1994. 18.50 (*81-7027-196-7*, Pub. by Radiant Pubs II) S Asia.

***China & the Law of the Sea Convention: Follow the Sea.** Elizabeth Van Wie Davis. LC 94-36474. (Illus.). 128p. 1995. text ed. 59.95 (*0-7734-9059-0*) E Mellen.

China & the Major Powers in East Asia. A. Doak Barnett. LC 77-21981. 416p. 1978. pap. 18.95 (*0-8157-0823-8*) Brookings.

China & the Manchus. H. A. Giles. 1972. lib. bdg. 250.00 (*0-87968-519-0*) Krishna Pr.

China & the Neutron Bomb. Liu Huaqiu. (Occasional Paper of Center for International Security & Arms Control, Stanford University Ser.). 49p. (Orig.). 1988. pap. 9.00 (*0-935371-20-6*) CFISAC.

China & the Origins of the Pacific War, 1931-41. Youli Sun. LC 92-36305. 256p. 1993. text ed. 45.00 (*0-312-09010-2*) St Martin.

China & the Overseas Chinese in Southeast Asia. Theresa C. Carino. vii, 115p. (Orig.). (C). 1986. pap. 7.50 (*971-10-0231-0*, Pub. by New Day Pub PH) Cellar.

China & the People's Democratic Republic of Yemen: A Report. Ed. by Hashim S. Behbehani. 425p. 1985. 45.00 (*0-7103-0097-2*, Pub. by Kegan Paul Intl UK) Routledge Chapman & Hall.

China & the Powers: A Narrative of the Outbreak of 1900. Harry C. Thomson. LC 79-2840. (Illus.). 285p. 1981. reprint ed. 28.00 (*0-8305-0017-0*) Hyperion Conn.

China & the Roman Orient. Friedrich Hirth. xvi, 329p. 1975. pap. 25.00 (*0-89005-093-7*) Ares.

China & the Roman Orient. Friedrich Hirth. 1976. lib. bdg. 59.95 (*0-8490-1607-X*) Gordon Pr.

China & the Soviet Union. A. K. Wu. 1976. lib. bdg. 69.95 (*0-8490-1608-8*) Gordon Pr.

China & the Taiwan Issue. Hungdah Chiu. LC 79-14270. (Praeger Special Studies). 310p. 1979. text ed. 65.00 (*0-275-90341-9*, C0341, Praeger Pubs) Greenwood.

China & the Third World: Champion or Challenger? Lillian C. Harris & Robert L. Worden. LC 85-30690. 154p. 1986. text ed. 55.00 (*0-86569-142-8*, Auburn Hse) Greenwood.

China & the Three Worlds: A Foreign Policy Reader. Ed. by King C. Chen. LC 78-51973. 396p. reprint ed. pap. 112.90 (*0-8357-2584-7*, 2040289) Bks Demand.

China & the U. S. S. R. Limits to Trade with the West. Georges Sokoloff & Francoise Lemoine. (Atlantic Papers: No. 46). 70p. (C). 1982. pap. text ed. 10.50 (*0-86598-104-3*) Rowman.

China & the United Nations. Yeshi Choedon. 1990. 17.50 (*81-7003-119-2*, Pub. by S Asia Pubs II) S Asia.

China & the United States, Nineteen Fifty-Five to Nineteen Sixty-Three. Ed. by Kwan H. Yim. LC 72-80832. 195p. reprint ed. pap. 55.60 (*0-317-20500-5*, 2022905) Bks Demand.

China & the United States, Nineteen Sixty-Four to Nineteen Seventy-Two. Ed. by Kwan H. Yim. LC 72-80832. 276p. reprint ed. pap. 78.70 (*0-317-20499-8*, 2022906) Bks Demand.

China & the West: Ideas & Activists. Ed. by David S. Goodman. LC 90-19673. (Studies on East Asia). 192p. 1991. text ed. 59.95 (*0-7190-2941-4*, Pub. by Manchester Univ Pr UK) St Martin.

China & the West, Eighteen Fifty-Eight to Eighteen Sixty-One: The Origins of the Tsungli Yamen. Masataka Banno. LC 64-13419. (Harvard East Asian Ser.: No. 15). 427p. reprint ed. pap. 121.70 (*0-317-08154-3*, 2006413) Bks Demand.

China & the World: Chinese Foreign Relations in the Post-Cold War Era. 3rd ed. Ed. by Samuel S. Kim. 315p. (C). 1994. text ed. 73.50 (*0-8133-1595-6*); pap. text ed. 24.95 (*0-8133-1596-4*) Westview.

China & the World Community. Ed. by Ian F. Wilson. LC 74-169719. (Illus.). 314p. reprint ed. pap. 89.50 (*0-685-23475-4*, 2056689) Bks Demand.

China & the World War. Thomas E. LaFargue. 45.00 (*0-86527-023-6*) Fertig.

China & Vietnam: The Roots of Conflict. William J. Duiker. LC 86-81534. (Indochina Research Monograph: No. 1). 136p. 1986. pap. 10.00 (*0-912966-89-0*) IEAS.

China Anthology: Lectures of the First Graphological Delegation to China 1987. Bolomet et al. (Illus.). 84p. (Orig.). 1988. pap. 10.00 (*0-939221-05-5*) Wellingham-Jones.

China, Around the World, Vol. 5. Betsy Franco. (Illus.). 48p. 1994. pap. text ed. 7.95 (*1-55799-270-3*) Evan-Moor Corp.

China As a Model of Development. Al Imfeld. LC 76-4827. 165p. reprint ed. pap. 47.10 (*0-8357-8843-1*, 2033472) Bks Demand.

China Assignment. Karl L. Rankin. LC 64-20488. (Illus.). 363p. 1964. 20.00 (*0-295-73742-5*) U of Wash Pr.

China at the Brink: The Political Economy of Reform & Retrenchment in the Post-Mao Era. Peter M. Lichtenstein. LC 91-9594. 176p. 1991. text ed. 45.00 (*0-275-94052-7*, C4052, Praeger Pubs) Greenwood.

China at the Conference: A Report. Westal W. Willoughby. LC 76-144850. 419p. 1972. reprint ed. text ed. 55.00 (*0-8371-5978-4*, WICH, Greenwood Pr) Greenwood.

China at the Crossroads. Ed. by Donald Altschiller. LC 94-9187. (Reference Shelf Ser.: Vol. 66, No. 3). 1994. 15.00 (*0-8242-0854-4*) Wilson.

China at the Crossroads: Reform after Tiananmen. Steven M. Goldstein. LC 92-72962. (Headline Ser.: No. 298). (Illus.). 128p. (Orig.). 1992. pap. 11.25 (*0-87124-148-X*) Foreign Policy.

China at the Threshold of a Market Economy. Michael W. Bell et al. LC 93-34529. (Occasional Paper Ser.: No. 107). 1993. pap. 15.00 (*1-55775-349-0*) Intl Monetary.

***China at War, 1901-1949.** Edward L. Dreyer. LC 94-32357. (Modern Wars in Perspective Ser.). 384p. (C). 1996. text ed. 55.95 (*0-582-05125-8*, 76985, Pub. by Longman UK); pap. text ed. 25.95 (*0-582-05123-1*, 76984, Pub. by Longman UK) Longman.

***China Atlas.** (Illus.). 100p. (Orig.). 1994. pap. 75.00 (*0-7605-0616-7*) Rector Pr.

***China Atlas.** (Illus.). 100p. (Orig.). (CHI.). 1994. pap. 45.00 (*0-7605-0614-0*) Rector Pr.

China Avante-Garde: Counter-Currents in Art & Culture. Haus der Kulturen der Welt Staff. (Illus.). 360p. 1994. 75.00 (*0-19-586423-9*) OUP.

China Beach. David Matlin. 112p. (Orig.). 1989. pap. 8.95 (*0-88268-066-8*) Station Hill Pr.

China Beginner's Traveler's Dictionary. Richard L. Kimball. 154p. pap. 6.95 (*0-685-06995-8*) Eurasia Pr NY.

China Between Revolutions: Photographs by Sidney D. Gamble, 1917-1927. Ed. by Nancy Jervis & May Wu. (Illus.). 32p. (Orig.). 1989. pap. 7.00 (*0-9622826-0-X*) S D Gamble FCS.

***China Bibliography: A Research Guide to Reference Works About China Past & Present.** Harriet T. Zurndorfer. LC 95-203. (Handbuch der Orientalistik; Vierte Abteilung: China: Vol. 9). 1995. write for info. (*90-04-10278-7*) E J Brill.

China Bloodhunt. Axel Kilgore. (They Call Me the Mercenary Ser.: No. 16). 1983. pap. 2.50 (*0-8217-1288-8*) Zebra.

China, Body & Soul. Ed. by Ernest R. Hughes. LC 78-117811. (Essay Index Reprint Ser.). 1977. 19.95 (*0-8369-1661-1*) Ayer.

China Bomb. Sid Campbell. (Orig.). 1989. pap. write for info. (*0-318-66712-6*) Gong Prods.

China Born: Adventures of a Maverick Bookman. Henry Noyes. LC 89-60880. 224p. (Orig.). 1989. reprint ed. 19.95 (*0-8351-2198-4*) China Bks.

China Bound: A Guide to Academic Life & Work in the PRC. Karen Turner-Gottschang. LC 94-736. 240p. reprint ed. pap. 68.40 (*0-7837-1297-9*, 2041438) Bks Demand.

An Asterisk (*) at the beginning of an entry indicates that the title is appearing in BIP for the first time.

China Bound, Revised: A Guide to Academic Life & Work in the PRC. Karen Turner-Gottschang & Linda A. Reed. LC 94-736. 252p. (C). 1994. pap. 24.95 (*0-309-04932-6*) Natl Acad Pr.

China Boy. Gus Lee. LC 93-27236. 336p. 1994. pap. 10.95 (*0-452-27158-4*, Plume) NAL-Dutton.

China Boy. Idwal Jones. LC 70-163033. (Short Story Index Reprint Ser.). 1977. reprint ed. 15.95 (*0-8369-3947-6*) Ayer.

China Briefing, 1994. Ed. by William A. Joseph. 200p. (C). 1994. text ed. 39.85 (*0-8133-2056-9*); pap. text ed. 15.85 (*0-8133-2057-7*) Westview.

China, Britain & Hong Kong: 1895-1945. Chan Lau Kit-Ching. 479p. 1990. 67.50 (*962-201-409-7*, Pub. by Chinese Univ HK) Coronet Bks.

China Builds for Democracy: A Story of Cooperative Industry. Nym Wales. Ed. by Helen F. Snow. LC 72-13495. (Illus.). xvi, 310p. 1976. reprint ed. 59.00 (*0-403-02253-3*) Scholarly.

China Builds the Bomb. John W. Lewis & Xue Litai. LC 87-30404. (ISIS Studies in International Security & Arms Control: Vol. 3). (Illus.). 352p. 1988. 45.00 (*0-8047-1452-5*); pap. 14.95 (*0-8047-1841-5*) Stanford U Pr.

China Business: The Portable Encyclopedia for Doing Business with China. Christine Genzberger et al. LC 93-45977. (World Trade Press Country Business Guides Ser.). 1994. 24.95 (*0-9631864-3-4*) Wrld Trade Pr.

***China Business Directory.** (Illus.). 300p. (Orig.). 1994. pap. 295.00 (*0-7605-0701-5*) Rector Pr.

China Business Directory, 1994 Edition. AT&T EastGate Services Staff. 4500p. 1994. 1,350.00 (*1-885530-18-8*) AT&T EastGate.

China Business Forecaster. Ed. by Lewis B. Sckolnick. 70p. (Orig.). (C). 1994. pap. 675.00 (*1-57205-335-6*) Rector Pr.

***China Business Guide.** 1995. lib. bdg. 256.75 (*0-8490-7409-6*) Gordon Pr.

China Business Guidebook. Ed. by Lewis B. Sckolnick. 400p. (Orig.). (C). 1994. pap. 125.00 (*1-57205-513-8*) Rector Pr.

China Business Handbook. Ed. by Lewis B. Sckolnick. (Illus.). 400p. (Orig.). (C). 1994. pap. 295.00 (*1-57205-691-6*) Rector Pr.

***China Business in the South-West Region: Investment Guide.** (Illus.). 60p. (Orig.). 1994. per., pap. 125.00 (*0-7605-0605-1*) Rector Pr.

***China Business Intelligence Handbook.** (Illus.). 70p. (Orig.). 1994. pap. 295.00 (*0-7605-1010-5*) Rector Pr.

***China Business Report Annual 1994.** (Illus.). 200p. (Orig.). 1995. pap. 695.00 (*0-7605-1447-X*) Rector Pr.

***China Business Report, '94.** 125p. (Orig.). 1994. pap. 495.00 (*0-7605-0510-1*) Rector Pr.

***China Business Review.** 100p. (Orig.). 1995. pap. 995.00 (*0-7605-1992-7*) Rector Pr.

***China Business Risk Outlook.** 70p. (Orig.). 1994. pap. 495.00 (*0-7605-1432-1*) Rector Pr.

***China Business Risks & Forecasts 1994-1995.** (Illus.). 175p. (Orig.). 1994. pap. 495.00 (*0-7605-0661-2*) Rector Pr.

China Business Unlocked. Ed. by Lewis B. Sckolnick. 140p. (Orig.). 1994. pap. 295.00 (*1-57205-281-3*) Rector Pr.

China by Bike: Taiwan, Hong Kong, China's East Coast. Roger Grigsby. (Illus.). 256p. 1994. pap. 14.95 (*0-89886-410-0*) Mountaineers.

China Calls: Paving the Way for Nixon's Historic Journey to China. Anne C. Walker. Ed. by Elizabeth C. Eastman. LC 92-27899. (Illus.). 446p. 1992. 24.95 (*0-8191-8619-8*) Madison Bks UPA.

China Caravans. Robert Easton. LC 81-21742. (Illus.). 156p. 1982. pap. 8.95 (*0-88496-179-6*) Capra Pr.

China Caravans: An American Adventurer in Old China. Robert Easton. LC 89-559. 156p. (C). 1988. reprint ed. lib. bdg. 23.00x (*0-8095-4034-7*) Borgo Pr.

***China Challenge.** (Proceedings of the Academy of Political Science Ser.: Vol. 38, No. 2). 1991. 14.95 (*0-614-04162-7*) Acad Poli Sci.

China Changes Face: The Road from Revolution, 1949-1989. John Gittings. (Illus.). 320p. 1989. 29.95 (*0-19-215887-2*) OUP.

China Chemical Industry: World Chemical Industry Yearbook, 1987. Ed. by Ministry of Chemical Industry, Scientific & Technical Information Research Institute Staff. 580p. 1987. lib. bdg. 275.00 (*0-89573-666-7*) VCH Pubs.

***China Chemical Industry Investment Handbook.** (Illus.). 240p. (Orig.). 1994. pap. 395.00 (*0-7605-1160-8*) Rector Pr.

China Clay. Charles Thurlow. (C). 1990. pap. 24.95 (*0-85025-323-3*, Pub. by Tor Mark Pr UK) St Mut.

China Clipper. Peter Guttmacher. LC 93-46204. (Those Daring Machines Ser.). (J). 1994. text ed. 13.95 (*0-89686-826-5*, Crstwood Hse) Silver Burdett Pr.

China Clipper: The Age of the Great Flying Boats. Robert L. Grandt. LC 91-15386. (Illus.). 320p. 1991. 29.95 (*0-87021-209-5*) Naval Inst Pr.

China Clippers. Basil Lubbock. (C). 1987. 126.00 (*0-85174-109-6*, Pub. by Brwn Son Ferg) St Mut.

China Coal Industry Yearbook: Nineteen Eighty-Three. Ed. by Gong Miao et al. Tr. by Chen Zunfang et al. (China Coal Industry Yearbooks Ser.). (Illus.). 304p. 1984. text ed. 50.00 (*0-918062-61-6*, Pub. by Economic Info HK) Colo Sch Mines.

China Coal Industry Yearbook Nineteen Eighty-Two. Ed. by Gong Miao et al. (China Coal Industry Yearbooks Ser.). (Illus.). 336p. 1983. text ed. 40.00 (*0-918062-60-8*, Pub. by Economic Info HK) Colo Sch Mines.

***China Commercial Law Encyclopedia, 4 vols.** 1600p. (C). 1994. 1,495.00 (*0-7605-0992-1*) Rector Pr.

China Connection. Warren I. Cohen et al. LC 77-18101. (Studies of the East Asian Institute). 322p. 1978. text ed. 46.00 (*0-231-04444-5*) Col U Pr.

China Connection. Emery Tang. LC 86-60169. (Illus.). 80p. 1986. 21.95 (*0-89390-080-X*) Resource Pubns.

China Connection: Finding Ancestral Roots for Chinese in America. 2nd rev. ed. Jeanie W. Low. LC 93-91747. (Illus.). 65p. 1994. per., pap. 11.95 (*0-9638835-1-8*) JWC Low.

China Connection: U. S. Policy & the People's Republic of China. A. James Gregor. 280p. 1986. pap. 15.95 (*0-8179-8292-2*, P329) Hoover Inst Pr.

China Consuls: British Consular Officers, 1843-1943. P. D. Coates. (Illus.). 624p. 1988. 45.00 (*0-19-584078-X*) OUP.

China Consumer Markets. Ed. by Lewis B. Sckolnick. 125p. (Orig.). 1994. pap. 550.00 (*1-57205-282-1*) Rector Pr.

***China Consumer 1994.** 300p. (Orig.). 1994. pap. 825.00 (*1-57205-805-6*) Rector Pr.

China Court: The Hours of a Country House. Rumer Godden. LC 92-20702. 1993. pap. 13.00 (*0-688-11722-8*, Quill) Morrow.

China Court: The Hours of a Country House. large type ed. Rumer Godden. LC 93-33462. 1994. 20.95 (*0-7862-0098-7*) Thorndike Pr.

China Crosses the Yalu: The Decision to Enter the Korean War. Allen S. Whiting. LC 68-13744. x, 219p. 1960. 35.00 (*0-8047-0627-1*); pap. 12.95 (*0-8047-0629-8*) Stanford U Pr.

China: Crossroads Socialism: An Unofficial Manifesto for Proletarian Democracy. Chen Erjin. Tr. & Intro. by Robin Munro. 263p. 1988. text ed. 32.95 (*0-86091-062-8*, A0863, Pub. by Verso UK); pap. text ed. 14.95 (*0-86091-762-2*, Pub. by Verso UK) Routledge Chapman & Hall.

China Day by Day. Eileen Hsu-Balzer et al. LC 73-89575. 248p. reprint ed. pap. 70.70 (*0-8357-8070-8*, 2033761) Bks Demand.

***China Deconstructs: Politics, Trade & Regionalism.** Ed. by Gerald Segal & David S. Goodman. LC 94-21698. (In Asia Ser.). (Illus.). 304p. 1995. 59.95x (*0-415-11833-6*, C0378); pap. 18.95 (*0-415-11834-4*, C0379) Routledge.

China Diary. Stephen Spender & David Hockney. LC 92-62209. (Illus.). 200p. 1993. reprint ed. pap. 24.95 (*0-500-27711-7*) Thames Hudson.

China Diplomacy, Nineteen Fourteen to Nineteen Eighteen. Madeleine Chi. LC 77-82302. (East Asian Monographs: No. 31). 213p. 1970. pap. 14.00 (*0-674-11825-1*) HUP.

China Directory of Industry & Commerce. 2nd ed. Ed. by Xinhua Publishing House Staff. 1794p. 1984. 354.00 (*0-442-20640-2*) Prof Bk Ctr Inc.

China Directory of Industry & Commerce & Economic Annual. 1983. 395.00 (*0-86720-500-8*) Key Bk Serv.

China Directory of Mechanical & Electrical Enterprises. China Machine Pr. Staff. 1500p. (C). 1988. 175.00 (*0-685-30212-1*, Pub. by China Machine Pr CH) St Mut.

China Doctor of John Day, Oregon. Jeffrey Barlow & Christine Richardson. LC 79-3300. (Illus.). 160p. 1979. pap. 9.95 (*0-8323-0346-1*) Binford Mort.

China Documents Annual, 1989-1990-1991-1992. Ed. by Peter R. Moody, Jr. 1992. 75.00 (*0-87569-160-9*) Academic Intl.

***China Dome.** Lovejoy. 1995. mass mkt. 5.99 (*0-7860-0111-9*, Pinnacle NY) Windsor NY.

***China Dome.** William H. Lovejoy. 544p. 1995. pap. 5.99 (*0-8217-0111-8*) Zebra.

China, During the War & since the Peace, 2 vols., Set. John F. Davis. LC 72-79816. (China Library Ser.). (Illus.). 1972. reprint ed. lib. bdg. 45.00 (*0-8420-1369-5*) Scholarly Res Inc.

***China Economic Atlas.** (Illus.). 300p. (C). 1994. text ed. 695.00 (*0-7605-0982-4*) Rector Pr.

China Economic Handbook. 2nd ed. 1994. write for info. (*0-8103-9798-6*, 072144, Pub. by Euromonitor Pubns UK) Gale.

China, Eighteen Ninety-Eight to Nineteen Twelve: The Xinzheng Revolution & Japan. Douglas R. Reynolds. (East Asian Monographs: No. 160). (Illus.). 332p. (C). 1993. text ed. 32.00 (*0-674-11660-7*) HUP.

China Emerges. rev. ed. Steven Warshaw et al. LC 86-16783. (Asia Emerges Ser.). (Illus.). 243p. 1994. 14.95 (*0-87297-000-0*); teacher ed, pap. 4.95 (*0-87297-001-9*, X1973) Diablo.

***China Employment Handbook, 3 Vols.** (Illus.). 1800p. (C). 1994. 3,600.00 (*0-7605-0668-X*) Rector Pr.

China Enters the Machine Age: A Study of Labor in Chinese War Industry. Ed. by Shih Kuo-Heng et al. LC 68-23327. 1968. reprint ed. 65.00 (*0-8371-0222-7*, SHCL, Greenwood Pr) Greenwood.

China Express. Nina Simonds. LC 92-46413. 1993. 25.00 (*0-688-11478-4*) Morrow.

China Faces Japan. Allen S. Whiting. 1989. 38.00 (*0-520-06511-5*) U CA Pr.

China Factor. Ed. by Richard H. Solomon. LC 81-10660. 1981. 11.95 (*0-13-132704-6*) Am Assembly.

China Factor: Peking & the Superpowers. Ed. by Gerald Segal. LC 81-6897. 180p. 1981. 34.50 (*0-8419-0735-8*) Holmes & Meier.

China Facts & Figures Annual, Vol. 6. Ed. by John L. Scherer. 1985. 95.00 (*0-87569-048-3*) Academic Intl.

China Facts & Figures Annual, Vol. 7. Ed. by John L. Scherer. 1987. 95.00 (*0-87569-077-7*) Academic Intl.

***China Facts & Figures Annual, Vol. 8.** Ed. by John L. Sherer. 1987. 95.00 (*0-87569-080-7*) Academic Intl.

China Facts & Figures Annual, Vol. 9. John L. Scherer. 1988. 95.00 (*0-87569-086-6*) Academic Intl.

China Facts & Figures Annual, Vol. 10. John L. Scherer. 1988. 95.00 (*0-87569-092-0*) Academic Intl.

China Facts & Figures Annual, Vol. 11. Charles E. Greer. 1989. 95.00 (*0-87569-107-2*) Academic Intl.

China Facts & Figures Annual, Vol. 12. Ed. by Charles E. Greer. 1989. 95.00 (*0-87569-112-9*) Academic Intl.

***China Facts & Figures Annual, Vol. 13.** Ed. by Charles E. Greer. 1989. 95.00 (*0-87569-118-8*) Academic Intl.

China Facts & Figures Annual, Vol. 14. Ed. by Charles E. Greer. 1989. 95.00 (*0-87569-155-2*) Academic Intl.

China Facts & Figures Annual, Vol. 15 Index Vols. 1-10. Ed. by Charles E. Greer. 1992. 97.00 (*0-87569-157-9*) Academic Intl.

China Facts & Figures Annual, Vol. 16. Ed. by Charles E. Greer. 1989. 95.00 (*0-87569-161-7*) Academic Intl.

China Facts & Figures Annual, Vols. 1-3. Ed. by John L. Scherer. (CHIFFA Ser.). 1987. 95.00 (*0-87569-071-8*) Academic Intl.

China Fax & Telex Directory, 1993. 230p. (Orig.). (C). 1993. pap. text ed. 145.00 (*0-934393-31-1*) Rector Pr.

***China Fax & Telex Directory 1995.** 300p. (Orig.). 1994. pap. 165.00 (*0-7605-1341-4*) Rector Pr.

China Fights Back, an American Woman with the Eighth Route Army. Agnes Smedley. LC 75-39034. (China Studies). (Illus.). xxii, 282p. 1977. reprint ed. lib. bdg. 27.50 (*0-88355-389-9*) Hyperion Conn.

***China Financial Law.** 700p. (C). 1994. 1,495.00 (*0-7605-0993-X*) Rector Pr.

China for America: Export Porcelain of the 18th & 19th Centuries. Herbert Peter & Nancy Schiffer. LC 79-88254. (Illus.). 224p. 1979. 27.50 (*0-916838-23-4*) Schiffer.

***China for Women: Travel & Culture.** (Feminist Press Travel Ser.). 328p. (Orig.). 1995. pap. 17.95 (*1-55861-112-6*) Feminist Pr.

China Foreign Business Survey. N. Campbell. Ed. by P. Adlington. 272p. 1988. text ed. 122.00 (*0-08-036748-8*, CRC Reprint) Franklin.

China from Mao to Deng: The Politics & Economics of Socialist Development. Bulletin of Concerned Asian Scholars Staff. LC 82-19668. 99p. reprint ed. pap. 28.30 (*0-318-34843-8*, 2030986) Bks Demand.

China from the 7th to 19th Century. Enrica C. Pischel. LC 93-40124. (History of the World Ser.). (J). 1994. lib. bdg. 25.67 (*0-8114-3329-3*) Raintree Steck-V.

China Governess. Margery Allingham. 224p. 1993. 19.95 (*1-56723-004-0*) Yestermorrow.

China Governess. Margery Allingham. 272p. 1990. mass mkt. 4.50 (*0-380-70578-8*) Avon.

China Guide. 8th rev. ed. Ruth L. Malloy. Ed. by Stein & Cardoza. (Passport Press Travel Guides Ser.). (Illus.). 704p. 1994. pap. 17.95 (*1-883323-06-1*, Passpt Pr) Open Rd Pub.

China Guidebook, 1985. Fredric M. Kaplan et al. (Illus.). 672p. (Orig.). 1985. pap. 14.95 (*0-932030-18-1*) Eurasia Pr NY.

China Guidebook, 1986. 7th ed. 1986. 14.95 (*0-932030-20-3*) Eurasia Pr NY.

China Guidebook, 1987. Fredric M. Kaplan et al. 1987. pap. 15.95 (*0-317-56461-7*) HM.

China Guidebook 1993-94. Fredric M. Kaplan et al. (Eurasia Travel Guides Ser.). (Illus.). 800p. 1993. pap. 19.95 (*0-395-67028-4*, Travl Guides) HM.

***China Guides: Beijing.** 3rd ed. Cohn. 1995. pap. 15.95 (*0-8442-9986-3*, Passport Bks) NTC Pub Grp.

China Half-Figures Called Pincushion Dolls. Frieda Marion. LC 74-178257. (Illus.). 1977. reprint ed. 7.95 (*0-89145-058-0*) J Palmer.

China Handbook, Nineteen Thirty-Seven to Nineteen Forty-Five: A Comprehensive Survey of Major Developments in China. enl. rev. ed. Ed. by Hollington K. Tong. (China in the 20th Century Ser.). (Illus.). xvi, 862p. 1975. reprint ed. lib. bdg. 95.00 (*0-306-70701-2*) Da Capo.

China Homecoming. Jean Fritz. LC 84-24775. (Illus.). 144p. (J). (gr. 5 up). 1985. 15.95 (*0-399-21182-9*, Putnam) Putnam Pub Group.

China-Hong Kong Connection: The Key to China's Open Door Policy. Yun-Wing Sung. (Trade & Development Ser.). 220p. (C). 1991. 54.95 (*0-521-38245-9*) Cambridge U Pr.

China, Hong Kong, Taiwan & the World Trading System. Penelope Hartland-Thunberg. LC 90-31060. 185p. 1990. text ed. 45.00 (*0-312-04756-8*) St Martin.

China House. Vincent Lardo. 204p. (Orig.). 1983. pap. 6.95 (*0-932870-30-9*) Alyson Pubns.

China Illustrata. Athanasius Kircher. Tr. by Charles D. Van Tuyl. (Illus.). 228p. (Orig.). 1987. pap. 20.00 (*0-940392-24-0*) Indian U Pr OK.

China Illustrata. Athanasius Kircher. (Orig.). 1979. 150.00 (*0-7855-0307-2*, Pub. by Ratna Pustak Bhandar) St Mut.

China Illustrata. Ed. by Athanasius Kircher. 294p. (Orig.). (C). 1979. reprint ed. 450.00 (*0-89771-106-8*, Pub. by Ratna Pustak Bhandar) St Mut.

China Images in the Life & Times of Henry Luce. Patricia Neils. 384p. 1990. lib. bdg. 50.50 (*0-8476-7634-X*) Rowman.

China in Ancient & Modern Maps. Comp. by Ancient Map Research Team of the Institute of Surveying & Mapping Sciences Staff. LC 93-21211. (Illus.). 288p. Date not set. 120.00 (*0-85667-413-3*, Pub. by P Wilson Pubs) Sothebys Pubns.

China in Books: A Basic Bibliography in Western Language. Norman E. Tanis & David L. Perkins. Ed. by Robert D. Stueart. LC 77-24396. (Foundations in Library & Information Science: Vol. 4). 328p. 1979. lib. bdg. 73.25 (*0-89232-071-0*) Jai Pr.

China in Convulsion, 2 vols., Set. Arthur H. Smith. LC 71-38086. (China Classic & Contemporary Works in Reprint Ser.). (Illus.). reprint ed. 125.20 (*0-404-56954-4*) AMS Pr.

China in Crisis: China's Policies in Asia & America's Alternatives, Vol. 2. Ed. by Tang Tsou. LC 68-20981. 1968. lib. bdg. 15.00 (*0-226-81519-6*) U Ch Pr.

China in Disintegration: The Republican Era in Chinese History, 1912-1949. James E. Sheridan. LC 74-28940. (Transformation of Modern China Ser.). 1977. 18.95 (*0-02-928610-7*); pap. 19.95 (*0-02-928650-6*) Free Pr.

China in Oregon: A Resource Directory. Jeffrey Barlow et al. (Illus.). 179p. (Orig.). 1988. pap. 14.95 (*0-87678-072-9*) PSU CE Pr.

China in our Time: The Epic Saga of the People's Republic, from the Communist Victory to Tiananmen Square & Beyond. Ross Terrill. (Illus.). 384p. 1992. 25.00 (*0-671-68096-X*) S&S Trade.

China in Pictures. Ed. by Lerner Publications, Department of Geography Staff. (Visual Geography Ser.). (Illus.). 64p. (YA). (gr. 5 up). 1989. 18.95 (*0-8225-1859-7*, Lerner Publctns) Lerner Group.

China in Revolt: How a Civilization Became a Nation. Leang-Li T'Ang. LC 75-32326. (Studies in Chinese History & Civilization). 176p. 1976. reprint ed. text ed. 45.00 (*0-313-26977-7*, U6977, Greenwood Pr) Greenwood.

China in Revolt & the Idea of Freedom. 1989. pap. 1.50 (*0-914441-39-6*) News & Letters.

China in Revolution: The First Phase, 1900-1913. Ed. by Mary C. Wright. LC 71-28206. 518p. reprint ed. pap. 147.70 (*0-7837-3315-1*, 2057718) Bks Demand.

***China in Revolution: The Yenan Way Revisited.** Mark Selden. (Socialism & Social Movements Ser.). (Illus.). 350p. (C). 1995. text ed. 55.00 (*1-56324-554-X*, East Gate Bk); pap. text ed. 22.50 (*1-56324-555-8*, East Gate Bk) M E Sharpe.

China in Search of Its Future: Years of Great Reform, 1982-87. John Woodruff. LC 88-29027. 1989. 22.50 (*0-295-96803-6*) U of Wash Pr.

China in Search of Its Future Reform vs. Repression, 1982-1989. John Woodruff. 1990. pap. 9.95 (*0-8184-0524-4*) Carol Pub Group.

China in Seventeen Hundred: Kangxi Porcelains at the Taft Museum. Sheila Keppel. LC 88-50970. (Illus.). 24p. (Orig.). 1988. pap. 3.00 (*0-915577-16-X*) Taft Museum.

China in the Era of Deng Xiaoping: A Decade of Reform. Ed. by Michael Y. Kau & Susan H. Marsh. (Studies on Contemporary China). 534p. (C). 1993. text ed. 72.95 (*1-56324-277-X*, East Gate Bk) M E Sharpe.

***China in the Era of Deng Xiaoping: A Decade of Reform.** Ed. by Michael Y. Kau & Susan H. Marsh. (Studies on Contemporary China). 534p. 1993. pap. 24.95 (*1-56324-278-8*, East Gate Bk) M E Sharpe.

China in the Nineteen Eighties & Beyond: Political & Cultural Developments. Ed. by Arendrup et al. (C). 1986. pap. 18.50 (*0-7007-0174-5*, Pub. by Curzon Pr UK) Humanities.

China in the Nineties: Crisis Management & Beyond. Ed. by David S. Goodman & Gerald Segal. (Illus.). 248p. 1992. pap. 22.00 (*0-19-827363-0*) OUP.

***China in the Sea.** Sheila Jordan. LC 95-10376. (Signatures Poetry Ser.: Vol. 1). 1995. write for info. (*0-930095-02-2*) Signal Bks.

China in the Tokugawa World. Marius B. Jansen. (Reischauer Lectures). (Illus.). 137p. (C). 1992. 27.00 (*0-674-11753-0*) HUP.

China in the World Economy. Nicholas R. Lardy. 156p. (Orig.). (C). 1994. pap. 16.95 (*0-88132-200-8*) Inst Intl Eco.

China in the World Today. Ed. by Richard D. Lambert. LC 72-78295. (Annals Ser.: 402). 300p. 1972. 27.00 (*0-685-00180-6*); pap. 18.00 (*0-87761-150-5*) Am Acad Pol Soc Sci.

China in Transformation. Ed. by Tu Wei-ming. LC 93-42866. 1994. 15.50 (*0-674-11754-9*) HUP.

***China in Transition.** (Illus.). 200p. (Orig.). 1994. pap. 125.00 (*0-7605-0986-7*) Rector Pr.

China in Transition. Ed. by William A. Robson & Bernard Crick. LC 75-11135. (Sage Contemporary Social Science Issues Ser.: No. 17). 120p. reprint ed. pap. 34.20 (*0-317-11057-8*, 2021945) Bks Demand.

China in Transition: Communism, Capitalism, & Democracy. Ronald M. Glassman. LC 91-11071. 304p. 1991. text ed. 55.00 (*0-275-93614-7*, C3614, Praeger Pubs) Greenwood.

China in Transition: Political & Social Developments. Ed. by George T. Yu. 314p. (Orig.). (C). 1993. lib. bdg. 57.50 (*0-8191-9166-3*); pap. text ed. 34.50 (*0-8191-9167-1*) U Pr of Amer.

***China in World History.** Samuel A. Adshead. LC 94-28743. 1995. write for info. (*0-312-12379-5*) St Martin.

***China in World Politics.** John R. Faust & Judith F. Kornberg. LC 94-38876. 250p. (C). 1995. lib. bdg. 48.00 (*1-55587-413-4*); pap. 19.95 (*1-55587-427-4*) Lynne Rienner.

China, India, Japan & the Security of Southeast Asia. Ed. by Jeshurun Chandran. 285p. 1993. pap. 43.00 (*981-3016-61-2*, Pub. by Inst SE Asian Studies SI) Ashgate Pub Co.

***China Intellectual Property Law.** 700p. (C). 1994. 1,495.00 (*0-7605-0994-8*) Rector Pr.

China International Conference on Circuits & Systems, Proceedings, 1991. IEEE Circuits & Systems Society Staff. Ed. by IEEE Staff. LC 91-65879. 1000p. 1991. pap. text ed. write for info. (*0-7803-0150-1*, 91TH0387-1); fiche write for info. (*0-7803-0151-X*, 91TH0387-1) Inst Electrical.

China Is Farther Than the Sun? A Beginning Chinese-English Reader. Florence C. Chang. LC 80-68256. (Chinese Can Be Fun Bks.: Level 2). (Illus.). 51p. (J). (gr. 3-4). 1980. student ed, pap. 6.00 (*0-936620-00-5*) Ginkgo Hut.

China, Japan & Korea. John O. Bland. LC 77-160959. (Select Bibliographies Reprint Ser.). 1977. reprint ed. 35.95 (*0-8369-5826-8*) Ayer.

C

An Asterisk (*) at the beginning of an entry indicates that the title is appearing in BIP for the first time.

China, Japan & the European Community. Robert Taylor. LC 90-55154. 168p. 1990. 38.50 (*0-8386-3428-1*) Fairleigh Dickinson.

China, Japan & the Powers: A History of the Modern Far East. 2nd ed. Meribeth E. Cameron et al. LC 60-7761. 726p. reprint ed. pap. 180.00 (*0-8357-9857-7*, 2012473) Bks Demand.

China Joins the U. N. Blythe F. Finke. Ed. by D. Steve Rahmas. LC 72-89215. (Events of Our Times Ser.: No. 1). 32p. (Orig.). (gr. 7-12). 1973. lib. bdg. 4.95 (*0-87157-701-1*); pap. 2.95 (*0-87157-201-X*) SamHar Pr.

***China Joint Venture Handbook.** 300p. (C). 1994. 295.00 (*0-7605-0524-1*) Rector Pr.

China Joint Venture Handbook. Ed. by Lewis B. Sckolnick. (Illus.). 270p. (C). Date not set. pap. 695.00 (*1-57205-023-3*) Rector Pr.

China Joint Ventures. Ed. by Lewis B. Sckolnick. 250p. (Orig.). 1994. pap. 695.00 (*1-57205-283-X*) Rector Pr.

China Journal: Glimpses of a Nation in Transition. Robert Lee. LC 80-52783. (Illus.). (Orig.). 1980. 9.25 (*0-934788-00-6*); pap. 5.25 (*0-686-96708-9*) E-W Pub Co.

China Journal 1889-1900: An American Missionary Family During the Boxer Rebellion. Eva J. Price. 320p. 1990. pap. 9.95 (*0-02-036065-7*, Collier S&S) S&S Trade.

China, Korea & Japan: The Rise of Civilization in East Asia. Gina L. Barnes. LC 93-60205. (Illus.). 304p. 1993. 45.00 (*0-500-05071-6*) Thames Hudson.

China Lake. Anthony Hyde. 1993. mass mkt. 5.99 (*0-345-37695-1*) Ballantine.

China Language Learning Kit. 12.95 (*0-686-47139-3*) Eurasia Pr NY.

China Law Review, 10 vols., Set, Vols. 1-10. Comparative Law School of China, Soochow University Law Dept. Staff. LC 74-28774. 1975. reprint ed. Set. lib. bdg. 450.00 (*0-379-20201-8*) Oceana.

China Learns English: Language Teaching & Social Change in the People's Republic. Heidi A. Ross. (Illus.). 320p. 1993. 35.00 (*0-300-05562-5*) Yale U Pr.

China Letters. David Lin. 470p. (Orig.). 1993. pap. 9.95 (*0-923309-05-5*) Hartland Pubns.

China Looks Forward. Sun Fo K'O. LC 74-31229. (China in the 20th Century Ser.). (Illus.). xvi, 276p. 1975. reprint ed. lib. bdg. 32.50 (*0-306-70696-2*) Da Capo.

China Machinery Industries Yearbook, 1987. Ed. by Compiling Committee Staff. 460p. 1988. 95.00 (*0-387-18725-1*) Spr-Verlag.

China Machinery Industries Yearbook 1988. China Machine Pr. Staff. (C). 1988. 150.00 (*0-685-30213-X*, Pub. by China Machine Pr CH) St Mut.

China Market: America's Quest for Informal Empire, 1893-1901. Thomas J. McCormick. 252p. 1990. pap. 9.95 (*0-929587-24-3*, Elephant Paperbacks) I R Dee.

***China, Marxism, & Democracy: Selections from "October Review"** Ed. & Intro. by Thomas Barrett. (Revolutionary Studies Ser.). 288p. (C). 1995. text ed. 55.00 (*0-391-03923-7*) Humanities.

China Memoirs. Owen Lattimore. 1991. text ed. 34.50 (*0-86008-468-X*, Pub. by U of Tokyo JA) Col U Pr.

China Men. Maxine H. Kingston. (International Ser.). 1989. pap. 10.00 (*0-679-72328-5*, Vin) Random.

China Mending for Beginners: A Practical Guide. Margot Wisler. (Illus.). 120p. 1987. 15.95 (*0-900873-46-9*, Pub. by Bishopsgte Pr UK); pap. 11.95 (*0-900873-47-7*, Pub. by Bishopsgte Pr UK) Intl Spec Bk.

China Miracle: A Silent Explosion. Arthur Wallis. 171p. (Orig.). 1986. reprint ed. pap. 5.95 (*0-939159-00-7*) Cityhill Pub.

China, Modernisation & the Goal of Prosperity: Government Administration & Economic Policy in the Late 1980s. Ed. by Kate Hannan. (Illus.). 384p. (C). 1995. 59.95 (*0-521-46043-3*) Cambridge U Pr.

***China, Modernisation & the Goal of Prosperity: Government Administration & Economic Policy in the Late 1980s.** Ed. by Kate Hannan. 1995. pap. 24.95 (*0-521-52660-4*) Cambridge U Pr.

China, Mongolia: Business Risk Overview. Ed. by Lewis B. Sckolnick. 125p. (Orig.). (C). 1994. pap. text ed. 495.00 (*1-57205-549-9*) Rector Pr.

China Moon. Alice Sharpe. 1993. 13.95 (*0-8034-9003-8*) Bouregy.

China Moon Cookbook. Barbara Tropp. LC 92-50283. (Illus.). 528p. 1992. 24.95 (*1-56305-315-2*, 3315); pap. 14.95 (*0-89480-754-4*, 1754) Workman Pub.

China, Mother of Gardens. Ernest H. Wilson. LC 73-172555. (Illus.). 1972. reprint ed. 33.95 (*0-405-09081-1*) Ayer.

China Mountain Zhang. Maureen F. McHugh. 320p. 1992. 19.95 (*0-312-85271-1*) Tor Bks.

China Mountain Zhang. Maureen F. McHugh. 320p. 1993. mass mkt. 3.99 (*0-8125-0892-0*) Tor Bks.

China Notebook, Nineteen Seventy-Five to Nineteen Seventy-Eight. Jan Myrdal. Tr. by Rolf Von Dorp. LC 79-88412. (Illus.). 1982. lib. bdg. 12.95 (*0-930720-59-8*) Lake View Pr.

China Now: An Introductory Survey with Readings. Ed. by D. J. Dwyer. LC 73-87225. (Illus.). 520p. reprint ed. pap. 148.20 (*0-317-11042-X*, 2022526) Bks Demand.

China of Confucius: A Critical Interpretation. Harold H. Sunoo. LC 85-7639. (Illus.). 208p. 1985. lib. bdg. 14.95 (*0-912617-00-4*); pap. 8.95 (*0-912617-01-2*) Heritage Res Hse.

China, Oil, & Asia: Conflict Ahead? Selig S. Harrison. LC 77-8185. 1977. text ed. 43.00 (*0-231-04378-3*) Col U Pr.

China on Our Shelves. Ed. by Edwin Wolf, II. LC 88-151990. (Illus.). 44p. (Orig.). 1984. pap. 1.00 (*0-914076-64-7*) Lib Co Phila.

China on the Edge: Crisis of Ecology & Development in China. He Bochuan. Tr. by China Books & Periodicals, Inc. Staff. LC 91-70073. 220p. 1992. 29.95 (*0-8351-2447-9*); pap. 16.95 (*0-8351-2448-7*) China Bks.

China Opens Its Doors: The Politics of Economic Transition. Jude Howell. LC 93-2538. 1993. pap. text ed. 25.00 (*1-55587-480-0*) Lynne Rienner.

China Paper Nineteen Eighty-Seven: International Pulp, Paper & Converting Exhibition & Conference, October 13-18, 1987, Shanghai. Technical Association of the Pulp & Paper Industry Staff. (Illus.). 198p. reprint ed. pap. 56.50 (*0-8357-6802-3*, 2035481) Bks Demand.

China Paper, 1989: Technical Conference Program, Great Wall Sheraton Hotel, Beijing, People's Republic of China, November 10-11, 1989. Technical Association of the Pulp & Paper Industry Staff. (TAPPI Proceedings Ser.). 140p. reprint ed. pap. 39.90 (*0-8357-7904-1*, 2036332) Bks Demand.

China, Parian & Bisque German Dolls. Lydia Richter. 1993. 39.95 (*0-87588-411-3*) Hobby Hse.

China Past - China Future. Alden R. Carter. LC 93-13537. (J). 1994. lib. bdg. 14.77 (*0-531-11161-X*) Watts.

China (People's Republic of) (Let's Visit Places & Peoples of the World Ser.). (Illus.). 128p. (J). (gr. 5 up). 1991. 14.95 (*0-7910-1368-5*) Chelsea Hse.

***China Pharmaceutical Law.** 700p. (C). 1994. 1,495.00 (*0-7605-0995-6*) Rector Pr.

China Phoenix. Peter Townsend. LC 75-37340. (China Studies). 1978. reprint ed. lib. bdg. 27.50 (*0-88355-398-8*) Hyperion Conn.

China Phonebook & Business Directory 1993 Edition. 230p. 1993. pap. 225.00 (*0-934393-26-5*) Rector Pr.

China Phonebook & Business Directory 1994 Edition. 230p. 1993. pap. 225.00 (*0-934393-28-1*) Rector Pr.

***China Pilot: Flying for Chiang & Chennault.** Felix Smith. (WWII Commemorative Ser.). (Illus.). 320p. 1995. 24.95 (*0-02-881126-7*) Brasseys Inc.

China Pocket Guide. 1993. pap. 10.95 (*2-8315-2324-9*) Berlitz.

China Poems. Willis Barnstone. LC 75-43525. (Breakthrough Bks.). 64p. 1976. 14.95 (*0-8262-0194-6*) U of Mo Pr.

China Poems. Josef Knoepfler. (Illus.). 16p. (Orig.). 1994. pap. 5.00 (*1-878888-14-5*) Nine Muses.

China Policy: New Priorities & Alternatives. Ed. by W. Meyers & M. V. Hayes. 96p. 1972. text ed. 76.00 (*0-677-12210-1*) Gordon & Breach.

China Policy: Old Problems & New Challenges. A. Doak Barnett. LC 76-51538. 130p. 1977. 26.95 (*0-8157-0822-X*); pap. 9.95 (*0-8157-0821-1*) Brookings.

China Policy & National Security. Ed. by Frederick T. Chen. 250p. 1984. lib. bdg. 35.00 (*0-941320-17-0*) Transnatl Pubs.

***China Pop: How Soap Operas, Tabloids, & Bestsellers Are Transforming a Culture.** Jianying Zha. LC 94-43004. 210p. 1995. 20.00 (*1-56584-249-9*) New Press NY.

China Press & Publishing Directory, 1985. Ed. by Gao Guo-Gan et al. 400p. 1986. 55.00 (*0-582-97819-X*, Pub. by Longman Grp UK) Gale.

China Question: Essays on Current Relations Between Mainland China & Taiwan. Yu San Wang. LC 85-12210. 188p. 1985. text ed. 49.95 (*0-275-90046-0*, C0046, Praeger Pubs) Greenwood.

China Race. large type ed. John Dyson. 512p. 1986. 23.95 (*0-7089-8337-5*, Charnwood) Ulverscroft.

China Reporting: An Oral History of American Journalism in the 1930's & 1940's. Stephen R. MacKinnon & Oris Friesen. 200p. (C). 1987. pap. 13.00 (*0-520-06967-6*) U CA Pr.

***China Retailing.** (Illus.). 400p. (Orig.). 1994. pap. 2,195.00 (*0-7605-0899-2*) Rector Pr.

***China Retailing.** 133p. (Orig.). 1995. pap. 2,195.00 (*0-7605-2124-7*) Rector Pr.

China Review. Ed. by Kuan Hsin-chi & Maurice Brosseau. (Illus.). 300p. 1991. 62.50 (*962-201-513-1*, Pub. by Chinese Univ HK) Coronet Bks.

China Review 1993. Ed. by Joseph C. Yu-Shek & Maurice Brosseau. (Illus.). xxxii, 700p. 1993. 82.50 (*962-201-570-0*, Pub. by Chinese Univ HK) Coronet Bks.

***China Review, 1994.** Ed. by Maurice Brosseau & Lo Chi-kin. 540p. 1994. 87.50x (*962-201-616-2*, Pub. by Chinese Univ HK) Coronet Bks.

China Rights Annals, Vol. 1: Human Rights Developments in the People's Republic of China from October 1993 Through September 1984. James D. Seymour. 200p. 1985. 51.95 (*0-87332-320-3*) M E Sharpe.

China Rising: The Meaning of Tiananmen. Lee Feigon. 288p. 1990. 19.95 (*0-929587-30-8*) I R Dee.

China Rose. Marsha Canham. 1991. 19.95 (*0-7278-4169-6*) Severn Hse.

China Rural Statistics, 1988. (China Statistics Ser.). 281p. 1989. text ed. 89.50 (*0-275-93346-6*, C3346, Praeger Pubs) Greenwood.

China Sailor. Alvin J. Bessee & K. J. Besse. LC 93-60730. (Illus.). 128p. (Orig.). 1995. pap. text ed. write for info. (*1-883141-01-X*) Victoria Pubns.

China Scapegoat: The Diplomatic Ordeal of John Carter Vincent. Gary May. 370p. (C). 1982. reprint ed. pap. 13.95 (*0-917974-98-0*) Waveland Pr.

China Sea. Barry Blair. (Illus.). 64p. 1989. pap. 6.95 (*0-944735-10-X*) Malibu Graphics.

China Sea: The American Stake in Its Future. Harold C. Hinton. 40p. 1981. pap. text ed. 19.95 (*0-87855-871-3*) Transaction Pubs.

***China, Search for Community.** fac. ed. Raymond L. Whitehead & Rhea M. Whitehead. LC 82-157730. 96p. 1994. pap. 27.40 (*0-7837-7710-8*, 2047469) Bks Demand.

***China, Seventy Years after the 1911 Hsin-Hai Revolution.** Ed. by Hungdah Chiu & Shao-Chuan Leng. LC 84-7217. 611p. 1984. reprint ed. pap. 174.20 (*0-7837-8572-0*, 2049387) Bks Demand.

China Shadow. Clarissa Ross. 448p. 1985. reprint ed. pap. 3.75 (*0-8439-2237-0*) Dorchester Pub Co.

China Shakes the World. Jack Belden. LC 77-105312. 544p. reprint ed. pap. 155.10 (*0-8357-6054-5*, 2034358) Bks Demand.

China Silk. large type ed. Anne Worboys. 755p. 1993. 21.95 (*0-7505-0457-9*) Ulverscroft.

China since Mao. Charles Bettelheim & Neil Burton. LC 78-15623. 130p. 1978. pap. 3.95 (*0-85345-475-2*) Monthly Rev.

China since Mao. Neill G. Burton & Charles Bettelheim. LC 78-15623. 130p. reprint ed. pap. 37.10 (*0-7837-6985-7*, 2046797) Bks Demand.

***China since the Cultural Revolution: From Totalitarianism to Authoritarianism.** Jie Chen & Peng Deng. LC 94-28006. 144p. 1994. text ed. 49.95 (*0-275-94647-9*, Praeger Pubs) Greenwood.

China since the Gang of Four. Ed. by Bill Brugger. LC 80-10251. 288p. 1980. text ed. 35.00 (*0-312-13323-5*) St Martin.

***China Since Tiananmen: Political, Economic, & Social Conflicts - Documents & Analysis.** Ed. by Lawrence R. Sullivan. 300p. (C). 1995. 60.00 (*1-56324-538-8*, East Gate Bk) M E Sharpe.

***China Since Tiananmen: Political, Economic, & Social Conflicts - Documents & Analysis.** Ed. by Lawrence R. Sullivan. 300p. (C). 1995. pap. text ed. 19.95 (*1-56324-539-6*, East Gate Bk) M E Sharpe.

China since 1978: Reform, Modernisation & Socialism with Chinese Characteristics. Colin Mackerras et al. LC 93-24509. 1994. text ed. 49.95 (*0-312-10252-6*); pap. write for info. (*0-312-10306-9*) St Martin.

China Social Statistics, 1986. Ed. by William T. Liu. (China Statistics Ser.). 294p. 1989. text ed. 95.00 (*0-275-93273-7*, C3273, Praeger Pubs) Greenwood.

China Space Report. Ed. by Wilbur L. Pritchard & James J. Harford. (Illus.). 200p. 25.00 (*0-317-32131-5*) AIAA.

China Spy. George Watt. 1979. pap. 3.95 (*0-88264-027-5*) Living Sacrifice Bks.

China Statistical Abstract, 1988. Ed. by William T. Liu. LC 88-28571. 144p. 1988. text ed. 55.00 (*0-275-93214-1*, C3214, Praeger Pubs) Greenwood.

China Statistical Abstract, 1989. (China Statistics Ser.). 122p. 1989. text ed. 75.00 (*0-275-93436-5*, C3436, Praeger Pubs) Greenwood.

China Statistical Abstract, 1990. (China Statistics Ser.). 128p. 1990. text ed. 75.00 (*0-275-93869-7*, C3869, Praeger Pubs) Greenwood.

China Statistical Handbook, 1987. Rock Creek Research Staff. Ed. by Albert Keidel. 25p. (Orig.). (C). 1987. pap. text ed. 4.50 (*0-943085-02-0*) Rock Creek Res.

China Statistical Yearbook, 1989. (China Statistics Ser.). 840p. 1990. text ed. 195.00 (*0-275-93636-8*, C3636, Praeger Pubs) Greenwood.

China Statistical Yearbook 1990. (China Statistics Ser.). 808p. 1991. text ed. 195.00 (*0-275-94000-4*, C4000, Praeger Pubs) Greenwood.

China Stories. Thomas D. Holmes & Lois M. Holmes. 1994. 11.95 (*0-533-10492-0*) Vantage.

China Struggles for Unity. J. M. Pringle. 1976. lib. bdg. 59.95 (*0-8490-1609-6*) Gordon Pr.

China Study, 1964. 2nd ed. Survey Research Center Staff. LC 75-38492. 1975. write for info. (*0-89138-001-9*) ICPSR.

China Supports the Arab People's Struggle for National Independence: A Selection of Important Documents. Chinese People's Institute of Foreign Affairs Staff. LC 75-38060. reprint ed. 39.50 (*0-404-56916-1*) AMS Pr.

China Syndrome. Burton Wohl. 18.95 (*0-8488-1224-7*) Amereon Ltd.

China, Taiwan, & the Offshore Islands. Thomas E. Stolper. LC 84-22124. 180p. (Orig.). 1985. 62.95 (*0-87332-311-4*) M E Sharpe.

China Takes Off: Technology Transfer & Modernization. E. E. Bauer. LC 85-17984. (Illus.). 260p. 1986. 22.50 (*0-295-96298-4*) U of Wash Pr.

China Tax Guide. 2nd ed. Michael J. Moser & Winston K. Zee. LC 92-29434. 328p. (C). 1993. 79.00 (*0-19-585724-0*) OUP.

China Tea Clippers. George Campbell. 1990. text ed. 27.95 (*0-87742-253-2*) Intl Marine.

China Teacup. Anthony Holcroft. LC 93-6620. (J). 1994. write for info. (*0-383-03682-8*) SRA Schl Grp.

China the Beautiful Cookbook. Kevin Sinclair. LC 86-7300. (Illus.). 256p. 1989. 45.00 (*0-00-215999-6*) Collins SF.

China: The Crisis of Nineteen Eighty-Nine: Origins & Implications, 2 vols., 1. Ed. by Roger Des Forges et al. (Council on International Studies & Programs Special Studies). 447p. 1990. pap. 10.00 (*0-924197-11-0*) SUNYB Coun Intl Studies.

China: The Crisis of Nineteen Eighty-Nine: Origins & Implications, 2 vols., 2. Ed. by Roger Des Forges et al. (Council on International Studies & Programs Special Studies). 447p. 1990. pap. 10.00 (*0-685-74308-X*) SUNYB Coun Intl Studies.

China, the Land & the People: A Human Geography. Leonard H. Buxton. LC 79-2818. (Illus.). 333p. 1983. reprint ed. 31.75 (*0-8305-0000-6*) Hyperion Conn.

China, the Struggle Within. 2nd ed. Sam Marcy et al. 116p. 1972. pap. 4.00 (*0-89567-008-9*) World View Forum.

China, the U. S. S. R., & Eastern Europe: A U. S. Trade Perspective. Ed. by John K. Ryans et al. LC 74-79995. 208p. reprint ed. pap. 59.30 (*0-685-16417-9*, 2027307) Bks Demand.

China, the United Nations, & World Order. Samuel S. Kim. LC 78-51174. (Center for International Studies). 1979. pap. 29.95 (*0-691-10076-4*) Princeton U Pr.

***China, the United Nations, & World Order.** Samuel S. Kim. LC 78-51174. reprint ed. pap. 172.80 (*0-7837-9359-6*, 2060101) Bks Demand.

China, the United States & the Soviet Union: Tripolarity & Policymaking in the Cold War. Ed. by Robert S. Ross. (Studies on Contemporary China). 224p. (C). 1993. text ed. 57.95 (*1-56324-253-2*, East Gate Bk); pap. text ed. 20.95 (*1-56324-254-0*, East Gate Bk) M E Sharpe.

China Theatre in World War II, 1939-1945. B. Sapozhnikov. 256p. (C). 1985. 40.00 (*0-685-31475-8*) St Mut.

China This Century. Ed. by Rafe De Crespigny. (Illus.). 368p. 1992. pap. 19.95 (*0-19-585164-1*) OUP.

China Through the Ages: History of a Civilization. Franz Michael. 278p. (C). 1986. pap. text ed. 21.50 (*0-86531-726-7*) Westview.

China Through Western Eyes: The Nineteenth Century: A Reader in History. Ed. by J. A. Roberts. 125p. 1991. text ed. 16.00 (*0-86299-828-X*) A Sutton Pub.

China to Me: A Partial Autobiography. Emily Hahn. LC 74-23432. (China in the 20th Century Ser.). 429p. 1975. reprint ed. lib. bdg. 45.00 (*0-306-70695-4*) Da Capo.

China to 1850: A Short History. Charles O. Hucker. LC 77-79998. xiv, 162p. 1978. 22.50 (*0-8047-0957-2*); pap. 8.95 (*0-8047-0958-0*) Stanford U Pr.

China Today. Ed. by Fran Ringold. 132p. 1986. pap. 5.50 (*0-317-60731-6*) Art & Human Council Tulsa.

China Today. Steve Stern. write for info. (*0-670-81388-5*) Viking Penguin.

***China Today: How Population Control, Human Rights, Government Repression, Hong Kong, & Democratic Reform Affect Life in China...& Will Shape World Events into the New Century.** Donald Shanor & constance Shanor. LC 94-46637. 259p. 1995. 22.95 (*0-312-11759-0*) St Martin.

China Trade. S. J. Rozan. 256p. 1994. 20.95 (*0-312-11254-8*) St Martin.

China Trade: A Guide to Doing Business with the People's Republic of China. Herbert B. Azif. LC 80-84105. (Illus.). 131p. (Orig.). 1981. pap. 17.50 (*0-9605190-0-9*) China Res.

China Trade & Price Statistics in 1988. (China Statistics Ser.). 229p. 1989. text ed. 79.50 (*0-275-93342-3*, C3342, Praeger Pubs) Greenwood.

China Trade & Price Statistics, 1989. State Statistical Bureau of the People's Republic of China Staff. (China Statistics Ser.). 200p. 1990. text ed. 115.00 (*0-275-93846-8*, C3846, Praeger Pubs) Greenwood.

***China Trade Handbook.** (Illus.). 600p. (Orig.). 1994. pap. 225.00 (*1-57205-777-7*) Rector Pr.

***China Trade Handbook.** 450p. (Orig.). 1995. pap. 750.00 (*0-7605-1866-1*) Rector Pr.

***China Trade Handbook.** (Illus.). 600p. (Orig.). 1994. pap. 225.00 (*0-7605-0672-8*) Rector Pr.

***China Trading Handbook.** (Illus.). 600p. (Orig.). 1994. pap. 195.00 (*1-57205-759-9*) Rector Pr.

***China Transportation Atlas.** (Illus.). 100p. (Orig.). (CHI.). 1994. pap. 45.00 (*0-7605-0615-9*) Rector Pr.

China Turned On: Television, Reform & Resistance. James Lull. (Illus.). 208p. 1991. 49.95 (*0-415-05215-7*, A6221); pap. 16.95 (*0-415-05216-5*, A6225) Routledge.

China Turned Rightside Up: Revolutionary Legitimacy in the Peasant World. Ralph Thaxton. LC 82-40165. (Illus.). 290p. 1983. text ed. 40.00 (*0-300-02707-9*) Yale U Pr.

China Turning Inward: Intellectual-Political Changes in the Early Twelfth Century, Vol. 132. James T. Liu. LC 80-3579. (East Asian Monographs). 225p. 1989. 28.00 (*0-674-11755-7*) HUP.

China under Communism. Michael G. Kort. LC 94-8312. (Illus.). 176p. (YA). (gr. 7 up). 1995. lib. bdg. 16.90 (*1-56294-450-9*) Millbrook Pr.

China under Deng. Kwan Ha Yim. 336p. (C). 1990. 27.95 (*0-8160-2315-8*) Facts on File.

China Under Deng Xiaoping: Political & Economic Reform. David Wen-Wei Chang. LC 87-34906. 328p. 1991. pap. 16.95 (*0-312-04811-4*) St Martin.

China under Jurchen Rule: Essays on Chin Intellectual & Cultural History. Ed. by Hoyt C. Tillman & Stephen H. West. LC 94-4812. (SUNY Series in Chinese Philosophy & Culture). (Illus.). 384p. 1995. text ed. 59.50x (*0-7914-2273-9*); pap. text ed. 19.95x (*0-7914-2274-7*) State U NY Pr.

China under Mongol Rule. Herbert Franke. LC 94-616. (Collected Studies Ser.). 1994. 89.95 (*0-86078-399-5*, Pub. by Variorum UK) Ashgate Pub Co.

China under Mongol Rule. Ed. by John D. Langlois, Jr. LC 80-8559. (Illus.). 515p. reprint ed. pap. 146.80 (*0-7837-6497-9*, 2046587) Bks Demand.

China under Reform. Lowell Dittmer. (Politics in Asia & the Pacific, Interdisciplinary Perspectives Ser.). 250p. (C). 1994. text ed. 63.00 (*0-8133-1119-5*); pap. text ed. 19.95 (*0-8133-1120-9*) Westview.

China under the Empress Dowager. J. O. Bland. 1972. lib. bdg. 250.00 (*0-87968-485-2*) Krishna Pr.

China under Threat: The Politics of Strategy & Diplomacy. Melvin Gurtov & Byong-Moo Hwang. LC 80-7990. 352p. 1981. text ed. 52.00x (*0-8018-2397-8*) Johns Hopkins.

China Urban Statistics, Nineteen Eighty-Six. 2nd ed. State Statistical Bureau Staff, People's Republic of China. 492p. 1987. 80.00 (*0-582-99756-9*, Pub. by Longman Grp UK) Gale.

China Urban Statistics 1988. 496p. 1990. text ed. 110.00 (*0-275-93514-0*, C3514, Praeger Pubs) Greenwood.

***China Voyage: Across the Pacific by Bamboo Raft.** Tim Severin. 1995. 24.00 (*0-201-48394-7*) Addison-Wesley.

China Wakes: The Struggle for the Soul of a Rising Power. Nicholas D. Kristof. LC 94-10609. 1994. 25.00 (*0-8129-2252-2*, Times Bks) Random.

China War Medal, Nineteen Hundred, to the Royal Navy & the Royal Marines. Ed. by J. W. Wilson. 164p. (C). 1987. 112.00 (*0-317-90451-5*, Pub. by Picton UK) St Mut.

C

An Asterisk (*) at the beginning of an entry indicates that the title is appearing in BIP for the first time.

China Watch. John K. Fairbank. LC 86-33570. 232p. 1987. text ed. 29.95 (*0-674-11765-4*) HUP.

China White. Peter Maas. 1994. 23.00 (*0-671-69417-0*) S&S Trade.

***China White.** Peter Maas. 320p. 1995. pap. 5.99 (*0-7860-0204-2*) Windsor NY.

***China White.** large type ed. Peter Maas. LC 95-5406. (Large Print Book Ser.). 1995. pap. write for info. (*1-56895-096-9*) Wheeler Pub.

China White Paper: August 1949. U. S. Department of State Staff. LC 67-26650. xlix, 1086p. 1967. reprint ed. 89.50 (*0-8047-0607-7*) Stanford U Pr.

China White Paper: August 1949, 2 vols., Set. U. S. Department of State Staff. LC 67-26650. xlix, 1086p. 1967. reprint ed. pap. 25.00 (*0-8047-0608-5*) Stanford U Pr.

China Without Mao: The Search for a New Order. 2nd ed. Immanuel C. Hsu. (Illus.). 352p. 1990. pap. 11.95 (*0-19-506056-3*) OUP.

China Year. Emily C. Neville. LC 90-39899. 256p. (J). (gr. 5-9). 1991. lib. bdg. 15.89 (*0-06-024384-8*) HarpC Child Bks.

China Year Book, 20 vols. Ed. by H. G. Woodhead. 1977. 3,500.00 (*0-8490-1610-X*) Gordon Pr.

***China 1994: Government, Economy & Business.** (Illus.). 225p. (Orig.). 1994. pap. 595.00 (*0-7605-0013-4*) Rector Pr.

Chinaberry Beads. Elaine C. Crump. LC 78-21581. (Illus.). (ENG & FRE.). pap. 7.95 (*0-88289-228-2*) Pelican.

***Chinaberry Tree.** Jessie R. Fauset. LC 94-42138. (African American Women Writers, 1910-1940, Ser.). 1995. write for info. (*0-8161-1627-X*) G K Hall.

***Chinaberry Tree.** Patsy B. O'Leary. LC 95-1666. (J). 1995. write for info. (*0-395-70557-6*) Ticknor & Flds Bks Yng Read.

Chinaberry Tree. Jessie R. Fauset. LC 70-95405. reprint ed. 29.50 (*0-404-00256-0*) AMS Pr.

Chinaberry Tree: A Novel of American Life. Jessie R. Fauset. 34.95 (*0-405-18503-0*) Ayer.

Chinaberry Tree: A Novel of American Life. Jessie R. Fauset. LC 74-89033. 341p. 1969. reprint ed. text ed. 35.00 (*0-8371-1919-7*, FAC&, Negro U Pr) Greenwood.

Chinaberry Tree & Selected Writings. Jessie R. Fauset. (Northeastern Library of Black Literature). 384p. 1994. reprint ed. pap. text ed. 13.95 (*1-55553-207-1*) NE U Pr.

Chinaman. Stephen Leather. Ed. by Bill Grose. 368p. 1993. mass mkt. 5.99 (*0-671-74302-3*) PB.

Chinaman As We See Him & Fifty Years of Work for Him. Ira M. Condit. Ed. by Roger Daniels. LC 78-54839. (Asian Experience in North America Ser.). (Illus.). 1979. reprint ed. lib. bdg. 23.95 (*0-405-11305-6*) Ayer.

Chinaman Pacific & Frisco R. R. Co. Frank Chin. LC 88-30326. 170p. (Orig.). 1988. pap. 10.95 (*0-918273-44-7*) Coffee Hse.

Chinaman's Chance. Ross Thomas. 352p. 1988. mass mkt. 4.99 (*0-445-40725-5*, Mysterious Paperbk) Warner Bks.

China's Agricultural Modernization: The Socialist Mechanization Scheme. On Kit Tam. LC 84-29333. 241p. 1985. 47.50 (*0-7099-2478-X*, Pub. by Croom Helm UK) Routledge Chapman & Hall.

China's Allocation of Fixed Capital Investment, 1952-1957. Chu-yuan Cheng. (Michigan Monographs in Chinese Studies: No. 17). 115p. 1974. pap. 1.50 (*0-89264-017-0*) Ctr Chinese Studies.

China's Art of Revolution: The Mobilization of Discontent, 1927-1928. Marcia R. Ristaino. LC 87-470. xv, 274p. (C). 1987. 50.50 (*0-8223-0718-9*) Duke.

China's Automobile Industry: Policies, Problems, & Prospects. Eric Harwit. LC 94-27011. (Studies on Contemporary China). (Illus.). 224p. (C). 1994. text ed. 55.00 (*1-56324-441-1*, East Gate Bk); pap. text ed. 22.50 (*1-56324-442-X*, East Gate Bk) M E Sharpe.

China's Bitter Victory: The War with Japan, 1937-1945. Ed. by James C. Hsiung & Steven I. Levine. LC 91-6961. 360p. 1992. 49.95 (*0-87332-708-X*) M E Sharpe.

China's Bitter Victory: The War with Japan, 1937-1945. Ed. by James C. Hsiung & Steven I. Levine. LC 91-6961. 360p. 1993. pap. text ed. 20.95 (*1-56324-246-X*) M E Sharpe.

China's Bloody Century: Genocide & Mass Murder since 1900. R. J. Rummel. 196p. (C). 1991. 39.95 (*0-88738-417-X*) Transaction Pubs.

China's Boundary Treaties & Frontier Disputes. Luke T. Chang. LC 82-3483. 443p. 1982. 45.00 (*0-379-20733-8*) Oceana.

***China's Brain Drain to the United States: Views of Overseas Chinese Students & Scholars in the 1990s.** David Zweig & Changgui Chen. LC 95-8737. (China Research Monographs: Vol. 47). 1995. write for info. (*1-55729-049-0*) IEAS.

China's Bravest Girl: The Legend of Hua Mu Lan. Charlie Chin. LC 93-15255. (Illus.). 32p. (YA). (gr. 6-12). 1993. 13.95 (*0-89239-120-0*) Childrens Book Pr.

China's Buried Kingdoms. Ed. by Dale Brown. LC 93-15068. (Lost Civilizations Ser.). (Illus.). 168p. 1993. 18.95 (*0-8094-9891-X*); lib. bdg. 25.93 (*0-8094-9892-8*) Time-Life.

China's Capital Market: A Systematic Introduction to China's Stock & Bond Markets. Hu Yebi. 166p. (Orig.). 1993. pap. 42.50 (*962-201-564-6*, Pub. by Chinese Univ HK) Coronet Bks.

China's Changing Population. Judith Banister. LC 82-60105. xviii, 488p. 1987. 65.00 (*0-8047-1155-0*); pap. 18.95 (*0-8047-1887-3*) Stanford U Pr.

China's Changing Relations with the Middle East. John Calabrese. 224p. 1991. text ed. 49.00 (*0-86187-138-3*, Pub. by Pinter Pubs UK) St Martin.

China's Civil & Commercial Law. Henry R. Zhang. 540p. 1988. 90.00 (*0-88063-733-1*) Butterworth Legal Pubs.

China's Coastal Cities: Catalysts for Modernization. Yue-man Yeung. Ed. by Xu-wei Hu. LC 91-28822. 352p. (C). 1992. text ed. 38.00 (*0-8248-1373-1*) UH Pr.

***China's Company Law.** Guiguo Wang & Roman Tomasic. 216p. 1994. pap. write for info. (*0-409-99732-3*) Butterworth Legal Pubs.

China's Continuous Revolution: The Postliberation Epoch, 1949-1981. Lowell Dittmer. 1987. pap. 15.00 (*0-520-06599-9*) U CA Pr.

***China's Conventional Military Studies: An Assessment.** John Caldwell. (CSIS Report Ser.). 29p. (C). 1994. pap. 14.95 (*0-89206-257-6*) CSI Studies.

China's Crisis: Dilemmas of Reform & Prospects for Democracy. Andrew J. Nathan. (Studies of the East Asian Institute). 256p. 1990. text ed. 26.00 (*0-231-07284-8*) Col U Pr.

China's Crisis: Dilemmas of Reform & Prospects for Democracy. Andrew J. Nathan. 1990. pap. 12.95 (*0-231-07285-6*) Col U Pr.

China's Crisis & Revolution Through American Lenses, 1944-1949. Peng Deng. LC 93-36355. (C). Date not set. write for info. (*0-8191-9313-5*) U Pr of Amer.

China's Crisis, China's Hope. Liu Binyan. (Interpretations of Asia Ser.). 192p. 1990. text ed. 25.00 (*0-674-11882-0*) HUP.

China's Cultural Development: From the Earliest Dynasties to the Present Day. Joseph D. Lowe. LC 90-91679. (Illus.). xxiv, 565p. 1994. text ed. 90.00 (*0-930325-15-X*) Lowe Pub.

China's Cultural Heritage: The Qing Dynasty, 1644-1912. 2nd ed. Richard J. Smith. LC 94-948. (C). 1994. text ed. 59.95 (*0-8133-1346-5*); pap. text ed. 21.50 (*0-8133-1347-3*) Westview.

China's Cultural Values. Benjamin Schwartz. LC 85-47931. (Arizona State University Center for Asian Studies Monograph Ser.: No. 18). 43p. (Orig.). 1985. pap. text ed. 6.00 (*0-939252-14-7*) ASU Ctr Asian.

China's Currency Reform, 1941 see History of China's Internal Loan Issues: Shanghai, 1934

China's Customs Revenue since the Revolution of 1911. rev. ed. Stanley F. Wright. LC 75-38095. (China Classic & Contemporary Works in Reprint Ser.). reprint ed. 115.00 (*0-404-56970-6*) AMS Pr.

China's Daughter. Fern Adams. 134p. (Orig.). (YA). (gr. 7-12). 1991. pap. 4.95 (*0-8474-6623-X*) Back to Bible.

China's Defense Modernisation & Military Leadership. Lee Ngok. (Illus.). 400p. 1990. 47.00 (*0-08-033046-0*, Pergamon Pr) Elsevier.

China's Destiny. Chiang Kai-Shek. LC 76-24849. 260p. 1976. reprint ed. lib. bdg. 32.50 (*0-306-70821-3*) Da Capo.

China's Destiny. Chiang Kai-Shek. Tr. by Wang Chung-Hui. LC 84-22503. xii, 260p. 1985. reprint ed. text ed. 59.75 (*0-313-24676-9*, CHCD, Greenwood Pr) Greenwood.

China's Development Experience in Comparative Perspective: A Social Science Research Council Study. Ed. by Robert Dernberger. LC 80-418. (East Asian Monographs: No. 93). 358p. 1980. 42.50 (*0-674-11890-1*) HUP.

Chinas, Dolls for Study & Admiration. Mona M. Borger. LC 83-91074. (Illus.). 160p. 1983. 21.95 (*0-9611838-0-2*) Borger Pubns.

***China's Domestic Economy in Regional Context.** Ding Jingping. (Significant Issues Ser.). (C). 1995. pap. 14.95 (*0-89206-318-1*) CSI Studies.

China's Economic Aid. Wolfgang Bartke. LC 74-78315. 206p. 1975. 30.00 (*0-8419-0179-1*) Holmes & Meier.

***China's Economic & Financial Future & Implications for East Asia.** Ting Ching-Ping. LC 95-2138. (Significant Issues Series: Vol. 17, No. 1). 1995. write for info. (*0-614-04411-1*) CSI Studies.

China's Economic Development: The Interplay of Scarcity & Ideology. Alexander Eckstein. LC 74-25951. (Studies on China). (Illus.). 1975. pap. 24.95 (*0-472-08310-4*) U of Mich Pr.

China's Economic Dilemmas in the 1990s: The Problems of Reforms, Modernization, & Interdependence. Joint Economic Committee Congress of the United States. LC 92-29068. 968p. 1992. reprint ed. text ed. 88.95 (*1-56324-158-7*); reprint ed. pap. text ed. 33.95 (*1-56324-159-5*) M E Sharpe.

China's Economic Evolution. Ed. by Piet Frantzen. 192p. 1994. pap. 25.00 (*90-5487-055-9*, Pub. by VUB Univ Pr BE) Paul & Co Pubs.

China's Economic Opening to the Outside World: The Politics of Empowerment. Jonathan R. Woetzel. LC 88-27577. 201p. 1989. text ed. 55.00 (*0-275-93163-3*, C3163, Praeger Pubs) Greenwood.

China's Economic Reform. Ed. by Walter Galenson. 296p. (C). 1993. text ed. 39.50x (*0-472-10473-X*) U of Mich Pr.

China's Economic Reform. Shangquan Gao. LC 93-38043. (Studies on the Chinese Economy). 1994. 69.95 (*0-312-12034-6*) St Martin.

China's Economic Reform: Administering the Introduction of the Market Mechanism. Ed. by George O. Totten & Shulian Zhou. 258p. (C). 1993. pap. text ed. 30.85 (*0-8133-8701-9*) Westview.

China's Economic Reforms. Ed. by Lin Wei & Arnold Chao. LC 82-60262. 352p. (CHI.). 1982. 47.95x (*0-8122-7857-7*) U of Pa Pr.

China's Economic System. Audrey G. Donnithorne. LC 67-23967. 592p. reprint ed. pap. 168.80 (*0-317-29979-4*, 2051762) Bks Demand.

China's Economy & the Maoist Strategy. John G. Gurley. LC 76-26314. 325p. 1976. 15.00 (*0-85345-395-0*) Monthly Rev.

China's Economy in Global Perspective. A. Doak Barnett. LC 81-1193. 752p. 1981. 39.95 (*0-8157-0826-2*); pap. 18.95 (*0-8157-0825-4*) Brookings.

China's Education & the Industrialized World: Studies in Cultural Transfer. Ed. by Ruth Hayhoe & Marianne Bastid. LC 87-4744. 382p. 1987. 46.95 (*0-87332-425-0*); pap. text ed. 20.95 (*0-87332-428-5*) M E Sharpe.

China's Education Reform in the 1980s: Policies, Issues, & Historical Perspectives, No. 36. Suzanne Pepper. (China Research Monographs). 195p. (Orig.). 1990. pap. 12.00 (*1-55729-020-2*) IEAS.

China's Electric Power Development. 1989. 210.00 (*0-317-99911-7*) Natl Coun US-China.

China's Entrance into the Family of Nations: The Diplomatic Phase, 1858-1880. Immanuel C. Hshu. LC 60-5738. (Harvard East Asian Studies: No. 5). 310p. reprint ed. pap. 88.40 (*0-7837-4111-1*, 2057934) Bks Demand.

China's Entry into the World Economy: Implicatioms for Northeast Asia & the U. S. Nicholas R. Lardy. (Asian Agenda Report Ser.: No. 11). (Illus.). 76p. (Orig.). (C). 1987. lib. bdg. 27.00 (*0-8191-6371-6*, The Asia Society); pap. text ed. 10.50 (*0-8191-6372-4*, The Asia Society) U Pr of Amer.

China's Environmental Crisis: An Inquiry into the Limits of National Development. Vaclav Smil. LC 91-20037. 280p. (C). 1993. 51.95 (*0-87332-819-1*); pap. text ed. 20.95 (*1-56324-041-6*) M E Sharpe.

China's Establishment Intellectuals. Carol L. Hamrin & Timothy Cheek. LC 85-22148. 296p. 1986. pap. text ed. 23.95 (*0-87332-367-X*) M E Sharpe.

China's Examination Hell: The Civil Service Examinations of Imperial China. Ichisada Miyazaki. Tr. by Conrad Schirokauer. LC 80-54223. Orig. Title: Kakyo-Chugoku No Shikenjigoku. 142p. 1981. reprint ed. pap. 12.00 (*0-300-02639-0*, Y-398) Yale U Pr.

China's Experience in Economic Development & Reforms. 166p. 19.00 (*92-1-119459-8*) UN.

China's External Trade since the Reforms. Ed. by Bibek Debroy. (C). 1991. 48.00 (*81-7169-107-2*, Pub. by Commonwealth II) S Asia.

China's Far West: Four Decades of Change. A. Doak Barnett. LC 93-4194. 688p. 1993. text ed. 63.00 (*0-8133-1773-8*) Westview.

China's Far West: Four Decades of Change. A. Doak Barnett. LC 93-4194. 688p. (C). 1994. pap. text ed. 24.95 (*0-8133-1774-6*) Westview.

China's Finance & Trade: A Policy Reader. Ed. by Gordon Bennett. LC 77-99080. 264p. reprint ed. pap. 75.30 (*0-8357-2626-6*, 2040114) Bks Demand.

China's First Hundred: Educational Mission Students in the United States, 1872-1881. Thomas E. LaFargue. LC 87-10404. (Washington State University Press Art Ser.). (Illus.). 184p. 1987. reprint ed. pap. 11.25 (*0-87422-035-1*) Wash St U Pr.

China's Folk Fine Arts of Shaanxi Province. Ed. by Wang Yaoan. Tr. by Zhang Long. (Illus.). 96p. (CHI & ENG.). 1992. 39.00 (*1-880132-07-9*) Sci Pr NY.

***China's Foreign Debt: Catalogue of Chinese Bonds.** (Illus.). 210p. (Orig.). 1994. pap. 145.00 (*0-7605-0865-8*) Rector Pr.

China's Foreign Economic Relations & Trade 1993-94. Ed. by Lewis B. Sckolnick. 300p. (Orig.). 1994. pap. 235.00 (*1-57205-001-2*) Rector Pr.

China's Foreign Policy in the Arab World 1955-75: Three Case Studies. Hashim S. Behbehani. (Illus.). 425p. 1981. pap. text ed. 29.95 (*0-7103-0125-1*, Pub. by Kegan Paul Intl UK) Routledge Chapman & Hall.

China's Foreign Policy Toward the Third World. Louise C. Harris. LC 84-23744. (Washington Papers: No. 112). 170p. 1985. pap. text ed. 9.95 (*0-275-91649-9*, B1649, Praeger Pubs) Greenwood.

China's Foreign Relations Conducted by the Warlords: 1916-1928. Joseph D. Lowe. LC 88-91012. (Illus.). xii, 52p. 1991. 15.00 (*0-930325-05-2*) Lowe Pub.

China's Foreign Relations in the Nineteen Eighties. Harry Harding. LC 84-3677. 256p. 1984. 30.00 (*0-300-03207-2*) Yale U Pr.

China's Foreign Relations in the Nineteen Eighties. Harry Harding. LC 84-3677. 256p. 1986. pap. 14.00 (*0-300-03628-0*, Y-566) Yale U Pr.

China's Foreign Relations, Nineteen Seventeen to Nineteen Thirty-One. Robert T. Pollard. LC 70-111745. (American Imperialism: Viewpoints of United States Foreign Policy, 1898-1941 Ser.). 1970. reprint ed. 23.95 (*0-405-02046-5*) Ayer.

China's Foreign Trade & Comparative Advantage: Prospects, Problems, & Policy Implications. Alexander J. Yeats. (Discussion Paper Ser.: No. 141). 101p. 1991. 7.95 (*0-8213-1960-4*, 11960) World Bank.

China's Foreign Trade Reforms: Impact on Growth & Stability. John C. Hsu. (Illus.). (C). 1990. 69.95 (*0-521-37197-X*) Cambridge U Pr.

China's Foreign Trade Statistics, 1864-1949. Liang-Lin Hsiao. LC 74-78789. (East Asian Monographs: No. 56). 285p. 1974. 26.00 (*0-674-11960-6*) HUP.

China's Forty Millions. June Dreyer. (East Asian Monographs: No. 87). 343p. 1976. 24.95 (*0-674-11964-9*) HUP.

China's Gentry: Essays in Rural-Urban Relations with Six Life-Histories of Chinese Gentry Families. Ed. by Hsiao-Tung Fei et al. LC 53-11440. (Midway Reprint Ser.). 296p. 1980. reprint ed. pap. text ed. 16.95 (*0-226-23957-8*) U Ch Pr.

China's Gifts to the West. Derk Bodde. LC 43-3077. (Asiatic Studies in American Education: No. 1). 47p. reprint ed. pap. 25.00 (*0-317-10030-0*, 2014507) Bks Demand.

China's Global Role: An Analysis of Peking's National Power Capabilities in the Context of an Evolving International System. John F. Copper. (Publication Ser.: No. 226). 181p. 1980. pap. 3.58 (*0-8179-7262-5*) Hoover Inst Pr.

China's Green Revolution. Benedict Stavis. LC 76-374877. (Cornell East Asia Ser.: No. 2). 58p. 1974. 7.00 (*0-939657-02-3*) Cornell East Asia Pgm.

China's Hand-Painted Marbles of the Late 19th Century. Jeff Carskadden & Richard Gartley. (Illus.). 100p. (Orig.). 1990. pap. 20.00 (*0-9626931-0-3*) Muskingum Val Arch.

China's Imperial Past: An Introduction to Chinese History & Culture. Charles O. Hucker. LC 74-25929. (Illus.). xviii, 474p. 1975. 55.00 (*0-8047-0887-8*); student ed, ring bd. 22.50 (*0-8047-0979-3*) Stanford U Pr.

***China's Imperial Past: An Introduction to Chinese History & Culture.** Charles O. Hucker. 1994. pap. 18.95 (*0-8047-2353-2*) Stanford U Pr.

China's Industrial Reform. Ed. by Gene Tidrick & Chen Jiyuan. (World Bank Publication Ser.). 392p. 1987. 35.00 (*0-19-520592-8*) OUP.

China's Inner Asian Frontier: Photographs of the Wulsin Expedition to Northwest China in 1923. Ed. by Mary E. Alonso. (Illus.). 108p. 1981. pap. 15.00 (*0-685-66764-2*) Pacific Asia.

China's Intellectuals: Advise & Dissent. Merle R. Goldman. LC 81-2945. 282p. (C). 1981. 29.00 (*0-674-11970-3*) HUP.

China's Intellectuals: Advise & Dissent. Merle R. Goldman. LC 81-2945. 282p. 1988. reprint ed. pap. 14.50 (*0-674-11971-1*) HUP.

China's Investment Laws: New Directions. Guiguo Wang. 260p. 1988. boxed 75.00 (*0-88063-734-X*) Michie Butterworth.

China's Island Frontier: Studies in the Historical Geography of Taiwan. Ed. by Ronald G. Knapp. LC 80-18578. 312p. 1980. text ed. 20.00 (*0-8248-0705-7*) UH Pr.

China's Just World: The Morality of Chinese Foreign Policy. Chih-yu Shih. LC 92-1774. 246p. 1993. lib. bdg. 40.00 (*1-55587-350-2*) Lynne Rienner.

***China's Legal Awakening: Legal Theory & Criminal Justice in Deng's Era.** Carlos Lo. 400p. 1995. pap. 67.50 (*962-209-342-6*, Pub. by Hong Kong Univ Pr HK) Coronet Bks.

China's Livestock & Related Agriculture. J. R. Simpson et al. 500p. 1994. 72.00x (*0-85198-891-1*) CAB Intl.

***China's Local Councils in the Age of Constitutional Reform, 1898-1911.** Roger R. Thompson. LC 94-49385. (Harvard East Asian Monographs: No. 161). 270p. (C). 1995. text ed. 38.00 (*0-674-11973-8*) HUP.

China's Long March: 6000 Miles of Danger. Jean Fritz. LC 87-31171. (Illus.). 128p. (J). (gr. 7 up). 1988. 15.95 (*0-399-21512-3*, Putnam) Putnam Pub Group.

***China's Long March to an Open Economy.** OECD Staff. 120p. (Orig.). 1994. pap. 19.00x (*92-64-14290-8*) OECD.

C

China's Media, Media's China. Chin-Chuan Lee. LC 94-949. (C). 1994. text ed. 59.95 (*0-8133-8800-7*) Westview.

China's Metals & Minerals. 1988. 200.00 (*0-317-99910-9*) Natl Coun US-China.

China's Military. Ed. by Richard H. Yang. (C). 1993. pap. text ed. 49.85 (*0-8133-8787-6*) Westview.

China's Military: The PLA in 1990-1991. Ed. by Richard H. Yang. 219p. (C). 1991. pap. text ed. 53.50 (*0-8133-8385-4*) Westview.

China's Military Modernization: International Implications. Larry M. Wortzel. LC 87-23657. (Contributions in Military Studies: No. 72). 224p. 1988. text ed. 55.00 (*0-313-25626-8*, WZC/, Greenwood Pr) Greenwood.

China's Millions: The Revolutionary Struggles from 1927 to 1935. Anna L. Strong. 1977. 23.95 (*0-8369-7170-1*, 8002) Ayer.

China's Minorities: Integration & Modernization in the Twentieth Century. Colin Mackerras. LC 93-43882. (Illus.). 364p. (C). 1994. 79.00 (*0-19-585988-X*) OUP.

China's Modern Economy. Raymond O. Farrish & James C. Hsiao. 256p. 1986. 29.95 (*0-03-063762-7*, Praeger Pubs); pap. text ed. 12.95 (*0-03-063763-5*, Praeger Pubs) Greenwood.

China's Modern Economy in Historical Perspective. Ed. by Dwight H. Perkins. LC 74-82779. 360p. 1975. 45.00 (*0-8047-0871-1*) Stanford U Pr.

China's Modernisation: Westernisation & Acculturation. Ed. by Kurt W. Radtke & Tony Saich. 202p. (Orig.). 1993. pap. 57.50 (*3-515-06406-0*) Coronet Bks.

***China's Motor: A Thousand Years of Petty Capitalism.** Hill Gates. (Illus.). 368p. 1996. 35.00 (*0-8014-3143-3*) Cornell U Pr.

China's Nation-Building Effort, 1927-1937: The Financial & Economic Record. Arthur N. Young. LC 70-123350. (Publication Ser.: No. 104). (Illus.). 553p. 1971. 22.50 (*0-8179-6041-4*) Hoover Inst Pr.

China's Nature Reserves. Li Wenhua & Xianying Zhao. (Illus.). 191p. 1989. pap. 12.95 (*0-8351-2108-9*) China Bks.

***China's New Art, Post-1989.** Valerie C. Doran. (Illus.). 348p. 1994. 135.00 (*962-7376-02-7*) U of Wash Pr.

China's New Constitution & International Problems. Min-Chi'En T. Tyau. LC 76-55090. (Studies in Chinese Government & Law). 286p. 1976. reprint ed. text ed. 55.00 (*0-313-27021-X*, U7021, Greenwood Pr) Greenwood.

China's New Creative Age. Hewlett Johnson. LC 72-11477. (Illus.). 192p. 1973. reprint ed. text ed. 35.00 (*0-8371-6671-3*, JOCN, Greenwood Pr) Greenwood.

China's New Development Strategy. Ed. by J. Gray & G. White. LC 81-68984. 1982. text ed. 85.00 (*0-12-296840-9*) Acad Pr.

***China's New Political Economy: The Giant Awakes.** Susumu Yabuki. Tr. by Stephen M. Harner. LC 94-28436. Orig. Title: Zusetsu Chugoku no Keizai. (C). 1994. text ed. 69.00 (*0-8133-2254-5*); pap. text ed. 23.95 (*0-8133-2255-3*) Westview.

An Asterisk (*) at the beginning of an entry indicates that the title is appearing in BIP for the first time.

China's New Social Fabric. Ed. by Godwin C. Chu & Francis L. Hsu. 1983. pap. 22.50 (*0-7103-0050-6*, 00506, Pub. by Kegan Paul Intl UK) Routledge Chapman & Hall.

China's Only Hope: An Appeal by Her Greatest Viceroy with the Sanction of the Present Emperor, Kwang Su. Chih-Tung Chang. LC 74-10099. (China Studies: from Confucius to Mao Ser.). (Illus.). 151p. 1975. reprint ed. 17.60 (*0-88355-164-0*) Hyperion Conn.

China's "Opening" to the Outside World: The Experiment with Foreign Capitalism. Robert Kleinberg. (Special Studies on China). 277p. (C). 1990. pap. text ed. 23.50 (*0-8133-8089-8*) Westview.

China's Own Critics. Shih Hu & Yu-T'Ang Lin. LC 79-2829. 166p. 1986. reprint ed. 22.00 (*0-8305-0006-5*) Hyperion Conn.

China's Participation in the IMF, the World Bank, & the GATT: Toward a Global Economic Order. Harold K. Jacobson & Micheal Oksenberg. LC 90-10727. 226p. 1990. text ed. 39.50 (*0-472-10177-3*) U of Mich Pr.

China's Pastoral Region: Sheep & Wool, Minority Nationalities, Rangeland Degradation & Sustainable Development. J. W. Longworth & G. J. Williamson. 370p. 1994. text ed. 85.50 (*0-85198-890-3*) CAB Intl.

China's Path to Modernization: A Historical Review from 1800 to the Present. 2nd ed. Ranbir Vohra. 336p. (C). 1991. pap. text ed. write for info. (*0-13-131525-0*) P-H.

China's Peasants: The Anthropology of a Revolution. Sulamith H. Potter & Jack M. Potter. (Illus.). (C). 1990. 74.95 (*0-521-35521-4*); pap. 17.95 (*0-521-35787-X*) Cambridge U Pr.

China's Picasso, Ch'i Pai-Shih: His Life & Works. Charles Chu. 1967. 7.95 (*0-88710-010-4*); audio write for info. (*0-88710-011-2*) Yale Far Eastern Pubns.

China's Policy in Africa, Nineteen Fifty-Eight to Nineteen Seventy-One. Alaba Ogunsanwo. LC 72-89810. (International Studies). 329p. reprint ed. pap. 93.80 (*0-317-27987-4*, 2025593) Bks Demand.

China's Policy Towards Territorial Disputes: The Case of the South China Seas. Chi Kin Lo. 256p. 1989. 57.50 (*0-415-00927-8*, A3431) Routledge.

China's Political Reforms: An Interim Report. Benedict Stavis. LC 87-7184. 176p. 1988. text ed. 45.00 (*0-275-92905-1*, C2905, Praeger Pubs) Greenwood.

China's Politics in Perspective. Harold S. Quigley. LC 72-14000. (Illus.). 266p. 1973. reprint ed. text ed. 67.50 (*0-8371-6745-0*, QUCP, Greenwood Pr) Greenwood.

China's Practice in the Law of the Sea. Jeanette Greenfield. (Oxford Monographs in International Law). (Illus.). 352p. 1992. 89.00 (*0-19-825618-3*) OUP.

China's Practice of International Law: Some Case Studies. Ed. by Jerome A. Cohen. LC 72-80656. (Studies in East Asian Law: No. 6). (Illus.). 429p. 1972. 40.00 (*0-674-11975-4*) HUP.

China's Provincial Statistics, 1949-1989. Ed. by Tien-tung Hsueh et al. LC 93-14244. 597p. (C). 1993. pap. text ed. 89.50 (*0-8133-8732-9*) Westview.

China's Quest for National Identity. Ed. by Lowell Dittmer & Samuel S. Kim. LC 92-27284. 320p. 1993. 42.50 (*0-8014-2785-1*); pap. 16.95 (*0-8014-8064-7*) Cornell U Pr.

China's Quiet Revolution: New Interactions Between State & Society. Ed. by David S. Goodman & Beverley Hooper. LC 93-26983. 290p. 1994. text ed. 49.95 (*0-312-10251-8*) St Martin.

China's Red Army Marches. Agnes Smedley. LC 75-39035. (China Studies). (Illus.). xxi, 311p. 1977. reprint ed. lib. bdg. 27.50 (*0-88355-390-2*) Hyperion Conn.

China's Reform Experience to Date. Peter Harrold. LC 92-32161. (Discussion Paper Ser.: No. 180). 56p. 1992. 6.95 (*0-8213-2233-8*, 12233) World Bank.

China's Regional Development. David S. Goodman. 208p. 1989. 66.50 (*0-415-03510-4*, A3274) Routledge.

China's Relations with Japan, Nineteen Forty-Five to Nineteen Eighty-Three: The Role of Liao Chengzhi. Kurt W. Radtke. LC 90-36569. (Studies on East Asia). 304p. 1990. text ed. 69.95 (*0-7190-2795-0*, Pub. by Manchester Univ Pr UK) St Martin.

China's Religious Heritage. Yung-Ch'Ing Yang. LC 72-4542. (Essay Index Reprint Ser.). 1977. reprint ed. 18.95 (*0-8369-2981-0*) Ayer.

China's Renaissance in Bronze: The Robert H. Clague Collection of Later Chinese Bronzes, 1100-1911. Robert D. Mowry. Ed. by Claudia Brown & Anne Gully. LC 93-20881. 256p. (Orig.). 1993. pap. 40.00 (*0-910407-29-0*) Phoenix Art.

***China's Republican Revolution.** Ed. by Eto Shinkichi & Harold Z. Schiffrin. 300p. 1994. 59.50 (*0-86008-513-9*) Col U Pr.

China's Republican Revolution: The Case of Kwangtung, 1895-1913. Edward J. Rhoads. LC 74-84090. (East Asian Monographs: No. 81). 392p. 1975. 25.00 (*0-674-11980-0*) HUP.

China's Response to the Downfall of Communism in Eastern Europe & the Soviet Union. Jialin Zhang. LC 94-6128. (Essays in Public Policy Ser.: Vol. 48). 1994. 5.00 (*0-8179-5532-1*) Hoover Inst Pr.

China's Response to the West: A Documentary Survey, 1839-1923. Teng Ssu-Yu et al. LC 53-5061. 235p. 1979. pap. 15.95 (*0-674-12025-6*) HUP.

China's Revolution, Nineteen Eleven to Nineteen Twelve. Edwin J. Dingle. LC 72-3486. (World History Ser.: No. 48). (Illus.). 1972. reprint ed. lib. bdg. 59.95 (*0-8383-1565-8*) M S G Haskell Hse.

China's Revolutionary War. Dick Wilson. 1991. text ed. 39.95 (*0-312-06709-7*) St Martin.

China's Rise to Commercial Maritime Power. Irwin M. Heine. LC 88-25095. (Contributions in Economics & Economic History Ser.: No. 87). 193p. 1989. text ed. 55.00 (*0-313-26454-6*, HCZ/, Greenwood Pr) Greenwood.

***China's Road to the Korean War: The Making of the Sino-American Confrontation.** Chen Jian. (Illus.). 352p. 1994. 37.50 (*0-231-10024-8*) Col U Pr.

China's Rural Development Miracle. Ed. by John W. Longworth. 1989. pap. 34.95 (*0-7022-2264-X*, Pub. by Univ Queensland Pr AT) Intl Spec Bk.

China's Rural Industry: Structure, Development & Reform. Ed. by William A. Byrd & Qingson Lin. 460p. 1990. 39.95 (*0-685-45122-4*, 60822) World Bank.

China's Satellite Parties. James D. Seymour. LC 86-31343. 164p. 1987. 62.95 (*0-87332-412-9*) M E Sharpe.

China's Science & Technology Policy 1949-1989. Yeu-Farn Wang. 181p. 1993. 58.95 (*1-85628-520-0*, Pub. by Avebury Pub UK) Ashgate Pub Co.

China's Search for Democracy: The Student & Mass Movement of 1989. Ed. by Suzanne Ogden et al. LC 91-26768. 488p. 1992. 57.95 (*0-87332-723-3*); pap. text ed. 20.95 (*0-87332-724-1*) M E Sharpe.

China's Second Revolution: Reform after Mao. Harry Harding. LC 87-27235. 369p. 1987. 36.95 (*0-8157-3462-X*); pap. 16.95 (*0-8157-3461-1*) Brookings.

China's Silk Trade: Traditional Industry in the Modern World, 1842-1937. Lillian M. Li. (East Asian Monographs: No. 97). 309p. 1981. 30.00 (*0-674-11962-2*) HUP.

China's Socialist Revolution. John Collier & Elsie Collier. LC 74-7782. 286p. 1976. pap. 4.95 (*0-85345-368-3*) Monthly Rev.

China's Southern Strategy: Encirclement & Counterencirclement. Yaacov Y. Vertzberger. LC 85-6275. 256p. 1985. text ed. 59.95 (*0-275-90176-9*, C0176, Praeger Pubs) Greenwood.

China's Spatial Economy: Recent Developments & Reforms. Ed. by Godfrey J. Linge & D. K. Forbes. (Illus.). 240p. 1991. 45.00 (*0-19-585296-6*) OUP.

China's Sports Medicine. Ed. by Q. Mianyu & Y. Changlong. (Medicine & Sport Science Ser.: Vol. 28). (Illus.). viii, 120p. 1989. 79.25 (*3-8055-4806-0*) S Karger.

China's Story in Myth, Legend, Art & Annals. W. E. Griffis. 1980. lib. bdg. 64.95 (*0-8490-3145-1*) Gordon Pr.

China's Strategic Demographic Initiative. H. Yuan Tien. LC 90-20614. 336p. 1991. text ed. 59.95 (*0-275-93824-7*, C3824, Praeger Pubs) Greenwood.

China's Strategic Seapower: The Politics of Force Modernization in the Nuclear Age. John W. Lewis & Xue Litai. LC 94-11688. (Studies in International Security & Arms Control). 1994. 45.00 (*0-8047-2303-6*) Stanford U Pr.

China's Struggle for Naval Development, 1839-1895. John L. Rawlinson. LC 66-10127. (Harvard East Asian Ser.: No. 25). 329p. reprint ed. pap. 93.80 (*0-7837-3962-1*, 2043791) Bks Demand.

China's Struggle for Railroad Development. Chang Kia-ngau, pseud. LC 74-34331. (China in the 20th Century Ser.). (Illus.). vii, 340p. 1975. reprint ed. lib. bdg. 39.50 (*0-306-70689-X*) Da Capo.

China's Struggle for the Rule of Law. Ronald C. Keith. LC 93-23256. 1994. text ed. 65.00 (*0-312-10669-6*) St Martin.

China's Struggle to Modernize. 2nd ed. Michael Gasster. LC 93-34052. (Illus.). 256p. (C). 1983. pap. text ed. write for info. (*0-07-554407-5*) McGraw.

China's Students: The Struggle for Democracy. Ruth Cherrington. 224p. 1991. 52.50 (*0-415-05291-2*, A4957) Routledge.

***China's Tang Dynasty.** Heather Millar. (Cultures of the Past Ser.). 80p. (J). (gr. 5-8). 1995. lib. bdg. write for info. (*0-7614-0074-5*, Benchmark NY) Marshall Cavendish.

China's Trade & Investment Organizations. 1989. 95.00 (*0-317-99912-5*) Natl Coun US-China.

China's Trade with the Industrialized Countries: Socio-Economic & Political Perspectives. Ed. by Anant R. Negandhi. (Research in International Business & International Relations Ser.: Vol. 2). 1986. 73.25 (*0-89232-530-5*) Jai Pr.

China's Traditional Rural Architecture: A Cultural Geography of the Common House. Ronald G. Knapp. LC 86-7003. (Illus.). 192p. 1986. text ed. 25.00 (*0-8248-1053-8*) UH Pr.

China's Transition from Socialism: Statist Legacies & Market Reforms, 1980-1990. Dorothy J. Solinger. LC 92-43250. (Socialism & Social Movements Ser.). 304p. (C). 1993. 57.95 (*1-56324-067-X*); pap. text ed. 23.95 (*1-56324-068-8*) M E Sharpe.

China's Transition to Industrialism: Producer Goods & Economic Development in the Twentieth Century. Thomas G. Rawski. (Studies on China). (Illus.). 226p. 1980. 32.50x (*0-472-08755-X*) U of Mich Pr.

China's Universities: Post-Mao Enrollment Policies & Their Impact on the Structure of Secondary Education. Suzanne Pepper. LC 83-25277. (Michigan Monographs in Chinese Studies: No. 46). xvi, 155p. (C). 1984. pap. 8.00 (*0-89264-046-4*) Ctr Chinese Studies.

China's Universities & the Open Door. Ruth Hayhoe. LC 88-18347. 264p. 1989. 51.95 (*0-87332-501-X*) M E Sharpe.

China's Unresolved Issues: Politics, Development, & Culture. 2nd ed. Suzanne Ogden. 400p. (C). 1991. pap. text ed. write for info. (*0-13-132747-X*) P-H.

***China's Unresolved Issues: Politics, Development, & Culture.** 3rd ed. Suzanne Ogden. LC 94-30959. 352p. 1994. pap. text ed. write for info. (*0-13-178591-5*) P-H.

***China's Urban Revolutionaries: Explorations in the History of Chinese Trotskyism, 1921-1952.** Gregor Benton. (Revolutionary Studies Ser.). 304p. (C). 1995. text ed. 55.00 (*0-391-03921-0*) Humanities.

China's Urban Villagers: Changing Life in a Beijing Suburb. 2nd ed. Norman A. Chance. Ed. by Louise Spindler. (Case Studies in Cultural Anthropology). (Illus.). 248p. (Orig.). (C). 1991. pap. text ed. 13.50 (*0-03-031333-3*) HB Coll Pubs.

China's Vernacular Architecture: House Form & Culture. Ronald G. Knapp. LC 89-4713. 1989. text ed. 38.00 (*0-8248-1204-2*) UH Pr.

China's War with Vietnam, 1979: Issues, Decisions, & Implications. King C. Chen. (Publication Ser.: No. 357). 234p. 1987. 31.95 (*0-8179-8571-9*); pap. 18.95 (*0-8179-8572-7*) Hoover Inst Pr.

***China's Warlords.** David Bonavia. (Oxford in Asia Paperbacks Ser.). (Illus.). 272p. 1995. pap. 23.00 (*0-19-586179-5*) OUP.

China's Wartime Finance & Inflation, 1937-1945. Arthur N. Young. LC 65-22049. (Harvard East Asian Ser.: No. 20). 439p. reprint ed. pap. 125.20 (*0-7837-4134-0*, 2057957) Bks Demand.

Chinas Weg in die Weltpolitik: Die Nationalen und Aussenpolitischen Konzeptionen Sun Yat-Sens, Chiang Kaisheks und Mao Tse-Tungs. Marie-Luise Naeth. (Beitraege zur Auswaertigen und Internationalen Politik Ser.: Vol. 7). (C). 1976. pap. 93.85 (*3-11-004737-3*) De Gruyter.

Chinatown: Economic Adaptation & Ethnic Identity of the Chinese. Bernard Wong. 160p. (C). 1982. pap. text ed. 13.50 (*0-03-058906-1*) HB Coll Pubs.

Chinatown: Most Time, Hard Time. Chalsa Loo. LC 91-27984. 384p. 1991. text ed. 59.95 (*0-275-93893-X*, C3893, Praeger Pubs) Greenwood.

***Chinatown: The Socioeconomic Potential of an Urban Enclave.** Min Zhou. (Conflicts in Urban & Regional Development Ser.). 300p. 1994. pap. write for info. (*0-614-03051-X*) Temple U Pr.

***Chinatown: The Socioeconomic Potential of an Urban Enclave.** Zhou. (C). 1995. pap. text ed. 18.95 (*1-56639-337-X*) Temple U Pr.

***Chinatown: The Socioeconomic Potential of an Urban Enclave.** Zhou. (C). 1995. pap. text ed. 18.95 (*0-614-05493-1*) Temple U Pr.

Chinatown: The Socioeconomic Potential of an Urban Enclave. Min Zhou. (Conflicts in Urban & Regional Development Ser.). 300p. (C). 1992. 44.95 (*0-87722-934-1*) Temple U Pr.

Chinatown, DC: A Photographic Journal. Wendy Lim. Ed. by Esther N. Chow & Chi-Kwan Ho. Tr. by Wei Li & Yumei Sun. (Illus.). 111p. (Orig.). (CHI.). (C). 1991. write for info. (*0-9629267-0-1*) Asian Amer Arts.

***Chinatown, New York: Labor & Politics, 1930-1950.** Peter Kwong. LC 79-2327. (Illus.). reprint ed. pap. 50.80 (*0-7837-9606-4*, 2060363) Bks Demand.

Chinatown No More: Taiwan Immigrants in Contemporary New York. Hsiang-shui Chen. LC 91-55547. (Anthropology of Contemporary Issues Ser.). (Illus.). 296p. 1992. 39.95 (*0-8014-2697-9*); pap. 14.95 (*0-8014-9989-5*) Cornell U Pr.

Chinatown Photographer: Louis J. Stellman. Ed. by Gary E. Strong. (Illus.). 139p. 1989. pap. 24.95 (*0-929722-20-5*) CA State Library Fndtn.

Chinatown, San Jose, U. S. A. Connie Y. Yu. Ed. by Kathleen Muller. (Illus.). 120p. 1991. write for info. (*0-914139-09-6*) San Jose His Mus Assn.

Chinatown; The Last Detail; Shampoo: Screenplays. Robert Towne. LC 94-8952. 288p. 1994. 12.00 (*0-8021-3401-7*, Grove) Grove-Atltic.

Chinatown's Angry Angel: The Story of Donaldina Cameron. Mildred C. Martin. LC 77-2151. (Illus.). 308p. 1986. pap. 10.95 (*0-87015-252-1*) Pacific Bks.

Chinch Bugs, Chinky Pins, & Chinie-Berry Beads. Faye Brown. (Illus.). 191p. (Orig.). (J). 1990. pap. 9.95 (*0-943487-24-2*) Sevgo Pr.

Chinchilla. Robert D. MacDonald. (Phoenix Theatre Ser.). 1982. pap. 2.95 (*0-912262-73-7*) Proscenium.

Chinchilla Farm. Judith Freeman. LC 90-50117. (Vintage Contemporaries Ser.). 308p. 1990. pap. 12.00 (*0-679-73052-4*, Vin) Random.

Chinchilla Farm. Judith Freeman. 1988. write for info. (*0-318-63678-6*) Viking Penguin.

Chinchilla Farm. Judith Freeman. 1989. 19.95 (*0-393-02722-8*) Norton.

Chinchillas: A Complete Introduction. Jack C. Harris. (Illus.). 93p. (Orig.). 1987. pap. 5.95 (*0-86622-393-2*, CO-042S) TFH Pubns.

Chinchillas: A Complete Pet Owner's Manual. Maike Roder-Thiede. LC 92-32050. (Complete Pet Owner's Manuals Ser.). 80p. 1993. pap. 5.95 (*0-8120-1471-5*) Barron.

***Chinchorro Mummies: The Dead among the Living in Arica, Chile.** Bernardo T. Arriaza. LC 94-39295. (Illus.). 176p. 1995. 39.95 (*1-56098-512-7*) Smithsonian.

Chindit War. large type ed. Shelford Bidwell. 514p. 1982. 15.95 (*0-7089-0770-9*) Ulverscroft.

***Chines Societies & Mental Health.** Ed. by Tsung-Yi Lin et al. (Illus.). 448p. 1995. 79.00 (*0-19-586399-2*) OUP.

Chinese. (Handy Dictionaries Ser.). 120p. (Orig.). 1991. pap. 8.95 (*0-87052-050-4*) Hippocrene Bks.

Chinese. David Bonavia. 320p. 1989. pap. 7.95 (*0-14-010479-8*, Penguin Bks) Viking Penguin.

Chinese. Jodine Mayberry. LC 90-17223. (Recent American Immigrants Ser.). (Illus.). 64p. (J). (gr. 5-8). 1990. lib. bdg. 14.21 (*0-531-10977-1*) Watts.

Chinese. Jerry Norman. (Cambridge Language Surveys Ser.). (Illus.). 310p. 1988. 74.95 (*0-521-22809-3*); pap. 27.95 (*0-521-29653-6*) Cambridge U Pr.

Chinese. Pamela Odijk. (Ancient World Ser.). (Illus.). 48p. (J). (gr. 5-8). 1991. lib. bdg. 14.95 (*0-382-09894-3*) Silver Burdett Pr.

***Chinese.** Pamela Odijk. (Ancient World Ser.). (Illus.). 48p. (J). (gr. 5-8). 1991. teacher ed 4.50 (*0-382-24285-8*); pap. 7.95 (*0-382-24271-8*) Silver Burdett Pr.

Chinese. rev. ed. David Bonavia. 1983. pap. 7.95 (*0-14-022394-0*, Penguin Bks) Viking Penguin.

Chinese. Robert Coltman. LC 72-4164. (Select Bibliographies Reprint Ser.). 1977. reprint ed. 25.95 (*0-8369-6874-3*) Ayer.

Chinese: A Study of a Hong Kong Community, 3 vols., Set. Cornelius Osgood. LC 74-77207. 1264p. (C). 1975. 135.00 (*0-8165-0418-0*) U of Ariz Pr.

Chinese: Adapting the Past, Facing the Future. 2nd ed. Ed. by Robert F. Dernberger et al. 802p. 1991. pap. text ed. 25.00 (*0-89264-100-2*) Ctr Chinese Studies.

Chinese: Speaking in China. Hsu Ying & Marvin J. Brown. 314p. 1983. Incl. 6 cassettes. audio 135.00 (*0-88432-150-9*, AFM320); 18.95 (*0-685-73879-5*, AFM995) Audio-Forum.

Chinese - English Medical Dictionary. Commercial Press Staff. (CHI & ENG.). 150.00 (*0-8288-2483-5*, F45700) Fr & Eur.

***Chinese Acquisitions of Weapons & Technologies from Abroad.** Bates Gill & Kim Taeho. (SIPRI Research Reports Ser.: No. 11). 100p. 1995. 39.95 (*0-19-829195-7*); pap. 21.00 (*0-19-829196-5*) OUP.

Chinese Acupuncture. George Soulie de Morant. Ed. by Paul Zmiewski. Tr. by Dhruva Grinnell et al. 916p. (ENG.). 1994. 125.00 (*0-912111-31-3*) Paradigm Publns.

Chinese Agent in Mongolia. Ho-t'ien Ma. Tr. by John De Francis. LC 49-11857. 231p. reprint ed. pap. 65.90 (*0-317-08380-5*, 2003913) Bks Demand.

Chinese Alchemy: Preliminary Studies. Nathan Sivin. LC 67-27093. (Harvard Monographs in the History of Science). (Illus.). 363p. reprint ed. pap. 104.10 (*0-7837-1724-5*, 2057254) Bks Demand.

Chinese Almanacs. Richard J. Smith. LC 92-16713. (Images of Asia Ser.). (C). 1993. 16.95 (*0-19-585288-5*) OUP.

Chinese Amerian Struggle for Equality. Franklin Ng. LC 92-7472. (Discrimination Ser.). (YA). 1992. 22.60 (*0-86593-181-X*); lib. bdg. 16.95 (*0-685-59290-1*) Rourke Corp.

Chinese America: Chinese Historical Society of America. 192p. 1990. pap. text ed. 12.00 (*0-9614198-5-7*) CHSA SF.

Chinese America: History & Perspectives, 1987. 187p. (Orig.). (C). 1987. pap. write for info. (*0-9614198-0-6*) CHSA SF.

Chinese America: History & Perspectives, 1988. (Illus.). 202p. (Orig.). (C). 1988. pap. write for info. (*0-9614198-1-4*) CHSA SF.

***Chinese America: History & Perspectives 1995.** Ed. by Marlon K. Hom et al. 217p. (Orig.). (C). Date not set. pap. 15.00 (*1-885864-00-0*) CHSA SF.

Chinese-American Experience. Dana Y. Wu & Jeffrey D. Tung. LC 92-15649. (Coming to America Ser.). (Illus.). 64p. (J). (gr. 4-6). 1993. lib. bdg. 15.40 (*1-56294-271-9*) Millbrook Pr.

Chinese American Family Album. Dorothy Hoobler & Thomas Hoobler. (American Family Albums Ser.). (Illus.). 128p. (J). 1994. 19.95 (*0-19-509123-X*); lib. bdg. 22.95 (*0-19-508130-7*) OUP.

Chinese American Food Practices, Customs, & Holidays. Kee M. Ma. (Ethnic & Regional Food Practices Ser.). 36p. 1990. ring bd. 5.75 (*0-88091-077-1*, 0868) Am Dietetic Assn.

Chinese-American Heritage. David M. Brownstone. (America's Ethnic Heritage Ser.). (Illus.). 144p. (YA). 1988. 16.95 (*0-8160-1627-5*) Facts on File.

Chinese-American Interactions: A Historical Summary. John K. Fairbank. LC 74-22192. (Brown & Haley Lectures: Yr. 1974). 96p. reprint ed. pap. 27.40 (*0-317-29961-1*, 2051726) Bks Demand.

Chinese American Intermarriage. Betty L. Sung. (Illus.). 252p. 1990. pap. text ed. 14.50 (*0-934733-48-1*) Ctr Migration.

Chinese American Intermarriage. Betty L. Sung. (Illus.). 252p. (C). 1990. text ed. 19.50 (*0-934733-47-3*) Ctr Migration.

Chinese Americans. Alexandra Bandon. LC 93-32711. (Footsteps to America Ser.). (Illus.). 112p. (J). (gr. 6 up). 1994. text ed. 14.95 (*0-02-768149-1*, New Dscvry Bks) Silver Burdett Pr.

Chinese Americans. William Daley. (Peoples of North America Ser.). (Illus.). 112p. (J). (gr. 5 up). 1988. lib. bdg. 17.95 (*0-87754-867-6*) Chelsea Hse.

Chinese Americans. William Daley. (J). (gr. 4-7). 1993. pap. 8.95 (*0-7910-0260-8*) Chelsea Hse.

***Chinese Americans.** William Daley. LC 94-45788. (Immigrant Experience Ser.). 1995. write for info. (*0-7910-3357-0*); pap. write for info. (*0-7910-3379-1*) Chelsea Hse.

Chinese Americans. Ed. by Integrated Education Associates Editorial Staff. LC 72-83395. pap. 2.70 (*0-912008-04-0*) Equity & Excel.

Chinese Americans. Tina Moy. LC 94-12601. (Cultures of America Ser.). 1994. 19.95 (*1-85435-785-9*) Marshall Cavendish.

Chinese Americans. Wilson. (American Voices Ser.). (J). 1991. 13.95 (*0-86593-135-6*) Rourke Corp.

Chinese & Dr. Fish: Two Plays. Murray Schisgal. 1970. pap. 4.75 (*0-8222-0207-7*) Dramatists Play.

Chinese & Gothic Architecture. William Halfpenny & John Halfpenny. LC 69-13237. (Illus.). 1972. reprint ed. 18.95 (*0-405-08588-5*, Pub. by Blom Pubns UK) Ayer.

Chinese & Japanese Calligraphy: Spanning Two Thousand Years-The Heinz Goetze Collection: Masterpieces of Two Thousand Years. Ed. by Shigemi Komatsu & Kwang S. Wong. 198p. 1989. 85.00 (*3-7913-1026-7*, Pub. by Prestel) TeNeues.

Chinese & Other Far Eastern Art. Contrib by Yamanaka & Co. Staff & C. T. Loo. (Illus.). 400p. reprint ed. 60.00 (*0-938290-09-6*) Apollo.

An Asterisk (*) at the beginning of an entry indicates that the title is appearing in BIP for the first time.

Chinese & South-East Asian White Ware Found in the Philippines. Rita C. Tan et al. LC 92-35122. (Illus.). 128p. 1993. 70.00 (*0-19-588615-1*) OUP.

Chinese & Their Future: Beijing, Taipei, & Hong Kong. Ed. by Zhiling Lin & Thomas W. Robinson. LC 93-21227. 536p. 1994. 39.75 (*0-8447-3805-0*, AEI Pr); pap. 19.95 (*0-8447-3804-2*, AEI Pr) Am Enterprise.

Chinese & Western Daily Practical Health Guide. Betty Y. Ho. LC 81-20848. (System of Government in the Living Body Ser.). (Illus.). 122p. (Orig.). 1982. pap. 9.00 (*0-9600148-4-5*) Juvenescent.

Chinese & Western Guide to Better Health & Longer Life. Betty Y. Ho. LC 74-12332. 50p. (Orig.). 1974. pap. 5.00 (*0-87576-046-5*) Juvenescent.

Chinese Appetizers & Garnishes. Huang Su Huei. Tr. by Chen Chang-Yen. (Illus.). 160p. (CHI & ENG.). 1982. pap. 19.95 (*0-941676-01-3*) Wei-Chuan Pub.

Chinese Approaches to Family Planning. Ed. by Leo A. Orleans. LC 79-64372. 232p. 1979. 49.95 (*0-87332-139-1*) M E Sharpe.

Chinese Approaches to Literature from Confucius to Liang Chi-Chao. Ed. by Adele A. Rickett. LC 77-7311. 282p. reprint ed. pap. 80.40 (*0-8357-6055-3*, 2034650) Bks Demand.

Chinese Archaeological Abstracts. Incl. Vol. 9. Prehistoric to Western Zhou. Ed. by Albert E. Dien et al. 618p. 1985. (*0-917956-55-9*); Vol. 10. Eastern Zhou to Han. Ed. by Albert E. Dien et al. 763p. 1985. (*0-917956-53-2*); Vol. 11. Post Han. Ed. by Nancy T. Price et al. 750p. 1985. (*0-917956-54-0*); (Monumenta Graeca et Romana Ser.: No. 9-11). (Illus.). 2131p. 1985. 75.00 (*0-685-11885-1*) UCLA Arch.

Chinese Architecture. Aleda Shirley. LC 86-4283. (Contemporary Poetry Ser.). 88p. 1986. 15.00 (*0-8203-0870-6*); pap. 7.95 (*0-8203-0871-4*) U of Ga Pr.

***Chinese Archives: An Introductory Guide.** Ed. by Ye Wa & Joseph Esherick. (China Research Monograph Ser.: No. 45). 1995. pap. 23.50 (*1-55729-047-4*) IEAS.

Chinese Arms Transfers: Purposes, Patterns, & Prospects in the New World Order. R. Bates Gill. LC 92-8386. 376p. 1992. text ed. 55.00 (*0-275-94279-1*, C4279, Praeger Pubs) Greenwood.

Chinese Army. Evans F. Carlson. LC 74-10097. (China Studies: from Confucius to Mao Ser.). (Illus.). 142p. 1975. reprint ed. 17.60 (*0-88355-162-4*) Hyperion Conn.

Chinese Army after Mao. Ellis Joffe. LC 87-131. 224p. 1987. 29.00 (*0-674-54849-3*) HUP.

Chinese Art. Mary Tregear. (World of Art Ser.). (Illus.). 216p. 1985. pap. 12.95 (*0-500-20178-1*) Thames Hudson.

Chinese Art, 2 vols., Set. S. W. Bushell. (C). 1988. 400.00 (*0-7855-0058-8*, Pub. by Print Hse II) St Mut.

Chinese Art: One Thousand Masterpieces from the Arthur M. Sackler Collection. Paul Singer. (Illus.). 560p. (Orig.). (C). 1989. pap. write for info. (*0-318-66604-9*) AMS Found Arts Sci.

Chinese Art & Design: Art Objects in Ritual & Daily Life. Ed. by Rose Kerr. (Illus.). 256p. 1991. 60.00 (*0-87951-437-X*) Overlook Pr.

Chinese Art in the Chrysler Museum. Shirley H. Ganse. (Illus.). 48p. 1976. pap. 1.00 (*0-940744-10-4*) Chrysler Museum.

Chinese Art Ivory. enl. rev. ed. Barry C. Eastham. LC 76-23710. (Illus.). 1976. 32.50 (*0-89344-003-5*) Ars Ceramica.

Chinese Art of Bonsai & Potted Landscapes. Y. C. Shen et al. LC 91-75245. 170p. 1991. 49.88 (*0-9630538-0-9*) Unison Grp.

Chinese Art of T'ai Chi Ch'uan: The Taoist Way to Mental & Physical Health. Chee Soo. LC 93-25026. (Illus.). 160p. 1993. reprint ed. pap. 9.95 (*0-8069-0554-9*) Sterling.

Chinese Art of the Warring States Period: Change & Continuity, 480-222 B.C. Thomas Lawton. LC 82-600184. (Illus.). 204p. (Orig.). 1982. 35.00 (*0-934686-39-4*); pap. 20.00 (*0-934686-50-5*) Freer.

Chinese Art Symbols. Hawley. 1993. pap. 6.95 (*0-910704-78-3*) Hawley.

Chinese Art under the Mongols: The Yuan Dynasty 1279-1368. Sherman E. Lee & Wai-Kam Ho. LC 68-9276. (Illus.). 415p. reprint ed. pap. 118.30 (*0-317-10189-7*, 2005108) Bks Demand.

Chinese Artistic Kites. Ha Kuiming & Ha Yiqi. Tr. by Ralph Kiggell. LC 89-60883. (Illus.). 160p. 1990. 16.95 (*0-8351-2279-4*) China Bks.

Chinese Astrology. Paul Carus. LC 73-20411. (Illus.). 114p. 1974. pap. 6.95 (*0-87548-155-8*) Open Court.

Chinese Astrology. rev. ed. Paula Delsol. 1986. mass mkt. 5.99 (*0-446-34300-5*) Warner Bks.

Chinese Astrology. Derek Walters. 368p. (Orig.). 1993. reprint ed. pap. 20.00 (*1-85538-232-6*, Pub. by Aquarian Pr UK) Thorsons SF.

Chinese at a Glance. (At a Glance Ser.). 272p. 1986. pap. 6.95 (*0-8120-2851-1*) Barron.

Chinese Attitudes Toward Nuclear Weapons: China & the United States during the Korean War. Mark A. Ryan. LC 89-4158. 256p. 1990. 51.95 (*0-87332-530-3*) M E Sharpe.

***Chinese Awakenings: Life Stories from the Unofficial China.** James L. Tyson, Jr. & Ann S. Tyson. LC 94-44056. 1995. text ed. 59.95 (*0-8133-2472-6*) Westview.

***Chinese Awakenings: Life Stories from the Unofficial China.** James L. Tyson, Jr. & Ann S. Tyson. LC 94-44056. (C). 1995. pap. text ed. 19.95 (*0-8133-2473-4*) Westview.

***Chinese Basics: Build 35 Picture-Blocks into 1000 Words.** Rudolf E. Klimes. 250p. (C). 1989. per., pap. text ed. 29.95 (*1-886304-04-1*) LearnWell Pr.

Chinese Baskets. Berthold Laufer. LC 28-1443. (Illus.). 42p. 1925. ring bd. 50.00 (*0-686-25961-0*) Rare Oriental Bk Co.

Chinese Baskets & Mats. Dieter Kuhn. (Illus.). 100p. (Orig.). 1980. pap. 25.00 (*3-515-03351-3*) Coronet Bks.

Chinese Batch: The Maynooth Mission to China, 1911-1920. Bernard T. Smyth. (Illus.). 128p. 1994. pap. 11.99 (*1-85182-142-2*, Pub. by Four Cts Pr IE) Intl Spec Bk.

Chinese Beggars' Den: Poverty & Mobility in an Underclass Community. David C. Schak. LC 87-16191. (Illus.). 258p. (C). 1988. 49.95 (*0-8229-3822-7*) U of Pittsburgh Pr.

***Chinese Beliefs & Superstitions.** Evelyn Lip. (Illus.). 80p. (Orig.). 1985. pap. 6.95 (*9971-947-88-9*) Heian Intl.

Chinese Bell Murders. Robert M. Van Gulik. LC 77-80378. (Illus.). x, 288p. 1977. pap. 6.95 (*0-226-84862-0*) U Ch Pr.

***Chinese Blue & White Porcelain.** Duncan Macintosh. 1994. 59.50 (*1-85149-210-0*) Antique Collect.

Chinese Blue Shirt Society: Fascism & Developmental Nationalism. Maria H. Chang. LC 85-80730. (China Research Monographs: No. 30). 144p. 1985. pap. 7.50 (*0-912966-81-5*) IEAS.

Chinese Bodywork: A Complete Manual of Chinese Therapeutic Massage. Ed. by Sun Chengnan. LC 93-85293. 328p. 1993. 50.00 (*1-881896-06-4*) Pacific View Pr.

Chinese Bondage in Peru: A History of the Chinese Coolie in Peru, 1849-1874. Watt Stewart. LC 70-100180. (Illus.). 247p. 1970. reprint ed. text ed. 59.75 (*0-8371-2977-X*, STCH, Greenwood Pr) Greenwood.

Chinese Boxing: Masters & Methods. 2nd ed. Robert Smith. (Illus.). 156p. 1990. reprint ed. text ed. 25.00 (*1-55643-095-7*); reprint ed. pap. 9.95 (*1-55643-085-X*) North Atlantic.

Chinese Boycotts vs. Japanese Bombs: The Failure of China's "Revolutionary Diplomacy", 1931-1932. Donald A. Jordan. 346p. (C). 1991. text ed. 49.50 (*0-472-10172-2*) U of Mich Pr.

Chinese Brain Twisters: Fifty-Six Fast, Fun Puzzles That Help Children Develop Quick, Logical Minds. Baifang. LC 93-10862. 1994. pap. text ed. 14.95 (*0-471-59505-5*) Wiley.

***Chinese Breakthrough: Learning Chinese Language Through TV & Newspapers.** Hong Gang Jin et al. (C&T Language Ser.). (Illus.). 219p. (CHI.). (C). 1995. pap. text ed. 27.95 (*0-88727-194-4*); student ed. pap. text ed. 17.95 (*0-88727-210-X*) Cheng & Tsui.

Chinese Bridges. Ronald G. Knapp. LC 92-30265. (Images of Asia Ser.). 1993. 15.95 (*0-19-585728-3*) OUP.

Chinese Bronzes. Helen Loveday. (Illus.). 48p. 1995. pap. 6.95 (*1-85444-003-9*, 003-9, Pub. by Ashmolean Mus UK) A Schwartz & Co.

Chinese Brush Painting. Jane Evans. (Illus.). 144p. 1987. 29.95 (*0-8230-0632-8*, Watsn-Guptill) Watsn-Guptill.

Chinese Brush Painting. I-Ching Hsu. (Workstations Ser.). (Illus.). 48p. (J). (gr. 4 up). 1995. pap. 21.95 (*0-8431-3753-3*) Price Stern.

Chinese Brush Painting. Lucy Wang. (How to Draw & Paint Ser.). (Illus.). 32p. 1992. pap. 5.95 (*1-56010-166-0*, HT233) W Foster Pub.

Chinese Brush Painting: An Instructional Guide. Ning Yeh. Ed. by Michael Werthman. Tr. by Judith McDuff. (Illus.). 190p. (Orig.). (C). 1987. pap. text ed. 18.00 (*0-9618305-0-6*) Silk Era.

Chinese Brush Strokes, An Introduction: The Scholarly Bamboo. June Greene. LC 81-69758. (Illus.). (Orig.). 1981. pap. 9.50 (*0-941284-11-5*) J Shaw Studio.

Chinese Brushwork in Calligraphy & Painting: Its History Aesthetics & Techniques. Kwo Da-wei. 1990. pap. 12.95 (*0-486-26481-5*) Dover.

Chinese Buddhist Apocrypha. Ed. by Robert E. Buswell, Jr. LC 89-20614. 376p. 1990. text ed. 37.50 (*0-8248-1253-0*) UH Pr.

Chinese Buddhist Bronzes. Hugo Munsterberg. LC 87-80393. (Illus.). 191p. 1988. reprint ed. lib. bdg. 50.00 (*0-87817-324-2*) Hacker.

Chinese Buddhist Monasteries: Their Plan & Function As a Setting for Buddhist Monastic Life. Johannes Prip-Moller. (Illus.). 410p. 1982. 127.50 (*962-209-067-2*, Pub. by Hong Kong Univ Pr HK) Coronet Bks.

Chinese Buddhist Sculpture under the Liao: Free Standing Works In Situ & Selected Examples from Public Collections. Marilyn L. Gridley. (Illus.). 1993. 110.00 (*81-85689-04-0*, Pub. by Aditya Prakashan II) S Asia.

Chinese Buddhist Verse. Ed. by J. L. Cranmer-Byng. Tr. by Richard H. Robinson. LC 79-8725. 85p. 1980. reprint ed. text ed. 35.00 (*0-313-22189-8*, ROCB, Greenwood Pr) Greenwood.

Chinese Burn. large type ed. Eric Clark. 528p. 1986. 15.95 (*0-7089-1454-3*) Ulverscroft.

***Chinese Business Enterprise in Asia.** Ed. by Rajeswary A. Brown. LC 94-33826. 1995. 75.00x (*0-415-11487-X*, C0441) Routledge.

Chinese Business (Taiwan) Guidebook. Ed. by Lewis B. Sckolnick. 130p. (Orig.). (C). 1994. pap. 225.00 (*1-57205-321-6*) Rector Pr.

Chinese Business under Socialism: The Politics of Domestic Commerce in Contemporary China. Dorothy J. Solinger. LC 83-17930. (Illus.). 400p. (C). 1985. pap. 15.00 (*0-520-06181-0*) U CA Pr.

Chinese Call Me Teacher. Raymond L. Malody. LC 92-61876. 192p. (Orig.). 1992. pap. 10.95 (*0-939644-89-4*) Media Pub.

Chinese Calligraphy. Yujiro Nakata et al. Tr. by Jeffrey Hunter. LC 83-3490. (History of the Art of China Ser.: Vol. 1). Orig. Title: Chugoku no bijutsu-shoseki. (Illus.). 240p. (C). 1983. 65.00 (*0-8348-1526-5*) Weatherhill.

Chinese Calligraphy: An Introduction to Its Aesthetic & Technique. 3rd ed. Chiang Yee. LC 72-75400. (Illus.). 270p. 1974. pap. 16.95 (*0-674-12226-7*) HUP.

Chinese Calligraphy: From Pictograph to Ideogram: The History of 214 Essential Chinese-Japanese Characters. Edoardo Fazzioli. (Illus.). 252p. 1987. 29.95 (*0-89659-774-1*) Abbeville Pr.

Chinese Camp & Other California Poems. John C. Pine. 28p. (Orig.). 1982. pap. 2.50 (*0-943430-00-3*) Moveable Feast Pr.

Chinese Camp & Other California Poems. John C. Pine. LC 85-22079. 64p. (Orig.). 1985. pap. 6.95 (*0-86534-078-1*) Sunstone Pr.

Chinese Carved Lacquer. Derek Clifford. (Illus.). 160p. 1992. 59.50 (*1-870076-20-6*, Pub. by Bamboo Pub UK) Antique Collect.

Chinese Cash. O. D. Cresswell. (Illus.). 1980. reprint ed. pap. 12.00 (*0-915262-41-X*) S J Durst.

Chinese Cassette Pack. Berlitz Editors. (Cassette Packs Ser.). (Illus.). 192p. (CHI.). 1994. audio, pap. 15.95 (*2-8315-1480-0*) Berlitz.

Chinese Celadon Wares. 2nd ed. G. St. Gompertz. (Monographs on Pottery & Porcelain). (Illus.). 224p. 1980. 55.00 (*0-571-18003-5*) Faber & Faber.

Chinese Ceramics. Ed. by Wolfgang Hageney. (Illus.). 120p. (ENG, FRE, GER, ITA & SPA.). 1983. pap. 21.95 (*88-7070-038-0*) Belvedere USA.

Chinese Ceramics from Japanese Collections. Seizo Hayashiya & Henry Trubner. LC 77-1654. (Illus.). 136p. 1977. 19.95 (*0-685-00530-5*) Asia Soc.

Chinese Ceramics from the Collection of the Baltimore Museum of Art. Frances Klapthor. LC 92-43490. 1993. 14.95 (*0-912298-65-0*) Baltimore Mus.

Chinese Ceramics in the Department of Eastern Art. M. Tregear. (Illus.). 32p. 1995. pap. 6.95 (*0-907849-57-1*, N571, Pub. by Ashmolean Mus UK) A Schwartz & Co.

Chinese Ceramics in the Topkapi Saray Museum, Istanbul: A Complete Catalogue, 3 vols., Set. Regina Krahl & Nurdan Erbahar. Ed. by John Ayers. LC 85-50982. (Illus.). 1384p. 1986. 990.00 (*0-85667-184-3*, Pub. by P Wilson Pubs) Sothebys Pubns.

Chinese Character Exercise Book for Practical Chinese Reader. Ed. by Beijing Language Institute Staff. (Practical Chinese Reader Ser.: No. 1). 208p. (Orig.). (C). 1982. pap. 4.95 (*0-8351-1146-6*) China Bks.

Chinese Character Exercise Book for Practical Chinese Reader. Ed. by Beijing Language Institute Staff. (Practical Chinese Reader Ser.: No. 2). 108p. (Orig.). (C). 1982. pap. 4.95 (*0-8351-1147-4*) China Bks.

Chinese Character Indexes: Vol. 1: Telegraphic Code Index. Vol. 2: Romanization Index. Vol. 3: Radical Index. Vol. 4: Total Stroke Count Index. Vol. 5: Four Corner System Index, Set. Ed. by Ching-yi Dougherty et al. 1963. 175.00 (*0-520-00346-2*) U CA Pr.

Chinese Characters, Their Origin, Etymology, History, Classification & Signification. 2nd ed. L. Wieger. Tr. by L. Davrout. (CHI.). 1927. pap. 13.95 (*0-486-21321-8*) Dover.

Chinese Chess. H. T. Lau. LC 84-52394. (Illus.). 248p. 1991. pap. 9.95 (*0-8048-1675-1*) C E Tuttle.

Chinese Children's Stories, Vol. 1: Two Bushels of Grain, Forget the Turnips! Hwa-I Publishing Co., Staff. Ed. by Emily Ching et al. Tr. by Wonder Kids Publications Staff. (Folklore Ser.). (Illus.). 28p. (J). (gr. 3-6). 1991. reprint ed. 7.95 (*1-56162-001-7*) Wonder Kids.

Chinese Children's Stories, Vol. 10: The Money Tree, The Coxcomb. Hwa-I Publishing Co., Staff. Ed. by Emily Ching et al. Tr. by Wonder Kids Publications Staff. LC 90-60792. (Tales about Plants Ser.). (Illus.). 28p. (J). (gr. 3-6). 1991. reprint ed. 7.95 (*1-56162-010-6*) Wonder Kids.

Chinese Children's Stories, Vol. 100: From Rice into Flowers, The Shy Rainbow. Hwa-I Publishing Co., Staff. Ed. by Emily Ching et al. Tr. by Wonder Kids Publications Staff. LC 90-60811. (Taiwanese Folklore Ser.). (Illus.). 28p. (J). (gr. 3-6). 1991. reprint ed. 7.95 (*1-56162-100-5*) Wonder Kids.

Chinese Children's Stories, Vol. 11: Ker-Plunk is Coming!, Baby Chicks' Revenge. Hwa-I Publishing Co., Staff. Ed. by Emily Ching et al. Tr. by Wonder Kids Publications Staff. (Animal Tales Ser.). (Illus.). 28p. (J). (gr. 3-6). 1991. reprint ed. 7.95 (*1-56162-011-4*) Wonder Kids.

Chinese Children's Stories, Vol. 12: The Snail & the Ox, Sparrows Can't Walk. Hwa-I Publishing Co., Staff. Ed. by Emily Ching et al. Tr. by Wonder Kids Publications Staff. LC 90-60793. (Animal Tales Ser.). (Illus.). 28p. (J). (gr. 3-6). 1991. reprint ed. 7.95 (*1-56162-012-2*) Wonder Kids.

Chinese Children's Stories, Vol. 13: Rooster Summons the Sun, The White-Haired Bird. Hwa-I Publishing Co., Staff. Ed. by Emily Ching et al. Tr. by Wonder Kids Publications Staff. LC 90-60793. (Animal Tales Ser.). (Illus.). 28p. (J). (gr. 3-6). 1991. reprint ed. 7.95 (*1-56162-013-0*) Wonder Kids.

Chinese Children's Stories, Vol. 14: Weasel Steals the Chickens, Why is the Crow Black? Hwa-I Publishing Co., Staff. Ed. by Emily Ching et al. Tr. by Wonder Kids Publications Staff. LC 90-60793. (Animal Tales Ser.). (Illus.). 28p. (J). (gr. 3-6). 1991. reprint ed. 7.95 (*1-56162-014-9*) Wonder Kids.

Chinese Children's Stories, Vol. 15: Jiggle in the Wind, The Bat Can't See the Sun. Hwa-I Publishing Co., Staff. Ed. by Emily Ching et al. Tr. by Wonder Kids Publications Staff. LC 90-60793. (Animal Tales Ser.). (Illus.). 28p. (J). (gr. 3-6). 1991. reprint ed. 7.95 (*1-56162-015-7*) Wonder Kids.

Chinese Children's Stories, Vol. 16: How to Build a Nest, Moving the Mountain. Hwa-I Publishing Co., Staff. Ed. by Emily Ching et al. Tr. by Wonder Kids Publications Staff. (Fables Ser.). (Illus.). 28p. (J). (gr. 3-6). 1991. reprint ed. 7.95 (*1-56162-016-5*) Wonder Kids.

Chinese Children's Stories, Vol. 17: The Monkey & the Fire, Lazy Wife & the Bread Ring. Hwa-I Publishing Co., Staff. Ed. by Emily Ching et al. Tr. by Wonder Kids Publications Staff. LC 90-60794. (Fables Ser.). (Illus.). 28p. (J). (gr. 3-6). 1991. reprint ed. 7.95 (*1-56162-017-3*) Wonder Kids.

Chinese Children's Stories, Vol. 18: The Little Bamboo Pole, The Wise Old Man. Hwa-I Publishing Co., Staff. Ed. by Emily Ching et al. Tr. by Wonder Kids Publications Staff. LC 90-60794. (Fables Ser.). (Illus.). 28p. (J). (gr. 3-6). 1991. reprint ed. 7.95 (*1-56162-018-1*) Wonder Kids.

Chinese Children's Stories, Vol. 19: Crow Moves Away, Baby Lion & Baby Rhino. Hwa-I Publishing Co., Staff. Ed. by Emily Ching et al. Tr. by Wonder Kids Publications Staff. LC 90-60794. (Fables Ser.). (Illus.). 28p. (J). (gr. 3-6). 1991. reprint ed. 7.95 (*1-56162-019-X*) Wonder Kids.

Chinese Children's Stories, Vol. 2: The Blind Man & the Cripple, Orchard Village. Hwa-I Publishing Co., Staff. Ed. by Emily Ching et al. Tr. by Wonder Kids Publications Staff. (Folklore Ser.). (Illus.). 28p. (J). (gr. 3-6). 1991. reprint ed. 7.95 (*1-56162-002-5*) Wonder Kids.

Chinese Children's Stories, Vol. 20: Ah-Liu Picks Corn, Cuckoo's Winter. Hwa-I Publishing Co., Staff. Ed. by Emily Ching et al. Tr. by Wonder Kids Publications Staff. LC 90-60794. (Fables Ser.). (Illus.). 28p. (J). (gr. 3-6). 1991. reprint ed. 7.95 (*1-56162-020-3*) Wonder Kids.

Chinese Children's Stories, Vol. 21: Seamless Clothing, The Big Clam & the Snipe. Hwa-I Publishing Co., Staff. Ed. by Emily Ching et al. Tr. by Wonder Kids Publications Staff. (Idioms Ser.). (Illus.). 28p. (J). (gr. 3-6). 1991. reprint ed. 7.95 (*1-56162-021-1*) Wonder Kids.

Chinese Children's Stories, Vol. 22: The Steal a Bell, The Dropout. Hwa-I Publishing Co., Staff. Ed. by Emily Ching et al. Tr. by Wonder Kids Publications Staff. LC 90-60796. (Idioms Ser.). (Illus.). 28p. (J). (gr. 3-6). 1991. reprint ed. 7.95 (*1-56162-022-X*) Wonder Kids.

Chinese Children's Stories, Vol. 23: Dummy Afa, The Fox in a Tiger's Suit. Hwa-I Publishing Co., Staff. Ed. by Emily Ching et al. Tr. by Wonder Kids Publications Staff. LC 90-60796. (Idioms Ser.). (Illus.). 28p. (J). (gr. 3-6). 1991. reprint ed. 7.95 (*1-56162-023-8*) Wonder Kids.

C

Chinese Children's Stories, Vol. 24: Running Fifty vs. One-Hundred Strides, Atu Yanks the Rice Seedlings. Hwa-I Publishing Co., Staff. Ed. by Emily Ching et al. Tr. by Wonder Kids Publications Staff. LC 90-60796. (Idioms Ser.). (Illus.). 28p. (J). (gr. 3-6). 1991. reprint ed. 7.95 (*1-56162-024-6*) Wonder Kids.

Chinese Children's Stories, Vol. 25: The Blindmen & the Elephant, Little Frog in the Well. Hwa-I Publishing Co., Staff. Ed. by Emily Ching et al. Tr. by Wonder Kids Publications Staff. LC 90-60796. (Idioms Ser.). (Illus.). 28p. (J). (gr. 3-6). 1991. reprint ed. 7.95 (*1-56162-025-4*) Wonder Kids.

Chinese Children's Stories, Vol. 26: Celebrating New York, Miss Yuan-Tsau. Hwa-I Publishing Co., Staff. Ed. by Emily Ching et al. Tr. by Wonder Kids Publications Staff. (Festivals Ser.). (Illus.). 28p. (J). (gr. 3-6). 1991. reprint ed. 7.95 (*1-56162-026-2*) Wonder Kids.

Chinese Children's Stories, Vol. 27: Sky-Mending Festival, Decorative Paper for Graves. Hwa-I Publishing Co., Staff. Ed. by Emily Ching et al. Tr. by Wonder Kids Publications Staff. LC 90-60797. (Festivals Ser.). (Illus.). 28p. (J). (gr. 3-6). 1991. reprint ed. 7.95 (*1-56162-027-0*) Wonder Kids.

Chinese Children's Stories, Vol. 28: Mih-Ro River, The Herder & the Seamstress. Hwa-I Publishing Co., Staff. Ed. by Emily Ching et al. Tr. by Wonder Kids Publications Staff. LC 90-60797. (Festivals Ser.). (Illus.). 28p. (J). (gr. 3-6). 1991. reprint ed. 7.95 (*1-56162-028-9*) Wonder Kids.

Chinese Children's Stories, Vol. 29: Moon Cake, Fei's Adventure. Hwa-I Publishing Co., Staff. Ed. by Emily Ching et al. Tr. by Wonder Kids Publications Staff. LC 90-60797. (Festivals Ser.). (Illus.). 28p. (J). (gr. 3-6). 1991. reprint ed. 7.95 (*1-56162-029-7*) Wonder Kids.

Chinese Children's Stories, Vol. 3: The Redbud Tree, Lazy Bones & the Magical Bowl. Hwa-I Publishing Co., Staff. Ed. by Emily Ching et al. Tr. by Wonder Kids Publications Staff. (Folklore Ser.). (Illus.). 28p. (J). (gr. 3-6). 1991. reprint ed. 7.95 (*1-56162-003-3*) Wonder Kids.

Chinese Children's Stories, Vol. 30: La-Ba Porridge, The Stove God. Hwa-I Publishing Co., Staff. Ed. by Emily Ching et al. Tr. by Wonder Kids Publications Staff. LC 90-60797. (Festivals Ser.). (Illus.). 28p. (J). (gr. 3-6). 1991. reprint ed. 7.95 (*1-56162-030-0*) Wonder Kids.

Chinese Children's Stories, Vol. 31: The Refugee Empress, Chi Jiguang Cookies. Hwa-I Publishing Co., Staff. Ed. by Emily Ching et al. Tr. by Wonder Kids Publications Staff. (Tales about Food Ser.). (Illus.). 28p. (J). (gr. 3-6). 1991. reprint ed. 7.95 (*1-56162-031-9*) Wonder Kids.

Chinese Children's Stories, Vol. 32: Dumplings, Ham. Hwa-I Publishing Co., Staff. Ed. by Emily Ching et al. Tr. by Wonder Kids Publications Staff. LC 90-60798. (Tales about Food Ser.). (Illus.). 28p. (J). (gr. 3-6). 1991. reprint ed. 7.95 (*1-56162-032-7*) Wonder Kids.

Chinese Children's Stories, Vol. 33: Noodles over the Bridge, Steamed Bread. Hwa-I Publishing Co., Staff. Ed. by Emily Ching et al. Tr. by Wonder Kids Publications Staff. LC 90-60798. (Tales about Food Ser.). (Illus.). 28p. (J). (gr. 3-6). 1991. reprint ed. 7.95 (*1-56162-033-5*) Wonder Kids.

An Asterisk (*) at the beginning of an entry indicates that the title is appearing in BIP for the first time.

Chinese Children's Stories, Vol. 34: The Stuffed Steamed Bao, Miss Freckle's Tofu. Hwa-I Publishing Co., Staff. Ed. by Emily Ching et al. Tr. by Wonder Kids Publications Staff. LC 90-60798. (Tales about Food Ser.). (Illus.). 28p. (J). (gr. 3-6). 1991. reprint ed. 7.95 (*1-56162-034-3*) Wonder Kids.

Chinese Children's Stories, Vol. 35: Monks' Beef Stew, Yue's Tofu Store. Hwa-I Publishing Co., Staff. Ed. by Emily Ching et al. Tr. by Wonder Kids Publications Staff. LC 90-60798. (Tales about Food Ser.). (Illus.). 28p. (J). (gr. 3-6). 1991. reprint ed. 7.95 (*1-56162-035-1*) Wonder Kids.

Chinese Children's Stories, Vol. 36: Lu Ban & Old Sir Lee, Umbrellas. Hwa-I Publishing Co., Staff. Ed. by Emily Ching et al. Tr. by Wonder Kids Publications Staff. (Inventions Ser.). (Illus.). 28p. (J). (gr. 3-6). 1991. reprint ed. 7.95 (*1-56162-036-X*) Wonder Kids.

Chinese Children's Stories, Vol. 37: Confucius' Bookkeeping, The Scissors Shop. Hwa-I Publishing Co., Staff. Ed. by Emily Ching et al. Tr. by Wonder Kids Publications Staff. LC 90-60799. (Inventions Ser.). (Illus.). 28p. (J). (gr. 3-6). 1991. reprint ed. 7.95 (*1-56162-037-8*) Wonder Kids.

Chinese Children's Stories, Vol. 38: The Peace Drum, Comb. Hwa-I Publishing Co., Staff. Ed. by Emily Ching et al. Tr. by Wonder Kids Publications Staff. LC 90-60799. (Inventions Ser.). (Illus.). 28p. (J). (gr. 3-6). 1991. reprint ed. 7.95 (*1-56162-038-6*) Wonder Kids.

Chinese Children's Stories, Vol. 39: Brush Pen, Duan's Ink-Slab. Hwa-I Publishing Co., Staff. Ed. by Emily Ching et al. Tr. by Wonder Kids Publications Staff. LC 90-6079. (Inventions Ser.). (Illus.). 28p. (J). (gr. 3-6). 1991. reprint ed. 7.95 (*1-56162-039-4*) Wonder Kids.

Chinese Children's Stories, Vol. 4: Golden Needles, Three Treasures. Hwa-I Publishing Co., Staff. Ed. by Emily Ching et al. Tr. by Wonder Kids Publications Staff. (Folklore Ser.). (Illus.). 28p. (J). (gr. 3-6). 1991. reprint ed. 7.95 (*1-56162-004-1*) Wonder Kids.

Chinese Children's Stories, Vol. 40: The Ink-Stick, Shiuan Paper. Hwa-I Publishing Co., Staff. Ed. by Emily Ching et al. Tr. by Wonder Kids Publications Staff. LC 90-60799. (Inventions Ser.). (Illus.). 28p. (J). (gr. 3-6). 1991. reprint ed. 7.95 (*1-56162-040-8*) Wonder Kids.

Chinese Children's Stories, Vol. 41: Brother Cat & Brother Rat, The Rooster's Antlers. Hwa-I Publishing Co., Staff. Ed. by Emily Ching et al. Tr. by Wonder Kids Publications Staff. (Twelve Beasts & the Years Ser.). (Illus.). 28p. (J). (gr. 3-6). 1991. reprint ed. 7.95 (*1-56162-041-6*) Wonder Kids.

Chinese Children's Stories, Vol. 42: Tiger Seeks a Master, Why Are Cats Afraid of Dogs? Hwa-I Publishing Co., Staff. Ed. by Emily Ching et al. Tr. by Wonder Kids Publications Staff. LC 90-60800. (Twelve Beasts & the Years Ser.). (Illus.). 28p. (J). (gr. 3-6). 1991. reprint ed. 7.95 (*1-56162-042-4*) Wonder Kids.

Chinese Children's Stories, Vol. 43: The Bunny's Tail, Fox, Monkey, Rabbit & Horse. Hwa-I Publishing Co., Staff. Ed. by Emily Ching et al. Tr. by Wonder Kids Publications Staff. LC 90-60800. (Twelve Beasts & the Years Ser.). (Illus.). 28p. (J). (gr. 3-6). 1991. reprint ed. 7.95 (*1-56162-043-2*) Wonder Kids.

Chinese Children's Stories, Vol. 44: Snake's Lost Drum, Ox & Buffalo Change Clothes. Hwa-I Publishing Co., Staff. Ed. by Emily Ching et al. Tr. by Wonder Kids Publications Staff. LC 90-60800. (Twelve Beasts & the Years Ser.). (Illus.). 28p. (J). (gr. 3-6). 1991. reprint ed. 7.95 (*1-56162-044-0*) Wonder Kids.

Chinese Children's Stories, Vol. 45: The Goat & the Camel, The Wolf & the Pig. Hwa-I Publishing Co., Staff. Ed. by Emily Ching et al. Tr. by Wonder Kids Publications Staff. LC 90-60800. (Twelve Beasts & the Years Ser.). (Illus.). 28p. (J). (gr. 3-6). 1991. reprint ed. 7.95 (*1-56162-045-9*) Wonder Kids.

Chinese Children's Stories, Vol. 46: Ma-Gu's Cock-a-Doodle-Doo, The Crippled God. Hwa-I Publishing Co., Staff. Ed. by Emily Ching et al. Tr. by Wonder Kids Publications Staff. (Fairy Tales Ser.). (Illus.). 28p. (J). (gr. 3-6). 1991. reprint ed. 7.95 (*1-56162-046-7*) Wonder Kids.

Chinese Children's Stories, Vol. 47: The Crane-Riding Immortal, Lyu Dungbin & Guanyin. Hwa-I Publishing Co., Staff. Ed. by Emily Ching et al. Tr. by Wonder Kids Publications Staff. LC 90-60801. (Fairy Tales Ser.). (Illus.). 28p. (J). (gr. 3-6). 1991. reprint ed. 7.95 (*1-56162-047-5*) Wonder Kids.

Chinese Children's Stories, Vol. 48: Sir Thunder & Lady Lightning, The Door Guards. Hwa-I Publishing Co., Staff. Ed. by Emily Ching et al. Tr. by Wonder Kids Publications Staff. LC 90-60801. (Folklore Ser.). (Illus.). 28p. (J). (gr. 3-6). 1991. reprint ed. 7.95 (*1-56162-048-3*) Wonder Kids.

Chinese Children's Stories, Vol. 49: The Slippery Nose Deity, Under the Moonlight. Hwa-I Publishing Co., Staff. Ed. by Emily Ching et al. Tr. by Wonder Kids Publications Staff. LC 90-60801. (Fairy Tales Ser.). (Illus.). 28p. (J). (gr. 3-6). 1991. reprint ed. 7.95 (*1-56162-049-1*) Wonder Kids.

Chinese Children's Stories, Vol. 5: Sun Valley, A Stone Carver's Dream. Hwa-I Publishing Co., Staff. Ed. by Emily Ching et al. Tr. by Wonder Kids Publications Staff. (Illus.). 28p. (J). (gr. 3-6). 1991. reprint ed. 7.95 (*0-685-49019-X*) Wonder Kids.

Chinese Children's Stories, Vol. 50: Zung Kuei & the Little Ghost, Earth God & Earth Goddess. Hwa-I Publishing Co., Staff. Ed. by Emily Ching et al. Tr. by Wonder Kids Publications Staff. LC 90-60801. (Fairy Tales Ser.). (Illus.). 28p. (J). (gr. 3-6). 1991. reprint ed. 7.95 (*1-56162-050-5*) Wonder Kids.

Chinese Children's Stories, Vol. 51: Moginlin Saves His Mother, Hwang Shun & His Father. Hwa-I Publishing Co., Staff. Ed. by Emily Ching et al. Tr. by Wonder Kids Publications Staff. (Filial Piety Ser.). (Illus.). 28p. (J). (gr. 3-6). 1991. reprint ed. 7.95 (*1-56162-051-3*) Wonder Kids.

Chinese Children's Stories, Vol. 52: Joining the Army, Beating up the Tiger. Hwa-I Publishing Co., Staff. Ed. by Emily Ching et al. Tr. by Wonder Kids Publications Staff. LC 90-60802. (Filial Piety Ser.). (Illus.). 28p. (J). (gr. 3-6). 1991. reprint ed. 7.95 (*1-56162-052-1*) Wonder Kids.

Chinese Children's Stories, Vol. 53: Meeting an Angel, The Child in the Deer Skin. Hwa-I Publishing Co., Staff. Ed. by Emily Ching et al. Tr. by Wonder Kids Publications Staff. LC 90-60802. (Filial Piety Ser.). (Illus.). 28p. (J). (gr. 3-6). 1991. reprint ed. 7.95 (*1-56162-053-X*) Wonder Kids.

Chinese Children's Stories, Vol. 54: The Story of Shun, Village of Filial Piety. Hwa-I Publishing Co., Staff. Ed. by Emily Ching et al. Tr. by Wonder Kids Publications Staff. LC 90-60802. (Filial Piety Ser.). (Illus.). 28p. (J). (gr. 3-6). 1991. reprint ed. 7.95 (*1-56162-054-8*) Wonder Kids.

Chinese Children's Stories, Vol. 55: Two Baskets of Mulberries, Trun's Little Daughter. Hwa-I Publishing Co., Staff. Ed. by Emily Ching et al. Tr. by Wonder Kids Publications Staff. LC 90-60802. (Filial Piety Ser.). (Illus.). 28p. (J). (gr. 3-6). 1991. reprint ed. 7.95 (*1-56162-055-6*) Wonder Kids.

Chinese Children's Stories, Vol. 56: Catching a Thief, The Plum Tree by the Road. Hwa-I Publishing Co., Staff. Ed. by Emily Ching et al. Tr. by Wonder Kids Publications Staff. (Wonder Kids Ser.). (Illus.). 28p. (J). (gr. 3-6). 1991. reprint ed. 7.95 (*1-56162-056-4*) Wonder Kids.

Chinese Children's Stories, Vol. 57: The Little-Boy God, A Rooster's Egg. Hwa-I Publishing Co., Staff. Ed. by Emily Ching et al. Tr. by Wonder Kids Publications Staff. LC 90-60803. (Wonder Kids Ser.). (Illus.). 28p. (J). (gr. 3-6). 1991. reprint ed. 7.95 (*1-56162-057-2*) Wonder Kids.

Chinese Children's Stories, Vol. 58: Three Princes & the Firewood, Wang's Memory. Hwa-I Publishing Co., Staff. Ed. by Emily Ching et al. Tr. by Wonder Kids Publications Staff. LC 90-60803. (Wonder Kids Ser.). (Illus.). 28p. (J). (gr. 3-6). 1991. reprint ed. 7.95 (*1-56162-058-0*) Wonder Kids.

Chinese Children's Stories, Vol. 59: A Tankful of Water, The Little Hero. Hwa-I Publishing Co., Staff. Ed. by Emily Ching et al. Tr. by Wonder Kids Publications Staff. LC 90-60803. (Wonder Kids Ser.). (Illus.). 28p. (J). (gr. 3-6). 1991. reprint ed. 7.95 (*1-56162-059-9*) Wonder Kids.

Chinese Children's Stories, Vol. 6: Miss Gold 'n' Silver, Pearl Rice. Hwa-I Publishing Co., Staff. Ed. by Emily Ching et al. Tr. by Wonder Kids Publications Staff. (Tales about Plants Ser.). (Illus.). 28p. (J). (gr. 3-6). 1991. reprint ed. 7.95 (*1-56162-006-8*) Wonder Kids.

Chinese Children's Stories, Vol. 60: Weighing an Elephant, The Distant Homeland. Hwa-I Publishing Co., Staff. Ed. by Emily Ching et al. Tr. by Wonder Kids Publications Staff. LC 90-60803. (Wonder Kids Ser.). (Illus.). 28p. (J). (gr. 3-6). 1991. reprint ed. 7.95 (*1-56162-060-2*) Wonder Kids.

Chinese Children's Stories, Vol. 61: Pan Koo Creates the World, A Hole in the Sky. Hwa-I Publishing Co., Staff. Ed. by Emily Ching et al. Tr. by Wonder Kids Publications Staff. (Mythology Ser.). (Illus.). 28p. (J). (gr. 3-6). 1991. reprint ed. 7.95 (*1-56162-061-0*) Wonder Kids.

Chinese Children's Stories, Vol. 62: To Catch the Suns, Two Quarrelsome Brothers. Hwa-I Publishing Co., Staff. Ed. by Emily Ching et al. Tr. by Wonder Kids Publications Staff. LC 90-60804. (Mythology Ser.). (Illus.). 28p. (J). (gr. 3-6). 1991. reprint ed. 7.95 (*1-56162-062-9*) Wonder Kids.

Chinese Children's Stories, Vol. 63: To Speak or Not, The Dark Village. Hwa-I Publishing Co., Staff. Ed. by Emily Ching et al. Tr. by Wonder Kids Publications Staff. LC 90-60804. (Mythology Ser.). (Illus.). 28p. (J). (gr. 3-6). 1991. reprint ed. 7.95 (*1-56162-063-7*) Wonder Kids.

Chinese Children's Stories, Vol. 64: Why Is the Sky So High?, Turning into Stone. Hwa-I Publishing Co., Staff. Ed. by Emily Ching et al. Tr. by Wonder Kids Publications Staff. LC 90-60804. (Mythology Ser.). (Illus.). 28p. (J). (gr. 3-6). 1991. reprint ed. 7.95 (*1-56162-064-5*) Wonder Kids.

Chinese Children's Stories, Vol. 65: Lugging Mountains, What's a Life Span? Hwa-I Publishing Co., Staff. Ed. by Emily Ching et al. Tr. by Wonder Kids Publications Staff. LC 90-60804. (Mythology Ser.). (Illus.). 28p. (J). (gr. 3-6). 1991. reprint ed. 7.95 (*1-56162-065-3*) Wonder Kids.

Chinese Children's Stories, Vol. 66: The Chiao Sisters, Zhou under the Bed. Hwa-I Publishing Co., Staff. Ed. by Emily Ching et al. Tr. by Wonder Kids Publications Staff. (Literature Ser.). (Illus.). 28p. (J). (gr. 3-6). 1991. reprint ed. 7.95 (*1-56162-066-1*) Wonder Kids.

Chinese Children's Stories, Vol. 67: The After-Meal Bell, Passing the Three Gorges. Hwa-I Publishing Co., Staff. Ed. by Emily Ching et al. Tr. by Wonder Kids Publications Staff. LC 90-60805. (Literature Ser.). (Illus.). 28p. (J). (gr. 3-6). 1991. reprint ed. 7.95 (*1-56162-067-X*) Wonder Kids.

Chinese Children's Stories, Vol. 68: The Donkey-Riding Poet, The Backyard Song. Hwa-I Publishing Co., Staff. Ed. by Emily Ching et al. Tr. by Wonder Kids Publications Staff. LC 90-60805. (Literature Ser.). (Illus.). 28p. (J). (gr. 3-6). 1991. reprint ed. 7.95 (*1-56162-068-8*) Wonder Kids.

Chinese Children's Stories, Vol. 69: The Young Family, Tsuei's Beautiful Bride. Hwa-I Publishing Co., Staff. Ed. by Emily Ching et al. Tr. by Wonder Kids Publications Staff. LC 90-60805. (Literature Ser.). (Illus.). 28p. (J). (gr. 3-6). 1991. reprint ed. 7.95 (*1-56162-069-6*) Wonder Kids.

Chinese Children's Stories, Vol. 7: Dragon Eye & Cassia Circle, The Conceited Barber. Hwa-I Publishing Co., Staff. Ed. by Emily Ching et al. Tr. by Wonder Kids Publications Staff. LC 90-60792. (Tales about Plants Ser.). (Illus.). 28p. (J). (gr. 3-6). 1991. reprint ed. 7.95 (*1-56162-007-6*) Wonder Kids.

Chinese Children's Stories, Vol. 70: Ji's Jokes, The Scrooge. Hwa-I Publishing Co., Staff. Ed. by Emily Ching et al. Tr. by Wonder Kids Publications Staff. LC 90-60805. (Literature Ser.). (Illus.). 28p. (J). (gr. 3-6). 1991. reprint ed. 7.95 (*1-56162-070-X*) Wonder Kids.

Chinese Children's Stories, Vol. 71: The Magic Glass Jar, The Pear Tree. Hwa-I Publishing Co., Staff. Ed. by Emily Ching et al. Tr. by Wonder Kids Publications Staff. (Popular Narratives Ser.). (Illus.). 28p. (J). (gr. 3-6). 1991. reprint ed. 7.95 (*1-56162-071-8*) Wonder Kids.

Chinese Children's Stories, Vol. 72: The Lotus Child, The Ghost in the Basin. Hwa-I Publishing Co., Staff. Ed. by Emily Ching et al. Tr. by Wonder Kids Publications Staff. LC 90-60806. (Popular Narratives Ser.). (Illus.). 28p. (J). (gr. 3-6). 1991. reprint ed. 7.95 (*1-56162-072-6*) Wonder Kids.

Chinese Children's Stories, Vol. 73: Walking through Walls, Who Is the Real Lord Ji? Hwa-I Publishing Co., Staff. Ed. by Emily Ching et al. Tr. by Wonder Kids Publications Staff. LC 90-60806. (Popular Narratives Ser.). (Illus.). 28p. (J). (gr. 3-6). 1991. reprint ed. 7.95 (*1-56162-073-4*) Wonder Kids.

Chinese Children's Stories, Vol. 74: Chaos in the Heavenly Palace, Eating the Ginseng Fruit. Hwa-I Publishing Co., Staff. Ed. by Emily Ching et al. Tr. by Wonder Kids Publications Staff. LC 90-60806. (Popular Narratives Ser.). (Illus.). 28p. (J). (gr. 3-6). 1991. reprint ed. 7.95 (*1-56162-074-2*) Wonder Kids.

Chinese Children's Stories, Vol. 75: Tang's Strange Journey, Dwarfs & Giants. Hwa-I Publishing Co., Staff. Ed. by Emily Ching et al. Tr. by Wonder Kids Publications Staff. LC 90-60806. (Popular Narratives Ser.). (Illus.). 28p. (J). (gr. 3-6). 1991. reprint ed. 7.95 (*1-56162-075-0*) Wonder Kids.

Chinese Children's Stories, Vol. 76: The Stinky Emperor, The Hero Who Crawled. Hwa-I Publishing Co., Staff. Ed. by Emily Ching et al. Tr. by Wonder Kids Publications Staff. (Heroes Ser.). (Illus.). 28p. (J). (gr. 3-6). 1991. reprint ed. 7.95 (*1-56162-076-9*) Wonder Kids.

Chinese Children's Stories, Vol. 77: Sir Guan's Big Red Face, Turning Cranes into Words. Hwa-I Publishing Co., Staff. Ed. by Emily Ching et al. Tr. by Wonder Kids Publications Staff. LC 90-60807. (Heroes Ser.). (Illus.). 28p. (J). (gr. 3-6). 1991. reprint ed. 7.95 (*1-56162-077-7*) Wonder Kids.

Chinese Children's Stories, Vol. 78: Tang Buohu's Drawings, The General & the Water Tank. Hwa-I Publishing Co., Staff. Ed. by Emily Ching et al. Tr. by Wonder Kids Publications Staff. LC 90-60807. (Heroes Ser.). (Illus.). 28p. (J). (gr. 3-6). 1991. reprint ed. 7.95 (*1-56162-078-5*) Wonder Kids.

Chinese Children's Stories, Vol. 79: Black-Faced Sir Bao, Doctor Hwa-Tuo. Hwa-I Publishing Co., Staff. Ed. by Emily Ching et al. Tr. by Wonder Kids Publications Staff. LC 90-60807. (Heroes Ser.). (Illus.). 28p. (J). (gr. 3-6). 1991. reprint ed. 7.95 (*1-56162-079-3*) Wonder Kids.

Chinese Children's Stories, Vol. 8: The Millets Won't Go Home, The Immortal Palm. Hwa-I Publishing Co., Staff. Ed. by Emily Ching et al. Tr. by Wonder Kids Publications Staff. LC 90-60792. (Tales about Plants Ser.). (Illus.). 28p. (J). (gr. 3-6). 1991. reprint ed. 7.95 (*1-56162-008-4*) Wonder Kids.

Chinese Children's Stories, Vol. 80: The Dwarf Minister, The Fabulous Chimera's Gift. Hwa-I Publishing Co., Staff. Ed. by Emily Ching et al. Tr. by Wonder Kids Publications Staff. LC 90-60807. (Heroes Ser.). (Illus.). 28p. (J). (gr. 3-6). 1991. reprint ed. 7.95 (*1-56162-080-7*) Wonder Kids.

Chinese Children's Stories, Vol. 81: The Emperor vs. the Rebel, The Queen & the Fire. Hwa-I Publishing Co., Staff. Ed. by Emily Ching et al. Tr. by Wonder Kids Publications Staff. (Historical Accounts Ser.). (Illus.). 28p. (J). (gr. 3-6). 1991. reprint ed. 7.95 (*1-56162-081-5*) Wonder Kids.

Chinese Children's Stories, Vol. 82: The Fish Minister, The Hidden Sword. Hwa-I Publishing Co., Staff. Ed. by Emily Ching et al. Tr. by Wonder Kids Publications Staff. LC 90-60808. (Historical Accounts Ser.). (Illus.). 28p. (J). (gr. 3-6). 1991. reprint ed. 7.95 (*1-56162-082-3*) Wonder Kids.

Chinese Children's Stories, Vol. 83: The Revenge of Chao's Orphan, Tien's Wonderful Strategies. Hwa-I Publishing Co., Staff. Ed. by Emily Ching et al. Tr. by Wonder Kids Publications Staff. LC 90-60808. (Historical Accounts Ser.). (Illus.). 28p. (J). (gr. 3-6). 1991. reprint ed. 7.95 (*1-56162-083-1*) Wonder Kids.

Chinese Children's Stories, Vol. 84: Who Is the Real Liu Bong?, Kong Borrows the East Wind. Hwa-I Publishing Co., Staff. Ed. by Emily Ching et al. Tr. by Wonder Kids Publications Staff. LC 90-60808. (Historical Accounts Ser.). (Illus.). 28p. (J). (gr. 3-6). 1991. reprint ed. 7.95 (*1-56162-084-X*) Wonder Kids.

Chinese Children's Stories, Vol. 85: The Battle of the Fei River, The Princess' Engagement. Hwa-I Publishing Co., Staff. Ed. by Emily Ching et al. Tr. by Wonder Kids Publications Staff. LC 90-60808. (Historical Accounts Ser.). (Illus.). 28p. (J). (gr. 3-6). 1991. reprint ed. 7.95 (*1-56162-085-8*) Wonder Kids.

Chinese Children's Stories, Vol. 86: From Crows into Bricks, Two Treasured Swords. Hwa-I Publishing Co., Staff. Ed. by Emily Ching et al. Tr. by Wonder Kids Publications Staff. (Chinese Sites Ser.). (Illus.). 28p. (J). (gr. 3-6). 1991. reprint ed. 7.95 (*1-56162-086-6*) Wonder Kids.

Chinese Children's Stories, Vol. 87: Fan Bridge & Escape Alley, The Stream of Flowers. Hwa-I Publishing Co., Staff. Ed. by Emily Ching et al. Tr. by Wonder Kids Publications Staff. LC 90-60809. (Chinese Sites Ser.). (Illus.). 28p. (J). (gr. 3-6). 1991. reprint ed. 7.95 (*1-56162-087-4*) Wonder Kids.

Chinese Children's Stories, Vol. 88: Five Stone Goats, Six-Foot Street. Hwa-I Publishing Co., Staff. Ed. by Emily Ching et al. Tr. by Wonder Kids Publications Staff. LC 90-60809. (Chinese Sites Ser.). (Illus.). 28p. (J). (gr. 3-6). 1991. reprint ed. 7.95 (*1-56162-088-2*) Wonder Kids.

Chinese Children's Stories, Vol. 89: Peach Blossom Cave, Mt. Lee. Hwa-I Publishing Co., Staff. Ed. by Emily Ching et al. Tr. by Wonder Kids Publications Staff. LC 90-60809. (Chinese Sites Ser.). (Illus.). 28p. (J). (gr. 3-6). 1991. reprint ed. 7.95 (*1-56162-089-0*) Wonder Kids.

Chinese Children's Stories, Vol. 9: The Story of Rice, The Cows & the Trumpet. Hwa-I Publishing Co., Staff. Ed. by Emily Ching et al. Tr. by Wonder Kids Publications Staff. LC 90-60792. (Tales about Plants Ser.). (Illus.). 28p. (J). (gr. 3-6). 1991. reprint ed. 7.95 (*1-56162-009-2*) Wonder Kids.

Chinese Children's Stories, Vol. 90: The Dragon Who Puts out Fires, The Golden Hairpin Well. Hwa-I Publishing Co., Staff. Ed. by Emily Ching et al. Tr. by Wonder Kids Publications Staff. LC 90-60809. (Chinese Sites Ser.). (Illus.). 28p. (J). (gr. 3-6). 1991. reprint ed. 7.95 (*1-56162-090-4*) Wonder Kids.

Chinese Children's Stories, Vol. 91: A Little City, Beating the Devil. Hwa-I Publishing Co., Staff. Ed. by Emily Ching et al. Tr. by Wonder Kids Publications Staff. (Taiwanese Sites Ser.). (Illus.). 28p. (J). (gr. 3-6). 1991. reprint ed. 7.95 (*1-56162-091-2*) Wonder Kids.

Chinese Children's Stories, Vol. 92: White-Rice Magic Cave, Sun-Moon Lake. Hwa-I Publishing Co., Staff. Ed. by Emily Ching et al. Tr. by Wonder Kids Publications Staff. LC 90-60810. (Taiwanese Sites Ser.). (Illus.). 28p. (J). (gr. 3-6). 1991. reprint ed. 7.95 (*1-56162-092-0*) Wonder Kids.

Chinese Children's Stories, Vol. 93: Mt. Anvil & the Sword Well, Two Waters. Hwa-I Publishing Co., Staff. Ed. by Emily Ching et al. Tr. by Wonder Kids Publications Staff. LC 90-60810. (Taiwanese Sites Ser.). (Illus.). 28p. (J). (gr. 3-6). 1991. reprint ed. 7.95 (*1-56162-093-9*) Wonder Kids.

Chinese Children's Stories, Vol. 94: Muddy Water Stream, Sister Lakes & Brother Trees. Hwa-I Publishing Co., Staff. Ed. by Emily Ching et al. Tr. by Wonder Kids Publications Staff. LC 90-60810. (Taiwanese Sites Ser.). (Illus.). 28p. (J). (gr. 3-6). 1991. reprint ed. 7.95 (*1-56162-094-7*) Wonder Kids.

Chinese Children's Stories, Vol. 95: Half-Shield Mountain, The Adopted Daughter Lake. Hwa-I Publishing Co., Staff. Ed. by Emily Ching et al. Tr. by Wonder Kids Publications Staff. LC 90-60810. (Taiwanese Sites Ser.). (Illus.). 28p. (J). (gr. 3-6). 1991. reprint ed. 7.95 (*1-56162-095-5*) Wonder Kids.

Chinese Children's Stories, Vol. 96: Tsi, the Cheat, The Mill in the Sea. Hwa-I Publishing Co., Staff. Ed. by Emily Ching et al. Tr. by Wonder Kids Publications Staff. (Taiwanese Folklore Ser.). (Illus.). 28p. (J). (gr. 3-6). 1991. reprint ed. 7.95 (*1-56162-096-3*) Wonder Kids.

Chinese Children's Stories, Vol. 97: Tiger Aunty, Ah-Long & Ah-Hwa. Hwa-I Publishing Co., Staff. Ed. by Emily Ching et al. Tr. by Wonder Kids Publications Staff. LC 90-60811. (Taiwanese Folklore Ser.). (Illus.). 28p. (J). (gr. 3-6). 1991. reprint ed. 7.95 (*1-56162-097-1*) Wonder Kids.

Chinese Children's Stories, Vol. 98: Ai-Yu Jello, Granny & the Fox. Hwa-I Publishing Co., Staff. Ed. by Emily Ching et al. Tr. by Wonder Kids Publications Staff. LC 90-60811. (Taiwanese Folklore Ser.). (Illus.). 28p. (J). (gr. 3-6). 1991. reprint ed. 7.95 (*1-56162-098-X*) Wonder Kids.

Chinese Children's Stories, Vol. 99: The Underground People, Half-Street Lai. Hwa-I Publishing Co., Staff. Ed. by Emily Ching et al. Tr. by Wonder Kids Publications Staff. LC 90-60811. (Taiwanese Folklore Ser.). (Illus.). 28p. (J). (gr. 3-6). 1991. reprint ed. 7.95 (*1-56162-099-8*) Wonder Kids.

Chinese Chronological History: From Prehistory Through 1950. Alfonz Lengyel. (Museum Study Ser.: No. 4). 108p. (Orig.). 1993. pap. 10.00 (*0-9626500-3-X*) Fudan Mus Fndtn.

Chinese Cinema: Culture & Politics since 1949. Paul Clark. (Cambridge Studies in Film). (Illus.). 256p. 1988. 65.00 (*0-521-32638-9*) Cambridge U Pr.

Chinese City Between Two Worlds. Ed. by Mark Elvin & G. William Skinner. LC 73-89858. (Studies in Chinese Society). 480p. 1974. 57.50 (*0-8047-0853-3*) Stanford U Pr.

Chinese Civil Law. V. A. Riasanovsky. LC 76-20214. (Studies in Chinese Government & Law). 310p. 1976. reprint ed. text ed. 55.00 (*0-313-26965-3*, U6965, Greenwood Pr) Greenwood.

***Chinese Civil Wars, 1911-1949.** Arthur N. Waldron. (Modern Wars Ser.). 256p. 1995. 49.95 (*0-340-64535-0*, Pub. by E Arnld UK); pap. 16.95 (*0-340-58264-2*, Pub. by E Arnld UK) St Martin.

C

An Asterisk (*) at the beginning of an entry indicates that the title is appearing in BIP for the first time.

Chinese Civilization. Marcel Granet. LC 74-38068. reprint ed. 42.50 (*0-404-56974-9*) AMS Pr.

Chinese Civilization: A Sourcebook. rev. ed. Ed. by Patricia B. Ebrey. LC 92-47017. 524p. 1993. pap. 19.95 (*0-02-908752-X*) Free Pr.

Chinese Civilization: An Introduction to Sinology. Kang-hu Kiang. 1972. lib. bdg. 79.95 (*0-87968-531-X*) Krishna Pr.

Chinese Civilization & Bureaucracy: Variations on a Theme. Etienne Balazs. Ed. by Arthur F. Wright. Tr. by H. M. Wright. LC 64-20909. 331p. reprint ed. pap. 94.40 (*0-8357-8712-5*, 2033665) Bks Demand.

Chinese Civilization & Society: A Sourcebook. Ed. by Patricia B. Ebrey. LC 80-639. 1981. 27.95 (*0-02-908750-3*); pap. 18.95 (*0-02-908760-0*) Free Pr.

Chinese Classical Gardens of Suzhou. China Architecture Building Inc. Staff. 1993. text ed. 65.00 (*0-07-010876-5*) McGraw.

Chinese Classical Work Commonly Called the Four Books, 1828. Ssu Shu. Ed. by David Collie. LC 75-122487. 1970. reprint ed. 50.00 (*0-8201-1079-5*) Schol Facsimiles.

Chinese Classics, 4 vols. Tr. by James Legge. (CHI & ENG.). 1991. reprint ed. Vol. I, Four Books of Chinese Classics: Confucian Analects; Great Learning: Doctrine of the Mean; Wo. 35.00 (*0-318-63251-9*); reprint ed. Vol. II, Sho King, or the Book of Historical Documents. 35.00 (*0-318-63252-7*) Oriental Bk Store.

Chinese Classics, 4 vols., Set. Tr. by James Legge. (CHI & ENG.). 1991. 135.00 (*0-685-65145-2*, Pub. by SMC Pub CC) Oriental Bk Store.

Chinese Classics, 4 vols., Set. Tr. by James Legge. (CHI & ENG.). 1991. reprint ed. 135.00 (*957-638-038-3*, Pub. by SMC Pub CC) Oriental Bk Store.

Chinese Classics, 4 vols., Vol. III: She King, or the Book of Poetry. Tr. by James Legge. (CHI & ENG.). 1991. reprint ed. Vol. III, She King, or the Book of Poetry. 35.00 (*0-318-63253-5*) Oriental Bk Store.

Chinese Classics, 4 vols., Vol. IV: Ch'un Ts'ew with the Tso Chuen. Tr. by James Legge. (CHI & ENG.). 1991. reprint ed. Vol. IV, Ch'un Ts'ew with the Tso Chuen. 35.00 (*0-318-63254-3*) Oriental Bk Store.

Chinese Classics: With a Translation, Critical & Exegetical Notes, Prolegomena, & Copious Indexes, 5 vols., Set. Tr. by James Legge. 3852p. (C). 1982. text ed. 600.00 (*962-209-102-4*, Pub. by Hong Kong U Pr HK) St Mut.

Chinese Clay Figures see Notes on Turquois in the East: 1913-1914, Field Museum of Natural History

Chinese Cloisonne. Helmut Brinker & Albert Lutz. (Illus.). 400p. 1989. 67.50 (*1-870076-12-5*, Pub. by Bamboo Pub UK) Antique Collect.

Chinese Cloisonne: The Clague Collection. Claudia Brown. LC 80-80709. (Illus.). 181p. (Orig.). 1980. 30.00 (*0-910407-05-3*); pap. 20.00 (*0-910407-04-5*) Phoenix Art.

Chinese Clothing: An Illustrated Guide. Valery M. Garrett. LC 93-42487. (Illus.). 304p. 1994. 65.00 (*0-19-586426-3*) OUP.

***Chinese Coffee.** Ira Lewis. 1995. pap. 4.75 (*0-8222-1426-1*) Dramatists Play.

***Chinese Commercial Laws, Vol. I.** 300p. (Orig.). 1995. pap. 795.00 (*0-7605-1498-4*) Rector Pr.

***Chinese Commercial Laws, Vol. II.** 300p. (Orig.). 1995. pap. 1,295.00 (*0-7605-1499-2*) Rector Pr.

Chinese Communism & the U. S. Proceedings of a Mini-Symposium, 1935-1936. Lord Lindsay & Donald Gillin. 69p. 1975. pap. 6.00 (*0-939252-03-1*) ASU Ctr Asian.

Chinese Communism, 1931-1934: Grass Roots History in Modern China. Lotveit. (C). 1979. pap. 29.95 (*0-7007-0065-X*, Pub. by Curzon Pr UK) Humanities.

Chinese Communist Army in Action. Alexander L. George. 1969. pap. text ed. 17.00 (*0-231-08595-8*) Col U Pr.

Chinese Communist Materials at the Bureau of Investigation Archives, Taiwan. Peter Donovan et al. (Michigan Monographs in Chinese Studies: No. 24). 105p. 1976. pap. 6.00 (*0-89264-024-3*) Ctr Chinese Studies.

Chinese Communist Movement: A Report of the U. S. War Department, July 1945. United States War Department Staff. Ed. by Lyman P. Van Slyke. LC 68-26783. xi, 274p. 1968. 37.50 (*0-8047-0639-5*) Stanford U Pr.

Chinese Communist Party in Power. P'eng Shu-Tse. Ed. by Leslie Evans. LC 79-92214. 1980. lib. bdg. 65.00 (*0-913460-75-3*); pap. 28.95 (*0-913460-76-1*) Pathfinder NY.

Chinese Communist Party's Nomenklatura System. Ed. & Intro. by John P. Burns. LC 88-35577. (Chinese Studies on China). 214p. (C). 1989. 62.95 (*0-87332-543-5*) M E Sharpe.

Chinese Communist Studies of Modern Chinese History. Albert Feuerwerke & Sally Cheng. LC 61-19595. (East Asian Monographs: No. 11). 312p. 1961. 11.00 (*0-674-12301-8*) HUP.

Chinese Communist Treatment of Counterrevolutionaries, 1924-1949. Patricia Griffin. LC 75-30193. (Studies in East Asian Law). 312p. 1976. text ed. 45.00 (*0-691-09232-X*) Princeton U Pr.

***Chinese Communist Treatment of Counterrevolutionaries, 1924-1949.** Patricia E. Griffin. LC 75-30193. (Studies in East Asian Law). reprint ed. pap. 77.00 (*0-7837-9346-4*, 2060087) Bks Demand.

Chinese Community in Vietnam under the French. Alain G. Margot. LC 93-24943. 196p. 1993. pap. 39.95 (*0-7734-1941-1*) E Mellen.

Chinese Complete Course Audio Pack. (Teach Yourself Ser.). 1993. audio, pap. 19.95 (*0-8442-3854-6*) NTC Pub Grp.

Chinese Conception of the Theatre. Tao-Ching Hsu. LC 83-5964. (Illus.). 676p. 1985. text ed. 40.00 (*0-295-96034-5*) U of Wash Pr.

Chinese Constitution: A Study of Forty Years of Constitution-Making in China. P'an Wei-Tung. LC 79-1639. 1985. reprint ed. 27.00 (*0-88355-942-0*) Hyperion Conn.

***Chinese Consumer Profile, 1994.** (Illus.). 60p. (Orig.). 1994. pap. 165.00 (*1-57205-778-5*) Rector Pr.

Chinese Cookbook. Craig Claiborne & Virginia Lee. LC 82-48827. 480p. (Orig.). 1992. reprint ed. pap. 18.00 (*0-06-092261-3*, PL) HarpC.

Chinese Cookery. Rose Cheng & Michele Morris. LC 81-80800. 192p. 1981. pap. 12.95 (*0-89586-088-0*) Price Stern.

***Chinese Cookery: Vegetarian Delicacies.** Sangeeta Khanna. (C). 1992. 9.50x (*81-207-0938-1*, Pub. by Sterling Plns Pvt II) S Asia.

Chinese Cooking. (Favorite All Time Recipes Ser.). (Illus.). 96p. 1993. spiral bd. 3.50 (*0-7853-0330-8*, 2007100) Pubns Intl Ltd.

Chinese Cooking. Constance D. Chang. (Quick & Easy Ser.). (Illus.). 32p. (Orig.). 1969. pap. 5.95 (*4-07-973719-X*, Pub. by Shufunomoto Co Ltd JA) C E Tuttle.

***Chinese Cooking.** Judith Ferguson. 64p. 1995. write for info. (*1-57215-013-0*) World Pubns.

Chinese Cooking. Jillian Stewart. 1993. 9.99 (*0-517-08750-2*) Random Hse Value.

Chinese Cooking: Favorite Home Dishes. Chen Hsueh-Hsia. Ed. by Huang Su-Huei & Chiu Cheng-Tzu. (Illus.). 112p. (CHI & ENG.). 1993. pap. 17.95 (*0-941676-38-2*) Wei-Chuan Pub.

Chinese Cooking at the Academy. Jay Harlow. LC 92-30276. (California Culinary Academy Ser.). 128p. 1993. reprint ed. pap. 11.95 (*1-56426-037-2*, Calif Culinary Acad) Cole Group.

Chinese Cooking Class Cookbook. Consumer Guide Editors. 1989. pap. 6.99 (*0-517-32245-5*) Random Hse Value.

Chinese Cooking, Family Style. Lily Ger. Ed. by Dianne Ooka. (Heian Asian Cooking Ser.). (Illus.). 96p. 1994. reprint ed. pap. 11.95 (*0-89346-796-0*) Heian Intl.

Chinese Cooking for Beginners. rev. ed. (CHI & ENG.). 1994. pap. 14.95 (*0-941676-30-7*); pap. 14.95 (*0-941676-33-1*) Wei-Chuan Pub.

Chinese Cooking for Pleasure. Yong Y. Cotterell. LC 88-33014. (Illus.). 252p. (C). 1989. 18.95 (*0-941533-62-X*) New Amsterdam Bks.

Chinese Cooking Made Easy. Wei-Chuan's Publishing Staff. 96p. (CHI & ENG.). 1991. pap. 14.95 (*0-941676-26-9*) Wei-Chuan Pub.

Chinese Cooking Made Easy. Cecilia H. Yang. LC 82-84700. (Illus.). 108p. (Orig.). 1985. pap. 12.00 (*0-9614902-0-9*) East Linden Pr.

Chinese Cooking, Restaurant Style. Lily Ger. Ed. by Dianne Ooka. (Heian Asian Cooking Ser.). (Illus.). 96p. 1994. reprint ed. pap. 11.95 (*0-89346-797-9*) Heian Intl.

Chinese Cooking the Micro-Way. M. L. Kao. 174p. 1984. pap. 6.95 (*0-932403-24-7*) Overview Pr.

Chinese Coolie Emigration to Countries Within the British Empire. Persia C. Campbell. LC 70-88402. 240p. 1969. reprint ed. text ed. 52.50 (*0-8371-1751-8*, CCE&, Negro U Pr) Greenwood.

Chinese Coolie Emigration to Countries Within the British Empire. Persia C. Campbell. 240p. 1971. reprint ed. 35.00 (*0-7146-2000-9*, Pub. by F Cass Pubs UK) Intl Spec Bk.

Chinese Cuisine. Huang Su Huei. Ed. by Chen Chang yen et al. (Illus.). 206p. (CHI & ENG.). 1972. pap. 23.95 (*0-941676-08-0*) Wei-Chuan Pub.

Chinese Cuisine - Taiwanese Style. Wei-Chuan Cultural & Educational Foundation Staff. 120p. (CHI & ENG.). 1991. pap. 19.95 (*0-941676-25-0*) Wei-Chuan Pub.

***Chinese Cuisine, Shanghai Style.** Wei-Chuan Cultural Educational Foundation. Ed. by Elizabeth L. Lin. (Illus.). 96p. (CHI.). 1995. pap. 19.95 (*0-941676-55-2*) Wei-Chuan Pub.

Chinese Culture & Mental Health. Ed. by Wen-Shing Tseng & David Y. Wu. 1985. pap. text ed. 49.00 (*0-12-701631-7*) Acad Pr.

Chinese Culture in a Kaleidoscope. H. J. Hsia & Alexander H. Hsia. (East-West Communication Ser.). 245p. 1993. 25.95 (*1-881673-02-2*); pap. 9.95 (*1-881673-03-0*) Amer Assoc Pub.

***Chinese Customs.** Henry Dore. (Illus.). 253p. 1987. pap. 19.95 (*9971-4-9215-6*) Heian Intl.

Chinese Cut-Out Design Book: Designs from the World of Nature. Ramona Jablonski. (International Design Library). (Illus.). 48p. (Orig.). 1980. pap. 5.95 (*0-916144-55-0*) Stemmer Hse.

Chinese Cut-Out Design Book: Designs from the World of People. Ramona Jablonski. (International Design Library). (Illus.). 48p. (Orig.). 1981. pap. 5.95 (*0-916144-83-6*) Stemmer Hse.

Chinese Cut-out Design Book: Designs of Costumes. Barbara Holdridge. (International Design Library). (Illus.). 48p. 1989. pap. 5.95 (*0-88045-111-4*) Stemmer Hse.

Chinese Cut Paper Designs. Ed. by Theodore Menten. LC 75-22240. (Pictorial Archive Ser.). (Illus.). 96p. (Orig.). 1975. pap. 5.95 (*0-486-23198-4*) Dover.

Chinese Debate about Soviet Socialism, 1978-1985. Gilbert Rozman. 416p. 1987. text ed. 62.50 (*0-691-09429-2*) Princeton U Pr.

Chinese Decorative Design, 2 vols., 1. Fu Jen Catholic University, Dept. of Textiles & Clothing Committee Editors. (Illus.). 466p. (CHI & ENG.). 1991. write for info. (*957-638-046-4*) Oriental Bk Store.

Chinese Decorative Design, 2 vols., 2. Fu Jen Catholic University, Dept. of Textiles & Clothing Committee Editors. (Illus.). 466p. (CHI & ENG.). 1991. write for info. (*957-638-048-0*) Oriental Bk Store.

Chinese Decorative Design, 2 vols., 3. Fu Jen Catholic University, Dept. of Textiles & Clothing Committee Editors. 466p. (CHI & ENG.). 1991. 85.00 (*0-685-72528-6*) Oriental Bk Store.

Chinese Decorative Design, 4 Vols., Set. Fu Jen Catholic University, Dept. of Textiles & Clothing Staff. (Illus.). 1054p. (CHI & ENG.). 1993. 150.00 (*0-295-97251-3*) U of Wash Pr.

Chinese Decorative Design, 2 vols., Vol. 3. Fu Jen Catholic University, Dept. of Textiles & Clothing Committee Editors. 466p. (CHI & ENG.). 1991. write for info. (*957-638-050-2*) Oriental Bk Store.

Chinese Decorative Design, 2 vols., Vol. 4. Fu Jen Catholic University, Dept. of Textiles & Clothing Committee Editors. 466p. (CHI & ENG.). 1991. write for info. (*957-638-052-9*) Oriental Bk Store.

Chinese Decorative Design, 2 vols., Vols. 1 & 2. Fu Jen Catholic University, Dept. of Textiles & Clothing Committee Editors. (Illus.). 466p. (CHI & ENG.). 1991. 85.00 (*0-685-72527-8*) Oriental Bk Store.

Chinese Defense & Foreign Policy. Ed. by Ilpyong J. Kim & June T. Dreyer. LC 88-22386. 357p. 1988. 29.95 (*0-943852-55-2*); pap. 14.95 (*0-943852-56-0*) Prof World Peace.

Chinese Democracy. Andrew J. Nathan. LC 85-40163. (Illus.). 336p. 1985. 22.95 (*0-394-51386-X*) Knopf.

Chinese Democracy. Andrew J. Nathan. 313p. (C). 1986. pap. 13.00 (*0-520-05933-6*) U CA Pr.

Chinese Democracy & the Crisis of 1989: Chinese & American Reflections. Ed. by Roger V. Des Forges et al. LC 91-45279. 371p. (C). 1993. 64.50 (*0-7914-1269-5*); pap. 21.95 (*0-7914-1270-9*) State U NY Pr.

Chinese Demon Tales: Meanings & Parallels in Oral Tradition. rev. ed. Alsace Ping-Chiu Yen. LC 90-22043. (Harvard Dissertations in Folklore & Oral Literature Ser.). 216p. 1991. reprint ed. lib. bdg. 50.00 (*0-8240-2529-6*) Garland.

Chinese Design & Pattern in Full Color. Owen Jones. 48p. 1981. pap. 6.95 (*0-486-24204-8*) Dover.

Chinese Destinies: Sketches of Present-Day China. Agnes Smedley. LC 75-39036. (China Studies). (Illus.). viii, 315p. 1977. reprint ed. lib. bdg. 29.00 (*0-88355-391-0*) Hyperion Conn.

Chinese Dialectology: A Selected & Classified Bibliography. Paul F. Yang. xxvii, 189p. 1981. text ed. 44.50 (*962-201-211-6*) Coronet Bks.

Chinese Dialogues. Fred Fang-Yu Wang. 1953. 15.95 (*0-88710-014-7*); audio write for info. (*0-88710-015-5*) Yale Far Eastern Pubns.

Chinese Diary & Album. Cecil Beaton. (Illus.). 184p. 1991. 24.95 (*0-19-585428-4*) OUP.

Chinese Dictionaries: An Extensive Bibliography of Dictionaries in Chinese & Other Languages. Ed. by Chinese-English Translation Assistance Group Staff. LC 82-923. xvi, 448p. (CHI & ENG.). 1982. text ed. 105.00 (*0-313-23505-8*, MDC/) Greenwood.

Chinese Dictionary: Cantonese Dialect, 3 pts. Ernest J. Eitel. (CHI.). 1977. reprint ed. 169.95 (*0-518-19009-9*) Ayer.

Chinese Dictionary of Verbs. 532p. 1989. pap. 17.50 (*0-89346-313-2*) Heian Intl.

Chinese Diet Cookbook. Pedro Chan. 91p. 10.00 (*0-317-31560-9*) Chans Corp.

Chinese Dim Sum; Wei-Chuan Cultural & Educational Foundation. Wei-Chuan Cultural & Educational Foundation Staff. 128p. (CHI & ENG.). 1990. pap. 19.95 (*0-941676-24-2*) Wei-Chuan Pub.

Chinese Divination. James Kao. 117p. reprint ed. pap. 33.40 (*0-317-26229-7*, 2055584) Bks Demand.

Chinese Domestic Furniture. Gustav Ecke. (Illus.). 210p. reprint ed. 55.00 (*957-638-100-2*, ATE009, Pub. by SMC Pub CC) Oriental Bk Store.

Chinese Domestic Furniture in Photographs & Measured Drawings. Ed. by Gustav Ecke. 224p. 1986. reprint ed. pap. 13.95 (*0-486-25171-3*) Dover.

Chinese Domestic Politics & Foreign Policy in the 1970s. Allen S. Whiting. LC 78-31865. (Michigan Monographs in Chinese Studies: No. 36). 85p. 1979. 6.00 (*0-89264-036-7*) Ctr Chinese Studies.

Chinese-Dougal Dixon's Dinosaurs: Simplified Language. Dougal Dixon. 1994. 19.95 (*1-56397-381-2*) Boyds Mills Pr.

Chinese Drama. Lewis C. Arlington. LC 65-19614. (Illus.). 1972. reprint ed. 46.95 (*0-405-08212-6*) Ayer.

Chinese Drama: An Annotated Bibliography of Commentary, Criticism, & Plays in English Translation. annot. ed. Manuel D. Lopez. LC 91-15902. 535p. 1991. 57.50 (*0-8108-2347-0*) Scarecrow.

Chinese Drugs of Plant Origin: Chemistry, Pharmacology, & Use in Traditional & Modern Medicine. W. Tang & G. Eisenbrand. (Illus.). ix, 1056p. 1992. 169.00 (*0-387-19309-X*) Spr-Verlag.

Chinese Dynasties. Hawley. 1993. pap. 5.95 (*0-910704-79-1*) Hawley.

Chinese Earth. Shen Ts'Ung-Wen. Ed. & Tr. by Robert Payne. Tr. by Ching Ti. LC 81-18150. 320p. 1982. pap. text ed. 18.50 (*0-231-05485-8*, Morningside Bkshop) Col U Pr.

Chinese Earth-Sheltered Dwellings: Indigenous Lessons for Modern Urban Design. Gideon S. Golany. LC 91-21496. (Illus.). 280p. (C). 1992. text ed. 44.00 (*0-8248-1369-3*) UH Pr.

Chinese Economic Activity in Netherlands India: Selected Translations from the Dutch. Ed. by M. R. Fernando & David Bulbeck. 275p. 1992. pap. 25.00 (*981-3016-21-3*, Pub. by Inst SE Asian Studies SI) Ashgate Pub Co.

Chinese Economic Planning: Transations from Chi-Hua Ching-Chi. Ed. by Nicholas R. Lardy. LC 78-52292. 280p. reprint ed. pap. 79.80 (*0-317-29625-6*, 2021858) Bks Demand.

Chinese Economic Planning & Input-Output Analysis. Karen R. Polenske & Chen Xikang. (Illus.). 368p. 1992. 65.00 (*0-19-585249-4*) OUP.

Chinese Economic Policy: Economic Reform at Midstream. Ed. by Ilpyong J. Kim & Bruce L. Reynolds. 318p. 1989. 29.95 (*0-943852-69-2*); pap. 14.95 (*0-943852-70-6*) Prof World Peace.

Chinese Economic Reform: How Far, How Fast? Ed. by Bruce Reynolds. 233p. 1988. text ed. 53.00 (*0-12-587045-0*) Acad Pr.

Chinese Economic Reforms. Athar Hussain. Ed. by Stephen Feuchtwang. LC 82-10703. 385p. 1983. text ed. 39.95 (*0-312-13385-5*) St Martin.

Chinese Economy. Gregory C. Chow. 320p. 1987. text ed. 93.00 (*9971-5-0466-9*); pap. text ed. 47.00 (*9971-5-0467-7*) World Scientific Pub.

Chinese Economy: A Bibliography of Works in English. Robert Goehlert. LC 93-329. (Reference Guides Ser.: No. 4). 200p. 1995. lib. bdg. write for info. (*0-8095-0700-5*); pap. write for info. (*0-8095-1700-0*) Borgo Pr.

***Chinese Economy: Changes & Challenges in the Post-Mao Era.** Kalipada Deb. (C). 1993. 28.00x (*81-207-1128-9*, Pub. by Sterling Plns Pvt II) S Asia.

Chinese Economy: Structure & Reform in the Economy & in Foreign Trade. Wolfgang Klenner & Kurt Wiesegart. 147p. (C). 1984. pap. 19.95x (*3-87895-233-3*) Transaction Pubs.

Chinese Economy & Its Future: Achievements & Problems of Post-Mao Reform. Ed. by Peter Nolan & Dong Fureng. 250p. (C). 1991. 47.95 (*0-7456-0522-2*) Blackwell Pubs.

Chinese Economy in the Early Twentieth Century: Recent Chinese Studies. Ed. by Tim Wright. LC 91-34667. 224p. 1992. text ed. 70.00 (*0-312-07547-2*) St Martin.

Chinese Economy in the 1990s. Ed. by Robert Ash & Y. Y. Kueh. (Studies on Contemporary China). (Illus.). 280p. 1995. pap. 23.00 (*0-19-828822-0*) OUP.

Chinese Education: Old & New, Radical & Reformed. Kuan Y. Chen. (TWEC World Education Monographs). 24p. 1980. 2.50 (*0-685-05136-6*) I N Thut World Educ Ctr.

Chinese Education: Problems, Policies, & Prospects. Ed. by Irving Epstein. LC 90-21938. (Books in International Education Ser.: Vol. 20). (Illus.). 544p. 1991. 60.00 (*0-8240-4382-0*, 585) Garland.

Chinese Education & Society: A Bibliographic Guide, the Cultural Revolution & Its Aftermath. Stewart E. Fraser & Kuang-Liang Hsu. LC 72-77206. 214p. reprint ed. pap. 61.00 (*0-317-10233-8*, 2015407) Bks Demand.

Chinese Education in Transition: Prelude to the Cultural Revolution. Julia Kwong. LC 80-451964. (Illus.). 319p. reprint ed. pap. 91.00 (*0-7837-1152-2*, 2041681) Bks Demand.

Chinese Elites & Political Change: Zhejiang Province in the Early Twentieth Century. R. Keith Schoppa. LC 81-7075. (East Asian Ser.: No. 96). (Illus.). 304p. 1982. 39.95 (*0-674-12325-5*) HUP.

Chinese Embroidered Purses. 120p. 1992. reprint ed. pap. 19.50 (*0-89346-383-3*) Heian Intl.

Chinese Emigration in the U. S., Eighteen Fifty to Eighteen Eighty. Kil Young Zo. Ed. by Roger Daniels. LC 78-54851. (Asian Experience in North America Ser.). 1979. lib. bdg. 21.95 (*0-405-11302-1*) Ayer.

Chinese Emperor. Jean Levi. 1989. pap. 8.95 (*0-394-75996-6*, Vin) Random.

Chinese Empire. Marinella Terzi. LC 92-7509. (World Heritage Ser.). (Illus.). 36p. (J). (gr. 3 up). 1992. lib. bdg. 15.00 (*0-516-08377-5*) Childrens.

Chinese Empire. Marinella Terzi. LC 92-7509. (World Heritage Ser.). 36p. (J). (gr. 3 up). 1993. pap. 6.95 (*0-516-48377-3*) Childrens.

Chinese-English: Classified & Ill. Guangzhou Inst. of Foreign Language. 897p. 1981. 22.00 (*962-04-0098-4*) IBD Ltd.

Chinese-English: New. 2nd ed. 1401p. 1990. reprint ed. 47.00 (*962-04-0398-3*) IBD Ltd.

Chinese-English Common Vocabulary of Civil Engineering. 249p. (CHI & ENG.). 1990. 24.00 (*962-07-0135-6*) IBD Ltd.

Chinese-English Dictionary. 27.50 (*0-685-04462-9*) Saphrograph.

Chinese-English Dictionary. Wu Jongrong & Ponxin. 976p. (CHI & ENG.). 1981. 150.00 (*0-8288-4428-3*, M9400) Fr & Eur.

Chinese-English Dictionary. Samuel W. Williams. (CHI & ENG.). 1977. reprint ed. 78.95 (*0-518-19007-2*) Ayer.

Chinese-English Dictionary: A Chinese-English Dictionary Compiled for the China Inland Mission. rev. ed. Robert H. Mathews. (Harvard-Yenching Institute Publications). 1250p. (C). 1943. 39.50 (*0-674-12350-6*) HUP.

Chinese-English Dictionary: Cantonese in Yale Romanization, Mandarin in Pinyin. Ed. by Chik Hon Man & Ng Lam Sim Yuk. 521p. (Orig.). (CHI & ENG.). 1989. pap. 42.50 (*962-7141-14-3*, Pub. by Chinese Univ HK) Coronet Bks.

Chinese-English Dictionary: Hakka-Dialect. D. MacIver. (CHI & ENG.). 1982. reprint ed. 45.00 (*0-89986-344-2*) Oriental Bk Store.

Chinese-English Dictionary of Architecture & Construction. Beijing Institute of Architectural Design & Research Staff. 1027p. (CHI & ENG.). 1992. 35.00 (*0-88431-150-3*) IBD Ltd.

***Chinese-English Dictionary of Architecture & Construction.** Beijing Institute Staff. (CHI & ENG.). 1992. 35.00 (*0-7859-8831-9*) Fr & Eur.

Chinese-English Dictionary of Chinese Law & Government. Phillip R. Bilancia. 822p. (CHI & ENG.). 1981. 125.00 (*0-8288-0972-0*, M3879) Fr & Eur.

Chinese-English Dictionary of Colloquial Terms Used in Modern Chinese Literature. David Collier. 1979. 15.95 (*0-88710-016-3*) Yale Far Eastern Pubns.

C

An Asterisk (*) at the beginning of an entry indicates that the title is appearing in BIP for the first time.

Chinese-English Dictionary of Contemporary Usage. Ed. by Chi Wen-Shun. (CHI & ENG.). 1977. 50.00 (*0-520-02655-1*) U CA Pr.

Chinese-English Dictionary of Current Affairs. deluxe ed. Commercial Press Staff. 594p. (CHI & ENG.). 1977. 49.95 (*0-8288-5297-9*, M9247) Fr & Eur.

Chinese-English Dictionary of Enigmatic Folk Similes (Xiehouyu) John S. Rohsenow. LC 90-25213. 325p. 1991. 50.00 (*0-8165-1031-8*) U of Ariz Pr.

Chinese-English Dictionary of Idioms: Compiled by Specialists of English from Sichuan Province. 2nd ed. 424p. 1988. 12.95 (*0-87052-454-2*, 0270) Hippocrene Bks.

Chinese-English Dictionary of Idioms & Proverbs. Xiao-jun Heng & Xue-sh Zhang. 511p. (CHI & ENG.). 1988. 250.00 (*0-8288-1002-8*, F 75130) Fr & Eur.

Chinese-English Dictionary of Military Terms. Commercial Press Staff. 366p. (CHI & ENG.). 1977. 59.95 (*0-8288-5298-7*, M9275) Fr & Eur.

Chinese-English Dictionary of Modern Usage. Lin Yutang. 1720p. 1990. 325.00 (*0-317-59312-9*) St Mut.

Chinese-English Dictionary of Physical Terms. S. Chang. 405p. (ENG & GER.). 1969. pap. 175.00 (*0-8288-9089-7*, M15363, Pub. by Harrassowitz) Fr & Eur.

Chinese-English Dictionary of the Vernacular or Spoken Language of Amoy. suppl. ed. Thomas Barclay & Carstairs Douglas. 276p. reprint ed. Incl. supplement by Rev. Thomas Barclay, 276p. 84.00 (*957-9482-32-2*, RFE007, Pub. by SMC Pub CC) Oriental Bk Store.

Chinese-English Dictionary of the Wu Dialect (Featuring the Dialect of the City of Shanghai) Ed. by Thomas Creamer et al. Tr. by Wu Ying et al. LC 91-70271. xi, 192p. (CHI & ENG.). 1992. 38.00 (*0-931745-81-0*) Dunwoody Pr.

Chinese-English Glossary of Astro-Science Terms. Chinese-English Translation Assistance Group. LC 86-71163. (Chinese-English Technical Glossary Ser.). 130p. (Orig.). 1986. pap. 18.75 (*0-931745-16-0*) Dunwoody Pr.

Chinese-English Glossary of Aviation Technology Terms. Ed. by Chinese-English Translation Assistance Group Staff. 205p. 1986. pap. 16.00 (*0-931745-32-2*) Dunwoody Pr.

Chinese-English Glossary of Computer Technology Terms. LC 86-71168. (Chinese-English Technical Glossary Ser.). 385p. (Orig.). (C). 1986. pap. 22.50 (*0-931745-17-9*) Dunwoody Pr.

Chinese-English Glossary of Cytology Terms. LC 86-71171. (Chinese-English Technical Glossary Ser.). 45p. (Orig.). (C). 1986. pap. 10.00 (*0-931745-18-7*) Dunwoody Pr.

Chinese-English Glossary of Demographic Terms Accompanied by Chinese-English Glossary of Selected U. S. Economic & Statistical Terms. Ed. by Chinese-English Translation Assistance Group. LC 86-71169. (Chinese-English Technical Glossary Ser.). 45p. (Orig.). 1986. pap. 10.00 (*0-931745-19-5*) Dunwoody Pr.

Chinese-English Glossary of Linguistic Terms. Ed. by Chinese-English Translation Assistance Group. LC 86-71174. (Chinese-English Technical Glossary Ser.). 130p. (Orig.). 1986. pap. 15.00 (*0-931745-21-7*) Dunwoody Pr.

Chinese-English Glossary of Military Affairs Terms with Diagrams. Ed. by Chinese-English Translation Assistance Group. LC 86-71176. (Chinese-English Technical Glossary Ser.). 200p. (Orig.). (C). 1986. pap. 17.50 (*0-931745-22-5*) Dunwoody Pr.

Chinese-English Glossary of Military Terms, 3 vols. Ed. by Chinese-English Translation Assistance Group Staff. 1988. Vol. I (A-Hei). write for info. (*0-318-65010-X*); Vol. II (Hen-Sheng). write for info. (*0-318-65011-8*); Vol. III (Shizuo). write for info. (*0-318-65012-6*) Dunwoody Pr.

Chinese-English Glossary of Military Terms, 3 vols., Set. Ed. by Chinese-English Translation Assistance Group Staff. 1988. pap. 100.00 (*0-931745-55-1*) Dunwoody Pr.

Chinese-English Glossary of Names of Foreign Arms Manufacturers & Satellite Systems. Ed. by Chinese-English Translation Assistance Group. LC 86-71173. (Chinese-English Technical Glossary Ser.). 35p. (Orig.). 1986. pap. 7.50 (*0-931745-23-3*) Dunwoody Pr.

Chinese-English Glossary of Oil Well Terms. Ed. by Chinese-English Translation Assistance Group. LC 86-71166. (Chinese-English Technical Glossary Ser.). 650p. (Orig.). (C). 1986. pap. 68.75 (*0-931745-24-1*) Dunwoody Pr.

Chinese-English Glossary of Particle Physics Supplement. Ed. by Chinese-English Translation Assistance Group. LC 86-71170. (Chinese-English Technical Glossary Ser.). 15p. (Orig.). (C). 1986. pap. 6.25 (*0-931745-29-2*) Dunwoody Pr.

Chinese-English Glossary of Petrochemical Terms. Ed. by Chinese-English Translation Assistance Group. LC 86-71164. (Chinese-English Technical Glossary Ser.). 110p. (Orig.). 1986. pap. 15.00 (*0-931745-26-8*) Dunwoody Pr.

Chinese-English Glossary of Selected Posts & Telecommunications Terms. Ed. by Chinese-English Translation Assistance Group. LC 86-71165. (Chinese-English Technical Glossary Ser.). 25p. (Orig.). 1986. pap. 6.25 (*0-931745-27-6*) Dunwoody Pr.

Chinese-English Glossary of Spectrum Analysis Terms. Ed. by Chinese-English Translation Assistance Group. LC 86-71175. (Chinese-English Technical Glossary Ser.). 30p. (Orig.). (C). 1986. pap. 7.50 (*0-931745-25-X*) Dunwoody Pr.

Chinese-English Glossary of the Mathematical Sciences. John F. De Francis. LC 64-16997. 286p. reprint ed. pap. 81.60 (*0-317-08625-1*, 2004670) Bks Demand.

Chinese-English Glossary of Thermal Power Terms. Ed. by Chinese-English Translation Assistance Group. LC 86-71167. (Chinese-English Technical Glossary Ser.). 45p. (Orig.). 1986. pap. 10.00 (*0-931745-30-6*) Dunwoody Pr.

Chinese-English Glossary of Naval Terms. Ed. by Chinese-English Translation Assistance Group. LC 86-71172. (Chinese-English Technical Glossary Ser.). 95p. (Orig.). (C). 1986. pap. 12.50 (*0-931745-28-4*) Dunwoody Pr.

Chinese-English Idioms & Phrases. S. M. Season. 311p. (CHI & ENG.). 1978. 29.95 (*0-8288-4868-8*, M9246) Fr & Eur.

Chinese-English-Japanese Glossary of Chemical Terms. S. Tamura & F. Shiratori. 661p. (CHI, ENG & JPN.). 1977. 95.00 (*0-8288-5299-5*, M9351) Fr & Eur.

Chinese-English Mathematical Dictionary. Science Press Staff. 1130p. (CHI & ENG.). 1990. 75.00 (*0-8288-6992-8*, 703001393X) Fr & Eur.

Chinese-English Medical Dictionary. 1835p. 1988. 73.00 (*962-07-0094-5*) IBD Ltd.

Chinese Enlightenment: Intellectuals & the Legacy of the May Fourth Movement of 1919. Vera Schwarcz. (Illus.). 409p. 1986. pap. 17.00 (*0-520-06837-8*, SCHENX) U CA Pr.

Chinese Enlightment's Intellectuals & the Legacy of the May 4th Movement of 1919. Vera Schwarcz. (Center for Chinese Studies, UC Berkeley: No. 27). 1986. 50.00 (*0-520-05027-4*) U CA Pr.

Chinese Enterprise Management: Reforms in Economic Perspective. Sukhan Jackson. LC 92-19467. (Studies in Organization: Vol. 41). xviii, 324p. (C). 1992. lib. bdg. 54.95 (*3-11-013480-2*) De Gruyter.

Chinese Ethical Ideals: A Study of the Ethical Values in China's Literary, Social & Religious Life. F. Rawlingson. 1972. lib. bdg. 79.95 (*0-87968-551-4*) Krishna Pr.

Chinese Etiquette & Ethics in Business. Boye De Mente. 1989. pap. 14.95 (*0-8442-8525-0*, Passport Bks) NTC Pub Grp.

Chinese Etiquette & Ethics in Business. Boye L. De Mente. LC 94-6700. 1994. 16.95 (*0-8442-8524-2*) NTC Pub Grp.

Chinese Eulogy & the Textual Variation. Don Y. Lee. LC 83-82652. 96p. (C). 1983. 32.50 (*0-939758-06-7*) Eastern Pr.

Chinese Eunuchs: The Structure of Intimate Politics. Taisuke Mitamura. 1992. 14.95 (*0-8048-1881-9*) C E Tuttle.

Chinese Exclusion vs. the Open Door Policy, 1900-1906: Clashes Over China Policy in the Roosevelt Era. Delber L. McKee. LC 76-47024. (Illus.). 293p. reprint ed. pap. 83.60 (*0-318-39774-9*, 2033176) Bks Demand.

Chinese Export Art & Design. Craig Clunas. (Illus.). 124p. 1990. pap. 24.95 (*1-85177-000-3*, Pub. by Victoria & Albert Mus UK) Trafalgar.

Chinese Export Porcelain: Ethel Liebmand & Arthur L. Liebman Porcelain Collection. Catherine C. Brawer. LC 92-52695. (Illus.). 160p. 1992. pap. 29.95 (*0-932900-30-5*, Antique Collect) Antique Collect.

Chinese Export Porcelain: Standard Patterns & Forms, 1780-1880. Herbert Schiffer et al. LC 75-21623. (Illus.). 256p. 1975. 37.50 (*0-916838-01-3*) Schiffer.

Chinese Export Porcelain for the American Trade, 1785-1835. Jean M. Mudge. LC 61-16518. (Illus.). 284p. 40.00 (*0-87413-102-2*) U Delaware Pr.

Chinese Export Porcelain for the American Trade, 1785-1835. rev. ed. Jean M. Mudge. LC 79-4713. (Illus.). 300p. 1980. 55.00 (*0-87413-166-9*) U Delaware Pr.

Chinese Export Porcelain in the 19th Century: Canton Famille Rose Porcelain. John Q. Feller. (Illus.). 52p. (Orig.). 1982. pap. 15.00 (*0-87577-069-X*, Peabody Museum) Peabody Essex Mus.

Chinese Export Porcelains from the Collection of Dr. & Mrs. Harold L. Tonkin: Exhibition Catalogue. Olga K. Preisner. (Illus.). 48p. 1980. pap. 4.50 (*0-911209-17-4*) Palmer Mus Art.

Chinese Export Silver: A Legacy of Luxury. H. Crosby Forbes. LC 84-82443. (Illus.). 20p. (Orig.). 1984. pap. 5.00 (*0-88397-082-1*) Art Srvc Intl.

Chinese Export Silver, Seventeen Eighty-Five to Eighteen Eighty-Five. H. A. Forbes. LC 85-12401. (Illus.). 1975. 95.00 (*0-937650-02-1*) Mus Am China Trade.

Chinese Export Silver, Seventeen Eighty-Five to Eighteen Eighty-Five. deluxe limited ed. H. A. Forbes. LC 85-12401. (Illus.). 1975. boxed 125.00 (*0-686-77324-1*) Mus Am China Trade.

Chinese Eyes. Marjorie Waybill. LC 74-5751. (Illus.). 32p. (J). (gr. k-2). 1974. 14.95 (*0-8361-1738-7*) Herald Pr.

Chinese Fables & Wisdom: Insights for Better Living. Tom Ma. 126p. 1995. pap. 16.95 (*0-89876-211-1*) Gardner Pr.

Chinese Fairy Tales & Fantasies. Ed. by Moss Roberts. (Fairy Tale & Folklore Library). (Illus.). 1980. pap. 14.00 (*0-394-73994-9*) Pantheon.

Chinese Families in the Post-Mao Era. Ed. by Deborah Davis & Stevan Harrell. LC 92-23163. (Studies on China: Vol. 17). (C). 1993. 55.00 (*0-520-07797-0*); pap. 17.00 (*0-520-08222-2*) U CA Pr.

Chinese Family & Kinship. Hugh Baker. LC 78-26724. 272p. 1980. text ed. 47.50 (*0-231-04768-1*); pap. text ed. 15.50 (*0-231-04769-X*) Col U Pr.

Chinese Family & Society. Olga Lang. (Illus.). 395p. 1985. reprint ed. pap. 18.00 (*0-89986-373-6*) Oriental Bk Store.

Chinese Family Law & Social Change in Historical & Comparative Perspective. Ed. by David C. Buxbaum. LC 76-7781. (Asian Law Ser.: No. 3). 582p. 1978. 50.00 (*0-295-95448-5*) U of Wash Pr.

Chinese Fatal Flute & Stick Forms. Chan Poi. LC 84-52680. (Illus.). 160p. (Orig.). 1985. pap. 8.95 (*0-86568-059-0*, 215) Unique Pubns.

Chinese Femme Fatale: Stories from the Ming Period. Anne McLaren. (University of Sydney East Asian Ser.: No. 8). 176p. (C). 1994. pap. text ed. 16.95 (*0-646-14924-5*, Pub. by Wild Peony Pty AT) UH Pr.

Chinese Fiction: A Bibliography of Books & Articles in Chinese & English. Tien-Yi Li. 1968. 21.95 (*0-88710-017-1*) Yale Far Eastern Pubns.

Chinese Fiction from Taiwan: Critical Perspectives. Symposium on Taiwan Fiction (1979: University of Texas at Austin), Staff. Ed. by Jeannette L. Faurot. LC 80-7490. (Studies in Chinese Literature & Society). 284p. reprint ed. pap. 81.00 (*0-685-23881-4*, 2056699) Bks Demand.

Chinese Filial Piety. Kenneth L. Traylor. Ed. by Don Y. Lee. LC 88-81825. (C). 1988. 37.50 (*0-939758-19-9*) Eastern Pr.

Chinese Film: The State of the Art in the People's Republic of China. Ed. by George S. Semsel. LC 87-6973. 208p. 1987. text ed. 49.95 (*0-275-92644-3*, C2644, Praeger Pubs) Greenwood.

Chinese Film Theory: A Guide to the New Era. Ed. by George S. Semsel et al. LC 89-23079. 256p. 1990. text ed. 49.95 (*0-275-93103-X*, C3103, Praeger Pubs) Greenwood.

Chinese Financial System. Cecil R. Dipchand et al. LC 93-50539. (Contributions in Economics & Economic History Ser.: No. 157). 240p. 1994. text ed. 59.95 (*0-313-29282-5*, Greenwood Pr) Greenwood.

Chinese-Finnish Dictionary: Kina-Suomi Sanakirja. A. Arponen. 485p. (CHI & FIN.). 1985. 125.00 (*0-8288-1004-4*, M2843) Fr & Eur.

Chinese Firms & the State in Transition: Property Rights & Agency Problems in the Reform Era. Keun Lee. LC 91-2075. (Studies on Contemporary China Ser.). 224p. 1992. 57.95 (*0-87332-850-7*) M E Sharpe.

***Chinese Firms Between Hierarchy & Market: The Contract Management Responsibility System in China.** Derong Chen. LC 94-9888. 1994. write for info. (*0-312-12221-7*) St Martin.

Chinese Flora & Fauna Designs. Ming-Ju Sun. (International Design Library). (Illus.). 48p. 1985. pap. 5.95 (*0-88045-062-2*) Stemmer Hse.

Chinese Floral & Animal Charted Designs. Barbara Christopher. LC 92-40611. (Needlework Ser.). 1993. pap. write for info. (*0-486-27537-X*) Dover.

Chinese Flower Painting. Jane Evans. 1990. pap. 4.95 (*0-85532-638-7*, Pub. by Search Pr UK) A Schwartz & Co.

Chinese Folk Designs: A Collection of 300 Cut-Paper Designs. Ed. by W. M. Hawley. (Pictorial Archive Ser.). (Illus.). 1971. reprint ed. pap. 7.95 (*0-486-22633-6*) Dover.

Chinese Folk Tales. Yuan Hsi Kuo & Louise Hsi Kuo. LC 75-9082. (YA). (gr. 7 up). 1976. pap. 5.95 (*0-89087-074-8*) Celestial Arts.

Chinese Foods for Longevity. Henry C. Lu. LC 90-40723. 192p. (Orig.). 1990. pap. 9.95 (*0-8069-5830-8*) Sterling.

Chinese for the English-Speaking Student: An Approach Through English Grammar, Vol. 1. Show-chih Rai Chu. LC 72-87136. 330p. 1973. 11.95 (*0-913973-00-9*); pap. 9.95 (*0-913973-01-7*); audio 14.95 (*0-913973-02-5*) Inst Sino-Amer.

Chinese for the English-Speaking Student: An Approach Through English Grammar, Vol. 2. Show-chih Rai Chu. 424p. 1976. 12.95 (*0-913973-10-6*); pap. 10.95 (*0-913973-03-3*); audio 19.95 (*0-913973-04-1*) Inst Sino-Amer.

Chinese for Today. 1988. 19.95 (*0-8351-1840-1*) China Bks.

Chinese for Today: Character Exercise Book. 1988. 10.95 (*0-8351-1841-X*); audio 49.95 (*0-8351-1842-8*) China Bks.

Chinese Foreign Economic Law. Ed. by Rui Mu & Wang Guiguo. 1990. 82.00 (*0-935328-62-9*) Intl Law Inst.

Chinese Foreign Policy: Development after Mao. Robert G. Sutter. LC 85-6450. 250p. 1985. text ed. 49.95 (*0-275-90231-5*, C0231, Praeger Pubs) Greenwood.

Chinese Foreign Policy: Theory & Practice. Ed. by Thomas Robinson & David Shambaugh. (Studies on Contemporary China). 640p. 1994. 65.00 (*0-19-828389-X*) OUP.

***Chinese Foreign Policy: Theory & Practice.** Ed. by Thomas W. Robinson & David Shambaugh. (Studies on Contemporary China). (Illus.). 664p. 1995. reprint ed. pap. 29.95 (*0-19-829016-0*) OUP.

Chinese Fortune-Telling Calendar for China & U. S. A. Daily Edition. Allen Tsai. LC 91-91212. 550p. (Orig.). (CHI.). 1993. pap. 19.95 (*1-880482-06-1*) Three Bs Bks.

Chinese Foundations for Moral Education & Character Development. Ed. by Tran Van Doan et al. (Cultural Heritage & Contemporary Change Series VI: Foundations of Moral Education,: Vol. III, No. 2). 200p. (Orig.). 1991. 45.00 (*1-56518-033-X*, LC315C6C447); pap. 14.00 (*1-56518-032-1*) Coun Res Values.

Chinese Geomancy. Derek Walters. 1989. pap. 15.95 (*1-85230-058-2*) Element MA.

Chinese-German Dictionary: Chinese-Deutsch Worterbuch. deluxe ed. Commercial Press Staff. 830p. (CHI & GER.). 1980. 49.95 (*0-7859-0653-3*, M9272) Fr & Eur.

Chinese-German Dictionary: Woerterbuch Chinesisch-Deutsch. 6th ed. Martin Piasek. 336p. (CHI & GER.). 1986. 69.95 (*0-8288-1008-7*, M7320) Fr & Eur.

Chinese Ghosts & ESP: A Study of Paranormal Beliefs & Experiences. Charles F. Emmons. LC 81-18236. 307p. 1982. 27.50 (*0-8108-1492-7*) Scarecrow.

***Chinese Gods of Wealth.** Basil M. Alexeiev. (Illus.). 62p. 1989. pap. 7.95 (*9971-4-9184-2*) Heian Intl.

Chinese Gold: The Chinese in the Monterey Bay Region. Sandy Lydon. LC 84-72699. (Illus.). 550p. (C). 1985. 29.95 (*0-932319-00-9*); pap. text ed. 24.95 (*0-932319-01-7*) Capitola Bk.

Chinese Gold Murders. Robert H. Van Gulik. LC 79-1536. x, 214p. 1979. pap. 6.95 (*0-226-84864-7*) U Ch Pr.

Chinese Goldfish. Li Zhen. (Illus.). 200p. 1991. 26.95 (*7-119-00408-5*, 16035) Tetra Pr.

Chinese Gourmet: Authentic Ingredients & Traditional Recipes from the Kitchens of China. William Mark. LC 94-14138. 1994. 39.95 (*1-57145-006-8*) Thunder Bay CA.

Chinese Government & Politics. Shibnath Banerjee. 175p. (C). 1980. 13.95 (*0-940500-04-3*) Asia Bk Corp.

Chinese Government in Ming Times: Seven Studies. Ed. by Charles O. Hucker. LC 69-14265. (Studies in Oriental Culture: No. 2). 301p. reprint ed. pap. 85.80 (*0-317-26650-0*, 2025106) Bks Demand.

Chinese Grain Economy & Policy. Chen L. Yu & A. Buckwell. 288p. 1991. text ed. 84.00 (*0-85198-642-0*) CAB Intl.

Chinese Grammar & English Grammar: A Comparative Study. Show-Chih Rai Chu. 417p. 1982. 12.95 (*0-913973-05-X*); pap. 10.95 (*0-913973-06-8*) Inst Sino-Amer.

***Chinese Grammar Flipper.** Flora Yang. 49p. (YA). (gr. 9 up). 1994. 6.25 (*1-878383-32-9*) C Lee Pubns.

Chinese Graphic Design. Scott Minick. 1990. text ed. 19.95 (*0-442-30364-5*) Van Nos Reinhold.

Chinese Grave: Sculptures of the Han Period. Berthold Laufer. (Illus.). 45p. 1911. 65.00 (*0-318-04695-4*) Rare Oriental Bk Co.

Chinese Gung Fu. Bruce Lee. LC 86-43242. (Specialties Ser.: No. 451). 112p. 1987. reprint ed. pap. 8.50 (*0-89750-112-8*) Ohara Pubns.

Chinese Hand Analysis. Terence Dukes. (Illus.). 362p. 1987. 15.95 (*0-87728-622-1*) Weiser.

Chinese Handcuffs. Chris Crutcher. (YA). 1991. mass mkt. 3.99 (*0-440-20837-8*, LFL) Dell.

Chinese Handcuffs. Chris Crutcher. LC 88-45809. 192p. 1989. 12.95 (*0-688-08345-5*) Greenwillow.

Chinese Healing Arts: Internal Kung Fu. William Berk. Ed. by William R. Berk. Tr. by John Dudgeon. LC 86-50612. 209p. (Orig.). 1986. reprint ed. pap. 9.95 (*0-86568-083-3*, 222) Unique Pubns.

Chinese Healing Foods & Herbs. Albert Y. Leung. Orig. Title: Chinese Herbal Remedies. (Illus.). 192p. reprint ed. pap. 10.95 (*0-9634979-0-1*) AYSL.

Chinese Health Balls: Practical Exercises. Hans Hoting. (Illus.). 118p. (Orig.). 1993. pap. 10.95 (*90-74597-03-3*, Pub. by Binkey Kok NE) Weiser.

***Chinese Herb Medicine & Therapy.** Hong-Yen Hsu. 1994. pap. 22.95 (*0-87983-653-9*) Keats.

Chinese Herb Medicine & Therapy. rev. ed. Hong-yen Hsu. 1993. 15.00 (*0-941942-12-0*) Orient Heal Arts.

Chinese Herbal Cures. Henry C. Lu. LC 93-43376. (Illus.). 160p. 1994. pap. 9.95 (*0-8069-0762-2*) Sterling.

Chinese Herbal Medicine. Daniel P. Reid. LC 86-17814. (Illus.). 180p. 1987. reprint ed. pap. 25.00 (*0-87773-398-8*) Shambhala Pubns.

Chinese Herbal Medicine: Formulas & Strategies. Dan Bensky & Randall Barolet. LC 89-81674. (Illus.). 592p. (C). 1990. text ed. 85.00 (*0-939616-10-6*) Eastland.

Chinese Herbal Medicine: Materia Medica. rev. ed. Ed. by Andrew Gamble & Ted Kaptchuk. LC 92-74516. (Illus.). 556p. (C). 1993. 75.00 (*0-939616-15-7*) Eastland.

Chinese Herbal Medicine & the Problems of Aging. Bokuso Terashi. 1993. pap. 12.00 (*0-941942-17-1*) Orient Heal Arts.

Chinese Herbal Remedies see Chinese Healing Foods & Herbs

***Chinese Herbal Science: Its Characteristics, Diagnosis & Treatment.** Hong-Yen Hsu. 1995. 6.95 (*0-941942-10-4*) Keats.

Chinese Herbal Therapy: A Guide to Its Principles & Practice. Takahide Kuwaki. 1993. pap. 19.95 (*0-941942-30-9*) Orient Heal Arts.

Chinese Herbalist's Handbook. Dagmar Ehling et al. 765p. 1993. pap. 34.95 (*1-56690-300-9*, OnWord Pr) High Mtn.

Chinese Herbology Made Easy. Maoshing Ni. (Illus.). 150p. 1986. pap. text ed. 14.50 (*0-937064-12-2*) SevenStar Comm.

Chinese Herbs: Their Botany, Chemistry & Pharmacodynamics. John E. Keys. 346p. 1991. pap. 14.95 (*0-8048-1667-0*) C E Tuttle.

Chinese Herbs Made Easy. Frank Miesse. 20p. pap. 2.95 (*0-913923-64-8*) Woodland UT.

Chinese Heroes. I. T. Headland. 1973. 59.95 (*0-87968-854-8*) Gordon Pr.

Chinese Higher Education: A Decade of Reform & Development (1978-88) Ruiqing Du. LC 91-24251. 176p. 1992. text ed. 59.95 (*0-312-06071-8*) St Martin.

Chinese Historic Sites & Pioneer Families of Rural Oahu. Wai J. Char & Tin-Yuke Char. LC 87-35501. (Illus.). 304p. 1988. pap. text ed. 26.00 (*0-8248-1113-5*, Hawaii Chinese Hist Ctr) UH Pr.

Chinese Historic Sites & Pioneer Families of the Island of Hawaii. Tin-Yuke Char & Waij J. Char. LC 83-9294. (Illus.). 247p. 1983. pap. text ed. 20.00 (*0-8248-0863-0*) UH Pr.

Chinese Historical Microdemography. Ed. by Stevan Harrell. LC 94-6116. (Studies on China: Vol. 20). 1994. 42.00 (*0-520-08306-7*) U CA Pr.

Chinese History: An Annotated Bibliography. Leona Phillips & Jill Phillips. 1978. lib. bdg. 250.00 (*0-8490-1391-7*) Gordon Pr.

Chinese History & Literature: Collection of Studies. Jaroslav Prusek. LC 77-733129. 586p. 1970. lib. bdg. 112.50 (*90-277-0175-X*) Kluwer Ac.

Chinese History in Economic Perspective. Ed. by Thomas G. Rawski & Lillian M. Li. (Studies on China: Vol. 13). (C). 1992. 45.00 (*0-520-07068-2*) U CA Pr.

Chinese Horoscopes. rev. ed. Lori Reid. (Illus.). 96p. 1994. pap. 6.95 (*0-7063-7222-0*, Pub. by Ward Lock UK) Sterling.

C

An Asterisk (*) at the beginning of an entry indicates that the title is appearing in BIP for the first time.

An Asterisk (*) at the beginning of an entry indicates that the title is appearing in BIP for the first time.

1225

Chinese New Year Fact & Folklore: Fact & Folklore. William C. Hu. LC 90-85200. (Foods & Snacks of Chinese Festivals Ser.). (Illus.). 1992. 39.95 (*0-89344-037-X*) Ars Ceramica.

*Chinese New Year Festivals.** rev. ed. Juliet Bredon. (Illus.). 29p. 1989. reprint ed. 19.95 (*9971-4-9124-9*) Heian Intl.

Chinese New Year's Dragon. Rachel Sing. (J). (ps-3). 1994. pap. 4.95 (*0-671-88602-9*, Half Moon Paper) S&S Childrens.

Chinese Nights Entertainment: Stories of Old China. Brian Brown. 1972. lib. bdg. 79.95 (*0-87968-491-7*) Krishna Pr.

Chinese Novel. P. S. Buck. LC 73-20425. (Studies in Asiatic Literature: No. 57). (C). 1974. lib. bdg. 75.00 (*0-8383-1766-9*) M S G Haskell Hse.

Chinese Novel at the Turn of the Century. Ed. by Milena Dolezelova-Velingerova. LC 79-22783. (Modern East Asian Studies: No. 1). (Illus.). 263p. reprint ed. pap. 75.00 (*0-8357-8071-6*, 2034060) Bks Demand.

Chinese Novels. John F. Davis. LC 76-43332. 1976. reprint ed. 50.00 (*0-8201-1278-X*) Schol Facsimiles.

Chinese Numbers: Significance, Symbolism & Traditions. Evelyn Lip. (Illus.). 121p. (Orig.). 1992. pap. 9.95 (*0-89346-376-0*) Heian Intl.

Chinese Nursery Rhymes - Animals & Riddles, Vol. 3. Headland. 1993. pap. 7.50 (*0-910704-74-0*) Hawley.

Chinese Nursery Rhymes - Family Relations, Vol. 1. Headland. 1993. pap. 7.50 (*0-910704-72-4*) Hawley.

Chinese Nursery Rhymes - Nineteenth Century Life, Vol. 2. Headland. 1993. pap. 7.50 (*0-910704-73-2*) Hawley.

Chinese of Early Tucson: Historic Archaeology from the Tucson Urban Renewal Project. Florence C. Lister & Robert H. Lister. LC 89-5105. (Anthropological Papers: No. 52). 131p. (Orig.). 1990. pap. 29.95 (*0-8165-1151-9*) U of Ariz Pr.

Chinese of Sarawak: A Study of Social Structure. Ju-K'ang T'ien. LC 77-87004. (London School of Economics & Political Science Monographs on Social Anthropology: No. 12). reprint ed. 42.50 (*0-404-16779-9*) AMS Pr.

Chinese of South East Asia. Lewis B. Sckolnick. (Civil Rights Reporter Ser.). (Illus.). 60p. (Orig.). (C). 1994. pap. 45.00 (*1-57205-116-7*) Rector Pr.

*Chinese One Dish Meals.** rev. ed. Huang Su-Huei. (Illus.). 96p. (CHI & SPA.). 1995. pap. 14.95 (*0-941676-57-9*) Wei-Chuan Pub.

Chinese Opium Wars. Jack Beeching. LC 76-40223. (Illus.). 1977. pap. 6.95 (*0-15-617094-9*, Harvest Bks) HarBrace.

Chinese Ornament: The Lotus & the Dragon. Jessica Rawson. LC 84-43047. (Illus.). 248p. 1985. 44.50 (*0-8419-1022-7*); pap. write for info. (*0-8419-1023-5*) Holmes & Meier.

Chinese Oxymoron. Veronica S. Pierce. LC 90-81818. (Brown Bag Mystery Line Ser.). 332p. 1990. 14.95 (*0-933031-29-7*) Coun Oak Bks.

Chinese Painted Quail (The Button Quail) Their Breeding & Care. Leland B. Hayes. (Illus.). 161p. 1992. pap. 13.95 (*0-9633196-1-2*) L B Hayes.

Chinese Painters. Raphael Petrucci. Tr. by Frances Seaver. LC 79-102253. (Select Bibliographies Reprint Ser.). 1977. 15.95 (*0-8369-5138-7*) Ayer.

Chinese Painting. Torao Miyagawa et al. Tr. by Alfred T. Birnbaum. LC 83-3505. (History of the Art of China Ser.). (Illus.). 232p. 1984. 65.00 (*0-8348-1527-3*) Weatherhill.

Chinese Painting. Skira-Rizzoli Staff & James Cahill. LC 76-62896. (Illus.). 216p. 1978. pap. 25.00 (*0-8478-0079-2*) Rizzoli Intl.

Chinese Painting: An Escape from the "Dusty" World. LC 81-65665. (Themes in Art Ser.). (Illus.). 74p. reprint ed. pap. 25.00 (*0-317-09307-X*, 2022659) Bks Demand.

*Chinese Painting: Ideas & Inspiration.** Marguerite Franklin-Carrier. (Illus.). 128p. 1995. 24.95 (*0-289-80131-1*, Pub. by Studio Vista Bks UK) Sterling.

Chinese Painting: The Complete Self Tutor. Francisca Ting. 1991. pap. 16.95 (*0-486-26785-7*) Dover.

Chinese Painting & Caligraphy. Fang Zhaoling. 93p. 1981. 35.00 (*0-87556-175-6*) Saifer.

Chinese Painting & Calligraphy, a Pictorical Survey: Sixty-Nine Fine Examples from the John M. Crawford Collection in 109 Photographs. Wan-Go H. Weng. (Illus.). 1978. pap. 9.95 (*0-486-23707-9*) Dover.

Chinese Painting Colors: Studies of Their Preparation & Application in Traditional & Modern Times. Yu Fei-an. Tr. by Jerome Silbergeld & Amy McNair. LC 85-24638. (Illus.). 128p. 1987. pap. 50.00 (*0-295-96356-5*) U of Wash Pr.

Chinese Painting, No. 1. Chows. (How to Draw & Paint Ser.). (Illus.). 32p. (Orig.). 1989. pap. 5.95 (*1-56010-016-8*, HT069) W Foster Pub.

Chinese Painting, No. 2. Chows. (How to Draw & Paint Ser.). (Illus.). 32p. (Orig.). 1989. pap. 5.95 (*1-56010-017-6*, HT128) W Foster Pub.

Chinese Painting Style: Media, Methods, & Principles of Form. Jerome Silbergeld. LC 81-21837. (Illus.). 132p. 1982. pap. 20.00 (*0-295-95921-5*) U of Wash Pr.

Chinese Painting Techniques: A Complete Course. Jean Long. (Illus.). 224p. 1994. 19.95 (*0-289-80114-1*, Pub. by Studio Vista Bks UK) Sterling.

Chinese Paintings. Susan Y. Kiang. LC 85-62610. 96p. 1986. text ed. 19.95 (*0-916301-01-X*) One World Pub.

Chinese Paintings & Mounted Rocks: Exhibition Catalogue. Walton J. Lord. (Illus.). 28p. 1979. pap. 2.00 (*0-911209-14-X*) Palmer Mus Art.

Chinese Paintings of the Middle Qing Dynasty. Jung Y. Tsao. LC 87-80626. 280p. (Orig.). 1987. 34.95 (*0-9618493-0-4*) Far East Fine Arts.

*Chinese Papercuts: A Selection.** (Exotic Miniatures Ser.). (Illus.). 160p. Date not set. 14.95 (*981-00-4410-0*) Heian Intl.

Chinese Patterns of Behavior: A Sourcebook of Psychological & Psychiatric Studies. Ed. by David Yau--Fai Ho et al. LC 88-32335. 512p. 1989. text ed. 155.00 (*0-275-93270-2*, C3270, Praeger Pubs) Greenwood.

Chinese Pavilion at Drottingholm. Ake Setterwall et al. (Illus.). 327p. 1974. 125.00 (*91-7004-024-9*, Pub. by Bamboo Pub UK) Antique Collect.

Chinese Pavilion at Drottningholm (Sweden) Ake Setterwall. (Illus.). 327p. 1974. 160.00 (*0-87556-739-8*) Saifer.

Chinese Peasant Economy: Agricultural Development in Hopei & Shantung, 1890-1949. Ramon H. Myers. LC 79-115189. (Harvard East Asian Ser.: No. 47). 410p. reprint ed. pap. 116.90 (*0-317-09167-0*, 2005498) Bks Demand.

Chinese Pediatric Massage Therapy: A Parent & Practitioner's Guide to the Treatment & Prevention of Childhood Diseases. Fan Ya-li. Ed. & Intro. by Bob Flaws. LC 93-74981. (Illus.). 151p. (Orig.). 1994. pap. 12.95 (*0-936185-54-6*) Blue Poppy.

Chinese People's Movement: Perspectives on Spring 1989. Ed. by Tony Saich. LC 90-41535. 224p. 1990. 44.95 (*0-87332-745-4*); pap. text ed. 20.95 (*0-87332-746-2*) M E Sharpe.

Chinese People's Republic. Dennis Doolin & Robert C. North. LC 65-19769. (Studies Ser.: No. 14). 68p. 1966. pap. 1.80 (*0-8179-3142-2*) Hoover Inst Pr.

Chinese Periodicals in the Library of Congress: A Bibliography. Ed. by David H. Hsu. LC 87-600394. 814p. 1988. 39.00 (*0-8444-0581-7*, 030-000-00207-5) Lib Congress.

Chinese Philosophy, Art, Life & Mathematics. Li-Chung Wang. 44p. (Orig.). (C). 1987. pap. text ed. 3.95 (*0-9624242-0-X*) L C Wang Pr.

Chinese Philosophy in Classical Times. Ed. by E. R. Hughes. 1977. lib. bdg. 59.95 (*0-8490-1611-8*) Gordon Pr.

Chinese Philosophy, 1949-1963: An Annotated Bibliography of Mainland China Publications. Wing-tsit Chan. LC 65-20582. 304p. reprint ed. pap. 86.70 (*0-317-55699-1*, 2029581) Bks Demand.

Chinese Phrase Book. (Hugo Ser.). (Illus.). 128p. (Orig.). 1991. pap. 4.95 (*0-85285-153-7*); audio, pap. 14.95 (*0-85285-156-1*) Hunter NJ.

Chinese Phrase Book & Dictionary. Berlitz Staff. LC 87-70573. (Phrase Book Ser.). 192p. 1994. pap. 6.95 (*2-8315-0909-2*) Berlitz.

Chinese Phrasebook. 2nd ed. Chris Taylor. 184p. 1991. pap. 4.95 (*0-86442-086-2*) Lonely Planet.

Chinese Physician: Dying & Loss in an American Perspective. Ed. by Clarence Chen et al. 120p. 1991. pap. 16.95 (*0-930194-48-9*) Ctr Thanatology.

Chinese Pictorial Art. R. H. Van Gulik. (Illus.). 537p. 1993. 65.00 (*957-638-153-3*) Oriental Bk Store.

Chinese Pictorial Art As Viewed by the Connoisseur. R. H. Van Gulik. LC 79-91820. (Illus.). 537p. 1980. reprint ed. lib. bdg. 90.00 (*0-87817-264-5*) Hacker.

Chinese Picture Cookbook, Pt. 2. Alan Ching. 72p. (Orig.). pap. 3.99 (*0-9619961-1-0*) Rising Co Inc.

Chinese Picture Cookbook, Bk. 1: Pork, Beef, Chicken & Dietetic Menu Recipes. Alan Ching. (Illus.). 72p. (Orig.). 1988. pap. 5.95 (*0-9619961-0-2*) Rising Co Inc.

Chinese Picture Cookbook, Bk. 2: Seafood, Appetizer, Vegetable, Dessert & Soup Recipes. Alan Ching. (Illus.). 72p. (Orig.). 1988. pap. 5.95 (*0-317-91108-2*) Rising Co Inc.

Chinese Pioneer Family: The Lins of Wu-feng, Taiwan, 1729-1895. Johanna M. Meskill. LC 78-70308. (Studies of the East Asian Institute, Columbia University). (Illus.). 392p. 1986. text ed. 59.50 (*0-691-03124-X*); pap. text ed. 16.95x (*0-691-00808-6*) Princeton U Pr.

Chinese Pioneers on the Sarawak Frontier, 1841-1941. Daniel Chew. (South-East Asian Historical Monographs). (Illus.). 302p. 1990. 29.95 (*0-19-588915-0*) OUP.

Chinese Poems in English Rhyme. Ts'ai T'ing-Kan. LC 73-137273. reprint ed. 22.50 (*0-404-06525-2*) AMS Pr.

Chinese Poetry. Ed. by Marina H. Sung. 105p. (Orig.). (C). 1990. pap. text ed. write for info. (*0-9630354-0-1*) Lao Lab.

Chinese Policy Toward Indonesia, 1949-1967. David Mozingo. LC 75-14719. 303p. 1976. 39.95 (*0-8014-0921-7*) Cornell U Pr.

Chinese Political Thought. Elbert D. Thomas. LC 73-102257. (Select Bibliographies Reprint Ser.). 1977. 31.95 (*0-8369-5142-5*) Ayer.

Chinese Politics after Mao: Development & Liberalization, 1976-1983. Peter R. Moody, Jr. LC 83-13925. 220p. 1983. text ed. 55.00 (*0-275-91046-6*, C1046, Praeger Pubs) Greenwood.

Chinese Politics & Christian Missions. Jessie G. Lutz. LC 87-72450. (Church & the World Ser., The West & the Wider World Ser.). xviii, 440p. 1988. 48.85 (*0-940121-05-0*) Cross Cultural Pubns.

Chinese Politics & Foreign Policy Reform. Ed. by Gerald Segal. 256p. 1990. 59.95 (*0-7103-0390-4*, A4803, Pub. by Kegan Paul Intl UK) Routledge Chapman & Hall.

Chinese Politics & the Succession to Mao. John Gardner. LC 82-6174. (Illus.). 217p. (C). 1982. pap. text ed. 19.50 (*0-8419-0809-5*) Holmes & Meier.

*Chinese Politics: Documents & Analysis: The Death of Mao (1976) to the Fall of Hua Kuo-feng (1980), Vol. 3.** Ed. by James T. Myers et al. Date not set. 69.95 (*1-57003-062-6*) U of SC Pr.

*Chinese Politics: Documents & Analysis: The Fall of Hua Kuo-feng (1980) to the Twelfth Party Congress (1982), Vol. 4.** Ed. by James T. Myers et al. Date not set. 69.95 (*1-57003-063-4*) U of SC Pr.

Chinese Politics: Documents & Analysis, Vol. 1: Cultural Revolution to 1969. James T. Myers et al. LC 85-22466. 433p. 1986. text ed. 69.95 (*0-87249-475-6*) U of SC Pr.

Chinese Politics: Documents & Analysis, Vol. 2: Ninth Party Congress (1969) to the Death of Mao (1976) James T. Myers et al. 467p. (C). 1989. text ed. 69.95 (*0-87249-601-5*) U of SC Pr.

Chinese Politics from Mao to Deng. Ed. by Ilpyong J. Kim & Vic Falkenheim. 347p. 1989. 29.95 (*0-943852-71-4*); pap. 15.95 (*0-943852-72-2*) Prof World Peace.

*Chinese Porcelains of the Seventeenth Century: Landscapes, Scholars' Motifs & Narratives.** Julia B. Curtis & Stephen Little. (Illus.). 168p. (C). 1995. pap. 35.00 (*0-295-97467-2*) U of Wash Pr.

Chinese Portraits. Dorothy Hoobler & Thomas Hoobler. LC 92-13617. (Images Across the Ages Ser.). (Illus.). 96p. (J). (gr. 7-8). 1992. lib. bdg. 24.26 (*0-8114-6375-3*) Raintree Steck-V.

Chinese Pottery & Porcelain. L. Zhiyan & C. Wan. (Illus.). 201p. (Orig.). (C). 1984. text ed. 100.00 (*0-685-40284-3*, Pub. by Collets) St Mut.

Chinese Pottery & Porcelain. R. L. Hobson. LC 75-21139. (Illus.). 563p. 1976. reprint ed. pap. 15.95 (*0-486-23253-0*) Dover.

Chinese Pottery & Porcelain: From Prehistory to the Present. Shelagh J. Vainker. (Braziller Library of Far Eastern Art). (Illus.). 255p. 1991. 45.00 (*0-8076-1260-X*) Braziller.

Chinese Pottery in the Philippines: The Wild Tribes of Davao District, Mindanao. F. C. Cole. (Chicago Field Museum of Natural History Fieldiana Anthropology Ser.: Vol. 12). 1913. 45.00 (*0-527-01872-4*) Periodicals Srv.

Chinese Primer: Character Text. Ta-tuan Chen et al. LC 93-45904. 1994. reprint ed. 15.00 (*0-691-03694-2*) Princeton U Pr.

Chinese Primer: GR Edition, 3 vols., Set. Ta-Tuan Ch'en et al. LC 89-2218. 590p. (C). 1989. pap. text ed. 42.00 (*0-674-12476-6*) HUP.

Chinese Primer: Pinyin Edition, 3 vols. Ta-Tuan Ch'en et al. LC 89-2218. 590p. (C). 1989. GR System, 632p. 37.50 (*0-685-28017-9*); Character Text, 144p. 10.50 (*0-685-28018-7*) HUP.

Chinese Primer: Pinyin Edition, 3 vols., Set. Ta-Tuan Ch'en et al. LC 89-2218. 608p. (C). 1989. pap. text ed. 42.00 (*0-674-12475-8*) HUP.

*Chinese Primer Vols. 1-3: Gr. Version, 3 vols., Set.** Ta-tuan Chen. 1994. 45.00 (*0-691-03696-9*) Princeton U Pr.

*Chinese Primer Vols. 1-3: Pinyin Version, 3 vols., Set.** Ta-tuan Chen. 1994. 45.00 (*0-691-03695-0*) Princeton U Pr.

Chinese Profile. Zhang Xinxin & Sang Ye. 376p. 1986. pap. 9.95 (*0-8351-1603-4*) China Bks.

*Chinese Profiles.** Zhang Xinxin & Sang Ye. 375p. 1995. lib. bdg. 29.00 (*0-8095-4508-X*) Borgo Pr.

*Chinese Propaganda Posters: From Revolution to Modernization.** Stefan L. Landsberger. (Illus.). 204p. 1995. 85.00 (*1-56324-688-0*) M E Sharpe.

Chinese Prose Literature of the T'ang Period: A.D. 618-906, 2 vols., Set. Evangeline D. Edwards. LC 70-38067. reprint ed. 67.50 (*0-404-56971-4*) AMS Pr.

Chinese Proverbs. Ruthanne L. McCunn. (Little Book Ser.). (Illus.). 60p. 1992. 6.95 (*0-8118-0083-0*) Chronicle Bks.

*Chinese Proverbs & Sayings.** Evelyn Lip. 111p. 1984. pap. 5.95 (*9971-947-61-7*) Heian Intl.

Chinese Province As a Reform Experiment: The Case of Hainan. Paul M. Cadario et al. LC 92-19133. (Discussion Paper Ser.: Vol. 170). 72p. 1992. 6.95 (*0-8213-2169-2*, 12169) World Bank.

Chinese Puzzle. Warren Murphy. (Destroyer Ser.: No. 3). (Orig.). 1988. pap. 3.50 (*1-55817-038-3*, Pinnacle NY) Windsor NY.

Chinese Qigong & the Science of Energy: Improving Mental & Physical Health & Increasing Longevity. (Alternative Medicine Ser.). 1992. lib. bdg. 93.95 (*0-8490-5391-9*) Gordon Pr.

Chinese Qigong Massage: General Massage. Yang Jwing-Ming. (Illus.). 332p. (Orig.). (C). 1992. 29.95 (*0-940871-26-2*) YMAA Pubn.

Chinese Qigong Massage: General Massage. Yang Jwing-Ming. Ed. by Alan Dougall. (Illus.). 332p. (Orig.). (C). 1992. pap. 24.95 (*0-940871-25-4*, B016SC) YMAA Pubn.

Chinese Radicals, Vol. 1. Tan Huay Peng. (Peng's Chinese Treasury Ser.). (Illus.). 144p. 1987. pap. 4.95 (*0-89346-291-8*) Heian Intl.

Chinese Radicals, Vol. 2. Tan Huay Peng. (Peng's Chinese Treasury Ser.). (Illus.). 136p. 1987. pap. 4.95 (*0-89346-292-6*) Heian Intl.

Chinese Railroad Workers. Susan Sinnott. LC 94-50. (First Book Ser.). (J). 1994. lib. bdg. 13.93 (*0-531-20169-4*) Watts.

Chinese Read, Vol. I. H. C. Fenn & M. G. Tewksbury. 236p. (C). 1961. audio 65.00 (*0-88432-090-1*, AFM301); 12.95 (*0-685-73534-6*, AFM993) Audio-Forum.

Chinese Read, Vol. II. H. C. Fenn & M. G. Tewksbury. 276p. (C). 1983. audio 55.00 (*0-88432-091-X*, AFM310); 12.95 (*0-685-73536-2*, AFM994) Audio-Forum.

Chinese Reader's Manual: A Handbook of Biographical, Historical, Mythological, & General Literary Reference. W. E. Mayers. 1972. 250.00 (*0-87968-855-6*) Gordon Pr.

*Chinese Reassessment of Socialism.** Yan Sun. LC 95-6349. 1995. write for info. (*0-691-02999-7*); pap. write for info. (*0-691-02998-9*) Princeton U Pr.

*Chinese Recipes.** Ed. by G & R Publishing Staff. (Uni-Book Ser.). 160p. (Orig.). 1994. pap. text ed. 3.00 (*1-56383-030-2*, 6100) G & R Pub.

*Chinese Recipes.** Ken Hom. 144p. 1995. 13.95 (*1-85145-388-1*, Pub. by Pavilion UK) Trafalgar.

*Chinese Recipes.** Ken Hom. 144p. 1995. 13.95 (*1-85793-388-5*, Pub. by Pavilion UK) Trafalgar.

Chinese Recipes. Stephen Yan. (Illus.). 146p. (Orig.). 1988. pap. 11.95 (*0-921053-01-0*) Gordon Soules Bk.

Chinese Recorder Index: A Guide to Christian Missions in Asia, 1867-1941, 2 vols. Ed. by Kathleen Lodwick. LC 85-26125. 1200p. 1986. 150.00 (*0-8420-2250-3*) Scholarly Res Inc.

Chinese Red Army, Nineteen Twenty-Seven to Nineteen Sixty-Three: An Annotated Bibliography. Edward J. Rhoads et al. LC 65-1422. (East Asian Monographs: No. 16). 202p. 1964. pap. 11.00 (*0-674-12500-2*) HUP.

Chinese Reflections: Americans Teaching in the People's Republic. Tani E. Balrow & Donald M. Lowe. LC 85-6467. (Illus.). 256p. 1985. text ed. 59.95 (*0-275-91759-2*, C1759, Praeger Pubs) Greenwood.

*Chinese Regional Specialties.** Sonia Allison. 1994. 9.95 (*0-572-01765-0*, Pub. by W Foulsham UK) Trans-Atl Phila.

Chinese Regionalism: The Security Dimension. Ed. by Richard H. Yang. LC 93-50193. (C). 1994. pap. text ed. 49.95 (*0-8133-8853-8*) Westview.

Chinese Religion: An Anthology of Sources. Ed. by Deborah Sommer. 416p. (C). 1994. pap. text ed. 24.00 (*0-19-508895-6*) OUP.

Chinese Religion: An Anthology of Sources. Ed. by Deborah Sommer. 416p. (C). 1995. 45.00 (*0-19-508894-8*) OUP.

Chinese Religion: An Introduction. 4th ed. Laurence G. Thompson. 184p. (C). 1989. pap. 19.95 (*0-534-09270-5*) Intl Thomson.

*Chinese Religion: An Introduction.** 5th ed. Laurence G. Thompson. LC 95-10344. 1996. pap. 19.95 (*0-534-25536-1*) Intl Thomson.

Chinese Religion: Publications in Western Languages, 1981 Through 1990. Ed. by Gary Seaman. LC 93-3757. (Monographs & Occasional Papers: No. 47). 280p. 1993. 32.00 (*0-924304-13-8*) Assn Asian Studies.

Chinese Religion & the Baha'i Faith. Phyllis G. Chew. 256p. (Orig.). 1993. pap. 12.95 (*0-85398-358-5*) G Ronald Pub.

Chinese Religion Through Hindu Eyes: A Study in the Tendencies of Asiatic Mentality. Benoy K. Sarkar. (C). 1988. reprint ed. 21.50 (*81-206-0415-6*, Pub. by Asian Educ Servs II) S Asia.

Chinese Religions. Julia Ching. LC 93-2896. 300p. 1993. pap. 18.95 (*0-88344-875-0*) Orbis Bks.

Chinese Religions: A Cultural Perspective. Christian Jochim. (Illus.). 224p. (C). 1985. pap. text ed. 19.33 (*0-13-132994-4*) P-H.

Chinese Restaurants Never Serve Breakfast: Murder in Carmel. Roy Gilligan. LC 91-72120. (Pat Riordan Mystery Ser.). 180p. 1986. reprint ed. pap. 8.95 (*0-9626136-2-2*) Brendan Bks.

Chinese Revolution. Anthony Weston. Ed. by Malcolm Yapp et al. (World History Ser.). (Illus.). 32p. (YA). (gr. 6-11). 1980. reprint ed. pap. text ed. 4.35 (*0-89908-114-2*) Greenhaven.

Chinese Revolution in Historical Perspective. John E. Schrecker. LC 90-40901. 264p. 1991. pap. text ed. 18.95 (*0-275-93646-5*, B3646, Praeger Pubs) Greenwood.

Chinese Revolution in Historical Perspective. John E. Schrecker. LC 90-38410. (Contributions to the Study of World History Ser.: No. 19). 264p. 1991. text ed. 49.95 (*0-313-27485-1*, SKB, Greenwood Pr) Greenwood.

Chinese Revolution, Nineteen Twenty-Six to Nineteen Twenty-Seven: A Record of the Period Under Communist Control As Seen from the Nationalist Capital. Herbert O. Chapman. LC 75-39022. (China Studies: from Confucius to Mao Ser.). (Illus.). xvii, 310p. 1977. reprint ed. lib. bdg. 25.85 (*0-88355-379-1*) Hyperion Conn.

Chinese Revolution, with Details of the Habits, Manners & Customs of China & the Chinese. Charles MacFarlane. 1972. 59.95 (*0-87968-856-4*) Gordon Pr.

Chinese Ring Daggers: The Ultimate Close-Quarter Weapons. Ricky Pickens. (Illus.). 104p. 1987. pap. 12.00 (*0-87364-444-1*) Paladin Pr.

Chinese Rites Controversy: From Its Beginnings to Modern Times. George Minamiki. 1985. 15.95 (*0-8294-0457-0*) Loyola Univ Pr.

Chinese Road to Socialism: Economics of the Cultural Revolution. E. L. Wheelwright & Bruce McFarlane. LC 76-124082. 256p. 1971. reprint ed. pap. 4.50 (*0-85345-194-X*) Monthly Rev.

Chinese Road to Socialism: Economics of the Cultural Revolution. Edward Wheelwright & Bruce McFarlane. LC 76-124082. reprint ed. pap. 69.20 (*0-7837-6987-3*, 204799) Bks Demand.

Chinese Romanization Self-Study Guide. Dennis K. Yee. Ed. by John DeFrancis. LC 74-189616. (PALI Language Texts, Chinese Ser.). 62p. (C). 1975. pap. text ed. 2.50 (*0-8248-0227-6*) UH Pr.

Chinese Roulette. Philip Kirk. (Butler Ser.). 208p. 1984. pap. 2.50 (*0-8439-2068-8*) Dorchester Pub Co.

Chinese Roundabout: Essays in History & Culture. Jonathan D. Spence. (Illus.). 384p. 1992. 24.95 (*0-393-03355-4*) Norton.

Chinese Roundabout: Essays in History & Culture. Jonathan D. Spence. (Illus.). 416p. 1993. pap. 12.95 (*0-393-30994-0*) Norton.

Chinese Rugs: A Buyer's Guide. Lee Allane. LC 92-80332. (Illus.). 136p. 1993. 24.95 (*0-500-01541-4*) Thames Hudson.

Chinese Rugs: A Buyer's Guide. Lee Allane. LC 92-80332. (Illus.). 144p. 1994. pap. 15.95 (*0-500-27701-X*) Thames Hudson.

Chinese Rural Development: The Great Transformation. Ed. by William L. Parish. LC 84-22193. 286p. 1985. pap. text ed. 25.95 (*0-87332-344-0*) M E Sharpe.

1226 An Asterisk (*) at the beginning of an entry indicates that the title is appearing in BIP for the first time.

Chinese-Russian Military & Technical Dictionary. I. D. Klein. 676p. (CHI & RUS.). 1985. 95.00 (*0-8288-1908-4*, M1986) Fr & Eur.
Chinese Sailing Rig: Designing & Building Your Own. rev. ed. Derek Van Loan & Dan Haggerty. (Illus.). 112p. (Orig.). 1993. pap. 15.95 (*0-939837-18-8*) Paradise Cay Pubns.
Chinese Sailing Rig: Designing & Building Your Own. 4th ed. Derek Van Loan. (Illus.). 79p. (Orig.). 1981. pap. 8.50 (*0-9614068-0-1*) Epoch Pr.
Chinese Scientific & Technical Research, Vol. 1. Ed. by R. J. Berry. 387p. 1994. lib. bdg. 245.00 (*1-56072-124-3*); disk 175.00 (*1-56072-125-1*); mac hd 175.00 (*1-56072-126-X*) Nova Sci Pubs.
Chinese Scientific & Technical Research, Vol. 2. Ed. by R. J. Berry. 412p. 1994. lib. bdg. 245.00 (*1-56072-127-8*); disk 175.00 (*1-56072-128-6*); mac hd 175.00 (*1-56072-129-4*) Nova Sci Pubs.
Chinese Sculpture in the Metropolitan Museum of Art. Metropolitan Museum of Art Staff & Alan Priest. 1974. 40.95 (*0-405-02264-6*, 16141) Ayer.
Chinese Seafood. Huang Su Huei. Tr. by Lai Yen-Jen. (Illus.). 104p. 1984. pap. 14.95 (*0-941676-09-9*) Wei-Chuan Pub.
Chinese Sedimentary Basins. Ed. by X. Zhu. (Sedimentary Basins of the World Ser.: No. 1). 256p. 1989. 128.25 (*0-444-43017-2*) Elsevier.
Chinese Shadow Theatre. Sven Broman. (Ethnographical Museum of Sweden Monograph: No. 15). (Illus.). 250p. 1981. 83.50x (*91-22-01370-9*, Pub. by Almqv & Wiksell SW) Coronet Bks.
Chinese Shar-Pei. Paul D. Strang & Eve C. Olsen. LC 79-55675. (Other Dog Bks.). (Illus.). 1980. 29.95 (*0-87714-072-3*); pap. 19.95 (*0-685-73228-2*) Denlingers.
***Chinese Shar Peis Today.** Julliette Cunliffe. (Illus.). 160p. 1995. 25.95 (*0-87605-095-X*) Howell Bk.
***Chinese Shawl.** P. Wentworth. 1994. pap. 3.99 (*0-517-13223-0*) Random Hse Value.
Chinese Shawl. large type ed. Patricia Wentworth. (General Ser.). 305p. 1992. pap. 14.95 (*0-8161-5314-0*, Large Print Bks) Hall.
Chinese "Shehuo" Art of Shaanxi Province. Ed. by Wang Yao'an. Tr. by Zhang Long. (Illus.). 96p. (CHI & ENG.). 1992. 39.00 (*1-880132-06-0*) Sci Pr NY.
Chinese Short Story: Studies in Dating, Authorship, & Composition. Patrick Hanan. LC 72-87776. (Harvard-Yenching Institute Monograph: No. 21). 320p. 1973. 20.00 (*0-674-12525-8*) HUP.
Chinese Siamese Cat. Amy Tan. LC 93-24008. (Illus.). 32p. (J). (gr. k-3). 1994. text ed. 16.95 (*0-02-788835-5*, Mac Bks Young Read) S&S Childrens.
Chinese Sites: Chinese Children's Stories, Vols. 86-90, 5 vols., Set. Wonder Kids Publications Group Staff (USA) et al. Ed. by Emily Ching et al. Tr. by Wonder Kids Publications Staff. LC 90-60809. (Illus.). (J). (gr. 3-6). 1991. reprint ed. Five vol. set, 28p. ea. bk. 39.75 (*0-685-58717-7*) Wonder Kids.
Chinese Snacks. rev. ed. Su Huei Huang. Ed. by Chen Chang-Yen & Gloria C. Martinez. Tr. by Lai Yen-Jen. (Illus.). 100p. (CHI & ENG.). (C). 1985. pap. 14.95 (*0-941676-11-0*) Wei-Chuan Pub.
Chinese Snuff Bottles. John G. Ford. (Edward Choate O'Dell Collection). (Illus.). 80p. (Orig.). 1982. 32.95 (*0-9609668-0-3*) Intl Chi Snuff.
Chinese Snuff Bottles. Robert L. Kleiner. (Images of Asia Ser.). (Illus.). 96p. 1994. 16.95 (*0-19-585756-9*) OUP.
Chinese Social & Economic History from the Song to 1900: Report of the American Delegation to a Sino-American Symposium. Ed. by Albert Feuerwerker. LC 83-1789. (Michigan Monographs in Chinese Studies: No. 45). vi, 182p. (Orig.). (C). 1982. pap. 8.00 (*0-89264-045-6*) Ctr Chinese Studies.
Chinese Society in the Eighteenth Century. Susan Naquin & Evelyn S. Rawski. LC 86-29007. 320p. (C). 1987. text ed. 32.00 (*0-300-03848-8*) Yale U Pr.
Chinese Society in the Eighteenth Century. Susan Naquin & Evelyn S. Rawski. 270p. (C). 1989. reprint ed. pap. 15.00 (*0-300-04602-2*) Yale U Pr.
Chinese Society on the Eve of Tiananmen: The Impact of Reform. Ed. by Deborah Davis & Ezra F. Vogel. (Harvard Contemporary China Ser.: No. 7). (Illus.). 401p. 1990. pap. 18.00 (*0-674-12535-5*) HUP.
Chinese Sources for the Taiping Rebellion, 1850-1864. James C. Cheng. LC 63-4982. 199p. reprint ed. pap. 56.80 (*0-7837-0117-9*, 2040394) Bks Demand.
Chinese-Soviet Relations, 1937-1945: The Diplomacy of Chinese Nationalism. John W. Garver. (Illus.). 320p. 1988. 49.95 (*0-19-505432-6*) OUP.
Chinese Spirit Medium Cults in Singapore. Alan J. Elliott. LC 90-35762. (Monographs on Social Anthropology: Vol. 14). 176p. (C). 1990. text ed. 70.00 (*0-485-19514-3*, Pub. by Athlone Pr UK) Humanities.
Chinese Spirit-Medium Cults in Singapore. Alan J. Elliott. 1981. reprint ed. 20.00 (*0-89986-347-7*) Oriental Bk Store.
Chinese Spirit Road: The Classical Tradition of Stone Tomb Statuary. Ann Paludan. (Illus.). 256p. (C). 1991. text ed. 45.00 (*0-300-04597-2*) Yale U Pr.
Chinese Spring Festival. Ming Tsow. (Way We Live Ser.). (Illus.). 25p. (J). (gr. 2-4). 1991. 13.95 (*0-237-60137-0*, Pub. by Evans Bros Ltd UK) Trafalgar.
Chinese State Enterprises: A Regional Property Rights Analysis. David Granick. LC 89-20166. (Illus.). 360p. 1990. 39.95 (*0-226-30588-0*) U Ch Pr.
Chinese State in the Era of Economic Reform: The Road to Crisis. Ed. by Gordon White. LC 90-29275. (Socialism & Social Movement Ser.). 352p. (C). 1991. 62.95 (*0-87332-853-1*) M E Sharpe.
Chinese Statelets & the Northern Barbarians in the Period 1400-300 B. C. Jaroslav Prusek. LC 70-154745. 312p. 1971. lib. bdg. 80.00 (*90-277-0225-X*) Kluwer Ac.
***Chinese Stories.** Cheng Mei. 1995. pap. 16.00 (*0-89410-796-8*) Three Continents.
***Chinese Stories.** rev. ed. Robert K. Douglas. (Illus.). 216p. 1990. reprint ed. pap. 9.95 (*9971-4-9165-6*) Heian Intl.
Chinese Stories from Taiwan, Nineteen Sixty to Nineteen Seventy. Ed. by Joseph S. Lau & Timothy A. Ross. LC 75-4391. 359p. 1976. text ed. 50.00 (*0-231-04007-5*) Col U Pr.
***Chinese Stories from the Fifties.** 239p. 1995. lib. bdg. 27.00 (*0-8095-4507-1*) Borgo Pr.
Chinese Students in America: Policies, Issues & Numbers. Leo A. Orleans. 156p. 1988. pap. 14.95 (*0-309-03886-3*) Natl Acad Pr.
Chinese Subculture & Criminality: Non-Traditional Crime Groups in America. Ko-Lin Chin. LC 89-71441. (Contributions in Criminology & Penology Ser.: No. 29). 192p. 1990. text ed. 49.95 (*0-313-27262-X*, CCK/, Greenwood Pr) Greenwood.
Chinese Supreme Court Decisions: Relating to General Principles of Civil Law, Obligations & Commercial Law. Tr. by F. T. Cheng. LC 76-11421. 229p. 1976. reprint ed. text ed. 55.00 (*0-313-26967-X*, U6967, Greenwood Pr) Greenwood.
Chinese Symbolism & Art Motifs. Charles A. Williams. LC 73-90237. (Illus.). 498p. 1989. reprint ed. pap. 29.95 (*0-8048-1586-0*) C E Tuttle.
Chinese System of Food Cures: Prevention & Remedies. Henry C. Lu. LC 86-5678. (Illus.). 192p. (Orig.). 1986. pap. 9.95 (*0-8069-6308-5*) Sterling.
Chinese System of Natural Cures. Henry C. Lu. LC 94-13706. 160p. 1994. pap. 9.95 (*0-8069-0616-2*) Sterling.
Chinese System of Public Education. Ping-Wan. 1977. lib. bdg. 59.95 (*0-8490-1612-6*) Gordon Pr.
Chinese System of Public Education. Ping-Wen Kuo. LC 72-176937. (Columbia University. Teachers College. Contributions to Education Ser.: No. 64). reprint ed. 37.50 (*0-404-55064-9*) AMS Pr.
Chinese Tales: Zhuangzi: Sayings & Parables & Chinese Ghost & Love Stories. Martin Buber. Tr. by Alex Page. LC 90-20517. 240p. (C). 1991. text ed. 39.95 (*0-391-03698-X*); pap. 15.00 (*0-391-03699-8*) Humanities.
Chinese Tarot. Stuart R. Kaplan. 24p. 1989. 14.00 (*0-88079-373-2*) US Games Syst.
Chinese Testament: The Autobiography of Tan Shi-Hua As Told to S. Tretiakov. Sergiei M. Tret'Tiakov. LC 75-39043. (China Studies). 383p. 1976. reprint ed. 27.50 (*0-88355-397-X*) Hyperion Conn.
Chinese Text: Studies in Comparative Literature. Ed. by Ying-hsiung Chou. xxii, 210p. 1986. text ed. 43.50 (*962-201-318-X*, Pub. by Chinese Univ HK) Coronet Bks.
Chinese Text for a Changing China, Revised Edition. rev. ed. Irene Liu & Li Xiaoqi. (C & T Asian Language Ser.). 250p. 1994. pap. text ed. 18.95 (*0-88727-199-5*) Cheng & Tsui.
Chinese Texts & Philosophical Contexts: Essays Dedicated to Angus C. Graham. Henry Rosemont, Jr. LC 90-41104. 352p. (C). 1991. 54.95 (*0-8126-9121-0*); pap. 24.95 (*0-8126-9122-9*) Open Court.
***Chinese, the Magic Ark.** 161p. Date not set. audio, text ed. 34.50 (*0-614-01439-5*, SCH210) Audio-Forum.
Chinese Theater: From Its Origins to the Present Day. Ed. by Colin Mackerras. LC 83-6687. (Illus.). 228p. (C). 1989. reprint ed. pap. 14.95 (*0-8248-1220-4*) UH Pr.
Chinese Theater in the Days of Kublai Khan. 2nd ed. James I. Crump. (Michigan Monographs in Chinese Studies: No. 62). 224p. (C). 1991. reprint ed. pap. text ed. 15.00 (*0-89264-093-6*) Ctr Chinese Studies.
Chinese Theater in the Days of Kublai Khan. James I. Crump. LC 79-20046. (Illus.). 439p. reprint ed. pap. 125.20 (*0-7837-1905-1*, 2042109) Bks Demand.
Chinese Theater, 1100-1450: A Source Book. Wilt L. Idema & Stephen H. West. 538p. (Orig.). 1982. pap. 67.50 (*3-515-03663-6*) Coronet Bks.
Chinese Theatre in Modern Times: From 1840 to the Present Day. Colin Mackerras. LC 75-13827. (Illus.). 260p. 1975. 30.00x (*0-87023-196-0*) U of Mass Pr.
Chinese Themes in American Verse. W. R. North. 1973. 59.95 (*0-87968-857-2*) Gordon Pr.
Chinese Theology in Construction. Wing-hung Lam. LC 81-15483. 308p. 1983. pap. 12.95 (*0-87808-180-1*) William Carey Lib.
Chinese Therapeutical Methods of Acupuncture & Moxibustion. 1991. lib. bdg. 75.00 (*0-87700-967-8*) Revisionist Pr.
Chinese Therapeutical Methods of Acupuncture & Moxibustion. Research Inst. of Acupuncture & Moxibustion, China Staff. 18p. 1994. reprint ed. spiral bd. 2.75 (*0-7873-1023-9*) Mokelumne.
Chinese Thought: An Exposition of the Main Characteristic Features of the Chinese World Conception. Paul Carus. LC 07-14567. (Illus.). 209p. reprint ed. pap. 59.60 (*0-317-11337-2*, 2050917) Bks Demand.
Chinese Thought: An Introduction. Ed. by Donald H. Bishop. 484p. 1985. 34.00 (*0-8364-1130-7*) S Asia.
***Chinese Thought: An Introduction.** Donald H. Bishop. (C). 1995. reprint ed. 22.50x (*81-208-1139-9*, Pub. by Motilal Banarsidass II) S Asia.
Chinese Thought & Institutions. John K. Fairbank. 455p. reprint ed. pap. 129.70 (*0-8357-8844-X*, 2056777) Bks Demand.
Chinese Thought from Confucius to Mao Tse-Tung. Herrlee G. Creel. LC 53-10054. 1971. reprint ed. pap. text ed. 13.95 (*0-226-12030-9*, P394) U Ch Pr.
Chinese Thought, Society & Science: The Intellectual & Social Background of Science & Technology in Pre-Modern China. Derk Bodde. LC 91-4437. 456p. 1991. text ed. 38.00 (*0-8248-1334-0*) UH Pr.
Chinese Tomb Figures: A Study in the Beliefs & Folklore of Ancient China. Carl Hentze & W. Perceval Yetts. LC 70-38072. (China Classic & Contemporary Works in Reprint Ser.). reprint ed. 145.00 (*0-404-56934-X*) AMS Pr.
Chinese Tomb Figurines. Ann Paludan. (Images of Asia Ser.). (Illus.). 96p. 1994. 16.95 (*0-19-585817-4*) OUP.
Chinese Tomb Pottery Figures: Catalogue of Exhibition, 26th-28th September, 1953. University of Hong Kong, Institute of Oriental Studies Staff. LC 55-25696. (Institute of Oriental Studies, Catalogue Ser.: No. 1). 42p. reprint ed. pap. 25.00 (*0-317-28811-3*, 2020771) Bks Demand.
Chinese Tonic Herbs. (Alternative Medicine Ser.). 1992. lib. bdg. 88.95 (*0-8490-5396-X*) Gordon Pr.
Chinese Tonis Herbs. Ron Teeguarden. LC 84-80650. (Illus.). 196p. (Orig.). 1985. pap. 17.00 (*0-87040-551-9*) Japan Pubns USA.
Chinese Trademarks. David B. Kay & Lee D. Green. 112p. (C). 1988. 120.00 (*962-318-001-2*) St Mut.
Chinese Traditional Historiography. rev. ed. Charles S. Gardner. LC 38-13532. (Historical Monographs: No. 11). 130p. 1938. 10.00 (*0-674-12550-9*) HUP.
Chinese Unmasked: Grammatical Principles & Applications; Simplified Character Edition, 2 vols., Set. Jing-heng Ma. 400p. (Orig.). (CHI & ENG.). 1994. Two-volume set. pap. text ed. 39.95 (*0-88727-198-7*) Cheng & Tsui.
Chinese Unmasked: Grammatical Principles & Applications; Traditional Character Edition, 2 vols., Set. Jing-heng Ma. 400p. (Orig.). (CHI & ENG.). 1994. Two-volume set. pap. text ed. 39.95 (*0-88727-190-1*) Cheng & Tsui.
Chinese Urban Reforms: What Model Now? Ed. by Yin-Wang Kwok et al. LC 89-24315. (Studies on Contemporary China). 270p. 1990. 57.95 (*0-87332-589-3*) M E Sharpe.
***Chinese Vegetable & Vegetarian Cooking.** Kenneth Lo. 176p. (Orig.). 1995. pap. 10.95 (*0-571-10652-8*) Faber & Faber.
Chinese Vegetarian Cookery. Jack Santa Maria. LC 86-26428. (Illus.). 159p. (Orig.). 1987. pap. 9.95 (*0-916360-36-9*) CRCS Pubns CA.
Chinese Vegetarian Cuisine. Wang Wenqiao & Gang Wenbin. (Illus.). 142p. (Orig.). 1990. pap. 16.95 (*0-8351-2446-0*) China Bks.
Chinese Vegetarian Delights: Sugar & Dairy-Free Cookbook. Lily Chuang. LC 87-60146. 112p. 1987. pap. text ed. 7.50 (*0-937064-13-0*) SevenStar Comm.
Chinese Vernacular Story. Patrick Hanan. LC 80-17840. (East Asian Monographs: No. 94). 286p. (C). 1981. 32.00 (*0-674-12565-7*) HUP.
***Chinese Views of Childhood.** Anne B. Kinney. LC 95-882. 1995. write for info. (*0-8248-1681-1*) UH Pr.
Chinese Village: Taitou, Shantung Province. Martin C. Yang. LC 45-4581. (C). 1965. pap. text ed. 16.50 (*0-231-08561-3*) Col U Pr.
Chinese Village Checkbook. R. Yee. 1983. pap. 5.95 (*0-912738-07-3*) Taylor & Ng.
Chinese Village Cookbook. Rhoda Yee. LC 75-18964. (Illus.). 1976. pap. 5.95 (*0-394-73152-2*, Random) Taylor & Ng.
Chinese Village in Early Communist Transition. Ch'ing-k'un Yang. LC 84-6618. xii, 284p. (C). 1984. reprint ed. text ed. 65.00 (*0-313-24456-1*, YACV, Greenwood Pr) Greenwood.
Chinese Village Politics in the Malaysian State. Judith Strauch. LC 80-20519. (East Asian Monographs: No. 95). (Illus.). 208p. (C). 1981. 29.50 (*0-674-12570-3*) HUP.
Chinese Village, Socialist State. Edward Friedman et al. (Illus.). 384p. (C). 1991. text ed. 45.00 (*0-300-04655-3*) Yale U Pr.
Chinese Village, Socialist State. Edward Friedman et al. (Illus.). 384p. (C). 1993. reprint ed. pap. text ed. 18.00 (*0-300-05428-9*) Yale U Pr.
***Chinese Virago: A Literary Theme.** Yenna Wu. LC 95-13353. (Harvard-Yenching Institute Monograph Ser.: No. 40). 280p. (C). 1995. text ed. 39.00 (*0-674-12572-X*) HUP.
Chinese Vocabulary Cards. rev. ed. Ed. by John S. Montanaro. (CHI & ENG.). 1987. 13.95 (*0-88710-126-7*) Yale Far Eastern Pubns.
Chinese Warlord: The Career of Feng Yu-hsiang. James E. Sheridan. LC 65-18978. (Illus.). xiv, 384p. 1966. 47.50 (*0-8047-0145-8*); pap. 16.95 (*0-8047-0146-6*) Stanford U Pr.
Chinese Watercolor Workbook: Grapes, Sunflowers, Waterlilies. Leslie T. Yu. (Illus.). 52p. (Orig.). 1993. pap. 29.00 (*0-9637389-0-9*) L Yu Prods.
Chinese Way in Religion. Ed. by Laurence G. Thompson. 241p. (C). 1973. pap. 19.95 (*0-8221-0109-2*) Intl Thomson.
Chinese Way to a Long & Healthy Life. Comp. by People's Medical Publishing House Staff. (Illus.). 320p. 1991. 4.99 (*0-517-64337-5*) Random Hse Value.
Chinese Ways in Warfare. Ed. by Frank A. Kierman, Jr. & John K. Fairbank. LC 73-80565. (Harvard East Asian Ser.: No. 74). (Illus.). 413p. reprint ed. pap. 118.60 (*0-7837-1711-3*, 2057240) Bks Demand.
***Chinese Weapons.** 2nd ed. E. T. Werner. (Illus.). 100p. 1989. reprint ed. pap. 12.95 (*9971-4-9116-8*) Heian Intl.
Chinese Welfare System, Nineteen Forty-Nine to Nineteen Seventy-Nine. John Dixon. LC 81-2822. 462p. 1981. text ed. 95.00 (*0-275-90605-1*, C0605, Praeger Pubs) Greenwood.
Chinese-Western Comparative Literature: Theory & Strategy. Ed. by John J. Deeney. 198p. (Orig.). 1980. pap. 29.50 (*962-201-228-0*, Pub. by Chinese Univ HK) Coronet Bks.
Chinese Whispers. Robert Sproat. 239p. 1989. pap. 8.95 (*0-571-15290-2*) Faber & Faber.
Chinese Wilson. Roy W. Briggs. 160p. 1993. 39.95 (*0-11-250017-X*, HM0017X, Pub. by HMSO UK) UNIPUB.
Chinese Winter's Tale. Yu Luojin. Tr. by Rachel May & Zhu Zhiyu. xix, 210p. 1990. reprint ed. pap. 9.50 (*962-201-383-X*, Pub. by Renditions Papbk HK) SPD-Small Pr Dist.
Chinese Woman in Iowa: Poems by Chang Shiang-hua. Chang Shiang-hua. Tr. by Valerie C. Doran. 125p. 1992. 12.95 (*0-88727-176-6*) Cheng & Tsui.
Chinese Women: Past & Present. Esther S. Lee Yao. (Woman in History Ser.: Vol. 82). (Illus.). 271p. (Orig.). 1983. lib. bdg. 30.00 (*0-86663-099-6*); pap. text ed. 15.00 (*0-86663-098-8*) Ide Hse.
Chinese Women: Yesterday & Today. Florence Ayscough. LC 74-32095. (China in the 20th Century Ser.). (Illus.). xiv, 324p. 1975. reprint ed. lib. bdg. 42.50 (*0-306-70700-4*) Da Capo.
Chinese Women & Christianity, 1860-1927. Kwok Pui-Lan. (American Academy of Religion Academy Ser.). 229p. (C). 1992. 29.95 (*1-55540-669-6*, 010175); pap. 19.95 (*1-55540-670-X*) Scholars Pr GA.
Chinese Women in a Century of Revolution, 1850-1950. Ono Kazuko. Ed. by Joshua A. Fogel. LC 88-8630. 288p. 1989. 37.50 (*0-8047-1496-7*); pap. 12.95 (*0-8047-1497-5*) Stanford U Pr.
Chinese Women in the Great Leap Forward. LC 75-36226. reprint ed. 32.50 (*0-404-14476-4*) AMS Pr.
Chinese Women of America: A Pictorial History. Judy Yung. LC 85-40974. (Illus.). 128p. (C). 1986. pap. 16.95 (*0-295-96358-1*) U of Wash Pr.
Chinese Women Through Chinese Eyes. Ed. by Li Yu-Ning. LC 91-11313. 282p. 1992. 46.95 (*0-87332-596-6*); pap. text ed. 20.95 (*0-87332-597-4*) M E Sharpe.
***Chinese Word Book.** Jiang An. LC 89-82132. (Rainbow Book Ser.). (Illus.). 106p. (Orig.). (CHI.). 1995. 15.95 (*1-57306-007-0*) Bess Pr.
Chinese Word Book. Jiang An. LC 89-82132. (Rainbow Book Ser.). (Illus.). 106p. (Orig.). (CHI & ENG.). 1990. pap. 11.95 (*0-935848-75-4*) Bess Pr.
Chinese Worker. Charles Hoffmann. LC 74-3053. 252p. 1974. 29.50 (*0-87395-238-3*) State U NY Pr.
Chinese Working-Class Lives: Getting By in Taiwan. Hill Gates. LC 87-47597. (Anthropology of Contemporary Issues Ser.). (Illus.). 264p. (C). 1987. pap. 16.95 (*0-8014-9461-3*) Cornell U Pr.
Chinese World. Richard Yang & Edward J. Lazzerini. LC 77-81184. (World of Asia Ser.). (Illus.). 1978. pap. text ed. write for info. (*0-88273-504-7*) Forum Pr IL.
Chinese World Order: Traditional China's Foreign Relations. Ed. by John K. Fairbank. LC 68-14255. (Harvard East Asian Ser.: No. 32). 426p. reprint ed. pap. 123.20 (*0-7837-1694-X*, 2057223) Bks Demand.
Chinese Written Character As a Medium for Poetry. Ernest Fenollosa. 64p. 1936. pap. 5.95 (*0-87286-014-0*) City Lights.
Chinese Written Characters: Their Wit & Wisdom. Rose Quong. (Illus.). 80p. 1994. 14.95 (*0-939218-01-1*) Chapman Billies.
Chinese Yearbook of International Law & Affairs, Vol.II. Hungdah Chiu. LC 82-645664. 432p. 1982. 24.00 (*0-942182-94-4*) Occasional Papers.
Chinese Yearbook of International Law & Affairs, 1981, Vol.I. Ed. by Hungdah Chiu. (Chinese Yearbook of International Law & Affairs Ser.). 392p. 1982. reprint ed. 24.00 (*0-942182-93-6*) Occasional Papers.
Chinese Yearbook of International Law & Affairs, 1983, Vol. 3. Hungdah Chiu. LC 82-645664. 350p. 1984. 24.00 (*0-942182-95-2*) Occasional Papers.
Chinese Yearbook of International Law & Affairs, 1984, Vol. 4. Hungdah Chiu. LC 82-645664. 400p. 1985. 24.00 (*0-942182-96-0*) Occasional Papers.
Chinese Yearbook of International Law & Affairs, 1985, Vol. 5. 390p. 1992. 24.00 (*0-942182-97-9*) Occasional Papers.
Chinese Yearbook of International Law & Affairs, 1986-1987, Vol. 6. 517p. 1992. 24.00 (*0-942182-98-7*) Occasional Papers.
Chinese Yearbook of International Law & Affairs, 1987-1988, Vol. 7. 548p. 1992. 24.00 (*0-942182-99-5*) Occasional Papers.
Chinese Yearbook of International Law & Affairs, 1988-1989, Vol. 8. 586p. 1992. 24.00 (*0-925153-90-7*) Occasional Papers.
Chinese Yearbook of International Law & Affairs, 1989-1990, Vol. 9. 664p. 1992. 24.00 (*0-925153-91-5*) Occasional Papers.
Chinese Zither Tutor: The Mei-an ch'in-p'u. Ed. by Fredric Lieberman. LC 82-4895. (Illus.). 156p. 1982. 40.00 (*0-295-95941-X*) U of Wash Pr.
Chinese Zoo: Fables & Proverbs. Illus. by Demi. LC 86-33562. 32p. (J). (ps-3). 1987. 14.95 (*0-15-217510-5*, HB Juv Bks) HarBrace.
Chineseness of China: Selected Essays. Wang Gungwu. (Illus.). 320p. 1992. 39.95 (*0-19-585332-6*) OUP.
Chinesisch-Deutsches Stilwoerterbuch fuer Konversation. Liu Mau-Tsai. 816p. (CHI & GER.). 1980. 185.00 (*0-8288-1007-9*, F34990) Fr & Eur.
***Chinesisch-Deutsches Woerterbuch.** 3rd ed. Werner Rudenberg. 821p. (CHI & GER.). 1963. 395.00 (*0-7859-8264-7*, 3110000202) Fr & Eur.
Chinesisch-Deutsches Woerterbuch. 3rd ed. Werner Ruedenberg. 821p. (CHI & GER.). (C). 1963. 173.50 (*3-11-000020-2*) De Gruyter.
Chinesische Anthologie: Ubersetzungen aus Dem Wen Hsuan, 2 Vols, Set. Ed. by Ilse M. Fang. Tr. by Erwin Von Zach. LC 58-6581. (Harvard-Yenching Institute Studies: No. 18). 1154p. 1958. pap. 30.00 (*0-674-12650-5*) HUP.

An Asterisk (*) at the beginning of an entry indicates that the title is appearing in BIP for the first time. 1227

Ch'ing Administration: Three Studies. John K. Fairbank & Teng Ssu-Yu. LC 60-7991. (Harvard-Yenching Institute Studies: No. 19). 228p. 1960. pap. 5.00 (0-674-12700-5) HUP.

Ch'ing Dynasty Enamelled Porcelain. (Collections of the National Palace Museum, Taipei). 285p. 1992. boxed 95.00 (957-562-125-5) Heian Intl.

Ch'ing Empire & the Russian State in the 17th Century. V. Miasnikov. 342p. (C). 1985. 80.00 (0-685-31474-X) St Mut.

Ch'ing Game: History & Simulation. Robert B. Oxnam. (Foreign Area Materials Center Ser.). 80p. 1972. pap. 2.00 (0-89192-138-9) Interbk Inc.

Ch'ing Ginseng Management: Ch'ing Monopolies in Microcosm. Van J. Symons. LC 80-71096. (Occasional Papers: No. 13). v, 121p. (Orig.). 1981. pap. text ed. 10.00 (0-939252-09-0) ASU Ctr Asian.

Ch'ing Imperial Household Department: A Study of Its Organization & Principal Functions, 1662-1976. Preston M. Torbert. (East Asian Monographs: No. 71). 350p. 1977. 26.00 (0-674-12761-7) HUP.

Ching Poems. William J. Lazo. (Minority Poet Ser.). 38p. (ENG & SPA.). 1990. pap. 5.00 (1-880046-02-4) Baculite Pub.

Ching-Te-Chen: Views of a Porcelain City. rev. ed. Robert Tichane. Tr. by S. W. Bushell & Delores Young. LC 83-62593. (Oriental Glaze Ser.). (Illus.). 468p. 1983. 32.00 (0-914267-02-7) NYS Inst Glaze.

Chingaira Makoni's Head: Myth, History & the Colonial Experience. Terence Ranger. (Hans Wolff Memorial Lecture Ser.). 27p. 1988. 5.00 (0-941934-52-7) Indiana Africa.

Chingis Khan. Demi. LC 90-28807. (Illus.). 64p. (J). (gr. 3-5). 1991. 19.95 (0-8050-1708-9, Bks Young Read) H Holt & Co.

Chinh Nghia Luu Vong Con Mot Chut Nay. Pham K. Vinh. 176p. (Orig.). (VIE.). 1991. pap. text ed. 12.00 (1-882273-23-0) P K Vinh Res.

Chinked with Oakum. Eve Hobson. LC 86-20619. (Illus.). 292p. 1986. 15.95 (0-939421-00-3) Admont Corp.

***Chinnamasta: The Aweful Buddhist & Hindu Tantri Goddess.** Elisabeth A. Benard. (C). 1994. 16.00x (81-208-1065-1, Pub. by Motilal Banarsidass II) S Asia.

Chinnery. Robert Hutcheon. (Illus.). 126p. 1994. 45.00 (962-7283-03-7) Weatherhill.

Chino. Allen Say. (Illus.). 32p. (J). (gr. 2-8). 1990. 14.95 (0-395-52023-1) HM.

Chinois Sans Peine (One) Chinese for French Speakers (1) Assimil Staff. (CHI & FRE.). 1990. 28.95 (0-8288-4379-1, M12639); audio, pap. 125.00 (0-8288-9036-6, M12634) Fr & Eur.

Chinois Sans Peine (Two) Chinese for French Speakers (2) Assimil Staff. (CHI & FRE.). 1990. 28.95 (0-8288-4381-3, M12650); audio 125.00 (0-8288-9037-4, M12651) Fr & Eur.

Chinoiserie. Dawn Jacobson. (Illus.). 240p. (C). 1993. 49.95 (0-7148-2883-1, Pub. by Phaidon Press UK) Chronicle Bks.

Chinoiserie for the Decorative Artist. Rena Friedman. (Illus.). (Orig.). 1983. pap. 5.50 (0-941284-18-2) J Shaw Studio.

Chinook. Jessie Marsh. (Indian Culture Ser.). 32p. (J). (ps-9). 1976. 4.95 (0-89992-041-1) Coun India Ed.

Chinook. Clifford E. Trafzer. (Indians of North America Ser.). (Illus.). 112p. (YA). (gr. 5 up). 1990. 17.95 (1-55546-698-2) Chelsea Hse.

Chinook! Michael O. Tunnell. LC 92-12711. (Illus.). 32p. (J). (gr. k up). 1993. 14.00 (0-688-10869-5, Tambourine Bks); lib. bdg. 13.93 (0-688-10870-9, Tambourine Bks) Morrow.

Chinook: A History & Dictionary. 2nd ed. Edward H. Thomas. LC 79-116971. 1970. 14.95 (0-8323-0217-1) Binford Mort.

***Chinook Christmas.** Rudy Wiebe. (Illus.). 32p. (J). 1995. 12.95 (0-88995-086-5, Pub. by Red Deer CN) BookWorld Dist.

Chinook Indians: Traders of the Lower Columbia River. Robert H. Ruby & John A. Brown. LC 79-34110. (Civilization of the American Indian Ser.: Vol. 138). (Illus.). 400p. 1988. pap. 19.95 (0-8061-2107-6) U of Okla Pr.

Chinook Jargon & How to Use It. George C. Shaw. (Shorey Indian Ser.). 79p. reprint ed. pap. 6.95 (0-8466-0065-X, S65) Shorey.

***Chinook Texts.** Franz Boas. (Bureau of American Ethnology Bulletins Ser.). 178p. 1995. lib. bdg. 79.00 (0-7812-4020-4) Rprt Serv.

***Chinook the Mustang.** Dayton O. Hyde. Tr. by Suzanne Royal. (Friends of the Forest Adenture Bks.). (Illus.). 24p. (J). (ps-4). Date not set. 16.95 (1-886738-06-8) Pequot Pubng.

CHINOPERL, No. 13. Ed. by Harold Shadick et al. (Chinoperl Papers). (Orig.). 1985. pap. 10.00 (0-318-04644-X) Chinoperl.

Chinoperl Papers,1982, No. 11. Ed Gunn et al. Ed. by Harold Shadick. (Chinoperl Papers). 177p. (Orig.). 1983. pap. 6.00 (0-318-23302-9) Chinoperl.

Chinoperl Papers,1983, No. 12. Lindy L. Marks et al. Ed. by Harold Shadick et al. (Chinoperl Papers). 171p. (Orig.). 1984. pap. 10.00 (0-318-23301-0) Chinoperl.

Chintaman & I. D. Deshmukh. 121p. 1980. 14.95 (0-318-37204-5) Asia Bk Corp.

Chinto, The Chaparral Cock. Emilie Toepperwein & Fritz Toepperwein. (J). (gr. 4-7). 2.95 (0-910722-04-8) Highland Pr.

***Chintz & Cotton: India's Textile Gift to the World.** Joyce Burnard. (Illus.). 92p. 1994. 24.95 (0-86417-597-3) Seven Hills Bk.

Chinua Achebe. C. L. Innes. (Cambridge Studies in African & Caribbean Literature). (Illus.). 210p. (C). 1990. 59.95 (0-521-35623-7) Cambridge U Pr.

Chinua Achebe. C. L. Innes. (Cambridge Studies in African & Caribbean Literature). (Illus.). 224p. (C). 1992. pap. 16.95 (0-521-42897-1) Cambridge U Pr.

Chinua Achebe: A Celebration. Ed. by A. Rutherford & K. H. Peterson. (Studies in African Literature). 165p. 1991. pap. 17.50 (0-435-08060-1, 08060) Heinemann.

Chinua Achebe: A Novelist & Portraitist of His Society. Christophe T. Kambaji. 1993. 13.95 (0-533-10615-X) Vantage.

Chinua Achebe: Critical Perspectives Past & Present. Ed. by Henry L. Gates, Jr. & K. A. Appiah. (Literary Ser.). 1994. 24.95 (1-56743-053-8); pap. 14.95 (1-56743-059-7) Amistad Pr.

***Chinua Achebe Revisited.** Echeruo. Date not set. 22.95 (0-8057-4591-2, Twayne) Macmillan.

Chinyanja Basic Course. 351p. 1992. 29.50 (0-88432-604-7, AFCY91); audio 185.00 (0-88432-374-9, AFCY10) Audio-Forum.

Chinye: A West African Folk Tale. Illus. by Evie Safarewicz. 32p. (J). (gr. k up). 1994. 14.99 (0-670-85115-9) Viking Child Bks.

Chioggia & the Villages of the Venetian Lagoon: Studies in History. Richard J. Goy. (Illus.). 350p. 1985. 89.95 (0-521-30275-7) Cambridge U Pr.

Chion of Heraclea. Ed. by W. R. Connor. LC 78-18571. (Greek Texts & Commentaries Ser.). 1979. reprint ed. lib. bdg. 21.95 (0-405-11415-X) Ayer.

Chios: A Conference at the Homereion in Chios, 1984. Ed. by John Boardman & C. E. Vaphopoulou-Richardson. 300p. 1987. 98.00 (0-19-814864-X) OUP.

Chiot. Mario Vargas Llosa. 126p. (FRE.). 1991. pap. 13.95 (0-7859-4382-X, 2070384357) Fr & Eur.

Chip & Dale. (Disney Learn to Draw Ser.). (Illus.). 28p. (J). 1991. pap. 5.95 (1-56010-091-5, DS04) W Foster Pub.

Chip & Dip Lovers Cook Book: More Than 150 Delectable Dip Recipes for Chips, Crackers. Susan K. Bollin. LC 93-36756. 128p. 1993. pap. 5.95 (0-914846-93-0) Golden West Pub.

Chip & How It Changed the World. Ian Locke. LC 94-15227. (History & Invention Ser.). 1995. write for info. (0-8160-3144-4) Facts on File.

Chip Carving. Harris W. Moore. LC 75-19755. (Illus.). 48p. 1976. reprint ed. pap. 2.95 (0-486-23256-5) Dover.

Chip Carving: Techniques & Patterns. Wayne Barton. LC 84-8779. (Illus.). 128p. (Orig.). 1985. pap. 12.95 (0-8069-7924-0) Sterling.

Chip Carving & Relief Carving. Josef Mader. (Illus.). 88p. 1987. pap. 14.95 (0-02-000720-5) Macmillan.

Chip Carving Patterns. Wayne Barton. LC 89-26174. (Illus.). 128p. (Orig.). 1990. pap. 12.95 (0-8069-5782-4) Sterling.

Chip Carving Patterns & Designs. Ivan H. Crowell. LC 77-78511. (Illus.). 1978. reprint ed. pap. 3.95 (0-486-23532-7) Dover.

***Chip Carving Pennsylvania Dutch Designs.** Pam Gresham. (Illus.). 64p. (Orig.). 1995. pap. 12.95 (0-88740-711-0) Schiffer.

Chip Carving the Southwest. Pam Gresham. LC 94-66373. (Illus.). 64p. (Orig.). 1994. pap. 12.95 (0-88740-699-8) Schiffer.

Chip in the Curtain: Computer Technology in the Soviet Union. David A. Wellman. LC 89-25309. (Illus.). 202p. 1989. per., pap. 4.75 (0-16-001706-8, S/N 008-020-011) USGPO.

Chip, of the Flying U. B. M. Bower. 1975. lib. bdg. 16.95 (0-89966-012-6) Buccaneer Bks.

***Chip, of the Flying U.** B. M. Bower. (Illus.). 272p. 1995. pap. 8.95 (0-8032-6121-7, Bison Books) U of Nebr Pr.

Chip on Board Technology. J. Lau. 1994. text ed. 64.95 (0-442-01441-4) Van Nos Reinhold.

Chip Preparation & Quality Seminar, 1992: Ramada Renaissance Hotel, Saratoga Springs, NY, June 23-24. Technical Association of the Pulp & Paper Industry Staff. (TAPPI Notes Ser.). reprint ed. pap. 96.70 (0-7837-3206-6, 2043202) Bks Demand.

Chip Quality Monograph. Ed. by J. V. Hatton. (Pulp & Paper Technology Ser.: No. 5). (Illus.). 333p. reprint ed. pap. 95.00 (0-685-20491-X, 2029929) Bks Demand.

Chip Seals, Friction Courses, & Asphalt Pavement Rutting 1990. (Transportation Research Record Ser.: No. 1259). 177p. 1990. 28.00 (0-309-05016-2) Transport Res Bd.

***Chip-Wrecked in Las Vegas.** Barney Vinson. Ed. & Illus. by Daniel R. Mead. LC 94-77468. 392p. (Orig.). 1994. pap. 19.95 (0-934422-07-9, 170079) Mead Pub Corp.

Chiparus: Master of Art Deco. Alberto Shayo. LC 93-16115. 1993. 75.00 (1-55859-475-2) Abbeville Pr.

Chipmakers. rev. ed. Time-Life Books Editors. (Understanding Computers Ser.). (Illus.). 128p. 1990. write for info. (0-8094-7618-5); lib. bdg. write for info. (0-8094-7619-3) Time-Life.

Chipmans of America. A. L. Chipman. (Illus.). 232p. 1993. reprint ed. lib. bdg. 44.50 (0-8328-1338-9); reprint ed. pap. 34.50 (0-8328-1339-7) Higginson Bk Co.

Chipmunk! Jessie Haas. LC 92-30080. (Illus.). 24p. (J). (ps up). 1993. 14.00 (0-688-11874-7); lib. bdg. 13.93 (0-688-11875-5) Greenwillow.

Chipmunk at Hollow Tree Lane. Victoria Sherrow. LC 93-27267. (Smithsonian's Backyard Ser.). (Illus.). 32p. (J). (ps-2). 1994. audio 19.95 (1-56899-043-X); 29.95 (1-56899-042-1); 4.95 (1-56899-029-4); 12.95 (1-56899-044-8); audio write for info. (1-56899-041-3) Soundprints.

Chipmunk at Hollow Tree Lane. Victoria Sherrow. LC 93-27267. (Smithsonian's Backyard Ser.). (Illus.). 32p. (J). (ps-2). 1994. 15.95 (1-56899-028-6) Soundprints.

Chipmunk Portrait. B. A. Henisch & H. K. Henisch. LC 78-88029. (Illus.). 198p. 1970. 15.00 (0-87601-003-6) Carnation.

Chipmunk Song. Joanne Ryder. LC 86-19786. (Illus.). 32p. (J). (ps-3). 1987. 14.99 (0-525-67191-9, Lodestar Bks); pap. 4.95 (0-525-67312-1, Lodestar Bks) Dutton Child Bks.

***Chipmunks ABC.** (J). Date not set. pap. 1.59 (0-307-02024-X, Golden Pr) Western Pub.

Chipmunks & the Siberian Chipmunk in Captivity. K. Elizabeth Gillett. (C). 1989. 35.00 (0-946873-97-6, Pub. by Basset Pubns UK) St Mut.

***Chipotle Chile Cookbook: Fire with Flavor.** Jacqueline H. McMahan. Ed. by Ruth Hightower. (Illus.). 172p. (Orig.). 1994. pap. 14.95 (1-881656-03-9) Olive Pr.

Chipped Chocolate. Lewis Sckolnick. 60p. (Orig.). 1981. pap. 14.95 (0-934393-01-X) Rector Pr.

Chipped Stone Raw Materials & the Study of Interaction on Black Mesa, Arizona. Margerie Green. LC 85-73325. (Center for Archaeological Investigations Research Paper Ser.: No. 11). xviii, 212p. 1985. pap. 10.00 (0-88104-051-7) Center Archaeo.

Chipped Stone Tools in Formative Oaxaca, Mexico: Their Procurement, Production & Use. William J. Parry. (Memoirs Ser.: No. 20). (Illus.). xvi, 178p. (Orig.). 1987. pap. 18.00 (0-915703-10-6) U Mich Mus Anthro.

Chippendale: Country Life Collectors Guides Ser. Edward T. Joy. 1972. 7.95 (0-600-43588-1) Transatl Arts.

Chippendale Period in English Furniture. Kate W. Clouston. (Illus.). 1976. reprint ed. 25.00 (0-7158-1127-4) Charles River Bks.

Chippewa. Jacqueline D. Green. LC 93-18371. (First Bks.). (Illus.). 64p. (J). (gr. 4-6). 1993. lib. bdg. 13.93 (0-531-20122-8); pap. 5.95 (0-531-15700-8) Watts.

Chippewa. Jacqueline D. Greene. (First Bks.). (Illus.). 64p. (J). (gr. 5-8). 1994. pap. 5.95 (0-531-15703-2) Watts.

Chippewa. Alice Osinski. LC 86-32687. (New True Bks.). (Illus.). 48p. (J). (gr. k-4). 1987. lib. bdg. 12.90 (0-516-01230-4); pap. 4.95 (0-516-41230-2) Childrens.

***Chippewa - Great Lakes.** Frank W. Porter, 3rd. (Indians of North America Ser.). (Illus.). 144p. (YA). (gr. 5 up). 1995. 18.95 (0-7910-2650-7) Chelsea Hse.

Chippewa & Their Neighbors: A Study in Ethnohistory. rev. ed. Harold Hickerson. (Illus.). 151p. (C). 1988. reprint ed. pap. text ed. 9.50 (0-88133-330-1) Waveland Pr.

Chippewa & Their Neighbors: A Study in Ethnohistory. Harold Hickerson. Ed. by George Spindler & Louise Spindler. (Studies in Anthropological Method). 144p. 1982. reprint ed. pap. text ed. 8.95 (0-8290-0305-3) Irvington.

***Chippewa Child Life & Its Cultural Background.** M. Inez Hilger. (Bureau of American Ethnology Bulletins Ser.). 204p. 1995. lib. bdg. 89.00 (0-7812-4146-4) Rprt Serv.

Chippewa Child Life & Its Cultural Background. Inez Hilger. LC 76-43740. (BAE. Bulletin Ser.: 146). reprint ed. 34.50 (0-404-15581-2) AMS Pr.

Chippewa Child Life & Its Cultural Background. Inez Hilger. LC 91-44657. 204p. 1992. reprint ed. pap. 10.95 (0-87351-271-5, Borealis Book) Minn Hist.

Chippewa Child Life & Its Cultural Background. Inez Hilger, Sr. 1988. reprint ed. lib. bdg. 49.00 (0-7812-0524-7) Rprt Serv.

Chippewa Child Life & Its Cultural Background. Inez Hilger. reprint ed. 49.00 (0-403-03555-4) Scholarly.

***Chippewa County Chronicle.** Michael J. Goc. (Illus.). 168p. Date not set. 40.00 (0-938627-28-7) New Past Pr.

***Chippewa Customs.** Frances Densmore. (Bureau of American Ethnology Bulletins Ser.). 204p. 1995. lib. bdg. write for info. (0-7812-4086-7) Rprt Serv.

Chippewa Customs. Frances Densmore. LC 79-15400. (Illus.). xxiv, 204p. 1979. reprint ed. pap. 9.95 (0-87351-142-5, Borealis Book) Minn Hist.

Chippewa Customs. Frances Densmore. 1988. reprint ed. lib. bdg. 75.00 (0-7812-0221-3) Rprt Serv.

Chippewa Customs. Frances Densmore. reprint ed. 49.00 (0-403-03556-2) Scholarly.

Chippewa Lake Park Chronicles. Sharon L. Kraynek. (Illus.). 208p. 1993. pap. 20.00 (0-9619905-1-1) Kraynek & Assocs.

Chippewa Lake Park Eighteen Hundred to Nineteen Seventy-Eight: Diary of an Amusement Park. Sharon L. Kraynek. (Illus.). 156p. 1987. 24.95 (0-9619905-0-3) Kraynek & Assocs.

***Chippewa Music.** Frances Densmore. (Bureau of American Ethnology Bulletins Ser.). 216p. 1995. lib. bdg. 89.00 (0-7812-4045-X); lib. bdg. 99.00 (0-7812-4053-0) Rprt Serv.

Chippewa Music. Francis Densmore. reprint ed. 49.00 (0-403-03557-0) Scholarly.

Chippewa Music, 2 vols, Set. Frances Densmore. LC 77-164513. (Illus.). 1972. reprint ed. lib. bdg. 55.00 (0-306-70459-5) Da Capo.

Chippewa Valley Office Supply. (C). 1993. text ed. 13.95 (0-538-83646-6) S-W Pub.

Chippewas of Lake Superior. Edmund J. Danziger, Jr. LC 78-58130. (Civilization of the American Indian Ser.: No. 148). (Illus.). 288p. (C). 1990. pap. 14.95 (0-8061-2246-3) U of Okla Pr.

Chipping Away at the Writer's Block. 1987. 6.95 (0-88047-134-4, D8708) DOK Pubs.

Chipping Campden. Catherine Gordon. (Towns & Villages of England Ser.). (Illus.). 1993. pap. write for info. (0-7509-0492-5) A Sutton Pub.

Chips. William H. Scott. 67p. (Orig.). 1987. pap. 5.75 (971-10-0331-7, Pub. by New Day Pub PH) Cellar.

Chips Around the World. Florence Manford. 1992. 10.95 (0-533-10057-7) Vantage.

Chips Chats. Ed. by Edward F. Gallenstein. (Illus.). 120p. 8.00 (0-318-15942-2) Natl Wood Carver.

Chips from a German Workshop: Volume I: Essays on the Science of Religion. Max Muller. (Reprints & Translations Ser.). 1985. pap. 16.95 (0-89130-890-3, 00-07-10) Scholars Pr GA.

Chips from My Chisel: An Autobiography. Grace H. Turnbull. LC 53-12776. 333p. reprint ed. pap. 95.00 (0-317-10540-X, 2006131) Bks Demand.

Chips from the Mathematical Log. Ed. by Josephine P. Andree. (J). (gr. 11-12). 1966. pap. 2.00 (0-686-00750-6) Mu Alpha Theta.

***Chips of Flint: A Collection of Poems & Thoughts.** Richard B. Thornton. (Illus.). 78p. (Orig.). 1994. pap. 12.50 (0-9637476-1-4) Flickwick.

Chips off the Old Benchley. Robert Benchley. (Illus.). 1976. reprint ed. lib. bdg. 21.95 (0-88411-301-9, Aeonian Pr) Amereon Ltd.

Chips off the Old Block. Ruth E. Turpin. 104p. 1990. 15.00 (0-8187-0119-6) Harlo Press.

Chips Quips. Clyde Geronimi. LC 83-72694. (Illus.). 55p. (J). (gr. 4 up). 1983. pap. 3.95 (0-939126-09-5) Back Bay.

Chiquita's Cocoon: A "Cinderella Complex" for the Latina Woman. Bettina Flores. Ed. by Marian Allison. LC 90-61448. (Illus.). 190p. (Orig.). 1990. pap. text ed. 13.50 (0-9625777-5-8) Pepper Vine Pr.

Chiquita's Cocoon: A Self-Help Guide for the Latina Woman. Bettina R. Flores. LC 93-25981. 1994. 13.50 (0-679-75044-4, Villard Bks); Spanish. pap. 13.50 (0-679-75073-8, Villard Bks) Random.

Chiquita's Cocoon: Un "Complejo de Cenicienta" Para la Mujer Latina. Bettina R. Flores. Tr. by Teresita J. Tibbetts. (Illus.). 190p. (Orig.). (SPA.). 1992. pap. text ed. 13.50 (0-9625777-6-6) Pepper Vine Pr.

***Chiquita's Diary Bk. I: The Escape.** Bettina R. Flora. Ed. by Marian Allison & Ruth Letner. LC 94-69171. (Illus.). (YA). 1995. pap. 13.50 (0-9625777-7-4) Soccer Bks.

Chirac's France, Nineteen Eighty-Six to Eighty-Eight: Contemporary Issues in French Society. John Tuppen. LC 89-70270. 236p. 1991. text ed. 55.00 (0-312-04489-5) St Martin.

Chiral Auxiliaries: Application in Organic Synthesis. Johann Mulzer & Eberhard Berger. 500p. 1993. 100.00 (3-528-06463-3, Pub. by Vieweg & Sohn GW) Ballen Bkslr.

***Chiral Auxiliaries & Ligands in Asymmetric Synthesis.** Jacqueline Seyden-Penne. LC 95-1600. (ENG & FRE.). 1995. text ed. 79.95 (0-471-11607-6) Wiley.

Chiral Dynamics. B. Lee. 130p. (C). 1972. pap. text ed. 121.00 (0-677-01385-X) Gordon & Breach.

Chiral Liquid Chromatography. Ed. by W. J. Lough. (Illus.). 256p. 1989. 112.00 (0-412-01741-5, A2081, Chap & Hall NY) Chapman & Hall.

Chiral Nuclear Dynamics. M. A. Nowak et al. 400p. 1995. text ed. 74.00 (981-02-1000-0) World Scientific Pub.

Chiral Separations. Ed. by D. Stevenson & I. D. Wilson. (Illus.). 220p. 1989. 59.50 (0-306-43252-8, Plenum Pr) Plenum.

Chiral Separations by Liquid Chromatography. Ed. by Satinder Ahuja. LC 91-4970. (ACS Symposium Ser.: No. 471). (Illus.). 239p. 1991. 59.95 (0-8412-2116-2) Am Chemical.

Chiral Solitons. Ed. by K. F. Liu. 578p. 1987. pap. 47.00 (9971-5-0323-9) World Scientific Pub.

Chirality - From Weak Bosons to the Alpha-Helix. Ed. by R. Janoschek. (Illus.). xi, 246p. 1991. 124.00 (0-387-53920-4) Spr-Verlag.

***Chirality & the Biological Activity of Drugs.** Roger J. Crossley. Ed. by Charles W. Rees. 224p. 1995. 125.00 (0-8493-9140-7, 9140) CRC Pr.

Chirality in Drug Design & Synthesis. Ed. by C. Brown. (Smith Kline & French Symposium Ser.). (Illus.). 243p. 1991. text ed. 88.00 (0-12-136670-7) Acad Pr.

Chirality in Industry: The Commercial Manufacture & Applications of Optically Active Compounds. Ed. by A. N. Collins et al. LC 92-16000. 300p. 1993. text ed. 150.00 (0-471-93595-6) Wiley.

Chiricahua & Mescalero Apache Texts. Harry Hoijer & Morris E. Opler. LC 76-43746. (Univ. of Chicago Pubns. in Anthropology, Linguistics Ser.). reprint ed. 55.00 (0-404-15783-1) AMS Pr.

Chiricahua National Monument. Janice E. Bowers. Ed. by T. J. Priehs & Carolyn Dodson. LC 88-62022. (Illus.). 64p. (Orig.). 1988. pap. 6.95 (0-911408-79-7) SW Pks Mnmts.

Chiricahua National Monument. Laurence E. Parent. Ed. by Sandra Scott & T. J. Priehs. LC 93-86935. (Illus.). 16p. (Orig.). (YA). 1994. pap. 2.95 (1-877856-41-X) SW Pks Mnmts.

Chiricahuas Sky Island. Weldon F. Heald. Ed. by Marguerite Bantlin. (Illus.). 148p. 1993. reprint ed. pap. 13.95 (0-9635103-1-2) M Bantlin Pub.

Chirologia, 2 vols. in 1. John Bulwer. LC 75-147955. (Language, Man & Society Ser.). reprint ed. 62.50 (0-404-08205-X) AMS Pr.

Chirologia: or the Natural Language of the Hand. Chironomia; or the Art of Manual Rhetoric. John Bulwer. Ed. by James W. Cleary. LC 76-132492. (Landmarks in Rhetoric & Public Address Ser.). 380p. 1974. 19.50 (0-8093-0497-X) S Ill U Pr.

Chiron: New Planet in the Horoscope. Richard Nolle. LC 83-70810. 160p. 1983. 12.00 (0-86690-236-8, N2281-014) Am Fed Astrologers.

Chiron: Rainbow Bridge Between the Inner & Outer Planets. exp. rev. ed. Barbara H. Clow. LC 87-45244. (Modern Astrology Library). (Illus.). 336p. (Orig.). 1993. pap. 12.00 (0-87542-094-X) Llewellyn Pubns.

Chiron & the Healing Journey: An Astrological & Psychological Perspective. Melanie Reinhart. 464p. 1990. pap. 12.00 (0-14-019209-3, Penguin Bks) Viking Penguin.

Chiron Dictionary of Greek & Roman Mythology: Gods & Goddesses, Heroes, Places, & Events of Antiquity. Tr. by Elizabeth Burr. (Illus.). 320p. (Orig.). 1994. pap. 14.95 (0-933029-82-9) Chiron Pubns.

An Asterisk (*) at the beginning of an entry indicates that the title is appearing in BIP for the first time.

C

An Asterisk (*) at the beginning of an entry indicates that the title is appearing in BIP for the first time.

1229

Chloride Channels & Their Modulation by Neurotransmitters & Drugs. Ed. by Giovanni Biggio & Erminio Costa. (Advances in Biochemical Psychopharmacology Ser.: Vol. 45). 400p. 1988. text ed. 121.50 (*0-88167-449-4*) Raven.

Chloride Corrosion of Steel in Concrete - STP 629. Ed. by D. E. Tonini & S. W. Dean, Jr. 196p. 1977. pap. 21.25 (*0-8031-0301-8*, 04-629000-27) ASTM.

Chloride Electrometallurgy: Proceedings of a Symposium. Ed. by Peter D. Parker. LC 82-63095. (Conference Proceedings Ser.). (Illus.). 243p. reprint ed. pap. 69.30 (*0-685-23389-8*, 2032593) Bks Demand.

Chloride Mines & Murals. Ed. by Stanley W. Paher. (Illus.). 1978. pap. 3.95 (*0-913814-15-6*) Nevada Pubns.

Chloride Removal Implementation Guide. Jack Bennett & Thomas J. Schue. 45p. (Orig.). (C). 1993. pap. text ed. 10.00 (*0-309-05606-3*, SHRP-S-347) SHRP.

Chloride Transport Coupling in Biological Membranes & Epithelia. George A. Gerencser. 1984. 189.75 (*0-444-80522-2*, I-182-84) Elsevier.

Chlorinated Dioxins & Dibenzofurans in Perspective. Ed. by C. Rappe et al. (Illus.). 589p. 1986. 86.95 (*0-87371-056-8*, TD196, CRC Reprint) Franklin.

Chlorinated Dioxins & Furans: Analytical Methods. Clement. 1995. write for info. (*0-87371-880-1*) Lewis Pubs.

Chlorinated Dioxins & Furans: Exposed Populations 1994. Patterson. 1995. write for info. (*0-87371-879-8*) Lewis Pubs.

Chlorinated Dioxins & Related Compounds 1984: Proceedings of the Fourth International Conference held at Ottawa, Canada, October 16-18, 1984. Ed. by M. J. Boddington et al. (Illus.). 420p. 1985. pap. 51.00 (*0-08-032608-0*, Pub. by PPL UK) Elsevier.

Chlorination By-Products: Production & Control. 216p. 1986. pap. 36.50 (*0-685-50833-1*, 90512) Am Water Wks Assn.

Chlorine: An Annotated Bibliography. Ralph G. Smith. LC 72-75586. 168p. 1971. reprint ed. pap. text ed. 12.00 (*0-686-32455-2*) Chlorine Inst.

Chlorine: An Annotated Bibliography Supplement. Ralph G. Smith. 1983. pap. 12.00 (*0-940230-03-8*) Chlorine Inst.

Chlorine: Its Manufacture, Properties & Uses. Ed. by J. S. Sconce. LC 62-20781. 912p. 1972. reprint ed. 90.50 (*0-88275-075-5*) Krieger.

C

Chlorine & the Chesapeake Bay: A Review of Research Literature. Linda L. Breisch et al. 6.00 (*0-943676-17-7*) MD Sea Grant Col.

Chlorine Bicentennial Symposium: Papers. Chlorine Bicentennial Symposium Staff. Ed. by Thomas C. Jeffery et al. LC 74-78467. (Illus.). 412p. reprint ed. pap. 117.50 (*0-8357-8072-4*, 2052292) Bks Demand.

Chlorine in Coal: Proc. of an Internat. Conf. Coal Science & Technology, Vol. 17. Ed. by J. Stringer & D. D. Banerjee. 520p. 1991. 200.00 (*0-444-87499-2*) Elsevier.

Chloris Andina: Essai d'une Flore de la Region alpine des Cordilleres de l'Amerique du Sud, 2 vols. in 1. H. A. Weddell. (Illus.). 1972. 150.00 (*3-7682-0729-3*) Lubrecht & Cramer.

Chloro-Organic Water Quality Changes Resulting from Modification of Water Treatment Practices. 196p. 1986. pap. 22.00 (*0-89867-391-7*, 90517) Am Water Wks Assn.

Chlorodioxins: Origin & Fate. Ed. by Ectyl H. Blair. LC 73-84139. (Advances in Chemistry Ser.: No. 120). 1973. 27.95 (*0-8412-0181-1*) Am Chemical.

Chlorofluorocarbons (CFCs) & the Building Services Industry. M. Johansson. (C). 1988. 150.00 (*0-86022-208-X*, Pub. by Build Servs Info Assn UK) St Mut.

Chloromethane. Ed. by GDCh-Advisory Committee on Existing Chemicals of Environmental Relevance. LC 93-2643. (BUA Report Ser.: Vol. 7). (ENG & GER.). 1993. 32.00 (*1-56081-734-8*); 25.00 (*0-685-63372-1*) VCH Pubs.

Chlorophyllfluoreszenz in der Oekologie. Ed. by D. Ernst. (Advances in Limnology Ser.: No. 29). (Illus.). 146p. (GER.). 1987. pap. text ed. 92.60 (*3-510-47027-3*, Pub. by E Schweizerbartsche GW) Lubrecht & Cramer.

Chlorophylls. Hugo Scheer. (Illus.). 152p. 1991. 345.00 (*0-8493-6842-1*, QP671) CRC Pr.

Chloroplast Biogenesis. Ed. by N. R. Baker & J. Barber. (Topics in Photosynthesis Ser.: Vol. 5). 380p. 1984. 166.25 (*0-444-80548-6*) Elsevier.

Chloroplast Metabolism: The Structure & Function of Chloroplasts in Green Leaf Cells. Ed. by Barry Halliwell. (Illus.). 1984. pap. 18.95 (*0-19-854585-1*) OUP.

Chloroplasts. J. Kenneth Hoober. LC 84-9934. (Cellular Organelles Ser.). 290p. 1984. 65.00 (*0-306-41643-3*, Plenum Pr); pap. 32.50 (*0-306-41686-7*, Plenum Pr) Plenum.

Chloroplasts. Ed. by J. Reinert. (Results & Problems in Cell Differentiation Ser.: Vol. 10). (Illus.). 280p. 1980. 59.00 (*0-387-10082-2*) Spr-Verlag.

Chlorotoluenes: Methylchlorobenzenes. (BUA Report Ser.: Vol. 38). 84p. 1993. pap. 48.00 (*1-56081-237-0*) VCH Pubs.

Choates in America, 1643-1896: John Choate & His Descendants Chebacco, Ipswich, Mass. E. O. Jameson. (Illus.). 474p. 1989. reprint ed. lib. bdg. 68.00 (*0-8328-0398-7*); reprint ed. pap. 58.00 (*0-8328-0399-5*) Higginson Bk Co.

Choc en Retour. Jean-Baptiste Cineas. (B. E. Ser.: No. 48). (FRE.). 1948. 24.00 (*0-8115-2999-1*) Periodicals Srv.

Chochmas Hamussar. A. H. Leibowitz. (Annual Fryer Memorial Lecture Ser.). 1.00 (*0-914131-11-7*, B150) Torah Umesorah.

Chocks Away. Gillian Simpson. 193p. (C). 1989. text ed. 59.00 (*1-872795-11-0*, Pub. by Pentland Pr UK) St Mut.

***Choco-Louie.** Jeffrey Kindley. LC 94-49334. (Bank Street Ready-to-Read Ser.). (Illus.). (J). 1996. text ed. write for info. (*0-553-09744-X*); pap. write for info. (*0-553-37576-8*) Bantam.

***Chococlate Lovers' Diet: Eat Chocolate, & Say Goodbye to Fat.** Robert F. Joseph. 150p. (Orig.). 1995. pap. 12.95 (*0-9634147-1-2*) Noble Porter Pr.

***Chocoholic: For the Addict.** Ed. by G & R Publishing Staff. (Uni-Book Ser.). 160p. (Orig.). 1994. pap. text ed. 3.00 (*1-56383-027-2*, 3500) G & R Pub.

***Chocolate.** Sonia Allison. 1994. 9.95 (*0-572-01823-1*, Pub. by W Foulsham UK) Trans-Atl Phila.

Chocolate. Lora Brody. Ed. by Laurie Wertz. LC 93-17990. (Williams-Sonoma Kitchen Library). (Illus.). 108p. 1993. 17.95 (*0-7835-0241-9*); lib. bdg. write for info. (*0-7835-0242-7*) Time-Life.

Chocolate. Jacqueline Dineen. (Foods We Eat Ser.). (Illus.). 32p. (J). (gr. 1-4). 1991. lib. bdg. 14.96 (*0-87614-657-4*, Carolrhoda) Lerner Group.

***Chocolate!** Carin Kuoni et al. (Illus.). 72p. 1995. write for info. (*1-884692-03-6*) Swiss Inst.

***Chocolate.** Murfitt. 1995. pap. text ed. 8.95 (*0-316-54806-5*) Little.

Chocolate. Aleksandr I. Tarasov-Rodionov. Tr. by Charles Malamuth. LC 72-90315. (Soviet Literature in English Translation Ser.). 311p. 1979. reprint ed. 23.60 (*0-88355-025-3*) Hyperion Conn.

Chocolate: Miniature Book of Food. Jane Donovan. 1991. 4.99 (*0-517-06540-1*) Random Hse Value.

Chocolate: The Consuming Passion. Sandra Boynton. LC 81-43781. (Illus.). 112p. 1982. pap. 6.95 (*0-89480-199-6*, 485) Workman Pub.

Chocolate Ain't Enough...No More: Every Woman's Choice. Arnie Wallace & Adryan Russ. LC 90-85214. 104p. (Orig.). 1991. pap. 9.95 (*0-9625341-2-9*) Challenger CA.

Chocolate & Chortles. Edwina G. Lashings. 64p. (Orig.). 1975. pap. 2.95 (*0-938758-02-0*) MTM Pub Co.

Chocolate & Cocoa to Copper see Encyclopedia of Chemical Technology

Chocolate & the Art of Low-Fat Desserts. Alice Medrich. (Illus.). 192p. 1994. 35.00 (*0-446-51666-X*) Warner Bks.

***Chocolate Bar Bust.** Miranda Barry & Corinne Jacker. (Ghostwriter Ser.). (J). (gr. 2-6). 1995. mass mkt. 3.50 (*0-553-48287-4*) Bantam.

Chocolate Book. Sara Perry. (Illus.). 72p. 1992. 9.95 (*0-8118-0246-9*) Chronicle Bks.

***Chocolate Box: Candies & Desserts Cakes & Cookies.** Joanna Farrow. (Illus.). 1995. 25.00 (*0-8478-5768-9*) Rizzoli Intl.

***Chocolate Box: Candies & Desserts; Cakes & Cookies, 2 Vol. Set, Set.** Joanna Farrow. LC 94-43379. (Illus.). 144p. 1995. 25.00 (*0-8478-1869-1*) Rizzoli Intl.

Chocolate by Hershey: A Story about Milton S. Hershey. Betty Burford. LC 93-43638. (Creative Minds Ser.). (Illus.). 64p. (J). (gr. 3-6). 1994. lib. bdg. 15.95 (*0-87614-830-5*, Carolrhoda) Lerner Group.

***Chocolate by Hershey: A Story about Milton S. Hershey.** Betty Burford. (Creative Minds Ser.). (Illus.). 64p. (J). (gr. 3-6). 1994. pap. 5.95 (*0-87614-641-8*, Carolrhoda) Lerner Group.

Chocolate Cake. Carolyn Graham. 1992. pap. text ed. write for info. (*0-13-131616-8*) P-H.

Chocolate Cake & Black Sand & Two Other Plays. Samuel M. Cauldwell. LC 79-50021. (One-Act Plays in Reprint Ser.). 1980. reprint ed. 18.50 (*0-8486-2045-3*) Roth Pub Inc.

Chocolate Cherry Tortes & Other Lowfat Desserts. Maureen Egan & Penny Ballantyne. (Illus.). 160p. 1990. pap. 6.95 (*0-911954-97-X*) Bristol Pub Ent CA.

Chocolate Chicanery. Gene Hatfield. 160p. 1993. 12.95 (*0-8059-3351-4*) Dorrance.

Chocolate Chip Cookies. Karen Wagner. (Illus.). 32p. (J). (ps-2). 1990. 14.95 (*0-8050-1268-0*, Bks Young Read) H Holt & Co.

***Chocolate Chip Cookies for Your Enemies.** Bill Holm. Tr. by Franz A. Richter. (Illus.). 56p. (Orig.). 1993. pap. 4.95 (*0-9638549-0-9*) Josephson Pubns.

Chocolate, Chipmunks, & Canoes: An American Indian Words Coloring Book. Juan Alvarez. LC 90-60331. (Illus.). 32p. (J). (gr. 1-3). 1991. pap. 3.95 (*1-878610-03-1*) Red Crane Bks.

Chocolate Chips & Trumpet Tricks. Nancy S. Levene. Ed. by Sue Reck. LC 93-36195. 192p. (J). (gr. 3-6). 1994. pap. 5.99 (*0-7814-0103-8*, Chariot Bks) Cook.

Chocolate, Chocolate A Gift of the Gods. Reba A. Karp. 1994. 17.95 (*1-885142-00-5*) J & B Editions.

Chocolate, Chocolate, Chocolate...with Love. Jeannine B. Browning. 1994. pap. write for info. (*0-9627729-7-6*) J B Browning.

Chocolate Classics. Barbara Grunes & Phyllis Magida. 96p. 1993. 9.95 (*0-8092-3700-8*) Contemp Bks.

Chocolate Cobweb. Armstrong. (Black Dagger Crime Ser.). 16.50 (*0-86220-750-9*, C0851, Black Dagger) Chivers N Amer.

Chocolate Cobweb. Charlotte Armstrong. LC 91-70603. 190p. 1991. reprint ed. pap. text ed. 7.95 (*1-55882-096-5*, Lib Crime Classics) Intl Polygonics.

Chocolate, Cocoa & Confectionary Science & Technology. 3rd ed. Bernard W. Minifie. (Illus.). 544p. 1988. text ed. 99.95 (*0-442-26521-2*) Chapman & Hall.

Chocolate Companion. Cynthia Shade Rogers. LC 93-74032. (Traditional Country Life Recipe Ser.). (Illus.). 96p. (Orig.). 1994. pap. 9.95 (*1-883283-02-7*) Brick Tower.

***Chocolate Companion: A Connoisseur's Guide to the World's Finest Chocolates.** Chantal Coady. LC 95-11529. 1995. 20.00 (*0-684-80374-7*) S&S Trade.

Chocolate Cookbook. Elizabeth W. Cohen. 1992. 12.99 (*0-517-07315-3*) Random Hse Value.

***Chocolate Cooking.** Judith Ferguson. 64p. 1995. write for info. (*1-57215-014-9*) World Pubns.

Chocolate-Covered Ants. Stephen Manes. (J). (gr. 4-7). 1993. pap. 2.95 (*0-590-40961-1*) Scholastic Inc.

Chocolate Covered Cherries: Esther Price's Memories. Esther Price & Linda O. Lipsett. (Illus.). 112p. 1992. pap. 11.99 (*0-9629399-1-9*) Halstead Meadows.

Chocolate Cow. Lilian Obligado. LC 91-27464. (Illus.). 48p. (J). (ps-2). 1993. pap. 14.00 (*0-671-73852-6*, S&S Bks Young Read) S&S Childrens.

Chocolate Creams & Dollars. Mohammed Mrabet. Ed. by Paola Igliori. Tr. by Paul Bowles. (Illus.). 192p. 1993. 29.95 (*0-9625119-6-X*) Inanout Pr.

Chocolate Delights. Aaron Maree. (Illus.). 64p. 1993. 10.00 (*0-207-18036-9*, Pub. by Angus & Robertson AT) HarpC.

Chocolate Desserts. Anne Willan. LC 91-58570. (Look & Cook Ser.). (Illus.). 128p. 1992. 19.95 (*1-56458-031-8*) Dorling Kindersley.

***Chocolate Dinosaurs.** Rochester Elementary School Third-Graders. (Wee Write Bks.: No. 1). (Illus.). 16p. (J). (ps-3). 1994. 32.95 (*1-884987-00-1*) WeWrite.

***Chocolate Dinosaurs.** Rochester Elementary School Third-Graders. (Wee Write Bks.: No. 1). (Illus.). 16p. (J). (ps-3). 1994. pap. text ed. 7.95 (*1-884987-02-8*) WeWrite.

***Chocolate Dinosaurs, Big Bk.** Rochester, Illinois, Elementary School Third-Graders Staff. (Wee Write Bks.: No. 1). (Illus.). 16p. (J). (ps-3). 1994. 32.95 (*1-884987-08-7*) WeWrite.

Chocolate Dreams. Arnold Adoff. LC 88-27208. (Illus.). 64p. (J). (gr. 3 up). 1989. 13.95 (*0-688-06822-7*); lib. bdg. 13.88 (*0-688-06823-5*) Lothrop.

Chocolate Egg Cream. Yankee Diablerie, pseud. 125p. (Orig.). 1990. pap. 5.95 (*0-9626578-0-8*) Savage Pubns.

Chocolate Fads, Folklore, & Fantasies: 1,000 Chunks of Chocolate. Linda K. Fuller. LC 92-19414. 1993. pap. 14.95 (*1-56023-027-4*) Harrington Pk.

Chocolate Fads, Folklore, & Fantasies: 1,000 Plus Chunks of Chocolate Information. Linda K. Fuller. LC 92-19440. (Original Book Ser.). (Illus.). 286p. 1993. lib. bdg. 39.95 (*1-56024-337-6*) Haworth Pr.

Chocolate Fever. Robert K. Smith. 96p. (J). (gr. 2-6). 1978. pap. 3.50 (*0-440-41369-9*, YB) Dell.

Chocolate Fever. Robert K. Smith. (J). (gr. 4-7). 1994. pap. 1.99 (*0-440-21949-3*) Dell.

Chocolate Has No Natural Enemies. Chef Cosmo Appleduck. 1985. pap. 6.95 (*0-911505-20-2*) Lifecraft.

***Chocolate Heaven.** Steven Wheeler. LC 95-67263. (Illus.). 80p. 1995. 12.95 (*0-8478-1896-9*) Rizzoli Intl.

Chocolate Horse. Bonnie Bryant. (Saddle Club Ser.: No. 32). (J). (gr. 4-7). 1994. pap. 3.50 (*0-553-48146-0*) Bantam.

***Chocolate Island.** K. Dolby & C. Church. (Young Puzzle Adventure Ser.). (Illus.). 32p. (J). (ps-1). 1995. lib. bdg. 12.96 (*0-88110-726-3*, Usborne); pap. 4.95 (*0-7460-1458-9*, Usborne) EDC.

***Chocolate Lovers Cookbook.** 1995. 12.99 (*0-88705-761-6*) Joshua Morris.

Chocolate Lover's Cookies & Brownies. (Illus.). 96p. 1993. 9.98 (*0-88176-851-0*); spiral bd. 3.50 (*1-56173-398-9*, 2001200) Pubns Intl Ltd.

Chocolate Lover's Cookies & Brownies. Consumer Guide Editors. 1990. 10.99 (*0-517-02739-9*) Random Hse Value.

Chocolate Lover's Guide to Silicon Valley. Mary Fischer et al. (Illus.). 64p. (Orig.). 1984. pap. 3.95 (*0-932161-00-6*) San Jose Face.

Chocolate Lover's Handbook: How to Eat & Enjoy Chocolate Without Guilt & Without Gaining Weight. rev. ed. Andrew M. Reenan. Ed. by Teresa J. Clark. LC 93-71146. (Illus.). 260p. 1993. pap. text ed. 14.95 (*0-9636482-0-9*) Action Pubns.

Chocolate Moose for Dinner. Fred Gwynne. LC 80-14150. (Illus.). (J). (gr. 1-6). 1988. pap. 13.00 (*0-671-66685-1*, S&S Bks Young Read); pap. 5.95 (*0-671-66741-6*, S&S Bks Young Read) S&S Childrens.

Chocolate Moulds: A History & Encyclopedia. Judene Divone. LC 86-28571. (Illus.). 168p. (Orig.). 1987. pap. 21.95 (*0-939047-02-0*) Oakton Hills Pubns.

Chocolate Mouse. Harriet Herbst. LC 87-29496. 213p. 1988. 17.95 (*0-916515-33-8*) Mercury Hse Inc.

Chocolate Mousse & Other Fabulous Chocolate Creations. Betty M. Potter. 220p. (Orig.). 1986. spiral bd. 9.95 (*0-913703-11-7*) Branches.

***Chocolate or Lollipops?** Antonietta Salvatore. (J). 1995. 7.95 (*0-533-10750-4*) Vantage.

Chocolate Quick Fix. Chocolate News Editors. Ed. by Milton Zelman & Jeannine Winquist. (Illus.). 56p. 1985. pap. 2.95 (*0-942320-18-2*) Am Cooking.

Chocolate Rabbit. Maria Claret. LC 84-24610. 28p. (J). (ps-3). 1985. 7.95 (*0-8120-5624-8*); pap. 5.95 (*0-8120-4926-8*) Barron.

Chocolate Sex: A Naughty Little Book. A. Richard Barber et al. (Illus.). 64p. 1994. 10.95 (*0-446-51812-3*) Warner Bks.

***Chocolate Soldier.** Cyrus Colter. 278p. Date not set. pap. 14.95 (*0-8101-5038-7*) TriQuarterly.

***Chocolate Sundae Mystery.** Gertrude C. Warner. LC 94-36418. (Boxcar Children Ser.: No. 46). (Illus.). (J). (gr. 4-7). 1995. 11.95 (*0-8075-1146-3*); pap. 3.50 (*0-8075-1145-5*) A Whitman.

Chocolate Touch. Patrick S. Catling. (J). 1984. 3.50 (*0-553-15639-X*) Bantam.

Chocolate Touch. Patrick S. Catling. LC 78-31100. (Illus.). 96p. (J). (gr. 4-6). 1979. reprint ed. lib. bdg. 12.93 (*0-688-32187-9*) Morrow Jr Bks.

Chocolate Touch: A Study Guide. Norma Marsh. (Novel-Ties Ser.). (J). (gr. 2-4). 1989. student ed, teacher ed 15.95 (*0-88122-043-4*) Lrn Links.

Chocolate Tree: A Natural History of Cacao. Allen M. Young. LC 93-44196. 1994. 24.95 (*1-56098-357-4*) Smithsonian.

Chocolate Tree: An African Folktale. Deborah Sandlain-Buchanan. (Illus.). 16p. (Orig.). (J). (gr. k-3). 1993. write for info. (*0-9639057-2-4*); lib. bdg. write for info. (*0-9639057-3-2*); pap. 3.99 (*0-9639057-0-8*); 5.00 (*0-9639057-1-6*) Chocolate Tree.

Chocolate Truffles. Carrie Huber. Ed. by Sheilah Kaufman. 64p. (Orig.). 1985. pap. 3.49 (*0-685-09728-5*, CH102) Am Cooking.

***Chocolate War.** Campbell. 1995. 26.95 (*0-8057-8808-5*, Twayne); pap. 12.95 (*0-8057-8809-3*, Twayne) Macmillan.

Chocolate War. Robert Cormier. 192p. (J). (gr. 6 up). 1986. mass mkt. 4.50 (*0-440-94459-7*, LFL) Dell.

Chocolate War. Robert Cormier. LC 73-15109. 272p. (J). (gr. 7-9). 1974. 20.00 (*0-394-82805-4*) Pantheon.

Chocolate War. Robert Cormier. 1993. reprint ed. lib. bdg. 18.95 (*1-56849-170-0*) Buccaneer Bks.

Chocolate War: A Study Guide. Crystal Norris. (Novel-Ties Ser.). (gr. 7-10). 1987. student ed, teacher ed 15.95 (*0-88122-108-2*) Lrn Links.

Chocolate Wildcat. Dorothy Hawthorne. LC 87-72602. (Illus.). (J). (gr. 4-6). 1988. pap. 5.95 (*0-931722-65-9*) Corona Pub.

Chocolates. A. Welch. 1993. text ed. write for info. (*0-442-00492-3*) Van Nos Reinhold.

Chocolates for My Wife. Todd Matshikiza. 128p. 1990. pap. 9.95 (*0-908396-83-X*, Pub. by D Philip SA) Interlink Pub.

Chocolates for the Pillows, Nightmares for the Guests: The Failure of the Hotel Industry to Protect the Traveling Public from Violent Crime. Kenneth L. Prestia. LC 93-5928. 1993. pap. 12.95 (*0-910155-25-9*) Bartleby Pr.

Chocorua & Other Poems. Cedric H. Whitman. LC 82-13910. 120p. 1983. 10.95 (*0-87233-070-2*); pap. 6.95 (*0-87233-069-9*) Bauhan.

Choctaw. Emilie U. Lepthien. LC 87-14583. (New True Bks.). (Illus.). 48p. (J). (gr. k-4). 1987. lib. bdg. 12.90 (*0-516-01240-1*); pap. 4.95 (*0-516-41240-X*) Childrens.

Choctaw. Jesse O. McKee. (Indians of North America Ser.). (Illus.). 104p. (J). (gr. 5 up). 1989. 17.95 (*1-55546-699-0*) Chelsea Hse.

Choctaw. Jesse O. McKee. 1994. pap. 7.95 (*0-7910-0375-2*) Chelsea Hse.

Choctaw Academy: Official Correspondence, 1825-1841. Joe R. Goss. 189p. 1992. 32.00 (*1-56869-000-2*); pap. 24.00 (*1-56869-001-0*) Oldbuck Pr.

Choctaw Before Removal. Ed. by Carolyn K. Reeves. LC 84-13090. 1985. 30.00 (*0-87805-244-5*) U Pr of Miss.

Choctaw Claimants & Their Heirs. Joe R. Goss. 193p. 1992. 34.00 (*1-56869-002-9*); pap. 26.00 (*1-56869-003-7*) Oldbuck Pr.

Choctaw County War. Peter McCurtin. (Sundance Ser.). 208p. 1982. pap. 2.25 (*0-8439-1101-8*) Dorchester Pub Co.

***Choctaw Genesis, 1500-1700.** Patricia Galloway. LC 95-1659. (Indians of the Southeast Ser.). 1996. write for info. (*0-8032-1510-X*) U of Nebr Pr.

Choctaw Laws: Passed at the Special Sessions in January, 1894, & April, 1894, & the Regular Session, October, 1894. LC 75-3690. (Constitutions & Laws of the American Indian Tribes Ser. 2: Vol. 23). 1975. reprint ed. 11.00 (*0-8420-1881-6*) Scholarly Res Inc.

Choctaw Music. Frances Densmore. LC 72-1883. (Music Ser.). (Illus.). 110p. 1972. reprint ed. lib. bdg. 22.50 (*0-306-70511-7*) Da Capo.

Choctaw Music. Frances Densmore. LC 90-44635. (Illus.). 100p. 1990. reprint ed. lib. bdg. 29.00 (*1-878592-22-X*); reprint ed. pap. 15.00 (*1-878592-21-1*) Native Amer Bk Pubs.

Choctaw Music & Dance. James H. Howard & Victoria L. Levine. 1990. 22.95 (*0-8061-2225-0*) U of Okla Pr.

***Choctaw of Bayou Lacomb, St. Tammany Parish, Louisiana.** David I. Bushnell, Jr. (Bureau of American Ethnology Bulletins Ser.). 99p. 1995. lib. bdg. 69.00 (*0-7812-4048-4*) Rprt Serv.

Choctaw Trail. Will Camp. 1994. mass mkt. 3.50 (*0-06-100729-3*, Harp PBks) HarpC.

Choctaw Verb Agreement & Universal Grammar. William D. Davies. 1985. lib. bdg. 101.50 (*90-277-2065-7*) Kluwer Ac.

***Choctaws & Missionaries in Mississippi, 1818-1918.** Clara S. Kidwell. LC 94-30374. (Illus.). 288p. 1995. 32.95x (*0-8061-2691-4*) U of Okla Pr.

Choe Notes: A Handbook of Pharmacology. Jae Y. Choe. LC 90-1787. 440p. (Orig.). (C). 1990. pap. 29.95 (*0-940473-14-3*) Wm Caxton.

Ch'oe Pu's Diary: A Record of Drifting Across the Sea. Pu Ch'oe. Tr. by John Meskill. LC 64-19165. (Association for Asian Studies, Monographs & Papers: No. 17). 185p. reprint ed. pap. 52.80 (*0-7837-1461-0*, 2055362) Bks Demand.

Choephores et les Eumerides d'Eschyle. Paul Claudel. 1952. pap. 8.95 (*0-686-50142-X*) Fr & Eur.

Choes & Anthesteria: Athenian Iconography & Ritual. Richard Hamilton. (Illus.). 230p. (C). 1992. text ed. 39.50 (*0-472-10280-X*) U of Mich Pr.

Choice. Rose Drachler. LC 77-70787. 1977. pap. 5.00 (*0-686-19541-8*) Tree Bks.

***Choice.** Claire Luckham. 1995. 5.00 (*0-87129-482-6*, C89) Dramatic Pub.

Choice. Philip MacDonald. 256p. 1994. 16.95 (*0-7451-8633-5*, Black Dagger) Chivers N Amer.

Choice. Og Mandino. 1986. mass mkt. 5.50 (*0-553-24576-7*) Bantam.

Choice. Michael McLaverty. 240p. 1991. pap. 12.95 (*1-85371-110-1*, Pub. by Poolbeg Pr IE) Dufour.

Choice. Barry Reed. 1992. mass mkt. 5.99 (*0-312-92883-1*) St Martin.

Choice: A Fable of Free Trade & Protectionism. Russell Roberts. 1993. pap. 11.95 (*0-13-083008-9*) P-H.

An Asterisk (*) at the beginning of an entry indicates that the title is appearing in BIP for the first time.

An Asterisk (*) at the beginning of an entry indicates that the title is appearing in BIP for the first time.

1231

C

Choice to Win in America. Gerald A. Cory, Jr. LC 92-72012. (Illus.). 240p. (Orig.). Date not set. pap. 19.95 (0-9631280-3-5) Ctr Behav Ecol.

***Choice, Welfare, & Development: Essays in Honour of Amartya K. Sen.** Ed. by K. Basu et al. (Illus.). 360p. 1995. text ed. 55.00 (0-19-828789-5) OUP.

Choice Years: Health, Happiness & Beauty Through Menopause & Beyond. Judith Paige & Pamela Gordon. 1992. mass mkt. 5.99 (0-449-22190-3, Crest) Fawcett.

Choicemaker. Elizabeth B. Howes & Sheila Moon. LC 76-54534. 1977. reprint ed. pap. 6.75 (0-8356-0492-6, Quest) Theos Pub Hse.

Choicemaking. Sharon Wegscheider-Cruse. 206p. 1985. pap. text ed. 9.95 (0-932194-26-5, 22H104) Health Comm.

Choices. 16p. (Orig.). 1984. pap. 1.55 (0-89486-248-0, 1225B) Hazelden.

Choices. Annette Broadrick. (Men Made in America Ser.). 1994. mass mkt. 3.59 (0-373-45175-X, 1-45175-6) Silhouette.

Choices. Mary Farrar. 1994. 16.99 (0-88070-662-7, Multnomah Bks) Questar Pubs.

Choices. Marie Ferrarella. 1993. mass mkt. 4.99 (0-06-108002-0, Harp PBks) HarpC.

Choices. Pat King. LC 83-90350. 128p. 1983. pap. 5.95 (0-9611532-0-2) King Bks.

Choices. George E. Lyon. LC 89-38082. 64p. 1989. pap. 4.50 (0-8131-0900-0) U Pr of Ky.

Choices. Elaine Scott. LC 88-34537. (Illus.). 192p. (YA). (gr. 7 up). 1989. 12.95 (0-688-07230-5) Morrow Jr Bks.

***Choices.** Mary L. Settle. LC 94-30097. 1995. 24.95 (0-385-47699-X) Doubleday.

Choices. Noreen Teachout. (Illus.). 90p. (Orig.). 1988. pap. 10.00 (0-317-93648-4) Peace Curriculum.

***Choices.** Buck Young. Ed. by Richard Courtney & Maryglenn McCombs. 176p. (Orig.). 1995. pap. 14.95 (1-886371-00-8) Eggman Pub.

Choices. Young Playwrights of Louisville Staff. 71p. 1991. pap. 4.95 (0-87129-096-0, C81) Dramatic Pub.

Choices. large type ed. Susan Goodman. 416p. 1986. 23.95 (0-7089-8349-9, Charnwood) Ulverscroft.

Choices. rev. ed. Marion Morra & Eve Potts. 976p. (Orig.). 1994. pap. 15.00 (0-380-77620-0) Avon.

Choices. Shad Helmstetter. Ed. by Olga Vezeris. 304p. 1990. reprint ed. mass mkt. 5.99 (0-671-67419-6) PB.

Choices. Nancy Toder. 250p. 1984. reprint ed. pap. 8.95 (0-932870-61-9) Alyson Pubns.

Choices: A Core Collection for Young Reluctant Readers, Vol. 3. Sharon Salluzzo. Ed. by Peg Glisson. 272p. 1994. 45.00 (0-934272-30-1) J G Burke Pub.

Choices: A Guide to Sex Counseling with Physically Disabled Adults. Maureen E. Neistadt & Maureen Freda. LC 86-2888. 132p. 1987. text ed. 14.50 (0-89874-903-4); pap. 9.95 (0-89464-201-4) Krieger.

Choices: A Stewardship Study for Teens. Helen Johns & Robert Leadley. Ed. by Glen A. Pierce. 32p. (Orig.). (YA). 1989. teacher ed 5.95 (0-916035-34-4); student ed 4.95 (0-916035-35-2) Evangel Indiana.

Choices: A Student Survival Guide for the 1990s. Bryna J. Fireside. LC 89-83639. 111p. (Orig.). 1989. pap. 10.95 (0-685-29201-0) Garrett Pk.

Choices: A Teen Woman's Journal for Self-Awareness & Personal Planning. Mindy Bingham et al. Ed. by Barbara Green & Kathleen Peters. (Illus.). 240p. (YA). (gr. 8 up). 1993. pap. 18.95 (0-911655-22-0) Advocacy Pr.

Choices: An Introduction to Decision Theory. Michael D. Resnik. LC 86-11307. 234p. 1987. text ed. 34.95 (0-8166-1439-3); pap. text ed. 14.95x (0-8166-1440-7) U of Minn Pr.

Choices: Decision Making Processes for Speakers. 2nd ed. Carl Johnson et al. 496p. 1993. per. 15.95 (0-8403-8476-9) Kendall-Hunt.

Choices: Ending Abuse in Intimate Relationships. M. Ciaro & Denton Hendershot. (Illus.). (Orig.). 1991. pap. write for info. (0-9629030-0-0) Denton Consulting.

Choices: Ethics & the Christian. David Brown. (Faith & the Future Ser.). 176p. 1984. pap. 21.95 (0-631-13222-8) Blackwell Pubs.

Choices: Exercise Workbook. Margy Hendershot & Denny Hendershot. 55p. (Orig.). 1993. pap. text ed. 25.00 (0-9629030-2-7) Denton Consulting.

Choices: Facilitator's Manual. Margy Hendershot & Denny Hendershot. 100p. (Orig.). 1993. pap. 20.00 (0-9629030-1-9) Denton Consulting.

Choices: Finding God's Way in Dating, Sex, Singleness & Marriage. Stacy Rinehart & Paula Rinehart. LC 82-62071. 170p. 1983. pap. 5.00 (0-89109-494-6) NavPress.

Choices: In a Crisis Pregnancy. Noreen Byrne. 80p. (Orig.). 1992. pap. 9.99 (1-85594-041-8, Pub. by Attic IE) InBook.

Choices: Making Right Decisions in a Complex World. Lewis B. Smedes. 1991. pap. 9.00 (0-06-067411-3) Harper SF.

Choices: Making Sure Your Everyday Decisions Move You Closer to God. Ronnie W. Floyd. LC 94-10245. 192p. 1994. 16.99 (0-8054-6152-3, 4261-52) Broadman.

Choices: Public Education for the 21st Century. Don L. Fuhr. 292p. (Orig.). (C). 1990. lib. bdg. 51.00 (0-8191-7879-9); pap. text ed. 25.00 (0-8191-7880-2) U Pr of Amer.

Choices: Realistic Alternatives in Cancer Treatment. rev. ed. Marion Morra & Eve Potts. 976p. 1980. pap. 12.95 (0-380-75308-1) Avon.

***Choices: Sex in the Age of Standards.** Jeffrey S. Nevid. 1995. pap. 15.95 (0-205-16941-4) Allyn.

Choices: Tales of the Human (& Inhuman) Condition. Charles I. Shade. 130p. 1992. pap. write for info. (0-9632405-0-1) C I Shade.

Choices: The Realistic & Moving Story of a Mother's Decision about Abortion. Dorothy W. Peterson. 9.95 (0-88494-675-4) Bookcraft Inc.

***Choices: Writing Projects for Students of ESL.** Carole Turkenik. 272p. (C). 1994. pap. text ed. 13.00 (0-312-09972-X) St Martin.

***Choices after Medical School.** Leonard Laster. 300p. (C). 1995. pap. write for info. (0-393-71030-0) Norton.

***Choices & Challenges: Stewardship Strategies for Youth.** LC 94-72155. 72p. 1994. pap. 8.95 (0-88177-135-X, DR135) Discipleship Res.

Choices & Chances: Sociology for Everyday Life. Lorne Tepperman & Angela Djao. 250p. (C). 1990. pap. text ed. 17.50 (0-15-507347-8) HB Coll Pubs.

Choices & Conflict: Explorations in Health Care Ethics. Ed. by Emily Friedman. LC 92-816. 221p. 1992. pap. 42.00 (1-55648-082-2, 025105) AHPI.

Choices & Consequences: Contemporary Policy Issues in Education. Ed. by Ronald G. Ehrenberg. 172p. 1994. 29.00 (0-87546-333-9) ILR Pr.

Choices & Consequences: What to Do When a Teenager Uses Alcohol-Drugs, A Step-By-Step System That Really Works. Dick Schaefer. 156p. (Orig.). 1987. pap. 10.95 (0-935908-42-0, P096) Johnsn Inst.

Choices & Constraints: Economic Decisionmaking. 2nd ed. Yung-Ping Chen & Robert C. De Vos. LC 94-70026. 207p. (C). 1994. pap. text ed. 22.00 (0-89463-065-2) Am Inst FCPCU.

Choices & Decisions in Health Care. Andrew Grubb. LC 92-49195. 200p. 1993. text ed. 69.95 (0-471-93621-9) Wiley.

Choices & Other Poems. Vincent Byrne. 1981. pap. 6.95 (0-8159-5223-6) Devin.

Choices & Other Stories from the Caribbean. Alma F. Ada et al. LC 92-43134. (J). 1993. pap. 6.95 (0-377-00257-7) Friendship Pr.

Choices for a Healthy Heart. Joseph Piscatella. LC 86-40199. 592p. (Orig.). 1987. pap. 15.95 (0-89480-138-4, 1138) Workman Pub.

Choices for Churches. Lyle E. Schaller. LC 89-27337. 176p. 1990. pap. 10.95 (0-687-06694-8) Abingdon.

Choices for Graduates. Al Janssen. 1989. 8.99 (0-8010-5225-4) Baker Bk.

Choices for Our Future: A Generation Rising for Life on Earth. Ocean Robbins & Sol Solomon. LC 94-29060. (Illus.). 192p. (Orig.). 1994. pap. 9.95 (1-57067-002-1) Book Pub Co.

Choices for the Heartland: Alternative Directions in Biotechnology & Implications for Family Farming, Rural Communities, & the Environment. Chuck Hassebrook & Gabriel Hegyes. (Studies in Technology & Social Change: No. 9). 113p. (Orig.). (C). 1989. pap. 12.00 (0-945271-13-1) ISU-TSCP.

Choices for the Journey: Durable Power of Attorney & Healthcare Decision Making for Religious. Peter Campbell. 60p. 1989. 6.00 (0-87125-163-9, 151) Cath Health.

Choices in Caring: Contemporary Approaches to Child & Youth Care Work. 1990. pap. 16.95 (0-87868-376-3) Child Welfare.

***Choices in Child Care: The Distribution of Child Care among Mothers, Fathers & Non-Parental Care Providers.** Liset Van Dijk. (ICS Ser.). 259p. 1994. pap. 25.00 (90-5170-311-2, Pub. by Thesis Pubs NE) IBD Ltd.

***Choices in Child Care: What's Best for Your Child.** Suzanne Laird. (Illus.). 138p. (Orig.). 1992. pap. 12.95 (1-55059-043-X) Temeron Bks.

Choices in Deafness: A Parents' Guide. Ed. by Sue Schwartz. LC 86-51221. (Illus.). 212p. (Orig.). 1987. pap. 14.95 (0-933149-09-3) Woodbine House.

Choices in Health & Fitness for Life. 2nd ed. Sally Althoff et al. 362p. (C). 1992. pap. text ed. 32.00 (0-89787-618-0) Gorsuch Scarisbrick.

***Choices in Health & Fitness for Life: Laboratory Manual.** 2nd ed. Ed. by Sally Althoff et al. 120p. 1992. pap. text ed. 15.00 (0-89787-622-9) Gorsuch Scarisbrick.

Choices in Marriage & Family. 2nd ed. J. Gipson Wells. (Illus.). 475p. (C). 1991. pap. text ed. 30.75 (0-939693-14-3) Collegiate Pr.

Choices in Modern Jewish Thought. Eugene B. Borowitz. 352p. (C). 1983. pap. text ed. 14.95x (0-87441-343-5) Behrman.

***Choices in Modern Jewish Thought: A Partisan Guide.** 2nd ed. Eugene B. Borowitz. Ed. by David Behrman. LC 95-2583. (Illus.). 1995. pap. 14.95 (0-87441-581-0) Behrman.

Choices in Relationships: An Introduction to Marriage & Family. 3rd ed. David Knox & Caroline Schacht. Ed. by Marshall. 621p. (C). 1991. text ed. 52.00 (0-314-78709-7) West Pub.

Choices in Relationships: An Introduction to Marriage & the Family. 4th ed. David Knox & Caroline Schacht. Ed. by Marshall. LC 93-30592. 600p. (C). 1993. text ed. 53.25 (0-314-02605-3) West Pub.

***Choices in Risk Assessment: The Role of Science Policy in the Environmental Risk Management Process.** Regulatory Impact Analysis Project, Inc. Staff. 300p. (Orig.). 1994. pap. write for info. (0-9643747-1-4) Regulatory Impact.

Choices in Schools: What's Ahead & What to Do. 1986. 18.95 (0-87545-047-4, 411-13366) Natl Sch PR.

Choices in Sexuality. Susan L. McCammon et al. Ed. by Marshall. LC 92-38235. 675p. (C). 1993. text ed. 54.50 (0-314-01267-2) West Pub.

Choices in the Hereafter. Janet Buell. LC 88-7551. (Illus.). 176p. (Orig.). 1988. pap. 7.95 (0-929551-02-8); audio 8.95 (0-929551-00-1) Ability Workshop Pr.

Choices in Vichy France: The French under Nazi Occupation. John F. Sweets. 320p. (C). 1994. reprint ed. pap. 13.95 (0-19-509052-7) OUP.

Choices in Your Life. Marian McKenzie. (Literacy Volunteers of America Readers Ser.). 32p. (Orig.). 1988. pap. text ed. 3.00 (0-8428-9620-1) Cambridge Bk.

Choices of Daniel Trigo. Joseph Neppe. 199p. 1992. 13.95 (0-944070-87-6); pap. 10.95 (0-685-65662-4) Targum Pr.

Choices of Power: Utilities Face the Environmental Challenge. Marc J. Roberts & Jeremy S. Bluhm. LC 80-20729. 468p. reprint ed. pap. 133.40 (0-7837-4110-3, 2057933) Bks Demand.

Choices of School in Six Nations: Canada, Great Britain & Four Western European Countries. 1990. lib. bdg. 75.00 (0-8490-4021-3) Gordon Pr.

Choices of the Heart. Kathy C. Miller. (Bible Study Series for Daughters of the King). 96p. 1993. pap. 4.95 (0-89636-295-7, AC244) Accent CO.

***Choices to Be Made: The Dunlop Commission Hearings & the State of Workplace Relations in the 1990s.** Richard N. Block et al. 1995. write for info. (0-614-06296-9) W E Upjohn.

Choices, Vol. 2: A Core Collection for Young Reluctant Readers. Ed. by Julie Cummins & Blair Cummins. 544p. 1990. 45.00 (0-934272-22-0) J G Burke Pub.

Choices We Made: Twenty-Five Women & Men Speak Out about Abortion. Angela Bonavoglia. LC 92-5363. 1992. pap. 10.00 (0-679-74247-6) Random.

Choices We Made: 25 Women & Men Speak Out about Abortion. Ed. by Angela Bonavoglia. 1991. 19.95 (0-394-58463-5) Random.

***Choices with Clout.** Wilbur Cross. 224p. (Orig.). 1995. pap. text ed. 5.99 (0-425-14538-7) Berkley Pub.

***Choir.** Joanna Trollope. LC 95-11612. 1995. write for info. (0-8129-2328-6) Random.

Choir. large type ed. Joanna Trollope. LC 94-11455. 1994. 20.95 (0-7927-2089-X, Eagle Lrg Print) Chivers N Amer.

***Choir.** large type ed. Joanna Trollope. LC 94-11455. 1994. pap. 19.95 (0-7927-2088-1, Eagle Lrg Print) Chivers N Amer.

Choir Accompaniment. Dudley Buck. 177p. 1992. pap. 29.95 (1-881162-01-X) W Leupold Edits.

Choir & Music, No. 1459. (Illus.). 48p. 1988. 5.95 (1-878259-14-8) Neibauer Pr.

Choir Director's Handbook. Charles Montgomery. Ed. by Jane Montgomery. (Illus.). 44p. (Orig.). 1984. pap. 3.95 (0-916043-01-0) Light Hearted Pub Co.

Choir Invisible. James L. Allen. 1897. 7.00 (0-403-00000-9) Scholarly.

Choir Invisible. Marianne Hauser. 1958. 14.95 (0-8392-1014-0) Astor-Honor.

Choir Invisible. James L. Allen. LC 73-86169. reprint ed. 22.50 (0-404-00327-3) AMS Pr.

Choir Invisible. James L. Allen. (Principle Works of James Lane Allen). 1989. reprint ed. lib. bdg. 79.00 (0-7812-1732-6) Rprt Serv.

Choir Prayers. Jeanne Hunt. 1986. 5.95 (0-912405-22-8) Pastoral Pr.

Choirboys. Joseph Wambaugh. 1976. mass mkt. 6.50 (0-440-11188-9) Dell.

Choiring of the Trees. Harington. 1991. 22.95 (0-15-117550-0) HarBrace.

Choiring of the Trees. Harington. 1992. pap. 9.95 (0-15-617099-X, Harvest Bks) HarBrace.

Choirs & Choral Music. Arthur Mees. LC 69-13995. 250p. 1970. reprint ed. text ed. 45.00 (0-8371-1967-7, MECM, Greenwood Pr) Greenwood.

Choirs & Choral Music. Arthur Mees. LC 68-25296. (Studies in Music: No. 42). 1969. reprint ed. lib. bdg. 59.95 (0-8383-0308-0) M S G Haskell Hse.

Choix de Lettres a Malwida Von Meysenburg. Romain Rolland. 336p. (FRE.). 1948. pap. 9.95 (0-7859-5443-0) Fr & Eur.

Choix de Poemes. Jules Romains. 286p. (FRE.). 1948. pap. 10.95 (0-7859-1309-2, 2070255220) Fr & Eur.

Choix de Poesies. Paul Verlaine. 336p. (FRE.). 1969. pap. 10.95 (0-7859-1256-8, 2038701806) Fr & Eur.

***Choix des Elues.** Jean Giraudoux. 240p. 1939. 26.95 (0-7859-5263-2) Fr & Eur.

Choix d'inscriptions de Delos. Ed. by F. Durrbach. xii, 288p. 1977. 30.00 (0-89005-190-9) Ares.

Choix d'Inscriptions de Delos. Felix Durrbach. (Subsidia Epigraphica Ser.: Vol. VI). iii, 294p. (GER.). 1976. reprint ed. write for info. (3-487-05998-3, Pub. by Georg Olms GW) Lubrecht & Cramer.

***Choke: A Novel.** Stuart Woods. 1995. 23.00 (0-06-017667-9, PL) HarpC.

Choking Doberman & Other "New" Urban Legends. Jan H. Brunvand. LC 83-22031. (Illus.). 1986. reprint ed. pap. 9.95 (0-393-30321-7) Norton.

Cholas Latino Girls & Gangs. Ed. by Mary G. Harris. LC 87-45784. (Immigrant Communities & Ethnic Minorities in the U. S. & Canada Ser.: No. 19). 1988. 42.50 (0-404-19429-X) AMS Pr.

Cholecystokinin. Ed. by Joseph R. Reeve, Jr. LC 94-4554. (Annals Ser.: Vol. 713). 1994. write for info. (0-89766-857-X); pap. 130.00 (0-89766-858-8) NY Acad Sci.

***Cholecystokinin & Anxiety: From Neuron to Behavior.** Jacques Bradwejn. (Neuroscience Intelligence Unit Ser.). 1995. write for info. (7-315-70592-9) R G Landes.

***Cholecystokinin & Anxiety: From Neuron to Behavior.** Jacques Bradwejn & Eero Vasar. (Neuroscience Intelligence Unit Ser.). 173p. 1995. write for info. (1-57059-293-4) R G Landes.

Cholecystokinin Antagonists in Gastroenterology: Basic & Clinical Status. Ed. by G. Adler & C. Beglinger. (Illus.). xiii, 233p. 1991. 109.00 (0-387-53582-9) Spr-Verlag.

Cholera. Ed. by D Barua & W. B. Greenough, III. (Current Topics in Infectious Disease Ser.). (Illus.). 396p. 1992. 59.50 (0-306-44077-6, Plenum Med Bk) Plenum.

Cholera. R. Pollitzer. (Monograph Ser.: No. 43). (Illus.). 1019p. (FRE.). 1959. 26.80 (92-4-140043-9) World Health.

Cholera & Related Diarrheas: Molecular Aspects of a Global Health Problem. WHO, 43rd Nobel Symposium, Stockholm, August 1978. Ed. by O. Ouchterlony & J. Holmgren. (Illus.). 1980. 92.00 (3-8055-3060-9) S Karger.

Cholera Bulletin. Association of Physicians. LC 77-180564. (Medicine & Society in America Ser.). 198p. 1972. reprint ed. 21.95 (0-405-03942-5) Ayer.

Cholera, Eighteen Thirty-Two: Social Response to an Epidemic. R. J. Morris. LC 76-25452. (Illus.). 230p. 1976. 39.50 (0-8419-0288-7) Holmes & Meier.

Cholera Immunology: Proceedings of the WHO Scientific Group, Teheran, 1968. WHO Staff. (Technical Report Ser.: No. 414). 1969. pap. 1.20 (92-4-120414-1) World Health.

Cholera in Africa: Diffusion of the Disease 1970-1975, with Particular Emphasis of West Africa. Robert F. Stock. LC 77-361351. (African Environment: Special Report Ser.: No. 3). 135p. reprint ed. pap. 38.50 (0-8357-6971-2, 2039031) Bks Demand.

Cholera on the American Continents. Ed. by A. F. De Castro & W. F. Almeida. LC 93-61303. (Illus.). 177p. 1993. pap. 37.50 (0-944398-12-X) ILSI.

Cholera Problem. Oscar Felsenfeld. LC 67-26004. (Illus.). 180p. 1967. 8.50 (0-87527-008-5) Green.

Cholera Years: The United States in 1832, 1849, & 1866. Charles E. Rosenberg. LC 62-18121. (Illus.). x, 266p. (C). 1987. pap. text ed. 11.95 (0-226-72677-0) U Ch Pr.

Cholescintigraphy: Developments in Nuclear Medicine, No. 1. Peter H. Cox. 250p. 1981. lib. bdg. 80.00 (90-247-2524-0) Kluwer Ac.

***Cholestatic Liver Diseases: New Strategies for Prevention & Treatment of Hepatobiliary & Cholestatic Liver Diseases.** Ed. by G. P. Van Berge Henegouwen. LC 94-23373. 352p. (C). 1994. lib. bdg. 86.50 (0-7923-8867-4) Kluwer Ac.

Cholesteatoma & Mastoid Surgery. Ed. by M. Tos et al. LC 89-19867. (Illus.). 1248p. 1989. lib. bdg. 250.00 (90-6299-056-8, Pub. by Kugler NE) Kugler Pubns.

Cholesteatoma & Mastoid Surgery: Proceedings of the Fourth International Conference, Nigata, Japan, September 8-12, 1993. Ed. by Yuichi Nakano. LC 93-41769. (Illus.). 1994. lib. bdg. 216.00 (90-6299-102-5, Pub. by Kugler NE) Kugler Pubns.

Cholesterol. Consumer Guide Editors. 1989. pap. 3.95 (0-451-15932-2, Sig) NAL-Dutton.

Cholesterol. John R. Sabine. LC 76-28905. (Illus.). 505p. reprint ed. pap. 144.00 (0-7837-0828-9, 2041142) Bks Demand.

Cholesterol: Friend or Foe? David G. Williams. 76p. 1988. pap. write for info. (0-944649-03-3) Mtn Home Pub.

Cholesterol: Your Guide for a Healthy Heart. Consumer Guide Editors. 256p. 1989. 7.98 (0-88176-584-8) Pubns Intl Ltd.

Cholesterol: Your Guide for a Healthy Heart. Consumer Guide Editors Staff. 256p. (Orig.). 1989. pap. 6.95 (0-451-82206-4, Sig) NAL-Dutton.

Cholesterol: Your Guide for a Healty Heart. rev. ed. Consumer Guide Editors. 256p. 1995. pap. 7.99 (0-451-82283-8, Sig) NAL-Dutton.

Cholesterol: Your Guide to a Healthy Heart. rev. ed. Consumer Guide Editors. 256p. 1993. pap. 7.99 (0-451-82268-4, Sig) NAL-Dutton.

Cholesterol & Coronary Heart Disease: The Great Debate. P. Gold et al. (Illus.). 500p. (C). 1992. text ed. 75.00 (1-85070-414-7) Prthnon Pub.

***Cholesterol & Red Meat: Fat Doesn't Cook, It Melts! And They Make Soap Out of It!** rev. ed. Date not set. write for info. (0-614-04565-7) Giovanni Pub.

Cholesterol & Sodium Book: A Guide to Dietary Cholesterol & Sodium for Health, Prevention & Diet Information. Andrew Goliszek. LC 84-70247. 66p. 1984. pap. 3.95 (0-916833-01-1) Bio-Pub.

Cholesterol & Your Health - the Great American Rip-Off!, Pt. 1. Chris Mudd. (Illus.). 170p. 1990. pap. write for info. (0-9624515-1-7) Am Lite Co.

Cholesterol & Your Health - the Great American Ripoff, Pt. 1. Chris Mudd. 125p. 1990. pap. 13.00 (0-685-29288-6) Am Lite Co.

Cholesterol Autoxidation. L. L. Smith. LC 81-10616. 692p. 1981. 125.00 (0-306-40759-0, Plenum Pr) Plenum.

Cholesterol Connections. Joan Bissen et al. 56p. 1990. student ed write for info. (1-884153-02-X) Prk Nicollet.

Cholesterol Conspiracy. Russell Smith. 400p. (Orig.). 1991. pap. text ed. 27.75 (0-87527-476-5) Green.

Cholesterol Content of Food. rev. ed. Corinne T. Netzer. 1992. mass mkt. 4.50 (0-440-20739-8) Dell.

Cholesterol Control Gram Counter. W. I. Kaufman. (Orig.). 1992. pap. 2.95 (0-515-09248-7) Jove Pubns.

Cholesterol Counter. 3rd rev. ed. Annette B. Natow & Jo-Ann Hesun. Ed. by Sally Peters. 592p. 1993. mass mkt. 5.99 (0-671-75173-5) PB.

Cholesterol Cure Made Easy. Sylvan R. Lewis. LC 92-34868. 1993. 4.99 (0-517-08904-1) Random Hse Value.

Cholesterol Cure Made Easy: A Doctor's Diet Plan to Lower Your Cholesterol Naturally. Sylvan R. Lewis. 122p. 1994. pap. 5.95 (0-8119-0182-3) LIFETIME.

Cholesterol-Free Cakes & Cookies: All-Time Favorite Recipes Adapted for a Low-Cholesterol Diet. Mabel Cavaiani. LC 92-8664. 320p. 1992. pap. 14.95 (0-8050-1739-9, Owl) H Holt & Co.

Cholesterol Handbook. Consumer Guide Editors. 160p. 1989. pap. 6.99 (0-517-68854-9) Random Hse Value.

Cholesterol in Children: Healthy Eating Is a Family Affair. (Illus.). 52p. (Orig.). (C). 1994. pap. text ed. 19.95 (0-7881-0329-6) Diane Pub.

Cholesterol in Membrane Models. Finegold. 1992. 79.95 (0-8493-4207-4, QP752) CRC Pr.

Cholesterol in School Age Children: A Program to Develop Awareness. Johanna C. Burani. (Illus.). 88p. 1990. spiral bd. 39.95 (1-879339-12-9) Infinity Impress.

An Asterisk (*) at the beginning of an entry indicates that the title is appearing in BIP for the first time.

Cholesterol Lowering & Controlling Three Week Plan Handbook & Cookbook. Patricia Krimmel & Edward Krimmel. (Illus.). 192p. (Orig.). 1994. pap. 12.95 (*0-916503-05-4*) Franklin Pubs.

Cholesterol Metabolism, LDL, & the LDL Receptor. Nicholas B. Myant. 465p. 1990. text ed. 88.00 (*0-12-512300-0*) Acad Pr.

Cholesterol Systems in Insects & Animals. Jacqueline Dupont. 160p. 1982. 79.95 (*0-8493-5315-7*, QL495) CRC Pr.

Cholesterol Treatment: User Guide to Lipid Disorder Management. 2nd ed. 1992. 12.95 (*0-929240-44-8*) Essential Med Info Syst Inc.

Cholesterol 7 Alpha & Hydroxylase (7 Alpha Monooxygenase) Robin Fears & John R. Sabine. 256p. 1986. 166.00 (*0-8493-6553-8*, QP603, CRC Reprint) Franklin.

Cholesterols: Causing Cancers & a Whole Lot More. Arthur Isbit & Nancy Buckner. 50p. (Orig.). 1984. pap. 5.50 (*0-917591-01-1*) Health Pub Co.

Cholesterosis - Membrane Cholesterol: Theoretical & Clinical Aspects. Ed. by Yu M. Lopukhin et al. (Physicochemical Biology Reviews Supplement Ser.: Soviet Scientific Reviews, Sect. D). 382p. 1984. text ed. 319.00 (*3-7186-0159-1*) Gordon & Breach.

Choline, Lecithin, Inositol. Jeffrey Bland. Ed. by Richard Passwater. (Good Health Guide Ser.). 1983. pap. 2.50 (*0-87983-277-0*) Keats.

Cholinergic Basis for Alzheimer Therapy. Ed. by Robert E. Becker & Ezio Giacobini. (Advances in Alzheimer Disease Therapy Ser.). (Illus.). x, 480p. 1991. 74.50 (*0-8176-3566-1*) Birkhauser.

Cholinergic Function & Dysfunction. Ed. by A. Claudio Cuello. LC 93-2319. (Progress in Brain Research Ser.: Vol. 98). 1993. write for info. (*0-444-89717-8*) Elsevier.

Cholinergic Neuron & Its Target: The Electromotor Innervation of the Electric Ray, Torpedo, As a Model System. V. P. Whittaker. (Illus.). xvi, 572p. 1992. 149.50 (*0-8176-3553-X*) Spr-Verlag.

Cholinergic Neurotransmission: Functional & Clinical Aspects. Ed. by S. M. Aquilonius & P. G. Gillberg. (Progress in Brain Research Ser.: No. 84). 516p. 1990. 165.75 (*0-685-39431-X*); 141.00 (*0-444-81148-6*) Elsevier.

Cholinergic Synapse. Ed. by V. P. Whittaker. (Handbook of Experimental Pharmacology Ser.: Vol. 86). (Illus.). 750p. 1988. 478.00 (*0-387-18613-1*) Spr-Verlag.

Cholinesterase. (Monographs in Human Genetics: Vol. 11). x, 134p. 1986. 104.00 (*3-8055-4257-7*) S Karger.

Cholinesterase Genes: Multileveled Regulation. Hermona Soreq. Ed. by H. Zakut. (Monographs in Human Genetics: Vol. 13). (Illus.). viii, 108p. 1990. 78.50 (*3-8055-5137-1*) S Karger.

Cholinesterases: Fundamental & Applied Aspects. Ed. by M. Brzin et al. LC 84-12062. xiv, 527p. 1984. 152.35 (*3-11-009873-3*) De Gruyter.

Cholinesterases: Histochemical Contribution Solution Functional Problems. M. Gerebitzoff & P. Alexander. LC 59-13813. (International Series of Monographs on Pure & Applied Mathematics: Vol. 3). 1959. 86.00 (*0-08-009234-9*, Pub. by Pergamon Repr UK) Franklin.

Cholinesterases: Structure, Function, Mechanism, Genetics, & Cell Biology. Ed. by Jean Massoulie et al. LC 91-12371. 414p. 1991. 89.95 (*0-8412-2008-5*) Am Chemical.

Chomsky Update: Linguistics & Politics. Raphael Salkie. 176p. (C). 1990. text ed. 39.95 (*0-04-445589-5*); pap. text ed. 14.95 (*0-04-445590-9*) Routledge Chapman & Hall.

Chomskyan Turn. Ed. by Asa Kasher. (Illus.). 416p. 1993. pap. 21.95 (*0-631-18734-0*) Blackwell Pubs.

***Chomsky's Politics.** Milan Rai. 160p. 1995. 59.95x (*1-85984-916-4*, Pub. by Verso UK); pap. 16.95 (*1-85984-011-6*, C0497, Pub. by Verso UK) Routledge Chapman & Hall.

Chomsky's Universal Grammar: An Introduction. V. J. Cook. (Applied Language Studies). (Illus.). 224p. pap. text ed. 19.95 (*0-631-15302-0*) Blackwell Pubs.

Chon-Ji of Tae Kwon Do Hyung. Jhoon Rhee. Tr. by Roberto Alvarez. LC 74-120124. (Korean Arts Ser.). (Illus.). (ENG & SPA.). 1970. pap. text ed. 13.95 (*0-89750-000-8*, 102, Wehman) Ohara Pubns.

Chondrichthyes I: Paleozoic Elasmobranchii. R. Zangerl. Ed. by O. Kuhn & H. P. Schultz. (Handbook of Paleoichthyology: Vol. 3A). (Illus.). 115p. 1981. text ed. 115.00 (*3-437-30337-6*) Lubrecht & Cramer.

Chondrichthyes II: Mesozoic & Genozoic Elasmobranhii. Henri Cappetta. (Handbook of Paleoichthyology Ser.: Vol. 3B). (Illus.). 193p. 1987. text ed. 160.80 (*3-437-30393-7*) Lubrecht & Cramer.

Chondrichthyes II, Vol. 3B. Henri Cappetta. LC 86-29568. (Handbook of Paleoichthyology Ser.). 193p. 1987. 215.00 (*0-89574-231-4*, Pub. by Gustav Fischer Verlag) VCH Pubs.

Chondrules & Their Origins. Ed. by E. A. King. LC 83-26818. 375p. 1984. 25.00 (*0-942862-01-5*) Lunar & Planet Inst.

***Chong Family History.** J. H. Kim On Chong-Gossard. 184p. 1992. pap. 35.00 (*0-9634186-0-2*) Chong Hee Bks.

Choo Choo. Virginia L. Burton. (Illus.). 48p. (J). (gr. k-3). 1973. 14.95 (*0-395-17684-0*) HM.

Choo Choo: The Story of a Little Engine Who Ran Away. Virginia L. Burton. LC 37-19461. (Illus.). 56p. (Orig.). (J). (gr. k-8). 1988. pap. 4.95 (*0-395-47942-8*) HM.

Choo-Choo, Peek-a-Boo. W. Awdry. LC 91-61250. (Peek-a-Boo Board Bks.). (Illus.). 14p. (J). (ps). 1992. 3.99 (*0-679-82262-3*) Random Bks Yng Read.

Chooch. Betty K. Schultz. LC 90-91639. (Illus.). 64p. (J). (gr. 3-8). 1990. boxed, lib. bdg. 14.95 (*0-929568-00-1*) Raspberry IL.

Choose a Career That Likes You: How to Predict Career Success. Vincent W. Kafka. 112p. 1993. pap. 19.95 (*0-913261-29-7*) Effect Learn Sys.

***Choose a Christian College: A Guide to Academically Challenging Colleges Committed to a Christ-Centered Campus Life.** 4th ed. Christian College Coalition Staff & Vere L. Oliver. LC 92-22622. 144p. 1994. 12.95 (*1-56079-434-8*) Petersons Guides.

Choose Costa Rica: A Guide to Retirement & Investment. 2nd ed. John Howells. LC 92-27009. (Illus.). 252p. 1994. pap. 13.95 (*0-933469-17-9*) Gateway Bks.

Choose Health, Choose Lean: A Guide for a Supermarket Lean Meat Nutrition Education Program. California Project Lean Staff. Ed. by Prudence Breitrose. 84p. (Orig.). 1992. pap. 19.50 (*1-879552-09-4*) Stanford CRDP.

Choose Life. Bernard Mandelbaum. 1972. pap. 8.95 (*0-8197-0006-1*) Bloch.

Choose Life. James J. Mulligan. 383p. 1991. pap. text ed. 17.95 (*0-935372-31-8*) Pope John Ctr.

Choose Life: Consistent Life Ethic & Political Responsibility. Kate Chambers & Patricia Natali. 40p. (Orig.). 1988. pap. 2.95 (*1-55612-150-4*) Sheed & Ward MO.

Choose Life: Knowing Your Purpose in Life. Ezriel Tauber. Ed. by Yaakov Astor. (Hashkafa Dialogue Ser.). (Orig.). 1991. pap. 15.00 (*1-878999-02-8*); pap. 12.00 (*1-878999-03-6*) Shelheves.

Choose Life & Not Death: A Primer on Abortion, Euthanasia, & Suicide. William F. Maestri. LC 85-28687. 1986. pap. 9.95 (*0-8189-0490-9*) Alba.

Choose Life! Unborn Children & the Right to Life. Pref. by Francis D. Kelly. (Illus.). 72p. (Orig.). (YA). (gr. 11-12). 1991. pap. 12.95 (*1-55833-106-9*) Natl Cath Educ.

Choose Love. Teddy Milne. LC 86-62021. 203p. 1986. pap. 10.95 (*0-938875-00-0*) Pittenbruach Pr.

Choose Love: A Jewish Buddhist Human Rights Activist in Central America. Joe Gorin. 224p. (Orig.). (C). 1993. pap. 12.00 (*0-938077-35-X*) Parallax Pr.

Choose Me. Marilyn Kaye. (Changes Romance Ser.: No. 8). (YA). 1992. mass mkt. 3.50 (*0-06-106714-8*, Harp PBks) HarpC.

Choose Me: Portraits of a Presidential Race. Arthur Grace. LC 89-5643. (Newsweek Bk.). (Illus.). 127p. 1989. pap. 19.95 (*0-87451-492-4*) U Pr of New Eng.

Choose Mexico: Live Well on Eight Hundred Dollars a Month. 4th ed. John Howells & Don Merwin. LC 92-14248. (Illus.). 252p. 1994. pap. 11.95 (*0-933469-18-7*) Gateway Bks.

Choose My Shoes: Dial the Answer. 1992. pap. 3.99 (*0-517-06616-5*) Random Hse Value.

Choose Once Again. Ed. by Julius J. Finegold & William N. Thetford. LC 76-20363. (Illus.). 112p. 1981. 7.95 (*0-89087-413-1*) Celestial Arts.

***Choose Peace.** Johan Galtung & Daisaku Ikeda. Ed. & Tr. by Richard L. Gage. LC 95-13591. 1995. write for info. (*0-7453-1040-0*, Pub. by Pluto Pr UK); pap. write for info. (*0-7453-1039-7*, Pub. by Pluto Pr UK) Westview.

Choose Spain: For Leisurely Vacations or Affordable Retirement. John Howells & Bettie Magee. LC 90-41031. (Illus.). 252p. (Orig.). 1990. pap. 11.95 (*0-933469-09-8*) Gateway Bks.

***Choose the Fate of Apollo 13.** Linda W. Aber. LC 95-13067. (J). 1995. write for info. (*0-448-41116-4*, G&D) Putnam Pub Group.

Choose the Perfect Name for Your Baby. Sarah B. Parsons. LC 92-10483. 1992. 4.95 (*0-681-41444-8*) Longmeadow Pr.

Choose the Right Mate, Lover or Friend Through Handwriting. Jess E. Dines. 1992. pap. 10.95 (*0-9627666-1-5*) Pantex.

***Choose the Right Move.** Daniel King & Peter Dove. 128p. 1995. 14.95 (*1-85744-135-4*, Pub. by Cadogan Books UK) Macmillan.

Choose the Right Word: A Contemporary Guide to Selecting the Precise Word for Every Situation. 2nd ed. S. I. Hayakawa. Ed. by Eugene Ehrlich. 608p. (Orig.). 1994. pap. 17.00 (*0-06-273131-9*, Harper Ref) HarpC.

Choose to Be Healthy. Susan S. Jones. LC 86-26842. 264p. 1987. 11.95 (*0-89087-482-4*) Celestial Arts.

Choose to Be Tobacco Free. Ed. by Jean Funk & Gretchen Griffin. LC 87-80985. 89p. 1987. teacher ed 20.00 (*0-89486-473-4*, 5709) Hazelden.

Choose to Live: An AIDS Healing Companion. Laurence E. Badgley. LC 87-81624. 70p. 1993. pap. 11.95 (*0-941523-01-2*) Human Energy Pr.

Choose to Live Each Day Fully: A 365 Day Guide to Transforming Your Life from Ordinary to Extraordinary. Susan S. Jones. LC 94-332. 1994. pap. 12.95 (*0-89087-713-0*) Celestial Arts.

Choose to Live Peacefully. Susan S. Jones. 310p. (Orig.). 1991. pap. 12.95 (*0-89087-615-0*) Celestial Arts.

Choose to Lose: A Food Lover's Guide to Permanent Weight Loss. rev. ed. Ron Goor & Nancy Goor. 416p. 1995. pap. 12.95 (*0-395-70814-1*) HM.

***Choose to Reuse: An Encyclopedia of Services, Products, Programs & Charitable Organizations That Foster Reuse.** Nikki Goldbeck & David Goldbeck. 400p. (Orig.). 1995. pap. 15.95 (*0-9606138-6-2*) Ceres Pr.

Choose, Use, Enjoy, Share: Library Media Skills for the Gifted Child. Phyllis Leonard. Ed. by Paula K. Montgomery. LC 85-4532. (Teaching Library Media Research & Information Skills Ser.). 153p. 1985. lib. bdg. 23.50 (*0-87287-417-6*) Libs Unl.

Choose Well, Be Well: A Curriculum for Junior High School. California Department of Education Staff. (Nutrition Education Ser.). (Illus.). 344p. 1984. pap. 6.50 (*0-8011-0229-4*) Calif Education.

Choose Well, Be Well: A Curriculum Guide for High School. California Department of Education Staff. (Nutrition Education Ser.). (Illus.). 381p. 1984. pap. 6.50 (*0-8011-0228-6*) Calif Education.

Choose Well, Be Well: A Curriculum Guide for Preschool & Kindergarten. California Department of Education Staff. (Nutrition Education Ser.). (Illus.). 204p. 1982. pap. 6.50 (*0-8011-0182-4*) Calif Education.

Choose Well, Be Well: A Curriculum Guide for the Primary Grades. California Department of Education Staff. (Nutrition Education Ser.). (Illus.). 208p. 1982. pap. 6.50 (*0-8011-0183-2*) Calif Education.

Choose Well, Be Well: A Curriculum Guide for the Upper Elementary Grades. California Department of Education Staff. (Nutrition Education Ser.). (Illus.). 237p. 1982. pap. 6.50 (*0-8011-0184-0*) Calif Education.

Choose Well, Be Well: Color Supplement to the Preschool & Kindergarten Curriculum Guide. California Department of Education Staff. (Nutrition Education Ser.). (Illus.). 48p. 1985. pap. 6.00 (*0-8011-0254-5*) Calif Education.

Choose Your Attitudes, Change Your Life. Robert Jeffress. 1992. pap. 8.99 (*0-89693-123-4*) SP Pubns.

Choose Your Own Adventure, 5 vols., Set, No. 1. (J). (gr. 4). Boxed Set. boxed, mass mkt. 9.75 (*0-553-30307-4*, Skylark) Bantam.

Choose Your Own Adventure, 5 vols., Set, No. 2. (J). (gr. 4). Boxed Set. boxed, mass mkt. 9.75 (*0-553-30308-2*, Skylark) Bantam.

Choose Your Own Adventure, 5 vols., Set, No. 3. (J). Boxed Set. boxed, mass mkt. 9.75 (*0-553-30310-4*, Skylark) Bantam.

Choose Your Own Adventure, 5 vols., Set, No. 4. (J). (gr. 4). Boxed Set. boxed, mass mkt. 9.75 (*0-553-30434-8*) Bantam.

***Choose Your Own Adventure Series.** large type ed. (Illus.). (J). (gr. 4 up). lib. bdg. 146.00 (*0-8368-1303-0*) Gareth Stevens Inc.

Choose-Your-Own-Ending Sex Ed Adventures. Carole Marsh. (Smart Sex Stuff Ser.). 60p. (Orig.). 1994. 24.95 (*1-55609-283-0*); pap. 14.95 (*1-55609-226-1*) Gallopade Pub Group.

Choose Your Own World. Edouard Roditi. LC 91-73681. (Illus.). 112p. (Orig.). 1992. 20.00 (*1-878580-40-X*); pap. 7.95 (*1-878580-39-6*) Asylum Arts.

Choosing. Corinne Sanders. 64p. (J). (gr. 3-8). 1985. student ed 8.95 (*0-86653-333-8*, GA 677) Good Apple.

Choosing: A Better Way to Live. Richard C. Nelson. LC 78-67188. (Illus.). 1978. pap. 5.95 (*0-932570-00-3*) Guidelines Pr.

Choosing: Cases in Moral Decision Making. Michael Pennock. LC 90-85155. (Friendship in the Lord Ser.). 160p. (Orig.). (YA). (gr. 9-12). 1991. spiral bd. 7.95 (*0-87793-446-0*) Ave Maria.

Choosing: Which Way Do I Go? Sandy Larsen. (Bible Discovery Guide for Campers Ser.). (Illus.). 32p. (J). (gr. 7-10). 1985. 1.50 (*0-87788-115-4*); 3.50 (*0-87788-116-2*) Shaw Pubs.

Choosing a Bibliographic Utility: User Views of Current Choices. Ed. by Leslie R. Morris. 200p. (Orig.). 1990. pap. text ed. 37.50 (*1-55570-044-6*) Neal-Schuman.

***Choosing a Career in the Law.** rev. ed. Dena O. Rakoff. 88p. 1991. pap. 13.00 (*0-943747-15-5*) Harvard OCS.

Choosing a College. Gordon P. Miller. 165p. 1990. pap. 9.95 (*0-87447-333-0*) College Bd.

Choosing a College Major: Humanities. Gummere. 1987. pap. 6.95 (*0-679-50953-4*) McKay.

Choosing a College Major: Social Sciences. Norma P. Simon & Robert G. Simon. 1986. pap. 7.95 (*0-679-50968-2*) McKay.

Choosing a College President: Opportunities & Constraints. Judith B. McLaughlin & David Riesman. LC 90-47689. 377p. (Orig.). 1991. pap. 8.00 (*0-931050-40-5*) Carnegie Fnd Advan Teach.

Choosing a Color Scheme: How to Handle Samples & Use Color Successfully in Your Home. Ed. by Kimberly Kerrigone. LC 91-71688. 96p. 1992. pap. 8.95 (*0-932944-98-1*) Creative Homeowner.

***Choosing a Faith.** Ninian Smart. LC 94-31505. (Briefings Ser.). 128p. 1995. pap. 14.95 (*0-7145-2982-6*) M Boyars Pubs.

***Choosing a "Human" Service Provider: Tips for Adult Students.** Margie Sherman. (Illus.). 8p. 1994. pap. 2.50 (*1-884241-21-2*) Energeia Pub.

***Choosing a Management Company No. 8: Choosing a Management Company.** 3rd rev. ed. Michael E. Packard. (GAP Ser.: No. 8). 16p. (C). 1994. pap. 14.50 (*0-944715-33-8*) CAI.

Choosing a Martial Arts School, Style or Teacher. Christopher J. Goedecke. 24p. (Orig.). 1986. pap. 3.00 (*0-9614046-1-2*) Martial Art Direct.

Choosing a Mate. K. Stewart. 80p. (Orig.). pap. 3.99 (*0-88368-252-4*) Whitaker Hse.

Choosing a Nurse-Midwife: Your Guide to Safe, Sensitive Care During Pregnancy & the Birth of Your Child. Catherine Poole & Elizabeth Parr. LC 93-33105. 1994. pap. text ed. 12.95 (*0-471-58452-5*) Wiley.

Choosing a Nursing Home: A Guidebook for Families. Marty Richards et al. LC 84-25651. (Illus.). 112p. (Orig.). 1985. pap. 9.95 (*0-295-96221-6*) U of Wash Pr.

Choosing a Path. David D. Moore. 1990. pap. 4.95 (*0-913543-17-9*) African Am Imag.

Choosing a Path. Swami Rama. LC 81-85538. 200p. (Orig.). 1982. pap. 9.95 (*0-89389-077-4*) Himalayan Pubs.

Choosing a Sex Ethic: A Jewish Inquiry. Eugene B. Borowitz. LC 73-79123. (gr. 10-12). 1987. pap. 6.95 (*0-8052-0276-5*) Schocken.

***Choosing A Shelter Dog: Complete Guide to Help You Rescue & Rehome a Dog.** Bob Christiansen. 128p. (Orig.). 1995. pap. 11.95 (*1-884421-66-0*) Canine Lrning.

Choosing a Sustainable Future: The Report of the National Commission on the Environment. National Commission on the Environment Staff. LC 92-35267. (Illus.). 190p. (C). 1992. 25.00 (*1-55963-231-3*); pap. 15.00 (*1-55963-232-1*) Island Pr.

Choosing a Vocation. Intro. by Frank Parsons & Carl McDaniels. LC 89-80556. 165p. (C). 1909. reprint ed. pap. 10.00 (*0-912048-65-4*) Garrett Pk.

Choosing a Wheelchair System. Ed. by Seldon P. Todd, Jr. (Illus.). 118p. (Orig.). (C). 1993. pap. text ed. 30.00 (*1-56806-213-3*) Diane Pub.

***Choosing a World Map: Attributes, Distortions, Aspects.** American Cartographics Association Staff. 15p. 1988. pap. 12.00 (*0-614-06090-7*, C168) Am Congrs Survey.

Choosing An Advertising Agency. William M. Weilbacher. 170p. 1983. pap. 19.95 (*0-8442-3082-0*, NTC Busn Bks) NTC Pub Grp.

Choosing an Airline Career: In-Depth Descriptions of Entry-Level Positions, Travel Benefits, How to Apply & Interview. Carol March. LC 91-77885. (Illus.). 160p. 1992. pap. 16.95 (*0-9631614-0-7*) Capri Pub.

Choosing an Alternative Transportation Fuel: Air Pollution & Greenhouse Gas Effects. Daniel Sperling & Mark DeLuchi. 149p. (Orig.). 1993. pap. text ed. 38.00 (*92-64-14004-2*, 97-93-12-1) OECD.

Choosing an Electoral System: Issues & Alternatives. Ed. by Arent Lijphart & Bernard Grofman. LC 84-18283. (American Political Parties & Elections Ser.). 286p. 1984. text ed. 75.00 (*0-275-91216-7*, C1216, Praeger Pubs) Greenwood.

Choosing an Exchange Rate Regime: The Challenge for Smaller Industrial Counties. Ed. by Victor Argy & Paul De Grauwe. LC 89-48328. v, 391p. 1990. pap. 19.50 (*1-55775-133-1*) Intl Monetary.

Choosing & Buying a Pony. Pony Club Training Committee Staff. (Illus.). 96p. 1990. 18.95 (*0-900226-38-2*, Pub. by Brit Horse Soc & Pony Club UK) Half Halt Pr.

***Choosing & Changing Jobs & Careers.** David F. Cox. LC 85-81875. 147p. 1985. pap. 8.95 (*0-9616213-0-3*) Empire Pub.

Choosing & Growing Australian Plants. Bill Molyneux & Sue Forrester. (Illus.). 192p. (Orig.). 1994. pap. 12.95 (*0-86417-516-7*, Pub. by Kangaroo Pr AT) Seven Hills Bk.

Choosing & Staging a Play. Guy Williams. (Illus.). 96p. (Orig.). 1990. pap. 16.00 (*0-333-39590-5*, Pub. by Macmillan Ed UK) Players Pr.

Choosing & Using a CCD Camera: Your Invitation to Join the CCD Revolution in Astronomical Imaging. Richard Berry. LC 92-586. 1992. 29.95 (*0-943396-39-5*) Willmann-Bell.

Choosing & Using ECL. P. Matthews. 1984. text ed. 40.00 (*0-07-040949-8*) McGraw.

Choosing & Using Educational Software: A Teachers Guide. David Squires & Anne McDougall. LC 93-30302. 1994. write for info. (*0-7507-0306-7*, Falmer Pr); pap. write for info. (*0-7507-0307-5*, Falmer Pr) Taylor & Francis.

Choosing & Using Four Bit Microcontrollers. Philip McDowell. LC 93-15660. 246p. 1993. 75.00 (*0-8247-9153-3*) Dekker.

Choosing & Using Management Consultants. Roger Bennett. 320p. 1990. pap. 49.95 (*0-8464-1340-X*) Beekman Pubs.

Choosing & Using the Right Medical Office Computer. Peter C. Tolos & Daniel J. Moody. 240p. 1986. 42.95 (*0-87489-434-4*) Med Economics.

Choosing & Using Training Consultants. Diane Bailey & Clare Sproston. 120p. 1993. 67.95 (*0-566-07328-5*, Pub. by Gower UK) Ashgate Pub Co.

Choosing & Using Your First CD-ROM Drive. Robert Mullen. LC 94-66140. 232p. 1994. cd-rom, pap. 19.99 (*0-7821-1526-8*) Sybex.

Choosing & Working with Your Advertising Agency. William M. Weilbacher. 220p. 1991. 39.95 (*0-8442-3468-0*, VGM Career Bks) NTC Pub Grp.

Choosing & Working with Your Public Relations Firm. Thomas Harris. 220p. 1992. 39.95 (*0-8442-3261-0*, NTC Busn Bks) NTC Pub Grp.

Choosing Big Technologies. Ed. by John Krige. LC 92-19366. 1993. text ed. 69.00 (*3-7186-5302-8*) Gordon & Breach.

Choosing Books for Young People: A Guide to Criticism & Bibliography, 1976-1984, Vol. 2. Diana L. Spirt & John R. Ettlinger. LC 86-42785. 168p. 1987. 43.50 (*0-89774-247-8*) Oryx Pr.

Choosing Childcare: Solving Your Childcare Problems. Ed. by Patricia Murray. 1992. 31.00 (*1-85549-062-5*, Pub. by Attic Pr IE) St Mut.

Choosing Childcare: Solving Your Childcare Problems. Patricia H. Murray. 144p. (Orig.). 1993. pap. 15.99 (*1-85594-062-0*, Pub. by Attic IE) InBook.

Choosing Christ in the World: Directing the Spiritual Exercises of St. Ignatius of Loyola. J. A. Tetlow. (Studies on Jesuit Topics Series IV: No. 12). 254p. 1989. ring bd. 21.95 (*0-912422-97-1*) Inst Jesuit.

Choosing College Major in Education. Miller. 1979. 10.95 (*0-679-50957-7*); pap. 5.95 (*0-679-50958-5*) McKay.

***Choosing Colors.** (Illus.). 14p. 1995. 5.99 (*0-525-45475-6*, DCB) Dutton Child Bks.

Choosing Crime: The Criminal Calculus of Property Offenders. Kenneth Tunnell. (Law, Crime, & Justice Ser.). 175p. (C). 1992. pap. text ed. 19.95 (*0-8304-1242-5*) Nelson-Hall.

Choosing Death: Active Euthanasia, Religion & the Public Debate. Ed. by Ron Hamel. LC 91-24448. 192p. (C). 1991. pap. 12.95 (*1-56338-031-5*) TPI PA.

***Choosing Democracy: A Practical Guide to Multicultural Education.** Duane E. Campbell. LC 95-7654. 1996. pap. write for info. (*0-13-351370-X*, Merrill Pub Co) Macmillan.

Choosing Effective Development Programs: An Appraisal Guide for Human Resources & Training Managers. James E. Gardner. LC 86-30604. 204p. 1987. text ed. 55.00 (*0-89930-182-7*, GCE/, Quorum Bks) Greenwood.

Choosing Equality: The Case for Democratic Schooling. Ann Bastian et al. 240p. 1986. pap. 18.95 (*0-87722-454-4*) Temple U Pr.

Choosing Family Child Care: A Handbook for Parents. National Council of Jewish Women Staff. (Illus.). 21p. 1990. 3.00 (*0-685-62941-4*) NCJW.

***Choosing Flower Essences: An Assessment Guide.** Patricia Kaminski. 36p. 1994. 1.95 (*0-9631306-3-3*) Flower Essence.

Choosing Foods for a Healthy Heart: Introducing the CEF Index. Michael Mogadam. LC 92-39213. 192p. 1993. 19.95 (*0-89043-633-9*) Consumer Reports.

Choosing for Children: Parents' Consent to Surgery. Priscilla Anderson. 272p. 1990. 41.00 (*0-19-217774-5*) OUP.

Choosing God's Way to See & Share. Beers. 1983. 14.99 (*0-88207-819-4*, Victor Books) SP Pubns.

Choosing Happiness: The Art of Living Unconditionally. Veronica Ray. LC 90-55300. 176p. (Orig.). 1991. pap. 10.00 (*0-06-255356-9*, Hazelden SF) Harper SF.

Choosing Health. Alan Collinson. LC 90-25849. (Facing the Future Ser.). (Illus.). 48p. (J). (gr. 5-8). 1991. lib. bdg. 22.80 (*0-8114-2801-X*) Raintree Steck-V.

Choosing Health for Yourself: A Clear & Practical Guide to Motivating Self-Care. Leonard G. Horowitz. (Illus.). 76p. (Orig.). 1981. pap. 4.25 (*0-9609386-0-5*) Tetrahedron.

Choosing Is Confusing: How to Make Good Choices, Not Bad Guesses. Claudine G. Wirths & Mary Bowman-Kruhm. 100p. (J). (gr. 6-10). 1994. pap. 11.95 (*0-89106-068-5*) Davies-Black.

***Choosing Is Confusing: How to Make Good Choices, Not Bad Guesses.** Claudine G. Wirths & Mary Bowman-Kruhm. 120p. (YA). (gr. 6-12). 1994. pap. 11.95 (*0-614-07134-8*, 7190) Davies-Black.

Choosing Joy for Lent. Marilyn N. Gustin. LC 90-70803. (Orig.). 1990. pap. 3.95 (*0-89243-331-0*) Liguori Pubns.

Choosing Judaism. Lydia Kukoff. 152p. (Orig.). 1983. pap. 7.95 (*0-87052-070-9*) Hippocrene Bks.

Choosing Judaism. Lydia Kukoff. (Orig.). 1981. 10.00 (*0-8074-0151-X*); pap. 6.95 (*0-8074-0150-1*) UAHC.

Choosing Justice: An Experimental Approach to Ethical Theory. Norman Frohlich & Joe A. Oppenheimer. LC 91-29059. (California Series on Social Choice & Political Economy: Vol. 22). (C). 1992. 45.00 (*0-520-07299-5*); pap. 15.00 (*0-520-08437-3*) U CA Pr.

Choosing Life's Best: The Success Plan of Proverbs. Lottie B. Hobbs. 166p. 1988. pap. 5.95 (*0-913838-13-6*) Harvest TX.

***Choosing Losing.** Julia Moore & Barbara Johnson. 1995. write for info. (*0-87397-998-2*) Strode.

Choosing Lovers. Martin Blinder. LC 88-83381. 222p. 1989. 18.95 (*0-944435-04-1*) Glenbridge Pub.

Choosing Lovers: Ten Steps to a Happier Relationship. Martin Blinder & Carmen Lynch. 192p. 1991. pap. 3.95 (*0-380-71201-6*) Avon.

Choosing Materials to Teach Reading. Kenneth S. Goodman et al. LC 66-19547. 158p. reprint ed. pap. 45.10 (*0-7837-3820-X*, 2043640) Bks Demand.

Choosing Medical Care in Old Age: What Kind, How Much, When to Stop. Muriel R. Gillick. LC 94-11333. 223p. 1994. text ed. 19.95 (*0-674-12812-5*, GILCHO) HUP.

***Choosing Mind & the Judging Will: An Analysis of Attention.** Clotilde Calabi. LC 94-255513. (European University Studies, Series XX, Philosophy: Vol. 432). 1994. write for info. (*3-631-47667-1*) P Lang Pubs.

Choosing NDT: Applications, Costs, & Benefits of Nondestructive Testing in Your Quality Assurance Program. Samuel A. Wenk & Robert C. McMaster. Ed. by Paul McIntire. (Illus.). 96p. 1987. 15.75 (*0-931403-09-X*) Am Soc Nondestructive.

Choosing Nonviolence: The Rainbow House Handbook to a Violence-Free Future for Young Children. Anne Parry et al. LC 90-62582. (Illus.). (Orig.). 1990. pap. 25.45 (*0-9627528-9-4*) Rainbow Hse.

Choosing Not Choosing: Dickinson's Fascicles. Sharon Cameron. LC 92-15544. (Illus.). 216p. 1993. lib. bdg. 45.00 (*0-226-09232-1*); pap. text ed. 16.95 (*0-226-09234-8*) U Ch Pr.

Choosing Options & Accommodations for Children: (COACH) A Guide to Planning Inclusive Education. Michael F. Giangreco et al. 208p. (Orig.). (C). 1992. spiral bd. 29.00 (*1-55766-106-5*) P H Brookes.

Choosing, Planting & Cultivating Herbs. Philippa Back. LC 76-58770. (Living with Herbs Ser.: Vol. 2). (Illus.). 100p. 1977. pap. 2.50 (*0-87983-149-9*) Keats.

Choosing Presidents: Symbols of Political Leadership. 2nd ed. Michael Novak. 402p. (C). 1991. pap. text ed. 21.95 (*1-56000-567-X*) Transaction Pubs.

Choosing Priorities in Science & Technology. OECD Staff. 91p. (Orig.). 1991. pap. 24.00 (*92-64-13499-9*) OECD.

***Choosing Quality Childcare.** Robert Schoelsel & Katherine Schoelsel. 75p. Date not set. student ed write for info. (*0-9643199-1-8*) P E R C.

Choosing Research Methods: Data Collection for Development Workers. Brian Pratt & Peter Lizos. 80p. (C). 1980. text ed. 80.00 (*0-85598-176-8*, Pub. by Oxfam Pubns UK); pap. text ed. 24.00 (*0-85598-177-6*, Pub. by Oxfam Pubns UK) St Mut.

Choosing Schools & Child Care Options: Answering Parents' Questions. Nancy H. Phillips. LC 94-19163. (Illus.). 112p. (C). 1994. 34.95 (*0-398-05923-3*) C C Thomas.

***Choosing Schools & Child Care Options: Answering Parents' Questions.** Nancy H. Phillips. LC 94-19163. (Illus.). 112p. (C). 1994. pap. 19.95 (*0-398-05969-1*) C C Thomas.

Choosing Sides. Ilene Cooper. LC 89-13669. 224p. (J). (gr. 4-7). 1990. 12.95 (*0-688-07934-2*) Morrow Jr Bks.

Choosing Sides. Carolyn Keene. Ed. by Anne Greenberg. (Nancy Drew Files Ser.: No. 84). 160p. (Orig.). (J). 1993. mass mkt. 3.99 (*0-671-73088-6*, Archway) PB.

Choosing Sides. Francine Pascal. (Sweet Valley Twins Ser.: No. 4). (Orig.). (J). 1986. pap. 3.25 (*0-553-15658-6*) Bantam.

Choosing Sides. large type ed. Jamie Suzanne. (Sweet Valley Twins Ser.: No. 4). 104p. (YA). (gr. 7-12). 1990. reprint ed. 9.95 (*1-55905-067-5*) Grey Castle.

Choosing Sides: Alignment & Realignment in the Third World. Steven R. David. LC 90-5297. 272p. 1991. text ed. 38.50 (*0-8018-4122-4*) Johns Hopkins.

Choosing Sides: Unions & the Team Concept. Mike Parker & Jane Slaughter. LC 88-80585. (Illus.). 240p. 1988. pap. 16.00 (*0-685-20979-2*) Labor Notes.

Choosing Sides: Unions & the Team Concept. Mike Parker & Jane Slaughter. LC 88-80585. (Illus.). 240p. 1988. pap. 16.00 (*0-89608-347-0*) Labor Notes.

Choosing Sorghum as Food in the Semi-Arid Tropics: Studies in Dryland Communities. P. Pushpamma. 91p. 1993. pap. 15.00 (*0-88936-657-8*, IDRC6578, Pub. by IDRC CN) UNIPUB.

***Choosing Staff: A Guide to Better Selection Interviewing.** Ian Mackay. 72p. (C). 1991. pap. 21.00x (*0-85171-092-1*, Pub. by IPM Hse UK) St Mut.

Choosing the Candidates. George Sullivan. (Ballots & Bandwagons Ser.). (Illus.). 128p. (J). (gr. 5 up). 1991. lib. bdg. 12.95 (*0-382-24314-5*); pap. 7.95 (*0-382-24319-6*) Silver Burdett Pr.

***Choosing the Chief: Presidential Elections in France & the United States.** Roy Pierce. 326p. 1995. text ed. 39.50x (*0-472-10559-0*) U of Mich Pr.

Choosing the Dream: The Future of Religion in American Public Life. Frederick M. Gedicks & Roger Hendrix. LC 91-10426. (Contributions to the Study of Religion Ser.: No. 32). 216p. 1991. text ed. 45.00 (*0-313-27809-1*, HCJ/, Greenwood Pr) Greenwood.

Choosing the Fulness: Wickedness or Righteousness. S. Michael Wilcox. 8.95 (*0-88494-654-1*) Bookcraft Inc.

Choosing the News: The Profit Factor in News Selection. Philip Gaunt. LC 89-23466. (Contributions to the Study of Mass Media & Communications Ser.: No. 16). 193p. 1990. text ed. 45.00 (*0-313-26847-9*, GCQ/, Greenwood Pr) Greenwood.

Choosing the Perfect Dog for You & Your Family. Mordecai Siegel. 192p. 1994. pap. 8.95 (*0-8092-3709-1*) Contemp Bks.

***Choosing the Players.** Penny Hackett. 98p. (C). 1994. pap. 18.00x (*0-85292-552-2*, Pub. by IPM Hse UK) St Mut.

Choosing the President, 1992. League of Women Voters Staff. 160p. 1992. pap. 9.95 (*1-55821-169-1*) Lyons & Burford.

Choosing the Right Camp: A Complete Guide to the Best Summer Camp for Your Child. Richard Kennedy. 1992. pap. 15.00 (*0-8129-1926-2*, Times Bks) Random.

***Choosing the Right Camp, 1995-96: The Complete Guide to the Best Summer Camp for Your Child.** Richard Kennedy. 1995. pap. 15.00 (*0-8129-2490-8*, Times Bks) Random.

Choosing the Right Cruise for You: The Bon Voyage Guide. John W. Macchi & Art Kane. LC 94-29665. (Illus.). 112p. 1994. pap. 9.95 (*0-942963-52-0*) Distinctive Pub.

Choosing the Right Health Care Plan. Henry Berman et al. (Illus.). 400p. 1989. pap. 14.95 (*0-89043-218-X*) Consumer Reports.

Choosing the Right Pond: Human Behavior & the Quest for Status. Robert H. Frank. (Illus.). 1987. reprint ed. pap. 16.95 (*0-19-504945-4*) OUP.

Choosing the Right School for Your Child: A Guide to Selected Elementary Schools in the Washington Area. Blythe Lyons & Missy Janes. 344p. (Orig.). 1990. pap. 14.95 (*0-8191-7682-6*) Madison Bks UPA.

Choosing the Right Stuff: The Psychological Selection of Astronauts & Cosmonauts. Patricia A. Santry. LC 93-22834. (Human Evolution, Behavior, & Intelligence Ser.). 324p. 1994. text ed. 65.00 (*0-275-94236-8*, C4236, Praeger Pubs) Greenwood.

Choosing the Type of Ownership Module, PACE: A Program for Acquiring Competence in Entrepreneurship, 3 levels. rev. ed. National Center for Research in Vocational Education Staff. 1983. 2.50 (*0-317-06028-7*) Ctr Educ Trng Employ.

Choosing the Type of Ownership Module, PACE: A Program for Acquiring Competence in Entrepreneurship, 3 levels, Level 1. rev. ed. National Center for Research in Vocational Education Staff. 1983. 2.50 (*0-317-06029-5*, RD240AB5) Ctr Educ Trng Employ.

Choosing the Type of Ownership Module, PACE: A Program for Acquiring Competence in Entrepreneurship, 3 levels, Level 2. rev. ed. National Center for Research in Vocational Education Staff. 1983. 2.50 (*0-317-06030-9*, RD240BB5) Ctr Educ Trng Employ.

Choosing the Type of Ownership Module, PACE: A Program for Acquiring Competence in Entrepreneurship, 3 levels, Level 3. rev. ed. National Center for Research in Vocational Education Staff. 1983. 2.50 (*0-317-06031-7*, RD240CB5) Ctr Educ Trng Employ.

Choosing to Co-Operate: How States Avoid Loss. Ed. by Janice G. Stein & Louis W. Pauly. LC 92-36269. 240p. 1993. text ed. 38.00 (*0-8018-4610-2*); pap. text ed. 13.95 (*0-8018-4611-0*) Johns Hopkins.

Choosing to Cope. Mary J. Beggs. LC 87-82988. 128p. (Orig.). 1988. pap. 2.95 (*0-88243-510-8*, 02-0510) Gospel Pub.

Choosing to Emerge As Readers & Writers: A Multicultural Reader. Marilyn S. Layton. LC 92-25113. (C). 1992. text ed. 26.00 (*0-06-500727-1*) HarpCollege.

Choosing to Lead. Kenneth E. Clark & Miriam B. Clark. LC 93-79886. 209p. (C). 1994. 35.00 (*0-9638301-0-4*) Ldrship Pr NC.

Choosing to Leave: Voluntary Retirement from the U. S. House of Representatives. John R. Hibbing. LC 81-40635. (Illus.). 162p. (Orig.). 1982. lib. bdg. 52.00 (*0-8191-2427-3*) U Pr of Amer.

Choosing to Love: A New Way to Respond. 3rd ed. Edward E. Ford. 149p. 1990. reprint ed. pap. 9.00 (*0-9616716-4-5*) Brandt Pub.

Choosing to Love Again. Gary Rosberg. 1992. 14.99 (*1-56179-095-8*) Focus Family.

Choosing to Love Again. Gary Rosberg. 1995. pap. 9.99 (*1-56179-257-8*) Focus Family.

Choosing Truman: The Democratic Convention of 1944. Robert H. Ferrell. LC 93-40833. 160p. 1994. 24.95 (*0-8262-0948-3*) U of Mo Pr.

***Choosing Unsafe Sex: AIDS-Risk Denial among Disadvantaged Women.** E. J. Sobo. (Illus.). 256p. 1995. text ed. 33.95 (*0-8122-3314-X*); pap. text ed. 14.95 (*0-8122-1553-2*) U of Pa Pr.

Choosing Using Four Bit Micro-Controllers. McDowell. 1994. pap. 34.95 (*0-7506-1916-3*) Buttrwrth-Heinemann.

Choosing Victory, Overcoming Defeat: Joshua, Judges, and Ruth. rev. ed. Emily Hunter & Wayne Hunter. (Illus.). 224p. 1975. reprint ed. teacher ed 8.99 (*0-89081-511-9*); reprint ed. student ed 6.99 (*0-89081-510-0*) Harvest Hse.

Choosing Victory, Overcoming Defeat: Joshua, Judges, and Ruth, Parchment. rev. ed. Kay Arthur. (International Inductive Study Ser.). 1995. reprint ed. pap. 4.99 (*1-56507-304-5*) Harvest Hse.

Choosing Your Boat. John Roberts & Maria Mann. 1986. 19.95 (*0-393-03315-5*) Norton.

Choosing Your Career: The Christian's Decision Manual. Martin E. Clark. 1981. pap. 6.99 (*0-87552-205-X*) Presby & Reformed.

Choosing Your Career, Finding Your Vocation: A Step-by-Step Guide for Adults & Counselors. Roy Lewis. 1989. pap. 9.95 (*0-8091-3099-8*) Paulist Pr.

Choosing Your Children's Books: Beginning Readers 5 to 8 Years Old. Valerie White. (Illus.). 32p. (Orig.). (J). (gr. k-3). 1993. pap. 4.95 (*1-882726-00-6*) Bayley & Musgrave.

Choosing Your Children's Books: Eight to Twelve Years Old. Valerie White. (Illus.). 80p. (Orig.). 1994. 13.95 (*1-882726-14-6*); per., pap. 5.95 (*1-882726-12-X*) Bayley & Musgrave.

Choosing Your Children's Books: Five to Eight Years Old. rev. ed. Valerie White. (Illus.). 80p. 1994. per., pap. 5.95 (*1-882726-11-1*) Bayley & Musgrave.

Choosing Your Children's Books: Five to Eight Years Old. 2nd rev. ed. Valerie White. (Illus.). 80p. 1994. 13.95 (*1-882726-13-8*) Bayley & Musgrave.

***Choosing Your Children's Books: 2 to 5 Years Old.** Valerie White. (Illus.). 80p. (Orig.). 1994. 13.95 (*1-882726-15-4*); per., pap. 5.95 (*1-882726-10-3*) Bayley & Musgrave.

***Choosing Your English.** BBC Staff. 342p. audio 44.50 (*0-88432-670-5*, S32590); audio 54.50 (*0-88432-672-1*, S32592) Audio-Forum.

Choosing Your Homebuilt. Kenneth D. Armstrong. (Illus.). 352p. (Orig.). 1991. pap. 19.95 (*0-932579-25-6*) Butterfield Pr.

Choosing Your New Home: A Consumer Guide to Living Styles for Retirees, New Jersey Edition, 1993. Barbara M. Lancaster. Ed. by Liane Gonzalez. 259p. (Orig.). 1993. pap. text ed. 19.95 (*1-57108-000-7*) Lancashire Intl.

Choosing Your New Home: A Consumer Guide to Living Styles for Retirees, New Jersey Edition, 1993. Barbara M. Lancaster. Ed. by Liane Gonzalez. Tr. & Illus. by Suzanne Pease. 268p. (Orig.). 1994. pap. 24.95 (*1-57108-001-5*) Lancashire Intl.

Choosing Your New Home: A Consumer Guide to Living Styles for Retirees, New Jersey Edition, 1993. Barbara M. Lancaster. LC 94-75143. (Illus.). 660p. (Orig.). 1994. pap. 29.95 (*1-57108-002-3*) Lancashire Intl.

Choosing Your Pet. Mark McPherson. LC 84-226. (Pet Library Ser.). (Illus.). 48p. (J). (gr. 3-7). 1985. lib. bdg. 9.89 (*0-8167-0111-3*) Troll Assocs.

Choosing Zero: Origins of the INF Treaty. Frederick Donovan & James E. Goodby. (Pew Case Studies in International Affairs). 87p. (C). 1988. pap. text ed. 2.50 (*1-56927-319-7*) Geo U Inst Dplmcy.

***Chop, Chop Chick: or We Are Not Our Own.** Everett W. Oliver. 1994. 13.95 (*0-533-11053-X*) Vantage.

Chop Shop. Kathy Braidhill. (Illus.). 384p. 1993. mass mkt. 4.99 (*1-55817-693-4*, Pinnacle NY) Windsor NY.

Chop Suey. Liu Kang. 96p. 1991. pap. text ed. 5.00 (*981-00-2730-3*) World Scientific Pub.

Chop to the Top: A Behind the Scenes Look at the Team & the Town That Turned Upside Down. Richard M. Sink. LC 92-60191. (Illus.). 336p. 1992. 19.95 (*0-9632624-0-8*) Tomahawk Pr.

Chop Wood, Carry Water: A Guide to Finding Spiritual Fulfillment in Everyday Life. Rick Fields et al. LC 84-23942. 304p. 1984. pap. 13.95 (*0-87477-209-5*) J P Tarcher.

Chopi Musicians: Their Music, Poetry & Instruments. Hugh Tracey. LC 78-558402. 234p. reprint ed. pap. 66.70 (*0-8357-6974-7*, 2039034) Bks Demand.

Chopin. (Portraits of Greatness Ser.: No. I). 1987. pap. 12.50 (*0-918367-03-4*) Elite.

Chopin. (Masterpieces of Piano Music Ser.). (Illus.). 192p. 1986. pap. 11.95 (*0-8256-2420-7*, AM37193) Music Sales.

Chopin. Gavoty. 1986. 14.95 (*0-684-14930-3*, Scribners) S&S Trade.

***Chopin.** Christopher Headington. LC 95-5612. (Compact Companions Ser.). 1995. 17.50 (*0-684-81356-4*) S&S Trade.

Chopin. Ates Orga. (Illustrated Lives of the Great Composers Ser.). (Illus.). 144p. pap. 14.95 (*0-7119-0247-X*, OP42332) Omnibus NY.

Chopin. Ann Rachlin. (Famous Children Ser.). (Illus.). 24p. (J). (gr. k-3). 1993. pap. 5.95 (*0-8120-1543-6*) Barron.

Chopin. James C. Hadden. LC 74-24094. (Master Musicians Ser.). (Illus.). reprint ed. 37.50 (*0-404-12939-0*) AMS Pr.

Chopin: "The Four Ballades" Ed. by Jim Samson. (Cambridge Music Handbooks Ser.). 136p. (C). 1992. pap. 10.95 (*0-521-38615-2*) Cambridge U Pr.

Chopin: "The Four Ballades" Ed. by Jim Samson. (Cambridge Music Handbooks Ser.). 136p. (C). 1992. 29.95 (*0-521-38461-3*) Cambridge U Pr.

Chopin: An Index of His Works in Chronological Order. 2nd ed. Maurice J. E. Brown. LC 70-39498. (Music Ser.). 1972. reprint ed. 32.50 (*0-306-70500-1*) Da Capo.

Chopin: His Life. William D. Murdoch. LC 70-136077. (Illus.). 410p. 1971. reprint ed. text ed. 65.00 (*0-8371-5227-5*, MUCH, Greenwood Pr) Greenwood.

Chopin: His Life. William D. Murdock. 1988. reprint ed. lib. bdg. 59.00 (*0-7812-0495-X*) Rprt Serv.

Chopin: His Life. William D. Murdock. LC 73-181213. 410p. 1935. reprint ed. 59.00 (*0-403-01625-8*) Scholarly.

Chopin: Pianist & Teacher As Seen by His Pupils. Jean-Jacques Eigeldinger. Ed. by Roy Howat. Tr. by Naomi Shohet & Krysia Osostowicz. (Illus.). 340p. (C). 1989. pap. 24.95 (*0-521-36709-3*) Cambridge U Pr.

Chopin: The Composer & His Music. John F. Porte. 1988. reprint ed. lib. bdg. 59.00 (*0-7812-0780-0*) Rprt Serv.

Chopin: The Man & His Music. James G. Huneker. Ed. by Herbert Weinstock. (Illus.). 1966. pap. 5.95 (*0-486-21687-X*) Dover.

Chopin: The Man & His Music. James G. Huneker. 415p. 1990. reprint ed. lib. bdg. 89.00 (*0-7812-9057-0*) Rprt Serv.

Chopin: The Man & His Music. James G. Huneker. LC 72-181182. 415p. 1900. reprint ed. 39.00 (*0-403-01587-1*) Scholarly.

Chopin: The Man & His Music. Herbert Weinstock. LC 80-27187. (Music Ser.). (Illus.). xiv, 336p. 1981. reprint ed. lib. bdg. 37.50 (*0-306-76081-9*) Da Capo.

Chopin & George Sand in Majorca. B. Ferra. LC 73-21620. (Studies in French Literature: No. 45). 1974. lib. bdg. 75.00 (*0-8383-1807-X*) M S G Haskell Hse.

Chopin, & Other Musical Essays. Henry T. Finck. LC 78-37471. (Essay Index Reprint Ser.). 1977. reprint ed. 19.95 (*0-8369-2548-3*) Ayer.

Chopin Companion: Profiles of the Man & the Musician. Ed. & Pref. by Alan Walker. 336p. 1973. reprint ed. pap. 7.95 (*0-393-00668-9*) Norton.

Chopin in Space. Phil Bosakowski. 1986. pap. 4.75 (*0-8222-0209-3*) Dramatists Play.

Chopin Playoffs. Israel Horovitz. 1987. pap. 4.75 (*0-8222-0210-7*) Dramatists Play.

Chopin Preludes: Opus Twenty-Eight. (C). 1974. pap. text ed. 6.95 (*0-393-09699-8*) Norton.

Chopin Studies. Ed. by Jim Samson. (Illus.). 300p. 1988. 69.95 (*0-521-30365-6*) Cambridge U Pr.

Chopin Studies 2, No. 2. Ed. by John Rink & Jim Samson. (Illus.). 300p. (C). 1995. 64.95 (*0-521-41647-7*) Cambridge U Pr.

Chopin, the Composer: His Structural Art & Its Influence on Contemporaneous Music. Edgar S. Kelley. 190p. 1990. reprint ed. lib. bdg. 59.00 (*0-7812-9048-1*) Rprt Serv.

Chopin the Composer & His Music. John F. Porte. 1976. lib. bdg. 25.00 (*0-403-03791-3*) Scholarly.

***Chopin, the Reluctant Romantic.** Jeremy Siepmann. LC 95-14504. 1995. write for info. (*1-55553-249-7*) NE U Pr.

Chopin's Letters. Frederic Chopin. 448p. 1988. reprint ed. pap. 8.95 (*0-486-25564-6*) Dover.

Chopin's Musical Style. Gerald E. Abraham. LC 79-25521. xii, 116p. 1980. reprint ed. text ed. 42.50 (*0-313-22251-7*, ABCM, Greenwood Pr) Greenwood.

***Chopper Boys: Helicopter Warfare in Africa.** Al J. Venter. (Illus.). 240p. 1995. 39.95 (*1-85367-177-0*) Stackpole.

Chopper Cops, No. 1: Fire Storm. Rick Mackin. 1990. pap. 2.95 (*1-55817-353-6*, Pinnacle NY) Windsor NY.

Chopping Down Trees. LC 78-5475. 1978. 2.00 (*0-936428-02-3*) Polygonal Pub.

Chopping Wood, Carrying Water. Lani Steele et al. 46p. 1988. pap. 5.00 (*0-9616635-1-0*) Oblong Pr.

Chopping Wood, Carrying Water. Carol Stetser. LC 77-83081. (Illus.). 1978. pap. 19.95 (*0-917960-02-5*) Padma.

Chopsticks! An Owner's Manual. Hashi-San. 96p. 1991. reprint ed. lib. bdg. 23.00x (*0-8095-5851-3*) Borgo Pr.

Chopsticks & Chips. Joan Solomon. (Way We Live Ser.). (Illus.). 25p. (J). (gr. 2-4). 1991. 12.95 (*0-237-60142-7*, Pub. by Evans Bros Ltd UK) Trafalgar.

Chopsticks, Cleaver & Wok: Homestyle Chinese Cooking. Jennie Low. LC 87-11655. (Illus.). 160p. (Orig.). 1987. pap. 9.95 (*0-87701-421-3*) Chronicle Bks.

Chopsticks from America. Elaine Hosozawa-Nagano. LC 93-45795. (Illus.). (J). 1994. 12.95 (*1-879965-11-9*) Polychrome Pub.

Chopstix: Quick Cooking with Pacific Flavors. Hugh Carpenter & Teri Sandison. LC 89-28334. (Illus.). 208p. 1990. 32.50 (*1-55670-133-0*) Stewart Tabori & Chang.

Choque de Dos Culturas Juridicas en Puerto Rico: El Caso de la Respons Civil Extracontrac. Jose T. Monge. 470p. 1991. 60.00 (*0-409-25574-2*) Michie Butterworth.

Choquet-Deny Type Functional Equations with Applications to Stochastic Models. C. Radhakrishna Rao & D. N. Shanbhag. LC 94-10080. (Series in Probability & Mathematical Statistics). 1994. text ed. 72.95 (*0-471-95104-8*) Wiley.

C

An Asterisk (*) at the beginning of an entry indicates that the title is appearing in BIP for the first time.

An Asterisk (*) at the beginning of an entry indicates that the title is appearing in BIP for the first time.

1235

C

Chosen Place, the Timeless People. Paule Marshall. LC 84-40073. (Vintage Contemporaries Ser.). 480p. 1984. pap. 13.00 (*0-394-72633-2*, Vin) Random.

Chosen Place, the Timeless People. Paule Marshall. LC 84-4007. 1992. pap. 13.00 (*0-394-23987-3*, Vin) Random.

Chosen Primate: Human Nature & Cultural Diversity. Adam Kuper. 285p. (C). 1994. text ed. 27.95 (*0-674-12825-7*) HUP.

Chosen Puppy: How to Select & Raise a Great Puppy from an Animal Shelter. Carol L. Benjamin. 1990. pap. 7.95 (*0-87605-417-3*) Howell Bk.

***Chosen Tales: Stories Told by Jewish Storytellers.** Ed. by Peninnah Schram. LC 94-43612. 480p. 1995. 30.00 (*1-56821-352-2*) Aronson.

Chosen to Fly: A Sixty Year Love Affair with Aviation - & Beyond. Josephine Halsmer. LC 92-71762. (Illus.). 208p. Date not set. pap. 14.95 (*0-9632834-4-8*) Apple Tree IN.

Chosen to Live. D. Kelton. 176p. pap. 2.99 (*0-88368-137-4*) Whitaker Hse.

Chosen to Salvation: Select Thoughts on the Doctrine of Election. David Nettleton. LC 83-11062. 180p. 1984. pap. 5.95 (*0-87227-094-7*) Reg Baptist.

Chosen to Walk. Maxine Roberson. LC 88-35643. (Orig.). 1988. pap. 4.00 (*0-915541-41-6*) Star Bks Inc.

Chosen Vessel: The Luke H. Wetherington Story. Cecil Cahoon, II. (Illus.). 117p. (Orig.). 1992. pap. 8.95 (*1-880994-02-X*) Mt Olive Coll Pr.

Chosen Vessels: Women of Color, Keys to Change. Rebecca F. Osaigbovo. LC 92-85567. (Illus.). 216p. (Orig.). 1993. pap. 9.95 (*1-880560-57-7*) DaBaR Srvs.

Chosen Voices: The Story of the American Cantorate. Mark Slobin. LC 88-17310. (Music in American Life Ser.). (Illus.). 368p. 1989. 32.50 (*0-252-01565-7*); audio 37.95 (*0-252-01567-3*); audio 9.95 (*0-252-01566-5*) U of Ill Pr.

Chosen Women in Korean Politics. 2nd ed. Chung-Hee S. Soh. LC 93-5956. (C). 1993. pap. text ed. 18.95 (*0-8133-2041-0*) Westview.

Chosen Women in Korean Politics: An Anthropological Study. Chung-Hee S. Soh. LC 90-28110. 184p. 1991. text ed. 45.00 (*0-275-93876-X*, C3876, Praeger Pubs) Greenwood.

Chosen Women of the Bible. Ethel Herr. LC 75-36503. 96p. (Orig.). 1976. pap. 5.99 (*0-8024-1297-1*) Moody.

C

Chosen Words. Ivor J. Brown. LC 78-26764. 304p. 1979. reprint ed. text ed. 59.75 (*0-313-20895-6*, BRCW, Greenwood Pr) Greenwood.

Chosen Words, Favorite Sayings of Famous People. Joseph L. Neely. 1994. 5.95 (*1-56245-163-4*) Great Quotations.

Choses. Georges Perec. (FRE.). 1987. pap. 8.95 (*0-7859-3222-4*, 2266025791) Fr & Eur.

Choses: Une Histoire des Annees Soixante. Georges Perec. Ed. by Jean M. Leblon. LC 71-84473. (Illus.). (Orig.). (FRE.). (C). 1969. pap. text ed. 14.95 (*0-89197-078-9*) Irvington.

Choses de la Vie. Paul Guimard. (Folio Ser.: No. 315). 149p. (FRE.). 1986. pap. 6.95 (*2-07-036315-5*) Schoenhof.

Choses de la Vie. Paul Guimard. (FRE.). 1973. pap. 10.95 (*0-7859-2301-2*, 2070363155) Fr & Eur.

Choses et Autres. Jacques Prevert. 264p. (FRE.). 1975. pap. 10.95 (*0-7859-2355-1*, 2070366464) Fr & Eur.

Choses et Autres. Jacques Prevert. (Folio Ser.: No. 646). (FRE.). 1975. pap. 8.95 (*2-07-036646-4*) Schoenhof.

Choses Nues. Andre Maurois. (Coll. Soleil). 284p. (FRE.). 1963. pap. 15.95 (*0-7859-1286-X*, 2070243125) Fr & Eur.

Choses Vues: 1870-1885 (Souvenirs, Journaux, Cahiers), 4 vols. Victor Hugo. Ed. by Hubert Juin. 544p. 1972. 3.95 (*0-685-73255-X*) Fr & Eur.

Choses Vues, Tome I (1830-1846) Victor Hugo. (FRE.). 1972. pap. 11.95 (*0-7859-2258-X*, 2070360113) Fr & Eur.

Choses Vues, Tome II (1847-1848) Victor Hugo. (FRE.). 1990. pap. 11.95 (*0-7859-2261-X*, 2070360474) Fr & Eur.

Choses Vues, Tome III (1849-1869) Victor Hugo. (FRE.). 1972. pap. 11.95 (*0-7859-2265-2*, 2070360911) Fr & Eur.

Choses Vues, Tome IV (1870-1885) Victor Hugo. 544p. (FRE.). 1972. pap. 11.95 (*0-7859-2268-7*, 2070361411) Fr & Eur.

Chosin: Heroic Ordeal of the Korean War. Eric Hammel. LC 89-27272. 1990. 24.95 (*0-89141-378-2*) Presidio Pr.

***Chosin: Heroic Ordeal of the Korean War.** Eric Hammel. LC 89-27272. 467p. 1994. pap. 14.95 (*0-89141-527-0*) Presidio Pr.

Chosin Few - North Korea. Turner Publishing Co., Staff. LC 89-50045. 248p. 1989. 48.00 (*0-938021-37-0*) Turner Pub KY.

Chosin Marine: Breakout from North Korea. W. J. Davis. 134p. 1985. pap. 11.00 (*1-885541-04-X*) Marine Bks.

Chosin Reservoir Campaign. 7th ed. Lynn Montross & Nicholas A. Canzona. (Elite Unit Ser.). 432p. 1986. reprint ed. 24.95 (*0-89839-098-2*) Battery Pr.

CHOSOVI of the Kachinas. Dean F. Herring. 275p. (Orig.). 1992. pap. 10.95 (*0-9621854-1-8*) Real Americana.

Chotankers: A Family History. A. Edward Foote. LC 82-6989. 336p. 1982. 19.95 (*0-943054-13-3*) Thornwood Bk.

Choteau Creek: A Sioux Reminiscence. Joseph Dudley. LC 91-39285. (Illus.). x, 179p. 1992. 22.50 (*0-8032-1690-4*) U of Nebr Pr.

Choteau Creek: A Sioux Reminiscence. Joseph I. Dudley. 176p. 1994. pap. 12.99 (*0-446-39519-6*) Warner Bks.

Chou-Yang Model for Elastic Reactions at High Energies. F. E-Aleem & M. Saleem. (Orig.). 1991. pap. text ed. 50.00 (*0-911767-51-7*) Hadronic Pr Inc.

Chouans. Honore De Balzac. (FRE.). 1972. pap. 12.95 (*0-7859-1694-6*, 2070360849) Fr & Eur.

Chouans. Honore De Balzac. (Folio Ser.: No. 84). (FRE.). pap. 9.95 (*2-07-036084-9*) Schoenhof.

Chouans. Honore De Balzac. (Classics Ser.). 1972. mass mkt. 9.95 (*0-14-044260-X*, Penguin Classics) Viking Penguin.

Chouinard: An Art Vision Betrayed. Robert Perine. LC 86-70036. (Illus.). 260p. 1986. 37.50 (*0-936725-00-1*) Artra Pub.

Choura: The Memoirs of Alexandra Danilova. Alexandra Danilova. LC 87-27496. (Illus.). 213p. 1988. reprint ed. pap. 11.95 (*0-88064-103-7*) Fromm Intl Pub.

Chow Chow. Anna K. Nicholas. (Illus.). 256p. 1989. 19.95 (*0-86622-029-1*, PS-812) TFH Pubns.

Chow Chow Champions, 1952-1982. Jan L. Freund. (Illus.). 170p. 1987. pap. 36.95 (*0-940808-35-8*) Camino E E & Bk.

Chow Chow Champions, 1983-1986. Camino E. E. & B. Co. Staff. (Illus.). 85p. 1988. pap. 28.95 (*0-940808-67-6*) Camino E E & Bk.

Chow-Chows. James Atkinson. (Pet Owner's Manuals Ser.). (Illus.). 80p. 1988. pap. 5.95 (*0-8120-3952-1*) Barron.

Chow Chows. Beverly Pisano. (Illus.). 125p. 1989. 11.95 (*0-86622-514-5*, KW089) TFH Pubns.

***Chowan County, North Carolina Marriage Bonds & Certificates, 1742-1868.** Francis T. Ingmire. 114p. 1994. lib. bdg. 37.00 (*0-8095-8024-1*); pap. 15.00 (*0-8095-8545-6*) Borgo Pr.

Choy Li Fut Kung Fu. Doc Fai Wong & Jane Hallander. LC 84-52683. (Illus.). 176p. (Orig.). 1985. pap. 9.95 (*0-86568-062-0*, 217) Unique Pubns.

CHP: The Conversational Historical Present in American English Narrative. Nessa Wolfson. 132p. 1982. 44.65 (*90-70176-61-0*); pap. 30.80 (*90-70176-60-2*) Mouton.

Chreia in Ancient Rhetoric, Vol. I: The Progymnasmata. Ronald F. Hock & Edward N. O'Neill. (Society of Biblical Literature Texts & Translations Ser.). (C). 1986. pap. 23.95 (*0-89130-847-4*) Scholars Pr GA.

Chrestomathia. Jeremy Bentham. Ed. by M. J. Smith & W. H. Burston. (Collected Works of Jeremy Bentham Ser.). (Illus.). 420p. 1984. 85.00 (*0-19-822610-1*) OUP.

Chrestomathie Arabe, 3 vols., Set. Antoine I. Silvestre De Sacy. LC 73-12556. reprint ed. 125.00 (*0-404-11233-1*) AMS Pr.

Chrestomathie de Papyrologie Arabe: Documents Relatis a la Vie Privee, Sociale et Administrative Dans les Premiers Siecles Islamiques. Raif G. Khoury. LC 91-32123. (Handbuch der Orientalistik Ser.: Vol. 1.2-2). (Illus.). xi, 260p. (ARA, FRE & GER.). 1993. 103.00 (*90-04-09551-9*) E J Brill.

Chrestomathie du Moyen Age. G. Paris & E. Langlois. 366p. 1970. 18.95 (*0-8288-7440-9*) Fr & Eur.

Chrestomathie Provencale. 6th ed. Karl F. Bartsch. LC 72-38500. (FRE.). reprint ed. 55.00 (*0-404-08346-3*) AMS Pr.

Chrestomathie Provencale (Tenth-Fifteenth Siecles) Karl Bartsch & Eduard Koschwitz. xi, 661p. 1971. reprint ed. write for info. (*0-318-71315-2*, Pub. by Georg Olms GW) Lubrecht & Cramer.

Chrestomathy of Vulgar Latin: With a Detailed Glossary & Bibliography. Henry F. Muller & Pauline Taylor. xvii, 315p. 1990. reprint ed. 54.60 (*3-487-09378-2*, Pub. by Georg Olms GW) Lubrecht & Cramer.

Chretien Bernanos. Hans U. Von Balthasar. 576p. (FRE.). 1970. pap. 31.95 (*0-7859-0926-5*, F87980) Fr & Eur.

Chretien de Troyes: Inventor of the Modern Novel. Foster E. Guyer. LC 73-168215. reprint ed. 19.50 (*0-404-02965-5*) AMS Pr.

Chretien de Troyes: The Story of the Grail or Perceval (Li Contesd del Graal) Ed. by Rupert T. Pickens. Tr. by William W. Kibler. LC 90-3025. (Library of Medieval Literature: Vol. 62A). 576p. 1990. 75.00 (*0-8240-4599-8*) Garland.

Chretien de Troyes & the German Middle Ages: Papers from an International Symposium. Ed. by Martin H. Jones & Roy Wisbey. (Arthurian Studies: No. XXVI). 352p. (ENG, FRE & GER.). (C). 1992. text ed. 71.00 (*0-85991-356-2*) Boydell & Brewer.

***Chretien de Troyes Revisited.** Karl D. Uitti & Michelle A. Freeman. (World Author Ser.: No. 841). 192p. 1994. text ed. 23.95x (*0-8057-4307-3*, Twayne) Macmillan.

Chris. Mark Dunster. (Rin Ser.: Pt. 14). (Orig.). 1978. pap. 4.00 (*0-89642-044-2*) Linden Pubs.

Chris Ahrens' Greenhouse. Chris Ahrens. (Illus.). 8p. 1990. 5.25 (*0-86619-136-4*) Vols Tech Asst.

Chris & Croc. Marcus Pfister. LC 93-46828. (Illus.). 32p. (J). (gr. k-3). 1994. 14.95 (*1-55858-273-8*); lib. bdg. 14.88 (*1-55858-274-6*) North-South Bks NYC.

Chris Batin's Twenty Great Alaska Fishing Adventures: A Travel - Planning Guide for Those Who Want the Best in Alaska Sportfishing Adventures. Christopher Batin. (Illus.). 224p. (Orig.). 1991. pap. 19.95 (*0-916771-09-1*) Alaska Angler.

Chris Burke. Bob Italia. LC 92-16037. (Reaching for the Stars Ser.). (J). 1992. lib. bdg. 12.94 (*1-56239-143-7*) Abdo & Dghtrs.

Chris Burke: Actor. Helen M. Geraghty. (Great Achievers: Lives of the Physically Challenged Ser.). (Illus.). (J). 1994. 18.95 (*0-7910-2081-9*, Am Art Analog); pap. write for info. (*0-7910-2094-0*, Am Art Analog) Chelsea Hse.

Chris Burke: He Overcame Down Syndrome. Gregory Lee. LC 93-18213. (Reaching Your Goal Bks.). (J). 1993. 14.60 (*0-86593-263-8*); 10.95 (*0-685-66611-5*) Rourke Corp.

Chris Chrisman Goes to College - & Faces the Challenges of Relativism, Individualism, & Pluralism. James W. Sire. LC 93-17816. 156p. (Orig.). 1993. pap. 9.99 (*0-8308-1656-9*, 1656) InterVarsity.

Chris Christophersen: A Play in Three Acts. Eugene O'Neill. LC 82-40135. 150p. 1982. 15.00 (*0-394-52531-0*) Random.

Chris de Burgh Story: From a Spark to a Flame. Dave Thompson. (Illus.). 96p. 1987. pap. 19.95 (*0-7119-0976-8*, OP43892) Omnibus NY.

Chris Finds the Answer. Sandra Klaus. (Illus.). 20p. (J). (gr. k-6). 1988. pap. text ed. 4.25 (*1-55976-127-X*) CEF Press.

***Chris Hani: Portrait of a South African Revolutionary.** Raymond Suttner. (Illus.). 160p. 1994. pap. 13.95 (*1-875284-81-8*, Pub. by Ocean Pr AT) Talman.

Chris Has An Accident. Jackie M. Kirby. Ed. by Nancy McCormack. (Illus.). 52p. (Orig.). (J). (gr. 3-4). 1987. pap. 5.95 (*0-942459-00-8*) McCormack Co.

Chris-in-the-Morning: Love, Life, & the Whole Karmic Enchilada. Ed. & Comp. by Louis Chunovic. LC 92-47372. 144p. 1993. pap. 8.95 (*0-8092-3762-8*) Contemp Bks.

Chris Mann on Grammar. Chris Mann. LC 90-61818. 90p. 1990. pap. 10.95 (*0-939044-30-7*) Lingua Pr.

***Chris McGregor & the Brotherhood of Breath.** Maxine McGregor. (Illus.). 260p. 1995. lib. bdg. 43.00 (*0-8095-6508-0*) Borgo Pr.

Chris McGregor & the Brotherhood of Breath: My Life with a South African Jazz Pioneer. Maxine McGregor. (Illus.). (Orig.). 1995. pap. write for info. (*0-318-72938-5*) Bamberger.

Chris Mullin: Star Forward. Michael J. Sullivan. LC 93-32727. (Sports Reports Ser.). (Illus.). 104p. (J). (gr. 4-10). 1994. lib. bdg. 17.95 (*0-89490-486-8*) Enslow Pubs.

Chris Mullin: Sure Shot. Terri Morgan & Shuel Thaler. LC 94-2704. (Achievers Ser.). (Illus.). 64p. (J). (gr. 4-9). 1994. lib. bdg. 13.50 (*0-8225-2882-7*, Lerner Publctns); pap. 5.95 (*0-8225-9664-4*, Lerner Publctns) Lerner Group.

Chris Sprague's Newcastle Inn Cookbook: Recipes & Menus from a Celebrated New England Inn. Chris Sprague. Ed. by Linda Ziedrich. LC 92-21366. (Illus.). 176p. (Orig.). 1992. 18.95 (*1-55832-050-4*); pap. 10.95 (*1-55832-049-0*) Harvard Common Pr.

Chrisgopher Columbus in Stowaway on the Santa Maria. Terry Cecil & Barbara Cecil. (Illus.). 32p. (Orig.). (J). (gr. k-6). 1992. lib. bdg. 4.00 (*0-9633016-0-8*) Infiniti.

Chrismon Service. James Edgar & Ellen Edgar. 20p. 1981. pap. text ed. 3.10 (*0-89536-500-6*, 0341) CSS OH.

ChrisNames: An Illustrated Guide to Chris Berman's Unique Characterizations of Sports Personalities. Chris Berman. (Illus.). 1994. pap. 8.95 (*0-8362-1753-5*) Andrews & McMeel.

Chrissy Cottontail. Dave Sargent & Pat Sargent. (Animal Pride Ser.). 64p. (J). (gr. 2-6). 1992. pap. write for info. (*1-56763-009-X*) Ozark Pub.

Christ. pap. 0.95 (*0-937408-14-X*) GMI Pubns Inc.

Christ. Charles Guignebert. (Citadel Library of the Mystic Arts). 1989. pap. 9.95 (*0-8065-1143-5*, Citadel Pr) Carol Pub Group.

Christ. John R. Stott. (Christian Basics Bible Studies). 64p. (Orig.). 1994. pap. 4.99 (*0-8308-2002-7*, 2002) InterVarsity.

***Christ: A Critical Review & Analysis of the Evidence of His Existence.** John E. Remsberg. 437p. (C). 1994. 29.95 (*0-87975-924-0*) Prometheus Bks.

Christ: The Experience of Jesus As Lord. Edward Schillebeeckx. 928p. 1983. pap. 19.95 (*0-8245-0605-7*) Crossroad NY.

Christ - Our Relationship with Everything. Bill Freeman. 40p. (Orig.). 1994. pap. 1.00 (*0-914271-57-1*) Mnstry Wrd.

Christ Above All. Robert C. Shannon. 224p. 1989. pap. 9.99 (*0-87403-568-6*, 3194) Standard Pub.

Christ All & in All. Ralph Robinson. 640p. 1992. reprint ed. 29.95 (*1-877611-49-2*) Soli Deo Gloria.

Christ All in All. Philip Henry. 10.99 (*0-87377-044-7*) GAM Pubns.

Christ among Other Gods. Erwin W. Lutzer. 1994. 12.99 (*0-8024-1648-9*) Moody.

Christ among the Welsh Miners. H. Elvit Lewis. 1987. pap. 8.99 (*0-88019-221-6*) Schmul Pub Co.

Christ among Us: A Modern Presentation of the Catholic Faith for Adults. 5th rev. ed. Anthony Wilhelm. LC 89-46468. 464p. 1990. pap. 9.95 (*0-00-001215-7*) Harper SF.

Christ & Baha'u'llah. George Townshend. LC 68-168. 116p. 1966. pap. 8.75 (*0-85398-005-5*) G Ronald Pub.

Christ & Christianity: Studies in the Formation of Christology. Reginald H. Fuller. Ed. by Robert Kahl. 144p. (Orig.). (C). 1994. pap. 15.00 (*1-56338-076-5*) TPI PA.

Christ & Christmas: A Poem. Mary M. Eddy. (Notable American Authors Ser.). 1992. reprint ed. lib. bdg. 75.00 (*0-7812-2755-0*) Rprt Serv.

Christ & Context: The Confrontation Between Gospel & Culture. Ed. by Hilary Regan & Alan J. Torrance. 288p. 1993. pap. text ed. 24.95 (*0-567-29235-5*, Pub. by T & T Clark UK) Bks Intl VA.

***Christ & Creation.** fac. ed. Colin E. Gunton. LC 92-43025. (Didsbury Lectures). 127p. 1992. reprint ed. pap. 36.20 (*0-7837-7956-9*, 2047712) Bks Demand.

Christ & Culture. H. Richard Niebuhr. 1956. pap. text ed. 13.00 (*0-06-130003-9*, TB3, Torch) HarpC.

Christ & His Associates in Voltairian Polemic: An Assault on the Trinity and the Two Natures. William H. Trapnell. (Stanford French & Italian Studies: Vol. 26). vi, 268p. 1982. pap. 46.50 (*0-915838-13-3*) Anma Libri.

Christ & His Church. Larry Christenson. (Trinity Bible Ser.). 160p. 1973. pap. 5.99 (*0-87123-550-1*) Bethany Hse.

Christ & His Church: Teacher Guide. Sandra Hall. 48p. (Orig.). 1985. pap. 9.99 (*0-87123-801-2*) Bethany Hse.

Christ & His Communities: Essays in Honor of Reginald H. Fuller. Ed. by Arland J. Hultgren & Barbara Hall. 184p. 1990. pap. 7.95 (*0-88028-104-9*, 1055) Forward Movement.

Christ & His Righteousness. E. J. Waggoner. (Pioneer Classics Ser.). 96p. (YA). (gr. 9 up). 1988. reprint ed. pap. 5.95 (*0-945460-01-5*) Upward Way.

Christ & Humanity. Ivar Asheim. LC 73-101426. 203p. (Orig.). reprint ed. pap. 57.90 (*0-685-15900-0*, 2026913) Bks Demand.

Christ & Krishna. J. M. Robertson. 1972. 59.95 (*0-87968-422-4*) Gordon Pr.

Christ & Krishna: The Path of Pure Devotion. Swami Bhaktipada. LC 87-17884. 190p. 1987. reprint ed. 10.95 (*0-932215-05-X*); reprint ed. pap. 4.95 (*0-932215-03-3*) Palace Pub.

Christ & Narcissus: Prayer in a Self-Centered World. Warren McWilliams. 160p. (Orig.). 1992. pap. 11.95 (*0-8361-3569-5*) Herald Pr.

Christ & Oriental Ideals. 5th ed. Swami Paramananda. 1989. pap. 5.95 (*0-911564-14-4*) Vedanta Ctr.

Christ & Reason: An Introduction to Ideas from Kant to Tyrrell. George W. Rutler. 212p. 1990. pap. 10.95 (*0-931888-38-7*) Christendom Pr.

Christ & the Bible. 3rd ed. John Wenham. LC 93-46090. 222p. 1994. reprint ed. pap. 10.99 (*0-8010-9733-9*) Baker Bk.

Christ & the Bodhisattva. Ed. by Donald S. Lopez, Jr. & Stephen C. Rockefeller. LC 86-14356. (Buddhist Studies). 274p. (C). 1987. 59.50 (*0-88706-401-9*); pap. 19.95 (*0-88706-402-7*) State U NY Pr.

Christ & the Church. Edward C. Wharton. 137p. (Orig.). 1981. pap. 7.95 (*1-878990-11-X*) Howard Pub LA.

Christ & the Colonel. Merrill Finley. 224p. 1993. pap. 10.00 (*0-911826-51-3*) Am Atheist.

Christ & the Cosmos. Edgar H. Andrews. 1986. pap. 7.99 (*0-85234-220-9*, Pub. by Evangel Pr UK) Presby & Reformed.

Christ & the Decree: Christology & Predestination in Reformed Theology from Calvin to Perkins. Richard A. Muller. LC 88-6296. 240p. 1988. pap. 12.99 (*0-8010-6231-4*) Baker Bk.

Christ & the Decree: Christology & Predestination in Reformed Theology from Calvin to Perkins. Richard A. Muller. LC 84-20117. (Studies in Historical Theology: Vol. 2). 244p. (C). 1986. lib. bdg. 30.00 (*0-939464-39-X*) Labyrinth Pr.

Christ & the Eastern Soul: Oriental Consciousness & Jesus. Charles C. Hall. 1977. lib. bdg. 59.95 (*0-8490-1613-4*) Gordon Pr.

Christ & the End of Meaning: The Theology of Passion. Paul Hessert. 256p. 1994. reprint ed. pap. text ed. 14.95 (*0-8264-0767-6*) Continuum.

Christ & the Gallows: Or, Reasons for the Abolition of Capital Punishment. Marvin H. Bovee. LC 82-45656. (Capital Punishment Ser.). 1983. reprint ed. 40.00 (*0-404-62403-0*) AMS Pr.

Christ & the Human Soul. 4th ed. Rudolf Steiner. 81p. 1984. pap. 10.95 (*0-85440-013-3*, Steinerbks) Anthroposophic.

Christ & the Inner Life. Truman G. Madsen. 6.95 (*0-88494-345-3*) Bookcraft Inc.

Christ & the Powers. rev. ed. Hendrik Berkhof. LC 62-13713. 80p. 1977. pap. 5.95 (*0-8361-1820-0*) Herald Pr.

Christ & the Spirit: Spirit-Christology in Trinitarian Perspectives. Ralph Del Colle. LC 92-47399. 1994. 39.95 (*0-19-507776-8*) OUP.

Christ & the Spiritual World: The Search for the Holy Grail. Rudolf Steiner. Tr. by C. Day & D. Osmond. 144p. 1983. reprint ed. pap. 12.95 (*0-88010-267-5*, Steinerbks) Anthroposophic.

Christ & Time: The Primitive Christian Conception of Time & History. Oscar Cullman. 1977. lib. bdg. 59.95 (*0-8490-1614-2*) Gordon Pr.

Christ & Violence. Ronald J. Sider. LC 79-9239. (Christian Peace Shelf Ser.). 104p. 1979. pap. 5.95 (*0-8361-1895-2*) Herald Pr.

***Christ & Your Problem.** Jay Adames. Tr. by Deborah Lau. 33p. (CHI.). 1993. pap. 1.50 (*1-56582-034-7*) Christ Renew Min.

Christ & Your Problems. Jay E. Adams. 33p. 1973. pap. 1.75 (*0-87552-011-1*) Presby & Reformed.

Christ as Common Ground: A Study of Christianity & Hinduism. Kathleen Healy. LC 90-34260. 224p. 1990. text ed. 24.95 (*0-8207-0227-7*) Duquesne.

Christ Ascended: A Study in the Significance of the Ascension of Jesus Christ in the New Testament. Brian K. Donne. 1983. pap. text ed. 11.95 (*0-85364-336-9*) Attic Pr.

Christ at the Centre: Selected Issues in Christology. Dermot Lane. 154p. 1989. pap. 24.00 (*1-85390-058-3*, Pub. by Veritas IE) St Mut.

Christ at the Crossroads. Chuck Swindoll. 1991. pap. 4.99 (*0-8499-8427-0*) Word Inc.

Christ, Avatar of Sacrificial Love. rev. ed. Torkom Saraydarian. LC 74-11760. 1994. pap. 12.00 (*0-911794-69-7*) Aqua Educ.

Christ, Avatar of Sacrificial Love. 2nd rev. ed. Torkom Saraydarian. LC 74-11760. 1994. 16.00 (*0-911794-70-0*) Aqua Educ.

Christ B. C. Becoming Closer Friends with the Hidden Christ of the Old Testament. Bill Myers. Ed. by Annette Parrish. LC 90-35816. 120p. (Orig.). 1990. pap. 6.99 (*0-8307-1304-2*, 5184459) Regal.

Christ before the Manger: The Life & Times of the Preincarnate Christ. Ron Rhodes. LC 92-23993. 288p. 1992. pap. 13.99 (*0-8010-7766-4*) Baker Bk.

Christ Book: What Did He Really Say? Christopher Hills. Ed. by Norah Hills. LC 80-5865. (Illus.). 224p. (C). 1980. 15.95 (*0-685-05195-1*); text ed. 10.95 (*0-916438-37-6*) Univ of Trees.

Christ-Care: Bible Study for Personal & Group Use. Lois Qualben. 124p. (Orig.). 1991. pap. text ed. 5.95 (*1-880292-01-7*) LangMarc.

Christ-Care Leaders Commentary. James Qualben. 150p. 1992. pap. 6.95 (*1-880292-06-8*) LangMarc.

Christ-Centered Family. Raymond T. Brock. LC 76-46036. (Radiant Life Ser.). 128p. 1977. teacher ed 4.50 (*0-88243-173-0*, 32-0173); pap. 2.95 (*0-88243-903-0*, 02-0903) Gospel Pub.

***Christ-Centered Living.** Robert L. Millet. 1994. 12.95 (*0-88494-934-6*) Bookcraft Inc.

Christ-Centered Personality Development: Looking Inward to Christ to Reach Outward the Process of Sanctification. Robert Abarno. 110p. 1991. pap. text ed. write for info. (*0-9631575-5-8*) R Abarno.

Christ-Centered Personality Development: Looking Inward to Christ to Reach Outward, the Process of Sanctification. 3rd ed. 1994. write for info. (*0-9631575-7-4*) R Abarno.

Christ-Centered Preaching: Redeeming the Expository Sermon. Bryan Chapell. LC 93-46468. (Illus.). 376p. (C). 1994. 24.99 (*0-8010-2586-9*) Baker Bk.

Christ Child Goes to Court. Wayne R. Swanson. 284p. (C). 1989. 39.95 (*0-87722-638-5*) Temple U Pr.

Christ Child Goes to Court. Wayne R. Swanson. 1992. pap. 22.95 (*0-87722-958-9*) Temple U Pr.

Christ, Church & Society: Essays on John Baillie & Donald Baillie. Ed. by David Fergusson. 307p. 1993. text ed. 39.95 (*0-567-09617-3*, Pub. by T & T Clark UK) Bks Intl VA.

Christ Church Cook Book. Comp. by Women's Auxillary of Christ's Church. 1950. pap. 4.50 (*0-87517-006-4*) Dietz.

***Christ Church, Frederica Cookbook.** Women of Christ Church, Frederica. (Illus.). 301p. Date not set. 20.00 (*0-9644973-0-1*) Christ Ch.

***Christ Church, Philadelphia: The Nation's Church in a Changing City.** Deborah M. Gough. (Illus.). 372p. 1995. text ed. 34.95 (*0-8122-3272-0*) U of Pa Pr.

***Christ Church, Philadelphia: The Nation's Church in a Changing City.** Deborah M. Gough. (Illus.). 372p. 1995. pap. text ed. 14.95 (*0-8122-1552-4*) U of Pa Pr.

Christ Commission. Og Mandino. 1983. mass mkt. 5.50 (*0-553-27742-1*) Bantam.

Christ Consciousness. Comp. by Association for Research & Enlightenment, Readings Research Dept. (Library: Vol. 11). 277p. 1980. 19.95 (*0-87604-124-1*, 1111) ARE Pr.

***Christ Consciousness: The Pure Self Within You.** Norman Paulsen. (Illus.). 496p. (Orig.). 1994. pap. 19.95 (*0-941848-05-1*) Builders Pub.

Christ Continuing. James A. Stewart. 1965. pap. 1.99 (*1-56632-039-9*) Revival Lit.

Christ Crucified. C. H. Spurgeon. 1978. pap. 0.50 (*1-56186-337-8*) Pilgrim Pubns.

Christ Crucified: Meditations of a Benedictine Monk. Monk of Farne. Ed. by Hugh Farmer. LC 93-74850. Orig. Title: Monk of Farne. 164p. 1994. reprint ed. pap. 12.95 (*0-87061-202-6*) Chr Classics.

Christ Dans la Theologie Byzantine see Christ in Eastern Christian Thought

Christ Denied. Paul A. Wickens. LC 82-50585. 49p. 1982. pap. 2.00 (*0-89555-183-7*) TAN Bks Pubs.

Christ Diet: Connect Your Cells to Your Soul. Charles J. Hunt, III. (Illus.). 224p. 1991. pap. 14.95 (*0-9630377-1-4*) HeartQuake.

Christ Enthroned in Man. Cora D. Fillmore. 112p. 1937. 5.95 (*0-87159-014-X*) Unity Bks.

Christ-Esteem. Don Matzat. LC 89-27039. 144p. 1990. pap. 7.99 (*0-89081-784-7*) Harvest Hse.

Christ, Ethics, & Tragedy: Essays in Honour of Donald MacKinnon. Ed. by Kenneth Surin. 224p. 1989. 64.95 (*0-521-34137-X*) Cambridge U Pr.

Christ, Faith & History. S. W. Sykes & J. P. Clayton. LC 70-176257. (Cambridge Studies in Christology). (Illus.). 280p. 1978. pap. 21.95 (*0-521-29325-1*) Cambridge U Pr.

***Christ for Real: How to Grow into God's Likeness.** Charles W. Price. 192p. 1995. pap. 4.99 (*0-8254-3550-1*) Kregel.

Christ for the World. Bertrand De Margerie. Tr. by Malachy Carroll. pap. 10.00 (*0-8199-0485-6*, Frncscn Herld) Franciscan Pr.

Christ Formed in Us. Bill Freeman. 25p. (Orig.). 1994. pap. 0.75 (*0-914271-56-3*) Mnstry Wrd.

Christ, God's Final Word to Man: An Exposition of the Epistle to the Hebrews. Herman A. Hoyt. pap. 7.99 (*0-88469-009-1*) BMH Bks.

Christ-Haunted Landscape: Faith & Doubt in Southern Fiction. Susan Ketchin. 352p. 1994. text ed. 40.00 (*0-87805-669-6*); pap. 16.95 (*0-87805-670-X*) U Pr of Miss.

Christ Highway. Genevah D. Seivertson. LC 81-69023. 184p. 1982. pap. 7.25 (*0-87516-465-X*) DeVorss.

Christ Idea. Max Kappeler. LC 79-868476. 32p. 1975. pap. 4.50 (*0-85241-079-4*) Kappeler Inst Pub.

Christ Impulse & the Development of the Ego-Consciousness. rev. ed. Rudolf Steiner. 100p. 1991. reprint ed. pap. 13.50 (*0-8334-2013-5*, Spir Rsch Edit) Garber Comm.

Christ in a Pluralistic Age. John B. Cobb, Jr. LC 74-820. 286p. 1976. pap. 15.99 (*0-664-24522-6*, Westminster) Westminster John Knox.

Christ in a Poncho: Testimonials of the Nonviolent Struggles in Latin America. Adolfo Perez Esquivel. Ed. by Charles Antoine. Tr. by Robert R. Barr. LC 82-18760. 143p. reprint ed. pap. 40.80 (*0-8357-8550-5*, 2034892) Bks Demand.

Christ in All the Scriptures. 7.99 (*1-55748-066-4*) Barbour & Co.

Christ in Catastrophe. Emil Fuchs. (C). 1949. pap. 3.00 (*0-87574-049-9*) Pendle Hill.

Christ in Christian Tradition: From the Apostolic Age to Chalcedon, Vol. 1. rev. ed. Aloys Grillmeier. Tr. by John S. Bowden. LC 75-13456. 451p. 1975. 38.00 (*0-8042-0492-6*, John Knox) Westminster John Knox.

Christ in Christian Tradition: From the Council of Chalcedon (451) to Gregory the Great (590-604), Vol. 2. Aloys Grillmeier & Theresia Hainthaler. Tr. by Paulin Allen & John Cawte. 544p. 1994. 50.00 (*0-664-21997-7*) Westminster John Knox.

Christ in Christmas: A Family Advent Celebration. James M. Boice et al. LC 89-62891. 80p. 1989. 7.00 (*0-89109-605-1*) NavPress.

Christ in Concrete. Pietro Di Donato. LC 39-10762. 320p. 1975. 8.95 (*0-672-52161-X*, Bobbs); pap. 5.95 (*0-672-52187-3*, Bobbs) Macmillan.

Christ in Concrete: A Novel. Pietro Di Donato. LC 92-39372. 1993. pap. 5.95 (*0-451-52575-2*, Sig Classics) NAL-Dutton.

Christ in East & West. Ed. by Paul R. Fries & Tiran Nersoyan. LC 87-7699. 240p. 1987. 18.95 (*0-86554-267-8*, H228) Mercer Univ Pr.

Christ in Easter: A Family Celebration of Holy Week. Charles M. Colson et al. LC 90-60399. 80p. (Orig.). 1990. pap. 7.00 (*0-89109-309-5*) NavPress.

Christ in Eastern Christian Thought. John Meyendorff. LC 75-31977. Orig. Title: Le Christ Dans la Theologie Byzantine. 248p. 1975. pap. 12.95 (*0-913836-27-3*) St Vladimirs.

Christ in His Time & Ours. Arthur A. Vogel. LC 92-8034. 112p. (Orig.). 1992. pap. 8.95 (*1-55612-555-0*, LL1555) Sheed & Ward MO.

Christ in India. Bede Griffiths. 1984. pap. 11.95 (*0-87243-134-7*) Templegate.

Christ in Islam & Christianity. Neal Robinson. LC 90-36383. 248p. 1991. 64.50 (*0-7914-0558-3*); pap. 21.95 (*0-7914-0559-1*) State U NY Pr.

***Christ in North American.** Delbert Curtis. 280p. (YA). Date not set. write for info. (*1-883266-24-6*) Srv Consolidate.

Christ in Our Place: The Humanity of God in Christ for the Reconciliation of the World: Essays Presented to Professor James Torrance. Ed. by T. A. Hart & Daniel P. Thimmell. LC 90-21238. (Princeton Theological Monograph Ser.: No. 25). (Orig.). 1991. pap. 25.00 (*1-55635-009-0*) Pickwick.

Christ in Relation to Lucifer & Ahriman. Rudolf Steiner. Tr. by Peter Mollenhauer. 1978. pap. 3.95 (*0-910142-77-7*) Anthroposophic.

Christ in Shakespeare's Dramas & Sonnets. C. Ellis. 1972. 59.95 (*0-87968-860-2*) Gordon Pr.

Christ in the Bible Commentary, Vol. 1: Genesis, Exodus, Leviticus, Numbers, Deuteronomy, 6 vols. LC 92-70937. 379p. 1992. reprint ed. 24.99 (*0-87509-490-2*) Chr Pubns.

Christ in the Bible Commentary, Vol. 2: Joshua, Judges, Ruth, 1 & 2 Samuel, 1 & 2 Kings, 1 & 2 Chronicles. rev. ed. A. B. Simpson. LC 92-70937. 415p. 1993. 24.99 (*0-87509-494-5*) Chr Pubns.

Christ in the Bible Commentary, Vol. 3: Kings, Prophets, Psalms, Isaiah. rev. ed. A. B. Simpson. LC 92-70937. 500p. 1993. 24.99 (*0-87509-500-3*) Chr Pubns.

Christ in the Bible Commentary, Vol. 4: Matthew, Mark, Luke, John, Acts. rev. ed. A. B. Simpson. LC 92-70937. 450p. 1993. 24.99 (*0-87509-501-1*) Chr Pubns.

Christ in the Bible Commentary, Vol. 5: Romans to Colossians. A. B. Simpson. LC 92-70937. 1994. text ed. 24.99 (*0-87509-502-X*) Chr Pubns.

Christ in the Bible Commentary, Vol. 6: Thessalonians to Revelation. A. B. Simpson. LC 92-70937. 1994. text ed. 24.99 (*0-87509-503-8*) Chr Pubns.

Christ in the Brother: According to the Rule of St. Benedict. rev. ed. Fidelis Ruppert & Anselm Gruen. Ed. by Alphonse M. Lauer. Tr. by Gregory J. Roettger. (Schuyler Spiritual Ser.: Vol. 2). 61p. 1992. pap. text ed. 3.60 (*1-56788-001-0*, 10-002) BMH Pubns.

Christ in the Christian Tradition, Vol. 2, Pt. 1. Aloys Grillmeier. Tr. by Pauline Allen & John Cawte. 1987. 38.00 (*0-8042-0493-4*, John Knox) Westminster John Knox.

Christ in the Communist Prisons see In God's Underground

Christ in the Drama: A Study of the Influence of Christ on the Drama of England & America. Fred Eastman. LC 79-167336. (Essay Index Reprints - Shaffer Lectures of Northwestern University, 1946). 1977. reprint ed. 18.95 (*0-8369-2647-1*) Ayer.

Christ in the Home. Robert Taylor, Jr. 1983. pap. 7.50 (*0-89137-314-4*) Quality Pubns.

Christ in the Passover. Ceil Rosen & Moishe Rosen. LC 77-10689. (C). 1978. pap. 5.99 (*0-8024-1392-7*) Moody.

Christ in the Psalms. Brian McNeil. 104p. (Orig.). 1980. pap. 4.95 (*0-905092-87-2*, Pub. by Veritas Publns IE) Ignatius Pr.

Christ in the Tabernacle. A. B. Simpson. LC 85-70720. 150p. 1985. pap. 6.99 (*0-87509-361-2*) Chr Pubns.

Christ in You. 224p. 1983. reprint ed. pap. 7.95 (*0-87516-506-0*) DeVorss.

***Christ Is a Native American.** Achiel Peelman. 285p. (Orig.). 1995. pap. 19.95 (*1-57075-047-5*) Orbis Bks.

Christ Is All. James A. Stewart. 1965. pap. 1.99 (*1-56632-038-0*) Revival Lit.

Christ Is Coming! Celebrating Advent, Christmas & Epiphany. Theresa Cotter. 134p. 1992. 6.95 (*0-86716-157-4*) St Anthony Mess Pr.

Christ Is Community: The Christologies of the New Testament. Jerome H. Neyrey. LC 85-47753. (Good News Studies: Vol. 13). 229p. 1985. pap. 12.95 (*0-8146-5465-7*) Liturgical Pr.

Christ Is in Our Midst: Letters from a Russian Monk. John Skhi-Igumen. Tr. by Esther Williams. LC 80-10530. 168p. (Orig.). 1980. reprint ed. pap. 7.95 (*0-913836-64-8*) St Vladimirs.

Christ Is Passing By. Josemaria Escriva. LC 74-78783. 276p. 1990. reprint ed. pap. 9.95 (*0-933932-04-9*) Scepter Pubs.

***Christ Is Risen: Celebrating Lent, Easter & Pentecost.** Theresa Cotter. 248p. 1994. 9.95 (*0-86716-200-7*) St Anthony Mess Pr.

Christ is Risen: The Paschal Sermons of Metropolitan Philaret of Moscow. Metropolitan of Moscow, Philaret Staff. 1991. pap. 5.95 (*0-89981-118-3*) Eastern Orthodox.

***Christ Jesus Lay Enchained by Death.** Johann S. Bach. 48p. 1994. 7.00 (*0-9643394-0-4*) Stonehill MI.

Christ, Justice & Peace: Toward a Theology of the State. Eberhard Jungel. Tr. by D. Bruce Hamill & Alan J. Torrance. 112p. 1992. pap. text ed. 17.95 (*0-567-29212-6*, Pub. by T & T Clark UK) Bks Intl VA.

Christ Krishna & You. Swami Venkatesananda. 168p. (Orig.). 1983. write for info. (*0-318-57642-2*) Chiltern Yoga.

***Christ Life.** A. B. Simpson. 120p. Date not set. pap. text ed. write for info. (*0-614-02761-6*) Christ Stewards.

Christ Life. Albert B. Simpson. LC 80-68837. 96p. 1980. pap. 2.99 (*0-87509-291-8*) Chr Pubns.

Christ Lore. F. W. Hackwood. 1972. 59.95 (*0-87968-861-0*) Gordon Pr.

Christ Loved the Church. William MacDonald. 1956. pap. 5.95 (*0-937396-09-5*) Walterick Pubs.

Christ Men Can Follow. Brown Landone. 24p. 1966. reprint ed. spiral bd. 2.20 (*0-7873-1255-X*) Mokelumne.

Christ Mystery in Relation to the Secret of Pentecost. Rudolf Steiner. 1986. pap. 2.50 (*0-916786-87-0*, Saint George Pubns) R Steiner Col Pubns.

***Christ Object Lessons.** Ellen G. White. (ASI Ser.). 184p. 1990. pap. 0.75 (*0-8163-0828-4*) Pacific Pr Pub Assn.

Christ of Cynewulf. Cynewulf. (BCL1-PR English Literature Ser.). 294p. 1992. reprint ed. lib. bdg. 79.00 (*0-7812-7164-9*) Rprt Serv.

Christ of Cynewulf: A Poem in Three Parts; the Advent, the Ascension, & the Last Judgement. Cynewulf. Ed. by Albert S. Cook. LC 74-114906. (Select Bibliographies Reprint Ser.). 1977. 28.95 (*0-8369-5310-X*) Ayer.

Christ of Cynewulf: A Poem in Three Parts; the Advent, the Ascension, & the Last Judgement. Albert S. Cook. (Select Bibliographies Reprint Ser.). 1982. reprint ed. lib. bdg. 13.95 (*0-8290-0846-2*) Irvington.

Christ of Cynewulf: A Poem in Three Parts; the Advent, the Ascension, & the Last Judgement. Cynewulf. Ed. by Albert S. Cook. LC 73-178524. reprint ed. 32.50 (*0-404-56538-7*) AMS Pr.

Christ of Michelangelo: An Essay on Carnal Spirituality. John W. Dixon, Jr. LC 93-47181. (USF South Florida - St. Louis - Rochester Studies on Religion & the Social Order: Vol. 6). 228p. 1994. 74.95 (*1-55540-944-X*, 245006) Scholars Pr GA.

Christ of the Apocalypse. C. Paul Willis. 210p. (Orig.). 1993. pap. 8.99 (*1-56043-104-0*) Destiny Image.

Christ of the Covenants. O. Palmer Robertson. 1981. pap. 9.99 (*0-87552-418-4*) Presby & Reformed.

Christ of the Twenty-First Century. Ewert H. Cousins. 224p. 1994. reprint ed. pap. text ed. 14.95 (*0-8264-0699-8*) Continuum.

Christ on the Jewish Road. Richard Wurmbrand. (Orig.). pap. text ed. 5.00 (*0-88264-015-1*) Living Sacrifice Bks.

***Christ on the Rue Jacob.** Severo Sarduy. Tr. by Juan Goytisolo et al. LC 94-37259. 144p. 1995. pap. 12.95 (*1-56279-075-7*) Mercury Hse Inc.

Christ or Aquinas? Exploring the New Age Movement. Godfred Danneels. 53p. 1991. 3.95 (*0-85390-109-0*, Pub. by Veritas Publns IE) Ignatius Pr.

Christ or Baal. Millie Smith. 128p. (Orig.). 1991. pap. 6.95 (*0-927022-03-6*) CHJ Pub.

Christ or Chaos? Kenneth T. Glasziou. 1994. pap. 13.95 (*0-533-10886-1*) Vantage.

Christ Our Example. Caroline Fry. 155p. 1976. reprint ed. pap. 4.99 (*0-87377-040-4*) GAM Pubns.

Christ, Our Mother of Mercy: Divine Mercy & Compassion in the Theology of the Shewings of Julian of Norwich. Margaret A. Palliser. LC 92-24301. xiv, 262p. (C). 1992. lib. bdg. 129.25 (*3-11-013558-2*) De Gruyter.

Christ, Our Pattern & Plan. John C. Whitcomb, Jr. 1979. pap. 1.50 (*0-88469-031-8*) BMH Bks.

Christ Our Savior. E. G. White. (Pioneer Ser.). (Illus.). 160p. (YA). (gr. 5 up). 1989. reprint ed. pap. 8.95 (*0-945460-05-8*) Upward Way.

Christ Our Savior. E. G. White. (Pioneer Ser.). (Illus.). 176p. (SPA.). (YA). (gr. 5 up). 1990. reprint ed. pap. 8.95 (*0-945460-10-4*) Upward Way.

***Christ Our Sure Foundation.** Marc Kolden. 1995. pap. write for info. (*0-7880-0499-9*) CSS OH.

Christ Outside the Gate: Mission Beyond Christendom. Orlando E. Costas. LC 82-7892. 272p. (Orig.). 1982. pap. 16.95 (*0-88344-147-0*) Orbis Bks.

Christ Papers, Vol. I. LC 82-90717. 150p. (Orig.). pap. 5.95 (*0-937408-22-0*) GMI Pubns Inc.

Christ, Plato, Hermes Trismegistus, Vol. 1, 2 pts. The Dawn of Printing. Catalogue of the Incunabula in the Bibliotheca Philosophica Hermetica. Ed. by Margaret L. Ford. (Illus.). 410p. 1990. 250.00 (*90-6004-406-1*, Pub. by B De Graaf NE) Coronet Bks.

Christ Principle & True Christianity to Be. Marie B. Hall. (Illus.). 1973. 27.50 (*0-938760-03-3*) Veritat Found.

Christ, Resurrection Life. Valarie Owen. 268p. (Orig.). 1985. pap. text ed. 7.95 (*0-914307-32-0*) R Tilton Ministries.

Christ Returns to the Soviets. Greg Gulley & Kim Parker. LC 93-77300. 1993. pap. 9.99 (*1-56384-041-3*) Huntington Hse.

Christ Revealed. Thomas Taylor. LC 79-10885. 1979. reprint ed. 60.00 (*0-8201-1334-4*) Schol Facsimiles.

Christ Revealed: The History of the Neotypological Lyric in the English Renaissance. Ira Clark. LC 82-2696. (University of Florida Humanities Monographs: No. 51). xiv, 218p. 1982. pap. 24.95 (*0-8130-0712-7*) U Press Fla.

Christ Reveals Himself to Daisy's Co-Workers. (Illus.). 100p. (Orig.). 1987. pap. 9.95 (*0-944039-04-9*) Van Winkle Pr.

Christ S'Est Arrete a Eboli. Carlo Levi. (FRE.). 1977. pap. 11.95 (*0-7859-4085-5*) Fr & Eur.

Christ Spirit: The Eschatology of Shaker Christianity. Kathleen P. Deignan. LC 91-40688. (American Theological Library Association Monograph: No. 29). 316p. 1992. 39.50 (*0-8108-2489-2*) Scarecrow.

Christ Stopped at Eboli. Carlo Levi. Tr. by Frances Frenaye. 268p. 1947. pap. 10.00 (*0-374-50316-8*) FS&G.

Christ the Center. Dietrich Bonhoeffer. 1978. pap. 11.00 (*0-06-060811-0*) Harper SF.

Christ the Center: A New Translation. Dietrich Bonhoeffer. LC 78-4747. (Harper's Ministers Paperback Library). 1978. pap. 7.95 (*0-06-060815-3*, RD 285) Harper SF.

Christ: The Christian Life: Important Steps for Our Growth in Christ. Kirk Eland. 210p. (Orig.). 1993. pap. 5.00 (*0-914271-50-4*) Mnstry Wrd.

Christ, the Divine Network: Reflections on the Gospels for the A-Cycle. Joseph G. Donders. LC 86-718. 224p. reprint ed. pap. 63.90 (*0-8357-4053-6*, 2034869) Bks Demand.

***Christ, the Educator.** Clement Alexandria. Tr. by Simon P. Wood. LC 66-20313. (Fathers of the Church Ser.: Vol. 23). 333p. Date not set. reprint ed. pap. 95.00 (*0-7837-9142-9*, 2049942) Bks Demand.

Christ the Eternal Son. A. W. Tozer. LC 91-58235. 1991. 7.99 (*0-87509-472-4*) Chr Pubns.

Christ the Fountaine of Life, Or, Sundry Choyce Sermons on Part of the Fifth Chapter of the First Epistle of St. John. John Cotton. LC 75-141107. (Research Library of Colonial Americana). 1972. reprint ed. 26.95 (*0-405-03321-4*) Ayer.

Christ the Great Physician. Gordon Lindsay. 1960. 1.95 (*0-89985-024-3*) Christ for the Nations.

Christ the Healer. F. F. Bosworth. LC 73-17492. 241p. 1980. pap. 8.99 (*0-8007-5124-8*) Revell.

Christ the Invisible Phenomena. Dia Baldwin. 80p. 1994. pap. 11.95 (*0-8059-3510-X*) Dorrance.

***Christ the King, Lord of History.** Anne W. Carroll. LC 93-61594. 472p. (YA). (gr. 10-12). 1994. pap. text ed. 20.00 (*0-89555-503-4*) TAN Bks Pubs.

Christ: The Living Water: The Catholic Church in Mississippi. Cleta S. Ellington. Ed. by Janna P. Avalon. LC 88-92391. (Illus.). 600p. (Orig.). 1989. pap. 17.95 (*0-9621536-0-5*) MS Today.

Christ the Lord: The Reformation & Lordship Salvation. Ed. by Michael S. Horton. LC 92-26910. (CURE Book Ser.). 304p. 1992. pap. 14.99 (*0-8010-4374-3*) Baker Bk.

Christ the Placenta. David Arthur Bickimer. LC 82-24097. 239p. (Orig.). 1983. pap. 12.95 (*0-89135-034-9*) Religious Educ.

Christ the Sacrament of the Encounter with God. E. Schillebeeckx. LC 63-17144. 240p. 1987. reprint ed. pap. 15.95 (*0-934134-72-3*) Sheed & Ward MO.

Christ the Savior & Christ Myth. rev. ed. Swami Prajnanananda. 1961. 7.95 (*0-87481-652-1*, Pub. by Advaita Ashrama II) Vedanta Pr.

Christ the Sum of All Spiritual Things. Watchman Nee. Tr. by Stephen Kaung. 96p. 1973. pap. 3.50 (*0-935008-14-4*) Christian Fellow Pubs.

Christ the Tiger: A Postscript to Dogma. 2nd ed. Thomas Howard. LC 89-81432. 148p. 1990. pap. 9.95 (*0-89870-279-8*) Ignatius Pr.

Christ the Way: The Christology of Guerric of Igny. John Morson. (Cistercian Studies: NO.25). 1978. 11.95 (*0-87907-825-1*) Cistercian Pubns.

Christ Unmasked: The Meaning of the Life of Jesus in German Politics. Marilyn C. Massey. LC 82-8547. (Studies in Religion). 192p. reprint ed. pap. 54.80 (*0-7837-2463-2*, 2042616) Bks Demand.

Christ We Know. John Booty. LC 87-6779. (Illus.). 174p. (Orig.). 1987. pap. 9.95 (*0-936384-48-4*) Cowley Pubns.

Christ Who Is Hidden. Burton F. Blair. 1991. pap. 5.75 (*1-55673-295-3*, 9128) CSS OH.

Christ Will See You Through. Richard M. Cromie. 60p. (Orig.). 1985. pap. 1.50 (*0-914733-04-4*) Desert Min.

Christ Without Absolutes: A Study of the Christology of Ernst Troeltsch. Sarah Coakley. 224p. 1995. reprint ed. pap. 19.95 (*0-19-826374-0*) OUP.

Christ Without Myth: A Study Based on the Theology of Rudolf Bultmann. Schubert M. Ogden. LC 79-10284. 192p. 1991. reprint ed. pap. text ed. 9.95 (*0-87074-172-1*) SMU Press.

Christ Yesterday & Today. Carol Cowgill & James P. Campbell. 141p. (Orig.). 1986. student ed 8.95 (*1-55588-125-4*) TEL Pubs.

Christa McAuliffe: A Teacher in Space. Corrine J. Naden. (J). (gr. 4-7). 1992. pap. 4.95 (*1-878841-58-0*) Millbrook Pr.

Christa McAuliffe: Teacher in Space. Corinne J. Naden & Rose Blue. (Gateway Biographies Ser.). (Illus.). 48p. (J). (gr. 2-4). 1991. lib. bdg. 12.90 (*1-56294-046-5*) Millbrook Pr.

Christa Naher. (Illus.). 104p. 1991. 55.00 (*3-89322-199-9*, Pub. by Edition Cantz GW) Dist Art Pubs.

Christa Wolf: Literature & the Conscience of History. Myra N. Love. LC 91-17401. (DDR-Studien - East German Studies: Vol. 6). 202p. (C). 1992. text ed. 42.95 (*0-8204-1651-7*) P Lang Pubs.

Christa Wolf's Utopian Vision: From Marxism to Feminism. Anna K. Kuhn. (Cambridge Studies in German). (Illus.). 296p. 1988. 69.95 (*0-521-32233-2*) Cambridge U Pr.

Christabel. Samuel Taylor Coleridge. LC 91-30898. 82p. 1991. reprint ed. 35.00 (*1-85477-063-2*, Pub. by Woodstock Bks UK) Cassell.

C

An Asterisk (*) at the beginning of an entry indicates that the title is appearing in BIP for the first time. 1237

Christabel Crocodile's Birthday Egg. Helga Knuppel. LC 92-24360. (Illus.). 32p. (J). (ps-3). 1993. 13.95 (1-56656-113-2, Crocodile Bks) Interlink Pub.
Christbook, Matthew, Vol. 1, 1-12. Frederick Bruner. 475p. 1987. write for info. (0-8499-0526-5) Word Inc.
Christchurch Priory: Theoretical Projects. Bernard Tschumi. (Illus.). 96p. 1994. pap. 25.00 (1-85490-382-9, Academy Edits) St Martin.
Christen Kobke. Sanford Schwartz. LC 92-20771. (Illus.). 144p. 1992. 35.00 (0-943221-15-3) Timken Pubs.
Christendom & Christianity in the Middle Ages: The Relations Between Religion, Church, & Society. Adriaan H. Bredero. Tr. by Diana L. Beitzel. 416p. 1994. 29.99 (0-8028-3692-5) Eerdmans.
***Christendom & Its Discontents: Exclusion, Persecution, & Rebellion, 1000-1500.** Ed. by Scott L. Waugh & Peter Diehl. 325p. (C). 1995. write for info. (0-521-47183-4) Cambridge U Pr.
Christened Chinaman. Andrei Bely. Tr. by Thomas R. Beyer. LC 91-32723. 187p. (Orig.). 1991. pap. 12.00 (1-55779-042-6) Hermitage.
Christening. Roger Elwood. 258p. 1989. pap. 8.99 (0-89081-736-7) Harvest Hse.
Christening: The Making of Christians. Mark Searle. LC 80-19454. (Illus.). 178p. (Orig.). (C). 1980. reprint ed. pap. text ed. 6.50 (0-8146-1183-4) Liturgical Pr.
Christening Day Murder. Lee Harris. 1993. mass mkt. 4.50 (0-449-14871-8) Fawcett.
Christening Pagan Mysteries: Erasmus in Pursuit of Wisdom. Marjorie O. Boyle. LC 81-134156. (Erasmus Studies: No. 5). 189p. reprint ed. pap. 53.90 (0-8357-4722-0, 2037637) Bks Demand.
Christensen's Physics of Diagnostic Radiology. 4th ed. Thomas S. Curry, III et al. LC 90-5586. 522p. 1990. text ed. 52.50 (0-8121-1310-1) Williams & Wilkins.
Christensen's Ultimate Movie, TV & Rock 'N' Roll Directory. 3rd ed. Roger Christensen & Karen Christensen. 1006p. 1988. 39.95 (0-9608038-3-1) Cardiff.
Christentum am Roten Meer, Vol. 1. Franz Altheim & Ruth Stiehl. (C). 1971. 346.15 (3-11-003790-4) De Gruyter.
Christentum am Roten Meer, Vol. 2. Franz Altheim & Ruth Stiehl. (C). 1973. 346.15 (3-11-003791-2) De Gruyter.
Christentumsgeschichte und Wahrheitsbewusstsein: Studien zur Theologie Emanuel Hirschs. Ed. by Joachim Ringleben. (Theologische Bibliothek Toepelmann Ser.: Vol. 50). vii, 254p. (GER.). (C). 1991. lib. bdg. 86.15 (3-11-012700-8) De Gruyter.
Christenverfolgung im roemischen Reich. 2nd ed. Jacques Moreau. 119p. (C). 1971. 22.30 (3-11-002456-X) De Gruyter.
Christgau's Record Guide: The Eighties. Robert Christgau. 525p. 1994. reprint ed. pap. 17.95 (0-306-80582-0) Da Capo.
Christgau's Record Guide: The '80s. Robert Christgau. LC 90-52512. 512p. 1990. pap. 17.95 (0-679-73015-X) Pantheon.
Christgau's Record Guide: Rock Albums of the 70's see Rock Albums of the Seventies: A Critical Guide
Christiada: Introduction & Text. Diego De Hojeda. Ed. by Mary H. Corcoran. LC 35-9384. (Catholic University of America. Studies in Romance Languages & Literatures: No. 11). reprint ed. 62.50 (0-404-50311-X) AMS Pr.
Christian. Hall Caine. 1976. 20.95 (0-8488-0255-1) Amereon Ltd.
Christian: Following Christ As Lord. William A. Webster. 160p. 1991. pap. 7.95 (0-85151-577-0) Banner of Truth.
Christian see Stephen Remarx: The Story of a Venture into Ethics, 1893
Christian - Marxist Studies in United States Higher Education: A Handbook of Syllabi. Ed. by Rom Maczka & Mark Elliott. 233p. 1991. pap. 20.00 (1-879089-06-8) B Graham Ctr.
Christian A. Herter. G. Bernard Noble. LC 73-122753. (American Secretaries of State & Their Diplomacy, New Ser. 1925-1961: Vol. 18). 1970. 60.50 (0-8154-0341-0) Cooper Sq.
Christian Adventure, Step 1: Beginning the Exciting Journey of Faith. Bill Bright. Ed. by Don Tanner et al. (Ten Basic Steps Toward Christian Maturity Ser.). (Illus.). 80p. (Orig.). 1994. pap. text ed. 4.99 (1-56399-030-X) NewLife Pubns.
Christian Agnostic. Weatherhead. (C). 1990. pap. 35.00 (0-85305-300-6, Pub. by J Arthur Ltd UK) St Mut.
Christian Agnostic. Leslie D. Weatherhead. LC 90-35764. (Abingdon Classics Ser.). 1990. pap. 5.95 (0-687-06980-7) Abingdon.
Christian Allusions in the Novels of Thomas Pynchon. Victoria H. Price. (American University Studies: English Language & Literature: Ser. IV, Vol. 89). 264p. (C). 1989. text ed. 37.95 (0-8204-0859-X) P Lang Pubs.
Christian America: Protestant Hopes & Historical Realities. enl. ed. Robert T. Handy. 1984. pap. 16.95 (0-19-503387-6) OUP.
Christian Anarchy: Jesus' Primacy over the Powers. Vernard Eller. LC 87-6734. 281p. reprint ed. pap. 80.10 (0-7837-0513-1, 2040837) Bks Demand.
Christian & Civil Disobedience. John H. Redekop. (Faith & Life Ser.). 42p. 1991. pap. text ed. 2.50 (0-921788-12-6) Kindred Prods.
Christian & Civil Government: Romans 13. John Weaver. 220p. (Orig.). 1991. pap. 12.95 (0-9626379-1-2) Custom Prints.
Christian & Giving, Step 8: Rejoicing in His Abundance, Sharing His Resources. Bill Bright. Ed. by Don Tanner et al. (Ten Basic Steps Toward Christian Maturity Ser.). (Illus.). 80p. (Orig.). 1994. pap. text ed. 4.99 (1-56399-037-7) NewLife Pubns.
Christian & His Money: Earning & Spending in the Light of the Gospel. 2nd rev. ed. John R. Crawford. 192p. reprint ed. pap. 5.95 (0-944990-00-2) Medcor Montreat.
Christian & Islamic Spirituality. Maria Jaoudi. LC 93-25368. 112p. (Orig.). 1993. pap. 7.95 (0-8091-3426-8) Paulist Pr.
Christian & Judaic Invention of History. Ed. by Jacob Neusner. 256p. 1991. 44.95 (1-55540-320-4, 01 00 55); pap. 29.95 (1-55540-321-2) Scholars Pr GA.
Christian & Jury Duty. Duane Ruth-Heffelbower. LC 91-13624. (Peace & Justice Ser.: Vol. 14). 104p. (Orig.). 1991. pap. 5.95 (0-8361-3562-8) Herald Pr.
Christian & Muslim Relations in Africa: The Cases of Northern Nigeria & Tanzania Compared. Lissi Rasmussen. 200p. 1993. text ed. 59.50 (1-85043-641-X, Pub. by I B Tauris UK) St Martin.
Christian & Obedience, Step 6: Living Daily in God's Grace. Bill Bright. Ed. by Don Tanner et al. (Ten Basic Steps Toward Christian Maturity Ser.). (Illus.). 64p. (Orig.). 1994. pap. text ed. 4.99 (1-56399-035-0) NewLife Pubns.
Christian & Oriental Philosophy of Art. Ananda K. Coomaraswamy. 1957. pap. 5.95 (0-486-20378-6) Dover.
Christian & Oriental Philosophy of Art. Ananda K. Coomaraswamy. 1974. reprint ed. 12.75 (0-8364-2574-X, Pub. by Munshiram Manoharial II) S Asia.
Christian & Politics. Robert L. Thoburn. 224p. (Orig.). 1984. pap. text ed. 4.95 (0-317-15003-0) Thoburn Pr.
Christian & Prayer, Step 4: Unlocking the Secrets of a Successful Prayer Life. Bill Bright. Ed. by Don Tanner et al. (Ten Basic Steps Toward Christian Maturity Ser.). (Illus.). 64p. (Orig.). 1994. pap. text ed. 4.99 (1-56399-033-4) NewLife Pubns.
***Christian & Revolution.** fac. ed. Melvin Gingerich. LC 68-12028. (Conrad Grebel Lectures: No. 1967). 229p. 1968. pap. 65.30 (0-7837-7326-9, 2047255) Bks Demand.
Christian & the Abundant Life, Step 2: Focusing on New Priorities. Bill Bright. Ed. by Don Tanner et al. (Ten Basic Steps Toward Christian Maturity Ser.). (Illus.). 64p. (Orig.). 1994. pap. text ed. 4.99 (1-56399-031-8) NewLife Pubns.
Christian & the Bible, Step 5: Growing Through the Study of God's Word. Bill Bright. Ed. by Don Tanner et al. (Ten Basic Steps Toward Christian Maturity Ser.). (Illus.). 80p. (Orig.). 1994. pap. text ed. 4.99 (1-56399-034-2) NewLife Pubns.
Christian & the Holy Spirit, Step 3: Moving Beyond Discouragement & Defeat. Bill Bright. Ed. by Don Tanner et al. (Ten Basic Steps Toward Christian Maturity Ser.). (Illus.). 80p. (Orig.). 1994. pap. text ed. 4.99 (1-56399-032-6) NewLife Pubns.
Christian & Warfare: The Roots of Pacifism in the Old Testament. Jacob J. Enz. LC 72-192756. (Christian Peace Shelf Ser.: No. 3). 96p. reprint ed. pap. 27.40 (0-7837-5120-6, 2044819) Bks Demand.
Christian & Witnessing, Step 7: Bringing Words of Hope to the World Around You. Bill Bright. Ed. by Don Tanner et al. (Ten Basic Steps Toward Christian Maturity Ser.). (Illus.). 80p. (Orig.). 1994. pap. text ed. 4.99 (1-56399-036-9) NewLife Pubns.
Christian Anti-Semitism & Paul's Theology. Sidney G. Hall, III. 208p. (Orig.). 1992. pap. 14.00 (0-8006-2654-0, 1-2654, Fortress Pr) Augsburg Fortress.
***Christian Antisemitism: A History of Hate.** William Nicholls. LC 92-35713. 532p. 1995. pap. 30.00 (1-56821-519-3) Aronson.
Christian Apologetics. Norman L. Geisler. LC 76-24706. 393p. (C). 1988. pap. text ed. 17.99 (0-8010-3822-7) Baker Bk.
Christian Apologetics. Cornelius Van Til. 1975. pap. 7.99 (0-87552-477-X) Presby & Reformed.
Christian Apologetics in a World Community. William A. Dyrness. LC 82-21383. 197p. 1983. pap. 21.99 (0-87784-399-6, 399) InterVarsity.
Christian Apologetics in France, 1730-1790: The Roots of Romantic Religion. William R. Everdell. LC 87-5706. (Texts & Studies in Religion: Vol. 31). 346p. 1987. lib. bdg. 99.95 (0-88946-819-2) E Mellen.
***Christian Apologetics in the Postmodern World.** Ed. by Timothy R. Phillips & Dennis L. Okholm. 240p. (Orig.). 1995. pap. text ed. 15.99 (0-8308-1860-X, 1860) InterVarsity.
Christian Approach to Muslims: Reflections from West Africa. James P. Dretke. LC 79-11912. (Islamic Studies). 261p. 1979. pap. 5.95 (0-87808-432-0) William Carey Lib.
Christian Approach to National Defense. rev. ed. A. Willmott. 122p. 1986. pap. 27.00 (0-7223-1968-1, Pub. by A H S Ltd UK) St Mut.
Christian Approach To Spiritual Warfare, Vol. 1. Frank M. Brim. Ed. by Connie Shoemaker. 280p. 1990. spiral bd. 35.00 (0-9612676-2-3) World Wide Mini.
Christian Approach to Work & Industry. Alexander J. Matejko. LC 88-13824. (Mellen Studies in Business: Vol. 4). 439p. 1989. lib. bdg. 109.95 (0-88946-156-2) E Mellen.
***Christian Approaches to Dialogue with Other Faith Communities.** Cornelius Mereweather-Thompson. LC 94-47432. 148p. 1995. text ed. 69.95 (0-7734-8979-7, Mellen Univ Pr) E Mellen.
Christian Approaches to Learning Theory - Freedom & Discipline: Major Papers Delivered at the Third Annual Conference, Trinity Christian College, Palos Heights, Illinois, November 1-2, 1985, Vol. III. Ed. by Norman De Jong. LC 84-20884. 118p. (Orig.). (C). 1987. pap. text ed. 21.00 (0-8191-6280-9, Trinity Christ Coll) U Pr of Amer.
Christian Arabic Apologetics During the Abbasid Period, 750-1258. Ed. by Samir K. Samir & Jurgen S. Nielsen. LC 93-38130. (Studies in the History of Religions: Vol. 63). 1993. 85.75 (90-04-09568-3) E J Brill.
Christian Argument for Gays & Lesbians in the Military: Essays by Mainline Church Leaders. Intro. by John J. Carey. LC 93-21573. 58p. 1993. text ed. 39.95 (0-7734-9315-8) E Mellen.
Christian Armory. Schwalb Creative Staff. 1992. pap. 3.50 (0-8024-1574-1) Moody.
Christian Arts & Crafts, Vol. I. Mari Gonzalez. 1991. pap. 9.95 (0-687-07020-1) Abingdon.
Christian Ashrams: A New Religious Movement in Contemporary India. Helen Ralston. LC 87-21019. (Studies in Religion & Society: Vol. 20). 150p. 1987. lib. bdg. 69.95 (0-88946-854-0) E Mellen.
Christian Astrology, 3 vols. William Lilly. (Illus.). 893p. (C). 1986. reprint ed. Vol. I, Introduction to Astrology. write for info. (0-318-68005-X); reprint ed. Vol. II, Horary Astrology. write for info. (0-318-68006-8); reprint ed. Vol. III, Natal Astrology & Predictive Astrology. write for info. (0-318-68007-6) JustUs & Assocs.
Christian Astrology, 3 vols., Set. William Lilly. (Illus.). 893p. (C). 1986. reprint ed. pap. text ed. 80.00 (1-878935-03-8) JustUs & Assocs.
Christian Astrology, Vol. I: Introduction to Astrology - The Basics. William Lilly. (Illus.). 147p. (C). 1985. reprint ed. pap. text ed. 20.00 (1-878935-00-3) JustUs & Assocs.
Christian Astrology, Vol. II: Horary Astrology (Traditional Method) William Lilly. (Illus.). 367p. (C). 1985. reprint ed. pap. 30.00 (1-878935-01-1) JustUs & Assocs.
Christian Astrology, Vol. III: Natal Astrology & Predictive Astrology. William Lilly. (Illus.). 379p. (C). 1986. reprint ed. pap. 30.00 (1-878935-02-X) JustUs & Assocs.
Christian at Play. Robert K. Johnston. LC 83-16552. 174p. reprint ed. 49.60 (0-685-15950-7, 2027548) Bks Demand.
Christian at Prayer: An Illustrated Prayer Manual Attributed to Peter the Chanter. Richard C. Trexler. LC 87-1591. (Medieval & Renaissance Texts & Studies: Vol. 44). (Illus.). 272p. 1987. 25.00 (0-86698-027-X) MRTS.
Christian Attitude Toward War. Loraine Boettner. LC 85-17039. 104p. 1986. pap. 4.99 (0-87552-118-5) Presby & Reformed.
Christian Attitudes & Racial Problems. rev. ed. Fred P. Miller. 60p. 1993. pap. 4.95 (1-883116-03-1) Moellerhaus.
Christian Attitudes Toward War & Peace. Roland H. Bainton. LC 60-12064. 1979. pap. 9.95 (0-687-07027-9) Abingdon.
Christian Attitudes Towards the Emperor in the Fourth Century. Kenneth M. Setton. LC 41-13567. (Columbia University. Studies in Social Sciences: No. 482). reprint ed. 26.00 (0-404-51482-0) AMS Pr.
Christian Authority: Essays in Honour of Henry Chadwick. Ed. by G. Rosemary Evans. (Illus.). 368p. 1988. 74.00 (0-19-826683-9) OUP.
Christian Authors Workshop. Arthur F. Hallam. LC 92-22226. 1992. 6.00 (0-938770-07-1) Capitalist Pr OH.
Christian Babysitter's Handbook. Sarah Fletcher. 1985. pap. 3.99 (0-570-03948-7, 12-2881) Concordia.
Christian Baptism. A. P. Gibbs. 1982. pap. 6.95 (0-937396-62-1) Walterick Pubs.
Christian Baptism. John Murray. 1974. pap. 5.99 (0-87552-343-9) Presby & Reformed.
Christian Baptism, Feet Washing & the Lord's Supper. H. M. Riggle. 264p. 5.00 (0-686-29105-0) Faith Pub Hse.
Christian Bases of World Order. H. A. Wallace et al. LC 75-134068. (Essay Index Reprint Ser.). 1977. reprint ed. 21.95 (0-8369-2490-8) Ayer.
***Christian Bashing: America's New National Pastime.** Jeremy Reynolds. 224p. 1995. pap. 10.99 (1-56384-084-7) Huntington Hse.
Christian Basics: A Handbook of Beginnings, Beliefs & Behaviour. John R. Stott. 160p. 1992. 9.99 (0-8010-8335-4) Baker Bk.
Christian Basics: A Primer for Pilgrims. Dorothy Fackre & Gabriel Fackre. (Illus.). 144p. (Orig.). 1991. pap. 10.99 (0-8028-0541-8) Eerdmans.
Christian Basics Bible Studies, 8 vols., Set. (Orig.). 1994. pap. 39.92 (0-8308-2000-0, 2000) InterVarsity.
Christian Bed & Breakfast Directory: 1992-1993 Edition. Ed. by Robyn Martins. 1992. pap. 8.95 (1-55748-289-6) Barbour & Co.
Christian Bed & Breakfast Directory, 1994-1995. Karen Carroll. 1994. pap. 3.97 (1-55748-459-7) Barbour & Co.
***Christian Bed & Breakfast Directory 1995-96.** Germany. 1995. pap. text ed. 3.97 (1-55748-596-8) Barbour & Co.
Christian Bed & Breakfast 1993-94. Ed. by Karen Carroll. 1993. pap. 3.97 (1-55748-341-8) Barbour & Co.
Christian Beginnings: Word & Community from Jesus to Post-Apostolic Times. Ed. by Jurgen Becker. Tr. by Annamarie Kidder & Reinhard Krauss. 336p. (Orig.). 1993. pap. 24.99 (0-664-25195-1) Westminster John Knox.
Christian Behind the Mask. Jim Toombs. 200p. 1994. pap. 8.99 (0-88070-676-7, Multnomah Bks) Questar Pubs.
Christian Belief in a Postmodern World: The Full Wealth of Conviction. Diogenes Allen. 240p. (Orig.). 1989. pap. 15.99 (0-8042-0625-2, John Knox) Westminster John Knox.
Christian Beliefs. Stephen D. Eyre. LC 89-15297. (LifeGuide Bible Studies). 64p. 1989. pap. 4.99 (0-8308-1061-7, 1061) InterVarsity.
Christian Believing. Urban T. Holmes, III & John H. Westerhoff. (Church's Teaching Ser.: Vol. 1). 144p. 1984. student ed 1.50 (0-8164-2221-4) Harper SF.
Christian Boltanski. Lynn Gumpert. (Illus.). 182p. Date not set. 24.95 (2-08-013559-7) Abbeville Pr.
Christian Boltanski & Jeff Wall. (Parkett Art Magazine Ser.: No. 22). (Illus.). 200p. 1989. 19.50 (3-907509-72-2, Pub. by Parkett Pubs SZ) Dist Art Pubs.
Christian Book of Mystical Verse. Ed. by A. W. Tozer. 1991. pap. 7.99 (0-87509-446-5) Chr Pubns.
Christian Book of Why. John C. McCollister. 340p. 1983. 12.95 (0-8246-0297-8) Jonathan David.
Christian Book of Why. John C. McCollister. 360p. 1986. pap. 12.95 (0-8246-0317-6) Jonathan David.
Christian Boy, 4 vols., 1. L. W. Hayhurst. (J). 1964. pap. 2.75 (0-685-74299-7, CB100) Quality Pubns.
Christian Boy, 4 vols., 2. L. W. Hayhurst. (J). 1964. pap. 2.75 (0-685-74300-4, CB200) Quality Pubns.
Christian Boy, 4 vols., 3. L. W. Hayhurst. (J). 1964. pap. 2.75 (0-685-74301-2, CB300) Quality Pubns.
Christian Boy, 4 vols., 4. L. W. Hayhurst. (J). 1964. pap. 2.75 (0-685-74302-0, CB400) Quality Pubns.
Christian Building: Final Report VIII, Part II. Carl H. Kraeling. LC 43-2669. 32.50 (0-685-71744-5) J J Augustin.
Christian Calendar & the Gregorian Reform. Peter Archer. LC 41-15354. (Illus.). 136p. reprint ed. pap. 38.80 (0-7837-5586-4, 2045379) Bks Demand.
Christian Call to Justice & Peace. Joseph Stoutzenberger. (Illus.). 288p. (Orig.). 1987. pap. text ed. 10.50 (0-88489-180-1); teacher ed, spiral bd. 17.95 (0-88489-181-X) St Marys.
Christian Capitalism. Arthur F. Hallam. 182p. (Orig.). 1981. pap. 14.95 (0-938770-00-4) Capitalist Pr OH.
Christian Capitalist Sermons One Thru Twenty-Six. Arthur F. Hallam. 232p. 1983. pap. 30.00 (0-938770-02-0) Capitalist Pr OH.
Christian Caregiving: A Way of Life. Kenneth C. Haugk. LC 84-24341. (Orig.). 1984. pap. 10.99 (0-8066-2123-0, 10-1103, Augsburg) Augsburg Fortress.
Christian Caregiving: A Way of Life - Leader's Guide. Kenneth C. Haugk & William J. McKay. 1994. pap. 10.99 (0-8066-2704-2, 9-2704, Augsburg) Augsburg Fortress.
Christian Case Against Abortion. 1992. lib. bdg. 149.95 (0-8490-5564-4) Gordon Pr.
Christian Case Against Abortion. Kenneth L. Gentry, Jr. 80p. Date not set. pap. 5.95 (1-877818-05-4) Footstool Pubns.
Christian Celebrations for Autumn & Winter. Mary McMillan. (Christian Parties & Celebrations Ser.). 96p. (J). (gr. 2-7). 1990. 10.95 (0-86653-546-2, SS1821, Shining Star Pubns) Good Apple.
Christian Century Reader: Representative Articles, Editorials, & Poems Selected from More Than Fifty Years of the Christian Century. Ed. by Harold E. Fey & Margaret Frakes. LC 72-331. (Essay Index Reprint Ser.). 1977. reprint ed. 26.95 (0-8369-2786-9) Ayer.
Christian Character. Andrea Sterk & Peter Scazzero. (LifeGuide Bible Studies). 60p. (Orig.). 1985. pap. 4.99 (0-8308-1054-4, 1054) InterVarsity.
Christian Character Bible Study Series, 8 vols., Set. Carolyn Nystrom et al. 1992. 39.92 (0-8308-1140-0) InterVarsity.
Christian Character Course. Keith L. Brooks. (Teach Yourself the Bible Ser.). (C). 1961. pap. 3.99 (0-8024-1301-3) Moody.
Christian Charm Course. rev. ed. Emily Hunter. 112p. 1986. reprint ed. teacher ed 8.99 (0-89081-509-7); reprint ed. student ed 6.99 (0-89081-508-9) Harvest Hse.
Christian Charm Course, Certificate. rev. ed. Emily Hunter. 1986. reprint ed. 0.25 (0-89081-003-6) Harvest Hse.
Christian Charm Notebook see Como Ser Encantadora (Para Alumna)
Christian Child Rearing & Personality Development. Paul D. Meier. LC 76-57501. 1977. pap. 7.99 (0-8010-6016-8) Baker Bk.
Christian Chronicles & Byzantine History, Fifth-Sixth Centuries. Brian Croke. (Collected Studies: No. CS386). 352p. 1992. 89.95 (0-86078-343-X, Pub. by Variorum UK) Ashgate Pub Co.
Christian Church. Fisher Humphreys. Orig. Title: The Doctrine of the Church. 48p. 1974. reprint ed. pap. 2.00 (0-914520-02-4) Insight Pr.
Christian Church: Its Rise & Progress. H. M. Riggle. 488p. 6.00 (0-686-29144-1) Faith Pub Hse.
Christian Church in the Cold War. Owen Chadwick. 240p. 1992. 25.00 (0-7139-9046-5, A Lane) Viking Penguin.
Christian Church in the Cold War. Owen Chadwick. (History of the Church Ser.: Vol. 7). 240p. 1993. reprint ed. pap. 12.00 (0-14-012540-X, Penguin Bks) Viking Penguin.
Christian Church Plea. H. Eugene Johnson. LC 75-12012. (New Life Bks.). 96p. 1975. pap. 2.99 (0-87239-053-5, 40028) Standard Pub.
Christian Church Women: Shapers of a Movement. Ed. by Debra B. Hull. 176p. (Orig.). 1994. pap. 14.99 (0-8272-0463-9) Chalice Pr.
***Christian Churches & the Democratisation of Africa.** Ed. by Paul Gifford. LC 95-7523. (Studies of Religion in Africa: Vol. 12). 1995. write for info. (90-04-10324-4) E J Brill.
Christian Churches at the Crossroads. Ben Coe. LC 80-27624. 135p. (Orig.). 1980. pap. 5.95 (0-87808-178-X) William Carey Lib.
Christian Churches of American Origins & Beliefs. rev. ed. Milton V. Backman, Jr. 278p. (C). 1983. reprint ed. pap. write for info. (0-02-305090-X, Scribners) S&S Trade.
Christian Classics in Modern English. Brother Lawrence et al. 272p. 1991. per., pap. 9.99 (0-87788-121-9) Shaw Pubs.
Christian Cline: Observations about Life & God. Kathy Merrifield. 250p. (Orig.). 1992. pap. write for info. (0-9630692-1-7) Selaginella.
Christian Clip & Copy Art. Susan Schneck. (Teacher Helper Ser.). 96p. (J). (ps-8). 1989. 10.95 (0-86653-503-9, SS1816, Shining Star Pubns) Good Apple.

An Asterisk (*) at the beginning of an entry indicates that the title is appearing in BIP for the first time.

Christian Clip & Copy Greeting Cards. Vanessa Filkins & Rebecca Daniel. (Bible Clip & Copy Ser.). 96p. 1991. 10.95 (*0-86653-631-0*, SS1890, Shining Star Pubns) Good Apple.

Christian Clip & Copy Messages & Awards. Rebecca Daniel & Janet Skiles. (Bible Clip & Copy Ser.). (Illus.). 96p. 1992. 10.95 (*0-86653-702-3*, SS2832, Shining Star Pubns) Good Apple.

Christian Clip & Copy Time-Savers. Corbin Hillam. (Teacher Helper Ser.). 96p. (J). (ps up). 1990. 10.95 (*0-86653-553-5*, SS1822, Shining Star Pubns) Good Apple.

Christian College Advantage: A Student-Parent Guide to Colleges Affiliated with the Churches of Christ. James I. Woodrow. 102p. (YA). (gr. 10-12). 1992. 11.95 (*0-9631429-0-9*) Inst Advan PHE.

Christian Commitment. Edward J. Carnell. (Illus.). 230p. Date not set. kivar 9.95 (*0-8010-2473-0*) Baker Bk.

Christian Commonwealth: Or, the Civil Policy of the Rising Kingdom of Jesus Christ. John Eliot. LC 77-141110. (Research Library of Colonial Americana). 1972. reprint ed. 20.95 (*0-405-03323-0*) Ayer.

Christian Communication: A Bibliographical Survey. Comp. by Paul A. Soukup. LC 89-12076. (Bibliographies & Indexes in Religious Studies: No. 14). 414p. 1989. text ed. 75.00 (*0-313-25673-X*, SKN/, Greenwood Pr) Greenwood.

***Christian Communicator's Handbook.** Tom Nash. 240p. 1995. 17.99 (*1-56476-384-6*, 6-3384, Victor Books) SP Pubns.

Christian Communities in Jerusalem & the West Bank since 1948: An Historical, Social, & Political Study. Daphne Tsimhoni. LC 92-23058. 264p. 1993. text ed. 57.95 (*0-275-93921-9*, C3921, Praeger Pubs) Greenwood.

Christian Community. Rob Suggs. (LifeGuide Bible Studies). 64p. (Orig.). 1994. pap. 4.99 (*0-8308-1071-4*, 1071) InterVarsity.

Christian Community: A Reporter's Inside Look. Ralph Rath. (Get the Facts Ser.: Series II). 32p. (Orig.). 1994. pap. 2.95 (*0-9640167-6-1*) Peter Pubns.

Christian Concept of History in the Chronicle of Sulpicius Severus. G. K. Andel. iv, 195p. (Orig.). 1976. pap. text ed. 54.00 (*0-317-57956-8*, Pub. by A M Hakkert SP) Coronet Bks.

Christian Concept of History in the Chronicle of Sulpicius Severus. G. K. Van Andel. 195p. (Orig.). 1976. pap. 47.00 (*90-256-0722-5*, Pub. by A M Hakkert NE) Benjamins North Am.

Christian Conspiracy: How the Teachings of Christ Have Been Altered by Christians. L. David Moore. LC 94-66236. 360p. (Orig.). 1994. pap. 14.95 (*0-9635665-2-0*) Pendulum Plus.

Christian Controversy in Alexandria: Clement's Polemic Against the Basilideans & Valentinians. Everett Procter. LC 93-37342. (AUS VII: Vol. 172). 136p. (C). 1995. text ed. 37.95 (*0-8204-2378-5*) P Lang Pubs.

Christian Conversion in Context. Hans Kasdorf. LC 88-12871. (Illus.). 220p. reprint ed. pap. 62.70 (*0-7837-5110-9*, 2044809) Bks Demand.

Christian Counseling. Gary Collins. 711p. 1988. write for info. (*0-8499-0692-X*); pap. write for info. (*0-8499-3124-X*) Word Inc.

Christian Counseling & Occultism. Kurt E. Koch. LC 65-23118. 340p. (C). 1973. pap. 12.99 (*0-8254-3010-0*) Kregel.

Christian Counseling & the Law. Steve Levicoff. 13.99 (*0-8024-1239-4*) Moody.

Christian Counsellor's Pocket Guide. Selwyn Hughes. (Orig.). 1977. pap. 9.95 (*0-86065-153-3*) Trans-Atl Phila.

Christian Counselor's Casebook. Jay E. Adams. LC 74-81707. 223p. 1974. pap. 14.99 (*0-87552-012-X*) Presby & Reformed.

Christian Counselor's Casebook. Jay E. Adams. (Jay Adams Library). 224p. 1986. pap. 14.99 (*0-310-51161-5*, 12128P) Zondervan.

***Christian Counselor's Commentary: Galatians, Ephesians, Colossians, Philemon.** Jay E. Adams. 190p. Date not set. 24.95 (*0-9643556-2-0*) Timeless Texts.

***Christian Counselor's Commentary: I & II Timothy & Titus.** Jay E. Adams. 144p. 1995. 24.95 (*0-9643556-5-5*) Timeless Texts.

***Christian Counselor's Commentary on I & II Corinthians.** Jay E. Adams. 190p. 1994. 24.95 (*0-9643556-1-2*) Timeless Texts.

Christian Counselor's Handbook. Ed. by Christian Broadcasting Network Staff. 240p. 1987. pap. 14.99 (*0-8423-0255-7*) Tyndale.

Christian Counselor's Manual. Jay E. Adams. LC 73-87752. 490p. 1973. 19.99 (*0-87552-013-8*) Presby & Reformed.

Christian Counselor's Manual: The Practice of Nouthetic Counseling. Jay E. Adams. (Jay Adams Library). 496p. 1986. 19.99 (*0-310-51150-X*, 12127) Zondervan.

Christian Counselor's Pocket Guide. rev. ed. Selwyn Hughes. LC 80-65443. 96p. 1985. reprint ed. pap. 4.99 (*0-87123-844-6*) Bethany Hse.

***Christian County, Kentucky, Deed Book G (1816-1817)** T. L.C. Genealogy Staff. 148p. (Orig.). 1994. spiral bd., pap. 15.00 (*1-886633-03-7*) TLC Genealogy.

Christian County Kentucky, Historical & Biographical. Ed. by William H. Perrin. 344p. 1993. reprint ed. pap. text ed. 26.50 (*1-55613-825-3*) Heritage Bk.

***Christian County, Kentucky, Wills & Estates, 1815-1823.** T.L.C. Genealogy Staff. 223p. (Orig.). 1993. spiral bd., pap. 20.00 (*1-886633-04-5*) TLC Genealogy.

Christian Couple. Larry Christenson & Nordis Christenson. LC 77-24085. 186p. 1977. pap. 7.99 (*0-87123-051-8*, 210046); student ed 1.50 (*0-87123-046-1*, 210046) Bethany Hse.

Christian Crafts - Paper Bag Puppets. Susan J. Stegenga. (Christian Craft Ser.). 64p. (J). (ps-5). 1990. 8.95 (*0-86653-552-7*, SS1881, Shining Star Pubns) Good Apple.

Christian Crafts for Holidays Hand-Shaped Art. Anita Stohs. (Christian Craft Ser.). 64p. (J). (ps-5). 1994. 7.95 (*1-56417-005-5*, SS3827, Shining Star Pubns) Good Apple.

Christian Crafts from Cardboard. Anita R. Stohs. (Christian Craft Ser.). (Illus.). 64p. (J). (ps-5). 1994. 7.95 (*0-86653-779-1*, SS3812, Shining Star Pubns) Good Apple.

Christian Crafts from Cardboard Containers. Rebecca Daniel & Susan J. Stegenga. (Christian Craft Ser.). (Illus.). 64p. (J). (ps-5). 1992. 8.95 (*0-86653-703-1*, SS2833, Shining Star Pubns) Good Apple.

Christian Crafts from Cardboard Tubes. Anita R. Stohs. (Christian Craft Ser.). 1992. 8.95 (*0-86653-708-2*, Shining Star Pubns) Good Apple.

Christian Crafts from Construction Paper. Lori Miescke. (Christian Craft Ser.). 64p. (J). (ps-5). 1992. 8.95 (*0-86653-707-4*, SS2843, Shining Star Pubns) Good Apple.

Christian Crafts from Eggs. Kim Rankin. (Christian Craft Ser.). (Illus.). 64p. 1992. 8.95 (*0-86653-642-6*, SS1899, Shining Star Pubns) Good Apple.

Christian Crafts from Folded Paper. Anita R. Stohs. (Christian Craft Ser.). (Illus.). 64p. (J). (ps-5). 1994. 7.95 (*0-86653-778-3*, SS3811, Shining Star Pubns) Good Apple.

Christian Crafts from Hand-Shaped Art. Mary McMillan. (Christian Craft Ser.). 64p. (J). (ps-5). 1991. 8.95 (*0-86653-629-9*, SS1886, Shining Star Pubns) Good Apple.

Christian Crafts from Milk Containers. Joanne Hooker. (Christian Craft Ser.). 64p. (J). (ps-5). 1994. 7.95 (*1-56417-007-1*, SS3829, Shining Star Pubns) Good Apple.

Christian Crafts from Paper Bags. Shery Borenstein. (Christian Craft Ser.). 64p. (J). (ps-5). 1994. 7.95 (*1-56417-006-3*, SS3828, Shining Star Pubns) Good Apple.

Christian Crafts from Paper Plates. Mary Currier. (Christian Craft Ser.). 64p. (J). (ps-5). 1989. 8.95 (*0-86653-494-6*, SS1880, Shining Star Pubns) Good Apple.

Christian Crafts with Egg Cartons. Marilyn Senterfitt. (Christian Craft Ser.). 64p. (J). (ps-5). 1991. 8.95 (*0-86653-574-8*, SS1882, Shining Star Pubns) Good Apple.

Christian Crafts Yarn Art. Anita Stohl. (Christian Craft Ser.). (Illus.). 64p. (J). (ps-5). 1992. 8.95 (*0-86653-701-5*, SS2831, Shining Star Pubns) Good Apple.

Christian Creed: A Meditative Path. Hans-Werner Schroeder. 112p. 1990. pap. 10.95 (*0-86315-032-2*, 1081, Pub. by Floris Books UK) Anthroposophic.

Christian Creed: Its Origin & Signification. C. W. Leadbeater. 172p. 1992. pap. 16.95 (*1-56459-238-3*) Kessinger Pub.

Christian Creed, Its Origin & Signification. C. W. Leadbeater. 109p. 1976. reprint ed. spiral bd. 3.85 (*0-7873-0541-3*) Mokelumne.

***Christian Critique of Art & Literature.** Calvin Seerveld. 1995. pap. write for info. (*0-932914-35-7*) Dordt Coll Pr.

Christian Critique of the University. Charles Malik. 118p. (C). 1987. reprint ed. lib. bdg. 16.00 (*0-921075-06-5*) N Waterloo Acad Pr.

Christian Cross Stitch. (Orig.). 1985. pap. 5.95 (*0-687-07033-3*) Abingdon.

Christian Cross Stitch, No. III. 24p. (Orig.). 1992. pap. 5.95 (*0-687-07038-4*) Abingdon.

Christian Crusader: Plague of Evil. John Celestri. (Illus.). 80p. (Orig.). (J). 1994. pap. 3.99 (*0-9634183-3-5*) CC Comics.

Christian Crusader: The Quest Begins. John Celestri. 72p. (J). (gr. 3-6). 1992. pap. 3.49 (*0-9634183-0-0*) CC Comics.

Christian Crusader: The Quest Begins. rev. ed. John Celestri. (Illus.). 80p. (J). 1992. pap. 3.99 (*0-9634183-1-9*) CC Comics.

Christian Crusader: Web of Lies...Chains of Sin. John Celestri. (Illus.). 80p. (Orig.). (J). 1993. pap. 3.99 (*0-9634183-2-7*) CC Comics.

***Christian Cybernetics.** William A. Ward. 168p. 1994. pap. 6.95 (*1-884369-19-7*, Treasures Pub) McDougal Pubng.

***Christian Cyberspace Companion: A Guide to the Internet & Christian Online Resources.** Jason D. Baker. LC 95-6936. 1995. pap. write for info. (*0-8010-5248-3*) Baker Bk.

Christian Democracy in Venezuela. Donald L. Herman. LC 79-24582. 303p. reprint ed. pap. 86.40 (*0-7837-3761-0*, 2043578) Bks Demand.

Christian Democracy in Western Europe, 1820-1953. Michael P. Fogarty. LC 73-11997. (Illus.). 448p. 1974. reprint ed. text ed. 38.50 (*0-8371-7114-8*, FOCH, Greenwood Pr) Greenwood.

Christian Democratic Parties of Western Europe. Ronald E. Irving. LC 78-41082. 360p. reprint ed. pap. 102.60 (*0-317-42290-1*, 2023267) Bks Demand.

Christian Development Course: A Reason of the Hope, 3 vols., Set, Vol. I. Crawford D. Coon. LC 87-71134. 313p. (C). 1987. Set 3 vol. ring bd. write for info. (*0-9618853-3-5*) Christian Development.

Christian Development Course: A Reason of the Hope, Vol. I. Crawford D. Coon. LC 87-71134. 313p. (C). 1987. 19.95 (*0-9618853-0-0*) Christian Development.

Christian Dietrich Grabbe. Roy C. Brown. LC 76-169639. (Twayne's World Authors Ser.). 176p. (C). text ed. 17.95 (*0-8290-1733-X*) Irvington.

Christian Dimension of Shakespearean Drama. Ed. by E. Beatrice Batson. LC 93-46262. 200p. 1994. 79.95 (*0-7734-9425-1*) E Mellen.

Christian Dior. Diana De Marly. LC 90-4061. (Illus.). 100p. 1990. 39.95 (*0-8419-1260-2*); pap. 23.95 (*0-8419-1278-5*) Holmes & Meier.

Christian Disciple's Manual: Life-Changing Truths for Every Believer. David S. Kirkwood. 294p. 1992. pap. 8.95 (*0-9629625-2-X*) Ethnos.

Christian Discipleship: Foundations for Maximum Spiritual Growth. Steven Collins. (Illus.). 304p. 1988. reprint ed. pap. text ed. 16.99 (*1-56322-022-9*) V Hensley.

Christian Discipleship & Sexuality. Frederick H. Borsch & M. R. Ritley. 80p. (Orig.). 1993. student ed, pap. 3.95 (*0-88028-141-3*, 1210) Forward Movement.

***Christian Disciplines.** Oswald Chambers. LC 94-30010. 1995. pap. 8.99 (*0-929239-64-4*) Discovery Hse Pubs.

Christian Disciplines: Living the Way God Wants You to Live. Andrea Sterk & Peter Scazzero. (LifeGuide Bible Studies). 64p. (Orig.). 1986. pap. 4.99 (*0-8308-1055-2*, 1055) InterVarsity.

Christian Discourses: And the Lilies of the Field & the Birds of the Air & Three Discourses at the Communion on Fridays. Soren Kierkegaard. Tr. by Walter Lowrie. 409p. reprint ed. pap. 116.60 (*0-7837-1945-0*, 2042160) Bks Demand.

Christian Discovery: The Road to Justice. James DiGiacomo & John J. Walsh. LC 91-41590. 1992. 10.95 (*0-88344-807-6*) Orbis Bks.

Christian Doctrine. French Arrington. 1992. pap. 13.99 (*0-87148-199-5*) Pathway Pr.

Christian Doctrine. John S. Whale. (C). 1941. pap. 17.95 (*0-521-09642-1*) Cambridge U Pr.

Christian Doctrine. rev. ed. Shirley C. Guthrie. LC 93-44988. 432p. 1994. pap. 17.99 (*0-664-25368-7*) Westminster John Knox.

Christian Doctrine: Lectures & Sermons. J. Allen Miller. 1946. 1.75 (*0-934970-01-7*) Brethren Church.

Christian Doctrine: Teachings of the Christian Church. Shirley C. Guthrie, Jr. (Illus.). (Orig.). 1969. pap. 11.99 (*0-8042-9051-2*, John Knox) Westminster John Knox.

Christian Doctrine: The Faith... Once Delivered. W. Richardson. LC 82-25598. (Bible College Textbooks Ser.). 448p. (Orig.). 1983. pap. 9.99 (*0-87239-610-X*, 88588) Standard Pub.

Christian Doctrine see Doctrina Cristiana

***Christian Doctrine-Are You Sure They Taught You the Truth?** Robert Goodhart. 134p. (Orig.). 1990. write for info. (*0-9627493-0-3*) Church of Phila.

Christian Doctrine for Everyman: Introduction to Baptist Beliefs. Jimmy A. Millikin. LC 78-10464. (Orig.). 1989. reprint ed. pap. 4.50 (*0-9621902-0-9*) KRB Bks.

Christian Doctrine for the Instruction & Information of the Indians. Pedro De Cordoba. Tr. by Sterling A. Stoudemire. LC 79-121681. 1970. 10.95 (*0-87024-159-1*) U of Miami Pr.

***Christian Doctrine in the Light of Michael Polanyi's Theory of Personal Knowledge: A Personalist Theology.** Joan O. Crewdson. LC 94-38970. (Toronto Studies in Theology: Vol. 66). 464p. 1994. text ed. write for info. (*0-7734-9150-3*) E Mellen.

Christian Doctrine of Creation & Redemption. Emil Brunner. Tr. by Olive Wyon. LC 50-6821. 396p. 1979. pap. 14.99 (*0-664-24248-0*, Westminster) Westminster John Knox.

Christian Doctrine of God. Emil Brunner. Tr. by Olive Wyon. LC 50-6821. 376p. 1980. pap. 13.99 (*0-664-24304-5*, Westminster) Westminster John Knox.

Christian Doctrine of Slavery. George D. Armstrong. LC 69-16595. 148p. 1969. reprint ed. text ed. 38.50 (*0-8371-0892-6*, ARC&, Negro U Pr) Greenwood.

Christian Doctrines: A Compendium of Theology. James H. Pendleton. 1957. 21.00 (*0-8170-0037-2*) Judson.

Christian Dogmatics, 4 Vols, 1. Francis Pieper. Tr. by Theodore Engelder et al. 1957. 19.95 (*0-570-06712-X*, 15-1001) Concordia.

Christian Dogmatics, 4 Vols, 2. Francis Pieper. Tr. by Theodore Engelder et al. 1957. 19.95 (*0-570-06713-8*, 15-1002) Concordia.

Christian Dogmatics, 4 Vols, 3. Francis Pieper. Tr. by Theodore Engelder et al. 1957. 19.95 (*0-570-06714-6*, 15-1003) Concordia.

Christian Dogmatics, 2 vols., Set. Ed. by Carl E. Braaten & Robert W. Jenson. LC 83-48007. 1984. 57.00 (*0-8006-0712-0*, 1-712, Fortress Pr) Augsburg Fortress.

Christian Dogmatics, 4 Vols., Set. Francis Pieper. Tr. by Theodore Engelder et al. 1957. 87.99 (*0-570-06715-4*, 15-1852) Concordia.

Christian Dogmatics, 2 vols., Vol 1. Ed. by Carl E. Braaten & Robert W. Jenson. LC 83-48007. 1984. Volume 1. 31.00 (*0-8006-0703-1*, 1-703, Fortress Pr) Augsburg Fortress.

Christian Dogmatics, 2 vols., Vol. 2. Ed. by Carl E. Braaten & Robert W. Jenson. LC 83-48007. 1984. Volume 2. 31.00 (*0-8006-0704-X*, 1-704, Fortress Pr) Augsburg Fortress.

Christian Dogmatics, 4 Vols, Vol. 4. Francis Pieper. Tr. by Theodore Engelder et al. 1957. 28.99 (*0-570-06711-1*, 15-1000) Concordia.

Christian Earthkeeper's Journal. Elizabeth W. Kreider. (Illus.). 96p. 1991. pap. 5.95 (*1-56148-053-3*) Good Bks PA.

Christian East & the Rise of the Papacy: The Church 1071-1453 A.D. Aristeides Papadakis. LC 94-16429. 434p. 1994. 29.95 (*0-88141-057-8*); pap. 16.95 (*0-88141-058-6*) St Vladimirs.

Christian Ecology: Toward an Environmental Ethic for the Twenty-First Century. Ed. by Frederick W. Krueger. LC 88-60520. (Illus.). 146p. (Orig.). 1988. pap. 10.00 (*0-9620248-0-5*) NACCE.

Christian Education: An Introduction to Its Scope. Ed. by Douglas J. Simpson. 1979. 8.95 (*0-89265-053-2*) Randall Hse.

Christian Education: Foundations for the Future. Ed. by Robert E. Clark et al. 1991. 29.99 (*0-8024-1647-0*) Moody.

Christian Education: Its History & Philosophy. Kenneth O. Gangel & Warren S. Benson. 1983. 24.99 (*0-8024-3561-0*) Moody.

Christian Education: Its Mandate & Mission. Ed. by Ronald A. Horton. LC 92-22625. 283p. (C). 1992. pap. 8.95 (*0-89084-639-1*) Bob Jones Univ Pr.

Christian Education: Modeling the Gift of New Life. Lawrence O. Richards. 336p. 1988. pap. 18.99 (*0-310-52081-9*, 18216P) Zondervan.

Christian Education: Total Task of the Church. H. D. Harrison. 28p. 1976. pap. 0.95 (*0-89265-101-6*) Randall Hse.

Christian Education & Computers. Marydel Frohne. 41p. (Orig.). 1994. pap. text ed. 9.00 (*1-878221-12-4*) Church Bytes.

Christian Education & the Search for Meaning. 2nd ed. Jim Wilhoit. LC 91-26232. 192p. 1991. pap. 7.99 (*0-8010-9711-8*) Baker Bk.

Christian Education As Evangelism. Steve Clapp. 154p. (Orig.). 1982. pap. 9.00 (*0-914527-11-8*) C-Four Res.

Christian Education for the Real World. Henry M. Morris. LC 77-78017. 295p. 1991. reprint ed. pap. 10.95 (*0-89051-160-8*) Master Bks.

***Christian Education for the 21st Century.** Michael Lawson & Robert Choun. 416p. 1995. pap. 13.99 (*0-8254-2348-1*) Kregel.

Christian Education Handbook. Ed. by Bruce P. Powers. LC 80-69522. 1991. pap. 12.99 (*0-8054-3229-9*) Broadman.

Christian Education in China: A Study. China Educational Commission. LC 75-36223. reprint ed. 34.50 (*0-404-14474-8*) AMS Pr.

Christian Education in Pluralist Society. V. Alan McClelland. 224p. (C). 1988. lib. bdg. 47.50 (*0-415-00540-X*, A1841) Routledge.

Christian Education in the Small Church. Ed. by Donald L. Griggs et al. 112p. 1988. pap. 10.00 (*0-8170-1103-X*) Judson.

Christian Education Made Easy. Howard Hanchey. LC 88-38710. 180p. (Orig.). 1989. pap. 12.95 (*0-8192-1446-9*) Morehouse Pub.

Christian Educator's Handbook on Adult Education. Jim Wilhoit. 416p. 1993. 22.99 (*1-56476-019-7*, Victor Books) SP Pubns.

***Christian Educator's Handbook on Spiritual Formation.** Kenneth O. Gangel. 1994. 22.99 (*1-56476-079-0*, Victor Books) SP Pubns.

Christian Educator's Handbook on Teaching. Kenneth D. Gangel & Howard Hendricks. 350p. 1988. text ed. 22.99 (*0-89693-489-6*, Victor Books) SP Pubns.

Christian Employee. Robert Mattox. LC 77-20588. 220p. 1978. pap. 5.95 (*0-88270-263-7*) Bridge Pub.

Christian Endeavor Stories, 3 vols. Grace L. Hill. reprint ed. lib. bdg. 43.95 (*0-89190-036-5*, Rivercity Pr) Amereon Ltd.

Christian Epigraphy. Orazio Marucchi. Tr. by J. Armine Willis. LC 74-82057. 472p. 1975. 30.00 (*0-89005-070-8*) Ares.

Christian Essence of Spanish Literature: An Historical Study. Lewis J. Hutton. LC 87-3535. (Studies in Art & Religious Interpretation: Vol. 9). 520p. 1987. lib. bdg. 119.95 (*0-88946-561-4*) E Mellen.

Christian Ethic as an Economic Factor. Josiah C. Stamp. LC 70-102256. (Select Bibliographies Reprint Ser.). 1977. 19.95 (*0-8369-5141-7*) Ayer.

Christian Ethics. J. Elliott Ross. 250p. 1951. 12.95 (*0-8159-5202-3*) Devin.

Christian Ethics. Ed. by Lane A. Scott & Leon O. Hynson. (Wesleyan Theological Perspectives Ser.: Vol. III). 1989. 14.95 (*0-87162-267-X*, D4852) Warner Pr.

Christian Ethics: A Case Method Approach. 2nd ed. Robert L. Stivers et al. LC 94-15929. 300p. (Orig.). 1994. pap. 16.95 (*0-88344-973-0*) Orbis Bks.

Christian Ethics: A Historical Introduction. J. Philip Wogaman. LC 93-3259. 352p. (Orig.). 1993. pap. 19.99 (*0-664-25163-3*) Westminster John Knox.

Christian Ethics: A Primer. William M. Tillman, Jr. & Timothy D. Gilbert. LC 85-25474. 1986. pap. 5.99 (*0-8054-6128-0*) Broadman.

Christian Ethics: An Introduction Through History & Current Issues. Denise L. Carmody. 256p. (C). 1992. pap. text ed. 19.25 (*0-13-131533-1*) P-H.

Christian Ethics: Foundations & Practice. Robert B. McLaren. 304p. (C). 1993. pap. text ed. write for info. (*0-13-132804-2*) P-H.

Christian Ethics: Options & Issues. Norman L. Geisler. LC 89-37974. 272p. (Orig.). 1989. pap. text ed. 17.99 (*0-8010-3832-4*) Baker Bk.

***Christian Ethics: Shaping Values, Visions, & Decisions.** Judith Caron. LC 95-60625. 256p. (Orig.). 1995. pap. 14.95 (*0-89622-658-1*) Twenty-Third.

Christian Ethics & Political Action. Donald E. Messer. 176p. 1984. pap. 13.00 (*0-8170-1018-1*) Judson.

***Christian Ethics & Political Economy in North America: A Critical Analysis.** P. Travis Kroeker. (McGill-Queen's Studies in the History of Religion). 224p. 1995. 44.95 (*0-7735-1267-5*, Pub. by McGill CN); pap. 18.95 (*0-7735-1268-3*, Pub. by McGill CN) U of Toronto Pr.

Christian Ethics & the Dilemmas of Foreign Policy. Kenneth W. Thompson. LC 59-15344. 160p. reprint ed. pap. 45.60 (*0-8357-9098-3*, 2017937) Bks Demand.

***Christian Ethics & the Global Economy.** Max Stackhouse & Peter Berger. 176p. (Orig.). 1995. pap. 14.95 (*0-687-00335-0*) Abingdon.

An Asterisk (*) at the beginning of an entry indicates that the title is appearing in BIP for the first time.

Christian Ethics in a Secular Arena. Josef Fuchs. LC 84-7964. 164p. (Orig.). reprint ed. pap. 46.80 (*0-7837-6452-9*, 2046451) Bks Demand.

Christian Ethics in an African Context: A Focus on Urban Zambia. Dick A. Rader. LC 90-21429. (American University Studies: Theology & Religion: Ser. VII, Vol. 128). 200p. (C). 1991. text ed. 36.95 (*0-8204-1453-0*) P Lang Pubs.

Christian Ethics in Health Care. John Wilkinson. (C). 1990. 95.00 (*0-85305-317-0*, Pub. by J Arthur Ltd UK); pap. 24.00 (*0-905312-35-X*, Pub. by J Arthur Ltd UK) St Mut.

Christian Ethics in Secular Worlds. Robin Gill. 160p. 1991. pap. text ed. 19.95 (*0-567-29198-7*, Pub. by T & T Clark UK) Bks Intl VA.

Christian Ethics in the Protestant Tradition. Waldo Beach. LC 88-8213. 132p. 1989. pap. 11.99 (*0-8042-0793-3*, John Knox) Westminster John Knox.

Christian Evidences - How We Know the Bible Is God's Revelation. Leland M. Haines. 128p. (Orig.). 1991. pap. 3.95 (*0-9616910-2-6*) L M Haines.

Christian Excellence. Jon Johnston. 1985. pap. 6.99 (*0-8010-5195-9*) Baker Bk.

Christian Existence Today: Essays on Church, World, & Living in Between. Stanley M. Hauerwas. LC 88-18774. x, 288p. 1988. 14.95 (*0-939464-48-9*) Labyrinth Pr.

Christian Experience. Donald MacDonald. 160p. 1988. 16.95 (*0-85151-527-4*) Banner of Truth.

Christian Experience. rev. ed. (Time of Life Learning Ser.). (Illus.). 32p. 1985. reprint ed. pap. 2.95 (*0-89622-246-2*) Twenty-Third.

Christian Experience & Teaching of Ellen G. White. Ellen G. White. 1940. reprint ed. 11.95 (*0-8163-0126-3*, 03310-0) Pacific Pr Pub Assn.

Christian Experience of Salvation. William E. Hull. LC 84-20501. (Layman's Library of Christian Doctrine Ser.). 1991. 7.99 (*0-8054-1639-0*) Broadman.

Christian Expressions, 14 vols. Carol Arida. Incl. Bk. 1. LC 94-94273. 1994. (*1-885493-00-2*); Bk. 2. LC 94-94273. 1994. (*1-885493-01-0*); Bk. 3. LC 94-94273. 1994. (*1-885493-02-9*); Bk. 4. LC 94-94273. 1994. (*1-885493-03-7*); Bk. 5. LC 94-94273. 1994. (*1-885493-04-5*); Bk. 6. LC 94-94273. 1994. (*1-885493-05-3*); Bk. 7. LC 94-94273. 1994. (*1-885493-06-1*); Bk. 8. LC 94-94273. 1994. (*1-885493-07-X*); Bk. 9. LC 94-94273. 1994. (*1-885493-08-8*); Bk. 10. LC 94-94273. 1994. (*1-885493-09-6*); Bk. 11. LC 94-94273. 1994. (*1-885493-10-X*); Bk. 12. LC 94-94273. 1994. (*1-885493-11-8*); Bk. 13. LC 94-94273. 1994. (*1-885493-12-6*); Bk. 14. LC 94-94273. 1994. (*1-885493-13-4*); LC 94-94273. 110p. (Orig.). 1994. Set pap. 2.50 (*0-685-75064-7*) C Arida Christian.

Christian Faith. Henri De Lubac. Tr. by Richard Arnandez. LC 84-80903. Orig. Title: La Foi Chretienne. 353p. (Orig.). 1986. pap. 16.95 (*0-89870-053-1*) Ignatius Pr.

Christian Faith. Friedrich Schleiermacher. Ed. by H. R. MacKintosh & J. S. Stewart. 772p. 1928. 39.95 (*0-567-02239-0*, Pub. by T & T Clark UK) Bks Intl VA.

Christian Faith. Ernst Troeltsch. Tr. by Garrett E. Paul. LC 90-19370. (Texts in Modern Theology Ser.). 320p. (Orig.). 1991. pap. 20.00 (*0-8006-3209-5*, 1-3209, Fortress Pr) Augsburg Fortress.

Christian Faith. large type ed. David H. Read. 1985. pap. 9.95 (*0-8027-2515-5*) Walker & Co.

Christian Faith. rev. ed. Ed. by J. Neuner & J. Dupuis. LC 82-22700. 740p. 1990. pap. 16.95 (*0-8189-0453-4*) Alba.

Christian Faith: Essays in Explanation & Defence. Ed. by W. R. Matthews. LC 73-152162. (Essay Index Reprint Ser.). 1977. reprint ed. 23.95 (*0-8369-2348-0*) Ayer.

Christian Faith & Beliefs. Morris Ashcraft. LC 83-71872. 1984. 12.99 (*0-8054-1603-X*) Broadman.

Christian Faith & Freedom: Proceedings. Fellowship of Catholic Scholars Staff. Ed. by Paul L. Williams. LC 82-81072. 128p. (Orig.). 1982. pap. text ed. 4.50 (*0-686-97454-9*) NE Bks.

Christian Faith & Greek Philosophy in Late Antiquity: Essays in Tribute to George Christopher Stead. Lionel R. Wickham & Caroline P. Bammel. LC 93-19426. (Supplements to Vigiliae Christianae Ser.: Vol. 19). x, 266p. (ENG & GER.). 1993. 71.50 (*90-04-09605-1*) E J Brill.

Christian Faith & Historical Understanding. 2nd ed. Ronald H. Nash. LC 89-48471. 169p. (C). 1989. reprint ed. pap. 11.99 (*0-945241-07-0*) Probe Bks.

***Christian Faith & Life.** William Temple. Ed. by Susan Howatch. (Yes: Library of Anglican Spirituality Ser.). 150p. 1995. pap. 9.95 (*0-8192-1631-3*) Morehouse Pub.

Christian Faith & My Everyday Life. Robert Faricy. (C). 1988. 39.00 (*0-85439-197-5*, Pub. by St Paul Pubns UK) St Mut.

Christian Faith & Natural Science. Karl Heim. 10.50 (*0-8446-0690-1*) Peter Smith.

Christian Faith & Other Faiths. Stephen Neill. LC 84-19123. 304p. 1984. pap. 15.99 (*0-87784-337-6*, 337) InterVarsity.

Christian Faith & Practice in the Modern World: Theology from an Evangelical Point of View. Ed. by Mark A. Noll & David F. Wells. LC 88-3635. 357p. reprint ed. pap. 101.80 (*0-7837-3197-3*, 2042802) Bks Demand.

Christian Faith & Practice of Samuel Johnson, Thomas De Quincey & Thomas Love Peacock. Neil Tomkinson. LC 92-32309. 284p. 1992. text ed. 89.95 (*0-7734-9194-5*) E Mellen.

Christian Faith & the Bible of Judaism: The Judaic Encounter with Scripture. Jacob Neusner. (Brown Judaic Studies). 232p. 1991. 59.95 (*1-55540-498-7*, 140208) Scholars Pr GA.

Christian Faith & the Bible of Judaism: The Judaic Encounter with Scripture. Jacob Neusner. LC 87-20177. 221p. reprint ed. pap. 63.00 (*0-8357-4366-7*, 2037195) Bks Demand.

Christian Faith & the Interpretation of History: A Study of St. Augustine's Philosophy of History. Gordon L. Keyes. LC 66-10314. 220p. reprint ed. pap. 62.70 (*0-8357-3804-3*, 2036532) Bks Demand.

Christian Faith & the Question of History. William N. Pittenger. LC 73-79353. 159p. reprint ed. pap. 45.40 (*0-685-15547-1*, 2026910) Bks Demand.

Christian Faith & War. Metropolitan Anthony Khrapovitsky. (Orig.). 1973. pap. 0.50 (*0-317-30278-7*) Holy Trinity.

Christian Faith, Health, & Medical Practice. Hessel Bouma, III et al. 352p. (Orig.). (C). 1989. pap. 24.99 (*0-8028-0369-5*) Eerdmans.

Christian Faith in a Religiously Plural World. Ed. by Donald G. Dawe & John B. Carman. LC 78-50927. 208p. (Orig.). reprint ed. pap. 59.30 (*0-8357-2671-1*, 2040207) Bks Demand.

Christian Faith in Dark Times: Theological Conflicts in the Shadow of Hitler. Jack Forstman. 240p. 1992. text ed. 23.00 (*0-664-21974-8*) Westminster John Knox.

Christian Faith vs. Unbelief. Constancio Amen. 1987. pap. 6.95 (*0-9618383-0-2*) GN Inc.

Christian Families in the Real World. Mitch Finley & Kathy Finley. 1984. pap. 11.95 (*0-88347-192-2*) Thomas More.

Christian Family. Larry Christenson. LC 75-324692. 224p. pap. 7.99 (*0-87123-114-X*) Bethany Hse.

Christian Family. Larry Christenson. LC 75-324692. 224p. 1970. 7.99 (*0-87123-071-2*) Bethany Hse.

Christian Family: In the Teachings of John Paul II. Pope John Paul, II. 1991. pap. 6.50 (*0-949080-13-6*) Alba.

Christian Family Christmas Book. Ed. by Ron Klug & Lyn Klug. LC 87-1391. (Illus.). 128p. (J). (ps-7). 1987. text ed. 14.99 (*0-8066-2270-9*, 10-1113, Augsburg) Augsburg Fortress.

Christian Family Living. John Coblentz. 1992. pap. 9.95 (*0-87813-541-3*) Christian Light.

Christian Family Living. Perry Gillum & Rob Allen. LC 85-1679. 125p. (Orig.). 1987. 3.95 (*0-934942-65-X*) White Wing Pub.

Christian Family Prepares for Christmas. Charles S. Mueller. 1965. 5.99 (*0-570-03023-4*, 6-1092) Concordia.

Christian Family Prepares for Easter. Ruth Geisler. 96p. (Orig.). 1985. pap. 9.99 (*0-570-03977-0*, 12-2893) Concordia.

Christian Fantasy: From Twelve Hundred to the Present. Colin Manlove. LC 91-47494. (C). 1992. text ed. 32.95 (*0-268-00790-X*) U of Notre Dame Pr.

Christian Father's Present to His Children. John A. James. 436p. 1993. reprint ed. 32.95 (*1-877611-70-0*) Soli Deo Gloria.

***Christian Feminist Theology: A Constructive Interpretation.** Denise L. Carmody. 304p. (C). 1995. write for info. (*1-55786-586-8*); pap. write for info. (*1-55786-587-6*) Blackwell Pubs.

Christian Financial Counselor's Manual. Larry Burkett. (Christian Financial Concepts Ser.). 73p. 1991. pap. 5.00 (*1-56427-075-0*) Christian Fin Concepts.

Christian Financial Counselor's Self-Study Course. Larry Burkett. (Christian Financial Concepts Ser.). 200p. 1991. ring bd. 50.00 (*1-56427-076-9*) Christian Fin Concepts.

Christian for All Christians: Essays in Honor of C. S. Lewis. Ed. by Andrew Walker & James Patrick. LC 91-46764. 258p. 1992. pap. 10.95 (*0-89526-735-7*) Regnery Pub.

Christian for All Christians: Essays in Honour of C. S. Lewis. Ed. by A. Walker & J. Patrick. 258p. (Orig.). 1990. pap. 22.95 (*0-340-51384-5*, Pub. by Hodder & Stoughton Ltd UK) Lubrecht & Cramer.

Christian Foundation of Criminal Responsibility: Historical-Comparative Approach to the Roots of Theological & Civil Law. John Quinn & J. M. Crawford. LC 90-5638. (Toronto Studies in Theology: Vol. 40). 640p. 1991. lib. bdg. 129.95 (*0-88946-979-2*) E Mellen.

***Christian Foundation Package.** Joseph Giles. 1994. 10.95 (*0-533-10919-1*) Vantage.

Christian Foundations. Lester Sumrall. 118p. (C). 1983. pap. text ed. 10.00 (*0-937580-74-0*) LeSEA Pub Co.

Christian Foundations, 2 vols., Set. Donald G. Bloesch. 1994. 46.99 (*0-8308-1410-8*, 1410) InterVarsity.

Christian Foundations: An Introduction to Faith in Our Time. Kathleen R. Fisher & Thomas N. Hart. 240p. 1986. pap. 9.95 (*0-8091-2817-9*) Paulist Pr.

Christian Frame of Mind: Reason, Order, & Openness in Theology & Natural Science. Thomas F. Torrance. 1989. 22.95 (*0-939443-09-0*) Helmers Howard Pub.

Christian Freedom: Essays by the Faculty of the Saint Meinrad School of Theology. Ed. by Clayton N. Jefford. LC 92-30406. (American University Studies: Theology & Religion: Ser. VII, Vol. 144). 228p. (C). 1993. pap. text ed. 26.95 (*0-8204-2061-1*) P Lang Pubs.

Christian Friendship in the Fourth Century. Carolinne White. 266p. (C). 1992. 59.95 (*0-521-41907-7*) Cambridge U Pr.

Christian Fudge Family. Frank Sellers. (Illus.). 631p. 1990. 35.00 (*0-685-45843-1*) F Sellers.

Christian Furchtegott Gellert Gesammelte Schriften, Band VI: Moralische Vorlesungen, Moralische Charaktere Kommentierte, Kritische Ausgabe, 6 vols., Set. Ed. by Sibylle Spath. vii, 526p. (GER.). (C). 1991. lib. bdg. 246.15 (*3-11-012818-7*) De Gruyter.

Christian Future. Eugen Rosenstock-Huessy. 248p. pap. 9.50 (*0-912148-10-1*) Argo Bks.

Christian Girl, 4 vols., 1. Mamie W. Hayhurst. (J). 1964. pap. 2.75 (*0-685-74303-9*, CG100) Quality Pubns.

Christian Girl, 4 vols., 2. Mamie W. Hayhurst. (J). 1964. pap. 2.75 (*0-685-74304-7*, CG200) Quality Pubns.

Christian Girl, 4 vols., 3. Mamie W. Hayhurst. (J). 1964. pap. 2.75 (*0-318-68055-6*, CG300) Quality Pubns.

Christian Girl, 4 vols., 4. Mamie W. Hayhurst. (J). 1964. pap. 2.75 (*0-685-74306-3*, CG400) Quality Pubns.

Christian Giving. John F. Hopkins. Tr. by David Agriesti. LC 92-27257. 160p. (Orig.). 1992. pap. 5.99 (*1-56722-003-7*) Word Aflame.

Christian God. Richard Swinburne. 256p. 1994. 55.00 (*0-19-823513-5*); pap. 22.00 (*0-19-823512-7*) OUP.

Christian Government: Its Scientific Evolution. 3rd ed. Max Kappeler. LC 58-26852. 106p. 1990. reprint ed. pap. 12.00 (*0-85241-070-0*) Kappeler Inst Pub.

Christian Guide to Parent Care. Robert Riekse & Henry Holstege. 1992. pap. 9.99 (*0-8423-0544-0*) Tyndale.

Christian Guide to Prosperity. 2nd ed. Michael Fries et al. Ed. by Diane Frank. LC 83-46178. (Illus.). 523p. 1984. pap. 9.95 (*0-9611910-5-8*) Comm Res.

Christian Harmony. Jeremiah Ingalls. LC 80-16558. (Earlier American Music Ser.). 1981. 29.50 (*0-306-79617-1*) Da Capo.

Christian Healing. Mary Baker Eddy. 1908. pap. 3.95 (*0-87952-058-2*) Christian Sci.

Christian Healing. Charles Fillmore. 172p. 1909. 7.95 (*0-87159-017-4*) Unity Bks.

Christian Healing. Mary M. Eddy. (Notable American Authors Ser.). 1992. reprint ed. lib. bdg. 75.00 (*0-7812-2748-8*) Rprt Serv.

Christian Healing. Charles Fillmore. reprint ed. pap. 14.95 (*1-872736-44-0*, Pub. by Mandrake Pr UK) Holmes Pub.

Christian Healing: A Practical, Comprehensive Guide. Mark A. Pearson. LC 90-35712. 1990. pap. 11.99 (*0-8007-9165-7*) Chosen Bks.

Christian Healing: A Practical, Comprehensive Guide. 2nd ed. Mark A. Pearson. LC 94-16615. 368p. 1995. pap. 11.99 (*0-8007-9221-1*) Chosen Bks.

Christian Healing after the New Testament: Some Approaches to Illness in the Second, Third, & Fourth Centuries. R. J. Barrett-Lennard. LC 93-3835. Date not set. 46.50 (*0-8191-9129-9*) U Pr of Amer.

Christian Healing Again & Again. Elaine M. Ward. 103p. (Orig.). 1992. pap. 10.95 (*1-877871-23-0*, 3345) Ed Ministries.

Christian Healing & Other Writings on Christian Science. Mary B. Eddy. 246p. (C). reprint ed. pap. 10.95 (*0-930227-19-0*) Bookmark CA.

Christian Hebraists & Dutch Rabbis: Seventeenth Century Apologetics & the Study of Maimonides' Mishneh Torah. Aaron L. Katchen. (Harvard Judaic Texts & Studies: No. 3). 430p. 1985. text ed. 28.00 (*0-674-12865-6*) Harvard U Ctr Jewish.

Christian Hedonism. Howard A. Redmond. LC 89-12344. (American University Studies: Theology & Religion: Ser. VII, Vol. 67). 156p. 1990. text ed. 34.95 (*0-8204-1117-5*) P Lang Pubs.

Christian Hellenism, Vol. Three: Essays & Studies in Continuity & Change. Demetrios J. Constantelos. (Hellenism: Ancient, Mediaeval, Modern Ser.: No. 13). 292p. (C). 1993. text ed. 60.00 (*0-89241-523-1*) Caratzas.

***Christian Hermeneutics: Paul Ricoeur & the Refiguring of Theology.** James Fodor. 400p. 1995. 65.00 (*0-19-826349-X*) OUP.

Christian Heroes of the Holocaust: The Righteous Gentiles. Joseph J. Carr. LC 85-70538. 189p. 1985. pap. 3.95 (*0-88270-582-2*) Bridge Pub.

Christian Higher Education in Changing China, 1880-1950. William P. Fenn. LC 75-43741. (Illus.). 256p. reprint ed. pap. 73.00 (*0-317-07969-7*, 2012769) Bks Demand.

Christian History & Interpretation: Studies Presented to John Knox. Ed. by William R. Farmer & C. F. Moule. LC 67-15306. 464p. reprint ed. pap. 132.30 (*0-317-08479-8*, 2022449) Bks Demand.

Christian History of the American Revolution: Consider & Ponder. Verna M. Hall. LC 75-18326. (Illus.). 736p. 1976. lib. bdg. 41.95 (*0-912498-04-8*) F A C E.

Christian History of the Constitution of the United States of America, Vol. 1: Christian Self-Government. Verna M. Hall. LC 61-16012. (Illus.). 545p. 1960. lib. bdg. 39.95 (*0-912498-00-5*) F A C E.

Christian History of the Constitution of the United States of America, Vol. 2: Christian Self-Government with Union. Verna M. Hall. LC 61-16012. (Illus.). 660p. 1962. lib. bdg. 39.95 (*0-912498-01-3*) F A C E.

Christian Holiday Verses. Elizabeth L. Nichols. (Illus.). 24p. (Orig.). 1993. pap. text ed. 3.95 (*1-880473-05-4*) Fam Hist Educ.

Inspirational Christian verses--ideal for devotionals, family sharing, or personal inspiration. Twelve simple-language poems about Jesus Christ as Savior & Redeemer--with emphasis on his birth, resurrection & love; & Christmas, & Easter. Ideal gift. Cardstock cover; four-color reproductions of two Harry Anderson paintings--"The Prophet Isaiah Foretells Christ's Birth" & "Second Coming;" worth its price just for these paintings. Reader Responses: "A MOST INSPIRING BOOKLET OF POETRY ON THE BIRTH & MISSION OF THE SAVIOR." "THE AUTHOR HAS BEEN GIVEN THE GIFT OF INSIGHT & THE POWER TO SHARE THAT INSIGHT IN VERSE." "THE FEELINGS IT EVOKES PREPARES ME FOR THE GLORIOUS CELEBRATION OF THE SAVIOR'S PRICELESS GIFT TO US." "WE JUST READ CHRISTIAN HOLIDAY VERSES FOR FAMILY HOME EVENING AN EVENING WHERE THE WHOLE FAMILY SHARES TOGETHER, & ENJOYED EVERY WORD OF IT." A few selected verses: "A child is born to Mary,/A baby dear & sweet;/An infant to be cared for/By loving hands petite"--(page 3). "It's true! 'tis true!/How can we know?/Kneel & pray, & ask for your heart/To know from within..."--(page 23). Order from: Family History Educators, Box 510606, Salt Lake City, UT 84151-0606. Phone & FAX: 801-359-7391. ***Publisher Provided Annotation.***

Christian Home. Mervin Baer. 1976. 2.00 (*0-686-11147-8*) Rod & Staff.

Christian Home. Carl R. Birchard & Delores S. Birchard. 39p. 1988. pap. 2.50 (*0-8341-1259-0*) Beacon Hill.

Christian Home. R. Campbell. pap. 4.95 (*0-88172-006-2*) Believers Bkshelf.

Christian Home Cookbook: Traditional Family Recipes. Hearth Publishing Committee Staff. 400p. 1991. 15.95 (*0-9627947-2-4*) Hearth KS.

***Christian Home Educator's Curriculum Manual: Elementary Grades.** Cathy Duffy. (Illus.). 328p. (Orig.). 1995. pap. 16.95 (*0-929320-05-0*) Home Run Enterprises.

***Christian Home Educators' Curriculum Manual: Junior-Senior High.** Cathy Duffy. 320p. 1995. pap. 16.95 (*0-929320-08-5*) Home Run Enterprises.

Christian Home Educators' Curriculum Manual: Junior-Senior High. Cathy Duffy. 224p. 1995. pap. 14.95 (*0-929320-04-2*) Home Run Enterprises.

Christian Home in Victorian America, 1840-1900. Colleen McDannell. LC 85-42947. (Religion in North America Ser.). (Illus.). 216p. 1986. 25.00 (*0-253-31376-7*); pap. 12.95 (*0-253-20882-3*) Ind U Pr.

Christian Hope. Morris Ashcraft. LC 87-29998. (Layman's Library of Christian Doctrine Ser.). 154p. (Orig.). 1991. 7.99 (*0-8054-1645-5*) Broadman.

Christian Humanism, a Critique of the Secular City & Its Ideology. Thomas Molnar. 1978. 8.95 (*0-8199-0694-8*, Frncscn Herld) Franciscan Pr.

Christian Humanism & the Puritan Social Order. Margo Todd. (Ideas in Context Ser.). 230p. 1988. 59.95 (*0-521-33129-3*) Cambridge U Pr.

Christian Humanism & the Reformation: Selected Writings of Erasmus. 3rd ed. John C. Olin. LC 65-10218. (Illus.). x, 221p. 1987. pap. 15.00 (*0-8232-1192-4*) Fordham.

Christian Humanism of Flannery O'Connor. David Eggenschwiler. LC 79-179560. 149p. reprint ed. pap. 42.50 (*0-7837-3775-0*, 2043593) Bks Demand.

Christian Iconography: A Study of Its Origins. Andre Grabar. LC 67-31114. (A. W. Mellon Lectures in the Fine Arts Bollingen Ser.: Vol. 35, No. 10). (Illus.). 432p. (Orig.). 1980. pap. 24.95 (*0-691-01830-8*) Princeton U Pr.

Christian Idea of Education. Ed. by Edmund Fuller. 1957. 27.50 (*0-685-45675-7*) Elliots Bks.

Christian Ideals. 1970. reprint ed. pap. 3.95 (*0-87813-501-4*) Christian Light.

Christian Identity & Theological Education. Joseph C. Hough, Jr. & John B. Cobb, Jr. (Studies in Religious & Theological Scholarship). 1985. pap. 14.95 (*0-89130-855-5*, 00-08-01) Scholars Pr GA.

Christian Images in Hispanic New Mexico: The Taylor Museum Collection of Santos. William Wroth. LC 82-4404. (Illus.). 227p. 1982. text ed. 35.00 (*0-685-19154-0*); pap. 20.00 (*0-317-64321-5*) CO Springs Fine Arts.

Christian in a Changing Society. Jon Johnston. (Christian Living Ser.). 47p. 1988. pap. 2.50 (*0-8341-1230-2*) Beacon Hill.

Christian in Complete Armour. abr. ed. William Gurnall. (Fifty Greatest Christian Classics Ser.). 640p. 1989. text ed. 19.95 (*0-685-30024-2*) Sovereign Grace Trust Fund.

Christian in Complete Armour. William Gurnall. 600p. 1989. reprint ed. 46.95 (*0-85151-196-1*) Banner of Truth.

Christian in Complete Armour, 3 vols., Set. abr. ed. William Gurnall. 1990. pap. 21.95 (*0-85151-568-1*) Banner of Truth.

Christian in Complete Armour, Vol. 3. abr. rev. ed. William Gurnall. 320p. 1989. reprint ed. pap. 7.50 (*0-85151-560-6*) Banner of Truth.

Christian in Complete Armour: A Modernised Abridgement, Vol. 1. abr. rev. ed. William Gurnall. 320p. 1986. pap. 7.50 (*0-85151-456-1*) Banner of Truth.

Christian in Complete Armour: Daily Readings in Spiritual Warfare. William Gurnall. Ed. by James S. Bell, Jr. 370p. 1994. 14.99 (*0-8024-1176-2*) Moody.

Christian in Complete Armour, Vol. 2: (A Modernised Abridgement) abr. rev. ed. William Gurnall. 396p. 1988. pap. 7.50 (*0-85151-515-0*) Banner of Truth.

Christian Initiation: A Comparative Study of the Interpretation of the Baptismal Liturgy in the Mystagogical Writing of Cyril of Jerusalem, John Chrysostom, Theodore of Mopsuetia, & Ambrose of Milan. Hugh M. Riley. LC 74-11191. (Catholic University of America Studies in Christian Antiquity: No. 17). 515p. reprint ed. pap. 146.80 (*0-317-27922-X*, 2025126) Bks Demand.

An Asterisk (*) at the beginning of an entry indicates that the title is appearing in BIP for the first time.

Christian Initiation & Baptism in the Holy Spirit. Kilian McDonnell & George T. Montague. 368p. (C). 1991. pap. 14.95 (*0-8146-5009-0*) Liturgical Pr.

Christian Initiation of Adults. rev. ed. Congregation for Divine Worship Staff. Tr. by International Committee on English in the Liturgy Staff. (Liturgy Documentary Ser.: No. 4). 138p. (Orig.). 1988. pap. 5.95 (*1-55586-895-9*) US Catholic.

Christian Initiation of Adults: A Commentary. rev. ed. Secretariat Staff et al. (Study Text Ser.: No. 10). 120p. (Orig.). 1988. pap. 7.95 (*1-55586-934-3*) US Catholic.

Christian Initiation of Children: Hope for the Future. Robert D. Duggan & Maureen A. Kelly. 1991. pap. 7.95 (*0-8091-3258-3*) Paulist Pr.

Christian Initiation of Older Children. Sandra Figgess. 88p. (C). 1990. text ed. 29.00 (*0-85439-340-4*, Pub. by St Paul Pubns UK) St Mut.

Christian Initiation of Older Children. rev. ed. Sandra Figgess. 96p. 1992. pap. text ed. 6.95 (*0-8146-2103-1*) Liturgical Pr.

***Christian Inscription at Pompeii.** Paul Berry. LC 95-19165. (Illus.). 84p. Date not set. text ed. 49.95 (*0-7734-8899-5*) E Mellen.

Christian Institute for the Study of Religion & Society, a Research Arm of Christian Churches in India. Frank Thompson. LC 92-28668. (Studies in the History of Missions: Vol. 9). 164p. 1992. text ed. 79.95 (*0-7734-9158-9*) E Mellen.

Christian Instruction, Admonition & Grace, The Christian Combat, Faith, Hope & Charity. Augustine. Tr. by John J. Gavigan et al. LC 66-20314. (Fathers of the Church Ser.: Vol. 2). 494p. 1950. 34.95 (*0-8132-0002-4*) Cath U Pr.

Christian Island. Beram Saklatvala. LC 75-92561. (Illus.). 150p. 1975. 24.50 (*0-8386-7571-9*) Fairleigh Dickinson.

***Christian Issues in the Gospels.** Eileen Bromley. 72p. (C). 1991. pap. 30.00x (*0-7478-0582-2*, Pub. by S Thornes Pubs UK) St Mut.

Christian Journey. Paul N. Howell. 1991. 13.95 (*0-533-09089-X*) Vantage.

***Christian Justice: Sharing God's Goodness.** Julia Ahlers & Michael Wilt. Ed. by Barbara Allaire. (Illus.). 304p. (Orig.). (YA). (gr. 11-12). 1995. pap. text ed. 12.50 (*0-88489-330-8*) St Marys.

***Christian Justice: Sharing God's Goodness.** Kevin Lanave. Ed. by Barbara Allaire. (Illus.). 51p. (Orig.). 1995. teacher ed, spiral bd. 24.95 (*0-88489-331-6*) St Marys.

Christian Law. S. Sebartin. (C). 1988. 136.00 (*0-685-36479-8*) St Mut.

Christian Leaders of the Eighteenth Century: Includes Whitefield, Wesley, Grimshaw, Romaine, Rowlands, Berridge, Venn, Walker, Harvey, Toplady, & Fletcher. J. C. Ryle. 1978. pap. 9.95 (*0-85151-268-2*) Banner of Truth.

Christian Leadership: The Source of the Vision. Samuel B. Casey. 24p. (Orig.). 1992. pap. text ed. 4.00 (*0-944561-21-7*) Chr Legal.

Christian Leadership Handbook. J. J. Turner. 255p. (Orig.). 1982. pap. 7.95 (*1-878990-10-1*) Howard Pub LA.

Christian Liberty. Martin Luther. Ed. by Harold J. Grimm. Tr. by W. A. Lambert. 1943. pap. 3.50 (*0-8006-0182-3*, 1-182, Fortress Pr) Augsburg Fortress.

Christian Liberty. Arthur W. Pink. pap. 0.99 (*0-87377-072-2*) GAM Pubns.

Christian Liberty: A New Testament Perspective. James D. Dunn. LC 94-16688. xii, 115p. (Orig.). 1994. pap. text ed. 10.99 (*0-8028-0796-8*) Eerdmans.

Christian Life. Perry Gillum. 151p. (Orig.). 1983. teacher ed write for info. (*0-318-58603-7*); pap. 3.95 (*0-934942-46-3*, 2418) White Wing Pub.

Christian Life. W. Graham Scroggie. pap. 1.99 (*1-56632-078-X*) Revival Lit.

Christian Life: A Doctrinal Introduction. Sinclair B. Ferguson. 201p. 1989. reprint ed. pap. 8.95 (*0-85151-516-9*) Banner of Truth.

***Christian Life: An Owner's Manual.** Scott McCallum. 128p. 1995. pap. 7.99 (*0-8254-3194-8*, 95-027) Kregel.

Christian Life: Church Dogmatics IV, 4: Lecture Fragments. Karl Barth. Tr. by Geoffrey W. Bromiley. LC 80-39942. 326p. reprint ed. pap. 93.00 (*0-8357-4352-7*, 2037179) Bks Demand.

Christian Life: Ethics, Morality, & Discipline in the Early Church. Ed. by Everett Ferguson. LC 92-41589. (Studies in Early Christianity: Vol. 16). 376p. 1993. 60.00 (*0-8153-1076-5*) Garland.

Christian Life: Traditional Metaphors & Contemporary Theologies. Harriet Crabtree. LC 91-27980. (Harvard Dissertations in Religion Ser.). 229p. (Orig.). 1991. pap. 15.00 (*0-8006-7083-3*, 1-7083, Fortress Pr) Augsburg Fortress.

***Christian Life - Master Outlines & Notes.** Porter Barrington. Tr. by Wesley Hsu. 129p. (CHI.). 1985. pap. 4.00 (*1-56582-044-4*) Christ Renew Min.

Christian Life & How to Live It. James A. Stewart. pap. 1.99 (*1-56632-065-8*) Revival Lit.

Christian Life & Salvation. Donald G. Bloesch. 168p. 1991. reprint ed. pap. 14.95 (*0-939443-24-4*) Helmers Howard Pub.

Christian Life & Worship. Gerald Ellard. 1978. 39.95 (*0-405-10819-2*) Ayer.

Christian Life Classics. deluxe ed. J. C. Ryle et al. Ed. by Jay P. Green. (Fifty Greatest Christian Classics Ser.: Vol. III). 768p. 1990. 24.95 (*1-878442-52-X*) Sovereign Grace Trust Fund.

Christian Life in Depth. Joseph A. Synan. 1970. 3.95 (*0-911866-60-4*); pap. 2.95 (*0-911866-87-6*) LifeSprings Res.

Christian Life in the Early Church & Today: According to St. Paul's First Epistle to the Corinthians. Barbara Pappas. xvi, 172p. (Orig.). 1989. pap. write for info. (*0-9623721-3-7*) Amnos Pubns.

Christian Life in the Primitive Church. Ernst Von Dobschutz. 1977. lib. bdg. 59.95 (*0-8490-1615-0*) Gordon Pr.

Christian Life Patterns: The Psychological Challenges & Religious Invitations of Adult Life. James D. Whitehead & Evelyn E. Whitehead. 192p. 1992. pap. 11.95 (*0-8245-1154-9*) Crossroad NY.

***Christian Life Style.** 115p. (CHI.). 1987. pap. 5.00 (*1-56582-104-1*) Christ Renew Min.

Christian Liturgy I. Theology. Edward J. Kilmartin. LC 87-61262. 418p. 1988. 26.95 (*1-55612-118-0*); pap. 16.95 (*1-55612-067-2*) Sheed & Ward MO.

Christian Living in the Home. Jay E. Adams. 1972. pap. 6.99 (*0-87552-016-2*) Presby & Reformed.

Christian Living in the Home. Jay E. Adams. 1974. reprint ed. pap. 6.99 (*0-8010-0052-1*) Baker Bk.

Christian Living in the U. S. Culture. Thomas E. Clarke. 36p. 1987. 2.95 (*1-55612-075-3*) Sheed & Ward MO.

Christian Looks at the Jewish Question. Jacques Maritain. LC 73-2216. (Jewish People; History, Religion, Literature Ser.). 1980. reprint ed. 19.95 (*0-405-05280-4*) Ayer.

Christian Love & Just War: Moral Paradox & Political Life in St. Augustine & His Modern Interpreters. William R. Stevenson, Jr. LC 87-15376. 256p. (C). 1987. 29.95 (*0-86554-272-4*, H235) Mercer Univ Pr.

***Christian Man.** Ed. by R. M. Davis & P. D. Buford. 160p. 1995. pap. 4.99 (*1-56722-033-9*) Word Aflame.

Christian Manifesto. Francis A. Schaeffer. LC 81-69737. 192p. 1981. pap. 7.99 (*0-89107-233-0*) Crossway Bks.

***Christian Marriage.** Chris S. Sherrerd. 294p. (Orig.). 1994. pap. 10.99 (*1-56043-806-1*) Destiny Image.

Christian Marriage. Worship for the Presbyterian Church (U. S. A.) Staff & Cumberland Presbyterian Church Staff. LC 85-29571. (Supplemental Liturgical Resource Ser.: 3). 120p. (Orig.). 1986. pap. 8.99 (*0-664-24033-X*, Westminster) Westminster John Knox.

Christian Marriage: A Handbook for Couples. Michael Baughen & Myrtle Baughen. (Illus.). 144p. 1994. 11.99 (*0-8010-1097-7*) Baker Bk.

Christian Marriage: A Journey Together. David M. Thomas. LC 82-84412. (Message of the Sacraments Ser.: Vol. 5). 1983. pap. 12.95 (*0-8146-5231-X*) Liturgical Pr.

Christian Marriage: Grace & Work. Robert E. Money. LC 89-28939. 1991. pap. 7.99 (*0-8054-3004-0*) Broadman.

***Christian Marriage: Sacrament of Abiding Friendship.** John Boucher & Therese Boucher. (Spirit Life Ser.). 64p. (Orig.). 1995. pap. 3.95 (*1-878718-25-8*) Resurrection.

Christian Marriage Today: Growth or Breakdown? Ed. by Joseph A. Buijs. LC 85-10466. (Symposium Ser.: Vol. 16). 168p. 1984. 79.95 (*0-88946-707-2*) E Mellen.

Christian Martyrs in Muslim Spain. Kenneth B. Wolf. (Cambridge Iberian & Latin American Studies). 160p. 1987. 49.95 (*0-521-34416-6*) Cambridge U Pr.

Christian Maturity. Bernard Haring. (C). 1988. 39.00 (*0-85439-223-8*, Pub. by St Paul Pubns UK) St Mut.

Christian Maturity. E. Stanley Jones. (Abingdon Classics Ser.). 364p. 1992. reprint ed. pap. 5.95 (*0-687-07662-5*) Abingdon.

Christian Maturity & Christian Success. Daniel T. Jenkins. LC 82-9759. (Laity Exchange Bks.). 157p. reprint ed. pap. 44.80 (*0-685-23490-8*, 2029095) Bks Demand.

Christian Meaning of Human Sexuality. Paul M. Quay. LC 88-81092. 121p. 1988. reprint ed. pap. 9.95 (*0-89870-212-7*) Ignatius Pr.

Christian Meditation. Hans U. Von Balthasar. Tr. by Mary T. Skerry. LC 88-83746. 97p. (Orig.). 1989. pap. text ed. 8.95 (*0-89870-235-6*) Ignatius Pr.

Christian Meditation & Inner Healing. Dwight H. Judy. 144p. (Orig.). 1991. pap. 10.95 (*0-8245-1090-9*) Crossroad NY.

Christian Meditation by Those Who Practice It. Ed. by Paul T. Harris. 1993. pap. 14.95 (*0-87193-281-4*) Dimension Bks.

Christian Meditations. Wilma Noell. Date not set. pap. 1.95 (*0-317-05928-9*) Crusade Pubs.

Christian Men Who Hate Women. Margaret Rinck. 208p. 1990. pap. 9.99 (*0-310-51751-6*) Zondervan.

Christian Men's Union Brotherhood Guide. J. R. Mosley, Sr. 51p. 1990. pap. text ed. 3.50 (*0-9627958-0-1*, TXU 371-442) J R Mosleys Pr.

Christian Message for the World Today. E. S. Jones et al. LC 77-152163. (Essay Index Reprint Ser.). 1977. 19.95 (*0-8369-2184-4*) Ayer.

Christian Message for Today. Thomas J. Cooper & Willia S. Cooper. (Guidebook to Biblical Truth Ser.: Vol. 3). 60p. (Orig.). 1984. pap. 4.50 (*0-931429-03-X*, TXU 109-949) Cooper & Cooper Pub.

Christian Metz & the Reality of Film. George A. Cozyris. Ed. by Garth S. Jowett. LC 79-6670. (Dissertation on Film, 1980 Ser.). 1980. lib. bdg. 15.95 (*0-405-12904-1*) Ayer.

***Christian Midwifery.** 2nd rev. ed. Betty Peckmann. (Illus.). 500p. 1994. pap. 19.95 (*0-934426-63-5*) NAPSAC Reprods.

Christian Mind. Harry Blamires. 1978. reprint ed. pap. 9.99 (*0-89283-049-2*, Vine Bks) Servant.

Christian Minister: A Practical Approach to the Preaching Ministry. rev. ed. Sam Stone. 272p. (C). 1991. pap. text ed. 9.99 (*0-87403-800-6*, 18-88594) Standard Pub.

Christian Ministerial Priesthood: A Search for Its Beginnings in the Primary Documents of the Apostolic Fathers. Ray R. Noll. 275p. 1993. 64.95 (*1-883255-07-4*); pap. 44.95 (*1-883255-00-7*) Intl Scholars.

Christian Minister's Manual. Rod Huron. (Illus.). 256p. (Orig.). 1984. 18.99 (*0-87239-753-X*, 3028); 24.99 (*0-87239-592-8*, 3029) Standard Pub.

Christian Ministries & the Law: What Church & Parachurch Leaders Should Know. H. Wayne House. LC 91-44969. 288p. 1992. pap. 15.99 (*0-8010-4365-4*) Baker Bk.

Christian Ministry. J. B. Lightfoot. LC 83-62042. 120p. 1983. pap. 8.95 (*0-8192-1331-4*) Morehouse Pub.

Christian Ministry. Charles Bridges. 390p. 1991. reprint ed. 24.95 (*0-85151-087-6*) Banner of Truth.

Christian Ministry of Spiritual Direction. Ed. by David L. Fleming. (Best of the Review Ser.: Bk. 3). 445p. (Orig.). (C). 1988. pap. text ed. 12.95 (*0-924768-05-3*) Review Relig.

Christian Minstrel. Jesse B. Aikin. (Earlier American Music Ser.). 1992. 39.50 (*0-306-77326-0*) Da Capo.

***Christian Mission: A Case Study Approach.** Alan Neely. (American Society of Missiology Ser.: No. 21). 250p. (Orig.). 1995. pap. 19.95 (*1-57075-008-4*) Orbis Bks.

Christian Mission - Jewish Mission. Ed. by Martin A. Cohen & Helga Croner. LC 82-60856. 1982. pap. 7.95 (*0-8091-2475-0*) Paulist Pr.

Christian Mission & Interreligious Dialogue. Ed. by Paul Mojzes & Leonard Swidler. LC 91-2010. (Religions in Dialogue Ser.: Vol. 4). 288p. 1991. lib. bdg. 89.95 (*0-88946-520-7*) E Mellen.

Christian Mission in a Pluralistic World. John P. Brennan. 144p. (C). 1990. 49.00 (*0-85439-326-9*, Pub. by St Paul Pubns UK) St Mut.

Christian Mission in Reconstruction: An Asian Analysis. Choan-Seng Song. LC 77-23237. 288p. pap. 82.10 (*0-8357-8845-8*, 2033473) Bks Demand.

Christian Mission in the Modern World: What the Church Shoud Be Doint Now! John R. Stott. LC 75-21455. 128p. (Orig.). 1975. pap. text ed. 8.99 (*0-87784-485-2*, 485) InterVarsity.

Christian Mission in the Twentieth Century. Timothy Yates. 293p. (C). 1994. 59.95 (*0-521-43493-9*) Cambridge U Pr.

Christian Missionaries & the Creation of Northern Rhodesia, 1880-1924. Robert I. Rotberg. LC 65-12993. (Illus.). 264p. reprint ed. pap. 75.30 (*0-8357-2924-9*, 2039163) Bks Demand.

Christian Missionaries in Orissa: Their Impact on 19th Century Society. D. Swaro. (C). 1990. text ed. 44.00 (*81-85094-35-7*, Pub. by Punthi Pus II) S Asia.

Christian Missionaries on the Indigo Question in Bengal (1855-1861) Abhijit Dutta. (C). 1989. 20.00 (*81-85195-23-4*, Pub. by Minerva II) S Asia.

Christian Missionary Activity in the Early Middle Ages. Richard E. Sullivan. LC 93-47057. 1994. 78.95 (*0-86078-402-9*, Pub. by Variorum UK) Ashgate Pub Co.

Christian Missionizing & Social Transformation: A History of Conflict & Change in Eastern Zaire. Jack E. Nelson. LC 91-46755. 224p. 1992. text ed. 49.95 (*0-275-94246-5*, C4246, Praeger Pubs) Greenwood.

Christian Missions & Colonialism. Lal Deena. 1988. 21.00 (*0-8364-2552-9*, Pub. by Usha II) S Asia.

Christian Missions in North India. Raj B. Sharma. (C). 1988. 22.00 (*0-317-93106-7*, Pub. by Mittal II) S Asia.

Christian Moral Judgment. J. Philip Wogaman. LC 88-27711. 192p. 1989. pap. 15.99 (*0-664-25004-1*) Westminster John Knox.

Christian Moral Principles. Germain Grisez. 1983. 35.00 (*0-8199-0861-4*, Frncscn Herld) Franciscan Pr.

Christian Morality: The Word Becomes Flesh. Josef Fuchs. LC 87-9138. 223p. (Orig.). 1987. pap. 11.95 (*0-87840-452-X*) Georgetown U Pr.

Christian Morality, Natural, Developing, Final. Herbert H. Henson. LC 77-27189. (Gifford Lectures: 1935-36). reprint ed. 27.00 (*0-404-60494-3*) AMS Pr.

***Christian Morgenstern: Lullabies, Lyrics & Gallows Songs.** Christian Morgenstern. Tr. by Anthea Bell. LC 94-40351. (Illus.). 48p. (J). (gr. 1-4). 1995. 16.95 (*1-55858-364-5*); lib. bdg. 16.88 (*1-55858-365-3*) North-South Bks NYC.

Christian Morgenstern's Galgenlieder (Gallows Songs) Christian Morgenstern. Tr. & Intro. by Max Knight. (Illus.). (ENG & GER.). 1963. pap. 11.00 (*0-520-00884-7*) U CA Pr.

Christian Mortalism from Tyndale to Milton. Norman T. Burns. LC 72-75406. 232p. reprint ed. pap. 66.20 (*0-8357-2537-5*, 2057158) Bks Demand.

Christian Mother Goose: Little Tommy Tucker. Marjorie Decker. (Christian Mother Goose Board Bks.). (J). (ps). 1989. 3.99 (*0-529-06685-8*) World Bible.

Christian Mother Goose Big Book. Marjorie A. Decker. LC 92-60502. (Illus.). 304p. (J). (ps-4). 1992. 16.99 (*0-529-07315-3*) World Bible.

Christian Mother Goose Humpty Dumpty. Marjorie Decker. (Christian Mother Goose Board Bks.). (J). (ps). 1989. 3.99 (*0-529-06683-1*) World Bible.

Christian Mother Goose Little Bo Peep. Marjorie Decker. (Christian Mother Goose Board Bks.). (J). (ps). 1989. 3.99 (*0-529-06687-4*) World Bible.

Christian Mother Goose Little Miss Muffet. Marjorie Decker. (Christian Mother Goose Board Bks.). (J). (ps). 1989. 3.99 (*0-529-06686-6*) World Bible.

Christian Mother Goose Piano Book. Marjorie Decker. (J). (gr. k-4). 1989. 8.99 (*0-529-06692-0*) World Bible.

Christian Mother Goose Pop-up Bedtime Animal Friends. Marjorie Decker. (Christian Mother Goose Pop-Up Bks.). (J). (ps). 1989. 6.99 (*0-529-06689-0*) World Bible.

Christian Mother Goose Pop-Up Bedtime Rhymes. Marjorie Decker. (Christian Mother Goose Pop-Up Bks.). (J). (ps). 1989. 6.99 (*0-529-06688-2*) World Bible.

Christian Mother Goose Pop-Up Favorite Rhymes. Marjorie Decker. (Christian Mother Goose Pop-Up Bks.). (J). (ps). 1989. 6.99 (*0-529-06691-2*) World Bible.

Christian Mother Goose Pop-Up Happy Rhymes. Marjorie Decker. (Christian Mother Goose Pop-Up Bks.). (J). (ps). 1989. 6.99 (*0-529-06690-4*) World Bible.

Christian Mother Goose Treasury. Marjorie A. Decker. (Illus.). 112p. 1987. reprint ed. 9.99 (*0-529-06477-4*) World Bible.

***Christian Multi-Media Catalogue for Multi-Lingual Ministries. Raffaele Manzi. Ed. by Sharon S. Ulrich. 384p. (Orig.). 1994. pap. 100.00 (*0-9644029-1-2*) Means NJ.**

If you are in an everyday process of attempting to disseminate Biblical truths to people of culture & language different from yourself, this soon-to-be-published book, CHRISTIAN MULTI-MEDIA CATALOGUE FOR MULTI-LINGUAL MINISTRIES, by Raffaele Manzi from MEANS' INC., is for you. This book will be available in two formats; computer diskettes 3 1/2 & 5 inches & hard page notebook. As this is a resource that will be revised & updated yearly, update information will be made available to original purchasers at a reduced price. THE CHRISTIAN MULTI-MEDIA CATALOGUE FOR MULTI-LINGUAL MINISTRIES, cites over 1,000 distributors & lists over 350 different languages. It indexes by languages, countries of origin, & countries by which these distributors are located, & also has an alphabetical index of all producers, publishers & distributors. The cost paid prior to publication is $75 to missionaries, & $100 to all other organizations & agencies. After publication, the price will be $100 for missionaries & $120 to organizations & agencies. For further information or order forms write MEANS' INC., 488 Parker Ave., Hackensack, NJ 07601; 201-488-6727.

Publisher Provided Annotation.

Christian Muslim Dialogue. H. M. Baagil. 47p. 1984. pap. write for info. (*1-882837-14-2*) Wamy Intl.

***Christian-Muslim Encounters.** Ed. by Yvonne Y. Haddad & Wadi Z. Haddad. LC 95-5178. 520p. 1995. lib. bdg. 49.95 (*0-8130-1356-9*); pap. 29.95 (*0-8130-1359-3*) U Press Fla.

Christian Mystery. Rodney Collin. 1984. pap. 4.95 (*0-916411-26-5*, Sure Fire) Holmes Pub.

Christian Mystery: From Pagan Myth to Christian Mysticism. Louis Bouyer. Tr. by Illtyd Trethowan. 312p. 1990. 39.95 (*0-567-09514-2*, Pub. by T & T Clark UK) Bks Intl VA.

Christian Mystery: From Pagan Myth to Christian Mysticism. Louis Bouyer. Tr. by Illtyd Trethowan. LC 94-17518. 1995. reprint ed. pap. write for info. (*1-879007-07-X*) St Bedes Pubns.

Christian Mystery in a Secular Age: The Foundation & Task of Theology. John Thornhill. LC 91-72128. 225p. (Orig.). 1991. pap. 19.95 (*0-87061-182-8*) Chr Classics.

Christian Mysticism. Harryl. Haywood. 1975. 250.00 (*0-87968-862-9*) Gordon Pr.

Christian Mysticism. William McNamara. (Wellspring Bks.). 176p. 1988. pap. 9.95 (*0-916349-29-2*) Amity Hse Inc.

Christian Mysticism: Psychotheology. William McNamara. LC 80-13139. 173p. 1981. pap. 9.50 (*0-8199-0793-6*, Frncscn Herld) Franciscan Pr.

Christian Mysticism: The Art of the Inner Way. William McNamara. 176p. 1994. reprint ed. pap. text ed. 12.95 (*0-8264-0763-3*) Continuum.

Christian Mysticism: The Future of a Tradition. Harvey Egan. 438p. 1992. pap. 16.50 (*0-8146-6063-0*, Pueblo Bks) Liturgical Pr.

Christian Myth & Ritual: A Historical Study. Edwin O. James. 11.25 (*0-8446-2307-5*) Peter Smith.

Christian Nationalism & the Rise of the Afrikaner Broederbond in South Africa, 1981-1948. Charles Bloomberg. Ed. by Saul Dubow. LC 89-11056. (Illus.). 278p. 1989. 35.00 (*0-253-31235-3*) Ind U Pr.

Christian Neighbor-Love: An Assessment of Six Rival Versions. Garth L. Hallett. LC 88-29182. 179p. 1989. pap. 12.95 (*0-87840-480-5*) Georgetown U Pr.

Christian Non-Resistance. Adin Ballou. LC 70-121104. (Civil Liberties in American History Ser.). 1970. reprint ed. lib. bdg. 35.00 (*0-306-71980-0*) Da Capo.

Christian Non-Resistance in All Its Important Bearings, Illustrated & Defended. Adin Ballou. LC 76-137527. (Peace Movement in America Ser.). 240p. 1972. reprint ed. lib. bdg. 27.95 (*0-89198-054-7*) Ozer.

Christian Nurture. Horace Bushnell. 432p. 1991. pap. 14.99 (*0-8010-0765-8*) Baker Bk.

Christian Nurture. Horace Bushnell. LC 94-6911. (William Bradford Collection). 432p. 1994. reprint ed. pap. 12.95 (*0-8298-1000-5*) Pilgrim OH.

***Christian Orchestra: And Other Plays for Church.** Robert A. Allen. (Christian Theatre Ser.). 40p. (Orig.). 1995. pap. 4.00 (*1-57514-107-8*) Encore Perform Pub.

Christian Origins & Judaism. W. D. Davies. LC 73-2192. (Jewish People; History, Religion, Literature Ser.). 1978. reprint ed. 24.95 (*0-405-05258-8*) Ayer.

C

Christian Pacifism. Daniel A. Dombrowski. (Ethics & Action Ser.). 240p. 1991. 34.95 (*0-87722-802-7*) Temple U Pr.

Christian Pacifism in History. Geoffrey Nuttall. pap. 1.25 (*0-912018-13-5*) World Without War.

Christian Pagan: A Naturalistic Survey of Christian History. John H. Burgess. (Illus.). 1968. 7.00 (*0-912084-04-9*) Mimir.

Christian Paganism. J. C. Metcalfe. 1964. pap. 2.25 (*0-947788-27-1*) Chr Lit.

Christian Palestinian Syriac Horologian (Berlin MS. OR. Oct. 1019) Ed. by M. Black. (Texts & Studies New Ser.). 1972. reprint ed. 52.00 (*0-8115-1714-4*) Periodicals Srv.

Christian Paradox. Cyril Scott. 144p. 1966. reprint ed. spiral bd. 5.50 (*0-7873-0749-1*) Mokelumne.

Christian Parenting. Ed. by Lee W. Carlson. 80p. 1985. pap. 8.00 (*0-8170-1072-6*) Judson.

Christian Parenting. Betsy D. Smylie & John S. Smylie. LC 91-65727. 128p. 1991. pap. 8.95 (*0-8358-0642-1*) Upper Room Bks.

Christian Parenting: Raising Children in the Real World. Donna Sinclair & Yvonne Stewart. 176p. (Orig.). 1992. pap. 11.99 (*0-664-25290-7*) Westminster John Knox.

Christian Parenting Answers. Debra Evans. Ed. by Cathy Davis. 400p. 1994. 24.99 (*0-7814-0182-8*, Chariot Bks) Chariot Family.

Christian Parties for Autumn & Winter. Mary McMillan. (Christian Parties & Celebrations Ser.). 96p. (J). (ps-3). 1989. 10.95 (*0-86653-497-0*, SS1815, Shining Star Pubns) Good Apple.

Christian Parties for Spring & Summer. Mary McMillan. (Illus.). 96p. (J). (ps-3). 1989. 10.95 (*0-86653-473-3*, SS1814, Shining Star Pubns) Good Apple.

Christian Pastor. 3rd rev. ed. Wayne E. Oates. LC 82-4933. 298p. 1982. pap. 10.99 (*0-664-24372-X*, Westminster) Westminster John Knox.

Christian Pattern. John Wesley. 1986. 4.99 (*0-88019-198-8*) Schmul Pub Co.

Christian Peacemaker's Journal. Elizabeth W. Kreider. (Illus.). 96p. (Orig.). 1991. pap. 5.95 (*1-56148-017-7*) Good Bks PA.

Christian Peacemaking: From Heritage to Hope. Daniel L. Buttry. 240p. 1994. pap. 14.00 (*0-8170-1213-3*) Judson.

Christian Peacemaking & International Conflict. Duane K. Friesen. LC 85-24803. (Christian Peace Shelf Ser.). 320p. (Orig.). 1986. pap. 19.95 (*0-8361-1273-3*) Herald Pr.

Christian Perfection. Francois Fenelon. Ed. by Charles F. Whiston. Tr. by Mildred W. Stillman. LC 75-22545. 208p. 1976. reprint ed. pap. 5.99 (*0-87123-083-6*) Bethany Hse.

Christian Perfection, Vol. 1. George Peck. 1990. pap. 9.99 (*0-88019-266-6*) Schmul Pub Co.

Christian Perfection, Vol. 2. George Peck. 1991. reprint ed. pap. 9.99 (*0-88019-271-2*) Schmul Pub Co.

Christian Periodical Index: Annual 1985. 1985. 50.00 (*0-318-04217-7*) Assn Chr Libs.

Christian Periodical Index: Cumulative, 1982-1984, Vol. 7. 1985. 60.00 (*0-318-04216-9*) Assn Chr Libs.

Christian Periodical Index: 1979-1981, Cumulated Vol. 45.00 (*0-318-00379-1*) Assn Chr Libs.

Christian Periodical Index: 1982-1984, Cumulated Vol. 60.00 (*0-318-41170-9*) Assn Chr Libs.

Christian Periodical Index: 1986 Annual. 52.00 (*0-318-41171-7*) Assn Chr Libs.

Christian Periodical Index: 1987 Annual. 75.00 (*0-318-41172-5*) Assn Chr Libs.

Christian Periodical Index: 1988 Tri Annual. 75.00 (*0-318-41173-3*) Assn Chr Libs.

Christian Periodical Index, 1976-1978. Cumulated vol. 40.00 (*0-686-37453-3*) Assn Chr Libs.

Christian Persecution & Genocide. William LeGrande. 1982. lib. bdg. 59.95 (*0-87700-392-0*) Revisionist Pr.

Christian Personality under Construction. (Dialog Ser.). 125p. 1988. student ed, pap. 4.95 (*0-8341-1153-5*); teacher ed, pap. 3.95 (*0-8341-1154-3*) Beacon Hill.

Christian Perspectives in Being Human: A Multidisciplinary Approach to Integration. Ed. by J. P. Moreland & David M. Ciocchi. LC 92-29773. 192p. (Orig.). 1993. pap. 15.99 (*0-8010-6300-0*) Baker Bk.

Christian Perspectives on Dating & Marriage. David Chadwell. 1980. pap. 6.50 (*0-89137-523-6*) Quality Pubns.

Christian Perspectives on Faith Development. Ed. by Jeff Astley & Leslie Francis. 435p. (Orig.). 1992. pap. 24.99 (*0-8028-0578-7*) Eerdmans.

Christian Perspectives on Human Development. LeRoy Aden et al. LC 91-31783. (Psychology & Christianity Ser.). 272p. (Orig.). 1992. pap. text ed. 14.99 (*0-8010-0225-7*) Baker Bk.

Christian Perspectives on Psychology. Ed. by Richard Ruble. LC 75-15956. 147p. (C). 1975. pap. text ed. 15.95 (*0-8422-0456-3*) Irvington.

Christian Perspectives on Religious Knowledge. Ed. by C. Stephen Evans & Merold Westphal. 288p. (Orig.). (C). 1993. pap. text ed. 16.99 (*0-8028-0679-1*) Eerdmans.

Christian Persuader. Leighton Ford. 1988. pap. 6.95 (*0-89066-093-X*) World Wide Pubs.

Christian Philosopher. Cotton Mather. LC 92-32064. 630p. (C). 1993. 49.95 (*0-252-01952-0*) U of Ill Pr.

Christian Philosopher: A Collection of the Best Discoveries in Nature, with Religious Improvements. Cotton Mather. LC 68-29082. 1968. reprint ed. 50.00 (*0-8201-1033-7*) Schol Facsimiles.

Christian Philosophy. Ed. by Thomas P. Flint. LC 89-40388. (Studies in Philosophy of Religion: Vol. 6). (C). 1991. pap. text ed. 12.95 (*0-268-00777-2*) U of Notre Dame Pr.

Christian Philosophy & Its Future. Gerard Smith. LC 75-140071. 144p. 10.00 (*0-87462-439-8*) Marquette.

Christian Philosophy of Education. 2nd rev. ed. Gordon H. Clark. Ed. & Intro. by John W. Robbins. 243p. (Orig.). 1988. pap. 8.95 (*0-940931-20-6*) Trinity Found.

Christian Philosophy of St. Thomas Aquinas. Etienne Gilson. (C). 1994. reprint ed. pap. text ed. 16.95 (*0-268-00801-9*) U of Notre Dame Pr.

Christian Pilgrimage in Modern Western Europe. Mary L. Nolan & Sidney Nolan. LC 88-14364. (Studies in Religion). (Illus.). xxii, 422p. (C). 1992. reprint ed. pap. 16.95 (*0-8078-4389-X*) U of NC Pr.

*__Christian Plain Style: The Evolution of a Spiritual Ideal.__ Peter Auksi. 384p. 1995. 49.95 (*0-7735-1220-9*) U of Toronto Pr.

Christian Platonists of Alexandria. Charles Bigg. xvii, 304p. 1981. reprint ed. 50.70 (*3-487-07044-8*, Pub. by Georg Olms GW) Lubrecht & Cramer.

Christian Platonists of Alexandria: Eight Lectures. Charles Bigg. LC 75-123764. reprint ed. 39.50 (*0-404-00799-6*) AMS Pr.

Christian Political Activism at a Crossroads. Ed. by William R. Stevenson, Jr. (Calvin College Ser.: Vol. III). 205p. (Orig.). Date not set. lib. bdg. 47.00 (*0-8191-9410-7*); pap. text ed. 19.50 (*0-8191-9411-5*) U Pr of Amer.

Christian Polity of John Calvin. Harro Hopfl. (Cambridge Studies in the History & Theory of Politics). 320p. 1985. pap. 21.95 (*0-521-31638-3*) Cambridge U Pr.

*__Christian Position, Conflict, & Hope 1995.__ 56p. Date not set. pap. text ed. 2.50 (*0-9640037-5-9*) Pres Truth.

Christian Prayer. 1976. 23.50 (*0-89942-406-6*, 406/10); 1.00 (*0-686-14264-0*, 406G) Catholic Bk Pub.

Christian Prayer: The Liturgy of the Hours. 1992. reprint ed. 21.95 (*0-8198-1448-2*) Pauline Bks.

Christian Preparation for Death. St. Cyprian. pap. 1.50 (*0-89981-010-1*) Eastern Orthodox.

*__Christian Priest Today.__ rev. ed. Michael Ramsey. 112p. 1994. pap. 9.95 (*1-56101-106-1*) Cowley Pubns.

Christian Primer. Louis Cassels. 112p. 1981. reprint ed. pap. 1.65 (*0-88028-012-3*, 665) Forward Movement.

Christian Primer: The Prayer, the Creed, the Commandments. Albert C. Winn. 204p. (Orig.). 1990. pap. 11.99 (*0-664-25101-3*) Westminster John Knox.

Christian Proficiency. Martin Thornton. LC 88-23768. 201p. 1988. reprint ed. pap. 8.95 (*0-936384-62-X*) Cowley Pubns.

Christian Protagonists for Jewish Restoration: An Original Anthology. Ed. by Moshe Davis. LC 77-70678. (America & the Holy Land Ser.). 1977. lib. bdg. 23.95 (*0-405-10221-6*) Ayer.

Christian Psychiatry. Frank Minirth. LC 76-57767. 1990. pap. 9.99 (*0-8007-5352-6*) Revell.

Christian Psychology. Walter E. Adams. Ed. by Candy L. Adams. 128p. (Orig.). 1990. pap. text ed. 5.95 (*0-937408-95-6*) GMI Pubns Inc.

Christian Psychology in a Course in Miracles. 2nd enl. ed. Kenneth Wapnick. LC 92-19498. 102p. 1992. 4.00 (*0-933291-14-0*) Foun Miracles.

Christian Psychology's War on God's Word: The Victimization of the Believer. James D. Owen. LC 93-70361. 218p. (Orig.). 1993. pap. 9.95 (*0-941717-08-9*) EastGate Pubs.

Christian Rakovski: A Political Biography. Frances Conte. (East European Monographs: No. 256). 550p. 1989. text ed. 77.00 (*0-88033-153-4*) East Eur Quarterly.

Christian Readings, 6 vols. Incl. Vol. 1. Easter to 17th Sunday, Year II. 4.00 (*0-89942-601-8*, 601/04); Vol. 2. Seventeenth Sunday to Advent, Year II. 4.00 (*0-89942-602-6*, 602/04); Vol. 4. Easter to 17th Sunday, Year I. 4.00 (*0-89942-604-2*, 604/04); Vol. 6. Advent to Easter, Year II. 4.00 (*0-89942-606-9*, 606/04); write for info. (*0-318-51309-9*) Catholic Bk Pub.

Christian Realism & Political Problems. Reinhold Niebuhr. LC 75-128062. 203p. 1977. reprint ed. 25.00 (*0-678-02757-9*) Kelley.

Christian Realism of Reinhold Niebuhr & the Political Theology of Jurgen Moltmann in Dialogue: The Realism of Hope. Robert T. Cornelison. LC 92-35175. 240p. 1993. text ed. 89.95 (*0-7734-9805-2*) E Mellen.

Christian Reconstruction: The American Missionary Association & Southern Blacks, 1861-1890. Joe M. Richardson. LC 85-13946. (Illus.). 352p. 1986. 30.00 (*0-8203-0816-1*) U of Ga Pr.

Christian Reconstruction: What It Is, What It Isn't. Gary DeMar & Gary North. LC 90-22956. 218p. 1991. 25.00 (*0-930464-52-4*); pap. 8.95 (*0-930464-53-2*) Inst Christian.

Christian Record Book: The Acivator's Calendar. rev. ed. Truman Massey. 246p. 1992. student ed 15.99 (*1-882844-01-7*) TRU Pubns.

Christian Recovery of Spain. H. E. Watts. 1972. 69.95 (*0-87968-863-7*) Gordon Pr.

Christian Reflections. C. S. Lewis. 1976. 18.95 (*0-8488-1077-5*) Amereon Ltd.

Christian Reflections. C. S. Lewis. 1967. pap. 9.99 (*0-8028-0869-7*) Eerdmans.

Christian Relief & Development. Edgar Elliston. 351p. 1989. pap. write for info. (*0-8499-3155-X*) Word Inc.

Christian Religion: An Introduction. Thomas E. Helm. 288p. (C). 1990. pap. text ed. write for info. (*0-13-133513-8*) P-H.

Christian Religion among the Stockbridge-Munsee Band of Mohican Indians. rev. ed. Thelma Putnam et al. (Illus.). 78p. (Orig.). (C). 1980. pap. text ed. 3.50 (*0-935790-01-2*) Muh-He-Con-Neew.

Christian Religion in Its Doctrinal Expression see Religion Cristiana En Su Expresion Doctrinal

Christian Religion in the Soviet Union: A Sociological Study. Christel Lane. LC 77-801. 256p. 1978. 59.50 (*0-87395-327-4*) State U NY Pr.

*__Christian Religion Ser.__ Date not set. pap. write for info. (*1-881309-09-6*) Orchid Land.

Christian Religious Education: Sharing Our Story & Vision. Thomas H. Groome. LC 81-47847. 320p. (C). 1982. pap. 16.00 (*0-06-063494-4*, RD 371) Harper SF.

Christian Religious Tradition. Stephen Reynolds. 232p. (C). 1977. pap. 19.95 (*0-8221-0204-8*) Intl Thomson.

Christian Response to Domestic Violence: A Reconciliation Model for Social Workers. (Practice Monograph Ser.: No. 1). 45p. 1985. 6.00 (*0-318-17617-3*) N American Assn.

Christian Revelation. Borden P. Bowne. LC 75-3069. reprint ed. 20.00 (*0-404-59068-3*) AMS Pr.

Christian Revelation & the Completion of the Aristotelian Revolution. Patrick Madigan. 136p. (Orig.). (C). 1988. lib. bdg. 34.00 (*0-8191-7090-9*); pap. text ed. 19.50 (*0-8191-7091-7*) U Pr of Amer.

Christian Revolt, Long Overdue: Toward American Freedom from Aliens. Ratibor-Ray M. Jurjevich. (Demonic Maladies in the Western Culture Ser.). 350p. 1990. 24.95 (*0-930711-11-4*); pap. 17.95 (*0-930711-10-6*) Ichthys Bks.

Christian Right & Congress. Matthew C. Moen. LC 88-34010. 248p. (C). 1989. pap. 19.95 (*0-685-67698-6*) U of Ala Pr.

Christian Rite & Christian Drama in the Middle Ages: Essays in the Origin & Early History of Modern Drama. O. B. Hardison, Jr. LC 83-10864. xiii, 328p. (C). 1983. reprint ed. text ed. 75.00 (*0-313-24121-X*, HCRI, Greenwood Pr) Greenwood.

Christian Ritual & the World of Shakespeare's Tragedies. Herbert R. Coursen, Jr. 441p. 1976. 45.00 (*0-8387-1518-4*) Bucknell U Pr.

Christian Rock: Friend Or Foe? Angelo De Simone. 259p. Date not set. pap. 9.95 (*0-925591-26-2*) Covenant Hse Bks.

Christian Rohlfs: Paintings. (Illus.). 224p. 1990. 55.00 (*3-89322-169-7*, Pub. by Edition Cantz GW) Dist Art Pubs.

Christian Rohlfs: The Complete Paintings. Paul Vogt. (Illus.). 280p. (GER.). 1978. 120.00 (*1-55660-004-6*) A Wofsy Fine Arts.

Christian Rosenkreutz: From the Works of Rudolf Steiner. Ed. by Steven Roboz. 20p. 1982. pap. 3.25 (*0-919924-16-6*, Pub. by Steiner Book Centre CN) Anthroposophic.

Christian Rosenkreutz Anthology, Vol. 10. 2nd rev. ed. Ed. by Paul M. Allen. LC 68-13130. (Spiritual Science Library). (Illus.). 640p. 1981. reprint ed. lib. bdg. 69.00 (*0-89345-009-X*, Spir Sci Lib) Garber Comm.

Christian Sacraments of Initiation, Baptism, Confirmation, Eucharist. Kenan B. Osborne. 256p. 1987. pap. 11.95 (*0-8091-2886-1*) Paulist Pr.

Christian Sacrifice: The Judaeo-Christian Background Before Origen. Robert J. Daly. LC 78-12004. (Catholic University of American Studies in Christian Antiquity: No. 18). 605p. reprint ed. pap. 172.50 (*0-7837-1001-1*, 2041308) Bks Demand.

Christian Salvation & Human Temporal Progress. Bonaventure Kloppenberg. 1979. 2.95 (*0-8199-0778-2*, Frncscn Herld) Franciscan Pr.

Christian Scholar in the Age of the Reformation. E. Harris Harbison. LC 80-20805. xi, 177p. 1981. reprint ed. lib. bdg. 29.50 (*0-87991-954-X*) Porcupine Pr.

Christian Scholar in the Age of the Reformation. Elmore H. Harbison. LC 83-16511. 187p. reprint ed. 53.30 (*0-685-15936-1*, 2027546) Bks Demand.

Christian School: An Introduction. Noel Weeks. 216p. (Orig.). 1988. pap. 13.95 (*0-85151-526-6*) Banner of Truth.

Christian School Curriculum. Chadwick. 15.99 (*0-88469-228-0*) BMH Bks.

Christian School Finance. James W. Deuink. (Illus.). 160p. 1985. pap. 6.95 (*0-89084-304-X*) Bob Jones Univ Pr.

Christian Science. Mary Baker Eddy. 1963. pap. 2.00 (*0-87516-021-2*) DeVorss.

Christian Science. Salem Kirban. LC 75-124142. (Illus.). 1974. pap. 4.95 (*0-912582-11-1*) Kirban.

Christian Science. Walter Martin. 32p. 1957. pap. 3.50 (*0-87123-064-X*) Bethany Hse.

Christian Science. Samuel L. Clemens. (Works of Mark Twain). 1988. reprint ed. lib. bdg. 79.00 (*0-7812-1130-1*) Rprt Serv.

Christian Science. Ed. by J. Gordon Melton. (Cults & New Religions Ser.: Vol. 12). 528p. 1990. reprint ed. 93.00 (*0-8240-4373-1*) Garland.

Christian Science. Mark Twain, pseud. 196p. (C). 1993. reprint ed. pap. 15.95 (*0-87975-825-2*) Prometheus Bks.

Christian Science: A Sourcebook of Contemporary Materials. LC 89-82094. 348p. 1990. pap. 12.95 (*0-87510-197-6*) Christian Sci.

Christian Science: Its "Clear, Correct Teaching" & Complete Writings. 2nd ed. Herbert W. Eustace. 1037p. 1985. 16.00 (*0-9611156-0-2*) H W Eustace.

Christian Science: Its Encounter with American Culture. R. Peel. 1986. pap. 9.95 (*0-933062-24-9*) R H Sommer.

Christian Science after 1910. Andrew W. Hartsook. LC 93-91745. 280p. (C). 1994. 24.95 (*0-930227-24-7*); pap. 12.95 (*0-930227-25-5*) Bookmark CA.

Christian Science & Its Discoverer. E. Mary Ramsay. LC 35-18957. 137p. 1963. 14.95 (*0-87510-162-3*); pap. 9.95 (*0-87510-108-9*) Christian Sci.

Christian Science & Its Discoverer. Mary Ramsay. (GER.). pap. 9.95 (*0-87510-280-8*); pap. 9.95 (*0-87510-281-6*) Christian Sci.

Christian Science & Liberty. Robert E. Merritt & Arthur Corey. LC 70-132847. 1970. 8.95 (*0-87516-060-3*) DeVorss.

*__Christian Science & Unity School.__ Todd Ehrenborg. LC 95-2140. (Guide to Cults & Religious Movements Ser.). 1995. pap. 4.99 (*0-310-48861-3*) Zondervan.

Christian Science Board of Directors Defying Mrs. Eddy's By-Laws in Taking & Holding Offices, for the Closing of Which She Provided in Her Church Are Not Legitimate: The Position in Christian Science of Augusta E. Stetson, C.S.D... Franklin Ford & Hickman Price. (Illus.). 30p. 1994. reprint ed. pap. 4.00 (*1-879135-12-4*) Emma Pub Soc.

Christian Science Healing, Its Principles & Practice. Frances Lord. 471p. 1972. reprint ed. spiral bd. 16.50 (*0-7873-0570-7*) Mokelumne.

Christian Science Hymnal. (Organist Edition Ser.). 640p. 1993. 79.95 (*0-87510-249-2*) Christian Sci.

Christian Science Hymnal. reprint ed. 14.95 (*0-87510-025-2*) Christian Sci.

Christian Science Hymnal. 1994. reprint ed. pap. 19.95 (*0-87510-071-6*) Christian Sci.

Christian Science in the Age of Mary Baker Eddy. Stuart E. Knee. LC 93-37506. (Contributions in American History Ser.: No 154). 176p. 1994. text ed. 49.95 (*0-313-28360-5*, Greenwood Pr) Greenwood.

Christian Science-Kingdom or Cult? Karl Roebling. 190p. 1984. 12.95 (*0-942910-09-5*) Dynapress.

Christian Science Today: Power, Policy, Practice. Charles S. Braden. LC 58-11399. 464p. reprint ed. pap. 132.30 (*0-8357-8846-6*, 2033413) Bks Demand.

Christian Science Treatment. Ann Beals. 26p. 1979. pap. 2.00 (*0-930227-06-9*) Bookmark CA.

Christian Science versus Pantheism. Mary Baker Eddy. reprint ed. pap. 2.95 (*0-87952-054-X*) Christian Sci.

Christian Science vs. Pantheism. Mary M. Eddy. (Notable American Authors Ser.). 1992. reprint ed. lib. bdg. 75.00 (*0-7812-2759-3*) Rprt Serv.

Christian Scripture. David S. Dockery. (Orig.). 1995. pap. text ed. 19.99 (*0-8054-1040-6*, 4210-40) Broadman.

Christian Search for a Philosophy of Science. Ed. by Bill Keeth. 180p. 1993. pap. write for info. (*1-882510-04-6*) Bible-Sci Asn.

*__Christian Seeker & the Contrary Church.__ Arthur Pickett. 1994. 12.95 (*0-533-10997-3*) Vantage.

Christian Sense of Sexuality. James D. Whithead & Evelyn E. Whitehead. (Illus.). 24p. 1991. 2.95 (*1-55612-365-5*) Sheed & Ward MO.

Christian Service: Workshop Models. Center for Learning Network Staff. (Junior High Religion Ser.). 101p. 1992. teacher ed 15.95 (*1-56077-182-8*) Ctr Learning.

Christian Settings in Shakespeare's Tragedies. D. Douglas Waters. LC 92-55115. 1994. write for info. (*0-8386-3528-8*) Fairleigh Dickinson.

Christian Short Story. Ruth O. Hobbs. 1980. 10.95 (*0-686-32320-3*) Rod & Staff.

Christian Singers of Germany. Catherine Winkworth. LC 72-1295. (Essay Index Reprint Ser.). 1977. reprint ed. 25.95 (*0-8369-2878-4*) Ayer.

Christian Singles Connection, October-November, 1991. 1991. write for info. (*0-89921-060-0*) Biblical News Serv.

Christian Social Ethics: A Reader. Ed. by John Atherton. LC 94-6913. 424p. (Orig.). 1994. pap. 24.95 (*0-8298-0999-6*) Pilgrim OH.

Christian Social Ministry: An Introduction. Derrel R. Watkins. LC 93-12388. 1994. 15.99 (*0-8054-1073-2*) Broadman.

Christian Social Reformers of the Nineteenth Century. Ed. by Hugh Martin. LC 70-107725. (Essay Index Reprint Ser.). 1977. 20.95 (*0-8369-1526-7*) Ayer.

Christian Socialism: An Informal History. John C. Cort. LC 87-14046. 416p. (Orig.). 1988. 39.95 (*0-88344-601-4*); pap. 16.95 (*0-88344-600-6*) Orbis Bks.

Christian Socialism 1848-1854. Charles E. Raven. LC 68-56058. xii, 396p. 1968. reprint ed. 45.00 (*0-678-05148-8*) Kelley.

Christian Socialism, 1848-1854. Charles E. Raven. 396p. 1968. reprint ed. 35.00 (*0-7146-2129-3*, Pub. by F Cass Pubs UK) Intl Spec Bk.

Christian Society & the Crusades, 1198-1229: Sources in Translation, Including the Capture of Damietta. Ed. by Edward Peters. LC 78-163385. (Middle Ages Ser.). 192p. (C). 1971. pap. text ed. 16.95 (*0-8122-1024-7*) U of Pa Pr.

Christian Soldier. Katherine Hershey. (Illus.). 10p. (J). (gr. k-6). 1981. pap. text ed. 4.25 (*1-55976-138-5*) CEF Press.

Christian Soldier. D. Martyn Lloyd-Jones. 1977. 24.99 (*0-8010-5583-0*) Baker Bk.

Christian Souls & Chinese Spirits: A Hakka Community in Hong Kong. Nicole Constable. LC 93-24006. 274p. 1994. 37.00 (*0-520-08384-9*) U CA Pr.

Christian Spiritual Formation in the Church & Classroom. Susanne Johnson. LC 89-31939. 176p. 1989. pap. 14.95 (*0-687-07590-4*) Abingdon.

Christian Spiritual Healing: A Psychological Study. Ideology & Experience in the British Healing Movement. Lars G. Lindstrom. (Psychologia et Sociologica Religionum Ser.: No. 7). 207p. (Orig.). 1992. pap. text ed. 46.50x (*91-554-2962-9*, Pub. by Almqv & Wiksell SW) Coronet Bks.

*__Christian Spirituality, Vol. 2.__ Raitt. Date not set. 43.50 (*0-8245-0765-7*) Crossroad NY.

*__Christian Spirituality, Vol. 3.__ Dupre. Date not set. 43.50 (*0-8245-0766-5*) Crossroad NY.

Christian Spirituality: A Theological History From the New Testament to Luther & St. John of the Cross. Rowan Williams. LC 80-82190. 201p. reprint ed. pap. 57.30 (*0-685-15262-6*, 2027154) Bks Demand.

Christian Spirituality: An Historical Sketch. George A. Lane. 88p. 1984. pap. 4.95 (*0-8294-0450-3*) Loyola Univ Pr.

Christian Spirituality: Five Views of Sanctification. Gerhard O. Forde et al. Ed. by Donald L. Alexander. LC 88-29023. 203p. (Orig.). 1989. pap. 11.99 (*0-8308-1278-4*, 1278) InterVarsity.

An Asterisk (*) at the beginning of an entry indicates that the title is appearing in BIP for the first time.

An Asterisk (*) at the beginning of an entry indicates that the title is appearing in BIP for the first time.

1243

C

Christianity - Teacher's Notes. Sacred Trinity R. E. Centre-Salford Staff. (C). 1989. Set of 4 filmstrips & 2 cass. audio, text ed. 720.00 (*0-86158-646-8*, Pub. by S Thornes Pubs UK) St Mut.

Christianity: A Clear Case of History. Edward C. Wharton. 185p. (Orig.). 1977. pap. 7.95 (*1-878990-09-8*) Howard Pub LA.

Christianity According to the Wesleys. Franz Hildebrandt. 90p. 1994. reprint ed. pap. 7.95 (*0-939464-54-3*) Labyrinth Pr.

***Christianity after Communism: Social, Political & Cultural Struggle in Russia.** Niels C. Nielsen, Jr. LC 94-29700. (C). 1994. text ed. 49.95 (*0-8133-2365-7*) Westview.

Christianity Amidst Apartheid: Selected Perspectives on the Church in South Africa. Ed. by Martin Prozesky. LC 89-34299. 256p. 1990. text ed. 39.95 (*0-312-03529-2*) St Martin.

Christianity among the Arabs in Pre-Islamic Times. Trimingham. 1990. 42.00 (*0-86685-533-5*) Intl Bk Ctr.

Christianity Among the New Zealanders. William Carlos Williams. (Illus.). 398p. (Orig.). 1989. 22.95 (*0-85151-566-5*) Banner of Truth.

Christianity & African Education: The Papers of a Conference at the University of Chicago. Robert P. Beaver. LC 65-25184. 233p. reprint ed. pap. 66.50 (*0-317-09800-4*, 2012940) Bks Demand.

Christianity & African Traditional Beliefs. Nano O. Dankwa, III. Ed. by John W. Branch. (Illus.). 70p. 1990. pap. text ed. 7.00 (*0-9626487-0-1*) Power Word NY.

Christianity & American Freemasonry. William J. Whalen. LC 86-62968. 180p. 1987. pap. 6.95 (*0-87973-484-1*) Our Sunday Visitor.

Christianity & Autosuggestion. Brooks & Charles. 158p. 1996. pap. 12.00 (*0-89540-198-3*, SB-198) Sun Pub.

Christianity & Capitalism: Perspectives on Religion, Liberalism, & the Economy. Ed. by Bruce Grelle & David A. Krueger. LC 85-73375. (Studies in Religion & Society). 189p. 1986. text ed. 30.95 (*0-913348-23-6*); pap. 17.95 (*0-913348-24-4*) Ctr Sci Study.

Christianity & Change. Ralph Armstrong. LC 89-61930. 256p. (Orig.). 1990. pap. 16.95 (*1-55612-308-6*) Sheed & Ward MO.

***Christianity & Civil Society: Theological Education for Public Life.** Ed. by Rodney L. Pertersen. LC 94-43405. (Boston Theological Institute Ser.: Vol. 4). 184p. (Orig.). 1995. pap. 16.95 (*1-57075-009-2*) Orbis Bks.

Christianity & Civilisation, 2 vols. in one. Heinrich E. Brunner. LC 77-27182. (Gifford Lectures: 1947-48). reprint ed. 55.00 (*0-404-60530-3*) AMS Pr.

Christianity & Civilization. Arnold J. Toynbee. (C). 1947. pap. 3.00 (*0-87574-039-1*) Pendle Hill.

Christianity & Classical Culture: The Metamorphosis of Natural Theology in the Christian Encounter with Hellenism. Jaroslav Pelikan. LC 92-42407. 416p. (C). 1993. 42.50 (*0-300-05554-4*) Yale U Pr.

***Christianity & Classical Culture: The Metamorphsis of Natural Theology in the Christian.** Pelikan. 1995. pap. text ed. 17.00 (*0-300-06255-9*) Yale U Pr.

***Christianity & Culture.** Virgil Elizondo. 198p. 1975. write for info. (*0-614-04872-9*) Mex Am Cult.

Christianity & Culture Change in India. Keshari N. Sahay. (C). 1986. 34.00 (*81-210-0173-0*, Pub. by Inter-India Pubns) S Asia.

Christianity & Cultures: A Mutual Enrichment - Concilium. Ed. by Norbert Greinacher & Norbert Mette. 1994. pap. 15.00 (*0-88344-877-7*) Orbis Bks.

Christianity & Democracy. Jacques Maritain. Bd. with Rights of Man & Natural Law. LC 83-80191. LC 83-80191. 250p. 1986. Set pap. 12.95 (*0-89870-030-2*) Ignatius Pr.

Christianity & Democracy. Jacques Maritain. Tr. by Doris C. Anson. LC 72-6765. (Essay Index Reprint Ser.). 1980. reprint ed. 18.95 (*0-8369-7243-0*) Ayer.

***Christianity & Democracy: A Theology for a Just World Order.** John W. De Gruchy. (Cambridge Studies in Ideology & Religion: No. 7). 307p. (C). 1994. 59.95 (*0-521-45216-3*); pap. 17.95 (*0-521-45841-2*) Cambridge U Pr.

Christianity & Democracy in Global Context. Ed. by John F. Witte, Jr. LC 93-9606. (C). 1993. text ed. 52.50 (*0-8133-1843-2*) Westview.

***Christianity & Economics in the Post-Cold War: The Oxford Declaration & Beyond.** Herbert Schlossberg. 1994. pap. 10.99 (*0-8028-0798-4*) Eerdmans.

Christianity & Education: A Manifesto. Jack H. Rose. LC 86-90551. 302p. (Orig.). 1986. pap. 34.95 (*0-9617430-0-X*) J H Rose.

Christianity & Education Provision. Ed. by Witold Tulasiewicz & Colin Brock. 256p. 1988. lib. bdg. 59.95 (*0-415-00568-X*, A1831) Routledge.

Christianity & Evolution. Pierre Teilhard De Chardin. LC 73-12926. 255p. 1974. pap. 8.95 (*0-15-617740-4*, Harvest Bks) HarBrace.

Christianity & Existentialism. Ed. by William Earle et al. (Studies in Phenomenology & Existential Philosophy). 1963. pap. 12.95 (*0-8101-0084-3*) Northwestern U Pr.

Christianity & Feminism in Conversation. Regina Coll. LC 93-79451. 208p. (Orig.). 1994. pap. 14.95 (*0-89622-579-8*) Twenty-Third.

Christianity & Hegemony: Christianity & Politics on the Frontiers of Social Change. Ed. by Jan N. Pieterse. 336p. 1992. 59.95 (*0-85496-749-4*) Berg Pubs.

Christianity & Humanism. Dale A. Jorgenson. LC 83-70878. 166p. (Orig.). (C). 1983. pap. 4.95 (*0-89900-149-1*) College Pr Pub.

Christianity & Incest. Annie F. Imbens. LC 91-42379. 332p. 1992. pap. 17.00 (*0-8006-2541-2*, 1-2541) Augsburg Fortress.

Christianity & Islam: A Battle for the True Image of Man. Rudolf Frieling. 144p. 1990. pap. 14.95 (*0-903540-18-5*, 249, Pub. by Floris Books UK) Anthroposophic.

Christianity & Islam: The Struggling Dialogue. Ed. by Richard W. Rousseau. (Modern Theological Themes: Selections from the Literature Ser.: Vol. 4). 220p. (Orig.). 1985. pap. 17.95 (*0-940866-03-X*) U Scranton Pr.

Christianity & Islam in Spain, A. D. 756-1031. Charles R. Haines. LC 76-144625. reprint ed. 34.00 (*0-404-03024-6*) AMS Pr.

Christianity & Judaism: Papers Read at the 1991 Summer Meeting & the 1992 Winter Meeting of the Ecclesiastical History Society. Ed. by Diana Wood. LC 92-15569. (Studies in Church History: Vol. 29). 1992. 59.95 (*0-631-18497-X*) Blackwell Pubs.

Christianity & Judaism: The Deepening Dialogue. Ed. by Richard Rousseau. (Modern Theological Themes: Selections from the Literature Ser.: Vol. 3). (Orig.). 1983. pap. 15.00 (*0-940866-02-1*) U Scranton Pr.

Christianity & Judaism: The Early Centuries. Ed. by Everett Ferguson. LC 92-41463. (Studies in Early Christianity: Vol. 6). (Illus.). 392p. 1993. 64.00 (*0-8153-1066-8*) Garland.

Christianity & Judaism: Two Covenants. Yehezkel Kaufman. xi, 230p. (C). 1988. text ed. 20.00 (*0-685-74245-8*, Pub. by Magnes Press IS) Eisenbrauns.

Christianity & Leisure: Issues in a Pluralistic Society. Ed. by Thomas L. Visker et al. 251p. (Orig.). 1994. pap. 13.25 (*0-932914-29-2*) Dordt Coll Pr.

Christianity & Liberalism. J. Gresham Machen. 1946. pap. 10.99 (*0-8028-1121-3*) Eerdmans.

Christianity & Marxism. Alan Scarfe & Patrick Sookhedo. 168p. 1982. pap. 12.95 (*0-85364-289-3*, Pub. by Paternoster UK) Attic Pr.

Christianity & Marxism Worldwide: An Annotated Bibliography. Intro. by Mark Elliott. 136p. (Orig.). 1988. pap. 15.00 (*1-879089-04-1*) B Graham Ctr.

Christianity & Modern Politics. Ed. by Louisa S. Hulett. LC 92-36923. ix, 453p. (C). 1993. lib. bdg. 64.95 (*3-11-013462-4*); pap. text ed. 29.95 (*3-11-013461-6*) De Gruyter.

Christianity & Modern Thought. Ralph H. Gabriel & Charles R. Brown. 1977. 13.95 (*0-8369-7217-1*, 8016) Ayer.

Christianity & Morals. Edward A. Westermarck. LC 78-80406. (Essay Index Reprint Ser.). 1977. 26.95 (*0-8369-1055-9*) Ayer.

Christianity & Nationalism in the Later Roman Empire. Ernest L. Woodward. LC 82-45828. (Orthodoxies & Heresies in the Early Christian Ser.). reprint ed. 21.50 (*0-404-62398-0*) AMS Pr.

Christianity & Native Traditions: Indigenization & Syncretism among the Inuit & Dene of the Western Arctic. Antonio R. Gualtieri. Ed. by Cyriac K. Pullapilly & George H. Williams. (Church & the World Ser.: Vol. II). xvi, 186p. 1984. 19.95x (*0-940121-03-4*) Cross Cultural Pubns.

Christianity & Other Faiths. Patrick Sookhdeo. 48p. 1983. pap. 3.95 (*0-85364-363-6*, Pub. by Paternoster UK) Attic Pr.

Christianity & Paganism, 350-750: The Conversion of Western Europe. rev. ed. Ed. by J. N. Hillgarth. LC 85-1154. (Middle Ages Ser.). 232p. (C). 1986. reprint ed. pap. 17.95 (*0-8122-1213-4*) U of Pa Pr.

***Christianity & Philosophy.** Keith E. Yandell. LC 83-14226. (Studies in a Christian World View: No. 2). 301p. 1984. pap. 85.80 (*0-7837-7982-8*, 2047738) Bks Demand.

Christianity & Politics in Doe's Liberia. Paul Gifford. LC 92-15834. (Cambridge Studies in Ideology & Religion: No. 2). (Illus.). 352p. (C). 1993. 64.95 (*0-521-42029-6*) Cambridge U Pr.

Christianity & Rabbinic Judaism: A Parallel History of Their Origins & Early Development. Louis Feldman et al. LC 92-39396. (Illus.). 380p. (C). 1992. 28.95 (*1-880317-03-6*, 7H71); pap. 16.95 (*1-880317-08-7*, 7H72) Biblical Arch Soc.

Christianity & Reincarnation. Rudolf Frieling. 118p. 1990. pap. 14.95 (*0-903540-05-3*, 250, Pub. by Floris Books UK) Anthroposophic.

Christianity & Revolution: Tomas Borge's Theology of Life. Tomas Borge. Ed. by Andrew Reding. LC 86-23788. 176p. reprint ed. pap. 50.20 (*0-8357-2688-6*, 2040224) Bks Demand.

Christianity & Romanticism in the Victorian Era: 1830-1880 see Religious Trends in English Poetry

Christianity & Russia. P. N. Fedoseyev. 176p. (C). 1988. 35.00 (*0-685-31476-6*) St Mut.

Christianity & Russian Culture in Soviet Society, Vol. 3. Ed. by Nicolai Petro. 244p. (C). 1990. pap. text ed. 47.50 (*0-8133-7742-0*) Westview.

Christianity & Sex Problems. 2nd ed. Hugh Northcote. LC 72-9668. reprint ed. 49.50 (*0-404-57486-6*) AMS Pr.

***Christianity & Social Change in Northeast India.** O. L. Snaitang. (C). 1993. 20.00x (*81-85408-12-2*, Pub. by Firma KLM) S Asia.

Christianity & Social Justice see How Christ Changed the World: The Social Principles of the Catholic Church

Christianity & Social Order. William Temple. 119p. 1976. pap. 9.95 (*0-85683-025-9*, Pub. by Shepheard-Walwyn Pubs UK) Paul & Co Pubs.

Christianity & Society. Nels F. Ferre. LC 78-117791. (Essay Index Reprint Ser.). 1977. 21.95 (*0-8369-1924-6*) Ayer.

Christianity & the Age of the Earth. Davis A. Young. LC 88-71400. (Illus.). 188p. 1988. reprint ed. pap. 8.00 (*0-934666-27-X*) Artisan Sales.

Christianity & the Classics: The Acceptance of a Heritage. Ed. by Wendy E. Helleman. LC 89-35897. (Christian Studies Today). 220p. (Orig.). (C). 1990. lib. bdg. 42.00 (*0-8191-7577-3*, Inst Christ Stud) U Pr of Amer.

Christianity & the Constitution: The Faith of Our Founding Fathers. John Eidsmoe. LC 87-70789. 442p. 1987. pap. 24.99 (*0-8010-3444-2*) Baker Bk.

***Christianity & the Constitution: The Faith of Our Founding Fathers.** John Eidsmoe. 448p. 1995. reprint ed. pap. 17.99 (*0-8010-5231-9*) Baker Bk.

Christianity & the Eastern Slavs Vol. II: Russian Culture in Modern Times. Ed. by Robert P. Hughes & Irina Paperno. LC 93-25779. (California Slavic Studies: Vol. 17). (C). 1994. 55.00 (*0-520-08175-7*) U CA Pr.

Christianity & the Encounter of World Religions. Paul Tillich. LC 94-9991. 1994. pap. 10.00 (*0-8006-2761-X*, Fortress Pr) Augsburg Fortress.

Christianity & the Hellenistic World Ser. see Gospel & the Greeks: Did the New Testament Borrow from Pagan Thought?

***Christianity & the Holocaust of Hungarian Jewry.** Moshe Y. Herczl. Tr. by Joel Lerner. LC 92-47500. 299p. 1995. pap. 17.95 (*0-8147-3520-7*) NYU Pr.

Christianity & the Holocaust of Hungarian Jewry. Moshe Y. Herczl. Tr. by Joel Lerner. LC 92-47500. 299p. (C). 1995. 45.00 (*0-8147-3503-7*) NYU Pr.

Christianity & the Intellectuals. Arther Trace. 208p. (Orig.). 1983. pap. 8.95 (*0-89385-018-7*) Sugden.

Christianity & the Kikuyu: Religious Divisions & Social Conflict. David P. Sandgren. (American University Studies: History: Ser. IX, Vol. 45). 201p. (C). 1989. text ed. 34.40 (*0-8204-0732-1*) P Lang Pubs.

Christianity & the Machine Age. Eric Gill. 1973. 59.95 (*0-87968-864-5*) Gordon Pr.

Christianity & the Nature of Science: A Philosophical Investigation. J. P. Moreland. LC 89-6719. 263p. (Orig.). 1989. pap. text ed. 14.99 (*0-8010-6249-7*) Baker Bk.

Christianity & the New Age Religion: A Bridge Toward Mutual Understanding. L. David Moore. LC 92-82117. 248p. 1993. pap. 12.95 (*0-9635665-0-4*) Pendulum Plus.

Christianity & the Paranormal, Set. Ed. by Frank C. Tribbe. (Spiritual Frontiers Fellowship Thirtieth Anniversary Booklet Ser.: Vol. I, No. 2). 1986. boxed 12.00 (*0-317-68870-7*) Spirit Front Fellow.

Christianity & the Race Problem. Joseph H. Oldham. LC 73-75534. 280p. 1969. reprint ed. text ed. 52.50 (*0-8371-1112-9*, OLC&, Negro U Pr) Greenwood.

Christianity & the Religions of the East: Models for a Dynamic Relationship. Ed. by Richard W. Rousseau. (Modern Theological Themes: Selections from the Literature Ser.: Vol. 2). 174p. (Orig.). (C). 1982. pap. 15.00 (*0-940866-01-3*) U Scranton Pr.

Christianity & the Renaissance: Image & Religious Imagination in the Quattrocento. Ed. by Timothy Verdon & John Henderson. LC 89-30918. (Illus.). 528p. (Orig.). 1990. text ed. 55.00 (*0-8156-2414-X*); pap. text ed. 18.95 (*0-8156-2456-5*) Syracuse U Pr.

***Christianity & the Rhetoric of Empire: The Development of Christian Discourse.** Averil Cameron. 1991. pap. 14.00 (*0-520-08923-5*) U CA Pr.

Christianity & the Rhetoric of Empire: The Development of Christian Discourse. Averil Cameron. LC 90-39376. (Sather Classical Lectures: No. 55). (Illus.). 275p. 1991. 40.00 (*0-520-07160-3*) U CA Pr.

Christianity & the Rights of Animals. Andrew Linzey. 224p. 1987. pap. 12.95 (*0-8245-0875-0*) Crossroad NY.

Christianity & the Social Crisis. Walter Rauschenbusch. (Library of Theological Ethics). 448p. 1992. reprint ed. pap. 14.99 (*0-664-25321-0*) Westminster John Knox.

Christianity & the Social Revolution. Ed. by John Lewis et al. LC 79-37892. (Select Bibliographies Reprint Ser.). 1977. reprint ed. 27.95 (*0-8369-6729-1*) Ayer.

Christianity & Traditional Religion in Western Zimbabwe, 1859-1923. Ngwabi Bhebe. LC 79-322844. 206p. reprint ed. pap. 58.80 (*0-8357-2966-4*, 2039228) Bks Demand.

***Christianity & Western Civilization.** Ed. by Wethersfield Institute Staff. 122p. Date not set. pap. 9.95 (*0-89870-534-7*) Ignatius Pr.

Christianity & Western Civilization. Carlton J. Hayes. LC 83-5680. vii, 63p. 1983. reprint ed. text ed. 49.75 (*0-313-23962-2*, HACW, Greenwood Pr) Greenwood.

Christianity & Western Thought: A History of Philosophers, Ideas & Movements, Vol. 1: From the Ancient World to the Age of Enlightenment. Colin Brown. LC 89-48564. 447p. 1990. text ed. 27.99 (*0-8308-1752-2*, 1752) InterVarsity.

Christianity & World Religion: Paths to Dialogue with Islam, Hinduism & Buddhism. Hans Kung et al. Tr. by Peter Heinegg. 480p. 1993. reprint ed. pap. 19.95 (*0-88344-858-0*) Orbis Bks.

Christianity & World Religions. rev. ed. Norman Anderson. LC 84-115291. 216p. 1984. pap. 13.99 (*0-87784-981-1*, 981) InterVarsity.

Christianity & World Religious see Cristianismo y Otras Religiones

Christianity As Mystical Fact & the Occult Mysteries of Antiquity. 3rd ed. Rudolf Steiner. Ed. by Paul M. Allen. 256p. 1980. pap. 12.50 (*0-89345-201-7*, Steinerbks) Garber Comm.

Christianity As Mystical Fact & the Occult Mysteries of Antiquity, Vol. 7. 3rd ed. Rudolf Steiner. Ed. by Paul M. Allen. LC 61-18165. 256p. 1980. lib. bdg. 19.50 (*0-89345-021-9*, Spir Sci Lib) Garber Comm.

Christianity at a Glance. R. E. McMaster. 1989. write for info. (*0-318-61880-X*) Reaper Pub.

Christianity at Rome in the Apostolic Age. Arthur S. Barnes. LC 72-114462. (Illus.). 222p. 1971. reprint ed. text ed. 59.50 (*0-8371-4760-3*, BACR, Greenwood Pr) Greenwood.

Christianity Before Christ. John G. Jackson. 237p. (Orig.). 1985. pap. 9.00 (*0-910309-20-5*, 5200) Am Atheist.

Christianity Before Christ. Charles J. Stone. 1977. lib. bdg. 59.95 (*0-8490-1616-9*) Gordon Pr.

Christianity Betrayed: The Name of the Beast (666) Revealed. Kenneth A. Schei. LC 89-90650. 115p. (Orig.). 1989. pap. 11.95 (*0-926491-00-8*) Synthesis.

Christianity Comes to the Americas, 1492-1776. Charles H. Lippy et al. (Illus.). 384p. 1992. 29.95 (*1-55778-234-2*) Paragon Hse.

Christianity Comes to the Americas, 1492-1776: 1492-1776. Charles H. Lippy et al. LC 92-8490. 400p. 1992. pap. 18.95 (*1-55778-501-5*) Paragon Hse.

Christianity, Communism & the Ideal Society: A Philosophical Approach to Modern Politics. James K. Feibleman. LC 75-3140. reprint ed. 52.50 (*0-404-59149-3*) AMS Pr.

Christianity Confronts Communism. Charles McFadden. 1983. 6.95 (*0-8199-0841-X*, Frncscn Herld) Franciscan Pr.

Christianity Confronts Culture. enl. rev. ed. Marvin K. Mayers. 1987. 22.99 (*0-310-28901-7*) Zondervan.

Christianity Crime Against Humanity. Arnold Gordon. 178p. 1992. pap. write for info. (*0-9632629-0-4*) Five Star IL.

Christianity for Modern Pagans: Pascal's Pensees. Comment by Peter Kreeft. LC 93-78533. 352p. 1993. 14.95 (*0-89870-452-9*) Ignatius Pr.

***Christianity for the Tough Minded: Essays in Support of an Intellectually Defensible Religious Commitment.** Ed. by John W. Montgomery. 296p. (C). 1994. pap. text ed. 14.95 (*1-885914-00-8*) Trinity Bible Coll.

Christianity Four Thousand Years Before Jesus. Walter A. Dawes. Ed. by Kathleen A. Dawes. (Illus.). 63p. (Orig.). 1982. pap. 4.95 (*0-938792-17-2*) New Capernaum.

Christianity in a Revolutionary Age, 5 vols., 3. Kenneth S. Latourette. 1973. reprint ed. lib. bdg. 34.75 (*0-8371-5703-X*, LACK) Greenwood.

Christianity in a Revolutionary Age, 5 vols., 4. Kenneth S. Latourette. 1973. reprint ed. lib. bdg. 34.75 (*0-8371-5704-8*, LACL) Greenwood.

Christianity in a Revolutionary Age, 5 vols., 5. Kenneth S. Latourette. 1973. reprint ed. lib. bdg. 34.75 (*0-8371-5705-6*, LACM) Greenwood.

Christianity in a Secularized World. Wolfhart Pannenberg. 96p. 1989. pap. 8.95 (*0-8245-0936-6*) Crossroad NY.

Christianity in China: A Scholar's Guide to Resources in the Libraries & Archives of the United States. Archie R. Crouch et al. LC 88-18524. 750p. 1989. 157.95 (*0-87332-419-6*) M E Sharpe.

Christianity in China: Early Protestant Missionary Writings. Ed. by Suzanne W. Barnett & John K. Fairbank. (Studies in American-East Asian Relations: No. 9). 280p. 1985. 20.00 (*0-674-12881-8*) HUP.

Christianity in Crisis. Hank Hanegraaff. 1993. 16.99 (*0-89081-976-9*) Harvest Hse.

Christianity in Crisis. Hank Hanegraaff. 1993. audio 16.99 (*1-56507-151-4*) Harvest Hse.

Christianity in Crisis Study Guide. Hank Hanegraaff. 1993. pap. 5.99 (*1-56507-191-3*) Harvest Hse.

Christianity in Culture. Charles H. Kraft. LC 78-13736. 463p. (Orig.). 1979. 19.95 (*0-88344-075-X*) Orbis Bks.

Christianity in East & West. Christopher Dawson. Ed. by John J. Mulloy. 224p. 1981. pap. 8.95 (*0-89385-015-2*) Sugden.

Christianity in History. A. Azhar. 14.50 (*0-935782-56-7*) Kazi Pubns.

Christianity in Human Evolution. Rudolf Steiner. 1979. reprint ed. pap. 3.95 (*0-88010-095-8*) Anthroposophic.

Christianity in India. Arthur B. Mayhew. (C). 1988. 32.50 (*81-212-0143-8*, Pub. by Gian Publng Hse II) S Asia.

Christianity in Modern Korea. Donald N. Clark. LC 86-9092. (Asian Agenda Report Ser.: No. 5). 70p. (Orig.). (C). 1986. lib. bdg. 27.00 (*0-8191-5384-2*); pap. text ed. 12.50 (*0-8191-5385-0*) U Pr of Amer.

Christianity in Oceania: Ethnographic Perspectives. Ed. by John Barker. (ASAO Monograph: No. 12). 330p. (C). 1990. lib. bdg. 51.00 (*0-8191-7906-X*, Assn Soc Anthrop Oceania) U Pr of Amer.

Christianity in Talmud & Midsrah. R. Travers Herford. reprint ed. 19.95 (*0-87068-479-5*) Ktav.

Christianity in the Modern World. David Field. 160p. (Orig.). 1983. pap. 17.95 (*0-7175-0974-5*, Pub. by Stanley Thornes UK) Trans-Atl Phila.

Christianity in the Non-Western World. Ed. by Charles W. Forman. LC 71-117792. (Essay Index Reprint Ser.). 1977. 19.95 (*0-8369-1806-1*) Ayer.

Christianity in the Twenty-First Century: Reflections on the Challenges Ahead. Robert Wuthnow. LC 92-28689. 256p. 1993. 25.00 (*0-19-507957-4*) OUP.

Christianity in the West, Fourteen Hundred to Seventeen Hundred. John Bossy. (Opus Ser.). 189p. 1985. pap. 16.95 (*0-19-289162-6*) OUP.

***Christianity in the 21st Century: Reflections on the Challenges Ahead.** Robert Wuthnow. 262p. 1995. pap. 11.95 (*0-19-509651-7*) OUP.

Christianity Is a Bridge. Kenna Farris. write for info. (*0-318-60370-5*) Port Love Intl.

Christianity Is All Talk. Paul Kelm. Ed. by William Fischer. (Bible Class Course for Young Adults Ser.). 64p. 1984. teacher ed, pap. text ed. 3.95 (*0-938272-17-9*) WELS Board.

Christianity Is All Talk. Paul Kelm. Ed. by William Fischer. (Bible Class Course for Young Adults Ser.). (Illus.). 44p. 1984. student ed, pap. text ed. 3.25 (*0-938272-16-0*) WELS Board.

Christianity Is Born. James P. Taylor. (C). 1988. 39.00 (*0-685-22278-0*, Pub. by St Paul Pubns UK) St Mut.

Christianity Is Born. James P. Taylor. 128p. (C). 1990. text ed. 39.00 (*0-85439-275-0*, Pub. by St Paul Pubns UK) St Mut.

Christianity Is Christ. W. Griffith Thomas. LC 80-85341. (Shepherd Illustrated Classics Ser.). 170p. pap. 5.95 (*0-8254-5323-2*) Kregel.

An Asterisk (*) at the beginning of an entry indicates that the title is appearing in BIP for the first time.

Christianity Is for You. Milton L. Rudnick. 1961. pap. 5.00 (*0-570-03503-1*, 14-1271) Concordia.
Christianity Is Jewish. Edith Schaeffer. 1977. pap. 8.99 (*0-8423-0242-5*) Tyndale.
Christianity, Islam & the Negro Race. Edward W. Blyden. 441p. reprint ed. pap. 14.95 (*0-933121-41-5*) Black Classic.
Christianity, Islam & the Negro Race. Edward W. Blyden. (African Heritage Classical Research Studies). 407p. reprint ed. 40.00 (*0-938818-36-8*) ECA Assoc.
Christianity, Islam & the Negro Race. Edward W. Blyden. 408p. (C). 1990. reprint ed. 34.95 (*0-685-45610-2*); reprint ed. pap. 21.95 (*0-685-45611-0*) J Richardson.
Christianity, Judaism, & Islam. Leonard Swidler. 1999. pap. text ed. 7.95 (*0-8146-2140-6*) Liturgical Pr.
Christianity Meets Buddhism. Heinrich Dumoulin. Tr. by John C. Maraldo. LC 73-82783. 216p. 1974. 26.95 (*0-87548-121-3*); pap. 13.95 (*0-8126-9110-5*) Open Court.
Christianity of Ignatius of Antioch. Cyril C. Richardson. LC 35-7948. reprint ed. 20.00 (*0-404-05297-5*) AMS Pr.
***Christianity on Trial: African-American Religious Thought Before & after Black Power.** Marc L. Chapman. (Bishop Henry McNeal Turner-Sojourner Truth Ser.: Vol. 10). 175p. (Orig.). 1995. pap. 18.95 (*1-57075-044-0*) Orbis Bks.
Christianity One Hundred One: Your Guide to Eight Basic Christian Beliefs. Gilbert Bilezikian. 288p. 1993. pap. 14.99 (*0-310-57701-2*) Zondervan.
Christianity or the Church? St. Hilary Troitsky. 48p. (Orig.). 1985. pap. 2.00 (*0-317-30269-8*) Holy Trinity.
Christianity or the Papacy: An Appeal to Roman Catholics. Alexey Young. 32p. (Orig.). 1990. pap. 2.00 (*0-912927-42-9*, X042) St John Kronstadt.
Christianity, Past & Present. Basil Willey. LC 78-65632. 1980. reprint ed. 16.50 (*0-88355-877-7*) Hyperion Conn.
Christianity, Patriarchy, & Abuse: A Feminist Critique. Ed. by Joanne C. Brown & Carole R. Bohn. LC 89-35505. 192p. (Orig.). (C). 1989. pap. 14.95 (*0-8298-0808-6*) Pilgrim OH.
Christianity Rediscovered. rev. ed. Vincent J. Donovan. LC 81-18992. 208p. 1982. pap. 12.95 (*0-88344-096-2*) Orbis Bks.
Christianity, Social Tolerance, & Homosexuality: Gay People in Western Europe from the Beginning of the Christian Era to the Fourteenth Century. John Boswell. LC 79-11171. (Illus.). xviii, 424p. 1981. pap. 18.95 (*0-226-06711-4*) U Ch Pr.
Christianity That Counts: Being a Christian in a Non-Christian World. Douglas Groothuis. 224p. (Orig.). 1994. pap. 11.99 (*0-8010-3868-5*) Baker Bk.
Christianity That Really Works. Ron Marr. 320p. 1993. pap. 5.99 (*0-88368-271-0*) Whitaker Hse.
Christianity the Deadliest Poison & Zen the Antidote to All Poisons. Osho Rajneesh. Ed. by Swami Krishna Prabhu. (Zen Ser.). 340p. 1990. 21.95 (*3-89338-071-X*, Pub. by Rebel Hse GW) Osho Chidvilas.
Christianity the Logic of Creation. Henry James, Sr. LC 72-921. (Selected Works of Henry James, Sr.: Vol. 1). 1983. reprint ed. 35.00 (*0-404-10081-3*) AMS Pr.
Christianity Through Jewish Eyes. Walter Jacob. 1974. pap. 11.95 (*0-685-56220-4*) Ktav.
Christianity Through Non-Christian Eyes. Paul J. Griffiths. LC 89-77870. (Faith Meets Faith Ser.). 1990. 39.95 (*0-88344-662-6*); pap. 16.95 (*0-88344-661-8*) Orbis Bks.
Christianity Through the Centuries. Earle E. Cairns. 544p. (C). 1981. 22.99 (*0-310-38360-9*, 9377) Zondervan.
Christianity Today in the U. S. S. R. Howard L. Parsons. LC 86-27320. 211p. (Orig.). reprint ed. pap. 60.20 (*0-7837-0582-4*, 2040926) Bks Demand.
***Christianity, Tragedy & Holocaust Literature.** Michael R. Steele. LC 95-5265. (Contributions to the Study of Religion Ser.: Vol. 41). 200p. 1995. text ed. 49.95 (*0-313-29512-3*, Greenwood Pr) Greenwood.
Christianity Unveiled. Paul H. D'Holbach. 1973. 250.00 (*0-87968-068-7*) Gordon Pr.
Christianity Versus Jesus: The Saga & Odyssey of a Postpagan Mystery Cult. Milton Aron. 1990. 19.95 (*0-533-08637-X*) Vantage.
Christianity vs. Islam. Elijah Muhammad. 37p. (Orig.). 1993. pap. text ed. 6.95 (*0-685-71988-X*) Untd Bros & Sis.
***Christianity vs. Islam: An Examination over the Black Religious Debate.** Scott A. Bradley. Ed. by Consuelo Divers. 47p. (Orig.). (C). Date not set. pap. text ed. 4.95 (*0-9636928-2-8*) Riv Life Min.
Christianity, Wilderness, & Wildlife: The Original Desert Solitaire. Susan P. Bratton. LC 91-67107. 352p. (C). 1993. 49.50 (*0-940866-14-5*) U Scranton Pr.
Christianity with Power: Your Worldview & Your Experience of the Supernatural. Charles Kraft. 230p. (Orig.). 1989. pap. 8.99 (*0-89283-396-3*, Vine Bks) Servant.
Christianity Without Antisemitism: James Parkes & the Jewish-Christian Encounter. Robert A. Everett. LC 93-9480. (Studies in Antisemitism). 1993. 79.00 (*0-08-041040-5*, Pergamon Pr) Elsevier.
Christianity Without Fetishes: An African Critique & Recapture of Christianity. Fabien Eboussi Boulaga. Tr. by Robert R. Barr. LC 84-5807. 255p. (Orig.). reprint ed. pap. 72.70 (*0-7837-5518-X*, 2045288) Bks Demand.
Christianity Without Morals. Blaine Taylor et al. Ed. by Jerry O. Cook. 96p. (Orig.). 1982. pap. 7.00 (*0-914527-16-9*) C-Four Res.
Christianity Without Religion. Manfred VerHulst. 177p. 1993. 12.95 (*0-9637416-0-8*) Schaefer Edits.
Christianity Without the Myths. S. Farrer. 1988. 39.00 (*0-317-43636-8*, Pub. by Regency Press) St Mut.
Christianity Without Ulcers. Edward Fudge. pap. 5.00 (*0-686-12686-6*) E Fudge.
***Christianity 101.** (Cross Training Ser.: Vol. 1). 76p. (YA). (gr. 10-12). 1994. 29.95 (*1-57405-008-7*) CharismaLife Pub.
***Christianity 201.** (Cross Training Ser.: Vol. 2). 76p. (YA). (gr. 10-12). 1994. 29.95 (*1-57405-016-8*) CharismaLife Pub.
***Christianity 301.** (Cross Training Ser.: Vol. 3). 72p. (YA). (gr. 10-12). 1995. 29.95 (*1-57405-024-9*) CharismaLife Pub.
***Christianization of Pyrrhonism: Scepticism & Faith in Pascal, Kierkegaard & Shestov.** Jose R. Neto. LC 95-1251. (International Archives of the History of Ideas Ser.: Vol. 144). 1995. lib. bdg. write for info. (*0-7923-3381-0*) Kluwer Ac.
Christianizing Death: The Creation of a Ritual Process in Early Medieval Europe. Frederick S. Paxton. LC 90-34072. (Illus.). 256p. 1990. 34.95 (*0-8014-2492-5*) Cornell U Pr.
Christianizing Homer: The Odyssey, Plato, & the Acts of Andrew. Dennis R. MacDonald. 384p. 1994. 45.00 (*0-19-508722-4*) OUP.
Christianizing the Roman Empire: A.D. 100-400. Ramsay MacMullen. LC 84-3694. 200p. 1984. 27.00 (*0-300-03216-1*) Yale U Pr.
Christianizing the Roman Empire: A.D. 100-400. Ramsay MacMullen. LC 84-3694. 200p. 1986. pap. 14.00 (*0-300-03642-6*, Y-571) Yale U Pr.
Christiano Wolff E il Razionalismo Precritico, 2 vols. in 1. Mariano Campo. (Wolff, Christian, Gesammelte Werke, Materialien und Dokumente Ser.: No. III, Vol. 9). xxxii, 718p. 1980. reprint ed. write for info. (*3-487-06968-7*, Pub. by Georg Olms GW) Lubrecht & Cramer.
Christians. John Drane. (Factfinder Ser.). (Illus.). 48p. (J). (gr. 3-6). 1993. 14.95 (*0-7459-2516-2*) Lion USA.
Christians & Churches in the GDR: A Report from the GDR. Collets Staff. (First-Hand Information Ser.). 64p. 1980. 7.50 (*0-317-53832-2*) St Mut.
***Christians & Jews: In the Twelfth Century Renaissance.** Anna S. Abulafia. LC 94-24560. (Illus.). 232p. 1995. 64.95 (*0-415-00012-2*, C0468) Routledge.
Christians & Jews in the Ottoman Empire: The Functioning of a Plural Society, 2 vols. Ed. by Benjamin Braude & Bernard Lewis. LC 80-11337. 1982. Vol. 1, The Central Lands, 450p. write for info. (*0-8419-0519-3*); Vol. 2, The Arabic-speaking Lands, 248p. write for info. (*0-8419-0520-7*) Holmes & Meier.
Christians & Jews in the Ottoman Empire: The Functioning of a Plural Society. abr. ed. Ed. by Bernard Lewis. 320p. (C). Date not set. pap. text ed. 24.95 (*0-8419-1138-X*) Holmes & Meier.
Christians & Jews in the Ottoman Empire: The Functioning of a Plural Society, 2 vols., Set. Ed. by Benjamin Braude & Bernard Lewis. LC 80-11337. 1982. 94.50 (*0-685-02331-1*) Holmes & Meier.
Christians & Money: A Guide to Personal Finance. Donald W. Joiner. LC 90-82876. 136p. 1991. pap. 9.95 (*0-88177-096-5*, DR096) Discipleship Res.
Christians & Moors in Spain, Vol. 2 1100-1614. Ed. by Smith. (Hispanic Classics Ser.). 1989. 49.95 (*0-85668-447-3*, Pub. by Aris & Phillips UK) David Brown.
Christians & Moors in Spain, Vol. 2 1195-1614. Ed. by Smith. (Hispanic Classics Ser.). 1989. pap. 22.00 (*0-85668-448-1*, Pub. by Aris & Phillips UK) David Brown.
Christians & Moors in Spain, Vol. 1 711-1150 AD: Texts of the Reconquest. Ed. by Smith. (Hispanic Classics Ser.). 1989. pap. 22.00 (*0-85668-411-2*, Pub. by Aris & Phillips UK) David Brown.
Christians & Moors in Spain, Vol. 3: Arabic Sources (711-1501) Ed. by Charles Melville & Smith. (Hispanic Classics Ser.). 1992. 49.95 (*0-85668-449-X*, Pub. by Aris & Phillips UK); pap. write for info. (*0-85668-450-3*, Pub. by Aris & Phillips UK) David Brown.
Christians & Moors in Spain 711-1100, Vol. 1: Texts of the Reconquest. Ed. by Smith. (Hispanic Classics Ser.). 1989. 49.95 (*0-85668-410-4*, Pub. by Aris & Phillips UK) David Brown.
***Christians & Muslims: From Double Standards to Mutual Understanding.** Hugh Goddard. 200p. 1995. 70.00 (*0-7007-0363-2*, Pub. by Curzon Pr UK) Humanities.
***Christians & Muslims: From Double Standards to Mutual Understanding.** Hugh Goddard. 1995. pap. 19.95 (*0-7007-0364-0*, Pub. by Curzon Pr UK) Humanities.
Christians & Muslims in Ottoman Cyprus & the Mediterranean World, 1571-1640. Ronald C. Jennings. (Studies in Near Eastern Civilization: No. 16). 416p. (C). 1992. text ed. 65.00 (*0-8147-4181-9*) NYU Pr.
Christians & Nonviolence in the Nuclear Age: Scripture, the Arms Race & You. Gerard A. Vanderhaar. LC 82-82388. 128p. 1982. pap. 5.95 (*0-89622-162-8*) Twenty-Third.
Christians & Pagans in Roman Britain. Dorothy Watts. (Illus.). 288p. 1991. 55.00 (*0-415-05071-5*, A6009) Routledge.
Christians & the American Revolution. Mark A. Noll. LC 77-23354. 195p. reprint ed. pap. 55.60 (*0-8357-9125-4*, 2016042) Bks Demand.
Christians & the Art of Caring. William V. Arnold & Margaret A. Fohl. LC 87-29394. 118p. (Orig.). 1988. pap. 9.99 (*0-664-24073-9*, Westminster) Westminster John Knox.
Christians & the Holy Places: The Myth of Jewish-Christian Origins. Joan E. Taylor. LC 92-20582. (C). 1993. 69.00 (*0-19-814785-6*, Clarendon Pr) OUP.
Christians & the New Creation: Genesis Motifs in the New Testament. Paul S. Minear. LC 93-42167. 176p. (Orig.). 1994. pap. 14.99 (*0-664-25531-0*) Westminster John Knox.
Christians & the Roman Empire. Marta Sordi. Tr. by Annabel Bedini. LC 86-40081. 224p. 1986. 29.95 (*0-8061-2011-8*) U of Okla Pr.
Christians & the Roman Empire. Marta Sordi. Tr. by Annabel Bedini. LC 86-40081. 224p. 1994. pap. 14.95 (*0-8061-2637-X*) U of Okla Pr.
Christians & the Sandinista Revolution: Interview with Luis Carrion. Marta Harnecker. Tr. by Kevan Insko. 16p. 1987. pap. 1.50 (*0-942638-16-6*, 36L) New Amer Pr.
Christians & the World of Computers: Professional & Social Excellence in the Computer World. Parker Rossman & Richard Kirby. LC 90-41636. 160p. (Orig.). (C). 1990. pap. 12.95 (*0-334-02468-4*) TPI PA.
Christians & Tyrants: The Prison Testimonies of Boethius, Thomas More, & Dietrich Bonhoeffer. Jamie S. Scott. LC 93-36535. (Toronto Studies in Religion: Vol. 19). 288p. (C). 1995. text ed. 49.95 (*0-8204-2274-6*) P Lang Pubs.
Christians Arise. Contrib by Tom Fettke. 1987. 5.25 (*0-685-68631-0*, MB-581); audio 10.98 (*0-685-68632-9*, TA-9090C) Lillenas.
Christians As Peacemakers. Henry Rust. 54p. (Orig.). 1983. pap. 7.95 (*0-940754-21-5*) Ed Ministries.
Christians As the Romans Saw Them. Robert L. Wilken. LC 83-12472. 218p. 1984. 30.00 (*0-300-03066-5*) Yale U Pr.
Christians As the Romans Saw Them. Robert L. Wilken. LC 83-12472. 218p. 1986. pap. 13.00 (*0-300-03627-2*, Y-575) Yale U Pr.
Christians at Work in a Hurting World. (Dialog Ser.). 124p. 1990. student ed, pap. 4.95 (*0-8341-1269-8*); teacher ed, pap. 3.95 (*0-8341-1270-1*) Beacon Hill.
Christian's Children: The Influence of John Bunyan's The Pilgrim's Progress on American Children's Literature. Ruth K. MacDonald. (American University Studies: American Literature: Ser. XXIV, Vol. 10). 208p. (C). 1989. text ed. 35.10 (*0-8204-1003-9*) P Lang Pubs.
Christians, Christians, Everywhere, How Do Your Gardens Grow? A Stewardship Service for Youth. Cynthia E. Cowen. (Orig.). 1994. pap. write for info. (*0-7880-0115-9*) CSS OH.
Christian's Edge. J. J. Turner. 1987. pap. 5.25 (*0-89137-324-1*) Quality Pubns.
Christian's Experience of the Holy Spirit see Espiritu Santo en la Experiencia del Cristiano
***Christians, Feminists, & the Culture of Pornography.** Arthur J. Mielke. 154p. (C). 1994. lib. bdg. 44.00 (*0-8191-9764-5*); pap. text ed. 28.50 (*0-8191-9765-3*) U Pr of Amer.
Christian's Freedom: The Doctrine of Christian Liberty. George Downame. 144p. 1994. reprint ed. 15.95 (*1-877611-75-1*) Soli Deo Gloria.
Christian's Future. George R. Brunk, III. (Mennonite Faith Ser.: No. 16). 96p. (Orig.). 1987. pap. 2.95 (*0-8361-3449-4*) Herald Pr.
Christian's Great Interest. William Guthrie. (Puritan Paperbacks Ser.). 208p. 1983. pap. 6.50 (*0-85151-354-9*) Banner of Truth.
Christians Grieve Too. Donald Howard. 1980. pap. 1.95 (*0-85151-315-8*) Banner of Truth.
***Christian's Guide to Designing a Loving Trust: The Smart Alternative to the Headaches & Heartaches of Wills & Probate.** 2nd ed. Robert A. Esperti & Renno L. Peterson. 400p. 1995. pap. 12.99 (*0-310-46161-8*) Zondervan.
Christian's Guide to Mental Wellness: How to Balance (Not Choose Between) Psychology & Religion. Richard P. Johnson. LC 90-61148. 192p. (Orig.). 1990. pap. 7.95 (*0-89243-325-6*) Liguori Pubns.
***Christian's Guide to Money Matters for Women.** Mary L. McDonald. 240p. 1995. pap. 14.99 (*0-310-50160-1*) Zondervan.
Christian's Guide to Today's Catholic Charismatic Movement. James A. Neher. vi, 134p. 1987. pap. 6.95 (*0-944788-99-8*) IBRI.
***Christian's Guide to Wise Investing.** rev. ed. Gary D. Moore. 336p. 1994. pap. 14.99 (*0-310-49261-0*) Zondervan.
Christian's Guide to Worry-Free Money Management: Ten Easy Steps. Kent E. Barber et al. 192p. 1994. 12.99 (*0-310-46231-2*) Zondervan.
Christians in a Crooked World. (Dialog Ser.). 111p. 1988. student ed, pap. 4.95 (*0-8341-1203-5*) Beacon Hill.
Christians in a Crooked World. (Dialog Ser.). 111p. 1988. teacher ed, pap. 4.95 (*0-8341-1204-3*) Beacon Hill.
Christians in a Non-Christian World. Rick Chromey. (Active Bible Curriculum Ser.). (Illus.). 48p. 1992. pap. 9.99 (*1-55945-224-2*) Group Pub.
Christians in China Before the Year 1550. A. C. Moule. 1972. 59.95 (*0-87968-865-3*) Gordon Pr.
Christians in Communion. Paul Avis. 150p. (Orig.). 1990. pap. 9.95 (*0-8146-1980-0*) Liturgical Pr.
Christians in Conflict. William C. Martin. LC 72-88018. (Studies in Religion & Society). 106p. 1972. 15.95 (*0-913348-01-5*); pap. 10.95 (*0-913348-10-4*) Ctr Sci Study.
Christians in Families: Genesis & Exodus. Ross T. Bender. LC 82-6058. (Conrad Grebel Lectures: No. 1981). 191p. reprint ed. pap. 54.50 (*0-7837-5122-2*, 2044821) Bks Demand.
Christians in Japan. Carolyn B. Francis & John M. Nakajima. (Orig.). 1991. pap. 7.95 (*0-377-00216-X*) Friendship Pr.
Christians in Romans Seven. Arthur W. Pink. pap. 0.99 (*0-87377-073-0*) GAM Pubns.
Christians in Secular India. Abraham V. Thomas. LC 72-420. 246p. 1973. 20.00 (*0-8386-1021-8*) Fairleigh Dickinson.
Christians in the Age of AIDS. Smith & Smith Staff. 192p. 1990. pap. text ed. 2.00 (*0-89693-196-X*) SP Pubns.
Christians in the Crossfire. Mark R. McMinn & James D. Foster. LC 90-82741. 180p. (Orig.). 1990. pap. 9.95 (*0-913342-68-8*) Barclay Pr.
Christians in the Marketplace. rev. ed. Bill Hybels. 1992. pap. 8.99 (*0-89693-073-4*, Victor Books) SP Pubns.
Christians in the Nicaraguan Revolution. Margaret Randall. (Illus.). 240p. (Orig.). 1984. pap. 4.00 (*0-919573-15-0*) Left Bank.
Christians in the Nicaraguan Revolution. Margaret Randall. 240p. (Orig.). (C). 1983. reprint ed. pap. 7.95 (*0-939306-48-4*) Left Bank.
Christians in the Technical & Social Revolutions of Our Times: World Conference on Church & Society, Geneva, July 12-26, 1966. World Conference on Church & Society Staff. LC 67-100995. 235p. reprint ed. pap. 67.00 (*0-7837-5991-6*, 2045801) Bks Demand.
Christians in the Third World. D. W. Edgington. 142p. 1982. pap. 11.95 (*0-85364-286-9*) Attic Pr.
***Christians Involved in the Political Process.** Whitehead. 1994. pap. 3.99 (*0-8024-1576-8*) Moody.
Christians, Jews & Other Worlds: Patterns of Conflict & Accommodation. Ed. by Philip F. Gallagher. LC 88-89. (Avery Lectures in History). 168p. (C). 1988. lib. bdg. 36.00 (*0-8191-6894-7*, Atlantic Rsch & Pubns Inc) U Pr of Amer.
Christians of Kerala: History, Belief & Ritual among the Yakoba. Susan Viswanathan. (Illus.). 297p. 1994. 27.00 (*0-19-563189-7*) OUP.
Christians Only: A Study in Prejudice. Heywood Broun & George Britt. LC 73-19688. (Civil Liberties in American History Ser.). 333p. 1974. reprint ed. lib. bdg. 39.50 (*0-306-70599-0*) Da Capo.
Christians Organizing for Political Service: A Study Guide Based on the Work of the Association for Public Justice. James W. Skillen. LC 80-66190. 113p. (Orig.). 1982. reprint ed. pap. 3.95 (*0-936456-01-9*) Ctr Pub Justice.
Christians, Politics & Violent Revolution. John Davies. LC 75-42517. 224p. reprint ed. pap. 63.90 (*0-317-26642-X*, 2025118) Bks Demand.
***Christian's Reasonable Service, Vol. 4.** Wilhemus A'Brakel. 580p. 1995. 27.00 (*0-614-06634-4*) Soli Deo Gloria.
Christian's Response to Islam. William M. Miller. 1976. pap. 4.99 (*0-87552-335-8*) Presby & Reformed.
Christian's Secret of a Happy Life. Hannah W. Smith. 224p. 1986. mass mkt. 4.95 (*0-345-33586-4*, Ballantine Epiphany) Ballantine.
Christian's Secret of a Happy Life. Hannah W. Smith. 9.95 (*1-55748-158-X*) Barbour & Co.
Christian's Secret of a Happy Life. Hanna W. Smith. LC 17-3740. 256p. 1968. reprint ed. pap. 4.99 (*0-8007-8007-8*) Revell.
Christian's Secret of a Happy Life. Hannah W. Smith. (Christian Library). 1985. reprint ed. 7.99 (*0-916441-21-0*); reprint ed. pap. 5.95 (*0-916441-27-X*) Barbour & Co.
Christian's Secret of a Holy Life: The Unpublished Personal Writings of Hannah Whitall Smith. Hannah W. Smith. Ed. by Melvin E. Dieter. 304p. 1994. pap. 14.99 (*0-310-39612-3*) Zondervan.
***Christian's Secret to a Happy Life.** Smith. 1995. pap. text ed. 7.99 (*1-55748-617-4*) Barbour & Co.
Christian's Secret to a Happy Life. Hannah W. Smith. 240p. 1983. pap. text ed. 3.99 (*0-88368-132-3*) Whitaker Hse.
Christians Should Be Prosperous. Victor P. Wierwille. 31p. 1971. pap. 1.00 (*0-910068-65-8*) Am Christian.
Christians True in China. James J. Liu & Stephen Wang. Ed. by Maynard Shelly. LC 88-80007. 114p. 1988. pap. 10.95 (*0-87303-127-X*) Faith & Life.
Christian's Two Chief Lessons, Viz. Selfe Deniall, & Selfe Tryall. Thomas Hooker. LC 74-14112. (Research Library of Colonial Americana). 1972. reprint ed. 37.95 (*0-405-03325-7*) Ayer.

***Christians under Construction: A Guide to Spiritual Growth. Staccato Powell & Dennis V. Proctor. (Illus.). 130p. 1995. pap. 10.00 (*0-9646729-0-1*) Kairos Pr. Have you ever thought you "had it all together" - only to discover you were not as "together" as you thought? You are not alone. If you are serious about delving into the realm of spirituality & becoming more intimate in your relationship with God. This work explores the challenges encountered in faith formation. It presents the dimensions of spiritual development in a very inspiring & illuminating fashion. Provides strategies for overcoming the obstacles to spiritual growth faced in everyday life. It reveals practical approaches & emphasizes the dynamic nature of spiritual maturation. CHRISTIANS UNDER CONSTRUCTION is a guide to help you pass inspection & hear those coveted words, "Well done, thou good & faithful servant." Order from: Kairos Press, P.O. Box 21237, Baltimore, MD 21228; 410-728-7416 or 314-533-0316.**
Publisher Provided Annotation.

C

An Asterisk (*) at the beginning of an entry indicates that the title is appearing in BIP for the first time. 1245

Christians Will Go Through the Tribulation. Jim McKeever. LC 78-55091. (Illus.). 1978. 10.95 (*0-931608-01-5*); pap. 5.95 (*0-931608-02-3*) Omega Pubns OR.

Christiansburg Montgomery County, Virginia in the Heart of the Alleghenies. Lula P. Givens. LC 80-68026. (Illus.). 256p. 1981. 12.00 (*0-9614765-1-6*) Walpa Pub.

Christiantown, U. S. A. Richard Stellway. LC 90-33833. (Marriage & the Family Review Ser.). (Illus.). 170p. 1990. text ed. 32.95 (*0-86656-903-0*); pap. text ed. 17.95 (*0-86656-908-1*) Haworth Pr.

***Christic & Patristic Baptism: Baptizo: An Inquiry into the Meaning of the Word in the Holy Scriptures.** James W. Dale. LC 94-44997. 670p. Date not set. pap. text ed. 25.00 (*0-86516-263-8*) Bolchazy-Carducci.

Christie Brinkley. Bob Italia. LC 92-13693. (Cover Girls Ser.). (J). 1992. lib. bdg. 12.94 (*1-56239-108-9*) Abdo & Dghtrs.

Christie Caper. Carolyn G. Hart. 1992. mass mkt. 4.99 (*0-553-29569-1*) Bantam.

Christie Malry's Own Double-Entry. B. S. Johnson. LC 85-71476. 192p. 1985. 14.95 (*0-8112-0953-9*); pap. 6.95 (*0-8112-0954-7*, NDP600) New Directions.

Christie on Employment Law in Canada. 2nd ed. England. 512p. Date not set. 145.00 (*0-409-88887-7*) Butterworth Legal Pubs.

Christie Seigneuries: Estate Management & Settlement in the Upper Richelieu Valley, 1760-1854. Francoise Noel. (Illus.). 256p. 1992. 44.95 (*0-7735-0876-7*, Pub. by McGill CN) U of Toronto Pr.

***Christie Whitman for the People: A Political Biography.** Sandy McClure. 270p. 1996. 24.95 (*1-57392-014-2*) Prometheus Bks.

***Christie's Old Organ.** O. F. Walton. LC 82-70861. (Victorian Children's Classics Ser.). 117p. 1982. pap. 4.95 (*0-88270-532-6*) Bridge Pub.

Christie's Rapture. Veronica Sattler. 528p. (Orig.). 1982. pap. 3.50 (*0-8217-1074-5*) Zebra.

Christie's Review of the Season. 70.00 (*0-317-57526-0*) Edns Publisol.

Christina & the Little Red Bird. Elizabeth J. Peterson. (Illus.). 23p. (Orig.). (J). (ps-1). 1984. pap. 4.95 (*0-938911-02-3*) Indiv Educ Syst.

Christina Katerina & Fats Watson's Finest Hour. Patricia L. Gauch. LC 94-9798. (J). 1996. write for info. (*0-399-22651-6*, Putnam) Putnam Pub Group.

Christina Katerina & the Box. Patricia L. Gauch. (J). (ps-3). 1993. pap. 6.95 (*0-698-20682-7*, Sandcastle Bks) Putnam Pub Group.

Christina Katerina & the Great Bear Train. Patricia L. Gauch. (Illus.). 32p. (J). 1990. 14.95 (*0-399-21623-5*, Putnam) Putnam Pub Group.

Christina Katerina & the Time She Quit the Family. Patricia L. Gauch. (Illus.). 32p. (J). (ps-3). 1987. 14.95 (*0-399-21408-9*, Putnam) Putnam Pub Group.

Christina of Denmark, Duchess of Milan & Lorraine, 1522-1590. Julia M. Ady. LC 73-154140. reprint ed. 49.50 (*0-404-09205-5*) AMS Pr.

Christina Rossetti. Intro. by Peter Porter & Geoffrey Moore. (Great Poets Ser.). (Illus.). 1986. 10.00 (*0-517-56288-X*, Crown) Crown Pub Group.

Christina Rossetti. M. Bell. LC 74-156294. (English Literature Ser.: No. 33). 1971. reprint ed. lib. bdg. 75.00 (*0-8383-1292-6*) M S G Haskell Hse.

Christina Rossetti. Dorothy M. Stuart. LC 74-160429. (English Literature Ser.: No. 33). 1971. reprint ed. lib. bdg. 49.95 (*0-8383-1299-3*) M S G Haskell Hse.

Christina Rossetti: A Biographical & Critical Study. Mackenzie Bell. LC 70-148747. reprint ed. 35.00 (*0-404-08724-8*) AMS Pr.

***Christina Rossetti: A Literary Biography.** Jan Marsh. 1995. 27.95 (*0-670-83517-X*, Viking) Viking Penguin.

Christina Rossetti: Critical Perspectives, 1862-1982. Edna K. Charles. LC 84-40392. (Illus.). 192p. 1985. 32.50 (*0-941664-06-6*) Susquehanna U Pr.

Christina Rossetti: Poet. Carol Greene. (Rookie Biographies Ser.). (Illus.). 48p. (J). (gr. k-3). 1994. lib. bdg. 12.90 (*0-516-04262-9*) Childrens.

***Christina Rossetti: Poet.** Carol Greene. LC 93-42862. (Rookie Biographies Ser.). (J). (ps-2). 1994. pap. 4.95 (*0-516-44262-7*) Childrens.

Christina Rossetti: The Poetry of Endurance. Dolores Rosenblum. LC 85-30739. (Ad Feminam: Women & Literature). 264p. 1987. text ed. 26.95 (*0-8093-1269-7*) S Ill U Pr.

Christina Rossetti & Her Poetry. Edith Birkhead. LC 75-148751. reprint ed. 16.00 (*0-404-52503-2*) AMS Pr.

Christina Rossetti & the Poetry of Discovery. Katherine J. Mayberry. LC 89-33163. 160p. 1989. text ed. 27.50 (*0-8071-1529-0*) La State U Pr.

Christina Rossetti in Context. Antony H. Harrison. LC 87-10773. xvi, 231p. (C). 1988. 37.50 (*0-8078-1755-4*); pap. 14.95 (*0-8078-4211-7*) U of NC Pr.

Christina Stead. Diana Brydon. LC 86-22307. (Women Writers Ser.). 250p. (C). 1987. 44.00 (*0-389-20689-X*, N8247); pap. 13.00 (*0-389-20690-3*, N8248) B&N Imports.

Christina Stead. Jennifer Gribble. (Australian Writers Ser.). 124p. 1994. pap. 19.95 (*0-19-553370-4*) OUP.

Christina Stead. Susan Sheridan. LC 88-10917. (Key Women Writers Ser.). 174p. 1988. 29.95 (*0-253-30106-8*) Ind U Pr.

Christina Stead: A Biography. Hazel Rowley. LC 94-14236. 1994. 37.50 (*0-8050-3411-0*) H Holt & Co.

Christina Stead's Heroine: The Changing Sense of Decorum. Kate M. Stern. (American University Studies: Ser. IV, Vol. 87). 295p. (C). 1989. text ed. 35.95 (*0-8204-0830-1*) P Lang Pubs.

Christina's Ghost. Betty R. Wright. LC 85-42880. 128p. (J). (gr. 3-7). 1985. 14.95 (*0-8234-0581-8*) Holiday.

Christina's Ghost. Betty R. Wright. 112p. (J). (gr. 3-7). 1987. pap. 2.75 (*0-590-42709-1*) Scholastic Inc.

Christine. Stephen King. LC 82-20105. 600p. 1983. pap. 25.00 (*0-670-22026-4*) Viking Penguin.

***Christine.** Raymond Wilson. 430p. 1995. pap. 12.95 (*1-56901-544-9*) NW Pub.

Christine. Stephen King. 528p. 1983. reprint ed. pap. 6.99 (*0-451-16044-4*, Sig) NAL-Dutton.

Christine Brooke-Rose & Contemporary Fiction. Sarah Birch. LC 93-24543. 1994. 45.00 (*0-19-812375-2*) OUP.

Christine de Pizan: A Bibliography. 2nd ed. Edith Yenal. LC 89-10718. (Author Bibliographies Ser.: No. 63). (Illus.). 213p. 1989. 25.00 (*0-8108-2248-2*) Scarecrow.

Christine de Pizan: Christine's Vision. Tr. by Glenda K. McLeod. LC 92-37726. (Library of Medieval Literature: Vol. 68B). 232p. 1993. 33.00 (*0-8240-6048-2*) Garland.

Christine de Pizan: Her Life & Works. Charity C. Willard. LC 84-1081. (Illus.). 266p. 1990. reprint ed. pap. 14.95 (*0-89255-152-6*) Persea Bks.

***Christine De Pizan: Le Livre du duc des vrais amans.** Ed. by Thelma S. Fenster. (Medieval & Renaissance Texts & Studies: Vol. 124). 272p. 1994. 24.00 (*0-86698-129-2*, MR124) MRTS.

Christine Lavin Songbook. Ed. by Milton Okun. pap. 17.95 (*0-89524-712-7*) Cherry Lane.

Christine McAuliffe: Reach for the Stars. Patricia S. Martin. (Reaching Your Goal Bks.). (Illus.). 24p. (J). (gr. 1-4). 1987. lib. bdg. 14.60 (*0-86592-172-5*) Rourke Corp.

Christine McAuliffe: Reach for the Stars, Set. Patricia S. Martin. (Reaching Your Goal Bks.). (Illus.). 24p. (J). (gr. 1-4). 1987. lib. bdg. 10.95 (*0-685-67566-1*) Rourke Corp.

Christkwanza. Ndugu T'Ofori-Atta. LC 90-26424. (Illus.). 100p. (Orig.). 1990. pap. text ed. 9.95 (*0-913491-13-6*) SCP Third.

Christliche Platonaneigunug in den Stromateis des Clemens von Alexandrien. Dietmar Wyrwa. 364p. (GER.). 1983. 72.30 (*3-11-008903-3*) De Gruyter.

Christliche Staatsphilosophie in Spanien. Alois Dempf. Ed. by J. P. Mayer. LC 78-67344. (European Political Thought Ser.). (GER.). 1979. reprint ed. lib. bdg. 15.95 (*0-405-11691-8*) Ayer.

Christliche Theologie und Philologie in der Spaetantike: Die schulwissenschaftlichen Methoden der Psalmenexegese Cassiodors. Reinhard Schlieben. LC 74-77213. (Arbeiten zur Kirchengeschichte Ser.: Vol. 46). 132p. (GER.). (C). 1974. 55.40 (*3-11-004634-2*) De Gruyter.

Christlichen Lehrer im Zweiten Jahrhundert: Ihre Lehrtatigkeit, ihr Selbstverstandnis und ihre Geschichte. Ulrich Neymeyr. LC 88-29247. (Supplements to Vigiliae Christianae Ser.: Vol. IV). 279p. (GER.). (C). 1989. text ed. 74.50 (*90-04-08773-7*) E J Brill.

Christlichen Sarkophage der vorkonstantinischen Zeit. Friedrich Gerke. (Studien zur Spaetantiken Kunstgeschichte: Vol. 11). (Illus.). viii, 432p. 1978. reprint ed. 315.40 (*3-11-004999-6*) De Gruyter.

Christlieb Family. Benjamin F. Christlieb. 52p. 1994. reprint ed. pap. 11.00 (*0-8328-4202-8*) Higginson Bk Co.

***Christlieb Family.** Benjamin F. Christlieb. 52p. 1994. reprint ed. lib. bdg. 21.00 (*0-8328-4513-2*) Higginson Bk Co.

***Christlieb Family.** Benjamin F. Christlieb. 52p. 1994. reprint ed. pap. 11.00 (*0-8328-4514-0*) Higginson Bk Co.

Christlike God. John V. Taylor. 320p. (Orig.). 1993. pap. 18.00 (*0-334-00179-X*, SCM Pr) TPI PA.

Christlike Leadership. Mark Gilroy. (Active Bible Curriculum Ser.). (Illus.). 48p. 1993. pap. 9.99 (*1-55945-231-5*) Group Pub.

Christmas. (Blank Bks.). 32p. (J). 1986. 2.95 (*0-88682-111-8*, 95162-098) Creative Ed.

Christmas. (Hidden Pictures Story Ser.). (Illus.). 48p. (J). (ps-2). 1993. pap. 2.95 (*0-8431-3606-5*) Price Stern.

***Christmas.** (Puzzle Fun Bks.). (J). Date not set. 7.95 (*1-56828-078-5*) Red Jacket Pr.

Christmas. Judy Beach & Kathleen Spencer. (Teachers' Holiday Helpers Ser.). (J). (gr. 1-3). 1987. pap. 6.99 (*0-8224-6773-9*) Fearon Teach Aids.

Christmas. Illus. by Frank Daniel. (Fun Shapes Ser.). 20p. (J). (ps). 1993. bds. 3.95 (*0-689-71734-2*, Aladdin Paperbacks) S&S Childrens.

Christmas. Jane Duden. LC 89-28520. (Holidays Ser.). (Illus.). 48p. (J). (gr. 5-6). 1990. text ed. 12.95 (*0-89686-497-9*, Crstwood Hse) Silver Burdett Pr.

***Christmas.** Ed. by Helen Exley. (So-Much-More-Than-a-Card Ser.). (Illus.). 28p. (Orig.). 1995. pap. 2.99 (*1-85015-653-0*) Exley Giftbooks.

Christmas. Dennis B. Fradin. LC 89-25634. (Best Holiday Books Ser.). (Illus.). 48p. (J). (gr. 1-4). 1990. lib. bdg. 15.95 (*0-89490-258-X*) Enslow Pubs.

Christmas. K. Gibson & R. Gee. (You & Your Child Ser.). (Illus.). 32p. (J). (ps-3). 1992. pap. 5.95 (*0-7460-1030-3*) EDC.

Christmas. Miriam Nerlove. Ed. by Kathy Tucker. LC 89-70737. (Illus.). 24p. (J). (ps-1). 1990. 11.95 (*0-8075-1148-X*) A Whitman.

Christmas. Shelly Nielsen. Ed. by Rosemary Wallner. LC 91-73034. (Holiday Celebrations Ser.). (J). 1992. lib. bdg. 13.99 (*1-56239-067-8*) Abdo & Dghtrs.

Christmas. Alana Willoughby. Ed. by Alton Jordan. (ARO Holidays Ser.). (Illus.) (J). (gr. k-3). 1984. 6.95 (*0-89868-025-5*, Read Res); pap. 3.50 (*0-89868-058-1*, Read Res) ARO Pub.

Christmas, Vol. 47. Ed. by Randolph Haugan. LC 32-30914. 64p. 1977. 22.95 (*0-8066-8951-X*, 10-17115, Augsburg); pap. 12.99 (*0-8066-8950-1*, 10-17114, Augsburg) Augsburg Fortress.

Christmas: A Celebration in Words & Paintings. Helen Exley. (Words & Paintings Ser.). (Illus.). 60p. 1993. 6.99 (*1-85015-444-9*) Exley Giftbooks.

Christmas: A Fresh Look. Steve Wamberg & Annie Wamberg. (Active Bible Curriculum Ser.). (Illus.). 48p. 1991. pap. 9.99 (*1-55945-124-6*) Group Pub.

***Christmas: A Holiday Treasury.** Mary Engelbreit. 1994. 4.95 (*0-8362-3086-8*) Andrews & McMeel.

Christmas: A Holiday Treasury. Ed. by Della Rowland. LC 93-16663. 1993. pap. 6.95 (*0-8362-4938-0*) Andrews & McMeel.

Christmas: A Joyful Heritage. Susan A. Madsen. LC 84-72519. (Illus.). xvi, 93p. 1984. reprint ed. pap. 3.95 (*0-87579-367-3*) Deseret Bk.

***Christmas: A Season of Traditions.** Ariel Books Staff. (Illus.). 32p. 1995. 6.95 (*0-8362-4741-8*) Andrews & McMeel.

Christmas: A Thematic Unit. Ireta S. Graube. (Thematic Units Ser.). (Illus.). 80p. (Orig.). (gr. 1-3). 1992. student ed 8.95 (*1-55734-259-8*) Tchr Create Mat.

Christmas: A Treasury of Verse & Prose. Sheila Pickles. 1994. 6.50 (*0-517-59900-7*, Harmony) Crown Pub Group.

Christmas: An Albert Whitman Prairie Book. Miriam Nerlove. (J). (ps-3). 1993. pap. 4.95 (*0-8075-1147-1*) A Whitman.

Christmas: An American Annual of Christmas Literature & Art, Vol. 46. Ed. by Randolph E. Haugan. LC 32-30914. 64p. 1976. 22.95 (*0-8066-8948-X*, 10-17113, Augsburg); pap. 11.95 (*0-8066-8947-1*, 10-17112, Augsburg) Augsburg Fortress.

Christmas: An American Annual of Christmas Literature & Art, Vol. 48. Ed. by Randolph E. Haugan. LC 32-30914. (Illus.). 64p. 1978. 22.95 (*0-8066-8953-6*, 10-17117, Augsburg); pap. 11.95 (*0-8066-8952-8*, 10-17116, Augsburg) Augsburg Fortress.

Christmas: An American Annual of Christmas Literature & Art, Vol. 49. Ed. by Randolph E. Haugan. LC 32-30914. (Illus.). 64p. 1979. 22.95 (*0-8066-8955-2*, 10-17119, Augsburg); pap. 11.95 (*0-8066-8954-4*, 10-17118, Augsburg) Augsburg Fortress.

Christmas: An Annual Treasury, Vol. 64. Augsburg Fortress Staff. 1994. 16.99 (*0-8066-8985-4*, Fortress Pr) Augsburg Fortress.

Christmas: An Illustrated Treasury. Comp. by Michelle Louric. (Courage Illustrated Treasuries Ser.). (Illus.). 48p. 1994. 6.98 (*1-56138-437-2*) Running Pr.

Christmas: Creative Image Bank. 96p. 1991. pap. 19.95 (*88-7070-156-5*) Belvedere USA.

Christmas: Cut & Color Activity Book. 1988. pap. 3.99 (*0-517-66282-5*) Random Hse Value.

Christmas: Facts & Fun. Jill Hierstein-Morris. (Facts & Fun Ser.). (Illus.). 72p. (Orig.). (J). (gr. 1 up). 1990. pap. 9.95 (*1-877588-02-4*) Creatively Yours.

Christmas: How Sweet It Is! rev. ed. Patricia B. Mitchell. 1991. pap. 4.00 (*0-925117-48-X*) Mitchells.

Christmas: Its Origin & Associations. W. F. Dawson. LC 89-63012. (Illus.). 366p. 1990. reprint ed. lib. bdg. 48.00 (*1-55888-842-X*) Omnigraphics Inc.

Christmas: Its Origin, Celebration & Significance As Related in Prose & Verse. Ed. by Robert H. Schauffler. LC 89-43063. 368p. 1990. reprint ed. lib. bdg. 48.00 (*1-55888-824-1*) Omnigraphics Inc.

Christmas: King James Version. Illus. by Jan Pienkowski. LC 84-5719. 32p. (J). (gr. 1 up). 1984. reprint ed. 18.95 (*0-394-86923-0*) Knopf Bks Yng Read.

Christmas: Make-Believe Or Discovery. Louis A. Michaux. Ed. by Evan Davies. LC 88-92481. (Illus.). 65p. (Orig.). 1989. pap. 7.50 (*0-317-93408-2*) L A Michaux.

Christmas: Mystical Interpretation Of. 7th ed. Max Heindel. Ed. by Rosicrucian Fellowship Staff. 51p. (C). 1987. reprint ed. pap. text ed. 3.50 (*0-911274-65-0*) Rosicrucian.

Christmas: One Hundred Seasonal Favorites. (Ultimate Ser.). 248p. (J). (gr. 4-12). 1985. 17.95 (*0-88188-158-9*, 00361399) H Leonard.

Christmas: Penhaligon's Scented Treasury of Verse & Prose. Ed. by Sheila Pickles. 1989. pap. 19.95 (*0-517-57367-9*, Harmony) Crown Pub Group.

Christmas: Recipes, Crafts & More. Barbara Randolph. (American Country Living Ser.). 1991. 14.99 (*0-517-02014-9*) Random Hse Value.

Christmas: The Annual of Christmas Literature & Art, Vol. 52. LC 32-30914. (Illus.). 64p. 1982. 22.95 (*0-8066-8961-7*, 10-17125, Augsburg); pap. text ed. 11.95 (*0-8066-8960-9*, 17-0124, Augsburg) Augsburg Fortress.

Christmas: The Annual of Christmas Literature & Art, Vol. 54. LC 32-30914. (Illus.). 64p. 1984. 22.95 (*0-8066-8965-X*, 10-17129, Augsburg); pap. text ed. 11.95 (*0-8066-8964-1*, 17-0128, Augsburg) Augsburg Fortress.

Christmas: The Annual of Christmas Literature & Art, Vol. 55. Leonard Flachman. LC 32-30914. 64p. 1985. text ed. 22.95 (*0-8066-8967-6*, 10-17131, Augsburg); pap. text ed. 11.95 (*0-8066-8966-8*, 10-17130, Augsburg) Augsburg Fortress.

Christmas: The Annual of Christmas Literature & Art, Vol. 56. Ed. by Leonard Flachman et al. LC 32-30914. 64p. 1986. text ed. 22.95 (*0-8066-8969-2*, 10-17133, Augsburg); pap. 11.95 (*0-8066-8968-4*, 10-17132, Augsburg) Augsburg Fortress.

Christmas: The Annual of Christmas Literature & Art, Vol. 57. Ed. by Leonard Flachman. LC 32-30914. (Illus.). 64p. 1987. text ed. 22.95 (*0-8066-8971-4*, 10-17135, Augsburg); pap. 11.95 (*0-8066-8970-6*, 10-17134, Augsburg) Augsburg Fortress.

Christmas: The Annual of Christmas Literature & Art, Vol. 58. LC 32-30914. 64p. 1988. 22.95 (*0-8066-8973-0*, 10-17137, Augsburg); pap. 11.95 (*0-8066-8972-2*, 10-17136, Augsburg) Augsburg Fortress.

Christmas: The Annual of Christmas Literature & Art, Vol. 59. Illus. by Audrey Teeple. LC 32-30914. 64p. 1989. 22.95 (*0-8066-8975-7*, 10-17139); pap. 11.95 (*0-8066-8974-9*, 10-17138) Augsburg Fortress.

Christmas: The Annual of Christmas Literature & Art, Vol. 60. David Augsburger. LC 32-30914. 64p. 1991. pap. 12.99 (*0-8066-8978-1*, 10-17140) Augsburg Fortress.

Christmas: The Annual of Christmas Literature & Art, Vol. 63. Augsburg Staff. 1993. pap. 12.99 (*0-8066-8982-X*) Augsburg Fortress.

Christmas: The Annual of Christmas Literature & Arts, Vol. 51. LC 32-30914. (Illus.). 64p. 1981. pap. text ed. 11.95 (*0-8066-8958-7*, 10-17122, Augsburg) Augsburg Fortress.

Christmas A-Z. Dee Leone. (Bible Crafts Ser.). 96p. (J). (gr. 2-7). 1989. 10.95 (*0-86653-499-7*, SS1892, Shining Star Pubns) Good Apple.

Christmas Accident & Other Stories. Annie E. Trumbull. LC 75-98601. (Short Story Index Reprint Ser.). 1977. 19.95 (*0-8369-3176-9*) Ayer.

Christmas Activities Around the World. Dianna Sullivan. (Illus.). 48p. (J). (gr. 1-4). 1985. student ed 6.95 (*1-55734-008-0*) Tchr Create Mat.

Christmas Activity Book. (J). 1989. pap. 3.99 (*0-517-69110-8*) Random Hse Value.

Christmas Activity Book. Catherine Bruzzone. (Illus.). 24p. (J). (gr. k-5). 1993. pap. 3.95 (*0-8120-1745-5*) Barron.

Christmas Activity Book. Stacy Venturi-Pickett. (Illus.). 24p. 1993. pap. 4.95 (*0-8249-8621-0*, Ideals Child) Hambleton-Hill.

Christmas Affair. Carole Mortimer. 1990. pap. 2.50 (*0-373-11325-0*) Harlequin Bks.

Christmas Album. Nancy Cogan & Roni Akmon. (Illus.). 84p. 1992. 32.95 (*0-926684-05-1*) Eclectic Oregon.

Christmas Album. John Griggs & Carlos Barbosa-Lima. Ed. by Aaron Stang. 40p. (Orig.). (YA). 1993. pap. text ed. 9.95 (*0-89898-641-9*) CPP Belwin.

Christmas All over the Place. Judith Martin & Donald Ashwander. 22p. (Orig.). (J). (ps-12). 1977. 4.00 (*0-87602-113-5*) Anchorage.

Christmas Alphabet. Robert Sabuda. LC 94-65106. (Illus.). 26p. (J). (ps up). 1994. 21.95 (*0-531-06857-9*) Orchard Bks Watts.

Christmas Alphabet. Carolyn Wells. (Illus.). 32p. (J). 1989. 15.95 (*0-399-21683-9*, Putnam) Putnam Pub Group.

***Christmas Alphabet.** deluxe limited ed. Robert Sabuda. LC 94-65106. (Illus.). 1995. 100.00 (*0-531-09492-8*) Orchard Bks Watts.

Christmas Alphabet Book. Patricia Whitehead. LC 84-8830. (ABC Adventures Ser.). (Illus.). 32p. (J). (gr. k-2). 1985. lib. bdg. 11.59 (*0-8167-0365-5*); pap. text ed. 2.95 (*0-8167-0366-3*) Troll Assocs.

Christmas Always. Peter Catalanotto. LC 90-28712. (Illus.). 32p. (J). (ps-1). 1991. 14.95 (*0-531-05946-4*); lib. bdg. 14.99 (*0-531-08546-5*) Orchard Bks Watts.

***Christmas Always...** Peter Catalanotto. LC 90-28712. (Illus.). 32p. (J). (ps-1). 1995. pap. 5.95 (*0-531-07066-2*) Orchard Bks Watts.

Christmas: An American Annual of Christmas Literature & Art, Vol. 50. Ed. by Randolph E. Haugan. LC 32-30914. (Illus.). 64p. 1980. 22.95 (*0-8066-8957-9*, 10-17121, Augsburg); pap. 12.99 (*0-8066-8956-0*, 17-0120, Augsburg) Augsburg Fortress.

Christmas & Advent. Ed. by Anthony Petti. (Chester's Books of Motets: Bk. 6). Date not set. pap. 7.50 (*0-685-69006-7*, Chester Music) Music Sales.

Christmas & Advent Book. Ed. by Anthony Petti. (Chester's Books of Motets: Bk. 12). Date not set. pap. 7.50 (*0-685-69007-5*, Chester Music) Music Sales.

Christmas & Advent Book. Ed. by Anthony Petti. (Chester's Books of Motets: Bk. 16). Date not set. pap. 7.50 (*0-685-69008-3*, Chester Music) Music Sales.

Christmas & Christmas Lore. Thomas G. Crippen. 1976. lib. bdg. 59.95 (*0-8490-1617-7*) Gordon Pr.

Christmas & Christmas Lore. Thomas G. Crippen. LC 89-43370. (Illus.). 1990. reprint ed. 42.00 (*1-55888-860-8*) Omnigraphics Inc.

Christmas & Easter in the Initiatic Tradition. rev. ed. Omraam M. Aivanhov. (Izvor Collection: Vol. 209). (Illus.). 154p. (Orig.). 1987. pap. 6.95 (*2-85566-397-0*, Pub. by Prosveta FR) Prosveta USA.

Christmas & the Old House. Tom T. Hall. (Illus.). 48p. (J). 1989. audio 21.00 (*0-934601-91-7*) Peachtree Pubs.

Christmas Angel. Jo Beverley. 320p. 1992. mass mkt. 3.99 (*0-8217-3976-X*) Zebra.

***Christmas Angel.** Pirkko Vainio. Tr. by Anthea Bell. LC 95-8435. (Illus.). (J). 1995. write for info. (*1-55858-499-4*) North-South Bks NYC.

***Christmas Angel.** Pirkko Vainio. Tr. by Anthea Bell. LC 95-8435. (Illus.). (J). 1995. lib. bdg. write for info. (*1-55858-500-1*) North-South Bks NYC.

Christmas Angel. Kaye J. Volk. pap. 2.95 (*1-55503-582-5*, 01111329) Covenant Comms.

Christmas Angel. Shannon Waverly. (Romance Ser.). 1993. mass mkt. 2.99 (*0-373-03292-7*, 1-03292-9) Harlequin Bks.

Christmas Angel. Joan G. Thomas. (Illus.). 20p. (J). (gr. 1-5). 1988. reprint ed. pap. 3.95 (*0-8192-1429-9*) Morehouse Pub.

***Christmas Angels.** Debra Dier et al. 448p. (Orig.). 1995. mass mkt., pap. 5.99 (*0-505-52062-1*) Dorchester Pub Co.

***Christmas Angels: A Pop-Up Book.** Ariel Books Staff. (Illus.). 8p. (J). (ps-3). 1994. 4.95 (*0-8362-3090-6*) Andrews & McMeel.

***Christmas Apple.** J. O. Schrag. (Illus.). 24p. (Orig.). (J). (gr. k-3). 1995. pap. 8.95 (*0-945530-11-0*) Wordsworth KS.

C

C

Christmas Classics. 1993. mass mkt. 4.99 (0-373-48265-5, 5-48265-8) Harlequin Bks.

Christmas Classics. Western Publishing Staff. (Illus.). (J). (gr. k-4). 1992. pap. 19.95 (1-882954-03-3) Aspen Press.

Christmas Classics for Children. John T. Moore et al. (J). (ps-00). 1981. 14.99 (0-570-04058-2, 56-1351) Concordia.

Christmas, Coins & Other Poems. Douglas Hawks, Jr. 40p. (Orig.). 1990. pap. 9.00 (0-9624156-1-8) Creekside Pubs.

*Christmas Collectibles. Cpp Belwin Staff. 1994. pap. 12.95 (0-89898-941-8) CPP Belwin.

Christmas Collectibles. Duncan Designers Staff. Ed. by Bill Thompson. 52p. 1993. pap. text ed. 9.95 (0-916809-71-4) Scott Pubns MI.

Christmas Collectibles. Beth Prince. 1993. 12.98 (1-55521-910-1) Bk Sales Inc.

Christmas Collectibles. Margaret Whitmyer. (Second Ser.). 1993. 24.95 (0-89145-558-2) Collector Bks.

*Christmas Collection. Susan Hill. (J). (ps-3). 1994. 19.95 (1-56402-341-9) Candlewick Pr.

Christmas Collection. (Easy ABC Music Ser.). 176p. 1990. reprint ed. pap. 12.95 (0-7935-0103-2, 00001255) H Leonard.

*Christmas Collections: A Book of Decorations & Design. Bob Hampton & Ralph Null. 128p. 1995. 39.95 (1-56469-027-X) Harmony Hse Pub LO.

Christmas Collie. Ted Paul. LC 89-17994. (Illus.). 42p. (J). (ps-7). 1989. 12.95 (0-89802-548-6) Beautiful Am.

Christmas Colt. Mallory Stevens. (J). (gr. 4-7). 1992. mass mkt. 3.50 (0-06-106721-0, Harp PBks) HarpC.

Christmas Comes Alive! Geneva M. Butz. LC 88-19587. (Illus.). 96p. (Orig.). 1988. pap. 9.95 (0-8298-0787-X) Pilgrim OH.

Christmas Comes in Assorted Sizes. Marguerite Goodman. Ed. by Sylvia Ashton. LC 77-80303. 1977. 22.95 (0-87949-111-6) Ashley Bks.

Christmas Comes to Lone Star Gulch. Paul M. Miller. (J). 1989. 4.95 (0-8341-9157-1, BCMC-67); 29.95 (0-685-68524-1, MC-67C); audio 10.98 (0-685-68525-X, TA-9060C) Lillenas.

Christmas Companion. Gloria Nichol. 96p. 1994. 10.98 (0-8317-1223-6) Smithmark.

Christmas Conference for the Foundation of the General Anthroposophical Society, 1923-1924. Rudolf Steiner. Tr. by Johanna Collis. 300p. 1990. 29.95 (0-88010-193-8) Anthroposophic.

Christmas Cook Book. June Dutton. (Illus.). 1978. pap. 2.50 (0-915696-06-1) Determined Prods.

*Christmas Cookbook: Over 150 Festive Recipes. Longmeadow Staff. 1994. 9.98 (0-681-45459-8) Longmeadow Pr.

Christmas Cookie Book. Judy Knipe & Barbara Marks. 1990. 14.95 (0-449-90509-8, Columbine) Fawcett.

Christmas Cookie Book. Joan W. Anglund. LC 77-78293. (Illus.). (J). 1982. reprint ed. 3.95 (0-915696-07-X) Determined Prods.

Christmas Cookies. (Favorite All Time Recipes Ser.). (Illus.). 96p. 1993. 7.98 (1-56173-785-2, 2012500) Pubns Intl Ltd.

Christmas Cookies. Margo Finch. 20p. (J). 1989. bds. 2.95 (0-8167-1892-X) Troll Assocs.

Christmas Cookies. Glorya Hale. 1990. 5.99 (0-517-02424-1) Random Hse Value.

Christmas Cookies. Wendy Lewison. (Wee Pudgy Board Bks.). (Illus.). 24p. (J). (ps). 1993. bds. 2.95 (0-448-40554-7, G&D) Putnam Pub Group.

Christmas Countdown. Troll Staff. 10p. (J). (ps). 1991. pap. 3.95 (0-8167-2183-1) Troll Assocs.

Christmas Countdown: A Story a Day for 25 Days for Everyone Who Just Can't Wait 'til Christmas. Steve Englehart. (Illus.). 64p. (Orig.). (J). 1993. reprint ed. mass mkt. 5.99 (0-380-76842-9, Camelot) Avon.

Christmas Countdown with Ruth J. Morehead's Holly Babes. Illus. by Ruth J. Morehead. LC 90-61905. (Chunky Shape Bks.). 22p. (J). (ps). 1991. bds. 2.95 (0-679-81417-5) Random Bks Yng Read.

*Christmas Counting. (J). 1994. bds. 2.95 (1-56458-823-8) Dorling Kindersley.

Christmas Counting. Lynn Reiser. LC 91-32501. (Illus.). 32p. (J). (ps-4). 1992. 14.00 (0-688-10676-5); lib. bdg. 13.93 (0-688-10677-3) Greenwillow.

Christmas Country Style. Ed. by Linda Piepenbrink. LC 91-62465. 98p. 1991. 14.98 (0-89821-096-8) Reiman Pubns.

*Christmas Cowboy. Suzannah Davis. (Desire Ser.). 1995. pap. 2.99 (0-373-05903-5, 1-05903-9) Silhouette.

Christmas Cowboy. Sarah Wilson. (J). (ps-6). 1993. pap. 14.00 (0-671-74780-0, S&S Bks Young Read) S&S Childrens.

Christmas Craft Book. 1991. 9.99 (0-517-06692-0) Random Hse Value.

Christmas Craft Book. Thomas Berger. Tr. by Polly Lawson. (Illus.). 86p. (J). 1990. reprint ed. pap. 12.95 (0-86315-110-8, Pub. by Floris Bks UK) Gryphon Hse.

*Christmas Craft Source Book: Over Two-Hundred Ideas & Motifs for the Festive Season. Gail Lawther. (Illus.). 144p. 1995. 24.95 (1-57076-019-5, Trafalgar Sq Pub) Trafalgar.

Christmas Crafts. Judith H. Corwin. LC 93-6366. (Holiday Crafts Ser.). (Illus.). (J). (gr. k-4). Date not set. lib. bdg. 13.37 (0-531-11149-0) Watts.

Christmas Crafts. Hilary Devonshire et al. LC 90-32522. (Fresh Start Ser.). (Illus.). 48p. (J). (gr. 5-8). 1990. lib. bdg. 12.95 (0-531-14073-3) Watts.

Christmas Crafts. Sabine Lohf. LC 89-22255. (Craft Bks.). 64p. (J). 1989. lib. bdg. 15.45 (0-516-09252-9); pap. 8.95 (0-516-49252-7) Childrens.

*Christmas Crafts. Carol McCleeve. LC 95-16921. (Illus.). 128p. 1995. 24.95 (0-8069-4214-2) Sterling.

Christmas Crafts: Merry Things to Make. Ed. by Colleen Van Blaricom. (Illus.). 32p. (Orig.). (J). (ps-5). 1993. pap. 3.95 (1-56397-083-X) Boyds Mills Pr.

Christmas Crafts: Over Fifty Festive Ideas for Every Room in the Home. Myra Davidson. (Illus.). 128p. 1994. 27.95 (0-304-34337-4, Pub. by Cassell UK) Sterling.

Christmas Crafts Book. (Illus.). 64p. 1993. spiral bd. 5.98 (1-56173-732-1, 3613700) Pubns Intl Ltd.

Christmas Creations. Ed. by Bill Thompson. (Illus.). 52p. 1984. pap. text ed. 2.98 (0-916809-12-9) Scott Pubns MI.

*Christmas Creche: O Holy Night. Bradley Clarke. (J). (ps-3). 1994. 16.99 (1-56476-419-2) SP Pubns.

Christmas Creche Pop-up Book. (Illus.). (J). (ps-3). 1992. 15.00 (1-56021-159-8) W J Fantasy.

*Christmas Crew Book Compendium. James Van Hise. 1994. pap. 19.95 (1-55698-345-X) Movie Pubs Servs.

Christmas Crib That Zack Built. Carol S. Wedeven. LC 89-263. (J). 1989. boxed 9.95 (0-687-07816-4) Abingdon.

Christmas Crimes. Simon Brett. 1993. mass mkt. 9.95 (0-440-50469-4, Dell Trade Pbks) Dell.

Christmas Cup. Nancy R. Patterson. LC 88-29112. (Illus.). 80p. (J). (gr. 3-5). 1989. 14.95 (0-531-05821-2); lib. bdg. 14.99 (0-531-08421-3) Orchard Bks Watts.

Christmas Cup. Nancy R. Patterson. 80p. (J). 1991. pap. 2.95 (0-590-43870-0, Apple Paperbacks) Scholastic Inc.

Christmas Customs & Traditions: Their History & Significance. Clement A. Miles. (Illus.). 19.75 (0-8446-5484-1) Peter Smith.

Christmas Customs & Traditions: Their History & Significance. Clement A. Miles. LC 76-9183. (Illus.). 1976. reprint ed. pap. 6.95 (0-486-23354-5) Dover.

Christmas Customs Around the World. Herbert H. Wernecke. LC 59-9581. 188p. 1979. pap. 10.99 (0-664-24258-8, Westminster) Westminster John Knox.

Christmas Customs Cookbook. Nan Lansing. 346p. 1993. lib. bdg. write for info. (0-9637976-3-8) Nickoli Pub.

Christmas Cycle: Advent, Christmas, Epiphany. Ed. by Blair G. Meeks & Virginia Sloyan. (Liturgy Ser.). (Illus.). 120p. (Orig.). 1991. pap. 10.95 (0-918208-54-8) Liturgical Conf.

Christmas Day Kitten. James Herriot. LC 86-13890. (J). (ps up). 1986. 12.95 (0-312-13407-X) St Martin.

Christmas Day Kitten. James Herriot. (Illus.). 32p. (J). (gr. 3 up). 1993. pap. 6.95 (0-312-09767-0) St Martin.

Christmas Death. Barbara McCoy. 1979. pap. 2.00 (0-913719-39-0) High-Coo Pr.

*Christmas Deck the Tree: Decorations, Gifts, & Food to Put Joy into Your Christmas. Lois Rock. (Illus.). 48p. (J). (gr. 3-5). 1995. pap. 8.99 (0-7459-3041-7) Lion USA.

Christmas Decoration: Eggshell-Wydmuski. Lester L. Wegrzecki. (Illus.). 88p. (J). (gr. 4 up). 1987. 9.50 (0-317-90582-1) L L Wegrzecki.

Christmas Decoration: Eggshell-Wydmuszki. Lester L. Wegrzecki. (Illus.). (Orig.). (J). (gr. 4 up). 1987. pap. write for info. (0-9620774-0-2) L L Wegrzecki.

Christmas Decorations. Francesca Crespi. 16p. (J). 1992. pap. 7.95 (0-8249-8529-X, Ideals Child) Hambleton-Hill.

Christmas Decorations. National Gallery, London. (Illus.). (J). (gr. 8 up). 1993. pap. 12.95 (0-316-59890-9) Little.

Christmas Decorations: Make & Color Your Own. (J). (ps-3). 1989. pap. 1.95 (0-89375-645-8) Troll Assocs.

Christmas Decorations from Williamsburg. Susan H. Rountree. LC 91-26438. (Illus.). 144p. 1991. 19.95 (0-87935-085-7) Colonial Williamsburg.

Christmas Decorations from Williamsburg's Folk Art Collection: Step by Step Instructions for Christmas Ornaments You Can Make at Home. Colonial Williamsburg Foundation Staff. LC 76-41253. (Illus.). 80p. (Orig.). 1976. pap. 9.95 (0-87935-040-7) Colonial Williamsburg.

*Christmas Deer. April Wilson. LC 94-49319. (Illus.). 40p. (J). 1995. 16.95 (1-55591-242-7) Fulcrum Pub.

Christmas Delights. (Illus.). 12p. (J). (gr. 1-6). 1971. reprint ed. pap. 3.25 (0-914510-02-9) Evergreen.

Christmas Delights for Two Violins, Pts. Violin I-II. Anne Baker. 25p. 1992. pap. text ed. 5.95 (0-87487-436-X) Summy-Birchard.

Christmas Delights for Two Violins, Pts. Violin I-II: Score. Anne Baker. 25p. 1992. pap. text ed. 8.95 (0-87487-437-8) Summy-Birchard.

Christmas Dinners. D. Barich. 1994. pap. 17.00 (0-06-095025-0) HarpC.

Christmas Displays & Promotions. Martin M. Pegler. 1993. 49.95 (0-934590-54-0) Retail Report.

Christmas Dolls. Carol B. York. (J). (gr. 4-7). 1994. pap. 2.75 (0-590-42435-1) Scholastic Inc.

Christmas Donkey. (Little Fish Books about Bible Animals). (J). 1991. 0.79 (0-8307-1061-2, 5608614) Regal.

*Christmas Donkey. Gillian McClure. (Illus.). 32p. Date not set. 4.95 (0-374-41191-3) FS&G.

Christmas Donkey: A New Version of the Nativity Story. Gillian McClure. (J). (ps-3). 1993. 15.00 (0-374-31261-3) FS&G.

*Christmas Doughcrafts: Salt Dough Projects for All Ages. Elisabeth Bang. (Illus.). 128p. 1995. 24.95 (0-304-34395-1, Pub. by Cassell UK) Sterling.

Christmas Dream. John Ciaravino. LC 88-51890. (Illus.). 44p. (J). (gr. k-3). 1989. 5.95 (1-55523-215-9) Winston-Derek.

Christmas Dream. I. E. Clark. (Illus.). 21p. 1970. pap. 5.00 (0-88680-026-9); pap. 2.50 (0-88680-025-0) I E Clark.

Christmas Dreaming. Edmund E. Wells. (Orig.). pap. 1.50 (0-686-30401-2) WOS.

Christmas Dreams. Cynthia H. Cummings. (Illus.). 112p. 1992. 35.00 (1-881811-09-3) H Peterson Pr.

Christmas Drum. Maureen Hooper. LC 93-73308. (Illus.). 32p. (J). (ps-3). 1994. 14.95 (1-56397-105-4) Boyds Mills Pr.

Christmas, Easter, Ascension & Burial Services for Knights Templar. rev. ed. Robert Macoy. 111p. 1978. pap. 4.60 (0-88053-011-1, M 036) Macoy Pub.

Christmas Embrace. Ed. by John Scognamiglio. 352p. 1994. mass mkt. 4.50 (0-8217-4761-4) Zebra.

*Christmas Embrace Vol. 1. Ellen T. Marsh. 1994. pap. 4.50 (0-312-92957-9) St Martin.

Christmas Entertainments. Alice M. Kellogg. LC 72-139764. (Granger Index Reprint Ser.). 1977. 18.95 (0-8369-6218-4) Ayer.

Christmas Escapade. Meg-Lynn Roberts. 320p. 1994. mass mkt. 3.99 (0-8217-4787-8) Zebra.

Christmas Eve. Henrietta Bredin. LC 92-1235. (J). 1992. 5.95 (0-85953-145-7) Childs Play.

Christmas Eve. Charnan Simon. 10p. (J). 1989. bds. 2.95 (0-8167-1884-9) Troll Assocs.

Christmas Eve. Sucie Stevenson. (Illus.). 32p. (J). (ps-2). 1992. mass mkt. 4.99 (0-440-40729-X, YB) Dell.

Christmas Eve: Dialogue on the Incarnation. Friedrich Schleiermacher. Tr. by Terrence N. Tice. LC 90-33285. 100p. 1990. lib. bdg. 59.95 (0-7734-9890-7) E Mellen.

*Christmas Eve Alphabet. Carole Gerber. (Illus.). 32p. 1994. pap. 6.95 (0-9643028-0-2) Sparrow Bks.

Christmas Eve & Christmas Day. Edward E. Hale. LC 71-101814. (Short Story Index Reprint Ser.). 1977. 20.95 (0-8369-3202-1) Ayer.

Christmas Eve Cattle Drive. George S. Smith. (Illus.). 32p. (J). (gr. 1-4). 1991. pap. 3.95 (0-89015-820-7) Sunbelt Media.

Christmas Eve Mystery. Joan L. Nixon. Ed. by Ann Fay. LC 81-345. (First Read-Alone Mysteries Ser.). (Illus.). 32p. (J). (gr. 1-3). 1981. lib. bdg. 8.95 (0-8075-1150-1) A Whitman.

Christmas Eve on Lonesome, & Other Stories. John Fox. LC 70-121546. (Short Story Index Reprint Ser.). (Illus.). 1977. 21.95 (0-8369-3500-4) Ayer.

Christmas Eve on Sesame Street. Jon Stone & Joe Bailey. LC 81-50247. (Illus.). 64p. (J). (ps-2). 1981. 7.95 (0-394-84733-4) Random Bks Yng Read.

Christmas Eve on the Big Bayou. Hasa Ortego. 1974. 3.95 (0-87511-091-6) Claitors.

*Christmas Eve Services: Turning Your Traditional Service into An Evangelistic Celebration. Robert L. Kintigh. Ed. by Cindy G. Spear. 88p. 1995. ring bd. 59.95 (1-57052-035-6) Chrch Grwth VA.

Christmas Eve Storyteller. Edward Hays. LC 92-73009. (Illus.). 92p. (Orig.). 1992. 16.95 (0-939516-16-0) Forest Peace.

Christmas Eve Tradition. R. W. Thompson, Jr. (North Pole Chronicles Ser.). (Illus.). 16p. (J). (ps-3). 1993. 8.95 (0-9636442-1-1) N Pole Chron.

Christmas Every Day. Marie Ferrarella. (Silhouette Intimate Moments Ser.). 1993. mass mkt. 3.50 (0-373-07538-3, 5-07538-7) Silhouette.

*Christmas Express. Pat Cook. Date not set. 5.00 (0-87129-562-8, C45) Dramatic Pub.

Christmas Fairy. 2nd ed. Debbie Hester & Bryan Brewer. LC 82-73313. (Illus.). 56p. (Orig.). 1982. pap. 5.00 (0-9609834-0-6) CIRI-BETH.

*Christmas Favorites. (Easy Guitar Ser.). 48p. (Orig.). 1994. pap. 7.95 (0-89724-384-6) Warner Brothers.

Christmas Favorites: Big Note. (Instant Play Ser.). 32p. (Orig.). 1993. disk, pap. 24.95 (0-89724-087-1, MW0901) Warner Brothers.

Christmas Festival. Otis Skillings & Jimmy Owens. 1972. 5.25 (0-685-68467-9, MC-24); audio 60.00 (0-685-68468-7, MU-7026C) Lillenas.

Christmas Fever. Grace Hawthorne & Larry Mayfield. (J). 1981. 4.95 (0-685-68515-2, MC-42); audio 10.98 (0-685-68516-0, TA-9022C) Lillenas.

Christmas for Andy. Teri Martini. (J). (gr. 3 up). 1991. pap. 3.95 (0-8091-6603-8) Paulist Pr.

Christmas for Carol. Julie Landry. 16p. (Orig.). 1991. pap. 2.50 (0-88680-360-8) I E Clark.

Christmas for Chabelita. Argentina Palacios. LC 94-9833. (Illus.). 32p. (J). (gr. k-4). 1994. lib. bdg. 14.95 (0-8167-3545-X) BrdgeWater.

Christmas for Chabelita. Argentina Palacios. LC 94-9833. (Illus.). 32p. (J). (gr. k-4). 1994. pap. 3.95 (0-8167-3541-7) BrdgeWater.

Christmas for Flute & Guitar. Jerry Willard. (Illus.). 48p. 1989. pap. 9.95 (0-8256-1120-2, AM67125) Music Sales.

Christmas for Holly. Dorothy Hamilton. LC 72-141831. (Illus.). 112p. (J). (gr. 4-9). 1971. pap. 4.95 (0-8361-1658-5) Herald Pr.

*Christmas for Polar Bear. Susanne S. Whayne. LC 95-3002. (Illus.). 24p. (J). (gr. k-2). 1995. pap. text ed. 2.95 (0-8167-3737-1, Whistlstop) Troll Assocs.

Christmas for Quilters. Betty Boyink. 72p. (Orig.). 1993. pap. 14.00 (0-925623-05-9) B Boyink.

Christmas for the World: A Gift to the Children. Ed. by Curtis Taylor & Stan Zenk. LC 91-76004. 341p. (Orig.). 1991. pap. 12.95 (1-56236-204-6) Aspen Bks.

Christmas Forever. Ed. by David G. Hartwell. 416p. 1993. 24.95 (0-312-85576-1) Tor Bks.

Christmas Foundation Meeting: Beginning of a New Cosmic Age. Rudolf Grosse. Tr. by Johanna Collis. 158p. (Orig.). 1984. pap. 14.95 (0-919924-23-9, Pub. by Steiner Book Centre CN) Anthroposophic.

*Christmas from the Heart: Home for the Holidays. Better Homes & Gardens Staff. 160p. 1994. 19.95 (0-696-20105-4) Meredith Bks.

Christmas from the Heart of Byfield. Susie Saunders. (Illus.). 48p. 1991. 10.95 (1-883406-05-6) Hrt of Byfield.

Christmas from the Heart of the Home. Susan Branch. (Illus.). 1990. 21.95 (0-316-10638-0) Little.

Christmas Fun. Judith H. Corwin. (Holiday Library). (Illus.). 64p. (J). (gr. 3 up). 1982. lib. bdg. 10.98 (0-671-45944-9, Julian Messner); lib. bdg. 5.95 (0-671-49583-6, Julian Messner); lib. bdg. 7.71 (0-685-47052-0, Julian Messner); pap. 4.46 (0-685-47053-9, Julian Messner) Silver Burdett Pr.

*Christmas Fun. Deri Robins. LC 95-2454. (Illus.). (J). 1995. pap. write for info. (1-85697-567-3) Kingfisher.

Christmas Fun: Holiday Crafts & Treats. Diane Cherkerzian. LC 92-75840. (Illus.). 32p. (J). (ps-5). 1994. pap. 4.95 (1-56397-277-8) Boyds Mills Pr.

Christmas Fun Mad Libs. Roger Price & Leonard Stern. (Mad Libs Ser.). 48p. (Orig.). (J). (gr. 3 up). 1985. bds. 2.95 (0-8431-1238-7) Price Stern.

Christmas Games for Adults & Children. Crispin DeFoyer. (Games & Pastimes Ser.: Vol. 7). (Illus.). 64p. 1982. 9.95 (0-906672-08-2); pap. 4.95 (0-906672-09-0) Oleander Pr.

Christmas Gang. James Duffy. 80p. (YA). 1991. pap. 2.99 (0-380-71149-4, Camelot) Avon.

*Christmas Garland. Celia Haddon. (Illus.). 64p. 1995. 8.95 (0-7181-3896-1, M Joseph) Viking Penguin.

Christmas Garland. Illus. by Kathy Orr. 40p. (J). 1991. lib. bdg. 8.95 (0-8378-2069-3) Gibson.

Christmas Gathering: The Sweet Nellie Book of Entertainment, Diversions, & Traditions of the Holiday Season. Pat Ross. LC 91-50164. (Illus.). 64p. 1991. 8.95 (0-670-83530-7, Viking Studio) Studio Bks.

Christmas Gatherings: An American Celebration. Joanne Lowery & Debra Anton. Ed. by Steve Slack. (Illus.). 118p. 1991. 19.95 (0-944493-05-X) Sampler Pubns.

Christmas Ghost. Francine Pascal. No. 1. (YA). (gr. 7-12). 1990. pap. write for info. (0-318-66852-1) Bantam.

Christmas Ghosts. Ed. by Mike Resnick & Martin H. Greenberg. 352p. 1993. mass mkt. 5.50 (0-88677-586-8) DAW Bks.

Christmas Gif' An Anthology of Christmas Poems, Songs, & Stories, Written by & about Black People. Ed. by Charlemae H. Rollins. LC 92-18976. (Illus.). 128p. (J). 1993. 14.00 (0-688-11667-1) Morrow Jr Bks.

Christmas Gift. Emily A. McCully. LC 87-45758. (Illus.). 32p. (J). (ps-1). 1988. lib. bdg. 12.89 (0-06-024212-4) HarpC Child Bks.

Christmas Gift! Ferrol Sams. LC 89-84528. 112p. 1989. 15.95 (0-929264-59-2) Longstreet Pr Inc.

Christmas Gift-Making Workshop. Mary J. Shannon. 1990. pap. 6.95 (0-940754-99-1) Ed Ministries.

Christmas Gifts of Good Taste. 1991. 19.95 (0-942237-13-7) Leisure AR.

Christmas Gifts That Didn't Need Wrapping. Dandi D. Mackall. LC 89-82553. (Illus.). 32p. (J). (ps-2). 1990. pap. 5.99 (0-8066-2466-3, 9-2466) Augsburg Fortress.

Christmas Goose. Geraldine Harder & Milton Harder. Ed. by Maynard Shelly. LC 90-84535. (Illus.). 80p. (Orig.). (J). (gr. k-6). 1990. pap. 5.95 (0-87303-146-6) Faith & Life.

*Christmas Greatest Hits. Cpp Belwin Staff. 1994. pap. 12.95 (0-7604-0018-0) CPP Belwin.

Christmas Guest. David La Rochelle. (Illus.). 32p. (J). (ps-3). 1988. lib. bdg. 18.95 (0-87614-325-7, Carolrhoda); pap. 5.95 (0-87614-506-3, Carolrhoda) Lerner Group.

Christmas Guest. David LaRochelle. (Carolrhoda Picture Bks.). (Illus.). 32p. (J). (ps-3). 1989. reprint ed. pap. 5.95 (0-685-25636-7, Lerner Publctns) Lerner Group.

Christmas Guitar. Stephen Siktberg. 1993. 9.95 (1-56222-015-2, 94428); audio 9.98 (1-56222-016-0, 94428) Mel Bay.

Christmas Handbook. Dotti Hannum. LC 83-26149. (Holiday Handbooks Ser.). (Illus.). 96p. (J). (ps-3). 1984. lib. bdg. 25.64 (0-89565-268-4) Childs World.

Christmas Handcrafts. LC 92-60993. 144p. 1993. pap. 14.95 (0-8487-1170-X) Oxmoor Hse.

Christmas Handcrafts. Sunset Publishing Staff. 144p. 1992. 24.99 (0-8487-1120-3) Oxmoor Hse.

Christmas Handcrafts, Bk. 2. LC 92-60993. 144p. 1993. pap. 14.95 (0-8487-1171-8) Oxmoor Hse.

Christmas Hero & Yuletide Tradition in Sir Gawain & the Green Knight. Walter S. Phelan. LC 92-28373. (Illus.). 325p. 1992. text ed. 99.95 (0-7734-9568-1) E Mellen.

Christmas Holiday. W. Somerset Maugham. LC 75-25351. (Works of W. Somerset Maugham Ser.). 1977. reprint ed. 23.95 (0-405-07809-9) Ayer.

Christmas Holiday Fun Book. 1990. pap. 4.99 (0-7459-1720-8) Lion USA.

Christmas Holiday Grab Bag. Judith Stamper. LC 92-13226. (Illus.). 48p. (J). (gr. 2-5). 1992. lib. bdg. 11.89 (0-8167-2908-5); pap. text ed. 3.95 (0-8167-2909-3) Troll Assocs.

Christmas Horse. Glenn Balch. (Illus.). (J). 1990. reprint ed. pap. 9.95 (0-931659-10-8) Limberlost Pr.

Christmas Hospital. large type ed. Pauline Ash. (Linford Romance Library). 272p. 1984. pap. 11.95 (0-7089-6037-5) Ulverscroft.

Christmas House. Ann Turner. LC 93-12740. (Illus.). 32p. (J). (gr. k-3). 1994. 15.00 (0-06-023429-6) HarpC Child Bks.

Christmas House. Ann Turner. LC 93-12740. (Illus.). 32p. (J). (gr. k-3). 1994. lib. bdg. 14.89 (0-06-023432-6) HarpC Child Bks.

Christmas Housewarming: A Collection of Christmas Memories to Benefit Habitat for Humanity. Ed. by Gene Stelten. LC 92-26187. (Illus.). 1992. 12.95 (1-56145-065-0) Peachtree Pubs.

*Christmas Humor: A Gift of Christmas Cheer. DeLoss Bell. 90p. (Orig.). 1994. pap. write for info. (1-885591-14-4) Morris Pubng.

*Christmas Humor II: A Gift of Christmas Cheer. DeLoss Bell. 90p. (Orig.). 1994. pap. write for info. (1-885591-15-2) Morris Pubng.

*Christmas Husband. Mary A. Wilson. 1995. pap. 3.50 (0-373-16609-5, 1-16609-9) Harlequin Bks.

C

An Asterisk (*) at the beginning of an entry indicates that the title is appearing in BIP for the first time.

Christmas I Remember Best. Ed. by J. Livingood et al. (Illus.). (Orig.). write for info. (*0-910901-00-7*); pap. 5.95 (*0-910901-01-5*) Deseret News.

Christmas Icon: A Theological & Historical Study. Date not set. write for info. (*0-9618545-5-3*) Oakwood Pubns.

Christmas Ideals Magazine, 1993. (Illus.). 80p. 1993. pap. 4.95 (*0-8249-1113-X*) Ideals.

Christmas Ideals Magazine, 1994. 1994. pap. 4.95 (*0-8249-1122-9*) Ideals.

*__Christmas Images for Two Vol. 2.__ Ed. by Carole Flodau. 24p. (Orig.). (YA). 1994. pap. text ed. 5.50 (*0-89898-918-3*) CPP Belwin.

*__Christmas in All Seasons.__ Geneva M. Butz. 136p. (Orig.). 1995. pap. 10.95 (*0-8298-1068-4*) Pilgrim OH.

Christmas in America. (Illus.). 128p. 1991. 15.99 (*0-517-06573-8*, Crescent) Random Hse Value.

Christmas in America. David C. Cohen. 1988. 14.95 (*0-00-215164-2*) Collins SF.

*__Christmas in America: A History.__ Penne L. Restad. (Illus.). 256p. 1995. 25.00 (*0-19-509300-3*) OUP.

Christmas in Arizona: Recipes, Traditions & Folklore for the Holiday Season. Lynn Nusom. Tr. by Steve Parker. LC 92-32251. (Illus.). 128p. 1992. pap. 8.95 (*0-914846-65-5*) Golden West Pub.

Christmas in Aspen. Jill Sheeley. (Illus.). 1982. reprint ed. write for info. (*0-9609108-0-8*) Courtney Pr.

Christmas in Aunt Lillies Kitchen. Illus. by Ralph Butz. 100p. 1978. pap. 4.00 (*0-931440-03-3*) Stoneback Pub.

*__Christmas in Canada.__ World Book Editors Staff. LC 94-60826. (Christmas Around the World Ser.). (Illus.). 80p. 1994. write for info. (*0-7166-0894-4*) World Bk.

*__Christmas in Colorado.__ Marie Cahill. LC 94-24481. (Illus.). 120p. (Orig.). 1994. pap. text ed. 8.95 (*0-914846-84-1*) Golden West Pub.

Christmas in France. (Christmas in...Ser.). (Illus.). 80p. 1991. 9.95 (*0-8442-1004-8*, Passport Bks) NTC Pub Grp.

Christmas in Georgia. 2nd ed. Celestine Sibley. LC 85-61978. 112p. 1985. 12.95 (*0-931948-83-5*) Peachtree Pubs.

Christmas in Germany. (Christmas in...Ser.). (Illus.). 80p. 1991. 9.95 (*0-8442-2110-4*, Passport Bks) NTC Pub Grp.

Christmas in Germany. 2nd ed. Thomas Cook. (Illustrated Travel Guides Ser.). 1995. 11.95 (*0-8442-2111-2*, Passport Bks) NTC Pub Grp.

Christmas in Ireland. Intro. by Colin Morrison. (Illus.). 94p. 1990. 26.00 (*0-85342-908-1*, Pub. by Mercier Pr IE); pap. 13.95 (*0-85342-950-2*, Pub. by Mercier Pr IE) Dufour.

Christmas in Italy. (Christmas in...Ser.). (Illus.). 1991. 9.95 (*0-8442-8071-2*, Passport Bks) NTC Pub Grp.

Christmas in July. Madeline Harper. (Temptation Ser.). 1994. mass mkt. 2.99 (*0-373-25599-3*, 1-25599-1) Harlequin Bks.

Christmas in July. Arthur Yorinks. LC 91-55244. (Michael di Capua Bks.). (Illus.). 32p. (J). (ps-3). 1991. 14.95 (*0-06-020256-4*); lib. bdg. 14.89 (*0-06-020257-2*) HarpC Child Bks.

Christmas in July: The Life & Art of Preston Sturges. Diane Jacobs. LC 92-19690. 1992. 30.00 (*0-520-07926-4*) U CA Pr.

*__Christmas in July: The Life & Art of Preston Sturges.__ Diane Jacobs. 1994. pap. 18.00 (*0-520-08928-6*) U CA Pr.

Christmas in July? The Political Economy of German Unification Reconsidered. Ullrich Heilemann & Reimut Jochimsen. 82p. (C). 1993. pap. 8.95 (*0-8157-3541-3*) Brookings.

Christmas in Latin America. 1976. reprint ed. pap. 1.00 (*0-8270-4365-1*) OAS.

Christmas in Legend & Story: A Book for Boys & Girls Illustrated from Famous Paintings. Comp. by Elva S. Smith & Alice I. Hazeltine. LC 72-39390. (Granger Index Reprint Ser.). (YA). (gr. 7 up). 1977. reprint ed. 20.95 (*0-8369-6353-9*) Ayer.

Christmas in Mexico. (Christmas in...Ser.). (Illus.). 80p. 1991. 9.95 (*0-8442-7209-4*, Passport Bks) NTC Pub Grp.

Christmas in Michigan: Tales & Recipes. Carole Eberly. (Illus.). 136p. (Orig.). 1987. pap. 7.95 (*0-932296-12-2*) Eberly Pr.

Christmas in My Bones. W. C. Burton. Ed. by Erik Bledsoe. (Illus.). 140p. 1991. 14.95 (*1-878086-11-1*) Down Home NC.

Christmas in My Heart. Comp. by Joe L. Wheeler. LC 92-27484. 1992. pap. 8.95 (*0-8280-0672-5*) Review & Herald.

Christmas in New Mexico: Recipes, Traditions & Folklore for the Holiday Season. Lynn Nusom. LC 91-34113. (Illus.). 144p. (Orig.). 1991. pap. 8.95 (*0-914846-59-0*) Golden West Pub.

Christmas in Noisy Village. Astrid Lindgren. LC 64-21473. (Picture Puffins Ser.). 32p. (J). (ps-3). 1981. pap. 4.99 (*0-14-050344-7*, Puffin) Puffin Bks.

Christmas in Oklahoma. Linda K. Rosser. (Illus.). 122p. 1982. 14.95 (*0-86546-041-8*) Bobwhite Pubns.

Christmas in Old Santa Fe. Pedro R. Ortega. LC 73-90581. (Illus.). 1982. pap. 8.95 (*0-913270-25-3*) Sunstone Pr.

Christmas in Other Lands. Janet McDonnell. LC 93-7632. (Circle the Year with Holidays Ser.). (Illus.). 32p. (J). (ps-2). 1993. lib. bdg. 12.30 (*0-516-00682-7*); pap. 3.95 (*0-516-40682-5*) Childrens.

Christmas in Oz. Val R. Cheatham. 1983. pap. 4.95 (*0-686-39595-6*) Eldridge Pub.

Christmas in Purgatory. Burton Blatt & Fred Kaplan. 1974. 5.25 (*0-937540-00-5*, HPP-3) Human Policy Pr.

Christmas in Ritual & Tradition: Christian & Pagan. Clement A. Miles. 1977. lib. bdg. 59.95 (*0-8490-1618-5*) Gordon Pr.

Christmas in Ritual & Tradition: Christian & Pagan. Clement A. Miles. LC 89-29299. (Illus.). 400p. 1990. reprint ed. lib. bdg. 42.00 (*1-55888-896-9*) Omnigraphics Inc.

Christmas in Russia. Passport Books Staff. 1993. 11.95 (*0-8442-4291-8*, Passport Bks) NTC Pub Grp.

Christmas in Russia. Ed. by World Book Staff. LC 92-64394. (Christmas Around the World Ser.). (Illus.). 80p. (YA). (gr. 6 up). 1992. write for info. (*0-7166-0892-8*) World Bk.

Christmas in Scandinavia. Melody Favish. (Illus.). 160p. 1982. write for info. (*0-9609890-0-5*) Trollpost.

Christmas in Song, Sketch & Story: Nearly Three Hundred Christmas Songs, Hymns & Carols. John P. McCaskey. 1980. lib. bdg. 67.95 (*0-8490-3175-3*) Gordon Pr.

Christmas in Spain. (Christmas in...Ser.). 1991. 9.95 (*0-8442-7205-1*, Passport Bks) NTC Pub Grp.

Christmas in Stained Glass. Carolyn Kyle. (Illus.). 48p. 1985. reprint ed. pap. 16.95 (*0-935133-01-1*) CKE Pubns.

Christmas in Stained Glass Two. Carolyn Kyle. (Illus.). 80p. 1985. reprint ed. pap. 17.95 (*0-935133-02-X*) CKE Pubns.

Christmas in Strawberryland see Strawberry Shortcake's Holiday Library

Christmas in Texas. Ed. by V. T. Abercrombie & Helen Williams. LC 79-66212. (Illus.). (Orig.). 1979. pap. 7.95 (*0-933988-00-1*) Brown Rabbit.

*__Christmas in Texas.__ Marie Cahill. LC 94-24483. (Illus.). 120p. (Orig.). 1994. pap. text ed. 8.95 (*0-914846-86-8*) Golden West Pub.

Christmas in Texas. Elizabeth Silverthorne. LC 90-10846. (Clayton Wheat Williams Texas Life Ser.: No. 3). (Illus.). 224p. 1990. 29.95 (*0-89096-446-7*) Tex A&M Univ Pr.

Christmas in Texas. Elizabeth Silverthorne. (Clayton Wheat Williams Texas Life Ser.: No. 3). (Illus.). 224p. 1994. pap. 17.95 (*0-89096-578-1*) Tex A&M Univ Pr.

Christmas in the Barn. Margaret W. Brown. (J). 1952. 14.00 (*0-690-19271-1*, Crowell Jr Bks) HarpC Child Bks.

Christmas in the Barn. Margaret W. Brown. LC 52-7858. (Illus.). 32p. (J). (gr. k-3). 1961. lib. bdg. 14.89 (*0-690-19272-X*, Crowell Jr Bks) HarpC Child Bks.

Christmas in the Barn. Margaret W. Brown. LC 85-42738. (Trophy Picture Bk.). (Illus.). 32p. (J). (ps-3). 1985. reprint ed. pap. 5.95 (*0-06-443082-0*, Trophy) HarpC Child Bks.

Christmas in the Big House, Christmas in the Quarters. Patricia C. McKissack & Frederick McKissack. LC 92-33831. (Illus.). (J). (gr. 2 up). 1994. 15.95 (*0-590-43027-0*) Scholastic Inc.

Christmas in the Big Woods. Laura I. Wilder. LC 94-14478. (My First Little House Bks.). (Illus.). 40p. (J). (ps-3). 1995. 11.95 (*0-06-024752-5*); lib. bdg. 11.89 (*0-06-024753-3*) HarpC Child Bks.

Christmas in the Good Old Days: A Victorian Album of Stories, Poems & Pictures of the Personalities Who Rediscovered Christmas. Daniel J. Foley. LC 93-28202. (Illus.). 224p. 1994. reprint ed. lib. bdg. 38.00 (*0-7808-0003-6*) Omnigraphics Inc.

Christmas in the Holy Land. Ed. by World Book Staff. LC 87-50393. (Christmas Around the World Ser.). (Illus.). 80p. (YA). (gr. 6 up). 1992. write for info. (*0-7166-2009-X*) World Bk.

Christmas in the Manger. Nola Buck. (Pat & Peek Book). (Illus.). 16p. (J). (ps). 1994. 9.95 (*0-694-00605-X*, Festival) HarpC Child Bks.

*__Christmas in the Manger: A Pat-&-Peek Book.__ Nola Buck. (Illus.). 16p. (J). (ps up). Date not set. 9.95 (*0-694-00836-2*, Festival) HarpC Child Bks.

Christmas in the Midwest: With Cookie Recipes. 1994. pap. 12.95 (*0-685-72930-3*) Penfield.

Christmas in the Stable. Beverly K. Duncan. (Illus.). 32p. (J). (ps up). 1990. 14.95 (*0-15-217758-2*) HarBrace.

Christmas in the Stable. Astrid Lindgren. (Sandcastle Ser.). (Illus.). 32p. (J). 1991. 5.95 (*0-698-20677-0*, Sandcastle Bks) Putnam Pub Group.

Christmas in the Theatre. Ed. by Patricia Whitton. 1985. pap. 9.95 (*0-932720-03-X*) New Plays Inc.

Christmas in the White House. Albert J. Menendez. LC 83-3629. (Illus.). 128p. 1983. 12.00 (*0-664-21392-8*, Westminster) Westminster John Knox.

Christmas in Today's Germany. Ed. by World Book Editors. LC 93-60510. (Christmas Around the World Ser.). (Illus.). 80p. (YA). (gr. 5 up). 1993. lib. bdg. write for info. (*0-7166-0893-6*) World Bk.

Christmas in Vermont: Three Stories. Margaret F. Carty. LC 83-62750. (Illus.). 48p. (Orig.). (J). (gr. 5 up). 1983. pap. 2.95 (*0-933050-21-6*) New Eng Pr VT.

Christmas in Wales: A Homecoming. Jane Maas & Michael Maas. (Illus.). 112p. 1994. 16.95 (*0-312-11464-8*, Pub. by Thomas Dunne Bks) St Martin.

Christmas Is a Quantum Leap: Sermons for Advent, Christmas, & Epiphany: Cycle B Gospel Texts. Glenn Schoonover. LC 93-18744. 1993. pap. 8.95 (*1-55673-606-1*, 9331) CSS OH.

Christmas Is a Time of Giving. Joan W. Anglund. LC 61-10106. (Illus.). 32p. (J). (ps up). 1961. 9.95 (*0-15-217863-5*, HB Juv Bks) HarBrace.

Christmas Is Coming. (Christmas Board Books Ser.: No. S8823-3). (Illus.). (J). (ps-00). 1990. bds. 3.95 (*0-7214-9133-2*) Ladybird Bks.

Christmas Is Coming! 1991. pap. 9.95 (*0-8487-1083-5*) Oxmoor Hse.

*__Christmas Is Coming.__ (J). 1994. bds. 2.95 (*1-56458-825-4*) Dorling Kindersley.

Christmas Is Coming. Susie Saunders. (Illus.). 48p. 1992. 12.95 (*1-883406-02-1*) Hrt of Byfield.

Christmas Is Coming, Vol. 2. Oxmoor House Editors. 144p. 1992. pap. 9.99 (*0-8487-1110-6*) Oxmoor Hse.

Christmas Is Coming, Vol. 3. LC 84-63030. 140p. 1993. pap. 9.99 (*0-8487-1161-0*) Oxmoor Hse.

*__Christmas is Coming: A Story & Project Book-Make Your Own Holiday Ornaments.__ Tsuneo Tanuchi. 48p. Date not set. 17.95 (*4-7700-1990-4*) FS&G.

Christmas Is Coming: Sixteen Fun Things to Make. Debbie T. O'Neal. (Illus.). 20p. 1993. pap. 6.99 (*0-8010-6755-3*) Baker Bk.

Christmas Is Coming with Ruth J. Morehead's Holly Babes: A Book of Poems & Songs. Illus. by Ruth J. Morehead. LC 89-3717. (Pictureback Ser.). 32p. (Orig.). (J). (ps-1). 1990. pap. 2.25 (*0-679-80075-1*) Random Bks Yng Read.

*__Christmas Is Coming, 1994 Vol. 4: Holiday Projects for Children & Parents.__ Oxmoor Staff. 1994. pap. 14.95 (*0-8487-1414-8*) Oxmoor Hse.

Christmas Is for Me. Christine H. Tangvald. LC 88-70665. (For Me Ser.). (Illus.). 24p. (J). (ps-1). 1988. pap. 3.99 (*1-55513-705-9*, Chariot Bks) Chariot Family.

Christmas Is Love. Joan W. Anglund. (Illus.). 32p. (J). (ps up). 1988. 7.95 (*0-15-200425-4*, Gulliver Bks) HarBrace.

Christmas Is Together Time. Charles M. Schulz. 1983. pap. 4.95 (*0-915696-76-2*) Determined Prods.

Christmas Is Together Time. Charles M. Schulz. LC 80-65226. 1982. reprint ed. 6.95 (*0-915696-30-4*) Determined Prods.

*__Christmas Journal.__ Mary Engelbreit. (Illus.). 96p. 1994. 12.95 (*0-8362-4623-3*) Andrews & McMeel.

Christmas Journey. Sally Fisher. (Illus.). 40p. (J). (ps-7). 1993. 19.99 (*0-670-85039-X*) Viking Child Bks.

Christmas Journey. Hans Wilhelm. (Illus.). Date not set. 4.50 (*0-8378-5878-X*) Gibson.

*__Christmas Journeys.__ Emma Richmond et al. 1995. pap. 4.99 (*0-373-15271-X*, 1-15271-9) Harlequin Bks.

Christmas Journeys with Howard Shuler. Ardath Olsen et al. Ed. by Bernadine Smith. 102p. 1987. 15.00 (*0-940696-16-9*) Monroe County Lib.

Christmas Joy. Cynthia H. Cummings. (Illus.). 84p. (J). 1986. 10.00 (*1-881811-05-0*) H Peterson Pr.

Christmas Joy. Ed. by Joanne Van Roden. 32p. (Orig.). 1985. pap. 2.95 (*0-940844-56-7*) Wellspring.

*__Christmas Joy: Favorite Holiday Stories.__ Ed. & Comp. by Noel Rogers. (Die-Cuts Ser.). (Illus.). 80p. (Orig.). 1995. pap. 6.99 (*0-88088-951-9*) Peter Pauper.

Christmas Joy, Level One. Comp. by Ethel T. Rogers. 1984. 6.50 (*0-685-68308-7*, BCMC-260) Lillenas.

Christmas Joy, Level Two. Contrib by Ethel T. Rogers. 1984. 6.50 (*0-685-68309-5*, BCMC-261) Lillenas.

Christmas Kalends of Provence: And Some Other Provencal Festivals. Thomas A. Janvier. (Illus.). vii, 262p. 1990. reprint ed. lib. bdg. 35.00 (*1-55888-823-3*) Omnigraphics Inc.

Christmas Keepsakes. 1990. 24.95 (*0-942237-08-0*) Leisure AR.

Christmas KidDoodles, Bk. 1. Emmi S. Herman. (KidDoodles Ser.). (Illus.). 64p. (Orig.). (J). (ps-2). 1991. pap. 0.99 (*1-56293-153-9*) McClanahan Bk.

Christmas KidDoodles, Bk. 2. Beth A. Wise. (KidDoodles Ser.). (Illus.). 64p. (Orig.). (J). (ps-2). 1991. pap. 0.99 (*1-56293-154-7*) McClanahan Bk.

Christmas KidDoodles, Bk. 3. Gail Tuchman. (KidDoodles Ser.). (Illus.). 64p. (Orig.). (J). (ps-2). 1991. pap. 0.99 (*1-56293-155-5*) McClanahan Bk.

Christmas KidDoodles, Bk. 4. Beth A. Wise. (KidDoodles Ser.). (Illus.). 64p. (Orig.). (J). (ps-2). 1991. pap. 0.99 (*1-56293-156-3*) McClanahan Bk.

Christmas KidDoodles, No. 5. Emmi Herman. (KidDoodles Ser.). (Illus.). 64p. (Orig.). (J). (ps-2). 1992. pap. 0.99 (*1-56293-270-5*) McClanahan Bk.

Christmas KidDoodles, No. 6. Emmi Herman. (KidDoodles Ser.). (Illus.). 64p. (Orig.). (J). (ps-2). 1992. pap. 0.99 (*1-56293-271-3*) McClanahan Bk.

Christmas KidDoodles, No. 7. Emmi Herman. (KidDoodles Ser.). (Illus.). 64p. (Orig.). (J). (ps-2). 1992. pap. 0.99 (*1-56293-269-1*) McClanahan Bk.

Christmas KidDoodles, No. 8. Emmi Herman. (KidDoodles Ser.). (Illus.). 64p. (Orig.). (J). (ps-2). 1992. pap. 0.99 (*1-56293-272-1*) McClanahan Bk.

Christmas Killer. Patricia Windsor. (YA). 1992. pap. 3.50 (*0-590-43310-5*) Scholastic Inc.

Christmas Kiss. Ed. by Ann LaFarge. 352p. 1992. mass mkt. 4.50 (*0-8217-3975-1*) Zebra.

Christmas Kiss. Elizabeth Mansfield. 1991. pap. 4.50 (*0-515-10520-1*) Jove Pubns.

*__Christmas Kisses for a Dollar.__ Laurie Paige. 1995. pap. 3.50 (*0-373-52009-3*, 1-52009-7) Silhouette.

Christmas Kitchen: A Sumptuous Treasury of Recipes, Menus, Gifts & Party Ideas. Lorraine Bodger. 1989. pap. 15.00 (*0-385-42431-0*) Doubleday.

*__Christmas Kitten.__ Mary Packard. (J). (ps-2). 1994. pap. 3.95 (*0-516-45364-5*) Childrens.

Christmas Kitten. Mary Packard. LC 94-12301. (My First Reader Ser.). (Illus.). 28p. (J). (ps-2). 1994. lib. bdg. 10.50 (*0-516-05364-7*) Childrens.

Christmas Knight. Jane L. Curry. LC 92-2277. (Illus.). 32p. (J). (gr. k-4). 1993. 14.95 (*0-689-50572-8*, McElderry) S&S Childrens.

Christmas Lamb. Anne Baird. LC 88-5137. (Illus.). 32p. (J). (ps-2). 1989. 12.95 (*0-688-07774-9*) Morrow Jr Bks.

Christmas Legend. Robert L. Merriam. (Illus.). 9p. (Orig.). 1970. pap. 1.50 (*0-686-32485-4*) R L Merriam.

Christmas Lessons. Janine Boissard. Tr. by Mary Feeney. 252p. 1984. 15.95 (*0-316-10097-8*) Little.

Christmas List Book. Nancy Cogan & Roni Akmon. 84p. 1993. 9.95 (*1-884807-07-0*) Blushing Rose.

Christmas List Organizer. Marylynn Anderson. 160p. 1991. pap. 12.95 (*0-9630945-0-5*) M L Pr.

Christmas Long Stocking. Kayla Braced. Ed. & Illus. by Joan Abell. 50p. (Orig.). (J). (gr. 1-6). 1993. lib. bdg. 25.00 (*1-56611-078-5*); pap. 15.00 (*1-56611-077-7*) Jonas.

Christmas Longing. Joni Eareckson-Tada. Ed. by Larry Libby. (Illus.). 80p. 1990. 17.99 (*0-88070-366-0*, Multnomah Bks) Questar Pubs.

Christmas Loon. Tom Martinson. (Illus.). 48p. (J). (gr. 1-3). 1990. 14.95 (*1-55971-092-6*); pap. 6.95 (*1-55971-124-8*) NorthWord.

Christmas Love. Kathleen Creighton. 1992. mass mkt. 3.99 (*0-312-92904-8*) St Martin.

Christmas Love. 5th ed. Cynthia H. Cummings. (Illus.). 80p. 1994. reprint ed. 10.00 (*1-881811-03-4*) H Peterson Pr.

Christmas Lover's Handbook. Lasley F. Gober. (Illus.). 256p. 1993. pap. 14.95 (*1-55870-313-6*) Betterway Bks.

Christmas Lullaby. Carlson. (Arch Bks.). 24p. (J). (gr. k-4). 1985. pap. 1.99 (*0-570-06195-4*, 59-1296) Concordia.

Christmas Lullaby. Nancy Jewell. LC 93-38786. (Illus.). (J). 1994. 14.95 (*0-395-66586-8*, Hills Med) HM.

Christmas Magic. Ed. by David G. Hartwell. 448p. (Orig.). 1994. mass mkt. 5.99 (*0-8125-3447-6*) Tor Bks.

Christmas Magic. Chris Sheehan. LC 94-75616. (Illus.). 5p. (J). (ps up). 1994. 16.95 (*1-85697-528-2*, Kingfisher LKC) LKC.

Christmas Magic: A Modern Christmas Fable. Mary M. Hamilton. Ed. by Leona Miles & Robert T. Kelly. (Illus.). 208p. (J). 1989. lib. bdg. 15.95 (*0-317-93677-8*) Havet Pr.

Christmas Magic: A Multi-Ethnic Christmas Fable. Mary M. Hamilton. Ed. by Robert T. Kelly. (Illus.). 310p. 1989. 17.95 (*0-9622528-0-8*) Havet Pr.

Christmas Magic: Christmas Story for Any Age Group. Eugene L. Vickery. (Illus.). 20p. (Orig.). 1986. pap. 1.95 (*0-937775-02-9*) Stonehaven Pubs.

*__Christmas Magic: Flute.__ (Supersound Easy Play Solos Ser.). 16p. (Orig.). 1994. pap. 5.95 (*0-89724-391-9*) Warner Brothers.

Christmas Make & Bake. Inge Relph. (Illus.). 48p. (J). (gr. 2-4). 1993. pap. 8.99 (*0-7459-2505-7*) Lion USA.

Christmas Makes Me Crazy: A Spiritual & Practical Guide to Enjoying the Holidays. Lucinda A. Dummer. LC 92-74211. (Illus.). 128p. (Orig.). 1992. pap. 9.95 (*0-9634533-0-0*) DTS Pr.

Christmas Memories. Alice S. Winter. (J). 1994. 7.95 (*0-533-10785-7*) Vantage.

Christmas Memories. deluxe ed. Carriage House Staff. 17.95 (*0-89786-031-4*); 17.95 (*0-89786-032-2*) CHP Ltd Redding.

Christmas Memories. 4th ed. Cynthia H. Cummings. (Illus.). 80p. 1990. reprint ed. 10.00 (*1-881811-02-6*) H Peterson Pr.

Christmas Memories: A Family Album of Christmas Celebrations. Illus. by George Hinke. 48p. (J). 1993. 17.95 (*0-8249-8567-2*, Ideals Child) Hambleton-Hill.

Christmas Memories: Room at the Inn; Woman Hater. Marilyn Pappano & Diana Palmer. (Harlequin Reprint Ser.). 1994. mass mkt. 4.99 (*0-373-15186-1*, 1-15186-9) Harlequin Bks.

Christmas Memories Cookbook. Ed. by Lois Klee & Connie Colom. (Illus.). 238p. 1985. pap. 12.95 (*0-939510-03-0*) Mystic Sea Mus.

Christmas Memories with Recipes. LC 94-10843. 1994. 9.99 (*0-517-10190-4*) Random Hse Value.

Christmas Memory. Truman Capote. 1966. boxed 19.95 (*0-394-41931-6*) Random.

Christmas Memory. Truman Capote. LC 88-36452. (Illus.). 48p. (J). (gr. 2 up). 1989. 17.00 (*0-679-80040-9*) Knopf Bks Yng Read.

Christmas Memory. Truman Capote. (Creative's Christmas Stories Ser.). (Illus.). 40p. (J). (gr. 4 up). 1984. lib. bdg. 13.95 (*0-87191-956-7*) Creative Ed.

*__Christmas Menorahs: How a Town Fought Hate.__ Janice Cohn. LC 95-2053. (Illus.). (J). 1995. write for info. (*0-8075-1152-8*) A Whitman.

*__Christmas Miracle of Jonathan Toomey.__ Susan Wojciechowski. LC 94-48917. (Illus.). (J). 1995. 15.95 (*1-56402-320-6*) Candlewick Pr.

Christmas Mix-Up. Margo Finch. (J). 1989. bds. 2.95 (*0-8167-1893-8*) Troll Assocs.

*__Christmas Moods Vol. III: An Extended Guide to the Fine Art of Wire Wrapping.__ 75p. (YA). (gr. 9-12). Date not set. write for info. (*0-9640483-2-9*) Orig Ellsworth.

Christmas Moon. Denys Cazet. LC 87-37434. (Illus.). 32p. (J). (ps-2). 1988. pap. 4.95 (*0-689-71259-6*, Aladdin Paperbacks) S&S Childrens.

Christmas Mouse. (Favorite Christmas Tales Ser.). (Illus.). 24p. (J). 1993. 4.98 (*0-7853-0271-9*) Pubns Intl Ltd.

Christmas Mouse. Miss Read. (J). 15.95 (*0-8488-1452-5*) Amereon Ltd.

Christmas Mouse. Read. 150p. 1986. reprint ed. lib. bdg. 16.95 (*0-89966-537-3*) Buccaneer Bks.

Christmas Mumming in Newfoundland: Essays in Anthropology, Folklore, & History. Ed. by Herbert Halpert & G. M. Story. LC 71-391290. 260p. reprint ed. pap. 74.10 (*0-317-42289-8*, 2055819) Bks Demand.

Christmas Music for Guitar from the Sixteenth & Seventeenth Centuries. E. James Kalal. (Editiones Classicae Ser.). 1993. 9.95 (*0-87166-141-1*, 94181); audio 19.50 (*0-87166-965-X*, 94181); audio 10.98 (*0-87166-142-X*, 94181) Mel Bay.

Christmas Nativity. Bishop. (Little Christmas Pop-Ups Ser.). (J). 1994. 4.95 (*0-671-89517-6*, Litl Simon S&S) S&S Childrens.

Christmas Nativity Diorama. Illus. by Carole Gray. (J). (ps-1). 1992. boxed 13.00 (*0-671-78513-3*, S&S Bks Young Read) S&S Childrens.

Christmas Naturals: Ornaments, Wreaths & Decorations. Carol Taylor. LC 91-17552. (Illus.). 128p. (YA). (gr. 8 up). 1992. pap. 14.95 (*0-8069-8361-2*) Sterling.

Christmas Needlepoint Designs. Rita Weiss. LC 74-21224. (Illus.). 48p. 1975. pap. 2.95 (*0-486-23161-5*) Dover.

*__Christmas Night in the Quarters.__ Irwin Russell. Date not set. pap. 1.00 (*0-87517-009-9*) Dietz.

*__Christmas Night Lights.__ Ann Fearrington. LC 94-25768. 1996. 13.95 (*0-395-71036-7*) Ticknor & Fields.

*__Christmas Night Murder.__ Lee Harris. (Orig.). 1994. mass mkt. 4.99 (*0-449-14922-6*, GM) Fawcett.

Christmas Night, O Night of Nights. Heini Arnold & Dwight Blough. 1976. pap. 1.50 (*0-87486-120-9*) Plough.

C

An Asterisk (*) at the beginning of an entry indicates that the title is appearing in BIP for the first time. 1249

Christmas Nightingale. Phylis Groff. (J). 1935. 5.00 (*0-87602-115-1*) Anchorage.

Christmas Nutshell Library, 4 bks., Set. Hilary Knight. Incl. Christmas Stocking Story. LC 63-18904. 1963. (*0-06-023205-6*); Firefly in a Fir Tree. LC 63-18904. 1963. (*0-06-023190-4*); Night Before Christmas. LC 63-18904. 1963. (*0-318-52915-7*); LC 63-18904. (Illus.). (J). (gr. 1 up). 1963. 11.95 (*0-06-023165-3*) HarpC Child Bks.

Christmas of Nineteen Sixty-One. John Carnuccio, Sr. 1993. 12.95 (*0-533-10219-7*) Vantage.

Christmas of the Reddle Moon. J. Patrick Lewis. LC 93-28049. (Illus.). (J). 1994. 15.99 (*0-8037-1566-8*); lib. bdg. 15.89 (*0-8037-1567-6*) Dial Bks Young.

Christmas on an Island. Gail Gibbons. LC 93-50111. (Illus.). 32p. (J). (ps up). 1994. 15.00 (*0-688-09678-6*); lib. bdg. 14.93 (*0-688-09679-4*) Morrow Jr Bks.

Christmas on Ganymede & Other Stories. Ed. by Martin H. Greenberg. 256p. (Orig.). 1990. pap. 3.50 (*0-380-76203-X*) Avon.

Christmas on Main Street. Bernie Fass & Mack Wolfson. 48p. (J). (gr. 3-12). 1986. pap. 16.95 (*0-86704-036-X*); student ed 2.95 (*0-86704-037-8*) Clarus Music.

Christmas on Mars. Harry Kondoleon. 1983. pap. 4.75 (*0-8222-0212-3*) Dramatists Play.

***Christmas on Miracle Lane.** Kaye J. Volk. 1994. pap. 2.95 (*1-55503-762-3*) Covenant Comms.

Christmas on Record: Best Selling Xmas Singles & Albums of the Past 40 Years. Craig W. Pattillo. 220p. 1983. pap. 14.50 (*0-9612044-0-0*) Braemar OR.

Christmas on Stage: An Anthology of Royalty-Free Christmas Plays for All Ages. Ed. by Theodore O. Zapel. LC 90-53278. 304p. (Orig.). 1990. pap. 14.95 (*0-916260-68-2*, B153) Meriwether Pub.

Christmas on the American Frontier, 1800-1900. John E. Baur. LC 93-8918. (Illus.). 320p. 1993. reprint ed. lib. bdg. 44.00 (*1-55888-171-9*) Omnigraphics Inc.

Christmas on the Prairie. Joan Anderson. LC 85-4095. (Illus.). 48p. (J). (gr. 2-6). 1985. 14.95 (*0-89919-307-2*, Clarion Bks) HM.

Christmas One Hundred Years Ago. Comp. by Skip Whitson. (Historical Ser.). (Illus.). (Orig.). 1976. pap. 3.50 (*0-89540-036-7*, SB-036) Sun Pub.

Christmas Onstage! Ed. by Paul M. Miller. 1993. 5.25 (*0-685-72866-8*, MC-277) Lillenas.

Christmas Oratorio. Goran Tunstrom. Tr. by Paul Hoover. (Verba Mundi Ser.). 320p. 1994. 23.95 (*1-56792-008-X*) Godine.

Christmas Origami No. 1. (Illus.). 14p. 1986. pap. 4.95 (*0-89346-280-2*) Heian Intl.

Christmas Origami No. 2. (Illus.). 16p. 1986. pap. 4.95 (*0-89346-281-0*) Heian Intl.

Christmas Origami No. 3. (Illus.). 16p. 1986. pap. 4.95 (*0-89346-282-9*) Heian Intl.

Christmas Origami No. 4. (Illus.). 16p. 1986. pap. 4.95 (*0-89346-283-7*) Heian Intl.

Christmas Ornaments. Ed. by Better Homes & Gardens Staff. (Illus.). 80p. 1991. pap. 9.95 (*0-696-01923-X*) Meredith Bks.

***Christmas Ornaments: A Festive Study.** Margaret Schiffer. (Illus.). 176p. (Orig.). 1995. pap. 29.95 (*0-88740-878-8*) Schiffer.

Christmas Ornaments: A Festive Study. Margaret B. Schiffer. LC 84-50805. (Illus.). 168p. 1984. pap. 19.95 (*0-88740-011-6*) Schiffer.

***Christmas Ornaments: Miss Flowers.** Joanne Wall. 34p. (Orig.). (J). 1994. pap. write for info. (*0-9644283-0-X*) M J Wall.

Christmas Ornaments: Twelve Punch-Out Designs. A. G. Smith. (Illus.). (J). (gr. 4-7). 1993. pap. 2.95 (*0-486-27623-6*) Dover.

Christmas Ornaments, Lights & Decorations. George W. Johnson. (Illus.). 318p. 1990. 19.95 (*0-89145-335-0*, 1752) Collector Bks.

Christmas Ornaments Made Easy. Consumer Guide Editors. 128p. (Orig.). 1994. pap. 6.99 (*0-451-82286-2*, Sig) NAL-Dutton.

Christmas Pageant. Jacqueline Rogers. (Sandcastle Ser.). (Illus.). 32p. (J). (ps-3). 1992. pap. 5.95 (*0-448-40256-4*, G&D) Putnam Pub Group.

Christmas Pageant. Helen Ward. (Illus.). 1994. 14.95 (*1-55859-894-4*) Abbeville Pr.

Christmas Pageant Board Book. Dana Stewart. (Illus.). 12p. 1992. bds. 4.99 (*0-87403-991-6*, 24-03111) Standard Pub.

Christmas Paintings of Norman Rockwell. Ariel Books Staff. (Illus.). 80p. 1993. 4.95 (*0-8362-3038-8*) Andrews & McMeel.

Christmas Parable. Boyd K. Packer. 1993. 9.95 (*0-88494-901-X*) Bookcraft Inc.

Christmas Party. 2nd ed. Adrienne Adams. LC 91-42159. (Illus.). 32p. (J). (ps-3). 1992. reprint ed. pap. 3.95 (*0-689-71630-3*, Aladdin Paperbacks) S&S Childrens.

Christmas Past. rev. ed. Robert Brenner. LC 85-61518. (Illus.). 192p. 1991. pap. 29.95 (*0-88740-363-8*) Schiffer.

Christmas Past & Christmas Presents. Catherine Austin. LC 93-7456. (Illus.). 144p. 1993. 24.95 (*0-8069-0404-6*, Chapelle) Sterling.

Christmas Past & Christmas Presents. Catherine Austin. (Illus.). 144p. 1994. pap. 14.95 (*0-8069-0405-4*, Chapelle) Sterling.

Christmas Patchwork Projects. Linda Seward. LC 86-5738. (Illus.). 144p. 1987. pap. 10.95 (*0-8069-6364-6*) Sterling.

Christmas Patterns. (Letts Pattern Library). (Illus.). 48p. 1992. pap. 6.95 (*1-85238-125-6*, Pub. by New Holland Pubs UK) Sterling.

Christmas People. Jack L. Summers. LC 88-51480. 180p. (YA). 1988. 7.95 (*1-55523-208-6*) Winston-Derek.

Christmas Piano. Date not set. 4.95 (*0-87166-075-X*, 94116) Mel Bay.

Christmas Pipe: A Collector's Celebration of Pipe Smoking at Yuletide. Richard C. Hacker. LC 86-70905. (Illus.). 156p. 1986. 27.95 (*0-931253-01-2*) Autumngold Pub.

Christmas Play Favorites for Young People. Ed. by Sylvia E. Kamerman. (Orig.). (J). (gr. 4-12). 1982. pap. 12.00 (*0-8238-0257-4*) Plays.

Christmas Plays for Young Audiences: 'Twas the Night Before Columbus Day...I Mean Christmas; The Angels' Greatest Message; How Santa Claus Discovered Christmas. Maggie Lawrence et al. (Illus.). 52p. (YA). (gr. 6-12). 1994. pap. 4.00 (*0-88680-391-8*) I E Clark.

Christmas Plays From Oberufer. 3rd ed. Tr. & Intro. by A. C. Harwood. 64p. 1973. pap. 6.95 (*0-85440-279-9*, Steinerbks) Anthroposophic.

Christmas Poems. Illus. by Trina S. Hyman. LC 83-18559. 32p. (J). (ps-3). 1984. lib. bdg. 14.95 (*0-8234-0508-7*) Holiday.

Christmas Poems & Stories. LC 92-505. 1992. 5.99 (*0-517-08138-5*, Pub. by Gramercy) Random Hse Value.

Christmas Polar Bear. Adela Bishop. (Illus.). 32p. (J). (gr. k-3). 1991. 12.95 (*0-9625620-2-5*) DOT Garnet.

Christmas Pop-up Counting Book. Chariot Staff. (J). (ps). 1993. 9.99 (*0-7814-0127-5*, Chariot Bks) Chariot Family.

Christmas Pop-up Set: The First Christmas Tree, Silent Night, The Shepherd's Christmas, Santa's Toy Shop, 4 bks., Set. (J). 1993. Boxed set. boxed 14.95 (*0-307-16300-8*, Artsts Writrs) Western Pub.

***Christmas Popular & Traditional.** Cpp Belwin Staff. 1994. pap. 12.95 (*0-89898-930-2*) CPP Belwin.

Christmas Portraits. 1991. 24.95 (*0-942237-12-9*) Leisure AR.

Christmas Praise: Worship Resources for the Seasons of Christmas. Ed. by Waldo Beach. 1991. text ed. 12.00 (*0-664-21939-X*) Westminster John Knox.

Christmas Prayers. Illus. by Paul Johnson. (Hands Together Ser.). 16p. (J). (ps). 1993. bds. 2.98 (*0-8317-4277-1*) Smithmark.

Christmas Preparations: A Christmas Pageant for Youth. Cynthia E. Cowen. (Orig.). 1994. pap. write for info. (*0-7880-0098-5*) CSS OH.

Christmas Present Mystery. Marion M. Markham. (Illus.). 64p. (J). 1990. pap. 2.95 (*0-380-70966-X*, Camelot) Avon.

Christmas Program Builder, No. 22. Comp. by Grace Ramquist. 1969. 4.25 (*0-685-68582-9*, MC-122) Lillenas.

Christmas Program Builder, No. 23. Comp. by Grace Ramquist. 1970. 4.25 (*0-8341-9138-5*, MC-123) Lillenas.

Christmas Program Builder, No. 24. Comp. by Grace Ramquist. 1971. 4.25 (*0-685-68580-2*, MC-124) Lillenas.

Christmas Program Builder, No. 25. Comp. by Grace Ramquist. 1972. 4.25 (*0-8341-9139-3*, MC-125) Lillenas.

Christmas Program Builder, No. 26. Comp. by Grace Ramquist. 1973. 4.25 (*0-685-68578-0*, MC-126) Lillenas.

Christmas Program Builder, No. 27. Comp. by Grace Ramquist. 1974. 4.25 (*0-8341-9140-7*, MC-127) Lillenas.

Christmas Program Builder, No. 28. Comp. by Grace Ramquist. 1975. 4.25 (*0-8341-9141-5*, MC-128) Lillenas.

Christmas Program Builder, No. 29. Comp. by Grace Ramquist. 1976. 4.25 (*0-685-68575-6*, MC-129) Lillenas.

Christmas Program Builder, No. 30. Comp. by Grace Ramquist. 1977. 4.25 (*0-8341-9142-3*, MC-130) Lillenas.

Christmas Program Builder, No. 31. Comp. by Grace Ramquist. 1978. 4.25 (*0-685-68573-X*, MC-131) Lillenas.

Christmas Program Builder, No. 32. Comp. by Grace Ramquist. 1979. 4.25 (*0-685-68572-1*, MC-132) Lillenas.

Christmas Program Builder, No. 33. Comp. by Evelyn Stenbock. 1980. 4.25 (*0-685-68571-3*, MC-133) Lillenas.

Christmas Program Builder, No. 34. Comp. by Evelyn Stenbock. 1981. 4.25 (*0-685-68570-5*, MC-134) Lillenas.

Christmas Program Builder, No. 35. Comp. by Paul M. Miller. 1982. 4.25 (*0-685-68569-1*, MC-135) Lillenas.

Christmas Program Builder, No. 36. Comp. by Paul M. Miller. 1983. 4.25 (*0-685-68568-3*, MC-136) Lillenas.

Christmas Program Builder, No. 37. Comp. by Paul M. Miller. 1984. 4.25 (*0-685-68567-5*, MC-137) Lillenas.

Christmas Program Builder, No. 38. Comp. by Paul M. Miller. 1985. 4.25 (*0-8341-9143-1*, MC-138) Lillenas.

Christmas Program Builder, No. 39. Comp. by Paul M. Miller. 1986. 4.25 (*0-685-68565-9*, MC-139) Lillenas.

Christmas Program Builder, No. 40. Comp. by Paul M. Miller. 1987. 4.25 (*0-685-68564-0*, MC-140) Lillenas.

Christmas Program Builder, No. 41. Comp. by Paul M. Miller. 1988. 4.25 (*0-8341-9144-X*, MC-141) Lillenas.

Christmas Program Builder, No. 42. Comp. by Paul M. Miller. 1989. 4.25 (*0-8341-9145-8*, MC-142) Lillenas.

Christmas Program Builder, No. 43. Comp. by Paul M. Miller. 1990. 4.25 (*0-685-68561-6*, MC-143) Lillenas.

Christmas Program Builder, No. 44. Comp. by Paul M. Miller. 1991. 4.25 (*0-685-68560-8*, MC-144) Lillenas.

Christmas Program Builder, No. 45. Comp. by Paul M. Miller. 1992. 4.25 (*0-685-68559-4*, MC-145) Lillenas.

Christmas Program Builder, No. 46. Comp. by Paul M. Miller. 1993. 4.25 (*0-685-72867-6*, MC-146) Lillenas.

Christmas Program Builder, No. 47. Comp. by Paul M. Miller. 1994. 4.25 (*0-8341-9104-0*, MC-147) Lillenas.

Christmas Program Builder: Resources for Inspiration, Outreach, & Fun. Comp. by Paul M. Miller. 1994. 4.25 (*0-8341-9053-2*, MP-110) Lillenas.

Christmas Programs for All Ages. Comp. by Grace Ramquist. 1978. 4.25 (*0-8341-9148-2*, MC-252) Lillenas.

Christmas Programs for Children. Comp. by Pat Fittro. 48p. pap. 3.50 (*0-7847-0070-2*, 21-08608) Standard Pub.

Christmas Programs for Children. Ed. by Pat Fittro. 48p. (J). (ps up). 1994. pap. 3.50 (*0-7847-0216-0*, 21-08609) Standard Pub.

***Christmas Programs for Children.** Ed. by Pat Fittro. (Yes Ser.). 48p. 1995. pap. 3.50 (*0-7847-0380-9*, 21-08610) Standard Pub.

Christmas Programs for the Church: Includes Thanksgiving Material. Comp. by Pat Fittro. 64p. 1992. pap. 4.50 (*0-87403-925-8*, 21-08625) Standard Pub.

Christmas Programs for the Church: Includes Thanksgiving Material. Comp. by Pat Fittro. 64p. 1993. pap. 4.50 (*0-7847-0069-9*, 21-08626) Standard Pub.

Christmas Programs for the Church: Includes Thanksgiving Material. Ed. by Pat Fittro. 64p. 1994. pap. 4.99 (*0-7847-0217-9*, 21-08627) Standard Pub.

***Christmas Programs for the Church: Includes Thanksgiving Material.** Ed. by Pat Fittro. (Yes Ser.). 64p. (YA). 1995. pap. 4.99 (*0-7847-0339-6*, 21-08628) Standard Pub.

Christmas Promise. Mary Balogh. (Signet Regency Romance Ser.). 224p. (Orig.). 1992. pap. 3.99 (*0-451-17360-0*, Sig) NAL-Dutton.

Christmas Promise. Mary Balogh. 256p. (Orig.). 1993. lib. bdg. 18.00 (*0-7278-4401-6*) Severn Hse.

Christmas Promise. Lark Carrier. LC 91-14556. (Pixies Miniature Reprint Ser.). (Illus.). 28p. (J). (gr. k up). 1991. pap. 4.95 (*0-88708-180-0*, Picture Book Studio) S&S Childrens.

Christmas Promise. Lark Carrier. LC 86-12356. (Illus.). 36p. (J). (ps up). 1991. pap. 15.95 (*0-88708-032-4*, Picture Book Studio) S&S Childrens.

Christmas Pudding. Nancy Mitford. 1987. pap. 4.95 (*0-88184-342-3*) Carroll & Graf.

Christmas Pudding. braille ed. Nancy Mitford. 338p. 1992. vinyl bd. 27.04 (*1-56956-046-3*, BR8647) W A T Braille.

Christmas Quilting: Twenty Decorative Projects. Terry T. Evans. 64p. 1988. pap. 5.95 (*0-486-25755-X*) Dover.

Christmas Quilts. Marsha McCloskey. 1990. pap. 6.95 (*0-486-26406-8*) Dover.

Christmas Quilts & Afghans. Better Homes & Gardens Editors. 80p. 1990. pap. 9.95 (*0-696-01857-8*) Meredith Bks.

Christmas Reader. LC 93-15526. 1993. 8.99 (*0-517-09338-3*, Pub. by Gramercy) Random Hse Value.

***Christmas Readings to Recapture the Wonder of the Season.** 150p. 1995. 14.99 (*0-87788-131-6*) Shaw Pubs.

Christmas Recipes from the Lion House. Ed. by Gloria W. Rytting. LC 89-35572. (Illus.). 214p. 1989. 12.95 (*0-87579-255-3*) Deseret Bk.

Christmas Recital. (Recital Notebooks Ser.: No. 12). 1967. pap. 3.95 (*0-8256-8061-1*, Yorktown Mus) Music Sales.

***Christmas Record Book.** Brent. 1992. 16.99 (*1-85145-607-4*, Pavilion Bks) Viking Penguin.

Christmas Reflections. Frances J. Roberts. 1982. pap. 3.25 (*0-932814-28-X*) Kings Farspan.

Christmas Reflections for Piano. Ed. by Teresa Wilhelmi. 1985. 7.95 (*0-685-71342-3*, MC-264) Lillenas.

Christmas Remembered. Ron DelBene et al. LC 91-75224. 128p. 1991. text ed. 12.95 (*0-8358-0650-2*) Upper Room Bks.

Christmas Remembered. Arthur R. Pitcher. 1985. pap. 5.95 (*0-86544-029-8*) Salv Army Suppl South.

Christmas Remembrance. May Gray. 64p. 1993. 10.00 (*0-8233-0487-6*) Golden Quill.

***Christmas Reminder.** Comp. by Society of Old Brooklynites Staff. 61p. (YA). 1995. pap. 15.00 (*1-878545-07-8*) ACETO Bookmen.

Christmas Rendezvous. 1992. mass mkt. 3.99 (*0-8217-3589-6*) Zebra.

Christmas Revisited. Robert Brenner. LC 86-61297. (Illus.). 206p. 1986. pap. 24.95 (*0-88740-067-1*) Schiffer.

Christmas Revolution. Barbara Cohen. LC 86-21340. (Illus.). 96p. (J). (gr. 3-6). 1987. 12.95 (*0-688-06806-5*) Lothrop.

Christmas Revolution. Barbara Cohen. (J). 1993. pap. 3.50 (*0-440-40871-7*) Dell.

Christmas Ribbons. 8th ed. Cynthia H. Cummings. (Illus.). 80p. 1990. reprint ed. 10.00 (*1-881811-01-8*) H Peterson Pr.

Christmas Riddle. Illus. by John Ward. LC 93-10713. (J). (gr. 2 up). 1995. 14.99 (*0-525-67469-1*, Lodestar Bks) Dutton Child Bks.

Christmas Robin. (Christmas Titles Ser.: No. S808-18). (Illus.). (J). 1989. 3.95 (*0-7214-5255-8*) Ladybird Bks.

***Christmas Rogues: The Christmas Stranger; The Homecoming; Bayberry & Mistletoe.** Anita Mills et al. 1995. 4.99 (*0-373-83297-4*) Harlequin Bks.

Christmas Romance. Maggie Daniels. (Orig.). 1991. mass mkt. 3.99 (*0-312-92669-3*) St Martin.

Christmas Roses & Other Stories. Anne D. Sedgwick. LC 70-152957. (Short Story Index Reprint Ser.). 1977. reprint ed. 20.95 (*0-8369-3872-0*) Ayer.

***Christmas Ruby.** Robert L. Holt. 158p. 1991. 14.95 (*0-930926-13-7*) Calif Fin Pubns.

Christmas Santa Almost Missed. 1986. pap. 1.95 (*0-8167-0028-1*) Troll Assocs.

Christmas Santa Almost Missed. Cathy E. Dubowski. (Storytime Christmas Bks.). (Illus.). 24p. (Orig.). (J). (gr. k-1). 1990. pap. 0.99 (*1-878624-48-2*) McClanahan Bk.

***Christmas Scene.** Neal A. Maxwell. 1994. pap. write for info. (*0-88494-962-1*) Bookcraft Inc.

Christmas Scene Revisited. Phyllis V. Wezeman. 1990. 5.50 (*1-877871-09-5*, 2562) Ed Ministries.

Christmas Scrapcrafts. Maggie Malone. LC 91-23273. (Illus.). 144p. 1991. 24.95 (*0-8069-6804-4*) Sterling.

Christmas Scrapcrafts. Maggie Malone. (Illus.). 136p. (J). (gr. 5-10). 1992. pap. 12.95 (*0-8069-6805-2*) Sterling.

Christmas Script Book. Comp. by Paul M. Miller. 1988. 5.25 (*0-685-68584-5*, MC-270) Lillenas.

Christmas Scroll Saw Patterns. Patrick Spielman & Patricia Spielman. LC 93-3417. (Illus.). 164p. 1993. pap. 12.95 (*0-8069-0308-2*) Sterling.

Christmas Search & Find. 1989. pap. 2.50 (*0-8167-1851-2*) Troll Assocs.

Christmas Season. Monks of New Skete Staff. Tr. by Laurence Mancuso. (Liturgical Music Series I: Great Feasts: Vol. 7). viii, 221p. (Orig.). 1990. pap. text ed. 50.00 (*0-935129-16-2*) Monks of New Skete.

Christmas Secret. David Delamare. LC 91-12779. (Illus.). 40p. (J). (ps-2). 1991. 15.00 (*0-671-74822-X*, Green Tiger S&S) S&S Childrens.

Christmas Secrets. Margo Finch. 1988. pap. 2.95 (*0-8167-1492-4*) Troll Assocs.

Christmas Secrets. Ann Schweninger. (Picture Puffins Ser.). (Illus.). 32p. (J). (ps-1). 1986. pap. 4.99 (*0-14-050577-6*, Puffin) Puffin Bks.

Christmas Selections: For Readings & Recitations. Comp. by Rosemond L. McNaught. LC 74-38601. (Granger Index Reprint Ser.). 1977. reprint ed. 15.95 (*0-8369-6333-4*) Ayer.

Christmas Serenity. Teddy Milne. 1990. pap. 3.50 (*0-938875-24-8*) Pittenbruach Pr.

Christmas Sermon. 2nd ed. Robert G. Ingersoll. 47p. 1988. 4.00 (*0-910309-56-6*, 5148) Am Atheist.

***Christmas Shapes.** (J). (ps). 1994. bds. 2.95 (*1-56458-822-X*) Dorling Kindersley.

Christmas Sing-Along. (Illus.). 5p. (J). (gr. k-3). 1991. 9.95 (*0-8167-2454-7*) Troll Assocs.

Christmas Snowman. Margery Cuyler. (Illus.). 32p. (J). (ps-3). 1992. 14.95 (*1-55970-066-1*) Arcade Pub Inc.

Christmas Solos for Beginning Cello. Craig Duncan. (Building Excellence Ser.). 1993. 4.95 (*1-56222-261-9*, 94670) Mel Bay.

Christmas Solos for Beginning Clarinet. Norman Heim. (Building Excellence Ser.). 1993. 4.95 (*1-56222-278-3*, 94653) Mel Bay.

Christmas Solos for Beginning Flute, Level 1. Dona Gilliam & Mizzy McCaskill. 1993. 4.95 (*1-56222-277-5*, 94654) Mel Bay.

Christmas Solos for Beginning Saxophone. Mike Buerk. (Building Excellence Ser.). 1993. 4.95 (*1-56222-422-0*, 94720) Mel Bay.

Christmas Solos for Beginning Trumpet. William Bay. 1993. 4.95 (*1-56222-279-1*, 94701) Mel Bay.

Christmas Solos for Beginning Viola. Craig Duncan. (Building Excellence Ser.). 1993. 4.95 (*1-56222-276-7*, 94669) Mel Bay.

Christmas Solos for Beginning Violin. Craig Duncan. (Building Excellence Ser.). 1993. 4.95 (*1-56222-260-0*, 94668) Mel Bay.

Christmas Solos for the Bb Saxophone. Sel. by Robin De Smet. (Illus.). 48p. 1987. pap. 7.95 (*0-8256-1164-4*, AM65061) Music Sales.

Christmas Solos for the Clarinet. Sel. by Robin De Smet. (Illus.). 48p. 1987. pap. 7.95 (*0-8256-1161-X*, AM65020) Music Sales.

Christmas Solos for the Flute. Sel. by Robin De Smet. (Illus.). 48p. 1987. pap. 7.95 (*0-8256-1160-1*, AM65038) Music Sales.

Christmas Solos for the Recorder. Sel. by Robin De Smet. (Illus.). 48p. 1987. pap. 7.95 (*0-8256-1163-6*, AM65046) Music Sales.

Christmas Solos for the Trumpet. Sel. by Robin De Smet. (Illus.). 48p. 1987. pap. 7.95 (*0-8256-1162-8*, AM65053) Music Sales.

Christmas Solos for the Violin. (Illus.). 60p. 1987. pap. 6.95 (*0-8256-1121-0*, AM67133) Music Sales.

Christmas Sonata. Gary Paulsen. LC 90-46891. (Illus.). 80p. (J). (gr. 3-7). 1992. 14.95 (*0-385-30441-2*) Delacorte.

Christmas Sonata. Gary Paulsen. 1994. mass mkt. 3.99 (*0-440-40958-6*) Dell.

Christmas Song of Old Boston. M. H. Maxwell. Ed. & Intro. by George Junghanns. (Illus.). 40p. 1973. reprint ed. 3.50 (*0-686-05469-5*) Gauntlet Bks.

Christmas Song of Old Boston: A String of Pearls, 1852 Replica. M. H. Maxwell. 31p. 1973. 10.00 (*1-881946-04-5*) Gauntlet Bks.

Christmas Songbook. (Illus.). 96p. 1993. pap. 12.95 (*0-8256-2107-0*) Music Sales.

Christmas Songs. (Sing 'n' Color Fun! Ser.). 32p. (J). (gr. 3 up). 1992. Incl. cass., songbk., crayons. 6.95 (*0-7935-1083-X*, 00850117) H Leonard.

Christmas Songs. (Recorder Fun! Ser.). (Illus.). 24p. (J). 1993. 9.95 (*0-7935-1826-1*, 00710372) H Leonard.

Christmas Songs. (Xylotone Fun! Ser.). (Illus.). 16p. (J). 1993. 9.95 (*0-7935-1781-8*, 00824021) H Leonard.

Christmas Songs. (Play - a - Song Ser.). (Illus.). 24p. (J). 1993. 12.98 (*0-7853-0135-6*) Pubns Intl Ltd.

Christmas Songs. Bishop. (Little Christmas Pop-Ups Ser.). (J). (gr. k up). 1994. 3.95 (*0-671-89516-8*, Litl Simon S&S) S&S Childrens.

Christmas Songs. Comp. by Jerry Silverman. (Traditional Black Music Ser.). (Illus.). 80p. (YA). (gr. 5 up). 1992. lib. bdg. 15.95 (*0-7910-1832-6*, Am Art Analog); pap. 9.95 (*0-7910-1848-2*, Am Art Analog) Chelsea Hse.

***Christmas Songs.** Viki Woodworth. (Umbrella Bks.). (Illus.). 32p. (J). (gr. 2-6). 1995. lib. bdg. 14.95 (*1-56766-117-3*) Childs World.

Christmas Songs & Stories for All the Family. (Illus.). 192p. 1993. pap. 17.95 (*0-8256-1368-X*) Music Sales.

Christmas Songs-Classic Guitar. Date not set. 3.95 (*0-87166-005-9*, 93789) Mel Bay.

Christmas Songs-Fingerstyle Guitar. Date not set. 3.95 (*0-87166-791-6*, 93788) Mel Bay.

Christmas Songs for Children. Jonathan Pickow. (Illus.). 56p. 1988. pap. 7.95 (*0-685-65822-8*, AM67117) Music Sales.

Christmas Songs for Piano (Big Note) Albert De Vito. 1968. pap. 4.95 (*0-934286-53-1*) Kenyon.

Christmas Songs for the Recorder. (Illus.). 32p. 1977. pap. 7.95 (*0-86001-473-8*, AM20167) Music Sales.

Christmas Songs in Spanish. Ina W. Ramboz. 32p. (SPA.). (J). (gr. 6-9). 1985. pap. 7.95 (*0-8442-7097-0*, Passport Bks) NTC Pub Grp.

1250 An Asterisk (*) at the beginning of an entry indicates that the title is appearing in BIP for the first time.

Christmas Thyme at Oak Hill Farm.

Marge Clark. LC 94-90065. (Illus.). 176p. 1994. 20.00 *(0-9640514-5-1)* Thyme Ckbks.

CHRISTMAS THYME AT OAK HILL FARM is a new book by Marge Clark, author of the popular book, IT'S ABOUT THYME (ISBN 0-9620692-0-5, $14.95). CHRISTMAS THYME AT OAK HILL FARM is a story about how Marge, her family & friends celebrate the holidays. She gives us menus & recipes for parties the Clarks host at Christmastime. Learn how to make Marge's CHRISTMAS POTPOURRI, GINGERBREAD BIRDHOUSES, a fresh ROSEMARY WREATH, a fabulous FRUIT, FLOWER & HERB TOPIARY, APPLE GARLANDS, an ADVENT WREATH & much more. And gifts - wonderful & homemade gifts! There is something here for everyone - HERBAL VINEGARS, HOMEMADE LIQUEURS, COOKIES, BREADS & CAKES. Linda Ligon, editor of THE HERB COMPANION says it best - "Marge Clark knows how to create the kind of homey, spicy, lovingly bountiful Christmases that memories are made of. Furthermore, she knows how to do it in smart, work-ahead ways that can take out the stress of holiday planning. CHRISTMAS THYME AT OAK HILL FARM is packed with inviting party menus, delicious home-style recipes that have a special flair, & a whole pantry full of great gift ideas. The next-best thing to owning this beautifully presented book would be to give it to a friend." Order from: Thyme Cookbooks, Oak Hill Farm, R.R. 1, P.O. Box 69, West Lebanon, IN 47991. Call 317-893-4270 or 1-800-930-3222.

Publisher Provided Annotation.

Christmas Tree That Cried. Bobbi McPeak-Bailey. (Illus.). 36p. (J). (gr. k-6). 1982. 11.95 (*0-9625005-0-X*) Wee Pr.

Christmas Trees. Robert Frost. LC 89-48899. (Illus.). 32p. (J). (gr. 2-4). 1990. 14.95 (*0-8050-1208-7*, Bks Young Read) H Holt & Co.

Christmas Trees. Kathy Henderson. LC 89-859. (New True Bks.). (Illus.). 48p. (J). (gr. k-4). 1989. lib. bdg. 12.90 (*0-516-01162-6*) Childrens.

Christmas Trees. Robert B. Hoffman, Jr. (Illus.). 62p. (Orig.). (J). (gr. 3 up). 1991. reprint ed. pap. 9.95 (*0-9633156-0-9*) R B Hoffman.

Christmas Trees: Growing & Selling Trees, Wreaths, & Greens. Lewis Hill. Ed. by Gwen Steege & Sarah M. Clarkson. LC 89-45222. (Illus.). 160p. (Orig.). 1989. pap. 9.95 (*0-88266-566-9*, Garden Way Pub) Storey Comm Inc.

Christmas Trees for Pleasure & Profit. rev. ed. Arthur G. Chapman & Robert D. Wray. 220p. 1984. pap. text ed. 18.95 (*0-8135-1074-0*) Rutgers U Pr.

Christmas Trilogy. Ann N. Parker. (Sandman Ser.: Pt. II). (Illus.). (J). (gr. k-4). 1988. pap. 3.95 (*0-943487-14-5*) Sevgo Pr.

Christmas Trims Kids Can Make. Better Homes & Gardens Editors. Date not set. pap. 9.95 (*0-696-01641-9*) Meredith Bks.

Christmas Trolls. Jan Brett. LC 93-10106. (Illus.). 32p. (J). (ps-3). 1993. lib. bdg. 15.95 (*0-399-22507-2*, Putnam) Putnam Pub Group.

Christmas Truce. Malcolm Brown & Shirley Seaton. 228p. (C). 1987. 105.00 (*0-317-90437-X*, Pub. by Picton UK) St Mut.

*__Christmas Twist.__ Illegitimate Players Staff. 50p. 1993. pap. 5.95 (*1-56850-039-4*) Chicago Plays.

*__Christmas Visitor.__ Anneliese Lussert. Tr. by Rosemary Lanning. LC 95-1642. (Illus.). (J). 1995. 14.95 (*1-55858-449-8*); lib. bdg. write for info. (*1-55858-450-1*) North-South Bks NYC.

Christmas, Vol. 60: The Annual of Christmas Literature & Art. LC 43-30914. (Illus.). 64p. 1990. 22.95 (*0-8066-8977-3*, 10-17141, Augsburg); pap. 11.95 (*0-8066-8976-5*, 10-17140, Augsburg) Augsburg Fortress.

Christmas, Vol. 62: The Annual of Christmas Literature & Art. 64p. (Orig.). 1992. pap. 11.95 (*0-8066-8980-3*, 10-17144, Augsburg) Augsburg Fortress.

*__Christmas Wedding.__ Pamela Macaluso. 1995. pap. 3.25 (*0-373-05970-1*, 1-05970-8) Silhouette.

Christmas Week at Bigler's Mill: A Sketch in Black & White. Dora F. Spratt. LC 72-2171. (Black Heritage Library Collection). 1977. reprint ed. 16.95 (*0-8369-9065-X*) Ayer.

Christmas Wife: Stories. Helen Norris. LC 84-24080. (Illinois Short Fiction Ser.). 144p. 1988. pap. 9.95 (*0-252-06041-5*) U of Ill Pr.

Christmas Windows. (Illus.). 1990. 7.95 (*0-922434-35-2*) Brighton & Lloyd.

Christmas Wish. Rexanne Becnel. 1993. mass mkt. 4.99 (*0-440-21672-9*) Dell.

*__Christmas Wish.__ Betty Neels. 1995. pap. 2.99 (*0-373-03389-3*, 1-03389-3) Harlequin Bks.

Christmas Wish. Ed. by Jennifer Sawyer. 352p. 1994. mass mkt. 4.50 (*0-8217-4762-2*) Zebra.

*__Christmas Wish: A Glow in the Dark Book.__ Justine Korman. (J). (ps). 1994. 2.95 (*0-8167-3511-5*) Troll Assocs.

Christmas Wishes. Alan Benjamin. (Chubby Board Bks.). 16p. (J). 1989. pap. 3.95 (*0-671-68268-7*, Litl Simon S&S) S&S Childrens.

Christmas Wishes. Cynthia H. Cummings. (Illus.). 80p. 1987. 10.00 (*1-881811-06-9*) H Peterson Pr.

*__Christmas Wishes.__ Ed. by Helen Exley. (So-Much-More-Than-a-Card Ser.). (Illus.). 28p. (Orig.). 1995. pap. 2.99 (*1-85015-654-9*) Exley Giftbooks.

Christmas Wishes. Barbara Metzger. (Orig.). 1992. mass mkt. 3.99 (*0-449-22078-8*, Crest) Fawcett.

Christmas Wishes. Barbara Metzger. (Orig.). 1993. mass mkt. 3.99 (*0-449-45241-7*, Crest) Fawcett.

Christmas Wishes: Under the Mistletoe. Moyra Tarling. (Silhouette Romance Ser.). 1993. pap. 2.75 (*0-373-08979-1*, 5-08979-2) Silhouette.

Christmas Witch. Steven Kellogg. LC 91-32688. (Illus.). 40p. (J). (gr. k-3). 1992. 15.00 (*0-8037-1268-5*); lib. bdg. 14.89 (*0-8037-1269-3*) Dial Bks Young.

Christmas Witch. Illus. by Annie Mitra. LC 92-562. (J). 1993. mass mkt. 3.99 (*0-553-37187-8*, Little Rooster) Bantam.

Christmas Witch. Illus. & Ret. by Ilse Plume. LC 91-71380. 32p. (J). (gr. k-3). 1991. 13.95 (*1-56282-077-X*); lib. bdg. 13.89 (*1-56282-078-8*) Hyprn Child.

Christmas Witch. Illus. & Ret. by Ilse Plume. LC 91-71380. 32p. (J). (gr. k-3). 1993. pap. 4.95 (*1-56282-524-0*) Hyprn Child.

Christmas with All the Trimmings: Original Stories & Crafts from Mickey Mouse & Friends. Katherine Applegate. LC 93-74420. (Illus.). 64p. (J). (ps-3). 1994. 12.95 (*0-7868-3003-4*) Disney Pr.

Christmas with Angelina. Katharine Holabird. LC 92-80523. (Angelina Board Bks.). (Illus.). 6p. (J). (ps-00). 1992. bds. 5.99 (*0-679-83485-0*) Random Bks Yng Read.

Christmas with Cesar & Ernestina - Christmas with Earnest & Celestine. Gabrielle Vincent. (SPA.). (J). 19.95 (*84-372-6600-9*) Santillana.

Christmas with Dickens: The Dickens' Family's 150th Anniversary Gift of A Christmas Carol for Modern-Day Families at Yuletide. Charles C. Dickens et al. LC 93-39711. 1993. 12.95 (*0-911057-02-1*) Belvedere Pr.

Christmas with Grandfather. Winfried Wolf. Tr. by J. A. James. LC 94-9315. (J). 1994. 14.95 (*1-55858-296-7*); lib. bdg. 14.88 (*1-55858-297-5*) North-South Bks NYC.

Christmas with Grandma. Frank McClanahan. (Storytime Christmas Bks.). (Illus.). 24p. (Orig.). (J). (gr. k-1). 1990. pap. 0.99 (*1-878624-46-6*) McClanahan Bk.

Christmas with Ida Early. Robert Burch. LC 85-5680. 158p. (J). (gr. 3-7). 1985. pap. 4.99 (*0-14-031971-9*, Puffin) Puffin Bks.

Christmas with Madonna: Holiday Recipes. Madonna S. Echols. LC 87-62187. 64p. (Orig.). 1987. pap. 2.95 (*0-915216-94-9*) Marathon Intl Bk.

Christmas with Mormon Handicraft. LC 92-15016. (Illus.). 168p. 1992. 16.95 (*0-87579-535-8*) Deseret Bk.

Christmas with Southern Living - 94. Southern Living Staff. 1994. 24.95 (*0-8487-1190-4*) Oxmoor Hse.

Christmas with Southern Living, 1992. Oxmoor House Editors. 160p. 1992. 24.99 (*0-8487-1091-6*) Oxmoor Hse.

Christmas with Southern Living 1993. LC 84-63032. 160p. 1993. 24.99 (*0-8487-1133-5*) Oxmoor Hse.

Christmas with the Classical Guitar. Des. by Charles Duncan. 48p. 1991. pap. text ed. 7.95 (*0-87487-408-4*) Summy-Birchard.

Christmas with the Santa Bears, A Christmas to Remember. (Illus.). 24p. (J). 1987. write for info. (*0-318-68584-1*, Honey Bear Bks); text ed. 3.95 (*0-87449-072-3*, Honey Bear Bks); text ed. 3.95 (*0-87449-112-6*, Honey Bear Bks) Modern Pub NYC.

Christmas with the Three Bears. R. Eugene Jackson. (Illus.). 48p. (Orig.). (J). (gr. 1-10). 1990. pap. 4.00 (*0-88680-326-8*); 10.00 (*0-88680-327-6*) I E Clark.

*__Christmas Without a Tree.__ Elizabeth Rodger. LC 94-44399. (J). 1995. pap. write for info. (*0-689-80157-2*, Aladdin Paperbacks) S&S Childrens.

Christmas Without Elizabeth. Francine Pascal. (Sweet Valley Twins & Friends Magna Ser.: No. 2). (J). (gr. 4-7). 1993. mass mkt. 3.99 (*0-553-15947-X*) Bantam.

Christmas Wolf. Karen Wantland. 1990. 6.95 (*0-533-08864-X*) Vantage.

Christmas Wonder: An Anthology of Verse & Song. Waldo Beach. LC 73-79038. 96p. reprint ed. pap. 27.40 (*0-685-15995-7*, 2026924) Bks Demand.

Christmas Wonder: From Ireland - For Children: Craftwork, Lore, Poems, Songs & Stories. Sean C. O'Leary. LC 89-50972. (Illus.). 98p. (Orig.). (J). 1989. pap. 12.95 (*0-86278-177-9*, Pub. by OBrien Pr IE) Dufour.

*__Christmas Wonderland.__ 160p. 1995. 20.85 (*0-9638031-6-6*) Needlecrft Shop.

Christmas Won't Wait. Eve Tharlet. Tr. by Andrew Clements. (Illus.). (J). (gr. k up). 1991. pap. 14.95 (*0-88708-151-7*, Picture Book Studio) S&S Childrens.

Christmas Wreath. James Hoffman. (J). (ps-3). 1993. 12.95 (*0-88743-575-0*) Sch Zone Pub Co.

Christmas Wreaths. Steve Sherman. 1987. 12.95 (*0-317-61854-7*) Viking Penguin.

*__Christmas Wreaths: Twenty-Seven Festive Easy-to-Make Wreaths, Garlands & Swags.__ Chris Rankin. LC 94-30697. 1995. write for info. (*0-8069-1279-0*) Sterling.

Christmas Wrinkle. Richard S. Kimball. LC 88-16310. (Illus.). 48p. (Orig.). (J). (gr. 3 up). 1988. pap. 4.95 (*0-944443-01-X*) Green Timber.

Christmas Year Round: A Guide to America's Christmas Shops. James R. Heintze. LC 91-5037. 175p. 1991. 10.95 (*0-89990-059-3*) Info Coord.

*__Christmas 1956: A Poem.__ Keith Denniston. Ed. by Gloria V. Hickok. 6p. (Orig.). 1995. pap. 2.50 (*1-884235-09-3*) Helicon Nine Eds.

*__Christmas 1995: Unlock the Secrets to a Truly Happy Holiday.__ Mary Thompson & Deborah Pike. 150p. 1995. pap. 7.95 (*0-8027-7467-9*) Walker & Co.

Christmastide: Its History, Festivities & Carols. William Sandys. 1973. 69.95 (*0-87968-867-X*) Gordon Pr.

Christmastime. Sandra Boynton. LC 87-6204. (Illus.). 112p. 1987. 12.95 (*0-89480-635-1*, 1635) Workman Pub.

Christmastime at Santa's Workshop. Peggy Kahn. (Pop-Up Bks.). (Illus.). 14p. (J). (ps-3). 1992. 7.99 (*0-679-82451-0*) Random Bks Yng Read.

Christmastime in Montana. Comp. by Dave Walters. (Illus.). 128p. (Orig.). 1990. pap. 19.95 (*0-938314-92-0*) Am Wrld Geog.

Christmastime in New York City. Roxie Munro. (Illus.). 32p. (J). (ps-3). 1994. pap. 5.99 (*0-14-050462-1*) Puffin Bks.

*__Christmastory.__ Thomas Williams. 40p. (J). 1995. 12.50 (*1-887495-02-9*) Coiny Pub.

Christo. Lady Marina Vaizey. LC 90-52615. (Twentieth Century Artists Ser.). (Illus.). 128p. 1990. 22.50 (*0-8478-1239-1*) Rizzoli Intl.

Christo: Collection on Loan Rothschild Bank. Sebastian Adler & Robert McDonald. LC 81-84093. (Illus.). 144p. 1981. 19.95 (*0-934418-12-8*) Mus Contemp Art.

Christo: Prints & Objects. Jorg Schellmann & Josephine Benecke. (Illus.). 176p. 1988. 29.98 (*0-89659-796-2*) Abbeville Pr.

Christo: Surrounded Islands: Biscayne Bay, Greater Miami, Florida, 1980-83. Photos by Wolfgang Volz. LC 85-28634. (Illus.). 696p. 1986. boxed 95.00 (*0-8109-0790-9*) Abrams.

Christo: The Pont-Neuf Wrapped, Project for Paris, 1975-1985. Photos by Wolfgang Volz. (Illus.). 592p. 1990. 95.00 (*0-8109-3164-8*) Abrams.

Christo: The Reichstag & Urban Projects. Ed. by Jacob Baal-Teshuva. (Illus.). 160p. 1993. pap. 35.00 (*3-7913-1323-1*, Pub. by Prestel) TeNeues.

*__Christo y Su Justicia.__ Ellet J. Waggoner. 95p. (SPA.). 1994. pap. 5.95x (*0-9635077-3-7*, 02102) Glad Tidngs.

Christodoulos the Counterfeiter. J. Svoronos. (Illus.). 38p. 1974. pap. 10.00 (*0-89005-040-6*) Ares.

Christoffel Functions & Orthogonal Polynomials for Exponential Weights. A. L. Levin & D. S. Lubinsky. LC 94-17089. (Memoirs of the American Mathematical Society Ser.: Vol. 535). 1994. write for info. (*0-8218-2599-2*) Am Math.

Christointegration: The Transforming Love of Jesus Christ. Bernard J. Tyrrell. 1989. pap. 9.95 (*0-8091-3098-X*) Paulist Pr.

Christological Catechism: New Testament Answers. 2nd ed. Joseph A. Fitzmyer. (Orig.). 1991. pap. 9.95 (*0-8091-3253-2*) Paulist Pr.

Christological Controversy. Ed. by Richard A. Norris, Jr. & William G. Rusch. LC 79-8890. (Sources of Early Christian Thought Ser.). 176p. 1980. pap. 13.00 (*0-8006-1411-9*, 1-1411, Fortress Pr) Augsburg Fortress.

Christological Foundation for Contemporary Theological Education. Ed. by Joseph D. Ban. LC 88-13315. 272p. (C). 1988. 30.00 (*0-86554-313-5*, MUP/H249) Mercer Univ Pr.

Christologie Emanuel Hirschs: Eine Systematische und Problemgeschichtliche Darstellung Ihrer Geschichtsmethodologischen, Erkenntniskritischen und Subjektivitatstheoretischen Grundlagen. Ulrich Barth. xvi, 669p. (C). 1992. lib. bdg. 163.10 (*3-11-012894-2*, 238-91) De Gruyter.

Christologische Schriftargumentation & Bildersprache: Zum Konflikt Zwischen Metapherninterpretation & Dogmatischen Schriftbeweistraditionen in Der Patristischen Auslegung Des 44. 45. Psalms. E. Von Grunbeck. LC 94-8574. (Supplements to Vigiliae Christianae Ser.: Vol. 26). 1994. 108.75 (*90-04-10021-0*) E J Brill.

Christology. L. Bouyer et al. LC 83-4420. (Word & Spirit Ser.: Vol. V). 1983. pap. 7.00 (*0-932506-28-3*) St Bedes Pubns.

Christology. David P. Scaer. Ed. by Robert D. Preus et al. LC 89-84112. (Confessional Lutheran Dogmatics Ser.: Vol. 6). 130p. (C). 1989. 10.00 (*0-9622791-6-1*) Luth Confess Res.

*__Christology: A Biblical, Historical, & System.__ Gerald O'Collins. 352p. 1995. text ed. 56.00 (*0-19-875501-5*); pap. 14.95 (*0-19-875502-3*) OUP.

Christology: Basic Texts in Focus. Leopold Sabourin. LC 84-12304. 259p. (Orig.). (C). 1984. pap. 9.95 (*0-8189-0471-2*) Alba.

Christology & a Modern Pilgrimage: A Discussion with Norman Perrin. rev. ed. Ed. by Hans D. Betz. LC 79-31605. 109p. reprint ed. pap. 31.10 (*0-317-28877-6*, 2020268) Bks Demand.

Christology & Cosmology: Models of Divine Activity in Origen, Eusebius, & Athanasius. J. Rebecca Lyman. LC 92-32481. (Oxford Theological Monographs). (C). 1993. 42.00 (*0-19-826745-2*, Clarendon Pr) OUP.

Christology & Eucharist in the Early Thought of Cyril of Alexandria. Lawrence J. Welch. 250p. 1994. 64.95 (*1-883255-13-9*, Cath Scholar Pr); pap. 44.95 (*1-883255-06-6*, Cath Scholar Pr) Intl Scholars.

Christology & Spirituality. William M. Thompson. 224p. 1991. 27.50 (*0-8245-1098-4*) Crossroad NY.

Christology & Transition in the Theology of Edwin Lewis. Stephen A. Seamands. LC 87-8255. 198p. (Orig.). (C). 1987. lib. bdg. 44.00 (*0-8191-6381-3*) U Pr of Amer.

Christology at the Crossroads: A Latin American Approach. Jon Sobrino. Tr. by John Drury. LC 77-25025. Orig. Title: Cristologia desde America Latina. 458p. (Orig.). 1978. pap. 16.95 (*0-88344-076-8*) Orbis Bks.

Christology Beyond Dogma: Matthew's Christ in Process Hermeneutic. Russell Pregeant. LC 77-78638. (Society of Biblical Literature. Semeia Supplements Ser.: No. 7). 176p. (Orig.). reprint ed. pap. 50.20 (*0-7837-5439-6*, 2045204) Bks Demand.

Christology in Context: The Earliest Christian Response to Jesus. Marinus DeJonge. LC 87-30878. 276p. 1988. pap. 17.99 (*0-664-25010-6*, Westminster) Westminster John Knox.

Christology in Dialogue. Ed. by Robert F. Berkey & Sarah A. Edwards. LC 92-47004. 400p. (Orig.). (C). 1993. pap. 24.95 (*0-8298-0956-2*) Pilgrim OH.

Christology in Paul & John. Robin Scroggs. (Proclamation Commentaries Ser.). 160p. 1988. pap. 11.00 (*0-8006-0599-3*, 1-599, Fortress Pr) Augsburg Fortress.

Christology in the Making. James D. Dunn. 480p. (Orig.). 1989. pap. 26.95 (*0-334-00215-X*, SCM Pr) TPI PA.

Christology of Casper Schwenckfeld: Spirit & Flesh in the Process of Life Tranformation. Andre Seguenny & Simone Nieuwwolt. LC 87-24675. (Texts & Studies in Religion: Vol. 35). 150p. 1987. lib. bdg. 69.95 (*0-88946-820-6*) E Mellen.

Christology of Hegel. James Yerkes. LC 82-5711. (Hegelian Studies). 288p. 1983. 64.50 (*0-87395-648-6*); pap. 21.95 (*0-87395-649-4*) State U NY Pr.

Christology of Jesus. Ben Witherington, III. LC 90-34896. 320p. 1990. lib. bdg. 30.00 (*0-8006-2430-0*, 1-2430) Augsburg Fortress.

Christology of Peace. James E. Will. 144p. 1989. pap. 11.99 (*0-8042-0540-X*, John Knox) Westminster John Knox.

Christology of Rosemary Radford Ruether: A Critical Introduction. Mary H. Snyder. LC 87-51564. 168p. (Orig.). 1988. pap. 12.95 (*0-89622-358-2*) Twenty-Third.

Christology of Solidarity: Jesus as the Representative of His People in Matthew. William L. Kynes. 262p. (C). 1991. lib. bdg. 46.50 (*0-8191-8097-1*); pap. text ed. 29.50 (*0-8191-8098-X*) U Pr of Amer.

Christology of St. Paul. S. Nowell Rostron. 1977. lib. bdg. 59.95 (*0-8490-1620-7*) Gordon Pr.

*__Christology of the Fourth Gospel.__ Paul N. Anderson. (WissUNT Zum Neuen Testament Ser.). 330p. (Orig.). 1994. pap. text ed. 88.50 (*3-16-145779-X*, Pub. by J C B Mohr GW) Coronet Bks.

Christology of the Later Fathers. Ed. by Edward R. Hardy. LC 54-9949. (Library of Christian Classics). 396p. 1977. pap. 14.99 (*0-664-24152-2*, Westminster) Westminster John Knox.

Christology of the New Testament. rev. ed. Oscar Cullmann. Tr. by Shirley C. Guthrie & Charles A. M. Hall. LC 59-10178. 364p. (C). 1980. pap. 14.99 (*0-664-24351-7*, Westminster) Westminster John Knox.

Christology of the Old Testament. E. W. Hengstenberg. LC 77-129739. 716p. pap. 24.99 (*0-8254-2835-1*) Kregel.

Christoph Blumhardt & His Message. R. Lejeune. LC 63-15816. 240p. 1963. 9.00 (*0-87486-200-0*) Plough.

*__Christoph Wants a Party.__ Mira Lobe. LC 95-8395. (Illus.). (J). 1995. write for info. (*0-916291-59-6*) Kane-Miller Bk.

Christopher. Geoffrey Drayton. (Caribbean Writers Ser.). 1972. pap. 7.95 (*0-435-98235-4*) Heinemann.

Christopher. Richard M. Koff. Ed. by Orly Kelly. LC 81-65885. (Illus.). 128p. (J). (gr. 7 up). 1981. 8.95 (*0-89742-050-0*) Celestial Arts.

Christopher. Regine Schindler. (Illus.). (C). 1990. text ed. 29.00 (*0-85439-306-4*, Pub. by St Paul Pubns UK) St Mut.

*__Christopher.__ Lauren L. Wohl. LC 94-26791. (J). (gr. 1-8). 1995. write for info. (*0-7868-0106-9*) Hyprn Child.

Christopher. Margaret Yorke. 192p. 1992. reprint ed. 18.00 (*0-7278-4359-1*) Severn Hse.

Christopher: The Holy Giant. Tomie DePaola. (Illus.). 32p. (J). (ps-3). 1994. lib. bdg. 15.95 (*0-8234-0862-0*) Holiday.

Christopher Alexander: The Search for a New Paradigm in Architecture. Stephen Grabow. (Illus.). 306p. 1983. 37.50 (*0-85362-199-3*) Routledge.

Christopher & Columbus. Elizabeth Von Arnim. 272p. 1994. pap. 10.95 (*1-85381-748-1*, Pub. by Virago Pr UK) Trafalgar.

Christopher & Cumulus Cloud. Fred D. Hill. Ed. by Elaine Young & Charlotte Hill. LC 90-80285. (Illus.). 28p. (Orig.). (J). (gr. k-4). 1990. pap. 5.95 (*0-9620182-1-X*) Charill Pubs.

*__Christopher & Grandma on Safari.__ Joan B. Barsotti. (Apple Hill Ser.). (Illus.). 24p. (Orig.). (J). (ps-2). Date not set. pap. 5.99 (*0-9642112-2-X*) Barsotti Bks.

Christopher & His Kind. Christopher Isherwood. (Michael di Capua Bks.). 352p. 1987. pap. 8.95 (*0-374-52036-4*) FS&G.

Christopher & Me. Carolyn Stewart. 128p. 1987. 7.95 (*0-9617491-0-5*) Hansen Pubns.

Christopher, & Other Stories. Amelia Barr. LC 72-167440. (Short Story Index Reprint Ser.). 1977. reprint ed. 23.95 (*0-8369-3966-2*) Ayer.

Christopher & Pony Boy. Rita Kerr. (Illus.). 96p. (J). (gr. 4-7). 1991. 10.95 (*0-89015-843-6*) Sunbelt Media.

Christopher & the Sycamore Tree. G. Van Denend & J. Vreeman. (Illus.). 16p. (Orig.). (J). 1985. pap. 3.95 (*0-918789-00-1*) FreeMan Prods.

*__Christopher Brown: Works on Paper.__ Signe Mayfield. Date not set. pap. text ed. write for info. (*0-9636922-3-2*) Palo Alto Cult.

Christopher C. Cat see There's a Skunk in My Trunk

Christopher C. Kidd. Gwen Starcher. LC 93-61445. (Illus.). 96p. (Orig.). (J). (gr. 2-6). 1994. pap. 4.95 (*1-878893-42-4*) Telcraft Bks.

Christopher Cartier of Hazelnut, Also Known As Bear. Antonine Maillet. 76p. 1984. 9.95 (*0-458-98110-9*, Pub. by Stoddart Pubng CN) Genl Dist Srvs.

Christopher Caudwell. Robert Sullivan. (Critics of the Twentieth Century Ser.). 208p. 1987. 49.95 (*0-7099-3881-0*, A3944, Pub. by Croom Helm UK) Routledge Chapman & Hall.

Christopher Caudwell: Towards a Dialectical Theory of Literature. Christopher Pawling. LC 88-35482. 208p. 1989. text ed. 39.95 (*0-312-03014-2*) St Martin.

Christopher Churchmouse Treasury. Barbara Davoll. (Illus.). (Orig.). (J). 1992. pap. 14.99 (*0-89693-078-5*, Victor Books) SP Pubns.

Christopher Codrington: Sixteen Sixty-Eight to Seventeen Hundred Ten. Vincent T. Harlow. 262p. 1990. 39.95 (*0-685-47233-7*) St Martin.

Christopher Columbus. Isaac Asimov. LC 90-25836. (Isaac Asimov's Pioneers of Science & Exploration Ser.). (Illus.). 64p. (J). (gr. 3-4). 1991. lib. bdg. 19.93 (*0-8368-0556-9*) Gareth Stevens Inc.

Christopher Columbus. Rae Bains. LC 84-2585. (Illus.). 32p. (J). (gr. 3-6). 1985. lib. bdg. 9.49 (*0-8167-0150-4*); pap. text ed. 2.95 (*0-8167-0151-2*) Troll Assocs.

Christopher Columbus. Christopher Columbus. (J). (gr. 1-9). 1992. pap. 2.50 (*0-88388-156-X*) Bellerophon Bks.

Christopher Columbus. Nonie Cox. (Illus.). 48p. (J). (gr. k-1). 1992. pap. 9.95 (*1-55799-240-1*) Evan-Moor Corp.

Christopher Columbus. Jan Gleiter & Kathleen Thompson. (Stories Ser.). (Illus.). 32p. (J). (gr. 2-5). 1986. lib. bdg. 19.97 (*0-8172-2643-5*); pap. text ed. 9.27 (*0-8172-2647-8*) Raintree Steck-V.

*__Christopher Columbus.__ Jan Gleiter & Kathleen Thompson. LC 94-41003. (First Biographies Ser.). (J). 1995. write for info. (*0-8114-8456-4*) Raintree Steck-V.

Christopher Columbus. David Goodnough. LC 78-18052. (Illus.). 48p. (J). (gr. 4-7). 1979. lib. bdg. 10.59 (*0-89375-170-7*); pap. 3.50 (*0-89375-162-6*) Troll Assocs.

Christopher Columbus. Bob Italia. Ed. by Rosemary Walner. LC 90-82621. (Explorers of the Past & Present Ser.). (Illus.). 32p. (J). (gr. 4). 1990. lib. bdg. 11.96 (*0-939179-94-6*) Abdo & Dghtrs.

Christopher Columbus. Ann McGovern. (J). 1992. 4.95 (*0-590-45765-9*, 051) Scholastic Inc.

Christopher Columbus. Lee Morgan & Claudio Solarino. (What Made Them Great Ser.). (Illus.). 104p. (J). (gr. 5-8). 1990. 12.95 (*0-382-09974-5*); pap. 5.95 (*0-382-24001-4*) Silver Burdett Pr.

An Asterisk (*) at the beginning of an entry indicates that the title is appearing in BIP for the first time.

Christopher Columbus. Carol Murphy. (Famous People Ser.). (Illus.). (J). (gr. k-6). 1991. 11.95 (*0-89868-228-2*); pap. 20.00 (*0-89868-229-0*) ARO Pub.

Christopher Columbus. Daniel C. Scavone. LC 92-29499. (Importance of Ser.). (Illus.). 112p. (J). (gr. 5-8). 1992. lib. bdg. 16.95 (*1-56006-034-4*) Lucent Bks.

Christopher Columbus. R. Conrad Stein. LC 91-34744. (Cornerstones of Freedom Ser.). (Illus.). 32p. (J). (gr. 3-6). 1992. lib. bdg. 12.30 (*0-516-04851-1*) Childrens.

Christopher Columbus. R. Conrad Stein. LC 91-34744. (Cornerstones of Freedom Ser.). (Illus.). 32p. (J). (gr. 3-6). 1992. pap. 3.95 (*0-516-44851-X*) Childrens.

Christopher Columbus. Robert Young. Ed. by Bonnie Brook. (Let's Celebrate Ser.). (Illus.). 32p. (J). (gr. k-2). 1990. 4.95 (*0-671-69110-4*); lib. bdg. 6.95 (*0-671-69104-X*) Silver Pr.

Christopher Columbus. Charles Bertin. Tr. & Intro. by William J. Smith. (Illus.). 85p. 1992. reprint ed. 120.00 (*0-937035-24-6*); reprint ed. 750.00 (*0-937035-25-4*) Stone Hse NY.

Christopher Columbus. Gianni Granzotto. Tr. by Stephen Sartarelli. LC 87-40206. (Illus.). 320p. (C). 1992. reprint ed. pap. 12.95 (*0-8061-2100-9*) U of Okla Pr.

Christopher Columbus. Meyer Kayserling. 190p. 1989. reprint ed. pap. 7.95 (*0-9620772-2-4*) Carmi Hse Pr.

Christopher Columbus. Bennie Rhodes. LC 76-5788. (Sower Ser.). (Illus.). (J). (gr. 3-6). 1977. reprint ed. pap. 6.95 (*0-915134-26-8*) Mott Media.

Christopher Columbus: A Great Explorer. Carol Greene. LC 88-37943. (Rookie Biographies Ser.). (Illus.). 48p. (J). (gr. k-3). 1989. lib. bdg. 12.90 (*0-516-04204-1*); pap. 4.95 (*0-516-44204-X*) Childrens.

Christopher Columbus: A Latter-Day Saint Perspective. Arnold K. Garr. 1992. 8.95 (*0-88494-842-0*) Bookcraft Inc.

Christopher Columbus: A Play. Joseph Chiari. LC 78-23741. 79p. 1979. 20.00 (*0-87752-216-2*) Gordian.

Christopher Columbus: A Step Two Book. Stephen Krensky. LC 89-62507. (Step into Reading Bks.). (Illus.). 48p. (Orig.). (J). (gr. 1-3). 1991. pap. 3.50 (*0-679-80369-6*) Random Bks Yng Read.

Christopher Columbus: A Step Two Book. Stephen Krensky. LC 89-62507. (Step into Reading Bks.). (Illus.). 48p. (Orig.). (J). (gr. 1-3). 1991. lib. bdg. 7.99 (*0-679-90369-0*) Random Bks Yng Read.

Christopher Columbus: Admiral of the Ocean Sea. Jim Haskins. (Illus.). 64p. (J). (gr. 2-5). 1991. pap. 2.95 (*0-590-42396-7*) Scholastic Inc.

Christopher Columbus: Admiral of the Sea. Mary P. Osborne. (Yearling Biography Ser.: No. 2). (Orig.). (J). (gr. k-6). 1987. pap. 3.50 (*0-440-41275-7*, YB) Dell.

Christopher Columbus: Being the Life of the Very Magnificent Lord Don Cristobal Colon. Salvador de Madariaga. LC 79-16973. (Illus.). 534p. 1979. reprint ed. text ed. 95.00 (*0-313-22031-X*, MACB, Greenwood Pr) Greenwood.

Christopher Columbus: Expeditions to the New World. Zachary Kent. LC 91-13863. (World's Greatest Explorers Ser.). 128p. (J). (gr. 3 up). 1991. lib. bdg. 20.55 (*0-516-03064-7*); pap. 9.95 (*0-516-43064-5*) Childrens.

Christopher Columbus: Explorer. Norman L. Macht. (Junior World Biographies Ser.). (Illus.). 80p. (J). (gr. 3-6). 1992. lib. bdg. 14.95 (*0-7910-1752-4*) Chelsea Hse.

Christopher Columbus: Explorer. Norman L. Macht. (Junior World Biographies Ser.). (J). (gr. 3-6). 1992. pap. 4.95 (*0-7910-1953-5*) Chelsea Hse.

Christopher Columbus: Four Voyages to the New World. Ed. & Tr. by R. H. Major. (Illus.). 240p. 1992. pap. 9.95 (*0-8065-1337-3*, Citadel Pr) Carol Pub Group.

Christopher Columbus: Great Explorer. David A. Adler. LC 90-28668. (Illus.). 48p. (J). (gr. 2-5). 1991. lib. bdg. 14.95 (*0-8234-0895-7*) Holiday.

Christopher Columbus: Green Sea of Darkness. Gardner Soule. LC 90-48975. (American Cavalcade Ser.). (Illus.). 112p. (J). (gr. 6-10). 1991. lib. bdg. 9.95 (*1-55905-076-4*) Marshall Cavendish.

Christopher Columbus: His Life & Discovery in the Light of His Prophecies. Kay Brigham. LC 90-198425. (Illus.). 174p. (SPA.). 1991. 16.95 (*84-7645-408-2*, 223538, Pub. by Edit Clie SP) TSELF.

Christopher Columbus: How He Did It. Charlotte Yue & David Yue. (Illus.). 144p. (J). (gr. 3-6). 1992. 14.95 (*0-395-52100-9*) HM.

Christopher Columbus: Master of the Atlantic. David A. Thomas. (Illus.). 1992. pap. 34.95 (*0-233-98724-X*, Pub. by A Deutsch UK) Trafalgar.

Christopher Columbus: Mini-Play & Activities. Lawrence Stevens. (World History Ser.). (YA). (gr. 7 up). 1981. 6.50 (*0-89550-344-1*) Stevens & Shea.

Christopher Columbus: Recognizing Stereotypes. Bonnie Szumski. LC 92-19873. (Opposing Viewpoints Juniors Ser.). (Illus.). 32p. (J). (gr. 4-7). 1992. lib. bdg. 11.95 (*0-89908-069-3*) Greenhaven.

Christopher Columbus: The Discovery of the Americas. Clint Twist. LC 93-19017. (Beyond the Horizons Ser.). (J). 1994. lib. bdg. 22.80 (*0-8114-7253-1*) Raintree Steck-V.

Christopher Columbus: The Dream That Changed the World. Ted DeZinno. (Illus.). (J). 1992. pap. 12.50 (*0-9632182-0-4*) McClain.

Christopher Columbus: The Great Adventure & How We Know about It. Delno C. West & Jean M. West. LC 90-936. (Illus.). 144p. (J). (gr. 5-9). 1991. text ed. 15.95 (*0-689-31433-7*, Atheneum Bks Young) S&S Childrens.

Christopher Columbus: Two Civilizations Come Together. Peter Mel. (Illus.). 192p. (Orig.). 1992. pap. 14.92 (*1-882234-03-0*) Heritage CA.

Christopher Columbus a Jew. Brother Nectario. 1992. lib. bdg. 79.95 (*0-8490-5345-5*) Gordon Pr.

Christopher Columbus & His Legacy: Opposing Viewpoints. Ed. by Mary E. Jones. LC 92-18160. (Opposing Viewpoints Ser.). (Illus.). 240p. (YA). (gr. 10 up). 1992. lib. bdg. 19.95 (*0-89908-196-7*); pap. text ed. 11.55 (*0-89908-171-1*) Greenhaven.

Christopher Columbus & the African Holocaust: Slavery & the Rise of European Capitalism. John H. Clarke. 123p. 1992. pap. text ed. write for info. (*1-881316-14-9*) A&B Bks.

Christopher Columbus & the First Voyages to the New World. Steven C. Dodge. Ed. by William H. Goetzmann. (World Explorers Ser.). (Illus.). 112p. (YA). (gr. 5 up). 1991. lib. bdg. 18.95 (*0-7910-1299-9*); pap. 9.95 (*0-7910-1522-X*) Chelsea Hse.

Christopher Columbus & the Great Voyage of Discovery: With a Message from President George Bush. JoAnne B. Weisman & Kenneth M. Deitch. LC 90-81362. (Picture-Book Biography Ser.: Vol. 1). 40p. (J). (gr. k-6). 1990. lib. bdg. 14.95 (*1-878668-00-5*); pap. 7.95 (*1-878668-01-3*) Disc Enter Ltd.

Christopher Columbus & the Portuguese, 1476-1498. Rebecca Catz. LC 93-18141. (Contributions to the Study of World History Ser.: No. 39). 144p. 1993. text ed. 47.95 (*0-313-28867-4*, GM8867, Gotham) Greenwood.

Christopher Columbus Comes to Alabama! Includes Reproducible Activities for Kids! Carole Marsh. (Carole Marsh Alabama Bks.). (Illus.). (J). (gr. 3-12). 1994. lib. bdg. 24.95 (*0-7933-3620-1*); pap. 14.95 (*0-7933-3621-X*); disk 29.95 (*0-7933-3622-8*) Gallopade Pub Group.

Christopher Columbus Comes to Alaska! Includes Reproducible Activities for Kids! Carole Marsh. (Carole Marsh Alaska Bks.). (Illus.). (J). (gr. 3-12). 1994. lib. bdg. 24.95 (*0-7933-3623-6*); pap. 14.95 (*0-7933-3624-4*); disk 29.95 (*0-7933-3625-2*) Gallopade Pub Group.

Christopher Columbus Comes to Arizona! Includes Reproducible Activities for Kids! Carole Marsh. (Carole Marsh Arizona Bks.). (Illus.). (J). (gr. 3-12). 1994. lib. bdg. 24.95 (*0-7933-3626-0*); pap. 14.95 (*0-7933-3627-9*); disk 29.95 (*0-7933-3628-7*) Gallopade Pub Group.

Christopher Columbus Comes to Arkansas! Includes Reproducible Activities for Kids! Carole Marsh. (Carole Marsh Arkansas Bks.). (Illus.). (J). (gr. 3-12). 1994. lib. bdg. 24.95 (*0-7933-3629-5*); pap. 14.95 (*0-7933-3630-9*); disk 29.95 (*0-7933-3631-7*) Gallopade Pub Group.

Christopher Columbus Comes to California! Includes Reproducible Activities for Kids! Carole Marsh. (Carole Marsh California Bks.). (Illus.). (J). (gr. 3-12). 1994. lib. bdg. 24.95 (*0-7933-3632-5*); pap. 14.95 (*0-7933-3633-3*); disk 29.95 (*0-7933-3634-1*) Gallopade Pub Group.

Christopher Columbus Comes to Colorado! Includes Reproducible Activities for Kids! Carole Marsh. (Carole Marsh Colorado Bks.). (Illus.). (J). (gr. 3-12). 1994. lib. bdg. 24.95 (*0-7933-3635-X*); pap. 14.95 (*0-7933-3636-8*); disk 29.95 (*0-7933-3637-6*) Gallopade Pub Group.

Christopher Columbus Comes to Connecticut! Includes Reproducible Activities for Kids! Carole Marsh. (Carole Marsh Connecticut Bks.). (Illus.). (J). (gr. 3-12). 1994. lib. bdg. 24.95 (*0-7933-3638-4*); pap. 14.95 (*0-7933-3639-2*); disk 29.95 (*0-7933-3640-6*) Gallopade Pub Group.

Christopher Columbus Comes to Delaware! Includes Reproducible Activities for Kids! Carole Marsh. (Carole Marsh Delaware Bks.). (Illus.). (J). (gr. 3-12). 1994. lib. bdg. 24.95 (*0-7933-3641-4*); pap. 14.95 (*0-7933-3642-2*); disk 29.95 (*0-7933-3643-0*) Gallopade Pub Group.

Christopher Columbus Comes to Florida! Includes Reproducible Activities for Kids! Carole Marsh. (Carole Marsh Florida Bks.). (Illus.). (J). (gr. 3-12). 1994. lib. bdg. 24.95 (*0-7933-3647-3*); pap. 14.95 (*0-7933-3648-1*); disk 29.95 (*0-7933-3649-X*) Gallopade Pub Group.

Christopher Columbus Comes to Georgia! Includes Reproducible Activities for Kids! Carole Marsh. (Carole Marsh Georgia Bks.). (Illus.). (J). (gr. 3-12). 1994. lib. bdg. 24.95 (*0-7933-3650-3*); pap. 14.95 (*0-7933-3651-1*); disk 29.95 (*0-7933-3652-X*) Gallopade Pub Group.

Christopher Columbus Comes to Hawaii! Includes Reproducible Activities for Kids! Carole Marsh. (Carole Marsh Hawaii Bks.). (Illus.). (J). (gr. 3-12). 1994. lib. bdg. 24.95 (*0-7933-3653-8*); pap. 14.95 (*0-7933-3654-6*); disk 29.95 (*0-7933-3655-4*) Gallopade Pub Group.

Christopher Columbus Comes to Idaho! Includes Reproducible Activities for Kids! Carole Marsh. (Carole Marsh Idaho Bks.). (Illus.). (J). (gr. 3-12). 1994. lib. bdg. 24.95 (*0-7933-3656-2*); pap. 14.95 (*0-7933-3657-0*); disk 29.95 (*0-7933-3658-9*) Gallopade Pub Group.

Christopher Columbus Comes to Illinois! Includes Reproducible Activities for Kids! Carole Marsh. (Carole Marsh Illinois Bks.). (Illus.). (J). (gr. 3-12). 1994. lib. bdg. 24.95 (*0-7933-3659-7*); pap. 14.95 (*0-7933-3660-0*); disk 29.95 (*0-7933-3661-9*) Gallopade Pub Group.

Christopher Columbus Comes to Indiana! Includes Reproducible Activities for Kids! Carole Marsh. (Carole Marsh Indiana Bks.). (Illus.). (J). (gr. 3-12). 1994. lib. bdg. 24.95 (*0-7933-3662-7*); pap. 14.95 (*0-7933-3663-5*); disk 29.95 (*0-7933-3664-3*) Gallopade Pub Group.

Christopher Columbus Comes to Iowa! Includes Reproducible Activities for Kids! Carole Marsh. (Carole Marsh Iowa Bks.). (Illus.). (J). (gr. 3-12). 1994. lib. bdg. 24.95 (*0-7933-3665-1*); pap. 14.95 (*0-7933-3666-X*); disk 29.95 (*0-7933-3667-8*) Gallopade Pub Group.

Christopher Columbus Comes to Kansas! Includes Reproducible Activities for Kids! Carole Marsh. (Carole Marsh Kansas Bks.). (Illus.). (J). (gr. 3-12). 1994. lib. bdg. 24.95 (*0-7933-3668-6*); pap. 14.95 (*0-7933-3669-4*); disk 29.95 (*0-7933-3670-8*) Gallopade Pub Group.

Christopher Columbus Comes to Kentucky! Includes Reproducible Activities for Kids! Carole Marsh. (Carole Marsh Kentucky Bks.). (Illus.). (J). (gr. 3-12). 1994. lib. bdg. 24.95 (*0-7933-3671-6*); pap. 14.95 (*0-7933-3672-4*); disk 29.95 (*0-7933-3673-2*) Gallopade Pub Group.

Christopher Columbus Comes to Louisiana! Includes Reproducible Activities for Kids! Carole Marsh. (Carole Marsh Louisiana Bks.). (Illus.). (J). (gr. 3-12). 1994. lib. bdg. 24.95 (*0-7933-3674-0*); pap. 14.95 (*0-7933-3675-9*); disk 29.95 (*0-7933-3676-7*) Gallopade Pub Group.

Christopher Columbus Comes to Maine! Includes Reproducible Activities for Kids! Carole Marsh. (Carole Marsh Maine Bks.). (Illus.). (J). (gr. 3-12). 1994. lib. bdg. 24.95 (*0-7933-3677-5*); pap. 14.95 (*0-7933-3678-3*); disk 29.95 (*0-7933-3679-1*) Gallopade Pub Group.

Christopher Columbus Comes to Maryland! Includes Reproducible Activities for Kids! Carole Marsh. (Carole Marsh Maryland Bks.). (Illus.). (J). (gr. 3-12). 1994. lib. bdg. 24.95 (*0-7933-3680-5*); pap. 14.95 (*0-7933-3681-3*); disk 29.95 (*0-7933-3682-1*) Gallopade Pub Group.

Christopher Columbus Comes to Massachusetts! Includes Reproducible Activities for Kids! Carole Marsh. (Massachuseets Bks.). (Illus.). (J). (gr. 3-12). 1994. lib. bdg. 24.95 (*0-7933-3683-X*); pap. 14.95 (*0-7933-3684-8*); disk 29.95 (*0-7933-3685-6*) Gallopade Pub Group.

Christopher Columbus Comes to Michigan! Includes Reproducible Activities for Kids! Carole Marsh. (Carole Marsh Michigan Bks.). (Illus.). (J). (gr. 3-12). 1994. lib. bdg. 24.95 (*0-7933-3686-4*); pap. 14.95 (*0-7933-3687-2*); disk 29.95 (*0-7933-3688-0*) Gallopade Pub Group.

Christopher Columbus Comes to Minnesota! Includes Reproducible Activities for Kids! Carole Marsh. (Carole Marsh Minnesota Bks.). (Illus.). (J). (gr. 3-12). 1994. lib. bdg. 24.95 (*0-7933-3689-9*); pap. 14.95 (*0-7933-3690-2*); disk 29.95 (*0-7933-3691-0*) Gallopade Pub Group.

Christopher Columbus Comes to Mississippi! Includes Reproducible Activities for Kids! Carole Marsh. (Carole Marsh Mississippi Bks.). (Illus.). (J). (gr. 3-12). 1994. lib. bdg. 24.95 (*0-7933-3692-9*); pap. 14.95 (*0-7933-3693-7*); disk 29.95 (*0-7933-3694-5*) Gallopade Pub Group.

Christopher Columbus Comes to Missouri! Includes Reproducible Activities for Kids! Carole Marsh. (Carole Marsh Missouri Bks.). (Illus.). (J). (gr. 3-12). 1994. lib. bdg. 24.95 (*0-7933-3695-3*); pap. 14.95 (*0-7933-3696-1*); disk 29.95 (*0-7933-3697-X*) Gallopade Pub Group.

Christopher Columbus Comes to Montana! Includes Reproducible Activities for Kids! Carole Marsh. (Carole Marsh Montana Bks.). (Illus.). (J). (gr. 3-12). 1994. lib. bdg. 24.95 (*0-7933-3698-8*); pap. 14.95 (*0-7933-3699-6*); disk 29.95 (*0-7933-3700-3*) Gallopade Pub Group.

Christopher Columbus Comes to Nebraska! Includes Reproducible Activities for Kids! Carole Marsh. (Carole Marsh Nebraska Bks.). (Illus.). (J). (gr. 3-12). 1994. lib. bdg. 24.95 (*0-7933-3701-1*); pap. 14.95 (*0-7933-3702-X*); disk 29.95 (*0-7933-3703-8*) Gallopade Pub Group.

Christopher Columbus Comes to Nevada! Includes Reproducible Activities for Kids! Carole Marsh. (Carole Marsh Nevada Bks.). (Illus.). (J). (gr. 3-12). 1994. lib. bdg. 24.95 (*0-7933-3704-6*); pap. 14.95 (*0-7933-3705-4*); disk 29.95 (*0-7933-3706-2*) Gallopade Pub Group.

Christopher Columbus Comes to New Hampshire! Includes Reproducible Activities for Kids! Carole Marsh. (Carole Marsh New Hampshire Bks.). (Illus.). (J). (gr. 3-12). 1994. lib. bdg. 24.95 (*0-7933-3707-0*); pap. 14.95 (*0-7933-3708-9*); disk 29.95 (*0-7933-3709-7*) Gallopade Pub Group.

Christopher Columbus Comes to New Jersey! Includes Reproducible Activities for Kids! Carole Marsh. (Carole Marsh New Jersey Bks.). (Illus.). (J). (gr. 3-12). 1994. lib. bdg. 24.95 (*0-7933-3710-0*); pap. 14.95 (*0-7933-3711-9*); disk 29.95 (*0-7933-3712-7*) Gallopade Pub Group.

Christopher Columbus Comes to New Mexico! Includes Reproducible Activities for Kids! Carole Marsh. (Carole Marsh New Mexico Bks.). (Illus.). (J). (gr. 3-12). 1994. lib. bdg. 24.95 (*0-7933-3713-5*); pap. 14.95 (*0-7933-3714-3*); disk 29.95 (*0-7933-3715-1*) Gallopade Pub Group.

Christopher Columbus Comes to New York! Includes Reproducible Activities for Kids! Carole Marsh. (Carole Marsh New York Bks.). (Illus.). (J). (gr. 3-12). 1994. lib. bdg. 24.95 (*0-7933-3716-X*); pap. 14.95 (*0-7933-3717-8*); disk 29.95 (*0-7933-3718-6*) Gallopade Pub Group.

Christopher Columbus Comes to North Carolina! Includes Reproducible Activities for Kids! Carole Marsh. (Carole Marsh North Carolina Bks.). (Illus.). (J). (gr. 3-12). 1994. lib. bdg. 24.95 (*0-7933-3719-4*); pap. 14.95 (*0-7933-3720-8*); disk 29.95 (*0-7933-3721-6*) Gallopade Pub Group.

Christopher Columbus Comes to North Dakota! Includes Reproducible Activities for Kids! Carole Marsh. (Carole Marsh North Dakota Bks.). (Illus.). (J). (gr. 3-12). 1994. lib. bdg. 24.95 (*0-7933-3722-4*); pap. 14.95 (*0-7933-3723-2*); disk 29.95 (*0-7933-3724-0*) Gallopade Pub Group.

Christopher Columbus Comes to Ohio! Includes Reproducible Activities for Kids! Carole Marsh. (Carole Marsh Ohio Bks.). (Illus.). (J). (gr. 3-12). 1994. lib. bdg. 24.95 (*0-7933-3725-9*); pap. 14.95 (*0-7933-3726-7*); disk 29.95 (*0-7933-3727-5*) Gallopade Pub Group.

Christopher Columbus Comes to Oklahoma! Includes Reproducible Activities for Kids! Carole Marsh. (Carole Marsh Oklahoma Bks.). (Illus.). (J). (gr. 3-12). 1994. lib. bdg. 24.95 (*0-7933-3728-3*); pap. 14.95 (*0-7933-3729-1*); disk 29.95 (*0-7933-3730-5*) Gallopade Pub Group.

Christopher Columbus Comes to Oregon! Includes Reproducible Activities for Kids! Carole Marsh. (Oregon Bks.). (Illus.). (J). (gr. 3-12). 1994. lib. bdg. 24.95 (*0-7933-3731-3*); pap. 14.95 (*0-7933-3732-1*); disk 29.95 (*0-7933-3733-X*) Gallopade Pub Group.

Christopher Columbus Comes to Pennsylvania! Includes Reproducible Activities for Kids! Carole Marsh. (Pennsylvania Bks.). (Illus.). (J). (gr. 3-12). 1994. lib. bdg. 24.95 (*0-7933-3734-8*); pap. 14.95 (*0-7933-3735-6*); disk 29.95 (*0-7933-3736-4*) Gallopade Pub Group.

Christopher Columbus Comes to Rhode Island! Includes Reproducible Activities for Kids! Carole Marsh. (Rhode Island Bks.). (Illus.). (J). (gr. 3-12). 1994. lib. bdg. 24.95 (*0-7933-3737-2*); pap. 14.95 (*0-7933-3738-0*); disk 29.95 (*0-7933-3739-9*) Gallopade Pub Group.

Christopher Columbus Comes to South Carolina! Includes Reproducible Activities for Kids! Carole Marsh. (South Carolina Bks.). (Illus.). (J). (gr. 3-12). 1994. lib. bdg. 24.95 (*0-7933-3740-2*); pap. 14.95 (*0-7933-3741-0*); disk 29.95 (*0-7933-3742-9*) Gallopade Pub Group.

Christopher Columbus Comes to South Dakota! Includes Reproducible Activities for Kids! Carole Marsh. (South Dakota Bks.). (Illus.). (J). (gr. 3-12). 1994. lib. bdg. 24.95 (*0-7933-3743-7*); pap. 14.95 (*0-7933-3744-5*); disk 29.95 (*0-7933-3745-3*) Gallopade Pub Group.

Christopher Columbus Comes to Tennessee! Includes Reproducible Activities for Kids! Carole Marsh. (Tennessee Bks.). (Illus.). (J). (gr. 3-12). 1994. lib. bdg. 24.95 (*0-7933-3746-1*); pap. 14.95 (*0-7933-3747-X*); disk 29.95 (*0-7933-3748-8*) Gallopade Pub Group.

Christopher Columbus Comes to Texas! Includes Reproducible Activities for Kids! Carole Marsh. (Texas Bks.). (Illus.). (J). (gr. 3-12). 1994. lib. bdg. 24.95 (*0-7933-3749-6*); pap. 14.95 (*0-7933-3750-X*); disk 29.95 (*0-7933-3751-8*) Gallopade Pub Group.

Christopher Columbus Comes to Utah! Includes Reproducible Activities for Kids! Carole Marsh. (Utah Bks.). (Illus.). (J). (gr. 3-12). 1994. lib. bdg. 24.95 (*0-7933-3752-6*); pap. 14.95 (*0-7933-3753-4*); disk 29.95 (*0-7933-3754-2*) Gallopade Pub Group.

Christopher Columbus Comes to Vermont! Includes Reproducible Activities for Kids! Carole Marsh. (Vermont Bks.). (Illus.). (J). (gr. 3-12). 1994. lib. bdg. 24.95 (*0-7933-3755-0*); pap. 14.95 (*0-7933-3756-9*); disk 29.95 (*0-7933-3757-7*) Gallopade Pub Group.

Christopher Columbus Comes to Virginia! Includes Reproducible Activities for Kids! Carole Marsh. (Virginia Bks.). (Illus.). (J). (gr. 3-12). 1994. lib. bdg. 24.95 (*0-7933-3758-5*); pap. 14.95 (*0-7933-3759-3*); disk 29.95 (*0-7933-3760-7*) Gallopade Pub Group.

Christopher Columbus Comes to Washington! Includes Reproducible Activities for Kids! Carole Marsh. (Washington Bks.). (Illus.). (J). (gr. 3-12). 1994. lib. bdg. 24.95 (*0-7933-3761-5*); pap. 14.95 (*0-7933-3762-3*); disk 29.95 (*0-7933-3763-1*) Gallopade Pub Group.

Christopher Columbus Comes to Washington D. C.! Includes Reproducible Activities for Kids! Carole Marsh. (Washington, D.C. Bks.). (Illus.). (J). (gr. 3-12). 1994. lib. bdg. 24.95 (*0-7933-3644-9*); pap. 14.95 (*0-7933-3645-7*); disk 29.95 (*0-7933-3646-5*) Gallopade Pub Group.

Christopher Columbus Comes to West Virginia! Includes Reproducible Activities for Kids! Carole Marsh. (West Virginia Bks.). (Illus.). (J). (gr. 3-12). 1994. lib. bdg. 24.95 (*0-7933-3764-X*); pap. 14.95 (*0-7933-3765-8*); disk 29.95 (*0-7933-3766-6*) Gallopade Pub Group.

Christopher Columbus Comes to Wisconsin! Includes Reproducible Activities for Kids! Carole Marsh. (Wisconsin Bks.). (Illus.). (J). (gr. 3-12). 1994. lib. bdg. 24.95 (*0-7933-3767-4*); pap. 14.95 (*0-7933-3768-2*); disk 29.95 (*0-7933-3769-0*) Gallopade Pub Group.

Christopher Columbus Comes to Wyoming! Includes Reproducible Activities for Kids! Carole Marsh. (Wyoming Bks.). (Illus.). (J). (gr. 3-12). 1994. lib. bdg. 24.95 (*0-7933-3770-4*); pap. 14.95 (*0-7933-3771-2*); disk 29.95 (*0-7933-3772-0*) Gallopade Pub Group.

Christopher Columbus, Cosmographer: A History of Metrology, Geodesy, Geography, & Exploration from Antiquity to the Columbian Era. Fred F. Kravath. (Illus.). 343p. 1988. 35.00 (*0-910845-32-8*, 530) Landmark Ent.

Christopher Columbus Encyclopedia, 2 vols., Set. Ed. by Silvio A. Bedini. (Illus.). 800p. 1991. 175.00 (*0-13-142662-1*) S&S Trade.

***Christopher Columbus Encyclopedia, Vol. I.** Bedini. 1991. 90.00 (*0-13-142670-2*) P-H.

C

An Asterisk (*) at the beginning of an entry indicates that the title is appearing in BIP for the first time.

*Christopher Columbus Encyclopedia, Vol. II. Bedini. 1991. 90.00 (0-13-142688-5) P-H.

Christopher Columbus: His Story. Lewis Hardee. (Illus.). 62p. (Orig.). 1991. 18.95 (0-88680-362-4); pap. 4.00 (0-88680-353-5) I E Clark.

Christopher Columbus in Philately. David E. Nye. (Illus.). 32p. 1992. pap. 6.00 (0-935991-16-6) Am Topical Assn.

Christopher Columbus in Poetry, History & Art. S. Ryan. 1976. lib. bdg. 250.00 (0-8490-1621-5) Gordon Pr.

Christopher Columbus in World Literature: An Annotated Bibliography. Moses M. Nagy. LC 93-24541. (Reference Library of the Humanities: Vol. 1629). (Illus.). 378p. 1994. 57.00 (0-8153-0927-9, H1629) Garland.

Christopher Columbus, Mariner. Samuel E. Morison. (Illus.). 192p. (YA). (gr. 9-12). 1983. pap. 9.00 (0-452-00992-8, Mer) NAL-Dutton.

Christopher Columbus Paper Dolls. Tom Tierney. (Illus.). 32p. 1992. pap. 3.95 (0-486-27098-X) Dover.

Christopher Columbus Revisited. Lois F. Roets. 32p. 1992. pap. 8.00 (0-911943-25-0) Leadership Pub.

Christopher Columbus's Book of Prophecies: Reproduction of the Original Manuscript with English Translation by Kay Brigham. Christopher Columbus. Tr. & Intro. by Kay Brigham. (Illus.). 286p. (Orig.). 1991. pap. text ed. 15.95 (84-7645-477-5, 223579, Pub. by Edit Clie SP) TSELF.

Christopher Columbus's Jewish Roots. Jane F. Amler. LC 91-16694. 304p. 1993. reprint ed. pap. 19.95 (1-56821-021-3) Aronson.

Christopher Dock. Martin G. Brumbaugh. 1993. reprint ed. lib. bdg. 89.00 (0-7812-5437-X) Rprt Serv.

Christopher Dock: Pioneer Schoolmaster on Skippack. John D. Martin. 1971. pap. 3.85 (0-87813-906-0) Christian Light.

Christopher Dock, Colonial Schoolmaster: The Biography & Writings of Christopher Dock. 2nd ed. Gerald C. Studer. (Illus.). 448p. 1993. pap. 17.95 (0-8361-3644-6) Herald Pr.

Christopher Dresser: A Pioneer of Modern Design. Widar Halen. (Illus.). 224p. (C). 1993. reprint ed. pap. 24.95 (0-7148-2952-8, Pub. by Phaidon Press UK) Chronicle Bks.

Christopher Dresser, 1834-1904. Stuart Durant. (Designer Monographs: No. 1). (Illus.). 144p. (Orig.). 1993. 55.00 (1-85490-145-1, Academy Edits); pap. 38.00 (1-85490-187-7, Academy Edits) St Martin.

*Christopher Durang Vol. 1: 20 Short Plays. Durang. (Contemporary Playwrights). 288p. 1995. pap. 16.95 (1-880399-89-X) Smith & Kraus.

*Christopher Durang Vol. 1: 20 Short Plays. (Contemporary Playwrights Ser.). 288p. 1995. 29.95 (1-57525-023-3) Smith & Kraus.

*Christopher Durang Vol. II: Collected Plays. (Contemporary Playwrights Ser.). 320p. 1996. pap. 16.95 (1-57525-000-4) Smith & Kraus.

*Christopher Durang Vol. II: Collected Plays. (Contemporary Playwrights Ser.). 320p. 1996. 29.95 (1-57525-017-9) Smith & Kraus.

Christopher Durang Explains It All for You. Christopher Durang. 240p. 1990. pap. 12.95 (0-8021-3232-4) Grove-Atltic.

Christopher Fry. Glenda Leeming. (Twayne's English Authors Ser.: No. 479). 200p. (C). 1990. text ed. 22.95 (0-8057-6998-6, Twayne) Macmillan.

Christopher G. Marlowe's Agonists: An Approach to the Ambiguity of His Plays. Fanta. LC 74-143220. (LeBaron Russell Briggs Prize Honors Essays in English Ser.). 68p. 1970. pap. 5.00 (0-674-55060-9) HUP.

Christopher Gadsden & the American Revolution. E. Stanly Godbold & Robert H. Woody. LC 82-6915. 315p. reprint ed. pap. 89.80 (0-7837-3029-2, 2042911) Bks Demand.

Christopher Gist's Journals. Ed. by William A. Darlington. LC 65-27166. 296p. 1971. reprint ed. 31.95 (0-405-03671-X) Ayer.

Christopher Hampton: A Casebook. Robert Gross. LC 89-39317. (Casebooks on Modern Dramatists Ser.). 176p. 1990. 27.00 (0-8240-0690-9, H989) Garland.

Christopher Hampton: An Introduction to His Plays. William J. Free. LC 93-345. (Milford Series: Popular Writers of Today: Popular Writers of Today: Vol. 49). 136p. (C). 1994. lib. bdg. 27.00x (0-8095-5206-X); pap. 17.00x (0-8095-5231-0) Borgo Pr.

Christopher Idone's Summer Salads. Christopher Idone. LC 86-29750. (Illus.). 144p. 1987. 19.95 (0-394-55377-2) Random.

Christopher Isherwood. Carolyn G. Heilbrun. LC 73-126543. (Columbia Essays on Modern Writers Ser.: No. 53). 48p. (Orig.). 1971. pap. text ed. 7.50 (0-231-03257-9) Col U Pr.

Christopher Isherwood. Stephen Wade. LC 90-24556. (Modern Novelists Ser.). 160p. 1992. text ed. 39.95 (0-312-06040-8) St Martin.

Christopher Isherwood: A Bibliography of His Personal Papers. Ed. by James White & William H. White. 1987. pap. 10.95 (0-916092-11-9) Tex Ctr Writers.

Christopher Isherwood: A World in Evening. Kay Ferres. LC 93-343. (Milford Ser.: Popular Writers of Today: Vol. 43). 152p. 1994. lib. bdg. 27.00x (0-8095-5202-7); pap. 17.00x (0-8095-5227-2) Borgo Pr.

Christopher Isherwood: Myth & Anti-Myth. Paul Piazza. LC 77-14271. 1978. text ed. 36.50 (0-231-04118-7) Col U Pr.

Christopher Lee & Peter Cushing & Horror Cinema: A Filmography of Their 22 Collaborations. Mark A. Miller. 480p. 1994. lib. bdg. 45.00 (0-89950-960-6) McFarland & Co.

Christopher Lloyd's Flower Garden. Christopher Lloyd. LC 92-53449. (Illus.). 192p. 1993. 29.95 (1-56458-167-5) Dorling Kindersley.

Christopher Marlowe. John Bakeless. LC 75-42103. (English Literature Ser.: No. 33). (C). 1974. lib. bdg. 75.00 (0-8383-1881-9) M S G Haskell Hse.

Christopher Marlowe. Intro. by Harold Bloom. (Modern Critical Views Ser.). 246p. 1986. 29.95 (0-87754-666-5) Chelsea Hse.

Christopher Marlowe. Thomas Healy. 1990. 40.00 (0-7463-0702-0, Pub. by Northcote UK); pap. 21.00 (0-685-67958-6, Pub. by Northcote UK) St Mut.

Christopher Marlowe. Thomas Healy. (Writers & Their Work Ser.). 96p. 1994. pap. text ed. 11.50 (0-7463-0707-1, Pub. by Northcote House UK) Trans-Atl Phila.

Christopher Marlowe. Roger Sales. 180p. 1991. text ed. 45.00 (0-312-06239-7) St Martin.

Christopher Marlowe: A Concordance to the Works of Christopher Marlowe. Louis Ule. (Elizabethan Concordance Ser.: Vol. 1). xv, 596p. 1979. lib. bdg. 83.20 (3-487-06820-6, Pub. by Georg Olms GW) Lubrecht & Cramer.

Christopher Marlowe: An Annotated Bibliography of Criticism since 1950. Kenneth Friedenreich. LC 79-17646. (Author Bibliographies Ser.: No. 43). 166p. 1979. 20.00 (0-8108-1239-8) Scarecrow.

Christopher Marlowe: Poet for the Stage. Clifford Leech. Ed. by Anne Lancashire. LC 83-45278. (Studies in the Renaissance: No. 11). 1986. 39.50 (0-404-62281-X) AMS Pr.

Christopher Marlowe: The Complete Poems & Translation. Stephen Orgel. (Poetry Library). 1980. pap. 9.95 (0-14-042267-6, Penguin Classics) Viking Penguin.

Christopher Marlowe: The Major Sources. Ed. by Vivien Thomas & William Tydeman. LC 93-34070. 1994. write for info. (0-415-04052-3, Routledge NY) Routledge.

Christopher Marlowe: The Muse's Darling. Charles Norman. LC 70-142471. 1971. 7.50 (0-672-51406-0, Bobbs) Macmillan.

Christopher Marlowe & the New London Theatre. Della Hilton. (C). 1989. text ed. 75.00 (1-85821-003-8, Pub. by Pentland Pr UK) St Mut.

Christopher Marlowe & Theatre of Cruelty & Violence: A Shaping Thought. N. S. Sahu. 240p. 1989. text ed. 30.00 (81-7045-033-0, Pub. by Associated Pub Hse II) Advent Bks Div.

Christopher Marlowe in the Eighties: An Annotated Bibliography of Marlowe Criticism from 1978 Through 1989. Bruce E. Brandt. LC 91-32885. 215p. (C). 1991. lib. bdg. 30.00 (0-933951-45-0) Locust Hill Pr.

Christopher Marlowe Poet & Playwright Studies in Poetical Method. Virginia M. Meehan. LC 74-79321. (De Proprietatibus Litterarum, Ser. Practica: No. 81). 100p. 1974. pap. text ed. 52.35 (90-279-3382-0) Mouton.

Christopher Marlowe 1564-1607. Louis Ule. 1994. 28.95 (0-8062-5028-3) Carlton.

Christopher Marlowe's Doctor Faustus. Intro. by Harold Bloom. (Modern Critical Interpretations Ser.). 160p. 1988. lib. bdg. 29.95 (0-87754-915-X) Chelsea Hse.

Christopher Morley's New York. Christopher Morley. LC 88-81015. (Illus.). xx, 379p. 1988. 19.95 (0-8232-1214-9) Fordham.

Christopher Morley's Philadelphia. Christopher Morley. Ed. by Ken Kalfus. LC 90-80081. (Illus.). xx, 329p. (C). 1993. pap. 15.00 (0-8232-1270-X) Fordham.

Christopher Park. Rosemary Clement. 220p. 1993. 20.00 (1-883285-00-3) Delphinium.

Christopher Park Regulars. Edward Swift. Ed. by Margaret Mirabelli. 192p. 1989. 17.95 (0-945167-16-4) British Amer Pub.

Christopher Pike, 5 vols. Christopher Pike. 1989. Boxed. boxed, pap. 11.80 (0-671-92249-1) PB.

Christopher Pike, 4 vols. Christopher Pike. (YA). 1990. boxed, pap. 11.80 (0-671-96377-5) S&S Trade.

Christopher Priest. Nicholas Ruddick. LC 88-16046. (Starmont Reader's Guide Ser.: Vol. 50). x, 104p. 1989. lib. bdg. 25.00x (1-55742-110-2); pap. 15.00x (1-55742-109-9) Borgo Pr.

Christopher Rich of Drury Lane: The Biography of a Theatre Manager. Paul Sawyer. 142p. (C). 1986. lib. bdg. 34.00 (0-8191-5499-7) U Pr of Amer.

Christopher Robin Gives Pooh a Party. A. A. Milne. (Pooh Jewelry Bks.). (Illus.). 32p. (J). (ps up). 1992. 13.95 (0-525-44871-3, DCB) Dutton Child Bks.

Christopher Robin Gives Pooh a Party. A. A. Milne. (Illus.). 32p. (J). 1993. 4.99 (0-525-45144-7, DCB) Dutton Child Bks.

Christopher Robin Leads an Expotition. A. A. Milne. (Illus.). 32p. (J). 1993. 4.99 (0-525-45142-0, DCB) Dutton Child Bks.

Christopher Samuel Youd: Master of All Genres: A Working Bibliography. 2nd ed. Phil Stephensen-Payne & Gordon Benson, Jr. (Galactic Central Bibliographies Ser.: No. 25). ix, 33p. (C). 1990. lib. bdg. 15.00x (0-8095-4723-6) Borgo Pr.

Christopher Sauers. Stephen Longenecker. 160p. (Orig.). 1981. 14.95 (0-87178-139-5); pap. 8.95 (0-87178-141-7) Brethren.

Christopher Saxton: Elizabethan Map-Maker, Vol. 6. Ifor M. Evans & Heather Lawrence. (Holland Press Cartographica Ser.). xvi, 186p. 1979. 45.00 (0-901869-06-6, Pub. by Holland Press UK) W G Arader.

Christopher Saxton's Sixteenth Century Maps. Christopher Saxton. (Illus.). 96p. 1992. 27.95 (1-85310-354-3, Pub. by Airlife Pub Ltd UK) Voyageur Pr.

*Christopher, the Holy Giant. Tomie DePaola. (Illus.). (J). (ps-3). 1995. pap. 6.95 (0-8234-1169-9) Holiday.

Christopher Unborn. Carlos Fuentes. Tr. by Alfred Mac Adam. 569p. 1989. 22.95 (0-374-12334-9) FS&G.

Christopher Unborn. Carlos Fuentes. LC 90-50296. (Vintage International Ser.). 544p. 1990. pap. 14.00 (0-679-73222-5, Vin) Random.

Christopher Weimann (1946-1988) A Tribute. Ingrid Weimann & Nedim Sonmez. (Illus.). 107p. 1991. 175.00 (0-685-65063-4); 350.00 (0-685-66558-5) Dawsons.

Christopher Williams: Angola to Vietnam. (Illus.). 86p. 1989. pap. 30.00 (90-72191-10-2, Pub. by Imschoot BE) Dist Art Pubs.

Christopher Wilmarth. Laura Rosenstock. (Illus.). 48p. (Orig.). 1989. pap. 9.95 (0-87070-644-6, 0-8109-6084-2) Mus of Modern Art.

Christopher's America on Fifteen to Twenty-Five Dollars a Night: Mid-West States. Bob Christopher & Ellen Christopher. 80p. (Orig.). 1983. pap. 4.95 (0-930570-04-9) Travel Discover.

Christopher's America on Fifteen to Twenty-Five Dollars a Night: Northwest States. Bob Christopher & Ellen Christopher. 80p. (Orig.). 1983. pap. 4.95 (0-930570-06-5) Travel Discover.

Christopher's America on Fifteen to Twenty-Five Dollars a Night Dining & Lodging Guide: Northeast States. Bob Christopher & Ellen Christopher. 80p. (Orig.). 1983. pap. 4.95 (0-930570-02-2) Travel Discover.

Christopher's America on Fifteen to Twenty-Five Dollars a Night Dining & Lodging Guide: Southern States. Bob Christopher & Ellen Christopher. 80p. (Orig.). 1983. pap. 4.95 (0-930570-03-0) Travel Discover.

Christopher's America on Fifteen to Twenty-Five Dollars a Night Dining & Lodging Guide: Southwest States. Bob Christopher & Ellen Christopher. 80p. (Orig.). 1983. pap. 4.95 (0-930570-05-7) Travel Discover.

Christopher's Bed & Breakfast Guide to U. S. & Canada. Bob Christopher & Ellen Christopher. 80p. (Orig.). 1983. pap. 4.95 (0-930570-07-3) Travel Discover.

Christopher's Dream Car. Andreas Greve. (Illus.). 32p. (J). (gr. 1-3). 1991. lib. bdg. 15.95 (1-55037-169-X, Pub. by Annick CN); pap. 5.95 (1-55037-166-5, Pub. by Annick CN) Firefly Bks Ltd.

*Christophers Genealogy: Jeffrey & Christopher Christophers of New London, CT; & Their Descendants. J. R. Totten. 178p. 1994. reprint ed. lib. bdg. 38.00 (0-8328-4307-5); reprint ed. pap. 28.00 (0-8328-4308-3) Higginson Bk Co.

Christopher's Light. Paul J. Leadem. LC 86-60839. 100p. (Orig.). 1986. pap. 7.95 (0-88100-053-1) Natl Writ Pr.

Christopher's Wife. large type ed. Renee Shann. 400p. 1984. 15.95 (0-7089-1119-6) Ulverscroft.

*Christopraxis: A Theology of Action. Edmund Arens. Tr. by John F. Hoffmeyer. LC 95-2302. 1995. write for info. (0-8006-2746-6, Fortress Pr) Augsburg Fortress.

Christos: The Religion of the Future. William Kingsland. 133p. 1992. pap. 14.95 (1-56459-297-9) Kessinger Pub.

Christos, the Religion of the Future. William Kingsland. 123p. 1971. reprint ed. spiral bd. 5.50 (0-7873-0498-0) Mokelumne.

Christowell: A Dartmoor Tale, 3 vols. in 2, Set. Richard D. Blackmore. LC 79-3327. reprint ed. 84.50 (0-404-61783-2) AMS Pr.

Christs & Other Poems. Jack Dann. 1978. 6.00 (0-686-21111-1) Bellevue Pr.

Christ's Appeal for Love. Josefa Menendez. Tr. by L. Keppel. 1975. reprint ed. pap. 5.50 (0-89555-013-X) TAN Bks Pubs.

Christ's Body: Identity, Gender & Society in Late Medieval Writings. Sarah Beckwith. LC 92-39188. 240p. 1993. 65.00 (0-415-04420-0, B0363) Routledge.

Christ's Body: The Good News. Joseph Stefanazzi. 101p. 1991. pap. 8.95 (1-85390-187-3, Pub. by Veritas Publns IE) Ignatius Pr.

Christ's Cabinet. rev. ed. William McIntyre. 143p. 1982. reprint ed. 4.95 (0-86544-017-4) Salv Army Suppl South.

Christ's Comfort for Those Who Sorrow. A. M. Coniaris. 1978. pap. 6.95 (0-937032-00-X) Light&Life Pub Co MN.

Christ's Commandment: "Love One Another"; an Examination of the Biblical Teaching on Unity. Bryan Conway. LC 92-22778. 60p. (Orig.). 1992. pap. text ed. 3.50 (1-880573-07-5) Grace WI.

Christ's Doctrine of the Atonement. George Smeaton. 520p. 1991. text ed. 23.95 (0-85151-600-9) Banner of Truth.

Christ's Eucharistic Presence: A History of the Doctrine. Paul H. Jones. LC 93-2970. (American University Studies: American Literature: Ser. VII, Vol. 157). 264p. (C). 1994. text ed. 48.95 (0-8204-2174-X) P Lang Pubs.

Christ's Hospital of London, 1552-1598: Passing Deed of Pity. Carol K. Manzione. LC 94-16865. 232p. 1995. 37.50 (0-945636-71-7) Susquehanna U Pr.

Christ's Incarnation-"Good Tidings of Great Joy" C. H. Spurgeon. 1978. pap. 3.95 (1-56186-328-9) Pilgrim Pubns.

Christ's Incredible Cross: Coming Back to the Core of Christianity. David S. Kirkwood. 168p. 1992. pap. 7.95 (0-9629625-1-1) Ethnos.

Christ's Life, Our Life. John B. Coburn. LC 77-17172. 112p. 1978. 4.00 (0-8164-0384-8); pap. 4.95 (0-8164-2616-3) Harper SF.

Christ's Lordship & Religious Pluralism. Ed. by Gerald H. Anderson & Thomas F. Stransky. LC 80-25406. 224p. (Orig.). reprint ed. pap. 63.90 (0-7837-5513-9, 2045283) Bks Demand.

Christ's Ministry. Robert Whitelaw. pap. 0.19 (0-87377-098-6) GAM Pubns.

Christ's Object Lessons. large type ed. 1980. pap. 7.95 (0-8280-0044-1, 03364-7) Review & Herald.

Christ's Person & Life-Work in the Theology of Albrecht Ritschl: With Special Attention to Munus Triplex. Gerald W. McCulloh. 234p. (Orig.). (C). 1990. lib. bdg. 49.00 (0-8191-7885-3) U Pr of Amer.

Christ's Three Days in Hell - Case of the Missing Messiah. Alvin B. Kuhn. reprint ed. 8.50 (0-685-71644-9) Mokelumne.

Christ's Three Days in Hell & Case of the Missing Messiah. Alvin B. Kuhn. 70p. reprint ed. spiral bd. 8.50 (0-7873-1188-X) Mokelumne.

Christ's Words from the Cross. Charles H. Spurgeon. (Charles H. Spurgeon Library). 120p. 1981. reprint ed. pap. 5.99 (0-8010-8207-2) Baker Bk.

Christus Faber: The Master-Builder & the House of God. Ben F. Meyer. (Princeton Theological Monograph Ser.: No. 29). (Orig.). 1992. pap. 27.50 (1-55635-014-7) Pickwick.

*Christus Interpres: Die Einheit Von Auslegung Und Verkuendigung in der Lukaserklaerung Des Ambrosius Von Mailand. Thomas Graumann. (Patristische Texte Und Studien Ser.: No. 41). xi, 477p. (GER.). (C). 1994. lib. bdg. 183.10 (3-11-014423-9) De Gruyter.

Christus Mediator. Eric O. Springstead. LC 82-16972. (American Academy of Religion Academy Ser.). 320p. (C). 1983. 27.95 (0-89130-596-3, 01 01 41) Scholars Pr GA.

Christus Praesens: A Reconsideration of Rudolf Bultmann's Christology. James F. Kay. LC 93-38658. 152p. (Orig.). (C). 1994. pap. text ed. 14.99 (0-8028-0131-5) Eerdmans.

Christus und die Caesaren. Bruno Bauer. iv, 387p. 1968. reprint ed. write for info. (0-318-70704-7, Pub. by Georg Olms GW) Lubrecht & Cramer.

Christus Victor. Gustav E. Aulen. 192p. (Orig.). 1969. pap. 10.95 (0-02-083400-4, Collier S&S) S&S Trade.

Christward Way. Flower A. Newhouse. 396p. 1984. pap. 14.00 (0-910378-19-3) Christward.

Christy. Catherine Marshall. 1976. mass mkt. 5.99 (0-380-00141-1) Avon.

*Christy. abr. ed. Catherine Marshall. (Illus.). 160p. (J). (gr. 4-7). 1995. 10.99 (0-8007-1708-2) Revell.

Christy. Catherine Marshall. 1994. reprint ed. lib. bdg. 27.95 (1-56849-309-6) Buccaneer Bks.

Christy Dancing. rev. ed. John Coriolan. LC 83-22665. 224p. 1984. pap. 7.95 (0-912516-87-9) Grey Fox.

Christy Lane's Complete Book of Line Dancing. Christy Lane. LC 94-18038. (Illus.). 160p. 1994. pap. 13.95 (0-87322-719-0, PLAN0719) Human Kinetics.

Christy Mathewson. Norm Macht. (Baseball Legends Ser.). (Illus.). 64p. (J). (gr. 3 up). 1991. lib. bdg. 14.95 (0-7910-1182-8) Chelsea Hse.

Christy Mathewson: A Game-by-Game Profile of a Legendary Pitcher. Ronald A. Mayer. LC 92-50890. (Illus.). 380p. 1993. lib. bdg. 29.95 (0-89950-821-9) McFarland & Co.

Christy's Chance. Bryan Strong & Christine DeVault. Ed. by Mary Nelson. (Illus.). 72p. (J). (gr. 5-8). 1987. pap. text ed. 3.95 (0-941816-33-8) ETR Assocs.

Christy's Choice see World of Christy

Christy's Love see World of Christy

Christy's Magic Glove. Gibbs Davis. (Never Sink Nine Ser.: No. 6). (J). (ps-3). 1992. 3.25 (0-553-15988-7) Bantam.

Christy's Pouting Again. Barbara Linville. (Ark Angel Bks.). (Illus.). 32p. (J). (gr. k-2). 1989. 2.99 (0-87403-627-5, 3891) Standard Pub.

Christy's Senior Year see World of Christy

*Chroma. Derek Jarman. 240p. 1995. 19.95 (0-87951-574-0) Overlook Pr.

Chromatic Hexachord Fantasy: Ut, Re, Mi, Fa, Sol, La for Four Viols. John Bull. Ed. by Walker Cunningham. (Viol Consort Ser.: No. 4). iii, 17p. 1990. 10.00 (1-56571-025-8) PRB Prods.

Chromaticism: Theory & Practice. Howard Boatwright. (Illus.). 300p. (C). 1994. text ed. 56.00 (0-8156-8118-6) Syracuse U Pr.

Chromaticism in the English Madrigal. Kian-Seng Teo. Ed. by John Caldwell. (British Music Theses Ser.). 386p. 1989. 30.00 (0-8240-2044-8) Garland.

Chromatin. Kensal E. Van Holde. (Molecular Biology Ser.). (Illus.). 530p. 1988. 119.00 (0-387-96694-3) Spr-Verlag.

Chromatin: Structure & Function. Alan Wolffe. (Illus.). 224p. 1992. pap. text ed. 37.50 (0-12-761911-9) Acad Pr.

*Chromatin: Structure & Function. Alan Wolffe. (Illus.). 356p. 1995. pap. write for info. (0-12-761913-5) Acad Pr.

*Chromatin: Structure & Function. 2nd ed. Alan Wolffe. (Illus.). 356p. 1995. boxed write for info. (0-12-761912-7) Acad Pr.

Chromatin Structure - DNA Replication - Repair - Gene Ex - Carcino. Teni Boulikas. 1994. write for info. (0-8493-4450-6) CRC Pr.

*Chromatin Structure & Gene Expression. Ed. by Sarah C. Elgin. (Frontiers in Molecular Biology Ser.). (Illus.). 250p. 1995. pap. text ed. 46.00 (0-19-963575-7, IRL Pr) OUP.

*Chromatin Structure & Gene Expression. Ed. by Sarah C. Elgin. (Frontiers in Molecular Biology Ser.). (Illus.). 250p. 1995. bds. 85.00 (0-19-963576-5, IRL Pr) OUP.

Chromatographic Analysis of Alkaloids. Popl et al. (Chromatographic Science Ser.: Vol. 53). 664p. 1990. 195.00 (0-8247-8140-6) Dekker.

Chromatographic Analysis of Pharmaceuticals. Ed. by Adamovics. (Chromatographic Science Ser.: Vol. 49). 688p. 1990. 165.00 (0-8247-7953-3) Dekker.

Chromatographic Analysis of the Environment. 2nd expanded rev. ed. Grob. 736p. 1983. 210.00 (0-8247-1803-8) Dekker.

Chromatographic & Membrane Processes in Biotechnology. Ed. by Carlos A. Costa & Joaquim S. Cabral. 488p. (C). 1991. lib. bdg. 151.50 (0-7923-1417-4) Kluwer Ac.

Chromatographic Chiral Separations. Zief & Crane. (Chromatographic Science Ser.: Vol. 40). 432p. 1988. 170.00 (0-8247-7786-7) Dekker.

An Asterisk (*) at the beginning of an entry indicates that the title is appearing in BIP for the first time.

C

An Asterisk (*) at the beginning of an entry indicates that the title is appearing in BIP for the first time.

1255

Chronic Back Pain: Assessment & Treatment from a Behavioral Rehabilitation Perspective. J. W. Vlaeyen. (Series in Rehabilitation Research: Vol. 1). 280p. 1991. pap. 42.00 (*90-265-1173-6*, Pub. by Swets Pub Serv NE) Taylor & Francis.

Chronic Bronchitis & Emphysema Handbook. Francois Haas & Shelia S. Haas. (Science Editions Ser.). 262p. 1990. pap. text ed. 14.95 (*0-471-62263-X*) Wiley.

Chronic Bronchitis in the 90's, Vol. 58, Supplement 1: Journal: Respiration. Ed. by D. Olivieri & J. A. Nadel. (Illus.). vi, 58p. 1991. pap. 25.75 (*3-8055-5452-4*) S Karger.

Chronic Cannabis Use, Vol. 282. Ed. by Rhea L. Dornbush et al. (Annals Ser.). 430p. 1976. 32.00 (*0-89072-028-2*) NY Acad Sci.

Chronic Childhood Disease: An Introduction to Psychological Theory & Research. Christine Eiser. 125p. (C). 1990. 64.95 (*0-521-38519-9*); pap. 14.95 (*0-685-45257-3*) Cambridge U Pr.

Chronic Constipation. 1991. lib. bdg. 250.00 (*0-8490-5120-7*) Gordon Pr.

Chronic Crisis in Psychological Measurement & Assessment: A Historical Survey. Scott T. Meier. (Illus.). 290p. 1994. text ed. 54.95 (*0-12-488440-7*) Acad Pr.

Chronic Disease & Disability: A Contemporary Rehabilitation Approach to Medical Practice. Hays et al. 1994. 29.95 (*0-939957-46-9*) Demos Vermande.

***Chronic Disease Epidemiology & Control. Ed. by Ross C. Brownson et al. 358p. 1993. pap. 35.00 (*0-87553-214-4*) Am Pub Health.**
Provides practical information intended to support a broad range of chronic disease control activities. The book is designed to serve as a quick reference guide for practicing health professionals who need critical background information for public & professional education & for developing appropriate interventions. Information for each disease is given in a standard format including significance, descriptive epidemiology, risk factors, & prevention & control measures. Contents: current issues; methods in epidemiology; surveillance; intervention methods for control; cardiovascular disease; high blood pressure; elevated blood cholesterol; cancer; chronic lung diseases; tobacco use; diabetes; cirrhosis & other chronic liver diseases; alcohol use; arthritis & other musculoskeletal diseases; neurologic disorders. Nonmembers: $35.00 APHA Members: $24.50 *Publisher Provided Annotation.*

C

Chronic Disease Modelling: Measurement & Evaluation of the Risks of Chronic Disease Processes. Kenneth G. Manton & Eric Stallard. (Charles Griffin Series--Mathematics in Medicine: No. 2). (Illus.). 288p. 1988. 69.00 (*0-19-520617-7*) OUP.

***Chronic Diseases.** Ed. by Marvin Stein & Andrew S. Baum. (Perspectives on Behavioral Medicine Ser.). 352p. 1995. text ed. 55.00 (*0-8058-1855-3*) L Erlbaum Assocs.

Chronic Diseases in the Year Two Thousand Five, Vol. 2: Scenarios on Chronic Non-Specific Lung Diseases 1990-2005 Scenario Report Commissioned by the Steering Committee on Future Health Scenarios. Chronic Diseases Scenario Committee Staff. 245p. (C). 1993. pap. text ed. 70.50 (*0-7923-2354-8*) Kluwer Ac.

Chronic Diseases in the Year 2005, Vol. 1. Chronic Diseases Scenario Committee Staff & A. F. Casparie. (C). 1991. pap. text ed. 64.50 (*0-7923-1377-1*) Kluwer Ac.

***Chronic Diseases in the Year 2005 Vol. 3: Scenarios on Rheumatoid Arthritis 1990-2005 Scenario Report Commissioned by the Steering Committee on Future Health Scenarios.** (Future Health Scenarios Ser.). 271p. (C). 1995. pap. text ed. 80.00 (*0-7923-3367-5*) Kluwer Ac.

Chronic Disorders & the Family. Ed. by Froma Walsh & Carol Anderson. LC 87-31196. (Journal of Psychotherapy & the Family: Vol. 3, No. 3). (Illus.). 183p. 1988. text ed. 37.95 (*0-86656-700-3*); pap. text ed. 19.95 (*0-86656-926-X*) Haworth Pr.

Chronic Ear Disease. Gordon D. Smyth. LC 80-17690. (Monographs in Clinical Otolaryngology: No. 2). (Illus.). 237p. reprint ed. pap. 67.60 (*0-7837-2574-4*, 2042733) Bks Demand.

***Chronic Emotional Fatigue.** Billie J Sahley. (Illus.). 40p. Date not set. pap. text ed. 3.95 (*0-9625914-2-4*) Pain & Stress.

Chronic Encephalitis & Seizures. Frederick Andermann & Theodore Rasmussen. (Illus.). 384p. 1991. text ed. 98.00 (*0-7506-9009-7*) Buttrwrth-Heinemann.

Chronic Epilepsy: Its Prognosis & Management. Ed. by Michael R. Trimble. 1989. text ed. 139.95 (*0-471-92464-4*) Wiley.

Chronic Fatigue: A Resource Guide to Chronic Fatigue Syndrome, Infectious Diseases Syndrome & Musculoskeletal Diseases. 1991. lib. bdg. 250.00 (*0-8490-5109-6*) Gordon Pr.

Chronic Fatigue: Your Complete Exercise Guide. Neil F. Gordon. LC 92-6295. (Cooper Clinic & Research Institute Fitness Ser.). 144p. 1993. pap. 11.95 (*0-87322-393-4*, PGOR0393) Human Kinetics.

Chronic Fatigue & Related Immune Deficiency Syndromes. Ed. by Paul J. Goodnick & Nancy G. Klimas. LC 93-9228. (Progress in Psychiatry Ser.: No. 40). 192p. 1993. text ed. 27.50 (*0-88048-468-3*) Am Psychiatric.

Chronic Fatigue & Tiredness. Susan M. Lark. 234p. 1993. pap. 12.95 (*0-917010-52-3*, Wstchstr Pub Co) Natl Nursing.

Chronic Fatigue Epidemic. 1992. lib. bdg. 250.00 (*0-8490-5240-8*) Gordon Pr.

Chronic Fatigue Story: Medical Cover-Up of the Century. Neenyah Ostrom. 60p. (Orig.). 1989. pap. 6.95 (*0-685-29178-2*) That New Mag.

Chronic Fatigue Syndrome. 1992. lib. bdg. 250.00 (*0-8490-8784-8*) Gordon Pr.

Chronic Fatigue Syndrome. CIBA Foundation Staff. LC 92-48772. (CIBA Foundation Symposia Ser.: No. 173). 357p. 1993. text ed. 72.00 (*0-471-93618-9*) Wiley.

Chronic Fatigue Syndrome. Ed. by David M. Dawson & Thomas D. Sabin. LC 92-49249. 300p. 1993. 71.95 (*0-316-17748-2*) Little.

***Chronic Fatigue Syndrome.** Ed. by Stephen E. Straus. LC 94-14914. (Infectious Disease & Therapy Ser.: Vol. 14). 456p. 1994. 135.00 (*0-8247-9187-8*) Dekker.

Chronic Fatigue Syndrome: A Victim's Guide to Understanding, Treating & Coping with This Debilitating Illness. Gregg C. Fisher et al. 224p. 1989. pap. 10.99 (*0-446-39004-6*) Warner Bks.

Chronic Fatigue Syndrome: How You Can Benefit from Diet, Vitamins, Minerals, Herbs, Exercise, & Other Natural Methods. Michael T. Murray. LC 94-7471. (Getting Well Naturally Ser.). 1994. write for info. (*1-55958-490-4*) Prima Pub.

Chronic Fatigue Syndrome: The Hidden Epidemic. Jesse A. Stoff. 1988. 18.95 (*0-318-40167-3*) Random.

Chronic Fatigue Syndrome: The Hidden Epidemic. Jesse A. Stoff & Charles R. Pellegrino. LC 91-50504. 352p. 1992. reprint ed. pap. 12.00 (*0-06-092260-5*, PL) HarpC.

Chronic Fatigue Syndrome, AIDS, & Immune Dysfunction Disease: The Cause & the Cure. Suzann M. Angelus. (Illus.). 240p. (Orig.). 1994. pap. 15.95 (*0-9640559-9-6*) Symbolic Prods.

Chronic Fatigue Syndrome & the Yeast Connection: A Get-Well Guide for People with this Often Misunderstood Illness & Those Who Care for Them. William C. Crook. (Illus.). 400p. (Orig.). 1992. pap. 14.95 (*0-933478-20-8*) Prof Bks Future Health.

Chronic Fatigue Syndrome Cookbook: Delicious, Wellness-Enhancing Recipes Created Especially for CFS Sufferers. Mary Hale & Chris Miller. LC 93-43775. 1994. 18.95 (*1-55972-220-7*, Birch Ln Pr) Carol Pub Group.

Chronic Fatigue Syndromes: The Limbic Hypothesis. Jay A. Goldstein. LC 92-48706. 234p. 1992. 89.95 (*1-56024-433-X*); pap. 49.95 (*1-56024-904-8*) Haworth Pr.

Chronic Fatigue Unmasked: What You & Your Doctor Should Know about the Adrenal Syndrome, Today's Most Misunderstood, Mistreated & Ignored Health Problem. Gerald E. Poesnecker. 204p. 1994. pap. 12.00 (*0-916285-39-1*) Humanitarian.

Chronic Gastritis-Achlorhydria in the Elderly. Holt. 1993. 161.00 (*0-8493-6970-3*, RC840) CRC Pr.

Chronic Granulocytic Leukemia. Ed. by Michael T. Shaw. LC 81-23356. 264p. 1982. text ed. 69.50 (*0-275-91379-1*, C1379, Praeger Pubs) Greenwood.

Chronic Granulomatous Disease. Ed. by John I. Gallin & Anthony S. Fauci. (Advances in Host Defense Mechanisms Ser.: Vol. 3). 272p. 1983. text ed. 104.00 (*0-89004-825-8*) Raven.

Chronic Hepatitis. Ed. by Y. F. Liaw. 292p. 1987. 106.25 (*0-444-80822-1*) Elsevier.

Chronic Hepatitis: Proceedings of the International Symposium on Problems of Chronic Hepatitis, Montecatini, 1975. International Symposium on Problems of Chronic Hepatitis Staff. Ed. by P. Gentilini. (Illus.). 208p. 1976. 78.50 (*3-8055-2321-1*) S Karger.

Chronic Hyperandrogenic Anovulation. Ed. by H. J. Coelingh-Bennink et al. (Illus.). 200p. (C). 1991. 78.00 (*1-85070-322-1*) Prthnon Pub.

Chronic Illness. 2nd ed. Ilene M. Lubkin. 480p. 1990. boxed 43.75 (*0-86720-430-3*) Jones & Bartlett.

***Chronic Illness: From Experience to Policy.** Ed. by S. Kay Toombs et al. LC 94-30389. (Medical Ethics Ser.). 1995. 27.95 (*0-253-36011-0*) Ind U Pr.

***Chronic Illness: Impact & Interventions.** 3rd ed. Ilene Morof Lubkin. LC 94-37265. (Series in Nursing). 1994. 43.75 (*0-86720-712-4*) Jones & Bartlett.

Chronic Illness & Disability Through the Life Span: Effects on Self & Family. Ed. by Myron G. Eisenberg et al. (Series on Rehabilitation: Vol. 4). 304p. (C). 1984. 29.95 (*0-8261-4180-3*) Springer Pub.

Chronic Illness During Childhood & Adolescence: Psychological Aspects. William T. Garrison & Susan McQuiston. (Developmental Clinical Psychology & Psychiatry Ser.: Vol. 19). 160p. (C). 1989. 37.00 (*0-8039-3332-0*) Sage.

Chronic Illness During Childhood & Adolescence: Psychological Aspects. William T. Garrison & Susan McQuiston. Ed. by Alan E. Kazdin. (Developmental Clinical Psychology & Psychiatry Ser.: Vol. 19). 160p. (C). 1989. pap. 16.95 (*0-8039-3333-9*) Sage.

Chronic Illness in a Health Care Crisis. Sally E. Thorne. (Illus.). 280p. (C). 1993. text ed. 44.00 (*0-8039-4917-0*); pap. text ed. 19.95 (*0-8039-4918-9*) Sage.

Chronic Illness in Children: Its Impact on Child & Family. Georgia Travis. LC 75-185. xviii, 556p. 1976. 62.50 (*0-8047-0893-2*) Stanford U Pr.

Chronic Illness in Young Children. Ed. by D. W. Kaplan. (Journal: Pediatrician: Vol. 15, No. 1-2). (Illus.). 108p. 1988. 58.50 (*3-8055-4813-3*) S Karger.

Chronic Illness Trajectory Frameworks: The Corbin & Strauss Nursing Model. Ed. by Pierre Woog. LC 91-5198. 112p. 1991. 23.50 (*0-8261-8000-0*) Springer Pub.

Chronic Inflammation of the Bronchi: Proceedings of the Gesellschaft fuer Lungen und Atmungsforschung, Bochum, 1969. Societas Europaea Physiologiae Clinicae Respiratoriae Staff. Ed. by W. T. Ulmer. (Progress in Respiration Research Ser.: Vol. 6). 1971. 128.00 (*3-8055-1189-2*) S Karger.

***Chronic Inflammatory Bowel Disease: Proceedings of the Falk Symposium Held in Lubeck, Germany, 4-5, March 1994.** Ed. by E. F. Stange. LC 94-39943. 224p. (C). 1995. lib. bdg. 88.00 (*0-7923-8876-3*) Kluwer Ac.

Chronic Inflation in an Industrializing Economy: The Brazilian Experience. Vincent Parkin. (Illus.). 275p. (C). 1991. 59.95 (*0-521-37540-1*) Cambridge U Pr.

Chronic Inflation in Latin America. Felipe Pazos. LC 71-180848. (Special Studies in International Economics & Development). 1972. 29.50 (*0-275-28282-1*) Irvington.

Chronic Juvenile Offenders: Final Results from the Skillman Aftercare Experiment. Peter W. Greenwood et al. LC 93-40155. 1994. write for info. (*0-8330-1477-3*, MR-220-SKF) Rand Corp.

Chronic Leukemia: Approach to Diagnosis. Harold R. Schumacher & James D. Cotelingam. LC 94-27327. (Illus.). 392p. 1995. 78.50 (*0-89640-220-7*) Igaku-Shoin.

Chronic Liver Disease. Ed. by M. U. Dianzani & P. Gentilini. (Frontiers of Gastrointestinal Research Ser.: Vol. 9). (Illus.). x, 282p. 1986. 157.00 (*3-8055-4205-4*) S Karger.

Chronic Lymphocytic Leukemia. A. Polliack & D. Catovsky. 400p. 1988. text ed. 149.00 (*3-7186-4802-4*) Gordon & Breach.

Chronic Lymphocytic Leukemia: Scientific Advances & Clinical Development. Ed. by Bruce D. Cheson. LC 92-49857. (Basic & Clinical Oncology Ser.: Vol. 1). 440p. 1992. 110.00 (*0-8247-8736-6*) Dekker.

Chronic Mental Illness in Children & Adolescents. John G. Looney. LC 87-1472. 284p. 1987. text ed. 38.50 (*0-88048-236-2*, 0-88048-236-2) Am Psychiatric.

Chronic Mental Patient-II. Ed. by W. Walter Menninger & Gerald Hannah. LC 87-1085. 224p. 1987. text ed. 33.00 (*0-88048-278-8*) Am Psychiatric.

Chronic Mental Patient in a Community Context. Ed. by Ranjit C. Chacko. LC 84-24542. (Clinical Insights Ser.). 96p. reprint ed. pap. 27.40 (*0-8357-7829-0*, 2036203) Bks Demand.

Chronic Mental Patient in the Community. Group for the Advancement of Psychiatry Staff. LC 78-55381. (Group for the Advancement of Psychiatry, Symposium Ser.: Vol. 10, No. 102). 103p. reprint ed. pap. 29.40 (*0-7837-2105-6*, 2042382) Bks Demand.

Chronic Mentally Ill: Treatment, Programs, Systems. Ed. by John Talbott. LC 80-24874. 374p. 1981. 45.95 (*0-87705-086-4*) Human Sci Pr.

Chronic Mercury Toxicity: New Hope Against an Endemic Disease. H. L. Queen. (Doctor's Guide for Lifestyle Counseling Ser.: Vol. 1). (Illus.). 302p. (C). 1988. text ed. 45.00 (*0-9620479-1-0*) Queen Co Hlth Comns.

Chronic Muscle Pain Syndrome. Paul Davidson. 1991. pap. 5.50 (*0-425-12775-3*) Berkley Pub.

Chronic Muscle Pain Syndrome: Understanding & Treating Fibrositis - The Body's Powerful Reaction to Deep Stress. Paul Davidson. LC 89-33981. 1990. 17.95 (*0-394-56860-5*, Villard Bks) Random.

Chronic Myelogenous Leukemia: Molecular Approaches. Deisseroth & Arlinghaus. (Hematology Ser.: Vol. 13). 504p. 1990. 170.00 (*0-8247-8352-2*) Dekker.

Chronic Neurological Disorders. Mary A. Watson & Helen Sinclair. 144p. (Orig.). 1990. text ed. 95.00 (*1-877592-20-X*) GSH&MC.

Chronic Obstructive Lung Disorders. Taussig. 1991. write for info. (*0-8151-8706-8*, Yr Bk Med Pubs) Mosby Yr Bk.

Chronic Obstructive Pulmonary Disease. 118p. (*0-318-62031-6*, 0160) Am Lung Assn.

Chronic Obstructive Pulmonary Disease. Louis Cherniack. (Illus.). 640p. 1990. text ed. 105.00 (*0-7216-2300-X*) Saunders.

Chronic Obstructive Pulmonary Disease. 2nd ed. Petty. (Lung Biology in Health & Disease Ser.: Vol. 28). 512p. 1985. 175.00 (*0-8247-7385-3*) Dekker.

Chronic Obstructive Pulmonary Disease: A Behavioral Perspective. McSweeny & Grant. (Lung Biology in Health & Disease Ser.: Vol. 36). 336p. 1988. 140.00 (*0-8247-7693-3*) Dekker.

Chronic Obstructive Pulmonary Disease: Current Concepts. John E. Hodgkin & Thomas L. Petty. (Illus.). 334p. 1987. pap. text ed. 45.50 (*0-7216-1897-9*) Saunders.

Chronic Pain. 1984. lib. bdg. 79.95 (*0-87700-540-0*) Revisionist Pr.

Chronic Pain. Randal D. France & K. Ranga Krishnan. LC 87-1480. 340p. 1988. text ed. 40.00 (*0-88048-206-0*, 48-206-0) Am Psychiatric.

Chronic Pain, Vol. I. Ed. by Thomas W. Miller. 400p. 1990. 52.50x (*0-8236-0850-6*) Intl Univs Pr.

Chronic Pain, Vol. II. Ed. by Thomas W. Miller. 550p. 1990. 67.50x (*0-8236-0851-4*) Intl Univs Pr.

Chronic Pain: Finding a Life Worth Living. Ed. by Jan Nyberg. 1994. 14.95 (*0-533-10868-3*) Vantage.

Chronic Pain: Its Social Dimensions. Joseph A. Kotarba. LC 82-16851. (Sociological Observations Ser.: No. 13). 224p. reprint ed. pap. 63.90 (*0-8357-8443-6*, 2034707) Bks Demand.

Chronic Pain: Psychosocial Factors in Rehabilitation. 2nd ed. Ed. by Eldon Tunks et al. LC 88-13252. 304p. (C). 1990. lib. bdg. 31.50 (*0-89464-221-9*) Krieger.

Chronic Pain: Reflex Sympathetic Dystrophy - Prevention & Management. Hooshang Hooshmand. LC 92-48334. 1993. 95.00 (*0-8493-8667-5*, RC422) CRC Pr.

***Chronic Pain: The Natural Way of Healing.** Natural. 1995. mass mkt. 4.99 (*0-440-21658-3*) Dell.

Chronic Pain: The Psychotherapeutic Spectrum. Anthony Bellissimo & Eldon Tunks. LC 84-9909. 384p. 1984. text ed. 89.50 (*0-275-91422-4*, C1422, Praeger Pubs) Greenwood.

Chronic Pain & the Family: A Problem-Centered Perspective. R. Roy. (Illus.). 256p. 1989. 32.95 (*0-89885-443-1*) Human Sci Pr.

Chronic Pain Control Workbook. Ellen Mohr-Catalano et al. (Illus.). 216p. 1987. 24.95 (*0-934986-46-0*); pap. 13.95 (*0-934986-45-2*) New Harbinger.

***Chronic Pain in Old Age: An Integrated Biopsychosocial Perspective.** Ed. by Ranjan Roy. 272p. 1995. 50.00 (*0-8020-2859-4*) U of Toronto Pr.

***Chronic Pain in Old Age: An Integrated Biopsychosocial Perspective.** Ed. by Ranjan Roy. 272p. 1995. pap. 19.95 (*0-8020-7359-X*) U of Toronto Pr.

Chronic Pain Patient. P. L. Gildenberg. Ed. by R. A. DeVaul. (Pain & Headache Ser.: Vol. 7). (Illus.). viii, 148p. 1984. 50.50 (*3-8055-3911-8*) S Karger.

Chronic Pain Primer. Ronald P. Pawl. LC 79-22621. (Illus.). 221p. reprint ed. pap. 63.00 (*0-8357-7627-1*, 2056950) Bks Demand.

***CHRONIC PAIN: Taking Command of Our Healing: Understanding the Emotional Trauma Underlying Chronic Pain. William R. B. Anderson & Jesse F. Taylor. (Illus.). 130p. (Orig.). 1995. pap. 10.95 (*0-9642979-0-6*) New Energy Pr.**
Over one hundred & sixty million Americans suffer from chronic pain. Mainstream medical techniques have few weapons in their arsenal to fight this insidious illness. Chronic pain patients are increasingly turning to alternative therapies in search of relief from the relentless & exhausting discomfort. CHRONIC PAIN: TAKING COMMAND OF OUR HEALING focuses on the effect of emotional trauma on chronic pain & suggests ways in which releasing emotional trauma can reduce or eliminate chronic pain. Based on the experiences of William Anderson, Ph.D., a pain management consultant & therapist, the book uses the experiences of Dr. Anderson & his patients to illustrate the types of personality profiles which people with chronic pain seem to fit & provides breathing, visualization, & relaxation exercises to begin the exploration of their pain & ways in which they can take command of their own healing. The book urges a heavy dependence on intuition in selecting therapies & a positive, clear-sighted view of how to deal with this intrusion of pain. *Publisher Provided Annotation.*

Chronic Pancreatitis: Research & Clinical Management. Ed. by H. G. Beger et al. (Illus.). xvi, 574p. 1990. 102.00 (*0-387-52034-1*) Spr-Verlag.

Chronic Physical Illness & Depression among Ethnic Minority Elderly. Janet L. Bell. LC 91-37482. (Studies on Elderly in America). 168p. 1992. 46.00 (*0-8153-0513-3*) Garland.

***Chronic Poverty & Lack of Basic Security: A Report of the Social & Economic Council of France.** Joseph Wresinski. Tr. by New Fourth World Movement Staff. LC 93-74805. 120p. (Orig.). 1994. pap. 10.00 (*0-934199-01-9*, Fourth Wrld Pubns) New Fourth Wrld.

Chronic Problem Wound. Ross Rudolph. 1983. 67.00 (*0-316-76110-9*) Little.

Chronic Progressive Deafness: Resume of World-Wide Publications 1952-1959. Bruce Proctor. LC 63-19171. 758p. pap. 180.00 (*0-685-15701-6*, 2027661) Bks Demand.

Chronic Prostatitis. Ed. by H. R. Brunner et al. 1984. pap. text ed. 154.95 (*0-471-56569-5*) Wiley.

Chronic Psychiatric Patient in the Community: Principles of Treatment. Ed. by I. Barofsky & R. D. Budson. LC 82-7338. 570p. 1983. text ed. 54.95 (*0-88331-117-8*) Luce.

Chronic Psychoses & Recovery: An Experiment in Socio-Environmental Treatment. Richard Sanders et al. LC 67-29135. (Jossey-Bass Behavioral Science Ser.). 368p. reprint ed. 104.90 (*0-8357-9304-4*, 2013912) Bks Demand.

Chronic Pulmonary Hyperinflation. Ed. by A. Grassino et al. (Current Topics in Rehabilitation Ser.). (Illus.). 200p. 1991. 59.00 (*0-387-19662-5*) Spr-Verlag.

Chronic Radiation Hazards: Experimental Study Fast Neutrons. G. Neary & R. Munson. LC 57-14862. 1957. 89.00 (*0-08-009053-2*, Pub. by Pergamon Repr UK) Franklin.

1256 An Asterisk (*) at the beginning of an entry indicates that the title is appearing in BIP for the first time.

An Asterisk (*) at the beginning of an entry indicates that the title is appearing in BIP for the first time.

1257

C

Chronicle of the Cid: El Cid Campeador. Ed. by Robert Southey. 1980. lib. bdg. 59.95 (*0-8490-3171-0*) Gordon Pr.

Chronicle of the Cinema. Ed. by Robyn Karney. (Illus.). 912p. 1994. 54.95 (*1-872031-22-6*) JL Intl Pub.

Chronicle of the Conquest of Granada, 2 Vols. W. Irving. 1986. write for info. (*0-318-62289-0*, Darf Pubs Ltd) St Mut.

Chronicle of the Conquest of Granada, 2 vols., Set. Washington Irving. 1980. lib. bdg. 200.00 (*0-8490-3144-3*) Gordon Pr.

Chronicle of the Conquest of Granada, 2 Vols, Set. Washington Irving. LC 73-120558. reprint ed. 124.50 (*0-404-03532-9*) AMS Pr.

Chronicle of the Conquest of Granada, 2 Vols., Vol. 1. W. Irving. 424p. 1986. 300.00 (*1-85077-107-3*, Darf Pubs Ltd) St Mut.

Chronicle of the Conquest of Granada, 2 Vols., Vol. 2. W. Irving. 432p. 1986. 300.00 (*1-85077-108-1*, Darf Pubs Ltd) St Mut.

Chronicle of the Conquest of Grenada. Ed. by Earl N. Harbert et al. (Works of Washington Irving). 75.00 (*0-685-40582-6*, 434, Twayne) Macmillan.

Chronicle of the First Crusade. Foucher De Chartres. Tr. by Martha E. McGinty. LC 76-29823. reprint ed. 22.50 (*0-404-15417-4*) AMS Pr.

Chronicle of the First Thirteen Years of the Reign of King Edward Fourth. John Warkworth. Ed. by J. O. Halliwell. (Camden Society, London. Publications, First Ser.: No. 10). reprint ed. 27.00 (*0-404-50110-9*) AMS Pr.

Chronicle of the First World War, Vol. II: 1917-1921. Randal Gray & Christopher Argyle. 352p. 1991. lib. bdg. 45.00 (*0-8160-2595-9*) Facts on File.

Chronicle of the First World War, Vol. 1: 1914-1916. Randal Gray & Christopher Argyle. 352p. 1990. 45.00 (*0-8160-2139-2*) Facts on File.

Chronicle of the Grey Friars of London. Ed. by John G. Nichols. (Camden Society, London. Publications, First Ser.: No. 53). reprint ed. 32.50 (*0-404-50153-2*) AMS Pr.

Chronicle of the Hungarians, Vol. 155. Janos Thuroczy. Ed. by Denis Sinor & Emmanuel Mickel. Tr. by Frank Mantello. (Uralic & Altaic Ser. - Mediaevalia Hungarica Subser.). xiv, 225p. 1991. 29.50 (*0-933070-27-6*) Ind U Res Inst.

Chronicle of the Hutterian Brethren, Vol. 1. Kasper Braitmichel et al. Ed. by Hutterian Brethren. LC 87-2464. (Illus.). 968p. 1987. 44.00 (*0-87486-021-0*) Plough.

Chronicle of the Kings of England. William of Malmesbury. Ed. by J. A. Giles. Tr. by J. Sharpe. LC 68-55558. (Bohn's Antiquarian Library). reprint ed. 75.00 (*0-404-50025-0*) AMS Pr.

Chronicle of the Kings of Scotland. John W. MacKenzie. LC 72-1037. (Maitland Club, Glasgow. Publications: No. 8). reprint ed. 18.00 (*0-404-52935-6*) AMS Pr.

Chronicle of the Last Pagans. Pierre Chuvin. Tr. by B. A. Archer. (Revealing Antiquity Ser.: No. 4). 188p. 1990. 29.95 (*0-674-12970-9*) HUP.

Chronicle of the Lodz Ghetto. Lucjan Dobroszycki. LC 84-3614. 565p. 1987. pap. 27.00 (*0-300-03924-7*, Y-637) Yale U Pr.

Chronicle of the Lodz Ghetto, 1941-1944. Ed. by Lucjan Dobroszycki. LC 84-3614. (Illus.). 603p. 1984. 55.00 (*0-300-03208-0*) Yale U Pr.

Chronicle of the Movies. 1991. 19.99 (*0-517-05689-5*, Crescent) Random Hse Value.

Chronicle of the Pharaohs. Peter A. Clayton. LC 94-60269. (Illus.). 224p. 1994. 29.95 (*0-500-05074-0*) Thames Hudson.

Chronicle of the Reign of King Pedro III of Aragon, 2 vols., Set. Bernardo Desclot. Tr. by F. L. Critchlow. LC 79-8360. reprint ed. 75.00 (*0-404-18340-9*) AMS Pr.

***Chronicle of the Roman Emperors.** Chris Scarre. LC 95-60277. (Illus.). 240p. 1995. 29.95 (*0-500-05077-5*) Thames Hudson.

Chronicle of the Royal Family. Chronicle Books Staff. 1993. 59.95 (*1-872031-20-X*) JL Intl Pub.

***Chronicle of the Thupa & the Thupavamsa.** Ed. & Tr. by N. A. Jayawickrama. (Illus.). 320p. (PLI.). (C). 1971. 37.00 (*0-7189-0485-0*) Wisdom MA.

Chronicle of the Twentieth Century. rev. ed. Ed. by Clifton Daniel. (Illus.). 1438p. 1992. 59.95 (*1-872031-02-1*) JL Intl Pub.

***Chronicle of the Worker-Priests.** Ed. & Tr. by Stanley Windass. 1967. 59.50 (*0-614-00163-3*) Elliots Bks.

***Chronicle of the World.** 1200p. Date not set. 59.95 (*0-7894-0334-X*, 6-70520) Dorling Kindersley.

Chronicle of the World. Ed. by Jerome Burne. (Illus.). 1296p. 1993. 59.95 (*1-872031-00-5*) JL Intl Pub.

Chronicle of the World. Ed. by Jerome Burne. 1990. 49.95 (*0-685-34644-7*) P-H.

Chronicle of the Year 1992. Chronicle Books Staff. 1993. 14.95 (*1-872031-75-7*) JL Intl Pub.

Chronicle of the Year 1993. 1994. 14.95 (*1-872031-32-3*) JL Intl Pub.

***Chronicle of the 20th Century.** 1200p. Date not set. 59.95 (*0-7894-0332-3*, 6-70519) Dorling Kindersley.

Chronicle of Twentieth Century Conflict. Neil Grant. LC 92-35674. (Illus.). 400p. 1993. 24.98 (*0-8317-1371-2*) Smithmark.

Chronicle of Western Fashion: From Ancient Times to the Present Day. John Peacock. (Illus.). 224p. 1991. 29.95 (*0-8109-3953-3*) Abrams.

Chronicle of William De Rishanger, of the Barons' Wars. William De Rishanger. Ed. by James O. Halliwell. (Camden Society, London. Publications, First Ser.: No. 15). reprint ed. 50.00 (*0-404-50115-X*) AMS Pr.

Chronicle of World War II. 1994. 59.95 (*1-872031-37-4*) JL Intl Pub.

***Chronicle of 20th Century Murder, Vol. II.** Brian Lane. 288p. 1995. pap. text ed. 7.99 (*0-425-14832-7*) Jove Pubns.

***Chronicle of 20th Century Murder Vol. I.** Brian Lane. 288p. (Orig.). 1995. pap. text ed. 5.99 (*0-425-14649-9*) Berkley Pub.

Chronicle, Together with a Little Romance, Regarding Rudolf & Jacob Naf, of Frankford Pennsylvania, & Their Descendants, Including an Account of the Neffs in Switzerland & America. E. C. Neff. (Illus.). 352p. 1989. reprint ed. lib. bdg. 65.50 (*0-8328-0898-9*); reprint ed. pap. 55.50 (*0-8328-0899-7*) Higginson Bk Co.

Chronicle Two-Year College Databook, 1994-95. rev. ed. Ed. by Paul A. Downes. LC 79-644821. 432p. (YA). (gr. 10-12). 1994. pap. text ed. 22.46 (*1-55631-224-5*) Chron Guide.

***Chronicle Vocational School Manual, 1994-95.** rev. ed. Ed. by Paul A. Downes. 360p. (YA). (gr. 10-12). 1994. pap. text ed. 22.48 (*1-55631-222-9*) Chron Guide.

Chronicle Vocational School Manual, 1994-95. rev. ed. Ed. by Patricia Hammon. LC 82-643014. 360p. 1994. pap. 22.48 (*0-685-73030-1*) Chron Guide.

Chronicler of Barsetshire: A Life of Anthony Trollope. R. H. Super. 544p. 1990. 44.50 (*0-472-10102-1*); pap. 18.95 (*0-472-08139-X*) U of Mich Pr.

Chronicler of Immigrant Life: Svein Nilsson's Articles in Billed-Magazin, 1868-1870. C. A. Clausen & Odd S. Lovoll. (Author's Ser.). (Illus.). 171p. 1982. 15.00 (*0-87732-067-5*) Norwegian-Am Hist Assn.

Chroniclers. (Old West Ser.). (Illus.). 240p. 1976. 19.93 (*0-8094-1531-3*); lib. bdg. 25.93 (*0-8094-1530-5*) Time-Life.

Chronicler's Use of the Deuteronomistic History. Steven L. McKenzie. (Harvard Semitic Monographs: No. 33). (C). 1985. 19.50 (*0-89130-828-8*, 04 00 33) Scholars Pr GA.

Chronicles. Froissart. Tr. by Geoffrey Brereton. (Classics Ser.). 1978. pap. 10.95 (*0-14-044200-6*, Penguin Classics) Viking Penguin.

Chronicles. J. G. McConville. 288p. 1993. pap. 25.00 (*0-7152-0527-7*) St Mut.

Chronicles & Annals of Medieval Ireland & Wales. Kathryn Grabowski & David Dumville. (Studies in Celtic History: Vol. IV). 242p. 1984. 53.00 (*0-85115-167-1*) Boydell & Brewer.

Chronicles & Dispatches. Alfredo N. Salanga. 187p. (Orig.). (C). 1992. pap. 11.00 (*971-10-0391-0*, Pub. by New Day Pub PH) Cellar.

Chronicles & Genealogy of the Jacob Dellinger Family of York County, Pennsylvania. Donald F. Billet & Edward A. Dellinger. 420p. 1993. 40.00 (*0-9638721-0-9*) Billet Pubng.

Chronicles & Memorials of the Reign of Richard I, 2 vols., Set. Ed. by William Stubbs. Incl. Vol. 1. Itinerarium Peregrinorum. 1972. (*0-8115-1090-5*); Vol. 2. Epistolae Cantuarienses, 1187-1199. 1972. (*0-8115-1091-3*); (Rolls Ser.: No. 38). 1972. reprint ed. 120.00 (*0-685-10002-2*) Periodicals Srv.

Chronicles Concerning Early Babylonian Kings, 2 vols., Set. Ed. by Leonard W. King. LC 78-72743. (Ancient Mesopotamian Texts & Studies). reprint ed. 55.00 (*0-404-18185-6*) AMS Pr.

Chronicles Concerning Early Babylonian Kings, Including Records of the Early History of the Kassites & the Country of the Sea. Leonard W. King. 1980. lib. bdg. 195.00 (*0-8490-3170-2*) Gordon Pr.

Chronicles I: Hebrew Text, English Translation & Commentary Digest. Tr. by A. J. Rosenberg. 1992. 17.95 (*0-910818-97-5*) Judaica Pr.

Chronicles I & II. Ed. by A. Cohen. 360p. (HEB.). 1952. 14.95 (*0-900689-37-4*) Soncino Pr.

Chronicles I & II: Critical & Exegetical Commentary. Edward L. Curtis & Albert A. Madsen. Ed. by Samuel R. Driver et al. LC 10-14958. (International Critical Commentary Ser.). 560p. 1910. 39.95 (*0-567-05007-6*, Pub. by T & T Clark UK) Bks Intl VA.

Chronicles I & II: Hebrew Text, English Translation & Commentary Digest. 2nd rev. ed. Ed. by A. J. Rosenberg. LC 93-8763. 1995. 14.95 (*1-871055-85-7*) Soncino Pr.

Chronicles I Diveri Hayamim I: A New Translation With A Commentary from Talmudic, Midrashic & Rabbinic Sources, I. Moshe Eisemann. Ed. by Y. Danziger. (ArtScroll Tanach Ser.). 492p. 1987. 32.95 (*0-89906-091-9*); pap. 25.95 (*0-89906-092-7*) Mesorah Pubns.

Chronicles I Diveri Hayamim I: A New Translation With A Commentary from Talmudic, Midrashic & Rabbinic Sources, II. Moshe Eisemann. Ed. by Y. Danziger. (ArtScroll Tanach Ser.). 492p. 1987. 32.95 (*0-89906-093-5*); pap. 25.95 (*0-89906-094-3*) Mesorah Pubns.

Chronicles II: Hebrew Text, English Translation & Commentary Digest. Tr. by A. J. Rosenberg. 1992. 17.95 (*0-910818-98-3*) Judaica Pr.

Chronicles of a Baby Carriage. F. A. Whitney. (Illus.). 46p. 1993. reprint ed. lib. bdg. 20.00 (*0-8328-3197-2*) Higginson Bk Co.

Chronicles of a Bow Street Police-Office, 2 vols. in 1. Percy Fitzgerald. LC 78-129313. (Criminology, Law Enforcement, & Social Problems Ser.: No. 136). (Illus.). 816p. 1972. reprint ed. 35.00 (*0-87585-136-3*) Patterson Smith.

***Chronicles of a Computer Game Addict: The Ultimate Game.** Terrance Dicks. LC 94-33293. (Arch Book Ser.). (Illus.). 1995. write for info. (*0-8120-9184-1*) Barron.

Chronicles of a Rural Journalist in America. Norbert Blei. (Illus.). 474p. (Orig.). 1990. pap. 11.95 (*0-9626140-3-3*) Door Reminder.

Chronicles of a Second African Trip. George Eastman. Ed. & Intro. by Kenneth M. Cameron. (Illus.). 136p. 1987. 20.00 (*0-9610824-1-0*) FURL.

Chronicles of a Virginia Family: The Klomans of Warrenton. Erasmus H. Kloman, Jr. (Illus.). xvi, 166p. (Orig.). 1991. pap. text ed. 15.50 (*1-55613-452-5*) Heritage Bk.

Chronicles of a Western Family. Phoebe E. DeHart. 113p. (Orig.). Date not set. pap. text ed. 9.95 (*0-685-70946-9*) Writers Pub Serv.

Chronicles of Adam de Salimbene. Ed. by Baird et al. 1986. 33.00 (*0-318-35493-4*) Franciscan Inst.

***Chronicles of Amber, Vol. I.** Roger Zelazny. 480p. 1979. 7.99 (*1-56865-001-9*, GuildAmerica) Dblday Bk Music.

***Chronicles of Amber, Vol. II.** Roger Zelazny. 480p. 1979. 7.99 (*1-56865-002-7*, GuildAmerica) Dblday Bk Music.

Chronicles of an American Home. John S. Coonley. (Illus.). 288p. 1991. reprint ed. 25.00 (*1-55787-079-9*, NY61028) Hrt of the Lakes.

Chronicles of an Old Inn: Or, a Few Words about Gray's Inn. Andree Hope. x, 252p. 1989. reprint ed. lib. bdg. 30.00 (*0-8377-2243-8*) Rothman.

Chronicles of Arkansas. Arthur W. Smith. LC 89-90982. (Illus.). 124p. (Orig.). 1989. pap. 14.95 (*0-9615146-1-2*) Silv Dollar Pr.

Chronicles of Auderlin. Walter Pyne. Ed. by James B. Van Treese. 354p. 1993. pap. 9.95 (*1-56901-003-X*) NW Pub.

Chronicles of Aunt Hilma & Other East Hillside Swedes. Michael Fedo. (Illus.). 128p. 1991. pap. 9.95 (*0-87839-068-5*) North Star.

Chronicles of Aunt Minerva Ann. Joel C. Harris. (Notable American Authors Ser.). 1992. reprint ed. lib. bdg. 75.00 (*0-7812-3021-7*) Rprt Serv.

Chronicles of Aunt Minervy Ann. Joel C. Harris. 1972. reprint ed. 27.00 (*0-8422-8070-7*) Irvington.

Chronicles of Avonlea. Lacy M. Montgomery. 1976. 22.95 (*0-8488-0719-7*) Amereon Ltd.

Chronicles of Avonlea. Lucy M. Montgomery. (J). 1988. 2.95 (*0-553-21378-4*, Bantam Classics) Bantam.

Chronicles of Avonlea. Lucy M. Montgomery. 224p. (YA). 1988. pap. 3.95 (*0-451-52233-8*, Sig Classics) NAL-Dutton.

Chronicles of Border Warfare. Alexander S. Withers. 1989. reprint ed. pap. 14.95 (*0-87012-000-X*) McClain.

Chronicles of Border Warfare; or, a History of the Settlement by the Whites of Northwestern Virginia. Alexander S. Withers. LC 75-146426. (First American Frontier Ser.). 1971. reprint ed. 39.95 (*0-405-02896-2*) Ayer.

Chronicles of Border Warfare: or A History of the Settlement by the Whites, of Northwestern Virginia: And of the Indian Wars & Massacres in That Section of the State; with Reflections, Anecdotes. Alexander S. Withers. 330p. 1993. reprint ed. pap. text ed. 23.00 (*1-55613-781-8*) Heritage Bk.

Chronicles of Border Warfare: Or a History of the Settlement by the Whites, of Northwestern Virginia & of the Indian Wars & Massacres in That Section of the State with Reflections, Anecdotes, etc. Alexander S. Withers. Ed. & Anno. by Reuben G. Thwaites. 467p. 1994. reprint ed. pap. 37.50 (*0-685-75103-1*, 9590) Clearfield Co.

Chronicles of Canada Series, 32 vols., Set. George M. Wrong. (BCL1 - History - Canada Ser.). 1991. reprint ed. lib. bdg. 3,200.00 (*0-7812-6347-6*) Rprt Serv.

Chronicles of Caroltune: Scherzo Finds a Home. Jimm Omodt. Ed. & Illus. by Mary Omodt. 40p. (Orig.). (J). (gr. 3-8). 1993. pap. text ed. 10.00 (*1-881026-05-1*) Scherzo Pub.

Chronicles of Childhood: Recording Your Child's Spiritual Journey. Elisa Morgan. LC 91-61427. 144p. 1991. 12.00 (*0-89109-630-2*) NavPress.

Chronicles of Clovis. Saki, pseud. 176p. 1989. mass mkt. 5.95 (*0-14-018349-3*, Penguin Bks) Viking Penguin.

Chronicles of Colorado. 2nd ed. Ed. by Frederick R. Rinehart. LC 83-62747. (Illus.). 1993. pap. 14.95 (*1-879373-65-3*) R Rinehart.

Chronicles of Core. 3rd ed. Earl L. Core. 1975. 10.00 (*0-87012-227-4*) McClain.

Chronicles of Corporate Change: Management Lessons from AT&T & Its Offspring. Leonard A. Schlesinger et al. LC 86-45555. 272p. 1987. text ed. 35.00 (*0-669-13685-9*) Free Pr.

Chronicles of Darkness. David Ward. 224p. 1989. 57.95 (*0-415-02995-3*, A3208) Routledge.

Chronicles of Dissent. Noam Chomsky & David Barsamian. 416p. (Orig.). 1993. 29.95 (*0-9628838-9-1*); pap. 16.95 (*0-9628838-8-3*) Common Courage.

Chronicles of Drug Discovery, Vol. 3. Ed. by Daniel Lednicer. LC 81-11471. (Illus.). 350p. 1993. 84.95 (*0-8412-2523-0*); pap. 34.95 (*0-8412-2733-0*) Am Chemical.

Chronicles of Faith: The Autobiography of Frederick D. Patterson. Ed. by Martia Goodson. 240p. 1991. 35.00 (*0-8173-0459-2*) U of Ala Pr.

Chronicles of Genghis Grimtoad. Alan Grant et al. 64p. 1990. 8.95 (*1-85400-222-8*) Marvel Entmnt.

Chronicles of Genius & Folly: R. Hoe & Company & the Printing Press As a Service to Democracy. Frank E. Comparato. LC 77-90647. (Illus.). 846p. 1979. 39.95 (*0-911437-00-2*); 24.95 (*0-911437-10-X*) Labyrinthos.

Chronicles of Golden Friars, 3 vols., 1. Joseph S. Le Fanu. Ed. by Devendra P. Varma. LC 76-4178. (Collected Works). 1977. reprint ed. 29.95 (*0-405-09199-0*) Ayer.

Chronicles of Golden Friars, 3 vols., 2. Joseph S. Le Fanu. Ed. by Devendra P. Varma. LC 76-4178. (Collected Works). 1977. reprint ed. 29.95 (*0-405-09200-8*) Ayer.

Chronicles of Golden Friars, 3 vols., 3. Joseph S. Le Fanu. Ed. by Devendra P. Varma. LC 76-4178. (Collected Works). 1977. reprint ed. 29.95 (*0-405-09201-6*) Ayer.

Chronicles of Golden Friars, 3 vols., Set. Joseph S. Le Fanu. Ed. by Devendra P. Varma. LC 76-4178. (Collected Works). 1977. reprint ed. 87.95 (*0-405-09198-2*) Ayer.

Chronicles of Golf: 1457-1857. Alastair J. Johnston & James F. Johnston. (Illus.). 776p. 1993. write for info. (*1-878843-07-9*) Intl Merc OH.

Chronicles of James the First, King of Aragon, 2 vols., Set. Jaime I King Of Aragon. Tr. by John Forster. LC 78-63501. reprint ed. 69.50 (*0-404-17190-7*) AMS Pr.

Chronicles of Jerahmeel. rev. ed. Moses Gaster. 1971. 45.00 (*0-87068-162-1*) Ktav.

Chronicles of King Arthur. Ed. by Andrea Hopkins. (Illus.). 190p. 1994. 25.00 (*0-670-85232-5*, Viking Studio) Studio Bks.

***Chronicles of Lake George: Journeys in War & Peace.** Russell P. Bellico. 416p. 1995. write for info. (*0-935796-62-2*); pap. 29.00 (*0-935796-63-0*) Purple Mnt Pr.

Chronicles of Little Nicholas. Jean-Jacques Sempe. (J). 1992. 15.00 (*0-374-31275-3*) FS&G.

Chronicles of London. Andrew Saint & Gillian Darley. LC 94-9977. 1994. 40.00 (*0-312-12213-6*) St Martin.

Chronicles of Martin Hewitt. Arthur Morrison. LC 74-144165. (Short Story Index Reprint Ser.). 1977. reprint ed. 18.95 (*0-8369-3780-5*) Ayer.

Chronicles of Milwaukee: Being a Narrative History of the Town from Its Earliest Years to the Present. A. C. Wheeler. 310p. 1990. reprint ed. pap. 22.50 (*1-55613-373-1*) Heritage Bk.

Chronicles of Mokelumne Hill. Lirrel Starling. 125p. 1979. 10.00 (*0-686-63645-7*) Byzantine Pr.

Chronicles of Mokelumne Hill II. Lirrel Starling. 150p. 1980. 10.00 (*0-686-64265-1*) Byzantine Pr.

Chronicles of Mokelumne Hill III. Lirrel Starling. 250p. 1983. 10.00 (*0-686-46916-X*) Byzantine Pr.

Chronicles of Narnia, 7 bks., Set. C. S. Lewis. (Illus.). (J). (gr. 3 up). 1994. boxed 105.00 (*0-06-024488-7*); boxed, pap. 27.65 (*0-06-447119-5*, Trophy); boxed, pap. 41.65 (*0-06-440537-0*, Trophy) HarpC Child Bks.

Chronicles of Narnia: The Patterning of a Fantastic World. Colin Manlove. (Masterwork Studies). 160p. 1993. text ed. 22.95 (*0-8057-8800-X*, Twayne); pap. 12.95 (*0-8057-8801-8*, Twayne) Macmillan.

Chronicles of Newgate. Arthur Griffiths. 289p. 1988. 22.95 (*0-317-67844-2*) Dorset Pr.

Chronicles of Notre Dame du Lac. Edward Sorin. Ed. by James T. Connelly. LC 91-51114. (C). 1992. text ed. 18.95 (*0-268-00789-6*) U of Notre Dame Pr.

Chronicles of Pantouflia. Ed. by Andrew Lang. 18.95 (*0-89190-088-8*, Am Repr) Amereon Ltd.

Chronicles of Pennsylvania from the English Revolution to the Peace of Aix-La-Chapelle 1688-1748, 2 Vols, Set. Charles P. Keith. LC 72-102270. (Select Bibliographies Reprint Ser.). 1977. 66.95 (*0-8369-5145-X*) Ayer.

Chronicles of Pern: First Fall. Anne McCaffrey. 1994. mass mkt. 5.99 (*0-345-36899-1*, Del Rey) Ballantine.

Chronicles of Pern: The First Fall. Anne McCaffrey. 1992. 22.00 (*0-345-36898-3*, Del Rey) Ballantine.

Chronicles of Pharmacy, 2 vols., Set. 1977. lib. bdg. 500.00 (*0-8490-1622-3*) Gordon Pr.

***Chronicles of Pride: A Journey of Discovery.** Patricia R. Logie. (Illus.). 196p. 1990. lib. bdg. 27.95x (*1-55059-012-X*, Pub. by Detselig CN) Temeron Bks.

***Chronicles of Pride: A Teacher Resource Guide.** Patricia R. Logie et al. 127p. 1991. 17.95x (*1-55059-027-8*) Temeron Bks.

Chronicles of Quincy Adams Sawyer, Detective. Charles F. Pidgin & J. M. Taylor. LC 75-32774. (Literature of Mystery & Detection Ser.). (Illus.). 1976. reprint ed. 28.95 (*0-405-07893-5*) Ayer.

Chronicles of Solar Pons. August Derleth. LC 73-169744. 1973. 8.95 (*0-87054-005-X*, Mycroft & Moran) Arkham.

Chronicles of St. Mark's Parish, Santee Circuit, & Williamsburg Township, South Carolina, 1731-1885. James M. Burgess. 108p. 1991. reprint ed. pap. 12.50 (*0-89308-458-1*, SC 92) Southern Hist Pr.

Chronicles of St. Tid. Eden Phillpotts. LC 78-132124. (Short Story Index Reprint Ser.). 1977. 20.95 (*0-8369-3681-7*) Ayer.

Chronicles of Tao: The Secret Life of a Taoist Master. Deng Ming-Dao. LC 92-56409. 640p. 1993. pap. 16.00 (*0-06-250219-0*) Harper SF.

Chronicles of the American Dance. Ed. by Paul Magriel. LC 77-25865. (Series in Dance). (Illus.). 1978. reprint ed. lib. bdg. 35.00 (*0-306-77566-2*) Da Capo.

Chronicles of the American Dance: From the Shakers to Martha Graham. Ed. by Paul Magriel. LC 78-9067. (Quality Paperbacks Ser.). (Illus.). 1978. reprint ed. pap. 7.95 (*0-306-80082-9*) Da Capo.

Chronicles of the Big Bend: A Photographic Memoir of Life on the Border. W. D. Smithers. LC 75-16939. (Illus.). 250p. 1976. 19.50 (*0-89052-016-X*) Madrona Pr.

Chronicles of the Cape Fear River. James Sprunt. (Illus.). 732p. 1992. reprint ed. 35.00 (*1-56837-050-4*) Broadfoot.

Chronicles of the Crusades. Geoffroi De Villehardouin & Jean De Joinville. Tr. by Margaret R. Shaw. (Classics Ser.). (Orig.). 1963. pap. 11.95 (*0-14-044124-7*, Penguin Classics) Viking Penguin.

Chronicles of the Crusades. Villehardouin & Joinville. Tr. by M. R. Shaw. 258p. 1985. 14.95 (*0-88029-037-4*) Dorset Pr.

Chronicles of the Crusades. Geoffrey De Vinsauf et al. Tr. by John A. Giles & Thomas Johnes. LC 73-84862. (Bohn's Antiquarian Library). reprint ed. 56.00 (*0-404-50014-5*) AMS Pr.

Chronicles of the Damned. Malcolm Cheney. (Illus.). 160p. (Orig.). 1992. pap. 9.95 (*0-9517700-3-9*, Pub. by Marston Hse UK) Seven Hills Bk.

Chronicles of the Doon Valley: An Environmental Expose. Prem K. Thadhani. (C). 1993. 44.00 (*81-85182-84-1*, Pub. by Indus Pub II) S Asia.

Chronicles of the Episcopal High School in Virginia, 1839-1989. John White. (Illus.). 1989. 25.00 (*0-87233-100-8*) Bauhan.

C

1258 An Asterisk (*) at the beginning of an entry indicates that the title is appearing in BIP for the first time.

C

An Asterisk (*) at the beginning of an entry indicates that the title is appearing in BIP for the first time.

1259

Chronology & Index of the Second World War, 1938-1945. Royal Institute of International Affairs. LC 89-48664. 448p. 1990. text ed. 99.50 (0-313-28072-X, RCQ/, Greenwood Pr) Greenwood.

Chronology & Process of Papermaking, 1876-1990. Joel Munsell. 263p. 1992. pap. 25.00 (0-87556-813-0) Saifer.

Chronology & Recensional Development in the Greek Text of Kings. James D. Shenkel. LC 68-21983. (Semitic Monographs: No. 1). (Illus.). 159p. 1968. 19.95 (0-674-13050-2) HUP.

Chronology, Migration & Drought in Interlacustrine Africa. Ed. by J. B. Webster. LC 78-7050. (Dalhousie African Studies). 345p. 1980. pap. 34.50 (0-8419-0388-3, Africana) Holmes & Meier.

Chronology, Migration & Drought in Interlacustrine Africa. Ed. by J. B. Webster. LC 78-7050. (Dalhousie African Studies). 345p. 1980. 59.50 (0-8419-0377-8, Africana) Holmes & Meier.

Chronology of African American History: Significant Events & People from 1400 to the Present. Ed. by Alton Hornsby, Jr. 570p. 1991. 60.00 (0-8103-7093-X) Gale.

Chronology of African-American History from 1445-1980. Ed. by Henry L. Gates, Jr. (Illus.). 320p. 1993. 29.95 (1-56743-023-6); pap. 16.95 (1-56743-024-4) Amistad Pr.

Chronology of Afro-American History. 2nd ed. Alton Hornsby, Jr. 1996. 60.00 (0-8103-8573-2, 003435) Gale.

Chronology of American Authors of Note. 2nd rev. ed. Comp. by LaVerne H. Ireland. 24p. 1985. pap. 6.00 (0-943932-25-4) Petervin Pr.

Chronology of American Constitutional History & Law. Irving J. Sloan. 54p. 1987. pap. text ed. 7.50 (0-379-20737-0) Oceana.

Chronology of an Oral Tradition: Quest for a Chimera. David P. Henige. LC 86-25673. (Oxford Studies in African Affairs). (Illus.). 278p. 1987. reprint ed. text ed. 69.50 (0-313-25654-3, HECO/, Greenwood Pr) Greenwood.

Chronology of Ancient Nations. Albiruni. Ed. by Edward C. Sachau. xvi, 464p. Date not set. reprint ed. lib. bdg. 90.00 (0-89241-178-3) Caratzas.

Chronology of Ancient Nations: An English Version of the Arab Text of Athar-ul-Bakiya of Albiruni. Al Biruni. Tr. by Edward C. Sachau. (Islam Ser.). 1976. lib. bdg. 59.95 (0-8490-1624-X) Gordon Pr.

***Chronology of Ancient World, 10,000 B.C. to A.D. 799.** H. E. Mellersh. LC 94-30474. 1994. 70.00 (0-13-326422-X) S&S Trade.

Chronology of Business Education in the U. S., 1635-1990. 37p. 1990. write for info. (0-933964-32-3) Natl Busn Ed Assoc.

Chronology of Conflict & Resolution, 1945-1985. John E. Jessup. LC 88-28974. 952p. 1989. text ed. 135.00 (0-313-24308-5, JWP, Greenwood Pr) Greenwood.

Chronology of Eclipses & Comets AD1-1000. D. J. Schove. (Illus.). 356p. 1985. 63.00 (0-85115-406-9) Boydell & Brewer.

Chronology of English Authors of Note. 2nd rev. ed. Comp. by LaVerne H. Ireland. 36p. 1985. pap. 7.00 (0-943932-26-2) Petervin Pr.

Chronology of Florida Post Offices. 2nd ed. Alford G. Bradbury & E. Story Hallock. 100p. 1993. reprint ed. pap. 10.00 (0-9630788-1-X) Sewalls Pt.

Chronology of Geological Thinking from Antiquity to 1899. Susan J. Thompson. LC 88-1493. 328p. 1988. 29.50 (0-8108-2121-4) Scarecrow.

***Chronology of Hispanic American History.** Nicolas Kanellos & Cristelia Perez. LC 95-7903. 1995. 49.95 (0-8103-9200-3) Gale.

Chronology of Indian History. C. Mabel Rickmers. 420p. reprint ed. text ed. 27.50 (0-685-13325-7) Coronet Bks.

Chronology of Irish History since Fifteen Hundred. J. E. Doherty & D. J. Hickey. 352p. (C). 1989. lib. bdg. 52.50 (0-389-20895-7, N8453) B&N Imports.

Chronology of Islamic History. Habib U. Rahman. 256p. (C). 1989. text ed. 45.00 (0-8161-9067-4, Hall Reference) Macmillan.

Chronology of Lope De Vega's Comedies. S. G. Morley & C. Bruerton. (MLA Ser.). 1940. 37.00 (0-527-65200-8) Periodicals Srv.

***Chronology of Municipal History & Election Statistics, Waterville, 1771-1908.** Ed. & Comp. by Clement M. Green. (Illus.). 282p. 1995. reprint ed. lib. bdg. 37.00 (0-8328-4690-2) Higginson Bk Co.

Chronology of Music in the Florentine Theater, 1590-1750. Robert Weaver & Norma Weaver. LC 77-74664. (Detroit Studies in Music Bibliography: No. 38). 421p. 1978. 30.00 (0-911772-83-9) Info Coord.

Chronology of Music in the Florentine Theater, 1751-1800, Vol. 2. Robert L. Weaver & Norma Weaver. (Detroit Studies in Music Bibliography: No. 70). 1993. 60.00 (0-89990-064-X) Info Coord.

Chronology of Native North American History: From Pre-Columbian Times to the Present. Ed. by Duane Champagne. LC 94-18455. 574p. (C). 1994. 59.95 (0-8103-9195-3) Gale.

***Chronology of Noteworthy Events in American Psychology.** Warren R. Street. LC 94-29690. 425p. 1994. 39.95 (1-55798-267-8); pap. text ed. 29.95 (1-55798-261-9) Am Psychol.

Chronology of Nuclear Medicine. Marshall Brucer. Ed. by Robert R. Buntaine. (Illus.). 514p. (C). 1990. lib. bdg. 55.00 (0-9625674-0-X) Heritage MO.

Chronology of Plato's Dialogues. Leonard Brandwood. (Illus.). 240p. (C). 1990. 64.95 (0-521-39000-1) Cambridge U Pr.

Chronology of Postwar British Politics Nineteen Forty-Five to Nineteen Eighty-Six. Geoffrey Foote. 224p. 1988. pap. text ed. 14.95 (0-7099-4922-7, Pub. by Croom Helm UK) Routledge Chapman & Hall.

Chronology of Texas History, Vol. II. Donald W. Whisenhunt. (Illus.). 168p. 1986. 12.95 (0-89015-577-1) Sunbelt Media.

Chronology of the American Indian. rev. ed. (American Indian Dictionary Ser.). (Illus.). 300p. 1984. lib. bdg. 75.00 (0-317-17414-2) Am Indian Pubs.

***Chronology of the American Indian.** rev. ed. (American Indian Dictionary Ser.). (Illus.). 300p. 1984. lib. bdg. 75.00 (0-937862-27-4) Am Indian Pubs.

Chronology of the American Indian: A Guide to Native Peoples of the Western Hemisphere. LC 94-6488. 1994. write for info. (0-403-09949-8) Somerset Pub.

Chronology of the Ancient World. 2nd ed. E. J. Bickerman. (Aspects of Greek & Roman Life Ser.). (Illus.). 260p. 1980. 39.95 (0-8014-1282-X) Cornell U Pr.

Chronology of the Belvidere Delaware Railroad & the Region Through Which It Operated. Warren F. Lee & Catherine T. Lee. (Illus.). 325p. (Orig.). 1988. pap. 19.95 (0-9616893-1-5) Bel-Del Ent.

Chronology of the Bible. Philip Mauro. 1980. lib. bdg. 49.95 (0-8490-3140-0) Gordon Pr.

Chronology of the Bible: Challenge to the Standard Version. Yosef Ben-Jochannan. 16p. 1991. reprint ed. pap. 3.00 (0-933121-28-8) Black Classic.

Chronology of the Death Valley Region in California, 1849-1949, & Place Names of the Death Valley Region in California & Nevada, 1845-1947. T. S. Palmer. LC 88-34098. (West Coast Studies: No. 3). 102p. (C). 1989. reprint ed. lib. bdg. 25.00x (0-89370-837-2); reprint ed. pap. 15.00x (0-89370-937-9) Borgo Pr.

Chronology of the Early Tamils. Sivaraja Pillai. (Illus.). 284p. 1986. 22.00 (0-8364-1713-5, Pub. by Manohar II) S Asia.

***Chronology of the Expanding World, 1492 to 1762.** Williams Neville. LC 94-30476. 1994. 75.00 (0-13-326406-8) S&S Trade.

Chronology of the Extant Plays of Euripides. Grace H. Macurdy. LC 68-936. (Studies in Drama: No. 39). 1969. reprint ed. lib. bdg. 44.95 (0-8383-0590-3) M S G Haskell Hse.

Chronology of the Federal Emergency Relief Administration: May 12, 1933 to December 31, 1935. Doris Carothers. LC 70-165681. (Research Monograph Ser.: Vol. 6). 1971. reprint ed. lib. bdg. 19.50 (0-306-70338-6) Da Capo.

Chronology of the Great War. Ed. by Edward Gleichen. 816p. 50.00 (1-85367-012-X, 5483) Stackpole.

Chronology of the Larsa Dynasty. Ettalene M. Grice. Bd. with Pt. 1 Ettalene M. Grice. LC 80-21416.; Patesis of the Ur Dynasty, Pt 2. Clarence E. Kelser. LC 80-21416.; Old Babylonian Version of the Gilgamesh Epic on the Basis of Recently Discovered Texts Pt. 3. Morris Jastrow & Albert T. Clay. LC 80-21416. LC 80-21416. (Yale Oriental Series: Researches). (C). 1979. 37.50 (0-404-60274-6) AMS Pr.

***Chronology of the Medieval World, 800 to 1491.** R. L. Storey. LC 94-30475. 1994. 75.00 (0-13-326465-3) S&S Trade.

***Chronology of the Modern World, 1763-1992.** 8th ed. Neville Williams & P. J. Waller. LC 94-30477. 1994. 90.00 (0-13-326695-8) S&S Trade.

Chronology of the North Indian Kings. Rai G. Prasad. 1990. 46.00 (81-7186-003-6, Pub. by Agam II) S Asia.

Chronology of the People's Republic of China, 1970-1979. Peter P. Cheng. LC 84-20231. 629p. 1984. 57.50 (0-8108-1751-9) Scarecrow.

Chronology of the Plays of D. Pedro Calderon de la Barca. Harry W. Hilborn. 1980. lib. bdg. 55.00 (0-8490-3188-5) Gordon Pr.

Chronology of the Public Ministry of Jesus. George Ogg. 1980. lib. bdg. 75.00 (0-8490-3142-7) Gordon Pr.

Chronology of the Spanish Civil War & Its Origins. J. Viadiu & P. Vallina. 1972. 250.00 (0-87700-129-4) Revisionist Pr.

Chronology of the War at Sea, 1939-1945: The Naval History of World War Two. Jurgen Rohwer & Gerhard Hummelchen. 416p. 1992. 55.00 (1-55750-105-X) Naval Inst Pr.

Chronology of the Works of Guillaume Dufay. Charles Hamm. LC 83-18991. (Music Reprint Ser.). 192p. 1986. reprint ed. lib. bdg. 25.00 (0-306-76225-0) Da Capo.

Chronology of Twentieth-Century Eastern European History. Ed. by Gregory C. Ference. 475p. 1994. 59.95 (0-8103-8879-0, 101534) Gale.

Chronology of Women's History. Kirstin Olsen. LC 93-50542. 528p. 1994. text ed. 39.95 (0-313-28803-8) Greenwood.

Chronology Papers. Walter R. Dolen. LC 89-85605. (Becoming-One Papers: Ser. 5000, Vol. 5). (Illus.). xii, 188p. 1989. 29.95 (1-877981-00-1); pap. 22.00 (1-877981-07-9) Becoming-One.

Chronology to Irish History to Nineteen Seventy-Six: A Companion to Irish History, Part 1. Ed. by T. W. Moody et al. (New History of Ireland Ser.: No. 8). (Illus.). 1983. 130.00 (0-19-821744-7) OUP.

Chronometer Makers of the World. Tony Mercer. (Illus.). 291p. 1991. 75.00 (0-7198-0240-7, Pub. by NAG Press UK) Antique Collect.

Chronometric Exploration of Mind. Michael I. Posner. (Illus.). 288p. 1986. reprint ed. pap. 19.95 (0-19-503999-8) OUP.

Chronopharmacology: Cellular & Biomedical Interactions. Lemmer. (Cellular Clocks Ser.: Vol. 3). 744p. 1989. 215.00 (0-8247-8103-1) Dekker.

Chronopharmacology: Proceedings of the International Congress of Pharmacology, 7th, Paris, 1978. International Congress of Pharmacology Staff. Ed. by Alain Reinberg & Franz Halberg. (Illus.). 1979. 96.00 (0-08-023215-9, Pergamon Pr) Elsevier.

Chronopharmacology in Therapy of the Epilepsies. F. E. Dreifuss et al. 204p. 1990. 105.00 (0-88167-626-8) Raven.

Chronos, Kairos, Christos: Nativity & Chronological Studies Presented to Jack Finegan. Ed. by Jerry Vardaman & Edwin M. Yamauchi. LC 89-34759. xxiii, 240p. 1989. text ed. 27.50 (0-931464-50-1) Eisenbrauns.

Chronosequence. Hilbert Schenck. 1990. pap. 3.95 (0-8125-0320-1) Tor Bks.

Chronotypes: The Construction of Time. Ed. by John Bender & David E. Wellbery. 276p. 1991. 39.50 (0-8047-1910-1); pap. 13.95 (0-8047-1912-8) Stanford U Pr.

***Chrsitian Labor & the Politics of Frustration in Imperial Germany.** Eric D. Brose. LC 83-25172. reprint ed. pap. 119.70 (0-7837-9190-9, 2049891) Bks Demand.

Chrysal: Or, the Adventures of a Guinea. Montague R. James. Ed. by R. Reginald & Douglas Menville. LC 75-46228. (Supernatural & Occult Fiction Ser.). (Illus.). 1976. reprint ed. lib. bdg. 50.95 (0-405-08142-1) Ayer.

Chrysalids. John Wyndham. 208p. 1993. 3.95 (0-7867-0041-6) Carroll & Graf.

Chrysalids. large type ed. John Wyndham. (Classics Ser.). 304p. 1983. 23.95 (0-7089-8131-3, Trail West Pubs) Ulverscroft.

Chrysalis. Aicha Lemsine. Tr. by Dorothy S. Blair. 189p. 1993. 19.95 (0-7043-7034-4, Pub. by Quartet UK) Interlink Pub.

Chrysalis. large type ed. Phyllis Demaine. (Linford Romance Library). 272p. 1992. pap. 14.95 (0-7089-7274-8, Trailtree Bookshop) Ulverscroft.

Chrysalis: Nurturing Creative & Independent Thought in Children. Micki McKisson. (Illus.). 225p. (Orig.). (J). (gr. 4-12). 1983. pap. text ed. 29.95 (0-913705-19-5) Zephyr Pr AZ.

Chrysalis: Willa Cather in Pittsburgh, 1896-1906. Kathleen D. Byrne & Richard C. Snyder. LC 80-80284. (Illus.). 160p. 1982. 14.95 (0-936340-00-2) Hist Soc West PA.

Chrysalis I. Ed. by Roy Torgeson. 288p. (Orig.). 1980. pap. 1.95 (0-89083-629-9) Zebra.

Chrysalis II. Ed. by Roy Torgeson. (Orig.). 1978. pap. 1.95 (0-89083-381-8) Zebra.

Chrysalis III. Ed. by Roy Torgeson. (Orig.). 1978. pap. 1.95 (0-89083-432-6) Zebra.

Chrysalis IV. Ed. by Roy Torgeson. (Orig.). 1979. pap. 1.95 (0-89083-449-0) Zebra.

Chrysalis IX. Ed. by Roy Torgeson. 1982. pap. 2.50 (0-8217-1077-X) Zebra.

Chrysalis V. Ed. by Roy Torgeson. (Orig.). 1979. pap. 1.95 (0-89083-518-7) Zebra.

Chrysalis VI. Ed. by Roy Torgeson. (Orig.). 1980. pap. 1.95 (0-89083-567-5) Zebra.

Chrysalis VII. Ed. by Roy Torgeson. (Orig.). 1980. pap. 1.95 (0-89083-575-6) Zebra.

Chrysalis VIII. Ed. by Roy Torgeson. 1982. pap. 2.50 (0-89083-959-X) Zebra.

Chrysanthemum. Kevin Henkes. LC 90-39803. (Illus.). 32p. (J). (ps up). 1991. 13.95 (0-688-09699-9); lib. bdg. 13.88 (0-688-09700-6) Greenwillow.

Chrysanthemum & the Eagle: The Future of U. S.-Japan Relations. Ryuzo Sato. LC 93-33592. 220p. 1994. 35.00 (0-8147-7971-9) NYU Pr.

***Chrysanthemum & the Eagle: The Future of U. S.-Japan Relations.** Ryuzo Sato. 220p. 1995. pap. 16.95 (0-8147-8021-0) NYU Pr.

Chrysanthemum & the Sword: Patterns of Japanese Culture. Ruth Benedict. 1989. pap. 11.95 (0-395-50075-3) HM.

Chrysanthemum Chain. large type ed. James Melville. 370p. 1982. 21.95 (0-7089-0758-X) Ulverscroft.

***Chrysanthemums: The Complete Guide.** Baden Locke. (Illus.). 192p. 1995. pap. 19.95 (1-85223-890-9, Pub. by Crowood Pr UK) Trafalgar.

Chrysanthemums & Thorns: The Untold Story of Modern Japan. Edwin Reingold. (Illus.). 384p. 1994. pap. 14.95 (0-312-10440-5) St Martin.

Chrysanthemums & Thorns: The Untold Story of Modern Japan. Edwin M. Reingold. (Illus.). 384p. 1992. 24.95 (0-312-08160-X) St Martin.

Chrysidid Wasps of the World. Lynn S. Kimsey & Richard M. Bohart. (Illus.). 664p. 1991. 140.00 (0-19-854010-8) OUP.

Chrysippe et L'ancien Stoicisme. E. Brehier. 300p. (FRE.). 1971. pap. text ed. 82.00 (0-677-50605-8) Gordon & Breach.

Chrysler & Imperial, 1946-1975: The Classic Postwar Years. Richard M. Langworth. LC 92-33788. (MBI Ser.). (Illus.). 200p. 1993. 24.95 (0-87938-728-9) Motorbooks Intl.

Chrysler Art Museum of Provincetown, Inaugural Exhibition. Bertina S. Manning. (Illus.). 115p. 1958. pap. 7.50 (0-940744-00-7) Chrysler Museum.

Chrysler Building. Paul Bentel. (Illus.). Date not set. 50.00 (0-910413-89-4); pap. 35.00 (1-878271-24-5) Princeton Arch.

***Chrysler Compact, 1987-95.** Ed. by Chilton Staff. 704p. 1995. pap. 21.95 (0-8019-8673-7) Chilton.

***Chrysler Compact, 1987-95.** Ed. by Chilton Staff. 448p. 1995. pap. 16.95 (0-8019-8678-8) Chilton.

***Chrysler Corp. A Report on the Company's Environmental Policies & Practices.** (Illus.). 50p. (C). 1994. reprint ed. pap. text ed. 200.00x (0-7881-0912-X, Coun on Econ) Diane Pub.

***Chrysler Engine Control Systems Manual 1983-1992.** Target Training Systems, Inc. Staff. 592p. 1995. 110.00 (1-887023-01-1) Target Trning.

Chrysler Engine Swapping. R. M. Clarke. (Brooklands Bks.). (Illus.). 128p. 1993. pap. 16.95 (1-85520-190-9) Motorbooks Intl.

Chrysler Front Wheel Drive 1981-92. 832p. 1992. pap. 21.95 (0-8019-8267-7) Chilton.

Chrysler Fuel Injection Systems: Diagnosis & Repair. David Cadden. 312p. (Orig.). 1992. student ed 39.95 (1-881483-02-9) HyperGraphics.

Chrysler Full Size Front Wheel Drive 1988-93. (Haynes Automotive Repair Manual Ser.). (Illus.). 324p. 1993. pap. text ed. 16.95 (1-56392-058-1, Pub. by J H Haynes & Co UK) Motorbooks Intl.

Chrysler Hemi. R. M. Clarke. (Muscle Car & High Powered Engines Ser.). (Illus.). 100p. 1991. pap. 16.95 (1-85520-101-1, Pub. by Brooklands Bks UK) Motorbooks Intl.

Chrysler LWD 81-92. Chilton Automotives Editorial Staff. 432p. 1993. pap. 16.95 (0-8019-8367-3) Chilton.

***Chrysler Mid-Size, 1981-95.** Ed. by Chilton Staff. 800p. 1995. pap. 21.95 (0-8019-8672-9) Chilton.

***Chrysler Mid-Size, 1981-95.** Ed. by Chilton Staff. 448p. 1995. pap. 16.95 (0-8019-8677-X) Chilton.

Chrysler Muscle Cars. Mike Mueller. LC 93-13064. (Enthusiast Color Ser.). 1993. pap. 12.95 (0-87938-817-X) Motorbooks Intl.

Chrysler Museum: Handbook of the European & American Collections, Selected Paintings, Sculpture & Drawings. Jefferson C. Harrison, Jr. LC 90-86394. (Illus.). 216p. 1991. 35.00 (0-940744-62-7); pap. 25.00 (0-940744-59-7) Chrysler Museum.

Chrysler Museum: Selections from the Permenant Collection. LC 81-71918. (Illus.). 168p. 1982. pap. 10.00 (0-940744-37-6) Chrysler Museum.

Chrysler Repair Manual 1988-92: Jumbo Maxi Manual. 736p. 1992. pap. 19.95 (0-8019-8320-7) Chilton.

Chrysler 3.5-140 hp, 66-84. 1991. 32.95 (0-89287-551-8, B-750) Intertec Pub.

Chrysler 350 & 400. R. M. Clarke. (Muscle Car & High Powered Engines Ser.). (Illus.). 100p. 1991. pap. 16.95 (1-85520-096-1, Pub. by Brooklands Bks UK) Motorbooks Intl.

Chrysobalanaceae. Ghillean T. Prance. LC 70-180014. (Flora Neotropica Monograph Ser.: No. 9). (Illus.). 410p. (Orig.). 1972. pap. 27.95 (0-89327-292-2) NY Botanical.

Chrysobalanaceae. Ghillean T. Prance. (Flora Neotropica Monographs: No. 9S). (Illus.). 268p. (Orig.). 1989. pap. text ed. 50.00 (0-89327-338-4) NY Botanical.

Chrysophyte Algae: Ecology, Phylogeny & Development. Ed. by Craig D. Sandgren et al. (Illus.). 304p. (C). 1995. 79.95 (0-521-46260-6) Cambridge U Pr.

Chrysophytes: Aspects & Problems. Ed. by Jorgen Kristiansen & Robert A. Andersen. (Illus.). 320p. 1986. 94.95 (0-521-32090-9) Cambridge U Pr.

Chrysophytes. Development & Perspectives: Proceedings of the 2nd International Chrysophyte Symposia Berlin, August 1987. Ed. by J. Kristiansen et al. (Nova Hedwigia Beiheft Ser.: No. 95). (Illus.). 288p. 1989. pap. text ed. 137.00 (3-443-51017-5, Pub. by Cramer GW) Lubrecht & Cramer.

Chrysostome, Severien, Proclus, Hesychius et Alii Patrisique et Hagiographie Grecques. Michel Aubineau. (Collected Studies: No. CS276). 380p. (C). 1988. reprint ed. lib. bdg. 124.95 (0-86078-224-7, Pub. by Variorum UK) Ashgate Pub Co.

Chrysostomus - Indices Chrysostomici, Vol. I: Lettres a Olympias. Lettre d'Exil. Sur La Providence De Dieu. Chrysostomus. Ed. by A. M. Malingrey. (Alpha-Omega, Reihe A Ser.: Vol. XXXI). xv, 462p. (GER.). 1978. write for info. (3-487-06635-1, Pub. by Georg Olms GW) Lubrecht & Cramer.

Chrysostomus - Indices Chrysostomici, Vol. II: De Sacerdotio. Chrysostomus. Ed. by A. M. Malingrey. (Alpha-Omega, Reihe A Ser.: Vol. XXXI). x, 330p. (GER.). 1988. write for info. (3-487-06636-X, Pub. by Georg Olms GW) Lubrecht & Cramer.

***Chto Emu Gekuba.** Alexey Kovalev. 172p. (Orig.). (RUS.). 1991. pap. 12.00 (1-880247-00-3) Clio & Co.

Chu Hsi: Life & Thought. Wing-tsit Chan. LC 86-6683. 250p. 1987. text ed. 39.95 (0-312-13470-3) St Martin.

Chu Hsi: New Studies. Wing-tsit Chan. LC 89-4799. 592p. 1989. text ed. 40.00 (0-8248-1201-8) UH Pr.

Chu Hsi & His Masters: An Introduction to Chu Hsi & the Sung School of Chinese Philosophy. Joseph P. Bruce. 1973. lib. bdg. 250.00 (0-87968-078-4) Krishna Pr.

Chu Hsi & His Masters, An Introduction to Chu Hsi & the Sung School of Chinese Philosophy. Joseph P. Bruce. LC 78-38050. (China Classic & Contemporary Works in Reprint Ser.). reprint ed. 42.50 (0-404-56904-8) AMS Pr.

Chu Hsi & Neo-Confucianism. Ed. by Wing-Tsit Chan. LC 85-24532. (Illus.). 672p. 1986. 30.00 (0-8248-0961-0) UH Pr.

Chu Hsi & the Ta-hsueh: Neo-Confucian Reflection on the Confucian Canon. Daniel K. Gardner. (East Asian Monographs: No. 118). 300p. 1986. 20.00 (0-674-13065-0) HUP.

Chu Hsi's Family Rituals: A Twelfth-Century Chinese Manual for the Performance of Cappings, Weddings, Funerals & Ancestral Rites. Tr. by Patricia B. Ebrey. (Library of Asian Translations). (Illus.). 276p. 1991. text ed. 45.00 (0-691-03149-5) Princeton U Pr.

***Chu Kinh Thuong Tung.** Chan Nhu & Thich Nu. LC 94-72617. 420p. (VIE.). 1995. text ed. write for info. (0-9645062-0-3) CCN Buddhist.

Chu-Shu-Chi-Nien As a Source to the Social History of Ancient China. LC 79-2822. 101p. 1988. reprint ed. 17.00 (0-8305-0002-2) Hyperion Conn.

Chuang Tsu - Inner Chapters. Chuang Tsu. Ed. by Gia-Fu Feng. Tr. by Jane English. (Giant Ser.). 1974. pap. 19.00 (0-394-71990-5, V-990, Vin) Random.

Chuang-Tzu: A New Selected Translation with an Exposition of the Philosophy of Kuo Hsiang. Yu-lan Fung. 1975. lib. bdg. 250.00 (0-87968-187-X) Krishna Pr.

An Asterisk (*) at the beginning of an entry indicates that the title is appearing in BIP for the first time.

Chuang Tzu: Basic Writings. Chuang Tzu. Tr. by Burton Watson. LC 64-21079. (Oriental Classics Ser.). 148p. 1964. pap. text ed. 12.00 (*0-231-08606-7*) Col U Pr.

Chuang Tzu: Mystic, Moralist, & Social Reformer. 2nd rev. ed. Chuang Tzu. Tr. by Herbert A. Giles. LC 70-38059. (China Classic & Contemporary Works in Reprint Ser.: No. II). reprint ed. 57.50 (*0-404-56915-3*) AMS Pr.

Chuang Tzu: World Philosopher at Play. Kuang-ming Wu. (American Academy of Religion, Studies in Religion). 1989. 23.95 (*0-89130-537-8*, 01-00-26) Scholars Pr GA.

Chuang-Tzu for Spiritual Transformation: An Analysis of the Inner Chapters. Robert E. Allinson. LC 88-19974. (SUNY Series in Philosophy). 203p. 1989. 69.50 (*0-88706-967-3*); pap. 24.95 (*0-88706-969-X*) State U NY Pr.

Chua's Circuit: A Paradigm for Chaos. R. Madan. 1088p. 1993. text ed. 213.00 (*981-02-1366-2*) World Scientific Pub.

Chubby Bear. (Chubby Shape Bks.). (J). 1984. pap. 2.95 (*0-671-50949-7*, Litl Simon S&S) S&S Childrens.

Chubby Cheek Dilemma. Jacquelyn R. Thrash. (YA). 1992. pap. 14.95 (*0-9635247-5-5*) Three Pines.

Chubby Chums: Chick, 3 bks., Set. (Illus.). 36p. (J). (ps). 1991. pap. 7.95 (*0-671-70802-3*, Litl Simon S&S) S&S Childrens.

Chubby Chums Christmas Tree: Christmas Wishes; Wheels That Work; A Little Book of Colors, 3 bks., Set. (Illus.). 12p. (J). (ps). 1992. boxed, pap. 7.95 (*0-671-79043-9*, Litl Simon S&S) S&S Childrens.

Chubby Chums Snowman: Jingle Bells; Opposites; Things I Like to Eat, 3 bks., Set. (Illus.). 12p. (J). (ps). 1992. boxed, pap. 7.95 (*0-671-79042-0*, Litl Simon S&S) S&S Childrens.

Chubby Engine. (Chubby Shape Bks.). (J). 1984. pap. 2.95 (*0-671-50951-9*, Litl Simon S&S) S&S Childrens.

Chubby Snowman. (Chubby Shape Bks.). (J). 1984. pap. 2.95 (*0-671-50948-9*, Litl Simon S&S) S&S Childrens.

Chubby Tugboat. (Chubby Shape Bks.). (J). 1984. pap. 3.50 (*0-671-50950-0*, Litl Simon S&S) S&S Childrens.

Chucaro: Wild Pony of the Pampa. Francis Kalnay. (Illus.). 115p. (J). 1993. pap. 6.95 (*0-8027-7387-7*) Walker & Co.

Chuck Amuck: The Life & Times of an Animated Cartoonist. Chuck Jones. 1990. pap. 12.95 (*0-380-71214-8*) Avon.

Chuck Amuck: The Life & Times of an Animated Cartoonist. Chuck Jones. 224p. 1989. 29.00 (*0-374-12348-9*) FS&G.

Chuck & Di Have a Baby. John Boswell et al. 1982. write for info. (*0-318-57011-4*) PB.

Chuck & Gail's Favorite Bike Rides: 75 Great Rides in the Mid-Atlantic from the Chesapeake Bay to the Shenandoah Valley. Chuck Helfer & Gail Helfer. LC 92-71424. (Illus.). 224p. (Orig.). 1992. pap. 16.95 (*0-9614137-8-6*) Cycleways Pubns.

Chuck Baird, Thirty-Five Plates. 64p. 1993. pap. 22.00 (*0-915035-18-9*) Dawn Sign.

Chuck Berry: Rock'N'Roll Music. 2nd ed. Howard A. De Witt. (Rock & Roll Reference Ser.: No. 12). 1985. 32.00 (*0-87650-171-4*) Popular Culture.

***Chuck Close.** Ed. by Rodney Sappington & William S. Bartman. (Illus.). 240p. 1995. text ed. write for info. (*0-614-02590-7*) ART Pr CA.

Chuck Close. Colin Westerbeck. LC 88-26868. (Illus.). 28p. 1989. pap. 11.95 (*0-86559-081-8*) Art Inst Chi.

***Chuck Close: Life & Work 1988-1995.** Text by John Guare. LC 95-60602. (Illus.). 128p. 1995. 35.00 (*0-500-09253-2*) Thames Hudson.

***Chuck Close: Works 1967-1992.** (Illus.). 200p. 1995. 49.95 (*3-89322-613-3*) Dist Art Pubs.

Chuck Close Editions: A Catalogue Raissone. James Pernotto. (Illus.). 32p. (Orig.). (C). 1989. pap. text ed. write for info. (*0-9624401-0-8*) Butler Inst.

Chuck Dougherty's Running Washington: A Guide to 101 Washington Area Running Trails. Chuck Dougherty. LC 84-52351. (Illus.). 124p. (Orig.). 1984. pap. 6.95 (*0-918339-01-4*) Vandamere.

Chuck Forsman: Meditations on Realist Form & Content. Howard E. Wooden. LC 81-85229. (Illus.). 24p. 1981. pap. 4.00 (*0-939324-04-0*) Wichita Art Mus.

Chuck Jones: A Flurry of Drawings. Hugh Kenner. LC 93-48418. (Portraits of American Genius Ser.: No. 3). (C). 1994. 16.00 (*0-520-08797-6*) U CA Pr.

Chuck Jones' Peter & the Wolf. George Daugherty & Janis Diamond. (Illus.). 96p. 1994. 29.95 (*0-446-51894-8*) Warner Bks.

Chuck Jones' Peter & the Wolf. deluxe limited ed. Chuck Jones. (Illus.). 96p. 1994. 100.00 (*0-446-51899-9*) Warner Bks.

Chuck Stewart's Jazz Files. Photos by Charles Stewart. (Quality Paperbacks Ser.). (Illus.). 144p. 1991. reprint ed. pap. 17.95 (*0-306-80442-5*) Da Capo.

***Chuck, the Horse Who Cared.** large type ed. William O. Beazley. (Illus.). 44p. (J). (gr. k-5). 1993. reprint ed. spiral bd., pap. 7.95 (*1-884758-03-7*) W O Beazley.

Chuck, the Unlucky Duck. Morgan Matthews. LC 88-1284. (Fiddlesticks Ser.). (Illus.). 48p. (Orig.). (J). (gr. 1-4). 1989. lib. bdg. 10.59 (*0-8167-1333-2*); pap. text ed. 3.50 (*0-8167-1334-0*) Troll Assocs.

Chuck Wagon Cookbook. Beth McElfresh. LC 60-8068. 75p. 1960. pap. 6.95 (*0-8040-0042-5*) Swallow.

Chuck Wagon Cookin' Stella Hughes. LC 74-78567. 170p. 1974. pap. 10.95 (*0-8165-0432-6*) U of Ariz Pr.

Chuck Wagon Gang: A Legend Lives On. Bob Terrell. (Illus.). 248p. 1990. 19.95 (*1-878894-01-3*, Hall Reference) Macmillan.

***Chuck Wagon Recipes & Others.** Sue Cunningham & Jean Cates. (Illus.). 115p. 1994. write for info. (*0-9645414-0-8*) Chuck Wagon.

Chuck Wagon Stew. E. J. Bird. (Good Time Library). (Illus.). 72p. (J). (gr. 2-6). 1988. 14.95 (*0-87614-313-3*, Carolrhoda); pap. 4.95 (*0-87614-498-9*, Carolrhoda) Lerner Group.

Chuck Williams' Thanksgiving & Christmas. Chuck Williams. Ed. by Laurie Wertz. LC 93-17988. (Williams-Sonoma Kitchen Library). (Illus.). 108p. 1993. 17.95 (*0-7835-0258-3*); lib. bdg. write for info. (*0-7835-0259-1*) Time-Life.

Chuck Yeager: First Man to Fly Faster than Sound. Timothy R. Gaffney. LC 86-9555. (People of Distinction Ser.). (Illus.). 128p. (J). (gr. 4 up). 1986. lib. bdg. 14.40 (*0-516-03223-2*) Childrens.

Chuck Yeager the Man Who Broke the Sound Barrier. Nancy S. Levinson. LC 87-25431. 133p. (J). (gr. 5 up). 1988. 13.95 (*0-8027-6781-8*); lib. bdg. 14.85 (*0-8027-6799-0*) Walker & Co.

***Chucker Jones' Adventures in Shadowland: What's It All about Chucker?** R. T. Richardson. Ed. by Bruce Dobie. (Illus.). 32p. (Orig.). (J). (gr. k-8). 1994. pap. 1.95 (*0-9643522-0-6*) R T Richardson.

Chuckle Mountain. Tammy Hunter. (Illus.). 64p. (Orig.). (J). (gr. 3-6). 1992. pap. 2.95 (*0-88625-280-6*) Durkin Hayes Pub.

Chuckles & Challenges. Annetta Dellinger. 96p. 1986. pap. 4.99 (*0-8010-2960-0*) Baker Bk.

Chuck's Story. Corbet Hanchett. LC 87-82034. 280p. (Orig.). 1987. pap. 6.25 (*0-9618961-0-8*) Hob Hill.

***Chuckwalla.** Edward R. Ricciuti. Ed. by Bruce Glassman. LC 94-28248. (What on Earth Is...? Ser). 32p. (J). (gr. 2-5). 1994. lib. bdg. 12.95 (*1-56711-089-4*) Blackbirch.

Chucky Bellman Was So Bad. Phyllis Green. Ed. by Judith Mathews. LC 90-26823. (Illus.). 32p. (J). (gr. k-3). 1991. 13.95 (*0-8075-1156-0*) A Whitman.

Chudesnaia Zhizn' Iosifa Bal'Zamo, Grafa Kaliostro. Mikhail A. Kuzmin & Gennady Smakov. LC 81-50873. 250p. (RUS.). 1982. reprint ed. pap. 9.95 (*0-89830-037-1*) Russica Pubs.

Chudesnyi Desant. Lev Loseff. LC 85-8721. 160p. 1985. pap. 9.00 (*0-938920-50-2*) Hermitage.

Chuetas of Majorca. rev. ed. Baruch Braunstein. 1971. 25.00 (*0-87068-147-8*) Ktav.

Chugoku no bijutsu-shoseki see Chinese Calligraphy

***Chui! A Guide to Hunting the African Leopard.** Lou Hallamore & Bruce Woods. LC 94-60940. 238p. 1994. 75.00 (*1-882458-06-0*) Trophy Rm Bks.

Chuk I Gek: An Easy Russian Reader. A. Gaidar. 55p. 1985. pap. 25.00 (*0-317-40649-3*, Pub. by Collets UK) St Mut.

Chukchee. Vladimir G. Bogoraz. LC 73-3527. (Jesup North Pacific Expedition. Publications: No. 7). reprint ed. 94.50 (*0-404-58107-2*) AMS Pr.

Chukchee Mythology. Vladimir G. Bogoraz. LC 73-3528. (Jesup North Pacific Expedition. Publications: Vol. 8, Pt. 1). reprint ed. 41.50 (*0-404-58108-0*) AMS Pr.

Chula Vista: The Early Years. Intro. by John Rojas, Jr. 80p. (Orig.). 1992. pap. 7.95 (*0-938711-14-8*) Tecolote Pubns.

Chula Vista: The Early Years, Vol. 2. Alfred Lansley et al. (Illus.). 80p. (Orig.). Date not set. pap. 7.95 (*0-938711-17-2*) Tecolote Pubns.

Chula Vista: The Early Years, Vol. 3. John Rojas, Jr. et al. (Illus.). 72p. (Orig.). Date not set. pap. 7.95 (*0-938711-24-5*) Tecolote Pubns.

Chulla Romero y Flores. Jorge Icaza. Ed. by Renaud Richard & Ricardo Descalzi. (Latin American Series - Coleccion Archivos). 342p. (C). 1988. pap. 27.95 (*84-00-06883-1*) U of Pittsburgh Pr.

Chulo: A Year among the Coatimundis. Bil Gilbert. LC 83-18299. (Illus.). 297p. 1984. reprint ed. pap. 14.95 (*0-8165-0842-9*) U of Ariz Pr.

Chultunes of Labna, Yucatan. E. H. Thompson. (HU PMM Ser.). 1972. reprint ed. 70.00 (*0-527-01152-5*) Periodicals Srv.

Chumash. Jill D. Duvall. LC 93-36672. (New True Bks.). (Illus.). 48p. (J). (gr. k-4). 1994. lib. bdg. 13.50 (*0-516-01052-2*) Childrens.

***Chumash.** Jill D. Duvall. LC 93-36672. (J). (ps-2). 1994. pap. 5.50 (*0-516-41052-0*) Childrens.

Chumash. Robert O. Gibson. (Indians of North America Ser.). (Illus.). (J). (gr. 5 up). 1991. 17.95 (*1-55546-700-8*); pap. 9.95 (*0-7910-0376-0*) Chelsea Hse.

Chumash. Gary Thompson. 400p. (Orig.). 1986. pap. 3.95 (*0-8439-2386-5*) Dorchester Pub Co.

Chumash: A Picture of Their World. Bruce W. Miller, III. (Illus.). 136p. (Orig.). 1988. pap. 8.95 (*0-944627-51-X*) Sand River Pr.

Chumash & Rashi Curriculum. Dov Leibenstein. (Orig.). 1990. Looseleaf Binder. ring bd. 28.00 (*0-914131-94-X*, C030) Torah Umesorah.

Chumash Healing. Phillip L. Walker & Travis Hudson. LC 92-62437. 1993. 16.95 (*0-939046-33-4*); pap. 12.95 (*0-939046-34-2*) Malki Mus Pr.

***Chumash Indians.** Martin Schwabacher. LC 94-17181. (Junior Library of American Indians). (Illus.). 80p. (J). (gr. 3-7). 1995. lib. bdg. 14.95 (*0-7910-2488-1*); pap. text ed. 6.95 (*0-7910-2490-3*) Chelsea Hse.

Chumash Indians of Southern California. Eugene Anderson. 1973. 2.00 (*0-939046-13-X*) Malki Mus Pr.

Chumash People. 2nd ed. Santa Barbara Museum of Natural History, Education Dept. Staff. (Illus.). 96p. (Orig.). (YA). (gr. 4 up). 1991. Grades 4 up. spiral bd. 12.95 (*0-945092-23-7*) EZ Nature.

Chumash Place Name Lists. Ed. by R. F. Heizer. 89p. reprint ed. pap. 25.40 (*0-7837-2612-0*, 2042776) Bks Demand.

Ch'un Ts'ew with the Tso Chuen, Vol. IV. Tr. by James Legge. (CHI & ENG.). 1991. 35.00 (*957-638-042-1*, Pub. by SMC Pub CC) Oriental Bk Store.

Chung-Gun & Toi Gye of Tae Kwon Do Hyung. Jhoon Rhee. LC 76-163381. (Series 108). (Illus.). 1971. pap. text ed. 14.95 (*0-89750-003-2*) Ohara Pubns.

Chung Kuo: The Middle Kingdom. David Wingrove. 1991. mass mkt. 5.99 (*0-440-20761-4*) Dell.

Chung-Kuo Ching-Chi Shih see Economic History of China

Chung Lee Loves Lobsters. High MacDonald. (Illus.). 24p. (J). (gr. k-3). 1992. lib. bdg. 14.95 (*1-55037-217-3*, Pub. by Annick CN); pap. 4.95 (*1-55037-214-9*, Pub. by Annick CN) Firefly Bks Ltd.

Chung, the China Gold, & Me. Eleanor Phillips. 150p. (Orig.). (J). (gr. 6-10). 1990. pap. 7.95 (*0-9624210-0-6*) Laurelwood Pr.

Chunky Tray Series. Target. Date not set. write for info. (*0-679-86120-3*) Random.

***Chunnel Handbook & Atlas.** (Illus.). 60p. (Orig.). 1994. pap. 24.95 (*0-7605-0638-8*) Rector Pr.

***Churban Europe - (Destruction History) Beir Yehuda.** Date not set. write for info. (*1-879515-02-4*) Beir Yehuda.

Church. Rick Bundschuh. LC 88-9692. (Light Force Ser.). (Illus.). 154p. (Orig.). (YA). (gr. 9-12). 1988. pap. 5.99 (*0-8307-1182-1*, S184102) Regal.

Church. Ernest A. Clevenger, Jr. (Bible Drill Flash Cards Flipbook Ser.). 104p. (J). (gr. 3 up). 1994. pap. 5.00 (*0-88428-016-0*) Parchment Pr.

***Church.** Edmund P. Clowney. Ed. by Gerald Bray. LC 94-45405. (Contours of Christian Theology Ser.). 240p. (Orig.). 1995. pap. text ed. 14.99 (*0-8308-1534-1*, 1534, Pub. by IVP UK) InterVarsity.

Church. Carol Crook. 42p. (Orig.). 1988. pap. 1.50 (*0-939399-01-6*) Bks of Truth.

Church. Ed. by Melvin E. Dieter & Daniel N. Berg. (Wesleyan Theological Perspectives Ser.: Vol. IV). 1989. 14.95 (*0-87162-406-0*, D4853) Warner Pr.

Church. Thomas Halton. LC 84-72860. (Message of the Fathers of the Church Ser.: Vol. 4). 239p. 1985. 15.95 (*0-8146-5344-8*); pap. 14.95 (*0-8146-5316-2*) Liturgical Pr.

Church. Russell P. Spittler. LC 77-83982. (Radiant Life Ser.). 126p. 1977. teacher ed 4.50 (*0-88243-180-3*, 32-0180); pap. 2.95 (*0-88243-910-3*, 02-0910) Gospel Pub.

Church. Richard E. Todd. (Wordbook Ser.). (Illus.). 26p. (J). (gr. 2-6). 1993. student ed 2.45 (*0-9605324-4-7*) Crosswalk Res.

***Church: A Spirited Communion.** Michael G. Lawler & Thomas J. Shanahan. LC 94-41758. (Theology & Life Ser.: Vol. 40). (Orig.). 1995. pap. text ed. 12.95 (*0-8146-5821-0*) Liturgical Pr.

Church: Charism & Power ... Liberation Theology & the Institutional Church. Leonardo Boff. Tr. by John Dierksmeyer. LC 84-21431. 192p. 1986. 14.95 (*0-8245-0726-6*) Crossroad NY.

Church: Its Beginning, Doctrine & Order. R. P. Daniel. 76p. pap. 3.95 (*0-88172-161-1*) Believers Bkshelf.

Church: Selected Writings of Arthur Carl Piepkorn. Arthur C. Piepkorn. Ed. by Michael P. Plekon & William S. Wiecher. 304p. (Orig.). (C). Date not set. pap. text ed. 12.00 (*0-9633142-2-X*) Am Luth Pub Bur.

Church: Simeon Church of Chester, Connecticut, 1708-1792, & His Descendants. Charles W. Church. 241p. 1993. reprint ed. lib. bdg. 48.00 (*0-8328-3280-4*); reprint ed. pap. 38.00 (*0-8328-3281-2*) Higginson Bk Co.

Church: The Human Story of God. Edward Schillebeeckx. Tr. by John Bowden. 268p. 1993. reprint ed. pap. 15.95 (*0-8245-1372-X*) Crossroad NY.

***Church: The Mystery of Christ.** Bill Freeman. 225p. (Orig.). 1994. pap. 6.00 (*0-914271-62-8*) Mnstry Wrd.

Church: The Universal Sacrament of Salvation. Johann Auer. Ed. by Hugh M. Riley. Tr. by Michael Waldstein. LC 91-44734. (Dogmatic Theology Ser.: Vol. 8). 541p. 1993. text ed. 39.95 (*0-8132-0684-7*); pap. text ed. 24.95 (*0-8132-0685-5*) Cath U Pr.

Church: Trampled or Triumphant? Earl Paulk. 240p. (Orig.). 1990. pap. 9.95 (*0-917595-35-1*) Kingdom Pubs.

***Church: What Am I Doing Here?** Group Publishing, Inc. Editors. Ed. by Paul Woods. (Adult Curriculum Ser.). 1995. 9.99 (*1-55945-513-6*) Group Pub.

Church - Gold Afternoon Fix. pap. 16.95 (*0-89524-582-5*) Cherry Lane.

***Church - No Spectator Sport.** Eric Wright. 1994. pap. 18.99 (*0-85234-314-0*, Pub. by Evangel Pr UK) Presby & Reformed.

Church - Starfish. pap. 14.95 (*0-89524-405-5*) Cherry Lane.

Church, a Believing Fellowship. John H. Leith. LC 80-82192. 192p. 1981. pap. 7.99 (*0-8042-0518-3*, John Knox) Westminster John Knox.

***Church, a Demon Lover: A Sartrean Analysis of an Institution.** Roberta Imboden. 170p. 1995. pap. 19.95 (*1-895176-55-7*, Pub. by Univ Calgary CN) Paul & Co Pubs.

Church Administration: A Handbook for Church Leaders. Walter H. Adams. 1979. pap. 2.95 (*0-88027-001-2*) Firm Foun Pub.

Church Administration: The Dollars & Sense of It. David R. Pollock. (Christian Financial Concepts Ser.). 96p. (Orig.). 1991. pap. 5.00 (*1-56427-084-X*) Christian Fin Concepts.

Church Administration - Effective Leadership for Ministry. Charles A. Tidwell. LC 85-6620. 1992. pap. 11.99 (*0-8054-3113-6*) Broadman.

Church Administration Handbook. Bruce P. Powers. LC 84-29249. 1992. pap. 12.99 (*0-8054-3112-8*) Broadman.

Church Administration in the Black Perspective. Floyd Massey, Jr. & Samuel B. McKinney. LC 76-9804. 176p. 1976. pap. 12.00 (*0-8170-0710-5*) Judson.

Church Administrator "How to" Manual. Donald Buckel & Barbara Buckel. LC 91-72790. 202p. 1991. ring bd. 49.95 (*0-935779-14-0*) Crown Min.

Church Agencies: Caring for Children & Families in Crisis. Diana S. Garland. 1993. 26.95 (*0-87868-532-4*) Child Welfare.

***Church Alive.** Harold E. Trammell. 154p. (Orig.). 1994. pap. 7.99 (*1-56043-820-7*) Destiny Image.

Church Alive & Growing. J. Terry Young. LC 78-50371. 222p. 1987. pap. 10.00 (*0-914520-25-3*) Insight Pr.

Church & Abortion. Paul Stallsworth. LC 92-40691. 144p. (Orig.). 1993. pap. 10.95 (*0-687-07852-0*) Abingdon.

Church & Age Unite! The Modernist Impulse in American Catholicism. R. Scott Appleby. LC 90-50976. (Studies in American Catholicism: Vol. 11). (C). 1991. text ed. 29.95 (*0-268-00782-9*) U of Notre Dame Pr.

Church & Canadian Culture. Ed. by Robert E. VanderVennen. 232p. (Orig.). (C). 1991. lib. bdg. 49.00 (*0-8191-8420-9*, Inst Christ Stud) U Pr of Amer.

***Church & Childhood.** Diana Wood. 512p. Date not set. text ed. 59.95 (*0-631-19586-6*); pap. text ed. 24.95 (*0-631-19587-4*) Blackwell Pubs.

Church & Chronicle in the Middle Ages: Essays Presented to John Taylor. Ed. by Ian Wood & G. H. Loud. 324p. 1991. boxed 60.00 (*1-85285-046-9*) Hambledon Press.

Church & City in Transition: The Social Composition of Religious Groups in Detroit, 1880-1940. Ralph Janis. LC 90-36710. (European Immigrants & American Society Ser.). 292p. 1990. reprint ed. 20.00 (*0-8240-0253-9*) Garland.

Church & City, 1000-1500: Essays in Honour of Christopher Brooke. Ed. by David Abulafia et al. (Illus.). 312p. (C). 1992. 79.95 (*0-521-35611-3*) Cambridge U Pr.

Church & Clergy in Sixteenth-Century Mexico. John F. Schwaller. LC 87-5942. 281p. reprint ed. pap. 80.10 (*0-7837-5856-1*, 2045575) Bks Demand.

Church & Clergy Tax Guide: 1992 Edition. rev. ed. Richard R. Hammar. 248p. 1991. pap. 14.95 (*1-880562-01-4*) Christ Minist.

***Church & Clergy Tax Guide: 1995 Edition.** Richard R. Hammar. 328p. 1994. pap. 14.95 (*1-880562-14-6*) Christ Minist.

Church & Communication. Ed. by Patrick Granfield. LC 93-46601. (Communication, Culture & Theology Ser.). 232p. (Orig.). 1994. pap. 24.95 (*1-55612-674-3*) Sheed & Ward MO.

Church & Community among Black Southerners, 1856-1900. Ed. by Donald G. Nieman. LC 93-37341. (African American Life in the Post-Emancipation South Ser.: No. 9). 424p. 1994. 73.00 (*0-8153-1446-9*) Garland.

***Church & Community in Crisis: The Gospel According to Matthew.** J. Andrew Overman. (New Testament in Context Ser.). 1995. pap. 24.00 (*1-56338-101-X*) TPI PA.

Church & Community in the Diocese of Lyon: 1500-1789. Philip T. Hoffman. LC 83-23404. (Historical Publications Ser.: No. 132). 256p. 1984. text ed. 35.00x (*0-300-03141-6*) Yale U Pr.

Church & Confession: Conservative Theologians in Germany, England, & America, 1815-1866. Walter H. Conser, Jr. LC 84-18990. viii, 360p. 1984. 28.95 (*0-86554-119-1*, MUP/H109) Mercer Univ Pr.

***Church & Creed in Scotland: The Free Church Case 1900-1904 & Its Origins.** Kenneth Ross. 400p. Date not set. 49.50 (*0-614-06084-2*) Attic Pr.

Church & Creed in Scotland: The Free Church Case 1900-1904 & Its Origins. Kenneth R. Ross. LC 92-5153. (Rutherford Studies in Historical Theology). 424p. 1992. reprint ed. lib. bdg. 109.95 (*0-7734-1647-1*) E Mellen.

Church & Culture: German Catholic Theology, 1860-1914. Thomas F. O'Meara. LC 90-50971. (C). 1992. text ed. 35.95 (*0-268-00783-7*) U of Notre Dame Pr.

***Church & Culture: Challenge & Confrontation: Inculturation & Evangelization.** Paul C. Poupard. Tr. by John H. Miller. 160p. 1994. pap. 15.00 (*0-9626257-7-9*) CBCCU Amer.

Church & Cultures: New Perspectives in Missiological Anthropology. rev. ed. Louis J. Luzbetak. LC 89-2880. (American Society of Missiology Ser.). 384p. 1989. pap. 21.95 (*0-88344-625-1*) Orbis Bks.

Church & Denominational Growth. C. Kirk Hadaway & David Roozen. LC 93-16698. 400p. (Orig.). 1993. pap. 21.95 (*0-687-15904-0*) Abingdon.

Church & Freemasonry. Church of Scotland Panel on Doctrine. (C). 1989. pap. 20.00 (*0-86153-115-9*, Pub. by St Andrew UK) St Mut.

Church & Gnosis: A Study of Christian Thought & Speculation in the Second Century. Francis C. Burkitt. LC 77-84696. (Morse Lectures: 1931). reprint ed. 26.00 (*0-404-16104-9*) AMS Pr.

Church & Government in the Middle Ages: Essays Presented to C. R. Cheney on His 70th Birthday. Ed. by Christopher N. Brooke et al. LC 75-41614. 332p. reprint ed. pap. 94.70 (*0-685-16331-8*, 2027285) Bks Demand.

***Church & Healing: Echoes from Africa.** Ed. by Emmanuel Y. Lartey et al. LC 94-26926. (African Pastoral Studies, Etudes Pastorales Africaines: 2). (ENG & FRE.). 1994. write for info. (*3-631-47227-7*) P Lang Pubs.

Church & Her Fellowship, Ministry, & Governance. Kurt Marquart. Ed. by Robert Preus et al. LC 89-84112. (Confessional Lutheran Dogmatics Ser.: Vol. 9). 280p. 1990. 14.50 (*0-9622791-9-6*) Luth Confess Res.

Church & Her Ideal Educational Situation. Henry E. Speck. Ed. by Jesse P. Sewell. 1933. 2.50 (*0-88027-083-7*); pap. 1.50 (*0-88027-084-5*) Firm Foun Pub.

Church & Human Rights. Jean F. Six. 128p. (C). 1990. 45.00 (*0-85439-368-4*, Pub. by St Paul Pubns UK) St Mut.

Church & Its Function in Society. W. A. Hooft & J. H. Oldham. 1977. lib. bdg. 59.95 (*0-8490-1625-8*) Gordon Pr.

Church & Its Order According to Scripture. Samuel Ridout. 1915. reprint ed. pap. 4.99 (*0-87213-711-2*) Loizeaux.

Church & Its Youth. Lamar Vest. (Church Training Course Ser.). 1980. 1.00 (*0-87148-170-7*) Pathway Pr.

An Asterisk (*) at the beginning of an entry indicates that the title is appearing in BIP for the first time. 1261

Church & Jewish People: New Considerations. Johannes C. Willebrands. LC 91-46374. 288p. 1992. pap. text ed. 14.95 (*0-8091-0456-3*) Paulist Pr.

Church & Labour in Colombia. Kenneth N. Medhurst. LC 82-62254. 320p. (C). 1988. text ed. 75.00 (*0-7190-0969-3*, Pub. by Manchester Univ Pr UK) St Martin.

Church & Law in the Balkan Peninsula during the Ottoman Rule. N. J. Pantazopoulos. (Illus.). 125p. 1983. reprint ed. pap. text ed. 24.00 (*0-317-54442-X*, Pub. by A M Hakkert SP) Coronet Bks.

Church & Liberation in Namibia. Peter Katjavivi et al. 240p. (C). 1989. pap. text ed. 19.50 (*1-85305-078-4*) Westview.

Church & Liberation in Namibia. Peter Katjavivi et al. 240p. (C). 1989. text ed. 49.00 (*1-85305-073-3*) Westview.

Church & Manor: A Study in English Economic History. Sidney O. Addy. LC 70-107902. (Reprints of Economic Classics Ser.). (Illus.). 1970. reprint ed. 49.50 (*0-678-00632-6*) Kelley.

Church & Ministry: The Role of Church, Pastor, & People from Luther to Walther. Eugene F. Klug. LC 93-25772. (Concordia Scholarship Today Ser.). 1993. write for info. (*0-570-04625-4*) Concordia.

Church & Ministry (Kirche Und Amt) Witnessess of the Evangelical Lutheran Church on the Question of Church & Ministry. C. F. Walther. 368p. 1987. 16.95 (*0-570-04241-0*, 15-2192) Concordia.

Church & Ministry Project Book. Greer Gordon. 56p. 1987. pap. 5.95 (*0-89505-555-4*) Tabor Pub.

Church & Ministry Strategic Planning: From Concept to Success. R. Henry Migliore et al. LC 93-17360. (Illus.). 172p. 1994. lib. bdg. 34.95 (*1-56024-346-5*) Haworth Pr.

Church & Missions Alive. rev. ed. Samuel J. Stoesz. LC 86-72257. 95p. 1987. teacher ed 0.99 (*0-87509-069-9*); pap. 2.99 (*0-87509-386-8*) Chr Pubns.

Church & Morality: An Ecumenical & Catholic Approach. Charles E. Curran. LC 92-47448. 1993. pap. 10.00 (*0-8006-2756-3*, Fortress Pr) Augsburg Fortress.

Church & Organization: A Sociological & Theological Inquiry. Joseph F. McCann. LC 91-68568. (Illus.). 256p. 1993. 39.50 (*0-940866-19-6*) U Scranton Pr.

Church & Organized Movements. Ed. by Randolph C. Miller. LC 76-134115. (Essay Index Reprint Ser.). 1977. 20.95 (*0-8369-1998-X*) Ayer.

Church & Parliament: The Reshaping of the Church of England, 1828-1860. Olive J. Bross. LC 59-7423. 120p. reprint ed. pap. 30.00 (*0-317-26542-3*, 2023992) Bks Demand.

Church & Persons with Handicaps. H. Oliver Ohsberg. LC 82-80342. 128p. 1982. pap. 7.95 (*0-8361-1996-7*) Herald Pr.

Church & Politics in a Secular Age. Kenneth H. Medhurst & George H. Moyser. (Illus.). 410p. 1988. 79.00 (*0-19-826454-2*) OUP.

Church & Politics in Chile: Challenges to Modern Catholicism. Brian H. Smith. LC 81-47951. 416p. 1982. 55.00x (*0-691-07629-4*) Princeton U Pr.

Church & Politics in Latin America. Ed. by Dermot F. Keogh. 320p. 1990. text ed. 39.95 (*0-312-02815-6*) St Martin.

Church & Politics in Renaissance Italy: The Life & Career of Cardinal Francesco Soderini, 1453-1524. K. J. Lowe. LC 92-33576. (Studies in Italian History & Culture). (Illus.). 308p. (C). 1993. 59.95 (*0-521-42103-9*) Cambridge U Pr.

Church & Politics in the Chilean Countryside. Hannah W. Stewart-Gambino. 200p. (C). 1992. text ed. 55.50 (*0-8133-7724-2*) Westview.

Church & Popular Education. Herbert B. Adams. LC 78-63876. (Johns Hopkins University. Studies in the Social Sciences. Thirtieth Ser. 1912: 8-9). reprint ed. 11.50 (*0-404-61132-X*) AMS Pr.

Church & Power in Brazil. Charles Antoine. Tr. by Peter Nelson. LC 72-93341. 287p. reprint ed. pap. 81.80 (*0-8357-8847-4*, 2033477) Bks Demand.

Church & Racial Hostility: A History of Interpretation of Ephesians 2, 11-22. William Rader. 282p. 1978. 55.00 (*3-16-140112-3*, Pub. by J C B Mohr GW) Coronet Bks.

Church & Racism. Veritas Publications Staff. 1989. pap. 15.00 (*1-85390-014-1*, Pub. by Veritas IE) St Mut.

Church & Religion in Rural England. Douglas Davies et al. (Illus.). 304p. 1991. pap. text ed. 27.95 (*0-567-29201-0*, Pub. by T & T Clark UK) Bks Intl VA.

Church & Residential Desegregation. Henry Clark. 1965. 22.95 (*0-8084-0076-2*) NCUP.

Church & Revolution in Nicaragua. Laura O'Shaughnessy & Luis Serra. LC 82-92625. (Monographs in International Studies, Latin America Ser.: No. 11). 118p. 1986. pap. 18.00 (*0-89680-126-8*, Ohio U Ctr Intl) Ohio U Pr.

Church & School in Scotland. Andrew M. Douglas. 104p. (C). 1988. pap. text ed. 25.00 (*0-7152-0584-6*) St Mut.

Church & Schools in Vichy France, 1940-1944. Nicholas Atkin & William McNeill. LC 91-32628. (Modern European History Ser.). 464p. 1991. 63.00 (*0-8153-0664-4*) Garland.

Church & Scottish Social Development, 1780-1870. Stewart Mechie. LC 75-3740. 181p. 1975. reprint ed. text ed. 49.75 (*0-8371-8060-0*, MECS, Greenwood Pr) Greenwood.

Church & Secular Education. Lewis B. Whittemore. LC 78-17152. 130p. 1978. reprint ed. text ed. 55.00 (*0-313-20540-X*, WHCS, Greenwood Pr) Greenwood.

Church & Slave in Perry County, Missouri, 1818-1865. Stafford Poole & Douglas J. Slawson. LC 86-16374. (Studies in American Religion: Vol. 22). (Illus.). 252p. 1988. lib. bdg. 89.95 (*0-88946-666-1*) E Mellen.

Church & Slavery. Albert Barnes. LC 79-82416. 15.00 (*0-403-00150-1*) Scholarly.

Church & Slavery. Albert Barnes. LC 71-98714. 204p. 1970. reprint ed. text ed. 45.00 (*0-8371-2771-8*, BAC&, Negro U Pr) Greenwood.

Church & Social Action: A Bibliographical Survey. Comp. by Roger T. Wolcott & Dorita E. Bolger. LC 89-25865. (Bibliographies & Indexes in Religious Studies: No. 15). 270p. 1990. text ed. 49.95 (*0-313-25086-3*, WCU/, Greenwood Pr) Greenwood.

Church & Social Reform. John Boojamra. 1993. 30.00 (*0-8232-1334-X*); pap. 19.95 (*0-8232-1335-8*) Fordham.

***Church & Society in Byzantium under the Comneni, 1081-1261.** Michael Angold. 656p. (C). 1995. 89.95 (*0-521-26432-4*) Cambridge U Pr.

Church & Society in Ireland, A. D. 400-1200. Kathleen Hughes. Ed. by David Dumville. (Collected Studies: No. CS258). 380p. (C). 1987. reprint ed. lib. bdg. 99.95 (*0-86078-206-9*, Pub. by Variorum UK) Ashgate Pub Co.

Church & Society in Late Medieval England. R. N. Swanson. 464p. 1989. text ed. 89.95 (*0-631-14659-8*) Blackwell Pubs.

Church & Society in Late Medieval England. R. N. Swanson. LC 92-33826. (Illus.). 464p. 1993. pap. 27.95 (*0-631-18643-3*) Blackwell Pubs.

Church & Sovereignty c.590-1915: Essays in Honour of Michael Wilks. Diana Wood. (Studies in Church History: Subsida Series No. 9). 500p. (C). 1991. text ed. 59.95 (*0-631-18042-7*) Blackwell Pubs.

***Church & State.** Steve Dolan. 232p. 1994. write for info. (*1-885845-00-6*) Leaflet Missal.

Church & State. Karl Barth. (Church Classics Ser.). 126p. (Orig.). 1991. reprint ed. pap. text ed. 9.95 (*0-9628455-4-X*) Smyth & Helwys.

Church & State: Government & Religion in the United States. Kathlyn Gay. LC 91-34753. (Issue & Debate Ser.). (Illus.). 128p. (YA). (gr. 7 up). 1992. lib. bdg. 15.90 (*1-56294-063-5*) Millbrook Pr.

Church & State from Constantine to Theodosius. Stanley L. Greenslade. LC 79-8712. 93p. 1981. reprint ed. text ed. 45.00 (*0-313-20793-3*, GRCS, Greenwood Pr) Greenwood.

Church & State in America: A Bibliographical Guide (The Colonial & Early National Periods). Ed. by John F. Wilson. LC 85-31698. 447p. 1986. text ed. 79.50 (*0-313-25236-X*, WNC/, Greenwood Pr) Greenwood.

Church & State in America: A Bibliographical Guide: The Civil War to Present Day. Ed. by John F. Wilson. LC 85-31698. 465p. 1987. text ed. 85.00 (*0-313-25914-3*, WNW/, Greenwood Pr) Greenwood.

Church & State in American History: The Burden of Religious Pluralism. 2nd ed. Ed. by John F. Wilson & Donald L. Drakeman. LC 86-47513. 237p. reprint ed. pap. 67.60 (*0-7837-1387-8*, 2041563) Bks Demand.

Church & State in Bourbon Mexico: The Diocese of Michoacan, 1749-1810. D. A. Brading. LC 93-44303. 304p. (C). 1994. 59.95 (*0-521-46092-1*) Cambridge U Pr.

Church & State in Early Christianity. Hugo Rahner. Tr. by Leo D. Davis. LC 91-76752. 342p. 1992. pap. 16.95 (*0-89870-377-8*) Ignatius Pr.

Church & State in Early Modern England, 1509-1640. Leo F. Solt. 288p. 1990. 42.00 (*0-19-505979-4*) OUP.

Church & State in Europe, 1864-1914. Ed. by Ernst Helmreich. LC 78-68021. (Problems in Civilization Ser.). 128p. 1979. pap. text ed. write for info. (*0-88273-405-9*) Forum Pr IL.

Church & State in Latin America: A History of Politico Ecclesiastical Relations. rev. ed. John L. Mecham. LC 66-15511. 477p. reprint ed. pap. 136.00 (*0-7837-0315-5*, 2040637) Bks Demand.

Church & State in Modern Britain 1700-1850. Richard Brown. (Illus.). 544p. 1991. 57.50 (*0-415-01122-1*, A4857); pap. 19.95 (*0-415-01123-X*, A4861) Routledge.

Church & State in New England. Paul E. Lauer. LC 78-63809. (Johns Hopkins University. Studies in the Social Sciences. Thirtieth Ser. 1912: 2-3). reprint ed. 11.50 (*0-404-61072-2*) AMS Pr.

Church & State in North Carolina. Stephen B. Weeks. LC 78-63820. (Johns Hopkins University. Studies in the Social Sciences. Thirtieth Ser. 1912: 6). reprint ed. 11.50 (*0-404-61082-X*) AMS Pr.

Church & State in Postwar Eastern Europe: A Bibliographical Survey. Comp. by Paul Mojzes. LC 87-8358. (Bibliographies & Indexes in Religious Studies: No. 11). 120p. 1987. text ed. 55.00 (*0-313-24002-7*, MOJ/, Greenwood Pr) Greenwood.

Church & State in Revolutionary Virginia, 1776-1787. Thomas E. Buckley. LC 77-4283. 213p. reprint ed. pap. 60.80 (*0-7837-1078-X*, 2041608) Bks Demand.

Church & State in Scripture, History, & Constitutional Law. James E. Wood, Jr. et al. LC 59-21543. (Institute of Church-State Studies). 171p. 1985. reprint ed. pap. 6.95 (*0-918954-01-0*) Baylor Univ Pr.

Church & State in the Early Church. Ed. by Everett Ferguson. LC 92-41857. (Studies in Early Christianity: Vol. 7). 432p. 1993. 67.00 (*0-8153-1067-6*) Garland.

Church & State in the Middle Ages. Arthur L. Smith. 245p. 1964. 30.00 (*0-7146-1514-5*, Pub. by F Cass Pubs UK) Intl Spec Bk.

***Church & State in the Modern Age: A Documentary History.** J. F. Maclear. 480p. 1995. text ed. 60.00 (*0-19-508681-3*) OUP.

Church & State in the Spanish Floridas (1783-1822) Michael J. Curley. LC 73-3584. (Catholic University of America. Studies in Romance Languages & Literatures: No. 30). reprint ed. 49.50 (*0-404-57780-6*) AMS Pr.

Church & State in the U. S.; or, the American Idea of Religious Liberty & Its... Philip Schaff. LC 75-38462. (Religion in America, Ser. 2). 188p. 1975. reprint ed. 19.95 (*0-405-04083-0*) Ayer.

Church & State in the United States. rev. ed. Anson Stokes & Leo Pfeffer. LC 73-15318. 660p. 1975. reprint ed. text ed. 55.50 (*0-8371-7186-5*, STCI, Greenwood Pr) Greenwood.

Church & State in the United States: With an Appendix on the German Population. Joseph P. Thompson. 166p. 1990. reprint ed. lib. bdg. 22.50 (*0-8377-1216-5*) Rothman.

Church & State in Tudor & Stuart England. Stuart E. Prall. Ed. by Keith Eubank. LC 92-35135. (European History Ser.). 190p. (C). 1993. pap. text ed. write for info. (*0-88295-904-2*) Harlan Davidson.

Church & State, Opening a New Ecumenical Discussion. World Council of Churches Staff. LC 79-313820. (Faith & Order Paper Ser.: No. 85). 183p. reprint ed. pap. 52.20 (*0-7837-6008-6*, 2045818) Bks Demand.

Church & State Through the Centuries. Sidney Z. Ehler & John B. Morrall. LC 66-30406. 1988. 20.00 (*0-8196-0189-6*) Biblo.

Church & Sunday School Hymnal with Supplement. Ed. by J. D. Brunk. LC 72-2053. 384p. 1902. 11.95 (*0-8361-1110-9*) Herald Pr.

***Church & Synagogue Affiliation: Theory, Research, & Practice.** Ed. by Amy L. Sales & Gary A. Tobin. LC 95-6671. (Contributions to the Study of Religion Ser.: No. 42). 208p. 1995. text ed. 55.00 (*0-313-29681-2*, Greenwood Pr) Greenwood.

Church & Synagogue Libraries. Ed. by John F. Harvey. LC 80-11736. 299p. 1980. 25.00 (*0-8108-1304-1*) Scarecrow.

Church & Synagogue Library Resources. 5th ed. Dorothy Rodda. LC 75-1178. 24p. 1992. pap. 6.00 (*0-915324-33-4*) CSLA.

Church & the Age of Reason. Gerald R. Cragg. (History of the Church Ser.: Vol. 4). (Orig.). 1961. mass mkt. 6.95 (*0-14-020505-5*, Penguin Bks) Viking Penguin.

Church & the American Teenager: What Works & Doesn't Work in Youth Ministry. Anthony Campolo. Orig. Title: Growing up in America. 224p. 1993. reprint ed. pap. 12.99 (*0-310-52471-7*) Zondervan.

***Church & the Arts.** Diana Wood. Ed. by Robert Swanson. (Studies in Church History). (Illus.). 585p. 1995. pap. write for info. (*0-631-19928-4*) Blackwell Pubs.

Church & the Arts. Diana Wood. Ed. by Robert Swanson. (Studies in Church History: No. 28). (Illus.). 585p. 1995. 59.95 (*0-631-18043-5*) Blackwell Pubs.

Church & the Children. Ed. by Jesse P. Sewell & Henry E. Speck. 1935. 1.50 (*0-88027-104-3*) Firm Foun Pub.

Church & the Churches: Toward an Ecumenical Ecclesiology. G. R. Evans. LC 93-42441. 362p. (C). 1994. 59.95 (*0-521-46286-X*) Cambridge U Pr.

Church & the City: 1865-1910. Ed. by Robert D. Cross. LC 66-17273. (Orig.). 1967. 49.50 (*0-672-50994-6*) Irvington.

Church & the City: 1865-1910. Ed. by Robert D. Cross. LC 66-17273. (Orig.). (C). 1967. pap. write for info. (*0-672-60094-3*, AHS61, Bobbs) Macmillan.

Church & the Country Community. Edwin V. O'Hara. 1978. 17.95 (*0-405-10846-X*, 11849) Ayer.

Church & the Disabled. Carl Fenn. 1985. pap. 6.25 (*0-8309-0414-X*) Herald Hse.

Church & the Homosexual. 4th ed. John J. McNeill. LC 93-7088. 288p. 1993. pap. 14.00 (*0-8070-7931-6*) Beacon Pr.

Church & the Jews in the Thirteenth Century, Vol. Two: 1254-1314. Solomon Grayzel. Ed. by Kenneth R. Stow. LC 89-8941. 380p. (C). 1989. 39.95 (*0-8143-2254-9*) Wayne St U Pr.

Church & the Law: The Seventh Proceedings of the Fellowship of Catholic Scholars. Ed. by Paul L. Williams. 128p. (Orig.). 1985. pap. 6.95 (*0-937374-01-6*) NE Bks.

Church & the Left. Adam Michnik. Ed. by David Ost. 280p. (C). 1992. 24.95 (*0-226-52424-8*) U Ch Pr.

Church & the National Security State. Joseph Comblin. LC 79-10881. 254p. (Orig.). reprint ed. pap. 72.40 (*0-7837-6415-4*, 2046395) Bks Demand.

Church & the New World Mind: The Drake Lectures for 1944. W. E. Hocking et al. LC 68-57311. (Essay Index Reprint Ser.). reprint ed. 20.95 (*0-8369-9698-4*) Ayer.

Church & the Oneness of the Triune God. Bill Freeman. 150p. (Orig.). 1992. pap. 5.00 (*0-914271-33-4*) Mnstry Wrd.

Church & the Powers: A Theology of Church Structure. James F. Cobbles, Jr. 176p. 1987. pap. 7.95 (*0-913573-50-7*) Hendrickson MA.

Church & the Public Conscience. Edgar M. Carlson. LC 79-8710. xii, 104p. 1981. reprint ed. text ed. 45.00 (*0-313-22195-2*, CACH, Greenwood Pr) Greenwood.

Church & the Rebellion. Robert L. Stanton. LC 70-168521. (Black Heritage Library Collection). 1977. reprint ed. 42.95 (*0-8369-8873-6*) Ayer.

Church & the Rebellion. Robert L. Stanton. LC 70-168521. 562p. 1982. reprint ed. lib. bdg. 19.00 (*0-8290-0475-0*) Irvington.

Church & the Second Sex: Including the Feminist Postchristian. rev. ed. Mary Daly. LC 85-47519. 240p. 1985. reprint ed. pap. 14.00 (*0-8070-1101-0*, BP 698) Beacon Pr.

Church & the Secular Order in Reformation Thought. John Tonkin. LC 73-143390. 233p. reprint ed. pap. 66.50 (*0-317-26653-5*, 2025107) Bks Demand.

Church & the Shaping of English Society, 1215-1535. Peter Heath. 224p. 1993. pap. 19.95 (*0-340-54005-2*, A9525, Pub. by E Arnold UK) Routledge Chapman & Hall.

***Church & the Shaping of English Society, 1215-1535.** Peter Heath. 224p. 1995. 49.95 (*0-340-64529-6*, Pub. by E Arnld UK) St Martin.

Church & the Social Question. Franz H. Mueller. 158p. 1984. 33.25 (*0-8447-3567-1*) Am Enterprise.

Church & the Society in Latin American. Ed. by Jeffrey A. Cole. 379p. 1984. pap. 12.00 (*0-317-43435-7*) Tulane Lat Am Lib.

Church & the Twentieth Century. Ed. by George L. Harvey. LC 67-26747. (Essay Index Reprint Ser.). 1977. 23.95 (*0-8369-0517-2*) Ayer.

Church & the Urban Challenge. Walter Kloetzli. LC 61-14757. 95p. reprint ed. pap. 27.10 (*0-685-15443-2*, 2027195) Bks Demand.

Church & the Welsh Border in the Central Middle Ages. Christopher Brooke. Ed. by D. N. Dunville & C. N. Brooke. (Studies in Celtic History). 1986. 55.00 (*0-85115-175-2*) Boydell & Brewer.

Church & the Work, 3 vols. Watchman Nee. Tr. by Stephen Kaung. 550p. (CHI.). 1982. reprint ed. 30.00 (*0-935008-57-8*); reprint ed. pap. text ed. 17.00 (*0-935008-58-6*) Christian Fellow Pubs.

Church & the Young People. Ed. by Jesse P. Sewell & Henry E. Speck. 1935. 1.50 (*0-88027-105-1*) Firm Foun Pub.

Church & Theology: Essays in Memory of Carl J. Peter. Ed. by Peter C. Phan. LC 93-41316. 320p. 1995. 59.95 (*0-8132-0798-3*) Cath U Pr.

Church & Third World Revolution. Pierre Bigo. LC 76-55388. 320p. reprint ed. pap. 91.20 (*0-8357-8848-2*, 2033476) Bks Demand.

Church & University in the Scottish Enlightenment: The Moderate Literati of Edinburgh. Richard B. Sher. LC 85-17911. (Illus.). 1985. text ed. 62.50x (*0-691-05445-2*) Princeton U Pr.

Church & Usury. Patrick Cleary. 1979. lib. bdg. 250.00 (*0-8490-2884-1*) Gordon Pr.

Church & Wealth. Ed. by W. J. Sheils & Diana Wood. (Studies in Church History: Vol. 25). (Illus.). 384p. 1987. text ed. 59.95 (*0-631-15901-0*) Blackwell Pubs.

Church & Women: A Compendium. Joseph C. Ratzinger et al. Tr. by Lothar Krauth et al. LC 88-81309. 277p. (Orig.). 1988. pap. 14.95 (*0-89870-164-3*) Ignatius Pr.

Church & World in the New Testament. Johannes Schneider. LC 82-25879. 59p. 1983. pap. 5.45 (*0-86554-063-2*, P11) Mercer Univ Pr.

***Church Anthem Handbook.** Lionel Dakers. 32p. 1995. pap. 5.95 (*0-19-353108-9*) OUP.

Church Architecture. Henry H. Holly. 1980. lib. bdg. 75.00 (*0-8490-3141-9*) Gordon Pr.

Church Architecture. Frederick C. Withers. 1980. lib. bdg. 64.95 (*0-8490-3198-2*) Gordon Pr.

Church Architecture of Robert Mills. Rhodri W. Liscombe. (Illus.). 160p. 1985. 30.00 (*0-89308-542-1*) Southern Hist Pr.

***Church As a Healing Community: Setting up Shop to Deal with the Pain of Life-Controlling Problems.** Mike S. O'Neil & Charles E. Newbold, Jr. 177p. (Orig.). 1995. pap. 19.95 (*0-9633454-1-9*) Sonlight Pub.

Church As Idea & Fact. Daniel Donovan. LC 88-81139. (Zacchaeus Studies). 95p. (Orig.). 1988. pap. 6.95 (*0-8146-5685-4*) Liturgical Pr.

Church As Partner in Community Economic Development: Proceedings from a Forum & Consultation. Theatrice Williams & B. Bakama. 128p. (Orig.). (C). 1994. pap. text ed. 60.00 (*0-7881-0752-6*) Diane Pub.

***Church As Polis: From Political Theology to Theological Politics.** Arne Rasmusson. LC 94-45054. (C). 1995. text ed. 34.95x (*0-268-00810-8*) U of Notre Dame Pr.

***Church as Polis: From Political Theology to Theological Politics as Exemplified by Jurgen Moltmann & Stanley Hauerwas.** Arne Rasmusson et al. LC 94-45054. 1995. write for info. (*0-268-00809-4*) U of Notre Dame Pr.

Church As Sacrament see Dogma

Church As the Body of Christ in the Pauline Corpus: A Re-Examination. Gosnell L. Yorke. 176p. (C). 1991. lib. bdg. 46.50 (*0-8191-8215-X*); pap. text ed. 26.00 (*0-8191-8216-8*) U Pr of Amer.

Church As the Fullness of Christ. Bill Freeman. 14p. (Orig.). 1992. pap. 1.00 (*0-914271-26-1*) Mnstry Wrd.

Church at Prayer: A Holy Temple of the Lord. 60p. 1983. pap. 2.50 (*1-55586-900-9*) US Catholic.

Church at Prayer: An Introduction to the Liturgy. Ed. by Aime G. Martimort. LC 92-28775. 1992. 49.95 (*0-8146-2209-7*) Liturgical Pr.

Church at Prayer: Principles of the Liturgy, Vol. 1. A. G. Martimort et al. Tr. by Matthew J. O'Connell. 316p. 1987. pap. 15.95 (*0-8146-1363-2*) Liturgical Pr.

Church at Prayer: The Eucharist, Vol. 2. Robert Cabie et al. Ed. by A. G. Martimort. Tr. by Matthew O'Connell. Orig. Title: L'Eglise en Priere: L'eucharistie. 287p. 1986. pap. 15.95 (*0-8146-1364-0*) Liturgical Pr.

Church at Prayer: The Sacraments, Vol. 3. Robert Cabie et al. Ed. by Damien Sicard. Tr. by Matthew O'Connell. 337p. 1988. pap. 15.95 (*0-8146-1365-9*) Liturgical Pr.

***Church at Risk: The Challenge of Spiritually Hungry Adults.** Marcel Dumestre. 192p. (Orig.). 1995. pap. 15.95 (*0-8245-1461-0*) Crossroad NY.

Church at Study. 96p. 1992. pap. text ed. 7.95 (*0-910566-51-8*); teacher ed, ring bd. 10.95 (*0-910566-52-6*) Evang Trg Assn.

Church at the End of the Twentieth Century: Including, the Church Before the Watching World. 2nd ed. Francis A. Schaeffer. LC 93-49997. (Illus.). 1994. pap. 9.99 (*0-89107-789-8*) Crossway Bks.

Church at Work in the Modern World. Ed. by William C. Bower. LC 67-26717. (Essay Index Reprint Ser.). 1977. 20.95 (*0-8369-0231-9*) Ayer.

Church Becoming Christ's Body: The Small Church's Manual of Dances for Holy Seasons. Dane Packard. Ed. by Doug Adams. 110p. (Orig.). 1985. pap. 7.95 (*0-941500-35-7*) Sharing Co.

***Church Before the Watching World.** Francis A. Schaeffer. Tr. by Anna C. Lee. 137p. (CHI.). 1975. pap. 3.25 (*1-56582-096-7*) Christ Renew Min.

An Asterisk (*) at the beginning of an entry indicates that the title is appearing in BIP for the first time.

C

An Asterisk (*) at the beginning of an entry indicates that the title is appearing in BIP for the first time.

1263

Church in Exile: God's Counter-Culture in a Non-Christian World. James Thompson. LC 89-81439. 140p. 1990. pap. 10.95 (*0-89112-096-3*) Abilene Christ U.

Church in God's Program. Robert L. Saucy. LC 70-175496. (Handbook of Bible Doctrine Ser.). 1972. pap. 9.99 (*0-8024-1544-X*) Moody.

Church in History. John E. Booty. (Church's Teaching Ser.: Vol. 3). 320p. 1984. pap. 13.00 (*0-8164-2216-8*) Harper SF.

Church in History. B. K. Kuiper. 1951. student ed 18.99 (*0-8028-1314-3*); pap. 19.99 (*0-8028-1777-7*) Eerdmans.

Church in Late Victorian Scotland, 1874-1900. Andrew L. Drummond & James Bulloch. 352p. (C). 1988. text ed. 80.00 (*0-7152-0371-1*) St Mut.

Church in Latin America, 1492-1992. Ed. by Enrique Dussel. LC 92-21631. 400p. (Orig.). 1992. 49.95 (*0-88344-820-3*) Orbis Bks.

Church in Mission. Wilbert R. Shenk. LC 84-81231. (Mennonite Faith Ser.: No. 15). 1984. pap. 1.95 (*0-8361-3377-3*) Herald Pr.

Church in Our Day. NCCB Staff. 78p. 1967. 1.25 (*1-55586-041-9*) US Catholic.

Church in Perspective: Standard Course for Layreaders. rev. ed. Edmund Partridge. LC 68-56918. 113p. 1976. pap. 5.95 (*0-8192-1210-5*) Morehouse Pub.

Church in Rome in the First Century. George Edmundson. 1976. lib. bdg. 59.95 (*0-8490-1627-4*) Gordon Pr.

Church in Soviet Russia. Matthew Spinka. LC 80-18191. xi, 179p. 1980. reprint ed. text ed. 59.75 (*0-313-22658-X*, SPCR, Greenwood Pr) Greenwood.

Church in Spain, Seventeen Thirty-Seven to Nineteen Thirty-Seven. Edgar A. Peers. 1980. lib. bdg. 44.95 (*0-8490-3149-4*) Gordon Pr.

Church in the African City. Aylward Shorter. LC 90-47577. 175p. (Orig.). 1991. pap. 19.95 (*0-88344-746-0*) Orbis Bks.

Church in the Age of Absolutism & Enlightenment. Hubert Jedin. Ed. by John P. Dolan. (History of the Church Ser.: Vol. 6). 1981. 59.50x (*0-8245-0010-5*) Crossroad NY.

Church in the Age of Liberalism, Vol. 8. Hubert Jedin. Ed. by John P. Dolan. (History of the Church Ser.: Vol. 8). 1981. 59.50x (*0-8245-0011-3*) Crossroad NY.

Church in the Bible. 9th ed. Don DeWelt. (Bible Study Textbook Ser.). (Illus.). 424p. 1988. pap. 10.99 (*0-89900-221-8*) College Pr Pub.

Church in the Bible & the World: An International Study. Ed. by D. A. Carson. LC 93-16687. (World Evangelical Fellowship Ser.). 368p. (Orig.). 1988. pap. 19.99 (*0-8010-2526-5*) Baker Bk.

Church in the Changing Community: An Area of Sociological Research. Fordham University, Department of Political Philosophy & the Social Sciences Staff. (Publications in the Social Sciences: No. 1). 83p. reprint ed. pap. 25.00 (*0-7837-5576-7*, 2045358) Bks Demand.

Church in the City: Samuel C. Kincheloe & the Sociology of the City Church. Samuel C. Kincheloe. LC 88-81958. (Studies in Ministry & Parish Life). 176p. 1989. text ed. 22.95 (*0-913552-40-2*) Exploration Pr.

Church in the Industrial Age, Vol. 9. Hubert Jedin. Ed. by John P. Dolan. (History of the Church Ser.: Vol. 9). 1981. 59.50x (*0-8245-0012-1*) Crossroad NY.

Church in the Life of the Black Family. Wallace C. Smith. (Family Life Ser.). 160p. 1985. pap. 11.00 (*0-8170-1040-8*) Judson.

Church in the Market Place. George Carey. LC 90-25405. 154p. 1991. reprint ed. pap. 7.95 (*0-8192-1562-7*) Morehouse Pub.

Church in the Market Place: Study Guide. Michael P. Knowles. LC 90-25405. 20p. (Orig.). 1993. pap. 3.95 (*0-8192-1607-0*) Morehouse Pub.

Church in the Marketplace. George Carey. (Orig.). 1989. pap. 16.95 (*0-86065-727-2*) Trans-Atl Phila.

Church in the Midst of Creation. Vincent J. Donovan. LC 88-35614. 150p. 1989. pap. 12.95 (*0-88344-366-X*) Orbis Bks.

Church in the Modern Age. Ed. by Hubert Jedin & John P. Dolan. (History of the Church Ser.: Vol. 10). 1980. 59.50 (*0-8245-0013-X*) Crossroad NY.

Church in the Movement of the Spirit. Ed. by William R. Barr & Rena M. Yocom. LC 94-5572. 1994. pap. 12.99 (*0-8028-0554-X*) Eerdmans.

Church in the Nineties: It's Legacy, It's Future. Ed. by Pierre M. Hegy. 352p. (Orig.). 1993. pap. text ed. 19.95 (*0-8146-2098-1*) Liturgical Pr.

Church in the Power of the Spirit: A Contribution to Messianic Ecclesiology. Jurgen Moltmann. Tr. by Margaret Kohl. LC 93-29951. 1993. 16.00 (*0-8006-2821-7*, Fortress Pr) Augsburg Fortress.

Church in the Round: Feminist Interpretation of the Church. Letty M. Russell. 272p. (Orig.). 1993. pap. 14.99 (*0-664-25070-X*) Westminster John Knox.

Church in the World. William R. Inge. LC 68-57324. (Essay Index Reprint Ser.). 1977. 19.95 (*0-8369-0080-4*) Ayer.

Church in Today's World. Ed. by Henry R. Rust. pap. 8.95 (*1-877871-29-X*, 3544) Ed Ministries.

*__Church in Transition.__ James S. Woodroof. 210p. (Orig.). 1990. pap. 6.95 (*0-9622649-1-1*) Bible Hse.

Church Is Christ. Bill Freeman. (Illus.). 238p. (Orig.). 1993. pap. 6.00 (*0-914271-42-3*) Mnstry Wrd.

Church is in a Stew: Developing Multi-Congregational Churches. Jerry Appleby. 144p. (Orig.). 1990. 6.95 (*0-8341-1357-0*) Beacon Hill.

Church Is One. Alexei Khomiakov. 1988. pap. 1.00 (*0-89981-215-5*) Eastern Orthodox.

Church Is One. Alexei S. Khomiakov. (Illus.). 1980. reprint ed. pap. 1.25 (*0-913026-23-9*) St Nectarios.

Church Is Stranger Than Fiction. Mary Chambers. LC 90-37194. (Illus.). 104p. (Orig.). 1990. pap. 6.99 (*0-8308-1326-8*, 1326) InterVarsity.

Church Is You & I. Carl B. Rife & Carolyn Bishop. 1984. 2.00 (*0-89536-658-4*, 0394) CSS OH.

Church Laces-Creative Crocheting. Mary E. Crockett. (Illus.). 125p. 1980. 9.00 (*0-8187-0037-8*) Harlo Press.

Church, Law & Society in Catalonia, 900-1500. Paul Freedman. (Collected Studies: No. CS 440). 288p. 1994. 77.50 (*0-86078-414-2*, Pub. by Variorum UK) Ashgate Pub Co.

Church Leaders in Primitive Times. William Lefroy. 1977. lib. bdg. 69.95 (*0-8490-1628-2*) Gordon Pr.

Church Leadership: Vision, Team, Culture, & Integrity. Lovett H. Weems, Jr. LC 93-18119. 144p. (Orig.). 1993. pap. 10.95 (*0-687-13341-6*) Abingdon.

Church Leadership, Call to Virtue. Calvin B. Rock. (Anchor Ser.). 96p. 1989. pap. 2.99 (*0-8163-0859-4*) Pacific Pr Pub Assn.

Church Library Promotion: A Handbook of How-Tos. Ginger Caughman. LC 89-43642. (Illus.). 264p. 1990. lib. bdg. 31.50 (*0-89950-288-1*) McFarland & Co.

Church Library Workbook. Francine E. Walls. 144p. 1980. pap. 3.00 (*0-89367-048-0*) Light & Life.

Church Life & Church Order During the First Four Centuries. James V. Bartlet. Ed. by Cecil J. Cadoux. 1980. lib. bdg. 59.95 (*0-8490-3147-8*) Gordon Pr.

Church Life Before Constantine. Graydon F. Snyder. LC 84-27328. 169p. (Orig.). 1991. pap. 19.95 (*0-940232-42-1*) Seedsowers.

Church Life in England in the Thirteenth Century. John R. Moorman. LC 76-29401. reprint ed. 49.50 (*0-404-15352-6*) AMS Pr.

Church Life in Norway: 1800-1950. Einar Molland. Tr. by Kaasa Harris. LC 78-2711. 120p. 1978. reprint ed. text ed. 45.00 (*0-313-20342-3*, MOCL, Greenwood Pr) Greenwood.

Church Maintained in Church. Hans Kung. 1980. 6.95 (*0-8164-0454-2*) Harper SF.

Church Meetings That Matter. enl. ed. Philip A. Anderson. LC 86-30262. 120p. 1987. pap. 9.95 (*0-8298-0752-7*) Pilgrim OH.

*__Church Meetings That Work.__ Gaylord Noyce. 1995. 9.95 (*1-56699-132-3*, AL153) Alban Inst.

Church Member's Handbook. Joe T. Odle. pap. 1.50 (*0-8054-9401-4*) Broadman.

Church Membership As a Catholic & Ecumenical Problem. Avery Dulles. (Pere Marquette Lectures). 1974. 10.00 (*0-87462-506-8*) Marquette.

*__Church Memorial Brasses & Brass Rubbing.__ Leigh Chapman. (C). 1989. pap. 25.00x (*0-85263-905-8*, Pub. by Shire UK) St Mut.

Church Mice & the Moon. Graham Oakley. LC 74-75569. (Illus.). 40p. (J). (gr. k-3). 1974. 13.95 (*0-689-30437-4*, Atheneum Bks Young) S&S Childrens.

Church Mice & the Ring. Graham Oakley. LC 91-45273. (Illus.). 32p. (J). (ps up). 1992. 14.95 (*0-689-31790-5*, Atheneum Bks Young) S&S Childrens.

Church Mice in Action. Graham Oakley. LC 82-11394. (Illus.). 32p. (J). (gr. k-3). 1983. 13.95 (*0-689-30949-X*, Atheneum Bks Young) S&S Childrens.

Church Mice Spread Their Wings. Graham Oakley. LC 75-15102. (Illus.). 40p. (J). (gr. k-3). 1976. 13.95 (*0-689-30496-X*, Atheneum Bks Young) S&S Childrens.

Church Militant & Iberian Expansion, 1440-1770. Charles R. Boxer. LC 77-18386. (Johns Hopkins Symposia in Comparative History Ser.: No. 10). 160p. reprint ed. pap. 45.60 (*0-8357-8074-0*, 2034135) Bks Demand.

Church Ministering to Adults. Jerry M. Stubblefield. LC 86-2299. (Orig.). 1986. pap. 9.99 (*0-8054-3235-3*) Broadman.

Church, Ministry, & Organization in the Early Church Era. Ed. by Everett Ferguson. LC 92-42822. (Studies in Early Christianity: Vol. 13). 408p. 1993. 58.00 (*0-8153-1073-0*) Garland.

*__Church, Ministry, & Sacraments in the New Testament.__ C. K. Barrett. 109p. (Orig.). Date not set. pap. 9.95 (*0-85364-406-3*) Attic Pr.

*__Church Misericords & Bench Ends.__ Richard Hayman. (C). 1989. pap. 25.00x (*0-85263-996-1*, Pub. by Shire UK) St Mut.

Church Monastery Cathedral: A Guide to the Symbolism of the Christian Tradition. Herbert Whone. 1990. pap. 15.95 (*1-85230-179-1*) Element MA.

*__Church Monuments.__ Brian Kemp. (C). 1989. pap. 25.00x (*0-85263-768-3*, Pub. by Shire UK) St Mut.

Church Monuments in Romantic England. Nicholas Penny. LC 76-58912. (Studies in British Art). (Illus.). 1977. 50.00 (*0-300-02075-9*) Yale U Pr.

Church Mouse. Graham Oakley. LC 72-75276. (Illus.). 40p. (J). (gr. k-3). 1972. 13.95 (*0-689-30058-1*, Atheneum Bks Young) S&S Childrens.

Church Multiplication Guide: Helping Churches to Reproduce Locally & Abroad. George Patterson & Richard Scoggins. LC 93-40678. 128p. 1994. pap. 5.95 (*0-87808-245-X*) William Carey Lib.

Church Music: An International Bibliography. Richard C. Von Ende. LC 79-23697. 473p. 1980. lib. bdg. 42.50 (*0-8108-1271-1*) Scarecrow.

Church Music: An International Bibliography. Richard C. Von Ende. LC 79-23697. 473p. reprint ed. pap. 134.90 (*0-317-52049-0*, 2027497) Bks Demand.

Church Music & Musical Life in Pennsylvania in the Eighteenth Century, 3 vols. in 4 pts. National Society of Colonial Dames of America Staff. LC 79-38037. (Illus.). reprint ed. Vol. 3, Pt. 1. write for info. (*0-404-08093-6*); reprint ed. Vol. 3, Pt. 2. write for info. (*0-404-08094-4*) AMS Pr.

Church Music & Musical Life in Pennsylvania in the Eighteenth Century, 3 vols. in 4 pts., 1. National Society of Colonial Dames of America Staff. LC 79-38037. (Illus.). reprint ed. write for info. (*0-404-08091-X*) AMS Pr.

Church Music & Musical Life in Pennsylvania in the Eighteenth Century, 3 vols. in 4 pts., 2. National Society of Colonial Dames of America Staff. LC 79-38037. (Illus.). reprint ed. write for info. (*0-404-08092-8*) AMS Pr.

Church Music & Musical Life in Pennsylvania in the Eighteenth Century, 3 vols. in 4 pts., Set. National Society of Colonial Dames of America Staff. LC 79-38037. (Illus.). reprint ed. 195.00 (*0-404-08090-1*) AMS Pr.

Church Music & the Christian Faith. Erik Routley. LC 78-110219. 156p. 1978. pap. 9.95 (*0-916642-10-0*) Agape IL.

Church Music & the Christian Faith. Erik Routley. LC 78-110219. 1979. 9.95 (*0-916642-11-9*) Hope Pub.

Church Music Handbook: For Pastors & Musicians. N. Lee Orr. 1991. 11.95 (*0-687-07853-9*) Abingdon.

Church Music Handbook: 1991-1992. 10th ed. Paul Hamill. (Illus.). 96p. 1991. pap. 10.95 (*0-9626099-1-9*) Gemini Pr MA.

Church Music Handbook: 1993-1994. 12th ed. Paul Hamill. (Illus.). 128p. 1993. pap. text ed. 11.95 (*0-9626099-3-5*) Gemini Pr MA.

Church Music Handbook, 1992-1993. Paul Hamill. 128p. 1992. pap. 11.95 (*0-9626099-2-7*) Gemini Pr MA.

Church Music Handbook, 1994-1995. Ed. by Paul Hamill. (Illus.). 128p. 1994. pap. 12.95 (*0-9626099-4-3*) Gemini Pr MA.

*__Church Music Handbook, 1995-1996.__ Paul Hamill. (Illus.). 133p. 1995. pap. 12.95 (*0-9626099-5-1*) Gemini Pr MA.

Church Music in America. Nathaniel D. Gould. 1980. lib. bdg. 59.75 (*0-8490-3192-3*) Gordon Pr.

Church Music in America, Comprising Its History & Its Peculiarities at Different Periods. Nathaniel D. Gould. LC 78-144620. reprint ed. 37.50 (*0-404-02888-8*) AMS Pr.

Church Music in History & Practice. Charles W. Douglas. (Music Book Index Ser.). 311p. 1992. reprint ed. lib. bdg. 89.00 (*0-7812-9474-6*) Rprt Serv.

Church Music in the Nineteenth Century. Arthur Hutchings. LC 77-7920. (Studies in Church Music). 166p. 1977. reprint ed. text ed. 35.00 (*0-8371-9695-7*, HUCMN, Greenwood Pr) Greenwood.

Church Music of Heinrich Biber. Eric T. Chafe. LC 86-30866. (Studies in Musicology: No. 95). reprint ed. pap. 85.60 (*0-8357-1770-4*, 2070661) Bks Demand.

Church Music of William Billings. James M. Barbour. LC 72-39000. 167p. 1972. reprint ed. lib. bdg. 27.50 (*0-306-70434-X*) Da Capo.

Church Musicians Enchiridion. A. Lehmann. 1979. 3.25 (*0-8100-0111-X*, 15N0369) Northwest Pub.

Church, Nation & State in Russia & Ukraine. Ed. by Geoffrey A. Hosking. LC 91-6751. 376p. 1991. text ed. 65.00 (*0-312-06092-0*) St Martin.

Church Needlepoint. 2nd ed. Carolyn H. Kerr & Louise A. Raynor. (Illus.). 80p. 1989. spiral bd. 10.95 (*0-8192-1436-1*) Morehouse Pub.

Church Needlework. Beryl Dean. (Illus.). 176p. 1991. 39.95 (*0-7134-6405-4*, Pub. by Batsford UK) Trafalgar.

Church of Christ. 227p. (SPA.). 1994. pap. 7.95 (*1-878990-33-0*) Howard Pub LA.

Church of Christ. Michael Richards. (C). 1988. 39.00 (*0-85439-203-3*, Pub. by St Paul Pubns UK) St Mut.

Church of Christ. Edward C. Wharton. 137p. (Orig.). 1981. pap. 7.95 (*1-878990-08-X*) Howard Pub LA.

Church of Christ Not An Ecclesiasticism: A Letter to a Sectarian. Henry James, Sr. LC 72-922. (Selected Works of Henry James, Sr.: Vol. 2). reprint ed. 27.50 (*0-404-10082-1*) AMS Pr.

Church of England & Social Reform since 1854. Donald O. Wagner. LC 77-127438. (Columbia University. Studies in the Social Sciences: No. 325). 22.50 (*0-404-51325-5*) AMS Pr.

Church of England, 1570-1640. Andrew Foster. LC 93-23462. (Seminar Studies in History). (C). 1995. pap. text ed. 11.95 (*0-582-35574-5*, Pub. by Longman UK) Longman.

Church of England, 1689-1833: From Toleration to Tractarianism. Ed. by John Walsh et al. LC 92-42707. 420p. (C). 1993. 69.95 (*0-521-41732-5*) Cambridge U Pr.

Church of God. Louis Bouyer. Tr. by Charles U. Quinn. 1983. 25.00 (*0-8199-0777-4*, Frncscn Herld) Franciscan Pr.

Church of God: A Social History. Mickey Crews. LC 89-38121. (Illus.). 272p. 1990. text ed. 36.00x (*0-87049-634-4*) U of Tenn Pr.

Church of God: History & Prophecy. Wade Phillips. (Systematic Ecclesiology Ser.). 120p. (Orig.). 1990. pap. 6.95 (*0-934942-82-X*, 2442) White Wing Pub.

Church of God & Saints of Christ: The Rise of Black Jews. Elly M. Wynia. LC 94-486. (Cults & Nonconventional Religious Groups Ser.). 1994. write for info. (*0-8153-0356-4*); 39.00 (*0-8153-1136-2*) Garland.

Church of God As Revealed in Scripture. Arlo Newell. 1983. pap. 1.95 (*0-87162-269-6*, D4775) Warner Pr.

Church of God Distinctives. Ray H. Hughes. 1989. 5.99 (*0-87148-192-8*) Pathway Pr.

Church of God Doctrines. C. C. Carver. 180p. 1948. pap. 2.50 (*0-686-29106-9*) Faith Pub Hse.

Church of God of Prophecy: History & Polity. James Stone. 1977. 12.95 (*0-934942-02-1*) White Wing Pub.

Church of God of Prophecy: Pastor. R. L. Black. 1977. 4.25 (*0-934942-29-3*) White Wing Pub.

Church of Ireland: Ecclesiastical Reform & Revolution, 1880-1885. Donald H. Akenson. LC 76-151565. 428p. reprint ed. pap. 122.00 (*0-317-08435-6*, 2013197) Bks Demand.

Church of Jesus Begins. Norman Bull. (C). 1984. pap. 10.95 (*0-7175-0983-4*, Pub. by S Thornes UK) Dufour.

Church of Jesus Grows. Norman Bull. (Bible Story & Its Background Ser.: Vol. 8). (J). (gr. 2-7). 1979. 10.95 (*0-7175-0454-9*) Dufour.

Church of Many Cultures: Selected Historical Essays on Ethnic American Catholicism. Ed. by Dolores Liptak. (Heritage of American Catholicism Ser.). 416p. 1988. lib. bdg. 20.00 (*0-8240-4081-3*) Garland.

Church of My Dreams. John Beaumont. 182p. (Orig.). 1988. pap. 6.99 (*0-914903-61-6*) Destiny Image.

Church of Notre-Dame in Montreal: An Architectural History. Franklin Toker. LC 70-98392. (Illus.). (C). 1970. 42.95 (*0-7735-0058-8*, Pub. by McGill CN) U of Toronto Pr.

Church of Notre-Dame in Montreal: An Architectural History. 2nd ed. Franklin Toker. (Illus.). 196p. (C). 1991. reprint ed. pap. text ed. 24.95 (*0-7735-0848-1*, Pub. by McGill CN) U of Toronto Pr.

Church of Our Fathers. Roland H. Bainton. 1987. pap. 8.99 (*0-88019-211-9*) Schmul Pub Co.

Church of Our Fathers. Roland H. Bainton. (Illus.). 222p. (C). 1978. pap. write for info. (*0-02-305450-6*, Scribners) S&S Trade.

Church of Our Fathers. Ronald H. Bainton. 1984. 32.25 (*0-8446-6120-1*) Peter Smith.

Church of Our Fathers: The Story of Old St. Michaels. 2nd ed. Dorothy Miles. Ed. by Alexander MacDonald. 112p. (Orig.). 1984. reprint ed. pap. write for info. (*0-318-65391-5*) D Miles.

*__Church of Power: The Invincible Movement of the Christian Church Through an Upside Down World: Completely Revised with Two New Exciting Chapters on the Acts of the Apostles.__ Amos Jones, Jr. 1994. write for info. (*0-9605592-0-5*) Amos Jones Jr.

Church of Power Is Emerging. Don Faix. 224p. (Orig.). 1993. pap. 8.99 (*1-56043-782-0*) Destiny Image.

Church of Salvation? J. Fred Farrell. 100p. 1991. pap. 7.95 (*0-685-46914-X*) Charlemagne Pr.

Church of Satan. Blanche Barton. (Illus.). 200p. (Orig.). 1990. pap. 8.95 (*0-9623286-2-6*) Hells Kitchen.

Church of Scientology & L. Ron Hubbard. June D. Littler. LC 92-15175. 400p. 60.00 (*0-8240-4345-6*, SS468) Garland.

Church of Scotland Year Book, 1992. Andrew Herron. 392p. (C). 1989. pap. 75.00 (*0-86153-144-2*, Pub. by St Andrew UK) St Mut.

Church of Scotland Yearbook 1993. James Black. 392p. 1993. pap. 40.00 (*0-86153-166-3*) St Mut.

Church of St. Helen, Bishopsgate, Pt. 1. Minnie Reddan & Alfred W. Clapham. LC 74-6179. (London County Council. Survey of London Ser.: No. 9). reprint ed. 84.50 (*0-404-51659-9*) AMS Pr.

Church of Sweden on the Delaware 1638-1831. Conrad Bergendoff. LC 87-71046. (Augustana Historical Society Publication Ser.: No. 37). 38p. 1988. pap. 5.00 (*0-910184-37-2*) Augustana.

Church of the Baptized: Overcoming Tension Between the Clergy & the Laity. Remi Parent. Tr. by Stephen W. Arndt. 1989. pap. 12.95 (*0-8091-3076-9*) Paulist Pr.

Church of the Brethren Yesterday & Today. Donald F. Durnbaugh. Ed. by David Eller. 192p. (Orig.). 1986. pap. 11.95 (*0-87178-151-4*) Brethren.

Church of the East & the Church of England. J. F. Coakley. (Illus.). 384p. 1992. 85.00 (*0-19-826744-4*) OUP.

Church of the Future: A Model for the Year 2001. Walbert Buhlmann. LC 86-178053. 221p. (Orig.). reprint ed. pap. 63.00 (*0-7837-5526-0*, 2045296) Bks Demand.

Church of the Holy Sepulchre. Henry T. Duckworth. LC 78-63361. (BCL Ser.). (Illus.). reprint ed. 39.50 (*0-404-17014-5*) AMS Pr.

Church of the Jews. Norman Bull. (Bible Story & Its Background Ser.: Vol. 4). (J). (gr. 2-7). 1975. 10.95 (*0-7175-0450-6*) Dufour.

Church of the Living God. R. K. Campbell. pap. 6.95 (*0-88172-007-0*) Believers Bkshelf.

Church of the Living God, the Pillar & Ground of the Truth, Inc. Constitution, Government, & General Decree Book. 1924. pap. write for info. (*0-910003-00-9*) New & Living.

Church of the Living God, the Pillar & Ground of the Truth, Inc: General Assembly Programs 1978-1987. Ed. by Helen M. Lewis & Meharry H. Lewis. (Illus.). 200p. 1987. lib. bdg. 35.00 (*0-910003-03-3*) New & Living.

Church of the Living God, the Pillar & Ground of the Truth, Inc. Minister's Guide & Handbook. Church of the Living God, the Pillar & Ground of the Truth, Inc. Supreme Executive Council Staff. LC 88-90896. 150p. 1988. 30.00 (*0-910003-04-1*) New & Living.

Church of the Living God, the Pillar & Ground of the Truth, Inc. Training Guide for Mission Workers & Missionaries. Church of the Living God, the Pillar & Ground of the Truth, Inc. Supreme Executive Council Staff. Ed. by Meharry H. Lewis et al. LC 89-92041. 51p. (Orig.). (C). 1989. pap. write for info. (*0-910003-06-8*) New & Living.

Church of the Living God, the Pillar & Ground of the Truth, Inc. 75th Anniversary Yearbook. 1978. 30.00 (*0-910003-02-5*) New & Living.

Church of the Poor Devil. Dunne. 1982. 14.38 (*0-02-533960-5*) Macmillan.

Church of the Poor Devil: Reflections on a Riverboat Voyage & a Spiritual Journey. John S. Dunne. LC 83-14548. (C). 1983. pap. text ed. 8.95 (*0-268-00746-2*) U of Notre Dame Pr.

An Asterisk (*) at the beginning of an entry indicates that the title is appearing in BIP for the first time.

***Church of the Sacred Heart: Prague 1922-33: Joze Plecnik.** Ivan Margolius. (Architecture in Detail Ser.). (Illus.). 60p. (Orig.). (C). 1995. pap. 29.95 (*0-7148-3351-7*, Pub. by Phaidon Press UK) Chronicle Bks.

Church of the Word: A Comparative Study of Word, Church & Office in the Thought of Karl Rahner & Gerhard Ebeling. John B. Ackley. LC 90-35342. (American University Studies: Theology & Religion: Ser. VII, Vol. 81). 381p. (C). 1993. text ed. 59.95 (*0-8204-1389-5*) P Lang Pubs.

Church Office Handbook: A Basic Guide to Keeping Order. Carol R. Shearn. LC 86-18200. 288p. (Orig.). 1986. pap. 12.95 (*0-8192-1391-8*) Morehouse Pub.

Church Office Handbook for Ministers. Betty Powers & E. Jane Mall. 80p. 1983. pap. 6.00 (*0-8170-1011-4*) Judson.

Church Officers at Work. Glenn H. Asquith. 1951. pap. 8.50 (*0-8170-0048-8*) Judson.

Church on Parade. John E. Walsh. LC 83-62517. 1984. pap. 7.95 (*0-89390-053-2*) Resource Pubns.

Church on the Way see Igreja do Caminho

Church or the Bible? Hubert J. Marshall. LC 93-91524. 167p. (Orig.). 1993. 9.95 (*0-9636743-4-X*) Marshall Pub.

Church Organ. Noel Bonavia-Hunt. 140p. 1991. reprint ed. text ed. 69.00 (*0-7812-9327-8*) Rprt Serv.

Church Organ Method. Mildred Andrews & Pauline Riddle. 123p. 1973. pap. 16.95 (*0-8258-0050-1*, 04904) Fischer Inc NY.

Church Organist. 2nd ed. Henry Coleman. 1968. 13.95 (*0-19-322100-4*) OUP.

Church Organization Development: Perspectives & Resources. H. Newton Malony. LC 86-81285. (Orig.). 1986. pap. 16.95 (*0-9609928-2-0*) Integ Pr.

Church Organs: A Guide to Selection & Purchase. John Ogasapian. (Illus.). 144p. (Orig.). 1991. reprint ed. pap. 6.95 (*0-913499-06-4*) Organ Hist Soc.

Church Papists: Catholicism, Conformity & Confessional Polemic in Early Modern England. Alexandra Walsham. (Royal Historical Society: Studies in History: Vol. 68). 160p. (C). 1993. text ed. 53.00 (*0-86193-225-0*) Boydell & Brewer.

Church Paraments in Needlework. William R. Doser & Mabel S. Doser. (Illus.). 180p. 1985. 14.50 (*0-9618948-1-4*) Doser Designs.

Church Peace Union: Visions of Peace in Troubled Times. Karen K. Sinclair. LC 92-36024. (Non-profit Institutions in America Ser.). 176p. 1993. 45.00 (*0-8153-0909-0*) Garland.

Church People Beware! William J. Carl, III. 1992. pap. 6.75 (*1-55673-426-3*, 9229) CSS OH.

Church People in the Struggle: The National Council of Churches & the Black Freedom Movement, 1950-1970. James Findlay. LC 92-27457. (Religion in America Ser.). 1993. 42.00 (*0-19-507967-1*) OUP.

***Church Philanthropy for Native Americans & Other Minorities: A Guide to Multicultural Funding from Religious Sources.** Phyllis A. Meiners & Greg A. Sanford. (Illus.). 350p. 1994. pap. 118.95 (*0-9633694-3-1*) CRC Pub CO.

***Church, Pilgrim of Centuries.** fac. ed. Thomas S. Molnar. LC 90-41597. 192p. 1990. reprint ed. pap. 54.80 (*0-7837-7965-8*, 2047721) Bks Demand.

Church Planning Questionnaire: Manual & Discoveries from 100 Churches. Grayson L. Tucker, Jr. 161p. (Orig.). 1983. pap. text ed. 11.00 (*0-9610706-0-9*) G L Tucker.

Church Planter's Dream. David Norris. 200p. (Orig.). 1992. pap. 6.95 (*1-56722-006-1*) Word Aflame.

Church Planter's Handbook. Larry L. Lewis. LC 92-25513. 1992. 8.99 (*0-8054-6068-3*) Broadman.

Church Planter's Training Manual. Fred King. LC 92-74653. 160p. (Orig.). 1993. pap. 9.99 (*0-87509-526-7*) Chr Pubns.

Church Planting at the End of the Twentieth Century. rev. ed. Charles L. Chaney. LC 92-29524. 1993. 14.99 (*0-8423-1113-0*) Tyndale.

Church Planting for a Greater Harvest: A Comprehensive Guide. C. Peter Wagner. LC 90-45513. 115p. 1990. pap. 8.99 (*0-8307-1435-9*, 5421305) Regal.

Church Planting for Reproduction. Samuel D. Faircloth. LC 90-44359. 208p. 1991. pap. 14.99 (*0-8010-3558-9*) Baker Bk.

Church Planting in the African-American Community. Joe S. Ratliff. (Orig.). 1993. pap. 6.95 (*0-8054-6071-3*) Broadman.

Church Planting in Uganda: A Comparative Study. Gailyn Van Rheenen. LC 76-20461. 153p. 1976. pap. 5.95 (*0-87808-314-6*) William Carey Lib.

Church Planting, Watering & Increasing in Kenya. Kenya Mission Team. Ed. by B. J. Humble. (Illus.). 130p. 1981. pap. 2.95 (*0-88027-002-0*) Firm Foun Pub.

Church, Politics & Patronage in the Fifteenth Century. Ed. by R. B. Dobson. LC 84-15102. 245p. 1985. text ed. 29.95 (*0-312-13481-9*) St Martin.

Church, Politics, & Society in Spain, 1750-1874. William J. Callahan. (Historical Monographs: No. 73). (Illus.). 336p. 1984. 25.00 (*0-674-13125-8*) HUP.

Church Polity: How the Clergy Run the Church. Marion R. Winkler. LC 82-91145. 271p. 1983. lib. bdg. 19.95 (*0-9610344-1-6*); pap. 12.95 (*0-9610344-2-4*) M R Winkler.

Church Polity & Church Politics: Issues in Contemporary American Catholicism. Mary C. Segers. LC 89-29915. 380p. 1990. 40.00 (*0-8240-4440-1*) Garland.

Church Property & the Mexican Reform, 1856-1910. Robert J. Knowlton. LC 74-28897. (Origins of Modern Mexico Ser.). (Illus.). 265p. 1976. 27.00 (*0-87580-055-6*) N Ill U Pr.

Church Puzzle Game. Energize Associates Staff. 36p. (Orig.). 1989. pap. 9.50 (*0-940576-09-0*) Energize.

Church Records of Killingly, Connecticut. E. D. Larned. 56p. 1984. pap. 7.00 (*0-912606-22-3*) Hunterdon Hse.

Church Records of Rochester, New Hampshire. Franklin McDuffee. 52p. 1984. pap. 6.50 (*0-912606-21-5*) Hunterdon Hse.

Church Records of Rochester, NH. Franklin McDuffee. 1986. reprint ed. pap. 6.50 (*0-935207-61-9*) Danbury Hse Bks.

Church Records of Saint Matthews Lutheran Church, Orangeburg, Co., S. C. Beginning in 1799, Giving Births, Christenings, Confirmations, Marriages, & Burials & "the Red Church", 1767-1838. Anne M. Haigler. (Illus.). 126p. 1985. 20.00 (*0-89308-563-4*) Southern Hist Pr.

***Church Records of St. David's Lutheran & Reformed Church at Hebe, Jordan Township, Northumberland County, PA.** Phillip A. Rice & Jean Dellock. 74p. 1995. pap. 9.95 (*1-55856-181-1*) Closson Pr.

***Church Records of the Bethany Evangelical Congregational Church (Formerly Bethany United Evangelical Church)** Phillip A. Rice. 197p. 1994. pap. 22.95 (*1-55856-179-X*) Closson Pr.

Church Reform of Peter the Great. James Cracraft. xx, 324p. 1971. 42.50 (*0-8047-0747-2*) Stanford U Pr.

Church Roll & Record. Comp. by T. O. Tollett. 1979. 13.50 (*0-89114-017-4*) Baptist Pub Hse.

Church Sale. Donald Pollins. (Illus.). 50p. 1989. pap. 5.00 (*0-923621-00-8*) Infinity MD.

Church School Teacher's Thirty Minute Craft Book. Phyllis Barker. 36p. (Orig.). 1989. pap. 4.95 (*0-8192-4107-5*) Morehouse Pub.

Church Schools & Public Money: The Politics of Parochiaid. Edd Doerr & Al Menendez. 156p. 1991. 14.95 (*0-87975-708-6*) Prometheus Bks.

Church Serves. Joan Huyser-Honig & Steve Huyser-Honig. 86p. (Orig.). (YA). (gr. 7-8). 1987. teacher ed 8.95 (*0-930265-39-4*); pap. text ed. 7.25 (*0-930265-38-6*) CRC Pubns.

Church Shall Be Free: A Glance at Eight Centuries of Church & State. Arthur E. Sutherland. LC 65-24000. 47p. reprint ed. pap. 25.00 (*0-685-07760-8*, 2017808) Bks Demand.

Church Slavonic - Russian - English Dictionary. Ed. by V. M. Kamensky et al. 44p. (Orig.). (ENG, RUS & SLA.). 1991. pap. 6.95 (*1-878997-36-X*) St Tikhons Pr.

Church, Society, & Hegemony: A Critical Sociology of Religion in Latin America. Carlos A. Torres. LC 92-9118. 240p. 1992. text ed. 47.95 (*0-275-93773-9*, C3773, Praeger Pubs) Greenwood.

Church Soloists Favorites, 2 bks., Bk. 1: High Voice. Ed. by Carl Fredrickson. (Illus.). 64p. 1963. Bk. 1, High Voice, 64p. pap. 10.95 (*0-8258-0228-8*, RB-65) Fischer Inc NY.

Church Soloists Favorites, 2 bks., Bk. 2: Low Voice. Ed. by Carl Fredrickson. (Illus.). 85p. 1963. Bk. 2, Low Voice, 85p. pap. 10.95 (*0-8258-0229-6*, RB-66) Fischer Inc NY.

Church Speaks about Sacraments with Children: Baptism, Confirmation, Eucharist, Penance. Ed. by Mark Searle. 66p. (Orig.). 1990. pap. 4.50 (*0-929650-26-3*) Liturgy Tr Pubns.

Church Sponsored Missions. Phillip W. Elkins. 1974. pap. 3.00 (*0-88027-003-9*) Firm Foun Pub.

Church Staff Administration: Practical Approaches. Leonard E. Wedel. LC 78-51490. 1991. 12.99 (*0-8054-3105-5*) Broadman.

Church, Stage, & Studio: Music & Its Contexts in Seventeenth-Century Germany. Ed. by Paul Walker. LC 89-4919. (Studies in Music: No. 107). 408p. 1991. 59.00 (*0-8357-1938-3*) Univ Rochester Pr.

Church, State, & Christian Society at the Time of the Investiture Contest. Gerd Tellenbach. Tr. by R. F. Bennett. (Medieval Academy Reprints for Teaching Ser.: No. 27). 224p. 1991. pap. 14.95 (*0-8020-6857-X*) U of Toronto Pr.

Church, State & Jew in the Middle Ages. Robert Chazan. Ed. by Neal Kozodoy. LC 78-27221. (Library of Jewish Studies). 1979. pap. text ed. 14.95x (*0-87441-302-8*) Behrman.

Church, State, & Nation in Ireland, 1898-1921. David W. Miller. LC 72-95453. 589p. reprint ed. pap. 167.90 (*0-318-34735-0*, 2031992) Bks Demand.

Church, State & Politics: Final Report of the 1981 Chief Justice Earl Warren Conference on Advocacy in the United States. Roscoe Pound-American Trial Lawyers Foundation Staff. LC 81-85556. (Annual Chief Earl Warren Conference on Advocacy in the U. S. Ser.). 147p. 1982. pap. 25.00 (*0-933067-03-8*) Roscoe Pound Found.

Church, State, & Politics: The Diaries of John Henry Smith. limited ed. Ed. by Jean B. White. LC 89-27212. (Significant Mormon Diaries Ser.). 700p. 1991. 75.00 (*0-941214-85-0*) Signature Bks.

Church, State, & Public Policy: The New Shape of the Church - State Debate. Jay Mechling. LC 79-17711. (AEI Symposia Ser.: No. 79F). (Illus.). 136p. reprint ed. pap. 38.80 (*0-8357-4449-3*, 2037286) Bks Demand.

Church, State, & Religious Dissent: A History of Seventh-Day Adventists in Austria, 1890-1975. Daniel Heinz. LC 93-3071. 1993. write for info. (*3-631-45553-4*) P Lang Pubs.

Church-State & School in Switzerland & the U. S. A Study in Comparative Constitutional Law. Walter A. Stoeckli. (European University Studies: Law: Ser. 2, Vol. 23). 50p. 1969. 8.60 (*3-261-00081-3*) P Lang Pubs.

Church, State, & Society: 1760-1850. William Gibson. LC 93-28945. (British History in Perspective Ser.). 176p. 1994. text ed. 39.95 (*0-312-10363-8*) St Martin.

Church, State & Society under the Bourbon Kings of France. Richard M. Golden et al. 378p. (C). 1982. 15.00 (*0-87291-161-6*) Coronado Pr.

Church, State, & the Control of Schooling in Ireland, 1900-1944. E. Brian Titley. 232p. 1983. 39.95 (*0-7735-0394-3*, Pub. by McGill CN) U of Toronto Pr.

Church-State Constitutional Issues: Making Sense of the Establishment Clause. Donald L. Drakeman. LC 90-45464. (Contributions in Legal Studies: No. 62). 152p. 1991. text ed. 45.00 (*0-313-27663-3*, DCS, Greenwood Pr) Greenwood.

Church, State, Morality & Law. Patrick Hannon. 160p. (Orig.). (C). 1992. pap. 19.95 (*0-7171-1978-5*) Chr Classics.

Church-State Relations: Tensions & Transitions. Ed. by Thomas Robbins & Roland Robertson. 380p. 1986. 39.95x (*0-88738-108-1*) Transaction Pubs.

Church-State Relationships in America. Gerard V. Bradley. LC 86-27149. (Contributions in Legal Studies: No. 37). 180p. 1987. text ed. 45.00 (*0-313-25494-X*, BYC/, Greenwood Pr) Greenwood.

Church Struggle in South Africa. 2nd ed. John W. DeGruchy. 300p. 1986. pap. 12.99 (*0-8028-0243-5*) Eerdmans.

Church Symbolism: An Explanation of the More Important Symbols of the Old & New Testament, the Primitive, the Mediaeval & the Modern Church. rev. ed. Frederick Webber. (Illus.). 1980. reprint ed. 62.00 (*1-55888-941-8*) Omnigraphics Inc.

***Church Tales of the Niagara Frontier.** Austin M. Fox. (Illus.). 128p. (Orig.). 1994. pap. 14.95 (*1-879201-13-5*) Meyer Enter.

Church Teaches: Documents of the Church in English Translation. St. Mary's College Jesuit Fathers, Kansas Staff. Ed. by John F. Clarkson et al. 1973. reprint ed. pap. 15.00 (*0-89555-011-3*) TAN Bks Pubs.

Church Teaching & Training. William W. Graves. Ed. by Weldon Viertel & Joyce Viertel. 152p. 1982. reprint ed. 12.50 (*0-311-72681-X*, Carib Pubns) Casa Bautista.

Church Teaching Authority: Historical & Theological Studies. John P. Boyle. LC 94-15468. (C). 1995. text ed. 38.95 (*0-268-00805-1*) U of Notre Dame Pr.

Church That Keeps Memories Alive: The Story of Christ Church, Alexandria, Virginia. 2nd rev. ed. Ellen E. Morrison. LC 79-114253. (Illus.). 12p. (J). (gr. 6). 1979. 1.75 (*0-9622537-0-7*) Morielle Pr.

Church, the Beautiful Bride of Christ. Ed. by Thomas B. Warren & Garland Elkins. 1980. 14.00 (*0-934916-27-6*) Natl Christian Pr.

Church, the State, & Education in Virginia. Sadie Bell. LC 78-89148. (American Education: Its Men, Institutions & Ideas, Ser.). 1977. reprint ed. 47.95 (*0-405-01385-X*) Ayer.

Church, the State & Society in the Thought of John Paul II. J. V. Schall. 1982. 9.95 (*0-8199-0838-X*, Frncscn Herld) Franciscan Pr.

Church Through the Centuries. Cyril C. Richardson. LC 72-6726. reprint ed. 34.50 (*0-404-10645-5*) AMS Pr.

Church Through the Years, Vol. 2. Richard P. Howard. 520p. 1993. 30.00 (*0-8309-0629-0*) Herald Hse.

Church Through the Years: RLDS Beginnings, to 1860, Vol. 1. Richard P. Howard. LC 92-9185. 400p. 1992. 30.00 (*0-8309-0556-1*) Herald Hse.

***Church Tiles of the Nineteenth Century.** Kenneth Beaulah. (C). 1989. pap. 25.00x (*0-85263-842-6*, Pub. by Shire UK) St Mut.

Church Time for Children. Dorothy G. Johnston & Kathleen Abbas. LC 80-67855. 120p. (Orig.). (J). (gr. 1-6). 1981. 10.95 (*0-89636-056-3*, 18630) Cook.

Church Time for Preschoolers. Leora W. Huttar. LC 75-17368. 1975. spiral bd. 6.95 (*0-916406-36-9*) Accent CO.

Church to Believe In. Peter Moore. 197p. (Orig.). 1994. pap. 9.95 (*0-917851-76-5*) Bristol Hse.

Church Today: Belonging & Believing. Anthony T. Padovano. (Catholic Home Library). (Illus.). 128p. 1989. 4.95 (*1-55944-001-5*) Franciscan Comns.

***Church, Tradition, Scripture, Truth, & the Christian Life: Some Heresies of Evangelicalism & an Orthodox Response.** Hiero D. Gregory. 54p. (Orig.). (C). 1995. pap. text ed. 5.00 (*0-911165-24-X*) Ctr Trad Orthodox.

Church Triumphant. A. L. Gill & Joyce Gill. 133p. 1990. student ed, spiral bd. 12.95 (*0-941975-08-8*) Power Hse Pub.

Church Triumphant at the End of the Age. Nate Krupp. 392p. (Orig.). 1989. pap. 11.99 (*0-914903-38-1*) Destiny Image.

Church Two Thousand One. Michael Richards. (C). 1988. 65.00 (*0-85439-202-5*, Pub. by St Paul Pubns UK) St Mut.

Church under Fire: Studies in the Book of Revelation. David Ewert. (Luminaire Ser.). 224p. (Orig.). 1988. pap. 7.95 (*0-919797-60-1*) Kindred Prods.

Church Unity. Warren Litzman et al. LC 91-76171. 87p. 1991. pap. 7.95 (*0-940232-47-2*) Seedsowers.

Church Universal & Triumphant: In Scholarly Perspective. Ed. by James R. Lewis & J. Gordon Melton. (Illus.). 174p. (C). 1994. pap. text ed. 20.00 (*0-8191-9634-7*) U Pr of Amer.

Church Usher: Servant of God. David R. Enlow. LC 80-66769. 64p. (Orig.). 1980. pap. 3.99 (*0-87509-402-3*) Chr Pubns.

Church Ushering. rev. ed. Paul H. Lang. 1957. pap. 1.95 (*0-570-03522-8*, 14-1141) Concordia.

Church Views of the Mexican American. Ed. by Carlos E. Cortes. LC 73-14198. (Mexican American Ser.). (Illus.). 58p. 1975. reprint ed. 49.95 (*0-405-05672-9*) Ayer.

***Church vs. Education: A Battle Lost.** J. Gordon Chamberlin. viii, 140p. (Orig.). 1994. pap. 13.95 (*0-915481-02-2*) Ed Pr.

***Church vs. Education: A Battle Lost.** J. Gordon Chamberlin. viii, 140p. (Orig.). Date not set. 16.95 (*0-915481-03-0*) Ed Pr.

Church We Believe In: One, Holy, Catholic & Apostolic. Francis A. Sullivan. 1989. pap. 11.95 (*0-8091-3039-4*) Paulist Pr.

Church Wealth in Mexico: A Study of the Juzgado de Capellanias in the Archbishopric of Mexico, 1800-1856. LC 67-18310. (Cambridge Latin American Studies: No. 2). 149p. reprint ed. pap. 42.50 (*0-317-26021-9*, 2024431) Bks Demand.

Church Wedding. Ewen Gilchrist. (Pocketbooks Ser.). 1992. pap. 2.99 (*0-7459-1649-X*) Lion USA.

Church Will Not Go Through the Tribulation. Franklin S. Logsdon. 24p. 1980. pap. 1.45 (*0-87227-077-7*, RBP5092) Reg Baptist.

Church with a Human Face: New & Expanded Theology of Ministry. Edward Schillebeeckx. Tr. by John Bowden. 400p. 1987. pap. 17.95 (*0-8245-0849-1*) Crossroad NY.

Church with AIDS: Renewal in the Midst of Crisis. Ed. by Letty M. Russell. 168p. (Orig.). 1990. pap. 11.99 (*0-664-25111-0*) Westminster John Knox.

Church with the Golden Roof. Joe Powlas. 1988p. 12.00 (*0-8187-0103-X*) Harlo Press.

Church Without Spot or Wrinkle. Traci Mize. 1993. pap. 6.95 (*0-933025-26-2*) Blue Bird Pub.

Church Without Walls. Thomas S. Goslin, II. LC 84-63037. 102p. (Orig.). 1985. pap. 7.95 (*0-932727-00-X*) Hope Pub Hse.

Church Without Walls. Jean Koberlein. 196p. (Orig.). 1990. pap. 8.99 (*1-56043-054-0*) Destiny Image.

Church Without Walls: Moving Beyond Traditional Boundaries. Jim Petersen. LC 91-67292. 240p. (Orig.). 1991. pap. 10.00 (*0-89109-663-9*) NavPress.

Church, Word, & Spirit: Historical & Theological Essays in Honor of Geoffrey W. Bromiley. Ed. by James E. Bradley & Richard A. Muller. LC 87-24447. 335p. reprint ed. pap. 95.50 (*0-8357-8559-9*, 2034908) Bks Demand.

Church, World, Mission. Alexander Schmemann. LC 79-27597. 227p. 1979. pap. 9.95 (*0-913836-49-4*) St Vladimirs.

Church Year I. Neibauer Press Staff. (Illus.). 48p. 1987. 5.95 (*0-685-28913-3*, 1451) Neibauer Pr.

Church Year One, No. 1451. (Illus.). 48p. 1987. reprint ed. 5.95 (*1-878259-04-0*) Neibauer Pr.

Church Year Two, No. 1455. (Illus.). 48p. 1987. reprint ed. 5.95 (*1-878259-10-5*) Neibauer Pr.

Churches. 1989. pap. 45.00 (*0-86022-235-7*, Pub. by Build Servs Info Assn UK) St Mut.

Churches Aflame: Asian Americans & United Methodism. Ed. by Artemio R. Guillermo. 176p. 1991. pap. 14.95 (*0-687-08383-4*) Abingdon.

Churches & Chapels: A Design & Development Guide. Martin Purdy. (Illus.). 128p. 1991. 54.95 (*0-7506-1222-3*) Buttrwrth-Heinemann.

Churches & Church Membership in the U. S. Bradley et al. LC 92-70469. 1990. pap. 36.00 (*0-914422-22-7*) Glenmary Res Ctr.

Churches & Church Membership in the U. S. 1980: An Enumeration by Region, State & County Based on Data Reported by 111 Church Bodies. Bernard Quinn et al. LC 82-81978. 1982. pap. 24.00 (*0-914422-12-X*) Glenmary Res Ctr.

Churches & Churchmen in China. Susan Woodaman. (Illus.). 96p. (Orig.). 1989. pap. 4.95 (*0-685-29099-9*) Intl Outreach.

Churches & Communities. George Lovell & Catherine Widdicombe. 222p. 1990. pap. 40.00 (*0-85532-387-6*, Pub. by Srch Pr UK) St Mut.

Churches & Health Care in the Third World. Ed. by Jean Pirotte & Henri Derroitte. LC 91-9389. (SCM Ser.: No. 5). xxi, 176p. (ENG & FRE.). 1991. 54.50 (*90-04-09470-9*) E J Brill.

Churches & Politics in Germany. Frederic Spotts. LC 72-11050. (Illus.). 431p. reprint ed. pap. 122.90 (*0-685-23467-3*, 2056668) Bks Demand.

Churches & Politics in Latin America. Ed. by Daniel H. Levine. LC 79-23827. (Sage Focus Editions Ser.: No. 14). 288p. reprint ed. pap. 82.10 (*0-8357-8489-4*, 2034762) Bks Demand.

Churches & Racism. Zolile Mbali. 240p. (C). 1987. pap. text ed. 17.95 (*0-334-01923-0*, SCM Pr) TPI PA.

Churches & Royal Patronage: A History of the Royal Patronage in the Churches of England & Wales. W. A. Salmon. 84p. (C). 1989. 60.00 (*0-685-61444-1*, Pub. by D Brown & Sons Ltd UK) St Mut.

Churches & the Indian Schools, 1888-1912. Francis P. Prucha. LC 79-12220. (Illus.). xiv, 278p. 1979. 30.00 (*0-8032-3657-3*) U of Nebr Pr.

Churches in Cultural Captivity: A History of the Social Attitudes of Southern Baptists. rev. ed. John L. Eighmy. LC 87-10892. 284p. 1987. reprint ed. text ed. 31.00x (*0-87049-547-X*); reprint ed. pap. text ed. 16.00x (*0-87049-548-8*) U of Tenn Pr.

Churches in Cultural Captivity: A History of the Social Attitudes of Southern Baptists. John L. Eighmy. LC 70-111047. 268p. reprint ed. pap. 76.40 (*0-317-55793-9*, 2029374) Bks Demand.

Churches in India. P. Thomas. 30p. 1981. 5.95 (*0-318-36670-3*) Asia Bk Corp.

Churches in Struggle: Liberation Theologies & Social Change in North America. Ed. by William K. Tabb. 331p. 1986. 27.00 (*0-85345-692-5*); pap. 13.00 (*0-85345-693-3*) Monthly Rev.

Churches in the Nineteenth Century. Josef L. Altholz. LC 66-30446. (Orig.). (C). 1967. write for info. (*0-672-51130-4*, Bobbs); pap. 6.95 (*0-672-60682-8*, Bobbs) Macmillan.

Churches, Ireland & the Irish. Ed. by W. J. Sheils & Diana Wood. (Studies in Church History). 320p. 1988. text ed. 59.95 (*0-631-16114-7*) Blackwell Pubs.

Churches Militant: The War of 1812 & American Religion. William Gribbin. LC 72-91313. 220p. reprint ed. pap. 62.70 (*0-317-29581-0*, 2022000) Bks Demand.

C

An Asterisk (*) at the beginning of an entry indicates that the title is appearing in BIP for the first time. 1265

Churches of Charleston & the Lowcountry. Preservation Society of Charleston Staff. Ed. by Mary M. Jacoby. LC 93-10057. 136p. (C). 1993. 39.95 (*0-87249-888-3*) U of SC Pr.

***Churches of Christ in the United States, 1994.** Mac Lynn. 750p. 1994. pap. 14.95 (*1-885836-00-7*) Morrison & Phillips.

Churches of Christ of the Congregational Way in New England. Richard H. Taylor. 320p. (C). 1989. text ed. 30.00 (*0-9622486-0-6*) Richard H Taylor.

Churches of Cornwall. Ed. by S. Daniell. (C). 1988. pap. 24.95 (*0-85025-300-4*, Pub. by Tor Mark Pr UK) St Mut.

Churches of Dedham, Mass., 1638-1844. Ed. by Robert B. Hanson. 149p. (Orig.). 1990. pap. 15.00 (*1-55613-403-7*) Heritage Bk.

Churches of Eastern Christendom from Four Hundred Fifty-One A.D. to the Present Time, 2 vols., Set. Beresford J. Kidd. 1980. lib. bdg. 195.00 (*0-8490-3196-6*) Gordon Pr.

Churches of Foster: A History of Religious Life in Rural Rhode Island. Margery I. Matthews et al. (Illus.). 169p. (Orig.). 1978. pap. 5.00 (*0-917012-20-8*) N Foster Baptist.

Churches of the Crusader Kingdom of Jerusalem: A Corpus, Vol. 1: A-K (Excluding Acre & Jerusalem) Denys Pringle. (Illus.). 352p. (C). 1993. 125.00 (*0-521-39036-2*) Cambridge U Pr.

Churches of the Not-So-Standing Order: 1809-1869. Peter J. Gomes. (Pilgrim Society Notes Ser.: No. 18). 1966. 2.00 (*0-940628-10-4*) Pilgrim Soc.

Churches of the Restoration: A Study in Origins. George A. Turner. LC 93-48201. 276p. 1993. 89.95 (*0-7734-9843-5*, Mellen Univ Pr) E Mellen.

Churches of Winchester, Virginia: A Brief History of Those Established Prior to 1825. 64p. 1960. pap. write for info. (*0-318-64325-1*) Winchester-Frederick Cty Hist Soc.

Churches Plea for Her Right. William Best. LC 76-57357. (English Experience Ser.: No. 776). 1977. reprint ed. lib. bdg. 25.00 (*90-221-0776-0*) Walter J Johnson.

Churches Quarrel Espoused, 1713. John Wise. LC 66-10006. 1966. 50.00 (*0-8201-1052-3*) Schol Facsimiles.

Churches' Response to the Holocaust. Ed. by Jack R. Fischel & Sanford Pinsker. (Holocaust Studies Annual: Vol. II). 200p. 1986. 20.00 (*0-913283-12-6*) Penkevill.

C

Churches Speak Series, Issue 1. J. Gordon Melton. 150p. 1989. pap. text ed. 39.00 (*0-8103-7218-5*) Gale.

Churches Speak Series, Issue 2. J. Gordon Melton. 1989. pap. text ed. 39.00 (*0-8103-7219-3*) Gale.

Churches Speak Series, Issue 3. J. Gordon Melton. 1989. pap. text ed. 39.00 (*0-8103-7220-7*) Gale.

Churches Speak Series, Issue 5. Ed. by J. Gordon Melton. 1990. pap. 39.00 (*0-8103-7646-6*) Gale.

Churches Speak Series, Issue 6. Ed. by J. Gordon Melton. 175p. 1991. 39.00 (*0-8103-7647-4*) Gale.

Churches Speak Series, Issue 7. Ed. by J. Gordon Melton. 175p. 1991. 39.00 (*0-8103-7648-2*) Gale.

Churches Speak Series, Issue No. 4. J. Gordon Melton. 150p. 1989. pap. text ed. 39.00 (*0-8103-7221-5*) Gale.

Churches Speak Series, Issues 5-8. Ed. by J. Gordon Melton. 1990. pap. 77.00 (*0-8103-7658-X*) Gale.

Churches Speak Series, Set. Ed. by J. Gordon Melton. 1989. pap. 95.00 (*0-8103-7158-8*, 30144-99728) Gale.

Churches That Abuse: Help for Those Hurt by Legalism, Authoritarian Leadership, Manipulation, Excessive Discipline. Ronald M. Enroth. 256p. 1992. 15.99 (*0-310-53290-6*) Zondervan.

Churches That Abuse: Help for Those Hurt by Legalism, Authoritarian Leadership, Manipulation, Excessive Discipline. Ronald M. Enroth. 1993. pap. 5.99 (*0-310-53292-2*) Zondervan.

Churches That Pray: How Prayer Can Help Revitalize Your Congregation & Break Down the Walls Between the Church & the Community. Peter Wagner. Ed. by Virginia Woodard. LC 93-5420. (Illus.). 192p. 1993. 15.99 (*0-8307-1598-3*, 5112281) Regal.

Churches the Apostles Left Behind. Raymond E. Brown. 160p. (Orig.). (C). 1984. pap. 7.95 (*0-8091-2611-7*) Paulist Pr.

Churchill. Ed. by Robert Blake & William R. Louis. LC 92-21814. 1993. 20.00 (*0-19-820317-9*) OUP.

Churchill. Ed. by Robert Blake & William R. Louis. 480p. 1993. 35.00 (*0-393-03409-7*) Norton.

Churchill. Keith Robbins. 1993. pap. text ed. 19.95 (*0-685-72550-2*, 79372) Longman.

Churchill: A Life. Martin Gilbert. (Illus.). 1088p. 1991. 34.50 (*0-8050-0615-X*) H Holt & Co.

Churchill: A Life. Martin Gilbert. (Illus.). 1088p. 1992. pap. 19.95 (*0-8050-2396-8*, Owl) H Holt & Co.

***Churchill: A Member for Woodford.** David A. Thomas. LC 94-31527. 1994. write for info. (*0-7146-4126-X*) Intl Spec Bk.

***Churchill: A Member for Woodford.** David A. Thorps & David A. Thomas. LC 94-31527. (Illus.). 256p. 1994. 35.00 (*0-7146-4586-9*, Pub. by F Cass Pubs UK) Intl Spec Bk.

Churchill: A Photographic Portrait. Martin Gilbert. LC 92-46175. 1993. 15.99 (*0-517-09297-2*, Pub. by Wings Bks) Random Hse Value.

***Churchill: An Unruly Life.** Norman Rose. LC 95-4125. 450p. 1995. 25.00 (*0-02-874009-2*) Free Pr.

Churchill: Plays Two. Caryl Churchill. (Methuen World Dramatists Ser.). 309p. (Orig.). (C). 1990. pap. 12.95 (*0-413-62270-3*, A0403, Pub. by Methuen UK) Heinemann.

Churchill: Retreat from Empire. Pref. by Raymond A. Callahan. LC 83-20285. 293p. 1984. lib. bdg. 40.00 (*0-8420-2210-4*) Scholarly Res Inc.

Churchill: Speaker of the Century. James C. Humes. LC 79-3812. 360p. Date not set. pap. 15.95 (*0-8128-6151-5*, Scrbrough Hse) Madison Bks UPA.

Churchill: Strategy & History. Tuvia Ben-Moshe. LC 90-26495. 397p. 1991. lib. bdg. 47.00 (*1-55587-142-9*) Lynne Rienner.

Churchill: The Diaries of Lord Moran: The Struggle for Survival, 1940-1965. Baron Charles McMoran Wilson Moran. LC 66-14761. (Illus.). 892p. 1976. reprint ed. 39.95 (*0-87797-189-7*) Cherokee.

***Churchill: An Uncomfortable Hero: An Address.** Caspar W. Weinberger. (Oral History Ser.: No. 1). (Illus.). 20p. 1986. pap. 15.00 (*0-614-04944-X*) Intl Churchill Soc.

Churchill & Hitler: Essays on the Political-Military Direction of Total War. David Jablonsky. LC 94-5767. (Cass Series on Politics & Military Affairs in the Twentieth Century: Vol. 5). 1994. 35.00 (*0-7146-4563-X*, Pub. by F Cass Pubs UK) Intl Spec Bk.

***Churchill & Hitler: Essays on the Political-Military Direction of Total War.** David Jablonsky. LC 94-5767. (Cass Political & Military Affairs Ser.). 327p. 1995. pap. 22.50 (*0-7146-4119-7*) Intl Spec Bk.

Churchill & Roosevelt at War: The War They Fought & the Peace They Hoped to Make. Keith Sainsbury. LC 93-36954. (C). 1994. 25.95 (*0-8147-7991-3*) NYU Pr.

Churchill & Roosevelt, the Complete Correspondence, 3 vols. Ed. by Warren F. Kimball. LC 83-43080. (Illus.). 2285p. 1984. pap. 79.50 (*0-691-00817-5*) Princeton U Pr.

Churchill & Roosevelt, the Complete Correspondence, 3 vols., Set. Ed. by Warren F. Kimball. LC 83-43080. (Illus.). 2285p. 1984. 325.00 (*0-691-05649-8*) Princeton U Pr.

Churchill & the Archangel Fiasco. Michael Kettle. LC 92-48092. 288p. 1992. 85.00 (*0-415-08286-2*, A9568) Routledge.

Churchill & the Jews. Michael J. Cohen. (Illus.). 408p. 1985. 37.50 (*0-7146-3254-6*, Pub. by F Cass Pubs UK) Intl Spec Bk.

Churchill & the Politics of War, 1940-1941. Sheila Lawlor. LC 93-28733. 308p. (C). 1994. 69.95 (*0-521-44545-0*); pap. 22.95 (*0-521-46685-7*) Cambridge U Pr.

Churchill & Yalta. Francis Neilson. (Revisionist Historiography Ser.). 1979. lib. bdg. 250.00 (*0-685-96613-5*) Revisionist Pr.

Churchill As War Leader. Richard Lamb. 416p. 1993. 22.95 (*0-88184-937-5*) Carroll & Graf.

Churchill As Warlord. Ronald Lewin. LC 72-96544. (Illus.). 308p. (C). 1982. pap. 10.95 (*0-8128-6099-3*, Scrbrough Hse) Madison Bks UPA.

Churchill at Chartwell. R. Fedden. LC 75-89777. 1969. 29.00 (*0-08-013053-4*, Pub. by Pergamon Repr UK) Franklin.

***Churchill Bibliographic Data: Surveys of Works by & about Sir Winston Churchill.** Richard M. Langworth & H. Ashley Redburn. (Educational Ser.: No. 4). (Illus.). 52p. 1992. pap. 10.00 (*0-614-04945-8*) Intl Churchill Soc.

Churchill Diamonds. Bob Langley. 240p. 1986. 15.95 (*0-8027-0934-6*) Walker & Co.

Churchill Diamonds. large type ed. Bob Langley. 448p. 1987. 16.95 (*0-7089-1687-2*) Ulverscroft.

Churchill Downs Museum Book. William Butt. (Illus.). 40p. (Orig.). 1986. pap. 4.95 (*0-685-13348-6*) Harmony Hse Pub LO.

Churchill-Eisenhower Correspondence, 1953-1955. Ed. by Peter G. Boyle. LC 89-77572. (Illus.). xx, 230p. (C). 1990. 27.50 (*0-8078-1910-7*) U of NC Pr.

Churchill Family in America. G. A. Churchill & N. W. Churchill. Ed. by G. M. Badge. (Illus.). 722p. 1989. reprint ed. lib. bdg. 99.50 (*0-8328-0400-2*); reprint ed. pap. 89.50 (*0-8328-0401-0*) Higginson Bk Co.

Churchill Family in America. Gardner A. Churchill & Nathaniel W. Churchill. (Illus.). 777p. 1991. reprint ed. pap. 34.50 (*1-55613-519-X*) Heritage Bk.

***Churchill Gold.** large type ed. James Follett. (Magna Large Print Ser.). 1994. 24.95 (*0-7505-0659-8*, Pub. by Magna Print Bks) Ulverscroft.

Churchill Infantry Tank 1941-51. Bryan Perrett. (New Vanguard Ser.: No. 4). (Illus.). 48p. pap. 11.95 (*1-85532-297-8*, 9339, Pub. by Osprey UK) Stackpole.

Churchill Lecture. deluxe ed. Gerald R. Ford. LC 83-83406. 25p. 1984. 100.00 (*0-935716-30-0*) Lord John.

Churchill Legend: Winston Churchill As Fraud, Fakir & War-Monger. Francis Neilson. 1983. lib. bdg. 79.95 (*0-87700-001-8*) Revisionist Pr.

Churchill Livingstone Nurse's Dictionary. 16th ed. Churchill Livingstone. 480p. 1989. pap. text ed. 7.00 (*0-443-02242-9*) Churchill.

Churchill Livingstone's Medical Word Guide. 340p. 1991. pap. text ed. 19.95 (*0-443-08833-0*) Churchill.

Churchill on the Home Front, 1900-1955. Paul Addison. (Illus.). 512p. 1994. pap. 19.95 (*0-7126-5826-2*, Pub. by Pimlico) Trafalgar.

Churchill Plays. Brenton. 1991. pap. 9.95 (*0-413-33906-8*, Methuen) Routledge Chapman & Hall.

Churchill Plays: One. Caryl Churchill. 320p. 1985. pap. 7.95 (*0-415-90196-0*, 9499, Routledge NY) Routledge.

Churchill Returns. Robert R. Leichtman. LC 81-66847. (From Heaven to Earth Ser.). (Illus.). 96p. (Orig.). 1981. pap. 3.50 (*0-89804-065-5*) Ariel GA.

Churchill Speaks: Winston S. Churchill in Peace & War Collected Speeches, 1897-1963. abr. ed. Ed. by Robert R. James. LC 80-21880. 1000p. 1980. pap. 25.00 (*0-87754-256-2*) Chelsea Hse.

Churchill, the End of Glory: A Politcal Biography. John Charmley. LC 93-12546. 1993. reprint ed. 34.95 (*0-15-117881-X*) HarBrace.

Churchill: The End of Glory: A Political Biography. John Charmley. 1994. pap. 17.95 (*0-15-600144-6*) HarBrace.

Churchill, the Great Game & Total War. David Jablonsky. (Illus.). 235p. 1991. text ed. 35.00 (*0-7146-3367-4*, Pub. by F Cass Pubs UK); pap. text ed. 18.00 (*0-7146-4078-6*, Pub. by F Cass Pubs UK) Intl Spec Bk.

***Churchill, the Member for Woodford.** David A. Thorps & David A. Thomas. LC 94-31527. (Illus.). 224p. 1994. pap. 19.50 (*0-7146-4143-X*, Pub. by F Cass Pubs UK) Intl Spec Bk.

Churchill the Playwright. Geraldine Cousin. (Methuen Theatre Profiles Ser.). (Illus.). 135p. (C). 1989. pap. 9.95 (*0-413-14790-8*, A0051, Pub. by Methuen UK) Heinemann.

***Churchill to Major: The British Prime Ministership since 1945.** R. L. Borthwick. Ed. by Donald Shell & Richard Hodder-Williams. LC 95-11511. 288p. 1995. 59.95 (*1-56324-635-X*) M E Sharpe.

***Churchill to Major: The British Prime Ministership since 1945.** Ed. by Donald Shell & Richard Hodder-Williams. LC 95-11511. 288p. 1995. pap. 21.95 (*1-56324-636-8*) M E Sharpe.

Churchill War Papers. Ed. by Martin Gilbert. 1322p. 1994. 75.00 (*0-393-03746-0*) Norton.

Churchill War Papers: At the Admiralty, Vol. 1. Comp. by Martin Gilbert. LC 92-44367. 1400p. 1993. 75.00 (*0-393-03522-0*) Norton.

Churchill's Deception: The Dark Secret That Destroyed Nazi Germany. Louis Kilzer. LC 94-3178. 1994. 23.00 (*0-671-76722-4*) S&S Trade.

Churchill's Desert Rats: From Normandy to Berlin with the 7th Armoured Division. Patrick Delaforce. (Illus.). 224p. 1993. 30.00 (*0-7509-0529-8*) A Sutton Pub.

Churchills Doctor: A Biography of Lord Moran. Richard Lovell. (Illus.). 480p. 1993. 49.00 (*1-85070-485-6*) Prthnon Pub.

Churchill's Generals. Ed. by John Keegan. (Illus.). 368p. 1992. pap. 13.00 (*0-688-11415-6*, Quill) Morrow.

Churchill's History of the English-Speaking Peoples. Henry S. Commager. 1987. 9.99 (*0-517-42283-2*) Random Hse Value.

***Churchill's History of the English-Speaking Peoples.** Henry S. Commager. 1994. 9.99 (*0-517-06019-1*) Random Hse Value.

***Churchill's House Physician's Survival Guide.** Roger A. Fisken. LC 94-26803. 271p. 1994. 22.95 (*0-443-04895-9*) Churchill.

Churchill's House Surgeon's Survival Guide. Henry K. Gompertz et al. LC 92-22883. 338p. 1992. 30.00 (*0-443-04342-6*) Churchill.

Churchill's Medical Dictionary. (Illus.). 2121p. 1989. 43.00 (*0-443-08691-5*) Churchill.

Churchill's Pocketbook of Medicine. Peter C. Hayes & Thomas W. MacKay. (Illus.). 256p. 1992. pap. text ed. 24.95 (*0-443-04213-6*) Churchill.

Churchill's Rhetoric & Political Discourse. Manfred Weidhorn. LC 87-10734. (Exxon Education Foundation Series on Rhetoric & Political Discourse: Vol. 17). 154p. (Orig.). 1988. pap. text ed. 20.00 (*0-8191-6436-4*) U Pr of Amer.

Churchill's Sacrifice of the Highland Division: France 1940. Saul David. (Illus.). 280p. 1994. 40.00 (*1-85753-039-X*) Macmillan.

Churchill's Speeches: His Complete Speeches; 1897-1963, 8 vols., Set. Ed. by R. R. James. 2766p. 1979. pap. 71.80 (*0-87754-128-0*) Chelsea Hse.

Churchill's War. David Irving. 696p. 1991. pap. 12.95 (*0-380-76314-1*) Avon.

Churchill's War Memoirs. Francis Neilson. (Revisionist Historiography Ser.). 1979. lib. bdg. 250.00 (*0-87700-275-4*) Revisionist Pr.

Churching of America, 1776-1990: Winners & Losers in Our Religious Economy. Roger Finke & Rodney Stark. (Illus.). 325p. (C). 1992. 30.00 (*0-8135-1837-7*) Rutgers U Pr.

Churching of America, 1776-1990: Winners & Losers in Our Religious Economy. Roger Finke & Rodney Stark. LC 91-45908. (Illus.). 328p. (Orig.). 1993. pap. 15.95 (*0-8135-1838-5*) Rutgers U Pr.

Churchmen & the Western Indians, 1820-1920. Ed. by Clyde A. Milner, II & Floyd A. O'Neil. LC 85-40477. (Illus.). 272p. 1985. 26.95 (*0-8061-1950-0*) U of Okla Pr.

Churchmouse Birthday. Barbara Davoll. (Christopher Churchmouse Classics Ser.). (Illus.). 24p. (J). 1994. 7.99 (*1-56476-277-7*, Victor Books); audio 11.99 (*7-900882-16-2*, Victor Books) SP Pubns.

Churchmouse Christmas. Barbara Davoll. (Christopher Churchmouse Classics Ser.). (Illus.). 24p. (J). 1994. 7.99 (*1-56476-276-9*, Victor Books); audio 11.99 (*7-900882-15-4*, Victor Books) SP Pubns.

***Churchmouse Christmas: A Musical for Children.** Barbara Davoll & Don Wyrtzen. 1994. 4.95 (*0-8341-9116-4*, MC-88); digital audio 10.98 (*0-614-01705-X*, TA-9173C); digital audio 60.00 (*0-614-01706-8*, MU-9173C); digital audio 60.00 (*0-614-01707-6*, MU-9173T); sl. write for info. (*0-614-01710-6*, MM-9173) Lillenas.

***Churchmouse Christmas: A Musical for Children.** suppl. ed. Barbara Davoll & Don Wyrtzen. 1994. 6.00 (*0-614-01708-4*, L-9173C); write for info. (*0-614-01709-2*, MC-88SF); 5.00 (*0-8341-9208-X*, MC-88A) Lillenas.

Church's Confession of Faith: A Catholic Catechism for Adults. Ed. by German Bishops' Conference Staff. LC 87-80530. (Communio Bk.). 378p. (Orig.). 1987. pap. 16.95 (*0-89870-162-7*) Ignatius Pr.

Church's Confession Under Hitler. 2nd ed. Arthur C. Cochrane. LC 76-57655. (Pittsburgh Reprint Ser.: No. 4). 1977. pap. text ed. 15.00 (*0-915138-28-X*) Pickwick.

Church's Desperate Need for Revival. David R. Barnhart. 163p. (Orig.). 1986. pap. 8.95 (*0-9617377-0-0*) Abiding Word Pubns.

Church's Educational Space: Creating Learning Environments for Teaching & Learning. J. Cy Rowell. 80p. (Orig.). 1989. pap. 6.99 (*0-8272-0454-X*) Chalice Pr.

Church's Great Picture: The Heart of the Andes. Kevin J. Avery. (Illus.). 64p. 1993. 10.95 (*0-685-71013-0*) Metro Mus Art.

Church's Ministry with Families. Diana Garland & Diane Pancoast. 258p. 1990. write for info. (*0-8499-3141-X*) Word Inc.

***Church's Peace Witness.** Ed. by Marlin E. Miller. 216p. 1994. pap. text ed. 14.99 (*0-8028-0555-8*) Eerdmans.

Church's Public Role: Retrospect & Prospect. Ed. by Dieter T. Hessel. LC 92-27234. 1992. pap. 14.99 (*0-8028-0647-3*) Eerdmans.

Church's Task Under the Roman Empire. Charles Bigg. 1977. lib. bdg. 59.95 (*0-8490-1629-0*) Gordon Pr.

Churchwardens' Accounts of the Town of Ludlow in Shropshire. Ed. by Thomas Wright. LC 17-1267. (Camden Society, London. Publications, First Ser.: No. 102). reprint ed. 45.00 (*0-404-50202-4*, A17-1267) AMS Pr.

Churchyard Carvers' Art. Martin C. Johnson. 104p. 1987. pap. 60.00 (*0-317-62080-0*) St Mut.

Churchyard Literature. J. R. Kippax. 1972. 59.95 (*0-87968-870-X*) Gordon Pr.

Churchyard Literature: A Choice Collection of American Epitaphs. John R. Kippax. 213p. 1978. reprint ed. 20.00 (*0-87928-087-5*) Corner Hse.

Churchyard Literature: A Choice Collection of American Epitaphs, with Remarks on Monumental Inscriptions & the Obsequies of Various Nations. Ed. by John R. Kippax. 213p. (Orig.). 1994. reprint ed. pap. text ed. 17.50 (*1-55613-951-9*) Heritage Bk.

Churgurgische Verbandlehre (Surgical Bandages) M. Troschel. (Illus.). 89p. 1987. reprint ed. pap. 25.00 (*0-87556-765-7*) Saifer.

Churlsgrace. William Hathaway. (University of Central Florida Contemporary Poetry Ser.). 106p. (C). 1992. lib. bdg. 18.95 (*0-8130-1125-6*); pap. text ed. 10.95 (*0-8130-1126-4*) U Press Fla.

Churn 'Em & Burn 'Em. Maurice D. Rutledge. 250p. (Orig.). 1992. pap. 7.95 (*0-9633311-0-8*) Rutledge Pub.

Chushingura: The Treasury of Loyal Retainers, a Puppet Play. Tr. by Donald Keene. LC 78-142283. 183p. 1971. text ed. 42.00 (*0-231-03530-6*); pap. text ed. 14.50 (*0-231-03531-4*) Col U Pr.

Chut, Chut, Charlotte! Rosemary Wells. (Folio - Benjamin Ser.: No. 1). (FRE.). (J). 1990. pap. 8.95 (*2-07-039001-2*) Schoenhof.

Chute. Albert Camus. (Folio Ser.: No. 10). (FRE.). 1956. 6.95 (*2-07-036010-5*) Schoenhof.

Chute. Albert Camus. (FRE.). 1972. pap. 10.95 (*0-8288-3662-0*, F90551) Fr & Eur.

Chute. Albert Camus. Ed. by Germaine Bree. 135p. (ENG & FRE.). 1986. 3.95 (*0-88332-465-2*) Schoenhof.

Chute. Albert Halper. LC 74-26109. reprint ed. 42.50 (*0-404-58434-9*) AMS Pr.

Chutes & Adders: A Robin Light Mystery. Barbara Block. 320p. 1994. 18.95 (*0-8217-4533-6*) Zebra.

Chutes & Ladders. Illus. by Carolyn Bracken. (Lift-&-Peek-a-Board Bks.). (J). (ps-00). 1994. bds. 4.50 (*0-679-86565-9*) Random Bks Yng Read.

***Chutney Complete.** R. Marilyn Schmidt. 76p. 1994. 7.95 (*0-614-00848-4*) Pine Barrens Pr.

***Chutneys & Relishes.** Lou S. Pappas. LC 94-43153. (Illus.). 1995. 9.95 (*0-8118-0840-8*) Chronicle Bks.

Chutneys, Relishes, & Table Sauces. Jay Solomon. 128p. (Orig.). 1990. pap. 8.95 (*0-89594-443-X*) Crossing Pr.

Chutzpah. Alan M. Dershowitz. 1991. 22.95 (*0-316-18137-4*) Little.

Chutzpah. Alan M. Dershowitz. (Illus.). 400p. 1992. pap. 13.00 (*0-671-76089-0*, Touchstone Bks) S&S Trade.

Chuvash Folk Art. Ed. by E. D. Medzhitova & A. A. Trofimov. (Illus.). 246p. (CHV & RUS.). 1981. 250.00 (*0-317-57298-9*, Pub. by Collets UK) St Mut.

***Chuvash Folksongs.** Ed. by L. Vikar & G. Bereczki. 580p. (C). 1979. 158.00x (*963-05-1460-5*, Pub. by Akad Kiado HU) St Mut.

Chuyen Ba Con Gau: The Three Bears. Hanna Hutchinson. Tr. by Christine Vu. (Interlingo Ser.). (Illus.). 22p. (Orig.). (VIE.). (J). (gr. k-12). 1990. pap. 2.95 (*0-922852-10-3*) AIMS Intl.

Chuzhie Kamni. Natalya Gorbanevskaya. (Russica Poetry Ser.: No. 3). 70p. (Orig.). (RUS.). 1983. 13.00 (*0-89830-077-0*); pap. 5.95 (*0-685-06192-2*) Russica Pubs.

***Chuzzlewit.** Charles Dickens. Ed. & Intro. by P. N. Furbank. 944p. 1995. 10.95 (*0-14-043574-3*, Penguin Classics) Viking Penguin.

Chymia Basiliensis. B. Prijs. (Illus.). x, 126p. 1983. 16.00 (*3-8055-3786-7*) S Karger.

Chymical Wedding. Lindsay Clarke. 512p. 1991. mass mkt. 5.95 (*0-8041-0702-5*) Ivy Books.

Chymical Wedding of Christian Rosencreuz Anno 1459. Jon Valentine. (Illus.). 1981. 21.95 (*0-916786-58-7*, Saint George Pubns) R Steiner Col Pubns.

Chymical Wedding of Christian Rosenkreutz: A Commentary. Ehrenfried Pfeiffer. 63p. (Orig.). 1984. pap. 6.50 (*0-936132-16-7*) Merc Pr NY.

Chymist's Key: The True Doctrine of Corruption & Generation, in Ten Brief Aphorisms Illustrated with the Pure Light of Nature. Henry Nollius. Tr. by Henry Vaughan. reprint ed. pap. 4.95 (*1-55818-187-3*) Holmes Pub.

Chymotrypsins: Real & Artificial. Valerian T. D'Souza. 1991. 115.00 (*0-8493-6433-7*, RC267) CRC Pr.

Chyrgeons: Or, an Antidotarie Chyrurgicall. Thomas Bonham. Ed. by E. Poeton. LC 68-54619. (English Experience Ser.: No. 31). 360p. 1968. reprint ed. 49.00 (*90-221-0031-6*) Walter J Johnson.

Chyrology for the Deaf: Reading, Spelling & Ciphering by the Fingers. T. M. Lucas. 1972. 250.00 (*0-87968-054-7*) Gordon Pr.

1266

An Asterisk (*) at the beginning of an entry indicates that the title is appearing in BIP for the first time.

Chytridiomycetarum Iconographia: Illustrated & Descriptive Guide to the Chytridiomycetous Genera with a Suppl. of the Hyphochytriomycetes. J. S. Karling. (Illus.). 1978. lib. bdg. 99.00 (*3-7682-1111-8*) Lubrecht & Cramer.

***CI Tools in Government.** Jerry Koehler. 200p. 1995. 29.95 (*1-884015-97-2*) St Lucie Pr.

CIA. Graham Yost. LC 88-25190. (World Espionage Ser.). (Illus.). 170p. reprint ed. pap. 48.50 (*0-7837-5342-X*, 2045084) Bks Demand.

CIA & American Democracy. Rhodri Jeffreys-Jones. 352p. (C). 1991. reprint ed. pap. 16.00 (*0-300-05017-8*) Yale U Pr.

CIA & the Cold War: A Memoir. Scott D. Breckinridge. LC 92-46554. 336p. 1993. text ed. 57.95 (*0-275-94547-2*, C4547, Praeger Pubs) Greenwood.

CIA & the Marshall Plan. Sallie Pisani. LC 91-16840. x, 190p. 1991. 25.00 (*0-7006-0502-9*) U Pr of KS.

CIA & the Third World. S. Kumar. 200p. 1981. 24.95 (*0-318-37230-4*) Asia Bk Corp.

CIA Catalog of Clandestine Weapons, Tools & Gadgets. 1991. lib. bdg. 250.00 (*0-87700-939-2*) Revisionist Pr.

CIA Catalog of Clandestine Weapons, Tools, & Gadgets. John Minnery. (Illus.). 128p. 1990. pap. 14.95 (*0-87364-576-6*) Paladin Pr.

CIA Catalog of Clandestine Weapons, Tools, & Gadgets. John Minnery. LC 92-15887. 1992. pap. 10.00 (*0-942637-69-0*) Barricade Bks.

***CIA Documents on the Cuban Missile Crisis.** (Illus.). 220p. (Orig.). (C). 1995. pap. text ed. 80.00 (*0-7881-1638-X*) Diane Pub.

CIA Entrance Examination. John Quirk. (Arco Professional Test Preparation Ser.). 1988. pap. 14.95 (*0-317-66872-2*, Arco Test) P-H Gen Ref & Trav.

CIA Field Expedient Incendiary Manual. 1986. lib. bdg. 250.00 (*0-8490-3542-2*) Gordon Pr.

CIA Field-Expedient Key Casting Manual. (Illus.). 48p. 1988. pap. 10.00 (*0-87364-495-6*) Paladin Pr.

CIA Field Expedient Key Casting Manual. 1991. lib. bdg. 75.95 (*0-8490-4753-6*) Gordon Pr.

CIA Flaps & Seals Manual. (Illus.). 56p. 1975. pap. 10.00 (*0-87364-039-X*) Paladin Pr.

CIA Improvised Sabotage Techniques. 1986. lib. bdg. 250. 00 (*0-8490-3543-0*) Gordon Pr.

CIA in Guatemala: The Foreign Policy of Intervention. Richard H. Immerman. (Texas Pan American Ser.). 302p. 1982. pap. 13.95 (*0-292-71083-6*) U of Tex Pr.

CIA Off Campus: Building the Movement Against Agency Recruitment & Research. Ami C. Mills. 210p. (Orig.). 1991. 25.00 (*0-89608-404-3*); pap. 10.00 (*0-89608-403-5*) South End Pr.

***CIA Response to the Aldrich Hazen Ames Case: Report of Investigation Abstract; Press Statements & Statements by Inspector General; Woolsey Mandates for Change.** (Nightmover Case Ser.: Vol. 4). 1995. 24.95 (*1-878292-14-5*) Natl Intel Bk Ctr.

CIA Review, Set. 6th ed. Irvin N. Gleim. LC 94-76179. (Illus.). 800p. (C). 1994. write for info. (*0-917537-67-X*) Gleim Pubns.

CIA Review, Vol. I. Irvin N. Gleim. LC 94-76179. (Illus.). 768p. (C). 1994. pap. 25.95 (*0-917537-65-3*) Gleim Pubns.

CIA Review, Vol. II. Irvin N. Gleim. LC 94-76179. (Illus.). 720p. (C). 1994. pap. text ed. 25.95 (*0-917537-66-1*) Gleim Pubns.

CIA Rocket Assisted Grenades. 1986. lib. bdg. 250.00 (*0-8490-3589-9*) Gordon Pr.

CIA Special Weapons & Equipment: Spy Devices of the Cold War. H. Keith Melton. (Illus.). 128p. 1994. pap. 11.95 (*0-8069-8733-2*) Sterling.

CIA Wife: One Woman's Life Inside the CIA. Florence F. Garbler. 168p. (Orig.). 1994. pap. 10.95 (*1-56474-089-7*) Fithian Pr.

CIAM, Dokumente 1928-1939. Ed. by Martin Steinmann. (Geschichte und Theorie der Architektur Ser.: No. 11). (Illus.). (FRE & GER.). 1980. 80.25 (*0-8176-1022-7*) Birkhauser.

Ciano's Diplomatic Papers. Galeazzo Ciano. Ed. by Malcolm Muggeridge. Tr. by Stuart Head. LC 83-45734. reprint ed. 41.50 (*0-404-20060-5*, DG575) AMS Pr.

Ciao! 2nd rev. ed. Carla Federici & Carla L. Riga. Ed. by Sharon Alexander. (Illus.). 480p. (C). 1990. text ed. 45. 25 (*0-03-026238-0*) HB Coll Pubs.

Ciao! 3rd ed. Carla Federici & Carla L. Riga. LC 93-37214. (ENG & ITA.). 1993. text ed. 46.75 (*0-15-500645-2*) HB Coll Pubs.

Ciao!, Level 1. Jackson et al. 1993. pap. 23.95 (*0-17-439224-9*) Heinle & Heinle.

Ciao!, Level 2. Jackson et al. 1992. pap. 23.95 (*0-17-439230-3*) Heinle & Heinle.

Ciao!, Level 3. Jackson et al. 1993. pap. 23.95 (*0-17-439557-4*) Heinle & Heinle.

Ciao! Level 1. Jackson et al. (Illus.). (ENG & ITA.). (C). 1992. Tchr's manual. teacher ed, pap. 24.95 (*0-17-439222-2*); Copymasters. pap. 47.95 (*0-17-439229-X*); Flashcards. 74.95 (*0-17-439227-3*) Heinle & Heinle.

Ciao! Level 1. Jackson et al. (Illus.). (ENG & ITA.). (C). 1993. Cassette. audio 25.95 (*0-17-439223-0*) Heinle & Heinle.

Ciao! Level 2. Jackson et al. (Illus.). (C). 1992. Copymasters. pap. 48.95 (*0-17-439232-X*) Heinle & Heinle.

Ciao! Level 2. Jackson et al. (Illus.). (C). 1993. Tchr's manual. teacher ed, pap. 24.95 (*0-17-439231-1*) Heinle & Heinle.

Ciao! Level 2, No. A. Jackson et al. (Illus.). (C). 1992. Cassette A. audio 25.95 (*0-17-439526-4*) Heinle & Heinle.

Ciao! Level 2, No. B. Jackson et al. (Illus.). (C). 1993. Cassette B. audio 25.95 (*0-17-439619-8*) Heinle & Heinle.

Ciao! Level 3. Jackson et al. (Illus.). (C). 1993. Tchr's manual. teacher ed, pap. 24.95 (*0-17-439653-8*); Cassettes. audio 74.95 (*0-17-439655-4*) Heinle & Heinle.

Ciao! Level 3. Jackson et al. (Illus.). (C). 1993. Copymasters. pap. 102.95 (*0-17-439654-6*) Heinle & Heinle.

***Ciao, Francesco.** Francis X. Medina & Dorothy B. Marra. 224p. 1995. 17.50 (*0-9645371-0-9*) F X Medina.

Ciao Italia: Traditional Italian Recipes from Family Kitchens. Mary A. Esposito. (Illus.). 288p. 1991. 20.00 (*0-688-10317-0*) Hearst Bks.

Ciao, Sweet Valley! Francine Pascal. (Sweet Valley Twins Ser.: No. 60). (J). (gr. 4-7). 1992. pap. 3.25 (*0-553-15940-2*) Bantam.

Ciarcia's Circuit Cellar, Vol. IV. Steve Ciarcia. (BYTE Bks.). (Illus.). 1984. pap. text ed. 28.95 (*0-07-010966-4*) McGraw.

Ciarcia's Circuit Cellar, Vol. VII. Steve Ciarcia. (BYTE Bks.). (Illus.). 256p. 1990. pap. text ed. 22.95 (*0-07-010969-9*) McGraw.

Ciardi Himself: Fifteen Essays in the Reading, Writing, & Teaching of Poetry. John Ciardi. LC 89-31386. 155p. 1989. 19.95 (*1-55728-084-3*); pap. 9.95 (*1-55728-085-1*) U of Ark Pr.

***CIA's Greatest Hits.** Mark Zepezauer. Ed. by Arthur Naiman. (Real Story Ser.). (Illus.). 96p. (Orig.). 1994. pap. 6.00 (*1-878825-30-5*) Odonian Pr.

CIBA Foundation: An Analytic History, 1949-1974. F. Peter Woodford. 210p. 1974. 28.25 (*0-444-15145-1*, Excerpta Medica) Elsevier.

***Ciba-Geigy Corporation: A Report on the Company's Environmental Policies & Practices.** (Illus.). 37p. (C). 1994. reprint ed. pap. text ed. 200.00x (*0-7881-0917-0*, Coun on Econ) Diane Pub.

Cibber & the Dunciad see Popeiana

Cibecue Apache. Keith H. Basso. (Illus.). 106p. (C). 1986. reprint ed. pap. text ed. 8.50 (*0-88133-214-3*) Waveland Pr.

Cibernetical Dictionary: E-G-F-R-Slovene. Achim Sydow. 171p. (ENG, FRE, GER, RUS & SLV.). 1974. 95.00 (*0-8288-5976-0*, M9895) Fr & Eur.

Cibola. William J. Fling. Ed. by Renais J. Hill. LC 92-53225. 160p. (Orig.). 1993. pap. 10.95 (*1-55666-083-9*) Pubs Grp Toluca.

Cicada Grove. Lindsey M. Bowen. 96p. (Orig.). 1992. pap. 7.50 (*1-881048-01-2*) Paladin Contemp.

Cicada Sing-Song. Densey Clyne. (J). (gr. 4-7). 1994. pap. 6.95 (*1-86373-131-8*, Pub. by Allen & Unwin Aust Pty AT) IPG Chicago.

Cicada Voices: Selected Haiku of Eric Amann, 1966-1979. Eric Amann. 64p. (Orig.). 1983. pap. 5.00 (*0-913719-25-0*) High-Coo Pr.

Cicada's Return. Jerry W. Hardin. 147p. 1992. 9.95 (*1-882446-09-7*); pap. 6.95 (*1-882446-08-9*) I p e Alliance.

Cicada's Return: O Retorno Das Cigarras Bi-Lingual Edition. Jerry W. Hardin & Camilo De Andrade. 294p. (ENG & POR.). 1992. 12.95 (*1-882446-07-0*); pap. 10. 95 (*1-882446-06-2*) I p e Alliance.

Cicadellidae of Hawaii. H. Osborn. (BMB Ser.). 1972. reprint ed. pap. 15.00 (*0-527-02240-3*) Periodicals Srv.

Cicatricial Xerosis of the Eye. Vladimir E. Shevalev. LC 61-17731. 138p. reprint ed. pap. 39.40 (*0-317-27108-3*, 2024706) Bks Demand.

Ciccimarra: A Biography. Frank Nowosad. LC 88-31037. (Illus.). 253p. 1988. 24.95 (*0-940537-04-4*) Fuller Tech.

Cicely Mary Barker & Her Art. Jane Laing. (Illus.). 128p. (J). 1995. 35.00 (*0-7232-4051-5*) Warne.

Cicero. George C. Richards. LC 79-109830. 298p. 1970. reprint ed. text ed. 55.00 (*0-8371-4321-7*, RCIC, Greenwood Pr) Greenwood.

Cicero: A Biography. Torsten Petersson. LC 63-10768. 1920. 25.00 (*0-8196-0119-5*) Biblo.

Cicero: De Legibus One. N. Rudd & T. Wiedemann. 90p. 1987. 14.95 (*0-86292-271-2*, Pub. by Brstl Class Pr UK) Focus Info Gr.

Cicero: In Catilinam One & Two. H. E. Gould & J. L. Whiteley. 148p. 1982. reprint ed. 14.95 (*0-86292-014-0*, Pub. by Brstl Class Pr UK) Focus Info Gr.

Cicero: In L. Calpurnium Pisonem Oratio. Ed. by Robin G. Nisbet. 240p. 1987. pap. 21.00 (*0-19-872131-5*) OUP.

Cicero: In Vatinium. Ed. by L. G. Pocock. vi, 200p. 1967. reprint ed. 30.00 (*0-685-54232-7*, Pub. by A M Hakkert NE) Benjamins North Am.

Cicero: Murder at Larinum: Selections from Pro Cluentio. H. Grose-Hodge. 112p. 1983. reprint ed. 14.95 (*0-86292-093-0*, Pub. by Brstl Class Pr UK) Focus Info Gr.

Cicero: Philippics. Cicero. Ed. & Tr. by D. R. Shackleton Bailey. LC 85-1029. xviii, 402p. 1986. 45.00 (*0-8078-1657-4*) U of NC Pr.

Cicero: Philippics One & Two. J. D. Denniston. 208p. 1978. reprint ed. 18.95 (*0-906515-08-4*, Pub. by Brstl Class Pr UK) Focus Info Gr.

Cicero: Pro Caelio. Walter Englert. 79p. 1991. pap. text ed. 6.00 (*0-929524-65-9*) Bryn Mawr Commentaries.

Cicero: Pro Milone. Ed. by F. H. Colson. 180p. 1893. 18.95 (*0-906515-50-5*, Pub. by Brstl Class Pr UK) Focus Info Gr.

Cicero: Pro Murena. C. MacDonald. 220p. 1982. reprint ed. 17.95 (*0-86292-010-8*, Pub. by Brstl Class Pr UK) Focus Info Gr.

Cicero: Select Letters: A Companion to the Translation by L. P. Wilkinson. M. M. Willcock. 84p. 1986. 17.95 (*0-86292-195-3*, Pub. by Brstl Class Pr UK) Focus Info Gr.

Cicero: Selections from Latin Readings. Robert P. Sonkowsky. (Living Voice of Greek & Latin Literature Ser.). 1985. audio 29.95 (*0-88432-126-6*, S23680) Audio-Forum.

Cicero: Verrine V. R. G. Levens. 250p. 1980. reprint ed. 14. 95 (*0-906515-74-2*, Pub. by Brstl Class Pr UK) Focus Info Gr.

Cicero - On Old Age-De Senectute: Cicero. Ed. by Charles E. Bennett. (Textbook Ser.). (Illus.). 446p. 1980. pap. text ed. 11.00 (*0-86516-001-5*) Bolchazy-Carducci.

Cicero & Sallust. E. J. Barnes & John T. Ramsey. 1988. pap. text ed. 14.88 (*0-582-36752-2*, 72528) Longman.

***Cicero & the End of the Roman Republic.** T. Wiedemann. (Classical World Ser.). 102p. 1994. pap. text ed. 13.95 (*1-85399-193-7*) Focus Info Gr.

Cicero & the Fall of the Roman Republic. James L. Strachan-Davidson. LC 72-2510. (Select Bibliographies Reprint Ser.). 1977. reprint ed. 41.95 (*0-8369-6866-2*) Ayer.

Cicero & the Roman Republic. Manfred Fuhrmann. 1992. 34.95 (*0-631-17879-1*) Blackwell Pubs.

Cicero & the State Religion. R. J. Goar. 141p. (Orig.). 1978. pap. 27.00 (*90-256-0804-3*, Pub. by A M Hakkert NE) Benjamins North Am.

Cicero: Back from Exile: Six Speeches upon His Return. Tr. by D. R. Bailey. 278p. 1991. 29.95 (*1-55540-626-2*, 40 07 04); pap. 19.95 (*1-55540-627-0*) Scholars Pr GA.

Cicero de Amicitia. Gould & Whiteley. 178p. 1983. 12.00 (*0-86516-042-2*) Bolchazy-Carducci.

Cicero. De Legibus. A Commentary on Book I. L. P. Kenter. xx, 257p. 1971. 54.00 (*90-256-0575-3*, Pub. by A M Hakkert NE) Benjamins North Am.

Cicero in the Courtroom of Saint Thomas Aquinas. Edward K. Rand. (Aquinas Lectures). 1945. 10.00 (*0-87462-109-7*) Marquette.

Cicero on Oratory & Orators. 2nd ed. Marcus T. Cicero. Ed. by J. S. Watson. LC 85-26258. (Landmarks in Rhetoric & Public Address Ser.). 432p. (C). 1986. reprint ed. pap. text ed. 19.95 (*0-8093-1293-X*) S Ill U Pr.

Cicero Pro Archia. Grace S. West. (Latin Commentaries Ser.). 49p. (Orig.). (C). 1988. pap. text ed. 6.00 (*0-929524-38-1*) Bryn Mawr Commentaries.

***Cicero the Philosopher.** Ed. & Intro. by Jonathan Powell. 376p. 1995. 65.00 (*0-19-814751-1*) OUP.

Cicero, the Senior Statesman. Thomas N. Mitchell. 360p. (C). 1991. text ed. 37.50 (*0-300-04779-7*) Yale U Pr.

Ciceron Et Ses Amis: Etude Sur La Societe Romaine Du Temps De Cesar. Gaston Boissier. 523p. 1976. reprint ed. write for info. (*3-487-05614-3*, Pub. by Georg Olms GW) Lubrecht & Cramer.

Ciceron, les Aratea. Cicero. xx, 403p. 1966. reprint ed. write for info. (*0-318-71089-7*, Pub. by Georg Olms GW) Lubrecht & Cramer.

Ciceron y el Imperio. Pedro Badillo Gerena. LC 76-10131. (UPREX, Humanidades Ser.: Serie Humanidades No. 50). 199p. (Orig.). 1976. pap. 1.50 (*0-8477-0050-X*) U of PR Pr.

Ciceronian Style in Fr. Luis De Granada. Rebecca Switzer. 159p. (SPA.). 1927. 1.90 (*0-318-14248-1*) Hispanic Inst.

Ciceronianus: Or, A Dialogue on the Best Style of Speaking. Desiderius Erasmus. Tr. by Izora Scott. LC 73-176755. (Columbia University. Teachers College. Contributions to Education Ser.: No. 21). reprint ed. 37. 50 (*0-404-55021-5*) AMS Pr.

Ciceronis Amor: Tullies Love (1589) & Quip for an Upstart (1592) Robert Greene. LC 54-11901. 1979. 50.00 (*0-8201-1224-0*) Schol Facsimiles.

Ciceronis Orationum Scholiastae. Cicero. 351p. 1964. reprint ed. write for info. (*0-318-71090-0*, Pub. by Georg Olms GW) Lubrecht & Cramer.

Cicero's Brutus: Or, History of Famous Orators. Marcus Cicero. Tr. by Ernest Jones. LC 72-158313. (Augustan Translators Ser.). reprint ed. 62.00 (*0-404-54106-2*) AMS Pr.

Cicero's Caesarian Speeches: A Stylistic Commentary. Harold C. Gotoff. LC 92-50816. xlvi, 310p. (C). 1993. 42.50 (*0-8078-2075-X*); pap. text ed. 15.95 (*0-8078-4407-1*) U of NC Pr.

Cicero's Knowledge of the Peripatos. Ed. by William W. Fortenbaugh & Peter Steinmetz. (Rutgers University Studies in Classical Humanities: Vol. IV). 324p. 1989. 49.95 (*0-88738-271-1*) Transaction Pubs.

Cicero's Letters to His Friends. D. R. Bailey. 1989. pap. 20.95 (*1-55540-264-X*, 40 07 01) Scholars Pr GA.

Cicero's Philippics & Their Demosthenic Model: The Rhetoric of Crisis. Cecil W. Wooten. LC 82-24857. xi, 199p. 1983. 29.95 (*0-8078-1558-6*) U of NC Pr.

Ciceros Philosophisches Spatwerk Als Aufruf Gegen die Herrschaft Caesars. Hermann Strasburger. Ed. by Gisela Strasburger. (Spudasmata Ser.: Bd. XLV). 92p. (GER.). 1990. write for info. (*3-487-09370-7*, Pub. by Georg Olms GW) Lubrecht & Cramer.

***Cicero's Pro Caelio.** Ed. by Stephen N. Ciraolo. Date not set. student ed, pap. text ed. 14.00 (*0-86516-264-6*); teacher ed, pap. text ed. 8.00 (*0-86516-265-4*) Bolchazy-Carducci.

Cicero's Return from Exile: The Orations Post Reditum. John Nicholson. LC 92-12191. (Classical Studies: Vol. 4). 174p. (C). 1992. text ed. 39.95 (*0-8204-1945-1*) P Lang Pubs.

Cicero's Social & Political Thought: An Introduction. Neal Wood. 301p. 1991. pap. 15.00 (*0-520-07427-0*) U CA Pr.

Cicero's Somnium Scipionis. Sally Davis & Gilbert Lawall. 1988. pap. text ed. 14.88 (*0-582-36751-4*, 72527) Longman.

Cicero's Verrine Oration, No. II.4: With Notes & Vocabulary. Sheila K. Dickison. LC 92-9058. (Classical Studies: Pedagogy Ser.). 270p. (LAT.). (C). 1992. pap. 17.95 (*0-8143-2382-0*) Wayne St U Pr.

Cichlid Aquarium. Paul Loiselle. (Illus.). 285p. Date not set. 23.95 (*3-923880-20-0*, 16077) Tetra Pr.

***Cichlid Aquarium.** Paul V. Loiselle. 1994. 39.95 (*1-56465-146-0*) Tetra Pr.

Cichlid Fishes: Behaviour, Ecology & Evolution. M. A. Keenleyside. 1991. 72.95 (*0-442-31157-5*) Chapman & Hall.

Cichlid Lexicon. Herbert R. Axelrod. (TS Ser.). (Illus.). 864p. 1993. text ed. 100.00 (*0-86622-422-X*, TS-190) TFH Pubns.

Cichlids: A Complete Pet Owners Manual. Georg Zurlo. 64p. 1991. pap. 5.95 (*0-8120-4597-1*) Barron.

Cichlids from Central America. Ad Konings. (Illus.). 224p. (C). 1988. lib. bdg. 39.95 (*0-86622-700-8*, TS-124) TFH Pubns.

Cichlids from Lake Malawi & Tanganyika, Success with. Sabine Melke. (Illus.). 192p. 1993. 24.95 (*0-86622-489-0*, TT030) TFH Pubns.

Cichlids of North & Central America. Donald Conkel. (TS Ser.). (Illus.). 191p. 1993. text ed. 49.95 (*0-86622-444-0*, TS-184) TFH Pubns.

Cichlids of Surinam: Teleostei: Labroidei. Sven O. Kullander & Han Nijssen. LC 89-33883. (Illus.). xxxii, 256p. (Orig.). 1989. pap. text ed. 59.50 (*90-04-09077-0*) E J Brill.

Cichlids of the World. Robert J. Goldstein. (Illus.). 382p. 1989. 34.95 (*0-86622-893-4*, H-945) TFH Pubns.

Ciclo De la Vida Victoriosa: Recyled for Living. Earl G. Lee. (SPA.). 3.25 (*84-7228-333-X*, 220153, Pub. by Edit Clie SP) TSELF.

Ciclo Villa. Raymond Plants. (Coleccion Rosa Ser.). (Illus.). 60p. (SPA.). (J). (gr. 5 up). 1994. pap. 5.95 (*958-07-0067-2*) Firefly Bks Ltd.

Ciclopidine. Ed. by J. R. O'Brien & M. Verstraete. (Journal: Haemostasis: Vol. 13, Suppl. 1). (Illus.). ii, 54p. 1983. pap. 38.50 (*3-8055-3816-2*) S Karger.

Ciclos De la Vida Animal: Aves, Anfibios, e Insectos. Joy Evans & Jo E. Moore. Tr. by Liz Wolfe & Dora Ficklin. (Science Mini-Unit Ser.). (Illus.). 16p. (SPA.). (J). (gr. 1-3). 1992. pap. text ed. 5.95 (*1-55799-232-0*) Evan-Moor Corp.

Ciclos De la Vida Animales: Mamiferos y Reptiles. Joy Evans & Jo E. Moore. Tr. by Liz Wolfe & Dora Ficklin. (Science Mini-Unit Ser.). (Illus.). 16p. (SPA.). (J). (gr. 1-3). 1992. pap. text ed. 5.95 (*1-55799-238-X*) Evan-Moor Corp.

Ciclosporin. Ed. by J. F. Borel. (Progress in Allergy Ser.: Vol. 38). (Illus.). vi, 474p. 1986. 156.00 (*3-8055-4221-6*) S Karger.

Ciclosporin in Pediatric Renal Transplantation. Ed. by Wolff & Provoost. (Clinical Research Ser.: No. 4). ix, 122p. (Orig.). (C). 1986. pap. text ed. 34.60 (*3-11-013367-9*) Mouton.

Ciclosporin in Renal Transplantation. Ed. by C. Ponticelli & A. De Vecchi. (Contributions to Nephrology Ser.: Vol. 51). (Illus.). viii, 168p. 1987. 107.25 (*3-8055-4357-3*) S Karger.

CICS: A Guide to Internal Structure. Eugene Hudders. 1993. pap. 39.95 (*0-89435-451-5*) Wiley.

CICS: A Guide to Internal Structure. Eugene S. Hudders. LC 94-18026. 1994. pap. text ed. 44.95 (*0-471-52172-8*) Wiley.

CICS: A Guide to Performance Tuning. Eugene S. Hudders. 1991. 39.95 (*0-89435-395-0*) Wiley.

CICS: A Guide to Performance Tuning. Eugene S. Hudders. 1993. pap. text ed. 39.95 (*0-471-56710-8*, GD3950) Wiley.

CICS: A How-to for COBOL Programmers. David S. Kirk. 1992. pap. 39.95 (*0-89435-428-0*) Wiley.

CICS: A How-to for COBOL Programmers. David S. Kirk. 1993. pap. text ed. 49.95 (*0-471-58021-X*, GD4280) Wiley.

CICS: Designing for Performance. Eric P. Emanuel. 1991. text ed. 49.95 (*0-07-019420-3*) McGraw.

***CICS - ESA Migration Notebook: An Inside Look at Versions 3 & 4.** Phyllis Donofrio. Ed. by Mascomm Associates Circle Education Staff. (Compuware Technology Update Ser.). Date not set. pap. text ed. 49. 95 (*0-923039-00-7*) CompuWare MI.

CICS - ESA Version 3.0: Architecture & Problem Detection. Bob Archambeault & Mardie Gibbs. 1994. text ed. 50.00 (*0-07-002744-7*) McGraw.

CICS - VS: A Guide to Application Debugging. Eugene S. Hudders. 1991. 39.95 (*0-89435-331-4*) Wiley.

CICS - VS: A Guide to Application Debugging. Eugene S. Hudders. 1992. 39.95 (*0-471-56660-8*, GD3314) Wiley.

CICS, a Programmer's Reference. Phyllis Donofrio. 480p. 1991. text ed. 45.00 (*0-07-017607-8*) McGraw.

CICS Application & System Programming: Tools & Techniques. Barry Nirmal. 1993. pap. text ed. 39.95 (*0-471-58477-0*, GD3934) Wiley.

CICS Application & System Programming: Tools & Techniques. Barry K. Nirmal. 1991. 39.95 (*0-89435-393-4*) Wiley.

CICS Application Design Handbook. Crownhart. (J. Ranade IBM Ser.). 1995. text ed. 50.00 (*0-07-014774-4*) McGraw.

CICS Capacity Planning & Performance Management. Thomas F. Keller. (IBM Ser.). 396p. 1993. text ed. 40.00 (*0-07-033783-7*) McGraw.

CICS Command Level Program. 2nd ed. Alida M. Jatich. 1991. pap. text ed. 44.95 (*0-471-52862-5*) Wiley.

CICS Essentials for Application Developers & Programmers. Joseph J. Le Bert. LC 92-25967. 384p. 1993. text ed. 45.00 (*0-07-035869-9*) McGraw.

CICS for Microcomputers. Joseph J. LeBert. 384p. 1989. pap. text ed. 32.95 (*0-07-036968-2*) McGraw.

CICS for the COBOL Programmer: An Advanced Course, Pt. 2. 2nd ed. Doug Lowe. LC 92-17814. 352p. 1992. 31.00 (*0-911625-67-4*) M Murach & Assoc.

An Asterisk (*) at the beginning of an entry indicates that the title is appearing in BIP for the first time.

1267

CICS for the COBOL Programmer: An Introductory Course, Pt. 1. 2nd ed. Doug Lowe. LC 92-17814. 409p. 1992. 31.00 (0-911625-60-7) M Murach & Assoc.

CICS Handbook. Yukihisa Kageyama. 1990. text ed. 54.50 (0-07-033637-7) McGraw.

***CICS Primer.** James G. Janossy. 1995. pap. text ed. 39.95 (0-471-30991-5) Wiley.

CICS Programmer's Desk Reference. 2nd ed. Doug Lowe. LC 92-38014. 507p. 1992. pap. 36.50 (0-911625-68-2) M Murach & Assoc.

CICS Programmer's Guide. Kelvin Kostohyrz. 286p. (Orig.). 1988. pap. 24.95 (0-938862-88-X) Weber Systems.

CICS-VS Command Level Programming with COBOL Examples. David L. Shyh-Yuan. 295p. 1983. per. 29.95 (0-9611810-1-X) CCD Online Syst.

CICS-VS Online System & Implementation Techniques. 420p. 1986. 29.95 (0-9611810-7-9) CCD Online Syst.

Cid. Pierre Corneille. 1965. pap. 5.95 (0-7859-0591-X, FC1219) Fr & Eur.

Cid. Pierre Corneille. Ed. & Tr. by John C. Lapp. (Crofts Classics Ser.). 96p. 1955. pap. text ed. write for info. (0-88295-026-6) Harlan Davidson.

Cid: A Translation in Rhymed Couplets. Pierre Corneille. Tr. by Vincent J. Cheng. LC 85-40877. 208p. 1987. 36.50 (0-87413-294-0) U Delaware Pr.

Cid: Spanish Military Leader. Philip Koslow. LC 92-33377. (Hispanics of Achievement Ser.). (Illus.). (J). 1993. lib. bdg. 18.95 (0-7910-1239-5, Am Art Analog); pap. write for info. (0-7910-1266-2, Am Art Analog) Chelsea Hse.

***Cid: The Text of the Original Edition, 1637.** fac. ed. Pierre Corneille. Ed. by Peter H. Nurse. LC 79-100489. (Illus.). 183p. 1978. reprint ed. pap. 52.20 (0-7837-7939-9, 2047695) Bks Demand.

Cid: Tragi-Comedie. Ed. by Milorad R. Margitic. LC 89-6655. (Purdue University Monographs in Romance Languages: Vol. 28). lxxxv, 302p. (FRE.). 1989. 106.00x (1-55619-067-0); pap. 27.95 (1-55619-068-9) Benjamins North Am.

Cid Campeador & the Waning of the Crescent in the West. Henry B. Clarke. LC 73-14438. (Heroes of the Nations Ser.). (Illus.). reprint ed. 49.50 (0-404-58256-7) AMS Pr.

Cid, Cinna, the Theatrical Illusion. Pierre Corneille. Tr. by John Cairncross. (Classics Ser.). 1976. pap. 9.95 (0-14-044312-6, Penguin Classics) Viking Penguin.

CIDA & Sustainable Development: How Canada's Aid Policies Can Support Sustainable Development in the Third World More Effectively. Jim MacNeill et al. 110p. 1990. pap. text ed. 17.95 (0-88645-097-7, Pub. by Inst Res Pub CN) Ashgate Pub Co.

Cidean Ballads, Ballads About the Great Spanish Hero, El Cid. 2nd ed. Merrill G. Christophersen & Adolfo Leon. Ed. by John E. Westburg. LC 74-24580. (Comparative Literature Studies). 180p. pap. 16.50 (0-87423-012-8) Westburg.

***Cider.** Paul Correnty. (Illus.). 86p. 1995. 9.95 (0-937381-42-X) Brewers Pubns.

Cider House Rules. John Irving. 1993. mass mkt. 6.99 (0-345-38765-1) Ballantine.

Cider House Rules. John Irving. LC 84-27195. 640p. 1985. 18.95 (0-688-03036-X) Morrow.

Cider Vinegar: Slimming Folk Remedy. Cyril Scott. 1982. pap. 2.95 (0-87904-011-4) Lust.

Cider with Rosie. Laurie Lee. (Chatto Pocket Library). 388p. 1994. 17.95 (0-7011-4973-6, Pub. by Chatto & Windus UK) Trafalgar.

Cidermaking. Michael B. Quinion. 1989. pap. 25.00 (0-85263-614-8, Pub. by Shire UK) St Mut.

CIDI Researcher's Manual. World Health Organization: CIDI Editorial Committee. 1994. text ed. write for info. (0-88048-982-0) Am Psychiatric.

CIE Guides to Insects of Importance to Man, No. 1: Lepidoptera. J. D. Holloway et al. 292p. (Orig.). 1987. pap. text ed. 38.00 (0-85198-594-7) CAB Intl.

CIE Guides to Insects of Importance to Man, No. 2: Thysanoptera. J. M. Palmer et al. 73p. (Orig.). 1989. pap. text ed. 24.00 (0-85198-634-X) CAB Intl.

***Ciel Ma Femme! Sky My Wife! Dictionnaire de l'Anglais Courant.** Jean-Loup Chiflet. 126p. (ENG & FRE.). 1991. pap. 12.95 (0-7859-7626-4, 2020125528) Fr & Eur.

Cielo: Heaven. John Zoller. (SPA.). 8.95 (84-7228-041-1, 220156, Pub. by Edit Clie SP) TSELF.

Cielo: Heaven: A Bright & Glorious. Betty Maltz. (SPA.). 5.00 (84-7645-493-7, 223584, Pub. by Edit Clie SP) TSELF.

Cielo & la Tierra en Sus Manos: Los Grandes Propietarios de Ponce, 1816-1830. Ivette Perez-Vega. LC 85-81454. 123p. (SPA.). 1985. pap. 5.95 (0-940238-22-5) Ediciones Huracan.

Cielo Azul de Shawna. Claire Blatchford. Tr. by C. C. Writer & Lisa C. Nielsen. (Hippy Ser.). (Illus.). 24p. (Orig.). (SPA.). (J). (ps). 1992. pap. text ed. 3.00 (1-56134-174-6) Dushkin Pub.

Cielo (Heaven) large type ed. R. C. Ryle. (SPA.). Date not set. 2.99 (1-56063-342-5, 494025) Editorial Unilit.

Cielo: un Lugar, una Ciudad... Heaven: a Place, a City, a Home. Edward M. Bounds. (SPA.). 4.25 (84-7228-667-3, 220152, Pub. by Edit Clie SP) TSELF.

Cielos Fueron Abiertos: The Heavens Were Opened. Jessie Penn-Lewis. (SPA.). 3.25 (84-7228-907-9, 222222, Pub. by Edit Clie SP) TSELF.

Cien Anos de Soledad. Gabriel Garcia Marquez. (Nueva Austral Ser.: Vol. 100). (SPA.). 1991. pap. text ed. 18.95x (84-239-1900-5) Elliots Bks.

Cien Anos De Soledad. 11th ed. Gabriel Garcia Marquez. 448p. (SPA.). 1990. pap. 19.95 (0-7859-5010-9) Fr & Eur.

Cien Bosquejos Ilustrados: 100 Illustrated Sermon Outlines. E. Lund. (SPA.). 5.95 (84-7645-468-6, 223340, Pub. by Edit Clie SP) TSELF.

Cien Cuartos. Chaya Shinhav. Tr. by C. C. Writer & Lisa C. Nielsen. (Hippy Ser.). (Illus.). 24p. (Orig.). (SPA.). (J). (ps). 1992. pap. text ed. 3.00 (1-56134-169-X) Dushkin Pub.

Cien Poesias de Cien Autores Hispanoamericanos. pap. 1.95 (0-685-11083-4) Fr & Eur.

Cien Poesias de Sarah Wekselbaum Luski. Sarah W. Luski. LC 80-69466. (Coleccion Espejo de Paciencia Ser.). (Illus.). 267p. (Orig.). (SPA.). 1981. pap. 14.95 (0-89729-272-3) Ediciones.

Cien Preguntas Acerca De Dios: 100 Questions about God. Edwin J. Orr. (SPA.). 4.95 (84-7228-143-4, 220159, Pub. by Edit Clie SP) TSELF.

Cien Vestidos. Eleanor Estes. Tr. by Teresa Mlawer. (Illus.). 80p. (SPA.). (J). (gr. 4). 1993. 13.95 (1-880507-06-4) Lectorum Pubns.

Cien y Uno Consejos: Como Ayudar a los Estudiantes a Lograr Sus Metas. Kristen Amundson. Ed. by American Assn. of School Administrators Staff. Tr. by Laredo Texas School District Staff & Victoria Barrosse. LC 92-73481. 28p. (Orig.). (SPA.). 1992. pap. 2.50 (0-87652-185-5, 21-00161) Am Assn Sch Admin.

Ciencia de la Economia Christiana. Lyndon H. LaRouche, Jr. Tr. by Dennis Small & Salvador Lozano. LC 93-83889. (Illus.). 300p. (Orig.). (SPA.). 1993. pap. 10.00 (1-882985-00-1) Schiller Inst.

Ciencia De la Oracion (The Science of Praying) Y. Avila. (SPA.). Date not set. 4.99 (1-56063-633-5, 550049) Editorial Unilit.

Ciencia de la Palabra Hablada. Elizabeth C. Prophet. 262p. 1991. pap. write for info. (0-318-71307-1) Edic Gran Dir.

Ciencia de la Palabra Hablada. Elizabeth C. Prophet. Tr. by Soledad Garces. 262p. (SPA.). 1991. pap. write for info. (1-883482-00-3) Edic Gran Dir.

Ciencia de la Palabra Hablada. Mark L. Prophet & Elizabeth C. Prophet. 1965. pap. 9.95 (0-922729-13-1) Summit Univ.

Ciencia De la Pedagogia. Eugenio M. De Hostos. 321p. 1991. 12.95 (0-8477-3663-6); pap. 8.50 (0-8477-3662-8) U of PR Pr.

Ciencia del Alma. R. Swinburne Clymer. Tr. by Fina Aparis. 272p. (Orig.). (SPA.). 1967. pap. 6.95 (0-932785-51-4) Philos Pub.

Ciencia, el Gobierno y la Industria Para el Desarrollo: El Foro de Texas. Interamerican Forum on Technological Development: Interactions of Science, Government, & Industry. Ed. by Earl Ingerson & Wayne G. Bragg. LC 75-620103. 467p. reprint ed. pap. 133.10 (0-685-17107-8, 2027323) Bks Demand.

Ciencia Interamericana. (Illus.). 71p. (SPA.). (C). 1981. pap. 1.00 (0-686-75079-9) OAS.

Ciencia Interamericana: Vol. 17, Nos. 3-4. 1977. pap. 1.00 (0-685-80053-9) OAS.

Ciencia Politica y Relaciones Internacionales: Political Science & International Relations. Conrad J. Schmitt. 1993. pap. text ed. 10.95 (0-07-056819-7) McGraw.

Ciencia Retorna a Dios. J. H. Jauncey. Tr. by Ana M. Swenson. 110p. (SPA.). 1981. reprint ed. pap. 2.25 (0-311-05004-2) Casa Bautista.

Ciencia y Arte del Verso Castellano. Luis Mario. LC 91-72151. (Coleccion Polymita Ser.). 506p. (Orig.). (SPA.). 1991. pap. 24.95 (0-89729-607-9) Ediciones.

Ciencia y Biblia, ? Se Contradicen? Science & Bible, Can We Believe. Larry Richards. (SPA.). 3.25 (84-7228-378-X, 220160, Pub. by Edit Clie SP) TSELF.

Cienciapoesia. Rafael Catala. LC 83-62040. (Serie de Poesia Guampara: No. 1). 128p. (Orig.). (SPA.). 1984. pap. text ed. 5.95 (0-910235-04-X) Prisma Bks.

Ciencias Fisicas. 9th ed. Departamento De Ciencias Fisicas. (C). 6.50 (0-8477-2340-2) U of PR Pr.

Ciencias Preguntan ? Es Cierta La? Science Asks: Is Evolution True? James L. Carder. (SPA.). 3.25 (84-7645-363-9, 223500, Pub. by Edit Clie SP) TSELF.

Ciento Cincuenta Cosas Que Hacer Con Papel. P. G. Patterson & D. G. Pettit. Orig. Title: One Hundred & Fifty Things to Make with Paper. 64p. 1985. reprint ed. pap. 3.50 (0-311-26604-5) Casa Bautista.

Ciento Tres Preguntas Comunes Acerca de Dios: (One Hundred Three Questions People Ask Most about God) Don Stewart. Tr. by Alicia Zorzoli. 128p. (SPA.). 1989. pap. 4.50 (0-311-09131-8) Casa Bautista.

Ciento Veinte Charlas de Sombremesa: Para la Ensenanza del Espanol en una Clase de Adultos. Ana L. Jaramillo. LC 89-81714. (Coleccion Textos Ser.). (Illus.). 338p. (Orig.). (SPA.). 1991. pap. 19.95 (0-89729-559-5) Ediciones.

Cierva Autogiros: The Development of Rotary-Wing Flight. Peter W. Brooks. LC 87-600310. (Illus.). 416p. (C). 1988. 42.50 (0-87474-268-4) Smithsonian.

CIFA - Report of the Eighth Session. (Fisheries Reports: No. 448). 50p. 1991. pap. 12.00 (92-5-003056-8, F0568) UNIPUB.

Cigale Chez les Fourmis. Eugene Labiche. (FRE.). pap. 10.95 (0-7859-5352-3) Fr & Eur.

Cigalon. Marcel Pagnol. 180p. 1978. 9.95 (0-686-54820-5) Fr & Eur.

Cigar Companion: A Connoisseur's Guide to the Pleasures of Cigar Smoking. Anwer Bati. LC 93-83532. (Illus.). 224p. 1993. 24.95 (1-56138-293-0) Running Pr.

***Cigar Killer.** Furst. 1995. pap. text ed. (0-8101-1261-2) Northwestern U Pr.

Cigar Means Never Having to Say You're Sorry. Jeff MacNelly. 128p. (Orig.). 1989. pap. 5.95 (0-312-02651-X) St Martin.

Cigar Smoker's Guide to Restaurants. (Orig.). 1993. pap. write for info. (0-9637403-0-X) Davidoff Geneva.

Cigares du Pharaon. Herge. 64p. (FRE.). (J). (gr. 7-9). 1992. reprint ed. write for info. (0-7859-4560-1) Fr & Eur.

Cigarette Cessation. 1985. student ed, audio 10.95 (0-393-70014-3) Norton.

Cigarette Makers Romance. Francis M. Crawford. (Works of Francis Marion Crawford Ser.). 1990. reprint ed. lib. bdg. 79.00 (0-7812-2537-X) Rprt Serv.

***Cigarette Sellers of Three Crosses Square.** Joseph Ziemian. LC 94-31368. 1995. write for info. (0-8225-3153-4, Lerner Publctns) Lerner Group.

***Cigarette Smoking.** Rita Milios & Marcia King. 88p. (YA). (gr. 7-12). 1994. pap. write for info. (1-57515-044-1) PPI Pubng.

***Cigarette Smoking: What Its Doing to Smokers & Nonsmokers.** Sukhraj S. Dhillon. 64p. (YA). (gr. 7-12). 1993. pap. write for info. (1-57515-037-9) PPI Pubng.

Cigarette Waltz: Seventeen Short Stories Adaptable for Theater. Philip-Dimitri Galas. (Illus.). 224p. (Orig.). 1992. pap. 11.95 (0-9632454-0-6) Dimitri Pubns.

Cigarettes Are Sublime. Richard Klein. LC 93-22621. (Illus.). 232p. 1993. 21.95 (0-8223-1401-0) Duke.

***Cigarettes Are Sublime.** Richard Klein. LC 93-22621. (Illus.). 232p. 1995. pap. 12.95 (0-8223-1641-2) Duke.

Cigarettes, Cigarettes. Pete Traynor. LC 92-31033. (Illus.). 28p. (J). 1994. 14.95 (0-9629978-7-0) Sights Prods.

***Cigarettes, Cigarettes.** Pete Traynor. (Illus.). 28p. (J). 1995. pap. 7.95 (1-886366-08-X) Sights Prods.

Cigarrillo: Contaminante, No. 1. Lindsay R. Curtis. 48p. 1986. reprint ed. pap. 2.25 (0-311-46073-9) Casa Bautista.

Cigarros del Faraon. Herge. (Illus.). 62p. (SPA.). (J). 19.95 (0-8288-5019-4) Fr & Eur.

Cigars du Pharon. Herge. (Illus.). 62p. (FRE.). (J). 19.95 (0-8288-5020-8) Fr & Eur.

Cigars of the Pharaoh. Herge. (Illus.). 62p. (J). 19.95 (0-8288-5021-6) Fr & Eur.

Cigars of the Pharoah. Herge. LC 74-21620. (Adventures of Tintin Ser.). (J). (gr. k up). 1975. mass mkt. 7.95 (0-316-35836-3, Joy St Bks) Little.

Ciguatera Seafood Toxins. Donald M. Miller & Donald R. Tindall. (Illus.). 378p. 1990. 133.00 (0-8493-6073-0, QP632) CRC Pr.

CIH Descriptions of Plant-Parasitic Nematodes, 8 vols., Set, Vols. 1-8. (C). 1985. Complete Set (1-8). 104.50 (0-685-44281-0) CAB Intl.

CIH Keys to the Nematode Parasites of Vertebrates, No. 1. Ed. by R. C. Anderson et al. 17p. (C). 1974. pap. 8.00 (0-685-44282-9) CAB Intl.

Cihuatan: An Early Postclassic Town of El Salvador: the 1977-78 Excavations. Karen O. Bruhns. Ed. by Lawrence Feldman. (Monographs in Anthropology: No. 5). (Illus.). vii, 171p. 1980. pap. 9.00 (0-913134-82-1) Mus Anthro MO.

Cihuatan, El Salvador: A Study in Intrasite Variability. Jane H. Kelley. Ed. by Ronald Spores et al. (Publications in Anthropology: No. 35). (Illus.). (Orig.). 1988. pap. text ed. 14.75 (0-935462-26-0) Vanderbilt Pubns.

Cilantro. P. J. Birosik. LC 93-46064. 160p. 1994. pap. 13.00 (0-02-016605-2, Collier S&S) S&S Trade.

Cilappatikaram of Ilanko Atikal: An Epic of South India. Tr. by R. Parthasarathy. 448p. 1992. text ed. 35.00 (0-231-07848-X) Col U Pr.

Cilia Ciliated Epithelium Ciliary Activity. J. Rivera. LC 61-14245. 1962. 79.00 (0-08-009623-9, Pub. by Pergamon Repr UK) Franklin.

Ciliary & Flagellar Membranes. Ed. by R. A. Bloodgood. LC 89-23227. (Illus.). 450p. 1990. 95.00 (0-306-43279-X, Plenum Pr) Plenum.

Ciliated Protozoa: An Illustrated Guide to the Species Used As Biological Indicators in Fresh Water Biology. H. Bick. 198p. 1972. pap. 9.60 (92-4-154028-1, 1308) World Health.

Ciliated Protozoa: Characterization, Classification & Guide to the Literature. 2nd ed. John O. Corliss. LC 78-41075. (Illus.). 1979. 188.00 (0-08-018752-8, Pub. by Pergamon Repr UK) Franklin.

Cilician Armenian Ordeal. Paren Kazanjian. 515p. (Orig.). 1989. pap. write for info. (0-318-65854-2) Hye Intentions.

CIM: Principles of Computer Integrated Manufacturing. J. B. Waldner. Tr. by W. J. Duffin. 189p. 1992. pap. text ed. 59.95 (0-471-93450-X) Wiley.

CIM & Manufacturing Automation Markets: 1992-1995. Ed. by Richard Miller & Terri C. Walker. (Orig.). 1992. pap. text ed. 485.00 (1-881503-02-X) R K Miller Assocs.

CIM Computer Integrated Manufacturing. August-Wilhelm Scheer. (Illus.). 215p. 1988. 45.00 (0-387-19191-7) Spr-Verlag.

CIM Computer Integrated Manufacturing: Towards the Factory of the Future. 2nd enl. rev. ed. August-Wilhelm Scheer. (Illus.). xii, 208p. 1991. 59.00 (0-387-53667-1) Spr-Verlag.

***CIM Computer Integrated Manufacturing: Towards the Factory of the Future.** 3rd ed. A W. Scheer. 287p. 1994. 59.00 (0-387-57964-8) Spr-Verlag.

CIM Handbook: The Opportunities for Rationalization Opened up by the Acquisition & Integration of Computer Automation. Ed. by M. Mesina et al. Tr. by Adrian Morris. LC 93-13855. 1994. 110.00 (0-7506-0820-X) Buttrwrth-Heinemann.

CIM Implementation Guide. 3rd ed. Ed. by Leonard Bertain. LC 91-60114. (Illus.). 170p. 1991. pap. text ed. 42.00 (0-87263-400-0) SME.

CIM in Process & Manufacturing Industries: IFAC Workshop, Espoo, Finland, 23-25 November 1992. Ed. by K. Leiviska. LC 93-17913. (IFAC Pre-Print Ser.). 1993. pap. 91.00 (0-08-042182-2, Pergamon Pr) Elsevier.

CIM in the Process Industries. J. W. Bernard. (Independent Learning Module Ser.). 240p. 1989. text ed. 50.00 (1-55617-167-6, A167-6) Instru Soc.

CIM Interfaces: Concepts, Standards & Problems of Interfaces in Computer Integrated Manufacturing. B. Scholz-Reiter. Tr. by Christoph Torring. LC 92-27392. (ENG & GER.). 1992. write for info. (0-442-31626-7) Chapman & Hall.

CIM Justification in the Process Industry: A Case Study. H. Lee Hales & Raymond C. Cole, Jr. Ed. by Claire Barth. (Illus.). 64p. (Orig.). 1991. pap. 12.50 (0-86641-195-X, 91257) Inst Mgmt Account.

CIM Systems: An Introduction to Computer Integrated Manufacturing. Fred H. Mitchell. 752p. 1990. text ed. 79.00 (0-13-133299-6) P-H.

CIM Systems Integrators. Richard K. Miller & Terri C. Walker. LC 88-81657. (Survey on Technology & Markets Ser.: No. 66). 50p. 1989. pap. text ed. 200.00 (1-55865-065-2) Future Tech Surveys.

CIM Technology: Fundamentals & Applications. Russell Biekert. LC 92-32085. 384p. 1993. 34.60 (0-87006-994-2) Goodheart.

Cimarron. Edna Ferber. 26.95 (0-88411-548-8, Aeonian Pr) Amereon Ltd.

Cimarron. Edna Ferber. 1992. reprint ed. lib. bdg. 27.95 (0-89968-279-0, Lghtyr Pr) Buccaneer Bks.

Cimarron Bride. Catherine Creel. 1989. pap. 3.95 (0-8217-2595-5) Zebra.

Cimarron Family Legends, Vol. 1. Ed. by Robert L. Evans & LaVeta Randall. (Illus.). 1978. 40.00 (0-934188-02-5) Evans Pubns.

Cimarron Family Legends, Vol. 2. Ed. by Robert L. Evans & Laveta Randall. LC 80-67133. (Illus.). 1979. 40.00 (0-934188-03-3) Evans Pubns.

Cimarron Kid. large type ed. Cy James. (Linford Western Library). 368p. 1986. pap. 11.95 (0-7089-6212-2, Linford) Ulverscroft.

Cimarron Seductress. Patricia Werner. 1991. mass mkt. 4.25 (0-8217-3587-X) Zebra.

CIME (Computers in Mechanical Engineering Magazine) Research Supplement, Vol. 1. Ed. by Ali A. Seireg. 79p. 1983. pap. text ed. 3.00 (0-317-02556-2, G00234) ASME.

Cimelio of Bodoni. Bodoni. 252p. 1991. write for info. (0-87923-924-7) Godine.

Cimetiere des Voitures. Fernando Arrabal. 192p. (FRE.). 1972. pap. 10.95 (0-8288-9025-0, FA783) Fr & Eur.

Cimmeride Orogenic System & the Tectonics of Eurasia. A. M. Celal Sengor. (Special Paper Ser.: No. 195). (Illus.). 92p. 1985. pap. 3.00 (0-8137-2195-4) Geol Soc.

CIMOSA: Open System Architecture for CIM. 2nd enl. rev. ed. Ed. by ESPRIT Consortium AMICE Staff. LC 93-1199. (Research Reports ESPRIT, Project 688, AMICE: Vol. 1). xi, 234p. 1993. pap. 39.00 (0-387-56256-7) Spr-Verlag.

Cincinnati: A Guide to the Queen City & Its Neighbors. Federal Writers' Project Staff. LC 72-84462. (American Guidebook Ser.). 1981. reprint ed. 89.00 (0-403-02201-0) Somerset Pub.

Cincinnati: A Pictorial History. Marilyn Green & Michael Bennett. 225p. 1987. 21.95 (0-89865-477-7) Donning Co.

Cincinnati: An Urban History Sourcebook, Bk. II. Ed. by Karen Regina & Gregory L. Rhodes. LC 87-72186. (Illus.). 88p. (Orig.). (YA). (gr. 7-8). 1988. pap. text ed. 6.95 (0-911497-02-1) Cinc Hist Soc.

Cincinnati: An Urban History Sourcebook, Bk. 1. Ed. by Karen Regina & Gregory L. Rhodes. LC 87-72186. (Illus.). 88p. (Orig.). (J). (gr. 4-6). 1988. pap. text ed. 6.95 (0-911497-01-3) Cinc Hist Soc.

Cincinnati: Paintings & Sketches. Clinton Orlemann & Hollis Stevenson. (Illus.). 116p. reprint ed. 24.95 (0-9618069-1-5) C Orlemann.

Cincinnati & the Big Red Machine. Robert H. Walker. LC 88-45166. (Illus.). 176p. 1988. 19.95 (0-253-32863-2); pap. 8.95 (0-253-21370-3) Ind U Pr.

Cincinnati Bengals. Richard Rambeck. (NFL Today Ser.). (J). (gr. 4 up). 1991. lib. bdg. 14.95 (0-88682-362-5) Creative Ed.

Cincinnati Chefs Books. William Struns. Ed. by Russ McMinn. 120p. (Orig.). 1988. pap. text ed. 5.95 (0-935201-72-6) Affordable Adven.

Cincinnati City Directory for 1825. Harvey Hall. Ed. by Karen M. Green. LC 88-72185. 86p. 1988. reprint ed. pap. 11.00 (0-932231-06-3) Frontier Pr.

Cincinnati, Columbus, Cleveland & Erie Railroad Guide. limited ed. (Illus.). 176p. 1989. 13.95 (0-913428-60-4) Landfall Pr.

Cincinnati Cookbook: Household Guide Embracing Menu, Daily Recipes, Doctors Prescriptions & Various Suggestions for the Coming Generation. Ed. by David E. Schoonover. LC 93-23630. (Iowa Szathmary Culinary Arts Ser.). (Illus.). 288p. 1994. reprint ed. 24.95 (0-87745-460-4) U of Iowa Pr.

Cincinnati Days in History: A Bicentennial Almanac. Ed. by Nancy Berliner & Peter Dantzler. (Illus.). 224p. (Orig.). 1988. pap. 9.00 (0-933002-04-1) Cin Post.

Cincinnati Fossils: An Elementary Guide to the Ordivician Rocks & Fossils of the Cincinnati, Ohio, Region. rev. ed. Ed. by R. A. Davis. (Illus.). 64p. reprint ed. pap. text ed. 6.95 (1-882151-00-3) Cinc Mus Nat Hist.

Cincinnati Game. Lonnie Wheeler & John Baskin. LC 88-60682. 270p. 1988. 29.95 (0-9619637-1-9) Orange Frazer.

Cincinnati German Imprints: A Checklist. Franziska C. Ott. LC 92-15690. (New German-American Studies: Vol. 7). 378p. 1992. 58.95 (0-8204-1900-1) P Lang Pubs.

Cincinnati in Eighteen Twenty. Benjamin Drake. (Notable American Authors Ser.). 1992. reprint ed. lib. bdg. 75.00 (0-7812-2683-X) Rprt Serv.

Cincinnati Kid. Richard Jessup. LC 85-80626. 154p. 1985. pap. 7.95 (0-917657-58-6, Primus Lib Contemp) D I Fine.

C

An Asterisk (*) at the beginning of an entry indicates that the title is appearing in BIP for the first time.

Cincinnati Kid. Richard Jessup. 1991. reprint ed. lib. bdg. 21.95 (*1-56849-043-7*) Buccaneer Bks.

Cincinnati Miscellany, or Antiquities of the West: Pioneer History & General & Local Statistics Compiled from the Western General Advertiser, 2 Vols. in 1. Charles Cist. LC 72-146381. (First American Frontier Ser.). 1971. reprint ed. 47.95 (*0-405-02832-6*) Ayer.

Cincinnati Observed: Architecture & History. John Clubbe. (Urban Life & Urban Landscape Ser.). (Illus.). 480p. 1992. 60.00 (*0-8142-0512-7*); pap. 27.50 (*0-8142-0514-3*) Ohio St U Pr.

***Cincinnati Opera: From the Zoo to Music Hall. Eldred A. Thierstein. LC 95-92158. (Illus.). 373p. 1995. 20.00 (*0-9646068-0-1*) Deerstone Bks. OPERA IN A ZOO? CINCINNATI OPERA: FROM THE ZOO TO MUSIC HALL is a fascinating narrative of how the CINCINNATI OPERA COMPANY, grew from a small local opera company with performances in the Zoo Pavilion (1920), to the international reputation of being one of the primary grand opera companies with its summer opera performances in the air-conditioned comfort of Cincinnati's Music Hall (1995). It relates stories of singers competing with the Zoo animals during the 50 years performances were given at the Zoo pavilion. The CINCINNATI OPERA COMPANY has had many of the world's greatest opera stars come to sing their first performance of a role or make their American. The second oldest continuing opera company in the U.S. has helped many young singers launch their professional careers. It has overcome many threats of financial disaster in its 75 year history. CINCINNATI OPERA: FROM THE ZOO TO MUSIC HALL also contains the Annals that list all of the 100 plus different operas given & all of the individuals involved. The Annals give a day-by- day listing, & an index of the opera performed, singers, conductors, stage directors, lighting & costume designers, ballet dancers & managers. To order contact: Eldred A. Thierstein, Deerstone Books, 2636 Lake Shore Dr., Hillsdale, MI 49242. (517) 437-3539.**

Publisher Provided Annotation.

Cincinnati, Queen City of the West, 1819-1838. Daniel Aaron. (Urban Life & Landscape Ser.). 416p. 1992. lib. bdg. 49.50 (*0-8142-0570-4*) Ohio St U Pr.

Cincinnati Recipe Treasury: Queen City's Culinary Heritage. Mary Anna DuSablon. Ed. by Robyn Browder. LC 82-14773. (Regional Cookbks.). (Illus.). 229p. 1983. pap. 8.95 (*0-89865-247-2*) Donning Co.

Cincinnati Recipe Treasury: The Queen City's Culinary Heritage. Mary A. DuSablon. LC 82-14773. (Illus.). 230p. 1989. reprint ed. pap. 12.95 (*0-8214-0933-6*) Ohio U Pr.

Cincinnati Reds. Michael Goodman. (Baseball: The Great American Game Ser.). 48p. (J). (gr. 4-10). 1992. Net. lib. bdg. 14.95 (*0-88682-462-1*) Creative Ed.

Cincinnati Reds: Memories & Memorabilia of the Big Red Machine. Bruce Chadwick. (Illus.). 156p. 1994. 29.95 (*1-55859-514-7*) Abbeville Pr.

Cincinnati Reds Trivia Book. David S. Neft et al. LC 92-44101. 1993. write for info. (*0-312-98736-6*, Pub. by Thomas Dunne Bks) St Martin.

Cincinnati Reds Trivia Book. David S. Neft. 1993. pap. 9.99 (*0-312-08736-5*) St Martin.

Cincinnati Run; Dallas Run, 2 vols. in 1. David Robbins. (Endworld Double Edition Ser.). 384p. 1992. pap. 4.50 (*0-8439-3359-3*) Dorchester Pub Co.

Cincinnati Scenes. Caroline Williams. (Illus.). 176p. 1975. 14.95 (*0-913428-12-4*) Landfall Pr.

Cincinnati Seasons: My Thirty-Four Years with the Reds. Earl Lawson. LC 87-15743. 218p. 1987. 16.95 (*0-912083-24-7*) Diamond Communications.

Cincinnati Seasons: My Thirty-Four Years with the Reds. Earl Lawson. LC 87-15943. 218p. 1990. pap. 9.95 (*0-912083-36-0*) Diamond Communications.

***Cincinnati Symphony Orchestra: Centennial Portraits.** Ed. by Sam Ashworth & Fran Norberg. 160p. 1995. 35.00 (*0-9643686-0-9*); pap. 20.00 (*0-9643686-1-7*) Cincinn Symp.

Cincinnati: The Queen City: Bicentennial Edition. 272p. (Orig.). 1988. 34.95 (*0-911497-11-0*) Cinc Hist Soc.

Cincinnati: The Queen City: Bicentennial Edition. deluxe ed. 272p. (Orig.). 1988. boxed 49.95 (*0-911497-14-5*) Cinc Hist Soc.

Cincinnati Today. Photos by Miles Wolf. (Urban Portrait Color Ser.). (Illus.). 96p. 1991. 22.50 (*1-878005-06-5*) Northmont Pub.

Cincinnati Women: Jewels in the Crown. Illus. by Judy Anderson. 104p. (Orig.). 1988. pap. 15.00 (*0-9622899-0-6*) Creative Consort Inc.

***Cincinnati Zoo & Botanical Garden: From Past to Present.** David Ehrlinger. (Illus.). 141p. 1993. 19.95 (*0-9636552-0-5*) Cinc Zoo.

***Cincinnati's German Heritage.** Don H. Tolzmann. (Illus.). 429p. (Orig.). 1994. pap. text ed. 28.00 (*1-55613-986-1*) Heritage Bk.

Cinco Cartas De Consuelo: Five Letters of Comfort. Basilea Schlink. (SPA.). 2.95 (*84-7228-469-7*, 220154, Pub. by Edit Clie SP) TSELF.

Cinco Ciento Palabras Nuevas Para Ti. Pilar De Cuenca. Tr. by Ines Alvarez. LC 81-13766. (Bilingual Picturebacks Ser.). (Illus.). 32p. (J). (ps-3). 1982. pap. 2.50 (*0-394-85145-5*) Random Bks Yng Read.

Cinco de Mayo. Janet Riehecky. LC 93-13249. (Circle the Year with Holidays Ser.). (Illus.). 32p. (J). (ps-2). 1993. lib. bdg. 12.30 (*0-516-00681-9*); pap. 3.95 (*0-516-40681-7*) Childrens.

Cinco de Mayo: A Review of the Battle of Puebla. 2nd ed. Maria V. De Marin & Reymundo Marin. (Illus.). 80p. (C). 1991. pap. 8.00 (*0-927065-03-7*) Marin Chula Vista.

Cinco de Mayo: An Epic Novel. David Monreal. 180p. 1990. 25.00 (*0-685-38354-7*) Floricanto Pr.

Cinco de Mayo: An Historical Play. Mignon L. Bradley. LC 81-8341. (Bilingual Plays by LUISA Ser.). (Illus.). 60p. (Orig.). (ENG & SPA.). (J). (gr. 4 up). 1981. pap. 6.95 (*0-939584-00-X*) LUISA Prods.

Cinco de Mayo: Symbol of National Self Determination. Luis L. Arroyo & Antonio Rios-Bustamante. (Illus.). 200p. 1990. 40.00 (*0-685-38355-5*) Floricanto Pr.

Cinco de Mayo en San Jose. Mary Andrade & Shirley I. Fisher. (Illus.). 115p. (Orig.). (SPA.). 1987. pap. 15.00 (*0-942607-00-7*) Hispanic Anglo Pubns.

Cinco Farsas Breves. Federico Garcia Lorca. 206p. (SPA.). 1968. 4.50 (*0-8288-7090-X*, S19949) Fr & Eur.

Cinco Maestros: Cuentos Modernos de Hispanoamerica. Ed. by Alexander Coleman. 328p. (SPA.). (C). 1969. pap. text ed. 22.75 (*0-15-507551-9*) HB Coll Pubs.

Cinco Pescadores Tontos. Roberta Edwards. Tr. by Paola B. Saunders. LC 93-48933. (Apriendiendo a Leer Ser.). (Illus.). (J). 1994. write for info. (*0-679-86543-8*) Random.

Cinco Poetas Disidentes Escrito en Cuba. Ed. by Ramon J. Sender. 118p. (SPA.). (C). 1978. pap. text ed. 18.95x (*84-359-0140-8*) Transaction Pubs.

Cinco Pollitos y Otras Poesias Favoritas. (Dias y Dias de Poesia (Tan Small Book) Ser.). (Illus.). 40p. (Orig.). (SPA.). (J). (gr. 1-4). 1991. pap. text ed. 7.00 (*1-56334-061-5*) Hampton-Brown.

Cinco Pollitos y Otras Poesias Favoritas: Tan Small Book Set, 6 bks., Set. Alma F. Ada. (Dias y Dias de Poesia Ser.). (Illus.). 40p. (Orig.). (SPA.). (J). (ps-6). 1991. pap. 42.00 (*1-56334-117-4*) Hampton-Brown.

Cinco Requisitos Esenciales Vida Crist. Secrets of Christian Living. F. B. Meyer. (SPA.). 3.25 (*84-7228-564-2*, 220155, Pub. by Edit Clie SP) TSELF.

***Cinco Tibetanos-The Five Tibetans.** Christopher S. Kilham. 1995. pap. 9.95 (*0-89281-466-7*) Inner Tradit.

Cinco Tractados. Juan Manuel. Ed. by Reinaldo Ayerbe-Chaux. (Spanish Ser.: No. 51). 1989. 25.00 (*0-940639-36-X*) Hispanic Seminary.

CINCOM: Courses in Communications - 1994. Communications Library Staff. Ed. by Theodore S. Connelly. LC 90-85811. 100p. (Orig.). 1994. pap. 35.00 (*0-934339-75-9*) Comm Lib.

***CINCOM: Courses in Communications - 1996.** Communications Library Staff. Ed. by Theodore S. Connelly. LC 90-85811. (Orig.). 1996. pap. 35.00 (*0-934339-76-7*) Comm Lib.

Cincuenta Anos De Guerra Encubierta: El FBI Contra los Derechos Democraticos. Larry Seigle et al. 70p. (SPA.). 1988. 6.95 (*0-87348-533-5*) Pathfinder NY.

Cincuenta Palabras Claves de la Biblia. Julian Charley. Tr. by Jorge E. Diaz & Myriam R. Diaz. Orig. Title: Fifty Key Words-The Bible. (Illus.). 112p. (SPA.). 1987. pap. 3.25 (*0-311-04029-2*) Casa Bautista.

Cincuenta Testimonios Urgentes (Denuncias en Ginebra sobe violaciones de los Derechos Humanos-Presidio Politico Hist. Cubano) Jose Carreno. LC 87-8224. (Coleccion Cuba y Sus Jueces Ser.). (Illus.). 171p. (Orig.). (SPA.). 1987. pap. 9.95 (*0-89729-459-9*) Ediciones.

Cincuenta y dos mensajes Biblicos - Fifty-Two Bible Messages. Preston A. Taylor. Tr. by Ruben A. Zorzoli. 160p. (Orig.). (SPA.). 1991. pap. 4.95 (*0-311-43043-0*) Casa Bautista.

CINDA - A, 1935-1987, Vol. 5: Z - 84-105, Rev. 1. IAEA Staff. 3000p. 1990. pap. 130.00 (*92-0-039590-2*, CIN/35/87/5) UNIPUB.

CINDA, IAEA, 1988-1991. 700p. 1991. pap. 55.00 (*92-0-039091-9*, CIN0910) UNIPUB.

Cinder Edna. Ellen Jackson. LC 92-44160. (Illus.). (J). (gr. 3 up). 1994. 15.00 (*0-688-12322-8*); lib. bdg. 14.93 (*0-688-12323-6*) Lothrop.

Cinder-Elly. Frances Minters. LC 93-14533. (Illus.). 32p. (J). (ps-3). 1994. lib. bdg. 13.99 (*0-670-84417-9*) Viking Child Bks.

Cinder Path. Catherine Cookson. 304p. 1983. pap. 4.95 (*0-552-11160-0*) Bantam.

Cinder Path. large type ed. Catherine Cookson. LC 93-47363. 1994. 22.95 (*0-7927-1955-7*, Eagle Lrg Print); pap. write for info. (*0-7927-1956-5*, Eagle Lrg Print) Chivers N Amer.

Cinderella. (Illus.). 16p. (J). 1991. audio write for info. (*1-880459-03-5*) Arrow Trad.

Cinderella. (Vocal Score Ser.). 1981. pap. 35.00 (*0-88188-012-4*, 00312092) H Leonard.

Cinderella. (Ladybird Stories Ser.). (Illus.). (ARA.). (J). (gr. 2-5). 1987. 3.95 (*0-86685-193-3*) Intl Bk Ctr.

Cinderella. (First Fairy Tales Ser.: No. S852-1). (Illus.). (J). (ps-2). 3.95 (*0-7214-5058-X*) Ladybird Bks.

Cinderella. (Fun-to-Read Fairy Tales Ser.). (Illus.). 24p. (J). 1992. pap. 2.50 (*1-56144-088-4*) Modern Pub NYC.

Cinderella. (Treasury of Fairy Tales Ser.). (Illus.). 24p. (J). (gr. 2-5). 1993. pap. 3.95 (*1-56144-359-X*, Honey Bear Bks) Modern Pub NYC.

Cinderella. (Classics Ser.). 96p. (J). 1986. 6.98 (*1-57082-017-1*) Mouse Works.

Cinderella. (Favorite Fairy Tales Ser.). (Illus.). 24p. (J). 1993. 4.98 (*1-56173-913-8*) Pubns Intl Ltd.

Cinderella. (Classic Fairytales Pop-Ups Ser.). (Illus.). (J). (ps-1). 1.98 (*0-517-39461-8*) Random Hse Value.

Cinderella. (Derrydale Fairytale Library). (Illus.). (J). (ps-3). 1985. 1.98 (*0-517-28807-9*) Random Hse Value.

Cinderella. (Disney Animated Ser.). (Illus.). 48p. (J). 1989. 5.99 (*0-517-67010-0*) Random Hse Value.

Cinderella. (Read Along With Me Ser.). (J). (ps-1). 1989. 2.99 (*0-517-69215-5*) Random Hse Value.

Cinderella. (Illus.). (J). 1990. 5.99 (*0-517-05142-7*) Random Hse Value.

***Cinderella.** (Paint with Water Fairy Tales Ser.). (Illus.). 32p. (Orig.). (J). (gr. k-2). 1994. pap. 1.95 (*1-56144-487-1*, Honey Bear Bks) Modern Pub NYC.

***Cinderella.** 1995. 2.98 (*1-85854-278-2*) Brimax Bks.

Cinderella. Berthe Amoss. (Illus.). 10p. (J). (ps-7). 1989. pap. 2.95 (*0-922589-04-6*) More than Card.

Cinderella. Ariel Books Staff. (J). (ps-3). 1993. 4.95 (*0-8362-3034-5*) Andrews & McMeel.

Cinderella. Birch Lane Press Staff. (Upside Down Tales Ser.). (J). (ps-3). 1990. 12.95 (*1-55972-054-9*, Birch Ln Pr) Carol Pub Group.

Cinderella. Marcia Brown & Charles Perrault. (Illus.). 32p. (J). (gr. 3). 1971. 13.95 (*0-684-12676-1*, C Scribner Sons Young) S&S Childrens.

Cinderella. Illus. by Lynn Bywaters. 32p. (J). (ps-3). 1992. 6.95 (*0-8362-4905-4*) Andrews & McMeel.

Cinderella. Charlotte B. Chorpenning. (J). (gr. 1-7). 1940. 5.00 (*0-87602-116-X*) Anchorage.

Cinderella. Ed. by Roger Culbertson. (Tell Tale Theater Pop-Up Book & Audiocassette Ser.). (Illus.). 12p. (J). 1994. 12.95 (*0-685-72753-X*) Running Pr.

Cinderella. Patricia Daniels. LC 79-28526. (Fairy Tale Clippers Ser.). (Illus.). 24p. (J). (gr. k-5). 1980. audio, lib. bdg. 29.28 (*0-8393-1834-0*); lib. bdg. 14.64 (*0-8393-0253-3*) Raintree Steck-V.

Cinderella. David Delamare. LC 92-25126. (J). 1993. 15.00 (*0-671-76944-8*, S&S Bks Young Read) S&S Childrens.

Cinderella. Walt Disney. (J). (ps-3). 1993. 6.98 (*0-453-03167-6*) Mouse Works.

Cinderella. C. S. Evans. (J). 1993. 12.95 (*0-679-42313-3*, Everymans Lib) Knopf.

Cinderella. Illus. by Mimi Everett. (Happytime Storybks.). 24p. (J). 1991. pap. 1.25 (*0-7214-5300-7*, S9016-1 SER.) Ladybird Bks.

***Cinderella.** Zoe Lewis. LC 94-70524. (Illustrated Classics Ser.). (Illus.). 96p. 1995. 14.95 (*0-7868-3014-X*) Disney Pr.

***Cinderella.** Zoe Lewis. LC 94-70524. (Illustrated Classics Ser.). (Illus.). 96p. 1995. lib. bdg. 14.89 (*0-7868-5008-6*) Disney Pr.

***Cinderella.** Zoe Lewis. LC 94-70523. (Junior Novel Ser.). (Illus.). 64p. (J). (gr. 2-6). 1995. pap. 3.50 (*0-7868-4009-9*) Disney Pr.

***Cinderella.** Little Golden Books Staff. (J). Date not set. 1.59 (*0-307-01035-X*) Western Pub.

Cinderella. Illus. by James Marshall. 32p. (J). (ps-3). 1992. mass mkt. 4.95 (*0-316-48303-6*) Little.

Cinderella. Ed McBain. 272p. 1994. mass mkt. 5.99 (*0-446-60134-9*) Warner Bks.

Cinderella. Patricia McKissack & Fredrick McKissack. LC 85-12764. (Start-Off Stories Ser.). (Illus.). (J). (gr. 1-2). 1985. lib. bdg. 10.35 (*0-516-02361-6*); pap. 3.95 (*0-516-42361-4*) Childrens.

***Cinderella.** Naomi McMillan. (Storytime Ser.). (Illus.). 24p. (J). (ps-2). 1995. pap. 0.99 (*1-56293-539-9*) McClanahan Bk.

Cinderella. Sally Netzel. (Illus.). 32p. (J). (ps up). 1981. pap. 3.00 (*0-88680-028-5*) I E Clark.

Cinderella. Illus. by Ogawa & Katayama. (Nihongo Folktales Ser.). (Illus.). 32p. (J). 1994. pap. 7.00 (*4-7700-1796-0*) Kodansha.

Cinderella. Outlet Staff. (J). 1993. 12.99 (*0-517-03707-6*) Random Hse Value.

Cinderella. Charles Perrault. (Creative's Collection of Fairy Tales). (Illus.). 32p. (J). (gr. 4 up). 1983. 13.95 (*0-87191-945-1*) Creative Ed.

Cinderella. Charles Perrault. LC 85-1685. (Illus.). 32p. (J). (ps-3). 1985. 16.99 (*0-8037-0205-1*) Dial Bks Young.

Cinderella. Charles Perrault. 55p. (FRE.). (J). (gr. 3-8). 1990. pap. 10.95 (*0-7859-1354-8*, 2070312224) Fr & Eur.

Cinderella. Charles Perrault. (J). (ps-3). 1990. pap. 4.95 (*0-8037-0830-0*, Puff Pied Piper) Puffin Bks.

Cinderella. Charles Perrault. (J). (ps-3). 1993. pap. 5.99 (*0-14-054618-9*, Puff Pied Piper) Puffin Bks.

Cinderella. Charles Perrault. LC 78-18067. (Illus.). 32p. (J). (gr. k-3). 1979. lib. bdg. 9.79 (*0-89375-120-0*); pap. 2.50 (*0-89375-098-0*) Troll Assocs.

Cinderella. Charles Perrault. (Tell Me a Story Ser.). (Illus.). 26p. (J). (ps). 1988. audio 9.95 (*1-55578-911-0*) Worlds Wonder.

Cinderella. Illus. by Debrah Santini. LC 92-73991. 32p. 1994. 14.95 (*1-56397-152-6*) Boyds Mills Pr.

Cinderella. Judy Sierra. LC 92-16476. (Multicultural Folktale Ser.). 184p. 1992. pap. 23.50 (*0-89774-727-5*) Oryx Pr.

Cinderella. Illus. by Susan Spellman & Sam Thiewes. (Favorite Fairy Tales Ser.). 24p. (J). (gr. k-4). 1993. lib. bdg. 10.95 (*1-56674-062-2*, HTS Bks) Forest Hse.

Cinderella. William Springer. 1979. pap. 1.75 (*0-686-38384-2*) Eldridge Pub.

***Cinderella.** Walt Disney Company Staff. (FRE.). Date not set. pap. 9.95 (*0-7859-8855-6*) Fr & Eur.

Cinderella. Walt Disney Staff. (Penguin-Disney Ser.). (J). 1987. 6.98 (*0-8317-1309-7*) Viking Child Bks.

Cinderella. William Wegman. LC 92-72028. (Fay's Fairy Tales Ser.). (Illus.). 40p. (J). 1993. 16.95 (*1-56282-348-5*); lib. bdg. 16.89 (*1-56282-349-3*) Hyprn Child.

Cinderella. rev. ed. William Glennon. 51p. 1991. pap. 3.45 (*0-87129-073-1*, C73) Dramatic Pub.

***Cinderella.** 2nd ed. Titian Beresford. 1995. pap. text ed. 4.95 (*1-56333-305-8*) Masquerade.

Cinderella. 2nd ed. Charles Perrault. Tr. & Illus. by Marcia Brown. LC 87-34920. 32p. (J). (ps-3). 1988. pap. 4.95 (*0-689-71261-8*, Aladdin Paperbacks) S&S Childrens.

Cinderella, Vol. 512. rev. ed. Alfred Lipton. Ed. & Illus. by Janice Caban. (Once upon a Tale Ser.). 10p. (J). (gr. k). 1989. pap. 2.00 (*1-878501-01-1*) Ntrl Science Indus.

Cinderella: A Casebook. Alan Dundes. LC 81-43334. (Folklore Casebooks Ser.). 331p. 1982. lib. bdg. 25.00 (*0-8240-9295-3*) Garland.

Cinderella: A Casebook. Alan Dundes. LC 88-40186. 328p. (C). 1988. pap. text ed. 14.95 (*0-299-11864-9*) U of Wis Pr.

Cinderella: A Retold Story. Fred Crump, Jr. LC 89-51789. (Illus.). 44p. (J). (gr. k-2). 1990. pap. 6.95 (*1-55523-299-X*) Winston-Derek.

Cinderella: And Other Tales from Perrault. Charles Perrault. (Illus.). 78p. (J). (ps-2). 1989. 18.95 (*0-8050-1004-1*, Bks Young Read) H Holt & Co.

Cinderella: Full Color Picture Book. J. Sainsbury's Pure Tea Staff. (Illus.). 12p. (Orig.). (J). 1993. pap. text ed. 1.00 (*0-486-27799-2*) Dover.

Cinderella: Heartbreak Station. (Recorded Versions - Guitar Ser.). (Illus.). 105p. 1991. pap. 18.95 (*0-7935-0399-X*, HL00694762) H Leonard.

Cinderella: Lamb Chop's Play-Along Fairy Tales. Shari Lewis. (J). (ps-3). 1994. pap. 2.99 (*0-553-37386-2*) Bantam.

***Cinderella: Pop-Up Book.** Illus. by Franc Mateu. LC 94-71482. 12p. (J). (ps-3). 1995. 12.95 (*0-7868-3025-5*) Disney Pr.

***Cinderella: Stand-Up Fairy Tale House.** Dial Books for Young Readers Staff. (Illus.). 1995. 6.95 (*0-8037-1844-6*) Dial Bks Young.

Cinderella: The Fairy Godmother's Magic. Illus. by Robbin Cuddy. LC 93-73820. (Surprise Lift-the-Flap Ser.). (J). 1994. 9.95 (*1-56282-624-7*) Disney Pr.

Cinderella: The Fairy Tale. Ret. by Carol A. Hanshaw. (Comes to Life Bks.). 16p. (J). (ps-2). 1993. write for info. (*1-883366-19-4*) YES Ent.

Cinderella: The Fairy Tale. YES! Entertainment Corporation Staff. (Pop-Up Sound-Up Bks.). 2p. (J). (ps-2). 1993. write for info. (*1-883366-11-9*) YES Ent.

Cinderella: The World's Favorite Fairy Tale. Lowell Swortzell. 92p. 1992. pap. 8.95 (*0-932720-84-6*) New Plays Inc.

Cinderella: Treasures from the Library of Congress. (Shape Bks.). (Illus.). 20p. (J). 1992. reprint ed. 3.95 (*1-55709-166-8*) Applewood.

Cinderella - Night Songs. (Recorded Versions Ser.). (Illus.). 72p. (YA). (gr. 9-12). 1988. 18.95 (*0-88188-766-8*, HL00692375) H Leonard.

***Cinderella - The Fairy Tale.** Ret. by Carol A. Hanshaw. (Comes to Life Bks.). 16p. (J). (ps-2). 1994. write for info. (*1-883366-78-X*) YES Ent.

Cinderella - Vocal Selections: Vocal Selections from the Show. rev. ed. Rodgers & Hammerstein. (Illus.). 1989. pap. 8.95 (*0-88188-069-8*, HL 00312091) H Leonard.

Cinderella & Cinderella's Stepsister. Russell Shorto. (Illus.). (J). (ps-2). 1990. 12.95 (*0-685-38933-2*, Birch Ln Pr) Carol Pub Group.

Cinderella & Her Sisters: The Envied & the Envying. Barry Ulanov & Ann Ulanov. LC 83-10463. 186p. 1983. pap. 11.99 (*0-664-24482-3*, Westminster) Westminster John Knox.

Cinderella & How the Elephant Got Its Trunk. Charles Perrault & Rudyard Kipling. (Upside Down Bks.). (Illus.). 48p. (J). (gr. 1-4). 1985. 5.95 (*0-88110-252-0*) EDC.

Cinderella, & Other Stories. Richard H. Davis. LC 70-90579. (Short Story Index Reprint Ser.). 1977. 19.95 (*0-8369-3062-2*) Ayer.

Cinderella & Other Stories. Illus. by Hilda Offen. LC 93-5770. (Little Library). (J). 1994. 3.95 (*1-85697-968-7*, Kingfisher LKC) LKC.

Cinderella & the Glass Slipper. (Favorite Fairy Tales Ser.). (J). 1991. 5.99 (*0-517-05649-6*) Random Hse Value.

Cinderella & the Glass Slipper: A Retelling. Marilyn J. Shearer. LC 90-60394. (Illus.). 16p. (J). (ps-6). 1990. 19.95 (*0-685-33063-X*); pap. 10.95 (*1-878389-02-5*) L Ashley & Joshua.

Cinderella at the Ball. Margaret Hillert. (Illus.). (J). (ps-00). 1970. lib. bdg. 8.99 (*0-8136-5032-1*, TK2282); pap. 4.79 (*0-8136-5532-3*, TK2283) Modern Curr.

Cinderella at the Firecracker Ball. Julie Kistler. (American Romance Ser.). 1993. mass mkt. 3.50 (*0-373-16511-0*, 1-16511-7) Harlequin Bks.

Cinderella Bride. large type ed. Jacqueline Fleury. LC 90-44507. 261p. 1990. reprint ed. lib. bdg. 17.95 (*1-56054-052-4*) Thorndike Pr.

Cinderella Coach. large type ed. Roz Denny. 328p. 1992. reprint ed. lib. bdg. 13.95 (*1-56054-408-2*) Thorndike Pr.

Cinderella Complex: Woman's Hidden Fear of Independence. Colette Dowling. 288p. 1990. mass mkt. 5.99 (*0-671-73334-6*) PB.

Cinderella Cracked. abr. ed. Kim Jacklin. 190p. 1995. pap. 8.95 (*1-56901-357-8*) NW Pub.

Cinderella Cycle. Anna Birgitta Rooth. Ed. by Richard M. Dorson. LC 80-748. (Folklore of the World Ser.). 1981. reprint ed. lib. bdg. 29.95 (*0-405-13322-7*) Ayer.

C

An Asterisk (*) at the beginning of an entry indicates that the title is appearing in BIP for the first time. 1269

Cinderella (Disney Movie) (Illus.). 1985. 5.95 (0-88188-850-8, 00359478) H Leonard.
***Cinderella Dressed in Yellow.** Rozanne Williams. (Emergent Reader Bks.). 16p. (J). (gr. k-2). 1994. 2.49 (0-916119-68-8) Creat Teach Pr.
Cinderella Goes to Market: Citizenship, Gender & the Women's Movement in East Central Europe. Barbara Einhorn. 256p. 1993. 59.95 (0-86091-410-0, B0516, Pub. by Verso UK); pap. 17.95 (0-86091-615-4, B0520, Pub. by Verso UK) Routledge Chapman & Hall.
Cinderella Had Two Sisters. large type ed. Jan Tempest. (Linford Romance Library). 400p. 1985. pap. 11.95 (0-7089-6052-9, Trailtree Bookshop) Ulverscroft.
Cinderella-Musical. Phyllis W. Fox & David Coleman. 69p. 1978. pap. 3.45 (0-87129-021-9, C74) Dramatic Pub.
***Cinderella of the New South: A History of the Cottonseed Industry, 1855-1955.** Lynette B. Wrenn. LC 94-18733. (Illus.). 296p. (C). 1995. text ed. 38.00x (0-87049-882-7) U of Tenn Pr.
Cinderella on the Ball. Attic Pr. Staff. (Fairytales for Feminists Ser.). 64p. (Orig.). 1991. pap. 7.99 (1-85594-027-2, Pub. by Attic IE) InBook.
Cinderella; or, The Little Glass Slipper. Charles Perrault. (Picture Puffins Ser.). (Illus.). (J). (gr. 1 up). 1977. pap. 3.95 (0-14-050137-1, Puffin) Puffin Bks.
***Cinderella Penguin.** Janet Perlman. (Illus.). 32p. (J). 1995. pap. 4.99 (0-14-055552-8) Puffin Bks.
Cinderella Penguin. Janet Perlman. (Illus.). 32p. (J). (ps-3). 1993. 13.99 (0-670-84753-4) Viking Child Bks.
Cinderella-Pop Up. 12p. (J). 1989. 9.95 (0-8167-0896-7) Troll Assocs.
Cinderella Rockefeller. Isabel L. Elmer. LC 86-29163. 224p. 1987. 18.95 (0-88191-052-X) Freundlich.
Cinderella Spy. large type ed. Philip Daniels. (Linford Mystery Library). 304p. 1989. pap. 11.95 (0-7089-6729-9, Linford) Ulverscroft.
Cinderella-Sticker Book. Chatham River Press. 1990. pap. 3.99 (0-517-69693-2) Random Hse Value.
Cinderella Stories: Transformations of Historic Birmingham Buildings. Marjorie L. White & Philip A. Morris. LC 90-61304. (Illus.). 64p. (Orig.). 1990. text ed. 28.00 (0-943994-16-0); pap. 14.95 (0-943994-17-9) Birmingham Hist Soc.
Cinderella Suicide. Joseph Malagon. LC 83-62348. (Illus.). 70p. (Orig.). 1984. pap. 6.00 (0-318-00451-8) Metropol Press.
Cinderella Summer. Elizabeth D'Anard. (Changes Romance Ser.: No. 5). (YA). (gr. 7 up). 1992. mass mkt. 3.50 (0-06-106776-8, Harp PBks) HarpC.
***Cinderella Syndrome: Discovering God's Plan When Your Dreams Don't Come True.** Lee Ezell. LC 94-26594. 171p. 1995. 8.99 (0-89283-897-3, Vine Bks) Servant.
Cinderella Tree: The Story of Mayr Bros. Logging. Werner Mayr. (Illus.). 208p. (Orig.). 1992. pap. 14.95 (1-879628-01-5) Keokee ID.
Cinderella Wore Combat Boots. Jerry Chase. 1979. pap. 2.75 (0-8222-0213-1) Dramatists Play.
***Cinderellas: Selected Poetry of Sekine Hiroshi.** Hiroshi Sekine. 250p. (C). 1995. 30.00x (1-880276-55-0) Yakusha.
***Cinderella's Coach.** (Rolling Wheels Book Ser.). 14p. (J). 1995. 6.98 (1-57082-106-2) Mouse Works.
***Cinderella's Dreams Come True.** (Picture Window Ser.). 30p. (J). 1995. 9.98 (1-57082-242-5) Mouse Works.
Cinderella's Gold Slipper. Dennis Fohr. 1991. pap. 11.95 (0-8356-0672-4, Quest) Theos Pub Hse.
***Cinderella's Revenge.** Samuele Mazza. Ed. by Jack Jensen. (Illus.). 192p. 1994. pap. text ed. 16.95 (0-8118-0681-2) Chronicle Bks.
Cinderfella & the Slam Dunk Contest. Ed. by A. Caso. (Illus.). 32p. (J). (gr. 2-6). 1994. pap. 13.95 (0-8283-1966-9) Branden Pub Co.
***Cinderhazel.** Deborah N. Lattimore. LC 95-13089. (J). 1996. write for info. (0-590-20232-4); pap. write for info. (0-590-20233-2) Scholastic Inc.
***Cinderina & the Corridors of Power.** Joanna M. Hempel. Date not set. 3.45 (0-87129-592-X, C92) Dramatic Pub.
Cinderman. Anne Stuart. (American Romance Ser.). 1994. mass mkt. 3.50 (0-373-16525-0, 1-16525-7) Harlequin Bks.
Cinders. Jacques Derrida. Tr. & Intro. by Ned Lukacher. LC 90-27742. xvi, 80p. 1991. 27.50 (0-8032-1689-0) U of Nebr Pr.
***Cinders & Smoke: A Mile by Mile Guide for the Durango & Silverton Narrow Gauge Railroad.** 7th rev. ed. Doris B. Osterwald. LC 68-4969. (Illus.). 168p. (YA). 1995. pap. 7.95 (0-931788-95-1) Western Guideways.
Cinders to Satin. Fern Michaels. 1986. mass mkt. 5.99 (0-345-33952-5) Ballantine.
Cinders to Satin. Fern Michaels. 512p. 1995. reprint ed. lib. bdg. 22.00 (0-7278-4502-0) Severn Hse.
CINDI: Country Integrated Noncommunicable Diseases Intervention Programme, Baseline Evaluation. Ed. by W. Morgenstern et al. (Sitzungsberichte der Heidelberger Akademie der Wissenschaften Ser., Mathematisch-Naturwissenschaftliche Klasse, Jahrgang 1991: Suppl. 3). (Illus.). 70p. 1991. pap. 14.00 (0-387-54646-4) Spr-Verlag.
Cindra Gold. Trudi Jordan. 1994. pap. 12.95 (0-533-10779-2) Vantage.
Cindy. Margaret A. Hooks. 1984. 11.25 (0-318-03658-4) Rod & Staff.
Cindy Crawford. Bob Italia. LC 92-13692. (Cover Girls Ser.). (J). 1992. lib. bdg. 12.94 (1-56239-106-2) Abdo & Dghtrs.
Cindy Sherman, No. 65. Kyoichi Tsuzuki. (Art Random Ser.). (Illus.). 48p. 1992. 32.95 (4-7636-8568-6, Pub. by Kyoto Shoin JA) Bks Nippan.
Cindy Sherman: Untitled Film Stills. Ed. by Arthur Danto. LC 90-60903. (Illus.). 120p. 1990. 37.50 (0-8478-1274-X) Rizzoli Intl.
Cindy Sherman, 1979-1993. Rosiland Krauss & Norman Bryson. LC 93-13557. (Illus.). 240p. 1993. 60.00 (0-8478-1756-3) Rizzoli Intl.
Cindy's Baby. Stacy Johnson. (YA). 1993. pap. 3.50 (0-553-56312-2) Bantam.
***Cindy's Itty Bitty Baking Book.** Cindy Brooks. LC 95-1008. 1995. 14.95 (0-688-13696-6) Hearst Bks.
***Cindy's Runaway Colt.** Campbell. (Thoroughbred Ser.: No. 13). (J). 1995. pap. text ed. 3.50 (0-06-106303-7, Harp PBks) HarpC.
Cine: Enciclopedia Salvat del Septimo Arte, 11 vols., Set. Salvat Staff. 3080p. 495.00 (0-7859-0444-1, S50550) Fr & Eur.
Cine Cubano, Nos. 101-103. (Illus.). 174p. 1983. 6.00 (0-686-38852-6) Smyrna.
Cine Cubano, Set, Nos. 101-103. (Illus.). 174p. 1983. Set. 15.00 (0-685-42541-X) Smyrna.
Cine de Federico Fellini. Luis Trelles Plazaola. (UPREX, Teatro y Cine Ser.: No. 14). 117p. (C). 1973. pap. 1.50 (0-8477-0014-3) U of PR Pr.
Cine Goes to Town: French Cinema 1896-1914. Richard L. Abel. LC 93-20640. 1994. 55.00 (0-520-07935-3) U CA Pr.
Cine-Lit: Essays on Peninsular Film & Fiction. George C. Castellet. Ed. by Jaume Marti-Olivella & Guy H. Wood. 240p. 1992. pap. text ed. 10.00 (0-9631927-0-1) OR St U Foreign Lang.
Cine Norteamericano. L. Mendez-Leite. 1976. lib. bdg. 250.00 (0-8490-1630-4) Gordon Pr.
Cine-Roman. Roger Grenier. 320p. (FRE.). 1975. pap. 10.95 (0-7859-2358-6, 2070366677) Fr & Eur.
Cine Sudamericano: Diccionario de Directores. Luis Trelles Plazaola. (UPREX, Teatro y Cine Ser.: No. 72). 373p. 1985. pap. 6.00 (0-8477-0072-0) U of PR Pr.
Cine Visto en Puerto Rico: 1962-1972. Luis Trelles Plazaola. (UPREX, Teatro y Cine Ser.: No. 44). 279p. (C). 1975. pap. 1.50 (0-8477-0044-5) U of PR Pr.
Cine y Mujer en America Latina. Luis T. Plazaola. 304p. 1991. pap. 17.50 (0-8477-2507-3) U of PR Pr.
Cineaste Interviews: The Art & Politics of the Cinema. Ed. by Dan Georgakas & Lenny Rubenstein. LC 82-83804. (Cineaste Reader Ser.). (Illus.). 416p. (C). 1982. 29.95 (0-941702-02-2); pap. 11.95 (0-941702-03-0) Lake View Pr.
Cinegramas Anthology, 3 vols. Ed. by R. Gordon. 1976. lib. bdg. 999.75 (0-8490-1631-2) Gordon Pr.
Cinema. Mesa L. Gomez. 1976. lib. bdg. 59.95 (0-8490-1632-0) Gordon Pr.
Cinema. C. A. Lejeune. 1972. 69.95 (0-87968-871-8) Gordon Pr.
Cinema: Concept & Practice. Edward Dmytryk. (Illus.). 150p. 1988. pap. 22.95 (0-240-80002-8, Focal) Buttrwrth-Heinemann.
Cinema: Its Present Position & Future Possibilities. Cinema Commission of Inquiry. LC 78-124002. (Literature of Cinema Ser.). 1970. reprint ed. 30.95 (0-405-01608-5) Ayer.
Cinema: The First Hundred Years. David Shipman. (Illus.). 384p. 1993. 50.00 (0-312-10013-2) St Martin.
Cinema & Fiction: New Modes of Adapting, 1950-1990. Ed. by Colin Nicholson & John Orr. 240p. 1992. 55.00 (0-7486-0356-5, Pub. by Edinburgh U Pr UK) Col U Pr.
Cinema & History. Marc Ferro. Tr. by Naomi Greene. LC 87-37213. (Contemporary Film Studies). (Illus.). 176p. 1988. 29.95 (0-8143-1904-1); pap. 15.95 (0-8143-1905-X) Wayne St U Pr.
Cinema & Ireland. Kevin Rockett et al. (Irish Studies). (Illus.). 288p. (C). 1988. text ed. 39.95x (0-8156-2424-7) Syracuse U Pr.
Cinema & Ireland. Kevin Rockett et al. LC 87-7121. (Irish Studies). (Illus.). 288p. 1989. reprint ed. pap. text ed. 15.95 (0-8156-2459-X) Syracuse U Pr.
Cinema & Language. Ed. by Stephen Heath & Patricia Mellencamp. LC 83-17020. 192p. (C). 1983. text ed. 42.95 (0-313-27004-X, U7004, Greenwood Pr); pap. text ed. 17.95 (0-313-26998-X, P6998, Greenwood Pr) Greenwood.
Cinema & Modernity. John Orr. (Illus.). 232p. 1994. text ed. 49.95 (0-7456-0631-8); pap. text ed. 19.95 (0-7456-1186-9) Blackwell Pubs.
Cinema & Social Change in Latin America: Conversations with Filmmakers. Ed. by Julianne Burton. LC 86-11297. (Institute of Latin American Studies Special Publication). 320p. 1986. text ed. 25.00 (0-292-72453-5); pap. 16.95 (0-292-72454-3) U of Tex Pr.
Cinema & Social Sciences: A Survey of Ethnographic & Sociological Films. Luc De Heusch. Bd. with International Directory of Sample Survey Centres (Outside the U. S. A.) International Committee for Social Sciences Documentation & Luc De Heusch.; Social Science Activities of Some Eastern European Academies of Science. Luc De Heusch.; Attitude Change; a Review & Bibliography of Selected Research. E. E. Davis & Luc De Heusch.; International Repertory of Sociological Research Centres (Outside the U. S. A.) Luc De Heusch.; International Organizations in the Social Sciences. rev. ed. Luc De Heusch. (UNESCO Social Science Clearing House Report Ser.: Nos. 16 & 21). 1962. Set pap. (0-317-16491-0) Periodicals Srv.
Cinema & Society: France & Germany During the Twenties. Paul Monaco. LC 75-40650. 194p. 1981. text ed. 35.00 (0-444-99019-4, MOC/) Greenwood.
Cinema & Soviet Society, 1917-1953. Peter Kenez. (Cambridge Studies in the History of Mass Communications). (Illus.). (C). 1992. 70.00 (0-521-41671-X); pap. 21.95 (0-521-42863-7) Cambridge U Pr.
Cinema & Spectatorship. Judith Mayne. LC 92-24927. (Sightlines Ser.). 192p. 1993. 49.95 (0-415-03415-9, A1707, Routledge NY); pap. 16.95 (0-415-03416-7, Routledge NY) Routledge.
Cinema & Television: Fifty Years of Reflection in France. Ed. by Jacques Kermabon & Kumar Shahani. x, 256p. 1991. text ed. 27.50 (0-86311-206-4, Pub. by Orient Longman Ltd II) Apt Bks.
***Cinema & the Invention of Modern Life.** Ed. by Leo Charney & Vanessa R. Schwartz. LC 95-10821. 1995. write for info. (0-520-20111-6); pap. write for info. (0-520-20112-4) U CA Pr.
Cinema & the Negro: Nineteen Five to Nineteen Forty-Eight. Peter Noble. (Film Ser.). 1980. lib. bdg. 69.95 (0-8490-3093-5) Gordon Pr.
Cinema & the Realms of Enchantment: Lectures, Seminars & Essays by Marina Warner & Others. Ed. by Duncan Petrie. (Illus.). 144p. 1994. pap. 16.95 (0-85170-405-0, Pub. by British Film Inst UK) Ind U Pr.
Cinema & the Urban Poor in South India. Sara Dickey. LC 92-32196. (Cambridge Studies in Social & Cultural Anthropology: No. 92). (Illus.). 224p. (C). 1993. 49.95 (0-521-44084-X) Cambridge U Pr.
Cinema & Theatre Organ: A Comprehensive Description of This Instrument, Its Constituent Parts, & Its Use. Reginald Whitworth. (Illus.). 144p. 1981. reprint ed. pap. 25.00 (0-913746-14-2) Organ Lit.
Cinema Book. Ed. by Pam Cook. (Illus.). 384p. 1992. pap. 35.00 (0-85170-144-2, Pub. by British Film Inst UK) Ind U Pr.
Cinema, Censorship & Sexuality, 1909-1925. Annette Kuhn. (Cinema & Society Ser.). (Illus.). 252p. 1988. text ed. 57.50 (0-415-00381-4) Routledge.
Cinema, Censorship & Sexuality 1909-1925. Annette Kuhn. 160p. 1990. pap. 16.95 (0-415-04303-4, A4313) Routledge.
Cinema, Censorship, & the State: The Writings of Nagisa Oshima. Nagisa Oshima. Tr. by Dawn Lawson. (October Bks.). (Illus.). 445p. 1992. pap. 37.50 (0-262-15040-9) MIT Pr.
Cinema, Censorship, & the State: The Writings of Nagisa Oshima. Nagisa Oshima. 320p. 1993. pap. 15.95x (0-262-65039-8) MIT Pr.
Cinema Century, Vol. I: The First Fifty Years. Celia Lighthill. 240p. (C). 1993. per., pap. text ed. 33.95 (0-8403-8788-1) Kendall-Hunt.
Cinema De la Cruaute see Cinema of Cruelty
Cinema Digest Anthology, 3 vols. Ed. by R. Gordon. 1972. lib. bdg. 995.00 (0-8490-1633-9) Gordon Pr.
Cinema East: A Critical Study of Major Japanese Films. Keiko I. McDonald. LC 81-65870. (Illus.). 280p. 1983. 45.00 (0-8386-3094-4) Fairleigh Dickinson.
Cinema Engage: Film in the Popular Front. Jonathan Buchsbaum. LC 87-19034. 320p. 1988. 29.95 (0-252-01485-5) U of Ill Pr.
Cinema Histories, Cinema Practices. Ed. by Patricia Mellencamp & Philip T. Rosen. LC 83-22457. 220p. (C). 1984. text ed. 42.95 (0-313-27037-6, U7037); pap. text ed. 17.95 (0-313-27003-1, P7003) Greenwood.
Cinema History of Burt Lancaster. David Fury. (Illus.). 336p. 1989. boxed 29.95 (0-924556-00-5) Artists Pr.
Cinema in Australia - A Documentary History. Ed. by Ina Bertrand. 448p. 1990. 39.95 (0-86840-075-0, Pub. by New South Wales Univ Pr AT) Intl Spec Bk.
***Cinema in Democratizing Germany: The Reconstruction of National Identity in the West, 1945-1962.** Heide Fehrenbach. LC 94-33816. (Illus.). 380p. 1995. lib. bdg. 49.95x (0-8078-2204-3); pap. text ed. 18.95x (0-8078-4512-4) U of NC Pr.
Cinema in Education. Ed. by James Marchant & Garth S. Jowett. LC 77-11381. (Aspects of Film Ser.). (Illus.). 1978. reprint ed. lib. bdg. 13.95 (0-405-11140-1) Ayer.
Cinema in France: After the New Wave. Jill Forbes. LC 93-1368. 1994. 35.00 (0-253-32367-3); pap. 14.95 (0-253-32368-1) Ind U Pr.
Cinema in Iran, Nineteen Hundred to Nineteen Seventy-Nine. M. Ali Issari. LC 88-18228. (Illus.). 458p. 1989. 45.00 (0-8108-2142-7) Scarecrow.
Cinema in Revolution: The Heroic Era of the Soviet Film. Ed. by Luda Schnitzer et al. 1987. pap. 10.95 (0-306-80285-6) Da Capo.
***Cinema Industry in India: Pricing & Taxation.** Ashok Mittal. (C). 1995. 28.00x (81-7387-023-3, Pub. by Indus Pub II) S Asia.
Cinema, Literature & Society: Elite & Mass Culture in Interwar Britain. Peter Miles & Malcolm Smith. (Film Ser.). 272p. 1987. lib. bdg. 35.00 (0-7099-3363-0, Pub. by Croom Helm UK) Routledge Chapman & Hall.
Cinema Mexicain. A. Camp. 1976. lib. bdg. 59.95 (0-8490-1634-7) Gordon Pr.
Cinema Novo x 5: Masters of Contempory Brazilian Film. Randal Johnson. LC 83-16685. (Institute of Latin American Studies: Vol. 60.). 262p. reprint ed. pap. 74.70 (0-685-23401-0, 2032610) Bks Demand.
Cinema of Adolescence. David M. Considine. LC 84-24604. (Illus.). 304p. 1985. lib. bdg. 29.95x (0-89950-123-0) McFarland & Co.
Cinema of Adventure, Romance & Terror. Contrib by George E. Turner et al. (Illus.). 304p. 1989. 39.95 (0-935578-09-9) ASC Holding.
Cinema of Andrei Tarkovsky. Mark Le Fanu. 156p. 1987. 39.95 (0-85170-193-0, Pub. by British Film Inst UK); pap. 16.95 (0-85170-194-9, Pub. by British Film Inst UK) Ind U Pr.
Cinema of Apartheid: Race & Class in South African Cinema. Keyan Tomaselli. 300p. 1988. 29.95 (0-941702-18-9) Lake View Pr.
Cinema of Apartheid: Race & Class in South African Films. Keyan Tomaselli. (Orig.). 1988. pap. 11.95 (0-918266-19-X) Smyrna.
Cinema of Baseball: Images of America 1929-1989. Gary E. Dickerson. (Baseball & American Society Ser.: No. 14). 175p. 1991. lib. bdg. 39.50 (0-88736-710-0) Mecklermedia.
***Cinema of Cruelty.** Andre Bazin. Tr. by Sabine D'Estree & Tiffany Fliss. LC 81-13545. Orig. Title: La Cinema De la Cruaute. 224p. (Orig.). (FRE.). 1992. pap. 9.95 (0-394-17826-2) Seaver Bks.
Cinema of Eisenstein. David Bordwell. LC 92-45678. 336p. (C). 1993. 68.50 (0-674-13137-1); pap. 32.00 (0-674-13138-X) HUP.
Cinema of Federico Fellini. Peter Bondanella. (Illus.). 392p. 1992. text ed. 55.00 (0-691-03196-7); pap. text ed. 18.95 (0-691-00875-2) Princeton U Pr.
Cinema of Isolation: A History of Physical Disability in the Movies. Martin F. Norden. LC 93-44547. (Illus.). 375p. (C). 1994. text ed. 48.00 (0-8135-2103-3); pap. 16.95 (0-8135-2104-1) Rutgers U Pr.
Cinema of Jean Genet: Un Chant d'Amour. Jane Giles. (Illus.). 80p. 1991. 29.95 (0-253-32584-6, Pub. by British Film Inst UK); pap. 12.95 (0-85170-289-9, Pub. by British Film Inst UK) Ind U Pr.
Cinema of John Marshall. Ed. by Jay Ruby. LC 92-28923. (Visual Anthropology Ser.: Vol. 3). 282p. 1993. text ed. 58.00 (3-7186-0557-0); pap. text ed. 24.00 (3-7186-0558-9) Gordon & Breach.
Cinema of Loneliness: Penn, Kubrick, Scorsese, Spielberg, Altman. 2nd ed. Robert P. Kolker. (Illus.). 464p. 1988. pap. 16.95 (0-19-505390-7) OUP.
***Cinema of Malcolm Lowry: A Scholarly Edition of Lowry's "Tender Is the Night"** Paul Tiessen & Miguel Mota. 276p. 1990. 65.00 (0-7748-0345-2) U of Wash Pr.
***Cinema of Max Ophuls: Magisterial Vision & the Figure of Woman.** Susan M. White. LC 94-30573. (Film & Culture Ser.). 1995. 59.50 (0-231-10112-0); pap. 18.50 (0-231-10113-9) Col U Pr.
Cinema of Nonfiction. William Guynn. LC 88-45736. (Illus.). 256p. 1990. 42.50 (0-8386-3340-4) Fairleigh Dickinson.
***Cinema of Oliver Stone, Vol. 1.** Norman Kagan. 304p. 1995. 27.95 (0-8264-0817-6) Continuum.
Cinema of Orson Welles. Peter Cowie. LC 83-10154. (Quality Paperbacks Ser.). (Illus.). 262p. 1983. pap. 12.95 (0-306-80201-5) Da Capo.
Cinema of Ousmane Sembene: A Pioneer of African Film. Francoise Pfaff. LC 84-3842. (Contributions in Afro-American & African Studies: No. 79). (Illus.). xx, 207p. 1984. text ed. 49.95 (0-313-24400-6, PCI/, Greenwood Pr) Greenwood.
Cinema of Paradox: French Filmmaking under the German Occupation. Evelyn Ehrlich. LC 84-28594. 240p. 1985. text ed. 37.50 (0-231-05926-4) Col U Pr.
***Cinema of Quebec: Masters in their Own House.** Janis L. Pallister. LC 94-43507. 1995. write for info. (0-8386-3562-8) Fairleigh Dickinson.
Cinema of Satyajit Ray. Chidananda D. Gupta. (Illus.). 105p. 1980. 19.95 (0-318-36279-1) Asia Bk Corp.
Cinema of Solitude: A Critical Study of Mexican Film, 1967-1983. Charles R. Berg. LC 92-7492. (Film Studies). (Illus.). 264p. (C). 1992. text ed. 35.00 (0-292-70791-6); pap. 15.95 (0-292-70795-9) U of Tex Pr.
Cinema of Stanley Kubrick. Norman Kagan. (Illus.). 250p. 1989. pap. text ed. 14.95 (0-8264-0422-7) Continuum.
Cinema of the Sea: A Critical Survey & Filmography, 1925-1986. Tony Thomas. LC 88-42571. 262p. 1988. lib. bdg. 32.50x (0-89950-342-X) McFarland & Co.
Cinema, Politics & Society in America. Ed. by Philip J. Davies & Brian Neve. LC 81-52234. 266p. 1985. pap. 12.95 (0-312-13902-0) St Martin.
Cinema Sequels & Remakes, 1903-1987. Robert A. Nowlan & Gwendolyn W. Nowlan. LC 88-42640. (Illus.). 966p. 1988. lib. bdg. 82.00x (0-89950-314-4) McFarland & Co.
Cinema Sheet Music: A Comprehensive Listing of Published Film Music from "Squaw Man" (1914) to "Batman" (1989) Donald J. Stubblebine. LC 91-52514. 640p. 1991. lib. bdg. 72.00x (0-89950-569-4) McFarland & Co.
Cinema Strikes Back: Radical Filmmaking in the United States, 1930-1942. Russell Campbell. LC 82-4819. (Studies in Cinema: No. 20). (Illus.). 397p. reprint ed. pap. 113.20 (0-685-20890-7, 2070319) Bks Demand.
Cinema Stylists. John Belton. LC 82-10793. (Filmmakers Ser.: No. 2). (Illus.). 384p. 1983. 27.50 (0-8108-1585-0) Scarecrow.
Cinema Without Walls: Movies & Culture after Vietnam. Timothy Corrigan. LC 90-48792. (Illus.). 250p. (C). 1991. text ed. 40.00 (0-8135-1667-6); pap. 13.95 (0-8135-1668-4) Rutgers U Pr.
Cinema 1: The Movement-Image. Gilles Deleuze. Tr. by Hugh Tomlinson & Barbara Habberjam. LC 85-28898. 263p. 1986. text ed. 34.95 (0-8166-1399-0) U of Minn Pr.
Cinema 1: The Movement-Image. Gilles Deleuze. Tr. by Hugh Tomlinson & Barbara Habberjam. LC 85-28898. 263p. 1989. pap. text ed. 15.95 (0-8166-1400-8) U of Minn Pr.
Cinema, 1950. Ed. by Roger Manvell & Garth S. Jowett. LC 77-11380. (Aspects of Film Ser.). (Illus.). 1978. reprint ed. lib. bdg. 18.95 (0-405-11139-8) Ayer.
Cinema, 1951. Ed. by Roger Manvell & Garth S. Jowett. LC 77-18644. (Aspects of Film Ser.). (Illus.). 1978. reprint ed. lib. bdg. 18.95 (0-405-11145-2) Ayer.
Cinema, 1952. Ed. by Roger Manvell & Garth S. Jowett. LC 77-18645. (Aspects of Film Ser.). (Illus.). 1978. reprint ed. lib. bdg. 18.95 (0-405-11146-0) Ayer.
Cinema 2: The Time-Image. Gilles Deleuze. Tr. by Hugh Tomlinson & Robert Galeta. 362p. 1989. text ed. 34.95 (0-8166-1676-0); pap. 17.95 (0-8166-1677-9) U of Minn Pr.
***Cinemas of the Black Diaspora: Diversity, Dependence, & Oppositionality.** Ed. by Michael T. Martin. (Contemporary Film & Television Ser.). 560p. (C). 1996. 49.95 (0-8143-2587-4); pap. 19.95 (0-8143-2588-2) Wayne St U Pr.

An Asterisk (*) at the beginning of an entry indicates that the title is appearing in BIP for the first time.

1271

Circle of Love. Romaine Stauffer. 1988. pap. 3.50 (*0-87813-528-6*) Christian Light.
Circle of Men: The Original Manual for Men's Support Groups. Bill Kauth. (Illus.). 224p. 1992. pap. 12.95 (*0-312-07247-3*) St Martin.
Circle of Mountains: A Basque Shepherding Community. Sandra Ott. LC 93-13842. (Basque Ser.). (Illus.). 272p. 1993. pap. 12.95 (*0-87417-224-1*) U of Nev Pr.
***Circle of Mysteries: The Woman's Rosary Book.** Christin L. Weber. 176p. (Orig.). 1995. pap. 12.95 (*0-936663-11-1*) Yes Intl.
Circle of Nations: Voices & Visions of American Indians. Leslie M. Silko et al. Ed. by John Gattuso. (Earthsong Collection Ser.). (Illus.). 128p. (C). 1993. 39.95 (*0-941831-90-6*) Beyond Words Pub.
Circle of Our Vision: Dante's Presence in English Romantic Poetry. Ralph Pite. (Illus.). 288p. 1994. 45.00 (*0-19-811294-7*) OUP.
Circle of Paradox: Time & Essence in the Poetry of Juan Ramon Jimenez. Paul R. Olson. LC 67-21581. 248p. reprint ed. pap. 70.70 (*0-317-28736-2*, 2020730) Bks Demand.
Circle of Peace: Reflections on the Baha'i Teachings. Ed. by Anthony A. Lee. (Orig.). 1986. 11.95 (*0-933770-48-0*) Kalimat.
Circle of Poison: Pesticides & People in a Hungry World. David Weir & Mark Schapiro. LC 81-13384. 99p. 1981. pap. 7.95 (*0-935028-09-9*) Inst Food & Develop.
Circle of Power. William F. Higbie. Ed. by Denise E. Knight. LC 90-82883. (Illus.). 96p. (J). (gr. 3 up). 1990. per., pap. 7.95 (*0-943604-27-3*) Eagles View.
Circle of Power: Tying down Strings of Energy. Heather Hughes-Calero. (Illus.). 144p. (Orig.). 1993. pap. 10.00 (*0-932927-09-2*) Higher Consciousness.
Circle of Protection for the Unborn. Jampa Thaye. 1993. spiral bd. 3.95 (*0-317-05522-4*) Atrium Pubs.
Circle of Protest: Political Ritual in the Tibetan Uprising, 1987-1992. Ronald D. Schwartz. LC 94-5522. 1994. write for info. (*0-231-10094-9*) Col U Pr.
***Circle of Protest: Political Ritual in the Tibetan Uprising, 1987-1992.** Ronald D. Schwartz. LC 94-5522. 1994. pap. 16.50 (*0-231-10095-7*) Col U Pr.
Circle of Quiet. Madeleine L'Engle. 246p. 1971. 20.00 (*0-374-12374-8*) FS&G.
Circle of Quiet. Madeleine L'Engle. 1984. pap. 12.00 (*0-06-254503-5*, PL) HarpC.
Circle of Quiet, 3 vols., Set. Madeleine L'Engle. (Crosswicks Journal Trilogy Ser.). 246p. 1977. 19.95 (*0-685-06341-0*) Harper SF.
Circle of Sacred Dance: Peter Deunov's Paneurythmy. Ed. by David Lorimer. (Illus.). 160p. 1991. pap. 14.95 (*1-85230-207-0*) Element MA.
Circle of Seasons. Corinne Linker. (Science & Nature Ser.). (Illus.). 32p. (J). (ps-2). Date not set. 11.95 (*1-56065-157-1*) Capstone Pr.
Circle of Seasons. Myra C. Livingston. LC 81-20305. (Illus.). 32p. (J). (ps-3). 1982. lib. bdg. 15.95 (*0-8234-0452-8*); pap. 5.95 (*0-8234-0656-3*) Holiday.
***Circle of Seasons.** Gerda Muller. LC 95-10382. (J). 1995. write for info. (*0-525-45394-6*, DCB) Dutton Child Bks.
Circle of Song - Songs, Chants & Dances for Ritual & Celebration. Kate Marks. LC 93-73300. (Illus.). 304p. (Orig.). 1994. pap. 17.95 (*0-9637489-0-4*) Full Circle MA.
Circle of Sovereignty: Plotting Politics in the Book of Daniel. Danna N. Fewell. 160p. 1991. pap. 12.95 (*0-687-08389-3*) Abingdon.
Circle of Stars. Roebuck. 1992. pap. 15.95 (*1-85230-303-4*) Element MA.
Circle of Stone. Poems. Miller Williams. LC 64-23149. xiv, 48p. 1970. pap. 6.95 (*0-8071-0202-4*) La State U Pr.
***Circle of Stones: Journeys & Meditations for Modern Celts.** Erynn R. Laurie. 112p. 1995. 9.95 (*1-57353-106-5*, Eschaton Bks) Eschaton Prods.
Circle of Stones: Woman's Journey to Herself. Judith Duerk. Ed. by Ruth Butler. LC 89-8120. (Women's Ser.). 96p. (Orig.). 1989. pap. 10.95 (*0-931055-66-0*) LuraMedia.
Circle of the Cosmic Muse: A Wiccan Book of Shadows. Maria K. Simms. LC 93-46303. (Illus.). 496p. 1994. pap. 17.95 (*1-56718-656-4*) Llewellyn Pubns.
Circle of the Gods. large type ed. Victor Canning. 380p. 1981. 12.00 (*0-7089-0571-4*) Ulverscroft.
Circle of the Spirit. Joan W. Anglund. 1983. 12.00 (*0-394-53080-2*) Random.
Circle of Totems. Peggy Shumaker. LC 87-25189. (Poetry Ser.). 60p. (C). 1988. pap. 10.95 (*0-8229-5402-8*) U of Pittsburgh Pr.
Circle of Toulouse-Lautrec: An Exhibition of the Work of the Artist & of His Close Associates. Philip D. Cate & Patricia E. Boyer. (Illus.). 203p. (Orig.). 1989. pap. 19.95 (*0-8135-1468-1*) Rutgers U Pr.
Circle of Unity: Baha'i Approaches to Current Social Issues. Ed. by Anthony A. Lee. 268p. (Orig.). 1984. pap. 11.95 (*0-933770-28-6*) Kalimat.
Circle of Women: An Anthology of Contemporary Western Women Writers. Ed. by Kim Barnes & Mary C. Blew. 320p. (Orig.). 1994. 11.95 (*0-14-023524-8*, Penguin Bks) Viking Penguin.
Circle of Women: Stories of the Sisterhood. LC 94-15049. (Icarus World Issues Ser.). 1994. write for info. (*0-8239-1811-4*); pap. write for info. (*0-8239-1812-2*) Rosen Group.
Circle of Wonder: A Native American Christmas Story. N. Scott Momaday. LC 93-5387. (Illus.). 82p. 1993. 14.95 (*0-940666-32-4*) Clear Light.
Circle Sarah Drew. Peter Barrett & Susan Barrett. Incl. Line Sophie Drew. LC 72-89449. 1973. 8.95 (*0-87592-029-2*); Square Ben Drew. LC 72-89449. 1973. 8.95 (*0-87592-049-7*); LC 72-89449. (Illus.). 32p. (J). (ps-2). 1973. write for info. (*0-87592-012-8*) Scroll Pr.
***Circle Stock Theater: Touring American Small Towns, 1900-1950.** Landis K. Magnuson. 192p. 1995. lib. bdg. 32.50 (*0-7864-0101-X*) McFarland & Co.
Circle (Ten Issues), 2 vols., 1. Ed. by George Leite & Bern Porter. (Avant-Garde Magazines Ser.). 890p. 1974. reprint ed. 30.95 (*0-405-01760-X*) Ayer.
Circle (Ten Issues), 2 vols., 2. Ed. by George Leite & Bern Porter. (Avant-Garde Magazines Ser.). 890p. 1974. reprint ed. 30.95 (*0-405-01761-8*) Ayer.
Circle (Ten Issues), 2 vols., Set. Ed. by George Leite & Bern Porter. (Avant-Garde Magazines Ser.). 890p. 1974. reprint ed. 60.95 (*0-405-01756-1*) Ayer.
***Circle the Number You Love, Cross Out the Number You Hate.** Dirk Wales. 96p. Date not set. 265.00 (*0-9632459-7-X*) Grt Plains IL.
***Circle Time.** (Bear Hugs Ser.). (Illus.). 24p. (J). 1995. teacher ed, pap. 3.95 (*0-614-06817-7*, WPH 2503) Totline Bks.
Circle Time Activities for Young Children. Ed. by Deya Brashears & Sharron W. Krull. (Illus.). 139p. (Orig.). 1981. pap. 14.95 (*0-9614717-1-9*) Deya Brashears.
Circle Time Book. Liz Wilmes & Dick Wilmes. LC 82-72304. (Illus.). 128p. (Orig.). (C). 1982. pap. 8.95 (*0-943452-00-7*) Building Blocks.
Circle Track Racing. Sallie Stephenson. (Fast Track Ser.). (Illus.). 48p. (J). (gr. 5). 1991. 12.95 (*0-89686-693-9*, Crstwood Hse) Silver Burdett Pr.
Circle Track Suspension. Forbes Aird. (Power Pro Ser.). (Illus.). 160p. 1994. pap. 17.95 (*0-87938-872-2*) Motorbooks Intl.
Circle Unbroken. Sollace Hotze. LC 88-2569. 224p. (YA). (gr. 7 up). 1988. 14.95 (*0-89919-733-7*, Clarion Bks) HM.
Circle Unbroken. Sollace Hotze. 244p. (J). (gr. 6 up). 1991. pap. 5.95 (*0-395-59702-1*, Clarion Bks) HM.
Circle with Two Corners. Ted B. Guevara. LC 93-93898. 152p. (Orig.). 1994. pap. text ed. 8.95 (*1-56002-337-6*, Univ Edtns) Aegina Pr.
Circle Within a Circle. Monte Killingsworth. LC 93-17244. 144p. (YA). (gr. 7 up). 1994. 14.95 (*0-689-50598-1*, McElderry) S&S Childrens.
Circle Without End: A Sourcebook of American Indian Ethics. Gerald S. Lombardi & Frances G. Lombardi. LC 82-12481. 208p. 1982. lib. bdg. 16.95 (*0-87961-114-6*); pap. 8.95 (*0-87961-115-4*) Naturegraph.
Circlebook: A Leader Handbook for Conducting Circletime - A Curriculum of Affect. Jim Ballard. LC 75-25396. (Mandala Series in Education). (Illus.). 60p. (Orig.). 1981. reprint ed. pap. 7.95 (*0-8290-0150-6*) Irvington.
***Circled in Red.** Mary Plutchak. 65p. 1995. pap. 8.00 (*0-9630322-1-6*) Carrousel Pr.
Circled Round with Awe. Mildred R. Trivers. 120p. 1993. 16.95 (*1-878208-22-5*) Guild Pr IN.
Circlemaker. Maxine R. Schur. LC 93-17983. (YA). 1994. 14.99 (*0-8037-1354-1*) Dial Bks Young.
Circles. Perry Brass. Ed. by Tom Laine. LC 93-70194. (Ki Chronicles Ser.: Bk. 2). 224p. (Orig.). 1993. pap. 11.95 (*0-9627123-3-7*) Belhue Pr.
Circles. Karen Callinan. (Concept Series for the Flannel Board). (Illus.). 32p. (J). (ps-2). Date not set. 11.95 (*1-56065-151-2*) Capstone Pr.
Circles. Theodore Enslin. 4.00 (*0-686-15295-6*) Great Raven Pr.
Circle's. Cherie J. Gierak. (Illus.). 384p. (Orig.). 1993. pap. 6.99 (*0-9636237-3-7*) Insight CA.
Circles. Rose Griffiths. LC 94-9592. (First Step Math Ser.). (Illus.). 32p. (J). (gr. 1 up). 1994. lib. bdg. 17.27 (*0-8368-1109-7*) Gareth Stevens Inc.
Circles. Martha McKee. 72p. 1976. pap. 4.95 (*0-913428-26-4*) Landfall Pr.
Circles. Doris Mortman. (Orig.). 1988. mass mkt. 6.50 (*0-553-27197-0*) Bantam.
Circles. Illus. by Frank Nichols. (Shape Play Ser.). (Orig.). (J). (ps-2). 1976. pap. 3.95 (*0-85953-047-7*) Childs Play.
Circles. Emily Pestana. Ed. by Robert Bixby. 17p. 1993. pap. 6.00 (*1-882983-03-3*) March Street Pr.
Circles. Marilyn Sachs. LC 90-37516. 144p. (J). (gr. 5-9). 1991. 15.00 (*0-525-44683-4*, DCB) Dutton Child Bks.
Circles. Marilyn Sachs. LC 92-20287. 144p. (J). (gr. 5 up). 1992. pap. 3.99 (*0-14-034931-6*) Puffin Bks.
Circles. Mavis Smith. (J). (ps-8). 1991. 3.95 (*1-55782-366-9*, Warner Juvenile Bks) Little.
Circles. Marion Smoothey. (Let's Investigate Ser.). (Illus.). 64p. (J). (gr. 4-8). 1992. text ed. 16.95 (*1-85435-456-6*) Marshall Cavendish.
Circles: Fun Ideas for Getting A-Round in Math. Catherine S. Ross. LC 92-40159. (Illus.). (J). (gr. 4-7). 1993. pap. 9.57 (*0-201-62268-8*) Addison-Wesley.
Circles see Key to Geometry Series
***Circles & Cycles QI Coloring Book: Systems Thinking Made Easy.** Lowell J. Arthur. (QI Coloring Book Ser.). 48p. 1995. student ed 9.95 (*1-884180-06-X*) LifeStar.
Circles & Settings: Role Changes of American Women. Helen Lopata. (SUNY Series in Gender & Society). 325p. 1994. 59.50 (*0-7914-1767-0*); pap. 19.95 (*0-7914-1768-9*) State U NY Pr.
Circles & Spheres. Sally Morgan. (World of Shapes Ser.). (Illus.). 32p. (J). (gr. 1-3). 1994. 14.95 (*1-56847-235-8*) Thomson Lrning.
Circles & Standing Stones: An Illustrated Exploration of Magalith Mysteries of Early Britain. Evan Hadingham. LC 74-82169. (Illus.). 224p. 1975. 12.50 (*0-8027-0463-8*) Walker & Co.
Circles, Consciousness, & Culture. James A. Mischke. 1984. pap. 2.50 (*0-912586-57-5*) Navajo Coll Pr.
Circles Cycles in the Air. Turgut A. Akter. 1993. 12.95 (*0-533-10172-7*) Vantage.
Circles Effect & Its Mysteries. George T. Meaden. 116p. (C). 1989. text ed. 80.00 (*0-9510590-3-3*, Pub. by Artetech Pub Co UK) St Mut.
Circles End. Michael Stephens. 1982. 6.00 (*0-686-34452-9*) S Duyvil.
Circles, Groves & Sanctuaries: Sacred Spaces of Today's Pagans. Pauline Campanelli & Dan Campanelli. LC 92-19357. (Practical Magick Ser.). (Illus.). 288p. 1992. 12.95 (*0-87542-108-3*) Llewellyn Pubns.
Circles I Move In: Short Stories. Diane Lefer. LC 94-14562. (Illus.). 192p. 1994. 19.95 (*0-944072-41-0*) Zoland Bks.
Circles in a Pool. Sally H. Schueler & Ellen Probert. Ed. by Sidney Probert. 1988. pap. 10.95 (*0-9621454-0-8*) Hogan Ministries.
Circles in a Square: A Book of Hours...Days...Years. Georgia M. Joyner. (Illus.). 71p. (Orig.). 1991. pap. 6.95 (*0-9627687-2-3*) Proctors Hall Pr.
Circles in the Sand. Philip Macht. LC 84-90597. (Illus.). 64p. (YA). (gr. 7 up). 1985. 12.95 (*0-930339-00-2*) Maxrom Pr.
Circles of Care: Work & Identity in Women's Lives. Ed. by Emily K. Abel & Margaret K. Nelson. LC 89-78197. (Women & Work Ser.). 326p. 1990. 69.50 (*0-7914-0263-0*); pap. 24.95 (*0-7914-0264-9*) State U NY Pr.
Circles of Care & Understanding: Support Groups for Fathers of Children with Special Needs. James May. 1992. pap. 6.95 (*0-937821-86-1*) Assn Care Child.
***Circles of Censorship: Censorship & Its Metaphors in French History, Literature & Theory.** Nicholas Harrison. 260p. 1995. 49.95 (*0-19-815909-9*) OUP.
***Circles of Compassion: A Collection of Humane Words & Work.** Photos by Sumner W. Fowler. LC 94-61221. (Illus.). 226p. (Orig.). 1995. pap. 12.00 (*0-9643033-5-3*) Voice & Vision.
Circles of Faces. Mary Dadswell. 192p. (Orig.). 1987. pap. 11.95 (*0-7022-1969-X*, Pub. by Univ Queensland Pr AT) Intl Spec Bk.
***Circles of Fantasy: Convention in the Plays of Chikamatsu.** Andrew C. Gerstle. (Harvard East Asian Monographs: No. 116). 248p. (C). 1995. pap. text ed. 19.00 (*0-674-13172-X*) HUP.
Circles of Fantasy: Convention in the Plays of Chikamatsu. C. Andrew Gerstle. (East Asian Monographs: No. 116). 312p. 1990. 25.00 (*0-674-13171-1*) HUP.
Circles of Fate. large type ed. Anne Saunders. LC 94-9784. 1994. 19.95 (*0-7927-2046-6*, Curley Lrg Print); pap. 18.95 (*0-7927-2045-8*, Curley Lrg Print) Chivers N Amer.
Circles of Friends: People with Disabilities & Their Friends Enrich the Lives of One Another. Robert Perske. LC 88-14616. (Illus.). 96p. 1988. pap. 11.95 (*0-687-08390-7*) Abingdon.
***Circles of Grace.** Paul N. Mason. 1995. 5.00 (*0-87129-563-6*, C91) Dramatic Pub.
Circles of Hope: Breathing Life & Spirit into a Wounded World. Bill Cane. LC 92-10629. (Illus.). 160p. (Orig.). 1992. pap. 9.95 (*0-88344-816-5*) Orbis Bks.
Circles of Influence: A Writer's Rhetoric. Michael J. Vivion & Sarah Morgan. LC 94-16652. 1994. pap. text ed. write for info. (*0-205-15103-5*) Allyn.
Circles of Influence: Expanding Your Leadership Capabilities in the Church. Robert C. Anderson. 1991. pap. 16.99 (*0-8024-1126-6*) Moody.
Circles of Kings: Political Dynamics in Early Continental Southeast Asia. Renee Hagesteijn. (KLTV Verhandelingen Ser.: No. 138). (Illus.). 186p. (Orig.). 1992. pap. 23.00 (*90-6765-451-5*, Pub. by KLTV Pr NE) Cellar.
Circles of Learning: Cooperation in the Classroom. David W. Johnson et al. LC 83-83395. 88p. 1984. pap. text ed. 8.50 (*0-87120-123-2*, 611-84324) Assn Supervision.
Circles of Life. Michael C. Giammatteo. (Illus.). (Orig.). 1973. pap. 8.95 (*0-918428-01-7*) Sylvan Inst.
Circles of Light: Poems. Florentin Smarandache. Ed. by Erhus University Press Staff & Constantin M. Popa. 120p. (Orig.). (C). 1992. pap. text ed. 9.99 (*1-879585-31-6*) Xiquan Pubng.
Circles of Madness: Mothers of the Plaza de Mayo. Marjorie Agosin. Tr. by Celeste Kostopulus-Cooperman. 128p. 1991. 13.00 (*1-877727-17-2*) White Pine.
Circles of Strength: Community Alternatives to Alienation. Helen Forsey. (New Catalyst Bioregional Ser.). 1992. 34.95 (*0-86571-258-1*); pap. 9.95 (*0-86571-259-X*) New Soc Pubs.
Circles of the World: Traditional Art of the Plains Indians. Richard Conn. LC 82-70497. (Illus.). 152p. 1982. pap. 24.95 (*0-914738-27-5*, U of Wash Pr) Denver Art Mus.
Circles of Tradition: Folk Arts in Minnesota. Willard B. Moore et al. LC 88-37753. (Illus.). 162p. 1989. pap. 18.95 (*0-87351-239-1*) Minn Hist.
Circles on the Water. Valerie Kane. 192p. 1994. pap. 7.95 (*1-56901-323-3*) NW Pub.
Circles on the Water: Selected Poems of Marge Piercy. Marge Piercy. 320p. 1982. pap. 16.00 (*0-394-70779-6*) Knopf.
Circle's Search for its Center: A Tale In Two Dimensions. David D. Thornburg. (Illus.). 28p. 1987. pap. 2.95 (*0-942207-04-1*) Starsong CA.
Circles, Triangles & Squares. Tana Hoban. LC 72-93305. (Illus.). 32p. (J). (ps-2). 1974. 13.95 (*0-02-744830-4*, Mac Bks Young Read) S&S Childrens.
Circles Without Center: Paths to the Discovery & Creation of Self in Modern Literature. Enrico Garzilli. LC 77-182814. 182p. reprint ed. pap. 51.90 (*0-7837-1699-0*, 2057228) Bks Demand.
Circling: A Cycle of Linked Hoops. Steve Sanfield & John Brandi. 24p. 1988. 5.00 (*1-882623-06-1*) Exiled-Am Pr.
Circling at the Chain's Length. C. J. Stevens. LC 91-65884. 77p. (Orig.). 1991. text ed. 12.95 (*0-9623934-5-2*); pap. text ed. 8.95 (*0-9623934-4-4*) J Wade.
***Circling Eden.** Carol Magun. 200p. 1995. 19.95 (*0-89733-412-4*) Academy Chi Pubs.
Circling Home. Cheryl B. Rush. 85p. 1990. 22.50 (*0-916379-59-0*) Scripta.
Circling Song. Nawal El Saadawi. LC 88-29782. 128p. (C). 1989. text ed. 15.00 (*0-86232-816-0*, Pub. by Zed Books UK); pap. 7.95 (*0-86232-817-9*, Pub. by Zed Books UK) Humanities.
Circling the Sun. Robert Pelton. 1986. 12.95 (*0-912405-14-7*) Pastoral Pr.
Circo. Clarisa Bell. (This Is Entertainment Ser.). (Illus.). 24p. (Orig.). (SPA.). (J). (gr. 2-6). 1992. lib. bdg. 9.95 (*1-56492-078-X*) Laredo.
Circuit Analysis. Irving L. Kosow. 115p. 1988. text ed. 49.50 (*0-471-03067-8*) P-H.
Circuit Analysis. Allan D. Kraus. Ed. by Michael Slaughter. 859p. (C). 1991. text ed. 74.75 (*0-314-79500-6*) West Pub.
Circuit Analysis. Elias M. Sabbagh. LC 61-6789. (Illus.). 465p. reprint ed. pap. 132.60 (*0-317-08887-4*, 2012458) Bks Demand.
Circuit Analysis: Theory & Practice. Allan Robbins & Wilhelm Miller. LC 94-10022. (Illus.). 1120p. 1995. 58.95 (*0-8273-5414-2*) Delmar.
Circuit Analysis by Computer: From Algorithms to Package. Robert Spence & John P. Burgess. (Illus.). 528p. (C). 1986. text ed. 61.60 (*0-13-134024-7*) P-H.
Circuit Analysis Exam File. Ed. by Artice M. Davis. LC 85-25346. (Exam File Ser.). 314p. (Orig.). 1986. pap. 14.50 (*0-910554-53-6*) Engineering.
Circuit Analysis, Simulation & Design. Ed. by A. E. Ruehli. (Advances in CAD for VLSI Ser.: Vol. 3, Part 2). 400p. 1987. 62.50 (*0-444-87889-0*, North Holland) Elsevier.
Circuit Analysis, Simulation & Design: General Aspects of Circuit Analysis & Design. Ed. by A. E. Ruehli. 1986. 57.50 (*0-444-87893-9*, North Holland) Elsevier.
Circuit & Family Court Management in the Second Judicial Circuit of Hawaii: A Technical Assistance Report. National Center for State Courts Staff. 42p. 1985. 3.00 (*0-685-15101-8*, WRO-057) Natl Ctr St Courts.
Circuit Cellar Project File, Vol. 1. Winefred Washington et al. (Illus.). 220p. (Orig.). 1991. pap. 17.95 (*0-9630133-0-0*) Circuit Cellar.
Circuit Cellar Project File, Vol. II. Ed. by Steve Ciarcia et al. (Illus.). 178p. (C). 1993. pap. text ed. 17.95 (*0-9630133-1-9*) Circuit Cellar.
Circuit Complexity & Neural Networks. Ian Parberry. (Foundations of Contemporary Interpretation Ser.). (Illus.). 296p. 1994. 37.50x (*0-262-16148-6*) MIT Pr.
Circuit Court Microfilming & Records Retention Project for the State of South Dakota. National Center for State Courts Staff. 213p. 1979. 12.78 (*0-685-16563-9*, NCRO-020) Natl Ctr St Courts.
Circuit Design & Analysis: Featuring C Routines. C. Britton Rorabaugh. 1992. pap. 34.95 (*0-07-053659-7*) McGraw.
Circuit Design & Analysis: Featuring C Routines. C. Britton Rorabaugh. 256p. 1992. pap. 34.95 (*0-8306-4275-7*, 4308) TAB Bks.
Circuit Design & Anaylsis: Featuring C Routine. C. Britton Rorabaugh. 240p. 1992. text ed. 50.00 (*0-07-053653-8*) McGraw.
Circuit Design for CMOS VLSI. John P. Uyremura. (C). 1991. lib. bdg. 99.00 (*0-7923-9184-5*) Kluwer Ac.
Circuit Design Using Personal Computers. Thomas R. Cuthbert, Jr. LC 91-22506. 512p. (C). 1994. reprint ed. text ed. 63.95 (*0-89464-637-0*) Krieger.
Circuit Designer's Companion. Tim Williams. 320p. 1991. text ed. 47.95 (*0-7506-1142-1*) Buttrwrth-Heinemann.
Circuit Hikes in Northern New Jersey. 3rd ed. Bruce Scofield. LC 90-33777. (Illus.). 128p. 1990. pap. 8.95 (*0-9603966-7-5*) NY-NJ Trail Confer.
Circuit Hikes in Shenandoah National Park. 13th ed. James Denton. LC 83-62223. 106p. 1990. pap. 5.00 (*0-915746-26-3*) Potomac Appalach.
Circuit Hikes in Virginia, West Virginia, Maryland & Pennsylvania. 4th ed. Jean Golightly. LC 85-60393. 88p. 1986. pap. text ed. 5.00 (*0-915746-29-8*) Potomac Appalach.
Circuit Interruption: Theory & Techniques. Browne, Jr. (Electrical Engineering & Electronics Ser.: Vol. 21). 720p. 1984. 150.00 (*0-8247-7177-X*) Dekker.
Circuit Modeling: Exercises & Software. 3rd ed. F. A. Ciccarelli. LC 94-9549. 208p. (C). 1994. pap. write for info. (*0-02-322473-8*) Macmillan.
Circuit Rider. Edward Eggleston. Ed. by William Randel. (Masterworks of Literature Ser.). 1966. 18.95x (*0-8084-0077-0*); pap. 14.95x (*0-8084-0078-9*) NCUP.
Circuit Rider. Robert Harris. LC 94-60481. (Land of the Sky Ser.: Vol. 1). (Illus.). 126p. (Orig.). 1991. pap. 8.95 (*1-56664-000-8*) WorldComm.
Circuit Rider. Edward Eggleston. 1988. reprint ed. lib. bdg. 75.00 (*0-7812-1175-1*) Rprt Serv.
Circuit Rider: A Tale of the Heroic Age. Edward Eggleston. 20.95 (*0-88411-529-1*, Aeonian Pr) Amereon Ltd.
Circuit Rider see Collected Works of Edward Eggleston
Circuit Rider Dismounts, a Social History of Southern Methodism 1865-1900. Hunter D. Farish. LC 77-87534. (American Scene Ser.). 1969. reprint ed. 45.00 (*0-306-71450-7*) Da Capo.
Circuit Riders of the Big Bend. W. D. Smithers. (Southwestern Studies: No. 64). 1981. pap. 10.00 (*0-87404-124-4*) Tex Western.
Circuit Rider's Wife. Cora Harris. LC 87-73216. 158p. 1988. reprint ed. pap. 5.95 (*0-917851-10-2*) Bristol Hse.
Circuit-Riding Combat Chaplain. Frank R. Griepp. 1991. pap. 9.95 (*0-9619858-0-1*) Griepp Pub.
Circuit Sense for Elementary Teachers & Students: Understanding & Building Simple Logic Circuits. Janaye M. Houghton & Robert S. Houghton. LC 93-30270. (Illus.). 64p. 1994. pap. 13.00 (*1-56308-149-0*) Teacher Ideas Pr.

An Asterisk (*) at the beginning of an entry indicates that the title is appearing in BIP for the first time.

C

An Asterisk (*) at the beginning of an entry indicates that the title is appearing in BIP for the first time.

1273

Circus. Marianne Anderson & Betty Greenwood. Ed. by Marianne Robb. (C). 1989. 40.00 (*1-85098-267-8*, Pub. by Jordanhill College UK) St Mut.

Circus. Rosemary Caggiano & Larry Martinez. 48p. (J). (gr. k-6). 1978. pap. 14.95 (*0-86704-000-9*) Clarus Music.

Circus. Lois Ehlert. LC 91-12067. (Illus.). 40p. (J). (ps-1). 1992. 15.00 (*0-06-020252-1*); lib. bdg. 14.89 (*0-06-020253-X*) HarpC Child Bks.

Circus. Heidi Goennel. LC 91-448. (Illus.). 32p. (J). (ps-3). 1992. 15.00 (*0-688-10883-0*, Tambourine Bks); lib. bdg. 14.93 (*0-688-10884-9*, Tambourine Bks) Morrow.

Circus. Mabel Harmer. LC 81-7709. (New True Bks.). (Illus.). 48p. (J). (gr. k-4). 1981. lib. bdg. 12.90 (*0-516-01610-5*) Childrens.

Circus. Gabriela Kohen. (This Is Entertainment Ser.). (Illus.). 24p. (Orig.). (J). (gr. 2-6). 1992. lib. bdg. 9.95 (*1-56492-023-2*) Laredo.

Circus. Richard L. Lessard. 32p. (J). 1993. pap. 4.95 (*1-883656-00-1*) Earth Bound.

Circus. Alistair MacLean. 22.95 (*0-89190-672-X*, Am Repr) Amereon Ltd.

Circus. Peggy Roalf. LC 92-52983. (Looking at Paintings Ser.). (Illus.). 48p. (Orig.). (J). (gr. 3-7). 1993. lib. bdg. 14.89 (*1-56282-304-3*); pap. 6.95 (*1-56282-305-1*) Hyprn Child.

Circus. William Saroyan. (Creative's Classic Short Stories Ser.). 32p. (J). (gr. 4 up). 1986. lib. bdg. 13.95 (*0-88682-066-9*) Creative Ed.

Circus. Charles Sullivan. LC 92-19430. (Adventures in Art Book Ser.). (Illus.). 48p. (J). 1992. 15.95 (*0-8478-1604-4*) Rizzoli Intl.

Circus. Brian Wildsmith. (Illus.). (J). (ps-3). 1980. pap. 7.50 (*0-19-272102-X*) OUP.

Circus! 2nd ed. Jack Prelutsky. (Illus.). 32p. (J). (ps-2). 1989. reprint ed. pap. 4.95 (*0-689-70806-8*, Aladdin Paperbacks) S&S Childrens.

Circus: Big Book. Gabriela Kohen. (This Is Entertainment Ser.). (Illus.). 24p. (J). (gr. 2-6). 1992. pap. 19.95 (*1-56492-024-0*) Laredo.

Circus: From Rome to Ringling. Marian Murray. LC 74-171420. (Illus.). 354p. 1973. reprint ed. text ed. 49.75 (*0-8371-6259-9*, MUCI, Greenwood Pr) Greenwood.

Circus Alphabets. Dan X. Solo. 104p. 1989. pap. 5.95 (*0-486-26155-7*) Dover.

Circus & a Byzantine Cemetary at Carthage, Vol. 1. John H. Humphrey. LC 88-27969. (Illus.). 608p. 1989. text ed. 95.00 (*0-472-10113-7*) U of Mich Pr.

Circus Animals: Essays on W. B. Yeats. A. Norman Jeffares. LC 73-13824. x, 186p. 1970. 27.50 (*0-8047-0754-5*) Stanford U Pr.

Circus Animals Stained Glass Coloring Book. John Green. (Illus.). (J). (gr. k-3). 1993. pap. 1.00 (*0-486-27529-9*) Dover.

Circus Baby. Maud Petersham & Miska Petersham. LC 50-9295. (Illus.). 32p. (J). (ps-1). 1968. 13.95 (*0-02-771670-8*, Mac Bks Young Read) S&S Childrens.

Circus Baby. Maud Petersham & Miska Petersham. LC 88-7369. (Illus.). 32p. (J). (ps-1). 1989. reprint ed. pap. 3.95 (*0-689-71295-2*, Aladdin Paperbacks) S&S Childrens.

Circus Baggage Stock: A Tribute to the Percheron Horse. Charles P. Fox. LC 82-7631. (Illus.). 252p. 1989. reprint ed. pap. 15.95 (*0-9622663-0-2*) Heart Prairie Pr.

***Circus Boy.** Patricia B. Rumble. 29p. (Orig.). (J). (gr. 3-8). 1993. pap. 3.00 (*1-57514-110-8*, 1100) Encore Perform Pub.

***Circus by the Cemetery.** Lewis P. Simpson. (Orig.). 1995. 15.00 (*1-884725-08-2*); pap. 8.00 (*0-614-04820-6*) Blue Heron LA.

Circus Cage: A Journey of Transformation. Rosalie Douglas. (Illus.). 100p. (Orig.). (C). 1992. pap. 10.00 (*0-944164-02-1*) Moon Bear Pr.

***Circus Circus Enterprises.** 60p. (Orig.). 1995. pap. 295.00 (*0-7605-2113-1*) Rector Pr.

Circus City PLAE Score: A Thematic Play & Learning Program for Children of All Abilities. Susan M. Goltsman et al. LC 94-21494. (Illus.). 1994. 14.95 (*0-944661-07-6*) MIG Comns.

Circus Comes Home. Lois Duncan. LC 92-7481. (Illus.). (J). 1993. 16.95 (*0-385-30689-X*) Doubleday.

Circus Days. R. Pare. (Illus.). 24p. (J). (ps-8). 1988. lib. bdg. 14.95 (*1-55037-021-9*, Pub. by Annick CN); pap. 4.95 (*1-55037-020-0*, Pub. by Annick CN) Firefly Bks Ltd.

Circus Days Cookbook. Ringling Bros. & Barnum & Bailey Combined Shows, Inc. Staff. Ed. by Kathy A. Self. LC 90-62393. (Orig.). (J). 1990. pap. 13.00 (*1-878163-00-0*) Ringling Bros.

Circus Dreams. Lynn Goldsmith. LC 91-52883. (Illus.). 128p. 1991. 17.50 (*0-8478-1447-5*) Rizzoli Intl.

Circus Dreams: The Making of a Circus Artist. Kathleen Cushman. (J). (gr. 4-7). 1990. 15.95 (*0-316-16561-1*, Joy St Bks) Little.

Circus for Love. large type ed. Barbara Cartland. 245p. 1992. 21.95 (*0-7505-0236-3*) Ulverscroft.

Circus Fun. Margaret Hillert. (Illus.). (J). (ps-00). 1969. lib. bdg. 8.99 (*0-8136-5011-9*, TK2284); pap. 4.79 (*0-8136-5511-0*, TK2285) Modern Curr.

Circus Girl. Michael Garland. LC 92-22270. (Illus.). 32p. (J). (ps-3). 1993. 14.99 (*0-525-45069-6*, DCB) Dutton Child Bks.

Circus Hidden Pictures. Ed. by Jody Taylor. 32p. (J). (ps-5). 1994. pap. 4.95 (*1-56397-358-8*) Boyds Mills Pr.

Circus in a Suitcase. Reg Bolton. (Illus.). 94p. 1982. pap. 8.95 (*0-932720-08-0*) New Plays Inc.

Circus in the Attic: And Other Stories. Robert Penn Warren. LC 83-8461. 288p. 1901. pap. 6.95 (*0-15-618002-2*, Harvest Bks) HarBrace.

Circus Lady. Josephine D. Robinson. Ed. by Annette K. Baxter. LC 79-8808. (Signal Lives Ser.). (Illus.). 1980. reprint ed. lib. bdg. 35.95 (*0-405-12854-1*) Ayer.

Circus Locomotive. Joanne Barkan. (Circus Train Come Aboard Bks.). (Illus.). 12p. (J). (ps). 1993. pap. 3.50 (*0-689-71674-5*, Aladdin Paperbacks) S&S Childrens.

Circus Master's Mission. Joel Brinkley. 1989. 18.95 (*0-394-57570-9*) Random.

Circus Moves by Rail. C. Fox & T. Parkinson. (Illus.). 400p. 1993. 54.95 (*0-911868-85-2*, C85); pap. 39.95 (*0-911868-84-4*, C84) Carstens Pubns.

Circus of Ambition: The Culture of Wealth & Power in the Eighties. John Taylor. 1990. pap. 12.95 (*0-446-39157-3*) Warner Bks.

Circus of Dr. Lao. Charles Finney. 1993. reprint ed. lib. bdg. 18.95 (*0-89968-402-5*, Lghtyr Pr) Buccaneer Bks.

Circus of Love. Mary A. Dasgupta. 8.00 (*0-89253-463-X*); 4.80 (*0-89253-464-8*) Ind-US Inc.

Circus of Needs. Stephen Dunn. LC 78-59800. (Poetry Ser.). 1978. 16.95 (*0-915604-50-7*); pap. 9.95 (*0-915604-15-9*) Carnegie-Mellon.

***Circus of the Damned.** Laurell K. Hamilton. 336p. (Orig.). 1995. pap. text ed. 5.50 (*0-441-00197-1*) Ace Bks.

Circus of the Earth & Air. Brooke Stevens. LC 93-19163. 1994. 23.95 (*0-15-117987-5*) HB Coll Pubs.

***Circus of the Earth & the Air.** Brooke Stevens. 1995. pap. 12.00 (*0-15-600206-X*) HarBrace.

Circus of the Mind in Motion: Postmodernism & the Comic Vision. Lance Olson. LC 89-39857. 172p. (C). 1990. text ed. 34.95 (*0-8143-2132-1*) Wayne St U Pr.

Circus of the Wolves. Jack Bushnell. LC 93-8092. (Illus.). (J). 1994. 15.00 (*0-688-12554-9*); lib. bdg. 14.93 (*0-688-12555-7*) Lothrop.

Circus of Unreasonable Acts: Poems & Photographs. Roger Pfingston. (Illus.). 44p. (Orig.). 1982. pap. 10.00 (*0-685-54971-2*) Years Pr.

Circus of Want: Poems. Kevin J. Stein. LC 92-12350. 64p. 1992. 18.95 (*0-8262-0843-6*); pap. 9.95 (*0-8262-0844-4*) U of Mo Pr.

Circus Songs. Ed. by Norbert Krapf. (Illus.). 32p. (Orig.). 1984. pap. 5.00 (*0-912449-12-8*) Floating Island.

Circus Star. Bill Graham. 18p. (J). (ps). 1987. 10.95 (*1-879680-00-9*) About You.

Circus Stars. Kyle Carter. LC 94-12385. (Performers Discovery Library). (J). 1994. write for info. (*1-57103-066-2*) Rourke Pr.

Circus Stickers. Nina Barbaresi. (Illus.). (J). (gr. k-3). 1991. pap. 1.00 (*0-486-26814-4*) Dover.

Circus Techniques: Juggling, Equilibristics, Vaulting. rev. ed. Hovey Burgess. LC 89-28751. (Illus.). 162p. 1990. pap. 19.95 (*0-917643-06-2*) B Dube.

***Circus Thru the Fog.** Bud Backen. Ed. by Patrick McKinnon. (Illus.). 24p. Date not set. pap. 3.95 (*0-9641986-3-0*) Poetry Harbor.

Circus Time. Harry Bornstein. (Signed English Ser.). (Illus.). 16p. (J). (ps). 1976. pap. 3.50 (*0-913580-51-1*) Gallaudet Univ Pr.

Circus Time Dot-To-Dot Activity Book. Barbara Soloff-Levy. 32p. (J). 1989. pap. 1.25 (*0-8167-0000-1*) Troll Assocs.

Circus Train Gift Pack, Set. Jennifer Daniel. (Illus.). 48p. (J). (ps). Date not set. bds. 9.95 (*1-56828-063-7*) Red Jacket Pr.

Circus Trains, Trucks & Models. Harold H. Carstens. (Illus.). 52p. 1990. pap. 12.95 (*0-911868-70-4*, C70) Carstens Pubns.

Circus Trip Nineteen Forty-Three. Gerald Williams. (Morning Coffee Chapbook Ser.). (Illus.). 19p. (Orig.). 1988. pap. 10.00 (*0-918273-48-X*) Coffee Hse.

CIRED Nineteen Seventy-Seven, London, Pt. 2. International Conference on Electricity Distribution Staff. LC 78-306506. (Institution of Electrical Engineers Conference Report Ser.: No. 151). 203p. pap. 57.90 (*0-317-10074-2*, 2012185) Bks Demand.

CIRED Nineteen Seventy-Three, London. International Conference on Electricity Distribution Staff. LC 74-154513. (Institution of Electrical Engineers Conference Report Ser.: No. 99). 290p. reprint ed. pap. 82.70 (*0-317-10082-3*, 2012133) Bks Demand.

***Cirmac-BF-Carbiosystem Upgrading of Land Fill-Gas into Psueudo-Natural Gas NL-EN.** European Commission Staff. 90p. 1994. pap. 16.00 (*92-826-6914-9*, CSNA150712MC, Pub. by Europ Com) UNIPUB.

Ciro & Sal's Cookbook: Recipes, Tips & Lore from the Acclaimed Chef of Provincetown's Famous Italian Restaurant, Ciro & Sal's. Ciro Cozzi & Alethea Cozzi. LC 86-82115. 244p. 1987. 18.95 (*1-55611-005-7*) D I Fine.

Ciro's Circus. Joyce Sanker & Gary M. Coates. 1984. pap. 4.95 (*0-912963-04-2*) Eldridge Pub.

***Ciro's Provincetown Kitchen: Italian Cooking by the Sea.** Cirro Cozzi. 1995. pap. 16.95 (*0-9635257-5-1*) Mt Ivy Pr.

Cirque Du Soleil. Lois Brown. (Illus.). 144p. 1993. pap. 40.00 (*0-8478-1793-8*) Rizzoli Intl.

Cirrhosis, Hepatic Encephalopathy, & Ammonium Toxicity, Vol. 272. Ed. by S. Grisolia et al. (Advances in Experimental Medicine & Biology Ser.). (Illus.). 270p. 1990. 79.50 (*0-306-43666-3*, Plenum Pr) Plenum.

Cirrhosis, Hyperammonemia, & Hepatic Encephalopathy. Ed. by S. Grisolia & V. Felipo. (Advances in Experimental Medicine & Biology Ser.: Vol. 341). (Illus.). 142p. 1993. 59.50 (*0-306-44595-6*, Plenum Pr) Plenum.

Cirrhosis of the Liver: Methods & Fields of Research. N. Tygstrup & F. Orlandi. 1987. 212.00 (*0-444-80892-2*) Elsevier.

Cirrhosis of the Liver & Alcoholism. (World Health Statistics Report Ser.: Vol. 21, No. 11). 80p. 1968. pap. 3.60 (*0-686-09007-1*, 79) World Health.

CIS: OECD Economic Survey. Ed. by Lewis B. Sckolnick. (Illus.). 200p. (Orig.). (C). 1994. pap. text ed. 165.00 (*1-57205-652-5*) Rector Pr.

CIS: United States Company Directory. Ed. by Lewis B. Sckolnick. 350p. (Orig.). (C). 1994. pap. 165.00 (*1-57205-416-6*) Rector Pr.

CIS - East European Business World Directory 1991. Ed. by Lewis B. Sckolnick. (Illus.). 800p. (C). 1991. 295.00 (*0-934393-72-9*) Rector Pr.

CIS - East European Business World Directory 1992. Ed. by Lewis B. Sckolnick. (Illus.). 810p. (C). 1992. 395.00 (*0-934393-73-7*) Rector Pr.

CIS - East European Business World Directory 1993. Ed. by Lewis B. Sckolnick. (Illus.). 820p. (C). 1993. 495.00 (*0-934393-74-5*) Rector Pr.

CIS American Business Handbook. Ed. by Lewis B. Sckolnick. 224p. (Orig.). (C). 1994. pap. 125.00 (*1-57205-419-0*) Rector Pr.

***CIS & East Europe Political Risk Handbook.** (Illus.). 300p. (Orig.). 1994. pap. 695.00 (*0-7605-1331-7*) Rector Pr.

CIS & Eastern Europe Annual Economic Outlook. Ed. by Lewis B. Sckolnick. 132p. (C). 1993. pap. 75.00 (*0-934393-97-4*) Rector Pr.

***CIS & Eastern Europe Banking Reform 1993.** (Illus.). 200p. (Orig.). 1994. pap. 295.00 (*1-57205-877-3*) Rector Pr.

***CIS & Eastern Europe Chemical Company Directory.** 190p. (Orig.). 1994. pap. 295.00 (*1-57205-874-9*) Rector Pr.

***CIS & Eastern Europe Labor Market Handbook.** (Illus.). 425p. (Orig.). 1995. pap. 295.00 (*0-7605-1554-9*) Rector Pr.

***CIS & Eastern Europe Labour Statistics.** (Illus.). 320p. (C). 1994. 175.00 (*0-7605-0426-1*) Rector Pr.

CIS & Eastern Europe on File. LC 93-29159. 1993. write for info. (*0-8160-2920-2*) Facts on File.

***CIS & Europe U. S. Non Profit Aid Handbook, 3 vols., Set.** 600p. (Orig.). 1995. pap. 295.00 (*0-7605-1532-8*) Rector Pr.

***CIS Atlas: Russia & the Post Soviet Republics.** (Illus.). 64p. (Orig.). 1995. pap. 195.00 (*0-7605-2109-3*) Rector Pr.

CIS Automobile Atlas. (Illus.). 166p. (C). 1993. 35.00 (*0-934393-63-X*) Rector Pr.

***CIS Banking & Private Financing.** 235p. (Orig.). 1994. pap. 145.00 (*0-7605-0598-5*) Rector Pr.

CIS Business Directory. 700p. (C). 1994. 495.00 (*1-57205-723-8*) Rector Pr.

CIS Business Guide. Ed. by Lewis B. Sckolnick. 450p. (Orig.). (C). 1994. pap. 925.00 (*1-57205-319-4*) Rector Pr.

CIS Business Handbook & Guide. Ed. by Lewis B. Sckolnick. 1300p. (Orig.). (C). 1994. pap. 425.00 (*1-57205-506-5*) Rector Pr.

CIS Business Names & Managerial Personnel Names Handbook: 1991 Edition. (Illus.). 600p. (Orig.). (C). 1991. pap. 395.00 (*1-57205-706-8*) Rector Pr.

CIS Business Names & Managerial Personnel Names Handbook: 1992-93 Edition, 2 vols., Set. (Illus.). 1000p. (Orig.). (C). 1993. pap. 495.00 (*1-57205-707-6*) Rector Pr.

***CIS Business Reference.** 100p. (Orig.). 1995. pap. 125.00 (*0-7605-1689-8*) Rector Pr.

CIS Commercial Overview. Ed. by Lewis B. Sckolnick. 325p. (Orig.). (C). 1994. pap. 145.00 (*1-57205-422-0*) Rector Pr.

***CIS Demographics, Economics & Trade Data.** (Illus.). 150p. (Orig.). 1994. pap. 125.00 (*0-7605-0666-3*) Rector Pr.

CIS Energy & Minerals Development: Prospects, Problems, & Opportunities for International Cooperation. Ed. by James P. Dorian et al. LC 93-19530. (GeoJournal Library: Vol. 25). 388p. (C). 1993. lib. bdg. 119.00 (*0-7923-2323-8*) Kluwer Ac.

***CIS Executive Branch Documents: Part 1.** Ed. by Congressional Information Service, Inc., Staff. write for info. (*0-88692-202-X*) Cong Info.

***CIS Executive Branch Documents: Part 2.** Ed. by Congressional Information Service, Inc., Staff. write for info. (*0-88692-225-9*) Cong Info.

***CIS Executive Branch Documents: Part 3.** Ed. by Congressional Information Service, Inc., Staff. write for info. (*0-88692-252-6*) Cong Info.

***CIS Executive Branch Documents: Part 4.** Ed. by Congressional Information Service, Inc., Staff. write for info. (*0-88692-274-7*) Cong Info.

***CIS Executive Branch Documents: Part 5.** Ed. by Congressional Information Service, Inc., Staff. write for info. (*0-88692-275-5*) Cong Info.

***CIS Federal Register Index: Jan-June 1984.** Ed. by Congressional Information Service, Inc., Staff. write for info. (*0-88692-074-4*) Cong Info.

***CIS Federal Register Index: Jan-June 1985.** Ed. by Congressional Information Service, Inc., Staff. write for info. (*0-88692-076-0*) Cong Info.

***CIS Federal Register Index: Jan-June 1986.** Ed. by Congressional Information Service, Inc., Staff. write for info. (*0-88692-100-7*) Cong Info.

***CIS Federal Register Index: Jan-June 1987.** Ed. by Congressional Information Service, Inc., Staff. write for info. (*0-88692-125-2*) Cong Info.

***CIS Federal Register Index: Jan-June 1988.** Ed. by Congressional Information Service, Inc., Staff. write for info. (*0-88692-149-X*) Cong Info.

***CIS Federal Register Index: Jan-June 1989.** Ed. by Congressional Information Service, Inc., Staff. write for info. (*0-88692-176-7*) Cong Info.

***CIS Federal Register Index: Jan-June 1990.** Ed. by Congressional Information Service, Inc., Staff. write for info. (*0-88692-198-8*) Cong Info.

***CIS Federal Register Index: Jan-June 1991.** Ed. by Congressional Information Service, Inc., Staff. write for info. (*0-88692-223-2*) Cong Info.

***CIS Federal Register Index: Jan-June 1992.** Ed. by Congressional Information Service, Inc., Staff. write for info. (*0-88692-250-X*) Cong Info.

***CIS Federal Register Index: Jan-June 1993.** Ed. by Congressional Information Service, Inc., Staff. write for info. (*0-88692-276-3*) Cong Info.

***CIS Federal Register Index: Jan-June 1994.** Ed. by Congressional Information Service, Inc., Staff. write for info. (*0-88692-304-2*) Cong Info.

***CIS Federal Register Index: July-Dec 1984.** Ed. by Congressional Information Service, Inc., Staff. write for info. (*0-88692-075-2*) Cong Info.

***CIS Federal Register Index: July-Dec 1985.** Ed. by Congressional Information Service, Inc., Staff. write for info. (*0-88692-081-7*) Cong Info.

***CIS Federal Register Index: July-Dec 1986.** Ed. by Congressional Information Service, Inc., Staff. write for info. (*0-88692-114-7*) Cong Info.

***CIS Federal Register Index: July-Dec 1987.** Ed. by Congressional Information Service, Inc., Staff. write for info. (*0-88692-131-7*) Cong Info.

***CIS Federal Register Index: July-Dec 1988.** Ed. by Congressional Information Service, Inc., Staff. write for info. (*0-88692-156-2*) Cong Info.

***CIS Federal Register Index: July-Dec 1989.** Ed. by Congressional Information Service, Inc., Staff. write for info. (*0-615-00804-6*) Cong Info.

***CIS Federal Register Index: July-Dec 1990.** Ed. by Congressional Information Service, Inc., Staff. write for info. (*0-88692-207-0*) Cong Info.

***CIS Federal Register Index: July-Dec 1991.** Ed. by Congressional Information Service, Inc., Staff. write for info. (*0-88692-229-1*) Cong Info.

***CIS Federal Register Index: July-Dec 1992.** Ed. by Congressional Information Service, Inc., Staff. write for info. (*0-88692-258-5*) Cong Info.

***CIS Federal Register Index: July-Dec 1993.** Ed. by Congressional Information Service, Inc., Staff. write for info. (*0-88692-293-3*) Cong Info.

***CIS Federal Register Index, July-December 1994.** Ed. by Congressional Information Service, Inc., Staff. 810p. 1995. write for info. (*0-88692-324-7*) Cong Info.

CIS Fiscal Reform. 149p. (Orig.). (C). 1993. pap. 75.00 (*0-934393-44-3*) Rector Pr.

***CIS Food & Agriculture Reforms.** (Illus.). 250p. (Orig.). 1994. pap. 145.00 (*0-7605-0869-0*) Rector Pr.

***CIS Foreign Direct Investment.** (Illus.). 140p. (Orig.). 1995. pap. 295.00 (*0-7605-1520-4*) Rector Pr.

CIS Foreign Direct Investment. Ed. by Lewis B. Sckolnick. 140p. (Orig.). (C). 1994. text ed. 35.00 (*1-57205-005-5*) Rector Pr.

CIS Foreign Trade. 106p. (Orig.). (C). 1993. pap. 75.00 (*0-934393-43-5*) Rector Pr.

CIS Former U.S.S.R. Military Technical Atlas Scale: 1: 100000. Ed. by Lewis B. Sckolnick. 17500p. (Orig.). (RUS.). (C). 1994. pap. text ed. 3,500.00 (*1-57205-472-7*) Rector Pr.

CIS Former U.S.S.R. Military Technical Atlas Scale: 1: 200000. Ed. by Lewis B. Sckolnick. 4500p. (Orig.). (RUS.). (C). 1994. pap. text ed. 900.00 (*1-57205-471-9*) Rector Pr.

CIS Former U.S.S.R. Military Technical Atlas Scale: 1: 50000. Ed. by Lewis B. Sckolnick. 70000p. (Orig.). (RUS.). (C). 1994. pap. text ed. 1,400.00 (*1-57205-473-5*) Rector Pr.

***CIS Geographical Perspective: Natural Resources & Industries.** (Illus.). 320p. (Orig.). 1995. 195.00 (*0-7605-1680-4*) Rector Pr.

***CIS Geographical Perspective: Natural Resources & Industries.** (Illus.). 320p. (Orig.). 1995. pap. 125.00 (*0-7605-1681-2*) Rector Pr.

CIS Index to Presidential Executive Orders & Proclamations Part II. Congressional Information Service Staff. LC 87-109975. write for info. (*0-88692-106-6*) Cong Info.

CIS Index to Unpublished U. S. Senate Committee Hearings: 18th Congress-88th Congress, 1823-1964. Congressional Information Service Staff. LC 86-210230. 2,085.00 (*0-88692-089-2*) Cong Info.

***CIS Index Volume 1981, 2 vols.** Ed. by Congressional Information Service, Inc., Staff. write for info. (*0-912380-92-6*) Cong Info.

***CIS Index 1970 Abstracts Volume.** Ed. by Congressional Information Service, Inc., Staff. write for info. (*0-912380-02-0*) Cong Info.

***CIS Index 1970-1974 Cumulative Index, 2 vols.** Ed. by Congressional Information Service, Inc., Staff. write for info. (*0-912380-28-4*) Cong Info.

***CIS Index 1971, Abstracts Volume.** Ed. by Congressional Information Service, Inc., Staff. write for info. (*0-912380-05-5*) Cong Info.

***CIS Index 1972 Abstracts Volume.** Ed. by Congressional Information Service, Inc., Staff. write for info. (*0-88692-073-6*) Cong Info.

***CIS Index 1973 Abstracts Volume.** Ed. by Congressional Information Service, Inc., Staff. write for info. (*0-912380-14-4*) Cong Info.

***CIS Index 1974 Abstracts Volume.** Ed. by Congressional Information Service, Inc., Staff. write for info. (*0-912380-22-5*) Cong Info.

***CIS Index 1975, 2 vols.** Ed. by Congressional Information Service, Inc., Staff. write for info. (*0-912380-32-2*) Cong Info.

***CIS Index 1975 Abstracts Volume.** Ed. by Congressional Information Service, Inc., Staff. write for info. (*0-912380-34-9*) Cong Info.

***CIS Index 1975 Index Volume.** Ed. by Congressional Information Service, Inc., Staff. write for info. (*0-912380-33-0*) Cong Info.

C

An Asterisk (*) at the beginning of an entry indicates that the title is appearing in BIP for the first time.

An Asterisk (*) at the beginning of an entry indicates that the title is appearing in BIP for the first time.

1275

***CIS Unpublished U. S. Senate Committee Hearings: 1823-1964 (Ref. Bib. 2)** Ed. by Congressional Information Service, Inc., Staff. write for info. (*0-88692-091-4*) Cong Info.

***CIS Unpublished U. S. Senate Committee Hearings: 1823-1964 (Subject Index 1)** Ed. by Congressional Information Service, Inc., Staff. write for info. (*0-88692-092-2*) Cong Info.

***CIS Unpublished U. S. Senate Committee Hearings: 1823-1964 (Subject Index 2)** Ed. by Congressional Information Service, Inc., Staff. write for info. (*0-88692-093-0*) Cong Info.

***CIS Unpublished U. S. Senate Committee Hearings: 1965-1968.** Ed. by Congressional Information Service, Inc., Staff. write for info. (*0-88692-174-0*) Cong Info.

***CIS U.S. Congressional Committee Hearings, Part I: 1833-1917 (Subject Index 1)** Ed. by Congressional Information Service, Inc., Staff. write for info. (*0-88692-053-1*) Cong Info.

***CIS U.S. Congressional Committee Hearings, Part I: 1833-1917 (Subject Index 2)** Ed. by Congressional Information Service, Inc., Staff. write for info. (*0-88692-054-X*) Cong Info.

***CIS U.S. Congressional Committee Hearings, Part II: 1917-1925, 5 vols.** Ed. by Congressional Information Service, Inc., Staff. write for info. (*0-88692-031-0*) Cong Info.

Cisalpine Gaul: Social & Economic History from 49 B.C. to the Death of Trajan. Guy E. Chilver. LC 75-7308. (Roman History Ser.). (Illus.). 1979. reprint ed. 26.95 (*0-405-07190-6*) Ayer.

Cisco & the Twin Foals. Arthur W. Field. LC 83-61713. (Illus.). 160p. (YA). (gr. 8 up). 1983. 12.00 (*0-935356-06-1*) Mills Pub Co.

Cisco Kid. Rod Reed. (U. S. Classics Ser.). (Illus.). 80p. (Orig.). 1983. pap. 5.95 (*0-912277-00-9*) K Pierce Inc.

Cisplatin derzeitiger Stand und neue Entwicklungen in der Chemotherapie maligner Neoplasien. Ed. by S. Seeber et al. (Beitraege zur Onkologie Ser.: Band 3). (Illus.). 184p. 1980. pap. 23.25 (*3-8055-1364-X*) S Karger.

Cistercian Art & Architecture in the British Isles. Ed. by Christopher Norton & David A. Park. (Illus.). 448p. 1986. 150.00 (*0-521-25475-2*) Cambridge U Pr.

Cistercian Finances in the Fourteenth Century. Peter King. 24.95 (*0-87907-885-5*) Cistercian Pubns.

Cistercian Ideals & Reality. Ed. by John R. Sommerfeldt. LC 78-16615. (Cistercian Studies: No. 60). 1978. pap. 8.95 (*0-87907-860-X*) Cistercian Pubns.

Cistercian Monasteries of Ireland. Roger Stalley. LC 86-26626. 296p. 1987. text ed. 50.00 (*0-300-03737-6*) Yale U Pr.

Cistercian Monasteries of Ireland. Roger Stalley. LC 86-26626. 296p. 1989. pap. 32.00 (*0-300-04546-8*) Yale U Pr.

Cistercian Settlements in Wales & Monmouthshire, 1140-1540. Jeremiah F. O'Sullivan. LC 48-6318. (Fordham University Studies. History Ser.: No. 2). 151p. reprint ed. pap. 43.10 (*0-7837-5577-5*, 2045359) Bks Demand.

Cistercian Sign Language. Robert Barakat. LC 70-152476. (Cistercian Studies: No. 11). 1976. 14.95 (*0-87907-811-1*) Cistercian Pubns.

Cistercian Spirit: A Symposium in Memory of Thomas Merton. Ed. by M. Basil Pennington. (Cistercian Studies: No. 3). xvi, 286p. 1973. reprint ed. 7.95 (*0-87907-803-0*) Cistercian Pubns.

Cistercian Way. Andre Louf. (Cistercian Studies: No. 76). pap. 7.95 (*0-87907-976-2*) Cistercian Pubns.

Cistercian World: Monastic Writings of the Twelfth Century. Ed. & Tr. by Pauline Matarasso. 336p. 1993. 12.95 (*0-14-043356-2*, Penguin Classics) Viking Penguin.

Cistercians. Basil Pennington. 136p. (Orig.). 1992. pap. text ed. 18.95 (*0-8146-5720-6*, M Glazier) Liturgical Pr.

Cistercians: Ideals & Reality. Louis J. Lekai. LC 77-3692. (Illus.). 534p. 1977. 35.00 (*0-87338-201-3*) Kent St U Pr.

Cistercians & Cluniacs: Apologia to Abbot William. Bernard. 1986. pap. 3.25 (*0-87907-102-8*) Cistercian Pubns.

Cistercians & Cluniacs: The Case for Citeaux. Idung Of Prufening. Tr. by Jeremiah F. O'Sullivan et al. LC 77-9289. 1977. 12.95 (*0-87907-633-X*) Cistercian Pubns.

Cistercians in Denmark: Their Attitudes, Roles, & Functions in Medieval Society. Brian P. McGuire. (Cistercian Studies: No. 35). 1982. 35.00 (*0-87907-835-9*) Cistercian Pubns.

Cistercians in the Late Middle Ages: Studies in Medieval Cistercian History. Ed. by E. Rozanne Elder et al. (Cistercian Studies: No. VI). 161p. (Orig.). 1981. pap. 8.95 (*0-87907-865-0*) Cistercian Pubns.

Cistophori of Hadrian. William E. Metcalf. (Numismatic Studies: NS-15). (Illus.). 195p. 1980. 65.00 (*0-89722-004-8*) Am Numismatic.

CIT Fourth National Conference Proceedings: "New Dimensions in Interpreter Education" Marina L. McIntire. LC 84-60332. 337p. 1984. pap. text ed. 10.95 (*0-317-06558-0*) RID Pubns.

Cita Con el Diablo. Francisco Quintana. LC 90-83578. 159p. 1991. 16.00 (*0-89729-576-5*) Ediciones.

Cita En Jerusalem: Appointment in Jerusalem. Derek Prince. (SPA.). 5.95 (*84-7228-360-7*, 360091, Pub. by Edit Clie SP) TSELF.

Citadel. (Fiction Ser.). (YA). 1993. pap. text ed. 6.50 (*0-582-09673-1*, 79817) Longman.

Citadel. A. J. Cronin. (J). 1983. 16.45 (*0-316-16158-6*); pap. 9.95i (*0-316-16183-7*) Little.

Citadel. Kevin Randle. 192p. (Orig.). 1994. pap. 4.50 (*0-441-00056-8*) Ace Bks.

Citadel. Kyle Stone. (Orig.). 1994. pap. 4.95 (*1-56333-198-5*) Masquerade.

Citadel. Paul J. Young, Jr. Ed. by Trevor M. Phillips. 1991. write for info. (*0-9622708-6-5*) Zubra Pub.

Citadel: The Battle of Kursk. Robin Cross. (Illus.). 288p. 1993. 24.95 (*0-962761З-6-2*) Sarpedon.

Citadel - Then & Now. Photos by Tommy Thompson. (Illus.). 112p. 1993. 39.00 (*1-56469-003-2*) Harmony Hse Pub LO.

Citadel Culture. O. K. Werckmeister. LC 90-20529. (Illus.). 232p. 1991. 24.95 (*0-226-89361-8*) U Ch Pr.

Citadel in Spring. Hiroyuki Agawa. Ed. by Jones. Tr. by Lawrence Rogers. 224p. 1991. 18.95 (*0-87011-960-5*) Kodansha.

Citadel, Market & Altar: Emerging Society. Spencer Heath. LC 57-14589. 1957. 17.95 (*0-9600300-1-8*) Heather Foun.

Citadel of Ethiopia. Max Gruhl. LC 74-15043. (ENG.). reprint ed. 55.00 (*0-404-12073-3*) AMS Pr.

Citadel of Fear. Francis Stevens. 272p. 1984. pap. 3.50 (*0-88184-038-6*) Carroll & Graf.

Citadel of God: A Novel of Saint Benedict. Louis De Wohl. LC 91-77212. 343p. Date not set. pap. 14.95 (*0-89870-404-9*) Ignatius Pr.

***Citadel of Love.** large type ed. Rose Dana. (Romance Library). 272p. 1995. pap. 14.95 (*0-7089-7660-3*, Linford) Ulverscroft.

Citadel of the Autarch. Gene Wolfe. LC 82-5964. 317p. 1983. 40.00 (*0-671-45251-7*) Ultramarine Pub.

Citadel of the Senses & Other Essays. Macdonald Critchley. (Illus.). 288p. 1986. text ed. 47.50 (*0-88167-105-3*) Raven.

Citadel Run. David Robbins. (Endworld Ser.: No. 6). 256p. (Orig.). 1987. pap. 2.95 (*0-8439-2507-8*) Dorchester Pub Co.

Citadel Treasury of Famous Movie Lines. Ted Gottfried. LC 94-17782. 1994. 29.95 (*0-8065-1590-2*, Citadel Pr); pap. 21.95 (*0-8065-1551-1*, Citadel Pr) Carol Pub Group.

Citadel'i Pisatel. Holger Siegel. (Slavistische Texte und Studien Ser.: Vol. 2). 356p. 1983. write for info. (*3-487-07288-2*, Pub. by Georg Olms GW) Lubrecht & Cramer.

Citadelle. Antoine de Saint-Exupery. 1972. write for info. (*0-318-63461-9*) Fr & Eur.

Citadelle. Antoine de Saint-Exupery. (FRE.). 1991. pap. 17.95 (*0-8288-3729-5*, F123521) Fr & Eur.

Citadelle. Antoine de Saint-Exupery. (Folio Ser.: No. 108). (FRE.). 1972. 14.95 (*2-07-036108-X*) Schoenhof.

Citadels of Mystery. L. Sprague De Camp. 1973. mass mkt. 4.95 (*0-345-23215-1*) Ballantine.

***Citaras Colgadas de Arboles.** 5th ed. A. Gala. 1989. pap. 10.95 (*0-7859-5180-6*) Fr & Eur.

Citaras Colgadas de los Arboles. Por Que Corres, Ulises? Antonio Gala. (Nueva Austral Ser.: Vol. 111). (SPA.). 1991. pap. text ed. 15.95 (*84-239-1911-0*) Elliots Bks.

Citation & Examination of William Shakespeare. Walter S. Landor. LC 73-16141. (Studies in Shakespeare: No. 24). 1974. reprint ed. lib. bdg. 59.95 (*0-8383-1721-9*) M S G Haskell Hse.

Citation & Modernity. Claudette Sartiliot & Brecht Derrida. LC 92-50721. 1993. 27.95 (*0-8061-2506-3*) U of Okla Pr.

***Citation & Modernity: Derroda, Joyce, & Brecht.** Claudette Sartiliot. LC 92-50721. (Oklahoma Project for Discourse & Theory Ser.: Vol. 13). 256p. Date not set. pap. 15.95 (*0-8061-2538-1*) U of Okla Pr.

Citations & Allusions to Jewish Scripture in Early Christian & Jewish Writings Through 180 C. E. Bradley H. McLean. LC 91-38309. 144p. 1992. lib. bdg. 69.95 (*0-7734-9430-8*) E Mellen.

Citation's Who's Who among Rising Young Americans 1991, Vol. 1. Citation Directories, Ltd., Inc. Staff. Ed. by Joseph W. Peed & Marilyn A. Riley. 1991. lib. bdg. 99.95 (*1-880486-00-8*) Citation Direct.

Citation's Who's Who among Rising Young Americans, 1992, Vol. 2. Citation Directories, Ltd., Inc. Staff. Ed. by Joseph W. Peed & Marilyn A. Riley. 1992. lib. bdg. 119.95 (*1-880486-01-6*) Citation Direct.

Citation's Who's Who Environmental Registry, 1992. Citation Directories, Ltd., Inc. Staff. Ed. by Joseph W. Peed & Marilyn A. Riley. (Environmental Ser.: Vol. 1). 750p. 1992. pap. 239.95 (*1-880486-02-4*) Citation Direct.

Citation's Who's Who Registry of Rising Young Americans, 1993. Citation Directories, Ltd. Inc. Staff. Ed. by Joseph W. Peed & Marilyn A. Riley. (Young American Ser.: Vol. 3). 1993. lib. bdg. 119.95 (*1-880486-03-2*) Citation Direct.

Cite Fertile. Andree Chedid. (FRE.). 1992. pap. 10.95 (*0-7859-3289-5*, 2277233196) Fr & Eur.

Cite Frages & Other Buildings & Projects 1923-1927. Alexander Tzonis. Ed. by H. Allen Brooks. LC 83-1584. (Le Corbusier Archieve Ser.). 1983. lib. bdg. 260.00 (*0-8240-5051-7*) Garland.

Cite Industrielle. Tony Garnier. 196p. 1989. reprint ed. 29.95 (*0-910413-47-9*) Princeton Arch.

Cite Your Sources: A Manual for Documenting Family Histories & Genealogical Records. Ed. by Richard S. Lackey. LC 85-20371. 94p. 1985. pap. 9.95 (*0-87805-286-0*) U Pr of Miss.

Citebook. 8th ed. Tony Darwin. Ed. by Barbara Fluharty. LC 90-71186. (Illus.). 270p. (C). 1990. pap. 16.95 (*0-9628328-0-4*, TX2-139-018) Starlite Inc.

Cites Charnelles. Zoe Oldenbourg. (FRE.). 1983. pap. 20.95 (*0-7859-4189-4*) Fr & Eur.

Cites Endangered Species Coloring Book. rev. ed. Conservation Treaty Support Group Staff. Ed. by Peter Dollinger. (Illus.). 72p. (J). 1993. pap. 4.95 (*1-56002-281-7*) Aegina Pr.

Citibank, 1812-1970. Harold Van B. Cleveland & Thomas F. Huertas. (Studies in Business History: No. 37). (Illus.). 512p. 1985. 25.00 (*0-674-13175-4*) HUP.

Cities. (Mix & Match Tracing Ser.). (Illus.). 44p. (J). (gr. k-5). 1988. pap. 2.95 (*0-8431-2248-X*) Price Stern.

Cities. Donna Bailey. LC 89-26153. (Facts About Ser.). (Illus.). 48p. (J). (gr. 2-6). 1990. lib. bdg. 21.36 (*0-8114-2515-0*) Raintree Steck-V.

Cities. Roger Barr. (Lucent Overview Ser.). (Illus.). (J). (gr. 5-8). 1994. 16.95 (*1-56006-158-8*) Lucent Bks.

Cities. William Carney. 80p. (Orig.). 1985. pap. 5.95 (*0-938190-58-X*) North Atlantic.

Cities. Richard C. Wade & Gene Brown. 1976. 27.95 (*0-405-09849-9*, 1756) Ayer.

Cities. John Yau & Chris Bruce. LC 87-83029. (Illus.). 48p. (Orig.). 1987. pap. 14.00 (*0-935558-25-X*) Henry Art.

Cities. Richard Tames. Ed. by Malcolm Yapp et al. (World History Ser.). (Illus.). 32p. (YA). (gr. 6-11). 1980. reprint ed. pap. text ed. 4.35 (*0-89908-115-0*) Greenhaven.

Cities: Citizens & Civilizations. Fiona MacDonald. LC 91-33498. (Timelines Ser.). (Illus.). 48p. (J). 1992. 13.95 (*0-531-15247-2*) Watts.

Cities: Missions' New Frontier. Roger S. Greenway & Timothy M. Monsma. LC 89-6962. 224p. 1989. pap. 18.99 (*0-8010-3831-6*) Baker Bk.

Cities: Through the Eyes of Artists. Wendy Richardson & Jack Richardson. LC 90-34277. (Artists of the World Ser.). 48p. (J). (gr. 4 up). 1991. lib. bdg. 15.45 (*0-516-09282-0*); pap. 7.95 (*0-516-49282-9*) Childrens.

Cities: U. S. A. A. Teplitsky & Ronald T. Hyman. 1976. pap. 5.48 (*0-13-134833-7*) P-H.

Cities Advocate: Whether Apprentiship Extinguisheth Gentry? Edmund Bolton. LC 74-28834. (English Experience Ser.: No. 715). 1975. reprint ed. 7.00 (*90-221-0715-9*) Walter J Johnson.

Cities Against Nature. Nancy Bruning. LC 91-34604. (Saving Planet Earth Ser.). 128p. (J). (gr. 4-8). 1992. lib. bdg. 21.23 (*0-516-05510-0*) Childrens.

Cities & Automobile Dependence: A Sourcebook. Peter W. Newman & Jeffrey R. Kenworthy. (Illus.). xviii, 388p. 1989. text ed. 79.95 (*1-85742-103-5*, Pub. by Ashgate UK) Ashgate Pub Co.

Cities & Bishoprics of Phrygia. William M. Ramsay. LC 75-7336. (Roman History Ser.). (Illus.). 1975. reprint ed. 63.95 (*0-405-07055-1*) Ayer.

Cities & Buildings: Skyscrapers, Skid Rows, & Suburbs. Larry R. Ford. LC 93-5752. (Creating the North American Landscape Ser.). 1994. text ed. 55.00 (*0-8018-4646-3*); pap. 19.95 (*0-8018-4647-1*) Johns Hopkins.

Cities & Caliphs: On the Genesis of Arab Muslim Urbanism. Nezar Alsayyad. LC 90-19913. (Contributions to the Study of World History Ser.: No. 26). 208p. 1991. text ed. 49.95 (*0-313-27791-5*, ASC/, Greenwood Pr) Greenwood.

Cities & Cemeteries of Etruria. George Dennis. LC 84-8431. (Illus.). 416p. 1985. 75.00 (*0-691-03575-X*) Princeton U Pr.

Cities & Cemeteries of Etruria. abr. ed. George Dennis. Ed. by Pamela Hemphill. LC 84-8431. (Illus.). 458p. pap. 130.60 (*0-7837-6495-2*, 2046585) Bks Demand.

Cities & Churches: An International Bibliography, 3 vols. Loyde H. Hartley. No. 31. 2793p. 1992. Vol. I: 1800-1959. write for info. (*0-318-69430-1*); Vol. II: 1960-1979. write for info. (*0-318-69431-X*); Vol. III: 1980-1991 & Indexes. write for info. (*0-318-69432-8*) Scarecrow.

Cities & Churches: An International Bibliography, 3 vols., Set. Loyde H. Hartley. LC 92-18819. (American Theological Library Association Monograph: No. 31). 2793p. 1992. 225.00 (*0-8108-2583-X*) Scarecrow.

Cities & City Planning. Lloyd Rodwin. LC 81-13956. (Environment, Development, & Public Policy: Public Policy & Social Services Ser.). 318p. (C). 1981. 49.50 (*0-306-40666-7*, Plenum Pr) Plenum.

Cities & Development in the Third World. Ed. by Robert B. Potter & Ademola T. Salau. (Illus.). 208p. 1990. text ed. 80.00 (*0-7201-2066-7*, Mansell Pub) Cassell.

***Cities & Disaster: North American Studies in Emergency Management.** Richard T. Sylves & William L. Waugh, Jr. (Illus.). 278p. 1990. pap. 33.95 (*0-398-06451-2*) C C Thomas.

Cities & Disaster: North American Studies in Emergency Management. Richard T. Sylves & William L. Waugh, Jr. (Illus.). 278p. (C). 1990. text ed. 55.95x (*0-398-05635-8*) C C Thomas.

Cities & Economic Development: From the Dawn of History to the Present. Paul Bairoch. LC 87-35484. (Illus.). xxii, 574p. 1988. pap. text ed. 21.95 (*0-226-03466-0*) U Ch Pr.

Cities & Economic Development: From the Dawn of History to the Present. Paul Bairoch. Tr. by Christopher Braider. (Illus.). 600p. 1988. 49.95 (*0-226-03465-8*) U Ch Pr.

Cities & Fiscal Choices: A New Model of Urban Public Investment. Michael A. Pagano & Richard Moore. LC 85-16211. (Duke Press Policy Studies). xii, 166p. 1985. 39.50 (*0-8223-0653-0*) Duke.

Cities & Frontiers in Brazil: Regional Dimensions of Economic Development. Martin T. Katzman. LC 77-23159. (Illus.). 255p. reprint ed. pap. 76.70 (*0-7837-1710-5*, 2057239) Bks Demand.

***Cities & Greed.** Francis K. Peddle. 255p. Date not set. 12.00 (*0-9698812-0-7*) Schalkenbach.

Cities & Housing: Perspectives on Urban Geography, Vol. 2. Ed. by C. S. Yadav. 307p. (C). 1987. 57.50 (*81-7022-030-0*, Pub. by Concept II) S Asia.

Cities & Immigrants: A Geography of Change in Nineteenth-Century America. David Ward. (Historical Geography of North America Ser.). (C). 1971. pap. text ed. 13.95 (*0-19-501284-4*) OUP.

***Cities & Natural Process.** Michael Hough. LC 94-31155. (Illus.). 272p. 1995. 59.95x (*0-415-12168-X*, C0139); pap. 22.95 (*0-415-12198-1*, C0443) Routledge.

Cities & New Technologies. OECD Staff. 289p. (Orig.). 1992. pap. 80.00 (*92-64-13591-X*) OECD.

Cities & People. Mark Girouard. LC 85-40461. (Illus.). 408p. 1987. pap. 27.50 (*0-300-03968-9*) Yale U Pr.

Cities & People: A Social & Architectural History. Mark Girouard. LC 85-40461. (Illus.). 416p. 1985. 55.00 (*0-300-03502-0*) Yale U Pr.

Cities & Regions in the New Europe: The Global-Local Interplay & Spatial Development Strategies. Mick Dunford & Grigorio Kafkalas. 339p. (Orig.). 1992. text ed. 69.95 (*0-470-21923-8*) Halsted Pr.

***Cities & Regions in the New Europe: The Global-Local Interplay & Spatial Development Strategies.** Ed. by Mick Dunford & Grigoris Kafkalas. 1993. text ed. 79.95 (*0-471-94525-0*) Wiley.

Cities & Scenes from the Ancient World. Roy G. Krenkel. LC 74-77464. (Illus.). 82p. 1974. 30.00 (*0-913896-02-0*) Owlswick Pr.

Cities & Sickness: Health Care in Urban America. Ed. by Ann L. Greer & Scott Greer. LC 83-15222. (Urban Affairs Annual Reviews Ser.: No. 25). (Illus.). 303p. reprint ed. pap. 86.40 (*0-8357-8424-X*, 2034687) Bks Demand.

Cities & Social Change in Early Modern France. Ed. by Philip Benedict. 272p. 1992. pap. 18.95 (*0-415-08161-0*, A9406) Routledge.

Cities & Social Change in Early Modern France. Ed. by Philip Benedict. 224p. 1989. text ed. 55.00 (*0-04-944017-9*) Routledge Chapman & Hall.

Cities & Society in Colonial Latin America. Ed. by Louisa S. Hoberman & Susan M. Socolow. LC 85-20855. (Illus.). 362p. (C). 1986. pap. 16.95 (*0-8263-0845-7*) U of NM Pr.

Cities & Space: The Future Use of Urban Land, Essays from the Fourth RFF Forum. Ed. by Lowdon Wingo et al. LC 63-18694. 275p. reprint ed. pap. 78.40 (*0-7837-3044-6*, 2042881) Bks Demand.

Cities & Subsurface Use: Proceedings of an International Conference, Bordeaux, 21-23 October 1987. Ed. by M. Legrand. 480p. (C). 1987. text ed. 155.00 (*90-6191-715-8*, Pub. by A A Balkema NE) Ashgate Pub Co.

Cities & Suburbs: Urban Life in West Africa. Margaret Peil. LC 80-26440. (New Library of African Affairs). 330p. (C). 1982. 49.50 (*0-8419-0685-8*) Holmes & Meier.

Cities & the Federal System. R. C. Martin. LC 77-74949. (American Federalism-the Urban Dimension Ser.). 1978. reprint ed. lib. bdg. 23.95 (*0-405-10495-2*) Ayer.

Cities & the Global Environment: Proceedings of a European Workshop. European Foundation Staff. 283p. 1992. pap. 35.00 (*92-826-3247-4*, SY-72-91-172-EN-C, Pub. by Europ Com) UNIPUB.

Cities & the International Division of Labor. Norman J. Glickman. (Working Paper Ser.: No. 31). 37p. 1985. 5.00 (*0-685-10698-5*) LBJ Sch Pub Aff.

Cities & the Rise of States in Europe, A. D. 1000-1800. Ed. by Charles Tilly & Wim P. Blockmans. LC 94-17378. (C). 1994. pap. text ed. 21.95 (*0-8133-8849-X*) Westview.

Cities & the Rise of States in Europe, A. D. 1000-1800. Ed. by Charles Tilly & Wim P. Blockmans. LC 94-17378. 1994. text ed. 65.00 (*0-8133-8848-1*) Westview.

Cities & the Sea: Port City Planning in Early Modern Europe. Josef W. Konvitz. LC 77-12976. (Illus.). 253p. reprint ed. pap. 72.20 (*0-8357-6618-7*, 2035263) Bks Demand.

Cities & the Wealth of Nations: Principles of Economic Life. Jane Jacobs. LC 83-43184. 251p. 1985. pap. 12.50 (*0-394-72911-0*, Vin) Random.

Cities & the 1936 Congress & Recent Federal-City Relations. Paul V. Betters et al. LC 77-74929. (American Federalism-the Urban Dimension Ser.). 1978. reprint ed. lib. bdg. 19.95 (*0-405-10478-2*) Ayer.

Cities & Their Vital Systems: Infrastructure Past, Present & Future. National Academy of Engineering. 368p. 1988. pap. text ed. 35.00 (*0-309-03786-7*) Natl Acad Pr.

Cities & Towns in American History: A Bibliography of Doctoral Dissertations. Comp. by Arthur P. Young. LC 89-11996. (Bibliographies & Indexes in American History Ser.: No. 13). 448p. 1989. text ed. 85.00 (*0-313-26588-7*, YCT/, Greenwood Pr) Greenwood.

Cities & Towns in Indonesia: Their Development, Current Positions & Functions with Regard to Administration & Regional Economy. Werner Rutz. Ed. by W. Tietze. (Urbanization of the Earth Ser.: Vol. 4). 292p. 1987. lib. bdg. 90.00 (*3-443-37006-3*) Lubrecht & Cramer.

Cities & Towns of China: A Geographical Dictionary. George M. Playfair. 1976. lib. bdg. 59.95 (*0-8490-1635-5*) Gordon Pr.

Cities & Towns of Early South Carolina: Articles from the South Carolina Historical (and Genealogical) Magazine, Vol. II. Henry A. Smith. LC 87-26623. (Historical Writings of Henry A. M. Smith). 256p. 1988. reprint ed. 25.00 (*0-87152-425-2*) Reprint.

Cities & Towns of Puerto Rico. Ed. by Raoul Gordon. 1976. lib. bdg. 59.95 (*0-87968-872-6*) Gordon Pr.

Cities & Trade: Consul Abbott on the Economy of Iran, 1847-1866. Abbas Amanat. 256p. 1984. 29.00 (*0-86372-006-4*, Pub. by Ithaca UK) Evergreen Dist.

Cities & Urban Living. Ed. by Mark Baldassare. LC 82-19875. 336p. 1983. text ed. 61.00 (*0-231-05502-1*); pap. text ed. 18.50 (*0-231-05503-X*) Col U Pr.

Cities & Urbanism. Ed. by W. Tietze. 104p. (C). 1975. pap. 29.00 (*0-08-019666-7*, Pergamon Pr) Elsevier.

Cities & Years. Konstantin Fedin. Tr. by Michael Scammell. (European Classics Ser.). 350p. 1993. reprint ed. pap. 15.95 (*0-8101-1066-0*) Northwestern U Pr.

Cities at War. Robin Cross. (World War II Ser.). (Illus.). 48p. (J). (gr. 5-9). 1994. 14.95 (*1-56847-179-3*) Thomson Lrning.

Cities at War: London. write for info. (*0-318-59717-9*) S&S Trade.

C

An Asterisk (*) at the beginning of an entry indicates that the title is appearing in BIP for the first time.

C

An Asterisk (*) at the beginning of an entry indicates that the title is appearing in BIP for the first time.

Citizen Participation Handbook for Public Officials & Other Professionals Serving the Public. Hans Bleiker & Annemarie Bleiker. 1990. ring bd. write for info. (*0-925368-00-8*) IPMP.

Citizen Participation Handbook, 1988: For Public Officials & Other Professionals Serving the Public. 6th ed. 1988. ring bd. write for info. (*0-318-64681-1*) IPMP.

Citizen Participation in Environmental Affairs, 1970-1986: A Bibliography. Ed. by Frederick Frankena & Joan K. Frankena. LC 87-45800. (Studies in Social History: No. 8). 1988. 45.00 (*0-404-61608-9*) AMS Pr.

Citizen Participation in Library Decision-Making: The Toronto Experience. Ed. by John Marshall. LC 84-10617. (Dalhousie University School of Library Service Ser.: No. 1). 436p. 1984. 35.00 (*0-8108-1709-8*) Scarecrow.

Citizen Participation in Local Planning in the U. K. & U. S. A. W. C. Johnson. 74p. 1984. pap. 22.00 (*0-08-031720-0*, Pergamon Pr) Elsevier.

Citizen Participation in Planning. Michael Fagence. 1977. pap. 36.00 (*0-08-020398-1*, Pergamon Pr) Elsevier.

Citizen Participation in Public Decision Making. Ed. by Jack DeSario & Stuart Langton. LC 86-7571. (Contributions in Political Science Ser.: No. 158). 249p. 1987. text ed. 55.00 (*0-313-25478-8*, DCZ/, Greenwood Pr) Greenwood.

Citizen Participation in Science Policy. Ed. by James C. Petersen. LC 84-246. 256p. 1984. lib. bdg. 30.00x (*0-87023-433-1*); pap. 16.95x (*0-87023-434-X*) U of Mass Pr.

Citizen Participation in Urban & Regional Planning: A Comprehensive Bibliography, No. 1297. John D. Hulchanski. 1977. 6.00 (*0-686-19696-1*) CPL Biblios.

*__Citizen Participation Specialist.__ (Career Examination Ser.: Series 1). Date not set. pap. 29.95 (*0-8373-3669-4*) Nat Learn.

Citizen-Patient in Revolutionary & Imperial Paris. Dora B. Weiner. LC 92-49007. (Henry E. Sigerist Series in the History of Medicine). 464p. (C). 1993. text ed. 48.50 (*0-8018-4483-5*) Johns Hopkins.

*__Citizen Politics in Western Democracies: Public Opinion & Political Parties in the United States, Great Britain, Germany, & France.__ Russell J. Dalton. LC 88-2830. 288p. (C). 1995. reprint ed. pap. text ed. 24.95x (*1-56643-020-8*) Chatham Hse Pubs.

Citizen R. K. Does Not Live: Poems of Ryszard Krynicki. Sel. by Stanislaw Baranczak. (Poetry Chapbook Ser.). 36p. 1985. 10.00 (*0-932191-06-1*, PG7170) Mr Cogito Pr.

Citizen Racing. John Caldwell & Michael Brady. (Orig.). 1983. 15.25 (*0-8446-6045-0*) Peter Smith.

Citizen Reclaimed. Eckhard Gerdes. 118p. (Orig.). 1996. pap. 9.95 (*1-884097-19-7*) Depth Charge.

Citizen Response to Volcanic Eruption: The Case of Mt. St. Helens. Ronald W. Perry & Marjorie Greene. 145p. 1983. text ed. 19.50 (*0-8290-1050-5*) Irvington.

Citizen Rights & Access to Electronic Information: The 1991 LITA President's Program Presentations & Background Papers. Ed. by Dennis J. Reynolds. LC 92-19782. 201p. 1992. pap. 22.00 (*0-8389-7601-8*) ALA.

Citizen Sailors in Changing Society: Policy Issues for Manning the United States Naval Reserve. Milton L. Boykin. Ed. by Louis A. Zurcher & Hardy L. Merritt. LC 85-14714. (Contributions in Military Studies: No. 50). (Illus.). 290p. 1986. text ed. 55.00 (*0-313-24476-6*, ZPE/) Greenwood.

*__Citizen Science: A Study of People, Expertise, & Sustainable Development.__ Alan Irwin. LC 94-49028. (Environment & Society Ser.). 1995. write for info. (*0-415-11548-5*); pap. write for info. (*0-415-13010-7*) Routledge.

Citizen Scientist. Frank Von Hippel. (Masters of Modern Physics Ser.). 1991. 24.95 (*0-88318-709-4*) Am Inst Physics.

Citizen Settlement Program: Mediation of Small Claims. National Center for State Courts. (Paul Reardon Ser.). 16p. 1982. 0.96 (*0-685-16810-7*, PRS-035) Natl Ctr St Courts.

Citizen Shakespeare: A Social & Political Portrait. James C. Humes. LC 92-3365. 192p. 1993. text ed. 42.95 (*0-275-94153-1*, C4153, Praeger Pubs) Greenwood.

*__Citizen Sherman.__ Michael Fellman. 576p. 1995. 30.00 (*0-679-42966-2*) Random.

Citizen Soldier: Opportunities in the Reserves. Carl P. White. Ed. by Ruth Rosen. (Military Opportunities Ser.). (YA). (gr. 7-12). 1990. lib. bdg. 14.95 (*0-8239-1023-7*) Rosen Group.

*__Citizen Soldier: The Fighting Style of Brigadier General Edward W. Bird.__ Robert J. Berens. LC 95-8424. 1995. write for info. (*0-9635812-7-9*) Sigler Print.

Citizen-Soldier of the American Revolution: The Diary of Benjamin Gilbert in Massachusetts & New York. Ed. by Rebecca D. Symmes. 1980. 8.95 (*0-917334-04-3*) Fenimore Hse Mus.

Citizen-Soldier Remembers 1942-1946: 149th Armored Signal Company of the 9th Armored Division. George E. McAvoy. (Illus.). 238p. 1991. 32.50 (*0-9630647-2-X*) Crawford Pr.

Citizen Soldiers: Oklahoma's National Guard. Kenny A. Franks. LC 83-40326. (Illus.). 264p. 1984. 28.95 (*0-8061-1862-8*) U of Okla Pr.

Citizen, State, & Social Welfare in Britain, 1830-1990. Geoffrey Finlayson. LC 93-28926. 1994. 69.00 (*0-19-822760-4*) OUP.

Citizen Survey Process. 1986. 11.95 (*0-88314-338-0*) AAHPERD.

Citizen Surveys: How to Do Them, How to Use Them, What They Mean. Thomas I. Miller & Michelle A. Miller. (Special Report Ser.). 213p. 1991. pap. 38.00 (*0-87326-920-9*) Intl City-Cnty Mgt.

Citizen Temple Community. J. Weinberg. Tr. by Daniel Smith-Christopher. (JSOT Supplement Ser.: No. 151). 140p. 1992. 20.00 (*1-85075-395-4*, Pub. by Sheffield Acad UK) CUP Services.

Citizen to Soldier: Australia Before the Great War: Recollections of Members of the First A.I.F. J. N. Dawes & L. L. Robson. 1977. 24.95 (*0-522-84124-4*) Intl Spec Bk.

Citizen Tom Paine. Howard Fast. 352p. 1987. pap. 10.95 (*0-8021-3064-X*) Grove-Atltic.

Citizen, Turn Back! A Russian-American Odyssey. Galina McVicker. (Illus.). 128p. (Orig.). 1993. 16.95 (*1-56474-076-5*); pap. 8.95 (*1-56474-070-6*) Fithian Pr.

*__Citizen Turner: The Wild Rise of an American Tycoon.__ Robert Goldberg & Gerald J. Goldberg. 672p. 1995. 27.00 (*0-15-118008-3*) HarBrace.

Citizen Worker: The Experience of Workers in the United States with Democracy & the Free Market During the Nineteenth Century. David Montgomery. 224p. (C). 1994. 22.95 (*0-521-42057-1*) Cambridge U Pr.

*__Citizen Worker: The Experience of Workers in the United States with Democracy & the Free Market During the Nineteenth Century.__ David Montgomery. 1995. pap. 13.95 (*0-521-48380-8*) Cambridge U Pr.

Citizen 13660. Mine Okubo. LC 82-20221. (Illus.). 226p. (Orig.). 1983. pap. 14.95 (*0-295-95989-4*) U of Wash Pr.

Citizen 13660. Ed. by Roger Daniels. LC 78-54830. (Asian Experience in North America Ser.). (Illus.). 1980. reprint ed. lib. bdg. 18.95 (*0-405-11287-4*) Ayer.

Citizens. Simon Schama. LC 89-40127. 976p. 1990. pap. 22.00 (*0-679-72610-1*, Vin) Random.

Citizens: A Chronicle of the French Revolution. Simon Schama. LC 88-45320. 512p. 1991. 39.50 (*0-394-55948-7*) Knopf.

Citizens: A Novel. Meyer Levin. LC 74-22793. reprint ed. 39.00 (*0-404-58447-0*) AMS Pr.

*__Citizens: Strengthening Global Civil Society.__ 1994. pap. 20.00 (*0-9644001-0-3*) CIVICUS.

Citizens Against Crime Vol. O2: An Assessment of the Neighborhood Watch Program in Washington, D.C. Jeffrey R. Henig. 1984. 4.00 (*0-317-04098-7*) GWU CWAS.

Citizens Against the MX: Public Languages in the Nuclear Age. Matthew Glass. 208p. (C). 1993. 29.95 (*0-252-01928-8*) U of Ill Pr.

Citizen's Alcohol & Other Drug Prevention Directory: Resources. 1991. lib. bdg. 75.00 (*0-8490-4351-4*) Gordon Pr.

Citizen's Alcohol & Other Drug Prevention Directory: Resources. 1993. lib. bdg. 350.00 (*0-8490-8919-0*) Gordon Pr.

Citizen's Alcohol & Other Drug Prevention Directory: Resources for Getting Involved. 261p. (C). 1992. pap. text ed. 39.95 (*1-56806-061-0*) Diane Pub.

Citizen's Alcohol & Other Drug Prevention Directory: Resources for Getting Involved. 1992. lib. bdg. 288.95 (*0-8490-8826-7*) Gordon Pr.

Citizen's Alcohol & Other Drug Prevention Directory: Resources for Getting Involved. 270p. 1990. per., pap. 13.00 (*0-16-021947-7*, S/N 017-024-013) USGPO.

Citizens Alert! Alternatives for Low-Profile Survival. Virgil A. Postlethwaite. Ed. by Paul M. Clemens. 80p. (Orig.). 1981. pap. text ed. 7.95 (*0-931892-02-3*) B Dolphin Pub.

Citizens & Clergy of Grasse: How Modernity Came to a Provencal Town. John F. Freeman & Roger L. Williams. LC 87-29811. (Studies in French Civilization: Vol. 2). (Illus.). 576p. 1989. lib. bdg. 119.95 (*0-88946-638-6*) E Mellen.

Citizens & Community: Political Support in a Representative Democracy. Allan Kornberg & Harold D. Clarke. (Studies in Comparative Politics). (Illus.). 304p. (C). 1992. 64.95 (*0-521-41678-7*) Cambridge U Pr.

Citizens & Foreigners of the Nacogdoches District, 1809-1836, Vol. II. Carolyn Ericson. LC 82-106713. 49p. (Orig.). 1985. pap. 7.50 (*0-911317-37-6*) Ericson Bks.

Citizens & Groups in Contemporary China. Ed. by Victor C. Falkenheim. (Michigan Monographs in Chinese Studies: No. 56). 320p. (Orig.). 1987. text ed. 17.50 (*0-89264-065-0*) Ctr Chinese Studies.

Citizens & Saints: Politics & Anti-Politics in Early British Socialism. Gregory Claeys. 384p. (C). 1989. 69.95 (*0-521-36490-6*) Cambridge U Pr.

Citizens & Soldiers: The Dilemmas of Military Service. Eliot A. Cohen. LC 84-14266. (Cornell Studies in Security Affairs). 227p. 1985. 39.95 (*0-8014-1581-0*) Cornell U Pr.

Citizens & Soldiers: The Dilemmas of Military Service. Eliot A. Cohen. LC 84-14266. (Cornell Studies in Security Affairs). 227p. 1990. reprint ed. pap. 13.95 (*0-8014-9719-1*) Cornell U Pr.

Citizens & Statesmen: A Study of Aristotle's Politics. Mary P. Nichols. 288p. 1991. pap. text ed. 22.00 (*0-8476-7703-6*) Rowman.

Citizens & Statesmen: A Study of Aristotle's Politics. Mary P. Nichols. 288p. (C). 1991. text ed. 54.50 (*0-8476-7702-8*) Rowman.

Citizens & Subjects: An Essay on British Politics. Anthony Wright. LC 93-12965. 256p. 1993. pap. 17.95 (*0-415-04964-4*, B2436) Routledge.

Citizens & the Environment: Case Studies in Popular Action. Lynton K. Caldwell et al. LC 75-31442. 479p. reprint ed. pap. 136.60 (*0-685-16401-2*, 2056222) Bks Demand.

Citizens & the Schools: Partners in Education. 12p. (Orig.). 1984. pap. 0.60 (*0-87652-068-9*, 021-00115) Am Assn Sch Admin.

*__Citizens & the State.__ Ed. by Hans-Dieter Klingemann & Dieter Fuchs. (Beliefs in Government Ser.: No. 1). (Illus.). 360p. 1995. 59.00 (*0-19-827955-8*) OUP.

Citizens & Waste. write for info. (*0-686-27466-0*) Tech Info Proj.

Citizens & Waste, 1. 2.00 (*0-686-27467-9*) Tech Info Proj.

Citizens Apart: A Portrait of Palestinians of Israel. Amina Minns & Nadia Hijab. 250p. 1990. 34.50 (*0-685-38700-3*, Pub. by I B Tauris UK) St Martin.

Citizens Apart: A Portrait of the Palestinians in Israel. Amina Minns & Nadia Hijab. 1991. 34.50 (*0-685-48183-2*, Pub. by I B Tauris UK) St Martin.

Citizens As Sovereigns. Paul H. Appleby. LC 62-10727. 224p. reprint ed. pap. 63.90 (*0-317-29314-1*, 2022378) Bks Demand.

Citizens at Last! The Woman Suffrage Movement in Texas. A. Elizabeth Taylor. (Illus.). 256p. 1987. 14.95 (*0-936650-04-4*) E C Temple.

Citizen's Charter: First Report 1992. HMSO Staff. (Command Paper Ser.: No. 2101). 80p. 1992. pap. 17.00 (*0-10-121012-4*, HM10124, Pub. by HMSO UK) UNIPUB.

Citizen's Choice. Ernest Barker. LC 72-300. (Essay Index Reprint Ser.). 1977. reprint ed. 19.95 (*0-8369-2784-2*) Ayer.

Citizens Club. Ted Meyer. 224p. (Orig.). 1983. pap. 2.50 (*0-9611140-0-2*) Mey-Hse Bks.

Citizens' Council: Organized Resistance to the Second Reconstruction, 1954-64. Neil R. McMillen. LC 94-18858. 1994. write for info. (*0-252-06441-0*) U of Ill Pr.

Citizen's Europe: Action Taken by the European Parliament to Create a European Community to Serve Its Citizens. European Communities Staff. 53p. 1992. pap. 7.00 (*92-823-0397-7*, AX-74-92-839-EN-C, Pub. by Europ Com) UNIPUB.

*__Citizens' Europe: In Search of a New Order.__ Ed. by Allan Rosas & Esko Antola. 272p. (C). 1995. 69.95 (*0-8039-7560-0*); pap. 21.95 (*0-8039-7561-9*) Sage.

*__Citizens for a Poodle-Free Montana.__ limited ed. Greg Leichner. Ed. by Tom Trusky. (Himingway Western Studies Ser.). (Illus.). 17p. (Orig.). 1995. 7.95 (*0-932129-22-6*) Heming W Studies.

Citizens for the Fatherland: Education, Educators, & Pedagogical Ideals in Eighteenth Century Russia. J. L. Black. (East European Monographs: No. 53). 273p. 1979. text ed. 57.00 (*0-914710-46-X*) East Eur Quarterly.

Citizen's Guide on How to Use the Freedom of Information Act & the Privacy Act in Requesting Government Documents. 1984. lib. bdg. 250.00 (*0-87700-532-X*) Revisionist Pr.

*__Citizen's Guide on Using the Freedom of Information Act & the Privacy Act of 1974 to Request Government Records.__ (Illus.). 70p. (Orig.). (C). 1994. pap. text ed. 20.00x (*0-7881-1298-8*) Diane Pub.

Citizen's Guide on Using the Freedom of Information Act & the Privacy Act of 1974 to Request Government Records, July 28, 1989. 3rd ed. 64p. 1989. pap. 1.75 (*0-16-006414-7*, S/N 052-071-008) USGPO.

Citizen's Guide to Air Pollution. David V. Bates. LC 72-75504. (Environmental Damage & Control in Canada Ser.: No. 2). (Illus.). 160p. reprint ed. pap. 45.60 (*0-7837-1162-X*, 2041691) Bks Demand.

Citizen's Guide to Cleveland. Leslie Kay. 56p. 1992. pap. 6.00 (*1-880746-06-9*) LOWV Cleve Educ.

Citizen's Guide to Fighting Government. Steven D. Symms. 1994. pap. 16.95 (*0-915463-63-6*, Jameson Bks) Green Hill.

*__Citizen's Guide to Guerrilla Warfare.__ 6th ed. Ed. by Alex Thorhoffen. (Illus.). 400p. (Orig.). 1994. pap. 45.00 (*1-877884-09-X*) Tech Group.

Citizen's Guide to Gun Control. Franklin E. Zimring & Gordon J. Hawkins. LC 87-5503. 224p. 1987. 19.95 (*0-02-934830-7*) Macmillan.

Citizen's Guide to Gun Control. Ed. by Franklin E. Zimring & Gordon J. Hawkins. 210p. 1992. pap. 14.95 (*0-02-897505-7*) Macmillan.

*__Citizen's Guide to NAFTA's Environmental Commission.__ Karl Spiecken et al. (Orig.). 1995. pap. 2.00 (*0-913890-93-6*) Friends of Earth.

Citizen's Guide to Planning. rev. ed. Herbert H. Smith. 208p. 1979. pap. 15.00 (*0-317-05973-4*) Am Plan Assn.

Citizen's Guide to Planning. 2nd rev. ed. Herbert H. Smith. 208p. 1979. pap. 16.95 (*0-318-12941-8*) Am Plan Assn.

Citizen's Guide to Planning. 3rd ed. Herbert H. Smith. LC 92-76067. 288p. 1993. lib. bdg. 36.00 (*0-918286-84-0*); pap. 24.95 (*0-918286-83-2*) Planners Pr.

Citizen's Guide to Plastic in the Ocean: More Than a Litter Problem. Kathryn J. O'Hara & Suzanne Iudicello. (Illus.). 140p. (Orig.). 1988. pap. write for info. (*0-9615294-2-3*) Ctr Env Educ.

Citizen's Guide to Promoting Toxic Waste Reduction. Lauren Kenworthy & Eric Schaeffer. LC 89-71650. 128p. 1990. pap. 15.00 (*0-918780-54-3*) INFORM NY.

Citizen's Guide to Radon: What It Is & What to Do about It. (OPA Ser.: No. 86-004). (Illus.). 13p. 1986. pap. 1.00 (*0-16-006440-6*, S/N 055-000-00258-4) USGPO.

Citizen's Guide to River Conservation. Rolf Diamant et al. LC 84-7799. (Illus.). 125p. (Orig.). reprint ed. pap. 35.70 (*0-7837-1210-3*, 2041742) Bks Demand.

Citizen's Guide to Scanning. Laura E. Quarantiello. 100p. 1992. pap. 19.95 (*0-936653-44-2*) Tiare Pubns.

Citizen's Guide to Sources for Marine & Coastal Information in Massachusetts. 5th ed. Ed. by Madeleine Hall-Arber & Karen Hartley. 179p. 1990. pap. text ed. 5.00 (*1-56172-000-3*) MIT Sea Grant.

Citizen's Guide to the Courts in the Washington Region. Council for Court Excellence Staff. (Illus.). 32p. (Orig.). 1990. pap. text ed. 5.00 (*0-940259-01-X*, TXU 399-229) Council Ct Excell.

Citizen's Guide to the Federal Budget: Understanding What Really Happens to Your Tax Dollars. John Heuser. Ed. by Diane Parker. LC 91-50985. 100p. 1992. pap. 9.95 (*0-88247-912-1*, 912) R & E Pubs.

Citizen's Guide to the New Tax Reforms: Fair Tax, Flat Tax, Simple Tax. Ed. by Joseph A. Pechman. 176p. 1985. 30.25 (*0-8476-7403-7*) Rowman.

Citizen's Guide to Zoning. Herbert H. Smith. LC 82-62237. (Illus.). 242p. 1983. pap. 22.95 (*0-918286-28-X*) Planners Pr.

Citizen's Guide to Zoning, 10 copies, Set. Herbert H. Smith. LC 82-62237. (Illus.). 242p. 1983. pap. 15.00 (*0-685-06455-7*) Planners Pr.

Citizen's Handbook. Larry Moffi. LC 89-8626. 48p. (Orig.). 1989. pap. 6.95 (*0-914061-10-0*) Orchises Pr.

Citizen's Handbook. T. J. Stiles. 288p. (Orig.). 1993. mass mkt. 4.99 (*0-425-13842-9*) Berkley Pub.

Citizen's Handbook. T. J. Stiles. 304p. (Orig.). 1994. pap. 12.00 (*0-425-14387-2*, Berkley Trade) Berkley Pub.

Citizen's Handbook on Jobs. Robert Stumberg. 80p. 1988. 10.00 (*0-685-56599-8*) CPA Washington.

Citizens Handbook on Maine Courts. National Center for State Courts Staff. 77p. 1976. write for info. (*0-318-61219-4*, MAB-021) Natl Ctr St Courts.

Citizen's Handbook on Solar Energy. rev. ed. Anita Gunn. 90p. 1977. 3.50 (*0-318-16178-8*); 15.00 (*0-318-16179-6*) USPIRG.

Citizen's Handbook on Water Quality Standards. Jessica Landman. 1987. 4.00 (*0-318-23632-X*) NRDC Newsletter.

Citizens in Action. League of Women Voters of Minnesota Staff. 1991. 7.50 (*1-877889-02-4*) LWV MN.

Citizens in Action. rev. ed. League of Women Voters of Minnesota Education Fund Staff. (Illus.). 78p. 1985. pap. text ed. 6.50 (*0-939816-03-2*) LWV MN.

Citizens in Conflict: Prints & Photographs of the American Civil War. Sally Pierce & Temple D. Smith. LC 81-70895. (Illus.). 50p. (Orig.). 1981. pap. 7.50 (*0-934552-38-X*) Boston Athenaeum.

Citizen's Inquiry: The Opsahl Report on Northern Ireland. Ed. by Andy Pollak. (Illus.). 464p. 1993. pap. 18.95 (*1-874675-08-2*, Pub. by Lilliput Pr Ltd IE) Irish Bks Media.

Citizens Media Directory. Ed. by Pamela Draves. 1977. pap. 3.50 (*0-9603466-3-5*) T R A C.

Citizens Media Directory. Ed. by Pamela Draves. 1980. write for info. (*0-318-54564-0*) T R A C.

Citizens of Long Ago: Essays on Life & Letters in the Roman Empire. Adeline B. Hawes. LC 67-23228. (Essay Index Reprint Ser.). 1977. reprint ed. 19.95 (*0-8369-0520-2*) Ayer.

Citizens of the Cosmos: Life's Unfolding from Conception Through Death to Rebirth. Beredene Jocelyn. (Freedeeds Library). (Illus.). 198p. 1983. reprint ed. 17.50 (*0-8334-1008-3*, Freedeeds Libr) Garber Comm.

Citizens of the Kingdom. Billie Friel. 1992. pap. 9.99 (*0-8054-6025-X*) Broadman.

*__Citizens of the World.__ Nicolas Faure & Andre Klopman. 192p. Date not set. 49.95 (*1-881616-52-5*) Dist Art Pubs.

*__Citizens of the World: London Merchants & the Integration of the British Atlantic Community, 1735-1785.__ David Hancock. (Illus.). 416p. (C). 1995. 59.95 (*0-521-47430-2*) Cambridge U Pr.

Citizens of This Country: The Asian-British. Mary Stopes-Roe & Raymond Cochrane. (Multilingual Matters Ser.: No. 68). 286p. 1990. 69.00 (*1-85359-101-7*, Pub. by Multilingual Matters UK); pap. 19.95 (*1-85359-100-9*, Pub. by Multilingual Matters UK) Taylor & Francis.

Citizen's Part in Government & Experiments in Government & the Essentials of the Constitution, 2 vols. in 1. Elihu Root. LC 73-19174. (Politics & People Ser.). 220p. 1974. reprint ed. 19.95 (*0-405-05895-0*) Ayer.

Citizens, Parties, & the State: A Reappraisal. Alan Ware. 275p. 1988. text ed. 45.00 (*0-691-07763-0*) Princeton U Pr.

Citizens, Political Communication & Interest Groups: Environmental Organizations in Canada & the United States. John C. Pierce et al. LC 92-15686. (Praeger Series in Political Communication). 256p. 1992. text ed. 49.95 (*0-275-93579-5*, C3579, Praeger Pubs) Greenwood.

*__Citizens, Politics, & Social Communication: Information & Influence in an Election Campaign.__ Robert Huckfeldt & John Sprague. (Illus.). 352p. (C). 1995. 49.95 (*0-521-45298-8*) Cambridge U Pr.

Citizens Suits: Private Enforcement of Federal Pollution Control Laws. Environmental Law Institute Staff & Jeffrey G. Miller. LC 86-2463. (Federal Practice Ser.). 306p. 1987. text ed. 125.00 (*0-471-85508-1*) Wiley.

Citizens Training Handbook-Manual de Formacion Ciudadana: Discipline-Moral-Covism-Urbanity. Demetrio Perez, Jr. (Illus.). 315p. (ENG & SPA.). (J). 1991. 25.00 (*0-9628780-0-6*) Ed Lncln-Mrt.

*__Citizen's Wage: The State & the Elderly in Canada, 1900-1951.__ James G. Snell. (Illus.). 338p. (C). 1995. 60.00 (*0-8020-0737-6*); pap. 18.95 (*0-8020-7792-7*) U of Toronto Pr.

Citizens Who Commit Murder: A Psychiatric Study. Warren S. Wille. LC 73-376. (Illus.). 280p. 1975. 10.60 (*0-87527-128-6*) Green.

Citizens Without Sovereignty: Equally & Sociability in French Thought, 1670-1789. Daniel Gordon. LC 94-5876. 1994. 39.50 (*0-691-05699-4*) Princeton U Pr.

Citizens 7 Cities: Urban Policy Reconsidered. Dilys Hill. 256p. 1994. pap. 39.00 (*0-13-302720-1*) P-H.

Citizenship. Ed. by Andrews. (C). 1991. pap. 19.95 (*0-85315-733-2*, Pub. by Lawrence & Wishart UK) Humanities.

Citizenship. J. M. Barbalet. LC 88-27718. (Concepts in Social Thought Ser.). 119p. (Orig.). 1989. text ed. 39.95 (*0-8166-1775-9*); pap. text ed. 13.95 (*0-8166-1776-7*) U of Minn Pr.

C

1278

An Asterisk (*) at the beginning of an entry indicates that the title is appearing in BIP for the first time.

An Asterisk (*) at the beginning of an entry indicates that the title is appearing in BIP for the first time.

1279

C

*City Boys: Cagney, Bogart, Garfield. Robert Sklar. 1994. pap. 14.95 (0-691-00614-8) Princeton U Pr.

City Bred Daughter. Jeanne L. Schuler. (Illus.). 12p. (Orig.). 1982. pap. 1.50 (0-910083-08-8) Heritage Trails.

City Builder. George Konrad. 192p. 1987. mass mkt. 6.95 (0-14-009947-6, Penguin Bks) Viking Penguin.

City Builders: One Hundred Years of Union Carpentry in Portland, Oregon 1883-1983. Craig Wollner. 180p. 1990. 24.95 (0-87595-198-8) Oregon Hist.

City Builders: Property, Politics, & Planning in London & New York. Susan S. Fainstein. LC 93-17858. (Studies in Urban & Social Change). 328p. 1994. 54.95 (0-631-18243-8); pap. 21.95 (0-631-18244-6) Blackwell Pubs.

*City-Building in America. Anthony M. Orum. LC 94-38969. (C). 1995. text ed. 65.00 (0-8133-0842-9); pap. text ed. 19.95 (0-8133-0843-7) Westview.

*City Business Profiles: Kansas City. Community Communications Staff. 1994. pap. 19.95 (0-9630029-9-6) Community Comm.

*City Business Profiles: Mobile. Community Communications Staff. 1994. pap. 19.95 (1-885352-02-6) Community Comm.

*City Business Profiles: Tuscaloosa. Community Communications Staff. 1994. pap. 19.95 (1-885352-05-0) Community Comm.

City by Design. Peter R. Moberly. LC 93-93802. 144p. (Orig.). 1994. pap. 9.50 (1-56002-326-0, Univ Edtns) Aegina Pr.

*City by Silt Sea. Shane Hensley. 1994. 25.00 (1-56076-882-7) TSR Inc.

City by the Bay. Elisa Kleven. (Art Card Ser.). 1994. boxed 5.95 (0-8118-0563-8) Chronicle Bks.

*City by the Bay. Antony Shuggar. 128p. 1994. 14.98 (0-8317-7981-0) Smithmark.

City by the Bay: A Magical Journey Around San Francisco. Junior League of San Francisco Staff & Tricia Brown. LC 92-32104. (Illus.). (J). 1993. 12.95 (0-8118-0233-7) Chronicle Bks.

City by the Sea. Debra Doyle & James Macdonald. LC 89-5213. (Circle of Magic Ser.). (Illus.). 144p. (J). (gr. 5-9). 1990. lib. bdg. 9.89 (0-8167-1830-X); pap. text ed. 2.95 (0-8167-1831-8) Troll Assocs.

City Called July. large type ed. Howard Engel. 481p. 1989. 17.95 (0-7089-1957-X) Ulverscroft.

City Car Book. Illus. by Mark Barry. 12p. (J). (ps). 1992. 3.95 (1-56828-004-1) Red Jacket Pr.

City Cat: How to Live Healthily & Happily with Your Indoor Pet. Roz Riddle. 1987. mass mkt. 4.99 (0-449-21022-7, Crest) Fawcett.

City Cat, Country Cat. Patricia Cleveland-Peck. LC 91-42402. (Illus.). 32p. (J). (ps). 1992. 14.00 (0-688-11644-2); lib. bdg. 13.93 (0-688-11645-0) Morrow Jr Bks.

*City Cat Goes to the Country. Dorothy Dunton. (J). 1995. 8.95 (0-8062-5150-6) Carlton.

City Cats. J. C. Suares. 1994. 14.95 (0-00-255251-5) Collins SF.

City Centre Planning & Public Transport. 1988. 69.95 (0-7476-0006-6) Chapman & Hall.

City Centre Redevelopment see Progress in Planning

City Chamberlain. Jack Rudman. (Career Examination Ser.: C-2981). 1994. pap. 34.95 (0-8373-2981-7) Nat Learn.

City Characteristics, Migration, & Urban Development Policies in India. Mahendra K. Premi & Judith A. Tom. LC 85-13102. (Papers of the East-West Population Institute: No. 92). vii, 127p. 1985. pap. 3.00 (0-86638-061-2) EW Ctr HI.

City Charter Revision. rev. ed. (Technical Topics Ser.: No. 38). 1993. pap. 5.00 (0-317-05700-6) MI Municipal.

City Choices: Education & Housing. Kenneth K. Wong. LC 89-4587. (SUNY Series in Urban Public Policy). 218p. 1990. 59.50 (0-7914-0225-8); pap. 19.95 (0-7914-0226-6) State U NY Pr.

City Class & Capital: New Developments in the Political Economy of Cities & Regions. Ed. by Michael Harloe & Elizabeth Lebas. LC 82-988. 224p. (Orig.). (C). 1982. pap. 18.50 (0-8419-0794-3) Holmes & Meier.

City, Class & Culture: Studies of Cultural Formation & Social Policy in Victorian Manchester. Ed. by Alan J. Kidd & Ken Roberts. LC 85-2988. (C). 1988. text ed. 49.95 (0-7190-1768-8, Pub. by Manchester Univ Pr UK) St Martin.

City, Class & Trade: Social & Economic Change in the Third World. Nigel Harris. 250p. 1991. text ed. 59.50 (1-85043-301-1, Pub. by I B Tauris UK) St Martin.

City Classification Handbook: Methods & Application. Ed. by Brian J. Berry. LC 71-171911. (Wiley Series in Urban Research). 406p. reprint ed. pap. 115.80 (0-317-09217-0, 2022500) Bks Demand.

*City Codes: Reading the Modern Urban Novel. Hana Wirth-Nesher. (Illus.). 256p. (C). 1995. write for info. (0-521-47314-4) Cambridge U Pr.

City Comes of Age: Chicago in the 1890's. Susan E. Hirsch. 1991. pap. 17.95 (0-913820-13-X) Chicago Hist.

*City Comforts: How to Build an Urban Village. David Sucher. (Illus.). 176p. (Orig.). 1994. pap. 18.00 (0-9642680-0-0) City Comforts Pr.

City Comptroller. Jack Rudman. (Career Examination Ser.: C-1746). 1994. pap. 39.95 (0-8373-1746-0) Nat Learn.

City Connection: Migration & Family Interdependence in the Philippines. Lillian Trager. 1988. pap. 15.95 (0-472-06390-1) U of Mich Pr.

City Country. Vyt Bakaitis. 146p. 1991. pap. 11.95 (0-9628181-2-7) Black Thistle Pr.

City-Country Miners: Some Northern California Veins. Ed. by Michael Helm. LC 82-11968. (Illus.). 256p. 1982. pap. 7.95 (0-933944-03-9) City Miner Bks.

City, County, Town & Township Index to the 1850 Federal Census Schedules. J. Carlyle Parker. (Gale Genealogy & Local History Ser.: Vol. 6). 215p. 1990. reprint ed. fiche 9.95 (0-934153-06-X, OCLZ 27863673) Marietta Pub.

*City Crime Rankings: Crime in Metropolitan America. Ed. by Kathleen O. Morgan et al. 300p. (Orig.). 1995. pap. 19.95 (1-56692-307-7) Morgan Quitno Corp.

*City Cuisine. Mary S. Milliken. 1994. pap. 14.95 (0-688-13177-8) Hearst Bks.

*City Culture & the Madrigal at Venice. Martha Feldman. LC 94-31376. 1995. 60.00 (0-520-08314-8) U CA Pr.

City Deal Making. Terry Lassar. LC 90-70877. 1990. 37.95 (0-87420-704-5) Urban Land.

City Different & the Palace. Rosemary Nusbaum. LC 78-17591. (Illus.). 1978. pap. 6.95 (0-913270-79-2) Sunstone Pr.

City Directories of the United States, Pre-1860 to 1901. Ed. by Research Publications, Inc. Staff. 487p. 1984. 155.00 (0-89235-081-4) Res Pubns CT.

City Dog. Karla Kuskin. LC 93-8252. (Illus.). (J). (ps-3). 1994. 14.95 (0-395-66138-2, Clarion Bks) HM.

City Dogs. J. C. Suares. 1994. 14.95 (0-00-255252-3) Collins SF.

City Executives: Leadership Roles, Work Characteristics, & Time Management. David N. Ammons & Charldean Newell. LC 88-15380. (Leadership Studies). 224p. (C). 1988. 64.50 (0-88706-957-6); pap. 21.95 (0-88706-958-4) State U NY Pr.

City Expenditures in the United States: Supplement, Appendix E. Harvey E. Brazer. (Occasional Papers: No. 66). 94p. 1959. reprint ed. 24.50 (0-87014-380-8); reprint ed. mic. film 20.00 (0-685-61321-6) Natl Bur Econ Res.

City Financial Insurance Register (U. K.), 1988-89 (United Kingdom) Witherby's Editorial Staff. (C). 1988. 500.00 (0-685-33734-0, Pub. by Witherby & Co UK) St Mut.

City for Lincoln. John R. Tunis. 392p. (J). (gr. 3-7). 1989. pap. 3.95 (0-15-218580-1, Odyssey) HarBrace.

City for Ransom. Judith A. Green. (Adult Basic Learner Ser.). (Illus.). 225p. (Orig.). 1981. pap. text ed. 6.50 (0-89061-216-1, 205) Jamestown Pubs.

City Form & Everyday Life: Toronto's Centrification & Critical Social Practice. Jon Caulfield. (Illus.). 256p. (C). 1994. 55.00 (0-8020-2997-3); pap. 17.95 (0-8020-7448-0) U of Toronto Pr.

City Form & Natural Process. Michael Hough. 304p. 1989. pap. 16.95 (0-415-04390-5, A3671) Routledge.

*City Full of People: Men & Women of London 1650-1750. Peter Earle. 321p. 1995. 50.00 (0-413-68170-X) Trafalgar.

City Fun. Margaret Hillert. (Illus.). (J). (ps-00). 1981. lib. bdg. 8.99 (0-8136-5071-2, TK2286); pap. 4.79 (0-8136-5571-4, TK2287) Modern Curr.

City Games: The Evolution of American Urban Society & the Rise of Sports. Steven A. Riess. (Sport & Society Ser.). (Illus.). 368p. 1991. pap. 13.95 (0-252-06216-7) U of Ill Pr.

City Gardener's Cookbook: Totally Fresh, Mostly Vegetarian, Decidedly Delicious Recipes from Seattle's P-Patches. Ed. by N. Allen et al. (Illus.). 256p. (Orig.). 1994. pap. 14.95 (0-912365-99-4) Sasquatch Bks.

City Gardener's Handbook: From Balcony to Backyard. Linda Yang. LC 89-43422. (Illus.). 304p. 1990. 26.95 (0-394-58371-X) Random.

City Gardens: A Survey of Open Spaces in the City of London. Ed. by Brian Plummer & Don Shewan. (Illus.). 256p. 1992. text ed. 65.00 (1-85293-219-8, Pub. by Pinter Pubs UK) St Martin.

City Girl. Mary L. Dille. 224p. (Orig.). 1993. pap. 2.95 (1-56597-094-2, Kismet) Meteor Pub.

City Girl. Linda Lerner. 32p. (Orig.). 1990. pap. text ed. 4.00 (0-935839-09-7) Vergin Pr.

City Girl, Country Girl. Marilyn Levy. (Orig.). 1993. mass mkt. 3.99 (0-449-70424-6, Juniper) Fawcett.

City Girl Who Went to Sea. Rosmarie Hausherr. LC 89-27236. (Illus.). 80p. (J). (gr. 3-6). 1990. text ed. 14.95 (0-02-743421-4, Four Winds Pr) S&S Childrens.

City Government: The Record of the Milwaukee Experiment. Daniel W. Hoan. LC 74-14353. 365p. 1975. reprint ed. text ed. 65.00 (0-8371-7793-6, HOCI, Greenwood Pr) Greenwood.

City Government Finances: A Statistical Profile (1990-91) (Illus.). 123p. (Orig.). (C). 1994. pap. text ed. 45.00 (0-7881-0235-4) Diane Pub.

City Government in the United States. Frank J. Goodnow. LC 73-11903. (Metropolitan America Ser.). 330p. 1974. reprint ed. 23.95 (0-405-05394-0) Ayer.

City Government in the United States. Frank J. Goodnow. LC 91-55449. (American State Ser.). 315p. 1991. reprint ed. lib. bdg. 53.00 (0-912004-98-3) W W Gaunt.

City Government of Philadelphia. Edward P. Allinson & Boies Penrose. LC 78-63768. (Johns Hopkins University. Studies in the Social Sciences. Thirtieth Ser. 1912: 1-2). reprint ed. 11.50 (0-404-61035-8) AMS Pr.

City Green. DyAnne DiSalvo-Ryan. LC 93-27117. (Illus.). 32p. (J). (gr. k up). 1994. 15.00 (0-688-12786-X); lib. bdg. 14.93 (0-688-12787-8) Morrow Jr Bks.

City Growth in the United States, England & Wales, 1820-1861: The Effects of Location, Size & Economic Structure on Interurban Variations in Demographic Growth. John B. Sharpless. Ed. by Stuart Bruchey. LC 76-45115. (Nineteen Seventy-Seven Dissertations Ser.). 1977. lib. bdg. 26.95 (0-405-09926-6) Ayer.

City Hall Goes Abroad: The Foreign Policy of Local Politics. Heidi H. Hobbs. 120p. (C). 1994. text ed. 29.95 (0-8039-5522-7); pap. text ed. 14.95 (0-8039-5523-5) Sage.

City High Schools: A Recognition of Progress. Ford Foundation Staff. LC 84-10258. (Ford Foundation Report Series on Higher Education in the Cities). (Illus.). 107p. (Orig.). 1984. pap. (0-916584-23-2) Ford Found.

City Homes on Country Lanes: Philosophy & Practice of the Home-in-a-Garden. William E. Smythe. LC 73-2912. (Metropolitan America Ser.). (Illus.). 332p. 1974. 23.95 (0-405-05425-4) Ayer.

City Hospitals: The Undercare of the Underprivileged. Harry F. Dowling. 256p. 1982. 34.50 (0-674-13197-5) HUP.

City in African-American Literature. Intro. by Yoshinobu Hakutani & Robert Butler. LC 94-17251. 272p. 1995. 39.50 (0-8386-3565-2) Fairleigh Dickinson.

City in Ancient Israel. Frank S. Frick. LC 77-21984. (Society of Biblical Literature. Dissertation Ser.: No. 36). 296p. reprint ed. pap. 84.40 (0-8357-9566-7, 2017500) Bks Demand.

City in Brazilian Literature. Elizabeth Lowe. LC 80-66823. 360p. 1982. 34.50 (0-8386-3009-X) Fairleigh Dickinson.

City in Communist China. Ed. by John W. Lewis. LC 78-130828. 120p. reprint ed. pap. 30.00 (0-8357-4633-X, 2037562) Bks Demand.

City in Crisis: A Report by the Special Advisor to the Board of Police Commissioners on the Civil Disorder in Los Angeles, 2 vols., Set. (Illus.). 464p. (Orig.). 1992. pap. 30.00 (1-884614-05-1) Police Found.

City in Crisis: A Report by the Special Advisor to the Board of Police Commissioners on the Civil Disorder in Los Angeles, 2 vols., Vol. 1. (Illus.). 222p. (Orig.). 1992. pap. write for info. (1-884614-07-8) Police Found.

City in Crisis: A Report by the Special Advisor to the Board of Police Commissioners on the Civil Disorder in Los Angeles, 2 vols., Vol. 2. (Illus.). 240p. (Orig.). 1992. pap. write for info. (1-884614-08-6) Police Found.

City in History: Its Origins, Its Transformations & Its Prospects. Lewis Mumford. LC 61-7689. 1968. reprint ed. pap. 22.95 (0-15-618035-9, Harvest Bks) HarBrace.

City in Indian History. Ed. by Indu Gan & Indu Banga. (C). 1991. 25.00 (0-945921-17-9, Pub. by S Asia Pubs II) S Asia.

City in Late Antiquity. Ed. by John Rich. LC 91-36367. (Leicester-Nottingham Studies in Ancient Society). 256p. 1992. 59.95 (0-415-06855-X, A7464) Routledge.

City in Late Imperial China. Ed. by G. William Skinner. LC 75-184. (Studies in Chinese Society). (Illus.). xviii, 820p. 1977. 79.50 (0-8047-0892-4) Stanford U Pr.

City in Late Imperial China. George W. Skinner. LC 75-184. (Studies in Chinese Society). 111p. reprint ed. pap. 30.00 (0-7837-6438-3, 2046438) Bks Demand.

City in Late Imperial Russia. Ed. by Michael F. Hamm. LC 84-43082. (Indiana-Michigan Series in Russian & East European Studies). (Illus.). 352p. 1986. 29.95 (0-253-31370-8) Ind U Pr.

City in Russian History. Ed. by Michael F. Hamm. LC 75-3544. 361p. reprint ed. pap. 102.90 (0-685-20787-0, 2030053) Bks Demand.

City in Slang: New York Life & Popular Speech. Irving L. Allen. LC 92-9377. (Illus.). 320p. (C). 1993. 30.00 (0-19-507591-9) OUP.

City in Slang: New York Life & Popular Speech. Irving L. Allen. (Illus.). 320p. 1995. reprint ed. pap. 12.95 (0-19-509265-1) OUP.

City in the Ancient World. Mason Hammond. Ed. by Lester Bartson. LC 73-180153. (Studies in Urban History). (Illus.). 633p. 1972. 46.50 (0-674-13180-0) HUP.

City in the Desert. Oleg Grabar et al. (Middle East Monographs: Vols. 23 & 24). 536p. 1978. pap. 45.00 (0-674-13195-9) HUP.

City in the Greek & Roman World. E. J. Owens. (Illus.). 224p. 1992. pap. 15.95 (0-415-08224-2, A7630) Routledge.

City in the Greek & Roman World: Ancient Town Planning. J. E. Owens. 224p. 1990. 52.50 (0-415-01896-X, A4870) Routledge.

*City in the Making: Progress, People & Perils in Victorian Toronto. Frederick H. Armstrong. (Illus.). 360p. Date not set. 29.99 (0-614-06784-7) Dun.

City in the Republic: Antebellum New York & the Origins of Machine Politics. Amy Bridges. LC 86-47994. (Illus.). 224p. 1987. reprint ed. pap. 13.95 (0-8014-9392-7) Cornell U Pr.

City in the Sahara. Jules Verne. 1960. 4.95 (0-685-06545-6) Assoc Bk.

City in the Sand: Ocean City, Maryland, & the People Who Built It. Mary Corddry. (Illus.). 207p. 1991. 19.95 (0-87033-420-4, Tidewtr Pubs) Cornell Maritime.

City in the Sun: The Japanese Concentration Camp at Poston, Arizona. Paul Bailey. (Illus.). 1979. 24.95 (0-87026-026-X) Westernlore.

City in the Village. Harold Brookfield et al. (Illus.). 212p. 1991. 56.00 (0-19-588976-2, 12239) OUP.

City in the Woods: The Life & Design of an American Camp Meeting on Martha's Vineyard. Ellen Weiss. (Illus.). 186p. 1987. 32.50 (0-19-504163-1) OUP.

City in Transition: Prospects & Policies for New York, Final Report of the Temporary Commission on City Finances. 1978. pap. 7.50 (0-685-48606-0) Ayer.

City in Transition: Prospects & Policies for New York, Final Report of the Temporary Commission on City Finances. 1978. lib. bdg. 18.95 (0-405-10526-6) Ayer.

City in War: American Views on Barcelona & the Spanish Civil War, 1936-39. Ed. by James W. Cortada. LC 84-20302. (Illus.). 224p. 1985. 40.00 (0-8420-2229-5) Scholarly Res Inc.

City in Which I Love You. Li-Young Lee. (American Poets Continuum Ser.: No. 20). 80p. 1991. 18.00 (0-918526-82-5); pap. 10.00 (0-918526-83-3) BOA Edns.

*City Invasions: 14 International Projects for Vienna. 272p. 1994. 89.00 (0-8176-5110-1) Birkhauser.

City Is Our Farm: Seven Migrant Ijebu Yoruba Families. 2nd ed. Dan R. Aronson. 224p. 1978. pap. text ed. 18.95 (0-87073-563-2) Transaction Pubs.

City Junket. Kenward Elmslie. LC 86-73202. 96p. (Orig.). 1987. pap. 8.50 (0-917453-13-1) Bamberger.

City Junket. limited ed. Kenward Elmslie. LC 86-73202. 96p. (Orig.). 1987. Signed Ltd. ed. student ed, pap. 25.00 (0-917453-14-X) Bamberger.

*City Junket: A Play. Kenward Elmslie. 87p. 1994. lib. bdg. 23.00 (0-8095-6510-2) Borgo Pr.

City Kids: Raise Kids in Urban Areas - From Cincinnati to Seattle & Have Fun Doing It. Susan P. Haven & Valerie Monroe. (Illus.). 256p. 1987. 15.95 (0-671-60208-X, Fireside) S&S Trade.

City Kid's Field Guide. Ethan Herberman. (J). (gr. 3 up). 1989. pap. 14.95 (0-671-67749-7, S&S Bks Young Read); pap. 5.95 (0-671-67746-2, S&S Bks Young Read) S&S Childrens.

City Kids Speak on Prejudice. (City Kids Speak Ser.). (Illus.). 48p. (J). (gr. 3-7). 1994. pap. 5.99 (0-679-86552-7) Random Bks Yng Read.

City Kids Speak on Real Love. (City Kids Speak Ser.). (Illus.). 48p. (J). (gr. 3-7). 1994. pap. 5.99 (0-679-86553-5) Random Bks Yng Read.

City Life: A Collection of Poetry. Frederick Feirstein. 85p. 1991. pap. 10.95 (0-934257-76-0) Story Line.

City Life: A Perspective from Baltimore, 1968-1978. Paul F. Evans. LC 79-54852. (Illus.). 1981. 20.00 (0-935132-01-5); pap. 15.00 (0-935132-00-7) C H Fairfax.

*City Life: Urban Expectations in a New World. Witold Rybczynski. 1995. 23.00 (0-684-81302-5) S&S Trade.

City Lights: An Introduction to Urban Studies. E. Barbara Phillips & Richard T. LeGates. (Illus.). (C). 1981. pap. text ed. 29.95 (0-19-502797-3) OUP.

*City Lights: Urban-Suburban Life in a Global Society. 2nd ed. E. Barbara Phillips. (Illus.). 544p. (C). 1995. pap. text ed. 35.00 (0-19-505689-2) OUP.

City Lights Books: A Descriptive Bibliography. Ralph T. Cook. Ed. by Lori A. Cook. (Illus.). 361p. 1992. 39.50 (0-8108-2621-6) Scarecrow.

City Lights (Five Issues), Set. Ed. by Peter Martin. (Avant-Garde Magazines Ser.). 368p. 1974. reprint ed. 36.95 (0-405-01758-8) Ayer.

City Lights Pocket Poets Series: A Descriptive Bibliography. Ralph T. Cook. 104p. 1982. lib. bdg. 22.50 (0-910938-90-3); pap. 12.50 (0-910938-89-X) McGilvery.

City Lights Review, No. 2. Ed. by Lawrence Ferlinghetti & Nancy J. Peters. (Illus.). 208p. 1988. pap. 9.95 (0-87286-221-6) City Lights.

City Lights Review, No. 3. Ed. by Lawrence Ferlinghetti & Nancy J. Peters. (Illus.). 214p. 1989. pap. 10.00 (0-87286-241-0) City Lights.

City Lights Review, No. 4. Ed. by Lawrence Ferlinghetti & Nancy Peters. 1990. pap. 10.95 (0-87286-253-4) City Lights.

City Limits. Paul E. Peterson. LC 80-29043. 288p. (C). 1981. lib. bdg. 27.50 (0-226-66292-6); pap. text ed. 11.95 (0-226-66293-4) U Ch Pr.

City Limits: Emerging Constraints on Urban Growth. Kathleen Newland. 1980. pap. write for info. (0-916468-37-2) Worldwatch Inst.

City Limits: Images of Boston in Transition. Kelly Wise et al. (Illus.). 160p. 1987. 30.00 (0-317-55341-0) NE U Pr.

City Limits Blues. Dale Pendell. 20p. 1986. 5.00 (1-882623-02-9) Exiled-Am Pr.

City Looking Glass: A Philadelphia Comedy. Robert M. Bird. LC 74-177511. 1972. reprint ed. 23.95 (0-405-08271-1, Pub. by Blom Pubns UK) Ayer.

*City Madam. fac. ed. Philip Massinger. Ed. by Cyrus Hoy. LC 64-11357. (Regents Renaissance Drama Ser.). 127p. 1994. pap. 36.20 (0-7837-7338-2, 2047291) Bks Demand.

City Magic. Jocobo. (Illus.). 66p. 1987. 6.95 (0-929436-00-8) Eyesburg Pr.

City Management Institute, First: Proceedings. 46p. 1975. pap. 3.00 (0-89940-053-1) LBJ Sch Pub Aff.

City Manager: A New Profession. Harry A. Toulmin, Jr. LC 73-11936. (Metropolitan America Ser.). 328p. 1974. reprint ed. 23.95 (0-405-05428-9) Ayer.

City Managers & School Superintendents: Response to Community Conflict. Harmon Zeigler & Jane Reisman. LC 84-15973. 224p. 1984. text ed. 55.00 (0-275-91296-5, C1296, Praeger Pubs) Greenwood.

City Managers in Politics: An Analysis of Manager Tenure & Termination. Gladys M. Kammerer et al. LC 62-63138. (University of Florida Monographs: Social Sciences: No. 13). 99p. reprint ed. pap. 28.30 (0-7837-4938-4, 2044604) Bks Demand.

City Man's Guide to the Farm Problem. Willard W. Cochrane. LC 65-20831. 262p. reprint ed. pap. 74.70 (0-7837-2968-5, 2057486) Bks Demand.

City, Marriage, Tournament: Arts of Rule in Late Medieval Scotland. Louise O. Fradenburg. LC 91-12976. (Illus.). 406p. (Orig.). 1991. lib. bdg. 49.75 (0-299-12950-0); pap. 19.95 (0-299-12954-3) U of Wis Pr.

City Money: Political Processes, Fiscal Strain, & Retrenchment. Terry Clark & Lorna Ferguson. LC 83-7735. 384p. 1983. text ed. 67.50 (0-231-05688-5) Col U Pr.

City Mouse - Country Mouse. John Wallner. (J). (ps-3). 1989. pap. 19.95 (0-590-73281-1) Scholastic Inc.

City Mouse - Country Mouse & Two More Mouse Tales from Aesop. Illus. by Marian Parry. (J). (gr. 2-3). 1989. 28.67 (0-590-65228-1) Scholastic Inc.

1280

An Asterisk (*) at the beginning of an entry indicates that the title is appearing in BIP for the first time.

An Asterisk (*) at the beginning of an entry indicates that the title is appearing in BIP for the first time.

1281

City of the Red Plague, Soviet Rule in Baltic Town. Georgii K. Popov. LC 75-35059. (Russian Studies: Perspectives on the Revolution). (Illus.). 343p. 1986. reprint ed. lib. bdg. 29.15 (*0-88355-439-9*) Hyperion Conn.

City of the Right: Urban Applications of American Conservative Thought. Gerald L. Houseman. LC 81-6345. (Contributions in Political Science Ser.: No. 67). ix, 209p. 1982. text ed. 55.00 (*0-313-23181-8*, HCI/, Greenwood Pr) Greenwood.

City of the Saints. Richard F. Burton. LC 72-134390. (BCL Ser. II). (Illus.). reprint ed. 82.50 (*0-404-08433-8*) AMS Pr.

City of the Saints. Richard F. Burton. (Illus.). 589p. 1990. reprint ed. pap. 19.95 (*0-87081-191-6*) Univ Pr Colo.

City of the Sorcerers. M. H. Herbert. 320p. (Orig.). 1994. pap. 4.95 (*1-56076-876-2*) TSR Inc.

City of the Sultan: And Domestic Manners of the Turks in 1836, 2 vols., Set. Julia Pardoe. LC 77-87633. reprint ed. 45.00 (*0-404-16540-0*) AMS Pr.

City of the Sun see Famous Utopias of the Renaissance

City of Tomorrow & Its Planning. Le Corbusier. 352p. 1987. reprint ed. pap. 8.95 (*0-486-25332-5*) Dover.

City of Trees: The Complete Field Guide to the Trees of Washington, D. C. rev. ed. Melanie Choukas-Bradley & Polly Alexander. LC 86-20912. (Illus.). 394p. 1987. pap. 14.95 (*0-8018-3320-5*) Johns Hopkins.

City of Trembling Leaves. Walter V. Clark. LC 91-31158. (Western Literature Ser.). 712p. 1991. reprint ed. pap. 21.00 (*0-87417-180-6*) U of Nev Pr.

City of Truth. James Morrow. LC 92-43161. 1993. pap. 7.95 (*0-15-618042-1*) HarBrace.

City of Victory: Vijayanagara, the Medieval Hindu Capital of Southern India. John Gollings. (Illus.). 128p. 1991. 49.95 (*0-89381-467-9*) Aperture.

***City of Villages: The Emergence of Colonial Madras, 1780-1840.** Susan N. Basu. 288p. 1995. 19.95 (*0-19-563553-1*) OUP.

City of Washington: An Illustrated History. Junior League of Washington Staff. (Illus.). 384p. 1992. reprint ed. 12.99 (*0-517-07390-0*, Pub. by Wings Bks) Random Hse Value.

City of Watts: Nineteen Seven to Nineteen Twenty-Six. MaryEllen B. Ray. LC 85-8336. (Illus.). 96p. (Orig.). 1985. pap. 6.95 (*0-917047-01-X*) Rising Pub.

City of Widows. Loren Estleman. 256p. 1995. pap. 4.99 (*0-8125-3538-3*) Forge NYC.

City of Widows. Loren Estleman. 256p. 1994. 20.95 (*0-312-85667-9*) Tor Bks.

***City of Widows.** large type ed. Loren Estelman. LC 94-21080. 309p. 1994. 19.95 (*0-7862-0295-5*) Thorndike Pr.

***City of Women.** Susan Anders. (Orig.). 1996. mass mkt., pap. 5.95 (*1-56333-375-9*) Masquerade.

City of Women. Ruth Landes. 287p. 1994. 35.00x (*0-8263-1555-0*); pap. 17.95 (*0-8263-1556-9*) U of NM Pr.

City of Women: A Sequence of Poems & Prose. Sherod Santos. LC 92-27431. 96p. 1993. 18.95 (*0-393-03475-5*) Norton.

City of Women: A Sequence of Poems & Prose. Sherod Santos. 1994. pap. 8.95 (*0-393-31175-9*) Norton.

City of Women: Sex & Class in New York, 1789-1860. Christine Stansell. LC 86-45283. 320p. 1986. 30.00 (*0-394-51534-X*) Knopf.

City of Women: Sex & Class in New York, 1789-1860. Christine Stansell. LC 87-16163. 320p. 1987. reprint ed. pap. 11.95 (*0-252-01481-2*) U of Ill Pr.

City of Woods & Fields: A Journey Through Britain from A to Z. Stephen Butler. (Illus.). 208p. 1992. 29.95 (*1-85158-354-8*, Pub. by Mnstream UK) Trafalgar.

***City of Wrong: A Friday in Jerusalem.** M. Kamel Hussein. 1995. pap. 12.95 (*1-85168-072-1*) Onewrld Pubns.

City of Zion-The Human Society in Christ, i.e., the Church Built upon a Rock. Apostolos Makrakis. Ed. by Orthodox Christian Educational Society Staff. Tr. by Denver Cummings. 109p. (C). 1958. pap. 6.95 (*0-938366-16-5*) Orthodox Chr.

City on a Hill. George V. Higgins. 1992. pap. 3.50 (*0-88184-181-1*) Carroll & Graf.

City on a Hill: A History of Ideas & Myths in America. Loren Baritz. LC 80-11468. xi, 367p. 1980. reprint ed. text ed. 35.00 (*0-313-22268-1*, BACI, Greenwood Pr) Greenwood.

City on a Mountain - Padre Pio. Pascal P. Parente. Orig. Title: Padre Pio. 154p. 1968. pap. 4.95 (*0-911988-35-1*) AMI Pr.

City on the Edge: The Transformation of Miami. Alejandro Portes & Alex Stepick. LC 92-39417. 1993. 25.00 (*0-520-08217-6*) U CA Pr.

***City on the Edge: The Transformation of Miami.** Alejandro Portes. 1994. pap. 15.00 (*0-520-08932-4*) U CA Pr.

City on the Edge of Forever. Harlan Ellison. 176p. 1995. 25.00 (*1-880325-02-0*) Borderlnds MD.

City on the Edge of Forever. Harlan Ellison. 176p. 1996. pap. 14.95 (*1-880325-03-9*) Borderlnds MD.

***City on the Edge of Forever.** limited ed. Harlan Ellison. 176p. 1995. 75.00 (*0-615-00696-5*) Borderlnds MD.

***City on the Hill: History of the Harrisburg State Hospital.** Ernest Morrison. 262p. 1995. 25.00 (*0-9644246-0-6*); pap. 10.00 (*0-9644246-1-4*) Hist Committ HSH.

City on the Lake: History & the Challenge of Change in Buffalo, New York. Mark Goldman. 324p. (Orig.). 1990. pap. 17.95 (*0-87975-579-2*) Prometheus Bks.

City on the Tiber: Spiritual Reflections on the Reality That Is Rome. Willard F. Jabusch. LC 90-753. 152p. (Orig.). 1990. pap. 7.95 (*0-8189-0572-7*) Alba.

City Once upon a Time. Gilchrist Waring. 1986. pap. 6.00 (*0-87517-012-9*) Dietz.

City Or Village Incorporation from an Unincorporated Area. rev. ed. (Technical Topics Ser.: No. 12). 1994. 5.00 (*0-318-02026-2*) MI Municipal.

***City Parks of Canada.** Linda Martin & Kerry Segrave. (Illus.). 128p. 1995. lib. bdg. 33.00 (*0-8095-4913-1*) Borgo Pr.

City People: The Rise of Modern City Culture in Nineteenth Century America. Gunther Barth. (Illus.). 1982. pap. 10.95 (*0-19-503194-6*) OUP.

City People Notebook. Will Eisner. (Illus.). 86p. 1989. pap. 8.95 (*0-87816-054-X*) Kitchen Sink.

City People Notebook. deluxe ed. Will Eisner. (Illus.). 86p. 1989. 25.00 (*0-87816-053-1*) Kitchen Sink.

City Peregrines. Saul Frank. 320p. 1994. 29.95 (*0-88839-330-X*) Hancock House.

City Planning. Ed. by Richard C. Wade. LC 73-11935. (Metropolitan America Ser.). 110p. 1974. reprint ed. 11.95 (*0-405-05430-0*) Ayer.

City Planning: Problems & Prospects. C. S. Yadav. 1987. 49.00 (*0-8364-2306-2*, Pub. by Concept II) S Asia.

City Planning Bibliography: A Basic Bibliography of Sources & Trends. 3rd ed. Ed. by George C. Bestor & Holway R. Jones. 534p. 1972. pap. 19.00 (*0-87262-036-0*) Am Soc Civil Eng.

City Planning in America: Between Promise & Despair. Mary E. Hommann. LC 92-35351. 168p. 1993. text ed. 47.95 (*0-275-94473-5*, C4473, Praeger Pubs) Greenwood.

City Planning Politics. Don T. Allenworth. LC 80-134. 286p. 1980. text ed. 55.00 (*0-275-90445-8*, C0445, Praeger Pubs) Greenwood.

City Play. Amanda Dargan & Steven Zeitlin. LC 90-30667. (Illus.). 220p. (C). 1990. 24.95 (*0-8135-1577-7*) Rutgers U Pr.

City Poet: The Life & Times of Frank O'Hara. Brad Gooch. LC 92-56766. (Borzoi Reader Ser.). 1993. 30.00 (*0-394-57118-5*) Knopf.

City Poet: The Life & Times of Frank O'Hara. Brad Gooch. (Illus.). 560p. 1994. reprint ed. pap. 15.00 (*0-06-097613-6*, PL) HarpC.

City Police. Jonathan Rubinstein. 498p. 1980. pap. 15.00 (*0-374-51555-7*) FS&G.

City Politics. Edward C. Banfield & James Q. Wilson. LC 63-19134. (Joint Center for Urban Studies Publications). (Illus.). 374p. 1963. 35.00 (*0-674-13250-5*) HUP.

City Politics: Hegemonic Projects & Discourse. Maarten A. Hajer. 152p. 1989. text ed. 63.95 (*0-566-05754-9*, Pub. by Avebury Pub UK) Ashgate Pub Co.

City Politics: Private Power & Public Policy. Dennis R. Judd & Todd Swanston. (C). 1993. text ed. 27.50 (*0-673-46962-X*) HarpCollege.

City Politics & Public Policy. Ed. by James Q. Wilson. LC 67-30636. (Illus.). 310p. reprint ed. pap. 88.40 (*0-317-09617-6*, 2012600) Bks Demand.

City Politics in Canada. Ed. by Warren Magnusson & Andrew Sancton. LC 83-196724. 346p. reprint ed. pap. 98.70 (*0-8357-3782-9*, 2036512) Bks Demand.

City Politics, Police Administrators, & Corruption Control. Lawrence W. Sherman. (Criminal Justice Center Monographs). 1977. pap. text ed. 3.25x (*0-318-37491-9*) John Jay Pr.

City Politiques. John Crowne. Ed. by John H. Wilson. LC 67-12641. x, 159p. 1967. pap. 7.95 (*0-8032-5355-9*) U of Nebr Pr.

City Primeval: High Noon in Detroit. Elmore Leonard. 224p. 1982. pap. 3.95 (*0-380-56952-3*) Avon.

***City Profiles U. S. A., 1995: A Traveler's Guide to Major U. S. Cities.** Ed. by Darren L. Smith. 400p. 1995. lib. bdg. 65.00x (*0-7808-0056-7*) Omnigraphics Inc.

City Psalms. Benjamin Zephaniah. 64p. 1993. pap. 14.95 (*1-85224-230-2*, Pub. by Bloodaxe Bks UK) Dufour.

City Quilts. Susan Greenhut & Diane Herbort. (Illus.). 160p. 1987. 18.95 (*0-13-134776-4*); pap. 12.95 (*0-13-134768-3*) P-H.

City Revolution: Causes & Consequences. Maximillian J. Hall. LC 87-9684. 120p. 1987. text ed. 39.95 (*0-312-00986-0*) St Martin.

***City Risk Kit.** James E. Loeb. 500p. 1991. 335.00 (*0-9628164-4-2*) Indep Risk Insur Mgmt.

City River of Voices. Ed. by Denise Bergman. (Illus.). 91p. (Orig.). 1992. pap. 9.95 (*0-931122-68-6*) West End.

City! San Francisco. Shirley Climo. LC 89-32912. (Illus.). 64p. (J). (gr. 3-7). 1990. text ed. 16.95 (*0-02-719030-7*, Mac Bks Young Read) S&S Childrens.

City School Attendance Service. Frederick E. Emmons. LC 79-176751. (Columbia University. Teachers College. Contributions to Education Ser.: No. 200). reprint ed. 37.50 (*0-404-55200-5*) AMS Pr.

City School Expenditures: Variability & Interrelations of the Principal Items. George D. Strayer. LC 76-177813. (Columbia University. Teachers College. Contributions to Education Ser.: No. 5). reprint ed. 37.50 (*0-404-55005-3*) AMS Pr.

City School Surveys: An Interpretation & Appraisal. Hollis L. Caswell. LC 70-176632. (Columbia University. Teachers College. Contributions to Education Ser.: No. 358). reprint ed. 37.50 (*0-404-55358-3*) AMS Pr.

City Schools: Leading the Way. Patrick B. Forsyth & Marilyn Tallerico. 352p. 1993. 46.95 (*0-8039-6065-4*); pap. 23.95 (*0-8039-6066-2*) Corwin Pr.

City Schools-Suburban Schools: A History of Fiscal Conflict. Seymour Sacks et al. LC 70-39585. (Education in Large Cities Ser.: No. 4). 219p. reprint ed. pap. 62.50 (*0-8357-3982-1*, 2036680) Bks Demand.

City Science, Grades 3-6. Peggy K. Perdue & Diane A. Vaszily. 1990. pap. 11.95 (*0-673-46430-X*) GdYrBks.

City Scriptures: Modern Jewish Writing. Murray Baumgarten. LC 81-6879. 293p. 1982. 30.00 (*0-674-13278-5*) HUP.

City Seen from A to Z. Rachel Isadora. LC 82-11966. (Illus.). 32p. (J). (gr. k-3). 1983. lib. bdg. 15.93 (*0-688-01803-3*) Greenwillow.

City Seen from A to Z. Rachel Isadora. Ed. by ALC Staff. LC 82-11966. (Illus.). 32p. (J). (gr. k up). 1992. pap. 3.95 (*0-688-12032-6*, Mulberry) Morrow.

City Sense & City Design: Writings & Projects of Kevin Lynch. Kevin Lynch. Ed. by Tribib Banerjee et al. (Illus.). 850p. 1990. 65.00x (*0-262-12143-3*) MIT Pr.

***City Sense & City Design: Writings & Projects of Kevin Lynch.** Kevin Lynch. (Illus.). 872p. 1995. pap. text ed. 29.95 (*0-262-62095-2*) MIT Pr.

City Shaped: Urban Patterns & Meanings Through History. Spiro Kostof. (Illus.). 352p. 1993. pap. 29.95 (*0-8212-2016-0*) Bulfinch Pr.

City Signs. Gaildeibler Finke. (Illus.). 192p. 1994. 45.00 (*0-942604-41-5*) Madison Square.

City Signs & Lights Prepared for the Boston Redevelopment Authority & U. S. Dept. of Housing & Urban Development. Stephen Carr. 1973. 19.95 (*0-262-02087-4*) MIT Pr.

City, Sing, for Me: A Country Child Moves to the City. Jane Jacobson. LC 77-11130. (Illus.). 32p. (J). (gr. 1-5). 1978. 16.95 (*0-87705-358-8*) Human Sci Pr.

City Sites. Skip Williams. (Advanced Dungeons & Dragons 2nd Ed. Accessory Ser.). 1995. pap. 12.95 (*1-56076-923-8*) TSR Inc.

City Size & the Quality of Life. Judith Bachman. (gr. 11 up). 1985. pap. 5.95 (*0-89420-060-7*, 480041); audio 101.30 (*0-89420-134-4*, 480020) Natl Book.

***City Sketches.** Ed. by B. Fleck. 248p. (ENG & POR.). 1994. 72.00 (*0-8176-2820-7*) Spr-Verlag.

City Slickers. William E. Geist. LC 87-9952. 384p. 1987. 16.95 (*0-8129-1633-6*, Times Bks) Random.

City Slickers. William E. Geist. 1989. pap. write for info. (*0-14-022580-3*, Penguin Bks) Viking Penguin.

City Sounds. Craig Brown. LC 90-25632. (Illus.). 24p. (J). (ps-4). 1992. 14.00 (*0-688-10028-7*); lib. bdg. 13.93 (*0-688-10029-5*) Greenwillow.

City Sounds. Rebecca Emberley. (Illus.). 32p. (J). (ps-1). 1989. 15.95 (*0-316-23635-7*) Little.

City Sourcebook. 128p. 1992. per., pap. 18.00 (*0-87431-341-4*, 20524) West End Games.

City Sports. Isidro Sanchez & Carme Peris. (World of Sports Ser.). 32p. (J). (ps-1). 1992. pap. 5.95 (*0-8120-4866-0*) Barron.

City Staged: Jacobean Comedy, 1603-1613. Theodore B. Leinwand. LC 86-1683. 240p. 1986. text ed. 27.50 (*0-299-10670-5*) U of Wis Pr.

City, State & Regional Media Directory. Ed. by Alan Green & Bill Hogan. 160p. ring bd. 46.00 (*0-9614280-0-7*) City Desk.

City State & World State. Mason Hammond. LC 66-23518. 1951. 18.00 (*0-8196-0176-4*) Biblo.

City-State Foundations of Western Thought. rev. ed. V. Tejera. LC 92-11143. 182p. (C). 1993. 38.50 (*0-8191-8746-1*); lib. bdg. 18.50 (*0-8191-8747-X*) U Pr of Amer.

City-State of Tyr. Walt Baas. (Dark Sun Accessory, Advanced Dungeons & Dragons 2nd Ed. Ser.: DSS1). 1993. pap. 10.95 (*1-56076-629-8*) TSR Inc.

City-State, 1500-1700: Republican Liberty in an Age of Princely Power. Richard Mackenney. LC 88-13075. (Studies in European History). (C). 1989. pap. 10.95 (*0-391-03598-3*) Humanities.

City, States & Market: The Political Economy of Urban Society. Michael P. Smith. (Ideas Ser.). 1991. pap. 21.95 (*0-631-18052-4*) Blackwell Pubs.

City-States in Classical Antiquity & Medieval Italy. Ed. by Anthony Molho et al. (Illus.). 500p. 1992. text ed. 62.50 (*0-472-10286-9*) U of Mich Pr.

***City States in the Global Economics.** Stephen Chiu. (Transitions). (C). 1995. text ed. 49.95 (*0-8133-8863-5*) Westview.

City Steeple, City Streets: Saints' Tales from Granada & a Changing Spain. Candace Slater. LC 89-27995. (Illus.). 250p. 1990. 37.50 (*0-520-06815-7*) U CA Pr.

City Street. Douglas Florian. LC 89-28694. (Illus.). 32p. (J). (ps up). 1990. 14.00 (*0-688-09543-7*); lib. bdg. 13.93 (*0-688-09544-5*) Greenwillow.

City Superintendent & the Board of Education. William W. Theisen. LC 70-177719. (Columbia University. Teachers College. Contributions to Education Ser.: No. 84). reprint ed. 37.50 (*0-404-55084-3*) AMS Pr.

City Surveyor. Jack Rudman. (Career Examination Ser.: C-1188). 1994. pap. 29.95 (*0-8373-1188-8*) Nat Learn.

City Survival. James E. Kennedy. 70p. 1993. pap. text ed. 4.95 (*0-9637843-0-7*) J E Kennedy.

City Symbols. Ed. by Marcia Divona & Barbara Shaw. LC 93-71360. (Illus.). 184p. 1993. text ed. 22.50 (*0-88108-115-9*); pap. text ed. 16.95 (*0-88108-116-7*) Art Dir.

City Tales. Mary R. Lansing. 1994. 8.95 (*0-8062-4806-8*) Carlton.

City Technology College. Geoffrey Walford & Henry Miller. 176p. 1991. pap. 34.00 (*0-335-09275-6*, Open Univ Pr) Taylor & Francis.

City That Disappeared: Glasgow's Demolished Architecture. Frank Wordsall. 160p. 1981. 45.00 (*0-904002-69-1*) St Mut.

***City That Never Sleeps.** Antony Shuggar. 1994. 14.98 (*0-8317-6256-X*) Smithmark.

City That Refused to Die: Glasgow: The Politics of Urban Regeneration. Michael Keating. 260p. 1988. text ed. 39.00 (*0-08-036412-8*, Pub. by Aberdeen U Pr) Macmillan.

City That She Loved: A Reflection... Janet Ross. LC 93-86933. (Illus.). 147p. (Orig.). 1993. pap. 7.95 (*0-9624229-6-7*) St Thomas Tech.

City Through the Ages. Philip Steele. LC 91-37350. (Illus.). 32p. (J). (gr. 3-6). 1993. lib. bdg. 11.89 (*0-8167-2727-9*); pap. text ed. 3.95 (*0-8167-2728-7*) Troll Assocs.

***City-to-City Atlas.** (Illus.). 1995. per. 17.95 (*0-933162-82-0*) Creative Sales.

City, Town & Countryside in the Early Byzantine Era. Robert L. Hohlfelder. (Brooklyn College Studies on Society in Change). 209p. 1983. text ed. 36.00 (*0-88033-013-9*) East Eur Quarterly.

City Trains: Moving Through America's Cities by Rail. Roger Yepsen. LC 92-2395. (Illus.). 96p. (J). (gr. 3-7). 1993. text ed. 14.95 (*0-02-793675-9*, Mac Bks Young Read) S&S Childrens.

City Transport in Developed & Developing Countries. Tom Rallis. LC 86-29789. 210p. 1988. text ed. 45.00 (*0-312-00450-8*) St Martin.

City Travel Kit: Paris. William Halden. 1990. pap. 16.95 (*0-385-26173-X*) Doubleday.

City Trenches: Urban Politics & the Patterning of Class in the United States. Ira Katznelson. LC 82-8392. xvii, 268p. 1982. pap. text ed. 14.95 (*0-226-42673-4*) U Ch Pr.

City under Siege. Mike Wright. Date not set. 19.95 (*1-56833-011-1*) Madison Bks UPA.

City Unions: Managing Discontent in New York City. Mark H. Maier. 214p. 1987. pap. text ed. 15.00 (*0-8135-1229-8*) Rutgers U Pr.

City University of New York English Forum, Vol. 1. Ed. by Saul N. Brody & Harold Schechter. LC 83-45285. (Illus.). 45.00 (*0-404-62451-0*) AMS Pr.

City upon a Hill: Testing the American Dream at City College. James Traub. (Illus.). 320p. 1994. 24.00 (*0-201-62227-0*) Addison-Wesley.

City Walks of London. Paul Begg. (Illus.). 181p. 1992. pap. 8.95 (*0-86051-647-4*, Robson-Parkwest) Parkwest Pubns.

City! Washington, D. C. Shirley Climo. LC 90-1785. (Illus.). 64p. (J). (gr. 3-7). 1991. text ed. 16.95 (*0-02-719036-6*, Mac Bks Young Read) S&S Childrens.

City Where No One Dies. Bernard B. Dadie. Tr. by Janis Mayes. LC 86-50451. 139p. (Orig.). (FRE.). 1986. 18.00 (*0-89410-498-5*); pap. 8.00 (*0-89410-499-3*) Three Continents.

City Who Fought. Anne McCaffrey & S. M. Stirling. LC 93-2651. 432p. 1993. 19.00 (*0-671-72166-6*) Baen Bks.

City Who Fought. Anne McCaffrey & S. M. Stirling. (Brain-Brawn Ser.). 448p. 1994. mass mkt. 5.99 (*0-671-87599-X*) Baen Bks.

City Wilderness: A Settlement Study by Residents & Associates of the South End House. Ed. by Robert A. Woods. LC 70-112584. (Rise of Urban America Ser.). (Illus.). 1970. reprint ed. 25.95 (*0-405-02485-1*) Ayer.

City Within a City: How Kids Live in New York's Chinatown. Kathleen Krull. LC 93-15846. (World of My Own Ser.). (J). 1994. 15.99 (*0-525-67437-3*, Lodestar Bks) Dutton Child Bks.

City Within a Park: One Hundred Years of Parks & Boulevards in Kansas City Missouri. Jane Mobley & Nancy W. Harris. (Illus.). 108p. 1991. 25.00 (*0-932845-52-5*) Lowell Pr.

City Without Jews. Hugo Bettauer. Tr. by Salomea N. Brainin. LC 91-24155. (Stadt Ohne Juden Ser.). 200p. reprint ed. pap. 9.95 (*0-8197-0594-2*) Bloch.

***City Without Women.** Mario Duliani. Tr. by Antonino Mazza. 220p. 1995. lib. bdg. 37.00 (*0-8095-4821-6*) Borgo Pr.

City Women. Cynthia Smith. LC 93-7411. 64p. (Orig.). 1993. pap. 7.95 (*0-940669-21-8*) Dramaline Pubns.

City Women, Vol. 2. Helena Z. Lopata. LC 84-15933. 576p. 1985. text ed. 75.00 (*0-275-90190-4*, C01902, Praeger Pubs) Greenwood.

City Women: Stories of the World's Great Cities by Djuna Barnes, Angela Carter, Tove Dilevsen, Hayashi Fumiko, Toni Morrison, Grace Paley, Dorothy Parker, Ann Petry, Alix Kates Shulman, Christa Wolf, Virginia Woolf & Others. Ed. by Liz Heron. LC 93-17591. 368p. 1993. 30.00 (*0-8070-8330-5*); pap. 15.00 (*0-8070-8331-3*) Beacon Pr.

City Women in America: Work, Jobs, Occupations, Careers. Helena Z. Lopata et al. LC 84-15933. 316p. 1984. text ed. 33.95 (*0-275-91218-3*, C12181, Praeger Pubs) Greenwood.

City Worker's World in America. Mary K. Simkhovitch. LC 70-156424. (American Labor Ser., No. 2). 1977. reprint ed. 21.95 (*0-405-02942-X*) Ayer.

City Year: On the Streets & in the Neighborhoods with Twelve Young Community Service Volunteers. Suzanne Goldsmith. LC 93-83617. 304p. 1993. 22.95 (*1-56584-093-3*) New Press NY.

City Zoning: The Once & Future Frontier. Clifford L. Weaver & Richard F. Babcock. LC 79-90347. 328p. (Orig.). (C). 1980. pap. 22.95 (*0-918286-17-4*) Planners Pr.

Citybook. Shelley Rotner & Ken Kreisler. LC 93-6350. (Illus.). 32p. (J). (ps-1). 1994. 14.95 (*0-531-06837-4*); lib. bdg. 14.99 (*0-531-08687-9*) Orchard Bks Watts.

Citybook 1: Butcher, Baker, Candlestick Maker. Ed. by Larry DiTillio. (Illus.). 1982. 14.95 (*0-940244-70-5*) Flying Buffalo.

Citybook 2: Port 'O Call. Ed. by Elizabeth Danforth & Michael Stackpole. (Illus.). 1984. 11.95 (*0-940244-71-3*) Flying Buffalo.

Citybook 3: Deadly Nightside. Ed. by Michael Stackpole. (Illus.). 1987. 11.95 (*0-940244-72-1*) Flying Buffalo.

Citybook 4: On the Road. Dennis McKiernan et al. Ed. & Illus. by Paul Jaquays. 96p. 1990. pap. 11.95 (*0-940244-73-X*) Flying Buffalo.

Citybook 5: Sideshow. Ed. & Illus. by Paul Jaquays. 1991. 11.95 (*0-940244-74-8*) Flying Buffalo.

Citybook 6: Uptown. Elizabeth Danforth et al. Ed. by Paul Jaquays. (Illus.). (Orig.). Date not set. pap. 11.95 (*0-940244-99-3*) Flying Buffalo.

Cityfile: Atlanta. Ed. by Metro Files, Inc. Staff. (City at Your Fingertips! Ser.). 475p. 1988. 35.00 (*0-942619-11-0*) Metro Files.

C

1282

An Asterisk (*) at the beginning of an entry indicates that the title is appearing in BIP for the first time.

Cityfile: Baltimore. Ed. by Metro Files, Inc. Staff. (City at Your Fingertips! Ser.). 475p. 1988. 35.00 (*0-942619-25-0*) Metro Files.

Cityfile: Boston - the City at Your Fingertips! Ed. by Metro Files, Inc. Staff. 475p. Directory. 35.00 (*0-942619-03-X*) Metro Files.

Cityfile: Chicago. Ed. by Metro Files, Inc. Staff. (City at Your Fingertips! Ser.). 475p. 1988. 35.00 (*0-942619-04-8*) Metro Files.

Cityfile: Cleveland. Ed. by Metro Files, Inc. Staff. (City at Your Fingertips! Ser.). 475p. 1988. 35.00 (*0-942619-12-9*) Metro Files.

Cityfile: Dallas. Ed. by Metro Files, Inc. Staff. (City at Your Fingertips! Ser.). 475p. 1988. 35.00 (*0-942619-08-0*) Metro Files.

Cityfile: Denver. Ed. by Metro Files, Inc. Staff. 475p. 1988. 35.00 (*0-942619-45-5*) Metro Files.

Cityfile: Houston. Ed. by Metro Files, Inc. Staff. (City at Your Fingertips! Ser.). 475p. 1988. 35.00 (*0-942619-07-2*) Metro Files.

Cityfile: Kansas City. Ed. by Metro Files, Inc. Staff. 475p. 1988. 35.00 (*0-942619-46-3*) Metro Files.

Cityfile: Los Angeles - the City at Your Fingertips! Ed. by Metro Files, Inc. Staff. 475p. Directory. 35.00 (*0-942619-02-1*) Metro Files.

Cityfile: Miami. Ed. by Metro Files, Inc. Staff. (City at Your Fingertips! Ser.). 475p. 1988. 35.00 (*0-942619-09-9*) Metro Files.

Cityfile: Minneapolis. Ed. by Metro Files, Inc. Staff. (City at Your Fingertips! Ser.). 475p. 1988. 35.00 (*0-942619-26-9*) Metro Files.

Cityfile: New York - the City at Your Fingertips! Ed. by Metro Files, Inc. Staff. 475p. Directory. 35.00 (*0-942619-00-5*) Metro Files.

Cityfile: Orange County, CA. Ed. by Metro Files, Inc. Staff. 475p. 1988. 35.00 (*0-942619-44-7*) Metro Files.

Cityfile: Peninsula. Ed. by Metro Files, Inc. Staff. (City at Your Fingertips! Ser.). 475p. 1988. 35.00 (*0-942619-29-3*) Metro Files.

Cityfile: Philadelphia. Ed. by Metro Files, Inc. Staff. (City at Your Fingertips! Ser.). 475p. 1988. 35.00 (*0-942619-06-4*) Metro Files.

Cityfile: Phoenix. Ed. by Metro Files, Inc. Staff. 475p. 1988. 35.00 (*0-942619-43-9*) Metro Files.

Cityfile: Pittsburgh. Ed. by Metro Files, Inc. Staff. (City at Your Fingertips! Ser.). 475p. 1988. 35.00 (*0-942619-27-7*) Metro Files.

Cityfile: San Diego. Ed. by Metro Files, Inc. Staff. (City at Your Fingertips! Ser.). 475p. 1988. 35.00 (*0-942619-10-2*) Metro Files.

Cityfile: San Francisco. Ed. by Metro Files, Inc. Staff. (City at Your Fingertips! Ser.). 475p. 1988. 35.00 (*0-942619-05-6*) Metro Files.

Cityfile: Seattle. Ed. by Metro Files, Inc. Staff. (City at Your Fingertips! Ser.). 475p. 1988. 35.00 (*0-942619-28-5*) Metro Files.

Cityfile: St. Louis. Ed. by Metro Files, Inc. Staff. (City at Your Fingertips! Ser.). 475p. 1988. 35.00 (*0-942619-13-7*) Metro Files.

Cityfile: Washington, D.C. - the City at Your Fingertips! Ed. by Metro Files, Inc. Staff. 475p. Directory. 35.00 (*0-942619-01-3*) Metro Files.

Cityguide: San Francisco Bay Area & Northern California, 1990. 14th ed. Ed. by Bella Whelan. 1990. pap. 9.95 (*0-940562-22-7*) Danella Pubns.

Cityguide: San Francisco Bay Area & Northern California, 1990. 15th ed. Ed. by Bella Whelan. 1991. pap. 9.95 (*0-940562-23-5*) Danella Pubns.

***CityGuide Locator: Denver.** (1995 Ser.). (Illus.). Date not set. pap. text ed. 7.95 (*0-9631668-0-8*) CtyGuide Loc.

CityGuide Locator of Denver. rev. ed. Patricia Montgomery. 64p. 1993. pap. text ed. 7.95 (*0-9631668-2-4*) CtyGuide Loc.

Cityguide to San Jose. Forbes & Zoltan. 1985. pap. 4.95 (*0-940562-06-5*) Danella Pubns.

Cityguide, 1989: San Francisco Bay Area & Northern California. Bella Whelan & Dan Whelan. (Illus.). 304p. 1988. pap. 7.95 (*0-940562-20-0*) Danella Pubns.

Cityless & Countryless World: An Outline of Practical Cooperative Individualism. Henry Olerich. LC 73-154455. (Utopian Literature Ser.). 1976. reprint ed. 35.95 (*0-405-03537-3*) Ayer.

***Citymaze! A Collection of Amazing City Mazes.** Wendy Madgwick. (Illus.). 40p. (J). (gr. 3 up). 1995. pap. 7.95 (*1-56294-846-6*) Millbrook Pr.

***Citymaze! A Collection of Amazing City Mazes.** Wendy Madgwick & Don Courtney. LC 94-26291. (Illus.). 40p. (YA). (gr. 8 up). 1995. lib. bdg. 12.90 (*1-56294-561-0*) Millbrook Pr.

Cityscape: The Art of Painting the Urban Environment. Frederick Sweney. (Illus.). 128p. 1985. 24.95 (*0-13-134503-6*) P-H.

Cityscape: The Art of Painting the Urban Environment. Frederick Sweney. 1985. 14.95 (*0-685-43062-6*) S&S Trade.

Cityscapes. (Illus.). 1991. text ed. write for info. (*1-56290-075-7*, 6006) Crystal.

Cityscapes. Algimantas Kezys. LC 88-23150. (Illus.). 144p. 1988. 19.95 (*0-8294-0595-X*) Loyola Univ Pr.

***Cityscapes & Capital: The Politics of Urban Development.** Michael A. Pagano & Ann O. Bowman. (Illus.). 224p. 1994. text ed. 32.50x (*0-8018-5034-7*) Johns Hopkins.

Cityscapes of Boston. Robert Campbell & Peter Vanderwarker. (Illus.). 240p. 1994. pap. 19.95 (*0-395-70065-5*, P Davison Bk) HM.

Cityshape: Research & References in Community Design. Sherwin Greene & Rita A. Calvan. (CPL Bibliographies Ser.: No. 119). 73p. 1983. 12.00 (*0-86602-119-1*) Coun Plan Librarians.

CityTech. 2nd ed. FASA Staff. (BattleTech Ser.). (Illus.). 1994. boxed, pap. 25.00 (*1-55560-239-8*, 1608) FASA Corp.

Cityward Migration: Swedish Data. Jane Moore. 1938. 69.50 (*0-686-51354-1*) Elliots Bks.

Citywide EDCs. 12p. 1976. 8.00 (*0-317-05059-1*) Natl Coun Econ Dev.

Citywide Targeting Strategies. Marianne Clarke. Ed. by Stephanie Bell. 8p. (Orig.). 1978. pap. 8.00 (*0-317-04866-X*) Natl Coun Econ Dev.

Ciucurencu. Illus. by Dan Grigorescu. (FRE, GER, RUM & RUS.). (C). 1965. text ed. 59.50 (*0-8290-0366-5*) Irvington.

Ciudad. Isidro Sanchez & Carme Peris. (World of Sports Ser.). 32p. (J). (ps-1). 1992. pap. 6.95 (*0-8120-4871-7*) Barron.

Ciudad (City) Maria Rius & Josep M. Parramon. (Let's Discover Ser.). 32p. (SPA.). (J). (ps-1). 1986. pap. 6.95 (*0-8120-3753-7*) Barron.

Ciudad De Dios En la Jungla: God's City in the Jungle. Sanna Barlow. (SPA.). 4.95 (*84-7228-847-1*, 222316, Pub. by Edit Clie SP) TSELF.

***Ciudad en la Antiguedad.** F. Kolb. 298p. (SPA.). 1993. 100.00 (*84-249-1488-0*) Elliots Bks.

Ciudad Que Me Habita. Magali Garcia-Ramis. (Illus.). 120p. (Orig.). (SPA.). 1993. pap. 7.50 (*0-929157-21-4*) Ediciones Huracan.

Ciudad Real, 1500-1750: Growth, Crisis, & Readjustment in the Spanish Economy. Carla R. Phillips. LC 78-9293. 208p. 1979. 25.00 (*0-674-13285-8*) HUP.

Ciudad y los Perros. 9th ed. Mario Vargas Llosa. (SPA.). 1989. pap. 16.95 (*0-8288-2583-1*) Fr & Eur.

Ciudadania en Puerto Rico. 2nd ed. Reece B. Bothwell. LC 78-24031. (Illus.). (SPA.). 1980. pap. 2.00 (*0-8477-2451-4*) U of PR Pr.

Ciudadanos Del Cielo: Citizens of Heaven. F. B. Meyer. (SPA.). 6.25 (*84-7228-916-8*, 223011, Pub. by Edit Clie SP) TSELF.

***Ciudades de Hormigas.** Arthur Dorros. Tr. by Daniel Santacruz. LC 94-35266. (Let's Read & Find Out Science, Stage 2). (Illus.). 32p. (SPA.). (J). (ps-3). 1995. 14.95 (*0-06-025360-6*); pap. 4.95 (*0-06-445137-2*, Trophy) HarpC Child Bks.

***Ciudades Desiertas.** Jose Agustin. 1995. pap. 12.50 (*0-679-76336-8*, Vin) Random.

Civic Attitudes in American School Textbooks. Bessie L. Pierce. LC 76-165727. (American Education, Ser, No. 2). 1972. reprint ed. 18.95 (*0-405-03716-3*) Ayer.

Civic Calvinism in Northwestern Germany & the Netherlands: Sixteenth to Nineteenth Centuries. Heinz Schilling. 240p. 1992. 35.00 (*0-940474-18-2*) Sixteenth Cent.

Civic Ceremonial. G. N. Waldram. (C). 1984. 100.00 (*0-7219-0162-X*, Scientific) St Mut.

Civic Culture: Political Attitudes & Democracy in Five Nations. Gabriel A. Almond & Sidney Verba. LC 63-12666. 576p. reprint ed. pap. 164.20 (*0-8357-3844-2*, 2036577) Bks Demand.

Civic Culture Revisited. Ed. by Gabriel A. Almond & Sidney Verba. 422p. (C). 1989. reprint ed. text ed. 49.95 (*0-8039-3559-5*); reprint ed. pap. text ed. 24.00 (*0-8039-3560-9*) Sage.

Civic Culture Study, 1959-1960. Gabriel Almond & Sidney Verba. 1974. write for info. (*0-89138-065-5*) ICPSR.

Civic Education: Its Limits & Conditions. Ed. by Susan D. Franzosa. LC 86-63414. 250p. (Orig.). 1987. pap. 20.00 (*0-911168-68-0*) Prakken.

Civic Education, Its Objectives & Methods for a Specific Case Group: A Study in Educational Sociology. Clyde B. Moore. LC 70-177080. (Columbia University. Teachers College. Contributions to Education Ser.: No. 151). reprint ed. 37.50 (*0-404-55151-3*) AMS Pr.

Civic Environmentalism: Alternatives to Regulation in States & Communities. DeWitt John. LC 93-27005. 1993. 41.95 (*0-87187-954-9*); pap. 22.95 (*0-87187-948-4*) Congr Quarterly.

Civic Freedom in Central Europe: Voices from Czechoslovakia. Ed. by H. Gordon Skilling & Paul Wilson. 176p. 1991. text ed. 49.95 (*0-312-05803-9*) St Martin.

Civic Frontier. Bernard Barrett. LC 79-670360. 1979. 34.95 (*0-522-84171-6*) Intl Spec Bk.

Civic Heraldry of England & Wales. rev. ed. Wilfrid Scott-Giles. LC 71-184280. (Illus.). 1972. reprint ed. lib. bdg. 42.95 (*0-405-08941-4*) Ayer.

Civic Imperative: Examining the Need for Civic Education. Richard Pratte. (Advances in Contemporary Educational Thought Ser.). 224p. (C). 1988. text ed. 23.95 (*0-8077-2922-1*) Tchrs Coll.

Civic Learning for Teachers: Capstone for Educational Reform. Ed. by Alan H. Jones. vii, 184p. (Orig.). 1985. pap. 10.00 (*0-911168-63-X*) Prakken.

Civic Learning in Teacher Education. R. Freeman Butts et al. (SPE Monograph Ser.). 1983. 3.00 (*0-933669-21-6*) Soc Profs Ed.

Civic Mission in Educational Reform: Perspectives for the Public & the Profession, P-377. R. Freeman Butts. (Publication Series: Education & Society). 361p. 1989. text ed. 32.95 (*0-8179-8771-1*); pap. text ed. 22.35 (*0-8179-8772-X*) Hoover Inst Pr.

Civic Politics in the Rome of Urban VIII. Laurie Nussdorfer. (Illus.). 296p. 1992. text ed. 45.00 (*0-691-03182-7*) Princeton U Pr.

***Civic Pride.** Blythe Durand. 140p. (Orig.). Date not set. pap. 7.95 (*0-7610-0362-2*) NW Pub.

Civic Ritual in Renaissance Venice. Edward Muir. LC 80-8568. (Illus.). 376p. 1986. pap. 19.95 (*0-691-10200-7*) Princeton U Pr.

Civic Sculpture in the Renaissance: Montorsoli's Fountains at Messina. Sheila Ffolliott. LC 84-141. (Studies in Renaissance Art History: No. 1). (Illus.). 268p. reprint ed. pap. 76.40 (*0-8357-1474-8*, 2070544) Bks Demand.

Civic Spectacle: Essays on Drama & Community. Mera J. Flaumenhaft. 120p. 1994. lib. bdg. 48.50 (*0-8476-7963-2*); pap. 18.50 (*0-8476-7964-0*) Rowman.

Civic Tradition & Roman Athens. James H. Oliver. LC 82-16180. 182p. reprint ed. pap. 51.90 (*0-7837-0338-4*, 2040657) Bks Demand.

Civic Virtue in the American Republic: Essays on Moral Philosophy & Public Administration. Ralph C. Chandler. LC 86-62855. 1987. pap. 9.95 (*0-932826-20-2*) New Issues MI.

Civic World of Early Renaissance Florence. Gene A. Brucker. LC 76-45891. 539p. reprint ed. pap. 153.70 (*0-8357-2612-6*, 2039932) Bks Demand.

Civic Writing in the Classroom. Sandra Stotsky. 78p. 1987. pap. 8.00 (*0-941339-01-7*) Ind U SSDC.

Civics: Citizens & Society. 2nd ed. Allan O. Kownslar & Terry L. Smart. (Illus.). 576p. (J). (gr. 7-8). 1983. text ed. 31.88 (*0-07-035433-2*) McGraw.

Civics & Law for Alabama Schools. 1986. write for info. (*0-932659-06-3*) Viewpoint Pubns.

Civics & Law in State & Nation. 1986. write for info. (*0-932659-04-7*) Viewpoint Pubns.

Civics, Commerce & Community: The History of the Greater Washington Board of Trade 1889-1989. C.W. A.S. Staff. 144p. 1989. pap. text ed. 15.95 (*0-8403-5678-1*) Kendall-Hunt.

Civics, Commerce & Community Vol. M15: The History of the Greater Washington Board of Trade, 1889-1989. Jessica I. Elfenbein et al. 1989. 14.95 (*0-317-04097-9*) GWU CWAS.

Civics for Democracy: A Journey for Teachers & Students. Katherine E. Isaac. LC 92-97031. (Illus.). 390p. 1992. pap. 17.50 (*0-936758-32-5*) Ctr Responsive Law.

Civics for Today. Margaret Branson & Fred Coombs. (Illus.). (J). (gr. 7-9). 1980. text ed. 43.76 (*0-395-26201-1*); student ed, pap. 13.48 (*0-395-26203-8*) HM.

***Civil Action.** Jonathan Harr. LC 95-2088. 1995. 25.00 (*0-394-56349-2*) Random.

Civil Action for Childhood Sexual Abuse. James Neeb & Shelly Harper. 392p. 1994. boxed 75.00 (*0-409-91493-2*, CN) Butterworth Legal Pubs.

Civil Actions Against State & Local Government, Its Divisions, Agencies, & Officers. 2nd ed. Shepard Editors. LC 92-26559. 1500p. 1992. text ed. 190.00 (*0-07-172447-8*) Shepards-McGraw.

Civil Actions Against State Government: Its Divisions, Agencies & Officers. Shepard's Citation, Inc. Staff. (Trial Publications). 939p. 1982. text ed. 95.00 (*0-07-056729-8*) Shepards-McGraw.

Civil Actions Against the United States: Its Agencies, Officers & Employees. Shepard's Editorial Staff. (Trial Publications). 544p. 1982. text ed. 95.00 (*0-07-056725-5*) Shepards-McGraw.

Civil Actions Against the United States, Its Agencies, Officers, & Employees. 2nd ed. Shepard Editors. LC 92-26558. 1000p. 1992. text ed. 190.00 (*0-07-172449-4*) Shepards-McGraw.

Civil Actions at Law in Alabama. 2nd ed. Grover S. McLeod. 686p. 1987. text ed. 75.00 (*1-884150-25-X*) Manchester AL.

Civil Actions at Law in Alabama: Pocket Parts, 1993. 2nd ed. Grover S. McLeod. 285p. (C). 1993. 32.00 (*1-884150-26-8*) Manchester AL.

Civil Aircraft. Joseph P. Juptner. (U. S. Civil Aircraft Ser.: Vol. 1). 1993. text ed. 29.95 (*0-07-032980-X*) McGraw.

Civil Aircraft. Joseph P. Juptner. (U. S. Civil Aircraft Ser.: Vol. 7). 1993. text ed. 29.95 (*0-07-032986-9*) McGraw.

Civil Aircraft. Joseph P. Juptner. (U. S. Civil Aircraft Ser.: Vol. 4). 1994. text ed. 29.95 (*0-07-032983-4*) McGraw.

Civil Aircraft. Joseph P. Juptner. (U. S. Civil Aircraft Ser.: Vol. 6). 1994. text ed. write for info. (*0-07-032985-0*) McGraw.

Civil Aircraft, Vol. 2. Joseph P. Juptner. (U. S. Civil Aircraft Ser.: Vol. 2). 1993. pap. text ed. 29.95 (*0-07-032981-8*) McGraw.

Civil Aircraft, Vol. 3. Joseph P. Juptner. (U. S. Civil Aircraft Ser.: Vol. 3). 1993. text ed. 29.95 (*0-07-032982-6*) McGraw.

Civil Aircraft, Vol. 5. Joseph P. Juptner. (U. S. Civil Aircraft Ser.: Vol. 5). 1993. text ed. 29.95 (*0-07-032984-2*) McGraw.

Civil Aircraft of the World. rev. ed. Gordon Swanborough. 1982. 4.95 (*0-684-16616-X*, Scribners) S&S Trade.

Civil & Criminal Forfeiture: Federal & State Practice, 3 vols. Steven L. Kessler. LC 93-29165. (Criminal Law Ser.). 1993. ring bd. 350.00 (*0-87632-910-5*) Clark Boardman Callaghan.

Civil & Criminal Liability of Bank Directors, Lawyers & Accountants in the 90's. (Commercial Law & Practice Course Handbook Ser.: Vol. 640). 508p. 1992. 70.00 (*0-685-65485-0*, A4-4406) PLI.

Civil & Criminal Liability of Officers, Directors & Professionals: Bank & Thrift Litigation in the 1990's. (Commercial Law & Practice Ser.). 876p. 1991. pap. text ed. 65.00 (*0-685-49876-X*, A4-4355) PLI.

Civil & Criminal Procedure. Ed. by Sarah Maguire. 265p. (C). 1991. 90.00 (*1-85352-864-1*, Pub. by HLT Pubns UK) St Mut.

Civil & Environmental Engineering Aspects of Energy Complexes: Proceedings of the Engineering Foundation Conference, August 1975. Ed. by Alvin S. Goodman. 450p. 1976. pap. 16.00 (*0-87262-153-7*) Am Soc Civil Eng.

Civil & Mexican Wars. (Papers of the Military Historical Society of Massachusetts: Vol. 13). (Illus.). 660p. 1990. reprint ed. 40.00 (*1-56837-017-2*) Broadfoot.

Civil & Military Clothing in Europe: From the First to the Eighteenth Century. Frederic Stibbert. LC 65-27918. (Illus.). 1972. reprint ed. 33.95 (*0-405-09001-3*) Ayer.

Civil & Military List of Rhode Island, 1647-1850, 3 vols., Set. Comp. by Joseph J. Smith. LC 74-25388. reprint ed. 122.00 (*0-404-13371-1*) AMS Pr.

Civil & Natural History of Jamaica. Patrick Browne. LC 71-141130. (Research Library of Colonial Americana). (Illus.). 1972. reprint ed. 72.95 (*0-405-03276-5*) Ayer.

Civil & Political History of the State of Tennessee from Its Earliest Settlement up to the Year 1796 Including the Boundaries of the State. John Haywood. LC 71-146397. (First American Frontier Ser.). 1971. reprint ed. 41.95 (*0-405-02851-2*) Ayer.

***Civil & Political Rights in the United States: Initial Report of the U. S. A. to the U. N. Rights Committee under the International Covenant on Civil & Political Rights.** John Shattuck. 240p. (Orig.). 1994. pap. text ed. 45.00 (*0-7881-1501-4*) Diane Pub.

Civil & Savage Encounters: The Worldly Travel Letters of an Imperial Russian Navy Officer, 1860-61. Pavel N. Golovin. Tr. by Basil Dmytryshyn & E. A. Crownhart-Vaughan. (North Pacific Studies: No. 5). (Illus.). 208p. (Orig.). 1983. 21.95 (*0-87595-067-1*); pap. 12.95 (*0-87595-095-7*) Oregon Hist.

Civil & Structural Details for Engineers & Architects: Industrial, Commercial, Residential. Franquintin Talania. LC 88-92277. (Illus.). 496p. 1989. 54.75 (*0-929176-02-2*) Burdick & Landreth Co.

Civil Appeal Procedures Worldwide. Ed. by Charles Platto. LC 92-18821. (International Bar Association Ser.). 448p. (C). 1992. lib. bdg. 170.00 (*1-85333-725-0*, Pub. by Graham & Trotman UK) Kluwer Ac.

***Civil Architecture: The New Public Infrastructure.** Richard Dattner. 1995. text ed. 46.95 (*0-07-015665-4*) McGraw.

Civil Aviation Authority. 167p. 1990. pap. 30.00 (*0-10-111222-X*, HM2220) UNIPUB.

Civil Aviation Development: A Policy & Operation Analysis. Arthur D. Little, Inc. et al. LC 70-185656. (Special Studies in U. S. Economic, Social & Political Issues). 1980. reprint ed. 49.50 (*0-89197-697-3*) Irvington.

Civil Blood: Poems & Prose. Jill Breckenridge. LC 86-60097. (Illus.). 216p. (Orig.). 1986. 19.50 (*0-915943-10-7*); pap. 9.50 (*0-915943-09-3*) Milkweed Ed.

Civil Case Backlog Reduction: San Diego Superior Court. National Center for State Courts. (Paul Reardon Ser.). 9p. 1982. 0.54 (*0-685-15472-6*, PRS-031) Natl Ctr St Courts.

Civil Case Scheduling in the Trumbull County (OH) Court of Common Pleas: Final Report. National Center for State Courts Staff. 52p. 1982. 3.12 (*0-685-15792-X*, NERO-122) Natl Ctr St Courts.

Civil Case Scheduling in the Trumbull County (OH) Court of Common Pleas: Findings & Recommendations. National Center for State Courts Staff. 85p. 1982. 5.10 (*0-685-15785-7*, NERO-111) Natl Ctr St Courts.

Civil Case Scheduling in the Trumbull County (Ohio) Court of Common Pleas: Final Report. David Steelman. 52p. 1982. 3.12 (*0-685-55348-5*, NERO122) Natl Ctr St Courts.

***Civil Code of Iran.** Tr. by M. A. Taleghany. LC 94-37658. 198p. 1995. 57.50x (*0-8377-1222-5*) Rothman.

Civil Code of Iran: (With Post-Revolution Amendments) 1987. 50.00 (*0-946706-34-4*, Pub. by Royston Ltd) St Mut.

***Civil Code of Spain.** Tr. by Julio Romanach, Jr. 521p. 1994. pap. text ed. 65.00 (*0-9633610-1-5*) Lawrence LA.

Civil Code of the Republic of China. Ching-Lin Hsia. Tr. by Yu-Kon Chang et al. LC 76-20213. (Studies in Chinese Government & Law). 400p. 1976. reprint ed. text ed. 65.00 (*0-313-26959-9*, U6959, Greenwood Pr) Greenwood.

***Civil Code of the Republic of Hungary.** 298p. (Orig.). (C). 1994. pap. text ed. 95.00x (*0-7881-1219-8*) Diane Pub.

***Civil Code of the Republic of Kazakhstan: General Part.** Tr. & Intro. by William E. Butler. 250p. 1995. pap. 62.00 (*1-898029-14-8*, Pub. by Simmonds & Hill Pubng UK) W W Gaunt.

Civil Code of the State of Louisiana: By Authority. Louisiana State Staff. LC 74-19620. reprint ed. 94.50 (*0-404-12456-9*) AMS Pr.

Civil Commitment in Minnesota. 2nd ed. Eric S. Janus. 300p. 1991. ring bd. 115.00 (*0-86678-314-8*) Michie Butterworth.

Civil Contract. Georgette Heyer. 1991. mass mkt. 3.99 (*0-06-100177-5*, Harp PBks) HarpC.

Civil Contract. large type ed. Georgette Heyer. LC 91-4318. 601p. 1991. reprint ed. lib. bdg. 18.95 (*1-56054-199-7*) Thorndike Pr.

Civil Contract. large type ed. Georgette Heyer. 601p. 1992. reprint ed. pap. 12.95 (*1-56054-951-3*) Thorndike Pr.

Civil Costumes of France of Thirteenth & Fourteenth Century. Camille Piton. (Illus.). 380p. 1986. reprint ed. pap. text ed. 35.00 (*0-87556-387-2*) Saifer.

***Civil Court.** David W. Felder. 44p. 1995. pap. text ed. 5.00 (*0-910959-97-8*, B&G 19C) Felder Bks.

Civil Court in Action. 2nd ed. David Barnard. 1985. 84.00 (*0-406-55622-9*); pap. 40.00 (*0-406-55623-7*) Butterworth Legal Pubs.

Civil Court Manual (Central Acts.) 12th ed. (C). 1988. 750.00 (*0-685-27953-7*) St Mut.

Civil Court Practice & Procedure. 11th ed. G. Ganguly. (C). 1989. 310.00 (*0-685-36557-3*) St Mut.

Civil Court Practice & Procedure Manual. S. Sarkar. (C). 1990. 125.00 (*0-89771-286-2*) St Mut.

Civil Defense: A Choice of Disasters. Intro. by John Dowling & Evans M. Harrell. LC 86-28785. (Monograph Ser.). (Illus.). 256p. 1987. text ed. 45.00 (*0-88318-512-1*) Am Inst Physics.

An Asterisk (*) at the beginning of an entry indicates that the title is appearing in BIP for the first time. 1283

Civil Defense in the Soviet Union. Leon Goure. LC 86-337. (Illus.). 221p. 1986. reprint ed. text ed. 59.75 (*0-313-25162-2*, GCDE, Greenwood Pr) Greenwood.

Civil Defense in War & Peace: Index of Modern Authors & Subjects with Guide for Rapid Research. rev. ed. Science & Life Consultants Association Staff. LC 92-42820. 170p. 1994. 44.50 (*1-55914-966-3*); pap. 39.50 (*1-55914-967-1*) ABBE Pubs Assn.

Civil Discovery & Depositions. 2nd ed. Reagan W. Simpson. LC 93-32350. (Trial Practice Library: Trial Techniques). 1994. text ed. 128.00 (*0-471-59326-5*) Wiley.

***Civil Discovery & Mandatory Disclosure: A Guide to Efficient Practice.** William W. Schwarzer & Lynn H. Pasahow. 536p. Date not set. 106.00 (*0-13-349606-6*) Aspen Law.

Civil Discovery Practice in California, 2 vols. 1200p. 1988. text ed. 155.00 (*0-88124-158-X*, CP-30760) Cont Ed Bar-CA.

Civil Disobedience. R. D. Dixit. 104p. 1980. 13.95 (*0-318-36847-1*) Asia Bk Corp.

Civil Disobedience. Ed. by Paul Harris. 302p. (Orig.). (C). 1989. pap. text ed. 24.00 (*0-8191-7443-2*) U Pr of Amer.

Civil Disobedience: Theory & Practice. Ed. by Hugo A. Bedau. LC 69-27984. (Orig.). 1969. pap. 10.28 (*0-672-63514-3*) Pegasus.

Civil Disobedience see Modern Essays

Civil Disobedience see Walden

Civil Disobedience & Beyond: Law, Resistance & Religion in South Africa. Charles Villa-Vicencio. LC 90-30862. 181p. reprint ed. pap. 51.60 (*0-7837-3173-6*, 2042805) Bks Demand.

Civil Disobedience & Moral Law in Nineteenth-Century American Philosophy. Edward H. Madden. LC 68-11043. 222p. 1970. pap. 9.00 (*0-295-95070-6*) U of Wash Pr.

Civil Disobedience, & Other Essays. Henry David Thoreau. LC 93-15708. (Thrift Editions Ser.). 96p. 1993. reprint ed. pap. 1.00 (*0-486-27563-9*) Dover.

Civil Disobedience & Political Obligation: A Study in Christian Social Ethics. James F. Childress. LC 75-158137. (Yale Publications in Religion: No. 16). 266p. reprint ed. pap. 75.90 (*0-317-09428-9*, 2021988) Bks Demand.

Civil Disobedience Enquiry Committee Report, 1922. Ed. by A. M. Zaidi. 1986. 38.50 (*0-8364-1866-2*, Pub. by Manohar II) S Asia.

Civil Disobedience in Focus. Ed. by Hugo A. Bedau. (Philosophers in Focus Ser.). 256p. 1991. 69.95 (*0-415-05054-5*, A5478); pap. 17.95 (*0-415-05055-3*, A5482) Routledge.

Civil Disorder: What Do We Know? How Should We Prepare? Intro. by Hubert Williams. LC 93-87557. (Illus.). 166p. (Orig.). 1994. pap. text ed. 27.95 (*1-884614-03-5*) Police Found.

Civil Disorder & Civil Liberties: Evidence to the Scarman Inquiry. NCCL. 1981. 30.00 (*0-901108-96-0*, Pub. by NCCL UK) St Mut.

Civil Disorder & the Agents of Social Control. Gary T. Marx. (Reprint Series in Sociology). (C). 1993. reprint ed. pap. text ed. 2.90 (*0-8290-2682-7*, S-731) Irvington.

Civil Disturbances. 1989. lib. bdg. 79.95 (*0-8490-3977-0*) Gordon Pr.

Civil Drafting Technology. 2nd ed. David Madsen & Terrance Shumaker. 294p. 1994. pap. text ed. 26.00 (*0-13-100785-8*) P-H.

Civil Elegies & Other Poems. Dennis Lee. 59p. (Orig.). 1972. 7.95 (*0-88784-123-6*, Pub. by Hse of Anansi Pr CN); pap. 7.95 (*0-88784-023-X*, Pub. by Hse of Anansi Pr CN) Genl Dist Srvs.

Civil Engineer. Jack Rudman. (Career Examination Ser.: C-136). 1994. pap. 27.95 (*0-8373-0136-X*) Nat Learn.

Civil Engineer I. Jack Rudman. (Career Examination Ser.: C-2158). 1994. reprint ed. pap. 27.95 (*0-8373-2158-1*) Nat Learn.

Civil Engineer I, II, III, IV, V. Jack Rudman. (Career Examination Ser.: C-2000). 1994. pap. 49.95 (*0-8373-2000-3*) Nat Learn.

Civil Engineer II. Jack Rudman. (Career Examination Ser.: C-2159). 1994. reprint ed. pap. 29.95 (*0-8373-2159-X*) Nat Learn.

Civil Engineer III. Jack Rudman. (Career Examination Ser.: C-2160). 1994. reprint ed. pap. 34.95 (*0-8373-2160-3*) Nat Learn.

Civil Engineer IV. Jack Rudman. (Career Examination Ser.: C-2161). 1994. reprint ed. pap. 34.95 (*0-8373-2161-1*) Nat Learn.

Civil Engineer (Materials) Jack Rudman. (Career Examination Ser.: C-3224). 1994. pap. 29.95 (*0-8373-3224-9*) Nat Learn.

Civil Engineer (Physical Research) Jack Rudman. (Career Examination Ser.: C-3225). 1994. pap. 29.95 (*0-8373-3225-7*) Nat Learn.

Civil Engineer (Planning) Jack Rudman. (Career Examination Ser.: C-3226). 1994. pap. 29.95 (*0-8373-3226-5*) Nat Learn.

Civil Engineer (Traffic) Jack Rudman. (Career Examination Ser.: C-3227). 1994. pap. 29.95 (*0-8373-3227-3*) Nat Learn.

Civil Engineer V. Jack Rudman. (Career Examination Ser.: C-2162). 1994. reprint ed. pap. 34.95 (*0-8373-2162-X*) Nat Learn.

Civil Engineering: CE1 - Hydraulic & Sanitary Engineering. Allen C. Chao. (Professional Engineering Exam Review Ser.). (Illus.). 179p. (Orig.). (C). 1983. pap. text ed. 16.00 (*1-56049-050-0*) NCSU CE IES.

Civil Engineering: CE2 - Transportation Engineering. Paul D. Cribbins. (Professional Engineering Exam Review Ser.). (Illus.). 100p. (Orig.). (C). 1983. pap. text ed. 30.00 (*1-56049-048-9*) NCSU CE IES.

***Civil Engineering: Problem Solving Flowcharts.** George L. Rodriquez. (Illus.). 110p. (Orig.). 1995. pap. 25.50 (*0-910554-07-2*, 072) Engineering.

Civil Engineering No. CE2A: Transportation Engineering: Highway Capacity Manual. Paul D. Cribbins. (Professional Engineering Exam Review Ser.). (Illus.). 100p. (Orig.). (C). 1983. pap. text ed. 20.00 (*1-56049-049-7*) NCSU CE IES.

Civil Engineering No. CE4: Structural Analysis-Design, Pt. 2. (Professional Engineering Exam Review Ser.). (Illus.). 570p. (Orig.). (C). 1986. pap. text ed. 16.00 (*1-56049-005-5*) NCSU CE IES.

Civil Engineering Pt. 1: CE3 - Structural Analysis-Design. D. James & M. May. (Professional Engineering Exam Review Ser.). (Illus.). 570p. (Orig.). (C). 1986. pap. text ed. 55.00 (*0-685-44687-5*) NCSU CE IES.

Civil Engineering & Nuclear Power, 6 vols. LC 80-67611. 1974p. 1980. pap. 110.00 (*0-87262-248-7*) Am Soc Civil Eng.

Civil Engineering Applications of Remote Sensing. ASCE Conference, Aerospace Division, 1980. Ed. by Ralph W. Kiefer. LC 80-67879. 199p. 1980. pap. 21.00 (*0-87262-253-3*) Am Soc Civil Eng.

Civil Engineering Applications of Remote Sensing & Geographic Information Systems. Ed. by Donald B. Stafford. LC 91-12166. 360p. 1991. pap. text ed. 35.00 (*0-87262-832-9*) Am Soc Civil Eng.

Civil Engineering Calculations Reference Guide. Tyler G. Hicks. 288p. 1987. text ed. 46.00 (*0-07-028798-8*) McGraw.

Civil Engineering Classics: Outstanding Papers of Thomas R. Camp. 418p. 1973. pap. 18.00 (*0-87262-053-0*) Am Soc Civil Eng.

Civil Engineering Contract Administration. A. Atkinson. (C). 1989. 110.00 (*0-685-37695-8*, Pub. by S Thornes Pubs UK) St Mut.

***Civil Engineering Contract Administration: North East Surrey College of Technology.** A. V. Atkinson. 160p. (C). 1992. 51.00x (*0-7487-1521-5*, Pub. by S Thornes Pubs UK) St Mut.

Civil Engineering Contracts. Karl Williams. LC 92-30470. (Ellis Horwood Series in Civil Engineering). 1992. 81.00 (*0-13-132986-3*, Tavistock-E Horwood) Routledge Chapman & Hall.

Civil Engineering Contracts: Practice & Procedure. 2nd ed. Charles K. Haswell & Douglas S. De Silva. 256p. 1989. text ed. 79.95 (*0-408-03201-4*) Buttrwrth-Heinemann.

Civil Engineering Contracts & Estimates. B. S. Patil. (Illus.). 586p. 1981. pap. text ed. 20.00 (*0-86125-036-2*, Pub. by Orient Longman Ltd II) Apt Bks.

Civil Engineering Design for Decommissioning of Nuclear Installations. A. A. Paton et al. 104p. 1984. pap. text ed. 67.50 (*0-86010-614-4*) G & T Inc.

Civil Engineering Drafting. J. R. Wirshing & R. H. Wirshing. LC 82-17195. 352p. 1983. text ed. 26.95 (*0-07-071127-5*) McGraw.

Civil Engineering Draftsman. Jack Rudman. (Career Examination Ser.: C-137). 1994. pap. 27.95 (*0-8373-0137-8*) Nat Learn.

Civil Engineering Draftsman I. Jack Rudman. (Career Examination Ser.: C-2154). 1994. pap. 27.95 (*0-8373-2154-9*) Nat Learn.

Civil Engineering Draftsman II. Jack Rudman. (Career Examination Ser.: C-2155). 1994. pap. 29.95 (*0-8373-2155-7*) Nat Learn.

Civil Engineering Draftsman III. Jack Rudman. (Career Examination Ser.: C-2156). 1994. 29.95 (*0-8373-2156-5*) Nat Learn.

Civil Engineering Education: Related to Engineering Practice & to the Nation's Needs, 2 Vols., Set. 1545p. 1974. pap. 52.00 (*0-87262-110-3*) Am Soc Civil Eng.

Civil Engineering Education: Responding to the Challenges of Engineering Practice, 2 vols., Set. 1119p. 1979. pap. 52.00 (*0-87262-195-2*) Am Soc Civil Eng.

Civil Engineering Education & Training. 190p. 1977. 14.50 (*0-7277-0042-1*, Pub. by T Telford UK) Am Soc Civil Eng.

Civil Engineering for the Community. Dennis A. Randolph. LC 93-12282. 96p. 1993. 20.00 (*0-87262-845-0*) Am Soc Civil Eng.

Civil Engineering for the Plant Engineer. 2nd ed. Max Schwartz. LC 79-21884. 416p. (C). 1984. lib. bdg. 36.50 (*0-89874-050-9*) Krieger.

Civil Engineering for Underground Rail Transport. Jack T. Edwards. 608p. 1990. text ed. 280.00 (*0-408-04343-1*) Buttrwrth-Heinemann.

Civil Engineering Guidelines for Planning & Designing Hydroelectric Developments, 5 vols., Set. LC 89-45882. 2052p. 1989. 250.00 (*0-87262-725-X*, 725) Am Soc Civil Eng.

Civil Engineering Guidelines for Planning & Designing Hydroelectric Developments, Vol. 1: Planning, Design of Dams & Related Features, & Environmental (Conventional Hydro Guidelines) LC 89-45882. 582p. 1989. 75.00 (*0-87262-726-8*, 726) Am Soc Civil Eng.

Civil Engineering Guidelines for Planning & Designing Hydroelectric Developments, Vol. 2: Waterways (Conventional Hydro Guidelines) LC 89-45882. 402p. 1989. 60.00 (*0-87262-727-6*, 727) Am Soc Civil Eng.

Civil Engineering Guidelines for Planning & Designing Hydroelectric Developments, Vol. 3: Powerhouses & Related Topics (Conventional Hydro Guidelines) LC 89-45882. 296p. 1989. 50.00 (*0-87262-728-4*, 728) Am Soc Civil Eng.

Civil Engineering Guidelines for Planning & Designing Hydroelectric Developments, Vol. 4: Small-Scale Hydro. LC 89-45882. 366p. 1989. 55.00 (*0-87262-729-2*, 729) Am Soc Civil Eng.

Civil Engineering Guidelines for Planning & Designing Hydroelectric Developments, Vol. 5: Pumped Storage & Tidal Power. LC 89-45882. 406p. 1989. 60.00 (*0-87262-730-6*, 730) Am Soc Civil Eng.

***Civil Engineering Handbook.** Ed. by W. F. Chen. 2000p. 1995. 99.95 (*0-8493-8953-4*, 8953) CRC Pr.

Civil Engineering Handbook. 4th ed. Leonard C. Urquhart. 1959. text ed. 97.50 (*0-07-066148-0*) McGraw.

Civil Engineering Heritage: Eastern & Central England. Ed. by E. A. Labrum. 288p. 1994. 24.00 (*0-685-75139-2*, 1970-X) Am Soc Civil Eng.

Civil Engineering Heritage: Southern England. Ed. by R. A. Otter. 304p. 1994. 24.00 (*0-685-75140-6*, 1971-8) Am Soc Civil Eng.

***Civil Engineering Hydraulics: Essential Theory with Worked Examples.** 3rd ed. R. E. Featherstone & C. Nalluri. LC 94-25122. 1995. write for info. (*0-632-03863-2*) Blackwell Sci.

Civil Engineering in the Arctic Offshore. 1260p. 1985. 108.00 (*0-87262-441-2*) Am Soc Civil Eng.

Civil Engineering in the Nuclear Industry. Ed. by R. Dexter-Smith. 372p. 1991. text ed. 97.00 (*0-7277-1643-3*, Pub. by T Telford UK) Am Soc Civil Eng.

Civil Engineering in the Oceans II. ASCE Technical Council on Ocean Engineering, Dec. 1969. 1277p. 1970. 42.00 (*0-87262-018-2*) Am Soc Civil Eng.

Civil Engineering in the Oceans IV, 2 vols., Set. 1092p. 1979. pap. 42.00 (*0-87262-191-X*) Am Soc Civil Eng.

Civil Engineering in the Oceans V: Proceedings of the International Conference, College Station, Texas, November 2-5, 1992. Ed. by Robert T. Hudspeth. LC 92-32385. 1088p. 1992. 82.00 (*0-87262-908-2*) Am Soc Civil Eng.

Civil Engineering Insurance & Bonding. Ed. by Peter Madge. 144p. 1987. 34.00 (*0-7277-0371-4*, Pub. by T Telford UK) Am Soc Civil Eng.

Civil Engineering Insurance & Bonding. Peter Madge. (C). 1987. 175.00 (*0-685-33733-2*, Pub. by Witherby & Co UK) St Mut.

Civil Engineering License Exam File. 11th ed. Donald G. Newnan & Robert E. Lindskog. LC 90-22318. (Exam File Ser.). (Illus.). 380p. 1991. pap. 39.50 (*0-910554-84-6*) Engineering.

Civil Engineering License Problems & Solutions: Problems & Solutions. 12th ed. Donald G. Newnan. (Illus.). 350p. 1995. 29.50 (*0-910554-91-9*, 919) Engineering.

Civil Engineering License Review: Text. 12th ed. Donald G. Newnan. (Illus.). 736p. 1995. 49.50 (*0-910554-90-0*, 900) Engineering.

Civil Engineering Materials. Shan Somayji. LC 09-415484. 1994. text ed. 60.00 (*0-13-177643-6*) P-H Gen Ref & Trav.

Civil Engineering Practice, 5 vols., Set. Incl. Vol. 1. Structures. Ed. by Paul N. Cheremisinoff et al. LC 87-50629. 832p. 1987. 49.00 (*0-87762-529-8*); Vol. 2. Hydraulics-Mechanics. Ed. by Paul N. Cheremisinoff et al. LC 87-50629. 850p. 1988. 38.00 (*0-87762-546-8*); Vol. 3. Geotechnical-Ocean Engineering. Ed. by Paul N. Cheremisinoff et al. LC 87-50629. 850p. 1988. 38.00 (*0-87762-554-9*); Vol. 4. Surveying-Construction-Transportation-Energy-Economics & Government-Computers. Ed. by Paul N. Cheremisinoff et al. LC 87-50629. 700p. 1987. 29.00 (*0-87762-537-9*); Vol. 5. Water Resources-Environmental. Ed. by Paul N. Cheremisinoff et al. LC 87-50629. 832p. 1988. 55.00 (*0-87762-540-9*); LC 87-50629. 199.00 (*0-87762-966-8*) Technomic.

Civil Engineering Practice: Engineering Success by Analysis of Failure. David D. Piesold. 1991. text ed. 49.00 (*0-07-707239-1*) McGraw.

Civil Engineering Procedure: Institution of Civil Engineers. 4th ed. Institution of Civil Engineers Staff. 128p. 1986. 13.00 (*0-7277-0363-3*, Pub. by T Telford UK) Am Soc Civil Eng.

Civil Engineering Project Procedure in the EC. Ed. by P. A. Cox. 214p. 1991. text ed. 76.00 (*0-7277-1639-5*, Pub. by T Telford UK) Am Soc Civil Eng.

Civil Engineering, Public Works & Infrastructure: A Resource Guide to the Rebuilding of America's Decaying Cities. 1991. lib. bdg. 79.95 (*0-8490-4913-X*) Gordon Pr.

Civil Engineering Quick Reference Cards. Michael R. Lindeburg. (Engineering Reference Manual Ser.). 48p. (Orig.). 1986. spiral bd. 19.95 (*0-932276-59-8*) Prof Pubns CA.

Civil Engineering Reference Manual. 6th ed. Michael R. Lindeburg. (Engineering Reference Manual Ser.). 712p. 1992. 51.95 (*0-912045-45-0*) Prof Pubns CA.

Civil Engineering Sample Examination. 3rd ed. Michael R. Lindeburg. (Engineering Reference Manual Ser.). 72p. 1992. pap. text ed. 13.95 (*0-912045-51-5*) Prof Pubns CA.

Civil Engineering Systems. Andrew B. Templeman. (Illus.). 375p. (C). 1983. pap. text ed. 39.95 (*0-333-28510-7*, Pub. by Macmill Press UK) Scholium Intl.

Civil Engineering Systems Analysis & Design. Alan A. Smith et al. LC 82-13640. 473p. 1983. pap. text ed. 79.95 (*0-471-90060-5*, Wiley-Interscience) Wiley.

Civil Engineering Trainee. Jack Rudman. (Career Examination Ser.: C-945). 1994. pap. 23.95 (*0-8373-0945-X*) Nat Learn.

Civil Engineering Work: A Compendium of Occupational Safety Practice. (Occupational Safety & Health Ser.: No. 45). viii, 153p. (Orig.). 1981. pap. 16.00 (*92-2-102577-2*) Intl Labour Office.

Civil Engineering 1839-1889. Mike Chrimes. (Illus.). 192p. 1991. text ed. 36.00 (*0-86299-933-2*) A Sutton Pub.

Civil Engineering 1839-1889: A Photographic History. Mike Chrimes. (Illus.). 181p. 1991. text ed. 41.00 (*0-685-59660-5*, AS933) Am Soc Civil Eng.

Civil Engineers for Management. 140p. 1987. 48.00 (*0-7277-0387-0*, Pub. by T Telford UK) Am Soc Civil Eng.

Civil Engineers for the 1990's, Conference: Proceedings. 190p. 1986. 50.00 (*0-7277-0264-5*, Pub. by T Telford UK) Am Soc Civil Eng.

Civil Engineers in the World Around Us. 299p. 1974. pap. 16.00 (*0-87262-069-7*) Am Soc Civil Eng.

***Civil Engineer's Reference Book.** 4th ed. Ed. by L. S. Blake. (Illus.). 1800p. 1994. pap. 69.95 (*0-7506-1964-3*) Buttrwrth-Heinemann.

Civil Engineers Reference Book. 4th ed. Leslie S. Blake. (Illus.). 960p. 1989. text ed. 180.00 (*0-408-01208-0*) Buttrwrth-Heinemann.

Civil Engineer's Role in Productivity in the Construction Industry, 2 vols., Set. ASCE Committee on Engineering Management, Aug. 1976. 402p. 1976. pap. 20.00 (*0-87262-075-1*) Am Soc Civil Eng.

Civil Evidence Trial Manual for Texas Lawyers, 1986-93. 2nd ed. Murl A. Larkin. 950p. 1991. ring bd. 170.00 (*0-409-25658-7*) Michie Butterworth.

Civil Evidence Trial Manual for Texas Lawyers, 1986-93. 2nd suppl. ed. Murl A. Larkin. 950p. 1994. 50.00 (*0-250-42764-8*) Butterworth Legal Pubs.

Civil False Claims & Qui Tam Actions. John T. Boese. 724p. 1993. ring bd. 126.00 (*0-13-241204-7*) Aspen Law.

Civil Government in the United States. John Fiske. (Notable American Authors Ser.). 1992. reprint ed. lib. bdg. 75.00 (*0-7812-2851-4*) Rprt Serv.

Civil Idolatry: Desacralizing & Monarchy in Spenser, Shakespeare, & Milton. Richard F. Hardin. LC 90-50937. 272p. 1992. 39.50 (*0-87413-426-9*) U Delaware Pr.

Civil Judgment Recognition & the Integration of Multiple-State Associations: Central America, the United States of America, & the European Economic Community. Robert C. Casad. LC 81-11926. xiv, 258p. 1982. 29.95 (*0-7006-0218-6*) U Pr of KS.

Civil Juries & the Politics of Reform. Stephen Daniels & Joanne Martin. (American Bar Foundation Ser.). 320p. 1995. 35.00 (*0-8101-1121-7*) Northwestern U Pr.

Civil Jurisdiction & Judgements: Maritime Claims. David Jackson. 1987. pap. 95.00 (*1-85044-144-8*) Lloyds London Pr.

Civil Jurisdiction & Judgments: Maritime Claims. David Jackson. (C). 1987. 340.00 (*0-685-33732-4*, Pub. by Witherby & Co UK) St Mut.

Civil Jurisdiction & Judgments in Europe. Ed. by Harry D. Tebbens et al. 1993. pap. 130.00 (*0-406-01651-8*, U.K.) Butterworth Legal Pubs.

Civil Jury: Trends in Trials & Verdicts, Cook County, Illinois 1960-1979 - Executive Summary. Institute for Civil Justice (U.S.) Staff et al. LC 82-534. 1982. 4.00 (*0-8330-0389-5*, R-2881/1-ICJ) Rand Corp.

Civil Jury Selection. 2nd ed. Arne Werchick. LC 93-10018. (Trial Practice Library). 416p. 1993. text ed. 128.00 (*0-471-58372-3*) Wiley.

Civil Justice & the Jury. Charles W. Joiner. LC 72-6684. 238p. 1973. reprint ed. text ed. 59.75 (*0-8371-6495-8*, JOCJ, Greenwood Pr) Greenwood.

***Civil Law.** Ed. by Ralf Rogowski. LC 95-8007. (International Library of Essays in Law & Legal Theory: No. 10). 500p. 1995. 150.00x (*0-8147-7465-2*) NYU Pr.

Civil Law in Its Natural Order, 2 vols., Set. Jean Domat. Ed. by Luther S. Cushing. Tr. by William Strahan. 1763p. 1981. reprint ed. lib. bdg. 97.50 (*0-8377-0511-8*) Rothman.

Civil Law in Qing & Republican China. Ed. by Kathryn Bernhardt & Philip C. Huang. LC 94-11687. (Law, Society, & Culture in China Ser.). 1994. 42.40 (*0-8047-2274-9*) Stanford U Pr.

Civil Law System: An Introduction to the Comparative Study of Law. 2nd ed. Arthur T. Von Mehren & James R. Gordley. 1977. 50.00 (*0-316-90754-5*) Little.

Civil Law Tradition: An Introduction to the Legal Systems of Western Europe & Latin America. 2nd ed. John H. Merryman. LC 84-50153. 184p. 1985. 27.50 (*0-8047-1247-6*); pap. 10.95 (*0-8047-1248-4*) Stanford U Pr.

Civil Liabilities: Enforcement & Litigation Under the 1933 Act, 2 vols. J. William Hicks. (Securities Law). 1989. ring bd. 250.00 (*0-87632-669-6*) Clark Boardman Callaghan.

Civil Liabilities of N. Y. Law Enforcement Officers. John J. Sullivan. 32p. 5.95 (*0-930137-80-9*) Looseleaf Law.

Civil Liability & the Police. Northwestern University Traffic Institute Staff. LC 83-114221. (Know the Law Ser.: No. 202). 1987. 12.00 (*0-685-07053-0*) Traffic Inst.

Civil Liability for Defective Premises. J. H. Holyoak & D. K. Allen. 1982. 90.00 (*0-406-23340-3*, U.K.) Butterworth Legal Pubs.

Civil Liability for Transfrontier Pollution: Dutch Environmental Tort Law in International Cases in the Light of Community Law. Gerrit Betlem. (International Environmental Law & Policy Ser.). 640p. (C). 1993. lib. bdg. 136.00 (*1-85333-951-2*, Pub. by Graham & Trotman UK) Kluwer Ac.

Civil Liability for Waste: A Legal Analysis of the Proposed EC Directive. Peter Von Wilmowsky & Gerhard Roller. LC 92-19027. (Studies of the Environmental Law Network International: Vol. 2). 1992. write for info. (*3-631-45172-5*) P Lang Pubs.

Civil Liability in Criminal Justice. H. E. Barrineau, III. 105p. 1987. pap. 14.95 (*0-932930-76-X*) Anderson Pub Co.

Civil Liability in Criminal Justice. 2nd rev. ed. H. E. Barrineau, III. LC 93-74613. 150p. (C). 1994. pap. text ed. write for info. (*0-87084-095-9*) Anderson Pub Co.

Civil Liablity Act, 1961 (Annotated) Antony Kerr. 192p. 1993. text ed. 65.00 (*1-85800-014-9*, Pub. by Round Hall) Intl Spec Bk.

An Asterisk (*) at the beginning of an entry indicates that the title is appearing in BIP for the first time.

Civil Liberties: Opposing Viewpoints. rev. ed. Ed. by Charles P. Cozic. LC 93-16419. (YA). 1994. lib. bdg. 19.95 (*1-56510-058-1*); pap. 11.55 (*1-56510-057-3*) Greenhaven.

Civil Liberties: Policy & Policy Making. Ed. by Stephen L. Wasby. LC 76-43318. 256p. 1977. pap. 18.95 (*0-8093-0817-7*) Transaction Pubs.

Civil Liberties: Policy & Policy Making. Stephen L. Wasby. 272p. 1985. reprint ed. pap. 17.50 (*0-8191-5153-X*, Pol Studies) U Pr of Amer.

Civil Liberties - Cases & Materials. 3rd ed. S. H. Bailey et al. 1991. U.K. pap. 54.00 (*0-406-55230-4*) Butterworth Legal Pubs.

Civil Liberties & Civil Rights. Ed. by Victor J. Stone. LC 77-9428. (David C. Baum Memorial Lecture Ser.). 156p. reprint ed. pap. 44.50 (*0-317-28790-7*, 2020224) Bks Demand.

Civil Liberties & Electronic Surveillance. 1991. lib. bdg. 300.00 (*0-8490-4766-8*) Gordon Pr.

Civil Liberties & Free Speech Policy. Ed. by Stephen Wasby. (C). 1975. pap. 12.00 (*0-918592-13-5*) Pol Studies.

Civil Liberties & Nazis: The Skokie Free-Speech Controversy. James L. Gibson & Richard D. Bingham. LC 84-26320. 240p. 1985. text ed. 55.00 (*0-275-90105-X*, C0105, Praeger Pubs) Greenwood.

Civil Liberties & the Arts: Selections from Twice a Year, 1938-1948. Ed. by William Wasserstrom. LC 64-23340. (Illus.). 1964. 19.95 (*0-8156-0039-9*) Syracuse U Pr.

Civil Liberties & the Constitution. 6th ed. Lucius J. Barker, Jr. & Twiley W. Barker. 656p. (C). 1989. Casebound. boxed, pap. text ed. write for info. (*0-13-134099-9*) P-H.

Civil Liberties & the Constitution. Paul G. Kauper. LC 79-26222. x, 237p. 1980. reprint ed. text ed. 35.00 (*0-313-22223-1*, KACL, Greenwood Pr) Greenwood.

Civil Liberties & the Constitution: Cases & Commentaries. 7th ed. Lucius J. Barker & Twiley W. Barker, Jr. LC 93-23785. 784p. 1994. pap. text ed. write for info. (*0-13-137209-2*) P-H.

Civil Liberties & the Miners' Dispute. NCCL. 40p. (C). 1988. 30.00 (*0-946088-11-X*, Pub. by NCCL UK) St Mut.

Civil Liberties at Work: A Guide to Your Rights as a Job Applicant or Employee. 1991. lib. bdg. 300.00 (*0-8490-5181-9*) Gordon Pr.

Civil Liberties in Conflict. Ed. by Larry Gostin. 224p. (C). 1988. text ed. 49.95 (*0-415-00679-1*); pap. text ed. 14.95 (*0-415-00680-5*) Routledge.

Civil Liberties under Attack: Publications of the William J. Cooper Foundation, Swarthmore College. Henry S. Commager et al. LC 68-14899. (Essay Index Reprint Ser.). 1977. 19.95 (*0-8369-0308-0*) Ayer.

Civil Liberties under the Constitution. 6th ed. M. Glenn Abernathy & A. Perry Barbara. LC 92-23581. 656p. (C). 1993. pap. 34.95 (*0-87249-854-9*) U of SC Pr.

Civil Liberties 1984. NCCL. Ed. by Peter Wallington. 1984. 40.00 (*0-317-54657-0*, Pub. by NCCL UK) St Mut.

Civil Liberty Briefings: Campaigning on the Public Order Bill, No. 2. NCCL. 40p. 1984. 20.00 (*0-317-54648-1*, Pub. by NCCL UK) St Mut.

Civil Liberty Briefings: Police Accountability, No. 3. NCCL. 40p. 1984. 25.00 (*0-317-54652-X*, Pub. by NCCL UK) St Mut.

Civil Liberty Briefings: Police & Criminal Evidence, No. 1. NCCL. 40p. 1984. 40.00 (*0-685-17736-X*, Pub. by NCCL UK) St Mut.

Civil Liberty under Indian Constitution. Jitendra Pandey. (C). 1992. 28.00 (*81-7100-383-4*, Pub. by Deep) S Asia.

***Civil Lines: New Writing from India.** Ed. by Rukun Advani et al. (C). 1994. pap. 9.50 (*0-86311-584-5*, Pub. by Ravi Dayal II) S Asia.

Civil Litigation. William V. Dorsaneo, III & Suzanne K. Griggs. LC 92-45068. (Texas Legal Assistant Education Ser.). 1993. write for info. (*0-8205-0652-4*) Bender.

Civil Litigation. Richard Ladmore. (C). 1992. text ed. 48.00 (*1-85431-231-6*, Pub. by Blackstone Pr UK) W W Gaunt.

Civil Litigation. Craig Osborne & Maria Tighe. 200p. 1993. 34.00 (*1-85431-292-8*, Pub. by Blackstone Pr UK) W W Gaunt.

Civil Litigation: A Practice Guide for Advocates. P. W. Young. 1986. Australia. 72.00 (*0-409-49234-5*) Butterworth Legal Pubs.

***Civil Litigation: Legal Practice Course Guides.** Craig Osborne. 424p. 1995. pap. 34.00 (*1-85431-367-3*, Pub. by Blackstone Pr UK) W W Gaunt.

Civil Litigation Action Guides: References & Key Words & Phrases, Summer 1992. Ed. by Suzanne E. Graber. 98p. 1992. pap. 47.00 (*0-88124-534-8*, CP-11541) Cont Ed Bar-CA.

Civil Litigation & Remedies. Blackstone Press Ltd. Staff. (C). 1991. text ed. 150.00 (*1-85431-159-X*, Pub. by Blackstone Pr UK) W W Gaunt.

Civil Litigation for the Paralegal. Peggy N. Kerley et al. 1991. text ed. 44.95 (*0-8273-4771-5*) Delmar.

Civil Litigation for the Paralegal New York State Student Pocket Part. Cathy Okrent. 1992. student ed 9.95 (*0-8273-5294-8*) Delmar.

Civil Litigation for the Paralegal Ohio Student Pocket Part. Paul A. Sukys. 1992. student ed 9.95 (*0-8273-5291-3*) Delmar.

Civil Litigation for the Paralegal Texas Student Pocket Part. Peggy N. Kerley. 1992. student ed 9.95 (*0-8273-5292-1*) Delmar.

Civil Litigation in Alaska: Improvement Through Simplification. National Center for State Courts Staff. 64p. 1983. 3.84 (*0-685-15477-7*, WRO-051) Natl Ctr St Courts.

Civil Litigation in New York. 2nd ed. Chase & Barker. 1972. write for info. (*0-8205-0251-0*, 472) Bender.

Civil Litigation in the Federal Courts: Increasing Role of U. S. Magistrates. 188p. 1982. pap. text ed. 5.00 (*1-56986-136-6*) Federal Bar.

Civil Litigation Instructors Guide. Peggy N. Kerley. 1991. teacher ed 12.00 (*0-8273-4772-3*) Delmar.

Civil Litigation Manual, 1982 & Supplement, 1990. Ed. by Randy Foster. write for info. (*0-318-61747-1*) OR Bar CLE.

Civil Litigation Research Project Final Report, 3 Pts. David M. Trubek et al. 1005p. 1983. fiche 10.00 (*0-915329-03-4*) Univ Wis-Mad Law.

Civil Litigation Research Project Final Report, 3 Pts., Set. David M. Trubek et al. 1005p. 1983. 50.00 (*0-915329-00-X*) Univ Wis-Mad Law.

Civil Litigation 1992: The Anatomy of a Civil Case. Wake Forest University School of Law Staff. 353p. 1992. pap. 65.00 (*0-942225-55-4*) Wake Forest Law.

Civil Magistrate's Power in Matters of Religion Modestly Debated, London, 1653. Thomas Cobbett. LC 74-141104. (Research Library of Colonial Americana). 1972. reprint ed. 26.95 (*0-405-03318-4*) Ayer.

Civil-Military Conflict in Imperial Russia, 1881-1914. William C. Fuller, Jr. LC 85-3493. (Illus.). 350p. 1985. text ed. 65.00 (*0-691-05452-5*) Princeton U Pr.

Civil Military Interaction in Asia & Africa. Ed. by Charles H. Kennedy & David J. Louscher. LC 90-24887. (International Studies in Sociology & Social Anthropology: No. 55). 154p. 1991. pap. 37.25 (*90-04-09359-1*) E J Brill.

***Civil-Military Relations.** Ed. by Constantine Danopoulos. (C). 1995. text ed. 49.95 (*0-8133-8846-5*) Westview.

Civil-Military Relations. Andrew J. Goodpaster & Samuel P. Huntington. LC 77-960. (AEI Studies: No. 141). 92p. reprint ed. pap. 26.30 (*0-8357-4450-7*, 2037287) Bks Demand.

Civil-Military Relations, an Annotated Bibliography, 1940-1952. Social Science Research Council Staff. LC 75-3796. 140p. 1975. reprint ed. text ed. 49.75 (*0-8371-8076-7*, CIMR, Greenwood Pr) Greenwood.

Civil-Military Relations & Militarism: A Classified Bibliography Covering the United States & Other Nations of the World (with Introductory Notes) Arthur D. Larson. LC 71-31050. (Libraries Bibliography: No. 9). 1971. reprint ed. 4.00 (*0-686-20807-2*) KSU.

Civil-Military Relations & National Security Thinking in Czechoslovakia: A Conference Report. Thomas S. Szayna & James B. Steinberg. LC 92-14545. 1992. write for info. (*0-8330-1245-2*, R-4195-OSD) Rand Corp.

***Civil-Military Relations & Nuclear Weapons.** Ed. by Scott Sagan. 164p. (Orig.). 1994. pap. 12.00 (*0-935371-31-1*) CFISAC.

***Civil-Military Relations in Israel.** Yehyda Ben Meir. LC 94-33142. 1995. write for info. (*0-231-09684-4*) Col U Pr.

Civil-Military Relations in Pakistan. Saeed Shafqat. 288p. (C). 1995. text ed. 49.95 (*0-8133-8809-0*) Westview.

Civil-Military Relations in Sierra Leone: A Case Study of African Soldiers in Politics. Thomas S. Cox. 283p. 1976. 32.00 (*0-674-13290-4*) HUP.

Civil-Military Relations in South Asia: Pakistan, Bangladesh & India. Veena Kukreja. (Illus.). 284p. 1992. 35.00 (*0-8039-9699-3*) Sage.

Civil-Military Relations in the Soviet Union. Ed. by Alexander Dallin. LC 91-44950. (Articles on Russian & Soviet History, 1500-1991 Ser.: Vol. 12). 312p. 1992. 51.00 (*0-8153-0569-9*) Garland.

Civil Noir. Melanie Neilson. LC 91-67073. 96p. (Orig.). 1992. pap. 8.95 (*0-937804-45-2*) Segue NYC.

Civil Obedience: An Oral History of School Desegregation in Fayetteville, Arkansas, 1954-1965. Ed. by Julianne L. Adams & Thomas A. DeBlack. (Illus.). 224p. (RUS.). 1994. 20.00 (*1-55728-358-3*); pap. 12.00 (*1-55728-359-1*) U of Ark Pr.

Civil Patrols in Guatemala. Americas Watch Staff. 105p. 1986. 8.00 (*0-938579-24-X*, Fund Free Exp); 6.00 (*0-938579-20-7*, Fund Free Exp) Hum Rts Watch.

Civil Peace & Sacred Order: Limits & Renewals, Vol. 1. Stephen R. Clark. 208p. 1989. 45.00 (*0-19-824446-0*) OUP.

Civil Poems. Josephine Miles. 1966. pap. 1.00 (*0-685-29875-2*) Oyez.

Civil, Political & Mechanical History of the Framwork-Knitters in Europe & America, Vol. 1. Gravenor Henson & Stanley D. Chapman. LC 70-97974. xx, 449p. 1970. reprint ed. lib. bdg. 49.50 (*0-678-05671-4*) Kelley.

Civil Practice Annual of New York. Bender's Editorial Staff. 1967. ring bd. write for info. (*0-8205-1205-2*) Bender.

***Civil Practice in the Southern District of New York.** Michael Silbergerg. LC 95-13189. (Federal Practice Ser.). 1995. write for info. (*0-07-172263-7*) Shepards-McGraw.

Civil Practice Law & Rules Plus Appendix, N.Y.S. 425p. 1994. ring bd. 18.95 (*0-930137-12-4*) Looseleaf Law.

Civil Practice of the Superior Courts of South Africa. 4th ed. L. De V Van Winsen et al. Date not set. write for info. (*0-318-72483-9*, Pub. by Juta SA) W W Gaunt.

Civil Practice of the Superior Courts of South Africa. 4th ed. Herbstein et al. 1993. write for info. (*0-318-72245-3*, Pub. by Juta SA) W W Gaunt.

Civil Prisoners. large type ed. Meriol Trevor. 350p. 1980. 21.95 (*0-7089-0526-9*) Ulverscroft.

Civil Procedure. Brousseau. 1982. write for info. (*0-8205-0071-2*, 157) Bender.

***Civil Procedure.** Katherine Delsack. (Education Ser.). 250p. (C). 1992. pap. text ed. 10.95 (*0-614-04992-X*) Lawprep Pr.

Civil Procedure. Ed. by P. Lemmens & S. Raes. 1991. ring bd. write for info. (*0-318-68488-8*) Kluwer Law Tax Pubs.

Civil Procedure. John Oakley & Rex Perschbacher. Ed. by Robert J. Switzer. (Law Outlines Ser.). 300p. (Orig.). 1993. pap. text ed. 16.95 (*0-87457-179-0*, 5040) Casenotes Pub.

Civil Procedure. C. K. Takwani. 570p. 1983. 120.00 (*0-317-57733-6*) St Mut.

Civil Procedure. Larry L. Teply & Ralph U. Whitten. (University Casebook Ser.). 983p. 1994. text ed. 37.00 (*1-56662-173-9*) Foundation Pr.

Civil Procedure. rev. ed. Steven Emanuel. 385p. 1993. pap. text ed. 16.95 (*1-56542-011-X*) E Law Outlines.

Civil Procedure. 2nd ed. Jack H. Friedenthal et al. (Hornbook Ser.). 777p. 1993. text ed. 38.50 (*0-314-01306-7*) West Pub.

Civil Procedure. 2nd ed. C. K. Takwani. (C). 1987. 60.00 (*0-685-37437-8*) St Mut.

Civil Procedure. 3rd ed. Kevin M. Clermont. LC 93-12068. (Black Letter Ser.). 350p. 1993. pap. text ed. 24.50 (*0-314-01868-9*) West Pub.

Civil Procedure. 3rd ed. Geoffrey C. Hazard, Jr. & James Fleming, Jr. LC 84-81753. 1985. 33.00 (*0-316-45693-4*) Little.

***Civil Procedure.** 4th ed. Kevin M. Clermont. (Black Letter Ser.). 304p. 1995. pap. text ed. write for info. (*0-314-06528-8*) West Pub.

Civil Procedure. 4th ed. Jack Friedanthal & Arthur Miller. (Sum & Substance Ser.). 1988. 19.95 (*0-940366-24-X*) Sum & Substance.

***Civil Procedure: A Modern Approach.** 2nd ed. Richard L. Marcus et al. (American Casebook Ser.). 1177p. (C). 1995. text ed. 51.00 (*0-314-06105-3*) West Pub.

Civil Procedure: A Modern Approach, 1991 Supplement. Richard L. Marcus et al. (American Casebook Ser.). 151p. (C). 1993. reprint ed. pap. text ed. 11.00 (*0-314-88748-2*) West Pub.

Civil Procedure: Adaptable to Courses Utilizing Cound, Friedenthal, Miller & Sexton's Casebook on Civil Procedure. Casenotes Publishing Co., Inc. Staff. Ed. by Norman S. Goldenberg et al. (Legal Briefs Ser.). 1993. pap. write for info. (*0-87457-013-1*, 1040) Casenotes Pub.

Civil Procedure: Adaptable to Courses Utilizing Field, Kaplan & Clermont's Casebook on Civil Procedure. Casenotes Publishing Co., Inc. Staff. Ed. by Norman S. Goldenberg et al. (Legal Briefs Ser.). 1990. pap. write for info. (*0-87457-014-X*, 1043) Casenotes Pub.

Civil Procedure: Adaptable to Courses Utilizing Hazard, Tait & Fletcher Casebook on Pleading & Procedure. Casenotes Publishing Co., Inc. Staff. Ed. by Norman S. Goldenberg et al. (Legal Briefs Ser.). 1994. pap. write for info. (*0-87457-017-4*, 1041) Casenotes Pub.

Civil Procedure: Adaptable to Courses Utilizing Materials by Field. LC 87-115178. (Legalines Ser.). 365p. 12.95 (*0-685-18523-0*) HarBrace.

Civil Procedure: Adaptable to Courses Utilizing Materials by Landers. Jonathan M. Landers. LC 87-130239. (Legalines Ser.). 257p. 10.95 (*0-685-19020-X*) HarBrace.

Civil Procedure: Adaptable to Courses Utilizing Rosenberg, Smit & Dreyfuss' Casebook on Civil Procedure. Casenotes Publishing Co., Inc. Staff. Ed. by Norman S. Goldenberg et al. (Legal Briefs Ser.). 1990. pap. write for info. (*0-87457-018-2*, 1044) Casenotes Pub.

Civil Procedure: Adaptable to Courses Utilizing Yeazell, Landers & Martin's Casebook on Civil Procedure. Casenotes Publishing Co., Inc. Staff. Ed. by Norman S. Goldenberg et al. (Legal Briefs Ser.). 1992. pap. write for info. (*0-87457-016-6*, 1046) Casenotes Pub.

Civil Procedure: Cases & Comments on the Process of Adjudication. 3rd ed. Paul Carrington & Barbara A. Babcock. 1250p. (C). 1983. 46.00 (*0-316-12988-7*) Little.

Civil Procedure: Cases & Materials. 2nd ed. Robert C. Casad et al. (Contemporary Legal Education Ser.). 1153p. 1989. 44.00 (*0-87473-439-8*) Michie Butterworth.

***Civil Procedure: Cases & Materials, Successor Edition, 1994 Supplement.** A. Leo Levin et al. (University Casebook Ser.). 80p. 1994. pap. text ed. 6.50 (*1-56662-206-9*) Foundation Pr.

Civil Procedure: Materials for a Basic Course, 1994 Supplement. 6th ed. Kevin M. Clermont. (University Casebook Ser.). (Illus.). 108p. 1994. pap. text ed. 7.50 (*1-56662-184-4*) Foundation Pr.

Civil Procedure: Statutes & Rules the Court. 2nd ed. Paul Carrington & Barbara A. Babcock. (C). 1983. pap. 19.00 (*0-316-12974-7*) Little.

Civil Procedure: Teacher's Manual to Accompany Materials for a Basic Course In. 6th ed. Richard H. Field et al. (University Casebook Ser.). 160p. 1990. pap. text ed. write for info. (*0-88277-823-4*) Foundation Pr.

***Civil Procedure, a Modern Approach, Teacher's Manual For.** 2nd ed. Richard L. Marcus et al. (American Casebook Ser.). 450p. (C). 1995. pap. text ed. write for info. (*0-314-06902-X*) West Pub.

Civil Procedure, a Modern Approach, 1994. suppl. ed. Richard L. Marcus. 200p. 1994. pap. text ed. 12.00 (*0-314-04320-9*) West Pub.

Civil Procedure Adaptable to Courses Utilizing Marcus, Redish & Sherman's Casebook on Civil Procedure. Casenotes Publishing Co., Inc. Staff et al. Ed. by Goldenberg et al. (Legal Briefs Ser.). 1990. pap. write for info. (*0-87457-163-4*, 1047) Casenotes Pub.

Civil Procedure, Basic. 2nd ed. Green. 1979. text ed. 22.75 (*0-88277-458-1*) Foundation Pr.

Civil Procedure, Cases & Materials. 6th ed. John J. Cound et al. (American Casebook Ser.). 1353p. 1993. text ed. 54.00 (*0-314-02219-8*) West Pub.

Civil Procedure, Cases & Materials. Richard L. Marcus et al. (American Casebook Ser.). 1027p. 1992. reprint ed. text ed. 46.00 (*0-314-49349-2*) West Pub.

Civil Procedure Code. C. K. Takwani. (C). 1987. 80.00 (*0-89771-772-4*, Pub. by Eastern Book II) St Mut.

Civil Procedure Code, 2 vols., Set. S. Sarkar. (C). 1989. 470.00 (*0-685-46478-4*) St Mut.

Civil Procedure in a Nutshell. 3rd ed. Mary K. Kane. (Nutshell Ser.). 303p. 1992. reprint ed. pap. text ed. 15.50 (*0-314-86282-X*) West Pub.

Civil Procedure in California: State & Federal, Supplemental Materials for Use with All Civil Procedure Casebooks, 1994 Edition. Mary K. Kane & David I. Levine. (American Casebook Ser.). 650p. 1994. pap. text ed. 21.50 (*0-314-04170-2*) West Pub.

Civil Procedure in California: State & Federal: Supplemental Materials for Use with All Civil Procedure Casebooks. Mary K. Kane & David I. Levine. (American Casebook Ser.). 551p. 1993. reprint ed. pap. text ed. 21.50 (*0-314-00770-9*) West Pub.

Civil Procedure in Japan. Takaaki Hattori & Dan F. Henderson. 1988. reprint ed. ring bd. 125.00 (*0-929179-01-3*) Transnatl Juris Pubns.

Civil Procedure Supplement for Use with All Pleading & Procedure Casebooks, 1993. John J. Cound et al. (American Casebook Ser.). 459p. (C). 1993. pap. text ed. 17.00 (*0-314-02528-6*) West Pub.

Civil Procedure Supplement for Use with All Pleading & Procedure Casebooks, 1994. John J. Cound et al. (American Casebook Ser.). 475p. 1994. pap. text ed. 17.00 (*0-314-04282-2*) West Pub.

Civil Procedure, Teacher's Manual for Cases & Materials on Civil Procedure Successor Edition. A. Leo Levin et al. (University Casebook Ser.). 106p. (C). 1992. pap. text ed. write for info. (*1-56662-032-5*) Foundation Pr.

Civil Procedure, 1987. 2nd ed. Ed. by C. K. Takwani. (C). 1990. 70.00 (*0-685-39785-8*) St Mut.

Civil Ready Referencer, 2 vols. 4th ed. N. Nandi. (C). 1989. 250.00 (*0-685-46480-6*) St Mut.

Civil Referencer. Bholeshwar Nath. 1733p. (C). 1989. 350.00x (*0-685-37464-5*); 175.00 (*0-685-38612-0*) St Mut.

Civil Religion & Moral Order: Theoretical & Historical Dimensions. Michael W. Hughey. LC 82-15429. (Contributions in Sociology Ser.: No. 43). 256p. 1983. text ed. 55.00 (*0-313-23522-8*, HUR/, Greenwood Pr) Greenwood.

Civil Religion & Political Theology. Ed. by Leroy S. Rouner. LC 86-11242. (Boston University Studies in Philosophy & Religion: Vol. 8). 240p. (C). 1986. text ed. 29.95x (*0-268-00757-8*) U of Notre Dame Pr.

Civil Religion & Political Theology. Ed. by Leroy S. Rouner. LC 86-11242. (Boston University Studies in Philosophy & Religion: Vol. 8). (C). 1994. reprint ed. pap. text ed. 10.95 (*0-268-00806-X*) U of Notre Dame Pr.

Civil Religion & Transcendent Experience: Studies in Theology & History, Psychology & Mysticism. Ed. by Ralph C. Wood & John E. Collins. LC 88-5166. (Luce Program on Religion & the Social Crisis Ser.: No. 3). vi, 167p. (C). 1988. 24.95 (*0-86554-295-3*, H254) Mercer Univ Pr.

Civil Religion, Church & State see Modern American Protestantism & Its World

Civil Religion in Israel: Traditional Judaism & Political Culture in the Jewish State. Charles S. Liebman & Eliezer Don-Yehiya. LC 82-17427. 270p. 1983. 45.00 (*0-520-04817-2*) U CA Pr.

***Civil Remedies, Vol. 1.** M. Tilbury. 350p. 1990. pap. 83.00 (*0-409-30078-0*, Austral); boxed 120.00 (*0-409-30077-2*, Austral) Butterworth Legal Pubs.

***Civil Remedies, Vol. 2.** M. Tilbury. 464p. 1993. pap. 83.00 (*0-409-30313-5*, Austral); boxed 120.00 (*0-409-30312-7*, Austral) Butterworth Legal Pubs.

Civil Reserve Air Fleet & Operation Desert Shield - Desert Storm. Mary E. Chenoweth. LC 93-28795. 1993. write for info. (*0-8330-1437-4*, MR-298-AF) Rand Corp.

Civil Resistance in the East European & Soviet Revolutions. Adam Roberts. (Einstein Institution Monograph Ser.). 43p. 1991. 3.00 (*1-880813-04-1*) A Einstein Inst.

Civil Rico. D. B. Smith & T. G. Reed. 1987. write for info. (*0-8205-1527-2*) Bender.

Civil RICO: A Research Guide to Civil Liability for Business Crimes. Peter S. Dickinson. LC 89-2099. (Legal Research Guides Ser.). iii, 32p. 1989. lib. bdg. 32.00 (*0-89941-668-3*, 305780) W S Hein.

Civil RICO Litigation, 3 vols. 2nd ed. John H. Sturc. 2590p. 1992. ring bd. 360.00 (*0-13-138546-1*) Aspen Law.

Civil RICO Litigation after Sedima, 2 Vols., 1. 60.00 (*0-317-01376-9*) RICO Law.

Civil RICO Litigation after Sedima, 2 Vols., 2. 80.00 (*0-317-01377-7*) RICO Law.

Civil RICO Litigation after Sedima, 2 Vols., Set. 126.00 (*0-317-01375-0*) RICO Law.

Civil RICO Practice: Causes of Action. Ed. by Harold Brown. (Business Litigation Library). 368p. 1991. text ed. 138.00 (*0-471-53275-4*) Wiley.

Civil RICO Practice Manual. Paul A. Batista. (Trial Practice Library). 1987. text ed. 138.00 (*0-471-84510-8*) Wiley.

Civil RICO Practice Manual. suppl. ed. Paul A. Batista. (Trial Practice Library). 1993. Cumulative supplement, 1993. pap. 75.00 (*0-471-59550-0*) Wiley.

***Civil Rights.** (Voices in African American History Ser.). (YA). 1994. lib. bdg. 11.95 (*0-8136-4975-7*) Modern Curr.

***Civil Rights.** (Voices in African American History Ser.). (YA). 1994. pap. 5.95 (*0-8136-4976-5*) Modern Curr.

Civil Rights. Michael L. Levine. Ed. by Nick Bakalar. (Social Issues in American History Ser.). (Illus.). 192p. 1996. 29.95 (*0-89774-859-X*, 2147) Oryx Pr.

Civil Rights. Ed. by Leonard W. Levy et al. (Readings from the Encyclopedia of the American Constitution Ser.). 350p. (C). 1989. pap. 12.95 (*0-02-897241-4*) Macmillan.

An Asterisk (*) at the beginning of an entry indicates that the title is appearing in BIP for the first time. 1285

Civil Rights: HIV Testing, Contact Tracing, & Quarantine. Neal A. Dickerson. LC 93-2598. (Politics of AIDS Ser.: Vol. 2). 1993. pap. 12.00 (*0-930383-34-6*) Monument Pr.

***Civil Rights: Index of Modern Information.** rev. ed. Daskin R. Durron. LC 88-47546. 153p. 1994. 39.50 (*0-7883-0680-4*); pap. 39.50 (*0-7883-0681-2*) ABBE Pubs Assn.

Civil Rights: Rhetoric or Reality? Thomas Sowell. LC 85-19131. 168p. 1985. pap. 6.95 (*0-688-06269-5*, Quill) Morrow.

Civil Rights: The Nineteen Sixties Freedom Struggle. Rhoda L. Blumberg. LC 84-3810. (Social Movements Past & Present Ser.). 1984. lib. bdg. 23.95 (*0-8057-9704-1*, Twayne); pap. 11.95 (*0-8057-9708-4*, Twayne) Macmillan.

Civil Rights: The 1960's Freedom Struggle. rev. ed. Rhoda L. Blumberg. (Twayne's Social Movements Past & Present Ser.: No. 248). 248p. (C). 1991. text ed. 27.95 (*0-8057-9733-5*, Twayne); pap. 13.95 (*0-8057-9734-3*, Twayne) Macmillan.

Civil Rights Act of Nineteen Ninety-One. (Monograph Ser.). 1991. 10.00 (*0-685-61707-6*) Intl Personnel Mgmt.

Civil Rights Act of Nineteen Ninety-One: Its Impact on Employment Discrimination Litigation. Susan Ritz. (Litigation & Administrative Practice Ser.). 304p. 1992. pap. text ed. 70.00 (*0-685-56924-1*, H4-5127) PLI.

Civil Rights Act of Nineteen Ninety-One: Law & Explanation. 120p. 1991. pap. 12.50 (*0-685-67122-4*, 4837) Commerce.

Civil Rights Act of 1991. David A. Cathcart et al. LC 93-71601. 478p. 1993. text ed. 95.00 (*0-8318-0696-6*, B696) Am Law Inst.

Civil Rights Act of 1991: Legislative History, 2 vols., Set. Ed. by Douglas S. McDowell. 1467p. (Orig.). 1992. pap. 120.00 (*0-916559-40-8*) EPF.

Civil Rights Actions, 7 vols. Joseph G. Cook & John L. Sobieski. 1983. Updates. ring bd. write for info. (*0-8205-1199-4*) Bender.

Civil Rights Actions: Section 1983 & Related Statutes. Peter Low & John Jeffries. (University Casebook Ser.). 290p. 1993. pap. text ed. 11.50 (*1-56662-107-0*) Foundation Pr.

Civil Rights Actions: Section 1983 & Related Statutes. Peter W. Low & John C. Jeffries, Jr. (University Casebook Ser.). 773p. 1988. text ed. 35.95 (*0-88277-635-5*) Foundation Pr.

Civil Rights Actions: Section 1983 & Related Statutes. 2nd ed. Peter W. Low & John C. Jeffries, Jr. LC 94-7715. (University Casebook Ser.). 953p. 1994. text ed. 42.50 (*1-56662-149-6*) Foundation Pr.

Civil Rights & African-Americans: A Documentary History. Ed. by Robert L. Zangrando. 681p. 1991. reprint ed. pap. 19.95 (*0-8101-0920-4*) Northwestern U Pr.

Civil Rights & Civil Liberties. Michael L. Benedict. LC 87-70965. (Bicentennial Essays on the Constitution Ser.). 77p. 1987. pap. 7.00 (*0-87229-038-7*) Am Hist Assn.

Civil Rights & Civil Liberties Litigation: The Law of Section 1983. 2nd ed. Sheldon H. Nahmod. LC 86-26080. (Individual Rights Ser.). 1050p. 1991. text ed. 170.00 (*0-07-172311-0*) Shepards-McGraw.

Civil Rights & Constitutional Litigation, Cases & Materials. 2nd ed. Charles F. Abernathy. (American Casebook Ser.). 753p. (C). 1992. text ed. 43.50 (*0-314-92683-6*) West Pub.

Civil Rights & Liberties. Domino. (C). 1993. text ed. 25.00 (*0-06-500612-7*) HarpCollege.

Civil Rights & the Reagan Administration. Norman C. Amaker. 1988. 46.00 (*0-87766-452-8*); pap. 25.00 (*0-87766-451-X*) U Pr of Amer.

Civil Rights & the Social Programs of the 1960s: The Social Justice Functions of Social Policy. Marcia Bok. LC 91-46996. 200p. 1992. text ed. 49.95 (*0-275-93654-6*, C3654, Praeger Pubs) Greenwood.

Civil Rights & the South: A Symposium. A. E. Sutherland, Jr. LC 78-151047. (Symposia on Law & Society Ser.). 1971. reprint ed. lib. bdg. 19.50 (*0-306-70116-2*) Da Capo.

Civil Rights & Wrongs: A Memoir of Race & Politics. Harry S. Ashmore. LC 93-30553. 1994. 25.00 (*0-679-43181-0*) Pantheon.

Civil Rights Compliance: An Update. Ed. by Frank Gonzales. (Illus.). 65p. (Orig.). 1988. pap. text ed. 7.50 (*1-878550-18-7*) Inter Dev Res Assn.

Civil Rights Decisions of the United States Supreme Court: The 19th Century. Ed. by Maureen Harrison & Steve Gilbert. (Civil Rights Decisions Ser.). 239p. (Orig.). 1994. pap. 16.95 (*1-880780-04-6*) Excellent Bks.

Civil Rights Decisions of the United States Supreme Court: The 20th Century. Ed. by Maureen Harrison & Steve Gilbert. (Civil Rights Decisions Ser.). 273p. (Orig.). 1994. pap. 16.95 (*1-880780-05-4*) Excellent Bks.

Civil Rights Era. abr. ed. Hugh D. Graham. 336p. (C). 1992. pap. text ed. 15.95 (*0-19-507322-3*) OUP.

Civil Rights Era: Origins & Development of National Policy, 1960-1972. Hugh D. Graham. 590p. 1990. 40.00 (*0-19-504531-9*) OUP.

Civil Rights for Civil Servants. NCCL. 95p. 1988. 35.00 (*0-946088-09-8*, Pub. by NCCL UK) St Mut.

Civil Rights for State & Federal Prisoners, Vol. III. Jack L. Kunsman, Jr. (Encyclopedia of Prisoner's Rights Ser.). 1982. pap. text ed. 11.50 (*0-914235-03-6*) J L Kunsman.

Civil Rights in Immigration. Milton R. Konvitz. LC 77-2605. (Cornell Studies in Civil Liberty). xii, 216p. 1977. reprint ed. text ed. 55.00 (*0-8371-9556-X*, KOCR, Greenwood Pr) Greenwood.

Civil Rights in the Federal Sector, a Look at H. R. 3613 (1992) 34p. 1992. pap. text ed. 15.00 (*1-56986-039-4*) Federal Bar.

Civil Rights in the United States. Ed. by Hugh D. Graham. (Issues in Policy History Ser.: No. 4). 160p. (C). 1994. pap. 13.95 (*0-271-01343-5*) Pa St U Pr.

***Civil Rights in the Workplace, 2 vols, Vol. 2.** 2nd rev. ed. Henry H. Perritt, Jr. Incl. Vol. 1. Civil Rights in the Workplace. 2nd rev. ed. LC 94-36366. 1994. (*0-471-10626-7*, Pub. by Wiley Law Pubns); Vol.2. Civil Rights in the Workplace. 2nd rev. ed. LC 94-36366. 1994. (*0-471-10624-0*, Pub. by Wiley Law Pubns); LC 94-36366. (Employment Law Library). 1994. Set text ed. 218.00 (*0-471-10632-1*, Pub. by Wiley Law Pubns) Wiley.

Civil Rights in Two Thousand Four: Where Will We Be? Derrick Bell, Jr. (Working Papers on Civil Rights). 1988. 2.50 (*0-318-33316-3*, CR2) IPPP.

Civil Rights Injunction. Owen M. Fiss. LC 78-2052. 123p. reprint ed. pap. 35.10 (*0-317-27816-9*, 2056034) Bks Demand.

Civil Rights Issues of Asian & Pacific Americans: Myths & Realities. U. S. Commission on Civil Rights. 854p. 1982. reprint ed. lib. bdg. 55.00 (*0-89941-216-5*, 201380) W S Hein.

Civil Rights Leaders. Ed. by Richard Rennert. LC 92-37655. (Profiles of Great Black Americans Ser.). (Illus.). (J). 1993. 13.95 (*0-7910-2051-7*, Am Art Analog); pap. 5.95 (*0-7910-2052-5*, Am Art Analog) Chelsea Hse.

Civil Rights Legislation: Case & Materials. 3rd ed. Theodore Eisenberg. (Contemporary Legal Education Ser.). 1343p. 1991. 38.00 (*0-87473-721-4*) Michie Butterworth.

***Civil Rights Legislation & Litigation, 1994.** Levinson & Bodensteiner. 682p. Date not set. ring bd. 48.50 (*1-879581-16-7*) Lupus Pubns.

***Civil Rights Litigation: Cases & Perspectives.** Roy L. Brooks et al. LC 94-73848. 1500p. (C). 1995. text ed. write for info. (*0-89089-692-5*) Carolina Acad Pr.

***Civil Rights Litigation & Attorney Fees Annual Handbook, Vol. 10.** National Lawyers Guild Staff. (Civil Rights Ser.). 1994. pap. 115.00 (*0-614-07303-0*) Clark Boardman Callaghan.

***Civil Rights Litigation under 42 USC Section 1983.** 307p. 1994. 35.00 (*1-56986-251-6*) Federal Bar.

Civil Rights Movement. Suzanne M. Coil. (Liberty & Justice For All Ser.). (Illus.). 64p. (J). (gr. 5-8). 1995. lib. bdg. 15.98 (*0-8050-2987-7*) TFC Bks NY.

***Civil Rights Movement.** Charles Patterson. LC 95-3027. (Social Reform Movements Ser.). 1995. 17.95 (*0-8160-2968-7*) Facts on File.

Civil Rights Movement. Sanford Wexler. (Eyewitness History Ser.). (Illus.). 304p. 1993. 45.00 (*0-8160-2748-X*) Facts on File.

Civil Rights Movement: References & Resources. Paul T. Murray. (G. K. Hall Reference Ser.). 280p. 1993. text ed. 40.00 (*0-8161-1837-X*) G K Hall.

Civil Rights Movement in America. Ed. by Charles W. Eagles. LC 86-5665. (Chancellor's Symposium on Southern History Ser.). (Orig.). 1986. 27.50 (*0-87805-297-6*); pap. 14.95 (*0-87805-298-4*) U Pr of Miss.

Civil Rights Movement in America. D. S. Gaikwad. (C). 1987. 31.00 (*81-7100-005-3*, Pub. by Deep) S Asia.

Civil Rights Movement in America from 1865 to the Present. 2nd ed. Patricia McKissack & Fredrick McKissack. LC 86-9636. (Civil Rights Ser.). (Illus.). 352p. (J). (gr. 4 up). 1991. 30.90 (*0-516-00579-0*) Childrens.

Civil Rights Movement in Florida & the United States. Charles U. Smith. 326p. 1989. 29.95 (*0-942407-09-1*) Father & Son.

***Civil Rights of Homeless People.** Madeleine Stoner. (Modern Applications of Social Work Ser.). 208p. 1995. lib. bdg. 38.95 (*0-202-30513-9*); pap. 19.95 (*0-202-30514-7*) Aldine de Gruyter.

Civil Rights Restoration Act. (Monograph Ser.). 1989. 10.00 (*0-685-61709-2*) Intl Personnel Mgmt.

Civil Rights Society: The Social Construction of Victims. Kristin Bumiller. LC 87-45485. 176p. 1988. text ed. 32.50 (*0-8018-3544-5*) Johns Hopkins.

Civil Rights Society: The Social Construction of Victims. Kristin Bumiller. LC 87-45485. 172p. 1992. reprint ed. pap. text ed. 12.95 (*0-8018-4510-6*) Johns Hopkins.

Civil Rights Struggle: Leaders in Profile. John D'Emilio. LC 79-18006. 201p. reprint ed. pap. 57.30 (*0-685-23986-1*, 2031556) Bks Demand.

Civil Rights, the Constitution & Congress, 1863-1869. Earl M. Maltz. LC 90-32818. xii, 196p. 1990. 25.00 (*0-7006-0467-7*) U Pr of KS.

Civil Rights, the Constitution, & the Courts. Archibald Cox et al. LC 67-20874. 76p. 1967. reprint ed. pap. 25.00 (*0-7837-1686-9*, 2057216) Bks Demand.

Civil Rights under Reagan. Robert Detlefsen. 300p. (C). 1991. 24.95 (*1-55815-111-7*) ICS Pr.

Civil Rules Annotated. Colorado Supreme Court Staff et al. write for info. (*0-318-59330-0*) West Pub.

Civil Servants & the Politics of Inflation in Germany, 1914-1924. Andreas Kunz. (Veroeffentlichungen der Historischen Kommission zu Berlin, Band 67, Beitraege zu Inflation und Wiederaufbau in Deutschland und Europa 1914-1924: Vol. 66). xxii, 428p. 1986. lib. bdg. 84.60 (*0-89925-222-2*) De Gruyter.

***Civil Servants & the Politics of Inflation in Germany, 1914-1924.** Andreas Kunz. (Veroeffentlichungen der Historischen Kommission Zu Berlin Ser.: Vol. 66). xxii, 428p. 1986. lib. bdg. 84.60 (*3-11-010482-2*) De Gruyter.

***Civil Service.** Keith Dowding. LC 94-48461. (Theory & Practice in British Politics Ser.). 1995. 59.95 (*0-415-07567-X*); pap. write for info. (*0-415-07568-8*) Routledge.

***Civil Service: Taking Forward Continuity & Change - White Paper.** (Command Paper Ser.: No. 2748). 55p. 1995. pap. 16.00 (*0-10-127482-3*, HM74823, Pub. by HMSO UK) UNIPUB.

***Civil Service Administration, Management & Supervision.** Jack Rudman. (General Aptitude & Abilities Ser.: CS-3). 1994. pap. 27.95 (*0-8373-6703-4*) Nat Learn.

Civil Service Administrative Tests. Ed. by Hy Hammer. LC 85-9046. 192p. 1985. pap. 12.00 (*0-668-05768-8*, Arco Test) P-H Gen Ref & Trav.

Civil Service & the Patronage. C. R. Fish. 1984. lib. bdg. 90.00 (*0-8490-3237-7*) Gordon Pr.

***Civil Service Arithmetic.** Jack Rudman. (General Aptitude & Abilities Ser.: CS-6). 1994. pap. 17.95 (*0-8373-6706-9*) Nat Learn.

Civil Service Arithmetic & Vocabulary. Barbara Erdsneker et al. 1993. pap. 12.00 (*0-671-86897-7*, Arco Test) P-H Gen Ref & Trav.

Civil Service, Business & Industry Tests: Clerical & Stenographic. 2nd ed. D. D. Mulkerne & M. E. Andrews. 1983. text ed. 14.56 (*0-07-043987-7*) McGraw.

***Civil Service Clerical Abilities.** Jack Rudman. (General Aptitude & Abilities Ser.: CS-12). 1994. pap. 17.95 (*0-8373-6712-3*) Nat Learn.

Civil Service Development in Louisiana, Vol. 3. L. V. Howard. LC 57-3262. 1956. 11.00 (*0-930598-02-4*) Tulane Stud Pol.

Civil Service Examination Passbook Series see Career Examination Series

***Civil Service General & Mental Abilities.** Jack Rudman. (General Aptitude & Abilities Ser.: CS-16). 1994. pap. 19.95 (*0-8373-6716-6*) Nat Learn.

***Civil Service Grammar & Usage.** Jack Rudman. (General Aptitude & Abilities Ser.: CS-7). 1994. pap. 19.95 (*0-8373-6707-7*) Nat Learn.

***Civil Service Graphs, Charts & Tables.** Jack Rudman. (General Aptitude & Abilities Ser.: CS-11). 1994. pap. 19.95 (*0-8373-6711-5*) Nat Learn.

Civil Service Handbook. 9th ed. Hy Hammer. (Arco Civil Service Ser.). 160p. 1988. pap. 8.95 (*0-13-135021-8*, Arco Test) P-H Gen Ref & Trav.

Civil Service Handbook: How to Get a Civil Service Job. 11th ed. Ed. by Hy Hammer. LC 93-27882. 1994. 10.00 (*0-671-87461-6*, Arco Test) P-H Gen Ref & Trav.

***Civil Service Home Study Course.** Jack Rudman. (General Aptitude & Abilities Ser.: CS-1). 1994. pap. 19.95 (*0-8373-6701-8*) Nat Learn.

Civil Service in Britain & France. Ed. by William A. Robson. LC 75-26777. 191p. 1975. reprint ed. text ed. 35.00 (*0-8371-8347-2*, ROCSB, Greenwood Pr) Greenwood.

Civil Service in Liberal Democracies: An International Survey. Ed. by John Kingdom. 240p. 1988. lib. bdg. 53.00 (*0-415-00493-4*, A0449); pap. 17.95 (*0-415-04456-1*) Routledge.

Civil Service Law in Ohio. Jonathan Downes & Marybeth Deavers. (Baldwin's Labor Law Ser.). 452p. 1993. ring bd. 72.00 (*0-8322-0439-0*) Banks-Baldwin.

Civil Service Law, N. Y. C. 200p. 1994. ring bd. 12.95 (*0-930137-53-1*) Looseleaf Law.

***Civil Service Mechanical Aptitude.** Jack Rudman. (General Aptitude & Abilities Ser.: CS-15). 1994. pap. 23.95 (*0-8373-6715-8*) Nat Learn.

Civil Service of Great Britain. Robert Moses. LC 14-2375. (Columbia University. Studies in the Social Sciences: No. 139). reprint ed. 34.50 (*0-404-51139-2*) AMS Pr.

Civil Service Pay in Africa. Derek Robinson. xi, 220p. (Orig.). 1990. lib. bdg. 22.00 (*92-2-106459-X*) Intl Labour Office.

Civil Service Pay in South Asia. David C. Chew. Ed. by International Labour Office Staff. v, 149p. (Orig.). 1992. pap. 18.00 (*92-2-107759-4*) Intl Labour Office.

***Civil Service Promotion Course.** Jack Rudman. (General Aptitude & Abilities Ser.: CS-2). 1994. pap. 23.95 (*0-8373-6702-6*) Nat Learn.

Civil Service Psychological & Psychiatric Tests. Mark L. Mendelsohn. 160p. 1990. pap. 10.95 (*0-13-136912-1*) P-H.

Civil Service Question Books, 6 bks., Set. 1994. 24.95 (*0-930137-55-8*) Looseleaf Law.

Civil Service Quizzer & Guide. 11th ed. Harry W. Koch. 1978. pap. 8.00 (*0-910553-12-2*) Ken-Bks.

***Civil Service Reading Comprehension.** Jack Rudman. (General Aptitude & Abilities Ser.: CS-8). 1994. pap. 19.95 (*0-8373-6708-5*) Nat Learn.

Civil Service Reading Comprehension Tests. Eve P. Steinberg. 1986. pap. 8.95 (*0-668-06486-2*) P-H.

Civil Service Reform Act of Nineteen Seventy-Eight: Tenth Anniversary Review & Assessment. Ed. by Elaine G. Goldberg. 228p. 1988. pap. 38.50 (*0-934753-35-0*) LRP Pubns.

Civil Service Reform Act of 1978. Ed. by Patricia Ingraham & David Rosenbloom. (Orig.). 1988. pap. 12.00 (*0-944285-04-X*) Pol Studies.

Civil Service Reform & the World Bank. Barbara Nunberg & John Nellis. LC 92-12847. (Discussion Paper Ser.: No. 161). 56p. 1993. 6.95 (*0-8213-2117-X*, 12117) World Bank.

***Civil Service Reform in Latin America & the Caribbean: Proceedings of a Conference.** Ed. by Shahid A. Chaudry et al. LC 94-35275. (Technical Papers: Vol. 259). 1994. write for info. (*0-8213-3041-1*) World Bank.

Civil Service Reform in Lebanon. Iskandar Bashir. 1977. 19.95 (*0-8156-6050-2*, Am U Beirut) Syracuse U Pr.

***Civil Service Secretary.** Jack Rudman. (General Aptitude & Abilities Ser.: CS-4). 1994. pap. 19.95 (*0-8373-6704-2*) Nat Learn.

***Civil Service Since 1945.** Kevin Theakston. (Making Contemporary Britain Ser.). 208p. 1995. pap. write for info. (*0-631-18825-8*) Blackwell Pubs.

***Civil Service since 1945.** Kevin Theakston. (Making Contemporary Britain Ser.). 208p. 1995. write for info. (*0-631-18824-X*) Blackwell Pubs.

***Civil Service Spelling.** Jack Rudman. (General Aptitude & Abilities Ser.: CS-9). 1994. pap. 17.95 (*0-8373-6709-3*) Nat Learn.

***Civil Service System & Economic Development: The Japanese Experience: Report on an International Colloquium in Tokyo, March 22-25, 1994.** Hyung-Ki Kim. LC 94-48164. (EDI Policy Seminar Report Ser.: No. 33). 1995. write for info. (*0-8213-3170-1*) World Bank.

***Civil Service Test Practice Book for 100 Civil Service Jobs.** Jack Rudman. (General Aptitude & Abilities Ser.: CS-5). 1994. pap. 23.95 (*0-8373-6705-0*) Nat Learn.

Civil Service Tests for Basic Skills Jobs. Ed. by Hy Hammer. LC 84-6342. 192p. (Orig.). 1985. pap. 9.95 (*0-668-06187-1*, 6187-1, Arco Test) P-H Gen Ref & Trav.

Civil Service Today. Gavin Drewry & Tony Butcher. (Illus.). 256p. 1991. pap. 24.95 (*0-631-18172-5*) Blackwell Pubs.

***Civil Service Verbal Abilities.** Jack Rudman. (General Aptitude & Abilities Ser.: CS-13). 1994. pap. 17.95 (*0-8373-6713-1*) Nat Learn.

***Civil Service Verbal & Clerical Abilities.** Jack Rudman. (General Aptitude & Abilities Ser.). 1994. pap. 19.95 (*0-8373-6714-X*) Nat Learn.

***Civil Service Vocabulary.** Jack Rudman. (General Aptitude & Abilities Ser.: CS-10). 1994. pap. 17.95 (*0-8373-6710-7*) Nat Learn.

Civil Service Yearbook, 1993. HMSO Staff. 372p. 1993. pap. 40.00 (*0-11-430075-5*, HM00755, Pub. by HMSO UK) UNIPUB.

Civil Service 2000. William B. Johnston. 54p. 1988. per., pap. 2.00 (*0-16-001227-9*, S/N 006-000-01337-6) USGPO.

***Civil Service 2000: A Report on the Long-Term Work Force Needs of the Federal Government.** William B. Johnston. (Illus.). 52p. (C). 1994. pap. text ed. 30.00 (*0-7881-1378-X*) Diane Pub.

Civil Services of the United Kingdom: 1885-1970. E. N. Gladden. (Illus.). 289p. 1967. 27.50 (*0-7146-1066-6*, Pub. by F Cass Pubs UK) Intl Spec Bk.

Civil Society. Keith Tester. 208p. 1992. 49.95 (*0-415-07516-5*, A9877); pap. 15.95 (*0-415-07517-3*, A9881) Routledge.

***Civil Society: Theory, History, Comparison.** 2nd ed. Ed. by John A. Hall. 342p. 1995. 45.00 (*0-7456-1061-7*, Pub. by Polity Pr UK) Blackwell Pubs.

***Civil Society: Theory, History, Comparison.** 2nd ed. Ed. by John A. Hall. 342p. 1995. pap. 13.95 (*0-7456-1456-6*, Pub. by Polity Pr UK) Blackwell Pubs.

Civil Society & Political Theory. Jean L. Cohen & Andrew Arato. (Studies in Contemporary German Social Thought). (Illus.). 800p. 1994. pap. 22.00 (*0-262-53121-6*) MIT Pr.

***Civil Society & State Relations in Sweden.** Michele Micheletti. 212p. (C). 1995. boxed, pap. text ed. 59.95 (*1-85972-037-4*, Pub. by Avebury Pub UK) Ashgate Pub Co.

Civil Society & the State: New European Perspectives. Ed. by John B. Keane. 416p. 1988. text ed. 55.00 (*0-86091-203-5*, Pub. by Verso UK); pap. text ed. 18.95 (*0-86091-921-8*, Pub. by Verso UK) Routledge Chapman & Hall.

Civil Society & the State in Africa. Ed. by John W. Harbeson et al. LC 93-42930. 312p. 1994. lib. bdg. 45.00 (*1-55587-360-X*) Lynne Rienner.

***Civil Society, Civil Religion.** Andrew Shooks. 288p. (C). 1995. write for info. (*0-631-19758-3*); pap. write for info. (*0-631-19759-1*) Blackwell Pubs.

***Civil Society in the Middle East.** Augustus R. Norton. LC 94-33780. (Social, Economic, & Political Studies of the Middle East: 50). 1994. 71.50 (*90-04-10037-7*) E J Brill.

Civil Space Systems: Implications for International Security. Stephen E. Doyle. LC 93-39213. 288p. 1994. 57.95 (*1-85521-431-8*, Pub. by Dartmth Pub UK) Ashgate Pub Co.

Civil Strife in Latin America: A Legal History of U. S. Involvement. William Everett Kane. LC 76-184954. 252p. reprint ed. pap. 71.90 (*0-8357-8075-9*, 2034129) Bks Demand.

Civil-Structural Inspection, Course 29. (Illus.). 260p. 1979. ring bd. 95.00 (*0-87683-115-3*) GP Pub.

Civil Structural Inspection, Course 29. Center for Occupational Research & Development Staff. (Nuclear Technology Ser.). (Illus.). 282p. (C). 1984. pap. text ed. 28.00 (*1-55502-118-2*) CORD Commns.

Civil to Strangers: And Other Writings. Barbara Pym. 396p. 1989. pap. 8.95 (*0-452-26138-4*, Plume) NAL-Dutton.

Civil Tongue. Edwin Newman. LC 76-11607. 1976. 9.95 (*0-672-52267-5*, Bobbs) Macmillan.

***Civil Tongue: Justice, Dialogue & the Politics of Pluralism.** Mark Kingwell. 272p. 1995. 37.50 (*0-271-01334-6*); pap. 16.95 (*0-271-01335-4*) Pa St U Pr.

Civil Trial & Appellate Procedure, Vol. 30-32. Jeremy C. Wicker. 1985. write for info. (*0-318-60692-5*) West Pub.

Civil Trial Manual. 2nd ed. Ralph C. McCullough. 908p. 1980. Suppl., 1987, 419p. & Rev. Contents Table, 34p. ring bd., pap. 95.00 (*0-685-00157-1*, B544/B603) Am Law Inst.

Civil Trial Manual. 2nd suppl. ed. Ralph C. McCullough. 908p. 1980. ring bd. 189.00 (*0-686-31970-2*, B108/B544/B603) Am Law Inst.

Civil Trial Manual II: 1987 Supplement. Ralph C. McCullough & James L. Underwood. 385p. 1987. pap. 86.00 (*0-8318-0544-7*, B544) Am Law Inst.

Civil Trials Benchbook. California Continuing Education of the Bar Staff. LC 81-67564. (California Judges Benchbook Civil Trials Ser.). 776p. 1981. 85.00 (*0-88124-080-X*, CP-34550) Cont Ed Bar-CA.

An Asterisk (*) at the beginning of an entry indicates that the title is appearing in BIP for the first time.

Civil Universities: Aspects of a British Tradition. W. H. Armytage. LC 76-55207. (Academic Profession Ser.). (Illus.). 1977. reprint ed. lib. bdg. 28.95 (*0-405-10031-0*) Ayer.

Civil Use of Government Helicopters. Crowell & Moring. Ed. by Frank L. Jensen, Jr. 82p. 1994. ring bd. write for info. (*0-9630326-4-X*) Helicopter Assn Intl.

Civil War. Timothy Biel. LC 91-29500. (America's Wars Ser.). (Illus.). 112p. (J). (gr. 5-8). 1991. lib. bdg. 19.95 (*1-56006-404-8*) Lucent Bks.

Civil War. Julias Caesar. Tr. by Jane F. Gardner. 400p. 1985. 16.95 (*0-88029-041-2*) Dorset Pr.

Civil War. Julius Caesar. Tr. by Jane F. Mitchell. (Classics Ser.). 1976. mass mkt. 8.95 (*0-14-044187-5*, Penguin Classics) Viking Penguin.

Civil War. Bruce Catton. LC 85-3969. (American Heritage Library). (Illus.). 320p. 1985. pap. 12.95 (*0-8281-0305-4*) HM.

Civil War. Taylor Downing & Maggie Millman. (Illus.). 192p. 1992. pap. 24.95 (*1-85585-094-X*) Trafalgar.

***Civil War.** David W. Felder. 52p. 1995. pap. text ed. 5.00 (*0-910959-62-5*) Felder Bks.

Civil War. Kathlyn Gay. (YA). (gr. 6 up). 1995. lib. bdg. 15.98 (*0-8050-2845-5*) H Holt & Co.

Civil War. Michael Golay. Ed. by John Bowman. (America at War Ser.). (Illus.). 192p. (YA). (gr. 6-12). 1992. lib. bdg. 17.95 (*0-8160-2514-2*) Facts on File.

Civil War. Hazel Jensen. (History of Iowa Ser.). (Illus.). 63p. (Orig.). (YA). (gr. 5 up). 1988. pap. text ed. 1.50 (*0-924702-11-7*) Grn Valley Area.

***Civil War.** David Johnson. (Jackdaws Ser.). (Illus.). 1991. 24.95 (*1-56696-045-2*); student ed 32.00 (*0-614-07312-X*) Golden Owl NY.

Civil War. Ed. by Raymond F. Locke. (Great Adventures of History Ser.). 1.75 (*0-87687-006-X*, BM006) Mankind Pub.

Civil War. Lucan. (Loeb Classical Library: No. 220). 658p. 1928. 18.95 (*0-674-99242-3*) HUP.

Civil War. Lucan. Ed. & Tr. by Susan H. Braund. (World's Classics Ser.). (Illus.). 384p. 1993. pap. 9.95 (*0-19-282994-7*) OUP.

***Civil War.** Martin W. Sandler. LC 95-1507. (J). 1996. 19.95 (*0-06-026024-6*); lib. bdg. 20.89 (*0-06-026027-0*) HarpC Child Bks.

***Civil War.** Brooks D. Simpson. Ed. by John H. Franklin & A. S. Eisenstadt. (American History Ser.). 175p. (C). 1996. pap. text ed. 11.95 (*0-88295-929-8*) Harlan Davidson.

Civil War. Carter Smith. (American Historical Images on File Collection). (Illus.). 320p. 1988. ring bd. 155.00 (*0-8160-1609-7*) Facts on File.

***Civil War.** Geoffrey C. Ward. 1994. pap. 13.00 (*0-679-75543-8*, Vin) Random.

Civil War. Eric Weiner. LC 92-9461. (Facts America Ser.). (Illus.). 64p. (J). (gr. 2-6). 1993. 7.98 (*0-8317-2312-2*) Smithmark.

Civil War, Bk. III. Caesar. Ed. by Carter. 1993. 49.95 (*0-85668-582-8*, Pub. by Aris & Phillips UK); pap. 24.95 (*0-85668-583-6*, Pub. by Aris & Phillips UK) David Brown.

Civil War, No. 1. 48p. 1992. 4.95 (*0-87135-918-9*) Marvel Entmnt.

Civil War, No. 2. 48p. 1992. 4.95 (*0-87135-919-7*) Marvel Entmnt.

Civil War, No. 3. 48p. 1992. 4.95 (*0-87135-920-0*) Marvel Entmnt.

Civil War, No. 4. 48p. 1992. 4.95 (*0-87135-921-9*) Marvel Entmnt.

Civil War, Vol. 1. Shelby Foote. 1974. 120.00 (*0-394-49517-9*) Random.

Civil War, Vol. I-II. Caesar. Ed. by J. M. Carter. (Classical Texts Ser.). 256p. (C). 1991. text ed. 49.95 (*0-85668-461-9*, Pub. by Aris & Phillips UK); pap. text ed. 24.95 (*0-85668-462-7*, Pub. by Aris & Phillips UK) David Brown.

Civil War, Vol. 2. Shelby Foote. 1963. 40.00 (*0-394-41951-0*) Random.

Civil War, Vol. 3. Shelby Foote. 1974. 40.00 (*0-394-46512-1*) Random.

Civil War: "A House Divided" Zachary Kent. LC 93-33622. (American War Ser.). (Illus.). 128p. (J). (gr. 5 up). 1994. lib. bdg. 17.95 (*0-89490-522-8*) Enslow Pubs.

***Civil War: A Collection of U. S. Commemorative Stamps.** Ed. by Time-Life Books Staff. LC 95-7484. 96p. 1995. 29.95 (*0-8094-9191-5*) Time-Life.

Civil War: A History. Harry Hansen. 664p. 1991. pap. 6.99 (*0-451-62840-3*, Ment) NAL-Dutton.

Civil War: A Narrative, 3 vols., Set. Shelby Foote. (Illus.). 1986. 72.00 (*0-394-74913-8*); pap. 72.00 (*0-685-04224-3*) Random.

Civil War: A Photographic History. Stan Schindler. (Illus.). 1991. 19.99 (*0-517-05418-3*) Random Hse Value.

Civil War: A Second American Revolution? Ed. by William E. Parrish. LC 77-15658. (American Problem Studies). 158p. (gr. 11-12). 1978. reprint ed. pap. text ed. 9.50 (*0-88275-637-0*) Krieger.

Civil War: A Soldier's View; A Collection of Civil War Writings. George F. Henderson. Ed. by Jay Luvaas. LC 57-11209. 337p. reprint ed. pap. 96.10 (*0-317-29793-7*, 2016995) Bks Demand.

Civil War: A Study Guide. Barbara Reeves. (Historical Ties Ser.). (J). (gr. 5-8). 1991. pap. text ed. 20.95 (*0-88122-688-2*) Lrn Links.

Civil War: A Thematic Unit. John Carratello & Patty Carratello. (Thematic Units Ser.). (Illus.). 80p. (gr. 5-8). 1991. student ed 8.95 (*1-55734-290-3*) Tchr Create Mat.

Civil War! America Becomes One Nation. James I. Robertson, Jr. LC 91-19177. (Illus.). 192p. (J). (gr. 5-9). 1992. lib. bdg. 16.99 (*0-394-92996-9*) Knopf Bks Yng Read.

Civil War: American Tragedy. Alden R. Carter. (First Bks.). (Illus.). 64p. (J). (gr. 5-8). 1992. lib. bdg. 13.93 (*0-531-20039-6*) Watts.

Civil War: American Tragedy. Alden R. Carter. (First Bks.). (Illus.). 64p. (J). (gr. 5-8). 1993. pap. 5.95 (*0-531-15653-2*) Watts.

Civil War: An Aerial Portrait. Photos by Sam Abell. LC 89-20467. (Illus.). 144p. 1990. 19.98 (*0-934738-61-0*) Thomasson-Grant.

Civil War: An Illustrated History. Geoffrey C. Ward et al. (Illus.). 1990. 60.00 (*0-394-56285-2*) Knopf.

Civil War: An Illustrated History. Geoffrey C. Ward et al. LC 89-43475. (Illus.). 448p. 1992. pap. 30.00 (*0-679-74277-8*) Knopf.

Civil War: Fort Sumter to Appomatax. William J. Bradley. (Illus.). 224p. 1990. 19.99 (*0-517-69325-9*) Random Hse Value.

***Civil War: Literature Units, Projects & Activities.** Janet Cassidy. 1999. pap. 9.95 (*0-590-49509-7*) Scholastic Inc.

Civil War: Opposing Viewpoints. Ed. by William Dudley. LC 94-9510. (American History Ser.). (Illus.). 312p. 1995. lib. bdg. 19.95 (*1-56510-225-8*, 2258); pap. text ed. 11.55 (*1-56510-224-X*, 224X) Greenhaven.

Civil War: Slavery & the Crisis of Union. 2nd ed. Laurel R. Singleton. (Public Issues Ser.). (Illus.). 68p. 1989. teacher ed 2.00 (*0-89994-340-3*); pap. 3.50 (*0-89994-339-X*) Soc Sci Ed.

Civil War: Strange & Fascinating Facts. Burke Davis. 1988. 6.99 (*0-517-37151-0*) Random Hse Value.

Civil War: The Best of American Heritage. Ed. by Stephen W. Sears. (American Heritage Library). 256p. 1993. pap. 9.95 (*0-395-61906-8*) HM.

***Civil War: The Nantucket Experience. Richard F. Miller & Robert F. Mooney. Ed. by Elizabeth Oldham. (Illus.). 208p. (Orig.). 1994. pap. 14.95 (*0-9627851-1-3*) Wesco Pub MA.**
"For Civil War buffs & all who love Nantucket, Miller & Mooney have given us a treasure of a book. Reminding us that Nantucketers were there - at Antietam, at Fredericksburg, at Gettysburg - it's an important piece of scholarship, & a fascinating read." - Russell Baker. "A superb & detailed story of one company of Nantucket men during the Civil War - Excellent." - Warren Wilkinson, Civil War historian & author of Mother, May You Never See the Sights I Have Seen. A chronicle of the war years as lived by the people of Nantucket including the memoirs & diary of Josiah Fitch Murphey, a Nantucketer of the famed Harvard Regiment, who was at Fredericksburg, Chancellorsville, the Wilderness, Spotsylvania, & Petersburg. THE CIVIL WAR: THE NANTUCKET EXPERIENCE also contains detailed biographies of the 80 Nantucketers who served with the 20th Massachusetts. 216 pages, complete with photographs & notes. Softcover (available immediately) $14.95. Send check or money order to: Wesco Publishing, P.O. Box 1540, Nantucket, MA 02554. ***Publisher Provided Annotation.***

Civil War: The Town of Prattsville, & the Neighboring Greene, Delaware, & Schoharie County Area. Gerald E. Sutch. xxvi, 15p. 1987. reprint ed. pap. 7.50 (*0-910746-22-2*, TCW01) Hope Farm.

Civil War Almanac. Ed. by John S. Bowman. 400p. 1986. pap. 14.95 (*0-345-35434-6*, World Almanac) Newspaper Ent.

Civil War Almanac. large type ed. Ed. by John S. Bowman. 828p. 1992. text ed. 39.95 (*0-8161-5339-6*) G K Hall.

Civil War & America's Wit. William Gibson & James Murfin. (Illus.). 432p. 1992. 19.95 (*0-685-45430-4*, 34546) Interp Mktg Prods.

Civil War & Miscellaneous Papers. (Papers of the Military Historical Society of Massachusetts: Vol. 14). 457p. 1990. reprint ed. 40.00 (*1-56837-018-0*) Broadfoot.

Civil War & National Park Wit. William Gibson & James Murfin. (Illus.). 432p. 1992. 19.95 (*0-317-91091-4*, 34541) Interp Mktg Prods.

Civil War & New York City. Ernest McKay. LC 90-32799. (New York State Bks.). (Illus.). 380p. 1991. text ed. 39.95x (*0-8156-0246-4*); pap. text ed. 15.95 (*0-8156-2545-6*) Syracuse U Pr.

Civil War & Readjustment in Kentucky. E. Merton Coulter. 1926. 12.75 (*0-8446-1131-X*) Peter Smith.

Civil War & Readjustment in Kentucky. Ellis M. Coulter. (History - United States Ser.). 468p. 1992. reprint ed. lib. bdg. 99.00 (*0-7812-6185-6*) Rprt Serv.

Civil War & Rebellion in the Roman Empire, A.D. 69-70. B. W. Henderson. 1977. lib. bdg. 59.95 (*0-8490-1636-3*) Gordon Pr.

***Civil War & Reconstruction.** (Voices in African American History Ser.). (YA). 1994. pap. 5.95 (*0-8136-4972-2*) Modern Curr.

***Civil War & Reconstruction.** (Voices in African American History Ser.). (YA). 1994. lib. bdg. 11.95 (*0-8136-4974-9*) Modern Curr.

Civil War & Reconstruction. Joe H. Kirchberger. (Eyewitness History Ser.). (Illus.). 400p. 1990. 45.00 (*0-8160-2171-6*) Facts on File.

Civil War & Reconstruction. 2nd rev. ed. James G. Randall & David H. Donald. 866p. (C). 1969. pap. text ed. 21.00 (*0-669-06428-9*) Heath.

Civil War & Reconstruction Era, 1861-1877. Ed. by Kenneth Kusmer. LC 91-3756. (Black Community & Urban Development in America Ser.: Vol. 3). 444p. 1991. reprint ed. 90.00 (*0-8153-0427-7*) Garland.

Civil War & Reconstruction in Alabama. Walter L. Fleming. (BCL1 - United States Local History Ser.). 815p. 1991. reprint ed. lib. bdg. 119.00 (*0-7812-6302-6*) Rprt Serv.

Civil War & Reconstruction, 1850-1877. Ed. by I. A. Newby. (Literature of History Ser.). (Orig.). (C). 1971. pap. text ed. 14.95 (*0-89197-081-9*) Irvington.

Civil War & Restoration in the Three Stuart Kingdoms: The Career of Randal MacDonnell, Marquis of Antrim, 1609-1683. Jane H. Ohlmeyer. LC 92-8873. (Cambridge Studies in Early Modern British History). (Illus.). 336p. (C). 1993. 69.95 (*0-521-41978-6*) Cambridge U Pr.

Civil War & the American System: America's Battle with Britain, 1860-1876. 2nd ed. Allen Salisbury. Ed. by Nancy B. Spannaus. 500p. 1992. reprint ed. pap. 15.00 (*0-943235-06-5*) Exec Intel Review.

Civil War Angel. Gary Lavetta. 128p. (Orig.). 1987. pap. 4.95 (*0-9618951-0-1*) Memory Ln Bks.

***Civil War Artillery, History of the 2nd Massachusetts Battery (Nim's Battery) of Light Artillery, 1861-1865.** Caroline E. Whitcomb. (Illus.). 111p. 1995. reprint ed. lib. bdg. 25.00 (*0-8328-4631-7*) Higginson Bk Co.

***Civil War Artillery, 1st Regiment of Heavy Artillery, Mass. Volunteers, (Formerly the 14th Regiment of Infantry), 1861-1865.** Alfred S. Roe & Chas. Nutt. 507p. 1995. reprint ed. lib. bdg. 55.00 (*0-8328-4640-6*) Higginson Bk Co.

Civil War As They Knew It. Pierce G. Fredericks. 18.95 (*0-88411-268-3*, Aeonian Pr) Amereon Ltd.

Civil War at Sea, 3 vols., Set. Virgil C. Jones. (Illus.). 1990. reprint ed. 60.00 (*0-916107-82-5*) Broadfoot.

Civil War Autographs & Manuscripts: A Guide to Autographs & Manuscripts of the War Between the States. rev. ed. Ronald R. Seagrave. (Illus.). xv, 401p. 1994. pap. 29.95 (*0-9632137-2-5*) Sergeant Kirk.

Civil War Autographs & Manuscripts Prices Current 1992. Ronald R. Seagrave. (Illus.). 172p. 1992. 39.95 (*0-9632137-0-9*) Sergeant Kirk.

Civil War Battlefield Guide. Conservationist Fund Staff. Ed. by Frances H. Kennedy. (Illus.). 320p. 1990. pap. 17.95 (*0-395-52283-8*) HM.

Civil War Battlefields. Bill Harris. Date not set. pap. 14.99 (*0-517-10054-1*) Random Hse Value.

***Civil War Battlefields: A Touring Guide.** David J. Eicher. 1995. write for info. (*0-87833-886-1*); pap. 14.95 (*0-87833-881-0*) Taylor Pub.

Civil War Battles. Curt Johnson & Mark McLaughlin. (Illus.). 1977. 9.99 (*0-517-52633-6*, 526336) Random Hse Value.

Civil War Battles in the West. 2nd ed. Ed. by LeRoy H. Fischer. (Illus.). 112p. 1981. pap. text ed., spiral bd. 17.00 (*0-89745-013-2*) Sunflower U Pr.

Civil War Battles in Winchester & Frederick County Virginia 1861-1865. 1988. pap. write for info. (*0-318-64333-2*) Winchester-Frederick Cty Hist Soc.

Civil War Book of Lists. Ed. by Combined Bks Staff. 240p. 1994. pap. 11.95 (*0-938289-43-8*, 7306) Stackpole.

Civil War Books: A Priced Checklist with Advice. 3rd ed. Tom Broadfoot. Ed. by Julia Nichols. 573p. 1990. 40.00 (*0-916107-85-X*) Broadfoot.

***Civil War Books Confederate & Union: A Bibliography & Price Guide.** Ronald R. Seagrave. Ed. by R. Douglas Sanders. (Illus.). 700p. 1995. pap. 34.95 (*0-9632137-5-X*) Sergeant Kirk.

Civil War Breech Loading Rifles: A Survey of the Innovative Infantry Arms of the American Civil War. John D. McAulay. LC 87-60724. (Illus.). 144p. 1987. pap. 15.00 (*0-917218-29-9*) A Mowbray.

Civil War Campaign Medal. John M. Carroll. 1976. 18.00 (*0-8488-0243-8*, J M C & Co) Amereon Ltd.

***Civil War Cavalry, the Third Mass. Cavalry in the War for the Union.** James K. Ewer. (Illus.). 566p. 1995. reprint ed. lib. bdg. 59.50 (*0-8328-4634-1*) Higginson Bk Co.

Civil War Chief of Sharpshooters, Hiram Berdan, Military Commander & Firearms Inventor. Roy M. Marcot. LC 89-92286. (Illus.). 342p. 1992. 59.95 (*0-9611494-1-8*) Northwood Heritage Pr.

Civil War Cinema: A Pictorial History of Hollywood & the War Between the States. John M. Cassidy. LC 86-60434. (Illus.). 1986. pap. 9.95 (*0-933126-74-3*) Pictorial Hist.

Civil War Collectibles see Official Price Guide to Civil War Colectibles

Civil War Collector's Encyclopedia, Vol. V. Marjorie F. Lord. 230p. 1989. lib. bdg. 35.00 (*0-916492-05-2*) Lord Americana.

Civil War Coloring Book. Peter Copeland. (Illus.). (YA). (gr. 7-10). 1990. pap. 2.95 (*0-486-26532-3*) Dover.

Civil War Command & Strategy: The Process of Victory & Defeat. Archer Jones. 256p. 1992. 29.95 (*0-02-916635-7*) Free Pr.

Civil War Commanders. Dean S. Thomas. (Illus.). 72p. 1986. pap. 5.95 (*0-939631-05-9*) Thomas Publications.

Civil War Cookbook. 2.00 (*0-936672-56-0*) Aerial Photo.

Civil War Cookbook. William C. Davis. LC 93-70599. (Illus.). 96p. 1993. 12.98 (*1-56138-287-6*) Courage Bks.

Civil War Cooking: The Housekeeper's Encyclopedia. E. F. Haskell. Ed. by R. L. Shep. LC 92-50431. Orig. Title: The Housekeeper's Encyclopedia. (Illus.). 464p. 1992. pap. 29.95 (*0-914046-16-0*) R L Shep.

Civil War Correspondence of Judge Thomas Goldsborough Odell. Ed. by Donald O. Virdin. xvi, 133p. (Orig.). 1992. pap. text ed. 13.50 (*1-55613-671-4*) Heritage Bk.

***Civil War Curiosities.** Webb Garrison. (Illus.). 256p. 1994. pap. 9.95 (*1-55853-315-X*) Rutledge Hill Pr.

Civil War Custer. Carroll. 1976. 10.00 (*0-685-71822-0*, J M C & Co) Amereon Ltd.

Civil War Day by Day: An Almanac 1861-1865. E. B. Long. (Quality Paperbacks Ser.). (Illus.). xiv, 1135p. 1985. reprint ed. pap. 19.95 (*0-306-80255-4*) Da Capo.

Civil War Diaries of Col. Theodore B. Gates, Twentieth New York State Militia. Ed. by Seward R. Osborne. (Illus.). 197p. (C). 1992. 25.00 (*0-944413-21-8*) Longstreet Hse.

***Civil War Diary.** Josiah Gorgas. (American Autobiography Ser.). 208p. 1995. reprint ed. lib. bdg. 79.00 (*0-7812-8533-X*) Rprt Serv.

Civil War Diary of Anne S. Frobel. Intro. by Mary H. Lancaster & Dallas M. Lancaster. LC 92-21439. 320p. 1992. pap. 14.95 (*0-939009-69-2*) EPM Pubns.

***Civil War Diary of Berea M. Willsey: The Intimate Daily Observations of a Massachusetts Volunteer in the Union Army, 1862-64.** Ed. by Jessica H. DeMay. 196p. (Orig.). 1995. pap. text ed. 17.50 (*0-7884-0168-8*) Heritage Bk.

Civil War Diary of Charles A. Leuschner. Ed. by Charles D. Spurlin. 128p. (C). 1992. 14.95 (*0-89015-853-3*) Sunbelt Media.

***Civil War Diary of Clara Solomon: Growing up in New Orleans, 1861-1862.** Ed. by Elliot Ashkenazi. (Library of Southern Civilization). (Illus.). 504p. 1995. 34.95 (*0-8071-1968-7*) La State U Pr.

Civil War Diary of Cyrus Pringle: Record of Quaker Conscience. Cyrus Pringle. LC 62-18328. Orig. Title: Record of a Quaker Conscience. (Orig.). 1962. pap. 3.00 (*0-87574-122-3*) Pendle Hill.

***Civil War Diary of Lieutenant J. E. Hodgkins 1862-1865.** Ed. by Kenneth C. Turino. LC 94-67828. (Illus.). 224p. 1994. 22.50x (*0-89725-177-6*, 523) Picton Pr.

***Civil War Diary of Martha Abernathy: Wife of Dr. C. C. Abernathy of Pulaski, Tennessee.** Ed. & Intro. by Elizabeth P. Dargan. (Illus.). 142p. (Orig.). (YA). (gr. 9 up). 1994. pap. 11.95 (*0-9644094-0-2*, TX3 851 802) E P Dargan.

Civil War Diary of Nelson Stauffer. Nelson Stauffer. Ed. by Norman E. Tanis. (American Classics Facsimile Ser.: Pt. IV). 1976. pap. 10.00 (*0-937048-03-8*) CSUN.

Civil War Diary of Sarah Morgan. Sarah Morgan. Ed. by Charles East. LC 91-2161. 688p. 1991. 34.95 (*0-8203-1357-2*) U of Ga Pr.

Civil War Dictionary. Mark M. Boatner, III. (Illus.). 1980. Incl. maps & diagrams. 25.00 (*0-679-50013-8*) McKay.

Civil War Dictionary. Mark M. Boatner, III. LC 91-50013. (Vintage Civil War Library). 1008p. 1991. pap. 19.00 (*0-679-73392-2*, Vin) Random.

Civil War Dictionary. rev. ed. Mark M. Boatner, III. (Illus.). 974p. 1988. write for info. (*0-8129-1726-X*, Times Bks); 30.00 (*0-8129-1689-1*, Times Bks) Random.

***Civil War Era: Historical Viewpoints.** Eugene H. Berwanger. LC 93-78909. 249p. 1995. pap. 25.75 (*0-15-501039-5*) HarBrace.

Civil War Era Etiquette: Martine's Handbook & Vulgarisms in Conversation. Ed. by R. L. Shep. LC 88-90814. (Illus.). 236p. 1988. pap. 12.95 (*0-914046-07-1*) R L Shep.

Civil War Era, 1850-1873 see History of the State of Ohio

Civil War Etchings. Edwin Forbes. (Illus.). 96p. 1994. reprint ed. pap. 6.95 (*0-486-28043-8*) Dover.

Civil War Extra: From the Pages of the Charleston Mercury & the New York Times. Charleston Mercury Staff & New York Times Staff The. Ed. by Eugene P. Moehring & Arleen Keylin. LC 75-20220. 310p. 1976. 16.95 (*0-405-06662-7*) Ayer.

Civil War Eyewitnesses: An Annotated Bibliography of Books & Articles, 1955-1986. Garold L. Cole. 359p. 1988. text ed. 49.95 (*0-87249-545-0*) U of SC Pr.

Civil War Flags. Whitney Smith. (J). (gr. 1-9). 1992. pap. 2.50 (*0-88388-094-6*) Bellerophon Bks.

Civil War Genealogy. 64p. 1988. pap. 12.00 (*0-913857-00-9*) Genealog Sources.

Civil War Genealogy. Ed. by Jane Hedlin. 80p. 1993. pap. 8.50 (*0-913233-27-7*) AFRA.

Civil War Generals: Categorical Listings & a Biographical Directory. Comp. by James Spencer. LC 86-19391. 344p. 1986. text ed. 55.00 (*0-313-25423-0*, SCW/, Greenwood Pr) Greenwood.

***Civil War Gentlemen: Eighteen Sixties Apparel Arts & Uniforms.** R. L. Shep et al. LC 94-37721. (Illus.). 208p. (Orig.). 1994. pap. 24.95 (*0-914046-22-5*) R L Shep.

Civil War Ghost Stories & Legends. Nancy Roberts. LC 92-10411. (Illus.). 192p. 1992. text ed. 19.95 (*0-87249-851-4*); pap. 9.95 (*0-87249-852-2*) U of SC Pr.

Civil War Ghosts. Ed. by Martin H. Greenberg et al. 216p. 1991. pap. 10.95 (*0-87483-173-3*) August Hse.

Civil War Handbook. 3.20 (*0-936672-25-0*) Aerial Photo.

Civil War Handbook: A Civil War Research Associates Series. William H. Price. (Illus.). 72p. reprint ed. pap. 2.95 (*1-879295-00-8*) L B Prince.

Civil War Heroes. Jill Canon & Alan Archambault. (Illus.). 48p. (Orig.). (J). (gr. 7). 1988. pap. 3.95 (*0-88388-130-6*) Bellerophon Bks.

Civil War Heroines. Jill Canon. (Illus.). (Orig.). (J). (gr. 7 up). 1989. pap. 3.95 (*0-88388-147-0*) Bellerophon Bks.

***Civil War II.** George Wright. 232p. 1995. pap. 8.95 (*1-56901-546-5*) NW Pub.

***Civil War in Bosnia, 1992-94.** Edgar O'Ballance. LC 94-32534. 1995. write for info. (*0-312-12503-8*) St Martin.

Civil War in Buchanan & Wise Counties: Bushwhackers' Paradise. Jeffrey C. Weaver. (Virginia Civil War Battles & Leaders Ser.). (Illus.). 323p. 1994. 25.00 (*1-56190-059-1*) H E Howard.

C

An Asterisk (*) at the beginning of an entry indicates that the title is appearing in BIP for the first time. 1287

Civil War in Cabell County West Virginia. Joe Geiger. 1991. pap. 9.95 (*0-929521-58-7*) Pictorial Hist.

Civil War in France. Karl Marx. 144p. 1934. 19.95 (*0-88286-035-6*) C H Kerr.

***Civil War in France.** Karl Marx. 91p. Date not set. pap. 5.00 (*0-614-04202-X*) Pathfinder NY.

Civil War in France: The Paris Commune. rev. ed. Karl Marx et al. LC 88-24454. 180p. (C). 1993. reprint ed. pap. text ed. 8.95 (*0-7178-0666-9*) Intl Pubs Co.

Civil War in Kentucky. 2nd ed. Lowell H. Harrison. LC 79-56829. (Illus.). 144p. 1987. reprint ed. 16.00 (*0-8131-1419-5*) U Pr of Ky.

Civil War in Lebanon: 1975-1976, A Bibliographical Guide. Ed. by Linda Sadaka & Nawaf Salam. (Illus.). 112p. 1982. pap. text ed. 9.95 (*0-8156-6064-2*, Am U Beirut) Syracuse U Pr.

Civil War in Louisiana. John D. Winters. LC 63-9647. (Illus.). 536p. 1979. pap. 16.95 (*0-8071-1725-0*) La State U Pr.

Civil War in Missouri As Seen From the Capital City. Dino Brugioni. LC 86-71353. 200p. (Orig.). 1986. pap. 14.95 (*0-916109-05-4*) Summers Pub.

***Civil War in Missouri Day by Day 1861-1865.** Carolyn M. Bartels. (Illus.). 230p. 1992. lib. bdg. 29.95 (*0-9636780-2-7*); spiral bd. 17.50 (*0-9636780-0-0*) C M Bartels.

***Civil War in Missouri Day by Day 1861-1865.** Carolyn M. Bartels. (Illus.). 1994. per. 17.50 (*0-9636780-1-9*) C M Bartels.

Civil War in Nicaragua: Inside the Sandinistas. Roger Miranda & William Ratliff. 298p. (C). 1992. 34.95 (*1-56000-064-3*) Transaction Pubs.

***Civil War in Nicaragua: Inside the Sandinistas.** Roger Miranda & William Ratliff. 298p. (C). 1994. pap. 21.95 (*1-56000-761-3*) Transaction Pubs.

Civil War in North Carolina. John G. Barrett. LC 63-22810. xi, 484p. 1963. 24.95 (*0-8078-0874-1*) U of NC Pr.

***Civil War in North Carolina.** John G. Barrett. LC 63-22810. 484p. 1995. pap. 16.95 (*0-8078-4520-5*) U of NC Pr.

Civil War in Popular Culture: A Reusable Past. Jim Cullen. LC 94-25072. 1995. 29.95 (*1-56098-459-7*) Smithsonian.

Civil War in Popular Culture: A Reusable Past. Lillian D. Kozloski. LC 94-25072. 1993. 39.95 (*0-87474-459-8*) Smithsonian.

Civil War in Ripley County, Missouri. Dorothy Ponder. Ed. by Prospect News Staff. LC 92-82882. (Illus.). 102p. (Orig.). (C). 1992. pap. 5.00 (*0-9623922-1-9*) Ponder Bks.

Civil War in Song & Story, 2 vols., Set. Frank Moore. 1980. lib. bdg. 195.75 (*0-8490-3130-3*) Gordon Pr.

***Civil War in St. Louis: A Guided Tour.** Ed. by William C. Winter. LC 94-22858. (Illus.). 189p. 1994. 22.95 (*1-883982-05-7*); pap. 22.95 (*1-883982-06-5*) MO Hist Soc.

Civil War in the American West. Alvin M. Josephy, Jr. LC 91-399. (Illus.). 464p. 1991. 27.00 (*0-394-56482-0*) Knopf.

Civil War in the American West. Alvin M. Josephy, Jr. LC 92-50622. 1993. pap. 15.00 (*0-679-74003-1*, Vin) Random.

***Civil War in the Indian Territory.** Steve Cottrell. (Illus.). 128p. 1995. pap. text ed. 8.95 (*1-56554-110-3*) Pelican.

Civil War in the Making, 1815-1860. Avery O. Craven. LC 59-7943. (Walter Lynwood Fleming Lectures). xiv, 116p. 1968. pap. text ed. 8.95 (*0-8071-0131-1*) La State U Pr.

Civil War in the Midlands, 1642-1651. Roy E. Sherwood. (Illus.). 250p. (C). 1992. text ed. 34.00 (*0-7509-0166-7*); pap. text ed. 20.00 (*0-7509-0167-5*) A Sutton Pub.

Civil War in the Ozarks. Phillip W. Steele & Steve Cottrell. LC 93-18337. (Illus.). 112p. 1993. pap. 8.95 (*0-88289-988-0*) Pelican.

Civil War in the Western Territories: Arizona, Colorado, New Mexico, & Utah. Ray C. Colton. LC 59-7964. (Illus.). 240p. (Orig.). 1984. pap. 12.95 (*0-8061-1902-0*) U of Okla Pr.

Civil War in West Virginia: A Story of the Industrial Conflict in the Coal Mines. Winthrop D. Lane. LC 76-89745. (American Labor Ser.). reprint ed. 17.95 (*0-405-02133-X*) Ayer.

***Civil War Infantry, History of the Fifth Massachusetts Battery, Organized Oct. 3, 1861, Mustered Out June 12, 1865.** Luther E. Cowles. (Illus.). 981p. 1995. reprint ed. lib. bdg. 99.00 (*0-8328-4635-X*) Higginson Bk Co.

***Civil War Infantry, History of the 50th Regiment, Mass. Volunteer Militia, in the Late War of the Rebellion.** Wm. B. Stevens. 399p. 1995. reprint ed. lib. bdg. 45.00 (*0-8328-4638-4*) Higginson Bk Co.

***Civil War Infantry, History of the 52nd Regiment, Mass. Volunteers.** J. F. Moors. (Illus.). 283p. 1995. reprint ed. lib. bdg. 38.00 (*0-8328-4628-7*) Higginson Bk Co.

***Civil War Infantry, the Eighth Regiment at Chickamauga Park, Historical & Pictorial, with Accurate Views of the Regiment & Complete History of Each Company from Foundation to Present Writing.** (Illus.). 155p. 1995. reprint ed. lib. bdg. 29.50 (*0-8328-4627-9*) Higginson Bk Co.

***Civil War Infantry, the Record of the 2nd Massachusetts Infantry, 1861-1865.** Alonzo H. Quint. (Illus.). 528p. 1995. reprint ed. lib. bdg. 55.00 (*0-8328-4633-3*) Higginson Bk Co.

***Civil War Infantry, the Story of the 32nd Massachusetts Infantry, Whence It Came, Where It Went, What It Saw & What It Did.** Francis J. Parker. (Illus.). 260p. 1995. reprint ed. lib. bdg. 35.00 (*0-8328-4632-5*) Higginson Bk Co.

***Civil War Infantry, the 10th Regiment, Mass. Volunteer Infantry, 1861-1864, a Western Massachusetts Regiment.** Alfred S. Roe. (Illus.). 535p. 1995. reprint ed. lib. bdg. 57.50 (*0-614-03921-5*) Higginson Bk Co.

***Civil War Infantry, the 20th Regiment of Massachusetts Volunteer Infantry, 1861-1865.** George A. Bruce. (Illus.). 519p. 1995. reprint ed. lib. bdg. 57.00 (*0-8328-4629-5*) Higginson Bk Co.

***Civil War Infantry, the 48th Regiment, M. V. M., During the Civil War.** Albert Plummer. (Illus.). 133p. 1995. reprint ed. lib. bdg. 29.50 (*0-8328-4636-8*) Higginson Bk Co.

***Civil War Infantry, the 57th Regiment of Massachusetts Volunteers in the War of the Rebellion, Army of the Potomac.** John Anderson. (Illus.). 512p. 1995. reprint ed. lib. bdg. 56.00 (*0-8328-4630-9*) Higginson Bk Co.

***Civil War Infantry, 5th Regiment, Mass. Volunteers Infantry, in Its Three Tours of Duty, 1861, 1862-3, 1864.** Alfred S. Roe. (Illus.). 510p. 1995. reprint ed. lib. bdg. 56.00 (*0-8328-4639-2*) Higginson Bk Co.

***Civil War Journal.** Nofi. 1995. 6.98 (*0-88394-090-6*) Promntory Pr.

Civil War Journal of Billy Davis: From Hopewell, Indiana to Port Republic, Virginia. Ed. by Richard S. Skidmore. LC 89-90126. (Illus.). 184p. (Orig.). 1989. pap. 16.95 (*0-9623292-0-7*) Nugget IN.

Civil War Justice: Union Army Executions under Lincoln. Robert I. Alotta. LC 88-36680. (Illus.). 245p. (C). 1989. 24.95 (*0-942597-10-9*) White Mane Pub.

Civil War Ladies: Fashions & Needle-Arts of the Early 1860's. Ed. by R. L. Shep. LC 89-91791. (Illus.). 348p. 1989. pap. 24.95 (*0-914046-09-8*) R L Shep.

Civil War Letters & Diary of Joshua Winters. Ed. by Elizabeth Swiger. 1975. pap. 10.00 (*0-9616245-3-1*) McClain.

Civil War Letters of Charles Barber, Private, 104th New York Volunteer Infantry. Raymond G. Barber & Gary E. Swinson. LC 91-909058. 256p. 1991. pap. 20.00 (*0-9629573-2-1*) G E Swinson.

Civil War Letters of Colonel Hans Christian Heg. Hans C. Heg. Ed. by Theodore C. Blegen. LC 36-7110. 280p. reprint ed. pap. 79.80 (*0-317-27957-2*, 2056020) Bks Demand.

Civil War Letters of Cpl. John H. Strathern: Eighth Pennsylvania Reserve Volunteer Corps. Marlene C. Bumbera. 146p. 1994. pap. 19.95 (*1-55856-175-7*) Closson Pr.

Civil War Letters of George Washington Whitman. George Whitman. Ed. by Jerome M. Loving. LC 74-83788. 197p. reprint ed. pap. 56.20 (*0-317-26119-3*, 2023763) Bks Demand.

Civil War Letters of Private Henry Kauffman (1862-1865) The Harmony Boys Are All Well. Ed. by David McCordick. LC 91-34380. (Illus.). 124p. 1991. lib. bdg. 59.95 (*0-7734-9684-X*) E Mellen.

Civil War Letters of the Tenure Family of Rockland County. Larry H. Whiteaker & W. Calvin Dickinson. LC 89-15301. (Illus.). 110p. 1990. pap. 5.00 (*0-911183-39-6*) Rockland County Hist.

Civil War Manuscripts. (Civil War Ser.). 1991. lib. bdg. 79.99 (*0-87700-926-0*) Revisionist Pr.

***Civil War Manuscripts, 2 vols., Set.** 1995. lib. bdg. 602.75 (*0-8490-6770-7*) Gordon Pr.

Civil War Manuscripts: A Guide to Collections in the Manuscript Division of the Library of Congress. LC 81-607105. 391p. 1986. 20.00 (*0-8444-0381-4*, 030-000-00159-1) Lib Congress.

***Civil War Maps, 2 vols., Set.** 1995. lib. bdg. 602.99 (*0-8490-6771-5*) Gordon Pr.

Civil War Maps: A Annotated List of Maps & Atlases in the Library of Congress. 2nd ed. Comp. by Richard W. Stephenson. LC 88-600031. 410p. 1989. 46.00 (*0-8444-0598-1*, 030-000-00209-1) Lib Congress.

Civil War Maps: A Graphic Index to the Atlas to Accompany the Official Records of the Union & Confederate Armies. Ed. by N. S. Reilly et al. (Illus.). 68p. 1987. pap. 8.00 (*0-911028-36-6*) Newberry.

Civil War Maps: An Annotated List of Maps & Atlases in the Library of Congress. 2nd ed. Comp. by Richard W. Stephenson. LC 88-600031. (Illus.). 418p. 1989. 46.00 (*0-16-004008-6*, S/N 030-000-00209-1) USGPO.

Civil War Maps: An Annotated Lists of Maps & Atlases in Map Collections of Library of Congress. United States Library of Congress, Map Division Staff. LC 78-14050. 138p. 1979. reprint ed. text ed. 38.50 (*0-313-20683-X*, STWM) Greenwood.

Civil War Maps: Annotated List. 1991. lib. bdg. 82.95 (*0-8490-4386-7*) Gordon Pr.

Civil War Medicine: Care & Comfort of the Wounded. Robert E. Denney. LC 94-16737. 422p. (Orig.). 1994. 27.95 (*0-8069-0879-3*) Sterling.

***Civil War Medicine: Care & Comfort of the Wounded.** Robert E. Denney. (Illus.). 408p. (Orig.). 1995. pap. 19.95 (*0-8069-0880-7*) Sterling.

***Civil War Memoir of Philip Dangerfield Stephenson, D. D. Private Company K, 13th Arkansas Volunteer Infantry, & Loader, Piece No. 4, 5th Company, Washington Artillery, Army of Tennessee.** Nathaniel C. Hughes, Jr. LC 94-34077. (J). 1995. 34.95 (*0-944436-24-2*) Univ Central AR Pr.

Civil War Memoirs: Grant & Sherman, 2 vols., Set. (Library of America). (Illus.). 1990. boxed 70.00 (*0-940450-69-0*) Library of America.

Civil War Memoirs of Captain William J. Seymour: Reminiscences of a Louisiana Tiger. Ed. by Terry L. Jones. LC 90-49919. (Illus.). 184p. 1991. 19.95 (*0-8071-1646-7*) La State U Pr.

Civil War Memoirs of Two Rebel Sisters. William Wintz. 1992. pap. 9.95 (*0-929521-24-2*) Pictorial Hist.

Civil War Memories of Elizabeth Bacon Custer: Reconstructed from Her Notes & Diaries. Ed. by Arlene Reynolds. LC 94-1759. 1994. 24.95 (*0-292-71168-9*) U of Tex Pr.

***Civil War Militia, History of the 45th Regiment, M. V. M., "The Cadet Regiment"** Albert W. Mann. (Illus.). 562p. 1995. reprint ed. lib. bdg. 62.00 (*0-8328-4626-0*) Higginson Bk Co.

Civil War Newspaper Maps: A Cartobibliography of the Northern Daily Press. Comp. by David Bosse. LC 92-43100. (Bibliographies & Indexes in Military Studies: No. 5). 288p. 1993. text ed. 75.00 (*0-313-28705-8*, GR8705, Greenwood Pr) Greenwood.

Civil War Newspaper Maps: A Historical Atlas. David Bosse. LC 92-33942. (Illus.). 160p. (C). 1993. 34.95 (*0-8018-4553-X*) Johns Hopkins.

Civil War Nurse: The Diary & Letters of Hannah Ropes. John R. Brumgardt. LC 79-28372. (C). 1992. pap. 11.95 (*0-87049-790-1*) U of Tenn Pr.

***Civil War on the Border Vol. 1: 1861-1862.** Wiley Britton. (Illus.). 473p. (C). 1995. pap. 22.95 (*1-878882-09-0*) KS Heritage Pr.

***Civil War on the Border Vol. 2: 1863-1865.** Wiley Britton. (Illus.). 546p. (C). 1995. pap. 22.95 (*1-878882-10-4*) KS Heritage Pr.

Civil War on the Western Border, 1854-1865. Jay Monaghan. LC 84-11856. viii, 454p. 1984. reprint ed. 40.00 (*0-8032-3091-5*); reprint ed. pap. 11.95 (*0-8032-8126-9*) U of Nebr Pr.

Civil War Paper Soldiers in Full Color. A. G. Smith. (J). 1985. pap. 4.95 (*0-486-24987-5*) Dover.

Civil War Papers of George B. McClellan: Selected Correspondence 1860-1865. George B. McClellan. Ed. by Stephen W. Sears. 669p. 1992. reprint ed. pap. 17.95 (*0-306-80471-9*) Da Capo.

Civil War Papers, Vol. 2: Commandery of the State of Massachusetts. (Military Order of the Loyal Legion of the United States Ser.: Vol. 53). 631p. 1993. reprint ed. 40.00 (*1-56837-245-0*) Broadfoot.

Civil War Parks: The Story Behind the Scenery. William C. Davis. LC 83-83006. (Illus.). 64p. (Orig.). 1984. pap. 6.95 (*0-916122-95-6*) KC Pubns.

Civil War Party System: The Case of Massachusetts, 1848-1876. Dale Baum. LC 83-19687. xviii, 289p. 1984. 39.95 (*0-8078-1588-8*) U of NC Pr.

Civil War Pictures. D. L. Corbitt & Elizabeth W. Wilborn. (Illus.). xiii, 55p. 1991. pap. 4.00 (*0-86526-074-5*) NC Archives.

Civil War Pistols. John D. McAulay. (Illus.). 1992. pap. 24.00 (*0-685-59082-8*) A Mowbray.

***Civil War Poetry & Prose.** unabridged ed. Walt Whitman. (Thrift Editions Ser.). 96p. 1995. pap. text ed. 1.00 (*0-486-28507-3*) Dover.

Civil War Postcard Book. (Illus.). 64p. (Orig.). 1991. pap. 10.00 (*0-345-37374-X*, Ballantine Trade) Ballantine.

Civil War Prisons. Ed. by William B. Hesseltine. LC 72-84195. 123p. 1972. reprint ed. pap. 8.00 (*0-87338-129-7*) Kent St U Pr.

Civil War Prisons: A Study in War Psychology. William B. Hesseltine. (History - United States Ser.). 290p. 1992. reprint ed. lib. bdg. 79.00 (*0-7812-6188-0*) Rprt Serv.

Civil War Prisons & Escapes: A Day by Day Chronicle. Robert E. Denney. LC 93-23889. (Illus.). 424p. 1993. 27.95 (*0-8069-0414-3*) Sterling.

***Civil War Prisons & Escapes: A Day-by-Day Chronicle.** Robert E. Denney. (Illus.). 408p. 1995. pap. 19.95 (*0-8069-0415-1*) Sterling.

Civil War Quiz & Fact Book. Rod Gragg. LC 84-48162. (Illus.). 224p. 1985. pap. 12.00 (*0-06-091226-X*, CN 1226, PL) HarpC.

Civil War Quiz & Fact Book. Rod Gragg. 1993. 6.98 (*0-88394-087-6*) Promntory Pr.

Civil War Quiz Book. John Malone. (Quill Quiz Bk.). (Illus.). 224p. 1992. pap. 9.00 (*0-688-11269-2*, Quill) Morrow.

***Civil War Quotations.** Lyman. 1995. pap. text ed. 11.95 (*0-938289-45-4*) Combined Bks.

***Civil War Record of the 144th Regiment NY Volunteer Infantry: Back "in War Times"** James H. McKee. (Illus.). 378p. 1994. pap. 28.00 (*0-7884-0007-X*) Heritage Bk.

Civil War Records of Jefferson County, Alabama. Comp. by Marilyn D. Barefield. LC 93-19970. 1993. 20.00 (*0-942301-22-6*) Birm Pub Lib.

Civil War Reenactments. Stephen W. Sylvia & Michael J. O'Donnell. (Illus.). 132p. (Orig.). 1985. pap. 17.95 (*0-943522-11-0*) Moss Pubns VA.

Civil War Remembered. Carl Lowe. LC 94-8757. 1994. write for info. (*1-56799-107-6*, Friedman-Fairfax) M Friedman Pub Grp Inc.

Civil War Reminiscences of Major Silas T. Grisamore, C. S. A. Ed. by Arthur W. Bergeron, Jr. LC 92-37038. (Illus.). 240p. 1993. 24.95 (*0-8071-1817-6*) La State U Pr.

***Civil War Reports.** Historical Briefs, Inc. Staff. Ed. by Thomas Antonucci & Michael Antonucci. 224p. 1994. pap. 24.95 (*0-89677-053-2*) Hist Briefs.

***Civil War, Revised Register of the Soldiers & Sailors of New Hampshire in the War of the Rebellion, 1861-1866.** Ed. by Augustus D. Ayling. (Illus.). 1347p. 1995. reprint ed. lib. bdg. 135.00 (*0-8328-4625-2*) Higginson Bk Co.

Civil War Round Table: Fifty Years of Scholarship & Fellowship. Barbara Hughett. LC 90-84288. (Illus.). xviii, 206p. 1990. 30.00 (*0-9630754-0-3*) Civil War RT.

***Civil War Sea Battles.** Miller. 1995. 24.95 (*0-938289-52-7*) Combined Bks.

Civil War Short Stories of Ambrose Bierce. Ambrose Bierce. Ed. by Ernest J. Hopkins. LC 87-27970. vi, 139p. 1988. pap. 7.95 (*0-8032-6087-3*, Bison Books) U of Nebr Pr.

Civil War Sites. Tom Weil. (U. S. A. Guides Ser.). (Illus.). 200p. (Orig.). 1994. pap. 14.95 (*0-7818-0302-0*) Hippocrene Bks.

Civil War Sites in Virginia: A Tour Guide. James I. Robertson, Jr. LC 81-7426. (Illus.). 108p. 1982. pap. 6.95 (*0-8139-0907-4*) U Pr of Va.

Civil War Sketches & Incidents: Papers Read by Companions of the Commandery of the State of Nebraska. (Military Order of the Loyal Legion of the United States Ser.: Vol. 25). 277p. 1992. reprint ed. 40.00 (*1-56837-180-2*) Broadfoot.

Civil War Soldier at Atlanta. (Soldier Ser.). 48p. (J). (gr. 5-6). 1991. lib. bdg. 11.95 (*1-56065-002-8*) Capstone Pr.

Civil War Soldiers. Reid Mitchell. 1989. pap. 9.95 (*0-671-68641-0*, Touchstone Bks) S&S Trade.

Civil War Soldiers. Catherine Reef. (African-American Soldiers Ser.). (Illus.). 80p. (J). (gr. 4-7). 1993. lib. bdg. 14.98 (*0-8050-2371-2*) TFC Bks NY.

Civil War Soldiers Coloring Book. Alan Archambault. (Illus.). (J). (gr. 4-7). 1985. pap. 3.95 (*0-88388-047-4*) Bellerophon Bks.

Civil War Soldier's Diary, Peter W. Funk, NY, Vol. 150. Margaret Herrick. 54p. 1991. pap. 13.50 (*1-56012-118-1*) Kinship Rhinebeck.

***Civil War Soldiers from New York: Origins & Nominal Lists.** Diane S. Ptak. 25p. 1995. pap. 14.00 (*1-886905-11-8*) D S Ptak.

Civil War Source Book. Philip Katcher. (Source Book Ser.). (Illus.). 320p. 1992. 35.00 (*0-8160-2823-0*) Facts on File.

Civil War Sourcebook: A Traveler's Guide. Chuck Lawliss. (Illus.). 320p. 1991. 20.00 (*0-517-57767-4*, Harmony) Crown Pub Group.

Civil War Spoken Here: A Dictionary of Mispronounced People, Places & Things of the 1860s. Robert D. Quigley. 216p. 1993. pap. 12.00 (*0-9637745-0-6*) C W Hist.

Civil War Stories. Ambrose Bierce. LC 93-46121. 128p. (Orig.). 1994. pap. 1.00 (*0-486-28038-1*) Dover.

Civil War Stories of Harold Frederic. Harold Frederic. Ed. by Thomas F. O'Donnell. (New York Classics Ser.). 360p. 1992. reprint ed. pap. 14.95 (*0-8156-2572-3*) Syracuse U Pr.

***Civil War Stories of Missouri.** Carolyn M. Bartels. 297p. 1994. pap. 13.95 (*0-9636780-3-5*) C M Bartels.

Civil War Sutler Tokens & Cardboard Scrip. David E. Schenkman. LC 82-83781. (Illus.). 103p. 1983. 27.50 (*0-942596-01-3*) Jade Hse Pubns.

***Civil War Tales.** (Illus.). 185p. (C). Date not set. reprint ed. 26.95 (*0-9617898-1-6*) A & W Enterprises.

***Civil War Tales, Vol. II.** (Illus.). 226p. (C). Date not set. reprint ed. 28.95 (*0-9617898-2-4*) A & W Enterprises.

Civil War Tennessee: Battles & Leaders. Thomas L. Connelly. LC 79-14885. (Tennessee Three Star Ser.). (Illus.). 114p. 1979. pap. 4.95 (*0-87049-261-6*) U of Tenn Pr.

Civil War Through the Camera. Henry W. Elson & Matthew B. Brady. (Orig.). 1979. 30.95 (*0-405-12294-2*) Ayer.

***Civil War Through the Camera.** Henry W. Elson. (Illus.). 256p. (Orig.). 1994. pap. text ed. 31.00 (*0-7884-0078-9*) Heritage Bk.

***Civil War Through the Camera: Hundreds of Vivid Photographs Actually Taken in Civil War Times, Together with Elson's New History, Vol. 1, Pts. 1-8.** Ed. by Henry W. Elson. (Illus.). 256p. (Orig.). 1994. pap. text ed. 31.00 (*0-7884-0039-8*) Heritage Bk.

Civil War Times: 30 Year Comprehensive Index, April 1959 - February 1989. Lee W. Merideth. LC 90-62096. 228p. (Orig.). 1990. pap. 29.95 (*0-9626237-0-9*) Hist Indexes.

***Civil War Times Illustrated Photographic History of the Civil War, 2, 1.** Ed. by William C. Davis & Bell I. Wiley. LC 94-30567. (Illus.). 1994. write for info. (*1-884822-09-6*) Blck Dog & Leventhal.

***Civil War Times Illustrated Photographic History of the Civil War, 2, 2.** Ed. by William C. Davis & Bell I. Wiley. LC 94-30567. 1994. write for info. (*1-884822-08-8*) Blck Dog & Leventhal.

Civil War Times in St. Augustine. Ed. by Jacqueline K. Fretwell. (Illus.). 122p. 1988. pap. 7.95 (*0-912451-23-8*) Florida Classics.

***Civil War to the Last Frontier, 1850-1880.** Katz. 1995. pap. text ed. (*0-8114-2914-8*) Raintree Steck-V.

***Civil War to the Last Frontier, 1850-1880.** William L. Katz. LC 92-17924. (History of Multicultural America Ser.). (Illus.). 96p. (J). (gr. 7-8). 1992. lib. bdg. 24.26 (*0-8114-6277-3*) Raintree Steck-V.

Civil War Treasury: Being a Miscellany of Arms & Artillery Facts & Figures, Legends & Lore, Etc. Albert A. Nofi. (Illus.). 432p. 1992. 24.95 (*0-938289-12-8*) Combined Bks.

***Civil War Treasury: Being a Miscellany of Arms & Artillery, Facts & Figures, Legends & Lore, Muses & Minstrels, Personalities & People.** Albert A. Nofi. LC 94-31227. 1995. 15.95 (*0-306-80622-3*) Da Capo.

Civil War Treasury of Tales. Ed. by B. A. Botkin. 34.95 (*0-88411-860-6*, Aeonian Pr) Amereon Ltd.

Civil War Treasury of Tales, Legends & Folklore. B. A. Botkin. 1981. 10.98 (*0-88394-049-3*) Promntory Pr.

Civil War Trivia & Fact Book. Webb Garrison. LC 92-7273. (Illus.). 240p. (Orig.). 1992. pap. 9.95 (*1-55853-160-2*) Rutledge Hill Pr.

Civil War Veterans of Winnebago Co, WI, Vol. I: A-H. David A. Langkau. 378p. (Orig.). 1994. pap. text ed. 27.50 (*1-55613-911-X*) Heritage Bk.

***Civil War Veterans of Winnebago County, Wisconsin Vol. 2, I-T.** David A. Langkau. 384p. (Orig.). 1994. pap. text ed. 27.50 (*0-7884-0035-5*) Heritage Bk.

Civil War Veterans Organization, Reunions & Badges. Turner E. Kirkland. 1991. 3.95 (*1-877704-99-7*) Pioneer Pr.

Civil War VI. Shelby Foote. 1958. 40.00 (*0-394-41948-0*) Random.

An Asterisk (*) at the beginning of an entry indicates that the title is appearing in BIP for the first time.

Civil War VIII. Lucan. Ed. by Mayer. (Classical Texts Ser.). 1981. 49.95 (*0-85668-155-5*, Pub. by Aris & Phillips UK); pap. 24.95 (*0-85668-176-8*, Pub. by Aris & Phillips UK) David Brown.

Civil War Virginia: Battleground for a Nation. James I. Robertson, Jr. (Illus.). 197p. (C). 1993. pap. text ed. 8.95 (*0-8139-1457-4*) U Pr of Va.

Civil War, Vol. 1: Fort Sumter to Perryville. Shelby Foote. LC 86-40135. 848p. 1986. pap. 24.00 (*0-394-74623-6*, Vin) Random.

Civil War, Vol. 2: Fredericksburg to Meridian. Shelby Foote. LC 86-40136. 1120p. 1986. pap. 24.00 (*0-394-74621-X*, Vin) Random.

Civil War, Vol. 3: Red River to Appomattox. Shelby Foote. LC 86-40137. 1008p. 1986. pap. 24.00 (*0-394-74622-8*, Vin) Random.

Civil War Weapons. 1991. lib. bdg. 79.95 (*0-8490-4985-7*) Gordon Pr.

Civil War Wit, No. I. William Gibson & James Murfin. (Illus.). 216p. 1992. 8.95 (*0-936023-02-3*, 34502) Interp Mktg Prods.

Civil War Within: Biblical "Facts of Life": the Struggle for Spirited Growth. Wayne Taylor. 108p. (Orig.). (C). 1989. pap. 4.95 (*0-9625475-0-6*) Calvary Fellowship.

Civil War Women. Frank Mcsherry. 1990. pap. 10.00 (*0-671-70248-3*) S&S Trade.

Civil War Wordbook: Including Sayings, Phrases, & Expletives. Darryl Lyman. 240p. 1993. pap. 11.95 (*0-938289-25-X*, 7305) Combined Bks.

Civil War World of Herman Melville. Stanton Garner. LC 93-640. (Illus.). 560p. 1993. 29.95 (*0-7006-0602-5*) U Pr of KS.

Civil War Years: A Day-by-Day Chronicle of the Life of a Nation. Robert E. Denney. (Illus.). 624p. 1994. pap. 19.95 (*0-8069-8515-1*) Sterling.

Civil War 1861-1865, Pt. 1. Ed. by Michael J. Matochik. (Bibliographic Guide to the Microfiche Collection Ser.). ix, 144p. reprint ed. 40.00 (*0-8357-0719-9*) Univ Microfilms.

Civil War, 1922-23. Eoin Neeson. 350p. 1988. pap. 19.95 (*1-85371-013-X*, Pub. by Poolbeg Pr IE) Dufour.

***Civil War 3-D.** James D. Van Eldik. (Illus.). (Orig.). 1995. pap. 6.95 (*0-9646665-0-2*) Civil War in Depth.

Civil Wars. Rosellen Brown. LC 83-48866. 512p. 1984. 16.95 (*0-394-53478-6*) Knopf.

Civil Wars. Rosellen Brown. 1994. mass mkt. 5.99 (*0-440-21695-8*) Dell.

Civil Wars. Julius Caesar. (Loeb Classical Library: No. 39). 382p. 1914. 18.95 (*0-674-99043-9*) HUP.

***Civil Wars: From L. A. to Bosnia.** Hans M. Enzensberger. Tr. by Martin Chalmers & Pier Spence. 144p. 1994. 18.00 (*1-56584-208-1*) New Press NY.

***Civil Wars: From L. A. to Bosnia.** Hans M. Enzensberger. Tr. by Martin Chalmers & Piers Spence. 144p. 1995. pap. 9.95 (*1-56584-209-X*) New Press NY.

Civil Wars: Women & the Crisis of Southern Nationalism. George C. Rable. (Women in American History Ser.). 416p. 1991. pap. 13.95 (*0-252-06212-4*) U of Ill Pr.

Civil Wars & Monarchy in France: In the Sixteenth & Seventeenth Centuries; A History of France Principally During That Period, 2 vols. Leopold Ranke. Tr. by M. A. Garvey. LC 78-38365. (Select Bibliographies Reprint Ser.). 1977. reprint ed. 57.95 (*0-8369-6782-8*) Ayer.

Civil Wars & Monarchy in France, in the Sixteenth & Seventeenth Centuries, 2 vols in 1. Leopold Von Ranke. Tr. by M. A. Garvey. LC 70-153634. reprint ed. 55.00 (*0-404-09254-3*) AMS Pr.

Civil Works Administration, 1933-1934: The Business of Emergency Employment in the New Deal. Bonnie F. Schwartz. LC 84-42560. 248p. 1984. text ed. 49.50 (*0-691-04718-9*) Princeton U Pr.

***Civil Works Administration, 1933-1934: The Business of Emergency Employment in the New Deal.** Bonnie F. Schwartz. LC 84-42560. Date not set. reprint ed. pap. 91.00 (*0-7837-9440-1*, 2060182) Bks Demand.

Civil Wrongs: What Went Wrong with Affirmative Action. Steven Yates. 1994. 22.95 (*1-55815-292-X*) ICS Pr.

Civil Wrongs & the Anatomy of a Jury Trial. Robert S. Sigman. (Law for the Layman Ser.). 85p. (C). 1991. pap. text ed. write for info. (*1-878135-11-2*) Legovac.

Civilacion y Cultura de Espana. Vicente Cantarino. LC 80-24839. 416p. (C). 1981. text ed. write for info. (*0-13-132846-8*) P-H.

Civile Conversation of M. Steeven Guazzo, 2 Vols. Stefano Guazzo. LC 25-14538. (Tudor Translations, Second Ser.: Nos. 7 & 8). reprint ed. Set. 115.00 (*0-404-51980-6*); reprint ed. 45.00 (*0-685-73115-4*) AMS Pr.

Civile Conversation of M. Steeven Guazzo, 2 Vols, 1. Stefano Guazzo. LC 25-14538. (Tudor Translations, Second Ser.: Nos. 7 & 8). reprint ed. 57.50 (*0-404-51981-4*) AMS Pr.

Civile Conversation of M. Steeven Guazzo, 2 Vols, 2. Stefano Guazzo. LC 25-14538. (Tudor Translations, Second Ser.: Nos. 7 & 8). reprint ed. 57.50 (*0-404-51982-2*) AMS Pr.

Civilian Administration in the Occupied West Bank: Analysis of Israeli Military Government Order No. 947- A Study Prepared for Law in the Service of Man. Jonathan Kuttab & Raja Shehadeh. LC 86-116238. 44p. reprint ed. pap. 25.00 (*0-685-16135-8*, 2027733) Bks Demand.

Civilian & the Military: A History of the American Anti-Militarist Tradition. Arthur A. Ekirch, Jr. LC 72-80273. 1972. pap. 3.00 (*0-87926-007-6*) R Myles.

Civilian-Based Defense: A Post-Military Weapon Defense. Gene Sharp. 180p. (C). 1990. text ed. 24.95 (*0-691-07809-2*) Princeton U Pr.

Civilian-Based Defense in a New Era. Johan J. Holst. (Monograph Ser.). 22p. 1990. 2.00 (*1-880813-01-7*) A Einstein Inst.

Civilian Career Guide. 4th ed. Ed. by James Grant. 220p. 1993. pap. 9.95 (*0-9620051-4-2*) Grants Guide.

Civilian Career Guide: A No Nonsense Guide for Veterans to Obtaining Civilian Employment. 3rd ed. James W. Grant. Ed. by Robert E. Grant. 240p. 1992. pap. 14.95 (*0-9620051-2-6*) Grants Guide.

Civilian Career Guide, 1988-1989. Ed. by James W. Grant. (Illus.). 250p. (Orig.). 1988. pap. 9.95 (*0-9620051-0-X*) Grants Guide.

Civilian Career Guide, 1990. Ed. by James W. Grant. 240p. 1990. pap. 11.95 (*0-9620051-1-8*) Grants Guide.

Civilian Conservation Corps: The Way We Remember It. Turner Publishing Co. Staff. LC 90-71685. 250p. 1990. 48.00 (*0-685-59052-6*) Turner Pub KY.

***Civilian Conservation Corps Camp Papers: A Guide.** 1991. 35.00 (*0-932486-37-1*) Ctr Res Lib.

Civilian Conservation Corps, 1933-1942: A New Deal Case. John A. Salmond. LC 66-30206. (Duke Historical Publications). 248p. reprint ed. pap. 70.70 (*0-317-26095-2*, 2023767) Bks Demand.

Civilian Control of the Military: Theory & Cases from Developing Countries. Ed. by Claude E. Welch, Jr. LC 76-40278. 337p. 1976. 49.50 (*0-87395-348-7*) State U NY Pr.

Civilian Elite of Cairo in the Later Middle Ages. Carl F. Petry. LC 80-8570. (Illus.). 450p. 1981. 70.00 (*0-691-05329-4*) Princeton U Pr.

Civilian Indoctrination of the Military: World War I & Future Implications for the Military-Industrial Complex. Penn Borden. LC 88-7700. (Contributions in Military Studies). 177p. 1989. text ed. 45.00 (*0-313-26381-7*, BCZ, Greenwood Pr) Greenwood.

Civilian. Military. Native American: Portraits of Fort Phil Kearny. Susan B. Doyle et al. (Illus.). 269p. (Orig.). 1993. pap. write for info. (*1-878856-14-6*) Ft P Kearney BT Assn.

Civilian Personnel Law Manual, Title 2: Leave. 3rd ed. 154p. 1990. ring bd. 10.00 (*0-16-022300-8*, S/N 020-000-002) USGPO.

Civilian Personnel Law Manual, Title 4: Relocation. 3rd ed. 546p. 1990. ring bd. 29.00 (*0-16-002851-5*, S/N 020-000-002) USGPO.

Civilian Population & the Warsaw Uprising of 1944. Joanna K. Hanson. LC 81-15545. (Illus.). 375p. 1982. 54.95 (*0-521-23421-2*) Cambridge U Pr.

Civilian Rule in the Developing World: Democracy on the March? Ed. by Constantine P. Danopoulos. 273p. (C). 1992. pap. text ed. 42.50 (*0-8133-8289-0*) Westview.

***Civilian Satellite Remote Sensing: A Strategic Approach.** (Illus.). 166p. (Orig.). (C). 1995. pap. text ed. 50.00 (*0-7881-1646-0*) Diane Pub.

Civilian Vascular Trauma. D. Preston Flanigan. (Illus.). 490p. 1992. text ed. 98.50 (*0-8121-1426-4*) Williams & Wilkins.

Civilians at Risk: Military & Police Abuses in the Mexican Countryside. Minnesota Advocates for Human Rights Staff. Date not set. pap. 5.00 (*0-929293-16-9*) MN Advocates.

Civilians at Risk: Military & Police Abuses in the Mexican Countryside. Eric Rosenthal. (North America Project Special Report Ser.). 37p. 1993. 5.00 (*0-911646-58-2*) World Policy.

Civilisation: Utopia & Tragedy. George Frankl. (Social History of the Unconscious Ser.: Vol. 2). 256p. 1993. pap. 18.95 (*1-871871-17-4*, Pub. by Open Gate Pr UK) Paul & Co Pubs.

Civilisation et Societe dans l'Occident Medieval. Aryeh Grabois. (Collected Studies: No. CS174). 334p. (FRE.). (C). 1983. reprint ed. lib. bdg. 105.00 (*0-86078-122-4*, Pub. by Variorum UK) Ashgate Pub Co.

Civilisation, ma Mere!... Driss Chraibi. (Folio Ser.: No. 1902). 180p. (FRE.). 1972. pap. 8.95 (*2-07-037902-7*) Schoenhof.

Civilisation, Ma Mere! Driss Chraibi. 180p. (FRE.). 1988. pap. 10.95 (*0-7859-2080-3*, 2070379027) Fr & Eur.

***Civilisation Phenicienne et Punique.** Ed. by Veronique Krings. 770p. (FRE.). 1994. 200.00 (*90-04-10068-7*) E J Brill.

Civilisations de L'Asie see Asian Civilizations

Civilising Caliban: The Misuse of Art 1875-1975. Frances Borzello. (Illus.). 192p. 1987. lib. bdg. 45.00 (*0-7102-0675-5*, RKP) Routledge.

Civilities & Civil Rights: Greensboro, North Carolina, & the Black Struggle for Freedom. William H. Chafe. (Illus.). 1981. pap. 9.95 (*0-19-502919-4*) OUP.

Civility & Citizenship. Ed. by Edward C. Banfield. 175p. 1992. 34.95 (*0-89226-104-8*) Paragon Hse.

Civility & Citizenship in Liberal Democratic Societies. Intro. by Edward C. Banfield. LC 91-11662. 165p. 1991. 35.95 (*0-943852-94-3*); pap. text ed. 17.95 (*0-943852-95-1*) Prof World Peace.

Civility & Disobedience. Burton Zwiebach. LC 74-12977. 251p. reprint ed. pap. 71.60 (*0-317-26356-0*, 2024568) Bks Demand.

Civility & Society in Western Europe, 1300-1600. Marvin B. Becker. LC 87-45262. 238p. 1988. 29.95 (*0-253-31118-7*) Ind U Pr.

Civilizacion de Occidente: Manual de Historia. 6th ed. William H. McNeill. 586p. (C). 1986. pap. 11.25 (*0-8477-0833-0*) U of PR Pr.

Civilizacion Espanola. rev. ed. Diego Marin. (Illus.). (C). 1969. text ed. 35.25 (*0-03-080033-1*) HB Coll Pubs.

Civilizaciones de Occidente: Introduccion a las Humanidades. 4th ed. Vicente Reynal. (Textbook Ser.). (Illus.). 470p. (Orig.). (SPA.). 1991. reprint ed. pap. text ed. 17.95 (*1-56328-006-X*) Edit Plaza Mayor.

Civilization: Contents, Discontents, Malcontents & Other Essays in Social Theory. Stanford M. Lyman. LC 89-20221. 352p. 1990. 30.00 (*1-55728-136-X*) U of Ark Pr.

Civilization: Death & Regeneration. (Institute of World Culture Ser.). 145p. 1985. pap. 8.75 (*0-88695-039-2*) Concord Grove.

Civilization: Its Cause & Cure. Edward Carpenter. 44p. 1972. pap. 3.50 (*0-934676-01-1*) Greenlf Bks.

Civilization: Tales of the Orient. Ellen N. La Motte. LC 76-122727. (Short Story Index Reprint Ser.). 1977. 19.95 (*0-8369-3560-8*) Ayer.

Civilization Analysis As a Sociology of Culture. Vytautas Kavolis. LC 94-12362. 233p. 1994. text ed. 89.95 (*0-7734-9083-3*) E Mellen.

Civilization & Barbarism: A Guide to the Teaching of Latin American Literature. Dave Oliphant. (Latin American Curriculum Units for Junior & Community Colleges Ser.). v, 94p. (Orig.). (C). 1979. pap. text ed. 4.95 (*0-86728-002-6*) U TX Inst Lat Am Stud.

***Civilization & Black Progress: Selected Writings of Alexander Crummell on the South.** Ed. by John Oldfield. 320p. (C). 1995. text ed. 38.50 (*0-8139-1602-X*) U Pr of Va.

Civilization & Capitalism, 15th-18th Century, 3 vols., Vol. 1: The Structures of Everyday Life. Fernand Braudel. Tr. by Sian Reynolds. LC 92-10173. (C). 1992. pap. 22.50 (*0-520-08114-5*) U CA Pr.

Civilization & Capitalism, 15th-18th Century, 3 vols., Vol. 2: The Wheels of Commerce. Fernand Braudel. Tr. by Sian Reynolds. LC 92-10173. (C). 1992. 22.50 (*0-520-08115-3*) U CA Pr.

Civilization & Capitalism, 15th-18th Century, 3 vols., Vol. 3: The Perspective of the World. Fernand Braudel. Tr. by Sian Reynolds. LC 92-10173. (C). 1992. 22.50 (*0-520-08116-1*) U CA Pr.

Civilization & Its Discontents. Sigmund Freud. pap. 17.00 (*0-679-43317-1*) Random.

Civilization & Its Discontents. unabridged ed. Sigmund Freud. 80p. 1994. pap. text ed. 1.00 (*0-486-28253-8*) Dover.

Civilization & Its Discontents. Sigmund Freud. Ed. by James Strachey. 128p. 1989. reprint ed. pap. 6.95 (*0-393-30158-3*) Norton.

Civilization & Religious Values. Henry D. Major. LC 77-27137. (Hibbert Lectures: 1946). reprint ed. 30.00 (*0-404-60431-5*) AMS Pr.

Civilization & Science in Conflict or Collaboration? Ciba Foundation Staff. LC 77-188826. (Ciba Foundation Symposium: New Ser.: No. 1). 237p. reprint ed. pap. 67.60 (*0-317-28331-6*, 2022134) Bks Demand.

Civilization & the Cripple. Frederick Watson. Ed. by William R. Phillips & Janet Rosenberg. LC 79-6927. (Physically Handicapped in Society Ser.). (Illus.). 1980. reprint ed. lib. bdg. 17.95 (*0-405-13134-8*) Ayer.

Civilization & the Growth of Law: Study of Relations Between Men's Ideas About the Universe & the Institutions of Law & Government. William A. Robson. LC 74-25779. (European Sociology Ser.). 374p. 1975. reprint ed. 31.95 (*0-405-06532-9*) Ayer.

Civilization & Transcendence. 78p. 1991. pap. 2.95 (*0-89213-298-1*) Bhaktivedanta.

Civilization Before Greece & Rome. H. W. Saggs. (Illus.). 352p. (C). 1991. reprint ed. pap. text ed. 18.00 (*0-300-05031-3*) Yale U Pr.

Civilization During the Middle Ages. G. B. Adams. 1972. 250.00 (*0-87968-873-4*) Gordon Pr.

Civilization Dynamics: Fundamentals of a Model-Oriented Description, No. 1. Norbert Muller. (Illus.). 239p. 1989. text ed. 68.95 (*0-566-05516-3*, Pub. by Avebury Pub UK) Ashgate Pub Co.

Civilization Dynamics, Vol. II: Nine Simulation Models. Norbert Muller. 435p. 1991. text ed. 68.95 (*1-85628-234-1*, Pub. by Avebury Pub UK) Ashgate Pub Co.

Civilization, Empires, Wars. William Eckhardt. 1992. write for info. (*0-318-68845-X*) Lentz Peace Res.

Civilization in Crisis: Human Prospects in a Changing World. Joseph A. Camilleri. LC 76-4240. 311p. reprint ed. pap. 88.70 (*0-317-09276-6*, 2022441) Bks Demand.

Civilization in the Buddhist Age (B.C. Three Hundred Twenty to Five Hundred A.D. Romesh C. Dutt. 1990. reprint ed. 7.50 (*81-85395-75-6*, Pub. by Low Price II) S Asia.

Civilization in the United States: An Inquiry by Thirty Americans. Ed. by Harold E. Stearns. (BCL1 - U. S. History Ser.). 577p. 1991. reprint ed. lib. bdg. 109.00 (*0-7812-6017-5*) Rprt Serv.

Civilization in the United States, An Inquiry by Thirty Americans. Harold E. Stearns. LC 71-109977. 577p. 1971. reprint ed. text ed. 38.50 (*0-8371-4483-3*, STCU, Greenwood Pr) Greenwood.

Civilization in the United States, First & Last Impressions. Matthew Arnold. 1972. 59.95 (*0-87968-874-2*) Gordon Pr.

***Civilization in the West.** 2nd ed. Mark Kishlansky et al. LC 94-22763. (C). 1995. text ed. 45.00 (*0-673-99226-8*); text ed. 7.20 (*0-673-99250-0*) HarpCollege.

Civilization in the West, 5 vols., A. Mark A. Kishlansky et al. (C). 1990. 38.50 (*0-673-46386-9*) HarpCollege.

Civilization in the West, 5 vols., B. Mark A. Kishlansky et al. (C). 1990. 40.00 (*0-673-46387-7*) HarpCollege.

Civilization in the West, 5 vols., C. Mark A. Kishlansky et al. (C). 1990. 28.25 (*0-673-46388-5*) HarpCollege.

Civilization in the West, 5 vols., II. Mark A. Kishlansky et al. (C). 1990. 40.00 (*0-673-46390-7*) HarpCollege.

Civilization in the West, Pt. 2. 4th ed. John B. Christopher et al. (Illus.). 512p. 1981. pap. text ed. write for info. (*0-13-134932-5*) P-H.

Civilization in the West, 5 vols., Set. Mark A. Kishlansky et al. (C). 1990. text ed. 63.50 (*0-673-18832-9*) HarpCollege.

***Civilization in the West, Vol. 1.** Kishlansky et al. (C). 1995. text ed. 30.50 (*0-673-99248-9*) HarpCollege.

Civilization in the West, Vol. I. Mark A. Kishlansky. (C). 1990. pap. text ed. 43.00 (*0-673-46389-3*) HarpCollege.

***Civilization in the West, Vol. 1.** 2nd ed. Bischoff. (C). 1995. student ed, text ed. 13.50 (*0-673-99266-7*) HarpCollege.

***Civilization in the West, Vol. 2.** 2nd ed. Bischoff. (C). 1995. student ed, text ed. 14.00 (*0-673-99267-5*) HarpCollege.

***Civilization in the West, Vol. 2.** 2nd ed. Kishlansky et al. (C). 1995. text ed. 30.50 (*0-673-99249-7*) HarpCollege.

***Civilization in the West, Vol. C.** 2nd ed. Kishlansky et al. (C). 1995. text ed. 28.25 (*0-673-99253-5*) HarpCollege.

***Civilization in the West, Vol. A.** 2nd ed. Kishlansky et al. (C). 1995. text ed. 28.25 (*0-673-99251-9*) HarpCollege.

***Civilization in the West: Renaissance to Present.** 2nd ed. Kishlansky et al. (C). 1995. text ed. 36.00 (*0-673-99254-3*) HarpCollege.

Civilization in the West: Study Guide, 2 vols., I. Mark A. Kishlansky. (C). 1991. 19.50 (*0-673-46418-0*) HarpCollege.

Civilization in the West: Study Guide, 2 vols., II. Mark A. Kishlansky. (C). 1991. 19.50 (*0-673-46419-9*) HarpCollege.

Civilization in the West: The Unfinished Legacy, a Brief History of Western Civilization. Mark A. Kishlansky. (C). 1993. 19.00 (*0-673-46696-5*) HarpCollege.

Civilization in the West: The Unfinished Legacy, a Brief History of Western Civilization, 2 vols., 1. Mark A. Kishlansky et al. LC 93-26228. (C). 1992. 39.50 (*0-673-46604-3*) HarpCollege.

Civilization in the West: The Unfinished Legacy, a Brief History of Western Civilization, 2 vols., 2. Mark A. Kishlansky et al. LC 93-26228. (C). 1993. 21.50 (*0-673-46605-1*) HarpCollege.

***Civilization in the West Vol. A: To 1550.** 2nd ed. Mark Kishlansky et al. 400p. 1995. reprint ed. pap. 38.50 (*1-886746-08-7*) Talman Pub.

***Civilization in the West Vol. B: 1350-1815.** 2nd ed. Mark Kishlansky et al. 400p. 1995. reprint ed. pap. 38.50 (*1-886746-09-5*) Talman Pub.

***Civilization in the West Vol. C: Since 1789.** 2nd ed. Mark Kishlansky et al. 400p. 1995. reprint ed. pap. 38.50 (*1-886746-10-9*) Talman Pub.

Civilization of Ancient Crete. R. F. Willets. 268p. 1992. pap. 46.00 (*90-256-0980-5*, Pub. by A M Hakkert NE) Benjamins North Am.

Civilization of Ancient Crete. R. F. Willetts. LC 76-55575. 679p. reprint ed. pap. 180.00 (*0-7837-4830-2*, 2044477) Bks Demand.

Civilization of Ancient Egypt. Johnson. Date not set. pap. 13.00 (*0-06-097548-2*) HarpC.

Civilization of Ancient Mexico. Lewis Spence. 121p. 1972. reprint ed. spiral bd. 4.95 (*0-7873-0810-2*) Mokelumne.

Civilization of Babylonia & Assyria. Morris Jastrow. LC 68-56504. (Illus.). 1980. reprint ed. 54.95 (*0-405-08668-7*, Pub. by Blom Pubns UK) Ayer.

Civilization of China see Civilizations of the East

Civilization of Europe in the Renaissance. John Hale. 649p. 1994. text ed. 35.00 (*0-689-12200-4*, Atheneum S&S) S&S Trade.

***Civilization of Europe in the Renaissance.** John Hale. 1995. pap. 18.00 (*0-684-80352-6*, Touchstone Bks) S&S Trade.

Civilization of Experience: A Whiteheadian Theory of Culture. David L. Hall. LC 72-83493. (Orestes Brownson Series on Contemporary Thought & Affairs: No. 8). 256p. reprint ed. pap. 73.00 (*0-7837-5603-8*, 2045509) Bks Demand.

Civilization of France: An Introduction. Ernst Robert Curtius. Tr. by Olive Wyon. LC 70-148877. (Select Bibliographies Reprint Ser.). 1977. reprint ed. 18.95 (*0-8369-5648-6*) Ayer.

Civilization of Greece in the Bronze Age. H. R. Hall. LC 78-124270. (Illus.). 1970. reprint ed. lib. bdg. 38.50 (*0-8154-0340-2*) Cooper Sq.

Civilization of Law: A Commentary on the Laws of Hammurabi & Magna Carta. Yousef Danesh-Khoshboo. LC 91-66748. 104p. (C). 1991. pap. text ed. 18.95 (*0-9628916-3-0*) Vande Vere.

Civilization of Rome. Donald R. Dudley. (Orig.). 1960. pap. 12.00 (*0-452-01016-0*, Mer); mass mkt. 4.95 (*0-452-00759-3*, Mer) NAL-Dutton.

Civilization of Sweden in Heathen Times. O. Montelius. LC 68-25251. (World History Ser.: No. 48). (Illus.). 1969. reprint ed. lib. bdg. 75.00 (*0-8383-0216-5*) M S G Haskell Hse.

Civilization of the Ancient Mediterranean, 3 vols., Set. Ed. by Michael Grant & Rachel Kitzinger. 1988. 195.00 (*0-318-32911-5*, Scribners) S&S Trade.

Civilization of the Ancient Mediterranean: Greece & Rome, 3 vols., Vol. 3. 2048p. 1988. Set. text ed. 275.00 (*0-684-17594-0*, Scribners) S&S Trade.

Civilization of the Goddess: The World of Old Europe. Marija Gimbutas. LC 90-55792. (Illus.). 544p. 1993. pap. 30.00 (*0-06-250804-0*) Harper SF.

Civilization of the Italian Renaissance: A Sourcebook. Ed. by Kenneth Bartlett. (Sources in Modern History Ser.). 441p. (C). 1992. pap. text ed. write for info. (*0-669-20900-7*) Heath.

Civilization of the Middle Ages. Norman F. Cantor. 1994. pap. 15.00 (*0-06-092553-1*) HarpC.

Civilization of the Old Northwest. Beverley W. Bond, Jr. LC 73-124226. (Select Bibliographies Reprint Ser.). 1977. 23.95 (*0-8369-5415-7*) Ayer.

Civilization of the Old Northwest. Beverly W. Bond, Jr. 1993. reprint ed. lib. bdg. 89.00 (*0-7812-5341-1*) Rprt Serv.

Civilization of the Renaissance in Italy. Jacob Burckhardt. 416p. 1990. pap. 10.95 (*0-14-044534-X*, Penguin Classics) Viking Penguin.

C

An Asterisk (*) at the beginning of an entry indicates that the title is appearing in BIP for the first time. 1289

Civilization of the Renaissance in Italy. Jacob Burckhardt. LC 54-6894. 424p. 1980. 16.00 (*0-394-60497-0*, Modern Lib) Random.

***Civilization of the Renaissance in Italy.** rev. ed. Jacob Burckhardt. Tr. by S. G. Middlemore. (Arts & Letters Ser.). (Illus.). 488p. (C). 1995. pap. 14.95 (*0-7148-3363-0*, Pub. by Phaidon Press UK) Chronicle Bks.

Civilization of the West, 5 vols., 1. Richard L. Greaves & Robert Zaller. (C). 1991. text ed. 41.50 (*0-06-047306-1*); 19.00 (*0-06-047298-7*) HarpCollege.

Civilization of the West, 5 vols., 2. Richard L. Greaves & Robert Zaller. (C). 1991. text ed. 41.50 (*0-06-047307-X*); 19.50 (*0-06-047297-9*) HarpCollege.

Civilization of the West, 5 vols., A. Richard L. Greaves & Robert Zaller. (C). 1991. text ed. 38.50 (*0-06-047303-7*) HarpCollege.

Civilization of the West, 5 vols., B. Richard L. Greaves & Robert Zaller. (C). 1991. text ed. 38.50 (*0-06-047304-5*) HarpCollege.

Civilization of the West, 5 vols., C. Richard L. Greaves & Robert Zaller. (C). 1991. text ed. 38.50 (*0-06-047305-3*) HarpCollege.

***Civilization of the West, Vol. B.** 2nd ed. Kishlansky et al. (C). 1995. text ed. 28.25 (*0-673-99252-7*) HarpCollege.

Civilization or Barbarism: An Authentic Anthropology. Cheikh A. Diop. Ed. by Harold J. Salemson & Marjolijn De Jager. Tr. by Yaa-Lengi Meema Ngemi. LC 90-4141. (Illus.). 461p. (C). 1991. 35.00 (*1-55652-049-2*); pap. 16.95 (*1-55652-048-4*) L Hill Bks.

Civilization Past & Present, 5 vols., A. 7th ed. T. Walter Wallbank. (C). 1991. text ed. 38.50 (*0-673-46581-0*) HarpCollege.

Civilization Past & Present, 5 vols., B. 7th ed. T. Walter Wallbank. (C). 1991. text ed. 38.50 (*0-673-46582-9*) HarpCollege.

Civilization Past & Present, 5 vols., C. 7th ed. T. Walter Wallbank. (C). 1991. text ed. 37.00 (*0-673-46583-7*) HarpCollege.

Civilization Past & Present, 5 vols., I. T. Walter Wallbank. (C). 1991. 21.00 (*0-673-46631-0*) HarpCollege.

Civilization Past & Present, 5 vols., I. 7th ed. T. Walter Wallbank. (C). 1991. text ed. write for info. (*0-318-68848-4*) HarpCollege.

Civilization Past & Present, 5 vols., II. T. Walter Wallbank. (C). 1991. 21.00 (*0-673-46632-9*) HarpCollege.

Civilization Past & Present, 5 vols., II. 7th ed. T. Walter Wallbank. (C). 1991. text ed. 45.00 (*0-673-38869-7*) HarpCollege.

Civilization Past & Present, 5 vols., Set. 7th ed. T. Walter Wallbank. (C). 1991. text ed. 60.50 (*0-673-38867-0*) HarpCollege.

Civilization Past & Present, Vol. 1. 6th ed. T. Walter Wallbank et al. (C). 1986. pap. text ed. 26.00 (*0-673-18348-3*) HarpCollege.

Civilization Past & Present, Vol. 2. 6th ed. T. Walter Wallbank et al. (C). 1986. pap. text ed. 26.00 (*0-673-18349-1*) HarpCollege.

Civilization Primer. 2nd ed. Edward M. Anson. 138p. (C). 1988. pap. text ed., spiral bd. 16.00 (*0-15-507596-9*) HB Coll Pubs.

Civilization Primer. 3rd ed. Edward Anson. 144p. (C). 1993. pap. text ed. 16.00 (*0-15-500261-9*) HB Coll Pubs.

Civilization, Science & Philosophy. Ed. by Collet's Holdings Limited Staff. 268p. 1983. 40.00 (*0-317-39487-8*, Pub. by Collets UK) St Mut.

Civilization, Science, Philosophy: Problems of the Contemporary World, No. 3. 268p. 1983. 40.00 (*0-685-17091-8*) St Mut.

Civilization Strategies & Secrets. Jason R. Rich. LC 93-83897. 235p. 1993. pap. 12.95 (*0-7821-1293-5*) Sybex.

Civilization Strategies & Secrets. 2nd ed. Jason Rich. LC 94-66850. 262p. 1994. 14.99 (*0-7821-1585-3*) Sybex.

Civilization West: Renaissance to Present. Richard L. Greaves & Robert Zaller. (C). 1991. text ed. 49.50 (*0-06-500787-5*) HarpCollege.

Civilization Without Sexes: Reconstructing Gender in Postwar France, 1917-1927. Mary L. Roberts. LC 93-26899. (Women in Culture & Society Ser.). 1994. lib. bdg. 48.00 (*0-226-72121-3*); pap. text ed. 18.95 (*0-226-72122-1*) U Ch Pr.

Civilizations & Other Living Systems. 3rd ed. Win Wenger & Susan Wenger. (Illus.). 120p. (C). 1985. reprint ed. pap. 12.00 (*0-931865-03-4*) Psychegenics.

Civilizations, Empires & Wars: A Quantitative History of War. William Eckhardt. LC 91-41450. 316p. 1992. lib. bdg. 49.95x (*0-89950-709-3*) McFarland & Co.

Civilizations in Desert Lands. Ed. by Richard B. Woodbury. (Utah Anthropological Papers). reprint ed. 18.50 (*0-404-60662-8*) AMS Pr.

Civilizations of Ancient America: Proceedings of the International Congress of Americanists, 29th. Americanists Staff. Ed. by Sol Tax. (Illus.). 328p. 1952. reprint ed. 55.50 (*0-8154-0231-7*) Cooper Sq.

Civilizations of Asia. (History of the World Ser.). (Illus.). 80p. (J). (gr. 4 up). 1988. lib. bdg. 25.67 (*0-8172-3302-4*) Raintree Steck-V.

Civilizations of Black Africa. Jacques P. Maquet. Tr. by Joan R. Rayfield. 1972. pap. 15.95 (*0-19-501464-2*) OUP.

Civilizations of Monsoon Asia. A. L. Basham. 1975. text ed. 22.95 (*0-685-14062-8*) Coronet Bks.

Civilizations of the Americas. (History of the World Ser.). (Illus.). 80p. (J). (gr. 4 up). 1988. lib. bdg. 25.67 (*0-8172-3306-7*) Raintree Steck-V.

***Civilizations of the Ancient Near East.** Ed. by Jack M. Sasson. LC 95-1712. 1995. 449.00 (*0-684-19279-9*, Scribners) S&S Trade.

Civilizations of the East. Rene Grousset. Tr. by Catherine Alison Phillips. Incl. Vol. 1. Near & Middle East. LC 66-30807. (Illus.). 404p. 1967. 37.50 (*0-8154-0093-4*); Vol. 3. Civilization of China. LC 66-30807. (Illus.). 363p. 1967. 57.00 (*0-8154-0095-0*); LC 66-30807. (ENG.). 1967. reprint ed. write for info. (*0-318-51441-9*) Cooper Sq.

Civilizations of the Middle East. (History of the World Ser.). (Illus.). 80p. (J). (gr. 4 up). 1988. lib. bdg. 25.67 (*0-8172-3303-2*) Raintree Steck-V.

Civilizations of the West, 2 Vols., 1. Richard L. Greaves et al. (C). 1993. text ed. 27.50 (*0-06-501260-7*) HarpCollege.

Civilizations of the West, 2 Vols., 2. Richard L. Greaves et al. (C). 1993. text ed. 27.50 (*0-06-501261-5*) HarpCollege.

Civilizations of the West, 2 Vols., Set. Richard L. Greaves et al. (C). 1993. text ed. 38.50 (*0-06-501259-3*) HarpCollege.

Civilizations of the World. 2nd ed. Richard L. Greaves. (C). 1993. 61.50 (*0-06-500674-7*) HarpCollege.

Civilizations of the World, 1. Richard L. Greaves. (C). 1993. 20.00 (*0-06-500855-3*) HarpCollege.

Civilizations of the World, 1. 2nd ed. Richard L. Greaves. (C). 1993. 45.00 (*0-06-500676-3*) HarpCollege.

Civilizations of the World, 2. Richard L. Greaves. (C). 1993. 19.50 (*0-06-500856-1*) HarpCollege.

Civilizations of the World, 2. 2nd ed. Richard L. Greaves. (C). 1993. 43.00 (*0-06-500677-1*) HarpCollege.

Civilizations of the World, A. 2nd ed. Richard L. Greaves. (C). 1993. 37.50 (*0-06-500678-X*) HarpCollege.

Civilizations of the World, B. 2nd ed. Richard L. Greaves. (C). 1993. 37.50 (*0-06-500679-8*) HarpCollege.

Civilizations of the World, C. 2nd ed. Richard L. Greaves. (C). 1993. 37.50 (*0-06-500680-1*) HarpCollege.

Civilizations of the World, Vol. 1. Richard L. Greaves. (C). 1990. pap. text ed. 26.75 (*0-06-047358-4*) HarpCollege.

Civilizations of the World: The Human Adventure (Combined) Richard L. Greaves et al. 1200p. (C). 1991. text ed. 60.50 (*0-06-047302-9*) HarpCollege.

Civilizations of the World: The Human Adventure from the Middle 1600's, Vol. 2. Richard L. Greaves et al. 600p. (C). 1990. pap. text ed. 26.75 (*0-06-047357-6*); Study Guide. student ed 12.50 (*0-06-047353-3*) HarpCollege.

Civilizations of the World: The Human Adventure: Volume A to 1500. Richard L. Greaves et al. 400p. (C). 1990. pap. text ed. 23.00 (*0-06-047356-8*) HarpCollege.

Civilizations of the World: The Human Adventure: Volume B from 1300-1800. Richard L. Greaves et al. 400p. (C). 1990. pap. text ed. 23.00 (*0-06-047355-X*) HarpCollege.

Civilizations of the World: The Human Adventure: Volume C from 1800. Richard L. Greaves et al. 400p. (C). 1990. pap. text ed. 23.00 (*0-06-047354-1*) HarpCollege.

Civilizations of the World: The Human Adventure Volume 1: To the Late 1600's. Richard L. Greaves et al. 600p. (C). 1990. pap. text ed. 36.25 (*0-06-047359-2*); Study Guide. student ed 13.00 (*0-06-047352-5*) HarpCollege.

Civilized Alternative. Jon Wynne-Tyson. 224p. 1972. 20.00 (*0-8464-0248-3*) Beekman Pubs.

Civilized Arrangement. large type ed. Catherine George. 1991. reprint ed. lib. bdg. 18.95 (*0-263-12562-9*, Pub. by Mills & Boon UK) Thorndike Pr.

Civilized Defense Plan. Howard S. Brembeck. 160p. 1989. 18.95 (*0-915979-25-X*) NOVA Pubns.

Civilized Engineer. Samuel C. Florman. LC 86-26183. 272p. 1987. pap. text ed. 8.95 (*0-685-17569-3*, Pub. by Thomas Dunne Bks) St Martin.

Civilized Engineer. Samuel C. Florman. 272p. 1988. pap. 10.95 (*0-312-02559-9*, Pub. by Thomas Dunne Bks) St Martin.

Civilized Imagination: A Study of Ann Radcliffe, Jane Austen, & Sir Walter Scott. Daniel Cottom. 224p. 1985. 14.95 (*0-521-30172-6*) Cambridge U Pr.

Civilized Shamans: Buddhism in Tibetan Societies. Geoffrey Samuel. LC 92-12590. (Illus.). 640p. 1993. 66.00 (*1-56098-231-4*) Smithsonian.

***Civilized Tribes: New & Selected Stories.** Jerry Bumpus. LC 95-10311. 1994. pap. 14.95 (*1-884836-08-9*) U Akron Pr.

***Civilized Tribes: New & Selected Stories.** Jerry Bumpus. LC 95-10311. 277p. (C). 1994. 24.95 (*1-884836-07-0*) U Akron Pr.

Civilized Wilderness: Backgrounds to American Literature, 1817-1860. Edward H. Foster. LC 74-33091. (Illus.). 1975. 16.95 (*0-02-910350-9*) Free Pr.

Civilized Women: Gender & Prestige in Southeastern Liberia. Mary H. Moran. LC 89-22398. (Anthropology of Contemporary Issues Ser.). (Illus.). 208p. (Orig.). 1990. 36.95 (*0-8014-2293-0*); pap. 13.95 (*0-8014-9554-7*) Cornell U Pr.

Civilizers: The Duvals of Texas. Roy L. Swift. (Illus.). 512p. 1992. 32.95 (*0-89015-840-1*) Sunbelt Media.

Civilizing Capitalism: The Beginnings of the Australian Labor Party. Bede Nairn. 1989. reprint ed. pap. 24.95 (*0-522-84382-4*) Intl Spec Bk.

***Civilizing Cyberspace: Policy, Power & the Information Superhighway.** Steven E. Miller. (C). 1996. text ed. write for info. (*0-201-84760-4*) Addison-Wesley.

Civilizing Mission: Exact Sciences & French Overseas Expansion, 1830-1940. Lewis Pyenson. LC 92-22577. (Illus.). 352p. 1993. text ed. 45.00 (*0-8018-4421-5*) Johns Hopkins.

Civilizing Process. Norbert Elias. 576p. 1994. text ed. 64.95 (*0-631-19221-2*); pap. text ed. 24.95 (*0-631-19222-0*) Blackwell Pubs.

***Civilizing Rituals: Inside Public Art Museums.** Carol Duncan. LC 94-31251. (Re Visions). (Illus.). 224p. 1995. 49.95x (*0-415-07011-2*, C0140); pap. 16.95 (*0-415-07012-0*, C0141) Routledge.

***Civilizing Terrains: Mountains, Mounds & Mesas.** William R. Morrish. (Illus.). 102p. (C). 1989. pap. text ed. 25.00 (*0-9625974-0-6*) Design Ctr Amer Urban Land.

Civilizing Your Puppy. Barbara J. Wrede. (Illus.). 96p. 1992. pap. 5.95 (*0-8120-4953-5*) Barron.

Civitas: Religious Interpretations of the City. Ed. by Peter S. Hawkins. LC 86-1836. (Studies in Humanities). 143p. 1986. 23.95 (*0-89130-987-X*, 00-01-10) Scholars Pr GA.

Civitas to Kingdom: British Political Continuity, 300-800. Kenneth R. Dark. (Studies in the Early History of Britain). 224p. 1994. 59.00 (*0-7185-1465-3*) St Martin.

Cizana. Rene De Goscinny & M. Uderzo. (Illus.). (SPA.). (J). 19.95 (*0-8288-4961-7*) Fr & Eur.

CJF Annual Report, 1990. 1990. write for info. (*0-318-68393-8*) Coun Jewish Feds.

CJF Directory of Jewish Federations, 1991. 1991. 10.00 (*0-317-03133-3*) Coun Jewish Feds.

CJS Purdy's Fine Art of Chess Annotation. Ralph Tykodi. (Illus.). 264p. (Orig.). 1992. pap. 16.95 (*0-938650-51-3*) Thinkers Pr.

CK & LD Isoenzymes: A Self-Instructional Text. Linda K. Brish. LC 84-9239. 146p. 1984. 22.00 (*0-89189-174-9*, 45-2-039-00) Am Soc Clinical.

CKBS '90: Proceedings of the International Working Conference on Cooperating Knowledge Based Systems, University of Keele, U. K. 3-5 October 1990. Ed. by S. M. Deen. xiv, 327p. 1991. pap. 59.00 (*0-387-19649-8*) Spr-Verlag.

***CL Cuisine: French.** Rosemary Moon. (Illus.). 256p. 1995. 7.98 (*0-8317-1121-3*) Smithmark.

***CL Cuisine: Pasta.** Rosemary Moon. (Illus.). 256p. 1995. 7.98 (*0-8317-1123-X*) Smithmark.

***CL Cuisine: Vegetarian.** Rosemary Moon. (Illus.). 256p. 1995. 7.98 (*0-8317-1122-1*) Smithmark.

***CL Programming: An Introduction.** Ed. by Catherine Rivera. (FastStart Ser.). (Illus.). 185p. (Orig.). 1994. pap. 59.00 (*1-884322-31-X*) Comp Applicatns.

CL Programming for the IBM AS-400. Greg Veal. Ed. by Robert Cozzi, Jr. 330p. 1992. pap. 56.00 (*0-9621825-2-4*) Cozzi Research.

CLA Computer Law Companion, 1993. Ed. by C. Ian Kyer & Christopher E. Erickson. 298p. Date not set. 15.00 (*1-885169-00-0*) Computer Law.

CLA Review Manual: A Practical Guide to CLA Exam Preparation. National Association of Legal Assistants, Inc. Staff & Virginia Koerselman. Ed. by Hannan. LC 93-8171. 700p. (C). 1993. pap. text ed. 67.00 (*0-314-01349-0*) West Pub.

CLA Study Guide, 1986-1991. Florida Legal Assistants, Inc. Staff. 400p. 1994. ring bd. 85.00 (*0-409-26545-4*) Michie Butterworth.

CLA Study Guide, 1986-1991. suppl. ed. Florida Legal Assistants, Inc. Staff. 400p. 1993. 23.50 (*0-685-44635-2*, D & S Pub) Butterworth Legal Pubs.

***CLA Study Guide, 1986-1991.** suppl. ed. Florida Legal Assistants, Inc. Staff. 1994. ring bd. 27.50 (*0-614-03177-X*) Butterworth Legal Pubs.

Claasified Directory of Artists' Signatures, Symbols & Monograms. 2nd ed. Ed. by H. H. Caplan. 850p. 1982. 220.00 (*0-8103-0977-7*) Gale.

Clabbered Dirt: Sweet Grass. Gary Paulsen. 1994. pap. 9.95 (*0-15-600052-0*) HarBrace.

Clabbered Dirt, Sweet Grass. Gary Paulsen. 144p. 1992. 19.95 (*0-15-118101-2*) HarBrace.

Clackamas. Gary Gildner. (Poetry Ser.). 64p. (Orig.). (C). 1991. lib. bdg. 16.95 (*0-88748-105-1*); pap. 9.95 (*0-88748-106-X*) Carnegie-Mellon.

Clackamas. Jana Harris. LC 79-65679. 68p. 1980. pap. 8.00 (*0-912292-59-8*) The Smith.

***Clackmannan & the Ochils: An Illustrated Architectural Guide.** Adam Swan. (Illus.). 112p. (C). 1987. pap. 35.00x (*1-873190-28-X*, Pub. by Rutland Pr UK) St Mut.

Clackshant. Alexander Blain. Ed. by K. R. Leo. LC 82-80034. (Illus.). (Orig.). 1982. pap. 5.00 (*0-9606678-1-4*) Sylvan Pubns.

***Clackymucky & the Bulldog.** Josephine Croser. 32p. (J). 1995. 12.95 (*0-908507-98-4*, Pub. by ERA Pubns AT); pap. 5.95 (*0-947212-43-4*, Pub. by ERA Pubns AT) Pubs Dist MI.

Cladding. 1992. text ed. 37.00 (*0-07-012534-1*) McGraw.

Cladding Materials for Industrial Buildings. EEMUA Staff. 1987. 125.00 (*0-85931-044-2*, Pub. by EEMUA UK) St Mut.

***Cladistic Analysis of North American Platynini & Revision of the Agonum Extensicolle Species Group (Coleoptera: Carabidae)** James K. Liebherr. LC 85-29034. (University of California Publications in Entomology: No. 106). 210p. 1986. pap. 59.90 (*0-7837-7490-7*, 2049212) Bks Demand.

Cladistics: A Practical Course in Systematics. Peter L. Forey et al. (Systematics Association Special Volume Ser.: Vol. 10). (Illus.). 208p. 1993. pap. 22.50 (*0-19-857766-4*) OUP.

Cladistics: Perspectives on the Reconstruction of Evolutionary History. Thomas Duncan & Tod F. Stuessy. LC 83-26178. (Illus.). 368p. 1984. text ed. 52.50 (*0-231-05430-0*) Col U Pr.

Cladocera. Ed. by L. Forro & D. G. Frey. (Developments in Hydrobiologia Ser.). 1987. lib. bdg. 202.50 (*90-6193-617-9*) Kluwer Ac.

***Cladocera as Model Organisms in Biology.** Ed. by Petter Larsson & Lawrence J. Weider. LC 95-13976. (Developments in Hydrobiology Ser.: No. 107). 1995. write for info. (*0-7923-3471-X*) Kluwer Ac.

Cladoniae of Connecticut. Alexander W. Evans. (Connecticut Academy of Arts & Sciences Ser., Trans.: Vol. 30). 1930. pap. 89.50 (*0-685-22803-7*) Elliots Bks.

Cladoniae of Florida. Alexander W. Evans. (Connecticut Academy of Arts & Sciences Ser., Trans.: Vol. 38). 1952. pap. 59.50 (*0-685-22897-5*) Elliots Bks.

Claes Oldenburg. Arne Glimcher. LC 92-61388. (Illus.). 110p. (Orig.). 1992. pap. write for info. (*1-878283-25-1*) PaceWildenstein.

Claes Oldenburg: Multiples in Retrospect, 1964-1990. Thomas Lawson. LC 90-50799. (Illus.). 1991. 65.00 (*0-8478-1335-5*) Rizzoli Intl.

***Claiborne Parish, Louisiana Newspaper Clippings, 1875-1882.** Wanda V. Head & Gloria L. Kerns. 125p. (Orig.). 1988. pap. 18.00 (*1-57088-015-8*) J&W Ent.

***Claiborne Parish, Louisiana 1830, 1840 & 1850 Censuses with 1850 Mortality Schedule & Slave Holders.** Wanda V. Head. 165p. (Orig.). 1991. pap. text ed. 17.00 (*1-57088-004-2*) J&W Ent.

***Claim.** Rob Robles. 1994. pap. 8.95 (*1-55503-743-7*) Covenant Comms.

***Claim: Nine Radical Claims of Jesus That Can Revolutionize Your Life.** Dwight K. Nelson. LC 94-26480. 1994. pap. 1.95 (*0-8163-1236-2*) Pacific Pr Pub Assn.

Claim Examiner. Jack Rudman. (Career Examination Ser.: C-139). 1994. pap. 27.95 (*0-8373-0139-4*) Nat Learn.

Claim Jumper. Doyle Trent. 1981. pap. 1.95 (*0-8439-0938-2*) Dorchester Pub Co.

Claim Jumpers. Stewart E. White. lib. bdg. 21.95 (*0-88411-828-2*, Aeonian Pr) Amereon Ltd.

Claim of Crofting. James Hunter. (Illus.). 224p. 1992. 34.95 (*1-85158-329-7*, Pub. by Mnstream UK) Trafalgar.

Claim of Dispossession: Jewish Land Settlement & the Arabs, 1878-1948. Arieh L. Avneri. 303p. 1982. pap. 19.95x (*0-87855-964-7*) Transaction Pubs.

Claim of Reason: Wittgenstein, Skepticism, Morality, & Tragedy. Stanley Cavell. 1982. pap. 14.95 (*0-19-503195-4*) OUP.

Claim Paid: A Consumer's Guide Through the Insurance Claims Maze. Frank R. Dumas. LC 89-51782. 191p. (Orig.). 1990. pap. 15.95 (*0-9624813-5-1*) Stratton Pr.

***Claim Prevention: A Self-Audit for Illinois Lawyers & Law Firms.** Robert S. Hunter. (Klear-E-Lex Ser.). 174p. (Orig.). 1992. pap. 19.95 (*1-884177-10-7*) Justice IL.

Claim Reserving in Non-Life Insurance. G. C. Taylor. (C). 1986. 500.00 (*0-685-33731-6*, Pub. by Witherby & Co UK) St Mut.

***Claim Simpli-filer.** Travis Gunn. 50p. 1995. 26.99 (*1-885518-03-X*) Crossfire Pubng.

Claim to Fame. William Appelman. 256p. 1993. 19.95 (*0-88184-935-9*) Carroll & Graf.

Claim to New Roles. Page P. Miller. LC 85-2249. (American Theological Library Association Monograph: No. 22). 253p. 1985. 25.00 (*0-8108-1809-4*) Scarecrow.

Claim Your Birthright. James McKeever. 1989. pap. 7.95 (*0-86694-112-6*) Omega Pubns OR.

Claim Your Money from Insurance Companies. Larry Lane. LC 93-85361. (Illus.). 310p. 1993. pap. 14.95 (*0-9622317-2-X*) Tailight Studio.

Claimant or Client? A Social Worker's View of the Supplementary Benefits Commission. Olive Stevenson. 1973. 30.00 (*0-317-05822-3*, Pub. by Natl Inst Soc Work) St Mut.

Claimed by Vesuvius. Walter H. Marx. (Illus.). 164p. (C). 1975. pap. text ed. 8.25 (*0-88334-069-0*) Longman.

***Claiming.** Patricia Ranzoni. Ed. by Constance Hunting. 65p. (Orig.). 1995. pap. 8.95 (*0-913006-59-9*) Puckerbrush.

Claiming a Frontier: Ministry & Older People. Robert W. McClellan & Carolyn E. Usher. LC 77-85413. 1977. 10.00 (*0-88474-040-4*, 05741-X) Free Pr.

Claiming Biotechnical Inventions. 1985. 25.00 (*0-318-20246-8*, P-9) Am IPLA.

Claiming Breath. Diane Glancy. LC 91-24637. (North American Indian Prose Award Ser.). xiv, 115p. 1992. 20.00 (*0-8032-2140-1*) U of Nebr Pr.

Claiming Earth: Race, Rape, Ritual, Richness in America & the Search for Enlightened Empowerment. Haki R. Madhubuti. 175p. 1994. 19.95 (*0-88378-095-X*) Third World.

Claiming God's Promise: A Guide to Discovering Your Spiritual Gifts. Thomas R. Hawkins. LC 92-13015. 128p. (Orig.). 1992. pap. 8.95 (*0-687-08397-4*) Abingdon.

Claiming Kin. Ellen B. Voigt. LC 76-5944. (Wesleyan Poetry Program Ser.: Vol. 83). 64p. 1976. 22.50 (*0-8195-2083-7*, Wesleyan Univ Pr); pap. 10.95 (*0-8195-1083-1*, Wesleyan Univ Pr) U Pr of New Eng.

Claiming of Sleeping Beauty. A. N. Roquelaure. 1983. pap. 10.95 (*0-452-26656-4*, Plume) NAL-Dutton.

Claiming on the Criminal Injuries Compensation Board. Dennis Foster. 265p. (C). 1991. 75.00 (*1-85190-122-1*, Pub. by Tolley Pubng UK) St Mut.

Claiming on the Motor Insurers Bureau: A Short Guide. Donald B. Williams. 59p. 1990. 30.00 (*1-85190-117-5*, Pub. by Tolley Pubng UK) St Mut.

Claiming Reality: Phenomenology & Women's Experience. Louise Levesque-Lopman. (New Feminist Perspectives Ser.). 208p. 1988. 50.00 (*0-8476-7580-7*, DR 7580); pap. 22.50 (*0-8476-7581-5*, DR 7581) Rowman.

Claiming the Dream: The Victorious Campaign of Douglas Wilder of Virginia. Margaret Edds. 383p. 1990. 17.95 (*0-912697-85-7*) Algonquin Bks.

Claiming the Heavens: The New York Times Complete Guide to the Star Wars Debate. William J. Broad et al. LC 87-40196. (Illus.). 304p. 1988. 17.95 (*0-8129-1647-6*, Times Bks) Random.

Claiming the Heritage: African-American Women Novelists & History. Missy D. Kubitschek. LC 90-44984. 1991. pap. 15.95 (*0-87805-475-8*) U Pr of Miss.

Claiming the High Ground: Sherpas, Subsistence, & Environmental Change in the Highest Himalaya. Stanley F. Stevens. (Illus.). 546p. (C). 55.00 (*0-520-07699-0*) U CA Pr.

Claiming the Promise. Doug Sparks. 32p. (Orig.). 1991. pap. 2.00 (*0-89109-624-8*, NavPr) NavPress.

C

An Asterisk (*) at the beginning of an entry indicates that the title is appearing in BIP for the first time.

Claiming the Promise: African Churches Speak. Musimbi Kanyoro et al. LC 93-40417. 128p. (Orig.). 1994. pap. 7.95 (*0-377-00267-4*) Friendship Pr.

***Claiming the Real: The Griersonian Documentary & Its Legitimations.** Brian Winston. 296p. 1995. text ed. 55.00 (*0-85170-463-8*); pap. 19.95 (*0-85170-464-6*) Ind U Pr.

Claiming Their Land: Women Homesteaders in Texas. Florence C. Gould & Patricia N. Pando. LC 89-52075. (Southwestern Studies: No. 93). (Illus.). 112p. 1991. pap. 10.00 (*0-87404-189-9*) Tex Western.

Claiming Your Destiny: The Path of Life Mastery. Richard Treadgold. Ed. by Lona Lyons. (Illus.). 250p. (Orig.). 1992. pap. 11.95 (*1-879647-33-8*) Essence Fndtn.

***Claiming Your Place: How to Find Where You Fit in the Life of the Church.** Ed. by Jeffrey A. Metzger. 1994. 5.99 (*0-7847-0284-5*, 11-40304) Standard Pub.

Claiming Your Self-Esteem: A Guide Out of Codependency, Addiction, & Other Useless Habits. Carolyn M. Ball. 224p. 1991. reprint ed. pap. 9.95 (*0-89087-645-2*) Celestial Arts.

Claims. Shirley Kaufman. LC 84-2146. 80p. 1984. 13.95 (*0-935296-53-0*) Sheep Meadow.

Claims & Changes: Handbook for Construction Contract Management. Paul Levin. Ed. by Bruce Jones & Angier Jones. (Illus.). 222p. 23.50 (*0-686-36279-9*) Constr Ind Pr.

Claims Clerk. Jack Rudman. (Career Examination Ser.: C-138). 1994. pap. 23.95 (*0-8373-0138-6*) Nat Learn.

Claims, Costs & Crimes. 2nd ed. 145p. 1990. pap. 12.95 (*0-939818-20-5*) Lee Bks.

Claims Environment. James J. Markham et al. LC 93-71086. 423p. (C). 1993. pap. text ed. 35.00 (*0-89462-078-9*) IIA.

Claims Examiner. Jack Rudman. (Career Examination Ser.: C-140). 1994. pap. 27.95 (*0-8373-0140-8*) Nat Learn.

Claims Examiner Aide. Jack Rudman. (Career Examination Ser.: C-948). 1994. pap. 23.95 (*0-8373-0948-4*) Nat Learn.

Claims for Missing Issues of Serials. (National Information Standards Ser.). 1983. 12.00 (*0-88738-961-9*, Z30.45) Transaction Pubs.

Claims for Poetry. Ed. by Donald Hall. 528p. (C). 1982. pap. text ed. 16.95 (*0-472-06308-1*) U of Mich Pr.

Claims Game - How to Play to Win: How to Present, Evaluate & Settle Your Automobile Injury Claim. Douglas L. LaFaive. Ed. by Vesta Urband. 80p. (Orig.). 1991. pap. 19.95 (*0-9629403-0-5*) Puck Pr.

Claims Investigator. Jack Rudman. (Career Examination Ser.: C-3324). 1994. pap. 23.95 (*0-8373-3324-5*) Nat Learn.

Claims Management: How to Select, Manage, & Save Money on Adjusting Services. Kevin M. Quinley. LC 92-18594. 252p. 1992. 46.50 (*0-934753-67-9*) LRP Pubns.

Claims Medical Manual. 4th rev. ed. Packard Thurber & Packard Thurber, Jr. LC 90-7652. (Illus.). 128p. (Orig.). 1991. pap. 9.95 (*0-87015-257-2*) Pacific Bks.

Claims of Feeling: Readings in Aesthetic Education. Ed. by Malcolm Ross. 240p. 1989. 75.00 (*1-85000-612-1*, Falmer Pr); pap. 38.00 (*1-85000-613-X*, Falmer Pr) Taylor & Francis.

Claims of French Poetry: Nine Studies in the Greater French Poets. John C. Bailey. LC 67-30195. (Essay Index Reprint Ser.). 1977. 20.95 (*0-8369-0168-1*) Ayer.

Claims Settlement Agent. Jack Rudman. (Career Examination Ser.: C-1189). 1994. pap. 27.95 (*0-8373-1189-6*) Nat Learn.

Claims to Fame: Celebrity in Contemporary America. Joshua Gamson. LC 93-28188. 270p. (C). 1994. 35.00 (*0-520-08352-0*); pap. 14.00 (*0-520-08353-9*) U CA Pr.

***Claims to Fame: The B-17 Flying Fortress.** Steve Birdsall & Roger A. Freeman. (Illus.). 192p. 1995. 24.95 (*1-85409-211-1*) Sterling.

***Claims to Fame: The Lancaster.** Norman Franks. (Illus.). 256p. 1995. 24.95 (*1-85409-220-0*) Sterling.

Claims to Name: Toponyms of St. Lawrence County. Ed. by Kelsie B. Harder & Mary H. Smallman. LC 92-43036. 1993. 25.00 (*0-925168-09-2*); pap. 14.95 (*0-925168-10-6*) North Country.

Claims to Territory in International Law & Relations. Norman L. Hill. LC 75-25488. (Illus.). 248p. 1976. reprint ed. text ed. 65.00 (*0-8371-8430-4*, HICT, Greenwood Pr) Greenwood.

Claims to the Possession of Land: The Law & Practice. Philip Walter & James Harris. 616p. 1987. 300.00 (*1-85190-000-4*, Pub. by Fourmat Pub UK) St Mut.

Claims to the Possession of Land the Law & Practice. 2nd ed. Philip Walter & James Harris. 882p. (C). 1991. 495.00 (*1-85190-101-9*, Pub. by Tolley Pubng UK) St Mut.

Claims upon My Heart. Kay D. Rizzo. LC 92-43931. 1993. pap. 10.95 (*0-8163-1133-1*) Pacific Pr Pub Assn.

Clair de Femme. Romain Gary. (FRE.). 1982. pap. 10.95 (*0-7859-2458-2*, 2070373673) Fr & Eur.

Clair de Femme. Romain Gary. (Folio Ser.: No. 1367). 167p. (FRE.). 1977. 8.95 (*2-07-037367-3*) Schoenhof.

Clair de Terre. Andre Breton. (Poesie Ser.). (FRE.). pap. 9.95 (*2-07-030045-5*) Schoenhof.

Claire: Theatre de Verdure. Rene Char. 112p. 1949. 8.95 (*0-7859-0684-3*, F93170) Fr & Eur.

Claire & the Friendly Snakes. Lindsey Tate. (J). (ps-3). 1993. 15.00 (*0-374-31337-7*) FS&G.

Claire Clairmont & the Shelleys, 1798-1879. Robert Gittings & Jo Manton. (Illus.). 265p. 1992. 45.00 (*0-19-818594-4*) OUP.

***Claire Clairmont & the Shelleys 1798-1879.** Robert Gittings & Jo Manton. (Illus.). 294p. 1995. pap. 21.00 (*0-19-818351-8*) OUP.

Claire de Terre, Mont de Piete, le Revolver a Cheveux Blancs, l'Air de l'Eau. Andre Breton. (FRE.). 1966. pap. 10.95 (*0-8288-3815-1*, F89480) Fr & Eur.

Claire Falkenstein: Chance & Choice. Maren Henderson. (Illus.). 33p. 1989. pap. 15.00 (*1-880566-07-9*) J Rutberg Fine Arts.

Claire Fejes Retrospective. Mary Goodwin. Ed. by Terry P. Dickey. (Illus.). 31p. (Orig.). 1991. pap. 8.00 (*0-931163-07-2*) U Alaska Museum.

Claire Gets Caught. Katherine Applegate. (Boyfriends & Girlfriends Ser.: No. 5). (J). (gr. 4-7). 1994. mass mkt. 3.99 (*0-06-106187-5*, Harp PBks) HarpC.

Claire H. Hewes: The Hofer Family of Carson City. Intro. by Mary E. Glass. 21p. 1966. lib. bdg. 16.00 (*1-56475-019-1*); fiche write for info. (*1-56475-020-5*) U NV Oral Hist.

Claire Leighton: Wood Engravings. Anne Stevens & David Leighton. (Illus.). 28p. 1995. pap. 12.95 (*1-85444-038-1*, 038-1, Pub. by Ashmolean Mus UK) A Schwartz & Co.

Claire of the Moon. Nicole Conn. 176p. 1993. pap. 10.95 (*1-56280-038-8*) Naiad Pr.

Claire of the Wild Rose Inn. Jennifer Armstrong. (Wild Rose Inn Ser.: No. 5). (YA). 1994. mass mkt. 3.99 (*0-553-29911-5*) Bantam.

Claire Shaeffer's Fabric Sewing Guide. Claire Shaeffer. 544p. 1994. pap. 32.95 (*0-8019-8628-1*) Chilton.

Claire's Corner Copia Cookbook: Two Hundred Twenty Five Homestyle Vegetarian Recipes from Claire's Family to Yours. Claire Criscuolo. LC 94-11882. 1994. 13.95 (*0-452-27176-2*, Plume) NAL-Dutton.

Claire's Girls. Don Winslow. (Orig.). 1993. pap. text ed. 4.95 (*1-56333-108-X*) Masquerade.

Clairmont Correspondence: Letters of Claire Clairemont, Charles Clairmont, & Fanny Imlay Godwin, 1808-1879, 2 vols., Set. Ed. by Marion K. Stocking. LC 94-789. (Illus.). 800p. 1994. text ed. 65.00x (*0-8018-4633-1*) Johns Hopkins.

Clairvoyance. Rudolf Steiner et al. 1973. lib. bdg. 79.95 (*0-87968-558-1*) Krishna Pr.

Clairvoyance. 10th ed. Charles W. Leadbeater. 1968. 8.95 (*81-7059-142-2*) Theos Pub Hse.

Clairvoyance. C. W. Leadbeater. 61p. 1959. reprint ed. spiral bd. 4.40 (*0-7873-1244-4*) Mokelumne.

Clairvoyance: Key to Spiritual Perspective. Mary E. Flora. LC 93-70667. (Illus.). 128p. (Orig.). 1993. pap. 10.00 (*0-9631993-5-8*) CDM Pubns.

Clairvoyance: The System of Philosophy Concerning the Divinity of Clairvoyance. J. F. Grumbine. reprint ed. pap. 14.95 (*1-872736-48-3*, Pub. by Mandrake Pr UK) Holmes Pub.

Clairvoyance & Clairaudience - Premonitions & Impressions. Edward B. Warman. 51p. 1994. pap. 5.00 (*0-89540-284-X*, SB-284) Sun Pub.

Clairvoyance & Materialisation: A Record of Experiments. Gustave Geley. Tr. by Stanley De Brath. LC 75-7381. (Perspectives in Psychical Research Ser.). (Illus.). 1975. reprint ed. 41.95 (*0-405-07031-4*) Ayer.

Clairvoyance & Occult Powers. Swami Panchadasi. 12.00 (*0-911662-35-9*) Yoga.

Clairvoyance & Thoughtography. T. Fukurai. LC 75-7379. (Perspectives in Psychical Research Ser.). (Illus.). 1975. reprint ed. 23.95 (*0-405-07029-2*) Ayer.

Clairvoyance, Its Nature & Unfoldment. J. C. Grumbine. 116p. 1968. reprint ed. spiral bd. 5.50 (*0-7873-0359-3*) Mokelumne.

Clairvoyant Countess. Dorothy Gilman. 224p. 1986. mass mkt. 4.95 (*0-449-21318-8*, Crest) Fawcett.

Clairvoyant Eye: The Poetry & Poetics of Wallace Stevens. Joseph N. Riddel. LC 91-15505. 308p. 1991. pap. text ed. 12.95 (*0-8071-0716-6*) La State U Pr.

Clairvoyant Investigations. Geoffrey Hodson. LC 84-40166. (Illus.). 160p. (Orig.). 1984. pap. 9.25 (*0-8356-0585-X*, Quest) Theos Pub Hse.

Clairvoyant Investigations of Christian Origins & Ceremonial. Geoffrey Hodson. (Orig.). 1977. pap. text ed. 3.25 (*0-918980-01-1*) St Alban Pr.

Clais & Clock: Poetry & Illustrations. Jean Kadman. (Illus.). 45p. 1988. 4.75 (*0-9615216-4-3*) Crones Own Pr.

Clam Mariculture in North America. Ed. by J. J. Manzi & M. Castagna. (Developments in Aquaculture & Fisheries Science Ser.: No. 19). 461p. 1989. 115.50 (*0-444-87300-7*) Elsevier.

Clambake: A History & Celebration of an American Tradition. Kathy Neustadt. LC 91-45599. (Illus.). 240p. 1992. lib. bdg. 40.00 (*0-87023-782-9*); pap. text ed. 16.95x (*0-87023-799-3*) U of Mass Pr.

Clambake: A Wampanoag Tradition. Russell Peters. (J). (gr. 3-6). 1992. pap. 6.95 (*0-8225-9621-0*, Lerner Publctns) Lerner Group.

Clambake: A Wampanoag Tradition. Russell M. Peters. (We Are Still Here: Native Americans Today Ser.). (Illus.). 48p. (J). (gr. 3-6). 1992. lib. bdg. 19.95 (*0-8225-2651-4*, Lerner Publctns) Lerner Group.

Clambake Sans Sand in Pots & Woks. Robert H. Robinson. 1983. pap. 2.95 (*0-911145-04-4*) Sussex Prints.

Clambakes & Fish Fries. Susn H. Loomis. LC 94-2420. 1994. 19.95 (*1-56305-671-2*); pap. 10.95 (*1-56305-295-4*) Workman Pub.

Clamdiggers & Downeast Country Stores: Eastern Maine's Vanishing Culture. Allan Lockyer. LC 93-84637. (Illus.). 12p. (Orig.). 1993. pap. 14.95 (*1-880811-12-X*) North Lights.

Clammer. William J. Hopkins. LC 79-116955. (Short Story Index Reprint Ser.). 1977. 20.95 (*0-8369-3458-X*) Ayer.

Clamor. Ann Lauterbach. 96p. 1992. pap. 11.00 (*0-14-058673-3*, Penguin Bks) Viking Penguin.

***Clamor De Mi Pueblo: Desde el Cautiverio En America Latina.** fac. ed. Esther Arias. LC 81-4816. (Illus.). 167p. 1994. pap. 47.60 (*0-7837-7707-8*, 2047466) Bks Demand.

Clamor en el Barrio. Freddie Garcia & Ninfa Garcia. 230p. (Orig.). (SPA.). (C). 1989. pap. text ed. 3.50 (*0-9619319-1-4*) F Garcia Ministries.

Clamor of Innocence: Central American Short Stories. Ed. by Barbara Paschke & David Volpendesta. 224p. (Orig.). 1988. pap. 9.95 (*0-87286-227-5*) City Lights.

Clamorous Voices: Shakespeare's Women Today. Carol Rutter et al. Ed. by Faith Evans. (Illus.). 131p. 1989. 39.95 (*0-87830-036-8*, A3685, Theatre Arts Bks); pap. 13.95 (*0-87830-037-6*, A3689, Theatre Arts Bks) Routledge Chapman & Hall.

Clams in Airtight Containers. (Latin American Products Included in the U. S. General System of Preferences Ser.). 33p. 1978. pap. 3.00 (*0-8270-3355-9*) OAS.

Clams, Mussels, Oysters, Scallops & Snails: A Cookbook & a Memoir. Howard Mitcham. (Illus.). 224p. 1990. pap. 12.50 (*0-940160-47-1*) Parnassus Imprints.

Clamshell Boy. Terri Cohlene. (Native American Legends Ser.). (Illus.). 48p. (J). (gr. 4-8). 1990. lib. bdg. 19.93 (*0-86593-001-5*); lib. bdg. 14.95 (*0-685-46446-6*) Rourke Corp.

Clamshell Boy: A Makah Legend. Terri Cohlene. 48p. (J). (gr. 4-7). 1990. pap. 3.95 (*0-8167-2361-3*) Troll Assocs.

Clan. William Kuhns. 410p. (FRE.). 1986. pap. 13.95 (*0-7859-2517-1*, 2070377385) Fr & Eur.

Clan Almanac. Charles MacLean. (Illus.). 144p. 1990. 5.99 (*0-517-05415-9*) Random Hse Value.

Clan Cameron. Charles I. Fraser. (Johnston & Bacon Clan Histories Ser.). (Illus.). 32p. 1993. reprint ed. pap. 8.95 (*0-685-69974-9*, 9607) Clearfield Co.

Clan Campbell. 2nd ed. Andrew McKerral. (Johnston & Bacon Clan Histories Ser.). (Illus.). 32p. 1993. reprint ed. pap. 8.95 (*0-685-69975-7*, 9617) Clearfield Co.

Clan Donald (Macdonalds, Etc.) I. F. Grant. (Johnston & Bacon Clan Histories Ser.). (Illus.). 32p. 1993. reprint ed. pap. 8.95 (*0-685-69982-X*, 9610) Clearfield Co.

Clan Fraser of Lovat. 2nd ed. Charles I. Fraser. (Johnston & Bacon Clan Histories Ser.). (Illus.). 32p. 1993. reprint ed. pap. 8.95 (*0-685-69977-3*, 9608) Clearfield Co.

Clan Gordon. Jean Dunlop. (Johnston & Bacon Clan Histories Ser.). (Illus.). 32p. 1993. reprint ed. pap. 8.95 (*0-685-69978-1*, 9601) Clearfield Co.

Clan Grant. I. F. Grant. (Johnston & Bacon Clan Histories Ser.). (Illus.). 32p. 1993. reprint ed. pap. 8.95 (*0-685-69980-3*, 9611) Clearfield Co.

Clan MacGregor. W. R. Kermack. (Johnston & Bacon Clan Histories Ser.). (Illus.). 32p. 1993. reprint ed. pap. 8.95 (*0-685-69983-8*, 9613) Clearfield Co.

Clan MacKay. Margaret O. MacDougall. (Johnston & Bacon Clan Histories Ser.). (Illus.). 32p. 1993. reprint ed. pap. 8.95 (*0-685-69984-6*, 9614) Clearfield Co.

Clan Mackay Society. Christian H. McKee. 54p. 1989. pap. 5.00 (*0-9611046-1-9*) C H McKee.

Clan MacKenzie. Jean Dunlop. (Johnston & Bacon Clan Histories Ser.). (Illus.). 32p. 1993. reprint ed. pap. 8.95 (*0-685-69985-4*, 9603) Clearfield Co.

Clan MacKintosh. Jean Dunlop. (Johnston & Bacon Clan Histories Ser.). (Illus.). 32p. 1993. reprint ed. pap. 8.95 (*0-685-69986-2*, 9602) Clearfield Co.

Clan MacLean. John Mackechnie. (Johnston & Bacon Clan Histories Ser.). (Illus.). 32p. 1993. reprint ed. pap. 8.95 (*0-685-69987-0*, 9615) Clearfield Co.

Clan MacLeod. I. F. Grant. (Johnston & Bacon Clan Histories Ser.). (Illus.). 32p. 1993. reprint ed. pap. 8.95 (*0-685-69988-9*, 9612) Clearfield Co.

Clan Morrison. Alick Morrison. (Johnston & Bacon Clan Histories Ser.). (Illus.). 32p. 1993. reprint ed. pap. 8.95 (*0-685-69989-7*, 9619) Clearfield Co.

Clan Munro. Charles I. Fraser. (Johnston & Bacon Clan Histories Ser.). (Illus.). 32p. 1993. reprint ed. pap. 8.95 (*0-685-69990-0*, 9609) Clearfield Co.

Clan of the Cave Bear. Jean M. Auel. 512p. 1984. mass mkt. 6.99 (*0-553-25042-6*) Bantam.

Clan of the Cave Bear. Jean M. Auel. 480p. 1980. 19.95 (*0-517-54202-1*, Crown) Crown Pub Group.

Clan of the Cave Bear. large type ed. Jean M. Auel. LC 83-445. 946p. 1983. reprint ed. lib. bdg. 22.95 (*0-89621-438-9*) Thorndike Pr.

Clan of the Cave Bear. large type ed. Jean M. Auel. LC 83-445. 946p. 1991. pap. 16.95 (*1-56054-983-1*) Thorndike Pr.

Clan of the Kerykeion. Clark. (J). Date not set. 15.00 (*0-06-021276-4*, HarpT); lib. bdg. 14.89 (*0-06-021277-2*, HarpT) HarpC.

Clan of the Shape-Changers. Robert Levy. LC 92-36010. (YA). 1994. 13.95 (*0-395-66602-3*) HM.

Clan of the Shape-Changers. Robert Levy. (J). (gr. 4-7). 1994. 13.95 (*0-395-66612-0*) HM.

Clan of the Warlords. 1992. mass mkt. 4.99 (*0-345-35966-6*, Del Rey) Ballantine.

***Clan Records: Five Stories of Korea.** Toshiyuki Kajiyama. Tr. by Yoshiko Dykstra. LC 94-42476. 192p. 1995. text ed. 18.00x (*0-8248-1532-7*) UH Pr.

Clan Ross. Donald Mackinnon. (Johnston & Bacon Clan Histories Ser.). (Illus.). 32p. 1993. reprint ed. pap. 8.95 (*0-685-69992-7*, 9616) Clearfield Co.

Clan Theory in African Development Studies: Reconsidering African Development Promotive Bases. E. D. Mwamula-Lubandi. 240p. (C). 1992. lib. bdg. 44.50 (*0-8191-8427-6*) U Pr of Amer.

Clan Traditions & Popular Tales of the Western Highlands & Islands. John G. Campbell. Ed. by Jessie Wallace & Duncan MacIsaac. LC 72-144458. (Waifs & Strays of Celtic Tradition: Argyllshire Ser.: No. 5). reprint ed. 29.50 (*0-404-53535-6*) AMS Pr.

***Clanbook: Assamite.** Graeme Davis. 72p. 1995. per., pap. 10.00 (*1-56504-214-X*, 04214) White Wolf.

***Clanbook: Brujah.** (Vampire Ser.). Date not set. per., pap. 10.00 (*1-56504-038-4*) White Wolf.

Clanbook: Gangrel. (Vampire). per., pap. 10.00 (*1-56504-046-5*, 2052) White Wolf.

***Clanbook: Malkavian.** White Wolf Staff. (Vampire Ser.). 1993. per., pap. 10.00 (*1-56504-052-X*, 2053) White Wolf.

Clanbook: Nosferatu. White Wolf Staff. (Vampire Ser.). 1994. per., pap. 10.00 (*1-56504-064-3*, 2054) White Wolf.

***Clanbook: Setite.** White Wolf Staff. (Vampire). 1995. per., pap. 10.00 (*1-56504-215-8*, 2060) White Wolf.

***Clanbook: Toreador.** White Wolf Staff. (Vampire). 1994. per., pap. 10.00 (*1-56504-095-3*, 20561) White Wolf.

Clanbook: Tremere. (Vampire). 1994. per., pap. 10.00 (*1-56504-115-1*, WW2057) White Wolf.

Clanbook: Ventrue. Andrew Greenberg. (Vampire). 72p. 1994. per., pap. 10.00 (*1-56504-129-1*, 2058) White Wolf.

Clancy & Tidepool Friends. Carol Batdorf. 76p. 1987. pap. 9.95 (*0-88839-336-9*) Hancock House.

Clancy Brothers & Tommy Makem Songbook. (Illus.). 64p. 1964. pap. 9.95 (*0-8256-0102-9*, OK61085, Oak) Music Sales.

***Clancy's Cabin.** Margaret Mahy. LC 94-46278. (Illus.). (J). 1995. 13.95 (*0-87951-592-9*) Overlook Pr.

Clancy's Treasure Book for Children. L. M. Boyd. (Illus.). 166p. (Orig.). (J). (gr. k-5). 1981. pap. 7.95 (*0-941620-34-4*) Carson Ent.

Clandestine. James Ellroy. 352p. 1982. mass mkt. 4.99 (*0-380-81141-3*) Avon.

Clandestine Affair. Sally James. (Coventry Romance Ser.: No. 64). 224p. 1980. pap. 1.75 (*0-449-50095-0*, Coventry) Fawcett.

Clandestine Affair. large type ed. Sally James. 1990. 21.95 (*0-7089-2235-X*) Ulverscroft.

Clandestine Broadcasting Directory. Mathias Kropf. 1994. pap. 12.95 (*0-936653-56-6*) Tiare Pubns.

Clandestine Building of Libya's Chemical Weapons Factory: A Study in International Collusion. Thomas C. Wiegele. LC 91-32975. 256p. (C). 1992. 29.95 (*0-8093-1775-3*) S Ill U Pr.

Clandestine Drug Laboratories: Their Construction & Operation. 1991. lib. bdg. 79.75 (*0-8490-4600-9*) Gordon Pr.

Clandestine Employment: The Situation in the Industrialised Market Economy Countries. Raffaele De Grazia. vii, 118p. 1984. pap. 14.00 (*92-2-103355-4*) Intl Labour Office.

Clandestine Erotic Fiction in English 1800-1930: A Bibliographic Study. Peter Mendes. 497p. 1993. 124.95 (*0-85967-919-5*, Pub. by Scolar Pr UK) Ashgate Pub Co.

Clandestine Essays. Ievhen Sverstiuk. Tr. by George S. Luckyj. Orig. Title: Ivan Kotliarevsky Smietsia. 100p. 1976. lib. bdg. 11.50 (*0-87287-151-7*); pap. 7.50 (*0-87287-158-4*) Ukrainian Acad.

Clandestine in Chile: The Adventures of Miguel Littin. Gabriel Garcia Marquez. Tr. by Asa Zatz. LC 87-39. (Owl Bks.). 128p. 1988. pap. 7.95 (*0-8050-0945-0*) H Holt & Co.

***Clandestine Marriage.** David Garrick & George Colman. Ed. by Noel Chevalier. 250p. 1995. pap. 12.95 (*1-55111-027-X*) Broadview Pr.

***Clandestine Marriage in England, 1500-1850.** R. B. Outhwaite. LC 95-13102. 1995. write for info. (*1-85285-130-9*) Hambledon Press.

Clandestine on the Morning Line. Josh Greenfield. 1961. pap. 4.75 (*0-8222-0214-X*) Dramatists Play.

Clandestine Poems. Roque Dalton. Ed. by Barbara Paschke & Jack Weaver. Tr. by Jack Hirschman. LC 83-51488. 208p. 1990. reprint ed. pap. 7.95 (*0-915306-91-3*) Curbstone.

Clandestine Poems--Poemas Clandestinos: Bilingual Edition. Roque Dalton. Ed. by Barbara Paschke & Eric Weaver. Tr. by Jack Hirschman. LC 83-51488. 224p. (Orig.). (ENG & SPA.). 1984. pap. 7.00 (*0-942638-07-7*, 26L) New Amer Pr.

Clandestine Radio Broadcasting. Lawrence C. Soley & John S. Nichols. LC 86-21169. 400p. 1986. text ed. 65.00 (*0-275-92259-6*, C2259, Praeger Pubs) Greenwood.

Clann Ag Urnaigh. Church of Scotland, Panel on Worship Staff. (C). 1992. pap. 39.00x (*0-86153-135-3*, Pub. by St Andrew UK) St Mut.

Clans & Families of Ireland. John Grenham. 1993. 19.98 (*1-55521-887-3*) Bk Sales Inc.

Clans & Families of Ireland & Scotland: An Ethnography of the Gael A.D. 500-1750. C. Thomas Cairney. LC 88-42644. 222p. 1989. lib. bdg. 28.50x (*0-89950-362-4*) McFarland & Co.

Clans & Tartans Library Style. R. R. Mcian. 1989. pap. 0.99 (*0-517-67590-0*) Random Hse Value.

Clans, Highland Games & Sporting Landlords. Grant Jarvie. 1991. text ed. 35.00 (*0-7486-0244-5*, Pub. by Edinburgh U Pr UK) Col U Pr.

***Clans of Many Nations: Selected Poems 1969-1994.** Peter B. Cloud. 128p. (Orig.). 1995. pap. 14.00 (*1-877727-47-4*) White Pine.

***Clans of Scotland.** Micheil MacDonald. 1994. 19.98 (*0-7858-0108-1*) Bk Sales Inc.

Clans of the Alphane Moon. Philip K. Dick. 269p. 1988. pap. 3.95 (*0-88184-436-5*) Carroll & Graf.

Clanship to Crofter's War: The Social Transformation of the Scottish Highlands. T. M. Devine. LC 93-30886. 1994. text ed. 69.95 (*0-7190-3481-7*, Pub. by Manchester Univ Pr UK); text ed. 29.95 (*0-7190-3482-5*, Pub. by Manchester Univ Pr UK) St Martin.

Clansman. Thomas Dixon, Jr. 1976. 25.95 (*0-8488-0263-2*) Amereon Ltd.

Clansman. Thomas Dixon, Jr. 400p. 1990. reprint ed. lib. bdg. 27.95 (*0-89966-677-9*) Buccaneer Bks.

Clansman. Thomas Dixon. 1973. reprint ed. lib. bdg. 250.00 (*0-87968-194-2*) Gordon Pr.

Clansman: An Historical Romance of the Ku Klux Klan. Thomas Dixon, Jr. LC 71-104761. 392p. 1980. reprint ed. pap. 12.00 (*0-8131-0126-3*) U Pr of Ky.

CLAO-Allergan. Dabezies. 1989. 130.00 (*0-316-17061-5*) Little.

C

An Asterisk (*) at the beginning of an entry indicates that the title is appearing in BIP for the first time. 1291

CLAO LL Set. 2nd ed. Dabezies. 1989. 85.00 (*0-316-17060-7*) Little.

CLAO Set. 2nd ed. Dabezies. 1989. 295.00 (*0-316-17055-0*) Little.

CLAO Update LL, No. 4. Dabezies. 1989. 45.00 (*0-316-17054-2*) Little.

CLAO Update LL, No. 5. Dabezies. 1989. 45.00 (*0-316-17062-3*) Little.

CLAO Update LL, No. 6. Dabezies. 1990. 45.00 (*0-316-17063-1*) Little.

CLAO Update LL, No. 7. Dabezies. 1990. 45.00 (*0-316-17065-8*) Little.

CLAO Update LL, No. 8. Dabezies. 1991. 45.00 (*0-316-17066-6*) Little.

Clap Clap! Mary C. Helldorfer. (Illus.). 32p. (J). (ps-2). 1993. 13.99 (*0-670-85155-8*) Viking Child Bks.

Clap Hands. Helen Oxenbury. (Macmillan Big Board Bks.). (Illus.). 10p. (J). (ps). 1987. pap. 6.95 (*0-02-769030-X*, Aladdin Paperbacks) S&S Childrens.

Clap Your Hands. Lorinda B. Cauley. (Illus.). 32p. (J). (ps-1). 1992. lib. bdg. 14.95 (*0-399-22118-2*, Putnam) Putnam Pub Group.

Clap Your Hands: Finger Rhymes. Sarah Hayes. LC 87-16958. (Illus.). (J). (ps-1). 1988. 13.00 (*0-688-07692-0*); lib. bdg. 12.88 (*0-688-07693-9*) Lothrop.

Clapp Memorial Record of the Clapp Family Containing Sketches of the Original Six Emigrants & a Genealogy of Their Descendants Bearing That Name; with Supplement & Proceedings at Two Family Meetings. Ed. by E. Clapp. (Illus.). 536p. 1989. reprint ed. lib. bdg. 87.00 (*0-8328-0402-9*); reprint ed. pap. 77.00 (*0-8328-0403-7*) Higginson Bk Co.

Clapper Rail. Mary Ketchum. (J). 1995. write for info. (*0-8050-2359-3*) H Holt & Co.

Clapton! Ray Coleman. 368p. (Orig.). 1988. pap. 13.99 (*0-446-38630-8*) Warner Bks.

***Clapton: The Authorized Biography.** Ray Coleman. (Illus.). 332p. 1994. 39.50 (*0-283-06211-8*, Pub. by Sidgwick & Jackson UK) Trans-Atl Phila.

Clara. (Orig.). 1991. pap. 4.95 (*1-878320-80-7*) Masquerade.

Clara & the Bookwagon. Nancy S. Levinson. LC 86-45773. (Harper I Can Read Bk.). (Illus.). 64p. (J). (gr. k-3). 1988. lib. bdg. 14.89 (*0-06-023838-0*) HarpC Child Bks.

Clara & the Bookwagon. Nancy S. Levinson. LC 86-45773. (Trophy I Can Read Bk.). (Illus.). 64p. (J). (gr. k-3). 1991. pap. 3.50 (*0-06-444134-2*, Trophy) HarpC Child Bks.

C

Clara Barton. Leni Hamilton. (American Women of Achievement Ser.). (Illus.). 112p. (J). (gr. 5 up). 1988. lib. bdg. 17.95 (*1-55546-641-9*) Chelsea Hse.

Clara Barton. Cynthia Klingel & Dan Zadra. (We the People Ser.). (Illus.). 32p. (J). 1987. lib. bdg. 14.95 (*0-88682-168-1*) Creative Ed.

Clara Barton: Angel of the Battlefield. Rae Bains. LC 81-23123. (Illus.). 48p. (J). (gr. 4-6). 1982. lib. bdg. 10.79 (*0-89375-752-7*); pap. text ed. 3.50 (*0-89375-753-5*) Troll Assocs.

Clara Barton: Founder, American Red Cross. Liz Sonneborn. (Junior World Biographies Ser.). (Illus.). 80p. (J). (gr. 3-6). 1991. lib. bdg. 14.95 (*0-7910-1565-3*) Chelsea Hse.

Clara Barton: Founder of the American Red Cross. Augusta Stevenson. LC 86-10750. (Childhood of Famous Americans Ser.). (Illus.). 192p. (J). (gr. 2-6). 1986. reprint ed. pap. 3.95 (*0-02-041820-5*, Aladdin Paperbacks) S&S Childrens.

Clara Barton: Healing the Wounds. Cathy E. Dubowski. (History of the Civil War Ser.). (Illus.). 160p. (J). (gr. 5 up). 1990. lib. bdg. 12.95 (*0-382-09940-0*); pap. 7.95 (*0-382-24049-9*) Silver Burdett Pr.

***Clara Barton: In the Service of Humanity.** David H. Burton. LC 94-37878. (Contributions in Women's Studies: Vol. 148). 192p. 1995. text ed. 49.95 (*0-313-28945-X*, Greenwood Pr) Greenwood.

Clara Barton: Soldier of Mercy. Mary C. Rose. (Discovery Biographies Ser.). (Illus.). 80p. (J). (gr. 2-6). 1991. reprint ed. lib. bdg. 12.95 (*0-7910-1403-7*) Chelsea Hse.

Clara Barton & Her Victory over Fear. Robert Quackenbush. LC 94-18168. (J). 1995. 14.00 (*0-671-86598-6*, S&S Bks Young Read) S&S Childrens.

***Clara Barton & Her Victory over Fear.** Robert Quackenbush. (Illus.). (J). (gr. 2-6). 1995. pap. 4.95 (*0-689-80124-6*, Aladdin Paperbacks) S&S Childrens.

***Clara Barton & Hightstown.** Ed. by David Martin. (Illus.). 32p. 1994. 6.00 (*0-944413-30-7*) Longstreet Hse.

Clara Barton, Founder of American Red Cross. Helen D. Boylston. (Landmark Ser.: No. 58). (Illus.). (J). (gr. 4-6). 1963. lib. bdg. 11.99 (*0-394-90358-7*) Random Bks Yng Read.

Clara Barton, Professional Angel. Elizabeth B. Pryor. LC 87-13868. (Studies in Health, Illness, & Caregiving). (Illus.). 450p. 1987. pap. text ed. 25.95 (*0-8122-1273-8*) U of Pa Pr.

Clara Butt: Her Life Story. Winifred Ponder. LC 77-16530. (Music Reprint Ser.: 1978). (Illus.). 1978. reprint ed. lib. bdg. 35.00 (*0-306-77529-8*) Da Capo.

***Clara Chicken.** Wendy Kanno. (Funny Farm Ser.). (Illus.). (J). (gr. k-3). 1994. lib. bdg. 9.25 (*0-89868-212-6*, Read Res); pap. 3.50 (*0-89868-213-4*, Read Res) ARO Pub.

***Clara d'Ellebeuse: Or the History of a Young Girl in the Past.** Francis Jammes. Tr. by Antony Oldknow. (Illus.). 68p. (Orig.). (C). 1992. pap. text ed. 7.50 (*1-881604-03-9*) Scopcraeft.

***Clara d'Ellebeuse 2.** Francis Jammes. Tr. by Antony Oldknow. 99p. (FRE.). 1993. pap. text ed. 7.50 (*1-881604-10-1*) Scopcraeft.

Clara Driscoll: An American Tradition. Martha A. Turner. LC 79-89214. (Illus.). 1980. 21.95 (*0-89052-025-9*) Madrona Pr.

Clara Driscoll: Savior of the Alamo: Her Life Story Presented Through the Clothes She Wore. Nelda Patteson. (Women of Texas Ser.: Bk. 1). (Illus.). 32p. (J). (gr. 4-7). 1991. pap. 14.95 (*0-9629001-0-9*) Smiley Originals.

Clara Hale: Mother to Those Who Needed One. Bob Italia. Ed. by Rosie Wallner. LC 93-15261. (Everyone Contributes Ser.). (J). 1993. lib. bdg. 12.94 (*1-56239-235-2*) Abdo & Dghtrs.

Clara Hopgood, 1896 see Catherine Furze, 1893

Clara Howard. Charles B. Brown. (Works of Charles Brockden Brown). 1989. reprint ed. lib. bdg. 79.00 (*0-7812-2070-X*) Rprt Serv.

Clara Joins the Circus. Michael Pellowski. LC 80-25602. (Illus.). 48p. (J). (ps-3). 1981. 5.95 (*0-8193-1057-3*); lib. bdg. 5.95 (*0-8193-1058-1*) Parents.

***Clara Joins the Circus.** Michael Pellowski. LC 94-34653. (Parents Magazine Read Aloud Original). (J). 1995. write for info. (*0-8368-0998-X*) Gareth Stevens Inc.

***Clara la Gallina: Libros de la Granja Loca.** Wendy Kanno. Tr. by Gloria Schaffer-Melendez. (Libro de Viente Palabras Ser.). (Illus.). (SPA.). (J). (gr. k-3). 1994. lib. bdg. 9.25 (*0-89868-263-0*, Read Res); pap. 3.50 (*0-89868-264-9*, Read Res) ARO Pub.

Clara Novello, Eighteen Eighteen to Nineteen Eight. Averil Mackenzie-Grieve. LC 79-24421. (Music Reprint Ser.). 1980. reprint ed. lib. bdg. 39.50 (*0-306-76009-6*) Da Capo.

Clara Schumann, 3 vols., Set. Berthold Litzmann. 1971. reprint ed. write for info. (*0-318-71925-8*, Pub. by Georg Olms GW) Lubrecht & Cramer.

Clara Schumann: An Artist's Life, 2 vols., Set. Berthold Litzmann. LC 79-20823. (Music Reprint Ser.). 1979. reprint ed. lib. bdg. 95.00 (*0-306-79582-5*) Da Capo.

Clara Schumann: The Artist & the Woman. Nancy B. Reich. LC 84-45798. (Illus.). 352p. 1987. pap. 15.95 (*0-8014-9388-9*) Cornell U Pr.

Clara Shumann, Dialectic of Education. Georges Ohsawa. 1992. pap. 9.50 (*0-685-57010-X*) Happiness Pr.

Clara Sipprell. Mary McCabe. LC 90-80190. (Illus.). 150p. 1990. 39.95 (*0-88360-064-1*) Amon Carter.

Clara the Juggling Cow. 1991. pap. 3.95 (*0-8167-2429-6*) Troll Assocs.

Clara Zetkin: Selected Writings. Clara Zetkin. Ed. by Philip S. Foner. Tr. by Kai Schoenhals. LC 84-4564. (Illus.). 208p. 1984. 14.00 (*0-7178-0620-0*); pap. 5.50 (*0-7178-0611-1*) Intl Pubs Co.

Clara Zetkin As a Socialist Speaker. Dorothea Reetz. LC 86-27178. 76p. 1987. pap. 3.95 (*0-7178-0649-9*) Intl Pubs Co.

Clara Zetkin und Brot und Rosen: Literaturpolitische Konflikte zwischen Partei und Frauenbewegung in der deutschen Vorkriegssozialdemokratie. Joan Reutershan. (New York University Ottendorfer Ser.: Vol. 20). 246p. (GER.). (C). 1985. text ed. 28.50 (*0-8204-0203-6*) P Lang Pubs.

Clara's Delicious Italian Recipes with a Regional Taste. Clara Facciani. LC 87-400820. (Illus.). 206p. 1986. 29.50 (*0-9617641-0-4*) Graph Arts Jrnl.

Clara's Delicious Italian Recipes with a Regional Taste. 2nd ed. Clara Facciani. LC 89-85788. (Illus.). 268p. 1990. 29.50 (*0-9617641-1-2*) Graph Arts Jrnl.

***Clara's Promise.** Hailstock. 1995. mass mkt. (*0-7860-0147-X*, Pinnacle NY) Windsor NY.

***Clara's Promise.** Shirley Hailstock. 416p. 1995. pap. 4.99 (*0-8217-0147-9*) Zebra.

Clara's Story. Clara Isaacman. LC 84-14339. 180p. (J). (gr. 3-7). 1984. 11.95 (*0-8276-0243-X*); pap. 9.95 (*0-8276-0506-4*) JPS Phila.

Clarastella Together with Poems Occasional, Elegies, Epigrams, Satyrs, 1650. Robert Heath. LC 74-119866. 1970. reprint ed. 50.00 (*0-8201-1073-6*) Schol Facsimiles.

Clare. Kent Gramm. (Northcote Bks.). 432p. (Orig.). 1991. pap. 11.99 (*0-87788-124-3*) Shaw Pubs.

Clare: A Light in the Garden. enl. rev. ed. Murray Bodo. 126p. 1992. 6.95 (*0-86716-122-1*) St Anthony Mess Pr.

Clare: A Novel. John MacKenna. 181p. 1994. pap. 13.95 (*0-85640-467-5*, Pub. by Blackstaff Pr IE) Dufour.

Clare: Her Light & Her Song. Mary Seraphim. 44p. 1983. 18.00 (*0-8199-0870-3*, Frncscn Herld) Franciscan Pr.

Clare among Her Sisters. Rene-Charles Dhont. LC 86-81344. (Franciscan Pathways Ser.). 1987. 9.00 (*0-318-35491-8*) Franciscan Inst.

Clare Booth Luce. Joseph Lyons. (American Women of Achievement Ser.). (Illus.). 112p. (YA). (gr. 5 up). 1989. lib. bdg. 17.95 (*1-55546-665-6*) Chelsea Hse.

***Clare Booth Luce: A Research & Production Sourcebook.** Mark Fearnow. LC 94-37080. (Modern Dramatists Research & Production Sourcebooks Ser.: Vol. 7). 208p. 1995. text ed. 65.00 (*0-313-29178-0*, Greenwood Pr) Greenwood.

Clare Leighton: Exhibition Catalogue. Anne Stevens. 1993. pap. 21.00 (*1-85183-038-3*) St Mut.

Clare Leighton an Exhibition: American Sheaves English Seed Corn. Frwd. by William D. Fletcher. (Illus.). pap. 3.00 (*0-685-85775-1*) Boston Public Lib.

Clare of Assisi. Marco Bartoli. Tr. by Frances Teresa. LC 93-10669. 1993. 21.95 (*0-8199-0963-7*) Franciscan Pr.

Clare of Assisi: A Biographical Study. Ingrid Peterson. LC 93-24140. 1993. 27.95 (*0-685-70885-3*); pap. 20.95 (*0-8199-0964-5*) Franciscan Pr.

***Clare Scares a Ghost.** Vicki Valentine. 32p. (J). (gr. 2-7). 1996. 17.95 (*1-886593-00-0*) Immac Heart Pr.

Clarel, 2 vols. Herman Melville. 1972. 400.00 (*0-87968-875-0*) Gordon Pr.

Clarel. Herman Melville. Ed. by Harrison Hayford et al. (Northwestern-Newberry Edition of the Writings of Herman Melville: Vol. 12). 893p. 1991. 82.95 (*0-8101-0906-9*); pap. 24.95 (*0-8101-0907-7*) Northwestern U Pr.

Clarel. annot. ed. Ed. by Walter E. Bezanson. (Complete Works of Herman Melville Ser.). 772p. 1959. 29.95 (*0-685-02254-4*) Hendricks House.

***Clarembald of Arras as a Boethian Commentator.** John R. Fortin. LC 95-5854. 1995. write for info. (*0-943549-27-2*) TJU Pr.

Claremont Colleges Faculty Exhibition. Marjorie H. Beebe. (Illus.). 1982. 4.00 (*0-915478-42-0*) Galleries Coll.

Claremont Colleges Faculty Exhibition. Intro. by David W. Steadman. (Illus.). 28p. 1977. 2.00 (*0-915478-36-6*) Galleries Coll.

Claremont Reading Conference Yearbook: Reading: A Literary Feast. Ed. by Malcolm P. Douglass. 260p. (Orig.). 1989. pap. 20.00 (*0-941742-07-5*) Claremont Grad.

Clarence A. Andrews "Christmas in the Midwest" rev. ed. Hamlin Garland et al. (Illus.). 144p. 1984. 8.95 (*0-934582-06-8*) Midwest Heritage.

Clarence & Corinne; Or God's Way. A. E. Johnson. (Schomburg Library of Nineteenth-Century Black Women Writers). 240p. 1992. pap. 10.95 (*0-19-507574-9*) OUP.

Clarence & Corrine: Or God's Way. Amelia A. Johnson. (Schomburg Library of Nineteenth-Century Black Women Writers). (Illus.). 240p. 1988. 27.00 (*0-19-505264-1*) OUP.

Clarence Darrow. John E. Driemen. (Library of Biography). (Illus.). 112p. (YA). (gr. 5 up). 1992. lib. bdg. 17.95 (*0-7910-1624-2*) Chelsea Hse.

Clarence Darrow: A Bibliography. Willard D. Hunsberger. LC 80-26317. viii, 215p. 1981. 20.00 (*0-8108-1384-X*) Scarecrow.

Clarence Darrow: Attorney for the Damned. Gerald Kurland. Ed. by D. Steve Rahmas. LC 75-190240. (Outstanding Personalities Ser.: No. 22). 32p. (Orig.). (J). (gr. 7-12). 1972. lib. bdg. 4.95 (*0-87157-522-1*) SamHar Pr.

Clarence Darrow: Mini-Play. (People of Conscience Ser.). (J). (gr. 5 up). 1978. 6.50 (*0-89550-312-3*) Stevens & Shea.

Clarence Darrow: The Creation of an American Myth. Richard J. Jensen. LC 90-20675. (Great American Orators: Critical Studies, Speeches & Sources: No. 12). 352p. 1992. text ed. 45.00 (*0-313-25990-9*, JCD/, Greenwood Pr) Greenwood.

Clarence Darrow in Hell: A Play. Kenan Heise & Dan Heise. 80p. (Orig.). 1992. pap. 7.95 (*0-924772-20-4*) CH Bookworks.

Clarence Darrow on Capital Punishment. Clarence Darrow. 192p. 1991. pap. 11.95 (*0-685-53600-9*) CH Bookworks.

***Clarence Dillon: A Wall Street Enigma.** Robert C. Perez & Edward F. Willett. LC 94-48138. 1995. write for info. (*1-56833-050-2*) Madison Bks UPA.

Clarence H. White: The Reverence for Beauty. Peter C. Bunnell. Ed. by Paul W. Richelson. LC 86-81613. (Illus.). 80p. (Orig.). 1986. pap. text ed. 19.95 (*0-933041-01-2*) Gallery Fine Art Ohio U.

***Clarence Honeybear Shines His Inner Light.** Jaclyn Catalfo. (Illus.). 1995. pap. 7.95 (*0-918915-00-7*) Inner Light Found.

Clarence John Laughlin: Visionary Photographer. Keith F. Davis et al. 1990. 40.00 (*0-87529-629-7*); pap. 25.00 (*0-87529-630-0*) Hallmark.

Clarence Jordan: Turning Dreams into Deeds. Henlee H. Barnette. 118p. (Orig.). 1992. pap. 8.95 (*1-880837-00-5*) Smyth & Helwys.

Clarence K. Jones: From Paperboy to Philanthropist. Ed. by Helen M. Blue & R. T. King. (Illus.). 210p. 1988. write for info. (*1-56475-337-9*); lib. bdg. 41.00 (*1-56475-336-0*); fiche write for info. (*1-56475-338-7*) U NV Oral Hist.

Clarence King. Peter Wild. LC 81-67302. (Western Writers Ser.: No. 48). (Illus.). 46p. (Orig.). 1981. pap. 3.95 (*0-88430-072-2*) Boise St U W Writ Ser.

Clarence N. Hickman: The Father of Scientific Archery. Maryanne M. Schumm. (Illus.). 173p. (Orig.). 1983. pap. 12.95 (*0-9613582-0-3*) M Schumm.

Clarence Ray: Black Politics & Gaming in Las Vegas, 1920s-1980s. Ed. by Helen M. Blue & Jamie Coughtry. (History of Las Vegas Black Community Ser.). (Illus.). 122p. 1991. lib. bdg. 30.00 (*1-56475-002-7*) U NV Oral Hist.

Clarence the Friendly Lion. D. Douglas Schneider. (Illus.). 24p. 1987. reprint ed. pap. 2.00 (*0-939169-02-9*) World Peace Univ.

Clarence Thomas. Paul Deegan. Ed. by Bob Italia. LC 92-13717. (Supreme Court Justices Ser.). (J). 1992. lib. bdg. 13.99 (*1-56239-088-0*) Abdo & Dghtrs.

***Clarence Thomas.** Norman L. Macht. Ed. by Nathan I. Huggins. LC 94-44353. (Black Americans of Achievement Ser.). (Illus.). 144p. (YA). (gr. 5 up). 1995. 18.95 (*0-7910-1883-0*) Chelsea Hse.

***Clarence Thomas.** Norman L. Macht. Ed. by Nathan I. Huggins. LC 94-44353. (Black Americans of Achievement Ser.). (YA). (gr. 5 up). 1995. pap. write for info. (*0-7910-1912-8*) Chelsea Hse.

Clarence Thomas: Confronting the Future. Intro. by L. Gordon Crovitz. LC 91-46764. 224p. 1992. pap. 7.95 (*0-89526-734-9*) Regnery Pub.

Clarence Thomas: Supreme Court Justice. Warren J. Halliburton. LC 92-30951. (People to Know Ser.). (Illus.). 104p. (J). (gr. 6 up). 1993. lib. bdg. 17.95 (*0-89490-414-0*) Enslow Pubs.

Clarence Thomas & the Tough Love Crowd: Counterfeit Heroes & Unhappy Truths. Ronald S. Roberts. 304p. 1994. 24.95 (*0-8147-7454-7*) NYU Pr.

Clarendon: Politics, History & Religion, 1640-1660. B. H. Wormald. 360p. (C). 1989. 64.95 (*0-521-37084-1*); pap. 24.95 (*0-521-37953-9*) Cambridge U Pr.

Clarendon & the English Revolution. R. W. Harris. LC 83-40092. 464p. 1983. 52.50 (*0-8047-1216-6*) Stanford U Pr.

Clarendon & the Rhetoric of Historical Form. Martine W. Brownley. LC 85-1197. (Illus.). 254p. 1985. text ed. 39.95 (*0-8122-7988-3*) U of Pa Pr.

Clarendon Guide to Kansas City Restaurants. Colin Clarendon & Sylvia Strock. (Illus.). 195p. (Orig.). pap. 7.50 (*0-9609028-0-5*) C & S Ent.

***Clare's Kitchen: The In Way to Eat.** Clare Latimer. (Illus.). 1995. 29.95 (*0-7475-1704-5*, Pub. by Bloomsbury Pub Ltd UK) Trafalgar.

***Clarice Cliff: The Bizarre Affair.** Leonard Griffin. 1994. 19.95 (*0-8109-2584-2*) Abrams.

Clarice Lispector: A Bio-Bibliography. Diane E. Marting. LC 93-28537. (Bio-Bibliographies in World Literature Ser.: Vol. 2). 368p. 1993. text ed. 85.00 (*0-313-27803-2*, Greenwood Pr) Greenwood.

Clariere. Therese De Saint Phalle. (FRE.). 1981. pap. 10.95 (*0-7859-4143-6*) Fr & Eur.

Clarification of Economic Questions: In Islamic Jurisprudence. Ayatullah Ruhullah Khomeini. Tr. by Laleh Bakhtiar. 160p. (Orig.). (C). 1989. pap. 10.00 (*1-871031-01-X*) Abjad Bk.

Clarification of Questions on Worship & Self-Development: In Islamic Jurisprudence. Ayatullah Ruhullah Khomeini. Tr. by Laleh Bakhtiar. 192p. (Orig.). (C). 1989. pap. 10.00 (*1-871031-02-8*) Abjad Bk.

Clarifier Design. Water Pollution Control Federation Staff. LC 85-51398. (Manual of Practice, Facilities Development Ser.: No. 8). 103p. 1985. pap. 21.50 (*0-943244-61-7*, MOPFD8) Water Environ.

Clarifier of the Sweet Meaning. Tr. by I. B. Horner. (C). 1978. 46.00 (*0-86013-069-X*, Pub. by Pali Text) Wisdom MA.

Clarifying & Summarizing the Fundamentals of Counseling: Hebrew Translation. Harvey Jackins. 1987. pap. 1.00 (*0-913937-22-3*) Rational Isl.

Clarifying Disability Insurance. William Houghton. 1992. 29.50 (*1-56461-107-8*, 46150) Rough Notes.

Clarifying Jewish Values: Clarification Strategies for Jewish Groups. Dov P. Elkins. LC 77-83774. 1977. pap. 10.00 (*0-918834-02-3*) Growth Assoc.

Clarifying McLuhan: An Assessment of Process & Product. S. D. Neill. LC 92-36609. (Contributions to the Study of Mass Media & Communications Ser.: No. 37). 168p. 1993. text ed. 47.95 (*0-313-28444-X*, NCM, Greenwood Pr) Greenwood.

Clarifying the Economics of Peace. Mildred Loomis. 1971. 250.00 (*0-87700-142-1*) Revisionist Pr.

Clarifying the Economics of War & Peace: Why the United States Must Fight in Iraq & the Middle East. M. Loomis. 1991. lib. bdg. 75.00 (*0-8490-4060-4*) Gordon Pr.

Clarinet. Date not set. pap. 0.95 (*0-87166-539-5*, 93744) Mel Bay.

***Clarinet Bk. 1.** (Breeze Easy Method Ser.). 32p. (Orig.). 1994. pap. 6.50 (*0-89724-365-X*) Warner Brothers.

***Clarinet Bk. 2.** (Breeze Easy Method Ser.). 32p. (Orig.). 1994. pap. 6.50 (*0-89724-366-8*) Warner Brothers.

Clarinet Acoustics. O. Lee Gibson. LC 94-75. (Illus.). 1994. 18.95 (*0-253-32576-5*) Ind U Pr.

Clarinet Articulation. Allen Sigel. 80p. (C). 1987. pap. text ed. 15.00 (*0-939103-02-8*) Roncorp.

Clarinet Duets, Vol. 1. Georgina Dobree. Date not set. pap. 7.95 (*0-685-69010-5*, Chester Music) Music Sales.

Clarinet Duets, Vol. 2. Georgina Dobree. Date not set. pap. 7.95 (*0-685-69009-1*, Chester Music) Music Sales.

Clarinet Duets, Vol. 3. Leon Lester. Date not set. pap. 7.95 (*0-685-69011-3*, Chester Music) Music Sales.

Clarinet Fingering Chart. Brenda Murphy. (Illus.). 1984. pap. 3.95 (*0-8256-2383-9*, AM35700) Music Sales.

Clarinet Handbook. Norman Heim. (Building Excellence Ser.). 1993. 5.95 (*0-87166-623-5*, 94133); audio 14.95 (*0-87166-640-5*, 94133); audio 9.98 (*0-87166-639-1*, 94133) Mel Bay.

Clarinet Method. Louis Hittler. 1993. 7.95 (*1-56222-006-3*, 93468) Mel Bay.

Clarinet Method, Bk. I. Leon Russianoff. (Illus.). Book I. write for info. (*0-318-56700-8*) Macmillan.

Clarinet Method, Bk. II. Leon Russianoff. (Schirmer Book Ser.). (Illus.). Book II. 14.95 (*0-685-05965-0*) Macmillan.

Clarinet One. Bram Wiggins. (Bandstand Junior Album Ser.). Date not set. pap. 5.95 (*0-685-69012-1*, Chester Music) Music Sales.

Clarinet Primer. Louis Hittler. (J). 1993. 3.50 (*0-87166-371-6*, 93406) Mel Bay.

***Clarinet Showstoppers.** rev. ed. Ed. by Carol Cuellar. (Showstoppers Ser.). 112p. (Orig.). (YA). 1995. pap. text ed. 12.95 (*0-89724-550-4*) Warner Brothers.

Clarinet Solos, EFS28. Sel. by Jay Arnold. (Illus.). 192p. 1987. pap. 9.95 (*0-8256-2028-7*, AM40155) Music Sales.

Clarinet Solos, Vol. 1. Thea King. Date not set. pap. 7.95 (*0-7119-2001-X*, Chester Music) Music Sales.

Clarinet Solos, Vol. 2. Thea King. Date not set. pap. 9.95 (*0-7119-2154-7*, Chester Music) Music Sales.

Clarinet Solos de Concours, 1897-1980: An Annotated Bibliography. Harry R. Gee. LC 80-8360. 128p. (C). 1981. 17.95 (*0-253-13577-X*) Ind U Pr.

Clarinet Three. Ed. by Bram Wiggins. (Bandstand Junior Album Ser.). Date not set. pap. 5.95 (*0-685-69013-X*, Chester Music) Music Sales.

Clarinet Two. Bram Wiggins. (Bandstand Junior Album Ser.). Date not set. pap. 5.95 (*0-685-69014-8*, Chester Music) Music Sales.

Clariodus: A Metrical Romance. Clariodus. Ed. by David Irving. LC 72-1035. (Maitland Club, Glasgow. Publications: No. 9). reprint ed. 49.50 (*0-404-52937-2*) AMS Pr.

An Asterisk (*) at the beginning of an entry indicates that the title is appearing in BIP for the first time.

An Asterisk (*) at the beginning of an entry indicates that the title is appearing in BIP for the first time.

1293

C

Class Act. Kathleen Eagle. 1995. mass mkt. 3.99 (0-373-45184-9, 1-45184-8) Harlequin Bks.

Class Act. Christie Wells. LC 88-16940. (Cranberry Cousins Ser.). 128p. (J). (gr. 5-8). 1989. lib. bdg. 9.89 (0-8167-1500-9); pap. text ed. 2.95 (0-8167-1501-7) Troll Assocs.

Class Act: A Creative Drama Guide for Teachers. Norman Delue. (Illus.). 80p. (J). (gr. 2-8). 1994. 8.95 (0-86653-783-X, GA1477) Good Apple.

***Class Act: Riddles for School.** John Jansen. LC 94-19554. (You Must Be Joking! Ser.). (Illus.). 32p. (J). (gr. 1-4). 1995. lib. bdg. 13.50 (0-8225-2345-0, Lerner Publctns); pap. 3.95 (0-8225-9673-3) Lerner Group.

Class Act Awards & Motivators: To Encourage School Spirit, Self-Esteem, & Attendance. Jan G. Philpot. Ed. by Jan Keeling. (Illus.). 80p. (Orig.). 1993. teacher ed 8.95 (0-86530-214-6) Incentive Pubns.

Class Act Reading Game. 2nd rev. ed. James Muckle. 16p. 1992. pap. 3.00 (0-9620445-3-9) KSJ Publishing.

Class Action: How to Create Accountability, Innovation, and Excellence in American Schools. John Katzman. 1995. 22.50 (0-679-43430-5, Villard Bks) Random.

Class Actions: Law & Practice with Forms, 1987-1988. Carl Aron et al. Treatise, 2 vols. 190.00 (0-685-24488-1); Forms, 2 vols. 190.00 (0-685-24489-X) Clark Boardman Callaghan.

Class Actions: Law & Practice with Forms, 1987-1988, Set. Carl Aron et al. 200.00 (0-685-24487-3) Clark Boardman Callaghan.

Class Actions: The Law of 50 States. Thomas A. Dickerson. 400p. 1988. ring bd. 85.00 (0-318-37786-1) NY Law Pub.

Class Activities Questionnaire. Joe Steele. 1982. pap. 8.95 (0-936386-20-7) Creative Learning.

Class Acts: Plays & Skits for Jewish Settings. Stan Beiner. LC 92-71967. 300p. (Orig.). 1992. pap. text ed. 9.75 (0-86705-028-4) A R E Pub.

Class Against Itself: Power & the Nationalisation of the British Steel Industry. Doug McEachern. LC 79-41766. 239p. reprint ed. pap. 68.20 (0-318-34822-5, 2031689) Bks Demand.

Class & Character in Faulkner's South. Myra Jehlen. 1978. pap. 3.95 (0-8065-0651-2, Citadel Pr) Carol Pub Group.

Class & Civil Society: The Limits of Marxian Critical Theory. Jean L. Cohen. LC 82-11104. 276p. 1987. lib. bdg. 30.00 (0-87023-380-7); pap. text ed. 16.95 (0-87023-572-9) U of Mass Pr.

Class & Class Conflict in Industrial Society. Ralf Dahrendorf. xvi, 336p. 1959. 45.00 (0-8047-0560-7); pap. 14.95 (0-8047-0561-5) Stanford U Pr.

Class & Class Struggle in Africa. Hashim Gibrill. Ed. by Omenana Collective Staff. (Etudes et Analyses Marxistes en Afrique Ser.). 30p. (Orig.). (C). 1983. pap. text ed. 3.00 (0-943324-07-6) Omenana.

Class & Client in Beirut. Johnson. 1991. 45.00 (0-86372-062-5, Pub. by Ithaca UK) Paul & Co Pubs.

Class & Community: The Industrial Revolution in Lynn. Alan Dawley. LC 75-29049. (Studies in Urban History). (Illus.). 315p. 1976. 34.00 (0-674-13390-0) HUP.

Class & Community: The Industrial Revolution in Lynn. Alan Dawley. LC 75-29049. (Studies in Urban History). (Illus.). 315p. 1979. pap. 15.95 (0-674-13395-1) HUP.

Class & Community in Frontier Colorado. Richard Hogan. LC 89-28317. (Illus.). x, 262p. 1990. 29.95 (0-7006-0462-6) U Pr of KS.

Class & Conformity: A Study in Values. 2nd ed. Melvin L. Kohn. LC 77-85194. (Midway Reprint Ser.). ix, 316p. 1989. reprint ed. pap. text ed. 16.95 (0-226-45026-0) U Ch Pr.

Class & Consciousness: The Black Petty Bourgeoisie in South Africa, 1924 to 1950. Alan G. Cobley. LC 89-11761. (Contributions in Afro-American & African Studies: No. 127). 272p. 1990. text ed. 55.00 (0-313-26708-1, CPH/, Greenwood Pr) Greenwood.

Class & Culture in Cold War America: A Rainbow at Midnight. George Lipsitz. 264p. 1981. 29.95 (0-03-059207-0, Bergin & Garvey) Greenwood.

Class & Culture in Urban India: Fundamentalism in a Christian Community. Lionel Caplan. 312p. 1988. 69.00 (0-19-823402-3) OUP.

Class & Economic Change in Kenya: The Making of an African Petite Bourgeoisie, 1905-1970. Gavin Kitching. LC 79-21804. 448p. 1980. text ed. 60.00 (0-300-02385-5, Y-444) Yale U Pr.

Class & Economic Change in Kenya: The Making of an African Petite Bourgeoisie, 1905-1970. Gavin Kitching. LC 79-21804. 448p. 1982. pap. text ed. 24.00 (0-300-02929-2) Yale U Pr.

Class & Ethnicity: Irish Catholics in England, 1880-1939. Steve Fielding. (Themes in the Twentieth Century Ser.). 192p. 1992. 95.00 (0-335-09993-9, Open Univ Pr); pap. 36.00 (0-335-09992-0, Open Univ Pr) Taylor & Francis.

Class & Ethnicity in the Pale: The Political Economy of Jewish Workers' Nationalism in Late Imperial Russia. Yoav Peled. LC 88-36892. 224p. 1989. text ed. 49.95 (0-312-03098-3) St Martin.

Class & Gender in Early English Literature: Intersections. Ed. by Britton J. Harwood & Gillian R. Overing. LC 93-14471. 1994. 25.00 (0-253-32734-2); pap. 10.95 (0-253-20858-0) Ind U Pr.

Class & Gender in India: Women & Their Organization in a South Indian City. Patricia Caplan. 264p. 1986. text ed. 37.50 (0-422-79970-X, 9610, Pub. by Tavistock UK); pap. text ed. 16.95 (0-422-79980-7, 9611, Pub. by Tavistock UK) Routledge Chapman & Hall.

Class & Inequality: In Pre-Industrial, Capitalist & Communist Societies. M. B. Hamilton & Maria Hirszowicz. LC 87-12751. 320p. 1987. text ed. 39.95 (0-312-01222-5) St Martin.

Class & Nation: Historically & in the Current Crisis. Samir Amin. LC 79-3022. 302p. reprint ed. pap. 86.10 (0-7837-3900-1, 2043748) Bks Demand.

Class & Nationality: English & American Studies. Joel B. Montague, Jr. 1963. pap. 16.95 (0-8084-0080-0) NCUP.

Class & Politics in Milan, 1881-1901. Louise A. Tilly. (Illus.). 352p. 1992. 49.95 (0-19-506683-9) OUP.

Class & Politics in the United States. R. F. Hamilton. LC 72-1951. 615p. reprint ed. 175.30 (0-8357-9858-5, 2051296) Bks Demand.

Class & Power in a Punjabi Village. Saghir Ahmad. LC 76-1663. 1977. 8.95 (0-85345-385-3) Monthly Rev.

Class & Power in a Punjabi Village. Saghir Ahmad. LC 76-1663. 174p. reprint ed. pap. 49.60 (0-7837-6986-5, 2046798) Bks Demand.

Class & Power in Sudan: The Dynamics of Sudanese Politics, 1898-1985. Tim Niblock. LC 86-23059. 370p. 1987. 64.50 (0-88706-480-9); pap. 21.95 (0-88706-481-7) State U NY Pr.

Class & Revolution in Ethiopia. John Markakis & Nega Ayela. LC 85-62178. 160p. 1986. 19.95 (0-932415-04-0); pap. 7.95 (0-932415-05-9) Red Sea Pr.

Class & Skill: Changing Divisions of Knowledge & Labor. Pat Ainley. 160p. 1993. text ed. 60.00 (0-304-32681-X); pap. text ed. 22.50 (0-304-32679-8) Cassell.

Class & Social Organisation in Finland, Sweden & Norway. Ed. by Goran Ahrne et al. (Acta Universitatis Upsaliensis Studia Sociologica: No. 28). 154p. (Orig.). 1988. pap. 37.50x (91-554-2196-2, Pub. by Uppsala Univ Acta Univ Uppsaliensis SW) Coronet Bks.

Class & Space: The Making of Urban Society. Ed. by Nigel J. Thrift & Peter Williams. (Illus.). 256p. 1987. lib. bdg. 62.50 (0-7102-0230-X, RKP) Routledge.

Class & Stratification: An Introduction to Current Debates. Rosemary Crompton. LC 92-41451. 1993. 49.95 (0-7456-0946-5); pap. 19.95 (0-7456-0947-3) Blackwell Pubs.

Class & Tennessee's Confederate Generation. Fred A. Bailey. LC 86-1407. (Fred W. Morrison Series in Southern Studies). x, 206p. 1987. 27.50 (0-8078-1703-1) U of NC Pr.

Class Apart. Susan Lewis. 1990. mass mkt. 4.95 (0-06-100093-0, Harp PBks) HarpC.

Class Apart: The Private Pictures of Montague Glover. James Gardiner. 1993. pap. 24.99 (1-85242-250-5) Serpents Tail.

Class Awareness in the United States. Mary R. Jackman & Robert W. Jackman. LC 82-2766. 300p. 1982. pap. 14.00 (0-520-05631-0) U CA Pr.

Class, Caste & Color: A Social & Economic History of the South African Western Cape. Ed. by Wilmot G. James & Mary Simons. 258p. (C). 1992. 34.95 (1-56000-035-X) Transaction Pubs.

Class, Caste, & Entrepreneurship: A Study of Indian Industrialists. E. Wayne Nafziger. LC 78-16889. 198p. 1978. text ed. 14.00 (0-8248-0575-5, Eastwest Ctr Pr) UH Pr.

Class Choregus. Dave Morine. 244p. 1993. 20.00 (1-55643-122-8) North Atlantic.

Class, Citizenship & Social Development: A Greenwood Archival Edition. T. H. Marshall. LC 73-2879. 334p. 1973. reprint ed. text ed. 55.00 (0-8371-6778-7, MACL, Greenwood Pr) Greenwood.

Class Clown. Johanna Hurwitz. LC 86-23624. (Illus.). 112p. (J). (gr. 1-4). 1987. 15.00 (0-688-06723-9) Morrow Jr Bks.

Class Clown. Johanna Hurwitz. 112p. (J). (gr. 2-5). 1988. pap. 2.75 (0-590-41821-1, Little Apple) Scholastic Inc.

Class Clown, No. 7. Michael J. Pellowski. LC 91-74005. (Riverdale High Ser.). (Illus.). 128p. (Orig.). (YA). (gr. 4-8). 1992. pap. 2.99 (1-56282-113-X) Hyprn Child.

Class, Community, & Collective Action: Social Change in Two British Coalfields, 1850-1926. David Gilbert. (Illus.). 304p. 1992. 72.00 (0-19-827364-9) OUP.

Class, Community & Culture in Tudor Wales. Ed. by J. Gwynfor Jones. xiii, 299p. 1989. 52.50 (0-7083-1031-1, Pub. by U of Wales UK) Bks Intl VA.

Class Conflict & Class Coalition in the California Woman Suffrage Movement, 1907-1912: The San Francisco Wage Earners' Suffrage League. Susan Englander. LC 91-39312. 200p. 1991. lib. bdg. 79.95 (0-7734-9845-1) E Mellen.

Class, Conflict, & Consensus: Antebellum Southern Community Studies. Ed. by Orville V. Burton & Robert C. McMath, Jr. LC 81-1071. (Contributions in American History Ser.: No. 96). (Illus.). xxvi, 308p. 1982. text ed. 69.50 (0-313-21310-0, BSC/) Greenwood.

Class Conflict & Cultural Consensus: The Making of a Mass Consumer Society in Flint, Michigan. Ronald W. Edsforth. (Class & Culture Ser.). 300p. (C). 1986. pap. text ed. 15.00 (0-8135-1105-4) Rutgers U Pr.

Class Conflict & Economic Development in Chile, 1958-1973. Barbara Stallings. LC 77-89181. xviii, 295p. 1978. 39.50 (0-8047-0978-5) Stanford U Pr.

Class, Conflict & Protest in the English Countryside, 1700-1800. Ed. by Mick Reed & Roger Wells. 236p. 1990. text ed. 35.00 (0-7146-3343-7, Pub. by F Cass Pubs UK) Intl Spec Bk.

Class Conflict & the Crisis of Capitalism: Essays in Medieval Social History. Rodney Hilton. 330p. (C). 1985. text ed. 55.00 (0-907628-36-2) Hambledon Press.

Class Conflict & the Crisis of Feudalism. Rodney H. Hilton. 320p. 1990. pap. 18.95 (0-86091-998-6, A4495, Pub. by Verso UK) Routledge Chapman & Hall.

Class Conflict in Chinese Socialism. Richard C. Kraus. LC 81-7754. 256p. 1981. text ed. 42.00 (0-231-05182-4) Col U Pr.

Class Conflict, Slavery & the United States Constitution: Ten Essays. Staughton Lynd. LC 80-18219. xiii, 288p. 1980. reprint ed. text ed. 55.00 (0-313-22672-5, LYCC, Greenwood Pr) Greenwood.

Class Construction in C & C Plus Plus Object-Oriented Programming Fundamentals. Roger Sessions. 192p. 1992. pap. text ed. 42.00 (0-13-630104-5) P-H.

Class, Control & Contestation in Educational Organisation. Ed. by Peter Watkins. 112p. (C). 1983. 60.00 (0-7300-0005-2, Pub. by Deakin Univ AT) St Mut.

Class Cooking: Family Recipes Celebrating Fred & Frances Sohn's 50th Wedding Anniversary, October 4, 1990. Mark F. Sohn. 150p. 1990. pap. 10.00 (0-9616911-4-X) M F Sohn Pubns.

Class, Culture & Curriculum: A Study of Continuity & Change in a Catholic School. Ed. by Lawrence Angus. 97p. (C). 1986. 55.00 (0-7300-0374-4, Pub. by Deakin Univ AT) St Mut.

***Class, Culture & Race in American Schools: A Handbook.** Stanley W. Rothstein. LC 94-38502. 272p. 1995. text ed. 69.50 (0-313-29102-0, Greenwood Pr) Greenwood.

***Class, Democracy & Labor in Contemporary Argentina.** rev. ed. Ed. by Peter Ranis. LC 94-26252. Orig. Title: Argentine Workers. 352p. 1994. pap. 21.95 (1-56000-775-3) Transaction Pubs.

Class Development & Gender Inequality in Kenya, 1963-1990. Bessie House-Midamba. LC 90-26100. (African Studies: Vol. 20). 168p. 1991. lib. bdg. 79.95 (0-7734-9754-4) E Mellen.

Class Dismissed! High School Poems. Mel Glenn. LC 81-38441. (Illus.). 112p. (YA). 1991. reprint ed. pap. 5.95 (0-395-58111-7, Clarion Bks) HM.

Class Dismissed Two: More High School Poems. Mel Glenn. LC 86-2671. (Illus.). 96p. (YA). (gr. 8 up). 1986. 13.95 (0-89919-443-5, Clarion Bks) HM.

Class Divided. William Peters. LC 87-50411. 172p. 1987. pap. 11.00 (0-300-04048-2) Yale U Pr.

***Class Enemy.** Nigel Williams. 96p. (Orig.). Date not set. pap. 10.95 (0-571-17474-4) Faber & Faber.

Class, Ethnicity, & Democracy in Nigeria: The Failure of the First Republic. Larry Diamond. (Illus.). 416p. (C). 1988. text ed. 45.00x (0-8156-2422-0) Syracuse U Pr.

Class, Ethnicity & Politics in Liberia: Analysis of Power Struggles in the Tubman & Tolbert Administrations from 1944-1975. Stephen S. Hlope. LC 79-63261. 1979. pap. text ed. 27.00 (0-8191-0721-2) U Pr of Amer.

Class, Ethnicity, & Social Inequality. Christopher McAll. (McGill-Queen's Studies in Ethnic History). 320p. (C). 1990. pap. 19.95 (0-7735-0923-2, Pub. by McGill CN) U of Toronto Pr.

Class Fertility Trends in Western Nations. Dennis H. Wrong. Ed. by Harriet Zuckerman & Robert K. Merton. LC 79-9039. (Dissertations on Sociology Ser.). 1980. lib. bdg. 29.95 (0-405-13006-6) Ayer.

Class Fictions: Shame & Resistance in the British Working-Class Novel, 1890-1945. Pamela Fox. (Post-Contemporary Interventions Ser.). 256p. 1994. lib. bdg. 45.95 (0-8223-1533-5); pap. text ed. 15.95 (0-8223-1542-4) Duke.

Class Field Theory. J. Neukirch. LC 85-14846. (Grundlehren der Mathematischen Wissenschaften Ser.: Vol. 280). 155p. 1986. 75.00 (0-387-15251-2) Spr-Verlag.

Class Five Chronicles: Things Mother Never Told You 'bout Whitewater. Ed. by Jeff Bennett. (Illus.). 256p. (Orig.). 1992. pap. text ed. 13.95 (0-9629843-3-7) Swiftwater Pub.

Class Formation & Peasantry. Bishnu C. Barik. (C). 1988. 24.50 (81-7033-045-9, Pub. by Rawat II) S Asia.

Class Formation & Urban Industrial Society: Bradford, 1750-1850. Theodore Koditschek. (Illus.). (C). 1990. 89.95 (0-521-32771-7) Cambridge U Pr.

Class Groups & Picard Groups of Group Rings & Orders. I. Reiner. LC 76-10337. (CBMS Regional Conference Series in Mathematics: Vol. 26). 44p. 1986. reprint ed. 21.00 (0-8218-1676-4, CBMS/26C) Am Math.

Class Ideologies & Educational Futures. David W. Livingstone. LC 83-8514. 250p. 1983. 36.00 (0-905273-40-0, Falmer Pr); pap. 20.00 (0-905273-39-7, Falmer Pr) Taylor & Francis.

Class Ideology & Community Action. Will Cowburn. Ed. by Jo Campling. (Radical Forum on Adult Education Ser.). 192p. 39.95 (0-7099-3497-1, Pub. by Croom Helm UK) Routledge Chapman & Hall.

Class, Ideology & the Nation: A Theory of Welsh Nationalism. David L. Adamson. vii, 224p. 1991. 57.00 (0-7083-1082-6, Pub. by U of Wales UK) Bks Intl VA.

Class, Ideology & the Rights of Nobles During the French Revolution. Patrice L. Higonnet. (Illus.). 1981. text ed. 74.00 (0-19-822583-0) OUP.

Class II Archaeological Reconnaissance of a Portion of Area 20, Nevada Test Site, Nye County, Nevada. Lonnie C. Pippin et al. (Illus.). 46p. 1987. 10.00 (0-945920-52-0) Desert Rsch Inst.

Class in American Society. Leonard Reissman. 1960. pap. 16.95 (0-02-926270-4) Free Pr.

Class in China: Stratification in a Classless Society. Larry M. Wortzel. LC 86-29394. (Contributions in Political Science Ser.: No. 168). (Illus.). 184p. 1987. text ed. 45.00 (0-313-25498-2, WCN, Greenwood Pr) Greenwood.

Class in Room Forty-Four: When a Classmate Dies. Lynn B. Blackburn. Ed. by Joy Johnson. (Illus.). 24p. (Orig.). (J). (gr. 1-6). 1990. pap. 3.60 (1-56123-025-1) Centering Corp.

Class in Twentieth-Century American Sociology: An Analysis of Theories & Measurement Strategies. Michael D. Grimes. LC 90-27840. 248p. 1991. text ed. 49.95 (0-275-93877-8, C3877, Praeger Pubs) Greenwood.

Class Joke. Trevor Raven. LC 92-62013. (Illus.). 64p. 1993. pap. 8.00 (1-56002-231-0, Univ Edtns) Aegina Pr.

Class, Kinship, & Power in an Ecuadorian Town: The Negroes of San Lorenzo. Norman E. Whitten, Jr. (Illus.). viii, 238p. 1965. 32.50 (0-8047-0087-7) Stanford U Pr.

Class Language & Education: Class Struggle & Sociolinguistics in an African Situation. H. E. Newsum. LC 89-81017. 97p. (C). 1989. 24.95 (0-86543-139-6); pap. 7.95 (0-86543-140-X) Africa World.

Class Leaders: Recovering a Tradition. David L. Watson. LC 90-82206. 192p. 1991. pap. 9.95 (0-88177-092-2, DR092) Discipleship Res.

Class Learning Log: Level 2. (Wonders! Ser.). (Illus.). 1992. 25.00 (1-56334-150-6) Hampton-Brown.

Class Mammalia: The Animal Kingdom Arranged in Conformity with Its Organization by the Baron Cuvier, 2. Georges Cuvier. Ed. by Keir B. Sterling. LC 77-81117. (Biologists & Their World Ser.). (Illus.). 1978. reprint ed. lib. bdg. 47.95 (0-405-10766-8) Ayer.

Class Mammalia: The Animal Kingdom Arranged in Conformity with Its Organization by the Baron Cuvier, 3. Georges Cuvier. Ed. by Keir B. Sterling. LC 77-81117. (Biologists & Their World Ser.). (Illus.). 1978. reprint ed. lib. bdg. 47.95 (0-405-10767-6) Ayer.

Class Mammalia: The Animal Kingdom Arranged in Conformity with Its Organization by the Baron Cuvier, 4. Georges Cuvier. Ed. by Keir B. Sterling. LC 77-81117. (Biologists & Their World Ser.). (Illus.). 1978. reprint ed. lib. bdg. 47.95 (0-405-10768-4) Ayer.

Class Mammalia: The Animal Kingdom Arranged in Conformity with Its Organization by the Baron Cuvier, 5. Georges Cuvier. Ed. by Keir B. Sterling. LC 77-81117. (Biologists & Their World Ser.). (Illus.). 1978. reprint ed. lib. bdg. 47.95 (0-405-10769-2) Ayer.

Class Mammalia: The Animal Kingdom Arranged in Conformity with Its Organization by the Baron Cuvier, Set, Vols 1-5. Georges Cuvier. Ed. by Keir B. Sterling. LC 77-81117. (Biologists & Their World Ser.). (Illus.). 1978. reprint ed. Set. lib. bdg. 237.95 (0-405-10746-3) Ayer.

Class Mammalia: The Animal Kingdom Arranged in Conformity with Its Organization by the Baron Cuvier, Vol. 1-5. Georges Cuvier. Ed. by Keir B. Sterling. LC 77-81117. (Biologists & Their World Ser.). (Illus.). 1978. reprint ed. Vol.1. lib. bdg. 47.95 (0-405-10765-X) Ayer.

Class Management. Ted Wragg. LC 92-20923. (Leverhulme Primary Project Classroom Skills Ser.). (Illus.). 80p. 1993. pap. 18.95 (0-415-08422-9, A9893, Routledge NY) Routledge.

Class Menagerie. Jill Churchill. 224p. (Orig.). 1994. mass mkt. 4.99 (0-380-77380-5) Avon.

Class Number Parity. P. E. Conner & J. Hurrelbrink. (Pure Mathematics Ser.: Vol. 8). 248p. 1988. text ed. 48.00 (9971-5-0669-6) World Scientific Pub.

Class of Functional Equations of Neutral Type. Jack Hale & K. R. Meyer. LC 52-42839. (Memoirs Ser.: No. 1/76). 65p. 1967. pap. 16.00 (0-8218-1276-9, MEMO 1/761) Am Math.

Class of Hybrid Finite Element Methods for Electromagnetics: A Review. rev. ed. John L. Volkais et al. (University of Michigan Report Ser.: No. 0289184-T). 36p. reprint ed. pap. 25.00 (0-7837-6285-2, 2046000) Bks Demand.

Class of the Carolinas. Mike Cheatham. 167p. 1992. pap. 6.95 (0-9634240-0-9) Bee Tree Bks.

Class of the Field: New Performance Ratings for the Thoroughbreds. James Quinn. LC 86-28464. (Illus.). 160p. 1987. 13.95 (0-688-06551-1) Morrow.

Class of the Field: New Performance Ratings for Thoroughbreds. James Quinn. (Illus.). 144p. 1992. pap. 10.00 (0-688-11277-3, Quill) Morrow.

Class of 1846: From West Point to Appomattox: Stonewall Jackson, George McClellan & Their Brothers. John C. Waugh. LC 92-50532. (Illus.). 672p. 1994. 29.95 (0-446-51594-9) Warner Bks.

***Class of 1994 Employment Report & Salary Survey.** 90p. (Orig.). 1995. pap. 60.00 (1-55733-008-5) NALP.

Class of '66: Living in Suburban Middle America. Paul Lyons. LC 93-50899. 272p. (C). 1994. text ed. 44.95 (1-56639-213-6); pap. text ed. 16.95 (1-56639-214-4) Temple U Pr.

Class, Party & the Political System in Britain 1867-1914. John Belchem. (Historical Association Studies). 96p. 1990. pap. text ed. 12.95 (0-631-15876-6) Blackwell Pubs.

Class Piano. Margaret S. McLain. LC 73-19659. 304p. 1974. pap. 8.95 (0-253-31357-0) Ind U Pr.

Class Piano for Adult Beginners. 4th ed. Russell N. Squire & Timothy Shafer. 208p. 1990. pap. text ed. 37.33 (0-13-136961-X) P-H.

Class Pictures. Marilyn Sachs. 144p. (J). (gr. 7 up). 1982. pap. 2.95 (0-380-61408-1, Flare) Avon.

Class Pictures. Marilyn Sachs. 144p. (J). (gr. 3-7). 1991. pap. 3.95 (0-14-034682-1, Puffin) Puffin Bks.

Class Play with Ms. Vanilla. Fred Ehrlich. (Hello Reading! Ser.). (Illus.). 32p. (J). (ps-3). 1992. pap. 3.50 (0-14-054580-8) Puffin Bks.

Class Play with Ms. Vanilla. Fred Ehrlich. (Puffin Easy-to-Read Level One Ser.). (Illus.). (J). (ps-2). 1994. pap. 3.25 (0-14-037142-7) Puffin Bks.

Class, Politics, & Early Industrial Capitalism: A Study of Mid-Nineteenth Century Toulouse, France. Ronald Aminzade. LC 80-28284. (European Social History Ser.). (Illus.). 334p. 1981. 74.50 (0-87395-528-5); pap. 24.95 (0-87395-529-3) State U NY Pr.

Class, Politics, & Ideology in the Iranian Revolution. Mansoor Moaddel. 300p. 1992. text ed. 37.50 (0-231-07866-8) Col U Pr.

Class, Politics & Popular Religion in Mexico & Central America. Ed. by Lynn Stephen & James Dow. 1990. write for info. (0-913167-40-1) Am Anthro Assn.

Class, Politics, & Sugar in Colonial Cuba. Anton Allahar. LC 90-22280. (Caribbean Studies: Vol. 2). 232p. 1990. lib. bdg. 89.95 (0-88946-217-8) E Mellen.

An Asterisk (*) at the beginning of an entry indicates that the title is appearing in BIP for the first time.

Class, Power & Austerity: The New York City Fiscal Crisis. Eric Lichten. LC 85-22954. (Critical Studies in Work & Community). 272p. (Orig.). 1986. text ed. 55.00 (*0-89789-090-6*, Bergin & Garvey); pap. text ed. 16.95 (*0-89789-091-4*, Bergin & Garvey) Greenwood.

Class Power & State Power: Political Essays. Ralph Miliband. 311p. 1985. pap. text ed. 14.95 (*0-86091-773-8*, Pub. by Verso UK) Routledge Chapman & Hall.

Class President. Johanna Hurwitz. LC 89-28600. (Illus.). 96p. (J). (gr. 2 up). 1990. 15.00 (*0-688-09114-8*) Morrow Jr Bks.

Class President. Johanna Hurwitz. 96p. (J). (gr. 3-7). 1991. reprint ed. pap. 2.75 (*0-590-44064-0*, Apple Paperbacks) Scholastic Inc.

Class Prophecy: Murder. Dean F. Du Vall. LC 80-65177. (Derek Dax Adventure Ser.: No. 2). (Illus.). 228p. 1982. pap. 6.95 (*0-931232-25-2*) Du Vall Financial.

Class, Race & Black Liberation. Henry Winston. LC 77-923. 252p. reprint ed. pap. 71.90 (*0-317-28795-8*, 2020638) Bks Demand.

Class, Race, & Gender in American Education. Ed. by Lois Weis. LC 87-21929. (Frontiers in Education Ser.). 329p. 1988. 59.50 (*0-88706-715-8*); pap. 19.95 (*0-88706-716-6*) State U NY Pr.

Class, Race & Gender in South Africa: The Nursing Profession & The Making of Apartheid. Shula Marks. LC 93-29470. 1994. 65.00 (*0-312-10643-2*) St Martin.

Class, Race, & the Civil Rights Movement: The Changing Political Economy of Southern Racism. Jack M. Bloom. LC 85-45983. (Blacks in the Diaspora Ser.). 278p. 1987. 35.00 (*0-253-31212-4*); 12.95 (*0-253-20407-0*, MB 407) Ind U Pr.

Class, Religion, & Local Politics: The Centre Party in Wurttemberg Before 1914. David Blackbourn. LC 80-11878. 288p. 1980. text ed. 55.00x (*0-300-02464-9*) Yale U Pr.

Class Reunion. Franz Werfel. Tr. by Whittaker Chambers. reprint ed. lib. bdg. 18.95 (*0-88411-718-9*, Aeonian Pr) Amereon Ltd.

Class Ring see Wildfire Bestsellers

Class, Sex, & the Woman Work. LC 76-15304. 253p. 1977. text ed. 59.95 (*0-8371-9032-0*, Greenwood Pr) Greenwood.

Class Size & Adaptability, Including Observations on Invention: A Study of Selected Elementary School Classes in New Jersey. Clarence A. Newell. LC 70-177119. (Columbia University. Teachers College. Contributions to Education Ser.: No. 894). reprint ed. 37.50 (*0-404-55894-1*) AMS Pr.

Class Society at War: England, Nineteen Fourteen to Eighteen. Bernard Waites. LC 87-6564. 304p. 1994. pap. 19.95 (*0-85496-674-9*) Berg Pubs.

Class, Sports, & Social Development. Richard Gruneau. LC 82-21896. 224p. 1983. pap. 15.95x (*0-87023-388-2*) U of Mass Pr.

Class, State & Democracy in Jamaica. Carl Stone. LC 85-19406. (Studies on Latin America, a Hoover Institution Ser.). 175p. 1986. text ed. 49.95 (*0-275-92013-5*, C2013, Praeger Pubs) Greenwood.

Class, State & Development in India. Berch Berberoglu. (Illus.). 330p. (C). 1992. text ed. 36.00 (*0-8039-9401-X*) Sage.

Class, State & Industrial Structure: The Historical Process of South American Industrial Growth. Frederick S. Weaver. LC 79-6571. (Contributions in Economics & Economic History Ser.: No. 32). (Illus.). xiv, 247p. 1980. text ed. 55.00 (*0-313-22114-6*, WCI/) Greenwood.

Class, State & Power in the Third World: With Case Studies in Class Conflict in Latin America. James Petras et al. LC 80-25938. 285p. 1981. pap. text ed. 25.50 (*0-86598-056-X*, R3748) Rowman.

Class Structure & Cultural Dynamics. Ed. by Virendra P. Singh. (C). 1992. 36.00 (*81-7169-243-5*, Commonwealth) S Asia.

Class Structure & Social Transformation. Berch Berberoglu. LC 94-12352. 144p. 1994. text ed. 45.00 (*0-275-94924-9*, Praeger Pubs) Greenwood.

Class Structure in Europe: New Findings from East-West Comparisons of Social Structure & Mobility. Ed. by Max Haller. LC 90-37798. 288p. 1990. 62.95 (*0-87332-722-5*) M E Sharpe.

Class Struggle & the Jewish Nation: Selected Essays in Marxist Zionism. Ber Borochov. Ed. by Mitchell Cohen. LC 83-4695. 358p. 1983. 37.95x (*0-87855-479-3*) Transaction Pubs.

Class Struggle & the New Deal: Industrial Labor, Industrial Capital, & the State. Rhonda F. Levine. LC 88-17183. (Studies in Historical Social Change). 232p. 1988. 29.95 (*0-7006-0373-5*); pap. 14.95 (*0-7006-0496-0*) U Pr of KS.

Class Struggle in Africa. Kwame Nkrumah. 96p. (C). 1970. text ed. 9.95 (*0-901787-12-4*, Pub. by Panaf Bks UK); pap. 3.95 (*0-901787-32-9*, Pub. by Panaf Bks UK) Humanities.

Class Struggle in Socialist Poland: With Comparisons to Yugoslavia. Albert Szymanski. LC 84-3158. 284p. 1984. text ed. 45.00 (*0-275-91283-3*, C1283, Praeger Pubs) Greenwood.

Class Struggle in the Ancient Greek World: From the Archaic Age to the Arab Conquests. G. E. de Ste. Croix. LC 81-66650. 732p. 1981. 81.50 (*0-8014-1442-3*); pap. 24.95 (*0-8014-9597-0*) Cornell U Pr.

Class Struggle, the State & Medicine: An Historical & Contemporary Analysis of the Medical Sector in Great Britain. Vicente Navarro. 1978. lib. bdg. 16.95 (*0-88202-122-2*) Watson Pub Intl.

Class Struggles & National Liberation in Africa. Nzongola Ntalaja. LC 82-81279. 175p. (Orig.). (C). 1982. pap. 6.95 (*0-943324-00-9*) Omenana.

Class Struggles in France. 2nd ed. Karl Marx. 220p. 1967. 3.50 (*0-935534-07-5*) NY Labor News.

Class Struggles in France, 1848-1850. Karl Marx. LC 64-19792. 158p. 1964. pap. text ed. 3.95 (*0-7178-0030-X*) Intl Pubs Co.

Class Struggles in the U. S. S. R. First Period, 1917-1923. Charles Bettelheim. Tr. by Brian Pearce. LC 76-28986. 567p. 1978. pap. 10.00 (*0-85345-434-5*) Monthly Rev.

Class Struggles in the U. S. S. R. Second Period: 1923-1930, Vol. 11. Charles Bettelheim. Tr. by Brian Pearce. LC 76-28976. 640p. 1978. pap. 8.95 (*0-85345-514-7*) Monthly Rev.

Class Struggles in Zambia, 1889-1989 & the Fall of Kenneth Kaunda; 1990-1991. Munyonzwe Hamalengwa. LC 92-14695. 194p. (Orig.). (C). 1992. lib. bdg. 46.50 (*0-8191-8741-0*) U Pr of Amer.

Class Study Guide for Physical Education. Floyd Hawkins. 150p. 1988. pap. 14.95 (*0-89697-307-7*) Intl Univ Pr.

***Class, the Labour-Process & Work: Focus on Education.** Peter Watkins. 182p. 1992. pap. 81.00 (*0-7300-1381-2*, ESA845, Pub. by Deakin Univ AT) St Mut.

Class Trip. Francine Pascal. (Sweet Valley Twins Super Chiller Ser.: Bk. 1). (Orig.). (YA). (gr. 7 up). 1988. pap. 3.50 (*0-553-15588-1*) Bantam.

Class Trip. Bebe F. Rice. (YA). 1993. mass mkt. 3.50 (*0-06-106731-8*, Harp PBks) HarpC.

***Class Trip Vol. II.** Bebe F. Rice. (YA). 1994. pap. 3.50 (*0-06-106195-6*) HarpC Child Bks.

Class Trip Chaos. Beth Cruise. LC 92-35523. (Saved by the Bell Ser.: No. 6). 144p. (YA). (gr. 5 up). 1992. pap. 2.95 (*0-02-042765-4*, Collier Bks Young) S&S Childrens.

Class Trips. Benjamin Piltch & Peter Smergut. (Skyview Ser.). 64p. (J). (gr. 4-8). 1983. 3.95 (*0-934618-00-3*) Learning Well.

Class Two Cultural Resources Survey for the Gila Land Disposal Project, Yuma County, Arizona. Jeffrey H. Altschul & Steven D. Shelley. (Statistical Research Technical Ser.: No. 8). 38p. 1987. spiral bd. 5.00 (*1-879442-48-5*) Stats Res.

Class Voice & the American Art Song: A Source Book & Anthology. Helen Lightner. LC 91-7428. (Illus.). 191p. 1991. 32.50 (*0-8108-2381-0*) Scarecrow.

Class War: A Decade of Disorder. Ed. by Ian Bone. (Illus.). 160p. 1991. pap. 16.95 (*0-86091-558-1*, A6245, Pub. by Verso UK) Routledge Chapman & Hall.

Class with the Summer Birthdays. Dian C. Regan. (Illus.). 80p. (J). (gr. 2-4). 1991. 13.95 (*0-8050-1657-0*, Redfeather BYR) H Holt & Co.

***Classbuilding: Cooperative Learning Activities.** Kagan et al. (Illus.). 100p. 1995. pap. text ed. 20.00 (*1-879097-29-X*) Kagan Cooperative.

Classe Ouvriere et les Niveaux de Vie. M. Halbwachs. (Reimpressions G & B Ser.). 512p. (FRE.). 1971. pap. text ed. 111.00 (*0-677-50365-2*) Gordon & Breach.

Classed Subject Catalog of the Engineering Societies Library, New York City, 12 vols. Ed. by Engineering Societies Library Staff. 1970. lib. bdg. 1,305.00 (*0-8161-0653-3*, Hall Library); lib. bdg. 110.00 (*0-8161-0237-6*, Hall Library) G K Hall.

Classed Subject Catalog of the Engineering Societies Library, New York City, 1st Supplement. Ed. by Engineering Societies Library Staff. 1970. lib. bdg. 120.00 (*0-8161-0700-9*, Hall Library) G K Hall.

Classed Subject Catalog of the Engineering Societies Library, New York City, 10th Supplement. Ed. by Engineering Societies Library Staff. 1974. lib. bdg. 70.00 (*0-8161-1123-5*, Hall Library) G K Hall.

Classed Subject Catalog of the Engineering Societies Library, New York City, 2nd Supplement. Ed. by Engineering Societies Library Staff. 1970. lib. bdg. 120.00 (*0-8161-0752-1*, Hall Library) G K Hall.

Classed Subject Catalog of the Engineering Societies Library, New York City, 3rd Supplement. Ed. by Engineering Societies Library Staff. 1970. lib. bdg. 120.00 (*0-8161-0756-4*, Hall Library) G K Hall.

Classed Subject Catalog of the Engineering Societies Library, New York City, 4th Supplement, 1968 & 5th Supplement, 1970. 4th suppl. ed. Ed. by Engineering Societies Library Staff. 1970. Fourth Suppl. lib. bdg. 120.00 (*0-8161-0817-X*, Hall Library) G K Hall.

Classed Subject Catalog of the Engineering Societies Library, New York City, 4th Supplement, 1968 & 5th Supplement, 1970. 5th suppl. ed. Ed. by Engineering Societies Library Staff. 1970. Fifth Suppl. lib. bdg. 120.00 (*0-8161-0836-6*, Hall Library) G K Hall.

Classed Subject Catalog of the Engineering Societies Library, New York City, 6th Supplement. Ed. by Engineering Societies Library Staff. 1970. lib. bdg. 120.00 (*0-8161-0883-8*, Hall Library) G K Hall.

Classed Subject Catalog of the Engineering Societies Library, New York City, 7th Supplement. Ed. by Engineering Societies Library Staff. 1971. lib. bdg. 120.00 (*0-8161-0913-3*, Hall Library) G K Hall.

Classed Subject Catalog of the Engineering Societies Library, New York City, 8th Supplement. Ed. by Engineering Societies Library Staff. 1972. lib. bdg. 120.00 (*0-8161-0982-6*, Hall Library) G K Hall.

Classed Subject Catalog of the Engineering Societies Library, New York City, 9th Supplement. Ed. by Engineering Societies Library Staff. 1973. lib. bdg. 120.00 (*0-8161-1050-6*, Hall Library) G K Hall.

Classen's Commercial Forms, 2 vols., Set. H. Ward Classen. 255p. 1991. ring bd. 128.00 (*0-929576-64-0*) Busn Laws Inc.

Classen's Mergers & Acquisitions Forms, No. 107. 300p. 1992. ring bd. 80.00 (*0-929576-81-0*) Busn Laws Inc.

Classes. Erik O. Wright. 342p. 1985. pap. text ed. 16.95 (*0-86091-812-2*, Pub. by Verso UK) Routledge Chapman & Hall.

Classes: A Marxist Critique. Paul Kamolnick. 250p. (Orig.). (C). 1988. text ed. 34.95 (*0-930390-84-9*) Gen Hall.

Classes & Conflits de Classes Dans la Societe Industrielle. Ralf Dahrendorf. (Oeuvre Sociologique Ser.: No. 1). 1972. pap. 26.95 (*90-279-7014-9*) Mouton.

Classes & the Class Struggle in the U. S. S. R. 1920's-1930's. Iu Mukhachev. 150p. (C). 1988. 30.00 (*0-685-31477-4*) St Mut.

Classes, Estates & Order in Early-Modern Brittany. James B. Collins. LC 93-18620. (Studies in Early Modern History). 288p. (C). 1994. 59.95 (*0-521-44072-6*) Cambridge U Pr.

Classes of Linear Operators, Vol. I. Ed. by I. Gohberg et al. (Operator Theory: Advances & Applications Ser.: Vol. 49). 488p. 1990. 155.50 (*0-8176-2531-3*) Birkhauser.

Classes of Linear Operators, Vol. 2. I. Gohberg et al. (Operator Theory: Advances & Applications Ser.: Vol. 63). 568p. 1993. 155.00 (*0-8176-2944-0*) Birkhauser.

Classes, Power & Conflict: Classical & Contemporary Debates. Ed. by Anthony Giddens & David Held. LC 81-43382. 640p. 1982. pap. 16.00 (*0-520-04627-7*) U CA Pr.

Classes Rurales et le Regime Domanial en France Au Moyen Age. Henri E. See. LC 80-2003. 1981. reprint ed. 61.50 (*0-404-18594-0*) AMS Pr.

***Classful of Gods & Goddesses in Nepal.** Higbie. 1988. pap. 12.50 (*0-940168-12-X*) Boxwood.

Classful of Gods & Goddesses in Nepal. R. Higbie. (C). 1991. text ed. 75.00 (*0-7855-0130-4*, Pub. by Ratna Pustak Bhandar) St Mut.

Classgroups & Hermitian Modules. A. Frohlich. (Progress in Mathematics Ser.: Vol. 48). 226p. 1984. 36.50 (*0-8176-3182-8*) Birkhauser.

Classgroups of Group Rings. Martin J. Taylor. LC 83-26167. (London Mathematical Society Lecture Note Ser.: No. 91). 134p. 1984. pap. 29.95 (*0-521-27870-8*) Cambridge U Pr.

Classic: A Christmas Carol. Charles Dickens. 64p. 1994. 4.98 (*0-8317-1258-9*) Smithmark.

Classic: Black Beauty. Anna Sewell. 64p. 1994. 4.98 (*0-8317-6578-X*) Smithmark.

Classic: Just So Stories. Rudyard Kipling. 64p. 1994. 4.98 (*0-8317-6581-X*) Smithmark.

Classic: Literary Images of Permanence & Change. Frank Kermode. 152p. 1983. pap. 11.50 (*0-674-13398-6*) HUP.

Classic: Thumbelina. Hans Christian Andersen. 64p. 1994. 4.98 (*0-8317-6580-1*) Smithmark.

Classic AC-DC. (Illus.). 172p. 1992. pap. 19.95 (*0-8256-1326-4*, AM87458) Music Sales.

Classic AC-DC: The Early Years. (Illus.). 172p. 1991. pap. 19.95 (*0-8256-1313-2*, AM85531) Music Sales.

Classic Adirondack Ski Tours. Tony Goodwin. LC 93-23288. (Illus.). 128p. 1994. pap. 10.95 (*0-935272-67-4*) ADK Mtn Club.

***Classic Aircraft Cutaways of World War II.** Bill Gunston. (Illus.). 160p. 1995. 29.95 (*0-7603-0029-1*) Motorbooks Intl.

Classic Aircraft in Aviation Art. Roger Markman. (Illus.). 96p. 1994. 49.95 (*0-943231-64-7*) Howell Pr VA.

Classic Aircraft of WWI. Richard Winslade & Melvin Hiscock. (Color Library). (Illus.). 128p. 1994. pap. 15.95 (*1-85532-407-5*, Pub. by Osprey Pubng Ltd UK) Motorbooks Intl.

Classic Airplanes of the Thirties - Aircraft of the Roaring Twenties. Antique Airplane Association Staff. Ed. by James B. Gilbert. LC 79-7238. (Flight: Its First Seventy-Five Years Ser.). (Illus.). 1980. reprint ed. lib. bdg. 19.95 (*0-405-12153-9*) Ayer.

Classic America: The Federal Style & Beyond. Wendell Garrett. LC 92-5577. (Illus.). 308p. 1992. 75.00 (*0-8478-1585-4*) Rizzoli Intl.

Classic American Autobiographies. Ed. by William L. Andrews. 464p. (Orig.). 1992. pap. 5.99 (*0-451-62852-7*, Ment) NAL-Dutton.

Classic American Cars. Richard Nichols. 1992. pap. 19.95 (*0-671-08193-4*) S&S Trade.

Classic American Cooking at the Academy. 2nd ed. Bruce Aidells et al. LC 93-37119. (California Culinary Academy Ser.). Orig. Title: Regional American Classics. 128p. 1993. reprint ed. pap. 11.95 (*1-56426-041-0*, Calif Culinary Acad) Cole Group.

Classic American Farm Tractors. Ed. by N. Baldwin. (Andrew Colar Library Ser.). (Illus.). 128p. 1985. pap. 15.95 (*0-85045-617-7*, Pub. by Osprey Pubng Ltd UK) Motorbooks Intl.

Classic American Folk Tales. Steven Zorn. LC 91-58125. (Courage Children's Classics Ser.). (Illus.). 56p. (J). 1992. 9.98 (*1-56138-062-8*) Courage Bks.

Classic American Furniture. James Clapper. Ed. by Roundtable Press Staff. LC 85-26976. (Illus.). 160p. 1986. pap. 9.95 (*0-932944-80-9*) Creative Homeowner.

Classic American Ghost Stories. Deborah A. Downer. 214p. 1990. 19.95 (*0-87483-115-6*); pap. 9.95 (*0-87483-118-0*) August Hse.

Classic American Graffiti: Lexical Evidence from Folk Epigraphy in Western North America; a Glossarial Study of the Low Element in the English Vocabulary. Allen W. Read. LC 76-5697. (Maledicta Press Publications Ser.: Vol. 6). 96p. (C). 1977. reprint ed. pap. 7.50 (*0-916500-06-3*) Maledicta.

Classic American Natural Desserts Cookbook. David Smither. LC 92-35089. 200p. 1993. pap. 9.95 (*0-89529-527-X*) Avery Pub.

***Classic American Quilt Collection: Baskets.** Ed. by Karen C. Soltys & Mary V. Green. LC 94-30877. (Illus.). 128p. 1995. 19.95 (*0-87596-644-6*) Rodale Pr Inc.

Classic American Quilt Collection: Log Cabin. Ed. by Mary V. Green. LC 94-8403. (Illus.). 128p. 1995. 19.95 (*0-87596-629-2*) Rodale Pr Inc.

Classic American Quilt Collection: Nine Patch. Ed. by Mary V. Green. LC 94-19175. 1994. 19.95 (*0-87596-643-8*) Rodale Pr Inc.

***Classic American Quilt Collection: Wedding Ring.** Ed. by Karen C. Soltys. (Illus.). 128p. 1995. 19.95 (*0-87596-683-7*) Rodale Pr Inc.

Classic American Short Stories. Ed. by Douglas Grant. 416p. 1990. pap. 11.95 (*0-19-282685-9*) OUP.

Classic & Romantic Music. Friedrich Blume. Tr. by M. D. Norton. LC 78-77390. (C). 1970. pap. text ed. 8.95 (*0-393-09868-0*) Norton.

Classic Animal Stories. Ed. by Lesley O'Mara. (Illus.). 160p. (J). (gr. 1 up). 1991. 18.95 (*1-55970-143-9*) Arcade Pub Inc.

Classic Approach to Make-up for Fashion, Film & Theatre. Mark Traynor. (Illus.). 191p. 1985. 29.93 (*0-317-59331-5*); pap. 14.00 (*0-912126-74-4*) Keystone Pubns.

Classic Arabian Horse. Judith Forbis. (Illus.). 416p. 1976. 34.95 (*0-87140-612-8*) Liveright.

Classic Architectural Birdhouses & Feeders. Malcolm Wells. (Illus.). 96p. (Orig.). 1988. pap. 9.95 (*0-9621878-0-1*) Malcolm Wells.

Classic Art: An Introduction to the Italian Renaissance. 5th ed. Heinrich Wolfflin. (Illus.). 320p. (C). 1994. reprint ed. pap. 19.95 (*0-7148-2974-9*, Pub. by Phaidon Press UK) Chronicle Bks.

Classic Atlanta: Landmarks of the Atlanta Spirit. William R. Mitchell, Jr. (Illus.). 208p. 1991. 60.00 (*0-932958-12-5*) Golden Coast.

Classic Atlanta: Landmarks of the Atlanta Spirit. William R. Mitchell, Jr. LC 91-71487. (Golden Coast Book Ser.). (Illus.). 224p. (C). 1991. 60.00 (*0-8203-1549-4*) U of Ga Pr.

Classic Austrian Cooking. Gretel Beer. 396p. 1994. 29.95 (*0-233-98827-0*, Pub. by A Deutsch UK) Trafalgar.

Classic Aviation Humor Bk. II. Sherm Morgan. 1989. pap. 5.95 (*0-944792-01-4*) Pendragon TX.

Classic Backcountry Skiing: A Guide to the Best Ski Tours in New England. David Goodman. LC 88-24260. (Illus.). 320p. (Orig.). 1989. 12.95 (*0-910146-74-8*) AMC Books.

Classic Ballet. Lincoln Kirstein. (Illus.). 1952. 35.00 (*0-394-40820-9*) Knopf.

Classic Ballroom Dances. C. Simic. (Ballroom Dance Ser.). 1986. lib. bdg. 79.95 (*0-8490-3327-6*) Gordon Pr.

Classic Ballroom Dances. C. Simic. (Ballroom Dance Ser.). 1985. lib. bdg. 78.00 (*0-87700-749-7*) Revisionist Pr.

Classic Bamboo Rodmakers: Past & Present. Dick Spurr. (Illus.). 96p. 1992. pap. 14.95 (*0-9629439-5-9*) Centenn Pubns.

Classic Baptism: An Inquiry into the Meaning of the Word Baptizo As Determined by the Usage of Classical Greek Writers. James W. Dale. LC 88-92850. 376p. 1989. reprint ed. pap. 25.00 (*0-86516-224-7*) Bolchazy-Carducci.

Classic Baptism: The Meaning of the Word in Classical Greek Writers. James W. Dale. 1989. pap. 19.99 (*0-87552-230-0*) Presby & Reformed.

Classic Baseball Cards. Bert R. Sugar. 1980. pap. 3.95 (*0-486-23498-3*) Dover.

Classic Basket Quilts. Elizabeth Porter. 1991. pap. 16.95 (*0-89145-973-1*) Collector Bks.

Classic Bear Style Series: Continental Pilsener. Dave Miller. (Classic Beer Style Ser.). (Illus.). 102p. 1990. pap. 11.95 (*0-937381-20-9*) Brewers Pubns.

Classic Beer Style Series: Lambic. Jean-Xavier Guinard. (Classic Beer Style Ser.). (Illus.). 160p. 1990. pap. 11.95 (*0-937381-22-5*) Brewers Pubns.

Classic Beer Style Series: Pale Ale. Terry Foster. (Classic Beer Style Ser.). (Illus.). 140p. 1990. pap. 11.95 (*0-937381-18-7*) Brewers Pubns.

Classic Bible Dictionary. Ed. by Jay P. Green, Sr. (Fifty Greatest Christian Classics Ser.). 1148p. 1989. text ed. 24.95 (*0-685-30025-0*) Sovereign Grace Trust Fund.

Classic Bible Stories for Jewish Children. Alfred J. Kolatch. LC 93-10165. (Illus.). 72p. (J). (gr. 3 up). 1994. 14.95 (*0-8246-0362-1*) Jonathan David.

Classic Bible Study Library for Today. Charles H. Spurgeon et al. LC 88-8814. 96p. pap. 3.99 (*0-8254-3762-8*) Kregel.

***Classic Bikes.** Henshaw. 1995. pap. text ed. 14.95 (*0-88317-183-X*) Stoeger Pub Co.

Classic Black African Poems. LC 75-152054. 61p. 1966. 20.00 (*0-87130-024-9*); pap. 12.50 (*0-87130-025-7*) Eakins.

***Classic Boat Seamanship.** Martin Tregoning. (Illus.). 192p. Date not set. 40.00 (*0-7136-3606-8*) Sheridan.

Classic Bonsai of Japan. Nippon Bonsai Association Staff. Tr. by John Bester. (Illus.). 176p. 1989. 100.00 (*0-87011-933-8*) Kodansha.

***Classic Border Designs.** Ed. by Clarence P. Hornung. (Illus.). 128p. 1995. pap. 8.95 (*0-486-28518-9*) Dover.

***Classic Brain Puzzlers.** Philip J. Carter et al. (Illus.). 128p. 1995. pap. 4.95 (*0-7063-7231-X*, Pub. by Ward Lock UK) Sterling.

Classic Brain Teasers of the Twentieth Century, Vols. 1 & 2: A Selection of the Best Puzzles in Logic, Math, & Deductive Reasoning, Vol. 1. Ed. by Richard J. Morway. 48p. 1992. pap. 2.95 (*0-9632528-0-1*) Madisn Hse NH.

Classic Brain Teasers of the Twentieth Century, Vols. 1 & 2: A Selection of the Best Puzzles in Logic, Math, & Deductive Reasoning, Vol. 2. Ed. by Richard J. Morway. 48p. 1992. pap. 2.95 (*0-9632528-1-X*) Madisn Hse NH.

Classic Brainteasers. Martin Gardner. LC 94-17524. 96p. 1994. 13.95 (*0-8069-1260-X*) Sterling.

***Classic Brainteasers.** Martin Gardner. (Illus.). 96p. (Orig.). 1995. pap. 4.95 (*0-8069-1261-8*) Sterling.

***Classic Breads.** Anne Willan. LC 94-31841. (Ann Willan's Look & Cook Ser.). (Illus.). 128p. 1995. 19.98 (*1-56458-866-1*) Dorling Kindersley.

C

An Asterisk (*) at the beginning of an entry indicates that the title is appearing in BIP for the first time. 1295

Classic Bulbs: Hidden Treasures for the Modern Garden. Katherine Whiteside. (Illus.). 272p. 1992. 40.00 (*0-394-58727-8*, Villard Bks) Random.

Classic Cajun: Culture & Cooking. Lucy H. Zaunbrecher. (Illus.). 160p. 1994. 12.95 (*0-9640748-0-X*) L Zaunbrecher.

Classic Cakes & Other Great Cuisinart Desserts. Carl G. Sontheimer & Cecily Brownstone. LC 93-28637. 1994. 15.00 (*0-688-12719-3*) Hearst Bks.

Classic Cakes Tempting Tortes. Jane Suthering. LC 93-37193. (Creative Cook Ser.). 1993. 16.95 (*1-56426-655-9*) Cole Group.

Classic Cameras. Kate Rouse. 1994. 10.98 (*0-7858-0177-4*) Bk Sales Inc.

***Classic Cameras.** Kate Rouse. 1994. 10.98 (*0-7858-0152-9*) Bk Sales Inc.

Classic Car. Ed. by Beverly R. Kimes. 48p. 1983. 7.00 (*0-685-06801-3*) Classic Car.

Classic Car: The Ultimate Book about the World's Grandest Automobiles. Ed. by Beverly R. Kimes. (Illus.). 752p. 1990. 69.95 (*0-9627868-0-2*) Classic Car.

Classic Car Profiles, 2 vols., Vol. 2. LC 87-80608. (Illus.). 148p. 1988. reprint ed. 34.95 (*0-85429-651-4*, F651, Pub. by G T Foulis Ltd) Haynes Pubns.

Classic Car Restoration Guide. Lindsay Porter. (Illus.). 224p. 1994. 34.95 (*1-85010-890-0*, Pub. by J H Haynes & Co UK) Motorbooks Intl.

Classic Car Restorer's Handbook: General Restoration Tips & Techniques for Owners & Restorers of Classic Automobiles. Jim Richardson. LC 94-19094. 176p. (Orig.). 1994. pap. 15.00 (*1-55788-194-4*, HP Books) Berkley Pub.

Classic Carousel Carving: From One-Eighth Scale to Full Size. H. LeRoy Marlow. LC 92-23217. (Illus.). 168p. 1993. pap. 19.95 (*0-8069-8252-7*) Sterling.

Classic Cars for Fun & Profit see Detroit Insider: How to Buy Three & Four Year Old Cars at Four Hundred & Less - How to Buy a New Car at Lowest Possible Prices - Classic Cars for Fun & Profit

Classic Carved Furniture: Making the Pie-Crust Teatable. Thomas Heller & Ronald Clarkson. Ed. by Douglas Congdon-Martin. LC 94-65627. (Illus.). 128p. (Orig.). 1994. pap. 19.95 (*0-88740-616-5*) Schiffer.

Classic Case of Murder: An Inspector Cross Mystery Jigsaw Puzzle Thriller. Henry Slesar. (Orig.). (C). 1992. pap. 20.00 (*0-922242-42-9*) Lombard Mktg.

Classic Cases in Medical Ethics. George Pence. 412p. (C). 1990. pap. text ed. write for info. (*0-07-038092-9*) McGraw.

***Classic Cases in Medical Ethics: Accounts of Cases That Have Shaped Medical Ethics, with Philosophical, Legal, & Historical Backgrounds.** 2nd ed. Gregory E. Pence. LC 94-41691. 1994. pap. text ed. 20.00 (*0-07-038094-5*) McGraw.

Classic Cat Stevens. (Illus.). 200p. 1991. pap. 19.95 (*0-8256-1285-3*, AM80029) Music Sales.

Classic Catfish: From the Crown at the Antique Mall. Evelyn Roughton & Tony Roughton. (Illus.). 160p. 1993. write for info. (*0-9635571-0-6*) Ant Mall & Crown.

Classic Catholic Poetry. Ed. by Thomas P. McDonnell. LC 88-60924. 144p. 1988. 13.95 (*0-87973-494-9*, 494) Our Sunday Visitor.

Classic Chess Problems. Kenneth S. Howard. (Orig.). 1970. pap. 3.95 (*0-486-22522-4*) Dover.

Classic Chinese & Oriental Cooking. Jeff Groman. 1992. 19.98 (*1-55521-811-3*) Bk Sales Inc.

Classic Chinese Cook Book. Mai Leung. LC 75-9354. (Illus.). 1976. 16.95 (*0-685-02047-9*, PL) HarpC.

Classic Chinese Cooking Vegetable Gourmet. Joanne Hush. Date not set. 7.99 (*0-517-10043-6*) Random Hse Value.

Classic Chinese Cuisine. rev. ed. Nina Simonds. LC 93-48261. (Illus.). 400p. 1994. reprint ed. 29.95 (*1-881527-31-X*); reprint ed. pap. 19.95 (*1-881527-32-8*) Chapters Pub.

Classic Chinese Furniture. Wang Shixiang. (Illus.). 328p. 1992. reprint ed. 110.00 (*0-685-59129-8*) Art Media Resources.

Classic Christian Faith: Chapel Meditations Based on Luther's Small Catechism. Edgar M. Carlson. LC 59-9093. 171p. reprint ed. pap. 48.80 (*0-685-15861-6*, 2026912) Bks Demand.

Classic Christian Hymn Writers. Elsie Houghton. 352p. 1992. pap. 10.95 (*0-87508-729-9*) Chr Lit.

Classic Christian Townsite at Arminna West. Kent R. Weeks. (Publications of the Penn-Yale Expedition to Egypt: No. 3). (Illus.). xv, 88p. 1967. 40.00 (*0-686-17769-X*) U PA Mus Pubns.

Classic Christian Townsite at Arminna West, Vol. 3. Kent R. Weeks. LC 67-26194. 1967. 25.00 (*0-686-00130-3*) Penn-Yale Expedit.

Classic Christianity. Bob George. LC 87-83230. 208p. (Orig.). 1992. pap. 7.99 (*0-89081-660-3*); audio 14.99 (*1-56507-017-8*) Harvest Hse.

Classic Christianity Illustrated. Bob George. LC 93-26329. (Illus.). 1993. pap. 6.99 (*1-56507-021-6*) Harvest Hse.

Classic Christianity Study Guide. Bob George. (Orig.). 1990. pap. 5.99 (*0-89081-845-2*) Harvest Hse.

***Classic Christmas Carols & Songs.** Donna Martin. 1994. 14.95 (*0-8362-4514-8*) Andrews & McMeel.

Classic Christmas Tales: The Elves & the Shoemaker; Twas the Night Before Christmas; The Little Drummer Boy; The Nutcracker; The Twelve Days of Christmas; Rudolph's Adventure, 6 bks., Set. (Illus.). 24p. (J). 1993. 9.98 (*0-7853-0276-X*) Pubns Intl Ltd.

Classic Christmas Treasury. Ed. by Ideals Staff. (Illus.). 1994. 22.95 (*0-8249-4064-4*) Ideals.

Classic Christmas Treasury for Children. Ed. by Armand Eisen. LC 89-43004. (Children's Classics Ser.). (Illus.). 56p. (J). (gr. 3 up). 1990. 9.98 (*0-89471-769-3*) Courage Bks.

Classic Climbs in the Caucasus. Friedrich Bender. (Illus.). 318p. 1992. 24.95 (*0-89732-116-2*) Menasha Ridge.

***Classic Climbs of the Northwest.** Alan Kearney. (Illus.). 256p. (Orig.). 1995. pap. 19.95 (*0-938567-35-7*) Cloudcap.

Classic Clint: The Laughs & Times of Clint Murchison, Jr. Dick Hitt. LC 91-23127. (Illus.). 278p. (Orig.). 1991. pap. 14.95 (*1-55622-146-0*) Wordware Pub.

Classic Clocks for Woodworkers: Complete Patterns for 21 Clocks. Raymond Haigh. (Illus.). 160p. 1994. 29.95 (*0-304-34205-X*, Pub. by Cassell UK) Sterling.

Classic Cocktails. T. Murphy. 234p. pap. 6.95 (*0-507-46050-2*, 217) Am Bartenders.

Classic Collection: Afghans to Crochet. Workbasket Magazine Staff. (Illus.). 96p. 1988. pap. 7.95 (*0-86675-302-8*) KC Pub.

Classic Collection: Collars to Knit & Crochet. Workbasket Magazine Staff. (Illus.). 72p. 1989. pap. 6.95 (*0-86675-303-6*) KC Pub.

Classic Collection: Tatting Patterns. Workbasket Magazine Staff. (Aunt Ellen's Treasury Ser.). (Illus.). 96p. (Orig.). 1990. pap. 6.95 (*0-86675-304-4*) KC Pub.

Classic Collection: U. S. State Quilt Blocks. Workbasket Magazine Staff. LC 87-34844. (Illus.). 96p. 1988. pap. 6.95 (*0-86675-300-1*) KC Pub.

Classic Comedies. Ed. by Maurice Charney. LC 94-18222. 1995. 11.95 (*0-452-01143-4*, Mer) NAL-Dutton.

Classic Comics & Their Creators. Martin Sheridan. LC 73-83508. (Illus.). 304p. 1973. 14.95 (*0-911160-59-0*) Post Group.

Classic Convertibles. Paul Badre. 1989. 9.98 (*0-671-09604-4*) S&S Trade.

Classic Convertibles. J. G. Newbery. (Illus.). 112p. 1995. 14.98 (*0-8317-1165-5*) Smithmark.

Classic Cooking with Coca-Cola. Elizabeth C. Graham & Ralph Roberts. Ed. by Carey E. Watson. (Illus.). 208p. (Orig.). 1994. pap. 14.95 (*1-57090-002-7*) Alexander Bks.

***Classic Cooking with Coca-Cola.** Elizabeth C. Graham & Ralph Roberts. (Illus.). 208p. (Orig.). 1994. pap. 12.95 (*1-57102-500-6*) Hambleton-Hill.

Classic Country. Ed. by Milton Okun. pap. 14.95 (*0-89524-595-7*) Cherry Lane.

Classic Country Encore. Ed. by Milton Okun. pap. 14.95 (*0-89524-755-0*) Cherry Lane.

Classic Country Quilts: Step-by-Step Directions for 25 All-Time Favorites. Quilter's Newsletter Magazine Editors & Jane Townswick. LC 92-29542. 256p. 1993. 26.95 (*0-87596-573-3*, 11-752-0) Rodale Pr Inc.

Classic Country Style: And How to Achieve It, Vol. 1. Mary Trewby. 1993. pap. 22.95 (*0-8212-2022-5*) Bulfinch Pr.

***Classic Cowboy Songs from the Minstrel of the Range.** Don Edwards. 1994. pap. 19.95 (*0-87905-617-7*, Peregrine Smith) Gibbs Smith Pub.

Classic Cracker: Florida's Wood-Frame Vernacular Architecture. Ronald W. Haase. LC 92-10189. (Illus.). 128p. 1992. 24.95 (*1-56164-013-1*); pap. 17.95 (*1-56164-014-X*) Pineapple Pr.

Classic Crews. Harry Crews. 1993. pap. 15.00 (*0-671-86527-7*) S&S Trade.

Classic Crib Quilts & How to Make Them. Thomas K. Woodard & Blanche Greenstein. (Illus.). 144p. 1994. reprint ed. pap. text ed. 11.95 (*0-486-27861-1*) Dover.

Classic Crime & Suspense Writers. Ed. by Harold Bloom. LC 93-22607. (Writers of English: Lives & Works). (Illus.). 1994. 24.95 (*0-7910-2206-4*, Am Art Analog); pap. write for info. (*0-7910-2231-5*, Am Art Analog) Chelsea Hse.

Classic Crimes: A Selection from Works of William Roughead. William Roughead. LC 74-10431. (Classics of Crime & Criminology Ser.). 449p. 1975. reprint ed. 18.25 (*0-88355-198-5*) Hyperion Conn.

Classic Crimes Omnibus. Ed. by Julian Symons. (Crime Ser.). 384p. 1984. mass mkt. 6.95 (*0-14-006739-6*, Penguin Bks) Viking Penguin.

Classic Crocheted Bedspread Designs. Ed. by Rita Weiss. 48p. (Orig.). 1987. pap. 2.95 (*0-486-25370-8*) Dover.

Classic Crosby, Stills, Nash & Young. (Authentic Guitar Tab Ser.). 192p. (Orig.). 1993. pap. 24.95 (*0-89724-098-7*, GF0511) Warner Brothers.

Classic Cuisine of Provence. Diane Holuigue. LC 93-19599. 1993. pap. 15.95 (*0-89815-562-2*) Ten Speed Pr.

Classic Cuisine of the Italian Jews, No. I. rev. ed. Edda S. Machlin. (Illus.). 254p. 1993. 27.50 (*1-878857-05-3*); pap. 18.95 (*1-878857-06-1*) Giro Pr.

Classic Cuisine of the Italian Jews, No. II. Edda S. Machlin. (Illus.). 272p. 1992. 27.50 (*1-878857-03-7*) Giro Pr.

Classic Cuisine of Vietnam. Bach Ngo & Gloria Zimmerman. 256p. 1986. pap. 9.95 (*0-425-25833-5*, Plume) NAL-Dutton.

Classic Cuisine of Vietnam. Bach Ngo & Gloria Zimmerman. 1986. pap. 11.00 (*0-452-25833-2*) NAL-Dutton.

Classic Cult Fiction: A Companion to Popular Cult Literature. Thomas R. Whissen. LC 91-25723. 368p. 1992. text ed. 69.50 (*0-313-26550-X*, WCQ, Greenwood Pr) Greenwood.

***Classic Cycle Races of Europe.** Rudolf Geser. (Illus.). 144p. 1995. 29.95 (*1-85688-028-1*) Lyons & Burford.

Classic Data Structures in C Plus Plus. Timothy A. Budd. (Illus.). 700p. (C). 1994. text ed. 48.50 (*0-201-50889-3*) Addison-Wesley.

Classic Decorative Details. Henrietta Spencer-Churchill. LC 94-8258. (Illus.). 192p. 1994. 45.00 (*0-8478-1808-X*) Rizzoli Intl.

Classic Delights for Easy Piano. 48p. Date not set. pap. 19.95 (*0-685-69015-6*) Music Sales.

Classic Descriptions of Disease: With Biographical Sketches of the Authors. 3rd ed. Ralph H. Major. (Illus.). 712p. 1978. Photocopy ed. 104.95 (*0-398-01202-4*) C C Thomas.

***Classic Descriptions of Disease: With Biographical Sketches of the Authors.** 3rd ed. Ralph H. Major. (Illus.). 712p. 1978. pap. 51.50 (*0-398-06265-X*) C C Thomas.

Classic Designs. Ed. by National Plan Service, Inc. Staff. (Illus.). 32p. reprint ed. pap. 3.95 (*0-934039-24-0*, A35) Natl Plan Serv.

Classic Desserts: Eagle Brand. Eagle Brand. 1989. 9.99 (*0-517-67592-7*) Random Hse Value.

Classic Desserts Eagle Brand. 1989. 6.99 (*0-517-69396-8*) Random Hse Value.

Classic Dialogues & Dramas. Comp. by J. W. Shoemaker. LC 70-109146. (Granger Index Reprint Ser.). 1977. 15.95 (*0-8369-6130-7*) Ayer.

***Classic Dinners in One Hour.** Tom Griffith. (Illus.). 176p. 1995. 19.95 (*1-883955-05-X*) Penmarin Bks.

Classic Discoveries of Neuroendocrine Syndromes of the Pancreas & Gut. Ed. by Stanley R. Friesen. 281p. 1993. 89.95 (*1-879702-63-0*, LN0263) CRC Pr.

Classic Dolls. Marco Tosa. (Illus.). 272p. 1989. 95.00 (*0-89659-972-8*) Abbeville Pr.

Classic Doll's Houses. Faith Eaton. 1994. 14.98 (*0-681-00452-5*) Longmeadow Pr.

Classic Dylan. (Illus.). 176p. 1991. pap. 19.95 (*0-8256-1289-6*, AM80185) Music Sales.

Classic Early African-American Writers. Intro. & Sel. by Anthony Appiah. 1990. mass mkt. 5.95 (*0-553-21379-2*) Bantam.

Classic Earring Designs. Nola May. (Illus.). 96p. (Orig.). 1994. pap. 9.95 (*0-943604-43-5*) Eagles View.

Classic Encyclopedia. D. Magner. 1988. pap. 6.99 (*0-517-32168-8*) Random Hse Value.

Classic Enemies. Scott Bennie. Ed. by Rob Bell et al. (Champions Ser.). (Illus.). 112p. (Orig.). (C). 1989. pap. 13.00 (*1-55806-044-8*, 403) Hero Games.

Classic English Crime. large type ed. Ed. by Tim Heald. (Keating's Choice Ser.). 290p. 1992. 11.97 (*1-85089-544-9*, Pub. by ISIS UK) Transaction Pubs.

Classic English Crime: Thirteen Stories for Christie Centenary from the Crime Writers' Association. Ed. by Tim Heald. 224p. 1992. mass mkt. 4.99 (*0-446-40158-7*, Mysterious Paperbk) Warner Bks.

Classic English Crime: Thirteen Stories for the Christie Centenary from the Crime Writers' Association. Tim Heald. 1991. 16.95 (*0-89296-456-1*) Mysterious Pr.

***Classic English Gardens.** Gertrude Jekyll. (Illus.). 192p. 1995. 24.98 (*0-8317-1310-0*) Smithmark.

Classic English Interiors. Henrietta Spencer-Churchill. LC 91-45614. (Illus.). 224p. 1992. 45.00 (*0-8478-1570-6*) Rizzoli Intl.

Classic English Short Stories, 1930-1955. Ed. by Derek Hudson. 384p. 1990. pap. 10.95 (*0-19-281121-5*) OUP.

***Classic Epic.** Thomas J. Sienkewicz. (Magill Bibliographies Ser.). 265p. 1991. 40.00 (*0-8108-2811-1*) Scarecrow.

***Classic Erotic Tales.** Ed L. Omara. 1994. 8.98 (*0-7858-0198-7*) Bk Sales Inc.

Classic Essays on Photography. Alan Trachtenberg. LC 78-61844. 1980. 12.95 (*0-918172-07-1*); pap. 8.95 (*0-918172-08-X*) Leetes Isl.

Classic European Racing Motorcycles. Mick Walker. (Osprey Ser.). (Illus.). 192p. 1993. pap. 24.95 (*1-85532-269-2*, Pub. by Osprey Pubng Ltd UK) Motorbooks Intl.

Classic European Short Stories. Ed. by Robert Beum. 276p. (Orig.). (C). 1984. pap. 8.95 (*0-89385-025-X*) Sugden.

Classic Failures in Product Marketing: Marketing Principles Violations & How to Avoid Them. Donald W. Hendon. 1992. pap. 14.95 (*0-8442-3458-3*, NTC Busn Bks) NTC Pub Grp.

Classic Failures in Production Marketing: Marketing Principle Violations & How to Avoid Them. Donald W. Hendon. LC 88-35469. 205p. 1989. text ed. 55.00 (*0-89930-304-8*, HPF/, Quorum Bks) Greenwood.

Classic Fairy Tales. Helen Cresswell. (Illus.). 64p. (J). (ps-3). 1994. 12.95 (*0-307-17503-0*, Artsts Writrs) Western Pub.

Classic Fairy Tales. Iona Opie & Peter Opie. (Illus.). 1980. pap. 11.95 (*0-19-520219-8*) OUP.

Classic Fairy Tales. Iona Opie & Peter Opie. (Illus.). 256p. 1992. 30.00 (*0-19-211559-6*) OUP.

Classic Fairy Tales Treasury: Cinderella; Little Red Riding Hood; The Sleeping Beauty; Jack & the Beanstalk; Rumpelstiltskin; The Ugly Duckling, 6 bks., Set. (Illus.). 24p. (J). 1993. boxed 9.98 (*0-7853-0070-8*) Pubns Intl Ltd.

Classic Fantasy Writers. Ed. by Harold Bloom. LC 93-8346. (Writers of English: Lives & Works). (Illus.). 1994. 24.95 (*0-7910-2204-8*, Am Art Analog); pap. write for info. (*0-7910-2229-3*, Am Art Analog) Chelsea Hse.

Classic Farber Nudes, 1970-1990. Robert Farber. (Illus.). 144p. 1991. pap. 24.95 (*0-8174-3670-7*, Amphoto) Watsn-Guptill.

Classic Farm Tractors. Randy Leffingwell. LC 92-1774. 1993. 19.98 (*0-87938-813-7*) Motorbooks Intl.

Classic Ferrari. Geoffrey Eaton. 1991. 9.99 (*0-517-06580-0*) Random Hse Value.

Classic Ferrari. Godfrey Eaton. 1985. 7.98 (*0-671-07534-9*) S&S Trade.

***Classic Festival Preludes.** Darhon Rees-Rohrbacher & Thomas Dutton. 67p. (Orig.). 1995. pap. 15.00 (*1-882712-42-0*) Dragonflower.

Classic Fiction of the Harlem Renaissance. William L. Andrews. 448p. (C). 1994. pap. 18.95 (*0-19-508196-X*) OUP.

Classic Fifties Cars. pap. 9.00 (*0-449-90581-0*, Columbine) Fawcett.

Classic Finishing Techniques. Sam Allen. LC 94-16844. (Illus.). 128p. 1994. 19.95 (*0-8069-0512-3*) Sterling.

Classic Foreign Films: From Nineteen Sixty to Today. James R. Paris. (Illus.). 256p. 1993. pap. 17.95 (*0-8065-1442-6*, Citadel Pr) Carol Pub Group.

***Classic Freight Cars Vol. 6: Loaded Flats & Gondolas.** Ed. by Henry Maywald. (Illus.). 64p. (Orig.). 1994. pap. text ed. 24.95 (*1-882608-06-2*) H & M Prods.

***Classic Freight Cars Vol. 7: More 40 Ft. Boxcars.** Ed. by Henry Maywald. (Illus.). 64p. (Orig.). 1994. pap. text ed. 24.95 (*1-882608-08-9*) H & M Prods.

Classic Freight Cars, Vol. 1: Forty Foot Boxcars. John Henderson. (Illus.). 64p. (C). 1992. pap. text ed. write for info. (*0-9629037-6-0*) H & M Prods.

Classic Freight Cars, Vol. 3: Forty Ft. Refrigerator Cars. John Henderson. LC 91-77924. (Illus.). 64p. (Orig.). 1993. pap. 23.95 (*1-882608-01-1*) H & M Prods.

Classic Freight Cars, Vol. 4: Four Feet or Less Open & Closed Hopper Cars. John Henderson. LC 91-77924. (Illus.). 64p. (Orig.). 1993. pap. 23.95 (*1-882608-02-X*) H & M Prods.

Classic French Cinema, 1930-1960. Colin Crisp. LC 92-21657. (C). 1993. 59.95 (*0-253-31550-6*) Ind U Pr.

Classic French Paperweights. Edith Mannoni. Ed. by Paul Jokelson & Lawrence H. Selman. LC 84-61013. (Illus.). 60p. 1984. 35.00 (*0-933756-06-2*) Paperwght Pr.

Classic Fretwork Scroll Saw Patterns. Patrick Spielman & James Reidle. LC 90-29137. (Illus.). 192p. 1991. pap. 12.95 (*0-8069-8254-3*) Sterling.

***Classic Frt. Cars Vol. 5: Northeast Work Equip.** Paul G. Yurko. (Illus.). 64p. (Orig.). 1994. pap. text ed. 24.95 (*1-882608-05-4*) H & M Prods.

Classic Gangster Films. Robert Bookbinder. (Illus.). 256p. 1993. pap. 16.95 (*0-8065-1467-1*, Citadel Pr) Carol Pub Group.

Classic Garden Design. Rosemary Verey. LC 84-9480. (Illus.). 160p. 1984. 24.95 (*0-86553-128-5*) Congdon & Weed.

Classic Garden Design. Rosemary Verey. 1989. 24.95 (*0-394-57558-X*) Random.

Classic Garden Design: How to Adapt & Recreate Garden Features of the Past. Rosemary Verey. 1989. 24.95 (*0-394-57830-9*) Random.

Classic Gardens. Erica Lennard. LC 83-80908. (Illus.). 128p. 1982. 27.95 (*0-912810-38-6*) Lustrum Pr.

Classic German Racing Motorcycles. Mick Walker. (Illus.). 192p. 1991. pap. 24.95 (*1-85532-141-6*, Pub. by Osprey Pubng Ltd UK) Motorbooks Intl.

Classic Ghost Stories. Charles Dickens et al. LC 74-12599. 330p. (Orig.). 1975. pap. 7.95 (*0-486-20735-8*) Dover.

Classic Glamour Photography. Iain Banks. (Illus.). 176p. 1989. pap. 22.50 (*0-8174-3672-3*, Amphoto) Watsn-Guptill.

Classic Golf Links of England, Scotland, Wales, & Ireland. Donald Steel. LC 92-27363. 1993. 34.95 (*0-88289-965-1*) Pelican.

Classic Golf Tips. Tommy Armour. 1994. 19.95 (*1-56943-009-8*, Tribune) Contemp Bks.

Classic Grimm's Fairy Tales. Jacob Grimm & Wilhelm K. Grimm. Ed. by L. Betts Egan. LC 89-43005. (Children's Classics Ser.). (Illus.). 56p. (J). (gr. 1-8). 1989. 9.98 (*0-89471-768-5*) Courage Bks.

Classic Groundwater Simulations: Proving & Improving Numerical Models. Genevieve Segol. LC 93-16938. 1993. text ed. 81.00 (*0-13-137993-3*) P-H.

Classic Guide to Fly-Fishing for Trout: The Fly-Fisher's Book of Quarry, Tackle & Techniques. Charles Jardine. 1991. 40.00 (*0-394-58719-7*) Random.

Classic Guitar Collection. Leonid Bolotine. (Illus.). 96p. 1977. pap. 12.95 (*0-8256-2268-9*, AM32657) Music Sales.

Classic Guitar Collection, Vol. 2. Leonid Bolotine. (Illus.). 128p. 1977. pap. 12.95 (*0-8256-2269-7*, AM32665) Music Sales.

Classic Guitar Collection, Vol. 3. Leonid Bolotine. (Illus.). 96p. 1977. pap. 12.95 (*0-8256-2270-0*, AM32673) Music Sales.

Classic Guitar Construction. rev. ed. Irving Sloane. (Illus.). 96p. 1989. reprint ed. pap. 13.95 (*0-933224-14-1*) Bold Strummer Ltd.

Classic Guitar Duets, MFM60. Harvey Vinson. (Illus.). 96p. 1973. pap. 12.95 (*0-8256-4060-1*, AM41724) Music Sales.

Classic Guitar in Tablature. Dennis Franco. (Editiones Classicae Ser.). (CHI, ENG, FRE, GER, JPN & SPA.). 1993. 5.95 (*0-87166-928-5*, 94098) Mel Bay.

Classic Guitar Manuscript Book. Date not set. 4.95 (*1-56222-995-8*, 95157) Mel Bay.

Classic Guitar Method, Vol. 1. Mel Bay. 1993. 4.95 (*0-87166-332-5*, 93207); audio 13.95 (*0-87166-334-1*, 93207); audio 9.98 (*0-87166-333-3*, 93207) Mel Bay.

Classic Guitar Method, Vol. 2. Mel Bay. 1993. 4.95 (*0-87166-335-X*, 93208) Mel Bay.

Classic Guitar Method, Vol. 3. Mel Bay. 1993. 4.95 (*1-56222-202-3*, 93209) Mel Bay.

Classic Guitar Solos in First & Second Position. Walt Lawry. 1993. 4.95 (*0-685-64357-3*, 93770) Mel Bay.

Classic Guitar Technique. Aaron Shearer. 82p. (Orig.). (YA). 1959. pap. text ed. 12.00 (*0-89898-572-2*) CPP Belwin.

Classic Guitar Technique, Vol. 2. Aaron Shearer. 160p. (Orig.). (YA). 1964. pap. 16.50 (*0-89898-573-0*) CPP Belwin.

Classic Guitars, U. S. A. A Primer for the Vintage Guitar Collector. Willie G. Moseley. LC 91-70519. (Illus.). 160p. (C). 1992. pap. text ed. 19.95 (*0-931759-52-8*, 00000139, Ctrstream) H Leonard.

Classic Haiku: A Master's Selection. Sel. by Yuzuru Miura. (Illus.). 120p. (Orig.). 1992. pap. 12.95 (*0-8048-1682-4*) C E Tuttle.

C

An Asterisk (*) at the beginning of an entry indicates that the title is appearing in BIP for the first time.

An Asterisk (*) at the beginning of an entry indicates that the title is appearing in BIP for the first time.

C

***Classic Search: 1920's-1948, Vol. 1.** 1994. per. 44.95 (*0-614-07082-1*) ADP-Hollander.

***Classic Search: 1946-1956, Vol. 2.** 1994. per. 44.95 (*0-614-07083-X*) ADP-Hollander.

Classic Sermons. Kenneth E. Hagin. 269p. 1992. pap. 6.95 (*0-89276-516-X*) Hagin Ministries.

Classic Sermons on Christian Service. Comp. by Warren W. Wiersbe. LC 90-36548. (Classic Sermons Ser.). 160p. 1990. pap. 8.99 (*0-8254-4041-6*) Kregel.

Classic Sermons on Faith & Doubt. Comp. by Warren W. Wiersbe. LC 85-9767. (Classic Sermons Ser.). 160p. 1985. pap. 8.99 (*0-8254-4028-9*) Kregel.

Classic Sermons on Family & Home. Warren W. Wiersbe. LC 92-39329. (Classic Sermons Ser.). 1993. 8.99 (*0-8254-4054-8*) Kregel.

Classic Sermons on Heaven & Hell. Warren W. Wiersbe. LC 94-3746. 160p. 1994. pap. 8.99 (*0-8254-3995-7*) Kregel.

Classic Sermons on Hope. Warren W. Wiersbe. LC 93-41452. 160p. 1994. pap. 8.99 (*0-8254-4045-9*) Kregel.

***Classic Sermons on Judas Iscariot.** Warren W. Wiersbe. LC 95-7814. (Classic Sermons Ser.). 160p. 1995. pap. 8.99 (*0-8254-4060-2*) Kregel.

Classic Sermons on Overcoming Fear. Warren W. Wiersbe. LC 91-111868. 160p. 1991. pap. 8.99 (*0-8254-4043-2*) Kregel.

Classic Sermons on Praise. Warren W. Wiersbe. LC 94-3745. 160p. 1994. pap. 8.99 (*0-8254-3994-9*) Kregel.

Classic Sermons on Prayer. Comp. by Warren W. Wiersbe. LC 87-3104. (Classic Sermons Ser.). 160p. 1987. pap. 8.99 (*0-8254-4029-7*) Kregel.

***Classic Sermons on Revival & Renewal.** Waren W. Wiersbe. 1995. pap. 8.99 (*0-8254-4062-9*) Kregel.

Classic Sermons on Spiritual Warfare. Comp. by Warren W. Wiersbe. LC 92-13765. (Classic Sermons Ser.). 160p. 1992. pap. 8.99 (*0-8254-4049-1*) Kregel.

Classic Sermons on Suffering. Comp. by Warren W. Wiersbe. LC 84-11260. (Classic Sermons Ser.). 204p. 1984. pap. 8.99 (*0-8254-4027-0*) Kregel.

***Classic Sermons on the Apostle Peter.** Warren W. Wiersbe. 160p. 1995. pap. 8.99 (*0-8254-3998-1*) Kregel.

Classic Sermons on the Attributes of God. Comp. by Warren W. Wiersbe. LC 88-12842. (Classic Sermons Ser.). 160p. 1989. pap. 8.99 (*0-8254-4038-6*) Kregel.

Classic Sermons on the Birth of Christ. Warren W. Wiersbe. LC 91-11816. (Classic Sermons Ser.). 160p. 1991. pap. 8.99 (*0-8254-4044-0*) Kregel.

Classic Sermons on the Cross of Christ. Comp. by Warren W. Wiersbe. LC 90-37887. (Classic Sermons Ser.). 160p. 1990. pap. 8.99 (*0-8254-4040-8*) Kregel.

***Classic Sermons on the Miracles of Jesus.** Warren W. Wiersbe. 160p. 1995. pap. 8.99 (*0-8254-3999-X*) Kregel.

Classic Sermons on the Names of God. Warren W. Wiersbe. LC 92-39330. (Classic Sermons Ser.). 1993. pap. 8.99 (*0-8254-4052-1*) Kregel.

Classic Sermons on the Prodigal Son. Comp. by Warren W. Wiersbe. LC 90-30403. (Classic Sermons Ser.). 153p. 1990. pap. 8.99 (*0-8254-4039-4*) Kregel.

Classic Sermons on the Resurrection of Christ. Comp. by Warren W. Wiersbe. LC 90-20619. 1991. pap. 8.99 (*0-8254-4042-4*) Kregel.

Classic Sermons on the Second Coming & Other Prophetic Themes. Comp. by Warren W. Wiersbe. LC 92-15173. (Classic Sermons Ser.). 1992. pap. 8.99 (*0-8254-4051-3*) Kregel.

Classic Sermons on the Sovereignty of God. Ed. by Warren W. Wiersbe. LC 93-41445. 160p. 1994. pap. 8.99 (*0-8254-4055-6*) Kregel.

Classic Sermons on Worship. Comp. & Intro. by Warren W. Wiersbe. LC 87-29721. (Classic Sermons Ser.). 160p. 1988. pap. 8.99 (*0-8254-4037-8*) Kregel.

Classic Shirley Temple-Paperdolls. Grayce Piemontes. (J). 1989. pap. 3.95 (*0-486-25193-4*) Dover.

***Classic Sitcoms: A Celebration of the Best in Prime-Time Comedy.** 2nd ed. Vince Waldron. (Illus.). 560p. 1995. pap. 18.95 (*1-879505-25-8*) Silman James Pr.

Classic Slave Narratives. Ed. by Henry L. Gates, Jr. 512p. 1987. pap. 5.99 (*0-451-62726-1*, Ment) NAL-Dutton.

***Classic Slum: Salford Life.** Robert Roberts. 1990. pap. 10.95 (*0-14-013624-X*, Penguin Bks) Viking Penguin.

Classic Slum: Salford Life in the First Quarter of the Century. Robert Roberts. 272p. 1973. pap. 7.95 (*0-14-021692-8*, Penguin Bks) Viking Penguin.

Classic Small Craft You Can Build. John Gardner. (Illus.). x, 194p. 1993. pap. 24.95 (*0-913372-66-8*) Mystic Seaport.

Classic Soul Winners New Testament with Helps, Black. 1989. 30.00 (*0-00-101988-0*) Anchor Bible Concepts.

***Classic Soul Winners New Testament with Helps, Burgundy.** 1989. 30.00 (*0-00-101984-8*) Anchor Bible Concepts.

Classic Southwest Cooking: Over 200 Succulent Recipes Celebrating America's Great Regional Cuisine. Carolyn Dille & Susan Belsinger. LC 92-39924. 264p. 1993. pap. 14.95 (*1-55958-291-X*) Prima Pub.

Classic Spanish Cooking with Chef Ef. Efrain Martinez. LC 93-20469. (Illus.). 288p. 1993. 21.95 (*1-56565-084-0*) Lowell Hse.

Classic Spanish Cooking with Chef Ef. Efrain Martinez. (Illus.). 288p. 1994. pap. 15.00 (*1-56565-119-7*) Lowell Hse.

Classic Standards: Piano - Vocal - Guitar. Ed. by Milton Okun. (Illus.). 111p. (Orig.). 1990. pap. text ed. 12.95 (*0-89524-365-2*) Cherry Lane.

***Classic Star Wars, Bk. 1.** 2nd ed. Archie Goodwin. (Illus.). 196p. 1995. pap. 16.95 (*1-56971-109-7*) Dark Horse Comics.

***Classic Star Wars: A New Hope.** George Lucas. 272p. 1995. 16.00 (*0-345-40077-1*, Del Rey) Ballantine.

***Classic Star Wars: Return of the Jedi.** James Kahn. 240p. 1995. 16.00 (*0-345-40079-8*, Del Rey) Ballantine.

***Classic Star Wars: The Empire Strikes Back.** Donald F. Glut. 224p. 1995. 16.00 (*0-345-40078-X*, Del Rey) Ballantine.

***Classic Star Wars: The Han Solo Adventures, 3 bks. in 1.** Brian Daley. 566p. 1994. pap. 10.00 (*0-345-39442-9*, Del Rey) Ballantine.

***Classic Star Wars: The Lando Calrissian Adventures, 3 bks. in 1.** Neil L. Smith & Crichton. 410p. 1994. pap. 10.00 (*0-345-39443-7*, Del Rey) Ballantine.

***Classic Star Wars Bk. 2: The Rebel Storm.** Archie Goodwin. (Illus.). 208p. 1995. pap. 16.95 (*1-56971-106-2*) Dark Horse Comics.

***Classic Star Wars Vol. 1.** Archie Goodwin. (Illus.). Date not set. pap. 15.95 (*1-56971-017-1*) Dark Horse Comics.

Classic Stenciling with Bronze Powders. Marie Skinner. (Illus.). 24p. 1985. pap. 5.95 (*0-941284-28-X*) J Shaw Studio.

***Classic Step by Step Cooking.** Moyra Fraser. 1994. 19.99 (*0-517-12116-6*) Random Hse Value.

Classic Studies in Abnormal Psychology. Steven Schwartz. LC 92-49375. 254p. (C). 1993. pap. text ed. 20.95 (*0-87484-866-0*) Mayfield Pub.

Classic Studies in American Foreign Relations (Vols. 1-6), 6 vols. 2096p. 1991. pap. write for info. (*1-879176-06-8*) Imprint Pubns.

Classic Studies in Psychology. Steven Schwartz. LC 86-62208. 196p. (C). 1986. pap. text ed. 19.95 (*0-87484-796-6*) Mayfield Pub.

Classic Studies on American Foreign Relations, 7 vols. 2432p. 1992. pap. 99.00 (*1-879176-13-0*) Imprint Pubns.

Classic Tailoring Techniques: A Construction Guide for Men's Wear. Roberto Cabrera & Patricia Meyers. (Illus.). 260p. (C). 1983. text ed. 26.50 (*0-87005-431-7*) Fairchild.

Classic Tailoring Techniques: A Construction Guide for Women's Wear. Roberto Cabrera & Patricia Meyers. (Illus.). 285p. (C). 1984. text ed. 26.50 (*0-87005-435-X*) Fairchild.

Classic Tale of the Velveteen Rabbit. Margery Williams. (J). 1991. 5.98 (*1-56138-069-5*) Courage Bks.

Classic Tales: 4,000 Years of Jewish Lore. Ellen Frankel. LC 88-35119. 704p. 1995. pap. 29.95 (*1-56821-038-8*) Aronson.

Classic Tales Literature Set, 6 stories. Ed. by L. Johnson. (Graphic Learning Literature Program Ser.). (Illus.). (ENG & SPA.). 1992. 225.00 (*0-87746-302-6*) Graphic Learning.

Classic Tales of Horror & the Supernatural. Ed. by Barry Malzberg & Martin H. Greenberg. 608p. 1991. pap. 15.00 (*0-688-10963-2*, Quill) Morrow.

Classic Tales of Mulla Nasreddin. Farzad Houman. Tr. by Diane L. Wilcox. (Illus.). 128p. (Orig.). 1990. pap. 8.00 (*0-939214-59-8*) Mazda Pubs.

Classic Tarot. Stuart R. Kaplan. 20p. 1971. 12.95 (*0-913866-54-7*) US Games Syst.

Classic Tarot Spreads. Sandor Konraad. Ed. by Marah Ren. LC 84-62282. (Illus.). 160p. (Orig.). 1985. pap. 12.95 (*0-914918-64-8*, Whitford Pr) Schiffer.

***Classic Teachings in Clinical Cardiology: A Tribute to W. Proctor Harvey.** Ed. by Michael A. Chizner. 1995. write for info. (*1-886128-06-5*) Laennec Pub.

***Classic Techniques for Fine Cooking.** Faye Levy. LC 94-28039. (California Culinary Academy Ser.). (Illus.). 128p. 1995. pap. 11.95 (*1-56426-071-2*) Cole Group.

***Classic Teddy Bear Designs: Heirlooms to Make & Dress.** Estelle Worrell. (Illus.). 150p. 1994. pap. 12.95 (*0-87588-283-8*, 3306) Hobby Hse.

Classic Textile Designs. 1989. 19.99 (*0-517-69329-1*) Random Hse Value.

Classic Texts & the Nature of Authority: An Account of a Principals' Institute Conducted by the Dallas Institute of Humanities & Culture on the Campus of the University of Dallas, June 22-July, 8, 1990. Ed. by Donald Cowan & Louise Cowan. LC 93-34910. 1993. write for info. (*0-911005-23-4*) Dallas Inst Pubns.

***Classic Texts in Mission & World Christianity.** Ed. by Norman E. Thomas. LC 94-44033. (American Society of Missiology Ser.: 20). 368p. (Orig.). 1995. pap. 24.95 (*1-57075-006-8*) Orbis Bks.

Classic Thai Cuisine. David Thompson. LC 93-1770. (Illus.). 1993. 15.95 (*0-89815-563-0*) Ten Speed Pr.

Classic Themes of Disciples Theology: Rethinking the Traditional Affirmations of the Christian Church (Disciples of Christ) Ed. by Kenneth Lawrence. LC 85-50712. 150p. 1986. text ed. 20.00 (*0-87565-024-4*) Tex Christian.

Classic Theory in Sociology. George Ritzer. 1992. text ed. write for info. (*0-07-052972-8*) McGraw.

Classic Touch. John K. Clemens. 240p. 1991. pap. 17.00 (*1-55623-685-9*) Irwin Prof Pubng.

Classic Toys in Wood: Projects & Plans. Janet A. Strombeck & Richard H. Strombeck. LC 94-25808. (Illus.). 96p. 1994. pap. 10.95 (*0-8069-0622-7*) Sterling.

***Classic Tractor Collectors: Restoring & Preserving Farm Power from the Past.** John Harvey. LC 94-78878. 128p. 1994. text ed. 26.50 (*0-929355-56-3*) Am Soc Ag Eng.

Classic Tractors in Australia. Ian M. Johnston. (Illus.). 192p. 1993. 32.50 (*0-86417-543-4*, Pub. by Kangaroo Pr AT) Seven Hills Bk.

Classic Treasury of Children's Poetry. Ed. by Louise B. Egan. LC 89-83327. (Illus.). 56p. (J). (gr. 1 up). 1990. 9.98 (*0-89471-802-9*) Courage Bks.

Classic Treasury of Christmas. Illus. by Lynn B. Ferris. LC 91-19276. 48p. (J). 1991. 13.95 (*0-8249-8524-9*, Ideals Child); audio 17.95 (*0-8249-7453-0*, Ideals Child) Hambleton-Hill.

Classic Trek Crew Book. James Van Hise. 1993. pap. 14.95 (*1-55698-368-9*) Movie Pubs Servs.

Classic Trilogy of the American Southwest, 3 vols., Set. William Eastlake. 1991. pap. write for info. (*0-9627387-6-X*) Seven Wolves.

***Classic Trucks.** Nicholas Faith. (Illus.). 144p. 1995. 24.95 (*0-7603-0023-2*) Motorbooks Intl.

Classic TV Westerns: A Pictorial History. Ronald Jackson. LC 93-45775. (Citadel Press Film Ser.). 1994. pap. 17.95 (*0-8065-1486-8*, Citadel Pr) Carol Pub Group.

***Classic Type Faces & How to Use Them: Including 91 Complete Fonts.** J. I. Biegeleisen. LC 95-15727. Orig. Title: Art Directors' Workbook of Type Faces. 1995. pap. write for info. (*0-486-28727-0*) Dover.

Classic U. S. Imperforate Stamps. Jon Rose. (Illus.). 100p. (Orig.). 1990. pap. 14.95 (*0-940403-29-3*) Linns Stamp News.

Classic Vegetable Cookbook: A Comprehensive Guide to Selecting & Preparing Vegetables of Every Variety. Ruth A. Spear. LC 84-48195. (Illus.). 432p. 1989. reprint ed. pap. 17.00 (*0-06-091628-1*, PL) HarpC.

Classic Vegetarian Cookbook. Rose Elliot. LC 93-6085. (Illus.). 160p. 1994. 24.95 (*1-56458-486-0*) Dorling Kindersley.

Classic Vision: The Retreat from Extremity see Visions of Extremity in Modern Literature

***Classic Watch Deluxe.** First Glance Staff. Date not set. 11.98 (*1-55521-437-1*) Bk Sales Inc.

Classic Welsh Short Stories. Ed. by Gwyn Jones. 256p. 1992. reprint ed. pap. 9.95 (*0-19-282940-8*) OUP.

Classic Western American Paintings. Gerald Peters. LC 78-58003. 22p. 1979. pap. 15.00 (*0-933052-00-6*) G Peters Gallery.

Classic Wheat for Man Cookbook: 300 Ways with Stone Ground Wheat. Vernice G. Rosenvall et al. LC 75-17276. (Illus.). 224p. (Orig.). 1975. pap. 5.95 (*0-912800-16-X*) Woodbridge Pr.

Classic Wicker Furniture: The Complete 1898-1899 Illustrated Catalog of the Heywood Brothers & Wakefield Company. Heywood Brothers & Wakefield Co. Staff. (Antiques Ser.). (Illus.). 128p. 1982. reprint ed. pap. 6.95 (*0-486-24355-9*) Dover.

Classic Wildfowl Decoy-Postcards. Karla Friedlich. 1989. pap. 3.95 (*0-486-26143-3*) Dover.

Classic Wildlife Photography. Intro. by David Hosking. 128p. (C). 1988. 130.00 (*1-85368-033-8*, Pub. by New Holland Pubs UK) St Mut.

Classic Wood Structures. Ed. by ASCE, Structural Division, Committee on Wood, Task Committee on Classic Wood Structures. 256p. 1989. pap. text ed. 22.00 (*0-87262-739-X*) Am Soc Civil Eng.

Classic Wreaths. Judi Williams. 1992. pap. 11.95 (*0-937769-24-X*) Mark Inc CA.

***Classic Writings of Oswald Chambers: Daily Meditations for Morning & Evening.** Oswald Chambers. 1994. 12.98 (*0-88486-102-3*) Arrowood Pr.

***Classic Writings on Instructional Technology.** Donald P. Ely & Tjeerd Plomp. (Instructional Technology Ser.). 225p. 1995. lib. bdg. 45.00 (*1-56308-230-6*) Libs Unl.

Classic Yacht Interiors: A Reissue. Jill Bobrow & Dana Jinkins. (Illus.). 256p. 1993. 50.00 (*0-393-03274-4*) Norton.

Classic Yamaha DX7. Lorenz Rychner. 93p. (C). 1987. pap. 19.95 (*0-939067-05-6*) Alexander Pub.

Classic Years of Robert A. Heinlein. George E. Slusser. LC 77-24626. (Milford Series: Popular Writers of Today: Popular Writers of Today: Vol. 11). 63p. 1977. lib. bdg. 20.00 (*0-89370-116-5*); pap. 10.00 (*0-89370-216-1*) Borgo Pr.

***Classic Yes - Selections from Yes Years.** (Authentic Guitar Tab Ser.). 112p. (Orig.). 1994. pap. 24.95 (*0-89724-252-1*) Warner Brothers.

***Classic Yiddish Fiction: Abromovitsch, Sholem Aleichem, & Peretz.** Ken Frieden. (Series in Modern Jewish Literature & Culture). (Illus.). 288p. (C). 1995. text ed. 59.50x (*0-7914-2601-7*); pap. 19.95x (*0-7914-2602-5*) State U NY Pr.

***Classic 1-2-3 Macros.** 3rd ed. E Michael Lunsford. 1995. pap. text ed. 24.95 (*0-471-06398-3*) Wiley.

Classic 1000 Baby Names. Foulsham Staff. 320p. 1993. 13.95 (*0-572-01838-X*, Pub. by W Foulsham UK) Trans-Atl Phila.

Classica Americana: The Greek & Roman Heritage in the United States. Meyer Reinhold. LC 83-197790. 370p. 1984. 34.95 (*0-8143-1744-8*) Wayne St U Pr.

Classical Abstract Algebra. Richard A. Dean. 576p. (C). 1990. text ed. 67.50 (*0-06-041601-7*) HarpCollege.

Classical Accounts of India: Rome, Greek. R. C. Majam-Majumdar. reprint ed. 18.50 (*0-8364-0704-0*, Pub. by Mukhopadhyaya II) S Asia.

Classical Age of German Literature, 1740-1815. Victor Lange. LC 82-15734. 256p. (Orig.). (C). 1982. 35.00 (*0-8419-0853-2*); pap. 19.50 (*0-8419-0854-0*) Holmes & Meier.

Classical Age of Islam see Venture of Islam

***Classical Algorithms in C++ With New Approaches to Sorting, Searching & Selection.** Nicholas Wilt. Date not set. text ed. 34.95 (*0-471-10985-1*) Wiley.

Classical American Philosophy: Essential Readings & Interpretive Essays. Ed. by John J. Stuhr. 496p. 1987. pap. 28.00 (*0-19-504198-4*) OUP.

Classical Analysis: Proceedings of 6th Symposium, Kazimierz Dolny, Poland, 23-29 September 1991. Ed. by T. Mazur. 400p. 1992. text ed. 109.00 (*981-02-0983-5*) World Scientific Pub.

***Classical Analysis on Normed Spaces.** Tsoy-Wo Ma. LC 94-44467. 376p. 1995. text ed. 74.00 (*981-02-2137-1*) World Scientific Pub.

Classical Anarchism: The Political Thought of Godwin, Proudhon, Bakunin, & Kropotkin. George Crowder. 224p. 1992. 49.95 (*0-19-827744-X*) OUP.

Classical Anatolia: The Glory of Hellenism. Harry Brewster. 224p. 1994. text ed. 49.50 (*1-85043-773-4*, Pub. by I B Tauris UK) St Martin.

Classical & Christian Ideas in English Renaissance Poetry. Isabel Rivers. 1979. pap. text ed. 15.95 (*0-04-807003-3*) Routledge Chapman & Hall.

Classical & Christian Ideas in English Renaissance Poetry: A Student's Guide. 2nd ed. Isabell Rivers. LC 94-12710. 240p. 1995. 59.00x (*0-415-10646-X*, B7069); pap. 16.95x (*0-415-10647-8*, B7073) Routledge.

Classical & Contemporary Italian Cooking. Bruno Ellmer. 1990. text ed. 44.95 (*0-442-20642-9*) Van Nos Reinhold.

Classical & Contemporary Readings in Philosophy of Religion. 3rd ed. John H. Hick. 176p. (C). 1989. Casebound. boxed, text ed. 48.00 (*0-13-136904-0*) P-H.

Classical & Contemporary Social Theory: A Critical Perspective. Berch Berberoglu. LC 92-76215. 166p. (Orig.). 1993. text ed. 34.95 (*1-882289-07-2*); pap. text ed. 16.95 (*1-882289-06-4*) Gen Hall.

***Classical & Fertility Dance Photos, with Dance Costume Index.** Marjorie M. Gilfillan. (Illus.). 200p. 1995. write for info. (*0-930887-24-7*) Wenzel Pr.

Classical & Foreign Quotations. W. F. King. 1972. lib. bdg. 59.95 (*0-87968-877-7*) Gordon Pr.

Classical & Marxian Political Economy. Ed. by Ian Bradley & Michael C. Howard. LC 81-14334. 296p. 1982. text ed. 32.50 (*0-312-14261-7*) St Martin.

Classical & Mediaeval Studies in Honor of Edward Kennard Rand, Presented upon the Completion of His Fortieth Year of Teaching. Ed. by L. W. Jones. LC 68-57312. (Essay Index Reprint Ser.). 1977. 23.95 (*0-8369-0312-9*) Ayer.

Classical & Medieval Literary Criticism, Vol. 1. Dennis Poupard & Jelena Kronick. 1987. 114.00 (*0-8103-2350-8*) Gale.

Classical & Medieval Literary Criticism, Vol. 4. Ed. by Jelena O. Krstovic. 500p. 1990. lib. bdg. 114.00 (*0-8103-2353-2*) Gale.

Classical & Medieval Literary Criticism, Vol. 6. Jelena O. Krstovic. 1991. 114.00 (*0-8103-7516-8*, 004207-M99406) Gale.

Classical & Medieval Literary Criticism, Vol. 7. Jelena O. Krstovic. 1991. 114.00 (*0-8103-7517-6*) Gale.

Classical & Medieval Literary Criticism, Vol. 8. Jelena O. Krstovic. 1992. 114.00 (*0-8103-7518-4*) Gale.

Classical & Medieval Literary Criticism, Vol. 9. Jelena O. Krstovic. 1992. 114.00 (*0-8103-7519-2*) Gale.

Classical & Medieval Literary Criticism, Vol. 10. Jelena O. Krstovic. 1993. 114.00 (*0-8103-7956-2*) Gale.

Classical & Medieval Literary Criticism, Vol. 11. Jelena O. Krstovic. 1993. 114.00 (*0-8103-7957-0*) Gale.

Classical & Medieval Literary Criticism, Vol. 12. Jelena O. Krstovic. 1994. 114.00 (*0-8103-2433-4*) Gale.

Classical & Medieval Literary Criticism, Vol. 13. Jelena O. Krstovic. 1994. 114.00 (*0-8103-2434-2*) Gale.

Classical & Medieval Literature Criticism, Vol. 2. Ed. by Jelena O. Krstovic. 1988. 114.00 (*0-8103-2351-6*) Gale.

Classical & Medieval Literature Criticism, Vol. 3. Ed. by Jelena O. Krstovic. 1989. 114.00 (*0-8103-2352-4*) Gale.

Classical & Medieval Literature Criticism, Vol. 5. Ed. by Jelena O. Krstovic. LC 88-658021. (Illus.). 490p. 1990. 114.00 (*0-8103-2354-0*) Gale.

***Classical & Medieval Literature Criticism, Vol. 14.** Jelena Krstovic. 450p. 1995. 114.00 (*0-8103-4877-2*) Gale.

Classical & Middle Armenian Bird Names. John A. Greppin. LC 77-25361. 1978. 35.00 (*0-88206-017-1*) Caravan Bks.

Classical & Modern Control Through Worked Examples. J. P. Elloy & J. M. Piasco. (International Series on Systems & Control: Vol. 3). (Illus.). 200p. 1981. text ed. 90.00 (*0-08-026745-9*, Pub. by Pergamon Repr UK) Franklin.

Classical & Modern Foreign Languages: Common Areas & Problems see Culture, Literature, & Articulation

Classical & Modern Interactions: Postmodern Architecture, Multiculturalism, Decline, & Other Issues. Karl Galinsky. LC 92-11516. (Illus.). 204p. 1992. text ed. 35.00 (*0-292-77053-7*) U of Tex Pr.

Classical & Modern Mechanisms for Engineers & Inventors. Preben W. Jensen. (Mechanical Engineering Ser.: Vol. 75). 616p. 1991. 125.00 (*0-8247-8527-4*) Dekker.

Classical & Modern Potential Theory & Applications: Proceedings of the NATO Advanced Research Workshop, Chateau de Bonas, France, July 25-31, 1993. Ed. by K. GowriSankaran. (NATO ASI Series C: Mathematical & Physical Sciences). 484p. (C). 1994. lib. bdg. 186.00 (*0-7923-2803-5*) Kluwer Ac.

Classical & New Inequalities in Analysis. D. S. Mitrinovic. (Mathematics & Its Applications East European Ser.). 760p. (C). 1992. lib. bdg. 285.00 (*0-7923-2064-6*) Kluwer Ac.

***Classical & Object-Oriented Software Engineering.** 3rd ed. Stephen R. Schach. LC 94-46905. 640p. (C). 1995. 55.00 (*0-256-18298-1*) Irwin.

Classical & Quantum Dynamics: From Classical Paths to Path Integrals. 2nd enl. ed. W. Dittrich & M. Reuter. ix, 361p. 1994. pap. 39.00 (*0-387-56245-1*) Spr-Verlag.

Classical & Quantum Effects in Electrodynamics. Ed. by A. A. Komar. (Proceedings of the Lebedev Physics Institute Ser.: Vol. 176). 281p. 1988. text ed. 116.00 (*0-941743-11-X*) Nova Sci Pubs.

Classical & Quantum Field Theory of Exactly Soluble Non-Linear Systems. P. Garbaczewski. 260p. 1985. text ed. 60.00 (*9971-966-55-7*) World Scientific Pub.

Classical & Quantum Gravity: Proceedings of the 1st Iberian Meeting on Gravity. M. C. Bento & O. Bertolami. 356p. 1993. text ed. 109.00 (*981-02-1369-7*) World Scientific Pub.

Classical & Quantum Systems - Foundations & Symmetries: Proceedings of the 2nd International Wigner Symposium. W. Scherer et al. 816p. 1993. text ed. 137.00 (*981-02-1099-X*) World Scientific Pub.

An Asterisk (*) at the beginning of an entry indicates that the title is appearing in BIP for the first time.

An Asterisk (*) at the beginning of an entry indicates that the title is appearing in BIP for the first time.

Classical Influence on the Public Architecture of Washington & Paris: A Comparison of Two Capital Cities. John E. Ziolkowski. (American University Studies: Fine Arts: Ser. XX, Vol. 4). 259p. (C). 1988. text ed. 42.50 (*0-8204-0598-1*) P Lang Pubs.

Classical Influences on English Prose. James A. Thomson. 1988. reprint ed. lib. bdg. 49.00 (*0-7812-0567-0*) Rprt Serv.

Classical Influences on English Prose. James A. Thomson. reprint ed. 49.00 (*0-403-07244-1*) Somerset Pub.

Classical Influences on European Culture, 1500-1700 A. D. Ed. by R. R. Bolgar. (Illus.). 300p. 1976. 79.95 (*0-521-20840-8*) Cambridge U Pr.

***Classical Ingenuity: The Legacy of Greek & Roman Architects, Artists, & Inventors.** Charles F. Baker, III & Rosalie F. Baker. (Illus.). 160p. 1994. pap. 17.50 (*0-942389-07-7*) Cobblestone Pub.

Classical Insurance Solvency Theory. Ed. by J. David Cummins & Richard A. Derrig. (C). 1988. lib. bdg. 54. 50 (*0-89838-272-6*) Huebner Foun Insur.

Classical Insurance Solvency Theory. J. David Cummins & R. A. Derrig. (C). 1988. 290.00 (*0-685-33730-8*, Pub. by Witherby & Co UK) St Mut.

Classical Introduction to Modern Number Theory. K. Ireland & Michael J. Rosen. (Graduate Texts in Mathematics Ser.: Vol. 84). (Illus.). 341p. 1982. 45.00 (*0-387-90625-8*) Spr-Verlag.

Classical Introduction to Modern Number Theory. 2nd ed. K. Ireland & Marcia Rosen. Ed. by J. H. Ewing et al. (Graduate Texts in Mathematics Ser.: Vol. 84). (Illus.). xiv, 392p. 1993. text ed. 49.95 (*0-387-97329-X*) Spr-Verlag.

Classical Italian Songs. A. M. Gisolfi & C. Coleman. 1955. 25.00 (*0-913298-64-6*) S F Vanni.

Classical Japanese Prose: An Anthology. Ed. by Helen C. McCullough. LC 89-78331. (Illus.). 596p. 1990. 65.00 (*0-8047-1628-5*); pap. 19.95 (*0-8047-1960-8*) Stanford U Pr.

Classical Keynesianism: Monetary Theory & the Price Level. Sidney Weintraub. LC 72-2573. (Illus.). 190p. 1973. reprint ed. text ed. 52.50 (*0-8371-6421-4*, WECK, Greenwood Pr) Greenwood.

Classical Kinetic Theory of Fluids. Pierre Resibois & M. DeLeener. LC 76-58852. 430p. reprint ed. pap. 122.60 (*0-317-55610-X*, 2056350) Bks Demand.

Classical King's Indian. John Nunn. 96p. 1990. pap. 14.95 (*0-02-035540-8*, Collier S&S) S&S Trade.

Classical Korean Poems (SIJO) rev. ed. Kim Unsong. LC 87-60115. (Illus.). 232p. 1987. 15.00 (*0-942049-00-4*) One Mind Pr.

Classical Korean Poetry. Tr. by Jaihiun Kim. LC 94-31949. 240p. (C). 1995. pap. text ed. 25.00 (*0-87573-056-6*, Asian Human Pr) Jain Pub Co.

Classical Language of Architecture. John Summerson. (Illus.). 1966. pap. 6.95 (*0-262-69012-8*) MIT Pr.

Classical Learning & Taoist Practices in Early Japan, with Translation of Books XVI & XX of the Engi-Shiki. Felicia G. Bock. LC 82-84464. (Occasional Paper Arizona State Univ., Center for Asian Studies: No. 17). 102p. 1985. pap. 10.00 (*0-939252-13-9*) ASU Ctr Asian.

Classical Legacy in Renaissance Poetry. Robin Sowerby. LC 93-34667. (Medieval & Renaissance Library). 320p. (C). 1994. pap. text ed. 29.25 (*0-685-72590-1*, 76456) Longman.

Classical Lexicon for Finnegans Wake: A Glossary of the Greek & Latin in the Major Works of Joyce, Including Finnegans Wake, the Poems, Dubliners, Stephen Hero, a Portrait of the Artist as a Young Man, Exiles, & Ulysses. Brendan O'Hehir & John M. Dillon. LC 77-372235. 675p. reprint ed. pap. 180.00 (*0-7837-4691-1*, 2044438) Bks Demand.

Classical Light Scattering from Polymer Solutions. P. Kratochvil. (Polymer Science Library: Vol. 5). 1987. 128.25 (*0-444-42890-9*) Elsevier.

Classical Literary Criticism. Incl. Aristotle Poetics, Longinus on the Sublime, Demetrius on Style. Aristotle. 1965. (*0-318-55019-9*); Ars Poetica. Horace. 1965. (*0-318-55020-2*); On the Sublime. Longinus. 1965. (*0-318-55021-0*); (Classics Ser.). 1965. Set mass mkt. 8.95 (*0-14-044155-7*, Penguin Classics) Viking Penguin.

Classical Literary Criticism. Ed. by Donald A. Russell & M. Winterbottom. (World's Classics Ser.). 272p. 1990. pap. 6.95 (*0-19-281830-9*) OUP.

***Classical Mandolin.** Paul Sparks. (Illus.). 240p. 1995. 44. 95 (*0-19-816295-2*) OUP.

***Classical Mechanics.** Tai L. Chow. LC 94-39839. 1995. text ed. write for info. (*0-471-04365-6*) Wiley.

Classical Mechanics. Brian Cowan. (Student Physics Ser.). (Illus.). 128p. (Orig.). 1984. pap. 12.95 (*0-7102-0280-6*, RKP) Routledge.

Classical Mechanics. Douglas A. Davis. 451p. (C). 1986. text ed. 59.00 (*0-15-507630-2*) SCP.

Classical Mechanics. K. M. Khanna. 240p. (Orig.). 1979. 19.00 (*0-317-64524-2*, Pub. by Today & Tomorrows P & P II) Scholarly Pubns.

Classical Mechanics. Lawrence Shepley & Richard Matzner. 256p. (C). 1991. text ed. 88.00 (*0-13-137076-6*, 530102) P-H.

Classical Mechanics. 2nd ed. H. C. Corben & Philip Stehle. (Illus.). 416p. 1994. reprint ed. pap. 10.95 (*0-486-68063-0*) Dover.

Classical Mechanics. 2nd ed. Herbert Goldstein. LC 79-23456. (Illus.). (C). 1980. text ed. 63.50 (*0-201-02918-9*) Addison-Wesley.

Classical Mechanics, Vol. 1. Edward A. Desloge. LC 88-12962. 538p. (C). 1989. reprint ed. lib. bdg. 57.50 (*0-89464-321-5*) Krieger.

Classical Mechanics, Vol. 2. Edward A. Desloge. LC 88-12969. 514p. (C). 1989. reprint ed. lib. bdg. 63.50 (*0-89464-322-3*) Krieger.

Classical Mechanics: A Modern Perspective. Vernon D. Barger & Martin G. Olsson. LC 72-5697. (Illus.). 352p. (C). 1973. text ed. write for info. (*0-07-003723-X*) McGraw.

***Classical Mechanics: A Modern Perspective.** 2nd ed. Vernon Barger. 1995. text ed. 60.75 (*0-07-003734-5*) McGraw.

***Classical Mechanics Simulations: The Consortium for Upper Level Physics Software.** Bruce Hawkins & Randall Jones. 1995. text ed. write for info. (*0-471-54881-2*) Wiley.

***Classical Mechanics with Maple.** Ronald L. Greene. LC 95-8322. 1995. write for info. (*0-387-94512-1*) Spr-Verlag.

Classical, Medieval, & Renaissance Foundations of Corasius' Systematic Methodology, Vol. 2. A. London Fell. LC 81-22332. (Origins of Legislative Sovereignty & the Legislative State Ser.: Vol. 2). 368p. 1991. text ed. 45.00 (*0-275-93972-3*, C3972, Praeger Pubs) Greenwood.

Classical Mediterranean Spirituality: Egyptian, Greek, Roman. Ed. by A. H. Armstrong. (World Spirituality Ser.). 499p. 1986. 49.50 (*0-8245-0764-9*) Crossroad NY.

Classical Methods, Pt. 1. John Mendham & David Derek. LC 86-28142. (Analytical Chemistry by Open Learning Ser.). 373p. 1987. pap. text ed. 63.95 (*0-471-91363-4*) Wiley.

Classical Methods, Vol. 2. John Mendham et al. (Analytical Chemistry by Open Learning Ser.). 351p. 1987. pap. text ed. 54.95 (*0-471-91365-0*) Wiley.

Classical Mind: Essays in Honour of Car Hoare. William Roscoe. 472p. 1994. text ed. 70.00 (*0-13-294844-3*) P-H.

Classical, Modern, & Humane: Essays in Chinese Literature. David Hawkes. Ed. by John Minford & Siu-kit Wong. 300p. 1986. text ed. 47.50 (*962-201-354-6*, Pub. by Chinese Univ HK) Coronet Bks.

Classical Modern Philosophers: Descartes to Kant. Richard Schacht. 270p. (Orig.). 1984. 15.95 (*0-7100-9959-2*, RKP) Routledge.

Classical Moment: Studies of Corneille, Moliere, & Racine. Martin Turnell. LC 79-138601. (Illus.). 261p. (C). 1971. reprint ed. text ed. 55.00 (*0-8371-5803-6*, TUCM, Greenwood Pr) Greenwood.

Classical Monologue: Men. Ed. by Michael Earley & Philippa Keil. 146p. 1992. pap. text ed. 9.95 (*0-87830-032-5*, A9674, Theatre Arts Bks) Routledge Chapman & Hall.

Classical Monologue: Women. Ed. by Michael Earley & Philipa Keil. 1992. pap. text ed. 9.95 (*0-87830-033-3*, A9678, Theatre Arts Bks) Routledge Chapman & Hall.

Classical Monologues for Men: From 16th, 17th & 18th Century Plays. Ed. by Kyle Donnelly. 130p. 1992. pap. 7.95 (*0-435-08619-7*, 08619) Heinemann.

Classical Monologues for Women: From 16th, 17th & 18th Century Plays. Ed. by Kyle Donnelly. 141p. 1992. pap. 7.95 (*0-435-08620-0*, 08620) Heinemann.

***Classical Moxibustion Skills in Contemporary Clinical Practice.** Sung Baek. Ed. & Pref. by James Ramholz. (Illus.). 59p. (Orig.). 1990. pap. 12.95 (*0-936185-16-3*) Blue Poppy.

Classical Music. Philip G. Downs. (C). 1992. text ed. 32.95 (*0-393-95191-X*) Norton.

Classical Music: A Concise History from Gluck to Beethoven. Julian Rushton. LC 86-50223. (World of Art Ser.). 192p. (Orig.). 1986. pap. 14.95 (*0-500-20210-9*) Thames Hudson.

***Classical Music: A New Way of Listening.** Alexander Waugh. LC 95-13143. 1995. write for info. (*0-02-860446-6*) Macmillan.

Classical Music: An Informal Guide. Richard Carlin. LC 92-1176. 1992. pap. 11.95 (*1-55652-148-0*) A cappella Bks.

Classical Music: An Introduction to Classical Music Through the Great Composers & Their Masterworks. John Stanley. LC 94-1931. (Illus.). 272p. 1994. 35.00 (*0-89577-606-5*) RD Assn.

Classical Music: The Fifty Greatest Composers & Their 1,000 Greatest Works. Phil G. Goulding. LC 92-90055. 688p. 1992. 25.00 (*0-449-90356-7*, Columbine) Fawcett.

***Classical Music: The 50 Greatest Composers & Their 1000 Greatest Works.** Phil G. Gooding. 656p. 1995. pap. 15. 00 (*0-449-91042-3*) Fawcett.

***Classical Music & Postmodern Knowledge.** Lawrence Kramer. (Illus.). 278p. 1995. 35.00 (*0-520-08820-4*) U CA Pr.

Classical Music Discographies, 1976-1988: A Bibliography. Comp. by Michael Gray. LC 89-11861. (Discographies Ser.: No. 34). 341p. 1989. text ed. 65.00 (*0-313-25942-9*, GCU/, Greenwood Pr) Greenwood.

Classical Music Fakebook. (Illus.). 160p. 1988. pap. 9.95 (*0-7119-1102-9*, AM65319) Music Sales.

Classical Music for Beginners. Stacy C. Lynch. 1994. pap. 9.95 (*0-86316-162-6*) Writers & Readers.

***Classical Music of North India.** George Ruckert. Ed. by Ali A. Khan. xiii, 367p. 1991. pap. 54.95 (*0-930997-02-6*) East Bay Bks.

***Classical Music Top 40.** Anthony J. Rudel. 1995. pap. 12. 00 (*0-671-79495-7*, Fireside) S&S Trade.

***Classical Myth.** Barry B. Powell. Ed. by Herbert M. Howe. LC 94-27441. 736p. 1994. pap. text ed. write for info. (*0-13-143470-5*) P-H.

Classical Myth & Legend in Renaissance Dictionaries. DeWitt T. Starnes & Ernest W. Talbert. LC 73-11753. (Illus.). 517p. 1973. reprint ed. text ed. 85.00 (*0-8371-7086-9*, STCM, Greenwood Pr) Greenwood.

Classical Myth & the "Polifemo" of Gongora. Melinda Lehrer. 130p. 1990. 39.50 (*0-916379-60-4*) Scripta.

Classical Mythology. 4th ed. Mark P. Morford & Robert J. Lenardon. 703p. (C). 1991. pap. text ed. 33.95 (*0-8013-0465-2*, 78280) Longman.

***Classical Mythology.** 5th ed. Mark Morford & Robert Lenardon. 608p. (C). 1994. text ed. 26.00 (*0-8013-1488-7*) Longman.

Classical Mythology. 5th ed. Mark P. Morford & Robert J. Lenardon. (Illus.). 608p. (C). 1995. pap. text ed. 31.95 (*0-8013-1138-1*) Longman.

***Classical Mythology: Images & Insights.** Stephen L. Harris & Gloria Platzner. LC 94-13224. 1065p. 1995. pap. text ed. 37.95 (*1-55934-146-7*) Mayfield Pub.

Classical Mythology in Shakespeare. Robert K. Root. LC 65-24996. 134p. 1965. reprint ed. 40.00 (*0-87752-096-8*) Gordian.

Classical Mythology in Shakespeare. Robert K. Root. (BCL1-PR English Literature Ser.). 134p. 1992. reprint ed. lib. bdg. 69.00 (*0-7812-7306-4*) Rprt Serv.

Classical Mythology in the Poetry of Edmund Spenser. Henry C. Lotspeich. LC 65-28856. (Princeton Studies in English: No. 9). 126p. 1965. reprint ed. 40.00 (*0-87752-064-X*) Gordian.

Classical Mythology in Twentieth-Century Thought & Literature. Ed. by Wendell M. Aycock & Theodore M. Klein. (Proceedings of the Comparative Literature Symposium Ser.: Vol. XI). (Illus.). 221p. (Orig.). 1980. pap. 12.00 (*0-89672-079-9*) Tex Tech Univ Pr.

Classical Mythology of Milton's English Poems. C. G. Osgood. (Reprints in History Ser.). reprint ed. lib. bdg. 36.00 (*0-697-00014-1*) Irvington.

Classical Mythology of Milton's English Poems. Charles G. Osgood. LC 64-8180. 198p. 1964. reprint ed. 50.00 (*0-87752-080-1*) Gordian.

Classical Mythology of Milton's English Poems. Charles G. Osgood. LC 65-15902. (Studies in Comparative Literature: No. 35). 1969. reprint ed. lib. bdg. 75.00 (*0-8383-0603-9*) M S G Haskell Hse.

Classical Mythology of Milton's English Poems. Charles G. Osgood. (BCL1-PR English Literature Ser.). 111p. 1992. reprint ed. lib. bdg. 69.00 (*0-7812-7387-0*) Rprt Serv.

Classical Myths in English Literature. Daniel S. Norton & Peters Rushton. LC 70-92305. 444p. 1969. reprint ed. text ed. 41.50 (*0-8371-2440-9*, NOCM, Greenwood Pr) Greenwood.

Classical No Theatre of Japan. Poh-Sim Plowright. (C). 1991. lib. bdg. 105.00 (*0-85964-203-8*) Chadwyck-Healey.

Classical Novels: The Macedonian & Scenes from the Life of Cleopatra. Mary Butts. 385p. 1994. 22.00 (*0-929701-43-7*); pap. 14.00 (*0-929701-42-9*) McPherson & Co.

Classical Organist, Vol. 2. Rick Parks. 1987. 8.95 (*0-685-71345-8*, MB-583) Lillenas.

Classical Organist, Vol. 3. Contrib by Rick Parks. 1989. 8.95 (*0-8341-9132-6*, MB-607) Lillenas.

Classical Organist, Vol. 4. Des. by Rick Parks. 1994. 8.95 (*0-8341-9029-X*, MB-675) Lillenas.

Classical Organist, Vol.1. Contrib by Rick Parks. 1985. 8.95 (*0-8341-9236-5*, MB-550) Lillenas.

Classical Orthogonal Polynomials of a Discrete Variable. A. F. Nikiforov et al. Ed. by R. Glowinski et al. (Computational Physics Ser.). (Illus.). 368p. 1992. text ed. 89.00 (*0-387-51123-7*) Spr-Verlag.

Classical Papers in Horticultural Science. Jules Janick. 450p. 1989. boxed 66.60 (*0-13-136847-8*) P-H.

Classical Papers of Gilbert Highet. Ed. by Robert J. Ball. LC 83-7181. 416p. 1983. text ed. 56.00 (*0-231-05104-2*) Col U Pr.

Classical Pastoral in the Visual Arts. Luba Freedman. (Hermeneutics of Art Ser.). 233p. (C). 1989. text ed. 51. 00 (*0-8204-1013-6*) P Lang Pubs.

Classical Period: Haydn, Mozart, Beethoven & Their Contemporaries. Denes Agay. (Anthology of Piano Music Ser.: Vol. 2). 236p. 1981. pap. 14.95 (*0-8256-8042-5*, Yorktown Mus) Music Sales.

Classical Period of the First British Empire, 1689-1783; The Foundations of a Colonial System of Government: Select Documents on the Constitutional History of the British Empire with Commonwealth, Vol. II. Ed. by Frederick Madden & David Fieldhouse. LC 84-21213. (Documents of Imperial History Ser.: No. 2). xxxvii, 628p. 1985. text ed. 105.00 (*0-313-25176-2*, MDL/) Greenwood.

***Classical Persian Literature.** Arberry. 1994. reprint ed. pap. 29.95 (*0-7007-0276-8*, Pub. by Curzon Pr UK) Humanities.

Classical Persian Music: An Introduction. Ella Zonis. LC 76-188350. (Illus.). 248p. reprint ed. pap. 71.60 (*0-7837-1740-7*, 2057270) Bks Demand.

Classical Persian Sufisu-from Its Origins to Rumi. Ed. by Leonard Lewisohn. (Illus.). 708p. 1994. 49.95 (*0-933546-50-5*); pap. 29.95 (*0-933546-51-3*) KNP.

Classical Philosophical Questions. 8th ed. James Gould. (Illus.). 640p. (C). 1995. pap. write for info. (*0-02-345474-1*) Macmillan.

***Classical Philosophy: Collected Papers, 8 vols.** Incl. Vol. 1. Philosophy Before Socrates. Ed. by Terence Irwin. LC 95-5168. 496p. 1995. 75.00 (*0-8153-1829-4*); Vol. 2. Socrates & His Contemporaries. Ed. by Terence Irwin. LC 95-5168. 560p. 1995. reprint ed. 84.00 (*0-8153-1830-8*); Vol. 3. Plato's Ethics. Ed. by Terence Irwin. LC 95-5168. 432p. 1995. reprint ed. 68.00 (*0-8153-1832-4*); Vol. 4. Plato's Metaphysics & Epistemology. Terence Irwin. LC 95-5168. 448p. 1995. 68.00 (*0-8153-1833-2*); Vol. 5. Aristotle's Ethics. Terence Irwin. LC 95-5168. 432p. 1995. 69.00 (*0-8153-1834-0*); Vol. 6. Aristotle: Substance, Form & Matter. Terence Irwin. LC 95-5168. 344p. 1995. 57.00 (*0-8153-1835-9*); Vol. 7. Aristotle: Metaphysics, Epistemology, Natural Philosophy. Terence Irwin. LC 95-5168. 456p. 1995. 72.00 (*0-8153-1836-7*); Vol. 8. Hellenistic Philosophy. Terence Irwin. LC 95-5168. 448p. 1995. 71.00 (*0-8153-1837-5*); LC 95-5168. write for info. (*0-614-03884-7*) Garland.

***Classical Piano Solos, Vol. 8.** Ed. by Stephen Harding. 48p. (Orig.). 1995. pap. 9.95 (*0-7119-4497-0*, AM 92420, Pub. by Wise Publns UK) Omnibus NY.

***Classical Piano Solos Collection, Vol. 7.** Ed. by Stephen Harding. 48p. (Orig.). 1995. pap. 9.95 (*0-7119-4496-2*, AM 92419, Pub. by Wise Publns UK) Omnibus NY.

Classical Piano Solos for Worship Settings. Comp. by Gail Smith. 1993. 6.95 (*1-56222-319-4*, 94672); audio 9.98 (*1-56222-459-X*, 94672) Mel Bay.

Classical Planar Scattering by Coulombic Potentials. M. Klein & A. Knauf. LC 92-36357. (Lecture Notes in Physics, Monographs: Vol. 13). 1992. 42.00 (*0-387-55987-6*) Spr-Verlag.

Classical Political Theories: From Plato to Marx. Robert Brown. Ed. by Paul Edwards. 807p. (C). 1990. pap. write for info. (*0-02-315591-4*) Macmillan.

Classical Potential Theory & Its Probabilistic Counterpart. Joseph L. Doob. (Grundlehren der Mathematischen Wissenschaften Ser.: Vol. 262). 750p. 1984. 108.00 (*0-387-90881-1*) Spr-Verlag.

Classical Principles & Optimization Problems. B. S. Razumikhin. (C). 1987. lib. bdg. 198.50 (*90-277-2605-1*) Kluwer Ac.

Classical Probability in the Enlightenment. Lorraine Daston. (Illus.). 400p. 1988. 60.00 (*0-691-08497-1*) Princeton U Pr.

Classical Real Analysis. Ed. by D. Waterman. LC 85-9241. (Contemporary Mathematics Ser.: No. 42). 216p. 1985. pap. text ed. 33.00 (*0-8218-5045-8*, CONM-42) Am Math.

Classical Records: Starting Your Collection. Gerald Brennan. LC 83-70327. 112p. (Orig.). 1983. pap. 6.95 (*0-89708-116-1*) And Bks.

Classical Recursion Theory: The Theory Functions & Sets of Natural Numbers. P. G. Odifreddi. (Studies in Logic & the Foundations of Mathematics: No. 125). 668p. 1989. 107.75 (*0-444-87295-7*, North Holland) Elsevier.

Classical Reproducing Piano Roll: A Catalogue - Index. Comp. by Larry Sitsky. LC 89-28651. (Music Reference Collection Ser.: No. 23). 1440p. 1990. text ed. 195.00 (*0-313-25496-6*, SCD/, Greenwood Pr) Greenwood.

Classical Reproducing Piano Roll, Vol. 1: A Catalogue-Index: Composers. Comp. by Larry Sitsky. LC 89-28651. (Music Reference Collection Ser.: No. 23). 632p. 1990. text ed. 195.00 (*0-313-27312-X*, SCD01, Greenwood Pr) Greenwood.

Classical Reproducing Piano Roll. Vol. 2: A Catalogue-Index: Pianists, Vol. 2. Comp. by Larry Sitsky. LC 89-28651. (Music Reference Collection Ser.: No. 23). 1990. text ed. 195.00 (*0-313-27313-8*, SCD02, Greenwood Pr) Greenwood.

Classical Rhetoric & Its Christian & Secular Tradition from Ancient to Modern Times. George A. Kennedy. LC 79-9295. xii, 291p. 1980. 32.50 (*0-8078-1401-6*); pap. 12.95 (*0-8078-4058-0*) U of NC Pr.

Classical Rhetoric & Medieval Historiography. Ed. by Ernst Breisach. LC 85-3055. (Studies in Medieval Culture: No. 19). 1985. 17.95 (*0-918720-56-7*); pap. 10. 95 (*0-918720-57-5*) Medieval Inst.

Classical Rhetoric for the Modern Student. 3rd ed. Edward P. Corbett. 616p. (C). 1990. text ed. 28.00 (*0-19-506293-0*) OUP.

Classical Rhetoric in English Poetry. 2nd ed. Brian Vickers. 1989. reprint ed. text ed. 24.50 (*0-8093-1495-9*); reprint ed. pap. text ed. 14.95 (*0-8093-1496-7*) S Ill U Pr.

Classical Riding Notebook. Michael J. Stevens. (Illus.). 128p. 1994. 34.95 (*1-872082-50-5*, Pub. by Kenilworth Pr UK) Half Halt Pr.

Classical Riffs for Guitar. Jesse Gress. (Illus.). 64p. 1989. pap. 12.95 (*0-8256-2543-2*, AM71291) Music Sales.

Classical Riffs for Rock Guitar. Wolf Marshall. (Illus.). 24p. 1990. audio, pap. 14.95 (*0-8256-1155-5*, AM67463) Music Sales.

Classical Rome. Ed. by John D. Clare. LC 92-30502. (Living History Ser.). (J). 1993. 16.95 (*0-15-200513-7*, Gulliver Bks) HarBrace.

Classical Rome Comes Alive. Ed. by Hildegarde W. Roberts. LC 92-13233. (Illus.). 200p. (Orig.). 1992. pap. text ed. 23.50 (*0-87287-915-1*) Teacher Ideas Pr.

Classical Roots of Ethnomethodology: Durkheim, Weber, & Garfinkel. Richard A. Hilbert. LC 91-47747. xviii, 260p. (C). 1992. 39.95 (*0-8078-2039-3*) U of NC Pr.

Classical Scientific Astrology. George Noonan. LC 83-71742. 176p. 1984. 16.00 (*0-86690-049-7*, N2344-014) Am Fed Astrologers.

Classical Sequences in Banach Spaces. Sylvie Guerre-Delabriere. LC 92-19239. (Pure & Applied Mathematics Ser.: Vol. 166). 232p. 1992. 110.00 (*0-8247-8723-4*) Dekker.

Classical Singers of the Opera & Recital Stages: A Bibliography of Biographical Materials. LC 94-6329. (Musica Ser.). 528p. 1994. text ed. 75.00 (*0-313-29332-5*, Greenwood Pr) Greenwood.

Classical Sociological Theory: A Positivist Perspective. Jonathan H. Turner. 200p. 1992. pap. text ed. 18.95 (*0-8304-1373-1*) Nelson-Hall.

Classical Solos Arranged for the Guitar, Vol. II. 2nd ed. Mike DiGiacomo. (C). 1991. reprint ed. pap. text ed. 12. 95 (*1-880462-05-2*); reprint ed. audio, pap. text ed. 22.95 (*0-685-50701-7*) Mad Music.

***Classical Southern: A Celebration of Cooking from the American South of the 19th Century.** Damon L. Fowler. LC 94-47268. 1995. 25.00 (*0-517-59353-X*, Crown) Crown Pub Group.

Classical Sparta: Techniques Behind Her Success. Ed. by Anton Powell. LC 88-20748. (Oklahoma Series in Classical Culture: Vol. 1). 210p. 1989. 38.95 (*0-8061-2177-7*) U of Okla Pr.

C

1300 An Asterisk (*) at the beginning of an entry indicates that the title is appearing in BIP for the first time.

Classical Spirit in American Portraiture. Brown University, Department of Art Staff. LC 76-380. (Illus.). 120p. (Orig.). 1976. pap. text ed. 14.00 (*0-933519-09-5*) D W Bell Gallery.

Classical Statistical Physics of Random Systems: An Introduction & Five Case Studies. Reiner Kree. 280p. (C). 1992. 62.00 (*3-528-06403-X*, Pub. by Vieweg & Sohn GW) Ballen Bkslr.

Classical Studies. Harvard University Library Staff. (Widener Library Shelflist: No. 57). 215p. 1979. text ed. 25.00 (*0-674-13461-3*) HUP.

Classical Studies. John W. Mackail. LC 68-16950. (Essay Index Reprint Ser.). 1977. 19.95 (*0-8369-0649-7*) Ayer.

***Classical Studies: A Guide to the Reference Literature.** Fred W. Jenkins. (Reference Sources in the Humanities Ser.). 275p. 1995. lib. bdg. 43.00 (*1-56308-110-5*) Libs Unl.

Classical Studies & Sketches. Joseph B. Pike. LC 67-23259. (Essay Index Reprint Ser.). 1977. 16.95 (*0-8369-0790-6*) Ayer.

Classical Studies in Honor of John C. Rolfe. Ed. by G. D. Hadzsits. LC 67-28747. (Essay Index Reprint Ser.). 1977. 23.95 (*0-8369-0311-0*) Ayer.

Classical Styles in Modern Architecture: From the Colonnade to Disjunctured Space. Thomas Doremus. 1994. pap. 39.95 (*0-442-01666-2*) Van Nos Reinhold.

Classical Swine Fever & Related Viral Infections. Ed. by B. Liese. (Developments in Veterinary Virology Ser.). (C). 1987. lib. bdg. 106.00 (*0-89838-969-0*) Kluwer Ac.

Classical Tamil Prosody: An Introduction. Kamil V. Zvelebil. (C). 1989. 12.75 (*0-8364-2459-X*, Pub. by New Era) S Asia.

Classical Taste in America, 1800-1840. Wendy A. Cooper. (Illus.). 256p. 1993. 55.00 (*1-55859-385-3*) Abbeville Pr.

Classical Tesselations & Three Manifolds. Jose M. Montesinos. (Universitext Ser.). (Illus.). xvii, 230p. 1987. pap. text ed. 44.00 (*0-387-15291-1*) Spr-Verlag.

Classical Texts & Their Traditions: Studies in Honor of C. R. Trahman. Ed. by David F. Bright & Edwin T. Ramage. LC 84-1326. (Homage Ser.). 270p. (C). 1984. text ed. 21.50 (*0-89130-729-X*, 00 16 06) Scholars Pr GA.

Classical Theatre & Art Song of South Fukien. Piet Van der Loon. 303p. (CHI & ENG). 1992. 48.00 (*957-638-107-X*, L1B001, Pub. by SMC Pub CC) Oriental Bk Store.

Classical Themes. Kenneth Baker. (Home Organist Library: Vol. 13). (Illus.). 80p. 1992. pap. 13.95 (*0-7119-2963-7*, AM88924) Music Sales.

Classical Themes: Level Two, Themes 4. Carmela Mercuri. (Dear Teacher, I've Always Wanted to Play the Piano Ser.). (Illus.). 32p. (Orig.). 1982. pap. 4.95 (*0-935474-07-2*, CAR1133) Carousel Pubns Ltd.

Classical Themes: Level Two, Themes 5. Carmela Mercuri. (Dear Teacher, I've Always Wanted to Play the Piano Ser.). (Illus.). 32p. (Orig.). 1982. pap. 3.95 (*0-685-73593-1*, CAR1134) Carousel Pubns Ltd.

Classical Themes for All Keyboards. Sel. by Daniel Scott. (Illus.). 80p. 1993. pap. 12.95 (*0-7119-2709-X*, AM85317) Music Sales.

Classical Themes for People Who Hate Classical Music. (Illus.). 126p. 1960. pap. 9.95 (*0-8256-2100-3*) Music Sales.

Classical Theories of Allegory & Christian Culture. Philip Rollinson. LC 81-4891. (Duquesne Studies: Language & Literature Ser.: Vol. 3). 196p. (C). 1981. text ed. 20.00 (*0-391-01712-8*) Duquesne.

Classical Theory of Electricity & Magnetism. A. K. Roychawdjuri. (Course of Lecture Ser.). (Illus.). 332p. 1991. 35.00 (*0-19-562578-1*, 10251) OUP.

Classical Theory of Relations. Constantine Cavarnos. LC 75-2659. 116p. 1975. pap. 5.00 (*0-914744-28-3*) Inst Byzantine.

Classical Thermodynamics. Arnold Munster. Tr. by E. S. Halberstadt. LC 71-122348. 401p. reprint ed. pap. 114. 30 (*0-317-12980-5*, 2020834) Bks Demand.

Classical Thought. Terence Irwin. (History of Western Philosophy Ser.: No. 1). 286p. (C). 1988. pap. text ed. 13.95 (*0-19-289177-4*) OUP.

Classical Tibetan Language. Stephan V. Beyer. LC 91-24499. (SUNY Series in Buddhist Studies). 503p. (C). 1992. 59.50 (*0-7914-1099-4*); pap. 19.95 (*0-7914-1100-1*) State U NY Pr.

Classical Topology & Combinatorial Group Theory. 2nd ed. John C. Stillwell. LC 92-40606. (Graduate Texts in Mathematics Ser.: Vol. 72). 360p. 1993. 49.90 (*0-387-97970-0*) Spr-Verlag.

Classical Topology & Quantum States. A. P. Balachandran et al. 376p. (C). 1991. text ed. 66.00 (*981-02-0329-2*); pap. text ed. 36.00 (*981-02-0330-6*) World Scientific Pub.

Classical Tradition: Greek & Roman Influences on Western Literature. Gilbert Highet. 802p. 1985. pap. 17.95 (*0-19-500206-7*) OUP.

Classical Tradition & the Americas, Vol. 1: European Images of the Americas & the Classical Tradition. Ed. by Wolfgang Haase & Meyer Reinhold. LC 93-35000. xxxviii, 682p. (C). 1993. lib. bdg. 249.00 (*3-11-011572-7*) De Gruyter.

Classical Tradition in Operation. Niall Rudd. (Robson Classical Lectures). 204p. 1994. 55.00 (*0-8020-0570-5*) U of Toronto Pr.

Classical Tradition in West European Farming. G. E. Fussell. LC 77-181502. 237p. 1972. 18.50 (*0-8386-1090-0*) Fairleigh Dickinson.

Classical Traditions in Early America. John W. Eadie. LC 76-51864. 265p. (Orig.). 1976. pap. 10.00 (*0-89824-000-X*) Trillium Pr.

Classical Tragedy: Greek & Roman. Intro. by Robert W. Corrigan. 576p. (Orig.). 1990. pap. 12.95 (*1-55783-046-0*) Applause Theatre Bk Pubs.

Classical Transmitters in the CNS, Pt. I. Ed. by Anders T. Bjorklund et al. (Handbook of Chemical Neuroanatomy Ser.: Vol. 2, pt. I). 1985. 250.75 (*0-444-90330-5*, Excerpta Medica) Elsevier.

Classical Transmitters in the CNS, Pt. II. Anders T. Bjorklund et al. (Handbook of Chemical Neuroanatomy Ser.: Vol. 3, pt. II). 1985. 239.50 (*0-444-90352-6*) Elsevier.

Classical Turkish Cooking: Traditional Turkish Food for the American Kitchen. Ayla E. Algar. LC 91-55096. 416p. 1991. 30.00 (*0-06-016317-8*, HarpT) HarpC.

***Classical Tutu Construction.** Kathryn K. Angleman. 42p. 1979. pap. text ed. 15.00 (*0-9646987-0-6*) K K Angleman.

***Classical Typography in the Computer Age.** Hermann Zapf & John Dreyfus. 36p. Date not set. pap. 15.00 (*0-614-07226-3*) Oak Knoll Pr.

Classical Utopian Theories of Education. Robert T. Fisher. 1963. pap. 15.95x (*0-8084-0395-8*) NCUP.

Classical Vases & Containers in the Collection of the Seattle Art Museum. Lawrence J. Bliquez. LC 85-50711. (Illus.). 32p. (Orig.). 1985. pap. 4.95 (*0-932216-19-6*) Seattle Art.

***Classical Vernacular: Architectural Principles in an Age of Nihilism.** Roger Scruton. LC 95-2604. 1995. write for info. (*0-312-12501-1*) St Martin.

Classical Violin Solos Arranged for the Guitar. Mike DiGiacomo. (Classical Solos Arranged for the Guitar Ser.: Vol. III). (C). 1991. pap. text ed. 12.95 (*1-880462-08-7*); audio, pap. text ed. 22.95 (*1-880462-10-9*) Mad Music.

***Classical Vocal Music in Print: Master Index 1995.** LC 76-29568. (Music in Print Ser.: Vol. 4X). 1995. lib. bdg. 95.00 (*0-88478-036-8*) Musicdata.

Classical Vocal Music in Print: Nineteen Eighty-Five Supplement. Ed. by Gary S. Eslinger & F. Mark Daugherty. LC 86-18088. (Music-in-Print Ser.: Vol. 4S). 245p. 1985. lib. bdg. 95.00 (*0-88478-018-X*) Musicdata.

***Classical Vocal Music in Print: 1995 Supplement.** Ed. by Mark Daugherty. LC 76-29568. (Vol. 4T: No. 4T). 279p. 1995. 95.00 (*0-88478-035-X*) Musicdata.

***Classical Wedding Hits for Piano Vol. 1: Easy-Intermediate.** Ed. by Tony Esposito. 28p. (YA). 1995. pap. text ed. 5.95 (*0-89724-687-X*) CPP Belwin.

Classical Woodwind Cadenza: A Workbook. David Lasocki & Betty B. Mather. 1978. 10.00 (*0-941084-06-X*) McGinnis & Marx.

Classical World. R. Peterson. (Atlas of Mankind Ser.: Vol. II). (Illus.). 112p. (C). 1985. 30.00 (*0-941694-15-1*) Cliveden Pr.

Classical Zeus: A Study in Art & Literature. Karim W. Arafat. (Oxford Monographs on Classical Archaeology). (Illus.). 286p. 1990. 110.00 (*0-19-814912-3*) OUP.

Classicism, Politics, & Kinship: The Ch'ang-Chou School of New Text Confucianism in Late Imperial China. Benjamin A. Elman. 1990. 48.00 (*0-520-06673-1*) U CA Pr.

***Classicist, Vol. 1.** Ed. by Institute for the Study of Classical Architecture Fellows. (Illus.). 96p. 1994. pap. 34.95 (*1-56000-804-0*) Transaction Pubs.

Classics. Library Service for the Blind & Physically Handicapped, Library of Congress Staff. LC 94-9204. 1994. write for info. (*0-8444-0811-5*) Lib Congress.

Classics: A Discipline & Profession in Crisis? Ed. by Phyllis Culham et al. LC 89-34188. (Illus.). 410p. (Orig.). (C). 1989. pap. text ed. 42.00 (*0-8191-7450-5*) U Pr of Amer.

Classics: Fisherman Knits. Janet W. Mysse. (Illus.). 206p. 1984. spiral bd. 14.50 (*0-934318-43-3*) Falcon Pr MT.

Classics: Major & Minor. Eric Blom. LC 74-166098. 212p. 1972. reprint ed. lib. bdg. 29.50 (*0-306-70293-2*) Da Capo.

Classics: Their History & Present Status in Education: A Symposium of Essays. Ed. by Felix M. Kirsch. LC 68-22104. (Essay Index Reprint Ser.). 1977. 23.95 (*0-8369-0600-4*) Ayer.

Classics: U. S. Aircraft of World War II. Photos by Mark Meyer. LC 87-80777. (Illus.). 224p. 1987. 45.00 (*0-9616878-6-X*) Howell Pr VA.

Classics: U. S. Aircraft of World War II. Mark Meyer. Ed. by Ross A. Howell, Jr. & Kathleen D. Valenzi. 1992. pap. 24.95 (*0-943231-41-8*) Howell Pr VA.

Classics & Cinema. Ed. by Martin A. Winkler. LC 90-55009. (Review Ser.: Vol. 35, No. 1). (Illus.). 272p. 1991. 22.00 (*0-8387-5198-9*) Bucknell U Pr.

Classics & Contemporaries. John W. Aldridge. 256p. 1992. 24.95 (*0-8262-0822-3*) U of Mo Pr.

Classics & English Renaissance Poetry: Three Case Studies. Gordon Braden. LC 77-10888. (Yale Studies in English: No. 187). 319p. reprint ed. pap. 91.00 (*0-8357-8693-5*, 2033678) Bks Demand.

***Classics & Feminism.** McManus. 1995. 26.95 (*0-8057-9757-2*, Twayne) Macmillan.

Classics & the Man of Letters. T. S. Eliot. LC 74-2409. (Studies in T. S. Eliot: No. 11). 1974. lib. bdg. 75.00 (*0-8383-2053-8*) M S G Haskell Hse.

Classics & Trash: Traditions & Taboos in High Literature & Popular Modern Genres. Harriet Hawkins. 238p. 1990. 65.00 (*0-8020-2767-9*); pap. 17.95 (*0-8020-6813-8*) U of Toronto Pr.

Classics Compendium: Everything You Always Wanted to Know about Classical Antiquity. Janise J. Gabbert. (Illus.). 390p. 1993. pap. text ed. 21.95 (*1-57074-061-5*) Greyden Pr.

***Classics Desecrated.** Doug Wheeler. 64p. 1995. pap. 8.95x (*1-56163-131-0*) NBM.

Classics from the New Yankee Workshop. Norman Abrams. 1990. pap. 19.95 (*0-316-00445-3*) Little.

Classics in American Government. Jay M. Shafritz & Lee S. Weinberg. 376p. 1994. pap. 20.95 (*0-534-20816-9*) Intl Thomson.

Classics in Austrian Economics: A Sampling in the History of a Tradition. Israel M. Kirzner. 1994. 295.00 (*1-85196-138-0*, Pub. by Pickering & Chatto UK) Ashgate Pub Co.

Classics in Child Development, 32 vols. Ed. by Judith K. Gardener & Howard Gardener. 924.00 (*0-405-06450-0*, 409) Ayer.

Classics in Commercial Bank Lending, Vol. 1. LC 81-83354. 556p. 1981. 26.50 (*0-936742-03-8*) Robt Morris Assocs.

Classics in Commercial Bank Lending, Vol. 2. Ed. by William W. Sihler. LC 81-83354. (Illus.). 568p. (Orig.). 1985. pap. text ed. 26.50 (*0-936742-24-0*) Robt Morris Assocs.

Classics in Coordination Chemistry: Twentieth-Century Papers (1904-1935), Pt. III. Ed. by George B. Kauffman. LC 67-26870. (Classics of Science Ser.). (Illus.). 1978. pap. text ed. 8.95 (*0-486-63496-5*) Dover.

Classics in Group Psychotherapy. K. Roy MacKenzie. LC 91-35412. 356p. 1992. lib. bdg. 45.00 (*0-89862-799-0*) Guilford Pr.

Classics in Obstetrics & Gynecology: Innovative Papers That Have Contributed to Current Clinical Practice. Ed. by T. K. Eskes & L. D. Longo. 350p. 1993. 78.00 (*1-85070-520-8*) Prthnon Pub.

Classics in Ophthalmology, 6 vols., Set. Paul Henkind. 1979. 150.00 (*0-88275-933-7*) Krieger.

Classics in Ophthalmology, 6 vols., Set. deluxe ed. Paul Henkind. 1979. 199.50 (*0-685-70911-6*) Krieger.

Classics in Paraphrase: Ezra Pound & Modern Translators of Latin Poetry. Daniel M. Hooley. LC 86-43216. 1988. 32.50 (*0-941664-82-1*) Susquehanna U Pr.

Classics in Psychiatry Ser., 46 vols. Ed. by Eric T. Carlson. 1976. 1,985.50 (*0-405-07410-7*) Ayer.

Classics in Psychoanalytic Technique. rev. ed. Ed. by Robert Langs. LC 90-38548. 512p. 1990. 80.00 (*0-87668-744-3*) Aronson.

Classics in Psychology, 42 bks., Set. Ed. by Howard Gardner & Judith K. Gardner. 1,047.50 (*0-405-05130-1*) Ayer.

Classics in Radio Astronomy. W. Sullivan, III. 1982. lib. bdg. 131.50 (*90-277-1356-1*) Kluwer Ac.

Classics in Russia, 1700-1855: Between Two Bronze Horsemen. Marinus A. Wes. LC 92-21784. (Brill's Studies in Intellectual History: Vol. 33). 1992. 94.50 (*90-04-09664-7*) E J Brill.

Classics in Semantics. Ed. by Donald E. Hayden & E. Paul Alworth. (Essay Index Reprint Ser.). 1977. 26.95 (*0-8369-1949-1*) Ayer.

Classics in Semantics. Ed. by Donald E. Hayden & E. Paul Alworth. (Essay Index Reprint Ser.). 1982. reprint ed. lib. bdg. 21.00 (*0-8290-0842-X*) Irvington.

Classics in the American Theater of the Nineteen Sixties & Early Nineteen Seventies. Marianthe Colakis. 96p. (C). 1993. lib. bdg. 34.50 (*0-8191-8972-3*) U Pr of Amer.

***Classics in the Classroom.** 2nd rev. ed. Michael Thompson. 137p. 1994. teacher ed, pap. 9.99 (*0-88092-220-6*) Royal Fireworks.

Classics in the Education of Girls & Women. Shirley N. Kersey. LC 80-20711. 335p. 1981. 32.50 (*0-8108-1354-8*) Scarecrow.

Classics in the Middle Ages. Ed. by Aldo S. Bernardo & Saul Levin. (Medieval & Renaissance Texts & Studies: Vol. 69). 432p. 1990. 25.00 (*0-86698-078-4*, MR69) MRTS.

Classics in the Theory of Public Finance. Ed. by Richard A. Musgrave & Alan T. Peacock. LC 94-1158. 1994. text ed. 69.95 (*0-312-12162-8*) St Martin.

Classics in Translation, 2 vols. Ed. by Paul L MacKendrick & Herbert M Howe. Incl. Vol. 1. Greek Literature. 444p. 1959. 14.95 (*0-299-80895-5*); Vol. 2. Latin Literature. 452p. 1959. 14.95 (*0-299-80896-3*); 1959. write for info. (*0-318-56167-0*) U of Wis Pr.

Classics in Voting Behavior. Ed. by Richard G. Niemi & Herbert F. Weisberg. LC 92-23085. 1992. 42.95 (*0-87187-705-8*); pap. 29.95 (*0-87187-651-5*) Congr Quarterly.

Classics Library, 4 vols. (Cliffs Notes Hardbound Library). 1989. lib. bdg. 219.25 (*0-931013-26-7*) Moonbeam Pubns.

Classics Library, Early Christian & European Classics: Collection of 14 Titles. (Cliffs Notes Softbound Literary Libraries). 1990. pap. text ed. 52.00 (*1-56271-287-X*) Moonbeam Pubns.

Classics Library, Greek & Roman Classics: Collection of 13 Titles. (Cliffs Notes Softbound Literary Libraries). 1990. pap. text ed. 55.50 (*1-56271-286-1*) Moonbeam Pubns.

Classics Library, Vol. 1: Greek & Roman Classics, Pt. 1. (Cliffs Notes Hardbound Library). 1989. lib. bdg. 85.25 (*0-931013-03-8*) Moonbeam Pubns.

Classics Library, Vol. 2: Greek & Roman Classics, Pt. 2. (Cliffs Notes Hardbound Library). 1989. lib. bdg. 25.50 (*0-931013-04-6*) Moonbeam Pubns.

Classics Library, Vol. 3: Early Christian & European Classics, Pt. 1. (Cliffs Notes Hardbound Library). 1989. lib. bdg. 54.25 (*0-931013-05-4*) Moonbeam Pubns.

Classics Library, Vol. 4: Early Christian & European Classics, Pt. 2. (Cliffs Notes Hardbound Library). 1989. lib. bdg. 54.25 (*0-931013-06-2*) Moonbeam Pubns.

Classics Library, 2 vols. Early Christian - European Classics. (Cliffs Notes Hardbound Library). 1989. lib. bdg. 108.50 (*0-931013-28-3*) Moonbeam Pubns.

Classics Library, 2 vols. Greek & Roman Classics. (Cliffs Notes Hardbound Library). 1989. lib. bdg. 100.75 (*0-931013-27-5*) Moonbeam Pubns.

Classics Made Easy: Level One. Brimhall. (Made Easy Ser.). 1990. 6.95 (*0-685-32065-0*, 8415) Hansen Ed Mus.

Classics No. II: The Most Interesting Ideas & Concepts from the Literature of Investing. Ed. by Charles D. Ellis & James R. Vertin. 480p. 1991. text ed. 49.00 (*1-55623-358-2*) Irwin Prof Pubng.

Classics of American Librarianship, 8 vols. A. E. Bostwick. 1973. 1,500.00 (*0-87968-879-3*) Gordon Pr.

Classics of American Psychiatry Eighteen-Ten to Nineteen Thirty-Four. John P. Brady. LC 72-85641. (Illus.). 336p. 1975. 12.75 (*0-87527-093-X*) Green.

Classics of Analytic Philosophy. Ed. by Robert R. Ammerman. LC 90-38344. (Hackett Classics Ser.). 424p. (C). 1990. reprint ed. lib. bdg. 32.50 (*0-87220-102-3*); reprint ed. pap. text ed. 14.50 (*0-87220-101-5*) Hackett Pub.

Classics of Cardiology, Pt. 1, Vol. 4. John A. Callahan et al. LC 82-7830. 600p. 1988. Pt. 1, 600 pgs. lib. bdg. 72.00 (*0-89874-872-0*) Krieger.

Classics of Cardiology, Pt. 2, Vol. 4. John A. Callahan et al. LC 82-7830. 514p. 1988. Pt. 2, 514 pgs. lib. bdg. 61.75 (*0-89464-265-0*) Krieger.

Classics of Cardiology, 5 vols., Set. Ed. by Thomas E. Keys & Fredrick A. Willius. LC 82-7830. 1536p. 1983. 235.00 (*0-89874-513-6*) Krieger.

Classics of Cardiology, 5 vols., Vol. 1: Repr. of 1941 Ed. Ed. by Thomas E. Keys & Fredrick A. Willius. LC 82-7830. 424p. 1983. Vol. 1, Repr. of 1941 ed., 424 pgs. 46. 75 (*0-89874-514-4*) Krieger.

Classics of Cardiology, 5 vols., Vol. 2: Repr. of 1941 Ed. Ed. by Thomas E. Keys & Fredrick A. Willius. LC 82-7830. 472p. 1983. Vol. 2, Repr. of 1941 ed., 472 pgs. 52. 25 (*0-89874-515-2*) Krieger.

Classics of Cardiology, 5 vols., Vol. 3. Ed. by John A. Callahan et al. LC 82-7830. 640p. 1983. 76.50 (*0-89874-516-0*) Krieger.

Classics of Children's Literature. rev. ed. John W. Griffith & Charles H. Frey. (Illus.). 1440p. (C). 1991. teacher ed write for info. (*0-318-69330-5*) Macmillan.

Classics of Children's Literature. 3rd rev. ed. John W. Griffith & Charles H. Frey. (Illus.). 1440p. (C). 1992. pap. write for info. (*0-02-347290-1*) Macmillan.

Classics of Civil War Fiction. Ed. by David Madden & Peggy Bach. LC 91-16947. 1991. 37.50 (*0-87805-522-3*); pap. 15.95 (*0-87805-541-X*) U Pr of Miss.

Classics of Criminology. 2nd ed. Ed. by Joseph E. Jacoby. (Illus.). 469p. (Orig.). (C). 1993. pap. text ed. 17.95 (*0-88133-769-2*) Waveland Pr.

Classics of Eastern Thought. Lynn H. Nelson & Patrick Peebles. 608p. (C). 1991. pap. text ed. 20.00 (*0-15-507655-8*) HB Coll Pubs.

Classics of Free Thought. Ed. by Paul Blanshard. LC 77-73846. (Skeptic's Bookshelf Ser.). 190p. 1977. pap. 18.95 (*0-87975-421-4*) Prometheus Bks.

Classics of Group Psychotherapy, 29 vols. 725.00 (*0-685-25825-4*); pap. 348.00 (*0-685-25826-2*) Beacon Hse.

Classics of Horror: Frankenstein - Dracula. Mary Wollstonecraft Shelley & Bram Stoker. (Classics - Bonded Leather Fibers Ser.). 656p. 1991. 18.95 (*0-681-41163-5*) Longmeadow Pr.

Classics of Indian Spirituality Series: The Bhagavad Gita, The Dhammapada, & The Upanishads, 3 bks. Eknath Easwaran. 1989. The/Bhagavad Gita, 248p., The Dhammapada, 208p., The Upanishads, 320p. 50.00 (*0-915132-45-1*); pap. 27.00 (*0-915132-44-3*) Nilgiri Pr.

Classics of International Relations. 2nd ed. John A. Vasquez. 400p. (C). 1989. pap. text ed. write for info. (*0-13-136888-5*) P-H.

Classics of Judaism: A Textbook & Reader. Jacob Neusner. LC 94-12970. 512p. (Orig.). (C). 1995. pap. 29.99 (*0-664-25455-1*) Westminster John Knox.

***Classics of Mathematics.** Ed. by Ronald Calinger. LC 94-25644. 1994. pap. text ed. 26.67 (*0-02-318342-X*) P-H.

Classics of Modern Fiction. 5th ed. Ed. by Irving Howe & Steve Welch. 750p. 1993. pap. text ed. 26.75 (*0-15-500171-X*) HarBrace.

Classics of Moral & Political Theory. Ed. by Michael L. Morgan. LC 91-38760. 1280p. (C). 1992. lib. bdg. 48.50 (*0-87220-127-9*); pap. text ed. 29.50 (*0-87220-126-0*) Hackett Pub.

Classics of Neurology. Ed. by Emerson C. Kelly. LC 78-158127. 384p. 1971. 35.50 (*0-685-55586-0*) Krieger.

Classics of Neurology. deluxe ed. Ed. by Emerson C. Kelly. LC 78-158127. 384p. 1971. 43.50 (*0-88275-029-1*) Krieger.

Classics of Organization Theory. 3rd ed. Jay M. Shafritz & J. Steven Ott. LC 91-32705. 534p. (Orig.). (C). 1992. pap. 30.95 (*0-534-17304-7*) Intl Thomson.

Classics of Organizational Behavior. Walter Natemeyer & Jay Gilberg. 370p. (Orig.). 1989. 21.95 (*0-8134-2814-9*) Interstate.

Classics of Polling. Ed. by Michael L. Young. LC 89-29320. (Illus.). 592p. 1990. 47.50 (*0-8108-2280-6*) Scarecrow.

Classics of Public Administration. 3rd ed. Jay M. Shafritz & Albert C. Hyde. LC 91-43241. 563p. (Orig.). (C). 1992. pap. 29.95 (*0-534-17310-1*) Intl Thomson.

Classics of Public Personnel Policy. 2nd rev. ed. Frank J. Thompson. 396p. (Orig.). (C). 1991. pap. 24.95 (*0-534-13938-8*) Intl Thomson.

Classics of Semiotics. Ed. by Martin Krampen et al. LC 87-2283. (Topics in Contemporary Semiotics Ser.). 288p. 1987. 59.50 (*0-306-42321-9*, Plenum Pr) Plenum.

Classics of Social Choice. Ed. by Iain McLean & Arnold B. Urken. 476p. (C). 1993. text ed. 49.50 (*0-472-10450-0*) U of Mich Pr.

Classics of Sociometry, Vols. XI-XVIII, Set. J. L. Moreno. pap. 110.00 (*0-685-22537-2*) Beacon Hse.

C

An Asterisk (*) at the beginning of an entry indicates that the title is appearing in BIP for the first time. 1301

Classics of Spanish Literature, 2 levels. Incl. Level 1, 4 bks. Adapt. by Alberto Romo. (0-318-55494-1); Bk. 1. Fuenteovejuna. 1963. pap. text ed. 3.50 (0-88345-057-7, 17449); Bk. 3. Pepita Jimenez. 1967. pap. text ed. 3.50 (0-88345-127-1, 17457); Bk. 4. Sombrero De Tres Picos. 1974. pap. text ed. 4.50 (0-88345-151-4, 17458); Level 2, 2 bks. Ed. by Juan Gamez-Garcia. pap. text ed. 3.95 (0-318-55495-X, 17763); Bk. 1. Amantes De Teruel. Juan E. Hartzenbusch. 1974. (0-318-55496-8); Bk. 2. Don Juan Tenorio. Jose Zorilla. 1974. pap. 4.50 (0-88345-042-9, 17764); (gr. 9 up). Set pap. text ed. write for info. (0-318-55493-3) Prentice ESL.

Classics of Texas Fiction. James W. Lee. 200p. (Orig.). (C). 1987. 15.95 (0-935014-09-8); pap. 9.95 (0-935014-10-1) E-Heart Pr.

Classics of the Courtroom, Vol. III: Clarence Darrow's Cross-Examination of William Jennings Bryan in Tennessee vs. John Thomas Scopes. Intro. by Irving Younger. 56p. 1987. pap. 12.00 (0-943380-09-X) PEG MN.

Classics of the Courtroom, Vol. XIV: Highlights from the Direct & Cross-Examination of Richard Hauptmann in the State of New Jersey vs. Hauptmann. Intro. by James W. McElhaney. 326p. 1988. pap. 20.00 (0-943380-20-0) PEG MN.

***Classics of the Courtroom Vol. XXIV: Pennzoil vs. Texaco, Inc.** Intro. by James W. McElhaney. 55p. 1992. pap. 12.00 (0-943380-30-8) PEG MN.

Classics of the Courtroom, Vol. I: The Summations of Max Steuer & Joseph Proskauer in Oppenheim vs. Metropolitan Street Railways. Intro. by Irving Younger. 63p. 1987. pap. text ed. 12.00 (0-943380-07-3) PEG MN.

Classics of the Courtroom, Vol. II: Robert Hanley's Summation in MCI vs. AT & T I. Intro. by Irving Younger. 86p. 1987. pap. 20.00 (0-943380-08-1) PEG MN.

Classics of the Courtroom, Vol. IV: Irving Younger's Opening Statement in Tavoulareas vs. the Washington Post Co. Intro. by Irving Younger. 24p. 1987. pap. 12.00 (0-943380-10-3) PEG MN.

Classics of the Courtroom, Vol. IX: James Brosnahan's Summation in U. S. vs. Aguilar (the Sanctuary Trial) Intro. by James W. Jeans, Sr. 70p. 1988. pap. 12.00 (0-943380-15-4) PEG MN.

Classics of the Courtroom, Vol. V: Thomas Murphy's Cross-Examination of Dr. Carl A. Binger in U. S. vs. Alger Hiss (Hiss II) Intro. by Irving Younger. 348p. 1987. pap. 20.00 (0-943380-11-1) PEG MN.

Classics of the Courtroom, Vol. VI: Edward Bennett Williams' Cross-Examination of Jake Jacobsen in U. S. vs. Connally. Intro. by Irving Younger. 163p. 1988. pap. 20.00 (0-943380-12-X) PEG MN.

Classics of the Courtroom, Vol. VII: Highlights from the Direct & Cross-Examination of Herman Goering in the Nuremberg Trial. Intro. by Irving Younger. 161p. 1988. pap. 20.00 (0-943380-13-8) PEG MN.

Classics of the Courtroom, Vol. VIII: Clarence Darrow's Sentencing Speech in State of Illinois vs. Leopold & Loeb. Intro. by Irving Younger. 89p. 1988. pap. 12.00 (0-943380-14-6) PEG MN.

Classics of the Courtroom, Vol. X: William H. Wallace's Summation in the State of Missouri vs. Frank James (1883) Intro. by James W. Jeans, Sr. 91p. 1988. pap. 12.00 (0-943380-16-2) PEG MN.

Classics of the Courtroom, Vol. XI: The Direct & Cross-Examination of John Dean in U. S. vs. Mitchell. Intro. by James W. Jeans, Sr. 227p. 1988. pap. 20.00 (0-943380-17-0) PEG MN.

Classics of the Courtroom, Vol. XII: Vincent Fuller's Summation in U. S. vs. Hinckley. Intro. by James W. McElhaney. 54p. 1988. pap. 12.00 (0-943380-18-9) PEG MN.

Classics of the Courtroom, Vol. XIII: Highlights from the Commonwealth of Massachusetts vs. Lizze Bordon. Intro. by James W. Jeans, Sr. 299p. 1988. pap. 20.00 (0-943380-19-7) PEG MN.

Classics of the Courtroom, Vol. XIX: Daniel K. Webb's Direct Examination of Oliver North & Summation in U. S. vs. John M. Poindexter. Intro. by James W. McElhaney. 348p. 1991. pap. 20.00 (0-943380-25-1) PEG MN.

Classics of the Courtroom, Vol. XV: Lantz Welch's Summation in Firestone vs. Crown Center Redevelopment Corp. Intro. by James W. Jeans, Sr. 27p. 1988. pap. 12.00 (0-943380-21-9) PEG MN.

Classics of the Courtroom, Vol. XVI: Ulysses in Court: the Litigation Surrounding the First Publication of James Joyce's Novel in the United States. Intro. by James W. McElhaney. 68p. 1988. pap. 12.00 (0-943380-22-7) PEG MN.

Classics of the Courtroom, Vol. XVII: Barry Slotnick's Summation in State of New York vs. Bernard H. Goetz. Intro. by William A. Barton. 90p. 1991. pap. 20.00 (0-943380-23-5) PEG MN.

Classics of the Courtroom, Vol. XVIII: Cross-Examinations of the Oscar Wilde Trials - a Comparison. Intro. by James W. Jeans, Sr. 66p. 1991. pap. 12.00 (0-943380-24-3) PEG MN.

Classics of the Courtroom, Vol. XX: Thurgood Marshall's Arguments Before the U. S. Supreme Court in Brown vs. the Board of Education. Intro. by James W. Jeans, Sr. 48p. 1992. pap. 12.00 (0-943380-26-X) PEG MN.

Classics of the Courtroom, Vol. XXI: Cruzan V. Director, Missouri Department of Health - an Overview & Analysis. Intro. by William A. Barton. 156p. 1992. pap. 20.00 (0-943380-27-8) PEG MN.

Classics of the Courtroom, Vol. XXII: Clarence Darrow's Summation in People vs. Henry Sweet (1926) Intro. by James W. McElhaney. 42p. 1992. pap. 12.00 (0-943380-28-6) PEG MN.

Classics of the Courtroom, Vol. XXIII: The Matter of Sacco & Vanzetti, an Ethical Dilemma. Intro. by James W. Jeans, Sr. 78p. 1991. pap. 20.00 (0-943380-29-4) PEG MN.

Classics of the Horror Film. William K. Everson. (Illus.). 256p. 1974. 15.95 (0-8065-0437-4, Citadel Pr); pap. 9.95 (0-8065-0900-7, Citadel Pr) Carol Pub Group.

Classics of the Modern Theater: Realism & After. Ed. by Alvin B. Kernan. 538p. (C). 1965. pap. text ed. 21.50 (0-15-507654-X) HB Coll Pubs.

Classics of the Silent Screen. Joe Franklin. (Illus.). 256p. 1983. pap. 9.95 (0-8065-0181-2, Citadel Pr) Carol Pub Group.

Classics of Western Philosophy. 3rd ed. Ed. by Steven M. Cahn. LC 90-39023. 1192p. (C). 1990. lib. bdg. 45.00 (0-87220-106-6); pap. text ed. 29.50 (0-87220-105-8) Hackett Pub.

***Classics of Western Philosophy.** 4th ed. Ed. by Steven M. Cahn. LC 94-46682. (Illus.). 1280p. (C). 1995. text ed. 45.00 (0-87220-301-8); pap. text ed. 29.50 (0-87220-300-X) Hackett Pub.

Classics of Western Thought, Vol. I: The Ancient World. 4th ed. Donald S. Gochberg. 642p. (C). 1988. pap. text ed. 20.00 (0-15-507682-5) HB Coll Pubs.

Classics of Western Thought, Vol. II: Middle Ages, Renaissance & Reformation. 4th ed. Ed. by Karl F. Thompson. 557p. (C). 1988. pap. text ed. 20.00 (0-15-507683-3) HB Coll Pubs.

Classics of Western Thought, Vol. III: The Modern World. 4th ed. Ed. by Edgar E. Knoebel. 665p. (C). 1988. pap. text ed. 20.00 (0-15-507684-1) HB Coll Pubs.

Classics of Western Thought, Vol. IV: The Twentieth Century. 3rd ed. Ed. by Thomas H. Greer & Donald Gochberg. 660p. (C). 1980. pap. text ed. 25.00 (0-15-507681-7) HB Coll Pubs.

Classics on Fractals. Gerald A. Edgar. (Illus.). 308p. (C). 1993. 59.95 (0-201-58701-7) Addison-Wesley.

Classics on the Trinity. abr. rev. ed. Goodwin Owen & Warfield Bickersteth. Ed. by Jay P. Green, Sr. (Fifty Greatest Christian Classics Ser.). 672p. 1991. 29.95 (1-878442-61-9) Sovereign Grace Trust Fund.

Classics Papercrafts. Jerome C. Brown. 1991. 8.99 (0-8224-1352-3) Fearon Teach Aids.

Classics Revisited. Kenneth Rexroth. LC 85-31088. (Revived Modern Classics Ser.). 256p. 1986. reprint ed. 23.95 (0-8112-0987-3); reprint ed. pap. 10.95 (0-8112-0988-1, NDP621) New Directions.

Classics-Romantics-Moderns. Paul Sheftel. (Carl Fischer's "All Time Favorites" Music Ser.). 1992. pap. 10.95 (0-8258-0344-6, XF1002) Fischer Inc NY.

Classics Staples & Precursors in Sociology, 40 vols. (Perspectives in Social Inquiry Ser.). 1974. 1,028.50 (0-405-05490-4) Ayer.

Classics Then & Now: Around the World in Eighty Days, the Prince & the Pauper, the Legend of Sleepy Hollow. Kay W. Wilson. Ed. by B. L. Kratoville. (Illus.). 112p. (J). (gr. 3 up). 1991. student ed 10.00 (0-87879-920-6); pap. text ed. 12.00 (0-87879-919-2, 919-2) High Noon Bks.

Classics to Read Aloud to Your Children. Sel. by William F. Russell. LC 84-7033. 320p. (J). (ps-5). 1984. 19.00 (0-517-55404-6, Crown) Crown Pub Group.

Classics to Read Aloud to Your Children. William F. Russell. 320p. 1992. 10.00 (0-517-58715-7, Crown) Crown Pub Group.

Classics We've Read, the Difference It's Made. Chrysostom Society Staff. LC 93-78994. 250p. 1993. pap. 12.95 (1-56977-503-6) McCracken Pr.

Classification. Lillian Lieberman. 64p. (J). (gr. 2-5). 1989. 6.95 (0-912107-89-8, MM1906) Monday Morning Bks.

Classification: A Tool for Managing Today's Offenders. 128p. (Orig.). 1993. pap. text ed. 17.00 (0-929310-90-X, 191) Am Correctional.

Classification: Its Kinds, Elements, Systems & Applications. Ed. by Derek Langridge. 100p. 1992. 50.00 (0-86291-622-4) Bowker-Saur.

***Classification: Options & Opportunities.** Ed. by Alan R. Thomas. (Cataloging & Classification Quarterly Ser.: Vol. 19, No. 3 & 4). 253p. 1995. 49.95 (1-56024-709-6); text ed. 24.95 (0-614-05608-X) Haworth Pr.

Classification Algorithms. Mike James. LC 86-4045. 209p. (Orig.). 1986. text ed. 60.00 (0-471-84799-2) Wiley.

Classification & Application of Welded Joints for Machinery & Equipment (D14.4-77) (Illus.). 74p. 1977. 28.00 (0-87171-118-4) Am Welding.

Classification & Cognition. William K. Estes. (Illus.). 336p. (C). 1994. 49.95 (0-19-507335-5, 12831) OUP.

Classification & Communication. S. R. Ranganathan. 291p. 1990. pap. 13.95 (81-85273-27-8, Pub. by Sarada Ranganathan Endowment for Library Science II) Advent Bks Div.

Classification & Definitions of Bulk Materials. American National Standard Institute Staff. (CEMA Standards Ser.: No. 550). 85p. 1988. 10.00 (0-318-13803-4) Conveyor Equip Mfrs.

Classification & Descriptions of Mixed Metal Oxide Inorganic Colored Pigments. 2nd ed. Dry Color Manufacturers' Association, Metal Oxides & Ceramic Colors Subcommittee. 68p. 1982. write for info. (0-318-60068-4) Dry Color Mfrs.

Classification & Diagnosis of Alzheimer Disease: An International Perspective. Ed. by T. Hovaguimian et al. LC 88-13716. (Illus.). 200p. (C). 1989. text ed. 68.00 (0-920887-31-7) Hogrefe & Huber Pubs.

Classification & Diagnostics of Soil of the U. S. S. R. (Russian Translation Ser.: Vol. 42). (Illus.). 297p. 1989. text ed. 75.00 (90-6191-465-5, Pub. by A A Balkema NE) Ashgate Pub Co.

***Classification & Dissimilarity Analysis.** Ed. by B. Van Cutsem et al. LC 94-35226. (Lecture Notes in Statistics: Vol. 93). 238p. 1994. pap. text ed. 39.00 (0-387-94400-1) Spr-Verlag.

Classification & Distribution of the Pit River Indian Tribes of California. Clinton H. Merriam. LC 76-43779. (Smithsonian Miscellaneous Collections: Vol. 78, No. 3). reprint ed. write for info. (0-404-15633-9) AMS Pr.

***Classification & Evaluation of Earthquake Records for Design.** Farzad Naeim & James C. Anderson. (Illus.). 288p. (Orig.). (C). 1994. pap. text ed. 75.00 (0-7881-0877-8) Diane Pub.

Classification & Fourier Inversion for Parabolic Subgroups with Square Integrable Nilradical. Joseph A. Wolf. LC 79-21155. (Memoirs Ser.: No. 22/225). 166p. 1979. pap. 19.00 (0-8218-2225-X, MEMO 22/225) Am Math.

Classification & Human Evolution. Ed. by Sherwood L. Washburn. LC 63-18184. (Viking Fund Publications in Anthropology: No. 37). 381p. reprint ed. pap. 108.60 (0-317-26251-3, 2052136) Bks Demand.

Classification & Labelling of Dangerous Preparations: Directive 88-379 EEC. European Communities Staff. 134p. 1992. 45.00 (92-826-4231-3, CD-73-91-813-EN-C, Pub. by Europ Com) UNIPUB.

Classification & Nomenclature of Beads & Pendants. Horace Beck. (Illus.). 80p. 1973. pap. 15.00 (0-87387-083-2) Shumway.

Classification & Nomenclature of Electroanalytical Techniques. International Union of Pure & Applied Chemistry. 1976. pap. 8.00 (0-08-021226-3, Pub. by Pergamon Repr UK) Franklin.

Classification & Nomenclature of Viruses. Ed. by R. E. Matthews. (Journal: Intervirology: Vol. 17, No. 1-3, 1982). (Illus.). 200p. 1982. 29.00 (3-8055-3557-0) S Karger.

Classification & Nomenclature of Viruses: Fifth Report of the International Committee on Taxonomy of Viruses. Ed. by R. I. Francki et al. (Archives of Virology Ser.: Supplementum 2). vii, 443p. 1991. pap. 71.00 (0-387-82286-0) Spr-Verlag.

Classification & Nomenclature of Viruses: Report of the International Committee on Taxonomy of Viruses, 3rd. Ed. by R. E. Matthews. (Intervirology Ser.: Vol. 12, Nos. 3-5, 1979). 1980. pap. 8.00 (3-8055-0523-X) S Karger.

***Classification & Properties of Matter.** Ed. by H. A. Neidig. (Modular Laboratory Program in Chemistry Ser.). 11p. (C). 1988. pap. text ed. 1.25x (0-87540-348-4) Chem Educ Res.

Classification & Related Methods of Data Analysis: Proceedings of the First Conference of the International Federation of Classification Societies, Aachen, FRG, 29 June-1 July, 1987. Ed. by H. H. Bock. 750p. 1988. 148.75 (0-444-70404-3, North Holland) Elsevier.

Classification & Structure of C-Algebra Bundles. M. J. Dupre. LC 79-17975. (Memoirs Ser.: No. 21/222). 77p. 1979. pap. 17.00 (0-8218-2222-5, MEMO 21/222) Am Math.

Classification & Subject Index for Cataloguing & Arranging the Books & Pamphlets of a Library. Melvil Dewey. 1979. lib. bdg. 250.00 (0-8490-1637-1) Gordon Pr.

Classification & Uses of Fingerprints see Origin of Fingerprinting

Classification As a Tool of Research. Ed. by W. Gaul & M. Schader. 502p. 1986. 133.50 (0-444-87980-3, North Holland) Elsevier.

Classification by Broad Economic Categories Defined in Terms of SITC. 86p. 1989. pap. 10.00 (92-1-161302-7, E.89.XVII.4) UN.

***Classification, Cladistics, & Natural History of Native North American Harpalus Latreille.** G. Noonan. (Thomas Say Monographs: Vol. 13). 310p. 1991. 50.00 (0-938522-35-3) Entomol Soc.

***Classification Cross-Reference.** 6th ed. International Risk Management Institute, Inc. Staff. 126p. 1994. pap. 29.95 (1-886813-04-3) Intl Risk Mgt.

Classification Decimale de Dewey et Index, 2 vols. Melvil Dewey. Incl. Vol. 1. Tables Generales. 1974. 32.00 (0-910608-14-8); Vol. 2. Index. 32.00 (0-910608-15-6); 1974. Set. 64.00 (0-910608-31-8) Forest Pr.

Classification, Etiological Factors & Associated Disturbances. Ed. by R. Noyes, Jr. et al. (Handbook of Anxiety Ser.: No. 2). 570p. 1989. 288.75 (0-444-90489-1, Excerpta Medica) Elsevier.

Classification, Evolution, & Phylogeny of the Families of Dicotyledons. Aaron Goldberg. LC 86-600058. (Smithsonian Contributions to Botany Ser.: No. 58). 318p. reprint ed. pap. 90.70 (0-317-55759-9, 2029363) Bks Demand.

Classification, Evolution, & Phylogeny of the Families of Monocotyledons. Aaron Goldberg. LC 89-600112. (Smithsonian Contributions to Botany Ser.: No. 71). (Illus.). 78p. reprint ed. pap. 25.00 (0-8357-7883-5, 2036301) Bks Demand.

Classification, Evolution, & the Nature of Biology. Alec L. Panchen. (Illus.). 350p. (C). 1992. pap. 34.95 (0-521-31578-6) Cambridge U Pr.

Classification in Congenitally Blind Children: An Examination of Inhelder & Piaget's Theory. Leslie C. Higgins. (American Foundation for the Blind Research Ser.: Vol. 25). 60p. reprint ed. pap. 25.00 (0-685-15713-X, 2027344) Bks Demand.

Classification in Mental Retardation. Ed. by Herbert J. Grossman. LC 83-8779. 228p. 1983. text ed. 5.00 (0-940898-12-8) Am Assn Mental.

Classification in Social Research. Ramkrishna Mukherjee. LC 82-682. 255p. (C). 1984. 64.50 (0-87395-607-9); pap. 21.95 (0-87395-608-7) State U NY Pr.

Classification Made Simple. Eric J. Hunter. 100p. 1988. pap. text ed. 12.95 (0-566-05605-4, Pub. by Gower UK) Ashgate Pub Co.

Classification, Management & Use Potential of Swell-Shrink & Soils: Transactions of the International Workshop at the National Bureau of Soil Survey & Land Use Planning, Nagpur, India, 24-28 October 1988. 277p. (C). 1989. text ed. 70.00 (90-6191-957-6, Pub. by A A Balkema NE) Ashgate Pub Co.

Classification, Management & Use Potential of Swell-Shrink Soils: Proceedings of the Transactions of International Workshop, Nagpur, October, 1988. Ed. by J. N. Sehgal. (C). 1988. 48.00 (81-204-0378-9, Pub. by Oxford IBH II) S Asia.

Classification Manual for the OAS Official Records Series: A Manual for the Maintenance of the Series. rev. ed. 1977. pap. text ed. 3.00 (0-8270-3065-7) OAS.

Classification, Monitoring & Evaluation of Cataracts: 4th Scheimpflug Club Meeting 1989 Gamagori, Japan, April 1989. Ed. by K. Sasaki. (Journal: Ophthalmic Research: Vol. 22, Suppl. 1, 1990). vi, 102p. 1990. pap. 30.50 (3-8055-5224-6) S Karger.

Classification of Algebraic & Analytic Manifolds. Ed. by Kenji Ueno. (Progress in Mathematics Ser.: Vol. 39). 1983. 57.50 (0-8176-3137-2) Birkhauser.

Classification of Algebraic Varieties: Proceedings of the Algebraic Geometry Conference on Classification of Algebraic Varieties, May 22-30, 1992, University of L'Aquila, L'Aquila, Italy. Ed. by Ciro Ciliberto et al. LC 93-44549. (Contemporary Mathematics Ser.: No. 162). 436p. 1994. 52.00 (0-8218-5179-9, CONM/162) Am Math.

Classification of Business Literature. Harvard University Graduate School of Business Administration Staff. LC 61-776. 274p. reprint ed. pap. 78.10 (0-317-10702-X, 2010207) Bks Demand.

Classification of Chronic Pain: Descriptions of Chronic Pain Syndromes & Definitions of Pain Terms. 2nd ed. Int'l Assoc. for the Study of Pain, Task Force on Taxonomy Staff. Ed. by Harold Merskey & Nikolai Bogduk. LC 94-8062. 238p. 1994. pap. 20.00 (0-931092-05-1) Intl Assn Study Pain.

Classification of Class I Hazardous Locations for Electrical Installations in Chemical Plants. National Fire Protection Association Staff. 40p. 1992. 20.25 (0-317-63463-1, 497A-92) Natl Fire Prot.

Classification of Consumer Goods: An Empirical Study. Barnett Greenberg & Danny Bellenger. LC 74-621745. (Research Monograph: No. 56). 72p. 1974. spiral bd. 19.95 (0-88406-022-5) GA St U Busn Pr.

Classification of Fiction: The Development of a System Based on Theoretical Principles. Clare Beghtol. LC 93-45409. 1993. 39.50 (0-8108-2828-6) Scarecrow.

Classification of Finite Simple Groups, Vol. 1: Groups of Noncharacteristic 2 Type. Ed. by Daniel Gorenstein. LC 83-4011. (University Series in Mathematics). (Illus.). 498p. 1983. 105.00 (0-306-41305-1, Plenum Pr) Plenum.

Classification of Floating Production Systems: A Cost Effective Verification System. Tore Baunan. 1989. 150.00 (90-6314-569-1, Pub. by Lorne & MacLean Marine) St Mut.

Classification of Flowering Plants, Vol. 1: Gymnosperms & Monocotyledons. 2nd ed. Alfred B. Rendle. 428p. reprint ed. pap. 122.00 (0-317-26387-0, 2024529) Bks Demand.

Classification of Flowering Plants, Vol. 2: Dicotyledons. 2nd ed. Alfred B. Rendle. 660p. reprint ed. pap. 180.00 (0-685-10694-2, 2024529) Bks Demand.

Classification of G-Spaces. 4th ed. Richard S. Palais. LC 52-42839. (Memoirs Ser.: No. 1/36). 72p. 1987. reprint ed. pap. 17.00 (0-8218-1236-X, MEMO 1/36) Am Math.

Classification of Gases, Vapors & Dusts for Electrical Equipment in Hazardous (Classified) Locations. National Fire Protection Association Staff. 1991. 16.75 (0-317-63466-6, 497M-91) Natl Fire Prot.

Classification of Igneous Rocks & Glossary of Terms. Comp. by Roger LeMaitre. (Illus.). 206p. (C). 1989. text ed. 55.00 (0-632-02593-X) Blackwell Sci.

Classification of Institutions of Higher Education, 1987. Carnegie Foundation for the Advancement of Teaching Staff. LC 85-28030. (Carnegie Foundation Technical Report Ser.). 154p. reprint ed. pap. 43.90 (0-7837-6303-4, 2046018) Bks Demand.

***Classification of Institutions of Higher Education, 1994.** Frwd. by Ernest L. Boyer. LC 94-36243. (Technical Reports Ser.). 1994. 12.00 (0-931050-46-4) Carnegie Fnd Advan Teach.

Classification of Instructional Programs. 1994. lib. bdg. 350.00 (0-8490-5773-6) Gordon Pr.

Classification of Irregular Varieties: Minimal Models & Abelian Varieties. Ed. by E. Ballico et al. (Lecture Notes in Mathematics Ser.: Vol. 1515). (Illus.). 149p. 1992. pap. 29.00 (0-387-55295-2) Spr-Verlag.

Classification of Jacobian Ideals Invariant by SL(2,C) Actions. S. Yau. LC 88-990. (MEMO Ser.: No. 72/384). 180p. 1988. pap. 25.00 (0-8218-2447-3, MEMO 72/384) Am Math.

Classification of Knots & Three-Dimensional Spaces. Geoffrey Hemion. LC 92-22277. 1993. 43.50 (0-19-859697-9) OUP.

Classification of Library Materials: Current & Future Potential for Providing Access. Ed. by Betty G. Bengtson & Janet S. Hill. 275p. (Orig.). 1990. pap. text ed. 39.50 (1-55570-027-6) Neal-Schuman.

Classification of Lower Organisms. Herbert F. Copeland. LC 56-7944. (Illus.). 1956. 24.95 (0-87015-059-6) Pacific Bks.

1302 An Asterisk (*) at the beginning of an entry indicates that the title is appearing in BIP for the first time.

C

An Asterisk (*) at the beginning of an entry indicates that the title is appearing in BIP for the first time.

1303

Classroom Classics: Macbeth, Sm. Set. Annabelle Howard. 1986. pap. text ed. 80.00 (*0-938735-85-3*) Classic Theatre Schl.

Classroom Classics: The Bourgeois Gentleman, Reg. Set. Annabelle Howard. 1986. pap. text ed. 120.00 (*0-938735-81-0*) Classic Theatre Schl.

Classroom Classics: The Bourgeois Gentleman, Sm. Set. Annabelle Howard. 1986. pap. text ed. 70.00 (*0-938735-89-6*) Classic Theatre Schl.

Classroom Classics: The Grouch, Reg. Set. Annabelle Howard. 1986. pap. text ed. 100.00 (*0-938735-76-4*) Classic Theatre Schl.

Classroom Classics: The Grouch, Sm. Set. Annabelle Howard. 1986. pap. text ed. 90.00 (*0-938735-84-5*) Classic Theatre Schl.

Classroom Communication: Collected Readings for Effective Discussion & Questioning. Ed. by Rose A. Neff & Maryellen Weimer. 93p. (Orig.). (C). 1989. pap. text ed. 22.50 (*0-912150-08-4*) Magna Pubns.

Classroom Communication Screening Procedure for Early Adolescents: A Handbook for Assessment & Intervention. rev. ed. Charlann S. Simon. 175p. (C). 1987. pap. 35.00 (*0-9619006-0-1*) Communicog Pubns.

Classroom Composition & Pupil Achievement: A Study of the Effect of Ability-Based Classes. Yehezkel Dar & Nura Resh. (Special Aspects of Education Ser.: Vol. 5). 208p. 1986. text ed. 58.00 (*0-677-21450-2*) Gordon & Breach.

Classroom Computers: A Practical Guide for Effective Teaching. Anthony C. Maffei. (Illus.). 266p. 1986. 38.95 (*0-89885-251-X*); pap. 20.95 (*0-89885-255-2*) Human Sci Pr.

Classroom Computers: A Triad of Creative Applications. Richard A. Shade. 1987. pap. 7.95 (*0-936386-46-0*) Creative Learning.

Classroom Context. (C). 1989. 40.00 (*1-85098-160-4*, Pub. by Jordanhill College UK) St Mut.

Classroom Creature Culture: Algae to Anoles. rev. ed. Carol Hampton et al. (Illus.). 96p. (Orig.). 1994. pap. text ed. 12.95 (*0-87355-120-6*) Natl Sci Tchrs.

Classroom Crucible: What Really Works, What Doesn't, & Why. Edward Pauly. LC 90-55591. 1992. pap. 14.00 (*0-465-01151-9*) Basic.

Classroom Crusaders: Eleven Teachers Who Are Trying to Change the System. Ed. by Ronald A. Wolk & Blake H. Rodman. LC 94-15536. (Education Ser.). 283p. 1994. 24.95 (*0-7879-0014-1*) Jossey-Bass.

Classroom Discipline: An Idea Handbook for Elementary School Teachers. 2nd ed. Dorothy Rogers. 288p. 1987. text ed. 24.95 (*0-87628-011-4*) P-H.

Classroom Discipline: Case Studies & Viewpoints. 2nd ed. Sylvester Kohut, Jr. & Dale G. Range. 112p. 1986. 10.95 (*0-8106-1486-3*) NEA.

Classroom Discipline & Control: One Hundred & One Practical Techniques. Fred B. Chernow & Carol Chernow. LC 80-21700. 204p. 1981. text ed. 24.95 (*0-13-136283-6*, Parker Publishing Co) P-H.

Classroom Discipline & Management. Clifford H. Edwards. 368p. (Orig.). (C). 1993. pap. write for info. (*0-02-331630-6*) Macmillan.

Classroom Discourse: The Language of Teaching & Learning. Courtney Cazden. LC 87-11874. viii, 230p. (Orig.). 1988. pap. text ed. 21.50 (*0-435-08445-3*) Heinemann.

Classroom Display. Noel Hodgson. (Illus.). 96p. (Orig.). 1988. teacher ed 19.95 (*0-906212-62-6*, Pub. by Tarquin UK) Parkwest Pubns.

Classroom Dulcimer. Lois Hornbostel. (Illus.). 64p. (J). (gr. 5-8). 1991. pap. text ed. 12.95 (*0-9614939-6-8*) Backyard Music.

Classroom Dynamics: Implementing a Technology-Based Learning Environment. Ellen B. Mandinach & Hugh F. Cline. 224p. 1993. text ed. 49.95 (*0-8058-0555-9*) L Erlbaum Assocs.

Classroom Encounters: Problems, Case Studies, Solutions. R. Baird Shuman. 256p. 1989. 19.95 (*0-8106-3001-X*) NEA.

Classroom Environment. (K-Three Curriculum Ser.). 156p. 1992. Field Test Ed. pap. 22.95 (*0-929816-39-0*) High-Scope.

Classroom Ethnography. Martyn Hammersley. 1990. 90.00 (*0-335-09236-5*, Open Univ Pr); pap. 32.00 (*0-335-09235-7*, Open Univ Pr) Taylor & Francis.

Classroom Exercises in General Semantics. Ed. by Mary Morain. LC 80-80100. 162p. 1980. pap. 10.00 (*0-918970-26-1*) Intl Gen Semantics.

Classroom Experiences: The Writing Process in Action. Ed. by Naomi Gordon. LC 84-6560. 118p. 1984. pap. text ed. 14.00 (*0-435-08210-8*, 08210) Heinemann.

Classroom Experiments in Hair Structure & Chemistry. Clarice Morris. (Illus.). 1976. 37.50 (*0-87350-068-7*) Milady Pub.

Classroom Ideas for Encouraging Thinking & Feeling, Vol. 2. Frank E. Williams. 170p. (Orig.). (gr. 1-12). 1982. teacher ed 14.00 (*0-88047-011-9*, 8215) DOK Pubs.

Classroom Ideas, Vol. Three: Curriculum Units. Frank Williams. 1991. 14.00 (*0-88047-203-0*, D9011) DOK Pubs.

Classroom in Conflict: Teaching Controversial Subjects in a Diverse Society. John A. Williams. LC 93-42768. (Philosophy of Education Ser.). 204p. 1994. 49.50 (*0-7914-2119-8*); pap. 18.95x (*0-7914-2120-1*) State U NY Pr.

Classroom Kickoff. Linda Milliken. 304p. 1992. pap. text ed. 21.50 (*1-56472-001-2*) Edupress.

Classroom Kit - Addition: Twenty-Eight Individual Sets. Marion W. Stuart. Date not set. student ed, text ed. write for info. (*0-943343-41-0*) Lrn Wrap-Ups.

Classroom Kit - Division: Twenty-Eight Individual Sets. Marion W. Stuart. Date not set. student ed, text ed. write for info. (*0-943343-44-5*) Lrn Wrap-Ups.

Classroom Kit - Multiplication: Twenty-Eighty Individual Sets. Marion W. Stuart. Date not set. student ed, text ed. write for info. (*0-943343-43-7*) Lrn Wrap-Ups.

Classroom Kit - Subtraction: Twenty-Eight Individual Sets. Marion W. Stuart. Date not set. student ed, text ed. write for info. (*0-943343-42-9*) Lrn Wrap-Ups.

Classroom, Laboratory, & Clinical Activities. Klingele. 1986. text ed. 33.00 (*0-205-10264-6*, H0264-5) Allyn.

Classroom Leadership Styles: IBM-PC Version. California State University Staff. 1984. 49.95 (*0-07-831047-4*) McGraw.

Classroom Learning Centers. John Morland et al. LC 73-77592. (J). (gr. 1-6). 1973. pap. 10.99 (*0-8224-1410-4*) Fearon Teach Aids.

Classroom Lessons: Integrating Cognitive Theory & Classroom Practice. Ed. by Kate McGilly. (Illus.). 450p. 1994. 45.00 (*0-262-13300-8*, Bradford Bks) MIT Pr.

Classroom Life as Civic Education: Individual Achievement & Student Cooperation in Schools. David C. Bricker. (Professional Ethics in Education Ser.: No. 2). 152p. 1989. text ed. 21.95 (*0-8077-2959-0*) Tchrs Coll.

Classroom Magic: Amazing Technology for Teachers & Homeschoolers. 4th ed. Linda Lloyd. (Illus.). 160p. (Orig.). 1982. reprint ed. pap. 15.95 (*1-55552-014-6*) Metamorphous Pr.

Classroom Management. Shirley Bull & Jonathan Solity. (Principles of Practice Ser.). 208p. 1987. lib. bdg. 55.00 (*0-7099-1415-6*, Pub. by Croom Helm UK) Routledge Chapman & Hall.

Classroom Management. Barbara Gruber. (Instant Idea Bks.). (Illus.). 64p. 1985. 7.95 (*0-86734-056-8*, FS-8306) Schaffer Pubns.

***Classroom Management.** William Martin. 176p. (C). 1995. pap. text ed., spiral bd. 30.95 (*0-7872-1030-7*) Kendall-Hunt.

Classroom Management. O'Leary. (C). 1977. 63.95 (*0-205-14430-6*, H4430) Allyn.

Classroom Management: A Guidebook for Success. Bonnie Williamson. (Illus.). 150p. (Orig.). 1992. pap. text ed. 12.95 (*0-937899-15-1*) Dynamic Teaching.

Classroom Management: Methods & Techniques for Elementary & Secondary Teachers. 2nd ed. Johanna K. Lemlech. (Illus.). 339p. (C). 1991. reprint ed. pap. text ed. 19.95x (*0-88133-620-3*) Waveland Pr.

Classroom Management: The Reflective Teacher-Leader. 2nd ed. Len A. Froyen. LC 92-19178. 496p. (C). 1993. pap. write for info. (*0-02-339791-8*) Macmillan.

Classroom Management see National Society for the Study of Education 78th Yearbook

***Classroom Management & Discipline: Methods to Facilitate Cooperation & Instruction.** Paul R. Burden. LC 94-5432. 400p. (C). 1995. pap. text ed. 31.95 (*0-8013-1185-3*) Longman.

Classroom Management Cases for Teacher Problem Solving. Rita Silverman et al. 1994. pap. text ed. write for info. (*0-07-057668-8*) McGraw.

Classroom Management for Elementary Teachers. Carolyn M. Evertson et al. (Illus.). 176p. (C). 1984. pap. text ed. 20.00 (*0-13-136127-9*) P-H.

Classroom Management for Elementary Teachers. 3rd ed. Carolyn M. Evertson et al. LC 93-1563. 1993. pap. text ed. 26.00 (*0-205-15426-3*) Allyn.

Classroom Management for Secondary Teachers. Edmund T. Emmer et al. Ed. by Murray E. Worsham. (Illus.). 160p. 1984. pap. text ed. 16.00 (*0-685-07854-X*) P-H.

Classroom Management for Secondary Teachers. 3rd ed. Edmund T. Emmer et al. LC 93-1564. 1993. pap. text ed. 26.00 (*0-205-15490-5*) Allyn.

Classroom Management from A to Z. Robert T. Tauber. Ed. by Jo-Anne Weaver & Dawn Youngblood. LC 89-15474. (Illus.). 320p. (C). 1990. pap. text ed. 18.75 (*0-03-030003-7*) HB Coll Pubs.

***Classroom Management in the Elementary School.** 2nd rev. ed. C. M. Charles & Gail W. Senter. LC 94-3648. 316p. (C). 1995. pap. text ed. 24.95 (*0-8013-1474-7*) Longman.

Classroom Management Strategies: Gaining & Maintaining Students' Cooperation. 2nd ed. James S. Cangelosi. 352p. (C). 1993. teacher ed write for info. (*0-8013-1090-3*, 79541); pap. text ed. 28.50 (*0-8013-0614-0*, 78547) Longman.

Classroom Management Survival Kit: Bulletin Boards, Student Activities & Teacher Ideas to Help You Motivate, Educate & Collaborate. Susanne Glover & Georgeann Grewe. (Illus.). 144p. (J). (gr. k-6). 1994. 11.95 (*0-86653-782-1*, GA1476) Good Apple.

Classroom Management Through Curricular Adaptations: Educating Minority Handicapped Students. John J. Hoover & Catherine Collier. LC 86-82580. 80p. 1986. pap. text ed. 8.50 (*0-940059-00-2*) Hamilton Pubns.

Classroom Management with Adolescents. Ed. by James D. Long & Robert L. Williams. LC 73-3077. 164p. 1973. pap. text ed. 12.95 (*0-8422-0288-9*) Irvington.

Classroom Measurement & Evaluation. 3rd ed. Charles D. Hopkins & Richard L. Antes. LC 89-63449. 571p. 1990. text ed. 45.00 (*0-87581-329-1*) Peacock Pubs.

Classroom Museums. Gloria McCarthy & Molly Marso. (Illus.). 56p. (gr. 3-6). 1983. 7.50 (*0-88047-027-5*, 8317) DOK Pubs.

Classroom Museums: Touchable Tables for Kids! Grades 3-6. Pamela Marx. (Illus.). 184p. (Orig.). (J). 1992. pap. 12.95 (*0-673-36040-7*) GdYrBks.

Classroom Newspaper Activities: A Resource for Teachers, Grades K-8. Frances J. Anderson. (Illus.). 276p. 1985. spiral bd., pap. 31.95x (*0-398-05145-3*) C C Thomas.

Classroom Nonverbal Communication. Sean Neill. (International Library of Psychology). (Illus.). 228p. (C). 1991. text ed. 65.00 (*0-415-02663-6*, A5247) Routledge.

Classroom Nursery Rhymes Activities Kit. Jody Carlisle et al. 232p. 1983. pap. text ed. 27.95 (*0-87628-228-1*) Ctr Appl Res.

Classroom Observation of Primary School Children see Observing Children in the Primary Classroom: All in a Day

Classroom Observation Tasks: A Resource Book for Language Teachers & Trainers. Ruth Wajnryb. (Cambridge Teacher Training & Development Ser.). 160p. (C). 1993. 37.95 (*0-521-40362-6*); pap. 16.95 (*0-521-40722-2*) Cambridge U Pr.

Classroom Observer: Developing Observation Skills in Early Childhood Settings. 2nd ed. Ann E. Boehm & Richard A. Weinberg. 176p. (C). 1987. pap. text ed. 15.95 (*0-8077-2874-8*) Tchrs Coll.

Classroom of the 21st Century: The Integrated Thematic Instruction Approach to a Brain-Compatible Environment. Robert Ellingsen. (Illus.). 72p. (Orig.). 1989. pap. 12.95 (*1-878631-03-9*) S Kovalik.

Classroom of the 21st Century: The Integrated Thematic Instruction Approach to Brain-Compatible Learning. Robert Ellingsen. (Illus.). 79p. (Orig.). 1992. Tchr.'s ed. teacher ed 15.95 (*1-878631-07-1*) S Kovalik.

***Classroom Organization - It Can Be Done Vol. 1: An Illustrated Guide to Dinah Zike's Classroom Organization.** Dinah Zike. Ed. by Earl Jordan. (Illus.). 122p. 1989. pap. 14.95 (*1-882796-06-3*, CCC 99) Dinah-Might Act.

Classroom Organizer: Two Hundred One Ready-to-Use Forms for K-8 Teachers & Administrators. Antonia Ballare & Angelique Lampros. 256p. 1989. pap. text ed. 24.95 (*0-13-136870-2*) P-H.

Classroom Parties. Susan Spaete. Ed. by Liz Wilmes & Dick Wilmes. (Illus.). 120p. (Orig.). 1987. pap. 8.95 (*0-943452-07-4*) Building Blocks.

Classroom Pedagogy & Primary Practice. David McNamara. LC 93-17212. 1994. write for info. (*0-415-08311-7*); pap. write for info. (*0-415-08312-5*) Routledge.

***Classroom Pet.** Grace Maccarone. LC 95-13151. (Hello Reader! Level 1: First Grade Friends Ser.: Bk. 3). (Illus.). (J). 1995. write for info. (*0-590-26264-5*) Scholastic Inc.

Classroom Practice: Teacher Images in Action. D. Jean Clandinin. 190p. 1986. 55.00 (*1-85000-037-9*, Falmer Pr); pap. 33.00 (*1-85000-038-7*, Falmer Pr) Taylor & Francis.

***Classroom Practice Ser. Mastering Mainstreaming.** Marjorie T. Goldstein & Susan Kuveke. (Classroom Practice Ser.). 80p. 1995. pap. 10.00 (*0-912099-40-2*) Kappa Delta Pi.

***Classroom Presentation Software.** Irwin Staff. (C). 1991. text ed. 30.00 (*0-256-11501-X*) Irwin.

Classroom Presents the Constitution of the United States: A Story for Elementary School Children. Janice Howes. LC 87-50078. (Illus.). 35p. (Orig.). (J). (gr. k-5). 1987. pap. 7.00 (*0-942431-00-6*) Teachers Pub Hse.

Classroom Processes: Study Guide. Ed. by Deakin University Press Staff. 417p. (C). 1989. 120.00 (*0-7300-0650-6*, Pub. by Deakin Univ AT); vhs 180.00 (*0-685-57277-3*, Pub. by Deakin Univ AT) St Mut.

Classroom Publishing: A Practical Guide to Enhancing Student Literacy. Laurie King & Dennis Stovall. 208p. (Orig.). 1992. pap. 22.95 (*0-936085-52-5*) Blue Heron OR.

Classroom Questions: What Kinds? Norris M. Sanders. (C). 1990. pap. text ed. 23.00 (*0-06-045712-0*) HarpCollege.

Classroom Reading Instruction. 2nd ed. Richard A. Thompson. 416p. 1991. per. 31.95 (*0-8403-6803-8*) Kendall-Hunt.

Classroom Reading Inventory. 6th ed. Nicholas J. Silvaroli. 176p. 1990. spiral bd. write for info. (*0-697-10421-4*) Brown & Benchmark.

Classroom Reading Inventory. 7th ed. Nicholas Silvaroli. 160p. 1994. spiral bd. write for info. (*0-697-12586-6*) Brown & Benchmark.

Classroom Reading Profiles: A Process Approach. Mary J. Gray & Dorothy Giroux. 244p. 1990. spiral bd. 25.95 (*0-8403-6192-0*) Kendall-Hunt.

Classroom Recorder, 2 bks., Bk. 1. Gerald Burakoff & Sonya Burakoff. 1970. 3.00 (*0-913334-00-6*, CM1001) Consort Music.

Classroom Recorder, 2 bks., Bk. 2. Gerald Burakoff & Sonya Burakoff. 1972. 3.25 (*0-685-51174-X*, CM1013) Consort Music.

Classroom Reference Collection - Math. 1990. pap. text ed. 137.75 (*0-201-28660-2*) Addison-Wesley.

Classroom Reference Collection - Reading. 1990. pap. text ed. 93.25 (*0-201-28662-9*) Addison-Wesley.

Classroom Relevant Research in the Language Arts. Harold G. Shane & James Walder. 1985. pap. 7.50 (*0-87120-090-2*, 611-78140) Assn Supervision.

Classroom Research: Early Lessons from Success. Ed. by Thomas A. Angelo. LC 85-644763. (New Directions for Teaching & Learning Ser.: No. 46). 1991. 16.95 (*1-55542-800-2*) Jossey-Bass.

Classroom Revisited see Foreign Language Learning: Research & Development

Classroom Set, Set. (Rimas y Risas Green Ser.). (Illus.). (ENG & SPA.). (J). (gr. k-3). 1988. teacher ed, ring bd. 316.00 (*0-917837-23-1*) Hampton-Brown.

Classroom Set, Set. (Cuento Mas Ser.). (Illus.). (ENG & SPA.). (J). 1989. teacher ed, ring bd. 315.00 (*0-917837-25-8*) Hampton-Brown.

Classroom Set, Set. (Rimas y Risas Red Ser.). (Illus.). (ENG & SPA.). (J). (gr. k-3). 1990. teacher ed, pap. text ed. 277.00 (*0-917837-60-6*) Hampton-Brown.

Classroom Set: Green Set, Set. Alma F. Ada. (Dias y Dias de Poesia Ser.). (Illus.). (Orig.). (SPA.). (J). (gr. 1-3). 1992. teacher ed, pap. 255.00 (*1-56334-120-4*) Hampton-Brown.

Classroom Set: Level 2, Set. (Wonders! Ser.). (Illus.). (Orig.). 1992. teacher ed, pap. 399.00 (*1-56334-220-0*); teacher ed, ring bd. 399.00 (*1-56334-207-3*) Hampton-Brown.

Classroom Set: Tan Set. Alma F. Ada. (Dias y Dias de Poesia Ser.). (Illus.). (Orig.). (SPA.). (J). (gr. 1-3). 1991. Set incl. anthology, 4 tapes, tan charts, 12 small bks. pap. 255.00 (*1-56334-119-0*) Hampton-Brown.

Classroom Skills in English Teaching: A Self-Appraisal Framework. Colin Peacock. 256p. 1990. 59.50 (*0-415-03633-X*, A4137); pap. 17.95 (*0-415-03634-8*, A4141) Routledge.

Classroom Starters for Any Occasion. Mary McMillan. 144p. 1989. 12.95 (*0-86653-508-X*, GA1130) Good Apple.

Classroom Strategies for Secondary Reading. 2nd ed. Ed. by W. John Harker. LC 84-28939. 149p. reprint ed. pap. 42.50 (*0-7837-0358-9*, 2040679) Bks Demand.

Classroom Strategies That Work: An Elementary Teacher's Guide to Process Writing. Frances Temple et al. LC 88-17602. (Illus.). xiv, 162p. (Orig.). (C). 1988. pap. text ed. 19.00 (*0-435-08479-8*, 08479) Heinemann.

Classroom Success for the Learning Disabled. Suzanne H. Stevens. LC 82-25726. xvi, 314p. 1984. 15.95 (*0-89587-036-3*); pap. 8.95 (*0-89587-035-5*) Blair.

***Classroom Talk.** Thornley-Hall & Booth. 118p. 1991. pap. text ed. 14.50 (*0-435-08596-4*, 08596) Heinemann.

Classroom Talk about Text. Ed. by Rosalind Horowitz. 64p. 1994. pap. 7.00 (*0-87207-399-8*) Intl Reading.

***Classroom Teachers ESL Survival Kit, No. 2.** Claire. 1995. pap. text ed. 31.50 (*0-13-299876-9*) P-H.

Classroom Teacher's ESL Survival Kit Number One. Elizabeth Claire & Judie Haynes. Ed. by John Chapman. LC 94-7447. 208p. 1994. write for info. (*0-13-137613-6*) P-H.

Classroom Teachers' Estimation of Intelligence & Industry of High School Students. Harry Eisner. LC 79-176743. (Columbia University. Teachers College. Contributions to Education Ser.: No. 726). reprint ed. 37.50 (*0-404-55726-0*) AMS Pr.

Classroom Teacher's Guide to Music Education. C. Vernon Burnsed. LC 92-38408. (Illus.). 174p. (C). 1993. pap. text ed., spiral bd. 31.95x (*0-398-05837-7*) C C Thomas.

Classroom Teaching & Learning. Robert L. Hohn. LC 94-4817. 425p. (C). 1995. teacher ed write for info. (*0-8013-0884-4*, 78986) Longman.

Classroom Teaching & Learning. Robert L. Hohn. LC 94-4817. 480p. (C). 1995. text ed. 45.95 (*0-8013-0879-8*, 78981) Longman.

Classroom Teaching Skills. 3rd ed. Kenneth D. Moore. LC 94-11081. 1994. pap. text ed. write for info. (*0-07-042922-7*) McGraw.

Classroom Teaching Skills. 4th ed. James A. Cooper et al. LC 89-85072. 415p. (C). 1990. pap. text ed. 25.00 (*0-669-20162-6*); Instr.'s guide. teacher ed 2.00 (*0-669-20163-4*) Heath.

***Classroom Teaching Skills.** 5th ed. Ed. by James M. Cooper. 408p. 1994. pap. text ed. write for info. (*0-669-34963-1*) Heath.

Classroom Techniques: Foreign Languages & English As a Second Language. Edward D. Allen & Rebecca M. Valette. 418p. (Orig.). (C). 1977. pap. text ed. 15.00 (*0-15-507674-4*) HB Coll Pubs.

***Classroom Techniques: Foreign Languages & English As a Second Language.** Edward D. Allen & Rebecca M. Valette. (Illus.). 418p. (Orig.). (C). 1994. pap. text ed. 18.95x (*0-88133-809-5*) Waveland Pr.

Classroom Technology: A Concise Overview for the Traditional & Non-Traditional Student Preliminary Edition. Judith E. Wakefield. 176p. (C). 1993. per., pap. text ed. 29.95 (*0-8403-8559-5*) Kendall-Hunt.

Classroom Testing. J. B. Heaton. (Keys to Language Teaching Ser.). 127p. 1990. pap. text ed. 17.95 (*0-582-74625-6*, 78666) Longman.

Classroom Testing: Construction. 2nd ed. Charles D. Hopkins & Richard L. Antes. LC 88-61530. 193p. 1989. pap. 14.00 (*0-87581-334-8*) Peacock Pubs.

Classroom Time Management, Bk. I: Organizing Self & Others. Dick Webster & Dave Bailey. 1992. pap. text ed. 13.95 (*1-881449-00-9*) Webley Assocs.

Classroom Time Management, Bk. II: Organizing Students. Dick Webster & Dave Bailey. 113p. 1992. pap. text ed. 12.95 (*1-881449-01-7*) Webley Assocs.

Classroom Time Management, Bk. III: Organizing Work. Dick Webster & Dave Bailey. 191p. 1992. pap. text ed. 14.95 (*1-881449-02-5*) Webley Assocs.

Classroom TOEFL. Lloyd Precious et al. 1993. teacher ed 14.95 (*0-8120-1517-7*); teacher ed 12.95 (*0-8120-1800-1*); teacher ed 79.95 (*0-8120-8027-0*) Barron.

Classroom TOEFL, 4 cass., Set. Lloyd Precious et al. 1993. audio 40.00 (*0-8120-1516-9*) Barron.

Classroom Visual Activities (CVA) Regina G. Richards. Ed. by Rick Brownell. (Illus.). 80p. (Orig.). 1988. pap. text ed. 12.00 (*0-87879-657-6*) Acad Therapy.

Classrooms & Literacy. David Bloome. LC 88-36906. 432p. (C). 1989. text ed. 59.50 (*0-89391-506-8*) Ablex Pub.

Classrooms & Staffrooms: The Sociology of Teachers & Teaching. Ed. by Andy Hargreaves & Peter Woods. 256p. 1984. pap. 29.00 (*0-335-10583-1*, Open Univ Pr) Taylor & Francis.

Classrooms in Crisis. Arnold Burron et al. LC 85-73068. 196p. (Orig.). 1992. pap. 8.99 (*0-89636-192-6*, LifeJourney) Chariot Family.

Classrooms in the Workplace: Workplace Literacy Programs in Small & Medium-Sized Firms. Kevin Hollenbeck. LC 93-45620. 130p. 1993. text ed. 20.00 (*0-88099-146-1*); pap. text ed. 10.00 (*0-88099-145-3*) W E Upjohn.

C

An Asterisk (*) at the beginning of an entry indicates that the title is appearing in BIP for the first time.

C

An Asterisk (*) at the beginning of an entry indicates that the title is appearing in BIP for the first time.

1305

Claudio Merulo: Il Secondo Libro de Madrigali a Cinque Voci (Venice, 1604) Ed. by Jessie A. Owens. LC 93-49757. (Sixteenth-Century Madrigal Ser.: Vol. 19). 208p. 1994. 71.00 (*0-8240-5519-5*) Garland.

Claudio Merulo: Ricercari da Cantare a Quattro Voci--Libro Terzo - Venice 1608, Vol. 7. Ed. by James Ladewig. LC 87-754765. (Italian Instrumental Music of the Sixteenth & Early Seventeenth Centuries Ser.). 1988. lib. bdg. 86.00 (*0-8240-4506-8*) Garland.

Claudio Merulo: Ricercari da Cantare a Quattro Voci... Libro Secondo, Venice, 1607. Ed. by James Ladewig. LC 87-752604. (Italian Instrumental Music of the Sixteenth & Early Seventeenth Centuries Ser.: Vol. 6). 1987. lib. bdg. 92.00 (*0-8240-4505-X*) Garland.

Claudio Merulo Il Primo Libro de Madrigali a Cinque Voci (Venice, 1566) Jessie A. Owens. LC 93-33356. (Sixteenth Century Madrigal Ser.: Vol. 18). 232p. 1994. 78.00 (*0-8240-5518-7*) Garland.

Claudio Monteverdi: A Guide to Research. Dyke Kiel & K. Gary Adams. LC 89-33040. (Composer Resource Manuals Ser.: Vol. 23). 292p. 1989. 47.00 (*0-8240-7743-1*, 792) Garland.

Claudio Rodriguez & the Language of Poetic Vision. Jonathan Mayhew. LC 89-42931. 160p. 1990. 32.50 (*0-8387-5174-1*) Bucknell U Pr.

Claudio Veggio: Madrigali a Guattro Voci (Venice, 1540) Ed. by Jessie A. Owens. LC 92-772058. (Sixteenth Century Madrigal Ser.: Vol. 4). (Illus.). 216p. 1992. 69.00 (*0-8240-5504-7*) Garland.

Claudius: The Corruption of Power. Barbara Levick. LC 89-51800. 272p. (C). 1993. pap. 16.00 (*0-300-05831-4*) Yale U Pr.

Claudius Crozet: French Engineer in America, 1790-1864. Robert F. Hunter & Edwin L. Dooley, Jr. LC 89-5312. (Illus.). 256p. 1989. 29.50 (*0-8139-1222-9*) U Pr of Va.

Claudius Galenus: Index in Galeni Libros. Ed. by C. G. Kuhn. Vol. XX. lxii, 676p. 1965. reprint ed. write for info. (*0-318-72024-8*, Pub. by Georg Olms GW) Lubrecht & Cramer.

Claudius Pontificals. Ed. by D. H. Turner. (Publications of the Henry Bradshaw Society Ser. No. XCIV (94)). 1970. 30.00 (*0-907077-14-5*) Boydell & Brewer.

Claudius Quadrigarius - Lexicon in Q. Claudium Quadrigarium. Ed. by Sonia Bastian. (Alpha-Omega, Reihe A Ser.: Bd. LXI). viii, 73p. 1983. write for info. (*3-487-07378-1*, Pub. by Georg Olms GW) Lubrecht & Cramer.

Claudius, the Emperor & His Achievement. rev. ed. Arnaldo D. Momigliano. Tr. by W. D. Hogarth. LC 80-26158. xv, 143p. 1981. reprint ed. text ed. 59.75 (*0-313-20813-1*, MOCE, Greenwood Pr) Greenwood.

Claudius the God. Robert Graves. LC 83-42945. 592p. 1983. 10.95 (*0-394-60812-7*, Modern Lib) Random.

Claudius the God. Robert Graves. (Vintage International Ser.). 1989. pap. 14.00 (*0-679-72573-3*, Vin) Random.

Claudius Tiberius Nero. LC 71-133646. (Tudor Facsimile Texts. Old English Plays Ser.: No. 117). reprint ed. 49.50 (*0-404-53417-1*) AMS Pr.

Claughton Pellew, Wood Engravings. Anne Stevens. 1993. pap. 21.00 (*0-907849-82-2*, Silent Bks) St Mut.

Claus Sluter: Artist at the Court of Burgundy. Kathleen Morand & David Finn. (Illus.). 400p. 1991. 75.00 (*0-292-71117-4*) U of Tex Pr.

Claus Spreckels, the Sugar King in Hawaii. Jacob Adler. 320p. 1989. 5.95 (*0-935180-76-1*) Mutual Pub HI.

Clausal Theory of Types. D. A. Wolfram. (Tracts in Theoretical Computer Science Ser.: No. 21). 250p. (C). 1993. 39.95 (*0-521-39538-0*) Cambridge U Pr.

Clausalform Logic: An Introduction to the Logic of Computer Reasoning. Thomas J. Richards. (International Computer Science Ser.). (Illus.). (C). 1989. pap. text ed. 38.75 (*0-201-12920-5*) Addison-Wesley.

***Clause by Clause: The Screenwriter's Legal Guide.** Stephen F. Breimer. LC 94-48672. 1995. write for info. (*0-440-50561-5*) Dell.

***Clause Combination in Chinese.** Halvor Eifring. LC 94-40785. (Sinica Leidensia, x069-9563 Ser.: Vol. 32). 1994. write for info. (*90-04-10146-2*) E J Brill.

Clause Combining in Grammar & Discourse. Ed. by John Haiman & Sandra A. Thompson. LC 88-35006. (Typological Studies in Language: No. 18). xiii, 428p. 1989. 112.00 (*1-55619-022-0*) Benjamins North Am.

Clause de Style. Frederic H. Fajardie. (FRE.). 1988. pap. 10.95 (*0-7859-2565-1*, 2070381218) Fr & Eur.

Clause, Sentence & Discourse Patterns in Selected Languages of Nepal, 15 fiches, Set. Ed. by Austin Hale. (Publications in Linguistics & Related Fields: No. 40). 1973. fiche 60.00 (*0-88312-442-4*) Summer Instit Ling.

Clause Structure & Language Change. Ed. by Adrian Battye & Ian Roberts. (Oxford Studies in Comparative Syntax). (Illus.). 304p. 1995. 60.00 (*0-19-508632-5*); pap. 38.00 (*0-19-508633-3*) OUP.

Clause Union in Chamorro & in Universal Grammar. Jeanne D. Gibson. LC 92-13238. (Outstanding Dissertations in Linguistics Ser.). 280p. 1992. 68.00 (*0-8153-0702-0*) Garland.

Clauses & Phrases. C. G. Cleveland. (Straight Forward Advanced English Ser.). 80p. 1993. student ed 6.95 (*0-931993-55-5*, GP-055) Garlic Pr OR.

***Clauses d'Exception En Matiere De Conflits De Lois et De Conflits De Jurisdictions - Ou le Principe De Proximite: Exception Clauses in Conflicts of Laws & Conflicts of Jurisdictions - or the Principle of Proximity.** Ed. by D. Kokkini-Iatridou. 352p. (C). 1994. lib. bdg. 99.00 (*0-7923-3017-X*) Kluwer Ac.

Clausewitz. Michael C. Howard. (Past Masters Ser.). 1983. pap. 7.95 (*0-19-287607-4*) OUP.

Clausewitz. Roger Parkinson. LC 79-150602. (Illus.). 1979. reprint ed. pap. 12.95 (*0-8128-6021-7*, Scrbrough Hse) Madison Bks UPA.

Clausewitz & Escalation: Classical Perspective on Nuclear Strategy. Stephen J. Cimbala. 218p. 1991. text ed. 7.95 (*0-7146-3420-4*, Pub. by F Cass Pubs UK) Intl Spec Bk.

Clausewitz & Modern Strategy. Ed. by Michael I. Handel. 352p. 1986. 30.00 (*0-7146-3294-5*, Pub. by F Cass Pubs UK); pap. 14.95 (*0-7146-4053-0*, Pub. by F Cass Pubs UK) Intl Spec Bk.

Clausewitz & the State: The Man, His Theories, & His Times. Peter Paret. LC 85-6570. 480p. 1985. pap. text ed. 18.95x (*0-691-00806-X*) Princeton U Pr.

Clausweitz in English: The Reception of Clausewitz in Britain & America, 1815-1945. Christopher Bassford. 320p. 1994. 47.00 (*0-19-508383-0*) OUP.

Clavaria of the Sikkim Himalayas. S. S. Rattan & I. P. S. Khurana. (Bibliotheca Mycologica Ser.: No. 66). (Illus.). 1978. pap. text ed. 18.00 (*3-7682-1212-2*) Lubrecht & Cramer.

Clavarias of the United States & Canada. W. C. Coker. 1932. reprint ed. 48.00 (*3-7682-0913-X*) Lubrecht & Cramer.

Clavarioid Fungi of New Zealand. Ronald H. Petersen. (Illus.). 170p. 1988. pap. 65.00 (*0-477-02514-5*) Lubrecht & Cramer.

***Clave.** Pierre Seghers & Pierre Cabanne. (Great Monographs). (Illus.). 424p. 1993. 250.00 (*84-343-0635-2*) Elliots Bks.

***Clave: Sculptor.** Lluis Permanyer. (Great Monographs). (Illus.). 288p. 1993. 250.00 (*84-343-0633-6*) Elliots Bks.

Clave de Cuaderno Taquigrafia Gregg S90. John R. Gregg. 1982. pap. text ed. 6.95 (*0-07-024485-5*) McGraw.

Clave De Visiones y Profecias Daniel: The Prophet Daniel. Arno C. Gaebelein. (SPA.). 5.95 (*84-7228-735-1*, 220232, Pub. by Edit Clie SP) TSELF.

Clave para Identificar los Peces Marinos del Peru. F. Norma Chirichigno. (Institut del Mar del Peru Ser.: Informe 44). (Illus.). 388p. (SPA.). 1978. reprint ed. pap. text ed. 65.00 (*3-87429-131-6*) Koeltz Sci Bks.

Claverack, Old & New. Franklin H. Webb. 1973. reprint ed. pap. 5.00 (*0-910746-23-0*, COA01) Hope Farm.

Claverings. Anthony Trollope. (Illus.). 448p. 1977. pap. 8.50 (*0-486-23464-9*) Dover.

Claverings. Anthony Trollope. Ed. & Intro. by David Skilton. (World's Classics Ser.). 560p. 1986. pap. 8.95 (*0-19-281727-2*) OUP.

Claverings. Anthony Trollope. 544p. 1994. pap. 8.95 (*0-14-043822-X*, Penguin Classics) Viking Penguin.

Claverleigh Curse. Sandra DuBay. (Orig.). 1982. pap. 2.50 (*0-89083-958-1*) Zebra.

Claves de Antonio Machado. Bernard Sese. Tr. by Soledad Garcia Mouton. (Nueva Austral Ser.: Vol. 178). (SPA.). 1991. pap. text ed. 29.95x (*84-239-1978-1*) Elliots Bks.

Claves de Interpretacion Biblica. Thomas Fountain. 148p. 1987. reprint ed. pap. 5.25 (*0-311-03653-8*) Casa Bautista.

Claves Psicologicas en Nuestra America, Vision Puertorriquena. Lester N. Allende et al. (Editorial Homines Ser.). 300p. (SPA.). 1991. pap. text ed. 20.00 (*0-9623590-3-3*) Libros-Ediciones.

Clavier-Buchlein Vor Wilhelm Friedemann Bach. Johann Sebastian Bach. (Music Reprint Ser.). 1979. reprint ed. 29.50 (*0-306-79558-2*) Da Capo.

Clavinova Sampler Pack Software. June Edison. (Peanuts Piano Course for Clavinova Ser.). (Illus.). 12p. (Orig.). (J). (gr. 1-6). 1992. pap. 19.95 (*1-56516-014-2*) Houston IN.

Clavis Mediaevalis: Kleines Woerterbuch der Mittelalterforschung. O. Meyer & R. Klauser. 312p. (GER.). 1966. 75.00 (*0-8288-6699-6*, M-7323, Pub. by Harrassowitz) Fr & Eur.

Clavis: or Key: An Exposition of Some Principal Matters & Words in the Writings of Jacob Boehme. Jacob Boehme. Tr. by John Sparrow. 63p. 1992. pap. 5.95 (*1-56459-267-7*) Kessinger Pub.

Clavis Philosophica. Jonas Hoecker. xvi, 674p. reprint ed. write for info. (*0-318-72031-0*, Pub. by Georg Olms GW) Lubrecht & Cramer.

Claw. Ken Eulo. 1994. 22.00 (*0-671-79963-0*) S&S Trade.

Claw. large type ed. Norah Lofts. 384p. 1983. 15.95 (*0-7089-1045-9*) Ulverscroft.

Claw Hammer. Paul D. Anderson. 1989. pap. 3.95 (*1-55817-281-5*, Pinnacle NY) Windsor NY.

Claw Your Way to the Top. Dave Barry. LC 86-13013. (Illus.). 96p. 1987. pap. 6.95 (*0-87857-652-5*, 20-564-1) Rodale Pr Inc.

***Clawhammer.** Sam Llewellyn. Ed. by Jane Chelius. 384p. 1995. mass mkt. 5.50 (*0-671-78994-5*) PB.

Clawhammer. large type ed. Sam Llewellyn. LC 94-10666. 516p. 1994. pap. 18.95 (*0-8161-7401-6*) Hall.

Clawhammer. large type ed. Sam Llewellyn. 548p. 1994. 26.95 (*0-7505-0684-9*) Ulverscroft.

Clawhammer Banjo. Miles Krassen. (Illus.). 80p. 1974. pap. 14.95 (*0-8256-0151-7*, OK63016, Oak) Music Sales.

Clawhammer Style Banjo. 2nd ed. Ken Perlman. 194p. 1989. reprint ed. pap. text ed. 16.95x (*0-931759-33-1*) Centerstream Pub.

Claws. D. Gunther Wilde. 1978. pap. 1.50 (*0-8439-0579-4*) Dorchester Pub Co.

Claws of Mercy. large type ed. John Harris. 1977. 15.95 (*0-7089-0004-6*) Ulverscroft.

Claws of the Crab: Georgia & Armenia in Crisis. Stephen Brook. (Illus.). 354p. 1993. 29.95 (*1-85619-161-3*, Sinclair-Stevenson) Trafalgar.

Claws of the Dragon: Kang Sheng - the Evil Genius Behind Mao - & His Legacy of Terror in People's China. John Byron & Robert Pack. (Illus.). 560p. 1993. pap. 14.00 (*0-671-79716-6*, Touchstone Bks) S&S Trade.

Claws of the Eagle. Ernest V. Correale. (Orig.). 1982. pap. 2.95 (*0-89083-957-3*) Zebra.

Claws of the Eagle. Andrew J. Fenady. 1990. pap. 3.95 (*1-55817-442-7*, Pinnacle NY) Windsor NY.

Claws of the Gryphon. large type ed. Peter Turnbull. 480p. 1988. 17.95 (*0-7089-1752-6*) Ulverscroft.

Claws, Paws, & Tales: Stories of Ordinary Pets with Extraordinary Ways. Ed. by Green & England. (Illus.). 86p. (Orig.). 1991. pap. 8.50 (*0-9625725-1-9*) Cat Tale Pr.

Clawson: Princess Eleanor, Being the Genealogy, Paternal & Maternal, of Mary Eleanor Clawson Knaus. Francis A. Knaus. (Illus.). 1109p. 1994. reprint ed. lib. bdg. 139.50 (*0-8328-4066-1*); reprint ed. pap. 129.50 (*0-8328-4067-X*) Higginson Bk Co.

Clay. Annabelle Dixon. Ed. by Rebecca Stefoff. LC 90-40369. (Threads Ser.). (Illus.). 22p. (J). (gr. 3-5). 1990. lib. bdg. 15.93 (*0-944483-69-0*) Garrett Ed Corp.

Clay. Mark Dunster. LC 74-165104. 1973. 4.00 (*0-89642-014-0*) Linden Pubs.

Clay. Jeannie Hull. LC 89-9959. (Fresh Start Ser.). (Illus.). 48p. (J). (gr. 3-6). 1989. lib. bdg. 12.95 (*0-531-10757-4*) Watts.

***Clay.** Ben Kelley. 330p. 1995. pap. 9.95 (*1-56901-557-0*) NW Pub.

Clay. Mike Roussel. (Craft Projects Ser.). (Illus.). 32p. (J). (gr. 2-6). 1990. lib. bdg. 15.94 (*0-86592-485-6*); lib. bdg. 11.95 (*0-685-36301-5*) Rourke Corp.

***Clay.** Lori V. Schue. (ArtWorks for Kids Ser.: Vol. 4). (Illus.). 48p. (J). (gr. k-6). 1995. pap. text ed. 9.95 (*1-55799-365-3*, EMC 294) Evan-Moor Corp.

Clay. Peter Whelan. (Royal Shakespeare Company PIT Playtext Ser.). 43p. (C). 1988. pap. 5.95 (*0-413-52580-5*, A0053) Heinemann.

Clay: Handbuilding. Maurice Sapiro. LC 78-72191. (Illus.). 88p. 1979. 14.50 (*0-87192-105-7*) Davis Mass.

Clay: The Potter's Wheel. Maurice Sapiro. LC 77-84480. (Illus.). 88p. 1978. 14.50 (*0-87192-095-6*) Davis Mass.

Clay & Cappuccino. Rena Kleefeld. LC 84-10378. (Illus.). xxvi, 246p. 1984. 18.00 (*0-911459-13-8*) Wedgestone Pr.

Clay & Clay Minerals of Japan. T. Sudo & S. Shimoda. (Developments in Sedimentology Ser.: Vol. 6). 326p. 1978. 123.00 (*0-444-99787-3*) Elsevier.

***Clay & Shale Slope Instability.** Ed. by William C. Haneberg & Scott A. Anderson. LC 94-49378. (Reviews in Engineering Geology Ser.: Vol. 10). 1995. write for info. (*0-8137-4110-6*) Geol Soc.

Clay & Star: Contemporary Bulgarian Poets. Ed. by Lisa Sapinkopf & Georgi Belev. Tr. by Georgi Belev. LC 92-4153. 232p. (Orig.). 1992. pap. 15.00 (*0-915943-85-9*) Milkweed Ed.

Clay Animation. Michael Frierson. (Twayne's Filmmakers Ser.). 304p. 1994. text ed. 29.95 (*0-8057-9327-5*, Twayne); pap. 18.95 (*0-8057-9328-3*, Twayne) Macmillan.

Clay Art of Adrian Saxe. Martha D. Lynn. LC 93-5654. (Illus.). 160p. 1994. 29.95 (*0-500-09238-9*) Thames Hudson.

Clay Babies & Other Puget Sound Stories. Jeffery H. Silver. 32p. (Orig.). (J). (gr. 5 up). 1982. pap. 4.00 (*0-910867-00-3*) Silver Seal Bks.

Clay Barriers for Embankment Dams. Institution of Civil Engineers Staff. 197p. 1990. text ed. 58.50 (*0-7277-1565-8*, Pub. by T Telford UK) Am Soc Civil Eng.

Clay-Based Materials for the Ceramics Industry: Proceedings for the Final Contractors' Meeting on Clay-Based Materials for the Ceramics Industry, Organized by the Commission of the European Communities Within the Raw Materials Sector (1982-85), Held in Brussels, Belgium, 11 Dec., 1986. Ed. by H. Nosbusch & I. V. Mitchell. 144p. 1989. 45.00 (*1-85166-315-0*) Elsevier.

Clay Bodies. Robert Tichane. LC 89-62305. (Ceramic Monographs). (Illus.). 339p. (C). 1990. 32.00x (*0-914267-06-X*) NYS Inst Glaze.

Clay Bonded Foundry Sand. W. B. Parkes. (Illus.). vii, 367p. 1971. 63.00 (*0-85334-833-2*, Pub. by Elsevier Applied Sci UK) Elsevier.

Clay Boy. Mirra Ginsburg. (Illus.). 32p. (J). (ps-3). 1993. lib. bdg. 14.95 (*0-399-21988-9*, Philomel Bks) Putnam Pub Group.

Clay Country. large type ed. Rowena Summers. 501p. 1992. 21.95 (*0-7505-0329-7*) Ulverscroft.

Clay Country Remembered: Recollections of a St. Austell Boyhood. Ed. by R. S. Best. (C). 1989. 50.00 (*1-85022-022-0*, Pub. by Dyllansow Truran UK) St Mut.

Clay County, Kansas Marriage Licenses (1866-1900) Topeka Genealogical Society Staff. LC 81-177136. 59p. 1980. pap. 7.75 (*0-943259-01-0*) Topeka Geneal Soc.

Clay County, Mississippi. Libby Bedford. (Illus.). 868p. 1988. 65.00 (*0-88107-125-0*) Curtis Media.

***Clay Dancers.** Cecil Dawkins. (Southwest Mysteries Ser.). (Orig.). 1994. mass mkt. 4.99 (*0-8041-1261-4*) Ivy Books.

***Clay Fighter II Official Game Secrets.** Ed Dille. 1994. pap. 9.95 (*1-55958-793-8*) Prima Pub.

Clay Figurines of Babylonia & Assyria. E. Douglas Van Buren. LC 78-63560. (Yale Oriental Series: Researches: No. 16). reprint ed. 57.50 (*0-404-60286-X*) AMS Pr.

***Clay from Molds: Multiples, Altered Castings, Combinations.** (Illus.). 56p. 1978. pap. 8.50 (*0-932718-03-5*) Kohler Arts.

Clay Hill. Tim Liardet. (Poetry Wales Poets Ser.: No. 12). 46p. (Orig.). 1988. pap. 8.95 (*0-907476-88-0*, Pub. by Poetry Wales Pr UK) Dufour.

Clay in Engineering Geology. 2nd rev. ed. J. E. Gillott. (Developments in Geotechnical Engineering Ser.: No. 41). (Illus.). 474p. 1987. 77.00 (*0-444-42758-9*) Elsevier.

Clay in the Classroom: Helping Children Develop Cognitive & Affective Skills for Learning. Sara Smilansky et al. 272p. 1989. reprint ed. pap. text ed. 18.95 (*0-8077-2965-5*) Tchrs Coll.

***Clay in the Master's Hands.** rev. ed. Donna Frank. Ed. by Andra Whitworth. LC 95-68808. (Illus.). 174p. 1995. pap. 14.95 (*0-9640706-2-6*) Cock-a-Hoop.

Clay Lifting. Anne A. Lohman. Ed. by Bill Thompson. LC 85-90939. 60p. (Orig.). 1985. pap. text ed. 7.95 (*0-685-71262-1*) Scott Pubns MI.

Clay Liners for Waste Management Facilities: Design, Construction & Evaluation. L. J. Goldman et al. LC 89-70985. (Pollution Technology Review Ser.: No. 178). (Illus.). 524p. 1990. 56.00 (*0-8155-1227-9*) Noyes.

Clay Marble. Minfong Ho. 160p. (YA). (gr. 7 up). 1991. 14.95 (*0-374-31340-7*) FS&G.

Clay Marble. Minfong Ho. (J). (gr. 4-7). 1993. pap. 4.50 (*0-374-41229-4*) FS&G.

Clay Microstructure. Richard Bennett & Matthew H. Hulbert. LC 85-11804. (Illus.). 150p. 1986. text ed. 39.00 (*0-88746-065-8*, QE471-3-B46) Intl Human Res.

Clay Mineralogy. Wilson. 1992. text ed. 105.00 (*0-442-30858-2*); text ed. 105.00 (*0-442-30859-0*) Van Nos Reinhold.

Clay Mineralogy. 2nd ed. Ralph E. Grim. LC 67-24951. (McGraw-Hill International Earth & Planetary Science Ser.). 596p. reprint ed. pap. 169.90 (*0-317-28217-4*, 2055969) Bks Demand.

***Clay Mineralogy: Spectroscopic & Chemical Determinative Methods.** Ed. by M. J. Wilson. LC 93-74207. 367p. 1994. 158.95 (*0-412-53380-4*) Chapman & Hall.

Clay Minerals. E. Nemecz. 548p. 1981. 227.00 (*0-569-08686-8*) St Mut.

Clay Minerals: A Physico-Chemical Explanation of Their Occurrence. Bruce Velde. (Developments in Sedimentology Ser.: Vol. 40). 428p. 1985. 89.75 (*0-444-42423-7*) Elsevier.

Clay Minerals & the Origin of Life. Ed. by A. G. Cairns-Smith & H. Hartman. 202p. 1987. 54.95 (*0-521-32408-4*) Cambridge U Pr.

Clay Minerals for Petroleum Geologists & Engineers. Ed. by Eric Eslinger & David Pevear. (Short Course Notes Ser.: No. 22). (Illus.). 428p. (Orig.). 1988. pap. text ed. 38.00 (*0-918985-73-0*) SEPM.

***Clay Minerals for Petroleum Geologists & Engineers.** Eric Eslinger & David Pevear. LC 89-157343. (SEPM Short Course Notes Ser.: No. 22). (Illus.). reprint ed. pap. 117.50 (*0-7837-9096-1*, 2049846) Bks Demand.

Clay Modelling for Everyone: Sculpture, Pottery & Jewellery Without a Wheel. Tr. by Charlotte De la Bedoyere. (Illus.). 112p. (Orig.). (YA). (gr. 7 up). 1988. pap. 16.95 (*0-85532-564-X*, Pub. by Search Pr UK) A Schwartz & Co.

Clay Pedestal: A Re-examination of the Doctor-Patient Relationship. Thomas Preston. LC 81-11742. 228p. 1981. 12.95 (*0-914842-68-4*) Madrona Pubs.

Clay Pigeon. Jose Maldonado. 1993. 17.95 (*0-533-10300-2*) Vantage.

Clay-Pot Cookbook: A New Way of Cooking in an Ancient Pot. Georgia Sales & Grover Sales. LC 74-81233. (Illus.). 256p. 1977. pap. 7.95 (*0-689-70547-6*, 228, Atheneum S&S) S&S Trade.

Clay Revisions: Plate, Cup, Vase. Vicki Halper. LC 87-82204. (Illus.). 64p. (Orig.). 1987. pap. 14.95 (*0-932216-26-9*) Seattle Art.

Clay Sedimentology. H. Chamley. (Illus.). 615p. 1989. 83.00 (*0-387-50889-9*, 2783) Spr-Verlag.

***Clay Sleeps: An Ethnoarchaeological Study of Three African Potters.** Richard A. Krause. LC 83-5077. (Illus.). 216p. 1985. pap. 61.60 (*0-7837-8389-2*, 2059200) Bks Demand.

Clay Target Handbook. Jerry Meyer. 220p. 1992. 22.95 (*1-55821-176-4*) Lyons & Burford.

***Clay-Target Handbook.** Jerry Meyer. 224p. 1995. pap. 16.95 (*1-55821-415-1*) Lyons & Burford.

Clay That Breathes: A Novella & Stories. Catherine Browder. LC 90-26184. 164p. (Orig.). 1991. pap. 9.95 (*0-915943-63-8*) Milkweed Ed.

Clay Tobacco Pipes in Cambridgeshire. Robert J. Flood. (Cambridge Town, Gown & County Ser.: Vol. 6). (Illus.). 40p. 1976. pap. 4.50 (*0-902675-70-2*) Oleander Pr.

Clay Today: Contemporary Ceramists & Their Work. Martha D. Lynn. LC 89-13731. (Illus.). 240p. 1990. 24.95 (*0-87701-756-5*) Chronicle Bks.

***Clay Vessels & Other Poems.** John P. McNamee & Robert McGovern. (Orig.). 1995. pap. write for info. (*1-55612-812-6*) Sheed & Ward MO.

Clay Walls. Kim Ronyoung. LC 86-60589. 304p. 1986. 22.00 (*0-932966-66-7*) Permanent Pr.

Clay Walls: A Novel. Ronyoung Kim. LC 89-39875. 306p. 1990. pap. 14.95 (*0-295-96927-X*) U of Wash Pr.

Clay-Water Interface & Its Rheological Implications. Ed. by N. Guven & R. M. Pollastro. (CMS Workshop Lectures: Vol. 4). (Illus.). 244p. (C). 1992. pap. text ed. 15.00 (*1-881208-04-4*) Clay Minerals.

Clayburn. Marvin Albert. 1989. pap. 2.95 (*0-449-13382-6*) Fawcett.

Clayey Reservoirs of Oil & Gas. T. T. Klubova. Tr. by S. Viswanathan. (Russian Translation Ser.: No. 85). (Illus.). 178p. (C). 1991. text ed. 70.00 (*90-6191-992-4*, Pub. by A A Balkema NE) Ashgate Pub Co.

Clayfeld Rejoices, Clayfeld Laments: A Sequence of Poems. Robert Pack. LC 87-7414. 112p. 1987. 14.95 (*0-87923-695-7*); pap. 9.95 (*0-87923-696-5*) Godine.

Clayhanger. Arnold Bennett. (Fiction Ser.). 528p. 1976. mass mkt. 5.95 (*0-14-000997-3*, Penguin Bks) Viking Penguin.

Clayhanger. braille ed. Arnold Bennett. 1058p. 1993. vinyl bd. 84.64 (*1-56956-435-3*, BR9121) W A T Braille.

Clayhanger. Arnold Bennett. LC 74-5390. (Collected Works of Arnold Bennett: Vol. 12). 1977. reprint ed. 47.95 (*0-518-19093-5*) Ayer.

Claymore Mines: Their History & Development. Larry Grupp. (Illus.). 152p. 1993. pap. 15.00 (*0-87364-715-7*) Paladin Pr.

1306

An Asterisk (*) at the beginning of an entry indicates that the title is appearing in BIP for the first time.

An Asterisk (*) at the beginning of an entry indicates that the title is appearing in BIP for the first time.

1307

Cleaner, Custodian USPS. Jack Rudman. (Career Examination Ser.: C-3315). 1994. pap. 23.95 (*0-8373-3315-6*) Nat Learn.

*__Cleaner Fuels, Cleaner Vehicles, & Altered Driving Habits: New Measures under the Clean Air Act to Control Pollution from Highway Vehicles.__ Heidi Snow. Ed. by Gerry Feinstein. 51p. (Orig.). 1992. pap. text ed. 18.95 (*1-55877-163-8*) Natl Governor.

Cleaner-Helper. Jack Rudman. (Career Examination Ser.: C-1195). 1994. pap. 19.95 (*0-8373-1195-0*) Nat Learn.

*__Cleaner Produciton in Industry: Integrating Business Goals & Environmental Management.__ Ian Christie. 160p. (C). 1995. pap. 17.95 (*0-85374-619-2*, Pub. by Pol Studies Inst UK) Brookings.

Cleaner (T. A.) Jack Rudman. (Career Examination Ser.: No. C-946). 1994. 19.95 (*0-8373-0946-8*) Nat Learn.

*__Cleaner Technologies & Cleaner Products for Sustainable Development.__ Ed. by Harry M. Freeman et al. LC 95-10170. (NATO ASI Ser.: Partnership Sub-Ser. 2; Environment: Vol. 2). 1995. write for info. (*3-540-59126-5*) Spr-Verlag.

Cleaner Technology. 76p. 1992. pap. 30.00 (*0-11-430069-0*, HM00690, Pub. by HMSO UK) UNIPUB.

*__Cleaners (Household) Market.__ 180p. (Orig.). 1995. pap. 1,995.00 (*0-7605-2047-X*) Rector Pr.

Cleaness: An Alliterative Tripartite Poem on the Deluge, the Destruction of Sodom, & the Death of Belshazzar, 2 vols., Set. Poet of Pearl. (BCL1-PR English Literature Ser.). 1992. reprint ed. lib. bdg. 150.00 (*0-7812-7181-9*) Rprt Serv.

Cleaning. (Home Repair & Improvement Ser.). (Illus.). 136p. 1982. 14.60 (*0-8094-3490-3*); lib. bdg. 20.60 (*0-8094-3491-1*) Time-Life.

*__Cleaning Agents (Household) International Market.__ 300p. (Orig.). 1995. pap. 3,195.00 (*0-7605-2050-X*) Rector Pr.

Cleaning & Conditioning Agents: Their Impact on the Environment in the EEC. Environment Resources, Ltd. Staff. 138p. 1978. lib. bdg. 46.00 (*0-86010-108-8*) G & T Inc.

Cleaning & Cooking Fish. Sylvia Bashline. LC 82-80889. (Hunting & Fishing Library). (Illus.). 160p. 1982. 19.95 (*0-86573-011-3*) Cy De Cosse.

*__Cleaning & Flushing Hydraulics Systems.__ James E. Anders, Sr. (Illus.). 100p. (Orig.). 1994. 45.00 (*0-9636737-1-8*) Hydraulics.

Cleaning & Lining Water Mains, No. M28. 40p. 1987. pap. 17.50 (*0-89867-425-5*, 30028) Am Water Wks Assn.

Cleaning & Lining Water Mains: The Answer to Some Transmission & Distribution Main Problems. 84p. 1989. pap. 16.00 (*0-89867-454-9*, 20241) Am Water Wks Assn.

Cleaning & Preservation of Coins & Medals. G. Welter. LC 76-3964. (Illus.). 1994. lib. bdg. 16.00 (*0-915262-03-7*) S J Durst.

Cleaning & Reconditioning of Spices, Seeds & Herbs. 40p. 20.00 (*0-318-21988-3*) Am Spice Trade.

Cleaning & Stain Removal. Time Life Staff. (Fix-It-Yourself Ser.). 1990. 18.60 (*0-8094-7400-X*); lib. bdg. 24.60 (*0-8094-7401-8*) Time-Life.

Cleaning Castings. 401p. 40.00 (*0-317-32561-2*, GM7706); 20.00 (*0-317-32562-0*); pap. 50.00 (*0-87433-009-2*, GM9205) Am Foundrymen.

*__Cleaning Closets: A Mother's Story.__ Beverly Cole. 152p. (Orig.). 1995. pap. 14.99 (*0-8272-0464-7*) Chalice Pr.

Cleaning Compounds, No. YC-174: Highlighting Additives to Surfactants in These Compounds. Dirk Muyskens. (Illus.). 179p. 1993. 2,650.00 (*1-56965-003-9*) BCC.

Cleaning Encyclopedia. Don Aslett. 1993. pap. 14.95 (*0-440-50481-3*) Dell.

Cleaning House: America's Campaign for Term Limits. James K. Coyne & John H. Fund. LC 92-19278. 352p. 1992. 21.95 (*0-89526-516-8*) Regnery Pub.

Cleaning Maintenance: Instructor's Manual. William Thomas. (Illus.). 240p. (C). 1988. lib. bdg. 45.00 (*0-943863-08-2*) Marsh-Wentworth.

Cleaning Nature Naturally. Kathlyn Gay. 144p. (J). (gr. 7-9). 1991. 15.95 (*0-8027-8118-5*); lib. bdg. 16.85 (*0-8027-8119-5*) Walker & Co.

Cleaning of Paintings: Problems & Potentialities. Helmut Ruhemann. LC 81-81722. (Illus.). 508p. 1982. reprint ed. lib. bdg. 75.00 (*0-87817-281-5*) Hacker.

Cleaning Operators Manual. Highfield Publications Staff. (C). 1989. 30.00 (*0-89771-816-X*, Pub. by Highfield Pubns UK) St Mut.

Cleaning Operators Manual. D. L. Williams. 1986. 40.00 (*0-317-61928-4*, Cresta Pub) St Mut.

Cleaning or Safeguarding Small Tanks & Containers. (Thirty Ser.). 1993. pap. 16.75 (*0-685-58110-1*, 327) Natl Fire Prot.

Cleaning Our Environment: A Chemical Perspective. LC 78-73104. 1978. 12.95 (*0-8412-0467-5*) Am Chemical.

Cleaning Out Congress: The Case for Term Limits. C. W. Griffin. 130p. 1992. pap. 9.95 (*0-9630270-0-X*) Griffin Assocs.

Cleaning Printed Wiring Assemblies. L. Hymes. 1991. text ed. 57.95 (*0-442-00275-0*) Van Nos Reinhold.

Cleaning Products from Nature: Vinegar, Baking Soda, Lemon Juice, & More - A Researcher's Guide & Workbook. Center for Self-Sufficiency, Research Division Staff. 18p. 1986. ring bd. 19.95 (*0-910811-55-5*) Ctr Self Suff.

*__Cleaning Products (Home) Market.__ 400p. (Orig.). 1994. pap. 1,295.00 (*1-57205-901-X*) Rector Pr.

*__Cleaning Products (Industrial) Market.__ 600p. (Orig.). 1994. pap. 1,295.00 (*1-57205-902-8*) Rector Pr.

Cleaning Professional Kitchens. Highfield Publications Staff. (C). 1989. 60.00 (*0-89771-812-7*, Pub. by Highfield Pubns UK) St Mut.

Cleaning Professional Kitchens. R. A. North. 1986. 75.00 (*0-317-61929-2*, Cresta Pub) St Mut.

Cleaning Proficiency Manual. Highfield Publications Staff. (C). 1989. 60.00 (*0-89771-817-8*, Pub. by Highfield Pubns UK) St Mut.

Cleaning, Repairing & Caring for Books. 4th enl. rev. ed. Robert L. Shep. (Illus.). 148p. 1991. 19.95 (*1-872699-02-2*) R L Shep.

*__Cleaning Services Market: Commerical U. S. A.__ 168p. (Orig.). 1995. pap. 1,195.00 (*0-7605-2119-0*) Rector Pr.

Cleaning Stainless Steel: A Symposium. American Society for Testing & Materials Staff. LC 73-80188. (American Society for Testing & Materials Special Technical Publication Ser.: 538). (Illus.). 238p. reprint ed. pap. 67.90 (*0-317-10763-1*, 2009068) Bks Demand.

Cleaning Stone & Masonry. Ed. by James R. Clifton. LC 86-25915. (Special Technical Publication Ser.: No. 935). (Illus.). 165p. 1986. text ed. 29.00 (*0-8031-0932-6*, 04-935000-10) ASTM.

Cleaning Supervisor's Handbook. J. K. Edwards. 1986. 75.00 (*0-317-61931-4*, Cresta Pub) St Mut.

Cleaning Supervisors Handbook. Highfield Publications Staff. (C). 1989. 45.00 (*0-89771-814-3*, Pub. by Highfield Pubns UK) St Mut.

Cleaning the Face of Morocco: Human Rights Abuses & Recent Developments. Lawyers Committee for Human Rights Staff. 51p. 1990. pap. 8.00 (*0-934143-36-6*) Lawyers Comm Human.

Cleaning Up: Basic American Work Language for ESL Students. Paul J. Hamel. (Illus.). 49p. (Orig.). 1988. pap. text ed. 11.50 (*0-937354-31-7*) Delta Systems.

Cleaning Up: How Trash Becomes Treasure. Eve Stwertka & Albert Stwertka. LC 91-28777. (At Home with Science Ser.). (Illus.). 40p. (J). (gr. 2-5). 1993. lib. bdg. 10.98 (*0-671-69461-8*, Julian Messner); pap. 5.95 (*0-671-69467-7*, Julian Messner) Silver Burdett Pr.

Cleaning Up: U. S. Waste Management Technology & Third World Development. John Elkington & Jonathan Shopley. 92p. (Orig.). 1989. pap. text ed. 10.00 (*0-915825-28-7*) World Resources Inst.

Cleaning up America the Poisoned: How to Survive Our Polluted Society. Lewis G. Regenstein. 1993. pap. 14.95 (*0-87491-999-1*) Acropolis.

Cleaning up Coal: A Study of Coal Cleaning & the Use of Cleaned Coal. Cynthia A. Hutton & Robert N. Gould. Ed. by Richard C. Allen. LC 82-81548. 412p. reprint ed. pap. 117.50 (*0-7837-0324-4*, 2040643) Bks Demand.

Cleaning up for a Living: Everything You Need to Know to Become a Successful Building Service Contractor. 2nd ed. Don Aslett & Mark Browning. (Illus.). 208p. (Orig.). 1991. pap. 12.95 (*1-55870-206-7*) Betterway Bks.

*__Cleaning up Industrial Waste: Gleanings from an Entrepreneur.__ Dale F. Galloway. 1995. pap. 10.00 (*0-8059-3729-3*) Dorrance.

Cleaning Up Our Water. Linda Goldman. LC 94-18025. (Restoring Nature: Success Stories Ser.). (Illus.). 96p. (J). (gr. 3-6). 1994. lib. bdg. 17.40 (*0-516-05543-7*) Childrens.

*__Cleaning up the Department of Energy's Nuclear Weapons Complex.__ Elizabeth Pinkston & Frances M. Lussier. (Illus.). 78p. (Orig.). (C). 1994. pap. text ed. 45.00x (*0-7881-0895-6*) Diane Pub.

Cleaning up the Mess: Implementation Strategies in Superfund. Thomas W. Church & Robert T. Nakamura. LC 92-39493. 209p. (C). 1993. 34.95 (*0-8157-1414-9*); pap. 14.95 (*0-8157-1413-0*) Brookings.

Cleaning up the Nation's Waste Sites: Markets & Technology Trends. 125p. (Orig.). (C). 1993. pap. text ed. 95.00 (*0-7881-0024-6*) Diane Pub.

*__Cleaning up the Nation's Watersites: Markets & Technology Trends.__ U. S. Environmental Protection Agency, Office of Wetlands, Oceans, & Watersheds Staff. 164p. (Orig.). 1994. pap. text ed. 79.00 (*0-86587-379-8*) Gov Insts.

Cleanroom Approach to Quality Software Development. Michael G. Dyer. (Series in Software Engineering Practice). 224p. 1992. text ed. 52.00 (*0-471-54823-5*) Wiley.

*__Cleanroom Microbiology for the Non-Microbiologist.__ David Carlberg. 254p. 1995. 97.00 (*0-935184-73-2*) Interpharm.

*__Cleanroom Operations.__ Inst. of Environmental Sciences Working Group 026. Ed. by Vinette Kopetz. (Recommended Practice Ser.). (Illus.). 24p. 1994. pap. text ed. 125.00 (*1-877862-25-8*, IES-RP-CC006.2) Inst Environ Sci.

Cleanroom Technology & Procedures Series. K. Evans et al. Ed. by Carol Rose. (Illus.). 1992. Cleanroom Technology Manual. student ed. pap. 12.50 (*0-9613880-5-6*) Semiconductor.

Cleanroom Technology & Procedures Series, Set. K. Evans et al. Ed. by Carol Rose. (Illus.). 1992. vhs 495.00 (*0-9613880-8-0*) Semiconductor.

Cleansing Flame. (Executioner Ser.). 1994. mass mkt. 3.50 (*0-373-61187-0*, 1-61187-0) Harlequin Bks.

Cleansing of the Sanctuary. D. S. Warner & H. M. Riggle. 541p. reprint ed. 6.00 (*0-686-29145-X*) Faith Pub Hse.

Cleansing the Fatherland: Nazi Medicine & Racial Hygiene. Gotz Aly et al. Tr. by Belinda Cooper. LC 93-42564. 1994. 48.50 (*0-8018-4775-3*); pap. 16.95 (*0-8018-4824-5*) Johns Hopkins.

Cleanth Brooks: An Annotated Bibliography. John M. Walsh. LC 89-23578. (Modern Critics & Critical Schools Ser.). 464p. 1990. 63.00 (*0-8240-4941-1*, H1208) Garland.

Cleanth Brooks: His Critical Formulations. Ed. by R. S. Singh. 1991. text ed. 35.00 (*81-85151-50-4*, Pub. by Harman Pub Hse II) Advent Bks Div.

*__Cleanup.__ (Bear Hugs Ser.). (Illus.). 24p. (J). 1995. teacher ed, pap. 3.95 (*0-614-06813-4*, WPH 2508) Totline Bks.

Cleanup of Releases from Petroleum USTs: Selected Technologies. (Illus.). 121p. 1988. per. pap. 7.50 (*0-16-006450-3*, S/N 055-000-002) USGPO.

Clear Air Turbulence & Its Detection: Proceedings of a Symposium. Ed. by Yih-Ho Pao & Arnold Goldburg. LC 73-76507. 556p. reprint ed. pap. 158.50 (*0-685-15683-4*, 2026290) Bks Demand.

Clear & Coherent Prose: A Functional Approach. William J. Vande Kopple. (C). 1988. pap. text ed. 22.00 (*0-673-39779-3*) HarpCollege.

*__Clear & Convincing Evidence: Measurement of Discrimination in America.__ Ed. by Michael Fix & Raymond J. Strayk. 440p. 1993. lib. bdg. 72.50 (*0-87766-599-0*) Urban Inst.

*__Clear & Convincing Evidence: Measurement of Discrimination in America.__ Ed. by Michael Fix & Raymond J. Strayk. 440p. 1993. pap. text ed. 34.50 (*0-87766-600-8*) Urban Inst.

Clear & Lively Writing: Language Games & Activities for Everyone. Priscilla L. Vail. LC 80-54818. 269p. 1981. 16.95 (*0-8027-0682-7*) Walker & Co.

*__Clear & Lively Writing: Language Games & Activities for Writers of All Ages.__ Priscilla L. Vail. 272p. 1994. pap. 14.95 (*0-8027-7436-9*) Walker & Co.

Clear & Present Danger. Tom Clancy. 1990. pap. 6.99 (*0-425-12212-3*) Berkley Pub.

Clear & Present Danger. Tom Clancy. 704p. 1994. pap. text ed. 6.99 (*0-425-14437-2*) Berkley Pub.

Clear & Present Danger. Tom Clancy. 544p. 1989. 21.95 (*0-399-13440-9*, Putnam) Putnam Pub Group.

Clear & Present Danger. large type ed. Tom Clancy. LC 89-27153. 1209p. 1990. lib. bdg. 21.95 (*0-89621-930-5*) Thorndike Pr.

Clear & Present Danger. large type ed. Tom Clancy. 1209p. 1990. reprint ed. pap. 15.95 (*0-89621-942-9*) Thorndike Pr.

Clear & Present Danger to Society. Illus. by Barry Lee. 24p. 1981. pap. 4.00 (*0-939622-10-6*) Four Zoas Night Ltd.

Clear & Present Dangers: The U.S. Military & the War on Drugs in the Andes. 154p. 1991. 12.00 (*0-685-59926-4*) WOLA.

Clear & Simple American History, Vol. I. Carolyn Pickering. 176p. 1986. pap. 5.95 (*0-671-60111-3*) S&S Trade.

Clear & Simple As the Truth: Writing Classic Prose. Francis-Noel Thomas & Mark Turner. LC 94-11752. 1994. 19.95 (*0-691-03667-5*) Princeton U Pr.

Clear & Simple Basic Algebra. Martin Lee. 1986. pap. 9.00 (*0-671-54555-8*) S&S Trade.

Clear & Simple Chemistry. James Berger. 212p. 1986. pap. 6.95 (*0-317-37777-9*) S&S Trade.

Clear & Simple Guide to Bookkeeping. B. G. Quint. (Clear & Simple Study Guides Ser.). (Illus.). 128p. (Orig.). (C). 1981. pap. 8.00 (*0-671-42108-5*, Arco Test) P-H Gen Ref & Trav.

Clear & Simple Intermediate Algebra. Martin Lee. 1986. 6.95 (*0-685-43080-4*) S&S Trade.

Clear & Simple Thesaurus Dictionary. Harriet Wittels & Joan Greisman. (Illus.). (J). (gr. 3 up). 1976. pap. 8.95 (*0-448-12198-0*, G&D) Putnam Pub Group.

Clear & Simple Wine Guide. Louis J. DiGiacomo. 160p. 1992. pap. 10.95 (*0-9633630-0-X*) Daylesford Pub.

Clear As Crystal, Red As Flame: Later Chinese Glass. Claudia Brown & Donald Rabiner. LC 89-82709. (Illus.). 104p. (Orig.). 1990. pap. 35.00 (*0-295-97029-4*) U of Wash Pr.

Clear Bad Credit . . . Build Great Credit! A Practical Guide for the Individual or Professional. Stephen Sharf. 192p. (Orig.). 1988. pap. 29.95 (*0-929747-00-3*) CPI Pubns Ltd.

Clear Blue Lobster-Water Country: A Trilogy. Leo Connellan. LC 84-12955. 160p. 1985. pap. 8.95 (*0-15-618054-5*, Harvest Bks) HarBrace.

Clear Body, Clear Mind. L. Ron Hubbard. 306p. 1990. 17.95 (*0-88404-549-8*) Bridge Pubns Inc.

Clear Body, Clear Mind: The Effective Purification Program. L. Ron Hubbard. 306p. 1990. 17.95 (*0-88404-588-9*) Bridge Pubns Inc.

*__Clear Body Clear Mind: The Effective Purification Program.__ L. Ron Hubbard. 360p. 1995. mass mkt. 6.99 (*0-88404-756-3*) Bridge Pubns Inc.

*__Clear Choices for Churches: Trends among Growing & Declining Churches of Christ.__ John W. Ellas. LC 94-72522. (Illus.). (Orig.). 1994. pap. write for info. (*0-9642447-1-3*) Ctr for Church.

Clear Coatings for Exposed Architectural Concrete. (PCI Journal Reprints Ser.). 9p. 1965. pap. 5.00 (*0-686-40000-3*, JR60) P-PCI.

*__Clear Conscience.__ Frances Fyfield. 224p. 1995. 20.00 (*0-679-42666-3*) Pantheon.

*__Clear Conscience.__ deluxe ed. Frances Fyfield. 1995. 20.00 (*0-676-50224-5*) Pantheon.

*__Clear Conscience.__ large type ed. Frances Fyfield. LC 95-7155. 304p. 1995. lib. bdg. 20.95 (*0-7862-0455-9*) Thorndike Pr.

Clear-Corneal Cataract Surgery & Topical Anesthesia. I. Howard Fine et al. LC 93-10591. 192p. 1993. 65.00 (*1-55642-226-1*) SLACK Inc.

*__Clear-Cut Murder.__ Lee Wallingford. (WWL Mystery Ser.). 1995. mass mkt. 3.99 (*0-373-26165-9*, 1-26165-0) Harlequin Bks.

Clear-Cut Murder: A Frank Carver - Ginny Trask Mystery. Lee Wallingford. LC 92-38254. 212p. 1993. 19.95 (*0-8027-3231-3*) Walker & Co.

Clear-Cut Pattern Making: By the Flat Pattern Method. Mary G. Wolfe. LC 81-16511. (Illus.). 221p. (C). 1982. reprint ed. pap. text ed. 25.00 (*0-471-09937-6*) M G Wolfe.

Clear for Action: A Biographical Novel about David Farragut. Noll B. Gerson. 20.95 (*0-88411-641-7*, Aeonian Pr) Amereon Ltd.

Clear Heads & Holy Hearts: The Religious & Theological Ideal of John Henry Newman. Terrence Merrigan. (Louvain Theological & Pastoral Monographs). 272p. (Orig.). 1991. pap. 24.99 (*0-8028-0567-1*) Eerdmans.

Clear Lacquers for Copper & Copper Alloys. British Non-Ferrous Metals Research Association Staff. 75p. 1965. 11.25 (*0-317-34498-6*, 5) Intl Copper.

Clear Light of Bliss: Mahamudra in Vajrayana Buddhism. Geshe Kelsang Gyatso. (Illus.). 320p. 1995. 24.95 (*0-948006-13-7*, Pub. by Tharpa UK); pap. 19.95 (*0-948006-21-8*, Pub. by Tharpa UK) Atrium Pubs.

Clear Light of Day. Anita Desai. 192p. 1989. pap. 10.00 (*0-14-010859-9*, Penguin Bks); mass mkt. 6.95 (*0-14-008670-6*, Penguin Bks) Viking Penguin.

Clear Mirror. G. Evelyn Hutchinson. LC 78-61845. 1979. pap. 4.95 (*0-918172-04-7*) Leetes Isl.

Clear Pictures: First Loves, First Guides. Reynolds Price. 288p. 1989. text ed. 19.95 (*0-689-12075-3*, Atheneum S&S) S&S Trade.

Clear Pond: The Reconstruction of a Life. Roger Mitchell. (Illus.). 201p. 1991. 19.95 (*0-8156-0257-X*) Syracuse U Pr.

Clear Red Stone: A Myth & the Meaning of Menstruation. Alexandra Kolkmeyer. Ed. by Lynn Goldstein. LC 82-2956. (Illus.). 64p. 1982. text ed. 9.50 (*0-942524-01-2*) In Sight Pr NM.

Clear Space on a Cold Day. Roger Mitchell. (CSU Poetry Ser.: No. XIX). 80p. (Orig.). 1986. 12.00 (*0-914946-65-X*); pap. 6.00 (*0-914946-55-2*) Cleveland St Univ Poetry Ctr.

Clear Speech: Pronunciation & Listening Comprehension in American English. 2nd ed. Judy B. Gilbert. 128p. (C). 1993. student ed, pap. 11.95 (*0-521-42118-5*); Set of 2 cassettes. pap. 29.95 (*0-521-42117-9*) Cambridge U Pr.

Clear Speech: Pronunciation & Listening Comprehension in American English. 2nd ed. Judy B. Gilbert. 128p. (C). 1993. teacher ed, pap. 12.95 (*0-521-42116-0*) Cambridge U Pr.

Clear Technical Communication: A Process Approach. 3rd ed. William A. Damerst & Arthur H. Bell. 491p. (C). 1989. pap. text ed. 28.00 (*0-15-507694-9*) Dryden Pr.

Clear Technical Writing. John A. Brogan. 1973. text ed. write for info. (*0-07-007983-8*) McGraw.

Clear Technical Writing. John A. Brogan. (C). 1973. text ed. 26.95 (*0-07-007974-9*) McGraw.

Clear the Bridge. Richard H. O'Kane. 1989. 24.95 (*0-89141-346-4*) Presidio Pr.

Clear the Cow Pasture: I'm Comin' In. Robert Quackenbush. LC 89-6164. (J). 1990. pap. 11.95 (*0-671-68548-1*, S&S Bks Young Read); pap. 3.95 (*0-671-69218-6*, S&S Bks Young Read) S&S Childrens.

Clear the Trail. Charles A. Seltzer. 1976. reprint ed. lib. bdg. 22.95 (*0-88411-120-2*, 120, Aeonian Pr) Amereon Ltd.

Clear the Way! A History of the 38th (Irish) Brigade, 1941-47. Richard Doherty. (Illus.). 352p. 1993. text ed. 39.95 (*0-7165-2504-6*, Pub. by Irish Acad Pr IE) Intl Spec Bk.

Clear Thinking. Columbia Pacific University Faculty Staff & Richard L. Crews. 115p. (C). 1989. student ed write for info. (*0-945864-26-4*); pap. text ed. write for info. (*0-945864-25-6*) Columbia Pacific U Pr.

Clear Thinking: A Practical Introduction. Hy Ruchlis. 271p. (Orig.). 1990. pap. 17.95 (*0-87975-594-6*) Prometheus Bks.

Clear Thinking - Preliminary Edition. Jason. 1991. pap. 30.00 (*0-86720-182-7*) Jones & Bartlett.

Clear Thinking about Sexual Deviations: A New Look at an Old Problem. James L. Mathis. LC 72-80165. 232p. 1972. 24.95 (*0-911012-40-0*) Nelson-Hall.

Clear Thinking for Composition. 5th ed. Ray Kytle, Jr. 176p. (C). 1987. pap. text ed. write for info. (*0-07-553969-1*) McGraw.

*__Clear to Chukchi: Poems of Alaska.__ Warren Woessner. 28p. (Orig.). 1995. pap. 3.95 (*0-9641986-8-1*) Poetry Harbor.

Clear View: Guide to Industrial Pollution Control. James S. Cannon. Ed. by Jean M. Halloran. LC 75-15321. 257p. reprint ed. pap. 73.30 (*0-7837-0325-2*, 2040644) Bks Demand.

Clear Water Repellent Treatments for Concrete Masonry. John A. Raeber. 62p. 1993. pap. 10.00 (*0-940116-25-1*) Masonry Inst Am.

Clear Writing. Diana Bonet. Ed. by W. Philip Gerould. LC 90-84924. (Fifty-Minute Ser.). 90p. (Orig.). 1991. pap. 9.95 (*1-56052-094-9*) Crisp Pubns.

Clear Writing. William Wood. LC 83-288. 360p. (C). 1984. pap. text ed. 20.75 (*0-03-060413-3*) HB Coll Pubs.

Clear Your Credit & Get Out of Debt: Five Easy Steps. Richard C. Applewhite. LC 93-94163. 160p. (Orig.). 1994. pap. 8.95 (*1-884148-25-5*) JaCee Pubng.

Clear Your Desk! Declan Treacy. 176p. 1992. pap. 14.95 (*0-936894-38-5*) Upstart Pub.

Clearance & Settlement Systems in the World Security Markets. Study Group Staff. (Special Report Ser.). 87p. 1989. pap. write for info. (*1-56708-076-6*) Grp of Thirty.

Clearance & Settlement Systems Status Reports: Spring 1990. Study Group Staff. (Special Report Ser.). 275p. 1990. pap. write for info. (*1-56708-078-2*) Grp of Thirty.

Clearance & Settlements Systems Status Reports: Year End 1990. Study Group Staff. (Special Report Ser.). 203p. 1991. pap. write for info. (*1-56708-079-0*) Grp of Thirty.

Clearburning: (For Felonies Compounded by the F. B. I. Etcetera) W. O. Dillard. (Illus.). 350p. (Orig.). 1993. pap. 19.95 (*0-9627737-2-7*) J Fraiser.

*__Clearcut.__ limited ed. Sandra Lopez. Ed. by Tom Trusky. (Hemingway Western Studies Ser.). (Illus.). 3p. (Orig.). 1994. 14.95 (*0-932129-23-4*) Heming W Studies.

Clearcut: The Tragedy of Industrial Forestry. Ed. by Bill Devall. LC 93-35989. (Illus.). 300p. 1994. 50.00 (*0-87156-494-7*) Sierra.

C

An Asterisk (*) at the beginning of an entry indicates that the title is appearing in BIP for the first time.

An Asterisk (*) at the beginning of an entry indicates that the title is appearing in BIP for the first time.

1309

C

***Cleopatra: Goddess of Egypt, Enemy of Rome.** Polly S. Brooks. LC 95-10688. (Illus.). 160p. (YA). (gr. 6 up). 1995. 15.95 (*0-06-023607-8*); lib. bdg. 15.89 (*0-06-023608-6*) HarpC Child Bks.

Cleopatra - Story of a Queen. Emil Ludwig. (African Studies). 221p. reprint ed. 25.00 (*0-938818-92-9*) ECA Assoc.

Cleopatra Gold. William J. Caunitz. LC 93-31057. 1994. 23.95 (*0-7927-1898-4*, Eagle Lrg Print) Chivers N Amer.

Cleopatra Gold. William J. Caunitz. LC 93-9966. 1993. 20.00 (*0-517-57498-5*, Crown) Crown Pub Group.

***Cleopatra Gold.** William J. Caunitz. 352p. 1994. pap. text ed. 6.99 (*0-425-14394-5*) Berkley Pub.

Cleopatra Kiss. George Junghanns. 162p. 1992. 14.50 (*1-881946-00-2*) Gauntlet Bks.

Cleopatra Needles & Other Egyptian Articles. E. Budge & A. Wallis. 1990. pap. 7.95 (*0-486-26347-9*) Dover.

Cleopatras. John Whitehorne. LC 93-5583. 1994. write for info. (*0-415-05806-6*, Routledge NY) Routledge.

Cleopatra's Carpet. Sarah Carlisle. (Regency Love Story Ser.). 1979. pap. 1.75 (*0-449-50009-8*, Coventry) Fawcett.

Cleopatra's Needles & Other Egyptian Obelisks. E. A. W. Budge. 308p. 1979. reprint ed. 35.00 (*0-89005-278-6*) Ares.

Cleopatra's Needles & Other Egyptian Obelisks. Ernest A. Budge. LC 73-18841. (Illus.). reprint ed. 27.50 (*0-404-11315-X*) AMS Pr.

Cleopatra's Nose, the Twinkie Defense, & Twelve Hundred Other Famous Catch Phrases. Jerome Agel. 1989. 18.95 (*0-13-216797-2*) P-H.

Cleopatra's Sister. large type ed. Penelope Lively. 1993. 23.95 (*1-56895-039-X*) Wheeler Pub.

Cleopatra's Sister: A Novel. Penelope Lively. 240p. 1994. pap. 11.00 (*0-06-092217-6*, PL) HarpC.

Cleora's Kitchens: The Memoir of a Cook & Eight Decades of Great American Food. 2nd ed. Cleora Butler. LC 90-80354. (Illus.). 213p. 1990. pap. 15.95 (*0-933031-11-4*) Coun Oak Bks.

Clerambard. Marcel Ayme. (FRE.). 1984. pap. 18.95 (*0-7859-3043-4*) Fr & Eur.

Clerambault, Destouches, & Rameau. Comment by David Tunley. (Eighteenth-Century French Cantata Ser.: Vol. 11). 248p. 1991. 95.00 (*0-8240-9665-7*) Garland.

Clerc: The Story of His Early Years. Cathryn Carroll. LC 91-7548. 185p. (Orig.). (gr. 7-12). 1991. pap. 7.95 (*0-930323-23-8*) Gallaudet Univ Pr.

Clergy & Chemical Dependency. Abraham J. Twerski. 1990. pap. 2.95 (*0-926028-11-1*) Edgehill Pubns.

Clergy & Teacher Malpractice Recognition & Prevention. R. W. McMenamin & William P. Kralovec. Ed. by JoAnn L. Lippert. 238p. 1987. 37.50 (*0-943279-00-3*); pap. 18.50 (*0-943279-01-1*) Jomac Pub.

Clergy & the Sexual Revolution. Ruth T. Barnhouse. LC 86-73243. 64p. (Orig.). 1987. pap. 9.95 (*1-56699-018-1*, AL96) Alban Inst.

Clergy Ethics in a Changing Society: Mapping the Terrain. Ed. by James P. Wind et al. 288p. (Orig.). 1991. pap. 18.99 (*0-664-25161-7*) Westminster John Knox.

***Clergy in the Classroom: The Religion of Secular Humanism.** David A. Noebel et al. 1995. pap. write for info. (*0-936163-27-5*) Summit Pr CO.

Clergy Malpractice. Robert W. McMenamin. LC 86-81075. 150p. 1986. lib. bdg. 35.00 (*0-89941-483-4*, 304100); pap. 20.00 (*0-89941-513-X*) W S Hein.

Clergy Malpractice: An Annotated Bibliography. Ed. by William J. Beintema. LC 90-80945. 82p. 1990. lib. bdg. 28.50 (*0-89941-738-8*, 306420) W S Hein.

Clergy Procedural Handbook. Randolph R. Calvo & Nevin J. Klinger. 283p. 1992. 18.00 (*0-943616-57-3*) Canon Law Soc.

Clergy Response to Suicidal Persons & Their Family Members: An Interfaith Resource Book for Clergy & Congregations. Ed. by David C. Clark. LC 93-72090. (Studies in Ministry & Parish Life). x, 219p. 1993. text ed. 30.95x (*0-913552-49-6*); pap. text ed. 17.95x (*0-913552-50-X*) Exploration Pr.

Clergy Search Dilemma: Pastors & Lay People Reflect on the Crisis of Clergy Deployment. Charles Crane & Diane Crane. LC 90-22731. 222p. 1991. pap. 11.95 (*1-56101-019-7*) Cowley Pubns.

Clergy Self-Care: Finding a Balance for Effective Ministry. Roy M. Oswald. LC 90-86201. 234p. (Orig.). 1991. pap. 17.95 (*1-56699-044-0*, AL125) Alban Inst.

***Clergy Sexual Misconduct: A Systems Perspective.** Ed. by Nancy M. Hopkins. Date not set. pap. 13.00 (*1-56699-119-6*, OD99) Alban Inst.

Clergy Stoles: Needlepoint or Cross Stitch. William R. Doser. 58p. 1981. 7.50 (*0-9618948-0-6*) Doser Designs.

Clergy Stress. Mary Anne Coate. 1989. pap. 13.95 (*0-687-85135-1*) Abingdon.

Clergy System. C. Ketcherside. pap. 0.99 (*0-87377-062-5*) GAM Pubns.

Clergy Women & Their Worldviews: Calling for a New Age. Martha L. Ice. LC 87-7001. 224p. 1987. text ed. 49.95 (*0-275-92643-5*, C2643, Praeger Pubs) Greenwood.

Clergyman & the Psychiatrist: When to Refer. Robert L. Mason et al. LC 77-22597. 248p. 1978. 29.95 (*0-88229-260-9*) Nelson-Hall.

Clergyman's Daughter. George Orwell. LC 60-10943. 320p. 1901. reprint ed. pap. 12.95 (*0-15-618065-0*, Harvest Bks) HarBrace.

Clerical & Administrative Support Positions. Jack Rudman. (Career Examination Ser.: C-314). 1994. pap. 19.95 (*0-8373-0314-1*) Nat Learn.

Clerical Associate. (Career Examination Ser.: Series 1). 1991. pap. 19.95 (*0-8373-3700-3*) Nat Learn.

Clerical Careers. (Career Examination Ser.: C-3434). 1994. pap. 19.95 (*0-8373-3434-9*) Nat Learn.

Clerical Employment & Technological Change. H. Allan Hunt & Timothy L. Hunt. LC 86-26556. 296p. 1986. text ed. 26.00 (*0-88099-043-0*); pap. text ed. 16.00 (*0-88099-042-2*) W E Upjohn.

Clerical Exams Handbook. Steinberg. 1994. pap. 12.00 (*0-671-87460-8*) P-H Gen Ref & Trav.

Clerical Operations of the Office of the Clerk of Courts for the Supreme Court & Court of Appeals of Alaska. National Center for State Courts Staff. 72p. 1982. 4.32 (*0-685-15216-2*, NERO-119) Natl Ctr St Courts.

Clerical Poll-Taxes of the Diocese of Lincoln, 1377-81. Intro. by A. K. McHardy. (Publications of the Lincoln Record Society: No. 81). (Illus.). 296p. (C). 1992. text ed. 35.00 (*0-901503-54-1*, Lincoln Record Soc) Boydell & Brewer.

Clerical Positions G-5. Jack Rudman. (Career Examination Ser.: C-1943). 1994. pap. 19.95 (*0-8373-1943-9*) Nat Learn.

Clerical Training Supervisor. Jack Rudman. (Career Examination Ser.: C-1194). 1994. pap. 29.95 (*0-8373-1194-2*) Nat Learn.

Cleric's Challenge. TSR, Inc. Staff. 1993. 6.95 (*1-56076-659-X*) TSR Inc.

Clerihews of Paul Horgan. Paul Horgan. LC 85-15780. (Illus.). 126p. 1985. pap. 12.95 (*0-8195-6157-6*, Wesleyan Univ Pr) U Pr of New Eng.

Clerk. Jack Rudman. (Career Examination Ser.: C-142). 1994. pap. 19.95 (*0-8373-0142-4*) Nat Learn.

Clerk - Part-Time. Jack Rudman. (Career Examination Ser.: C-1191). 1994. pap. 19.95 (*0-8373-1191-8*) Nat Learn.

Clerk - Typist - Steno. 1991. pap. 10.00 (*0-910553-28-9*) Ken-Bks.

Clerk-Carrier (U. S. P. S.) Jack Rudman. (Career Examination Ser.: C-143). 1994. pap. 19.95 (*0-8373-0143-2*) Nat Learn.

Clerk GS1-4. Jack Rudman. (Career Examination Ser.: C-144). 1994. pap. 19.95 (*0-8373-0144-0*) Nat Learn.

Clerk GS5-7. Jack Rudman. (Career Examination Ser.: C-145). 1994. pap. 19.95 (*0-8373-0145-9*) Nat Learn.

Clerk I. Jack Rudman. (Career Examination Ser.: C-3271). 1994. pap. 19.95 (*0-8373-3271-0*) Nat Learn.

Clerk II. Jack Rudman. (Career Examination Ser.: C-3272). 1994. pap. 16.00 (*0-8373-3272-9*) Nat Learn.

Clerk III. Jack Rudman. (Career Examination Ser.: C-3273). 1994. pap. 27.95 (*0-8373-3273-7*) Nat Learn.

Clerk (Income Maintenance) Jack Rudman. (Career Examination Ser.: C-1642). 1994. reprint ed. pap. 23.95 (*0-8373-1642-1*) Nat Learn.

Clerk IV. Jack Rudman. (Career Examination Ser.: C-3274). 1994. pap. 27.95 (*0-8373-3274-5*) Nat Learn.

Clerk-Laborer. Jack Rudman. (Career Examination Ser.: C-1190). 1994. 23.95 (*0-8373-1190-X*) Nat Learn.

Clerk of Courts Office, Cleveland Municipal Court: Technical Assistance Report. 116p. 1978. 6.96 (*0-685-18273-8*, NCRO,T/A-507) Natl Ctr St Courts.

Clerk of the District Court Manual, State of Idaho. National Center for State Courts Staff. 354p. 1978. 21.24 (*0-685-15219-7*, WRO-005) Natl Ctr St Courts.

Clerk of the Works. Jack Rudman. (Career Examination Ser.: C-3230). 1994. pap. 27.95 (*0-8373-3230-3*) Nat Learn.

Clerk-Seasonal. Jack Rudman. (Career Examination Ser.: C-1192). 1994. pap. 19.95 (*0-8373-1192-6*) Nat Learn.

Clerk-Stenographer. Jack Rudman. (Career Examination Ser.: C-146). 1994. pap. 19.95 (*0-8373-0146-7*) Nat Learn.

Clerk-Stenographer I. Jack Rudman. (Career Examination Ser.: C-2339). 1994. pap. 19.95 (*0-8373-2339-8*) Nat Learn.

Clerk-Stenographer II. Jack Rudman. (Career Examination Ser.: C-1650). 1994. pap. 23.95 (*0-8373-1650-2*) Nat Learn.

Clerk-Stenographer III. Jack Rudman. (Career Examination Ser.: C-1651). 1994. pap. 23.95 (*0-8373-1651-0*) Nat Learn.

Clerk-Stenographer IV. Jack Rudman. (Career Examination Ser.: C-1652). 1994. pap. 23.95 (*0-8373-1652-9*) Nat Learn.

Clerk-Technician (U. S. P. S.) Jack Rudman. (Career Examination Ser.: C-1633). 1994. reprint ed. pap. 27.95 (*0-8373-1633-2*) Nat Learn.

Clerk-Typist. Jack Rudman. (Career Examination Ser.: C-147). 1994. pap. 19.95 (*0-8373-0147-5*) Nat Learn.

Clerk, Typist & Steno Examination. Harry W. Koch. 1984. pap. 8.00 (*0-910553-01-7*) Ken-Bks.

Clerk-Typist II. Jack Rudman. (Career Examination Ser.: C-3572). 1994. 23.95 (*0-8373-3572-8*) Nat Learn.

Clerk-Typist Trainee. Jack Rudman. (Career Examination Ser.: C-1193). 1994. pap. 19.95 (*0-8373-1193-4*) Nat Learn.

Clerkly Maker: Langland's Poetic Art. A. V. Schmidt. 176p. 1987. text ed. 71.00 (*0-85991-233-7*) Boydell & Brewer.

Clerk's Journal. Conrad Aiken. LC 70-152799. 1971. 40.00 (*0-87130-022-2*) Eakins.

Clerk's Journal. deluxe limited ed. Conrad Aiken. LC 70-152799. 1971. 70.00 (*0-87130-023-0*) Eakins.

Clerks of Court in New Jersey: Final Report. National Center for State Courts Staff. 321p. 1981. 19.26 (*0-685-15220-0*, NERO-083) Natl Ctr St Courts.

Clerk's Prologue & Tale. Geoffrey Chaucer. Ed. by J. Winny. (Selected Tales from Chaucer Ser.). 1966. pap. 9.95 (*0-521-04632-7*) Cambridge U Pr.

Clermont County, Ohio Land Records 1787-1812: Surveys, Patents, Deeds & Mortgages with Index of Grantors & Grantees. Alma A. Smith. LC 90-61674. (Illus.). vi, 168p. (C). 1990. text ed. 30.00 (*0-9614863-3-3*); pap. 20.00 (*0-9614863-4-1*) Alma Smith.

Clermont-Gem of the Hills: A History of the Clermont, Florida, & Neighboring Communities. Miriam W. Johnson & Rosemary Y. Young. LC 83-82290. (Illus.). 344p. 1984. 15.00 (*0-9612626-0-5*) M W Johnson.

Clery Castle. large type ed. Monica Heath. 1990. 18.95 (*0-7927-0398-7*, C0256, Curley Lrg Print) Chivers N Amer.

Clery Castle. large type ed. Monica Heath. 1990. pap. 16.95 (*0-7927-0399-5*, C0484, Curley Lrg Print) Chivers N Amer.

Cleve Gray: Paintings, 1966-1977. Thomas B. Hess, Jr. & Robert T. Buck. LC 77-81576. (Illus.). 1977. 5.95 (*0-914782-13-4*) Buffalo Acad.

Cleveland: A Concise History, 1796-1990. Carol P. Miller & Robert Wheeler. LC 89-24580. (Encyclopedia of Cleveland History Ser.). (Illus.). 208p. 1990. 29.95 (*0-253-33841-7*); pap. 10.95 (*0-253-20572-7*, MB-572) Ind U Pr.

***Cleveland: A Metropolitan Reader.** Ed. by W. Dennis Keating et al. LC 95-5535. (Illus.). 512p. (Orig.). 1995. pap. text ed. 35.00x (*0-87338-492-X*) Kent St U Pr.

Cleveland: A Tradition of Reform. Ed. by David D. Van Tassel & John J. Grabowski. LC 85-8165. 226p. reprint ed. pap. 64.50 (*0-7837-2996-0*, 2042945) Bks Demand.

Cleveland: Confused City on a Seesaw. Philip W. Porter. LC 76-21700. (Illus.). 332p. 1976. 36.50 (*0-8142-0264-0*) Ohio St U Pr.

Cleveland: Shaping the Vision. Ned Whelan. 1989. 34.95 (*0-89781-320-0*) Preferred Mktg.

Cleveland: The Making of a City (1950) 1,950th ed. William G. Rose. LC 90-4853. (Black Squirrel Bks.: No. 1). (Illus.). 1286p. 1990. 75.00 (*0-87338-428-8*) Kent St U Pr.

Cleveland: Where the East Coast Meets the Midwest. Peter Jedick. (Illus.). 105p. (Orig.). 1980. pap. 11.95 (*0-9605508-1-X*) Jedick Ent.

Cleveland: Where the East Coast Meets the Midwest. 2nd rev. ed. Peter Jedick. (Illus.). 109p. (Orig.). 1993. pap. 19.95 (*0-9605508-2-8*) Jedick Ent.

Cleveland, a Portrait of the City: Photographs. Jonathan Wayne. LC 93-34215. (Illus.). 1993. write for info. (*0-9631738-4-7*) Gray & Co Pubs.

***Cleveland As a Center of Regional American Art.** Ed. by Sandy Richert. 153p. (Orig.). (C). 1994. pap. 12.50 (*0-9639562-3-X*) Clevelnd Art.

Cleveland Bay Horses. Anthony Dent. 87p. 1990. pap. 21.00 (*0-85131-283-7*, Pub. by J A Allen & Co UK) St Mut.

Cleveland Benjamin's Dead! A Struggle for Dignity in Louisiana's Cane Country. Patsy Sims. LC 93-15731. (Illus.). 296p. 1994. Alk. paper. 24.95 (*0-8203-1581-8*) U of Ga Pr.

Cleveland Browns. Richard Rambeck. (NFL Today Ser.). 48p. (J). (gr. 4 up). 1991. lib. bdg. 14.95 (*0-88682-363-3*) Creative Ed.

Cleveland Builds an Art Museum: Patronage, Politics, & Architecture, 1884-1916. Walter C. Leedy, Jr. LC 91-3424. (Illus.). 104p. 1991. pap. 14.50 (*0-940717-09-3*) Cleveland Mus Art.

Cleveland Cavaliers. rev. ed. Richard Rambeck. (NBA Today Ser.). (Illus.). 32p. (J). (gr. 4 up). 1993. lib. bdg. 14.95 (*0-88682-527-X*) Creative Ed.

Cleveland Chefs Book. William Struns. Ed. by R. McMinn. 120p. (Orig.). 1989. pap. text ed. 6.95 (*0-935201-85-8*) Affordable Adven.

Cleveland Clinic Foundation Creative Cooking for Renal Diabetic Diets. Cleveland Clinic Foundation, Department of Nutrition Services Staff & Pat Ellis. LC 87-4934. 178p. (Orig.). 1987. pap. 14.95 (*0-941511-01-4*) Senay Pub.

Cleveland Clinic Foundation Creative Cooking for Renal Diets. Cleveland Clinic Foundation, Department of Nutrition Services Staff & Pat Ellis. LC 87-4575. 280p. (Orig.). 1987. pap. 14.95 (*0-941511-00-6*) Senay Pub.

Cleveland Clinic Home Care Services: Home Therapy Standards, Policies, & Procedures. Ed. by Charlene L. Szunyog. LC 92-10859. 1992. ring bd. 160.00 (*0-8342-0330-8*) Aspen Pub.

Cleveland Collection. Junior League of Cleveland, Inc. Staff. (Illus.). 200p. 1992. 24.95 (*0-9619027-0-1*) Jr Leag of Cleve.

Cleveland Connection. Les Roberts. LC 92-42606. 1993. 19.95 (*0-312-08746-2*, Pub. by Thomas Dunne Bks) St Martin.

***Cleveland Discovery Guide: Greater Cleveland's Best Family Recreation.** Jennifer Stoffel & Stephen Phillips. (Illus.). 208p. 1994. per., pap. 12.95 (*0-9631738-5-5*) Gray & Co Pubs.

Cleveland Era: Chronicle of the New Order in Politics. Henry J. Ford. (History - United States Ser.). 232p. 1992. reprint ed. lib. bdg. 79.00 (*0-7812-6209-7*) Rprt Serv.

Cleveland for Kids: A "Let's-Have-Fun" Guide to Cultural Cleveland for Children, Families & Friends. Tricia Springstubb. (Illus.). 172p. 1993. pap. 15.00 (*0-9630961-0-9*) CL Arts Consort.

***Cleveland Garden Handbook: Expert Local Advice on Growing a Beautiful Lawn & Garden in Northeast Ohio.** 2nd rev. ed. Susan McClure et al. (Illus.). 256p. 1995. pap. 12.95 (*1-886228-00-0*) Gray & Co Pubs.

Cleveland Golfer's Bible. 2nd ed. John H. Tidyman. LC 94-19845. Orig. Title: Cleveland's Public Golf Courses. (Illus.). 240p. 1994. pap. 12.95 (*0-9631738-6-3*) Gray & Co Pubs.

Cleveland Herbal, Botanical, & Horticultural Collections: A Descriptive Bibliography of Pre-1830 Works from the Libraries of the Holden Arboretum, the Cleveland Medical Library Association, & the Garden Center of Greater Cleveland. Comp. by Stanley H. Johnston, Jr. LC 90-5383. (Illus.). 1032p. 1992. lib. bdg. 85.00 (*0-87338-433-4*) Kent St U Pr.

Cleveland in Picture Postcards, 1900-1930. Ralph B. Thompson. LC 92-15449. (Illus.). 112p. (Orig.). 1992. pap. 11.95 (*0-911572-90-2*) Vestal.

Cleveland Indian: The Legend of King Saturday. Luke Salisbury. LC 92-80448. 288p. (Orig.). 1992. 24.95 (*0-912292-95-4*) The Smith.

Cleveland Indian: The Legend of King Saturday. Luke Salisbury. LC 94-66402. 288p. (Orig.). 1995. pap. 14.95 (*1-882986-14-8*) The Smith.

Cleveland Indians. Richard Rambeck. (Baseball: The Great American Game Ser.). 48p. (J). (gr. 4-10). 1992. lib. bdg. 14.95 (*0-88682-439-7*) Creative Ed.

***Cleveland Lee's Beale Street Band.** Arthur Flowers. (Illus.). 32p. (J). (gr. k-3). 1995. lib. bdg. 13.95 (*0-8167-3652-9*) BridgeWater.

Cleveland Museum of Art's Tuti-Nama: Tales of a Parrot. Ziya'u'd-din Nakhshabi. Tr. by Muhammed A. Simsar. LC 76-55714. (Illus.). 362p. 1978. 35.00 (*0-910386-29-3*) Cleveland Mus Art.

Cleveland, OH: Cleveland & Vicinity, OH. (Streetfinder Ser.). (Illus.). 1994. pap. 9.95 (*0-528-91760-9*) Rand McNally.

Cleveland on Foot: A Guide to Walking & Hiking in Cleveland & Vicinity. Patience Cameron & Harry Cameron. LC 92-90252. (Illus.). 156p. (Orig.). 1992. pap. 11.95 (*0-9632979-0-2*) H&P Pub Co.

***Cleveland on Foot: A Guide to Walking & Hiking in Cleveland & Vicinity.** 2nd ed. Patience Cameron & Harry Cameron. LC 95-1337. (Illus.). 256p. (Orig.). 1995. 12.95 (*0-9631738-9-8*) Gray & Co Pubs.

***Cleveland Rocks: A Bicentennial Political & Social History of Cleveland 1796-1996.** Damon Stakes. 160p. (Orig.). Date not set. pap. 12.95 (*0-9634940-4-X*) York Pub.

Cleveland School Survey: Summary Volume. Leonard P. Ayres. LC 72-112539. (Rise of Urban America Ser.). (Illus.). 1970. reprint ed. 23.95 (*0-405-02433-9*) Ayer.

Cleveland Sports Legacy since 1945. Intro. by Mark Hodermarsky. LC 91-77472. (Illus.). 135p. (Orig.). 1991. pap. 14.95 (*0-936760-06-0*) Cleveland Landmarks.

Cleveland Stadium: Sixty Years of Memories. James A. Toman. LC 91-71939. (Illus.). 114p. 1991. reprint ed. pap. 19.95 (*0-936760-05-2*) Cleveland Landmarks.

Cleveland Symposium on Behavioral Research in Rehabilitation. rev. ed. Ed. by William R. Phillips & Janet Rosenberg. LC 79-6898. (Physically Handicapped in Society Ser.). 1980. reprint ed. lib. bdg. 25.95 (*0-405-13110-0*) Ayer.

Cleveland Union Station: Cleveland, Ohio. (Illus.). 1979. reprint ed. pap. 4.50 (*0-934906-00-9*) R J Liederbach.

***Cleveland Way.** Ian Sampson. (National Gravel Guides Ser.). (Illus.). 168p. Date not set. pap. 19.95 (*1-85410-021-1*, London Bridge) Genl Dist Srvs.

Cleveland Way - One Hundred Miles. 64p. 1987. 29.00 (*0-907496-70-9*, Pub. by JNM Pubns UK) St Mut.

Cleveland's Bottle Pricing Guide. 3rd rev. ed. Hugh Cleveland. (Illus.). 256p. 1988. pap. 7.95 (*0-89145-137-4*) Collector Bks.

Cleveland's Changing Skyline. Jim Toman & Dan Cook. Ed. by Tom Luckay. LC 84-72385. (Cleveland Landmarks Ser.: Vol. 3). (Illus.). 118p. (Orig.). 1984. pap. 14.50 (*0-936760-03-6*) Cleveland Landmarks.

Cleveland's Children & Youth: A Status Report, 1993. Ed. by Wornie L. Reed & Mary E. Simon. 175p. 1993. pap. write for info. (*0-9638675-0-4*) CSU Urban Chld.

***Cleveland's Ethnic Eats: A Guide to Cleveland's Authentic Restaurants & Food Stores.** Laura Taxel. 1995. pap. 12.95 (*0-9631738-7-1*) Gray & Co Pubs.

Cleveland's Flats on Tour: A Self Guide to the Riverfront. Joan M. Schattinger & Ann T. Lawrence. LC 87-81299. (Illus.). 80p. (Orig.). 1987. pap. 9.95 (*0-317-60668-9*) Hist Assocs.

Cleveland's Public Golf Courses: A Player's Guide. John H. Tidyman. LC 92-10056. 248p. 1992. 12.95 (*0-9631738-0-4*) Gray & Co Pubs.

Cleveland's Public Golf Courses see Cleveland Golfer's Bible

Clever Advertising: Getting the Most from Your Advertising Dollar. Brett W. Lowe. 152p. 1993. pap. 16.95 (*1-875680-06-3*, Pub. by Busn & Prof Pubng AT) Pubs Dist MI.

Clever Bridge Tricks. Brian Senior & Terence Reese. 144p. (Orig.). 1988. pap. 10.95 (*0-571-14919-7*) Faber & Faber.

Clever Crafts to Decorate Your Home. Tonia Todman. 1993. 12.98 (*1-55521-851-2*) Bk Sales Inc.

Clever Cryptograms. Louise B. Moll. LC 94-17397. (Illus.). 128p. 1994. pap. 5.95 (*0-8069-0756-8*) Sterling.

***Clever Curriculum Crafts from Recycled Materials.** Deborah Whitacre & Becky Radtke. Ed. by Judy Mitchell. (Illus.). 80p. (Orig.). 1995. pap. 8.95 (*1-57310-026-9*) Teachng & Lrning Co.

Clever Dick. Charles Marowitz. 1989. pap. 4.75 (*0-8222-0216-6*) Dramatists Play.

Clever Folk: Tales of Wisdom, Wit, & Wonder. Ruthilde M. Kronberg. (Illus.). 120p. 1993. lib. bdg. 21.00 (*1-56308-139-3*) Libs Unl.

Clever Foxes & Lucky Klutzes. William J. O'Malley. 169p. 1993. 12.95 (*0-7829-0364-9*, 22055) Tabor Pub.

Clever Gretchen & Other Forgotten Folktales. Alison Lurie. LC 78-22512. (Illus.). 128p. (J). (gr. 4-6). 1980. lib. bdg. 13.89 (*0-690-03944-1*, Crowell Jr Bks) HarpC Child Bks.

Clever Hans Phenomenon: Communication with Horses, Whales, Apes, & People. Ed. by Thomas A. Sebeok & Robert Rosenthal. LC 81-2806. 311p. 1981. pap. 62.00 (*0-89766-114-1*, VOL. 364P) NY Acad Sci.

Clever Hearts: Desmond & Molly MacCarthy - A Biography. Hugh Cecil & Mirabel Cecil. (Illus.). 320p. 1991. 39.95 (*0-575-03622-2*, Pub. by V Gollancz UK) Trafalgar.

An Asterisk (*) at the beginning of an entry indicates that the title is appearing in BIP for the first time.

An Asterisk (*) at the beginning of an entry indicates that the title is appearing in BIP for the first time.

1311

Clifford Numbers & Spinors: With Riesz's Private Lectures to E. Folke Bolinder & a Historical Review by Pertti Lounesto. Marcel Riesz. Ed. by E. Folke Bolinder & Pertti Lounesto. LC 93-1381. (Fundamental Theories of Physics Ser.: Vol. 54). 256p. (C). 1993. lib. bdg. 98.50 (*0-7923-2299-1*) Kluwer Ac.

Clifford Odets. Gabriel Miller. (Literature & Life Ser.). 192p. (C). (gr. 12). 1989. 19.95 (*0-8044-2632-5*) Continuum.

Clifford Odets: A Research & Production Sourcebook. William W. Demastes. LC 91-3757. (Modern Dramatists Research & Production Sourcebooks Ser.: No. 1). 224p. 1991. text ed. 49.95 (*0-313-26294-2*, DCO, Greenwood Pr) Greenwood.

Clifford Odets: An Annotated Bibliography of Criticism, 1935-1989. Robert Cooperman. 160p. 1990. text ed. 49.95 (*0-313-27669-2*) Greenwood.

***Clifford Selbert Design.** Date not set. 34.99 (*1-56496-168-0*) Rockport Pubs.

Clifford Sifton in Relation to His Times. John W. Dafoe. LC 79-157331. (Select Bibliographies Reprint Ser.). 1977. reprint ed. 35.95 (*0-8369-5791-1*) Ayer.

Clifford Simak. Robert J. Ewald. (Milford Series: Popular Writers of Today: Vol. 71). (Orig.). Date not set. lib. bdg. write for info. (*1-55742-218-4*); pap. write for info. (*1-55742-217-6*) Borgo Pr.

Clifford Takes a Trip. Norman Bridwell. (J). (ps-3). 1985. pap. 2.50 (*0-590-44260-0*) Scholastic Inc.

Clifford Takes a Trip. Norman Bridwell. (J). 1991. audio, pap. 5.95 (*0-590-63823-8*) Scholastic Inc.

Clifford the Big Red Dog. Norman Bridwell. (Illus.). (J). (ps-3). 1985. 2.50 (*0-590-44297-X*) Scholastic Inc.

Clifford the Big Red Dog. Norman Bridwell. (Illus.). (J). (ps-3). 1988. audio, pap. 5.95 (*0-590-63212-4*) Scholastic Inc.

Clifford the Big Red Dog. Norman Bridwell. (Illus.). 32p. (J). (ps-3). 1988. 10.95 (*0-590-40743-0*, Scholastic Hardcover) Scholastic Inc.

***Clifford, the Big Red Dog.** Garrett Christopher. Ed. by J. Friedland & R. Kessler. (Novel-Ties). (J). (gr. k-1). 1992. student ed, pap. text ed. 14.95 (*0-88122-733-1*) Lrn Links.

Clifford the Firehouse Dog. Norman Bridwell. (Illus.). 32p. (J). (ps-3). 1994. 2.50 (*0-590-48419-2*, Cartwheel); Spanish ed. 2.95 (*0-590-48808-2*, Cartwheel) Scholastic Inc.

Clifford the Small Red Puppy. Norman Bridwell. (J). (ps-2). 1985. 2.50 (*0-590-44294-5*) Scholastic Inc.

Clifford the Small Red Puppy. Norman Bridwell. (J). (ps-2). 1988. audio 5.95 (*0-590-63211-6*) Scholastic Inc.

Clifford the Small Red Puppy. Norman Bridwell. (J). (ps-3). 1990. 10.95 (*0-590-43496-9*) Scholastic Inc.

Clifford the Small Red Puppy Follows His Nose. Norman Bridwell. 32p. (J). 1992. bds. 5.95 (*0-590-44345-3*, Scholastic Hardcover) Scholastic Inc.

Clifford Theory for Group Representations. Gregory Karpilovsky. (Mathematics Studies: No. 156). 364p. 1989. 107.75 (*0-444-87377-5*, North Holland) Elsevier.

Clifford Treasury, No. I: Small Puppy - Big Red - Pals - Grouchy - Neighbors. Norman Bridwell. (J). 1991. pap. 9.00 (*0-590-63953-6*) Scholastic Inc.

Clifford Treasury, No. II: Birthday - Puppy - Days - Family - Kitten. Norman Bridwell. (J). 1991. pap. 9.00 (*0-590-63952-8*) Scholastic Inc.

Clifford Va de Viaje. rev. ed. Norman Bridwell. Tr. by Argentina Palacios. (Illus.). 32p. (SPA.). (J). (gr. k-3). 1987. pap. 2.50 (*0-590-40844-5*) Scholastic Inc.

Clifford W. Beers: Advocate for the Insane. Norman Dain. LC 79-24290. (Contemporary Community Health Ser.). 1980. 49.95 (*0-8229-3419-1*) U of Pittsburgh Pr.

Clifford Wants a Cookie. Norman Bridwell. (Clifford Activity Bks.). (Illus.). 16p. (J). (ps-3). 1988. Book & Cookie Cutter Package. pap. 3.95 (*0-590-63282-5*) Scholastic Inc.

Clifford Wavelets, Singular Integrals, & Hardy Spaces. Marius Mitrea. LC 94-9648. (Lecture Notes in Mathematics: Vol. 1575). 1994. 23.00 (*0-387-57884-6*) Spr-Verlag.

Clifford, We Love You. Norman Bridwell. (J). (ps-3). 1991. pap. 2.50 (*0-590-43843-3*); audio, pap. 5.95 (*0-590-63604-9*) Scholastic Inc.

Clifford, We Love You. Norman Bridwell. LC 94-4005. (J). (gr. 2 up). 1994. 10.95 (*0-590-48612-8*) Scholastic Inc.

Clifford Years: The University of North Dakota, 1971-1992. Daniel R. Rice. (Illus.). 224p. 1992. pap. 10.00 (*0-9608700-9-1*) U NDak Pres.

Clifford's ABC. Norman Bridwell. (J). (ps-3). 1986. pap. 2.50 (*0-590-44286-4*) Scholastic Inc.

Clifford's ABC. Norman Bridwell. LC 94-9787. (J). 1994. 10.95 (*0-590-48694-2*) Scholastic Inc.

Clifford's Animal Sounds. Norman Bridwell. (J). (ps). 1991. 3.95 (*0-590-44734-3*) Scholastic Inc.

Clifford's Bathtime. Norman Bridwell. (J). (ps). 1991. 3.95 (*0-590-44735-1*) Scholastic Inc.

Clifford's Bedtime. Norman Bridwell. (J). (ps). 1991. 3.95 (*0-590-44736-X*) Scholastic Inc.

Clifford's Big Book of Stories. Norman Bridwell. LC 93-31367. (Illus.). 64p. (J). (ps-3). 1994. 9.95 (*0-590-47925-3*, Cartwheel) Scholastic Inc.

Clifford's Birthday Party. Norman Bridwell. (Cliffords Bks.). (Illus.). 32p. (Orig.). (J). (gr. k-3). 1988. audio, pap. 5.95 (*0-590-63237-X*) Scholastic Inc.

Clifford's Christmas. Norman Bridwell. (Clifford Ser.). (Illus.). 32p. (J). (gr. k-3). 1984. 2.50 (*0-590-44288-0*) Scholastic Inc.

Clifford's Christmas. Norman Bridwell. (Clifford Ser.). (Illus.). 32p. (J). (gr. k-3). 1987. audio 5.95 (*0-590-63210-8*) Scholastic Inc.

Clifford's Family. Norman Bridwell. (J). (ps-3). 1993. pap. 19.95 (*0-590-71584-4*) Scholastic Inc.

Clifford's Family. Norman Bridwell. (Clifford Story Bks.). (Illus.). 32p. (Orig.). (J). (gr. k-3). 1984. pap. 2.50 (*0-590-44290-2*) Scholastic Inc.

Clifford's First Christmas. Norman Bridwell. (Illus.). 32p. (Orig.). (J). (ps-3). 1994. pap. 2.25 (*0-590-48420-6*, Cartwheel); Spanish ed. pap. 2.95 (*0-590-48852-X*, Cartwheel) Scholastic Inc.

***Clifford's First Easter.** Norman Bridwell. (J). (ps-3). 1995. 7.95 (*0-590-22241-4*, Cartwheel) Scholastic Inc.

Clifford's Good Deeds. Norman Bridwell. (Clifford Story Bks.). (Illus.). 32p. (J). (gr. k-3). 1985. pap. 2.50 (*0-590-44292-9*) Scholastic Inc.

Clifford's Good Deeds. Norman Bridwell. (J). 1991. audio, pap. 5.95 (*0-590-63824-6*) Scholastic Inc.

Clifford's Good Deeds see Buenas Acciones de Clifford

Clifford's Halloween. Norman Bridwell. (Clifford Story Bks.). (Illus.). 32p. (J). (gr. k-3). 1986. pap. 2.50 (*0-590-44287-2*) Scholastic Inc.

Clifford's Halloween. Norman Bridwell. (Clifford Story Bks.). (Illus.). 32p. (J). (gr. k-3). 1989. pap. 5.95 (*0-590-63436-4*) Scholastic Inc.

Clifford's Happy Days: A Pop-up Book. Norman Bridwell. (Clifford Activity Bks.). (Illus.). 16p. (Orig.). (J). (gr. k-3). 1990. pap. 12.95 (*0-590-42926-4*) Scholastic Inc.

Clifford's Happy Easter. Norman Bridwell. (Illus.). 32p. (J). (ps-3). 1994. pap. 2.25 (*0-590-47782-X*, Cartwheel) Scholastic Inc.

Clifford's I Love You. Norman Bridwell. (Illus.). 10p. (J). (ps up). 1994. 4.95 (*0-590-47309-3*, Cartwheel) Scholastic Inc.

Clifford's Kitten. Norman Bridwell. (Clifford Story Bks.). (Illus.). 32p. (Orig.). (J). (gr. k-3). 1984. pap. 2.50 (*0-590-44280-5*) Scholastic Inc.

Clifford's Manners. Norman Bridwell. (Clifford Story Bks.). (Illus.). 32p. (J). (gr. k-3). 1987. pap. 2.50 (*0-590-44285-6*) Scholastic Inc.

Clifford's Manners. Norman Bridwell. LC 94-4004. (J). 1994. 10.95 (*0-590-48697-7*) Scholastic Inc.

Clifford's Noisy Day. Norman Bridwell. (Illus.). (J). 1992. bds. 3.95 (*0-590-45737-3*, 036, Cartwheel) Scholastic Inc.

Clifford's Pals. Norman Bridwell. (Clifford Story Bks.). (Illus.). 32p. (J). (gr. k-3). 1985. pap. 2.50 (*0-590-44295-3*) Scholastic Inc.

Clifford's Peekaboo. Norman Bridwell. (J). (ps). 1991. 3.95 (*0-590-44737-8*) Scholastic Inc.

Clifford's Puppy Days. Norman Bridwell. (J). (ps-3). 1988. pap. 2.25 (*0-590-44262-7*) Scholastic Inc.

Clifford's Puppy Days. Norman Bridwell. (J). 1989. pap. 1.95 (*0-590-42189-1*) Scholastic Inc.

Clifford's Puppy Days. Norman Bridwell. (Big Book Ser.). (J). (ps-3). 1992. pap. 19.95 (*0-590-72612-9*) Scholastic Inc.

Clifford's Puppy Days. Norman Bridwell. LC 93-1802. (Illus.). 32p. (J). (ps-6). 1994. 10.95 (*0-590-43339-3*, Cartwheel) Scholastic Inc.

Clifford's Riddles. Norman Bridwell. (Clifford Story Bks.). (Illus.). 32p. (Orig.). (J). (gr. k-3). 1984. pap. 2.50 (*0-590-44282-1*) Scholastic Inc.

Clifford's Springtime. Norman Bridwell. (Illus.). 10p. (J). (ps up). 1994. 4.95 (*0-590-47293-3*, Cartwheel) Scholastic Inc.

Clifford's Thanksgiving Visit. Norman Bridwell. (Illus.). 32p. (J). (ps-3). 1993. pap. 2.25 (*0-590-46987-8*, Cartwheel) Scholastic Inc.

Clifford's Tricks. Norman Bridwell. (Clifford Story Bks.). (Illus.). 32p. (J). (gr. k-3). 1986. pap. 2.50 (*0-590-44291-0*) Scholastic Inc.

Clifford's Word Book. Norman Bridwell. (Illus.). 32p. (Orig.). (J). (ps-1). 1990. pap. 2.50 (*0-590-43095-5*) Scholastic Inc.

Clifford's Word Book. Norman Bridwell. LC 94-4003. (J). (J). 1994. 10.95 (*0-590-48696-9*) Scholastic Inc.

***Cliffs Graduate Management Admission Test (GMAT) Preparation Guide.** Jerry Bobrow. (Cliffs Test Preparation Guides Ser.). (Illus.). 431p. (Orig.). (C). 1994. pap. text ed. 9.95 (*0-8220-2061-0*) Cliffs.

***Cliffs Graduate Record Examination - General Test Preparation Guide.** rev. ed. Jerry Bobrow. (Cliffs Test Preparation Guides Ser.). (Illus.). 454p. 1995. pap. text ed. 9.95 (*0-8220-2073-4*) Cliffs.

Cliffs Notes Hardbound Authors Library Complete Set, 13 Vols. (C). 1990. lib. bdg. 635.00 (*0-931013-65-8*) Moonbeam Pubns.

Cliffs Notes Hardbound Literary Library: Complete 24 Vol. Set. 1989. lib. bdg. 1,668.50 (*0-931013-24-0*) Moonbeam Pubns.

Cliffs of Aries. Thom Nickels. LC 88-71119. 192p. (Orig.). 1989. pap. 10.00 (*0-916383-68-5*) Aegina Pr.

Cliffs of Dread. large type ed. Virginia Coffman. 1983. 15.95 (*0-7089-0944-2*) Ulverscroft.

Cliffs of Moher. Tony Whilde. (Irish Pocket Guide Ser.). (Illus.). 72p. (Orig.). 1987. pap. 7.95 (*0-86281-196-1*, Pub. by Appletree Pr IE) Irish Bks Media.

***Cliffs Police Officer Examination Preparation Guide.** Larry F. Jetmore. (Cliffs Test Preparation Guides Ser.). (Illus.). 403p. (Orig.). 1994. pap. text ed. 14.95 (*0-8220-2047-5*) Cliffs.

***Cliffs Postal Examinations Preparation Guide.** rev. ed. Jerry Bobrow. (Cliffs Test Preparation Guides Ser.). (Illus.). 307p. 1994. pap. text ed. 10.95 (*0-8220-2076-9*) Cliffs.

Cliff's Test Preparation Guides Library: Collection of 19 Guides. 1990. pap. text ed. 151.60 (*1-56271-300-0*) Moonbeam Pubns.

Clifton Fadiman's Fireside Reader. Ed. by Clifton Fadiman. 23.95 (*0-88411-546-1*, Aeonian Pr) Amereon Ltd.

Cliges. Chretien de Troyes & Alexandre Micha. 187p. 1969. 9.95 (*0-8288-9098-6*, F26532) Fr & Eur.

Cliges. Chretien De Troyes. Ed. by Stewart Gregory & Claude Luttrell. (Arthurian Studies: No. XXVIII). 431p. (C). 1993. text ed. 53.00 (*0-85991-383-X*) Boydell & Brewer.

Climacteric: An Update. Ed. by H. B. Van Herendael et al. 180p. 1984. lib. bdg. 45.00 (*0-85200-852-X*) Kluwer Ac.

Climacteric & Beyond. Ed. by L. Zichella et al. (Illus.). 190p. 1988. 55.00 (*1-85070-176-8*) Prthnon Pub.

Climacteric Hot Flush. Ed. by E. Schoenbaum. (Progress in Basic & Clinical Pharmacology Ser.: Vol. 6). (Illus.). x, 166p. 1991. 127.25 (*3-8055-5260-2*) S Karger.

Climacteric in Perspective. Ed. by M. Notevitz & P. A. Van Keep. 1986. lib. bdg. 259.50 (*0-85200-919-4*) Kluwer Ac.

Climate: Designing a Practical Tax System. OECD Staff. 276p. (Orig.). 1992. pap. text ed. 35.00 (*92-64-13776-9*, 02-92-07-1) OECD.

Climate: History, Periodicity, & Predictability. Ed. by Michael R. Rampino et al. (Illus.). 608p. 1987. text ed. 95.00 (*0-442-27866-7*) Chapman & Hall.

Climate: Present, Past & Future, Vol. 1. Hubert H. Lamb. (Illus.). 1972. 165.00 (*0-416-11530-6*, NO.2785) Routledge Chapman & Hall.

Climate: Present, Past & Future, Vol. 2. H. H. Lamb. 835p. 1977. 150.00 (*0-416-11540-3*, NO.2283) Routledge Chapman & Hall.

Climate - Our Future? rev. ed. Ulrich Schotterer. Tr. & Frwd. by Kerry Kelts. (Illus.). 175p. (C). 1992. 39.95 (*0-8166-2130-6*) U of Minn Pr.

Climate & Agricultural Land Use in Monsoon Asia. Masatoshi M. Yoshino. 398p. 1984. 82.50 (*0-86008-357-8*, Pub. by U of Tokyo JA) Col U Pr.

Climate & Architecture. 2nd ed. J. Aronin. 1984. write for info. (*0-442-28267-2*); pap. write for info. (*0-442-28266-4*) Van Nos Reinhold.

Climate & Circulation of the Tropics. Stefan Hastenrath. 1985. lib. bdg. 164.00 (*90-277-2026-6*) Kluwer Ac.

Climate & Culture: A Philosophical Study, 10 vols., Set. Tetsuro Watsuji. Tr. by Geoffrey Bownas. (Documentary Reference Collections). 1988. 395.00 (*0-318-35986-3*, CMJ03) Greenwood.

Climate & Culture: A Philosophical Study, 10 vols., Vol. 3. Tetsuro Watsuji. Tr. by Geoffrey Bownas. LC 88-21985. (Documentary Reference Collections). 235p. 1988. text ed. 45.00 (*0-313-26558-5*, WJC/) Greenwood.

Climate & Development. A. Biswag. 154p. 1983. pap. text ed. 50.00 (*0-907567-37-1*, Tycooly Pub) Weidner & Sons.

Climate & Development. H. J. Karpe & D. Otten. (Illus.). 449p. 1990. pap. 65.00 (*0-387-51269-1*, 3837) Spr-Verlag.

Climate & Economic Development in the Tropics. Douglas H. Lee. LC 76-56184. 182p. 1977. reprint ed. text ed. 49.75 (*0-8371-9410-5*, LECE, Greenwood Pr) Greenwood.

Climate & Energy: The Feasibility of Controlling CO2 Emissions. Ed. by P. A. Okken et al. (C). 1989. lib. bdg. 105.50 (*0-7923-0519-1*) Kluwer Ac.

Climate & Evolution. William D. Matthew. LC 73-17830. (Natural Sciences in America Ser.). (Illus.). 150p. 1974. reprint ed. 15.95 (*0-405-05748-2*) Ayer.

Climate & Fisheries. D. H. Cushing. 1983. text ed. 112.00 (*0-12-199720-0*) Acad Pr.

Climate & Geo-Sciences. Ed. by A. L. Berger et al. (C). 1989. lib. bdg. 186.50 (*0-7923-0404-7*); pap. text ed. 99.00 (*0-7923-0412-8*) Kluwer Ac.

Climate & Geology of Kashmir & Central Asia. Ed. by D. P. Agarwal et al. (Current Trends in Geology Ser.: Vol. 6). xvi, 247p. 1985. 59.00 (*1-55528-064-1*, Pub. by Today & Tomorrows P & P II) Scholarly Pubns.

Climate & Global Change Proceedings of the European School of Climatology, No. EUR 13149. Ed. by J. C. Duplessy et al. 358p. 1991. pap. 45.00 (*92-826-2779-9*, CD-NA-13149-EN-C) UNIPUB.

Climate & Health Implications of Bubble-Mediated Sea-Air Exchange. Ed. by Edward C. Monahan & Margaret A. Van Patten. (Illus.). (Orig.). (C). 1989. pap. 12.50 (*0-685-29355-6*) CT Sea Grant.

Climate & Human Ecology. Jim Norwine. LC 78-52975. (Illus.). 1978. pap. 9.95 (*0-918464-19-6*) D Armstrong.

Climate & Moisture Variability in a Tropical Forest: Long-Term Records from Barro Colorado Island, Panama. Donald M. Windsor. LC 89-600304. (Smithsonian Contributions to the Earth Sciences Ser.: No. 29). 149p. reprint ed. pap. 42.50 (*0-8357-2749-1*, 2039863) Bks Demand.

Climate & Plant Distribution. F. I. Woodward. (Cambridge Studies in Ecology). (Illus.). 225p. 1987. pap. 22.95 (*0-521-28214-4*) Cambridge U Pr.

Climate & Sea Level Change: Observations, Projections & Implications. Ed. by R. A. Warrick & T. M. Wigley. (Illus.). 250p. (C). 1993. 69.95 (*0-521-39516-X*) Cambridge U Pr.

Climate & the Affairs of Men. 2nd ed. Nels Winkless, III & Iben Browning. LC 74-27305. 1980. 16.00 (*0-87034-059-X*) Fraser Pub Co.

Climate & the Dolores River Anasazi: A Paleoenvironmental Reconstruction from a 10,000 Year Pollen Record, La Plata Mountains, Southwest Colorado. Kenneth L. Peterson. (Anthropological Papers: No. 113). 160p. (Orig.). 1988. pap. 25.00 (*0-87480-303-9*) U of Utah Pr.

Climate & the Energy of Nations. Sydney F. Markham. LC 77-10234. 248p. reprint ed. 42.50 (*0-404-16214-2*) AMS Pr.

Climate & the World Order. J. Bandopadhyaya. 178p. 1983. 23.95 (*0-318-37227-4*) Asia Bk Corp.

Climate & Weather. H. Dickson. 1976. lib. bdg. 59.95 (*0-8490-1638-X*) Gordon Pr.

Climate & Weather of Florida. James A. Henry et al. Ed. by Jan Coyne. LC 93-48077. (Illus.). 279p. 1994. 27.95 (*1-56164-036-0*) Pineapple Pr.

Climate & Weather of Florida. James A. Henry et al. Ed. by Jan Coyne. (Illus.). 200p. 1994. pap. 17.95 (*1-56164-037-9*) Pineapple Pr.

Climate-Biosphere Interactions: Biogenic Emissions & Environmental Effects of Climate Change. Richard G. Zepp. 1994. text ed. 110.00 (*0-471-58932-2*) Wiley.

Climate Change: Designing a Tradeable Permit System. OECD Staff. 282p. (Orig.). 1992. pap. 31.00 (*92-64-13731-9*) OECD.

Climate Change: Evaluating the Socio-Economic Impacts. Organisation for Economic Cooperation & Development Staff. 110p. (Orig.). 1991. pap. 27.00 (*92-64-13462-X*) OECD.

***Climate Change: Global Observation.** (Illus.). 500p. (C). 1994. 295.00 (*0-7605-0039-8*) Rector Pr.

Climate Change: Glossary. United Nations Staff. 143p. 1990. 59.95 (*0-8288-7362-3*, 9210020367) Fr & Eur.

Climate Change: Impact on Coastal Habitation. Eisma. 1995. write for info. (*0-87371-301-X*) Lewis Pubs.

Climate Change: Policy Initiatives. OECD Staff. 184p. (Orig.). 1992. pap. 37.00 (*92-64-13754-8*) OECD.

Climate Change: Significance for Agriculture & Forestry: Systems Approaches Arising from an IPCC Meeting. Ed. by David H. White & S. Mark Howden. LC 94-17899. 1994. lib. bdg. 68.50 (*0-7923-2933-3*) Kluwer Ac.

Climate Change: The IPCC Response Strategies. Intergovernmental Panel on Climate Change Staff. LC 90-26690. 272p. (Orig.). 1991. 60.00 (*1-55963-103-1*); pap. 39.95 (*1-55963-102-3*) Island Pr.

Climate Change: The IPCC Scientific Assessment. Ed. by John T. Houghton et al. (Illus.). 403p. (C). 1990. 79.95 (*0-521-40360-X*); pap. 39.95 (*0-521-40720-6*) Cambridge U Pr.

Climate Change - Glossary: 1990. 143p. 1990. 30.00 (*92-1-002036-7*, GV.90.0.12) UN.

***Climate Change - the U. K. Programme.** HMSO Staff. (Command Paper Ser.: No. 2427). 80p. 1994. pap. 19.00 (*0-10-124272-7*, HM42727, Pub. by HMSO UK) UNIPUB.

***Climate Change & Agriculture: Analysis of Potential International Impacts: Proceedings of a Symposium.** Ed. by Cynthia Rosenzweig et al. LC 95-14069. (Special Publication Ser.: Vol. 59). 1995. write for info. (*0-89118-126-1*) Am Soc Agron.

Climate Change & Energy Policy. Ed. by Louis Rosen & Robert Glasser. 564p. 1992. pap. 55.00 (*1-56396-017-6*) Am Inst Physics.

Climate Change & Human Impact on the Landscape. Ed. by F. M. Chambers. 304p. 1992. 79.95 (*0-412-46200-1*, A9444) Chapman & Hall.

Climate Change & Its Biological Consequences. David M. Gates. LC 92-36886. (Illus.). 280p. (Orig.). (C). 1993. pap. text ed. 19.95 (*0-87893-224-0*) Sinauer Assocs.

***Climate Change & Rice.** Ed. by S. Peng et al. LC 95-12491. 1995. write for info. (*3-540-58906-6*) Spr-Verlag.

Climate Change & the Agenda for Research. Ed. by Ted Hanisch. LC 94-13943. (C). 1994. text ed. 45.00 (*0-8133-8791-4*) Westview.

Climate Change & U. S. Water Resources. Paul E. Waggoner. 1990. text ed. 89.95 (*0-471-61838-1*) Wiley.

***Climate Change Atlas: Greenhouse Simulations from the Model Evaluation Consortium for Climate Assessment.** Ann Henderson-Sellers & Ann-Maree Hansen. LC 95-13512. (Atmospheric & Oceanographic Sciences Library: Vol. 17). (Illus.). 172p. (C). 1995. lib. bdg. 155.00 (*0-7923-3465-5*) Kluwer Ac.

Climate Change in Continental Isotopic Records. Ed. by P. K. Swart et al. LC 93-37709. (Geophysical Monograph Ser.: Vol. 78). 1993. 57.00 (*0-87590-037-2*) Am Geophysical.

***Climate Change Policy Initiatives 1994 Vol. 1: Update.** OECD Staff. 217p. (Orig.). 1994. pap. 53.00x (*92-64-14142-1*) OECD.

Climate Change to the Year 2000. 1905. write for info. (*0-8103-4325-8*) Gale.

***Climate Change World Economy.** Martin Parry. Date not set. 24.95 (*1-85383-109-3*, Pub. by Erthscan Pubns UK) Island Pr.

Climate Change 1992. Ed. by John T. Houghton. (Illus.). 150p. (C). 1992. pap. 19.95 (*0-521-43829-2*) Cambridge U Pr.

***Climate Change 1994: Radiative Forcing of Climate & an Evaluation of the IPCC IS92 Emission Scenarios.** Ed. by John T. Houghton et al. (Illus.). 250p. (C). 1995. 59.95 (*0-521-55055-6*); pap. 24.95 (*0-521-55962-6*) Cambridge U Pr.

Climate, Climatic Change & Water Supply. National Research Council Staff. (Studies in Geophysics). 132p. 1977. pap. 14.95 (*0-309-02625-3*) Natl Acad Pr.

Climate, Considered Especially in Relation to Man. 2nd rev. ed. Robert D. Ward. LC 77-10242. 400p. 1983. reprint ed. 42.50 (*0-404-16220-7*) AMS Pr.

Climate Control & Automotive Cabin Air Filtration: SAE International Congress & Exposition 1994, 16 papers. (Special Publications). 1994. pap. 45.00 (*1-56091-492-0*, SP-1040) Soc Auto Engineers.

Climate Crisis. 105p. 1987. pap. 20.00 (*92-807-1169-5*, E.87.III.D.9) UN.

Climate Data & Resources: A Reference & Guide. Edward Linacre. (Illus.). 384p. (C). 1992. 75.00 (*0-415-05702-7*, A6535); pap. 31.50 (*0-415-05703-5*, A6539) Routledge.

Climate Dynamics of the Tropics: From Climate & Circulation of the Tropics. (C). 1991. lib. bdg. 151.50 (*0-7923-1213-9*); pap. text ed. 58.00 (*0-7923-1346-1*) Kluwer Ac.

Climate, Earth Processes & Earth History. Richard J. Huggett. (Illus.). 260p. 1991. 89.00 (*0-387-53419-9*) Spr-Verlag.

An Asterisk (*) at the beginning of an entry indicates that the title is appearing in BIP for the first time.

Climate for Appeasement. Terrance L. Lewis. LC 90-6166. (Studies in History & Culture: Vol. 3). 263p. (C). 1990. text ed. 44.95 (0-8204-1314-3) P Lang Pubs.
Climate for Art: The History of the Boston Athenaeum Gallery 1827-1873. Pamela Hoyle et al. LC 80-69027. (Illus.). 41p. 1980. 7.50 (0-934552-34-7) Boston Athenaeum.
Climate for Conspiracy. large type ed. Palma Harcourt. 1981. 12.00 (0-7089-0703-2) Ulverscroft.
Climate for Creativity. Ed. by C. W. Taylor. 312p. 1972. 140.00 (0-08-016329-7, Pub. by Pergamon Repr UK) Franklin.
Climate for Learning. Mike Torbe & Peter Medway. LC 82-14768. 149p. (C). 1982. reprint ed. pap. text ed. 16.00 (0-86709-041-3) Boynton Cook Pubs.
Climate, History & the Modern World. H. H. Lamb. (Illus.). 480p. 1982. pap. 29.95 (0-416-33440-7, NO. 3696) Routledge Chapman & Hall.
***Climate, History & the Modern World.** 2nd ed. H. H. Lamb. LC 94-44666. 1995. write for info. (0-415-12734-3); pap. write for info. (0-415-12735-1) Routledge.
Climate Impact Assessment. Ed. by Robert W. Kates et al. LC 84-20922. (Scientific Committee on Problems of the Environment Ser.: No. 27). 625p. 1985. text ed. 395.00 (0-471-90634-4) Wiley.
Climate in Crisis: The Greenhouse Effect & What We Can Do. Albert Bates. LC 89-17890. (Illus.). 228p. (Orig.). 1990. pap. 11.95 (0-913990-67-1) Book Pub Co.
Climate in Earth History. National Research Council (U. S.), Geophysics Study Committee Staff. LC 82-18857. (Studies in Geophysics). 212p. reprint ed. pap. 60.50 (0-7837-0349-X, 2040668) Bks Demand.
Climate in Human Perspective: A Tribute to Helmut A. Landsberg. Ed. by F. Baer et al. (Atmospheric Sciences Library). 156p. 1991. lib. bdg. 61.50 (0-7923-1072-1) Kluwer Ac.
Climate, Incorporated: Classic Science Fiction. John R. Fearn. LC 87-33748. 36p. 1987. lib. bdg. 20.00x (0-8095-6650-8) Borgo Pr.
***Climate Model Applications in Paleoenvironmental Analysis.** Eric J. Barron & George T. Moore. (SEPM Short Course Notes Ser.: No. 33). (Illus.). 344p. 1994. pap. text ed. 49.00 (1-56576-012-3) SEPM.
Climate Modelling Primer. A. Henderson-Sellers & K. McGuffie. LC 86-32505. 250p. 1988. text ed. 95.00 (0-471-91462-2) Wiley.
Climate Modes of the Phanerozoic. Lawrence A. Frakes et al. (Illus.). 170p. (C). 1992. 69.95 (0-521-36627-5) Cambridge U Pr.
Climate near the Ground. 4th ed. Rudolf Geiger. LC 64-23191. (Illus.). 625p. reprint ed. pap. 178.70 (0-7837-1700-8, 2057229) Bks Demand.
Climate-Ocean Interaction. Ed. by M. E. Schlesinger. (C). 1990. lib. bdg. 136.50 (0-7923-0859-X) Kluwer Ac.
Climate of Africa: Air Temperature & Precipitation. Ed. by A. N. Lebedev. 488p. 1970. text ed. 110.00 (0-7065-0733-9, Pub. by Keter Pub IS) Coronet Bks.
Climate of Antarctica. Ed. by I. M. Dolgin. Tr. by P. Datta. 224p. (ENG.). (C). 1986. text ed. 95.00 (90-6191-463-9, Pub. by A A Balkema NE) Ashgate Pub Co.
Climate of Antarctica. I. M. Dolgin. 1986. 24.00 (81-205-0055-5, Pub. by Oxford IBH II) S Asia.
Climate of China. Jiacheng Zhang & Zhiguang Lin. 400p. 1992. text ed. 119.95 (0-471-51913-8) Wiley.
Climate of China & Global China. Ed. by D. Ye et al. (Illus.). xv, 441p. 1988. 99.00 (0-387-16718-8) Spr-Verlag.
***Climate of Extremes: Landscape & Imagination.** Marilyn Stablein. 160p. 1995. 20.95 (0-930773-38-1); pap. 12.95 (0-930773-39-X) Black Heron Pr.
Climate of Monastic Prayer. Thomas Merton. (Cistercian Studies: No. 1). 154p. 1973. reprint ed. 7.95 (0-87907-801-4) Cistercian Pubns.
Climate of the Arctic: Twenty-Fourth Alaska Science Conference, August 1973. 915th ed. Gunter Weller & Sue A. Bowling. LC 53-481. 436p. 1975. 10.00 (0-915360-01-2) Geophysical Inst.
Climate of the Free Atmosphere. Ed. by D. F. Rex. (World Survey of Climatology Ser.: Vol. 4). 450p. 1969. 174.50 (0-444-40703-0) Elsevier.
Climate of the United States & Its Endemic Influences. Samuel Forry. LC 77-10224. reprint ed. 49.50 (0-404-16205-3) AMS Pr.
Climate of Workplace Relations. Ali Dastmalchian et al. 240p. 1991. 74.50 (0-415-03738-7, A5925) Routledge.
Climate Processes & Climate Sensitivity, Maurice Ewing Vol. 5. Ed. by J. E. Hansen & T. Takahashi. (Geophysical Monograph Ser.: Vol. 29). 336p. 1984. 28. 00 (0-87590-404-1) Am Geophysical.
Climate Related Landscapes in World Mountains. Will E. Thompson. (Annals of Geomorphology Ser.: Suppl. 78). (Illus.). 92p. 1990. pap. 50.00 (0-685-64747-1, Pub. by Gebrueder Borntraeger GW) Lubrecht & Cramer.
Climate Related Landscapes in World Mountains: Criteria & Map, 1990. W. F. Thompson. (Annals of Geomorphology Ser.: Suppl. 78). (Illus.). 92p. 1990. pap. 55.00 (3-443-21078-3, Pub. by Gebrueder Borntraeger GW) Lubrecht & Cramer.
Climate Shocks, Natural & Anthropogenic. K. Y. Kondratyev. LC 87-21551. (Climate & the Biosphere Ser.). 296p. 1988. text ed. 82.95 (0-471-83019-4) Wiley.
***Climate since AD 1500.** Ed. by R. A. Bradley & P. D. Jones. (Illus.). 724p. 1995. pap. 39.95 (0-415-12030-6, C0551) Routledge.
Climate since AD 1500. R. S. Bradley & P. B. Jones. (Illus.). 704p. (C). 1992. text ed. 100.00 (0-415-07593-9, A8238) Routledge.
Climate Systems Modeling. Ed. by Kevin E. Trenberth. LC 92-22275. (Illus.). 600p. (C). 1993. 49.95 (0-521-43231-6) Cambridge U Pr.
Climate under Cover: Digital Dynamic Simulation in Plant Bio-Engineering. Tadashi Takakura. LC 92-41727. 150p. (C). 1993. lib. bdg. 84.00 (0-7923-2104-9); pap. text ed. 46.50 (0-7923-2105-7) Kluwer Ac.
Climate Variability, Climate Change & Fisheries. Ed. by Michael H. Glantz. (Illus.). 360p. (C). 1992. 74.95 (0-521-41440-7) Cambridge U Pr.
***Climate Variability, Climate Change & Social Vulnerability in the Semi-Arid Tropics.** Ed. by Jesse C. Ribot et al. (Internationsl Hydrology Ser.). (Illus.). 270p. (C). 1995. write for info. (0-521-48074-4) Cambridge U Pr.
Climates. Ruth Fainlight. 1983. pap. 4.95 (0-906427-34-7, Pub. by Bloodaxe Bks UK) Dufour.
Climates of Australia & New Zealand. Ed. by J. Gentilli. (World Survey of Climatology Ser.: Vol. 13). 405p. 1971. 182.00 (0-444-40827-4) Elsevier.
Climates of Central & South America. Ed. by W. Schwerdtfeger. (World Survey of Climatology Ser.: Vol. 12). 532p. 1976. 174.50 (0-444-41271-9) Elsevier.
Climates of Central & Southern Europe. Ed. by H. E. Landsberg & C. C. Wallen. (World Survey of Climatology Ser.: Vol. 6). 1977. 146.25 (0-444-41336-7) Elsevier.
Climates of Hunger: Mankind & the World's Changing Weather. Reid A. Bryson & Thomas J. Murray. LC 76-53649. (Illus.). 190p. 1979. pap. 14.95 (0-299-07374-2) U of Wis Pr.
Climates of Love. Andre Maurois. Ed. by Michael Levien. Tr. by Violet Schiff & Esme Cook. LC 87-60486. (Modern Romance Classics Ser.). 214p. 1986. reprint ed. 25.00 (0-7206-0671-3, Pub. by P Owen Ltd UK) Dufour.
Climates of North America. Ed. by R. A. Bryson & F. Hare. LC 74-477739. (World Survey of Climatology Ser.: Vol. 11). 420p. 1974. 164.00 (0-444-41062-7) Elsevier.
Climates of Northern & Eastern Asia. Ed. by H. Arakawa. (World Survey of Climatology Ser.: Vol. 8). 248p. 1970. 148.75 (0-444-40704-9) Elsevier.
Climates of Northern & Western Europe. Ed. by C. C. Wallen. (World Survey of Climatology Ser.: Vol. 5). 253p. 1971. 146.25 (0-444-40705-7) Elsevier.
Climates of Southern & Western Asia. Ed. by Koichiro Takahashi & H. Arakawa. (World Survey of Climatology Ser.: Vol. 9). 334p. 1981. 169.25 (0-444-41861-X) Elsevier.
Climates of States. 5th ed. Bair. 1999. 255.00 (0-8103-7109-X) Gale.
Climates of Texas Counties. John Griffiths & Janine Bryan. Ed. by Deanna Schexnayder. (Illus.). 569p. (Orig.). 1987. pap. 20.00 (0-87755-301-7) Bureau Busn UT.
***Climates of the Mind.** Carolyn Kleefeld. LC 78-73648. 240p. 1981. reprint ed. pap. 16.95 (0-9602214-2-5) Atoms Mirror.
Climates of the Ocean. H. Van Loon. (World Survey of Climatology Ser.: Vol. 15). 300p. 1984. 243.75 (0-444-41337-5, I-090-84) Elsevier.
Climates of the Polar Region. S. Orvig. Ed. by H. E. Lansberg. (World Survey of Climatology Ser.: Vol. 14). 370p. 1971. 174.50 (0-444-40828-2) Elsevier.
Climates of the Soviet Union. P. E. Lydolph. (World Survey of Climatology Ser.: Vol. 7). 444p. 1977. 174.50 (0-444-41516-5) Elsevier.
Climates of the States, 2 vols. 4th ed. Ed. by Frank E. Bair. 1575p. 1996. 255.00 (0-8103-0449-X) Gale.
Climates of the States, 2 vols., Set. Officials of the National Oceanic & Atmospheric Administration Staff. LC 73-93482. (Illus.). 1004p. 1974. 75.00 (0-912394-09-9) Water Info.
Climates of the States, 2 Vols., Vol. 1. 3rd ed. Frank E. Bair. 1588p. 1985. 245.00 (0-8103-1042-2) Gale.
Climates Throughout Geologic Time. L. A. Frakes. 310p. 1980. pap. 69.25 (0-444-41925-X) Elsevier.
Climatic Atlas of Michigan. Ed. by Val L. Eichenlaub. LC 89-40020. (Illus.). 160p. (C). 1989. text ed. 49.95 (0-268-00773-X) U of Notre Dame Pr.
Climatic Atlas of the Indian Ocean, 3 vols., Pt. III: Upper Ocean Structure. Stefan Hastenrath et al. LC 78-65016. (Illus.). 230p. 1989. pap. 40.00 (0-299-12154-2) U of Wis Pr.
Climatic Atlas of the Indian Ocean, 3 vols., Set. Stefan Hastenrath et al. LC 78-65016. (Illus.). 230p. 1989. pap. 100.00 (0-299-07814-0) U of Wis Pr.
Climatic Atlas of the Outer Continental Shelf Waters & Coastal Regions of Alaska, Vol. 1: Gulf of Alaska. rev. ed. William A. Brower, Jr. et al. (NAVAIR 50-1C-551. MMS 87-0011 Ser.). (Illus.). 553p. 1988. pap. 61.00 (0-16-000404-7, S/N 003-017-00527-5) USGPO.
Climatic Atlas of the Outer Continental Shelf Waters & Coastal Regions of Alaska, Vol. 2: Bering Sea. William A. Brower, Jr. (NAVAIR 50-1C-552. MMS 87-0012 Ser.). (Illus.). 549p. (Orig.). 1989. pap. 61.00 (0-16-000405-5, S/N 003-017-00528-3) USGPO.
Climatic Atlas of the Outer Continental Shelf Waters & Coastal Regions of Alaska, Vol. 3: Chukchi-Beaufort Sea. William A. Brower, Jr. (NAVAIR 50-1C-553. MMS 87-0013 Ser.). (Illus.). 525p. (Orig.). 1988. pap. 61.00 (0-16-000406-3, S/N 003-017-00529-1) USGPO.
Climatic Atlas of the Tropical Atlantic & Eastern Pacific Oceans, 2 vols. Stefan Hastenrath & Peter J. Lamb. 114p. 1977. pap. 50.00 (0-299-07234-7) U of Wis Pr.
Climatic Building Design: Energy-Efficient Building Principles & Practice. Donald A. Watson. 1993. pap. text ed. 29.95 (0-07-068488-X) McGraw.
Climatic Change & Food Production. Ed. by Koichiro Takahashi & Masatoshi M. Yoshino. 433p. 1978. 82.50 (0-86008-205-9, Pub. by U of Tokyo JA) Col U Pr.
Climatic Change & Impacts: A General Introduction. Ed. by R. Fantechi & G. Maracchi. 464p. 1991. pap. 50.00 (92-826-0564-7, CD-NA-11943-EN-C) UNIPUB.
Climatic Change & Plant Genetic Resources. Ed. by M. Jackson et al. (Illus.). 242p. 1992. text ed. 57.95 (1-85293-102-7, Pub. by Pinter Pubs Ltd UK) CRC Pr.
Climatic Change & Plant Genetic Resources. M. Jackson. 242p. (C). 1991. text ed. 265.00 (0-89771-540-3, Pub. by Intl Bk Distr II) St Mut.
***Climatic Change & Plant Genetic Resources.** Ed. by M. T. Jackson et al. 1994. text ed. 55.00 (0-471-94694-X) Wiley.
Climatic Change & the Mediterranean. Ed. by John D. Milliman. (Climatic Change & the Level of Seas Ser.). 550p. 1991. 120.00 (0-340-55329-4, A6222, Pub. by E Arnold UK) Routledge Chapman & Hall.
***Climatic Change & the Mediterranean: Environmental & Societal Impacts of Climatic Change & Sea-Level Rise in the Mediterranean Region.** Ed. by Jeftic et al. 1995. text ed. 129.00 (0-470-24975-7) Wiley.
Climatic Change & Variability in Southern Africa. P. D. Tyson. (Illus.). 232p. 1987. 29.95 (0-19-570430-4) OUP.
Climatic Change & World Affairs. rev. ed. Crispin Tickell. (Illus.). 92p. 1986. lib. bdg. 44.50 (0-8191-5105-X) U Pr of Amer.
***Climatic Change in the Intra-Americas Sea.** Ed. by Maul. 1995. text ed. 99.95 (0-470-24973-0) Wiley.
Climatic Change in the Intra-Americas Sea. Ed. by George A. Maul. LC 93-6852. 1993. write for info. (0-340-58981-7, Pub. by E Arnold UK) Routledge Chapman & Hall.
Climatic Changes. M. I. Budyko. Tr. by R. Zolina. (Illus.). 261p. 1977. 24.00 (0-87590-206-5) Am Geophysical.
Climatic Changes: Their Nature & Causes. Ellsworth Huntington & Stephen S. Visher. LC 77-10231. reprint ed. 84.50 (0-404-16211-8) AMS Pr.
Climatic Changes: Evidence, Causes, & Effects. Harlow Shapley. LC 53-9041. 336p. reprint ed. pap. 95.80 (0-317-08408-9, 2006045) Bks Demand.
Climatic Changes from Fourteen Thousand to Nine Thousand Years Ago: Proceedings of the American Quaternary Association, Biennial Meeting, 1st, 1970. American Quaternary Association Staff. 167p. 1970. 10. 00 (0-318-13126-9) Am Quaternary Assn.
Climatic Constraints & Human Activities. J. Ausebel & Asit K. Biswas. LC 80-41073. (ITASA Proceedings Ser.: Vol. 10). (Illus.). 215p. 1980. 95.00 (0-08-026721-1, Pub. by Pergamon Repr UK) Franklin.
Climatic Controls on Erosion in the Rolling Plains along the Caprock Escarpment of the Texas Panhandle. R. J. Finley & T. C. Gustavson. (Geological Circular Ser.: GC 80-11). (Illus.). 50p. 1980. 1.75 (0-686-36578-X) Bur Econ Geology.
Climatic Cycle & Tree Growth, 3 vols. in one, Vol 1 & 2. A. E. Douglass. 1971. Vols. 1 & 2: A Study of the Annual Rings of Trees in Relation to Climate & Solar Activity. 98.00 (3-7682-0720-X) Lubrecht & Cramer.
Climatic Cycle & Tree Growth, 3 vols. in one, Vol 3. A. E. Douglass. 1971. write for info. (0-318-54135-1) Lubrecht & Cramer.
Climatic Data Handbook for Europe: Climatic Data for the Design of Solar Energy Buildings. Ed. by Bernard Bourges. 300p. (C). 1992. lib. bdg. 94.00 (0-7923-1716-5) Kluwer Ac.
***Climatic Dwelling: An Introduction to Climate-Responsive Residential Architecture.** E. O'Cofaigh et al. (Illus.). 176p. (Orig.). 1994. pap. 50.00 (1-873936-39-7, Pub. by J & J Sci Pubs UK) Bks Intl VA.
***Climatic Dwelling: An Introduction to Climate-Responsive Residential Architecture.** E. O'Cofaigh et al. (Illus.). 40p. (Orig.). (C). 1994. 240.00 (1-873936-35-4, Pub. by J & J Sci Pubs UK) Bks Intl VA.
***Climatic Effects on Individual, Social & Economic Behavior: A Physioeconomic Review of Research Across Disciplines.** Philip M. Parker. LC 94-41521. (Bibliographies & Indexes in Geography Ser.: Vol. 2). 304p. 1995. text ed. 79.50 (0-313-29400-3, Greenwood Pr) Greenwood.
Climatic Environmental Testing Procedures. Jon C. Wilson. (Illus.). 284p. (C). 1991. student ed 75.00 (0-918247-11-X) Tustin Tech.
Climatic Factor As Illustrated in Arid America. Ellsworth Huntington. LC 77-10230. reprint ed. 59.50 (0-404-16210-X) AMS Pr.
Climatic Fluctuations & Water Management. Ed. by Mahmoud A. Abu-Zeid & Asit K. Biswas. 351p. 1992. 60.00 (0-7506-1320-3) Intl Water Resc.
Climatic Geomorphology. Julius Budel. Tr. by Lenore Fischer & Detlef Busche. LC 81-47909. (Illus.). 443p. 1982. 95.00 (0-691-08294-4); pap. 29.95x (0-691-08295-2) Princeton U Pr.
***Climatic Geomorphology.** Julius Budel. LC 81-47909. reprint ed. pap. 133.40 (0-7837-9307-3, 2060047) Bks Demand.
Climatic History & the Future. H. H. Lamb. LC 84-15955. (Illus.). 884p. 1985. pap. text ed. 39.50x (0-691-02387-5) Princeton U Pr.
Climatic Laws: Ninety Generalizations with Numerous Corollaries As to the Graphic Distribution of Temperature, Wind, Moisture, Etc. Stephen S. Visher. LC 77-10241. reprint ed. 24.95 (0-404-16219-3) AMS Pr.
Climatic Perspective of Louisiana Floods, 1982-1983. Ed. by Robert A. Muller & Gregory E. Faiers. (Illus.). 56p. (C). 1984. pap. text ed. 4.00 (0-938909-62-2) Geosci Pubns LSU.
Climatic Races & Descent Groups. Grover S. Krantz. 288p. (C). 1980. 14.95 (0-8158-0390-7) Chris Mass.
Climatic Risk in Crop Production: Models & Management for the Semiarid Tropics & Subtropics. Ed. by Russell C. Muchow & J. A. Bellamy. 550p. 1991. text ed. 94.00 (0-85198-665-X) CAB Intl.
Climatic Variation & Change: Implications for Agriculture in the Pacific Rim. Ed. by Shu Geng & Casey W. Cady. 245p. (Orig.). 1992. pap. text ed. 35.00 (0-9631410-0-7) U CA Dept Agr & RS.
Climatology. Karl Von Schilling. 12p. 1965. reprint ed. spiral bd. 3.30 (0-7873-0915-X) Mokelumne.
Climatology: An Atmospheric Science. John J. Hidore & John E. Oliver. (Illus.). 448p. (C). 1993. text ed. write for info. (0-02-354515-1) Macmillan.
Climatology: The Chemistry of Life & the Seasons of the Year. Karl Von Schilling. 1991. lib. bdg. 59.95 (0-8490-5002-2) Gordon Pr.
Climatology - Meteorology. Jack Rudman. (DANTES Ser.: No. 9). 1994. pap. 23.95 (0-8373-6609-7) Nat Learn.
***Climatology - Meteorology.** Jack Rudman. (DANTES Ser.: No. 9). 1994. 39.95 (0-8373-6509-0) Nat Learn.
Climatology of West Africa. D. Hayward & J. Oguntoyinbo. LC 87-1219. 288p. (C). 1987. text ed. 65.00 (0-389-20721-7, N8279) B&N Imports.
***Climatron.** Robert Stewart. Ed. by Gloria V. Hickok. 8p. (Orig.). 1994. pap. 3.00 (1-884235-03-4) Helicon Nine Eds.
Climats. Andre Maurois. 9.95 (0-686-55489-2) Fr & Eur.
Climats. Andre Maurois. (Coll. Diamant). (FRE.). 1955. 39. 95 (0-7859-0049-7, FC1394) Fr & Eur.
Climax of Capitalism: The U. S. Economy in the Twentieth Century. Tom Kemp. 251p. (C). 1990. pap. text ed. 23. 95 (0-582-49423-0, 78597) Longman.
Climax of French Imperial Expansion, 1914-1924. Christopher M. Andrew & A. S. Kanya-Forstner. LC 80-53435. 302p. 1981. 39.50 (0-8047-1101-1) Stanford U Pr.
***Climax of Passion.** Emma Darcy. 1995. mass mkt. 3.25 (0-373-11771-X, 1-11771-2) Harlequin Bks.
Climax of Prophecy: Studies on the Book of Revelation. Richard Bauckham. 512p. 1993. text ed. 59.95 (0-567-09620-3, Pub. by T & T Clark UK) Bks Intl VA.
Climax of the Covenant: Christ & the Law in Pauline Theology. N. T. Wright. LC 91-28454. 336p. (C). 1992. text ed. 26.00 (0-8006-2632-X, 1-2632, Fortress Pr) Augsburg Fortress.
Climax of the Risen Life. Jessie Penn-Lewis. 1992. pap. 4.95 (0-87508-941-0) Chr Lit.
***Climaxx!! Orgasmic Sex.** Celina Poy-Wing. 220p. 1995. pap. 9.95 (0-9638783-1-X) All Womens Hlth.
Climb Aboard. Rose Greydanus. LC 87-19150. (Giant First Start Reader Ser.). (Illus.). 32p. (J). (gr. k-2). 1988. lib. bdg. 11.59 (0-8167-1099-6); pap. text ed. 2.95 (0-8167-1100-3) Troll Assocs.
***Climb Away: Chasing the Dream.** Deborah Parks. LC 95-8684. 1995. write for info. (0-382-39093-8); pap. write for info. (0-382-39094-6) Silver Burdett Pr.
Climb Mount Moriah. Pat Brooks. 128p. 1993. pap. 2.99 (0-88368-024-6) Whitaker Hse.
Climb Nova Scotia: A Rock-Climbing Guide. Sean Willett. (Illus.). 112p. 1994. 9.95 (1-55109-087-2, Pub. by Nimbus Publishing Ltd CN) Chelsea Green Pub.
Climb or Die. Edward Myers. LC 93-44861. 192p. (J). (gr. 5-9). 1995. 14.95 (0-7868-0026-7) Hyprn Child.
Climb Parnassus & Behold! Albert Steffen. Tr. by Daisy Aldan. (Illus.). 48p. Date not set. pap. 7.95 (0-932776-20-5) Adonis Pr.
Climb That Barbed Wire Fence. Bessie Frazier. (Illus.). 40p. (Orig.). 1992. pap. text ed. 6.95 (1-56315-069-7) Sterling Hse.
Climb the Highest Mountain. Gene Edwards. (Orig.). 1984. pap. 8.95 (0-940232-11-1) Seedsowers.
Climb the Highest Mountain. Mark L. Prophet & Elizabeth C. Prophet. LC 72-175101. (Illus.). 700p. 1978. pap. 16. 95 (0-916766-26-8) Summit Univ.
Climb the Highest Mountain. 2nd ed. Mark L. Prophet & Elizabeth C. Prophet. LC 72-175101. (Illus.). 700p. 1973. 21.95 (0-916766-02-0) Summit Univ.
Climb the Joyous Mountain: Living the Meditative Way. rev. ed. Justin F. Stone. (Illus.). 94p. 1992. reprint ed. pap. 9.95 (0-9620812-5-6) Good Karma.
Climb the Waterfall & the Days of Rye. Eugenia Moore. Ed. by Elizabeth Derman. LC 86-28061. (Illus.). 216p. 1987. 14.95 (0-9617284-1-8); pap. 9.95 (0-9617284-0-X) Sand & Silk.
Climb to the High Country: New Poems. Bill Hotchkiss. 1978. pap. 2.95 (0-393-04500-5) Norton.
***Climb up to the Sunshine.** Judy Miller. 244p. 1993. 8.95 (0-942341-06-6) Dawn Pubns TX.
Climb Your Own Ladder: 101 Home Businesses that Can Make You Wealthy. Allen Lieberoff. 224p. 1982. pap. 7.95 (0-686-46704-3, Fireside) S&S Trade.
Climb Your Own Mountain. John F. Zaccaro. 341p. 1986. 16.95 (0-88282-014-1) New Horizon NJ.
Climb Your Own Mountain: The Ultimate Guide to Personal & Career Success. John F. Zaccaro. LC 91-33224. 1992. pap. 13.95 (0-88282-106-7) New Horizon NJ.
Climber & Pruner. Jack Rudman. (Career Examination Ser.: C-148). 1994. pap. 39.95 (0-8373-0148-3) Nat Learn.
Climbers. Jillian Powell. (J). (ps-2). 1992. 15.95 (0-87614-700-7, Carolrhoda) Lerner Group.
***Climbers: A History of Mountaineering.** Chris Bonington. 1995. 29.95 (0-563-20918-6) Parkwest Pubns.
Climbers: Scaling the Heights with the Sport's Elite. Steven Boga. (Adventure Athletes Ser.). (Illus.). 240p. 1994. pap. 14.95 (0-8117-2415-8) Stackpole.
Climbers & Hikers Guide to the World's Mountains. 3rd ed. Michael R. Kelsey. (Illus.). 928p. 1990. pap. 34.95 (0-944510-02-7) Kelsey Pub.
Climbers & Wall Plants for Year Round Colour. Jane Taylor. (Illus.). 128p. 1994. pap. 14.95 (0-7063-7236-0, Pub. by Ward Lock UK) Sterling.
***Climber's First Aid: What to Do While Waiting for Help.** Mark S. Fleming. (Illus.). (Orig.). 1995. spiral bd. 29.95 (0-614-07192-5) Rhache Pubs.

C

An Asterisk (*) at the beginning of an entry indicates that the title is appearing in BIP for the first time. 1313

***Climber's Guide to American Fork Canyon.** Stuart Ruckman & Bret Ruckman. (Illus.). 220p. (Orig.). 1995. pap. 18.00 (0-934641-88-9) Chockstone Pr.

Climber's Guide to Devil's Lake. William Widule & Sven O. Swartling. LC 78-65017. (Illus.). 208p. 1979. pap. 12.95 (0-299-07804-3) U of Wis Pr.

***Climber's Guide to Devil's Lake.** 2nd ed. Sven O. Swartling. LC 94-24116. (Illus.). 256p. 1995. pap. text ed. 16.95 (0-299-14594-8) U of Wis Pr.

***Climber's Guide to Gibraltar Rock.** 2nd ed. Eric Landmann & Don Hynek. (Illus.). 64p. 1993. pap. text ed. write for info. (0-9619571-5-8) Granite WI.

Climber's Guide to Glacier National Park. rev. ed. J. Gordon Edwards. LC 84-14787. (Illus.). 352p. 1984. pap. 12.95 (0-87842-177-7) Mountain Pr.

***Climber's Guide to Pinnacles National Monument.** 2nd ed. David Rubine. (Illus.). 220p. (Orig.). 1995. pap. 20.00 (0-934641-89-7) Chockstone Pr.

***Climber's Guide to Rocky Mountain National Park: The Crags.** Richard Rossiter. (Illus.). 300p. 1995. pap. 20.00 (0-934641-34-X) Chockstone Pr.

***Climber's Guide to Rocky Mountain National Park: The High Peaks.** Richard Rossiter. (Illus.). 144p. (Orig.). 1995. pap. 15.00 (0-614-07053-8) Chockstone Pr.

***Climber's Guide to Sedona & Oak Creek Canyon: Better Way to Die.** Tim Toula. (Illus.). 80p. (Orig.). 1995. pap. 12.95 (0-934641-16-1) Chockstone Pr.

***Climber's Guide to Smith Rock.** Alan Watts. (Illus.). 336p. 1994. pap. 22.00 (0-934641-18-8) Chockstone Pr.

Climber's Guide to Southern California. 2nd ed. Paul Hellweg & Nathan Warstler. LC 87-73435. (Illus.). 224p. 1993. pap. 12.95 (0-942568-26-5) Canyon Pub Co.

***Climbers Guide to Tahoe Rock.** Mike Carville. (Illus.). 200p. 1994. pap. 22.00 (0-934641-33-1) Chockstone Pr.

***Climber's Guide to Tahquitz & Suicide.** 2nd ed. Randy Vogel & Bob Gaines. (Illus.). 200p. 1994. pap. 20.00 (0-934641-31-5) Chockstone Pr.

Climbers' Guide to the Great Falls of the Potomac. James Eakin. LC 85-61503. 104p. 1985. pap. 6.00 (0-915746-30-1) Potomac Appalach.

Climber's Guide to the High Sierra. rev. ed. Steve Roper. LC 75-45108. (Totebook Ser.). (Illus.). 384p. 1976. pap. 12.00 (0-87156-147-6) Sierra.

Climber's Guide to the Olympic Mountains. 3rd ed. Olympic Mountain Rescue Staff. LC 88-17636. (Illus.). 260p. (Orig.). 1988. pap. 12.95 (0-89886-154-3) Mountaineers.

Climbers Guide to Yosemite Valley. Steve Roper. LC 71-157530. (Totebook Ser.). (Illus.). 320p. 1971. pap. 10.95 (0-87156-048-8) Sierra.

Climber's Lob. Kenneth Hukari & Scott Griebel. 1993. write for info. (0-318-72466-9) Wy East Log.

Climbie. Bernard B. Dadie. Tr. by Karen Chapman. LC 77-161231. 157p. 1971. 14.50 (0-8419-0080-9, Africana) Holmes & Meier.

***Climbing.** Steve Ashton. (All Action Ser.). (Illus.). 48p. (J). (gr. 4 up). 1993. 17.50 (0-8225-2480-5) Lerner Group.

***Climbing: The Complete Reference.** Greg Child. LC 94-33254. (Illus.). 304p. 1994. 39.95x (0-8160-2692-0) Facts on File.

Climbing Aconcagua. Frances Mayes. (Sansfolio Ser.: No. 1). 8p. 1977. pap. 1.75 (0-913282-11-1) Seven Woods Pr.

Climbing Adventures: A Climber's Passion. Jim Bridwell & Keith Peall. Ed. by Sally Moser. LC 92-17929. (Illus.). 214p. (Orig.). 1992. pap. 16.50 (0-934802-22-X) ICS Bks.

Climbing Anchors. John Long. (How to Rock Climb Ser.). (Illus.). 120p. (Orig.). 1993. pap. 11.95 (0-934641-37-4) Chockstone Pr.

***Climbing & Hiking in Ecuador.** 3rd ed. Rob Rachowiecki & Betsy Wagenhauser. (Illus.). 240p. 1995. pap. text ed. 15.95 (1-56440-612-1, Pub. by Bradt Pubns UK) Globe Pequot.

***Climbing & Hiking in the Wind River Mountains.** Joe Kelsey. (Illus.). 400p. 1994. pap. 25.00 (0-934641-70-6) Chockstone Pr.

***Climbing Art.** Ed. by Scott Titterington. (Illus.). 160p. (Orig.). 1995. pap. 9.95 (1-881663-00-0) Advent Mean Pr.

Climbing Back. Mark Wellman & John Flinn. (Illus.). 256p. 1992. 19.95 (0-941539-88-1) WRS Group.

Climbing Big Walls. Michael Strassman. LC 90-34049. (Illus.). 128p. (Orig.). 1990. pap. 9.99 (0-934802-59-9) ICS Bks.

Climbing down the Ladder: A Teacher & Pastor Reflects on His Retirement. Linden M. Wenger. LC 93-1338. 183p. (Orig.). 1993. pap. 8.95 (1-56148-079-7) Good Bks PA.

Climbing Fit. Martyn Hurn & Pat Ingle. (Illus.). 144p. 1989. pap. 14.95 (0-938567-14-4) Cloudcap.

Climbing Garden. Judy Horton. (Illus.). 96p. 1993. 14.95 (0-86417-473-X, Pub. by Kangaroo Pr AT) Seven Hills Bk.

***Climbing Green Ladders.** Michael Walsh. (C). 1994. pap. text ed. 5.00 (1-878173-39-1) Birnham Wood.

Climbing Guide to Colorado's Fourteeners. 3rd ed. Walter R. Borneman & Lyndon J. Lampert. LC 93-47980. 1994. pap. 16.95 (0-87108-850-9) Pruett.

Climbing Guide to Scotland. Tom Prentice. (Illus.). 205p. 1992. pap. 34.95 (1-85223-527-6, Pub. by Crowood Pr UK) Trafalgar.

Climbing Ice. Yvon Chouinard. LC 77-19137. (Illus.). 192p. 1978. pap. 20.00 (0-87156-208-1) Sierra.

***Climbing in Santa Barbara, Ventura, & San Luis Obispo.** Steve Tucker & Kevin Steele. 256p. 1994. pap. 12.00 (0-9642499-0-1) S Tucker & K Steele.

***Climbing in the Adirondacks: A Guide to Rock & Ice Routes.** 3rd ed. Don Mellor. (Illus.). 320p. Date not set. pap. 24.95 (0-935272-79-8) ADK Mtn Club.

Climbing in the Adirondacks: A Guide to Rock & Ice Routes in Adirondack Park. Don Mellor. (Illus.). 240p. (Orig.). 1986. pap. 15.95 (0-685-11832-0) Lake Placid Climb.

Climbing in the Adirondacks: A Guide to Rock & Ice Routes in Adirondack Park. suppl. ed. Don Mellor. (Illus.). 240p. (Orig.). 1986. Supplement. 4.50 (0-9615992-1-9) Lake Placid Climb.

Climbing Jacob's Ladder: Heroes of the Bible in African-American Spirituals. John Langstaff & Ashley Bryan. LC 90-27297. (Illus.). 24p. (J). 1991. text ed. 14.95 (0-689-50494-2, McElderry) S&S Childrens.

Climbing Jacob's Ladder: The Enduring Legacy of African-American Families. Andrew Billingsley. 1994. 14.00 (0-671-67709-8, Touchstone Bks) S&S Trade.

Climbing Jacob's Ladder: The Future of the African-American Family. Andrew Billingsley. 1993. 27.50 (0-671-67708-X) S&S Trade.

Climbing Jacob's Ladder: The Rise of Black Churches in Eastern American Cities, 1740-1877. Edward D. Smith. (Illus.). 144p. 1988. pap. 19.95 (0-87474-829-1) Smithsonian.

Climbing Kansas Mountains. George Shannon. LC 89-38197. (Illus.). 32p. (J). (ps-2). 1993. text ed. 15.95 (0-02-782181-1, Bradbury S&S) S&S Childrens.

Climbing Mount Whitney. rev. ed. Walt Wheelock & T. Condon. (Illus.). 36p. 1986. 2.50 (0-910856-02-8) La Siesta.

Climbing Olympus. Kevin J. Anderson. 304p. (Orig.). 1994. mass mkt. 5.50 (0-446-60158-6, Aspect) Warner Bks.

Climbing over Thorns. Richard E. Stephens. Tr. by Bill Harris Studios. (Orig.). 1983. pap. 4.00 (0-9611220-1-3) Crnrstn Cmns.

Climbing Plants: A Kew Gardening Guide. Jane Taylor. (Illus.). 124p. 1992. 19.95 (0-88192-221-8) Timber.

Climbing Plants & Wall Shrubs. Stephen Taffler. (Crowood Gardening Guides Ser.). (Illus.). 128p. 1991. pap. 16.95 (1-85223-165-3, Pub. by Crowood Pr UK) Trafalgar.

Climbing Prayer Mountain. Robert Tilton. 95p. (Orig.). 1988. pap. text ed. 6.95 (0-914307-73-8) R Tilton Ministries.

Climbing Rock & Ice: Learning the Vertical Dance. Jerry Cinnamon. 1993. pap. text ed. 19.95 (0-87742-405-5) Intl Marine.

Climbing Rock & Ice: Learning the Vertical Dance. Jerry Cinnamon. 1993. pap. text ed. 19.95 (0-07-011078-6) McGraw.

Climbing Roses. Stephen Scanniello & Tania Baynard. LC 92-32101. 1994. 30.00 (0-671-85046-6, P-H Gardening) P-H Gen Ref & Trav.

Climbing Roses. Christopher Warner. LC 87-32547. (Classic Garden Plants Ser.). (Illus.). 144p. 1988. 19.95 (0-87106-731-5) Globe Pequot.

Climbing School. John Barry. (Illus.). 192p. 1989. 19.95 (0-8120-5969-7) Barron.

Climbing Tales of Terror. Tami Knight. 128p. 1990. pap. 6.95 (0-89732-102-2) Menasha Ridge.

Climbing the Beanstalk: A Woman's Quest for Empowerment. Virginia H. Davis. (Illus.). 170p. (Orig.). 1993. pap. 18.95 (1-882275-02-0) Rnd Table Pr.

Climbing the Blue Mountain: A Guide for the Spiritual Journey. 2nd ed. Eknath Easwaran. LC 92-10306. Orig. Title: The Supreme Ambition. 176p. 1992. text ed. 22.00 (0-915132-71-0); pap. 12.95 (0-915132-70-2) Nilgiri Pr.

Climbing the Church Walls. Rob Portlock. LC 91-17872. (Illus.). 104p. (Orig.). 1991. pap. 6.99 (0-8308-1830-8, 1830) InterVarsity.

Climbing the Family Tree with Nancy. Nancy E. Carlberg. LC 87-400889. 142p. (Orig.). 1986. pap. 15.00 (0-944878-00-8) Carlberg Pr.

Climbing the Heights. Al Bryant. LC 91-24339. 384p. 1991. reprint ed. pap. 11.99 (0-8254-2286-8) Kregel.

Climbing the Ladder. Tom Edmonds. Ed. by John Honea. (Orig.). 1994. pap. write for info. (0-9636072-2-7) J Honea Pubs.

Climbing the Ladder: An Update on the Status of Doctoral Women Scientists & Engineers. Ed. by Office of Scientific & Engineering Personnel, National Research Council. 112p. (C). 1983. pap. text ed. 14.95 (0-309-03341-1) Natl Acad Pr.

Climbing the Ladder of Success in Highheels: Backgrounds of Professional Women. Jill A. Steinberg. LC 83-15921. (Research in Clinical Psychology Ser.: No. 9). 194p. reprint ed. pap. 55.30 (0-8357-1491-8, 2070418) Bks Demand.

***Climbing the Mississippi River Bridge by Bridge.** Mary C. Aubry-Costello. (Illus.). 110p. (Orig.). 1995. 39.95 (0-9644518-1-6) Aubry Costello.

***Climbing the Mississippi River Bridge by Bridge, Vol. I.** Mary C. Aubry-Costello. (Illus.). 110p. (Orig.). 1995. pap. text ed. 24.95 (0-9644518-0-8) Aubry Costello.

Climbing the Money Tree: Your Ladder to Financial Success. June Taylor. 128p. (Orig.). 1993. pap. 12.95 (0-9616108-7-5) Beaumont Bks.

Climbing the Mountain: A Journey in Prayer. Mary Meegan. (Illus.). 107p. (Orig.). 1984. pap. 9.95 (0-89505-132-X, 21080) Tabor Pub.

Climbing the Mountain, Teacher's Guide. Mary Meegan. (Illus.). 112p. 1984. pap. 9.95 (0-317-60039-7) Tabor Pub.

Climbing the Rainbow. Joy N. Hulme. LC 92-1109. 186p. (Orig.). (J). (gr. 3-7). 1992. pap. 4.95 (0-87579-584-6) Deseret Bk.

Climbing the Rainbow. Lloyd Ogilvie. 224p. 1993. 15.99 (0-8499-0762-4) Word Inc.

Climbing the Sacred Ladder. Horace L. Patterson. LC 91-74114. (Illus.). 70p. 1992. pap. 6.95 (1-55523-468-2) Winston-Derek.

Climbing the Stairs. Mark Vinz. 64p. 1983. pap. text ed. 4.95 (0-933180-50-0) Spoon Riv Poetry.

Climbing the Third Stair. Leah Paransky. 64p. (Orig.). 1981. pap. 3.95 (0-931642-09-4) Lintel.

***Climbing to the Sun: A Maya Boy Discovers His Heritage.** Guy Garcia. LC 94-44813. (Illus.). 48p. (J). (gr. 2-6). 1995. 15.95 (0-8027-8379-1); lib. bdg. 16.85 (0-8027-8380-5) Walker & Co.

Climbing Toward the Light: A Journey of Growth, Understanding & Love. Ardath Rodale. LC 89-32896. (Illus.). 240p. 1989. 17.95 (0-87857-834-X, 05-406-0) Rodale Pr Inc.

Climbing Tree. large type ed. Carol Mcafee. 1991. 21.95 (0-7089-2502-2) Ulverscroft.

Climbing Turns: A Pilot's Story in War & Peace. Patrick Foss. (Illus.). 260p. (Orig.). 1990. pap. 8.95 (0-948747-06-4, Pub. by Linden Hall UK) Grosvenor USA.

Climbing up & down the Ladder. Grace I. Krumwiede. 1979. 4.95 (0-686-26073-2) G I Krumwiede.

***Climbing Up the Mountain: The Musical Life & Times of Dr. Mattie Moss Clark.** Eugene B. McCoy. LC 94-35097. 1994. write for info. (0-917143-32-9) Sparrow TN.

Climbing Vines: Simple Secrets for Glorious Gardens, Indoors & Out. Mimi Luebbermann. LC 94-13127. 1995. 12.95 (0-8118-0723-1) Chronicle Bks.

Climbing Your Family Tree. Melba Tomeo. 52p. 1991. student ed 6.00 (1-55856-058-0) Closson Pr.

***Climbing 1996 Wall Calendar.** Ed. by Jeff Achey. 1995. 14.95 (1-887216-02-2) Elk Mtn Pr.

Clin d'Oeil de l'Ange. Francoise Mallet-Joris. (FRE.). 1985. pap. 12.95 (0-7859-2909-6) Fr & Eur.

Clincal of Erythropoieses. Feig. 1993. 149.95 (0-8493-6678-X, R) CRC Pr.

Clincal Psychopharmacology for the Busy Practitioner. 2nd rev. ed. Hugo Rosen. Ed. by Susan E. Wills. LC 93-76875. (Illus.). 362p. 1993. lib. bdg. 88.00 (1-883122-01-5) Pearce Pub.

***Clincial Measurement in Drug Evaluation.** Ed. by Walter S. Nimmo & Geoffrey T. Tucker. LC 94-40650. 1994. text ed. 79.95 (0-471-94391-6) Wiley.

***Clincopathologic Correlations in Dermatopathology.** Clay J. Cockerell. 1995. write for info. (0-89640-270-3) Igaku-Shoin.

Clingan Clan: Family History 1600-1981 (Clingan Family & Descendants) J. Floyd Bullock. 1981. pap. 17.00 (0-916660-21-4) Hse of York.

Clingan Clan Family Tree Chart 1600-1982. Courtney York. 1982. pap. 10.00 (0-916660-22-2) Hse of York.

Clingan's Chronicles. Clingan Jackson. Ed. by Andrea Wood. (Illus.). 1991. 16.95 (0-9631243-0-7) Youngstown Pub.

Clingers. Elaine Grant. 50p. 1994. spiral bd. 12.95 (0-9632722-1-7) Arteg Creations.

Clingin' Vines & Climbin' Roses: Little Agnes. Alleen Scanlon. 45p. 1987. pap. 6.95 (0-933865-12-0) Doris Pubns.

Clinging: The Experience of Prayer. Emilie Griffin. LC 83-48989. 96p. 1984. 11.45i (0-685-08081-1) Harper SF.

Clinging: The Experience of Prayer. Emilie Griffin. (Illus.). 112p. 1994. pap. 8.95 (1-56977-506-0) McCracken Pr.

Clinging to a Myth: The Story Behind Evolution. T. H. Janabi. 166p. 1991. pap. 10.00 (0-89259-109-9) Am Trust Pubns.

***Clinging to a Ray.** Riyad Y. Hamzah. LC 93-94208. 64p. (Orig.). 1994. pap. 6.00 (1-56002-396-1, Univ Edtns) Aegina Pr.

Clinging to Grandeur: British Attitudes & Foreign Policy in the Aftermath of the Second World War. Michael Blackwell. LC 92-30012. (Contributions to the Study of World History Ser.: No. 36). 208p. 1993. text ed. 52.95 (0-313-28616-7, BGZ/, Greenwood Pr) Greenwood.

Clinging to the Wreckage. John Mortimer. 1987. pap. 8.00 (0-14-006383-8, Penguin Bks) Viking Penguin.

Clinging to the Wreckage: A Part of Life. John Mortimer. LC 83-13078. 224p. 1984. mass mkt. 11.95 (0-14-006860-0, Penguin Bks) Viking Penguin.

Clinic. Christine Johnson. 266p. (Orig.). 1985. 13.95 (0-916485-03-X); pap. 6.95 (0-916485-04-8) Alexand Press.

Clinic Administrator. Jack Rudman. (Career Examination Ser.: C-915). 1994. pap. 39.95 (0-8373-0915-8) Nat Learn.

Clinic for Murder. Marsha Landreth. LC 93-1440. (Dr. Sam Turner Mystery Ser.). 1993. 19.95 (0-8027-3241-0) Walker & Co.

Clinic Habit. Camille Lambert, Jr. & Howard E. Freeman. 1967. pap. 17.95x (0-8084-0083-5) NCUP.

Clinic Supervisor (Drug Abuse) Jack Rudman. (Career Examination Ser.: C-3007). 1994. pap. 39.95 (0-8373-3007-6) Nat Learn.

Clinical Acupuncture: A Practical Japanese Approach. Katsuuke Serizawa & Mari Kusumi. (Illus.). 272p. 1989. 39.95 (0-87040-782-1) Japan Pubns USA.

Clinical Administration in Audiology & Speech-Language Pathology. Ed. by Stephen R. Rizzo, Jr. & Michael D. Trudeau. LC 93-25798. (Illus.). 320p. (Orig.). (C). 1993. pap. text ed. 59.95 (1-56593-088-6) Singular Publishing.

Clinical Advances in Monoamine Oxidase Inhibitor Therapies. Ed. by Sidney H. Kennedy. LC 93-46268. (Progress in Psychiatry Ser.: Vol. 43). 322p. 1994. text ed. 36.50 (0-88048-474-8) Am Psychiatric.

Clinical Alteration of the Growing Face: Proceedings of a Sponsored Symposium Honoring Professor Robert E. Moyers, Held February 26 & 27, 1982, in Ann Arbor, MI. Ed. by James A. McNamara, Jr. et al. LC 83-147016. (Craniofacial Growth Monograph Ser.: No. 14). (Illus.). 339p. reprint ed. pap. 96.70 (0-8357-7561-5, 2052325) Bks Demand.

Clinical Ambulatory Monitoring. W. A. Littler. (Illus.). 174p. 1981. 60.00 (0-8151-5482-8, ACT-1, Yr Bk Med Pubs) Mosby Yr Bk.

Clinical Anatomy. Harold H. Lindner. (Illus.). 690p. 1988. pap. text ed. 29.00 (0-8385-1259-3, A1259-9) Appleton & Lange.

Clinical Anatomy. 3rd ed. Richard S. Snell. 1986. 45.00 (0-316-80217-4) Little.

Clinical Anatomy. 8th ed. H. Ellis. (Illus.). 512p. 1992. pap. 49.95 (0-632-02409-7) Blackwell Sci.

Clinical Anatomy & Pathophysiology for the Health Professional. Joseph V. Stewart. (Illus.). 260p. (Orig.). (C). 1994. pap. text ed. 17.95 (0-940780-06-2) MedMaster.

Clinical Anatomy for Anesthesiologists. Richard S. Snell & Jordan Katz. (Illus.). 328p. 1988. boxed 115.00 (0-8385-1258-5, A1258-1) Appleton & Lange.

Clinical Anatomy for Emergency Medicine. Richard S. Snell & Mark S. Smith. LC 92-49973. 672p. 1993. 125.00 (0-8016-6549-3) Mosby Yr Bk.

***Clinical Anatomy for Laparoscopic & Thoracoscopic Surgery.** Ed. by Raghu Savalgi & Harold Ellis. 1995. 170.00 (1-85775-070-5) Scovill Paterson.

***Clinical Anatomy for Medical Students.** 5th ed. Richard S. Snell. LC 94-40606. 1995. 52.95 (0-316-80135-6) Little.

Clinical Anatomy for Orthopaedic Surgery. Snell & Wiesel. 704p. Date not set. 115.00 (0-8016-4710-X) Mosby Yr Bk.

Clinical Anatomy Made Ridiculously Simple. Stephen Goldberg. (Illus.). 175p. 1991. pap. text ed. 17.95 (0-940780-02-X) MedMaster.

Clinical Anatomy of the Cervical Spine. Johannes Lang. (Illus.). 188p. 1993. text ed. 129.00 (0-86577-486-2) Thieme Med Pubs.

Clinical Anatomy of the Eye. Ed. by Richard Snell & Michael Lemp. 1989. text ed. 99.95 (0-86542-053-X); pap. text ed. 65.00 (0-86542-086-6) Blackwell Sci.

Clinical Anatomy of the Lumbar Spine. 2nd ed. Nikolai Bogduk & Lance T. Twomey. (Illus.). 200p. 1991. pap. text ed. 41.95 (0-443-04339-6) Churchill.

***Clinical Anatomy of the Masticatory Apparatus & the Peripharyngeal Spaces.** Johannes Lang. (Illus.). 220p. 1994. 149.00 (0-86577-551-6) Thieme Med Pubs.

***Clinical Anatomy of the Masticatory Apparatus & the Peripharyngeal Spaces.** Johannes Lang. Tr. by Terry C. Telger. 1994. write for info. (3-13-799101-3) Thieme Med Pubs.

Clinical Anatomy of the Nose & Paranasal Sinuses. J. Lang. (Illus.). 144p. 1989. text ed. 119.00 (0-86577-330-0) Thieme Med Pubs.

Clinical Anatomy of the Posterior Cranial Fossa & Its Forimina. Johannes Lang. (Illus.). 166p. 1991. text ed. 109.00 (0-86577-379-3) Thieme Med Pubs.

Clinical & Abnormal Psychology, Vol. 9: Proceedings of the 24th International Congress of Psychology of the International Union of Psychological Science, Sydney, Australia, Aug. 28-Sept. 2, 1988. Ed. by P. Lovibond & P. Wilson. 504p. 1990. 107.75 (0-444-88527-7, North Holland) Elsevier.

Clinical & Basic Neurology for Health Professionals. Kenneth R. Magee & Joel R. Saper. LC 80-27146. 311p. reprint ed. pap. 88.70 (0-318-34979-5, 2030792) Bks Demand.

Clinical & Basic Science Aspects of Immunohematology. Sandra J. Nance. LC 91-31709. (Illus.). (C). 1991. text ed. 45.00 (1-56395-006-5) Am Assn Blood.

Clinical & Biochemical Luminescence. Ed. by Larry J. Kricka & Timothy J. Carter. LC 82-8976. (Clinical & Biochemical Analysis Ser.: No. 12). (Illus.). 303p. reprint ed. pap. 86.40 (0-7837-0635-9, 2040979) Bks Demand.

Clinical & Biological Aspects of Dentifrices. G. Embery & G. Rolla. (Illus.). 416p. 1992. 73.00 (0-19-262211-0) OUP.

Clinical & Diagnostic Interviewing. Ed. by Robert J. Craig. LC 89-29. 355p. 1989. 40.00 (0-87668-848-2) Aronson.

***Clinical & Diagnostic Interviewing.** Ed. by Robert J. Craig. LC 89-29. 380p. 1995. reprint ed. pap. 35.00 (1-56821-526-6) Aronson.

Clinical & Diagnostic Procedures in Obstetrics & Gynecology, Pt. A: Obstetrics. Ed. by E. Malcolm Symonds & Frederick P. Zuspan. LC 83-5341. (Reproductive Medicine Ser.: No. 4). (Illus.). 487p. 1994. pap. 138.80 (0-7837-4300-9, 2043992) Bks Demand.

Clinical & Diagnostic Procedures in Obstetrics & Gynecology, Pt. B: Gynecology. Ed. by E. Malcolm Symonds & Frederick P. Zuspan. LC 83-5341. (Reproductive Medicine Ser.: No. 4). (Illus.). 463p. 1994. pap. 132.00 (0-7837-4301-7, 2043992) Bks Demand.

Clinical & Educational Applications of Temperament Research. Ed. by W. B. Carey & S. C. McDevitt. 280p. 1989. 39.00 (90-265-0971-5, Pub. by Swets Pub Serv NE) Taylor & Francis.

Clinical & Educational Manual for Use with the Uzgiris & Hunt Scales of Infant Psychological Development. Carl J. Dunst. LC 80-131. (Illus.). 124p. 1980. pap. 24.00 (0-89079-100-7, 1187) PRO-ED.

***Clinical & Experimental Dermatology: Festschrift to Professor Kint.** Ed. by J. De Bersaques. (Journal Ser.: Vol. 189, Supplement 2, 1994). (Illus.). iv, 72p. 1994. pap. 30.50 (3-8055-6099-0) S Karger.

Clinical & Experimental Hypnosis: In Medicine, Dentistry & Psychology. 2nd ed. William S. Kroger. LC 77-10320. 1977. text ed. 57.50 (0-397-50377-6, 05-62678, Lippincott Medical) Lippincott.

Clinical & Experimental Pathology of Lung Cancer. Ed. by J. G. McVie et al. (Developments in Oncology Ser.). 1985. lib. bdg. 105.50 (0-89838-764-7) Kluwer Ac.

Clinical & Experimental Restricted Environmental Stimulation: New Developments & Perspectives. Ed. by Arreed F. Barabasz & Marianne Barabasz. 1993. write for info. (0-318-69808-0) Spr-Verlag.

An Asterisk (*) at the beginning of an entry indicates that the title is appearing in BIP for the first time.

An Asterisk (*) at the beginning of an entry indicates that the title is appearing in BIP for the first time.

1315

Clinical Audiometry & Masking. Frederick N. Martin. LC 74-183115. (Studies in Communicative Disorders). (C). 1972. pap. 3.25 (*0-672-61282-8*, Bobbs) Macmillan.

***Clinical Audit in Palliative Care.** Ed. by Irene Higginson. 1995. 24.95 (*1-870905-64-4*) Scovill Paterson.

***Clinical Auscultation of the Cardiovascular System.** W. Proctor Harvey & David C. Canfield. 1989. audio 95.00 (*1-886128-01-4*) Laennec Pub.

Clinical Autonomic Disorders: Evaluation & Management. Phillip A. Low. LC 92-49907. 600p. 1992. 190.00 (*0-316-53390-4*) Little.

Clinical Autonomic Failure: Practical Concepts. O. Appenzeller. 472p. 1986. pap. 45.50 (*0-444-80710-1*) Elsevier.

Clinical Avian Medicine & Surgery: Including Aviculture. Greg J. Harrison & Linda R. Harrison. (Illus.). 717p. 1986. text ed. 105.00 (*0-7216-1241-5*) Saunders.

Clinical Behavior Therapy. M. R. Goldfried & Gerald C. Davison. LC 75-25665. (C). 1976. text ed. 44.75 (*0-03-008151-3*) HB Coll Pubs.

Clinical Behavior Therapy. Marvin R. Goldfried & Gerald C. Davison. LC 94-16335. (Wiley Series in Clinical Psychology). 1994. pap. text ed. 29.95 (*0-471-07633-3*) Wiley.

Clinical Behavior Therapy with Children. Thomas H. Ollendick & Jerome A. Cerny. LC 81-17891. (Applied Clinical Psychology Ser.). 364p. (C). 1981. 49.50 (*0-306-40774-4*, Plenum Pr) Plenum.

Clinical Behavioral Medicine: Some Concepts & Procedures. Ian E. Wickramasekera. LC 88-1055. 334p. 1988. 42.50 (*0-306-42734-6*, Plenum Pr) Plenum.

Clinical Behavioral Pediatrics. James W. Varni. (C). 1983. 45.95 (*0-205-14492-6*, H4492) Allyn.

Clinical Benefits of Leukodepleted Blood Products. Ed. by Joseph Sweeney & Andrew Heaton. (Medical Intelligence Unit Ser.). 198p. 1995. 79.00 (*1-57059-122-9*) R G Landes.

Clinical Biochemical & Hematological Reference Values in Normal Experimental Animals & Normal Humans. 2nd exp. ed. Brij M. Mitruka & Howard M. Rawnsley. LC 81-17157. (Illus.). 432p. 1981. lib. bdg. 68.50 (*0-89352-163-9*, Yr Bk Med Pubs) Mosby Yr Bk.

Clinical Biochemistry & the Sick Child. 2nd ed. Ed. by Barbara E. Clayton & Joan M. Round. LC 93-38329. (Illus.). 640p. 1994. write for info. (*0-632-03681-8*, Pub. by Blckwell Sci Pubns UK) Blackwell Sci.

Clinical Biochemistry in Hepatobiliary Diseases. (Progress in Clinical Biochemistry & Medicine Ser.: Vol. 8). (Illus.). 180p. 1989. 95.00 (*0-387-50705-1*, 2622) Spr-Verlag.

Clinical Biochemistry Made Ridiculously Simple. Stephen Goldberg. (Illus.). 95p. (Orig.). 1993. 21.95 (*0-940780-10-0*) MedMaster.

Clinical Biochemistry of Cancer: Proceedings of the Second Arnold O. Beckman Conference in Clinical Chemistry. Ed. by Martin Fleisher. LC 79-14027. 405p. 1979. 20.00 (*0-915274-09-4*) Am Assn Clinical Chem.

Clinical Biochemistry of Domestic Animals. 4th ed. Ed. by Jiro J. Kaneko. 932p. 1989. text ed. 139.95 (*0-12-396304-4*) Acad Pr.

Clinical Biochemistry of Lipids. A. Dubin. Ed. by M. E. Rafelson. (Journal: Clinical Physiology & Biochemistry: Vol. 2, No. 2-3). (Illus.). 80p. 1984. pap. 64.00 (*3-8055-3859-6*) S Karger.

Clinical Biochemistry: Principals, Methods, Applications, Vol. 2: Data Presentation - Interpretaion. Ed. by H. Keller & C. Trendelenburg. xxii, 479p. (C). 1989. lib. bdg. 211.55 (*0-89925-550-7*) De Gruyter.

***Clinical Biochemistry: Principles - Methods - Applications Vol. 1: Mass Spectrometry.** Ed. by A. M. Lawson et al. (Illus.). xx, 745p. (C). 1989. 253.85 (*3-11-007751-5*) De Gruyter.

Clinical Biochemistry: Principles - Methods - Applications, Vol. 1: Mass Spectrometry. Ed. by A. M. Lawson et al. (Illus.). xx, 745p. (C). 1989. Series. 253.85 (*0-89925-581-7*); Single volume. 210.70 (*0-89925-488-8*) De Gruyter.

***Clinical Biochemistry: Principles, Methods, Applications Vol. 3: Human Plasma Lipoproteins.** Ed. by J. C. Fruchart & J. Shepherd. xix, 398p. (C). 1989. lib. bdg. 169.25 (*3-11-010734-1*) De Gruyter.

Clinical Biochemistry: Principles, Methods, Applications, Vol.3: Human Plasma Lipoproteins. Ed. by J. C. Fruchart & J. Shepherd. xix, 398p. (C). 1989. lib. bdg. 169.25 (*0-89925-549-3*) De Gruyter.

***Clinical Biochemistry Synopsis.** Ed. by Dean K. Sorenson et al. LC 89-16421. (Illus.). 146p. 1989. reprint ed. pap. 41.70 (*0-7837-8569-0*, 2049384) Bks Demand.

Clinical Bioenergetics. Michael Galitzer. (Illus.). 36p. (Orig.). 1994. pap. 3.95 (*1-885325-00-2*) IAMB.

Clinical Bioethics: For Doctors, Nurses & Ethics Committee Members. James F. Drane. LC 93-46600. (Orig.). 1994. pap. 24.95 (*1-55612-612-3*) Sheed & Ward MO.

***Clinical Biology of Sodium: The Physiology & Pathophysiology of Sodium in Mammals.** A. R. Michel. LC 95-2407. 1995. write for info. (*0-08-840842-6*, Pergamon Pr) Elsevier.

Clinical Biomechanics: A Case History Approach. Ed. by Jonathan Black & John H. Dumbleton. LC 80-23094. 432p. reprint ed. pap. 123.20 (*0-7837-2554-X*, 2042713) Bks Demand.

***Clinical Biomechanics & Related Research.** Ed. by Y. Hierasawa et al. LC 94-36332. 1994. write for info. (*3-540-70144-3*) Spr-Verlag.

***Clinical Biomechanics & Related Research.** Ed. by Y. Hierasawa et al. LC 94-36332. 1994. write for info. (*0-387-70144-3*) Spr-Verlag.

Clinical Biomechanics of the Lower Extremity. Valmassy. 1995. 75.00 (*0-8016-7986-9*) Mosby Yr Bk.

Clinical Biomechanics of the Spine. 2nd ed. White & Panjabi. (Illus.). 700p. 1990. text ed. 135.00 (*0-397-50720-8*) Lippincott.

Clinical Biophysics. Michael Anbar. Ed. by Alvin F. Gardner. (Allied Health Professions Monograph). (Illus.). 772p. 1985. 75.00 (*0-87527-316-5*) Green.

Clinical Blood Gases: Invasive & Noninvasive Techniques & Applications. Malley. (Illus.). 400p. 1990. text ed. 44.00 (*0-7216-5861-X*) Saunders.

Clinical Blood Rheology. Ed. by Gordon D. Lowe. 1988. write for info. (*0-318-62927-5*) CRC Pr.

Clinical Blood Rheology, Vol. I. Ed. by Gordon D. Lowe. 224p. 1988. 177.00 (*0-8493-4598-7*, RB45) CRC Pr.

Clinical Blood Rheology, Vol. II. Ed. by Gordon D. Lowe. 240p. 1988. 146.00 (*0-8493-4599-5*, RB45, CRC Reprint) Franklin.

Clinical Bone Marrow Transplantation: A Reference Textbook. Kerry Atkinson. (Illus.). 700p. (C). 1994. 195.00 (*0-521-42073-3*) Cambridge U Pr.

Clinical Brain Imaging: Normal Structure & Function. Hayman. 449p. 1992. 135.00 (*0-8151-4180-7*, Yr Bk Med Pubs) Mosby Yr Bk.

Clinical Brain Imaging: Normal Structure & Functional Anatomy. L. Anne Hayman & Vincent C. Hinck. 1992. write for info. (*0-318-69314-3*) Mosby Yr Bk.

Clinical Brain Imaging: Principles & Applications. Ed. by John C. Mazziotta & Sid Gilman. (Contemporary Neurology Ser.: No. 39). iii, 480p. (C). 1992. text ed. 120.00 (*0-8036-5944-X*) Davis Co.

Clinical Breast Radiology. E. J. Roebuck & Blam. 1990. text ed. 95.00 (*0-433-00066-X*) Buttrwrth-Heinemann.

Clinical Calculations: A Unified Approach. Joanne M. Daniels & Loretta M. Smith. LC 86-2131. 272p. (C). 1986. pap. text ed. 24.95 (*0-8273-2517-7*); Apple II 49.95 (*0-8273-2516-9*) Delmar.

Clinical Calculations: A Unified Approach. 3rd ed. Joanne M. Daniels & Loretta M. Smith. LC 93-19225. 375p. 1994. pap. text ed. 24.95 (*0-8273-5945-4*) Delmar.

Clinical Calculations: A Unified Approach - Instructor's Guide. 3rd ed. Joanne M. Daniels & Loretta M. Smith. 132p. 1994. 14.00 (*0-8273-5946-2*) Delmar.

Clinical Calculations for Nurses with Basic Mathematics Review. 3rd ed. Mary J. Cordon. (Illus.). 300p. 1994. pap. text ed. 26.50 (*0-8385-1367-0*, A1367-0) Appleton & Lange.

Clinical Cancer: Principle Sites 2. A. Canonico et al. (Advances in Medical Oncology Ser.: Vol. 11). 1979. 154.00 (*0-08-024394-0*, Pub. by Pergamon Repr UK) Franklin.

Clinical Cancer - Principal Sites One: International Cancer Congress, 12th, Buenos Aires, 1978. Ed. by A. Canonico et al. LC 79-40710. (Advances in Medical Oncology, Research & Education Ser.: Vol. X). (Illus.). 1979. 118.00 (*0-08-024393-2*, Pub. by Pergamon Repr UK) Franklin.

Clinical Capillaroscopy: A Guide for Its Use in Clinical Research & Practice. Ed. by Alfred Bollinger & Bengt Fagrell. LC 90-5052. (Illus.). 250p. 1990. text ed. 64.00 (*0-88937-048-6*) Hogrefe & Huber Pubs.

Clinical Cardiac Assessment, Interventions, & Assist-Technology. Ed. by D. N. Ghista. (Advances in Cardiovascular Physics Ser.: Vol. 7). (Illus.). xii, 178p. 1990. 174.50 (*3-8055-5024-3*) S Karger.

Clinical Cardiac Electrophysiology: Perioperative Considerations. Ed. by Carl Lynch, III. (Illus.). 300p. 1994. 49.95 (*0-397-51405-0*) Lippincott.

Clinical Cardiac Electrophysiology: Techniques & Interpretations. 2nd ed. Mark E. Josephson. (Illus.). 839p. 1992. 105.00 (*0-8121-1201-6*) Williams & Wilkins.

Clinical Cardiac Pacing. Ellen Bogen et al. (Illus.). 736p. 1994. text ed. 165.00 (*0-7216-5462-2*) Saunders.

Clinical Cardiac Radiology. 2nd ed. Keith Jefferson. LC 79-40913. (Illus.). 1980. text ed. 85.00 (*0-407-13576-6*) Buttrwrth-Heinemann.

Clinical Cardiac Rehabilitation. Frederic J. Pashkow. (Illus.). 416p. 1992. 62.00 (*0-683-06780-X*) Williams & Wilkins.

Clinical Cardiac Roentgen Diagnosis. Alphons Jacob. LC 70-96985. (Illus.). 322p. 1971. 20.80 (*0-87527-044-1*) Green.

Clinical Cardiology. 3rd ed. Peter C. Gazes. LC 89-12512. (Illus.). 594p. 1990. text ed. 69.95 (*0-8121-1235-0*) Williams & Wilkins.

Clinical Cardiology. 5th ed. E. Chesler. (Illus.). 416p. 1992. 98.00 (*0-387-97712-0*) Spr-Verlag.

Clinical Cardiology. 6th ed. Melvin D. Cheitlin & Maurice Sokolow. 672p. 1993. 39.95 (*0-8385-1093-0*, A1093-2) Appleton & Lange.

Clinical Cardiology: A Bedside Approach. 2nd ed. Peter C. Gazes. LC 82-13418. (Illus.). 610p. reprint ed. pap. 173.90 (*0-8357-7591-7*, 2056912) Bks Demand.

Clinical Cardiology in the Elderly. Ed. by Elliot Chesler. (Illus.). 624p. 1994. 95.00 (*0-87993-585-5*) Futura Pub.

Clinical Cardiovascular & Pulmonary Physiology. Clive Rosendorff. (Illus.). 382p. 1983. pap. 39.50 (*0-89004-919-X*) Raven.

Clinical Cardiovascular Pharmacology. Frishman. 1990. 70.00 (*0-8151-3359-6*, Yr Bk Med Pubs) Mosby Yr Bk.

Clinical Care & Information Systems in Psychiatry. Ed. by Juan E. Mezzich. LC 86-1193. (Clinical Insights Ser.). 145p. reprint ed. pap. 41.40 (*0-8357-7851-7*, 2036228) Bks Demand.

Clinical Care of the Aged Person: An Interdisciplinary Perspective. David G. Satin. (Illus.). 640p. 1994. 65.00 (*0-19-505290-0*) OUP.

Clinical Care of the Terminal Cancer Patient. Ed. by Barrie R. Cassileth & Peter A. Cassileth. LC 82-15222. 286p. reprint ed. pap. 81.60 (*0-7837-1482-3*, 2057177) Bks Demand.

Clinical Care Plans: Medical Nursing. Marlene G. Mayers. 141p. (Orig.). (C). 1989. pap. text ed. 19.95 (*0-939605-01-5*) Markham-McKenzie.

Clinical Care Plans: Orthopedic & Neurologic Nursing. Marlene G. Mayers. 119p. (C). 1989. pap. text ed. 19.95 (*0-939605-03-1*) Markham-McKenzie.

Clinical Care Plans: Pediatric Nursing. Marlene G. Mayers. 340p. (Orig.). (C). 1991. pap. 32.50 (*0-939605-04-X*) Markham-McKenzie.

Clinical Care Plans: Perinatal Nursing. Marlene G. Mayers. (Illus.). 280p. (Orig.). (C). 1991. pap. 32.50 (*0-939605-05-8*) Markham-McKenzie.

Clinical Care Plans: Surgical Nursing. Marlene Mayers. 157p. (Orig.). (C). 1989. pap. text ed. 19.95 (*0-939605-02-3*) Markham-McKenzie.

Clinical Care Plans for Perinatal-Neonatal Nursing. Ed. by Marlene G. Mayers & Annette L. Jacobson. (McGraw-Hill Clinical Care Plans Ser.). 298p. 1995. pap. 22.00 (*0-07-105463-4*) Hlth Prof Div.

Clinical Career Ladder: Planning & Implementation. Laura Merker et al. 176p. 1985. pap. 19.95 (*0-8261-4611-2*) Springer Pub.

Clinical Case Management. Ed. by Maxine Harris & Leona L. Bachrach. LC 87-646993. (New Directions for Mental Health Services Ser.: No. MHS 40). 1988. 17.95 (*1-55542-893-2*) Jossey-Bass.

Clinical Case Management: An Approach to Comprehensive Treatment of Serious Mental Illness. Ed. by Robert W. Surber. (Focus Editions Ser.: Vol. 167). (C). 1993. text ed. 49.95 (*0-8039-4386-5*); pap. text ed. 24.95 (*0-8039-4387-3*) Sage.

Clinical Case Studies in the Behavioral Treatment of Alcoholism. Ed. by William H. Hay & Peter E. Nathan. LC 82-18048. 324p. 1982. 55.00 (*0-306-40940-2*, Plenum Pr) Plenum.

Clinical Cases in Anesthesia. Alan P. Reed & Joel A. Kaplan. (Illus.). 344p. 1989. pap. text ed. 39.95 (*0-443-08595-1*) Churchill.

***Clinical Cases in Anesthesia.** 2nd ed. Ed. by Allan P. Reed. LC 94-23730. 1995. write for info. (*0-443-08899-3*) Churchill.

Clinical Cases in Neuroradiology. James M. Provenzale & Juan M. Taveras. LC 93-629. (Illus.). 400p. 1993. 125.00 (*0-8121-1590-2*) Williams & Wilkins.

***Clinical Cases in Ophthalmology.** H. B. Hoh & D. L. Easty. LC 94-44574. 1995. pap. write for info. (*0-7506-2102-8*, Focal) Buttrwrth-Heinemann.

***Clinical Cases in Physical Therapy.** Mark A. Brimer & Michael L. Moran. LC 95-13055. 1995. write for info. (*0-7506-9637-0*) Buttrwrth-Heinemann.

Clinical Cellular Immunology. Ed. by Albert A. Luderer & Howard H. Weetall. LC 81-83307. (Contemporary Immunology Ser.). (Illus.). 416p. 1982. 89.50 (*0-89603-011-3*) Humana.

Clinical Chairside Assisting. 3rd ed. William D. Strickland & Aldridge D. Wilder, Jr. (Dental Assisting Manuals Ser.: No. 8). ix, 225p. (C). 1980. pap. 18.00 (*0-8078-1382-6*) U of NC Pr.

Clinical Challenges in Psychiatry. Ed. by William Sledge & Allan Tasman. 384p. 1993. 45.00 (*0-88048-510-8*) Am Psychiatric.

Clinical Chemistry. Ed. by Donald T. Forman & Richard W. Mattoon. LC 76-49983. (ACS Symposium Ser.: No. 36). 1976. 29.95 (*0-8412-0345-8*) Am Chemical.

Clinical Chemistry. Muriel Kanter. LC 75-4050. (Allied Health Ser.). 1975. pap. 12.04 (*0-672-61380-8*, Bobbs) Macmillan.

Clinical Chemistry. Jack Rudman. (College Level Examination Ser.: CLEP-32). 1994. 39.95 (*0-8373-5382-3*); pap. 23.95 (*0-8373-5332-7*) Nat Learn.

Clinical Chemistry. E. Howard Taylor. (Chemistry & Its Applications Ser.). 1989. text ed. 140.00 (*0-471-85342-9*) Wiley.

Clinical Chemistry. 3rd ed. Bishop. Date not set. write for info. (*0-397-55167-3*) Lippincott.

Clinical Chemistry: An Overview. Ed. by N. C. den Boer et al. (Illus.). 874p. 1989. 155.00 (*0-306-43093-2*, Plenum Pr) Plenum.

Clinical Chemistry: Concepts & Applications. Shauna C. Anderson & Susan Cockayne. (Illus.). 768p. 1992. text ed. 55.50 (*0-7216-3372-2*) Saunders.

Clinical Chemistry: Interpretation & Techniques. 2nd ed. Alex Kaplan & LaVerne L. Szabo. LC 82-17249. (Illus.). 446p. reprint ed. pap. 127.20 (*0-8357-8686-2*, 2056843) Bks Demand.

Clinical Chemistry: Interpretation & Techniques. 4th ed. Alex Kaplan et al. LC 93-32472. (Illus.). 450p. 1994. text ed. 39.50 (*0-683-04560-1*) Williams & Wilkins.

Clinical Chemistry: Principles, Procedures, Correlations. 2nd ed. Michael L. Bishop et al. (Illus.). 720p. 1991. text ed. 53.50 (*0-397-54824-9*) Lippincott.

Clinical Chemistry: Theory, Analysis & Correlation. 2nd ed. Kaplan & Pesce. (Illus.). 1248p. 1989. 65.95 (*0-8016-2704-4*) Mosby Yr Bk.

Clinical Chemistry: Theory, Practice, & Interpretation. Roland Richterich & J. P. Colombo. LC 80-40286. (Illus.). 790p. reprint ed. pap. 180.00 (*0-685-20605-X*, 2030539) Bks Demand.

Clinical Chemistry: 1973-1980 Cumulative Index with Citations. Ed. by J. Stanton King. 227p. 1981. 25.00 (*0-915274-41-8*) Am Assn Clinical Chem.

Clinical Chemistry & Chemical Toxicology. Ed. by S. S. Brown. 1977. 47.00 (*0-444-41601-3*) Elsevier.

Clinical Chemistry in Diagnosis & Treatment. 5th ed. Zilva et al. 1988. 39.95 (*0-8151-9871-X*, Yr Bk Med Pubs) Mosby Yr Bk.

Clinical Chemistry Instrumentation & Reagents Markets. (Market Research Reports: No. 262). (Illus.). 146p. 1992. 295.00 (*0-317-04987-9*) Theta Corp.

Clinical Chemistry of Laboratory Animals. Walter Loeb & Fred W. Quimby. 519p. 1989. text ed. 69.50 (*0-07-105293-3*) Hlth Prof Div.

***Clinical Chemistry Profile Data for Hispanics.** 1995. lib. bdg. 250.00 (*0-8490-6524-0*) Gordon Pr.

Clinical Chemistry Profile Data for Hispanics, 1982-84. 53p. (Orig.). (C). 1993. pap. text ed. 25.00 (*1-56806-505-1*) Diane Pub.

Clinical Chemistry Profile Data for Hispanics, 1982-84. Matthew F. Najjar. LC 92-48934. (Vital & Health Statistics Ser. 11: Data from the National Health Survey: No. 241). 1992. write for info. (*0-8406-0467-X*) Natl Ctr Health Stats.

Clinical Chemistry Review Notes & Clinical Chemistry Review Questions, 2 vols., Set. Seymour Bakerman. 1182p. 1986. pap. text ed. 90.00 (*0-945577-02-8*) Interpret Lab Data.

Clinical Chemistry Self-Assessment. 2nd ed. Ed. by Marge A. Brewster et al. LC 89-7043. 158p. 1989. 30.00 (*0-915274-50-7*) Am Assn Clinical Chem.

Clinical Chemistry, 1981-1985: Cumulative Index. Ed. by J. Stanton King. 274p. 1986. 40.00 (*0-915274-37-X*) Am Assn Clinical Chem.

Clinical Child Interview. Jan N. Hughes & David B. Baker. LC 91-6501. (Guilford School Practitioner Ser.). 230p. 1991. lib. bdg. 45.00 (*0-89862-361-8*); pap. text ed. 19.95 (*0-89862-240-9*) Guilford Pr.

***Clinical Child Neuropsychiatry.** Christopher Gillberg. (Illus.). 300p. (C). 1995. 79.95 (*0-521-43388-6*) Cambridge U Pr.

Clinical Child Psychology: Social Learning, Development, & Behaviour. Martin Herbert. (Clinical Psychology Ser.). 1991. text ed. 78.50 (*0-471-92166-1*) Wiley.

Clinical Chiropractic Care No. 1: Clinical Care. Phillips et al. 400p. 1994. pap. 45.00 (*0-8016-6822-0*) Mosby Yr Bk.

Clinical Chiropractic: The Management of Pain & Disability: Upper Body Complaints. R. C. Schafer. LC 90-61201. (Illus.). 528p. (C). 1990. 59.00 (*0-924889-01-2*) Motion Palpat Inst.

Clinical Chronopharmacology. Ed. by B. Lemmer & H. Huller. (Clinical Pharmacology Ser.: Vol. 6). (Illus.). 208p. 1990. text ed. 48.00 (*3-88603-374-0*, Pub. by W Zuckschwerdt GW) Scholium Intl.

Clinical Chronopharmacology. Alain Reinberg. 260p. 1990. 93.00 (*0-89116-943-1*) Hemisp Pub.

Clinical Clerking: A Short Introduction to Clinical Skills. 2nd ed. Carol A. Seymour & Paul Siklos. LC 93-46628. (Illus.). 180p. (C). 1994. 19.95 (*0-521-46235-5*) Cambridge U Pr.

Clinical Clerkship Manual. Ed. by Larry E. Boh. 250p. (Orig.). (C). 1992. pap. text ed. 38.50 (*0-915486-17-2*) Applied Therapeutics.

Clinical Coding Compendium. rev. ed. Deborah Day-Oliver. 415p. (C). 1994. pap. text ed. 54.00 (*1-884103-00-6*) Hlth Data Concepts.

Clinical Competencies for the Medical Assistant. Kathy Bonewit. 359p. 1981. 17.95 (*0-8036-0963-9*) Davis Co.

***Clinical Computer Tomography for the Technologist.** 2nd ed. Ed. by Lee C. Chiu et al. LC 94-3656. 224p. 1995. 65.00 (*0-7817-0235-6*) Raven.

Clinical Computers in Nuclear Medicine. Ed. by Katherine L. Rowell. LC 91-5207. (Illus.). 86p. 1992. text ed. 50.00 (*0-932004-40-7*) Soc Nuclear Med.

Clinical Concepts in Arrhythmias: An Annual Review, 1988. Ed. by Jerry C. Griffin & William J. Mandel. 322p. 1988. 38.00 (*0-87993-333-X*) Futura Pub.

Clinical Considerations in Neuroanesthesia & Neurosurgery. Jane Matjasko & Jordan Katz. 288p. 1986. text ed. 59.95 (*0-8089-1817-6*, 792797, Grune) Saunders.

Clinical Considerations in Perioperative Nursing. Edwina A. McConnell. LC 64-4347. 1987. text ed. 24.95 (*0-397-54494-4*, Lippincott Nursing) Lippincott.

Clinical Consultation & Letters by Ippolito Francesco Albertini, Francesco Torti, & Other Physicians. Francesco Albertini et al. (Illus.). lxix, 356p. 1989. 24.95 (*0-88135-089-3*, Sci Hist) Watson Pub Intl.

Clinical Consultations: The Edition of Enrico Benassi (1935) rev. ed. Giambattista Morgagni. Tr. by Saul Jarcho. 450p. 1984. 25.00 (*0-317-04057-X*) F A Countway.

Clinical Consultations of Giambattista Morgagni: The Edition of Enrico Benassi, 1935. Giambattista Morgani. Tr. & Intro. by Saul Jarcho. c, 450p. 1984. 25.00 (*0-88135-103-2*, Sci Hist) Watson Pub Intl.

Clinical Consultations of Ippolito Francesco Albertini. Ippolio F. Albertini. Tr. & Intro. by Saul Jarcho. (Illus.). 356p. 1990. lib. bdg. 24.95 (*0-317-03952-0*, Watson Pub Intl) F A Countway.

Clinical Coronary Angioplasty: A Text. Jeffrey Brinker. Date not set. 44.95 (*0-8151-1234-3*, Yr Bk Med Pubs) Mosby Yr Bk.

Clinical Coronary Angioplasty: A Text & Atlas. Jeffrey A. Brinker. (Illus.). 208p. 1987. 49.95 (*0-8151-1235-1*, GKB-1, Yr Bk Med Pubs) Mosby Yr Bk.

Clinical Correlations in the Head & Neck, Vol. 1: The Larynx. William Hanafee & Paul Ward. (Illus.). 128p. 1990. text ed. 61.00 (*0-86577-309-2*) Thieme Med Pubs.

Clinical Cosmetology: A Medical Approach to Esthetics Procedures. Victoria Rayner. (Illus.). 440p. (C). 1993. text ed. 39.95 (*1-56253-056-9*) Milady Pub.

Clinical Cosmetology: A Medical Approach to Esthetics Procedures. Victoria Raynor. 1993. 34.95 (*1-56293-056-7*) Phoenix Soc.

Clinical Criteria & Indicators for Nutrition Services in Developmental Disabilities, Psychiatric Disorders, & Substance Abuse. LC 93-31212. 1993. write for info. (*0-88091-127-1*) Am Dietetic Assn.

Clinical Cytometry, Vol. 468. Ed. by Michael Andreeff. 101.00 (*0-89766-332-2*); pap. 101.00 (*0-317-47639-4*) NY Acad Sci.

An Asterisk (*) at the beginning of an entry indicates that the title is appearing in BIP for the first time.

***Clinical Faces of Childhood Volume I: The Oppositional Child, The Inhibited Child, The Depressed Child.** Ed. by E. James Anthony & Doris C. Gilpin. LC 94-72350. 272p. 1994. pap. text ed. 25.00 (*1-56821-334-4*) Aronson.

***Clinical Faces of Childhood Volume II: The Hysterical Child, The Anxious Child, The Borderline Child.** Ed. by E. James Anthony & Doris C. Gilpin. LC 94-72350. 336p. 1994. pap. text ed. 25.00 (*1-56821-335-2*) Aronson.

Clinical Facts & Curios: A Compendium of Unique Insights from the Medical Literature. James A. Stockton, III. LC 94-11041. 1994. write for info. (*1-885046-00-6*) Am Bd Pediatrics.

***Clinical Facts & Curios: A Compendium of Unique Insights from the Medical Literature, Vol. 1.** James A. Stockman, III. (Illus.). 458p. 1994. cd-rom write for info. (*1-885046-02-2*) Am Bd Pediatrics.

***Clinical Facts & Curios: A Compendium of Unique Insights from the Medical Literature, Vol. 1.** James A. Stockman, III. 1994. cd-rom write for info. (*1-885046-01-4*) Am Bd Pediatrics.

Clinical Fetal Monitoring. Schifrin. 1993. 34.95 (*0-8151-7564-7*, Yr Bk Med Pubs) Mosby Yr Bk.

Clinical Flow Cytometry. Ed. by Alan L. Landay et al. LC 93-9300. (Annals Ser.: Vol. 677). 1993. write for info. (*0-89766-767-0*); pap. write for info. (*0-89766-768-9*) NY Acad Sci.

Clinical Flow Cytometry: Principles & Applications. Ed. by Kenneth D. Bauer et al. LC 92-13746. (Illus.). 660p. 1993. 120.00 (*0-683-00480-8*) Williams & Wilkins.

Clinical Foot Roentgenology. 2nd ed. Felton O. Gamble & Irving Yale. LC 74-15632. (Illus.). 448p. 1976. reprint ed. 48.50 (*0-88275-102-6*) Krieger.

Clinical Forensic Medicine. Ed. by W. D. McLay. 376p. 1991. pap. text ed. 39.50 (*0-86187-155-3*, Pub. by Pinter Pubs UK) St Martin.

Clinical Gastroenterology. Ed. by Richard G. Farmer et al. (Illus.). 608p. 1983. text ed. 119.00 (*0-89004-780-4*) Raven.

Clinical Gastroenterology. 2nd ed. Edgar Achkar et al. (Illus.). 1992. text ed. 115.00 (*0-8121-1363-2*) Williams & Wilkins.

Clinical Gastroenterology. 4th ed. Howard M. Spiro et al. LC 93-21707. (Illus.). 1360p. 1993. text ed. 139.00 (*0-07-105434-0*) Hlth Prof Div.

Clinical Gastroenterology: A Problem-Oriented Approach. Ed. by Sidney Cohen. LC 82-10926. 464p. 1983. 42.00 (*0-471-08071-3*) Churchill.

***Clinical Gastroenterology: A Problem-Oriented Approach.** fac. ed. Ed. by Sidney Cohen. LC 82-10926. (Wiley Medical Publication Ser.). (Illus.). 478p. 1983. reprint ed. pap. 136.30 (*0-7837-7879-1*, 2047636) Bks Demand.

Clinical Gastroenterology: Companion Handbook. 4th ed. Basil Rigas & Howard M. Spiro. (Illus.). 384p. 1995. pap. text ed. 27.50 (*0-07-003341-2*) Hlth Prof Div.

Clinical Gastroenterology in the Dog & Cat. Murdoch. 1991. write for info. (*0-632-01402-4*) Mosby Yr Bk.

Clinical Genetics Handbook. 2nd ed. Arthur Robinson. 1993. 39.95 (*0-86542-194-3*, 93-010567) Blackwell Sci.

Clinical Geriatric Eyecare. Sheree J. Aston & Joseph H. Maino. (Illus.). 157p. 1993. 39.95 (*0-7506-9320-7*) Buttrwrth-Heinemann.

Clinical Geriatric Neurology. Ed. by Laurie Barclay. LC 92-20248. (Illus.). 513p. 1993. text ed. 98.00 (*0-8121-1610-0*) Williams & Wilkins.

Clinical Geriatric Otorhinolaryngology. 2nd ed. Kashima & Goldstein. 143p. 1991. 59.00 (*1-55664-313-6*) Mosby Yr Bk.

Clinical Geriatric Psychopharmacology. 2nd ed. Carl Salzman. (Illus.). 392p. 1992. 62.00 (*0-683-07495-4*) Williams & Wilkins.

Clinical Geriatrics. 3rd ed. Ed. by Isadore Rossman. LC 65-8386. (Illus.). 742p. 1986. text ed. 79.50 (*0-397-50672-4*, Lippincott Medical) Lippincott.

Clinical Gerontological Nursing: A Guide to Advanced Practice. W. Carole Chenitz et al. (Illus.). 672p. 1990. text ed. 50.00 (*0-7216-2299-2*) Saunders.

Clinical Gerontology: A Guide to Assessment & Intervention. Ed. by T. L. Brink. LC 86-240. (Clinical Gerontologist Ser.: Vol. 5, Nos. 1-4). 517p. 1986. 75.00 (*0-86656-536-1*) Haworth Pr.

Clinical GI Physiology for the Exam Taker. Eugene D. Jacobson & Joel S. Levine. LC 93-8348. (Illus.). 128p. 1993. pap. text ed. 21.00 (*0-7216-3701-9*) Saunders.

Clinical Glaucoma. George Gorin. LC 76-56700. (Ophthalmology Ser.: No. 1). (Illus.). 423p. reprint ed. pap. 120.60 (*0-7837-3375-5*, 2043333) Bks Demand.

Clinical Gross Anatomy: A Guide to Dissection, Study, & Review. Ed. by Gene L. Colborn & John E. Skandalakis. LC 93-11127. (Illus.). 581p. (Orig.). (C). 1993. pap. text ed. 29.95 (*1-85070-522-4*) Prthnon Pub.

Clinical Guide for Contraception. Leon Speroff & Philip Darney. (Illus.). 360p. 1992. pap. 29.00 (*0-683-07889-5*) Williams & Wilkins.

Clinical Guide for the Care of Older Women. Richard L. Byyny & Leon Speroff. (Illus.). 384p. 1990. 65.00 (*0-683-01150-2*) Williams & Wilkins.

Clinical Guide for the Treatment of Schizophrenia. Ed. by Alan S. Bellack. LC 88-32137. (Illus.). 344p. 1989. 49.50 (*0-306-43064-9*, Plenum Pr) Plenum.

Clinical Guide to Anaerobic Infections. Sydney M. Finegold et al. (Illus.). 160p. 1991. 29.95 (*0-89863-162-9*) Star Pub CA.

***Clinical Guide to Cancer Nursing: A Companion to Cancer Nursing.** 3rd ed. Susan L. Groenwald et al. LC 95-180. (Nursing Ser.). 400p. 1995. spiral bd., pap. 44.95 (*0-86720-708-6*) Jones & Bartlett.

Clinical Guide to Child Psychiatry. Ed. by David Shaffer et al. LC 84-57887. 624p. (C). 1984. text ed. 55.00 (*0-02-929020-1*) Free Pr.

Clinical Guide to Depression in Children & Adolescents. Ed. by Mohammad Shafii & Sharon L. Shafii. LC 91-22112. 450p. 1991. text ed. 39.50 (*0-88048-356-3*) Am Psychiatric.

Clinical Guide to Drug & Alcohol Problems. Joseph Westermeyer. LC 86-530. 336p. 1986. text ed. 65.00 (*0-275-92162-X*, C2162, Praeger Pubs) Greenwood.

***Clinical Guide to Laboratory Tests.** 3rd ed. Ed. by Norbert W. Tietz. LC 94-33795. 1997. pap. text ed. write for info. (*0-7216-5052-X*) Saunders.

***Clinical Guide to Ling. Profilin.** Ball. 1992. 41.50 (*1-56593-559-4*, 0486) Singular Publishing.

***Clinical Guide to Nursing Diagnosis: Data - Diagnosis.** Leslie D. Atkinson & Mary E. Murray. LC 94-34820. (Illus.). 336p. 1995. pap. text ed. 18.95 (*0-07-105466-9*) Hlth Prof Div.

Clinical Guide to Nutrition Care in End-Stage Renal Disease. American Dietetic Association Staff. Ed. by Diane Gillet et al. LC 87-19353. 200p. (Orig.). 1987. pap. 20.90 (*0-88091-033-X*, 0149) Am Dietetic Assn.

Clinical Guide to Nutrition Care in End Stage Renal Disease. 2nd ed. Ed. by Jean Stover. LC 93-31214. 1993. write for info. (*0-88091-124-7*) Am Dietetic Assn.

Clinical Guide to Periodontics. Murray Schwartz et al. LC 94-4810. 1994. pap. text ed. 30.00 (*0-7216-4823-1*) Saunders.

Clinical Guide to Reproductive & Developmental Toxicology. Anthony R. Scialli. 304p. 1991. 110.00 (*0-8493-6737-9*) CRC Pr.

Clinical Guide to the Treatment of the Human Stress Response. George S. Everly, Jr. (Stress & Coping Ser.). (Illus.). 406p. 1989. 34.50 (*0-306-43068-1*, Plenum Pr) Plenum.

Clinical Guide to the Use of Vitamin C: Abstracts of Dr. Frederick R. Klenner, M.D. rev. ed. Ed. by L. H. Smith. 66p. 1988. pap. 4.95 (*0-943685-13-3*) Life Sci Pr.

Clinical Guidelines: Diagnostic & Treatment Manual. Ed. by J. C. Desenclos. (Medecins Sans Frontieres - Hatier Ser.). 283p. 1988. vinyl bd. 27.95 (*2-218-01752-0*) Hatier Pub.

Clinical Guidelines for Involuntary Outpatient Treatment. J. Reid Meloy et al. Ed. by Harold H. Smith, Jr. LC 89-43652. (Practitioner's Resource Ser.). 78p. (Orig.). 1990. pap. 14.70 (*0-943158-45-1*, GGIBP) Pro Resource.

***Clinical Guidelines in Adult Health.** Constance R. Uphold & Mary V. Graham. (Illus.). 729p. (Orig.). (C). 1994. pap. text ed. 45.00 (*0-9646151-2-6*) Barmarrae Bks.

***Clinical Guidelines in Child Health.** 2nd ed. Mary V. Graham & Constance R. Uphold. (Illus.). 660p. (C). 1994. pap. text ed. 45.00 (*0-9646151-1-8*) Barmarrae Bks.

Clinical Guidelines in Cross-Cultural Mental Health. Lillian Comas-Diaz & Ezra E. Griffith. LC 87-25314. (Psychiatry Ser.). 384p. 1988. text ed. 60.00 (*0-471-83231-6*) Wiley.

***Clinical Guidelines in Family Practice.** 2nd ed. Constance R. Uphold & Mary V. Graham. (Illus.). 852p. (C). 1994. pap. text ed. 50.00 (*0-9646151-0-X*) Barmarrae Bks.

Clinical Gynecologic Endocrinology & Infertility. 5th ed. Leon Speroff et al. (Illus.). 1000p. 1994. 109.00 (*0-683-07899-2*) Williams & Wilkins.

***Clinical Gynecologic Endocrinology & Infertility: Self Assessment & Study Guide.** David B. Seifer & Leon Speroff. 441p. 1995. pap. 35.00 (*0-683-07901-8*) Williams & Wilkins.

Clinical Gynecologic Oncology. 4th ed. Disaia & Creasman. 743p. 1992. 89.00 (*0-8016-6756-9*) Mosby Yr Bk.

Clinical Gynecologic Oncology Review. Tung Van Dinh et al. Ed. by Philip J. DiSaia & William T. Creasman. LC 92-49305. 137p. 1992. pap. 19.95 (*0-8016-6986-3*) Mosby Yr Bk.

***Clinical Gynecologic Pathology.** Enrique Hernandez & Barbara Atkinson. (Illus.). 416p. 1995. text ed. write for info. (*0-7216-5170-4*) Saunders.

Clinical Gynecological Oncology. 2nd ed. Ed. by J. H. Shepherd & J. M. Monaghan. (Illus.). 520p. 1990. 160.00 (*0-632-02733-9*) Blackwell Sci.

Clinical Gynecology. K. Bhasker Rao & N. N. Chowdhury. 360p. 1984. pap. text ed. 25.00 (*0-86131-471-9*, Pub. by Orient Longman Ltd II) Apt Bks.

Clinical Haematology. Ed. by Christopher A. Ludlam. (Illus.). 496p. 1990. pap. text ed. 59.00 (*0-443-03834-1*) Churchill.

***Clinical Handbook of Ambulatory Medicine.** Ed. by Philip D. Zieve. LC 94-47181. Orig. Title: Principles of Ambulatory Medicine. 1995. text ed. write for info. (*0-683-09374-6*) Williams & Wilkins.

Clinical Handbook of Anxiety Disorders in Children & Adolescents. Ed. by Andrew R. Eisen et al. LC 94-18064. 624p. 1995. 50.00 (*1-56821-294-1*) Aronson.

Clinical Handbook of Behavior Therapy, Vol. 1: Adult Medical Disorders. Gerald Tarlow. 221p. 1988. text ed. 39.95 (*0-914797-39-5*) Brookline Bks.

Clinical Handbook of Behavior Therapy, Vol. 2: Adult Psychological Disorders, 2 vols., Set. Gerald Tarlow. 360p. 1990. text ed. 49.95 (*0-914797-40-9*) Brookline Bks.

Clinical Handbook of Child Abuse & Neglect. Lane J. Veltkamp & Thomas W. Miller. LC 93-15721. 188p. 1994. 25.00 (*0-8236-0950-2*) Intl Univs Pr.

Clinical Handbook of Child Psychiatry & the Law. Diane H. Schetky & Elissa P. Benedek. 352p. 1992. 58.00 (*0-683-07589-6*) Williams & Wilkins.

Clinical Handbook of Chinese Prepared Medicine. Chun-Han Zhu. Ed. by Richard Feit. pap. 25.00 (*0-912111-43-7*) Paradigm Publns.

***Clinical Handbook of Couples Therapy.** Neil S. Jacobson & Alan S. Gurman. 1995. lib. bdg. 55.00 (*0-89862-855-5*, C2855) Guilford Pr.

Clinical Handbook of Depression. 386p. (C). 1991. pap. text ed. 32.50 (*0-89876-174-3*) Gardner Pr.

Clinical Handbook of Family Nursing. Judith M. McFarlane. LC 85-31446. 562p. 1986. pap. text ed. 32.95 (*0-8273-4304-3*) Delmar.

Clinical Handbook of Marital Therapy. Ed. by Neil S. Jacobson & Alan S. Gurman. LC 85-31539. (Guilford Family Therapy Ser.). 657p. 1986. lib. bdg. 49.95 (*0-89862-067-8*) Guilford Pr.

Clinical Handbook of Ocular Microbiology. Haesaert. 154p. 1992. spiral bd. 29.95 (*0-685-65101-0*) Mosby Yr Bk.

Clinical Handbook of Ocular Microbiology. Susan P. Haesaert. LC 92-22538. 154p. 1992. spiral bd. 29.95 (*0-8016-6575-2*) Mosby Yr Bk.

Clinical Handbook of Ophthalmology. Robert G. Small. LC 94-10570. (Clinical Handbook Ser.). (Illus.). 200p. 1994. pap. 23.95 (*1-85070-584-4*) Prthnon Pub.

Clinical Handbook of Pastoral Counseling. Ed. by Robert J. Wicks & Richard D. Parsons. (Integration Ser.: Vol. 2). 752p. (Orig.). 1993. pap. 25.00 (*0-8091-3325-3*) Paulist Pr.

Clinical Handbook of Pastoral Counseling. enl. ed. Ed. by Robert J. Wicks et al. LC 92-30017. (Integration Ser.: Vol. 1). 720p. (Orig.). 1993. pap. 19.95 (*0-8091-3351-2*) Paulist Pr.

Clinical Handbook of Pediatric Infectious Disease. Russell W. Steele. LC 94-8896. (Clinical Handbook Ser.). (Illus.). 340p. 1994. pap. 26.95 (*1-85070-575-5*) Prthnon Pub.

Clinical Handbook of Pediatric Nursing. 2nd ed. Wong & Whaley. 1986. 24.95 (*0-8016-5638-9*) Mosby Yr Bk.

***Clinical Handbook of Pediatrics.** Ed. by M. W. Schwartz & A. B. Allen. LC 94-42130. 1995. write for info. (*0-683-07624-8*) Williams & Wilkins.

Clinical Handbook of Psychiatry & the Law. 2nd ed. Paul S. Appelbaum & Thomas G. Gutheil. 408p. 1991. 58.00 (*0-683-00237-6*) Williams & Wilkins.

Clinical Handbook of Psychological Disorders: A Step-by-Step Treatment Manual. 2nd ed. Ed. by David H. Barlow. LC 93-849. 534p. 1993. lib. bdg. 49.95 (*0-89862-129-1*) Guilford Pr.

Clinical Handbook of Psychotropic Drugs. 4th ed. Ed. by Kalyna Z. Bezchlibnyk-Butler & J. Joel Jeffries. LC 93-78026. (Illus.). 132p. 1994. reprint ed. spiral bd., pap. 29.50 (*0-88937-115-6*) Hogrefe & Huber Pubs.

Clinical Handbook of Respiratory Care. Eubanks et al. Date not set. pap. 49.95 (*0-8016-1653-0*) Mosby Yr Bk.

Clinical Handbook of Sleep Disorders in Children. Charles E. Schaefer. LC 94-19702. 360p. 1995. 45.00 (*1-56821-324-7*) Aronson.

***Clinical Handbook to Accompany Health Assessment in Nursing.** Sims et al. LC 94-45761. (C). 1995. pap. text ed. 23.75 (*0-8053-7349-7*) Addison-Wesley.

Clinical Handling of Dental Materials. Bernard G. Smith et al. (Dental Practitioners' Handbook Ser.: No. 12). 278p. 1986. 34.95 (*0-7236-0833-4*, Pub. by John Wright UK) Buttrwrth-Heinemann.

***Clinical Health Psychology in Medical Settings: A Practitioner's Handbook.** rev. ed. Cynthia Belar & William W. Deardorff. 184p. 1995. text ed. 40.00 (*1-55798-277-5*); pap. text ed. 24.95 (*1-55798-287-2*) Am Psychol.

Clinical Hematology. D. L. Barnard et al. (Mainstream Medicine Ser.). 416p. 1989. pap. text ed. 55.00 (*0-433-00068-6*) Buttrwrth-Heinemann.

Clinical Hematology. 7th ed. R. D. Eastham & Slad. 1992. pap. text ed. 50.00 (*0-7506-1339-4*, Pub. by John Wright UK) Buttrwrth-Heinemann.

Clinical Hematology: A Problem-Oriented Approach. James Isbister & D. Harmening Pittiglio. (Illus.). 264p. 1988. pap. 35.00 (*0-683-04349-8*) Williams & Wilkins.

Clinical Hematology: Principles, Procedures, Correlations. Cheryl A. Lotspeich-Steininger et al. LC 65-9558. (Illus.). 720p. 1991. 49.95 (*0-397-50790-9*, Lippincott Medical) Lippincott.

Clinical Hematology: Principles, Procedures, Correlations. Cheryl A. Lotspeich-Steininger & E. Anne Stiene-Martin. (Illus.). 800p. 1991. text ed. 49.95 (*0-397-54806-0*) Lippincott.

Clinical Hematology: Theory & Procedures. 2nd ed. Mary L. Turgeon. LC 92-48491. (Illus.). 450p. 1993. 55.95 (*0-316-85611-8*) Little.

Clinical Hematology & Fundamentals of Hemostasis. 2nd ed. Ed. by Denise M. Harmening. LC 91-20053. 657p. (C). 1992. text ed. 54.95 (*0-8036-4603-8*) Davis Co.

Clinical Hematology for Blood Bankers: A Case History Approach to Hemolytic Anemia. Denise H. Pottiglio & Lawerence W. Powers. Ed. by Betty Ciesla et al. (S.U.C.C.E.S.S. Program Ser.: No. 1). (Illus.). 64p. (Orig.). 1987. student ed 19.95 (*0-943903-00-9*) DH Pub PA.

Clinical Hemorheology. Ed. by S. Chein et al. 1987. lib. bdg. 147.00 (*0-89838-807-4*) Kluwer Ac.

Clinical Hemotasis Handbook. LaPosata. 348p. 1989. pap. 29.95 (*0-8151-5540-9*, Yr Bk Med Pubs) Mosby Yr Bk.

Clinical Hypertension. 6th ed. Norman M. Kaplan & Ellin Lieberman. Ed. by William W. Neal. LC 93-27557. (Illus.). 504p. 1994. 75.00 (*0-683-04544-X*) Williams & Wilkins.

Clinical Hypertension & Hypotension. Ed. by Hans R. Brunner & Haralambos Gavras. LC 81-19430. (Illus.). 521p. reprint ed. pap. 148.50 (*0-7837-0910-2*, 2041215) Bks Demand.

Clinical Hyperthermia. Ed. by F. N. Gilly et al. (Journal: Oncology: Vol. 50, No. 5, 1993). (Illus.). 64p. 1993. pap. 81.75 (*3-8055-5854-6*) S Karger.

Clinical Hypnosis: A Case Management Approach. 370p. 1987. 35.00 (*0-317-68234-2*) Behav Sci Ctr Pubs.

Clinical Hypnosis: A Multidisciplinary Approach. 636p. 1987. 25.00 (*0-938837-00-1*) Behav Sci Ctr Pubs.

Clinical Hypnosis: A Multidisciplinary Approach. William C. Wester, II & Alexander H. Smith, Jr. (Illus.). 660p. (C). 1991. reprint ed. pap. 25.00 (*0-938837-06-0*) Behav Sci Ctr Pubs.

***Clinical Hypnosis & Memory: Guidelines for Clinicians & for Forensic Hypnosis.** D. Corydon Hammond et al. LC 95-6572. 1995. write for info. (*1-886610-01-0*) Am Soc Clin Hyp Pr.

Clinical Hypnosis & Therapeutic Suggestion in Patient Care. Ed. by Rothlyn P. Zahourek. LC 90-2235. 270p. 1990. pap. 26.95 (*0-87630-606-7*) Brunner-Mazel.

Clinical Hypnosis Primer. George J. Pratt et al. LC 79-92665. (C). 1984. 36.00 (*0-930626-07-9*) Psych & Consul Assocs.

Clinical Hypnosis Primer. enl. rev. ed. George J. Pratt et al. LC 88-5566. 407p. 1988. text ed. 74.95 (*0-471-61384-3*) Wiley.

Clinical Hypnosis with Children. Ed. by William C. Wester & Donald J. O'Grady. LC 90-15157. 288p. 1991. 33.95 (*0-87630-605-9*) Brunner-Mazel.

Clinical Hypnotherapy: The Application of Ideometer Technicians. 2nd ed. David B. Cheek. 320p. Date not set. write for info. (*0-205-18595-9*) Allyn.

***Clinical Imaging: An Atlas of Differential Diagnosis.** 2nd ed. Ronald L. Eisenberg. 1152p. 1991. 173.50 (*0-7817-0208-9*) Raven.

Clinical Imaging: An Introduction to the Role of Imaging in Clinical Practice. Ed. by Matthew Freedman. LC 87-22986. (Illus.). 634p. reprint ed. pap. 180.00 (*0-7837-2582-5*, 2042741) Bks Demand.

Clinical Imaging of the Colon & Rectum. Frederick M. Kelvin & Richard Gardiner. (Clinical Imaging of the Gastrointestinal Tract Ser.). (Illus.). 528p. 1987. text ed. 113.00 (*0-88167-251-3*) Raven.

Clinical Imaging of the Pancreas. Gerald May & Richard Gardiner. (Clinical Imaging of the Gastrointestinal Tract Ser.). (Illus.). 192p. 1987. text ed. 66.00 (*0-88167-265-3*) Raven.

Clinical Immunology: Proceedings of the 1st IUIS Conf. on Clinical Immunology, Toronto, 6-11 July 1986. Ed. by W. Pruzanski & M. Seligmann. 472p. 1987. 160.50 (*0-444-80885-X*, Excerpta Medica) Elsevier.

Clinical Immunochemistry: Chemical & Cellular Bases & Applications in Disease. Samuel Natelson et al. LC 78-72879. 505p. 1978. 25.00 (*0-915274-07-8*) Am Assn Clinical Chem.

Clinical Immunodermatology. 2nd ed. Ed. by Mark V. Dahl. (Illus.). 420p. 1987. 69.00 (*0-8151-2247-0*, MMN-2, Yr Bk Med Pubs) Mosby Yr Bk.

Clinical Immunodermatology. Mark V. Dahl. LC 80-19466. (Illus.). 292p. reprint ed. pap. 83.30 (*0-8357-6311-0*, 2035584) Bks Demand.

Clinical Immunology. WHO Staff. (Technical Report Ser.: No. 496). 50p. 1972. pap. 1.60 (*92-4-120496-6*, 78) World Health.

***Clinical Immunology: A Laboratory Perspective.** Christine Stevens. (Illus.). 525p. (C). 1995. pap. text ed. 29.95 (*0-8036-0050-X*) Davis Co.

Clinical Immunology: A Practical Approach. H. C. Gooi & H. Chapel. (Practical Approach Ser.). (Illus.). 296p. 1990. 88.00 (*0-19-963086-0*, IRL Pr); pap. 48.00 (*0-19-963087-9*, IRL Pr) OUP.

Clinical Immunology: Principles & Laboratory Diagnosis. Sheehan. (Illus.). 480p. 1990. text ed. 29.95 (*0-397-50890-5*) Lippincott.

Clinical Immunology: Principles & Laboratory Diagnosis. Catherine Sheehan. (Illus.). 480p. 1990. 32.95 (*0-397-54809-5*) Lippincott.

Clinical Immunology: Principles & Practice. Rich. 2000p. 1995. 225.00 (*0-8016-7636-3*) Mosby Yr Bk.

Clinical Immunology & Allergology. Ed. by C. Steffen & Hans E. Ludwig. (Developments in Immunology Ser.: Vol. 14). 422p. 1981. 112.00 (*0-444-80312-2*) Elsevier.

Clinical Immunotherapy. Ed. by Albert F. LoBuglio. LC 80-15386. (Immunology Ser.: No. 11). (Illus.). 351p. reprint ed. pap. 100.10 (*0-8357-6057-X*, 2034546) Bks Demand.

Clinical Immunotoxicology. Ed. by David S. Newcombe et al. 464p. 1992. 100.00 (*0-88167-830-9*) Raven.

Clinical Impact of Bone & Connective Tissue Markers. Ed. by E. Lindh & Jan Thorell. 350p. 1989. text ed. 92.00 (*0-12-450740-9*) Acad Pr.

Clinical Impact of H Plus, K Plus-ATP-ase Inhibitors: Journal: Digestion, Vol. 44, Suppl. 1, 1989. Ed. by C. B. Lamers. 98p. 1989. pap. 29.75 (*3-8055-5111-8*) S Karger.

Clinical Impact of the Monitoring of Allergic Inflammation. Ed. by Per Matsson et al. (Illus.). 272p. 1991. text ed. 72.00 (*0-12-480265-6*) Acad Pr.

Clinical Implant Materials: Proceedings of the 8th European Conference on Biomaterials, Heidelberg, FRG, September 7-9, 1989. Ed. by G. Heimke et al. (Advances in Biomaterials Ser.: No. 9). 690p. 1990. 202.75 (*0-444-88226-X*, ABM 9) Elsevier.

Clinical Implications of Abnormal Digestive Tract Radiographs. David A. Morowitz. LC 89-12982. (Illus.). 235p. 1990. text ed. 45.00 (*0-8121-1268-7*) Williams & Wilkins.

Clinical Implications of Attachments. Ed. by Jay Belsky & Teresa Nezworski. (Palermo Ser.). 448p. 1987. text ed. 79.95 (*0-89859-778-1*) L Erlbaum Assocs.

Clinical Implications of Drug Use, 2 vols., Vol. 1. T. K. Basu. 160p. 1980. 46.95 (*0-8493-5391-2*, RM300) CRC Pr.

Clinical Implications of Drug Use, 2 vols., Vol. 2. T. K. Basu. 144p. 1980. 54.00 (*0-8493-5392-0*, RM300) CRC Pr.

Clinical Implications of Laboratory Tests. 4th ed. Tilkian et al. 688p. 1987. pap. 24.95 (*0-8016-4959-5*) Mosby Yr Bk.

Clinical Implications of Normal Biomechanical Stresses on Spinal Function. Herbert Junghanns. Ed. by Hans Hager. 410p. (C). 1990. text ed. 125.00 (*0-8342-0109-7*) Aspen Pub.

1318 An Asterisk (*) at the beginning of an entry indicates that the title is appearing in BIP for the first time.

An Asterisk (*) at the beginning of an entry indicates that the title is appearing in BIP for the first time.

1319

C

Clinical Management of Urticaria & Anaphpylaxis. Ed. by Alan L. Schocket. LC 92-49730. 264p. 1992. 110.00 (*0-8247-8632-7*) Dekker.
Clinical Management of Voice Disorders. 2nd ed. James Case. LC 90-14313. 348p. 1991. pap. text ed. 37.00 (*0-89079-425-1*, 1945) PRO-ED.
***Clinical Management of Voice Disorders.** 3rd ed. James L. Case. LC 95-10794. 1995. write for info. (*0-89079-674-2*) PRO-ED.
Clinical Manifestations of Respiratory Disease. Terry Des Jardins. (Illus.). 433p. 1984. 39.95 (*0-8151-2433-3*, JEF-1, Yr Bk Med Pubs) Mosby Yr Bk.
Clinical Manifestations of Respiratory Disease. 2nd ed. Terry Des Jardins. 406p. 1990. 35.95 (*0-8151-2432-5*, Yr Bk Med Pubs) Mosby Yr Bk.
Clinical Manifestations of Respiratory Disease. 3rd ed. Des Jardins. 1994. 34.95 (*0-8016-7988-5*) Mosby Yr Bk.
Clinical Manual for Binocular Vision. Scheiman. 1993. text ed. 49.95 (*0-397-51133-7*) Lippincott.
Clinical Manual for Care of the Adult Patient with HIV Infection see HIV Infection: A Clinical Manual
Clinical Manual for Essentials of Maternity Nursing: Family-Centered Care. Leonide L. Martin & Sharon J. Reeder. (Illus.). 352p. 1991. text ed. 18.50 (*0-397-54897-4*) Lippincott.
Clinical Manual for Laryngectomy & Head - Neck Cancer: Rehabilitation. Janina K. Casper & Raymond H. Colton. (Clinical Competence Ser.). (Illus.). 210p. (Orig.). (C). 1992. pap. text ed. 34.95 (*1-879105-61-6*) Singular Publishing.
Clinical Manual for Laryngectomy & Head-Neck Cancer Rehabilitation. Janina K. Casper & Raymond H. Colton. 1992. write for info. (*0-318-69438-7*) Singular Publishing.
Clinical Manual for Nursing Assistants. Sharon McClelland. LC 84-11985. 440p. (C). 1985. pap. text ed. 32.50 (*0-86720-365-X*) Jones & Bartlett.
Clinical Manual of Chemical Dependence. Ed. by Domenic A. Ciraulo & Richard I. Shader. LC 90-14511. 475p. 1991. text ed. 46.50 (*0-88048-280-X*) Am Psychiatric.
Clinical Manual of Contact Lenses. Ed. by Edward S. Bennett & Vinita A. Henry. (Illus.). 469p. 1994. text ed. 49.95 (*0-397-51139-6*, Lippincott Medical) Lippincott.
Clinical Manual of Electrophysiology. Igor Singer & Joel Kupersmith. (Illus.). 496p. 1993. 70.00 (*0-683-07735-X*) Williams & Wilkins.
Clinical Manual of Emergency Pediatrics. 2nd ed. Ellen F. Crain et al. LC 92-17267. (Clinical Manual Ser.). (Illus.). 550p. 1992. pap. text ed. 29.50 (*0-07-105429-4*) Hlth Prof Div.
Clinical Manual of Gerontological Nursing. Mildred Hogstel. 301p. 1991. spiral bd. 27.95 (*0-8016-2814-8*) Mosby Yr Bk.
Clinical Manual of Gynecology. 2nd ed. Thomas G. Stovall et al. (Clinical Manual Ser.). (Illus.). 680p. 1992. pap. text ed. 32.00 (*0-07-105389-1*) Hlth Prof Div.
Clinical Manual of Health Assessment. 4th ed. Arden C. Bowers. 657p. 1991. pap. 40.95 (*0-8016-0826-0*) Mosby Yr Bk.
Clinical Manual of Maternity & Gynecologic Nursing. Weiner. (Illus.). 384p. 1989. spiral bd. 28.95 (*0-8016-5741-5*) Mosby Yr Bk.
Clinical Manual of Medical-Surgical Nursing. Sands. 1994. 27.95 (*0-8016-7889-7*) Mosby Yr Bk.
Clinical Manual of Medical-Surgical Nursing. 2nd ed. Sands & Phipps. 304p. 1991. spiral bd. 27.95 (*0-8016-4107-1*) Mosby Yr Bk.
Clinical Manual of Neonatology. 3rd ed. Gomella. (C). 1994. pap. text ed. 24.95 (*0-8385-1331-X*) Appleton & Lange.
Clinical Manual of Obstetrics. 2nd ed. Sharon T. Phelan et al. Ed. by David C. Shaver et al. LC 92-49503. (Clinical Manual Ser.). (Illus.). 640p. 1993. pap. 32.00 (*0-07-105401-4*) Hlth Prof Div.
Clinical Manual of Otolaryngology. 2nd ed. Terence M. Davidson. LC 91-3857. (Clinical Manual Ser.). (Illus.). 267p. 1992. pap. text ed. 27.00 (*0-07-105399-9*, RF56) Hlth Prof Div.
Clinical Manual of Pediatric Anesthesia. Deborah K. Rasch & Dawn E. Webster. (Clinical Manual Ser.). (Illus.). 624p. 1994. pap. text ed. 37.50 (*0-07-051119-5*) Hlth Prof Div.
Clinical Manual of Pediatric Nursing. Wong & Whaley. (Illus.). 632p. 1990. spiral bd. 28.95 (*0-8016-6144-7*) Mosby Yr Bk.
Clinical Manual of Psychiatric Diagnosis & Treatment: A Biopsychosocial Approach. Ronald W. Pies. 1994. boxed 49.95 (*0-88048-534-5*) Am Psychiatric.
Clinical Manual of Psychiatric Nursing. 2nd ed. Ruth P. Rawlins. LC 92-12910. 401p. 1992. spiral bd. 27.95 (*0-8016-6333-4*) Mosby Yr Bk.
Clinical Manual of Substance Abuse, No. 1. Kinney. 512p. 1991. spiral bd. 27.95 (*0-8016-2680-3*) Mosby Yr Bk.
Clinical Manual of Supportive Psychotherapy. Peter N. Novalis et al. LC 92-18064. 384p. 1993. spiral bd. 44.00 (*0-88048-403-9*) Am Psychiatric.
Clinical Manual of Urology. 2nd ed. Philip M. Hanno & Alan J. Wein. (Clinical Manual Ser.). (Illus.). 672p. 1994. pap. text ed. 37.50 (*0-07-105435-9*) Hlth Prof Div.
Clinical Marker hCG. Robert O. Hussa. LC 87-2434. 290p. 1987. text ed. 79.50 (*0-275-92365-7*, C2365, Praeger Pubs) Greenwood.
Clinical Maternal & Fetal Medicine. Hoskins & Young. 750p. 1995. 99.00 (*1-55664-388-8*) Mosby Yr Bk.
Clinical Maternal-Fetal Nutrition. Barbara Luke et al. LC 92-48905. (Illus.). 368p. 1993. 79.95 (*0-316-53614-8*) Little.
Clinical Measurement in Coloproctology. Ed. by Devinder Kumar et al. (Illus.). xiv, 216p. 1991. 120.00 (*0-387-19643-9*) Spr-Verlag.
***Clinical Measurement of Joint Motion.** Ed. by Walter B. Greene & James D. Hickman. 152p. 1994. 25.00 (*0-89203-090-9*) Amer Acad Ortho Surg.
Clinical Measurement of Speech & Voice. R. J. Baken. 518p. (Orig.). (C). 1991. pap. text ed. 60.00 (*0-205-13554-4*) Allyn.
***Clinical Measures of Functional Outcomes: The Functional Tool Box.** Carole B. Lewis. Ed. by Therese McNerney. 240p. 1994. student ed 149.00 (*0-9643582-0-4*) Learn Pubns.
Clinical Mechanics of the Hand. 2nd ed. Paul W. Brand & Hollister. 386p. 1992. 67.00 (*0-8016-6978-2*) Mosby Yr Bk.
Clinical Medical Assistant. Mary A. Woods. (Illus.). 512p. 1993. text ed. 28.50 (*0-7216-5235-2*) Saunders.
Clinical Medical Ethics. Ed. by Edwin Salzman. (Medical Ethics Ser.). (Illus.). 109p. 1986. pap. text ed. 15.00 (*0-910133-17-4*) MA Med Soc.
***Clinical Medical Ethics: Cases & Readings.** David C. Thomasma. LC 94-22890. 1994. write for info. (*0-8191-9725-4*) U Pr of Amer.
Clinical Medical Ethics: Cases in Practice. Terry M. Perlin. LC 92-12544. 1992. 33.95 (*0-316-69959-4*) Little.
Clinical Medicine. Bhattacharyya. (C). 1989. 500.00 (*0-89771-372-9*, Current Dist) St Mut.
Clinical Medicine. Peter C. Hayes & Niall D. Finlayson. LC 94-4031. (Colour Guide, Picture Tests Ser.). 1994. 19.95 (*0-443-04957-2*) Churchill.
Clinical Medicine: Selected Problems with Pathophycology. Barnes. 1987. 49.95 (*0-8151-0489-8*, Yr Bk Med Pubs) Mosby Yr Bk.
Clinical Medicine: Self-Assessment Questions in Colour. Pierre-Mare G. Bouloux. 1994. pap. 29.95 (*1-56375-613-7*, Wolfe Pub) Mosby Yr Bk.
Clinical Medicine for Physical Therapists. Catherine Certo. 400p. 1994. pap. 39.95 (*0-8016-6979-0*) Mosby Yr Bk.
Clinical Medicine for the Occupational Physician. Alderman & Hanley. (Occupational Safety & Health Ser.: Vol. 7). 552p. 1982. 170.00 (*0-8247-7957-6*) Dekker.
Clinical Medicine in Optometric Practice. Muchnick. 352p. 1994. 45.95 (*0-8016-6306-7*) Mosby Yr Bk.
Clinical Method: A General Practice Approach. 2nd ed. Ed. by Robin C. Fraser. LC 92-11420. 1992. 30.00 (*0-7506-1448-X*) Buttrwrth-Heinemann.
Clinical Method & Analysis. James R. Critser, Jr. (Ser. 10-CMA-87). 371p. (Orig.). 1988. pap. 180.00 (*0-88178-063-4*) Lexington Data.
Clinical Methods: The History, Physical, & Laboratory Examinations. 3rd ed. H. Kenneth Walker et al. (Illus.). 1200p. 1990. text ed. 80.00 (*0-409-90077-X*) Buttrwrth-Heinemann.
Clinical Methods & Apparatus. James R. Critser, Jr. (Ser. 10CA-79). 122p. 1980. pap. 90.00 (*0-914428-65-9*) Lexington Data.
Clinical Methods & Apparatus. James R. Critser, Jr. (Ser. 10CA 80). 1981. pap. 100.00 (*0-914428-78-0*) Lexington Data.
Clinical Methods & Apparatus. James R. Critser, Jr. (Ser. 10CA-81). 1982. pap. 110.00 (*0-914428-88-8*) Lexington Data.
Clinical Methods & Apparatus. James R. Critser, Jr. (Ser. 10CA-82). 1983. pap. 120.00 (*0-88178-003-0*) Lexington Data.
Clinical Methods & Apparatus. James R. Critser, Jr. (Ser. 10CA-83). 200p. 1984. pap. 130.00 (*0-88178-014-6*) Lexington Data.
Clinical Methods & Apparatus. James R. Critser, Jr. (Ser. 10CA-85). 239p. 1986. pap. 140.00 (*0-88178-035-9*) Lexington Data.
Clinical Methods & Apparatus. James R. Critser, Jr. (Ser. 10CA-86). 281p. 1987. pap. 160.00 (*0-88178-043-X*) Lexington Data.
Clinical Methods & Apparatus, Ser. 10CA-84. James R. Critser, Jr. 261p. 1985. pap. 140.00 (*0-88178-051-0*) Lexington Data.
Clinical Methods & Practicum in Audiology. Ben R. Kelly et al. LC 93-28364. (Singular Textbook Ser.). (Illus.). 288p. (Orig.). (C). 1993. pap. text ed. 39.95x (*1-56593-161-0*, 0471) Singular Publishing.
Clinical Methods & Practicum in Speech-Language Pathology. M. N. Hegde & Deborah Davis. (Illus.). 304p. (Orig.). (C). 1991. pap. text ed. 39.95x (*1-879105-42-X*, 0226) Singular Publishing.
***Clinical Methods & Practicum in Speech-Language Pathology.** 2nd ed. M. N. Hegde & Deborah Davis. (Textbook Ser.). 288p. (Orig.). (C). 1995. text ed. 42.50x (*1-56593-507-1*, 1170) Singular Publishing.
Clinical Methods in Communication Disorders. 2nd ed. William R. Leith. LC 92-17022. 288p. 1993. pap. text ed. 27.00 (*0-89079-568-1*, 4047) PRO-ED.
Clinical Methods in Study of Cholesterol Metabolism. H. S. Sodhi et al. (Monographs on Atherosclerosis: Vol. 9). (Illus.). 1979. pap. 65.75 (*3-8055-2986-4*) S Karger.
Clinical Microbiology. Roger Silletti & Victor Lorian. (Illus.). 512p. 1994. 55.00 (*0-683-07712-0*) Williams & Wilkins.
Clinical Microbiology. Von Graevenitz & D. Seligson. LC 76-27688. (Handbook Series Clinical Laboratory Science: Vol. 1, Sec. E). 1977. 210.00 (*0-8493-7032-9*, CRC Reprint) Franklin.
Clinical Microbiology & Infectious Diseases of the Dog & Cat. Craig E. Greene. (Illus.). 610p. 1984. text ed. 98.00 (*0-7216-4251-9*) Saunders.
Clinical Microbiology Made Ridiculously Simple. Mark Gladwin & Bill Trattler. (Illus.). 275p. (Orig.). (C). 1995. pap. text ed. 21.95 (*0-940780-20-8*) MedMaster.
Clinical Microbiology Procedures Handbook, 2 vols., Set. Ed. by Henry D. Isenberg et al. (Illus.). 2468p. 1992. 240.00 (*1-55581-038-1*) Am Soc Microbio.
Clinical Monitoring for Anesthesia & Critical Care. 2nd ed. Ed. by Carol Lake. 1994. write for info. (*0-318-72429-4*) Saunders.
Clinical Musculoskeletal Anatomy. Neal E. Pratt. (Illus.). 333p. 1991. text ed. 39.95 (*0-397-54825-7*, Lippincott Medical) Lippincott.
Clinical Musculoskeletal Pathology. 3rd rev. ed. William F. Enneking. 508p. (C). 1990. lib. bdg. 42.95 (*0-8130-1016-0*) U Press Fla.
Clinical Nephrology: Immunologic Considerations, Invasive Techniques and Dialytic Strategies. Ed. by G. Colasanti & G. D'Amico. (Contributions to Nephrology Ser.: Vol. 69). (Illus.). 1989. 117.75 (*3-8055-4857-5*) S Karger.
Clinical Nephrology in Medical Practice. Gavin J. Becker et al. (Essentials Ser.). (Illus.). 400p. 1992. 95.00 (*0-632-03167-0*) Blackwell Sci.
Clinical Nephrology; Pathophysiology of Hypertension. Jean-Pierre Grunfeld et al. (Current Opinion in Nephrology & Hypertension Ser.). (Illus.). 236p. (Orig.). 1994. pap. text ed. 49.95 (*1-85922-613-2*) Current Science.
Clinical Neuro-Urology. 2nd ed. Krane. 1991. 120.00 (*0-316-50332-0*) Little.
Clinical Neuroanatomy for Medical Students. 2nd ed. Richard S. Snell. 1986. 35.50 (*0-316-80198-4*) Little.
Clinical Neuroanatomy for Medical Students. 3rd ed. Richard S. Snell. LC 91-44527. 653p. 1992. pap. 45.00 (*0-316-80244-1*, QM451, Little Med Div) Little.
Clinical Neuroanatomy Made Ridiculously Simple. Stephen Goldberg. (Illus.). 89p. (Orig.). 1993. reprint ed. pap. text ed. 11.95 (*0-940780-00-3*) MedMaster.
Clinical Neuroanesthesia. Ed. by Roy F. Cucchiara & John D. Michenfelder. (Illus.). 555p. 1990. text ed. 95.00 (*0-443-08719-9*) Churchill.
Clinical Neurochemistry, Vol. 1. Ed. by Herman S. Bachelard et al. 1986. text ed. 97.00 (*0-12-070101-4*) Acad Pr.
Clinical Neurochemistry, Vol. 2. Ed. by Herman S. Bachelard et al. 1986. text ed. 97.00 (*0-12-070102-2*) Acad Pr.
Clinical Neuroendocrinology. 2nd ed. Joseph B. Martin & Seymour Reichlin. LC 87-563. (Contemporary Neurology Ser.: No. 28). (Illus.). 759p. 1987. 79.00 (*0-8036-5886-9*) Davis Co.
***Clinical Neuroendocrinology: A Pathophysiological Approach.** fac. ed. Ed. by George Tolis et al. LC 78-64844. (Illus.). 492p. Date not set. pap. 140.30 (*0-7837-7262-9*, 2047043) Bks Demand.
Clinical Neurology, 4 vols. Ed. by Robert J. Joynt. (Annual Revision Service Ser.). ring bd. 450.00 (*0-06-148006-1*) Lippincott.
Clinical Neurology. Ed. by C. David Marsden & Timothy J. Fowler. 460p. 1989. 47.00 (*0-88167-527-X*) Raven.
Clinical Neurology. Ed. by Michael Swash & John Oxbury. (Illus.). 1776p. 1991. text ed. 220.00 (*0-443-03221-1*) Churchill.
Clinical Neurology, 4 vols. rev. ed. Ed. by Robert J. Joynt. (Annual Revision Service Ser.). 75.00 (*0-686-97872-2*) Lippincott.
Clinical Neurology. 2nd ed. David A. Greenberg & Roger P. Simon. (Illus.). 336p. (C). 1993. pap. text ed. 31.95 (*0-8385-1311-5*, A1311-8) Appleton & Lange.
Clinical Neurology: A Modern Approach. Anthony Hopkins. (Illus.). 600p. 1993. 86.50 (*0-19-261474-6*); pap. 39.95 (*0-19-262262-5*) OUP.
***Clinical Neurology & the Pathomechanical Lesion.** True & Durrant. 300p. 1995. 63.00 (*0-8342-0559-9*) Aspen Pub.
Clinical Neurology for Psychiatrists. 3rd ed. Joseph J. Kaufman. (Illus.). 544p. 1989. text ed. 90.50 (*0-7216-3123-1*) Saunders.
***Clinical Neurology for Psychiatrists.** 4th ed. David M. Kaufman. LC 94-46917. (Illus.). 592p. 1995. text ed. write for info. (*0-7216-5829-6*) Saunders.
Clinical Neurology of Aging. rev. ed. Ed. by Martin L. Albert & Janice E. Knoefel. (Illus.). 784p. 1994. reprint ed. 125.00 (*0-19-507167-0*) OUP.
Clinical Neurology of Old Age. R. Tallis. 1989. text ed. 321.95 (*0-471-91108-9*) Wiley.
Clinical Neuropathology. James S. Nelson & Paul E. McKeever. (C). 1994. disk 600.00 (*1-56815-020-2*) Image Premast.
Clinical Neuropharmacology, Vol. 2. Ed. by Harold L. Klawans. LC 75-14581. 218p. 1977. 66.50 (*0-89004-171-7*) Raven.
***Clinical Neuropharmacology Vol. 3.** fac. ed. Ed. by Harold L. Klawans. LC 76-644724. (Illus.). 221p. Date not set. pap. 63.00 (*0-7837-7152-5*, 2047144) Bks Demand.
Clinical Neuropharmacology, Vol. 13, Supp. 2, 1990: Proceedings of the 17th Collegium Internationale Neuro-Psychopharmacologicum Congress. Ed. by Yamashita et al. 718p. 1990. pap. 129.00 (*0-88167-732-9*) Raven.
Clinical Neurophysiological Aspects of Psychopathological Conditions. Ed. by C. Perris et al. (Advances in Biological Psychiatry Ser.: Vol. 4). (Illus.). viii, 192p. 1980. pap. 49.00 (*3-8055-0604-X*) S Karger.
***Clinical Neurophysiology.** Jasper R. Daube et al. (Contemporary Neurology Ser.: Vol. 46). (Illus.). 575p. (C). 1995. 90.00 (*0-8036-0073-9*) Davis Co.
Clinical Neurophysiology in Parkinsonism: Restorative Neurology, Vol. 2. P. J. Delwaide. Ed. by A. Agnoli. 192p. 1985. 82.75 (*0-444-80679-2*) Elsevier.
Clinical Neurophysiology in Peripheral Neuropathies. Ed. by P. J. Delwaide & A. Gorio. (Restorative Neurology Ser.: Vol. 3). 174p. 1986. 79.50 (*0-444-80693-8*) Elsevier.
Clinical Neurophysiology in Spasticity: Restorative Neurology, Vol. 1. Ed. by P. J. Delwaide & R. R. Young. 228p. 1985. 119.00 (*0-444-80653-9*) Elsevier.
Clinical Neurophysiology of Epilepsy: Handbook of Electroencephalography & Clinical Neurophysiology, No. 4. Ed. by J. A. Wada & R. J. Ellingson. 508p. 1990. 238.75 (*0-444-81241-5*) Elsevier.
Clinical Neurophysiology of the Vestibular System. 2nd ed. Robert W. Baloh & Vicente Honrubia. LC 89-16897. (Contemporary Neurology Ser.: No. 32). (Illus.). 301p. (C). 1990. 72.00 (*0-8036-0584-6*) Davis Co.
***Clinical Neurophysiology of the Vestibular System.** 2nd ed. Robert W. Baloh & Vicente Honrubia. LC 89-16897. (Contemporary Neurology Ser.: No. 32). (Illus.). 301p. (C). 1990. 32.00 (*0-8036-0585-4*) Davis Co.
***Clinical Neuropsychological Assessment: A Cognitive Approach.** Ed. by Robert L. Mapou & Jack Spector. (Critical Issues in Neuropsychology Ser.: Vol. 1). 360p. 1995. 65.00 (*0-306-44869-6*, Plenum Pr) Plenum.
Clinical Neuropsychology. Ed. by Kenneth M. Heilman & Edward Valenstein. LC 92-49919. 1993. 65.00 (*0-19-508123-4*) OUP.
***Clinical Neuropsychology: Behavioral & Brain Science.** John L. Bradshaw & Jason B. Mattingley. (Illus.). 402p. 1995. pap. text ed. write for info. (*0-12-124545-4*) Acad Pr.
Clinical Neuropsychology: Current Status & Applications. Ed. by Ralph M. Reitan & Leslie A. Davison. LC 66-40726. 417p. 1974. pap. 40.00 (*0-89116-367-0*) Hemisp Pub.
Clinical Neuropsychology: Interface with Neurological & Psychiatric Disorders. Ed. by Charles J. Golden et al. 1983. text ed. 32.95 (*0-8089-1541-X*, 791623, Grune) Saunders.
Clinical Neuropsychology & Brain Function: Research, Measurement, & Practice. Ed. by Thomas Boll & Brenda Bryant. LC 88-14558. (Master Lecture Ser.: Vol. 7). 202p. (Orig.). 1988. pap. 24.95 (*1-55798-038-1*) Am Psychol.
Clinical Neuropsychology of Attention. Adriaan H. Van Zomeren & Wiebo H. Brouwer. (Illus.). 256p. 1994. 35.00 (*0-19-506373-2*) OUP.
***Clinical Neuroradiology: A Textbook.** Ed. by Eberhard Lohr et al. LC 94-35189. (Illus.). 336p. 1995. text ed. 135.00 (*0-88937-132-6*) Hogrefe & Huber Pubs.
Clinical Neuroscience: From Neuroanatomy to Psychodynamics. Jay E. Harris. 304p. 1985. 45.95 (*0-89885-238-2*) Human Sci Pr.
Clinical Neurosis. 2nd ed. Philip Snaith. (Illus.). 256p. 1991. pap. 32.50 (*0-19-262067-3*) OUP.
Clinical Neurosurgery, Vol. 34. John Little. (Illus.). 718p. 1987. 64.95 (*0-683-02029-3*) Williams & Wilkins.
Clinical Neurosurgery, Vol. 35. Ed. by Peter Black. (Proceedings of the Congress of Neurological Surgeons Ser.). (Illus.). 576p. 1988. 65.00 (*0-683-02032-3*) Williams & Wilkins.
Clinical Neurosurgery, Vol. 39. Warren R. Selman. (Illus.). 602p. 1993. 85.00 (*0-683-02036-6*) Williams & Wilkins.
Clinical Neurosurgery: Proceedings of the Congress of Neurological Surgeons, Vol. 32. Ed. by John R. Little. (Illus.). 680p. 1985. 54.00 (*0-683-02027-7*) Williams & Wilkins.
Clinical Neurosurgery: Proceedings of the Congress of Neurological Surgeons, Vol. 33. John R. Little. (Illus.). 702p. 1986. write for info. (*0-683-02028-5*) Williams & Wilkins.
Clinical Neurosurgery: Proceedings of the Congress of Neurological Surgeons, Vol. 36. Peter M. Black. (Illus.). 512p. 1989. 65.00 (*0-683-02033-1*) Williams & Wilkins.
Clinical Neurosurgery: Proceedings of the Congress of Neurological Surgeons, Vol. 40. Warren Selman. 600p. 1994. 85.00 (*0-683-02037-4*) Williams & Wilkins.
Clinical Neurosurgery, Vol. 37: Proceedings of the Congress of Neurological Surgeons. Peter M. Black. (Illus.). 844p. 1990. 66.00 (*0-683-02034-X*) Williams & Wilkins.
Clinical Neutron Dosimetry, Part 1: Determination of Absorbed Dose in a Patient Treated by External Beams of Fast Neutrons. ICRU Staff. LC 88-25113. (ICRU Report Ser.: No. 45). 1989. pap. text ed. 40.00 (*0-913394-39-4*) Intl Comm Rad Meas.
Clinical NMR Imaging. Bryan et al. Date not set. pap. 49.95 (*0-8016-0830-9*) Mosby Yr Bk.
***Clinical Nuclear Cardiology.** George A. Beller. LC 94-25345. (Illus.). 336p. 1995. text ed. 95.00 (*0-7216-3332-3*) Saunders.
Clinical Nuclear Medicine. M. N. Maisey. 1983. 97.50 (*0-7020-1243-2*) Saunders.
Clinical Nuclear Medicine. M. N. Maisey et al. (Illus.). 525p. 1983. text ed. 121.00 (*0-7216-1087-0*) Saunders.
Clinical Nuclear Medicine. 2nd ed. M. N. Maisey et al. (Illus.). 650p. 1991. text ed. 149.50 (*0-397-58327-3*) Lippincott.
Clinical Nurse. Jack Rudman. (Career Examination Ser.: C-947). 1994. pap. 29.95 (*0-8373-0947-6*) Nat Learn.
Clinical Nurse Specialist: An Experiment in Role Effectiveness & Role Development. Rachel Ayers et al. 75p. 1972. pap. 5.00 (*0-940876-02-7*) City Hope.
Clinical Nurse Specialist: Implementation & Impact. Patricia S. Sparacino et al. (Illus.). 323p. 1990. pap. text ed. 34.95 (*0-8385-1278-X*, A1278-9) Appleton & Lange.
Clinical Nurse Specialist: Perspectives on Practice. Ed. by Shirley W. Menard. 1987. pap. text ed. 29.95 (*0-8273-4311-6*) Delmar.
Clinical Nurse Specialist in Theory & Practice. 2nd ed. Hamric & Spross. 1989. text ed. 40.95 (*0-7216-4486-4*) Saunders.
Clinical Nurse Specialist Role in Critical Care. American Association of Critical-Care Nurses Staff. Ed. by Anna Gawlinski & Leslie S. Kern. LC 93-30391. 1994. text ed. 47.50 (*0-7216-3715-9*) Saunders.
Clinical Nursing Interventions with Critical Elements. Mary A. Riley & Mary J. Beltran. LC 85-20360. 385p. 1986. pap. text ed. 26.95 (*0-8273-4338-8*) Delmar.

C

An Asterisk (*) at the beginning of an entry indicates that the title is appearing in BIP for the first time.

C

Clinical Pharmacology, Scope, Organization, Training: Proceedings of the WHO Scientific Group, Geneva, 1969. WHO Staff. (Technical Report Ser.: No. 446). 1970. pap. 1.20 (*92-4-120446-X*) World Health.

Clinical Pharmacy & Therapeutics. Ed. by Roger Walker & Cliv Edwards. LC 93-20832. 1994. 65.50 (*0-443-04553-4*) Churchill.

Clinical Phenomenology & Cognitive Psychology. David Fewtrell & Kieron O'Connor. LC 94-8923. (International Library of Psychology). 224p. 1994. 59.95x (*0-415-06946-7*, B4043, Routledge NY) Routledge.

Clinical Phonetics. Lawrence D. Shriberg & Raymond D. Kent. LC 81-15988. (Wiley Communications Ser.). 481p. (C). 1982. pap. write for info. (*0-02-410200-8*) Macmillan.

Clinical Phonetics. 2nd ed. Lawrence D. Shriberg & Ray Kent. LC 81-15988. 512p. (C). 1995. pap. write for info. (*0-02-410213-X*) Macmillan.

Clinical Photography in Plastic Surgery. Gerald D. Nelson & John L. Krause. (Illus.). 176p. 1987. 79.95 (*0-316-60315-5*, Little Med Div) Little.

Clinical Photomedicine. Lim & Soter. (Basic & Clinical Dermatology Ser.: Vol. 6). 428p. 1993. 140.00 (*0-8247-8862-1*) Dekker.

Clinical Physiology in Obstetrics. 2nd ed. Ed. by G. Chamberlain & F. E. Hytten. 512p. 1990. 160.05 (*0-632-02142-X*) Blackwell Sci.

***Clinical Physiology Made Ridiculously Simple.** Stephen Goldberg. 160p. (Orig.). (C). 1995. pap. text ed. 17.95 (*0-940780-21-6*) MedMaster.

Clinical Physiology of Acid-Base & Electrolyte Disorders. 4th ed. Burton D. Rose. (Illus.). 915p. 1994. pap. text ed. 37.00 (*0-07-053663-5*) Hlth Prof Div.

Clinical Physiology of Sleep. Ed. by Ralph Lydic & Julian F. Biebuyck. (Clinical Physiology Series - An American Physiological Society Book). (Illus.). 253p. 1988. 49.00 (*0-19-520780-7*) OUP.

Clinical Policies & Procedures for Home Health. Ed. by Judith M. Bulau. 288p. 1986. 95.00 (*0-87189-361-4*, 89361) Aspen Pub.

Clinical Positron Emission Tomography. Karl F. Hubner. 183p. 1991. 129.00 (*0-8151-4744-9*) Mosby Yr Bk.

Clinical Positron Emission Tomography. Mehr. 1991. 74.95 (*0-8151-5875-0*, Yr Bk Med Pubs) Mosby Yr Bk.

Clinical Potential of Interferons: Treatment of Viral Diseases & Malignant Tumors. Ed. by Reisaku Kono & Jan Vilcek. 404p. 1982. 79.50 (*0-86008-313-6*, Pub. by U of Tokyo JA) Col U Pr.

Clinical Practice & Cost Containment: A Physician's Perspective. Henry A. Shenkin. LC 85-25589. 160p. 1985. text ed. 55.00 (*0-275-92045-3*, C2045, Praeger Pubs) Greenwood.

Clinical Practice & Economics. C. I. Phillips & J. N. Wolfe. pap. 25.00 (*0-8464-0251-3*) Beekman Pubs.

***Clinical Practice & the Architecture of the Mind.** Robert Langs. 160p. 1995. pap. 22.95 (*1-85575-088-0*) Brunner-Mazel.

Clinical Practice Examination. Howard S. Barrows et al. (Illus.). 192p. (Orig.). (C). 1992. pap. 20.95 (*0-931369-24-X*) Southern IL Univ Sch.

Clinical Practice Guideline on Depression in Primary Care, 2 vols., Set. 1994. lib. bdg. 499.75 (*0-8490-9058-X*) Gordon Pr.

Clinical Practice Guidelines: Directions for a New Program. Institute of Medicine, Committee to Advise the Public Health Service of Clinical Practice Guidelines Staff. 168p. (C). 1990. pap. text ed. 30.00 (*0-309-04346-8*) Natl Acad Pr.

Clinical Practice Improvement: A New Technology for Developing Cost-Effective Quality Health Care. Susan D. Horn & David S. Hopkins. (Medical Outcomes & Practice Guidelines Library: Vol. I). 266p. 1994. pap. 125.00 (*1-881393-25-9*) Faulkner & Gray.

Clinical Practice in Adoption. Winkler. (C). 1988. 29.95 (*0-205-14513-2*, H4513) Allyn.

Clinical Practice in Adoption. Winkler. (Practitioner Guidebook Ser.). (C). 1988. pap. 19.95 (*0-205-14512-4*, H4512, Longwood Div) Allyn.

Clinical Practice in Music Education. Joseph W. Landon. (Contemporary Music Education Ser.). (Illus.). 128p. (Orig.). 1988. pap. 8.95 (*0-943988-03-9*, 943E) Music Educ Pubns.

Clinical Practice Management. Robert J. Solomon. 480p. (C). 1991. 70.00 (*0-8342-0224-7*) Aspen Pub.

Clinical Practice of Career Assessment: Abilities, Interests, & Personality. Rodney L. Lowman. (Illus.). 333p. (C). 1991. 37.50 (*1-55798-106-X*); pap. 19.50 (*1-55798-119-1*) Am Psychol.

Clinical Practice of Emergency Medicine. Harwood-Nuss et al. (Illus.). 1249p. 1990. text ed. 155.00 (*0-397-50896-4*) Lippincott.

Clinical Practice of Glaucoma. William C. Stewart. LC 89-43488. (Illus.). 363p. (C). 1989. text ed. 75.00 (*1-55642-055-2*) SLACK Inc.

Clinical Practice of Hypnotherapy. M. Erik Wright. LC 86-18473. (Guilford Clinical & Experimental Hypnosis Ser.). 292p. 1987. lib. bdg. 33.50 (*0-89862-337-5*) Guilford Pr.

Clinical Practice of Neurological & Neurosurgical Nursing. 3rd ed. Joanne Hickey. (Illus.). 608p. 1992. text ed. 57.95 (*0-397-54822-2*) Lippincott.

Clinical Practice of Nuclear Medicine. Ed. by Andrew Taylor, Jr. & Frederick L. Datz. (Illus.). 471p. 1991. text ed. 103.00 (*0-443-08384-3*) Churchill.

Clinical Practice of Psychology. Barbara G. Walker. (C). 1976. 96.95 (*0-205-14495-0*, H4495); pap. 40.95 (*0-205-14496-9*, H4496) Allyn.

Clinical Practice of Regional Anesthesia. Ed. by P. Prithvi Raj. (Illus.). 543p. 1991. text ed. 124.00 (*0-443-08685-0*) Churchill.

Clinical Practice of Sports Injury Prevention & Care. 2nd ed. Ed. by Per A. Renstrom. LC 93-39208. (Encyclopedia of Sports Medicine Ser.: Vol. V). (Illus.). 748p. 1993. text ed. 79.00x (*0-632-03785-7*, BREN3785) Blackwell Sci.

Clinical Practice of the Dental Hygienist. 6th ed. Esther M. Wilkins. (Illus.). 802p. 1989. text ed. 52.50 (*0-8121-1181-8*) Williams & Wilkins.

Clinical Practice of the Dental Hygienist. 7th ed. Esther M. Wilkins. LC 93-39743. 1994. 54.95 (*0-683-09078-X*) Williams & Wilkins.

Clinical Practice of Transfusion Medicine. 2nd ed. Ed. by Lawrence D. Petz & Scott Swisher. (Illus.). 790p. 1989. text ed. 142.00 (*0-443-08548-X*) Churchill.

Clinical Practitioners Pocket Guide to Respiratory Care. 3rd ed. Dana Oakes. (Illus.). 300p. 1994. ring bd. 18.95 (*0-932887-05-8*) Health Ed Pubns.

Clinical Pre-Computer Proforma for the International Computer Database for Radiation Exposure Case Histories. A. E. Baranov et al. (Illus.). 128p. 1994. pap. 53.00 (*0-387-57596-0*) Spr-Verlag.

Clinical Preventive Medicine. Matzen-Lang. 1312p. 1993. 85.00 (*0-8016-3176-9*) Mosby Yr Bk.

Clinical Preventive Medicine: Health Promotion & Disease Prevention. T. Warner Hudson. 768p. 1988. 56.95 (*0-316-37909-3*, Little Med Div) Little.

***Clinical Preventive Services.** (Medical Science Ser.). 1995. lib. bdg. 250.99 (*0-8490-7576-9*) Gordon Pr.

Clinical Primer of Psychopharmacology: A Practical Guide. 2nd ed. Donald M. Pirodsky & Jerry S. Cohn. (Illus.). 144p. 1992. pap. text ed. 24.95 (*0-07-105388-3*) Hlth Prof Div.

Clinical Problem-Based Learning 1988. Waterman et al. 322p. pap. 29.95 (*0-685-59493-9*) Springer Pub.

Clinical Problems in Acute Care Medicine. Heffernan et al. 688p. 1989. pap. text ed. 45.50 (*0-7216-1155-9*) Saunders.

Clinical Problems in Basic Pharmacology. Nierenberg & Smith. (Illus.). 336p. 1988. pap. text ed. 19.95 (*0-8016-3860-7*) Mosby Yr Bk.

Clinical Problems in Gastroenterology. Rhodes. 224p. 1994. pap. 39.95 (*0-8151-7334-2*, Yr Bk Med Pubs) Mosby Yr Bk.

Clinical Problems in General Surgery. Hunt & Marsh. 1991. pap. text ed. 145.00 (*0-409-49213-2*) Buttrwrth-Heinemann.

Clinical Problems in Neuropanes & Neuro-Intensive Care. Bedford. 1991. 49.95 (*0-8151-0628-9*, Yr Bk Med Pubs) Mosby Yr Bk.

Clinical Problems in Oncology. Carol S. Portlock. 1986. 10.95 (*0-316-71427-5*) Little.

Clinical Problems in Pediatrics. Ed. by Herbert C. Miller & Leone Mattioli. LC 77-89459. 251p. reprint ed. pap. 71.60 (*0-8357-6760-4*, 2035421) Bks Demand.

***Clinical Problems in Rheumatology.** Anthony Clarke & Frank D. Hart. 1994. pap. 74.95 (*1-85317-125-5*) Scovill Paterson.

Clinical Problems in Sexually Transmitted Diseases. D. Taylor-Robinson. LC 85-4924. (New Perspectives in Clinical Microbiology Ser.). 1985. lib. bdg. 162.50 (*0-89838-720-5*) Kluwer Ac.

***Clinical Problems, Injuries & Complications of Gynecologic & Obstetric Surgery.** rev. ed. Ed. by David H. Nichols & John O. L. Delancey. LC 94-44911. 453p. 1995. 85.00 (*0-683-06497-5*) Williams & Wilkins.

Clinical Problems, Injuries & Complications of Gynecologic Surgery. 2nd ed. David H. Nichols & George W. Anderson. 360p. 1988. 75.00 (*0-683-06496-7*) Williams & Wilkins.

Clinical Procedures for Medical Assistants. 3rd ed. Kathy Bonewit-West. 624p. 1989. text ed. 35.50 (*0-7216-2895-8*) Saunders.

Clinical Procedures for Medical Assistants. 4th ed. Kathy Bonewit-West. LC 94-10991. (Illus.). 480p. 1995. text ed. 32.50 (*0-7216-5413-4*) Saunders.

Clinical Procedures for Medical Assisting. David R. Frew & Mary A. Frew. LC 90-2929. (Illus.). 535p. 1990. Lilly & Frew wkbk. student ed 13.95 (*0-8036-3852-3*) Davis Co.

Clinical Procedures for Medical Assisting. Mary A. Frew & David R. Frew. LC 90-2929. (Illus.). 535p. 1990. pap. 33.95 (*0-8036-3851-5*) Davis Co.

Clinical Procedures for Ocular Examination. Nancy B. Carlson et al. (Illus.). 251p. (C). 1990. spiral bd. 37.95 (*0-8385-1328-X*, A1328-2) Appleton & Lange.

Clinical Procedures for Third Molar Surgery. Karl Koerner. 214p. 1986. 49.95 (*0-87814-311-4*, D4249) PennWell Bks.

Clinical Procedures in Anesthesia & Intensive Care. Benumof. (Illus.). 992p. 1991. text ed. 135.00 (*0-397-50950-2*) Lippincott.

Clinical Procedures in Emergency Medicine. James R. Roberts & Jerris R. Hedges. (Illus.). 1184p. 1991. text ed. 175.00 (*0-7216-7611-1*) Saunders.

Clinical Procedures in Optometry. J. Boyd Eskridge et al. (Illus.). 808p. 1991. text ed. 125.00 (*0-397-50984-7*) Lippincott.

Clinical Procedures in Therapeutic Exercise. Patricia E. Sullivan & Prudence D. Markos. (Illus.). 249p. 1987. pap. text ed. 38.95 (*0-8385-1272-0*, A1272-2) Appleton & Lange.

Clinical Process in Psychiatry: Diagnosis & Management Planning. Barry Nurcombe & Rollin M. Gallagher. (Illus.). 520p. 1986. pap. 44.95 (*0-521-28928-9*) Cambridge U Pr.

Clinical Processes. (Medical Ser.). (Illus.). 144p. 1983. pap. text ed. 12.95 (*0-935920-08-0*, Ntl Pubs Blck) P-H.

Clinical Processes for Medical Assisting. 3rd ed. LC 92-48262. (Regents - Prentice-Hall Medical Assistant Kit Ser.). 240p. 1993. pap. 16.65 (*0-13-722885-6*) P-H.

Clinical Profiles of Diffuse Interstitial Pulmonary Disease. Richard A. DeRemee. (Illus.). 208p. 1990. 43.00 (*0-87993-387-9*) Futura Pub.

Clinical Progress in Nutrition Research. Ed. by A. Sitges-Serra et al. (Illus.). viii, 282p. 1988. 93.75 (*3-8055-4683-1*) S Karger.

Clinical Psychiatry. Ed. by Sidney Bloch & Bruce S. Singh. 471p. (C). Date not set. pap. text ed. 59.95 (*0-522-84531-2*) Intl Spec Bk.

Clinical Psychiatry. Emil Kraepelin. LC 80-25289. (History of Psychology Ser.). 1981. 75.00 (*0-8201-1352-2*) Schol Facsimiles.

Clinical Psychiatry. Howard S. Sudak. 512p. 1985. 55.00 (*0-87527-333-5*) Green.

Clinical Psychiatry. 3rd ed. W. Mayer-Gross et al. (Illus.). 1969. text ed. 115.00 (*0-7020-0001-9*, Bailliere-Tindall) Saunders.

Clinical Psychiatry & the Law. 2nd ed. Robert I. Simon. LC 91-31031. 652p. 1992. 47.50 (*0-88048-401-2*) Am Psychiatric.

Clinical Psychiatry & the Law. Robert I. Simon. LC 86-17234. 557p. reprint ed. pap. 158.80 (*0-7837-2091-2*, 2042367) Bks Demand.

Clinical Psychiatry for Medical Students. 2nd ed. Ed. by Alan Stoudemire. LC 93-34226. 1994. 37.50 (*0-397-51338-0*); pap. 37.50 (*0-397-51388-7*) Lippincott.

Clinical Psychoanalysis. Ed. by Shelly Orgel & Bernard D. Fine. LC 79-51910. (Downstate Psychoanalytic Institute Twenty-Fifth Anniversary Ser: Vol. III). 360p. 1979. 45.00 (*0-87668-368-5*) Aronson.

Clinical Psychologist. Jack Rudman. (Career Examination Ser.: C-149). 1994. pap. 34.95 (*0-8373-0149-1*) Nat Learn.

Clinical Psychologist Intern. Jack Rudman. (Career Examination Ser.: C-1196). 1994. pap. 29.95 (*0-8373-1196-9*) Nat Learn.

Clinical Psychology. Dennis P. Saccuzzo. (C). 1984. text ed. 50.00 (*0-205-08075-8*, H80757) Allyn.

Clinical Psychology. 2nd ed. Julian B. Rotter. LC 74-110493. (Foundations of Modern Psychology Ser.). (Illus.). 1971. pap. 8.95 (*0-685-03791-6*) P-H.

Clinical Psychology. 4th ed. E. Jerry Phares. 640p. (C). 1992. text ed. 51.95 (*0-534-16830-2*) Brooks-Cole.

Clinical Psychology: Expanding Horizons. 2nd ed. Norman D. Sundberg et al. (Century Psychology Ser.). (Illus.). 1973. 32.95 (*0-685-03792-4*) P-H.

Clinical Psychology: Historical & Research Foundations. Ed. by C. E. Walker. (Applied Clinical Psychology Ser.). (Illus.). 600p. 1991. 75.00 (*0-306-43757-0*, Plenum Pr) Plenum.

Clinical Psychology: Research & Developments. Ed. by Helen Dent. 368p. 1987. lib. bdg. 59.50 (*0-7099-4544-2*, Pub. by Croom Helm UK) Routledge Chapman & Hall.

Clinical Psychology: Scientific & Professional Dimensions. Philip C. Kendall & Julian D. Norton-Ford. 699p. (C). 1982. Net. write for info. (*0-318-56421-1*); text ed. write for info. (*0-471-04350-8*) Wiley.

Clinical Psychology: Theory & Practice. R. M. Verma. xii, 212p. 1985. 8.00 (*81-208-0025-7*, Pub. by Motilal Banarsidass II) S Asia.

Clinical Psychology & Medicine: A Behavioral Perspective. Ed. by Chris J. Main et al. LC 81-19978. 384p. 1981. 65.00 (*0-306-40900-3*, Plenum Pr) Plenum.

Clinical Psychology & Personality: The Selected Papers of George Kelly. Ed. by Brendon Maher. LC 78-10716. 372p. 1979. reprint ed. lib. bdg. 29.50 (*0-88275-772-5*) Krieger.

Clinical Psychology Handbook. Ed. by Michel Hersen et al. (General Psychology Ser.: No. 120). 864p. 1983. 150.00 (*0-08-028058-7*, Pergamon Pr) Elsevier.

Clinical Psychology in Transition. Auerbach. 1994. 59.50 (*1-56032-228-4*); pap. 29.50 (*1-56032-229-2*) Hemisp Pub.

Clinical Psychology Observed. David Pilgrim & Andy Treacher. LC 91-25281. 208p. 1992. write for info. (*0-415-07227-1*, A5927) Routledge.

Clinical Psychology since 1917: Science, Practice, & Organization. Donald K. Routh. LC 93-50551. (Applied Clinical Psychology Ser.). 281p. 1994. 45.00 (*0-306-44452-6*) Plenum.

Clinical Psychopharmacology, Pt. 2. David G. Grahame-Smith. Vol. 2, Pt. 2. write for info. (*0-318-58437-9*) Elsevier.

Clinical Psychopharmacology: A Practical Reference for Nonmedical Psychotherapists. Gary W. Lawson & Craig C. Cooperrider. LC 87-33480. 375p. (C). 1988. 65.00 (*0-87189-751-2*) Aspen Pub.

***Clinical Psychopharmacology Made Ridiculously Simple.** 2nd ed. John Preston & James Johnson. (Illus.). 62p. 1995. pap. text ed. 10.95 (*0-940780-23-2*) MedMaster.

Clinical Pulmonary Medicine. Ed. by Lyle D. Victor. LC 92-23693. 1992. 72.00 (*0-316-90246-2*) Little.

Clinical Radioassay Procedures: A Compendium. Paige Besch. LC 74-28803. 338p. 1975. 10.00 (*0-915274-01-9*) Am Assn Clinical Chem.

Clinical Radiobiology. 2nd ed. A. H. Nias. (Illus.). 304p. 1989. text ed. 59.00 (*0-443-03340-4*) Churchill.

Clinical Radioimmunoimaging. Grossman & Rosebrough. 1987. text ed. 39.95 (*0-8089-1894-X*, Grune) Saunders.

Clinical Radiology. Richard H. Daffner. LC 92-12314. (Illus.). 408p. 1993. 32.00 (*0-683-02330-6*) Williams & Wilkins.

Clinical Radiology & Endoscopy of the Colon. Jacques W. Reeders & Gerd Rosenbusch. Ed. by Peter Winter. Tr. by Clifford Bergman et al. LC 93-30486. (Illus.). 1993. 199.00 (*0-86577-508-7*) Thieme Med Pubs.

Clinical Radiology for Medical Students. 2nd ed. K. T. Evans et al. (Illus.). 1987. pap. text ed. 34.95 (*0-407-01621-X*) Buttrwrth-Heinemann.

Clinical Radiology in Postgraduate Surgery. M. A. Al-Fallouji. (Illus.). 299p. 1992. 90.00 (*0-7506-0303-8*) Buttrwrth-Heinemann.

Clinical Radiology in the Tropics. Peter Cockshott & Howard Middlemiss. LC 79-40190. 244p. reprint ed. pap. 69.60 (*0-8357-3379-3*, 2039625) Bks Demand.

Clinical Radiology of the Horse. Janet A. Butler et al. (Illus.). 560p. (C). 1992. text ed. 268.95 (*0-8464-4162-4*) Beekman Pubs.

Clinical Radiology of the Horse. Janet A. Butler et al. (Illus.). 560p. 1993. 150.00 (*0-632-03271-5*) Blackwell Sci.

Clinical Radiology of the Liver, Pt. A. Ed. by Hans Herlinger et al. LC 82-14878. (Diagnostic Radiology Ser.: No. 1). (Illus.). 599p. reprint ed. pap. 170.80 (*0-7837-4308-4*, 2043999) Bks Demand.

Clinical Radiology of the Liver, Pt. B. Ed. by Hans Herlinger et al. LC 82-14878. (Diagnostic Radiology Ser.: No. 1). (Illus.). 583p. reprint ed. pap. 166.20 (*0-7837-4309-2*, 2043999) Bks Demand.

Clinical Radiology of the Small Intestine. Herlinger & Maglinte. 544p. 1989. text ed. 169.00 (*0-7216-4608-5*) Saunders.

Clinical Radiotherapy Physics. Lanzl. 1994. write for info. (*0-8493-6891-X*) CRC Pr.

Clinical Reactions to Food. M. H. Lessof. LC 82-11101. 222p. 1983. text ed. 99.95 (*0-471-10436-1*, A R Liss) Wiley.

Clinical Reasoning: Forms of Inquiry in Occupational Therapy. Cheryl Mattingly & Maureen H. Fleming. (Illus.). 378p. (C). 1993. text ed. 29.00 (*0-8036-5937-7*) Davis Co.

***Clinical Reasoning in Physical Disabilities.** Rebecca Dutton. LC 94-24714. 1995. write for info. (*0-683-02740-9*) Williams & Wilkins.

***Clinical Reasoning in the Health Professions.** Ed. by Joy Higgs & Mark Jones. LC 94-44572. 347p. 1995. 65.00 (*0-7506-0787-4*) Buttrwrth-Heinemann.

Clinical Recognition of Congenital Heart Disease. 4th ed. Joseph K. Perloff. LC 93-32195. 1994. text ed. 119.00 (*0-7216-5504-1*) Saunders.

Clinical Reference Cards. Children's Hospital Staff. 32p. (C). 1990. 12.50 (*0-8403-6166-1*) Kendall-Hunt.

Clinical Rehabilitation Assessment & Hearing Impairment: A Guide to Quality Assurance. Larry Stewart. 9.95 (*0-913072-69-9*, RB017) Natl Assn Deaf.

Clinical Relationship. Michael Kahn. 192p. (C). 1995. pap. text ed. write for info. (*0-7167-2194-5*) W H Freeman.

Clinical Relaxation Strategies. Kenneth L. Lichstein. LC 87-25296. (Personality Processes Ser.). 426p. 1988. text ed. 69.95 (*0-471-81592-6*) Wiley.

Clinical Relevance of Hemostaseological Findings: Abstracts. Ed. by E. Wenzel & P. Hellstern. (Journal: Haemostasis: Vol. 15). 88p. 1985. pap. 32.00 (*3-8055-4068-X*) S Karger.

Clinical Relevance of "Kindling" Ed. by Tom G. Bolwig & Michael R. Trimble. 1989. text ed. 114.00 (*0-471-92449-0*) Wiley.

***Clinical Relevance of the Self.** Kenneth Bragan. 160p. 1995. 55.00x (*0-415-12787-4*, C0569); pap. 16.95 (*0-415-12788-2*, C0570) Routledge.

Clinical Removable Partial Prosthodontics. 2nd ed. Kenneth L. Stewart et al. Ed. by Gregory Hacke. (Illus.). 695p. (C). 1992. text ed. 59.50 (*0-912791-98-5*) Ishiyaku Euro.

Clinical Repertory. John H. Clarke. 346p. (C). 1979. text ed. 39.95 (*0-8464-1000-1*) Beekman Pubs.

Clinical Repertory to the Dictionary of Materia Medica. John H. Clarke. 1979. 15.95 (*0-85032-061-5*) Formur Intl.

Clinical Reproductive Endocrinology. Ed. by Rodney P. Shearman. LC 84-12156. (Illus.). 776p. 1985. text ed. write for info. (*0-443-02645-9*) Churchill.

Clinical Reproductive Neuroendocrinology: Proceedings of the International Seminar on Reproductive Physiology & Sexual Endocrinology, 6th, Brussels, May-June, 1976. International Seminar on Reproductive Physiology & Sexual Endocrinology Staff. Ed. by P. O. Hubinont. (Progress in Reproductive Biology & Medicine Ser.: Vol. 2). (Illus.). 1977. 93.00 (*3-8055-2382-3*) S Karger.

Clinical Research As the Basis of Clinical Practice. Antczak-Bouckoms et al. Ed. by Katherine D. Vig & Peter S. Vig. (Craniofacial Growth Ser.: Vol. 25). (Illus.). 222p. 1991. 49.00 (*0-929921-21-6*) UM CHGD.

Clinical Research Careers in Psychiatry. Ed. by Harold A. Pincus & Herbert Pardes. LC 86-17249. (Issues in Psychiatry Ser.). 144p. 1986. pap. text ed. 21.00 (*0-88048-094-7*, 48-094-7) Am Psychiatric.

Clinical Research in Communicative Disorders. 2nd ed. M. N. Hegde. LC 93-41146. (Illus.). 485p. (C). 1994. text ed. 39.00 (*0-89079-594-0*, 6691) PRO-ED.

Clinical Research in Communicative Disorders: Principles & Strategies. M. N. Hegde. LC 90-9187. (Illus.). 451p. (C). 1987. text ed. 38.00 (*0-89079-349-2*, 1681) PRO-ED.

Clinical Research in Essential Hypertension. Michel E. Safar. 151p. 1989. pap. text ed. 65.95 (*0-471-56514-8*) Wiley.

Clinical Research in Gastroenterology, Vol. I. Ed. by S. Matern. (C). 1987. lib. bdg. 78.00 (*0-85200-696-9*) Kluwer Ac.

Clinical Research in Gastroenterology 2. Ed. by S. Matern. (C). 1989. lib. bdg. 60.00 (*0-7923-8906-9*) Kluwer Ac.

***Clinical Research Method Com.** Lewith. 1993. 144.50 (*1-56593-128-9*, 0449) Singular Publishing.

***Clinical Research Opportunities.** Matthew Heller & Anthony Boyle. Ed. by Kathy Swanson. 175p. 1995. pap. write for info. (*1-57066-030-1*) Practice Mgmt Info.

An Asterisk (*) at the beginning of an entry indicates that the title is appearing in BIP for the first time.

An Asterisk (*) at the beginning of an entry indicates that the title is appearing in BIP for the first time.

C

Clinical Ultrasound: Cardiac Ultrasound: A Comprehensive Text. Ed. by Peter Wilde. (Illus.). 550p. 1992. text ed. 165.00 (*0-443-04280-2*) Churchill.

Clinical Ultrasound: Ultrasound in Obstetrics & Gynaecology: A Comprehensive Text. Ed. by Keith Dewbury et al. (Illus.). 600p. 1993. text ed. 165.00 (*0-443-04279-9*) Churchill.

Clinical Urography: An Atlas & Textbook of Urological Imaging, 3 vols., 1. Pollack. 3168p. 1989. text ed. 185.00 (*0-7216-1556-2*) Saunders.

Clinical Urography: An Atlas & Textbook of Urological Imaging, 3 vols., 2. Pollack. 3168p. 1989. text ed. 185.00 (*0-7216-1557-0*) Saunders.

Clinical Urography: An Atlas & Textbook of Urological Imaging, 3 vols., 3. Pollack. 3168p. 1989. text ed. 185.00 (*0-7216-1558-9*) Saunders.

Clinical Urography: An Atlas & Textbook of Urological Imaging, 3 vols., Set. Pollack. 3168p. 1989. 475.00 (*0-7216-1555-4*) Saunders.

Clinical Urogynecology. Mark D. Walters & Mickey M. Karram. LC 93-18612. 432p. 1993. 65.00 (*0-8016-5673-7*) Mosby Yr Bk.

***Clinical Urologic Practice.** Ed. by Barry S. Stein et al. LC 94-22583. (Medical Bks.). 1600p. (C). 1995. 150.00 (*0-393-71023-8*) Norton.

Clinical Urology. Robert J. Krane et al. (Illus.). 1250p. (C). 1993. text ed. 175.00 (*0-397-51161-2*, Lippincott Medical) Lippincott.

***Clinical Use & Interpretation of the Wechsler Intelligence Scale for Children.** 3rd rev. ed. Shawn Cooper. LC 95-14202. 1995. write for info. (*0-398-06523-3*); pap. write for info. (*0-398-06524-1*) C C Thomas.

***Clinical Use & Interpretation of the Wechsler Intelligence Scale for Children-Revised.** Shawn Cooper. (Illus.). 310p. 1982. pap. 29.95 (*0-398-06075-4*) C C Thomas.

Clinical Use & Interpretation of the Wechsler Intelligence Scale for Children-Revised. Shawn Cooper. (Illus.). 310p. (C). 1982. 48.95x (*0-398-04750-2*) C C Thomas.

Clinical Use of Antibodies: Tumors, Infection, Infarction, Rejection in the Diagnosis of AIDS. Ed. by R. P. Baum et al. (C). 1991. lib. bdg. 80.50 (*0-7923-1424-7*) Kluwer Ac.

Clinical Use of Anticonvulsants in Psychiatric Disorders. Robert Post et al. LC 89-50472. (Illus.). 184p. 1989. 29.95 (*0-939957-20-5*) Demos Vermande.

Clinical Use of Antiviral Drugs. Ed. by Erik DeClerq. (Developments in Medical Virology Ser.). 416p. 1988. lib. bdg. 127.00 (*0-89838-357-9*) Kluwer Ac.

Clinical Use of Calcium Antagonist Drugs. Lionel H. Opie. (C). 1989. lib. bdg. 97.00 (*0-7923-0155-2*) Kluwer Ac.

Clinical Use of Dreams. Walter Bonime. (Psychoanalysis: Examined & Re-Examined Ser.). 343p. (C). 1982. reprint ed. lib. bdg. 35.00 (*0-306-79710-0*) Da Capo.

Clinical Use of Electron Microscopy in Dermatology. 5th ed. Alvin S. Zelickson. Ed. by Jess H. Mottaz. LC 90-71875. (Illus.). 79p. 1990. reprint ed. 40.00 (*0-9628449-0-X*) Westwood-Squibb Pharm.

Clinical Use of Intravenous Immunoglobulins. U. E. Nydegger & A. Morell. 1986. text ed. 105.00 (*0-12-523282-9*) Acad Pr.

Clinical Use of Mechanical Ventilation. 2nd ed. C. C. Rattenborg. (Illus.). 1989. pap. 24.95 (*0-8151-7071-8*, Yr Bk Med Pubs) Mosby Yr Bk.

Clinical Use of Mechanical Ventilation. Ed. by Christen C. Rattenborg. LC 80-25269. (Illus.). 383p. reprint ed. pap. 109.20 (*0-8357-7629-8*, 2056952) Bks Demand.

***Clinical Use of Mitoxantrone for Injection Concentrate: Clinical Use in Advanced Breast Cancer.** Ed. by Chris Fellner. (Orig.). 1994. write for info. (*1-57130-009-0*) Medicine Grp USA.

***Clinical Use of Mitoxantrone for Injection Concentrate: Clinical Use in Lymphoma.** Ed. by Chris Fellner. (Orig.). 1994. pap. write for info. (*1-57130-012-0*) Medicine Grp USA.

Clinical Use of Neuroleptic Plasma Levels. Ed. by Stephen R. Marder et al. LC 93-16126. 144p. 1993. text ed. 26.00 (*0-88048-524-8*) Am Psychiatric.

Clinical Use of Sex Steroids: Based on the Proceedings of the Fourth Annual Symposium on Gynecologic Endocrinology, Held May 7-9, 1979 at the University of Tennessee, Memphis, Tennessee. Symposium on Gynecologic Endocrinology Staff. LC 80-53576. (Illus.). 390p. reprint ed. pap. 111.20 (*0-8357-8579-3*, 2034945) Bks Demand.

Clinical Use of Story Telling: Emphasizing the TAT with Children & Adolescents. Hedwig Teglasi. LC 92-10779. 1992. 50.95 (*0-205-13938-8*, Longwood Div) Allyn.

Clinical Use of the Palmaz-Schatz Intracoronary Stent. Ed. by Howard C. Herrmann & John W. Hirshfeld, Jr. LC 93-11237. (Illus.). 208p. 1993. 45.00 (*0-87993-565-0*) Futura Pub.

Clinical Uses of Cerebral, Brainstem & Spinal Somatosensory Evoked Potentials. Ed. by John E. Desmedt. (Progress in Clinical Neurophysiology Ser.: Vol. 7). (Illus.). 1979. 110.50 (*3-8055-2936-8*) S Karger.

Clinical Uses of Fluorides: A State of the Art Conference on the Uses of Fluorides in Clinical Dentistry. Ed. by Stephen H. Wei. LC 84-19374. 250p. reprint ed. pap. 71.30 (*0-7837-2753-4*, 2043133) Bks Demand.

Clinical Uses of Radionuclides: Critical Comparison with Other Techniques: Proceedings. Ed. by Francis A. Goswitz et al. LC 72-660271. (AEC Symposium Ser.). 718p. 1972. 26.00 (*0-87079-002-1*, CONF-711101); fiche 9.00 (*0-87079-164-8*, CONF-711101) DOE.

Clinical Utilization of Microcomputer. Romanczyk. (C). 1986. pap. 19.95 (*0-205-14468-3*, H4468) Allyn.

Clinical Vademecum of the Medical Practice: Vademecum Clinico del Medico Practico, del Sintoma a la Receta. 5th ed. 1398p. 1982. 95.00 (*0-8288-1861-4*, S25225) Fr & Eur.

Clinical Vademecum of the Medical Practice (Vademecum Clinique du Medecin Practicien) 13th ed. V. Fattorusso & Otto Ritter. 1760p. (FRE.). 1990. boxed 125.00 (*0-7859-4631-4*, F137430) Fr & Eur.

Clinical Vascular Disease. Ed. by John A. Spittell, Jr. LC 82-12974. (Cardiovascular Clinics Ser.: Vol. 13, No. 2). (Illus.). 346p. 1983. text ed. 45.00 (*0-8036-8087-2*) Davis Co.

Clinical Vectorcardiography & Electrocardiography. Cooksey. Date not set. write for info. (*0-8151-1852-X*, Yr Bk Med Pubs) Mosby Yr Bk.

Clinical Venereology for Nurses & Students. B. Schwartz & R. Robinson. LC 65-27381. (Commonwealth & International Library). 1966. pap. 66.00 (*0-08-011602-7*, Pub. by Pergamon Repr UK) Franklin.

Clinical Versus Statistical Prediction: A Theoretical Analysis & a Review of the Evidence. Paul E. Meehl. LC 54-11774. 159p. reprint ed. pap. 45.40 (*0-317-29449-0*, 2055890) Bks Demand.

Clinical Veterinary Dentistry. Wiggs. 1995. text ed. write for info. (*0-397-51385-2*) Lippincott.

Clinical Virology in Oral Medicine & Dentistry. Crispian Scully & Lakshman Samaranayake. (Illus.). 448p. (C). 1992. 175.00 (*0-521-40102-X*) Cambridge U Pr.

Clinical Virology Manual. Steven Specter & Gerald J. Lancz. 554p. 1986. 79.25 (*0-444-01085-8*) Elsevier.

Clinical Virology Manual. 2nd ed. Ed. by Steven Specter & Gerald J. Lancz. (Illus.). 699p. 1992. boxed 85.00 (*0-8385-1257-7*, A1257-3) Appleton & Lange.

Clinical Visual Optics. 2nd ed. A. G. Bennett & R. B. Rabbetts. (Illus.). 529p. 1990. text ed. 110.00 (*0-7506-0454-9*) Buttrwrth-Heinemann.

Clinical Vitaminology: Methods & Interpretation. Herman Baker & Oscar Frank. LC 68-24678. 250p. reprint ed. pap. 71.30 (*0-317-28628-5*, 2051326) Bks Demand.

Clinical Voice Disorders. 3rd ed. Arnold E. Aronson. (Illus.). 398p. 1990. text ed. 45.00 (*0-86577-337-8*) Thieme Med Pubs.

Clinical Voice Pathology: Theory & Management. Joseph Stemple. (C). 1984. write for info. (*0-675-20128-4*, Merrill Pub Co) Macmillan.

***Clinical Voice Pathology: Theory & Management.** 2nd ed. Joe Stemple et al. (Illus.). 352p. (C). 1994. 49.95 (*1-56593-342-7*, 0640) Singular Publishing.

Clinical Work with Adolescents. Judith M. Mishne. 320p. 1986. text ed. 29.95 (*0-02-921260-X*) Free Pr.

Clinical Work with Children. Judith M. Mishne. 1983. text ed. 29.95 (*0-02-921630-3*) Free Pr.

Clinical Work with Maltreated Children & Their Families. Ed. by Shirley M. Ehrenkranz et al. (Psychoanalytic Crosscurrents Ser.). 224p. 1989. 45.00x (*0-8147-2174-5*) NYU Pr.

Clinical Work with Substance-Abusing Clients. Ed. by Shulamith L. Straussner. LC 92-1574. (Substance Abuse Ser.). 420p. 1992. lib. bdg. 35.95 (*0-89862-193-3*) Guilford Pr.

Clinical Workbook for Psychotherapists. Robert Langs. 506p. 1992. pap. 52.50 (*1-85575-004-X*, Pub. by Karnac Bks UK) Brunner-Mazel.

***Clinical Wound Management.** Prem P. Gogia. 300p. 1995. pap. 35.00 (*1-55642-234-2*, 42342) SLACK Inc.

Clinically Adapted Instruments for the Multiply Handicapped: A Sourcebook. rev. ed. Comp. by Cynthia Clark & Donna Chadwick. (Illus.). 200p. 1980. pap. 9.95 (*0-918812-13-5*, ST 032) MMB Music.

Clinically Applied Anthropology. Noel Chrisman & Thomas Maretski. 1982. lib. bdg. 149.50 (*90-277-1418-5*) Kluwer Ac.

Clinically Applied Microcirculation Research. Ed. by John H. Barker et al. 560p. 1995. 250.00 (*0-8493-4870-6*, 4870) CRC Pr.

Clinically Important Adverse Drug Interactions, Vol. 3: Gastrointestinal, Haematological & Infectious Disease Therapy. J. C. Petrie & L. E. Cluff. 1985. 153.50 (*0-444-80606-7*) Elsevier.

***Clinically Organ-Confined Adenocarcinoma of the Prostate: Natural History, Selection Criteria for Radical Prostatectomy & Prognostic Factors Based on Long-Term Follow-Up.** Ed. by H. P. Schmid. 74p. 1994. pap. 23.00 (*3-7985-0998-0*) Spr-Verlag.

Clinically Oriented Anatomy. 3rd ed. Keith L. Moore. (Illus.). 930p. 1992. 53.00 (*0-683-06133-X*) Williams & Wilkins.

Clinica's Factbook 1993 Medical Device & Diagnostics Industry Data. (Market Research Reports: No. 378). 220p. 1993. 475.00 (*0-317-05488-0*) Theta Corp.

Clinician. Jack Rudman. (Career Examination Ser.: C-150). 1994. pap. 34.95 (*0-8373-0150-5*) Nat Learn.

Clinician & Chemist: The Relationship of the Laboratory to the Physician: Proceedings of the First Arnold O. Beckman Conference in Clinical Chemistry. Donald Young et al. LC 78-72880. 375p. 1979. 20.00 (*0-915274-08-6*) Am Assn Clinical Chem.

Clinician, Part-Time. Jack Rudman. (Career Examination Ser.: C-1197). 1994. pap. 29.95 (*0-8373-1197-7*) Nat Learn.

Clinician's Companion: A Study Guide for Effective & Humane Patient Care. David H. Alpers & Wittenberg. (Illus.). 224p. 1986. 29.95 (*0-316-03511-4*, Little Med Div) Little.

Clinician's Guide to Ace Inhibition. Ed. by John Cleland. (Illus.). 224p. 1993. text ed. 36.00 (*0-443-04855-X*) Churchill.

***Clinician's Guide to Child Custody Evalutions.** 19th ed. Marc J. Ackerman. 49.95 (*0-615-00189-0*) Wiley.

Clinician's Guide to Cocaine Addiction: Theory, Research, & Treatment. Ed. by Thomas R. Kosten & Herbert D. Kleber. LC 92-1521. (Substance Abuse Ser.). 404p. 1992. lib. bdg. 42.00 (*0-89862-192-5*) Guilford Pr.

Clinician's Guide to Cognitive Assessment. John R. Hodges. LC 93-28360. 1994. pap. 27.95 (*0-19-262394-X*) OUP.

Clinician's Guide to Diagnostic Cytology. Gilbert B. Schumann & V. Franklin Colon. LC 82-2783. (Illus.). 291p. reprint ed. pap. 83.00 (*0-8357-6762-0*, 2035423) Bks Demand.

Clinician's Guide to Diagnostic Imaging: Cost-Effective Pathways. 2nd ed. Zachary D. Grossman et al. 288p. 1987. pap. text ed. 33.50 (*0-88167-285-8*) Raven.

Clinician's Guide to Forensic Psychological Assessment. Michael P. Maloney. 288p. (C). 1985. text ed. 35.00 (*0-02-919850-X*) Free Pr.

Clinician's Guide to Fungal Disease. Roberts et al. LC 84-14932. (Infectious Diseases & Antimicrobial Agents Ser.: Vol. 5). (Illus.). 264p. 1984. 110.00 (*0-8247-7190-7*) Dekker.

Clinician's Guide to Managed Mental Health Care. Norman Winegar. LC 91-22226. 342p. 1992. lib. bdg. 39.95 (*1-56024-204-3*) Haworth Pr.

Clinician's Guide to Neuropsychological Assessment. Ed. by Rodney D. Vanderploeg. 320p. 1993. text ed. 69.95 (*0-8058-1253-9*); pap. text ed. 27.50 (*0-8058-1254-7*) L Erlbaum Assocs.

Clinician's Guide to Non-Insulin-Dependent Diabetes Mellitus Pathogenesis & Treatment. Reaven. 152p. 1989. 65.00 (*0-8247-8083-3*) Dekker.

Clinician's Guide to Psychodrama. 2nd ed. Eva Leveton. LC 91-4823. Orig. Title: Psychodrama for the Timid Clinician. (Illus.). 192p. 1991. pap. 24.95 (*0-8261-2262-0*) Springer Pub.

Clinician's Guide to Reading Freud. Peter L. Giovacchini. LC 82-14891. 272p. 1982. 35.00 (*0-87668-484-3*) Aronson.

Clinician's Guide to Sexually Transmitted Infections. Stuart A. Levin et al. (Illus.). 150p. 1987. 31.95 (*0-8151-5401-1*, TID-1, Yr Bk Med Pubs) Mosby Yr Bk.

***Clinician's Guide to the Personality Profiles of Alcohol & Drug Abusers: Typological Descriptions Using the MMPI.** Donald J. Tosi et al. LC 93-24274. (Illus.). 156p. 1993. pap. 22.95 (*0-398-06463-6*) C C Thomas.

Clinician's Guide to the Personality Profiles of Alcohol & Drug Abusers: Typological Descriptions Using the MMPI. Donald J. Tosi et al. LC 93-24274. (Illus.). 156p. (C). 1993. text ed. 37.95 (*0-398-05885-7*) C C Thomas.

Clinician's Guide to Ulcerative Colitis & Crohn's Disease. P. P. Jewell et al. (Illus.). 80p. (Orig.). 1992. pap. text ed. 36.00 (*0-443-04803-7*) Churchill.

Clinician's Handbook: Integrated Diagnostic, Assessment, & Intervention in Adult & Intervention in Adult & Adolescent Psychopathology. 3rd ed. Robert G. Meyer. LC 92-21932. 496p. 1992. boxed write for info. (*0-205-14230-3*) Allyn.

***Clinician's Handbook: Integrated Diagnostics, Assessment, & Intervention in Adult & Adolescent Psychopathology.** 4th ed. Robert G. Meyer & Sarah E. Deitsch. 1995. text ed. 66.95 (*0-205-17181-8*) Allyn.

***Clinician's Handbook of Childhood Psychopathology.** Ed. by Martin M. Josephson & Robert T. Porter. LC 78-24831. 516p. 1995. pap. 45.00 (*1-56821-552-5*) Aronson.

***Clinician's Handbook of Preventive Services, 2 vols., Set.** (Medical Ser.). 1995. lib. bdg. 627.95 (*0-8490-7514-9*) Gordon Pr.

Clinician's Pocket Guide to Home Parenteral Medications. Date not set. pap. text ed. 12.95 (*1-883202-01-9*) Spec Clin Srvs.

Clinician's Pocket Guide to Home Parenteral Medications. 2nd ed. Roger S. Klotz & Kathryn T. Andrusko-Furphy. 233p. 1993. pap. text ed. 8.95 (*1-883202-00-0*) Spec Clin Srvs.

Clinician's Pocket Reference. 7th ed. Leonard G. Gomella. (Illus.). 636p. (C). 1993. pap. text ed. 24.95 (*0-8385-1222-4*, A1222-7) Appleton & Lange.

Clinician's Reading List on Alcohol & Other Drug Dependencies. 1992. lib. bdg. 88.95 (*0-8490-8746-5*) Gordon Pr.

Clinician's Thesaurus: A Guidebook for Wording Psychological Reports & Other Evaluations. Edward L. Zuckerman. 140p. 1989. spiral bd. 19.95 (*0-685-45115-1*, XTCTBP) Three Wishes.

Clinician's Thesaurus: A Guidebook to Wording Psychological Reports & Other Evaluations. 2nd ed. Edward L. Zuckerman. (Clinician's Toolbox Ser.). 174p. 1992. reprint ed. pap. text ed. 19.95 (*0-9622281-2-5*) Three Wishes.

***Clinician's Thesaurus: The Guidebook for Writing Psychological Reports.** 4th ed. Edward L. Zuckerman. 1995. pap. text ed. 29.95 (*0-89862-842-3*) Guilford Pr.

Clinician's Thesaurus Three: Electronic Edition. 3rd ed. Edward Zuckerman. 288p. (C). 1993. Incl. computer disk version for IBM & compatibles 3.5" or 5.25" disks. 3.5 hd, 5.25 hd 149.95 (*0-9622281-6-8*) Three Wishes.

Clinician's Thesaurus Three: The Guidebook for Wording Psychological Reports & Other Evaluations. 3rd ed. Edward Zuckerman. 288p. (C). 1993. pap. text ed., spiral bd. 24.95 (*0-9622281-4-1*) Three Wishes.

Clinician's View of Neuromuscular Disease. 2nd ed. Michael H. Brooke. (Illus.). 388p. 1986. 55.00 (*0-683-01064-6*) Williams & Wilkins.

Clinico-Pathological Atlas of Congenital Fundus Disorders. Juan Orellana & Alan H. Friedman. LC 92-49529. 1993. 150.00 (*0-387-97936-0*) Spr-Verlag.

Clinico-Pharmacological Models for the Assay of Topical Corticoids. H. Wendt & P. J. Frosch. (Illus.). 64p. 1982. pap. 26.50 (*3-8055-3538-4*) S Karger.

Clinicopathologic Principles for Veterinary Medicine. Ed. by Wayne F. Robinson & Clive R. Huxtable. (Illus.). 452p. 1988. 69.95 (*0-521-30883-6*) Cambridge U Pr.

Clinicopathological Aspects of Creutzfeld-Jacob Disease. Ed. by T. Mizutani & H. Shiraki. 325p. 1986. 147.25 (*0-444-80694-6*) Elsevier.

Clinics, Contraception & Communication: Evaluation Studies of Family Planning Programs in Four Latin American Countries. Ed. by J. Mayone Stycos. LC 79-184865. (Illus.). 1973. 26.00 (*0-89197-625-6*) Irvington.

Clinimetrics. Alvan R. Feinstein. LC 86-28241. 288p. 1987. text ed. 35.00 (*0-300-03806-2*) Yale U Pr.

Clinker Boatbuilding. John Leather. (Illus.). 224p. 1987. pap. 19.95 (*0-229-11818-6*, Adlard Coles) Sheridan.

Clinker Islands: A Complete History of the Galapagos Archipelago. Lillian Otterman. LC 92-62391. 276p. 1993. pap. 16.95 (*1-881117-03-0*) McGuinn & McGuire.

Clinker Storage Silo for Canada Cement Lafarge. (PCI Journal Reprints Ser.). 12p. 1981. pap. 6.00 (*0-686-40154-9*, JR251) P-PCI.

Clint. James A. McClintock. 1991. 8.95 (*0-533-09260-4*) Vantage.

***Clint Black: One Emotion.** Ed. by Carol Cuellar. (Illus.). 48p. (Orig.). (YA). 1995. pap. text ed. 16.95 (*0-89724-503-2*) Warner Brothers.

***Clint Eastwood.** RH Value Publishing Staff. 1995. pap. 9.99 (*0-517-12137-9*) Random.

***Clint Eastwood.** Robert Tanitch. (Illus.). 192p. 1995. 24.95 (*0-289-80132-X*, Pub. by Studio Vista Bks UK) Sterling.

***Clint Eastwood: A Biography.** Minty Clinch. (Illus.). 248p. 1995. 22.95 (*0-450-59439-4*, Pub. by Hodder & Stoughton Ltd UK) Trafalgar.

Clint Eastwood: A Cultural Production. Paul Smith. LC 92-34015. (American Culture Ser.: Vol. 8). 310p. (C). 1993. text ed. 44.95 (*0-8166-1958-1*); pap. 17.95 (*0-8166-1960-3*) U of Minn Pr.

Clint Eastwood: Hollywood's Loner. Michael Munn. (Illus.). 258p. 1993. 24.95 (*0-86051-790-X*, Robson-Parkwest) Parkwest Pubns.

Clint Eastwood: Malpaso. Fuensanta Plaza. LC 91-71749. (Illus.). 256p. (Orig.). 1991. pap. 24.95 (*0-9629481-9-5*) Ex Libris CA.

Clint Eastwood: Riding High. Douglas Thompson. LC 92-46897. 224p. 1993. 18.95 (*0-8092-3767-9*) Contemp Bks.

Clint Eastwood: The Man & His Films. Edward Gallafent. (Illus.). 256p. 1994. 24.95 (*0-8264-0665-3*) Continuum.

Clinton. Sterling Plump. 1976. 2.00 (*0-910296-43-X*) Broadside Pr.

Clinton: Young Man in a Hurry. Jim Moore. (Illus.). 290p. 1992. 22.95 (*1-56530-006-8*) Summit TX.

Clinton Adams: Paintings & Watercolors 1945-1987. Ed. by Peter Walch. (Illus.). 32p. (Orig.). (C). 1987. pap. 6.00 (*0-944282-00-8*) UNM Art Mus.

***Clinton Budget 1996.** 400p. (Orig.). 1995. pap. 195.00 (*0-7605-1677-4*) Rector Pr.

***Clinton Chronicle Trading Card Set.** 1995. boxed 12.95 (*1-56060-217-1*) InBook.

***Clinton Chronicles.** Patrick Matrisciana. 320p. (Orig.). 1994. pap. 12.95 (*1-878993-63-1*) Jeremiah Pubs.

***Clinton Confidential: The Climb to Power - The Unauthorized Biography of Bill & Hillary Clinton.** George Carpozi, Jr. LC 94-61245. (Illus.). 540p. 1995. 23.95 (*0-9640479-0-X*) E Dalton Bks.

***Clinton Countdown to 1997 - the Final Year 1996 Desk Calendar.** 3rd rev. ed. C. W. Kendall, 3rd. 386p. Date not set. pap. write for info. (*0-9636611-3-2*) Lame Duck.

***Clinton Health Care Plan: Dead on Arrival.** Colin Gordon. (Open Magazine Pamphlet Ser.: No. 32). 29p. (Orig.). (C). 1995. pap. text ed. 4.00 (*1-884519-12-1*) Open Media.

Clinton Health Plan. John C. Goodman et al. (Illus.). 48p. (Orig.). 1994. pap. text ed. 10.00 (*1-56808-018-2*, 184) Natl Ctr Pol.

Clinton Health Plan: Both Sides. Ed. by Lewis B. Sckolnick. (Illus.). 350p. (Orig.). (C). 1994. pap. 45.00 (*1-57205-284-8*) Rector Pr.

***Clinton Presidency: Campaigning, Governing & the Psychology of Leadership.** Stanley A. Renshon. LC 94-27952. (C). 1994. pap. text ed. 19.95 (*0-8133-1977-3*) Westview.

***Clinton Presidency: Campaigning, Governing & the Psychology of Leadership.** Stanley A. Renshon. LC 94-27952. (C). 1994. text ed. 64.95 (*0-8133-1976-5*) Westview.

***Clinton Presidency: First Appraisals.** Colin Campbell et al. (Illus.). 350p. (C). 1995. 30.00x (*1-56643-013-5*) Chatham Hse Pubs.

***Clinton Presidency: First Appraisals.** Colin Campbell et al. (Illus.). 350p. (C). 1995. pap. text ed. 19.95x (*1-56643-014-3*) Chatham Hse Pubs.

Clinton Revolution: An Inside Look at the New Administration. Koichi Suzuki et al. LC 93-1821. 162p. (Orig.). (C). 1993. lib. bdg. 47.95 (*0-8191-9171-X*); pap. text ed. 25.95 (*0-8191-9172-8*) U Pr of Amer.

Clinton Silver Rush: A Second Chance for Silver Investors. James Digeorgia. Ed. by Martin D. Weiss. 69p. (Orig.). Date not set. pap. text ed. 72.00 (*0-941739-03-1*) M D Weiss Pub.

Clinton Street Crime Wave. Laban C. Hill. (J). (gr. 4-7). 1994. 3.50 (*0-553-48186-X*) Bantam.

Clinton Tax Plan: What It Will Cost You--& Tax Saving Steps You Can Take. J K Lasser Editors. 1993. mass mkt. 4.99 (*0-671-87990-1*) PB.

Clinton Twins, & Other Stories. Archibald Marshall. LC 70-130062. (Short Story Index Reprint Ser.). 1977. 19.95 (*0-8369-3661-2*) Ayer.

ClintonCare: Putting Government in Charge of Your Health. Barry Asmus. 101p. (Orig.). 1994. pap. 9.95 (*0-9640421-0-X*) Ameripress.

Clintons: Meet the First Family. Chip Eliot. LC 93-14027. (Illus.). 24p. (J). (gr. 2-6). 1993. pap. text ed. 1.95 (*0-8167-3243-4*) Troll Assocs.

Clintons, & Others. Archibald Marshall. LC 73-130063. (Short Story Index Reprint Ser.). 1977. 24.95 (*0-8369-3662-0*) Ayer.

An Asterisk (*) at the beginning of an entry indicates that the title is appearing in BIP for the first time.

C

An Asterisk (*) at the beginning of an entry indicates that the title is appearing in BIP for the first time.

1325

***Clips & Quips: Copyright-Free Drawings for Libraries & Schools.** Sherry L. Watson. (Illus.). 64p. 1994. write for info. (0-9638913-0-8) Central Colo Lib.

Clips from Tom M. Olson: Nuggets from the Writings of Tom M. Olson Provide the Only-Way to View Events. Ed. by Louise L. Dick. LC 86-90141. (LeTourneau One-Way Ser.: Vol. 10). 251p. (Orig.). 1986. pap. 6.95 (0-935899-06-5) LeTourneau Pr.

Cliques & Clones. Fran Sciacca & Jill Sciacca. (Lifelines Ser.). (YA). (gr. 7 up). 1987. pap. 3.95 (0-89066-100-6) World Wide Pubs.

Cliques & Clones: Facing Peer Pressure. Fran Sciacca & Jill Sciacca. (Lifelines Ser.). 64p. (YA). 1992. pap. 3.99 (0-310-48031-0) Zondervan.

Clitandre ou l'Innocence Delivree. Pierre Corneille. 151p. (FRE.). 1949. pap. 24.95 (0-7859-5372-8) Fr & Eur.

***Clitics: A Comprehensive Bibliography 1892-1991.** Ed. by Joel A. Nevis et al. LC 94-27029. (Library & Information Sources in Linguistics). xxvii, 233p. 1994. lib. bdg. 69.00 (1-55619-252-5) Benjamins North Am.

Clitophon & Leucippe. Achilles Tatius. (Loeb Classical Library: No. 45). 478p. 18.95 (0-674-99050-1) HUP.

Clitoral Kiss: A Fun Guide to Oral Sex, Oral Massage & Other Oral Delights for Men & Women. Kenneth R. Stubbs & Chyrelle D. Chasen. (Illus.). 88p. (Orig.). 1993. pap. 16.95 (0-939263-08-4) Secret Garden.

Clitoris. Thomas P. Lowry. LC 73-704. (Illus.). 304p. 1976. 22.50 (0-87527-112-X) Green.

Clitoris Lost. Lynn Lonidier. 1989. pap. 11.95 (0-317-04319-6) Man-Root.

***Clivage et Integration du Moi Chez Julien Green.** Flavia Vernescu. LC 93-87000. 136p. (FRE.). 1994. lib. bdg. 29.95 (0-917786-99-8) Summa Pubns.

Clive & Duplix: The Beginning of Empire. Henry Dodwell. (C). 1989. reprint ed. 20.00 (81-206-0394-X, Pub. by Asian Educ Servs II) S Asia.

Clive Barker, Illustrator. Clive Barker & Fred Burke. 1990. pap. 19.95 (1-56060-028-4) Eclipse Bks.

Clive Barker, Illustrator. Clive Barker & Fred Burke. 1990. 40.00 (1-56060-027-6) Eclipse Bks.

Clive Barker Illustrator, No. 2: The Art of Clive Barker. Clive Barker. (Illus.). 1993. pap. 19.95 (1-56060-199-X) Eclipse Bks.

Clive Barker's Books of Blood, Vol. 1. Clive Barker. 224p. 1986. mass mkt. 5.99 (0-425-08389-6) Berkley Pub.

Clive Barker's Books of Blood, Vol. I. large type ed. Clive Barker. 1990. pap. 17.95 (0-7927-0295-6, C0397, Curley Lrg Print) Chivers N Amer.

Clive Barker's Books of Blood, Vol. 2. Clive Barker. 208p. 1986. mass mkt. 5.99 (0-425-08739-5) Berkley Pub.

Clive Barker's Books of Blood, Vol. 3. Clive Barker. 208p. 1986. mass mkt. 5.99 (0-425-09347-6) Berkley Pub.

Clive Barker's Shadows in Eden. Ed. by Stephen Jones. (Illus.). 504p. 1991. 39.95 (0-88733-073-8) Underwood-Miller.

Clive Barker's Shadows in Eden: The Books, Films, & Art of Clive Barker. Ed. by Stephen Jones. (Illus.). 512p. 1993. pap. 15.95 (0-88733-171-8) Underwood-Miller.

Clive Barker's Short Stories: Imagination As Metaphor in the Books of Blood & Other Works. Gary Hoppenstand. LC 94-8010. 232p. 1994. lib. bdg. 32.50 (0-89950-984-3) McFarland & Co.

Clive Bell's Eye. William G. Bywater. LC 74-23853. (Illus.). 250p. reprint ed. pap. 71.30 (0-318-39775-7, 2033177) Bks Demand.

Clive Eats Alligators. Alison Lester. (J). (ps). 1991. pap. 4.95 (0-395-58408-6) HM.

Clive M. Schmithoff's Select Essays on International Trade Law. Ed. by Chia-Jui Cheng. (C). 1988. lib. bdg. 322.50 (90-247-3702-8) Kluwer Ac.

Clive McCay, Nutrition Pioneer: Biographical Memoirs by His Wife. Jeanette B. McCay. LC 94-10013. 1994. write for info. (1-881539-04-0) Tabby Hse Bks.

***Cliveden.** Jonathan Marsden. (Illus.). 96p. 1995. pap. 10.95 (0-7078-0245-8, Pub. by Natl Trust UK) Trafalgar.

***Cliveden: The Place & the People.** James Crathorne. (Illus.). 240p. 1995. 55.00 (1-85585-223-3, Pub. by Coll & Brown) Trafalgar.

Clixi: Exploring Shape & Space. Peter Patilla. Ed. by Meg Stillman. 48p. (YA). 1994. student ed 7.95 (1-884461-09-3) NES Arnold.

***Clixi Technology.** Eric Parkinson. Ed. by Meg Stillman. (Illus.). 25p. (J). (gr. 3-9). 1994. 9.95 (1-884461-10-7) NES Arnold.

Clizek, Be Strong. Yitzchack Pomerantz. LC 93-72594. (Illus.). 300p. 1993. 18.95 (1-56062-225-3) CIS Comm.

CLMA Guide to Managing a Clinical Laboratory. Ed. by Bettina G. Martin. (Illus.). 95p. (Orig.). 1991. pap. text ed. 35.00 (0-9625414-1-9) Clinical Lab Mgmnt Assn.

Cloak & Dagger: Predator & Prey. Mantlo et al. 64p. 1988. 5.95 (0-87135-125-0) Marvel Entmnt.

Cloak & Dagger Fiction: A Guide to Spy Thrillers. 2nd ed. Myron J. Smith, Jr. 431p. 1982. 16.95 (0-87436-328-4) Regina Bks.

Cloak & Dagger Fiction: An Annotated Guide to Spy Thrillers. Myron J. Smith & Terry White. LC 94-22017. (Bibliographies & Indexes in World Literature Ser.: Vol. 45). 896p. 1995. text ed. 95.00 (0-313-27700-1, Greenwood Pr) Greenwood.

Cloak & Gavel: FBI Wiretaps, Bugs, Informers, & the Supreme Court. Alexander Charns. (Illus.). 240p. (C). 1992. 24.95 (0-252-01871-0) U of Ill Pr.

Cloak for the Dreamer. Aileen Friedman. LC 94-11274. (Brainy Day Bks.). (Illus.). (J). 1995. 14.95 (0-590-48987-9) Scholastic Inc.

Cloak of Aesir. John W. Campbell. LC 75-10664. (Classics of Science Fiction Ser.). 255p. 1976. reprint ed. 15.00 (0-88355-359-7); reprint ed. pap. 10.00 (0-88355-449-6) Hyperion Conn.

Cloak of Competence. rev. ed. Robert B. Edgerton. 276p. (C). 1993. 35.00 (0-520-08225-7); pap. 15.00 (0-520-08226-5) U CA Pr.

Cloak of Competence: Stigma in the Lives of the Mentally Retarded. Robert B. Edgerton. LC 67-14116. 1967. pap. 13.00 (0-520-01899-0) U CA Pr.

Cloak of Consciousness. Harold Klemp. (Mahanta Transcripts Ser.: Bk. 5). 294p. 1991. pap. 14.00 (1-57043-006-3) ECKANKAR.

Cloak of Consciousness. Harold Klemp. LC 91-70143. (Illus.). 1991. pap. 14.00 (0-88155-088-4) Illum Way Pub.

Cloak of Darkness. Ann Brahms. 1992. mass mkt. 4.50 (0-8217-3697-3) Zebra.

Cloak of Darkness. Sara Wood. (Presents Ser.). 1993. mass mkt. 2.99 (0-373-11573-3, 1-11573-2) Harlequin Bks.

Cloak of Illusion. John M. Roberts. 288p. (Orig.). 1985. 2.95 (0-8125-5202-4) Tor Bks.

***Cloak of Shadows.** Ed Greenwood. (Shadow of Avatar Ser.). 320p. (Orig.). 1995. pap. 4.95 (0-7869-0301-5) TSR Inc.

Clochards Celestes. Jack Kerouac. 384p. (FRE.). 1974. pap. 11.95 (0-7859-2340-3, 2070365654) Fr & Eur.

Cloches. Iris Murdoch. 416p. (FRE.). 1985. pap. 17.95 (0-7859-4222-X, 2070376508) Fr & Eur.

Cloches de Bale. Louis Aragon. (Folio Ser.: No. 791). (FRE.). pap. 10.95 (2-07-036791-6) Schoenhof.

Cloches De Bales (Le Monde Reel) Louis Aragon. 437p. (FRE.). 1978. pap. 13.95 (0-7859-1825-6, 2070367916) Fr & Eur.

Cloches de Bales (Le Monde Reel) A. Araneo. 287p. (SPA.). 1989. 39.95 (0-7859-6405-3, 8486761115) Fr & Eur.

***Clock.** James L. Collier. (J). (gr. 4-7). 1995. pap. 3.99 (0-440-40999-3) Dell.

Clock. James Lincoln. (J). 1992. pap. 15.00 (0-385-30037-9, Delta) Dell.

Clock. R. W. Whitfield. 300p. (Orig.). Date not set. pap. write for info. (0-9635750-1-5) Mobius Pr.

Clock. Aleksei M. Remizov. Tr. by John Cournos. LC 76-23894. (Classics of Russian Literature Ser.). 1993. reprint ed. lib. bdg. 24.50 (0-88355-509-3) Hyperion Conn.

Clock & How It Changed the World. Michael Pollard. LC 94-15225. (History & Invention Ser.). 1995. write for info. (0-8160-3142-8) Facts on File.

Clock & Time Related Problems. Fred Justus. (Math Ser.). 24p. (gr. 4-8). 1976. student ed 5.00 (0-8209-0115-6, A-25) ESP.

***Clock & Watch Escapements.** W. J. Gazeley. (Illus.). 294p. Date not set. 29.50 (0-7090-4738-X, Pub. by R Hale Ltd UK) Antique Collect.

Clock & Watch Pronunciary. Malcolm C. Gerschler. LC 82-91052. (Illus.). 256p. 1983. pap. 11.95 (0-9609628-1-6) Wag On Wall.

Clock & Watch Repairing. 2nd ed. Donald De Carle. (Illus.). 309p. 1983. 25.00 (0-7091-9436-6, Pub. by R Hale Ltd UK) Antique Collect.

***Clock & Watch Trademark Index, 1994 Edition - European Origin: Austria - England - France - Germany - Switzerland.** enl. ed. 965p. 1994. per. 38.50 (0-933396-32-5) Antique Clocks.

Clock Book. Harry Bornstein. (Signed English Ser.). (Illus.). 36p. (J). (ps-2). 1976. pap. 5.95 (0-913580-48-1) Gallaudet Univ Pr.

Clock Book. Wallace Nutting. 1975. 15.00 (0-685-56448-7) Assoc Bk.

Clock Decorating Stencils. 1991. write for info. (0-930476-17-4) Am Clock & Watch.

Clock, Desperadoes, & Jeremy: The 1992 Zapizdat Anthology. Kevin Arnold et al. LC 92-62706. 112p. (Orig.). 1992. pap. 5.95 (1-880964-03-1) Zapizdat Pubns.

***Clock Distribution Networks in VLSI Circuits & Systems.** Ed. by Eby G. Friedman. LC 95-14764. 1995. text ed. write for info. (0-7803-1058-6) Inst Electrical.

Clock Drawing: A Neuropsychological Analysis. Morris Freedman et al. (Illus.). 256p. (C). 1994. 35.00 (0-19-505906-9, 9427) OUP.

Clock-Hand Turning: Too Late - Too Soon. Jack Hedger. (Illus.). 200p. (Orig.). 1993. 19.95 (0-9634007-7-0); pap. 14.95 (0-9634007-6-2) Akela West Pubs.

Clock Identification & Price Guide, Bk. 1. rev. ed. Roy Ehrhardt & Malvern Rabeneck. (Illus.). 198p. 1977. reprint ed. ring bd. 25.00 (0-913902-23-3) Heart Am Pr.

Clock Identification & Price Guide, Bk. 2. Roy Erhardt & Malvern Rabeneck. 192p. 1979. ring bd. 25.00 (0-913902-27-6) Heart Am Pr.

Clock Identification & Price Guide, Bk. 3. Roy Ehrhardt & Red Rabeneck. 1983. ring bd. 25.00 (0-913902-50-0) Heart Am Pr.

Clock Making for the Woodworker. Wayne L. Kadar. (Illus.). 192p. 1984. 14.95 (0-8306-0648-3) TAB Bks.

***Clock Market.** (Orig.). 1995. pap. 995.00 (0-7605-2086-0) Rector Pr.

Clock of Clay: New & Selected Poems by Robert Hazel. Robert Hazel. LC 91-33749. 64p. 1992. text ed. 14.95 (0-8071-1738-2) La State U Pr.

Clock of Clay: New & Selected Poems by Robert Hazel. abr. ed. Robert Hazel. LC 91-33749. 64p. 1992. pap. 27.50 (0-8071-1739-0) La State U Pr.

Clock of Dreams. deluxe limited ed. Brian Lumley. LC 91-75683. (Illus.). 1994. reprint ed. boxed 42.50 (0-932445-52-7) Ganley Pub.

Clock of Dreams. Brian Lumley. LC 91-75683. (Illus.). 1994. reprint ed. 26.50 (0-932445-51-9) Ganley Pub.

Clock of Moss. Judson Crews. Ed. by Carol Berge & Dale Boyer. LC 82-73828. (Ahsahta Press Modern & Contemporary Poets of the West Ser.). 60p. (Orig.). 1983. pap. 6.95 (0-916272-21-4) Ahsahta Pr.

Clock Repair: Part-Time Hours, Full-Time Pay. John R. Pierson. LC 91-78023. 160p. 1992. 24.95 (0-9631669-6-4); pap. 19.95 (0-9631669-5-6) Clockwks Pr.

Clock Repair First Reader: Second Steps for the Beginner. Philip E. Balcomb. (Illus.). 160p. (Orig.). (YA). (gr. 9 up). 1989. pap. 14.95 (0-9620456-1-6) Tempus Pr.

Clock Repair Primer: The Beginner's Handbook. 6th ed. Philip E. Balcomb. (Illus.). (Orig.). 1988. reprint ed. pap. 14.95 (0-9620456-0-8) Tempus Pr.

Clock Repairer. Jack Rudman. (Career Examination Ser.: C-151). 1994. pap. 39.95 (0-8373-0151-3) Nat Learn.

Clock Repairer's Handbook. Laurie Penman. (Illus.). 176p. 1993. 29.95 (0-7153-0054-7, Pub. by D & C Pub UK) Sterling.

Clock Repairing As a Hobby. Kelly. LC 81-85509. 1972. pap. 6.95 (0-8329-1118-6) New Win Pub.

Clock Runs Backward: A Chapbook of Poetry. Carl Djerassi. 55p. 1991. 8.00 (0-934257-75-2) Story Line.

Clock Shop. Simon Henwood. 1989. 15.00 (0-374-31380-6) FS&G.

Clock Strikes Twelve. Patricia Wentworth. 19.95 (0-89190-923-0, Am Repr) Amereon Ltd.

Clock Strikes Twelve. Patricia Wentworth. LC 92-54859. 1993. pap. 8.00 (0-06-092408-X, PL) HarpC.

Clock Strikes Twelve. large type ed. Patricia Wentworth. 1981. 12.00 (0-7089-0604-4) Ulverscroft.

Clock That Went Meow. Betty Marrapodi. (Illus.). 31p. (J). (gr. k up). 1970. pap. 7.50 (0-88680-030-7); pap. 2.50 (0-88680-029-3) I E Clark.

Clock That Wouldn't Stop. large type ed. Elizabeth X. Ferrars. (Scarlet Dagger Ser.). 1993. 18.95 (0-7451-6440-4, Scarlet Dagger Lrg Print) Chivers N Amer.

Clock Wheel & Pinion Cutting. J. Malcolm Wild. (Illus.). 48p. 1988. pap. 11.95 (0-930163-13-3) Arlington Bk.

Clock Winder. Anne Tyler. 1992. reprint ed. mass mkt. 5.99 (0-8041-0885-4) Ivy Books.

Clock Wise Cuisine. Junior League of Detroit Staff. (Illus.). 298p. reprint ed. 13.95 (0-9613728-0-X) Jr League Detroit.

***Clock Works: Over 40 Original Craft Projects to Create at Home.** Juliet Bawden. (Illus.). 160p. 1995. 29.95 (1-57076-013-6, Trafalgar Sq Pub) Trafalgar.

Clockers. Richard Price. 640p. 1993. mass mkt. 5.99 (0-380-72081-7) Avon.

Clockers. Richard Price. 592p. 1992. 22.95 (0-395-53761-4) HM.

Clocker's Fancy Site (18ST1-65) on St. Andrew's Freehold: An Archaeological Survey. Garry W. Stone et al. (Research Papers Ser.: No. 4). 51p. 1987. 6.00 (1-878399-36-5) Div Hist Cult Progs.

Clockmaker. Gustav Meyrinck. (Orig.). 1987. pap. 4.50 (0-317-56165-0) Rosycross Pr.

Clockmaker. Georges Simenon. LC 77-4646. 124p. 1977. pap. 2.95 (0-15-618170-3, Harvest Bks) HarBrace.

Clockmakers & Craftsmen of the Avery Family in Connecticut. Amos G. Avery & Connecticut Historical Society Staff. 165p. 1988. write for info. (0-940748-94-0) Conn Hist Soc.

Clockmaking: Eighteen Antique Designs for the Woodworker. John A. Nelson. (Illus.). 240p. (Orig.). 1994. pap. 16.95 (0-8117-2526-X) Stackpole.

Clockmaking: Eighteen Antique Designs for the Woodworker. John A. Nelson. (Illus.). 176p. (Orig.). 1989. 25.95 (0-8306-9164-2); pap. 18.95 (0-8306-3164-X) TAB Bks.

Clocks. 1991. 14.99 (0-517-05239-3) Random Hse Value.

Clocks. Agatha Christie. 1991. mass mkt. 4.99 (0-06-100279-8, Harp PBks) HarpC.

Clocks: Chronicling Time. A. J. Brackin. LC 91-16713. (Encyclopedia of Discovery & Invention Ser.). (Illus.). 96p. (J). (gr. 5-8). 1991. lib. bdg. 17.95 (1-56006-208-8) Lucent Bks.

***Clocks: Full-Size Designs, Ready to Cut.** John A. Nelson. (Scroll Saw Pattern Book Ser.). (Illus.). 96p. 1995. pap. 14.95 (0-8117-3073-5) Stackpole.

Clocks! How Time Flies. Siegfried Aust. (Fun with Technology Ser.). 32p. (J). (gr. 2-5). 1991. lib. bdg. 21.50 (0-8225-2154-7, Lerner Publctns) Lerner Group.

Clocks & Clock Repairing. 2nd ed. Eric Smith. 1990. 22.95 (0-8306-0276-3); pap. 14.95 (0-685-26865-9) TAB Bks.

***Clocks & Clockmakers of Colonial Fairfield Connecticut 1736-1813.** Winthrop D. Warren & Christopher B. Nevins. (Illus.). 182p. Date not set. pap. 8.95 (0-614-05156-8) Fairfield Hist.

Clocks & More Clocks. 2nd ed. Pat Hutchins. LC 93-86027. (Illus.). 32p. (J). (ps-3). 1994. text ed. 13.95 (0-02-745921-7, Mac Bks Young Read) S&S Childrens.

Clocks & More Clocks. Pat Hutchins. LC 93-11208. (Illus.). 32p. (J). (ps-3). 1994. reprint ed. pap. 4.95 (0-689-71769-5, Aladdin Paperbacks) S&S Childrens.

Clocks & Watches. Hugh Tait. (Illus.). 72p. (C). 1983. pap. 10.95x (0-674-13571-7) HUP.

Clocks & Watches: Antique Collector's Guide. Alan Smith. 1989. 7.99 (0-517-68478-0) Random Hse Value.

Clocks & Watches: 1874-1990. 6th ed. Edmond Beckett. (Illus.). 322p. 1991. pap. 25.00 (0-87556-182-9) Saifer.

Clocks & Watches from the Landrock Collection. W. Polte & J. Hein. (Illus.). 296p. (C). 1988. 350.00 (0-569-21424-6) St Mut.

Clocks Are Neat. Muriel Vallet. (Illus.). 10p. (J). (gr. k-3). 1994. pap. 10.95 (1-895583-69-1) MAYA Pubs.

Clocks from the Hunter Collection. Frederick C. Holtz & Frances S. Ridgely. (Scientific Papers: Vol. IX). (Illus.). 64p. 1957. pap. 2.00 (0-89792-017-1) Ill St Museum.

Clocks of Iraz. L. Sprague De Camp. (Reluntant King Ser.: Vol. 2). 176p. 1987. pap. 3.95 (0-345-35212-2, Del Rey) Ballantine.

Clocks of Shenandoah. Philip Whitney. (Illus.). 93p. (Orig.). 1983. pap. 16.95 (0-9612992-0-7) Arlington Bk.

***Clocks of the Last 24 Hours of the Earthly Life of Jesus of Nazareth.** (Walk with Jesus Ser.). 20p. 1993. pap. 5.00 (1-57277-410-X) Truth Center.

Clocks That Time Us: Physiology of the Circadian Timing System. Martin C. Moore-Ede et al. LC 81-6780. (Commonwealth Fund Publications). 464p. 1984. pap. 18.95 (0-674-13581-4) HUP.

Clockwise User Manual. Eldon D. Hearn & Larry G. Lankford. (Illus.). 66p. (Orig.). 1987. 235.00 (0-317-93234-9) Geocomp Ltd.

Clockwise, Vol. One: Quotes on Life. Woody Young. (Illus.). 50p. (Orig.). (YA). 1984. pap. text ed. 4.95 (0-939513-01-3) Joy Pub SJC.

Clockwise, Vol. Two: Learn to Tell Time. Woody Young. (Illus.). 48p. (Orig.). (J). 1985. pap. text ed. 4.95 (0-939513-02-1) Joy Pub SJC.

Clockwork. Pat Cook. 67p. (Orig.). 1990. pap. 4.95 (0-87129-007-3, C76) Dramatic Pub.

Clockwork. large type ed. Neville Steed. 1991. 21.95 (0-7089-2379-8) Ulverscroft.

Clockwork: Timepieces by Artists, Architects & Industrial Designers. Dana Friis-Hansen et al. LC 88-63752. (Illus.). 44p. 1989. pap. 7.50 (0-938437-22-4) MIT List Visual Arts.

Clockwork Factory: Women & Work in Fascist Italy. Perry R. Willson. 294p. 1994. 55.00 (0-19-822732-9) OUP.

Clockwork Garden: On the Mechanistic Reduction of Living Things. Roger J. Faber. LC 85-28408. 280p. 1986. text ed. 30.00 (0-87023-521-4) U of Mass Pr.

***Clockwork Orange.** Burgess. 208p. 1995. pap. 10.00 (0-393-31283-6, Norton Paperbks) Norton.

***Clockwork Orange.** Anthony Burgess. 1994. lib. bdg. 24.95x (1-56849-511-0) Buccaneer Bks.

Clockwork Orange. Anthony Burgess. 1987. 14.95 (0-393-02439-3) Norton.

Clockwork Sparrow. Sue A. Binkley. 1989. 24.95 (0-13-073701-1) P-H.

Clockwork Universe. Ed. by Otto Mayr. 1980. lib. bdg. 55.00 (0-88202-188-5); write for info. (0-686-77549-X) Watson Pub Intl.

Clockwork Universe of Anthony Burgess. Richard Mathews. LC 78-14552. (Milford Ser.: Popular Writers of Today: Vol. 19). 63p. 1978. lib. bdg. 20.00 (0-89370-127-0); pap. 10.00 (0-89370-227-7) Borgo Pr.

Clockwork Worlds: Mechanized Environments in SF. Ed. by Richard D. Erlich & Thomas P. Dunn. LC 83-1718. (Contributions to the Study of Science Fiction & Fantasy Ser.: No. 7). xii, 369p. 1983. text ed. 55.00 (0-313-23026-9, DCW/, Greenwood Pr) Greenwood.

Clockworks: A Multimedia Bibliography of Works Useful for the Study of the Human - Machine Interface in SF. Ed. by Thomas P. Dunn. LC 93-1069. (Bibliographies & Indexes in World Literature Ser.: No. 37). 352p. 1993. Alk. paper. text ed. 79.50 (0-313-27305-7, DWG/, Greenwood Pr) Greenwood.

Clofibrate & Related Analogs: A Comprehensive Review. Donald T. Witiak et al. LC 77-13057. (Medicinal Research Ser.: No. 7). (Illus.). 301p. reprint ed. pap. 85.80 (0-7837-0808-4, 2041123) Bks Demand.

Cloisonne Enameling & Jewelry Making. Felicia Liban. 1989. pap. 8.95 (0-486-25971-4) Dover.

Cloister & the Flame. large type ed. Philippa Wiat. 448p. 1994. 21.95 (0-7089-3124-3) Ulverscroft.

Cloister Design & Monastic Reform in Toulouse: The Romanesque Sculpture of la Daurade. Kathryn Horste. (Clarendon Studies in the History of Art). (Illus.). 416p. 1992. 155.00 (0-19-817508-6) OUP.

Cloistered Virtue: Freedom of Speech & the Administration of Justice in the Western World. Barend Van Niekerk. LC 86-25570. 427p. 1987. text ed. 75.00 (0-275-92082-8, C2082, Praeger Pubs) Greenwood.

Cloisters: Papers in Honor of the Fiftieth Anniversary. Elizabeth C. Parker. 1994. 50.00 (0-8109-6453-8) Abrams.

Cloisters: Studies in Honor of the Fiftieth Anniversary. (Illus.). 484p. 1992. 55.00 (0-87099-635-5, Abrams) Metro Mus Art.

Cloisters Cross: Its Art & Meaning. Elizabeth C. Parker & Charles T. Little. LC 93-8585. (Illus.). 336p. 1993. 60.00 (0-87099-682-7, Abrams) Metro Mus Art.

Cloisters Cross: Its Art & Meaning. Elizabeth C. Parker. 1994. 60.00 (0-8109-6434-1) Abrams.

Cloister's Pale: A Biography of the University of Bombay. Aroon Tikekar. 1986. 36.00 (0-8364-1662-7, Pub. by Somaiya) S Asia.

Cloitre de la Rue D'Ulm: Avec: Journal de Romain Rolland a l'Ecole Normal (1886-1899) Romain Rolland. 416p. (FRE.). 1952. pap. 9.95 (0-7859-5444-9) Fr & Eur.

Clonal Culture of Hemopoietic Cells: Techniques & Applications. Donald Metcalf. 168p. 1984. pap. 63.75 (0-444-80565-6) Elsevier.

Clonal Forestry. Ed. by M. R. Ahuja & W. J. Libby. LC 92-25603. 1993. 139.00 (0-387-52501-7) Spr-Verlag.

Clonal Forestry II: Conservation & Application. Ed. by M. R. Ahuja & W. J. Libby. (Illus.). ix, 292p. 1993. 139.00 (0-387-55714-8) Spr-Verlag.

Clonal Growth in Plants: Regulation & Function. Ed. by J. Van Groenendael & H. De Kroon. (Illus.). ix, 196p. 1990. pap. 45.00 (90-5103-056-8, Pub. by SPB Acad Pub NE) Koeltz Sci Bks.

Clone Crisis. Lee McKeone. 224p. (Orig.). 1992. mass mkt. 4.99 (0-446-36321-9, Aspect) Warner Bks.

Cloning: Of Frogs, Mice & Other Animals. rev. ed. Robert G. McKinnell. LC 84-7514. (Illus.). 158p. (C). 1985. text ed. 15.95 (0-8166-1360-5) U of Minn Pr.

Cloning Agricultural Plants via In Vitro Techniques. Ed. by B. V. Conger. 280p. 1981. 152.00 (0-8493-5797-7, SB123, CRC Reprint) Franklin.

Cloning & Genetic Engineering: Social & Legal Implications. Phyllis P. McDonald. 82p. 1978. student ed 18.90 (1-877960-02-0, 2-505) Kemtec Educ.

An Asterisk (*) at the beginning of an entry indicates that the title is appearing in BIP for the first time.

Cloning & the Constitution: An Inquiry into Govermental PolicyMaking & Genetic Experimentation. Ira H. Carmen. LC 85-40363. (Illus.). 240p. 1986. text ed. 22. 50 (0-299-10340-4) U of Wis Pr.

Cloning Around: A Guide to PC Compatibles. Walter Stagner. 200p. (Orig.). 1988. pap. 24.95 (0-938862-94-4) Weber Systems.

Cloning the Genes for Excitatory Amino Acid Receptors. R. C. Henneberry. (Molecular Biology Intelligence Unit Ser.). write for info. (1-57059-141-5) R G Landes.

Cloportes see **Oeuvres**

Clore Gallery. (Architecture in Detail Ser.). (Illus.). 60p. 1993. pap. 29.99 (0-7148-2762-2, Pub. by Phaidon Press UK) Chronicle Bks.

***Clorox Company: A Report on the Company's Environmental Policies & Practices.** (Illus.). 19p. (C). 1994. reprint ed. pap. text ed. 200.00x (0-7881-0927-8, Coun on Econ) Diane Pub.

Close Any Deal: A. David Silver's Six-Step Formula for Success. A. David Silver. 1992. 21.95 (0-13-138306-X, Busn) P-H.

Close at Hand. Kim Gregory. LC 91-93065. (Illus.). 36p. (Orig.). (J). (ps-3). 1992. pap. text ed. 10.98 (0-9630898-0-3) K T Kids.

Close Binary Stars: Proceeding of the I.A.U. Symposium, No. 88, Toronto, Canada, Aug. 7-10, 1979. International Astronomical Union Staff. Ed. by Mirek J. Plavec & R. K. Ulrich. (International Astronomical Union Symposia Ser.: No. 88). 580p. 1980. lib. bdg. 136.50 (90-277-1116-X) Kluwer Ac.

Close Brush with Reality: Photographs & Writings, 1970-1981. Bart Parker. LC 81-51478. (Artist's Bks.). (Illus.). 56p. (Orig.). 1981. pap. 12.95 (0-89822-018-1) Visual Studies.

Close, but Not Touching. Jai Brett & Nancy Nunn. LC 86-90546. 64p. (Orig.). 1986. pap. write for info. (0-9617480-0-1) Spindrift Pr WI.

***Close Call.** Vivien Armstrong. 1995. lib. bdg. 20.00 (0-7278-4708-2) Severn Hse.

Close Call. Sally H. Reid. 320p. 1994. mass mkt. 4.50 (0-8217-4627-8) Zebra.

Close Call. Lauraine Snelling. (Golden Filly Ser.: No. 9). (YA). 1994. pap. 5.99 (1-55661-488-8) Bethany Hse.

Close Calls: From the Brink of Ruin to Business Success. Nathan Aaseng. (Inside Business Ser.). (Illus.). 80p. (J). (gr. 5 up). 1990. lib. bdg. 18.95 (0-8225-0682-3, Lerner Publctns) Lerner Group.

Close Calls: The Autobiography of a Survivor. Felicia B. Hyatt. Ed. by Sol Lewis. LC 91-9331. (Illus.). 210p. 1991. pap. 13.95 (0-89604-138-7) Holocaust Pubns.

Close Calls: Two Tours with the 35th SQ, 353rd Fighter Group WWII. Bill Price. Ed. by Tom Frisque. (Illus.). 128p. (Orig.). 1992. pap. 14.95 (0-9623080-3-X) Aviation Usk.

Close! Close! Close! How to Make the Sale. John Fenton. LC 92-50994. 128p. 1993. pap. 12.95 (0-89384-217-6) Pfeiffer & Co.

***Close Combat.** W. Griffin. Date not set. 5.98 (0-517-12999-X) Random Hse Value.

Close Combat. large type ed. W. E. B. Griffin. LC 93-153. (Corps Ser.: Bk. 6). 1994. 22.95 (0-7927-1660-4, Paragon Lrg Print) Chivers N Amer.

Close Combat: The Corps, Bk. VI. W. E. B. Griffin. 416p. (Orig.). 1993. mass mkt. 5.99 (0-515-11269-0) Jove Pubns.

Close Connections: Caroline Gordon & the Southern Renaissance. Ann Waldron. LC 88-20706. 416p. 1989. reprint ed. pap. 16.95 (0-87049-594-1) U of Tenn Pr.

***Close Contacts: The Joys & Tears of Contact Lenses - a User's Guide.** Caroline Archer. (Illus.). 152p. 1995. 17. 50 (0-86051-751-9, Robson-Parkwest) Parkwest Pubns.

Close Corp, 2 vols., 1. 3rd ed. Painter. 1991. 175.00 (0-316-68874-6) Little.

Close Corp, 2 vols., 2. 3rd ed. Painter. 1991. 175.00 (0-316-68879-7) Little.

Close Corp, 2 vols., Set. 3rd ed. Painter. 1991. 325.00 (0-316-68880-0) Little.

***Close Corporations: A Comprehensive Guide.** 2nd ed. H. S. Cillers. 280p. 1993. pap. 63.00 (0-409-01997-6, SA) Butterworth Legal Pubs.

Close Cover Before Striking: The Golden Age of Matchbook Art. H. Thomas Steele et al. LC 86-28787. (Illus.). 96p. 1987. 21.95 (0-89659-695-8) Abbeville Pr.

Close-Cropped Tales. John Baldessari. LC 81-50892. (Illus.). 88p. (Orig.). 1981. pap. 12.00 (0-939784-00-9) CEPA Gall.

***Close Encounter.** Kim Hansen. 1995. mass mkt. 3.50 (0-373-16604-4, 1-16604-0) Harlequin Bks.

Close Encounters: A Journey of Spiritual Discovery & Adventure. Roxi I. McNay. (Illus.). 320p. (Orig.). 1991. pap. 14.95 (0-9517206-1-9) Roximillion Pubns.

Close Encounters: A Relational View of the Therapeutic Process. Robert Winer. LC 93-5090. 296p. 1994. 35.00 (0-87668-165-8) Aronson.

Close Encounters: Film, Feminism, & Science Fiction. Constance Penley. Ed. by Lynn Speigel et al. (Camera Obscura Book Ser.). (Illus.). 313p. (C). 1990. reprint ed. pap. text ed. 15.95 (0-8166-1912-3) U of Minn Pr.

Close Encounters? Science & Science Fiction. R. Lambourne et al. (Illus.). 200p. 1990. pap. 29.90 (0-85274-141-3) IOP Pub.

Close Encounters: Systems & Interactions. Mary Leontovich. (Explore! Science Ser.). (Illus.). 48p. (J). (gr. 3-6). 1995. 12.95 (0-673-36220-5); pap. 4.95 (0-673-36215-9) GdYrBks.

***Close Encounters of the Fourth Kind: Alien Abduction, U. F.O.s & the Conference at M.I.T.** C. D. Bryan. 1995. 25.00 (0-679-42975-1) Knopf.

Close Encounters with Insects & Spiders. Jim Nardi. LC 87-26284. (Illus.). 204p. (Orig.). 1988. 17.95 (0-8138-1978-4) Iowa St U Pr.

Close Encounters with the Deity. Michael Bishop. LC 86-61070. 306p. (Orig.). 1986. 15.95 (0-931948-96-7); pap. 8.95 (0-934601-07-0) Peachtree Pubs.

Close Encounters with the New Age. Kevin Logan. (Orig.). 1991. pap. 15.95 (0-86065-879-1) Trans-Atl Phila.

Close Enough to Care. Pat Springle. 250p. 1991. pap. 9.99 (0-945276-18-4) Rapha Pub.

Close Enough to Touch. Richard Peck. LC 81-65498. 192p. (J). (gr. 7 up). 1981. 15.00 (0-385-28145-5) Delacorte.

Close Enough to Touch. Richard Peck. (Young Love Romance Ser.). 144p. (J). (gr. 7 up). 1982. pap. 3.50 (0-440-91282-2, LFL) Dell.

Close Extraterrestrial Encounters: Positive Experiences with Mysterious Visitors. Richard J. Boylan. (Illus.). 220p. 1994. pap. 12.95 (0-926524-26-7, Wild Flower Pr) Blue Wtr Pubng.

Close for Success: The Key to Real Estate Sales. Jim Londay. 162p. 1989. 18.95 (0-88462-739-X, 1913-04) Dearborn Finan.

Close Friends. Peter Jenkins. 1991. mass mkt. 5.99 (0-449-21970-4) Fawcett.

Close Friends. Peter Jenkins. LC 89-13039. (Illus.). 320p. 1989. 19.95 (0-688-08527-X) Morrow.

Close Friends. large type ed. Peter Jenkins. (Large Print Books General Ser.). 354p. 1990. lib. bdg. 20.95 (0-8161-5009-5) G K Hall.

Close Friendships: Making Them. Marie Chapian. LC 89-8406. 1989. pap. 7.99 (0-8007-5318-6) Revell.

***Close Friendships in Adolescence.** Ed. by Brett Laursen. LC 85-644581. (New Directions for Child Development Ser.: No. 60). 110p. (Orig.). 1993. pap. 17.95 (1-55542-689-1) Jossey-Bass.

Close Imaging: An Introduction to Literature. Benjamin Demott. 1440p. (C). 1988. pap. text ed. 28.00 (0-312-00336-6); teacher ed, pap. text ed. 0.43 (0-312-00337-4) St Martin.

Close Look at MVS Systems: Mechanisms, Performance & Security. R. Paans. 572p. 1986. 123.00 (0-444-70008-0, North Holland) Elsevier.

Close My Eyes. Stephen Poliakoff. 102p. (Orig.). 1991. pap. 11.95 (0-413-64920-2, AO581, Pub. by Methuen UK) Heinemann.

Close Neighbors, Distant Friends: United States-Central American Relations. John E. Findling. LC 86-19403. (Contributions in American History Ser.: No. 122). 260p. 1987. text ed. 49.95 (0-313-23679-8, FCL/, Greenwood Pr) Greenwood.

Close of Play. Simon Gray. 1982. pap. 4.75 (0-8222-0219-0) Dramatists Play.

Close of Play & Pig in a Poke. Simon Gray. (Methuen Modern Plays Ser.). 92p. (Orig.). 1988. pap. 8.95 (0-413-46960-3, A0055, Pub. by Methuen UK) Heinemann.

***Close Proximity.** large type ed. Elizabeth Oldfield. (Magna Large Print Ser.). 1994. 18.95 (0-7505-0739-X, Pub. by Magna Print Bks) Ulverscroft.

Close Quarters. Gilbert. (Black Dagger Crime Ser.). 16.50 (0-86220-805-X, BD011, Black Dagger) Chivers N Amer.

Close Quarters. William Golding. 224p. 1987. 16.95 (0-374-12510-4) FS&G.

Close Quarters. Victor Milan. 288p. (Orig.). 1994. pap. 4.99 (0-451-45378-6, ROC) NAL-Dutton.

Close Quarters. Marissa Piesman. LC 93-42215. 1994. 19. 95 (0-385-30538-9) Delacorte.

Close-Quarters Combat for Police & Security Forces. Robert K. Spear. (Illus.). 128p. (Orig.). 1990. pap. 19.95 (0-9622627-4-9) U Force Dynamics.

Close-Range Photogrammetry Meets Machine Vision (Sept. 1990, Zurich), Vol. 1395. 1990. 154.00 (0-685-39186-8) SPIE.

Close Relations. Susan Isaacs. 320p. 1981. mass mkt. 4.95 (0-380-55681-2) Avon.

Close Relations. Susan Isaacs. 1992. mass mkt. 6.50 (0-06-109947-3, Harp PBks) HarpC.

Close Relations. large type ed. Susan Isaacs. LC 93-8597. 1993. 23.95 (1-56895-028-4) Wheeler Pub.

Close Relationship Loss: Theoretical Approaches. Ed. by T. L. Orbuch. (Illus.). xvi, 233p. 1992. 83.00 (0-387-97727-9) Spr-Verlag.

Close Relationships. Ed. by Clyde Hendrick. (Review of Personality & Social Psychology Ser.: Vol. 10). 320p. (C). 1989. text ed. 49.95 (0-8039-3377-0); pap. text ed. 24.00 (0-8039-3378-9) Sage.

Close Relationships: Family, Friendship, Marriage. Eleanor Bertine. 1995. pap. 16.00 (0-919123-58-9) Atrium Pubs.

Close Relationships: Perspectives on the Meaning of Intimacy. Ed. by George Levinger & Harold L. Raush. LC 77-900. (Illus.). 208p. 1977. 27.50x (0-87023-238-X) U of Mass Pr.

***Close Relationships: What Couple Therapists Can Learn.** Susan S. Hendrick. LC 94-26025. 1995. pap. 17.95 (0-534-25434-9) Brooks-Cole.

***Close Relationships & Socioemotional Development.** Sidney Strauss et al. Ed. by Shmuel Shulman. (Human Development Ser.: Vol. 7). (Illus.). 256p. 1995. 49.50 (1-56750-114-1) Ablex Pub.

***Close Scrutiny: The Art of Joan Tanner.** Hunter Drohojowska-Philip. (Illus.). 48p. (Orig.). 1995. pap. write for info. (1-880658-07-0) San Barb CAF.

Close Sesame. Nuruddin Farah. 256p. 1992. pap. 12.00 (1-55597-162-8) Graywolf.

Close Shaves. (Illus.). 85p. (Orig.). 1979. pap. text ed. 10.00 (1-55950-008-5) Loompanics.

Close Softly the Doors. Ronald C. Roat. (First Stuart Mallory Mystery Ser.). 160p. 1993. pap. 12.95 (0-934257-96-5) Story Line.

Close Softly the Doors: A Mystery. 2nd ed. Ronald C. Roat. (First Stuart Mallory Mystery Ser.). 148p. 1991. 18.95 (0-934257-48-5) Story Line.

Close Support: A History of the Cannon Company of the "Go for Broke" 442d Combat Team As Told by the Men Who Fought & Died for It in Bloody Conflict. Tooru J. Kanazawa. (Illus.). 150p. (Orig.). 1994. pap. 25.00 (0-9641146-0-7, TXU 577 116) Cannon Co.

Close the Back Door. Alan F. Harre. 1984. pap. 7.95 (0-570-03932-0, 12-2867) Concordia.

Close the Door So It Can't Get in Your Room. Ev Miller. (Illus.). 52p. (Orig.). 1986. pap. 4.00 (0-88680-265-2) I E Clark.

Close the Forty-Ninth Parallel Etc. The Americanization of Canada. Ed. by Ian Lumsden. LC 79-477171. 343p. reprint ed. pap. 97.80 (0-8357-6385-4, 2023645) Bks Demand.

Close Ties. Elizabeth Diggs. 1982. pap. 4.75 (0-8222-0220-4) Dramatists Play.

Close Ties: Railways, Government, & the Board of Railway Commissioners, 1851-1933. Ken Cruikshank. 1991. text ed. 49.95 (0-7735-0854-6, Pub. by McGill CN) U of Toronto Pr.

Close to Death. Patricia Smith. LC 93-14215. 128p. 1993. pap. 10.95 (0-944072-35-6) Zoland Bks.

Close to Glory: Yank Correspondents' Untold Stories of World War II. Ed. by Art Weithas. 1992. 24.95 (0-89015-825-8) Sunbelt Media.

Close to Ground. Del M. Rogers. LC 90-61426. (Poets Ser.: No. 8). 68p. (Orig.). 1991. pap. 6.95 (0-931722-85-3) Corona Pub.

Close to His Majesty: An Invitation to Walk with God. David C. Needham. Ed. by Larry R. Libby. LC 87-11298. 154p. 1987. pap. 8.99 (0-88070-332-6, Multnomah Bks) Questar Pubs.

Close to Home. Bonnie Bruno. LC 93-22187. 1993. pap. 9.99 (0-7814-0925-X, Chariot Bks) Chariot Family.

Close to Home. Ellen Goodman. 1987. pap. 3.95 (0-449-21325-0) Fawcett.

***Close to Home.** Great Quotations Staff. 78p. 1995. 7.95 (1-56245-196-0) Great Quotations.

Close to Home. Gladys Hunt. 1990. 7.99 (0-929239-16-4) Discovery Hse Pubs.

Close to Home. John McPherson. 1994. pap. 6.95 (0-8362-1750-0) Andrews & McMeel.

Close to Home: A Materialist Analysis of Women's Oppression. Christine Delphy. Ed. & Tr. by Diana Leonard. LC 84-40285. 240p. 1984. pap. 16.95x (0-87023-454-4) U of Mass Pr.

Close to Home: A Story of the Polio Epidemic. Lydia Weaver. LC 92-25937. (Once Upon America Ser.). (Illus.). 64p. (J). (gr. 2-6). 1993. lib. bdg. 12.99 (0-670-84511-6) Viking Child Bks.

Close to Home: Colorado's Urban Wildlife. Ed. by Wendy Shattil et al. (Illus.). 200p. 1990. 19.95 (0-911797-70-X) R Rinehart.

Close to Home: Women Reconnect Ecology, Health & Development Worldwide. Ed. by Vandana Shiva. 176p. 1994. 39.95 (0-86571-263-8) New Soc Pubs.

Close to Home: Women Reconnect Ecology, Health & Development Worldwide. Ed. by Vandana Shiva. 176p. 1994. pap. 12.95 (0-86571-264-6) New Soc Pubs.

***Close to Home Revisited.** John McPherson. (Illus.). 1995. pap. 12.95 (0-8362-0427-1) Andrews & McMeel.

Close to Home, Seven Documentary Photographers. Pref. by David Featherstone. LC 88-83257. (Untitled Ser.: No. 48). (Illus.). 64p. 1988. pap. 17.95 (0-933286-52-X) Frnds Photography.

***Close to Me & Closer...(The Language of Heaven) & Desamere.** Alice Motley. 1995. write for info. (1-882022-26-2) O Bks.

Close to Power: Setting Priorities with City Officials. William Lucy. LC 87-71119. 289p. (Orig.). (C). 1988. lib. bdg. 44.95 (0-685-18627-X); pap. 26.95 (0-918286-49-2) Planners Pr.

Close to the Bone. Betty Andrews. (Illus.). 18p. 1984. 100. 00 (0-9614597-1-9); pap. 15.00 (0-9614597-0-0) Ninja Pr.

Close to the Bone. David Wiltse. 1993. mass mkt. 5.50 (0-425-13976-X) Berkley Pub.

Close to the Bone. David Wiltse. 304p. 1992. 21.95 (0-399-13718-1, Putnam) Putnam Pub Group.

***Close to the Bone: Selected Poems.** Enid Rutland. 80p. 1995. lib. bdg. 33.00 (0-8095-4833-X) Borgo Pr.

Close to the Customer: 25 Management Tips from the Other Side of the Counter. James H. Donnelly, Jr. 214p. 1991. text ed. 21.00 (1-55623-569-0) Irwin Prof Pubng.

Close to the Knives: A Memoir of Disintegration. David Wojnarowicz. LC 90-50210. 288p. (Orig.). 1991. pap. 11.00 (0-679-73227-6, Vin) Random.

Close to the Land: The Way We Lived in North Carolina, 1820-1870. Thomas H. Clayton. Ed. by Sydney Nathans. LC 82-20143. (Way We Lived in North Carolina Ser.). (Illus.). viii, 98p. (gr. 8-12). 1983. pap. 9.95 (0-8078-4103-X) U of NC Pr.

Close to the Stars. large type ed. Meredith B. Brucker. (Dales Romance Ser.). 299p. 1993. pap. 16.95 (1-85389-370-6, Medcom-Trainex) Ulverscroft.

Close to the Truth: An Anthology Featuring the Creative Works of Women & Men with Disabilities. braille ed. Intro. by Cheryl M. Wade. (Anthology Ser.). (Illus.). 80p. (Orig.). 1989. Avail. in Braille & audiotape. audio, pap. 10.00 (1-878458-50-7) Squeaky Wheels Pr.

Close to the Wild: Siberian Tigers in a Zoo. Thomas Cajacob & Teresa Burton. (Nature Watch Bks.). (Illus.). 48p. (J). (gr. 2-5). 1986. lib. bdg. 19.95 (0-87614-227-7, Carolrhoda); pap. 6.95 (0-87614-451-2, Carolrhoda) Lerner Group.

Close to Thee. Dick Bolks. 1977. 5.25 (0-685-74871-5, MB-420) Lillenas.

Close-up. Len Deighton. 1992. mass mkt. 5.50 (0-06-100505-3, Harp PBks) HarpC.

Close-up: A Magazine Devoted to the Art of Films, Set, Vols 1-10. Ed. by Kenneth MacPherson & Winifred Bryher. LC 70-88572. (Contemporary Art Ser.). reprint ed. Set. 300.00 (0-405-00732-9) Ayer.

Close-up: How to Read the American City. Grady Clay. LC 79-26307. (Illus.). 1980. reprint ed. pap. 13.95 (0-226-10945-3, P863) U Ch Pr.

Close Up: Microscopic Photographs of Everyday Stuff. Frank B. Edwards. (Illus.). 48p. (J). 1992. lib. bdg. 17.95 (0-921285-25-6, Pub. by Bungalo Bks CN); pap. 6.95 (0-921285-24-8, Pub. by Bungalo Bks CN) Firefly Bks Ltd.

***Close-up Colors.** (Changing Picture Bks.). (Illus.). 20p. (J). (ps-1). 1995. 6.95 (1-56458-959-5) Dorling Kindersley.

Close-up Nineteen-NIKKA. LC 79-89872. 1978. 6.95 (0-914144-19-7) Monogram Aviation.

Close-Up, No. 20: BLOHM & VOSS 155. Thomas H. Hitchcock. LC 85-63202. 1990. 7.95 (0-914144-20-0) Monogram Aviation.

Close-Up, No. 24: TA152. Jeffrey L. Ethell. LC 85-63203. 1990. 7.95 (0-914144-24-3) Monogram Aviation.

Close-Up, No. 9: BF109F. Thomas H. Hitchcock. LC 85-63198. 1990. 7.95 (0-914144-09-X) Monogram Aviation.

Close-up of the German Peasants' War. Hermann J. Weigand. (Connecticut Academy of Arts & Sciences Ser., Trans.: Vol. 35). 1942. pap. 39.50 (0-685-22912-2) Elliots Bks.

***Close-up on Cakes: Easy Recipes for Every Occasion.** Suzie Smith. LC 94-35428. (Illus.). 160p. 1995. 25.00 (0-8478-1856-X) Rizzoli Intl.

***Close-up Photography (KW-22)** William White. (Illus.). 96p. 1995. 14.95 (0-87985-750-1) Saunders Photo.

Close-Ups. Sandra Thompson. LC 83-4981. (Flannery O'Connor Award for Short Fiction Ser.). 128p. 1984. 15. 95 (0-8203-0683-5) U of Ga Pr.

Close Viewings: An Anthology of Film Criticism. Ed. by Peter Lehman. 464p. 1990. 49.95 (0-8130-0967-7); pap. 22.95 (0-8130-0991-X) U Press Fla.

Close Your Eyes. Jean Marzollo. LC 76-42935. (Pied Piper Bks.). (Illus.). (J). (ps-2). 1978. lib. bdg. 12.89 (0-8037-1610-9) Dial Bks Young.

Close Your Eyes. Jean Marzollo. (Pied Piper Bks.). (Illus.). (J). (ps-00). 1981. 4.95 (0-8037-1617-6) Dial Bks Young.

Close Your Eyes & Think of Dublin: Portrait of a Girl. Kathryn A. Thompson. 197p. 1991. 18.95 (0-932511-41-4); pap. 8.95 (0-932511-42-2) Fiction Coll.

Closed: Ninety-Nine Ways to Stop Abortion. Joseph M. Scheidler. 350p. (Orig.). 1985. pap. 9.95 (0-919225-24-1) Life Cycle Bks.

Closed: Ninety Nine Ways to Stop Abortion. rev. ed. Joseph M. Scheidler. LC 93-60573. (Illus.). 377p. 1993. pap. 13.50 (0-89555-493-3) TAN Bks Pubs.

Closed All Night. Paul Morand. LC 78-130067. (Short Story Index Reprint Ser.). 1977. 16.95 (0-8369-3648-5) Ayer.

Closed Borders. Alan Dowty. LC 86-23399. 272p. 1987. 35. 00x (0-300-03824-0) Yale U Pr.

Closed Borders: The Contemporary Assault on Freedom of Movement. Alan Dowty. LC 86-23399. 287p. (C). 1989. reprint ed. pap. 17.00 (0-300-04498-4) Yale U Pr.

Closed Circle. Robert Goddard. 1994. 22.00 (0-671-75072-0) S&S Trade.

Closed Circuit: The Poetry of Shadab Vajdi. Shadab Vajdi. Tr. by Lotfali Khonji. LC 89-85181. 96p. 1990. pap. 16. 95 (0-948259-78-7, Pub. by Forest Bks UK) Dufour.

Closed Circuit History. Frwd. by Ramsey Clark. LC 89-34243. (Illus.). 232p. 1989. boxed 50.00 (0-934211-18-3) Mage Pubs Inc.

Closed-Conduit Flow. M. H. Chaudhry & V. Yevjevich. LC 81-51337. 1981. 40.00 (0-918334-41-1) WRP.

***Closed Doors, Opportunities Lost: The Costs of Housing Discrimination.** John Yinger. 1995. 29.95 (0-87154-967-0) Russell Sage.

Closed-End Investment Companies: Issues & Answers. Seth C. Anderson. 160p. (C). 1992. lib. bdg. 62.50 (0-7923-9229-9) Kluwer Ac.

Closed Enterprise System. Ed. by Mark Green. 288p. 1972. pap. 1.95 (0-686-36547-X) Ctr Responsive Law.

Closed Eye. Anita Brookner. 1992. 20.50 (0-679-40447-3) Random.

Closed Eye. Anita Brookner. LC 92-56358. (Contemporaries Ser.). 1993. 11.00 (0-679-74340-5) Vintage NY.

Closed Eye. large type ed. Anita Brookner. LC 93-16778. 346p. 1993. pap. 16.95 (0-8161-5592-5) Hall.

Closed Eye. large type ed. Anita Brookner. 336p. 1994. 25. 95 (0-7089-8767-2, Trail West Pubs) Ulverscroft.

***Closed Eyes Have Visions: A Collection of Poems.** H. Yamasheta Wilson. 1994. 10.00 (0-938818-86-4) ECA Assoc.

Closed for Business. Steve Ward. Ed. by Ida W. Unton et al. (Illus.). 96p. 1992. 14.95 (1-879535-02-5) Skipjack Pr.

Closed Fraternity of Police & the Development of the Corrupt Atttitude. Herbert Beigel. (Criminal Justice Center Monographs). 1978. pap. text ed. 3.25x (0-318-37485-4) John Jay Pr.

Closed Functional Treatment of Fractures. Augusto Sarmiento & L. Latta. (Illus.). 608p. 1981. 231.00 (0-387-10384-8) Spr-Verlag.

Closed Geodesics on Riemannian Manifolds. Wilhelm Klingenberg. LC 83-5979. (CBMS Regional Conference Series in Mathematics: No. 53). 79p. 1983. pap. 21.00 (0-8218-0703-X, CBMS-53) Am Math.

Closed Graph & P-Closed Graph Properties in General Topology. T. R. Hamlett & L. L. Herrington. LC 81-10888. (Contemporary Mathematics Ser.: Vol. 3). 68p. 1981. pap. 16.00 (0-8218-5004-0, CONM-3) Am Math.

C

An Asterisk (*) at the beginning of an entry indicates that the title is appearing in BIP for the first time.

Closed Head Injury. D. Eugene Wiley & Carol E. Roberts. Ed. by Oliver D. Grin & Dorothy L. Bouwman. (Patient Education Ser.). (Illus.). 26p. (Orig.). 1992. pap. text ed. 3.00 (*0-929689-46-1*) Ludann Co.

***Closed-Head Injury: A Clinical Source Book.** Peter G. Bernad. 400p. 1994. 95.00 (*1-55834-155-2*) Michie Butterworth.

Closed Labor Markets: Underrepresentation of Blacks, Hispanics & Women in New York City's Core Industries & Jobs. Walter W. Stafford. LC 85-186853. 225p. (Orig.). 1985. pap. 15.00 (*0-88156-025-1*) Comm Serv Soc NY.

Closed List Classes of Colloquial Egyptian Arabic. Zaki N. Abdel-Malek. (Janua Linguarum, Ser. Practica: No. 128). 240p. (Orig.). 1972. pap. text ed. 76.15 (*90-279-2322-1*) Mouton.

Closed-Loop - Ground-Source Heat Pump System Installation Guide. James Bose et al. Ed. by Irene Fisher. (Orig.). 1988. pap. text ed. 75.00 (*0-685-22518-6*) GSHP Pubns.

Closed Loop Electrohydraulic Systems Manual. Richard J. Long & Stephen C. Skinner. (Illus.). (C). 1992. text ed. write for info. (*0-9634162-1-9*) Vickers Inc Trng Ctr.

***Closed Object Boundaries from Scattered Points.** Remco C. Veltkamp. LC 94-43968. (Lecture Notes in Computer Science: Vol. 885). viii, 144p. 1994. 33.00 (*0-387-58808-6*) Spr-Verlag.

Closed Opening in Action. Anatoly Karpov. 144p. 1990. pap. 14.95 (*0-02-033985-2*, Collier S&S) S&S Trade.

Closed Spanish Karpov-Zaitsev Systems. Anatoly Bikhovsky. 136p. 1993. pap. 14.95 (*0-8050-2938-9*) H Holt & Co.

Closed Strings in a Closed Space-Time. Sean Sheeter. (Projective - Elliptic Geometry & Unified Space-Time Ser.: Vol. IIA). (Illus.). 400p. (Orig.). 1995. pap. 25.00 (*0-685-40770-5*) Process Pr.

Closedown? The BBC & Government Broadcasting Policy 1979-92. Tom O'Malley. LC 94-18521. (C). 1994. text ed. 49.95 (*0-7453-0570-9*, Pub. by Pluto Pr UK) Westview.

Closely Held Business, 1992: Estate Freezes, Buy-Sell Agreements, Corporate & Tax Planning. (Tax Law & Estate Planning Ser.). 210p. 1992. pap. text ed. 70.00 (*0-685-56941-1*, D4-5228) PLI.

Closely Held Corporation: Planning & Operation. Ed. by Stephen J. Anderson. 1988. 150.00 (*0-916592-47-2*) Panel Pubs.

Closely Held Corporations: Forms & Checklists. James A. Douglas et al. 1989. 115.00 (*0-685-32303-X*); ring bd. 115.00 (*0-685-69643-X*, CHCF) Warren Gorham & Lamont.

Closely Held Corporations: Forms & Checklists, No. 1. suppl. ed. James A. Douglas et al. 1992. Supplemented semi-annually, write for info. 51.50 (*0-685-56112-7*) Warren Gorham & Lamont.

Closely Held Corporations: Forms & Checklists, No. 2. suppl. ed. James A. Douglas et al. 1992. 54.00 (*0-685-58525-5*) Warren Gorham & Lamont.

Closely Held Corporations in Business & Estate Planning, 2. Edwin T. Hood et al. 1982. 175.00 (*0-316-37218-8*) Little.

Closely Held Corporations in Business & Estate Planning, Set. Edwin T. Hood et al. 1982. Vol. 1. 160.00 (*0-316-37223-4*) Little.

Closely Observed Children: The Diary of a Primary Classroom. Michael Armstrong. (Chameleon Education Ser.). (Illus.). 224p. (Orig.). 1981. 12.95 (*0-906495-04-0*, Writers & Readers); pap. 5.95 (*0-906495-21-0*, Writers & Readers) Writers & Readers.

Closely Watched Films: The Czechoslovak Experience. Antonin J. Liehm. LC 72-94987. 495p. reprint ed. 141.10 (*0-685-16318-0*, 2027619) Bks Demand.

***Closely Watched Trains.** Bohumil Hrabal. Tr. by Edith Pargeter. LC 95-1209. (European Classics Ser.). 1995. write for info. (*0-8101-1278-7*) Northwestern U Pr.

Closeness: A Dictionary of Ideas, Set, Vol. I. Harry A. Wilmer. (Illus.). (Orig.). 1989. Set. write for info. (*0-9623336-0-3*) IH Salado.

Closeness: A Dictionary of Ideas, Vol. I. Harry A. Wilmer. (Illus.). (Orig.). 1989. text ed. write for info. (*0-9623336-2-X*); pap. write for info. (*0-9623336-1-1*) IH Salado.

Closeout. Donald Conger. 1980. pap. 1.75 (*0-8439-0722-3*) Dorchester Pub Co.

Closeout Merchandise: How to Buy Merchandise for Pennies on the Dollar, a Directory & Guide to Closeout Dealers. 1992. lib. bdg. 188.95 (*0-8490-8885-2*) Gordon Pr.

Closeout Merchandise Moneymaking Manual. 1987. lib. bdg. 65.50 (*0-8490-3912-6*) Gordon Pr.

Closeout Moneymaking Merchandise Handbook. 1992. lib. bdg. 88.00 (*0-8490-5470-2*) Gordon Pr.

Closer. Dennis Cooper. 144p. 1990. pap. 8.95 (*0-8021-3212-X*) Grove-Atltic.

***Closer & Closer Apart: Jealousy in Literature.** Rosemary Lloyd. 224p. 1995. 32.50 (*0-8014-3151-4*) Cornell U Pr.

Closer Look. (Illus.). 93p. (Orig.). 1981. pap. 6.95 (*0-9616013-4-5*) Midwest Media.

Closer Look. Laura C. Baer. 1992. pap. 9.95 (*1-55673-499-9*, 7947) CSS OH.

Closer Look at Catholicism: A Guide for Protestants. Bob Moran. 192p. 1986. write for info. (*0-8499-0514-1*) Word Inc.

Closer Look at Comparable Worth: A Study of the Basic Questions to be Addressed in Approaching Pay Equity. Robert E. Williams & Lorence L. Kessler. LC 84-60714. (Orig.). 1984. pap. 15.00 (*0-916559-00-9*) EPF.

Closer Look at Faith, Hope, & Love. Bob George. (Classic Christianity Study Ser.). 1994. pap. 4.99 (*1-56507-175-1*) Harvest Hse.

Closer Look at Jesus Christ. rev. ed. Bob George. (Classic Christianity Study Ser.). 144p. 1992. pap. 4.99 (*0-89081-948-3*) Harvest Hse.

Closer Look at Law & Grace. rev. ed. Bob George. (Classic Christianity Study Ser.). 1993. pap. 4.99 (*1-56507-083-6*) Harvest Hse.

Closer Look at the Enneagram. Dorothy G. Ranaghan. LC 89-83732. 42p. (Orig.). 1989. pap. 3.95 (*0-937779-10-5*) Greenlawn Pr.

Closer Look at the Finality of the Cross. rev. ed. Bob George. (Classic Christianity Study Ser.). 144p. 1992. pap. 4.99 (*0-89081-951-3*) Harvest Hse.

Closer Look at the Reality of the Resurrection. rev. ed. Bob George. (Classic Christianity Study Ser.). 144p. 1992. pap. 4.99 (*0-89081-950-5*) Harvest Hse.

Closer Look at the Truth about Prayer. Bob George. (Classic Christianity Study Ser.). (Orig.). 1994. pap. 4.99 (*1-56507-174-3*) Harvest Hse.

Closer Look at the Word of God. rev. ed. Bob George. (Classic Christianity Study Ser.). 144p. 1992. pap. 4.99 (*0-89081-949-1*) Harvest Hse.

Closer Look at Your Identity in Christ. rev. ed. Bob George. (Classic Christianity Study Ser.). 1993. pap. 4.99 (*1-56507-084-4*) Harvest Hse.

Closer to a Stranger. large type ed. Lilian Darcy. (Medical Science Ser.). 1993. 17.95 (*0-263-13511-X*, Pub. by Mills & Boon Ltd UK) Chivers N Amer.

Closer to Home. Roger Sale. LC 86-12067. 168p. 1986. 24.95 (*0-674-13625-X*) HUP.

Closer to Home: Bisexuality & Feminism. Ed. by Elizabeth R. Weise. LC 91-48262. 320p. (Orig.). 1992. pap. 14.95 (*1-878067-17-6*) Seal Pr Feminist.

Closer to Houston. Richard Fagen. LC 90-2790. 160p. (Orig.). 1990. pap. 8.95 (*0-936784-83-0*) J Daniel.

Closer to Shakespeare. David Honneyman. (C). 1989. 59.00 (*0-86303-482-9*, Pub. by Merlin Bks UK) St Mut.

Closer to the Light: Learning from Near Death Experiences of Children. Melvin Morse. 1991. mass mkt. 5.99 (*0-8041-0832-3*) Ivy Books.

Closer to the Light: Learning from the Near-Death Experiences of Children. large type ed. Melvin L. Morse & Paul J. Perry. (General Ser.). 293p. 1991. text ed. 20.95 (*0-8161-5183-0*, Large Print Bks) Hall.

Closer Walk. Catherine Marshall. Ed. by Leonard LeSourd. 251p. 1986. 12.99 (*0-8007-9065-0*) Chosen Bks.

***Closer Walk.** Catherine Marshall. 224p. 1994. pap. 9.00 (*0-380-72378-6*) Avon.

Closer Walk: A Spiritual Lifeline to God. Catherine Marshall. 224p. 1987. mass mkt. 4.99 (*0-380-70390-4*) Avon.

Closer Walk: Three Hundred Sixty-Five Daily Devotions That Nurture a Heart for God. 448p. 1992. pap. 12.99 (*0-310-54221-9*) Zondervan.

Closers. James W. Pickens. (Illus.). 1988. reprint ed. pap. 19.95 (*0-9620915-7-X*) Cobra Pub.

Closers: Sales Closer's Bible. 2nd ed. Jim Pickens. Ed. by Ben Gay, III. LC 87-81170. 320p. 1987. reprint ed. pap. 19.95 (*0-942645-00-6*) Hampton Hse Pub.

Closers: Sales Closer's Bible, 15 cass., Set. 2nd ed. Jim Pickens. Ed. by Ben Gay, III. LC 87-81170. 320p. 1987. reprint ed. audio 99.95 (*0-942645-01-4*) Hampton Hse Pub.

Closers, Pt. 2: Sales Closers Bible. Ben Gay, III. 300p. 1990. pap. 19.95 (*0-942645-08-1*) Hampton Hse Pub.

Closers, Pt. 2: Sales Closers Bible, 15 cass., Set. Ben Gay, III. 300p. 1990. audio 99.95 (*0-942645-09-X*) Hampton Hse Pub.

***Closest Companion: A Love Story: An Account of the Remarkable Friendship of Franklin D. Roosevelt & Margaret Suckley.** Geoffrey C. Ward. (Illus.). 384p. 1995. 24.95 (*0-395-66080-7*) HM.

Closest of Enemies: A Personal & Diplomatic History of U. S. Cuban Relations since 1957. Wayne S. Smith. (Illus.). 1988. pap. 8.95 (*0-393-30530-9*) Norton.

Closest of Strangers: Liberalism & the Politics of Race in New York. Jim Sleeper. 352p. 1991. pap. 11.95 (*0-393-30799-9*) Norton.

Closest to God: Humankind's Search for the Supreme Being. Richard Burrill. (Illus.). (C). 1989. write for info. (*0-318-66611-1*) Anthro Co.

Closest to God: The Life-Stories of Muhammad & the Five God-Men of History. Ed. by Richard Burrill. (YA). (gr. 9-12). Date not set. 17.95 (*1-878464-06-X*); pap. 10.95 (*1-878464-07-8*) Anthro Co.

Closet. Gary De Maria. LC 80-11677. (Illus.). (Orig.). 1980. pap. 5.95 (*0-89407-020-7*) Strawberry Hill.

Closet Case: A Novel. Robert Rodi. LC 93-47343. 336p. 1994. pap. 10.95 (*0-452-27211-4*, Plume) NAL-Dutton.

Closet Cultivator. Ed Rosenthal. 1991. pap. 16.95 (*0-86719-359-X*) Last Gasp.

Closet Entrepreneur: Three Hundred Thirty-Seven Ways to Start Your Successful Business with Little or No Money. Neil Balter. 288p. (Orig.). 1994. pap. 14.95 (*1-56414-138-1*) Career Pr Inc.

Closet Full of Clothes & Something to Wear. Betsy Chapman & Barbara Bookman. (Illus.). 40p. 1987. pap. 4.95 (*0-685-19172-9*); pap. text ed. 2.97 (*0-685-19173-7*) Chapman & Bkman.

Closet Full of Clothes & Something to Wear. Betsy Chapman & Barbara Bookman. (Illus.). 40p. 1987. reprint ed. pap. 4.95 (*0-9613544-8-8*); reprint ed. pap. text ed. 2.97 (*0-685-09075-2*) Chapman & Bkman.

***Closet Gorilla.** F. Weller. 1994. pap. 4.99 (*0-517-13317-2*) Random.

Closet Hanging. Tony Fennelly. (Matt Sinclair Ser.). 224p. 1987. 14.95 (*0-88184-306-7*); pap. 3.50 (*0-88184-393-8*) Carroll & Graf.

Closet Is No Place for a Computer. Karen M. Foley. 1985. teacher ed 7.20 (*0-201-20113-5*); Atari. pap. text ed., spiral bd. 10.95 (*0-201-20114-3*); TRS-80. pap. text ed. 10.15 (*0-318-37368-8*); Apple. Apple II, spiral bd. 10.95 (*0-201-20116-X*) Addison-Wesley.

***Closet of Identities.** Michael C. Giammatteo. (Illus.). (Orig.). 1994. pap. 8.95 (*0-918428-17-3*) Sylvan Inst.

Closet Writing - Gay Reading: The Case of Melville's Pierre. James Creech. LC 93-11176. (Illus.). 216p. 1993. lib. bdg. 36.00 (*0-226-12020-1*); pap. text ed. 14.95 (*0-226-12022-8*) U Ch Pr.

Closeted Screams: A Service Provider Handbook for Same-Sex Domestic Violence Issues. Sharon Daugherty. 250p. (Orig.). 1992. pap. text ed. 20.00 (*0-9633940-0-2*) Smith-Fliesher Soria.

Closets: Designing & Organizing the Personalized Closet. Patricia Coen & Bryan Milford. LC 87-8252. (Illus.). 128p. 1988. pap. 14.95 (*0-8021-3228-6*) Grove-Atltic.

Closets Are Empty...the Dining Room's Full: An Autobiographical Legacy. Ace Lundon. 384p. 1993. 24.95 (*0-9635670-4-7*) Ponderosa NV.

Closeup: Lessons in the Art of Seeing African Sculpture. Anne D'Alleva. Ed. by Susan Vogel et al. (Illus.). 196p. 1991. 65.00 (*3-7913-1150-6*, Pub. by Prestel) TeNeues.

Closeup: Lessons in the Art of Seeing African Sculpture. Jerry L. Thompson & Susan Vogel. LC 90-42065. (Illus.). 1990. 65.00 (*0-945802-07-2*); pap. 33.00 (*0-945802-08-0*) Museum African.

***Closing: A Process, Not a Problem.** Virden Thornton. Ed. by Philip Gerould. (Fifty-Minute Ser.). (Illus.). 100p. (Orig.). 1995. pap. 9.95 (*1-56052-318-2*) Crisp Pubns.

Closing Argument, 1969-1990. Jacob Stein. LC 85-7735. 130.00 (*0-317-12047-6*) Clark Boardman Callaghan.

***Closing Arguments.** Geoffrey Lavelle. LC 94-41938. 1995. 7.95 (*0-943512-49-2*) Linwood Pub.

Closing Chapter. Lord Denning. 1983. U.K. pap. 26.00 (*0-406-17612-4*) Butterworth Legal Pubs.

***Closing Date.** Stig B. Hedqvist. 540p. 1995. pap. 12.95 (*1-56901-869-3*) NW Pub.

Closing Door. Institute for the Preservation of Wealth Staff et al. 243p. 1989. pap. text ed. 68.00 (*0-938689-03-7*) Inst Preserv Wealth.

Closing Door: Conservative Policy & Black Opportunity. Gary Orfield & Carole Ashkinaze. LC 90-48542. (Illus.). 232p. 1991. 22.50 (*0-226-63272-5*) U Ch Pr.

Closing Door: Conservative Policy & Black Opportunity. Gary Orfield & Carole Ashkinaze. LC 90-48542. (Illus.). xx, 254p. 1993. pap. 11.95 (*0-226-63273-3*) U Ch Pr.

Closing Doors Behind Me. John Drogas. Ed. by Bradford White. LC 88-80001. 321p. (Orig.). 1988. pap. 7.90 (*0-9620016-0-0*) Grt Lakes MI.

Closing Doors, Opening Worlds: Looking Beyond the Retirement Horizon. Vern Drilling. 160p. 1993. pap. 9.95 (*0-925190-63-2*) Fairview Press.

***Closing of American Library Schools: Problems & Opportunities.** Larry J. Ostler et al. LC 94-46942. (Contributions in Librarianship & Information Science Ser.: No. 85). 176p. 1995. text ed. 49.95 (*0-313-28461-X*, Greenwood Pr) Greenwood.

Closing of Man's History. Ludie J. Wright. (Bible Prophecy Ser.: No. 1). (Illus.). 209p. (Orig.). 1986. 15.95 (*0-9617290-0-7*); pap. 12.95 (*0-9617290-1-5*) Hse Better Sales.

Closing of the American Heart: What's Really Wrong with America's Schools. Ronald H. Nash. LC 90-30823. 1990. 14.99 (*0-945241-11-9*) Probe Bks.

Closing of the American Mind. Allan Bloom. 1988. pap. 10.95 (*0-671-65715-1*, Touchstone Bks) S&S Trade.

Closing of the Public Domain: Disposal & Reservation Policies, 1900-50. E. Louise Peffer. LC 72-2862. (Use & Abuse of America's Natural Resources Ser.). 388p. 1972. reprint ed. 25.95 (*0-405-04528-X*) Ayer.

Closing of the Public Domain: Disposal & Reservation Policies, 1900-50. E. Louise Peffer. 120p. reprint ed. pap. 30.00 (*0-317-29829-1*, 2051958) Bks Demand.

Closing Officer's Guide: Washington, 1983-1993. Fred B. Phillips, Jr. 550p. 1994. ring bd. 90.00 (*0-409-20149-9*) Michie Butterworth.

Closing Officer's Guide: Washington, 1983-1993. suppl. ed. Fred B. Phillips, Jr. 550p. 1993. Latest suppl. 12/93. 45.00 (*1-56257-816-2*) Butterworth Legal Pubs.

Closing Pandora's Box: Arms Races, Arms Control, & the History of the Cold War. Patrick Glynn. LC 91-55464. 464p. 1993. pap. 17.00 (*0-465-01187-X*) Basic.

Closing Plants: Planning & Implementing Strategies. Coopers & Lybrand. LC 86-80051. 104p. 1986. 6.00 (*0-910586-57-8*) Finan Exec.

Closing, Servicing, & Enforcement of Mortgage. Ed. by Doris Stokes. (Correspondence Course Ser.). 26p. (C). Date not set. pap. text ed. write for info. (*0-945359-23-3*) Mortgage Bankers.

Closing, Shipping, & Warehousing. Anita W. Boyland. Ed. by Bob Linthicum. 75p. (Orig.). 1991. pap. 35.00 (*0-945359-05-5*) Mortgage Bankers.

***Closing Statement: A Schuyler Ridgway Mystery.** Tierney McClellan. 288p. (Orig.). 1995. mass mkt. 4.99 (*0-451-18464-5*, Sig) NAL-Dutton.

Closing System of Academic Employment. Cameron L. Fincher et al. 1978. pap. text ed. 4.00 (*0-686-23578-9*) S Regional Ed.

Closing Tactics: How to Use Fast & Effective Closing Techniques. Andoni Lizardy. 192p. 1993. pap. 12.95 (*0-89384-235-4*) Pfeiffer & Co.

***Closing Techniques: That Really Work!** Stephan Schiffman. LC 94-3726. 1994. pap. text ed. 7.95 (*1-55850-410-9*) Adams Pubng.

***Closing the Borders.** Wendy Davies. (Global Issues Ser.). (Illus.). 64p. (J). (gr. 7-9). 1995. 15.95 (*1-56847-335-4*) Thomson Lrning.

Closing the Circle: A Cultural History of the Rock Revolution. Herbert I. London. LC 84-2016. 208p. 1984. pap. 19.95 (*0-8304-1118-6*) Nelson-Hall.

Closing the Circle: War in the Pacific: 1945. Edwin P. Hoyt. 264p. 1984. pap. 3.95 (*0-380-67983-3*) Avon.

***Closing the Circle on the Splitting of the Atom: The Environmental Legacy of Nuclear Weapons Production in the U. S. & What the Department of Energy Is Doing about It.** (Illus.). 106p. (Orig.). (C). 1995. pap. text ed. 40.00 (*0-7881-1636-3*) Diane Pub.

Closing the Corporate Library: Case Studies on the Decision Making Process. James M. Matarazzo. LC 81-14452. 160p. reprint ed. pap. 45.60 (*0-317-26315-3*, 2025207) Bks Demand.

Closing the Door on the Poor: The Dismantling of California's County Hospitals. 230p. 7.50 (*0-318-14226-0*) Health PAC.

Closing the Door to Destitution: The Shaping of the Social Security Acts of the United States & New Zealand. Raymond Richards. 1994. 42.50 (*0-271-01060-6*) Pa St U Pr.

Closing the Door to Destitution: The Shaping of the Social Security Acts of the United States & New Zealand. Raymond Richards. LC 92-41698. 208p. (C). 1994. 42.50 (*0-271-01061-4*) Pa St U Pr.

Closing the Forbidden Door: An Expose of the Demonic. James D. Marocco & Paul Yonggi Cho. 160p. (Orig.). 1992. pap. 9.95 (*1-881227-01-4*) Bartimaeus.

Closing the Frontier: Radical Response in Oklahoma, 1889-1923. John Thompson. LC 86-1609. (Illus.). 288p. 1986. 24.95 (*0-8061-1996-9*) U of Okla Pr.

Closing the Gap. 2nd ed. Leslie L. Kossoff. 164p. 1994. pap. 14.00 (*0-945320-43-4*) SPC Pr.

***Closing the Gap: Meeting the Small Business Training Challenge in Connecticut.** Richard C. Harwood. 37p. 1989. pap. 10.00 (*1-887410-60-0*) Jobs for Future.

Closing the Gap: Symbolic vs. Subsymbolic Processing. Ed. by John Dinsmore. (Technical Monographs & Edited Collections in Cognitive Science). 280p. (C). 1992. text ed. 59.95 (*0-8058-1079-X*); pap. 29.95 (*0-8058-1080-3*) L Erlbaum Assocs.

Closing the Gap: The Coast Line & Its Bridges in Ventura & Santa Barbara Counties. Nan Lawler. (Illus.). 19p. (Orig.). 1984. reprint ed. pap. 2.00 (*0-911773-03-7*) Inst Am Res.

Closing the Gap: The Handbook for Total Quality Implementation. Leslie L. Kossoff. LC 91-93082. 128p. (Orig.). 1992. pap. 12.95 (*0-9630724-0-4*) LLK Assocs.

Closing the Gap Between Technology & Application: Proceedings. 215p. 20.00 (*0-318-14008-X*); 10.00 (*0-318-14009-8*) EDUCOM.

Closing the Gap for U. S.-Hispanic Youth Public-Private Strategies. Hispanic Policy Development Project Staff. LC 88-36539. (Illus.). 78p. (Orig.). (C). 1989. pap. text ed. 11.00 (*0-8191-7362-2*) U Pr of Amer.

Closing the Gate. Beverly Merrick. Ed. by Roy Zarucchi & Carolyn Page. (Illus.). 48p. (Orig.). 1993. pap. 7.95 (*1-879205-41-6*) Nightshade Pr.

Closing the Literacy Gap in American Business: A Guide for Trainers & Human Resource Specialists. Edward E. Gordon et al. LC 91-22016. 224p. 1991. text ed. 49.95 (*0-89930-621-7*, GCW, Quorum Bks) Greenwood.

Closing the Male-Female Earnings Gap in Pennsylvania. Pennsylvania State Data Center Staff. 16p. (Orig.). 1994. pap. text ed. 15.00 (*0-939667-29-0*, SDC1P2-94) Penn State Data Ctr.

Closing the Productivity Gap: A Comparison of Northern Ireland, the Republic of Ireland, Britain & West Germany. D. M. Hitchens & K. Wagner. Ed. by J. E. Birnie. 341p. 1990. text ed. 72.95 (*1-85628-098-5*, Pub. by Avebury Pub UK) Ashgate Pub Co.

Closing the Quality Gap: Lessons from America's Leading Companies. Conference Board Inc., Staff & Alexander Hiam. 1992. 22.95 (*0-13-138413-9*, Busn) P-H.

Closing the Ring. Winston S. Churchill. 1986. pap. 14.95 (*0-395-41059-2*) HM.

Closing the Ring see Second World War

Closing the Sea. Katzier. 1992. 18.95 (*0-15-118200-0*) HarBrace.

***Closing the Shop: Conversion from Sheltered to Integrated Work.** Murphy & Rogan. 240p. 1995. pap. 26.00 (*1-55766-153-7*) P H Brookes.

Closing the Space: Human Rights in Guatemala. Americas Watch Staff. 136p. 1988. pap. 6.00 (*0-929692-08-X*, Am Watch) Hum Rts Watch.

***Closing the Technology Gap: Change in India's Computer Industry.** Hans-Peter Brunner. LC 95-13140. 1995. write for info. (*0-8039-9251-3*); pap. write for info. (*0-8039-9252-1*) Sage.

Closing Time. Joseph Heller. 1994. 24.00 (*0-671-74604-9*) S&S Trade.

***Closing Time.** Joseph Heller. 1995. pap. 13.00 (*0-684-80450-6*, Scribners) S&S Trade.

Closing with the Enemy: How GIs Fought the War in Europe, 1944-1945. Michael D. Doubler. (Modern War Studies). (Illus.). 400p. (Orig.). 1994. 40.00 (*0-7006-0675-0*) U Pr of KS.

***Closing with the Enemy: How GIs Fought the War in Europe, 1944-1945.** Michael D. Doubler. LC 95-25067. (Modern War Studies). (Illus.). 368p. (Orig.). (C). 1995. 40.00x (*0-614-06489-9*); pap. 17.95 (*0-614-06490-2*) U Pr of KS.

Closing Your Practice. 1990. 22.95 (*0-89970-455-7*, OP381689) AMA.

Clostridia. Ed. by N. P. Minton & D. J. Clarke. (Biotechnology Handbooks Ser.: Vol. 3). (Illus.). 318p. 1989. 65.00 (*0-306-43261-7*, Plenum Pr) Plenum.

Clostridia & Biotechnology. David R. Woods. (Biotechnology Ser.). 459p. 1993. 129.00 (*0-7506-9004-6*) Buttrwrth-Heinemann.

C

An Asterisk (*) at the beginning of an entry indicates that the title is appearing in BIP for the first time.

An Asterisk (*) at the beginning of an entry indicates that the title is appearing in BIP for the first time.

1329

C

Cloud on Sand. Gabriella DeFerrari. Ed. by Jane Rosenman. 336p. 1992. reprint ed. pap. 9.00 (*0-671-73463-6*) PB.
Cloud over Bhopal: Causes, Consequences, & Constructive Solutions. Alfred De Grazia. 145p. 1992. pap. 20.00 (*0-940268-27-2*) Metron Pubns.
Cloud over Bhopal-Causes, Consequences. Alfred De Grazia. 145p. 1985. 12.95 (*0-318-37222-3*) Asia Bk Corp.
Cloud over Kuwait. Marwan Iskandar. 1992. pap. 11.95 (*0-533-09593-X*) Vantage.
Cloud over Malverton. large type ed. Nancy Buckingham. 1990. 21.95 (*0-7089-2278-3*) Ulverscroft.
Cloud Peak Primitive Area: Trail Guide, History & Photo Odyssey. Michael M. Melius. Ed. by Kenneth W. Melius. LC 93-60487. (Illus.). 120p. (Orig.). 1993. pap. 11.95 (*0-937603-12-0*) Melius Pub.
Cloud People. Robert Kelly. LC 90-71515. 320p. (Orig.). 1991. pap. 3.95 (*1-56076-077-X*) TSR Inc.
Cloud People: The Divergent Evolution of the Zapotic & Mixte Civilizations. Ed. by Kent V. Flannery & Joyce Marcus. 1983. text ed. 59.00 (*0-12-259860-1*) Acad Pr.
Cloud Physics. A. M. Borovikov. 402p. 1963. text ed. 102.00 (*0-7065-0259-0*, Pub. by Keter Pub IS) Coronet Bks.
Cloud Physics. D. W. Perrie. LC 51-9779. (Scholarly Reprint Ser.). 155p. reprint ed. pap. 44.20 (*0-317-08820-3*, 2020512) Bks Demand.
Cloud Physics: Experimental Investigations. Ed. by O. A. Volkovskii. 128p. 1974. text ed. 41.00 (*0-7065-1442-4*, Pub. by Keter Pub IS) Coronet Bks.
Cloud Physics & Cloud Seeding. Louis J. Battan. LC 78-25711. (Illus.). 144p. 1979. reprint ed. text ed. 49.75 (*0-313-20770-4*, BACL, Greenwood Pr) Greenwood.
Cloud Physics & Weather Modification. Y. S. Sedunova. 112p. 1974. text ed. 40.00 (*0-7065-1441-6*, Pub. by Keter Pub IS) Coronet Bks.
Cloud Reflections in My Soup. Jim DeWitt. LC 83-90475. (Poetry for Schools Ser.). (Illus.). 64p. (Orig.). (gr. 3-12). 1984. pap. text ed. 5.95 (*0-915199-01-7*) Pen-Dec.
Cloud Seven. Max Wilk. 1958. pap. 4.75 (*0-8222-0222-0*) Dramatists Play.
Cloud Shadows. Jane B. Gillespie. 1992. pap. 8.95 (*0-87233-101-6*) Bauhan.
Cloud Shadows: Word Paintings. Lesley Einer. 15p. (Orig.). 1989. pap. 2.50 (*0-9620822-1-X*) Sage Shadow Pr.
Cloud Song. A. Child. (Cityscapes Ser.). 15p. (J). (gr. 1). 1992. pap. text ed. 23.00 (*1-56843-023-X*); pap. text ed. 4.50 (*1-56843-073-6*) BGR Pub.
Cloud Train. Joan Aleshire. LC 82-80305. 58p. 1982. 8.95 (*0-89672-099-3*); pap. 4.95 (*0-89672-098-5*) Tex Tech Univ Pr.
Cloud upon the Sanctuary. Karl Von Eckartshausen. 92p. 1992. pap. 14.95 (*1-56459-126-3*) Kessinger Pub.
Cloud upon the Sanctuary. Karl Von Eckarthausen. Tr. by Isabel De Steiger & A. E. Waite. reprint ed. pap. 12.95 (*1-55818-143-1*, Sure Fire) Holmes Pub.
***Cloud 9.** Caryl Churchill. 104p. (Orig.). 1995. pap. 9.95 (*1-55936-099-2*) Theatre Comm.
Cloudburst. Ryne D. Pearson. LC 92-30489. 1993. 23.00 (*0-688-12246-9*) Morrow.
Clouded Dreams. Deborah Insel. 288p. 1995. 19.95 (*1-883285-04-6*) Delphinium.
Clouded Hills. Elizabeth Vermorcken. 1993. reprint ed. lib. bdg. 89.00 (*0-7812-5850-2*) Rprt Serv.
***Clouded Land.** Mary Mackie. 608p. 1995. pap. 10.95 (*0-7472-4684-X*, Pub. by Headline UK) Trafalgar.
Clouded Vision: The Student Movement in the United States in the 1960's. David L. Westby. 291p. 1976. 35.00 (*0-8387-1521-4*) Bucknell U Pr.
Clouded Witness: Initiation in the Church of England in the Mid-Victorian Period 1850-1875. Peter J. Jagger. LC 82-22465. (Pittsburgh Theological Monographs, New Ser.: No. 1). vii, 221p. (Orig.). 1982. pap. 10.00 (*0-915138-51-4*) Pickwick.
Cloudesley: A Tale, 3 vols. in 1. William Godwin. LC 79-8270. reprint ed. 44.50 (*0-404-61863-4*) AMS Pr.
Cloudless at First. Hilda Morley. 302p. 1989. 22.50 (*0-918825-71-7*); pap. 12.95 (*0-918825-72-5*) Moyer Bell.
Cloudless Sky: The Mahamudra Path of the Tibetan Buddhist Kagyu School. Jamgon Kongtrul. LC 92-50119. 128p. (Orig.). 1993. pap. 10.00 (*0-87773-694-4*) Shambhala Pubns.
Clouds. Aristophanes. Ed. by Kenneth J. Dover. (Illus.). 416p. 1989. pap. 24.95 (*0-19-814395-8*) OUP.
C.L.O.U.D.S. Pat Cummings. LC 85-9719. (Illus.). 32p. (J). (ps-3). 1986. 12.95 (*0-688-04682-7*); lib. bdg. 12.88 (*0-688-04683-5*) Lothrop.
Clouds. Michael George. (Images Ser.). (J). 1992. lib. bdg. 16.95 (*0-88682-435-4*) Creative Ed.
Clouds. Jenny Hessell. LC 92-27099. (Voyages Ser.). (Illus.). (J). 1993. 3.75 (*0-383-03561-9*) SRA Schl Grp.
Clouds. Jenny Markert. (J). (gr. 4-7). 1993. 15.95 (*1-56846-060-0*) Creative Ed.
Clouds. Ann Merk & Jim Merk. LC 94-13324. (Weather Report Ser.). (J). (gr. 2 up). 1994. write for info. (*0-86593-389-8*) Rourke Corp.
Clouds. Ina R. Walker. 1994. 7.95 (*0-8062-4889-0*) Carlton.
Clouds. Roy Wandelmaier. LC 84-8643. (Now I Know Ser.). (Illus.). 32p. (J). (gr. k-2). 1985. lib. bdg. 11.59 (*0-8167-0338-8*); pap. text ed. 2.95 (*0-8167-0441-4*) Troll Assocs.
Clouds. abr. ed. Aristophanes & Kenneth J. Dover. 1969. pap. 14.95 (*0-19-912009-9*) OUP.
Clouds. Aristophanes. Tr. by W. J. Starkie. 420p. reprint ed. lib. bdg. 67.50x (*0-685-13326-5*, Pub. by A M Hakkert SP) Coronet Bks.
Clouds: Biography of a Country House. Caroline Dakers. (Illus.). 224p. 1993. 45.00 (*0-300-05776-8*) Yale U Pr.
Clouds: The Comedies of Aristophanes. Aristophanes. Ed. by Sommerstein. (Classical Texts Ser.: Vol. 3). 1980. 49.95 (*0-85668-209-8*, Pub. by Aris & Phillips UK); pap. 24.95 (*0-85668-210-1*, Pub. by Aris & Phillips UK) David Brown.
Clouds: The Realm of the Air. Luke Howard. (Essay on the Modification of the Clouds Ser.). 1987. pap. 7.95 (*0-916786-95-1*, Saint George Pubns) R Steiner Col Pubns.
Clouds: Their Formation, Optical Properties & Effects. Ed. by Peter V. Hobbs & Adarsh Deepak. LC 81-3491. 1981. text ed. 99.00 (*0-12-350720-0*) Acad Pr.
Clouds & Clocks: A Story for Children Who Soil. Matthew R. Galvin. LC 89-12278. (Illus.). 48p. (J). 1989. 16.95 (*0-945354-18-5*); pap. 8.95 (*0-945354-15-0*) Magination Pr.
Clouds & Numbers - My Me. David Felder. Ed. by Barbara Truncellito. (Illus.). 85p. (Orig.). (C). 1992. pap. 9.95 (*0-9631101-1-X*) Fragile Twilight.
Clouds & Rain: A China-to-America Memoir. Edna Wu. (Illus.). 224p. (Orig.). 1994. pap. 9.95 (*1-879260-22-0*) Evanston Pub.
Clouds & Skyscapes. William Powell. (How to Draw & Paint Ser.). (Illus.). 32p. (Orig.). 1989. pap. 5.95 (*0-929261-48-8*, HT206) W Foster Pub.
***Clouds & Storms.** Audubon Society Staff. (National Audubon Society Pocket Guides Ser.). 1995. pap. 7.99 (*0-679-77999-X*) Knopf.
Clouds & Storms: The Behavior & Effect of Water in the Atmosphere. F. H. Ludlam. LC 77-22281. (Illus.). 1980. 65.00 (*0-271-00515-7*) Pa St U Pr.
Clouds & Sunshine. Sarah L. Fleming. LC 70-173606. (Black Heritage Library Collection). 1977. reprint ed. 13.95 (*0-8369-8916-3*) Ayer.
Clouds & The Pot of Gold. Aristophanes & Plautus. Ed. & Tr. by Peter D. Arnott. (Crofts Classics Ser.). 128p. 1967. pap. text ed. write for info. (*0-88295-005-3*) Harlan Davidson.
***Clouds Before the Storm.** Sigmund A. Boloz. Ed. by Donna Muri. (Illus.). 36p. (Orig.). 1994. pap. text ed. 6.00 (*1-886635-02-1*) Wooded Hill AZ.
Clouds Blur the Rainbow: The Other Side of the New Alliance Party. Chip Berlet. 15p. (Orig.). 1987. spiral bd. 3.50 (*0-915987-03-1*) Political Rsch Assocs.
Clouds, Clowns, & Rainbows. Joseph W. Barnett. LC 89-52186. 53p. 1990. pap. 5.95 (*1-55523-315-5*) Winston-Derek.
Clouds from Both Sides: An Autobiography. Julie Tullis. LC 87-4510. (Illus.). 336p. 1987. 17.95 (*0-87156-716-4*) Sierra.
Clouds in a Glass of Beer: Simple Experiments in Atmospheric Physics. Craig F. Bohren. LC 87-13375. 192p. 1987. pap. text ed. 17.95 (*0-471-62482-9*) Wiley.
Cloud's Journey. Sigrid Heuck. (Illus.). 28p. (J). (ps-2). 1991. pap. 9.95 (*1-56182-021-0*) Atomium Bks.
Clouds (Oblaka) Alexsandr Ostrovsky. (Childrens Ser.). (Illus.). 16p. (Orig.). (RUS.). (J). 1984. pap. 14.95 (*0-934393-20-6*) Rector Pr.
***Clouds of Glory.** Alan Robinson. 94p. 1992. pap. text ed. 24.95x (*0-85439-480-X*, Pub. by St Paul Pubns UK) St Mut.
Clouds of Secrecy: The Army's Germ Warfare Tests over Populated Areas. Leonard A. Cole. LC 89-24225. 204p. (C). 1990. pap. 14.95 (*0-8226-3001-X*) Littlefield.
Clouds of Secrecy: The Army's Germ Warfare Tests over Populated Areas. Leonard A. Cole. LC 87-12777. 188p. 1988. 38.50 (*0-8476-7579-3*) Rowman.
Clouds of Terror. Catherine A. Welch. LC 93-18416. (Carolrhoda On My Own Bks.). (J). (gr. k-3). 1993. 15.95 (*0-87614-771-6*, Carolrhoda) Lerner Group.
Clouds of Terror. Catherine A. Welch. (J). (ps-3). 1994. pap. 5.95 (*0-87614-639-6*, Carolrhoda) Lerner Group.
Clouds of That Country. Jack Anderson. 1982. pap. 7.00 (*0-914610-29-5*) Hanging Loose.
Clouds of War. LC 89-110893. (Moments in American History Ser.). (Illus.). 48p. (J). (gr. 4-10). 1990. lib. bdg. 19.97 (*0-8114-2670-X*) Raintree Steck-V.
***Clouds of Witness.** Sayers. 1995. mass mkt. 4.99 (*0-06-104353-2*, Harp PBks) HarpC.
***Clouds of Witness.** Dorothy L. Sayers. 746p. 1992. Not sold separately (*0-615-00015-0*) Random Hse Value.
Clouds of Witness. large type ed. Dorothy L. Sayers. LC 92-32136. (Eagle Large Print Ser.). 1993. 21.95 (*0-7927-1435-0*, Eagle Lrg Print); pap. write for info. (*0-7927-1434-2*, Eagle Lrg Print) Chivers N Amer.
Clouds on the Moon. large type ed. Kay Winchester. 400p. 1988. 17.95 (*0-7089-1780-1*) Ulverscroft.
Clouds, Rain, & Rainmaking. 2nd ed. Basil J. Mason. LC 74-16991. 197p. reprint ed. pap. 56.20 (*0-317-20591-9*, 2024497) Bks Demand.
Clouds, Rain, Wind & Snow. Marti Abbott & Betty J. Polk. 1991. 10.99 (*0-8224-1351-5*) Fearon Teach Aids.
Clouds Without Water. Aleister Crowley. 1973. lib. bdg. 250.00 (*0-87968-111-X*) Krishna Pr.
Clouds Without Water. Aleister Crowley. Ed. by C. Verey. 140p. 1986. reprint ed. pap. 14.95 (*0-934781-00-1*) Bk Look.
Clouds Without Water. Aleister Crowley. 139p. 1973. reprint ed. pap. text ed. 6.00 (*0-911662-50-2*) Yoga.
Cloudstreet. Tim Winton. 432p. 1993. 20.00 (*1-55597-158-X*); pap. 12.50 (*1-55597-183-0*) Graywolf.
Cloudy Day. Jane Stroschin. 32p. (J). (gr. k-6). 1989. lib. bdg. 15.00 (*1-883960-00-2*) Henry Quill.
Cloudy Day in Gray Minor. Gregory Rabassa. Ed. by Stanley M. Barkan. (Review Chapbook Ser.: No. 35: American Poetry 8). 48p. 1989. 15.00 (*0-89304-870-4*); 15.00 (*0-685-26627-3*); pap. 5.00 (*0-89304-871-2*); pap. 5.00 (*0-685-26628-1*) Cross-Cultrl NY.
Cloudy Jewel. Grace L. Hill. reprint ed. lib. bdg. 23.95 (*0-89190-037-3*, Rivercity Pr) Amereon Ltd.
Cloudy Jewel, No. 184. Grace L. Hill. 1989. pap. 4.99 (*0-8423-0474-6*) Tyndale.
***Cloudy Mirror: Tension & Conflict in the Writings of Sima Qian.** Stephen W. Durrant. (SUNY Series in Chinese Philosophy & Culture). 224p. (C). 1995. text ed. 49.50x (*0-7914-2655-6*); pap. 16.95x (*0-7914-2656-4*) State U NY Pr.
Cloudy with a Chance of Brimstone. David Willingham. LC 92-31391. (Devotions for Today Ser.). 1992. pap. text ed. 6.25 (*1-56212-026-3*, 1701-0430) CRC Pubns.
Cloudy with a Chance of Meatballs. Judi Barrett. (J). (gr. 2-5). 1985. audio, lib. bdg. 19.95 (*0-941078-93-0*); audio, pap. 12.95 (*0-941078-91-4*) Live Oak Media.
Cloudy with a Chance of Meatballs. Judi Barrett. LC 78-2945. (Illus.). 32p. (J). (ps-3). 1978. text ed. 14.95 (*0-689-30647-4*, Atheneum Bks Young) S&S Childrens.
Cloudy with a Chance of Meatballs. Judith Barrett. LC 87-29643. (Illus.). 32p. (J). (ps-3). 1982. pap. 3.95 (*0-689-70749-5*, Aladdin Paperbacks) S&S Childrens.
Cloudy with a Chance of Meatballs, 4 bks., Set. Judi Barrett. (J). (gr. 2-5). 1985. audio, pap. 27.95 (*0-941078-92-2*) Live Oak Media.
Clough: Selected Poems. Ed. by J. P. Phelan. LC 94-20379. (Annotated Texts Ser.). 304p. (C). 1996. text ed. 51.95 (*0-582-05113-4*, 77035, Pub. by Longman UK); pap. text ed. 21.95 (*0-582-05112-6*, 77034, Pub. by Longman UK) Longman.
Clough: The Critical Heritage. Ed. by Michael Thorpe. 1972. 69.50 (*0-7100-7156-6*, 71566, RKP) Routledge.
Clough, Charles. Charles Clough et al. (Illus.). 36p. 1983. pap. 7.50 (*0-914782-49-5*) Buffalo Acad.
Clough's Sinhala-English Dictionary. 2nd ed. B. Clough. 848p. 1982. 95.00 (*0-8288-1762-6*, M14116) Fr & Eur.
Clover. McKenna. (Illus.). 40p. 1994. pap. 10.95 (*0-8059-3532-0*) Dorrance.
Clover. Dori Sanders. 196p. 1990. 13.95 (*0-945575-26-2*) Algonquin Bks.
Clover. Dori Sanders. Date not set. pap. write for info. (*0-449-45355-3*) Fawcett.
Clover. Dori Sanders. 192p. 1994. pap. 10.00 (*0-449-90624-8*, Columbine) Fawcett.
Clover. large type ed. Dori Sanders. (General Ser.). 224p. 1990. 17.95 (*0-8161-5048-6*, Large Print Bks) G K Hall.
Clover & the Bee: A Book of Pollination. Anne O. Dowden. LC 87-30116. (Illus.). 96p. (J). (gr. 5 up). 1990. 18.00 (*0-690-04677-4*, Crowell Jr Bks); lib. bdg. 17.89 (*0-690-04679-0*, Crowell Jr Bks) HarpC Child Bks.
Clover County Carrot Contest. John Himmelman. (Fix-It Family Ser.). (Illus.). 48p. (J). (ps-3). 1991. lib. bdg. 5.95 (*0-671-69637-8*); pap. 2.95 (*0-671-69641-6*) Silver Pr.
Clover Science & Technology. Ed. by N. L. Taylor. 1985p. 1985. 40.00 (*0-89118-083-4*) Am Soc Agron.
Cloverdale Review of Criticism & Poetry: James Joyce (1882-1941) in Memoriam. Ed. by John H. Morgan. (Nineteen Ninety-One Ser.). 104p. (Orig.). (C). 1992. pap. text ed. 14.95 (*1-55605-199-9*) Wyndhall Pr.
Cloverdale Review of Poetry & Criticism, 1992-1993. Ed. by John H. Morgan. (Illus.). 178p. (C). Date not set. pap. text ed. 14.95 (*1-55605-227-8*) Wyndhall Pr.
Clovernook Sketches & Other Stories. Alice Cary. Ed. by Judith Fetterly. (American Women Writers Ser.). 314p. (C). 1987. text ed. 35.00 (*0-8135-1250-6*); pap. text ed. 15.00 (*0-8135-1251-4*) Rutgers U Pr.
Clovin's Head. Raymond DiZazzo. 1976. pap. 2.50 (*0-88031-027-8*) Invisible-Red Hill.
Clovis. Michael Fessier. 160p. (Orig.). 1993. pap. 8.95 (*0-9627987-1-1*) Turtle Point Pr.
Clovis: Origins & Adaptations. Ed. by Robson Bonnichsen & Karen L. Turnmire. 344p. 1991. 38.00 (*0-912933-08-9*) Ctr Study First Am.
Clovis Caper. Jane Trahey. 144p. 1990. pap. 2.95 (*0-380-75914-4*, Camelot) Avon.
Clovis Crawfish & Batiste Bete Puante. Mary A. Fontenot. LC 93-1249. (Illus.). 32p. (J). (gr. k-3). 1993. 14.95 (*0-88289-952-X*) Pelican.
Clovis Crawfish & Bertile's Bon Voyage. Mary A. Fontenot. LC 90-22160. (Clovis Crawfish Ser.). (Illus.). 32p. (J). (ps-3). 1991. 12.95 (*0-88289-825-6*) Pelican.
Clovis Crawfish & Bidon Box Turtle. Mary A. Fontenot. LC 93-44340. (Illus.). (J). 1996. 12.95 (*1-56554-057-3*) Pelican.
Clovis Crawfish & Etienne Escargot. Mary A. Fontenot. LC 91-26896. (Clovis Crawfish Ser.). (Illus.). 32p. (J). (ps-3). 1992. 12.95 (*0-88289-826-4*) Pelican.
Clovis Crawfish & His Friends. Mary A. Fontenot. 1962. 4.95 (*0-87511-045-2*) Claitors.
Clovis Crawfish & His Friends. rev. ed. Mary A. Fontenot. LC 85-16994. (Clovis Crawfish Ser.). (Illus.). 32p. (J). (ps-3). 1985. 12.95 (*0-88289-479-X*) Pelican.
Clovis Crawfish & His Friends: French Edition. Mary A. Fontenot. (Illus.). 32p. (FRE.). (J). (ps-3). 1995. 12.95 (*0-318-68830-1*) Pelican.
Clovis Crawfish & Michelle Mantis. Mary A. Fontenot. 2.00 (*0-87511-050-9*) Claitors.
Clovis Crawfish & Michelle Mantis. Mary A. Fontenot. LC 88-30305. (Clovis Crawfish Ser.). (Illus.). 32p. (J). (ps-3). 1989. 12.95 (*0-88289-730-6*) Pelican.
Clovis Crawfish & Petit Papillon. Mary A. Fontenot. LC 83-27325. (Clovis Crawfish Ser.). (Illus.). 32p. (J). (ps-3). 1985. reprint ed. 12.95 (*0-88289-448-X*) Pelican.
Clovis Crawfish & Simeon Suce-Fleur. Mary A. Fontenot. LC 89-35370. (Clovis Crawfish Ser.). (Illus.). 32p. (J). (ps-3). 1990. 12.95 (*0-88289-751-9*) Pelican.
Clovis Crawfish & the Big Betail. Mary A. Fontenot. 1963. 4.95 (*0-87511-046-0*) Claitors.
Clovis Crawfish & the Big Betail. Mary A. Fontenot. LC 87-36557. (Clovis Crawfish Ser.). (Illus.). 1988. 12.95 (*0-88289-689-X*) Pelican.
Clovis Crawfish & the Curious Crapaud. Mary A. Fontenot. LC 86-4997. (Clovis Crawfish Ser.). (Illus.). 32p. (J). (ps-3). 1986. 12.95 (*0-88289-610-5*) Pelican.
Clovis Crawfish & the Orphan Zo Zo. Mary A. Fontenot. LC 81-17740. (Clovis Crawfish Ser.). (Illus.). 32p. (J). (ps-3). 1983. 12.95 (*0-88289-312-2*) Pelican.
Clovis Crawfish & the Singing Cigales. Mary A. Fontenot. LC 81-5608. (Clovis Crawfish Ser.). (Illus.). 32p. (J). (ps-3). 1981. 12.95 (*0-88289-270-3*) Pelican.
Clovis Crawfish & the Spinning Spider. Mary A. Fontenot. LC 86-23778. (Clovis Crawfish Ser.). (Illus.). 32p. (J). (ps-3). 1987. 12.95 (*0-88289-644-X*) Pelican.
Clowes Collection. A. Ian Fraser. (Illus.). 1973. 4.00 (*0-317-29197-1*) Ind Mus Art.
***Clown.** Quentin Blake. LC 95-12811. 1995. write for info. (*0-8050-4399-3*) H Holt & Co.
Clown. Heinrich Boll. Tr. by Leila Vennewitz. 272p. 1994. 10.95 (*0-14-018726-X*, Penguin Classics) Viking Penguin.
***Clown.** Ivan Bulloch & Diane James. (I Want to Be Ser.). (Illus.). 32p. (J). (gr. 1-3). 1995. 13.95 (*1-56847-362-1*) Thomson Lrning.
Clown: My Life in Tatters & Smiles. F. Beverly Kelley. 1976. 22.95 (*0-8488-1397-9*) Amereon Ltd.
Clown: My Life in Tatters & Smiles. Emmett Kelly & F. Beverly Kelley. (Illus.). 272p. 1991. reprint ed. lib. bdg. 23.95 (*0-89966-812-7*) Buccaneer Bks.
Clown Act Omnibus. Wes McVicar. LC 87-42958. (Illus.). 192p. 1986. reprint ed. pap. 10.95 (*0-916260-41-0*, B-118) Meriwether Pub.
Clown-Arounds. Joanna Cole. LC 81-4662. (Illus.). 48p. (J). (ps-3). 1981. 5.95 (*0-8193-1059-X*); lib. bdg. 5.95 (*0-8193-1060-3*) Parents.
Clown-Arounds. Joanna Cole. LC 94-16228. (Parents Magazine Read Aloud Original Ser.). (J). 1994. write for info. (*0-8368-0995-5*) Parents.
Clown-Arounds. Joanna Cole. (Sunny Day Bks.). (Illus.). 48p. (J). (ps-2). 1992. pap. 2.95 (*0-448-40321-8*, G&D) Putnam Pub Group.
Clown-Arounds Go on Vacation. Joanna Cole. LC 93-15471. (Parents Magazine Read Aloud Original Ser.). (Illus.). (J). 1993. 14.60 (*0-8368-0966-1*) Gareth Stevens Inc.
Clown-Arounds Go on Vacation. Joanna Cole. LC 83-13480. (Illus.). 48p. (J). (ps-3). 1984. 5.95 (*0-8193-1120-0*) Parents.
Clown-Arounds Have a Party. Joanna Cole. LC 82-2128. (Illus.). 48p. (J). (ps-3). 1982. 5.95 (*0-8193-1085-9*); lib. bdg. 5.95 (*0-8193-1086-7*) Parents.
***Clown-Arounds Have a Party.** Joanna Cole. LC 94-34652. (Parents Magazine Read Aloud Original Ser.). (Illus.). (J). 1995. write for info. (*0-8368-0999-8*) Gareth Stevens Inc.
Clown Caboose. Joanne Barkan. (Circus Train Come Aboard Bks.). (Illus.). 12p. (J). (ps). 1993. bds. 3.50 (*0-689-71675-3*, Aladdin Paperbacks) S&S Childrens.
Clown Faces Stickers. Nina Barbaresi. (Illus.). (J). (gr. k-3). 1993. pap. 1.00 (*0-486-27248-6*) Dover.
Clown Games. Harriet Ziefert. (Hello Reading! Ser.). (Illus.). 32p. (J). (ps-3). 1993. pap. 3.50 (*0-14-054581-6*) Puffin Bks.
Clown Games. Harriet Ziefert. (Hello Reading! Ser.). (Illus.). 32p. (J). (ps-3). 1993. 9.00 (*0-670-84652-X*) Viking Child Bks.
Clown in Modern Anglo-Irish Drama. Elizabeth H. Winkler. (European University Studies: Ser. 14, Vol. 50). 298p. 1977. pap. 45.75 (*3-261-02903-X*) P Lang Pubs.
Clown Magic. David Ginn. LC 92-46228. (Illus.). 160p. (Orig.). 1993. pap. 16.95 (*0-941599-21-3*) Piccadilly Bks.
Clown Masks Punch Out Stencils. Theodore Menten. (Toy Bks.). (Illus.). 16p. 1984. pap. 3.50 (*0-486-24633-7*) Dover.
Clown Ministry. Floyd Shaffer & Penne Sewall. 112p. (Orig.). 1984. pap. 11.99 (*0-936664-18-5*) Group Pub.
Clown Ministry Handbook. 4th ed. Janet Litherland. Ed. by Sheila Meyer & Arthur L. Zapel. LC 82-61091. (Illus.). 160p. (Orig.). 1982. pap. text ed. 9.95 (*0-916260-20-8*, B-163) Meriwether Pub.
***Clown Ministry Organizer.** Chuck Amos & Sheila Amos. Ed. by Penny Lent. LC 94-79468. (Illus.). 210p. 1994. ring bd. 15.99 (*1-885371-06-3*) Kldoscope Pr.
Clown Ministry Skits for All Seasons. Floyd Shaffer. 96p. (Orig.). 1990. pap. 11.99 (*1-55945-051-3*) Group Pub.
Clown Must Die. Birdella Stewart & Dennis Baker. 143p. (Orig.). 1988. pap. 8.95 (*0-930397-12-6*) Inspiratnl Pub.
Clown of God. Tomie De Paola. LC 78-3845. (Illus.). (J). (gr. k up). 1978. 13.95 (*0-15-219175-5*, HB Juv Bks) HarBrace.
Clown of God. Tomie De Paola. LC 78-3845. (Illus.). 45p. (J). (ps-3). 1978. pap. 5.95 (*0-15-618192-4*, Voyager Bks) HarBrace.
Clown Plays. F. K. Waechter & Ken Campbell. (Methuen Young Drama Ser.). (Illus.). 129p. (J). 1992. reprint ed. pap. 11.95 (*0-413-66550-X*, A0661) Heinemann.
Clown Prince of Baseball. Max Patkin & Stan Hochman. LC 93-43574. (Illus.). 192p. 1994. 19.95 (*1-56796-036-7*, B0367) WRS Group.
Clown Skits for Everyone. Happy Jack Feder. Ed. by Arthur Zapel. LC 90-29297. (Illus.). 176p. 1990. reprint ed. pap. 9.95 (*0-916260-75-5*, B147) Meriwether Pub.
Clownin' Around. Janet Schrader. (Illus.). 56p. 1988. pap. text ed. 14.95 (*0-935133-21-6*) CKE Pubns.
Clowning Around! Jokes about the Circus. Rick Walton & Ann Walton. (Make Me Laugh! Joke Bks.). (Illus.). 32p. (J). (gr. 1-4). 1989. 11.95 (*0-8225-0975-X*, Lerner Publctns) Lerner Group.
Clowning As Critical Practice: Performance Humor in the South Pacific. Ed. by William E. Mitchell. LC 92-50195. (Association for Social Anthropology in Oceania Monographs). 272p. (C). 1993. text ed. 49.95 (*0-8229-3734-4*); pap. text ed. 19.95 (*0-8229-5487-7*) U of Pittsburgh Pr.

C

An Asterisk (*) at the beginning of an entry indicates that the title is appearing in BIP for the first time.

---

*Clueless in Seattle. Steve Oliver. (Illus.). 137p. (Orig.). 1995. pap. 10.95 (0-9644138-6-8) OffByOne
Simon, in the title story, was very proud of his personals ad. The only problem was that it took over 700 words to describe him & his needs. Simon is only one of the typically angst-ridden middle-class men in this wonderful collection of tongue-in-cheek short stories, mostly set in rainy, latte-addicted Seattle. Other stories feature a terribly tall man given to relationships with incredibly short

---

women, a military robot who is converted into a cybernetic chimp named Bonzo, & Milo & his too-silent girlfriends. Tongue-in-cheek, hilarious stories, these will tickle your funnybone every time. Oliver's offbeat characters are lovingly nerdy (sometimes just plain nerdy!) guys suffering through the male-female relationship pains of unrequited (or occasionally incorrectly requited) love. Copies may be ordered by sending either check or money order for $10.95 plus $3.00 shipping to: OffByOne Press, 9594 1st Avenue N.E. #322, Seattle, WA 98115-2012. Phone: (206) 528-0185; FAX: (206) 528-0147. *Publisher Provided Annotation.*

C

An Asterisk (*) at the beginning of an entry indicates that the title is appearing in BIP for the first time.

1331

Clumsy Construction in Mark's Gospel: A Critique of Form & Redaktionsgeschichte. John C. Meagher. LC 79-66373. (Toronto Studies in Theology: Vol. 3). 178p. 1979. lib. bdg. 79.95 (*0-88946-876-1*) E Mellen.

***Clumsy Crocodile.** F. Everett. (Reading for Beginners Ser.). (Illus.). 24p. (J). (gr. k-3). 1995. lib. bdg. 11.96 (*0-88110-743-3*, Usborne); pap. 4.95 (*0-7460-1533-X*, Usborne) EDC.

Clumsy Custard Horror Show. William Gleason. 1979. 4.95 (*0-87129-229-7*, C46) Dramatic Pub.

Cluny under Saint Hugh, Ten Forty-Nine to Eleven Hundred Nine. Noreen Hunt. LC 68-11411. 240p. reprint ed. pap. 68.40 (*0-317-29696-5*, 2022064) Bks Demand.

Clusiidae-Chloropidae. A. Soos & L. Papp. (Catalogue of Palaearctic Diptera Ser.: Vol. 10). 1984. 152.75 (*0-685-09920-2*) Elsevier.

Cluster. Piers Anthony. (Cluster Ser.: No. 1). 256p. 1977. pap. 3.95 (*0-380-01755-5*) Avon.

Cluster Analysis. Mark S. Aldenderfer & Roger K. Blashfield. (Quantitative Applications in the Social Sciences Ser.: Vol. 44). 96p. (C). 1984. pap. text ed. 9.95 (*0-8039-2376-7*) Sage.

Cluster Analysis. 3rd ed. Brian S. Everitt. 170p. 1993. text ed. 64.95 (*0-470-22043-0*) Halsted Pr.

Cluster Analysis & Data Analysis. Michel Jambu & M. O. Lebeaux. 1991. 145.75 (*0-685-50933-8*, I153-83) Elsevier.

Cluster Analysis for Applications. Michael R. Anderberg. (Probability & Mathematical Statistics Ser.: Vol. 19). 1973. text ed. 77.00 (*0-12-057650-3*) Acad Pr.

Cluster Analysis for Researchers. H. Charles Romesburg. LC 89-24453. 350p. (C). 1990. reprint ed. lib. bdg. 46.50 (*0-89464-426-2*) Krieger.

Cluster Analysis for Social Scientists. Maurice Lorr. LC 82-49283. (Jossey-Bass Social & Behavioral Science Ser.). (Illus.). 251p. reprint ed. pap. 71.60 (*0-8357-4905-3*, 2037835) Bks Demand.

Cluster Analysis in Clinical Chemistry: A Model. M. Vogt et al. LC 87-8288. 180p. 1987. text ed. 85.00 (*0-471-91554-8*) Wiley.

***Cluster & Colloids: From Theory to Applications.** Ed. by Gunter Schmid. 555p. 1994. 145.00 (*1-56081-753-4*) VCH Pubs.

Cluster Approach to Elementary Vocabulary Instruction. Robert J. Marzano & Jana S. Marzano. LC 88-2923. (Reading Aids Ser.). (Illus.). 270p. reprint ed. pap. 77.00 (*0-7837-4589-3*, 2044308) Bks Demand.

Cluster Chemistry: An Introduction to the Chemistry of Transition Metal & Main Group Element Molecular Clusters. Guillermo Gonzalez-Moraga. LC 93-12644. 1993. 59.00 (*0-387-56470-5*) Spr-Verlag.

Cluster College. Jerry Gaff et al. LC 77-110641. (Jossey-Bass Higher Education Ser.). 268p. reprint ed. 76.40 (*0-8357-9306-0*, 2013940) Bks Demand.

Cluster Command. David Drake & Bill Dietz. (Crisis of Empire Ser.: Vol. II). 288p. (Orig.). 1989. pap. 3.50 (*0-671-69817-6*) Baen Bks.

Cluster Headache. Ed. by Ninan Mathew. LC 84-4925. 176p. 1984. text ed. 40.00 (*0-89335-204-7*) PMA Pub Corp.

Cluster Ions. Ed. by Cheuk-Yiu Ng. LC 93-10286. (Current Topics in Ion Chemistry & Physics Ser.: Vol. 1). 400p. 1993. text ed. 144.00 (*0-471-93830-0*) Wiley.

Cluster Ions & Van Der Waal's Molecules. B. M. Smirnov. 284p. 1992. text ed. 150.00 (*2-88124-697-4*) Gordon & Breach.

Cluster Model & Other Topics. Y. Akaishi et al. (International Review of Nuclear Physics Ser.: Vol. 4). 520p. 1987. pap. 46.00 (*9971-5-0078-7*) World Scientific Pub.

Cluster Models for Surface & Bulk Phenomena. Ed. by G. Pacchioni et al. (NATO ASI Series B, Physics: Vol. 283). (Illus.). 678p. 1992. 149.50 (*0-306-44102-0*, Plenum Pr) Plenum.

Cluster Molecules of the p-Block Elements. Catherine E. Housecroft. (Oxford Chemistry Primers Ser.: No. 14). (Illus.). 96p. (C). 1994. 29.95 (*0-19-855699-3*); pap. 9.95 (*0-19-855698-5*) OUP.

Cluster of Jesse Mercer. C. Ray Brewster. (Illus.). 226p. 1983. 12.00 (*0-914707-01-9*) Ren Pr GA.

Cluster of Separate Sparks. large type ed. Joan Aiken. 387p. 1992. pap. 15.95 (*0-8161-5513-5*, Nightingale) Hall.

Cluster Representations of Nuclei. K. Wildermuth & W. McClure. (Tracts in Modern Physics Ser.: Vol. 41). (Illus.). 1966. 43.00 (*0-387-03670-9*) Spr-Verlag.

Clustering Algorithms. John A. Hartigan. LC 74-14573. (Wiley Series in Probability & Mathematical Statistics). 365p. reprint ed. pap. 104.10 (*0-317-09401-7*, 2019502) Bks Demand.

Clustering & Aggregation in Economics. Walter D. Fisher. LC 68-55610. 208p. reprint ed. pap. 59.30 (*0-317-42286-3*, 2023095) Bks Demand.

Clustering & Classification. P. Arabie et al. 550p. 1995. text ed. 109.00 (*981-02-1287-9*); pap. text ed. 61.00 (*981-02-1354-9*) World Scientific Pub.

Clustering Approach to Better Essay Writing. Char Large. 59p. 1987. student ed, pap. 9.99 (*0-89824-146-4*) Trillium Pr.

Clustering Aspects of Nuclear Reactions 1978. No. 47. write for info. (*0-318-68039-4*) Am Inst Physics.

Clustering Aspects of Nuclear Structure & Nuclear Reactions, Winnipeg, 1978. Ed. by Willem T. Van Oers et al. LC 78-64942. (AIP Conference Proceedings Ser.: No. 47). (Illus.). 1978. lib. bdg. 26.75 (*0-88318-146-0*) Am Inst Physics.

Clustering of Large Data Sets. Jure Zupan. (Chemometrics Research Studies: No. 2). (Illus.). 140p. reprint ed. pap. 39.90 (*0-8357-6058-8*, 2034246) Bks Demand.

Clustering Phenomena in Atoms & Nuclei: Proceedings of the International Conference on Nuclear & Atomic Clusters 1991, 3-7 June 1991, Turku, Finland. Ed. by M. Brenner et al. (Series in Nuclear & Particle Physics). (Illus.). 640p. 1992. 98.00 (*0-387-55101-8*) Spr-Verlag.

Clusters & Fullerenes: Proceedings of the Adriatico Research Conference. V. Kumar et al. 472p. 1993. text ed. 109.00 (*981-02-1084-1*) World Scientific Pub.

Clusters & Groups of Galaxies. Ed. by F. Mardirossian et al. 704p. 1984. lib. bdg. 204.50 (*90-277-1772-9*) Kluwer Ac.

Clusters & Superclusters of Galaxies: Proceedings of the NATO Advanced Study Institute, Cambridge, U. K. July 1-10, 1991. Ed. by Andrew C. Fabian. LC 92-5511. (NATO Advanced Science Institutes Series C: Mathematical & Physical Sciences). 384p. (C). 1992. lib. bdg. 122.00 (*0-7923-1702-5*) Kluwer Ac.

Clusters of Atoms & Molecules: Theory, Experiment, & Clusters of Atoms. Ed. by Hellmut Haberland. LC 93-28934. (Chemical Physics Ser.: Vol. 56). 1995. text ed. 89.00 (*0-387-53332-X*) Spr-Verlag.

Clusters of Galaxies. Ed. by W. Oegerle et al. (Space Telescope Science Institute Symposium Ser.). (Illus.). 408p. (C). 1990. 59.95 (*0-521-38462-1*) Cambridge U Pr.

Clusters of Galaxies & Extragalactic Radio Sources. Ed. by A. D. Kuz'min. Tr. by Paul Makinen. (Proceedings of the Lebedev Physics Institute Ser.: Vol. 189). 326p. (C). 1989. text ed. 145.00 (*0-941743-69-1*) Nova Sci Pubs.

Clusters of Galaxies & Large Scale Structure: The Minnesota Lectures. Ed. by J. Dickey. (ASP Conference Series Publications: Vol. 5). 250p. 1988. 25.00 (*0-937707-22-8*) Astron Soc Pacific.

Clutch & Differential. George A. Weller. LC 79-130078. (Short Story Index Reprint Ser.). 1977. 23.95 (*0-8369-3659-0*) Ayer.

Clutch & Flywheel Handbook. rev. ed. Tom Monroe. 184p. 1991. reprint ed. pap. 14.95 (*1-55788-030-1*) Price Stern.

Clutch Hitter. Clair Bee. 15.95 (*0-8488-1246-8*) Amereon Ltd.

Clutch Hitter! Clair Bee. (Illus.). 208p. 1990. reprint ed. lib. bdg. 25.95 (*0-89966-739-2*) Buccaneer Bks.

Clutch of Constables. Ngaio Marsh. 224p. 1986. pap. 3.99 (*0-515-08775-0*) Jove Pubns.

Clutch of Constables. Ngaio Marsh. 1976. reprint ed. lib. bdg. 20.95 (*0-88411-473-2*, Aeonian Pr) Amereon Ltd.

Clutch of Constables. Ngaio Marsh. 1994. reprint ed. lib. bdg. 27.95 (*1-56849-308-8*) Buccaneer Bks.

Clutch of Fables. 4th ed. Teo Savory. LC 73-76686. (Illus.). 100p. 1976. 15.00 (*0-87775-043-2*); pap. 7.95 (*0-87775-104-8*) Unicorn Pr.

Clutches & Brakes: Design & Selection. Orthwein. (Mechanical Engineering Ser.: Vol. 50). 368p. 1986. 125.00 (*0-8247-7393-4*) Dekker.

Clutter Control. Jeff Campbell. 1992. mass mkt. 7.99 (*0-440-50339-6*, Dell Trade Pbks) Dell.

***Cluttering: A Clinical Perspective.** Myers. 146p. 1992. pap. 38.25 (*1-56593-543-8*, 0488) Singular Publishing.

Clutter's Last Stand. Don Aslett. 280p. 1984. pap. 10.95 (*0-89879-137-5*) Writers Digest.

C.L.U.T.Z. Marilyn Z. Wilkes. LC 81-68786. (Illus.). 128p. (J). (gr. 3-7). 1982. 9.95 (*0-8037-1157-3*, 0966-290) Dial Bks Young.

Clyack Sheaf: Sketches of Life & Characters in Northeast Scotland. Ed. by D. Toulmin. 152p. 1987. text ed. 23.95 (*0-08-034526-3*, Pub. by Aberdeen U Pr); pap. text ed. 14.00 (*0-08-034517-4*, Pub. by Aberdeen U Pr) Macmillan.

***Clyde.** Jack Q. May. 1994. 15.95 (*0-533-11140-4*) Vantage.

Clyde Aspevig. Ed. by Thomas A. Nygard. (Illus.). 36p. 1994. pap. 10.00 (*0-9620327-4-3*) Nygard Pub.

Clyde Aspevig: Field Studies. Intro. by Thomas S. Buechner. (Illus.). 40p. (Orig.). 1991. pap. 3.00 (*0-9622038-2-3*) Rockwell NY.

Clyde Butcher, Portfolio I: Florida Landscapes. 2nd deluxe limited ed. Clyde Butcher. Ed. by Malcolm E. Reding. (Illus.). 100p. 1994. reprint ed. boxed 125.00 (*0-9638703-3-5*) Shade Tree Pr.

Clyde Butcher, Portfolio I: Florida Landscapes. 2nd ed. Clyde Butcher. Ed. by Malcolm E. Reding. (Illus.). 80p. 1994. reprint ed. 45.00 (*0-9638703-2-7*) Shade Tree Pr.

Clyde Connell: The Art & Life of a Louisiana Woman. Charlotte Moser. (Illus.). 94p. 1991. pap. 19.95 (*0-292-71141-7*) U of Tex Pr.

Clyde Hare's Pittsburgh: Four Decades of Pittsburgh, Frozen in Light. LC 94-67891. (Illus.). 168p. (C). 1994. pap. text ed. 65.00 (*0-916670-16-3*) Pitt Hist & Landmks Found.

Clyde McPhatter: Michael Jackson's U. S. A. Roots, Durham, NC (Unauthorized) James M. DeVone. LC 90-93013. (Illus.). (Orig.). 1990. pap. text ed. 9.95 (*0-9625092-4-8*) Schl Univ Studies.

Clyde McPhatter: Michael Jackson's U. S. A. Roots, Durham, NC (Unauthorized) James M. DeVone, Sr. LC 90-93013. (Illus.). (Orig.). 1990. pap. text ed. 9.95 (*0-685-35357-5*) Schl Univ Studies.

Clyde Monster. Robert L. Crowe. LC 76-10733. (Unicorn Paperbacks Ser.). (Illus.). 32p. (J). (ps-3). 1987. pap. 3.95 (*0-525-44289-8*, DCB) Dutton Child Bks.

Clyde Monster. Robert L. Crowe. (J). (ps-3). 1993. pap. 4.99 (*0-14-054743-6*) Puffin Bks.

Clyde Passenger Steamer: Its Rise & Progress During the Nineteenth Century from the "Comet" of 1812 to the King Edward of 1901. Ed. by James Williamson. 200p. (C). 1986. 90.00 (*0-907590-19-5*) St Mut.

Clyde River & Other Steamers: Supplement. C. L. Duckworth & G. E. Lanmuir. (C). 1987. 24.00 (*0-85174-421-4*, Pub. by Brwn Son Ferg) St Mut.

Clyde, the Cloud Who Always Cried. Kymberli M. Dyson. (Illus.). 28p. (Orig.). (J). (gr. k-4). 1994. Saddle-stitched. 5.00 (*1-885282-00-1*) This Little.

Clyde Tombaugh: Discoverer of Planet Pluto. David H. Levy. LC 90-48545. (Illus.). 212p. 1992. reprint ed. pap. 15.95 (*0-8165-1317-1*) U of Ariz Pr.

Clyde Wells: A Political Biography. Claire Hoy. 368p. 1992. 27.95 (*0-7737-2652-7*, Pub. by Stoddart Pubng CN) Genl Dist Srvs.

Clyde Wells Cartoon Book. Clyde Wells. LC 89-18036. (Illus.). 200p. (Orig.). 1989. 14.95 (*0-9618270-3-3*); pap. 9.95 (*0-9618270-4-1*) Morris Comms.

***Clydesdale Horses.** Janet L. Gammie. LC 95-5447. (Horses Ser.). (J). 1995. lib. bdg. 9.95 (*1-56239-441-X*) Abdo & Dghtrs.

Clydesiders: A Left-Wing Struggle for Parliamentary Power. Robert K. Middlemas. LC 66-2916. (Illus.). 307p. 1965. 39.50 (*0-678-08040-2*) Kelley.

Clyfford Still. Michael Auping. pap. 35.00 (*0-914782-86-X*) Buffalo Acad.

Clyfford Still. Susan Landauer et al. Ed. by Thomas Kellein. (Illus.). 176p. 1992. 60.00 (*3-7913-1187-5*, Pub. by Prestel) TeNeues.

***Clymer Kawasaki EX500, 1987-1991.** Clymer Staff. LC 91-75947. 1993. pap. 24.95 (*0-89287-562-3*) Clymer Pub.

Clyomon & Clamydes. LC 76-133737. (Tudor Facsimile Texts. Old English Plays Ser.: No. 85). reprint ed. 49.50 (*0-404-53385-X*) AMS Pr.

CMA Review, 2 vols., Set. 6th ed. Irvin N. Gleim & Dale L. Flesher. LC 94-75280. 1994. pap. write for info. (*0-917537-70-X*) Gleim Pubns.

CMA Review, 2 vols., Vol. I. 6th ed. Irvin N. Gleim & Dale L. Flesher. LC 94-75280. 760p. 1994. pap. 25.95 (*0-917537-68-8*) Gleim Pubns.

CMA Review, 2 vols., Vol. II. 6th ed. Irvin N. Gleim & Dale L. Flesher. LC 94-75280. 760p. 1994. pap. 25.95 (*0-917537-69-6*) Gleim Pubns.

CMEA: Energy Nineteen Eighty to Nineteen Ninety. Ed. by NATO Economic Directorate Staff. (NATO Colloquia Ser.). 337p. 1982. 45.00 (*0-89250-341-6*) Orient Res Partners.

***CMEA Chemotherapy Symposium, 1984.** S. Eckhardt & E. Kerpel-Fronius. 646p. (C). 1985. 135.00x (*963-05-4188-2*, Pub. by Akad Kiado HU) St Mut.

CMEA Economic Integration: Soviet-Romanian Economic Relations: A Personal Account. Joseph Savu. Ed. by Jonathan Gallant. 105p. (Orig.). 1989. pap. text ed. 75.00 (*1-55831-104-1*) Delphic Associates.

CMEA in Crisis: Toward a New European Order? Vlad Sobell. LC 90-2196. 128p. 1990. text ed. 39.95 (*0-275-93730-5*, C3730, Praeger Pubs); pap. text ed. 11.95 (*0-275-93731-3*, B3731, Praeger Pubs) Greenwood.

CMEA in Theory & Practice. Petre Nicolae. Ed. by Steven Jones. 90p. (Orig.). 1984. pap. text ed. 75.00 (*1-55831-032-0*) Delphic Associates.

***CMG94 Proceedings: Resource Management & Performance Evaluation of Enterprise Computing Systems, Vol. 1.** CMG94 Program Committee Staff. 700p. 1994. pap. write for info. (*1-886241-03-1*) The Computer Meas.

***CMG94 Proceedings: Resource Management & Performance Evaluation of Enterprise Computing Systems, Vol. 2.** CMG94 Program Committee Staff. 700p. 1994. pap. write for info. (*1-886241-04-X*) The Computer Meas.

CMO Portfolio Management. Ed. by Frank J. Fabozzi. (Illus.). 348p. (Orig.). (C). 1994. pap. write for info. (*1-883249-01-5*) F J Fabozzi.

C'mon Get Happy: Fear & Loathing on the Partridge Family Bus. David Cassidy & Chip Deffaa. 256p. (Orig.). 1994. pap. 11.99 (*0-446-39531-5*) Warner Bks.

CMOS Analog Circuit Design. Phillip E. Allen & Douglas R. Holberg. 500p. (C). 1987. text ed. 68.00 (*0-03-006587-9*); Solutions manual. write for info. (*0-03-006588-7*) SCP.

CMOS Cookbook. 2nd ed. Donald E. Lancaster. 528p. 1988. pap. 24.95 (*0-672-22459-3*) Sams.

***CMOS Designers' Primer & Handbook.** Jack Streater & Robert M. Glorioso. LC 77-26750. 1978. pap. text ed. 9.00 (*0-89704-020-1*) E&L Instru.

CMOS Devices: 1986 Source Book. Technipubs, Inc. Staff & Harry L. Helms. 560p. 1987. 36.95 (*0-13-138892-4*) P-H.

CMOS Digital Circuit Technology. Masakazu Shoji. (Illus.). 448p. 1987. text ed. 78.00 (*0-13-138850-9*) P-H.

CMOS Digital Techniques. rev. ed. Heath Company Staff. (Illus.). 698p. 1983. ring bd. 89.95 (*0-87119-035-4*, EE-3203A) Heathkit-Zenith Ed.

***CMOS Handbook.** 200p. (Orig.). 1995. pap. 125.00 (*0-7605-1832-7*) Rector Pr.

CMOS-TTL Digital Systems Design. James E. Buchanan. 1990. text ed. 50.00 (*0-07-008711-3*) McGraw.

CMOS3 Cell Library. Dennis Heinbuch. LC 86-21355. (VLSI Systems Ser.). 512p. (C). 1987. pap. text ed. 58.25 (*0-201-11257-4*) Addison-Wesley.

CMR: Contracts for the International Carriage of Goods by Road. D. J. Hill & A. D. Messent. 1984. 100.00 (*0-907432-55-7*) Lloyds London Pr.

CMR Index. rev. ed. 120p. (C). 1994. 79.95 (*0-916812-52-9*) Weil Pub.

CMS Archival Series. Incl. Vol. 1. A.C.I.M Records, Farfariello, ICM Documents, Italian Labor Movement Materials, Italian Welfare League Records, Juvenal Marchisio Papers, St. Raphael Society Records. Ed. by Olha D Cava. 38p. 1974. (*0-913256-18-8*); Vol. 2. Ethnic Press Holdings, AIHA Records, Casa Italiana of Columbia University Records, Papers of DeBiasi Family, V. Bocchimuzzo, Rev. N. DeCarlo, Frank DeLuca, & G. Zapulla, & Italian American Writers. Ed. by Olha D. Cava. 38p. 1977. (*0-318-64742-7*); Vol. 4. Archivio del Commissariato Generale dell'Emigrazione. Ed. by Maria R. Ostuni. 44p. 1981. (*0-318-64743-5*); Vol. 5. Records of the Commissariato Generale & Direzione Generale degli Italiani all'Estero. Ed. by Gianfusto Rosoli. 84p. 1986. (*0-913256-85-4*); Vol. 6. Records of the Apostleship of the Sea & Catholic Maritime Clubs. Ed. by Diana Zimmerman. 40p. 1989. (*0-913256-86-2*); Vol. 7. Papers of Congressman Victor Anfuso & Mayor Alex Pisciotta, Ethnic Press. Ed. by Diana Zimmerman. 30p. 1989. (*0-318-64744-3*); Vol. 8. Records of the Missionaries of St. Charles (Scalabrinians) in North America. Ed. by Nicholas Falco. 80p. 1988. (*0-934733-36-8*); Vol. 9. Records of the Italian Welfare League, Inc. Ed. by Nicholas Falco. 108p. 1988. (*0-934733-37-6*); Vol. 1. A.C.I.M Records, Farfariello, ICM Documents, Italian Labor Movement Materials, Italian Welfare League Records, Juvenal Marchisio Papers, St. Raphael Society Records. Ed. by Olha D Cava. 38p. 1974. (*0-913256-18-8*); Vol. 2. Ethnic Press Holdings, AIHA Records, Casa Italiana of Columbia University Records, Papers of DeBiasi Family, V. Bocchimuzzo, Rev. N. DeCarlo, Frank DeLuca, & G. Zapulla, & Italian American Writers. Ed. by Olha D. Cava. 38p. 1977. (*0-318-64742-7*); Vol. 4. Archivio del Commissariato Generale dell'Emigrazione. Ed. by Maria R. Ostuni. 44p. 1981. (*0-318-64743-5*); Vol. 5. Records of the Commissariato Generale & Direzione Generale degli Italiani all'Estero. Ed. by Gianfusto Rosoli. 84p. 1986. (*0-913256-85-4*); Vol. 6. Records of the Apostleship of the Sea & Catholic Maritime Clubs. Ed. by Diana Zimmerman. 40p. 1989. (*0-913256-86-2*); Vol. 7. Papers of Congressman Victor Anfuso & Mayor Alex Pisciotta, Ethnic Press. Ed. by Diana Zimmerman. 30p. 1989. (*0-318-64744-3*); Vol. 8. Records of the Missionaries of St. Charles (Scalabrinians) in North America. Ed. by Nicholas Falco. 80p. 1988. (*0-934733-36-8*); Vol. 9. Records of the Italian Welfare League, Inc. Ed. by Nicholas Falco. 108p. 1988. (*0-934733-37-6*); 9.95 (*0-685-74069-2*) Ctr Migration.

CMS User's Guide. Paul E. Hoffman & G. Mack Hicks. 1989. 24.95 (*0-13-187725-9*) P-H.

CMSAP Users' Manual, 2 disks, Set. G. David Peters. 1992. disk 20.00 (*0-317-05166-0*) U IL Sch Music.

CMU Computer Science: A Twenty-Fifth Anniversary Commemorative. Ed. by Richard F. Rashid. (ACM Press Anthology Ser.). (Illus.). 448p. (C). 1991. text ed. 44.25 (*0-201-52899-1*) Addison-Wesley.

CNC Handbook Series, 3 bks., Set. Josef Franz & Hans Frommer. (C). 1985. pap. text ed. 175.50 (*1-56990-114-7*) Hanser-Gardner.

CNC Lathe. Leo Rizzo. 1985. student ed 8.00 (*0-8064-0255-5*, 519); audio 369.00 (*0-8064-0256-3*) Bergwall.

CNC Machining: The Handbook on Turning & Machining Centres. Graham T. Smith. LC 92-27175. 1993. 98.00 (*0-387-19586-6*) Spr-Verlag.

***CNC Machining Handbook.** James Madison. (Illus.). 280p. (C). 1995. text ed. 38.95 (*0-8311-3064-4*) Indus Pr.

CNC Machining Technology, 1. Graham T. Smith. LC 93-19295. 1993. 29.00 (*0-387-19828-8*) Spr-Verlag.

CNC Machining Technology, 2. Graham T. Smith. LC 93-19295. 1993. 29.00 (*0-387-19829-6*) Spr-Verlag.

CNC Machining Technology, 3. Graham T. Smith. LC 93-19295. 1993. 29.00 (*0-387-19830-X*) Spr-Verlag.

***CNC Process Modeling Using SmartCAM.** S. C. Lin et al. Ed. by Karen L. Sterzik. (Illus.). 700p. (C). 1995. pap. 65.00 (*1-886552-02-9*) Scholars Intl.

***CNC Programming Using Mastercam Version Four & Five.** Jonathon Lin & Tony Shiue. Ed. by Karen L. Sterzik. (Illus.). 880p. (C). 1995. pap. text ed. 55.00 (*1-886552-00-2*) Scholars Intl.

CNC Workbook: Computer Numerical Control Programming Made Easy. Frank Nanfara. (Illus.). 320p. (C). 1995. pap. text ed. 32.25 (*0-201-65600-0*) Addison-Wesley.

***CNE Short Course.** New Riders Development Group Staff. (Illus.). 800p. (Orig.). 1995. pap. text ed. 60.00 (*1-56205-446-5*) New Riders Pub.

***CNJ-LV Color Guide to Freight & Passenger Equipment.** C. T. Bossler. (Illus.). 128p. 1995. 49.95 (*1-878887-38-6*) Morning NJ.

CNL-Quarterly World Report: Proceedings of CNL-MLA Meeting December 1982. Walter H. Sokel et al. Ed. by Elizabeth W. Trahan. 1983. pap. 6.95 (*0-918680-21-2*) Bagehot Council.

CNL-Quarterly World Report: Shakespeare & the World, Vol. 4. Comment by Rosette Lamont et al. (Illus.). 40p. 1982. pap. 4.95 (*0-918680-19-0*) Bagehot Council.

CNL-World Report III: Selected Papers on Columbus & His Time. 80p. 1989. 15.00 (*0-918680-40-9*) Bagehot Council.

CNL-World Report IV: The Doctor of Arts Degree: Reassessing Teaching & Research Priorities. 102p. 1989. 15.00 (*0-918680-42-5*) Bagehot Council.

CNL-World Report V: Modern Views of Columbus & His Time. annuals 112p. 1990. Annual. 15.00 (*0-918680-46-8*) Bagehot Council.

CNL-World Report VI: Multicultural Perspectives: New Approaches. 116p. 1993. 18.00 (*0-918680-52-2*) Bagehot Council.

An Asterisk (*) at the beginning of an entry indicates that the title is appearing in BIP for the first time.

An Asterisk (*) at the beginning of an entry indicates that the title is appearing in BIP for the first time.

1333

C

Coaching: Ideas & Ideals. 2nd ed. Arthur J. Gallon. (Illus.). 322p. (C). 1989. reprint ed. pap. text ed. 16.95 (*0-88133-461-8*) Waveland Pr.

***Coaching: Realizing the Potential.** Paul Kalinauckas & Helen King. 160p. (C). 1994. pap. 30.00x (*0-85292-555-7*, Pub. by IPM Hse UK) St Mut.

Coaching a Championship High School Track & Field Team. Dick Collins. LC 83-19385. 230p. 1984. text ed. 21.95 (*0-13-138967-X*, Parker Publishing Co) P-H.

Coaching Advanced Baseball. Technical Staff of Baseball Canada. LC 85-31233. (Illus.). 176p. (Orig.). 1986. pap. 20.00 (*0-88011-269-7*, PCOA0269) Human Kinetics.

Coaching & Counseling. Marianne Minor. Ed. by Michael G. Crisp. LC 88-72253. (Fifty Minute Ser.). (Illus.). 96p. (Orig.). 1989. pap. 9.95 (*0-931961-68-8*) Crisp Pubns.

***Coaching & Counseling: The McGraw-Hill One-Day Workshop.** 1995. text ed. 99.95 (*0-07-912092-X*) McGraw.

Coaching & Counseling in the Workplace. Donald H. Weiss. LC 93-10602. (Successful Office Skills Ser.). 64p. 1993. 4.00 (*0-8144-7818-2*) AMACOM.

***Coaching & Mentoring.** Nigel MacLennan. 200p. 1995. 42.95 (*0-566-07562-8*, Pub. by Gower Pub UK) Human Res Dev Pr.

Coaching & Motivation. William E. Warren. 1991. 9.95 (*0-13-140203-X*) P-H.

Coaching & Motivation: A Practical Guide to Maximum Athletic Performance. William E. Warren. LC 83-9671. 201p. 1983. 21.95 (*0-13-138990-4*) P-H.

Coaching & Supervising Teachers. National School Services Staff. (C). 1991. teacher ed 85.00 (*0-932957-80-3*) Natl School.

***Coaching & Supervising Teachers: Guidebook.** National School Services Staff. (C). Date not set. 25.00 (*0-932957-59-5*) Natl School.

Coaching & Training Techniques for Triathletes & Duathletes. Marc Evans. (Illus.). 282p. (Orig.). 1994. pap. 32.95 (*0-9640515-0-8*) Triathlet West.

Coaching & Winning. William E. Waren. 192p. 1989. 9.95 (*0-13-140005-3*) P-H.

Coaching & Winning: For Coaches of All Sports. William E. Warren. 180p. 1988. text ed. 21.95 (*0-13-138983-1*) P-H.

C

Coaching Baseball: Skills & Drills. Bragg A. Stockton. LC 84-6563. (American Coaching Effectiveness Program Ser.). 168p. (C). 1984. pap. text ed. 18.00 (*0-931250-65-X*, BST00065) Human Kinetics.

Coaching Baseball Effectively. Steven D. Houseworth. LC 85-24836. (Illus.). 176p. 1986. pap. 18.00 (*0-87322-037-4*, BHOU0037) Human Kinetics.

Coaching Basketball. 2nd rev. ed. Ed. by Jerry Krause. LC 94-5765. 320p. 1994. pap. 19.95 (*0-940279-86-X*) Masters Pr IN.

Coaching Basketball: The Complete Book from Beginning to Championship Play. Russell B. De Vette & William R. Vanderbilt. (Illus.). 254p. (C). 1986. pap. 14.95x (*0-89641-157-5*) American Pr.

Coaching Basketball Successfully. Morgan Wootten. LC 91-21041. (Illus.). 240p. (Orig.). 1992. pap. 18.95 (*0-88011-446-0*, PWOO0446) Human Kinetics.

Coaching Beginning Basketball. Jim Pruitt. (Coaching Ser.). (Illus.). 138p. 1980. 12.95 (*0-8092-7089-7*); pap. 11.95 (*0-8092-7088-9*) Contemp Bks.

***Coaching Cards for Soccer: Practice in a Box.** Colin Schmidt. 250p. 1995. 25.95 (*0-9646321-5-2*) Coaching Cards.

***Coaching Careers & Performance.** Gerald M. Sturman. 1992. 24.95 (*0-9626887-2-X*) Bierman Hse.

Coaching Champions. Jess Gibson. LC 93-87254. 200p. (Orig.). 1994. pap. 9.95 (*0-89221-257-8*) New Leaf.

Coaching Children in Sport: Principles & Practice. Ed. by Martin Lee. LC 93-18009. 1993. write for info. (*0-419-18250-0*, E & FN Spon) Routledge Chapman & Hall.

***Coaching Education Manual: Level One.** U. S. Amateur Boxing, Inc. Staff. (Illus.). 250p. (Orig.). 1994. pap. text ed. write for info. (*1-884125-25-5*) Cooper Pubng.

Coaching Evelyn: Fast, Faster, Fastest Woman in the World. Pat Connolly. LC 90-4835. (Illus.). 224p. (YA). (gr. 7 up). 1991. lib. bdg. 15.89 (*0-06-021283-7*) HarpC Child Bks.

Coaching Excellence. Keith Bell. LC 85-51524. 153p. (Orig.). 1989. pap. 19.95 (*0-945609-03-5*) Keel Pubns.

Coaching Flag Football. John Ferrell & MaryAnn Ferrell. 56p. 1980. pap. 5.00 (*0-88035-027-X*, LFER4226, YMCA USA) Human Kinetics.

Coaching Football. Tom Flores & Bob O'Connor. LC 93-5185. (Spalding Sports Library). (Illus.). 192p. 1993. pap. 14.95 (*0-940279-71-1*) Masters Pr IN.

Coaching Football Successfully. Bob Reade. LC 93-1272. (Illus.). 192p. 1994. pap. 18.95 (*0-87322-518-X*, PREA0518) Human Kinetics.

Coaching for Commitment: Managerial Strategies for Obtaining Superior Performance. Dennis C. Kinlaw. LC 89-50029. 125p. 1989. text ed. 29.95 (*0-88390-227-3*) Pfeiffer & Co.

Coaching for Commitment: Obtaining Superior Employee Performance. Dennis C. Kinlaw. LC 92-51083. 132p. 1993. pap. 14.95 (*0-89384-216-8*) Pfeiffer & Co.

Coaching for Commitment Trainer's Package. Dennis C. Kinlaw. LC 89-40172. 1990. ring bd. 295.00 (*0-88390-228-1*) Pfeiffer & Co.

***Coaching for Development.** Marianne Minor. Ed. by Philip Gerould. (Fifty-Minute Ser.). (Illus.). 100p. (Orig.). 1995. pap. 9.95 (*1-56052-319-0*) Crisp Pubns.

Coaching for Improved Teaching. Theodore Forte & Peggy S. Griffith. Ed. by Millicent T. Fazey. 59p. 1986. student ed 15.00 (*0-910475-34-2*) KET.

Coaching for Improved Work Performance. Ferdinand F. Fournies. LC 77-25199. 214p. 1987. 21.95 (*0-917472-11-X*) F Fournies.

Coaching for Improved Work Performance. Ferdinand F. Fournies. 1988. pap. 12.95 (*0-07-156032-7*) McGraw.

Coaching for Improved Work Performance. Ferdinand F. Fournies. 1987. pap. 12.95 (*0-8306-3054-6*, 30054) TAB Bks.

Coaching for Performance: A Practical Guide to Growing Your Own Skills. John Whitmore. 138p. 1993. pap. 12.95 (*0-89384-238-9*) Pfeiffer & Co.

Coaching Girls' Basketball Successfully. Jill Hutchison. LC 88-32972. 288p. 1989. pap. 20.00x (*0-88011-343-X*, PHUT0343) Human Kinetics.

Coaching Golf Effectively. DeDe Owens & Linda K. Bunker. LC 88-13843. (Coaching Effectively Ser.). (Illus.). 200p. 1989. pap. text ed. 18.00 (*0-88011-345-6*, POWE0345) Human Kinetics.

Coaching Hockey. Gerald A. Walford & Gerald E. Walford. LC 93-43065. (Illus.). 160p. (Orig.). 1993. pap. 12.95 (*0-940279-79-7*) Masters Pr IN.

Coaching Hockey. David Whitaker. (Illus.). 160p. 1991. pap. 29.95 (*1-85223-556-X*, Pub. by Crowood Pr UK) Trafalgar.

Coaching in Supervision. rev. ed. Richard P. Calhoon & Thomas H. Jerdee. 191p. (C). 1981. student ed 3.00 (*1-56011-014-7*, 80.34) Institute Government.

Coaching Intermediate Synchronized Swimming Effectively. U. S. Synchronized Swimming, Inc. Staff. 156p. (Orig.). pap. 16.00 (*0-317-61568-9*) US Synch Swim.

Coaching Intermediate Synchronized Swimming Effectively. Kim E. Van Buskirk. LC 86-21343. (Illus.). 144p. (Orig.). (C). 1987. pap. text ed. 18.00 (*0-87322-086-2*, BVAN0086) Human Kinetics.

Coaching Interscholastic Sports. Penelope A. Trojan & Linda Matthews. 100p. (C). 1994. pap. text ed., spiral bd. 13.95 (*0-8403-9441-1*) Kendall-Hunt.

Coaching Kids Lowhoop Basketball. Mike Daney. (Illus.). 117p. (Orig.). 1989. pap. 8.50 (*0-933715-01-3*) Am Youth Sports Pub.

Coaching Kids Teeball. Mike Daney. (Illus.). 117p. (Orig.). 1985. pap. 7.50 (*0-933715-00-5*) Am Youth Sports Pub.

Coaching Kids to Play Soccer. Kurt Ascherman & Jun San Marco. 1987. pap. 7.95 (*0-671-63936-6*, Fireside) S&S Trade.

***Coaching Mental Excellence: It Does Matter Whether You Win Or Lose...** Ralph Vernacchia et al. 172p. (Orig.). (C). 1995. pap. 17.95 (*1-886346-02-X*) Warde Pubs.

Coaching Mental Excellence: It Does Matter Whether You Win or Lose... Ralph A. Vernacchia et al. 184p. (C). 1992. pap. text ed. write for info. (*0-697-14848-3*) Brown & Benchmark.

***Coaching Mentoring & Assessing.** 2nd ed. Eric Parsloe. 1995. pap. text ed. 29.95 (*0-89397-442-0*) Nichols Pub.

Coaching, Mentoring, & Assessing: A Practical Guide to Developing Competence. Eric Parsloe. 220p. (C). 1993. pap. text ed. 25.95 (*0-89397-381-5*) Nichols Pub.

Coaching, Mentoring, & Assessing: A Practical Guide to Developing Competence. Eric Parsloe. LC 92-44135. 1992. pap. 23.95 (*0-7494-0664-X*, Pub. by Kogan Page Educ UK) Taylor & Francis.

Coaching Modern Soccer: Attack. Eric Batty. (Illus.). 128p. 1980. pap. 9.95 (*0-571-11605-1*) Faber & Faber.

Coaching Ms. Parker. Carla Heymsfeld. LC 91-28484. (Illus.). 96p. (J). (gr. 3-5). 1992. text ed. 12.95 (*0-02-743715-9*, Bradbury S&S) S&S Childrens.

***Coaching Ms. Parker.** Carla Heymsfeld. (Illus.). (J). (gr. 2-5). 1995. pap. 3.95 (*0-689-71830-6*, Aladdin Paperbacks) S&S Childrens.

Coaching Pitchers. 2nd ed. Joe S. McFarland. LC 89-37721. (Illus.). 152p. 1990. pap. text ed. 20.95 (*0-88011-368-5*, PMCF0368) Human Kinetics.

Coaching Run-&-Shoot Football. Al Black. (Illus.). 112p. (Orig.). 1991. pap. text ed. 12.00 (*0-9624779-2-3*) Harding Pr.

Coaching Science Stars: Pep Talk & Play Book for Real-World Problem Solving. Robert C. Barkman. 164p. (J). (gr. 6-12). 1991. pap. text ed. 17.95 (*0-913705-60-8*) Zephyr Pr AZ.

Coaching Self-Directed Workteams: Building Winning Teams in Today's Changing Workplace. Peter R. Garber. LC 92-62476. 109p. (Orig.). 1993. pap. text ed. 10.95 (*0-925652-17-2*) Orgn Design & Dev.

***Coaching Skills.** Kent W. Jones. Ed. by Dave Kirchner. (AMI How-to Ser.). 100p. 1995. 9.95 (*1-884926-39-8*) Amer Media.

Coaching Skills: A Guide for Supervisors. Robert W. Lucas. LC 93-44766. (Business Skills Express Ser.). 112p. 1994. 10.00 (*0-7863-0220-8*) Irwin Prof Pubng.

Coaching Skills see Productive Supervisor: A Program of Practical Managerial Skills

Coaching Soccer. Robert Lauffer. LC 89-37639. (Illus.). 160p. 1990. pap. 12.95 (*0-8069-6923-7*) Sterling.

***Coaching Soccer.** Robert Lauffer. 160p. 1994. lib. bdg. 33.00 (*0-8095-7620-1*) Borgo Pr.

Coaching Soccer Effectively. Christopher A. Hopper & Michael S. Davis. LC 86-34268. (Illus.). 200p. (Orig.). 1988. pap. text ed. 18.00 (*0-87322-112-5*, BHOP0112) Human Kinetics.

Coaching Softball Effectively. Steven D. Houseworth & Francine V. Rivkin. LC 85-7667. 176p. (C). 1985. pap. 18.00 (*0-87322-003-X*, BHOU0003) Human Kinetics.

Coaching Swimming Effectively. Jean G. Larrabee. LC 86-18594. (Illus.). 112p. (Orig.). 1987. pap. 18.00 (*0-87322-080-3*, BLAR0080) Human Kinetics.

Coaching Swimming Successfully. Dick Hannula. LC 94-10232. 176p. 1995. pap. 18.95 (*0-87322-492-2*, PHAN0492) Human Kinetics.

Coaching Synchronized Swimming Effectively. Margaret S. Forbes. 134p. pap. 14.00 (*0-317-61567-X*) US Synch Swim.

Coaching Synchronized Swimming Effectively. 2nd rev. ed. Margaret S. Forbes. LC 88-22964. (Illus.). 136p. 1989. pap. text ed. 18.00x (*0-88011-340-5*, PFOR0340) Human Kinetics.

Coaching Teaching: Clinical Supervision in Action. Robert H. Anderson & Karolyn J. Snyder. 256p. (C). 1988. text ed. write for info. (*0-394-37010-4*) Random.

***Coaching Team Defense.** 2nd ed. Fritz Shurmur. LC 94-22699. (Illus.). 112p. 1994. pap. text ed. 12.00 (*0-9624779-6-6*) Harding Pr.

***Coaching Tennis Successfully.** United States Tennis Association Staff. LC 94-41682. (Illus.). 200p. (Orig.). 1995. pap. write for info. (*0-87322-461-2*, PUST0461) Human Kinetics.

Coaching the Defensive Backfield. Greg McMackin. LC 91-43957. (Illus.). 128p. (Orig.). 1992. 12.00 (*0-9624779-3-1*) Harding Pr.

Coaching the Defensive Secondary. Mark A. Schuster. 183p. 1984. text ed. 21.95 (*0-13-138942-4*, Parker Publishing Co) P-H.

Coaching the Female Gymnast. fac. ed. Sandra J. Hartley-O'Brien. (Illus.). 402p. (C). 1983. spiral bd., pap. 45.95x (*0-398-04687-5*) C C Thomas.

Coaching Through Effective Feedback: A Practical Guide to Successful Communication. Paul J. Jerome. (Management Skills Ser.). (Illus.). 120p. 1994. pap. 12.95 (*1-883553-50-4*) R Chang Assocs.

Coaching Volleyball Successfully. United States Volleyball Association Staff & William J. Neville. LC 89-32987. (Illus.). 224p. 1990. pap. text ed. 18.00 (*0-88011-362-6*, PNEV0362) Human Kinetics.

Coaching Winning Basketball in the Offensive Zone. Jim Satalin & Fred Handler. 190p. 1985. 19.95 (*0-13-139361-8*, Parker Publishing Co) P-H.

Coaching Writers: Editors & Reporters Working Together. Peter Clark & Don Fry. LC 91-61444. 160p. (Orig.). (C). 1991. pap. text ed. 12.50 (*0-312-04937-4*) St Martin.

Coaching Writers: The Essential Guide for Editors & Reporters. Roy P. Clark. 1991. 19.95 (*0-312-06842-5*) St Martin.

Coaching Youth Baseball. Bob Kirchmer & Bryan Kirchmer. 122p. 1993. spiral bd. 15.95 (*0-9637236-0-X*) Baseball Adv.

***Coaching Youth Basketball.** 2nd rev. ed. American Sport Education Program Staff. LC 95-14388. (Coaching Youth Sport Ser.). 160p. 1995. pap. 12.95 (*0-87322-892-8*, ACEP0421) Human Kinetics.

***Coaching Youth Football.** 2nd rev. ed. John P. McCarthy, Jr. LC 95-14391. (Coaching Kids Ser.). Orig. Title: A Parent's Guide to Coaching Football. (Illus.). 160p. 1995. pap. 12.99 (*1-55870-395-0*) Betterway Bks.

Coaching Youth Football Defense. John T. Reed. LC 92-93048. 220p. (Orig.). 1993. pap. 19.95 (*0-939224-27-5*) John T Reed.

***Coaching Youth Hockey: American Sport Education Program.** LC 95-10269. 200p. 1995. 12.95 (*0-87322-964-9*) Human Kinetics.

***Coaching Youth Soccer.** 2nd ed. American Sport Education Program Staff. (Illus.). 160p. 1995. pap. 12.95 (*0-87322-831-6*, ACEP0420) Human Kinetics.

Coaching Youth Soccer. 2nd ed. Neil B. Ingels, Jr. (Illus.). 177p. (Orig.). 1982. pap. 9.95 (*0-943752-01-9*) Soccer Pubns Inc.

Coaching Youth Soccer Vol. 2: Attacking the Goal. Neil B. Ingels, Jr. (Illus.). 222p. 1985. pap. 8.95 (*0-943752-03-5*) Soccer Pubns Inc.

Coachmakers. Harold Nockolds. 240p. 1990. 60.00 (*0-85131-270-5*, Pub. by J A Allen & Co UK) St Mut.

Coachman & the Bells. Ted C. Hindmarsh. 64p. 1988. pap. 4.98 (*0-88290-340-3*) Horizon Utah.

Coachmen of Nineteenth-Century Paris: Service Workers & Class Consciousness. Nicholas Papayanis. LC 93-834. 269p. (C). 1993. text ed. 45.00 (*0-8071-1814-1*) La State U Pr.

Coach's Clipboards. Anne M. Riede. (Illus.). 306p. (Orig.). (J). (gr. 5-8). 1986. 10.95 (*0-931983-02-9*, BCLTXT-3) Basic Comp Lit.

Coach's Guide to Developing an Explosive Multi-Set Offense. Ron Gratz. LC 81-86511. (Illus.). 128p. (C). 1982. pap. 12.95 (*0-88011-038-4*, PGRA0038) Human Kinetics.

Coach's Pocket Planner. Roger Bakken. (Illus.). 72p. 1983. spiral bd. 7.95 (*0-930097-00-9*) Sportsrite Pub Co.

Coach's Wife: A Memoir. Teresa G. Phelps. LC 93-13148. 1994. 23.00 (*0-393-03470-4*) Norton.

Coactive Forest Management. John Hof. (Illus.). 189p. 1992. text ed. 39.95 (*0-12-351820-2*) Acad Pr.

Coadsorption, Promoters, & Poisons. Ed. by D. A. King & D. P. Woodruff. (Chemical Physics of Solid Surfaces Ser.: vol. 6). xiv, 348p. 1993. 182.75 (*0-444-81468-X*) Elsevier.

Coagulant Recovery: A Critical Assessment. 290p. 1991. pap. 37.00 (*0-89867-533-2*, 90565) Am Water Wks Assn.

***Coagulants & Flocculants.** Yong H. Kim. 88p. 1995. pap. 24.00 (*0-927188-04-X*) Tall Oaks Pub.

Coagulase-Negative Staphylococci. Ed. by P. A. Mardh & K. H. Schleifer. (Illus.). 222p. (Orig.). 1986. 71.00x (*91-22-00783-0*, Pub. by Almqv & Wiksell SW) Coronet Bks.

Coagulation & Bleeding Disorders: The Role of Factor VIII & Von Willebrand Factor. Zimmerman & Ruggeri. (Hematology Ser.: Vol. 9). 392p. 1989. 175.00 (*0-8247-8013-2*) Dekker.

Coagulation & Blood Transfusion. Ed. by C. Th. Smit Sibinga. (Developments in Hematology & Immunology Ser.). (C). 1991. lib. bdg. 60.50 (*0-7923-1331-3*) Kluwer Ac.

Coagulation & Cancer. Ed. by Maria B. Donati. (Journal: Haemostasis: Vol. 18, No. 1, 1988). (Illus.). 72p. 1988. pap. 28.00 (*3-8055-4768-4*) S Karger.

Coagulation & Filtration: Back to the Basics. 168p. 1981. pap. 21.00 (*0-89867-257-0*, 20155) Am Water Wks Assn.

Coagulation & Filtration: Pilot- to Full-Scale. 200p. 1987. pap. 22.00 (*0-89867-412-3*, 20017) Am Water Wks Assn.

Coagulation & Flocculation. Dobias. (Surfactant Science Ser.: Vol. 47). 720p. 1993. 215.00 (*0-8247-8797-8*) Dekker.

Coagulation & Lipids. Ed. by Robert F. Zwaal. 208p. 1988. 135.00 (*0-8493-6762-X*, QP93, CRC Reprint) Franklin.

Coagulation Kinetics & Structure Formation. H. Sonntag & K. Strenge. LC 85-63436. (Illus.). 194p. 1987. 75.00 (*0-306-42298-0*, Plenum Pr) Plenum.

Coagulations: New & Selected Poems. Jayne Cortez. LC 83-24180. 96p. (Orig.). 1984. pap. 8.95 (*0-938410-20-2*) Thunders Mouth.

Coal. rev. ed. J. Jason Grant. (Orig.). 1985. pap. 2.95 (*0-87067-718-7*, BH718) Holloway.

Coal: Classification, Coalification, Mineralogy, Trace-Element Chemistry, & Oil & Gas Potential. Ed. by P. C. Lyon & B. Alpern. 600p. 1990. 172.00 (*0-444-88011-9*) Elsevier.

***Coal: Energy for the Future.** National Research Council Staff. 320p. (Orig.). (C). 1995. text ed. 39.95 (*0-309-05232-7*) Natl Acad Pr.

Coal: Its Role in Tomorrow's Technology. Charles Simeons. 1978. 132.00 (*0-08-022712-0*, Pub. by Pergamon Repr UK) Franklin.

Coal: Modern Technology & Economics. L. Grainger. 300p. 1982. lib. bdg. 105.50 (*0-86010-266-1*) G & T Inc.

Coal: The Energy Source of the Past & Future. Harold H. Schobert. LC 87-11433. (Illus.). xi, 280p. 1987. 29.95 (*0-8412-1171-X*); pap. 14.95 (*0-8412-1172-8*) Am Chemical.

Coal: Topology, Chemistry, Physics & Constitution. Van Krevelen. (Coal Science & Technology Ser.: Vol. 3). 514p. 1981. 159.00 (*0-444-40600-X*) Elsevier.

Coal: Topology Chemistry Physics & Constitution. Van Krevelen. (CST Ser.: Vol. 3). 1991. 185.75 (*0-685-50937-0*) Elsevier.

Coal: Typology - Physics - Chemistry - Constitution. 3rd ed. D. W. Van Krevelen. 1008p. 1993. 397.00 (*0-444-89586-8*) Elsevier.

Coal: Yesterday's Energy Today, Vol. 2. Arthur F. Ide. LC 81-20012. (Illus.). 60p. 1982. lib. bdg. 8.00 (*0-86663-804-0*); pap. text ed. 1.00 (*0-86663-805-9*) Ide Hse.

Coal: Yesterday's Energy Tomorrow. Arthur F. Ide. (Energy: Management, Conservation & Communication Ser.: Vol. 2). (Illus.). 60p. (Orig.). 1981. lib. bdg. 18.50 (*0-86663-808-3*); pap. text ed. 1.00 (*0-86663-809-1*) Ide Hse.

Coal Age Empire: Pennsylvania Coal & Its Utilization to 1860. Frederick M. Binder. LC 75-621822. 184p. 1974. 7.95 (*0-911124-75-6*) Pa Hist & Mus.

Coal Age Fossils from Mazon Creek. F. M. Carpenter et al. (Scientific Papers: Vol. III, Nos. 1-4). (Illus.). 140p. 1979. pap. 4.00 (*0-89792-082-1*) Ill St Museum.

Coal & Ash Handling. (Principles of Steam Generation Ser.: Module 13). (Illus.). 200p. 1982. spiral bd. 34.50 (*0-87683-263-X*) GP Pub.

Coal & Canada - U. S. Energy Relations. Richard L. Gordon. LC 76-20420. (Canadian-American Committee Ser.). 76p. 1976. 3.00 (*0-88806-017-3*) Natl Planning.

Coal & Coal-Bearing Strata: Recent Advances. Ed. by A. C. Scott. 332p. 1993. pap. 34.00 (*1-897799-01-2*, Pub. by Geol Soc Pub Hse UK) AAPG.

Coal & Coal-Bearing Strata As Oil-Prone Source Rocks. Ed. by A. C. Scott & A. J. Fleet. (Geological Society Special Publications: No. 77). (Illus.). 208p. (C). 1994. 75.00 (*0-903317-99-0*, Pub. by Geol Soc Pub Hse UK) AAPG.

Coal & Coal Products: Analytical Characterization Techniques. Ed. by E. L. Fuller, Jr. LC 82-18442. (ACS Symposium Ser.: No. 205). 326p. 1982. lib. bdg. 54.95 (*0-8412-0748-8*) Am Chemical.

Coal & Fuel-Oil Burners & Ignitors. Center for Occupational Research & Development Staff. (EUTEC Power Plant Operator Curriculum Ser.). (Illus.). 38p. (C). 1985. pap. text ed. write for info. (*1-55502-209-X*) CORD Commns.

***Coal & Methane Industry International.** (Illus.). 70p. (Orig.). 1994. pap. 125.00 (*0-7605-0675-2*) Rector Pr.

Coal & Modern Coal Processing: An Introduction. Ed. by G. J. Pitt & G. R. Milward. 1979. text ed. 61.00 (*0-12-557850-4*) Acad Pr.

Coal & Politics in Late Imperial Russia: Memoirs of a Russian Mining Engineer. Aleksandr I. Fenin. Ed. by Susan P. McCaffray. Tr. by Alexandre Fediaevsky. (Illus.). 255p. 1990. 30.00 (*0-87580-153-6*) N Ill U Pr.

Coal & Tobacco: The Lowthers & the Economic Development of West Cumberland, 1660-1760. J. V. Beckett. LC 80-40785. 295p. reprint ed. pap. 84.10 (*0-318-34760-1*, 2031620) Bks Demand.

Coal Bearing Depositional Systems. C. F. Diessel. (Illus.). 664p. 1993. 138.00 (*0-387-52516-5*) Spr-Verlag.

Coal-Blending & Switching of Low-Sulfur Western Coals. Ed. by Richard W. Bryers & N. S. Harding. LC 93-74945. 476p. 1994. pap. 75.00 (*0-7918-1200-6*, 100363) ASME.

Coal Burning Issues: A Monograph Reporting the Results of the Scoping Phase of an Interdisciplinary Assessment of the Impact of the Increased Use of Coal. Alex E. Green. LC 79-25376. (Illus.). 400p. reprint ed. pap. 114.00 (*0-7837-4905-8*, 2044570) Bks Demand.

***Coal Burning Technologies.** (Illus.). 70p. (Orig.). 1994. pap. 125.00 (*0-7605-0676-0*) Rector Pr.

An Asterisk (*) at the beginning of an entry indicates that the title is appearing in BIP for the first time.

Coal Camp Kids, Coming up Hard & Making It. Barbara F. Ritch. 352p. 1991. 29.95 (*0-942407-12-1*) Father & Son.

Coal, Capital & Culture: A Sociological Analysis of Mining Communities in West Yorkshire. Dennis Warwick & Gary Littlejohn. 240p. 1992. 82.50 (*0-415-05015-4*, A6849) Routledge.

Coal Car Equipment. 24p. 1992. pap. 5.95 (*0-911581-26-X*) Heimburger Hse Pub.

Coal Carbonization Products. D. McNeil. LC 66-6880. 1966. 76.00 (*0-08-011446-6*, Pub. by Pergamon Repr UK) Franklin.

Coal Characterisation for Conversion Processes, 1986: Proceedings of the First International Rolduc Symposium, Rolduc, The Netherlands, April 28-May 1, 1986. Ed. by J. A. Moulijn & F. Kapteijn. 440p. 1987. 154.00 (*0-444-42742-2*) Elsevier.

Coal, Cinders & Parlor Cars. William F. Gale et al. LC 70-102682. (Colorado Rail Annual Ser.: No. 19). (Illus.). 236p. 1991. 39.95 (*0-918654-19-X*) CO RR Mus.

Coal, Class, & Color: Blacks in Southern West Virginia, 1915-32. Joe W. Trotter, Jr. (Blacks in the New World Ser. & The Working Class in American History Ser.). (Illus.). 320p. 1990. 44.95 (*0-252-01707-2*); pap. text ed. 14.95 (*0-252-06119-5*) U of Ill Pr.

Coal Cleaning Technology. Ed. by D. L. Khoury. LC 81-14225. (Pollution Technology Review Series & Energy Technical Review Ser.: Nos. 86 & 72). (Illus.). 368p. 1982. 45.00 (*0-8155-0875-1*) Noyes.

Coal Combustion. Jerzy Tomeczek. LC 91-46266. 182p. (Orig.). 1994. lib. bdg. 42.50 (*0-89464-651-6*) Krieger.

Coal Combustion: Science & Technology of Industrial & Utility Applications. Junkai Feng. 1050p. 1988. 194.00 (*0-89116-757-9*) Hemisp Pub.

Coal Combustion & Conversion Technology. David Merrick. 1984. 107.25 (*0-444-00933-7*) Elsevier.

Coal Combustion & Gasification. L. Douglas Smoot & Philip J. Smith. LC 84-17937. (Chemical Engineering Ser.). 460p. 1985. 120.00 (*0-306-41750-2*, Plenum Pr) Plenum.

Coal Combustion Chemistry: Correlation Aspects. E. J. Badin. (Coal Science & Technology Ser.: Vol. 6). 260p. 1984. 102.75 (*0-444-42318-4*, I-132-84) Elsevier.

Coal Conversion. E. J. Hoffman. LC 77-93533. (Illus.). 464p. 1978. 65.00 (*0-9601552-1-X*) Energon Co.

Coal Conversion & the Environment: Chemical, Biomedical, & Ecological Considerations. Ed. by Dennis D. Mahlum et al. LC 81-607088. (DOE Symposium Ser.: Proceedings). 622p. 1981. pap. 24.75 (*0-87079-128-1*, CONF-801039); fiche 9.00 (*0-87079-401-9*, CONF-801039) DOE.

Coal Conversion at New Jersey Utilities: A Study of the Conversion Prospects & Obstacles at Seven Power Plants. James S. Cannon. Ed. by Perrin Stryker. LC 83-82880. (INFORM Report Ser.). 144p. reprint ed. pap. 41.10 (*0-7837-0326-0*, 2040645) Bks Demand.

Coal Conversion Technology: Problems & Solutions. Ed. by Arnold Pelofsky. LC 79-17936. (ACS Symposium Ser.: No. 110). 257p. 1979. 36.95 (*0-8412-0516-7*) Am Chemical.

Coal Cutting by Winning Machines. E. Posin et al. Tr. by S. D. Sarve. (Russian Translation Ser.: No. 74). (Illus.). 288p. (C). 1990. text ed. 90.00 (*90-6191-909-6*, Pub. by A A Balkema NE) Ashgate Pub Co.

***Coal Data: A Reference.** 1995. lib. bdg. 250.00 (*0-8490-6462-7*) Gordon Pr.

Coal Demand in the Electric Utility Industry, Nineteen Forty-Six to Nineteen Ninety. Charles J. Johnson. Ed. by Stuart Bruchey. LC 78-22689. (Energy in the American Economy Ser.). (Illus.). 1979. lib. bdg. 25.95 (*0-405-11992-5*) Ayer.

Coal Desulfurization. Robert A. Meyers. LC 77-9928. (Illus.). 270p. reprint ed. pap. 77.00 (*0-8357-6059-6*, 2034552) Bks Demand.

Coal Desulfurization: A Bibliography. DOE Technical Information Center Staff. 510p. 1983. pap. 24.75 (*0-87079-514-7*, DOE/TIC-3400); fiche 9.00 (*0-87079-515-5*, DOE/TIC-3400) DOE.

Coal Desulfurization: Chemical & Physical Methods. Ed. by Thomas D. Wheelock. LC 77-17216. (ACS Symposium Ser.: No. 64). 1977. 39.95 (*0-8412-0400-4*) Am Chemical.

Coal Diamond. Shirley Lauro. 1979. pap. 2.75 (*0-8222-0223-9*) Dramatists Play.

Coal Dust. Shirley Swiesz. Ed. by James B. Van Treese. 354p. 1993. pap. 9.95 (*1-56901-011-0*) NW Pub.

Coal Dust in Their Blood: The Work & Lives of Underground Coal Miners. Bruce T. Williams. LC 89-31159. (Studies in Anthropology: No. 6). 1991. 59.50 (*0-404-62606-8*) AMS Pr.

Coal Exploration, Mine Planning, & Development. Roy D. Merritt. LC 85-25869. (Illus.). 464p. 1986. 64.00 (*0-8155-1070-5*) Noyes.

Coal Exports & Port Development. 2nd ed. Ed. by John H. Leeper & Mark Tomassoni. LC 81-71245. (Illus.). 116p. 1982. pap. text ed. 10.00 (*0-87033-286-4*) Cornell Maritime.

Coal-Fired Magnetohydrodynamic (MHD) Electric Power Generation, EUR 13928. Ed. by P. E. Sens. 243p. 1992. 30.00 (*92-826-3712-3*, CD-NA-13928-EN-C, Pub. by Europ Com) UNIPUB.

Coal Fired Power Plants & Aquatic Environment: IAWPRC International Conference on Coal Fired Power Plants & the Aquatic Environment, 16-18 August 1982, Copenhagen. Ed. by S. H. Jenkins & P. Schjodtz Hansen. (Illus.). 678p. 1984. pap. 130.00 (*0-08-031019-2*, Pergamon Pr) Elsevier.

Coal Fired Ships, 3 vols. Ed. by Lorne & MacLean Marine Staff. 1987. 210.00 (*0-317-43652-X*, Pub. by Lorne & MacLean Marine) St Mut.

Coal-Fired Ships, 3 vols. OCS Marine Staff. (C). 1989. text ed. 395.00 (*0-906314-39-9*, Pub. by Lorne & MacLean Marine) St Mut.

Coal Fired Ships, 3 vols., Set. (C). 1989. 280.00 (*0-89771-713-9*) St Mut.

Coal Firms under the New Social Regulation. Richard A. Harris. LC 85-13056. (Duke Press Policy Studies). (Illus.). x, 188p. 1985. 37.00 (*0-8223-0648-4*) Duke.

Coal Fouling & Slagging Parameters - Prepared by the ASME Research Committee on Corrosion & Deposits from Combustion Gases. American Society of Mechanical Engineers Research Committee on Corrosion & Deposits from Combustion Gases Staff. Ed. by E. C. Winegartner. LC 75-323625. 42p. reprint ed. pap. 25.00 (*0-685-23491-6*, 2014919) Bks Demand.

Coal-Fueled Diesel Engines - 1993. Ed. by J. A. Caton & H. A. Webb. (ICE Ser.: Vol. 19). 72p. 1993. 35.00 (*0-7918-0947-1*, 100352) ASME.

Coal, Gas & Electricity Industries. D. J. Harris et al. (Reviews of United Kingdom Statistical Sources Ser.: Vol. 11). 1979. 130.00 (*0-08-022461-X*, Pub. by Pergamon Repr UK) Franklin.

Coal Gasification: Direct Applications & Synthesis of Chemicals & Fuels, Vol. 12. Ed. by S. S. Penner. (International Journal of Energy: Vol. 12). 296p. 1987. 75.00 (*0-317-66175-2*, Pergamon Pr) Elsevier.

Coal Gasification Chemistry: Flash Hydrogenation of Coal; Pyrolysis Reactions of Coal; Government Role in Fuel R & D; Henry H. Storch Award Symposium (&) General Papers Presented at Washington, D. C., September 10-14, 1979. American Chemical Society, Division of Fuel Chemistry Staff. (Preprints of Papers Ser.: Vol. 24, No. 3). 308p. reprint ed. pap. 87.80 (*0-317-29986-7*, 2051824) Bks Demand.

Coal Gasification-Existing Processes & New Developments. H. D. Schilling et al. 330p. 1981. 56.00 (*0-86010-243-2*) G & T Inc.

Coal Gasifiers. E. J. Hoffman. LC 81-68121. (Illus.). 723p. 1981. 225.00 (*0-9601552-2-8*) Energon Co.

Coal Handbook. Ed. by Robert A. Meyers. LC 81-7824. (Energy, Power, & Environment Ser.: No. 11). (Illus.). 868p. reprint ed. pap. 180.00 (*0-7837-5175-3*, 2044905) Bks Demand.

Coal Handling: The Yard & Outside Equipment. Center for Occupational Research & Development Staff. (EUTEC Power Plant Operator Curriculum Ser.). (Illus.). 70p. (C). 1985. pap. text ed. write for info. (*1-55502-227-8*) CORD Commns.

Coal House. large type ed. Andrew Taylor. (J). (gr. 1-8). 1991. 16.95 (*0-7451-0761-3*, Galaxy Child Lrg Print) Chivers N Amer.

Coal in Appalachia: An Economic Analysis. Curtis E Harvey. LC 86-13294. 232p. 1986. 25.00 (*0-8131-1577-9*) U Pr of Ky.

Coal in My Blood. Fred R. Toothman. (Illus.). 140p. 1986. pap. 6.95 (*0-9617545-0-8*) F R Toothman.

Coal in Queensland: From Federation to the Twenties. R. L. Whitmore. 1991. 49.95 (*0-7022-2262-3*, Pub. by Univ Queensland Pr AT) Intl Spec Bk.

Coal Industry in America: Bibliography & Guide to Studies. 2nd ed. Robert F. Munn. LC 77-77913. 351p. 1977. 30.00 (*0-930284-00-3*) West Va U Pr.

Coal Industry in West Bengal. P. K. Chakrabarti. 1989. 19.00 (*81-85119-61-9*, Pub. by Northern Bk Ctr II) S Asia.

Coal Industry of India. Anubhuti K. Prasad. 515p. 1986. 58.50 (*81-7024-055-7*, Pub. by Ashish II) S Asia.

Coal Information Nineteen Ninety-Two. OECD Staff. 542p. (Orig.). 1992. pap. 125.00 (*92-64-13679-7*) OECD.

Coal Information, 1992: 1993 Edition. OECD Staff. 500p. (Orig.). 1993. pap. 125.00 (*92-64-13941-9*) OECD.

***Coal Information 1993.** OECD Staff. 605p. (Orig.). 1994. pap. 125.00x (*92-64-14185-5*) OECD.

Coal, Iron, & Slaves: Industrial Slavery in Maryland & Virginia, 1715-1865. Ronald L. Lewis. LC 78-55333. (Contributions in Labor Studies: No. 6). (Illus.). 283p. 1979. text ed. 59.95 (*0-313-20522-1*, LCI/, Greenwood Pr) Greenwood.

Coal Liquefaction Fundamentals. Ed. by D. D. Whitehurst. LC 80-20585. (ACS Symposium Ser.: No. 139). 1980. 49.95 (*0-8412-0587-6*) Am Chemical.

Coal Liquid Mixtures: Proceedings of the European Conference, 3rd. Ed. by T. J. Pierce. (European Federation of Chemical Engineering Ser.). 356p. 1988. 113.00 (*0-89116-843-5*) Hemisp Pub.

Coal Mine Directory 1990-91. 550p. 1990. pap. 110.00 (*0-929531-13-2*) MacLn Hunter Pub.

Coal Mine Directory 1991-92. 550p. 1990. pap. 120.00 (*0-929531-16-7*) MacLn Hunter Pub.

***Coal Mine Directory 1995.** 300p. 1995. pap. text ed. 140.00 (*0-929531-26-4*) MacLn Hunter Pub.

***Coal Mine Scream.** Virden (Illinois) Giften Program Students. (Wee Write Bks.: No. 18). (Illus.). 40p. (J). (ps-3). 1995. 32.95 (*1-884987-60-5*); lib. bdg. 18.95 (*1-884987-58-3*); pap. 8.95 (*1-884987-59-1*) WeWrite.

Coal Mine Subsidence: Proceedings from a Citizens' Conference. 2nd ed. Pamela Mavrolas & Michael Schechtman. Ed. by Harold Henderson. 46p. 1982. reprint ed. 4.00 (*0-943724-01-5*) Illinois South.

Coal Miner Preacher: A Testimony of Faith, Healings, Miracles, Angels, & Prophecies. James O. Russell & Georgia Smelser. LC 93-23506. 150p. (Orig.). pap. 6.99 (*1-56722-014-2*) Word Aflame.

Coal Miners. Gail Stewart. LC 88-11860. (At Risk Ser.). (Illus.). 48p. (J). (gr. 5-6). 1988. text ed. 11.95 (*0-89686-395-6*, Crstwood Hse) Silver Burdett Pr.

Coal Miner's General Strike of Nineteen Forty-Nine to Fifty & the Birth of Marxist-Humanism in the United States. Andy Phillips & Raya Dunayevskaya. (Illus.). 50p. 1984. pap. 2.00 (*0-914441-21-3*) News & Letters.

Coal Miner's Son. John G. Mattone. LC 93-92783. 104p. (Orig.). 1994. pap. 8.00 (*1-56002-374-0*, Univ Edtns) Aegina Pr.

Coal Miners' Struggle for Industrial Status. Arthur E. Suffern. (Brookings Institution Reprint Ser.). reprint ed. lib. bdg. 34.50 (*0-697-00170-9*) Irvington.

***Coal Miners' Wives: Portrait of Endurance.** Carol A. Gieson. LC 94-37966. (Illus.). 184p. 1995. text ed. 30.00 (*0-8131-1903-0*); pap. 14.95 (*0-8131-0845-4*) U Pr of Ky.

Coal Mines. Nathaniel Harris. (Working Lives Ser.). (Illus.). 64p. (YA). (gr. 7-12). 1986. 19.95 (*0-7134-5097-5*, Pub. by Batsford UK) Trafalgar.

Coal Mining: A PETEX Primer. Ed. by Jean Pietrobono. (Illus.). 87p. (Orig.). 1985. pap. text ed. 30.00 (*0-88698-087-9*, 6.00010) PETEX.

Coal Mining in China's Economy & Society, 1895-1937. Tim Wright. (Illus.). 260p. 1985. 69.95 (*0-521-25878-2*) Cambridge U Pr.

Coal-Mining Safety in the Progressive Period: The Political Economy of Reform. William Graebner. LC 75-38215. 256p. reprint ed. pap. 73.00 (*0-7837-5782-4*, 2045448) Bks Demand.

Coal Mining Technology: Theory & Practice. Robert Stefanko. Ed. by Christopher J. Bise & Thomas V. Falkie. LC 82-71995. (Illus.). 410p. (C). 1983. 15.00 (*0-89520-404-5*, 404-5) SMM&E Inc.

Coal Models & Their Use in Government Planning. Ed. by James Quirk et al. LC 81-21153. 288p. 1982. text ed. 55.00 (*0-275-90880-1*, C0880, Praeger Pubs) Greenwood.

Coal of El Cerrejon: Dependent Bargaining & Colombian Policy Making. Harvey F. Kline. LC 86-43038. 224p. 1987. 30.00 (*0-271-00491-6*) Pa St U Pr.

Coal-Oil Mixture Combustion Technology. Ed. by M. M. Schumacher. (Energy Technology Review Ser.: No. 73). (Illus.). 481p. 1982. 48.00 (*0-8155-0878-6*) Noyes.

***Coal on the Move Via the Virginia Railway.** (Illus.). 32p. 1995. pap. text ed. write for info. (*0-9633254-2-6*) Norfolk & Wstrn HS.

Coal Overburden: Geological Characterization & Premine Planning. Roy D. Merrit. LC 83-13093. (Energy Technology Review Ser.: No. 88). (Illus.). 343p. 1984. 39.00 (*0-8155-0964-2*) Noyes.

Coal Preparation. 5th ed. Ed. by J. W. Leonard, III. LC 91-61678. (Illus.). 1131p. (C). 1991. 83.50 (*0-87335-104-5*) SMM&E Inc.

Coal Preparation: Proceedings of an Information Symposium Organized by the Commission of the European Communities, Held in Luxembourg on 15 November 1984. Ed. by J. K. Wilkinson. 156p. (C). 1985. text ed. 95.00 (*90-6191-598-8*, Pub. by A A Balkema NE) Ashgate Pub Co.

Coal Preparation & Use--A World Review: International Coal Preparation Congress, New Delhi, India, 9th, 1982. Ed. by S. R. Rao. 259p. (C). 1982. text ed. 160.00 (*90-6191-256-3*, Pub. by A A Balkema NE) Ashgate Pub Co.

Coal Preparation Plants. National Fire Protection Association Staff. 1994. 16.75 (*0-317-63317-1*, 120-94) Natl Fire Prot.

Coal Preparation Technology, 2 vols., Set, Vols. 1 & 2. D. G. Osborne. (C). 1988. Set. lib. bdg. 563.50 (*1-85333-092-2*, Pub. by Graham & Trotman UK) Kluwer Ac.

Coal Pricing in China: Issues & Reform Strategy. Yves Albouy. (Discussion Paper Ser.: No. 138). 36p. 1991. 6.95 (*0-8213-1953-1*, 11953) World Bank.

Coal Processing: Gasification, Liquefaction, Desulfurization. A Bibliography, 1930-1974. DOE Technical Information Center Staff. 766p. 1974. pap. 34.00 (*0-87079-165-6*, TID-3349); fiche 9.00 (*0-87079-409-4*, TID-3349) DOE.

***Coal Processing & Pollution Control.** fac. ed. Thomas F. Edgar. LC 83-10725. (Illus.). 600p. Date not set. pap. 171.00 (*0-7837-7435-4*, 2047230) Bks Demand.

***Coal Production.** 1995. lib. bdg. 250.00 (*0-8490-6463-5*) Gordon Pr.

Coal Pyrolysis. G. S. Javalas. (Coal Science & Technology Ser.: No. 4). 168p. 1982. 89.75 (*0-444-42107-6*) Elsevier.

Coal Quality & Combustion Performance: An International Perpsective. J. F. Unsworth et al. (Coal Science & Technology Ser.: Vol. 19). 1991. 223.00 (*0-444-88703-2*) Elsevier.

Coal Question: An Inquiry Concerning the Progress of the Nation & the Probable Exhaustion of Our Coal-Mines. 3rd rev. ed. William S. Jevons. Ed. by A. W. Flux. LC 65-24371. (Reprints of Economic Classics Ser.). 467p. 1965. reprint ed. 45.00 (*0-678-00107-3*) Kelley.

Coal Question: Political Economy & Industrial Change from the Nineteenth Century to the Present Day. Ben Fine. 256p. 1990. 55.00 (*0-415-04384-0*, A4099) Routledge.

Coal Research. A. Macek. 140p. 1977. pap. text ed. 205.00 (*0-677-40255-4*) Gordon & Breach.

Coal Reserves of the Boltsfork Quadrangle, Kentucky: A Coal Recoverability Study. Timothy J. Rohrbacher et al. 1993. write for info. (*0-318-72293-3*) US Interior.

Coal Resource Recoverability: A Methodology. T. J. Rohrbacher et al. 1993. write for info. (*0-318-70285-1*) US Interior.

Coal Resources of Greene County, Pennsylvania, Pt. 1: Coal Crop Lines, Mined--outAreas, & Structure Contours. Clifford H. Dodge & Albert D. Glover. (Mineral Resource Report Ser.: No. 86). (Illus.). 67p. (Orig.). 1984. pap. 6.35 (*8-8182-0055-3*) Commonweal PA.

Coal Resources of the Americas: Selected Papers. Ed. by Frank E. Kottlowski et al. LC 78-57145. (Special Paper Ser.: No. 179). (Illus.). 96p. 1978. pap. 2.00 (*0-8137-2179-2*) Geol Soc.

Coal River Special. Michael H. Cary. LC 92-84108. 143p. 1993. 7.95 (*1-55523-550-6*) Winston-Derek.

Coal Sampling & Analysis: Methods & Models. Alan Gleit et al. LC 86-5160. (Illus.). 188p. 1986. 36.00 (*0-8155-1089-6*) Noyes.

Coal Science, No. II. Ed. by Harold H. Schobert et al. LC 91-11387. (ACS Symposium Ser.: No. 461). (Illus.). 352p. 1991. 77.95 (*0-8412-2005-0*) Am Chemical.

Coal Science & Chemistry. Ed. by A. Volborth. (Coal Science & Technology Ser.: No. 10). 490p. 1986. 138.50 (*0-444-42702-3*) Elsevier.

Coal Society: A History of the South Wales Mining Valleys 1840-1980. David Egan. (Illus.). 153p. (C). 1987. pap. 22.00x (*0-86383-239-3*, Pub. by Gomer Pr UK) St Mut.

Coal, Steel & the Rebirth of Europe, 1945-1955: The Germans & French from Ruhr Conflict to Economic Community. John Gillingham. 336p. (C). 1991. 59.95 (*0-521-40059-7*) Cambridge U Pr.

Coal Structure. Ed. by Martin L. Gorbaty & K. Ouchi. LC 80-24104. (ACS Advances in Chemistry Ser.: No. 192). 1981. 43.95 (*0-8412-0524-8*) Am Chemical.

Coal Tar Epoxy Coatings: A State-of-the-Art Review, TPC 12. 45p. 1991. 32.00 (*0-685-50987-7*) NACE Intl.

Coal Town: The Life & Times of Dawson, New Mexico. Toby Smith. LC 93-43245. (Illus.). 154p. (Orig.). 1994. pap. 15.95 (*0-941270-82-3*) Ancient City Pr.

***Coal Towns: Life, Work, & Culture in Company Towns of Southern Appalachia, 1850-1960.** Shifflett. LC 90-41458. 280p. (C). 1995. pap. text ed. 16.00x (*0-87049-885-1*) U of Tenn Pr.

Coal Towns: Life, Work & Culture in Company Towns of Southern Appalachia, 1880-1960. Crandall A. Shifflett. LC 90-41458. (Illus.). 280p. 1991. text ed. 34.95 (*0-87049-678-6*) U of Tenn Pr.

Coal Trans, '84. Ed. by Cargo Systems Staff. 1984. 195.00 (*0-907499-43-0*, Pub. by Cargo Systs UK) St Mut.

Coal, Uranium, & Oil & Gas in Mesozoic Rocks of the San Juan Basin: Anatomy of a Giant Energy-Rich Basin. Ed. by Finch. (IGC Field Trip Guidebooks Ser.). 112p. 1989. 28.00 (*0-87590-573-0*, T120) Am Geophysical.

Coal Viewer & Engine Builder's Practical Companion. 2nd ed. John Curr. 96p. 1970. reprint ed. 28.50 (*0-7146-2492-6*, Pub. by F Cass Pubs UK) Intl Spec Bk.

Coal War. Upton Sinclair. Ed. & Intro. by John Graham. LC 75-40885. 335p. 1976. text ed. 25.00 (*0-87081-067-7*) Univ Pr Colo.

Coal-Water Mixtures: Proceedings of a Contractor's Meeting Organized by the Commission of the European Communities, Directorate-General for Science, Research & Development, held in Brussels, Belgium, 26 May 1988. Ed. by P. F. Sens & J. K. Wilkinson. 100p. 1989. 36.00 (*1-85166-323-1*) Elsevier.

Coal Winning: Proceedings of the Information Symposium New Methods & Techniques of Coal Winning in the European Community, Held in Luxembourg from 23-25 April 1986. Ed. by F. W. Kindermann. 257p. (C). 1987. text ed. 140.00 (*90-6191-696-8*, Pub. by A A Balkema NE) Ashgate Pub Co.

Coalbed Gas Development - East & West. (Mineral Law Ser.). 1992. student ed 125.00 (*0-929047-30-3*) Rocky Mtn Mineral Law Found.

Coalbed Methane: Hazard of the Past, Energy for the Future. Jeanne G. Howard & Marcia S. Irvin. LC 92-12362. (CPL Bibliographies Ser.: No. 281). 1992. 18.00 (*0-86602-281-3*) Coun Plan Librarians.

***Coalbed Methane in the Upper Cretaceous Fruitland Formation, San Juan Basin, New Mexico & Colorado.** Ed. by W. B. Ayers, Jr. & W. R. Kaiser. (Illus.). 216p. 1994. 15.00 (*0-614-01867-6*) Bur Econ Geology.

***Coalbed Methane Resources of the United States.** Ed. by Craig T. Rightmire et al. (AAPG Studies in Geology: No. 17). (Illus.). viii, 378p. 1984. pap. 33.00 (*0-89181-023-4*) AAPG.

Coalbed Methane Technology. Rudy E. Rogers. 368p. 1994. text ed. 89.00 (*0-13-016353-8*) P-H.

Coalescence. Hatonn. (Phoenix Journals). 224p. 1993. pap. 6.00 (*1-56935-012-4*) Phoenix Source.

Coalinga, California Earthquake of May 2, 1983: A Reconaissance Report. Ed. by Roger Scholl & James Stratta. 312p. 1984. 12.00 (*0-685-14391-0*) Earthquake Eng.

Coalition & Coalescence: Berkeley Links Ecology & Ethnicity. Rosalind Lepawsky & Albert Lepawsky. (Environmental Studies: No. 1). 8p. 1972. 1.00 (*0-912102-46-2*) Cal Inst Public.

Coalition & Connection in Games. S. Guiasu & M. Malitza. 1980. 80.00 (*0-08-023033-4*, Pub. by Pergamon Repr UK) Franklin.

Coalition Bargaining. Philip J. Schwarz. (Key Issues Ser.: No. 5). 44p. 1970. pap. 2.00 (*0-87546-241-3*) ILR Pr.

***Coalition Compendium: A Guide to School Health Instructional Materials.** 1994. 14.50 (*0-614-06292-6*) Am Sch Health.

Coalition Formation. Ed. by A. A. Wilke. (Advances in Psychology Ser.: Vol. 24). 1985. 64.00 (*0-444-87702-9*) Elsevier.

Coalition Formation by Sophisticated Players. A. Rapoport et al. (Lecture Notes in Economics & Mathematical Systems Ser.: Vol. 169). 1979. pap. 27.00 (*0-387-09249-8*) Spr-Verlag.

Coalition Forming Behavior. Heinz Sauermann. (Contributions to Experimental Economics Ser.). 385p. 1978. lib. bdg. 62.50 (*3-16-340982-2*, Pub. by J C B Mohr GW) Coronet Bks.

Coalition Government in Western Europe. Vernon Bogdanor. 282p. 1983. text ed. 58.95 (*0-435-83104-6*) Ashgate Pub Co.

Coalition Strategies of Marxist Parties. Ed. by Trond Gilberg. LC 88-9579. (Duke Press Policy Studies). ix, 376p. (C). 1988. lib. bdg. 58.00 (*0-8223-0849-5*) Duke.

C

An Asterisk (*) at the beginning of an entry indicates that the title is appearing in BIP for the first time.

Coalition War Plans & Hemispheric Defense Plans, 1940-1941. Ed. by Steven T. Ross. LC 92-20669. (American War Plans, 1919-1941 Ser.: Vol. 4). 392p. 1992. 127.00 (*0-8153-0692-X*) Garland.

Coalitional Behaviour in Theory & Practice: An Inductive Model for Western Europe. Ed. by Geoffrey Pridham. (Illus.). 320p. 1986. 69.95 (*0-521-30537-3*) Cambridge U Pr.

Coalitions & Alliances in Humans & Other Animals. Ed. by Alexander H. Harcourt & Fans B. De Waal. (Illus.). 512p. 1992. 87.00 (*0-19-854273-9*) OUP.

Coalitions & Collaboration in International Business. Ed. by Geoffrey Jones. (International Library of Critical Writings in Business History: Vol. 7). (Illus.). 500p. 1993. 179.95 (*1-85278-747-3*, Pub. by E Elgar Pub UK) Ashgate Pub Co.

Coalitions & Competition: The Globalization of Professional Business Services. Ed. by Yair Aharoni. LC 93-6937. 256p. 1993. 65.00 (*0-415-08228-5*, B0181) Routledge.

Coalitions in British Politics. Ed. by David E. Butler. LC 77-17791. 1978. text ed. 29.95 (*0-312-14503-9*) St Martin.

Coalitions in Parliamentary Government. Lawrence C. Dodd. LC 75-2986. 184p. 1975. 47.50 (*0-691-07564-6*) Princeton U Pr.

***Coalitions in Parliamentary Government.** Lawrence C. Dodd. LC 75-2986. reprint ed. pap. 86.70 (*0-7837-9331-6*, 2060072) Bks Demand.

Coalitions, Politicians, & Generals: Some Aspects of Command in Two World Wars. Dominick Grahan & Shelford Bidwell. 260p. 1993. 35.00 (*1-85753-007-1*, Pub. by Brasseys UK) Brasseys Inc.

Coalminers of Durham. Norman Emery. (Illus.). 198p. 1992. text ed. 34.00 (*0-7509-0030-X*) A Sutton Pub.

Coalmining Women: Victorian Lives & Campaigns. Angela John. (Women in History Ser.). (Illus.). 48p. 1984. pap. 7.95 (*0-521-27872-4*) Cambridge U Pr.

Coalport, 1795-1926. Michael Messenger. (Illus.). 350p. 1993. 59.50 (*1-85149-112-0*) Antique Collect.

CoalPower, '87. Ed. by Cargo Systems Staff. 1987. 195.00 (*0-907400-59-0*, Pub. by Cargo Systs UK) St Mut.

Coal's Contribution to U. K. Self-Sufficiency. 2nd ed. Louise Turner. (Joint Energy Programme Ser.). 65p. (Orig.). 1985. text ed. 55.95 (*0-566-05016-1*) Ashgate Pub Co.

Coals of Fire. Elizabeth H. Bauman. LC 53-12197. (Christian Peace Shelf Ser.). (Illus.). (J). (gr. 5-9). 1954. pap. 5.95 (*0-8361-1957-6*) Herald Pr.

Coals of Fire. G. D. Watson. pap. 4.99 (*0-88019-009-4*) Schmul Pub Co.

Coals of Fire: The "Alton Telegraph" Libel Case. Thomas B. Littlewood. LC 87-9844. 247p. 1988. text ed. 24.50 (*0-8093-1401-0*) S Ill U Pr.

Coalseam: Poems from the Anthracite Region. Ed. by Karen Blomain. LC 92-60481. (C). 1993. 19.95 (*0-940866-21-8*) U Scranton Pr.

CoalTrans, '81. Ed. by Cargo Systems Staff. 1981. 195.00 (*0-907499-19-8*, Pub. by Cargo Systs UK) St Mut.

CoalTrans, '82. Ed. by Cargo Systems Staff. 1982. 195.00 (*0-907499-29-5*, Pub. by Cargo Systs UK) St Mut.

Coarse Cohomology & Index Theory on Complete Riemannian Manifolds. John Roe. LC 93-17166. (Memoirs of the American Mathematical Society Ser.: No. 497). 90p. 1993. pap. 29.00 (*0-8218-2559-3*) Am Math.

Coarse Fishing. Peter Collins & Colin Graham. (Know the Game Ser.). (Illus.). 1975. pap. 2.50 (*0-7158-0209-7*) Charles River Bks.

Coarse Fishing for Beginners. Kenneth Mansfield. (Illus.). 160p. (Orig.). 1974. pap. 14.95 (*0-572-01176-8*) Trans-Atl Phila.

***Coarse Fishing with Matt Hayes.** Matt Hayes. (Illus.). 192p. 1995. 39.95 (*1-85223-866-6*, Pub. by Crowood Pr UK) Trafalgar.

Coase Theorum: A Study in Economic Epistemology. Gary North. LC 91-40767. 128p. 1992. 25.00 (*0-930464-61-3*) Inst Christian.

Coast. Marius Kociejowski. (C). 1990. 35.00 (*0-906887-42-9*, Pub. by Greville Pr UK) St Mut.

Coast: A Journey Down the Atlantic Shore. Joseph J. Thorndike. (Illus.). 256p. 1994. pap. 12.95 (*0-312-10953-9*, Pub. by Thomas Dunne Bks) St Martin.

Coast: A Journey down the Atlantic Shore from Maine to Florida. Joseph J. Thorndike. LC 92-41223. 1993. 19.95 (*0-312-08700-4*) St Martin.

Coast Adventures. Pete Rehnberg. (Illus.). 40p. 1992. pap. 6.95 (*1-878175-17-3*) F Amato Pubns.

Coast & Geodetic Survey: Its History, Activities & Organization. Gustavus A. Weber. LC 72-3034. (Brookings Institution. Institute for Government Research. Service Monographs of the U. S. Government: No. 16). reprint ed. 21.50 (*0-404-57116-6*) AMS Pr.

Coast & Harbor Defences. Charles Ellet. (Notable American Authors Ser.). 1992. reprint ed. lib. bdg. 75.00 (*0-7812-2795-X*) Rprt Serv.

Coast Guard: Its History, Activities & Organization. Darrell H. Smith & Fred W. Powell. LC 72-3067. (Brookings Institution. Institute for Government Research. Service Monographs of the U. S. Government: No. 51). reprint ed. 34.50 (*0-404-57151-4*) AMS Pr.

Coast Guard & You. Dorothy Hole. LC 92-9775. (Armed Forces Ser.). (Illus.). 48p. (J). (gr. 5-6). 1993. text ed. 12.95 (*0-89686-766-8*, Crstwood Hse) Silver Burdett Pr.

Coast Guard City U. S. A. A History of the Port of Grand Haven. David S. Seibold. (Illus.). 340p. (Orig.). 1990. pap. 23.00 (*0-9614344-7-3*) Historical Soc MI.

***Coast Guard Combat.** Turner Publishing Company Staff. LC 94-60147. 144p. 1994. 48.00 (*1-56311-104-7*) Turner Pub KY.

Coast Guard License - From Six Pac to Master 100 Tons: Ed. 14-D. 14th rev. ed. Budd Gonder. LC 92-38247. (Illus.). 224p. (C). 1995. pap. text ed. 29.95 (*1-880093-03-0*) Charters W.

Coast Guard under Sail: The U. S. Revenue Cutter Service, 1789-1865. Irving H. King. LC 89-12445. 288p. 1989. 31.95 (*0-87021-234-6*) Naval Inst Pr.

Coast Guard's House. Eugenio Montale & Jeremy Reed. 224p. 1990. pap. 18.95 (*1-85224-100-4*, Pub. by Bloodaxe Bks UK) Dufour.

Coast Guardsman's Manual. 8th ed. George E. Krietemeyer. LC 91-10944. (Illus.). 736p. 1991. pap. 17.95 (*1-55750-450-4*) Naval Inst Pr.

Coast Miwok Indians of the Point Reyes Area. Sylvia B. Thalman. Ed. by Barbara Edmonds. (Illus.). 40p. (Orig.). 1992. pap. write for info. (*0-911235-04-3*) Pt Reyes Natl.

Coast of Bohemia. William Dean Howells. (Notable American Authors Ser.). 1992. reprint ed. lib. bdg. 75.00 (*0-7812-3248-1*) Rprt Serv.

Coast of Chi, Bk. 2. Stuart Dybek. 1986. write for info. (*0-670-81356-7*) Viking Penguin.

Coast of Chicago. Stuart Dybek. LC 90-50499. 192p. 1991. pap. 10.00 (*0-679-73334-5*, Vin) Random.

Coast of Illyria: A Play in Three Acts. Dorothy Parker & Ross Evans. LC 89-20251. (Illus.). 232p. (Orig.). 1990. 29.95x (*0-87745-273-3*); pap. 15.95 (*0-87745-288-1*) U of Iowa Pr.

Coast of Maine. Wayne Barrett et al. 96p. 1984. 19.95 (*1-55652-087-5*) Chicago Review.

Coast of Maine: A Complete Guide. Rick Ackermann & Kathryn Buxton. (Illus.). 1992. pap. 14.95 (*0-936399-24-4*) Berkshire Hse.

Coast of Maine: An Informal History & Guide. Louise D. Rich. LC 93-30612. 400p. 1993. reprint ed. pap. 13.95 (*0-89272-342-4*) Down East.

Coast of Malabar. John Maher. 176p. 1988. pap. 9.95 (*0-86278-166-3*, Pub. by OBrien Pr IE) Dufour.

Coast of Puget Sound: Its Processes & Development. John Downing. LC 82-10961. (Illus.). 142p. 1985. pap. 8.95 (*0-295-95944-4*) U of Wash Pr.

Coast of Summer: Sailing New England Waters from Shelter Island to Cape Cod. Antony Bailey. (Illus.). 320p. 1994. 23.00 (*0-06-118004-1*, HarpT) HarpC.

Coast of Victoria: Shaping of Scenery. Eric C. Bird. (Illus.). 324p. 1993. 49.95 (*0-522-84544-4*) Intl Spec Bk.

Coast of West Cork. Peter Somerville-Large. 128p. 1991. pap. 14.95 (*0-86281-282-8*, Pub. by Appletree Pr IE) Irish Bks Media.

Coast Salish. Reg Ashwell. (Illus.). 88p. pap. 6.95 (*0-88839-009-2*) Hancock House.

Coast Salish of British Columbia. Homer G. Barnett. LC 75-25251. (Univ. of Oregon Monographs, Studies in Anthropology: No. 4). (Illus.). 320p. 1975. reprint ed. text ed. 35.00 (*0-8371-8381-2*, BACSB, Greenwood Pr) Greenwood.

Coast Salish Peoples. Frank W. Porter. (Indians of North America Ser.). (Illus.). 104p. (J). (gr. 5 up). 1989. 17.95 (*1-55546-701-6*) Chelsea Hse.

Coast to Coast. Bruce Bawer. 75p. (Orig.). 1993. pap. 11.95 (*0-934257-51-5*) Story Line.

Coast to Coast. Betsy Byars. (J). (gr. 4-7). 1994. mass mkt. 3.99 (*0-440-40926-8*) Dell.

***Coast to Coast.** Guy Harriton. 1995. 14.95 (*0-8062-5250-2*) Carlton.

Coast to Coast: Facts & Fun about the Fifty States. S. Black & D. Newberger. 64p. (J). (gr. 3-7). 1991. 1.95 (*0-590-43970-7*) Scholastic Inc.

Coast to Coast: The Best of Travel Decal Art. Rod Dyer et al. (Illus.). 96p. 1991. 21.95 (*1-55859-156-7*) Abbeville Pr.

Coast to Coast - Level 1. Harmer & Surguine. (Illus.). 1987. teacher ed 18.95 (*0-582-90731-4*, 75242); student ed 8.95 (*0-582-90734-9*, 75245); pap. text ed. 12.95 (*0-582-90728-4*, 75239) Longman.

Coast to Coast - Level 1, No. 1. Harmer & Surguine. (Illus.). 1987. audio 49.95 (*0-582-00233-8*, 70397); audio 24.95 (*0-582-90737-3*, 75248) Longman.

Coast to Coast - Level 2. Harmer & Surguine. (Illus.). 1987. teacher ed 18.95 (*0-582-90732-2*, 75243); student ed 8.95 (*0-582-90735-7*, 75246); pap. text ed. 12.95 (*0-582-90729-2*, 75240) Longman.

Coast to Coast - Level 2, No. 2. Harmer & Surguine. (Illus.). 1987. audio 24.95 (*0-582-90738-1*, 75249); audio 49.95 (*0-582-00234-6*, 70398) Longman.

Coast to Coast - Level 3. Harmer & Surguine. (Illus.). 1987. teacher ed 18.95 (*0-582-90733-0*, 75244); student ed 8.95 (*0-582-90736-5*, 75247); pap. text ed. 12.95 (*0-582-90730-6*, 75241) Longman.

Coast to Coast - Level 3, No. 3. Harmer & Surguine. (Illus.). 1987. audio 24.95 (*0-582-90739-X*, 75250) Longman.

Coast to Coast in a Cab. Ed Byars. (Illus.). 117p. 1988. 17.95 (*0-9619264-0-6*) E F Byars.

Coast to Coast Walk: A Serendipitous Journey Across England. Richard Hayward. (Illus.). 100p. (Orig.). 1994. pap. 6.95 (*1-880848-03-1*) Brit Footpaths.

***Coast to Coast with Alice.** Pat R. Hyatt. LC 94-25750. (J). 1995. write for info. (*0-87614-789-9*, Carolrhoda) Lerner Group.

Coast Walks: One Hundred Adventures along the California Coast. John McKinney. (Illus.). 264p. (Orig.). 1988. pap. 10.95 (*0-934161-03-8*) Olympus Pr.

Coast Watching in the Solomon Islands: The Bougainville Reports, December 1941-July 1943. Ed. by A. B. Feuer. LC 91-40548. (Bougainville Reports of Jack Read & Paul Mason, December 1941-July 1943). 208p. 1992. text ed. 49.95 (*0-275-94203-1*, C4203, Praeger Pubs) Greenwood.

Coast Way. Louise Abbott. (Illus.). 156p. (C). 1988. 60.00 (*0-7735-0654-3*, Pub. by McGill CN); 125.00 (*0-7735-0671-3*, Pub. by McGill CN) U of Toronto Pr.

Coastal Affair. Jennifer Miller. (Southern Exposure Ser.). (Illus.). 120p. (Orig.). 1982. pap. 4.00 (*0-943810-13-2*) Inst Southern Studies.

Coastal Alert: Ecosystems, Energy, & Offshore Oil Drilling. Dwight Holing. LC 90-41293. 122p. 1990. pap. 11.95 (*1-55963-050-7*) Island Pr.

Coastal & Deep Ocean Dredging. John B. Herbich. LC 74-4828. (Illus.). 639p. reprint ed. pap. 180.00 (*0-685-44469-4*, 2032997) Bks Demand.

Coastal & Deep Sea Navigation for Yachtsmen. C. A. Lund. (C). 1987. 35.00 (*0-85174-119-3*, Pub. by Brwn Son Ferg) St Mut.

Coastal & Inland Periglacial Processes Canadian Arctic: Canadian Arctic. H. Hagedorn. (Zeitschrift Fuer Geomorphologie Ser.: Suppl. 47). (Illus.). 136p. 1983. pap. 49.00 (*3-443-21047-3*, Pub. by Cramer-Borntraeger GW) Lubrecht & Cramer.

Coastal & Maritime Archaeology: A Bibliography. Jordan E. Kerber. LC 91-25506. 408p. 1991. 42.50 (*0-8108-2465-5*) Scarecrow.

Coastal & Ocean Engineering, Eleventh Australasian Conference, 1993: Coastal Engineering - a Partnership with Nature, 2 vols., Set. Intro. by Dean Patterson. (National Conference Publication Ser.: No. 93-4). (Illus.). (Orig.). 1993. pap. 120.00 (*0-85825-574-X*, Pub. by Inst Engrs Aust-EA Bks AT) Accents Pubns.

***Coastal & Ocean Law.** 2nd ed. J. Kalo et al. LC 94-72966. 532p. 1994. 58.75 (*0-916081-36-2*) J Marshall Pub Co.

Coastal & Ocean Management Law in a Nutshell. Donna R. Christie. LC 93-48713. (Nutshell Ser.). 365p. 1994. pap. text ed. 18.00 (*0-314-03353-X*) West Pub.

Coastal & Offshore Navigation. Tom Cunliffe. 64p. (C). 1990. text ed. 59.00 (*0-906754-55-0*, Pub. by Fernhurst Bks UK) St Mut.

Coastal & Port Engineering in Developing Countries 1987: Proceedings, 2 vols. Ed. by Nanjing Hydraulic Research Institute. 2250p. (C). 1987. pap. 98.00 (*7-5027-0052-8*, Pub. by A A Balkema NE) Ashgate Pub Co.

Coastal Aquaculture Engineering. A. N. Bose. 1991. 64.00 (*81-204-0500-5*, Pub. by Oxford IBH II) S Asia.

Coastal Aquaculture in Developing Countries: Problems & Perspectives. Ed. by Richard B. Pollnac & Priscilla Weeks. (Illus.). 183p. (Orig.). (C). 1992. pap. text ed. write for info. (*1-882027-06-X*) URI ICMRD.

Coastal Area Management in Southeast Asia. Ed. by Chua Thia-Eng & Daniel Pauly. 1989. pap. 15.00 (*971-10-2261-3*, Pub. by ICLARM PH) Intl Spec Bk.

Coastal Area Resource Development: Energy in Small Islands. 94p. 1988. pap. 12.00 (*92-1-104220-8*, E.88.II. A.2) UN.

***Coastal Atlantic Sea Creatures: A Natural History.** Robert G. Bachand. Ed. by Michelle O'Conner. (Illus.). 194p. (Orig.). 1994. pap. 16.95 (*0-9616399-5-4*) Sea Sports Pubns.

Coastal Barriers: Development Occurring Despite Prohibitions Against Federal Assistance. 65p. (Orig.). (C). 1993. pap. text ed. 30.00 (*0-7881-0157-9*) Diane Pub.

Coastal Birds: A Guide to Birds of Maine's Beautiful Coastline. Al Kidwell. (Maine Geographic Ser.). (Illus.). 48p. 1983. pap. 4.95 (*0-89933-052-5*) DeLorme Map.

Coastal Bottom Boundary Layers & Sediment Transport. P. Nielsen. 250p. 1992. text ed. 64.00 (*981-02-0472-8*); pap. text ed. 32.00 (*981-02-0473-6*) World Scientific Pub.

***Coastal California: A Camping Guide.** George Cagala. (Camping Guide Ser.). (Illus.). 288p. (Orig.). 1995. pap. 11.95 (*1-55650-679-1*) Hunter NJ.

Coastal Carolina: From the Outer Banks to Hilton Head Isle. 32p. (J). (ps-12). 1986. 2.95 (*0-936672-67-6*) Aerial Photo.

Coastal Carolina Cookbook. 2.49 (*0-936672-04-8*) Aerial Photo.

Coastal Carolina Cooking. Nancy Davis & Kathy Hart. LC 85-22265. (Illus.). xvii, 179p. 1986. pap. 12.95 (*0-8078-4152-8*) U of NC Pr.

Coastal Changes. William W. Williams. LC 75-3873. (Illus.). 220p. 1975. reprint ed. text ed. 65.00 (*0-8371-8088-0*, WICOC, Greenwood Pr) Greenwood.

***Coastal Colors.** Gay H. Kovach. (Illus.). 30p. (Orig.). (J). (gr. k-6). 1995. pap. 3.95 (*0-87844-128-X*) Sandlapper Pub Co.

***Coastal Companion: A Guide for the Alaska Bound Traveler.** Joe Upton. (Illus.). 220p. (Orig.). 1995. pap. 16.95 (*0-9645682-0-9*) Coastal Pub.

Coastal Cook of West Marin: Kitchen Conversations & Recipes. Laura Riley. (Illus.). 240p. (Orig.). 1991. pap. text ed. 12.95 (*0-9628426-0-5*) Riley & Co.

Coastal Crude: In a Sea of Conflict. Robert E. Kallman & Eugene D. Wheeler. (Illus.). 144p. 1984. 11.95 (*0-918303-00-1*); pap. 7.95 (*0-918303-01-X*) Blake Pub.

Coastal Daytrips in New England. 2nd ed. Harriet Webster. LC 86-51012. 176p. 1987. pap. 9.95 (*0-89909-126-1*, 80-650-4) Yankee Bks.

Coastal Decisions: Difficult Choices. 2nd ed. Louis A. Iozzi. (Preparing for Tomorrow's World Ser.). 158p. 1992. reprint ed. teacher ed 80.00 (*0-944584-62-4*) Sopris.

Coastal Depositional Systems, Northwestern Gulf of Mexico, No. T370. Ed. by Suter. (IGC Field Trip Guidebooks Ser.). 56p. 1989. 21.00 (*0-87590-669-9*) Am Geophysical.

Coastal Disturbances: Four Plays by Tina Howe. Tina Howe. LC 88-37053. 240p. 1989. 22.95 (*0-930452-85-2*); pap. 11.95 (*0-930452-86-0*) Theatre Comm.

Coastal Dunes: Form & Process. Ed. by Karl Nordstrom et al. (Coastal Morphology & Research Ser.). 392p. 1991. text ed. 195.00 (*0-471-91842-3*) Wiley.

Coastal Dunes: Geomorphology, Ecology & Management for Conservation - Proceedings of the Third European Congress, Galway, Ireland, 17-21 June 1991. Ed. by R. W. Carter et al. (Illus.). 544p. (C). 1992. text ed. 130.00 (*90-5410-058-3*, Pub. by A A Balkema NE) Ashgate Pub Co.

Coastal Dunes of California. William S. Cooper. LC 67-29290. (Geological Society of America, Memoir Ser.: No. 104). 189p. reprint ed. pap. 53.90 (*0-318-34699-0*, 2031806) Bks Demand.

***Coastal Dynamics '94: Proceedings of an International Conference on the Role of the Large-Scale Experiments in Coastal Research, Universitat Politecnica de Catalunya, Barcelona, Spain, February 21-25, 1994.** Ed. by A. S. Arcilla et al. LC 94-5424. 1994. write for info. (*0-7844-0043-1*) Am Soc Civil Eng.

Coastal Ecology Coloring Book. Vickie Shufer. (Environmental Education Ser.). (Illus.). 1986. pap. 2.50 (*0-938423-00-2*) Eco Images.

Coastal Economies, Cultural Accounts: Human Ecology & Icelandic Discourse. Gisli Palsson. LC 90-29067. 224p. 1991. text ed. 69.95 (*0-7190-3543-0*, Pub. by Manchester Univ Pr UK) St Martin.

Coastal Economies, Cultural Accounts: Human Ecology & Icelandic Discourse. Gisli Palsson. (Themes in Social Anthropology Ser.). 224p. 1994. text ed. 29.95 (*0-7190-4386-7*, Pub. by Manchester Univ Pr UK) St Martin.

Coastal Engineering: Proceedings of 10th Conference, Tokyo, Japan, September, 1966, 2 vols., Vols. 1 & 2. American Society of Civil Engineers Staff. reprint ed. pap. 160.00 (*0-685-73721-7*, 2019545) Bks Demand.

***Coastal Engineering: Waves, Beaches, Wave Structure Interactions.** T. Sawaragi. LC 95-9722. (Developments in Geotechnical Engineering Ser.: Vol. 78). 1995. write for info. (*0-444-82068-X*) Elsevier.

Coastal Engineering: 1974, 3 vols. Comp. by American Society of Civil Engineers Staff. 2705p. 1975. pap. 120.00 (*0-87262-113-8*) Am Soc Civil Eng.

Coastal Engineering: 1976, 4 vols., Set. Comp. by American Society of Civil Engineers Staff. 2242p. 1977. pap. 120.00 (*0-87262-083-2*) Am Soc Civil Eng.

Coastal Engineering: 1978, 3 vols. Comp. by American Society of Civil Engineers Staff. 3094p. 1979. pap. 120.00 (*0-87262-190-1*) Am Soc Civil Eng.

Coastal Engineering: 1980, 3 vols. LC 81-69156. 3249p. 1981. pap. 165.00 (*0-87262-264-9*) Am Soc Civil Eng.

Coastal Engineering: 1982, 3 Vols. 18th ed. Ed. by Billy L. Edge. 2844p. 1983. pap. 180.00 (*0-87262-373-4*) Am Soc Civil Eng.

Coastal Engineering - 1992: Proceedings of the Twenty-Third International Conference, October 4-9, 1992, Venice, Italy. Ed. by Billy L. Edge. LC 93-7616. 3616p. 1993. 250.00 (*0-87262-933-3*) Am Soc Civil Eng.

Coastal Engineering Considerations in Coastal Zone Management. Steven A. Hughes. LC 93-2251. (Coastlines of the World Ser.). 312p. 1993. 26.00 (*0-87262-958-9*) Am Soc Civil Eng.

Coastal Engineering Nineteen Eighty-Eight, 3 vols. Ed. by Billy L. Edge. 3092p. 1989. 240.00 (*0-87262-687-3*) Am Soc Civil Eng.

Coastal Engineering Nineteen Ninety. Ed. by Billy L. Edge. LC 91-9069. 3424p. 1991. pap. text ed. 250.00 (*0-87262-776-4*) Am Soc Civil Eng.

Coastal Engineering Practice '92. Ed. by Steven A. Hughes. LC 92-931. 1104p. 1992. pap. text ed. 83.00 (*0-87262-866-3*) Am Soc Civil Eng.

Coastal Engineering Research. 114p. 1985. 48.00 (*0-7277-0241-6*, Pub. by T Telford UK) Am Soc Civil Eng.

Coastal Engineering Specialty Conference, Santa Barbara, October 1965. Coastal Engineering Conference Staff. LC 66-7562. 1017p. reprint ed. pap. 180.00 (*0-317-42285-5*, 2020835) Bks Demand.

Coastal Engineering, Vol. 2: Sedimentation, Estuaries, Tides, Effluents, Modelling. Richard Silvester. LC 72-97435. (Developments in Geotechnical Engineering Ser.: Vol. 4B). 338p. 1974. 100.00 (*0-444-41102-X*) Elsevier.

Coastal Engineering 1984, 3 vols., Set. 3282p. 1984. 245.00 (*0-87262-438-2*) Am Soc Civil Eng.

Coastal Engineering 1986, 3 vols., Set. Ed. by Billy L. Edge. 2888p. 1987. 215.00 (*0-87262-600-8*) Am Soc Civil Eng.

Coastal Environment Profile of Segara Anakan-Cilacap, South Java, Indonesia. Ed. by A. T. White et al. 1990. pap. text ed. 7.00 (*971-10-2254-0*, Pub. by ICLARM PH) Intl Spec Bk.

Coastal Environmental Profile of Brunel Darussalam: Resource Assessment & Management Issues. T. E. Chua et al. (ICLARM Technical Reports: No. 18). 1988. 12.00 (*971-10-2238-9*, Pub. by ICLARM PH); pap. 10.00 (*971-10-2237-0*, Pub. by ICLARM PH) Intl Spec Bk.

Coastal Environments: An Introduction to the Physical, Ecological & Cultural Systems of Ocean Sciences, Resources & Technology Coastlines. R. W. Carter. 640p. 1990. pap. text ed. 61.00 (*0-12-161856-0*) Acad Pr.

Coastal Erosion: Has Retreat Sounded? Rutherford H. Platt et al. LC 92-34852. (Program on Environment & Behavior Monograph Ser.: No. 53). 1992. 10.00 (*1-877943-07-X*) Natural Hazards.

Coastal, Estuarial, & Harbour Engineer's Reference Book. Ed. by M. B. Abbott & W. A. Price. LC 93-6888. 1993. write for info. (*0-419-15430-2*, E & FN Spon) Routledge Chapman & Hall.

Coastal Evaporite & Tidal-Flat Sediments of the Upper Clear Fork & Glorieta Formations, Texas Panhandle. M. W. Presley & K. A. McGillis. (Report of Investigations Ser.: RI 115). (Illus.). 50p. 1982. 2.00 (*0-318-03248-1*) Bur Econ Geology.

An Asterisk (*) at the beginning of an entry indicates that the title is appearing in BIP for the first time.

C

An Asterisk (*) at the beginning of an entry indicates that the title is appearing in BIP for the first time.

Coastwise Craft: The Development of the Sailing Vessel. Thomas C. Lethbridge. 1977. lib. bdg. 75.00 (0-8490-1639-8) Gordon Pr.

Coat. Connie Korda. (Illus.). 28p. (Orig.). (J). (gr. k-4). 1993. pap. 7.95 (1-879418-09-6) Biddle Pub.

Coat Holder. Mike Phillips. LC 84-24251. 1986. 13.95 (0-87949-248-1) Ashley Bks.

Coat of Arms. Chris Tysh. LC 92-16318. 1992. write for info. (0-88268-111-7) Station Hill Pr.

Coat of Arms. large type ed. Sims. 1991. 17.95 (0-7451-9951-8, AH010, Atlantic Lrg Print); pap. 15.95 (0-7927-0413-4, AS046, Atlantic Lrg Print) Chivers N Amer.

Coat of Many Colors. Behn Boruch. 1959. 3.95 (0-88482-728-3) Hebrew Pub.

Coat of Many Colors. Dawn Cahoon-Kniff. LC 90-70672. (Illus.). 94p. (Orig.). 1991. pap. 6.00 (1-56002-013-X) Aegina Pr.

Coat of Many Colors. Dolly Parton. LC 93-3866. (Illus.). 32p. (J). (gr. 1 up). 1994. 14.00 (0-06-023413-X); lib. bdg. 13.89 (0-06-023414-8) HarpC Child Bks.

Coat of Many Colors: Jewish Subcommunities in the United States. Ed. by Abraham D. Lavender. LC 77-71865. (Contributions in Family Studies: No. 1). 324p. 1977. text ed. 59.95 (0-8371-9539-X, LCM/, Greenwood Pr) Greenwood.

Coat of Many Colors: Osip Mandelstam & His Mythologies of Self-Presentation. Gregory Freidin. LC 85-16440. 450p. 1988. 55.00 (0-520-05438-5) U CA Pr.

Coat of Many Colors: Reflections on Diversity by a Minority of One. Eugene Eoyang. LC 94-13421. 224p. 1994. 24.00 (0-8070-0420-0) Beacon Pr.

Coat Pocket Bird Book. John Gillette. LC 83-62005. 160p. 1984. pap. 12.95 (0-685-10767-1) Mich Nat Res.

Coated Abrasives Reference Manual: Woodworking & Furniture Industries. Doug Washer. (Illus.). 64p. (Orig.). 1991. pap. 9.95 (0-9629717-0-7) Klingspor Abrasives.

Coated Fabrics: Meeting the Challenge of the 90's. (Symposium Papers). 166p. 1992. 55.00 (0-685-57401-6) AATCC.

Coated Grains. Ed. by T. Peryt. (Illus.). 600p. 1983. 107.00 (0-387-12071-8) Spr-Verlag.

Coated Paperboard Short Course, 1991: Sheraton Centre, Montreal, Quebec, May 23-24. Technical Association of the Pulp & Paper Industry Staff. (TAPPI Notes Ser.). reprint ed. pap. 40.50 (0-7837-1276-6, 2041417) Bks Demand.

Coated Paperboard Short Course, 1992: Holiday Inn Genesee Plaza, Rochester, NY, October 4-6. Technical Association of the Pulp & Paper Industry Staff. (TAPPI Notes Ser.). reprint ed. pap. 37.60 (0-7837-3939-7, 2043694) Bks Demand.

Coated Vesicles. Ed. by C. D. Ockleford & A. Whyte. LC 79-17280. 400p. reprint ed. pap. 114.00 (0-685-16174-9, 2027260) Bks Demand.

***Coating & Drying Defects: Troubleshooting Operating Problems.** Edgar B. Gutoff & Edward D. Cohen. LC 94-21972. 1995. text ed. 69.95 (0-471-59810-0) Wiley.

***Coating & Paint Market.** 400p. (Orig.). 1994. pap. 2,000.00 (0-7605-0003-7) Rector Pr.

Coating Binders Seminar, 1986: Proceedings of Notes of TAPPI, Washington Hilton Hotel, Washington, D.C., May 8, 1986. Technical Association of the Pulp & Paper Industry Staff. 71p. pap. 25.00 (0-685-17827-7, 2029185) Bks Demand.

Coating Binders Short Course, 1990: Boston Marriott, Copley Place, Boston, MA, May 17-18. Technical Association of the Pulp & Paper Industry Staff. (TAPPI Notes Ser.). 123p. reprint ed. pap. 35.10 (0-8357-4302-0, 2037099) Bks Demand.

Coating Binders Short Course, 1992: Stouffer Orlando Hotel, Orlando, FL May 21-22. Technical Association of the Pulp & Paper Industry Staff. (TAPPI Notes Ser.). reprint ed. pap. 29.20 (0-7837-3167-1, 2042811) Bks Demand.

Coating Conference, 1984: Proceedings. Technical Association of the Pulp & Paper Industry Staff. 177p. reprint ed. pap. 50.50 (0-317-20758-X, 2024784) Bks Demand.

Coating Conference, 1985: Proceedings of TAPPI, Atlanta Hilton Hotel, Atlanta, GA, May 19-23. Technical Association of the Pulp & Paper Industry Staff. 255p. reprint ed. pap. 72.70 (0-317-26860-0, 2025290) Bks Demand.

Coating Conference, 1986: Proceedings of TAPPI, Hilton Hotel, Washington, DC, May 4-7. Technical Association of the Pulp & Paper Industry Staff. 143p. pap. 40.80 (0-685-17830-7, 2029186) Bks Demand.

Coating Conference, 1989: Chicago Hilton & Towers, Chicago, IL, May 14-17. Technical Association of the Pulp & Paper Industry Staff. (TAPPI Proceedings Ser.). (Illus.). 215p. reprint ed. pap. 61.30 (0-8357-6320-X, 2035594) Bks Demand.

Coating Conference, 1990: Boston Marriott, Copley Place, Boston, MA, May 13- 16. Technical Association of the Pulp & Paper Industry Staff. (TAPPI Proceedings Ser.). (Illus.). 499p. reprint ed. pap. 142.30 (0-8357-4223-7, 2037011) Bks Demand.

Coating Conference, 1991: Le Centre Sheraton, Montreal, Quebec, May 19-22. Technical Association of the Pulp & Paper Industry Staff. (TAPPI Proceedings Ser.). reprint ed. pap. 147.20 (0-7837-1271-5, 2041412) Bks Demand.

Coating Conference, 1992: Stouffer Orlando Hotel, Orlando, FL, May 17-20. Technical Association of the Pulp & Paper Industry Staff. (TAPPI Proceedings Ser.). reprint ed. pap. 133.40 (0-7837-3168-X, 2042810) Bks Demand.

Coating, Converting & Specialty Processes. 3rd ed. Ed. by M. J. Kocurek & M. Kouris. (Pulp & Paper Manufacture Ser.: Vol. 8). 386p. 1990. 100.00 (0-919893-91-0, 0202MS08) TAPPI.

Coating Fundamentals: Suspension Rheology for Coating. Technical Association of the Pulp & Paper Industry Staff. Ed. by Brian G. Higgins. (Illus.). 44p. reprint ed. pap. 20.00 (0-318-39737-4, 2033109) Bks Demand.

Coating of Copper Wire for Severe Environment Electrical Insulation. Alloyd Corporation Staff. 56p. 1962. 8.40 (0-317-34499-4, 19) Intl Copper.

Coating Technology: Ion Beam Deposition. L. Pranevicius. 458p. 1993. text ed. 79.00 (0-9637993-0-4) Satas & Assocs.

Coating Thickness Measurement. H. Plogg. (C). 1988. 150.00 (0-85218-036-5, Pub. by Fuel Metallurgical Jrnl UK) St Mut.

Coatings: Film Formation, Components & Appearance, Science & Technology, Vol. 1. Zeno W. Wicks et al. (Society of Plastics Engineers Monographs). 368p. 1992. text ed. 89.95 (0-471-61406-8) Wiley.

Coatings & Bimetallics for Aggressive Environments: Conference Proceedings: Hilton Head, South Carolina, 12-14 November, 1984. Conference on Coatings & Bimetallics for Energy Systems & Chemical Process Environments Staff. LC 85-72288. (Illus.). 237p. reprint ed. pap. 67.60 (0-8357-6060-X, 2034325) Bks Demand.

Coatings & Liners for Pipes & Tanks, No. GB-143. Business Communications Co., Inc. Staff. 177p. 1991. 2,350.00 (0-89336-838-5) BCC.

Coatings & Linings for Immersion Service (TPC-2) (Illus.). 146p. 1972. 41.00 (0-915567-70-9) NACE Intl.

Coatings for Concrete & Cathodic Protection. Institution of Civil Engineers Staff. 50p. 1989. pap. text ed. 52.00 (0-7277-1500-3, Pub. by T Telford UK) Am Soc Civil Eng.

Coatings for Energy Efficiency & Solar Applications. J. J. Mason. (C). 1984. 100.00 (0-685-33082-6, Pub. by Interntl Solar Energy Soc UK) St Mut.

Coatings for Energy Efficiency & Solar Applications (C38) J. J. Mason. 89p. (C). 1984. 95.00 (0-685-30225-3, Pub. by Interntl Solar Energy Soc UK) St Mut.

Coatings for High Temperature Applications. Ed. by E. Lang. (Illus.). 448p. 1984. 124.25 (0-85334-221-0, Pub. by Elsevier Applied Sci UK) Elsevier.

Coatings for Potable Water Tank Interiors: A 33-Year Evaluation. John D. Keane et al. (Illus.). 25p. 1984. pap. text ed. 30.00 (0-938477-07-2) SSPC.

Coatings of High-Temperature Materials. Ed. by Henry H. Hausner. LC 65-12156. 305p. reprint ed. pap. 87.00 (0-685-15824-1, 2056106) Bks Demand.

Coatings on Glass. H. K. Pulker. (Thin Films Science & Technology Ser.: Vol. 6). 484p. 1984. 133.50 (0-444-42360-5, I-230-84) Elsevier.

Coatings on Glass. H. K. Pulker. 484p. 1987. pap. 79.00 (0-444-42834-8) Elsevier.

Coatings Technology Handbook. Ed. by D. Satas. 800p. 1991. 225.00 (0-8247-8410-3) Dekker.

Coatings Tribology: Properties, Techniques, & Applications in Surface Engineering. Kenneth Holmberg & Allan Matthews. LC 94-17684. (Tribology Ser.: Vol. 28). 1994. write for info. (0-444-88870-5) Elsevier.

Coattails. Margaret L. Kiely. 320p. (Orig.). 1991. pap. 12.95 (0-9612106-1-3) Codornices Pr.

Coaxial AC Bridges. B. P. Kibble & B. H. Rayner. (Illus.). 210p. 1984. 106.00 (0-85274-389-0) IOP Pub.

Coba: A Classical Maya Metropolis. William J. Folan et al. (Studies in Archaeology). 224p. 1983. text ed. 72.00 (0-12-261880-7) Acad Pr.

***Cobain.** Rolling Stones Editors. 1994. 24.95 (0-316-88034-5) Little.

Cobalamin: Biochemistry & Pathophysiology. Ed. by Bernard M. Babior. LC 74-32499. 489p. reprint ed. pap. 139.40 (0-317-07781-3, 2017398) Bks Demand.

Cobalt. (Metals & Minerals Ser.). 1993. lib. bdg. 250.75 (0-8490-8998-0) Gordon Pr.

Cobalt. I. V. Pyatniskii. (Analytical Chemistry of the Elements Ser.). 264p. 1970. text ed. 66.00 (0-7065-0746-0, Pub. by Keter Pub IS) Coronet Bks.

Cobalt, No. 1. Vaughn Bode. (Illus.). 48p. 1992. reprint ed. 3.95 (1-879450-35-6) Tundra MA.

Cobalt & Lustre: The First Centuries of Islamic Pottery. Ernst J. Grube. (Nasser D. Khalili Collection of Islamic Art: Vol. IX). (Illus.). 320p. (C). 1995. 245.00 (0-19-727607-5, 10948) OUP.

***Cobalt Blue.** Dorothy R. Lykes. (Illus.). 64p. 1995. 20.00 (0-933313-24-1); pap. 12.95 (0-933313-25-X) SUN Gemini Pr.

***Cobalt Blue.** deluxe limited ed. Dorothy R. Lykes. (Illus.). 64p. 1995. 30.00 (0-933313-23-3) SUN Gemini Pr.

Cobalt Facts. (Illus.). 225p. (C). 1994. pap. 75.00 (1-57205-715-7) Rector Pr.

***Cobalt Handbook: Update October 1994.** 70p. (Orig.). 1994. pap. 125.00 (0-7605-1163-2) Rector Pr.

Cobalt in Catalyst. 225p. (Orig.). (C). 1994. pap. 75.00 (1-57205-710-6) Rector Pr.

Cobalt in Chemicals. 225p. (Orig.). (C). 1994. pap. 75.00 (1-57205-708-4) Rector Pr.

Cobalt in Electronic Technology. (Illus.). 225p. (Orig.). (C). 1994. pap. 75.00 (1-57205-714-9) Rector Pr.

Cobalt in Medicine, Agriculture & the Environment. 225p. (Orig.). (C). 1994. pap. 75.00 (1-57205-709-2) Rector Pr.

Cobalt in Superalloys. 225p. (Orig.). (C). 1994. pap. 75.00 (1-57205-711-4) Rector Pr.

Cobalt 60. Vaughn Bode. (Illus.). 1988. pap. 7.95 (0-318-37685-7, Starblaze) Donning Co.

Cobalt Sixty. Vaughn Bode. 1988. pap. 7.95 (0-89865-677-X) Donning Co.

Cobalt Sixty, Bk. 2. Vaughn Bode. (Illus.). 48p. 1992. reprint ed. pap. 4.95 (1-879450-36-4) Tundra MA.

Cobalt Sixty, Bk. 3. Vaughn Bode. (Illus.). 48p. 1992. pap. 4.95 (1-879450-37-2) Tundra MA.

Cobalt Speciation & Mobility in Glacial Sand, EUR 13278. J. Higgo et al. 54p. 1991. pap. 9.00 (92-826-0517-5, CD-NA-13278-EN-C) UNIPUB.

Coban & the Verapaz: History & Cultural Process in Northern Guatemala. Arden R. King. (Publication Ser.: No. 37). (Illus.). 283p. 1974. 25.00 (0-939238-42-X) Tulane MARI.

Cobayos. Kate Petty. LC 90-71412. (First Pets Ser.). (Illus.). 24p. (SPA.). (J). (gr. k-4). 1991. lib. bdg. 11.62 (0-531-07914-7) Watts.

***Cobb.** Gorman Bechard. 1999. pap. 4.99 (0-451-18437-8, Sig) NAL-Dutton.

Cobb. Lee Blessing. 1991. pap. 4.75 (0-8222-0224-7) Dramatists Play.

***Cobb: The Life & Times of the Meanest Man Who Ever Played Baseball.** Al Stump. LC 94-26122. 436p. 1994. 24.95 (0-945575-64-5) Algonquin Bks.

Cobb Chronicles: An Overview of the Clan. John E. Cobb, Jr. LC 85-71704. (Illus.). 291p. 1985. 15.00 (0-9606128-5-8) Durant Pub.

Cobb County . . . a Portrait. John Rossino. 95p. (Orig.). 1988. pap. write for info. (0-318-64426-6) CCCC.

Cobb County, Georgia Cemeteries, Vol. II. Ed. by Elizabeth L. Parker. LC 81-45599. (Illus.). 756p. 1991. lib. bdg. 65.00 (1-879768-00-3) Cobb Cnty Geneal.

Cobb County, Georgia, Cemeteries, Vol. 3: Marietta National Cemetery. Ed. by Mimi J. Butler et al. LC 94-72040. (Illus.). 450p. 1994. lib. bdg. 45.00 (1-879768-01-1) Cobb Cnty Geneal.

***Cobb County, Georgia Marriages White 1865-1937, Colored 1865-1966.** Mary Hancock. 496p. 1995. lib. bdg. 24.00 (1-879768-02-X) Cobb Cnty Geneal.

Cobb of the World: A Leader in Liberalism. John L. Heaton. LC 78-175700. (Select Bibliographies Reprint Ser.). 1977. reprint ed. 24.95 (0-8369-6615-5) Ayer.

Cobb Would Have Caught It: The Golden Age of Baseball in Detroit. Richard Bak. LC 91-4156. (Illus.). 385p. 1991. 24.95 (0-8143-2355-3) Wayne St U Pr.

Cobb Would Have Caught It: The Golden Age of Baseball in Detroit. Richard Bak. LC 91-4156. (Illus.). 385p. 1993. pap. 14.95 (0-8143-2356-1) Wayne St U Pr.

Cobbett & His Times. John W. Osborne & Karl W. Schweizer. 192p. (C). 1990. text ed. 61.00 (0-389-20932-5) B&N Imports.

Cobbett in Ireland. Cobbett. (C). 1984. text ed. 49.95 (0-85315-588-7, Pub. by Lawrence & Wishart UK); pap. 19.95 (0-85315-596-8, Pub. by Lawrence & Wishart UK) Humanities.

Cobbett's Cyclopedic Survey of Chamber Music, 3 vols., Set. 2nd ed. Ed. by Walter W. Cobbett & Colin Mason. (Illus.). 1987. 275.00 (0-19-318306-4) OUP.

Cobbett's Cyclopedic Survey of Chamber Music, 3 vols., Vol. 1: A-H. 2nd ed. Ed. by Walter W. Cobbett & Colin Mason. (Illus.). 592p. 1987. 125.00 (0-19-318303-X) OUP.

Cobbett's Cyclopedic Survey of Chamber Music, 3 vols., Vol. 2: I-Z. 2nd ed. Ed. by Walter W. Cobbett & Colin Mason. (Illus.). 642p. 1987. 125.00 (0-19-318304-8) OUP.

Cobbett's Political Register (b), Vols. 37-89, Vols. 1-89. Incl. Vol. 37. 1835. lib. bdg. 39.00 (0-313-21901-X, PR30, Greenwood Pr); Vols. 38 & 39. 1835. lib. bdg. 50.00 (0-313-21902-8, PR31, Greenwood Pr); Vol. 40. 1835. lib. bdg. 39.00 (0-313-21903-6, PR32, Greenwood Pr); Vols. 41 & 42. 1835. lib. bdg. 44.00 (0-313-21904-4, PR33, Greenwood Pr); Vols. 43 & 44. 1835. lib. bdg. 40.00 (0-313-21905-2, PR34, Greenwood Pr); Vols. 45 & 46. 1835. lib. bdg. 40.00 (0-313-21906-0, PR35, Greenwood Pr); Vols. 47 & 48. 1835. lib. bdg. 40.00 (0-313-21907-9, PR36, Greenwood Pr); Vols. 49 & 50. 1835. lib. bdg. 40.00 (0-313-21908-7, PR37, Greenwood Pr); Vols. 51 & 52. 1835. lib. bdg. 40.00 (0-313-21909-5, PR38, Greenwood Pr); Vols. 53 & 54. 1835. lib. bdg. 40.00 (0-313-21910-9, PR39, Greenwood Pr); Vols. 55 & 56. 1835. lib. bdg. 40.00 (0-313-21911-7, PR40, Greenwood Pr); Vols. 57 & 58. 1835. lib. bdg. 40.00 (0-313-21912-5, PR41, Greenwood Pr); Vols. 59 & 60. 1835. lib. bdg. 40.00 (0-313-21913-3, PR42, Greenwood Pr); Vols. 61 & 62. 1835. lib. bdg. 44.00 (0-313-21914-1, PR43, Greenwood Pr); Vols. 63 & 64. 1835. lib. bdg. 50.00 (0-313-21915-X, PR44 , Greenwood Pr); Vols. 65 & 66. 1835. lib. bdg. 45.00 (0-313-21916-8, PR45, Greenwood Pr); Vols. 67 & 68. 1835. lib. bdg. 45.00 (0-313-21917-6, PR46, Greenwood Pr); Vols. 69 & 70. 1835. lib. bdg. 45.00 (0-313-21918-4, PR47, Greenwood Pr); Vols. 71 & 72. 1835. lib. bdg. 45.00 (0-313-21919-2, PR48, Greenwood Pr); Vols. 73 & 74. 1835. lib. bdg. 45.00 (0-313-21920-6, PR49, Greenwood Pr); Vols. 75 & 76. 1835. lib. bdg. 45.00 (0-313-21921-4, PR50, Greenwood Pr); Vols. 77 & 78. 1835. lib. bdg. 45.00 (0-313-21922-2, PR51, Greenwood Pr); Vols. 79 & 80. 1835. lib. bdg. 45.00 (0-313-21923-0, PR52, Greenwood Pr); Vols. 81 & 82. 1835. lib. bdg. 45.00 (0-313-21924-9, PR53, Greenwood Pr); Vols. 83 & 84. 1835. lib. bdg. 45.00 (0-313-21925-7, PR54, Greenwood Pr); Vols. 85 & 86. 1835. lib. bdg. 45.00 (0-313-21926-5, PR55, Greenwood Pr); Vols. 87 & 88. 1835. lib. bdg. 50.00 (0-313-21927-3, PR56, Greenwood Pr); Vol. 89. 1835. lib. bdg. 33.00 (0-313-21928-1, PR57, Greenwood Pr); 1835. reprint ed. Set. lib. bdg. 2,145.00 (0-317-64769-5, PR00, Greenwood Pr) Greenwood.

Cobbett's Tour in Scotland. Ed. by D. Green. 224p. 1984. text ed. 28.00 (0-08-030376-5, Pergamon Pr); pap. text ed. 17.90 (0-08-030384-6, Pergamon Pr) Elsevier.

Cobbler Crusade. Irene Ritter. LC 92-12019. (Illus.). 144p. (Orig.). 1992. pap. 9.95 (1-55561-044-7) Fisher Bks.

***Cobblers, Crisps, & Deep Dish Pies.** Lisa Yockelson. LC 94-23771. 1995. 15.00 (0-06-016749-1) HarpC.

Cobblers, Crumbles, & Crisps: And Other Old-Fashioned Fruit Desserts. Linda Zimmerman & Peggy Mellody. (Illus.). 128p. 1991. 11.00 (0-517-57489-6, C P Pubs) Crown Pub Group.

Cobbler's Guest. Lorraine Pooley & Fred Pooley. 1975. 4.25 (0-8341-9147-4, MC-246) Lillenas.

Cobblestone: A Detective Novel. Peter Lengyel. Tr. by John Batki. 528p. (Orig.). (C). 1993. pap. 14.95 (0-930523-86-5) Readers Intl.

Cobblestone Landmarks of New York State. Olaf W. Shelgren, Jr. et al. (Illus.). 176p. 1978. pap. 16.95 (0-8156-0149-2) Syracuse U Pr.

Cobblestone Leadership: Majority Rule, Minority Power. James M. Burns & L. Marvin Overby. LC 90-50229. (Julian J. Rothbaum Distinguished Lecture Ser.: Vol. 3). 160p. (C). 1990. 19.95 (0-8061-2314-1) U of Okla Pr.

Cobblestones. Wanda K. Patterson. (Illus.). 66p. 1983. 10.95 (0-9618774-0-5) W K Patterson.

Cobb's Baptist Church Manual. J. E. Cobb. 193p. 1979. reprint ed. pap. 3.00 (0-89114-056-5) Baptist Pub Hse.

Cobb's Cave. Heidi Henken. Ed. by Betty L. Kratoville. (Meridian Bks.). (Illus.). 64p. (J). (gr. 3-9). 1989. lib. bdg. 4.95 (0-87879-655-X) High Noon Bks.

***Cobbstone Project.** Donald R. Fessler. LC 94-43084. (Illus.). 400p. (Orig.). 1995. pap. 11.95 (0-936015-54-3) Pocahontas Pr.

Cobden's Cottage. large type ed. Jean Innes. 1990. pap. 12.95 (0-7089-6922-4, Trailtree Bookshop) Ulverscroft.

Cobh's Contribution to the Fight for Irish Freedom: 1913-1990. Kieran McCarthy & Maj-Britt Christensen. 223p. (Orig.). 1992. pap. 13.95 (0-685-67431-2, Pub. by Oileann Mor IR) Irish Bks Media.

Coblentz Society Desk Book of Infrared Spectra. 2nd ed. 1986. 130.00 (0-685-41067-6, CSC-1) Coblentz Soc.

Cobler's Prophecy. Robert Wilson. LC 74-133766. (Tudor Facsimile Texts. Old English Plays Ser.: No. 71). reprint ed. 49.50 (0-404-53371-X) AMS Pr.

COBOL. Jean Longhurst & Audrey Longhurst. (Illus.). 656p. (C). 1989. pap. text ed. 34.00 (0-13-139387-1) P-H.

COBOL: A Guide to Structured, Portable, Maintainable, & Efficient Prog Design. Eric G. Vesely. 320p. 1989. boxed 43.00 (0-13-854050-0) P-H.

COBOL: A Self-Instructional Manual. 2nd ed. James A. Saxon. 1971. pap. text ed. write for info. (0-13-139469-X) P-H.

COBOL: A Software Engineering Approach. James C. Janossy. 496p. (C). 1989. pap. text ed. 39.00 (0-03-014258-X) Dryden Pr.

COBOL: An Introduction to Structured Logic & Modular Program Design. William S. Davis & Richard H. Fisher. 1979. teacher ed write for info. (0-201-01432-7); pap. text ed. 31.25 (0-201-01431-9) Addison-Wesley.

COBOL: From Micro to Mainframe. 2nd ed. Robert T. Grauer. 1994. Incl. diskette. disk, pap. 62.00 (0-13-310764-7) P-H.

COBOL: From Micro to Mainframe, Vol. II: The IBM Environment. Robert T. Grauer. 208p. 1990. pap. text ed. 42.67 (0-13-016114-4) P-H.

COBOL: Structured Programming Techniques for Solving Problems. George Fowler. 720p. (C). 1989. pap. text ed. write for info. (0-318-65185-8, BF3291) S-W Pub.

COBOL: Structured Programming Techniques for Solving Problems. George C. Fowler. 728p. 1990. 35.00 (0-87835-329-1) Boyd & Fraser.

COBOL Application Debugging under MVS: COBOL & COBOL II. Alan Friend. 1992. text ed. 49.00 (0-07-022453-6) McGraw.

COBOL Basics. 2nd ed. Gerry Manning. 400p. 1984. pap. text ed. write for info. (0-394-33572-4) Random.

COBOL Book of Practice & Reference. Robert T. Grauer. (Software Ser.). (Illus.). 352p. (C). 1981. pap. text ed. 37.00 (0-13-139717-6) P-H.

COBOL by Design. Gary Klein. LC 93-18268. 1993. 39.95 (0-938661-60-4) Franklin Beedle.

COBOL 85 for Programmers. I. Inglis. 250p. 1989. pap. text ed. 58.50 (0-471-92156-4) Wiley.

COBOL 85 for Programmers. Donald F. Nelson. 250p. 1988. pap. 26.75 (0-444-01232-X) Elsevier.

COBOL for Students. 3rd ed. A. Parkin et al. 288p. 1990. pap. text ed. 16.95 (0-340-51798-0, A4401, Pub. by E Arnold UK) Routledge Chapman & Hall.

COBOL for the Eighties. 2nd ed. J. Wayne Spence. (Illus.). 883p. (Orig.). (C). 1985. pap. text ed. 37.00 (0-314-85303-0) West Pub.

COBOL for the IBM PC. Pacifico A. Lim. 292p. 1986. text ed. 49.95 (0-442-25970-0) Van Nos Reinhold.

COBOL for the IBM Personal Computer. Kip R. Irvine. (Illus.). 592p. (C). 1988. pap. text ed. 49.00 (0-13-139734-6) P-H.

COBOL for Today. 3rd ed. J. Wayne Spence & John C. Windsor. Ed. by Clyde Perlee. 732p. (C). 1989. pap. text ed. 53.75 (0-314-68967-2) West Pub.

COBOL from BASIC: A Short Self-Instructional Course. M. Oatey & C. Payne. 144p. (Orig.). (C). 1986. pap. text ed. 25.00 (0-273-02495-7) Trans-Atl Phila.

COBOL from Pascal. A. J. Tyrrell. Ed. by F. H. Sumner. (Computer Science Ser.). 224p. 1989. text ed. 56.00 (0-333-48302-2, Pub. by Macmill Press UK); pap. text ed. 30.00 (0-333-48303-0, Pub. by Macmillan UK) Scholium Intl.

COBOL Handbook: A Modular Approach. Linda Belcher. 650p. (C). 1989. pap. 50.95 (0-534-10038-4) PWS Pubs.

COBOL II: Programming Techniques, Efficiency Considerations, Debugging Techniques. Harvey Bookman. 1990. text ed. 45.00 (0-07-006533-0) McGraw.

COBOL II Quick Reference Guide. David S. Kirk. 1992. 9.95 (0-89435-345-4); pap. 9.95 (0-471-57628-X) Wiley.

An Asterisk (*) at the beginning of an entry indicates that the title is appearing in BIP for the first time.

Cochran's German Review Grammar. 4th ed. Jonathan B. Conant. 352p. (C). 1990. text ed. write for info. (*0-13-139965-9*) P-H.

Cociete Integree: De la Circulation Des Biens, Des Idees et Des Personnes. Simon Laflamme. LC 91-45433. (Worcester Polytechnic Institute Studies in Science, Technology, & Culture: Vol. 12). 328p. (FRE.). 1993. 54.95 (*0-8204-1869-2*) P Lang Pubs.

Cocina Criolla (Spanish Version of Puerto Rican Cookery) Carmen A. Valldejuli. LC 83-17178. (Illus.). 469p. 1983. 18.95 (*0-88289-429-3*) Pelican.

Cocina de la Frontera: Mexican-American Cooking from the Southwest. James W. Peyton. (Illus.). 352p. 1994. pap. 22.50 (*1-878610-34-1*) Red Crane Bks.

Cocina Dominicana: Edicion Para Coleccionistas. Maria Ramirez de Carias. (Illus.). 200p. (SPA.). 1993. write for info. (*0-318-69984-2*) Pilon FL.

Cocina Latino Americana. Ed. by Maria E. Alvarez del Real. (Illus.). 304p. (Orig.). (SPA.). (YA). 1988. pap. 4.50 (*0-944499-44-9*) Editorial Amer.

Cocina Prehispanica. Ana M. De Benitez. (Illus.). (ENG & SPA.). 1977. pap. 36.25 (*968-414-015-0*) Adlers Foreign Bks.

***Cocinando des de la Fortaleza.** Kate Donnelly de Romero. (Illus.). 232p. (SPA.). Date not set. reprint ed. ring bd. 24.95 (*0-89825-008-0*) Pub Resces PR.

***Cocinando Desde la Fortaleza.** Kate Donnelly de Romero. (SPA.). 1994. spiral bd., pap. 19.95 (*0-89882-500-8*) Pub Resces PR.

Cocine a Gusto. Berta Cabanillas et al. (Illus.). 326p. 1991. 9.50 (*0-8477-2779-3*) U of PR Pr.

***Cocine Conmigo.** rev. ed. Dora R. De Romano. (Illus.). 678p. (SPA.). 1970. write for info. (*0-9633449-0-0*) D R de Romano.

Cock-a-Doodle Dandy. Sean O'Casey. LC 90-41574. (Irish Dramatic Texts Ser.). 119p. 1991. 24.95 (*0-8132-0741-X*) Cath U Pr.

Cock-a-Doodle-Doo! Emma Harding. LC 93-11030. (J). 1994. 15.95 (*0-8050-3059-X*) H Holt & Co.

Cock-A-Doodle-Doo. Juliet Kepes. LC 76-44433. (J). (ps-2). 1978. 6.95 (*0-394-83867-X*) Pantheon.

***Cock-a-Doodle-Doo!** Illus. by Maureen Roffey. (Duplo Playbks.). 14p. (J). (ps up). 1995. bds. 7.50 (*0-316-72384-3*) Little.

***Cock-a-Doodle-Doo.** Phillip Weiss. LC 94-30187. 1995. 21.00 (*0-374-12515-5*) FS&G.

Cock-a-Doodle Doo! What Does It Sound Like to You? Marc Robinson. LC 92-30961. (Illus.). 32p. (J). 1993. 12.95 (*1-55670-267-1*) Stewart Tabori & Chang.

Cock-a-Doodle Dudley. Bill Peet. (Illus.). 48p. (J). (gr. k-3). 1990. 14.95 (*0-395-55331-8*) HM.

Cock-a-Doodle Dudley. Bill Peet. (Illus.). 48p. (J). (gr. k-3). 1993. pap. 4.95 (*0-395-65745-8*) HM.

Cock & Anchor: Being a Chronicle of Old Dublin City, 3 vols., 1. Joseph S. Le Fanu. Ed. by Devendra P. Varma. LC 76-4606. (Collected Works). 1977. reprint ed. 30.95 (*0-405-09203-2*) Ayer.

Cock & Anchor: Being a Chronicle of Old Dublin City, 3 vols., 2. Joseph S. Le Fanu. Ed. by Devendra P. Varma. LC 76-4606. (Collected Works). 1977. reprint ed. 30.95 (*0-405-09204-0*) Ayer.

Cock & Anchor: Being a Chronicle of Old Dublin City, 3 vols., 3. Joseph S. Le Fanu. Ed. by Devendra P. Varma. LC 76-4606. (Collected Works). 1977. reprint ed. 30.95 (*0-405-09205-9*) Ayer.

Cock & Anchor: Being a Chronicle of Old Dublin City, 3 vols., Set. Joseph S. Le Fanu. Ed. by Devendra P. Varma. LC 76-4606. (Collected Works). 1977. reprint ed. 90.95 (*0-405-09202-4*) Ayer.

Cock & Bull. Will Self. 1994. pap. 11.00 (*0-679-75092-4*, Vin) Random.

Cock Lane & Common-Sense. Andrew Lang. LC 74-110572. reprint ed. 39.50 (*0-404-03846-8*) AMS Pr.

Cock, the Mouse, & the Little Red Hen. Illus. by Graham Percy. LC 91-71857. 32p. (J). (ps up). 1992. 14.95 (*1-56402-008-8*) Candlewick Pr.

Cock, the Mouse, & the Little Red Hen. Graham Percy. LC 91-71857. 32p. (J). (ps up). 1994. pap. 5.99 (*1-56402-268-4*) Candlewick Pr.

Cockatiel Color Genetics: Advanced Topics. Robin L. Duis. (Illus.). 38p. (C). 1989. pap. text ed. write for info. (*0-318-66536-0*, 1020) Starbird Pubns.

Cockatiel Color Genetics: The Basics. David M. Slater. 14p. (C). 1989. pap. text ed. write for info. (*0-318-66535-2*, 1010) Starbird Pubns.

Cockatiel Handbook. Gerald R. Allen. 16.95 (*0-87666-956-9*, PS-741) TFH Pubns.

Cockatiels. W. A. Starika. (Illus.). 80p. 1989. 5.95 (*0-86622-200-6*, PB-104) TFH Pubns.

Cockatiels. Laura M. Tartak. 1989. 9.95 (*0-86622-847-0*, KW-057) TFH Pubns.

Cockatiels: A Complete Pet Owner's Manual. Annette Wolter. 64p. 1991. pap. 5.95 (*0-8120-4610-2*) Barron.

Cockatiels: Look & Learn. L. Lindner. (Illus.). 64p. 1993. 7.95 (*0-7938-0069-2*, KD009) TFH Pubns.

Cockatiels! Pets - Breeding - Showing. Nancy A. Reed. Ed. by Rainer R. Erhart. (Illus.). 256p. 1990. lib. bdg. 19.95 (*0-86622-640-0*, TS-140) TFH Pubns.

Cockatiels As a Hobby. Jack C. Harris. (TT Ser.). (Illus.). 98p. 1992. pap. 7.95 (*0-86622-423-8*) TFH Pubns.

Cockatiels As a New Pet. John Coborn. (Illus.). 64p. (Orig.). 1990. pap. 5.95 (*0-86622-612-5*, TU-005) TFH Pubns.

Cockatiels for Those Who Care. Floyd Young. (Illus.). 32p. 1994. 3.95 (*0-7938-1387-5*, B109) TFH Pubns.

Cockatoo Crime. large type ed. Bill Knox. 1989. 17.95 (*0-7089-2091-8*) Ulverscroft.

Cockatoos. Werner Lantermann & Susanne Lantermann. (Illus.). 56p. 1989. pap. 5.95 (*0-8120-4159-3*) Barron.

Cockatoos: Shorter Novels & Stories. Patrick White. 288p. 1993. 10.95 (*0-14-018582-8*, Penguin Classics) Viking Penguin.

***Cockatoos As a Hobby.** Coborn. 1995. pap. text ed. (*0-7938-0091-9*) TFH Pubns.

Cockatoos in Aviculture. Rosemary Low. (Illus.). 160p. 1994. 24.95 (*0-7137-2322-X*, Pub. by Blandford Pr UK) Sterling.

Cockburn in Spain: Despatches from the Spanish Civil War. Ed. by James Pettifer. 208p. (C). 1986. pap. 19.95 (*0-85315-668-9*, Pub. by Lawrence & Wishart UK) Humanities.

Cockburn Sums Up. Claude Cockburn. 1981. 17.95 (*0-7043-2266-8*, Pub. by Quartet UK) Charles River Bks.

Cockcrow at Night, the Heroic Journey, & 18 Other Stories. Lawrence Lee. (Illus.). 250p. (Orig.). 1973. 6.00 (*0-910286-35-3*) Boxwood.

Cocker Connection: Yorkshire, Van Diemen's Land Melbourne, British Columbia, Mexico, Tonga & Michigan. Ed. by Mark Dalby. 160p. (C). 1989. 34.00 (*0-7212-0784-7*, Pub. by Regency Press) St Mut.

Cocker Spaniel. George Caddy. 1994. 49.95 (*0-86622-470-X*) TFH Pubns.

***Cocker Spaniel.** Judy Iby. (Owner's Guide to a Happy, Healthy Pet Ser.). 160p. Date not set. 12.95 (*0-87605-381-9*) Howell Bk.

Cocker Spaniel. H. S. Lloyd. 1991. lib. bdg. 75.00 (*0-8490-5208-4*) Gordon Pr.

Cocker Spaniel. William Sanford & Carl Green. LC 90-34059. (Top Dog Ser.). (Illus.). 48p. (J). (gr. 4-5). 1990. text ed. 12.95 (*0-89686-531-2*, Crstwood Hse) Silver Burdett Pr.

Cocker Spaniel (English) George Caddy. (Illus.). 352p. 1993. 49.94 (*0-86620-470-9*, TS196) TFH Pubns.

Cocker Spaniel Handbook. Ernest H. Hart. text ed. 14.95 (*0-86622-099-2*, H-923) TFH Pubns.

Cocker Spaniel Owners' Medical Manual. Robert M. Brown. LC 87-71369. 305p. (Orig.). 1988. pap. 18.00 (*0-938681-01-X*) Breed Manual Pubns.

Cocker Spaniels. Jennifer L. Carey. (Owner's Companion Ser.). (Illus.). 272p. 1993. 39.95 (*1-85223-488-1*, Pub. by Crowood Pr UK) Trafalgar.

***Cocker Spaniels.** Stuart A. Kallen. LC 95-2238. (Dogs Ser.). 1995. lib. bdg. 9.95 (*1-56239-452-5*) Abdo & Dghtrs.

Cocker Spaniels. Bart King. 1989. 11.95 (*0-86622-167-0*, KW043) TFH Pubns.

Cocker Spaniels: A Complete Pet Owner's Manual. Jaime Sucher. (Complete Pet Owner's Manuals Ser.). 80p. 1993. pap. 5.95 (*0-8120-1478-2*) Barron.

Cockeyed Boom Shack Cat & Other Stories. Florence Morrison. (Illus.). 48p. 1974. 5.00 (*0-87881-009-9*) Mojave Bks.

Cockfight: A Casebook. Ed. by Alan Dundes. LC 93-30545. 1994. 58.00 (*0-299-14050-4*); pap. 19.95 (*0-299-14054-7*) U of Wis Pr.

Cockfighter. Charles Willeford. LC 90-50596. 240p. 1991. 9.00 (*0-679-73471-6*, Vin) Random.

Cockfighter. Charles Willeford. LC 86-71888. 224p. reprint ed. pap. 3.95 (*0-88739-026-9*, Blk Lizard) Creat Arts Bk.

Cockies Is Convenient. Bette Meyrick. 160p. (C). 1981. pap. 20.00x (*0-85088-615-5*, Pub. by Gomer Pr UK) St Mut.

Cockleshell Girl. large type ed. Emma Stirling. (General Ser.). 672p. 1993. 21.95 (*0-7089-2887-0*) Ulverscroft.

Cockney & the Crocodile. large type ed. Caroline Gye. (Non-Fiction Ser.). 544p. 1992. 21.95 (*0-7089-2640-1*) Ulverscroft.

Cockney, Past & Present. W. Matthews. 1972. 150.00 (*0-87968-881-5*) Gordon Pr.

***Cockney Rabbit: A Dick'n'Arry of Rhyming Slang.** Ray Puxley. 230p. 1995. pap. 10.95 (*0-86051-827-2*, Robson-Parkwest) Parkwest Pubns.

Cockney Soldier Duty Before Pleasure: An Autobiography 1918-46. William Harding. (C). 1989. 59.00 (*0-86303-452-7*, Pub. by Merlin Bks UK) St Mut.

Cockpit. Jerzy Kosinski. 272p. 1989. pap. 8.95 (*1-55970-022-X*, 1-55970-022-X) Arcade Pub Inc.

Cockpit Classroom. Harold J. Holmes. 116p. (Orig.). (C). 1987. pap. text ed. 15.95 (*0-940766-09-4*) Haldon Bks.

Cockpit Displays & Visual Simulation: Proceedings of a Conference Held April 1990, Orlando, Vol. 1290. Ed. by Harry M. Assenheim & Herbert H. Bell. 200p. 1990. 42.00 (*0-8194-0340-7*) SPIE.

Cockpit Monitoring & Alerting Systems. Paul M. Satchell. 194p. 1993. 49.95 (*1-85742-109-4*, Pub. by Ashgate UK) Ashgate Pub Co.

Cockpit Quiz Book: Two Hundred Sixty Puzzlers to Amuse, Annoy & Enlighten You & Your Shipmates. C. Dale Nouse. 144p. 1989. pap. text ed. 8.95 (*0-915160-97-8*) Seven Seas.

Cockpit Resource Management. Ed. by Earl L. Wiener et al. (Illus.). 519p. 1993. text ed. 75.00 (*0-12-750025-1*) Acad Pr.

***Cockpit Resource Management: The Private Pilot's Guide.** Thomas P. Turner. 1995. pap. text ed. 19.95 (*0-07-065604-5*) TAB Bks.

Cockroach Basketball League. Charles Rosen. LC 92-53074. 288p. 1992. 21.00 (*1-55611-329-3*) D I Fine.

Cockroach Crawl. Al Blair. 4p. 1990. pap. 3.95 (*0-930366-25-5*) Northcountry Pub.

Cockroach Dance. Meja Mwangi. (C). 1988. pap. text ed. 9.95 (*0-582-00392-X*, 76410) Longman.

Cockroach Dance. Meja Mwangi. 1990. pap. 9.95 (*0-582-64276-0*) Longman.

Cockroach Hall of Fame: And One Hundred One Other Off-the-Wall Museums. Sandra Gurvis. LC 93-42126. 1994. 14.95 (*0-8065-1501-5*, Citadel Pr) Carol Pub Group.

Cockroaches. Mona Kerby. LC 88-37857. (First Bks.). (Illus.). 64p. (J). (gr. 3 up). 1989. lib. bdg. 13.93 (*0-531-10689-6*) Watts.

Cockroaches As Models for Neurobiology, 2 vols., I. Ed. by Huber. 1990. 190.00 (*0-8493-4838-2*, QP357) CRC Pr.

Cockroaches As Models for Neurobiology, 2 vols., II. Ed. by Huber. 1990. 190.00 (*0-8493-4839-0*, QP357) CRC Pr.

Cockroaches As Models for Neurobiology, 2 vols., Set. Ed. by Huber. 1990. 159.95 (*0-685-74312-8*) CRC Pr.

Cockroaches of Stay More. Donald Harington. 337p. 1989. 19.95 (*0-15-118270-1*) HarBrace.

Cocks & Hens. Ian Taylor. 111p. (Orig.). 1986. pap. 4.95 (*0-685-22963-7*) Broadway Play.

Cocktail Bar: A Collection of Four Hundred Recipes. Charles. Ed. by Carlos. (Illus.). 120p. (Orig.). 1977. pap. 8.95 (*0-572-00995-X*, Pub. by W Foulsham UK) Trans-Atl Phila.

Cocktail Hour. A. R. Gurney. 1989. pap. 4.75 (*0-8222-0225-5*) Dramatists Play.

Cocktail Hour in Jackson Hole. Donald Hough. LC 93-77110. (Illus.). 254p. 1993. reprint ed. pap. 11.95 (*1-881019-02-0*) High Plns WY.

Cocktail Party. T. S. Eliot. LC 50-14646. 192p. 1964. pap. 7.00 (*0-15-618289-0*, Harvest Bks) HarBrace.

***Cocktail Party: A Comedy.** T. S. Eliot. 167p. 1950. 17.95 (*0-910278-97-0*) Boulevard.

Cocktail Time. P. G. Wodehouse. 224p. 1991. mass mkt. 8.95 (*0-14-008505-X*, Penguin Bks) Viking Penguin.

Cocktail Waitress: Woman's Work in a Man's World. James P. Spradley & Brenda J. Mann. LC 74-28048. 154p. (C). 1975. pap. text ed. write for info. (*0-07-554764-3*) McGraw.

Cocktailing.... The American Bartenders' Association Complete Guide of Professional Cocktailing. American Bartenders' Association Staff. Ed. by James P. Starcevic. 11p. (Orig.). 1986. pap. text ed. 2.95 (*0-916689-85-9*) Am Bartenders.

Cocktails & Hors D'Oeuvres. Ina C. Boyd. Ed. by Jackie Walsh. LC 77-93841. (Illus.). 1978. pap. 5.95 (*0-911954-45-7*) Bristol Pub Ent CA.

Cocktails with Mimi. Mary Chase. 1974. pap. 4.75 (*0-8222-0226-3*) Dramatists Play.

Cocle: An Archaeological Study of Central Panama, 2 vols., 1. K. S. Lothrop et al. (HU PMM Ser.). 1972. reprint ed. 90.00 (*0-527-01169-X*) Periodicals Srv.

Cocle: An Archaeological Study of Central Panama, 2 vols., 2. K. S. Lothrop et al. (HU PMM Ser.). 1972. reprint ed. 110.00 (*0-527-01170-3*) Periodicals Srv.

Coco: A Story for Dog Lovers. Theron A. Newell. (Illus.). 16p. (Orig.). 1986. pap. 2.00 (*0-9610080-1-6*) Dentan Pr.

Coco Can't Wait. Taro Gomi. (Illus.). (J). (ps-1). 1985. pap. 3.95 (*0-14-050522-9*, Puffin) Puffin Bks.

Coco Chanel. Alice Mackrell. LC 91-40599. (Fashion Designers Ser.). (Illus.). 96p. (Orig.). 1993. pap. 25.95 (*0-8419-1301-3*) Holmes & Meier.

Coco Grimes. Mary Stolz. LC 93-34153. 128p. (J). (gr. 3-6). 1994. 14.00 (*0-06-024232-9*) HarpC Child Bks.

Coco Grimes. Mary Stolz. LC 93-34153. 128p. (J). (gr. 3-6). 1994. lib. bdg. 13.89 (*0-06-024233-7*) HarpC Child Bks.

Coco Loco: A Treasury of Humor, Travel & Angling Adventures. Van S. Fulton. LC 94-10142. (Illus.). 224p. (Orig.). 1994. pap. 12.95 (*1-877633-18-6*) Luthers.

Coco Perdu. Louis Guilloux. (FRE.). 1990. pap. 10.95 (*0-7859-2586-4*, 2070382362) Fr & Eur.

Coco, the Novel. Patricia B. Soliman. 1991. mass mkt. 5.99 (*0-06-100268-2*, Harp PBks) HarpC.

Cocoa. 4th ed. G. A. Wood & R. A. Lass. 640p. 1986. text ed. 175.00 (*0-470-20618-7*) Halsted Pr.

***Cocoa: New York Cafes & Coffee Bars Appointment Book 1995.** Ed. by Zachary Soreff. (Illus.). 112p. (Orig.). 1994. pap. write for info. (*0-9640926-3-8*) Seen Pubng.

Cocoa & Chaos in Ghana. Gwendolyn Mikell. 288p. 1992. pap. 18.95 (*0-88258-153-8*) Howard U Pr.

Cocoa & Chocolate Painting. Marsha Winbeckler. (Illus.). 24p. (Orig.). 1987. pap. 8.95 (*0-930113-08-X*) Winbeckler.

Cocoa & Kinship in Ghana: The Matrilineal Akan of Ghana. Christine Okali. 200p. 1983. pap. 25.00 (*0-7103-0041-7*, Pub. by Kegan Paul Intl UK) Routledge Chapman & Hall.

Cocoa Butter. (Latin American Products Included in the U. S. General System of Preferences Ser.). 31p. 1978. pap. text ed. 3.00 (*0-8270-3415-6*) OAS.

Cocoa Diseases & Politics in Ghana, 1910-1966. Francis Danquah. LC 93-34296. (American University Studies: History: Ser. IX, Vol. 143). 1994. write for info. (*0-8204-2190-1*) P Lang Pubs.

***Cocoa Market.** 100p. (Orig.). 1995. pap. 1,295.00 (*0-7605-2154-9*) Rector Pr.

Cocoa Production & Marketing in India. V. N. Asopa & S. Narayanan. 1990. 14.00 (*81-204-0485-8*, Pub. by Oxford IBH II) S Asia.

Cocoa Puppy. Timothy Burke. LC 89-50890. (Illus.). 32p. (Orig.). (J). (ps-3). 1989. 5.00 (*0-9623227-0-9*) Thunder & Ink.

Cocodrilos y Caimanes. Norman S. Barrett. LC 90-71415. (Picture Library). (Illus.). 32p. (SPA.). (J). (gr. k-4). 1991. lib. bdg. 12.60 (*0-531-07919-8*) Watts.

Cocolat: Extraordinary Chocolate Desserts. Alice Medrich. (Illus.). 1990. 35.00 (*0-446-51419-5*) Warner Bks.

Coconut Crab: Aspects of Birgus Latro Biology & Ecology in Vanuatu. I. W. Brown & D. R. Fielder. 136p. (C). 1992. text ed. 160.00 (*1-86320-054-1*, Pub. by ACIAR) St Mut.

Coconut Germplasm in the South Pacific Islands. M. A. Foale. (C). 1986. text ed. 40.00 (*0-949511-35-8*, Pub. by ACIAR) St Mut.

Coconut Killings. Patricia Moyes. LC 76-29910. 224p. 1985. pap. 5.95 (*0-8050-0754-7*, Owl) H Holt & Co.

Coconut Kind of Day. Lynn Joseph. 32p. (J). 1990. 13.95 (*0-688-09119-9*); lib. bdg. 13.88 (*0-688-09120-2*) Lothrop.

***Coconut Mon.** Linda B. Milstein. LC 94-27171. (J). (gr. 1-8). 1995. write for info. (*0-688-12862-9*); write for info. (*0-688-12863-7*) Morrow.

Coconut Production: Present Status & Priorities for Research. large type ed. Ed. by Alan H. Green. (Technical Paper Ser.: No. 136). 162p. 1991. 10.95 (*0-8213-1809-8*, 11809) World Bank.

Coconut Rhinoceros Beetle with Particular Reference to the Palau Islands. J. L. Gressitt. (BMB Ser.). 1972. reprint ed. 25.00 (*0-527-02320-5*) Periodicals Srv.

Coconut Uses: Uses for the Coconut. rev. ed. Recycling Consortium Staff. 1992. pap. text ed. 14.95 (*0-317-04791-4*, Recycling Consort) Prosperity & Profits.

Coconuts: A Sea Story. David Z. Giffin. Ed. by James B. Van Treese. 166p. 1994. pap. 7.95 (*1-56901-112-5*) NW Pub.

Coconuts for the Saint. Debra Spark. 276p. 1994. 22.95 (*0-571-19846-5*) Faber & Faber.

Cocoon. Lindley Bhanji. Ed. by Chris Winkler. (Illus.). 28p. (Orig.). (YA). (gr. 10 up). 1988. pap. 2.00 (*0-929611-00-4*) Plutonium Pr.

***Cocopa Dictionary.** James M. Crawford. LC 89-5151. (University of California Publications in Entomology: No. 114). 546p. 1989. pap. 155.70 (*0-7837-7477-X*, 2049199) Bks Demand.

Cocopa Ethnography. William H. Kelly. LC 76-18469. (Anthropological Papers: No. 29). 150p. 1977. pap. 16.50 (*0-8165-0367-2*) U of Ariz Pr.

***Cocopa Texts.** James M. Crawford. LC 81-24046. (University of California Publications in Entomology: No. 100). 618p. 1983. pap. 176.20 (*0-7837-7478-8*, 2049200) Bks Demand.

Cocos Berry Party. Bob Reese. (Grand Canyon Ser.). (Illus.). (J). (gr. k-6). 1987. 7.95 (*0-89868-193-6*); pap. 2.95 (*0-89868-194-4*) ARO Pub.

Cocos Island Venture. Marie Briggs. 1950. 4.95 (*0-87505-120-0*) Borden.

Cocrete Mathematics. Ronald L. Graham et al. (Illus.). 640p. (C). 1989. text ed. 51.75 (*0-201-14236-8*) Addison-Wesley.

Cocteau: A Biography. Francis Steegmuller. LC 76-117039. 608p. 1986. pap. 17.95 (*0-87923-606-X*) Godine.

Cocteau et les Mythes. Jean J. Kihm & Michel Decaudin. 196p. (FRE.). 1972. pap. 28.95 (*0-7859-4876-7*) Fr & Eur.

Cod Fisheries: A History of an International Economy. Harold A. Innis. 1978. pap. 16.95 (*0-8020-6344-6*) U of Toronto Pr.

Coda. Thea Astley. 192p. 1994. 24.95 (*0-399-13966-4*, Putnam) Putnam Pub Group.

CODASYL Approach to Data Base Management. T. William Olle. LC 77-12375. 307p. reprint ed. pap. 87.50 (*0-685-44427-9*, 2032663) Bks Demand.

CODASYL COBOL Committee Journal of Development, 1988. rev. ed. CODASYL COBOL Committee Staff. Ed. & Illus. by Donald Nelson. 1200p. 1988. pap. 40.00 (*0-9621665-0-2*) D Nelson.

***CODATA Directory of Data Sources for Science & Technology in Asian-Oceanic Countries.** Ed. by Yaruo Hu & Edgar F. Westrum, Jr. LC 94-72548. (Monograph Ser.: Vol. 2). 176p. (Orig.). 1994. pap. 33.00 (*1-884893-09-0*) CODATA.

Codata Key Values for Thermodynamics. Ed. by John D. Cox et al. 285p. 1989. 81.00 (*0-89116-758-7*) Hemisp Pub.

Codata Thermodynamic Tables: Selections for Some Compounds of Calcium & Related Mixtures: A Prototype Set of Tables. Ed. by D. Garvin et al. 300p. 1987. 100.00 (*0-89116-730-7*) Hemisp Pub.

Code. Pat Califia. (Orig.). 1995. pap. 12.95 (*1-56333-237-X*) Masquerade.

Code. Nick Power. (Illus.). 16p. 1985. 0.75 (*0-938822-44-6*) USTA.

Code: Law in Traditional Vietnam, 3 vols., Set. Tr. by Nguyen Ngoc Huy et al. LC 86-8371. 1735p. 1987. text ed. 175.00 (*0-8214-0630-2*) Ohio U Pr.

Code Administration & Enforcement: Problems & Promises. Ed. by Gerard Hoetmer & Dennis Kouba. 112p. (Orig.). 1987. pap. 24.00 (*0-87326-942-X*) Intl City-Cnty Mgt.

Code & Cypher Puzzles. M. Fowler & R. Parekh. (Super Puzzles Ser.). (Illus.). 48p. (YA). (gr. 6 up). 1995. lib. bdg. 12.96 (*0-88110-526-0*, Usborne); pap. 6.95 (*0-7460-0675-6*, Usborne) EDC.

Code Blue. Charlotte White. 320p. 1992. mass mkt. 4.50 (*1-55817-644-6*, Pinnacle NY) Windsor NY.

Code Blue: Cardiac Arrest & Resuscitation. Mickey S. Eisenberg et al. (Blue Book Ser.). 272p. 1987. pap. text ed. 27.95 (*0-7216-1822-7*) Saunders.

Code Blue: Health Care in Crisis. Edward R. Annis. LC 92-44875. 288p. 1993. 21.95 (*0-89526-515-X*) Regnery Pub.

***Code Blue: Urgent Care for the American Youth Emergency.** Nicky Cruz. 361p. 1995. pap. 10.99 (*0-89283-904-X*, Vine Bks) Servant.

Code Blue: Uniting for Healthier Youth: The Report of the National Commision on the Role of the School & Community in Improving Adolescent Health. 52p. 1990. 13.50 (*0-317-05338-8*) NASBE.

Code Book: Amateur Radio CW Operating. Robert J. Halprin. LC 93-514. 1993. 17.95 (*0-936653-48-5*) Tiare Pubns.

Code Book: Cryptology. M. E. Marotta. 1986. lib. bdg. 79.95 (*0-8490-3567-8*) Gordon Pr.

***Code Book of America.** 2nd ed. Ed. & Intro. by Scott Morrison. (Illus.). (Orig.). 1995. pap. 6.95 (*0-929150-50-3*) Castalia CA.

1340 An Asterisk (*) at the beginning of an entry indicates that the title is appearing in BIP for the first time.

An Asterisk (*) at the beginning of an entry indicates that the title is appearing in BIP for the first time.

1341

Code of Practice for Occupational Fire Brigades. Fire Protection Association Staff. (C). 1990. 95.00 (*0-902167-12-X*, Pub. by Fire Protect Assn UK) St Mut.

***Code of Practice for the Design & Operation of On-Board Truck Computer Systems for Road Tankers.** Institute of Petroleum Staff. LC 94-46447. 1995. pap. text ed. 125.00 (*0-471-95709-7*) Wiley.

Code of Practice for the Identifications & Checking of Materials of Construction in Pressurized Systems in Process Plants. EEMUA Staff. 1986. 125.00 (*0-85931-123-6*, Pub. by EEMUA UK) St Mut.

Code of Practice for the Safe Construction & Installation of Electric Passenger Goods & Service Lifts. International Committee for Lift Regulations. (ILO Code of Practice Ser.). 108p. 1972. 6.40 (*92-2-100159-8*) Intl Labour Office.

Code of Professional Ethics of the American Institute for Property & Liability Underwriters. 3rd ed. LC 90-83980. 88p. (C). 1993. pap. text ed. 4.00 (*0-89463-057-1*) Am Inst FCPCU.

Code of Professional Reponsibility & Opinions of the D.C. Bar's Legal Ethics Committee. Through 1991. 43.75 (*0-317-62706-6*) DC Bar.

Code of Rhode Island Rules, 22 vols., Set. rev. ed. Weil Publishing Co., Inc. Staff. 30170p. (C). 1992. 2,700.00 (*0-916812-48-0*) Weil Pub.

Code of Rhode Island Rules, Vol. 1. rev. ed. Weil Publishing Co., Inc. Staff. 1500p. (C). 1992. 189.00 (*0-916812-28-6*) Weil Pub.

Code of Rhode Island Rules, Vol. 2. rev. ed. Weil Publishing Co., Inc. Staff. 1650p. (C). 1992. 189.00 (*0-916812-29-4*) Weil Pub.

Code of Rhode Island Rules, Vol. 3. rev. ed. Weil Publishing Co., Inc. Staff. 1500p. (C). 1992. 189.00 (*0-916812-30-8*) Weil Pub.

Code of Rhode Island Rules, Vol. 4. rev. ed. Weil Publishing Co., Inc. Staff. 1400p. (C). 1992. 189.00 (*0-916812-31-6*) Weil Pub.

C

Code of Rhode Island Rules, Vol. 5. rev. ed. Weil Publishing Co., Inc. Staff. 1400p. (C). 1992. 189.00 (*0-916812-32-4*) Weil Pub.

Code of Rhode Island Rules, Vol. 6. rev. ed. Weil Publishing Co., Inc. Staff. 1250p. (C). 1992. 189.00 (*0-916812-33-2*) Weil Pub.

Code of Rhode Island Rules, Vol. 7. rev. ed. Weil Publishing Co., Inc. Staff. 1250p. (C). 1992. 189.00 (*0-916812-34-0*) Weil Pub.

Code of Rhode Island Rules, Vol. 8. rev. ed. Weil Publishing Co., Inc. Staff. 1400p. (C). 1992. 189.00 (*0-916812-35-9*) Weil Pub.

Code of Rhode Island Rules, Vol. 9. rev. ed. Weil Publishing Co., Inc. Staff. 1150p. (C). 1992. 189.00 (*0-916812-36-7*) Weil Pub.

Code of Rhode Island Rules, Vol. 10. rev. ed. Weil Publishing Co., Inc. Staff. 1400p. (C). 1992. 189.00 (*0-916812-37-5*) Weil Pub.

Code of Rhode Island Rules, Vol. 11. rev. ed. Weil Publishing Co., Inc. Staff. 1400p. (C). 1992. 189.00 (*0-916812-38-3*) Weil Pub.

Code of Rhode Island Rules, Vol. 12. rev. ed. Weil Publishing Co., Inc. Staff. 1500p. (C). 1992. 189.00 (*0-916812-39-1*) Weil Pub.

Code of Rhode Island Rules, Vol. 13. rev. ed. Weil Publishing Co., Inc. Staff. 1250p. (C). 1992. 189.00 (*0-916812-40-5*) Weil Pub.

Code of Rhode Island Rules, Vol. 14. rev. ed. Weil Publishing Co., Inc. Staff. 1400p. (C). 1992. 189.00 (*0-916812-41-3*) Weil Pub.

Code of Rhode Island Rules, Vol. 15. rev. ed. Weil Publishing Co., Inc. Staff. 1200p. (C). 1992. 189.00 (*0-916812-42-1*) Weil Pub.

Code of Rhode Island Rules, Vol. 16. rev. ed. Weil Publishing Co., Inc. Staff. 1400p. (C). 1992. 189.00 (*0-916812-43-X*) Weil Pub.

Code of Rhode Island Rules, Vol. 17. rev. ed. Weil Publishing Co., Inc. Staff. 1400p. (C). 1992. 189.00 (*0-916812-44-8*) Weil Pub.

Code of Rhode Island Rules, Vol. 18. rev. ed. Weil Publishing Co., Inc. Staff. 1150p. (C). 1992. 189.00 (*0-916812-45-6*) Weil Pub.

Code of Rhode Island Rules, Vol. 19. rev. ed. Weil Publishing Co., Inc. Staff. 1500p. (C). 1992. 189.00 (*0-916812-46-4*) Weil Pub.

Code of Rhode Island Rules, Vol. 20. rev. ed. Weil Publishing Co., Inc. Staff. 1400p. (C). 1992. 189.00 (*0-916812-47-2*) Weil Pub.

Code of Rhode Island Rules, Vol. 21. rev. ed. Weil Publishing Co., Inc. Staff. 1250p. (C). 1992. 189.00 (*0-916812-50-2*) Weil Pub.

Code of Rhode Island Rules, Vol. 22. rev. ed. Weil Publishing Co., Inc. 1250p. (C). 1992. 189.00 (*0-916812-51-0*) Weil Pub.

Code of Safe Practice for Cargo Stowage & Securing. International Maritime Organization Staff. (C). 1992. 125.00 (*0-7855-0039-1*, Pub. by Intl Maritime Org UK) St Mut.

Code of Safe Practice for Ships Carrying Timber Deck Cargoes. International Maritime Organization Staff. (C). 1992. 110.00 (*0-7855-0038-3*, Pub. by Intl Maritime Org UK) St Mut.

Code of Safe Practice for Solid Bulk Cargoes (BC Code) International Maritime Organization Staff. 1991. text ed. 150.00 (*0-89771-876-3*, Pub. by Intl Maritime Org UK) St Mut.

Code of Safety for Diving Systems. International Maritime Organization Staff. 1985. text ed. 45.00 (*0-89771-996-4*, Pub. by Intl Maritime Org UK) St Mut.

Code of Safety for Dynamically Supported Craft. International Maritime Organization Staff. 1978. text ed. 40.00 (*0-89771-994-8*, Pub. by Intl Maritime Org UK) St Mut.

Code of Safety for Fishermen & Fishing Vessels, Pt. A: Safety & Health Practices for Skippers & Crews. International Maritime Organization Staff. 1975. text ed. 40.00 (*0-89771-984-0*, Pub. by Intl Maritime Org UK) St Mut.

Code of Safety for Fishermen & Fishing Vessels, Pt. B: Safety & Health Requirements for the Construction & Equipment of Fishing Vessels. International Maritime Organization Staff. 1975. text ed. 30.00 (*0-89771-985-9*, Pub. by Intl Maritime Org UK) St Mut.

Code of Safety for Nuclear Merchant Ships. IMO Staff. (FRE & SPA.). (C). 1982. French ed. 60.00 (*0-7855-0007-3*, IMO 852F, Pub. by Intl Maritime Org UK); Spanish ed. 60.00 (*0-685-74524-4*, IMO 853S, Pub. by Intl Maritime Org UK) St Mut.

Code of Safety for Special Purpose Ships. International Maritime Organization Staff. 1984. text ed. 30.00 (*0-89771-999-9*, Pub. by Intl Maritime Org UK) St Mut.

Code of Signals: Recent Writings in Poetics. Intro. by Michael Palmer. 275p. (Orig.). 1983. 25.00 (*0-938190-26-1*); pap. 12.95 (*0-938190-22-9*) North Atlantic.

Code of Standard Practice for Steel Buildings & Bridges. 52p. 1992. 5.00 (*1-56424-038-X*, 5303) Am Inst Steel Construct.

Code of the Gun. large type ed. Gordon D. Shirreffs. (Linford Western Library). 288p. 1988. pap. 11.95 (*0-7089-6491-5*, Trailtree Bookshop) Ulverscroft.

Code of the Lifemaker. James P. Hogan. 416p. 1995. mass mkt., pap. 4.99 (*0-345-30549-3*, Del Rey) Ballantine.

Code of the Mountain Man. William W. Johnstone. 288p. 1991. pap. 3.50 (*0-8217-3342-7*) Zebra.

Code of the Prophets. Madeleine L. Burman. LC 84-90888. (Illus.). 112p. (Orig.). 1984. 4.95 (*0-9613283-0-4*); pap. 6.95 (*0-317-00778-5*) M L Burman.

Code of the Samurai. Daidoji Yuzan. Tr. by A. L. Sadler. LC 87-51232. 108p. 1988. reprint ed. 14.95 (*0-8048-1535-6*) C E Tuttle.

Code of the Warrior: A Way of Personal Development Through Classic Warrior Traditions: Japanese Samurai, Plains Indians, & Medieval Knights. Rick Fields. LC 90-55986. (Illus.). 320p. 1991. pap. 16.00 (*0-06-096605-X*, PL) HarpC.

Code of the West. Zane Grey. 1991. mass mkt. 3.99 (*0-06-100173-2*, Harp PBks) HarpC.

Code of the West. Bruce A. Rosenberg. LC 81-47014. (Illus.). 213p. reprint ed. pap. 60.80 (*0-7837-1760-1*, 2057297) Bks Demand.

Code of the Woosters. P. G. Wodehouse. 1975. pap. 8.00 (*0-394-72028-8*, Vin) Random.

Code of the Woosters. P. G. Wodehouse. reprint ed. lib. bdg. 19.95 (*0-89190-291-0*, Rivercity Pr) Amereon Ltd.

Code of Vermont Rules. rev. ed. Weil Publishing Co., Inc. Staff. 1000p. (C). 1989. 168.00 (*0-916812-49-9*) Weil Pub.

Code of Vermont Rules, 9 vols., Set. rev. ed. Weil Publishing Co., Inc. Staff. 11560p. (C). 1989. 1,290.00 (*0-916812-27-8*) Weil Pub.

Code of Vermont Rules, Vol. 1. rev. ed. Weil Publishing Co., Inc. Staff. 1400p. (C). 1989. 168.00 (*0-916812-19-7*) Weil Pub.

Code of Vermont Rules, Vol. 2. rev. ed. Weil Publishing Co., Inc. Staff. 1750p. (C). 1989. 168.00 (*0-916812-20-0*) Weil Pub.

Code of Vermont Rules, Vol. 3. rev. ed. Weil Publishing Co., Inc. Staff. 1500p. (C). 1989. 168.00 (*0-916812-21-9*) Weil Pub.

Code of Vermont Rules, Vol. 4. rev. ed. Weil Publishing Co., Inc. Staff. 1500p. (C). 1989. 168.00 (*0-916812-22-7*) Weil Pub.

Code of Vermont Rules, Vol. 5. rev. ed. Weil Publishing Co., Inc. Staff. 1000p. (C). 1989. 168.00 (*0-916812-23-5*) Weil Pub.

Code of Vermont Rules, Vol. 6. rev. ed. Weil Publishing Co., Inc. Staff. 1250p. (C). 1989. 168.00 (*0-916812-24-3*) Weil Pub.

Code of Vermont Rules, Vol. 7. rev. ed. Weil Publishing Co., Inc. Staff. 1250p. (C). 1989. 168.00 (*0-916812-25-1*) Weil Pub.

Code of Vermont Rules, Vol. 8. rev. ed. Weil Publishing Co., Inc. Staff. 1000p. (C). 1989. 168.00 (*0-916812-26-X*) Weil Pub.

***Code of Virginia.** Date not set. write for info. (*0-614-05793-0*) Michie Butterworth.

Code of Virginia, 1950, 25 vols. Michie Company Editorial Staff. write for info. (*0-318-54327-3*) Michie Butterworth.

Code of Virginia, 1950, 25 vols., Set. Michie Company Editorial Staff. write for info. (*0-87215-137-9*) Michie Butterworth.

***Code of Washington.** annot. rev. ed. Date not set. write for info. (*0-614-05777-9*) Michie Butterworth.

Code Poems. Hannah Weiner. 32p. 1982. 3.50 (*0-940170-03-5*) Open Bk Pubns.

Code Practice for the Construction of Buildings. Fire Protection Association Staff. (C). 1992. 95.00 (*0-902167-00-6*, Pub. by Fire Protect Assn UK) St Mut.

Code Recognition & Set Selection with Neural Networks. C. Jeffries. (Mathematical Modeling Ser.: Vol. 7). viii, 166p. 1991. 49.50 (*0-8176-3585-8*) Spr-Verlag.

***Code Red: The Silent Emergency.** Sydne Johansen. Date not set. pap. 7.95 (*0-614-04786-2*) NW Pub.

Code Requirements for Nuclear Safety Related Concrete Structures: ACI 349-85(90) ACI Committee 349. 1985. 110.50 (*0-685-85087-0*, 349-85) ACI.

Code Talkers. Chuck Bianchi. 1990. pap. 3.95 (*1-55817-448-6*, Pinnacle NY) Windsor NY.

***Code 3.** Robert R. Easland. LC 93-94212. 168p. (Orig.). 1994. pap. 9.00 (*1-56002-393-7*, Univ Edtns) Aegina Pr.

Code to Keep. Ernest C. Brace. 1989. mass mkt. 4.95 (*0-312-91501-2*) St Martin.

Code Zero. Jonathan Cain. (Saigon Commandos Ser.: No. 2). 1984. pap. 2.50 (*0-8217-1329-9*) Zebra.

Codebreaker in the Far East. Alan Stripp. 1989. lib. bdg. 32.50 (*0-7146-3363-1*, F3363, Pub. by F Cass Pubs UK) Intl Spec Bk.

***Codebreaker in the Far East.** Alan Stripp. (Illus.). 224p. 1995. pap. 12.95 (*0-19-285316-3*) OUP.

Codebreaker Kids. George E. Stanley. 112p. (J). (gr. 3-7). 1987. pap. 2.95 (*0-380-75228-X*, Camelot) Avon.

Codebreaker Kids Return. George E. Stanley. 128p. (J). (gr. 3-7). 1989. pap. 2.50 (*0-380-75608-0*, Camelot) Avon.

Codebreakers. Harry Hinsley & Alan Stripp. LC 92-42502. 1993. 25.00 (*0-19-820327-6*) OUP.

Codebreakers. David Kahn. 1184p. 1967. text ed. 60.00 (*0-02-560460-0*) Macmillan.

Codebreakers: The Inside Story of Bletchley Park. Ed. by F. H. Hinsley & Alan Stripp. (Illus.). 352p. 1994. reprint ed. pap. 13.95 (*0-19-285304-X*) OUP.

Codebreaking & Signals Intelligence. Ed. by Christopher Andrew. 144p. 1986. 32.50 (*0-7146-3299-6*, Pub. by F Cass Pubs UK) Intl Spec Bk.

Coded-Character Sets: History & Development. Charles E. Mackenzie. LC 77-90165. (IBM Systems Programming Ser.). 1980. text ed. write for info. (*0-201-14460-3*) Addison-Wesley.

Coded Encounters: Writing, Gender, & Ethnicity in Colonial Latin America. Ed. by Francisco J. Cevallos-Candau et al. LC 93-24562. (Illus.). 312p. 1994. lib. bdg. 45.00 (*0-87023-885-X*); pap. 16.95 (*0-87023-886-8*) U of Mass Pr.

Coded Frequency Shift Keyed Sequences with Applications to Low Data Rate Communication & Radar. Michael J. Sites. LC 75-136728. 107p. 1969. 19.00 (*0-685-38428-4*) Scholarly.

Coded-Modulation Techniques for Fading Channels. S. Hamidreza Jamali & Tho Le-Ngoc. LC 94-2903. (International Series in Engineering & Computer Science, VLSI, Computer Architecture, & Digital Screen Processing: Vol. 268). 504p. (C). 1994. lib. bdg. 110.00 (*0-7923-9421-6*) Kluwer Ac.

Coded Workbook of Birds of the World Vol. 1: Non-Passerines. 2nd ed. Ernest P. Edwards. LC 82-82891. (Illus.). xxi, 134p. 1982. spiral bd. 7.50 (*0-911882-07-3*) E P Edwards.

Coded Workbook of Birds of the World Vol. 2: Passerines. 2nd ed. Ernest P. Edwards. LC 82-82891. (Illus.). 170p. 1986. spiral bd. 11.50 (*0-911882-10-3*) E P Edwards.

Codeine & Its Alternatives for Pain & Cough Relief. N. B. Eddy et al. (Bulletin of WHO Ser.: Vol. 38, No. 5 & Vol. 40, Nos. 1, 3 & 5). 253p. 1970. reprint ed. pap. 8.00 (*92-4-056005-X*, 94) World Health.

***Codelink for Ophthalmology, 1995.** rev. ed. Context Software Systems, Inc. Staff. 450p. 1995. pap. 99.95 (*0-07-600765-0*) Hlthcare Mgmt Grp.

***Codelink for Oral & Maxillofacial Surgery, 1995.** rev. ed. Context Software Systems, Inc. Staff. 450p. 1995. pap. 99.95 (*0-07-600764-2*) Hlthcare Mgmt Grp.

***Codelink for Orthopaedics, 1995.** rev. ed. Context Software Systems, Inc. Staff. 1050p. 1995. pap. 129.95 (*0-07-600766-9*) Hlthcare Mgmt Grp.

***Codelink for Otolaryngology, 1995.** Context Software Systems, Inc. Staff. 450p. 1995. pap. 99.95 (*0-07-600762-6*) Hlthcare Mgmt Grp.

***Codelink for Plastic Surgery, 1995.** Context Software Systems, Inc. Staff. 1050p. 1995. pap. 149.95 (*0-07-600763-4*) Hlthcare Mgmt Grp.

Codemaster: Secrets of Making & Breaking Codes. Hamilton Nickels. 144p. 1990. pap. 16.00 (*0-87364-564-2*) Paladin Pr.

Codename: Cipher. Chuck Freadhoff. 224p. 1991. 19.95 (*0-8027-1150-2*) Walker & Co.

Codename: Sand Castle, No. 2. Ned Bannister. 1988. pap. 2.95 (*0-345-35116-9*) Ballantine.

***Codename: Strykeforce.** Marc Silverstri. (Illus.). 96p. (Orig.). (YA). Date not set. pap. 9.95 (*1-887279-03-2*) Image Comics.

***Codename: The Long Sobbing.** Arnold Schwartzman. (Illus.). 160p. 1994. 29.95 (*0-943058-18-X*) S Wiesenthal Ctr.

Codename Dora. Sandor Rado. Tr. by J. A. Underwood. (Classics of World War II: The Secret War Ser.). (Illus.). 298p. 1990. reprint ed. write for info. (*0-8094-8566-4*); reprint ed. lib. bdg. write for info. (*0-8094-8567-2*) Time-Life.

***Codename: Mule: Fighting the Secret War in Laos for the C.I.A.** James E. Parker, Jr. Ed. by Mark Gatlin. LC 94-48538. (Naval Institute Special Warfare Ser.). (Illus.). 232p. 1995. 27.95 (*1-55750-668-X*) Naval Inst Pr.

Codename Quicksilver. S. Dixon. (Advanced Puzzle Adventures Ser.). (Illus.). 48p. (J). (gr. 6 up). 1992. lib. bdg. 11.96 (*0-88110-517-1*, Usborne); pap. 4.95 (*0-7460-0688-8*, Usborne) EDC.

Codependence in the Workplace Trainer's Package. Jeanette Goodstein & Earnie Larsen. 146p. 1993. ring bd. 129.00 (*0-88390-386-5*) Pfeiffer & Co.

Codependency. Pat Springle. 66p. 1991. pap. 2.99 (*0-945276-26-5*) Rapha Pub.

Codependency: A Christian Perspective. Pat Springle. 299p. 1990. pap. 10.99 (*0-945276-12-5*) Rapha Pub.

Codependency: A Christian Perspective Small Group Leader's Guide. Pat Springle. 51p. 1990. pap. 5.00 (*0-945276-08-7*) Rapha Pub.

Codependency: A Second-Hand Life. Stephanie Abbott. 11p. (Orig.). 1985. pap. 1.40 (*0-89486-317-7*, 5450B) Hazelden.

***Codependency: Feminist Critiques.** Ed. by Marguerite Babcock & Christine McKay. 224p. 1995. 60.00 (*0-8020-0440-7*) U of Toronto Pr.

***Codependency: Feminist Critiques.** Ed. by Marguerite Babcock & Christine McKay. 224p. 1995. pap. 19.95 (*0-8020-7230-5*) U of Toronto Pr.

***Codependency: PowerLoss, SoulLoss.** Dorothy May. 320p. 1994. pap. 12.95 (*0-8091-3532-9*) Paulist Pr.

***Codependency: PowerLoss SoulLoss.** Dorothy May. 300p. 1994. pap. 12.95 (*1-882195-02-7*) Whales Tale Pr.

Codependency Confusion: Developing Healthy Relationships. Randy Reynolds & David Lynn. (Recovery Discovery Ser.). 96p. 1992. pap. 4.99 (*0-310-57361-0*) Zondervan.

Codependency Conspiracy: How to Break the Recovery Habit & Take Charge of Your Life. Stan J. Katz & Aimee E. Liu. 256p. 1991. 18.95 (*0-446-51595-7*) Warner Bks.

Codependency in the Workplace: A Guide for Employee Assistance & Human Resource Professionals. Seth Allcorn. LC 91-39807. 224p. 1992. text ed. 49.95 (*0-89930-644-6*, ACD, Quorum Bks) Greenwood.

Codependency Issues in Treatment. Carruth et al. 1991. 39.95 (*0-86656-920-0*); pap. 12.95 (*0-86656-942-1*) Haworth Pr.

Codependency, Sexuality & Depression. William E. Thornton. 144p. (Orig.). 1990. pap. 7.95 (*0-929162-18-8*) PIA Pr.

Codependent Counselor: Guidelines for Self-Assessment & Change. Philip J. Beebe. 178p. 1990. 13.00 (*0-8309-0560-X*) Herald Hse.

Codependent for Sure! An Original Jokebook. Jann Mitchell. 104p. 1992. pap. 6.95 (*0-8362-7998-0*) Andrews & McMeel.

***Codependent No More.** Melody Beattie. 1987. digital audio 10.00 (*0-89486-633-8*) Hazelden.

Codependent No More: How to Stop Controlling Others & Start Caring for Yourself. Melody Beattie. (Orig.). 1987. pap. 11.00 (*0-06-255446-8*, Hazelden SF) Harper SF.

Codependent No More: How to Stop Controlling Others & Start Caring for Yourself. Melody Beattie. LC 86-82660. 208p. (Orig.). 1987. pap. 11.00 (*0-89486-402-5*, 5014A) Hazelden.

Codependent No More: How to Stop Controlling Others & Start Caring for Yourself. large type ed. Melody Beattie. (Orig.). 1989. pap. 14.95 (*0-8027-2631-3*) Walker & Co.

Codependent Parent: Free Yourself by Freeing Your Child. Barbara C. Becnel. 1991. pap. 12.00 (*0-06-250126-7*) Harper SF.

Codependents' Guide to the Twelve Steps. Melody Beattie. 224p. 1990. pap. 11.00 (*0-671-72606-4*, Fireside) S&S Trade.

Codes. Nigel Nelson. LC 93-40962. (Nonverbal Communications Ser.). (Illus.). 32p. (J). (gr. k-2). 1994. 12.95 (*1-56847-157-2*) Thomson Lrning.

Codes. L. Spellman. (Enrichment & Gifted Ser.). 40p. (J). (gr. 4-8). 1992. 6.95 (*0-88160-253-1*, LW1402) Learning Wks.

Codes & Ciphers: An A to Z of Covert Communication, from the Clay Tablet to the Microdot. Fred B. Wrixon. (Illus.). 288p. (YA). 1992. pap. 18.00 (*0-13-277047-4*) P-H Gen Ref & Trav.

Codes & Ciphers: Hundreds of Unusual & Secret Ways to Send Messages. Christina Ashton. (Illus.). 112p. (Orig.). (YA). (gr. 7 up). 1993. pap. 7.95 (*1-55870-292-X*) Betterway Bks.

Codes & Cryptography. Dominic Welsh. (Illus.). 272p. 1988. pap. 32.50 (*0-19-853287-3*) OUP.

Codes & Customs: Millennial Perspectives. Ed. by Roberta Kevelson. LC 93-37632. (Critic of Institutions Ser.: Vol. 1). 296p. (C). 1994. text ed. 49.95 (*0-8204-1979-6*) P Lang Pubs.

***Codes & Sequences.** Marion Smoothey. LC 94-13134. (Let's Investigate Ser.). (Illus.). (J). 1994. lib. bdg. 16.95 (*1-85435-774-3*) Marshall Cavendish.

***Codes & Standards for Quality Engineering: Proceedings of the Pressure Vessels & Piping Conference, Minneapolis, MN, 11994.** Ed. by K. R. Rao. LC 94-71664. (PVP Ser.: vol. 285). 279p. 1994. pap. 60.00 (*0-7918-1358-4*) ASME.

Codes & Standards in a Global Environment. Ed. by J. E. Staffiera. (PVP Ser.: Vol. 259). 244p. 1993. 55.00 (*0-7918-0986-2*, H00818) ASME.

Codes, Ciphers, & Secret Languages: A User's Manual & History. Fred B. Wrixon. LC 87-32580. 1989. 7.98 (*0-517-65704-X*) Random Hse Value.

Codes, Ciphers & Secret Writing. Martin Gardner. 96p. 1984. reprint ed. pap. 3.50 (*0-486-24761-9*) Dover.

Codes for Boundary-Value Problems in Ordinary Differential Equations. Ed. by Barton Childs et al. (Lecture Notes in Computer Science Ser.: Vol. 76). 388p. 1979. pap. 32.00 (*0-387-09554-3*) Spr-Verlag.

Codes for Detecting & Correcting Unidirectional Errors. Mario Blaum. LC 93-17499. 224p. 1993. reprint ed. 44.00 (*0-8186-4182-7*, 4182) IEEE Comp Soc.

Codes for Error Control & Synchronization. Djimitri Wiggert. LC 88-6339. (Artech House Communication & Electronic Defense Library). (Illus.). 211p. reprint ed. pap. 60.20 (*0-7837-5393-4*, 2045157) Bks Demand.

Codes for the Representation of Languages for Information Interchange. (National Information Standards Ser.). 1987. 30.00 (*0-88738-955-4*, Z39.53) Transaction Pubs.

Codes for the Representation of Names of Countries: ANSI-NISO-ISO 3166. National Information Standards Organization Staff. 76p. (C). 1993. pap. 50.00 (*0-88738-937-6*) Transaction Pubs.

***Codes Guidebook for Interiors.** Sharon K. Harmon. 1994. text ed. 34.95 (*0-471-00618-1*) Wiley.

Codes of Advertising: Fetishism & the Political Economy on Meaning in the Consumer Society. Sut Shally. 320p. 1990. pap. 13.95 (*0-415-90353-X*, A4804, Routledge NY) Routledge.

Codes of Conduct. Gallup Organization Staff & Philip Cochran. LC 94-70910. 100p. (Orig.). 1994. pap. 15.00 (*0-910586-92-6*) Finan Exec.

An Asterisk (*) at the beginning of an entry indicates that the title is appearing in BIP for the first time.

An Asterisk (*) at the beginning of an entry indicates that the title is appearing in BIP for the first time.

CoDominium: Revolt on War World. Created by Jerry Pournelle. 480p. (Orig.). 1992. mass mkt. 5.99 (0-671-72126-7) Baen Bks.

Cody. Keith Hale. 192p. (Orig.). 1994. reprint ed. pap. 5.95 (1-55583-601-1, AlyCat) Alyson Pubns.

Cody: A Novel That Motivates Towards Success. David K. Draper. 88p. (Orig.). (YA). (gr. 9-12). 1990. pap. 8.98 (0-88290-409-4) Horizon Utah.

Cody Angel. Joanne Whitfield. LC 90-26553. 225p. (Orig.). 1991. pap. 8.95 (0-934678-28-6) New Victoria Pubs.

Cody Family in America, 1698: Descendants of Philip & Martha of Massachusetts, Biographical & Genealogical. Comp. by Cody Fam Assoc Staff. (Illus.). 257p. 1991. reprint ed. lib. bdg. 51.00 (0-8328-2116-0); reprint ed. pap. 41.00 (0-8328-2117-9) Higginson Bk Co.

Cody Firearms Museum. Herbert G. Houze. (Illus.). 80p. 1992. 24.95 (0-931618-39-8); pap. 14.95 (0-931618-33-9) U of Wash Pr.

*Cody's Christmas Wish. Sally Carleen. 1995. pap. 2.99 (0-373-19124-3, 1-19124-6) Silhouette.

*Cody's Law. Matthew S. Hart. (Red Moon's Raid Ser.: No. 11). 1994. 3.99 (0-553-56107-3) Bantam.

Cody's Ride. Stan Wiseman. LC 92-35804. 182p. 1993. 19.95 (0-8027-1266-5) Walker & Co.

Cody's Ride. large type ed. Stan Wiseman. LC 93-43625. 1994. pap. 15.95 (0-8161-5929-7, Large Print Bks) Hall.

Codyview, Buffalo Bill's Link with Duluth. 3rd ed. Claire W. Schumacher. (Illus.). 25p. 1993. 4.00 (0-917378-03-2) Zenith City.

Coe - Ward Memorial & Immigrant Ancestors. L. E. Coe. (Illus.). 136p. 1991. reprint ed. lib. bdg. 31.50 (0-8328-1750-3); reprint ed. pap. 21.50 (0-8328-1751-1) Higginson Bk Co.

Coe the Good Dragon at the Center of the World. 6th ed. Jai. LC 85-71009. (Illus.). (ENG & FRE.). (J). (ps up). 1985. 11.00 (0-934003-00-9) Bluebird Pr CA.

Coe the Good Dragon at the Center of the World. 6th ed. Jai. LC 85-71009. (Illus.). (ENG & FRE.). (J). (ps up). 1985. French ed. 5.50 (0-934003-01-7) Bluebird Pr CA.

Coeducation in Its Historical & Theoretical Setting. Reginald Snell. LC 79-2952. 208p. 1980. reprint ed. 20.10 (0-8305-0115-0) Hyperion Conn.

Coefficient Plane Models for Control System Analysis & Design. Denis R. Towill. LC 80-41695. (Mechanical Engineering Research Studies Ser.: No. 1). (Illus.). 287p. reprint ed. pap. 81.80 (0-8357-6062-6, 2034241) Bks Demand.

Coefficient Regions for Schlicht Functions. A. C. Schaeffer & D. C. Spencer. Bd. with Chapter on the Region of Values of the Derivative of a Schlicht Function. LC 51-944. LC 51-944. (Colloquium Publications: Vol. 35). 311p. 1950. 34.00 (0-8218-1035-9, COLL-35) Am Math.

Coelebs in Search of a Wife: Comprehending Observations on Domestic Habits & Manners, Religion & Morals, 2 vols. in 1. Hannah More. LC 79-8178. reprint ed. 44.50 (0-404-62052-3) AMS Pr.

Coelenterata, Polyzoa: Freshwater Sponges, Hydroids, & Polyzoa. N. Annandale. (Fauna of British India Ser.). (Illus.). vii, 262p. 1972. reprint ed. 20.00 (0-88065-015-X, Messers Today & Tomorrow) Scholarly Pubns.

Coelenterate Biology: Recent Research on Cnidaria & Ctenophora. Ed. by R. B. Williams et al. (Developments in Hydrobiologia Ser.). (C). 1900. lib. bdg. 338.50 (0-7923-1241-4) Kluwer Ac.

*Coelestis: Man into Beast. Paul Park. 288p. 1995. 21.95 (0-312-85899-X) Tor Bks.

Coeli et Terra: Poems of Thirty-Five Years. Brian L. Pearce. LC 93-1884. 1993. pap. 4.00 (0-940895-09-9) Cornerstone IL.

Coeliac Disease. W. T. Hekkens & A. S. Pena. 1974. lib. bdg. 99.00 (90-207-0463-X) Kluwer Ac.

Coeliac Disease. M. N. Marsh. (Illus.). 352p. 1992. 175.00 (0-632-03097-6) Blackwell Sci.

Coelomycetes. B. C. Sutton. 696p. 1980. 78.00 (0-85198-446-0) CAB Intl.

*Coelophysis. Janet Riehecky. (Dinosaur Bks.). (Illus.). 32p. (ENG & SPA.). (J). (ps-2). 1990. lib. bdg. 21.36 (1-56766-136-X) Childs World.

Coelophysis. Janet Riehecky. (Dinosaur Bks.). (Illus.). 32p. (ENG & SPA.). (J). (ps-2). 1990. lib. bdg. 21.36 (0-89565-623-X) Childs World.

Coelum Philosophorum: Or the Book of Vexations. Paracelsus. Tr. by A. E. Waite. reprint ed. pap. 3.95 (0-916411-13-3) Holmes Pub.

Coelum Philosophorum: The Seven Canons of the Metals. Paracelsus. Tr. by Arthur E. Waite. 1982. reprint ed. pap. 4.50 (0-945303-08-4) Evanescent Pr.

Coelum Terrae: The Magician's Heavenly Chaos & First Matter of All Things. Thomas Vaughan. 1986. pap. 5.95 (0-916411-65-6, Sure Fire) Holmes Pub.

Coelura. Anne McCaffrey. 176p. 1989. pap. 3.95 (0-8125-0297-3) Tor Bks.

Coenties Slip. Mildred Glimcher. LC 92-84083. 72p. (Orig.). 1993. pap. write for info. (1-878283-27-8) PaceWildenstein.

Coenzyme Contents of Arterial Tissue. J. E. Kirk. (Monographs on Atherosclerosis: Vol. 4). (Illus.). 130p. 1974. 43.25 (3-8055-1670-3) S Karger.

Coenzyme Q-10. William H. Lee. Ed. by Richard Passwater & Earl Mindell. (Good Health Guide Ser.). 32p. (Orig.). 1987. pap. 2.50 (0-87983-427-7) Keats.

Coercion. Alan Wertheimer. Ed. by Marshall Cohen. (Studies in Moral, Political, & Legal Philosophy). (Illus.). 336p. (Orig.). 1990. text ed. 49.50 (0-691-07759-2); pap. text ed. 15.95 (0-691-02322-0) Princeton U Pr.

Coercion & Autonomy: Philosophical Foundations, Issues & Practices. Alan S. Rosenbaum. LC 86-7578. (Contributions in Philosophy Ser.: No. 31). 208p. 1986. text ed. 49.95 (0-313-22819-1, RHA/, Greenwood Pr) Greenwood.

*Coercion & Consent: Studies on the Modern State. John Hall. Ed. by Sue Leigh. 240p. 1995. text ed. 49.95 (0-7456-1194-X) Blackwell Pubs.

*Coercion & Consent: Studies on the Modern State. John Hall. Ed. by Sue Leigh. 240p. 1995. pap. text ed. 19.95 (0-7456-1195-8) Blackwell Pubs.

Coercion & Control in Communist Society: The Visible Hand in a Command Economy. Maria Hirszowicz. LC 85-14538. 233p. 1986. text ed. 32.50 (0-312-14639-6) St Martin.

Coercion & Its Fallout. Murray Sidman. LC 89-83719. xiii, 263p. 1989. 26.95 (0-9623311-1-2); pap. 16.95 (0-9623311-2-0) Authors Coop.

Coercion & Market: Silver Mining in Colonial Potosi, 1692-1826. Enrique Tandeter. LC 93-14687. 347p. 1993. 50.00x (0-8263-1430-9) U of NM Pr.

*Coercion & Punishment in Long-Term Perspectives. Ed. by Joan McCord. (Illus.). 400p. (C). 1995. 59.95 (0-521-45069-1) Cambridge U Pr.

Coercion, Capital, & European States, A.D. 990-1992. Charles Tilly. 1992. pap. 21.95 (1-55786-368-7) Blackwell Pubs.

Coercion, Freedom & Exploitation. Michael Gorr. (American University Studies: Philosophy: Ser. V, Vol. 65). 206p. (C). 1989. text ed. 32.50 (0-8204-0786-0) P Lang Pubs.

Coercion or Persuasion? Propaganda in Britain after 1945. William Crofts. 200p. 1989. 65.00 (0-415-02903-1, A3471) Routledge.

Coercion to Love. Michelle Reid. (Presents Ser.). 1993. mass mkt. 2.99 (0-373-11597-0, 1-11597-1) Harlequin Bks.

Coercion to Speak: Conrad's Poetics of Dialogue. Aaron Fogel. 304p. 1985. 35.00 (0-674-13639-X) HUP.

Coercive Cooperation: Explaining Multilateral Economic Sanctions. Lisa L. Martin. (Illus.). 1992. text ed. 45.00 (0-691-08624-9) Princeton U Pr.

Coercive Cooperation: Explaining Multilateral Economic Sanctions. Lisa L. Martin. (C). 1994. pap. 16.95 (0-691-03476-1) Princeton U Pr.

Coercive Egalitarianism: A Study of Discrimination Against Gifted Children. Stephen Schroeder-Davis. 1993. 13.00 (0-910609-25-X) Gifted Educ Pr.

Coeur Absolu. Phillipe Sollers. (FRE.). 1989. pap. 13.95 (0-7859-2917-7) Fr & Eur.

Coeur Aride. Carlo Cassola. (FRE.). 1975. pap. 10.95 (0-7859-1796-9, 2070366456) Fr & Eur.

Coeur D'Alene. Mary H. Foote. LC 74-22783. (Labor Movement in Fiction & Non-Fiction Ser.). reprint ed. 39.50 (0-404-58430-6) AMS Pr.

Coeur D'Alene Indian Story. Thomas E. Connolly. 85p. (J). pap. 4.50 (0-87770-483-X) Ye Galleon.

Coeur En Poche. Christine Aventin. (FRE.). 1989. pap. 10.95 (0-7859-2132-X, 2070382079) Fr & Eur.

Coeur Perdu; Meurtre a 45 Tours. Boileau-Narcejac. (FRE.). 1987. pap. 10.95 (0-7859-3990-3) Fr & Eur.

Coeur Simple. Gustave Flaubert & Sylvia E. Douyere. 160p. (FRE.). 1992. pap. 8.95 (0-7859-4760-4) Fr & Eur.

Coeurs Purs. Joseph Kessel. (Folio Ser.: No. 1905). (FRE.). pap. 8.95 (2-07-037905-1) Schoenhof.

Coeurs Purs. Joseph Kessel. 178p. (FRE.). 1988. pap. 10.95 (0-7859-2549-X, 2070379051) Fr & Eur.

Coevolution: Genes, Culture, & Human Diversity. William H. Durham. (C). pap. 22.50 (0-8047-2156-4) Stanford U Pr.

Coevolution: Genes, Culture, & Human Diversity. William H. Durham. xxiv, 651p. 1991. 69.50 (0-8047-1537-8) Stanford U Pr.

Coevolution of Animals & Plants. rev. ed. Ed. by Lawrence E. Gilbert & Peter H Raven. (Illus.). 277p. 1980. pap. 9.95 (0-292-71056-9) U of Tex Pr.

Coevolution of Fungi with Plants & Animals. Ed. by K. A. Pirozynski & David L. Hawksworth. 490p. 1988. text ed. 102.00 (0-12-557365-0) Acad Pr.

*Coevolutionary Economics: The Economy, Society & the Environment. John Gowdy. LC 94-28210. (Natural Resource Management & Policy Ser.). 264p. (C). 1994. lib. bdg. 99.95 (0-7923-9488-7) Kluwer Ac.

Coevolutionary Process. John N. Thompson. LC 94-14140. 1994. lib. bdg. 49.00 (0-226-79759-7); pap. text ed. 19.95 (0-226-79760-0) U Ch Pr.

Coexistence: Economic Challenge & Response. Henry G. Aubrey. LC 75-28675. 323p. 1976. reprint ed. text ed. 65.00 (0-8371-8471-1, AUCO, Greenwood Pr) Greenwood.

Coexistence, Cooperation & Common Security. Ed. by Joseph Rotblat & Laszlo Valki. LC 88-1956. 340p. 1988. text ed. 59.95 (0-312-01875-4) St Martin.

Coexistence of Neuronal Messengers: A New Principle in Chemical Transmission: Proceedings of the Marcus Wallenberg Symposium, Saltsjobaden, Stockholm, June 26-28, 1986. Ed. by Tomas B. Hokfelt et al. (Progress in Brain Research Ser.: Vol. 68). 411p. 1987. 173.50 (0-444-80762-4) Elsevier.

Coextrusion Coating & Film Fabrication. Ed. by R. H. Cramm & W. R. Sibbach. (Illus.). 251p. 1983. 37.00 (0-89852-412-1, 0101R112) TAPPI.

Coextrusion Coating & Film Fabrication. Technical Association of the Pulp & Paper Industry Staff. LC 83-50018. reprint ed. pap. 64.50 (0-317-20539-0, 2022831) Bks Demand.

Coextrusion Seminar: A Coextrusion Overview Regarding Real World Problems in Coextrusion. Society of Plastics Engineers Staff. (Illus.). 114p. reprint ed. pap. 32.50 (0-7837-1789-X, 2041988) Bks Demand.

Coextrusion Seminar, 1986: Proceedings Notes of TAPPI, Marriott Hilton Head, Hilton Head, SC, April 1-3, 1986. Technical Association of the Pulp & Paper Industry Staff. 138p. pap. 39.40 (0-685-17812-9, 2029183) Bks Demand.

Coextrusion Seminar, 1989: Marriott's Hilton Head, Hilton Head, SC, March 28-31. Technical Association of the Pulp & Paper Industry Staff. (TAPPI Notes Ser.). (Illus.). 105p. reprint ed. pap. 30.00 (0-8357-6321-8, 2035595) Bks Demand.

Coextrusion Short Course, 1992: Hyatt Regency Hotel, Savannah, GA, April 22-24. Technical Association of the Pulp & Paper Industry Staff. (TAPPI Notes Ser.). reprint ed. pap. 63.00 (0-7837-2437-3, 2042589) Bks Demand.

Coextrusion V: Explosion of Coextrusion: A Regional Technical Conference, October 23-25, 1989, Woodfield Hilton & Towers, Arlington Heights, IL. Society of Plastics Engineers Staff. (Illus.). 338p. reprint ed. pap. 96.40 (0-8357-3626-1, 2036327) Bks Demand.

Coextrusion VI: The Real World of Coextrusion: A Regional Technical Conference, October 14-16, 1991, Woodfield Hilton & Towers, Arlington Heights, IL. Society of Plastics Engineers Staff. (Illus.). 220p. reprint ed. pap. 62.70 (0-7837-1786-5, 2041985) Bks Demand.

Cofactors in HIV-1 Infection & AIDS. Ed. by Ronald R. Watson. 240p. 1989. text ed. 180.00 (0-8493-5845-0, QD431) CRC Pr.

Cofan Art of Hammock Making. M. B. Borman. LC 92-70219. (International Museum of Cultures Publications: No. 25). vi, 30p. (Orig.). 1992. pap. 2.00 (0-88312-185-9); fiche 4.00 (0-88312-936-1) Summer Instit Ling.

*Cofederate Memories. Phyllis Phillips. 520p. 1995. pap. 12.95 (0-7610-0154-9) NW Pub.

Coffee. Suzanne T. Moore. (Illus.). 144p. 1974. pap. 4.95 (0-938758-00-4) MTM Pub Co.

Coffee. Claudia Roden. (Handbook Ser.). 144p. (Orig.). 1981. mass mkt. 8.00 (0-14-046489-1, Penguin Bks) Viking Penguin.

Coffee. Violet Schafer & Charles Schafer. LC 76-14182. (Illus.). 1976. pap. 5.95 (0-912738-08-1, Random) Taylor & Ng.

Coffee: A Connoisseur's Companion. rev. ed. Claudia Roden. LC 94-18119. (Illus.). 1994. 15.00 (0-679-43739-8) Random.

*Coffee: A Guide to Buying, Brewing & Enjoying. Kenneth Davids. (One Hundred One Productions Ser.). 1991. pap. text ed. 10.95 (1-56426-500-5, One Hund One Prods) Cole Group.

*Coffee: A Guide to Buying, Brewing, & Enjoying. 4th ed. Kenneth Davids. (One Hundred One Productions Ser.). 1994. pap. 11.95 (1-56426-555-2, One Hund One Prods) Cole Group.

Coffee: Commercial & Technico-Legal Aspects, Vol. 6. Ed. by R. J. Clarke & Robert Macrae. 226p. 1989. 68.50 (1-85166-237-5) Elsevier.

*Coffee: Delectables for All Seasons. Maryjo Koch. LC 94-31807. 1995. 15.00 (0-00-255479-8) Harper SF.

Coffee: Miniature Book of Food. Jane Donovan. 1992. 4.99 (0-517-06542-8) Random Hse Value.

Coffee: Physiology, Vol. 3. Ed. by R. J. Clarke & Robert Macrae. 386p. 1989. 93.75 (1-85166-186-7) Elsevier.

*Coffee: The Bean of My Existence. R. D. Thomas. (Illus.). 96p. (Orig.). 1995. pap. 8.95 (0-8050-3769-1, Owl) H Holt & Co.

Coffee: The Bean of My Existence, a True Story. R. D. Thomas. LC 93-36952. Date not set. write for info. (0-688-13340-1) Hearst Bks.

Coffee: The Essential Guide to the Essential Bean. LC 94-8503. 1994. 20.00 (0-688-13328-2) Hearst Bks.

Coffee: The Political Economy of an Export Industry in Papua New Guinea. Randal G. Stewart. 316p. (C). 1992. pap. text ed. 54.50 (0-8133-8525-3) Westview.

Coffee: Volume Four - Agronomy. Ed. by R. J. Clarke & Robert Macrae. 330p. 1988. 88.25 (1-85166-132-8) Elsevier.

Coffee & Coffee Houses. Ulla Heise. LC 87-60529. (Illus.). 240p. 1987. 35.00 (0-88740-101-5, 101-5) Schiffer.

Coffee & Coffeehouses: The Origins of a Social Beverage in the Medieval Near East. Ralph S. Hattox. LC 84-40675. (Near Eastern Studies: No. 3). (Illus.). 192p. (Orig.). 1986. pap. text ed. 12.95 (0-295-96231-3) U of Wash Pr.

Coffee & Conflict in Colombia 1886-1910. Charles W. Bergquist. LC 78-59581. xiv, 277p. 1986. reprint ed. pap. 17.00 (0-8223-0735-9) Duke.

Coffee & Democracy in Modern Costa Rica. Anthony Winson. LC 88-23361. 250p. 1989. text ed. 45.00 (0-312-02521-1) St Martin.

Coffee & Health. Ed. by Brian MacMahon & Takashi Sugimura. LC 84-14199. (Banbury Report Ser.: Vol.17). 259p. 1984. 47.50 (0-87969-217-0) Cold Spring Harbor.

*Coffee & Tea Market. 217p. (Orig.). 1995. pap. 2,295.00 (0-7605-2151-4) Rector Pr.

Coffee & the Growth of Agrarian Capitalism in Nineteenth-Century Puerto Rico. Laird W. Bergad. LC 82-61354. 271p. reprint ed. pap. 77.30 (0-7837-0082-2, 2040343) Bks Demand.

Coffee Book. Dawn Campbell & Janet Smith. LC 92-45038. (Illus.). 176p. 1993. 16.95 (0-88289-950-3) Pelican.

Coffee Book. Melissa Clark. 272p. (Orig.). 1994. pap. 4.99 (0-425-14121-7) Berkley Pub.

Coffee Book: Featuring a Section on Teas. Christie Katona & Thomas Katona. (Illus.). 192p. (Orig.). 1992. pap. 8.95 (1-55867-051-3, Nitty Gritty Ckbks) Bristol Pub Ent CA.

Coffee, Brandy & Cigars: A Kaleidoscope of the Arts & That Strange Thing Called Life. Herman G. Weinberg. 96p. 1982. 16.00 (0-911689-13-3); pap. 8.00 (0-911689-12-5) Anthology Film.

*Coffee Break Book: Brief Diversions for Your Busy Day. Vicki Rottman. LC 94-96366. (Illus.). 112p. (Orig.). 1994. pap. 12.95 (0-9642517-0-1) VR Prodns.

Coffee Break in Latte Land. Kathrine J. Dietz. 64p. (Orig.). 1994. pap. text ed. 9.95 (0-89716-512-8) P B Pubng.

Coffee Cantata. Harvey Hess. Bd. with Kona Coffee Cantata. 24p. 1986. Set pap. 3.00 (0-685-19246-6) Malama Arts.

Coffee Cantata. Picander. Tr. by Harvey Hess. Bd. with Kona Coffee Cantata. 24p. (GER.). 1986. Set pap. 3.00 (0-931909-05-8) Malama Arts.

Coffee Co-Operatives & Culture: An Anthropological Study of a Coffee Co-Operative in Kenya. Hans Hedlund. 206p. (C). 1993. 26.00 (0-19-572758-4, 6319) OUP.

Coffee Companion. Dennis L. Boyer. Ed. by John O. Davies. 166p. 1992. 14.95 (0-9635222-0-5); pap. 9.95 (0-9635222-1-3) Entreper Pr.

Coffee, Contention & Change: In the Politics in Modern Brazil. Mauricio A. Font. 320p. 1990. text ed. 49.95 (1-55786-042-4) Blackwell Pubs.

*Coffee Cookbook. William Kauffman. 200p. Date not set. pap. 7.95 (0-7610-0313-4) NW Pub.

*Coffee Crazy: A Guide to the One Hundred Best Coffee Houses in America. Marybeth Bizjak. 192p. 1995. pap. 9.95 (0-929999-15-0) Tzedakah Pubns.

Coffee Exchange. George Monteiro. LC 82-81571. (Illus.). 77p. (Orig.). (C). 1982. pap. 3.50 (0-943722-02-0) Gavea-Brown.

*Coffee Heaven: Divine Coffee Libation & Dessert Recipes. Kimberly E. Kennedy. 52p. 1994. pap. 5.95 (0-9645647-1-8) Am Creat Concepts.

Coffee House Cookbook. Associated Students of the University of California, Davis. LC 86-50606. (Illus.). 105p. (Orig.). 1986. pap. 7.95 (0-934189-02-1) Unique Pub CA.

Coffee in the Gourd. Ed. by J. Frank Dobie. (Texas Folklore Society Publications: No. 2). (Illus.). 120p. 1979. reprint ed. 11.95 (0-87074-039-3) UNTX Pr.

Coffee Made Her Insane: And Other Nuggets from Old Minnesota Newspapers. Peg Meier. (Illus.). 314p. 1988. pap. 14.95 (0-933387-01-6) Neighbors Pub.

*Coffee Market. 100p. (Orig.). 1995. pap. 1,295.00 (0-7605-2152-2) Rector Pr.

Coffee Rust: Epidemiology, Resistance, & Management. Ed. by A. C. Kushalappa & A. B. Eskes. 336p. 1989. 234.00 (0-8493-6899-5, SB608) CRC Pr.

*Coffee Shop. Carlo Goldoni. Tr. by Robert Cornthwaite. (Great Translations for Actors Ser.). 112p. 1995. 11.95 (1-57525-004-7) Smith & Kraus.

Coffee, Society, & Power in Latin America. Ed. by William Roseberry et al. LC 94-14193. (Johns Hopkins Studies in Atlantic History & Culture Ser.). 304p. 1995. text ed. 48.50 (0-8018-4884-9); pap. text ed. 15.95 (0-8018-4887-3) Johns Hopkins.

*Coffee Substitutes - Poetry, Greetings, Etc. Lamp Light Press Staff. (Illus.). 18p. (Orig.). (C). 1995. pap. text ed. 6.95 (0-917593-37-5, Lamp Light Pr) Prosperity & Profits.

Coffee Substitutes with Medicinal Additives: A Recipe Book. Cookbook Consortium Staff. 1993. pap. text ed. 19.95 (0-318-04305-X, Cookbk Consort) Prosperity & Profits.

*Coffee Talk. Donna L. Montgomery. (Illus.). 204p. (Orig.). 1995. pap. 12.95 (0-938577-09-3) St Johns Pub.

*Coffee Talk. Mike Myers & Robin Ruzan. 96p. 1997. pap. 8.95 (0-7868-8085-6) Hyperion.

Coffee, Tea, & Chocolate Wares in the Collection of the Seattle Art Museum. Julie Emerson. (Illus.). 40p. (Orig.). 1991. pap. 6.95 (0-932216-38-2) Seattle Art.

Coffee, Tea, & Cocoa: An Economic & Political Analysis. Vernon D. Wickizer. 512p. 1951. 57.50 (0-8047-0420-1) Stanford U Pr.

Coffee, Tea, & Cocoa: Market Prospects & Development Lending. Shamsher Singh et al. LC 76-17239. 239p. reprint ed. pap. 68.20 (0-7837-4269-X, 2043961) Bks Demand.

Coffee, Three A.M. Brenda Hillman. 1982. pap. 22.50 (0-686-37138-0) Penumbra Press.

Coffee, Three A.M. deluxe ed. Brenda Hillman. 1982. 45.00 (0-686-37137-2) Penumbra Press.

Coffee Too. Suzanne T. Moore. 64p. (Orig.). 1975. pap. 3.95 (0-938758-03-9) MTM Pub Co.

Coffee, Volume 2: Technology. Ed. by R. J. Clarke & Robert Macrae. 312p. 1987. 84.75 (1-85166-034-8, Pub. by Elsevier Applied Sci UK) Elsevier.

*Coffee Will Make You Black. April Sinclair. 256p. 1995. pap. 10.00 (0-380-72459-6) Avon.

Coffee Will Make You Black: A Novel. April Sinclair. LC 93-13271. 256p. 1994. 19.95 (1-56282-796-0) Hyperion.

Coffee with Mama. Karen B. Douglas. 160p. 1994. write for info. (0-9639947-1-9) Suomi-Suerige.

*Coffeebreak Poems. Steven Hartman. (Backpocket Poets Ser.). 28p. (Orig.). 1994. pap. 1.75 (0-916155-27-7) Trout Creek.

*Coffeemakers. rev. ed. Ambrogio Fumagalli. (Bella Cosa Library). (ITA.). 1995. pap. 12.95 (0-8118-1082-8) Chronicle Bks.

Coffey Files. Joseph Coffey. 1993. mass mkt. 4.99 (0-312-92922-6) St Martin.

Coffey Pott Meets the Wolf Man. R. Eugene Jackson. 64p. (J). (gr. 3 up). 1982. pap. 3.00 (0-88680-031-5) I E Clark.

*Coffin. Diane Hoh. (Nightmare Hall Ser.: No. 19). (YA). 1995. pap. 3.50 (0-590-20297-9) Scholastic Inc.

Coffin & Co. Njami Simon. Tr. by Marlene Raderman. 176p. (Orig.). 1988. pap. 3.95 (0-88739-049-8, Blk Lizard) Creat Arts Bk.

Coffin & the Paper Man. Gwendoline Butler. (Worldwide Library Mystery). 1993. mass mkt. 3.99 (0-373-26133-0, 1-26133-8) Harlequin Bks.

*Coffin Creek. large type ed. Matt Logan. (Western Library). 272p. 1995. pap. 14.95 (0-7089-7686-7, Linford) Ulverscroft.

*Coffin Drop. J. Van Dyke. 236p. 1994. pap. write for info. (0-9642734-0-3)

An Asterisk (*) at the beginning of an entry indicates that the title is appearing in BIP for the first time.

Squeek-by Grphs. A fast-paced, suspense-filled mystery set near Ann Arbor, Michigan & centered around the thrilling equestrian sport of combined training. David Breton is the primary suspect in a shooting that crippled his step-father. When tragic accidents happen to the only people who can testify in his behalf, David must prove his innocence by discovering who did the shooting. In order to find answers, David & his mother need to examine the terrors & passions of their past with David's father Marc Breton, a European soccer star & international drug agent. Suspense builds rapidly when David & his mother learn that a stranger is stalking David. A horse trial David rides in turns dangerous when his life is threatened. A review by Rosemary Gordon, a Wayne County Prosecutor in Detroit, Michigan & president of Horse Show Management, Inc. states: "This is an excellent suspense novel with a delightfully accurate setting in the horse world. Horses, riding, & the excitement of competition are accurately portrayed. I picked it up for a cursory sampling & was late to court when I couldn't put it down." Call or write for information to order, Squeek-by Graphics Publications, 9571 Joy Rd., Plymouth, MI 48170-5026. 313-453-2586. ***Publisher Provided Annotation.***

Coffin Family. Ed. by Louis Coffin. LC 62-18214. 576p. 1962. 20.00 (*0-317-47143-0*) Nantucket Hist Assn.

Coffin for Baby. Gwendoline Butler. (Black Dagger Crime Ser.). 192p. 1993. 16.50 (*0-7451-8606-8*, Black Dagger) Chivers N Amer.

Coffin for Baby. large type ed. Gwendoline Butler. 1994. 18.95 (*0-7451-6458-7*, Scarlet Dagger Lrg Print) Chivers N Amer.

Coffin for Charley. Gwendoline Butler. LC 94-12920. 256p. 1994. 20.95 (*0-312-11466-4*, Pub. by Thomas Dunne Bks) St Martin.

Coffin for Dimitrios. Eric Ambler. 1990. pap. 3.95 (*0-88184-619-8*) Carroll & Graf.

Coffin for Dimitrios. Eric Ambler. 214p. reprint ed. lib. bdg. 20.95 (*0-89190-461-1*, Rivercity Pr) Amereon Ltd.

Coffin for Dimitrios. Eric Ambler. 1990. reprint ed. lib. bdg. 18.95 (*0-89968-471-8*) Buccaneer Bks.

Coffin from the Past. large type ed. Gwendoline Butler. 1992. 18.95 (*0-7451-6413-7*, Scarlet Dagger Lrg Print) Chivers N Amer.

Coffin from the Past. large type ed. Gwendoline Butler. 1993. pap. 16.95 (*0-7451-6419-6*, Scarlet Dagger Lrg Print) Chivers N Amer.

Coffin Hollow & Other Ghost Tales. Ruth A. Musick. LC 76-51157. (Illus.). 216p. 1977. pap. 11.00 (*0-8131-1416-0*) U Pr of Ky.

Coffin in the Museum of Crime. Gwendoline Butler. (Mystery Ser.). 1993. mass mkt. 3.99 (*0-373-26121-7*, 1-26121-3) Harlequin Bks.

Coffin in the Museum of Crime. braille ed. Gwendoline Butler. 353p. 1991. vinyl bd. 28.24 (*1-56956-210-5*, BR8445) W A T Braille.

Coffin of Clearwater. Anthony Fitzherbert. (C). 1989. 40.00 (*0-7223-2394-8*, Pub. by A H S Ltd UK) St Mut.

Coffin on a Case. Eve Bunting. LC 92-855. 112p. (J). (gr. 4-7). 1992. 13.95 (*0-06-020273-4*); lib. bdg. 13.89 (*0-06-020274-2*) HarpC Child Bks.

Coffin on a Case. Eve Bunting. LC 92-855. (Trophy Bk.). 112p. (J). (gr. 4-7). 1993. pap. 3.95 (*0-06-440461-7*, Trophy) HarpC Child Bks.

Coffin on Murder Street. Gwendoline Butler. (Mystery Ser.). 1994. mass mkt. 3.99 (*0-373-26147-0*, 1-26147-8) Harlequin Bks.

Coffin on Murder Street. Gwendoline Butler. 224p. 1992. 17.95 (*0-312-07673-8*, Pub. by Thomas Dunne Bks) St Martin.

Coffin Ship. Peter Tonkin. 1992. mass mkt. 4.99 (*0-8041-0872-2*) Ivy Books.

Coffin Ship. large type ed. Peter Tonkin. 1991. 21.95 (*0-7089-2488-3*) Ulverscroft.

*__Coffin to Let.__ large type ed. Freda Bream. (Mystery Ser.). 1994. pap. 14.95 (*0-7089-7624-7*, Linford) Ulverscroft.

*__Coffin Tree.__ large type ed. Gwendoline Butler. LC 95-7486. 1996. write for info. (*0-7862-0456-7*) Thorndike Pr.

Coffin Underground. Gwendoline Butler. 1992. mass mkt. 3.99 (*0-373-26110-1*, 1-26110-6) Harlequin Bks.

Coffinberry: Genealogy of the Coffinberry Family, Descendants of George Lewis Coffinberry, & His Wife Elizabeth (Little) Coffinberry, with Related Families Coffenberry, Gilkison, Keasey, Platt, 1760-1851. Comp. by B. B. Scott. (Illus.). 64p. 1994. reprint ed. lib. bdg. 23.00 (*0-8328-3945-0*); reprint ed. pap. 13.00 (*0-8328-3946-9*) Higginson Bk Co.

Coffin's Overtones of Bel Canto: Phonetic Basis of Artistic Singing with One Hundred Chromatic Vowel-Chart Exercises. Berton Coffin. LC 80-21958. 254p. (C). 1980. Vowel chart only. 10.00 (*0-8108-2028-5*) Scarecrow.

Coffin's Overtones of Bel Canto: Phonetic Basis of Artistic Singing with One Hundred Chromatic Vowel-Chart Exercises, Set. Berton Coffin. LC 80-21958. 254p. (C). 1980. text ed. 42.50 (*0-8108-1370-X*) Scarecrow.

Coffin's Sounds of Singing: Principles & Applications of Vocal Techniques Chromatic Vowel Chart. 2nd ed. Berton Coffin. LC 86-15491. (Illus.). 314p. 1987. 37.50 (*0-8108-1933-3*) Scarecrow.

Cofused Dream. Sandro Penna. Tr. by George Scrivani. 92p. (Orig.). 1988. 5.95 (*0-937815-15-2*) Hanuman Bks.

*__Cog Train to the Zoo.__ (Illus.). 16p. Date not set. pap. 2.95 (*0-614-04446-4*, 25) Mntn Automation.

*__Cog Train to the Zoo.__ Mary Humphreys. (Illus.). 16p. 1990. pap. 2.95 (*0-936206-25-X*) Mntn Automation.

*__Cog Wheel Route.__ (Illus.). 28p. Date not set. pap. 3.95 (*0-614-04444-8*, 33) Mntn Automation.

Cog Wheel Route. Claude Wiatrowski & Margaret Wiatrowski. (Illus.). 28p. 1989. pap. 3.95 (*0-936206-33-0*) Mntn Automation.

Cogadh Mor Nineteen Fourteen to Nineteen Eighteen. Ed. by Acair Ltd. Staff. 1985. 40.00 (*0-86152-016-5*, Pub. by Acair Ltd UK) St Mut.

Cogan's Trade. George V. Higgins. 216p. 1985. pap. 3.50 (*0-88184-150-1*) Carroll & Graf.

Cogel Blue Book: Campaign Finance, Ethics & Lobby Law. 9th ed. Council on Governmental Ethics Laws & Council of State Governments. 1992. 59.00 (*0-87292-968-X*) Coun State Govts.

COGEL Blue Book, 1990-91: Campaign Finance, Ethics & Lobby Law. 8th ed. Ed. by Joyce Bullock. 200p. 1990. pap. 45.00 (*0-87292-956-6*, C-173 090) Coun State Govts.

COGEL Compaign Financing & Lobbying Bibliography. 136p. 1992. pap. 25.00 (*0-87292-967-1*, C-022-91) Coun State Govts.

*__Cogeneration.__ Horlock. 232p. 1995. write for info. (*0-89464-928-0*) Krieger.

Cogeneration. David Hu. (C). 1985. text ed. 59.00 (*0-8359-0771-6*, Reston) P-H.

Cogeneration. Richard K. Miller & Marcia E. Rupnow. (Survey on Technology & Markets Ser.: No. 207). 50p. 1993. pap. text ed. 200.00 (*1-55865-238-8*) Future Tech Surveys.

Cogeneration: Current Prospects & Future Opportunities. 6th ed. Government Institutes, Inc. Staff. 267p. 1987. pap. 72.00 (*0-86587-490-5*) Gov Insts.

Cogeneration: Watt's Around the Corner. (Illus.). 1985. pap. 1.00 (*0-317-39785-0*) Reddy Comm.

Cogeneration: Why, When & How to Assess & Implement a Project. Ed. by Richard H. McMahan, Jr. LC 86-19795. (Series of Special Reports: No. 16). (Illus.). 367p. reprint ed. pap. 104.60 (*0-7837-0684-7*, 2041017) Bks Demand.

Cogeneration & Small Power Production Manual. 3rd ed. Scott A. Spiewak. (Illus.). 664p. 1991. pap. 95.00 (*0-88173-109-9*, P7800) Fairmont Pr.

*__Cogeneration & Small Power Production Manual.__ 4th ed. Spiewak & Fairmont. (Illus.). 308p. (C). 1994. pap. text ed. 95.00 (*0-13-324443-1*) P-H.

Cogeneration District Heating Applications: Papers Presented at the Winter Annual Meeting of the American Society of Mechanical Engineers, San Francisco, California, December 10-15, 1978. American Society of Mechanical Engineers Staff. Ed. by I. Oliker. LC 78-68082. (Illus.). 49p. reprint ed. pap. 25.00 (*0-8357-2869-2*, 2039105) Bks Demand.

Cogeneration Feasibility. Ron L. Highnote. 130p. 1990. student ed 49.95 (*1-880168-04-9*) Inst Applied Sci.

Cogeneration in the Cane Sugar Industry. J. H. Payne. (Sugar Ser.: No. 12). 338p. 1990. 141.00 (*0-444-88826-8*) Elsevier.

Cogeneration of Electricity & Useful Heat. Bruce W. Wilkinson & Richard W. Barnes. 272p. 1980. 119.00 (*0-8493-5615-6*, TK1005, CRC Reprint) Franklin.

Cogeneration Planner's Handbook. Joseph A. Orlando. 1991. 74.00 (*0-88173-111-0*) Fairmont Pr.

Cogenerational & Small Power Production Manual. Scott A. Spiewalk & Larry Weiss. LC 94-7353. 1994. write for info. (*0-88173-200-1*) Fairmont Pr.

Cogent Communication: Overcoming Reading Overload. Charles L. Bernier & A. Neil Yerkey. LC 78-73794. (Contributions in Librarianship & Information Science Ser.: No. 26). (Illus.). xii, 280p. 1979. text ed. 59.95 (*0-313-20893-X*, BEC/) Greenwood.

Cogewea, the Half-Blood. Mourning Dove. LC 80-29687. xxx, 302p. 1981. 30.00 (*0-8032-3069-9*); pap. 9.95 (*0-8032-8110-2*) U of Nebr Pr.

COGFNS Study Guide: 1990 Edition. 2nd ed. Nancy Engel et al. LC 86-72568. 205p. 1990. pap. text ed. 30.00 (*0-937126-15-X*) Am Journal Nurse.

Coggeshalls in America: Genealogy of the Descendants of John Coggeshall of Newport with a Brief Notice of Their English Antecedents. Charles P. Coggeshall & Thellwell R. Coggeshall. LC 83-3163. (Illus.). 424p. 1983. reprint ed. 65.00 (*0-87152-374-4*) Reprint.

Cogitat Ergo Erst: An Introductory Course in Computer Literacy. Columbia Pacific University Faculty Staff & Richard L. Crews. 45p. (C). 1989. pap. text ed. write for info. (*0-945864-21-3*) Columbia Pacific U Pr.

Cogitations. Wilfred R. Bion. 416p. 1992. pap. 59.95 (*0-946439-98-2*, Pub. by Karnac Bks UK) Brunner-Mazel.

Cogitations: A Study of the Cogito in Relation to the Philosophy of Logic & Language, & a Study of Them in Relation to the Cogito. Jerrold J. Katz. (Illus.). 226p. 1988. pap. 19.95 (*0-19-505550-0*) OUP.

Cogito & Hermeneutics: The Question of the Subject in Ricoeur. Domenico Jervolino. (C). 1990. lib. bdg. 85.50 (*0-7923-0824-7*) Kluwer Ac.

*__Cogito, Ergo, Sum: I Think, Therefore, I Exist.__ John E. Blunt & Kathryn L. Murray-Blunt. 32p. 1995. write for info. (*1-887401-01-6*) Essence Immort.

Cogito Seventy-Five: Meditations Metaphysiques. Julien Gracq. 156p. (FRE.). 1992. 24.95 (*0-7859-1199-5*, 2714303366) Fr & Eur.

Cogito 75: Meditations Metaphysiques. Rene Descartes & Andre Robinet. 152p. (FRE.). 1976. 19.95 (*0-7859-1196-0*, 2711601897) Fr & Eur.

Cognac & Collard Greens. A. H. Reynolds. 138p. (Orig.). 1986. 7.00 (*0-938887-00-9*) Ngomas Gourd.

Cognetics: Thinking Skills in Language Arts & Social Sciences. Judith Burr et al. 117p. 1991. teacher ed 89.95 (*1-56602-041-7*); student ed write for info. (*1-56602-054-9*) Research Better.

Cognetics, No. Two: Thinking Skills in Mathematics & Science. Judith Burr et al. 121p. 1992. teacher ed 89.95 (*1-56602-052-2*); student ed write for info. (*1-56602-053-0*) Research Better.

Cognition. John G. Benjafield. 496p. (C). 1991. text ed. 33.00 (*0-13-140211-0*, 670701) P-H.

Cognition. 2nd ed. Arnold L. Glass et al. 522p. (C). 1985. pap. text ed. write for info. (*0-07-554878-X*) McGraw.

Cognition. 2nd ed. Margaret Matlin. 448p. (C). 1989. text ed. 44.00 (*0-03-021658-3*) HB Coll Pubs.

Cognition. 3rd ed. Margaret W. Matlin. LC 92-75763. 554p. 1994. 46.25 (*0-15-500571-5*) HarBrace.

Cognition: An Epistemological Inquiry. Joseph Owens. LC 92-70254. (C). 1992. text ed. 29.95 (*0-268-00792-6*); pap. text ed. 14.95 (*0-268-00791-8*) U of Notre Dame Pr.

Cognition: Conceptual & Methodological Issues. Ed. by Herbert L. Pick, Jr. et al. (Illus.). 374p. 1992. text ed. 40.00 (*1-55798-165-5*) Am Psychol.

Cognition: Theory & Applications. 3rd ed. Stephen K. Reed. LC 91-14250. 400p. (C). 1992. text ed. 47.95 (*0-534-14760-7*) Brooks-Cole.

*__Cognition: Theory & Applications.__ 4th ed. Stephen K. Reed. LC 95-15683. 1996. text ed. 47.95 (*0-534-21954-3*) Brooks-Cole.

Cognition see Reasoning & Decision Making

Cognition & Action in Skilled Behaviour. Ed. by A. M. Colley & John R. Beech. (Advances in Psychology Ser.: No. 55). 426p. 1988. 105.25 (*0-444-70493-0*, North Holland) Elsevier.

Cognition & Action, Vol. 5, No. 3: Social Cognition. Ed. by Daniel M. Wegner & Robin R. Vallacher. 144p. 1988. pap. 15.00 (*0-89862-582-3*) Guilford Pr.

Cognition & Affect: A Developmental Psychology. Laurence R. Simon. LC 86-18659. 280p. 28.95x (*0-87975-340-4*) Prometheus Bks.

Cognition & Categorization. Ed. by Eleanor Rosch & Barbara B. Lloyd. LC 78-6570. 336p. reprint ed. pap. 95.80 (*0-8357-3404-8*, 2039661) Bks Demand.

Cognition & Communication see Knowledge & Symbolization in Saint John of the Cross

Cognition & Computer Programming. Ed. by Karl F. Wender et al. LC 93-44140. (Series in Computational Science). 424p. 1994. 75.00 (*1-56750-094-3*); pap. 79.50 (*1-56750-095-1*) Ablex Pub.

Cognition & Culture: A Cross-Cultural Approach to Cognitive Psychology. Ed. by Jeanette Altarriba. LC 93-36251. (Advances in Psychology Ser.: Vol. 103). 405p. 1993. 140.00 (*0-444-89639-2*, North Holland) Elsevier.

Cognition & Dream Research. Ed. by Robert E. Haskell. LC 82-642121. 332p. 1986. 18.00 (*0-930195-02-7*) Inst Mind Behavior.

Cognition & Emotional Disturbance. Ed. by Russell Grieger & Ingrid Z. Grieger. LC 81-6461. 232p. 1982. 35.95 (*0-89885-022-3*) Human Sci Pr.

Cognition & Environment: Functioning in an Uncertain World. Stephen Kaplan & Rachel Kaplan. 287p. (C). 1989. reprint ed. pap. text ed. 18.95 (*0-914004-50-6*) Ulrich.

Cognition & Eros: A Critique of the Kantian Paradigm. Robin M. Schott. LC 92-34926. 264p. (C). 1993. reprint ed. pap. 13.95 (*0-271-00936-5*) Pa St U Pr.

Cognition & Eye Movements. Ed. by R. Groner & Fraisse. 224p. 1983. 92.50 (*0-444-86354-0*, I-110-82, North Holland) Elsevier.

Cognition & Fact: Materials on Ludwik Fleck. Ed. by Robert S. Cohen & Thomas Schnelle. 1986. lib. bdg. 133.00 (*90-277-1902-0*) Kluwer Ac.

Cognition & Image Formation in Literature. Louk Wijsen. (European University Studies: German Language & Literature: Ser. 1, Vol. 311). 174p. 1980. pap. 33.60 (*3-8204-6598-7*) P Lang Pubs.

Cognition & Instruction. Ed. by D. Klahr. 361p. 1976. 79.95 (*0-89859-434-0*) L Erlbaum Assocs.

Cognition & Instruction. Ed. by Ronna F. Dillon & Robert J. Sternberg. 390p. 1988. reprint ed. pap. text ed. 44.00 (*0-12-216406-7*) Acad Pr.

Cognition & Learning: A Review of the Literature with Reference to Ethnolinguistic Minorities. Patricia M. Davis. LC 91-75098. x, 90p. (Orig.). 1991. pap. 6.00 (*0-88312-100-X*) Summer Instit Ling.

Cognition & Learning: A Review of the Literature with Reference to Ethnolinguistic Minorities, 2 fiche, Set. Patricia M. Davis. LC 91-75098. x, 90p. (Orig.). 1991. fiche 8.00 (*0-88312-935-3*) Summer Instit Ling.

Cognition & Motor Processes. Ed. by W. Prinz & A. F. Sanders. (Illus.). 385p. 1984. 80.00 (*0-387-12855-7*) Spr-Verlag.

Cognition & Perception in the Stroke Patient: A Guide to Functional Outcomes in Occupational Therapy. Kathleen Okkema. LC 92-48191. (Rehabilitation Institute of Chicago Publication Ser.). 250p. 1993. boxed 59.00 (*0-8342-0362-6*, 20362) Aspen Pub.

Cognition & Personal Structure: Computer Access & Analysis. Ed. by James C. Mancuso & Mildred L. Shaw. LC 87-13770. 352p. 1988. text ed. 65.00 (*0-275-92606-0*, C2606, Praeger Pubs) Greenwood.

Cognition & Psychotherapy. Ed. by Michael J. Mahoney & Arthur Freeman. LC 85-3370. 370p. 1985. 60.00 (*0-306-41858-4*, Plenum Pr) Plenum.

Cognition & Rationality in Negotiation. Margaret A. Neale & Max H. Bazerman. 240p. 1991. text ed. 42.95 (*0-02-922515-9*) Free Pr.

*__Cognition & Representation in Linguistic Theory.__ Antoine Culioli. Ed. by Michel Liddle & John T. Stonham. Tr. by John T. Stonham. LC 95-2051. (Current Issues in Linguistic Theory Ser.: No. 112). 160p. 1995. lib. bdg. 45.00x (*0-614-04789-7*) Benjamins North Am.

Cognition & Representation Reconsidered. 2nd ed. Elliot W. Eisner. LC 94-320. 120p. (C). 1994. text ed. 34.00 (*0-8077-3311-3*); pap. text ed. 14.95 (*0-8077-3310-5*) Tchrs Coll.

Cognition & Sentence Production. S. N. Sridhar. (Language & Communication Ser.). (Illus.). 150p. 1988. 64.00 (*0-387-96572-6*) Spr-Verlag.

Cognition & Social Behavior. John S. Carroll & John W. Payne. LC 76-48939. 290p. 1976. text ed. 59.95 (*0-89859-111-2*) L Erlbaum Assocs.

Cognition & Symbolic Structures. Robert E. Haskell. LC 87-11486. 320p. 1987. text ed. 55.00 (*0-89391-368-5*) Ablex Pub.

Cognition & the Development of Language. Ed. by John R. Hayes. LC 71-105383. 382p. reprint ed. pap. 108.90 (*0-317-07748-1*, 2012611) Bks Demand.

Cognition & the Menstrual Cycle. Ed. by J. T. Richardson. (Contributions to Psychology & Medicine Ser.). (Illus.). xi, 216p. 1991. 65.00 (*0-387-97612-4*) Spr-Verlag.

Cognition & the Symbolic Processes, Vol. 2. Ed. by Walter B. Weimer & David S. Palermo. 416p. 1982. 89.95 (*0-89859-066-3*) L Erlbaum Assocs.

Cognition & the Symbolic Processes, Vol. 3: Applied & Ecological Perspectives. Ed. by R. R. Hoffman. 552p. (C). 1991. pap. 39.95 (*0-8058-0904-X*) L Erlbaum Assocs.

Cognition & the Symbolic Processes, Vol. 3: Applied & Ecological Perspectives. Ed. by R. R. Hoffman & D. S. Palermo. 552p. (C). 1991. text ed. 99.95 (*0-8058-0903-1*) L Erlbaum Assocs.

Cognition & the Visual Arts. Robert L. Solso. (Cognitive Psychology Ser.). (Illus.). 264p. 1994. 42.50 (*0-262-19346-9*, Bradford Bks) MIT Pr.

Cognition As Intuitive Statistics. Gerd Gigerenzer & David Murray. 232p. 1987. text ed. 39.95 (*0-89859-570-3*) L Erlbaum Assocs.

Cognition, Computing & Cooperation. Scott P. Robertson et al. LC 89-14895. (Cognition & Computing Ser.: Vol. 2). 440p. (C). 1990. text ed. 59.50 (*0-89391-536-X*); pap. text ed. 29.50 (*0-89391-615-3*) Ablex Pub.

Cognition, Convention, & Communication. Mark H. Bickhard. LC 80-20799. 288p. 1980. text ed. 65.00 (*0-275-90455-5*, C0455, Praeger Pubs) Greenwood.

*__Cognition, Culture & Language in Bilingual Children: Conceptual & Semantic Development in a Multicultural America.__ Virginia Gonzalez. 265p. (C). Date not set. text ed. 64.95 (*1-57292-013-0*); pap. text ed. 44.95 (*1-57292-012-2*) Austin & Winfield.

Cognition, Curriculum, & Comprehension. Ed. by John T. Guthrie. LC 77-24012. 314p. reprint ed. pap. 89.50 (*0-685-23492-4*, 2027915) Bks Demand.

Cognition, Curriculum & Literacy. Ed. by Carolyn Hedley et al. LC 89-78061. 240p. (C). 1990. text ed. 39.50 (*0-89391-617-X*); pap. 24.50 (*0-89391-673-0*) Ablex Pub.

Cognition, Development & Instruction. Ed. by John R. Kirby & John B. Biggs. LC 80-523. (Educational Psychology Ser.). 1980. text ed. 46.00 (*0-12-409550-X*) Acad Pr.

Cognition, Education, & Deafness: Directions for Research & Instruction. Ed. by David S. Martin. LC 85-12992. 232p. 1985. text ed. 21.95 (*0-930323-12-2*) Gallaudet Univ Pr.

Cognition, Education, & Multimedia: Exploring Ideas in High Technology. Ed. by Don Nix & Rand Spiro. 232p. 1990. 49.95 (*0-8058-0036-0*) L Erlbaum Assocs.

Cognition in Action. Ed. by Mary Smyth et al. 360p. 1987. text ed. 69.95 (*0-86377-039-8*) L Erlbaum Assocs.

*__Cognition in Action.__ Ed. by Mary Smyth et al. 464p. 1994. pap. 29.95 (*0-86377-348-6*) L Erlbaum Assocs.

*__Cognition in Action.__ 2nd ed. Ed. by Mary Smyth et al. 464p. 1994. 89.95 (*0-86377-347-8*) L Erlbaum Assocs.

Cognition in Close Relationships. Ed. by Garth Fletcher & Frank D. Fincham. 360p. 1991. text ed. 69.95 (*0-8058-0568-0*) L Erlbaum Assocs.

Cognition in Early Childhood. Janie D. Osborn & D. Keith Osborn. LC 83-71727. (Illus.). 237p. (C). 1983. lib. bdg. 15.95 (*0-918772-11-7*); pap. text ed. 9.95 (*0-918772-12-5*) Daye Pr.

Cognition in Human Motivation & Learning. Ed. by Gery D'Ydewalle & Willy Lens. LC 80-23715. 304p. 1981. text ed. 59.95 (*0-89859-067-1*) L Erlbaum Assocs.

Cognition in Individual & Social Contexts, Vol. 3: Proceedings of the 24th International Congress of Psychology of the International Union of Psychological Science, Sydney, Australia, Aug. 28-Sept. 2, 1988. Ed. by A. F. Bennett & K. M. McConkey. 608p. 1990. 125.75 (*0-444-88521-8*, North Holland) Elsevier.

Cognition in Learning & Memory: Symposium on Cognition 5th: 1969: Pittsburgh. Ed. by Lee W. Gregg. LC 72-6107. (Illus.). 271p. reprint ed. pap. 77.30 (*0-317-08284-1*, 2012427) Bks Demand.

Cognition in Practice: Mind, Mathematics & Culture. Jean Lave. (Illus.). 264p. 1988. pap. 18.95 (*0-521-35734-9*) Cambridge U Pr.

C

An Asterisk (*) at the beginning of an entry indicates that the title is appearing in BIP for the first time. 1345

Cognition in Practice: Mind, Mathematics & Culture. Jean Lave. (Illus.). 264p. 1988. 64.95 (0-521-35015-8) Cambridge U Pr.

Cognition in Schizophrenia & Paranoia: The Integration of Cognitive Processes. Peter A. Magaro. LC 80-13870. 351p. 1980. text ed. 69.95 (0-89859-028-0) L Erlbaum Assocs.

Cognition in Social Worlds. Ed. by Angus Gellatly et al. (Keele Cognition Seminar Ser.: No. 2). (Illus.). 272p. 1989. 70.00 (0-19-852173-1) OUP.

Cognition in Special Children: Comparative Approaches to Retardation, Learning Disabilities & Giftedness. Ed. by John D. Borkowski & Jeanne D. Day. LC 87-11421. 256p. (C). 1987. text ed. 39.50 (0-89391-296-4) Ablex Pub.

*Cognition in the Wild. Edwin Hutchins. LC 94-21562. 1994. 45.00x (0-262-08231-4, Bradford Bks) MIT Pr.

Cognition Information Processing & Motivation see International Congress of Psychology of the International Union of Psychological Science, XXIII, Acapulco, Mexico, 2-7 September 1984: Proceedings

Cognition, Information Processing, & Psychophysics: Basic Issues. Hans-Georg Geissler et al. 334p. 1991. text ed. 69.95 (0-8058-0995-3) L Erlbaum Assocs.

Cognition, Language, & Consciousness: Integrative Levels. Ed. by Gary Greenberg & Ethel Tobach. (T. C. Schneirla Conference Ser.: Vol. 2). 312p. 1987. 69.95 (0-89859-722-6) L Erlbaum Assocs.

Cognition, Metacognition & Reading. D. L. Forrest-Pressley & T. Gary Waller. (Language & Communication Ser.: Vol. 18). (Illus.). 440p. 1984. 71.00 (0-387-90983-4) Spr-Verlag.

Cognition of the Literary Work of Art. Roman Ingarden. Tr. by Ruth A. Crowley & Kenneth R. Olsen. LC 73-80117. (Studies in Phenomenology & Existential Philosophy). 436p. (C). 1974. pap. 19.95 (0-8101-0599-3) Northwestern U Pr.

Cognition, Personality, & Clinical Psychology: A Symposium Held at the University of Colorado. Ed. by Richard Jessor & Seymour Feshbach. LC 67-21106. (Jossey-Bass Behavioral Science Ser.). 240p. reprint ed. pap. 68.40 (0-317-08236-1, 2013854) Bks Demand.

Cognition, Semantics & Philosophy: Proceedings of the First International Colloquium on Cognitive Science. (Philosophical Studies in Philosophy Ser.). 344p. (C). 1991. lib. bdg. 115.50 (0-7923-1538-3) Kluwer Ac.

*Cognition, Teaching & Assessment. Pressley & McCormick. (C). 1995. text ed. 34.00 (0-673-99400-7) HarpCollege.

Cognition Through Color. Jules Davidoff. (Issues in the Biology of Language Ser.). (Illus.). 200p. 1991. 37.50 (0-262-04115-4, Bradford Bks) MIT Pr.

Cognition, Value, & Price: A General Theory of Value. Henry K. Woo. 200p. (C). 1992. text ed. 39.50 (0-472-10331-8) U of Mich Pr.

Cognitive-Affective Processes: New Ways of Psychoanalytic Modeling. Ed. by U. Moser & I. Von Zeppelin. (Monographien der Breuninger-Stiffung Stuttgart Ser.). (Illus.). vii, 183p. 1991. pap. 51.00 (0-387-53993-X) Spr-Verlag.

Cognitive Analysis of Dyslexia. Philip H. Seymour. (International Library of Psychology). 368p. 1986. text ed. 59.95 (0-7100-9841-3, 98413, RKP) Routledge.

Cognitive Analysis of Social Behavior. J. P. Codol & J. P. Leyens. 1982. lib. bdg. 94.00 (90-247-2701-4) Kluwer Ac.

Cognitive-Analytic Therapy: Active Participation in Change - A New Integration in Brief Psychotherapy. Anthony Ryle et al. 267p. 1992. reprint ed. pap. text ed. 38.95 (0-471-93069-5) Wiley.

*Cognitive Analytic Therapy: Developments in Theory & Practice. Ed. by Anthony Ryle. LC 94-45112. (Psychotherapy & Counselling Ser.). 1995. write for info. (0-471-95602-3); pap. text ed. 29.95 (0-471-94355-X) Wiley.

Cognitive & Affective Learning Strategies. Ed. by Harold F. O'Neil, Jr. & Charles D. Spielberger. LC 79-18162. (Educational Technology Ser.). 1979. text ed. 52.00 (0-12-526680-4) Acad Pr.

Cognitive & Affective Responses to Advertising. Ed. by Patricia Cafferata & Alice M. Tybout. 432p. 1988. text ed. 65.00 (0-669-14830-X) Free Pr.

Cognitive & Behavioral Interventions: An Empirical Approach to Mental Health Problems. Ed. by Linda Craighead et al. 464p. 1993. 38.95 (0-205-14586-8) Allyn.

Cognitive & Behavioral Performance Factors in Atypical Aging. Ed. by M. L. Howe et al. (Illus.). 288p. 1990. 60.00 (0-387-97129-7, 3321) Spr-Verlag.

Cognitive & Behavioral Treatment: Methods & Application. Ed. by Donald K. Granvold. LC 93-24064. 1994. text ed. 48.95 (0-534-19194-0) Brooks-Cole.

*Cognitive & Computational Aspects of Face Recognition: Explorations in Face Space. Ed. by Tim Valentine. LC 94-41142. (International Library of Psychology). 1995. write for info. (0-415-11493-4) Routledge.

Cognitive & Constructive Psychotherapies: Theory, Research, & Practice. Ed. by Michael J. Mahoney. (Illus.). 232p. 1994. 38.95 (0-8261-8610-6) Springer Pub.

Cognitive & Emotional Disturbance in the Elderly: Clinical Issues. Ed. by Carl Eisdorfer & Robert O. Friedel. LC 77-77488. 183p. reprint ed. pap. 52.20 (0-8357-7613-1, 2056936) Bks Demand.

Cognitive & Instructional Processes in History & the Social Sciences. Ed. by Mario Carretero & James F. Voss. 456p. 1994. text ed. 89.95 (0-8058-1564-3); pap. 34.50 (0-8058-1565-1) L Erlbaum Assocs.

Cognitive & Linguistic Analyses of Test Performance. Ed. by Roy O. Freedle & Richard Duran. LC 86-10888. (Advances in Discourse Processes Ser.: Vol. 22). 416p. 1987. text ed. 85.00 (0-89391-295-6); pap. text ed. 39.50 (0-89391-366-9) Ablex Pub.

Cognitive & Motivational Aspects of Action. Ed. by W. Hacker et al. 174p. 1983. 74.50 (0-444-86348-6, North Holland) Elsevier.

Cognitive & Motivational Aspects of Instruction. Glaser & Lompscher. 190p. 1983. 84.75 (0-444-86351-6, I-109-82, North Holland) Elsevier.

Cognitive & Neurological Approaches to Mental Imagery. Ed. by Michel Denis et al. 1988. lib. bdg. 140.00 (90-247-3659-5) Kluwer Ac.

Cognitive & Psychometric Analysis of Analogical Problem Solving. I. I. Bejar et al. (Recent Research in Psychology Ser.). (Illus.). 224p. 1990. pap. 43.00 (0-387-97321-4) Spr-Verlag.

*Cognitive & Social Action. Rosaria Conte & Christiano Castelfranchi. 192p. 1995. 54.95 (1-85728-186-1, Pub. by UCL Pr UK) Taylor & Francis.

*Cognitive Appraisal, Emotion, & Empathy. Becky Omdahl. 288p. 1995. text ed. 59.95 (0-8058-1479-5) L Erlbaum Assocs.

Cognitive Approach to Learning Disabilities. 2nd ed. D. Kim Reid et al. LC 90-19787. 495p. 1991. text ed. 39.00 (0-89079-421-9, 1941) PRO-ED.

Cognitive Approaches in Neuropsychological Rehabilitation. Ed. by X. Seron & G. Deloche. (Neuropsychology & Neurolinguistics Ser.). 416p. 1989. 79.95 (0-89859-615-7) L Erlbaum Assocs.

Cognitive Approaches in Special Education. David A. Sugden. 220p. 1989. 75.00 (1-85000-419-6, Falmer Pr); pap. 35.00 (1-85000-418-8, Falmer Pr) Taylor & Francis.

Cognitive Approaches to Automated Instruction. Ed. by J. Wesley Regian & Valerie Shute. 264p. 1992. text ed. 59.95 (0-8058-0992-9) L Erlbaum Assocs.

Cognitive Approaches to Human Perception. Ed. by Soledad Ballesteros. LC 93-6805. 304p. 1993. 69.95 (0-8058-1043-9) L Erlbaum Assocs.

Cognitive Approaches to Neuropsychology. Ed. by J. Mark Williams & C. J. Long. LC 88-25178. (Human Neuropsychology Ser.). (Illus.). 374p. 1988. 95.00 (0-306-43024-X, Plenum Pr) Plenum.

Cognitive Approaches to Reading. Ed. by John R. Beech & Ann M. Colley. 1987. text ed. 132.00 (0-471-91169-0) Wiley.

Cognitive Approaches to Special Education. Ed. by David A. Sugden. 220p. 1988. write for info. (0-318-65442-3, Falmer Pr) Taylor & Francis.

*Cognitive Approaches to the Seriously Mentally Ill: Dialogue Across the Barrier. Barbara A. Olevitch. LC 95-6348. 192p. 1995. text ed. 55.00 (0-275-95244-4, Praeger Pubs) Greenwood.

Cognitive Aspects of Visual Languages & Visual Interfaces. Ed. by Michael J. Tauber et al. LC 94-2522. 1994. write for info. (0-444-89947-2, North Holland) Elsevier.

Cognitive Aspects of Computer-Supported Tasks. Yvonne Waern. 375p. 1989. text ed. 112.50 (0-471-91141-0) Wiley.

*Cognitive Aspects of Human-Computer Interaction for Geographic Information Systems: Proceedings of the NATO Advanced Research Workshop, Palma de Mallorca, Spain, March 20-25, 1994. Ed. by Timothy L. Nyerges. (NATO Advanced Science Institutes Series C). 448p. (C). 1995. lib. bdg. 225.00 (0-7923-3595-3) Kluwer Ac.

Cognitive Aspects of Language Use. Ed. by A. Kasher. 290p. 1989. 97.50 (0-444-87150-0, North Holland) Elsevier.

Cognitive Aspects of Religious Symbolism. Ed. by Pascal Boyer. LC 92-15803. (Illus.). 230p. (C). 1993. 44.95 (0-521-43288-X) Cambridge U Pr.

*Cognitive Aspects of Reporting Cancer Prevention Examinations & Tests. National Center for Health Statistics Staff. (Series Reports: Series 6, No. 7). 161p. Date not set. write for info. (0-614-02905-8) Natl Ctr Health Stats.

*Cognitive Aspects of Reporting Cancer Prevention Examinations & Tests. Seymour Sudman et al. LC 94-35224. (Vital & Health Statistics, Series 6, Cognition & Survey Measurement: No. 7). 1994. 12.00 (0-8406-0499-8) Natl Ctr Health Stats.

Cognitive Aspects of Skilled Typewriting. Ed. by William E. Cooper. (Illus.). 417p. 1983. 81.00 (0-387-90774-2) Spr-Verlag.

Cognitive Aspects of Social Behaviour in the Domestic Fowl. Ed. by R. Zayan & I. J. Duncan. 508p. 1987. 143.75 (0-444-42756-2) Elsevier.

Cognitive Aspects of Stimulus Control. Ed. by Vern Honig & J. Gregor Fetterman. 456p. 1991. text ed. 89.95 (0-8058-0983-X) L Erlbaum Assocs.

Cognitive Assessment. Carol R. Glass & Myles Genest. Ed. by Thomas V. Merluzzi et al. LC 85-32041. 532p. 1986. pap. 25.00x (0-8147-5425-2) NYU Pr.

Cognitive Assessment. Ed. by Thomas V. Merluzzi et al. LC 80-24870. (Guilford Clinical Psychology & Psychotherapy Ser.). (Illus.). 548p. reprint ed. pap. 156.20 (0-7837-0689-8, 2041022) Bks Demand.

Cognitive Assessment: A Multidisciplinary Perspective. Ed. by Cecil R. Reynolds. (Perspectives on Individual Differences Ser.). (Illus.). 265p. (C). 1994. 45.00 (0-306-44434-8, Plenum Pr) Plenum.

Cognitive Assessment of Language & Math Outcomes. Ed. by Sue M. Legg et al. LC 90-36747. (Advances in Discourse Processes Ser.: Vol. 36). 304p. (C). 1990. text ed. 65.00 (0-89391-541-6); pap. text ed. 39.50 (0-89391-542-4) Ablex Pub.

Cognitive Bases of Interpersonal Communication. Ed. by Dean E. Hewes. (Communication Ser.). 248p. 1994. text ed. 49.95 (0-8058-0469-2) L Erlbaum Assocs.

Cognitive Bases of Mental Disorders. Ed. by Peter A. Magaro. (Annual Review of Psychopathology Ser.: Vol. 1). 352p. (C). 1990. text ed. 49.95 (0-8039-4009-2); pap. text ed. 24.00 (0-8039-4010-6) Sage.

Cognitive Bases of Musical Communication. Ed. by Mari R. Jones & Susan Holleran. (Science Ser.). (Illus.). 298p. (C). 1992. 40.00 (1-55798-127-2) Am Psychol.

Cognitive Behavior Therapy in School. Hughes. (C). 1988. 40.95 (0-205-14375-X, H4375); pap. 21.95 (0-205-14376-8, H4376) Allyn.

Cognitive Behavior Therapy with Children. Ed. by Andrew W. Meyers & W. Edward Craighead. LC 83-16116. (Applied Clinical Psychology Ser.). 514p. 1984. 75.00 (0-306-41291-8, Plenum Pr) Plenum.

Cognitive-Behavior Therapy with Women: A Special Issue of Journal of Rational-Emotive & Cognitive-Behavior Therapy. Ed. by Susan Walen & Russell M. Grieger. 120p. 1987. pap. 16.95 (0-89885-384-2) Human Sci Pr.

Cognitive-Behavioral Approach to Counseling Psychology: Implications for Practice, Research, & Training. Gerald L. Stone. LC 80-21344. 208p. 1980. text ed. 55.00 (0-275-90557-8, C0557, Praeger Pubs) Greenwood.

Cognitive-Behavioral Approaches to Psychotherapy. Ed. by Wendy Dryden & William L. Golden. 392p. 1987. 55.00 (0-89116-774-9) Hemisp Pub.

Cognitive-Behavioral Assessment & Therapy with Adolescents. Janet M. Zarb. LC 92-16165. 272p. 1992. 29.50 (0-87630-685-7) Brunner-Mazel.

*Cognitive-Behavioral Coping Skills Therapy Manual: A Clinical Research Guide for Therapists Treating Individuals with Alcohol Abuse & Dependence. Ed. by Ronald Kadden et al. (Illus.). 101p. (Orig.). (C). 1994. pap. text ed. 75.00x (0-7881-0899-9) Diane Pub.

Cognitive-Behavioral Interventions. Clive R. Hollin. (Practitioner Guidebook Ser.). (C). 1989. pap. 25.95 (0-205-14368-7, H4368, Longwood Div) Allyn.

Cognitive Behavioral Interventions: Theory, Research & Procedures. Ed. by Philip C. Kendall & Steven D. Hollon. (Personality & Psychopathology Ser.). 1979. text ed. 85.00 (0-12-404480-8) Acad Pr.

Cognitive-Behavioral Interviewing for Adult Disorders. Peter H. Wilson et al. LC 88-45397. 192p. 1989. text ed. 37.50x (0-8018-3740-5) Johns Hopkins.

Cognitive-Behavioral Marital Therapy. Donald H. Baucom & Norman Epstein. LC 89-7279. 448p. 1990. 49.95 (0-87630-558-3) Brunner-Mazel.

Cognitive-Behavioral Play Therapy. Susan M. Knell. LC 92-49558. 304p. 1994. 35.00 (0-87668-089-9) Aronson.

Cognitive Behavioral Procedure with Children & Adolescents: A Practical Guide. Ed. by A. J. Finch et al. 444p. 1992. 43.95 (0-205-13435-1, Longwood Div) Allyn.

Cognitive-Behavioral Psychology in the Schools: A Comprehensive Handbook. Ed. by Jan N. Hughes & Robert J. Hall. LC 88-23598. 581p. 1989. lib. bdg. 55.00 (0-89862-736-2) Guilford Pr.

Cognitive-Behavioral Relaxation Training: A New System of Strategies for Treatment & Assessment. Jonathan Smith. 176p. 1990. 25.95 (0-8261-7070-6) Springer Pub.

Cognitive-Behavioral Strategies in Crisis Intervention. Ed. by Frank M. Datilio & Arthur Freeman. 412p. 1994. lib. bdg. 37.95 (0-89862-221-2) Guilford Pr.

Cognitive-Behavioral Therapy for Impulsive Children. 2nd ed. Philip C. Kendall & Lauren Braswell. LC 92-49966. 290p. 1993. lib. bdg. 27.95 (0-89862-013-9) Guilford Pr.

Cognitive-Behavioral Therapy of Schizophrenia. David G. Kingdon & Douglas Turkington. LC 93-31476. 224p. 1993. lib. bdg. 27.50 (0-89862-335-9) Guilford Pr.

Cognitive-Behavioral Therapy with ADHD Children: Child, Family & School Interventions. Lauren Braswell & Michael L. Bloomquist. LC 91-16596. 391p. 1991. lib. bdg. 40.00 (0-89862-764-8) Guilford Pr.

Cognitive-Behavioral Therapy with Families. Ed. by Norman B. Epstein et al. LC 87-36809. 392p. 1988. 47.95 (0-87630-503-6) Brunner-Mazel.

Cognitive Behavioral Treatment of Borderline Personality Disorder. Marsha M. Linehan. LC 93-20483. (Diagnosis & Treatment of Mental Disorders Ser.). 558p. 1993. lib. bdg. 39.50 (0-89862-183-6) Guilford Pr.

Cognitive Behaviour Therapy for Psychiatric Problems: A Practical Guide. Ed. by Keith E. Hawton et al. (Illus.). 472p. 1989. pap. 35.00 (0-19-261587-4) OUP.

Cognitive-Behavioural Approach to Clients' Problems. Mike Scott. (Tavistock Library of Social Work Practice). 224p. 1989. 45.00 (0-415-01740-8, A3275); pap. 19.95 (0-415-01741-6, A3279) Routledge.

Cognitive-Behavioural Counselling in Action. Peter Trower et al. (Counselling in Action Ser.). 160p. (C). 1988. text ed. 44.00 (0-8039-8047-7); pap. text ed. 19.95 (0-8039-8048-5) Sage.

*Cognitive-Behavioural Interventions with Psychotic Disorders. Ed. by Gillian Haddock & Peter D. Slade. LC 95-16043. 1995. write for info. (0-415-10289-8); pap. write for info. (0-415-10290-1) Routledge.

Cognitive-Behavioural Therapy. enl. rev. ed. Brian Sheldon. LC 94-18585. Orig. Title: Behaviour Modification. 256p. 1994. 59.95x (0-415-09373-2, B3993); pap. 18.95 (0-415-09374-0, B3997) Routledge.

Cognitive Biases. Ed. by J. P. Caverni et al. (Advances in Psychology Ser.: No. 68). 576p. 1990. 130.75 (0-444-88413-0, North Holland) Elsevier.

Cognitive Brain. Arnold Trehub. (Illus.). 344p. 1994. pap. 18.00 (0-262-70049-2, Bradford Bks) MIT Pr.

*Cognitive Carpentry: A Blueprint for How to Build a Person. John Pollock. 354p. 1995. 34.95x (0-262-16152-4, Bradford Bks) MIT Pr.

Cognitive Challenge Cards. Catherine Ross. 1976. pap. 12.00 (0-87879-188-4) Acad Therapy.

Cognitive Classroom Learning. Gary D. Phye & Thomas Andre. (Educational Psychology Ser.). 1986. text ed. 61.00 (0-12-554252-6) Acad Pr.

Cognitive Coaching: Approaching Renaissance Schools. Arthur L. Costa & Robert J. Garmston. (Illus.). 252p. (Orig.). (C). 1994. text ed. 32.95 (0-926842-37-4) CG Pubs Inc.

*Cognitive-Communicative Abilities Following Brain Injury: A Functional Approach. Leila L. Hartley. (Neurogenic Communication Disorders Ser.). (Illus.). 384p. (Orig.). (C). 1994. pap. text ed. 45.00 (1-56593-102-5, 0405) Singular Publishing.

Cognitive Components in Cerebral Event Related Potentials & Selective Attention. Ed. by J. E. Desmedt. (Progress in Clinical Neurophysiology Ser.: Vol. 6). (Illus.). 1979. 94.50 (3-8055-2760-8) S Karger.

Cognitive Computer: On Language, Learning, & Artificial Intelligence. Roger C. Schank & Peter Childers. 288p. 1985. write for info. (0-201-06446-4) Addison-Wesley.

Cognitive Control: A Study of Individual Consistencies in Cognitive Behavior. Riley W. Gardner et al. (Psychological Issues Monograph: No. 4, Vol. 1, No. 4). 85p. (Orig.). 1959. text ed. 26.00 (0-8236-1000-4) Intl Univs Pr.

Cognitive Control Therapy. Santostefano. (C). 1985. 31.95 (0-205-14476-4, H4476); pap. 21.95 (0-205-14475-6, H4475) Allyn.

Cognitive Coping, Families, & Disability. Ed. by Ann P. Turnbull et al. 304p. (C). 1993. pap. text ed. 29.00 (1-55766-114-6, 1146) P H Brookes.

Cognitive Counseling & Persons with Special Needs: Adapting Behavioral Approaches to the Social Context. Herbert Lovett. LC 85-3495. 160p. 1985. pap. text ed. 19.95 (0-275-91651-0, B1651, Praeger Pubs) Greenwood.

Cognitive Developement. Marvin W. Daehler & Danuta Bukatko. 432p. (C). 1985. text ed. write for info. (0-07-554432-6) McGraw.

Cognitive Development. Thomas F. Gross. LC 84-14982. (Psychology Ser.). 255p. (C). 1985. pap. 24.95 (0-534-03363-6) Brooks-Cole.

Cognitive Development. Aleksandr R. Luria. 180p. 1982. pap. 12.00 (0-674-13732-9) HUP.

Cognitive Development. Melinda Small. 530p. (C). 1990. text ed. 40.00 (0-15-507858-5) HB Coll Pubs.

Cognitive Development. 3rd ed. John H. Flavell et al. LC 92-24487. 384p. 1992. pap. text ed. 31.60 (0-13-140039-8) P-H.

Cognitive Development: An Information Processing Approach. John McShane. (Illus.). 288p. (Orig.). (C). 1991. pap. text ed. 24.95 (0-631-17019-7) Blackwell Pubs.

Cognitive Development: Psychological & Biological Perspectives. Rosemary A. Rosser. 1993. pap. text ed. 33.75 (0-205-13965-5) Allyn.

Cognitive Development: Research Based on a Neo-Piagetian Approach. Ed. by John A. Keats et al. LC 77-1717. 478p. reprint ed. pap. 136.30 (0-318-34687-7, 2031759) Bks Demand.

Cognitive Development among Sioux Children. Gilbert Voyat. LC 83-2463. (Cognition & Language Ser.). 172p. 1983. 49.50 (0-306-41276-4, Plenum Pr) Plenum.

Cognitive Development & Child Psychotherapy. Ed. by S. R. Shirk. LC 88-17854. (Perspectives in Developmental Psychology Ser.). (Illus.). 360p. 1988. 59.50 (0-306-42880-6, Plenum Pr) Plenum.

Cognitive Development & the Acquisition of Language. Ed. by Timothy E. Moore. 1973. text ed. 55.00 (0-12-505850-0) Acad Pr.

Cognitive Development in Adulthood. Ed. by M. L. Howe & Charles J. Brainerd. (Cognitive Development Ser.). (Illus.). 400p. 1988. 128.00 (0-387-96697-8) Spr-Verlag.

Cognitive Development in Atypical Children: Progress in Cognitive Development Research. Ed. by L. S. Siegel & F. J. Morrison. (Cognitive Development Ser.). (Illus.). 190p. 1984. 58.00 (0-387-96008-2) Spr-Verlag.

Cognitive Development in Infancy. Ed. by John Oates & Sue Sheldon. 320p. 1988. 69.95 (0-86377-085-1); pap. text ed. 34.50 (0-86377-086-X) L Erlbaum Assocs.

Cognitive Development to Adolescence. Ed. by Ken Richardson & Sue Sheldon. 336p. 1988. 69.95 (0-86377-087-8); pap. text ed. 29.95 (0-86377-088-6) L Erlbaum Assocs.

Cognitive Development Today: Piaget & His Critics. Peter Sutherland. 192p. 1992. pap. 24.95 (1-85396-133-7, Pub. by Paul Chapman UK) Taylor & Francis.

Cognitive-Developmental Psychology of James Mark Baldwin: Current Theory & Research in Genetic Epistemology. John M. Broughton & John D. Freeman-Moir. LC 81-7885. (Publications for the Advancement of Theory & History in Psychology, the PATH Ser.). 386p. 1982. 55.00 (0-89391-043-0) Ablex Pub.

Cognitive Disorders: Pathophysiology & Treatment. Ed. by Thal et al. (Neurological Disease & Therapy Ser.: Vol. 11). 400p. 1992. 150.00 (0-8247-8601-7) Dekker.

*Cognitive Ecology. 2nd ed. Ed. by Morton P. Friedman et al. (Handbook of Perception & Cognition Ser.). (Illus.). 430p. 1995. boxed write for info. (0-12-161966-4) Acad Pr.

Cognitive Economy: The Economic Dimension of the Theory of Knowledge. Nicholas Rescher. LC 89-5425. 178p. 1989. 49.95 (0-8229-3617-8) U of Pittsburgh Pr.

Cognitive Education & Testing: A Methodological Approach. Eugene J. Meehan. LC 91-3. (Contributions to the Study of Education Ser.: No. 47). 224p. 1991. text ed. 49.95 (0-313-27889-X, MGN, Greenwood Pr) Greenwood.

Cognitive Effects of Early Brain Injury. Casey Dorman & Bilha Katzir. LC 94-6782. (Johns Hopkins Series in Psychiatry & Neuroscience). 1994. text ed. 55.00x (0-8018-4856-3) Johns Hopkins.

Cognitive Electrophysiology. Ed. by H. J. Heinze et al. xiii, 383p. 1993. 99.00 (0-8176-3726-5) Birkhauser.

An Asterisk (*) at the beginning of an entry indicates that the title is appearing in BIP for the first time.

Cognitive Engineering in Complex Dynamic Worlds: From a Special Issue of the International Journal of Man-Machine Studies. Ed. by Erik Hollnagel et al. (Computers & People Ser.). 300p. 1989. text ed. 60.00 (*0-12-352655-8*) Acad Pr.

Cognitive Engineering in the Design of Human-Computer Interaction & Expert Systems, Vol. 2: Proceedings of the Second International Conference, Honolulu, HI, August 10-14, 1987. Ed. by Gavriel Salvendy. (Advances in Human Factors-Ergonomics Ser.: No. 10B). 592p. 1987. 156.50 (*0-444-42848-8*); Set (with Vol. 1). 231.00 (*0-444-42849-6*) Elsevier.

*__Cognitive Environment Simulation As a Tool for Modeling Human Performance & Reliability.__ 1995. lib. bdg. 251.95 (*0-8490-6738-3*) Gordon Pr.

Cognitive Ergonomics: Understanding, Learning & Designing Human-Computer Interaction. Ed. by Pierre Falzon. (Computers & People Ser.). 261p. 1990. text ed. 66.00 (*0-12-248290-5*) Acad Pr.

Cognitive Ergonomics & Human Computer Interaction. Ed. by J. Long & A. Whitefield. (Cambridge Series on Human-Computer Interaction: No. 1). 250p. (C). 1989. 64.95 (*0-521-37179-1*) Cambridge U Pr.

Cognitive Ethology: The Minds of Other Animals Essays in Honor of Donald R. Griffin. Ed. by Carolyn Ristau. (Comparative Cognition & Neuroscience Ser.). 344p. 1990. text ed. 69.95 (*0-8058-0251-7*); pap. 29.95 (*0-8058-0252-5*) L Erlbaum Assocs.

Cognitive-Experiential Therapy: An Integrative Ego Psychotherapy. Melvin L. Weiner. LC 85-11030. (Illus.). 264p. 1985. 39.95 (*0-87630-382-3*) Brunner-Mazel.

Cognitive Foundations of Calculated Speech: Controlling Understandings in Conversation & Persuasion. Robert Sanders. LC 86-5869. (Series in Human Communication Processes). 273p. (C). 1986. 74.50 (*0-88706-350-0*); pap. 24.95 (*0-88706-351-9*) State U NY Pr.

Cognitive Foundations of Clinical Psychology. Chris R. Brewin. 224p. 1988. 59.95 (*0-86377-098-3*) L Erlbaum Assocs.

Cognitive Foundations of Musical Pitch. Carol L. Krumhansl. (Oxford Psychology Ser.: No. 17). (Illus.). 318p. 1990. 45.00 (*0-19-505475-X*) OUP.

Cognitive Foundations of Natural History: Towards an Anthropology of Science. Scott Atran. (Illus.). 360p. (C). 1990. 74.95 (*0-521-37293-3*) Cambridge U Pr.

Cognitive Foundations of Natural History: Towards an Anthropology of Science. Scott Atran. (C). 1993. pap. 24.95 (*0-521-43871-3*) Cambridge U Pr.

Cognitive Foundations of Personality Traits. S. Kreitler & H. Kreitler. LC 89-38261. (Emotions, Personality, & Psychotherapy Ser.). (Illus.). 422p. 1990. 59.50 (*0-306-43179-3*, Plenum Pr) Plenum.

Cognitive Functioning & Social Structure over the Life Course. Ed. by Carmi Schooler & K. Warner Schaie. LC 86-32056. 304p. (C). 1987. text ed. 42.50 (*0-89391-410-X*) Ablex Pub.

Cognitive Gerontology: A Special Issue. Ed. by P. Rabbitt & L. Backman. 112p. 1990. pap. 19.95 (*0-86377-157-2*) L Erlbaum Assocs.

Cognitive Harmony: An Adventure in Mental Fitness. Jerry Stocking. Ed. by Jackie Stocking & Roger Anderson. (Illus.). 200p. 1991. pap. 22.50 (*0-9629593-0-8*) Moose Ear Pr.

*__Cognitive Information Processing.__ I. Tahara. LC 94-76151. 220p. 1994. 59.00 (*90-5199-162-2*) IOS Press.

*__Cognitive Interference: Theories, Methods, & Findings.__ Ed. by Irwin G. Sarason et al. (Personality & Clinical Psychology Ser.). 350p. 1995. text ed. 55.00 (*0-8058-1624-0*) L Erlbaum Assocs.

Cognitive Issues in Motor Expertise. Ed. by Janet L. Starkes & Fran Allard. LC 93-29187. 375p. 1993. 140.00 (*0-444-89302-4*, North Holland) Elsevier.

Cognitive Learning & Memory in Children. Ed. by M. Pressley & Charles J. Brainerd. (Cognitive Development Ser.). (Illus.). 290p. 1985. 69.00 (*0-387-96076-7*) Spr-Verlag.

Cognitive Learning in Children: Theories & Strategies. Ed. by J. R. Levin & Vernon L. Allen. (Educational Psychology Ser.). 1976. text ed. 51.00 (*0-12-444850-X*) Acad Pr.

Cognitive Learning Strategies for Minority Handicapped Students. Catherine Collier & John J. Hoover. LC 87-81734. 81p. 1987. pap. text ed. 8.50 (*0-940059-02-9*) Hamilton Pubns.

*__Cognitive Learning Theory & Cane Travel Instruction: A New Paradigm.__ Richard Mettler. LC 95-69567. 110p. 1995. pap. 10.00 (*0-9646058-0-5*) St NE DPI DRSVI.

Cognitive-Linguistic Improvement Program CLIP: A Program for Speech-Language Pathologists Treating Neuropathologies of Speech & Language & Learning Disabilities. (Illus.). 259p. (Orig.). (C). 1992. pap. text ed. 45.00 (*1-879105-62-4*, 0276) Singular Publishing.

Cognitive Microgenesis: A Neuropsychological Perspective. Ed. by R. E. Hanlon. (Illus.). 328p. 1991. 87.00 (*0-387-97407-5*) Spr-Verlag.

Cognitive Modelling & Interactive Environments in Language Learning. Ed. by F. L. Engel et al. LC 92-25229. (NATO ASI Series F: Computer & Systems Sciences, Special Programme AET: Vol. 87). ix, 311p. 1992. write for info. (*3-540-55559-5*) Spr-Verlag.

Cognitive Modelling & Interactive Environments in Language Learning, 2 diskettes, Set. Ed. by F. L. Engel et al. LC 92-25229. (NATO ASI Series F: Computer & Systems Sciences, Special Programme AET: Vol. 87). ix, 311p. 1992. 3.5 hd 103.00 (*0-387-55559-5*) Spr-Verlag.

Cognitive Models & Intelligent Environments for Learning Programming. Ed. by Enrica Lemut et al. LC 93-25348. (NATO ASI Series F: Computer & Systems Sciences, Special Programme AET: Vol. 111). 315p. 1993. 69.00 (*0-387-56580-9*) Spr-Verlag.

Cognitive Models of Psychological Time. Ed. by R. A. Block. 304p. 1990. text ed. 69.95 (*0-8058-0359-9*) L Erlbaum Assocs.

Cognitive Models of Science. Ed. by Ronald N. Giere. (Illus.). 512p. (C). 1992. text ed. 44.95 (*0-8166-1979-4*) U of Minn Pr.

Cognitive Models of Speech Processing: Psycholiguistic & Computational Perspectives. Gerry T. Altmann. (ACL-MIT Press Series in Natural Language Processing). 500p. 1990. 67.50x (*0-262-01117-4*) MIT Pr.

*__Cognitive Models of Speech Processing: Psycholinguistic & Computational Perspectives.__ Ed. by Gerry T. Altmann. (ACL Series in Natural Language Processing). 552p. 1995. pap. 20.00x (*0-262-51084-7*, Bradford Bks) MIT Pr.

Cognitive Neuropsychology: A Clinical Introduction. Rosaleen A. McCarthy & Elizabeth K. Warrington. 428p. 1990. text ed. 79.95 (*0-12-481845-5*); pap. text ed. 39.95 (*0-12-481846-3*) Acad Pr.

Cognitive Neuropsychology & Neurolinguistics: Advances in Models of Cognitive Function & Impairment. Ed. by Alfonso Caramazza. 312p. 1990. 59.95 (*0-89859-892-3*) L Erlbaum Assocs.

Cognitive Neuropsychology in Clinical Practice. Ed. by David I. Margolin. (Illus.). 560p. 1992. 60.00 (*0-19-506422-4*) OUP.

Cognitive Neuroscience: Research Directions in Cognitive Science. Ed. by Guy A. Orban & W. Singer. 192p. 1991. text ed. 45.00 (*0-86377-114-9*) L Erlbaum Assocs.

Cognitive Neurosciences. Ed. by Michael S. Gazzaniga et al. LC 93-40288. 1296p. (C). 1994. 95.00 (*0-262-07157-6*, Bradford Bks) MIT Pr.

Cognitive Organization & Change: An Information-Processing Approach. Robert S. Wyer, Jr. LC 74-12312. 502p. (C). 1974. text ed. 89.95 (*0-89859-200-3*) L Erlbaum Assocs.

Cognitive Paradigm. Marc De Mey. 1982. lib. bdg. 94.00 (*90-277-1382-0*) Kluwer Ac.

Cognitive Paradigm. Marc De Mey. 1984. pap. text ed. 44.50 (*90-277-1600-5*) Kluwer Ac.

Cognitive Paradigm. Marc De Mey. LC 82-10162. (Illus.). xxvi, 314p. 1992. pap. text ed. 15.95 (*0-226-14259-0*) U Ch Pr.

Cognitive Perceptual Motor Dysfunction: From Research to Practice. Eli Z. Rubin et al. LC 77-157415. (Lafayette Clinic Monographs in Psychiatry: No. 5). 173p. reprint ed. pap. 49.40 (*0-685-15707-5*, 2027662) Bks Demand.

Cognitive Perspectives on Children's Social & Behavioral Development: The Minnesota Symposia on Child Psychology, Vol. 18. Ed. by Marian Perlmutter. 352p. (C). 1986. text ed. 69.95 (*0-89859-546-0*) L Erlbaum Assocs.

Cognitive Perspectives on Educational Leadership. Ed. by Philip Hallinger et al. LC 93-22705. (Critical Issues in Educational Leadership Ser.). 312p. (C). 1993. text ed. 44.00 (*0-8077-3278-8*); pap. text ed. 20.95 (*0-8077-3277-X*) Tchrs Coll.

Cognitive Practices: Human Language & Human Knowledge. Rita Nolan. 200p. 1994. 44.95 (*0-631-18973-4*); pap. 21.95 (*0-631-18974-2*) Blackwell Pubs.

Cognitive Process Instruction: Research on Teaching Thinking Skills. Ed. by Jack Lochhead & John Clement. LC 78-22122. (Illus.). 339p. 1979. pap. 59.95 (*0-89859-729-3*) L Erlbaum Assocs.

Cognitive Processes & Emotional Disorders: A Structural Approach to Psychotherapy. Vittorio F. Guidano & G. Liotti. LC 83-13188. (Guilford Clinical Psychology & Psychotherapy Ser.). 347p. 1986. reprint ed. lib. bdg. 40.00 (*0-89862-006-6*); reprint ed. pap. text ed. 22.95 (*0-89862-907-1*) Guilford Pr.

Cognitive Processes & Pavlovian Conditioning in Humans. Ed. by Graham C. Davey. 298p. 1987. text ed. 165.00 (*0-471-90791-X*) Wiley.

*__Cognitive Processes & Pavlovian Conditioning in Humans.__ fac. ed. Graham Davey. LC 86-19036. 308p. 1987. reprint ed. pap. 87.80 (*0-7837-8282-9*, 2049063) Bks Demand.

*__Cognitive Processes in Children's Learning: Practical Applications in Educational Practice & Classroom Management.__ Prem S. Fry & Judy L. Lupart. (Illus.). 268p. 1987. pap. 28.95 (*0-398-06135-1*) C C Thomas.

Cognitive Processes in Children's Learning: Practical Applications in Educational Practice & Classroom Management. Prem S. Fry & Judy L. Lupart. (Illus.). 268p. (C). 1987. 46.95x (*0-398-05270-0*) C C Thomas.

Cognitive Processes in Choice & Decision Behavior. Ed. by Thomas S. Wallsten. LC 79-27553. (Illus.). 304p. 1980. text ed. 59.95 (*0-89859-054-X*) L Erlbaum Assocs.

Cognitive Processes in Comprehension. Ed. by M. A. Just & P. A. Carpenter. 352p. 1977. text ed. 69.95 (*0-89859-127-9*) L Erlbaum Assocs.

Cognitive Processes in Education. Sylvia Farnham-Diggory. (C). 1992. text ed. 51.50 (*0-06-042004-9*) HarpCollege.

Cognitive Processes in Mathematics. John A. Sloboda & Don Rogers. (Keele Cognition Seminar Ser.: No. 1). (Illus.). 218p. 1987. 65.00 (*0-19-852163-4*) OUP.

Cognitive Processes in Stereotyping & Intergroup Behavior. Ed. by David L. Hamilton. LC 80-29408. 378p. reprint ed. pap. 107.80 (*0-7837-1239-1*, 2041376) Bks Demand.

Cognitive Processes in the Perception of Art. Ed. by W. R. Crozier & A. J. Chapman. (Advances in Psychology Ser.: Vol. 19). 448p. 1984. 84.75 (*0-444-87501-8*, I-239-84) Elsevier.

Cognitive Processing for Vision & Voice: Proceedings of the Fourth NEC Research Symposium. Ed. by T. Ishiguro. LC 94-18674. (Proceedings in Applied Math Ser.: No. 71). 1994. 35.00 (*0-89871-335-8*) Soc Indus-Appl Math.

Cognitive Processing in the Right Hemisphere. Ed. by Ellen Perecman. (Perspectives in Neurolinguistics, Neuropsychology & Psycholinguistics Ser.). 1983. text ed. 54.00 (*0-12-550680-5*) Acad Pr.

Cognitive Processing Therapy for Rape Victims: A Treatment Manual. Patricia A. Resick & Monica K. Schnicke. (Interpersonal Violence Practice Ser.: Vol. 4). (Illus.). 174p. (C). 1993. text ed. 42.95 (*0-8039-4901-4*); pap. text ed. 18.95 (*0-8039-4902-2*) Sage.

Cognitive Psychology. Karl Haberlandt. LC 93-19505. 1993. text ed. write for info. (*0-205-13939-6*) Allyn.

*__Cognitive Psychology.__ Ronald T. Kellogg. LC 95-11732. (Advanced Psychology Texts Ser.: Vol. 2). 544p. (C). 1995. 43.95 (*0-8039-5329-1*) Sage.

Cognitive Psychology. Douglas L. Medin & Brian H. Ross. 450p. (C). 1992. text ed. 46.75 (*0-15-507872-0*) HB Coll Pubs.

Cognitive Psychology. Wayne A. Wickelgren. (Illus.). 1979. 29.95 (*0-685-03793-2*) P-H.

Cognitive Psychology. 2nd ed. John B. Best. Ed. by Baxter. 583p. (C). 1989. text ed. 45.00 (*0-314-46934-6*) West Pub.

Cognitive Psychology. 3rd ed. John B. Best. Ed. by Baxter & Crochiere. 550p. (C). 1992. text ed. 48.75 (*0-314-90894-3*) West Pub.

*__Cognitive Psychology.__ 4th ed. John B. Best. LC 94-31727. 500p. 1994. text ed. 51.50 (*0-314-04445-0*) West Pub.

*__Cognitive Psychology.__ 4th ed. Robert L. Solso. 1994. text ed. write for info. (*0-205-15831-5*) Allyn.

Cognitive Psychology: A Computerized Laboratory Course. Ian W. Bushnell & Jim T. Mullin. 272p. 1988. student ed, pap. text ed. 29.95 (*0-86377-060-6*) L Erlbaum Assocs.

Cognitive Psychology: A Neural-Network Approach. Colin Martindale. 320p. (C). 1991. text ed. 23.95 (*0-534-14130-7*) Brooks-Cole.

Cognitive Psychology: An Essay in Cognitive Science. George Mandler. 144p. (C). 1985. text ed. 29.95 (*0-89859-537-1*); pap. 6.95 (*0-89859-659-9*) L Erlbaum Assocs.

Cognitive Psychology: An International Review. Ed. by Michael W. Eysenck. 312p. 1990. text ed. 114.50 (*0-471-92757-0*) Wiley.

Cognitive Psychology: An Overview for Cognitive Scientists. Lawrence Barsalou. 424p. 1992. text ed. 79.95 (*0-8058-0691-1*); pap. 36.00 (*0-89859-966-0*) L Erlbaum Assocs.

Cognitive Psychology: Memory, Language, & Thought. Darlene Howard. 592p. (C). 1983. text ed. write for info. (*0-02-357320-1*) Macmillan.

Cognitive Psychology Vol. 1. Alan Baddeley & Niels O. Bernsen. 168p. 1989. 45.00 (*0-86377-111-4*) L Erlbaum Assocs.

Cognitive Psychology & Artificial Intelligence: Theory & Research in Cognitive Science. Morton Wagman. LC 92-1751. 192p. 1993. text ed. 55.00 (*0-275-94302-X*, C4302, Praeger Pubs) Greenwood.

Cognitive Psychology & Emotional Disorders. J. Mark Williams et al. LC 08-731739. (Clinical Psychology Ser.: No. 1837). 226p. 1991. pap. text ed. 36.95 (*0-471-92966-2*) Wiley.

*__Cognitive Psychology & Emotional Disorders.__ 2nd ed. MacLeod & Mathews. (Clinical Psychology Ser.). Date not set. pap. text ed. 39.95 (*0-471-94430-0*) Wiley.

Cognitive Psychology & Information Processing: An Introduction. Roy Lachman et al. 592p. (C). 1979. text ed. 69.95 (*0-89859-131-7*) L Erlbaum Assocs.

Cognitive Psychology & Instruction. Ed. by Alan M. Lesgold et al. LC 77-27133. (NATO Conference Series III, Human Factors: Vol. 5). 540p. 1978. 75.00 (*0-306-32886-0*, Plenum Pr) Plenum.

*__Cognitive Psychology & Instruction.__ 2nd ed. Roger Bruning & Gregg Schraw. (Illus.). 464p. 1995. pap. text ed. write for info. (*0-02-315911-1*, Merrill Pub Co) Macmillan.

*__Cognitive Psychology & Its Implications.__ 4th ed. John R. Anderson. LC 94-39006. (C). 1995. text ed. 45.95 (*0-7167-2385-9*) W H Freeman.

Cognitive Psychology & Reading in the U. S. S. R. J. Downing. (Advances in Psychology Ser.: Vol. 49). 472p. 1988. 105.25 (*0-444-70374-8*, North Holland) Elsevier.

Cognitive Psychology Applied: A Symposium at the 22nd International Congress of Applied Psychology. Ed. by Chizuko Izawa. 256p. 1993. text ed. 59.95 (*0-8058-0830-2*) L Erlbaum Assocs.

Cognitive Psychology for Teachers. John A. Glover et al. 464p. (C). 1990. pap. write for info. (*0-02-344133-X*) Macmillan.

Cognitive Psychology In & Out of the Laboratory. Kathleen M. Galotti. LC 93-26748. 1994. text ed. 47.95 (*0-534-21054-6*) Brooks-Cole.

Cognitive Psychology in the Seminar Room. Helen Abadzi. (EDI Seminar Paper Ser.: No. 41). 100p. 1990. 7.95 (*0-8213-1333-9*, 11333) World Bank.

Cognitive Psychology of Knowledge. Ed. by Gerhard Strube & Karl F. Wender. LC 93-29886. (Advances in Psychology Ser.: Vol. 101). 1993. write for info. (*0-444-89942-1*, North Holland) Elsevier.

Cognitive Psychology of Mass Communication. 2nd ed. Richard J. Harris. (Mass Communiciation Ser.). 328p. 1993. text ed. 32.50 (*0-8058-1264-4*) L Erlbaum Assocs.

Cognitive Psychology of Planning. Ed. by Jean-Michel Hoc. (Computers & People Ser.). 200p. 1988. text ed. 66.00 (*0-12-350770-7*) Acad Pr.

Cognitive Psychology of School Learning. Ellen D. Gagne. (C). 1987. text ed. 31.25 (*0-673-39153-1*) HarpCollege.

Cognitive Psychology of School Learning. Ellen D. Gagne. (C). 1993. 56.00 (*0-673-46416-4*) HarpCollege.

Cognitive Psychology of School Learning. Ellen D. Gagne. (C). 1985. text ed. 27.95 (*0-316-30165-5*) Little.

Cognitive Psychology with a Frame of Reference. J. P. Guilford. LC 78-74137. 1979. 16.00 (*0-912736-22-4*) EDITS Pubs.

Cognitive Psychophysiology: Event-Related Potentials & the Study of Cognition, the Carmel Conferences, Vol. 1. Ed. by E. Donchin. (Illus.). 448p. (C). 1984. text ed. 89.95 (*0-89859-150-3*) L Erlbaum Assocs.

Cognitive Psychophysiology: Principles of Covert Behavior. Frank J. McGuigan. LC 78-18542. (Century Psychology Ser.). 1978. 34.95 (*0-13-139519-X*) P-H.

Cognitive Psychophysiology: Principles of Covert Behavior. Frank J. McGuigan. LC 78-18542. (Century Psychology Ser.). 544p. reprint ed. pap. 155.10 (*0-8357-3403-X*, 2039660) Bks Demand.

Cognitive Psychotherapy. Ed. by Carlo Perris et al. (Illus.). 480p. 1988. 111.00 (*0-387-18870-3*) Spr-Verlag.

Cognitive Psychotherapy: Stasis & Change. Ed. by Windy Dryden & Peter Trower. 208p. 1989. 27.95 (*0-8261-6970-8*) Springer Pub.

Cognitive Rehabilitation: Conceptualization & Intervention. Ed. by Lance Trexler. LC 82-7619. 292p. 1982. 63.00 (*0-306-41016-8*, Plenum Pr) Plenum.

Cognitive Rehabilitation: Frameworks in Occupational Therapy. Ed. by Noomi Katz. 328p. 1992. 39.95 (*1-56372-038-8*, Andover Med Pubs) Buttrwrth-Heinemann.

Cognitive Rehabilitation in Perspective. Rodger L. Wood & Ian Fussey. 280p. 1990. text ed. 59.95 (*0-86377-192-0*); pap. 29.95 (*0-86377-193-9*) L Erlbaum Assocs.

Cognitive Rehabilitation of Closed Head Injured Patients: A Dynamic Approach. Brenda B. Adamovich et al. LC 90-50381. 160p. (Orig.). (C). 1989. pap. text ed. 27.95 (*0-89079-389-1*, 1600) PRO-ED.

Cognitive Rehabilitation of Memory: A Practical Guide. Minnie Harrell et al. LC 91-31706. 261p. 1992. 57.00 (*0-8342-0285-9*) Aspen Pub.

Cognitive Rehabilitation Resources for the Apple II Computer. Jeffrey S. Kreutzer et al. (Orig.). 1987. student ed 19.95 (*0-9618050-0-5*) NeuroSci Pubs.

Cognitive Rehabilitation Workbook: A Dynamic Assessment for Adults with Brain Injury. 2nd ed. Pamela M. Dougherty & Mary V. Radomski. 330p. 1993. pap. 73.00 (*0-8342-0357-X*, 20357) Aspen Pub.

Cognitive Relativism & Social Science. Ed. by Diederick Raven et al. 150p. (C). 1992. 39.95 (*0-88738-425-0*) Transaction Pubs.

Cognitive Reorganization: A Stimulus Handbook. Elizabeth J. Bressler & Sharon M. Holloran. 198p. 1983. spiral bd. 59.00 (*0-88120-190-1*, 2670) PRO-ED.

Cognitive Research in Psychology. Ed. by F. Klix et al. 204p. 1983. 84.75 (*0-444-86350-8*, I-116-82, North Holland) Elsevier.

Cognitive Research on Response Error in Survey Questions on Smoking. 97p. (Orig.). (C). 1993. pap. text ed. 30.00 (*1-56806-502-7*) Diane Pub.

Cognitive Responses in Persuasion. Ed. by Richard E. Petty et al. LC 80-26388. 512p. 1981. text ed. 49.95 (*0-89859-025-6*) L Erlbaum Assocs.

Cognitive Revolution in Psychology. Bernard J. Baars. LC 84-25311. 443p. 1986. pap. text ed. 25.95 (*0-89862-912-8*) Guilford Pr.

*__Cognitive Revolution in Western Culture.__ Don LePan. 388p. 1989. pap. 19.95 (*1-55111-081-4*, Pub. by Macmillan UK) Broadview Pr.

*__Cognitive Science, 3 vols., Set.__ Noel Sheehy & Antony J. Chapman. (International Library of Critical Writings in Psychology: No. 6). 1632p. 1995. 495.00 (*0-8147-8020-2*) NYU Pr.

Cognitive Science: An Introduction. Neil Stillings et al. 650p. 1987. 37.50x (*0-262-19257-8*) MIT Pr.

*__Cognitive Science: An Introduction.__ 2nd ed. Neil Stillings et al. (Bradford Bks.). (Illus.). 544p. 1995. 45.00x (*0-262-19353-1*) MIT Pr.

Cognitive Science: The Science of Intelligent Systems. George F. Luger. (Illus.). 666p. 1994. boxed 49.95 (*0-12-459570-7*) Acad Pr.

Cognitive Science & Clinical Disorders. Ed. by Daniel L. Stein & Jeffrey Young. LC 92-11148. (Illus.). 399p. 1992. text ed. 64.95 (*0-12-664720-8*) Acad Pr.

Cognitive Science & Concepts of Mind: Toward a General Theory of Human & Artificial Intelligence. Morton Wagman. LC 91-10585. 208p. 1991. text ed. 55.00 (*0-275-94044-6*, C4044, Praeger Pubs) Greenwood.

Cognitive Science & Genetic Epistemology: A Case Study of Understanding. D. Leiser & C. Gillieron. LC 89-22970. (PATH in Psychology Ser.). (Illus.). 216p. 1990. 45.00 (*0-306-43193-9*, Plenum Pr) Plenum.

Cognitive Science & Instruction. Robert Brien & Nick Eastmond. LC 93-40707. 192p. 1994. 34.95 (*0-87778-272-5*) Educ Tech Pubns.

Cognitive Science & Its Applications for Human-Computer Interaction. Ed. by Raymonde Guindon. 368p. 1988. text ed. 79.95 (*0-89859-884-2*) L Erlbaum Assocs.

Cognitive Science & Mathematics Education. Ed. by Alan H. Schoenfeld. 312p. 1987. pap. text ed. 27.50 (*0-8058-0057-3*) L Erlbaum Assocs.

Cognitive Science & Psychoanalysis. Kenneth M. Colby & R. J. Stoller. 176p. 1988. 34.50 (*0-8058-0177-4*); pap. 19.95 (*0-88163-076-4*) L Erlbaum Assocs.

Cognitive Science Foundations of Instruction. Ed. by Mitchell Rabinowitz. 248p. 1993. text ed. 49.95 (*0-8058-1279-2*) L Erlbaum Assocs.

Cognitive Science in Europe. Ed. by M. Imbert et al. (Recent Research in Psychology Ser.). 236p. 1987. pap. 46.00 (*0-387-96595-5*) Spr-Verlag.

Cognitive Science in Medicine: Biomedical Modeling. Ed. by David A. Evans & Vimla Patel. (DNA Ser.). 350p. 1989. 42.00 (*0-262-05037-4*, Bradford Bks) MIT Pr.

Cognitive Science Projects in Prolog. Peter Scott & Rod Nicolson. 296p. 1991. pap. 34.50 (*0-86377-182-3*) L Erlbaum Assocs.

Cognitive Science Society: Proceedings of the Eighth Annual Conference of the Cognitive Science Society, 1986. 882p. 1986. pap. 125.00 (*0-89859-864-8*) L Erlbaum Assocs.

Cognitive Science Society: Proceedings of the Eleventh Annual Conference of the Cognitive Science Society, August 16-19, 1989. 1032p. 1989. pap. 125.00 (*0-8058-0684-9*) L Erlbaum Assocs.

Cognitive Science Society: Proceedings of the Fifth Annual Conference of the Cognitive Science Society, 1983. 388p. 1983. pap. 79.95 (*0-89859-941-5*) L Erlbaum Assocs.

Cognitive Science Society: Proceedings of the Fourth Annual Conference of the Cognitive Science Society, 1982. 216p. 1982. pap. 49.95 (*0-89859-940-7*) L Erlbaum Assocs.

Cognitive Science Society: Proceedings of the Ninth Annual Conference of the Cognitive Science Society, 1987. 1008p. 1987. pap. 125.00 (*0-8058-0166-9*) L Erlbaum Assocs.

Cognitive Science Society: Proceedings of the Seventh Annual Conference of the Cognitive Science Society, 1985. 388p. 1985. pap. 125.00 (*0-89859-942-3*) L Erlbaum Assocs.

Cognitive Science Society: Proceedings of the Sixth Annual Conference of the Cognitive Science Society, 1984. 388p. 1984. pap. 79.95 (*0-89859-976-8*) L Erlbaum Assocs.

Cognitive Science Society: Proceedings of the Tenth Annual Conference of the Cognitive Science Society, 1988. 788p. 1988. 125.00 (*0-8058-0436-6*) L Erlbaum Assocs.

Cognitive Sciences: Basic Problems, New Perspectives. Maria Nowakowska. 1986. pap. text ed. 58.00 (*0-12-522621-7*) Acad Pr.

Cognitive Self-Instruction (CSI) for Classroom Processes. Brenda H. Manning. LC 90-32701. 370p. (C). 1991. 89.50 (*0-7914-0479-X*); pap. 29.95 (*0-7914-0480-3*) State U NY Pr.

Cognitive Skills & Their Acquisition. Ed. by John R. Anderson. (Carnegie-Mellon Symposia on Cognition Ser.). 384p. 1981. text ed. 69.95 (*0-89859-093-0*) L Erlbaum Assocs.

Cognitive Skills Assessment Battery. 2nd ed. Ann E. Boehm & Barbara R. Slater. 1981. 51.95 (*0-8077-5975-9*); 8.95 (*0-8077-5976-7*); teacher ed 3.50 (*0-8077-5977-5*); 3.95 (*0-8077-5978-3*) Tchrs Coll.

Cognitive Skills for Community Living: Teaching Students with Moderate to Severe Disabilities. Sandra McClennen. LC 90-27494. (Illus.). 402p. (C). 1991. pap. text ed. 34.00 (*0-89079-459-6*, 1591) PRO-ED.

Cognitive Social Factors in Early Deception. Ed. by Stephen J. Ceci et al. 192p. 1992. text ed. 39.95 (*0-8058-0953-8*) L Erlbaum Assocs.

Cognitive Social Psychology. A. H. Hastorf & Alice M. Isen. 362p. 1981. 66.50 (*0-444-00617-6*) Elsevier.

***Cognitive Space & Linguistic Case: Semantic & Syntactic Categories in English.** Izchak M. Schlesinger. (Studies in English Language). 241p. (C). 1995. 54.95 (*0-521-43436-X*) Cambridge U Pr.

Cognitive Strategies & Educational Performance. Ed. by John R. Kirby. (Educational Psychology Ser.). 1983. text ed. 72.00 (*0-12-409580-1*) Acad Pr.

Cognitive Strategies in Stochastic Thinking. Roland W. Scholz. 1987. lib. bdg. 88.00 (*90-277-2454-7*) Kluwer Ac.

Cognitive Strategies Special Education. Adrian F. Ashman & Robert N. Conway. 250p. 1988. text ed. 49.95 (*0-415-00594-9*, A1690); pap. text ed. 15.95 (*0-415-00595-7*, A1694) Routledge.

***Cognitive Strategy Instruction for Middle & High Schools.** Ed. by Eileen Wood et al. LC 95-2144. 1995. pap. 26.95 (*1-57129-007-9*) Brookline Bks.

***Cognitive Strategy Instruction That Really Improves Children's Academic Performance.** 2nd ed. Michael Pressley & Vera Woloshyn. LC 95-2310. (Cognitive Strategy Training Ser.). 1995. pap. text ed. 27.95 (*1-57129-005-2*) Brookline Bks.

Cognitive Strategy Instruction That Really Improves Children's Academic Performances. Michael Pressley et al. (Illus.). 200p. 1990. text ed. 24.95 (*0-914797-66-2*) Brookline Bks.

Cognitive Strategy Research. Ed. by C. B. McCormick et al. (Illus.). 345p. 1989. 68.00 (*0-387-96869-5*) Spr-Verlag.

Cognitive Strategy Research 1: Psychological Foundations. Ed. by M. Presley & J. R. Levin. (Cognitive Development Ser.). (Illus.). 350p. 1983. 73.00 (*0-387-90818-8*) Spr-Verlag.

Cognitive Structure & Development in Nonhuman Primates. Francesco Antinucci. 272p. (C). 1989. text ed. 49.95 (*0-8058-0242-8*); pap. 29.95 (*0-8058-0544-3*) L Erlbaum Assocs.

Cognitive Structure of Emotions. Andrew Ortony et al. (Illus.). 224p. (C). 1990. pap. 19.95 (*0-521-38664-0*) Cambridge U Pr.

Cognitive Structures. David G. Hays. (General Theory Ser.). 1981. 22.00 (*0-317-37053-7*) HRAFP.

Cognitive Studies of Southern Mesoamerica. Helen L. Neuenswander & Dean E. Arnold. LC 77-80015. (Museum of Anthropology Publications: No. 3). 283p. 1977. 10.95 (*0-88312-152-2*) Summer Instit Ling.

Cognitive Studies of Southern Mesoamerica, 4 fiche, Set. Helen L. Neuenswander & Dean E. Arnold. LC 77-80015. (Museum of Anthropology Publications: No. 3). 283p. 1977. fiche 16.00x (*0-88312-250-2*) Summer Instit Ling.

Cognitive Style & Cognitive Development. Ed. by Tamar Globerson et al. LC 88-24248. (Human Development Ser.: Vol. 3). 240p. (C). 1989. text ed. 39.50 (*0-89391-519-X*) Ablex Pub.

Cognitive Styles: A Primer to the Literature. Robert M. Hashway & L. Irene Duke. LC 91-46416. 132p. 1992. lib. bdg. 69.95 (*0-7734-9930-X*) E Mellen.

Cognitive Styles: Essence & Origins- Field Dependence & Field Independence. Herman A. Witkin & Donald R. Goodenough. LC 80-39995. (Psychological Issues Monograph: No. 51). (Illus.). 130p. 1981. text ed. 26.00 (*0-8236-1003-9*) Intl Univs Pr.

Cognitive Styles & Adult Learning. G. Squires. (C). 1988. text ed. 32.00 (*0-685-22142-3*, Pub. by Univ Nottingham UK) St Mut.

Cognitive Styles & Adult Learning. Geoffrey Squires. (C). 1986. reprint ed. 35.00 (*0-902031-48-1*, Pub. by Univ Nottingham UK) St Mut.

Cognitive Styles in Law Schools. Alfred G. Smith et al. LC 78-12521. 190p. reprint ed. pap. 54.20 (*0-8357-7763-4*, 2036121) Bks Demand.

Cognitive Styles in Personal & Cultural Adaptation. Herman A. Witkin. (Heinz Werner Lecture Ser.: No. 11). 1977. pap. 6.00 (*0-914206-10-9*) Clark U Pr.

Cognitive Systems Engineering. Jens Rasmussen et al. LC 93-46162. (A Wiley-Interscience Publication Ser.). 378p. 1994. text ed. 59.95 (*0-471-01198-3*) Wiley.

Cognitive Systems Engineering: Interface Design, Prototyping, & Evaluation. Stephen Andriole & Leonard Adelman. 280p. 1995. text ed. 59.95 (*0-8058-1244-X*) L Erlbaum Assocs.

Cognitive Technology in Psychiatric Rehabilitation. Ed. by William D. Spaulding. LC 93-23685. (Illus.). xviii, 246p. 1994. text ed. 36.50 (*0-8032-4224-7*) U of Nebr Pr.

Cognitive Testing Methodology: Proceedings of a Workshop Held on June 11-12, 1984. National Research Council (U. S.), Committee on Military Nutrition & Research. 214p. reprint ed. pap. 61.00 (*0-8357-7688-3*, 2036039) Bks Demand.

Cognitive Theory, Vol. 1. Ed. by F. Restle et al. LC 74-14293. 320p. 1975. text ed. 59.95 (*0-89859-436-7*) L Erlbaum Assocs.

Cognitive Theory, Vol. 3. Ed. by N. J. Castellan, Jr. & F. Restle. 336p. 1978. 69.95 (*0-89859-438-3*) L Erlbaum Assocs.

Cognitive Theory of Borderline Personality Disorder. Mary A. Layden et al. 256p. Date not set. write for info. (*0-318-71704-2*) Allyn.

Cognitive Theory of Consciousness. Bernard J. Baars. (Illus.). 452p. 1989. 59.95 (*0-521-30133-5*) Cambridge U Pr.

Cognitive Theory of Consciousness. Bernard J. Baars. (Illus.). 452p. (C). 1993. pap. 21.95 (*0-521-42743-6*) Cambridge U Pr.

Cognitive Theory of Metaphor. Earl R. MacCormac. 264p. 1989. reprint ed. pap. 14.95x (*0-262-63124-5*) MIT Pr.

Cognitive Therapies in Action: Evolving Innovative Practice. Kevin T. Kuehlwein & Hugh Rosen. LC 92-30055. (Social & Behavioral Sciences Ser.). 485p. 1993. 37.95 (*1-55542-496-1*) Jossey-Bass.

Cognitive Therapy: Applications in Psychiatric & Medical Settings. Ed. by Arthur Freeman & Vincent Greenwood. (Illus.). 234p. 1986. 42.95 (*0-89885-285-4*); 20.95 (*0-89885-311-7*) Human Sci Pr.

***Cognitive Therapy: Basics & Beyond.** Judith S. Beck. 1995. lib. bdg. 35.00 (*0-89862-847-4*) Guilford Pr.

Cognitive Therapy & Emotional Disorders. Aaron T. Beck. LC 75-33518. 365p. (Orig.). 1976. text ed. 50.00 (*0-8236-1005-5*) Intl Univs Pr.

Cognitive Therapy & the Emotional Disorders. Aaron T. Beck. 1979. pap. 12.95 (*0-452-00928-6*); mass mkt. 6.95 (*0-452-00788-7*, Mer) NAL-Dutton.

Cognitive Therapy & the Emotions. Beck. 1976. 45.00 (*0-8236-0990-1*) Intl Univs Pr.

Cognitive Therapy for Depressed Adolescents. T. C. R. Wilkes et al. LC 94-13340. (Mental Health & Psychopathology Ser.). 396p. 1994. lib. bdg. 36.95 (*0-89862-119-4*, C2119) Guilford Pr.

Cognitive Therapy for Depression & Anxiety: A Practitioners Guide. Ed. by Ivy-Marie Blackburn & Kate Davidson. (Illus.). 256p. 1990. 65.00 (*0-632-02636-7*) Blackwell Sci.

Cognitive Therapy for Personality Disorders: A Schema-Focused Approach. Jeffrey E. Young. Ed. by Harold H. Smith, Jr. LC 89-43704. (Practitioner's Resource Ser.). 90p. 1990. pap. 13.95 (*0-943158-46-X*, CTPDBP) Pro Resource.

Cognitive Therapy for Personality Disorders: A Schema-Focused Approach. rev. ed. Jeffrey E. Young. LC 94-1388. (Practitioner's Resource Ser.). 104p. 1995. pap. 14.70 (*1-56887-006-X*, CTPDBP, Prof Resc Pr) Pro Resource.

Cognitive Therapy in Clinical Practice. Ed. by Jan Scott et al. 256p. (C). 1989. lib. bdg. 39.95 (*0-415-00518-3*, A2736) Routledge.

Cognitive Therapy in Clinical Practice: An Illustrative Casebook. Ed. by Jan Scott et al. (Illus.). 263p. 1991. pap. 16.95 (*0-415-06242-X*, A5721) Routledge.

Cognitive Therapy in Practice: A Case Formulation Approach. Jacqueline B. Persons. (C). 1989. 25.95 (*0-393-70077-1*) Norton.

Cognitive Therapy of Borderline Personality Disorder. Mary A. Layden et al. LC 93-16298. (Practitioner Guidebook Ser.). 218p. 1993. 29.95 (*0-205-14807-7*, Longwood Div) Allyn.

Cognitive Therapy of Depression. Aaron T. Beck et al. LC 79-19967. (Guilford Clinical Psychology & Psychotherapy Ser.). 425p. 1987. lib. bdg. 45.00 (*0-89862-000-7*); pap. text ed. 23.95 (*0-89862-919-5*) Guilford Pr.

Cognitive Therapy of Personality Disorders. Aaron T. Beck & Arthur Freeman. LC 90-33575. 396p. 1990. lib. bdg. 36.95 (*0-89862-434-7*) Guilford Pr.

Cognitive Therapy of Substance Abuse. Aaron T. Beck et al. 354p. 1993. lib. bdg. 35.00 (*0-89862-115-1*) Guilford Pr.

Cognitive Therapy of Suicidal Behavior: A Manual for Treatment. Arthur Freeman & Mark Reinecke. LC 92-48342. (Death & Suicide Ser.: Vol. 12). 1993. 37.95 (*0-88616-500-8*) Springer Pub.

Cognitive Therapy with Couples. Frank M. Dattilio & Christine A. Padesky. LC 90-52991. 150p. 1990. pap. 19.20 (*0-943158-49-4*, CTCBP) Pro Resource.

Cognitive Therapy with Couples & Groups. Ed. by Arthur Freeman. LC 83-13210. 350p. 1983. 65.00 (*0-306-41149-0*, Plenum Pr) Plenum.

Cognitive Therapy with Inpatients: Developing a Cognitive Milieu. Ed. by Jesse H. Wright et al. LC 92-1529. 445p. 1992. lib. bdg. 38.95 (*0-89862-890-3*) Guilford Pr.

Cognitive Therapy with Schizophrenic Patients. Carlo Perris. LC 88-24467. 240p. 1989. lib. bdg. 32.00 (*0-89862-737-0*) Guilford Pr.

Cognitive Tools for Learning. Ed. by P. A. Kommers et al. (NATO ASI Series F: Computer & Systems Sciences, Special Programme AET: Vol. 81). x, 278p. 1992. 74.00 (*0-387-55045-3*) Spr-Verlag.

Cognitive Training for Children: A Developmental Program of Inductive Reasoning & Problem Solving. Karl J. Klauer & Gary D. Phye. LC 93-6025. (Illus.). 120p. 1994. pap. 290.00 (*0-88937-118-0*); student ed, pap. 26.00 (*0-685-70137-9*) Hogrefe & Huber Pubs.

Cognitive Turn: Sociological & Psychological Perspectives on Science. Ed. by Steve Fuller et al. (Sociology of the Sciences Yearbook Ser.: No. 13). 272p. 1989. lib. bdg. 99.00 (*0-7923-0306-7*) Kluwer Ac.

Cognitive Turn: The Interdisciplinary Story of Thought in Western Culture. Charlotte A. Frick. LC 94-3909. 168p. (Orig.). Date not set. lib. bdg. 43.50 (*0-8191-9473-5*); pap. text ed. 26.50 (*0-8191-9474-3*) U Pr of Amer.

Cognitive Unconscious: A Piagetian Approach to Psychotherapy. Melvin L. Weiner. LC 75-12937. (Illus.). 202p. 1975. 17.50 (*0-915662-01-9*) Intl Psych Pr.

Cognitive Views of Human Motivation. Ed. by Bernard Weiner. 1974. text ed. 44.00 (*0-12-741950-0*) Acad Pr.

Cognitively Diagnostic Assessment. Ed. by Paul D. Nichols et al. 480p. 1995. 89.95 (*0-8058-1588-0*); pap. 39.95 (*0-8058-1589-9*) L Erlbaum Assocs.

Cognitivity Paradox: An Inquiry Concerning the Claims of Philosophy. John Lange. LC 72-90952. 1970. 29.95 (*0-691-07159-4*); pap. 12.95 (*0-691-01967-3*) Princeton U Pr.

Cognizer Almanac: The First Stop for Information on Emerging Computing Technologies. R. Colin Johnson. 807p. 1994. ring bd. 395.00 (*0-9639899-1-X*) Cognizer.

Cognizers: Neural Networks & Machines That Work. R. Colin Johnson & Chappell Brown. 1988. text ed. 29.95 (*0-471-61161-1*) Wiley.

Cogs, Caravels & Galleons: The Sailing Ship, 1000-1650. Ed. by Richard W. Unger. (Conway's History of the Ship Ser.). (Illus.). 208p. 1993. 44.95 (*1-55750-124-6*) Naval Inst Pr.

Cogs in the Soviet Wheel: The Formation of Soviet Man. Mikhail Heller. LC 87-46075. 320p. 1988. 22.95 (*0-394-56926-1*) Knopf.

Cogswells in America. E. O. Jameson. (Illus.). 707p. 1989. reprint ed. lib. bdg. 98.00 (*0-8328-0410-X*); reprint ed. pap. 88.00 (*0-8328-0411-8*) Higginson Bk Co.

***Cogwheels & Other Stories.** Akutagawa Ryunosuke. Tr. by Howard Norman. 80p. 1995. lib. bdg. 27.00 (*0-8095-4874-7*) Borgo Pr.

Cogwheels of Democracy: A Study of the Precinct Captain. Sonya Forthal. LC 71-138232. 106p. 1972. reprint ed. text ed. 35.00 (*0-8371-5589-4*, FOCD, Greenwood Pr) Greenwood.

Cohabitation Contracts. Christopher Barton. LC 84-6102. 138p. 1985. text ed. 55.95 (*0-566-00711-8*) Ashgate Pub Co.

Cohabitation, Marriage, Marital Dissolution, & Remarriage: United States, 1988: PHS 91-1250. No. 194. 1991. write for info. (*0-318-69599-5*) Natl Ctr Health Stats.

Cohabitation Without Marriage. Michael D. Freeman & Christina M. Lyon. 256p. 1983. text ed. 52.95 (*0-566-00455-0*) Ashgate Pub Co.

***Cohassett Beach Chronicles: World War II in the Pacific Northwest.** Kathy Hogan. Ed. by Klancy De Nevers & Lucy Hart. LC 94-47571. (Illus.). 256p. 1995. 25.95 (*0-87071-384-1*) Oreg St U Pr.

Cohealing: Overcoming the Legacy of the Past & Reclaiming Your Life. Hope Sinclair. (Illus.). 321p. (Orig.). 1993. pap. 14.95 (*0-916147-39-8*) Regent Pr.

Coheleth & Song of Songs, with a Commentary Historical & Critical, 2 Vols. in 1. rev. ed. David C. Ginsburg. (Library of Biblical Studies). 1970. 69.50 (*0-87068-059-5*) Ktav.

Cohen & Cohen's Readings in Jurisprudence & Legal Philosophy. 2nd ed. Philip Shuchman. 1099p. 1979. 45.00 (*0-316-78877-5*) Little.

Cohen & Troeltsch: Ethical Monotheistic Religion & Theory of Culture. Wendell S. Dietrich. (Brown Judaic Studies). 1986. text ed. 24.95 (*1-55540-017-5*, 14-01-20); pap. 18.95 (*1-55540-018-3*) Scholars Pr GA.

Cohen Diabetic Rat. Ed. by A. M. Cohen & E. Rosenmann. (Illus.). xii, 200p. 1991. pap. 53.75 (*3-8055-5025-1*) S Karger.

Cohen-Macaulay & Gorenstein Rees Algebras Associated to Filtrations. Shiro Goto & Koji Nishida. LC 94-14402. (Memoirs of the American Mathematical Society Ser.: No. 526). 1994. write for info. (*0-8218-2584-4*) Am Math.

Cohen-Macaulay Rings. Winifrid Bruns & Jurgen Herzog. LC 93-16069. (Cambridge Studies in Advanced Mathematics: No. 39). 400p. (C). 1993. 84.95 (*0-521-41068-1*) Cambridge U Pr.

Cohencidents: Cartoons by David Cohen. David Cohen. (Illus.). 64p. 1987. pap. 3.95 (*0-9619739-0-0*) D Cohen.

Cohens of Tzefat. Miriam S. Zakon. (ArtScroll Youth Ser.). (Illus.). 128p. (YA). (gr. 6-12). 1985. 13.95 (*0-89906-783-2*); pap. 10.95 (*0-89906-784-0*) Mesorah Pubns.

Coherence. David Antin et al. Ed. by Don Wellman. Tr. by Rosmarie Waldrop. (Illus.). 208p. 1981. pap. 6.95 (*0-942030-01-X*) O ARS.

Coherence, Amplification & Quantum Effects in Semiconductor Lasers. Ed. by Yoshihisa Yamamoto. (Series In Pure & Applied Optics). 646p. 1991. text ed. 125.00 (*0-471-51249-4*) Wiley.

Coherence & Grounding in Discourse: Outcome of a Symposium, Eugene, Oregon, June, 1984. Ed. by Russell S. Tomlin. LC 87-898. (Typological Studies in Language: No. 11). x, 512p. (C). 1987. 130.00x (*0-915027-85-2*) Benjamins North Am.

Coherence & NMR. M. Munowitz. LC 88-10605. 289p. 1988. text ed. 74.95 (*0-471-61523-4*) Wiley.

Coherence & Non-Commutative Diagrams in Closed Categories. R. Voreadou. LC 76-50058. (Memoirs Ser.: No. 9/182). 93p. 1977. 21.00 (*0-8218-2182-2*, MEMO 9/182) Am Math.

Coherence & Quantum Optics Five. Ed. by L. Mandel & E. Wolf. LC 83-23067. 1280p. 1984. 160.00 (*0-306-41517-8*, Plenum Pr) Plenum.

Coherence & Quantum Optics Six. Ed. by J. H. Eberly et al. (Illus.). 1312p. 1990. 195.00 (*0-306-43485-7*, Plenum Pr) Plenum.

Coherence & Time Delay Estimation: An Applied Tutorial for Research, Development, Test, & Evaluation Engineers. Intro. by G. Clifford Carter. LC 92-46209. (Illus.). 528p. (C). 1993. text ed. 69.95 (*0-7803-1006-3*, PC03558) Inst Electrical.

Coherence & Verification in Ethics. Ralph D. Ellis. 250p. (Orig.). (C). 1991. lib. bdg. 50.50 (*0-8191-8410-1*); pap. text ed. 20.50 (*0-8191-8411-X*) U Pr of Amer.

***Coherence, Continuity & Cohesion: Theoretical Foundations for Document Design.** Kim S. Campbell. 128p. 1994. 29.95 (*0-8058-1301-2*); pap. 17.95 (*0-8058-1703-4*) L Erlbaum Assocs.

Coherence, Counterpoint, Instrumentation, Instruction in Form: Zusammenhang, Kontrapunkt, Instrumentation, Formenlehre. Arnold Schoenberg. Tr. by Severine Neff & Charlotte M. Cross. LC 92-46699. (Illus.). 135p. 1994. 40.00 (*0-8032-4230-1*) U of Nebr Pr.

Coherence in Art. Karl Aschenbrenner. 1985. lib. bdg. 121.50 (*90-277-1959-4*) Kluwer Ac.

Coherence in Atomic Collision Physics. Ed. by H. J. Beyer et al. LC 88-9796. (Physics of Atoms & Molecules Ser.). (Illus.). 368p. 1988. 95.00 (*0-306-42842-3*, Plenum Pr) Plenum.

Coherence in Psychotic Discourse. Branca T. Ribeiro. LC 92-49156. (Oxford Studies in Sociolinguistics). 1994. 49.95 (*0-19-506597-2*); pap. 22.00 (*0-19-506615-4*) OUP.

Coherence in Spoken & Written Discourse. Ed. by Deborah Tannen. LC 84-2970. (Advances in Discourse Processes Ser.: Vol. 12). 304p. 1984. text ed. 75.00 (*0-89391-097-X*); pap. text ed. 39.50 (*0-89391-098-8*) Ablex Pub.

***Coherence in Spontaneous Text.** Ed. by M. A. Gernsbacher & T. Givon. LC 94-49702. (Typological Studies in Language: No. 31). x, 267p. 1995. lib. bdg. 80.00x (*1-55619-637-7*) Benjamins North Am.

***Coherence in Spontaneous Text.** Ed. by M. A. Gernsbacher & T. Givon. LC 94-49702. (Typological Studies in Language: No. 31). x, 267p. 1995. pap. 32.95x (*1-55619-638-5*) Benjamins North Am.

Coherence in the Qur'an. Mustansir Mir. Ed. by American Trust Publications. 125p. 1987. pap. 7.00 (*0-89259-065-3*) Am Trust Pubns.

Coherence in Writing: Research & Pedagogical Perspectives. Ed. by Ulla Conner & Ann M. Johns. LC 88-50781. 272p. (Orig.). 1990. pap. 14.95 (*0-939791-34-X*) Tchrs Eng Spkrs.

Coherence of Gothic Conventions. Eve K. Sedgwick. Ed. by Devendra P. Varma. LC 79-8462. (Gothic Studies & Dissertations). 1980. lib. bdg. 23.95 (*0-405-12650-6*) Ayer.

Coherence of Gothic Conventions. rev. ed. Eve K. Sedgwick. 150p. 1986. pap. 10.95 (*0-416-01411-9*, 9923) Routledge Chapman & Hall.

Coherence of Kant's Doctrine of Freedom. Bernard Carnois & David Booth. LC 86-15935. xvi, 174p. (C). 1987. 23.95 (*0-226-09394-8*) U Ch Pr.

Coherence of Life Without God Before God: The Problem of Earthly Desires in the Later Theology of Dietrich Bonhoeffer. Terrence Reynolds. 190p. (C). 1989. lib. bdg. 39.00 (*0-8191-7237-5*) U Pr of Amer.

Coherence of Light. Jan Perina. (Orig.). 1985. lib. bdg. 145.50 (*90-277-2004-5*) Kluwer Ac.

Coherence of the Book of Micah: A Literary Analysis. David Hagstrom. LC 86-26107. (Society of Biblical Literature Ser.). 162p. 1988. pap. 11.95 (*0-89130-973-X*, 06 01 89) Scholars Pr GA.

***Coherence of the Pacifism of Walter George Muelder: With His Social Ethics.** Michael D. Blackwell. LC 94-37006. 472p. 1995. text ed. 109.95 (*0-7734-2283-8*, Mellen Univ Pr) E Mellen.

Coherence of Theism. rev. ed. Richard Swinburne. LC 92-30981. (Clarendon Library of Logic & Philosophy). 328p. 1993. 49.95 (*0-19-824069-4*); pap. 19.95 (*0-19-824070-8*) OUP.

Coherence Phenomena in Atoms & Molecules in Laser Fields. Ed. by A. D. Bandrauk & S. C. Wallace. (NATO ASI Series B, Physics: Vol. 287). (Illus.). 402p. (C). 1992. 120.00 (*0-306-44190-X*, Plenum Pr) Plenum.

1348 An Asterisk (*) at the beginning of an entry indicates that the title is appearing in BIP for the first time.

An Asterisk (*) at the beginning of an entry indicates that the title is appearing in BIP for the first time.

1349

Coinage of Nepal. E. H. Walch. (C). 1990. 7.00 (*81-85395-66-7*, Pub. by BR Pub II) S Asia.

Coinage of Nero. E. Sydenham. (Illus.). 1982. reprint ed. lib. bdg. 25.00 (*0-942666-02-X*) S J Durst.

Coinage of Parthia. 2nd ed. David Sellwood. (Illus.). 1980. 35.00 (*0-686-64675-4*) S J Durst.

Coinage of Pharaonic Egypt. J. W. Curtis. 1979. 5.00 (*0-89005-283-2*) Ares.

Coinage of Roman Britain. 2nd ed. Gilbert Askew. 1980. 12.00 (*0-900652-53-5*) Numismatic Fine Arts.

Coinage of Septimius Severus of the Mint of Rome. P. V. Hill. 1977. 12.00 (*0-685-51524-9*) S J Durst.

Coinage of Sybaris after 510 B.C. Colin Kraay. (Illus.). 1977. 2.50 (*0-915018-26-8*) Attic Bks.

Coinage of the Americas. Ed. by Theodore V. Buttrey, Jr. LC 73-75064. (Illus.). 139p. reprint ed. pap. 39.70 (*0-7837-6999-7*, 2046812) Bks Demand.

Coinage of the Arab Amirs of Crete. George C. Miles. (Numismatic Notes & Monographs: 160). (Illus.). 95p. 1960. pap. 12.00 (*0-89722-059-5*) Am Numismatic.

Coinage of the Armenian Kingdoms of Sophene & Commagene. Paul Bedoukian. (Illus.). 39p. (ARM & ENG.). 1985. 6.00 (*0-9606842-3-9*) ANS.

Coinage of the Bar Kokhba War: Typos VI. Leo Mildenberg. 1984. 95.00 (*3-7941-2634-3*) Numismatic Fine Arts.

Coinage of the Civil Wars of 68-69 A.D. Harold Mattingly. 1977. 3.75 (*0-915018-21-7*) Attic Bks.

Coinage of the Crusader States, 1098-1291. Irene F. Preston & Arthur J. Seltman. (Illus.). 1994. write for info. (*0-915018-39-X*) Attic Bks.

Coinage of the Eastern Seleucid Mints, from Seleucus I to Antiochus III. Edward T. Newell. (Numismatic Studies: No. 1). (Illus.). 363p. 1978. reprint ed. 40.00 (*0-89722-174-5*) Am Numismatic.

Coinage of the Greeks. N. J. Stillman. (Illus.). 20p. 1975. pap. 3.00 (*0-916710-22-X*) Obol Intl.

Coinage of the Lycian League. Hyla A. Troxell. (Numismatic Notes & Monographs: No. 162). (Illus.). 299p. 1983. 35.00 (*0-89722-192-3*) Am Numismatic.

Coinage of the Roman Republic. rev. ed. Edward A. Sydenham. Ed. by L. Forrer & C. A. Hersh. LC 75-7345. (Roman History Ser.). (Illus.). 1975. reprint ed. 51.95 (*0-405-07066-7*) Ayer.

Coinage of the Roman Republic. Edward Sydenham. LC 76-12921. (Illus.). 1976. reprint ed. lib. bdg. 40.00 (*0-915262-04-5*) S J Durst.

Coinage of the Western Seleucid Mints, from Seleucus I to Antiochus III. Edward T. Newell. (Numismatic Studies: No. 4). (Illus.). 552p. 1977. reprint ed. 50.00 (*0-89722-183-4*) Am Numismatic.

Coinage of Triumvirs, Antony, Lepidus & Octavian, Illustrative of the History of the Times. H. A. Grueber. (Illus.). 1977. 3.75 (*0-915018-31-4*) Attic Bks.

Coinage of Vindex & Galba, A.D. 68, & the Continuity of the Augustan Principate. Colin M. Kraay. (Illus.). 1977. 3.75 (*0-915018-20-9*) Attic Bks.

Coinage of William Wood. Illus. by Philip Nelson. 1978. reprint ed. pap. 8.00 (*0-915262-21-5*) S J Durst.

Coinages of Alexander the Great. Ed. by Soterios Gardiakos. (Illus.). 1007p. 1981. 295.00 (*0-916710-82-3*) Obol Intl.

Coinages of Demetrius Poliorcetes. E. T. Newell. (Illus.). 1978. 70.00 (*0-916710-36-X*) Obol Intl.

Coinages of Edward I & II. J. J. North. 1968. 4.00 (*0-685-51543-5*) S J Durst.

Coinages of Latin America & the Caribbean. Ed. by E. A. Furber. LC 74-78127. (Gleanings from the Numismatist Ser.: Vol. 5). (Illus.). 385p. 1974. 35.00 (*0-88000-041-4*) Quarterman.

Coincidance. Robert A. Wilson. LC 88-80256. 192p. (Orig.). 1991. pap. 12.95 (*1-56184-004-1*) New Falcon Pubns.

***Coincide: The Orton System of Pest Management.** Donald A. Orton & Thomas L. Green. 189p. (Orig.). (C). Date not set. pap. text ed. 20.95 (*1-887619-03-8*) Plantsm ns Pubns.

Coincidence. Jane McLoughlin. 256p. 1992. 24.95 (*1-85381-478-4*, Pub. by Virago Pr UK) Trafalgar.

Coincidence. Jane McLoughlin. 240p. 1993. pap. 13.95 (*1-85381-603-5*, Pub. by Virago Pr UK) Trafalgar.

Coincidence of Dry & Wet Bulb Temperatures. M. Holmes & S. Adams. (C). 1977. 50.00 (*0-86022-042-7*, Pub. by Build Servs Info Assn UK) St Mut.

Coincidence or Conspiracy? Bernard Fensterwald. (Illus.). 1977. pap. 2.50 (*0-89083-232-3*) Zebra.

***Coincidences: Chance or Fate?** Ken Anderson. 320p. 1995. pap. 12.95 (*0-7137-2523-0*, Pub. by Blandford Pr UK) Sterling.

Coincident Particle Emission from Continuum States in Nuclei (COPECOS) Proceedings of the Workshop on Coincident Particle Emission from Continuum States in Nucle (COPECOS), F R, Germany, June 1984. Ed. by H. Machner & J. Jahn. 642p. 1984. 121.00 (*9971-966-98-0*) World Scientific Pub.

***Coincidental Art of Charles Brockden Brown.** fac. ed. Norman S. Grabo. LC 80-39797. 223p. 1981. reprint ed. pap. 63.60 (*0-7837-8056-7*, 2047809) Bks Demand.

Coiners of Language. Jean-Joseph Goux. Tr. by Jennifer C. Gage. LC 94-8098. (Oklahoma Project for Discourse & Theory Ser.: Vol. 16). 192p. (ENG & FRE.). 1994. 29. 95x (*0-8061-2657-4*) U of Okla Pr.

Coinology. Mort Reed. 1985. 4.50 (*0-89637-005-4*) American Numismatic.

Coins. Carol Benanti. (Collector's Kits Ser.). (Illus.). 32p. (J). (gr. 3 up). 1994. 10.00 (*0-679-85069-4*) Random Bks Yng Read.

Coins. Andrew Burnett. LC 91-9181. (Interpreting the Past Ser.: No. 3). (Illus.). 64p. 1991. pap. 11.00 (*0-520-07628-1*) U CA Pr.

Coins: Facts & Feats. Kames A. Mackay. (Illus.). 1992. 34. 95 (*1-85264-025-1*, Pub. by Seaby UK) Trafalgar.

Coins & Coinages of the Straits Settlements & British Malaya, 1786-1951. F. Pridmore. 1968. 35.00 (*0-685-51510-9*) S J Durst.

Coins & Collectors. Q. David Bowers. (Illus.). 216p. 1988. reprint ed. pap. 9.95 (*0-943161-11-8*) Bowers & Merena.

Coins & Costume in Late Antiquity. Jutta A. Bruhn. LC 93-30777. (Byzantine Collection Publications Ser.: No. 9). (Illus.). 68p. 1993. pap. 12.00 (*0-88402-219-6*) Dumbarton Oaks.

Coins & Currency. Brenda R. Lewis. LC 92-46359. (Hobby Handbooks Ser.). (Illus.). 80p. (J). (gr. 5 up). 1993. lib. bdg. 13.99 (*0-679-92662-3*) Random Bks Yng Read.

***Coins & Currency Systems of Post-Gupta Bengal: (c. AD 550-700)** B. N. Mukherjee. (C). 1993. 19.50x (*81-215-0563-1*, Pub. by Munshiram Manoharial II) S Asia.

Coins & Documents from the Medieval Middle East. S. M. Stern. (Collected Studies: No. CS238). 330p. (C). 1986. reprint ed. lib. bdg. 95.00 (*0-86078-186-0*, Pub. by Variorum UK) Ashgate Pub Co.

Coins & Medals of the English Civil War. Edward Besley. (Illus.). 121p. 1992. 39.95 (*1-85264-065-0*, Pub. by Seaby UK) Trafalgar.

Coins & Medals of the Knights of Malta. H. C. Schembri. 1966. 40.00 (*0-685-51537-0*) S J Durst.

Coins & Medals of the Vatican. Joseph Sadow & Thomas Sarro, Jr. LC 76-40814. (Illus.). 1977. lib. bdg. 15.00 (*0-915262-06-1*) S J Durst.

Coins & Minting. Denis R. Cooper. 1989. pap. 25.00 (*0-7478-0069-3*, Pub. by Shire UK) St Mut.

Coins & the Archaeologist. rev. ed. Ed. by Richard Reece & John Casey. (Illus.). 306p. 1988. reprint ed. 39.95 (*1-85264-011-1*, Pub. by Seaby UK) Trafalgar.

Coins & Their Cities: Architecture on the Ancient Coins of Greece, Rome, & Palestine. Martin J. Price & Bluma L. Trell. LC 78-321015. (Illus.). 300p. reprint ed. pap. 85. 50 (*0-7837-3593-6*, 2043457) Bks Demand.

Coins & Tokens of Ireland. P. Seaby. 1972. lib. bdg. 8.00 (*0-686-45261-5*, Pub. by Seaby UK) S J Durst.

Coins & Tokens of Nova Scotia. E. Courteau. (Illus.). 1982. reprint ed. pap. 8.00 (*0-942666-09-7*) S J Durst.

Coins & Tokens of Scotland. A. Purvey. 1976. lib. bdg. 8.00 (*0-686-45253-4*, Pub. by Seaby UK) S J Durst.

Coins-Coins-Coins: The Collector's Guide. Joseph Lamagna & Carmen T. Pisano. 56p. (Orig.). 1988. pap. 8.50 (*0-9610464-1-4*) J Lamagna.

Coins, Culture, & History in the Ancient World: Numismatic & Other Studies in Honor of Bluma L. Trell. Ed. by Lionel Casson & Martin Price. LC 81-10491. (Illus.). 205p. reprint ed. pap. 58.50 (*0-7837-3590-1*, 2043454) Bks Demand.

Coins Exhibited in the Archaeological Museum of the American University of Beirut. Dimitri Baramki. (Illus.). 1968. pap. 22.95 (*0-8156-6010-3*, Am U Beirut) Syracuse U Pr.

Coin's Financial School. William H. Harvey. Ed. by Richard Hofstadter. LC 63-20768. (Illus.). 263p. reprint ed. pap. 75.00 (*0-7837-1515-3*, 2041792) Bks Demand.

Coins of Alexander the Great. L. Mueller et al. Ed. by A. Oikonomides. (Illus.). 173p. 1981. pap. 15.00 (*0-89005-382-0*) Ares.

Coins of Ancient Lycia. Charles Fellows. (Illus.). 1976. 8.00 (*0-916710-25-4*) Obol Intl.

Coins of Ancient Meiron. Joyce Raynor et al. LC 87-19135. (Meiron Excavation Project Ser.: Vol. 4). vii, 140p. 1988. text ed. 27.50 (*0-89757-208-4*); pap. text ed. 19.50 (*0-89757-209-2*) Am Sch Orient Res.

Coins of Ancient Sicily. G. F. Hill. Bd. with Catalog of Greek Coins in the British Museum: Sicily. (Illus.). 1985. reprint ed. Set lib. bdg. 50.00 (*0-915262-96-7*) S J Durst.

Coins of Bible Days. F. Banks. LC 84-71643. 1985. reprint ed. pap. 16.00 (*0-942666-41-0*) S J Durst.

Coins of Colonial Virginia. 2nd ed. Eric P. Newman. (Illus.). 1990. pap. 20.00 (*0-915262-67-3*) S J Durst.

Coins of Cyprus, Fourteen Eighty-Nine to Fifteen Seventy-One. 2nd ed. Soterios Gardiakos. (Illus.). 1975. pap. 5.00 (*0-916710-19-X*) Obol Intl.

Coins of England & the United Kingdom. P. F. Purvey. (Illus.). 1991. lib. bdg. 22.00 (*0-900652-69-1*, Pub. by Seaby UK) S J Durst.

Coins of India. C. J. Brown. (C). 1988. reprint ed. 14.50 (*81-206-0345-1*, Pub. by Asian Educ Servs II) S Asia.

Coins of Japan. Ng Munroe. 1990. reprint ed. lib. bdg. 40. 00 (*0-942666-49-6*) S J Durst.

Coins of Medieval Europe. Philip Grierson. (Illus.). 248p. 1991. 75.00 (*1-85264-058-8*, Pub. by Seaby UK) Trafalgar.

Coins of Mexico. Frank W. Grove. LC 80-54430. 480p. 1981. lib. bdg. 60.00 (*0-88000-123-2*) Quarterman.

Coins of New Jersey. Edward Maris. (Illus.). 1987. reprint ed. pap. 15.00 (*0-685-05536-1*) S J Durst.

Coins of Roman Britain. G. Askew. (Illus.). 1981. pap. 16. 00 (*0-686-45246-1*, Pub. by Seaby UK) S J Durst.

Coins of South Germany in the Thirteenth Century. D. M. Metcalf. 1961. 15.00 (*0-685-51539-7*) S J Durst.

Coins of the Ancient Celts. Derek Allen & Dephne Nash. (Illus.). 265p. 1980. 26.50 (*0-85224-371-5*, Pub. by Edinburgh U Pr UK) Col U Pr.

Coins of the British Commonwealth of Nations to the End of the Reign of George VI, 4 vols. Incl. Vol. I. Europe. 20.00 (*0-686-52274-5*); Vol. III. West Indies. F. Pridmore. 30.00 (*0-686-52275-3*); Vol. IV, Part I. India. 70.00 (*0-686-52276-1*); Vol. IV, Pt. II. India. Vol. IV, Part II. 75.00 (*0-685-04430-0*); write for info. (*0-318-55577-8*) S J Durst.

Coins of the Genoese Rulers of Chios (1314-1429) Paul Lambros. Tr. by A. Barozzi. (Illus.). 27p. 1968. pap. 5.00 (*0-916710-00-9*) Obol Intl.

Coins of the Hapsburg Emperors & Related Issues 1619-1919. S. R. Mort. (Illus.). 1990. reprint ed. lib. bdg. 30. 00 (*0-942666-15-1*) S J Durst.

Coins of the Isle of Man. pap. 7.50 (*0-89979-067-4*) British Am Bks.

Coins of the Jews. Frederic W. Madden. (International Numismata Orientalia Ser.: Vol. II). (Illus.). viii, 1703p. 1976. reprint ed. write for info. (*3-487-06006-X*, Pub. by Georg Olms GW) Lubrecht & Cramer.

Coins of the Mughal Emperors. H. Nelson Wright. (C). 1980. reprint ed. 14.00 (*0-8364-2388-7*, Pub. by Usha II) S Asia.

Coins of the Nomes & Prefecture of Roman Egypt. J. DeRouge & F. Feaurdent. (Illus.). (FRE.). 1979. reprint ed. 20.00 (*0-916710-41-6*); reprint ed. pap. 10.00 (*0-685-95531-1*) Obol Intl.

Coins of the Roman Empire. Robert B. Carson. (Illus.). 480p. 1990. 199.50 (*0-415-01591-X*, A3727) Routledge.

Coins of the Seleucid Empire from the Collection of Arthur Houghton. Arthur Houghton. LC 84-672605. (Ancient Coins in North American Collections 4: No. 4). (Illus.). 225p. reprint ed. pap. 64.20 (*0-7837-5974-6*, 2045778) Bks Demand.

Coins of the Twelve Caesars: A Numismatic History of Rome. David Van Meter. (Illus.). 195p. (Orig.). 1990. pap. 19.95 (*1-878420-01-1*) Laurion Pub.

Coins Question & Answer. Whitman Coin Products Staff. 1993. pap. 5.95 (*0-307-09359-X*) Western Pub.

Coinshooter's Manual, Poor Man's Guide to Financial Independence: Profession Secrets for Profitable Coinshooting. Karl Von Mueller. (Coin Collecting Ser.). (Illus.). 48p. 1984. pap. 5.00 (*0-89316-632-4*) Exanimo Pr.

Coinshooting, How & Where to Do It: Using a Metal Detector Effectively. H. Glenn Carson. (Illus.). 63p. (Orig.). 1971. reprint ed. pap. text ed. 6.95 (*0-941620-30-1*) Carson Ent.

Coinshooting II: Digging Deeper Coins. H. Glenn Carson. (Illus.). 106p. (Orig.). 1982. pap. 7.95 (*0-941620-17-4*) Carson Ent.

Cointegration: Expository Essays for the Applied Economist. Ed. by B. Bhaskara Rao. LC 94-5981. 1994. text ed. 75.00 (*0-312-12177-6*) St Martin.

Cointelpro: The FBI's Secret War on Political Freedom. Nelson Blackstock. LC 88-62040. 1990. reprint ed. lib. bdg. 45.00 (*0-937091-05-7*); reprint ed. pap. 15.95 (*0-937091-04-9*) Pathfinder NY.

COINTELPRO Papers: Documents from the FBI's Secret Wars Against Dissent in the United States. Ward Churchill & Jim VanderWall. 320p. (Orig.). 1990. 40.00 (*0-89608-360-8*); pap. 16.00 (*0-89608-359-4*) South End Pr.

COIS, '90: Conference on Office Information Systems, Held in Cambridge, MA, April 25-27, 1990. Ed. by Frederick H. Lochovsky & Robert Allen. (Illus.). viii, 291p. 1990. pap. text ed. 22.00 (*0-89791-358-2*, 611900) Assn Compu Machinery.

Coit Family: or the Descendants of John Coit, at Salem, Mass., in 1638, at Gloucester in 1644, & at New London, Connecticut, in 1650. F. W. Chapman. (Illus.). 341p. 1993. reprint ed. lib. bdg. 64.00 (*0-8328-1362-1*); reprint ed. pap. 54.00 (*0-8328-1363-X*) Higginson Bk Co.

Coit Tower, San Francisco: Its History & Art. Masha Z. Jewett. LC 83-5814. (Illus.). 136p. (Orig.). 1983. pap. 10.00 (*0-912078-75-8*) Volcano Pr.

Coke: Quality & Production. 2nd ed. R. Loison et al. (Illus.). 555p. 1989. text ed. 270.00 (*0-408-02870-X*) Butterworth-Heinemann.

Coke en Stock. Herge. (Illus.). 64p. (FRE.). (J). (gr. 7-9). 1992. reprint ed. write for info. (*0-7859-4563-6*) Fr & Eur.

Coke Formation on Metal Surfaces. Ed. by Lyle F. Albright & R. T. Baker. LC 82-16335. (ACS Symposium Ser.: No. 202). 321p. 1982. lib. bdg. 42.95 (*0-8412-0745-3*) Am Chemical.

Coke of Norfolk: A Financial & Agricultural Study, 1707-1842. R. A. Parker. (Illus.). 1975. 39.00 (*0-19-822403-6*) OUP.

Coke on Magna Carta: The Common Law. Edward Coke. 1979. lib. bdg. 300.00 (*0-8490-2885-X*) Gordon Pr.

Coke Oven Techniques. Ed. by Graham & Trotman Ltd. Staff. 350p. 1982. pap. text ed. 79.00 (*0-86010-366-8*) G & T Inc.

Coke Oven Wall Pressure: Measurement, Cause & Effect. LC 90-80538. 192p. 1990. 30.00 (*0-932897-52-5*) Iron & Steel.

Coke Reactivity & Its Effect on Blast Furnace Operation. LC 90-80539. 164p. 1990. 30.00 (*0-932897-51-7*) Iron & Steel.

Coker Creek: Cross Roads to History. Fred Brown. 128p. 1991. pap. 9.95 (*0-9630962-0-6*) C C Ruritan.

Coker's Survey of Dorsetshire. Thomas Gerard. 176p. 1987. 55.00 (*0-686-75652-5*) Dorset Pr.

Cokesbury Worship Hymnal. 288p. 1976. reprint ed. 7.50 (*0-687-08863-1*); reprint ed. 9.95 (*0-687-08866-6*); reprint ed. pap. 4.95 (*0-687-08865-8*) Abingdon.

Cokolina & the Wild Island. Dorothee Bohlke. Ed. by Jill Max & Elizabeth Bradford. Tr. by Mangold Verlag. LC 91-24337. (Magic Mountain Fables Ser.). (Illus.). 24p. (J). (gr. k-3). 1991. lib. bdg. 14.60 (*1-56074-032-9*) Garrett Ed Corp.

Col Dave & the Schroff Connection: Chronicles of a Hoosier Patriot. David M. Williams. 512p. 1993. pap. 19.95 (*0-9637702-0-9*) Keap Pub.

Col. Don Jose Cadalso. Russell P. Sebold. LC 72-125247. (Twayne's World Authors Ser.). 187p. (C). 1971. lib. bdg. 15.95 (*0-8290-1741-0*) Irvington.

Col. George Rogers Clark's Sketch of His Campaign in the Illinois in 1778-9 with an Introduction by Hon. Henry Pirtle. George R. Clark. LC 73-146384. (First American Frontier Ser.). 1975. reprint ed. 24.95 (*0-405-02835-0*) Ayer.

Col. George Stewart & His Wife Margaret Harris: Their Ancestors & Descendants. R. Stewart. (Illus.). 522p. reprint ed. lib. bdg. 89.50 (*0-8328-1672-8*); reprint ed. pap. 79.50 (*0-8328-1673-6*) Higginson Bk Co.

***Col. P. W. Norris: Yellowstone's Greatest Superintendent: America's Early Environmental Champion, 1877-1882.** Don Binkowski. 396p. (Orig.). 1995. pap. write for info. (*0-9646527-0-6*) D Binkowski.

Col. Weatherford & His Friends. Gordon Grand. (Fifty Greatest Bks.). (Illus.). 242p. (YA). (gr. 10 up). 1991. reprint ed. 40.00 (*1-56416-026-2*) Derrydale Pr.

Cola Cowboys. large type ed. Franklyn Wood. 560p. 1984. 15.95 (*0-7089-1094-7*) Ulverscroft.

Cola Magica de Marjorie. Marc P. Mannino & Angelica L. Mannino. Tr. by Patricia Norman-Grumbley. LC 93-86116. (Illus.). 32p. (Orig.). (SPA.). (J). (gr. k-3). 1993. pap. 7.95 (*0-9638340-1-0*) Sugar Sand.

***Colar Yo Quiero.** Judy Barron. (J). (ps-3). 1995. pap. 4.95 (*0-590-25011-6*) Scholastic Inc.

Colas Breugnon. Romain Rolland. 280p. (FRE.). 1988. 28. 95 (*0-686-55241-5*); pap. 10.95 (*0-7859-5445-7*) Fr & Eur.

Colbert. Ines Murat. Tr. by Robert F. Cook & Jeannie Van Asselt. LC 84-2194. (Illus.). 308p. reprint ed. pap. 87.80 (*0-8357-3134-0*, 2039397) Bks Demand.

Colbert's Medico English - Spanish Instant Communication for the Medical Profession. Roman Colbert. 322p. 1991. Incls. Mult-media Software. pap. write for info. (*0-9630253-0-9*) R Colbert.

Colby, Kerr, & Robinson's Color Atlas of Oral Pathology. 5th ed. Robinson & Miller. (Illus.). 198p. 1989. text ed. 57.50 (*0-397-51043-8*) Lippincott.

Colchester Past. Patrick Denney. 1993. pap. 16.00 (*0-86025-421-6*, Pub. by Ian Henry Pubns UK) Empire Pub Srvs.

Cold: The Record of an Antarctic Sledge Journey. limited ed. Laurence M. Gould. LC 84-217845. (Illus.). 213p. 1984. reprint ed. 19.95 (*0-9613911-2-X*) Carleton Coll.

Cold Allies. Patricia Anthony. 304p. 1994. pap. text ed. 4.99 (*0-441-00018-5*) Ace Bks.

Cold Allies. Patricia Anthony. LC 92-16195. 1993. 21.95 (*0-15-118503-4*) HarBrace.

Cold & Chilled Storage Technology. Dellino. 1990. text ed. 134.95 (*0-442-20673-9*) Chapman & Hall.

Cold & Flu Fighter see Jane Brody's Cold & Flu Fighter

Cold & Hot Winter. Johanna Hurwitz. LC 88-5144. (Illus.). 144p. (J). (gr. 3-7). 1988. 12.95 (*0-688-07839-7*) Morrow Jr Bks.

Cold & Hot Winter. Johanna Hurwitz. (J). (gr. 3-7). 1989. pap. 3.25 (*0-590-42619-2*, Apple Paperbacks) Scholastic Inc.

Cold Anger: A Story of Faith & Power Politics. Mary B. Rogers. LC 90-35619. 320p. (Orig.). 1990. pap. 14.95 (*0-929398-13-0*) UNTX Pr.

Cold As Ice. Carolyn Keene. Ed. by Ann Greenberg. (Nancy Drew Files Ser.: No. 54). 160p. (Orig.). (YA). (gr. 7 up). 1990. pap. 3.75 (*0-671-70031-6*, Archway) PB.

Cold As Ice. Elizabeth Levy. 176p. 1989. pap. 2.95 (*0-380-70315-7*, Flare) Avon.

Cold As Ice. Charles Sheffield. 384p. 1993. mass mkt. 4.99 (*0-8125-1163-8*) Tor Bks.

Cold Asylum. James Axler. (Deathlands Ser.). 1994. mass mkt. 4.99 (*0-373-62520-0*, 1-62520-1) Harlequin Bks.

Cold Before Morning: A Heart-Warming Novel of Pioneer Life in Florida. John P. Jones, Jr. 240p. 1992. 15.95 (*0-942407-18-0*) Father & Son.

***Cold Beverage Market.** 292p. (Orig.). 1995. pap. 795.00 (*0-7605-2136-0*) Rector Pr.

Cold Black Preach. Robert H. DeCoy. 224p. 1983. pap. 2.25 (*0-87067-220-7*, BH220) Holloway.

Cold Blood. large type ed. Leo Bruce. 320p. 1983. 15.95 (*0-7089-0968-X*) Ulverscroft.

***Cold Blood, Vol. III.** Ed. by Peter Sellers. 208p. 1995. lib. bdg. 37.00 (*0-8095-4848-8*) Borgo Pr.

***Cold Blood, Vol. V.** Ed. by Peter Sellers & John North. 240p. 1995. lib. bdg. 37.00 (*0-8095-4847-X*) Borgo Pr.

***Cold Blood: Murder in Canada.** Ed. by Peter Sellers. 250p. 1995. lib. bdg. 33.00 (*0-8095-4533-0*) Borgo Pr.

Cold Blood: New Tales of Mystery & Horror. Ed. by Richard T. Chizmar. LC 90-72038. 408p. 1990. 25.00 (*0-929480-57-0*) Mark Ziesing.

Cold Blood: New Tales of Mystery & Horror. limited ed. Ed. by Richard T. Chizmar. LC 90-72038. 408p. 1990. 75.00 (*0-929480-60-0*) Mark Ziesing.

Cold-Blooded Animals. (Illus.). 80p. (J). (gr. k-6). 1986. pap. 14.95 (*0-318-65617-5*) Raintree Steck-V.

Cold-Blooded Animals. Maurice Burton. (World of Science Ser.). (Illus.). 64p. 1985. 15.95 (*0-8160-1074-9*) Facts on File.

Cold-Blooded Animals, Set. LC 80-24150. (Let's Discover Library). (Illus.). 80p. (J). (gr. k-6). 1986. pap. 199.00 (*0-8172-2603-6*) Raintree Steck-V.

Cold-Blooded Business. Dana Stabenow. LC 93-32315. (Kate Shugak Mystery Ser.). (Orig.). 1994. 17.95 (*0-425-14173-X*) Berkley Pub.

***Cold-Blooded Business.** Dana Stabenow. 240p. (Orig.). 1994. pap. text ed. 17.95 (*0-425-15849-7*, Prime Crime) Berkley Pub.

***Cold Boiled Potatoes & Buttermilk.** Cliff Morrow. 1994. 12.95 (*0-533-11142-0*) Vantage.

Cold Call. Dianne G. Pugh. Ed. by Dana Isaacson. LC 92-40549. 288p. 1993. 20.00 (*0-671-77841-2*) PB.

Cold Call. Dianne G. Pugh. Ed. by Dana Isaacson. 288p. 1994. mass mkt. 5.50 (*0-671-77842-0*) PB.

Cold Calling Techniques (That Really Work!) 3rd ed. Stephan Schiffman. 1991. pap. 7.95 (*1-55850-860-0*) Adams Pubng.

Cold Cash War. Robert Asprin. 224p. (Orig.). 1992. pap. 4.50 (*0-441-11382-6*) Ace Bks.

C

An Asterisk (*) at the beginning of an entry indicates that the title is appearing in BIP for the first time.

Cold Chills. Adam Mills. (Twin Connection Ser.: No. 10). (J). (gr. 4 up). 1989. pap. 2.95 (*0-345-35929-1*) Ballantine.
Cold Choice: Pictures of a South African Reality. Struan Robertson. 1991. 24.95 (*0-86543-217-1*) Africa World.
Cold Choice: Pictures of a South African Reality. Struan Robertson. 128p. reprint ed. pap. 36.50 (*0-7837-6567-3*, 2046132) Bks Demand.
Cold Cleaning with Halogenated Solvents - STP 403A. 52p. 1981. pap. 7.25 (*0-8031-0758-7*, 04-403010-15) ASTM.
***Cold Clear Day: The Athletic Biography of Buddy Edelen.** 2nd ed. Frank J. Murphy. LC 91-9113. (Illus.). 200p. (Orig.). 1995. pap. 11.95 (*0-614-06930-0*) Wind Sprint.
Cold-Climate Gardening: How to Extend Your Growing Season by at Least 30 Days. Lewis Hill. LC 86-45712. 320p. 1987. pap. 14.95 (*0-88266-441-7*, Garden Way Pub) Storey Comm Inc.
Cold Climate Hydrometeorology. D. S. Upadhyay. 600p. 1995. text ed. 44.95 (*0-470-21955-6*) Halsted Pr.
***Cold Climate Landforms.** Ed. by David J. A. Evans. 1994. text ed. 165.00 (*0-471-94043-7*) Wiley.
Cold Climbs in Britain: The Great Snow & Ice Climbs of the British Isles. Ken Wilson et al. (Illus.). 280p. 1983. 50.00 (*0-906371-16-3*, Pub. by H & S UK) Trafalgar.
Cold Coffin. large type ed. Erica Quest. (General Ser.). 432p. 1993. 21.95 (*0-7089-2830-7*) Ulverscroft.
Cold, Cold Heart. James Elliot. LC 94-1261. 1994. 21.95 (*0-385-31329-2*) Delacorte.
***Cold Cold Heart.** Elliott. 1995. mass mkt. (*0-440-21863-2*) Dell.
Cold, Cold Heart. Ann Williams. (Silhouette Intimate Moments Ser.). 1993. mass mkt. 3.39 (*0-373-07487-5*, 5-07487-7) Silhouette.
Cold, Cold Heart. large type ed. James Elliott. LC 94-21913. 534p. 1994. 23.95 (*0-7862-0287-4*) Thorndike Pr.
Cold, Cold Heart. large type ed. James Elliott. LC 94-21913. 1995. pap. 18.95 (*0-7862-0288-2*) Thorndike Pr.
Cold Comfort. Maggie Anderson. LC 86-7004. (Poetry Ser.). 64p. 1986. 19.95 (*0-8229-3542-2*); pap. 10.95 (*0-8229-5384-6*) U of Pittsburgh Pr.
Cold Comfort. M. D. Lake. 1990. mass mkt. 4.99 (*0-380-76032-0*) Avon.
Cold Comfort: Keeping Warm in the Outdoors. Glenn Randall. (Illus.). 144p. (Orig.). 1987. pap. 10.95 (*0-941130-46-0*) Lyons & Burford.
Cold Comfort Farm. Stella Gibbons. 19.00 (*0-8446-6148-1*) Peter Smith.
Cold Comfort Farm. Stella Gibbons. 1977. mass mkt. 7.00 (*0-14-000140-9*, Penguin Bks) Viking Penguin.
Cold Coming. Tony Harrison. 1991. pap. 6.95 (*1-85224-186-1*) Dufour.
Cold Coming. large type ed. Mary Kelly. 1990. 21.95 (*0-7089-2192-2*) Ulverscroft.
Cold Copper Tears. Glen Cook. 256p. 1988. pap. 3.50 (*0-451-15773-7*, ROC) NAL-Dutton.
Cold Cuisine. Helen Hecht. 352p. 1990. pap. 9.95 (*0-88001-254-4*) Ecco Pr.
Cold Cures. Michael Castleman. (Orig.). 1987. mass mkt. 5.95 (*0-449-90225-0*, Columbine) Fawcett.
***Cold Day.** Roderick Hunt. (Oxford Reading Tree Ser.). (Illus.). 16p. (J). (gr. k-k). 1994. pap. 1.99 (*0-19-916307-3*) OUP.
Cold Day for Murder. Dana Stabenow. 1992. pap. 4.99 (*0-425-13301-X*) Berkley Pub.
Cold Deception. Shirley R. Wood. LC 89-36786. 227p. 1991. pap. 13.95 (*0-87949-311-9*) Ashley Bks.
Cold Downdraughts. 1991. 120.00 (*0-86022-253-5*, Pub. by Build Servs Info Assn UK) St Mut.
Cold Dread. Barbara Siegal & Scott Seigel. Ed. by Pat MacDonald. (Ghostworld Ser.: No. 4). 176p. (Orig.). (YA). 1992. pap. 2.99 (*0-671-75946-9*) PB.
Cold Eye. Giles Blunt. 288p. 1990. pap. 3.95 (*0-380-70876-0*) Avon.
Cold Face - Warm Heart. Nellie McCaslin. LC 93-5273. 20p. (J). 1993. pap. 4.00 (*0-88734-440-2*) Players Pr.
Cold Feet. Kerry Tucker. 1993. mass mkt. 4.50 (*0-06-109985-6*, Harp PBks) HarpC.
***Cold Feet II: Beginning Waltz & Two-Step Basics.** Kaye Anderson. (Fancy Dancing Ser.). (Illus.). 164p. (Orig.). Date not set. pap. 15.95 (*0-9625895-7-8*) Dance Action.
Cold Fire. Dean Koontz. 432p. 1991. pap. text ed. 6.99 (*0-425-13071-1*) Berkley Pub.
Cold Fire. large type ed. Dean R. Koontz. 1991. reprint ed. lib. bdg. 21.95 (*1-56054-179-2*) Thorndike Pr.
Cold Fire. large type ed. Dean R. Koontz. 652p. 1992. pap. 14.95 (*1-56054-978-5*) Thorndike Pr.
Cold Fire: Alienation & the Myth of Culture. Stanley D. Rosenberg & Bernard J. Bergen. LC 76-3918. 224p. reprint ed. pap. 63.90 (*0-317-41766-5*, 2025637) Bks Demand.
Cold-Formed Steel Design. 2nd ed. Wei-Wen Yu. LC 84-27048. 656p. 1991. text ed. 94.95 (*0-471-61970-1*) Wiley.
Cold-Formed Steel in Tall Buildings. Council on Tall Buildings Staff. 224p. 1993. text ed. 45.00 (*0-07-012529-5*) McGraw.
Cold Frame. Carol Frost. (Poetry Chapbook Ser.). 28p. (Orig.). 1982. pap. 4.00 (*0-937669-06-7*) Owl Creek Pr.
Cold Front. William H. Lovejoy. 1990. mass mkt. 4.50 (*0-8217-3041-X*) Zebra.
Cold Fusion: A Challenge to United States Science Policy. Lyndon H. LaRouche, Jr. Ed. by Paul Gallagher. LC 92-60722. (Illus.). 173p. (Orig.). (C). 1992. pap. 20.00 (*0-9621095-7-6*) Schiller Inst.
Cold Fusion: The Scientific Fiasco of the Century. John R. Huizenga. LC 93-28865. 1994. pap. 15.95 (*0-19-855817-1*) OUP.
Cold Fusion Impact in the Enhanced Energy Age. Hall Fox. 100p. 1992. pap. 19.95 (*0-9634978-0-4*) Fusion Info.
Cold Hand in Mine. Robert Aickman. 1993. reprint ed. lib. bdg. 18.95 (*0-89968-416-5*, Lghtyr Pr) Buccaneer Bks.
Cold Harbors. C. W. Truesdale. 1973. 4.50 (*0-686-27598-5*); write for info. (*0-686-27599-3*) Latitudes Pr.
Cold Harbour. Jack Higgins. 1990. write for info. (*0-671-94343-X*) S&S Trade.
Cold Harbour. large type ed. Jack Higgins. LC 90-11021. 426p. 1990. reprint ed. lib. bdg. 21.95 (*1-56054-021-4*) Thorndike Pr.
Cold Harbour. large type ed. Jack Higgins. 393p. 1991. reprint ed. pap. 13.95 (*0-89621-998-4*) Thorndike Pr.
Cold Harbour. Jack Higgins. Ed. by Bill Grose. 1990. reprint ed. mass mkt. 5.99 (*0-671-68426-4*) PB.
Cold Hearths & Barren Slopes: Woodfuel Crisis in the Third World. Bina Agarwal. LC 85-61078. 209p. (C). 1986. 21.00 (*0-913215-03-1*) Riverdale Co.
***Cold Hearts & Gentle People.** John R. Riggs. LC 94-25441. 1994. 17.95 (*1-56980-021-9*) Barricade Bks.
***Cold Hearts & Gentle People.** large type ed. John R. Riggs. 1995. 19.95 (*0-7862-0317-X*) Thorndike Pr.
Cold Heaven. Camille Roy. LC 93-84574. 89p. 1993. 9.00 (*1-882022-15-7*) O Bks.
Cold in July. Joe R. Lansdale. 208p. 1995. mass mkt. 5.50 (*0-446-40430-6*, Mysterious Paperbk) Warner Bks.
Cold in the Earth. Ann Granger. 256p. 1994. mass mkt. 4.99 (*0-380-72213-5*) Avon.
Cold in the Earth. large type ed. Ann Granger. 576p. 1994. 23.95 (*0-7089-3111-1*) Ulverscroft.
Cold in the Earth: A Mitchell & Markby Village Mystery. Ann Granger. LC 92-41833. 1993. 17.95 (*0-312-08747-0*) St Martin.
Cold Irish Earth. Knute Skinner. LC 93-60594. 1993. pap. 5.00 (*0-932264-04-2*) Trask Hse Bks.
Cold Iron. Nicolas Freeling. 240p. 1988. pap. 3.95 (*0-14-009252-8*, Penguin Bks) Viking Penguin.
Cold Is Nothing to Sneeze At. Susan Perry. (Umbrella Bks.). (Illus.). (J). (gr. 2-6). 1992. lib. bdg. 21.36 (*0-89565-819-4*) Childs World.
Cold Is the Sea. Edward L. Beach. 416p. 1988. pap. 3.95 (*0-8217-2507-6*) Zebra.
Cold Kill. Jack Olsen. 1988. mass mkt. 5.95 (*0-440-20212-4*) Dell.
***Cold Kiss.** Roxanne Longstreet. 256p. 1995. mass mkt. 4.50 (*0-8217-4812-2*) Windsor NY.
Cold Light. John Harvey. LC 93-6263. 1994. 22.00 (*0-8050-2046-2*) H Holt & Co.
Cold Light of Dawn: A History of Canadian Astronomy. Richard A. Jarrell. (Illus.). 264p. (C). 1988. text ed. 40.00 (*0-8020-2653-2*) U of Toronto Pr.
Cold Mind. David L. Lindsey. 352p. 1990. mass mkt. 5.99 (*0-671-73338-9*) PB.
Cold Mind. David L. Lindsey. 1994. mass mkt. 6.50 (*0-553-56081-6*) Bantam.
Cold Morning Sky. Marya Zaturenska. LC 79-127827. 62p. 1970. reprint ed. text ed. 38.50 (*0-8371-3061-1*, ZACM, Greenwood Pr) Greenwood.
Cold-Moulded & Strip-Planked Wood Boatbuilding. Ian Nicolson. (Illus.). 187p. 1991. 34.95 (*0-924486-14-7*) Sheridan.
Cold Mountain: One Hundred One Chinese Poems. 2nd rev. ed. Han-shan. Tr. by Burton Watson. LC 91-53227. (Pocket Classics Ser.). 112p. 1992. reprint ed. 6.00 (*0-87773-668-5*) Shambhala Pubns.
Cold Mountain: One Hundred Poems by the Tang Poet Han Shan. Han Shan. Tr. by Burton Watson. LC 62-15847. 118p. 1970. reprint ed. pap. text ed. 13.00 (*0-231-03450-4*) Col U Pr.
Cold Neutron Research in the U. S. Government. H. J. Prask et al. (Illus.). 145p. (Orig.). (C). 1993. pap. text ed. 50.00 (*0-7881-0046-7*) Diane Pub.
***Cold Night, Brittle Light.** Richard Thompson. (Illus.). 32p. (Orig.). (J). (gr. 1-4). 1994. pap. 5.95 (*1-55143-009-6*) Orca Bk Pubs.
Cold Nights, Fast Trails. Dave Olesen. 224p. 1989. 16.95 (*1-55971-041-1*, 0184) NorthWord.
Cold of Poetry. Lyn Hejinian. (Sun & Moon Classics Ser.: No. 42). 204p. (Orig.). 1994. pap. 12.95 (*1-55713-063-9*) Sun & Moon CA.
Cold One. Christopher Pike. 352p. 1994. 21.00 (*0-312-85117-0*) Tor Bks.
***Cold One.** Christopher Pike. 416p. 1995. mass mkt. write for info. (*0-614-05506-7*) Tor Bks.
Cold Paper: A Mother's Search for Her Daughter. Joannie Liesenfelt. 285p. 1992. pap. 14.95 (*0-9637547-1-8*) Arbor Hill Pr.
Cold Pasta. James McNair. LC 85-363. (Illus.). 96p. 1985. pap. 11.95 (*0-87701-353-5*) Chronicle Bks.
Cold Peace: America, Japan, Germany, & the Struggle for Supremacy. Jeffrey E. Garten. LC 91-58013. 204p. 1993. pap. 12.00 (*0-8129-2205-0*, Times Bks) Random.
Cold Peace: The Struggle for Supremacy in the Post-Cold War World. Jeffrey E. Garten. 1992. 22.00 (*0-8129-1979-3*, Times Bks) Random.
Cold Plasma in Materials Technology: From Fundamentals to Applications. Alfred Grill. LC 93-42135. 1994. 69.95 (*0-7803-1055-1*, PC04093) Inst Electrical.
Cold Plasma Waves. Henry G. Booker. LC 84-9018. 1984. lib. bdg. 140.00 (*90-247-2977-7*) Kluwer Ac.
Cold-Pressing Technology. C. Iliescu. (Studies in Mechanical Engineering: No. 9). 560p. 1990. 161.75 (*0-444-98865-3*) Elsevier.
Cold Rain. Vic Tapner. 304p. 1988. pap. 3.95 (*0-380-75483-5*) Avon.
***Cold Reading: Poems.** Laurence Goldstein. LC 95-3622. 64p. (Orig.). 1995. pap. 9.95 (*0-914278-66-5*) Copper Beech.
Cold Reality: How to Get & Keep a Black Man in a Relationship. Alvis O. Davis. Ed. by Paul Weisser. 105p. (Orig.). 1990. pap. text ed. 9.95 (*0-9627656-0-0*) Zevon Pubns.
Cold-Recycled Bituminous Concrete Using Bituminous Materials. (National Cooperative Highway Research Program Report Ser.: No. 160). 105p. 1990. 11.00 (*0-309-04911-3*) Transport Res Bd.
Cold, Red Sunrise. Stuart M. Kaminsky. 1989. mass mkt. 4.99 (*0-8041-0428-X*) Ivy Books.
Cold Regions Construction. Ed. by Darryl F. Jordan & Giles N. McDonald. 127p. 1983. pap. 18.00 (*0-87262-387-4*) Am Soc Civil Eng.
Cold Regions Engineering. Ed. by Radoslaw L. Michalowski. 408p. 1989. 40.00 (*0-87262-680-6*) Am Soc Civil Eng.
Cold Regions Engineering: Proceedings. Ed. by William L. Ryan. 788p. 1986. 66.00 (*0-87262-513-3*) Am Soc Civil Eng.
Cold Regions Engineering: Proceedings of a Conference, 1991. Ed. by Devinder S. Sodhi. 800p. 1991. 70.00 (*0-87262-798-5*) Am Soc Civil Eng.
Cold Regions Hydrology: Proceedings of the Symposium. Cold Regions Hydrology Symposium Staff. Ed. by Douglas L. Kane. LC 86-70416. (American Water Resources Association Technical Publication Ser.: No. TPS-86-1). 624p. reprint ed. pap. 177.90 (*0-8357-3171-5*, 2039434) Bks Demand.
Cold Regions Hydrology & Hydraulics. Ed. by William L. Ryan & Randy D. Crissman. LC 90-41156. 840p. 1990. pap. text ed. 72.00 (*0-87262-773-X*) Am Soc Civil Eng.
Cold River. William Judson. 1976. pap. 3.50 (*0-451-16164-5*, Sig) NAL-Dutton.
Cold Rolled Flat Steel Wire. 42p. 1981. 8.00 (*0-685-62289-4*) Iron & Steel.
Cold Rolling of Steel. William L. Roberts. (Manufacturing Engineering & Materials Processing Ser.: Vol. 2). (Illus.). 808p. 1978. 199.00 (*0-8247-6780-2*) Dekker.
Cold Running River. David N. Cassuto. 150p. (C). 1993. text ed. 29.95 (*0-472-10474-8*); pap. 15.95 (*0-472-08238-8*) U of Mich Pr.
Cold Sassy Tree. Olive A. Burns. LC 84-8570. 392p. 1984. 21.95 (*0-89919-309-9*) Ticknor & Fields.
Cold Sheet Treatment. John R. Christopher. 1991. 1.75 (*1-879436-07-8*, 99107) Dr Chris Pubns.
Cold Shocks. Ed. by Timothy R. Sullivan. 320p. (Orig.). 1991. mass mkt. 4.50 (*0-380-76160-2*) Avon.
Cold Smoked. K. K. Beck. 1995. write for info. (*0-89296-537-1*) Mysterious Pr.
***Cold Smoked.** K. K. Beck. 1996. mass mkt. write for info. (*0-446-40351-2*, Mysterious Paperbk) Warner Bks.
***Cold Snap: Stories.** Thom Jones. LC 94-49539. 1995. 19.95 (*0-316-47307-3*) Little.
Cold Soups. Nina Graybill et al. LC 88-21286. 181p. (Orig.). 1989. pap. 10.95 (*0-918535-07-7*) Farragut Pub.
***Cold Soups.** Linda Ziedrich. Ed. by Dan Rosenberg. LC 95-7394. (Illus.). 144p. 1995. 19.95 (*1-55832-077-6*) Harvard Common Pr.
***Cold Soups.** Linda Ziedrich. Ed. by Dan Rosenberg. LC 95-7394. (Illus.). 144p. 1995. pap. 10.95 (*1-55832-078-4*) Harvard Common Pr.
Cold Spaghetti at Midnight: Feel-Good Foods to Heal Your Body & Soothe Your Soul. Maggie Waldron. (Illus.). 356p. 1992. 19.00 (*0-688-09188-1*) Morrow.
Cold Spring Harbor Symposia on Quantitative Biology: Chromatin, Vol. 42. LC 34-8174. (Illus.). 1260p. 1978. 139.00 (*0-87969-041-0*) Cold Spring Harbor.
Cold Spring Harbor Symposia on Quantitative Biology: Exchange of Genetic Material, Vol. 23. LC 34-8174. (Illus.). 449p. 1959. 38.00 (*0-87969-022-4*) Cold Spring Harbor.
Cold Spring Harbor Symposia on Quantitative Biology: Origins of Lymphocyte Diversity, 2 bks., Set, Vol. 41. LC 34-8174. (Illus.). 1024p. 1977. Set. 107.50 (*0-87969-040-2*) Cold Spring Harbor.
Cold Spring Harbor Symposia on Quantitative Biology: Sensory Receptors, Vol. 30. LC 34-8174. (Illus.). 663p. 1966. 38.00 (*0-87969-029-1*) Cold Spring Harbor.
Cold Spring Harbor Symposia on Quantitative Biology: Structure & Function of Proteins at the Three-Dimensional Level, Vol. 36. LC 34-8174. (Illus.). 669p. 1972. 44.00 (*0-87969-035-6*) Cold Spring Harbor.
Cold Spring Harbor Symposia on Quantitative Biology: The Mechanism of Muscle Contraction, Vol. 37. LC 34-8174. (Illus.). 728p. 1973. 44.00 (*0-87969-036-4*) Cold Spring Harbor.
Cold Spring Harbor Symposia on Quantitative Biology: The Synapse, Vol. 40. LC 34-8174. (Illus.). 694p. 1976. 88.50 (*0-87969-039-9*) Cold Spring Harbor.
Cold Spring Harbor Symposia on Quantitative Biology: Tumor Viruses, 2 bks., Set., Vol. 39. LC 34-8174. (Illus.). 1258p. 1975. Set. 120.00 (*0-87969-038-0*) Cold Spring Harbor.
Cold Spring Harbor Symposia on Quantitative Biology: Viral Oncogenes, 2 bks., Set. LC 34-8174. (Illus.). 1322p. 1980. 164.50 (*0-87969-043-7*) Cold Spring Harbor.
Cold Spring Harbor Symposia on Quantitative Biology: Viruses, Vol. 18. LC 34-8174. 1954. 38.00 (*0-87969-017-8*) Cold Spring Harbor.
Cold Stars & Fireflies: Poems for the Four Seasons. Barbara J. Esbensen. LC 83-45051. (Illus.). 80p. (J). (gr. 3-7). 1984. lib. bdg. 14.89 (*0-690-04363-5*, Crowell Jr Bks) HarpC Child Bks.
Cold Steal. Phoebe A. Taylor. 21.95 (*0-8488-1200-X*) Amereon Ltd.
Cold Steel. John Styers. Ed. by Karl Schuon. LC 74-81801. (Illus.). 178p. 1974. reprint ed. 17.95 (*0-87364-025-X*) Paladin Pr.
Cold Steel: A Leonidas Witherall Mystery. Alice Tilton, pseud. (Leonidas Witherall Mystery Ser.). 288p. 1993. pap. 6.00 (*0-88150-269-3*, Foul Play) Countryman.
Cold Steel Third: Third Airborne Ranger Company Korean War (1950-1951) Robert I. Channon. LC 93-79557. (Illus.). 832p. 1993. lib. bdg. 39.95 (*1-881851-02-8*) Genealogy Pub.
Cold Stove League. Thomas Boyle. (Academy First Mystery Ser.). 221p. 1987. pap. 5.95 (*0-89733-259-8*) Academy Chi Pubs.
Cold Summer. Edward R. Brown. 1993. 14.95 (*0-533-10439-4*) Vantage.
Cold Summer. Alice H. Orr. (Intrigue Ser.). 1993. pap. 2.89 (*0-373-22216-5*, 1-22216-5) Harlequin Bks.
Cold Summer Wind. Clayton Klein. LC 83-50047. (Illus.). 280p. 1983. boxed 13.95 (*0-9611596-0-X*) Wilderness Adventure Bks.
Cold Surveillance: The Jake Lorenzo Wine Columns. Jake Lorenzo. (Orig.). 1993. pap. 9.95 (*0-9637438-4-8*) Wine Patrol Pr.
Cold Sweat. Neal Bell. 1988. pap. 4.75 (*0-8222-0227-1*) Dramatists Play.
Cold Sweat. Franklin W. Dixon. Ed. by Anne Greenberg. (Hardy Boys Casefiles Ser.). 160p. (Orig.). (J). 1992. pap. 3.75 (*0-671-73099-1*) PB.
Cold Tales. Virgilio Pinera. Tr. by Mark Schafer. LC 88-80807. 304p. 1988. 24.00 (*0-941419-18-5*, Eridanos Library); pap. 15.00 (*0-941419-80-0*, Eridanos Library) Marsilio Pubs.
***Cold Toes & Busted TVs.** Doug McGuinn. 128p. (Orig.). 1994. pap. 8.95 (*0-614-01954-0*) Dan River Pr.
Cold Tracks. Lee Wallingford. 192p. 1991. 18.95 (*0-8027-5783-9*) Walker & Co.
Cold Victory. Poul Anderson. (Orig.). 1985. pap. 2.95 (*0-8125-3057-8*) Tor Bks.
Cold War. Michael G. Kort. LC 93-1934. (Illus.). 160p. (YA). (gr. 7 up). 1994. lib. bdg. 16.90 (*1-56294-353-7*) Millbrook Pr.
Cold War. Martin Walker. 1994. 30.00 (*0-8050-3190-1*) H Holt & Co.
Cold War. Alasdair Nicholson. Ed. by Malcolm Yapp et al. (World History Ser.). (Illus.). 32p. (YA). (gr. 6-11). 1980. reprint ed. pap. text ed. 4.35 (*0-89908-211-4*) Greenhaven.
Cold War: A Conflict of Ideology & Power. 2nd ed. Norman A. Graebner. (Problems in European Civilization Ser.). 206p. (C). 1976. pap. text ed. 8.50 (*0-669-81984-0*) Heath.
***Cold War: A History.** Martin Walker. 416p. 1995. pap. 14.00 (*0-8050-3454-4*, Owl) H Holt & Co.
Cold War: Fifty Years of Conflict. William G. Hyland. LC 91-50182. 256p. 1991. pap. 12.00 (*0-8129-1932-7*, Times Bks) Random.
Cold War: Opposing Viewpoints. Ed. by William Dudley. LC 92-21797. (American History Ser.). 288p. (YA). 1992. lib. bdg. 19.95 (*1-56510-009-3*); pap. 11.55 (*1-56510-008-5*) Greenhaven.
Cold War: Past & Present. Ed. by Richard Crockatt & Steve Smith. 272p. 1987. pap. 19.95 (*0-04-327102-2*) Routledge Chapman & Hall.
Cold War: Retrospect & Prospect. 2nd ed. Frederick L. Schuman. LC 62-16466. 152p. reprint ed. pap. 43.40 (*0-317-28754-0*, 2051667) Bks Demand.
Cold War: Retrospect & Prospect. Frederick L. Schuman. LC 62-16466. (Edward Douglass White Lectures). 124p. 1962. reprint ed. pap. 35.40 (*0-317-29853-4*, 2019592) Bks Demand.
***Cold War: The American Crusade Against the Soviet Union & World Communism, 1945-1990.** James A. Warren. LC 94-24554. (J). 1995. write for info. (*0-688-10596-3*) Lothrop.
***Cold War: The Fifties.** Robert Vaughan. (American Chronicles Ser.: No. 7). 1995. mass mkt. 5.50 (*0-553-56077-8*) Bantam.
Cold War: 1945-1963. Michael L. Dockrill. LC 88-12838. (Studies in European History). (C). 1988. pap. 10.95 (*0-391-03592-4*) Humanities.
Cold War: 1945-1965. Joseph Smith. (Historical Association Studies). 96p. 1989. pap. text ed. 10.95 (*0-631-15816-2*) Blackwell Pubs.
Cold War: 1945-1987. 2nd ed. Ralph B. Levering. Ed. by John H. Franklin & A. S. Eisenstadt. LC 87-25459. (American History Ser.). (Illus.). 240p. (C). 1988. pap. text ed. write for info. (*0-88295-858-5*) Harlan Davidson.
Cold War: 1945-1991. Ed. by Benjamin Frankel. LC 92-30496. 1992. write for info. (*0-8103-8927-4*) Gale.
Cold War Against Labor, 2 vols., Set. Ed. by Ann F. Ginger & David Christiano. (Studies in Law & Social Change: No. 3). (Illus.). 950p. (Orig.). 1987. 39.95 (*0-913876-19-4*); pap. 19.95 (*0-913876-20-8*) Meiklejohn Civ Lib.
Cold War America: From Hiroshima to Watergate. Lawrence S. Wittner. LC 77-89742. (C). 1978. pap. text ed. 26.00 (*0-03-022211-7*) HB Coll Pubs.
Cold War Analytical Structures & the Post Post-War World: A Critique of Deterrence Theory. Cori E. Dauber. LC 92-28475. (Political Communication Ser.). 224p. 1993. text ed. 47.95 (*0-275-94419-0*, C4419, Praeger Pubs) Greenwood.
Cold War & Academic Governance: The Lattimore Case at Johns Hopkins. Lionel S. Lewis. LC 92-24053. (SUNY Series, Frontiers in Education). 318p. (C). 1993. 59.50 (*0-7914-1493-0*); pap. 19.95 (*0-7914-1494-9*) State U NY Pr.
Cold War & After: Prospects for Peace. 2nd ed. Ed. by Sean M. Lynn-Jones. (Illus.). 400p. 1993. pap. 18.00 (*0-262-62088-X*) MIT Pr.
Cold War & American Science. Stuart W. Leslie. 320p. 1993. text ed. 42.00 (*0-231-07958-3*) Col U Pr.
Cold War & American Science. Stuart W. Leslie. 1994. pap. 16.50 (*0-231-07959-1*) Col U Pr.

C

An Asterisk (*) at the beginning of an entry indicates that the title is appearing in BIP for the first time.

Cold War & Black Liberation: The United States & White Rule in Africa, 1948-1968. Thomas J. Noer. LC 84-19665. 288p. 1985. text ed. 30.00 (*0-8262-0458-9*) U of Mo Pr.

Cold War & Defense. Ed. by Keith Neilson & Ronald G. Haycock. LC 90-30926. 224p. 1990. text ed. 49.95 (*0-275-93556-6*, C3556, Praeger Pubs) Greenwood.

Cold War & Revolution: Soviet-American Rivalry & the Origins of the Chinese Civil War. Odd A. Westad. (United States & Pacific Asia: Studies in Social, Economic & Political Interaction). 260p. (C). 1993. text ed. 50.00 (*0-231-07984-2*); pap. 16.50 (*0-231-07985-0*) Col U Pr.

Cold War As Cooperation. Roger E. Kanet & Edward A. Kolodziej. LC 90-21345. 384p. 1991. text ed. 55.00x (*0-8018-4206-9*) Johns Hopkins.

Cold War As Rhetoric: The Beginnings, 1945-1950. Lynn B. Hinds et al. LC 91-445. 304p. 1991. text ed. 55.00 (*0-275-93578-7*, C3578, Praeger Pubs) Greenwood.

Cold War Begins in Asia: American East Asian Policy & the Fall of the Japanese Empire. Marc S. Gallicchio. 240p. 1988. text ed. 33.50 (*0-231-06502-7*) Col U Pr.

***Cold War Canada: The Making of a National Insecurity State, 1945-1957.** Reg Whitaker & Gary Marcuse. (Illus.). 544p. 1995. 35.00 (*0-8020-5935-X*) U of Toronto Pr.

***Cold War Capitalism: The View from Moscow, 1945-1975.** Richard B. Day. 384p. 1995. 85.00 (*1-56324-660-0*); pap. 34.95 (*1-56324-661-9*) M E Sharpe.

Cold War Casualty: The Court-Martial of Major General Robert W. Grow. George F. Hofmann. LC 92-30839. (Illus.). 264p. 1993. 26.00 (*0-87338-462-8*) Kent St U Pr.

Cold War Chronology: Soviet-American Relations 1945-1991. Kenneth Hill. 362p. 1993. 58.95 (*0-87187-921-2*) Congr Quarterly.

Cold War, Cold Peace. Bernard A. Weisberger. LC 81-29495. (American Heritage Library). (Illus.). 341p. 1985. pap. 9.95 (*0-8281-1164-2*) HM.

Cold War Criticism & the Politics of Skepticism. Tobin Siebers. LC 92-23376. (Odeon Ser.). 1993. 39.95 (*0-19-507964-7*); pap. 14.95 (*0-19-507965-5*) OUP.

Cold War Debated. David Carlton & Herbert M. Levine. 384p. 1988. pap. text ed. write for info. (*0-07-027990-X*) McGraw.

***Cold War Droppings.** George Wilbur. 48p. (Orig.). 1995. pap. 12.00 (*0-9634503-1-X*) Randatamp Pr.

Cold War Encyclopedia. Thomas Parrish. 544p. 1996. pap. 60.00 (*0-8050-2778-5*) H Holt & Co.

Cold War Europe, 1945-1989: A Political History. John W. Young. (Illus.). 256p. 1991. 59.50 (*0-340-55142-9*, A6226, Pub. by E Arnold UK); pap. 17.95 (*0-340-55324-3*, A6230, Pub. by E Arnold UK) Routledge Chapman & Hall.

***Cold War Exile: The Unclosed Case of Maurice Halperin.** Don S. Kirschner. 344p. 1995. 29.95 (*0-8262-0989-0*) U of Mo Pr.

Cold War File. Andy East. LC 83-7584. 376p. 1983. 32.50 (*0-8108-1641-5*) Scarecrow.

Cold War Fugitive. Gil Green. LC 84-22433. 288p. 1984. pap. 6.95 (*0-7178-0616-2*) Intl Pubs Co.

Cold War Guerrilla: Jonas Savimbi, the U. S. Media & the Angolan War. Elaine Windrich. LC 91-25444. (Contributions to the Study of Mass Media & Communications Ser.: No. 31). 200p. 1992. text ed. 49.95 (*0-313-27989-6*, WWR, Greenwood Pr) Greenwood.

***Cold War Illusions.** Dana H. Allin. LC 94-28776. 1995. text ed. 39.95 (*0-312-12374-4*) St Martin.

Cold War in Europe. Ed. by Charles S. Maier. LC 90-13075. 420p. (Orig.). (C). 1991. 38.95 (*1-55876-029-6*); pap. text ed. 18.95 (*1-55876-034-2*) Wiener Pubs Inc.

Cold War in the Balkans: American Foreign Policy & the Emergence of Communist Bulgaria, 1943-1947. Michael M. Boll. LC 84-7438. 264p. 1984. 29.00 (*0-8131-1527-2*) U Pr of Ky.

Cold War in the Working Class: The Rise & Decline of the United Electrical Workers. Ronald L. Filippelli & Mark D. McColloch. LC 93-50828. (American Labor History Ser.). 296p. 1995. text ed. 59.50 (*0-7914-2181-3*); pap. text ed. 19.95 (*0-7914-2182-1*) State U NY Pr.

Cold War Is Over. William G. Hyland. 1990. 18.95 (*0-8129-1871-1*, Times Bks) Random.

Cold War Is over - Again. Allen Lynch. 208p. 1992. text ed. 49.00 (*0-8133-1470-4*) Westview.

Cold War Is over - Again. Allen Lynch. 208p. (C). 1992. pap. text ed. 19.95 (*0-8133-1471-2*) Westview.

Cold War Legacy. Thomas H. Naylor. 224p. 1991. text ed. 24.95 (*0-669-24984-X*) Free Pr.

Cold War Legacy in Europe: Challenges & Opportunities. Otto Pick. 1992. text ed. 55.00 (*0-312-06543-4*) St Martin.

Cold War on Campus: A Study of the Politics of Organizational Control. Lionel S. Lewis. 314p. 1987. 37.95x (*0-88738-178-2*) Transaction Pubs.

Cold War on the Campus: Academic Freedom at the University of Washington, 1946-64. Jane Sanders. LC 78-21755. 252p. 1979. 20.00 (*0-295-95652-6*) U of Wash Pr.

Cold War on the Periphery: The United States, India, & Pakistan, 1947-1965. Robert J. McMahon. LC 93-38724. 431p. 1993. 30.00 (*0-231-08226-6*) Col U Pr.

Cold War or Detente in the Nineteen Eighties: The International Politics of American-Soviet Relations. Peter Savigear. 265p. 1987. text ed. 39.95 (*0-312-00437-0*) St Martin.

Cold War Patriot & Statesman: Richard M. Nixon. Ed. by Leon Friedman & William F. Levantrosser. LC 92-30011. (Contributions in Political Science Ser.: No. 312). 392p. 1993. text ed. 65.00 (*0-313-28787-2*, FXW/, Greenwood Pr) Greenwood.

Cold War Poems. Stafford L. Battle. 50p. 1985. pap. 5.95 (*0-943454-03-4*) Jotarian.

Cold War Political Justice: The Smith Act, the Communist Party, & American Civil Liberties. Michal R. Belknap. LC 77-4566. (Contributions in American History Ser.: No. 66). xiv, 322p. 1977. text ed. 47.95 (*0-8371-9692-2*, BCW/, Greenwood Pr) Greenwood.

Cold War Politician of Nevada in the Fifties: Rodney J. Reynolds. Ed. by Mary E. Glass. 70p. 1977. lib. bdg. 22.00 (*1-56475-167-8*); fiche write for info. (*1-56475-168-6*) U NV Oral Hist.

Cold War Rhetoric: Strategy, Metaphor & Ideology. Martin J. Medhurst et al. LC 89-25906. (Contributions to the Study of Mass Media & Communications Ser.: No. 19). 248p. 1990. text ed. 49.95 (*0-313-26766-9*, MCX/, Greenwood Pr) Greenwood.

Cold War Romance of Lillian Hellman & John Melby. Robert P. Newman. LC 88-22659. (Illus.). xvi, 376p. (C). 1989. 29.95 (*0-8078-1815-1*) U of NC Pr.

Cold War Swap. Ross Thomas. 1992. mass mkt. 5.99 (*0-446-40168-4*, Mysterious Paperbk) Warner Bks.

Cold War Theatre. John Elsom. LC 91-47104. 256p. 1992. 59.95 (*0-415-00167-6*, A7661); pap. 15.95 (*0-415-08108-4*, A7665) Routledge.

Cold War Theories, Vol. 1: World Polarization, 1943-1953. Kenneth W. Thompson. LC 81-6001. 262p. (C). 1981. pap. text ed. 11.95 (*0-8071-1744-7*) La State U Pr.

Cold War, 1945-1991: A Post-Cold War History. Ralph B. Levering. Ed. by John H. Franklin & A. S. Eisenstadt. (American History Ser.). (Illus.). 200p. (C). 1994. pap. text ed. write for info. (*0-88295-912-3*) Harlan Davidson.

Cold Warrior. Ed. by Richard Sapir. (Destroyer Ser.: No. 91). 256p. (Orig.). 1993. pap. 4.50 (*0-451-17484-4*, Sig) NAL-Dutton.

Cold Warriors: A Policy-Making Elite. John C. Donovan. 288p. (C). 1974. pap. text ed. 12.50 (*0-669-83931-0*) Heath.

Cold Warriors: Eisenhower's Generation & American Foreign Policy. H. W. Brands, Jr. (Contemporary American History Ser.). (Illus.). 304p. 1988. text ed. 38.00 (*0-231-06526-4*) Col U Pr.

Cold Warriors & Coups d'Etat: Brazilian-American Relations, 1945-1964. W. Michael Weis. LC 92-21712. 273p. (C). 1993. 39.95x (*0-8263-1400-7*) U of NM Pr.

Cold Water Cure. Vincent Priessnitz. 48p. 1976. reprint ed. spiral bd. 8.80 (*0-7873-0677-0*) Mokelumne.

Cold Weather Activities: A Coloring Book with Games & Projects That Kids Can Do Again & Again. Jennifer W. McIntosh. Ed. by Kathleen Gavin & Marshall Gavin. (Kids on the Go Ser.). (Illus.). 56p. (J). (ps-8). 1994. pap. 3.95 (*1-885437-02-1*) B dazzle.

Cold Weather Cooking. Sarah L. Chase. LC 90-50359. (Illus.). 432p. 1990. 22.95 (*0-89480-844-3*, 1844); pap. 13.95 (*0-89480-752-8*, 1752) Workman Pub.

***Cold Weather Emergencies: Principles of Patient Management.** Ed. by Andrew D. Weinberg et al. 64p. 1990. pap. text ed. 15.00 (*1-887272-00-3*) Amer Med Pub.

Cold Weather Flying. Bill Clarke. (Practical Flying Ser.). (Illus.). 160p. 1989. pap. 15.95 (*0-8306-9442-0*, 2442) TAB Bks.

Cold Weather Survival. 1986. lib. bdg. 79.95 (*0-8490-3581-3*) Gordon Pr.

Cold Whisper. Rick Hautala. 1991. mass mkt. 5.95 (*0-8217-3464-4*) Zebra.

Cold Will: The Defence of Finland. Tomas Ries. (Illus.). 394p. 1988. 52.00 (*0-08-033592-6*, Pub. by Brasseys UK) Brasseys Inc.

Cold Wind from Orion. Scott Asnin. 288p. (Orig.). 1980. pap. 2.25 (*0-345-28498-4*) Ballantine.

Colden Country Cookbook. 4th ed. Colden United Methodist Women Staff. 360p. 1985. write for info. (*0-9615568-0-3*) Colden UMW.

Colder Eye: The Modern Irish Writers. Hugh Kenner. LC 88-46119. 320p. 1989. reprint ed. pap. 12.95 (*0-8018-3838-X*) Johns Hopkins.

Colder Fire: The Poetry of Robert Penn Warren. Victor Strandberg. LC 73-15319. 292p. 1975. reprint ed. text ed. 59.75 (*0-8371-7180-6*, STCF, Greenwood Pr) Greenwood.

Coldest Harbour in the Land: Simon Stock & Lord Baltimore's Colony in Newfoundland, 1621-1649. Luca Codignola. 240p. 1988. 49.95 (*0-7735-0540-7*, Pub. by McGill CN) U of Toronto Pr.

Coldest War. James P. Brady. Ed. by Paul McCarthy. 312p. 1991. reprint ed. pap. 6.50 (*0-671-72525-4*) PB.

Coldest Winter. Samuel Freilich. 1989. pap. 10.95 (*0-89604-127-1*) Holocaust Pubns.

Coldest Winter. Elizabeth Lutzeier. LC 91-7159. 160p. (YA). (gr. 5-9). 1991. 13.95 (*0-8234-0899-X*) Holiday.

Coldest Year of Grace: Selected Poems of Giovanni Raboni. Giovanni Raboni. Tr. by Stuart Friebert & Vinio Rossi. LC 84-7363. (Wesleyan Poetry in Translation Ser.). 104p. 1985. 12.95 (*0-8195-5114-7*, Wesleyan Univ Pr) U Pr of New Eng.

Colditz Story. P. R. Reid. (Classics of World War II Ser.). 278p. reprint ed. write for info. (*0-8094-8733-0*); reprint ed. lib. bdg. write for info. (*0-8094-8734-9*) Time-Life.

Colds (Acute Coryza) & Related Subjects. H. M. Shelton et al. 65p. 1958. reprint ed. spiral bd. 5.50 (*0-7873-1017-4*) Mokelumne.

Colds & Fever Cures Story Poem: Rye the Rhyming Detective in "Therm the Cold Germ" Data Notes Staff. 18p. 1986. pap. text ed. 3.50 (*0-911569-68-5*) Prosperity & Profits.

Colds & Flu & You. Linda Rector-Page. (Healthy Healing Library Ser.). 32p. 1993. pap. 2.95 (*1-884334-03-2*) Hlthy Healing.

***Colds & Flu & You.** rev. ed. Linda R. Page. (Healthy Healing Library Ser.). (Illus.). 32p. 1994. pap. 2.95 (*1-884334-28-8*) Hlthy Healing.

***Colds & Flu, Natural Way.** Penny Davenport. 1995. pap. text ed. 5.95 (*1-85230-630-0*) Element MA.

Coldwater Indian Artifacts Price Guide. Doug Puckett. 1994. pap. 20.00 (*0-9637157-2-0*) D Puckett Ent.

Cole: The Descendants of Elisha Cole, Who Came from Cape Cod to What Is Now Putnam County, N.Y., about 1745. Joseph O. Cole. (Illus.). 237p. 1994. reprint ed. lib. bdg. 47.00 (*0-8328-4070-X*); reprint ed. pap. 37.00 (*0-8328-4071-8*) Higginson Bk Co.

Cole Family of Stark, NH: Descendants of Solomon Cole of Beverly, Massachusetts. H. W. Hardon. 90p. 1991. reprint ed. pap. 17.50 (*0-8328-1805-4*) Higginson Bk Co.

Cole Porter: A Biography. Charles Schwartz. LC 78-20840. (Quality Paperbacks Ser.). 1979. reprint ed. pap. 13.95 (*0-306-80097-7*) Da Capo.

Cole Porter: Twenty-Two Clever & Funny Songs. (Illus.). 112p. (Orig.). 1994. pap. 10.95 (*0-7935-2632-9*, 00311627) H Leonard.

Colebrooke's Translation of the Lilavati. H. C. Banerji. (C). 1993. 17.00 (*81-206-0840-2*, Pub. by Asian Educ Servs II) S Asia.

Coleccion De Autos, Farsas y Coloquios Del Siglo, 4 vols., Set, XVI. Leo Rouanet. xxviii, 2124p. 1979. reprint ed. Set. write for info. (*3-487-06804-4*, Pub. by Georg Olms GW) Lubrecht & Cramer.

Coleccion de Documentos del Archivo General de la Nacion para la Etnohistoria de la Mixteca de Oaxaca en el Siglo XVI. Ed. by Ronald Spores. (Publications in Anthropology: No. 41). 125p. (Orig.). (SPA.). 1992. pap. 14.00 (*0-935462-32-5*) Vanderbilt Pubns.

Coleccion Mi Mundo, 29 bks. rev. ed. (Illus.). (Orig.). (SPA.). (J). (ps-2). 1991. Set of 29 bks. 32 pgs. ea. pap. 232.00 (*1-56334-017-8*) Hampton-Brown.

Coleccion Navidena, 1. J. W. Blair. 1986. reprint ed. pap. 2.50 (*0-311-08201-7*) Casa Bautista.

Coleccion Navidena, 2. J. W. Blair. 1986. reprint ed. pap. 1.95 (*0-311-08202-5*) Casa Bautista.

***Coleccion Salud Tomo I: La Dieta Feliz - Impireno en la Tierra.** Leon C. Delgadillo. Ed. by Janett Camps & Maggie Ghezi. 200p. (Orig.). Date not set. pap. text ed. write for info. (*0-9641506-3-8*) Edit Interamerica.

Coleco Adam BASIC. Richard E. Haskell. 230p. 1985. pap. 10.95 (*0-685-08089-7*) P-H.

Colefax & Fowler: The Best in English Interior Decoration. Chester Jones. (Illus.). 1989. 40.00 (*0-8212-1746-1*) Bulfinch Pr.

Coleldraw 5 Made Easy: The Basics Beyond. Martin S. Matthews. 1994. pap. 29.95 (*0-07-882066-9*) McGraw.

Coleman vs. Block. James Massey & Lynne Hayes. 94p. 1986. pap. 5.00 (*0-685-23186-0*, 40,781) NCLS Inc.

Coleman Young & Detroit Politics: From Social Activist to Power Broker. Wilbur Rich. LC 88-39480. (African American Life Ser.). 298p. (C). 1989. 29.95 (*0-8143-2093-7*) Wayne St U Pr.

***Colenso 1899.** Ian Knight. (Campaign Ser.). (Illus.). 96p. 1995. pap. 14.95 (*1-85532-466-0*, Pub. by Osprey UK) Stackpole.

Coleoptera: Carabidae-Carabinae. H. E. Andrews. (Fauna of British India Ser.: Vol. 1). (Illus.). xxvii, 433p. 30.00 (*0-88065-006-0*, Messers Today & Tomorrow) Scholarly Pubns.

Coleoptera: Carabidae-Harpalinae 1. Ed. by H. E. Andrews. (Fauna of British India Ser.: Vol. 2). (Illus.). xvi, 340p. 1977. reprint ed. 25.00 (*0-88065-009-5*, Messers Today & Tomorrow) Scholarly Pubns.

Coleoptera: Clavicornia, Erotylidae, Languriidae & Endomychidae. G. J. Arrow. (Fauna of British India Ser.). (Illus.). xvi, 416p. 1976. reprint ed. 25.00 (*0-88065-016-8*, Messers Today & Tomorrow) Scholarly Pubns.

Coleoptera: General Introduction & Cicindelidae & Paussidae. W. W. Fowler. (Fauna of British India Ser.). xx, 530p. 1973. reprint ed. 20.00 (*0-88065-085-0*, Messers Today & Tomorrow) Scholarly Pubns.

Coleoptera: Lamellicornia, Cetoniinae, & Dynastinae. G. J. Arrow. (Fauna of British India Ser.). (Illus.). xiv, 328p. 1976. reprint ed. 25.00 (*0-88065-017-6*, Messers Today & Tomorrow) Scholarly Pubns.

Coleoptera: Lamellicornia, Coprinae, Pt. III. G. J. Arrow. (Fauna of British India Ser.). (Illus.). xii, 452p. 1977. reprint ed. 25.00 (*0-88065-019-2*, Messers Today & Tomorrow) Scholarly Pubns.

Coleoptera: Lamellicornia, Rutelinae, Desmonoycinae & Euchirinae. G. J. Arrow. (Fauna of British India Ser.). (Illus.). xiv, 400p. 1974. reprint ed. 50.00 (*0-88065-018-4*, Messers Today & Tomorrow) Scholarly Pubns.

Coleoptera - Phytophaga - Chrysomelidae: Chrysomelinae & Halticinae. S. Maulik. (Fauna of British India Ser.). (Illus.). xiv, 442p. 1977. reprint ed. 30.00 (*0-88065-156-3*, Messers Today & Tomorrow) Scholarly Pubns.

Coleoptera - Phytophaga - Chrysomelidae: Eupides, Camptromes, Cyclica. M. Jacoby. (Illus.). xx, 538p. 1975. reprint ed. 25.00 (*0-88065-135-0*, Messers Today & Tomorrow) Scholarly Pubns.

Coleoptera - Phytophaga - Chrysomelidae: Galerucinae. S. Maulik. (Fauna of British India Ser.). (Illus.). xiv, 658p. 1979. reprint ed. 30.00 (*0-88065-157-1*, Messers Today & Tomorrow) Scholarly Pubns.

Coleoptera - Phytophaga - Chrysomelidae: Hispinae & Cossidinae. S. Maulik. (Fauna of British India Ser.). xii, 442p. 1973. reprint ed. 16.00 (*0-88065-155-5*, Messers Today & Tomorrow) Scholarly Pubns.

Coleoptera - Rhynchophora - Curculionidae. G. A. Marshall. (Fauna of British India Ser.). xvi, 370p. 1977. reprint ed. 30.00 (*0-88065-154-7*, Messers Today & Tomorrow) Scholarly Pubns.

Coleoptera - Staphylinidae: Staphylinidae, Vol. I. M. Cameron. (Fauna of British India Ser.). (Illus.). xviii, 478p. 1978. reprint ed. 30.00 (*0-88065-026-5*, Messers Today & Tomorrow) Scholarly Pubns.

Coleoptera - Staphylinidae: Staphylinidae, Vol. II. M. Cameron. (Fauna of British India Ser.). (Illus.). vii, 260p. 1978. reprint ed. 30.00 (*0-88065-027-3*, Messers Today & Tomorrow) Scholarly Pubns.

Coleoptera - Staphylinoidea: Staphylinidae, Vol. 4, Pt. 2. M. Cameron. (Fauna of British India Ser.). (Illus.). 691p. 1977. reprint ed. 40.00 (*0-88065-030-3*, Messers Today & Tomorrow) Scholarly Pubns.

Coleoptera-Phytophaga-Cerambycidae. C. J. Gahan. (Fauna of British India Ser.). xviii, 330p. 1974. reprint ed. 16.00 (*0-88065-090-7*, Messers Today & Tomorrow) Scholarly Pubns.

Coleoptera-Staphylinoidea: Staphy-linoidea, Vol. 3. M. Cameron. (Fauna of British India Ser.). (Illus.). 1978. reprint ed. 30.00 (*0-88065-028-1*, Messers Today & Tomorrow) Scholarly Pubns.

Coleoptera-Staphylinoidea: Staphylinodea, Vol. 4, Pt. 1. M. Cameron. (Fauna of British India Ser.). (Illus.). reprint ed. 30.00 (*0-88065-029-X*, Messers Today & Tomorrow) Scholarly Pubns.

Coleoptra. Dermaptera-Earwigs. M. Burr. xviii, 217p. 1990. reprint ed. 20.00 (*81-7019-047-9*, Messers Today & Tomorrow) Scholarly Pubns.

Coleoptra, Lamellicornia, Lucanidae & Passalidae. G. J. Arrow. 274p. 1976. reprint ed. write for info. (*0-88065-020-6*, Pub. by Today & Tomorrows P & P II) Scholarly Pubns.

Colere De Maigret. Georges Simenon. 192p. (FRE.). 1963. pap. 11.95 (*0-7859-1472-2*, 2258001730) Fr & Eur.

Colere de Maigret; La Rue aux Trois Poussins; La Chambre Bleue; L'Homme au Petit Chien; Maigret et le Fantome; Maigret se Defend; Le Petit Saint; Le Train de Venise. Georges Simenon. 900p. (FRE.). 1990. 49.95 (*0-685-64847-8*, 2258031575) Fr & Eur.

Coleres. Jean Vercors. 360p. (FRE.). 1956. pap. 10.95 (*0-7859-5407-4*) Fr & Eur.

Coleridge. W. Jackson Bate. LC 86-22848. 256p. 1987. pap. 15.95 (*0-674-13680-2*) HUP.

Coleridge. H. D. Traill. Ed. by John Morley. LC 68-58402. (English Men of Letters Ser.). reprint ed. lib. bdg. 27.50 (*0-404-51735-8*) AMS Pr.

Coleridge: Critic of Shakespeare. Muhammad M. Badawi. LC 72-86417. 230p. reprint ed. pap. 65.60 (*0-317-28014-7*, 2025575) Bks Demand.

Coleridge: Poems & Prose. Samuel Taylor Coleridge. (Poetry Library). 304p. 1985. mass mkt. 8.95 (*0-14-058501-X*, Penguin Bks) Viking Penguin.

Coleridge: The Critical Heritage. J. R. Jackson. (Critical Heritage Ser.: Vol. 2). 320p. (C). 1991. text ed. 129.00 (*0-415-04746-3*, A5651) Routledge.

Coleridge: The Early Family Letters. Samuel Taylor Coleridge. Ed. by James Engell. (Illus.). 176p. 1995. 39.95 (*0-19-818244-9*) OUP.

Coleridge: The Sublime Somnambulist. J. Charpentier. LC 74-130259. (Studies in Coleridge: No. 7). 1970. reprint ed. lib. bdg. 49.95 (*0-8383-1163-6*) M S G Haskell Hse.

Coleridge & His Poetry. Kathleen E. Royds. LC 76-120990. (Poetry & Life Ser.). reprint ed. 27.50 (*0-404-52532-6*) AMS Pr.

Coleridge & Mill: A Study of Influence. Christopher C. Turk. 277p. 1988. text ed. 63.95 (*0-566-05668-2*, Pub. by Avebury Pub UK) Ashgate Pub Co.

Coleridge & Textual Instability: The Multiple Versions of the Major Poems. Jack Stillinger. (Illus.). 288p. 1994. 47.00 (*0-19-508583-3*) OUP.

Coleridge & the Armoury of the Human Mind: Essays on His Prose Writings. Ed. by Peter J. Kitson & Thomas N. Corns. 128p. 1991. text ed. 30.00 (*0-7146-3426-3*, Pub. by F Cass Pubs UK) Intl Spec Bk.

Coleridge & the Concept of Nature. Raimonda Modiano. LC 84-8043. xiv, 270p. 1985. 34.95 (*0-8130-0808-5*) U Press Fla.

Coleridge & the Friend (1809-1810) Deirdre Coleman. (Oxford English Monographs). 248p. 1989. 59.00 (*0-19-812957-2*) OUP.

Coleridge & the Inspired Word. Anthony J. Harding. 208p. 1985. 44.95 (*0-7735-1008-7*, Pub. by McGill CN) U of Toronto Pr.

Coleridge & Wordsworth: A Lyrical Dialogue. Paul Magnuson. 352p. 1988. text ed. 47.50 (*0-691-06732-5*) Princeton U Pr.

Coleridge & Wordsworth in the West Country. Tom Mayberry. (Illus.). 224p. (YA). (gr. 11-12). 1992. 30.00 (*0-86299-896-4*) A Sutton Pub.

Coleridge & Wordsworth in the West Country. Tom Mayberry. (Illus.). 224p. 1994. pap. 26.00 (*0-7509-0628-6*) A Sutton Pub.

Coleridge As Critic. Herbert Read. LC 65-15891. 40p. (C). 1964. text ed. 75.00 (*0-8383-0613-6*) M S G Haskell Hse.

Coleridge As Poet & Religious Thinker. David Jasper. (Pittsburgh Theological Monographs: No. 15). 1984. 20.00 (*0-915138-70-0*) Pickwick.

Coleridge Connection: Essays for Thomas McFarland. Ed. by Richard Gravil & Molly Lefebure. 350p. 1990. text ed. 49.95 (*0-312-03705-8*) St Martin.

Coleridge, Keats, & the Imagination: Romanticism & Adam's Dream: Essays in Honor of Walter Jackson Bate. Ed. by J. Robert Barth & John L. Mahoney. LC 89-4840. 237p. reprint ed. pap. 67.60 (*0-7837-2362-8*, AU00427) Bks Demand.

Coleridge, Lamb, Hazlitt & the Reader of Drama. Janet R. Heller. (Illus.). 240p. 1990. text ed. 32.50 (*0-8262-0718-9*) U of Mo Pr.

An Asterisk (*) at the beginning of an entry indicates that the title is appearing in BIP for the first time.

C

An Asterisk (*) at the beginning of an entry indicates that the title is appearing in BIP for the first time.

1353

Collaborative & Community-Based Management of Coral Reefs: Lessons from Experience. Ed. by Alan T. White et al. LC 94-3142. (Library of Management for Development). (Illus.). 144p. 1994. pap. 21.95 (1-56549-032-0) Kumarian Pr.

Collaborative-Apprenticeship Learning: Language & Thinking Across the Curriculum, K-12. Ann Shea Bayer. 146p. (C). 1990. pap. text ed. 20.95 (0-87484-882-2) Mayfield Pub.

Collaborative Care: Interprofessional, Interagency, & Interpersonal. Sally Hornby. LC 93-2406. 1993. write for info. (0-632-03725-3) Blackwell Sci.

Collaborative Care: Nursing Case Management. Center for Nursing Case Management Staff. Ed. by Mary L. Etheredge. LC 89-281. 134p. (Orig.). 1989. pap. 40.00 (1-55648-032-6, 154151) AHPI.

Collaborative Classroom: A Guide to Co-Operative Learning. Susan Hill & Tim Hill. LC 89-77378. 152p. 1990. pap. text ed. 18.50 (0-435-08525-5, 08525) Heinemann.

Collaborative Clinical Education: The Foundation of Effective Health Care. Jane Westberg & Hilliard Jason. LC 92-49817. (Medical Education Ser.: Vol. 16). 432p. 1992. 49.95 (0-8261-8030-2) Springer Pub.

Collaborative Communities: Cohousing, Central Living, & Other New Forms of Housing. Dorit Fromm. LC 90-44673. (Illus.). 256p. 1991. text ed. 49.95 (0-442-23785-5) Van Nos Reinhold.

***Collaborative Computing: Multimedia Across the Network.** Jeffrey A. Shapiro. (Illus.). 300p. 1995. disk, pap. write for info. (0-12-638675-7) Acad Pr.

Collaborative Construction of Pretend: Social Pretend Play Functions. Carollee Howes. LC 90-10330. (Children's Play in Society Ser.). 168p. 1992. 64.50 (0-7914-0755-1) State U NY Pr.

Collaborative Construction of Pretend: Social Pretend Play Functions. Carollee Howes et al. LC 90-10330. (Children's Play in Society Ser.). 168p. 1992. pap. 21.95 (0-7914-0756-X) State U NY Pr.

Collaborative Consultation. 2nd ed. Lorna Idol et al. LC 92-42907. (C). 1993. 36.00 (0-89079-583-5, 6598) PRO-ED.

Collaborative Data Base. Chris Bigum. (C). 1987. 30.00 (0-7300-0515-1, Pub. by Deakin Univ AT) St Mut.

***Collaborative Dialogue Technologies in Distance Learning.** Ed. by Felisa M. Verdejo & Stefano A. Cerri. (Computer & Systems Ser.: 133). 1994. write for info. (3-540-58249-5) Spr-Verlag.

***Collaborative Dialogue Technologies in Distance Learning, 1.** Ed. by Felisa M. Verdejo & Stefano A. Cerri. LC 94-33116. (Computer & Systems Ser.: Vol. 133). 1994. write for info. (0-387-58249-5) Spr-Verlag.

Collaborative Dimensions of Learning. Mary Hamm & Dennis Adams. 160p. (C). 1992. text ed. 39.50 (0-89391-754-0) Ablex Pub.

***Collaborative Discipline for At-Risk Students: Peer Support Activities Program for Grades 7-12.** George H. Byers. LC 94-23390. 1994. spiral bd. 29.95 (0-87628-122-6) Ctr Appl Res.

Collaborative Form: Studies in the Relations of the Arts. Thomas J. Hines. LC 90-46804. (Illus.). 224p. 1991. 28.00 (0-87338-417-2) Kent St U Pr.

Collaborative Health Care: A Family-Oriented Model. Michael M. Glenn. LC 87-2420. 235p. 1987. text ed. 65.00 (0-275-92319-3, C2319, Praeger Pubs) Greenwood.

Collaborative Language Learning & Teaching. Ed. by David Nunan. (Cambridge Language Teaching Library). 224p. (C). 1992. 42.95 (0-521-41687-6); pap. 16.95 (0-521-42701-0) Cambridge U Pr.

Collaborative Latin American Popular Theatre: From Theory to Form, from Text to Stage. Elena De Costa. LC 91-17087. (American University Studies: Romance Languages & Literature: Ser. II, Vol. 179). 175p. (C). 1992. text ed. 36.95 (0-8204-1653-3) P Lang Pubs.

***Collaborative Leader: Listening to the Wisdom of God's People.** Loughlan Sofield & Donald H. Kuhn. LC 94-79357. 224p. (Orig.). 1995. pap. 8.95 (0-87793-544-0) Ave Maria.

Collaborative Leadership: How Citizens & Civic Leaders Can Make a Difference. David D. Chrislip & Carl E. Larson. LC 94-10751. (Public Administration-Nonprofit Ser.). 200p. 1994. 24.95 (0-7879-0003-6) Jossey-Bass.

***Collaborative Leadership & Shared Decision Making: Teachers, Principals & University Professors.** Renee Clift et al. 192p. (C). 1995. text ed. 36.00x (0-8077-3394-6); pap. text ed. 17.95x (0-8077-3393-8) Tchrs Coll.

Collaborative Learning: Higher Education, Interdependence, & the Authority of Knowledge. Kenneth A. Bruffee. LC 93-15073. 264p. (C). 1993. text ed. 29.95 (0-8018-4642-0) Johns Hopkins.

***Collaborative Learning: Higher Education, Interdependence, & the Authority of Knowledge.** Kenneth A. Bruffee. 256p. 1995. reprint ed. pap. text ed. 15.95x (0-8018-5232-3) Johns Hopkins.

***Collaborative Learning: Underlying Processes & Effective Techniques.** Ed. by Kris Bosworth & Sharon J. Hamilton. LC 85-644763. (New Directions for Teaching & Learning Ser.: No. 59). 106p. (Orig.). 1994. pap. 16.95 (0-7879-9998-9) Jossey-Bass.

***Collaborative Learning in Staffrooms & Classrooms.** Colin Biott & Patrick Easen. (Primary Curriculum Ser.). 176p. 1994. pap. 29.00x (1-85346-201-2, Pub. by D Fulton UK) Taylor & Francis.

Collaborative Learning Through Computer Conferencing: The Najaden Papers. Ed. by Anthony R. Kaye. LC 92-22011. (NATO ASI Series F Computer & Systems Sciences, Special Programme AET: Vol. 90). x, 260p. 1992. 74.00 (0-387-55755-5) Spr-Verlag.

Collaborative Management in Health Care: Implementing the Integrative Organization. Martin P. Charns & Laura J. Tewksbury. LC 92-26467. (Health-Management Ser.). 341p. 1992. 35.95 (1-55542-483-X) Jossey-Bass.

Collaborative Ministry: Communion, Contention, Commitment. Norman P. Cooper. LC 92-38074. 192p. 1993. pap. 14.95 (0-8091-3376-8) Paulist Pr.

Collaborative Ministry: Skills & Guidelines. Loughlan Sofield & Carroll Juliano. LC 87-70901. 136p. (Orig.). 1987. pap. 6.95 (0-87793-360-X) Ave Maria.

Collaborative Nursing Case Management: A Handbook for Development & Implementation. Virginia Del Togno-Armanasco et al. LC 93-14984. 200p. 1993. 27.95 (0-8261-8110-4, 93-14984) Springer Pub.

***Collaborative Peer Review: The Role of Faculty in Improving Education.** Larry Keig & Michael D. Waggoner. Ed. & Frwd. by Jonathan D. Fife. (ASHE-ERIC Higher Education Report: No. 2, 1994). 166p. (Orig.). (C). 1995. pap. 18.00x (1-878380-58-3) GWU Schl E&HD.

Collaborative Planning for Wetlands & Wildlife: Issues & Examples. Ed. by Douglas R. Porter & David A. Salveson. LC 94-30143. 352p. (C). 1995. pap. text ed. 29.50 (1-55963-287-9) Island Pr.

Collaborative Practitioners, Collaborative Schools. Marleen C. Pugach & Lawrence J. Johnson. LC 94-75177. 224p. (Orig.). (C). 1994. pap. text ed. 24.95 (0-89108-234-4) Love Pub Co.

Collaborative Programming in Nonformal Education. Gail Von Hahmann. 76p. 1978. pap. 4.00 (0-932288-51-0) Ctr Intl Ed U of MA.

Collaborative Psychoanalysis: Anxiety, Depression, Dreams & Personality Change. Walter Bonime. LC 86-46161. 416p. 1989. 55.00 (0-8386-3298-X) Fairleigh Dickinson.

Collaborative Research in Developmental Therapy: A Model with Studies of Learning Disabled Children. Ed. by Margaret A. Short-DeGraff & Kenneth Ottenbacher. LC 86-11978. 157p. 1986. text ed. 39.95 (0-86656-570-1) Haworth Pr.

Collaborative School: A Work Environment for Effective Instruction. Stuart C. Smith & James J. Scott. LC 87-81544. xii, 77p. (Orig.). 1990. pap. 9.00 (0-86552-092-5) U of Oreg ERIC.

Collaborative Selling: How to Gain the Competitive Advantage in Sales. Anthony J. Alessandra & Rick Barrera. 208p. 1993. text ed. 37.50 (0-471-59664-7); pap. text ed. 14.95 (0-471-59665-5) Wiley.

***Collaborative Social Studies Classroom: A Resource for Teachers.** Joseph Nowicki & Kerry F. Meehan. LC 95-13741. 1995. write for info. (0-205-17391-8) Allyn.

Collaborative Teams for Students with Severe Disabilities: Integrating Therapy & Educational Services. Beverly Rainforth et al. 304p. (Orig.). (C). 1992. pap. text ed. 32.00 (1-55766-088-3) P H Brookes.

Collaborative Work, Social Communications & Information Systems: Proc. of the IFIP TC8 Conf., Helsinki, Hanassaari, Finland, 27-29 Aug., 1991. Ed. by R. Stamper et al. 404p. 1991. 100.00 (0-444-89211-7, North Holland) Elsevier.

Collaborative Writing in Industry: Investigations in Theory & Practice. Ed. by Mary M. Lay & William M. Karis. (Technical Communications Ser.). 284p. 1991. text ed. 29.95 (0-89503-071-3); pap. text ed. 22.50 (0-89503-070-5) Baywood Pub.

Collaborators. Janet Kauffman. LC 85-45595. 136p. 1986. 13.95 (0-394-55080-3) Knopf.

Collaborators. Janet Kauffman. LC 92-39288. 144p. 1993. reprint ed. pap. 11.00 (1-55597-185-7) Graywolf.

Collage. Mwatabu Okantah. LC 83-82776. 68p. 1984. per., pap. 5.00 (0-916418-56-1) Lotus.

Collage. Philip Steele. LC 92-42678. (Step-by-Step Ser.). 40p. (J). (gr. 3-7). 1993. 10.95 (1-85697-921-0, Kingfisher LKC); pap. 5.95 (1-85697-920-2, Kingfisher LKC) LKC.

Collage. Sue Stocks. LC 93-46891. (First Arts & Crafts Ser.). (Illus.). 32p. (J). (gr. 1-4). 1994. 14.95 (1-56847-161-0) Thomson Lrning.

Collage. Ruth Thomson. LC 94-12305. (Get Set--Go!). (Illus.). 24p. (J). (ps-3). 1994. lib. bdg. 10.80 (0-516-07988-3); pap. 4.95 (0-516-47988-1) Childrens.

Collage. 3rd ed. L. F. Baker et al. 1990. Revision de grammaire. pap. text ed. write for info. (0-07-540835-X) McGraw.

Collage, Vol. 2. 3rd ed. L. F. Baker et al. 1990. Lectures Litteraires. student ed. pap. text ed. write for info. (0-07-540836-8) McGraw.

Collage, Vol. 3. 3rd ed. L. F. Baker et al. 1990. Varietes Culturelles. pap. text ed. write for info. (0-07-540837-6) McGraw.

Collage, Vol. 4. 3rd ed. L. F. Baker et al. 1990. Conversation/Activites. student ed, pap. text ed. write for info. (0-07-540838-4) McGraw.

Collage: A Shattered Story. James J. LaVeck. Ed. by Jenny Stein. LC 93-10083. (Illus.). 150p. (Orig.). 1993. pap. 9.00 (1-882979-07-9) What the Heck.

Collage: An Intermediate French Program, 5 readers. 2nd ed. Incl. Reader 2. Literary Reader. Laura L. Border et al. 1985. pap. text ed. (0-318-57754-2); Reader 3. Cultural Reader. Laura L. Border et al. 1985. pap. text ed. 9.00 (0-685-08394-2); (C). 1985. Set pap. text ed. write for info. (0-318-57753-4) Random.

Collage: Critical Views. Ed. by Katherine Hoffman. LC 88-37072. (Studies in the Fine Arts: Criticism: No. 31). 456p. reprint ed. 130.00 (0-8357-1933-2, 2070722) Bks Demand.

Collage: Feminae Vitae. Judy B. Jason. LC 84-51944. (Womanlore Ser.). 76p. (Orig.). 1986. pap. 2.95 (0-317-52833-5) Sideling Pr.

Collage: Landscapes, Portraits, Abstracts, Still Life, Colors. Leonard Cirino. Ed. by Ray Zarucchi & Carolyn Page. (Chapbook Ser.). (Illus.). 24p. (Orig.). 1990. pap. 5.00 (0-9623862-9-4) Nightshade Pr.

Collage; A Resource Book for Christian Youth Groups. Jim O'Hara & Grace Walle. 86p. (Orig.). 1976. pap. 4.00 (0-9608124-5-8) Marianist Com Ctr.

Collage & Assemblage. (Illus.). Date not set. text ed. write for info. (1-56290-067-6) Crystal.

Collage & Assemblage. John Elderfield. (Studies in Modern Art: No. 2). 1992. 40.00 (0-8109-6112-1) Abrams.

Collage, Assemblage, & the Found Object. Diane Waldman. (Illus.). 336p. 1992. 85.00 (0-8109-3183-4) Abrams.

Collage City. Colin Rowe & Fred Koetter. 1978. pap. 19.95x (0-262-68042-4) MIT Pr.

Collage of Crafts. Charlie Guerrier. LC 93-24968. (Young Artisan Ser.). (Illus.). 60p. (J). (gr. 3 up). 1994. 12.95 (0-395-68377-7) Ticknor & Flds Bks Yng Read.

Collage One: Poems by Poets of St. Croix, 1990. Ed. by Arnold R. Highfield. 81p. (Orig.). 1990. pap. text ed. 10.00 (0-916611-02-7) Antilles Pr.

***Collage Techniques: A Guide for Artists & Illustrators.** Gerald F. Brommer. LC 94-7775. (Illus.). 160p. 1994. pap. 27.50 (0-8230-0655-7) Watsn-Guptill.

***Collage with Photoshop.** 205p. 1995. pap. 39.99 (1-56496-210-5) Rockport Pubs.

Collagen: Biochemistry, Biomechanics, Biotechnology, Vol. I. Ed. by Marcel E. Nimni. 384p. 1988. 175.00 (0-8493-4601-0, QP552, CRC Reprint) Franklin.

Collagen: Biochemistry, Biomechanics, Biotechnology, Vol. II. Ed. by Marcel E. Nimni. 336p. 1988. 239.00 (0-8493-4602-9, QP552) CRC Pr.

Collagen: Biochemistry, Biomechanics, Biotechnology, Vol. III. Ed. by Marcel E. Nimni. 368p. 1988. 176.00 (0-8493-4603-7, QP552, CRC Reprint) Franklin.

Collagen Vol. IV: Molecular Biology. Ed. by Marcel E. Nimni & Bjorn R. Olsen. 208p. 1989. 179.00 (0-8493-4604-5, QP552) CRC Pr.

Collagen Vol. V: Pathobiochemistry. Marcel E. Nimni & Andrew H. Kang. 288p. 1991. 205.00 (0-8493-4605-3, QP552) CRC Pr.

Collagen in Aging & Disease Studie CSAV, 1982, Pt. 11. Z. Deyl & M. Adam. 198p. 1982. 97.00 (0-317-89597-4) St Mut.

Collagenase. Ed. by Ines Mandl. LC 73-173997. (Illus.). 222p. 1972. text ed. 169.00 (0-677-15190-X) Gordon & Breach.

Collagenase in Normal & Pathological Connective Tissues. Ed. by David E. Woolley & John M. Evanson. LC 79-40821. (Illus.). 302p. reprint ed. pap. 86.10 (0-685-20655-6, 2030441) Bks Demand.

Collagens: Biochemistry & Pathophysiology. E. J. Kucharz. (Illus.). 304p. 1992. 149.00 (0-387-53323-0) Spr-Verlag.

Collages. Mila Boutan. (Illus.). (J). (ps-1). 1992. 4.50 (1-56021-196-2) W J Fantasy.

Collages. Anais Nin. LC 64-25338. (Illus.). 122p. 1964. 6.95 (0-8040-0045-X) Swallow.

Collages of Benny Andrews. Studio Museum in Harlem Staff. 28p. (Orig.). 1988. pap. 15.00 (0-942949-02-1) Studio Mus Harlem.

***Collages of Kurt Schwitters: Tradition & Innovation.** Dorothea Dietrich. (Illus.). 310p. (C). Date not set. pap. write for info. (0-521-49891-0) Cambridge U Pr.

Collages of Kurt Schwitters: Tradition & Innovation. Dorothea Dietrich. LC 92-44956. (Illus.). 310p. (C). 1993. 65.00 (0-521-41936-0) Cambridge U Pr.

Collapse: The Buckling of Structures in Theory & Practice. J. M. Thompson & G. W. Hunt. LC 83-5190. 480p. 1984. 100.00 (0-521-25102-8) Cambridge U Pr.

Collapse & Reorganization of the Latin Nominal Flection As Reflected in Epigraphic Sources. Paul A. Gaeng & Jeffrey T. Chamberlain. 24.00 (0-916379-06-X) Scripta.

***Collapse of a Single Party System: The Disintegration of the Communist Party of the Soviet Union.** Graeme Gill. (Cambridge Russian, Soviet & Post-Soviet Studies: 94). (Illus.). 269p. (C). 1994. pap. 18.95 (0-521-46943-0) Cambridge U Pr.

***Collapse of a Single Party System: The Disintegration of the Communist Party of the Soviet Union.** Graeme Gill. (Cambridge Russian, Soviet & Post-Soviet Studies: 94). (Illus.). 269p. (C). 1994. 59.95 (0-521-46537-0) Cambridge U Pr.

Collapse of an Industry: Nuclear Power & the Contradictions of U. S. Policy. John L. Campbell. LC 87-47856. (Cornell Studies in Political Economy). 1988. 39.95 (0-8014-2111-X); pap. 16.95 (0-8014-9500-8) Cornell U Pr.

Collapse of Ancient States & Civilizations. Ed. by Norman Yoffee & George L. Cowgill. LC 88-1347. (Illus.). 333p. (C). 1991. reprint ed. pap. 15.95 (0-8165-1249-3) U of Ariz Pr.

Collapse of Burning Buildings: A Guide to Fireground Survival. Vincent Dunn. (Illus.). 287p. (C). 1988. student ed 20.00 (0-87814-903-1); text ed. 37.75 (0-87814-902-3) Fire Eng.

Collapse of Canada? Ed. by R. Kent Weaver. 200p. (C). 1992. 28.95 (0-8157-9254-9); pap. 11.95 (0-8157-9253-0) Brookings.

Collapse of Chaos: Discovering Simplicity in a Complex World. Jack Cohen & Ian Stewart. 352p. 1994. 23.95 (0-670-84983-9, Viking) Viking Penguin.

***Collapse of Chaos: Discovering Simplicity in a Complex World.** Jack Cohen & Ian Stewart. (Illus.). 512p. 1995. 13.95 (0-14-017874-0, Penguin Bks) Viking Penguin.

Collapse of Communism. Ed. by Bernard Gwertzman & Michael T. Kaufman. 1990. pap. 9.95 (0-8129-1872-X, Times Bks) Random.

Collapse of Communism. Ed. by Bernard Gwertzman & Michael T. Kaufman. LC 91-50183. 480p. 1991. pap. 13.00 (0-8129-1941-6, Times Bks) Random.

***Collapse of Communism in Eastern Europe.** Martyn Rady. LC 95-11728. (Causes & Consequences Ser.). 1995. write for info. (0-8172-4052-7) Raintree Steck-V.

Collapse of Complex Societies. Joseph A. Tainter. (New Studies in Archaeology). (Illus.). 272p. (C). 1990. pap. 24.95 (0-521-38673-X) Cambridge U Pr.

Collapse of Cotton Tenancy. Charles S. Johnson & Edwin R. Embree. (Select Bibliographies Reprint Ser.). 1977. reprint ed. 15.95 (0-8369-6830-1) Ayer.

Collapse of Development Planning. Ed. by Peter J. Boettke. LC 93-51051. (Political Economy of the Austrian School Ser.). (C). 1994. 55.00 (0-8147-1216-9); pap. 20.00 (0-8147-1225-8) NYU Pr.

Collapse of East German Communism: The Year the Wall Came Down, 1989. David Keithly. LC 92-2686. 256p. 1992. text ed. 49.95 (0-275-94261-9, C4261, Praeger Pubs) Greenwood.

Collapse of Evolution. 2nd ed. Scott M. Huse. 208p. 1993. reprint ed. pap. 9.99 (0-8010-4384-0) Baker Bk.

Collapse of Evolution. Scott M. Huse. 192p. 1986. reprint ed. pap. 7.99 (0-8010-4310-7) Baker Bk.

Collapse of Federally Insured Depositories: The Savings & Loans As Precursor. rev. ed. R. Dan Brumbaugh, Jr. LC 92-22996. (Financial Sector of the American Economy Ser.). 272p. 1992. 67.00 (0-8153-0956-2) Garland.

Collapse of History: Reconstructing Old Testament Theology. Leo G. Perdue. LC 94-2824. 1994. 14.00 (0-8006-1563-8, Fortress Pr) Augsburg Fortress.

Collapse of Liberal Empire: Science & the Revolution in the Twentieth Century. Paul N. Goldstene. (Political Science Ser.). 160p. 1980. reprint ed. pap. 9.95 (0-88316-540-6) Chandler & Sharp.

Collapse of Real Socialism in Poland. Jacek Tittenbrun. 272p. (Orig.). 1993. pap. 18.95 (1-85756-043-4, Pub. by Janus Pubng UK) Paul & Co Pubs.

***Collapse of Soviet Communism: A View from the Information Society.** Manuel Castells & Emma Kiseleva. LC 95-13474. (Exploratory Essays Ser.: No. 2). 1995. pap. write for info. (0-87725-704-3) U of Cal IAS.

Collapse of State Socialism: The Case of Poland. Bartlomiej Kaminski. 252p. 1991. text ed. 42.50 (0-691-07880-7); pap. text ed. 15.95 (0-691-02335-2) Princeton U Pr.

Collapse of the Anglo-French Alliance, 1727-1731. Jeremy Black. LC 87-40237. 236p. 1987. text ed. 39.95 (0-312-01211-X) St Martin.

Collapse of the Brass Heaven: Rebuilding Our Worldview to Embrace the Power of God. Zeb B. Long & Douglas McMurry. 272p. (Orig.). 1994. pap. 11.99 (0-8007-9215-7) Revell.

Collapse of the German War Economy, 1944-1945: Allied Air Power & the German National Railway. Alfred C. Mierzejewski. LC 88-4777. xxi, 285p. (C). 1988. 39.95 (0-8078-1792-9) U of NC Pr.

Collapse of the Grand Alliance, 1945-1948. James L. Gormly. LC 86-27438. (Political Traditions in Foreign Policy Ser.). 224p. 1987. text ed. 30.00 (0-8071-1320-4) La State U Pr.

Collapse of the Middle Way: Senate Republicans & the Bipartisan Foreign Policy. David R. Kepley. LC 87-23665. (Contributions in American History Ser.: No. 126). 208p. 1988. text ed. 49.95 (0-313-25784-1, KYR/, Greenwood Pr) Greenwood.

***Collapse of the Soviet Empire: Managing the Regional Fallout.** Ed. by Trevor Taylor. 1992. 15.95 (0-905031-54-7) Brookings.

Collapse of the Soviet Union. Brenda Smith. LC 93-17097. (Overview Ser.: World in Conflict). (J). (gr. 6-9). 1994. 16.95 (1-56006-142-1) Lucent Bks.

Collapse of the Third Republic: An Inquiry into the Fall of France in 1940. William L. Shirer. (Illus.). 1082p. reprint ed. pap. 22.95 (0-306-80562-6) Da Capo.

Collapse of the Tokugawa Bakufu: Eighteen Sixty-Two to Eighteen Sixty-Eight. Conrad Totman. LC 79-22094. (Illus.). 612p. 1980. text ed. 25.00 (0-8248-0614-X) UH Pr.

Collapse of the Weimar Republic: Political Economy & Crisis. rev. ed. David Abraham. LC 86-27033. 366p. (C). 1986. 45.00 (0-8419-1083-9); pap. 18.95 (0-8419-1084-7) Holmes & Meier.

Collapse of the World Financial System 1919-1939. Barry Eichengreen. (Illus.). 560p. 1992. 39.95 (0-685-49841-7) OUP.

Collapse of Tori & Genesis of Chaos in Dissipative Systems. K. Kaneko. 276p. 1986. text ed. 41.00 (9971-978-61-X) World Scientific Pub.

***Collapsed States: The Disintegration & Restoration of Legitimate Authority.** Ed. by I. William Zartman. LC 94-25734. (SAIS African Studies Library). 330p. 1995. lib. bdg. 49.95 (1-55587-518-1); pap. text ed. 22.00 (1-55587-560-2) Lynne Rienner.

Collapsible Basket Patterns. Rick Longabaugh & Karen Longabaugh. (Illus.). 128p. 1992. pap. 12.95 (0-9633112-0-4) Berry Basket.

Collapsing Space & Time: Geographic Aspects of Communications & Information. S. Brunn & T. Leinbach. 384p. 1989. 75.00 (0-04-910119-6); pap. 24.95 (0-04-910120-X) Routledge Chapman & Hall.

Collapsing Spaces, Tilting Times. George Bailin. (Poetry Ser.: No. 11). 48p. (Orig.). 1981. pap. 5.95 (0-930020-10-3) Stone Country.

Collapsing Universe. Lars Wahlin. LC 85-71749. (Illus.). 1985. reprint ed. lib. bdg. 12.00 (0-933407-00-9) Colutron Research.

Collar the Lot: How Britain Interned & Expelled Its Wartime Refugees. Peter Gillman & Leni Gillman. (Illus.). 228p. 1981. 17.95 (0-7043-2244-7, Pub. by Quartet UK) Charles River Bks.

An Asterisk (*) at the beginning of an entry indicates that the title is appearing in BIP for the first time.

C

An Asterisk (*) at the beginning of an entry indicates that the title is appearing in BIP for the first time.

1355

Collected Essays of Joseph Murphy. Joseph Murphy. LC 87-70783. (Mentors of New Thought Ser.). 192p. (Orig.). 1987. pap. 8.95 (0-87516-592-3) DeVorss.

***Collected Essays of Meghnad Desai, 2 Vols., Set.** Meghnad Desai. (Economists of the Twentieth Century Ser.). 1995. write for info. (1-85898-095-X, Pub. by E Elgar Pub UK) Ashgate Pub Co.

***Collected Essays of Meghnad Desai, Vol. I.** Meghnad Desai. (Economists of the Twentieth Century Ser.). 384p. 1995. 71.95 (1-85278-689-2, Pub. by E Elgar Pub UK) Ashgate Pub Co.

Collected Essays of Richard E. Quandt, 2 vols., Set. Richard E. Quandt. (Economists of the Twentieth Century Ser.). 800p. 1992. 149.95 (1-85278-605-1, Pub. by E Elgar Pub UK) Ashgate Pub Co.

Collected Essays of Robert Bitzer. Robert Bitzer. LC 89-51300. (Mentors of New Thought Ser.). 192p. (Orig.). 1990. pap. 8.95 (0-87516-620-2) DeVorss.

Collected Essays of Robert Creeley. Robert Creeley. 1989. 45.00 (0-520-06150-0) U CA Pr.

***Collected Essays of Stuart Grayson.** Stuart Grayson. LC 95-68672. (Mentors of New Thought Ser.). 149p. (Orig.). 1995. pap. 9.95 (0-87516-679-2) DeVorss.

Collected Essays of Thomas Troward. Thomas Troward. LC 87-70911. (Mentors of New Thought Ser.). 192p. 1987. reprint ed. pap. 8.95 (0-87516-593-1) DeVorss.

Collected Essays of Virginia Woolf: 1904-1912, Vol. 1. Virginia Woolf. Ed. by Andrew McNeillie. 416p. 1987. 19.95 (0-15-129055-5) HarBrace.

Collected Essays on Economic Theory, Vol. 1: Wealth & Welfare. John Hicks. 320p. (C). 1981. 47.00 (0-674-13741-8) HUP.

Collected Essays on Economic Theory, Vol. 2: Money, Interest & Wages, Vol. 2. John Hicks. 366p. 1982. 47.00 (0-674-13742-6) HUP.

Collected Essays on Economic Theory, Vol. 3: Classics & Moderns, Vol. 2. John Hicks. 408p. 1983. 47.00 (0-674-13743-4) HUP.

Collected Essays on One Hundred One Art Works: From the Permanent Collection of the Wichita Art Museum. Howard E. Wooden. LC 88-51543. (Illus.). 216p. 1988. pap. 15.00 (0-939324-39-3) Wichita Art Mus.

Collected Essays on Public Health & Epidemiology, 2 Vols. Rudolf Virchow. LC 85-2042. (Illus.). 1985. 50.00 (0-317-38928-9) Watson Pub Intl.

Collected Essays on Public Health & Epidemiology, 2 Vols, 1. Rudolf Virchow. LC 85-2042. (Illus.). 1985. write for info. (0-88135-076-1) Watson Pub Intl.

Collected Essays on Public Health & Epidemiology, 2 Vols, 2. Rudolf Virchow. LC 85-2042. (Illus.). 1985. write for info. (0-88135-077-X) Watson Pub Intl.

Collected Essays, Papers, Etc. 30 Parts in 1. Robert Bridges. reprint ed. 188.00 (3-487-04382-3) Adlers Foreign Bks.

Collected Experimental Papers, 7 Vols, Set. Percy W. Bridgman. LC 64-16060. (Illus.). 4800p. 1964. 355.00 (0-674-13750-7) HUP.

Collected Fat Freddy's Cat, Vol. 1. Gilbert Shelton & Dave Sheridan. Ed. by Guy Colwell. (Illus.). 96p. 1989. reprint ed. pap. 8.95 (0-89620-096-5) Rip off.

Collected Fat Freddy's Cat, Vol. 2. Gilbert Shelton & Dave Sheridan. Ed. by Guy Colwell. (Illus.). 96p. 1989. reprint ed. pap. 8.95 (0-89620-097-3) Rip off.

Collected Fiction. Louis Zukofsky. LC 89-23697. 311p. 1990. reprint ed. pap. 9.95 (0-916583-59-7) Dalkey Arch.

Collected Fruits of Occult Teaching. A. P. Sinnett. 308p. 1964. reprint ed. spiral bd. 11.00 (0-7873-0797-1) Mokelumne.

Collected Ghost Stories. Mary E. Wilkins-Freeman. LC 73-88393. 1974. 8.95 (0-87054-065-3) Arkham.

Collected Ghost Stories of E. F. Benson. E. F. Benson. Ed. by Richard Dalby. 672p. 1992. pap. 10.95 (0-88184-857-3) Carroll & Graf.

Collected Ghost Stories of Mrs J. H. Riddell. 24.95 (0-89190-864-1, Am Repr) Amereon Ltd.

Collected Ghost Stories of Mrs. Riddell. E. F. Bleiler. 25.95 (0-89190-696-7) Amereon Ltd.

Collected Greed, Pts. 1-13. Diane Wakoski. LC 84-12416. 252p. (Orig.). 1984. pap. 10.00 (0-87685-462-5) Black Sparrow.

Collected in Himself: Essays, Critical, Biographical & Bibliographical on Pope & Some of His Contemporaries. Maynard Mack. LC 79-57524. 576p. 1982. 70.00 (0-87413-182-0) U Delaware Pr.

Collected Legal Essays. Boris I. Bittker. 730p. 1989. 42.50 (0-8377-0358-1) Rothman.

Collected Legal Papers. Oliver W. Holmes, Jr. 17.00 (0-8446-1241-3) Peter Smith.

Collected Legislation of Russia. Ed. & Tr. by William E. Butler. 1992. Annual releases. ring bd. 150.00 (0-379-10401-6) Oceana.

Collected Legislation of the U. S. S. R. The Constituent Union Republics, Legislation & Constitutions, Set. William E. Butler. Incl. Constituent Union Republics, legislation & Constitutions, 2 binders. LC 78-24391. 1978. (0-318-56891-8); Constitutions, 1 binder. LC 78-24391. 1978. (0-318-56892-6); Union Republic Legis, 4 binders legislative. LC 78-24391. 1978. (0-318-56893-4); LC 78-24391. 1978. Closed set. 500.00 (0-379-20450-9) Oceana.

Collected Letters: 1861-1897, Vol. 1. Joseph Conrad. Ed. by Frederick R. Karl & Laurence Davies. LC 82-14643. (Illus.). 480p. 1983. 94.95 (0-521-24216-9) Cambridge U Pr.

Collected Letters: 1898-1902, Vol. 2. Joseph Conrad. Ed. by Frederick R. Karl & Laurence Davies. (Illus.). 450p. 1986. 94.95 (0-521-25748-4) Cambridge U Pr.

Collected Letters: 1903-1907, Vol. 3. Joseph Conrad. Ed. by Frederick R. Karl & Laurence Davies. (Illus.). 500p. 1988. 94.95 (0-521-32387-8) Cambridge U Pr.

Collected Letters: 1908-1911, Vol. 4. Joseph Conrad. Ed. by Frederick R. Karl & Laurence Davies. (Illus.). 550p. (C). 1991. 94.95 (0-521-32388-6) Cambridge U Pr.

Collected Letters of Antoni van Leeuwenhoek, 12 vols. Antoni Van Leeuwenhoek. Incl. Vol. 1. 454p. 1939. text ed. 180.00 (0-317-05959-9); Vol. 2. 506p. 1941. (90-265-0041-6); Vol. 3. 560p. 1948. text ed. 180.00 (0-317-05960-2); Vol. 4. 383p. 1952. text ed. 180.00 (90-265-0043-2); Vol. 5. 457p. 1958. text ed. 180.00 (90-265-0044-0); Vol. 6. 425p. 1961. text ed. 180.00 (90-265-0045-9); Vol. 7. 427p. 1965. text ed. 180.00 (90-265-0046-7); Vol. 8. 383p. 1967. text ed. 180.00 (90-265-0047-5); Vol. 9. 482p. 1976. text ed. 180.00 (90-265-0220-6); Vol. 10. 362p. 1979. text ed. 180.00 (90-265-0285-0); Vol. 11. 384p. 1983. text ed. 180.00 (90-265-0446-2); Illus.). (DUT & ENG.). Set text ed. write for info. (0-318-55897-1) Swets North Am.

***Collected Letters of Antoni van Leeuwenhoek Pt. XIII.** Ed. by L. C. Palm. 444p. 1994. 265.00 (90-265-1239-2, Pub. by Swets Pub Serv NE) Taylor & Francis.

Collected Letters of Colin MacLaurin. Ed. by Stella Mills. 560p. (C). 1982. text ed. 35.00 (0-906812-08-9) Birkhauser.

***Collected Letters of George Gissing: 1897-1899, Vol. 7.** George Gissing. Ed. by Paul F. Mattheisen et al. LC 89-26577. (Illus.). 400p. (C). 1995. text ed. 60.00 (0-8214-1123-3) Ohio U Pr.

Collected Letters of George Gissing, Vol. I: 1863-1880. Ed. by Paul F. Mattheisen et al. LC 89-26577. 600p. (C). 1990. text ed. 70.00x (0-8214-0955-7) Ohio U Pr.

Collected Letters of George Gissing, Vol. IV: 1889-1891. George Gissing et al. Ed. by Paul F. Mattheisen et al. LC 89-26577. 400p. (C). 1993. text ed. 60.00 (0-8214-1054-7) Ohio U Pr.

Collected Letters of George Gissing, Vol. 5: 1892-1895. Ed. by Paul F. Mattheisen et al. LC 89-26577. 400p. (C). 1994. text ed. 60.00 (0-8214-1067-9) Ohio U Pr.

Collected Letters of George Gissing, 1881-1885, Vol. II. Ed. by Paul F. Mattheisen et al. (Illus.). 429p. (C). 1991. text ed. 60.00 (0-8214-0984-0) Ohio U Pr.

Collected Letters of George Gissing, 1886-1888. George Gissing et al. Ed. by Paul F. Mattheisen et al. LC 89-26577. (Collected Letters of George Gissing Ser.: Vol. III). 390p. (C). 1992. text ed. 60.00 (0-8214-1014-8) Ohio U Pr.

Collected Letters of George Gissing, 1895-1897, Vol. 6. Ed. by Paul F. Mattheisen et al. LC 89-26577. (Illus.). 390p. 1994. text ed. 60.00 (0-8214-1098-9) Ohio U Pr.

Collected Letters of John Millington Synge, 1871-1907, Vol. I. John Millington Synge. Ed. by Ann Saddlemyer. LC 82-14535. (Illus.). (C). 1983. 85.00 (0-19-812678-6) OUP.

Collected Letters of John Randolph to John Brockenbrough. Ed. by Russell A. Kirk & Kenneth Shorey. (Library of Conservative Thought). 192p. 1987. 39.95 (0-88738-194-4) Transaction Pubs.

Collected Letters of Katherine Mansfield, Vol. III: 1919-1920. Katherine Mansfield. Ed. by Vincent O'Sullivan & Margaret Scott. 328p. 1993. 55.00 (0-19-812615-8) OUP.

Collected Letters of Mary Wollstonecraft. Mary Wollstonecraft. Ed. by Ralph M. Wardle. LC 78-15641. (Illus.). 488p. 1979. 49.95 (0-8014-1164-5) Cornell U Pr.

Collected Letters of Sir Arthur Pinero. Arthur W. Pinero. Ed. by J. P. Wearing. LC 74-76742. 314p. reprint ed. pap. 89.50 (0-318-39674-2, 2033245) Bks Demand.

Collected Letters of Thomas & Jane Welch Carlyle, Vols. 13-15. Clyde de L. Ryals. Ed. by Kenneth J. Fielding. 1988. lib. bdg. 41.95 (0-318-61460-X); Vol. 13, 333p. write for info. (0-8223-0702-2); Vol. 14, 248p. write for info. (0-8223-0703-0); Vol. 15, 293p. write for info. (0-8223-0704-9) Duke.

Collected Letters of Thomas & Jane Welsh Carlyle, 1. Ed. by Charles R. Sanders. LC 71-101132. (Illus.). 1954p. 1970. write for info. (0-8223-0467-8) Duke.

Collected Letters of Thomas & Jane Welsh Carlyle, 3. Ed. by Charles R. Sanders. LC 71-101132. (Illus.). 1954p. 1970. write for info. (0-8223-0469-4) Duke.

Collected Letters of Thomas & Jane Welsh Carlyle, Set. Ed. by Charles R. Sanders. LC 71-101132. 1981. 85.00 (0-8223-0472-4) Duke.

Collected Letters of Thomas & Jane Welsh Carlyle, Set, Vols. 1-4. Ed. by Charles R. Sanders. LC 71-101132. (Illus.). 1954p. 1970. Set. 125.00 (0-8223-0240-3) Duke.

Collected Letters of Thomas & Jane Welsh Carlyle, Vol. 8, 1835-1836. Ed. by Charles R. Sanders. LC 71-101132. 1981. 39.95 (0-8223-0433-3) Duke.

Collected Letters of Thomas & Jane Welsh Carlyle, Vol. 9, 1836-1837. Ed. by Charles R. Sanders. LC 71-101132. 1981. 41.95 (0-8223-0434-1) Duke.

Collected Letters of Thomas & Jane Welsh Carlyle, 3 vols., Vol. 10. Ed. by Charles R. Sanders et al. 280p. 1985. 41.95 (0-685-73685-7) Duke.

Collected Letters of Thomas & Jane Welsh Carlyle, 3 vols., Vol. 11. Ed. by Charles R. Sanders et al. 256p. 1985. 41.95 (0-8223-0612-3) Duke.

Collected Letters of Thomas & Jane Welsh Carlyle, 3 vols., Vol. 12. Ed. by Charles R. Sanders et al. 312p. 1985. 41.95 (0-8223-0613-1) Duke.

Collected Letters of Thomas & Jane Welsh Carlyle, Vol. 16. Clyde de L. Ryals et al. Ed. by Kenneth J. Fielding et al. 424p. (Orig.). 1990. lib. bdg. 41.95 (0-8223-0919-X) Duke.

Collected Letters of Thomas & Jane Welsh Carlyle, Vol. 17. Clyde de L. Ryals et al. Ed. by Kenneth J. Fielding et al. 384p. (Orig.). 1990. lib. bdg. 41.95 (0-8223-0924-6) Duke.

Collected Letters of Thomas & Jane Welsh Carlyle, Vol. 18. Clyde de L. Ryals et al. Ed. by Kenneth J. Fielding et al. 384p. (Orig.). 1990. lib. bdg. 41.95 (0-8223-0936-X) Duke.

Collected Letters of Thomas & Jane Welsh Carlyle, Vols. 16-18. Clyde de L. Ryals et al. Ed. by Kenneth J. Fielding et al. (Orig.). 1990. lib. bdg. write for info. (0-318-65458-X) Duke.

Collected Letters of Thomas & Jane Welsh Carlyle: Duke-Edinburgh Edition, 5. Ed. by Charles R. Sanders. LC 71-101132. (Illus.). 1977. 41.95 (0-8223-0369-8) Duke.

Collected Letters of Thomas & Jane Welsh Carlyle: Duke-Edinburgh Edition, 6. Ed. by Charles R. Sanders. LC 71-101132. (Illus.). 1977. 41.95 (0-8223-0370-1) Duke.

Collected Letters of Thomas & Jane Welsh Carlyle: Duke-Edinburgh Edition, 7. Ed. by Charles R. Sanders. LC 71-101132. (Illus.). 1977. 41.95 (0-8223-0371-X) Duke.

Collected Letters of Thomas & Jane Welsh Carlyle: Duke-Edinburgh Edition, Set, Vols. 5-7. Ed. by Charles R. Sanders. LC 71-101132. (Illus.). 1977. Set. 100.00 (0-8223-0471-6) Duke.

Collected Letters of Thomas & Jane Welsh Carlyle, Vol. 19: January to September, 1845. Ed. by Clyde D. Ryals & Kenneth J. Fielding. LC 71-101323. 263p. 1993. lib. bdg. 45.00 (0-8223-1286-7) Duke.

Collected Letters of Thomas & Jane Welsh Carlyle, Vol. 20: October 1845 to July 1846. Ed. by Clyde D. Ryals & Kenneth J. Fielding. LC 71-101323. 269p. 1993. lib. bdg. 45.00 (0-8223-1287-5) Duke.

Collected Letters of Thomas & Jane Welsh Carlyle, Vol. 21: August 1846 to June 1847. Ed. by Clyde D. Ryals & Kenneth J. Fielding. LC 71-101323. 285p. 1993. lib. bdg. 45.00 (0-8223-1288-3) Duke.

Collected Letters of Thomas Hardy, Vol. 4: 1909-1913. Thomas Hardy. Ed. by Richard L. Purdy & Michael Millgate. (C). 1984. 59.00 (0-19-812621-2) OUP.

Collected Letters of Thomas Hardy, Vol. 5: 1914-1919. Thomas Hardy. Ed. by Richard L. Purdy & Michael Millgate. (Illus.). 304p. 1985. 59.00 (0-19-812622-0) OUP.

Collected Letters of Thomas Hardy, Vol. 6: 1920-1925. Thomas Hardy. Ed. by Richard L. Purdy & Michael Millgate. 370p. 1987. 72.00 (0-19-812623-9) OUP.

Collected Letters of Thomas Hardy, Vol. 7: 1926-1927 (with Addenda, Corringenda, & General Index) Thomas Hardy. Ed. by Richard L. Purdy & Michael Millgate. (Illus.). 322p. 1988. 69.00 (0-19-812624-7) OUP.

Collected Letters of Thomas Hardy, Vols. 1, 2 & 3: 1840-1842, Vol. 1. Thomas Hardy. Ed. by Richard L. Purdy. (Illus.). 1978. 85.00 (0-19-812470-8) OUP.

Collected Letters of Thomas Hardy, Vols. 1, 2 & 3: 1840-1842, Vol. 3. Thomas Hardy. Ed. by Richard L. Purdy. (Illus.). 1982. 88.00 (0-19-812620-4) OUP.

Collected Letters of W. B. Yeats: Vol. III: 1901-1904. Ed. by John Kelly. (Illus.). 600p. 1994. 55.00 (0-19-812683-2) OUP.

Collected Letters of W. B. Yeats, Vol. 1: 1865-1895. William Butler Yeats. Ed. by Eric Domville & John Kelly. (Illus.). 548p. 1986. text ed. 55.00 (0-19-812679-4) OUP.

Collected Letters of William Morris Vol. 2, Pt. A: 1881-1888. Ed. by Norman Kelvin. (Illus.). 450p. 1987. text ed. 55.00 (0-691-06600-0) Princeton U Pr.

Collected Letters of William Morris Vol. 2, Pt. B: 1881-1888. Ed. by Norman Kelvin. (Illus.). 550p. 1987. text ed. 67.50 (0-691-06723-6) Princeton U Pr.

Collected Letters of William Morris, Vol. 1. William Morris. Ed. by Norman Kelvin. LC 82-47604. (Collected Letters of William Morris Ser.). (Illus.). 626p. 1984. 87.50 (0-691-06501-2) Princeton U Pr.

Collected Lichenological Papers, 2 vols., 1. E. Tuckerman. Ed. by W. L. Culberson. 1964. 54.00 (3-7682-0221-6) Lubrecht & Cramer.

Collected Lichenological Papers, 2 vols., 2. E. Tuckerman. Ed. by W. L. Culberson. 1964. 66.00 (3-7682-0222-4) Lubrecht & Cramer.

Collected Lichenological Papers, 2 vols., Set. E. Tuckerman. Ed. by W. L. Culberson. 1964. 118.80 (3-7682-0220-8) Lubrecht & Cramer.

Collected Lichenological Papers. Including a Biography & Bibliography, Vol. 1: Papers 1852-1862. William Nylander. Ed. by Teuvi Ahti. 732p. 1990. reprint ed. lib. bdg. 210.00 (3-443-50013-7, Pub. by Cramer-Borntraeger GW) Lubrecht & Cramer.

Collected Lichenological Papers, Vol. 2: Papers 1863-1868 with Addenda Nova ad Lichenographiam Europaeam 1865-1887. William Nylander. Ed. by Teuvi Ahti. 801p. (LAT.). 1990. reprint ed. lib. bdg. 210.00 (3-443-50014-5, Pub. by Cramer-Borntraeger GW) Lubrecht & Cramer.

Collected Lichenological Papers, Vol. 3: Papers 1869-1887. William Nylander. Ed. by Teuvi Ahti. 560p. (LAT.). 1990. reprint ed. lib. bdg. 210.00 (3-443-50015-3, Pub. by Cramer-Borntraeger GW) Lubrecht & Cramer.

Collected Lichenological Papers, Vol. 4: Papers 1888-1900. William Nylander. Ed. by Teuvi Ahti. 826p. 1967. reprint ed. lib. bdg. 90.00 (3-7682-0434-0, Pub. by Cramer GW) Lubrecht & Cramer.

Collected Lichenological Papers, Vol. 5: Synopsis Methodica Lichenum 1958-69 & G. Lindau's Index Nominum Nylanderi Synopsis Lichenum 1907- William Nylander. Ed. by Teuvi Ahti. 556p. (LAT.). 1967. reprint ed. lib. bdg. 90.00 (3-7682-0435-9, Pub. by Cramer GW) Lubrecht & Cramer.

Collected Lichenological Papers, Vol. 6: Prodromus Lichenographiae Galliae et Algeriae 1857; Lichenes Scandinaviae 1861; Lichenes Lapponiae Orientalis 1862. William Nylander. Ed. by Teuvi Ahti. 636p. (LAT.). 1967. lib. bdg. 90.00 (3-7682-0436-7, Pub. by Cramer GW) Lubrecht & Cramer.

Collected Longer Poems. Hayden Carruth. LC 93-11404. 240p. (Orig.). 1993. 25.00 (1-55659-058-X); pap. 14.00 (1-55659-059-8) Copper Canyon.

Collected Longer Poems. Kenneth Rexroth. LC 68-25549. 1970. reprint ed. pap. 12.95 (0-8112-0177-5, NDP309) New Directions.

Collected Lyrics. Edna St. Vincent Millay. LC 75-6348. 304p. 1981. pap. 12.00 (0-06-090863-7, CN863, PL) HarpC.

Collected Lyrics & Epigrams. Oscar Mandel. LC 81-410. 104p. 1982. 9.50 (0-89807-025-2) Spectrum Prods.

Collected Mathematical Papers. I. R. Shafarevich. 780p. 1989. 128.00 (0-387-13618-5) Spr-Verlag.

Collected Mathematical Papers, 2 Vols. Henry J. Smith. LC 65-11859. 99.50 (0-8284-0187-X) Chelsea Pub.

Collected Mathematical Papers, 4 Vols. James J. Sylvester. LC 76-250188. 1973. reprint ed. text ed. 195.00 (0-8284-0253-1) Chelsea Pub.

Collected Mathematical Papers, 2 pts., Pts. 1 & 2. A. Adrian Albert. LC 92-28744. 743p. 1992. Pt. 1, 743p. 100.00 (0-8218-0005-1, CWORKS-3); Pt. 2, 938p. 117.00 (0-8218-0007-8) Am Math.

Collected Mathematical Papers, 2 pts., Set, Pts. 1 & 2. A. Adrian Albert. LC 92-28744. 1992. Set. 206.00 (0-8218-0003-5) Am Math.

Collected Mathematical Papers, Set, Vols. I-VI. Leonard E. Dickson. Ed. by A. Adrian Albert. LC 69-19943. 4000p. 1983. Set. text ed. 295.00 (0-8284-0273-6) Chelsea Pub.

Collected Memoirs of Central School: Kirkland, Washington, 1890-1980. Ed. by Kenfield Olson. 67p. (Orig.). (YA). (gr. 9-12). 1982. pap. 5.00 (0-685-28866-8) Marymoor Mus.

Collected Memoranda & Reports of the National Center for State Courts to the New York City Felony Backlog Reduction Program, October 1981-January 1982. National Center for State Courts Staff. 201p. 1983. 12.06 (0-685-15483-1, NERO-128) Natl Ctr St Courts.

Collected Moments of Spirituality. Hazelden. Date not set. pap. 10.00 (0-06-255310-0, PL) HarpC.

Collected Narrative & Lyrical Poetry. Aleksandr Pushkin. Tr. by Walter Arndt. 475p. 1984. pap. 18.95 (0-88233-826-9) Ardis Pubs.

Collected Novellas. Arno Schmidt. Tr. by John E. Woods. LC 94-8747. (Illus.). 432p. 1994. 22.95 (1-56478-066-X) Dalkey Arch.

Collected Novellas. Gabriel Garcia Marquez. Tr. by Gregory Rabassa & J. S. Bernstein. LC 89-46106. 304p. 1991. reprint ed. pap. 12.00 (0-06-092128-5, PL) HarpC.

Collected Novels, 2 Vols., 1. Thomas Hardy. 1993. 20.00 (0-679-60077-9, Modern Lib) Random.

Collected Novels, 2 Vols., 2. Thomas Hardy. 1993. 19.00 (0-679-60078-7, Modern Lib) Random.

Collected Novels & Memoirs of William Godwin. Ed. by Mark Philp et al. (Pickering Masters Ser.). 1992. 575.00 (1-85196-007-4, Pub. by Pickering & Chatto UK) Ashgate Pub Co.

Collected Nursery Rhymes: Four Verses. Ed. by Malachi McCormick. 80p. (J). 1985. boxed 20.00 (0-943984-21-1) Stone St Pr.

Collected Omaha, Vol. II. Reed Waller & Kate Worley. (Illus.). 130p. 1988. 25.00 (0-87816-048-5); pap. 12.95 (0-87816-049-3) Kitchen Sink.

Collected Omaha, Vol. III. Reed Waller & Kate Worley. (Collected Omaha the Cat Dancer Ser.: Vol. III). (Illus.). 126p. 1990. pap. 14.95 (0-87816-086-8) Kitchen Sink.

Collected Omaha, Vol. III. deluxe limited ed. Reed Waller & Kate Worley. (Collected Omaha the Cat Dancer Ser.: Vol. III). (Illus.). 126p. 1990. 27.95 (0-87816-085-X) Kitchen Sink.

Collected Omaha, Vol. 4. Reed Waller & Kate Worley. (Omaha, the Cat Dancer Ser.). (Illus.). 135p. 1990. 28.95 (0-87816-121-X); pap. 15.95 (0-87816-122-8) Kitchen Sink.

Collected Omaha the Cat Dancer. Reed Waller & Kate Worley. Ed. by Denis Kitchen & David Schreiner. (Illus.). 128p. 1987. pap. 15.95 (0-87816-031-0) Kitchen Sink.

Collected Omaha the Cat Dancer, Vol. 5. deluxe limited ed. Reed Waller & Kate Worley. Ed. by Dave Schreiner. (Illus.). 136p. 1993. 28.95 (0-87816-258-5) Kitchen Sink.

Collected Omaha the Cat Dancer, Vol. 5. Reed Waller & Kate Worley. Ed. by Dave Schreiner. (Illus.). 136p. 1993. reprint ed. pap. 15.95 (0-87816-257-7) Kitchen Sink.

Collected Paintings of the Tianpinglou Studio: Paintings of Zhang Slaeveheng, Zhang Loh Xiuping, Zhang Zhav & Zhang Yuan, Vol. I. Zhang Shoucheng. (Illus.). 132p. 1994. 120.00 (7-80512-765-4, 4/J636) S Zhang.

Collected Papers. Emil Artin. Ed. by Serge A. Lang & J. T. Tate. (Illus.). 576p. 1988. 72.00 (0-387-90686-X) Spr-Verlag.

Collected Papers. Harish Chandra. Ed. by V. S. Varadarajan. (Illus.). 2400p. 1983. 326.00 (0-387-90782-3) Spr-Verlag.

Collected Papers. N. Denholm-Young. 317p. 1969. 28.50 (0-904730-21-2, Pub. by U of Wales UK) Bks Intl VA.

Collected Papers. Gareth Evans. 1985. 69.00 (0-19-824737-0) OUP.

Collected Papers. I. M. Gelfand. x, 1039p. 1988. 216.00 (0-387-19035-X) Spr-Verlag.

Collected Papers. I. M. Gelfand. 1040p. 1989. 208.00 (0-387-19399-5) Spr-Verlag.

Collected Papers. P. L. Hsu. (Illus.). 589p. 1982. 119.00 (0-387-90725-4) Spr-Verlag.

Collected Papers, 8 vol. set. John G. Kirkwood. 1951p. 1968. text ed. 1,033.00 (0-677-01720-0) Gordon & Breach.

Collected Papers. Wilhelm Magnus. Ed. by B. Chandler & Gilbert Baumslag. (Illus.). 735p. 1983. 73.00 (0-387-90879-X) Spr-Verlag.

Collected Papers. Lloyd A. Metzler. LC 79-184108. (Economic Studies: No. 140). (Illus.). 614p. 1973. 35.00 (0-674-13775-2) HUP.

C

An Asterisk (*) at the beginning of an entry indicates that the title is appearing in BIP for the first time.

Collected Papers. Mitio Nagumo. Ed. by Masaya Yamaguti et al. LC 93-9561. (ENG, FRE & GER.). 1993. 132.00 (0-387-70112-5) Spr-Verlag.

Collected Papers. Emmy Noether. 776p. 1983. 116.00 (0-387-11504-8) Spr-Verlag.

Collected Papers. K. Oka. 245p. 1984. 119.00 (0-387-13240-6) Spr-Verlag.

Collected Papers. J. H. Polotsky. xi, 724p. 1971. text ed. 35.00 (0-685-74253-9, Pub. by Magnes Press IS) Eisenbrauns.

Collected Papers. Eric K. Van Douwen. Ed. by Jan Van Mill. LC 93-43644. 1994. 320.00 (0-444-81625-9, North Holland) Elsevier.

Collected Papers. Kosaku Yosida. Ed. by Kiyoski Ito. LC 92-30119. 1993. write for info. (4-431-70111-7); 149.00 (0-387-70111-7) Spr-Verlag.

Collected Papers. Ed. by Teiji Takagi et al. (Illus.). xv, 376p. 1990. reprint ed. 142.00 (0-387-70057-9) Spr-Verlag.

Collected Papers, 2 vols., 1. Friedrichs. (Contemporary Mathematicians Ser.). 1987. 115.00 (0-8176-3268-9) Birkhauser.

Collected Papers, 2 vols., 2. Friedrichs. (Contemporary Mathematicians Ser.). 1987. 150.00 (0-8176-3269-7) Birkhauser.

Collected Papers, 2 vols., Set. Friedrichs. (Contemporary Mathematicians Ser.). 1986. lib. bdg. 220.00 (0-8176-3270-0) Birkhauser.

Collected Papers, 6 vols., Set, Vol. 4, X-XII. Alexander Ostrowski. 600p. (ENG, FRE & GER.). 1983. Six-vol. set. 530.00 (0-8176-1512-1) Birkhauser.

Collected Papers, Vol. I. K. R. Norman. 271p. (C). 1990. 36.95 (0-86013-295-1, Pub. by Pali Text) Wisdom MA.

Collected Papers, Vol. 1. A. Selberg. (Illus.). vi, 711p. 1989. 159.00 (0-387-18389-2) Spr-Verlag.

Collected Papers, Vol. II. K. R. Norman. 271p. 1991. write for info. (0-86013-296-X) Wisdom MA.

Collected Papers, Vol. 3. J. C. Kiefer et al. Ed. by L. B. Brown et al. (Illus.). 720p. 1984. 81.00 (0-387-96004-X) Spr-Verlag.

Collected Papers, Vol. III. K. R. Norman. 271p. 1992. write for info. (0-86013-299-4) Wisdom MA.

Collected Papers, Vol. IV. K. R. Norman. 271p. 1993. write for info. (0-86013-306-0) Wisdom MA.

Collected Papers, Vol. 4, X-XII. Alexander Ostrowski. 600p. (ENG, FRE & GER.). 1984. 77.00 (0-8176-1509-1) Birkhauser.

Collected Papers, Vol. 5. Alexander Ostrowski. (Contemporary Mathematicians Ser.). 560p. 1985. text ed. 72.00 (0-8176-1510-5) Birkhauser.

Collected Papers, Vols. 1 & 2. J. C. Kiefer et al. Ed. by L. B. Brown et al. (Illus.). xliv, 1092p. 1984. 175.00 (0-387-96003-1) Spr-Verlag.

Collected Papers: Alexander Ostrowski, Vol. 6. Alexander Ostrowski. (Contemporary Mathematicians Ser.). 720p. 1985. pap. 93.00 (0-8176-1511-3) Birkhauser.

***Collected Papers: Mathematics.** Florentin Smarandache. Ed. by R. Muller. (Illus.). 300p. (C). 1996. pap. 9.99 (1-879585-44-8) Xiquan Pubng.

Collected Papers: Sieve Methods, No. II. A. Selberg. (Illus.). 272p. 1991. 103.00 (0-387-50626-8) Spr-Verlag.

Collected Papers see Psychodrama

Collected Papers in Physics & Engineering. James Thomson. LC 70-137300. reprint ed. 65.00 (0-404-06422-1) AMS Pr.

Collected Papers of Albert Einstein, Vol. 1: The Early Years: 1879-1902. Ed. by John Stachel et al. (Illus.). 375p. 1987. 85.00 (0-691-08407-6); pap. 29.95 (0-691-08475-0) Princeton U Pr.

Collected Papers of Albert Einstein, Vol. 2: The Swiss Years: Writings, 1900-1909. Ed. by John Stachel. 656p. (C). 1989. text ed. 85.00 (0-691-08526-9); pap. 29.95 (0-691-08549-8) Princeton U Pr.

Collected Papers of Albert Einstein, Vol. 3: The Swiss Years: Writings, 1909-1911. Ed. by Martin Klein et al. (Illus.). 550p. 1993. text ed. 85.00 (0-691-08772-5) Princeton U Pr.

Collected Papers of Albert Einstein, Vol. 5: The Swiss Years: Correspondence, 1902-1914. Ed. by Martin Klein et al. (Illus.). 780p. 1993. lib. bdg. 85.00 (0-691-03322-6); pap. text ed. 27.95 (0-691-00099-9) Princeton U Pr.

Collected Papers of Alfred Young, 1873-1940. Alfred Young. LC 78-306195. (Mathematical Expositions Ser.: No. 21). 712p. reprint ed. pap. 180.00 (0-7837-4282-7, 2043974) Bks Demand.

Collected Papers of Bertrand Russell: Philosophical Papers, 1896-1899, Vol. II. Nicholas Griffin & Albert C. Lewis. 672p. (C). 1990. text ed. 140.00 (0-04-920068-2) Routledge Chapman & Hall.

***Collected Papers of Bertrand Russell Vol. 14: The No-Conscription Fellowship: Pacifism & Revolution 1916-18.** Richard Rempel et al. 640p. 1995. 165.00x (0-415-09410-0, C0233) Routledge.

Collected Papers of Bertrand Russell, Vol. XIII: Prophesy & Dissent, 1914-1916. Ed. by Richard A. Rempel & Margaret Moran. 774p. 1988. text ed. 150.00 (0-04-920079-8, A9421) Routledge Chapman & Hall.

Collected Papers of Charles Sanders Peirce, 6 vols. Charles S. Peirce. Ed. by Charles Hartshorne & Paul Weiss. Incl. Vol. 1 (bk. 1). Principles of Philosophy. LC 60-9172. 1934. (0-318-53025-2); Vol. 2 (bk. 1). Elements of Logic. LC 60-9172. 1934. (0-318-53026-0); Vol. 3 (bk. 2). Exact Logic. LC 60-9172. 1934. (0-318-53027-9); Vol. 4 (bk. 2). Simplest Mathematics. LC 60-9172. 1934. (0-318-53028-7); Vol. 5 (bk. 3). Pragmatism & Pragmaticism. LC 60-9172. 1934. (0-318-53029-5); Vol. 6 (bk. 3). Scientific Metaphysics. LC 60-9172. 1934. (0-318-53030-9); LC 60-9172. 1934. write for info. (0-318-53024-4, Belknap Pr); Incl. Vol. 1 (bk. 1). (0-318-53025-2); Vol. 2 (bk. 1). (0-318-53026-0); Vol. 3 (bk. 2). (0-318-53027-9); Vol. 4 (bk. 2). (0-318-53028-7); Vol. 5 (bk. 3). (0-318-53029-5); Vol. 6 (bk. 3). (0-318-53030-9); Bk. 1. 70.00 (0-674-13800-7, Belknap Pr) HUP.

Collected Papers of Charles Sanders Peirce, 6 vols, Vol. 2. Charles S. Peirce. Ed. by Charles Hartshorne & Paul Weiss. Incl. Vol. 1 (bk. 1). Principles of Philosophy. LC 60-9172. 1934. (0-318-53025-2); Vol. 2 (bk. 1). Elements of Logic. LC 60-9172. 1934. (0-318-53026-0); Vol. 3 (bk. 2). Exact Logic. LC 60-9172. 1934. (0-318-53027-9); Vol. 4 (bk. 2). Simplest Mathematics. LC 60-9172. 1934. (0-318-53028-7); Vol. 5 (bk. 3). Pragmatism & Pragmaticism. LC 60-9172. 1934. (0-318-53029-5); Vol. 6 (bk. 3). Scientific Metaphysics. LC 60-9172. 1934. (0-318-53030-9); LC 60-9172. 1934. Bk. 2. 75.00 (0-674-13801-5, Belknap Pr) HUP.

Collected Papers of Charles Sanders Peirce, 6 vols, Vol. 3. Charles S. Peirce. Ed. by Charles Hartshorne & Paul Weiss. Incl. Vol. 1 (bk. 1). Principles of Philosophy. LC 60-9172. 1934. (0-318-53025-2); Vol. 2 (bk. 1). Elements of Logic. LC 60-9172. 1934. (0-318-53026-0); Vol. 3 (bk. 2). Exact Logic. LC 60-9172. 1934. (0-318-53027-9); Vol. 4 (bk. 2). Simplest Mathematics. LC 60-9172. 1934. (0-318-53028-7); Vol. 5 (bk. 3). Pragmatism & Pragmaticism. LC 60-9172. 1934. (0-318-53029-5); Vol. 6 (bk. 3). Scientific Metaphysics. LC 60-9172. 1934. (0-318-53030-9); LC 60-9172. 1934. Bk. 3. 70.00 (0-674-13802-3, Belknap Pr) HUP.

Collected Papers of Charles Sanders Peirce, 6 vols, Vol. 4. Charles S. Peirce. Ed. by Charles Hartshorne & Paul Weiss. Incl. Vol. 1 (bk. 1). Principles of Philosophy. LC 60-9172. 1934. (0-318-53025-2); Vol. 2 (bk. 1). Elements of Logic. LC 60-9172. 1934. (0-318-53026-0); Vol. 3 (bk. 2). Exact Logic. LC 60-9172. 1934. (0-318-53027-9); Vol. 4 (bk. 2). Simplest Mathematics. LC 60-9172. 1934. (0-318-53028-7); Vol. 5 (bk. 3). Pragmatism & Pragmaticism. LC 60-9172. 1934. (0-318-53029-5); Vol. 6 (bk. 3). Scientific Metaphysics. LC 60-9172. 1934. (0-318-53030-9); LC 60-9172. 1934. Bk. 4. 65.00 (0-674-13803-1, Belknap Pr) HUP.

Collected Papers of Charles Sanders Peirce, Vols. 1 & 2, 5 & 6. Charles S. Peirce. Ed. by Charles Hartshorne & Paul Weiss. LC 60-9172. (Illus.). 959p. reprint ed. Vol. 1-2: Principles of Philosophy & Elements of Logic, 667p. pap. 180.00 (0-7837-1682-6, 2057213); reprint ed. Vol. 5-6: Pragmatism & Pragmaticism & Scientific Metaphysics, 667p. pap. 180.00 (0-7837-1683-4, 2057213) Bks Demand.

Collected Papers of Charles Sanders Peirce, Vol. 3-4: Exact Logic (Published Papers) & the Simplest Mathematics. Ed. by Charles Hartshorne & Paul Weiss. LC 60-9172. (Illus.). 1061p. reprint ed. pap. 180.00 (0-7837-1508-0, 2041731) Bks Demand.

Collected Papers of Charles Sanders Peirce, Vol. 7-8: Science & Philosophy & Reviews, Correspondence, & Bibliography. Ed. by Charles Hartshorne & Paul Weiss. LC 60-9172. (Illus.). 795p. reprint ed. pap. 180.00 (0-7837-1509-9, 2041731) Bks Demand.

Collected Papers of Charles Willson Peale & His Family. Ed. by Lillian B. Miller. 1980. 1,500.00 (0-527-99008-6) Kraus Intl.

Collected Papers of Clarence Irving Lewis. Ed. by John D. Goheen & John L. Mothershead, Jr. LC 73-97913. x, 444p. 1970. 52.50 (0-8047-0717-0) Stanford U Pr.

Collected Papers of Dan Usher, 2 Vols. Dan Usher. (Economists of the Twentieth Century Ser.). 900p. 1994. Vol 1., National Accounting & Economic Theory; Vol. 2, Welfare Economics & Public Finance. 149.95 (1-85278-993-X, Pub. by E Elgar Pub UK) Ashgate Pub Co.

Collected Papers of Franco Modigliani, 3 vols., Vol. 1: Essays in Macroeconomics. Franco Modigliani. Ed. by Andrew Abel. 1980. Vol. 1, Essays In Macroeconomics. 52.50x (0-262-13150-1) MIT Pr.

Collected Papers of Franco Modigliani, Vol. 4: Monetary Theory & Stabilization Policies. Franco Modigliani. Ed. by Simon Johnson. 350p. 1989. 47.50 (0-262-13244-3) MIT Pr.

Collected Papers of Franco Modigliani, Vol. 5: Saving, Deficits, Inflation, & Financial Theory. Franco Modigliani. Ed. by Simon Johnson. 450p. 1989. 52.50 (0-262-13245-1) MIT Pr.

Collected Papers of Frederick G. Kilgour, 2 vols. Frederick G. Kilgour. Ed. by Lois L. Yoakam. (Illus.). (Orig.). 1984. Vol. 1, Early Years, 370 pgs. write for info. (0-933418-50-7); Vol. 2, OCLC Years, 370 pgs. write for info. (0-933418-49-3) OCLC Online Comp.

Collected Papers of Frederick G. Kilgour, 2 vols. deluxe ed. Frederick G. Kilgour. Ed. by Lois L. Yoakam. (Illus.). (Orig.). 1984. 75.00 (0-685-10824-4) OCLC Online Comp.

Collected Papers of Frederick G. Kilgour, 2 vols., Set. Frederick G. Kilgour. Ed. by Lois L. Yoakam. (Illus.). (Orig.). 1984. pap. 57.50 (0-685-10823-6) OCLC Online Comp.

Collected Papers of Frederick William Maitland, 3 vols., Set. Ed. by H. A. Fisher et al. LC 80-84867. (Historical Writings in Law & Jurisprudence Ser.: Title No. 20, Bks. 28-30). 1596p. 1981. reprint ed. lib. bdg. 195.00 (0-89941-241-6, 302160) W S Hein.

Collected Papers of Gabor Szego, 3 vols., Set. Ed. by R. Askey. (C). 1980. text ed. 260.00 (0-8176-3063-5) Birkhauser.

Collected Papers of Gabor Szego, Vol. I. Ed. by R. Askey. 872p. (C). 1982. text ed. 95.00 (0-8176-3056-2) Birkhauser.

Collected Papers of Gabor Szego, Vol. 2. Ed. by R. Askey. 894p. (C). 1982. text ed. 95.00 (0-8176-3060-0) Birkhauser.

Collected Papers of Gabor Szego, Vol. 3. Ed. by R. Askey. 892p. (C). 1982. text ed. 95.00 (0-8176-3061-9) Birkhauser.

Collected Papers of Hans Rademacher, 2 vols., 2. Hans Rademacher. Ed. by Emil Grosswald. (Mathematicians of Our Time Ser.: Vols. 1 & 2). 1356p. 1974. 70.00x (0-262-07055-3) MIT Pr.

Collected Papers of Hans Rademacher, 2 vols., Set. Hans Rademacher. Ed. by Emil Grosswald. (Mathematicians of Our Time Ser.: Vols. 1 & 2). 1356p. 1974. 135.00 (0-685-03383-X) MIT Pr.

Collected Papers of Hans Rademacher, 2 vols., Vol. 1. Hans Rademacher. Ed. by Emil Grosswald. (Mathematicians of Our Time Ser.: Vols. 1 & 2). 1356p. 1974. 70.00 (0-262-07054-5) MIT Pr.

Collected Papers of Hassler Whitney, 2 vols. Ed. by James Eells & D. Toledo. (Contemporary Mathematicians Ser.). xiv, 592p. 1991. Vol. 1, xiv, 592p. 120.00 (0-8176-3558-0); Vol. 2, xv, 600p. 120.00 (0-8176-3559-9) Birkhauser.

Collected Papers of Hassler Whitney, 2 vols., Set. Ed. by James Eells & D. Toledo. (Contemporary Mathematicians Ser.). xxxi, 1192p. 1991. 198.00 (0-8176-3560-2) Birkhauser.

Collected Papers of J. E. Littlewood, 2 vols., 1. J. E. Littlewood. Ed. by J. W. Cassels. 1983. 175.00 (0-19-853353-5) OUP.

Collected Papers of Jacob Guttmann: An Original Anthology. Ed. by Steven Katz. LC 79-7172. (Jewish Philosophy, Mysticism & History of Ideas Ser.). 1980. lib. bdg. 44.95 (0-405-12231-4) Ayer.

Collected Papers of James Meade, Set, Vols. I-IV. Ed. by Susan Howson. 1989. Set. 375.00 (0-04-445076-1) Routledge Chapman & Hall.

Collected Papers of James Meade, Vol. II: Value, Distribution & Growth. Ed. by Susan Howson. 496p. 1988. text ed. 110.00 (0-04-445073-7) Routledge Chapman & Hall.

Collected Papers of James Meade, Vol. IV: The Cabinet Office Diary, 1944-46. Ed. by Susan Howson & Donald Moggeridge. 400p. 1989. 110.00 (0-04-445075-3) Routledge Chapman & Hall.

Collected Papers of Jara Tomasek. Ed. by Hana Tomasek. LC 93-15897. 1993. 19.95 (1-882768-55-8) Queue Pub.

Collected Papers of Jay W. Forrester. Jay W. Forrester. LC 73-89547. 284p. (C). 1975. text ed. 65.00 (0-262-06065-5) Prod Press.

Collected Papers of Kenneth E. Boulding, 2. Kenneth E. Boulding. LC 77-135288. (Illus.). pap. 134.70 (0-8357-5525-8, 2035142) Bks Demand.

Collected Papers of Kenneth E. Boulding, 3. Kenneth E. Boulding. LC 77-135288. (Illus.). 624p. pap. 177.90 (0-8357-5526-6) Bks Demand.

Collected Papers of Kenneth E. Boulding, 4. Kenneth E. Boulding. LC 77-135288. (Illus.). 631p. pap. 179.90 (0-8357-5527-4) Bks Demand.

Collected Papers of Kenneth E. Boulding, 5. Kenneth E. Boulding. LC 77-135288. (Illus.). 438p. pap. 124.90 (0-8357-5528-2) Bks Demand.

Collected Papers of Kenneth E. Boulding, 6. Kenneth E. Boulding. LC 77-135288. (Illus.). 703p. pap. 180.00 (0-8357-5529-0) Bks Demand.

Collected Papers of Kenneth J. Arrow, Vol. 3: Individual Choice under Certainty & Uncertainty, Vol. 3. Kenneth J. Arrow. (Illus.). 288p. 1984. 36.00 (0-674-13762-0) Belknap Pr.

Collected Papers of Kenneth J. Arrow, Vol. 4: The Economics of Information, Vol. 4. Kenneth J. Arrow. (Illus.). 296p. 0194. 36.00 (0-674-13763-9) Belknap Pr.

Collected Papers of Kenneth J. Arrow, Vol. 5: Production & Capital, Vol. 5. Kenneth J. Arrow. (Illus.). 496p. 1985. 45.00 (0-674-13777-9) Belknap Pr.

Collected Papers of Kenneth J. Arrow, Vol. 6: Applied Economics, Vol. 6. Kenneth J. Arrow. (Illus.). 280p. 1985. 36.00 (0-674-13778-7) Belknap Pr.

Collected Papers of Kenneth J. Arrow, Vols. 1 & 2: Social Choice & Justice; General Equilibrium, 1. Kenneth J. Arrow. 240p. 1984. 32.00 (0-674-13760-4) HUP.

Collected Papers of Kenneth J. Arrow, Vols. 1 & 2: Social Choice & Justice; General Equilibrium, Vol. 2. Kenneth J. Arrow. 320p. 1984. 37.50 (0-674-13761-2) HUP.

Collected Papers of L. D. Landau. D. Ter Haar. LC 64-17191. 1965. 344.00 (0-08-010586-6, Pub. by Pergamon Repr UK) Franklin.

Collected Papers of L. D. Landau. D. Ter Haar. 856p. 1965. text ed. 398.00 (0-677-20550-3) Gordon & Breach.

Collected Papers of Marston Morse, 6 vols. 3612p. 1987. text ed. 426.00 (9971-978-94-6) World Scientific Pub.

Collected Papers of P. L. Kapitza, 2 vols, Vol. 1. P. L. Kapitza. Ed. by D. Ter Haar. 1965. 214.00 (0-08-010744-3, Pub. by Pergamon Repr UK) Franklin.

Collected Papers of P. L. Kapitza, 2 vols, Vol. 2. P. L. Kapitza. Ed. by D. Ter Haar. 1965. 205.00 (0-08-010973-X, Pub. by Pergamon Repr UK) Franklin.

Collected Papers of P. L. Kapitza, Vol. 3. D. Ter Haar. LC 64-15735. 1967. 107.00 (0-08-011947-6, Pub. by Pergamon Repr UK) Franklin.

Collected Papers of P. L. Kapitza, Vol. 4. Ed. by D. Ter Haar. (Illus.). 384p. 1986. 285.00 (0-08-026505-7, Pergamon Pr) Elsevier.

Collected Papers of Paul Ehrlich. F. Himmelweit. (Histology Biochemistry & Pathology Ser.: Vol. 1). 1956. 274.00 (0-08-009054-0, Pub. by Pergamon Repr UK) Franklin.

Collected Papers of Paul Ehrlich: Complete Bibliography, 3 vols., Set. F. Himmelweit & M. Marquardt. 1957. 769.00 (0-08-013123-9, Pub. by Pergamon Repr UK) Franklin.

Collected Papers of Peter J. W. Debye. Peter J. Debye. LC 87-36895. xxi, 700p. 1988. reprint ed. 90.00 (0-918024-58-7) Ox Bow.

Collected Papers of R. H. Bing, 2 vols. Ed. by S. Armentrout et al. LC 88-14445. 1654p. 1988. text ed. 188.00 (0-8218-0117-1, CWORKS-1) Am Math.

Collected Papers of Robert Park, 3 vols., Set. Incl. Vol. 1. Race & Culture. Ed. by Everett C. Hughes et al. LC 73-14174. 1974. (0-318-50800-1); Vol. 2. Human Communities: The City & Human Ecology. Ed. by Everett C. Hughes et al. LC 73-14174. 1974. (0-318-50801-X); Vol. 3. Society: Collective Behavior, News & Opinion, Sociology & Modern Society. Ed. by Everett C. Hughes et al. LC 73-14174. 1974. (0-318-50802-8); LC 73-14174. (Perspectives in Social Inquiry Ser.). 1066p. 1974. reprint ed. 60.95 (0-405-05517-X) Ayer.

***Collected Papers of Roger Harrison.** Roger Harrison. (Management Ser.). 416p. 1995. 34.95 (0-7879-0083-4) Jossey-Bass.

Collected Papers of Salomon Bochner, Pt. I, Vol. 2.1. 762p. 1992. 113.00 (0-8218-0174-0, CWORKS-2.1) Am Math.

Collected Papers of Salomon Bochner, Pt. II, Vol. 2.2. 790p. 1992. 116.00 (0-8218-0175-9, CWORKS-2.2) Am Math.

Collected Papers of Salomon Bochner, Pt. III, Vol. 2.3. 732p. 1992. 108.00 (0-8218-0176-7, CWORKS-2.3) Am Math.

Collected Papers of Salomon Bochner, Set. Gunning. LC 91-31045. 2840p. 1992. 367.00 (0-8218-0161-9, CWORKS-2) Am Math.

Collected Papers of Sigmund Freud, 5 Vols. Sigmund Freud. Ed. by Ernest Jones. LC 61-15950. (International Psycho-Analytic Library, Nos. 7, 8, 9, 10, 37). 1959. 50.00 (0-685-73182-0) Basic.

Collected Papers of Sigmund Freud, 5 Vols, Vol. 1. Sigmund Freud. Ed. by Ernest Jones. LC 61-15950. (International Psycho-Analytic Library, Nos. 7, 8, 9, 10, 37). 359p. 1959. text ed. 55.00 (0-465-01249-3) Basic.

Collected Papers of Sigmund Freud, 5 Vols, Vol. 3. Sigmund Freud. Ed. by Ernest Jones. LC 61-15950. (International Psycho-Analytic Library, Nos. 7, 8, 9, 10, 37). 608p. 1959. text ed. 55.00 (0-465-01251-5) Basic.

Collected Papers of Sigmund Freud, 5 Vols, Vol. 5. Sigmund Freud. Ed. by Ernest Jones. LC 61-15950. (International Psycho-Analytic Library, Nos. 7, 8, 9, 10, 37). 396p. 1959. text ed. 55.00 (0-465-01253-1) Basic.

Collected Papers of Sir Harold Jeffreys on Geophysics & Other Sciences, 6 vols., Vol. 6. H. Jeffreys & B. Jeffreys. Incl. Vol. I. 556p. 1971. text ed. 352.00 (0-677-03170-X); Vol. 2. 730p. 1973. text ed. 449.00 (0-677-03180-7); Vol. 3. 680p. 1974. text ed. 449.00 (0-677-03190-4); Vol. 4. 542p. 1975. text ed. 380.00 (0-677-03200-5); Vol. 5. 512p. 1976. text ed. 429.00 (0-677-03210-2); Vol. 6. 640p. 1977. text ed. 447.00 (0-677-03220-X); 3660p. 1977. Set. Set text ed. 1,727.00 (0-677-03230-7) Gordon & Breach.

Collected Papers of T. W. Anderson, 1943-1985, 2 vols., Vol. 2. Styan. (Probability & Mathematical Statistics Ser.). 1990. Set. text ed. 185.00 (0-471-62422-5) Wiley.

Collected Papers of Y. Matsushima. (Series in Pure Mathematics: Vol. 15). 780p. (C). 1992. text ed. 109.00 (981-02-0814-6) World Scientific Pub.

Collected Papers on Accounting: Original Anthology. William T. Baxter. Ed. by Richard P. Brief. LC 77-87311. (Contemporary Accounting Thought Ser.). 1978. lib. bdg. 37.95 (0-405-10924-5) Ayer.

Collected Papers on Acoustics. Wallace C. Sabine. 304p. 1993. reprint ed. 35.95 (0-932146-60-0) Peninsula CA.

Collected Papers on Cathodic Protection Current Distribution. LC 89-50422. (Illus.). 110p. 1989. 48.00 (0-915567-41-5) NACE Intl.

Collected Papers on Epistemology, Philosophy of Science & History of Philosophy, 2 vols, 2. Ed. by Wolfgang Stegmuller. (Synthese Library: No. 101). 1977. lib. bdg. 84.00 (90-277-0643-3) Kluwer Ac.

Collected Papers on Geology of the Atlantic Region: Hugh Lilly Memorial Volume. Ed. by Ernest R. Neale & H. Williams. LC 77-433692. (Geological Association of Canada. Special Paper Ser.: No. 4). 293p. reprint ed. pap. 83.60 (0-685-17109-4, 2027839) Bks Demand.

Collected Papers on Greek Tragedy. T. C. Stinton. (Illus.). 528p. 1990. 130.00 (0-19-814054-1) OUP.

***Collected Papers on Latin Literature.** R. G. Nisbet. 456p. 1995. 80.00 (0-19-814948-4) OUP.

Collected Papers on Marine Claims. J. Kenneth Goodacre. 244p. 1980. 145.00 (0-900886-47-1, Pub. by Witherby & Co UK) St Mut.

Collected Papers on Marine Claims, Vol. 2. J. Kenneth Goodacre. 108p. 1992. 37.50 (1-85609-040-X, Pub. by Witherby & Co UK) St Mut.

Collected Papers on Schizophrenia & Related Subjects. Harold F. Searles. LC 65-21320. 798p. 1966. text ed. 72.50x (0-8236-0980-4) Intl Univs Pr.

An Asterisk (*) at the beginning of an entry indicates that the title is appearing in BIP for the first time.

1357

Collected Papers on Wave Mechanics. 3rd ed. Erwin Schroedinger. LC 78-11493. 1978. text ed. 19.95 (0-8284-1302-9) Chelsea Pub.

Collected Papers Supplementary Volume. J. C. Keifer. Ed. by L. D. Brown et al. 64p. 1986. 36.00 (0-387-96383-9) Spr-Verlag.

Collected Papers, Vol. I: The Problem of Social Reality. 4th ed. Alfred Schutz. (Phaenomenologica Ser.: No. 11). 1972. pap. text ed. 25.50 (90-247-3046-5) Kluwer Ac.

Collected Papers, Vol. I: The Problem of Social Reality. 4th ed. Alfred Schutz. (Phaenomenologica Ser.: No. 11). 1974. lib. bdg. 74.50 (90-247-5089-X) Kluwer Ac.

Collected Papers, Vol. II. Alfred Schutz. (Phaenomenologica Ser.: No. 15). 1976. lib. bdg. 51.50 (90-247-0248-8) Kluwer Ac.

Collected Papers, Vol. III. Alfred Schutz. (Phaenomenologica Ser.: No. 22). 1975. lib. bdg. 47.00 (90-247-5090-3) Kluwer Ac.

Collected Performance Texts. Richard Kostelanetz. 154p. (Orig.). 1991. pap. 30.00 (0-685-50707-6) Archae Edns.

Collected Perspectives: Choosing & Using Books for the Classroom. 2nd ed. Ed. by Hughes Moir. 417p. (Orig.). (J). (gr. k-12). 1991. pap. text ed. 38.95 (0-926842-12-9) CG Pubs Inc.

Collected Philosophical Papers. Emmanuel Levinas. Ed. by Alphonso Lingis. 1987. lib. bdg. 95.00 (90-247-3272-7) Kluwer Ac.

Collected Plays. Ronald Duncan. 368p. 1971. 19.95 (0-246-64004-9) Boulevard.

Collected Plays. Nathalie Sarraute. Tr. by Maria Jolas & Barbara Wright. LC 78-7111. 107p. (C). 1981. pap. 5.95 (0-8076-0940-4) Braziller.

Collected Plays, 2 vols, 1. Oscar Mandel. LC 70-134738. 1971. write for info. (0-87775-000-9) Spectrum Prods.

Collected Plays, 2 vols, 2. Oscar Mandel. LC 70-134738. 1971. write for info. (0-87775-001-7) Spectrum Prods.

Collected Plays, 2 vols, Set. Oscar Mandel. LC 70-134738. 1971. 24.00 (0-914502-04-2); pap. 16.00 (0-914502-05-0) Spectrum Prods.

Collected Plays, Vol. 1. Wole Soyinka. 1973. pap. 12.95 (0-19-281136-3) OUP.

Collected Plays, Vol. 2. Wole Soyinka. 1975. pap. 12.95 (0-19-281164-9) OUP.

***Collected Plays Vol. 1.** Steven Berkoff. 400p. (Orig.). 1995. pap. 14.95 (0-571-16903-1) Faber & Faber.

***Collected Plays Vol. II, Vol. 2.** Steven Berkoff. 400p. (Orig.). Date not set. pap. 14.95 (0-571-17102-8) Faber & Faber.

Collected Plays & Poems, 1958-1988. J. P. Clark-Bekederemo. LC 91-14580. 1991. 34.95 (0-88258-128-7); pap. 16.95 (0-88258-136-8) Howard U Pr.

Collected Plays & Poems, 1958-1988. J. P. Clark-Bekederemo. LC 91-14580. 1991. pap. 17.95 (0-88258-129-5) Howard U Pr.

Collected Plays & Short Stories, 2 vols., Set. Sri Aurobindo. 1088p. 33.00 (0-89071-260-3) Aurobindo Assn.

Collected Plays & Writings on Theater. Karol Wojtyla. Tr. by Boleslaw Taborski. 450p. 1987. 45.00 (0-520-05289-7) U CA Pr.

Collected Plays of Eugene O'Neill, Vol. II. Eugene O'Neill. 1986. pap. 17.95 (0-452-26358-1, Plume) NAL-Dutton.

Collected Plays of Lady Gregory, Vol. 1: Comedies, 1971. Lady Gregory. Ed. by Ann Saddlemyer. 1979. 40.00 (0-900675-29-2, Pub. by Colin Smythe Ltd UK); pap. 13.95 (0-86140-016-X, Pub. by Colin Smythe Ltd UK) Dufour.

Collected Plays of Lady Gregory, Vol. 2: Tragedies & Tragic Comedies, 1971. Lady Gregory. Ed. by Ann Saddlemyer. 1979. 45.00 (0-900675-30-6, Pub. by Colin Smythe Ltd UK); pap. 15.95 (0-86140-017-8, Pub. by Colin Smythe Ltd UK) Dufour.

Collected Plays of Lady Gregory, Vol. 3: Wonder & Supernatural Plays, 1971. Lady Gregory. Ed. by Ann Saddlemyer. 1979. 50.00 (0-900675-31-4, Pub. by Colin Smythe Ltd UK); pap. 18.95 (0-86140-018-6, Pub. by Colin Smythe Ltd UK) Dufour.

Collected Plays of Lady Gregory, Vol. 4: Collaborations Adaptations & Translations, 1971. Lady Gregory. Ed. by Ann Saddlemyer. 1979. 45.00 (0-900675-32-2, Pub. by Colin Smythe Ltd UK); pap. 16.95 (0-86140-019-4, Pub. by Colin Smythe Ltd UK) Dufour.

Collected Plays of Neil Simon, Vol. 1. Neil Simon. LC 86-12639. 672p. 1986. pap. 17.95 (0-452-25870-7, Plume) NAL-Dutton.

Collected Plays of Neil Simon, Vol. 2. Neil Simon. 1980. pap. 7.95 (0-380-51904-6) Avon.

Collected Plays of Neil Simon, Vol. 2. Neil Simon. LC 86-12639. 752p. 1986. pap. 12.95 (0-452-25871-5, Plume) NAL-Dutton.

Collected Plays of Neil Simon, Vol. 2. Neil Simon. LC 79-5081. 1979. 29.95 (0-394-50770-3) Random.

Collected Plays of Neil Simon, Vol. III. Neil Simon. 1992. 34.50 (0-679-40889-4) Random.

Collected Plays of Peter Barnes. Peter Barnes. 468p. (Orig.). 1981. pap. 10.00 (0-435-18281-1) Heinemann.

Collected Plays of Ronald Harwood. Ronald Harwood. 400p. (Orig.). 1994. pap. 14.95 (0-571-17001-3) Faber & Faber.

Collected Plays of William Butler Yeats. William Butler Yeats. 1990. 40.00 (0-02-632941-7, Scribners) S&S Trade.

Collected Plays, Vol. 1: Contains Claw, No End of Blame, The Castle, Scenes from an Execution, & Victory. Howard Barker. 260p. (Orig.). 1990. pap. 15.95 (0-7145-4161-3) Riverrun NY.

Collected Plays, Vol. 2: Includes Love of a Good Man, The Possibilities, Brutopia, Rome, Uncle Vanga, & Ten Dilemmas. Howard Barker. 260p. (Orig.). 1993. pap. 16.50 (0-7145-4182-6) Riverrun NY.

Collected Poems. George Abbe. 1961. 5.95 (0-87233-800-2) Bauhan.

Collected Poems. Y. Amichai. 1994. 30.00 (0-06-019039-6, HarpT) HarpC.

Collected Poems. W. H. Auden. LC 90-50192. (Vintage International Ser.). 960p. 1991. pap. 22.50 (0-679-73197-0, Vin) Random.

Collected Poems. Ursula Bethell. Ed. by Vincent O'Sullivan. 128p. 1986. teacher ed write for info. (0-318-60424-8); pap. 15.95 (0-19-558139-3) OUP.

Collected Poems. Kay Boyle. LC 90-85089. 192p. (Orig.). 1991. pap. 10.00 (1-55659-039-3) Copper Canyon.

Collected Poems. Basil Bunting. 180p. 1985. 22.50 (0-918825-27-X); pap. 12.95 (0-918825-16-4) Moyer Bell.

Collected Poems. Joseph Chiari & Hugh Macdiarmid. LC 77-26826. 200p. 1978. 45.00 (0-87752-213-8) Gordian.

Collected Poems. Padraic Colum. 25.00 (0-8159-5203-1) Devin.

Collected Poems, 4 vols. Ernest Crosby. 1973. 400.00 (0-87968-882-3) Gordon Pr.

Collected Poems. Donald Davie. (Phoenix Poets Ser.). 480p. 1991. lib. bdg. 40.00 (0-226-13760-0); pap. 14.95 (0-226-13761-9) U Ch Pr.

Collected Poems. Samuel Davies. Ed. by Richard B. Davis. LC 68-17019. 1968. 50.00 (0-8201-1011-6) Schol Facsimiles.

Collected Poems. Walter De La Mare. LC 79-670359. 480p. 1979. pap. 19.95 (0-571-11382-6) Faber & Faber.

Collected Poems. Desmond Egan. LC 83-62144. (Irish Art & Man & Poet Ser.). (Illus.). 220p. 1983. 15.00 (0-915032-17-1); pap. 8.95 (0-915032-18-X) Natl Poet Foun.

Collected Poems. William Empson. LC 49-7861. 1901. pap. 4.95 (0-15-618839-2, Harvest Bks) HarBrace.

Collected Poems. Roy Fuller. LC 62-51612. 1962. 18.95 (0-8023-1046-X) Dufour.

Collected Poems. Federico Garcia Lorca. Ed. by Christopher Maurer. 1991. 50.00 (0-374-12624-0) FS&G.

Collected Poems. Louis Ginsberg. Ed. by Michael Fournier. 440p. 1992. 37.95 (1-880811-04-9) North Lights.

Collected Poems. Thom Gunn. 1994. 35.00 (0-374-12621-6) FS&G.

***Collected Poems.** Thom Gunn. 495p. 1995. pap. 14.00 (0-374-52433-5, Noonday) FS&G.

Collected Poems. Gwen Harwood. 232p. 1991. pap. 14.95 (0-19-282882-7) OUP.

Collected Poems. Robert Hayden. Ed. by Frederick Glaysher. 1985. pap. 10.95 (0-87140-138-X) Liveright.

Collected Poems. Frances Horovitz. 150p. 1985. 30.00 (0-906427-86-X, Pub. by Bloodaxe Bks UK); pap. 17.95 (0-906427-87-8, Pub. by Bloodaxe Bks UK) Dufour.

Collected Poems. A. E. Housman. 1976. 17.95 (0-8488-1373-1) Amereon Ltd.

Collected Poems. John Jordan. Ed. by Hugh McFadden. 140p. (C). 1991. 30.00 (0-685-60826-3, Pub. by Dedalus Pr IE); pap. 18.00 (0-685-60827-1, Pub. by Dedalus Pr IE) St Mut.

Collected Poems. Philip Larkin. 1993. pap. 15.00 (0-374-52275-8, Noonday) FS&G.

Collected Poems. James Liddy. 300p. (C). 1994. 24.95 (1-881871-09-6); pap. 14.95 (1-881871-08-8) Creighton U Pr.

Collected Poems. Martin Lings. (Illus.). 51p. (Orig.). 1987. pap. 14.95 (0-900588-28-4) S Perennis.

Collected Poems. Norman MacCaig. 456p. 1991. 39.95 (0-7011-3713-4, Pub. by Chatto & Windus UK) Trafalgar.

Collected Poems. Louis MacNeice. Ed. by E. R. Dodds. 593p. 1979. pap. 18.95 (0-571-11353-2) Faber & Faber.

***Collected Poems.** Stephane Mallarme. Tr. & Comment by Henry Weinfield. LC 94-26794. 1994. 25.00 (0-520-08188-9) U CA Pr.

Collected Poems. David Markson. LC 92-18999. 96p. (Orig.). 1993. pap. 9.95 (1-56478-033-3) Dalkey Arch.

Collected Poems. E. L. Mayo. Ed. by David Ray. LC 80-84519. (New Letters Ser.). 272p. (Orig.). 1981. pap. text ed. 20.00 (0-938652-00-1) New Letters MO.

Collected Poems. A. J. McGeoch. 125p. 1986. 30.00 (0-905075-22-6, Pub. by Wilfion Bks UK) Dufour.

Collected Poems. Samuel Menashe. 220p. 1986. pap. 12.95 (0-915032-43-0) Natl Poet Foun.

Collected Poems. May Miller. LC 88-83172. 235p. (YA). (gr. 7-12). 1989. 18.00 (0-916418-70-7) Lotus.

Collected Poems. Czeslaw Milosz. 528p. 1990. pap. 14.95 (0-88001-174-2) Ecco Pr.

***Collected Poems.** John Montague. 300p. (C). 1995. text ed. 16.95 (0-916390-68-3) Wake Forest.

***Collected Poems.** John Montague. 300p. (C). 1995. 24.95 (0-916390-69-1) Wake Forest.

Collected Poems. George Oppen. LC 75-6965. 1976. pap. 10.95 (0-8112-0615-7, NDP418) New Directions.

Collected Poems. Kenneth Patchen. LC 67-23487. 512p. 1969. pap. 16.95 (0-8112-0140-6, NDP284) New Directions.

Collected Poems. Sylvia Plath. LC 75-25075. 288p. 1981. pap. 17.00 (0-06-090900-5, CN 900, PL) HarpC.

Collected Poems. Peter Porter. 352p. 1984. pap. 7.95 (0-19-211965-6) OUP.

Collected Poems. Carl Rakosi. LC 84-62266. (Poets Ser.). 550p. (Orig.). 1986. 35.00 (0-915032-35-X); pap. 15.95 (0-915032-36-8) Natl Poet Foun.

Collected Poems. Henry Reed. Ed. by Jon Stallworthy. 192p. 1988. pap. 14.95 (0-19-282072-9) OUP.

Collected Poems. Henry Reed. Ed. by Jon Stallworthy. 192p. 1991. 42.50 (0-19-212298-3) OUP.

Collected Poems. Edwin Rolfe. Ed. by Cary Nelson & Jefferson Hendricks. LC 92-42324. (American Poetry Recovery Ser.). 352p. 1993. 34.95 (0-252-02026-X) U of Ill Pr.

Collected Poems. James Schuyler. LC 92-40977. 1993. 35.00 (0-374-12618-6) FS&G.

Collected Poems. James Schuyler. 256p. 1995. pap. 14.00 (0-374-52403-3) FS&G.

Collected Poems. Simpson. 1994. pap. 12.95 (1-56924-919-9) Marlowe & Co.

Collected Poems. Sri Aurobindo. 625p. 1979. text ed. 17.50 (0-89744-904-5, Pub. by Sri Aurob Ashram Trust II) Auromere.

Collected Poems. Wallace Stevens. LC 82-40031. 560p. 1982. pap. 11.95 (0-394-71180-7) Random.

Collected Poems. Wallace Stevens. 1990. pap. 15.00 (0-679-72669-1, Vin) Random.

Collected Poems. Dylan Thomas. LC 53-7766. 224p. 1971. pap. 9.95 (0-8112-0205-4, NDP316) New Directions.

Collected Poems. Edward Thomas. 192p. 1979. pap. 8.95 (0-571-11368-0) Faber & Faber.

Collected Poems. Tomas Transtromer. Tr. by Robin Fulton. LC 88-70238. 159p. (Orig.). 1988. pap. 17.95 (1-85224-023-7, Pub. by Bloodaxe Bks UK) Dufour.

Collected Poems. Donald Wandrei. (Illus.). 100p. (Orig.). 1988. pap. 8.95 (0-940884-04-6) Necronomicon.

Collected Poems. Philip Ward. 1960. pap. 4.95 (0-902675-40-0) Oleander Pr.

Collected Poems. John Wheelwright. Ed. by Alvin H. Rosenfeld. LC 79-175817. 304p. 1972. pap. 10.00 (0-8112-0849-4, NDP544) New Directions.

***Collected Poems.** Rosemary R. Wilkinson. (Illus.). 240p. (Orig.). 1994. pap. 10.00 (0-9642261-3-8) EJ Co.

Collected Poems. Lulu M. Winters. 1993. 8.95 (0-533-10443-2) Vantage.

Collected Poems. James Wright. LC 70-142727. (Wesleyan Poetry Ser.). 229p. 1971. pap. 16.95 (0-8195-6022-7, Wesleyan Univ Pr) U Pr of New Eng.

Collected Poems. James Wright. LC 70-142727. (Wesleyan Poetry Ser.). 229p. 1972. 30.00 (0-8195-4031-5, Wesleyan Univ Pr) U Pr of New Eng.

Collected Poems. Yevgeny Yevtushenko. 576p. 1991. 29.95 (0-8050-0696-6) H Holt & Co.

Collected Poems. rev. ed. Wilfred Owen. Ed. by C. Day Lewis. LC 64-10290. 1964. pap. 8.95 (0-8112-0132-5, NDP210) New Directions.

Collected Poems. Richard Aldington. LC 78-64002. (Des Imagistes: Literature of the Imagist Movement Ser.). 248p. reprint ed. 34.50 (0-404-17075-7) AMS Pr.

Collected Poems. Isabella Crawford. LC 72-91689. (Literature of Canada, Poetry & Prose in Reprint Ser.). 352p. reprint ed. pap. 100.40 (0-317-26928-3, 2023607) Bks Demand.

Collected Poems. Cecil Day-Lewis. LC 78-14113. 1995. reprint ed. 35.00 (0-88355-785-1) Hyperion Conn.

Collected Poems. Alfred B. Douglas. (BCL1-PR English Literature Ser.). 125p. 1992. reprint ed. lib. bdg. 69.00 (0-7812-7519-9) Rprt Serv.

Collected Poems. Alan Dugan. LC 76-89903. 212p. reprint ed. pap. 60.50 (0-8357-8694-3, 2033712) Bks Demand.

Collected Poems. Ford Madox Ford. LC 78-64033. (Des Imagistes: Literature of the Imagist Movement Ser.). reprint ed. 21.00 (0-404-17114-1) AMS Pr.

Collected Poems. John Freeman. 1971. reprint ed. 29.00 (0-403-00596-5) Scholarly.

Collected Poems. Robert Frost. 319p. 1983. reprint ed. lib. bdg. 27.95 (0-89966-442-3) Buccaneer Bks.

***Collected Poems.** Robert Hayden. Ed. by Frederick Glaysher. 225p. 1995. reprint ed. 23.00 (0-87140-651-9) Liveright.

Collected Poems. Ernest Hemingway. LC 79-100764. (American Literature Ser.: No. 49). (C). 1970. reprint ed. lib. bdg. 59.95 (0-8383-0334-X) M S G Haskell Hse.

Collected Poems. A. E. Housman. 138p. 1983. reprint ed. lib. bdg. 23.95 (0-89966-451-2) Buccaneer Bks.

Collected Poems. Philip B. Marston. LC 72-148816. reprint ed. 49.50 (0-404-04192-2) AMS Pr.

Collected Poems. Herman Melville. (BCL1-PS American Literature Ser.). 548p. 1993. reprint ed. lib. bdg. 99.00 (0-7812-6987-3) Rprt Serv.

Collected Poems. Edna St. Vincent Millay. LC 75-6348. 1992. reprint ed. lib. bdg. 35.95x (0-89968-266-9, Lghtyr Pr) Buccaneer Bks.

Collected Poems. Edna St. Vincent Millay. Ed. by Norma Millay. LC 75-6348. 760p. (YA). 1981. reprint ed. pap. 22.50 (0-06-090889-0, CN-889, PL) HarpC.

Collected Poems. Theodore Roethke. LC 65-23785. 288p. 1975. reprint ed. 12.95 (0-385-08601-6, Anchor NY) Doubleday.

Collected Poems. George E. Russel. 1988. reprint ed. lib. bdg. 59.00 (0-7812-0480-1) Rprt Serv.

Collected Poems. George W. Russel. LC 73-131821. 1970. reprint ed. 29.00 (0-403-00708-9) Scholarly.

Collected Poems. Sacheverell Sitwell. LC 75-41254. reprint ed. 37.50 (0-404-14604-X) AMS Pr.

Collected Poems. Stevie Smith. Ed. by James MacGibbon. LC 83-43008. 592p. 1983. reprint ed. pap. 18.95 (0-8112-0882-6, NDP562) New Directions.

Collected Poems. John C. Squire. LC 81-13489. (Illus.). xvii, 241p. 1982. reprint ed. text ed. 55.00 (0-313-23319-5, SQCP, Greenwood Pr) Greenwood.

Collected Poems, 2. Jonathan Griffin. (Poets Ser.). pap. 25.00 (0-943373-08-5) Natl Poet Foun.

Collected Poems, 2 vols., Set. Otto Fenichel. Ed. by Hanna Fenichel & Stanley Rapaport. 782p. (C). 1987. text ed. 75.00x (0-393-01505-X) Norton.

Collected Poems, Set, Vol. 1 & 2. Jonathan Griffin. (Poets Ser.). Set. 99.00 (0-685-53997-0) Natl Poet Foun.

Collected Poems, Set, Vol. 1 & 2. Jonathan Griffin. (Poets Ser.). 1989. Set. pap. 45.00 (0-685-53998-9) Natl Poet Foun.

Collected Poems, 2 vols., VI. Fenichel. (C). 1987. text ed. 37.50 (0-393-01055-4) Norton.

Collected Poems, 2 vols., VII. Fenichel. (C). 1987. text ed. 37.50 (0-393-01070-8) Norton.

Collected Poems, Vol. 1. Jonathan Griffin. (Poets Ser.). 406p. 1989. 62.50 (0-943373-05-0) Natl Poet Foun.

Collected Poems, Vol. 1. Jonathan Griffin. (Poets Ser.). 1990. pap. 25.00 (0-943373-06-9) Natl Poet Foun.

Collected Poems, Vol. 1. Vasyl Pachovsky. 420p. 1984. 12.00 (0-930013-00-X) Assn Ukrainian Writers.

Collected Poems, Vol. 2. Jonathan Griffin. (Poets Ser.). 577p. 1990. 62.50 (0-943373-07-7) Natl Poet Foun.

Collected Poems, Vol. 2. Michael Hartnett. LC 84-72523. 104p. 1986. pap. 12.95 (1-85186-009-6) Dufour.

Collected Poems, Vol. II. Jocelyn Hollis. LC 86-32194. 158p. 1988. 14.95 (0-930933-04-4); lib. bdg. 14.95 (0-930933-03-6); pap. text ed. 7.95 (0-930933-05-2) Am Poetry & Lit.

Collected Poems: From the Personal to the Universal. Marta Mitrovich. 80p. (Orig.). 1990. pap. 6.00 (0-9624205-1-4) Inevitable Pr.

Collected Poems: Moore. Moore. 1981. 10.95 (0-02-586170-0) Macmillan.

Collected Poems: New Edition. 2nd ed. Primo Levi. Tr. by Ruth Feldman & Brian Swann. 128p. (Orig.). 1992. pap. 10.95 (0-571-16539-7) Faber & Faber.

Collected Poems: Nineteen Twenty-Eight to Nineteen Eighty-Five. Stephen Spender. 1986. 19.95 (0-394-54601-6) Random.

Collected Poems: Norman Nicholson. Ed. by Neil Curry. 480p. 1994. 29.95 (0-571-17004-8) Faber & Faber.

***Collected Poems: Updike, 1953-1993.** John Updike. 1995. pap. 15.00 (0-679-76204-3) Knopf.

Collected Poems: 1930-1993. May Sarton. LC 92-32688. 576p. 1993. 27.50 (0-393-03493-3) Norton.

Collected Poems: 1937-1971. John Berryman. 512p. 1991. pap. 14.95 (0-374-52281-2, Noonday) FS&G.

Collected Poems: 1956-1974. Edward Dorn. LC 74-27227. (Writing Ser.: No. 34). 288p. 1975. 15.00 (0-87704-030-3); pap. 10.00 (0-87704-029-X) Four Seasons Foun.

***Collected Poems & One Essay.** Kathleen B. Maddox. Ed. by Jane Orth. (Illus.). 97p. 1995. pap. 6.00 (1-885761-01-5) Turner Geriatric.

Collected Poems & Plays. Rabindranath Tagore. LC 92-33702. 466p. 1993. pap. 14.00 (0-02-082455-6, Collier S&S) S&S Trade.

Collected Poems & Translations. Veronica Forrest-Thomson. 288p. 1990. 30.00 (0-907954-08-1, Pub. by Allardyce Barnett UK) SPD-Small Pr Dist.

Collected Poems by Mavis Clare Barnett. Ed. by Carey B. Dupret et al. 162p. 1991. 16.95 (1-882063-17-1, Heritage Hse) Cottage Pr MA.

Collected Poems (except Clarel) annot. ed. Herman Melville. Ed. by Howard P. Vincent. (Complete Works of Herman Melville Ser.). reprint ed. pap. write for info. (0-87532-007-4) Hendricks House.

Collected Poems for Fifty Years, Pt. 1. Victor Urin. 1988. 16.95 (0-685-44311-6) RWCPH.

Collected Poems in English. Samuel Beckett. 61p. 1989. 10.00 (0-8021-1186-6) Grove-Atltic.

Collected Poems in English & French. Samuel Beckett. LC 77-77855. 147p. 1977. pap. 8.95 (0-8021-3096-8) Grove-Atltic.

Collected Poems Nineteen Eighty-Nineteen Ninety. David Moe. Ed. by Mary Caroland. LC 90-70974. 94p. 1990. pap. 5.95 (1-55523-362-7) Winston-Derek.

Collected Poems, Nineteen Fifty-Three to Nineteen Eighty-Three. Lucien Stryk. LC 84-2583. 198p. 1985. pap. 12.95 (0-8040-0856-6, Swallow) Ohio U Pr.

Collected Poems, Nineteen Forty-Eight to Nineteen Eighty-Four. Derek Walcott. 1986. 30.00 (0-374-12626-7) FS&G.

Collected Poems Nineteen Forty-Eight to Nineteen Eighty-Four. Derek Walcott. 1987. pap. 17.00 (0-374-52025-9) FS&G.

Collected Poems, Nineteen Forty-Seven - Nineteen Eighty. Allen Ginsberg. 860p. 1991. reprint ed. lib. bdg. 49.00x (0-8095-9132-4) Borgo Pr.

Collected Poems, Nineteen Forty to Nineteen Ninety. Maurice Lindsay. 270p. 1990. pap. text ed. 25.00 (0-08-040910-5, Pub. by Aberdeen U Pr) Macmillan.

Collected Poems of A. E. Housman. LC 65-19348. 254p. 1971. pap. 12.95 (0-8050-0547-1, Owl) H Holt & Co.

Collected Poems of A. G. Prys-Jones. A. G. Prys-Jones. (C). 1989. pap. 21.00x (0-86383-419-1, Pub. by Gomer Pr UK) St Mut.

***Collected Poems of A. K. Ramanujan.** A. K. Ramanujan. 300p. 1995. 29.95 (0-19-563561-2) OUP.

***Collected Poems of Ann Fields.** Ed. by Michael Rothenberg. 281p. (Orig.). Date not set. pap. 12.95 (1-878471-02-3) Big Bridge Pr.

Collected Poems of Arturo Giovannitti. Arturo Giovannitti. LC 74-17931. (Italian American Experience Ser.). 240p. 1975. reprint ed. 20.95 (0-405-06403-9) Ayer.

Collected Poems of Austin Clarke. Austin Clarke. LC 75-41061. (BCL Ser.: No. II). reprint ed. 41.50 (0-404-14523-X) AMS Pr.

***Collected Poems of Barbara Howes, 1945-1990.** Barbara Howes. LC 94-32343. 1995. write for info. (1-55728-335-4); pap. write for info. (1-55728-336-2) U of Ark Pr.

Collected Poems of Beatrice Hawley. Beatrice Hawley. LC 89-50430. 192p. (Orig.). 1989. 17.95 (0-944072-08-9); pap. 9.95 (0-944072-09-7) Zoland Bks.

Collected Poems of Canon Richard Watson Dixon, (1833-1900) Shirley M. Johnson & Todd K. Bender. (Studies in Gerard Manley Hopkins: Vol. 1). 172p. (C). 1989. text ed. 39.95 (0-8204-0947-2) P Lang Pubs.

Collected Poems of Charles Olson. Charles Olson. Ed. by George F. Butterick. LC 86-14652. 609p. 1987. 60.00 (0-520-05764-3) U CA Pr.

Collected Poems of Denis Devlin. Denis Devlin. Ed. by J. C. Mays. LC 89-51505. 365p. 1990. 29.95 (0-916390-37-3) Wake Forest.

An Asterisk (*) at the beginning of an entry indicates that the title is appearing in BIP for the first time.

Collected Poems of Denis Devlin. Intro. & Notes by J. C. Mays. 366p. (C). 1989. 63.00 (*0-948268-50-6*, Pub. by Dedalus Pr IE) St Mut.

Collected Poems of Emily Dickinson. Emily Dickinson. 320p. 1982. 5.99 (*0-517-36242-2*) Random Hse Value.

Collected Poems of Ernest Hemingway. Ernest Hemingway. LC 71-188093. 1972. 250.00 (*0-87968-002-4*) Gordon Pr.

Collected Poems of George Butterick. George Butterick. Ed. by Richard Blevins. 256p. (Orig.). (C). 1988. pap. 8.00 (*0-922668-00-0*) SUNYB Poetry Rare Bks.

Collected Poems of George F. Butterick. George F. Butterick. Ed. by Richard Blevins. 240p. (Orig.). (C). 1988. pap. 8.00 (*0-685-44372-8*) SUNYB Poetry Rare Bks.

Collected Poems of Harold Monro. Harold Monro. 217p. 1933. reprint ed. 39.00 (*0-403-08943-3*) Somerset Pub.

Collected Poems of Harold Monro. Harold Monro. 1988. reprint ed. lib. bdg. 59.00 (*0-7812-0007-5*) Rprt Serv.

Collected Poems of Harold Monro. Harold Monro. 1971. reprint ed. 49.00 (*0-403-03562-7*) Scholarly.

Collected Poems of Henri Coulette. Ed. by Robert Mezey. 270p. 1990. 24.95 (*1-55728-144-0*); pap. 14.95 (*1-55728-145-9*) U of Ark Pr.

Collected Poems of Henry Thoreau. enl. ed. Henry David Thoreau. Ed. by Carl Bode. LC 64-12730. 432p. reprint ed. pap. 123.20 (*0-685-20478-2*, 2029910) Bks Demand.

Collected Poems of Howard Nemerov. Howard Nemerov. LC 77-544. 536p. 1981. pap. 16.95 (*0-226-57259-5*) U Ch Pr.

Collected Poems of Idris Davies. Ed. by Islwyn Jenkins. 190p. (C). 1980. pap. 20.00x (*0-85088-141-2*, Pub. by Gomer Pr UK) St Mut.

Collected Poems of Ivor Gurney. Ivor Gurney. Ed. by Patrick J. Kavanagh. 1982. 24.95 (*0-19-200940-0*) OUP.

Collected Poems of James Laughlin. James Laughlin. (Illus.). 608p. 1995. 34.95 (*1-55921-067-2*) Moyer Bell.

***Collected Poems of James Laughlin.** James Laughlin. 608p. 1995. pap. 16.95 (*1-55921-128-8*) Moyer Bell.

Collected Poems of Jean Toomer. Jean Toomer. Ed. by Robert B. Jones & Margery T. Latimer. LC 87-19203. xxxvi, 112p. (C). 1988. 22.50 (*0-8078-1773-2*); pap. 10.95 (*0-8078-4209-5*) U of NC Pr.

Collected Poems of John Hewitt. Ed. by Frank Ormsby. 708p. 1991. 50.00 (*0-85640-459-4*, Pub. by Blackstaff Pr IE) Dufour.

Collected Poems of John Hewitt. Ed. by Frank Ormsby. 708p. 1993. pap. 35.00 (*0-85640-494-2*, Pub. by Blackstaff Pr IE) Dufour.

Collected Poems of Joseph Hall, Bishop of Exeter & Norwich. Joseph Hall. LC 75-161969. 309p. 1949. reprint ed. 39.00 (*0-403-01340-2*) Scholarly.

Collected Poems of Joseph S. Cotter, Sr. Joseph S. Cotter, Sr. LC 75-179298. (Black Heritage Library Collection). 1977. reprint ed. 16.95 (*0-8369-8919-8*) Ayer.

Collected Poems of Kenneth Fearing. Kenneth Fearing. LC 75-41089. reprint ed. 28.50 (*0-404-14661-9*) AMS Pr.

Collected Poems of Langston Hughes. Ed. by Arnold Rampersad & David Roessel. LC 94-14509. 1994. 30.00 (*0-679-42631-0*) Knopf.

Collected Poems of Lord Alfred Douglas. Alfred Douglas. LC 75-41079. reprint ed. 29.50 (*0-404-14659-7*) AMS Pr.

Collected Poems of Lucio Piccolo. Lucio Piccolo. Ed. by Brian Swann & Ruth Feldman. LC 74-37576. 215p. reprint ed. pap. 61.30 (*0-7837-1407-6*, 2041761) Bks Demand.

Collected Poems of Marsden Hartley: 1904-1943. Marsden Hartley. Ed. by Gail R. Scott. LC 86-26338. (Illus.). 364p. (Orig.). 1987. 20.00 (*0-87685-681-4*); pap. 12.50 (*0-87685-680-6*) Black Sparrow.

Collected Poems of Maurice Baring. Maurice Baring. LC 75-41018. 28.50p. reprint ed. 16.00 (*0-404-14756-9*) AMS Pr.

Collected Poems of Nikos Kavadis. Tr. by Gail Holst-Warhaft. 256p. 1987. pap. 19.00 (*90-256-0924-4*, Pub. by A M Hakkert NE) Benjamins North Am.

Collected Poems of Paul Blackburn. Paul Blackburn. Ed. by Edith Jarolim. LC 85-9309. (Lamplighter Ser.). 728p. 1985. 37.50 (*0-89255-086-4*) Persea Bks.

Collected Poems of Peter Lott: Unionville Farmer Poet. Ed. by Jane L. Fleming & Irene P. Gilman. (Illus.). 192p. 1983. pap. 11.50 (*0-9612800-0-X*) J L Gilman.

Collected Poems of Richard Church. Richard Church. LC 75-41058. reprint ed. 42.50 (*0-404-14522-1*) AMS Pr.

Collected Poems of Robert Creeley, 1945-1975. Robert Creeley. LC 81-19668. 576p. 1982. 42.50 (*0-520-04243-3*); pap. 15.00 (*0-520-04244-1*) U CA Pr.

***Collected Poems of Robert Louis Stevenson, Vol. 1.** John Manning & Elizabeth Waterston. (Collected Works of Robert Louis Stevenson: Vol. 1). (Illus.). 300p. 1994. 35.00 (*0-7486-0503-7*, Pub. by Edinburgh U Pr UK) Col U Pr.

Collected Poems of Robert Service. Robert Service. (Robert Service Ser.). 1989. 21.95 (*0-399-15015-3*, Putnam) Putnam Pub Group.

Collected Poems of Robert Service. Robert Service. 732p. 1990. reprint ed. lib. bdg. 38.95 (*0-89966-754-6*) Buccaneer Bks.

Collected Poems of Rose Drachler. Rose Drachler. Ed. by Jacob Drachler & Rochelle Ratner. (Illus.). 240p. 1983. 20.00 (*0-915066-61-0*); pap. 10.00 (*0-685-65167-3*) Assembling Pr.

Collected Poems of Sam Ragan: Poet Laureate of North Carolina. Sam Ragan. Ed. by Marsha W. Warren. LC 91-60872. 286p. 1990. 14.95 (*0-932662-94-3*); pap. 9.95 (*0-932662-95-1*) St Andrews NC.

Collected Poems of Sara Teasdale. Sara Teasdale. 15.95 (*0-02-616890-1*) Macmillan.

Collected Poems of Sara Teasdale. Sara Teasdale. 1994. reprint ed. lib. bdg. 32.95 (*1-56849-345-2*) Buccaneer Bks.

Collected Poems of Sidney Keyes. Sidney Keyes. Ed. by Michael Meyer. 134p. 1988. pap. text ed. 14.95 (*0-415-00218-4*, A1456) Routledge.

Collected Poems of Sterling A. Brown. Sterling A. Brown. LC 82-48230. 268p. 1990. pap. 9.95 (*0-929968-07-7*) Another Chicago Pr.

Collected Poems of T. Harri Jones. T. Harri Jones. Ed. by Julian Croft & Don D. Jones. 267p. (C). 1987. pap. 20.00x (*0-85088-412-8*, Pub. by Gomer Pr UK) St Mut.

Collected Poems of Thomas & Jane Welsh Carlyle. Ed. by Rodger L. Tarr & Fleming McClelland. 304p. 1986. lib. bdg. 30.00 (*0-913283-09-6*) Penkevill.

Collected Poems of Thomas MacGreevy. Thomas MacGreevy. Ed. by Susan Schreibman. 180p. 1992. text ed. 24.95 (*0-8132-0756-8*) Cath U Pr.

Collected Poems of Thomas Merton. Thomas Merton. LC 77-9902. 1088p. 1980. 37.50 (*0-8112-0643-2*); pap. 29.95 (*0-8112-0769-2*, NDP504) New Directions.

Collected Poems of Thomas Parnell. Ed. by Claude Rawson & F. P. Lock. LC 85-41023. (Illus.). 720p. 1989. 89.50 (*0-87413-154-5*) U Delaware Pr.

Collected Poems of Virgil Geddes. Virgil Geddes. LC 78-55723. 1978. 9.95 (*0-915032-24-4*) Natl Poet Foun.

Collected Poems of W. B. Yeats. William Butler Yeats. 544p. 1989. pap. 17.00 (*0-02-055650-0*, Collier S&S) S&S Trade.

Collected Poems of Wallace Stevens. Wallace Stevens. 1954. 35.00 (*0-394-40330-4*) Knopf.

Collected Poems of Weldon Kees. rev. ed. Weldon Kees. Ed. by Donald Justice. LC 75-3567. 197p. reprint ed. pap. 56.20 (*0-8357-7935-1*, 2057008) Bks Demand.

Collected Poems of Weldon Kees. rev. ed. Weldon Kees. Ed. by Donald Justice. LC 75-3567. xvii, 180p. 1992. reprint ed. pap. 9.95 (*0-8032-5828-3*) U of Nebr Pr.

Collected Poems of Wendell Berry 1957-1982. Wendell Berry. LC 84-62305. 288p. 1985. 19.95 (*0-86547-189-4*) Gnomon Pr.

Collected Poems of Wendell Berry, 1957-1982. Wendell Berry. LC 84-62305. 288p. 1987. pap. 11.00 (*0-86547-197-5*, North Pt Pr) FS&G.

Collected Poems of William Carlos Williams, Vol. I: 1909-1939. William Carlos Williams. Ed. by A. Walton Litz & Christopher MacGowan. LC 86-5448. 600p. 1991. 35.00 (*0-8112-0999-7*); pap. 20.95 (*0-8112-1187-8*, NDP730) New Directions.

Collected Poems of William Carlos Williams, Vol. II: 1939-1962. William Carlos Williams. Ed. by Christopher MacGowan. LC 86-5448. 576p. 1991. 37.00 (*0-8112-1063-4*); pap. 19.95 (*0-8112-1188-6*, NDP731) New Directions.

Collected Poems of William Corbett. William Corbett. LC 84-71923. (Poets Ser.). 153p. (Orig.). 1984. 15.95 (*0-915032-45-7*); pap. 9.95 (*0-915032-46-5*) Natl Poet Foun.

Collected Poems of Yvor Winters. Yvor Winters. LC 78-51596. 230p. 1980. 22.95 (*0-8040-0799-3*) Swallow.

***Collected Poems, Plays & Prose.** Robert Frost. LC 94-43696. (Library of America: Vol. 81). 1995. write for info. (*1-883011-06-X*) Library of America.

Collected Poems, Stories, & Collages. George Hitchcock. 300p. (Orig.). 1983. 17.95 (*0-685-05528-0*); pap. 12.95 (*0-685-05529-9*) Panjandrum.

Collected Poems. The Complete Poetical Works. Sri Aurobindo. 631p. 1986. 21.50 (*81-7058-330-6*); pap. 17.50 (*81-7058-016-1*) Aurobindo Assn.

Collected Poems, Vol. 3: Father & Child, & a Play. Jocelyn Hollis. LC 86-32194. 80p. 1990. text ed. 14.95 (*0-930933-10-9*); lib. bdg. 14.95 (*0-930933-09-5*); pap. text ed. 7.95 (*0-930933-11-7*) Am Poetry & Lit.

Collected Poems, 1800-1822, 5 vols. in 1. Robert Bloomfield. Ed. & Intro. by Jonathan N. Lawson. LC 79-161927. 704p. 1971. 90.00 (*0-8201-1088-4*) Schol Facsimiles.

Collected Poems, 1817-1901. William E. Channing. Ed. by Walter Harding. LC 67-21749. 1967. 100.00 (*0-8201-1009-4*) Schol Facsimiles.

Collected Poems, 1835-1892. Christopher P. Cranch. Ed. by Joseph DeFalco. LC 70-161930. 744p. 1971. 90.00 (*0-8201-1091-4*) Schol Facsimiles.

Collected Poems, 1905-1925. Wilfrid Gibson. LC 71-145042. 1971. reprint ed. 70.00 (*0-403-00988-X*) Scholarly.

Collected Poems, 1908-1956. Siegfried Sassoon. 317p. 1986. pap. text ed. 15.95 (*0-571-13262-6*) Faber & Faber.

Collected Poems, 1909-1962. T. S. Eliot. LC 63-21424. 221p. 1963. 19.00 (*0-15-118978-1*) HarBrace.

Collected Poems, 1912-1944. Hilda Doolittle. Ed. by Louis L. Martz. LC 83-6380. 672p. 1986. pap. 21.95 (*0-8112-0971-7*, NDP611) New Directions.

Collected Poems, 1915-1967. Kenneth Burke. LC 67-29786. 318p. reprint ed. pap. 90.70 (*0-7837-4756-X*, 2044503) Bks Demand.

Collected Poems, 1916-1970. 2nd ed. Conrad P. Aiken. LC 79-120179. 1970. 45.00 (*0-19-501258-5*) OUP.

Collected Poems, 1919-1976. Allen Tate. LC 88-27385. x, 218p. 1989. pap. 9.95 (*0-8071-1533-9*) La State U Pr.

Collected Poems, 1930-1986. Richard Eberhart. 464p. 1988. 35.00 (*0-19-504055-4*) OUP.

Collected Poems, 1930-1989. Samuel Beckett. 350p. 1997. 29.95 (*0-7145-4186-9*) Riverrun NY.

Collected Poems, 1935-1992. F. T. Prince. LC 92-33032. 275p. (C). 1993. 13.95 (*1-878818-16-3*) Sheep Meadow.

Collected Poems 1936-1986. Gwyn Williams. 184p. (C). 1987. 33.00x (*0-86383-324-1*, Pub. by Gomer Pr UK) St Mut.

Collected Poems, 1939-1989. William J. Smith. 224p. 1990. text ed. 24.95 (*0-684-19167-9*, Scribners) S&S Trade.

Collected Poems, 1942-1968. William Hull. 20.00 (*0-89253-473-7*); 10.00 (*0-89253-474-5*) Ind-US Inc.

Collected Poems 1946-86. Raymond Garlick. 165p. (C). 1987. pap. 20.00x (*0-86383-318-7*, Pub. by Gomer Pr UK) St Mut.

Collected Poems, 1947-1980. Allen Ginsberg. LC 84-47573. (Illus.). 864p. 1988. pap. 22.50 (*0-06-091494-7*, PL-1494, PL) HarpC.

Collected Poems, 1952-1990: Yevgeny Yevtushenko. Ed. by Albert C. Todd & James Ragan. 688p. 1992. pap. 18.95 (*0-8050-2378-X*, Owl) H Holt & Co.

Collected Poems, 1953-1993. John Updike. LC 92-28957. 1993. 27.50 (*0-679-42221-8*) Knopf.

***Collected Poems (1953-1995)** David Galler. LC 94-69017. 288p. 1995. pap. 17.95 (*0-9640977-8-8*) Crane & Hopper.

Collected Poems, 1957-1987: Bilingual Edition. Octavio Paz. Ed. & Tr. by Eliot Weinberger. Tr. by Elizabeth Bishop et al. LC 87-23989. 688p. 1987. 37.50 (*0-8112-1037-5*); pap. 21.00 (*0-8112-1173-8*, NDP719) New Directions.

Collected Poems, 1960-1984. Francis Warner. 1985. 24.00 (*0-86140-206-5*, Pub. by Colin Smythe Ltd UK) Dufour.

Collected Poems, 1969-1982. Constance Hunting. LC 83-62145. (Poets Ser.). 212p. (Orig.). 1983. 18.00 (*0-915032-44-9*); pap. 12.95 (*0-915032-19-8*) Natl Poet Foun.

Collected Poems, 1979. Mary Barnard. LC 79-54693. 101p. 1979. pap. 8.95 (*0-932576-09-5*) Breitenbush Bks.

Collected Poems 1980-1990. Gavin Ewart. 488p. 1992. pap. 19.95 (*0-09-174756-2*, Pub. by Hutchnson UK) Trafalgar.

Collected Poems, 1987. D. J. Enright. 384p. 1987. pap. 12.95 (*0-19-282061-3*) OUP.

Collected Poems, 1988. David Gascoyne. 256p. 1988. pap. 14.95 (*0-19-281972-0*) OUP.

Collected Poetical Works, 6 vols., Set. Algernon C. Swinburne. (BCL1-PR English Literature Ser.). 1992. reprint ed. lib. bdg. 450.00 (*0-7812-7675-6*) Rprt Serv.

***Collected Poetry.** Steve H. Ali. 36p. (Orig.). Date not set. pap. 7.00 (*1-56167-207-6*) Am Literary Pr.

Collected Poetry of Aime Cesaire. Tr. by Clayton Eshleman & Annette Smith. LC 82-17394. (Illus.). 432p. (C). 1983. 42.00 (*0-520-04347-2*); pap. 17.00 (*0-520-05320-6*) U CA Pr.

***Collected Poetry of Malcolm Lowry.** Ed. by Kathleen D. Scherf. 438p. 1992. 60.00 (*0-7748-0362-2*) U of Wash Pr.

Collected Poetry of Paul Laurence Dunbar. Paul L. Dunbar. LC 92-37190. 354p. (C). 1993. text ed. 40.00 (*0-8139-1454-X*); pap. 14.95 (*0-8139-1438-8*) U Pr of Va.

Collected Poetry of Robinson Jeffers: Vol. I, 1920-1928. Robinson Jeffers. Ed. by Tim Hunt. LC 87-18083. 552p. 1988. 65.00 (*0-8047-1414-2*) Stanford U Pr.

Collected Poetry of Robinson Jeffers: Vol. II, 1928-1938. Robinson Jeffers. Ed. by Tim Hunt. 635p. 1989. 65.00 (*0-8047-1723-0*) Stanford U Pr.

Collected Poetry of Robinson Jeffers, Vol. 3: 1939-1962, Vol. 3. Ed. by Tim Hunt. (Illus.). 512p. 1991. 65.00 (*0-8047-1847-4*) Stanford U Pr.

Collected Poetry of Ron Dultz. Ron Dultz. Ed. by Ruth Towbin. LC 84-91082. (Illus.). 165p. 1984. 12.00 (*0-9601636-2-X*); pap. 7.00 (*0-9601636-3-8*) R Dultz.

Collected Poetry of Thomas A. Ekkens: Early Works. Thomas Ekkens. Ed. by Joanne Shwed. LC 86-70951. (Illus.). 96p. 1986. 12.00 (*0-9616675-0-8*, 1130) Backspace Ink.

Collected Practical Problems. Lemon. (C). 1959. 110.00 (*0-685-36030-X*, Pub. by British Textile Tech UK) St Mut.

Collected Practical Problems. Ed. by R. Lemon. 1959. 80.00 (*0-317-43607-4*) St Mut.

Collected Properties & Writings of J. G. Gallimore. J. G. Gallimore. (Handbook of Unusual Energies Ser.: Vol. 2). 249p. 1977. reprint ed. spiral bd. 41.25 (*0-7873-1234-7*) Mokelumne.

Collected Prose. Elizabeth Bishop. Ed. by Robert Giroux. LC 83-16418. 278p. 1984. 17.50 (*0-374-12628-3*); pap. 14.00 (*0-374-51855-6*) FS&G.

Collected Prose. Paul Celan. Tr. by Rosmarie Waldrop. LC 90-30112. 67p. 1990. 15.95 (*0-935296-92-1*) Sheep Meadow.

Collected Prose. Robert Creeley. 1988. pap. 15.00 (*0-520-06151-9*) U CA Pr.

Collected Prose. Robert Hayden. Ed. by Frederick Glaysher. (Poets on Poetry Ser.). 285p. 1984. pap. 13.95 (*0-472-06351-0*) U of Mich Pr.

Collected Prose. Robert Lowell. 350p. 1987. 25.00 (*0-374-12625-9*); pap. 14.95 (*0-374-52267-7*) FS&G.

Collected Prose. James Wright. Ed. by Anne Wright. (Poets on Poetry Ser.). 352p. 1983. pap. 13.95 (*0-472-06344-8*) U of Mich Pr.

Collected Prose. James E. Flecker. LC 75-41096. (BCL Ser.: II). reprint ed. 42.50 (*0-404-14541-8*) AMS Pr.

Collected Prose of Carl Rakosi. Carl Rakosi. LC 83-62144. 150p. 1984. pap. 12.95 (*0-915032-21-X*) Natl Poet Foun.

***Collected Questions & Answers.** 4th ed. Ed. by Richard J. Davey & Ann McMican. (C). 1994. pap. text ed. 28.00 (*1-56395-036-7*) Am Assn Blood.

Collected Questions & Answers, Vol. 3. Joel Umlas et al. LC 88-659936. (C). 1991. pap. text ed. 25.00 (*0-915355-94-9*) Am Assn Blood.

Collected Raffles. E. W. Hornung. Ed. by Jeremy Lewis. 470p. 1993. pap. 8.95 (*0-460-87393-8*, Everyman's Classic Lib) C E Tuttle.

Collected Reprints from Sing Out, Vols. 1-6. 2nd ed. Ed. by Sing Out Magazine Staff. (Illus.). 384p. 1990. spiral bd. 17.50 (*0-9626704-0-5*) Sing Out Corp.

Collected Reprints from Sing Out! Vol. 7-12: The Folk Song Magazine, 1964-1973. Intro. by Happy Traum. (Illus.). 384p. 1992. pap. text ed. 17.50 (*1-881322-00-9*) Sing Out Corp.

Collected Rituals from the T. O. T. & Other Sources. Nelson White & Anne White. LC 82-50719. 100p. (Orig.). 1982. pap. 25.00 (*0-939856-28-X*) Tech Group.

Collected Satires & Poems of Osbert Sitwell. Osbert Sitwell. LC 75-41252. reprint ed. 29.50 (*0-404-14602-3*) AMS Pr.

Collected Satires of Lord Alfred Douglas. Alfred Douglas. LC 75-41081. reprint ed. 27.50 (*0-404-14730-5*) AMS Pr.

***Collected Scientific Papers of Paul Samuelson, Vol. 1.** Paul Samuelson. 1966. 70.00 (*0-262-19021-4*) MIT Pr.

***Collected Scientific Papers of Paul Samuelson, Vol. 2.** Paul A. Samuelson. 1966. 70.00 (*0-262-19022-2*) MIT Pr.

***Collected Scientific Papers of Paul Samuelson, Vol. 3.** Paul Samuelson. 1972. 70.00 (*0-262-19080-X*) MIT Pr.

***Collected Scientific Papers of Paul Samuelson, Vol. 4.** Paul Samuelson. 1978. 70.00 (*0-262-19167-9*) MIT Pr.

***Collected Scientific Papers of Paul Samuelson, Vol. 5.** Paul Samuelson. 1986. 70.00 (*0-262-19251-9*) MIT Pr.

***Collected Short Fiction of Bruce Jay Friedman.** Bruce J. Friedman. 400p. 1995. 25.00 (*1-55611-462-1*) D I Fine.

Collected Short Stories. Robert Graves. 304p. 1993. 11.95 (*0-14-018484-8*, Penguin Classics) Viking Penguin.

Collected Short Stories. W. Somerset Maugham. 448p. 1992. pap. 9.95 (*0-14-018589-5*, Penguin Classics) Viking Penguin.

Collected Short Stories. Michael McLaverty. 278p. 1978. pap. 10.95 (*0-905169-14-X*, Pub. by Poolbeg Pr IE) Dufour.

Collected Short Stories. Anthony Trollope. (Illus.). 397p. 1987. pap. text ed. 8.95 (*0-486-25484-4*) Dover.

Collected Short Stories. Aldous Huxley. 396p. 1992. reprint ed. pap. 14.95 (*0-929587-81-2*, Elephant Paperbacks) I R Dee.

Collected Short Stories, Vol. 2. W. Somerset Maugham. 1991. mass mkt. 4.95 (*0-14-001872-7*, Penguin Bks) Viking Penguin.

Collected Short Stories, Vol. 2. W. Somerset Maugham. 256p. 1992. 10.95 (*0-14-018590-9*, Penguin Classics) Viking Penguin.

Collected Short Stories, Vol. 3. W. Somerset Maugham. 256p. 1984. mass mkt. 5.95 (*0-14-001873-5*, Penguin Bks) Viking Penguin.

Collected Short Stories, Vol. 4. W. Somerset Maugham. 464p. 1993. 11.95 (*0-14-018592-5*, Penguin Classics) Viking Penguin.

Collected Short Stories by Soviet Writers. Russkii Iazyk. 278p. 1983. 30.00 (*0-317-39491-6*, Pub. by Collets UK) St Mut.

Collected Short Stories of Edith Wharton, Vol. 1. Ed. by R. W. Lewis. (Hudson River Editions Ser.). 752p. 1987. text ed. 60.00 (*0-02-570600-4*, Scribners) S&S Trade.

Collected Short Stories of Edith Wharton, Vol. 2. Ed. by C. S. Lewis. (Hudson River Editions Ser.). 908p. 1989. text ed. 50.00 (*0-02-626161-8*, Scribners) S&S Trade.

Collected Short Stories of George W. Williams, Jr. George W. Williams, Jr. LC 90-80360. 72p. 1990. pap. 12.95 (*0-942963-02-4*) Distinctive Pub.

Collected Short Stories of Khushwant Singh. Khushwent Singh. (C). 1989. 12.50 (*0-86311-063-0*, Pub. by Ravi Dayal II) S Asia.

Collected Short Stories of Mary Johnston. Ed. by Annie Woodbridge & Hensley C. Woodbridge. LC 80-54204. (C). 1982. 25.00 (*0-87875-204-8*) Whitston Pub.

Collected Short Stories of Maxim Gorki. Maxim Gorki. Ed. by Avram Yarmolinsky--Baroness Moura Budberg. 400p. 1988. reprint ed. pap. 9.95 (*0-8065-1075-7*, Citadel Pr) Carol Pub Group.

Collected Short Works, 1907-1919. Bess S. Aldrich. LC 94-19005. 1995. text ed. 40.00 (*0-8032-1038-8*) U of Nebr Pr.

Collected Shorter Plays of Samuel Beckett. Samuel Beckett. 320p. (Orig.). 1984. pap. 15.95 (*0-8021-5055-1*) Grove-Atltic.

Collected Shorter Poems. Nelson Bentley. 192p. (Orig.). 1988. pap. 10.00 (*0-944920-01-2*) Bellowing Ark Pr.

Collected Shorter Poems. Kenneth Rexroth. LC 66-17818. 1967. pap. 14.95 (*0-8112-0178-3*, NDP243) New Directions.

Collected Shorter Poems, 1946-1991. Hayden Carruth. LC 92-3389. 432p. (Orig.). 1992. 28.00 (*1-55659-048-2*); pap. 14.00 (*1-55659-049-0*) Copper Canyon.

Collected Shorter Prose, 1945-1988. Samuel Beckett. 320p. 1997. pap. 19.95 (*0-7145-4211-3*) Riverrun NY.

Collected Shorter Works from the T. O. T. Frater Zarathustra, pseud. LC 87-50738. 56p. (Orig.). 1987. pap. 15.00 (*0-939856-77-8*) Tech Group.

Collected Sonnets. Edna St. Vincent Millay. LC 83-48369. 176p. 1988. pap. 11.00 (*0-06-091091-7*, CN 1091, PL) HarpC.

Collected Sonnets of Charles (Tennyson) Turner. Ed. by Marjorie Pinion & Frank B. Pinion. LC 87-12521. 256p. 1988. text ed. 35.00 (*0-312-01193-8*) St Martin.

Collected Stories. Isaac Babel. Ed. & Tr. by Walter Morison. (C). 1974. pap. 12.50 (*0-452-00798-4*, Mer) NAL-Dutton.

***Collected Stories.** Isaac Babel. Ed. & Intro. by David McDuff. 400p. 1995. 11.95 (*0-14-018462-7*, Penguin Classics) Viking Penguin.

Collected Stories. R. V. Cassill. LC 88-28614. 657p. 1989. pap. 14.95 (*1-55728-071-1*) U of Ark Pr.

Collected Stories. William Faulkner. 1956. 22.95 (*0-394-41967-7*) Random.

Collected Stories. Gabriel Garcia Marquez. pap. 11.00 (*0-685-51775-6*, PL) HarpC.

An Asterisk (*) at the beginning of an entry indicates that the title is appearing in BIP for the first time. 1359

Collected Stories. Gabriel Garcia Marquez. Tr. by Gregory Rabassa & S. J. Bernstein. LC 84-47826. 320p. 1985. pap. 13.00 (*0-06-091306-1*, PL 1306, PL) HarpC.

Collected Stories. Graham Greene. 400p. 1987. pap. 8.95 (*0-14-008070-8*, Penguin Bks) Viking Penguin.

Collected Stories. O. Henry. 448p. 1991. pap. 5.95 (*0-553-21396-2*, Bantam Classics) Bantam.

***Collected Stories.** Langston Hughes. Ed. by Akiba S. Harper. 320p. 1995. 24.00 (*0-8090-3541-3*) Hill & Wang.

Collected Stories. Franz Kafka. LC 93-1858. 1993. 20.00 (*0-679-42303-6*, Everymans Lib) Knopf.

Collected Stories. Rudyard Kipling. LC 94-5854. (Everyman's Library of Children's Classics). 1994. 20.00 (*0-679-43592-1*) Knopf.

Collected Stories. Richard Matheson. 920p. 1989. lib. bdg. 39.95 (*0-910489-10-6*, Dream Pr) Scream Pr.

Collected Stories. Carson McCullers. 1987. pap. 12.95 (*0-395-44243-5*) HM.

Collected Stories. John McGahern. 1993. 24.00 (*0-679-41913-6*) Knopf.

Collected Stories. John McGahern. LC 93-43483. 1994. pap. 12.00 (*0-679-74401-0*, Vin) Random.

Collected Stories. Kenneth Morris. 1995. pap. 13.95 (*0-312-89029-X*) Orb NYC.

Collected Stories. Amado Muro. 1979. 10.00 (*0-914476-82-3*) Thorp Springs.

Collected Stories. Frank O'Connor. LC 81-1253. 702p. 1981. 20.00 (*0-394-51602-8*) Knopf.

Collected Stories. Frank O'Connor. LC 82-40039. 736p. 1982. pap. 18.00 (*0-394-71048-7*, Vin) Random.

Collected Stories. Grace Paley. LC 93-42230. 1994. 27.50 (*0-374-12636-4*) FS&G.

***Collected Stories.** Grace Paley. 386p. 1995. pap. 14.00 (*0-374-52431-9*, Noonday) FS&G.

***Collected Stories.** Dorothy Parker. Ed. by Mikki Breese. LC 95-15524. 1995. pap. write for info. (*0-14-018939-4*, Penguin Bks) Viking Penguin.

Collected Stories. Harry M. Petrakis. LC 86-20859. 376p. 1987. 29.95 (*0-941702-14-6*); pap. 14.95 (*0-941702-23-5*) Lake View Pr.

Collected Stories. Reynolds Price. 640p. 1994. pap. 12.95 (*0-452-27218-1*, Plume) NAL-Dutton.

Collected Stories. Victor S. Pritchett. 1982. pap. 20.00 (*0-394-52417-9*) Random.

Collected Stories. Dylan Thomas. LC 84-6822. 384p. 1984. pap. 11.95 (*0-8112-0998-9*, NDP626) New Directions.

Collected Stories. Tennessee Williams. 1986. mass mkt. 5.95 (*0-345-33587-2*) Ballantine.

Collected Stories. Gabriel Garcia Marquez. 311p. 1991. reprint ed. lib. bdg. 25.00x (*0-8095-9051-4*) Borgo Pr.

Collected Stories. Tennessee Williams. LC 85-10642. 608p. 1994. reprint ed. pap. 14.95 (*0-8112-1269-6*, NDP784) New Directions.

Collected Stories, Vol. 1. T. D. Agcaoili. 128p. (Orig.). 1993. pap. 8.50 (*971-10-0479-8*, Pub. by New Day Pub PH) Cellar.

***Collected Stories: 1970 to 1995.** Janette T. Hospital. 1995. pap. 16.95 (*0-7022-2836-2*, Pub. by Univ Queensland Pr AT) Intl Spec Bk.

***Collected Stories Vol. 2: Stories of War.** T. D. Agcaoili. 149p. (Orig.). 1994. pap. 11.00 (*971-10-0539-5*, Pub. by New Day Pub PH) Cellar.

Collected Stories: D. H. Lawrence. D. H. Lawrence. 1994. 25.00 (*0-679-43135-7*, Everymans Lib) Knopf.

Collected Stories fo Philip K. Dick, Vol. 5: The Eye of the Sibyl. Philip K. Dick. 408p. 1992. pap. 12.95 (*0-8065-1328-4*, Citadel Pr) Carol Pub Group.

Collected Stories of Caroline Gordon. Caroline Gordon. LC 90-5709. 352p. 1990. pap. 16.95 (*0-8071-1630-0*) La State U Pr.

Collected Stories of Charles W. Chesnutt. Intro. by William L. Andrews. 288p. 1992. pap. 5.99 (*0-451-62843-8*, Ment) NAL-Dutton.

Collected Stories of Chester Himes. Chester Himes. 440p. (Orig.). 1991. pap. 14.95 (*1-56025-021-6*) Thunders Mouth.

Collected Stories of Colette. Colette. Ed. by Robert G. Phelps. Tr. by Matthew Ward et al. LC 83-16449. 605p. 1984. pap. 16.00 (*0-374-51865-3*) FS&G.

Collected Stories of Elizabeth Bowen. Elizabeth Bowen. LC 80-8729. 784p. 1981. 25.00 (*0-394-51666-4*) Knopf.

Collected Stories of Elizabeth Bowen. Elizabeth Bowen. 784p. 1989. reprint ed. pap. 13.95 (*0-88001-224-2*) Ecco Pr.

Collected Stories of Eudora Welty. Eudora Welty. LC 80-7947. 640p. 1982. pap. 12.95 (*0-15-618921-6*, Harvest Bks) HarBrace.

Collected Stories of Eudora Welty. Eudora Welty. LC 80-7947. 576p. 1980. 29.95 (*0-15-118994-3*) HarBrace.

Collected Stories of Isaac Babel. Isaac Babel. LC 60-6743. 199p. 1994. 32.95 (*0-87599-009-6*) S G Phillips.

Collected Stories of Isaac Bashevis Singer. Isaac Bashevis Singer. LC 81-12436. 614p. 1983. pap. 17.00 (*0-374-51788-6*) FS&G.

Collected Stories of Jean Stafford. Jean Stafford. LC 91-31221. 475p. 1992. reprint ed. pap. 15.95 (*0-292-71145-X*) U of Tex Pr.

Collected Stories of Jessamyn West. Jessamyn West & Julian P. Muller. 352p. 1987. pap. 10.95 (*0-15-618979-8*, Harvest Bks) HarBrace.

Collected Stories of John O'Hara. John O'Hara. Ed. by Frank MacShane. LC 84-42661. 1985. 19.95 (*0-394-54083-2*) Random.

Collected Stories of John William Corrington. Ed. by John W. Corrington. 528p. 1990. 24.95 (*0-8262-0753-7*) U of Mo Pr.

Collected Stories of Katherine Anne Porter. Katherine A. Porter. LC 79-10398. 495p. 1979. pap. 11.95 (*0-15-618876-7*, Harvest Bks) HarBrace.

Collected Stories of Lewis Carroll. Lewis Carroll. LC 94-18191. 1994. 12.95 (*0-8065-1552-X*, Citadel Pr) Carol Pub Group.

Collected Stories of Louis Auchincloss. Louis Auchincloss. LC 94-14364. 1994. 24.95 (*0-395-71039-1*) HM.

Collected Stories of Max Brand. Ed. by Jane Easton. LC 93-43938. 416p. (C). 1994. text ed. 35.00 (*0-8032-1244-5*) U of Nebr Pr.

Collected Stories of O. Henry. 1986. 9.98 (*0-685-43724-8*, 618397) Random Hse Value.

Collected Stories of O. Henry. O. Henry. 22.95 (*0-89190-397-6*, Am Repr) Amereon Ltd.

Collected Stories of O. Henry. O. Henry. 1993. 12.99 (*0-517-09340-5*) Random Hse Value.

Collected Stories of O. Henry. rev. ed. O. Henry. Ed. by P. Horowitz. (Illus.). 1008p. 1986. 12.99 (*0-517-61839-7*) Random Hse Value.

Collected Stories of Paul Bowles. Paul Bowles. LC 79-4569. 420p. 1994. reprint ed. 25.00 (*0-87685-397-1*); reprint ed. pap. 15.00 (*0-87685-396-3*) Black Sparrow.

Collected Stories of Peter Taylor. Peter Taylor. (Contemporary American Fiction Ser.). 544p. 1986. pap. 14.00 (*0-14-008361-8*, Penguin Bks) Viking Penguin.

Collected Stories of Philip K. Dick, Vol. 3. Philip K. Dick. 1991. pap. 12.95 (*0-8065-1226-1*, Citadel) Carol Pub Group.

Collected Stories of Philip K. Dick, Vol. 2: We Can Remember It for You Wholesale. Philip K. Dick. 1990. pap. 12.95 (*0-8065-1209-1*, Citadel Pr) Carol Pub Group.

Collected Stories of Philip K. Dick, Vol. 4: The Minority Report. Philip K. Dick. 1991. pap. 12.95 (*0-8065-1276-8*, Citadel Pr) Carol Pub Group.

Collected Stories of Reynolds Price. Reynolds Price. 672p. 1993. text ed. 25.00 (*0-689-12147-4*, Atheneum S&S) S&S Trade.

Collected Stories of Wallace Stegner. Wallace Stegner. 1990. 21.95 (*0-394-58409-0*) Random.

Collected Stories of Wallace Stegner. Wallace Stegner. (Contemporary American Fiction Ser.). 544p. 1991. pap. 12.95 (*0-14-014774-8*, Penguin Bks) Viking Penguin.

Collected Stories of Wallace Stegner. Wallace E. Stegner. LC 94-6607. 1994. 13.99 (*0-517-12188-3*, Pub. by Wings Bks) Random Hse Value.

Collected Stories of Willa Cather. Willa Cather. LC 92-5006. 1992. pap. 14.00 (*0-679-73648-4*, Vin) Random.

Collected Stories of William Faulkner. William Faulkner. (YA). (gr. 9 up). 1977. pap. 18.00 (*0-394-72257-4*) Random Bks Yng Read.

Collected Stories of Wolfgang Hildesheimer. Wolfgang Hildesheimer. Tr. by Joachim Neugroschel. 200p. 1987. 17.00 (*0-88001-131-9*) Ecco Pr.

Collected Stories of Wolfgang Hildesheimer. Wolfgang Hildesheimer. Tr. by Joachim Neugroschel. 197p. (C). 1988. pap. 9.95 (*0-88001-132-7*) Ecco Pr.

Collected Stories, 1893-1897., 4 Vols. in 1. Hubert Crackanthorpe. LC 74-75379. 1969. 90.00 (*0-8201-1056-6*) Schol Facsimiles.

Collected Stories, 1948-1986. Wright Morris. LC 88-45282. 274p. 1989. pap. 10.95 (*0-87923-752-X*) Godine.

Collected Studies. Chester N. Greenough. LC 78-128253. (Essay Index Reprint Ser.). 1977. 21.95 (*0-8369-1879-7*) Ayer.

Collected Studies I: Studies in Greek Literature & History, Excluding Epirus & Macedonia. N. G. Hammond. viii, 558p. 1993. pap. 90.00 (*90-256-1043-9*, Pub. by A M Hakkert NE) Benjamins North Am.

Collected Studies II: Studies Concerning Epirus & Macedonia Before Alexander. N. G. Hammond. 355p. 1994. pap. 68.00 (*90-256-1050-1*, Pub. by A M Hakkert NE) Benjamins North Am.

***Collected Studies III: Alexander & His Successors in Macedonia.** N. G. Hammond. 472p. 1994. pap. 128.00 (*90-256-1051-X*) Benjamins North Am.

Collected Studies on the Dionne Quintuplets. William E. Blatz. LC 74-21401. (Classics in Child Development Ser.). (Illus.). 294p. 1975. reprint ed. 31.95 (*0-405-06454-3*) Ayer.

Collected Studies on the Pathology of War Gas Poisoning. Milton C. Winternitz. (Illus.). 1920. 250.00 (*0-685-69885-8*) Elliots Bks.

Collected Subconscious: An Anthology of Subconscious Comics by Tim Eagan. Tim Eagan. LC 90-82903. (Illus.). 120p. (Orig.). 1990. 9.95 (*0-9626272-0-8*) Gray Matter Pr.

Collected Tales. Pierre Louys. LC 70-160941. (Short Story Index Reprint Ser.). (Illus.). 1977. reprint ed. 22.95 (*0-8369-3920-4*) Ayer.

Collected Tales & Stories: With Original Engravings. Mary Wollstonecraft Shelley. Ed. by Charles E. Robinson. LC 75-36931. 422p. reprint ed. pap. 120.30 (*0-317-30463-1*, 2024833) Bks Demand.

Collected Tales of A. E. Coppard. Alfred E. Coppard. Ed. by R. Reginald & Douglas Menville. LC 75-26260. (Supernatural & Occult Fiction Ser.). 1976. reprint ed. lib. bdg. 44.95 (*0-405-08119-7*) Ayer.

Collected Tales, Sketches, Speeches, & Essays, 2 vols. Mark Twain. Ed. by Louis J. Budd. LC 92-52657. 1070p. 1992. Vol. 1: 1852-1890, 1070p. 35.00 (*0-940450-36-4*); Vol. II: 1891-1910, 1050p. 35.00 (*0-940450-73-9*) Library of America.

Collected Teenage Mutant Ninja Turtles Adventures, Vol. 1. Ryan Brown & Dean Clarrian. (Illus.). 96p. (YA). 1991. pap. 5.95 (*1-879450-03-8*) Tundra MA.

Collected Teenage Mutant Ninja Turtles Adventures, Vol. 2. Ryan Brown & Dean Clarrian. (Illus.). 88p. (YA). 1991. pap. 5.95 (*1-879450-04-6*) Tundra MA.

Collected Teenage Mutant Ninja Turtles Adventures, Vol. 3. Dean Clarrain & Ryan Brown. (Illus.). 88p. (YA). 1991. pap. 5.95 (*1-879450-05-4*) Tundra MA.

Collected Teenage Mutant Ninja Turtles Adventures, Vol. 4. Dean Clarrain & Ryan Brown. (Illus.). 88p. (YA). 1991. pap. 5.95 (*1-879450-06-2*) Tundra MA.

Collected Translations. William J. Smith. 1985. pap. 8.00 (*0-89823-070-5*) New Rivers Pr.

Collected Travel Writings, 2 vols. Henry James. Ed. by Richard Howard. LC 93-9192. 850p. 1993. Vol. 1: Great Britain & America. 35.00 (*0-940450-76-3*); Vol. 2: The Continent. 35.00 (*0-940450-77-1*) Library of America.

Collected Verse. Archer M. Huntington. 1953. 10.00 (*0-87535-076-3*) Hispanic Soc.

Collected Verse. Archer M. Huntington. 100p. 1955. 10.00 (*0-317-00543-X*, Hispanic Soc) Interbk Inc.

Collected Verse. Edgar Guest. 1994. reprint ed. lib. bdg. 49. 95x (*1-56849-108-5*) Buccaneer Bks.

Collected Verse of Lewis Carroll see Humorous Verse of Lewis Carroll

Collected Vietnam Poems & Other Poems. Jocelyn Hollis. LC 85-20013. 168p. (C). 1986. lib. bdg. 14.95 (*0-933486-92-8*); pap. 7.95 (*0-933486-93-6*) Am Poetry & Lit.

Collected Visions: Women Artist at the Bunting Institute, 1961-1986. Mary Ingraham Bunting Institute of Radcliffe College Staff. 96p. 1986. pap. 7.95 (*0-9601774-2-6*) Radcliffe Coll.

Collected Werke, 8 vols. in 4. Georg Wickram. Ed. by Johannes Bolte & Willy Scheel. Nr. 222, 223, 229, 230, 232, 236, 237, 241. 1974. reprint ed. Bd. I: Galmy - Gabriotto. write for info. (*0-318-71289-X*, Pub. by Georg Olms GW); reprint ed. Bd. II: Knabenspiegel - Vomungeratenen Sohn - Von Guten und Bosen Nachbarn - Der Goldfaden. write for info. (*0-318-71290-3*, Pub. by Georg Olms GW); reprint ed. Bd. III: Rollwagenbuchlein - Die Sieben Hauptlaster. write for info. (*0-318-71291-1*, Pub. by Georg Olms GW); reprint ed. Bd. IV: Losbuch - Von der Trunkenheit - Der Irr - Reitende Pilger. write for info. (*0-318-71292-X*, Pub. by Georg Olms GW); reprint ed. Bd. V: Die Zehn Alter - Der Treue Eckart - Das Narrengieben - Der Verlorene Sohn - Weiberlist. write for info. (*0-318-71293-8*, Pub. by Georg Olms GW); reprint ed. Bd. VI: Tobias - Knabenspiegel. write for info. (*0-318-71294-6*, Pub. by Georg Olms GW); reprint ed. Bd. VII/VIII: Ovids Metamorphosen, Buch 1-15. write for info. (*0-318-71295-4*, Pub. by Georg Olms GW) Lubrecht & Cramer.

Collected Werke, 8 vols. in 4, Set. Georg Wickram. Ed. by Johannes Bolte & Willy Scheel. (Bibliothek Des Literarischen Vereins in Stuttgart Ser.: Nr. 222, 223, 229, 230, 232, 236, 237, 241). 1974. reprint ed. write for info. (*3-487-04478-1*, Pub. by Georg Olms GW) Lubrecht & Cramer.

Collected William Faulkner: The Sound & the Fury, Light in August, As I Lay Dying. William Faulkner. (Illus.). 676p. 1992. reprint ed. 9.99 (*0-517-07234-3*) Random Hse Value.

Collected Wisdom. Raymond C. Barker. Ed. by Jill Kramer. 256p. (Orig.). 1994. pap. 10.95 (*1-56170-097-5*, 160) Hay House.

Collected Women. limited ed. Patricia Beam. 1985. 19.50 (*0-935239-02-2*) Seajay Society.

Collected Wonderword, Vol. 3. Jo Ouellet. 104p. 1982. pap. 4.95 (*0-8362-2501-5*) Andrews & McMeel.

Collected Words 1953-81. Richard Hamilton. LC 82-50573. (Illus.). 1983. 35.00 (*0-500-97301-6*) Thames Hudson.

Collected Work of Samuel Taylor Coleridge, Vol. 14: Table Talk. Ed. by Carl Woodring. (Bollingen Ser.: Vol. 75, No. 14). (Illus.). 1288p. (C). 1989. text ed. 135.00 (*0-691-09881-6*) Princeton U Pr.

Collected Works. Lord Acton. 1974. 600.00 (*0-87968-883-1*) Gordon Pr.

Collected Works, 12 vols. Ambrose Bierce. 1972. 5,000.00 (*0-87968-884-X*) Gordon Pr.

Collected Works, 6 vols. Henry C. Carey. 1972. 600.00 (*0-87968-885-8*) Gordon Pr.

Collected Works. Edward Carpenter. 1972. 600.00 (*0-87968-886-6*) Gordon Pr.

Collected Works, 13 vols in 5. Muzio Clementi. LC 70-75299. (Music Reprint Ser.). 1973. 69.50 (*0-306-77260-4*); 18.50 (*0-306-77267-1*); 18.50 (*0-306-77268-X*) Da Capo.

Collected Works. Paul L. Dunbar. 1972. 600.00 (*0-87968-888-2*) Gordon Pr.

Collected Works, 6 vols. Johann L. Dussek. LC 79-75313. (Music Ser.). 1978. 59.50 (*0-685-74233-4*) Da Capo.

Collected Works. Annie Fields. 1990. Letters of Sarah Orne Jewett, 1911. write for info. (*0-318-67811-X*) Rprt Serv.

Collected Works, 6 vols. Harrison Fisher. 1972. 600.00 (*0-87968-889-0*) Gordon Pr.

Collected Works, 6 vols. Sadakichi Hartmann. 1972. 1,200. 00 (*0-87968-890-4*) Gordon Pr.

Collected Works. Lafcadio Hearn. 1972. 200.00 (*0-87968-891-2*) Gordon Pr.

Collected Works. Richard Hildreth. 1990. Theory of Morals, 1844. write for info. (*0-318-67479-3*) Rprt Serv.

Collected Works. Edward Lear. 1973. 59.95 (*0-87968-892-0*) Gordon Pr.

Collected Works. Alexander D. Mar. 1972. 500.00 (*0-87968-887-4*) Gordon Pr.

Collected Works. John Stuart Mill. 1972. 600.00 (*0-87968-893-9*) Gordon Pr.

Collected Works. Maria Montessori. 1973. 500.00 (*0-87968-894-7*) Gordon Pr.

Collected Works. William Morris. 1973. 600.00 (*0-87968-895-5*) Gordon Pr.

Collected Works. Flannery O'Connor. Ed. by Sally Fitzgerald. Incl. Wise Blood. LC 87-37829. 1988. (*0-318-62912-7*); Good Man Is Hard to Find. LC 87-37829. 1988. (*0-318-62913-5*); Violent Bear It Away. LC 87-37829. 1988. (*0-318-62914-3*); Everything That Rises Must Converge. LC 87-37829. 1988. (*0-318-62915-1*); LC 87-37829. 1281p. 1988. 35.00 (*0-940450-37-2*) Library of America.

Collected Works. J. M. Robertson. 1973. 400.00 (*0-87968-896-3*) Gordon Pr.

Collected Works, 3 vols. Morris Rosenfeld. 1972. 300.00 (*0-87968-897-1*) Gordon Pr.

Collected Works. Rabindranath Tagore. 1972. 300.00 (*0-87968-898-X*) Gordon Pr.

Collected Works. John Taylor. 1972. 600.00 (*0-87968-899-8*) Gordon Pr.

Collected Works. William E. Channing. (Works of William Ellery Channing II). 1990. reprint ed. lib. bdg. 79.00 (*0-7812-2474-8*) Rprt Serv.

Collected Works. James D. Dana. 1990. reprint ed. Zoophytes, 1846. lib. bdg. 75.00 (*0-7812-2603-1*); reprint ed. Geology, 1849. write for info. (*0-318-67673-7*); reprint ed. Crustacea, 1852-54. write for info. (*0-318-67674-5*); reprint ed. Corals & Coral Islands, 1872. write for info. (*0-318-67675-3*); reprint ed. Characteristacts of Volcanoes, 1890. write for info. (*0-318-67676-1*) Rprt Serv.

Collected Works. Richard H. Dana. 1990. reprint ed. The Buccaneer & Other Poems, 1827. lib. bdg. 75.00 (*0-7812-2609-0*); reprint ed. Two Years Before the Mast, 1840. lib. bdg. 75.00 (*0-7812-2612-0*); reprint ed. Poems & Prose Writings, 1833. write for info. (*0-318-67677-X*); reprint ed. The Seaman's Friend, 1841. write for info. (*0-318-67678-8*); reprint ed. To Cuba & Back, 1859. write for info. (*0-318-67679-6*) Rprt Serv.

Collected Works. Thomas Davidson. 1990. reprint ed. The Parthenon Frieze & Other Essays, 1882. lib. bdg. 75.00 (*0-7812-2616-3*, 1504); reprint ed. The Place of Art in Education, 1886. write for info. (*0-318-67680-X*); reprint ed. Prolegomena to In Memoriam, 1889. write for info. (*0-318-67681-8*); reprint ed. Aristotle & Ancient Educational Ideals, 1892. write for info. (*0-318-67682-6*); reprint ed. The Education of the Greek People & Its Influence on Civilization, 1894. write for info. (*0-318-67683-4*); reprint ed. Rousseau & Education According to Nature, 1898. write for info. (*0-318-67684-2*); reprint ed. A History of Education, 1900. write for info. (*0-318-67685-0*); reprint ed. The Education of the Wage Earner, 1905. write for info. (*0-318-67686-9*) Rprt Serv.

Collected Works. Joseph Dennie. 1990. reprint ed. The Lay Preacher, 1796. lib. bdg. 75.00 (*0-7812-2626-0*, 1506) Rprt Serv.

Collected Works. Emily E. Dickinson. 1990. reprint ed. Poems, 1890. lib. bdg. 75.00 (*0-7812-2627-9*, 1507); reprint ed. Poems: Second Series, 1891. write for info. (*0-318-67687-7*); reprint ed. Letters of Emily Dickinson, 1894. write for info. (*0-318-67688-5*); reprint ed. Poems: Third Series, 1896. write for info. (*0-318-67689-3*); reprint ed. The Single Hound, 1914. write for info. (*0-318-67690-7*); reprint ed. Complete Poems, 1924. write for info. (*0-318-67691-5*); reprint ed. Further Poems, 1929. write for info. (*0-318-67692-3*); reprint ed. Complete Letters, 1931. write for info. (*0-318-67693-1*) Rprt Serv.

Collected Works. John Dickinson. 1990. reprint ed. Letters from a Farmer in Pennsylvania to the Inhabitants of the British Colonies, 1768. lib. bdg. 75.00 (*0-7812-2636-8*, 1508); reprint ed. The Political Writings of John Dickinson, Esq., 1801. write for info. (*0-318-67694-X*) Rprt Serv.

Collected Works. Ignatius Donnelly. 1990. reprint ed. Atlantis: The Antediluvian World, 1882. lib. bdg. 75.00 (*0-7812-2666-X*, 1509); reprint ed. Ragnarok: The Age of Fire & Gravel, 1883. write for info. (*0-318-67695-8*); reprint ed. The Great Cryptogram, 1888. write for info. (*0-318-67696-6*); reprint ed. Caesar's Column: A Story of the Twentieth Century, 1891. write for info. (*0-318-67697-4*); reprint ed. The American People's Money, 1895. write for info. (*0-318-67698-2*); reprint ed. The Cipher in the Plays & on the Tombstone, 1899. write for info. (*0-318-67699-0*) Rprt Serv.

Collected Works. Frederick Douglass. 1990. reprint ed. The Narrative of the Life of Frederick Douglass: An American Slave, 1845. lib. bdg. 75.00 (*0-7812-2673-2*, 1510); reprint ed. My Bondage & My Freedom, 1855. write for info. (*0-318-67700-8*); reprint ed. Life & Times of Frederick Douglass, 1881. write for info. (*0-318-67701-6*) Rprt Serv.

Collected Works. William Douglass. 1990. reprint ed. The Practical History of a New Epidemical Eruptive Miliary Fever...in Boston New England in the Year. lib. bdg. 75. 00 (*0-7812-2677-5*, 1511); reprint ed. A Discourse Concerning the Currencies of the British Plantations in America, etc., 1739. write for info. (*0-318-67702-4*); reprint ed. Mercurius Nov-Anglicanus, 1743. write for info. (*0-318-67703-2*); reprint ed. A Summary: Historical & Political, of the First Planting, Progressive Improvements, & Present State. write for info. (*0-318-67704-0*) Rprt Serv.

C

An Asterisk (*) at the beginning of an entry indicates that the title is appearing in BIP for the first time.

TITLE INDEX COLLECTED WORKS

Collected Works. John W. Draper. 1990. reprint ed. A Treatise on the Forces Which Produce the Organization of Plants, 1844. lib. bdg. 75.00 (*0-685-37638-9*, 1513); reprint ed. Scientific Memoirs, 1878. lib. bdg. 75.00 (*0-7812-2695-3*, 1513); reprint ed. Treatise on Chemistry, 1846. write for info. (*0-318-67706-7*); reprint ed. Treatise on Natural History, 1849. write for info. (*0-318-67707-5*); reprint ed. Human Physiology: Statical & Dynamical, 1856. write for info. (*0-318-67708-3*); reprint ed. History of the Intellectual Development of Europe, 1863. write for info. (*0-318-67709-1*); reprint ed. Thoughts on the Future Civil Policy of America, 1865. write for info. (*0-318-67710-5*); reprint ed. History of the American Civil War, 1867-70. write for info. (*0-318-67711-3*); reprint ed. Contributions to Chemistry, 1874. write for info. (*0-318-67712-1*); reprint ed. History of the Conflict Between Religion & Science, 1874. write for info. (*0-318-67713-X*) Rprt Serv.

Collected Works. Paul L. Dunbar. 1990. reprint ed. Oak & Ivy, 1893. lib. bdg. 75.00 (*0-7812-2706-2*, 1514); reprint ed. Majors & Minors, 1895. write for info. (*0-318-67714-8*); reprint ed. Lyrics of Lowly Life, 1896. write for info. (*0-318-67715-6*); reprint ed. Complete Poems, 1913. write for info. (*0-318-67716-4*); reprint ed. The Uncalled, 1896. write for info. (*0-318-67717-2*); reprint ed. The Love of Landry, 1900. write for info. (*0-318-67718-0*); reprint ed. The Fanatics, 1901. write for info. (*0-318-67719-9*); reprint ed. The Sport of the Gods, 1902. write for info. (*0-318-67720-2*); reprint ed. Best Stories of Paul Laurence Dunbar (ed. by B. Brawley) 1938. write for info. (*0-318-67721-0*) Rprt Serv.

Collected Works. William Dunlap. 1990. reprint ed. Memoir of George Fred. Cooke, 1813. lib. bdg. 75.00 (*0-7812-2716-X*, 1515); reprint ed. Life of Charles Brockden Brown, 1815. write for info. (*0-318-67722-9*); reprint ed. History of the American Theater, 1832. write for info. (*0-318-67723-7*); reprint ed. History of the Rise & Progress of the Arts of Design in the United States, 1834. write for info. (*0-318-67724-5*); reprint ed. Thirty Years Ago: or, The Memoirs of a Water-Drinker (novel) 1836. write for info. (*0-318-67725-3*); reprint ed. A History of New York, for Schools, 1837. write for info. (*0-318-67726-1*); reprint ed. History of the New Netherlands, 1839-41. write for info. (*0-318-67727-X*) Rprt Serv.

Collected Works. Theodore Dwight. 1990. reprint ed. Things as They Are, 1834. lib. bdg. 75.00 (*0-7812-2727-5*, 1516); reprint ed. Dictionary of Roots & Derivations, 1837. write for info. (*0-318-67728-8*); reprint ed. History of Connecticut, 1840. write for info. (*0-318-67729-6*); reprint ed. Life of General Garibaldi: Translated from His Private Papers, 1861. write for info. (*0-318-67730-X*) Rprt Serv.

Collected Works. Timothy Dwight. 1990. reprint ed. The Conquest of Canaan, 1785. lib. bdg. 75.00 (*0-7812-2735-6*, 1517); reprint ed. Greenfield Hill, 1794. write for info. (*0-318-67731-8*); reprint ed. The Triumph of Infidelity, 1788. write for info. (*0-318-67732-6*); reprint ed. A Discourse on the Genuineness & Authenticity of the New Testament, 1794. write for info. (*0-318-67733-4*); reprint ed. The Nature, & Danger, of Infidel Philosophy, 1798. write for info. (*0-318-67734-2*); reprint ed. The Duty of Americans, at the Present Crisis, 1798. write for info. (*0-318-67735-0*); reprint ed. Discourse on the Character of George Washington, 1800. write for info. (*0-318-67736-9*); reprint ed. Theology Explained & Defended, 1818-19. write for info. (*0-318-67737-7*); reprint ed. Travels in New England & New York, 1821-22. write for info. (*0-318-67738-5*) Rprt Serv.

Collected Works. Mary M. Eddy. 1990. reprint ed. Science & Health, 1875. lib. bdg. 75.00 (*0-7812-2745-3*, 1518); reprint ed. Christ & Christmas: A Poem, 1893. lib. bdg. 75.00 (*0-685-37645-1*, 1518); reprint ed. The Science of Man, 1876. write for info. (*0-318-67739-3*); reprint ed. Christian Healing, 1886. write for info. (*0-318-67740-7*); reprint ed. The People's Idea of God, 1886. write for info. (*0-318-67741-5*); reprint ed. Unity of Good, 1887. write for info. (*0-318-67742-3*); reprint ed. Historical Sketch of Christian Science Healing, 1888. write for info. (*0-318-67743-1*); reprint ed. Retrospection & Introspection, 1891. write for info. (*0-318-67744-X*); reprint ed. No & Yes, 1891. write for info. (*0-318-67745-8*); reprint ed. Rudimental Divine Science, 1891. write for info. (*0-318-67746-6*); reprint ed. Poems, c.1894. write for info. (*0-318-67747-4*); reprint ed. Manual of the Mother Church, 1895. write for info. (*0-318-67748-2*); reprint ed. Miscellaneous Writings, 1896. write for info. (*0-318-67749-0*); reprint ed. Christian Science Versus Pantheism, 1898. write for info. (*0-318-67750-4*) Rprt Serv.

Collected Works. Jonathan Edwards. 1990. reprint ed. God Glorified in the Work of Redemption, 1731. lib. bdg. 75.00 (*0-7812-2760-7*, 1519); reprint ed. Misrepresentations Corrected & Truth Vindicated, 1752. lib. bdg. 75.00 (*0-685-37647-8*, 1519); reprint ed. A Devine & Supernatural Light, 1734. write for info. (*0-318-67751-2*); reprint ed. A Faithful Narrative of the Surprising Work of God, 1737. write for info. (*0-318-67752-0*); reprint ed. Discourses on Various Important Subjects, 1738. write for info. (*0-318-67753-9*); reprint ed. Sinners in the Hands of an Angry God, 1741. write for info. (*0-318-67754-7*); reprint ed. The Distinguishing Marks of a Work of the Spirit of God, 1741. write for info. (*0-318-67755-5*); reprint ed. Some Thoughts Concerning the Present Revival of Religion in New England, 1742. write for info. (*0-318-67756-3*); reprint ed. A Treatise Concerning Religious Affections, 1746. write for info. (*0-318-67757-1*); reprint ed. An Humble Inquiry into the Rules of the Word of God, 1749. write for info. (*0-318-67758-X*); reprint ed. A Careful & Strict Enquiry into . . . Freedom of the Will, 1754. write for info. (*0-318-67759-8*); reprint ed. The Great Christian Doctrine of Original Sin Defended, 1758. write for info. (*0-318-67760-1*); reprint ed. Two Dissertations, 1765. write for info. (*0-318-67761-X*); reprint ed. A History of the Work of Redemption (unfinished) 1774. write for info. (*0-318-67762-8*) Rprt Serv.

Collected Works. George C. Eggleston. 1990. reprint ed. The History of the Confederate War, 1910. lib. bdg. 180.00 (*0-7812-2785-2*, 1520) Rprt Serv.

Collected Works. George C. Eggleston. 1992. reprint ed. A Man of Honor, 1873. lib. bdg. 75.00 (*0-7812-2775-5*, 1520); reprint ed. Juggernaut (with D. Marbourg) 1891. write for info. (*0-318-67763-6*); reprint ed. Dorothy South, 1902. write for info. (*0-318-67764-4*); reprint ed. Evelyn Byrd, 1904. write for info. (*0-318-67765-2*); reprint ed. Big Brother Series, 1875-1882. write for info. (*0-318-67766-0*); reprint ed. Strange Stories from History, 1886. write for info. (*0-318-67767-9*); reprint ed. A Rebel's Recollections, 1874. write for info. (*0-318-67768-7*); reprint ed. The First of the Hoosiers: Reminiscences of Edward Eggleston, 1903. write for info. (*0-318-67769-5*); reprint ed. Recollections of a Varied Life, 1910. write for info. (*0-318-67770-9*) Rprt Serv.

Collected Works. Samuel Eliot. 1990. reprint ed. Passages from the History of Liberty, 1847. lib. bdg. 75.00 (*0-7812-2786-0*, 1521); reprint ed. The Liberty of Rome (2 vols.) 1849 (later republished in 4 vols., with title change). write for info. (*0-318-67771-7*); reprint ed. Selections from American Authors, 1879. write for info. (*0-318-67772-5*); reprint ed. Poetry for Children, 1879. write for info. (*0-318-67773-3*) Rprt Serv.

Collected Works. Jonathan Elliot. 1990. reprint ed. Debates, Resolutions, & Other Proceedings in Convention on the Adoption of the Federal Constitution,. lib. bdg. 75.00 (*0-7812-2797-6*, 1522); reprint ed. Diplomatic Code of the United States of America, 1827 (as American Diplomatic Code, 1834). write for info. (*0-318-67774-1*); reprint ed. Historical Sketches of the Ten Miles Square Forming the District of Columbia, 1830. write for info. (*0-318-67775-X*); reprint ed. The Funding System of the United States & Great Britain, 1845. write for info. (*0-318-67776-8*) Rprt Serv.

Collected Works. Ralph Waldo Emerson. 1990. reprint ed. Nature, 1836. lib. bdg. 75.00 (*0-7812-2802-6*, 1523); reprint ed. May Day & Other Pieces (Poems), 1867. lib. bdg. 75.00 (*0-685-47259-0*, 1523); reprint ed. The American Scholar, 1837. write for info. (*0-318-67777-6*); reprint ed. Address Before the Senior Class in Divinity College, Cambridge, 1838. write for info. (*0-318-67778-4*); reprint ed. Essays: First Series, 1841, Second Series, 1844. write for info. (*0-318-67779-2*); reprint ed. Poems, 1847. write for info. (*0-318-67780-6*); reprint ed. Miscellanies, 1849. write for info. (*0-318-67781-4*); reprint ed. Representative Men, 1850. write for info. (*0-318-67782-2*); reprint ed. English Traits, 1856. write for info. (*0-318-67783-0*); reprint ed. The Conduct of Life, 1860. write for info. (*0-318-67784-9*); reprint ed. Society & Solitude, 1870. write for info. (*0-318-67785-7*); reprint ed. Letters & Social Aims, 1876. write for info. (*0-318-67786-5*); reprint ed. Complete Works, 1884. write for info. (*0-318-67787-3*); reprint ed. Journals, 1909-1914. write for info. (*0-318-67788-1*); reprint ed. Uncollected Writings, 1912. write for info. (*0-318-67789-X*) Rprt Serv.

Collected Works. Eugene Field. 1990. reprint ed. Tribune Primer, 1882. lib. bdg. 75.00 (*0-685-47260-4*, 1524); reprint ed. The Holy Cross & Other Tales, 1893. lib. bdg. 75.00 (*0-685-47261-2*, 1524); reprint ed. Culture's Garland, 1887. write for info. (*0-318-67790-3*); reprint ed. A Little Book of Western Verse, 1889. write for info. (*0-318-67791-1*); reprint ed. Echoes from the Sabine Farm (with R. M. Field) 1892. write for info. (*0-318-67792-X*); reprint ed. With Trumpet & Drum, 1892. write for info. (*0-318-67793-8*); reprint ed. Second Book of Verse, 1892. write for info. (*0-318-67794-6*); reprint ed. Love Songs of Children, 1894. write for info. (*0-318-67795-4*); reprint ed. Lullaby Land, 1897. write for info. (*0-318-67796-2*); reprint ed. A Little Book of Profitable Tales, 1890. write for info. (*0-318-67797-0*); reprint ed. Dibdin's Ghost, 1893. write for info. (*0-318-67798-9*); reprint ed. Second Book of Tales, 1896. write for info. (*0-318-67799-7*); reprint ed. Love Affairs of a Bibliomaniac, 1896. write for info. (*0-318-67800-4*); reprint ed. Facts, Confessions, & Observations, 1894. write for info. (*0-318-67801-2*); reprint ed. Auto-Analysis, 1896. write for info. (*0-318-67802-0*) Rprt Serv.

Collected Works. Annie Fields. 1990. reprint ed. Under the Olive, 1880. lib. bdg. 75.00 (*0-7812-2819-0*, 1525); reprint ed. The Singing Shepherd & Other Poems, 1895. write for info. (*0-318-67803-9*); reprint ed. Orpheus: A Masque, 1900. write for info. (*0-318-67804-7*); reprint ed. James T. Fields: Biographical Notes & Personal Sketches, 1881. write for info. (*0-318-67805-5*); reprint ed. Whittier: Notes of His Life & of His Friendship, 1893. write for info. (*0-318-67806-3*); reprint ed. A Shelf of Old Books, 1894. write for info. (*0-318-67807-1*); reprint ed. Authors & Friends, 1896. write for info. (*0-318-67808-X*); reprint ed. Life & Letters of Harriet Beecher Stowe, 1897. write for info. (*0-318-67809-8*); reprint ed. Nathaniel Hawthorne (in Beacon Biographies), 1899. write for info. (*0-318-67810-1*) Rprt Serv.

Collected Works. James T. Fields. 1990. reprint ed. A Few Verses for a Few Friends, 1858. lib. bdg. write for info. (*0-318-67812-8*); reprint ed. Underbrush, 1877. write for info. (*0-318-67813-6*); reprint ed. Ballads & Other Verses, 1881. write for info. (*0-318-67814-4*); reprint ed. Yesterdays with Authors, 1872. write for info. (*0-318-67815-2*); reprint ed. Hawthorne, 1876. write for info. (*0-318-67816-0*); reprint ed. In & Out of Doors with Charles Dickens, 1876. write for info. (*0-318-67817-9*) Rprt Serv.

Collected Works. John Fiske. 1990. reprint ed. The Beginnings of New England, 1889. lib. bdg. 75.00 (*0-685-47263-9*, 1527); reprint ed. A Century of Science & Other Essays, 1899. lib. bdg. 75.00 (*0-685-47264-7*, 1527); reprint ed. The Outlines of Cosmic Philosophy, 1874. write for info. (*0-318-67818-7*); reprint ed. The Unseen World, 1876. write for info. (*0-318-67819-5*); reprint ed. Darwinism & Other Essays, 1879. write for info. (*0-318-67820-9*); reprint ed. Excursions of an Evolutionist, 1884. write for info. (*0-318-67821-7*); reprint ed. The Destiny of Man Viewed in the Light of His Origin, 1884. write for info. (*0-318-67822-5*); reprint ed. American Political Ideas Viewed from the Standpoint of Universal History, 1885. write for info. (*0-318-67823-3*); reprint ed. The Idea of God as Affected by Modern Knowledge, 1886. write for info. (*0-318-67824-1*); reprint ed. The Critical Period of American History, 1783-89, 1888. write for info. (*0-318-67825-X*); reprint ed. The War of Independence, 1889. write for info. (*0-318-67826-8*); reprint ed. Civil Government in the United States, 1890. write for info. (*0-318-67827-6*); reprint ed. The American Revolution, 1891. write for info. (*0-318-67828-4*); reprint ed. The Discovery of America, 1892. write for info. (*0-318-67829-2*); reprint ed. A History of the United States for Schools, 1894. write for info. (*0-318-67830-6*); reprint ed. Old Virginia & Her Neighbors, 1897. write for info. (*0-318-67831-4*); reprint ed. Dutch & Quaker Colonies, 1899. write for info. (*0-318-67832-2*); reprint ed. The Origin of Evil, 1899. write for info. (*0-318-67833-0*); reprint ed. Through Nature to God, 1899. write for info. (*0-318-67834-9*); reprint ed. Life Everlasting, 1901. write for info. (*0-318-67835-7*); reprint ed. The Mississippi Valley in the Civil War, 1900. write for info. (*0-318-67836-5*); reprint ed. Essays: Historical & Literary, 1902. write for info. (*0-318-67837-3*); reprint ed. New France & New England, 1902. write for info. (*0-318-67838-1*); reprint ed. How the United States Became a Nation, 1904. write for info. (*0-318-67839-X*) Rprt Serv.

Collected Works. Peter Force. 1990. reprint ed. Documentary History of the Revolution, 1843 (?). lib. bdg. 75.00 (*0-7812-2865-4*, 1528); reprint ed. Tracts & Other Papers, 1836-46. write for info. (*0-318-67840-3*); reprint ed. American Archives, 1837-53. write for info. (*0-318-67841-1*); reprint ed. Grinnell Land: Remarks on English Maps of Arctic Discoveries, 1852. write for info. (*0-318-67842-X*); reprint ed. Record of Auroral Phenomena, 1856. write for info. (*0-318-67843-8*) Rprt Serv.

Collected Works. Paul L. Ford. 1990. reprint ed. The Honorable Peter Stirling & What People Thought of Him, 1894. lib. bdg. 75.00 (*0-7812-2871-9*, 1529); reprint ed. The New England Primer: A History of Its Origin & Development, 1897. lib. bdg. 75.00 (*0-685-47265-5*, 1529); reprint ed. The Great K. & A. Train Robbery, 1897. write for info. (*0-318-67844-6*); reprint ed. The Story of an Untold Love, 1897. write for info. (*0-318-67845-4*); reprint ed. Tattle Tales of Cupid, 1898. write for info. (*0-318-67846-2*); reprint ed. Janice Meredith: A Story of the American Revolution, 1899. write for info. (*0-318-67847-0*); reprint ed. Wanted: A Match-Maker, 1900. write for info. (*0-318-67848-9*); reprint ed. Wanted: A Chaperone, 1902. write for info. (*0-318-67849-7*); reprint ed. Essays on the Constitution, 1892. write for info. (*0-318-67850-0*); reprint ed. The True George Washington, 1896. write for info. (*0-318-67851-9*); reprint ed. The Many-Sided Franklin, 1899. write for info. (*0-318-67852-7*) Rprt Serv.

Collected Works. Benjamin Franklin. 1990. reprint ed. A Dissertation on Liberty, Necessity, Pleasure, & Pain, 1725. lib. bdg. 75.00 (*0-7812-2883-2*, 1530); reprint ed. Political, Miscellaneous, & Philosophical Pieces, 1779. lib. bdg. 75.00 (*0-685-47266-3*, 1530); reprint ed. Articles of Belief & Acts of Religion, 1728. write for info. (*0-318-67853-5*); reprint ed. Reflection on Courtship & Marriage, 1746. write for info. (*0-318-67854-3*); reprint ed. Plain Truth: or, Serious Considerations on the Present State of the City of Philadelphia & Province. write for info. (*0-318-67855-1*); reprint ed. Experiments & Observations on Electricity, 1751-54. write for info. (*0-318-67856-X*); reprint ed. Poor Richard Improved, 1757. write for info. (*0-318-67857-8*); reprint ed. The Interest of Great Britain Considered with Regard to Her Colonies, 1760. write for info. (*0-318-67858-6*); reprint ed. Cool Thoughts on the Present Situation of Our Public Affairs, 1764. write for info. (*0-318-67859-4*); reprint ed. The True Sentiments of America, 1768. write for info. (*0-318-67860-8*); reprint ed. Autobiography, 1791-1828 (first published in full, 1868). write for info. (*0-318-67861-6*); reprint ed. Complete Works, 1806 (best later editions 1850, 1889, 1905-07). write for info. (*0-318-67862-4*) Rprt Serv.

Collected Works. John C. Fremont. 1990. reprint ed. Report of the Exploring Expedition to the Rocky Mountains, 1843. lib. bdg. 75.00 (*0-7812-2896-4*, 1531); reprint ed. Defence of Lieut. Col. J. C. Fremont, 1848. write for info. (*0-318-67863-2*); reprint ed. Geographical Memoir upon Upper California, 1849. write for info. (*0-318-67864-0*); reprint ed. Daring Adventures of Kit Carson & Fremont, 1878. write for info. (*0-318-67865-9*); reprint ed. Memoirs, 1887. write for info. (*0-318-67866-7*) Rprt Serv.

Collected Works. Octavius B. Frothingham. 1990. reprint ed. The Religion of Humanity, 1872. lib. bdg. 75.00 (*0-685-47267-1*, 1532); reprint ed. Recollections & Impressions, 1822-1890, 1891. lib. bdg. 75.00 (*0-7812-2902-2*, 1532); reprint ed. The Safest Creed, 1874. write for info. (*0-318-67867-5*); reprint ed. Theodore Parker: A Biography, 1874. write for info. (*0-318-67868-3*); reprint ed. Transcendentalism in New England: A History, 1876. write for info. (*0-318-67869-1*); reprint ed. Gerrit Smith: A Biography, 1877. write for info. (*0-318-67870-5*); reprint ed. George Ripley, 1882. write for info. (*0-318-67871-3*); reprint ed. Memoir of William Henry Channing, 1886. write for info. (*0-318-67872-1*); reprint ed. Boston Unitarianism, 1820-1850. write for info. (*0-318-67873-X*); reprint ed. A Study of the Life & Work of Nathaniel Langdon Frothingham, 1890. write for info. (*0-318-67874-8*) Rprt Serv.

Collected Works. Henry George. 1990. reprint ed. Our Land & Land Policy, 1871. lib. bdg. 75.00 (*0-7812-2912-X*, 1533); reprint ed. Progress & Poverty, 1879. write for info. (*0-318-67875-6*); reprint ed. The Irish Land Question, 1881. write for info. (*0-318-67876-4*); reprint ed. Social Problems, 1883. write for info. (*0-318-67877-2*); reprint ed. Protection or Free Trade, 1886. write for info. (*0-318-67878-0*); reprint ed. An Open Letter to Pope Leo XIII, 1891. write for info. (*0-318-67879-9*); reprint ed. A Perplexed Philosopher, 1892. write for info. (*0-318-67880-2*); reprint ed. The Science of Political Economy, 1897. write for info. (*0-318-67881-0*) Rprt Serv.

Collected Works. Edwin L. Godkin. 1990. reprint ed. The History of Hungary & the Magyars, 1853. lib. bdg. 75.00 (*0-7812-2921-9*, 1534); reprint ed. Government (American Science Series) 1871. write for info. (*0-318-67882-9*); reprint ed. Reflections & Comments, 1895. write for info. (*0-318-67883-7*); reprint ed. Problems of Modern Democracy, 1896. write for info. (*0-318-67884-5*); reprint ed. Unforeseen Tendencies of Democracy, 1898. write for info. (*0-318-67885-3*); reprint ed. Retrospect of Forty Years, 1899. write for info. (*0-318-67886-1*) Rprt Serv.

Collected Works. Henry W. Grady. 1990. reprint ed. Complete Orations & Speeches, 1910. write for info. (*0-318-67887-X*) Rprt Serv.

Collected Works. Asa Gray. 1990. reprint ed. Elements of Botany, 1836. lib. bdg. 75.00 (*0-685-47268-X*, 1536); reprint ed. Flora of North America (with J. Torrey) 1838-43. write for info. (*0-318-67888-8*); reprint ed. Botanical Text Book, 1842 (as Structural Botany, 1879). write for info. (*0-318-67889-6*); reprint ed. First Lessons in Botany & Vegetable Physiology, 1857. write for info. (*0-318-67890-X*); reprint ed. How Plants Grow, 1858. write for info. (*0-318-67891-8*); reprint ed. Manual of the Botany of the Northern United States, 1848-67. write for info. (*0-318-67892-6*); reprint ed. Field, Forest, & Garden Botany, 1868. write for info. (*0-318-67893-4*); reprint ed. How Plants Behave, 1872. write for info. (*0-318-67894-2*); reprint ed. Darwiniana, 1876. write for info. (*0-318-67895-0*); reprint ed. Elements of Botany (new) 1887. write for info. (*0-318-67896-9*); reprint ed. Scientific Papers (ed. by C. S. Sargent) 1888. write for info. (*0-318-67897-7*) Rprt Serv.

Collected Works. Horatio Greenough. (Notable American Authors Ser.). 1990. reprint ed. Aesthetics in Washington, 1851. lib. bdg. 75.00 (*0-7812-2952-9*, 1537); reprint ed. Essays on Art (in Memoir by H. T. Tuckerman) 1853. write for info. (*0-318-67898-5*); reprint ed. Letters of Horatio Greenough to His Brother Henry Greenough (ed. by F. B. Greenough) 1887. write for info. (*0-318-67899-3*) Rprt Serv.

Collected Works. Josiah Gregg. (Notable American Authors Ser.). 1990. reprint ed. Commerce of the Prairies: or, The Journal of a Santa Fe Trader, 1844. lib. bdg. 75.00 (*0-7812-2956-1*, 1538) Rprt Serv.

C

An Asterisk (*) at the beginning of an entry indicates that the title is appearing in BIP for the first time. 1361

Collected Works. William E. Griffis. 1990. reprint ed. The Mikado's Empire, 1876. lib. bdg. 75.00 (0-685-47269-8, 1539); reprint ed. The Japanese Nation in Evolution, 1907. lib. bdg. 75.00 (0-7812-2957-X, 1539); reprint ed. Corea: The Hermit Nation, 1882. write for info. (0-318-67900-0); reprint ed. Matthew Calbraith Perry: A Typical American Naval Officer, 1887. write for info. (0-318-67901-9); reprint ed. Japan in History, Folk-lore, & Art, 1892. write for info. (0-318-67902-7); reprint ed. The Religions of Japan from the Dawn of History to the Era of Meiji, 1895. write for info. (0-318-67903-5); reprint ed. Townsend Harris: First American Envoy to Japan, 1895. write for info. (0-318-67904-3); reprint ed. America in the East, 1899. write for info. (0-318-67905-1); reprint ed. Verbeck of Japan, 1900. write for info. (0-318-67906-X); reprint ed. A Maker of the New Orient: Samuel Robbins Brown, 1902. write for info. (0-318-67907-8); reprint ed. A Modern Pioneer in Korea: The Life Story of Henry G. Appenzeller, 1912. write for info. (0-318-67908-6); reprint ed. Hepburn of Japan, 1913. write for info. (0-318-67909-4); reprint ed. The Mikado-Institution & Person, 1915. write for info. (0-318-67910-8) Rprt Serv.

Collected Works. Edward E. Hale. 1990. reprint ed. If, Yes, & Perhaps: Four Possibilities & Six Exaggerations, 1868. lib. bdg. 75.00 (0-685-47270-1, 1540); reprint ed. Poems & Fancies, 1901. lib. bdg. 75.00 (0-7812-2971-5, 1540); reprint ed. Back to Back, 1878. write for info. (0-318-67911-6); reprint ed. East & West, 1892. write for info. (0-318-67912-4); reprint ed. Ninety Days' Worth of Europe, 1861. write for info. (0-318-67913-2); reprint ed. A New England Boyhood, 1892. write for info. (0-318-67914-0); reprint ed. Memories of a Hundred Years, 1904. write for info. (0-318-67915-9); reprint ed. Kansas & Nebraska, 1854. write for info. (0-318-67916-7); reprint ed. The Ingham Papers, 1869. write for info. (0-318-67917-5); reprint ed. Franklin in France, 1887-88. write for info. (0-318-67918-3) Rprt Serv.

Collected Works. James Hall. 1990. reprint ed. Letters from the West, 1828. lib. bdg. 75.00 (0-7812-2982-0, 1541); reprint ed. Legends of the West, 1832. write for info. (0-318-67919-1); reprint ed. The Soldier's Bride & Other Tales, 1833. write for info. (0-318-67920-5); reprint ed. Sketches of History, Life, & Manners in the West, 1834. write for info. (0-318-67921-3); reprint ed. History of the Indian Tribes of North America (in collaboration with Thomas L. McKenney) 1836. write for info. (0-318-67922-1) Rprt Serv.

Collected Works. Fitz-Greene Halleck. 1990. reprint ed. Alnwick Castle, with Other Poems, 1827. lib. bdg. 75.00 (0-7812-2988-X, 1542); reprint ed. Selections from British Poets, 1840. write for info. (0-318-67923-X); reprint ed. Poetical Works of Fitz-Greene Halleck, 1847. write for info. (0-318-67924-8); reprint ed. Connecticut (second part), 1852. write for info. (0-318-67925-6); reprint ed. Young America, 1864. write for info. (0-318-67926-4) Rprt Serv.

Collected Works. Alexander Hamilton. 1990. reprint ed. Itinerarium, 1744. lib. bdg. 75.00 (0-7812-2999-5, 1544); reprint ed. A Defense of Dr. Thomson's Discourse, 1752. write for info. (0-318-67930-2) Rprt Serv.

Collected Works. Alexander Hamilton. (Notable American Authors Ser.). 1992. reprint ed. Works (various compilations of state papers, pamphlets, etc.) 1850, 1885, 1904. lib. bdg. 75.00 (0-7812-3002-0, 1545) Rprt Serv.

Collected Works. Henry Harbaugh. 1990. reprint ed. The Heidelberg Catechism, 1849. lib. bdg. 75.00 (0-685-47271-X, 1546); reprint ed. Hymns & Chants, 1861. lib. bdg. 75.00 (0-7812-3003-9, 1546); reprint ed. The Sainted Dead, 1848. write for info. (0-318-67931-0); reprint ed. Heavenly Recognition, 1851. write for info. (0-318-67932-9); reprint ed. The Heavenly Home, 1853. write for info. (0-318-67933-7); reprint ed. Union with the Church, 1853. write for info. (0-318-67934-5); reprint ed. Birds of the Bible, 1854. write for info. (0-318-67935-3); reprint ed. Life of Michael Schlatter, 1857. write for info. (0-318-67936-1); reprint ed. Fathers of the German Reformed Church in Europe & America (2 vols.) 1857-1858. write for info. (0-318-67937-X); reprint ed. Poems, 1860. write for info. (0-318-67938-8); reprint ed. Youth in Earnest, 1867. write for info. (0-318-67939-6) Rprt Serv.

Collected Works. George W. Harris. 1990. reprint ed. Sut Lovingood Yarns, 1867. lib. bdg. 75.00 (0-7812-3015-2, 1547) Rprt Serv.

Collected Works. Joel C. Harris. 1990. reprint ed. Uncle Remus Series, 1880-1918. lib. bdg. 75.00 (0-685-47272-8, 1548); reprint ed. Mingo & Other Sketches in Black & White, 1884. write for info. (0-318-67940-X); reprint ed. Free Joe & Other Georgian Sketches, 1887. write for info. (0-318-67941-8); reprint ed. Balaam & His Master, 1891. write for info. (0-318-67942-6); reprint ed. Tales of the Home Folks in Peace & War, 1898. write for info. (0-318-67943-4); reprint ed. Chronicles of Aunt Minerva Ann, 1899. write for info. (0-318-67944-2); reprint ed. On the Wing of Occasions, 1900. write for info. (0-318-67945-0); reprint ed. The Making of a Statesman, 1902. write for info. (0-318-67946-9); reprint ed. Sister Jane: Her Friends & Acquaintances, 1896. write for info. (0-318-67947-7) Rprt Serv.

Collected Works. Joel C. Harris. 1992. reprint ed. Gabriel Tolliver: A Story of Reconstruction, 1902. lib. bdg. 75.00 (0-7812-3016-0, 1548) Rprt Serv.

Collected Works. Francis L. Hawks. (Notable American Authors Ser.). 1990. reprint ed. Contributions to the Ecclesiastical History of the U. S., 1836 & 1839. lib. bdg. 75.00 (0-7812-3027-6, 1549); reprint ed. Documentary History of the Protestant Episcopal Church (2 vols.) 1863-64. write for info. (0-318-67948-5); reprint ed. Early History of the Southern States, 1832. write for info. (0-318-67949-3); reprint ed. The Mecklenburg Declaration of Independence, 1836. write for info. (0-318-67950-7); reprint ed. History of North Carolina (2 vols.) 1857-58. write for info. (0-318-67951-5); reprint ed. Monuments of Egypt, 1850. write for info. (0-318-67952-3); reprint ed. Peruvian Antiquities, 1853. write for info. (0-318-67953-1); reprint ed. Romance of Biography, 1855. write for info. (0-318-67954-X); reprint ed. Poems Hitherto Uncollected, 1873. write for info. (0-318-67955-8) Rprt Serv.

Collected Works. John M. Hay. 1990. reprint ed. Pike County Ballads & Other Pieces, 1871. lib. bdg. 75.00 (0-7812-3053-5, 1551); reprint ed. Poems, 1890. write for info. (0-318-67956-6); reprint ed. The Breadwinners, 1883. write for info. (0-318-67957-4); reprint ed. Abraham Lincoln: A History (with John G. Nicolay) 1890. write for info. (0-318-67958-2); reprint ed. Castilian Days, 1871. write for info. (0-318-67959-0); reprint ed. Addresses, 1906. write for info. (0-318-67960-4) Rprt Serv.

Collected Works. Paul H. Hayne. (Notable American Authors Ser.). 1990. reprint ed. Poems, 1855, 1857, 1860. lib. bdg. 75.00 (0-7812-3060-8, 1552); reprint ed. Legends & Lyrics, 1872. write for info. (0-318-67961-2); reprint ed. Mountain of the Lovers, 1875. write for info. (0-318-67962-0) Rprt Serv.

Collected Works. Lafcadio Hearn. (Notable American Authors Ser.). 1990. reprint ed. Chita: A Story of Last Island, 1886. lib. bdg. 75.00 (0-7812-3064-0, 1553); reprint ed. Some Chinese Ghosts, 1887. write for info. (0-318-67963-9); reprint ed. Two Years in the French West Indies, 1890. write for info. (0-318-67964-7); reprint ed. One of Cleopatra's Nights, 1882. write for info. (0-318-67965-5); reprint ed. Stray Leaves from Strange Literatures, 1884. write for info. (0-318-67966-3); reprint ed. Gombo Zhebes, 1885. write for info. (0-318-67967-1); reprint ed. La Cuisine Creole, 1885. write for info. (0-318-67968-X); reprint ed. Glimpses of Unfamiliar Japan, 1894. write for info. (0-318-67969-8); reprint ed. Japan: An Attempt at Interpretation, 1904. write for info. (0-318-67970-1) Rprt Serv.

Collected Works. Hinton R. Helper. (Notable American Authors Ser.). 1990. reprint ed. Land of Gold: Reality Versus Fiction, 1855. lib. bdg. 75.00 (0-7812-3074-8, 1554); reprint ed. The Impending Crisis of the South: How to Meet It, 1857. write for info. (0-318-67971-X); reprint ed. Nojoque: A Question for a Continent, 1867. write for info. (0-318-67972-8); reprint ed. The Negroes in Negroland..., 1868. write for info. (0-318-67973-6); reprint ed. Noonday Exigencies, 1871. write for info. (0-318-67974-4); reprint ed. The Three Americas Railway, 1881. write for info. (0-318-67975-2) Rprt Serv.

Collected Works. Daniel M. Henderson. (Notable American Authors Ser.). 1990. reprint ed. Poems: Scottish & American, 1888. lib. bdg. 75.00 (0-7812-3081-0, 1555); reprint ed. A Bit Bookie of Verse, 1906. write for info. (0-318-67976-0) Rprt Serv.

Collected Works. Caroline L. Hentz. (Notable American Authors Ser.). 1990. reprint ed. De Lara: or, The Moorish Bride, 1843. lib. bdg. 75.00 (0-7812-3084-5, 1556); reprint ed. Aunt Patty's Scrap Bag, 1846. write for info. (0-318-67977-9); reprint ed. Linda: or, The Young Pilot of the Belle Creole, 1850. write for info. (0-318-67978-7); reprint ed. Rena: or, The Snow Bird, 1851. write for info. (0-318-67979-5); reprint ed. The Planter's Northern Bride (2 vols.) 1854. write for info. (0-318-67980-9); reprint ed. Ernest Linwood, 1856. write for info. (0-318-67981-7); reprint ed. The Banished Son & Other Stories of the Heart, 1856. write for info. (0-318-67982-5) Rprt Serv.

Collected Works. Henry W. Herbert. (Notable American Authors Ser.). 1990. reprint ed. The Brothers: A Tale of the Fronde, 1835. lib. bdg. 75.00 (0-7812-3092-6, 1557); reprint ed. The Warwick Woodlands..., 1845. write for info. (0-318-67356-8); reprint ed. My Shooting Box, 1846. write for info. (0-318-67357-6); reprint ed. The Deerstalkers, 1849. write for info. (0-318-67358-4); reprint ed. Prometheus & Agamemnon of Aeschylus: Translated into English Verse, 1849. write for info. (0-318-67359-2); reprint ed. Frank Forester's Field Sports of the United States & Brit- Translated into English Verse, 1849. write for info. (0-318-67360-6); reprint ed. Frank Forester's Fish & Fishing of the United States & British Provinces of North America (London) 1. write for info. (0-318-67361-4); reprint ed. The Quorndon Hounds..., 1852. write for info. (0-318-67362-2); reprint ed. Frank Forester's Horse & Horsemanship of the United States & British Provinces of North America (2 v. write for info. (0-318-67363-0) Rprt Serv.

Collected Works. Thomas W. Higginson. 1990. reprint ed. Army Life in a Black Regiment, 1870. lib. bdg. 75.00 (0-7812-3101-9, 1558); reprint ed. Cheerful Yesterdays, 1898. lib. bdg. 75.00 (0-7812-3103-5, 1558); reprint ed. Cheerful Yesterdays, 1898. write for info. (0-318-67364-9); reprint ed. Harvard Memorial Biographies (2 vols.) 1866. write for info. (0-318-67365-7); reprint ed. Margaret Fuller Ossoli, 1884. write for info. (0-318-67366-5); reprint ed. Life of Francis Higginson: First Minister in the Massachusetts Bay Colony, 1891. write for info. (0-318-67367-3); reprint ed. Henry Wadsworth Longfellow (in American Men of Letter Series) 1902. write for info. (0-318-67368-1); reprint ed. John Greenleaf Whittier (in English Men of Letters Series) 1902. write for info. (0-318-67369-X); reprint ed. Life & Times of Stephen Higginson, 1907. write for info. (0-318-67370-3); reprint ed. Atlantic Essays, 1871. write for info. (0-318-67371-1); reprint ed. Carlyle's Laugh & Other Surprises, 1909. write for info. (0-318-67372-X); reprint ed. Oldport Days, 1873. write for info. (0-318-67373-8); reprint ed. Young Folks History of the United States, 1875. write for info. (0-318-67374-6); reprint ed. Larger History of the United States, 1885. write for info. (0-318-67375-4); reprint ed. A Reader's History of American Literature, 1903. write for info. (0-318-67376-2); reprint ed. Letters & Journals of Thomas Wentworth Higginson, 1921. write for info. (0-318-67377-0); reprint ed. Malbone, 1869. write for info. (0-318-67378-9); reprint ed. Writings of Thomas Wentworth Higginson (7 vols.) 1900. write for info. (0-318-67379-7) Rprt Serv.

Collected Works. Richard Hildreth. (Notable American Authors Ser.). 1990. reprint ed. The Slave: or, Memoirs of Archy Moore (novel) 1836 (as The White Slave, 1852; as Archy Moore, 1855). lib. bdg. 75.00 (0-7812-3121-3, 1559); reprint ed. History of Banks, 1837. write for info. (0-318-67476-9); reprint ed. Banks, Banking, & Paper Currencies, 1840. write for info. (0-318-67477-7); reprint ed. Despotism in America, 1840. write for info. (0-318-67478-5); reprint ed. History of the United States, 1849-52. write for info. (0-318-67480-7); reprint ed. Theory of Politics, 1853. write for info. (0-318-67481-5); reprint ed. Japan as It Was & Is, 1855. write for info. (0-318-67482-3) Rprt Serv.

Collected Works. Charles F. Hoffman. (Notable American Authors Ser.). 1990. reprint ed. A Winter in the West, 1835. lib. bdg. 75.00 (0-7812-3132-9, 1560); reprint ed. Wild Scenes in the Forest & Prairie, 1839. write for info. (0-318-67483-1); reprint ed. Greyslaer: A Romance of the Mohawk, 1839. write for info. (0-318-67484-X); reprint ed. The Vigil of Faith & Other Poems, 1842. write for info. (0-318-67485-8); reprint ed. The Echo: or, Borrowed Notes for Home Circulation, 1844. write for info. (0-318-67486-6); reprint ed. Love's Calendar, Lays of the Hudson, & Other Poems, 1847. write for info. (0-318-67487-4); reprint ed. The Pioneers of New York, 1848. write for info. (0-318-67488-2); reprint ed. Poems (ed. by E. F. Hoffman) 1873. write for info. (0-318-67489-0) Rprt Serv.

Collected Works. John Hogan. (Notable American Authors Ser.). 1990. reprint ed. Tempest & Sunshine, 1854. lib. bdg. 75.00 (0-7812-3141-8, 1561); reprint ed. Thoughts about the City of St. Louis, 1854. write for info. (0-318-67490-4) Rprt Serv.

Collected Works. Mary J. Holmes. 1990. reprint ed. Tempest & Sunshine, 1854. lib. bdg. 75.00 (0-7812-3140-X, 1562); reprint ed. English Orphans, 1855. lib. bdg. 75.00 (0-7812-3142-6, 1562); reprint ed. The English Orphans, 1855. write for info. (0-318-67491-2); reprint ed. The Homestead on the Hillside, 1856. write for info. (0-318-67492-0); reprint ed. Lena Rivers, 1856. write for info. (0-318-67493-9); reprint ed. Dora Deane, 1858. write for info. (0-318-67494-7); reprint ed. Hugh Worthington, 1865. write for info. (0-318-67495-5); reprint ed. Ethelyn's Mistake, 1869. write for info. (0-318-67496-3); reprint ed. Daisy Thornton, 1878. write for info. (0-318-67497-1); reprint ed. Queenie Hetherton, 1883. write for info. (0-318-67498-X); reprint ed. Mrs. Hallam's Companion, 1894. write for info. (0-318-67499-8); reprint ed. Dr. Hathern's Daughter, 1895. write for info. (0-318-67500-5); reprint ed. The Tracy Diamonds, 1899. write for info. (0-318-67501-3); reprint ed. Rena's Experiment, 1904. write for info. (0-318-67502-1); reprint ed. The Abandoned Farm & Connie's Mistake, 1905. write for info. (0-318-67503-X) Rprt Serv.

Collected Works. Oliver W. Holmes. 1990. reprint ed. The Autocrat of the Breakfast-Table, 1857. lib. bdg. 75.00 (0-685-47258-2, 1563); reprint ed. The Professor at the Breakfast Table, 1860. lib. bdg. 75.00 (0-7812-3157-4, 1563); reprint ed. The Professor at the Breakfast-Table, 1860. write for info. (0-318-67504-8); reprint ed. The Poet at the Breakfast-Table, 1872. write for info. (0-318-67505-6); reprint ed. Pages from an Old Volume of Life, 1883. write for info. (0-318-67506-4); reprint ed. Over the Teacups, 1890. write for info. (0-318-67507-2); reprint ed. Poems, 1836. write for info. (0-318-67508-0); reprint ed. Songs in Many Keys, 1862. write for info. (0-318-67509-9); reprint ed. Songs of Many Seasons, 1875. write for info. (0-318-67510-2); reprint ed. The Iron Gate & Other Poems, 1880. write for info. (0-318-67511-0); reprint ed. Before the Curfew & Other Poems, 1887. write for info. (0-318-67512-9); reprint ed. Elsie Venner, 1861. write for info. (0-318-67513-7); reprint ed. The Guardian Angel, 1867. write for info. (0-318-67514-5); reprint ed. A Mortal Antipathy, 1884-85. write for info. (0-318-67515-3); reprint ed. John Lothrop Notley, 1879. write for info. (0-318-67516-1); reprint ed. Ralph Waldo Emerson, 1885. write for info. (0-318-67517-X); reprint ed. Our Hundred Days in Europe, 1887. write for info. (0-318-67518-8) Rprt Serv.

Collected Works. James K. Hosmer. 1990. reprint ed. Samuel Adams, 1885. lib. bdg. 75.00 (0-7812-3172-8, 1564); reprint ed. The Life of Young Sir Henry Vane, 1888. lib. bdg. 75.00 (0-7812-3174-4, 1564); reprint ed. The Life of Young Sir Henry Vane, 1888. write for info. (0-318-67519-6); reprint ed. The Life of Thomas Hutchinson, 1896. write for info. (0-318-67520-X); reprint ed. A Short History of German Literature, 1878. write for info. (0-318-67521-8); reprint ed. The Story of the Jews, 1885. write for info. (0-318-67522-6); reprint ed. A Short History of Anglo-Saxon Freedom, 1890. write for info. (0-318-67523-4); reprint ed. A Short History of the Mississippi Valley, 1901. write for info. (0-318-67524-2); reprint ed. The History of the Louisiana Purchase, 1902. write for info. (0-318-67525-0); reprint ed. The Appeal to Arms, 1861-63, 1907. write for info. (0-318-67526-9); reprint ed. Outcome of the Civil War, 1863-65, 1907. write for info. (0-318-67527-7); reprint ed. The Color Guard. write for info. (0-318-67528-5); reprint ed. The King Bayonet, 1865. write for info. (0-318-67529-3); reprint ed. How Mankind was Bewitched, 1894. write for info. (0-318-67530-7); reprint ed. The Last Leaf, 1912. write for info. (0-318-67531-5) Rprt Serv.

Collected Works. Richard Hovey. (Notable American Authors Ser.). 1990. reprint ed. The Laurel, 1889. lib. bdg. 75.00 (0-7812-3188-4, 1565); reprint ed. Launcelot & Guinevere, 1891, 1895, 1898, 1907. write for info. (0-318-67614-1); reprint ed. Seaward: An Elegy, 1893. write for info. (0-318-67615-X); reprint ed. Songs of Vagabondia (with Bliss Carman) 1891. write for info. (0-318-67616-8); reprint ed. Taliesin: A Masque, 1896. write for info. (0-318-67617-6); reprint ed. More Songs of Vagabondia (with Bliss Carman) 1898. write for info. (0-318-67618-4); reprint ed. Last Songs of Vagabondia (with Bliss Carman) 1901. write for info. (0-318-67619-2); reprint ed. To the End of the Trail, 1908. write for info. (0-318-67620-6) Rprt Serv.

Collected Works. Henry Howe. 1990. reprint ed. Eminent Mechanics, 1839. lib. bdg. 75.00 (0-7812-3196-5, 1566); reprint ed. Collections of the State of New York (with J. W. Barber), 1841. lib. bdg. 75.00 (0-7812-3198-1, 1566); reprint ed. Historical Collections of the State of New York (with J. W. Barber) 1841. write for info. (0-318-67532-3); reprint ed. Memoir of the Most Eminent American Mechanics, 1843. write for info. (0-318-67533-1); reprint ed. Historical Collections of the State of New Jersey (with J. W. Barber) 1844. write for info. (0-318-67534-X); reprint ed. Historical Collections of Virginia, 1845. write for info. (0-318-67535-8); reprint ed. Historical Collections of Ohio, 1847. write for info. (0-318-67536-6); reprint ed. Historical Collections of the Great West, 1851. write for info. (0-318-67537-4); reprint ed. The Travels & Adventures of Celebrated Travelers, 1853. write for info. (0-318-67538-2); reprint ed. Life & Death on the Ocean, 1855. write for info. (0-318-67539-0); reprint ed. Adventures & Achievements of Americans, 1859. write for info. (0-318-67540-4); reprint ed. Our Whole Country (with J. W. Barber) 1861 (in part, as All the Western States & Territories, 1867). write for info. (0-318-67541-2); reprint ed. The Times of the Rebellion in the West, 1867. write for info. (0-318-67542-0); reprint ed. Over the World, 1883. write for info. (0-318-67543-9) Rprt Serv.

C

An Asterisk (*) at the beginning of an entry indicates that the title is appearing in BIP for the first time.

Collected Works. Julia Howe. 1990. reprint ed. Passion Flowers, 1854. lib. bdg. 75.00 (*0-685-37605-2*, 1567); reprint ed. Words for the Hour, 1857. lib. bdg. 75.00 (*0-7812-3213-9*, 1567); reprint ed. Words for the Hour, 1857. write for info. (*0-318-67544-7*); reprint ed. The World's Own (play) 1857. write for info. (*0-318-67545-5*); reprint ed. Later Lyrics, 1868. write for info. (*0-318-67546-3*); reprint ed. From Sunset Ridge: Poems Old & New, 1898. write for info. (*0-318-67547-1*); reprint ed. A Trip to Cuba, 1860. write for info. (*0-318-67548-X*); reprint ed. From the Oak to the Olive, 1868. write for info. (*0-318-67549-8*); reprint ed. Memoir of Dr. Samuel Gridley Howe, 1876. write for info. (*0-318-67550-1*); reprint ed. Modern Society, 1881. write for info. (*0-318-67551-X*); reprint ed. Margaret Fuller, 1883. write for info. (*0-318-67552-8*); reprint ed. Is Polite Society Polite?, 1895. write for info. (*0-318-67553-6*); reprint ed. Reminiscences, 1899. write for info. (*0-318-67554-4*); reprint ed. Sketches of Representative New England Women, 1905. write for info. (*0-318-67555-2*); reprint ed. At Sunset, 1910. write for info. (*0-318-67556-0*) Rprt Serv.

Collected Works. Jedediah V. Huntington. 1990. reprint ed. The Northern Dawn & Other Poems, 1843. lib. bdg. 75.00 (*0-7812-3228-7*, 1569); reprint ed. Lady Alice, 1849. write for info. (*0-318-67557-9*); reprint ed. Alban: or, The History of a Young Puritan, 1851. write for info. (*0-318-67558-7*); reprint ed. The Forest (sequel) 1852. write for info. (*0-318-67559-5*); reprint ed. The Pretty Plate (juvenile) 1852. write for info. (*0-318-67560-9*); reprint ed. St. Vincent de Paul & the Fruits of His Life, 1852. write for info. (*0-318-67561-7*); reprint ed. America Discovered: A Poem, 1852. write for info. (*0-318-67562-5*); reprint ed. Blonde & Brunette, 1859. write for info. (*0-318-67563-3*); reprint ed. Rosemary, 1860. write for info. (*0-318-67564-1*) Rprt Serv.

Collected Works. Thomas Hutchinson. (Notable American Authors Ser.). 1990. reprint ed. A Brief Statement of the Claims of the Colonies, 1764. lib. bdg. 75.00 (*0-7812-3297-X*, 1570); reprint ed. History of the Colony of Massachusetts Bay, 1764-1828. write for info. (*0-318-67565-X*); reprint ed. Collection of Original Papers Relative to the History of the Colony of Massachusetts Bay, 1769. write for info. (*0-318-67566-8*); reprint ed. Copy of Letters Sent to Great-Britain, 1773. write for info. (*0-318-67567-6*); reprint ed. Strictures upon the Declaration of the Congress at Philadelphia, 1776. write for info. (*0-318-67568-4*); reprint ed. The Witchcraft Delusion of 1692, 1780. write for info. (*0-318-67569-2*); reprint ed. Diary & Letters: With an Account of His Administration. write for info. (*0-318-67570-6*) Rprt Serv.

Collected Works. Laurence Hutton. 1990. reprint ed. Plays & Players, 1875. lib. bdg. 75.00 (*0-7812-3303-8*, 1571); reprint ed. Portraits in Plaster, 1894. lib. bdg. 75.00 (*0-685-37610-9*, 1571); reprint ed. Talks in a Library, 1905. lib. bdg. 75.00 (*0-7812-3305-4*, 1571); reprint ed. Artists of the Nineteenth Century (with C. E. C. Waters) 1879. write for info. (*0-318-67571-4*); reprint ed. Literary Landmarks of London, 1885. write for info. (*0-318-67572-2*); reprint ed. Actors...of Great Britain & the United States from the Days of David Garrick to the Present Time (wi. write for info. (*0-318-67573-0*); reprint ed. Opening Addresses of the American Stage (with William Carey) 1887. write for info. (*0-318-67574-9*); reprint ed. Occasional Addresses (with William Carey) 1890. write for info. (*0-318-67575-7*); reprint ed. Curiosities of the American Stage, 1891. write for info. (*0-318-67576-5*); reprint ed. Literary Landmarks of Edinburgh, 1891. write for info. (*0-318-67577-3*); reprint ed. Edwin Booth, 1893. write for info. (*0-318-67578-1*); reprint ed. Other Times & Other Seasons, 1895. write for info. (*0-318-67579-X*); reprint ed. Literary Landmarks of Jerusalem, 1895. write for info. (*0-318-67580-3*); reprint ed. Literary Landmarks of Venice, 1896. write for info. (*0-318-67581-1*); reprint ed. Literary Landmarks of Rome, 1897. write for info. (*0-318-67582-X*); reprint ed. Literary Landmarks of Florence, 1897. write for info. (*0-318-67583-8*); reprint ed. A Boy I Knew, 1898. write for info. (*0-318-67584-6*); reprint ed. Literary Landmarks of Oxford, 1903. write for info. (*0-318-67585-4*); reprint ed. Literary Landmarks of the Scottish Universities, 1904. write for info. (*0-318-67586-2*) Rprt Serv.

Collected Works. Robert Ingersoll. (Notable American Authors Ser.). 1992. reprint ed. lib. bdg. 75.00 (*0-7812-3334-8*) Rprt Serv.

Collected Works. Robert G. Ingersoll. 1990. reprint ed. The Gods, 1872. lib. bdg. 75.00 (*0-7812-3323-2*, 1572); reprint ed. Collected Works, 1900. lib. bdg. 75.00 (*0-7812-3325-9*, 1572); reprint ed. Some Mistakes of Moses, 1879. write for info. (*0-318-67587-0*); reprint ed. What Must We Do to Be Saved? 1880. write for info. (*0-318-67588-9*); reprint ed. About the Holy Bible, 1894. write for info. (*0-318-67589-7*); reprint ed. Why I Am an Agnostic, 1896. write for info. (*0-318-67590-0*); reprint ed. Superstition, 1898. write for info. (*0-318-67591-9*); reprint ed. The Devil, 1899. write for info. (*0-318-67592-7*); reprint ed. Lectures Complete, 1883. write for info. (*0-318-67593-5*); reprint ed. Prose Poems & Selections, 1884. write for info. (*0-318-67594-3*) Rprt Serv.

Collected Works. William Ioor. 1990. reprint ed. Independence: or, Which Do You Like Best, the Peer or the Farmer, 1805. lib. bdg. 75.00 (*0-7812-3326-7*); reprint ed. The Battle of Eutaw Springs, 1807. write for info. (*0-318-67595-1*) Rprt Serv.

Collected Works. Joseph N. Ireland. 1990. reprint ed. Records of the New York Stage from 1750 to 1860 (2 vols.) 1866-67. lib. bdg. 75.00 (*0-7812-3327-5*); reprint ed. Mrs. Duff, 1882. write for info. (*0-318-67596-X*); reprint ed. A Memoir of the Professional Life of Thomas Abthorpe Cooper, 1888. write for info. (*0-318-67597-8*) Rprt Serv.

Collected Works. William Irving. 1990. reprint ed. Salmagundi (contributor) 1807. lib. bdg. 75.00 (*0-7812-3328-3*) Rprt Serv.

Collected Works. Helen M. Jackson. 1990. reprint ed. In the White Mountains, 1866. lib. bdg. 75.00 (*0-7812-3329-1*, 1576); reprint ed. Verses, 1870. write for info. (*0-318-67598-6*); reprint ed. Bits of Travel, 1872. write for info. (*0-318-67599-4*); reprint ed. Bits of Talk about Home Matters, 1873. write for info. (*0-318-67600-1*); reprint ed. Saxe Holm's Stories (?) 1874-78. write for info. (*0-318-67601-X*); reprint ed. The Story of Boon (verse) 1874. write for info. (*0-318-67602-8*); reprint ed. Mercy Philbrick's Choice, 1876. write for info. (*0-318-67603-6*); reprint ed. Hetty's Strange History, 1877. write for info. (*0-318-67604-4*); reprint ed. Nelly's Silver Mine, 1878. write for info. (*0-318-67605-2*) Rprt Serv.

Collected Works. Helen M. Jackson. (Notable American Authors Ser.). 1992. reprint ed. Bits of Travel at Home, 1878. lib. bdg. 75.00 (*0-7812-3343-7*); reprint ed. A Century of Dishonor, 1881. write for info. (*0-318-67606-0*); reprint ed. The Training of Children, 1882. write for info. (*0-318-67607-9*); reprint ed. Ramona, 1884. write for info. (*0-318-67608-7*); reprint ed. Glimpses of California & the Missions, 1885. write for info. (*0-318-67609-5*); reprint ed. Zeph, 1885. write for info. (*0-318-67610-9*); reprint ed. Glimpses of Three Coasts, 1886. write for info. (*0-318-67611-7*); reprint ed. Sonnets & Lyrics, 1886. write for info. (*0-318-67612-5*); reprint ed. Between Whiles, 1887. write for info. (*0-318-67613-3*) Rprt Serv.

Collected Works. Henry James, Jr. (Notable American Authors Ser.). 1992. reprint ed. lib. bdg. 75.00 (*0-7812-3422-0*) Rprt Serv.

Collected Works. John W. Rochester. (BCL1-PR English Literature Ser.). 407p. 1992. reprint ed. lib. bdg. 99.00 (*0-7812-7398-6*) Rprt Serv.

Collected Works, 6 vols., 1. Johann L. Dussek. LC 79-75313. (Music Ser.). 1978. 59.50 (*0-306-77271-X*) Da Capo.

Collected Works, 6 vols., 2. Johann L. Dussek. LC 79-75313. (Music Ser.). 1978. 59.50 (*0-306-77272-8*) Da Capo.

Collected Works, 6 vols., 3. Johann L. Dussek. LC 79-75313. (Music Ser.). 1978. 59.50 (*0-306-77273-6*) Da Capo.

Collected Works, 6 vols., 4. Johann L. Dussek. LC 79-75313. (Music Ser.). 1978. 59.50 (*0-306-77274-4*) Da Capo.

Collected Works, 6 vols., 5. Johann L. Dussek. LC 79-75313. (Music Ser.). 1978. 59.50 (*0-306-77275-2*) Da Capo.

Collected Works, 6 vols., 6. Johann L. Dussek. LC 79-75313. (Music Ser.). 1978. 59.50 (*0-306-77276-0*) Da Capo.

Collected Works, 3 vols., Set. Ethan Allen & Ira Allen. LC 91-77183. 1992. 96.00 (*1-56541-210-9*) Chalidze.

Collected Works, 6 vols., Set. Johann L. Dussek. LC 79-75313. (Music Ser.). 1978. 325.00 (*0-685-45906-3*) Da Capo.

Collected Works, Set. Stanislaw Lesniewski. Ed. by S. J. Surma et al. (Nijhoff International Philosophy Ser.: No. 44). 620p. 1991. lib. bdg. 309.00 (*0-7923-1512-X*) Kluwer Ac.

Collected Works, 6 vols., Set. John Von Neumann. Ed. by A. W. Taub. Incl. Vol. 1. Logic, Theory of Sets & Quantum Mechanics. 1961. 274.00 (*0-08-009567-4*); Vol. 3. Rings of Operators. 1962. 242.00 (*0-08-009569-0*); Vol. 4. 1961. 326.00 (*0-08-009570-4*); Vol. 5. Von Newmann Collect Wks. 1961. 322.00 (*0-08-009571-2*); Vol. 6. Theory of Games, Astrophysics, Hydrodynamics & Meteorology. 1963. 228.00 (*0-08-009572-0*); 1963. 1,390.00 (*0-08-009566-6*, Pub. by Pergamon Repr UK) Franklin.

Collected Works, 17 vols., Set. John W. De Forest. (Collected Works of John W. De Forest). 1988. reprint ed. lib. bdg. 895.00 (*0-7812-1151-4*) Rprt Serv.

Collected Works, 12 vols., Set. Edward Eggleston. (Collected Works of Edward Eggleston). 1988. reprint ed. lib. bdg. 948.00 (*0-7812-1169-7*) Rprt Serv.

Collected Works, 14 vols., Set. Harold Frederic. (Collected Works of Harold Frederic). 1988. reprint ed. lib. bdg. 1,160.00 (*0-7812-1182-4*) Rprt Serv.

Collected Works, 15 vols., Set. Henry B. Fuller. (Collected Works of Henry B. Fuller). 1988. reprint ed. lib. bdg. 700.00 (*0-7812-1197-2*) Rprt Serv.

Collected Works, 9 vols., Set. Joseph Glanvill. Ed. by Bernhard Fabian. 1970. reprint ed. 513.50 (*0-685-66469-4*, Pub. by Georg Olms GW) Lubrecht & Cramer.

Collected Works, 3 vols., Set. Joseph Kirkland. (Collected Works of Joseph Kirkland). 1988. reprint ed. lib. bdg. 240.00 (*0-7812-1316-9*) Rprt Serv.

Collected Works, 22 vols., Set. David C. Phillips. 1988. reprint ed. lib. bdg. 2,054.00 (*0-7812-1320-7*) Rprt Serv.

Collected Works, 2 vols., Set. Dante G. Rossetti. (BCL1-PR English Literature Ser.). 1992. reprint ed. lib. bdg. 150.00 (*0-7812-7626-8*) Rprt Serv.

Collected Works, 3 vols., Vol. 1. Kunihiko Kodaira. 540p. 1975. 85.00 (*0-691-08158-1*) Princeton U Pr.

Collected Works, 3 vols., Vol. 2. Kunihiko Kodaira. 540p. 1975. 65.00 (*0-691-08163-8*) Princeton U Pr.

Collected Works, 3 vols., Vol. 3. Kunihiko Kodaira. 540p. 1975. 65.00 (*0-691-08164-6*) Princeton U Pr.

***Collected Works, Vol. 47.** Karl Marx & Frederick Engels. 750p. Date not set. write for info. (*0-85315-623-9*, Pub. by Lawrence & Wishart UK) Humanities.

Collected Works: Illustrated London News, 1926-1928, Vol. XXXIV. G. K. Chesterton. Ed. by Lawrence Clipper. LC 85-81511. 669p. (Orig.). 1991. 39.95 (*0-89870-293-3*); Illustrated London News, 1926-1928. pap. 24.95 (*0-89870-294-1*) Ignatius Pr.

Collected Works: The Collected Works of E. W. Howe, 1891-1920, 15 vols. E. W. Howe. 1988. lib. bdg. 750.00 (*0-7812-1285-5*) Rprt Serv.

Collected Works: The Collected Works of Robert Herrick, 1897-1933, 25 vols. Robert Herrick. 1988. lib. bdg. 1,200.00 (*0-7812-1259-6*) Rprt Serv.

Collected Works: The Collected Works of Sarah O. Jewett, 1881-1901, 14 vols. Sarah O. Jewett. 1988. lib. bdg. 700.00 (*0-7812-1301-0*) Rprt Serv.

Collected Works Vol. II: A Treatise of the Hypochondriack & Hysterick Passions, Vulgarly Call'd the Hypo in Men an Vapours in Women. Bernard Mandeville. xxiv, 288p. 1981. reprint ed. write for info. (*3-487-07037-5*, Pub. by Georg Olms GW) Lubrecht & Cramer.

Collected Works Vol. III: The Fable of the Bees: or, Private Vices Publick Benefits. Bernard Mandeville. 404p. 1983. reprint ed. write for info. (*3-487-07177-0*, Pub. by Georg Olms GW) Lubrecht & Cramer.

***Collected Works Vol. III: Unpublished Essays & Lectures.** Kurt Godel. Ed. by S. Feferman et al. (Illus.). 560p. 1995. 59.95 (*0-19-507255-3*) OUP.

Collected Works Vol. IV: The Fable of the Bees, Pt. II. Bernard Mandeville. 456p. 1980. reprint ed. write for info. (*3-487-07038-3*, Pub. by Georg Olms GW) Lubrecht & Cramer.

Collected Works Vol. V: Free Thoughts on Religion, the Church, & National Happiness. Bernard Mandeville. xxii, 364p. 1987. reprint ed. write for info. (*3-487-07782-5*, Pub. by Georg Olms GW) Lubrecht & Cramer.

Collected Works Vol. VI: An Enquiry into the Origin of Honour, & the Usefulness of Christianity in War. Bernard Mandeville. xi, 240p. 1990. reprint ed. write for info. (*3-487-09315-4*, Pub. by Georg Olms GW) Lubrecht & Cramer.

Collected Works Vol. VII: Early Verse Drama & Prose Plays. Johann Wolfgang Von Goethe. Ed. by Cyrus Hamlin & Frank Ryder. Tr. by Frank Ryder et al. LC 88-2193. (Illus.). viii, 298p. 1988. 40.00 (*3-518-02564-3*, Pub. by Suhr Verlag GW) Intl Bk Import.

Collected Works by & about Blanche Evan: Dancer, Teacher, Writer. Blanche Evan. LC 91-35002. (Illus.). 213p. (C). 1991. 34.95 (*0-9630763-0-2*, GV1783.062 1991) B Evan Dance.

Collected Works: Drama, Verse, Novels, 2 vols., Set. Horatio Colony. 1500p. 1982. Vol. 1. 60.95 (*0-8283-1741-0*) Branden Pub Co.

Collected Works in Eight Volumes. Mikhail Sholokhov. 1985. 190.00 (*0-317-42830-6*, Pub. by Collets UK) St Mut.

Collected Works in Mesoamerican Linguistics & Archaeology, 6 vols. 2nd ed. Eduard Seler. Ed. by Frank E. Comparato. LC 88-82627. (Illus.). 1990. text ed. 250.00x (*0-911437-32-0*) Labyrinthos.

Collected Works in Twelve Volumes. Johann Wolfgang Von Goethe. 1989. 432.00 (*3-518-03056-6*, Pub. by Suhr Verlag GW) Intl Bk Import.

Collected Works of Abraham Cowley, Vol. 1. Ed. by Thomas O. Calhoun et al. LC 87-40005. (Illus.). 448p. 1990. 68.50 (*0-87413-282-7*) U Delaware Pr.

Collected Works of Abraham Cowley, Vol. 2: Poems (1656), Part I; the Mistress. Ed. by Thomas O. Calhoun et al. LC 87-40005. (Illus.). 656p. 1993. 80.00 (*0-87413-408-0*) U Delaware Pr.

Collected Works of Abraham Lincoln, Vol. 10, 1st Supplement. Roy P. Basler. 320p. (C). 1990. reprint ed. text ed. 50.00 (*0-8135-1552-1*) Rutgers U Pr.

Collected Works of Ada Jack Carver. Ed. by Mary D. Fletcher. LC 80-52636. 212p. (Orig.). 1980. 12.00 (*0-917898-04-4*); pap. 5.95 (*0-317-47700-5*) NSU Pr LA.

Collected Works of Aga Khan Third: Speeches & Writings of Sir Sultan Muhammod Shah, 2 vols., Set. Ed. by K. K. Aziz. 800p. 1993. 105.00 (*0-7103-0427-7*, A6948, Pub. by Kegan Paul Intl UK) Routledge Chapman & Hall.

Collected Works of Alan Rickard. Alan Rickard. 24.49 (*0-936128-50-X*) De Young Pr.

Collected Works of Aleister Crowley, 3 vols., Set. Aleister Crowley. 1974. lib. bdg. 900.00 (*0-8490-3962-2*) Krishna Pr.

Collected Works of Aleister Crowley, 3 vols, Vol. 1. Aleister Crowley. 269p. 1974. reprint ed. 15.00 (*0-911662-51-0*) Yoga.

Collected Works of Aleister Crowley, 3 vols, Vol. 2. Aleister Crowley. 282p. 1974. reprint ed. 15.00 (*0-911662-52-9*) Yoga.

Collected Works of Aleister Crowley, 3 vols, Vol. 3. Aleister Crowley. 248p. 1974. reprint ed. 15.00 (*0-911662-53-7*) Yoga.

Collected Works of Alexander Csoma De Koros, Set. J. Terjek. 1014p. 1984. 400.00 (*0-569-08809-7*) St Mut.

***Collected Works of Alexander Csoma De Koros, 4 vols., Set.** J. Terjek. (Bibliotheca Orientalis Hungarica Ser.: No. 35). (C). 1984. 360.00 (*963-05-4361-3*, Pub. by Akad Kiado HU) St Mut.

***Collected Works of Alexander Csoma de Koros Vol. 2: Grammar of the Tibetan Language.** J. Terjek. 204p. (C). 1986. 75.00x (*963-05-4362-1*, Pub. by Akad Kiado HU) St Mut.

***Collected Works of Alexander Csoma de Koros Vol. 4: Tibetan Studies.** Ed. by J. Terjek. 459p. (C). 1986. 132.00 (*963-05-4363-X*, Pub. by Akad Kiado HU) St Mut.

Collected Works of Alfred B. Sedgwick. Ed. by Michael Meckna. LC 94-707. (Nineteenth-Century American Musical Theater Ser.: No. 7). 488p. 1994. reprint ed. 130.00 (*0-8153-1369-1*) Garland.

Collected Works of Ambrose Bierce, 1909-1912, 12 Vols, Set. Ambrose Bierce. LC 66-14638. 1966. 500.00 (*0-87752-010-0*) Gordian.

Collected Works of Arnold Bennett, 90 vols, Set. Arnold Bennett. 1976. reprint ed. 1,897.50 (*0-8369-7057-8*) Ayer.

Collected Works of Arthur Symons, 9 Vols, Set. Arthur Symons. LC 74-148314. reprint ed. 645.00 (*0-404-08940-2*) AMS Pr.

Collected Works of Asa Gray. Asa Gray. 1992. reprint ed. lib. bdg. write for info. (*0-7812-2939-1*) Rprt Serv.

Collected Works of Bernard J. Lonergan. Bernard J. Lonergan. Ed. by Frederick E. Crowe & Robert M. Doran. 349p. 1988. 37.50 (*0-8020-3438-1*) U of Toronto Pr.

Collected Works of Bernard Lonergan, No. 4: Collection. Ed. by Frederick E. Crowe & Robert M. Doran. 368p. (Orig.). (C). 1994. pap. 19.95 (*0-8020-3439-X*) U of Toronto Pr.

Collected Works of Billy Graham. Billy Graham. 1993. 12.98 (*0-88486-087-6*) Arrowood Pr.

Collected Works of Billy the Kid. Michael Ondaatje. 112p. 1984. pap. 10.00 (*0-14-007280-2*, Penguin Bks) Viking Penguin.

Collected Works of C. B. Morrey. (Collected & Selected Works). 1994. write for info. (*1-57146-014-4*) Intl Pr Boston.

Collected Works of C. C. Parlin: An Original Anthology. Ed. by Henry Assael. LC 78-260. (Century of Marketing Ser.). (Illus.). 1979. lib. bdg. 24.95 (*0-405-11159-2*) Ayer.

Collected Works of C. G. Jung, No. 10: Civilization in Transition. 2nd ed. C. G. Jung et al. Ed. by Gerhard Adler et al. Tr. by R. F. Hull. (Bollingen Ser.: No. 20). 630p. 1970. 69.50 (*0-691-09762-3*) Princeton U Pr.

Collected Works of C. G. Jung, No. 11: Psychology & Religion - West & East. 2nd ed. C. G. Jung et al. Ed. by Gerhard Adler et al. Tr. by R. F. Hull. (Bollingen Ser.: No. 20). 712p. 1969. 69.50 (*0-691-09772-0*) Princeton U Pr.

Collected Works of C. G. Jung, No. 12: Psychology & Alchemy. 2nd ed. C. G. Jung et al. Ed. by Gerhard Adler et al. Tr. by R. F. Hull. (Bollingen Ser.: No. 20). 617p. 1968. 69.50 (*0-691-09771-2*); pap. 17.95 (*0-691-01831-6*) Princeton U Pr.

Collected Works of C. G. Jung, No. 13: Alchemical Studies. C. G. Jung et al. Ed. by Gerhard Adler et al. Tr. by R. F. Hull. (Bollingen Ser.: No. 20). 617p. 1968. 69.50 (*0-691-09760-7*); pap. 19.95 (*0-691-01849-9*) Princeton U Pr.

Collected Works of C. G. Jung, No. 14: Mysterium Coniunctionis. 2nd ed. C. G. Jung et al. Ed. by Gerhard Adler et al. Tr. by R. F. Hull. (Bollingen Ser.: No. 20). 714p. 1970. 65.00 (*0-691-09766-6*); pap. 19.95 (*0-691-01816-2*) Princeton U Pr.

Collected Works of C. G. Jung, No. 15: The Spirit in Man, Art, & Literature. C. G. Jung et al. Ed. by Gerhard Adler et al. Tr. by R. F. Hull. (Bollingen Ser.: No. 20). 176p. 1966. 27.50 (*0-691-09773-9*); pap. 10.95 (*0-691-01775-1*) Princeton U Pr.

Collected Works of C. G. Jung, No. 16: The Practice of Psychotherapy. 2nd ed. Ed. by Gerhard Adler et al. Tr. by R. F. Hull. (Bollingen Ser.: No. 20). 1966. 49.50 (*0-691-09767-4*) Princeton U Pr.

Collected Works of C. G. Jung, No. 17: The Development of Personality. Ed. by Gerhard Adler et al. Tr. by R. F. Hull. (Bollingen Ser.: No. 20). 1024p. 1985. 39.50 (*0-691-09763-1*); pap. 14.95 (*0-691-01838-3*) Princeton U Pr.

Collected Works of C. G. Jung, No. 18: The Symbolic Life. C. G. Jung et al. Ed. by Gerhard Adler et al. Tr. by R. F. Hull. (Bollingen Ser.: No. 20). 1024p. 1976. 85.00 (*0-691-09892-1*) Princeton U Pr.

Collected Works of C. G. Jung, No. 19: Bibliography of Jung's Writings. Lisa Ress et al. Ed. by Gerhard Adler et al. Tr. by R. F. Hull. (Bollingen Ser.: No. 20). 366p. 1979. 35.00 (*0-691-09893-X*) Princeton U Pr.

Collected Works of C. G. Jung, No. 2: Experimental Researches. C. G. Jung et al. Ed. by G. Adler et al. (Bollingen Ser.: No. 20). 1973. 69.50 (*0-691-09764-X*) Princeton U Pr.

Collected Works of C. G. Jung, No. 20: General Index. Ed. by Gerhard Adler et al. Tr. by R. F. Hull. (Bollingen Ser.: No. 20). 1979. 80.00 (*0-691-09867-0*) Princeton U Pr.

Collected Works of C. G. Jung, No. 3: The Psychogenesis of Mental Disease. C. G. Jung et al. Ed. by G. Adler et al. (Bollingen Ser.: No. 20). 1960. 47.50 (*0-691-09769-0*); pap. 14.95 (*0-691-01859-6*) Princeton U Pr.

Collected Works of C. G. Jung, No. 4: Freud & Psychoanalysis. Carl G. Jung. Ed. by G. Adler. Tr. by R. F. Hull. LC 52-8757. (Bollingen Ser.: No. 20). 392p. 1985. 59.50 (*0-691-09765-8*); pap. 16.95 (*0-691-01864-2*) Princeton U Pr.

Collected Works of C. G. Jung, No. 5: Symbols of Transformation. 2nd ed. C. G. Jung et al. Ed. by G. Adler et al. (Bollingen Ser.: No. 20). 597p. 1967. text ed. 69.50 (*0-691-09775-5*); pap. 19.95 (*0-691-01815-4*) Princeton U Pr.

Collected Works of C. G. Jung, No. 6: Psychological Types. C. G. Jung et al. Ed. by Gerhard Adler et al. Tr. by R. F. Hull & H. G. Baynes. (Bollingen Ser.: No. 20). 1971. 69.50 (*0-691-09770-4*); pap. 18.95 (*0-691-01813-8*) Princeton U Pr.

C

Collected Works of C. G. Jung, No. 7: Two Essays on Analytical Psychology. 2nd ed. C. G. Jung et al. Ed. by Gerhard Adler et al. Tr. by R. F. Hull. (Bollingen Ser.: No. 20). 396p. 1966. 45.00 (0-691-09776-3); pap. 14.95 (0-691-01782-4) Princeton U Pr.

Collected Works of C. G. Jung, No. 8: The Structure & Dynamics of the Psyche. 2nd ed. Carl G. Jung. Ed. by Gerhard Adler et al. Tr. by R. F. Hull. (Bollingen Ser.: No. 20). 606p. 1969. 69.50 (0-691-09774-7) Princeton U Pr.

Collected Works of C. G. Jung, No. 9, Pt. 1: The Archetypes & the Collective Unconscious. 2nd ed. C. G. Jung et al. Ed. by Gerhard Adler et al. Tr. by R. F. Hull. (Bollingen Ser.: No. 20). 474p. 1968. 65.00 (0-691-09761-5); pap. 18.95 (0-691-01833-2) Princeton U Pr.

Collected Works of C. G. Jung, No. 9, Pt. 2: Aion - Researches into the Phenomenology of the Self. 2nd ed. Ed. by Gerhard Adler et al. Tr. by R. F. Hull. (Bollingen Ser.: No. 20). 1968. 45.00 (0-691-09759-3); pap. 13.95 (0-691-01826-X) Princeton U Pr.

Collected Works of C. G. Jung, Vol. 1: Psychiatric Studies. C. G. Jung. Ed. by G. Adler & R. F. Hull. 238p. 1970. text ed. 55.00 (0-691-09768-2); pap. 16.95 (0-691-01855-3) Princeton U Pr.

Collected Works of Caroline Lee Whiting Hentz. Caroline L. Hentz. (Notable American Authors Ser.). 1992. reprint ed. lib. bdg. write for info. (0-7812-3083-7) Rprt Serv.

Collected Works of Charles Fenno Hoffman. Charles F. Hoffman. (Notable American Authors Ser.). 1992. reprint ed. lib. bdg. write for info. (0-7812-3130-2) Rprt Serv.

Collected Works of Charles Graham Halpine: Baked Meats of the Funeral. Charles G. Halpine. 1992. reprint ed. 1866. lib. bdg. write for info. (0-318-67928-0) Rprt Serv.

Collected Works of Charles Graham Halpine: Lyrics of the Letter H. Charles G. Halpine. 1992. reprint ed. 1854. lib. bdg. 75.00 (0-7812-2994-4, 1543) Rprt Serv.

Collected Works of Charles Graham Halpine: Poetical Works. Charles G. Halpine. Ed. by R. B. Roosevelt. 1992. reprint ed. 1869. lib. bdg. write for info. (0-318-67929-9) Rprt Serv.

Collected Works of Charles Graham Halpine: The Life & Adventures, Songs, Services & Speeches of Private Miles O'Reilly. Charles G. Halpine. 1992. reprint ed. 1864. lib. bdg. 75.00 (0-318-67927-2) Rprt Serv.

Collected Works of Count Rumford, 5 vols. Benjamin T. Rumford. Ed. by Sanborn C. Brown. Incl. Vol. 1. Nature of Heat. LC 68-17633. (Illus.). 521p. 1968. 42.50 (0-674-13951-8); Vol. 4. Light & Armament. LC 68-17633. (Illus.). 511p. 1970. 42.50 (0-674-13954-2); Vol. 5. Public Institutions. LC 68-17633. (Illus.). 524p. 1970. 39.95 (0-674-13955-0); LC 68-17633. write for info. (0-318-53031-7) HUP.

Collected Works of David Daube: New Testament Judaism, Vol. 2. David Daube. Ed. by Calum M. Carmichael. (Studies in Comparative Legal History). 1000p. (C). 1994. text ed. 60.00 (1-882239-04-0) U CA Schl Law.

Collected Works of David Daube: Talmudic Law. David Daube. Ed. by Calum M. Carmichael. Tr. by Colum M. Carmichael. LC 92-61641. (Studies in Comparative Legal History: Vol. 1). (Illus.). 527p. (ARC, ENG, GER, GRE, HEB & LAT.). (C). 1992. text ed. 32.50 (1-882239-00-8) U CA Schl Law. This is the first of a series of volumes to be published by the Robbins Religious & Civil Law Collection, School of Law, University of California, Berkeley, that brings together the writings of David Daube. These writings extend over a time span that began in 1932 &, at this point in time, the year 1992, continue to appear in scholarly journals worldwide. Volume one is divided into four sections dealing respectively with "Institutions, Practices & Principles," "Gender Matters," "The Perspective of Comparative Law," & "Canons of Interpretation." It includes fundamental studies such as Collaboration with Tyranny in Rabbinic Law, Texts & Interpretation in Roman & Jewish Law, The Civil Law of the Mishnah: The Arrangement of Three Gates. Edited by Calum Carmichael, this volume includes an index of the references, a subject index, & a select bibliography of the works of David Daube. Calum Carmichael is Professor of Comparative Literature & Biblical Studies at Cornell University, Ithaca & a Fellow of the Oxford Centre for Postgraduate Hebrew Studies. He is a graduate of the Universities of Edinburgh, Glasgow & Oxford where he studied under David Daube. He has published extensively on the history of Biblical law. *Publisher Provided Annotation.*

Collected Works of David Daube: Talmudic Law, Set. David Daube. Ed. by Calum M. Carmichael. Tr. by Colum M. Carmichael. LC 92-61641. (Studies in Comparative Legal History: Vol. 1). (Illus.). 527p. (ARC, ENG, GER, GRE, HEB & LAT.). (C). 1992. text ed. write for info. (1-882239-01-6) U CA Schl Law.

Collected Works of David G. Phillips, 11 vols., Set. David G. Phillips. Incl. Old Wives for New. 1908. reprint ed. 39.00 (0-686-01742-0); Worth of a Woman. 1908. reprint ed. 39.00 (0-686-01743-9); Fashionable Adventures of Joshua Craig. 1909. reprint ed. 39.00 (0-403-03157-5); Hungry Heart. 1909. reprint ed. 40.00 (0-686-01745-5); Husband's Story. 1910. reprint ed. 38.00 (0-686-01746-3); Grain of Dust. 1911. reprint ed. 39.00 (0-685-04693-1); Price She Paid. 1912. reprint ed. 39.00 (0-403-02960-0); George Helm. 1912. reprint ed. 29.00 (0-403-02999-6); Degarmo's Wife & Other Stories. 1913. reprint ed. 26.00 (0-686-01750-1); Susan Lenox: Her Fall & Rise, 2 vols. 1917. reprint ed. 79.00x (0-686-01751-X); 785.00 (0-686-01741-2) Somerset Pub.

Collected Works of Dr. Davudi. Ed. by Vahid Rafati. (Illus.). (PER.). 1987. 22.50 (0-933770-58-8) Kalimat.

Collected Works of E. W. Howe, 15 vols., Set. E. W. Howe. Incl. Story of a Country Town. 1884. reprint ed. 39.00 (0-403-03053-6); Mystery of the Locks. 1885. reprint ed. 59.00 (0-403-04641-6); Moonlight Boy. 1886. reprint ed. 59.00 (0-403-04642-4); Man Story. 1889. reprint ed. 59.00 (0-403-02961-9); Ante-Mortem Statement. 1891. reprint ed. 59.00 (0-403-04643-2); Daily Notes on a Trip Around the World. 1907. reprint ed. 59.00 (0-403-02284-3); Trip to the West Indies. 1910. reprint ed. 59.00 (0-403-04644-0); Country Town Sayings. 1911. reprint ed. 59.00 (0-686-01372-7); Travel Letters from New Zealand, Australia & Africa. 1913. reprint ed. 69.00 (0-403-04646-7); Success Easier Than Failure. 1917. reprint ed. 29.00 (0-403-04647-5); Blessing of Business. 1918. reprint ed. 59.00 (0-403-04648-3); Ventures in Common Sense. 1919. reprint ed. 29.00 (0-403-04649-1); Anthology of Another Town. 1920. reprint ed. 69.00 (0-403-03192-3); Plain People. 1929. reprint ed. 49.00 (0-403-02963-5); Indignations of E. W. Howe. 1933. reprint ed. 69.00 (0-403-04624-6); 650.00 (0-685-04692-3) Somerset Pub.

Collected Works of Edgar Allan Poe, Vol. 1: Poems. Edgar Allan Poe. Ed. by Thomas O. Mabbott. LC 68-17627. (Illus.). 657p. 1969. 50.00 (0-674-13935-6) Belknap Pr.

Collected Works of Edward Eggleston, 12 vols., Set. Edward Eggleston. Incl. Book of Queer Stories & Stories Told on a Cellar Door. 1871. reprint ed. 69.00 (0-403-04578-9); Hoosier School Master. 1871. reprint ed. 69.00 (0-685-04689-3); End of the World. 1872. reprint ed. 69.00 (0-403-04579-7); Mystery of Metropolisville. 1873. reprint ed. 69.00 (0-403-02977-5); Circuit Rider. 1874. reprint ed. 49.00 (0-403-02989-9); Schoolmaster's Stories for Boys & Girls. 1874. reprint ed. 59.00 (0-685-04690-7); Hoosier Schoolboy. 1883. reprint ed. 59.00 (0-403-04580-0); Roxy. 1878. reprint ed. 59.00 (0-403-04581-9); Graysons. 1888. reprint ed. 39.00 (0-403-00207-9); Faith Doctor. 1891. reprint ed. 34.00 (0-403-04582-7); Duffels. 1893. reprint ed. 22.00 (0-403-03158-3); 650.00x (0-403-03456-6) Somerset Pub.

Collected Works of Edward Sapir, 16 vols. Ed. by Edward Sapir. lib. bdg. write for info. (0-89925-138-2) Mouton.

***Collected Works of Edward Sapir Vol. 4: Ethnology.** Ed. by Regna Darnell & Judith T. Irvine. LC 94-26271. (Collected Works of Edward Sapir Ser.: Vol. 4). 963p. (C). 1994. lib. bdg. 260.00 (3-11-012858-6) Mouton.

Collected Works of Edward Sapir, Vol. VI: American Indian Languages II, 16 vols. Ed. by Victor Golla. LC 89-13233. 559p. (C). 1991. lib. bdg. 170.00 (3-11-012572-2) Mouton.

Collected Works of Edward Sapir, Vol. VII: Wishram Texts & Ethnography, 16 vols. Ed. by William Bright & Philip Sapir. 518p. (C). 1990. lib. bdg. 117.00 (3-11-012328-2) Mouton.

Collected Works of Edward Sapir, Vol. 10: Southern Paiute & Ute Linguistics & Ethnography. Ed. by William Bright. (Illus.). 932p. 1992. lib. bdg. 290.00 (3-11-013543-4) Mouton.

Collected Works of Effie Waller Smith. Effie W. Smith. (Schomburg Library of Nineteenth-Century Black Women Writers). 386p. 1991. 29.95 (0-19-506197-7) OUP.

Collected Works of Erasmus, Vol. 71. Ed. by J. K. Sowards. LC 74-6326. 190p. 1993. 85.00 (0-8020-2869-1) U of Toronto Pr.

Collected Works of Erasmus: Literary & Educational Writings, 2 vols., Set. Desiderius Erasmus. Ed. by J. Kelley Sowards. (Collected Works of Erasmus: Vols. 25 & 26). 752p. 1985. 110.00 (0-8020-5521-4) U of Toronto Pr.

***Collected Works of Erasmus: Paraphrase on The Acts of The Apostles.** Erasmus. Ed. by John J. Bateman. Tr. by Robert D. Sider. Vol. 50. 389p. 1995. 95.00 (0-8020-0664-7) U of Toronto Pr.

Collected Works of Erasumus, Vol. 56: New Scholarship. Desiderius Erasmus. LC 74-6326. 480p. 1994. 110.00 (0-8020-2803-9) U of Toronto Pr.

Collected Works of Eugene Arden. Eugene Arden. (Illus.). 112p. (Orig.). 1990. write for info. (0-933691-03-3) U Mich-Dearborn.

Collected Works of Eugene Paul Wigner. Ed. & Anno. by Alvin M. Weinberg. LC 92-38376. 1992. 129.00 (0-387-55343-6) Spr-Verlag.

Collected Works of Eugene Paul Wigner. Ed. by Arthur S. Wightman. LC 93-14276. 1993. 149.00 (0-387-56560-4) Spr-Verlag.

***Collected Works of Eugene Paul Wigner Vol VI, Pt. B: Historical Reflections & Syntheses.** J. Mehra. 640p. 1994. 148.00 (0-387-56986-3) Spr-Verlag.

Collected Works of Ezra H. Heywood. Ed. by Martin Blatt. 392p. 1985. 35.00 (0-87730-013-5) M&S Pr.

Collected Works of Freeman Dyson. Freeman Dyson. (Collected & Selected Works). 500p. (C). 1994. text ed. 30.00 (1-57146-004-7) Intl Pr Boston.

Collected Works of G. K. Chesterton. G. K. Chesterton. Ed. by Lawrence Clipper. LC 85-81511. Vol. XXXV. 650p. (Orig.). 1992. 39.95 (0-89870-366-2) Ignatius Pr.

Collected Works of G. K. Chesterton, Vol. XXXV. G. K. Chesterton. Ed. by Lawrence Clipper. LC 85-81511. 650p. (Orig.). 1992. pap. 24.95 (0-89870-367-0) Ignatius Pr.

Collected Works of G. K. Chesterton: Collected Poetry, Vol. X, Pt. 1. Ed. by Aidan Mackey. 565p. Date not set. 39.95 (0-89870-390-5); pap. 24.95 (0-89870-391-3) Ignatius Pr.

Collected Works of G. K. Chesterton, Vol. I: Heretics, Orothodoxy, Blatchford Controversies. G. K. Chesterton. LC 85-81511. 397p. 1986. 29.95 (0-89870-077-9); pap. 16.95 (0-89870-079-5) Ignatius Pr.

Collected Works of G. K. Chesterton, Vol. II: The Everlasting Man, St. Francis of Assisi, St. Thomas Aquinas, Vol. II. G. K. Chesterton. Ed. by George Marlin & Rutler Azar. LC 85-81511. 553p. 1986. 39.95 (0-89870-116-3); pap. 19.95 (0-89870-117-1) Ignatius Pr.

Collected Works of G. K. Chesterton, Vol. III: The Catholic Church & Conversion; Where All Roads Lead; The Well & the Shallows & Others. G. K. Chesterton. Ed. by George Marlin. LC 85-81511. 579p. (Orig.). 1990. text ed. 39.95 (0-89870-310-7); pap. text ed. 24.95 (0-89870-311-5) Ignatius Pr.

Collected Works of G. K. Chesterton, Vol. IV: What's Wrong with the World, Superstition of Divorce, Etc. G. K. Chesterton & James V. Schall. LC 85-81511. 443p. 1987. 39.95 (0-89870-146-5); pap. 24.95 (0-89870-147-3) Ignatius Pr.

Collected Works of G. K. Chesterton, Vol. V: Outline of Sanity, Etc. G. K. Chesterton. Ed. by George Marlin et al. LC 85-81511. 663p. (Orig.). 1987. 39.95 (0-89870-171-6); pap. 24.95 (0-89870-170-8) Ignatius Pr.

Collected Works of G. K. Chesterton, Vol. VI: The Club of Queer Trades; The Man Who Was Thursday; The Ball & the Cross. G. K. Chesterton. Ed. by George Marlin. LC 85-81511. (Illus.). 636p. (Orig.). 1991. 39.95 (0-89870-364-6); pap. 24.95 (0-89870-365-4) Ignatius Pr.

Collected Works of G. K. Chesterton, Vol. XI: Collected Plays & Chesterton on Shaw. G. K. Chesterton. Ed. by Dennis J. Conlon. LC 85-81511. (Illus.). 611p. 1989. 39.95 (0-89870-231-3); pap. 24.95 (0-89870-237-2) Ignatius Pr.

Collected Works of G. K. Chesterton, Vol. XIV: Short Stories, Fairy Tales, Mystery Stories. G. K. Chesterton. LC 85-81511. (Illus.). 808p. 1992. 39.95 (0-89870-400-6); pap. 29.95 (0-89870-401-4) Ignatius Pr.

Collected Works of G. K. Chesterton, Vol. XVI: The Autobiography, Vol. XVI. G. K. Chesterton. Ed. by George Marlin. LC 85-81511. (Illus.). 341p. 1988. 29.95 (0-89870-200-3); pap. 16.95 (0-89870-199-6) Ignatius Pr.

Collected Works of G. K. Chesterton, Vol. XVIII: Robert Louis Stevenson, Chaucer, Leo Tolstoy, Thomas Carlyle. G. K. Chesterton. LC 85-81511. 375p. 1991. 29.95 (0-89870-373-5); pap. 19.95 (0-89870-374-3) Ignatius Pr.

Collected Works of G. K. Chesterton, Vol. XXI: What I Saw in America, The Resurrection of Rome, Sidelights. G. K. Chesterton. Ed. by George Marlin. LC 85-81511. 667p. (Orig.). 1990. 34.95 (0-89870-271-2); pap. 24.95 (0-89870-272-0) Ignatius Pr.

Collected Works of G. K. Chesterton, Vol. XXIX: The Illustrated London News, 1911-1913. G. K. Chesterton. LC 85-81511. 617p. (Orig.). 1988. 39.95 (0-89870-173-2); pap. 24.95 (0-89870-172-4) Ignatius Pr.

Collected Works of G. K. Chesterton, Vol. XXVII: The Illustrated London News, 1905-1907. G. K. Chesterton. Ed. by Lawrence Clipper. LC 85-81511. 623p. 1986. 39.95 (0-89870-118-X); pap. 24.95 (0-89870-119-8) Ignatius Pr.

Collected Works of G. K. Chesterton, Vol. XXVIII: The Illustrated London News, 1908-1910. G. K. Chesterton. Ed. by Lawrence Clipper. LC 85-81511. 669p. 1987. 39.95 (0-89870-137-6); pap. 24.95 (0-89870-138-4) Ignatius Pr.

Collected Works of G. K. Chesterton, Vol. XXX: Illustrated London News, 1914-1916. Gilbert K. Chesterton. Ed. by Lawrence Clipper. LC 85-81511. 579p. 1988. 39.95 (0-89870-198-8); pap. text ed. 24.95 (0-89870-197-X) Ignatius Pr.

Collected Works of G. K. Chesterton, Vol. XXXI: Illustrated London News, 1917-1919. G. K. Chesterton. Ed. by Lawrence Clipper. LC 85-81511. (Illus.). 597p. (Orig.). 1989. 39.95 (0-89870-232-1); pap. 24.95 (0-89870-238-0) Ignatius Pr.

Collected Works of G. K. Chesterton, Vol. XXXII: Illustrated London News, 1920-1922. G. K. Chesterton. Ed. by Lawrence Clipper. LC 85-81511. 609p. (Orig.). 1989. text ed. 39.95 (0-89870-245-3); pap. text ed. 24.95 (0-89870-244-5) Ignatius Pr.

Collected Works of G. K. Chesterton, Vol. XXXIII: The Illustrated London News, 1923-1925. G. K. Chesterton. Ed. by Lawrence Clipper. LC 85-81511. 699p. (Orig.). 1990. text ed. 39.95 (0-89870-273-9); pap. text ed. 24.95 (0-89870-274-7) Ignatius Pr.

Collected Works of G. K. Chesterton, Volume XV: Chesterton on Dickens. G. K. Chesterton. LC 85-81511. 573p. (Orig.). 1989. 39.95 (0-89870-257-7); pap. text ed. 24.95 (0-89870-258-5) Ignatius Pr.

Collected Works of George E. P. Box, Vol. I. George E. Box. Ed. by George C. Tiao. 688p. (C). 1984. text ed. 59.95 (0-534-03307-5) Chapman & Hall.

Collected Works of George E. P. Box, Vol. II. George E. Box. Ed. by George C. Tiao. 736p. (C). 1984. text ed. 59.95 (0-534-03308-3) Chapman & Hall.

Collected Works of George W. Cable, 19 vols., Set. George W. Cable. Incl. Old Creole Days. 1879. reprint ed. 10.00 (0-403-03056-0); Grandissimes. 1880. reprint ed. 79.00 (0-403-02979-1); Madame Delphine. 1881. reprint ed. 9.00 (0-403-02287-8); Creoles of Louisiana. 1884. reprint ed. 69.00 (0-403-04550-9); Doctor Sevier. 1885. reprint ed. 19.00 (0-685-04688-5); Silent South. 1885. reprint ed. 49.00 (0-403-04551-7); Bonaventure. 1888. reprint ed. 10.00 (0-403-02974-0); Strange True Stories of Louisiana. 1889. reprint ed. 69.00 (0-403-02952-X); Negro Question. 1890. reprint ed. 59.00 (0-403-04553-3); John March, Southerner. 1894. reprint ed. 69.00 (0-403-04554-1); Strong Hearts. 1899. reprint ed. 29.00 (0-403-02990-2); Cavalier. 1901. reprint ed. 14.00 (0-403-02956-2); Bylow Hill. 1902. reprint ed. 14.00 (0-403-02297-5); Kinkaid's Battery. 1908. reprint ed. 49.00 (0-403-04555-X); Posson Jone & Pere Raphael. 1909. reprint ed. 29.00 (0-403-02950-3); Gideon's Band: A Tale of the Mississippi. 1914. reprint ed. 69.00 (0-403-02959-7); Amateur Garden. 1914. reprint ed. 89.00 (0-686-01561-4); Flower of the Chapdelaines. 1918. reprint ed. 69.00 (0-403-02991-0); Lovers of Louisiana. 1918. reprint ed. 69.00 (0-403-04557-6); 995.00 (0-686-01544-4) Somerset Pub.

Collected Works of Gustav Stickley. rev. ed. Ed. by Stephen Gray. (Mission Furniture Catalogues Ser.: No. 5). 176p. 1989. pap. 20.00 (0-940326-14-0) Turn of Cent.

Collected Works of Hamlin Garland, 45 vols. Hamlin Garland. 2,395.00x (0-403-03459-0) Somerset Pub.

Collected Works of Hamlin Garland. Incl. Boy Life on the Prairie. Hamlin Garland. 1899. reprint ed. 59.00 (0-403-04596-7); Her Mountain Lover. Hamlin Garland. 1901. reprint ed. 59.00 (0-403-04597-5); Captain of the Grayhorse Troop. Hamlin Garland. 1902. reprint ed. 39.00 (0-403-02966-X); Hesper. Hamlin Garland. 1903. reprint ed. 39.00 (0-403-02951-1); Light of the Star. Hamlin Garland. 1904. reprint ed. 29.00 (0-403-02980-5); Tyranny of the Dark. Hamlin Garland. 1905. reprint ed. 39.00 (0-403-02283-5); Witch's Gold. Hamlin Garland. 1906. reprint ed. 59.00 (0-686-01489-8); Long Trail. Hamlin Garland. 1907. reprint ed. 39.00 (0-686-01490-1); Money Magic. Hamlin Garland. 1907. reprint ed. 39.00 (0-403-02988-0); Shadow World. Hamlin Garland. 1908. reprint ed. 69.00 (0-403-04600-9); Moccasin Ranch. Hamlin Garland. 1909. reprint ed. 25.00 (0-403-02282-7); Cavanaugh, Forest Ranger. Hamlin Garland. 1910. reprint ed. 25.00 (0-403-02985-6); Other Main Travelled Roads. Hamlin Garland. 1910. reprint ed. 69.00 (0-403-02975-9); Victor Ollnee's Disciple. Hamlin Garland. 1911. reprint ed. 25.00 (0-403-02970-8); Forester's Daughter. Hamlin Garland. 1914. reprint ed. 24.00 (0-403-04601-7); Under the Wheel. 1890. reprint ed. 59.00 (0-403-04602-5); Main Travelled Roads. 1891. reprint ed. 69.00 (0-403-02981-3); Member of the Third House. 1892. reprint ed. 69.00 (0-403-04603-3); Jason Edwards. 1892. reprint ed. 69.00 (0-403-04604-1); Little Norsk. 1892. reprint ed. 59.00 (0-403-04605-X); Spoil of Office. 1892. reprint ed. 69.00 (0-403-04606-8); Prairie Folks. 1899. reprint ed. 59.00 (0-403-04607-6); Prairie Songs. 1893. reprint ed. 59.00 (0-403-04608-4); Crumbling Idols. 1894. reprint ed. 59.00 (0-403-04609-2); Rose of Dutcher's Cooly. 1895. reprint ed. 10.00 (0-403-00211-7); Wayside Courtships. 1897. reprint ed. 16.00 (0-403-04610-6); Ulysses S. Grant. 1898. reprint ed. 79.00 (0-403-04611-4); Spirit of Sweetwater. 1898. reprint ed. 59.00 (0-403-04612-2); Trail of the Goldseekers. 1899. reprint ed. 39.00 (0-403-04613-0); Eagle's Heart. 1900. reprint ed. 39.00 (0-403-02987-2); They of the High Trails. 1916. reprint ed. 39.00 (0-403-04614-9); Son of the Middle Border. 1917. reprint ed. 39.00 (0-403-02998-8); Daughter of the Middle Border. 1921. reprint ed. 79.00 (0-403-02968-6); Pioneer Mother. 1922. reprint ed. 59.00 (0-403-04615-7); Book of the American Indian. 1923. reprint ed. 79.00 (0-403-04616-5); Trail Markers of the Middle Border. 1926. reprint ed. 69.00 (0-403-00984-7); Westward March of American Settlement. 1927. reprint ed. 39.00 (0-403-04617-3); Back Trailers from the Middle Border. 1928. reprint ed. 69.00 (0-403-02986-4); Roadside Meetings. 1930. reprint ed. 39.00 (0-403-02982-1); Companions of the Trail. 1931. reprint ed. 69.00 (0-403-02978-3); My Friendly Contemporaries. 1932. reprint ed. 69.00 (0-403-00982-0); Afternoon Neighbors. 1934. reprint ed. 69.00 (0-403-04618-1); Iowa, O Iowa. reprint ed. 69.00 (0-403-04619-X); Forty Years of Psychic Research. 1936. reprint ed. 69.00 (0-403-04620-3); Mystery of the Buried Crosses. 1939. reprint ed. 59.00x (0-403-04621-1); write for info. (0-318-55748-7) Somerset Pub.

Collected Works of Hamlin Garland, 45 vols. Hamlin Garland. 1988. reprint ed. lib. bdg. 1,900.00x (0-7812-1213-8) Rprt Serv.

Collected Works of Harold Clurman. Ed. by Glenn Young & Marjorie Loggia. (Illus.). 1008p. 1994. 49.95 (1-55783-132-7) Applause Theatre Bk Pubs.

An Asterisk (*) at the beginning of an entry indicates that the title is appearing in BIP for the first time.

Collected Works of Harold Frederic, 14 vols., Set. Harold Frederic. Incl. Seth's Brother's Wife. 1887. reprint ed. 13.00 (*0-686-01530-4*); Lawton Girl. 1890. reprint ed. 69.00 (*0-686-01531-2*); In the Valley. 1890. reprint ed. 69.00 (*0-686-01532-0*); Young Emperor: William the Second of Germany. 1891. reprint ed. 69.00 (*0-686-01533-9*); Return of O'Mahony. 1892. reprint ed. 69.00 (*0-686-01534-7*); New Exodus. 1892. reprint ed. 69.00 (*0-686-01535-5*); Copperhead. 1893. reprint ed. 69.00 (*0-686-01536-3*); Marsena & Other Stories of the Wartime. 1894. reprint ed. 69.00 (*0-686-01537-1*); Mrs. Albert Grundy. 1896. reprint ed. 69.00 (*0-686-01538-X*); Damnation of Theron Ware. 1896. reprint ed. 69.00 (*0-686-01539-8*); March Hares. 1896. reprint ed. 69.00 (*0-686-01540-1*); Deserter & Other Stories. 1898. reprint ed. 69.00 (*0-686-01541-X*); Gloria Mundi. 1898. reprint ed. 69.00 (*0-686-01542-8*); Market Place. 1899. reprint ed. 69.00x (*0-686-01543-6*); 895.00x (*0-686-01529-0*) Somerset Pub.

Collected Works of Henry Woodfin Grady. Henry W. Grady. 1992. reprint ed. lib. bdg. 75.00 (*0-7812-2936-7*) Rprt Serv.

Collected Works of Hidehiko Yamabe. R. P. Boas. 154p. 1967. text ed. 119.00 (*0-677-00610-1*) Gordon & Breach.

Collected Works of J. G. Frazer, 28 vols. Intro. by Robert Ackerman. 11670p. (C). 1994. text ed. 2,750.00 (*0-7007-0318-7*, Pub. by Curzon Pr UK) Humanities.

Collected Works of J. Krishnamurti, 17 vols. J. Krishnamurti. Ed. by Krishnamurti Foundation of America Staff. (Orig.). (C). 1992. Per vol. pap. 14.95 (*0-685-60161-7*) Kendall-Hunt.

Collected Works of J. Krishnamurti, Vol. 1: 1933-1934. Krishnamurti. 224p. (C). 1991. per., pap. text ed. 14.95 (*0-8403-6341-9*) Kendall-Hunt.

Collected Works of J. Krishnamurti, Vol. 12: 1961. J. Krishnamurti. 368p. 1992. per., pap. text ed. 14.95 (*0-8403-6286-2*) Kendall-Hunt.

Collected Works of J. Krishnamurti, Vol. 7: 1952-1953. J. Krishnamurti. 368p. (C). 1991. per., pap. text ed. 14.95 (*0-8403-6257-9*) Kendall-Hunt.

Collected Works of J. Krishnamurti, (1934-1935), Vol. 2. J. Krishnamurti. 272p. (C). 1991. per., pap. text ed. 14.95 (*0-8403-6235-8*) Kendall-Hunt.

Collected Works of J. Krishnamurti, (1936-1944), Vol. 3. J. Krishnamurti. 288p. (C). 1991. per., pap. text ed. 14.95 (*0-8403-6236-6*) Kendall-Hunt.

Collected Works of J. Krishnamurti, (1945-1948), Vol. 4. J. Krishnamurti. 240p. (C). 1991. per., pap. text ed. 14.95 (*0-8403-6237-4*) Kendall-Hunt.

Collected Works of J. Krishnamurti, (1948-1949), Vol. 5. J. Krishnamurti. 400p. (C). 1991. per., pap. text ed. 14.95 (*0-8403-6238-2*) Kendall-Hunt.

Collected Works of J. Krishnamurti, (1949-1952), Vol. 6. J. Krishnamurti. 400p. (C). 1991. per., pap. text ed. 14.95 (*0-8403-6262-5*) Kendall-Hunt.

Collected Works of J. Krishnamurti, (1953-1955), Vol. 8. J. Krishnamurti. 384p. (C). 1991. per., pap. text ed. 14.95 (*0-8403-6266-8*) Kendall-Hunt.

Collected Works of J. Krishnamurti, (1955-1956), Vol. 9. J. Krishnamurti. 320p. (C). 1991. per., pap. text ed. 14.95 (*0-8403-6260-9*) Kendall-Hunt.

Collected Works of J. Krishnamurti, (1956-1957), Vol. 10. J. Krishnamurti. 204p. (C). 1991. per., pap. text ed. 14.95 (*0-8403-6268-4*) Kendall-Hunt.

Collected Works of J. Krishnamurti, (1958-1960), Vol. 11. J. Krishnamurti. 432p. (C). 1991. per., pap. text ed. 14.95 (*0-8403-6272-2*) Kendall-Hunt.

Collected Works of J. Krishnamurti, (1962-1963), Vol. 13. J. Krishnamurti. 384p. (C). 1992. per., pap. text ed. 14.95 (*0-8403-6287-0*) Kendall-Hunt.

Collected Works of J. Krishnamurti, (1963-1964), Vol. 14. J. Krishnamurti. 352p. (C). 1992. per., pap. text ed. 14.95 (*0-8403-6288-9*) Kendall-Hunt.

Collected Works of J. Krishnamurti, (1964-1965), Vol. 15. J. Krishnamurti. 384p. (C). 1992. per., pap. text ed. 14.95 (*0-8403-6282-X*) Kendall-Hunt.

Collected Works of J. Krishnamurti, (1965-1966), Vol. 16. J. Krishnamurti. 336p. (C). 1992. per., pap. text ed. 14.95 (*0-8403-6307-9*) Kendall-Hunt.

Collected Works of J. Krishnamurti, (1966-1967), Vol. 17. J. Krishnamurti. 320p. (C). 1992. per., pap. text ed. 14.95 (*0-8403-6314-1*) Kendall-Hunt.

***Collected Works of J. R. McCulloch, 8 vols., Set.** 1995. boxed 820.00 (*0-415-11352-0*, C0433, Pub. by Thoemmes Pr UK) Routledge.

Collected Works of J. Richard Buchi. Ed. by S. MacLane & D. J. Siefkes. (Illus.). 705p. 1989. 69.00 (*0-387-97064-9*, 3061) Spr-Verlag.

Collected Works of Jack London. Jack London. Ed. by Steven J. Kasdin. 1058p. 1991. 24.95 (*0-88029-596-1*) Marboro Bks.

Collected Works of James Rush, 4 vols., Set. James Rush. Ed. by Melvin H. Bernstein. 1925p. 1974. 115.00 (*0-87730-008-9*) M&S Pr.

***Collected Works of James Steuart, 7 vols., Set.** 3000p. 1995. boxed 720.00 (*0-415-11353-9*, C0431, Pub. by Thoemmes Pr UK) Routledge.

Collected Works of John Adolphus Etzler. John A. Etzler. LC 77-7124. 1977. reprint ed. 75.00x (*0-8201-1290-9*) Schol Facsimiles.

Collected Works of John Beauchamp Jones. John B. Jones. (Notable American Authors Ser.). 1992. reprint ed. lib. bdg. write for info. (*0-7812-3511-1*) Rprt Serv.

Collected Works of John Dewey, 1882-1953: Index. Ed. by Anne S. Sharpe et al. 440p. 1991. 50.00 (*0-8093-1728-1*) S Ill U Pr.

Collected Works of John Hill Hewitt. Ed. by N. Lee Orr & Lynn W. Bertrand. LC 94-76. (Nineteenth-Century American Musical Theater Ser.: No. 6). 328p. 1994. reprint ed. 102.00 (*0-8153-1370-5*) Garland.

Collected Works of John Jay Chapman, 12 vols., Set. John J. Chapman. Ed. by Melvin H. Bernstein. (Illus.). 4350p. 1970. 265.00 (*0-87730-003-8*) M&S Pr.

Collected Works of John Millington Synge, 4 Vols. Incl. Vol. I. Poems. Ed. by Robin Skelton. 128p. 1982. 16.95 (*0-8132-0563-8*); Vol. I. Poems. Ed. by Robin Skelton. 128p. 1982. pap. 8.95 (*0-8132-0562-X*); Vol. II. Prose. Ed. by Alan Price. 412p. 1982. 30.95 (*0-8132-0565-4*); Vol. II. Prose. Ed. by Alan Price. 412p. 1982. pap. 10.95 (*0-8132-0564-6*); Vol. III. Plays. Ed. by Ann Saddlemyer. 282p. 1982. 21.95 (*0-8132-0567-0*); Vol. III. Plays BK. 1. Ed. by Ann Saddlemyer. 282p. 1982. pap. 10.95 (*0-8132-0566-2*); Vol. IV. Plays. Ed. by Ann Saddlemyer. 394p. 1982. 30.95 (*0-8132-0569-7*); Vol. IV. Plays BK. 2. Ed. by Ann Saddlemyer. 394p. 1982. pap. 10.95 (*0-8132-0568-9*); (Illus.). 1982. write for info. (*0-318-56581-1*) Cath U Pr.

Collected Works of John P. Kennedy, 10 vols., Set. John P. Kennedy. 4566p. reprint ed. lib. bdg. 616.20 (*0-685-13863-1*, 05102665, Pub. by Georg Olms GW) Lubrecht & Cramer.

***Collected Works of John Reed.** John Reed. LC 94-32160. 1995. write for info. (*0-679-60114-7*, Modern Lib) Random.

***Collected Works of John Reed.** John Reed. 1995. 20.00 (*0-679-60144-9*, Modern Lib) Random.

Collected Works of John W. De Forest, 17 vols., Set. John W. De Forest. Incl. History of the Indians of Connecticut. 1851. reprint ed. 69.00 (*0-403-00426-8*); Oriental Acquaintance. 1856. reprint ed. 59.00 (*0-403-04562-2*); European Acquaintance. 1858. reprint ed. 59.00 (*0-403-04563-0*); Seacliff. 1859. reprint ed. 59.00 (*0-403-04564-9*); Miss Ravenel's Conversion from Secession to Loyalty. 1867. reprint ed. 69.00 (*0-403-03090-0*); Overland. 1871. reprint ed. 69.00 (*0-403-04565-7*); Kate Beaumont. 1872. reprint ed. 69.00 (*0-403-04566-5*); Wetherel Affair. 1873. reprint ed. 69.00 (*0-403-04567-3*); Honest John Vane. 1875. reprint ed. 69.00 (*0-403-04568-1*); Playing the Mischief. 1875. reprint ed. 69.00 (*0-403-04569-X*); Justine's Lovers. 1878. reprint ed. 69.00 (*0-403-04570-3*); Irene, the Missionary. 1879. reprint ed. 69.00 (*0-403-04571-1*); Bloody Chasm. 1881. reprint ed. 69.00 (*0-403-04572-X*); Lover's Revolt. 1898. reprint ed. 69.00 (*0-403-04573-8*); Deforests of Avesnes. 1900. reprint ed. 69.00 (*0-403-04574-6*); Downing Legends. 1901. reprint ed. 59.00 (*0-403-04575-4*); Poems: Medley & Palestina. 1902. reprint ed. 69.00x (*0-403-04576-2*); 995.00x (*0-403-03455-8*) Somerset Pub.

Collected Works of John W. Tukey, 6 vols., Vol. I. John W. Tukey. Ed. by William S. Cleveland et al. LC 84-15277. 689p. (C). 1984. 59.95 (*0-534-03303-2*) Chapman & Hall.

Collected Works of John W. Tukey, 6 vols., Vol. II. John W. Tukey. Ed. by William S. Cleveland et al. LC 84-15277. 642p. (C). 1985. 59.95 (*0-534-03304-0*) Chapman & Hall.

Collected Works of John W. Tukey, 6 vols., Vol. III. John W. Tukey. Ed. by William S. Cleveland et al. LC 84-15277. 640p. (C). 1986. 59.95 (*0-534-03305-9*) Chapman & Hall.

Collected Works of John W. Tukey, 6 vols., Vol. IV. John W. Tukey. Ed. by William S. Cleveland et al. LC 84-15277. 624p. (C). 1986. 59.95 (*0-534-05101-4*) Chapman & Hall.

Collected Works of John W. Tukey, 6 vols., Vol. V. John W. Tukey. Ed. by William S. Cleveland et al. LC 84-15277. 464p. (C). 1988. 59.75 (*0-534-05102-2*) Chapman & Hall.

Collected Works of John W. Tukey, 6 vols., Vol. VI. John W. Tukey. Ed. by William S. Cleveland et al. LC 84-15277. 736p. (C). 1990. 59.95 (*0-534-05103-0*) Chapman & Hall.

***Collected Works of John W. Tukey: Multiple Comparisons, 1948-1983, 8 Vols.** John W. Tukey & John Tukey Wilder. Ed. by Henry I. Braun. LC 84-15277. 485p. 1994. 62.95 (*0-412-05121-4*) Chapman & Hall.

Collected Works of John W. Tukey, Vol. 7: Factorial & Anova. John W. Tukey. Ed. by D. R. Cox. 305p. (C). 1992. text ed. 54.95 (*0-534-05104-9*) Chapman & Hall.

Collected Works of Joseph Kirkland, 3 vols., Set. Joseph Kirkland. Incl. Zury, the Meanest Man in Spring County. 1887. reprint ed. 69.00 (*0-685-73438-2*); McVeys. 1888. reprint ed. 69.00 (*0-685-73439-0*); Captain of Company K. 1890. reprint ed. 69.00 (*0-685-73440-4*); 195.00x (*0-686-01679-3*); Incl. reprint ed. 69.00 (*0-685-73438-2*); reprint ed. 69.00 (*0-685-73439-0*); reprint ed. 69.00 (*0-685-73440-4*); 69.00 (*0-318-55751-7*) Somerset Pub.

Collected Works of Joseph Norton Ireland. Joseph N. Ireland. (Notable American Authors Ser.). 1992. reprint ed. lib. bdg. write for info. (*0-7812-3338-0*) Rprt Serv.

Collected Works of Joseph Rodman Drake: Life & Works. Joseph R. Drake. Ed. by F. L. Pleadwell. (Notable American Authors Ser.). 1992. reprint ed. 1936. lib. bdg. 75.00 (*0-318-67705-9*) Rprt Serv.

Collected Works of Joseph Rodman Drake: The Culprit Fay & Other Stories. Joseph R. Drake. (Notable American Authors Ser.). 1992. reprint ed. 1835. lib. bdg. 75.00 (*0-7812-2692-9*, 1512) Rprt Serv.

Collected Works of Joseph Sheridan Le Fanu. Joseph S. Le Fanu. Ed. by Devendra P. Varma. (Illus.). 1977. 1,327.50 (*0-405-09190-7*) Ayer.

Collected Works of Josiah Tucker. (Collected Works). 3008p. 1993. 500.00 (*0-415-08306-0*, B2564) Routledge.

Collected Works of Julia (Ward) Howe. Julia W. Howe. (Notable American Authors Ser.). 1992. reprint ed. lib. bdg. write for info. (*0-7812-3211-2*) Rprt Serv.

Collected Works of Justice Holmes: Complete Published Writings & Selected Judicial Opinions of Oliver Wendell Holmes. Oliver W. Holmes, Jr. 1995. lib. bdg. 175.00 (*0-226-34966-7*) U Ch Pr.

Collected Works of Justice Holmes Vols. 1-3: The Complete Public Writings of Oliver Wendell Holmes. Ed. by Sheldon M. Novick. 1994. write for info. (*0-226-34965-9*) U Ch Pr.

***Collected Works of Karl Marx & Frederick Engels Vol. 36, Vol. 36.** (Das Kaptal Ser.: Vol. 2). Date not set. 24.95 (*0-614-01877-3*) Intl Pubs Co.

Collected Works of Karl Marx & Frederick Engels: Correspondence, Vols. 38-46. Incl. Vol. 38. 1844-1851. Karl Marx & Friedrich Engels. LC 73-84671. (Illus.). 712p. 1982. 24.95 (*0-7178-0538-7*); Vol. 39. 1852-55. Karl Marx & Friedrich Engels. LC 73-84671. (Illus.). 764p. 1983. 24.95 (*0-7178-0539-5*); Vol. 40. 1856-59. Karl Marx & Friedrich Engels. LC 73-84671. (Illus.). 780p. 1983. 24.95 (*0-7178-0540-9*); Vol. 41. 1860-1864. Karl Marx & Friedrich Engels. LC 73-84671. 24.95 (*0-7178-0541-7*); Vol. 42. Karl Marx & Friedrich Engels. Tr. by Christopher Upward & John Peet. LC 73-84671. (Illus.). xl, 768p. 1988. 24.95 (*0-7178-0542-5*); Vol. 43. 1868-1870. Karl Marx & Friedrich Engels. LC 73-84671. xxxix, 760p. 1988. 24.95 (*0-7178-0543-3*); Vol. 44. 1870-1873. Karl Marx & Friedrich Engels. LC 73-84671. (Illus.). 800p. 1990. 24.95 (*0-7178-0544-1*); Vol. 45. 1874-1879. Karl Marx & Friedrich Engels. LC 73-84671. 623p. 1992. 24.95 (*0-7178-0545-X*); Vol. 46. 1880-83. Karl Marx & Friedrich Engels. LC 73-84671. xxx, 606p. 1993. (*0-7178-0546-8*); LC 73-84671. 24.95 (*0-318-65971-9*) Intl Pubs Co.

Collected Works of Karl Marx & Frederick Engels: Economic Writings, Vols. 28-34. Incl. Vol. 28. Karl Marx. Tr. by Ernst Wangermann. LC 73-84671. (Illus.). 590p. 1987. 24.95 (*0-7178-0528-X*); Vol. 29. Karl Marx. Ed. by Lev Golman. Tr. by Victor Schnittke & Kuri Sdobnikov. LC 73-84671. (Illus.). xxiv, 592p. 1988. 24.95 (*0-7178-0529-8*); Vol. 30. Karl Marx & Frederick Engels. LC 73-84671. 1989. (*0-7178-0530-1*); Vol. 31. Karl Marx & Frederick Engels. LC 73-84671. 1989. (*0-7178-0531-X*); Vol. 32. Karl Marx. LC 73-84671. 1990. (*0-7178-0532-8*); Vol. 33. 1861-63. LC 73-84671. 1992. (*0-7178-0533-6*); Vol. 34. LC 73-84671. 560p. 1993. (*0-7178-0534-4*); LC 73-84671. 24.95 (*0-318-65883-6*) Intl Pubs Co.

***Collected Works of Karl Marx & Frederick Engels Vol. 47: Engels Letters 1883-1886.** Friedrich Engels. 760p. 1994. 24.95 (*0-7178-0547-6*) Intl Pubs Co.

Collected Works of Karl Marx & Frederick Engels, Vols. 1-27: General Works. Incl. Vol. 1. Marx, 1835-43. Karl Marx. LC 73-84671. (Illus.). 840p. 1975. 24.95 (*0-7178-0407-0*); Vol. 2. Engels, 1838-42. Frederick Engels. LC 73-84671. (Eng & Ger., Illus.). 703p. 1975. 24.95 (*0-7178-0413-5*); Vol. 3. 1843-44. Karl Marx & Frederick Engels. LC 73-84671. (Illus.). 694p. 1975. (*0-7178-0414-3*); Vol. 4. 1844-45. Karl Marx & Frederick Engels. LC 73-84671. (Illus.). 808p. 1975. (*0-7178-0455-0*); Vol. 5. 1845-47. Karl Marx & Frederick Engels. LC 73-84671. (Illus.). 687p. 1976. (*0-7178-0505-0*); Vol. 6. 1845-48. Karl Marx & Frederick Engels. LC 73-84671. (Illus.). 805p. 1976. (*0-7178-0506-9*); Vol. 7. 1848. Karl Marx & Frederick Engels. LC 73-84671. (Illus.). 750p. 1977. (*0-7178-0507-7*); Vol. 8. 1848-49. Karl Marx & Frederick Engels. LC 73-84671. (Illus.). 688p. 1977. (*0-7178-0508-5*); Vol. 9. 1849. Karl Marx & Frederick Engels. LC 73-84671. (Illus.). 662p. 1978. (*0-7178-0509-3*); Vol. 10. 1849-51. Karl Marx & Frederick Engels. LC 73-84671. (Illus.). 814p. 1978. (*0-7178-0510-7*); Vol. 11. 1851-53. Karl Marx & Frederick Engels. LC 73-84671. (Illus.). 796p. 1979. (*0-7178-0511-5*); Vol. 12. 1853-54. Karl Marx & Frederick Engels. LC 73-84671. (Illus.). 816p. 1979. (*0-7178-0512-3*); Vol. 13. 1854-55. Karl Marx & Frederick Engels. LC 73-84671. (Illus.). 826p. 1980. (*0-7178-0513-1*); Vol. 14. 1855-56. Karl Marx & Frederick Engels. LC 73-84671. (Illus.). 810p. 1980. (*0-7178-0514-X*); Vol. 15. 1856-58. Karl Marx & Frederick Engels. LC 73-84671. 1986. (*0-7178-0515-8*); Vol. 16. 1857-62. Karl Marx & Frederick Engels. LC 73-84671. (Illus.). 682p. 1982. (*0-7178-0518-2*); Vol. 17. 1858-60. Karl Marx & Frederick Engels. LC 73-84671. (Illus.). 800p. 1980. (*0-7178-0516-6*); Vol. 18. 1859-60. Karl Marx & Frederick Engels. LC 73-84671. (Illus.). 704p. 1981. (*0-7178-0517-4*); Vol. 19. 1861-64. Karl Marx & Frederick Engels. LC 73-84671. (Illus.). 456p. 1982. (*0-7178-0519-0*); Vol. 20. 1864-68. Karl Marx & Frederick Engels. LC 73-84671. (Illus.). 614p. 1986. (*0-7178-0520-4*); Vol. 21. 1867-70. Karl Marx & Frederick Engels. LC 73-84671. 645p. 1986. (*0-7178-0521-2*); Vol. 22. 1870-71. Karl Marx & Frederick Engels. Tr. by Barry Selman. LC 73-84671. (Illus.). 785p. 1987. (*0-7178-0522-0*); Vol. 23. 1871-74. Karl Marx & Frederick Engels. LC 73-84671. (Illus.). xxxv, 808p. 1988. (*0-7178-0523-9*); Vol. 24. Karl Marx & Frederick Engels. LC 73-84671. 1989. (*0-7178-0524-7*); Vol. 25. Frederick Engels & Karl Marx. Tr. by Clemens Dutt & Emile Burns. LC 73-84671. (Illus.). 776p. 1987. (*0-7178-0525-5*); Vol. 26. Engels 1882-1889. Karl Marx & Frederick Engels. LC 73-84671. 1991. (*0-7178-0526-3*); Vol. 27. Engels 1890-95. Karl Marx. Tr. by Tatiana Chikileva. Tr. by Ben Fowkes & S. Ryazanskaya. LC 73-84671. (Illus.). 728p. 1992. (*0-7178-0527-1*); LC 73-84671. 24.95 (*0-318-65882-8*) Intl Pubs Co.

Collected Works of Kate Chopin, 4 vols., Set. Kate Chopin. Incl. At Fault. LC 72-78673. 1890. reprint ed. 65.00 (*0-403-04558-4*); Bayou Folk. LC 72-78673. 1894. reprint ed. 65.00 (*0-403-04559-2*); Night at Acadie. LC 72-78673. 1899. 65.00 (*0-403-04560-6*); LC 72-78673. 1899. 225.00 (*0-403-03454-X*) Somerset Pub.

Collected Works of Kurt Godel, Vol. 1. Kurt Godel. Ed. by Solomon Feferman et al. 320p. 1986. 65.00 (*0-19-503964-5*) OUP.

Collected Works of L. S. Vygotsky, Vol. 1: Problems of General Psychology, Including the Volume Thinking & Speech. L. S. Vygotsky. Ed. by R. W. Reiber & A. Carton. Tr. by N. Minick. (Cognition & Language Ser.). 406p. 1988. 49.50 (*0-306-42441-X*, Plenum Pr) Plenum.

Collected Works of L. S. Vygotsky, Vol. 2: Fundamentals of Defectology (Abnormal Psychology & Learning Disabilities. L. S. Vygotsky. (Cognition & Language: A Series in Psycholinguistics). (Illus.). 306p. 1993. 49.50 (*0-306-42442-8*, Plenum Pr) Plenum.

Collected Works of Lawrence W. Macdonald. Lawrence W. Macdonald. Ed. by Abraham Shapiro. (Illus.). 299p. (C). 1992. lib. bdg. 15.00 (*0-943599-56-3*) OEPF.

Collected Works of Lawrence W. Macdonald, Set. Lawrence W. Macdonald. Ed. by Abraham Shapiro. (Illus.). 299p. (C). 1992. lib. bdg. write for info. (*0-943599-55-5*) OEPF.

Collected Works of Lawrence W. Macdonald, Vol. II. Lawrence W. Macdonald. Ed. by Ira Schwartz & Abraham Shapiro. (Illus.). 350p. (C). 1992. lib. bdg. 18.00 (*0-943599-58-X*) OEPF.

Collected Works of Leif Johansen, 2 vols., 1. Ed. by F. R. Forsund. 940p. 1987. 64.00 (*0-444-87859-9*, North Holland) Elsevier.

Collected Works of Leif Johansen, 2 vols., 2. Ed. by F. R. Forsund. 940p. 1987. 64.00 (*0-444-87860-2*, North Holland) Elsevier.

Collected Works of Leif Johansen, 2 vols., Set. Ed. by F. R. Forsund. 940p. 1987. 95.00 (*0-444-87833-5*, North Holland) Elsevier.

Collected Works of Leo Szilard: Scientific Papers. Leo Szilard. Ed. by Bernard T. Feld & Gertrud W. Szilard. 1972. 60.00 (*0-262-06039-6*) MIT Pr.

Collected Works of Lewis Fry Richardson, 2 vols. Lewis F. Richardson. Ed. by O. M. Ashford et al. (Illus.). 500p. (C). 1993. Vol. 1, 500p. 150.00 (*0-521-38297-1*); Vol. 2, 500p. 150.00 (*0-521-38298-X*) Cambridge U Pr.

Collected Works of Lewis George Janes. Lewis G. Janes. (Notable American Authors Ser.). 1992. reprint ed. lib. bdg. write for info. (*0-7812-3485-9*) Rprt Serv.

Collected Works of Lydia Sicher: An Adlerian Perspective. Lydia Sicher. Ed. by Adele K. Davidson. LC 90-26254. 572p. (Orig.). 1991. pap. 24.95 (*0-936609-22-2*) QED Ft Bragg.

Collected Works of Lysander Spooner, 6 vols., Set. Lysander Spooner. Ed. by Charles Shively. 2400p. 1971. 175.00 (*0-87730-006-2*) M&S Pr.

Collected Works of Mahatma Gandhi, 95 vols., Set. Mahatma Gandhi. 48000p. 1983. 1,600.00 (*0-934676-35-6*) Greenlf Bks.

Collected Works of Mahatma Gandhi, 90 vols., Set. Mahatma K. Gandhi. 1,600.00 (*0-318-36652-5*) Asia Bk Corp.

Collected Works of Max Muller, 4 Vols. F. Max Muller. 1986. 140.00 (*0-685-14469-0*, Pub. by Manohar II) S Asia.

Collected Works of Mel C. Thompson, Vol. 3. Mel C. Thompson. 102p. (Orig.). 1991. pap. text ed. 5.00 (*1-879665-09-3*) Cyborg Prods.

Collected Works of Mel C. Thompson: Marching with Idiots. Mel C. Thompson. 101p. (Orig.). 1991. pap. text ed. 5.00 (*1-879665-08-5*) Cyborg Prods.

Collected Works of Mel C. Thompson Vol. 9: Performing Without an Audience. Mel C. Thompson. (Mel C. Thompson's Collected Works). 112p. (Orig.). Date not set. pap. 3.50 (*1-879665-15-8*) Cyborg Prods.

Collected Works of Mel C. Thompson, Vol. IV: God's Magnificent Coward. Mel C. Thompson. 99p. (Orig.). 1991. pap. text ed. 5.00 (*1-879665-10-7*) Cyborg Prods.

Collected Works of Mel C. Thompson, Vol. 1: Things I Wrote Before I Learned to Write. Mel C. Thompson. 98p. (Orig.). 1991. pap. 5.00 (*1-879665-06-9*) Cyborg Prods.

Collected Works of Michal Kalecki, Vol. 2: Capitalism: Economic Dynamics. Michal Kalecki. Ed. by Jerzy Osiatynski. Tr. by Chester A. Kisiel. (Illus.). 650p. 1991. 135.00 (*0-19-828664-3*) OUP.

Collected Works of Michal Kalecki, Vol. 3: Socialism: Functioning & Long-Run Planning. Michal Kalecki. Ed. by Jerzy Osiatynski. Tr. by Bohdan Jimg. (Illus.). 464p. 1993. 89.00 (*0-19-828665-1*) OUP.

Collected Works of Michal Kalecki, Vol. 5: Developing Economies. Michal Kalecki. Ed. by Jerzy Osiatynski. Tr. by Chester A. Kisiel. (Illus.). 272p. (C). 1993. 55.00 (*0-19-828667-8*, 6011) OUP.

Collected Works of Olivia Ward Bush-Banks. Olivia W. Bush-Banks. (Schomburg Library of Nineteenth-Century Black Women Writers). (Illus.). 368p. 1991. 39.95 (*0-19-506196-9*) OUP.

***Collected Works of Oscar Wilde, 15 vols., Set.** (Collected Works). 4918p. 1993. 1,440.95 (*0-415-10584-6*, B3682, Pub. by Thoemmes Pr UK) Routledge.

Collected Works of P. Griffiths. (Collected & Selected Works). 1994. write for info. (*1-57146-015-2*) Intl Pr Boston.

***Collected Works of Paddy Chayefsky, Set.** Paddy Chayefsky. (Orig.). Date not set. boxed, pap. 59.80 (*1-55783-195-5*) Applause Theatre Bk Pubs.

C

An Asterisk (*) at the beginning of an entry indicates that the title is appearing in BIP for the first time. 1365

***Collected Works of Paddy Chayefsky: Screenplays II, Vol. 2.** Paddy Chayefsky. Incl. Vol. 1. Collected Works of Paddy Chayefsky: Screenplays I. 344p. (Orig.). 1994. pap. 16.95 (*1-55783-193-9*); (Collected Works of Paddy Chayefsky: Vol. 3 & 4). 344p. (Orig.). 1994. Set pap. 16.95 (*1-55783-194-7*) Applause Theatre Bk Pubs.

***Collected Works of Paddy Chayefsky: Stage Plays.** Paddy Chayefsky. 448p. (Orig.). 1994. pap. 12.95 (*1-55783-192-0*) Applause Theatre Bk Pubs.

***Collected Works of Paddy Chayefsky: The Screenplays, 2.** Paddy Chayefsky. LC 94-185845. 288p. (Orig.). 1994. pap. 12.95 (*1-55783-191-2*) Applause Theatre Bk Pubs.

Collected Works of Padraic H. Pearse. Padraic H. Pearse. LC 75-28838. reprint ed. 35.00 (*0-404-13827-6*) AMS Pr.

***Collected Works of P.A.M. Dirac: 1924-1948.** P. A. Dirac. Ed. by R. H. Dalitz. (Illus.). 1152p. (C). 1992. write for info. (*0-521-36231-8*) Cambridge U Pr.

***Collected Works of Pat Robertson.** Pat Robertson. 1994. 14.98 (*0-88486-106-6*) Arrowood Pr.

Collected Works of Paul Valery: Monsieur Teste. Tr. by Jackson Mathews. (Bollingen Ser.). 180p. 1989. pap. text ed. 9.95 (*0-691-01879-0*) Princeton U Pr.

Collected Works of Paul Valery: The Outlook for Intelligence. Tr. by Denise Folliot & Jackson Mathews. (Bollingen Ser.). 258p. 1989. pap. text ed. 9.95 (*0-691-01881-2*) Princeton U Pr.

Collected Works of Paul Valery Degas, Manet, Morisot. Tr. by David Paul. (Bollingen Ser.). 298p. 1989. pap. text ed. 9.95 (*0-691-01882-0*) Princeton U Pr.

Collected Works of Paul Valery, Vol. 15: MOI. Paul Valery. Tr. by Marthiel & Jackson Mathews. LC 56-9337. (Bollingen Ser.: Vol. 45). 464p. 1975. 55.00 (*0-691-09936-7*) Princeton U Pr.

Collected Works of Paul Valery, Vol. 3: Plays. Paul Valery. Ed. by Jackson Matthews. (Bollingen Ser.: Vol. 45). 1960. 47.00 (*0-691-09844-1*) Princeton U Pr.

Collected Works of Paul Valery, Vol. 4: Dialogues. Paul Valery. Ed. by Jackson Matthews. (Bollingen Ser.: Vol. 45). 1957. 29.95 (*0-691-09840-9*) Princeton U Pr.

Collected Works of Paul Valery, Vol. 7: Art of Poetry. Paul Valery. Ed. by Jackson Matthews. Tr. by Denise Folliot. LC 84-42940. (Bollingen Ser.: No. 45). 369p. 1985. 47.50 (*0-691-09838-7*) Princeton U Pr.

Collected Works of Paul Valery, Vol. 9: Masters & Friends. Paul Valery. Ed. by Jackson Mathews. Tr. by Martin Turnell. LC 56-9337. (Bollingen Ser.: Vol. 45). 1968. 52.50 (*0-691-09843-3*) Princeton U Pr.

***Collected Works of Pere Menal.** Ed. by M. Castellet & W. Dicks. 656p. 1995. 69.00 (*0-8176-5147-0*) Spr-Verlag.

Collected Works of Philip Hall. Philip Hall. Ed. by Karl W. Gruenberg & James E. Roseblade. (Illus.). 802p. 1988. 125.00 (*0-19-853254-7*) OUP.

Collected Works of Phillis Wheatley. Phillis Wheatley. Ed. by John Shields. (Schomburg Library of Nineteenth-Century Black Women Writers). 384p. 1988. 29.95 (*0-19-505241-2*) OUP.

Collected Works of Phillis Wheatley. Phillis Wheatley. 1989. pap. 11.95 (*0-19-506085-7*) OUP.

Collected Works of Phillis Wheatley. Phillis Wheatley. Ed. by John Shields. (Schomburg Library of Nineteenth-Century Black Women Writers). 384p. 1989. reprint ed. pap. 9.95 (*0-685-37795-4*) OUP.

Collected Works of Ralph Waldo Emerson Vol. 1, Vol. 1. Ralph Waldo Emerson. LC 70-158429. (Illus.). 371p. 1979. reprint ed. pap. 108.10 (*0-7837-1691-5*, 2057221) Bks Demand.

Collected Works of Ralph Waldo Emerson Vol. 2, Vol. 2. Ralph Waldo Emerson. LC 70-158429. (Illus.). 418p. 1979. reprint ed. pap. 120.38 (*0-7837-1692-3*, 2057221) Bks Demand.

Collected Works of Ralph Waldo Emerson, Vol. 3: Essays: Second Series, Vol. 3. Ralph Waldo Emerson. Ed. by Alfred R. Ferguson & Jean F. Carr. (Illus.). 352p. 1984. 39.95 (*0-674-13990-9*) Belknap Pr.

Collected Works of Ralph Waldo Emerson, Vol. 4: Representative Men, Vol. 4. Ralph Waldo Emerson. Ed. by Douglas E. Wilson. (Illus.). 576p. 1987. 42.50 (*0-674-13991-7*) Belknap Pr.

Collected Works of Raoul Bott, Set. Ed. by Robert D. MacPherson. LC 93-36938. (Contemporary Mathematicians Ser.). 1993. write for info. (*0-8176-3701-X*); write for info. (*3-7643-3701-X*) Birkhauser.

Collected Works of Raoul Bott: Topology of Lie Groups - the 1950s, Vol. 1. Ed. by R. D. MacPherson. (Contemporary Mathematicians Ser.). (Illus.). 450p. 1995. 95.00 (*0-8176-3613-7*) Birkhauser.

Collected Works of Richard Hovey. Richard Hovey. (Notable American Authors Ser.). 1992. reprint ed. lib. bdg. write for info. (*0-7812-3187-6*) Rprt Serv.

***Collected Works of Robert Burns, 6 vols., Set.** Ed. by William S. Douglas. (Collected Works). (Illus.). 2550p. 1993. 635.00 (*0-415-09918-8*, B3778, Pub. by Thoemmes Pr UK) Routledge.

Collected Works of Robert Herrick, 25 vols., Set. Robert Herrick. Incl. Man Who Wins. 1897. reprint ed. 29.00 (*0-403-04625-4*); Literary Love Letters & Other Stories. 1897. reprint ed. 69.00 (*0-403-04626-2*); Gospel of Freedom. 1898. reprint ed. 69.00 (*0-403-04627-0*); Love's Dilemmas. 1898. reprint ed. 69.00 (*0-403-04628-9*); Web of Life. 1900. reprint ed. 69.00 (*0-403-04629-7*); Real World. 1901. reprint ed. 69.00 (*0-403-04630-0*); Their Child. 1903. reprint ed. 69.00 (*0-403-04631-9*); Common Lot. 1904. reprint ed. 20.00 (*0-403-04632-7*); Memoirs of an American Citizen. 1905. reprint ed. 29.00 (*0-403-02969-4*); Master of the Inn. 1908. reprint ed. 10.00 (*0-403-03055-2*); Together. 1908. reprint ed. 59.00 (*0-403-03198-2*); Life for a Life. 1910. reprint ed. 49.00 (*0-403-03197-4*); Healer. 1911. reprint ed. 49.00 (*0-403-03193-1*); His Great Adventure. 1913. reprint ed. 59.00 (*0-403-04633-5*); One Woman's Life. 1913. reprint ed. 25.00 (*0-403-04634-3*); Clark's Field. 1914. reprint ed. 69.00 (*0-403-04635-1*); Conscript's Mother. 1916. reprint ed. 59.00 (*0-403-04636-X*); World Decision. 1916. reprint ed. 29.00 (*0-403-03074-9*); Homely Lilla. 1923. reprint ed. 49.00 (*0-403-03050-1*); Waste. 1924. reprint ed. 59.00 (*0-686-01400-6*); Wanderings. 1925. reprint ed. 39.00 (*0-403-04637-8*); Chimes. 1926. reprint ed. 29.00 (*0-403-03194-X*); Little Black Dog. 1931. reprint ed. 39.00 (*0-403-04638-6*); End of Desire. 1932. reprint ed. 30.00 (*0-403-03195-8*); Sometime. 1933. reprint ed. 69.00 (*0-686-01405-7*); 850.00 (*0-685-04691-5*) Somerset Pub.

Collected Works of Rudyard Kipling, 28 Vols, Set. Rudyard Kipling. LC 75-120920. reprint ed. 1,750.00 (*0-404-03740-2*) AMS Pr.

Collected Works of Salomon Bochner, Pt. IV, Vol. 2.4. 446p. 1992. 67.00 (*0-8218-0177-5*, CWORKS-2.4) Am Math.

Collected Works of Samuel Johnson. Samuel Johnson. (Notable American Authors Ser.). 1992. reprint ed. lib. bdg. write for info. (*0-7812-3490-5*) Rprt Serv.

Collected Works of Samuel T. Coleridge, Vol. 1. Samuel Taylor Coleridge. Ed. by K. Coburn & B. Winer. LC 68-10210. (Collected Works of Samuel T. Coleridge). 1970. 75.00x (*0-691-09861-1*) Princeton U Pr.

Collected Works of Samuel T. Coleridge, Vols. 1-4 & 6. Incl. Vol. 1. Collected Works of Samuel T. Coleridge. Samuel Taylor Coleridge. Ed. by K. Coburn & B. Winer. LC 68-10210. 1970. 75.00x (*0-691-09861-1*); Vol. 2. Watchman. Samuel Taylor Coleridge. Ed. by Lewis Patton et al. LC 68-10210. 490p. 1970. 70.00 (*0-691-09719-4*); Vol. 3. Essays on His Time, 3 vols. Samuel Taylor Coleridge. Ed. by D. V. Erdman et al. LC 68-10210. 1975. 190.00x (*0-691-09871-9*); Set, Vol. 4. Friend, 2 vols. Samuel Taylor Coleridge. Ed. by B. Rooke et al. LC 68-10210. 1969. Set. 160.00 (*0-691-09854-9*); Vol. 6. Lay Sermons. Samuel Taylor Coleridge. Ed. by R. J. White et al. LC 68-10210. 1972. 49.50 (*0-691-09873-5*); Vol. 7. Biographia Literaria. Samuel Taylor Coleridge. Ed. by K. Coburn & B. Winer. LC 68-10210. 1982. pap. 110.00x (*0-691-09874-3*); Vol. 7. Biographia Literaria. Samuel Taylor Coleridge. Ed. by K. Coburn & B. Winer. LC 68-10210. 1982. pap. 29.95 (*0-691-01861-8*); LC 68-10210. (Bollingen Ser.: Vol. 75). write for info. (*0-318-55351-1*) Princeton U Pr.

Collected Works of Samuel Taylor Coleridge: Aids of Reflection. Ed. by John Beer. (Bollingen Ser.: Vol. LXXV, No. 9). (Illus.). 950p. 1992. text ed. 125.00 (*0-691-09876-X*) Princeton U Pr.

Collected Works of Samuel Taylor Coleridge: Logic, Vol. 13. Samuel Taylor Coleridge. Ed. by J. R. Jackson. LC 68-10201. (Bollingen Ser.: No. LXXV). 1981. 75.00 (*0-691-09880-8*) Princeton U Pr.

Collected Works of Samuel Taylor Coleridge, Vol. 10: On the Constitution of the Church & State. Samuel Taylor Coleridge. Ed. by J. Colmer & B. Winer. (Bollingen Ser.: No. 75). (Illus.). 245p. 1975. 49.50 (*0-691-09877-8*) Princeton U Pr.

Collected Works of Samuel Taylor Coleridge, Vol. 12: Marginalia III. Ed. by H. J. Jackson & George Whalley. (Bollingen Ser.: LXXV). (Illus.). 1300p. 1992. text ed. 135.00 (*0-691-09954-5*) Princeton U Pr.

Collected Works of Samuel Taylor Coleridge, Vol. 12, Pt. 1: Marginalia. Samuel Taylor Coleridge & George Whalley. LC 68-10201. 1152p. 1980. 135.00x (*0-691-09879-4*) Princeton U Pr.

Collected Works of Samuel Taylor Coleridge, Vol. 12, Pt. 2: Marginalia. Ed. by Kathleen Coburn et al. LC 68-10201. (Bollingen Ser.: Vol. 75). (Illus.). 1280p. 1985. 135.00x (*0-691-09889-1*) Princeton U Pr.

Collected Works of Samuel Taylor Coleridge, Vol. 5: Lectures On Literature,1808-1819, 2 Vols. Samuel Taylor Coleridge. Ed. by Kathleen Coburn et al. LC 85-43198. (Bollingen Ser.: No. 75). 1175p. 1987. text ed. 135.00 (*0-691-09872-7*) Princeton U Pr.

Collected Works of Sarah Orne Jewett, 14 vols., Set. Sarah O. Jewett. Incl. Deephaven. 1877. reprint ed. 59.00 (*0-403-03190-7*); Old Friends & New. 1879. reprint ed. 59.00 (*0-403-03182-6*); Country By-Ways. 1881. reprint ed. 59.00 (*0-403-03183-4*); Mate of the Daylight & Friends Ashore. 1884. reprint ed. 59.00 (*0-403-03185-0*); Country Doctor. 1884. reprint ed. 59.00 (*0-403-03191-5*); Marsh Island. 1885. reprint ed. 59.00 (*0-403-03186-9*); White Heron & Other Stories. 1886. reprint ed. 59.00 (*0-403-03187-7*); King of Folly Island & Other People. 1888. reprint ed. 59.00 (*0-403-03188-5*); Strangers & Wayfarers. 1890. reprint ed. 59.00 (*0-403-03184-2*); Native of Winby & Other Tales. 1893. reprint ed. 59.00 (*0-403-03189-3*); Life of Nancy. 1895. reprint ed. 59.00 (*0-403-03181-8*); Country of the Pointed Firs. 1896. reprint ed. 59.00 (*0-403-03174-5*); Queen's Twin & Other Stories. 1899. reprint ed. 59.00 (*0-403-03180-X*); Tory Lover. 1901. reprint ed. 69.00x (*0-403-02994-5*); 895.00x (*0-403-03462-0*) Somerset Pub.

Collected Works of Sardar Vallabhbhai Patel, Vol. II (1926-1929) Sardar V. Patel. Ed. by P. N. Chopra. 432p. (C). 1992. text ed. 60.00 (*81-220-0252-8*, Pub. by Konark Pubs Pvt Ltd II) Advent Bks Div.

Collected Works of Sardar Vallabhbhai Patel: Volume 3: 1930-1931. Ed. by P. N. Chopra & Prabha Chopra. 1993. 60.00 (*81-220-0307-9*, Pub. by Konark Pubs Pvt Ltd II) Advent Bks Div.

Collected Works of Sardar Vallabhbhai Patel, 1918-1925, Vol. I. Sardar V. Patel. (Illus.). 500p. 1990. text ed. 60.00 (*81-220-0179-3*, Pub. by Konark Pubs Pvt Ltd II) Advent Bks Div.

***Collected Works of Sardar Vallabhbhai Patel 1932-1934 Vol. IV.** Ed. by P. N. Chopra & Prabha Chopra. (C). 1994. text ed. 42.00 (*81-220-0343-5*, Pub. by Konark Pubs II) S Asia.

Collected Works of Sir William Jones, 13 vols., Set. Intro. by Garland Cannon. LC 93-3862. 6240p. 1993. reprint ed. text ed. 995.00 (*0-8147-4199-1*) NYU Pr.

Collected Works of Siskiyou Poets, 1992: Sponsored by the Siskiyou Chapter of the National Writers Club. Ed. by Gail Jenner. 140p. (Orig.). (C). 1992. pap. 10.00 (*0-9628801-4-0*) Coyote Pub.

Collected Works of Spinoza, Vol. I. Baruch Spinoza. Ed. by Edwin Curley. LC 84-11716. (Illus.). 720p. 1985. text ed. 75.00 (*0-691-07222-1*) Princeton U Pr.

Collected Works of St. John of the Cross. rev. ed. Tr. by Kieran Kavanaugh & Otilio Rodriguez. LC 90-26713. (Illus.). 816p. (SPA.). 1991. 26.95 (*0-935216-15-4*); pap. 17.95 (*0-935216-14-6*) ICS Pubns.

Collected Works of St. Teresa of Avila, Vol. 2. Tr. by Kieran Kavanaugh & Otilio Rodriguez. LC 75-31305. 560p. 1980. pap. 11.95 (*0-9600876-6-4*) ICS Pubns.

Collected Works of St. Teresa of Avila, Vol. 3. Tr. by Kieran Kavanaugh & Otilio Rodriguez. LC 75-31305. (Illus.). 504p. 1985. pap. 11.95 (*0-935216-06-5*) ICS Pubns.

***Collected Works of St. Teresa of Avila: The Book of Her Life, Spiritual Testimonies, Soliloquies, Vol. 1.** Kieran Kavanaugh. Tr. by Otillo Rodriquez. LC 75-31305. 504p. 1976. pap. 10.95x (*0-9600876-2-1*) ICS Pubns.

Collected Works of the Caravan of Dreams Theater, Vol. 1: Gilgamesh, Marouf the Cobbler, Faust: Part One. Johnny Dolphin. 224p. 1983. pap. 5.95 (*0-907791-01-8*) Synerg AZ.

Collected Works of the Caravan of Dreams, Vol. 2: Billy the Kid, Metal Woman, Tin Can Man. Johnny Dolphin. 152p. 1984. pap. 5.95 (*0-907791-02-6*) Synerg AZ.

Collected Works of the Mother, 16 vols. 1978. Set, Life Companion travel-size. 100.00 (*0-89744-033-1*) Auromere.

Collected Works of the Mother, 16 vols., Set. 1978. 200.00 (*0-317-17487-8*) Auromere.

Collected Works of Thomas Muntzer. Ed. & Tr. by Peter Matheson. 544p. 1988. 59.95 (*0-567-09495-2*, Pub. by T & T Clark UK) Bks Intl VA.

***Collected Works of Thomas Muntzer.** Ed. & Tr. by Peter Matheson. 504p. 1994. pap. text ed. 39.95 (*0-567-29252-5*, Pub. by T & T Clark UK) Bks Intl VA.

Collected Works of Velimir Khlebnikov, Vol. 1: Letters & Theoretical Writings. Velimir Khlebnikov. Ed. by Charlotte Douglas. Tr. by Paul Schmidt. LC 87-8399. (Illus.). 416p. 1988. 45.00 (*0-674-14045-1*) HUP.

Collected Works of Velimir Khlebnikov, Vol. 2: Prose, Plays, & Supersagas, Vol. 2. Velimir Khlebnikov. Ed. by Ronald Vroon. Tr. by Paul Schmidt. LC 87-8399. (Illus.). 416p. 1989. 45.00 (*0-674-14046-X*) HUP.

Collected Works of Viginius Dabney: Gold That Did Not Glitter, 2 vols. Viginius Dabney. 1990. reprint ed. 1889. lib. bdg. 75.00 (*0-318-67672-9*) Rprt Serv.

Collected Works of Viginius Dabney: The Story of Don Miff, 2 vols. Viginius Dabney. (Notable American Authors Ser.). 1990. reprint ed. 1886. lib. bdg. 75.00 (*0-7812-2600-7*) Rprt Serv.

Collected Works of W. B. Yeats Vol. V: Later Essays, Vol. 5. Ed. by William H. O'Donnell. 296p. 1994. text ed. 35.00 (*0-02-632702-3*, Scribners) S&S Trade.

Collected Works of W. B. Yeats Vol. VIII: The Irish Dramatic Movement, Vol. 8. Ed. by Editor Fitzgerald. 1995. text ed. 35.00 (*0-02-538482-1*) Macmillan.

Collected Works of W. B. Yeats, Vol. XII: John Sherman & Dhoya. Ed. by Richard J. Finneran. 384p. 1993. text ed. 30.00 (*0-02-632703-1*) Macmillan.

Collected Works of W. B. Yeats, Vol. 1: The Poems. 2nd rev. ed. Ed. by Richard J. Finneran. 784p. 1989. text ed. 35.00 (*0-02-632701-5*) Macmillan.

Collected Works of W. B. Yeats, Vol. 6: Prefaces & Introductions, Vol. 6. Ed. by William H. O'Donnell. 370p. 1990. text ed. 35.00 (*0-02-592551-2*) Macmillan.

Collected Works of Walter Bagehot, Set, Vols 3 & 4. Walter Bagehot. Ed. by Norman St. John-Stevas. LC 66-1165. 1097p. 1968. Set. 100.00 (*0-674-14002-8*) HUP.

Collected Works of Wassily Hoeffding. Wassily Hoeffding. Ed. by P. K. Sen. LC 94-15495. (Statistics Ser.; Perspectives in Statistics). 1994. 49.00 (*0-387-94310-2*) Spr-Verlag.

Collected Works of William Henry Hudson, 24 Vols, Set. William H. Hudson. reprint ed. 1,480.00 (*0-404-03390-3*) AMS Pr.

Collected Works of William Ioor. William Ioor. (Notable American Authors Ser.). 1992. reprint ed. lib. bdg. 75.00 (*0-7812-3335-6*) Rprt Serv.

Collected Works of William Morris, 24 vols., Set. William Morris. (BCL1-PR English Literature Ser.). 1992. reprint ed. lib. bdg. 1,800.00 (*0-7812-7608-X*) Rprt Serv.

Collected Works of William Morris: Introductions by His Daughter, May Morris, 24 vols., Set. Ed. by May Morris. 8000p. 1992. Boxed set. boxed 2,650.00 (*0-415-07972-1*, B0563, Pub. by Thoemmes Pr UK) Routledge.

***Collected Works of Witold Hurewicz.** Witold Hurewicz. Ed. by Krystyna Kuperberg. LC 94-45887. (ENG & GER.). 1995. write for info. (*0-8218-0011-6*) Am Math.

Collected Works on Abraham Lincoln, 1848-1865, Vol. II, 2nd Supplement. Ed. by Roy P. Basler & Christian O. Basler. 130p. (C). 1990. text ed. 40.00 (*0-8135-1532-7*) Rutgers U Pr.

Collected Works: Tarski, 4 vols., Set. Ed. by Ralph McKenzie & Steven Givant. 1986. 650.00 (*0-8176-3284-0*) Birkhauser.

Collected Works: Tarski, 4 vols., Vol. 1: 1921-1934. Ed. by Ralph McKenzie & Steven Givant. 1987. 190.00 (*0-8176-3280-8*) Birkhauser.

Collected Works: Tarski, 4 vols., Vol. 2: 1935-1944. Ed. by Ralph McKenzie & Steven Givant. 1987. 190.00 (*0-8176-3281-6*) Birkhauser.

Collected Works: Tarski, 4 vols., Vol. 3: 1945-1957. Ed. by Ralph McKenzie & Steven Givant. 1987. 190.00 (*0-8176-3282-4*) Birkhauser.

Collected Works: Tarski, 4 vols., Vol. 4: 1958-1979. Ed. by Ralph McKenzie & Steven Givant. 1987. 190.00 (*0-8176-3283-2*) Birkhauser.

Collected Writing of Jellicoe, Vol. I. Geoffrey Jellicoe. (Illus.). 226p. 1994. 75.00 (*1-870673-04-2*) Antique Collect.

Collected Writing of Jellicoe: The Studies of a Landscape Designer over 80 Years, Vol. II. Geoffrey Jellicoe. (Illus.). 250p. 1995. 75.00 (*1-870673-07-7*) Antique Collect.

Collected Writings. Arno Breker. Ed. by Volker G. Probst. Tr. by Benjiman D. Webb. (Illus.). 256p. (Orig.). 1990. pap. 15.00 (*0-914301-13-6*) West-Art.

Collected Writings, 6 vols. V. F. Calverton. 1972. 600.00 (*0-87968-900-5*) Gordon Pr.

Collected Writings. Willem De Kooning. 200p. (Orig.). 1988. 5.95 (*0-937815-13-6*) Hanuman Bks.

Collected Writings. C. H. Douglas. 1972. 600.00 (*0-87968-901-3*) Gordon Pr.

Collected Writings. Zelda Fitzgerald. Ed. by Matthew J. Bruccoli. 448p. 1992. pap. 14.00 (*0-02-019883-3*, Collier S&S) S&S Trade.

Collected Writings, 4 vols. Charles Fort. 1972. 800.00 (*0-87968-902-1*) Gordon Pr.

Collected Writings. Edward M. Gallaudet. 1972. 600.00 (*0-87968-903-X*) Gordon Pr.

Collected Writings. Silvio Gesell. 1972. 600.00 (*0-87968-904-8*) Gordon Pr.

Collected Writings. James M. Gillis. 1972. 600.00 (*0-87968-905-6*) Gordon Pr.

***Collected Writings.** Paul R. Harrington. (Illus.). 376p. 1992. 100.00 (*0-932845-56-8*) Lowell Pr.

Collected Writings. Sidney Lanier. 1972. 600.00 (*0-87968-906-4*) Gordon Pr.

Collected Writings. Olive Moore. LC 91-29755. 424p. 1992. 22.95 (*1-56478-000-7*) Dalkey Arch.

Collected Writings. deluxe ed. Arno Breker. Ed. by Volker G. Probst. Tr. by Benjiman D. Webb. (Illus.). 256p. (Orig.). 1990. 85.00 (*0-914301-12-8*) West-Art.

1366

An Asterisk (*) at the beginning of an entry indicates that the title is appearing in BIP for the first time.

Collected Writings, 30 vols. John Maynard Keynes. Ed. by Donald Moggridge. Incl. Vol. 1. Indian Currency & Finance. 184p. 1978. reprint ed. 69.95 (0-521-22093-9); Vol. 2. Economic Consequences of the Peace. 192p. 1978. reprint ed. 69.95 (0-521-22094-7); Vol. 3. Revision of the Treaty. 158p. 1978. 69.95 (0-521-22095-5); Vol. 4. Tract on Monetary Reform. 172p. 1978. 69.95 (0-521-22096-3); Vol. 5. Pt. 1. Treatise on Money, the Pure Theory of Money. 336p. 1978. 64.95 (0-521-22097-1); Vol. 6, Pt.2. Treatise on Money, the Applied Theory of Money. 390p. 1978. 74.95 (0-521-22098-X); Vol. 7. General Theory of Employment, Interest, & Money. 428p. 1978. 74.95 (0-521-22099-8); Vol. 7. General Theory of Employment, Interest, & Money. 428p. 1978. pap. 19.95 (0-521-29382-0); Vol. 8. Treatise on Probability. 514p. 1978. 69.95 (0-521-22100-5); Vol. 9. Essays & Persuasions. 451p. 1978. 69.95 (0-521-22101-3); Vol. 10. Essays in Biography. 460p. 1978. 74.95 (0-521-22102-1); Vol. 13. General Theory & After, Pt. One: Preparation. 653p. 1978. 69.95 (0-521-22103-X); Vol. 14. General Theory & After, Pt. Two: Defence & Development. 584p. 1978. 74.95 (0-521-22104-8); Vol. 15. Activities: Nineteen Six to Nineteen Fourteen: India & Cambridge. 312p. 1978. 69.95 (0-521-22105-6); Vol. 16. Activities, Nineteen Fourteen to Nineteen Nineteen: The Treasury & Versailles. 488p. 1978. 64.95 (0-521-22106-4); Vol. 17. Activities Nineteen Twenty to Twenty-Two: Treaty Revision & Reconstruction. 1978. 69.95 (0-521-21874-8); Vol. 18. Activities Nineteen Twenty-Two to Thirty-Two: The End of Reparations. 1978. 69. 95 (0-521-21875-6); Set, Vol. 19. Activities Nineteen Twenty-Two to Twenty-Nine: The Return to Gold & Industrial Policy, 2 vols. 519p. 1981. Set. 140.00 (0-521-23071-3); Vol. 20. Activities Nineteen Twenty-Nine to Thirty-One: Rethinking Employment & Unemployment Policies. 330p. 1982. 74.95 (0-521-23072-1); Vol. 21. Activities Nineteen Thirty-One to Thirty Nine: World Crises & Policies in Britain & America. 688p. 1982. 69.95 (0-521-23073-X); Vol. 22. Activities Nineteen Thirty-Nine to Forty-Five: Internal War Finance. 1978. 69.95 (0-521-21876-4); Vol. 23. Activities Nineteen Forty to Forty-Three: External War Finance. 368p. 1979. 69.95 (0-521-22016-5); Vol. 24. Activities Nineteen Forty-Four to Forty-Six: The Transition to Peace. 1979. 74.95 (0-521-22017-3); Vol. 25. Activities Nineteen Forty to Nineteen Forty-Four: Shaping the Postwar World: The Clearing Union. 360p. 1980. 69.95 (0-521-22018-1); Vol. 26. Activities Nineteen Forty-One to Nineteen Forty-Six: Shaping the Postwar World: Bretton Woods & Reparations. 360p. 1980. 69.95 (0-521-22939-1); Vol. 27. Activities Nineteen Forty to Nineteen Forty-Six: Shaping the Postwar World: Employment & Commodities. 424p. 1980. 74.95 (0-521-23074-8); Vol. 29. General Theory & After - a Supplement. 1988. 64.95 (0-521-22949-9); write for info. (0-318-51276-9) Cambridge U Pr.

Collected Writings, 14 vols, Set. Thomas De Quincey. Ed. by David Masson. LC 68-58566. reprint ed. 975.00 (0-404-02100-X) AMS Pr.

Collected Writings, 14 vols., Set. Thomas De Quincey. (BCL1-PR English Literature Ser.). 1992. reprint ed. lib. bdg. 1,050.00 (0-7812-7508-3) Rprt Serv.

Collected Writings: 1947-1994. Nicholas V. Riasanovsky. (Illus.). viii, 312p. (C). 1993. 39.95 (1-884445-00-4) C Schlacks Pub.

Collected Writings Vol. 8: Treatise on Probability. John Maynard Keynes. Ed. by Donald Moggridge. 514p. (C). 1990. pap. 22.95 (0-521-37986-5) Cambridge U Pr.

Collected Writings Vol. 30: Bibliography & Index. John Maynard Keynes. Ed. by Donald Moggridge. 573p. (C). 1990. 89.95 (0-521-23076-4) Cambridge U Pr.

Collected Writings of Aleister Crowley, 3 vols. Aleister Crowley. 1973. 900.00 (0-685-01965-9) Gordon Pr.

***Collected Writings of Alice.** Alice V. Ambulator. iii, 215p. (Orig.). 1995. pap. text ed. 10.00 (0-9639719-2-1) Lambs Fold Ranch.

***Collected Writings of Alice.** Alice V. Ambulator. iii, 184p. (Orig.). 1995. pap. text ed. 10.00 (0-614-03520-1) Lambs Fold Ranch.

Collected Writings of Ambrose Bierce. A. Bierce. 39.95 (0-88411-859-2, Aeonian Pr) Amereon Ltd.

Collected Writings of Ambrose Bierce. Ambrose Bierce. 832p. 1983. pap. 11.95 (0-8065-0180-4, 70, Citadel Pr) Carol Pub Group.

Collected Writings of Ambrose Bierce. Ambrose Bierce. LC 72-13283. (Biography Index Reprint Ser.). 1977. reprint ed. 45.95 (0-8369-8141-3) Ayer.

Collected Writings of Edgar Allan Poe: Poe's Nonfiction in the Broadway Journal, Set, Vols. 3 & 4. Ed. by Burton R. Pollin. 760p. 1986. Set. 125.00 (0-87752-232-4) Gordian.

Collected Writings of Edgar Allan Poe, Vol. 2: The Brevities. Ed. by Burton R. Pollin. 640p. 1985. 75.00 (0-87752-229-4) Gordian.

Collected Writings of Frank Lloyd Wright, Vol. 3: 1931-1939. Frank Lloyd Wright. Ed. by Bruce B. Pfeiffer. (Illus.). 356p. 1994. 60.00 (0-8478-1699-0); pap. 40.00 (0-8478-1700-8) Rizzoli Intl.

Collected Writings of Frank Lloyd Wright, Vol. 4: 1939-1949. Frank Lloyd Wright. Ed. by Bruce B. Pfeiffer. (Illus.). 368p. 1994. 60.00 (0-8478-1803-9); pap. 40.00 (0-8478-1804-7) Rizzoli Intl.

Collected Writings of Frank Lloyd Wright, 1894-1931, Vol. I. Ed. by Bruce B. Pfeiffer. LC 91-40987. (Illus.). 400p. 1992. 60.00 (0-8478-1546-3); pap. 40.00 (0-8478-1547-1) Rizzoli Intl.

Collected Writings of Frank Lloyd Wright, 1931-1932, Vol. II. Ed. by Bruce B. Pfeiffer. LC 91-40987. (Illus.). 400p. 1992. 60.00 (0-8478-1548-X); pap. 40.00 (0-8478-1549-8) Rizzoli Intl.

Collected Writings of H. P. Blavatsky, 14 vols. Helena P. Blavatsky. Incl. Vol. 1. 1874-1878. rev. ed. 24.00 (0-8356-0082-3); Vol. 2. 1879-1880. 24.00 (0-8356-0091-2); Vol. 3. 1881-1882. 24.00 (0-8356-0099-8); Vol. 4. 1882-1883. 24.00 (0-8356-0106-4); Vol. 5. 1883. 24.00 (0-8356-0117-X); Vol. 6. 1883-1885. 24.00 (0-8356-0125-0); Vol. 7. 1886-1887. 24.00 (0-8356-7155-0); Vol. 8. 1887. 24.00 (0-8356-0224-9); Vol. 9. 1888. 24.00 (0-8356-0217-6); Vol. 10. 1888-1889. 24.00 (0-8356-7188-7); Vol. 11. 1889. 24.00 (0-8356-0215-X); Vol. 12: 1889-1890. 24.00 (0-8356-0228-1); Vol. 13: 1890-1891. 24.00 (0-8356-0229-X); Vol. 14: Miscellaneous. 24.00 (0-8356-0234-6); (Illus.). write for info. (0-318-55927-7, Quest) Theos Pub Hse.

Collected Writings of James Henley Thornwell, 4 vols., Set. James H. Thornwell. 1986. reprint ed. 122.95 (0-85151-197-X) Banner of Truth.

Collected Writings of James T. Hickey. James T. Hickey. 235p. 1990. 25.00 (0-912226-27-7); pap. 13.40 (0-912226-26-9) Ill St Hist Soc.

Collected Writings of Jessie Forsyth, 1847-1937: The Good Templars & Temperance Reform on Three Continents. Ed. by David M. Fahey. LC 87-35002. (Interdisciplinary Studies in Alcohol Use & Abuse: Vol. 1). 522p. 1988. 119.95 (0-88946-296-8) E Mellen.

Collected Writings of John Maynard Keynes, 30 vols., Vols. 1-30. John Maynard Keynes. Ed. by Donald Moggridge. 1992. 2,089.00 (0-521-30766-X) Cambridge U Pr.

Collected Writings of John Murray, 4 vols., Set. John Murray. 1976. 139.95 (0-85151-396-4) Banner of Truth.

Collected Writings of John Murray, Vol. 1: Claims of Truth. John Murray. 374p. 1976. 37.95 (0-85151-241-0) Banner of Truth.

Collected Writings of John Murray, Vol. 2: Lectures in Systematic Theology. John Murray. 1978. 37.95 (0-85151-242-9) Banner of Truth.

Collected Writings of John Murray, Vol. 3: To Serve the Living God. 1984. 37.95 (0-85151-337-9) Banner of Truth.

Collected Writings of John Murray, Vol. 4: Studies in Theology. John Murray. 390p. 1983. 37.95 (0-85151-340-9) Banner of Truth.

Collected Writings of Michael Snow. Michael Snow. 304p. (C). 1994. pap. 29.95 (0-88920-243-5, Pub. by Wilfrid Laurier CN) Humanities.

Collected Writings of Plotinus. Tr. by Thomas Taylor. (Thomas Taylor Ser.: No. 3). 1994. 36.00 (1-898910-02-2) Minerva CA.

Collected Writings of Robert Motherwell. Robert Motherwell. Ed. by Stephania Terenzio. LC 92-13639. (Illus.). 448p. 1993. 45.00 (0-19-507700-8) OUP.

Collected Writings of Robert Motherwell. Robert Motherwell. Ed. by Stephanie Terenzio. (Illus.). 358p. 1994. reprint ed. pap. 21.95 (0-19-509047-0) OUP.

***Collected Writings of Rousseau Vol. 5: The Confessions & Correspondence, Including the Letters to Malesherbes.** Ed. by Christopher Kelly et al. (Illus.). 624p. 1995. 60. 00x (0-87451-707-9) U Pr of New Eng.

Collected Writings of S. R. Hirsch, Vol. 4: Commentary on Isaiah & Additional Commentary on Psalms. 1986. 22. 95 (0-87306-950-1) Feldheim.

Collected Writings of S. R. Hirsch, Vol. 7: Jewish Education. 22.95 (0-87306-961-7) Feldheim.

Collected Writings of Samson Raphael Hirsch, Vol. I: The Jewish Year, Nissan-Av. Ed. by Breuer, Joseph, Foundation Staff. (Hirsch Heritage Ser.). 391p. 1984. 22. 95 (0-87306-364-3) Feldheim.

Collected Writings of Samson Raphael Hirsch, Vol. III: Jewish Symbolism. Ed. by Breuer, Joseph, Foundation Staff. (Hirsch Heritage Ser.). 260p. 1984. 22.95 (0-87306-924-2) Feldheim.

Collected Writings of Samson Raphael Hirsch, Vol. 2: The Jewish Year, Elul-Adar. S. R. Hirsch. (Hirsch Heritage Ser.). 1985. 22.95 (0-87306-951-X) Feldheim.

Collected Writings of Samson Raphael Hirsch, Vol. 6: Jewish Communal Life & Independent Orthodoxy. 1990. 22.95 (0-87306-948-X) Feldheim.

Collected Writings of T. E. Hulme. Ed. by Karen Csengeri. LC 93-43811. 540p. 1994. 85.00 (0-19-811234-3, Clarendon Pr) OUP.

Collected Writings of Warren J. Samuels, 5 vols., Set. Warren J. Samuels. 1792p. (C). 1992. text ed. 398.00 (0-8147-7944-1) NYU Pr.

Collected Writings on Edgar Allan Poe Vol. 1: The Imaginary Voyages; The Narrative of Arthur Gordon Pym; The Unparalleled Adventure of One Hans Pfaall; The Journal of Julius Rodman. rev. ed. Ed. by Burton R. Pollin. LC 81-2915. 667p. 1992. 70.00 (0-87752-238-3) Gordian.

Collected Writings on Samson Raphael Hirsch: Origin of the Oral Law, Vol. 5. 1988. 22.95 (0-87306-949-8) Feldheim.

***Collected Writings on the Gods & the World.** Tr. by Thomas Taylor. (Thomas Taylor Ser.: Vol. 4). Date not set. 32.00 (1-898910-03-0) Minerva CA.

Collectible Aluminum. Everett Grist. 1993. pap. 16.95 (0-89145-559-0) Collector Bks.

Collectible American Coins. Kenneth Bressett. 1991. 19.99 (0-517-03587-1) Random Hse Value.

Collectible American Coins. Kenneth E. Bressett. (Illus.). 320p. 1993. 19.98 (1-56173-300-8, 3600500) Pubns Intl Ltd.

Collectible & Classic Trucks. Consumer Guide Auto Editors. (Illus.). 96p. 1993. 12.98 (0-7853-0108-9, 1013100) Pubns Intl Ltd.

Collectible Aunt Jemima. Jean W. Turner. LC 94-65621. (Illus.). 128p. (Orig.). 1994. pap. 14.95 (0-88740-644-0) Schiffer.

***Collectible Beads.** Robert K. Liu. LC 94-68696. 256p. 1995. text ed. 44.95 (0-9641023-0-7) Ornament.

***Collectible Beer Trays.** Gary Straub. LC 95-9043. (Illus.). 160p. (Orig.). 1995. pap. 29.95 (0-88740-840-0) Schiffer.

Collectible Cars. Consumer Guide Auto Editors. (Illus.). 320p. 1993. 29.95 (0-88176-934-7, 1010200) Pubns Intl Ltd.

Collectible Cars. Poole. 1991. 29.99 (0-517-03594-4) Random Hse Value.

Collectible Coca-Cola Toy Trucks. Gael De Courtivron. 1994. 24.95 (0-89145-606-6) Collector Bks.

Collectible Coloring Books. Dian Zillner. LC 91-67780. (Illus.). 124p. 1992. pap. 24.95 (0-88740-393-X) Schiffer.

Collectible Compact Disc Price Guide. Gregory Cooper. (Illus.). 600p. 1993. pap. 24.95 (1-883907-10-1) Special Collectibles.

Collectible Correctibles. John Artman. 64p. (J). (gr. 4-8). 1984. student ed 8.95 (0-86653-214-5, GA 559) Good Apple.

Collectible Costume Jewelry, 1990. rev. ed. S. Sylvia Henzel. (Illus.). 120p. 1990. pap. 16.95 (0-87069-574-6, Wallace-Hmestead) Chilton.

Collectible Dolls & Accessories of the Twenties & Thirties from Sears, Roebuck & Co. Catalogs, 1921-1939. Ed. by Margaret Adams. 144p. (Orig.). 1986. pap. 9.95 (0-486-25107-1) Dover.

***Collectible Dolls-Facts & Trivia, Vol. 1.** Betty O. Bennett. Ed. by Michael J. Dugay. 160p. (Orig.). 1995. pap. 5.95 (0-9645218-0-6) Hipp-Daniel.

Collectible Florida Shells. R. Tucker Abbott. (Illus.). 68p. 1985. pap. 4.95 (0-915826-11-9) Am Malacologists.

Collectible Fountain Pens: Parker, Sheaffer, Wahl-Eversharp, Waterman. Glen Bowen. LC 82-90494. (Illus.). 320p. (Orig.). 1986. pap. 17.95 (0-910173-00-1) Wrld Pubns.

Collectible German Animals Value Guide, 1948-1968. Dee Hockenberry. (Illus.). 200p. (Orig.). (C). 1988. pap. 9.95 (0-87588-337-0, 3726) Hobby Hse.

Collectible Glassware from the 40's, 50's & 60's II. Gene Florence. 1993. 19.95 (0-89145-553-1) Collector Bks.

Collectible Golfing Novelties. Beverly Robb. LC 92-60627. (Illus.). 160p. (Orig.). 1992. pap. 29.95 (0-88740-423-5) Schiffer.

Collectible Magazines: Identification & Price Guide. David K. Henkel. (Illus.). 728p. (Orig.). 1993. pap. 15.00 (0-380-76926-3, Confident Collect) Avon.

Collectible Male Action Figures: G.I. Joe, Captain Action, & Ken. Paris Manos & Susan Manos. 1990. pap. 14.95 (0-89145-411-X) Collector Bks.

***Collectible Market Guide & Price Index: Limited Edition: Plates, Figurines, Bells, Graphics, Ornaments, Dolls & Steins.** 11th ed. Ed. by Diane C. Jones & Cindy Zagumny. (Illus.). 648p. 1993. pap. 22.95 (0-930785-15-0) Collectors Info.

Collectible Maxfield Parrish. William R. Holland & Douglas L. Congdon-Martin. (Illus.). 214p. 1993. 59.95 (0-88740-536-3) Schiffer.

Collectible Pin-Back Buttons, 1896-1986: An Illustrated Price Guide. Ted Hake & Russ King. LC 86-80807. (Illus.). 336p. (Orig.). 1986. 45.00 (0-918708-10-9) Hake.

***Collectible Plastic Kitchenware & Dinnerware, 1935-1965.** Michael J. Goldberg. LC 95-15968. (Illus.). 192p. (Orig.). 1995. pap. 29.95 (0-88740-843-5) Schiffer.

***Collectible Quilts.** Clark. 1995. 12.98 (1-56138-567-0) Courage Bks.

Collectible Rabbits. Herbert N. Schiffer. LC 90-61744. (Illus.). 96p. (Orig.). 1990. pap. 16.95 (0-88740-268-2) Schiffer.

Collectible Steins. Sally A. Denno. 40p. 1992. pap. text ed. 9.95 (0-916809-55-2) Scott Pubns MI.

Collectible Toys & Games of the Twenties & Thirties from Sears, Roebuck & Co. Catalogs. Ed. by James Spero. 128p. 1989. pap. 9.95 (0-486-25827-0) Dover.

Collectible Vernon Kilns. Maxine F. Nelson. 1994. pap. 18. 95 (0-89145-584-1) Collector Bks.

Collectibles. Nancy Dunnan. Ed. by Emily Raston. (Inside Track Library). (Illus.). 128p. (YA). (gr. 7 up). 1990. pap. 5.96 (0-685-47045-8) Silver Burdett Pr.

Collectibles. Nancy Dunnan. Ed. by Emily Raston. (Inside Track Library). (Illus.). 128p. (YA). (gr. 7 up). 1990. lib. bdg. 12.95 (0-382-09918-4); pap. 5.95 (0-382-24029-4) Silver Pr.

Collectibles Market Guide & Price Index: Limited Edition Plates, Figurines, Bells, Dolls, Graphics, Ornaments. 9th ed. Ed. by Diane C. Jones. (Illus.). 433p. 1991. pap. 19.95 (0-930785-08-8) Collectors Info.

Collectibles Market Guide & Price Index: Limited Edition Plates, Figurines, Bells, Graphics, Ornaments, Dolls & Steins. 10th ed. Diane C. Jones. (Illus.). 592p. 1992. pap. 19.95 (0-930785-12-6) Collectors Info.

***Collectibles Market Guide & Price Index: Limited Edition: Plates, Figurines, Cottages, Bells, Graphics, Ornaments, Dolls & Steins.** 12th ed. (Illus.). 700p. 1994. pap. 22.95 (0-930785-18-5) Collectors Info.

Collectibles Market Guide & Price Index: To Limited Edition Plates, Figurines, Bells, Graphics, Christmas Ornaments & Dolls. 6th ed. Ed. by Diane Carnevale. (Illus.). 312p. 1989. pap. 14.95 (0-930785-04-5) Collectors Info.

Collectibles Market Guide & Price Index: To Limited Edition Plates, Figurines, Bells, Graphics, Christmas Ornaments & Dolls. 7th ed. Ed. by Diane Carnevale. (Illus.). 395p. 1989. pap. 16.95 (0-930785-05-3) Collectors Info.

***Collectibles Market Guide & Price Index: To Limited Edition Plates, Figurines, Bells, Graphics, Steins & Dolls.** Ed. by Susan K. Jones & Diane Carnevale. (Illus.). 218p. 1985. pap. 13.95 (0-930785-01-0) Collectors Info.

***Collectibles Market Guide & Price Index: To Limited Edition Plates, Figurines, Bells, Graphics, Steins & Dolls.** Ed. by Susan K. Jones & Diane Cornevale. (Illus.). 222p. 1987. pap. 13.95 (0-930785-02-9) Collectors Info.

***Collectibles Market Guide & Price Index: To Limited Edition Plates, Figurines, Bells, Graphics, Steins & Dolls.** 2nd ed. Ed. by Susan K. Jones. (Illus.). 200p. 1984. pap. 13.95 (0-614-04574-6) Collectors Info.

Collectibles Market Guide & Price Index: 70 Limited Edition Plates, Figurines, Bells, Graphics, Christmas Ornaments & Dolls. 8th ed. Ed. by Diane Carnevale. (Illus.). 420p. 1990. pap. 18.95 (0-930785-06-1) Collectors Info.

Collectibles Market Guide & Price Index, 1988. 5th ed. Diane Carnevale. (Illus.). 256p. 1988. pap. 14.95 (0-930785-03-7) Collectors Info.

Collectibles Market Index Price Guide: To Limited Edition Plates, Figurines, Bells, Graphics, Steins & Dolls. Ed. by Susan K. Jones. LC 83-61660. (Illus.). 185p. 1983. pap. 13.95 (0-916838-85-4) Schiffer.

Collectibles Poems. Robert Hahn. (Illus.). 1976. pap. 2.95 (0-685-68422-9) Pygmalion Pr.

***Collectibles Price Guide: Your Guide to Current Prices for Limited Edition Plates, Figurines, Bells, Graphics, Ornaments, Dolls & Steins.** 4th ed. Ed. by Diane C. Jones. 208p. 1994. pap. 10.95 (0-930785-16-9) Collectors Info.

Collectibles Price Guide 1991: Comprehensive Value Guide Limited Edition: Plates, Figurines, Bells, Graphics, Ornaments & Dolls. 8th ed. Susan K. Jones. Ed. by Diane Carnevale. (Illus.). 109p. 1991. pap. 6.95 (0-930785-07-X) Collectors Info.

Collectibles Price Guide, 1992: Comprehensive Value Guide to Limited Edition Plates, Figurines, Bells, Graphics, Ornaments, Dolls & Steins. Ed. by Diane C. Jones. 132p. 1992. pap. 7.95 (0-930785-09-6) Collectors Info.

***Collectibles Price Guide 1993: Comprehensive Value Guide Limited Edition: Plates, Figurines, Bells, Graphics, Ornaments, Dolls & Steins.** 3rd ed. Ed. by Diane C. Jones. 164p. 1993. pap. 9.95 (0-930785-13-4) Collectors Info.

***Collectibles Price Guide 1995.** 5th ed. 160p. 1995. pap. 9.95 (0-87069-739-0) Chilton.

***Collectibly Mad: The Mad & EC Collectibles Guide.** Grant Geissman. Ed. by Chris Couch. LC 95-2612. (Illus.). 320p. 1995. pap. 25.00 (0-87816-202-X) Kitchen Sink.

***Collectibly Mad: The Mad & EC Collectibles Guide.** Grant Geissman. Ed. by Chris Couch. LC 95-2612. (Illus.). 320p. (YA). 1995. 200.00 (0-87816-343-3); pap. 40.00 (0-87816-203-8) Kitchen Sink.

Collecting. Bonnie Dobkin. (Rookie Reader Ser.). (Illus.). 32p. (J). (ps-2). 1993. lib. bdg. 10.95 (0-516-02015-3); pap. 3.50 (0-516-42015-1) Childrens.

Collecting: An Unruly Passion: Psychological Perspectives. Werner Muensterberger. LC 93-2174. 203p. 1994. text ed. 29.95 (0-691-03361-7) Princeton U Pr.

Collecting American. Stellinger. 1996. 29.95 (0-8050-1621-X) H Holt & Co.

Collecting American Brilliant Cut Glass. Louise Boggess & William Boggess. LC 91-67002. (Illus.). 320p. 1992. text ed. 59.95 (0-88740-383-2) Schiffer.

Collecting American Country: How to Select, Maintain & Display Country Pieces. Mary E. Emmerling & Richard Trask. LC 83-2207. (Illus.). 276p. 1983. 45.00 (0-517-54957-3, C P Pubs) Crown Pub Group.

Collecting & Analyzing Court Statistics: Handbook Prepared for the New Hampshire Judicial Council. National Center for State Courts Staff. 68p. 1976. 4.08 (0-685-16630-9, MAB-022) Natl Ctr St Courts.

Collecting & Constructing Model Buses. 96p. 1984. 25.00 (0-905418-44-1, Pub. by Gresham Bks UK) St Mut.

Collecting & Investing in U. S. Small Cents. 2nd ed. Thomas K. Schmeider. 1985. pap. 10.00 (0-942666-40-2) S J Durst.

Collecting & Managing Rare Law Books: Papers Presented at a Conference Celebrating the Dedication of the New Tarlton Law Library, the University of Texas at Austin School of Law, January 7-8, 1981. Ed. by Roy M. Mersky. LC 81-18820. 568p. 1981. lib. bdg. 45.00 (0-87802-070-5) Glanville.

Collecting & Managing Rare Law Books: Papers Presented at a Conference Celebrating the Dedication of the New Tarlton Law Library, the University of Texas at Austin School of Law, January 7-8, 1981. Ed. by Roy M. Mersky et al. LC 81-18820. 568p. 1982. lib. bdg. 45.00 (0-379-20740-0) Oceana.

Collecting & Preparing Study Specimens of Vertebrates. E. Raymond Hall. (Miscellaneous Publications: No. 30). 46p. 1962. pap. 2.25 (0-686-79807-4) U of KS Mus Nat Hist.

Collecting & Preserving Plants. unabridged ed. Ruth B. MacFarlane. LC 94-11884. (Illus.). 192p. 1994. pap. text ed. 5.95 (0-486-28281-3) Dover.

Collecting & Restoring Antique Fire Engines. Robert Lichty. (Illus.). 224p. 1981. pap. 9.95 (0-8306-2099-0) TAB Bks.

Collecting & Using Classic Cameras. Ivor Matanle. LC 91-75054. (Illus.). 224p. 1992. pap. 24.95 (0-500-27656-0) Thames Hudson.

Collecting & Valuing Fountain Pens. abr. ed. Paul Erano. 240p. 1995. pap. 8.95 (1-56901-133-8) NW Pub.

Collecting Antique Dolls. Lydia Richter. (Illus.). 124p. (Orig.). 1989. pap. 12.95 (0-87588-362-1) Hobby Hse.

Collecting Antique Linens Lace, Needlework. Frances Johnson. LC 91-16703. (Illus.). 208p. 1991. pap. 18.95 (0-87069-633-5) Chilton.

Collecting Antique Stickpins. Jack Kerins. 1994. pap. 19.95 (0-89145-607-4) Collector Bks.

C

An Asterisk (*) at the beginning of an entry indicates that the title is appearing in BIP for the first time.

Collecting Antique Tools. Herbert Kean & Emil Pollak. (Illus.). 208p. 1990. pap. 24.95 (*0-9618088-5-3*) Astragal Pr.

***Collecting Art: A Basic Need.** Ken Gilbert. (Petite Ser.). 56p. 1994. pap. 5.00 (*1-884754-11-2*) Potpourri Pubns.

Collecting Art Deco. Kevin McConnell. LC 90-62902. (Illus.). 144p. 1990. 49.95 (*0-88740-279-8*) Schiffer.

Collecting Assessments: An Operational Guide. 3rd ed. Ed. by Stan Rice & Alan S. More. (GAP Report Ser.: No. 10). 20p. (C). 1994. reprint ed. pap. 14.50 (*0-944715-29-X*) CAI.

Collecting Autographs & Manuscripts. rev. ed. Charles Hamilton. (Illus.). 448p. (C). 1993. reprint ed. pap. 40.00 (*0-929246-05-5*) Modoc Pr.

Collecting Baseball, Basketball, Football, Hockey Cards. Paul Green & Tony Galovich. 224p. 1992. pap. 8.95 (*0-929387-84-8*) Bonus Books.

Collecting Baseball Cards. Thomas S. Owens. LC 92-18166. (Illus.). 80p. (J). (gr. 4 up). 1993. lib. bdg. 15.40 (*1-56294-254-9*); pap. 8.95 (*1-56294-713-3*) Millbrook Pr.

Collecting Baseball Cards. 3rd ed. Donn Pearlman. LC 87-73307. (Illus.). 123p. 1990. pap. 7.95 (*0-929387-20-1*) Bonus Books.

Collecting Baseball Player Autographs. Don Raycraft. 1991. pap. 9.95 (*0-89145-445-4*) Collector Bks.

Collecting Books & Pamphlets Signed by the Presidents of the United States. Stephen Koschal. LC 82-90035. (Illus.). 84p. (Orig.). 1982. pap. 5.75 (*0-9608188-1-2*) Patriotic Pubs.

Collecting Books & Pamphlets Signed by the Presidents of the United States. limited ed. Stephen Koschal. LC 82-90035. (Illus.). 84p. (Orig.). 1982. 10.75 (*0-9608188-0-4*) Patriotic Pubs.

Collecting Bugs & Things: A Science Activity Storybook. Julia S. Moutron. (Illus.). 48p. (J). (gr. k up). 1988. pap. 2.95 (*0-8431-2226-9*) Price Stern.

Collecting Cigarette Cards. Gordon Howsden. 144p. 1994. pap. 19.95 (*1-883685-05-2*) Pincushion Pr.

Collecting Clues: Margaret Atwood's Bodily Harm. Lorna Irvine. (Canadian Fiction Studies: No. 28). (C). 1993. pap. text ed. 14.95 (*1-55022-150-7*, Pub. by ECW Press CN) Genl Dist Srvs.

Collecting Coins. Frank Purvey. 1985. 15.00 (*0-900652-75-6*) Numismatic Fine Arts.

Collecting Coins & Common Sense: A Complete Survival Guide for Today's Collector & Investor. David Van Meter. (Illus.). 120p. (Orig.). 1990. pap. 12.95 (*1-878420-03-8*) Laurion Pub.

Collecting Coins for Pleasure & Profit: A Comprehensive Guide & Handbook for Collectors & Investors. Barry Krause. (Illus.). 224p. (Orig.). 1991. pap. 18.95 (*1-55870-207-5*) Betterway Bks.

***Collecting Comic Books: A Young Person's Guide.** Thomas S. Owens. LC 94-48117. (Illus.). 80p. (YA). (gr. 4 up). 1995. lib. bdg. 18.90 (*1-56294-580-7*) Millbrook Pr.

***Collecting Comic Books: A Young Person's Guide.** Thomas S. Owens. LC 94-48117. (Illus.). 80p. (J). (gr. 4 up). 1995. pap. 8.95 (*1-56294-904-7*) Millbrook Pr.

Collecting Comic Character Clocks & Watches. Howard Brenner. (Illus.). 122p. 1986. pap. 14.95 (*0-89689-062-7*, 1797) Bks Americana.

Collecting, Cooking & Eating Shellfish: A Forager's Guide to Cape Cod, the Islands, & the Northeastern Shores. Ted Fenton et al. LC 84-72992. 1986. pap. 9.95 (*0-88748-010-1*) Carnegie-Mellon.

Collecting Dead Relatives. Laverne Galeener-Moore. 155p. 1992. reprint ed. 8.95 (*0-8063-1181-9*, 2105) Genealog Pub.

Collecting Doll Houses & Miniatures. Pam Hebbs. 144p. 1993. pap. 19.95 (*1-883685-03-6*) Pincushion Pr.

***Collecting Dolls.** Nora Earnshaw. (Pincushion Press Collectibles Ser.). (Illus.). 144p. Date not set. pap. 19.95 (*1-872727-81-6*) Pincushion Pr.

Collecting Evidence. Hugh Seidman. 78p. 1987. pap. 35.00 (*0-934450-12-9*) Unmuzzled Ox.

***Collecting Figural Tape Measures.** Elizabeth Arbitter et al. (Illus.). 128p. (Orig.). 1995. pap. 19.95 (*0-88740-866-4*) Schiffer.

Collecting Fishing Tackle: A Beginner's Guide. Tom Quinn. (Illus.). 80p. 1994. pap. 17.95 (*0-948253-68-1*, Pub. by Sportsmans Pr UK) Trafalgar.

***Collecting Football Cards: A Complete Guide with Prices.** Mike Bonner. LC 95-8016. 256p. 1995. pap. 15.95 (*0-87069-737-4*, Wallace-Hmestead) Chilton.

Collecting Football Cards for Fun & Profit: How to Buy, Store & Trade Them - & Keep Track of Their Value As Investments. Chuck Bennett & Don Butler. (Illus.). 158p. (Orig.). 1991. pap. 8.95 (*0-929387-32-5*) Bonus Books.

***Collecting for a College: Gifts from David P. Becker.** Marjorie B. Cohn & David P. Becker. LC 95-755252. (Illus.). 64p. 1995. pap. 15.00 (*0-916606-28-7*) Bowdoin Coll.

Collecting for Clio: An Exhibition of Representative Materials from the Holdings of the Massachusetts Historical Society. Frwd. by Stephen T. Riley. (Illus.). 73p. 1969. pap. 7.50 (*0-934909-02-4*) Mass Hist Soc.

Collecting German Dolls. Jean Bach. (Illus.). 192p. 1983. 20.00 (*0-8184-0333-0*) Carol Pub Group.

Collecting Glass, Vol. 3. William Heacock. 1986. pap. 13.95 (*0-915410-33-8*) Antique Pubns.

Collecting Gramophone Records. Eric T. Bryant. LC 77-28263. (Illus.). 153p. 1978. reprint ed. text ed. 38.50 (*0-313-20258-3*, BRCGR, Greenwood Pr) Greenwood.

Collecting Grand Army of the Republic Memorabilia. 2nd ed. R. Brad Long. (Illus.). 52p. 1991. reprint ed. pap. 8.95 (*0-9627584-1-8*) R B Long.

Collecting Greek Coins: A Complete Guide to Beginning & Enjoying a Collection of Classical Greek Coins. David A. Van Meter. (Illus.). 160p. (Orig.). 1990. pap. 17.95 (*1-878420-05-4*) Laurion Pub.

Collecting Guide: Holiday Paper Honeycomb-Cards, Garlands, Centerpieces, & Other Tissue-Paper Fantasies of the 20th Century. Jeannette Lasansky. Ed. by Joseph G. Foster. LC 92-44577. (Illus.). 48p. (Orig.). 1993. pap. 15.00 (*0-917127-07-2*) Oral Traditions.

Collecting Historical Documents: A Guide to Owning History. Todd M. Ayelrod. (How to...Ser.). (Illus.). 192p. 1984. 29.95 (*0-86622-008-9*, HT-1002) TFH Pubns.

***Collecting Hollywood: The Movie Poster Price Guide.** Jon R. Warren. 1994. pap. 18.95 (*0-9634319-1-9*) Am Collect Exch.

Collecting Hull Pottery's "Little Red Riding Hood" A Pictorial Reference & Price Guide. Mark E. Supnick. (Illus.). 62p. (Orig.). 1988. pap. 12.95 (*0-9611446-1-0*) M Supnick.

***Collecting in a Consumer Society.** Russell W. Belk. LC 94-39979. (Collecting Cultures Ser.). 224p. 1995. 39.95 (*0-415-10534-X*, C0484) Routledge.

Collecting Indian Knives. Lar Hothem. (Illus.). 152p. (Orig.). 1986. pap. 14.95 (*0-89689-059-7*, 1766) Bks Americana.

Collecting Jukeboxes - Slots. 3rd ed. Jerry Ayliffe. 352p. 1991. 14.95 (*0-89689-082-1*) Bks Americana.

Collecting Little Golden Books. 2nd ed. Sarte. 320p. 1994. 22.95 (*0-89689-105-4*) Bks Americana.

***Collecting Local Taxes: A Management Handbook.** HMSO Staff. 160p. 1995. pap. 35.00 (*0-11-886408-4*, HM64084, Pub. by HMSO UK) UNIPUB.

Collecting Lustreware. Geoffrey A. Godden & Michael Gibson. (Illus.). 384p. 1993. 150.00 (*0-7126-4682-5*, Pub. by Barrie & Jenkins) Trafalgar.

Collecting Medals & Decorations. Alec A. Purves. 237p. (C). 1987. 85.00 (*0-317-90453-1*, Pub. by Picton UK) St Mut.

Collecting Metal Shoulder Titles. Ray Westlake. 187p. (C). 1987. 91.00 (*0-317-90436-1*, Pub. by Picton UK) St Mut.

Collecting Model Farm Toys of the World. Raymond E. Crilley & Charles E. Burkholder. LC 78-55487. (Illus.). 1989. reprint ed. pap. 19.95 (*0-89404-011-1*) Aztex.

Collecting Moon Coins, Vol. II: Poems from the Heartland. Ed. by Diane Frank. (Illus.). 120p. (Orig.). 1991. pap. 8.00 (*0-9619744-5-1*) Blue Light Pr.

Collecting Myself: A Writer's Retrospective. A. Roy Eckardt. Ed. by Alice L. Eckardt et al. LC 93-28414. (Homage Ser.). 400p. 1993. 64.95 (*1-55540-898-2*, 000119) Scholars Pr GA.

Collecting Old Cameras. Cyril Permutt. LC 76-14888. (Photography Ser.). 1977. lib. bdg. 29.50 (*0-306-70855-8*) Da Capo.

Collecting Paper Money. Colin Narbeth. (Illus.). 168p. (Orig.). 1986. pap. 19.95 (*0-900652-89-6*, Pub. by Seaby UK) Trafalgar.

Collecting Paper Money for Pleasure & Profit: A Comprehensive Guide & Handbook for Collectors & Investors. Barry Krause. (Illus.). 240p. (Orig.). 1992. pap. 18.99 (*1-55870-256-3*) Betterway Bks.

***Collecting Personal Computers & Pocket Calculators, 1956-1991.** Thomas F. Haddock. (Illus.). 377p. 1994. pap. 14.95 (*0-89689-098-8*) Bks Americana.

***Collecting PEZ.** David Welch. (Illus.). 350p. (Orig.). 1995. pap. 39.95 (*1-879776-07-3*) JEM Commns.

***Collecting PEZ. David Welch. 344p. 1995. pap. 39.95 (*0-9644956-0-0*) Bubba Scrubba. Already referred to as "the Bible" on the subject, COLLECTING PEZ is the result of a 2-1/2 year research effort. If someone has interest in PEZ, no other publication provides even one-tenth the information contained here! Exhaustive historical information from the 1920s to present is presented in over 24 ex-employee interviews (hear stories of PEZ'S U.S. beginnings in 1953, live T.V. ads, company "mysteries" revealed), 275 photos(many color), company documents, old ads, & candy industry publications. State-of-the-art collectors information found nowhere else is included. Price guide, checklist, dispenser timeline, & answers to common questions assist collectors in this red-hot field where rarities can fetch $2,000+. With the first PEZ book ever, PICTORIAL GUIDE TO PLASTIC CANDY DISPENSERS FEATURING PEZ, the author is now considered the foremost authority on PEZ. Here he has created a definitive historical & collector-oriented work that will remain the standard on the subject. If libraries or individuals only acquire one PEZ book, COLLECTING PEZ should be it -- it'll make anyone an instant expert on the subject! To order contact: Bubba Scrubba Publications, P.O. Box 714, Murphysboro IL 62966. (618) 687-2286.** *Publisher Provided Annotation.*

Collecting Phil Spector: The Man, the Legend, & the Music. John J. Fitzpatrick & James E. Fogerty. LC 89-91180. (Illus.). 132p. 1990. 37.50 (*0-9622446-0-0*) Spectacle Pr.

***Collecting Plant Genetic Diversity: Technical Guidelines.** Ed. by L. Guarino et al. 760p. 1995. 120.00x (*0-85198-964-0*) CAB Intl.

Collecting Plastics: A Handbook & Price Guide. Jan Lindenberger. LC 91-65648. (Illus.). 144p. 1991. pap. 15.95 (*0-88740-335-2*) Schiffer.

Collecting Political Americana. Edmund B. Sullivan. LC 90-83146. 1991. 40.00 (*0-8158-0462-8*) Chris Mass.

Collecting Prang Mark Greeting Cards. L. Freeman. 1974. pap. 3.50 (*0-87282-042-4*) Am Life Foun.

Collecting, Processing & Germinating Seeds of Wildland Plants. James A. Young & Cheryl G. Young. (Illus.). 236p. 1986. 24.95 (*0-88192-057-6*) Timber.

Collecting Quimper. Joan Datesman. (Quimper Collections Ser). (Illus.). 96p. 1987. 50.00 (*0-9618593-0-X*) Merry Walk.

Collecting Rhinestone & Colored Jewelry. 3rd ed. Dolan. 384p. 1993. 22.95 (*0-89689-099-6*) Bks Americana.

Collecting Roman Coins: The Key to Identifying, Pricing & Building a Valuable Collection. Michael J. Kiely & David C. Van Meter. (Illus.). 92p. (Orig.). 1989. pap. 14.95 (*0-685-44888-6*) Laurion Pub.

***Collecting Romance Novels.** Dawn Reno & Jacque Tiegs. (Instant Expert Ser.). 120p. 1995. pap. 12.00 (*0-9641509-5-6*) Allian Pubng.

Collecting Russian Art & Antiques. Marina Bowater. (Illus.). 300p. 1991. 25.00 (*0-87052-897-1*) Hippocrene Bks.

Collecting Sensitive Data by Randomized Response: An Annotated Bibliography. Wayne W. Daniel. 113p. 1979. 20.00 (*0-88406-127-2*, RM85) GA St U Busn Pr.

Collecting Sensitive Data by Randomized Response: An Annotated Bibliography. 2nd ed. Wayne W. Daniel. LC 93-18343. (Research Monograph: No. 107). 134p. 1993. 20.00 (*0-88406-262-7*) GA St U Busn Pr.

***Collecting Shane Stevens a.k.a. J. W. Rider.** John Legg. 88p. 1995. pap. 24.95 (*0-9644069-0-X*) Black Diamond.

Collecting Shawnee Pottery: A Pictorial Reference & Price Guide. Mark Supnick. (Illus.). 64p. (Orig.). 1983. pap. 12.95 (*0-9611446-0-2*) M Supnick.

Collecting Shrill Shadows. Diana Dilemma, pseud. (Adult Poetry Ser.). (Illus.). 96p. (Orig.). 1987. pap. 6.95 (*0-915199-02-5*) Pen-Dec.

Collecting Silver. Elizabeth De Castres. (Illus.). 157p. 1987. 17.95 (*0-900873-71-X*, Pub. by Bishopsgte Pr UK) Intl Spec Bk.

***Collecting Societies in the Music Business.** Ed. by David Peeperkorn & Cees Van Rij. 160p. 1989. pap. 95.00 (*90-6215-228-7*, Pub. by Maklu Uitgevers BE) W W Gaunt.

***Collecting South Carolina Folk Art: A Guide.** Date not set. pap. 5.95 (*0-87249-958-8*) U of SC Pr.

Collecting Sports Autographs: Fun & Profit from This Easy-to-Learn Hobby. Tom Owens. 131p. (Orig.). (YA). (gr. 7 up). 1989. pap. 6.95 (*0-933893-79-5*) Bonus Books.

Collecting Stocks & Bonds, 3 vols., Set. George H. LaBarre. (Illus.). 368p. 1981. pap. 14.85 (*0-941538-00-1*) G H LaBarre.

Collecting Stocks & Bonds, Vol. I. rev. ed. George H. LaBarre. (Illus.). 108p. 1981. pap. 4.95 (*0-941538-01-X*) G H LaBarre.

Collecting Stocks & Bonds, Vol. II. George H. LaBarre. (Illus.). 128p. 1981. pap. 4.95 (*0-941538-02-8*) G H LaBarre.

Collecting Stocks & Bonds, Vol. III. George H. LaBarre. (Illus.). 132p. 1981. pap. 4.95 (*0-941538-03-6*) G H LaBarre.

***Collecting Teddy Bears.** Pam Hebbs. (Pincushion Press Collectibles Ser.). (Illus.). 144p. Date not set. pap. 19.95 (*1-872727-91-3*) Pincushion Pr.

Collecting the Beatles, Vol. 2. Barbara Fenick. (Rock & Roll Reference Ser.: No. 16). (Illus.). 320p. 1985. 34.50 (*0-87650-176-5*) Popular Culture.

Collecting the Edged Weapons of Imperial Germany. Thomas M. Johnson et al. Tr. by Mark Ready. LC 87-72171. (Illus.). 364p. 1988. 39.50 (*0-9600906-0-6*) Johnson Ref Bks.

Collecting the Edged Weapons of the Third Reich, Vol. I. 3rd ed. Thomas M. Johnson. LC 75-15486. (Illus.). 343p. 1975. 48.50 (*0-9600906-1-4*) Johnson Ref Bks.

Collecting the Edged Weapons of the Third Reich, Vol. II. 2nd ed. Thomas M. Johnson. LC 75-15486. (Illus.). 349p. 1976. 48.50 (*0-9600906-2-2*) Johnson Ref Bks.

Collecting the Edged Weapons of the Third Reich, Vol. III. 2nd ed. Thomas M. Johnson. LC 75-15486. (Illus.). 362p. 1978. 48.50 (*0-9600906-3-0*) Johnson Ref Bks.

Collecting the Edged Weapons of the Third Reich, Vol. IV. 2nd ed. Thomas M. Johnson. LC 75-15486. (Illus.). 343p. 1981. 48.50 (*0-944432-03-4*) Johnson Ref Bks.

Collecting the Edged Weapons of the Third Reich, Vol. V. Thomas M. Johnson. LC 75-15486. (Illus.). 330p. 1985. 48.50 (*0-9600906-8-1*) Johnson Ref Bks.

Collecting the Edged Weapons of the Third Reich, Vol. VI. Thomas M. Johnson. Ed. by Johnson Reference Books Staff. LC 75-15486. (Illus.). 365p. 1992. 48.50 (*0-944432-01-8*) Johnson Ref Bks.

Collecting the Edged Weapons of the Third Reich, Vol. VII. Thomas M. Johnson. Ed. by Johnson Reference Books Staff. Tr. by Mark Ready et al. LC 75-15486. (Illus.). 365p. 1994. 58.50 (*0-944432-04-2*) Johnson Ref Bks.

Collecting the Edged Weapons of the Third Reich: Five Volume Cross-Index. Thomas M. Johnson & A. Wasmus. Ed. by Johnson Reference Bks. Staff. LC 87-91108. 100p. 1988. pap. 15.00 (*0-944432-00-X*) Johnson Ref Bks.

Collecting the Empties: Poems. Larry Rapant. LC 92-20423. 64p. 1992. pap. 12.95 (*0-7734-9519-3*) E Mellen.

Collecting the Fifties & Sixties: A Handbook & Price Guide. Jan Lindenberger. (Illus.). 160p. 1993. pap. 16.95 (*0-88740-543-6*) Schiffer.

Collecting the Light. Markham Johnson. LC 93-1389. (University of Central Florida Contemporary Poetry Ser.). 72p. 1993. lib. bdg. 16.95 (*0-8130-1229-5*); pap. 10.95 (*0-8130-1230-9*) U Press Fla.

Collecting the Mercedes-Benz SL, 1954-1993. John R. Olson. 235p. 1993. 19.95 (*0-9635394-0-X*); pap. 16.95 (*0-9635394-1-8*) SL Mkt Letter.

***Collecting the Natural World: Legal Requirements & Personal Liability for Collecting Plants, Animals, Rocks, Minerals, Fossils & Artifacts.** Wolberg & Reinard. (Illus.). 288p. (Orig.). 1995. pap. 21.00 (*0-945005-20-2*) Geoscience Pr.

Collecting the Navajo Child's Blanket. Joshua Baer. (Illus.). 60p. (Orig.). 1986. pap. 21.00 (*0-9617085-0-6*) Morning Star Gal.

Collecting the Pre-Columbian Past: A Symposium at Dumbarton Oaks, 6th & 7th October 1990. Ed. by Elizabeth H. Boone. LC 92-12125. (Illus.). 368p. 1993. 30.00 (*0-88402-208-0*, BOCP, Dumbarton Rsch Lib) Dumbarton Oaks.

Collecting the Space Race. Stuart Scheider. (Illus.). 176p. 1993. pap. 34.95 (*0-88740-535-5*) Schiffer.

Collecting the Tin Toy Car, 1950-1970. Dale Kelley. LC 84-51183. (Illus.). 200p. 1984. 29.95 (*0-88740-012-4*) Schiffer.

Collecting the West: The C. R. Smith Collection of Western American Art. Richard H. Saunders. (Illus.). 224p. 1988. 35.00 (*0-292-71112-3*) U of Tex Pr.

***Collecting Things.** Kate Needham & Gay Gibson. (How to Make Ser.). (Illus.). 32p. (J). (gr. 2-6). 1995. lib. bdg. 12.96 (*0-88110-774-3*, Usborne); pap. 5.95 (*0-7460-2081-3*, Usborne) EDC.

Collecting Tin Toys. Jack Tempest. 144p. 1993. pap. 19.95 (*1-883685-02-8*) Pincushion Pr.

***Collecting Toy Airplanes: An Identification & Value Guide.** Ron Smith. (Illus.). 300p. (Orig.). 1995. pap. 22.95 (*0-89689-111-9*) Bks Americana.

***Collecting Toy Seven: A Collector's Identification & Value Guide.** 6th rev. ed. Richard O'Brien. (Collecting Toys Ser.). (Illus.). 600p. 1995. pap. 22.95 (*0-89689-114-3*) Bks Americana.

***Collecting Toy Soldiers.** James Opie. (Pincushion Press Collectibles Ser.). 144p. Date not set. pap. 19.95 (*1-872727-76-X*) Pincushion Pr.

Collecting Toy Soldiers. 2nd ed. Richard O'Brien. 512p. 1992. 29.95 (*0-89689-089-9*) Bks Americana.

Collecting Toy Trains. Pierce Carlson. 144p. 1993. pap. 19.95 (*1-883685-01-X*) Pincushion Pr.

Collecting Toy Trains. 3rd ed. Richard O'Brien. 360p. 1991. 22.95 (*0-89689-084-8*) Bks Americana.

Collecting U. S. Coins: A Guide for Beginners. Kenneth E. Bressett. (Illus.). 64p. 1993. spiral bd. 5.98 (*1-56173-745-3*, 3614900) Pubns Intl Ltd.

Collecting Victorian Tiles. Terence A. Lockett. (Illus.). 235p. 1979. 29.50 (*0-902028-82-0*) Antique Collect.

***Collecting Whistles.** James Dundas. (Illus.). 128p. (Orig.). 1995. pap. 19.95 (*0-88740-859-1*) Schiffer.

Collecting World Paper Money. 32p. 1992. pap. 2.00 (*0-931960-34-7*) BNR Pr.

Collecting Writing Instruments. Dietmar Geyer. LC 90-61508. (Illus.). 176p. 1990. 49.95 (*0-88740-272-0*) Schiffer.

Collecting Yelloware. Michel. 128p. 1992. pap. 16.95 (*0-89145-521-3*) Collector Bks.

Collectio Decem Carminum Gallicorum, Alias Chansons Francaises 4-5 Vocum see Complete Works of Philippe de Monte

Collectio Decem Motettorum 5-6-7 et 8 Vocum see Complete Works of Philippe de Monte

***Collectio Tripartita: Justinian on Religious & Ecclesiastical Affairs.** Ed. by N. Van der Wal & B. H. Stolte. lx, 176p. (GEC.). 1995. lib. bdg. 57.00 (*90-6980-042-X*, Pub. by Egbert Forsten NE) Benjamins North Am.

Collection. Hamlin Garland. reprint ed. lib. bdg. write for info. (*0-318-68142-0*) Scholarly.

Collection see Three Plays

Collection Agency Directory. Albert W. Scace. 220p. 1995. pap. text ed. 195.00 (*0-9630819-9-3*) First Detroit.

Collection, Analysis, & Use of Monitoring & Evaluation Data. Dennis J. Casley & Krishna Kumar. LC 87-16375. 208p. 1988. pap. text ed. 14.95 (*0-8018-3669-7*) Johns Hopkins.

Collection Analysis for the School Library Media Center: A Practical Approach. Ed. by Carol A. Doll & Pamela P. Barron. LC 90-40208. (C). 1990. pap. text ed. 15.00 (*0-8389-3390-4*, 3390-4) ALA.

Collection & Civil Prosecution Specialist. Jack Rudman. (Career Examination Ser.; Series 1). 1991. pap. 29.95 (*0-8373-3702-X*) Nat Learn.

Collection & Enforcement of Judgments Form Book 1992. Wake Forest University School of Law Staff. 186p. 1992. pap. 65.00 (*0-942225-52-X*) Wake Forest Law.

Collection & Enforcement of Judgments Handbook 1992. Wake Forest University School of Law Staff. (Illus.). 239p. 1992. pap. 65.00 (*0-942225-51-1*) Wake Forest Law.

Collection & Evaluation of Intelligence for the German Air Force High Command: Karlsruhe Study. Andreas L. Nielsen. (USAF Historical Studies: No. 171). 224p. 1955. reprint ed. pap. text ed. 27.00 (*0-89126-143-5*) MA-AH Pub.

Collection & Portfolio of Golf Humor. Ed. by John De Monte. 18p. (Orig.). 1984. pap. 3.00 (*0-9605176-2-6*) Raycol Prods.

An Asterisk (*) at the beginning of an entry indicates that the title is appearing in BIP for the first time.

C

An Asterisk (*) at the beginning of an entry indicates that the title is appearing in BIP for the first time.

1369

Collection of Old English Plays, 7 vols. in 4, 4. Ed. by Arthur H. Bullen. LC 64-14699. 1972. reprint ed. 48.95 (0-405-08329-7, Pub. by Blom Pubns UK) Ayer.

Collection of Old English Plays, 7 vols. in 4, Set. Ed. by Arthur H. Bullen. LC 64-14699. reprint ed. 176.00 (0-405-08325-4, Pub. by Blom Pubns UK) Ayer.

Collection of Old Irish Hymns, Vol. 1. Ed. by Ernst W. Windisch & Whitley Stokes. LC 78-72655. (Irische Texte). 70.00 (0-404-18231-3) AMS Pr.

Collection of Original Instructions to Surveyors of the Public Lands 1815-1881. Government Land Office Staff. Ed. by Roy Minnicic. (Illus.). 517p. 1982. reprint ed. 40.00 (0-910845-08-5, 520) Landmark Ent.

Collection of Original Papers Relative to the History of the Colony of Massachusetts Bay. Thomas Hutchinson. (Notable American Authors Ser.). 1992. reprint ed. lib. bdg. 75.00 (0-7812-3298-8) Rprt Serv.

Collection of Original Voyages. William Hacke. LC 93-24426. (Scholars' Facsimiles & Reprints, Maritime History Ser.: Vol. 483). 1993. reprint ed. 100.00 (0-8201-1483-9) Schol Facsimiles.

Collection of Osteological Material from Machu Picchu. George F. Eaton. (Connecticut Academy of Arts & Sciences Ser., Trans.: Vol. 5). 1916. pap. 200.00 (0-685-22868-1) Elliots Bks.

***Collection of Paper Ducks.** Amy L. Freeman. 45p. (Orig.). 1994. 9.00 (0-9641971-0-3) A L Freeman.

Collection of Papers from the All-Union School on Function Theory: Proceedings of the Steklov Institute of Mathematics, Vol. 189. Ed. by S. B. Stechkin. 234p. 1990. pap. text ed. 111.00 (0-8218-3136-4, STEKLO-189) Am Math.

***Collection of Papers Relating to the History of the Town of Groton, 4 vols., Set.** Samuel A. Green. (Groton Historical Ser.). 1970p. 1995. reprint ed. lib. bdg. 200.00 (0-8328-4594-9) Higginson Bk Co.

Collection of Papers Relative to the Dispute Between Great Britain & America, 1764-1775. Ed. by John Almon. LC 70-146272. (Era of the American Revolution Ser.). 1971. reprint ed. lib. bdg. 39.50 (0-306-70127-8) Da Capo.

Collection of Poems, 6 vols. Robert Dodsley. 1972. reprint ed. 40.00 (0-318-68141-2) Scholarly.

Collection of Poems, 6 vols., Set. Robert Dodsley. (BCL1-PR English Literature Ser.). 1992. reprint ed. lib. bdg. 450.00 (0-7812-7130-4) Rprt Serv.

Collection of Poems, 6 vols., Set. Robert Dodsley. LC 78-144978. 1972. reprint ed. 195.00 (0-686-66734-4) Scholarly.

***Collection of Poems for & about Children, 4 bks., Set.** Emory H. Jennings. 273p. (J). (gr. k-6). 1994. pap. 24.95 (1-885754-04-3) E H Jennings.

***Collection of Poems from the Heart.** Sherron D. Harris. 1995. 8.95 (0-533-10637-0) Vantage.

Collection of Poems on American Affairs & Variety of Other Subjects. Philip M. Freneau. LC 76-15581. 1976. reprint ed. lib. bdg. 60.00 (0-8201-1174-0) Schol Facsimiles.

***Collection of Poetry.** Richard Chittock. 40p. 1995. pap. 11.00 (0-8059-3692-0) Dorrance.

Collection of Poetry. Don Moon & Ruth Moon. LC 85-63483. (Illus.). 64p. 7.95 (0-9615098-0-5) Prairie Imp.

***Collection of Poetry.** Charles Stebbins, Sr. 56p. 1995. per., pap. 7.00 (0-8059-3638-6) Dorrance.

Collection of Points. Stuart Dods. 1988. student ed, pap. 8.00 (0-89824-161-8); teacher ed, pap. 10.00 (0-89824-162-6) Trillium Pr.

***Collection of Pop Psychology Articles.** George Borelli. 1994. pap. text ed. 12.95 (1-885792-07-7) Gemini Pubng.

Collection of Preacher Told Tall Tales. Ed. by William S. Deal. pap. 5.99 (0-685-70971-X) Schmul Pub Co.

Collection of Problems in Classical Mechanics. G. I. Kotkin & V. G. Serbo. 1971. 116.00 (0-08-015843-9, Pub. by Pergamon Repr UK) Franklin.

Collection of Problems in Math. 1988. pap. 15.95 (0-486-65806-6) Dover.

Collection of Problems of Complex Analysis. L. I. Volkovyskii et al. 438p. 1992. reprint ed. pap. 11.95 (0-486-66913-0) Dover.

Collection of Problems of Mechanics. I. Meshcherskii & R. Romicki. LC 63-15496. (International Series of Monographs on Pure & Applied Mathematics: Vol. 65). 1965. 220.00 (0-08-010145-3, Pub. by Pergamon Repr UK) Franklin.

Collection of Problems on a Course of Mathematical Analysis. Gerald Berman & D. Brown. LC 63-11927. (International Series of Monographs on Pure & Applied Mathematics: Vol. 64). 1965. 241.00 (0-08-013502-1, Pub. by Pergamon Repr UK) Franklin.

Collection of Problems on Complex Analysis. L. Volkovskii & G. Lunts. LC 63-10082. (International Series of Monographs on Pure & Applied Mathematics: Vol. 68). 1965. 180.00 (0-08-010250-6, Pub. by Pergamon Repr UK) Franklin.

Collection of Problems on the Equations of Mathematical Physics. Ed. by V. S. Vladimirov. 300p. 1986. 42.00 (0-387-16647-5) Spr-Verlag.

Collection of Recipes for the Use of Special Diet Kitchens in Military Hospitals. Helen Wittenmyer. 11.95 (0-8488-0006-0, J M C & Co) Amereon Ltd.

Collection of Sacred Hymns for the Use of the Latter Day Saints. 82p. reprint ed. pap. text ed. 4.95 (1-877869-25-2) Mason Cnty Hist Proj.

Collection of Sewing Ideas: For Children, Ladies & Dolls. June H. Fleming. LC 93-79249. (Illus.). 100p. 1995. pap. 24.95 (1-883165-34-2) Fernholm Pub.

Collection of Short Stories. Lincoln Hanks. Ed. by James B. Van Treese. 192p. (Orig.). 1993. pap. 7.95 (1-880416-48-4) NW Pub.

Collection of Short Stories. Jean McPherson. 56p. 1993. pap. 10.95 (0-8059-3363-8) Dorrance.

Collection of Short Stories: Love, Romance & Desire. Veronica L. Cook. 200p. (Orig.). 1989. pap. 10.00 (0-685-29995-3) Ronnie Two Pub.

Collection of Sonnets. Yenny Toybner. 88p. (J). 1994. pap. 10.95 (0-8059-3535-5) Dorrance.

Collection of Southwestern Cowboy Poetry: A Working Cowboy's Poetry. Bill Beam. LC 93-90945. (Illus.). 80p. (Orig.). 1994. pap. 24.95 (0-9639786-3-2) Shadow Rider.

Collection of Stories. Elena Kluyeva. 1988. write for info. (0-318-64031-7) RWCPH.

Collection of Surveys. Ed. by R. L. Dobrushin. 1986. lib. bdg. 136.50 (90-277-2183-1) Kluwer Ac.

Collection of Teaching Documents & Case Studies: Industrial Relations in Engineering. A. Marsh. LC 66-21142. 1966. 60.00 (0-08-011606-X, Pub. by Pergamon Repr UK) Franklin.

Collection of Telugu Proverbs Translated, Illustrated & Explained Together with Some Sanskrit Proverbs Printed in the Devanagari & Telugu Characters. M. W. Carr. (C). 1988. reprint ed. 29.50 (81-206-0261-7, Pub. by Asian Educ Servs II) S Asia.

Collection of Temne Traditions, Fables & Proverbs, with an English Translation; & also Some Specimens of the Author's Own Temne Compositions & Translations; to Which Is Appended a Temne-English Vocabulary. Christian F. Schlenker. (B. E. Ser.: No. 35). 1861. 26.00 (0-8115-2986-X) Periodicals Srv.

Collection of Test Problems for Constrained Global Optimization Algorithms. C. A. Floudas & Panos M. Pardalos. Ed. by G. Goos & J. Hartmanis. (Lecture Notes in Computer Science Ser.: Vol. 455). xiv, 180p. 1990. pap. 28.00 (0-387-53032-0) Spr-Verlag.

Collection of the Chronicles & Ancient Histories of Great Britain, Now Called England, Albina-1431, 3 vols., 1. Jehan De Waurin. Ed. by William Hardy & Edward L. Hardy. (Rolls Ser.: No. 40). 1972. reprint ed. write for info. (0-8115-1097-2) Periodicals Srv.

Collection of the Chronicles & Ancient Histories of Great Britain, Now Called England, Albina-1431, 3 vols., 2. Jehan De Waurin. Ed. by William Hardy & Edward L. Hardy. (Rolls Ser.: No. 40). 1972. reprint ed. write for info. (0-8115-1098-0) Periodicals Srv.

Collection of the Chronicles & Ancient Histories of Great Britain, Now Called England, Albina-1431, 3 vols., 3. Jehan De Waurin. Ed. by William Hardy & Edward L. Hardy. (Rolls Ser.: No. 40). 1972. reprint ed. write for info. (0-8115-1099-9) Periodicals Srv.

Collection of the Chronicles & Ancient Histories of Great Britain, Now Called England, Albina-1431, 3 vols., Set. Jehan De Waurin. Ed. by William Hardy & Edward L. Hardy. (Rolls Ser.: No. 40). 1972. reprint ed. 135.00 (0-8115-3576-2) Periodicals Srv.

Collection of the Facts & Documents, Relative to the Death of Major-General Alexander Hamilton. Alexander Hamilton. Ed. by William Coleman. LC 72-95068. (Select Bibliographies Reprint Ser.). 1977. 30.95 (0-8369-5025-9) Ayer.

Collection of the Historie of England. Samuel Daniel. LC 86-10208. 1986. reprint ed. 60.00 (0-8201-1413-8) Schol Facsimiles.

Collection of the Inscriptions on Copper Plates & Stones in the Nellore District, 3 vols., Set. A. Butterworth et al. 1990. reprint ed. 140.00 (81-206-0279-X, Pub. by Asian Educ Servs II) S Asia.

Collection of the Laws & Canons of the Church of England: Theological Works, 4 Vols, Set. John Johnson. LC 72-1032. (Library of Anglo-Catholic Theology: No. 10). reprint ed. 115.00 (0-404-52110-X) AMS Pr.

Collection of the Moral & Instructive Sentiments, Maxims, Cautions, & Reflections, Contained in the Histories of Pamela, Clarissa, & Sir Charles Grandison. Samuel Richardson. LC 92-9738. (Clarissa Project Ser.: Vol. 11). 1992. 76.50 (0-404-64111-3) AMS Pr.

Collection of the Moral & Instructive Sentiments, Maxims, Cautions, & Reflexions, Contained in the Histories of Pamela, Clarissa, & Sir Charles Grandison. Samuel Richardson. LC 80-22492. 1980. reprint ed. 75.00 (0-8201-1357-3) Schol Facsimiles.

Collection of the Political Writings of William Leggett. William Leggett. LC 76-125702. (American Journalists Ser.). 1971. reprint ed. 30.95 (0-405-01681-6) Ayer.

Collection of the "Very Finest Recipes" Ever Assembled into One Cookbook. rev. ed. David B. Schecter. LC 80-123367. 270p. reprint ed. pap. 12.00 (0-940115-00-X) Becker Pubns.

Collection of the Works of John Milton & Miltoniana in the Margaret I. King Library. John T. Shawcross. LC 84-822272. (University of Kentucky Libraries Occasional Papers). 229p. 1985. lib. bdg. 15.00 (0-917519-03-5) U of KY Libs.

Collection of the Works of William Penn, 2 vols. William Penn. LC 79-173942. reprint ed. 495.00 (0-404-04982-6) AMS Pr.

Collection of the Writings of John James Ingalls. John J. Ingalls. LC 77-170062. reprint ed. 57.50 (0-404-03483-7) AMS Pr.

***Collection of Trademarks & Logotypes in Japan.** Ed. by Sumio Hasegawa & Shigeji Kobayashi. (Illus.). 460p. 1995. pap. 55.00 (4-7661-0809-4, Pub. by Graphic Sha JA) Bks Nippan.

Collection of Trademarks & Logotypes in Japan, 1982-83. Ed. by Sumio Hasegawa & Shigeji Kobayashi. (Illus.). 480p. 1986. pap. 36.00 (0-8161-8806-8) G K Hall.

Collection of Translations into Latin & Neo-Latin Poetry - Original Compositions. Paul Murgatroyd. LC 91-31508. 120p. 1991. lib. bdg. 59.95 (0-7734-9750-1) E Mellen.

Collection of Treaties & Other Documents Affecting the States of Malayasia, 1761-1963, 2 vols., Set. J. Dev Allen et al. LC 80-24804. 1980. 85.00 (0-379-00781-9) Oceana.

Collection of Upper South Carolina Genealogical & Family Records, Vol. 1. Ed. by James E. Wooley & Vivian F. Wooley. 416p. 1980. 37.50 (0-89308-157-4) Southern Hist Pr.

Collection of Upwards of Thirty Thousand Names of German, Swiss, Dutch, French & Other Immigrants in Pennsylvania from 1727 to 1776. Israel D. Rupp. LC 65-26916. (Illus.). 583p. 1994. reprint ed. 30.00 (0-8063-0302-6, 5045) Genealog Pub.

Collection of Valuable Documents, Being Birney's Vindication of Abolitionists. James G. Birney. reprint ed. 12.50 (0-404-00247-1) AMS Pr.

Collection of Victorian Poems, 1894-1895. Marie-Louise Reeves. 1991. 8.95 (0-533-09373-2) Vantage.

Collection of Works of Phil King. Phil King. LC 78-60042. 1978. 5.00 (0-9601900-1-5) Phil King.

Collection of Yiddish Proverbs. Malachi McCormick. (Proverbs of the World Ser.). (Illus.). 60p. (Orig.). 1982. pap. text ed. 15.00 (0-943984-02-5) Stone St Pr.

Collection Policies & Procedures see Installment Credit Series

Collection Practice. Thomas A. Clark, III. (Illus.). 61p. 1992. pap. 35.00 (0-685-14624-3) NJ Inst CLE.

Collection Program in Schools: Concepts, Practices & Information Sources. Phyllis J. Van Orden. 347p. 1988. lib. bdg. 27.50 (0-87287-572-5) Libs Unl.

***Collection Program in Schools: Concepts, Practices & Information Sources.** 2nd ed. Phyllis J. Van Orden. LC 94-32233. (Library Science Text Ser.). 400p. 1995. pap. text ed. 32.50 (1-56308-334-5) Libs Unl.

***Collection Program in Schools: Concepts, Practices & Information Sources.** 2nd ed. Phyllis J. Van Orden. LC 94-32233. (Library Science Text Ser.). 400p. 1995. lib. bdg. 42.50 (1-56308-120-2) Libs Unl.

Collection Series Dirt Bikes, Vol. II. 1992. pap. 29.95 (0-89287-574-7, M301) Clymer Pub.

Collection Strategies & Techniques. R. D. Rutherford. Ed. by James J. Andover. LC 85-25835. 120p. 1985. pap. 20.95 (0-934914-66-4) NACM.

***Collection Supervisor (Revenue)** (Career Examination Ser.: Series 1). Date not set. pap. 27.95 (0-8373-3672-4) Nat Learn.

Collection Systems: Operations & Maintenance. 1993. pap. 150.00 (1-881369-24-2) Water Environ.

Collection Systems Digest. 327p. Date not set. pap. 70.00 (1-881369-29-3) Water Environ.

Collection Systems Symposia, Vol. 6: WEF 1992 Annual Conference. 1992. pap. 150.00 (1-881369-09-9) Water Environ.

Collection Systems Symposium, Vol. 6: WEF Annual Conference, 1993. 378p. 1993. pap. 150.00 (1-881369-46-3) Water Environ.

Collection Techniques for Small Business. 2nd ed. Gini G. Scott & John J. Harrison. (Successful Business Library). 250p. 1994. pap. 19.95 (1-55571-171-5); ring bd. 39.95 (1-55571-312-2) Oasis Pr OR.

Collection, Transport, & Preparation of Blood Specimens for Coagulation Testing & Performance of Coagulation Assays. 2nd ed. (Approved Guideline Ser.: Vol. 6). 1991. 40.00 (1-56238-129-6, H21-A2) Natl Comm Clin Lab Stds.

***Collection Works, 45 Vols. Plus 2 Vol. Index.** 4th ed. V. I. Lenin. Date not set. lib. bdg. 500.00 (0-8285-1588-3) Pathfinder NY.

Collections. Boy Scouts of America Staff. (Illus.). 48p. (YA). (gr. 6-12). 1991. pap. 1.85 (0-8395-3242-3, 33242) BSA.

Collections. Dorothy M. Center. 48p. (Orig.). 1994. pap. write for info. (1-56167-139-8) Am Literary Pr.

Collections. David Drew. LC 93-16141. (J). 1994. write for info. (0-383-03683-6) SRA Schl Grp.

Collections: Pitkin Papers - Correspondence & Documents During William Pitkin's Governorship of the Colony of CT, 1766-1769, Vol. 19. 311p. 1921. 10.00 (0-940748-71-1) Conn Hist Soc.

Collections: Rolls of Connecticut Men in the French & Indian War, 1755-1757, Vol. 9. 354p. 1903. 10.00 (0-940748-63-0) Conn Hist Soc.

Collections: Vol. 20, Huntington Papers - Correspondence of the Brothers Joshua & Jedediah Huntington During the Period of the Revolution. 514p. 1923. 6.00 (0-940748-72-X) Conn Hist Soc.

Collections: Vol. 21, Wyllys Papers - Correspondence & Papers of the Wyllys Family of Hartford, 1590-1796. 567p. 1924. 10.00 (0-940748-73-8) Conn Hist Soc.

Collections: Vol. 22, Records of the Particular Court of Connecticut, 1639-1663. 302p. 1928. 10.00 (0-940748-74-6) Conn Hist Soc.

Collections: Vol. 23, Deanne Papers - Correspondence Between Silas Deanne, His Brothers & Their Business & Political Associates, 1771-1795. 277p. 1930. 10.00 (0-940748-75-4) Conn Hist Soc.

Collections: Vol. 24, Hoadly Memorial - Early Letters & Documents Relating to Connecticut. 210p. 1932. 10.00 (0-940748-76-2) Conn Hist Soc.

Collections: Vol. 3, Pierson's Some Help for the Indians; Gersham Bulkeley's Will & Doom; Trumbull's Extracts from Letters to T. Prince... 340p. 1895. 10.00 (0-940748-61-4) Conn Hist Soc.

Collections: Vol. 4, Talcott Papers - Correspondence & Documents During Joseph Talcott's Governorship of the Colony of Connecticut 1724-1736. 417p. 1892. 10.00 (0-940748-62-2) Conn Hist Soc.

Collections: Wolcott Papers - Correspondence & Documents During Roger Wolcott's Governorship of the Colony of CT, 1750-1754, Vol. 16. 557p. 1916. 10.00 (0-940748-68-1) Conn Hist Soc.

Collections & Programs of the American Antiquarian Society: A 175th-Anniversary Guide. American Antiquarian Society Staff. (Illus.). 194p. 1987. pap. text ed. 12.50 (0-912296-93-3) Am Antiquarian.

Collections & the Enforcement of Money Judgements. New York State Bar Association Staff. Ed. by Jack Getman et al. LC 84-60393. 467p. 1985. text ed. 60.00 (0-942954-05-X) NYS Bar.

Collections Conservation. R. DeCandido. 134p. 1993. pap. 15.00 (0-918006-67-8) ARL.

Collections Des Memoires Relatifs a L'histoire De France, 31 Vols, Set. Ed. by Francois P. Guizot. LC 75-88788. (FRE.). reprint ed. 1,999.50 (0-404-02970-1) AMS Pr.

Collections, Fitch Papers: Correspondence & Documents During Thomas Fitch's Governorship of the Colony of Connecticut. Incl. Vol. 17. 1750 to 1754. 402p. 1918. 10.00 (0-940748-69-X); Vol. 18. 1750 to 1754, Conclusion. 457p. 1920. 10.00 (0-940748-70-3); Vol. 17. 1750 to 1754. 402p. 1918. 10.00 (0-940748-69-X); Vol. 18. 1750 to 1754, Conclusion. 457p. 1920. 10.00 (0-940748-70-3); write for info. (0-318-51428-1) Conn Hist Soc.

Collections for the Future: Archivists, Curators, Historians, Bibliographers Speak. Geoscience Information Society Staff. Ed. by Jean T. Eaglesfield. (Geoscience Information Society Proceedings Ser.: No. 18). 170p. reprint ed. pap. 48.50 (0-8357-2798-X, 2039925) Bks Demand.

***Collections Guide: Moving Image Collections of Northeast Historic Film.** Patricia Burdick et al. (Illus.). 64p. (Orig.). 1995. pap. 9.95 (0-9646933-0-5) NE Historic.

Collections, Law Papers: Correspondence & Documents During Jonathan Law's Governorship of Connecticut. Incl. Vol. 13. 1740 to 1750, Continued. 398p. 1911. 10.00 (0-940748-65-7); Vol. 15. 1740 to 1750, Concluded. 531p. 1914. 10.00 (0-940748-67-3); Vol. 13. 1740 to 1750, Continued. 398p. 1911. 10.00 (0-940748-65-7); Vol. 15. 1740 to 1750, Concluded. 531p. 1914. 10.00 (0-940748-67-3); write for info. (0-318-51427-3) Conn Hist Soc.

Collections Made Easy! Michael J. Berry. Ed. by Melanie C. Karaffa. 142p. 1992. 39.95 (1-878487-48-5) Practice Mgmt Info.

Collections Management. Ed. by Anne Fahy. LC 94-15725. (Leicester Readers in Museum Studies Ser.). 240p. 1994. 65.00x (0-415-11282-6, B4646); pap. 25.00 (0-415-11283-4, B4650) Routledge.

Collections of Brown University: A Twentieth Anniversary Exhibition. Diana L. Johnson et al. (Illus.). 64p. (Orig.). 1992. pap. 8.00 (0-933519-22-2) D W Bell Gallery.

Collections of Designs for Cross Stitches. Ondori Publishing Company Staff. LC 80-81038. (Illus.). 1980. pap. 11.95 (0-87040-486-5) Japan Pubns USA.

Collections of Frozen Tissues: Value, Management, Field & Laboratory Procedures, & Directory of Existing Collections. Ed. by Herbert C. Dessauer & Mark S. Hafner. (Illus.). 74p. (Orig.). 1984. pap. 4.00 (0-942924-10-X) Assn Syst Coll.

Collections of Lyrics & Poems: Sixteenth & Seventeenth Centuries, 6 vols. Ed. by Arthur H. Bullen. Incl. Lyrics from the Song-Books of the Elizabethan Age. LC 70-164695. reprint ed. 34.50 (0-404-01221-3); More Lyrics from the Song-Books of the Elizabethan Age. LC 70-164695. reprint ed. 34.50 (0-404-01222-1); Lyrics from the Dramatists of the Elizabethan Age. LC 70-164695. reprint ed. 34.50 (0-404-01223-X); Musa Proterva: Love Poems of the Restoration. LC 70-164695. reprint ed. 34.50 (0-404-01224-8); Speculum Amantis: Love Poems from Rare Song-Books & Miscellanies of the Seventeenth Century. LC 70-164695. reprint ed. 34.50 (0-404-01225-6); Poems, Chiefly Lyrical, from Romances & Prose-Tracts of the Elizabethan Age: With Chosen Poems of Nicholas Breton. LC 70-164695. reprint ed. 34.50 (0-404-01226-4); LC 70-164695. write for info. (0-318-50541-X) AMS Pr.

Collections of Lyrics & Poems: Sixteenth & Seventeenth Centuries, 6 vols, Set. Ed. by Arthur H. Bullen. Incl. Lyrics from the Song-Books of the Elizabethan Age. LC 70-164695. reprint ed. 34.50 (0-404-01221-3); More Lyrics from the Song-Books of the Elizabethan Age. LC 70-164695. reprint ed. 34.50 (0-404-01222-1); Lyrics from the Dramatists of the Elizabethan Age. LC 70-164695. reprint ed. 34.50 (0-404-01223-X); Musa Proterva: Love Poems of the Restoration. LC 70-164695. reprint ed. 34.50 (0-404-01224-8); Speculum Amantis: Love Poems from Rare Song-Books & Miscellanies of the Seventeenth Century. LC 70-164695. reprint ed. 34.50 (0-404-01225-6); Poems, Chiefly Lyrical, from Romances & Prose-Tracts of the Elizabethan Age: With Chosen Poems of Nicholas Breton. LC 70-164695. reprint ed. 34.50 (0-404-01226-4); LC 70-164695. 207.00 (0-404-01220-5) AMS Pr.

***Collections of Paintings in Madrid, 1601-1755.** Marcus B. Burke & Peter G. Cherry. Ed. by Maria L. Gilbert. 900p. 1995. 150.00 (3-598-21696-3, Getty Art Hist) J P Getty Trust.

Collections of Selected Pamphlets. W. Kelly. pap. text ed. 7.95 (0-88172-093-3) Believers Bkshelf.

Collections of the British Museum. Ed. by David H. Wilson. (Illus.). (C). 1989. 64.95 (0-521-37539-8) Cambridge U Pr.

Collections of the Budapest Museum of Applied Arts. Pal Mikos. 376p. 1981. 165.00 (0-317-57235-0, Pub. by Collets UK) St Mut.

Collections of the Connecticut Historical Society, 20 vols., Set. Connecticut Historical Society Staff. LC 74-19612. reprint ed. write for info. (0-404-12383-X) AMS Pr.

Collections of the Maine Historical Society, 10 vols., Set. Maine Historical Society. reprint ed. 345.00 (0-404-11059-2) AMS Pr.

***Collections of the Maine Historical Society, Vol. IV.** Maine Historical Society Staff. (Illus.). 433p. (Orig.). 1995. pap. text ed. 28.00 (0-7884-0172-6) Heritage Bk.

C

An Asterisk (*) at the beginning of an entry indicates that the title is appearing in BIP for the first time.

C

An Asterisk (*) at the beginning of an entry indicates that the title is appearing in BIP for the first time.

1371

Collective Self-Help in Brazil. Henk Gilhuis & Sjouke Volbeda. 196p. (Orig.). 1992. pap. 44.50 (*90-6275-672-7*, Pub. by Delft U Pr NE) Coronet Bks.
Collective Silence: German Identity & the Legacy of Shame. Ed. by Barbara HeimannsBerg & Christoph J. Schmidt. Tr. by Gordon Wheeler & Cynthia Oudejans Harris. 235p. 1993. 29.95 (*1-55542-556-9*) Jossey-Bass.
Collective Violence & Sacrifice in Shakespeare's Julius Caesar. Rene Girard. (Chapbooks in Literature Ser.). (Illus.). 36p. (Orig.). 1990. pap. text ed. 5.00 (*1-878603-00-0*) Bennington Coll.
Collective Vision: Clarence H. White & His Students. Museum Studies Class et al. Ed. by Lucinda Barnes. LC 85-16558. (Illus.). 72p. (Orig.). 1985. pap. 35.00 (*0-936270-24-1*) CA St U LB Art.
Collective Wisdom. Robert Wiltenberg & Sondra J. Stang. 352p. (C). 1988. text ed. write for info. (*0-07-554961-1*) McGraw.
***Collective Works Vol. 1: Osprey.** George F. Brown, Sr. 34p. 1993. 10.00 (*0-9645242-0-1*) G F Brown.
Collective Works of Robert E. Watlington. Robert E. Watington & Robert E. Watlington. 56p. (Orig.). 1981. pap. 10.95 (*0-940762-24-2*) Funky-Punky-Chic.
***Collectively Bargained Multi-Employer Pension Plans.** Joseph J. Melone. (C). 1963. 11.50 (*0-256-00654-7*) Irwin.
Collectives in the Spanish Revolution. Gaston Leval. Tr. by Vernon Richards. 368p. 1975. 15.00 (*0-900384-11-5*) Left Bank.
Collectivity in Social Group Work: Concept & Practice. Ed. by Norma C. Lang & Joanne Sulman. LC 86-31898. (Social Work with Groups Ser.: Vol. 9, No. 4). 125p. 1987. text ed. 29.95 (*0-86656-661-9*) Haworth Pr.
Collectivization, Convergence & Capitalism: Political Economy in a Divided World. Michael Ellman. 1984. text ed. 115.00 (*0-12-237520-3*) Acad Pr.
Collector. John Fowles. 256p. 1981. mass mkt. 5.99 (*0-440-31335-X*) Dell.
Collector Car Digest. Ed. by John Gunnell. LC 93-77545. 344p. 1993. pap. 24.95 (*0-87341-257-5*) Krause Pubns.
Collector of Characters: Reminiscences of Theodore Spicer-Simson. Theodore Spicer-Simson. LC 62-15965. (Illus.). 1962. 10.95 (*0-87024-015-3*) U of Miami Pr.
Collector of Cold Weather. Lawrence Raab. LC 76-3301. (American Poetry Ser.: Vol.9). 1976. pap. 9.95 (*0-912946-45-8*) Ecco Pr.
***Collector of Treasures: And Other Botswana Village Tales.** Head. (African Writers Ser.). 109p. (C). 1992. pap. 9.95 (*0-435-90981-9*) Heinemann.
Collector Steiff Values. Peter Consalvi. 128p. 1993. 19.95 (*0-87588-404-0*, 4528) Hobby Hse.
***Collectors.** Robert Carter. LC 94-75333. (J). (gr. 4-7). 1994. 14.00 (*0-688-13763-6*) Lothrop.
Collectors: Anecdotes & Answers about Antiques & Collectibles. Bob Rau. Ed. by Karla Powell. LC 88-82193. (Illus.). 104p. 1988. 19.95 (*0-932575-98-6*) Gr Arts Ctr Pub.
Collectors & Curiosities: Paris & Venice, 1500-1800. Krzystof Pomian. 348p. 1991. 47.95 (*0-7456-0680-6*) Blackwell Pubs.
Collector's Bach. Nathan Broder. LC 77-28265. (Keystone Books in English Ser.). 192p. 1978. reprint ed. text ed. 49.75 (*0-313-20240-0*, BRBAC, Greenwood Pr) Greenwood.
Collector's Bag: Traveller's Tales from India & Elsewhere. R. V. Vernede. (Illus.). 267p. 1993. 29.00 (*0-86140-352-5*, Pub. by Colin Smythe Ltd UK) Dufour.
Collector's Book Doll Clothes, Vol. I. Coleman. 1976. 130.95 (*0-8488-1533-5*) Amereon Ltd.
Collectors Book Doll Clothes, Patterns. Coleman. 1976. 40.95 (*0-8488-1534-3*) Amereon Ltd.
Collector's Book of Doll Poems. Ed. by Elaine Gilmore & Lachlan MacDonald. (Illus.). 1990. 14.95 (*0-937480-04-5*) Intl Resources.
Collector's Book of Fluorescent Minerals. Manuel A. Robbins. 320p. 1983. text ed. 69.95 (*0-442-27506-4*) Chapman & Hall.
Collector's Bookshelf: A Comprehensive Listing of Authors, Their Pseudonyms, & Their Books. Joseph R. LeFontaine. 333p. (C). 1990. 73.95 (*0-87975-605-5*) Prometheus Bks.
Collector's Bookshelf Value Guide. Joseph R. LeFontaine. 113p. (Orig.). (C). 1990. pap. 19.95 (*0-87975-606-3*) Prometheus Bks.
Collector's Cabinet: Flemish Paintings from New England Private Collections. James A. Welu. (Illus.). 144p. (Orig.). 1983. pap. 19.95 (*0-87023-420-X*) U of Mass Pr.
Collector's Choices: Asian Art from the Collection of Dr. Walter A. Compton. James Robinson & Yutaka Mino. LC 82-84073. (Illus.). 72p. (Orig.). 1983. pap. text ed. 9.00 (*0-936260-08-4*) Ind Mus Art.
Collector's Chopin & Schumann. Harold C. Schonberg. LC 77-28257. (Keystone Books in English Ser.: No. KB 8). 256p. 1978. reprint ed. text ed. 59.75 (*0-313-20242-7*, SCCC, Greenwood Pr) Greenwood.
Collector's Club Philatelist, Cumulative Index to Vols. 1-50, 1922-1971. Ernest C. Wilkens & John D. Dowd. 71p. 1972. pap. 12.50 (*0-912574-00-3*) Collectors.
***Collectors' Compendium of Roseville Pottery, Vol. 1.** Randall B. Monsen. (Illus.). 128p. 1995. 35.00 (*0-9636102-2-8*) Monsen & Baer.
Collector's Digest on German Character Dolls. Robert MacDowell & Karin MacDowell. (Illus.). 160p. (Orig.). 1981. pap. text ed. 9.95 (*0-87588-177-7*, 422) Hobby Hse.
Collectors Encyclopedia American Furniture. Robert Swedberg. 1991. 24.95 (*0-89145-441-1*) Collector Bks.
Collector's Encyclopedia of Akro Glassware. Cathy Florence. (Illus.). 80p. 1982. 14.95 (*0-89145-487-X*) Collector Bks.
Collector's Encyclopedia of American Dinnerware. Jo Cunningham. (Illus.). 320p. 1982. 24.95 (*0-89145-199-4*) Collector Bks.
Collector's Encyclopedia of American Furniture, Vol. II. Swedberg. 1991. 24.95 (*0-89145-480-2*) Collector Bks.
Collector's Encyclopedia of American Furniture Vol. 3: Country Furniture of the 18th & 19th Centuries. Robert W. Swedberg. 1993. 24.95 (*0-89145-560-4*) Collector Bks.
Collector's Encyclopedia of Barbie Dolls. Sybil DeWein & Joan Ashabraner. 312p. 1990. 19.95 (*0-89145-052-1*) Collector Bks.
Collector's Encyclopedia of Buttons. Sally C. Luscomb. LC 67-27049. (Illus.). 256p. 1993. 24.95 (*0-88740-500-2*) Schiffer.
Collector's Encyclopedia of California Pottery. Chipman. 1991. 24.95 (*0-89145-481-0*) Collector Bks.
Collectors Encyclopedia of Children's Dishes. Whitmyer. 176p. 1992. 19.95 (*0-89145-524-8*) Collector Bks.
Collector's Encyclopedia of Colorado Pottery. Carol Carlton. 1994. 24.95 (*0-89145-600-7*) Collector Bks.
Collector's Encyclopedia of Compacts: Carryalls & Face Powder Boxes. Laura M. Mueller. 1993. 24.95 (*0-89145-562-0*) Collector Bks.
Collectors Encyclopedia of Cookie Jars. Fred Roerig. 1991. 24.95 (*0-89145-438-1*) Collector Bks.
Collector's Encyclopedia of Cookie Jars, Vol. 2. Fred Roerig. 1993. 24.95 (*0-89145-563-9*) Collector Bks.
Collector's Encyclopedia of Cowan Pottery: Identification & Values. Tim Saloff & Jamie Saloff. 176p. 1993. 24.95 (*0-89145-533-7*, 3429) Collector Bks.
Collector's Encyclopedia of Depression Glass. 11th ed. Gene Florence. 1993. 19.95 (*0-89145-554-X*) Collector Bks.
Collectors Encyclopedia of Disneyana. Michael Stern. 272p. 1992. 24.95 (*0-89145-500-0*) Collector Bks.
Collector's Encyclopedia of Dolls, Vol. 1. Dorothy S. Coleman et al. (Illus.). 1986. 45.00 (*0-517-00059-8*, Crown) Crown Pub Group.
***Collector's Encyclopedia of Dolls, Vol. 2.** Colman. 1995. (*0-517-00796-7*) Crown Pub Group.
***Collector's Encyclopedia of Early Noritake.** Aimee N. Alden. 216p. 1995. 24.95 (*0-89145-637-6*, 3961) Collector Bks.
Collector's Encyclopedia of Fiesta. 7th ed. Bob Huxford. 1991. 19.95 (*0-89145-449-7*) Collector Bks.
Collector's Encyclopedia of Figural & Novelty Salt & Pepper Shakers, Vol. II. Melva Davern. 212p. 1990. 19.95 (*0-89145-407-1*) Collector Bks.
Collector's Encyclopedia of Flow Blue China. Mary F. Gaston. (Illus.). 160p. 1989. 19.95 (*0-89145-236-2*, 1439) Collector Bks.
Collector's Encyclopedia of Fostoria: An Identification & Value Guide of Pressed, Molded And. Ann Kerr. 1993. 24.95 (*0-89145-564-7*) Collector Bks.
Collector's Encyclopedia of Geisha Girl Porcelain. Elyce Litts. (Illus.). 176p. 1988. 19.95 (*0-89145-353-9*, 1813) Collector Bks.
Collector's Encyclopedia of Granite Ware. Helen Greguire. 416p. 1990. 24.95 (*0-89145-412-8*) Collector Bks.
Collector's Encyclopedia of Granite Ware, Bk. 2: Colors, Shapes, & Values. Helen Greguire. 384p. 1993. 24.95 (*0-89145-534-5*, 3430) Collector Bks.
Collector's Encyclopedia of Hall China. 2nd ed. Margaret Whitmyer. 1994. 24.95 (*0-89145-581-7*) Collector Bks.
Collector's Encyclopedia of Heisey Glass 1925-1938. Neila Bredehoft. (Illus.). 462p. 1991. 24.95 (*0-89145-307-5*) Collector Bks.
Collector's Encyclopedia of Homer Laughlin China: Reference & Value Guide. Joanne Jasper. 208p. 1993. 24.95 (*0-89145-535-3*, 3431) Collector Bks.
Collector's Encyclopedia of Hull Pottery. Roberts. 1990. 19.95 (*0-89145-149-8*) Collector Bks.
***Collector's Encyclopedia of Lefton China.** Loretta DeLozier. 144p. 1995. 19.95 (*0-89145-640-6*, 3962) Collector Bks.
Collectors Encyclopedia of Limoges Porcelain. 2nd ed. Mary F. Gaston. 1991. 24.95 (*0-89145-461-6*) Collector Bks.
Collectors Encyclopedia of Madame Alexander Dolls. Patricia Smith. 1991. 24.95 (*0-89145-453-5*) Collector Bks.
Collectors' Encyclopedia of Majolica. Katz-Marks. 1992. 19.95 (*0-89145-496-9*) Collector Bks.
Collector's Encyclopedia of McCoy Pottery. Sharon Huxford & Bob Huxford. (Illus.). 248p. 1991. 19.95 (*0-89145-068-8*) Collector Bks.
***Collector's Encyclopedia of Metlox Potteries.** Carl Gibbs, Jr. 288p. 1995. 24.95 (*0-89145-643-0*, 3963) Collector Bks.
Collector's Encyclopedia of Milk Glass. Betty Newbound. 1994. pap. 24.95 (*0-89145-626-0*) Collector Bks.
Collectors Encyclopedia of Niloak. Gifford. 176p. 1992. 19.95 (*0-89145-526-4*) Collector Bks.
Collector's Encyclopedia of Nippon: Third Series, Vol. III. Joan Van Patten. (Illus.). 320p. 1986. 24.95 (*0-89145-308-3*, 1665) Collector Bks.
Collector's Encyclopedia of Nippon Porcelain: Second Series, Vol. II. Joan Van Patten. (Illus.). 240p. 1982. 24.95 (*0-89145-186-2*, 1350) Collector Bks.
Collector's Encyclopedia of Noritake. Joan Van Patten. (Illus.). 200p. 1990. 24.95 (*0-89145-244-3*, 1447) Collector Bks.
Collector's Encyclopedia of Noritake Second Series. Joan Van Patten. 264p. 1993. 24.95 (*0-89145-536-1*, 3432) Collector Bks.
Collector's Encyclopedia of Occupied Japan Collectibles. Gene Florence. (Illus.). 108p. 1990. 14.95 (*0-89145-004-1*) Collector Bks.
Collectors Encyclopedia of Occupied Japan Collectibles, Series 5. Gene Florence. 1992. pap. 14.95 (*0-89145-497-7*) Collector Bks.
Collector's Encyclopedia of Occupied Japan Collectibles II. Gene Florence. (Illus.). 112p. 1990. 14.95 (*0-89145-111-0*) Collector Bks.
Collector's Encyclopedia of Occupied Japan III. Gene Florence. (Illus.). 144p. 1990. 14.95 (*0-89145-321-0*) Collector Bks.
Collector's Encyclopedia of Occupied Japan, 4th Series. Gene Florence. 128p. 1990. pap. 14.95 (*0-89145-401-2*) Collector Bks.
Collector's Encyclopedia of Pattern Glass. Mollie Helen McCain. (Illus.). 544p. 1990. pap. 12.95 (*0-89145-211-7*, 1380) Collector Bks.
***Collector's Encyclopedia of Pickard China.** Alan B. Reed. 216p. 1995. 24.95 (*0-89145-646-5*, 3964) Collector Bks.
Collector's Encyclopedia of R. S. Prussia. Mary F. Gaston. (Third Ser.). 1993. 24.95 (*0-89145-565-5*) Collector Bks.
Collector's Encyclopedia of R. S. Prussia. Mary F. Gaston. 1994. 24.95 (*0-89145-609-0*) Collector Bks.
Collector's Encyclopedia of R. S. Prussia: Second Series. Mary F. Gaston. (Illus.). 232p. 1986. 24.95 (*0-89145-317-2*) Collector Bks.
Collector's Encyclopedia of Roseville Pottery. Sharon Huxford & Bob Huxford. (Illus.). 192p. 1991. 19.95 (*0-89145-015-7*) Collector Bks.
Collector's Encyclopedia of Roseville Pottery: Second Series. Sharon Huxford & Bob Huxford. (Illus.). 208p. 1991. 19.95 (*0-89145-139-0*) Collector Bks.
Collector's Encyclopedia of Russel Wright. Ann Kerr. 1990. 19.95 (*0-89145-423-3*) Collector Bks.
Collector's Encyclopedia of Salt & Pepper Shakers. Melva Davern. (Illus.). 160p. 1991. 19.95 (*0-89145-291-5*) Collector Bks.
***Collector's Encyclopedia of Sascha Brastoff.** Steve Conti et al. 320p. 1995. 24.95 (*0-89145-647-3*, 3965) Collector Bks.
Collector's Encyclopedia of Toys & Dolls. Lydia Darbyshire. 1990. 19.98 (*1-55521-667-6*) Bk Sales Inc.
Collectors Encyclopedia of Van Briggle Art Pottery. Sasicki. 144p. 1992. 24.95 (*0-89145-519-1*) Collector Bks.
Collector's Encyclopedia of Weller Pottery. Huxford. 375p. 1990. 29.95 (*0-89145-114-5*) Collector Bks.
Collector's Eye: Japanese Art Lent by Friends of Japan Society Gallery. Anthony Derham et al. LC 89-84125. (Illus.). 25p. 1995. pap. 25.00 (*0-913304-27-1*, 271X) Japan Soc.
Collector's Guide to American Pressed Glass, 1825-1915. Kyle Hudson. LC 91-50682. (Illus.). 208p. 1992. pap. 18.95 (*0-87069-612-2*, Wallace-Hmestead) Chilton.
Collector's Guide to American Toy Trains. Sue Bagdade & Al Bagdade. LC 89-51556. (Illus.). 244p. 1990. pap. 16.95 (*0-87069-532-0*, Wallace-Hmestead) Chilton.
Collector's Guide to Ames U. S. Contract Military Edged Weapons: 1832-1906. rev. ed. Ron G. Hickox. 1992. 14.95 (*1-877704-11-3*) Pioneer Pr.
Collector's Guide to Anchor Hocking's Fire-King Glassware. Garry Kilgo et al. 176p. 1991. 24.95 (*0-9635119-0-4*) K&W Collect.
Collector's Guide to Antique Paper Dolls. Clara H. Fawcett. 1989. pap. 6.95 (*0-486-25956-0*) Dover.
Collector's Guide to Art Deco. Mary F. Gaston. (Illus.). 136p. 1989. pap. 14.95 (*0-89145-377-6*) Collector Bks.
Collectors Guide to Black Glass. Marlene Toohey. Ed. by Tom Klopp. 112p. 1988. 19.95 (*0-915410-48-6*); pap. 15.95 (*0-915410-47-8*) Antique Pubns.
Collector's Guide to Blue Ridge Dinnerware. Betty Newbound. 1994. pap. 18.95 (*0-89145-583-3*) Collector Bks.
***Collector's Guide to British Dolls since 1920.** Colette Mansell. (Illus.). 390p. Date not set. 45.00 (*0-7091-9380-7*, Pub. by R Hale Ltd UK) Antique Collect.
***Collector's Guide to Burnt Wood Antiques.** Frank L. Hawn. 1994. pap. text ed. 14.95 (*0-926110-05-5*) Golden Era Pubns.
Collectors Guide to Buttons. Diana Epstein. (Illus.). 84p. (Orig.). 1990. pap. 10.95 (*0-8027-7342-7*) Walker & Co.
Collector's Guide to Civil War Period Bottles & Jars. 2nd ed. George M. Russell. (Illus.). 96p. Date not set. pap. 15.95 (*1-880365-27-8*) Prof Pr NC.
Collector's Guide to Clocks. Derek Roberts. 1992. 12.98 (*1-55521-778-8*) Bk Sales Inc.
Collector's Guide to Colt Forty-Five Service Pistols: Models of 1911 & 1911A1. Charles W. Clawson. (Illus.). 96p. (Orig.). 1993. pap. 19.95 (*0-9633971-5-X*) C W Clawson.
Collector's Guide to Comic Books. John Hegenberger. LC 89-51561. (Illus.). 248p. 1990. pap. 12.95 (*0-87069-548-7*, Wallace-Hmestead) Chilton.
Collector's Guide to Country Stoneware. Carol Raycraft. 1990. pap. 14.95 (*0-89145-420-9*) Collector Bks.
Collectors Guide to Decoys. Bob Huxford. 1990. pap. 14.95 (*0-89145-389-X*) Collector Bks.
Collectors Guide to Diesinger Steins. Patricia L. Manusov & Eugene V. Manusov. (Illus.). 96p. (Orig.). 1991. pap. 24.95 (*0-9629458-0-3*) Bristol Pr.
***Collector's Guide to Dolls in Uniform.** Joseph Bourgeois. 1995. pap. 18.95 (*0-89145-659-7*) Collector Bks.
Collectors Guide to Early Photographs. O. Henry Mace. 224p. 1990. pap. 16.95 (*0-87069-547-9*, Wallace-Hmestead) Chilton.
Collector's Guide to Fossil Sharks & Rays from the Cretaceous of Texas. Bruce J. Wezton & Roger F. Farish. (Illus.). 204p. (Orig.). Date not set. pap. 24.95 (*0-9638394-0-3*) Before Time.
Collector's Guide to Games & Puzzles. Caroline Goodfellow. 1991. 12.98 (*1-55521-727-3*) Bk Sales Inc.
Collector's Guide to German WW Two Combat Medals & Political Awards. Chris Ailsby. (Illus.). 160p. (Orig.). 1994. pap. 19.95 (*0-7818-0225-3*) Hippocrene Bks.
Collector's Guide to Harker Pottery, U. S. A. Identification & Values. Neva Colbert. 128p. 1993. pap. 17.95 (*0-89145-537-X*, 3433) Collector Bks.
Collector's Guide to Heisey & Heisey by Imperial Glass Animals. Frank L. Hahn & Paul Kikeli. 76p. (Orig.). 1991. pap. text ed. 19.95 (*0-926110-01-2*) Golden Era Pubns.
Collector's Guide to History & Uniforms Od Das Heer: 1933-1945. Chris Ellis. (Illus.). 160p. (Orig.). 1994. pap. 19.95 (*0-7818-0226-1*) Hippocrene Bks.
Collector's Guide to Hull Pottery - the Dinnerware Lines: Identification & Values. Barbara L. Gick-Burke. 168p. 1993. pap. 16.95 (*0-89145-538-8*, 3434) Collector Bks.
Collector's Guide to Ideal Dolls. Judith Izen. 1993. pap. 18.95 (*0-89145-566-3*) Collector Bks.
***Collector's Guide to Inkwells.** Veldon Badders. 176p. 1995. pap. 18.95 (*0-89145-639-2*, 3966) Collector Bks.
Collector's Guide to Japanese Cameras. Ed. by Koich Sugiyama et al. LC 85-40113. (Illus.). 328p. 1985. 85.00 (*0-87011-743-2*) Kodansha.
Collector's Guide to Kodak Cameras. James M. McKeown & Joan C. McKeown. (Illus.). 176p. (Orig.). 1981. pap. 16.95 (*0-931838-02-9*, CP3802, Amphoto) Watson-Guptill.
***Collectors Guide to Kuribayashi - Petri Cameras.** John R. Baird. LC 91-71476. (Illus.). 288p. 1991. 34.95 (*0-931838-16-9*) Centennial Photo Serv.
Collector's Guide to Lu-ray Pastels: Ts&T Premier Potters of America. Bill Meehan. 1994. pap. 17.95 (*0-89145-608-2*) Collector Bks.
Collector's Guide to Luger Values. Michael Reese. 1972. pap. 2.00 (*0-911116-79-6*) Pelican.
Collector's Guide to Made in Japan Ceramics. Carole B. White. 1994. pap. 18.95 (*0-89145-582-5*) Collector Bks.
Collectors Guide to Magazine Paper. Mary Young. 1990. pap. 14.95 (*0-89145-424-1*) Collector Bks.
Collector's Guide to Masks. Timothy Teuten. 1990. 12.98 (*1-55521-543-2*) Bk Sales Inc.
Collector's Guide to Miniature Teddy Bears. Cynthia Powell. 1993. pap. 17.95 (*0-89145-567-1*) Collector Bks.
Collector's Guide to Modern Australian Ceramics. J. Mansfield. (Illus.). 128p. 1989. text ed. 60.00 (*0-947131-09-4*) Gordon & Breach.
Collector's Guide to Monster, Science Fiction & Fantasy Film Magazines. Robert V. Michelucci. LC 85-82030. (Illus.). 250p. (Orig.). 1988. pap. 9.95 (*0-911137-06-8*) Imagine.
Collector's Guide to Novelty Radios. Marty Bunis. 1994. pap. 18.95 (*0-89145-612-0*) Collector Bks.
Collector's Guide to Oak Furniture. Jennifer George. 1994. pap. 12.95 (*0-89145-623-6*) Collector Bks.
Collector's Guide to Old Fishing Reels. Dan Homel. (Illus.). 96p. 1991. pap. 9.95 (*1-879522-01-2*) Forrest Pk.
Collector's Guide to Paperweights. Sara Rossi. 1990. 12.98 (*1-55521-541-6*) Bk Sales Inc.
Collector's Guide to Post Cards. Jane Wood. (Illus.). 174p. (Orig.). 1991. pap. 9.95 (*0-89145-241-9*, 1441) Collector Bks.
Collector's Guide to Postwar Tin Toys, with Prices. Jack Tempest. (Illus.). 128p. 1991. 24.95 (*0-87069-632-7*) Chilton.
Collector's Guide to Quilts. Suzy M. Anderson. LC 89-51551. (Illus.). 200p. 1991. pap. text ed. 17.95 (*0-87069-534-7*, Wallace-Hmestead) Chilton.
Collector's Guide to Rollei Cameras. Arthur Evans. LC 86-70749. (Illus.). 272p. 1986. 22.95 (*0-931838-06-1*, CP3806, Amphoto) Watson-Guptill.
Collectors Guide to SA Insignia. David Fuller. (Illus.). 177p. 1985. 35.00 (*0-931065-04-6*) Matthaus Pubs.
Collector's Guide to Seashells of the World. Jerome M. Eisenberg. (Illus.). 224p. 1989. 15.99 (*0-517-69096-9*) Random Hse Value.
Collectors Guide to Shawnee Pottery. Duane Vanderbilt. 144p. 1992. 19.95 (*0-89145-501-9*) Collector Bks.
Collector's Guide to Snow Domes. Helene Guarnaccia. 1993. pap. 18.95 (*0-89145-568-X*) Collector Bks.
Collector's Guide to Swords, Daggers & Cutlasses. Gerald Weland. 1991. 12.98 (*1-55521-726-5*) Bk Sales Inc.
Collector's Guide to the American Musical Theatre, 2 vols., Set. David Hummel. LC 83-7520. 940p. 1984. 98.50 (*0-8108-1637-7*) Scarecrow.
Collector's Guide to the American Musical Theatre, 2 vols., Vol. 1: The Shows. David Hummel. 940p. 1984. Vol. 1, The Shows. write for info. (*0-318-57597-3*) Scarecrow.
Collector's Guide to the American Musical Theatre, 2 vols., Vol. 2: Index. David Hummel. 940p. 1984. Vol. 2, Index. write for info. (*0-318-57598-1*) Scarecrow.
Collector's Guide to the M1 Garand & the M1 Carbine. Bruce N. Canfield. LC 87-63578. (Illus.). 144p. 1988. pap. 22.00 (*0-917218-32-9*) A Mowbray.
***Collector's Guide to the Waffen-SS.** Lumsden. 1995. pap. (*0-7818-0357-8*) Hippocrene Bks.
Collector's Guide to the '03 Springfield. Bruce N. Canfield. LC 87-63578. 160p. 1989. pap. 22.00 (*0-917218-40-X*) A Mowbray.
Collectors Guide to Tootsietoys. David Richter. 1991. pap. 16.95 (*0-89145-442-X*) Collector Bks.
Collector's Guide to Trading Cards: Identification & Values. Robert Reed. 128p. 1993. pap. 17.95 (*0-89145-542-6*, 3438) Collector Bks.
Collector's Guide to Transistor Radios. Marty Bunis. 1993. pap. 15.95 (*0-89145-569-8*) Collector Bks.
Collectors Guide to Trivets & Stands. Rob R. Kelly & James Ellwood. 264p. 1990. text ed. 39.95 (*0-926110-00-4*) Golden Era Pubns.
***Collector's Guide to Trolls, Identification & Values.** Pat Peterson. 384p. 1995. pap. 18.95 (*0-89145-649-X*, 3967) Collector Bks.

An Asterisk (*) at the beginning of an entry indicates that the title is appearing in BIP for the first time.

An Asterisk (*) at the beginning of an entry indicates that the title is appearing in BIP for the first time.

1373

College Algebra. 2nd ed. Dennis T. Christy. 496p. (C). 1992. student ed write for info. (*0-697-12354-5*) Wm C Brown Pubs.

College Algebra. 2nd ed. Stanley I. Grossman. 688p. (C). 1992. teacher ed write for info. (*0-03-075511-5*); text ed. 46.75 (*0-03-052168-8*) SCP.

College Algebra. 2nd ed. Marshall D. Hestenes & Richard O. Hill, Jr. (Illus.). 448p. (C). 1986. text ed. write for info. (*0-13-140856-9*) P-H.

College Algebra. 2nd ed. Thomas W. Hungerford & Richard Mercer. 512p. (C). 1991. teacher ed write for info. (*0-03-054243-X*); text ed. 46.75 (*0-03-054229-4*) SCP.

College Algebra. 2nd ed. Jerome E. Kaufmann. 528p. (C). 1990. text ed. 48.95 (*0-534-92095-0*) PWS Pubs.

College Algebra, 2 Vols. 2nd ed. Timothy J. Kelly et al. (C). 1991. pap. 57.16 (*0-395-43215-4*) HM.

College Algebra. 2nd ed. Roland E. Larson. 576p. (C). 1990. student ed 8.50 (*0-669-16275-2*); teacher ed 10.50 (*0-669-16276-0*); teacher ed 2.00 (*0-669-16274-4*); text ed. 32.50 (*0-669-16273-6*) Heath.

College Algebra. 2nd ed. Louis Leithold. (Illus.). (C). 1980. text ed. write for info. (*0-02-369580-3*) Macmillan.

College Algebra. 2nd ed. Arnold R. Steffensen & L. Murphy Johnson. (C). 1992. text ed. 57.50 (*0-673-46455-5*) HarpCollege.

College Algebra. 2nd ed. Ralph C. Steinlage. (Illus.). 509p. (C). 1986. text ed. 45.00 (*0-314-29531-3*) West Pub.

College Algebra. 2nd ed. Dennis Zill & Jacqueline Dewar. 576p. (C). 1990. teacher ed 19.95 (*0-07-557008-4*); teacher ed write for info. (*0-318-65087-8*); text ed. write for info. (*0-07-557097-1*); student ed, pap. text ed. 11.84 (*0-07-557009-2*) McGraw.

College Algebra. 2nd suppl. ed. Dennis T. Christy. 496p. (C). 1992. write for info. (*0-697-16429-2*) Wm C Brown Pubs.

College Algebra. 2nd suppl. ed. Dennis T. Christy. 100p. (C). 1992. spiral bd. write for info. (*0-697-17095-0*) Wm C Brown Pubs.

College Algebra. 3rd ed. David C. Cohen. Ed. by Marshall. 592p. (C). 1992. text ed. 58.50 (*0-314-93362-X*) West Pub.

College Algebra. 3rd ed. Roland E. Larson & Robert P. Hostetler. 620p. (C). 1993. Instr.'s annotated ed. student ed write for info. (*0-669-33235-6*); text ed. write for info. (*0-669-28304-5*); Study & solutions guide. student ed, text ed. write for info. (*0-669-28306-1*); Complete solutions guide. teacher ed, text ed. write for info. (*0-669-28307-X*); Transparencies. trans. write for info. (*0-669-28322-3*); College Algebra videotapes. vhs write for info. (*0-669-28580-3*); Test item file/Resource guide. write for info. (*0-669-28309-6*) Heath.

College Algebra. 3rd ed. Max A. Sobel & Norbert Lerner. 640p. (C). 1991. text ed. write for info. (*0-13-142118-2*) P-H.

College Algebra. 3rd ed. Ralph C. Steinlage. Ed. by Marshall. 500p. (C). 1990. text ed. 57.50 (*0-314-57827-7*) West Pub.

College Algebra. 3rd ed. Michael Sullivan. 784p. (C). 1992. write for info. (*0-02-418471-3*) Macmillan.

College Algebra. 4th ed. Raymond A. Barnett & Michael R. Ziegler. 640p. 1989. Student solution manual. student ed, pap. text ed. write for info. (*0-07-003933-X*) McGraw.

College Algebra. 4th ed. R. David Gustafson & Peter D. Frisk. LC 89-31887. 480p. (C). 1989. text ed. 51.95 (*0-534-10380-4*) Brooks-Cole.

College Algebra. 4th ed. Max Sobel & Norbert Lerner. LC 94-11437. 1995. text ed. write for info. (*0-13-311614-X*) P-H.

College Algebra. 5th ed. Raymond A. Barnett & Michael R. Zielgler. LC 92-11134. 1993. Dittomaster. write for info. (*0-07-005000-7*) McGraw.

College Algebra. 5th ed. Raymond A. Barnett & Michael R. Zielgler. LC 92-11134. 1993. text ed. write for info. (*0-07-004995-5*) McGraw.

College Algebra. 5th ed. Raymond A. Barnett & Michael R. Zielgler. LC 92-11134. 1993. Solution manual. pap. text ed. write for info. (*0-07-005008-2*) McGraw.

College Algebra. 5th ed. R. David Gustafson & Peter D. Frisk. LC 93-8376. 1994. text ed. 53.95 (*0-534-20880-0*) Brooks-Cole.

College Algebra. 5th ed. Leonard I. Holder. 414p. (C). 1991. text ed. 53.95 (*0-534-13902-7*) PWS Pubs.

College Algebra. 5th ed. Margaret L. Lial & Charles D. Miller. (C). 1988. text ed. 39.00 (*0-673-38245-1*) HarpCollege.

College Algebra. 6th ed. Margaret L. Lial et al. LC 92-13866. (Illus.). (C). 1992. text ed. 42.50 (*0-673-46648-5*) HarpCollege.

College Algebra. 6th ed. Margaret L. Liall et al. (C). 1992. student ed 14.00 (*0-673-46816-X*); teacher ed 15.00 (*0-673-46817-8*) HarpCollege.

College Algebra. 8th ed. Michael D. Grady et al. 541p. (C). 1992. text ed. 53.95 (*0-534-16110-3*) PWS Pubs.

***College Algebra.** 9th ed. Michael D. Grady & Irving Drooyan. LC 94-39522. 540p. 1995. text ed. 34.95 (*0-534-94386-1*) PWS Pubs.

College Algebra. 10th ed. Paul K. Rees et al. 576p. (C). 1990. text ed. write for info. (*0-07-051741-X*); Student solutions manual. student ed, pap. text ed. 13.96 (*0-07-051744-4*) McGraw.

College Algebra. Charles H. Lehmann. LC 62-8778. 444p. reprint ed. pap. 126.60 (*0-317-09369-X*, 2055102) Bks Demand.

College Algebra: A Functions Approach. 4th ed. Mervin L. Keedy & Marvin L. Bittinger. (C). 1986. teacher ed write for info. (*0-201-13291-5*); teacher ed write for info. (*0-201-13293-1*); pap. text ed. 45.25 (*0-201-13290-7*); Student guide. student ed 19.50 (*0-201-13292-3*) Addison-Wesley.

College Algebra: A Functions Approach. 5th ed. Robert Mergener. 480p. 1993. per. 49.95 (*0-8403-7764-9*) Kendall-Hunt.

College Algebra: A Graphics Approach. M. G. Settle. LC 93-33045. 550p. 1994. text ed. 54.75 (*0-314-02841-2*) West Pub.

College Algebra: A Graphing Approach. Roland E. Larson et al. 688p. (C). 1993. text ed. write for info. (*0-669-28294-4*); Instr.'s guide. teacher ed write for info. (*0-669-33231-3*); Study & solutions guide. write for info. (*0-669-28295-2*); Test item file/Resource guide. write for info. (*0-318-70105-7*) Heath.

College Algebra: A Graphing Approach. 2nd ed. Ed. by Franklin D. Demana et al. (Illus.). 600p. (C). 1992. text ed. 46.95 (*0-201-57267-2*) Addison-Wesley.

College Algebra: A Problem Solving Approach. 4th ed. Walter Fleming et al. 576p. (C). 1991. text ed. write for info. (*0-13-142977-9*) P-H.

College Algebra: A Step-by-Step Approach. Kuen H. Lee. (Illus.). 658p. 1992. 38.90 (*0-9618665-3-5*) Edmund Pub.

College Algebra: A Straightforward Approach. Martin M. Zuckerman. LC 83-23548. 445p. (C). 1989. teacher ed write for info. (*0-471-87922-3*) Ardsley.

College Algebra: A Straightforward Approach. Martin M. Zuckerman. LC 83-23548. 445p. (C). 1989. reprint ed. student ed 14.95x (*0-471-09630-X*); reprint ed. teacher ed 14.95x (*0-471-87975-4*); reprint ed. text ed. 28.95x (*0-471-09619-9*) Ardsley.

College Algebra: Concepts & Models. Roland E. Larson et al. 678p. (C). 1992. text ed. write for info. (*0-669-18758-5*); Instr.'s guide. teacher ed write for info. (*0-669-18759-3*); Transparencies. trans. write for info. (*0-318-70102-2*); Study & solutions guide. write for info. (*0-669-18760-7*); Complete solutions guide. write for info. (*0-669-18761-5*); Test item file. write for info. (*0-669-28087-9*) Heath.

***College Algebra: With Problems & Solutions (Pre-Calculus Algebra)** 2nd ed. Irwin K. Feinstein & Kenneth H. Murphy. (Quality Paperback Ser.: No. 39). 486p. (Orig.). 1981. pap. text ed. 16.00 (*0-8226-0002-1*) Littlefield.

College Algebra Activities for the TI-81 Graphing Calculator. Larry Huff & David Peterson. 60p. 1992. pap. 15.95 (*0-534-93003-4*) PWS Pubs.

***College Algebra & Its Applications.** 2nd ed. Larry J. Goldstein. 192p. (C). 1995. student ed write for info. (*0-697-26530-7*) Wm C Brown Pubs.

***College Algebra & Its Applications.** 2nd ed. Larry J. Goldstein. 576p. (C). 1995. text ed. write for info. (*0-697-26527-7*) Wm C Brown Pubs.

College Algebra & Trig SG - Solution Manual. Bray. (C). 1987. pap. text ed. 14.25 (*0-673-18926-0*) HarpCollege.

College Algebra & Trignometry. Mark Dugopolski. LC 93-46705. (C). 1995. text ed. 52.75 (*0-201-52619-0*) Addison-Wesley.

***College Algebra & Trigonometry.** Arthur Goodman. LC 94-37422. 1995. pap. text ed. 57.75 (*0-13-031725-X*) P-H.

College Algebra & Trigonometry. Adelbert F. Hackert & Gene R. Sellers. 723p. (C). 1988. pap. text ed. 17.00 (*0-15-507922-0*) SCP.

College Algebra & Trigonometry. Adelbert F. Hackert & Gene R. Sellers. 723p. (C). 1988. student ed write for info. (*0-318-63358-2*); text ed. 47.00 (*0-15-507920-4*); disk write for info. (*0-318-63359-0*) SCP.

College Algebra & Trigonometry. Adelbert F. Hackert & Gene R. Sellers. 723p. (C). 1988. pap. text ed. 9.50 (*0-15-507921-2*) SCP.

College Algebra & Trigonometry. Louis Leithold. (Illus.). 702p. (C). 1989. teacher ed 12.95 (*0-201-15731-4*); student ed 18.25 (*0-201-15732-2*); teacher ed 12.95 (*0-201-15733-0*); text ed. 50.50 (*0-201-15730-6*); teacher ed, disk 12.95 (*0-201-15700-4*) Addison-Wesley.

College Algebra & Trigonometry. Steven Roman. 702p. (C). 1987. teacher ed write for info. (*0-15-507914-X*); text ed. 41.25 (*0-15-507911-5*); student ed, pap. text ed. 17.00 (*0-15-507913-1*) SCP.

College Algebra & Trigonometry. Michael Sentlowitz & Margaret Trivisone. (C). 1981. text ed. write for info. (*0-201-06676-9*) Addison-Wesley.

College Algebra & Trigonometry. Ralph C. Steinlage. LC 86-19099. (Illus.). 701p. (C). 1984. text ed. 37.50 (*0-314-77821-7*); Solutions manual. pap. text ed. 21.75 (*0-314-77824-1*) West Pub.

College Algebra & Trigonometry. David E. Stevens. Ed. by Pullins. LC 92-35659. 700p. (C). 1994. text ed. 59.75 (*0-314-01222-2*) West Pub.

College Algebra & Trigonometry. 2nd ed. John R. Durbin. LC 87-28039. 500p. 1988. Net. text ed. write for info. (*0-471-62545-0*) Wiley.

College Algebra & Trigonometry. 2nd ed. William L. Hart & Bert K. Waits. 1978. teacher ed 2.00 (*0-669-01462-1*); text ed. 26.00 (*0-669-01460-5*) Heath.

College Algebra & Trigonometry. 2nd ed. Jerome E. Kaufmann. 736p. (C). 1990. text ed. 50.95 (*0-534-92104-3*) PWS Pubs.

College Algebra & Trigonometry, 2 Vols. 2nd ed. Timothy J. Kelly et al. (C). 1991. pap. 55.56 (*0-395-43216-2*) HM.

College Algebra & Trigonometry. 2nd ed. Bernard Kolman & Arnold Shapiro. 624p. (C). 1986. text ed. 51.00 (*0-15-507915-8*) HB Coll Pubs.

College Algebra & Trigonometry. 3rd ed. R. David Gustafson & Peter D. Frisk. LC 89-34069. 688p. (C). 1989. text ed. 52.95 (*0-534-11832-1*) Brooks-Cole.

College Algebra & Trigonometry. 3rd ed. Jerome E. Kaufmann. LC 93-6078. 1994. text ed. 57.95 (*0-534-93525-7*) PWS Pubs.

College Algebra & Trigonometry. 3rd ed. Michael Sullivan. 1056p. (C). 1993. write for info. (*0-02-418305-9*) Macmillan.

College Algebra & Trigonometry. 4th ed. R. David Gustafson & Peter D. Frisk. LC 93-8375. 1994. text ed. 55.95 (*0-534-20862-2*) Brooks-Cole.

College Algebra & Trigonometry. David C. Cohen. (Illus.). 475p. (C). 1989. reprint ed. text ed. 40.75 (*0-314-93165-1*) West Pub.

College Algebra & Trigonometry: A Graphing Approach. 2nd ed. Franklin D. Demana et al. (Illus.). 750p. (C). 1992. text ed. 48.95 (*0-201-56294-4*) Addison-Wesley.

College Algebra & Trigonometry: Basics Through Precalculus. 2nd ed. John J. Schiller & Marie A. Wurster. 752p. (C). 1994. per., pap. text ed. 45.95 (*0-8403-9102-1*) Kendall-Hunt.

College Algebra & Trigonometry: Graph Calculator. Dennis C. Ebersole. (C). 1993. text ed. 19.00 (*0-06-500888-X*) HarpCollege.

***College Algebra & Trigonometry Plus.** Ronald D. Ferguson. LC 94-22907. (Illus.). 850p. (C). 1994. text ed. 58.75 (*0-314-04227-X*) West Pub.

College Algebra & Trigonometry with Applications. Jose Barros-Neto. (Illus.). 696p. (C). 1985. text ed. 38.75 (*0-314-85218-2*); pap. text ed. 16.50 (*0-314-87211-6*) West Pub.

College Algebra & Trigonometry with Applications. T. Koshy. 688p. 1986. text ed. write for info. (*0-07-035471-5*) McGraw.

College Algebra & Trigonometry with Applications. Terry H. Wesner et al. 800p. (C). 1993. boxed, text ed. write for info. (*0-697-11655-7*) Wm C Brown Pubs.

College Algebra & Trigonometry with Applications. Terry H. Wesner et al. 800p. (C). 1994. teacher ed write for info. (*0-697-11694-8*) Wm C Brown Pubs.

College Algebra & Trigonometry with Applications. suppl. ed. Terry H. Wesner et al. 800p. (C). 1993. write for info. (*0-697-16779-8*); write for info. (*0-697-16780-1*) Wm C Brown Pubs.

College Algebra & Trigonometry with Applications. 2nd ed. Jose Barros-Neto. Ed. by Ricci. 628p. (C). 1988. text ed. 57.50 (*0-314-59695-X*) West Pub.

College Algebra Exam File. Ed. by Eric M. Lederer. LC 89-17085. (Exam File Ser.). 410p. (Orig.). 1990. pap. 15.50 (*0-910554-77-3*) Engineering.

College Algebra for Management, Social, & Biological Sciences. Larry J. Goldstein. 672p. (C). 1994. text ed. write for info. (*0-697-21669-1*) Wm C Brown Pubs.

College Algebra for Management, Social, & Biological Sciences. Larry J. Goldstein. 192p. (C). 1995. student ed, pap. text ed. write for info. (*0-697-21673-X*) Wm C Brown Pubs.

***College Algebra Plus.** Ronald D. Ferguson. LC 94-22908. (Illus.). 675p. (C). 1994. text ed. 54.75 (*0-314-04228-8*) West Pub.

College Algebra Primer. Dale P. Hawkinson. 96p. (C). 1990. pap. text ed. 8.95 (*0-8403-6014-2*) Kendall-Hunt.

College Algebra Study Guide - Solution Manual. Bray. (C). 1987. pap. text ed. 13.25 (*0-673-18927-9*) HarpCollege.

College Algebra-Trigonometry. Jack Rudman. (College Level Examination Ser.: CLEP-7). 1994. pap. 23.95 (*0-8373-5307-6*) Nat Learn.

College Algebra with Applications. Jagdish C. Arya & Robin W. Lardner. (Illus.). 560p. (C). 1983. text ed. write for info. (*0-13-140699-X*) P-H.

College Algebra with Applications. L. Murphy Johnson & Arnold R. Steffensen. (C). 1987. text ed. 36.50 (*0-673-18354-8*) HarpCollege.

College Algebra with Applications. Terry H. Wesner et al. 576p. (C). 1993. boxed, text ed. write for info. (*0-697-11654-9*) Wm C Brown Pubs.

College Algebra with Applications. Terry H. Wesner et al. 576p. (C). 1993. Calculator View Using the Casio 7700. write for info. (*0-697-16785-2*) Wm C Brown Pubs.

College Algebra with Applications. Terry H. Wesner et al. 576p. (C). 1993. Calculator View Using the TI-81, TI-82, & TI-85. write for info. (*0-697-16784-4*) Wm C Brown Pubs.

College Algebra with Applications. Terry H. Wesner et al. 576p. (C). 1994. Solutions manual. write for info. (*0-697-11701-4*) Wm C Brown Pubs.

College Algebra with Applications. 2nd ed. Jose Barros-Neto. 452p. (C). 1988. text ed. 57.50 (*0-314-59696-8*) West Pub.

College Algebra with Applications. 3rd ed. James W. Hall. 656p. 1992. text ed. 55.95 (*0-534-92788-2*) PWS Pubs.

College Algebra with Applications. 3rd ed. M. A. Munem & David Foulis. 452p. 1991. student ed 11.95x (*0-87901-515-2*); text ed. 53.95x (*0-87901-499-7*) Worth.

College Algebra with Calculator Applications. Joseph Elich & Carletta J. Elich. (Math-Mallion Ser.). (Illus.). 480p. (C). 1982. teacher ed write for info. (*0-201-13341-5*); teacher ed write for info. (*0-201-13342-3*); student ed write for info. (*0-201-13343-1*); text ed. write for info. (*0-201-13340-7*) Addison-Wesley.

College Algebra with Graphing & Problem Solving. Karl J. Smith. LC 93-30496. 1994. text ed. 55.95 (*0-534-19374-9*) Brooks-Cole.

College Algebra with Graphing Calculators. Joan E. Girard & Michael Sullivan. 704p. (C). 1996. text ed. write for info. (*0-02-343751-0*) Macmillan.

College Algebra with Review. 2nd ed. Michael Sullivan. LC 92-19022. (Precalculus Ser.). 864p. (C). 1993. write for info. (*0-02-418371-7*) Macmillan.

College Algebra with Trigonometry. Linda Gilbert & Jimmie Gilbert. LC 94-13265. 1994. text ed. write for info. (*0-07-023586-4*) McGraw.

College Algebra with Trigonometry. Paul K. Rees et al. 736p. (C). 1991. text ed. write for info. (*0-07-051737-1*) McGraw.

College Algebra with Trigonometry. 5th ed. Raymond A. Barnett & Michael R. Ziegler. LC 92-14680. (Barnett & Ziegler's College Algebra - Precalculus Ser.). (C). 1993. text ed. write for info. (*0-07-004989-0*) McGraw.

College Algebra with Trigonometry. 5th ed. Raymond A. Barnett & Michael R. Ziegler. LC 92-14680. (Barnett & Ziegler's College Algebra - Precalculus Ser.). (C). 1993. Solution manual. pap. text ed. write for info. (*0-07-005006-6*) McGraw.

College Algebra with Trigonometry. Joseph B. Rosenbach. LC 73-79572. 512p. reprint ed. pap. 146.00 (*0-317-09359-2*, 2055103) Bks Demand.

College Algebra with Unit-Circle Trigonometry. David C. Cohen. Ed. by Marshall. LC 92-16241. 725p. (C). 1993. text ed. 60.75 (*0-314-93361-1*) West Pub.

College Alumni & Military Publications Directory, 1988. Ed. by Judith Drake. 1988. 87.00 (*0-935224-39-4*) Larimi Comm.

College & Career Directories of Maryland, Delaware & D. C., 1985. Ed. by Robert A. Wittman. 6.95 (*0-318-03286-4*) Wittman Pubns.

College & Character. Joseph Axelrod. Ed. by R. Nevitt Sanford. 1979. pap. 11.95 (*0-917430-01-8*) Montaigne.

College & Commonwealth, & Other Educational Papers & Addresses. John H. MacCracken. LC 67-26757. (Essay Index Reprint Ser.). 1977. 21.95 (*0-8369-0644-6*) Ayer.

College & Community Development: A Socioeconomic Analysis for Urban & Regional Growth. Julian M. Laub. LC 75-166397. (Special Studies in U. S. Economic, Social & Political Issues). 1972. 39.50 (*0-275-28207-4*) Irvington.

College & Jobs: Conservations with Recent Graduates. Steve R. Baumgardner. LC 87-25374. (Insight Book Ser.). 196p. 1988. 30.95 (*0-89885-413-X*); pap. 14.95 (*0-89885-416-4*) Human Sci Pr.

College & Research Libraries & College & Research Libraries News Index for Volumes 41-50 (1980-89) Comp. by Eldon W. Tamblyn. 176p. (Orig.). 1992. pap. text ed. 29.95 (*0-8389-7487-2*) ALA.

College & Student: Selected Readings in the Social Psychology of Higher Education. Ed. by Kenneth A. Feldman. 502p. (C). 1974. pap. 32.00 (*0-08-016788-8*, Pergamon Pr) Elsevier.

College & University Administrators Directory 1979-1980. 950p. 1980. 160.00 (*0-8103-1133-X*) Gale.

College & University Archives: Guidelines. Committee on College & University Archives. 10p. (Orig.). 1979. pap. text ed. 3.50 (*0-931828-32-5*) Soc Am Archivists.

College & University Basic Competency Tests (BCT-C&U) Jack Rudman. (Admission Test Ser.: ATS-58). 1994. pap. 23.95 (*0-8373-5058-1*) Nat Learn.

College & University Budget Information Systems. Archie W. Earl, Sr. (Higher Education Ser.). 610p. (C). 1993. lib. bdg. 62.95 (*1-884169-20-1*); pap. text ed. 47.95 (*1-884169-21-X*) Intl Educ Improve.

College & University Budgeting: An Introduction for Faculty & Academic Administrators. 2nd ed. Richard J. Meisinger, Jr. LC 94-20513. 1994. 60.00 (*0-915164-94-9*) NACUBO.

College & University Business Administration, 3 vols., Set. 5th ed. Ed. by Deirdre M. Greene. LC 82-2210. 527p. 1992. 195.00 (*0-915164-71-X*) NACUBO.

College & University Correspondence Courses Canada. abr. ed. Joseph E. Smart. 115p. (Orig.). 1987. pap. 13.88 (*0-917619-09-9*) SMARTCO.

College & University Correspondence Courses Canada. unabridged ed. Joseph E. Smart. 435p. (Orig.). 1987. pap. 40.15 (*0-917619-08-0*) SMARTCO.

College & University Correspondence Courses United States. abr. ed. Joseph E. Smart. 385p. (Orig.). 1987. pap. 29.95 (*0-917619-05-6*) SMARTCO.

College & University Correspondence Courses United States, 2 vols. unabridged ed. Joseph E. Smart. 2000p. (Orig.). 1987. pap. 169.50 (*0-917619-02-1*) SMARTCO.

College & University Food Service Manual. Paul Fairbrook. LC 79-50956. (Illus.). 1979. pap. 19.00 (*0-9602456-0-X*) Colman Pubs.

College & University Magazines: Building Credibility to Advance Your Institution. Patricia A. LaSalle. 121p. 1991. 32.00 (*0-89964-284-5*) Coun Adv & Supp Ed.

College & University Organization. James L. Bess. 1984. 45.00 (*0-8147-1049-2*); pap. 22.50x (*0-8147-1056-5*) NYU Pr.

College & University Press. (Illus.). 1982. write for info. (*0-318-58300-3*) Loyola LA Law.

College & University Trustee. Louis H. Heilbron. LC 72-5888. (Jossey-Bass Higher Education Ser.). 256p. reprint ed. 73.00 (*0-8357-9307-9*, 2013815) Bks Demand.

College Applications & Essays: A How-To Handbook. 2nd rev. ed. Susan D. Van Raalte. LC 92-35211. 1993. pap. 9.00 (*0-671-86644-3*, Arco Test) P-H Gen Ref & Trav.

College Arithmetic. 2nd ed. William I. Layton. LC 73-155121. 244p. reprint ed. pap. 69.60 (*0-317-08545-X*, 2055108) Bks Demand.

College Athletic Scholarships: A Complete Guide. Bob Mauro. LC 87-43210. 157p. 1988. lib. bdg. 18.95x (*0-89950-328-4*) McFarland & Co.

College Basics: How to Start Right & Finish Strong. Marvin Lunenfeld. 144p. (C). 1993. per., pap. text ed. 12.95 (*0-8403-8655-9*) Kendall-Hunt.

College Basics: How to Start Right & Finish Strong. 2nd ed. Marvin Lunenfeld & Peter B. Lunenfeld. LC 91-90353. (Illus.). 144p. 1991. pap. 11.95 (*0-9629783-0-2*) Semester Pr.

College Basics: How to Start Right & Finish Strong. 2nd ed. Marvin Lunenfeld & Peter Lunenfeld. LC 91-90353. (Illus.). 144p. 1992. pap. 12.95 (*0-9629783-1-0*) Semester Pr.

College Basketball Scorebook. Kenneth N. Carlson. (Illus.). 984p. (Orig.). 1990. pap. 22.50 (*0-938428-10-1*) Rain Belt.

1374

An Asterisk (*) at the beginning of an entry indicates that the title is appearing in BIP for the first time.

C

College Graduate Careers Examination. Jack Rudman. (Career Examination Ser.: Series 1). 1991. pap. 29.95 (*0-8373-3703-8*) Nat Learn.

College Grammar of English. Sidney Greenbaum. 340p. (C). 1989. text ed. 40.95 (*0-582-28597-6*, 71623) Longman.

***College Guide for American Indians: Info for Counselors, Parents, Students.** 96p. 1994. pap. 5.00 (*0-614-04177-5*) Am Indian Sci.

College Guide for Parents. rev. ed. Charles J. Shields. 197p. 1988. pap. 12.95 (*0-87447-316-0*) College Bd.

***College Guide for Parents.** 3rd ed. Charles J. Shields. Ed. by Renee Gernand. LC 88-70580. 200p. (Orig.). 1994. pap. 14.00 (*0-87447-474-4*) College Bd.

***College Handbook & College Explore.** (C). 1995. 35.00 (*0-87447-531-7*) College Bd.

***College Handbook for Transfer Students, 1996.** College Board Staff. LC 91-71255. 540p. 1995. pap. 17.00 (*0-87447-510-4*) College Bd.

College Handbook Foreign Student Supplement, 1995. 8th ed. College Board Staff. LC 87-70964. 320p. 1994. pap. 16.00 (*0-87447-494-9*) College Bd.

***College Handbook Foreign Student Supplement, 1996.** College Board Staff. LC 87-70964. 288p. 1995. pap. 16.00 (*0-87447-509-0*) College Bd.

College Handbook of Creative Writing. Robert De Maria. 384p. (C). 1990. pap. text ed. 16.00 (*0-15-509040-2*) HB Coll Pubs.

College Handbook of Creative Writing. 2nd rev. ed. Robert DeMaria. LC 94-17973. 416p. (C). 1994. pap. text ed. write for info. (*0-15-501187-1*) HB Coll Pubs.

***College Handbook, 1996.** College Board Staff. 1664p. 1995. pap. 20.00 (*0-87447-506-6*) College Bd.

College Handbook '95. 15th ed. College Board Staff. LC 80-648095. 336p. 1994. pap. 16.00 (*0-87447-492-2*) College Bd.

College Hill Chronicles: How the University of Alaska Came of Age. Neil Davis. LC 93-16969. 1993. 30.00 (*1-883309-01-8*) U AK Fnd.

College History of the United States, 2 vols. David Burner et al. (Illus.). 1219p. (C). 1991. Net. pap. text ed. 9.56 (*0-685-74365-9*) Brandywine Press.

College History of the United States, 2 vols., Set. David Burner et al. (Illus.). 1219p. (C). 1991. write for info. (*0-9603726-6-0*) Brandywine Press.

College History of the United States, 2 vols., Vol. 1. David Burner et al. (Illus.). 614p. (C). 1991. pap. text ed. 9.56 (*0-9603726-7-9*) Brandywine Press.

College History of the United States, 2 vols., Vol. 2. David Burner et al. (Illus.). 640p. (C). 1991. pap. text ed. 9.56 (*0-9603726-8-7*) Brandywine Press.

College in a Yard II. Ed. by David Aloian. (Alumni Association Ser.). (Illus.). 215p. 1986. 14.50 (*0-674-14151-2*) HUP.

College in Black & White: African American Students in Predominantly White & in Historically Black Public Universities. Ed. by Walter R. Allen et al. LC 90-32306. (Philosophy of Education Ser.). 322p. (C). 1991. 69.50 (*0-7914-0485-4*); pap. 24.95 (*0-7914-0486-2*) State U NY Pr.

College in California, the Inside Track: The Comprehensive & Practical Guide for Students, Parents, & Educators. Rochelle S. Rosen. LC 92-96890. (Illus.). 576p. (Orig.). 1992. pap. 24.95 (*1-880403-11-0*) Baywood.

College in California, the Inside Track, 1994 Edition: The Comprehensive & Practical Guide for Students, Parents, & Educators. Rochelle S. Rosen. LC 93-72476. (Illus.). 592p. (YA). (gr. 8 up). 1993. pap. 24.95 (*1-880403-12-9*) Baywood.

***College in California: The Inside Track 1995: Comprehensive Guide for Students, Parents, & Educators.** 3rd ed. Rochelle S. Rosen. 592p. (YA). (gr. 9-12). 1994. per., pap. 24.95 (*1-880403-13-7*) Baywood.

***College in Your Future: 140 Questions & Answers about Getting In-Staying In.** Henry Klein. LC 94-36250. (Illus.). 164p. (Orig.). (YA). (gr. 11-12). 1995. pap. 12.95 (*1-880774-08-9*) Garrett Pk.

College Instructor's Guide to Teaching & Academia. Roy Udolf. LC 76-7462. 168p. 1976. text ed. 28.95 (*0-88229-241-2*) Nelson-Hall.

College Is Only the Beginning: A Student Guide to Higher Education. 2nd ed. Ed. by John N. Gardner & A. Jerome Jewler. 327p. (C). 1989. pap. 19.95 (*0-534-09642-5*) Intl Thomson.

College Journal. Horace G. Nelson & Carol F. Nelson. 320p. 1994. 28.95 (*0-9638311-0-0*) Primary Publns.

***College Journals 1936-42, Vol. 1.** Gascoyne. 1995. pap. 19.95 (*1-871438-50-0*) Atrium Pubs.

College Keyboarding: Formatting with WordPerfect 5.1. 13th ed. Charles H. Duncan et al. LC 93-5224. 1994. text ed. 31.95 (*0-538-70867-0*) S-W Pub.

College Keyboarding - Typewriting: Formatting Course. 13th ed. Charles H. Duncan et al. LC 93-13638. 1994. text ed. 31.95 (*0-538-70808-5*) S-W Pub.

College Keyboarding - Typewriting: Intensive Course. 13th ed. Charles H. Duncan et al. LC 93-1744. 1994. text ed. 40.95 (*0-538-70805-0*) S-W Pub.

College Keyboarding - Typewriting: Introductory Course - Lessons 1-60. 13th ed. Charles H. Duncan. LC 92-40382. 1994. text ed. 31.95 (*0-538-70807-7*) S-W Pub.

***College Keyboarding for Windows Formatting with Microsoft Word 6.0 & WordPerfect 6.0.** 13th ed. Charles H. Duncan et al. 1996. text ed. 31.95 (*0-538-70868-9*) S-W Pub.

College Keyboarding-Typewriting. 11th ed. C. H. Duncan et al. (C). 1985. text ed. 45.95 (*0-538-20750-7*, T75) S-W Pub.

College Keyboarding-Typewriting. 12th ed. Charles H. Duncan. 428p. (C). 1990. text ed. 47.95 (*0-538-20860-0*, T86) S-W Pub.

College Keyboarding-Typewriting, Intensive Course. 11th ed. C. H. Duncan et al. 1986. text ed. 43.95 (*0-538-20270-X*, T27) S-W Pub.

College Kid's Cookbook. Marion Hodgson. (Illus.). pap. 3.95 (*0-912848-01-4*) Coll Kids Cook.

***College Knowledge: What You Need to Know Before You Go. Jennifer Trussell. Ed. by Paul D. Adams. 160p. (Orig.). 1995. pap. 9.00 (*0-9643862-0-8*) Carnegie NY.**
Going to college has been characterized as a right, a privilege, a social obligation, a career imperative, a rite of passage. But among the 2-million students who trudge off to college each year, only a little over half will graduate from the institution they entered as freshmen. Why? Many students simply find the transition from high school & family life difficult. Colleges now see 'retaining' students as a real institutional imperative & they realize that their success is proportional to the effort they make to help students work through their anxieties, their academic challenges & their social adjustments. Hence, a flood of books addressing this topic in recent years. But loaded with text, case histories, checklists & worksheets, these books themselves pose a problem: students are overwhelmed & rarely READ them. In COLLEGE KNOWLEDGE: WHAT YOU NEED TO KNOW BEFORE YOU GO, Jennifer Trussell addresses the issue briefly & from the STUDENT'S point of view, in their language & with humor & insight. A great gift from family or friends, Trussell's book is also one that a first semester college kid won't be embarrassed to be seen reading as he/she walks, tentatively, to that first class in the fall. To order contact: Carnegie Communications, Inc., 244 Winchester Ave., Suite 217, White Plains, NY 10604. 914-946-9638. ***Publisher Provided Annotation.***

College Korean. Michael C. Rogers et al. 380p. 1991. pap. 25.00 (*0-520-06994-3*) U CA Pr.

College Latin. Norman J. Dewitt et al. (C). 1954. text ed. 23.75 (*0-673-05105-6*) HarpCollege.

***College Latin.** Norman J. De Witt et al. LC 54-4228. (Illus.). 451p. 1954. reprint ed. pap. 128.60 (*0-7837-8853-3*, 2049547) Bks Demand.

College Law. Albert S. Miles. LC 87-61790. (Illus.). 121p. (Orig.). (C). 1987. pap. 19.95 (*0-943487-01-3*) Sevgo Pr.

College Law Digest, 12 vols., Set, 1971-1982. 290.00 (*0-685-07508-7*) Rothman.

College Law Digest, 12 vols., Vols. 1 & 2. 25.00 (*0-685-07509-5*) Rothman.

College Law Digest, 12 vols., Vols. 3-5. 20.00 (*0-318-57423-3*) Rothman.

College Law Digest, 12 vols., Vols. 6-9. 25.00 (*0-318-57425-X*) Rothman.

College Law Digest, 12 vols., Vols. 10-12. 35.00 (*0-318-57424-1*) Rothman.

College Law Digest, 1935-1970. Ed. by Thomas E. Blackwell. xi, 256p. 1974. pap. 12.00 (*0-8377-0307-7*) Rothman.

College Law Guide. Ivan Fox & Jesse Raphael. 5.85 (*0-914770-05-5*) Littoral Develop.

College Leadership for Community Renewal. James F. Gollattscheck & Ervin L. Harlacher. LC 76-19497. (Jossey-Bass Higher Education Ser.). 174p. reprint ed. pap. 49.60 (*0-685-16266-4*, 2027753) Bks Demand.

College Learning: Ways & Whys. Frank A. Logan. 320p. (C). 1991. pap. text ed. 17.95 (*0-8403-6861-5*) Kendall-Hunt.

College Learning Resources Programs. AECT Program Standards Committee Task Force & Howard B. Hitchens. 1977. pap. 7.95 (*0-89240-005-6*) Assn Ed Comm Tech.

***College Level Academic Skills Test (CLAST)** (Admission Test Ser.). Date not set. pap. 23.95 (*0-8373-5811-6*) Nat Learn.

***College Level Academic Skills Test (CLAST)** (Admission Test Ser.). Date not set. 39.95 (*0-8373-5861-2*) Nat Learn.

College Level Examination Program (CLEP) The Five General Examinations. LC 81-7895. (Illus.). 480p. 1982. pap. 8.00 (*0-668-05143-4*, Arco Test) P-H Gen Ref & Trav.

College-Level Examination Series. Jack Rudman. (Entire Ser.). 1994. pap. write for info. (*0-8373-5300-9*) Nat Learn.

College Level Program for Learning Disabled Students. John R. Moss et al. (C). 1980. pap. 15.95 (*0-937660-01-9*) PIP.

College-Level Vocabulary & Etymology. Elton F. Henley. 256p. (C). 1990. pap. text ed. 28.95 (*0-8403-6396-6*) Kendall-Hunt.

College Librarianship. Ed. by William Miller & D. Stephen Rockwood. LC 80-25546. 290p. 1981. 29.50 (*0-8108-1383-1*) Scarecrow.

College Library Newsletters. Patricia S. Butcher & Susan M. Campbell. (CLIP Notes Ser.: No. 13). 154p. 1990. pap. text ed. 18.95 (*0-8389-7445-7*) ALA.

College Life. Ellen Rosenberg. 416p. (Orig.). 1992. pap. 12.00 (*0-14-014484-6*, Penguin Bks) Viking Penguin.

College Life: Essays Reprinted from "School, College, & Character," & "Routine & Ideals" Le Baron R. Briggs. (Select Bibliographies Reprint Ser.). 1977. 19.95 (*0-8369-5039-9*) Ayer.

College Life in the Old South. 2nd ed. E. Merton Coulter. LC 83-9210. (Brown Thrasher Bks.). 336p. 1983. reprint ed. pap. 11.95 (*0-8203-0684-3*) U of Ga Pr.

College Major Handbook. 1990. 9.95 (*0-934783-12-8*); write for info. (*0-317-31634-6*) CFKR Career.

College Majors: A Complete Guide from Accounting to Zoology. Ellen Lederman. LC 89-29540. 140p. 1990. lib. bdg. 20.95x (*0-89950-462-0*) McFarland & Co.

College Majors & Careers: A Resource Guide for Effective Life Planning. rev. ed. Paul Phifer. LC 93-19213. 166p. 1993. 15.00 (*0-912048-46-8*) Garrett Pk.

College Man & Our Rural Civilization. Rupert N. Richardson. Ed. by Lawrence R. Clayton. 1989. write for info. (*0-910075-12-3*) Hardin-Simmons.

College Match, 1994-95: A Blueprint for Choosing the School That's Best for You. 3rd ed. Steven R. Antonoff. 1993. pap. 7.00 (*0-945981-81-3*, TN7675) Octameron Assocs.

***College Match, 1996-97.** 4th ed. 1995. pap. 7.50 (*1-57509-004-X*, TN67504) Octameron Assocs.

College Matchmaker. Charles W. Blaker. LC 80-67604. (Illus.). 56p. (Orig.). (YA). (gr. 11-12). 1980. pap. text ed. 3.50 (*0-9604614-0-X*) Rekalb Pr.

College Math: A Space Odyssey. Joseph Nelan. 180p. (Orig.). (C). 1994. pap. text ed. 25.00 (*1-878045-24-5*) Whittier Pubns.

College Mathematics. Richard J. Coppins & Paul M. Umberger. LC 85-26884. (C). 1986. student ed write for info. (*0-201-10319-2*); teacher ed write for info. (*0-201-10314-1*); text ed. write for info. (*0-201-10311-7*) Addison-Wesley.

College Mathematics. 2nd ed. S. T. Tan. 1120p. (C). 1988. text ed. 67.95 (*0-534-91791-7*) PWS Pubs.

College Mathematics. 3rd ed. S. T. Tan. LC 93-33270. 1995. text ed. 67.95 (*0-534-93549-4*) PWS Pubs.

College Mathematics & Calculus: With Applications to Management, Life & Social Sciences. 2nd ed. Karl J. Smith. 752p. (C). 1992. text ed. 65.95 (*0-534-16872-8*) Brooks-Cole.

College Mathematics for Business. Don Busche & Flora Locke. LC 83-6640. 632p. (C). 1984. text ed. 14.95 (*0-471-08995-8*) P-H.

College Mathematics for Business. 3rd ed. J. Dennis Hart & B. J. Landwehr. (Illus.). 375p. (C). 1988. pap. text ed. 20.00 (*0-923231-07-2*) Mohican Pub.

College Mathematics for Business, Economics, Life Sciences, & Social Sciences. 6th ed. Raymond A. Barnett & Michael R. Ziegler. LC 92-27502. 1200p. (C). 1993. write for info. (*0-02-306231-2*) Dellen Pub.

College Mathematics for Technology. 3rd rev. ed. Cheryl Cleaves et al. LC 94-5641. Orig. Title: Basic Mathematics for Trades & Technologies. 1024p. 1994. text ed. 63.00 (*0-13-336553-0*) P-H Gen Ref & Trav.

College Mathematics Review. 3rd ed. Robert Blitzer & Jack C. Gill. Ed. by Robert Hackworth & Joseph Howland. (Illus.). 349p. 1987. pap. text ed. 26.95 (*0-943202-25-6*) H & H Pub.

College Mathematics Review. 4th ed. Robert Blitzer & Jack Gill. Ed. by Robert Hackworth & Karen Davis. (Illus.). 460p. (C). 1992. pap. text ed. 33.95 (*0-943202-40-X*) H & H Pub.

College Mathematics with a Programming Language. E. J. LeCuyer. (Undergraduate Texts in Mathematics Ser.). 1978. 35.00 (*0-387-90280-5*) Spr-Verlag.

College Media Directory. 1989. 125.00 (*0-917460-21-9*) Oxbridge Comm.

College Men: Their Making & Unmaking. Dom Proface. LC 67-26772. (Essay Index Reprint Ser.). 1977. 20.95 (*0-8369-0803-1*) Ayer.

College Money Book: How to Get A High-Quality Education at the Lowest Possible Cost. David M. Brownstone & Gene R. Hawes. LC 83-15582. 256p. 1984. pap. write for info. (*0-672-52772-3*) Macmillan.

***College Money in Florida 1995.** rev. ed. Robert L. Burke. 216p. 1995. pap. 15.95 (*0-8119-0799-6*) LIFETIME.

***College Money in Florida: 1996: Scholarships, Grants, Loans & Awards.** Robert L. Burke & Anna Burke. 304p. (Orig.). (YA). 1995. pap. 15.95 (*0-8119-0813-5*) LIFETIME.

***College Money in New England: 1996: Scholarships, Grants, Loans & Awards.** Robert L. Burke & Anna Burke. 496p. (Orig.). (YA). 1995. pap. 18.95 (*0-8119-0815-1*) LIFETIME.

***College Money in New York-New Jersey: 1996: Scholarships, Awards, Grants & Loans.** Robert L. Burke & Anna Burke. 496p. (Orig.). (YA). 1995. pap. 18.95 (*0-8119-0814-3*) LIFETIME.

***College Newspaper Advertising Managers Handbook.** Ernest F. Larkin & Susan S. Larkin. 60p. 1994. pap. text ed. 25.00 (*0-9644192-0-3*) Assoc Collegiate Pr.

College Newspaper Critique. Ed. by Nancy L. Green. 20p. (Orig.). (C). 1986. student ed 2.50 (*0-916084-18-3*) Columbia Scholastic.

College Nicknames & Other Interesting Sports Traditions. Joanne Sloan & Cheryl Watts. LC 92-23714. (Illus.). 357p. (Orig.). 1992. pap. 13.95 (*0-9630700-3-7*) Vision AL.

College Nisei. Robert W. O'Brien & Roger Daniels. LC 78-54829. (Asian Experience in North America Ser.). (Illus.). 1979. reprint ed. lib. bdg. 15.95 (*0-405-11286-6*) Ayer.

College Nisei Revisited. Robert W. P'Brien & Amy Iwasaki. (Illus.). 1994. 21.95 (*0-87015-254-8*) Pacific Bks.

***College Not Required.** Leonard Corwen. LC 95-15933. 1995. write for info. (*0-02-860561-6*) Macmillan.

College of Character. Warren B. Martin. LC 82-48392. (Jossey-Bass Series in Higher Education). 247p. reprint ed. pap. 70.40 (*0-8357-4689-5*, 2052344) Bks Demand.

College of Earth & Mineral Sciences at Penn State. E. Willard Miller. (Illus.). 400p. 1992. 45.00 (*0-271-00796-6*) Pa St U Pr.

College of Franchise Knowledge: What You Should Know about Choosing & Buying a Franchise. Donald J. Foltz. 192p. (Orig.). 1992. pap. 49.95 (*0-9634671-0-7*) Franchise Centre.

College of Idaho 1891-1991: A Centennial History. Louie W. Attebery. 410p. 1991. write for info. (*0-9630028-0-5*) Albertson Col ID.

College of Life or Practical Self Educator. Henry D. Northrop. LC 71-79014. (Black Heritage Library Collection). (Illus.). 1977. 54.95 (*0-8369-8638-5*) Ayer.

College of Magics. Caroline Stevermer. 384p. 1994. 22.95 (*0-312-85689-X*) Tor Bks.

College of Magics. Caroline Stevermer. 384p. 1995. mass mkt. 4.99 (*0-8125-3005-5*) Tor Bks.

College of New Rochelle, 1904-1994: An Extraordinary Story. James T. Schleifer. LC 94-7549. 1994. write for info. (*0-89865-895-0*) Donning Co.

College of Philadelphia, 1749-1779: Impact of an Institution. Ann D. Gordon. (Outstanding Studies in Early American History). 352p. 1989. reprint ed. 25.00 (*0-8240-6182-9*) Garland.

College of Physicians of Philadelphia: A Bicentenial History. Whitfield J. Bell, Jr. LC 87-20570. 326p. 1987. 40.00 (*0-88135-003-6*) Watson Pub Intl.

College of Sociology, 1937-1939. Ed. by Denis Hollier. Tr. by Betsy Wing. LC 87-13557. (Theory & History of Literature Ser.: Vol. 41). 487p. (Orig.). 1988. text ed. 44.95 (*0-8166-1591-8*); pap. text ed. 19.95 (*0-8166-1592-6*) U of Minn Pr.

College of the City of New York: A History, 1847-1947. S. Willis Rudy. Ed. by Walter P. Metzger. LC 76-55189. (Academic Profession Ser.). (Illus.). 1977. lib. bdg. 42.95 (*0-405-10014-0*) Ayer.

College of William & Mary. Dan Dry. (Illus.). 112p. 1987. 37.50 (*0-916509-12-5*) Harmony Hse Pub LO.

College of William & Mary. Herbert B. Adams. (Principle Works of Herbert Baxter Adams). 1989. reprint ed. lib. bdg. 79.00 (*0-7812-1468-8*) Rprt Serv.

College of William & Mary: A History. Susan H. Godson et al. 1000p. 1993. boxed 50.00 (*0-9615670-4-X*) Soc Alu Wm.

College of Wooster - Then & Now. Photos by Scott Goldsmith. (First Edition Ser.). (Illus.). 112p. 1992. 42.50 (*0-916509-96-6*) Harmony Hse Pub LO.

College Office Assistant A. Jack Rudman. (Career Examination Ser.: C-153). 1994. pap. 23.95 (*0-8373-0153-X*) Nat Learn.

College Office Assistant B. Jack Rudman. (Career Examination Ser.: C-154). 1994. pap. 23.95 (*0-8373-0154-8*) Nat Learn.

College on the Hill: A Dartmouth Chronicle. Ralph N. Hill. LC 64-16542. 369p. reprint ed. 105.20 (*0-685-15815-2*, 2027532) Bks Demand.

College 101: A Freshman Reader. Lawry. 316p. 1992. text ed. write for info. (*0-07-036733-7*) McGraw.

College Peer Groups: Problems & Prospects for Research. Ed. by Theodore M. Newcomb & Everett K. Wilson. LC 65-29033. (Monographs in Social Research: No. 8). 1966. 10.95 (*0-202-09002-7*) NORC.

College Physics. Coletta. 944p. 1993. 61.00 (*0-8016-7722-X*) Mosby Yr Bk.

***College Physics.** Doug Davis. LC 94-26395. (C). 1995. pap. text ed. 22.50 (*0-03-007488-6*) SCP.

College Physics. Francis W. Sears et al. LC 79-20729. (Physics Ser.). 1980. teacher ed write for info. (*0-201-07566-0*) Addison-Wesley.

College Physics. Robert W. Stanley. (College Outline Ser.). 398p. (C). 1987. pap. text ed. 12.50 (*0-15-601662-1*) HB Coll Pubs.

College Physics. Paul A. Tipler. 932p. (C). 1987. text ed. 59.95x (*0-87901-268-4*); student ed, pap. 13.95x (*0-87901-269-2*) Worth.

College Physics. Jerry D. Wilson. 896p. 1990. write for info. (*0-318-66354-6*, H21124); student ed 24.00 (*0-685-29830-2*, H21173); text ed. write for info. (*0-205-12110-1*, H21108); teacher ed, disk write for info. (*0-318-66355-4*, H21124); teacher ed, disk write for info. (*0-318-66356-2*, H21132) P-H.

College Physics. annot. ed. Jerry D. Wilson. 896p. 1990. teacher ed write for info. (*0-318-66353-8*, H21165) P-H.

College Physics. 2nd ed. Jerry D. Wilson. LC 93-42566. 1993. text ed. 51.75 (*0-13-145269-X*) P-H.

College Physics. 3rd ed. Raymond A. Serway & Jerry Faughn. 1216p. (C). 1992. text ed. 68.00 (*0-03-073331-6*) SCP.

College Physics. 5th ed. Francis W. Sears et al. LC 79-20729. (Physics Ser.). 1980. student ed write for info. (*0-201-07682-9*); teacher ed write for info. (*0-201-07687-X*); text ed. write for info. (*0-201-07200-9*) Addison-Wesley.

College Physics. 6th ed. Franklin Miller, Jr. et al. 869p. (C). 1987. teacher ed 4.00 (*0-15-511747-5*); text ed. 61.25 (*0-15-511743-2*) SCP.

An Asterisk (*) at the beginning of an entry indicates that the title is appearing in BIP for the first time.

C

College Writing Skills: A Text with Exercises. 3rd ed. Peder Jones & Jay Farness. 395p. (C). 1991. pap. 25.75 (0-939693-01-1) Collegiate Pr.

College Writing Skills with Readings. 3rd ed. John Langan. LC 92-9865. 1992. pap. text ed. write for info. (0-07-036384-6) McGraw.

College Yearbook: Making It Through the First Year. Jackson C. Hardin. 1988. 22.25 (0-536-57194-5) Ginn Pr.

College Yearbook Fundamentals. Ed. by Charles E. Savedge. (Illus.). 44p. (Orig.). 1984. pap. text ed. 8.50 (0-916084-14-0) Columbia Scholastic.

College Years. Ed. by Auguste C. Spectorsky. LC 75-167422. (Essay Index Reprint Ser.). 1977. reprint ed. 44.95 (0-8369-2443-6) Ayer.

College Yiddish; An Introduction to the Yiddish Language & to Jewish Life & Culture. 5th ed. Uriel Weinreich. LC 76-88208. 399p. (C). 1979. 25.00 (0-914512-04-8) Yivo Inst.

***College Youth, Drugs & Alcohol: A Resource Guide.** 1995. lib. bdg. 251.95 (0-8490-6788-X) Gordon Pr.

College Zoology. 10th ed. Richard A. Boolootian & Karl A. Stiles. (Illus.). 768p. (C). 1981. text ed. write for info. (0-02-311990-X) Macmillan.

Collegefields: Youth from Delinquency to Freedom. Robert F. Allan et al. 176p. (Orig.). 1981. text ed. 22.00 (0-8290-0273-1); pap. text ed. 9.95 (0-8290-0274-X) Irvington.

Colleges & Money: A Faculty Guide to Academic Economics. George W. Bonham et al. LC 76-2872. 1976. pap. 18.95 (0-915390-04-3, Pub. by Change Mag) Transaction Pubs.

Colleges & Universities: A Strategic Marketing Analysis on the Business of Higher Education in the 1980's. 1983. 495.00 (0-318-00518-2) Busn Trend.

Colleges & Universities for Change: America's Comprehensive Public State Colleges & Universities. Fred F. Harcleroad & Allan W. Ostar. 238p. (Orig.). (C). 1987. lib. bdg. 41.25 (0-88044-085-6); pap. text ed. 19.75 (0-88044-086-4) AASCU Press.

Colleges & Universities in World War II. V. R. Cardozier. LC 92-18877. 264p. 1993. text ed. 52.95 (0-275-94432-8, C4432, Praeger Pubs) Greenwood.

Colleges & Universities to Avoid: From Case Western Reserve University to University of Waterloo. Chris Pupkiewicz. 97p. 1992. pap. text ed. 88.59 (1-895583-97-7) MAYA Pubs.

Colleges in Consort: Institutional Cooperation Through Consortia. Franklin K. Patterson. LC 73-20964. (Jossey-Bass Higher Education Ser.). 200p. reprint ed. pap. 57.00 (0-317-41809-2, 2025666) Bks Demand.

Colleges in Controversy: The Jesuit Schools in France from Revival to Suppression, 1815-1880. John W. Padberg. LC 75-78523. (Historical Studies: No. 83). 347p. 1969. 25.00 (0-674-14160-1) HUP.

Colleges in War Time & After: A Contemporary Account of the Effect of the War upon Higher Education in America. Parke R. Kolbe. LC 74-75247. (United States in World War I Ser.). (Illus.). xx, 320p. 1974. reprint ed. lib. bdg. 38.95 (0-89198-106-3) Ozer.

Colleges of Choice: The Enabling Impact of the Community College. Judith S. Eaton. (ACE-Oryx Series on Higher Education). 272p. 1987. 27.95 (0-02-908790-2, ACE-Oryx) Oryx Pr.

Colleges of Education: Perspectives on Their Future. Ed. by Charles W. Case & William A. Matthes. LC 84-61701. (National Society for the Study of Education Publication Ser.). 206p. (C). 1985. 29.75 (0-8211-0230-3); text ed. write for info. (0-685-10261-0) McCutchan.

Colleges of Podiatry Admission Test (CPAT) Jack Rudman. (Admission Test Ser.: ATS-37). 1994. reprint ed. pap. 29.95 (0-8373-5037-9) Nat Learn.

Colleges That Offer Credit for Life Experience: A How to Find or Locate Workbook. Data Notes Publishing Staff. 300p. 1983. text ed. 16.95 (0-911569-07-3) Prosperity & Profits.

Colleges, Their Constituencies, & the Courts. Robert M. Hendrickson. 167p. (Orig.). (C). 1992. pap. text ed. 27.95 (1-56534-033-7) NOLPE.

Colleges Today & Tomorrow. Lewis B. Mayhew. LC 74-75939. (Jossey-Bass Higher Education Ser.). 272p. reprint ed. 77.60 (0-8357-9308-7, 2013952) Bks Demand.

Colleges With Fences: A Handbook for Improving Corrections Education Programs. Brian E. Simms et al. 82p. 1987. 8.75 (0-318-23419-X, RD 266) Ctr Educ Trng Employ.

Collegeville Bible Commentary. Ed. by Dianne Bergant & Robert J. Karris. 1344p. 1989. 54.95 (0-8146-1484-1) Liturgical Pr.

Collegeville Bible Commentary: Based on the New American Bible. Ed. by Dianne Bergant & Robert J. Karris. LC 92-23578. 880p. 1992. Old Testament, 880p. 21.95 (0-8146-2210-0); New Testament, 464p. 16.95 (0-8146-2211-9) Liturgical Pr.

Collegeville Bible Commentary Series: New Testament, 11 Vols., Set. Ed. by Robert J. Karris. 1983. pap. 36.95 (0-8146-1312-8) Liturgical Pr.

Collegeville Bible Study Atlas. Illus. by Carta Staff. 18p. 1990. pap. text ed. 6.95 (0-8146-1976-2) Liturgical Pr.

Collegeville Bible Time-Line. Tim Dowley. LC 93-19614. (Illus.). 32p. 1994. pap. text ed. 7.95 (0-8146-2275-5) Liturgical Pr.

Collegeville Concise Dictionary of Biblical Terms. Dianne Bergant. 112p. (Orig.). 1994. pap. text ed. 7.95 (0-8146-2239-9) Liturgical Pr.

Collegeville Hymnal. Ed. by Edward McKenna. 768p. 1990. text ed. 11.95 (0-8146-1569-4) Liturgical Pr.

Collegeville Pastoral Dictionary of Biblical Theology. Ed. by Carol Stuhlmueller. (Orig.). 1996. pap. text ed. write for info. (0-8146-1996-7) Liturgical Pr.

Collegial Collectors: American Art from the Class of 1967. Mead Art Museum Staff. (Illus.). 12p. (Orig.). 1992. pap. 5.00 (0-914337-15-7) Mead Art Mus.

Collegial Discourse: Professional Conversation among Peers. Allen D. Grimshaw. Ed. by Roy O. Freedle. LC 88-10556. (Advances in Discourse Processes Ser.: Vol. 32). 640p. (C). 1989. text ed. 95.00 (0-89391-470-3) Ablex Pub.

Collegiality & Bureaucracy in the Modern University: The Influence of Information & Power on Decision-Making Structures. James L. Bess. 208p. (C). 1987. text ed. 26.95 (0-8077-2868-3) Tchrs Coll.

Collegiate Business Mathematics. 5th ed. Hyman M. Berston & Paul Fisher. 544p. (C). 1989. pap. text ed. 48.95 (0-256-08028-3) Irwin.

Collegiate Business Series: Syllabus. Richard R. Gallagher. 1977. pap. text ed. 8.25 (0-89420-011-9, 104021); audio 120.25 (0-89420-135-2, 104000) Natl Book.

Collegiate Church of Wimborne Minster. Patricia H. Coulstock. LC 93-31431. (Studies in the History of Medieval Religion: Vol. V). (Illus.). 256p. 1993. text ed. 63.00 (0-85115-339-9, Boydell Pr) Boydell & Brewer.

Collegiate Construction Education Directory. 4th ed. 55p. 1984. 5.00 (0-318-13515-9) Assn Gen Con.

Collegiate Cookbook. Lyn Shinn. (Illus.). 96p. (Orig.). 1986. pap. 7.95 (0-9618661-0-1) Cookbook CA.

Collegiate Culture & Leadership Strategies. Ellen E. Chaffee & William G. Tierney. (ACE-Oryx Series on Higher Education). 288p. (C). 1988. 27.95 (0-02-905291-2, ACE-Oryx) Oryx Pr.

Collegiate Dictionary of Zoology. Robert W. Pennak. LC 85-23983. 594p. (C). 1987. reprint ed. pap. text ed. 33.50 (0-89874-921-2) Krieger.

Collegiate English Handbook. 3rd ed. Francis L. Fennell. 450p. pap. 19.75 (0-939693-20-8) Collegiate Pr.

Collegiate Function of Community Colleges: Fostering Higher Learning Through Curriculum & Student Transfer. Arthur M. Cohen & Florence B. Brawer. LC 87-45430. (Higher Education Ser.). 269p. 1987. 35.95x (1-55542-047-8) Jossey-Bass.

Collegiate Gothic: The Architecture of Rhodes College. William Morgan. LC 89-4861. (Illus.). 128p. 1989. text ed. 28.00 (0-8262-0699-9) U of Mo Pr.

Collegiate Peaks-Buena Vista, CO. rev. ed. Ed. by Trails Illustrated Staff. 1992. 8.99 (0-925873-49-7) Trails Illustrated.

***Collegiate Reader.** Chris Robinson. 1995. pap. text ed. write for info. (1-56226-228-9) CT Pub.

Collegiate Reader. rev. ed. Christine Robinson. 252p. (C). 1990. pap. text ed. 18.15 (1-56226-021-9) CT Pub.

Collegiate Slang: Aspects of Word Formation & Semantic Change see Terms Used in Whitewater Kayaking in Colorado

Collegium: A Handbook. Edward Kottick. 1978. 15.00 (0-8079-0189-X) October.

Collegium Internationale Neuro-Psychopharmacologicum, 10th Congress: Proceedings, 2 vols., Set. Ed. by P. Deniker. 1978. 722.00 (0-08-021506-8, Pub. by Pergamon Repr UK) Franklin.

Collegium Phaenomenologicum. Ed. by Giuseppina Moneta et al. (C). 1988. lib. bdg. 133.00 (90-247-3709-5) Kluwer Ac.

Collembola of North America, North of the Rio Grande: A Taxonomic. Kenneth Christiansen & Peter Bellinger. (Illus.). 1322p. 1981. 35.00 (0-686-34383-2) Grinnell Coll.

Colle's Chess Masterpieces. Fred Reinfeld. 106p. 1984. reprint ed. pap. 3.95 (0-486-24757-0) Dover.

Colletotrichum: Biology, Pathology & Control. Ed. by J. A. Bailey & M. J. Jeger. 416p. 1992. 114.00 (0-85198-756-7) CAB Intl.

Colley Cibber. Leonard R. Ashley. LC 64-8324. (Twayne's English Authors Ser.). 224p. (C). 1965. 17.95 (0-8290-1730-5) Irvington.

Colley Cibber. rev. ed. Leonard R. Ashley. 200p. 1988. text ed. 25.95 (0-8057-6969-2, TEAS 17, Twayne) Macmillan.

Colley Cibber: A Biography. Helene Koon. LC 85-17899. 264p. 1986. 29.00 (0-8131-1551-5) U Pr of Ky.

Collezione Di Varie Scene Teatrali. Antonio Basoli. LC 68-21205. (Illus.). (ITA.). 1972. reprint ed. 26.95 (0-405-08241-X, Pub. by Blom Pubns UK) Ayer.

Collider Physics: Proceedings of the Lake Louise Winter Institute. A. Astbury et al. 560p. 1994. text ed. 121.00 (981-02-1598-3) World Scientific Pub.

Colliders Physics: Current Status & Future Prospects: Proceedings of the 8th Vanderbilt High Energy Physics Conference, Nashville, Tennesse, U. S. A. R. S. Parvini & J. Brau. 508p. (C). 1988. pap. 52.00 (9971-5-0544-4) World Scientific Pub.

Collidescope. Grace Chetwin. LC 89-38255. 240p. (J). (gr. 5-9). 1990. text ed. 14.95 (0-02-718316-5, Bradbury S&S) S&S Childrens.

Colliding Galaxies: The Universe in Turmoil. Barry Parker. LC 90-40651. (Illus.). 310p. 1990. 23.95 (0-306-43566-7, Plenum Pr) Plenum.

Colliding Plane Waves in General Relativity. J. B. Griffiths. (Oxford Mathematical Monographs). (Illus.). 248p. 1991. 49.95 (0-19-853209-1) OUP.

Collie. Anna K. Nicholas. (Illus.). 320p. 1986. 19.95 (0-86622-723-7, PS-825) TFH Pubns.

Collie: A Veterinary Reference for the Professional Breeder. Sharon L. Vanderlip. LC 83-73019. (Illus.). 296p. (ENG & GER.). 1984. 85.00 (0-89612-556-0-X) Biotech Vet.

Collie Concept. rev. ed. George H. Roos. (Illus.). 232p. 1988. 26.95 (0-931866-36-7) Alpine Pubns.

***Collier.** A. R. Griffin. (C). 1989. pap. 25.00x (0-85263-590-7, Pub. by Shire UK) St Mut.

Collier Bankruptcy Cases: Second Series, 30 vols. Roy Babbit & Lawrence P. King. 1979. Incl. 1 year's service. ring bd. write for info. (0-8205-1222-2) Bender.

Collier Bankruptcy Compensation Guide, No. 536. Stanley Bernstein. 1988. write for info. (0-8205-1536-1) Bender.

Collier Bankruptcy Exemption Guide. Lawrence P. King. 1982. Updates available. ring bd. write for info. (0-8205-1126-9) Bender.

Collier Bankruptcy Forms Manual, 2 vols. 3rd ed. Collier Staff & Lawrence P. King. 1979. Updates. ring bd. write for info. (0-8205-1215-X) Bender.

Collier Bankruptcy Manual, 3 vols. 3rd ed. Collier et al. 1979. Updates available. ring bd. write for info. (0-8205-1224-9) Bender.

Collier Bankruptcy Practice Guide, 8 vols. Collier Staff et al. 1981. Updates. ring bd. write for info. (0-8205-1200-1) Bender.

Collier Business Workout Guide. 1992. write for info. (0-8205-1177-3) Bender.

Collier, Coleridge & Shakespeare. Andrew E. Brac. LC 70-113562. reprint ed. 45.00 (0-404-01061-X) AMS Pr.

Collier Companion to African American Writers. rev. ed. Ed. by Lea Baechler. LC 93-6909. 416p. 1993. pap. 15.00 (0-02-082125-5, Collier S&S) S&S Trade.

Collier Companion to Modern American Women Writers. Ed. by Lea Baechler. LC 93-22193. 432p. 1993. pap. 15.00 (0-02-082025-9, Collier S&S) S&S Trade.

Collier de la Reine. Alexandre Dumas. (FRE.). 1973. 23.95 (0-8288-9739-5, 2070501337) Fr & Eur.

Collier de la Reine, Vol. 1. Alexandre Dumas. (FRE.). 1989. pap. 23.95 (0-7859-3313-1, 2870272928) Fr & Eur.

Collier de la Reine, Vol. 2. Alexandre Dumas. (FRE.). 1989. pap. 23.95 (0-7859-3314-X, 2870272936) Fr & Eur.

Collier Family Law & Bankruptcy Code, Vol. 1. H. Sommer et al. 1991. write for info. (0-8205-1125-0) Bender.

Collier Farm Bankruptcy Guide. Randy Rogers. 1989. Updates. ring bd. write for info. (0-8205-1233-8) Bender.

Collier Handbook for Creditors' Committees. 1988. write for info. (0-8205-1231-1) Bender.

Collier Handbook for Trustees & Debtors in Possession. Collier Staff & Irving Sulmeyer. LC 82-72098. (Illus.). 1985. Updates. ring bd. write for info. (0-8205-1149-8) Bender.

Collier Labor Law & the Bankruptcy Code. Pulliam et al. 1989. Updates. ring bd. write for info. (0-8205-1132-3) Bender.

Collier Lending Institutions & the Bankruptcy Code. Robert J. Rosenberg et al. 1986. write for info. (0-8205-1119-6) Bender.

Collier on Bankruptcy, 16 vols. 15th ed. Collier Staff et al. 1979. ring bd. write for info. (0-8205-1219-2) Bender.

Collier Pamphlet Edition. A. Herzog et al. 1988. write for info. (0-8205-1221-4) Bender.

Collier Real Estate Transactions & the Bankruptcy Code. Lawrence D. Cherkis et al. LC 84-70341. 1984. Updates. ring bd. write for info. (0-8205-1131-5) Bender.

Collier Tax & Bankruptcy. Fred T. Witt, Jr. et al. 1992. write for info. (0-8205-1861-1) Bender.

Collier Tracts 1698: Immorality of the English Pulpit. Bd. with Letter to A. H. Esq.; Concerning the Stage. Charles Hopkins. LC 76-170453.; Letter to Mr. Congreve on His Pretended Amendments. LC 76-170453.; Occasional Paper. Richard Willis. LC 76-170453.; Some Remarks Upon Mr. Collier's Defence of His Short View of the English Stage. LC 76-170453.; Vindication of the Stage. LC 76-170453. LC 76-170453. (English Stage Ser.: Vol. 27). 1973. Set lib. bdg. 61.00 (0-8240-0610-0) Garland.

Collier's Encyclopedia, 1991, 24 vols., Set. Macmillan Educational Company Staff. 1991. text ed. 959.00 (0-02-942517-4) Macmillan.

Collier's Encyclopedia, 1995 Edition, 24 vols., Set. P. F. Collier Staff. LC 94-70743. (Illus.). 19900p. 1995. write for info. (1-57161-003-0) P F Collier.

Collier's Encyclopedia, 1995 Edition, Vol. 1. P. F. Collier Staff. LC 94-70743. (Illus.). 628p. 1995. 35.00 (1-57161-004-9) P F Collier.

Collier's Encyclopedia, 1995 Edition, Vol. 2. P. F. Collier Staff. LC 94-70743. (Illus.). 780p. 1995. 35.00 (1-57161-005-7) P F Collier.

Collier's Encyclopedia, 1995 Edition, Vol. 3. P. F. Collier Staff. LC 94-70743. (Illus.). 783p. 1995. 35.00 (1-57161-006-5) P F Collier.

Collier's Encyclopedia, 1995 Edition, Vol. 4. P. F. Collier Staff. LC 94-70743. (Illus.). 764p. 1995. 35.00 (1-57161-007-3) P F Collier.

Collier's Encyclopedia, 1995 Edition, Vol. 5. P. F. Collier Staff. LC 94-70743. (Illus.). 726p. 1995. 35.00 (1-57161-008-1) P F Collier.

Collier's Encyclopedia, 1995 Edition, Vol. 6. P. F. Collier Staff. LC 94-70743. (Illus.). 762p. 1995. 35.00 (1-57161-009-X) P F Collier.

Collier's Encyclopedia, 1995 Edition, Vol. 7. P. F. Collier Staff. LC 94-70743. (Illus.). 772p. 1995. 35.00 (1-57161-010-3) P F Collier.

Collier's Encyclopedia, 1995 Edition, Vol. 8. P. F. Collier Staff. LC 94-70743. (Illus.). 788p. 1995. 35.00 (1-57161-011-1) P F Collier.

Collier's Encyclopedia, 1995 Edition, Vol. 9. P. F. Collier Staff. LC 94-70743. (Illus.). 760p. 1995. 35.00 (1-57161-012-X) P F Collier.

Collier's Encyclopedia, 1995 Edition, Vol. 10. P. F. Collier Staff. LC 94-70743. (Illus.). 740p. 1995. 35.00 (1-57161-013-8) P F Collier.

Collier's Encyclopedia, 1995 Edition, Vol. 11. P. F. Collier Staff. LC 94-70743. (Illus.). 761p. 1995. 35.00 (1-57161-014-6) P F Collier.

Collier's Encyclopedia, 1995 Edition, Vol. 12. P. F. Collier Staff. LC 94-70743. (Illus.). 793p. 1995. 35.00 (1-57161-015-4) P F Collier.

Collier's Encyclopedia, 1995 Edition, Vol. 13. P. F. Collier Staff. LC 94-70743. (Illus.). 766p. 1995. 35.00 (1-57161-016-2) P F Collier.

Collier's Encyclopedia, 1995 Edition, Vol. 14. P. F. Collier Staff. LC 94-70743. (Illus.). 766p. 1995. 35.00 (1-57161-017-0) P F Collier.

Collier's Encyclopedia, 1995 Edition, Vol. 15. P. F. Collier Staff. LC 94-70743. (Illus.). 760p. 1995. 35.00 (1-57161-018-9) P F Collier.

Collier's Encyclopedia, 1995 Edition, Vol. 16. P. F. Collier Staff. LC 94-70743. (Illus.). 754p. 1995. 35.00 (1-57161-019-7) P F Collier.

Collier's Encyclopedia, 1995 Edition, Vol. 17. P. F. Collier Staff. LC 94-70743. (Illus.). 774p. 1995. 35.00 (1-57161-020-0) P F Collier.

Collier's Encyclopedia, 1995 Edition, Vol. 18. P. F. Collier Staff. LC 94-70743. (Illus.). 776p. 1995. 35.00 (1-57161-021-9) P F Collier.

Collier's Encyclopedia, 1995 Edition, Vol. 19. P. F. Collier Staff. LC 94-70743. (Illus.). 760p. 1995. 35.00 (1-57161-022-7) P F Collier.

Collier's Encyclopedia, 1995 Edition, Vol. 20. P. F. Collier Staff. LC 94-70743. (Illus.). 716p. 1995. 35.00 (1-57161-023-5) P F Collier.

Collier's Encyclopedia, 1995 Edition, Vol. 21. P. F. Collier Staff. LC 94-70743. (Illus.). 721p. 1995. 35.00 (1-57161-024-3) P F Collier.

Collier's Encyclopedia, 1995 Edition, Vol. 22. P. F. Collier Staff. LC 94-70743. (Illus.). 763p. 1995. 35.00 (1-57161-025-1) P F Collier.

Collier's Encyclopedia, 1995 Edition, Vol. 23. P. F. Collier Staff. LC 94-70743. (Illus.). 800p. 1995. 35.00 (1-57161-026-X) P F Collier.

Collier's Encyclopedia, 1995 Edition, Vol. 24. P. F. Collier Staff. LC 94-70743. (Illus.). 1049p. 1995. 35.00 (1-57161-027-8) P F Collier.

***Collier's Encyclopedia, 1996, 24 vols., Set.** (Illus.). 19,900p. 1996. text ed. 1,499.00 (1-57161-046-4) P F Collier.

***Collier's Encyclopedia, 1996, Vol. 1.** LC 95-68867. (Illus.). 628p. 1996. text ed. 35.00 (1-57161-047-2) P F Collier.

***Collier's Encyclopedia, 1996, Vol. 2.** LC 95-68867. (Illus.). 780p. 1996. text ed. 35.00 (1-57161-048-0) P F Collier.

***Collier's Encyclopedia, 1996, Vol. 3.** LC 95-68867. (Illus.). 783p. 1996. text ed. 35.00 (1-57161-049-9) P F Collier.

***Collier's Encyclopedia, 1996, Vol. 4.** LC 95-68867. (Illus.). 764p. 1996. text ed. 35.00 (1-57161-050-2) P F Collier.

***Collier's Encyclopedia, 1996, Vol. 5.** LC 95-68867. (Illus.). 726p. 1996. text ed. 35.00 (1-57161-051-0) P F Collier.

***Collier's Encyclopedia, 1996, Vol. 6.** LC 95-68867. (Illus.). 774p. 1996. text ed. 35.00 (1-57161-052-9) P F Collier.

***Collier's Encyclopedia, 1996, Vol. 7.** LC 95-68867. (Illus.). 772p. 1996. text ed. 35.00 (1-57161-053-7) P F Collier.

***Collier's Encyclopedia, 1996, Vol. 8.** LC 95-68867. (Illus.). 788p. 1996. text ed. 35.00 (1-57161-054-5) P F Collier.

***Collier's Encyclopedia, 1996, Vol. 9.** LC 95-68867. (Illus.). 760p. 1996. text ed. 35.00 (1-57161-055-3) P F Collier.

***Collier's Encyclopedia, 1996, Vol. 10.** LC 95-68867. (Illus.). 740p. 1996. text ed. 35.00 (1-57161-056-1) P F Collier.

***Collier's Encyclopedia, 1996, Vol. 11.** LC 95-68867. (Illus.). 761p. 1996. text ed. 35.00 (1-57161-057-X) P F Collier.

***Collier's Encyclopedia, 1996, Vol. 12.** LC 95-68867. (Illus.). 793p. 1996. text ed. 35.00 (0-571-61058-7) P F Collier.

***Collier's Encyclopedia, 1996, Vol. 13.** LC 95-68867. (Illus.). 766p. 1996. text ed. 35.00 (1-57161-059-6) P F Collier.

***Collier's Encyclopedia, 1996, Vol. 14.** LC 95-68867. (Illus.). 766p. 1996. text ed. 35.00 (1-57161-060-X) P F Collier.

***Collier's Encyclopedia, 1996, Vol. 15.** LC 95-68867. (Illus.). 760p. 1996. text ed. 35.00 (1-57161-061-8) P F Collier.

***Collier's Encyclopedia, 1996, Vol. 16.** LC 95-68867. (Illus.). 754p. 1996. text ed. 35.00 (1-57161-062-6) P F Collier.

***Collier's Encyclopedia, 1996, Vol. 17.** LC 95-68867. (Illus.). 774p. 1996. text ed. 35.00 (1-57161-063-4) P F Collier.

***Collier's Encyclopedia, 1996, Vol. 18.** LC 95-68867. (Illus.). 776p. 1996. text ed. 35.00 (1-57161-064-2) P F Collier.

***Collier's Encyclopedia, 1996, Vol. 19.** LC 95-68867. (Illus.). 760p. 1996. text ed. 35.00 (1-57161-065-0) P F Collier.

***Collier's Encyclopedia, 1996, Vol. 20.** LC 95-68867. (Illus.). 728p. 1996. text ed. 35.00 (1-57161-066-9) P F Collier.

***Collier's Encyclopedia, 1996, Vol. 21.** LC 95-68867. (Illus.). 721p. 1996. text ed. 35.00 (1-57161-067-7) P F Collier.

***Collier's Encyclopedia, 1996, Vol. 22.** LC 95-68867. (Illus.). 763p. 1996. text ed. 35.00 (1-57161-068-5) P F Collier.

***Collier's Encyclopedia, 1996, Vol. 23.** LC 95-68867. (Illus.). 800p. 1996. text ed. 35.00 (1-57161-069-3) P F Collier.

***Collier's Encyclopedia, 1996, Vol. 24.** LC 95-68867. (Illus.), 1,049p. 1996. text ed. 35.00 (1-57161-070-7) P F Collier.

Colliers Row. large type ed. Jan Webster. 475p. 1981. 12.00 (0-7089-0656-7) Ulverscroft.

Collier's Rules for Desktop Design & Typography. David Collier. (C). 1991. text ed. 16.25 (0-201-54416-4) Addison-Wesley.

C

An Asterisk (*) at the beginning of an entry indicates that the title is appearing in BIP for the first time.

C

An Asterisk (*) at the beginning of an entry indicates that the title is appearing in BIP for the first time.

Colloid Chemistry of Silica & Silicates. Ralph K. Iler. LC 55-1415. 335p. reprint ed. pap. 95.50 (0-317-09823-3, 2000877) Bks Demand.

Colloid Electro-Optics: Theory, Techniques, Applications. S. P. Stoylov. (Colloid Science Ser.). (Illus.). 280p. 1991. text ed. 88.00 (0-12-672965-4) Acad Pr.

Colloid-Polymer Interactions: Particulate, Amphiphilic, & Biological Surfaces. Ed. by Paul L. Dubin & Penger Tong. LC 93-8495. (ACS Symposium Ser.: Vol. 532). (Illus.). 300p. 1993. 74.95 (0-8412-2696-2) Am Chemical.

Colloidal Dispersions. W. B. Russel et al. (Cambridge Monographs on Mechanics & Applied Mathematics). (Illus.). 525p. (C). 1992. pap. 42.95 (0-521-42600-6) Cambridge U Pr.

Colloidal Dispersions & Micellar Behavior: Papers from A Symposium Honoring Robert D. Vold & Marjorie J. Vold. Ed. by K. L. Mittal. LC 74-34072. (American Chemical Society ACS Symposium Ser.: No. 9). (Illus.). 362p. reprint ed. pap. 103.20 (0-317-09351-7, 2015233) Bks Demand.

Colloidal Domain: Where Physics, Chemistry, Biology, & Technology Meet. D. Fennell Evans & Hakan Wennerstrom. LC 94-2013. 1994. write for info. (1-56081-525-6) VCH Pubs.

Colloidal Drug Delivery Systems. Kreuter. (Drugs & the Pharmaceutical Sciences Ser.: Vol. 66). 368p. 1994. 125.00 (0-8247-9214-9) Dekker.

Colloidal Gold Vol. 1: Principles, Methods & Applications. Ed. by M. A. Hayat. 680p. 1989. text ed. 128.00 (0-12-333927-8) Acad Pr.

Colloidal Gold Vol. 2: Principles, Methods, & Applications. Ed. by M. A. Hayat. 380p. 1989. text ed. 128.00 (0-12-333928-6) Acad Pr.

Colloidal Gold Vol. 3: Principles, Methods & Applications. Ed. by M. A. Hayat. 421p. 1990. text ed. 128.00 (0-12-333929-4) Acad Pr.

Colloidal Hydrodynamics. T. G. Van de Ven. (Colloid Science Ser.). 582p. 1989. text ed. 113.00 (0-12-710770-3) Acad Pr.

***Colloidal Polymer Particles.** Ed. by J. W. Goodwin & R. Buscall. (Illus.). 300p. 1995. text ed. 90.00 (0-12-290045-6) Acad Pr.

***Colloidal Silver: The Natural Antibiotic Alternative.** Zane Baranowski. (Orig.). 1995. pap. 3.50 (0-9647080-1-9) Healing Wisdom.

Colloidal Systems & Interfaces. Sydney Ross & Ian Morris. LC 87-30529. 422p. 1988. text ed. 110.00 (0-471-82848-3) Wiley.

Colloids & Surfaces in Reprographic Technology. Ed. by Michael Hair & Melvin D. Croucher. LC 82-13931. (ACS Symposium Ser.: No. 200). 591p. 1982. lib. bdg. 71.95 (0-8412-0737-2) Am Chemical.

Colloids in Food. E. Dickinson & G. Stainsby. (Illus.). xiv, 532p. 1982. 142.25 (0-85334-153-2, I-357-82, Pub. by Elsevier Applied Sci UK) Elsevier.

Colloids in the Aquatic Environment. Ed. by T. F. Tadros & J. Gregory. LC 93-30149. 1993. write for info. (1-85861-038-9, Pub. by Elsevier Applied Sci UK) Elsevier.

Colloque International sur la Thrombolyse Paris, Mars 1985. Ed. by A. Serradimigni. (Journal: Haemostasis: Vol. 16, Suppl. 4, 1986). (Illus.). 160p. 1986. pap. 46.50 (3-8055-4375-1) S Karger.

Colloques Phytosociologiqeus Vol. XIV: Phytosociologie et Foresterie. Ed. by J. M. Gehu. 814p. (FRE.). 1988. 143.00 (3-443-70003-9) Lubrecht & Cramer.

Colloques Phytosociologique Vol. XIX: Vegetation et Qualite de l'Environnement Cotier Mediterranee. 760p. (FRE.). 1992. lib. bdg. 187.95 (3-443-70008-X, Pub. by E Schweizerbartsche GW) Lubrecht & Cramer.

Colloques Phytosociologiques: La Vegetation des Pelouses Calcaires, Vol. XI. Ed. by J. M. Gehu. (Illus.). 684p. 1982. lib. bdg. 108.00 (3-7682-1425-7) Lubrecht & Cramer.

Colloques Phytosociologiques: Les Vegetation Nitrophiles et Anthropogenes, Bailleul 1983 - Seminaire les Megamosphiaies, Bailleul 1984, Vol. XII. Ed. by J. M. Gehu. 805p. (FRE.). 1986. lib. bdg. 115.00 (3-443-70001-2) Lubrecht & Cramer.

Colloques Phytosociologiques: Les Vegetations Aquatiques et Amphibiens, Lille, 1981, Vol. X. Ed. by M. J. Gehu. (Illus.). (FRE.). 1983. lib. bdg. 90.00 (3-7682-1383-8) Lubrecht & Cramer.

Colloques Phytosociologiques No. XVIII: Phytosociologie Littotale & Taxonomie. Ed. by J. M. Gehu. (Illus.). 350p. (FRE.). 1993. lib. bdg. 110.00 (3-443-70007-1, Pub. by Cramer-Borntraeger GW) Lubrecht & Cramer.

***Colloques Phytosociologiques Vol. 20: Phytodynamique et Biogeographie Historique des Forets, Bailleul 1991.** Ed. by J. M. Gehu. (Illus.). 416p. (FRE.). 1993. lib. bdg. 135.00x (3-443-00090-8) Lubrecht & Cramer.

Colloques Phytosociologiques Vol. VII: Lille 1978, le Vegetation des Sols Tourbeux. Ed. by J. M. Gehu. 556p. (FRE.). 1981. lib. bdg. 90.00 (3-7682-1260-2) Lubrecht & Cramer.

Colloques Phytosociologiques Vol. XVI: Phytosociologie et Pastoralisme. Ed. by J. M. Gehu. 859p. (ENG, FRE & SPA.). 1990. lib. bdg. 175.00 (3-443-70005-5, Pub. by Gebruder Borntraeger GW) Lubrecht & Cramer.

Colloques Phytosociologiques Vol. XVII: Phytosociologie & Paysage. Ed. by J. M. Gehu. (Illus.). 519p. (FRE.). 1991. lib. bdg. 162.50 (0-685-50521-9, Pub. by Cramer-Borntraeger GW) Lubrecht & Cramer.

Colloques Phytosociologiques, Strasbourg 1980: La Vegetation des Forets Alluviales, Vol. IX. Ed. by J. M. Gehu. (Illus.). 774p. (ENG, FRE & GER.). 1984. lib. bdg. 120.00 (3-7682-1382-X) Lubrecht & Cramer.

***Colloques Phytosociologiques XXII: La Syntaxonomie et la Synsystematique Europeanes Comme Base Typologique des Habitats Bailleul 1993.** Ed. by J. N. Gehu. 743p. (FRE.). 1994. lib. bdg. 198.00 (3-443-70011-X, Pub. by Cramer-Borntraeger GW) Lubrecht & Cramer.

Colloques Phytosocioloques, Volume XIII: Vegetation et Geomorphologie. Ed. by J. M. Gehu. (Illus.). 870p. (FRE.). 1986. lib. bdg. 132.00 (0-685-17959-1) Lubrecht & Cramer.

Colloquial Albanian. Isa Zymberi. (Colloquial Ser.). 336p. 1991. pap. 19.95 (0-415-05663-2, A5077); audio, pap. 35.00 (0-415-05665-9, A5085) Routledge.

***Colloquial Amharic: A Complete Language Course.** David Appleyard. (Colloquial Ser.). 1995. 39.95 (0-415-10005-4, B4037); pap. 18.95 (0-415-10003-8, B4029); audio 22.95 (0-415-10004-6, B4033) Routledge.

Colloquial Arabic: An Oral Approach. Raja Nasr. (ARA.). 1968. 16.95 (0-86685-044-9) Intl Bk Ctr.

Colloquial Arabic of Egypt. Russell McGuirk. 320p. 1986. audio 29.95 (0-415-00072-6, RKP); pap. 14.95 (0-7100-9936-3, A2559, RKP) Routledge.

Colloquial Arabic of Egypt: Hermeneutics As Method, Philosophy, & Critique. Russell McGuirk. 1986. pap. 14.95 (0-415-05172-X, Pub. by Tavistock UK) Routledge Chapman & Hall.

Colloquial Arabic of the Gulf & Eastern Saudi Arabia. Clive Holes. (Colloquial Ser.). 220p. (Orig.). 1984. pap. 15.95 (0-7100-9709-3, RKP); audio 15.00 (0-7100-9769-7, RKP) Routledge.

Colloquial Arabic of the Gulf & Saudi Arabia. Clive Holes. (Colloquial Ser.). 326p. 1988. audio 27.50 (0-415-00074-2) Routledge.

Colloquial Arabic of the Levant. Leslie McLoughlin. (Colloquial Ser.). 152p. 1988. pap. 14.95 (0-7100-0668-3, RKP); audio 14.95 (0-415-01854-4, RKP) Routledge.

Colloquial Arabic of the Levant. Leslie McLoughlin. (Colloquial Ser.). 152p. 1988. audio 27.50 (0-415-00073-4, A2571, RKP); 14.95 (0-415-05107-X, RKP) Routledge.

Colloquial Bulgarian. George D. Papantchev. LC 93-26730. 1994. write for info. (0-415-07963-2, Routledge NY); audio write for info. (0-415-07965-9, Routledge NY); write for info. (0-415-07964-0, Routledge NY) Routledge.

Colloquial Cambodian: A Complete Language Course. David Smyth. LC 94-14337. (Colloquial Ser.). 1994. Pack. 35.00 (0-415-10008-9, B4189); pap. 16.95 (0-415-10006-2, B4045); Cassettes. audio 18.95 (0-415-10007-0, B4049) Routledge.

Colloquial Chinese. P. C. Tung & D. E. Pollard. (Colloquial Ser.). 300p. (Orig.). 1982. pap. 14.95 (0-7100-0891-0, RKP); audio 14.95 (0-7100-9428-0, RKP) Routledge.

Colloquial Chinese. P. C. T'ung & D. E. Pollard. 328p. 1982. audio 24.95 (0-415-00075-0, A2563); pap. 14.95 (0-415-01860-9, 08910) Routledge.

***Colloquial Chinese: A Complete Language Course.** Qian Kan. LC 94-49639. (Colloquial Ser.). (Illus.). 288p. (CHI.). 1995. pap. 15.95 (0-415-11386-5, C0611); audio, pap. 34.95 (0-415-11388-1, C0610); audio 22.95 (0-415-11387-3, C0609) Routledge.

Colloquial Czech. James Naughton. (Colloquial Ser.). 320p. 1988. audio 29.95 (0-415-00076-9, A2567, RKP); pap. 16.95 (0-7102-0857-X, 08575, RKP); audio 15.95 (0-7102-1104-X, 1104X, RKP) Routledge.

Colloquial Danish. W. Glyn Jones & Kristen Gade. LC 93-22098. (Colloquial Ser.). 288p. 1994. pap. 18.95 (0-415-07966-7, B2413, Routledge NY); audio 19.95 (0-415-07968-3, B2405, Routledge NY) Routledge.

Colloquial Danish, Set. W. Glyn Jones & Kristen Gade. LC 93-22098. (Colloquial Ser.). 288p. 1994. audio 35.00 (0-415-07967-5, B2409, Routledge NY) Routledge.

Colloquial Dutch. Fernand G. Renier. 1986. pap. 13.95 (0-7100-0785-X, RKP) Routledge.

Colloquial Dutch. Fernand G. Renier. (Colloquial Ser.). 1992. audio 29.95 (0-415-07424-X, A6896); audio 14.95 (0-415-07423-1, A6892) Routledge.

Colloquial Dutch. 3rd ed. Fernand G. Renier. 256p. 1983. pap. 14.95 (0-415-04039-6) Routledge.

Colloquial English. Graham Coe. (Illus.). 192p. (Orig.). 1981. pap. 14.95 (0-415-02769-1) Routledge.

Colloquial Estonian. Chris Moseley. LC 93-11594. (Colloquial Ser.). 1994. write for info. (0-415-08743-0, Routledge NY); audio write for info. (0-415-08744-9, Routledge NY); audio write for info. (0-415-08745-7, Routledge NY) Routledge.

Colloquial Expressions in Euripides. Philip T. Stevens. 83p. (Orig.). 1976. pap. text ed. 47.50 (3-515-02489-1) Coronet Bks.

Colloquial French. Flavio Andreis & Robert A. Humphreys. (Colloquial Ser.). 174p. 1981. audio 29.95 (0-415-03890-1, A3332); pap. 14.95 (0-415-03945-2, 04508); audio 15.50 (0-415-03889-8, A3561) Routledge.

Colloquial French. Routledge. 1985. pap. 12.95 (0-7100-0450-8, RKP) Routledge.

***Colloquial French: A Complete Language Course.** Alan Moys. LC 95-16104. (ENG & FRE.). 1995. write for info. (0-415-12089-6); audio write for info. (0-415-12091-8) Routledge.

Colloquial French: A Guide to Understanding Typical, Informal & Everyday French. C. W. Kirk-Greene. 160p. (Orig.). 1992. pap. 11.95 (0-572-01533-X, Pub. by W Foulsham UK) Trans-Atl Phila.

Colloquial German. Uhlich. 1985. pap. 14.95 (0-415-05891-0) Routledge.

Colloquial German. rev. ed. Inge Hubmann-Uhlich. (Colloquial Ser.). 1980. pap. 14.95 (0-7100-0482-6, RKP) Routledge.

Colloquial Greek. Niki Watts. LC 93-34818. (Colloquial Ser.). 1994. Bk. only. write for info. (0-415-08690-6, Routledge NY); write for info. (0-415-08691-4, Routledge NY) Routledge.

Colloquial Greek. 2nd ed. Katerina Harris. (Colloquial Ser.). 258p. 1987. pap. 15.95 (0-7100-8814-0, A3878) Routledge.

Colloquial Greek, Set. Niki Watts. LC 93-34818. (Colloquial Ser.). 1994. Bk. & cass. set. write for info. (0-415-08692-2, Routledge NY) Routledge.

***Colloquial Gujarati.** Jagdish Dave. 1994. audio, pap. 39.95 (0-415-09198-5, Pub. by Tavistock UK) Routledge Chapman & Hall.

Colloquial Gujarati: A Complete Language Course. Jagdish Dave. LC 94-3969. 1994. write for info. (0-415-09196-9); write for info. (0-415-09197-7) Routledge.

***Colloquial Hindi: A Complete Language Course.** Tej K. Bhatia. LC 95-14790. 1996. audio, pap. write for info. (0-415-11089-0); pap. write for info. (0-415-11087-4); audio write for info. (0-415-11088-2) Routledge.

Colloquial Hungarian. Jerry Payne. 1987. pap. 14.95 (0-7102-0636-4, RKP) Routledge.

Colloquial Hungarian. 2nd ed. Jerry Payne. (Colloquial Ser.). 240p. 1987. audio 29.95 (0-415-00077-7, A2575, RKP); pap. 15.95 (0-415-04589-4, 06364, RKP); audio 15.95 (0-7102-0984-3, 09843, RKP) Routledge.

Colloquial Indonesian. Sutanto Atmosumarto. LC 93-44403. 1994. pap. write for info. (0-415-09199-3, Routledge NY); audio write for info. (0-415-09200-0, Routledge NY) Routledge.

Colloquial Italian. Flavio Andreis. (Orig.). 1986. 13.95 (0-7100-0876-7, RKP) Routledge.

Colloquial Italian. Flavio Andreis. (Colloquial Ser.). 256p. (Orig.). 1989. audio 29.95 (0-415-03892-8, A3336); pap. 14.95 (0-415-03946-0, 08767); audio 14.95 (0-415-03891-X, A3557) Routledge.

Colloquial Italian. Flavio Andreis. (Colloquial Ser.). 244p. (Orig.). 1983. pap. 14.95 (0-685-04385-1) Routledge Chapman & Hall.

Colloquial Japanese. Clarke. (Orig.). 1986. pap. 14.95 (0-7100-0595-4, RKP) Routledge.

Colloquial Japanese. H. D. Clarke & Motoko Hamamura. (Colloquial Ser.). 346p. (Orig.). 1981. audio, pap. 29.95 (0-415-04741-2, 05954); pap. 14.95 (0-415-04544-4, A4363); audio 14.95 (0-685-04383-5, A4359) Routledge.

Colloquial Japanese: With Important Construction & Grammar Notes. Noboru Inamoto. LC 71-133865. 436p. 1988. reprint ed. pap. 16.95 (0-8048-1581-X) C E Tuttle.

***Colloquial Langauge in Ulysses: A Reference Tool.** R. W. Dent. (Illus.). 296p. 1994. 38.50 (0-87413-546-X) U Delaware Pr.

Colloquial Language in Literature see Needed Words

***Colloquial Malay: A Complete Language Course.** Zaharah Othman & Sutanto Atmosumarto. (Colloquial Ser.). 1995. 39.95 (0-415-11014-9, B4024); pap. 18.95 (0-415-11012-2, B4538) Routledge.

Colloquial Navajo Dictionary. Robert Young & William Morgan. 461p. 1994. reprint ed. pap. 16.95 (0-7818-0278-4) Hippocrene Bks.

Colloquial Nepali. G. G. Rogers. (C). 1991. reprint ed. 16.00 (81-206-0634-5, Pub. by Asian Educ Servs II) S Asia.

Colloquial Norwegian: A Complete Language Course. Kari Bratveit et al. LC 94-14197. (Colloquial Ser.). 1995. audio write for info. (0-415-11011-4, B4038, Routledge NY); pap. write for info. (0-415-11009-2, B4030, Routledge NY); audio write for info. (0-415-11010-6, B4034, Routledge NY) Routledge.

***Colloquial Panjabi: A Complete Language Course.** Mangat Bhardwaj. (Colloquial Ser.). 1995. 39.95 (0-415-10193-X, B4039); pap. 18.95 (0-415-10191-3, B4031); audio write for info. (0-415-10192-1, B4035) Routledge.

Colloquial Persian. 2nd ed. Leila Moshiri. 200p. 1988. pap. 17.95 (0-415-00886-7, A1402); audio 17.95 (0-415-00887-5, A1406) Routledge.

Colloquial Persian, Set. 2nd ed. Leila Moshiri. 200p. 1988. audio 29.95 (0-415-02618-0, A2659) Routledge.

Colloquial Polish. B. W. Mazur. (Colloquial Ser.). 224p. 1983. pap. 14.95 (0-7100-9030-7, RKP); audio 14.95 (0-7100-9387-X, RKP) Routledge.

Colloquial Polish. B. W. Mazur. (Colloquial Ser.). 282p. 1988. audio 24.95 (0-415-00078-5, A2583) Routledge.

Colloquial Portugese. Maria E. Naar. (Trubner's Colloquial Manuals Ser.). 192p. 1983. pap. 14.95 (0-7100-7450-6, RKP) Routledge.

Colloquial Romanian. Dennis Deletant. (Colloquial Ser.). (Orig.). 1983. audio 29.95 (0-415-05849-X); pap. 15.95 (0-7100-0834-1) Routledge.

Colloquial Russian. William Harrison et al. (Colloquial Ser.). 440p. 1974. pap. 14.95 (0-415-02530-3, 89651) Routledge.

Colloquial Russian. Svetlana Le Fleming & Susan Kay. LC 93-16782. (Colloquial Ser.). 306p. 1993. pap. 16.95 (0-415-05784-1, B2374); audio 17.95 (0-415-05785-X, B2366) Routledge.

Colloquial Russian, Set. Svetlana Le Fleming & Susan Kay. LC 93-16782. (Colloquial Ser.). 306p. 1993. Incl. cassette. audio 35.00 (0-415-05786-8, B2370) Routledge.

Colloquial Serbo-Croat. Celia Hawkesworth. 320p. 1986. pap. 15.95 (0-7100-9920-7, RKP); audio 15.95 (0-415-01859-5, 05805, RKP) Routledge.

Colloquial Serbo-Croat. Celia Hawkesworth. (Colloquial Ser.). 320p. 1988. 29.95 (0-415-00079-3, A2587) Routledge.

Colloquial Serbo-Croat, Set. Celia Hawkesworth. 320p. 1988. audio write for info. (0-318-63150-4) Routledge.

Colloquial Sinhalese Clause Structures. James W. Gair. (Janua Linguarum, Ser. Practica: No. 83). 1970. text ed. 70.80 (90-279-0733-1) Mouton.

***Colloquial Slovene: A Complete Language Course.** Andrea Albretti. LC 95-3675. (Colloquial Ser.). (ENG & SLO.). 1995. write for info. (0-415-08946-8) Routledge.

***Colloquial Somali: A Complete Language Course.** Martin Orwin. (Colloquial Ser.). 272p. (SOM.). 1995. pap. 18.95 (0-415-10009-7, B4032); audio, pap. 39.95 (0-415-10011-9, B4040); audio 24.95 (0-415-10010-0, B4036) Routledge.

Colloquial Spanish. Francine Patterson. 1979. pap. 13.95 (0-415-05908-9) Routledge.

Colloquial Spanish. rev. ed. W. R. Patterson. (Colloquial Ser.). pap. 13.95 (0-7100-6385-7, RKP) Routledge.

***Colloquial Spanish: A Complete Language Course.** Untza Sale. (Colloquial Ser.). 1995. (0-415-03026-9, B4054); pap. 14.95 (0-415-03024-2, B4046); audio write for info. (0-415-03025-0, B4050) Routledge.

Colloquial Spanish of Latin America. Roberto Rodriguez-Saona. (Colloquial Ser.). 1994. write for info. (0-415-08952-2); Incl. casette. audio write for info. (0-415-08954-9) Routledge.

Colloquial Swedish. Philip Holmes & Gunilla Serin. (Colloquial Ser.). 352p. 1990. pap. 18.95 (0-415-02803-5, A4365); audio, pap. 37.50 (0-415-04939-3, A4369); audio 17.95 (0-415-02804-3, 4361) Routledge.

Colloquial Thai: A Complete Language Course. John Moore & Soawalak Rodchue. LC 94-11582. 1994. write for info. (0-415-09574-3); Cassettes. audio write for info. (0-415-09575-1) Routledge.

Colloquial Turkish. Sinan Bayraktaroglu & Arin Bayraktaroglu. (Colloquial Ser.). 240p. 1992. audio write for info. (0-415-04075-2, A6953); pap. write for info. (0-415-04073-6, A6957); audio write for info. (0-415-04074-4, A6949) Routledge.

Colloquial Turkish. Yusuf Mardin. (Trubner's Colloquial Manuals Ser.). 1976. pap. 14.95 (0-7100-8415-3, RKP) Routledge.

Colloquial Ukrainian. Ian Press & Stefan Pugh. LC 93-38897. 1994. write for info. (0-415-09202-7); audio write for info. (0-415-09204-3) Routledge.

Colloquial Vietnamese. John Moore & Tuan D. Vuong. LC 93-33737. 1994. write for info. (0-415-09205-1); audio write for info. (0-415-09206-X) Routledge.

Colloquial Vietnamese. John Moore. 1994. pap. 35.00 (0-415-09207-8, Pub. by Tavistock UK) Routledge Chapman & Hall.

Colloquial Welsh: A Complete Language Course. Gary King. LC 94-16232. (Colloquial Ser.). 1994. Pack. write for info. (0-415-10785-7, B4055); pap. write for info. (0-415-10783-0, B4047); Cass. audio write for info. (0-415-10784-9, B4051) Routledge.

Colloquial Who's Who. William Abbat. LC 65-27204. 256p. 1969. reprint ed. 18.95 (0-405-03660-4, Pub. by Blom Pubns UK) Ayer.

Colloquies on the Simples & Drug of India. G. D. Orta. (C). 1988. 100.00 (0-317-92358-7, Scientific) St Mut.

Colloquies on the Simples & Drugs of India. G. D. Orta. 509p. (C). 1985. text ed. 300.00 (0-89771-616-7, Pub. by Intl Bk Distr II) St Mut.

Colloquies on the Simples & Drugs of India. G. D. Orta. 509p. (C). 1979. reprint ed. 300.00 (0-685-21866-X, Pub. by Intl Bk Distr II) St Mut.

Colloquium in Memory of George Carpenter Miles, 1904-1975. (Illus.). 47p. 1976. pap. 1.50 (0-89722-064-1) Am Numismatic.

Colloquium in South America, 1990. IEEE Staff. LC 90-85145. 400p. 1990. pap. text ed. write for info. (0-87942-610-1, 90TH0344-2); fiche write for info. (0-87942-611-X, 90TH0344-2) Inst Electrical.

Colloquium of the Seven about Secrets of the Sublime: Colloquium Heptaplomeres de Rerum Sublimium Arcanis Abditis. Jean Bodin. Tr. & Anno. by Marion L. Kuntz. LC 73-2453. 592p. reprint ed. pap. 168.80 (0-8357-3302-5, 2039525) Bks Demand.

Colloquium on Foreign Languages in the Elementary Schools: Proceedings. Intro. by Marcia Rosenbusch. (Illus.). 110p. (C). 1992. pap. text ed. 15.00 (0-942017-10-2) Amer Assn Teach German.

Colloquium on Hispanic Linguistics, 1975. Colloquium on Hispanic Linguistics Staff. Ed. by Frances M. Aid et al. LC 76-53729. 163p. reprint ed. pap. 46.50 (0-7837-6759-5, 2059158) Bks Demand.

Colloquium on Large Scale Finite Mathematics in the U. S. S. R. Goldberg et al. 120p. (Orig.). 1984. pap. text ed. 100.00 (1-55831-063-0) Delphic Associates.

Colloquium on Renal Lithiasis: Proceedings of an International Colloquium on Renal Lithiasis, Gainesville, Florida, 1975. International Colloquium on Renal Lithiasis Staff. Ed. by Birdwell Finlayson & William C. Thomas, Jr. LC 77-7779. 386p. reprint ed. pap. 110.10 (0-7837-5824-3, 2045496) Bks Demand.

Colloquium on Spanish & Luso-Brazilian Linguistics. Colloquium on Hispanic & Luso-Brazilian Linguistics Staff. Ed. by James P. Lantolf et al. LC 79-18824. 167p. reprint ed. pap. 47.60 (0-7837-6332-8, 2046045) Bks Demand.

Colloquium on Spanish & Portuguese Linguistics, 1974. Colloquium on Spanish & Portuguese Linguistics Staff. LC 75-28427. 154p. reprint ed. pap. 43.90 (0-7837-6333-6, 2046046) Bks Demand.

Colloquium on the History of Landscape Architecture, 8 vols. Incl. Vol. 2. Picturesque Garden & Its Influence Outside the British Isles. Ed. by Nikolaus Pevsner. (Illus.). 1974. 24.50 (0-88402-050-9); Vol. 4. Islamic Garden. Ed. by Elisabeth B. MacDougall & Richard Ettinghausen. (Illus.). 100p. 1976. 20.00 (0-88402-064-9); write for info. (0-318-51783-3) Dumbarton Oaks.

Colloquium on the History of Landscape Architecture Vol. 5: Fons Sapientiae: Renaissance Garden Fountains. Ed. by Elisabeth B. MacDougall. LC 78-55012. (Illus.). 212p. 1979. 25.00 (0-88402-080-0) Dumbarton Oaks.

An Asterisk (*) at the beginning of an entry indicates that the title is appearing in BIP for the first time.

Colloquium on the History of Landscape Architecture Vol. 7: Ancient Roman Gardens. Ed. by Elisabeth B. MacDougall & Wilhelmina F. Jashemski. LC 81-4510. (Illus.). 212p. 1981. 22.00 (*0-88402-100-9*) Dumbarton Oaks.

Colloquium on the Law of Outer Space: Proceedings, 22nd. (Illus.). 339p. 1980. 50.00 (*0-915928-37-X*, P801) AIAA.

Colloquium on the Law of Outer Space: Proceedings, 23rd. (Illus.). 296p. 1981. 50.00 (*0-915928-50-7*, P811) AIAA.

Colloquium on the Law of Outer Space: Proceedings, 27th. International Institute of Space Law Staff. LC 86-109602. 1984. 50.00 (*0-915928-93-0*) AIAA.

Colloquium on the Law of Outer Space: Proceedings, 28th. (Illus.). 350p. 1986. 59.50 (*0-930403-08-8*) AIAA.

Colloquium on the Law of Outer Space: Proceedings, 29th. 351p. 1987. 59.50 (*0-930403-27-4*) AIAA.

Colloquium on the Law of Outer Space: Proceedings, 31st. 1989. 59.50 (*0-930403-49-5*) AIAA.

Colloquium on the Law of Outer Space: Proceedings, 32nd. 1990. 59.50 (*0-685-40125-1*) AIAA.

Colloquium on the Law of Outer Space: Proceedings, 33rd. 428p. 1991. 59.50 (*0-930403-99-1*, P911) AIAA.

Colloquium on the Law of Outer Space: Proceedings, 34th. 420p. 1992. 59.50 (*1-56347-039-X*) AIAA.

Colloquium on the Law of Outer Space: Proceedings, 35th. 550p. 1993. 84.95 (*1-56347-062-4*, P931) AIAA.

Colloquium on the Law of Outer Space: Proceedings, 36th. 1994. 84.95 (*1-56347-104-3*) AIAA.

Colloquium on the Use of Embryonic Cell Transplantation for Correction of CNS Disorders. Ed. by V. H. Mark et al. (Journal: Applied Neurophysiology: Vol 47, No. 1-2). (Illus.). 96p. 1984. pap. 28.00 (*3-8055-3952-5*) S Karger.

Colloquium Paedolinguisticum. Ed. by Karel Ohnesorg. (Janua Linguarum, Ser. Minor: No. 133). 1972. pap. text ed. 45.50 (*90-279-2315-9*) Mouton.

Colloquium Uber Schaltkreis-und Schaltwerk Theorie: 1st Colloquium Bonn 1960. Ed. by E. Poeschel & H. Unger. (International Series of Numerical Mathematics: No. 3). 198p. (GER.). 1980. 28.75 (*0-8176-0187-2*) Birkhauser.

Colloquy. Aelfric. Ed. by G. N. Garmonsway. (Old English Ser.). 1966. pap. text ed. 2.95 (*0-89197-563-2*) Irvington.

Colloquy of Montbeliard: Religion & Politics in the Sixteenth Century. Jill Raitt. 304p. 1993. 49.95 (*0-19-507566-8*) OUP.

Colloquy on New Testament Studies: A Time for Reappraisal & Fresh Approaches. Ed. by Bruce C. Corley. LC 83-8192. xiv, 370p. 1983. 21.50 (*0-86554-082-9*, H54) Mercer Univ Pr.

Collusion Across the Jordan: King Abdullah, the Zionist Movement, & the Partition of Palestine. Avi Shlaim. 600p. 1988. text ed. 57.00 (*0-231-06838-7*) Col U Pr.

Collusion for Conformity. Andrew Slaby & Lawrence Tancredi. LC 75-5989. 224p. 1984. reprint ed. 25.00 (*0-87668-709-5*) Aronson.

Collusive Tendering. 36p. 1986. pap. 6.00 (*92-1-112197-3*, E.85.II.D.11) UN.

Colmena. Cela Trulock & Jose Camilo. (SPA.). 1989. 8.25 (*0-8288-2559-9*) Fr & Eur.

Colmillo Del Tigre. Paul Twitchell. Tr. by Lottie Gilpatrick et al. 180p. (Orig.). (SPA.). 1980. pap. 5.00 (*0-914766-52-X*, 0906) Illum Way Pub.

Colo-Proctology. Ed. by J. C. Givel & F. Saegesser. (Illus.). 190p. 1984. pap. 46.00 (*0-387-12557-4*) Spr-Verlag.

Colobine Monkeys: Their Evolutionary Ecology. Ed. by Glyn Davies & John Oates. (Illus.). 310p. (C). 1995. 79.95 (*0-521-33153-6*) Cambridge U Pr.

Colocando los Fundamentos: Laying the Foundation. James L. Beall. (SPA.). 7.50 (*84-7228-436-0*, 360100, Pub. by Edit Clie SP) TSELF.

Cologne. (Panorama Bks.). (Illus.). (FRE.). 1964. 3.95 (*0-685-11092-3*) Fr & Eur.

Cologne. (Insight Guides Ser.). 1993. pap. 21.95 (*0-395-66432-2*) HM.

Cologne: The History & Anthropology of a Rural Texas African American Community. Kwame M. Nash. (Illus.). 100p. (Orig.). (C). 1990. pap. 10.00 (*0-9623350-0-2*) M C Nash Pubns.

Cologne Atherosclerosis Conference No. 2: Lipids. Michael J. Parnham. (Agents & Actions Supplements Ser.: No. 16). 1984. text ed. 57.50 (*0-8176-1645-4*) Birkhauser.

Cologne Atherosclerosis Conference Three: Platelets. Ed. by Michael J. Parnham & G. Prop. (Agents & Actions Supplements Ser.: No. 20). 278p. 1986. 65.00 (*0-8176-1805-8*) Birkhauser.

Cologne Communist Trial. Karl Marx & Frederick Engels. Ed. & Tr. by Rodney Livingstone. LC 75-168986. 298p. 1971. 8.50 (*0-7178-0240-X*) Intl Pubs Co.

Cologne Mani Codex (P. Colon, Inv. Nr. 4780) Concerning the Origin of His Body. Cologne Mani Codex, English & Greek Staff. Tr. by Ron Cameron & Arthur J. Dewey. LC 79-14743. (Texts & Translations Ser.: No. 15). 87p. reprint ed. pap. 25.00 (*0-7837-5423-X*, 2045187) Bks Demand.

Colomb De la Lune. Rene Barjavel. 185p. (FRE.). 1977. pap. 10.95 (*0-7859-1853-1*, 2070369552) Fr & Eur.

Colomba. Prosper Merimee. (Coll. GF). 247p. (FRE.). 1992. pap. 11.95 (*0-7859-4765-5*) Fr & Eur.

Colomba. Prosper Merimee & Pierre Jourda. (Folio Ser.: No. 819). 188p. (FRE.). 1947. 10.95 (*2-07-036819-X*) Schoenhof.

Colomba - Mateo Falcone. Prosper Merimee & Pierre Jourda. 188p. (FRE.). 1989. reprint ed. pap. 10.95 (*0-7859-3227-5*, 2266030728) Fr & Eur.

Colomba et Autre Nouvelles. Prosper Merimee. (FRE.). 1973. pap. 10.95 (*0-7859-3064-7*) Fr & Eur.

Colombe. Jean Anouilh. (FRE.). 1963. pap. 10.95 (*0-685-58340-6*, M2956) Fr & Eur.

Colombe. Jean Anouilh. 158p. (FRE.). 1973. pap. 10.95 (*0-7859-1729-2*, M2957) Fr & Eur.

Colombe see Pieces Brillantes

Colombia. Jill DuBois. LC 90-22468. (Cultures of the World Ser.: Group 2: Colombia). (Illus.). 128p. (YA). (gr. 5-9). 1991. lib. bdg. 21.95 (*1-85435-384-5*) Marshall Cavendish.

Colombia. Phanor J. Eder. 1976. lib. bdg. 59.95 (*0-8490-1640-1*) Gordon Pr.

Colombia. V. Levine. 1976. lib. bdg. 59.95 (*0-8490-1641-X*) Gordon Pr.

Colombia. Rosa Q. Mesa. LC 68-56197. (Latin American Serial Documents Ser.: Vol. 1). 150p. pap. 42.80 (*0-317-10293-1*, 2013543) Bks Demand.

Colombia. Marion Morrison. LC 90-36528. (Enchantment of the World Ser.). (Illus.). 128p. (J). (gr. 5-9). 1990. lib. bdg. 20.55 (*0-516-02722-0*) Childrens.

Colombia. B. Niles. 1976. lib. bdg. 59.95 (*0-8490-1642-8*) Gordon Pr.

Colombia. Gail B. Stewart. LC 90-47694. (Places in the News Ser.). (Illus.). 48p. (J). (gr. 6-7). 1991. text ed. 4.95 (*0-89686-603-3*, Crstwood Hse) Silver Burdett Pr.

Colombia. Stanley Wellington. LC 84-6444. (World Education Ser.). (Illus.). 144p. (Orig.). 1984. pap. text ed. 12.00 (*0-910054-80-0*) Am Assn Coll Registrars.

Colombia. annot. ed. Ed. by Robert H. Davis. (World Bibliographical Ser.: No. 112). 206p. 1990. lib. bdg. 60.00 (*1-85109-093-2*) ABC-CLIO.

Colombia. Carlos F. Diaz Alejandro. LC 75-24035. (Foreign Trade Regimes & Economic Development Ser.: No. 9). (Illus.). 309p. reprint ed. pap. 88.10 (*0-8357-7567-4*, 2056888) Bks Demand.

Colombia. Carlos F. Diaz-Alejandro. (Special Conference Series on Foreign Trade Regimes & Economic Development: No. 9). 309p. 1976. reprint ed. 80.40 (*0-87014-509-6*) Natl Bur Econ Res.

Colombia. John D. Martz. LC 75-15694. (Illus.). 384p. 1975. reprint ed. text ed. 65.00 (*0-8371-8215-8*, MACOL, Greenwood Pr) Greenwood.

Colombia: A General Survey. W. O. Galbraith. 1976. lib. bdg. 59.95 (*0-8490-1643-6*) Gordon Pr.

Colombia: A New Vision. Tr. by Norman T. Di Giovanni. LC 92-43127. 1993. 45.00 (*1-55859-498-1*) Abbeville Pr.

Colombia: A Travel Survival Kit. Krzysztof Dydynski. (Illus.). 368p. (Orig.). 1988. pap. 11.95 (*0-86442-002-1*) Lonely Planet.

Colombia: Armed Forces & Society. J. Mark Ruhl. LC 80-18762. (Foreign & Comparative Studies Program, Latin American Ser.: No. 1). iv, 53p. (Orig.). 1980. pap. 5.00 (*0-915984-92-X*) Syracuse U Foreign Comp.

Colombia: Briefing. 1988. 5.00 (*0-939994-35-6*) Amnesty Intl USA.

***Colombia: Business Financing Handbook.** (Illus.). 70p. (Orig.). 1994. pap. 295.00 (*0-7605-1187-X*) Rector Pr.

***Colombia: Commercial Law.** 300p. (Orig.). 1994. pap. 295.00 (*0-7605-1239-6*) Rector Pr.

Colombia: Country Reporter. Lewis B. Sckolnick. (Illus.). 60p. 1994. pap. 895.00 (*1-57205-176-0*) Rector Pr.

***Colombia: Democracy under Assault.** 2nd ed. Harvey F. Kline. LC 95-8136. (Nations of the Modern World Ser.: Latin America). 1995. text ed. 59.95 (*0-8133-1071-7*) Westview.

Colombia: Foreign Financing Reporter. Ed. by Lewis B. Sckolnick. (Illus.). 60p. (Orig.). 1994. pap. 225.00 (*1-57205-246-5*) Rector Pr.

Colombia: Industrial Competition & Performance. (Country Study Ser.). 173p. 1991. 10.95 (*0-8213-1985-X*, 11985) World Bank.

***Colombia: Process of Tax Reform.** (Occasional Paper Ser.). Date not set. pap. 15.00 (*1-55775-464-0*) Intl Monetary.

Colombia: Social Programs for the Alleviation of Poverty. 102p. 1990. 7.95 (*0-8213-1573-0*, 11573) World Bank.

Colombia: Social Structure & the Process of Development. Thomas L. Smith. LC 67-26603. (Illus.). 405p. reprint ed. pap. 115.50 (*0-7837-4993-7*, 2044660) Bks Demand.

Colombia: The Rights to Justice. Comision Andina de Juristas Staff. 150p. 1991. pap. text ed. 12.00 (*0-934143-32-3*) Lawyers Comm Human.

***Colombia: Travel Survival Kit.** 2nd ed. Krzysztof Dydynski. (Illus.). 400p. 1995. pap. 15.95 (*0-86442-234-2*) Lonely Planet.

Colombia: Voyage of a Summer Sun. Robin Cody. LC 94-15527. 1995. 23.00 (*0-679-41768-0*) Knopf.

Colombia see American Nations Past & Present

Colombia see Statements of the Laws of the OAS Member States in Matters Affecting Business

Colombia & the United States. Taylor E. Parks. 1976. lib. bdg. 59.95 (*0-8490-1644-4*) Gordon Pr.

Colombia & the United States. E. Taylor Parks. LC 77-111728. (American Imperialism: Viewpoints of United States Foreign Policy, 1898-1941 Ser.). 1970. reprint ed. 34.95 (*0-405-02043-0*) Ayer.

Colombia & the United States: Hegemony & Interdependence. Stephen J. Randall. LC 91-17739. (United States & the Americas Ser.). (Illus.). 344p. 1992. 40.00 (*0-8203-1401-3*); pap. 17.50 (*0-8203-1402-1*) U of Ga Pr.

Colombia & the United States, 1765-1934. E. Taylor Parks. (History - United States Ser.). 554p. 1993. reprint ed. lib. bdg. 99.00 (*0-7812-4865-5*) Rprt Serv.

Colombia Before Independence: Economy, Society, & Politics under Bourbon Rule. Anthony McFarlane. LC 92-42299. (Cambridge Latin American Studies: No. 75). (Illus.). 400p. (C). 1993. 59.95 (*0-521-41641-8*) Cambridge U Pr.

Colombia Besieged: Political Violence & State Responsibility. Washington Office on Latin America Staff. 142p. (Orig.). (C). 1989. pap. text ed. 10.00 (*0-929513-11-8*) WOLA.

Colombia Business Forecaster. Ed. by Lewis B. Sckolnick. 70p. (Orig.). (C). 1994. pap. 675.00 (*1-57205-369-0*) Rector Pr.

***Colombia Business Intelligence Handbook.** (Illus.). 70p. (Orig.). 1994. pap. 295.00 (*0-7605-1074-1*) Rector Pr.

***Colombia Business Risk Outlook.** 70p. (Orig.). 1994. pap. 495.00 (*0-7605-1395-3*) Rector Pr.

Colombia in Pictures. Ed. by Lerner Publications, Department of Geography Staff. (Visual Geography Ser.). (Illus.). 64p. (YA). (gr. 5 up). 1987. lib. bdg. 18.95 (*0-8225-1810-4*, Lerner Publctns) Lerner Group.

Colombian Entrepreneur in Bogota. Aaron Lipman. LC 69-15926. (Hispanic-American Studies Ser.: No. 22). (Illus.). 1969. 9.95 (*0-87024-111-7*) U of Miami Pr.

Colombian Jungle Escape. Ed Dulka & Doreen Dulka. 175p. (Orig.). 1992. pap. 4.95 (*0-87508-092-8*) Chr Lit.

Colombian National Police, Human Rights & U. S. Drug Policy. Washington Office on Latin America Staff. 66p. (Orig.). 1993. pap. 6.00 (*0-929513-24-X*) WOLA.

Colombian Novel, 1844-1987. Raymond L. Williams. (Texas Pan American Ser.). 295p. (C). 1991. text ed. 35.00x (*0-292-75542-2*) U of Tex Pr.

Colombian Penal Code. Intro. by Phanor Eder. (American Series of Foreign Penal Codes: Vol. 14). xviii, 138p. 1967. 15.00 (*0-8377-0034-5*) Rothman.

***Colombian Policy in the Mid-1990s: A Report of the CSIS Americas Program.** Lowell Fleischer & Eduardo Lora. (CSIS Report Ser.). 60p. (C). 1994. pap. text ed. 10.95 (*0-89206-272-X*) CSI Studies.

Colombia's Foreign Trade & Economic Integration in Latin America. J. Kamal Dow. LC 71-631067. (Latin American Monographs: Ser. 2, No. 9). 95p. reprint ed. pap. 27.10 (*0-7837-4975-9*, 2044641) Bks Demand.

***Colombo Yellow Pages.** (Illus.). 300p. (Orig.). 1994. pap. 295.00 (*0-7605-0702-3*) Rector Pr.

Colombus County North Carolina Census 1810. Courtney York & Gerlene York. (Orig.). 1970. pap. 12.00 (*0-916660-11-7*) Hse of York.

Colometry in Ugaritic & Biblical Poetry: Introduction, Illustrations & Topical Bibliography. Oswald Loretz & Ingo Kottseiper. (Ugaritisch-Biblische Literatur Ser.: Vol. 5). 166p. 1987. text ed. 33.00 (*3-88733-074-9*, Pub. by UGARIT GW) Eisenbrauns.

***Colometry of Latin Prose.** Thomas N. Habinek. LC 85-1135. (University of California Publications: No. 25). 234p. 1985. pap. 66.70 (*0-7837-7484-2*, 2049206) Bks Demand.

Colon: Structure & Function. Ed. by Luis Bustos-Fernandez. (Topics in Gastroenterology Ser.). 326p. 1983. 69.50 (*0-306-41056-7*, Plenum Med Bk) Plenum.

Colon & Rectal Cancer. John M. MacKeigan & Kathleen M. Hillary. Ed. by Oliver D. Grin & Dorothy L. Bouwman. (Patient Education Ser.). (Illus.). 30p. 1990. pap. text ed. 3.00 (*0-929689-44-5*) Ludann Co.

Colon & Rectal Surgery. 3rd ed. Corman. (Illus.). 1100p. 1992. text ed. 180.00 (*0-397-51178-7*) Lippincott.

***Colon Cancer & the Polyps Connection.** Fisher. 1995. pap. text ed. 16.95 (*1-55561-080-3*) Fisher Bks.

Colon Cell Cancer. Ed. by Mary P. Moyer & George H. Poste. (Cell Biology Ser.). 620p. 1989. text ed. 241.00 (*0-12-509375-6*) Acad Pr.

Colon Classification. rev. ed. S. R. Ranganathan. 400p. (C). 1988. reprint ed. pap. text ed. 50.00 (*81-85273-11-1*, Pub. by Sarada Ranganathan Endowment for Library Science II) Advent Bks Div.

Colon Classification: Some Perspectives. Ed. by M. P. Satija. 250p. 1992. text ed. 27.95 (*81-207-1120-3*) Apt Bks.

Colon Cleanse the Easy Way. Vena Burnett & Jennifer Weiss. 15p. pap. 2.95 (*0-913923-42-7*) Woodland UT.

Colon Effect. Lupe Sampato. LC 88-72338. 126p. (Orig.). 1990. pap. 7.95 (*0-916383-74-1*) Aegina Pr.

Colon Handbook: A Guide to Health. 1991. lib. bdg. 75.00 (*0-8490-5119-3*) Gordon Pr.

Colon Health: Key to a Vibrant Life. N. W. Walker. 1979. pap. 5.95 (*0-89019-069-0*) Norwalk Pr.

***Colon Health Handbook.** 12th rev. ed. Robert Gray. 80p. 1991. pap. 7.95 (*0-9615757-2-7*) Emerald NV.

Colon Nunca Estuvo en San Salvador. Alejandro R. Perez. (Illus.). 150p. 1990. 37.50 (*1-55914-106-9*); pap. 29.50 (*1-55914-107-7*) ABBE Pubs Assn.

Colonat Romain. Numa D. Fustel De Coulanges. Ed. by Moses Finley. LC 79-4974. (Ancient Economic History Ser.). (FRE.). 1979. reprint ed. lib. bdg. 20.95 (*0-405-12362-0*) Ayer.

Colonel. Laisdell Mitchell. LC 72-1512. (Black Heritage Library Collection). 1977. reprint ed. 21.95 (*0-8369-9037-4*) Ayer.

Colonel: The Life & Wars of Henry Stimson, 1867-1950. Godfrey Hodgson. 402p. 1992. reprint ed. pap. 16.95 (*1-55553-127-X*) NE U Pr.

Colonel Alexander K. McClure's Recollections of Half a Century. Alexander K. McClure. LC 76-172762. reprint ed. 34.75 (*0-404-00086-X*) AMS Pr.

Colonel Came to Stay. Robert P. Dews. 192p. 1986. pap. 6.00 (*0-940184-09-5*) R P Dews.

Colonel Carter of Cartersville. Francis H. Smith. LC 73-104566. (Illus.). reprint ed. lib. bdg. 16.00 (*0-8398-1867-X*) Irvington.

Colonel Chabert. Honore De Balzac. 1964. 10.95 (*0-685-58341-4*, 207036593X) Fr & Eur.

Colonel Chabert. Honore De Balzac. (Folio Ser.: No. 593). (FRE.). 1964. pap. 9.95 (*2-07-036593-X*) Schoenhof.

Colonel Chabert, el Verdugo, Adieu, le Requisitionnaire. Honore De Balzac. 320p. (FRE.). 1974. pap. 11.95 (*0-7859-2207-5*, 207036593X) Fr & Eur.

Colonel Chabert; Le Contrat de Marriage. Honore De Balzac. (FRE.). 1984. pap. 10.95 (*0-7859-3119-8*) Fr & Eur.

Colonel Coggeshall - The Man Who Saved Lincoln. Freda P. Koch. Ed. by Katharine Koch. LC 84-62613. (Illus.). 262p. (Orig.). 1985. pap. 11.95 (*0-9616929-0-1*) Poko Press.

***Colonel Dick Thompson, the Persistent Whig.** Charles Roll. 315p. 1948. 2.50 (*1-885323-11-5*) IN Hist Bureau.

***Colonel Edward Saunderson 1837-1920: Land & Loyalty in Victorian Ireland.** Alvin Jackson. 330p. 1995. 59.00 (*0-19-820498-1*) OUP.

Colonel Effingham's Raid. Berry Fleming. LC 87-62811. 287p. 1988. 22.00 (*0-933256-67-1*) Second Chance.

Colonel Greene & the Copper Skyrocket. C. L. Sonnichsen. LC 74-77205. 325p. 1974. 45.00 (*0-8165-0429-6*) U of Ariz Pr.

***Colonel Grenfell's Wars: The Life of a Soldier of Fortune.** Stephen Z. Starr. 360p. (C). 1995. reprint ed. pap. 14.95 (*0-8071-2034-0*) La State U Pr.

Colonel Hawker's Shooting Diaries. 2nd ed. Eric Parker. (Fifty Greatest Bks.). (Illus.). 300p. 1990. reprint ed. 35.00 (*1-56416-000-9*) Derrydale Pr.

Colonel House in Paris: A Study of American Policy at the Paris Peace Conference, 1919. Igwa Floto. LC 79-24059. (Papers of Woodrow Wilson Supplementary Volume). 376p. 1981. reprint ed. 49.50 (*0-691-04662-X*) Princeton U Pr.

Colonel House in Paris: A Study of American Policy at the Paris Peace Conference, 1919. Inga Floto. LC 79-24059. 382p. reprint ed. pap. 108.90 (*0-7837-6499-5*, 2046589) Bks Demand.

Colonel Jack. Daniel DeFoe. 1976. 23.95 (*0-8488-0979-3*) Amereon Ltd.

Colonel John Pelham: Lee's Boy Artillerist. William W. Hassler. LC 60-10349. xiii, 185p. 1960. 22.50 (*0-8078-0974-8*) U of NC Pr.

Colonel Joseph Bampfield's Apology: "Written by Himself & Printed at His Desire," 1865. Ed. by John C. Loftis & Paul H. Hardacre. LC 91-58963. (Illus.). 312p. 1993. Incl. "Bampfield's Later Career: A Biographical Supplement" by John Loftis. 48.50 (*0-8387-5231-4*) Bucknell U Pr.

Colonel Neverfail's Christmas. Barbara Coltharp. Ed. by Shannon Sandifer & Doug Woolfolk. (Illus.). (Orig.). (J). (gr. 1-3). 1981. 7.95 (*0-86518-019-9*) Moran Pub Corp.

Colonel Nicolae Plesoianu & the National Regeneration Movement in Walachia. Dan V. Pleshoyano. 200p. 1991. text ed. 28.00 (*0-88033-207-7*) Col U Pr.

Colonel Noah Lee of Salisbury, Conn. & Castleton, Vt. & His Descendants: A 1990 Supplement to the 1897 Edition of John Lee of Farmington, Conn., & His Descendants - Thomas Branch. Robert E. Lee. (Illus.). 171p. (Orig.). 1990. per., pap. 20.00 (*0-9625530-0-X*) R E Lee.

Colonel Parke of Virginia: The Greatest Hector in the Town. Helen H. Miller. (Illus.). 210p. 1989. 19.95 (*0-912697-87-3*) Algonquin Bks.

Colonel Samuel Bagshawe & the Army of George the Second: 1731-1762. Ed. by Alan J. Guy. (Illus.). 326p. 1993. text ed. 66.00 (*0-370-31501-4*) A Sutton Pub.

Colonel Sanchez Traditional Foods Cookbook. Kathryn O. Bennett. 113p. (Orig.). 1989. pap. 9.95 (*0-89708-176-5*) And Bks.

Colonel Sandhurst. large type ed. Marion Chesney. LC 94-17135. 250p. 1995. pap. 17.95 (*0-8161-7415-6*, Large Print Bks) Hall.

***Colonel Sandhurst to the Rescue.** Chesney. 1995. mass mkt. 4.50 (*0-312-95337-2*) St Martin.

Colonel Sandhurst to the Rescue: Being the Fifth Volume of The Poor Relation. Marion Chesney. (Poor Relation Ser.: Vol. 5). 160p. 1994. 17.95 (*0-312-10444-8*) St Martin.

Colonel Starbottle's Client & Some Other People. Bret Harte. LC 70-110196. (Short Story Index Reprint Ser.). 1977. 20.95 (*0-8369-3347-8*) Ayer.

Colonel Stephen Kemble's Journals & British Army Orders, 1775-1778. New York Historical Society Staff. Ed. by George Billias. LC 72-8999. (American Revolutionary Ser.). reprint ed. lib. bdg. 35.00 (*0-8398-1355-4*) Irvington.

Colonel Sun. Robert Markham. 1993. mass mkt. 4.99 (*0-06-100568-1*, Harp PBks) HarpC.

Colonel Weatherford's Young Entry: Being an Account of the South Dorchester Ratters & Other Genteel Diversions Suitable for Children. Gordon Grand. (Illus.). 214p. (YA). (gr. 10 up). 1991. reprint ed. 40.00 (*1-56416-028-9*) Derrydale Pr.

Colonels & Cadres: War & Gender in South Africa. Jacklyn Cock. (Contemporary South African Debates Ser.). 264p. 1994. pap. 14.95 (*0-19-570706-0*) OUP.

Colonel's Christmas Dinner, & Other Stories, 2 Vols. in 1. Ed. by Charles King. LC 75-98581. (Short Story Index Reprint Ser.). 1977. 23.95 (*0-8369-3155-6*) Ayer.

Colonel's Daughter. Rita C. Estrada. (Temptation Ser.). 1994. mass mkt. 2.99 (*0-373-25574-8*, 1-25574-4) Harlequin Bks.

Colonel's Dream. Charles W. Chesnutt. LC 73-83928. (Black Heritage Library Collection). 1977. 28.95 (*0-8369-8538-9*) Ayer.

Colonel's Dream. Charles W. Chesnutt. 15.00 (*1-56675-005-9*) Mnemosyne.

Colonel's Dream. Charles W. Chesnutt. LC 77-100261. 294p. 1970. reprint ed. text ed. 35.00 (*0-8371-2857-9*, CCD, Negro U Pr) Greenwood.

Colonel's Dream. Charles W. Chesnutt. LC 68-57517. (Muckrakers Ser.). reprint ed. lib. bdg. 16.00 (*0-8398-0257-9*) Irvington.

Colonel's Lady on the Western Frontier: The Correspondence of Alice Kirk Grierson. Alice Grierson. LC 88-27912. (Illus.). xiv, 256p. 1989. pap. 9.95 (*0-8032-7929-9*) U of Nebr Pr.

Colonel's Opera Cloak. Christine Brush. LC 78-137723. (American Fiction Reprint Ser.). 1977. reprint ed. 19.95 (*0-8369-7022-5*) Ayer.

Colonel's Table: Recipes & Tales. Henry Stanhope et al. (Illus.). 192p. 1994. 45.00 (*1-85753-006-3*) Macmillan.

C

Colonia Baron Hirsch: A Jewish Agricultural Colony in Argentina. Morton D. Winsberg. LC 64-63523. (University of Florida Monographs: Social Sciences: No. 19). (Illus.). 80p. reprint ed. pap. 25.00 (*0-7837-5000-5*, 2044667) Bks Demand.

***Colonia Boer, an Afrikaner Settlement in Chubut, Argentina: An Afrikaner Settlement in Chubut, Argentina.** Brian M. Du Toit. LC 94-39217. (Illus.). 488p. 1995. text ed. 109.95 (*0-7734-8975-4*) E Mellen.

Colonial Administration of Great Britain. Sydney S. Bell. LC 74-114023. 1970. reprint ed. lib. bdg. 50.00 (*0-678-00639-3*) Kelley.

Colonial Administrations of Sir Thomas Maitland. C. Willis Dixon. LC 74-94534. 1969. reprint ed. lib. bdg. 39.50 (*0-678-05099-6*) Kelley.

Colonial Agents of New England. James J. Burns. LC 75-29253. (Perspectives in American History Ser.: No. 26). 156p. 1975. reprint ed. lib. bdg. 27.50 (*0-87991-350-9*) Porcupine Pr.

Colonial Agents of the British West Indies: A Study in Colonial Administration, Mainly in the Eighteenth Century. Lilliam M. Penson. 128p. 1971. reprint ed. 37.50 (*0-7146-1944-2*, Pub. by F Cass Pubs UK) Intl Spec Bk.

Colonial America. 1977. text ed. 30.00 (*0-684-12657-5*, Scribners) S&S Trade.

Colonial America. Ronald P. Dufour. Ed. by Baxter. LC 93-37278. 550p. (C). 1993. pap. text ed. 32.25 (*0-314-02749-1*) West Pub.

Colonial America. 3rd ed. Jerome R. Reich. LC 92-46073. 1993. pap. text ed. write for info. (*0-13-088808-7*) P-H.

Colonial America: A History, 1607-1760. Richard Middleton. (Illus.). 436p. 1992. pap. 19.95 (*1-55786-259-1*) Blackwell Pubs.

***Colonial America: A Traveler's Guide.** Robert Foulke & Patricia Foulke. (Discover Historic America Ser.). (Illus.). 384p. 1995. pap. 14.95 (*1-56440-520-6*) Globe Pequot.

***Colonial America: Cooperative Learning Activities.** Mary Strohl. 1993. pap. 12.95 (*0-590-49133-4*) Scholastic Inc.

Colonial America: English Colonies. rev. ed. Ed. by Margaret Fisher & Mary J. Fowler. LC 87-81353. (Story of America Ser.). (Illus.). 128p. (J). (gr. 4 up). 1988. 14.95 (*0-934291-23-3*); 11.95 (*0-317-91141-4*) Gateway Pr MI.

Colonial America: Essays in Politics & Social Development. 4th ed. Ed. by Douglas Greenberg et al. LC 92-16316. 1992. pap. text ed. write for info. (*0-07-033748-9*) McGraw.

Colonial America: 1607-1763. Harry M. Ward. 400p. (C). 1990. pap. text ed. write for info. (*0-13-142449-1*) P-H.

***Colonial America & the Revolution.** Joyce Friedland & Rikki Kessler. (Novel-Ties Ser.). (J). (gr. 4-7). 1985. student ed, pap. text ed. 20.95 (*1-56982-044-9*) Lrn Links.

Colonial American Activity Book: Art, Crafts, Cooking. 52p. 1992. teacher ed 5.95 (*1-56472-003-9*) Edupress.

Colonial American Crafts: The Home. Judith H. Corwin. LC 89-8958. (Illus.). 48p. (J). (gr. 3-6). 1989. lib. bdg. 13.23 (*0-531-10713-2*) Watts.

Colonial American Crafts: The School. Judith H. Corwin. LC 89-32542. (Illus.). 48p. (J). (gr. 3-6). 1989. lib. bdg. 13.23 (*0-531-10714-0*) Watts.

Colonial American Craftspeople. Bernardine S. Stevens. (Colonial America Ser.). (Illus.). 112p. (J). (gr. 5-8). 1993. lib. bdg. 13.72 (*0-531-12536-X*) Watts.

Colonial American English: A Glossary. Richard M. Lederer, Jr. LC 85-50954. 1985. 24.95 (*0-930454-19-7*) Verbatim Bks.

Colonial American Family: Collected Essays. 1978. 26.95 (*0-405-03880-1*, 13326) Ayer.

Colonial American Holidays & Entertainment. Karen H. Lizon. LC 92-40262. (Colonial America Ser.). (YA). 1993. lib. bdg. 13.72 (*0-531-12546-7*) Watts.

Colonial American Home Life. John F. Warner. (Colonial America Ser.). (Illus.). 112p. (J). (gr. 5-8). 1993. lib. bdg. 13.72 (*0-531-12541-6*) Watts.

Colonial American Jew, 1492-1776, Vols. I, II, & III. Jacob R. Marcus. 1650p. 1994. reprint ed. text ed. 75.00 (*0-8143-1403-1*) Wayne St U Pr.

Colonial American Medicine. Susan N. Terkel. LC 92-43988. (Colonial America Ser.). (J). 1993. lib. bdg. 13.72 (*0-531-12539-4*) Watts.

***Colonial American Photo Fun Activities.** Deneen Celecia. Ed. by Linda Milliken. (Illus.). 8p. (J). (gr. 3-6). 1994. 5.95 (*1-56472-040-3*) Edupress.

Colonial American Travel Narratives. Mary Rowlandson et al. 336p. 1994. 11.95 (*0-14-039088-X*, Penguin Classics) Viking Penguin.

Colonial American Writers, 1606-1734, Vol. 24. Ed. by Emory Elliot. (Dictionary of Literary Biography Ser.: Vol. 24). (Illus.). 350p. 1984. 128.00 (*0-8103-1703-6*) Gale.

Colonial American Writing. Intro. by Giles Gunn. 720p. 1994. 12.95 (*0-14-039087-1*, Penguin Classics) Viking Penguin.

Colonial Ancestors: Four Lineal Genealogies of Eastern Connecticut Families. Mary N. Foster & Edward H. Little. LC 91-61549. (Illus.). 384p. 1991. 30.00 (*0-929539-85-0*, Penobscot Pr) Picton Pr.

Colonial & Early American Lighting. 3rd ed. Arthur H. Hayward. 1962. pap. 6.95 (*0-486-20975-X*) Dover.

Colonial & Early National Period. Ed. by Kenneth Kusmer. LC 91-3756. (Black Community & Urban Development in America Ser.: Vol. 1). 328p. 1991. 75.00 (*0-8153-0425-0*) Garland.

Colonial & Gender Relations from Mary Wollstonecraft to Jamaica Kincaid: East Caribbean Connections. Moira Ferguson. LC 92-39302. 175p. 1993. 29.50 (*0-231-08222-3*) Col U Pr.

Colonial & Historic Homes of Maryland. Don Swann. Ed. by Don Swann, Jr. LC 90-28979. (Illus.). 224p. 1991. reprint ed. pap. 15.95 (*0-8018-4247-6*) Johns Hopkins.

***Colonial & Postcolonial Literature.** Elleke Boehmer. 256p. 1995. pap. 12.95 (*0-19-289232-0*) OUP.

Colonial & Revolutionary America. Carter Smith. (American Historical Images on File Collection). (Illus.). 288p. 1990. ring bd. 155.00 (*0-8160-2226-7*) Facts on File.

Colonial & Revolutionary American Literature: Recent Scholarship, since Nineteen Seventy-Five. Larry L. Carey. (C). 1989. text ed. 22.95 (*0-8290-0742-3*) Irvington.

***Colonial & Revolutionary Families of Pennsylvania, 3 vols., Set.** John W. Jordan. 1706p. 1994. pap. 125.00 (*0-614-00888-3*, 3120) Clearfield Co.

***Colonial & Revolutionary History of Upper South Carolina.** John Landrum. LC 61-1396. (Illus.). 376p. 1995. 35.00 (*0-87152-001-X*) Reprint.

Colonial & State Records of North Carolina: Index A-L, Index M-Z, 4 vols. in 2 bks., Set. Ed. by Stephen B. Weeks. 1993. reprint ed. 200.00 (*1-56837-252-3*) Broadfoot.

Colonial & State Records of North Carolina: 1662-1790, 28 bks. 1994. Set, colonial records, 10 vols., state records, 16 vols., index 4 vols. 1,200.00 (*1-56837-200-0*) Broadfoot.

Colonial Anglicanism in North America. John F. Woolverton. LC 83-27400. 332p. 1984. 39.95 (*0-8143-1755-3*); pap. 18.95 (*0-8143-1797-9*) Wayne St U Pr.

Colonial Architecture of Antigua, Guatemala. Sidney D. Markman. LC 66-13634. (American Philosophical Society, Memoirs Ser.: No. 64). 355p. reprint ed. pap. 101.20 (*0-7837-2681-3*, 2043058) Bks Demand.

Colonial Architecture of Cape Cod, Nantucket & Martha's Vineyard. Alfred E. Poor. (Illus.). 1970. reprint ed. pap. 5.95 (*0-486-22375-2*) Dover.

Colonial Architecture of Mexico. James Early. LC 93-42991. (Illus.). 233p. 1994. 55.00x (*0-8263-1474-0*) U of NM Pr.

Colonial Architecture of Salem. Frank Cousins & Phil M. Riley. (Illus.). 282p. 1989. reprint ed. lib. bdg. 39.00 (*0-8328-1400-8*) Higginson Bk Co.

Colonial Architecture of the Mid-Atlantic. Ed. by Lisa C. Mullins. (Architectural Treasures of Early America Ser.). (Illus.). 246p. 1987. 19.95 (*0-918678-23-4*) Natl Hist Soc.

Colonial Arkansas, 1686-1804: A Social & Cultural History. Morris S. Arnold. (Illus.). 296p. 1991. pap. 18.00 (*1-55728-317-6*) U of Ark Pr.

Colonial Art, 4 vols. Incl. Vol. 1. Architecture. 1979. Span. ed. pap. 1.00 (*0-8270-4225-6*); Vol. 2. Baroque in Brazil. 1976. Eng. ed. pap. 1.00 (*0-8270-4240-X*); Vol. 2. Baroque in Brazil. 1976. Span. ed. pap. 1.00 (*0-8270-4235-3*); Vol. 3. Hispano-Guarani Baroque. 1976. Eng. ed. pap. 1.00 (*0-8270-4245-0*); Vol. 3. Hispano-Guarani Baroque. 1976. Span. ed. pap. 1.00 (*0-8270-4250-7*); Vol. 4. Early Vision of Imperial Brazil. 1977. Eng.ed. pap. 1.00 (*0-8270-4260-4*); Vol. 4. Early Vision of Imperial Brazil. 1977. Span. ed. pap. 1.00 (*0-8270-4255-8*); (ENG & SPA.). Set pap. write for info. (*0-318-54728-7*) OAS.

Colonial Art in Mexico. Manuel Toussaint. Ed. by Elizabeth W. Weismann. LC 66-15696. (Texas Pan-American Ser.). (Illus.). 537p. reprint ed. pap. 153.10 (*0-317-10453-5*, 2016009) Bks Demand.

Colonial Atlas. Rob Caswell. (Twenty-Three Hundred AD Ser.). (Illus.). 96p. (Orig.). 1988. pap. 10.00 (*0-943580-58-7*) Game Designers.

Colonial Autocracy: New South Wales under Governor Macquarie, 1810-1821. Marion Phillips. 336p. 1971. reprint ed. 35.00 (*0-7146-2658-9*, Pub. by F Cass Pubs UK) Intl Spec Bk.

***Colonial Auxiliary Forces Long Service Medal.** Roberts Staff. (C). 1989. 90.00x (*1-873058-56-X*, Pub. by Roberts UK) St Mut.

Colonial Background of the American Revolution: Four Essays in American Colonial History. rev. ed. Charles M. Andrews. LC 31-2404. (C). 1961. pap. 14.00 (*0-300-00004-9*, Y44) Yale U Pr.

Colonial Baptists: Massachusetts & Rhode Island. John Clarke & William G. McLoughlin. Ed. by Edwin S. Gaustad. LC 79-52586. (Baptist Tradition Ser.). 1980. lib. bdg. 19.95 (*0-405-12453-8*) Ayer.

Colonial Baptists & Southern Revivals: An Original Anthology. William L. Lumpkin & Lyman Butterfield. Ed. by Edwin S. Gaustad. LC 79-52585. (Baptist Tradition Ser.). 1980. lib. bdg. 28.95 (*0-405-12452-X*) Ayer.

Colonial Blockade & Neutral Rights 1739-1763. Richard Pares. LC 75-25796. (Perspectives in European History Ser.: No. 10). vii, 323p. 1975. reprint ed. lib. bdg. 37.50 (*0-87991-616-8*) Porcupine Pr.

Colonial Brazil. Ed. by Leslie Bethell. 448p. 1987. 74.95 (*0-521-34127-2*); pap. 18.95 (*0-521-34925-7*) Cambridge U Pr.

Colonial British America: Essays in the New History of the Early Modern Era. Ed. by Jack P. Greene & J. R. Pole. LC 83-48060. 520p. 1984. pap. 16.95 (*0-8018-3055-9*) Johns Hopkins.

Colonial British Caribbean Newspapers: A Bibliography & Directory. Comp. by Howard S. Pactor. LC 90-35630. (Bibliographies & Indexes in World History Ser.: No. 19). 160p. 1990. text ed. 65.00 (*0-313-27232-8*, PBC/, Greenwood Pr) Greenwood.

Colonial Bureaucrats & the Mexican Economy: The Growth of a Patrimonial State, 1763-1821. John S. Leiby. (American University Studies: History: Ser. IX, Vol. 13). 252p. 1986. text ed. 32.00 (*0-8204-0239-7*) P Lang Pubs.

Colonial Burying Grounds of Eastern Connecticut & the Men Who Made Them. James A. Slater. LC 87-11815. (Memoirs of the Connecticut Academy of Arts & Sciences Ser.: Vol. 21). (Illus.). 326p. 1987. 75.00 (*0-208-02160-4*) CT Acad Arts & Sciences.

***Colonial Burying Grounds of Eastern Connecticut & the Men Who Made Them.** 2nd ed. James Slater. (Memoirs of the Connecticut Academy of Arts & Sciences Ser.: Vol. 21). (Illus.). 1995. text ed. write for info. (*1-878508-10-5*) CT Acad Arts & Sciences.

Colonial Cadet in Nigeria. John H. Smith. LC 68-8589. (Duke University Commonwealth-Studies Center Publication Ser.: No. 34). 216p. reprint ed. pap. 61.60 (*0-317-28782-6*, 2017930) Bks Demand.

Colonial Cakchiquels: Highland Maya Adaptations to Spanish Rule, 1600-1700. Robert M. Hill, II. (Case Studies in Cultural Anthropology). (Illus.). 235p. (Orig.). (C). 1992. pap. text ed. 13.50 (*0-03-073444-4*) HB Coll Pubs.

Colonial Caroline: A History of Caroline County, Virginia. T. E. Campbell. 1974. reprint ed. 30.00 (*0-87517-039-0*) Dietz.

Colonial Casualties: Chinese in Early Victoria. Kathryn Cronin. (Illus.). 175p. 1983. 27.50 (*0-522-84221-6*) Intl Spec Bk.

Colonial Cavalier: Or, Southern Life Before the Revolution. Maud W. Goodwin. LC 75-1849. (Leisure Class in America Ser.). (Illus.). 1975. reprint ed. 23.95 (*0-405-06916-2*) Ayer.

Colonial Central America: A Bibliography. Sidney D. Markman. LC 76-23299. 360p. 1977. 5.00 (*0-87918-023-4*) ASU Lat Am St.

Colonial Chesapeake Society. Ed. by Lois G. Carr et al. LC 88-4719. (Institute of Early American History & Culture Ser.). (Illus.). xii, 512p. (C). 1988. 39.95 (*0-8078-1800-3*) U of NC Pr.

Colonial Chesapeake Society. Ed. by Lois G. Carr et al. LC 88-4719. (Institute of Early American History & Culture Ser.). (Illus.). xii, 512p. 1991. pap. 16.95 (*0-8078-4343-1*) U of NC Pr.

Colonial Christmas Cooking. rev. ed. Patricia B. Mitchell. 1991. pap. 4.00 (*0-925117-43-9*) Mitchells.

Colonial Classics: Woodworking Projects from the Original Thirteen Colonies. Gloria Saberin. 1993. pap. 14.95 (*0-8306-4197-1*) TAB Bks.

Colonial Classics: Woodworking Projects from the Original 13 Colonies. Gloria Saberin. 1993. pap. text ed. 14.95 (*0-07-054940-0*) McGraw.

Colonial Classics You Can Build Today: Plans & Drawings for 80 Authentic Projects, All Exact Replicas of Early American Antiques. John Nelson. LC 85-26171. (Illus.). 256p. (Orig.). 1986. pap. 19.95 (*0-8117-2025-X*) Stackpole.

Colonial Clergy of Maryland, Deleware & Georgia. Frederick L. Weis. 104p. 1991. reprint ed. pap. 12.50 (*0-685-60327-X*, 6200) Clearfield Co.

Colonial Clergy of Virginia, North Carolina & South Carolina. Frederick L. Weis. 100p. 1990. reprint ed. 16.00 (*0-685-60328-8*, 6210) Clearfield Co.

Colonial Clippers. Basil Lubbock. (C). 1987. 126.00 (*0-85174-110-X*, Pub. by Brwn Son Ferg) St Mut.

Colonial Coins of Vermont. Hillyer Ryder. Bd. with Vermont Coinage. (Illus.). (Illus.). 1982. Set pap. 10.00 (*0-915262-65-7*) S J Durst.

Colonial Coins of Virginia. 2nd ed. E. Newman. 1990. pap. 15.00 (*0-942666-50-X*) S J Durst.

Colonial Colors. Colonial Williamsburg Foundation Staff. (Illus.). 8p. (J). (ps). 1993. bds. 3.95 (*0-87935-094-6*) Colonial Williamsburg.

Colonial Connecticut: A History. Robert J. Taylor. LC 79-1099. (History of the American Colonies Ser.). 285p. 1979. lib. bdg. 35.00 (*0-527-18710-0*) Kraus Intl.

Colonial Conscripts: The Tirailleurs Senegalais in French West Africa, 1857-1960. Myron Echenberg. (Social History of Africa Ser.). (Illus.). 236p. (Orig.). (C). 1990. 45.00 (*0-435-08048-2*, 08048); pap. 22.95 (*0-435-08052-0*, 08052) Heinemann.

Colonial Cookbook. Lucille R. Penner. (Illus.). 128p. (J). (gr. 4 up). 1976. 14.95 (*0-8038-1202-7*) Hastings.

Colonial Crafts. Bobbie Kalman. (Historic Communities Ser.). (Illus.). 32p. (J). (gr. k-9). 1992. lib. bdg. 15.95 (*0-86505-490-8*); pap. 7.95 (*0-86505-510-6*) Crabtree Pub Co.

Colonial Craftsman. Carl Bridenbaugh. 1990. pap. 6.95 (*0-486-26490-4*) Dover.

Colonial Craftsman. Carl Bridenbaugh. LC 50-7479. 240p. reprint ed. pap. 68.40 (*0-685-15677-X*, 2026767) Bks Demand.

Colonial Culhuacan, 1580-1600: A Social History of an Aztec. S. L. Cline. LC 86-7114. 276p. reprint ed. pap. 78.70 (*0-7837-5857-X*, 2045576) Bks Demand.

Colonial Currency Reprints, Sixteen Eighty-Two to Seventeen Fifty-One, 4 vols., Set. Ed. by Andrew M. Davis. LC 64-14707. (Reprints of Economic Classics Ser.). 1964. reprint ed. 195.00 (*0-678-00041-7*) Kelley.

Colonial Dames & Goodwives. Alice M. Earle. 322p. 1988. reprint ed. pap. 20.00 (*1-55613-150-X*) Heritage Bk.

Colonial Days & Dames. Anne H. Wharton. LC 77-173127. (Illus.). 1972. reprint ed. 17.95 (*0-405-09062-5*) Ayer.

Colonial Days & the Revolutionary War: An Annotated Bibliography. Leona Phillips. 1976. lib. bdg. 250.00 (*0-87968-337-6*) Gordon Pr.

Colonial Days in Old New York. Alice M. Earle. 322p. 1990. reprint ed. pap. 20.00 (*1-55613-368-5*) Heritage Bk.

Colonial Days in Old New York. Alice M. Earle. LC 89-63011. 312p. 1990. reprint ed. lib. bdg. 42.00 (*1-55888-838-1*) Omnigraphics Inc.

Colonial Days in Old New York. Alice M. Earle. 312p. 1993. reprint ed. lib. bdg. 89.00 (*0-7812-5173-7*) Rprt Serv.

Colonial Delaware: A History. John A. Munroe. LC 78-18738. (History of the American Colonies Ser.). 292p. 1978. lib. bdg. 35.00 (*0-527-18711-9*) Kraus Intl.

***Colonial Delaware Wills & Estates to 1800: An Index.** Donald O. Virdin. 191p. (Orig.). 1994. teacher ed, pap. 17.00 (*0-7884-0020-7*) Heritage Bk.

Colonial Desire: Hybridity in Theory, Culture & Race. Robert J. Young. LC 94-15815. 224p. 1995. 55.00x (*0-415-05373-0*, A5167); pap. write for info. (*0-415-05374-9*, A5171) Routledge.

Colonial Dilemma: Critical Perspectives on Contemporary Puerto Rico. Ed. by Edwin Melendez & Edgardo Melendez. 350p. (Orig.). 1992. 40.00 (*0-89608-442-6*); pap. 16.00 (*0-89608-441-8*) South End Pr.

Colonial Discourse & Post-Colonial Theory: A Reader. Ed. by Patrick Williams & Laura Chrisman. LC 93-36929. 570p. 1994. 55.00 (*0-231-10020-5*); pap. 17.50 (*0-231-10021-3*) Col U Pr.

Colonial Disease: A Social History of Sleeping Sickness in Northern Zaire, 1900-1940. Maryinez Lyons. (History of Medicine Ser.). (Illus.). 338p. (C). 1992. 79.95 (*0-521-40350-2*) Cambridge U Pr.

Colonial Education for Africans: George Stark's Policy in Zimbabwe. Dickson A. Mungazi. LC 91-2273. 176p. 1991. text ed. 45.00 (*0-275-94029-2*, C4029, Praeger Pubs) Greenwood.

Colonial Elite of Caracas: Formation & Crisis, 1567-1767. Robert J. Ferry. 245p. (C). 1989. 47.50 (*0-520-06399-6*) U CA Pr.

Colonial Encounters. Peter Hulme. 350p. 1987. text ed. 32.50 (*0-416-41860-0*, 1004) Routledge Chapman & Hall.

Colonial Encounters: Europe & the Native Caribbean, 1492-1797. Peter Hulme. LC 92-10513. 368p. 1992. pap. 16.95 (*0-415-01146-9*, A7893) Routledge.

Colonial Epoch in Africa. Ed. by Gregory Maddox. LC 93-17822. (Articles on Colonialism & Nationalism in Africa Ser.: Vol. 2). 408p. 1993. 69.00 (*0-8153-1389-6*) Garland.

Colonial Era. 2nd ed. Herbert Aptheker. LC 59-11215. 158p. (C). 1966. pap. 2.25 (*0-7178-0033-4*) Intl Pubs Co.

Colonial Evangelism: A Socio-Historical Study of an East African Mission at the Grassroots. T. O. Beidelman. LC 81-47771. (Illus.). 296p. 1982. 35.00 (*0-253-31386-4*) Ind U Pr.

Colonial Families of the Southern States of America: A History and Genealogy of Colonial Families Who Settled in the Colonies Prior to the Revolution. Stella P Hardy. LC 65-8785. 643p. 1991. reprint ed. 35.00 (*0-8063-0620-3*) Genealog Pub.

***Colonial Families of the United States of America Vol. I: Main Families.** George N. Mackenzie. (Illus.). 730p. 1995. reprint ed. 45.00 (*0-8063-0223-2*) Genealog Pub.

***Colonial Families of the United States of America Vol. II: Main Families.** George N. Mackenzie. (Illus.). 941p. 1995. reprint ed. 50.00 (*0-8063-0224-0*) Genealog Pub.

***Colonial Families of the United States of America Vol. III: Main Families.** George N. Mackenzie. (Illus.). 740p. 1995. reprint ed. 45.00 (*0-8063-0225-9*) Genealog Pub.

***Colonial Families of the United States of America Vol. IV: Main Families.** George N. Mackenzie. (Illus.). 684p. 1995. reprint ed. 40.00 (*0-8063-0226-7*) Genealog Pub.

***Colonial Families of the United States of America Vol. V: Main Families.** George N. Mackenzie. (Illus.). 719p. 1995. reprint ed. 40.00 (*0-8063-0227-5*) Genealog Pub.

***Colonial Families of the United States of America Vol. VI: Main Families.** George N. Mackenzie. (Illus.). 600p. 1995. reprint ed. 40.00 (*0-8063-0228-3*) Genealog Pub.

***Colonial Families of the United States of America Vol. VII: Main Families.** George N. Mackenzie. (Illus.). 605p. 1995. reprint ed. 40.00 (*0-8063-0229-1*) Genealog Pub.

Colonial Fireplace Cooking & Early American Recipes. Margaret T. Chalmers. (Illus.). 96p. (Orig.). 1979. pap. 7.95 (*0-932296-04-1*) Eberly Pr.

Colonial Frontier Guns. T. M. Hamilton. 1987. 13.95 (*0-913150-61-4*) Pioneer Pr.

Colonial Frontiers: Art & Life in Spanish New Mexico. Christine Mather. (Illus.). 120p. 1983. text ed. 29.95 (*0-89013-185-6*); pap. text ed. 19.95 (*0-89013-186-4*) Museum NM Pr.

Colonial Georgia: A History. Kenneth Coleman. LC 75-37534. (History of the American Colonies Ser.). 331p. 1976. lib. bdg. 35.00 (*0-527-18712-7*) Kraus Intl.

Colonial Georgia Genealogical Data 1748-1783. William H. Dumont. 77p. 6.50 (*0-915156-36-9*) Natl Genealogical.

Colonial Government, an Introduction to the Study of Colonial Institutions. Paul S. Reinsch. LC 72-107829. (Select Bibliographies Reprint Ser.). 1977. 29.95 (*0-8369-5221-9*) Ayer.

Colonial Governors from the Fifteenth Century to the Present. Ed. by David P. Henige. LC 73-81320. 482p. 1970. 50.00 (*0-299-05440-3*) U of Wis Pr.

Colonial Green Revolution? Food, Irrigation & the State in Colonial Malaya. John Overton. 250p. 1994. 54.00x (*0-85198-912-8*) CAB Intl.

Colonial Harem. Malek Alloula. Tr. by Myrna Godzich & Wlad Godzich. LC 85-16527. (Theory & History of Literature Ser.: Vol. 21). (Illus.). 135p. (Orig.). 1986. text ed. 39.95 (*0-8166-1383-4*); pap. text ed. 19.95x (*0-8166-1384-2*) U of Minn Pr.

Colonial Heritage of Latin America: Essays on Economic Dependence in Perspective. Stanley J. Stein & Barbara H. Stein. (C). 1970. pap. text ed. 14.95 (*0-19-501292-5*) OUP.

Colonial History: City of San Francisco. 4th ed. John W. Dwinelle. 497p. 1978. 10.00 (*0-937106-03-8*) Ross Valley.

Colonial History of Hartford (Conn.) William D. Love. (Illus.). 368p. 1993. reprint ed. lib. bdg. 42.00 (*0-8328-3130-1*) Higginson Bk Co.

An Asterisk (*) at the beginning of an entry indicates that the title is appearing in BIP for the first time.

***Colonial History of the Parish of Mount Carmel, Ct. As Read in Its Geologic Formations, Records & Traditions.** J. Dickerman. 109p. 1994. reprint ed. pap. 17.50 (*0-8328-4410-1*) Higginson Bk Co.

Colonial Houses: Modern Floor Plans & Authentic Exteriors for 161 Historical Colonial Homes. (Illus.). 208p. 1990. pap. 10.95 (*0-918894-82-4*) Home Planners.

Colonial Identity in the Atlantic World, 1500-1800. Ed. by Nicholas Canny & Anthony Pagden. (History of Rhetoric Ser.). 303p. 1990. pap. 15.95 (*0-691-00840-X*) Princeton U Pr.

Colonial Idiom. Ed. by David Potter & Gordon L. Thomas. LC 71-83669. (Landmarks in Rhetoric & Public Address Ser.). 653p. 1970. 25.00 (*0-8093-0431-7*); pap. 7.00 (*0-8093-9100-7*) S Ill U Pr.

***Colonial Idiom.** Ed. by David Potter & Gordon L. Thomas. LC 71-83669. (Landmarks in Rhetoric & Public Address Ser.). 653p. 1970. pap. 7.00 (*0-8093-9700-5*) S Ill U Pr.

Colonial Image Australian Painting 1800-1880. Tim Bonyhady. 112p. 1988. text ed. 67.50 (*0-7103-0320-3*, Pub. by Kegan Paul Intl UK) Routledge Chapman & Hall.

Colonial Immigration Laws. Emberson E. Proper. LC 04-2636. (Columbia University. Studies in the Social Sciences: No. 31). reprint ed. 31.50 (*0-404-51031-0*) AMS Pr.

Colonial Improver: A Life of Edward Deas Thomson. S. G. Foster. 1978. 27.50 (*0-522-84136-8*) Intl Spec Bk.

***Colonial Inscriptions: Race, Sex & Class in Kenya.** Carolyn M. Shaw. LC 94-36180. 1995. text ed. 49.95 (*0-8166-2524-7*); pap. text ed. 23.95 (*0-8166-2525-5*) U of Minn Pr.

Colonial Ireland in Medieval English Literature. Elizabeth L. Rambo. LC 93-46784. 1994. write for info. (*0-945636-61-X*) Susquehanna U Pr.

Colonial Justice in Western Massachusetts, 1639-1702: The Pynchon Court Record. Ed. by Joseph H. Smith. LC 61-7394. (Illus.). 435p. 1961. 32.50 (*0-674-14250-0*) HUP.

Colonial Keyboard Tunes. Ed. by J. S. Darling. LC 80-12691. 24p. 1980. pap. 4.95 (*0-87935-055-5*) Colonial Williamsburg.

Colonial Labor Policy & Administration 1910-1941. J. Norman Parmer. 6.00 (*0-685-71735-6*) J J Augustin.

Colonial Latin America. Mark A. Burkholder & Lyman L. Johnson. LC 93-6759. 1994. pap. 17.95 (*0-19-508089-0*) OUP.

Colonial Latin America. 2nd ed. Mark A. Burkholder & Lyman L. Johnson. LC 93-6759. 1994. 45.00 (*0-19-508088-2*) OUP.

Colonial Law: A Bibliography with Special Reference to Native African Systems of Law & Land Tenure. Charles K. Meek. LC 78-14383. xiii, 58p. 1979. text ed. 49.75 (*0-313-21011-X*, MECL, Greenwood Pr) Greenwood.

Colonial Law & Practice in New South Wales. 2nd ed. K. M. Waller. xvi, 215p. 1982. 64.50 (*0-455-20365-2*, Pub. by Law Bk Co) W W Gaunt.

***Colonial Laws of Massachusetts, Bk. 1.** xvi, 312p. 1995. lib. bdg. write for info. (*0-8377-2053-2*) Rothman.

***Colonial Laws of Massachusetts, Bk. 2.** 1995. lib. bdg. write for info. (*0-8377-2054-0*) Rothman.

***Colonial Laws of Massachusetts, 2 bks., Set.** 1995. lib. bdg. 137.50x (*0-614-03187-7*) Rothman.

Colonial Legacy in Caribbean Literature. Amon S. Saakana. LC 87-71877. 128p. 1988. 24.95 (*0-86543-059-4*); pap. 7.95 (*0-86543-060-8*) Africa World.

Colonial Leviathan: State Formation in Nineteenth-Century Canada. Ed. by Allan Greer & Ian Radforth. 360p. 1992. 55.00 (*0-8020-5931-7*); pap. 22.95 (*0-8020-6871-5*) U of Toronto Pr.

Colonial Liberalism: Lost Word of Three Victorian Visionaries. Stuart McIntyre. 264p. 1991. 29.95 (*0-19-554760-8*) OUP.

Colonial Life. Bobbie Kalman. (Historic Communities Ser.). (Illus.). 32p. (J). 1992. (gr. k-9). 1992. lib. bdg. 15.95 (*0-86505-491-6*); pap. 7.95 (*0-86505-511-4*) Crabtree Pub Co.

Colonial Life in America. Louis Sabin. LC 84-2669. (Illus.). 32p. (J). (gr. 3-6). 1985. lib. bdg. 9.49 (*0-8167-0138-5*); pap. text ed. 2.95 (*0-8167-0139-3*) Troll Assocs.

Colonial Lighthouses. Margaret P. Hassert. (Illus.). 64p. 1985. 28.00 (*0-88014-072-0*) Mosaic Pr OH.

Colonial Long Island Folklife. John H. Braunlein. (Illus.). 38p. (Orig.). 1976. pap. 2.50 (*0-943924-00-6*) Mus Stony Brook.

Colonial Louisiana Marriage Contracts: Pointe Coopee, Vol 3. Winston De Ville. Bd. with Vol. 4. Avoyelles. 10.00 (*0-685-01104-6*) Claitors.

Colonial Loves: Courtship & Marriage of the 1700s. Elizabeth A. Goesel. (Illus.). 70p. 1993. reprint ed. 5.95 (*0-9638427-1-4*, TX 3 520-127) E A Goesel.

Colonial Manila: The Context of Hispanic Urbanism & Process of Morphogenesis. Robert R. Reed. LC 77-80476. (University of California Publications in Social Welfare: No. 22). 143p. reprint ed. pap. 40.80 (*0-685-23993-4*, 2031576) Bks Demand.

Colonial Maryland: A History. Aubrey C. Land. LC 80-21732. (History of the American Colonies Ser.). 367p. 1981. lib. bdg. 35.00 (*0-527-18713-5*) Kraus Intl.

Colonial Maryland Naturalizations. Jeffrey A. Wyand & Florence L. Wyand. 104p. 1986. 12.50 (*0-8063-0680-7*, 6520) Genealog Pub.

***Colonial Masculinity: The Manly Englishman & the Effeminate Bengali.** Mrinalini Sinha. LC 94-41728. (Studies in Imperialism). 1995. text ed. write for info. (*0-7190-4285-2*); text ed. write for info. (*0-7190-4653-X*) St Martin.

Colonial Massachusetts: A History. Benjamin Labaree. LC 79-33. (History of the American Colonies Ser.). 349p. 1979. lib. bdg. 35.00 (*0-527-18714-3*) Kraus Intl.

Colonial Merchants & the American Revolution. Arthur Schlesinger. 647p. 1993. reprint ed. lib. bdg. 109.00 (*0-7812-5220-2*) Rprt Serv.

Colonial Mexican & Popular Religious Art. Ramon Favela. (Illus.). 48p. 1990. pap. 12.95 (*0-9605194-7-5*) Mexican Museum.

Colonial Mind. Ed. by Daniel Shanahan. (Illus.). 104p. (Orig.). 1989. pap. 7.95 (*0-940237-03-2*) ND Qtr Pr.

Colonial Mind: 1620-1800 see Main Currents in American Thought

Colonial Mobile: An Historical Study, Largely from Original Sources, of the Alabama-Tombigbee Basin of the Old South West from the Discovery of the Espiritu Santo in 1519 until the Demolition of Fort Charlotte in 1821. Peter J. Hamilton. (Illus.). 767p. 1991. reprint ed. pap. 40.00 (*1-55613-453-3*) Heritage Bk.

Colonial Moment in Africa: Essays on the Movement of Minds & Materials, 1900-1940. Ed. by Andrew Roberts. (Illus.). 304p. (C). 1990. pap. 21.95 (*0-521-38674-8*) Cambridge U Pr.

Colonial Moment in Africa: Essays on the Movement of Minds & Materials, 1900-1940. Ed. by Andrew Roberts. (Illus.). 304p. (C). 1990. 69.95 (*0-521-39090-7*) Cambridge U Pr.

Colonial Mosaic: American Women, 1600-1760. Robert Jakoubek. (Young Oxford History of Women in the United States Ser.: Vol. 2). (Illus.). 144p. (J). 1995. lib. bdg. 20.00 (*0-19-508015-7*) OUP.

Colonial Nails from Michilimackinac: Differentiation by Chemical & Statistical Analysis. David J. Frurip et al. LC 83-109676. (Archaeological Completion Report Ser.: No. 7). (Illus.). 83p. (Orig.). 1983. pap. 7.00 (*0-911872-47-7*) Mackinac Island.

Colonial National Historical Park: The Story Behind the Scenery. James N. Haskett. LC 90-60042. (Illus.). 48p. 1990. pap. 6.95 (*0-88714-044-0*) KC Pubns.

Colonial New Hampshire: A History. Jere R. Daniell. LC 81-6046. (History of the American Colonies Ser.). 279p. 1982. lib. bdg. 35.00 (*0-527-18715-1*) Kraus Intl.

Colonial New Jersey: A History. John E. Pomfret. LC 72-1228. (History of the American Colonies Ser.). 327p. 1973. lib. bdg. 35.00 (*0-527-18716-X*) Kraus Intl.

Colonial New York: A History. Michael Kammen. LC 75-5693. (History of the American Colonies Ser.). 426p. 1975. lib. bdg. 35.00 (*0-527-18717-8*); pap. 17.00 (*0-685-42229-1*) Kraus Intl.

Colonial North Carolina: A History. Hugh T. Lefler & William S. Powell. LC 73-5188. (History of the American Colonies Ser.). 318p. 1973. lib. bdg. 35.00 (*0-527-18718-6*) Kraus Intl.

Colonial Office. Charles J. Jeffries. LC 83-10876. 222p. (C). 1983. reprint ed. text ed. 59.75 (*0-313-24122-8*, JECO, Greenwood Pr) Greenwood.

Colonial Office & Nigeria, 1898-1914. John Carland. (Publication Ser.: No. 314). 258p. 1985. lib. bdg. 26.95 (*0-8179-8141-1*) Hoover Inst Pr.

Colonial Office, Eighteen Sixty Eight to Eighteen Ninety-Two. Brian L. Blakeley. LC 71-161357. 211p. reprint ed. pap. 60.20 (*0-317-42242-1*, 2026188) Bks Demand.

Colonial Origins of Korean Enterprise. Dennis L. McNamara. (Illus.). 240p. (C). 1990. 64.95 (*0-521-38565-2*) Cambridge U Pr.

Colonial Overlords. Time Life Staff. (Time Frame Ser.). 1990. 22.60 (*0-8094-6466-7*); lib. bdg. 28.60 (*0-8094-6467-5*) Time-Life.

Colonial Panorama Seventeen Seventy Five: Dr. Robert Honyman's Journal for March & April. Robert Honyman. Ed. by Philip Padelford. LC 70-164609. (Select Bibliographies Reprint Ser.). 1977. reprint ed. 20.95 (*0-8369-5893-4*) Ayer.

Colonial Pennsylvania: A History. Joseph E. Illick. LC 75-37551. (History of the American Colonies Ser.). 359p. 1976. lib. bdg. 35.00 (*0-527-18719-4*) Kraus Intl.

Colonial People. Sarah Howarth. (People & Places Ser.). (Illus.). 48p. (J). (gr. 4-6). 1994. lib. bdg. 14.90 (*1-56294-512-2*) Millbrook Pr.

Colonial Period of American History, Vol. 2: The Settlements. Charles M. Andrews. LC 64-54917. 417p. reprint ed. pap. 118.90 (*0-8357-8695-1*, 2033661) Bks Demand.

Colonial Petitions for Land Resurveys, Land Warrants, & Caveats. A. B. Pruitt. 142p. (YA). (gr. 12). 1993. pap. 14.50 (*0-944992-47-1*) ABP Abstracts.

Colonial Physician & Other Essays. Whitfield J. Bell, Jr. LC 75-6652. (Illus.). 236p. 1975. text ed. 16.00 (*0-88202-024-2*, Sci Hist) Watson Pub Intl.

Colonial Placer Mining in Columbia. Robert C. West. LC 52-14234. (Louisiana State University Studies, Social Science Ser.: No. 2). 189p. reprint ed. pap. 53.90 (*0-317-29939-5*, 2051689) Bks Demand.

Colonial Places. Sarah Howarth. (People & Places Ser.). (Illus.). 48p. (J). (gr. 4-6). 1994. lib. bdg. 14.90 (*1-56294-513-0*) Millbrook Pr.

Colonial Plantation Cookbook: The Receipt Book of Harriott Pickney Horry, 1770. Ed. by Richard J. Hooker. LC 84-12016. 159p. 1984. 16.95 (*0-87249-437-3*) U of SC Pr.

Colonial Plunder of Puerto Rico: Why Puerto Rico Is the Most Profitable Address in the U. S. A. Gus Hall. 16p. 1972. pap. 0.25 (*0-87898-095-4*) New Outlook.

Colonial Policies in Africa. Heinrich A. Wieschhoff. LC 44-5178. (African Handbooks: No. 5). 146p. reprint ed. pap. 41.70 (*0-317-11261-9*, 2022380) Bks Demand.

Colonial Policies of the United States. Theodore Roosevelt, Jr. LC 71-111705. (American Imperialism: Viewpoints of United States Foreign Policy, 1898-1941 Ser.). 1977. reprint ed. 19.95 (*0-405-02048-1*) Ayer.

Colonial Policy & Conflict in Zimbabwe: A Study of Cultures in Collision, 1890-1979. Dickson A. Mungazi. 200p. 1991. 47.00 (*0-8448-1703-1*, Crane Russak) Taylor & Francis.

Colonial Policy of Lord John Russell's Administration, 2 vols. in 1. Charles E. Grey. LC 79-118121. 1970. reprint ed. lib. bdg. 75.00 (*0-678-00660-1*) Kelley.

Colonial Policy of William Third in America & West Indies. George H. Guttridge. 190p. 1966. 35.00 (*0-7146-1478-5*, Pub. by F Cass Pubs UK) Intl Spec Bk.

Colonial Postal System & Postage Stamps of Vancouver Island & British Columbia Eighteen Forty-Nine to Eighteen Seventy-One. Alfred S. Deaville. LC 79-67392. 224p. 1980. reprint ed. lib. bdg. 35.00 (*0-88000-111-9*) Quarterman.

Colonial Precedents of Our National Land System As It Existed in 1800. Amelia C. Ford. LC 76-54887. (Perspectives in American History Ser.: No. 44). 157p. 1977. reprint ed. lib. bdg. 27.50 (*0-87991-368-1*) Porcupine Pr.

Colonial Printer. Jon Zonderman. LC 94-4015. (How They Lived Ser.). (J). (gr. 4 up). 1994. write for info. (*1-55916-042-X*) Rourke Bk Co.

***Colonial Printer.** unabridged ed. Lawrence C. Wroth. LC 94-32382. (Illus.). 368p. 1994. pap. text ed. 9.95 (*0-486-28294-5*) Dover.

Colonial Production in Provincial Java: The Sugar Industry in Pekalongan-Tegal 1800-1942. G. R. Knight. 96p. 1994. pap. 17.50 (*90-5383-260-2*, Pub. by VU Univ Pr NE) Paul & Co Pubs.

Colonial Profiles Series, 4 bks., Set. Dennis B. Fradin. (Illus.). (J). (gr. 3-6). lib. bdg. 59.80 (*0-89490-341-1*) Enslow Pubs.

Colonial Prose & Poetry, 3 Vols, Set. Ed. by William P. Trent & Benjamin W. Wells. LC 71-123763. reprint ed. 112.50 (*0-404-06620-8*) AMS Pr.

***Colonial Psychiatry & 'The African Mind'** Jock McCulloch. 192p. (C). 1995. 54.95 (*0-521-45330-5*) Cambridge U Pr.

Colonial Reckoning: End of Imperial Rule in Africa in the Light of British Experience. Margery F. Perham. LC 76-25998. 203p. 1976. reprint ed. text ed. 55.00 (*0-8371-9016-9*, PECR, Greenwood Pr) Greenwood.

Colonial Records of North Carolina: Second Series, 8 vols. Incl. Vol. 1. North Carolina Charters & Constitutions, 1578-1698. Ed. by Mattie E. Parker et al. xxii, 247p. 1963. 15.00 (*0-86526-022-2*); Vol. 3. North Carolina Higher-Court Records, 1697-1701. Ed. by Mattie E. Parker et al. (Illus.). lxviii, 620p. 1971. 15.00 (*0-86526-024-9*); Vol. 4. North Carolina Higher-Court Records, 1702-1708. Ed. by William S. Price, Jr. et al. (Illus.). xxxix, 533p. 1974. 16.00 (*0-86526-025-7*); Vol. 5. North Carolina Higher-Court Minutes, 1709-1723. Ed. by Mattie E. Parker et al. xliii, 631p. 1977. 21.00 (*0-86526-026-5*); Vol. 6. North Carolina Higher-Court Minutes, 1724-1730. Ed. by Robert J. Cain et al. lxi, 791p. 1981. 30.00 (*0-86526-027-3*); Vol. 7. Records of the Executive Council, 1664-1734. Ed. by Robert J. Cain et al. (Illus.). lxvii, 763p. 1984. 25.00 (*0-86526-210-1*); Vol. 8. Records of the Executive Council, 1735-1754. Ed. by Robert J. Cain et al. (Illus.). lxxvii, 723p. 1988. 45.00 (*0-86526-251-9*); Set. write for info. (*0-86526-020-6*) NC Archives.

Colonial Records of North Carolina: 1662-1712. Ed. by William L. Saunders. (Colonial & State Records of North Carolina Ser.). 992p. 1993. reprint ed. 50.00 (*1-56837-201-9*) Broadfoot.

Colonial Records of North Carolina: 1662-1776, 10 Vols, Set. North Carolina General Assembly Staff. Ed. by William L. Saunders. LC 72-130612. reprint ed. 1,800.00 (*0-404-05590-7*) AMS Pr.

Colonial Records of North Carolina: 1713-1728. Ed. by William L. Saunders. (Colonial & State Records of North Carolina Ser.: Vol. 2). 923p. 1993. reprint ed. 50.00 (*1-56837-202-7*) Broadfoot.

Colonial Records of North Carolina: 1728-1734. Ed. by William L. Saunders. (Colonial & State Records of North Carolina Ser.: Vol. 3). 664p. 1993. reprint ed. 50.00 (*1-56837-203-5*) Broadfoot.

Colonial Records of North Carolina: 1734-1752. Ed. by William L. Saunders. (Colonial & State Records of North Carolina Ser.: Vol. 4). 1376p. 1993. reprint ed. 50.00 (*1-56837-204-3*) Broadfoot.

Colonial Records of North Carolina: 1752-1759. Ed. by William L. Saunders. (Colonial & State Records of North Carolina Ser.: Vol. 5). 1228p. 1993. reprint ed. 50.00 (*1-56837-205-1*) Broadfoot.

Colonial Records of North Carolina: 1759-1765. Ed. by William L. Saunders. (Colonial & State Records of North Carolina Ser.: Vol. 6). 1322p. 1993. reprint ed. 50.00 (*1-56837-206-X*) Broadfoot.

Colonial Records of North Carolina: 1765-1768. Ed. by William L. Saunders. (Colonial & State Records of North Carolina Ser.: Vol. 7). 1046p. 1993. reprint ed. 50.00 (*1-56837-207-8*) Broadfoot.

Colonial Records of North Carolina: 1769-1771. Ed. by William L. Saunders. (Colonial & State Records of North Carolina Ser.: Vol. 8). 844p. 1993. reprint ed. 50.00 (*1-56837-208-6*) Broadfoot.

Colonial Records of North Carolina: 1771-1775. Ed. by William L. Saunders. (Colonial & State Records of North Carolina Ser.: Vol. 9). 1334p. 1993. reprint ed. 50.00 (*1-56837-209-4*) Broadfoot.

Colonial Records of North Carolina: 1775-1776. Ed. by William L. Saunders. (Colonial & State Records of North Carolina Ser.: Vol. 10). 1088p. 1993. reprint ed. 50.00 (*1-56837-210-8*) Broadfoot.

***Colonial Records of North Carolina Vol. 9: Records of the Executive Council, 1755-1775.** Ed. & Intro. by Robert J. Cain. (Colonial Records of North Carolina, Second Ser.). (Illus.). lxxix, 870p. 1994. 75.00x (*0-86526-261-6*) NC Archives.

Colonial Records of Pennsylvania, 16 Vols. Pennsylvania Colony Staff. LC 01-10370. student ed 47.50 (*0-404-05020-4*) AMS Pr.

Colonial Records of Pennsylvania, 16 Vols. Pennsylvania Colony Staff. LC 01-10370. reprint ed. 95.00 (*0-685-73116-2*) AMS Pr.

Colonial Records of Pennsylvania, 16 vols., Set. Pennsylvania Colony Staff. LC 01-10370. reprint ed. 1, 520.00 (*0-404-05000-X*) AMS Pr.

Colonial Records of Spanish Florida: Letters & Reports of Governors & Secular Persons, 2 vols., Set. Ed. by Jeannette M. Connor. LC 74-19720. reprint ed. 55.00 (*0-404-12475-5*) AMS Pr.

Colonial Records of the State of Georgia, Vol. 20. Ed. by Kenneth Coleman & Milton Ready. LC 82-2573. (Colonial Records Ser.). 536p. 1982. 35.00 (*0-8203-0598-7*) U of Ga Pr.

Colonial Records of the State of Georgia, Vol. 27. Ed. by Kenneth Coleman & Milton Ready. LC 77-6466. (Colonial Records Ser.). 320p. 1978. 30.00 (*0-8203-0423-9*) U of Ga Pr.

Colonial Records of the State of Georgia, Vol. 28, Pt I. Ed. by Kenneth Coleman & Milton Ready. LC 74-30679. (Colonial Records Ser.). 496p. 1975. 35.00 (*0-8203-0379-8*) U of Ga Pr.

Colonial Records of the State of Georgia, Vol. 28, Pt. II. Ed. by Kenneth Coleman & Milton Ready. LC 79-14348. (Colonial Records Ser.). 446p. 1979. 35.00 (*0-8203-0481-6*) U of Ga Pr.

Colonial Records of the State of Georgia, Vol. 29. Ed. by Kenneth Coleman & Milton Ready. LC 84-24142. 392p. 1985. 35.00 (*0-8203-0773-4*) U of Ga Pr.

Colonial Records of the State of Georgia, Vol. 30. Ed. by Kenneth Coleman. LC 84-24141. (Colonial Records Ser.). 392p. 1985. 35.00 (*0-8203-0774-2*) U of Ga Pr.

Colonial Records of the State of Georgia, Vol. 31. Ed. by Kenneth Coleman. LC 84-24142. (Colonial Records Ser.). 320p. 1986. 35.00 (*0-8203-0852-8*) U of Ga Pr.

Colonial Records of the State of Georgia, Vol. 32. Ed. by Kenneth Coleman. LC 88-27790. (Colonial Records Ser.). 312p. 1989. 35.00 (*0-8203-1079-4*) U of Ga Pr.

Colonial Records of the State of Georgia 1732-1782, 26 vols. in 28 pts., Set. Georgia Colony Staff. Ed. by Allen D. Candler. LC 70-138087. reprint ed. 3,326.40 (*0-404-07260-7*) AMS Pr.

Colonial Records of Virginia. Committee on State Library Staff. 106p. 1992. reprint ed. 17.50 (*0-685-60451-9*, 6090) Clearfield Co.

Colonial Revival Furniture with Prices. David P. Lindquist & Caroline C. Warren. LC 92-50671. 184p. 1993. pap. 14.95 (*0-87069-660-2*) Chilton.

Colonial Revival in America: A Winterthur Book. Ed. by Alan Axelrod. (Illus.). (Orig.). (C). 1986. reprint ed. pap. text ed. 14.95 (*0-393-95583-4*) Norton.

Colonial Rhode Island: A History. Sydney V. James. LC 75-9685. (History of the American Colonies Ser.). 423p. 1975. lib. bdg. 35.00 (*0-527-18720-8*) Kraus Intl.

Colonial Rise of the Novel: From Aphra Behn to Charlotte Bronte. Firdous Azim. LC 92-40810. 240p. 1993. 59.95 (*0-415-07024-4*, B0370); pap. 16.95 (*0-415-09569-7*, B0374) Routledge.

Colonial Rule & Political Development in Tanzania: The Case of the Makonde. J. Gus Liebenow. LC 72-126898. 374p. reprint ed. pap. 106.60 (*0-8357-9449-0*, 2014777) Bks Demand.

Colonial Rule in Africa: Readings from Primary Sources. Ed. by Bruce Fetter. LC 78-65020. (Illus.). 238p. 1979. 29.50 (*0-299-07780-2*); pap. 14.95 (*0-299-07784-5*) U of Wis Pr.

Colonial Search for a Southern Eden. L. B. Wright. LC 72-7521. (American History & Americana Ser.: No. 47). 1972. reprint ed. lib. bdg. 36.95 (*0-8383-1596-8*) M S G Haskell Hse.

Colonial Self-Government, 1652-1689. Charles M. Andrews. LC 04-32334. 1904. 11.00 (*0-403-00138-2*) Scholarly.

Colonial Self-Government, 1652-1689. Charles M. Andrews. LC 73-98630. reprint ed. 37.50 (*0-404-00359-1*) AMS Pr.

Colonial Self-Government, 1652-1689. Charles M. Andrews. (BCL1 - U. S. History Ser.). 369p. 1991. reprint ed. lib. bdg. 89.00 (*0-7812-6094-9*) Rprt Serv.

***Colonial Settlers (1634-1780) St. Clement's Bay St. Mary's County, Maryland.** Mary L. Donnelly. (Illus.). 250p. 1995. 30.00 (*0-939142-15-5*) M L Donnelly.

***Colonial Silversmith: His Techniques & His Products.** Henry J. Kauffman. (Illus.). 176p. 1995. pap. 22.95 (*1-879335-65-4*) Astragal Pr.

Colonial Situations: Essays on the Contextualization of Ethnographic Knowledge. Ed. by George W. Stocking, Jr. LC 91-50327. (History of Anthropology Ser.: Vol. 7). (Illus.). 348p. (C). 1992. 25.00 (*0-299-13120-3*) U of Wis Pr.

Colonial Situations: Essays on the Contextualization of Ethnographic Knowledge. Ed. by George W. Stocking, Jr. (History of Anthropology Ser.: Vol. 7). (Illus.). 348p. 1993. pap. 12.95 (*0-299-13124-6*) U of Wis Pr.

Colonial South. Anne H. Brown. LC 93-49008. (American Food Library). (J). 1994. write for info. (*0-86625-509-5*) Rourke Pubns.

Colonial South Carolina: A History. Robert H. Weir. LC 82-48990. (History of the American Colonies Ser.). 409p. (Orig.). 1983. lib. bdg. 35.00 (*0-527-18721-6*) Kraus Intl.

C

An Asterisk (*) at the beginning of an entry indicates that the title is appearing in BIP for the first time. 1383

Colonial South Carolina: A Political History, 1663-1763. Marion E. Sirmans. LC 66-25363. 414p. reprint ed. pap. 118.00 (*0-8357-3918-X*, 2036653) Bks Demand.

Colonial Southern Slavery. Ed. by Paul Finkelman. (Articles on American Slavery Ser.). 504p. 1990. reprint ed. 43.00 (*0-8240-6783-5*) Garland.

Colonial Spanish America. Ed. by Leslie Bethell. 455p. 1987. 74.95 (*0-521-34126-4*); pap. 18.95 (*0-521-34924-9*) Cambridge U Pr.

Colonial St. Louis: Building a Creole Capital. Charles E. Peterson. (Illus.). 112p. 1993. reprint ed. pap. 9.95 (*1-880397-00-5*) Patrice Pr.

Colonial Stencils: Stencils of Colonial America. Sherrie A. Styx. (Illus.). (Orig.). 1992. pap. text ed. 3.50 (*1-882121-09-0*) Styx Enter.

Colonial Surry, Virginia. John B. Boddie. 249p. 1992. reprint ed. 25.00 (*0-685-60496-9*, 498) Clearfield Co.

Colonial Tavern: A Glimpse of New England Town Life in the Seventeenth & Eighteenth Centuries. Edward Field. 304p. 1990. reprint ed. pap. 18.00 (*1-55613-274-3*) S B Paoli.

***Colonial Technology: Science & the Transfer of Innovation to Australia.** Jan Todd. (Studies in Australian History). (Illus.). 310p. (C). 1995. write for info. (*0-521-46138-3*) Cambridge U Pr.

Colonial Times. (C. C. Publications Social Studies Ser.). (Illus.). 64p. 1985. pap. text ed. 7.30 (*0-574-51757-X*) SRA.

Colonial Town: Williamsburg. Bobbie Kalman. (Historic Communities Ser.). (Illus.). 32p. (J). (gr. k-9). 1992. lib. bdg. 15.95 (*0-86505-489-4*); pap. 7.95 (*0-86505-509-2*) Crabtree Pub Co.

Colonial Trade of Maryland, 1689-1715. Margaret S. Morriss. LC 76-49477. (Perspectives in American History Ser.: No. 46). viii, 157p. 1977. reprint ed. lib. bdg. 27.50 (*0-87991-370-3*) Porcupine Pr.

Colonial Travelers in Latin America. Ed. by Irving Leonard. 236p. 1986. 15.00 (*0-936388-29-3*); pap. 10.50 (*0-936388-30-7*) Juan de la Cuesta.

Colonial Vestbook: Wit & Wisdom of the 1700s. Elizabeth A. Goesel. (Illus.). 70p. 1993. reprint ed. 5.95 (*0-9638427-0-6*, TX 3 470-472) E A Goesel.

Colonial Virginia: A History. Thad W. Tate et al. (History of the American Colonies Ser.). 420p. 1986. lib. bdg. 35.00 (*0-527-18722-4*) Kraus Intl.

Colonial Virginia: Its People & Customs. Mary N. Stanard. LC 89-29236. (Illus.). xv, 360p. 1991. reprint ed. lib. bdg. 40.00 (*1-55888-897-7*) Omnigraphics Inc.

Colonial Virginia Register: A List of Governors ... & Other Higher Officials ... of the Colony of Virginia. William G. Stanard & Mary N. Stanard. 249p. 1989. reprint ed. 17.95 (*0-685-60456-X*, 5540) Clearfield Co.

Colonial Virginians & Their Maryland Relatives: A Genealogy of the Tucker Family & Also Families of Allen, Blackistone, Chandler, Ford, Gerard, Harmor, Hume, Monroe, Skaggs, Smith, Stevesson, Stone, Sturman, Thompson, Ward, Yowell. Norma Tucker. 270p. 1994. pap. 25.00 (*0-685-75106-6*, 9570) Clearfield Co.

Colonial Virginians at Play. Jane Carson. (Illus.). 132p. 1989. reprint ed. pap. 14.95 (*0-87935-122-5*) U Pr of Va.

Colonial Virginia's Coastwise & Grain Trade. David C. Klingaman. LC 75-2584. (Dissertations in American Economic History Ser.). (Illus.). 1975. 20.95 (*0-405-07204-X*) Ayer.

Colonial Voices: Letter, Diaries, Journalism & Other Accounts of Nineteenth-Century Australia. Ed. by Elizabeth Webby. (UQP Australian Authors Ser.). 400p. (Orig.). 1989. pap. text ed. 18.95 (*0-7022-2171-6*, Pub. by Univ Queensland Pr AT) Intl Spec Bk.

Colonial Wars: Clashes in the Wilderness. Alden R. Carter. LC 92-9906. (First Book Ser.). (Illus.). 64p. (J). (gr. 5-8). 1992. lib. bdg. 13.93 (*0-531-20079-5*) Watts.

Colonial Wars: Clashes in the Wilderness. Alden R. Carter. (First Bks.). (Illus.). 64p. (J). (gr. 5-8). 1993. pap. 5.95 (*0-531-15654-0*) Watts.

Colonial Wars & the Politics of Third World Nationalism. Frank Furedi. 256p. 1994. text ed. 49.50 (*1-85043-784-X*, Pub. by I B Tauris UK) St Martin.

Colonial Wars, 1689-1762. Howard H. Peckham. LC 64-12606. (Chicago History of American Civilization Ser.). (Illus.). 1965. pap. text ed. 13.95 (*0-226-65314-5*, CHAC21) U Ch Pr.

Colonial Williamsburg. Philip Kopper. (Illus.). 320p. 1986. 60.00 (*0-8109-0787-9*) Abrams.

Colonial Williamsburg. Sandra Steen & Susan Steen. LC 92-26192. (Places in American History Ser.). (Illus.). 72p. (J). (gr. 4 up). 1993. text ed. 14.95 (*0-87518-546-0*, Dillon Silver Burdett) Silver Burdett Pr.

Colonial Williamsburg ABC. Amy Z. Watson. (Illus.). 28p. (J). (ps-00). 1994. 9.95 (*0-87935-127-6*) Colonial Williamsburg.

Colonial Williamsburg Activities Book: Fun Activities for Young Visitors. Pat Fortunato. (Illus.). 48p. (Orig.). (J). (gr. 1-4). 1982. pap. 4.25 (*0-87935-062-8*) Colonial Williamsburg.

Colonial Williamsburg Activities Book: Fun Things to Do for Children 4 & Up. Jean Bethell & Susan Axtell. (Illus.). 40p. (J). (ps). 1984. pap. 4.25 (*0-87935-068-7*) Colonial Williamsburg.

Colonial Williamsburg Coloring Book. Vernon Wooten. (Activity Bks. for Young Readers Ser.). (Illus.). 36p. (Orig.). (J). (gr. 1). 1979. pap. 3.95 (*0-87935-052-0*) Colonial Williamsburg.

Colonial Williamsburg Decorates for Christmas: Step-by-Step Illustrated Instructions for Christmas Decorations That You Can Make for Your Home. Libbey H. Oliver. LC 81-10103. (Illus.). 80p. 1981. 15.95 (*0-87935-056-3*); pap. 10.95 (*0-87935-058-X*) Colonial Williamsburg.

Colonial Williamsburg Historic Trades Annual, Vol. I. Colonial Williamsburg Staff. (Illus.). 77p. (Orig.). 1988. pap. 7.95 (*0-685-48222-7*) Colonial Williamsburg.

Colonial Williamsburg Historic Trades Annual, Vol. II. Colonial Williamsburg Staff. (Illus.). 91p. (Orig.). 1990. pap. 7.95 (*0-685-48223-5*) Colonial Williamsburg.

Colonial Williamsburg Music: A Descriptive Catalogue of the Printed Eighteenth & Nineteenth Century Music in the Collections of the Colonial Williamsburg Foundation. Cynthia Z. Stiverson. LC 88-15733. 189p. 1988. lib. bdg. 25.00 (*0-933951-18-3*) Locust Hill Pr.

***Colonial Wills of Henrico County, Virginia, 1677-1737.** Benjamin B. Weisiger, 3rd. 214p. 1976. lib. bdg. 47.00 (*0-8095-8255-4*); pap. 20.00 (*0-8095-8547-2*) Borgo Pr.

***Colonial Wills of Henrico County, Virginia, 1737-1781, with Addenda.** rev. ed. Benjamin B. Weisiger, 3rd. 185p. 1985. lib. bdg. 47.00 (*0-8095-8256-2*); pap. 20.00 (*0-8095-8548-0*) Borgo Pr.

Colonial Woman: The Life & Times of Mary Braidwood Mowle 1827-1857. Patricia Clarke. (Illus.). 316p. 1986. text ed. 34.95 (*0-04-909025-9*) Routledge Chapman & Hall.

Colonial Yorktown. Clyde F. Trudell. (Illus.). 192p. (C). 1992. reprint ed. pap. text ed. 7.95 (*0-939631-58-X*) Thomas Publications.

Colonialism & After: An Algerian Jewish Community. Elizabeth Friedman. LC 87-36791. (Critical Studies in Work & Community). 170p. 1988. text ed. 55.00 (*0-89789-095-7*, Bergin & Garvey) Greenwood.

Colonialism & Agrarian Transformation in Bolivia: Cochabamba, 1550-1900. Brooke Larson. (Illus.). 424p. 1988. pap. text ed. 26.95 (*0-691-10241-4*) Princeton U Pr.

Colonialism & Change: Essays Presented to Lucy Mair. Ed. by Maxwell Owuso. LC 74-83128. (Studies in Anthropology: No. 4). (Illus.). 264p. 1975. pap. text ed. 44.65 (*90-279-3187-9*) Mouton.

Colonialism & Cold War: The United States & the Struggle for Indonesian Independence, 1945-49. Robert J. McMahon. LC 81-66648. 338p. 1981. 39.95 (*0-8014-1388-5*) Cornell U Pr.

Colonialism & Culture. Ed. by Nicholas B. Dirks. LC 92-3315. (Comparative Studies in Society & History). 400p. (C). 1992. text ed. 59.50 (*0-472-09434-3*); pap. text ed. 20.95 (*0-472-06434-7*) U of Mich Pr.

Colonialism & Culture: Hispanic Modernisms & the Social Imaginary. Iris M. Zavala. LC 91-31785. 256p. 1992. 35.00 (*0-253-36861-8*) Ind U Pr.

Colonialism & Development: Britain & Its Tropical Colonies, 1850-1960. Michael Havinden & David Meredith. LC 92-40809. (Illus.). 448p. 1993. 65.00 (*0-415-02043-3*, A5036, Routledge NY) Routledge.

Colonialism & Development in the Contemporary World. Ed. by Chris Dixon & Michael Heffernan. (Illus.). 240p. 1991. text ed. 80.00 (*0-7201-2072-1*, Mansell Pub) Cassell.

***Colonialism & Gender from Mary Wollstonecraft to Jamaica Kincaid: East Carribean Connections.** Moira Ferguson. 1994. pap. 14.50 (*0-231-08223-1*) Col U Pr.

Colonialism & Language Policy in Viet Nam. John De Francis. 1977. 37.50 (*90-279-7643-0*) Mouton.

Colonialism & Nationalism in Asian Cinema. Ed. by Wimal Dissanayake. LC 93-51497. 1994. 29.95 (*0-253-31804-1*); pap. 13.95 (*0-253-20895-5*) Ind U Pr.

Colonialism & Revolution in the Middle East: Social & Cultural Origins of Egypt's Urabi Movement. Juan R. Cole. LC 92-11115. (Studies in the Near East). (Illus.). 416p. (C). 1993. text ed. 55.00 (*0-691-05683-8*) Princeton U Pr.

Colonialism & Science: Saint Domingue in the Old Regime. James E. McClellan, III. (Illus.). 416p. 1992. text ed. 55.00x (*0-8018-4270-0*) Johns Hopkins.

Colonialism & Underdevelopment: Processes of Political Economic Change in British Honduras. Norman Ashcraft. LC 72-92055. (Columbia University, Center for Education in Asia, Publications). 192p. reprint ed. pap. 54.80 (*0-317-41936-6*, 2025989) Bks Demand.

Colonialism & Underdevelopment in East Africa. E. A. Brett. LC 72-97704. 330p. 1973. text ed. 18.95 (*0-88357-000-9*); pap. 7.95 (*0-88357-001-7*) NOK Pubs.

Colonialism & Underdevelopment in East Africa: The Politics of Economic Change. E. A. Brett. (Modern Revivals in African Studies). 330p. 1992. 59.95 (*0-7512-0080-8*, Pub. by Gregg Revivals UK) Ashgate Pub Co.

Colonialism, Catholicism, & Contraception: A History of Birth Control in Puerto Rico. Annette B. Ramirez de Arellano & Conrad Seipp. LC 82-13646. xiv, 219p. 1983. 29.95 (*0-8078-1544-6*) U of NC Pr.

***Colonialism, Catholicism, & Contraception: A History of Birth Control in Puerto Rico.** Annette B. Ramirez de Arellano & Conrad Seipp. LC 82-13646. reprint ed. pap. 65.90 (*0-7837-9029-5*, 2049780) Bks Demand.

Colonialism, Chemical Technology & Industry in Southern India, 1880-1937. Nasir Tyabji. (Illus.). 360p. 1995. 26.00 (*0-19-563124-2*) OUP.

Colonialism, Class & Nation: The Confrontation in Bombay 1930. Georges K. Leiten. 1985. 22.50 (*0-8364-1274-5*, Pub. by KP Bagchi IA) S Asia.

Colonialism, Class Formation & Underdevelopment in Sierra Leone. Eliphas G. Mukonoweshuro. 268p. (Orig.). (C). 1991. lib. bdg. 45.00 (*0-8191-8282-6*); pap. text ed. 23.50 (*0-8191-8283-4*) U Pr of Amer.

***Colonialism, Health, & Illness in French Equatorial Africa, 1885-1935.** Rita Headrick. Ed. by Daniel R. Headrick. LC 94-29444. 1994. 48.00 (*0-918456-71-1*) African Studies Assn.

Colonialism in Africa, 1870-1960, 5 vols. Ed. by Peter Duignan & Lewis H. Gann. Incl. Vol. 4. Economics of Colonialism. 1975. 145.00 (*0-521-08641-8*); Vol. 5. Bibliography. 1974. 125.00 (*0-521-07859-8*); write for info. (*0-318-51277-7*) Cambridge U Pr.

Colonialism in Africa: 1870-1960, Vol. 4: The Economics of Colonialism. Ed. by Peter Duignan & L. H. Gann. (Publication Ser.: No. 127). 736p. 1975. reprint ed. pap. text ed. 18.95 (*0-8179-6272-7*) Hoover Inst Pr.

Colonialism in an Indian Hinterland: The Central Provinces, 1820-1920. D. E. Baker. (Illus.). 384p. (C). 1993. 29.95 (*0-19-563049-1*, 14338) OUP.

Colonialism in East-West Relations: A Study of Soviet Policy Towards India & Anglo-Soviet Relations 1917-47. Zafar Imam. 560p. (C). 1987. 48.00 (*81-7050-045-1*, Patriot) S Asia.

Colonialism in Sri Lanka: The Political Economy of the Kandyan Highlands, 1833-1886. Asoka Bandarage. LC 83-17274. (Studies in the Social Sciences: No. 39). xiv, 404p. 1983. 120.00 (*90-279-3080-5*) Mouton.

Colonialism in the Congo Basin, 1880-1940. Samuel H. Nelson. LC 94-18278. (Monographs in International Studies, Africa Ser.: No. 64). 248p. (Orig.). (C). 1994. pap. text ed. 23.00x (*0-89680-180-2*) Ohio U Pr.

Colonialism on Trial: Indigenous Land Rights & the Gitksan-We'suwet'en Sovereignty Case. Don Monet & Ardythe Wilson. 224p. 1991. lib. bdg. 49.95 (*0-86571-218-2*); pap. 17.95 (*0-86571-219-0*) New Soc Pubs.

Colonialism, Tradition & Reform: An Analysis of Gandhi's Political Discourse. Bhikhu Parekh. 288p. (C). 1989. text ed. 24.00 (*0-8039-9605-5*) Sage.

***Colonialism, Tropical Disease, & Imperial Medicine: Rockefeller Philanthropy in Sri Lanka.** Soma Hewa. LC 95-13578. 1995. write for info. (*0-8191-9939-7*) U Pr of Amer.

Colonialismo Interno en la Narrativa Chicana. Manuel De Jesus Hernandez-Gutierrez. 232p. 1994. pap. 20.00 (*0-927534-21-5*) Biling Rev-Pr.

***Colonialism's Culture: Anthropology, Travel & Government.** Nicholas Thomas. LC 94-32823. 1994. 49.95 (*0-691-03732-9*); pap. 16.95 (*0-691-03731-0*) Princeton U Pr.

Colonic Diverticular Disease. Veidenheimer & Roberts. (Illus.). 173p. 1991. 65.00 (*0-86542-136-6*) Blackwell Sci.

Colonic Drug Absorption & Metabolism. Ed. by Peter R. Bieck. LC 93-17265. (Drugs & the Pharmaceutical Sciences Ser.: Vol. 60). 240p. 1993. 125.00 (*0-8247-9013-8*) Dekker.

Colonie Penitentiaire et Autres Recits. Franz Kafka. 192p. (FRE.). 1972. pap. 10.95 (*0-7859-2276-8*, 2070361926) Fr & Eur.

***Colonies.** (Voices in African American History Ser.). (YA). 1994. lib. bdg. 11.95 (*0-8136-4959-5*) Modern Curr.

***Colonies.** (Voices in African American History Ser.). (YA). 1994. pap. 5.95 (*0-8136-4960-9*) Modern Curr.

Colonies: An Educational Coloring Book. Peter M. Spizzirri. Ed. by Linda Spizzirri. (Illus.). 32p. (J). (gr. 1-8). 1989. pap. 1.75 (*0-86545-137-0*) Spizzirri.

Colonies: Canada to 1867. David Bercuson et al. 1993. pap. text ed. write for info. (*0-07-551013-8*) McGraw.

Colonies & Democracy: Color & Race. W. E. B. Du Bois. (African Heritage Classical Research Studies). 143p. reprint ed. 20.00 (*0-938818-55-4*) ECA Assoc.

***Colonies, Commerce, & Constitutional Law: Rid Yourselves of Ultramaria & Other Writings on Spain & Spanish America.** Jeremy Bentham. Ed. by Philip Schofield & F. Rosen. 480p. 1996. 90.00 (*0-19-822612-8*) OUP.

Colonies Franques De Syrie Aux Dix-Septieme & Dix-Huitieme Siecles. Emmanuel Rey. LC 75-168087. reprint ed. 55.00 (*0-404-05285-1*) AMS Pr.

Colonies in America. Marilyn Thypin & Lynne Glasner. (History of the United States Ser.: Bk. 1). (Illus.). 96p. (Orig.). 1982. pap. text ed. 5.45 (*0-941342-01-8*, 1021) Entry Pub.

Colonies to Nation, Seventeen Sixty-Three to Seventeen Eighty-Nine: A Documentary History of the American Revolution. Ed. by Jack P. Greene. 608p. (C). 1975. reprint ed. pap. text ed. 18.95 (*0-393-09229-1*) Norton.

Colonies Under the House of Hanover see English in America

Colonisation de la Nouvelle-France: Etude sur les origines de la nation canadienne-francaise. 3rd ed. Emile Salone. (French-Canadian Cilivization Ser.). reprint ed. lib. bdg. 44.00 (*0-697-00056-7*) Irvington.

***Colonisation of Indo-China.** Joseph C. Bert. (C). 1993. 14.00x (*81-85557-21-7*, Pub. by Low Price II) S Asia.

Colonisation of Land: Origins & Adaptations of Terrestrial Animals. Colin Little. LC 83-1787. (Illus.). 480p. 1984. 145.00 (*0-521-25218-0*) Cambridge U Pr.

Colonising Egypt. Timothy Mitchell. (Illus.). 230p. 1991. reprint ed. pap. 14.00 (*0-520-07568-4*, MITCOX) U CA Pr.

***Colonists.** Jack Cavanaugh. (American Family Portrait Ser.). 500p. (Orig.). 1995. pap. 11.99 (*1-56476-346-3*, Victor Books) SP Pubns.

Colonists. Norman K. Risjord. (Representative Americans Ser.: Vol. 1). 253p. (C). 1981. pap. text ed. 13.50 (*0-669-02831-2*) Heath.

***Colonists from Scotland: Emigration to North America, 1707-1783.** Ian C. Graham. 223p. 1994. pap. 21.50 (*0-614-00924-3*, 9129) Clearfield Co.

Colonization: Particularly in South Australia, with Some Remarks on Small Farms & Overpopulation. Charles J. Napier. LC 68-56551. (Reprints of Economic Classics Ser.). xxxii, 269p. 1969. reprint ed. 39.50 (*0-678-00575-3*) Kelley.

Colonization & Environment: Land Settlement Projects in Central America. 170p. 1990. 30.00 (*92-808-0653-X*, 90.III.A.5) UN.

Colonization Control of Human Bacterial Enteropathogens in Poultry. Ed. by Leroy C. Blankenship. (Food Science & Technology Ser.). (Illus.). 395p. 1991. text ed. 55.00 (*0-12-104280-4*) Acad Pr.

Colonization of New Zealand. Johannes S. Marais. LC 77-137258. reprint ed. 24.75 (*0-404-04184-1*) AMS Pr.

Colonization of the Amazon. Anna L. Ozorio de Almeida. LC 92-5938. (Translations from Latin America Ser.). (Illus.). 389p. (C). 1992. text ed. 30.00 (*0-292-71146-8*) U of Tex Pr.

Colonization of the Pacific: A Genetic Trail. Adrian V. Hill & Susan W. Serjeantson. (Research Monographs on Human Population Biology: No. 7). (Illus.). 308p. 1989. 90.00 (*0-19-857695-1*) OUP.

***Colonization Strategies & Secrets.** Gary Meredith. 1995. 12.99 (*0-7821-1672-8*) Sybex.

Colonization to American Renaissance, 1640-1865. (Concise Dictionary of American Literary Biography Ser.). 1988. 70.00 (*0-8103-1819-9*) Gale.

***Colonization, Violation, & Narration in White South African Writing: Andre Brink, Breyten Breytenbach, & J. M. Coetzee.** Rosemary Jolly. 320p. (C). 1995. text ed. 44.95 (*0-8214-1130-6*); pap. text ed. 18.95 (*0-8214-1131-4*) Ohio U Pr.

Colonizer & the Colonized. rev. ed. Albert Memmi. LC 90-24035. 208p. 1991. pap. 14.00 (*0-8070-0301-8*) Beacon Pr.

Colonizer's Model of the World: Geographical Diffusionism & Eurocentric History. James M. Blaut. LC 93-22346. 246p. 1993. lib. bdg. 40.00 (*0-89862-349-9*); pap. text ed. 17.95 (*0-89862-348-0*) Guilford Pr.

Colonizing the Body: State Medicine & Epidemic Disease in Nineteenth-Century India. David Arnold. LC 92-25623. (C). 1993. 45.00 (*0-520-08124-2*); pap. 18.00 (*0-520-08295-8*) U CA Pr.

Colonos of Apostoles: Adaptive Strategy & Ethnicity in a Polish-Ukrainian. Leopoldo J. Bartolome. LC 89-6617. (Studies in Anthropology: No. 9). 1990. 59.50 (*0-404-62609-2*) AMS Pr.

***Colonoscopy: Principles & Techniques.** Nord Raskin. 1995. write for info. (*0-89640-277-0*) Igaku-Shoin.

Colonus: Private Farm Tenancy in Roman Italy During the Republic & the Early Principate. P. W. De Neeve. viii, 273p. (C). 1984. 50.00 (*90-70265-15-X*, Pub. by Gieben NE) Benjamins North Am.

Colony. Anne R. Siddons. 1993. mass mkt. 6.99 (*0-06-109970-8*, Harp PBks) HarpC.

Colony: A Novel. large type ed. Anne R. Siddons. LC 92-31897. (General Ser.). 705p. 1993. lib. bdg. 23.95 (*0-8161-5615-8*); pap. 17.95 (*0-8161-5616-6*) G K Hall.

Colony & Commonwealth: Massachusets Bay, 1649-1660. Timothy J. Sehr. (Outstanding Studies in Early American History). 328p. 1989. reprint ed. 20.00 (*0-8240-6196-9*) Garland.

Colony & Empire: The Capitalist Transformation of the American West. William G. Robbins. LC 94-11029. (Development of Western Resources Ser.). 274p. (Orig.). (C). 1995. 29.95x (*0-7006-0645-9*) U Pr of KS.

***Colony & Empire: The Capitalist Transformation of the American West.** William G. Robbins. LC 94-11029. (Development of Western Resources Ser.). (Orig.). (C). 1995. pap. 14.95 (*0-7006-0750-1*) U Pr of KS.

Colony & Mother City in Ancient Greece. Graham. xxxvi, 259p. 1983. pap. 20.00 (*0-89005-520-3*) Ares.

***Colony in Japan.** Kenichi Yoshida. 160p. 1995. pap. 18.50 (*1-873410-46-8*, Pub. by Japan Library) Humanities.

Colony of New Sweden. Bill Albensi. 37p. 1987. pap. 3.00 (*0-930950-27-5*) Nopoly Pr.

Colony of One. Elizabeth Boyer. LC 83-50742. (Illus.). 1983. 30.00 (*0-915964-05-8*) Veritie Pr.

Colony of Sierra Leone Vindicated from the Misrepresentations of Mr. MacQueen of Glasgow. Kenneth Macaulay. 127p. 1968. reprint ed. 35.00 (*0-7146-1831-4*, Pub. by F Cass Pubs UK) Intl Spec Bk.

Colony Olivenhain. Richard L. Bumann. LC 81-90363. (Illus.). 112p. 1981. 15.95 (*0-9607112-0-1*) Bumann Spec Works.

Colony Stimulating Factors: Molecular & Cellular Biology. Dexter et al. (Immunology Ser.: Vol. 49). 416p. 1990. 190.00 (*0-8247-8094-9*) Dekker.

Colophons of Armenian Manuscripts, 1301-1480: A Source for Middle Eastern History. Ed. by Avedis K. Sanlian. LC 69-18044. (Harvard Armenian Texts & Studies: No. 2). 479p. reprint ed. pap. 136.60 (*0-317-08390-2*, 2003783) Bks Demand.

Coloproctology. J. Nicholls & R. Glass. (Illus.). 244p. 1985. pap. 51.00 (*0-387-15140-0*) Spr-Verlag.

Coloproctology & the Pelvic Floor. 2nd ed. Ed. by M. M. Henry & M. Swash. (Illus.). 416p. 1992. 220.00 (*0-7506-1236-3*) Buttrwrth-Heinemann.

Coloquio del Azogamiento. Jorge V. Arango. 112p. (Orig.). (SPA.). 1988. pap. 8.00 (*0-917049-18-7*) Saeta.

Color. Alison Cole. LC 93-8066. (Eyewitness Art Ser.). (Illus.). 64p. 1993. 16.95 (*1-56458-332-5*) Dorling Kindersley.

Color. Hilary Devonshire. LC 91-11871. (Science Through Art Ser.). (Illus.). 32p. (J). (gr. 5-8). 1992. lib. bdg. 13.23 (*0-531-14221-3*) Watts.

Color. Barbara Einzig. 1976. pap. 5.00 (*0-87924-020-2*) Membrane Pr.

***Color.** Ruth Heller. LC 94-29097. (J). 1995. 18.95 (*0-399-22815-2*, G&D) Putnam Pub Group.

Color. Werner Kirst & Ulrich Diekmayer. (Illus.). 1978. 11.95 (*0-8464-0257-2*) Beekman Pubs.

Color. Sheila Metzner. 172p. 1991. 50.00 (*0-944092-15-2*) Twin Palms Pub.

Color. Christina Rossetti. LC 90-25588. (Illus.). 40p. (J). (ps-1). 1994. pap. 4.95 (*0-06-443361-7*, Trophy) HarpC Child Bks.

An Asterisk (*) at the beginning of an entry indicates that the title is appearing in BIP for the first time.

Color. Diana Saville. (Letts Guides to Garden Design Ser.). (Illus.). 64p. 1993. 9.95 (*1-55859-551-1*, Canopy Bks) Abbeville Pr.

Color. limited ed. Sheila Metzner. 172p. 1991. 150.00 (*0-944092-16-0*) Twin Palms Pub.

Color. rev. ed. Rudolf Steiner. 176p. 1992. reprint ed. pap. 15.00 (*0-89345-264-5*, Steinerbks) Garber Comm.

***Color.** 2nd ed. Zelanski & Fisher. (Illus.). 160p. 1994. pap. text ed. write for info. (*0-13-310715-9*) P-H.

Color. Countee Cullen. LC 70-101515. (American Negro: His History & Literature, Ser. No. 3). 1970. reprint ed. 14.00 (*0-405-01919-X*) Ayer.

Color: A Survey in Words & Pictures. Faber Birren. (Illus.). 256p. 1984. reprint ed. pap. 14.95 (*0-8065-0849-3*, Citadel Pr) Carol Pub Group.

Color: A Thematic Unit. Cheryl Russell. (Thematic Units Ser.). (Illus.). 80p. 1993. student ed 8.95 (*1-55734-279-2*) Tchr Create Mat.

Color: How to See It & How to Use It. Judy Martin. 1994. 19.98 (*0-7858-0053-0*) Bk Sales Inc.

Color: Light, Sight, Sense. Moritz Zwimpfer. LC 88-61471. (Illus.). 256p. 1988. 49.95 (*0-88740-139-2*) Schiffer.

Color: Natural Palettes for Painted Rooms. Donald Kaufman & Taffy Dahl. 224p. 1992. 50.00 (*0-517-57660-0*, C P Pubs) Crown Pub Group.

Color: Suite in Four Parts. deluxe limited ed. Harry Rand. (Illus.). 56p. 1993. ring bd. 3,000.00 (*0-9638014-0-6*) Dov Press.

***Color: Using Color to Decorate Your Home.** Laura Ashley. 1995. 40.00 (*0-517-70190-1*) Random Hse Value.

Color - on White Campus: The Education of a Racial World. (Orig.). 1992. pap. write for info. (*1-56411-042-7*) Untd Bros & Sis.

Color a Story: Adam. (J). (ps). Date not set. pap. 3.50 (*0-934905-10-X*) Kazi Pubns.

Color a Story: Nuh. Jeanette Hablallah. 32p. (J). (ps). 1989. pap. 3.50 (*1-56744-251-X*) Kazi Pubns.

Color Aerial Photography in the Plant Sciences & Related Fields: A Compendium, 1967-1988. 306p. 1988. pap. 10.00 (*0-944426-01-8*) ASP & RS.

Color Analysis Workbook Course: To Teach You How to Do Color Analysis. Bernice Kentner. (Illus.). 108p. 1982. student ed 15.00 (*0-941522-03-2*) Ken Kra Pubs.

Color Analyzers. Cary Sneider & Cheryll Hawthorne. Ed. by Lincoln Bergman & Kay Fairwell. (Great Explorations in Math & Science (GEMS) Ser.). (Illus.). 70p. 1989. pap. 15.00 (*0-912511-14-1*) Lawrence Science.

Color & Black & White Television Theory & Servicing. Alvin A. Liff. (Illus.). 1979. text ed. 29.95 (*0-685-03795-9*) P-H.

Color & Black & White Television Theory & Servicing. 3rd ed. Alvin A. Liff & Sam Wilson. 608p. 1993. text ed. 65.00 (*0-13-150012-0*) P-H.

Color & Cloth: The Quiltmaker's Ultimate Workbook. Mary C. Penders. LC 89-10448. (Illus.). 136p. (Orig.). 1989. pap. 21.95 (*0-913327-20-4*) Quilt Digest Pr.

Color & Color Perception: A Study in Anthropocentric Realism. David R. Hilbert. LC 87-27643. (CSLI Lecture Notes Ser.: No. 9). 146p. 1988. 24.95 (*0-937073-15-6*); pap. 11.95 (*0-937073-16-4*) Ctr Study Language.

Color & Color Vision. Ed. by Paul L. Pease. 136p. 1982. 18.00 (*0-318-41404-X*, RB-33) Am Assn Physics.

Color & Consciousness: An Essay in Metaphysics. Charles Landesman. LC 88-29442. 149p. (C). 1989. 24.95 (*0-87722-616-4*) Temple U Pr.

***Color & Context: The Architecture of Perry Dean Rodgers.** Date not set. 39.99 (*1-56496-138-9*) Rockport Pubs.

***Color & Context: The Architecture of Perry Dean Rogers & Partners.** Michael J. Crosbie. (Illus.). 192p. 1995. 39.95 (*1-55835-136-1*) AIA Press.

Color & Crystals: A Journey Through the Chakras. Joy Gardner. 112p. (Orig.). 1988. pap. 10.95 (*0-89594-258-5*) Crossing Pr.

Color & Culture: Practice & Meaning from Antiquity to Abstraction, Vol. 1. John Gage. (Illus.). 336p. 1993. 65.00 (*0-8212-2043-8*) Bulfinch Pr.

Color & Democracy: Colonies & Peace. W. E. B. Du Bois. LC 45-35105. 1975. reprint ed. 10.00 (*0-527-25290-5*) Kraus Intl.

Color & Discover: A Children's Guide to the North Carolina Museum of Art. Diana Suarez. LC 87-62986. (Illus.). 40p. (Orig.). (J). (ps-6). 1987. pap. 3.50 (*0-88259-956-9*) NCMA.

Color & Dyeing. Harriet Tidball. LC 76-24007. (Guild Monographs: No. 16). (Illus.). 53p. 1965. pap. 8.95 (*0-916658-16-3*) Shuttle Craft.

Color & Fiber. P. Lambert et al. LC 86-61295. (Illus.). 255p. 1986. 49.50 (*0-88740-065-5*) Schiffer.

Color & Form: A Retrospective. Nassos Daphnis. 1994. pap. 29.95 (*0-936859-10-5*) Boca Raton Museum.

Color & Healing. Gladys Mayer. 1973. lib. bdg. 250.00 (*0-87968-309-0*) Krishna Pr.

Color & How to Use It. William F. Powell. (Artist's Library). (Illus.). 64p. (Orig.). 1989. pap. 6.95 (*0-929261-05-4*, AL05) W Foster Pub.

Color & Human Response. Faber Birren. LC 77-12505. (Illus.). 120p. 1978. pap. 24.95 (*0-442-20961-4*) Van Nos Reinhold.

Color & Image: Recent American Enamels. Lloyd Herman. (Illus.). 63p. 1988. 15.00 (*0-934483-11-6*) Gal Assn NY.

Color & Its Reproduction. Gary G. Field. LC 86-82528. (Illus.). 386p. (Orig.). (C). 1988. pap. text ed. 65.00 (*0-88362-088-X*) Graphic Arts Tech Found.

Color & Learn Islamic Terms. M. A. Qazi. pap. 3.50 (*0-935782-57-5*) Kazi Pubns.

Color & Learn Muslim Names. 32p. (J). (ps). Date not set. pap. 3.50 (*0-933511-03-5*) Kazi Pubns.

Color & Learn Salat. P. Ahmad. (J). pap. 3.50 (*0-935782-58-3*) Kazi Pubns.

Color & Learn the Names of Animals. N. Hijazi. (Orig.). (J). (ps). Date not set. pap. 3.50 (*0-934905-12-6*) Kazi Pubns.

Color & Learn the Names of the Family of Prophet Muhammad. S. Ameer Ali. 32p. (Orig.). (J). (ps). Date not set. pap. 3.50 (*0-934905-13-4*) Kazi Pubns.

Color & Learn the Names of the Prophets. A. Hamza. (Orig.). (J). (ps). Date not set. pap. 3.50 (*0-934905-11-8*) Kazi Pubns.

Color & Light. David Evans & Claudette Williams. LC 92-53480. (Let's Explore Science Ser.). (Illus.). 24p. (J). (gr. k-3). 1993. 9.95 (*1-56458-207-8*) Dorling Kindersley.

Color & Light: Influences & Impact. Barbara Colby. 100p. (Orig.). 1990. pap. 14.50 (*0-9628138-0-X*) Chroma Prods.

Color & Light in Man Made Environments. R. Mahnke. 1993. pap. 39.95 (*0-442-01322-1*) Van Nos Reinhold.

Color & Light in Nature. David K. Lynch & William Livingston. LC 93-46711. (Illus.). 288p. (C). 1995. 69.95 (*0-521-43431-9*); pap. 29.95 (*0-521-46836-1*) Cambridge U Pr.

Color & Light in the Writings of Eduard von Keyserling. Richard A. Weber. LC 90-6053. (Studies in Modern Literature: Vol. 39). 375p. (C). 1990. text ed. 61.95 (*0-8204-1255-4*) P Lang Pubs.

Color & Meaning: Practice & Theory in Renaissance Painting. Marcia B. Hall. (Illus.). 288p. (C). 1992. 64.95 (*0-521-39222-5*) Cambridge U Pr.

Color & Meaning: Practice & Theory in Renaissance Painting. Marcia B. Hall. (Illus.). 288p. (C). 1994. pap. 19.95 (*0-521-45733-5*) Cambridge U Pr.

Color & Method in Painting. Ernest W. Watson. LC 72-117858. (Essay Index Reprint Ser.). 1977. 27.95 (*0-8369-1733-2*) Ayer.

Color & Music in the New Age. 8th ed. Corinne Heline. 139p. 1981. reprint ed. pap. 8.95 (*0-87516-432-3*) DeVorss.

Color & Personality. Audrey Kargere. 144p. 1979. pap. 7.95 (*0-87728-478-4*) Weiser.

Color & Personality. Tricia Nickel. 68p. 1989. spiral bd. 9.95 (*0-941522-08-3*) Ken Kra Pubs.

Color & Spectral Doppler Ultrasound of the Carotid Artery & Peripheral Vessels. E. Meredith James et al. (C). 1991. disk 700.00 (*1-56815-006-7*) Image Premast.

Color & Symmetry. Arthur L. Loeb. LC 78-13084. 196p. 1978. reprint ed. 26.50 (*0-88275-745-8*) Krieger.

Color & the Computer. Ed. by H. John Durrett. LC 86-17344. (Illus.). 299p. 1987. text ed. 92.00 (*0-12-225210-1*) Acad Pr.

Color & the Edgar Cayce Readings. Roger Lewis. 48p. 1973. pap. 4.00 (*0-87604-068-7*, 264) ARE Pr.

Color & the Human Soul. Gladys Mayer. 1973. lib. bdg. 250.00 (*0-87968-542-5*) Krishna Pr.

***Color & Weave II.** Margaret B. Windeknecht. (Illus.). 128p. (Orig.). 1995. pap. text ed. 18.95 (*0-9618797-3-4*) T G Windeknecht.

Color & You: A Guide to Determining Your Best Colors. rev. ed. Clare Revelli. (Illus.). 96p. 1994. reprint ed. pap. 7.99 (*0-9608092-3-6*) Revelli.

Color Appearance. LC 87-60498. (Technical Digest Series, 1987: Vol. 15). 117p. (Orig.). 1987. lib. bdg. 66.00 (*0-936659-77-7*); pap. 43.00 (*0-936659-57-2*) Optical Soc.

Color As Form: A History of Color Photography. International Museum of Photography, George Eastman House Staff. LC 82-81231. (Illus.). 40p. (Orig.). 1982. 12.00 (*0-935398-05-8*) G Eastman Hse.

Color at Home & Abroad. George Mallison. LC 72-132388. reprint ed. 39.50 (*0-404-00198-X*) AMS Pr.

Color Atlanta. Claire Keys & Kathleen Sawyer. 1988. pap. 2.95 (*0-88289-704-7*) Pelican.

Color Atlas: Test of Flow Cytometric Analysis of Hematologic Neoplasms. Tsieh Sun. LC 92-3103. (Illus.). 232p. 1993. 148.50 (*0-89640-232-0*) Igaku-Shoin.

Color Atlas: Text of Ureteroscopy. Lawrence B. Kandel. LC 92-48832. (Illus.). 336p. 1993. 159.95 (*0-89640-210-X*) Igaku-Shoin.

Color Atlas - Text of Advanced Laparoscopy for Surgeons. Barry A. Salky. LC 94-9399. 1995. write for info. (*0-89640-224-X*) Igaku-Shoin.

Color Atlas - Text of Excimer Laser Surgery: The Cornea. Frank B. Thompson & Peter J. McDonnell. LC 92-1551. (Illus.). 176p. 1993. 125.00 (*0-89640-225-8*) Igaku-Shoin.

Color Atlas - Text of Ophthalmic Parasitology. B. H. Kean et al. LC 90-5173. (Illus.). 248p. 1991. text ed. 130.00 (*0-89640-193-6*) Igaku-Shoin.

Color Atlas & Instruction Manual of Peripheral Blood Morphology. Barbara H. O'Connor. (Illus.). 316p. (C). 1984. pap. text ed. 45.00 (*0-683-06624-2*) Williams & Wilkins.

Color Atlas & Synopsis of Clinical Dermatology. 2nd ed. Thomas B. Fitzpatrick et al. 824p. 1992. pap. text ed. 48.00 (*0-07-021209-0*) Hlth Prof Div.

Color Atlas & Synopsis of Pigmented Lesions. Raymond L. Barnhill et al. (Illus.). 250p. 1995. 39.00 (*0-07-005110-0*) Hlth Prof Div.

Color Atlas & Synopsis of Sexually Transmitted Diseases. H. Hunter Handsfield. 224p. 1992. pap. text ed. 38.00 (*0-07-026006-0*) Hlth Prof Div.

***Color Atlas & Text of Adult Dementias.** David M. Mann et al. LC 94-43604. 1994. 99.95 (*0-7234-1784-9*) Wolfe Pub.

Color Atlas & Text of Complete Prosthodontics. Grant. 1993. 45.00 (*0-8151-3546-7*, Yr Bk Med Pubs) Mosby Yr Bk.

Color Atlas & Text of Dental Care for the Elderly. Yemm. 256p. 1994. 60.00 (*0-8151-9751-9*, Yr Bk Med Pubs) Mosby Yr Bk.

Color Atlas & Text of Ear Diseases in the Dog. Little. 1994. 99.50 (*0-8151-5445-3*, Yr Bk Med Pubs) Mosby Yr Bk.

***Color Atlas & Text of Equine Ophthalmology.** K. C. Barnett et al. 1994. 110.00 (*0-7234-1925-6*) Wolfe Pub.

Color Atlas & Text of Surgical Pathology of the Dog & Cat, 1. Julie A. Yager. LC 93-2094. 1993. write for info. (*0-7234-1827-6*, Wolfe Pub) Mosby Yr Bk.

Color Atlas & Textbook of Diagnostic Microbiology. 4th ed. Elmer W. Koneman et al. LC 92-6383. 1992. 59.95 (*0-397-51201-5*) Lippincott.

Color Atlas & Textbook of Diagnostic Parasitology. Tsieh Sun. LC 87-29308. (Illus.). 328p. 1988. 125.00 (*0-89640-135-9*) Igaku-Shoin.

Color Atlas & Textbook of Equine Ophthalmology. Barnett. 1994. 89.00 (*0-8151-0420-0*, Yr Bk Med Pubs) Mosby Yr Bk.

Color Atlas & Textbook of Human Anatomy: Locomotor System, Vol. I. 4th ed. Werner Platzer. (Illus.). 440p. 1992. pap. 27.00 (*0-86577-423-4*) Thieme Med Pubs.

Color Atlas & Textbook of Human Anatomy: Nervous System & Sensory Organs, Vol. III. 3rd ed. Werner Kahle. (Illus.). 360p. 1978. pap. 25.95 (*0-86577-251-7*) Thieme Med Pubs.

Color Atlas & Textbook of Oral Anatomy, Histology, & Embryology. 2nd rev. ed. B. K. Berkovitz et al. LC 92-12712. 328p. 1992. 65.00 (*0-8151-0697-1*) Mosby Yr Bk.

Color Atlas & Textbook of the Histopathology of Mycotic Diseases. Francis W. Chandler et al. (Illus.). 333p. 1980. 129.00 (*0-8151-1637-3*, DGD-1, Yr Bk Med Pubs) Mosby Yr Bk.

Color Atlas for General Biology. Gerald Etra. Ed. by Katherine Kelly. (Illus.). 96p. (Orig.). (C). 1994. pap. text ed. 15.00 (*1-878045-44-X*) Whittier Pubns.

***Color Atlas Human Anatomy.** Vannini. 12.99 (*0-517-14640-1*) Random Hse Value.

Color Atlas of Aesthetic Surgery of the Abdomen. Jorge Psillakis et al. (Illus.). 96p. 1991. text ed. 105.00 (*0-86577-343-2*) Thieme Med Pubs.

Color Atlas of Aids. Freidman-Kien. 160p. 1989. text ed. 54.50 (*0-7216-2759-5*) Saunders.

Color Atlas of AIDS & HIV Disease. Charles A. Farthing. 1988. 46.95 (*0-8151-3246-8*, Yr Bk Med Pubs) Mosby Yr Bk.

Color Atlas of Allergic Skin Disorders. Cerio. (Illus.). 128p. 1992. 45.00 (*0-8151-1504-0*) Mosby Yr Bk.

Color Atlas of Allergy. Jackson. 1988. 56.95 (*0-7234-0914-5*, Wolfe Pub) Mosby Yr Bk.

Color Atlas of Anatomy: A Photographic Study of the Human Body. Johannes W. Rohen et al. LC 92-49387. (Illus.). 494p. 1993. 59.00 (*0-89640-228-2*) Igaku-Shoin.

Color Atlas of Applied Anatomy. McMinn et al. (Illus.). 214p. 1984. pap. 64.95 (*0-8151-5827-0*, QMM-1, Yr Bk Med Pubs) Mosby Yr Bk.

Color Atlas of Arthropods in Clinical Medicine. Peters. (Illus.). 256p. 1992. 140.00 (*0-8151-6679-6*, Yr Bk Med Pubs) Mosby Yr Bk.

Color Atlas of Avian Anatomy. McLelland. 1991. text ed. 84.00 (*0-7216-3536-9*) Saunders.

Color Atlas of Baby Delivery. Morris. (Illus.). 1991. write for info. (*0-8151-5953-6*, Yr Bk Med Pubs) Mosby Yr Bk.

Color Atlas of Basic Histology. Irwin Berman. (Illus.). 336p. (C). 1993. pap. text ed. 36.00 (*0-8385-0445-0*, A0445-5) Appleton & Lange.

Color Atlas of Bone & Joint Disease in the Elderly. Chakravorty. 160p. Date not set. 60.00 (*0-8151-1613-6*, Yr Bk Med Pubs) Mosby Yr Bk.

Color Atlas of Bone Marrow Transplantation. Treleaven. 240p. 1993. 85.00 (*0-8151-8848-X*, Yr Bk Med Pubs) Mosby Yr Bk.

Color Atlas of Brain Disorders in the Newborn. Devries. (Illus.). 1990. 99.95 (*0-8151-2964-5*, Yr Bk Med Pubs) Mosby Yr Bk.

Color Atlas of Breast Diseases. Mansel. 128p. 1993. 49.50 (*0-8151-5756-8*, Yr Bk Med Pubs) Mosby Yr Bk.

***Color Atlas of Breast Diseases.** Robert E. Mansel & Nigel J. Bundred. LC 94-44123. (Illus.). (J). 1994. 45.00 (*0-7234-1721-0*, Yr Bk Med Pubs) Mosby Yr Bk.

Color Atlas of Breast Histopathology. M. Trojani. (Illus.). 223p. 1991. text ed. 165.00 (*0-397-58319-2*) Lippincott.

Color Atlas of Cancer Cytology. 2nd ed. Masayoshi Takahashi. LC 80-85297. (Illus.). 580p. 1981. 160.00 (*0-89640-050-6*) Igaku-Shoin.

Color Atlas of Ceramo-Metal Technology, Vol. 1. Masahiro Kuwata. Ed. by Monika E. Strong. (Illus.). 330p. 1986. 95.00 (*0-912791-12-8*) Ishiyaku Euro.

Color Atlas of Child Sexual Abuse. Chadwick. 176p. 1989. pap. 37.00 (*0-8151-1605-5*, Yr Bk Med Pubs) Mosby Yr Bk.

Color Atlas of Childbirth & Obstetric Techniques. Al-Azzawi. 144p. 1991. pap. 45.00 (*0-8016-6287-7*) Mosby Yr Bk.

Color Atlas of Clinical Embryology. Keith L. Moore et al. LC 93-26435. 1994. text ed. 93.50 (*0-7216-4663-8*) Saunders.

Color Atlas of Clinical Gonioscopy. Alward. 1993. 65.00 (*0-8151-0112-0*, Yr Bk Med Pubs) Mosby Yr Bk.

Color Atlas of Clinical Gynecology. V. R. Tindall. (Illus.). 131p. 1981. 79.95 (*0-8151-8204-X*, GI-1, Yr Bk Med Pubs) Mosby Yr Bk.

Color Atlas of Clinical Hematology. Bong H. Hyun et al. LC 84-25275. (Illus.). 285p. 1986. 120.00 (*0-89640-110-3*) Igaku-Shoin.

Color Atlas of Clinical Medicine. Forbes. (SPA.). 1993. 153.70 (*84-8086-068-5*) Mosby Yr Bk.

Color Atlas of Clinical Medicine. Charles D. Forbes. LC 92-8667. 528p. 1992. 39.95 (*0-8151-3271-9*) Mosby Yr Bk.

Color Atlas of Clinical Neurology. 2nd ed. Malcolm Parsons. (Illus.). 320p. 1992. 95.00 (*0-8151-6613-3*) Mosby Yr Bk.

Color Atlas of Clinical Operative Dentistry: Crowns & Bridges. Grundy. 192p. 1992. 65.00 (*0-8151-3622-6*) Mosby Yr Bk.

Color Atlas of Clinical Oral Pathology. Brad W. Neville et al. LC 89-13980. (Illus.). 385p. 1991. text ed. 99.50 (*0-8121-1311-X*) Williams & Wilkins.

Color Atlas of Colposcopy. Hanskurt Bauer. (Illus.). 221p. 1990. 98.50 (*0-89640-182-0*) Igaku-Shoin.

Color Atlas of Common Oral Diseases. Robert P. Langlais & Craig S. Miller. LC 89-12561. (Illus.). 182p. 1992. text ed. 36.95 (*0-8121-1249-0*) Williams & Wilkins.

Color Atlas of Comparative Veterinary Hematology: Normal & Abnormal Blood Cells in Mammals, Birds & Reptiles. C. M. Hawkey et al. (Illus.). 192p. 1989. text ed. 97.95 (*0-8138-0449-3*) Iowa St U Pr.

Color Atlas of Complete Dentures. John A. Hobkirk. (Illus.). 1991. write for info. (*0-8151-4475-X*, Yr Bk Med Pubs) Mosby Yr Bk.

Color Atlas of Congenital Heart Disease. Shapiro & Warnes. (SPA.). 1991. 46.65 (*0-7234-1766-0*, Wolfe Pub) Mosby Yr Bk.

Color Atlas of Congenital Heart Surgery. Litwin. 1994. 195.00 (*0-8151-5511-5*, Yr Bk Med Pubs) Mosby Yr Bk.

Color Atlas of Contact Lenses & Prosthetics, No. 2. Ruben. (Illus.). 1992. 59.10 (*0-7234-1761-X*) Mosby Yr Bk.

Color Atlas of Corneal Dystrophies & Degenerations. Casey. 126p. 1991. 82.00 (*0-8151-1445-1*) Mosby Yr Bk.

Color Atlas of Corneal Topography: Interpreting Videokeratography. Yaron S. Rabinowitz et al. LC 93-208. (Illus.). 96p. 1993. 125.00 (*0-89640-235-5*) Igaku-Shoin.

Color Atlas of CO2 Laser Surgical Techniques. Rochester General Hospital Laser Group Staff. Ed. by Raymond Lanzafame. (Illus.). 300p. 1988. 145.00 (*0-912791-34-9*) Ishiyaku Euro.

Color Atlas of Cutaneous Disorders of the Lower Extremities. Joseph A. Witkowski & Harvey Lemont. LC 92-48718. (Illus.). 144p. 1993. 98.50 (*0-89640-233-9*) Igaku-Shoin.

***Color Atlas of Cutaneous Infections.** Lawrence Charles Parish et al. 1995. write for info. (*0-86542-435-7*) Blackwell Sci.

Color Atlas of Dangerous Marine Animals. Halstead. 1990. 62.95 (*0-8493-7139-2*, QH) CRC Pr.

Color Atlas of Dental Medicine Two: Removable Partial Dentures. George Graber. (Illus.). 216p. 1988. 149.00 (*0-86577-276-2*) Thieme Med Pubs.

Color Atlas of Dermatology. Jeffrey P. Callen et al. (Illus.). 368p. 1993. text ed. 155.00 (*0-7216-3756-6*) Saunders.

Color Atlas of Dermatology. G. M. Levene & D. C. Calnan. (Year Book Color Atlas Ser.). (Illus.). 368p. 1985. reprint ed. 51.95 (*0-8151-1441-9*, CLP-1, Yr Bk Med Pubs) Mosby Yr Bk.

Color Atlas of Diabetes. 2nd ed. Bloom. (Illus.). 145p. 1991. 59.95 (*0-8151-0943-1*, Yr Bk Med Pubs) Mosby Yr Bk.

Color Atlas of Diabetes. 2nd ed. Bloom. (Illus.). 145p. 1991. 59.95 (*0-8151-0944-X*) Mosby Yr Bk.

Color Atlas of Diagnostic & Experimental Hematology. Smith. 184p. 1993. 85.00 (*0-8151-7848-4*, Yr Bk Med Pubs) Mosby Yr Bk.

Color Atlas of Diagnostic Histopathology. Howard C. Tseng. 352p. 1986. 186.00 (*0-8493-6438-8*, RB33, CRC Reprint) Franklin.

Color Atlas of Diagnostic Histopathology of Dog. Yager. 1993. 95.00 (*0-8151-9752-7*, Yr Bk Med Pubs) Mosby Yr Bk.

Color Atlas of Diagnostic Laparascopy. Harald Henning, Jr. et al. Tr. by Cedric Morris. LC 93-37719. (Illus.). 1994. 169.00 (*0-86577-289-4*) Thieme Med Pubs.

Color Atlas of Difficult Diagnoses in Dermatology. Lawrence C. Parish et al. LC 92-1573. (Illus.). 184p. 1993. 135.00 (*0-89640-226-6*) Igaku-Shoin.

Color Atlas of Diseases & Disorders in the Horse. Knottenbelt. 224p. 1993. 75.00 (*0-8151-5117-9*, Yr Bk Med Pubs) Mosby Yr Bk.

Color Atlas of Diseases & Disorders of Cattle. R. W. Blowey & A. D. Weaver. LC 90-85771. (Illus.). 224p. (C). 1991. text ed. 89.95 (*0-8138-0487-6*) Iowa St U Pr.

Color Atlas of Diseases & Disorders of Sheep. Linklater. 304p. 1993. 89.00 (*0-8151-5438-0*, Yr Bk Med Pubs) Mosby Yr Bk.

Color Atlas of Diseases & Disorders of the Domestic Fowl & Turkey. 2nd ed. C. J. Randall. LC 90-85707. (Illus.). 176p. (C). 1991. text ed. 79.95 (*0-8138-0376-4*) Iowa St U Pr.

Color Atlas of Diseases & Disorders of the Horse. Derek C. Knottenbelt & Reg R. Pascoe. LC 93-2092. 1994. write for info. (*0-7234-1702-4*) Mosby Yr Bk.

Color Atlas of Diseases & Disorders of the Pig. W. J. Smith et al. LC 89-81873. (Illus.). 192p. (C). 1990. 87.95 (*0-8138-0069-2*) Iowa St U Pr.

Color Atlas of Ear, Nose, & Throat Diagnosis. 2nd ed. T. R. Bull. (Illus.). 368p. 1987. pap. text ed. 45.95 (*0-8151-1317-X*, Yr Bk Med Pubs) Mosby Yr Bk.

Color Atlas of Emergencies. 2nd ed. Mills. 1993. 99.95 (*0-8151-5912-9*, Yr Bk Med Pubs) Mosby Yr Bk.

Color Atlas of Endocrinology. 2nd ed. Hall. (Illus.). 1990. 95.00 (*0-8151-4249-8*, Yr Bk Med Pubs) Mosby Yr Bk.

Color Atlas of Endocrinology: Spanish Edition. 2nd ed. Hall. (SPA.). 1992. 87.50 (*0-7234-1780-6*) Mosby Yr Bk.

Color Atlas of Endoscopic Diagnosis in Early Stage Lung Cancer. Harubumikato. 176p. 1992. 145.00 (*0-8151-4982-4*) Mosby Yr Bk.

Color Atlas of Endovascular Surgery: Interventional Techniques in Vascular Disease. White. (Illus.). 157p. 1990. text ed. 140.00 (*0-397-58328-1*) Lippincott.

C

An Asterisk (*) at the beginning of an entry indicates that the title is appearing in BIP for the first time. 1385

Color Atlas of ENT Diagnosis. Bull. (SPA.). 1991. 27.00 (*0-7234-1737-7*) Mosby Yr Bk.

Color Atlas of ENT Diagnosis. Bull. 1989. 175.00 (*0-7234-1506-4*) Wolfe Pub.

Color Atlas of Eruption of Permanent Teeth. Sadakatsu Sato & P. Parsons. (Illus.). 100p. 1990. 50.00 (*0-912791-44-6*) Ishiyaku Euro.

*__Color Atlas of Fetal Cardiology.__ L. D. Allan et al. LC 94-46128. 1994. 100.00 (*0-7234-1698-2*) Mosby Yr Bk.

Color Atlas of Fiberoptic Bronchoscopy. Ed. by Satoshi Kitamura. (Illus.). 282p. 1990. 128.00 (*0-8151-5141-1*, Yr Bk Med Pubs) Mosby Yr Bk.

Color Atlas of Fiberoptic Endoscopy of the Upper Respiratory Tract. John D. Shaw. (Illus.). 96p. 1987. text ed. 76.00 (*0-8151-7720-8*, Yr Bk Med Pubs) Mosby Yr Bk.

Color Atlas of Flourescein Angiography. Harney. 160p. 1993. 85.00 (*0-8151-4155-6*, Yr Bk Med Pubs) Mosby Yr Bk.

Color Atlas of Foot & Ankle Anatomy. R. M. McMinn et al. (Illus.). 96p. 1982. 54.95 (*0-8151-5829-7*, GZF-1, Yr Bk Med Pubs) Mosby Yr Bk.

Color Atlas of Foot Conditions. Zatouroff. (Illus.). 264p. 1991. 80.00 (*0-8151-9878-7*, Yr Bk Med Pubs) Mosby Yr Bk.

Color Atlas of Foot Disorders. Jose R. Luces. (Illus.). 152p. 1990. Monograph. 149.00 (*0-87993-369-0*) Futura Pub.

Color Atlas of Forefoot Surgery. Roger Butterworth. (Illus.). 264p. 1992. 99.00 (*0-8151-1387-0*) Mosby Yr Bk.

Color Atlas of Gastric Fundoplication. Cumming. (Single Surgical Procedure Ser.: No. 46). (Illus.). 1988. 56.95 (*0-8151-9081-6*, Yr Bk Med Pubs) Mosby Yr Bk.

Color Atlas of Gastrointestinal Pathology. Morson. 300p. 1988. text ed. 205.00 (*0-7216-2607-6*) Saunders.

Color Atlas of Gastrointestinal Surgery, 2 vols., Set. C. Cordiano & G. L. Nardi. 896p. 1989. text ed. 480.00 (*1-57235-039-3*) Piccin NY.

Color Atlas of General Pathology. 2nd ed. Gresham. 1992. write for info. (*0-8151-3989-6*) Mosby Yr Bk.

Color Atlas of General Surgical Diagnosis. William F. Walker. (Year Book Color Atlas Ser.). (Illus.). 1976. 71.50 (*0-8151-9086-7*, Yr Bk Med Pubs) Mosby Yr Bk.

Color Atlas of Geriatric Medicine. 2nd ed. Kamal Asif. (Illus.). 224p. 1991. 65.00 (*0-8151-0325-5*) Mosby Yr Bk.

C

Color Atlas of Gross Placental Pathology. Cynthia G. Kaplan. LC 93-33096. (Illus.). 128p. 1994. 99.50 (*0-89640-249-5*) Igaku-Shoin.

Color Atlas of Gynecologic Cytology. Husain. 1989. 82.00 (*0-8151-4732-5*, Yr Bk Med Pubs) Mosby Yr Bk.

Color Atlas of Gynecological Surgery Vol. 3: Operations for Malignant Diseases. David H. Lees & Albert Singer. (Illus.). 1979. 117.00 (*0-8151-5353-8*, Yr Bk Med Pubs) Mosby Yr Bk.

Color Atlas of Gynecological Surgery Vol. 4: Surgery of Vulva & Lower Genital Tract. David H. Lees & Albert Singer. (Illus.). 1980. 116.50 (*0-8151-5354-6*, Yr Bk Med Pubs) Mosby Yr Bk.

Color Atlas of Gynecological Surgery Vol. 6: Surgical Conditions Complicating Pregnancy. David H. Lees & Albert Singer. (Illus.). 1983. 117.00 (*0-8151-5356-2*, Yr Bk Med Pubs) Mosby Yr Bk.

Color Atlas of Hair & Nail Diagnosis. Levene. (Illus.). 1991. write for info. (*0-8151-5437-2*, Yr Bk Med Pubs) Mosby Yr Bk.

*__Color Atlas of Hair Restoration Surgery.__ Swinehart. (C). 1995. text ed. 125.00 (*0-8385-3567-4*) Appleton & Lange.

Color Atlas of Head & Neck Anatomy. R. M. McMinn. (Illus.). 240p. 1981. 69.95 (*0-8151-5826-2*, BKW-1, Yr Bk Med Pubs) Mosby Yr Bk.

Color Atlas of Head & Neck Surgery, Vol. 1. Shah. (Illus.). 1991. write for info. (*0-8151-7723-2*, Yr Bk Med Pubs) Mosby Yr Bk.

Color Atlas of Heart Disease: Pathological, Clinical & Investigatory Features. Sutton & Fox. (Illus.). 276p. 1990. text ed. 89.50 (*0-397-58318-4*) Lippincott.

Color Atlas of Hematological Cytology. 3rd ed. Hayhoe & Flemans. 384p. 1992. 125.00 (*0-8151-4218-8*) Mosby Yr Bk.

Color Atlas of Hematology: Atlas de Hematologia en Color. W. R. Platt. 645p. 1982. 175.00 (*0-8288-1873-8*) Fr & Eur.

Color Atlas of Histology. Erlandsen. (SPA.). 1993. 69.55 (*84-8086-059-6*) Mosby Yr Bk.

Color Atlas of Histology. Stanley L. Erlandsen & Magney. 196p. 1991. spiral bd. 35.95 (*0-8016-1560-7*) Mosby Yr Bk.

*__Color Atlas of Histology.__ Strete. (Illus.). (C). 1995. text ed. write for info. (*0-673-99190-3*) HarpCollege.

Color Atlas of Histology. 2nd ed. M. B. L. Craigmyle. (Illus.). 300p. 1986. 45.95 (*0-8151-1889-9*, CQ-2, Yr Bk Med Pubs) Mosby Yr Bk.

Color Atlas of Histology. 2nd ed. Leslie Gartner & James L. Hiatt. (Illus.). 400p. 1994. 38.00 (*0-683-03428-6*) Williams & Wilkins.

Color Atlas of Histology: International Student Edition. Erlandsen. 1991. 18.50 (*0-8016-6884-0*) Mosby Yr Bk.

Color Atlas of Histopathology. Ivan Damjanov. 300p. 1994. write for info. (*0-683-02334-9*) Williams & Wilkins.

Color Atlas of Histopathology. 2nd ed. Gresham. 160p. 1992. 34.95 (*0-685-65365-X*, Yr Bk Med Pubs) Mosby Yr Bk.

Color Atlas of Histopathology. 3rd ed. R. C. Curran. 300p. 1994. pap. 35.00 (*0-19-261794-X*) OUP.

Color Atlas of Histopathology of the Skin. Gundula Schaumburg-Lever & Walter F. Lever. LC 65-9970. (Illus.). 320p. 1988. text ed. 165.00 (*0-397-50832-8*, Lippincott Medical) Lippincott.

Color Atlas of Human Anatomy. Thompson. 1993. write for info. (*0-8016-7772-6*) Mosby Yr Bk.

Color Atlas of Human Anatomy. Ed. by Vanio Vannini & Giuliano Pogliani. 112p. 1981. 12.00 (*0-517-54514-4*, Harmony) Crown Pub Group.

Color Atlas of Human Anatomy. 2nd ed. McMinn & R. T. Hutchings. (Illus.). 352p. 1988. 53.95 (*0-8151-5854-8*, AJ-2, Yr Bk Med Pubs); pap. 37.95 (*0-8151-5855-6*, AJP-2, Yr Bk Med Pubs) Mosby Yr Bk.

Color Atlas of Human Dissection. 2nd ed. C. C. Chumbley. (Illus.). 192p. 1992. pap. 29.95 (*0-8151-1661-6*) Mosby Yr Bk.

Color Atlas of Human Form & Function. McMinn. Date not set. write for info. (*0-8151-5853-X*, Yr Bk Med Pubs) Mosby Yr Bk.

Color Atlas of Hypertension. 2nd ed. Leonard M. Shapiro. 159p. 1991. 49.95 (*0-8151-7663-5*) Mosby Yr Bk.

Color Atlas of Hypertension: Spanish Edition. 2nd ed. Shapiro & Fox. (SPA.). 1992. 57.25 (*0-7234-1758-X*) Mosby Yr Bk.

Color Atlas of Infectious & Inflammatory Diseases of the External Eye. H. Bruce Ostler et al. LC 86-15941. (Illus.). 166p. 1987. 145.00 (*0-683-06650-1*) Williams & Wilkins.

Color Atlas of Infectious Diseases. Emond. (SPA.). 1992. 32.70 (*0-7234-1736-9*) Mosby Yr Bk.

Color Atlas of Infectious Diseases. R. T. Emond. (Year Book Color Atlas Ser.). (Illus.). 384p. 1984. 47.95 (*0-8151-3118-6*, Yr Bk Med Pubs); pap. 36.75 (*0-8151-3121-6*, Yr Bk Med Pubs) Mosby Yr Bk.

Color Atlas of Infectious Diseases. Ronald T. Emond. (Illus.). 400p. 1987. pap. 45.95 (*0-8151-3122-4*, Yr Bk Med Pubs) Mosby Yr Bk.

Color Atlas of Inherited Connective Tissue Disease. Pope. 1994. 80.00 (*0-8151-6731-8*, Yr Bk Med Pubs) Mosby Yr Bk.

Color Atlas of Injury in Sport. 2nd ed. J. G. Williams. (Illus.). 216p. 1990. 80.00 (*0-8151-9338-6*, Yr Bk Med Pubs) Mosby Yr Bk.

Color Atlas of Intestinal Parasites. 2nd ed. Francis M. Spencer & Lee S. Monroe. (Illus.). 176p. (C). 1982. 52.95 (*0-398-04557-7*) C C Thomas.

Color Atlas of Laparoscopic Surgery. Friedrich Goetz et al. Ed. by A. Pier et al. LC 92-49502. (Illus.). 100p. 1992. text ed. 67.00 (*0-86577-470-6*) Thieme Med Pubs.

Color Atlas of Lens Implantation. Percival. 1991. 145.00 (*0-8151-6664-8*, Yr Bk Med Pubs) Mosby Yr Bk.

Color Atlas of Life Before Birth. England. 528p. 1990. pap. 36.95 (*0-8151-3074-0*, Yr Bk Med Pubs) Mosby Yr Bk.

Color Atlas of Life Before Birth. England. (SPA.). 1991. 56.00 (*0-7234-1722-9*, Wolfe Pub) Mosby Yr Bk.

Color Atlas of Life Before Birth: Normal Fetal Development. Marjorie A. England. (Illus.). 224p. 1983. 61.95 (*0-8151-3119-4*, FUL-1, Yr Bk Med Pubs) Mosby Yr Bk.

Color Atlas of Liver Disease. Sherlock. 248p. 1991. 89.00 (*0-8151-7658-9*) Mosby Yr Bk.

Color Atlas of Liver Disease: Spanish Edition. 2nd ed. Sherlock. (SPA.). 1992. 73.65 (*0-7234-1782-2*) Mosby Yr Bk.

Color Atlas of Liver Pathology. R. S. Patrick. (Oxford Color Atlases of Pathology Ser.). (Illus.). 1983. 85.00 (*0-19-921033-0*) OUP.

Color Atlas of Livestock Breeds. Sambereus. 272p. 1992. 35.00 (*0-8151-7533-7*, Yr Bk Med Pubs) Mosby Yr Bk.

Color Atlas of Low Back Pain. Kenneth Mills et al. (Illus.). 92p. 1990. text ed. 39.00 (*0-8036-9858-5*) Davis Co.

Color Atlas of Mammaplasty. P. McKissock. Ed. by J. M. Goin. (Operative Techniques in Plastic Surgery Ser.). (Illus.). 144p. 1991. text ed. 99.00 (*0-86577-385-8*) Thieme Med Pubs.

*__Color Atlas of Micromycetes.__ W. Juelich. (Illus.). 1994. 85.00 (*3-437-30726-6*) Lubrecht & Cramer.

Color Atlas of Microneurosurgery: Intracranial Tumors, Vol. 1. 2nd enl. rev. ed. Wolfgang T. Koos et al. LC 93-20014. (Illus.). 704p. 1993. text ed. 330.00 (*0-86577-477-3*) Thieme Med Pubs.

Color Atlas of Microscopic Anatomy. P. Motta. 268p. 1990. text ed. 40.00 (*1-57235-011-3*) Piccin NY.

Color Atlas of Microsurgery. Sun Lee et al. Ed. by Gregory Hacke. LC 92-56746. (Illus.). 388p. 1993. text ed. 145.00 (*0-912791-64-0*); pap. 120.00 (*0-685-70856-X*) Ishiyaku Euro.

Color Atlas of Microsurgery. Sun Lee. 385p. 1993. 145.00 (*0-318-72976-8*, D7066) PennWell Bks.

Color Atlas of Multiple Sclerosis. Adams. (Illus.). 1991. write for info. (*0-8151-0095-7*, Yr Bk Med Pubs) Mosby Yr Bk.

Color Atlas of Muscle Disorders in Childhood. Dubowitz. 1989. 94.95 (*0-8151-2967-X*, Yr Bk Med Pubs) Mosby Yr Bk.

Color Atlas of Muscle Disorders in Childhood: Spanish Edition. Dubowitz. (SPA.). 1992. 60.45 (*0-7234-1759-8*) Mosby Yr Bk.

Color Atlas of Muscle Histochemistry. Roger A. Brumback & Richard Leech. (Illus.). 118p. 1984. 79.95 (*0-88416-493-4*, Yr Bk Med Pubs) Mosby Yr Bk.

*__Color Atlas of Muscle Pathology.__ W. J. Cumming. LC 94-42133. (Illus.). 1995. 120.00 (*0-7234-2016-3*) Wolfe Pub.

Color Atlas of Nails. Beaven. 1990. pap. 45.95 (*0-7234-1532-3*) Mosby Yr Bk.

Color Atlas of Neoplastic & Non-Neoplastic Lesions in Aging Mice. C. H. Frith & J. M. Ward. 154p. 1988. 115.50 (*0-444-42850-X*) Elsevier.

Color Atlas of Neuropathology. C. S. Treip. (Illus.). 208p. 1978. 99.95 (*0-8151-8841-2*, NQ-1, Yr Bk Med Pubs) Mosby Yr Bk.

Color Atlas of Neuropathology. R. O. Weller. (Oxford Color Atlases of Pathology Ser.). (Illus.). 207p. 1984. 85.00 (*0-19-921044-6*) OUP.

Color Atlas of Neuropathology. 2nd ed. Graham. 1995. 79.50 (*0-8151-3855-5*, Yr Bk Med Pubs) Mosby Yr Bk.

Color Atlas of Obesity. Jung. (Illus.). 1991. 76.95 (*0-8016-6296-6*) Mosby Yr Bk.

*__Color Atlas of Obstetrics & Gynecology.__ E. Malcolm Symonds & Marion M. Macpherson. LC 94-43602. 1994. 67.50 (*0-7234-1589-7*) Wolfe Pub.

Color Atlas of Occlusion & Malocclusion. Howat. (SPA.). 1992. 65.45 (*0-7234-1764-4*) Mosby Yr Bk.

*__Color Atlas of Ocular Manifestations of AIDS: Diagnosis & Management.__ Juan Orellana et al. LC 94-33155. 105p. 1995. 98.50 (*0-89640-273-8*) Igaku-Shoin.

Color Atlas of Operative Gynecologic Laparoscopy. Peter Dottino & T. Jennings. 1995. write for info. (*0-318-72288-7*) Igaku-Shoin.

Color Atlas of Ophthalmic Surgery, 6 vols., Set. Ed. by Kenneth W. Wright. (Illus.). 1991. 499.00 (*0-397-51021-7*) Lippincott.

Color Atlas of Ophthalmological Diagnosis. 2nd ed. Ed. by Michael Bedford. (Illus.). 184p. 1986. 54.95 (*0-8151-0622-X*, OH-2, Yr Bk Med Pubs) Mosby Yr Bk.

Color Atlas of Oral Disease in Children. Scully. (Illus.). 160p. 1994. 59.95 (*0-8151-7589-2*, Yr Bk Med Pubs) Mosby Yr Bk.

Color Atlas of Oral Diseases. Crispian Scully & Flint. (Illus.). 256p. 1989. text ed. 99.00 (*0-397-58310-9*) Lippincott.

*__Color Atlas of Oral Diseases.__ 2nd ed. George Laskaris. LC 94-9767. (Illus.). 400p. Date not set. 99.00 (*0-614-02693-8*) Thieme Med Pubs.

Color Atlas of Oral Manifestations of AIDS. Silverman. 113p. 1990. 39.95 (*1-55664-199-0*) Mosby Yr Bk.

Color Atlas of Oral Pathology. Crispian Scully. 137p. 1994. 49.95 (*0-8151-7590-6*, Yr Bk Med Pubs) Mosby Yr Bk.

Color Atlas of Oral Pathology. G. Ishikawa. Ed. by James R. Newland & Charles A. Waldron. Tr. by C. Rosa Wen. 193p. 1987. 47.50 (*0-912791-25-X*) Ishiyaku Euro.

Color Atlas of Oro-Facial Diseases. Tyldesley. (Illus.). 286p. 1988. 35.95 (*0-8151-4999-9*, OF-2, Yr Bk Med Pubs) Mosby Yr Bk.

Color Atlas of Orthognathic Surgery: The Surgery of Facial Skeletal Deformity. Derek Henderson. (Illus.). 336p. 1986. 249.00 (*0-8151-4252-8*, CAO-1, Yr Bk Med Pubs) Mosby Yr Bk.

Color Atlas of Osteochondrosis in the Dog. Carmichael. (Illus.). 1993. write for info. (*0-8151-1438-9*) Mosby Yr Bk.

Color Atlas of Osteoporosis. Aloia. 1993. 85.00 (*0-8151-0107-4*, Yr Bk Med Pubs) Mosby Yr Bk.

Color Atlas of Otorhinolaryngology. Bruce Benjamin et al. (Illus.). 352p. 1994. 195.00 (*0-397-51422-0*) Lippincott.

Color Atlas of Paediatric Haematology. 2nd ed. Ian M. Hann et al. (Illus.). 168p. 1990. 125.00 (*0-19-261893-8*) OUP.

Color Atlas of Pathology of the Nervous System. 2nd ed. Asao Hirano et al. LC 88-12812. (Illus.). 248p. 1988. 165.00 (*0-89640-148-0*) Igaku-Shoin.

Color Atlas of Pediatric Dermatology. 2nd ed. Samuel Weinberg & Neil S. Prose. 264p. 1990. text ed. 72.00 (*0-07-069089-8*) Hlth Prof Div.

Color Atlas of Pediatric Diseases. 2nd ed. Simon Janner. 400p. 1990. 99.50 (*1-55664-201-6*) Mosby Yr Bk.

Color Atlas of Pediatric Emergencies. Beattie. 160p. 1993. 65.00 (*0-8151-0550-9*, Yr Bk Med Pubs) Mosby Yr Bk.

Color Atlas of Pediatric Infectious Disease. C. A. Hart. 208p. 1992. 62.00 (*0-8151-4143-2*) Mosby Yr Bk.

*__Color Atlas of Pediatric Neurology.__ Ed. by Richard W. Newton. LC 94-42132. (Illus.). 1994. 72.00 (*0-7234-1879-9*) Mosby Yr Bk.

Color Atlas of Pediatric Rheumatology. Ansell. (Illus.). 208p. 1991. 92.00 (*0-8151-0221-6*) Mosby Yr Bk.

Color Atlas of Pediatrics. Martha Dynski-Klein. (Illus.). 416p. 1986. 55.95 (*0-7234-0924-2*, DVP-1, Yr Bk Med Pubs) Mosby Yr Bk.

Color Atlas of Periodontics. Shiro Kinoshita & Rosa Wen. (Illus.). 404p. 1985. 157.50 (*0-912791-16-0*) Ishiyaku Euro.

Color Atlas of Periodontology. Ian M. Waite. (Illus.). 184p. 1990. 70.00 (*0-8151-8140-X*, AGP-2, Yr Bk Med Pubs) Mosby Yr Bk.

Color Atlas of Periodontology. 2nd rev. ed. K. Rateitschak et al. Tr. by Thomas Hassell. (Dental Medicine Ser.). (Illus.). 400p. 1989. text ed. 159.00 (*0-86577-318-1*) Thieme Med Pubs.

Color Atlas of Peripheral Vascular Diseases. William F. Walker. (Illus.). 112p. 1980. 89.95 (*0-8151-9083-2*, ACV-1, Yr Bk Med Pubs) Mosby Yr Bk.

*__Color Atlas of Pests of Ornamental Trees, Shrubs & Flowers.__ David V. Alford. LC 94-46507. 1995. text ed. 84.95 (*0-470-23494-6*) Halsted Pr.

Color Atlas of Physical Signs in Dermatology. Lawrence. 192p. 1993. 75.00 (*0-8151-5333-3*, Yr Bk Med Pubs) Mosby Yr Bk.

Color Atlas of Physical Signs in General Medicine. M. A. Zatouroff. (Year Book Color Atlas Ser.). (Illus.). 464p. 1985. 39.95 (*0-8151-9856-6*, ZG-1, Yr Bk Med Pubs); sl. 445.50 (*0-685-05478-0*, Yr Bk Med Pubs) Mosby Yr Bk.

Color Atlas of Physical Signs in General Medicine: Spanish Edition. Zatouroff. (SPA.). 1991. 36.00 (*0-7234-1752-0*) Mosby Yr Bk.

Color Atlas of Physiology. 4th rev. ed. A. Despopoulos & S. Silbernagl. Tr. by Joy Wieser. (Flexibook Ser.). (Illus.). 369p. 1991. pap. 27.00 (*0-86577-382-3*) Thieme Med Pubs.

Color Atlas of Porcelain Laminate Veneers. G. Freedman & G. L. McLaughlin. (Illus.). 250p. 1990. 99.00 (*0-912791-52-7*) Ishiyaku Euro.

Color Atlas of Preprosthetic Oral Surgery. Russell Hopkins. (Illus.). 193p. 1987. text ed. 85.00 (*0-8121-1097-8*) Williams & Wilkins.

Color Atlas of Pulmonary Cytopathology. Jennifer A. Young. (Oxford Color Atlases of Pathology Ser.). (Illus.). 1986. 95.00 (*0-19-921045-4*) OUP.

Color Atlas of Radical Hysterectomy with Pelvic Lymph Node Dissection. Ed. by Heung-Tat Ng. (Illus.). 120p. (C). 1993. 150.00 (*1-899015-01-9*, Pub. by Euromed Communs UK) St Mut.

Color Atlas of Reducing Operations for Lymphedema of the Lower Limb, Vol. 39. Ed. by Norman Browse. (Single Surgical Procedure Ser.). (Illus.). 78p. 1986. 43.50 (*0-8151-1288-2*, RAL-1, Yr Bk Med Pubs) Mosby Yr Bk.

Color Atlas of Removable Partial Dentures. Davenport. 1988. pap. 55.00 (*0-7234-1620-6*) Mosby Yr Bk.

Color Atlas of Renal Diseases. 2nd ed. Williams. 160p. 1994. 75.00 (*0-8151-9337-8*, Yr Bk Med Pubs) Mosby Yr Bk.

Color Atlas of Respiratory Disease. James. (Illus.). (SPA.). 1993. 66.00 (*0-7234-1756-3*) Mosby Yr Bk.

Color Atlas of Respiratory Disease. 2nd ed. James. (Illus.). 366p. 1992. 99.00 (*0-7234-1695-8*) Mosby Yr Bk.

Color Atlas of Rheumatology. 3rd ed. Michael Shipley. 176p. 1992. 35.00 (*0-8151-7660-0*) Mosby Yr Bk.

Color Atlas of Rocks & Minerals in Thin Section. W. S. MacKenzie & A. E. Adams. LC 93-6167. (Illus.). 1994. pap. text ed. 29.95 (*0-470-23338-9*) Wiley.

Color Atlas of Scleritis. Watson. Date not set. 70.00 (*0-8151-9185-5*, Yr Bk Med Pubs) Mosby Yr Bk.

Color Atlas of Sexually Transmitted Diseases. Lawrence Parish et al. LC 90-5080. (Illus.). 184p. 1991. 110.00 (*0-89640-192-8*) Igaku-Shoin.

Color Atlas of Sexually Transmitted Diseases. Wisdom. (Illus.). 1989. 46.95 (*0-8151-9241-X*, Yr Bk Med Pubs) Mosby Yr Bk.

Color Atlas of Sexually Transmitted Diseases: Spanish Edition. Wisdom. 1992. 36.80 (*0-7234-1783-0*) Mosby Yr Bk.

*__Color Atlas of Skin Diseases.__ Goh C. Leok & Tham S. Nee. (Illus.). 300p. 1995. pap. text ed. write for info. (*0-07-113839-0*) Hlth Prof Div.

Color Atlas of Small Animal Applied Anatomy. J. S. Boyd. (Illus.). 190p. 1991. 65.00 (*0-8151-1105-3*) Mosby Yr Bk.

Color Atlas of Small Animal Dermatology. Kummel. 288p. 1989. 89.00 (*0-8016-2910-1*) Mosby Yr Bk.

Color Atlas of Small Animal Dermatology: A Guide to Diagnosis. 2nd ed. George T. Wilkinson & Richard G. Harvey. LC 93-2093. 1994. write for info. (*0-7234-1898-5*) Mosby Yr Bk.

Color Atlas of Small Animal Endoscopy. Brearly. 128p. 1991. 75.00 (*0-8151-1195-9*, Yr Bk Med Pubs) Mosby Yr Bk.

Color Atlas of SMAS Rhytidectomy. Ed. by J. Goin & M. Lemmon. LC 93-8232. (Operative Techniques in Plastic Surgery Ser.). (Illus.). 148p. 1993. text ed. 95.00 (*0-86577-485-4*) Thieme Med Pubs.

Color Atlas of Surface Anatomy: Clinical & Applied. Kenneth M. Backhouse & Ralph Hutchings. (Illus.). 312p. (C). 1986. pap. text ed. 33.00 (*0-683-00307-0*) Williams & Wilkins.

Color Atlas of Surgery for the Removal of Melanoma, Vol. 40. McCarthy. (Illus.). 1991. write for info. (*0-8151-5859-9*, Yr Bk Med Pubs) Mosby Yr Bk.

Color Atlas of Surgery of Faecal Incontinence, Vol. 32. Henry. 1988. 49.95 (*0-8151-4281-1*, Yr Bk Med Pubs) Mosby Yr Bk.

Color Atlas of Surgical Anatomy for Esophageal Cancer. Ed. by T. Sato & T. Iizuka. LC 92-49824. (Illus.). 1993. 225.00 (*0-387-70100-1*) Spr-Verlag.

Color Atlas of Temporal Bone Surgical Anatomy. Richard T. Counter. (Illus.). 77p. 1980. 69.95 (*0-8151-1869-4*, CQX-1, Yr Bk Med Pubs) Mosby Yr Bk.

Color Atlas of the Brain & Spinal Cord. England. (Illus.). 288p. 1991. pap. 42.95 (*0-8151-3068-6*, Yr Bk Med Pubs) Mosby Yr Bk.

Color Atlas of the Brain & Spinal Cord. England. (SPA.). 1992. 55.60 (*0-7234-1755-5*) Mosby Yr Bk.

Color Atlas of the Brain & Spinal Cord. England. 288p. 1991. boxed 65.00 (*0-8016-6288-5*) Mosby Yr Bk.

Color Atlas of the Digestive System. Pounder. 1989. 75.95 (*0-8151-6789-X*, Yr Bk Med Pubs) Mosby Yr Bk.

Color Atlas of the Eye & Systemic Disease. Kritzinger & Barry E. Wright. (Illus.). 128p. 1984. 49.95 (*0-8151-5171-3*, QLP-1, Yr Bk Med Pubs) Mosby Yr Bk.

Color Atlas of the Hair, Scalp & Nails. Baran. (Illus.). 192p. 1991. 65.00 (*0-8151-0417-0*) Mosby Yr Bk.

Color Atlas of the Horse's Foot. Pollitt. Date not set. 95.00 (*0-8151-6743-1*, Yr Bk Med Pubs) Mosby Yr Bk.

Color Atlas of the Nail in Clinical Dignosis. D. W. Beaven & S. E. Brooks. (Illus.). 240p. 1984. 44.95 (*0-8151-0586-X*, QMF-1, Yr Bk Med Pubs) Mosby Yr Bk.

Color Atlas of the Surface Forms of the Earth. Helmut Blume. Ed. by Rita Gardner & Andrew S. Goudie. Tr. by Bjorn Wygrala. (Illus.). 140p. (C). 1992. 75.00 (*0-674-14306-X*) HUP.

Color Atlas of the Surgery & Management of Intestinal Stomas. L. R. Celestin. (Illus.). 96p. 1987. text ed. 89.95 (*0-8151-1484-2*, CAC-1, Yr Bk Med Pubs) Mosby Yr Bk.

Color Atlas of the Temporomandibular Joint. Norman. (SPA.). 1992. write for info. (*0-8151-6430-0*) Mosby Yr Bk.

Color Atlas of the Tongue in Clinical Diagnosis. Bevan. 1988. 36.95 (*0-8151-0587-8*, Yr Bk Med Pubs) Mosby Yr Bk.

Color Atlas of Tomato Diseases: Observation, Identification and Control. D. Blancard. LC 94-10363. 1994. text ed. 89.95 (*0-470-23417-2*) Halsted Pr.

An Asterisk (*) at the beginning of an entry indicates that the title is appearing in BIP for the first time.

An Asterisk (*) at the beginning of an entry indicates that the title is appearing in BIP for the first time.

1387

Color Me Beautiful. Carole Jackson. 1987. pap. 14.00 (*0-345-34588-6*, Ballantine Trade) Ballantine.

Color Me Beautiful Color Me Black. Vousette T. Miller. (Illus.). 32p. (J). (ps-6). 1988. student ed 4.00 (*0-9619641-0-3*) Vous Etes Tres Belle.

Color Me Beautiful Eyewear. 1992. pap. write for info. (*0-345-37760-5*, Ballantine Trade) Ballantine.

Color Me Beautiful Make-up Book. Carole Jackson. LC 87-91179. 1987. pap. 12.00 (*0-345-34842-7*, Ballantine Trade) Ballantine.

Color Me Bright. Shirley Greenway. (Illus.). 16p. (J). (ps-3). 1992. bds. 3.95 (*1-879085-53-4*) Whsprng Coyote Pr.

Color Me Brown. rev. ed. Lucille Giles. (Illus.). 47p. (J). (gr. k-6). 1974. pap. 5.00 (*0-87485-017-7*) Johnson Chi.

Color Me Changing - Succeeding: Personality Language Development. Stefan Neilson & Shay Thoelke. (Personality Language Ser.). (Illus.). 55p. (Orig.). 1988. pap. write for info. (*1-880830-23-X*); spiral bd. 15.00 (*1-880830-00-0*) AEON-Hierophant.

Color Me Cleveland: A Cleveland Coloring Book. Illus. by Thomas Judson. 32p. (J). 1993. pap. 4.95 (*0-9631738-2-0*) Gray & Co Pubs.

Color Me Greene. Illus. by Linda Tomcsanyi. 1980. 6.00 (*0-686-26237-9*) E S Cunningham.

Color Me Happy: It's Rosh Hashannah & Yom Kippur. Norman Geller. (Illus.). 36p. (J). (gr. k-4). 1986. pap. 2.95 (*0-915753-10-3*) N Geller Pub.

Color Me Happy It's Passover. Norman Geller. (Illus.). 23p. (J). (gr. k-2). pap. 2.95 (*0-915753-14-6*) N Geller Pub.

Color Me Justice, 2 vols., Set. Kenneth F. McLaughlin. 1987. 30.00 (*0-685-19455-8*) Equity Pubng NH.

Color Me Love. Sally Baker. LC 75-27766. (Illus.). 1975. pap. 4.50 (*0-930422-08-2*) Dennis-Landman.

Color Me Love. Alberta Ristich. Ed. by Alexis Satchell. LC 84-91395. (Illus.). 50p. (Orig.). 1984. pap. 6.25 (*0-931841-01-1*) Satchells Pub.

Color Me Natural with Wholesome, Homemade Food Coloring. Mary Lou Emami & Suzanne Coulson. (Illus.). 117p. (Orig.). 1978. pap. 5.95 (*0-686-74777-1*) Emami-Coulson.

Color Me One. Leia Stinnett. (Little Angel Books Ser.). (Illus.). 36p. (J). (gr. 3 up). 1993. pap. text ed. 4.95 (*1-880737-13-2*) Crystal Jrns.

***Color Me Proud: A Self-Esteem Coloring Book.** Deborah Easton. (Illus.). (Orig.). 1994. pap. 4.99 (*1-885821-00-X*) Identity Toys.

Color Me Red. abr. ed. Kalli Deschamps. 260p. 1994. pap. 8.95 (*1-56901-313-6*) NW Pub.

Color Me Right...Then Frame Me in Motion. Malachi Andrews. Ed. by Kim Warnette. LC 90-60395. (Illus.). 80p. (Orig.). (C). 1989. pap. text ed. 14.95 (*0-685-44910-6*) Seymour-Smith.

Color Me Safe. Rosalind Weber. Ed. by Janice Leader. (Illus.). 20p. 1992. pap. 9.95 (*0-9631694-0-8*) Weble Pub.

Color Me Special. Sue Shepherd et al. (Illus.). (J). (ps-3). 1982. pap. text ed. 4.00 (*0-937423-02-5*) U M H & C.

Color Me Truth: Elementary Level Coloring Book (Based on the Life of Mary Lena Tate, 1871-1930) 18p. 1992. pap. 3.00 (*0-910003-07-6*) New & Living.

Color Me Well. Geneva Butz. 24p. 1986. pap. 1.75 (*0-8298-0742-X*) Pilgrim OH.

***Color Me White.** Joseph Trevino. 1995. 13.95 (*0-8062-5294-4*) Carlton.

Color Me Winning. Stefan Neilson & Shay Thoelke. (Personality Language Ser.). (Illus.). 50p. (J). (gr. 4-6). 1989. spiral bd. 20.00 (*1-880830-02-7*) AEON-Hierophant.

Color Measurement. 2nd rev. ed. D. L. MacAdam. (Optical Sciences Ser.: Vol. 27). (Illus.). 256p. 1985. pap. 63.00 (*0-387-15573-2*) Spr-Verlag.

Color Measurement Principles & the Textile Industry, October, 1991. American Association of Textile Chemists & Colorists Staff. (Symposium Papers). 159p. 1991. 45.00 (*0-685-57399-0*) AATCC.

Color Me...Cuddly! Carolyn Owens. (Illus.). 32p. (J). (ps-4). 1982. pap. 1.19 (*0-87123-695-8*) Bethany Hse.

***Color Medicine: The Secrets of Color Vibrational Healing.** Charles Klotsche. 113p. (Orig.). 1993. pap. 11.95 (*0-929385-27-6*) Light Tech Comns Servs.

***Color Medicine: The Secrets of Color-Vibrational Healing.** Charles Klotsche. (Illus.). 114p. Date not set. pap. text ed. 11.95 (*0-9645472-3-6*) Metaterra Pubns.

Color Microforms: AIIM TR9-1989. Association for Information & Image Management Staff. 1990. pap. 30.00 (*0-89258-188-3*, TR09) Assn Inform & Image Mgmt.

Color Mixing in Action. Helen Van Wyk. Ed. by Herbert Rogoff. (Illus.). 112p. (Orig.). 1990. pap. 19.95 (*0-929552-06-7*) Art Instr Assocs.

***Color Mixing Recipes for Successful Painting.** rev. ed. Helen Van Wyk. Ed. by Herbert Rogoff. (Illus.). 128p. 1996. 27.95 (*0-929552-10-5*) Art Instr Assocs.

Color Mixing the Van Wyk Way: A Manual for Artists. rev. ed. Helen Van Wyk. Ed. by Herbert Rogoff. (Illus.). 144p. 1995. 27.95 (*0-929552-09-1*) Art Instr Assocs.

Color Monkeys. William R. Johnson. Ed. by Pauline Johnson. (BLIP Production Reference Board Bks.). (Illus.). 48p. (J). (ps-2). 1989. write for info. (*0-936917-05-9*, B608) Blip Prods.

Color, Music & Vibration. Bernard Jensen. 1988. pap. 7.95 (*0-932615-19-8*) B Jensen.

Color Mutations in Modern Cockatiels. David M. Slater. 8p. (C). 1989. pap. text ed. write for info. (*0-318-66534-4*, 1001) Starbird Pubns.

Color My Classics. (Children's Classics Ser.). 1990. 4.95 (*0-685-32042-1*, T751) Hansen Ed Mus.

***Color of Blood.** Hodgman. (Stakeout Squad Ser.: Vol. 3). 1995. mass mkt. 4.99 (*0-373-63412-9*) Harlequin Bks.

Color of Culture. Mona L. Jones. (Illus.). 80p. (Orig.). 1993. pap. 10.95 (*0-9635605-9-X*) IMPACT Comm.

Color of Darkness. James Purdy. LC 74-26739. 175p. 1975. reprint ed. text ed. 49.75 (*0-8371-7874-6*, PUCD, Greenwood Pr) Greenwood.

Color of Evil. Ed. by David G. Hartwell. (Dark Descent Ser.: No. 1). 448p. 1991. mass mkt. 4.99 (*0-8125-1898-5*) Tor Bks.

Color of Fashion. Lona Benney et al. LC 92-14676. (Illus.). 256p. 1992. 65.00 (*1-55670-311-2*) Stewart Tabori & Chang.

***Color of Fear.** (Destroyer Ser.). 1995. mass mkt. 4.99 (*0-373-63214-2*, 1-63214-0) Harlequin Bks.

Color of Gender: Reimaging Democracy. Zillah R. Eisenstein. LC 93-23836. 274p. 1994. 45.00 (*0-520-08338-5*); pap. 15.00 (*0-520-08422-5*) U CA Pr.

Color of God: The Concept of God in Afro-American Religious Thought. Major J. Jones. LC 87-18449. 160p. (C). 1987. pap. 14.95 (*0-86554-276-7*, P46) Mercer Univ Pr.

Color of His Own. Leo Lionni. LC 75-28456. (Illus.). 40p. (J). (ps-00). 1993. 8.99 (*0-679-84197-0*); lib. bdg. 9.99 (*0-679-94197-5*) Knopf Bks Yng Read.

***Color of Hunger: Race & Hunger in National & International Perspective.** Ed. by David L. Shields. LC 94-46882. 240p. (C). 1995. text ed. 56.50 (*0-8476-8004-5*); pap. text ed. 21.95 (*0-8476-8005-3*) Rowman.

Color of Legends, the Weight of Dreams: Selected Poems. James R. Hurst. Ed. by John E. Westburg. 1978. pap. 5.00 (*0-87423-024-1*) Westburg.

Color of Light. Nomi Joval. (Concept Books Ser.). (Illus.). 16p. (J). (ps-4). 1993. lib. bdg. 13.95 (*1-879567-19-9*, Valeria Bks) Wonder Well.

Color of Light: Meditations for All of Us Living with AIDS. Perry Tilleraas. (Illus.). 400p. (Orig.). 1988. pap. 9.00 (*0-89486-511-0*, 5056A) Hazelden.

***Color of Love.** Sandra Kitt. 398p. (Orig.). 1995. pap. 5.99 (*0-451-18427-0*, Sig) NAL-Dutton.

***Color of Love.** braille ed. Binnie Syril. 339p. 1994. text ed. 27.12 (*1-56956-448-5*, BR9313) W A T Braille.

Color of Mesabi Bones: Poems & Prose Poems. John Caddy. LC 89-36393. 136p. (Orig.). 1989. pap. 8.95 (*0-915943-40-9*) Milkweed Ed.

Color of Mesabi Bones: Poems & Prose Poems. braille ed. John Caddy. 154p. 1991. vinyl bd. 12.32 (*1-56956-212-1*, BR8448) W A T Braille.

Color of Music. Phillip Schreibman. 64p. 1992. pap. 34.95 (*0-9634620-0-8*) P Schreibman.

Color of My Fur. Nannette Brophy. LC 91-65704. (Illus.). 44p. (J). (gr. k-3). 1992. lib. bdg. 12.95 (*1-55523-456-9*); pap. 8.95 (*1-55523-443-7*) Winston-Derek.

Color of Rome, Historic, Personal & Local. O. M. Potter. 1977. lib. bdg. 59.95 (*0-8490-1645-2*) Gordon Pr.

Color of Strangers, the Color of Friends: The Play of Ethnicity in School & Community. Alan Peshkin. LC 90-19765. 320p. 1991. pap. text ed. 15.95 (*0-226-66201-2*) U Ch Pr.

Color of the Air: Scenes from the Life of an American Jew, Vol. 1. John Sanford. LC 85-13514. 305p. (Orig.). 1985. pap. 12.50 (*0-87685-643-1*) Black Sparrow.

Color of the Crown. 54.95 (*0-317-59507-5*) P-H.

Color of the Heart: Writing from Struggle & Change, 1959-1990. Susan Sherman. LC 90-81429. (Illus.). 234p. (Orig.). 1990. pap. 10.95 (*0-915306-90-5*) Curbstone.

Color of the Sky: A Study of Stephen Crane. David Halliburton. (Cambridge Studies in American Literature & Culture: No. 30). 336p. (C). 1989. 54.95 (*0-521-36274-1*) Cambridge U Pr.

Color of the Snow. Rudiger Kremer. Tr. by Breon Mitchell. LC 91-44000. 128p. 1992. 19.95 (*0-8112-1200-9*); pap. 9.95 (*0-8112-1208-4*, NDP743) New Directions.

Color of the Star. Gilbert Morris & Bobby Funderburk. LC 92-44518. (Price of Liberty Ser.: No. 2). 1993. pap. 8.99 (*0-8499-3495-8*) Word Pub.

Color of the Star. Gilbert Morris & Bobby Funderburk. No. 2. 220p. 1993. pap. write for info. (*0-318-70296-7*) Word Inc.

Color of Their Skin: A History of School Desegregation in Richmond, Virginia, 1954-89. Robert A. Pratt. (Carter G. Woodson Institute Series in Black Studies). (C). 1992. text ed. 24.95 (*0-8139-1372-1*) U Pr of Va.

Color of Their Skin: Education & Race in Richmond, Virginia, 1954-89. Robert A. Pratt. 151p. (C). 1994. pap. text ed. 10.95 (*0-8139-1481-7*) U Pr of Va.

***Color of Things.** Vivienne Shalom & Dusan Petricic. LC 94-32416. (Illus.). 32p. (J). (PS-4). 1995. 15.95 (*0-8478-1866-7*) Rizzoli Intl.

Color of Trees. Canaan Parker. LC 92-30486. 221p. (Orig.). 1992. pap. 8.95 (*1-55583-207-5*) Alyson Pubns.

Color on Color: Overprinting Two Colors to Create a New Third Color. North Light Books Staff. 160p. 1993. 34.99 (*1-56496-033-1*, 30467) Rockport Pubs.

***Color PC: Production Techniques.** Miller & Zaucha Staff. (Illus.). 400p. (Orig.). 1995. pap. 40.00 (*1-56830-179-0*) Alpha Bks IN.

Color Perception in Art. Faber Birren. LC 86-61199. (Illus.). 88p. 1986. pap. 10.95 (*0-88740-064-7*) Schiffer.

***Color Photographs: A Postcard Folio Book.** Ansel Adams. (Illus.). 64p. 1995. 9.95 (*0-8212-2240-6*) Bulfinch Pr.

Color Photographs of the Ruins. Elton Glaser. LC 91-50758. (Poetry Ser.). 67p. 1992. 19.95 (*0-8229-3705-0*); pap. 10.95 (*0-8229-5468-0*) U of Pittsburgh Pr.

Color Photography. Herb Taylor et al. LC 81-71037. (Modern Photo Guides Ser.). (Illus.). 120p. (Orig.). 1982. pap. 7.95 (*0-385-18152-3*) Avalon Comm.

Color Photography: A Basic Manual, Vol. 1. Henry Horenstein. 1995. 40.00 (*0-316-37317-6*); pap. 21.95 (*0-316-37316-8*) Little.

Color Portraits of Outstanding Plants. Briggs Nursery, Inc. Staff & Henny, Thomas, Nursery Staff. 1986. ring bd. 15.00 (*0-910013-01-2*) Offshoot Pub.

Color Primer 1 & 2. Richard Zakia & Hollis Todd. LC 74-83103. (Illus.). 152p. 1974. 18.00 (*0-87100-021-0*, 2021) Morgan.

Color Print Book: A Survey of Contemporary Photographic Printmaking Methods for the Creative Photographer. Arnold Gassan. LC 80-28859. (Extended Photo Media Ser.: No. 3). (Illus.). (Orig.). (C). 1981. pap. 9.95 (*0-87992-023-8*) Light Impressions.

Color Printing in England, 1486-1870. Joan M. Friedman. LC 78-50990. (Illus.). 72p. (Orig.). 1978. pap. 18.50 (*0-930606-12-4*) Yale Ctr Brit Art.

Color Psychology & Color Therapy. Faber Birren. (Illus.). 302p. 1984. pap. 12.95 (*0-8065-0653-9*, Citadel Pr) Carol Pub Group.

Color Publishing on the Macintosh: From Desktop to Print Shop. Kim Baker & Sunny Baker. 1992. disk, pap. 45.00 (*0-679-73977-7*) Random.

Color Publishing on the PC: From Desktop to Print Shop. Kim Baker & Sunny Baker. LC 92-28098. 1993. pap. 45.00 (*0-679-74215-8*) Random.

Color Purple. Alice Walker. LC 81-48242. 204p. 1982. 15.95 (*0-15-119153-0*) HarBrace.

Color Purple. Alice Walker. LC 81-48242. 1988. pap. 12.00 (*0-671-66878-1*, WSP) PB.

Color Purple. Alice Walker. Ed. by Julie Rubenstein. LC 81-48242. 1990. pap. 6.99 (*0-671-72779-6*) PB.

Color Purple. 10th aniversary ed. Alice Walker. LC 81-48242. 1992. pap. 19.95 (*0-15-119154-9*) HarBrace.

Color Purple & All That Jazz. Carole Marsh. (Our Black Heritage Ser.). (J). (gr. 3-12). 1994. lib. bdg. 24.95 (*1-55609-315-2*); pap. 14.95 (*1-55609-314-4*); disk 29.95 (*1-55609-316-0*) Gallopade Pub Group.

Color Purple Notes. Gloria Rose. 74p. (Orig.). (C). 1986. pap. text ed. 3.75 (*0-8220-0308-2*) Cliffs.

Color Research & Application, Vol. 12. 1987. 98.00 (*0-471-62664-3*) Wiley.

Color Resource Complete Color Glossary: From Desktop to Color Electronic Prepress. Miles Southworth et al. (Illus.). 222p. (C). 1992. 24.95 (*1-879847-01-9*) Graph Arts Pub.

Color Revolution. Phillip D. Cate & Sinclair H. Hitchings. 1985. pap. 12.00 (*0-87905-032-2*) Boston Public Lib.

Color Right from the Start: Progressive Lessons in Seeing & Understanding Color. Hilary Page. LC 93-48927. (Illus.). 144p. 1994. 29.95 (*0-8230-0751-0*, Watsn-Guptill) Watsn-Guptill.

Color Round the Year. Reader's Digest Editors. LC 93-45391. (Successful Gardening Ser.). (Illus.). 176p. 1994. 18.98 (*0-89577-602-2*) RD Assn.

Color Sampler. Illus. & Text by Kathleen Westray. LC 93-19967. 32p. (J). (gr. 1-4). 1993. lib. bdg. 14.95 (*0-395-65940-X*) Ticknor & Flds Bks Yng Read.

Color Scanner Book. 2nd ed. James Cavuoto & Stephen Beale. 1995. 27.95 (*0-941845-11-7*) Micro Pub Pr.

Color Scanning & Imaging Systems. Gary G. Field. Ed. by Ann Mertz. LC 89-86025. 1990. pap. text ed. 65.00 (*0-88362-120-7*) Graphic Arts Tech Found.

Color Scheme, 5 bks., Set. (Networks Ser.). (J). (gr. 2). 1991. 21.25 (*0-88106-752-0*) Charlesbridge Pub.

Color Science: Concepts & Methods, Quantitative Data & Formulae. 2nd ed. Gunter Wyszecki & W. S. Stiles. LC 82-2794. (Pure & Applied Optics Ser.). 950p. 1982. text ed. 210.00 (*0-471-02106-7*, Wiley-Interscience) Wiley.

Color Sedona. Bobbi Salts. (Illus.). 32p. (Orig.). (J). (ps-6). 1991. pap. 2.95 (*0-929526-10-4*) Double B Pubns.

Color Sensors & Instrumentation. Richard K. Miller & Terri C. Walker. LC 88-84060. (Survey on Technology & Markets Ser.: No. 85). 50p. 1989. pap. text ed. 200.00 (*1-55865-112-8*) Future Tech Surveys.

Color Separation Scanner Comparison Charts 1994. Harold C. Durbin. 1994. pap. 29.95 (*0-936786-10-8*) Durbin Assoc.

Color Separation Techniques. Miles Southworth. LC 88-83912. (Illus.). 271p. (Orig.). 1979. 23.00 (*0-933600-04-6*) Tech & Ed Ctr Graph Arts RIT.

Color Separations on the Desktop: How to Get Good Reproductions. LC 93-73114. (Illus.). 1993. pap. 16.95 (*0-933600-08-9*) Graph Arts Pub.

Color, Sex, & Poetry: Three Women Writers of the Harlem Renaissance. Gloria T. Hull. LC 86-45580. (Everywoman Studies in History, Literature & Culture; Blacks in the Diaspora Ser.). (Illus.). 256p. 1987. 35.00 (*0-253-34974-5*); 12.95 (*0-253-20430-5*, MB-430) Ind U Pr.

***Color, Shape & Season Rhymes.** (Take-Home Rhyme Bks.). (Illus.). 160p. (J). (ps-1). 1995. 14.95 (*0-614-06833-9*, WPH 1103) Totline Bks.

Color, Shape & Season Rhymes: Reproducible Pre-Reading Books for Young Children. Jean Warren. Ed. by Gayle Bittinger. (Take-Home Ser.). (Illus.). 160p. (Orig.). (J). (ps-1). 1989. pap. text ed. 14.95 (*0-911019-28-6*) Warren Pub Hse.

Color-Sonics, Inc. COMBI-150 Audio Visual Entertainment Center Service Manual. rev. ed. Ed. by Frank Adams. (Illus.). 82p. reprint ed. 35.00 (*1-56642-016-4*, R-46) AMR Pub Co.

Color Source Book for Graphic Designers. Sadao Nakamura. (Illus.). 116p. (Orig.). (C). 1992. pap. 19.95 (*4-8381-0110-4*, Pub. by Mitsumura Suiko Shoin JA) Weatherhill.

Color Source Book of Authentic Art Nouveau Designs: 146 Motifs. Max Benirschke. (Illus.). 32p. 1984. reprint ed. pap. 5.95 (*0-486-24547-0*) Dover.

Color Sourcebook No. I: A Complete Guide to Using Color in Patterns. AIM Creative Products Co. Ltd Staff. (Illus.). 108p. 1989. pap. 15.95 (*0-935603-28-X*, 30167) Rockport Pubs.

Color Sourcebook No. II: A Complete Guide to Using Color in Patterns. AIM Creative Products Co. Ltd Staff. (Illus.). 108p. 1989. pap. 15.95 (*0-935603-29-8*, 30168) Rockport Pubs.

Color Stages of Alchemy & Behavioral Change. James F. Skinner. 1991. 40.00 (*0-938434-86-1*); pap. 18.95 (*0-938434-85-3*) Sigo Pr.

Color Stripping: A Guide for Process Color Image Assembly. Malcolm G. Keif. 60p. 1992. pap. 12.50 (*1-882602-02-1*) Graphic Srvs.

Color Studies. Thomas A. Janvier. 1972. reprint ed. 19.00 (*0-8422-8080-4*) Irvington.

Color Symbolism: Six Excerpts from the Eranos Yearbook 1972. Portmann et al. Tr. by Jennings et al. LC 87-28764. 202p. 1983. pap. 18.00 (*0-88214-400-6*) Spring Pubns.

Color Symphony. 280p. 1992. 69.95 (*88-7070-132-8*) Belvedere USA.

Color Technology in the Textile Industry. Ed. by Gultekin Celikiz & Rolf G. Kuehni. 210p. 1983. 45.00 (*0-318-12152-2*); 25.00 (*0-318-12153-0*) AATCC.

Color Television. T. Rzeszewski. LC 83-7894. 400p. 1983. 59.95 (*0-87942-168-1*, PC01610) Inst Electrical.

Color Television Picture Tubes: Advances in Image Pick up Supplement I. Merrill. Benjamin Kazan. 1974. text ed. 143.00 (*0-12-022151-9*) Acad Pr.

Color Textbook of Pediatric Dermatology. Weston. 320p. 1993. 74.00 (*0-8151-9236-3*, Yr Bk Med Pubs) Mosby Yr Bk.

Color Textbook of Pediatric Dermatology: Spanish Edition. Weston. (SPA.). 1992. 60.90 (*0-8016-6708-9*) Mosby Yr Bk.

Color the Ancient Forest. Wilderness Society Staff. (Illus.). 48p. (Orig.). (J). (ps-3). 1991. 4.95 (*1-879326-07-8*) Living Planet Pr.

***Color the Classics No. 2: The Hymn Writer.** Carmen Ziarkowski. (Illus.). 56p. (J). (gr. k-6). 1993. 12.95 (*1-881153-18-5*) Color Class.

***Color the Classics No. 3: The Christmas Carols.** Carmen Ziarkowski. (Illus.). 56p. (J). (gr. k-6). 1994. 12.95 (*1-881153-23-1*) Color Class.

***Color the Classics No. 4: The Patriotic Songs.** Carmen Ziarkowski. (Illus.). 56p. (J). (gr. k-6). 1994. 12.95 (*1-881153-00-2*) Color Class.

***Color the Classics (Composers), No. 1.** Carmen Ziarkowski. (Illus.). 56p. (J). (gr. k-6). 1993. 12.95 (*1-881153-03-7*) Color Class.

Color the Inside of Your Brain. Lee Magdanz. (Illus.). 22p. 1989. pap. 9.95 (*0-9613949-2-7*) R S Pr.

Color the Rainforest. Mothers & Others for a Livable Planet. 48p. 1990. pap. 4.95 (*0-9626072-4-X*) Living Planet Pr.

***Color the Wind.** Robert B. Fox. LC 94-79129. 1995. 7.95 (*0-8158-0510-1*) Chris Mass.

Color Theory. Jose M. Parramon. (Artist's Library). (Illus.). 112p. 1989. pap. 14.95 (*0-8230-0755-3*, Watsn-Guptill) Watsn-Guptill.

Color Theory & Its Application in Art & Design. 2nd rev. ed. G. A. Agoston. (Optical Sciences Ser.: Vol. 19). (Illus.). 300p. 1987. pap. 66.00 (*0-387-17095-2*) Spr-Verlag.

Color Therapy. Reuben Amber. 207p. 1983. pap. 14.00 (*0-943358-04-3*) Aurora Press.

Color Therapy. Linda Clark. LC 74-75389. 1975. 12.95 (*0-8159-5206-6*) Devin.

Color Therapy: The Application of Color for Healing, Diagnosis, & Well-Being. Mary Anderson. 112p. 1991. pap. 6.95 (*1-85538-010-2*, Pub. by Aquarian Pr UK) Thorsons SF.

Color Therapy Workbook. Theo Gimbel. 1993. pap. 16.95 (*1-85230-388-3*) Element MA.

Color Thick & Thin. William Powell. (How to Draw & Paint Ser.). (Illus.). 32p. (Orig.). 1989. pap. 5.95 (*1-56010-048-6*, HT182) W Foster Pub.

Color to Be. Clifford M. Lauderdale. Ed. by David Hwayer. (Poetry Ser.). (Illus.). 39p. (Orig.). 1994. pap. text ed. 8.00 (*1-882300-03-3*) Willo Trees.

Color to Color: The Black Woman's Guide to the Rainbow for Fashion & Beauty. Jean Patton. (Illus.). 128p. (Orig.). 1991. pap. 13.00 (*0-671-69386-7*, Fireside) S&S Trade.

Color to Read, Vol. Aleph. Tom Foster. Ed. by L. LuBin. (Illus.). 72p. (J). (ps-1). 1990. teacher ed write for info. (*0-318-67150-6*); lib. bdg. write for info. (*0-318-67149-2*) Lubin Pr.

Color Tolerances: Measuring up to Today's Standards: Regional Technical Conference, September 14, 15, & 16, 1992, Cherry Hill Hyatt, Cherry Hill, NJ. Society of Plastics Engineers Staff. 176p. reprint ed. pap. 50.20 (*0-7837-4493-5*, 2044270) Bks Demand.

Color Tree. Denise Bennett. LC 93-77606. 32p. (J). (gr. 4-5). 1993. 12.95 (*1-880851-07-5*) Greene Bark Pr.

Color TV Servicing. Newt Smelser. LC 80-26523. (Illus.). 260p. 1981. 44.95 (*0-88229-549-7*) Nelson-Hall.

Color U. S. Yellow. Donald C. Kipfer. 114p. (Orig.). 1993. pap. text ed. 7.50 (*1-56002-272-8*, Univ Edtns) Aegina Pr.

Color Us Rational. Virginia Waters. LC 78-71011. (Illus.). (J). (ps-3). 1979. pap. 3.00 (*0-917476-15-8*) Inst Rational-Emotive.

Color Vision. Joe Marvullo. (Illus.). 144p. 1989. 29.95 (*0-8174-3675-8*, Amphoto); pap. 22.50 (*0-8174-3676-6*, Amphoto) Watsn-Guptill.

Color Vision Deficiencies. Ed. by Y. Ohta. LC 90-5233. (Illus.). 267p. 1990. lib. bdg. 67.50 (*90-6299-063-0*, Pub. by Kugler NE) Kugler Pubns.

Color Vision Deficiencies VIII. Ed. by G. Verriest. (Documenta Ophthalmologica Proceedings Ser.). 1987. lib. bdg. 202.50 (*0-89838-801-5*) Kluwer Ac.

Color Vision Deficiency & Color Blindness. Mary M. Olsen & Kenneth R. Harris. 62p. (Orig.). 1988. pap. 8.50 (*0-9615332-2-6*) Fern Ridge Pr.

Color War! Marilyn Kaye. (Camp Sunnyside Friends Ser.: No. 3). 128p. (Orig.). (J). (gr. 3 up). 1989. pap. 3.50 (*0-380-75702-8*, Camelot) Avon.

An Asterisk (*) at the beginning of an entry indicates that the title is appearing in BIP for the first time.

An Asterisk (*) at the beginning of an entry indicates that the title is appearing in BIP for the first time.

1389

C

Colorado Gold. Marian Wells. LC 87-35333. 302p. (Orig.). (YA). (gr. 9-12). 1988. pap. 8.99 (0-87123-966-3) Bethany Hse.

Colorado Gold: From the Pike's Peak Rush to the Present. Stephen M. Voynick. Ed. by Mark Waltermire. (Illus.). 224p. (Orig.). 1992. pap. 12.00 (0-87842-282-X) Mountain Pr.

***Colorado Golf Directory.** annuals 144p. 1995. write for info. (1-887351-03-5) Pastime CO.

Colorado Golf Highlights, 1992. Ed. by C. R. Goeldner et al. 133p. 1992. pap. text ed. 48.00 (0-89478-051-4) U CO Busn Res Div.

Colorado Gonzo Rides Vol. 1: A Mountain Biker's Guide to Colorado's Best Single Track Trails. Michael Merrifield. LC 91-71647. 192p. 1991. pap. write for info. (0-9628867-0-X) Blue Clover.

Colorado Governments Performance Standards, 1990. Ed. by Greg Michels. (Governments Performance Standards Ser.). (Illus.). 150p. 1990. text ed. 125.00 (1-55507-477-4) Municipal Analysis.

Colorado Guide. 3rd ed. Bruce Caughey & Dean Winstanley. (Illus.). 660p. 1994. pap. 18.95 (1-55591-152-8) Fulcrum Pub.

Colorado Gun. Edwin Booth. 224p. (Orig.). reprint ed. pap. 2.25 (0-8439-2296-6) Dorchester Pub Co.

Colorado Handbook. 2nd ed. Stephen Metzger. LC 93-30739. (Illus.). 430p. (Orig.). 1994. pap. 17.95 (1-56691-013-7) Moon Pubns CA.

Colorado Health Care Perspective, 1994. Ed. by Kathleen O. Morgan et al. 24p. 1994. 18.00 (1-56692-155-4) Morgan Quitno Corp.

***Colorado Health Care Perspective 1995.** Ed. by Kathleen O. Morgan et al. 24p. 1995. 18.00 (1-56692-405-7) Morgan Quitno Corp.

Colorado Health Correspondence Course. James J. Smith. 1991. 32.00 (1-56461-057-8, 26249) Rough Notes.

Colorado Health Insurance Licensing Course. James J. Smith. 1991. ring bd. 32.00 (1-877723-50-9, 26754) Rough Notes.

Colorado Heritage Series, 10 vols., Set. Jane V. Barker & Sybil Downing. (Illus.). (J). (ps-8). reprint ed. pap. 39.50 (1-878611-00-3) Silver Rim Pr.

***Colorado High.** Joyce C. Ware. (To Love Again Ser.). 512p. 1995. mass mkt. 4.99 (0-8217-4904-8) Zebra.

***Colorado High-The Official Guide to the Colorado Trail.** 3rd rev. ed. Randy Jacobs. (Illus.). 240p. 1992. pap. 12.95 (0-614-06596-8) CO Trail Fnd.

Colorado Hispanic Leadership Profiles: "Who's Who among Colorado's Outstanding Leaders" Doug McNair & Wallace Y. McNair. 186p. 1991. 40.00 (0-9627600-1-3) Wstrn Images.

Colorado Historical Tour Guide. D. Ray Wilson. LC 90-80022. (Illus.). 448p. (Orig.). 1990. pap. text ed. 12.95 (0-916445-26-7) Crossroads Comm.

***Colorado History.** 7th ed. Carl Ubbelohde et al. (Illus.). 422p. (Orig.). 1995. pap. 20.00 (0-87108-844-4) Pruett.

***Colorado History: Creative Activities for Curious Kids.** Phyllis J. Perry. 85p. 1994. ring bd. 12.00 (0-931510-55-4) Hi Willow.

***Colorado History of the Centennial State.** University Press of Colorado Staff. 1994. 22.50 (0-87081-344-7) Univ Pr Colo.

***Colorado Home Owner's Guide to Paying Less Property Taxes: Complete Step by Step Instructions to Lower Current Year Property Taxes, Receive Refunds for Past Years, Plus Interest.** Victoria M. Lewis. 216p. (C). 1995. pap. text ed. 24.95 (0-9645932-0-3) Xenia Pubns.

Colorado Homes. Sandra Dallas. LC 86-40070. (Illus.). 288p. 1986. 24.95 (0-8061-2004-5) U of Okla Pr.

Colorado Hot Air Balloon Mystery. Carole Marsh. (Carole Marsh Colorado Bks.). (Illus.). (J). (gr. 2-9). 1994. 24.95 (0-7933-2363-0); pap. 14.95 (0-7933-2364-9); disk 29.95 (0-7933-2365-7) Gallopade Pub Group.

Colorado Hut to Hut: Skiing & Biking Colorado's Back Country. Brian Litz. (Illus.). 240p. (Orig.). 1992. pap. 19.95 (0-929969-85-5) Westcliffe Pubs Inc.

Colorado in Perspective, 1994. Ed. by Kathleen O. Morgan et al. 26p. 1994. 18.00 (1-56692-205-4) Morgan Quitno Corp.

***Colorado in Perspective 1995.** Ed. by Kathleen O. Morgan et al. 26p. 1995. pap. 18.00 (1-56692-455-3) Morgan Quitno Corp.

Colorado Is for Kids! An Activity Book for Kids! Ed. by Lee Fischer. (Illus.). 32p. (J). (gr. 1-6). 1990. pap. 2.95 (0-929526-05-8) Double B Pubns.

Colorado Jeopardy! Answers & Questions about Our State! Carole Marsh. (Carole Marsh Colorado Bks.). (Illus.). (J). (gr. 3-12). 1994. lib. bdg. 24.95 (0-7933-4094-2); pap. 14.95 (0-7933-4095-0); disk 29.95 (0-7933-4096-9) Gallopade Pub Group.

Colorado Jewel. Cate Brandt. 1989. pap. 3.75 (0-8217-2639-0) Zebra.

Colorado "Jography" A Fun Run Thru Our State! Carole Marsh. (Carole Marsh Colorado Bks.). (Illus.). (YA). (gr. 3-12). 1994. lib. bdg. 24.95 (1-55609-525-2); pap. 14.95 (1-55609-524-4); disk 29.95 (0-7933-1407-0) Gallopade Pub Group.

Colorado Judicial Department: Personnel Technical Assistance on Job Classification, Pay, Salary Survey, & Human Resource Division Staffing. 52p. 1988. 3.00 (0-685-24112-2, WRO, T/A-508) Natl Ctr St Courts.

Colorado Jury Instructions: Civil, 2 binders. 3rd ed. Supreme Court Committee on Civil Jury Instructions Staff. 1989. 210.00 (0-318-43156-4); Suppl. 1993. 65.00 (0-317-03343-3) Lawyers Cooperative.

***Colorado Kids: A Family Activity Guide.** Linda Collison & Bob Russell. (Illus.). 128p. (Orig.). 1996. pap. 15.00 (0-87108-862-2) Pruett.

Colorado Kid's Cookbook: Recipes, How-to, History, Lore & More! Carole Marsh. (Carole Marsh Colorado Bks.). (Illus.). (YA). (gr. 3-12). 1994. lib. bdg. 24.95 (0-7933-0202-1); pap. 14.95 (0-7933-0201-3); disk 29.95 (0-7933-0203-X) Gallopade Pub Group.

Colorado Killzone. Don Pendleton. (Executioner Ser.: No. 25). 1989. pap. 3.50 (1-55817-275-0, Pinnacle NY) Windsor NY.

Colorado Kind of Christmas: Treasured Rocky Mountain Yuletide Traditions. Ed. by Dirks & Daniel. (Illus.). 112p. 1993. 35.00 (1-56579-048-0); pap. 25.00 (1-56579-049-9) Westcliffe Pubs Inc.

Colorado Lady. Smith. LC 86-72145. 1992. pap. 6.99 (0-7814-0523-8, LifeJourney) Chariot Family.

Colorado, Lakes & Creeks. John Fielder. LC 86-50066. (Illus.). 64p. 1986. pap. 10.95 (0-929969-64-2) Westcliffe Pubs Inc.

***Colorado Land Surveying Law: Questions & Answers.** John E. Keen. 42p. 1995. pap. text ed. 20.00 (1-56569-018-4) Land Survey.

Colorado Law Annotated, 2 vols., Set. 2nd ed. Bruce D. Pringle. LC 84-71934. 1991. 230.00 (0-317-04259-9) Lawyers Cooperative.

Colorado Law Office Handbook. Colorado Assoc. of Legal Secretaries Staff & Donna L. Pritchard. 420p. 1994. ring bd. 75.00 (1-55943-129-6) Michie Butterworth.

Colorado Law Office Handbook. suppl. ed. Colorado Assoc. of Legal Secretaries Staff. Ed. by Donna L. Pritchard. 1993. 42.50 (0-685-74404-3) Butterworth Legal Pubs.

Colorado Library Book: A Surprising Guide to the Unusual Special Collections in Libraries Across Our State for Students, Teachers, Writers & Publishers - Includes Reproducible Mailing Labels Plus Activities for Young People! Carole Marsh. (Carole Marsh Colorado Bks.). (Illus.). 1994. lib. bdg. 24.95 (0-7933-3023-8); pap. 14.95 (0-7933-3024-6); disk 29.95 (0-7933-3025-4) Gallopade Pub Group.

Colorado Life Correspondence Course. James J. Smith. 1991. 32.00 (1-56461-056-X, 26208) Rough Notes.

Colorado Life Insurance Licensing Course. James J. Smith. 1991. ring bd. 32.00 (1-877723-14-2, 26354) Rough Notes.

Colorado, Lost Places & Forgotten Words. John Fielder. (Illus.). 160p. 1989. 45.00 (0-942394-88-7) Westcliffe Pubs Inc.

Colorado, Magnificent Wilderness. John Ward. (Illus.). 112p. 1984. 29.95 (0-942394-07-0); pap. 19.95 (0-942394-36-4) Westcliffe Pubs Inc.

Colorado Manhunt. Dick Taylor. 208p. (Orig.). 1982. pap. 2.25 (0-8439-1181-6) Dorchester Pub Co.

Colorado Mathematical Olympiad: The First Ten Years & Further Explorations. Alexander Soifer. (Illus.). 200p. (Orig.). (YA). (gr. 7-12). 1994. pap. 19.95 (0-940263-03-3) Ctr Excel Math.

Colorado Media Book: A Surprising Guide to the Amazing Print, Broadcast & Online Media of Our State for Students, Teachers, Writers & Publishers - Includes Reproducible Mailing Labels Plus Activities for Young People! Carole Marsh. (Carole Marsh Colorado Bks.). (Illus.). 1994. lib. bdg. 24.95 (0-7933-3176-5); pap. 14.95 (0-7933-3177-3); disk 29.95 (0-7933-3178-1) Gallopade Pub Group.

Colorado Memories of the Narrow Gauge. Krause & Grenard. (Carstens Hobby Bks.). (Illus.). 132p. 1988. pap. 15.95 (0-911868-59-3, C59) Carstens Pubns.

Colorado Moonfire. Charlotte Hubbard. 1992. mass mkt. 4.25 (0-8217-3730-9) Zebra.

Colorado Mortality Schedule, 1885. 1991. 30.00 (0-89593-630-5) Accelerated Index.

Colorado Mountain Hikes for Everyone: Routes & Maps to 105 Named Summits. Dave Muller. LC 87-92198. (Illus.). 196p. (Orig.). 1987. pap. 10.95 (0-9619666-0-2) D J Muller.

Colorado Mountain Ranges. Jeff Rennicke. LC 86-81754. (Colorado Geographic Ser.). (Illus.). 104p. 1986. 14.95 (0-934318-92-1); pap. 9.95 (0-934318-66-2) Falcon Pr MT.

Colorado Mountain Ski Tours & Hikes: A Year Round Guide. Dave Muller. (Illus.). 224p. (Orig.). 1993. pap. 14.95 (0-9619666-1-0) D J Muller.

Colorado Mystery Van Takes Off! Bk. 1: Handicapped Colorado Kids Sneak Off on a Big Adventure. Carole Marsh. (Carole Marsh Colorado Bks.). (Illus.). (J). (gr. 3-12). 1994. 24.95 (0-7933-4979-6); pap. 14.95 (0-7933-4980-X); disk 29.95 (0-7933-4981-8) Gallopade Pub Group.

Colorado National Monument, CO. rev. ed. Ed. by Trails Illustrated Staff. (Illus.). 1993. Folded topographical map. 7.95 (0-925873-08-X) Trails Illustrated.

Colorado, Nineteen Ninety. Jane Fudge. Ed. by Marlene Chambers & Steve Grinstead. LC 90-80935. (Illus.). 144p. (Orig.). 1990. pap. text ed. 24.95 (0-914738-39-9) Denver Art Mus.

Colorado No-Trap Tourist Guide: How to Leave the Beaten Path & See the Real Colorado. Discover Hundreds of New & Interesting Adventures, & Most at Little or No Cost. This Book Tells It All! Tamara F. Kunz. LC 87-8373. (Illus.). 256p. (Orig.). 1987. pap. 12.95 (0-942125-00-2) V H Hedley Pub.

***Colorado: Off the Beaten Path: A Guide to Unique Places.** 3rd ed. Curtis W. Casewit. LC 94-11981. (Off the Beaten Path Ser.). (Illus.). 159p. 1994. pap. 9.95 (1-56440-399-8) Globe Pequot.

Colorado on Foot. Robert L. Brown. LC 91-8054. (Illus.). 1991. pap. 10.95 (0-87004-336-6) Caxton.

Colorado on My Mind. (On My Mind Ser.). 120p. 1994. 29.50 (1-56044-272-7) Falcon Pr MT.

Colorado One Hundred Years Ago. Comp. by Skip Whitson. (Historical Ser.). (Illus.). (Orig.). 1976. pap. 3.50 (0-89540-031-6, SB-031) Sun Pub.

***Colorado Outdoor Activity Guide.** Claire Walters. LC 94-46636. (Outdoor Activity Guide Ser.). (Illus.). 180p. (Orig.). 1995. pap. 9.95 (1-56626-082-5) Country Rds.

Colorado Outdoor Education Center Teacher's Field Guide. Colorado Outdoor Education Center Staff. (Illus.). 280p. 1985. reprint ed. pap. 15.00 (0-910715-06-8) Search Public.

Colorado Parent's Directory: 1992 Edition. 2nd ed. Denver Parent, Inc. Staff & Barbara Padgett. Ed. by Edith Sheldon. 126p. 1992. pap. 4.95 (0-9634804-0-5) Denver Parent.

Colorado Parklands. Stewart Green. Ed. by Marnie Hagman. LC 88-80071. (Colorado Geographic Ser.). (Illus.). 120p. 1988. 14.95 (0-937959-38-3); pap. 14.95 (0-937959-37-5) Falcon Pr MT.

Colorado Pass Book: A Guide to Colorado's Backroad Mountain Passes. 2nd ed. Don Koch. LC 87-16677. (Illus.). 162p. 1992. pap. 18.95 (0-87108-827-4) Pruett.

Colorado Passion. Veronica Blake. 384p. 1992. mass mkt. 4.25 (0-8217-4004-0) Zebra.

Colorado PC Correspondence Course. James Smith. 1991. 32.00 (1-877723-79-7, 26959) Rough Notes.

Colorado Personnel Review. Larry Henderson & Monica Lee. 50p. 1990. 3.00 (0-685-38115-3, WRO-114) Natl Ctr St Courts.

Colorado Place Names. William Bright. LC 93-777. (Illus.). 144p. (Orig.). 1993. pap. 11.95 (1-55566-102-5) Johnson Bks.

Colorado Placers & Placering. Ben H. Parker, Jr. Ed. by Mary Carson. (Illus.). 112p. 1994. reprint ed. pap. 10.95 (0-941620-61-1) Carson Ent.

Colorado Plateau: A Geologic History. rev. ed. Donald L. Baars. LC 83-1349. (Illus.). 279p. (Orig.). 1983. pap. 14.95 (0-8263-0599-7) U of NM Pr.

Colorado Poetry: And Thoughts of Yesteryear. Glen Allen. 86p. (Orig.). 1989. pap. 4.95 (0-9622131-0-1) McKee Bks.

Colorado Politics & Government: Governing the Centennial State. Thomas E. Cronin & Robert D. Loevy. LC 93-6587. (Politics & Governments of the American States Ser.). (Illus.). xxxii, 362p. 1993. 40.00 (0-8032-1451-0); pap. 15.95 (0-8032-6358-9) U of Nebr Pr.

Colorado Post Offices, 1859-1989. William H. Bauer et al. LC 90-34759. (Illus.). 280p. 1990. 39.95 (0-918654-42-4) CO RR Mus.

Colorado Pride: A Commemorative History of the Colorado Air National Guard. Charles G. Whitley, Jr. Ed. by Gary Watson. LC 89-60294. (Illus.). 352p. 1989. text ed. 60.00 (0-9621980-0-5) CO Air Natl.

Colorado Private Elementary & Secondary Schools, 1992-93. Margerie Hicks & Robert W. McBride. 96p. 1992. pap. 9.95 (1-880197-00-6) Gylantic Pub.

***Colorado Private Elementary & Secondary Schools, 1995-96.** 3rd ed. Hicks. 190p. 1995. pap. text ed. 10.95 (0-9635280-5-X) Magnolia St.

Colorado Profiles: Men & Women Who Shaped the Centennial State. John H. Monnett & Michael McCarthy. (Illus.). 350p. (Orig.). 1987. pap. 14.95 (0-917895-19-3) Cordillera CO.

Colorado Property & Casualty Insurance Licensing Course. James J. Smith. 1991. 50.00 (0-942326-72-5, 26843) Rough Notes.

Colorado Quarry. Jon Sharpe. (Trailsman Ser.: No. 124). 176p. (Orig.). 1992. pap. 3.50 (0-451-17213-2, Sig) NAL-Dutton.

Colorado Quiz Bag. E. Richard Churchill. 1978. 2.00 (0-913488-04-6) Timberline Bks.

Colorado Quiz Bowl Crash Course! Carole Marsh. (Carole Marsh Colorado Bks.). (Illus.). (YA). (gr. 3-12). 1994. lib. bdg. 24.95 (0-685-45927-6); pap. 14.95 (1-55609-531-7); disk 29.95 (0-7933-1416-X) Gallopade Pub Group.

Colorado Railroads & the Colorado Railroad Museum. Text by Cornelius W. Hauck & Charles Albi. (Illus.). 63p. 1989. pap. 4.95 (0-918654-41-6) CO RR Mus.

Colorado Ransom. Susan Harmon. 192p. 1991. 19.95 (0-8027-4125-8) Walker & Co.

Colorado Ransom. large type ed. Susan Harmon. 261p. 1992. reprint ed. lib. bdg. 14.95 (1-56054-403-1) Thorndike Pr.

Colorado Ransom. large type ed. Bill Wade. (Dales Western Ser.). 189p. 1993. pap. 16.95 (1-85389-406-0, Medcom-Trainex) Ulverscroft.

Colorado Real Estate: An Introduction to the Profession. Richard O. Jones & Bruce M. Harwood. LC 79-939. (Illus.). 1979. text ed. 28.00 (0-8359-0883-6, Reston) P-H.

Colorado Real Estate Forms, 3 vols. suppl. ed. Beverly J. Quail. 1993. 80.00 (0-685-74607-0) Butterworth Legal Pubs.

Colorado Real Estate Forms, 3 vols., Set. Beverly J. Quail. 1660p. 1993. 5.25 hd, ring bd. 299.00 (0-87189-058-5) Michie Butterworth.

Colorado Real Estate Transactions. Owen L. Oliver. LC 85-80619. (Practice Systems Library Manual). 1985. 120.00 (0-318-18298-X); Suppl. 1993. 67.50 (0-317-03274-7) Lawyers Cooperative.

Colorado Recreational Road Atlas. 1994. pap. 11.95 (0-914449-41-9) Pierson Graph.

***Colorado Reel & Old Fishing Tackle: A Collector's Guide.** Gary Carbaugh & Dick Spurr. 128p. 1994. pap. 16.00 (1-882418-14-X) Centenn Pubns.

Colorado Reflections. John Fielder. (Illus.). 60p. 1994. 14.95 (1-56579-054-5) Westcliffe Pubs Inc.

Colorado Remembrances. Marvin N. Cameron. (Illus.). 8p. 1988. pap. 2.00 (0-944653-01-4) Silver State Pub.

***Colorado Review: A Journal of Contemporary Literature.** Ed. by David Milofsky. 200p. 1995. write for info. (0-614-00687-2) CO St U Ctr Literary.

***Colorado Revised Statutes: 1995 Vehicles & Traffic.** State of Colorado by & Through Revisor of Statutes under Committee on Legal Services Staff. 347p. Date not set. pap. 9.50 (1-883726-02-6) Bradford Pub.

Colorado River: Instability & Basin Management. William L. Graf. LC 84-28336. (Resource Publications in Geography). 86p. (Orig.). (C). 1985. pap. 10.00 (0-89291-186-7) Assn Am Geographers.

Colorado River Compact. Reuel L. Olson. LC 26-15594. xxiv, 527p. 1983. reprint ed. lib. bdg. 53.00x (0-89370-777-5) Borgo Pr.

Colorado River Controversies. Robert B. Stanton. Ed. by James M. Chalfant. LC 82-60295. (Illus.). 310p. 1982. reprint ed. pap. 14.95 (0-916370-09-7) Westwater.

Colorado River Ecology & Dam Management. Commission on Geosciences, Environment, & Resources; National Research Council Staff,. 288p. 1991. pap. 29.00 (0-309-04535-5) Natl Acad Pr.

Colorado River Ghost Towns. Stanley W. Paher. (Illus.). 80p. 1976. pap. 14.95 (0-913814-08-3) Nevada Pubns.

***Colorado River in Grand Canyon: A Comprehensive Guide to Its Natural & Human History.** rev. ed. Larry Stevens. LC 83-61589. (Illus.). 115p. 1983. 12.95 (0-9611678-6-6) Red Lake Bks.

Colorado River Survey: Robert B. Stanton & the Denver, Colorado Canyon & Pacific Railroad. Robert B. Stanton. Ed. by C. Gregory Crampton & Dwight L. Smith. LC 84-22530. (Illus.). 319p. 1987. 29.95 (0-935704-24-8) Howe Brothers.

Colorado River Through Grand Canyon: Natural History & Human Change. Steven W. Carothers & Bryan T. Brown. LC 90-46390. (Illus.). 235p. (Orig.). 1991. 45.00 (0-8165-1131-4); pap. 19.95 (0-8165-1232-9) U of Ariz Pr.

Colorado Rivers of the Rockies. John Fielder. (Illus.). 128p. 1993. pap. 22.50 (1-56579-045-6) Westcliffe Pubs Inc.

Colorado Road Atlas. Susan Farewell et al. (State Road Atlases Ser.). 56p. 1990. pap. 4.95 (0-13-151275-7, H M Gousha) P-H Gen Ref & Trav.

Colorado Rockhounding: A Guide to Minerals, Gemstones, & Fossils. Stephen M. Voynick. (Illus.). 392p. (Orig.). 1993. pap. 15.00 (0-87842-292-7) Mountain Pr.

Colorado Rockies - The Inaugural Season: The Official Commemorative Edition. Fulcrum Staff. (Illus.). 180p. 1994. 39.95 (1-55591-175-7) Fulcrum Pub.

Colorado Rollercoasters! Carole Marsh. (Carole Marsh Colorado Bks.). (Illus.). (YA). (gr. 3-12). 1994. lib. bdg. 24.95 (0-7933-5239-8); pap. 14.95 (0-7933-5240-1); disk 29.95 (0-7933-5241-X) Gallopade Pub Group.

Colorado R.R. Guide. 120p. 1883. 8.00 (0-318-18048-0) Mobile PO.

***Colorado Rules of Evidence.** 5th annot. ed. Ethan A. Jacobson & Alan H. Bucholtz. Ed. by Robert L. Tonsing. 377p. 1994. student ed 91.00 (0-936381-14-0) CO Legal Pub.

***Colorado RV Parks - A Pictorial Guide: Modern Facilities, Full Hookups & Pull Thru Sites.** Jenny Fitt-Peaster. (Illus.). 288p. (Orig.). 1995. pap. 15.95 (1-883087-01-5) Rocky Mtn Vac.

Colorado Scenic Drives. Stewart M. Green. (FalconGuide Ser.). 240p. (Orig.). 1994. pap. 14.95 (1-56044-228-X) Falcon Pr MT.

***Colorado Scenic Guide: Northern Region.** 3rd ed. Lee Gregory. (Illus.). 240p. (Orig.). 1995. pap. 14.95 (1-55566-144-0) Johnson Bks.

***Colorado Scenic Guide: Southern Region.** 3rd ed. Lee Gregory. (Illus.). 240p. (Orig.). 1995. pap. 14.95 (1-55566-145-9) Johnson Bks.

Colorado School Trivia: An Amazing & Fascinating Look at Our State's Teachers, Schools & Students! Carole Marsh. (Carole Marsh Colorado Bks.). (Illus.). (YA). (gr. 3-12). 1994. lib. bdg. 24.95 (0-7933-0199-8); pap. 14.95 (0-7933-0198-X); disk 29.95 (0-7933-0200-5) Gallopade Pub Group.

Colorado Security Law. Frederic P. Storke & Don W. Sears. x, 396p. 1992. reprint ed. lib. bdg. 42.50 (0-8377-2651-4) Rothman.

Colorado Silly Basketball Sportsmysteries, Vol. I. Carole Marsh. (Carole Marsh Colorado Bks.). (Illus.). (YA). (gr. 3-12). 1994. lib. bdg. 24.95 (0-7933-0196-3); pap. 14.95 (0-7933-0195-5); disk 29.95 (0-7933-0197-1) Gallopade Pub Group.

Colorado Silly Basketball Sportsmysteries, Vol. II. Carole Marsh. (Carole Marsh Colorado Bks.). (Illus.). (YA). (gr. 3-12). 1994. lib. bdg. 24.95 (0-7933-1577-8); pap. 14.95 (0-7933-1578-6); disk 29.95 (0-7933-1579-4) Gallopade Pub Group.

Colorado Silly Football Sportsmysteries, Vol. I. Carole Marsh. (Carole Marsh Colorado Bks.). (Illus.). (YA). (gr. 3-12). 1994. lib. bdg. 24.95 (1-55609-528-7); pap. 14.95 (1-55609-527-9); disk 29.95 (0-7933-1409-7) Gallopade Pub Group.

Colorado Silly Football Sportsmysteries, Vol. II. Carole Marsh. (Carole Marsh Colorado Bks.). (Illus.). (YA). (gr. 3-12). 1994. lib. bdg. 24.95 (0-7933-1410-0); pap. 14.95 (0-7933-1411-9); disk 29.95 (0-7933-1412-7) Gallopade Pub Group.

Colorado Silly Trivia! Carole Marsh. (Carole Marsh Colorado Bks.). (Illus.). (YA). (gr. 3-12). 1994. lib. bdg. 24.95 (1-55609-523-6); pap. 14.95 (1-55609-522-8); disk 29.95 (0-7933-1406-2) Gallopade Pub Group.

***Colorado Silver Bullets: The Women Who Go Toe-to-Toe with the Men.** Dave Kindred. 144p. 1995. 19.50 (1-56352-199-7) Longstreet Pr Inc.

Colorado Ski Country. Charlie Meyers. Ed. by Marnie Hagmann. LC 86-82747. 104p. 1987. 14.95 (0-937959-17-0); pap. 14.95 (0-937959-16-2) Falcon Pr MT.

Colorado Ski Industry: Highlights of the 1986-87 Season. rev. ed. Kathleen O'Brien. 27p. 1987. pap. text ed. 15.00 (0-89478-000-X) U CO Busn Res Div.

An Asterisk (*) at the beginning of an entry indicates that the title is appearing in BIP for the first time.

An Asterisk (*) at the beginning of an entry indicates that the title is appearing in BIP for the first time.

1391

Colorful Streetcars We Rode Bulletin, No. 125. LC 85-81490. (Illus.). 112p. 1986. 45.00 (*0-915348-08-X*); pap. 28.00 (*0-915348-25-X*) Central Electric.

Colorful U. S. Navy A-4 Skyhawks. Bert Kinzey & Ray Leader. (Colors & Markings Ser.: Vol. 18). (Illus.). 64p. 1991. pap. 12.95 (*0-8306-4542-X*, 24542) TAB Bks.

Colorimetric & Fluorimetric Analysis of Organic Compounds & Drugs. Maurice Pesez & J. Bartos. LC 73-84815. (Clinical & Biochemical Analysis Ser.: No. 1). 688p. reprint ed. pap. 180.00 (*0-7837-5176-1*, 2044906) Bks Demand.

***Colorimetric Determination of Aspirin in Commercial Preparations.** Robert P. Pinnell. Ed. by H. A. Neidig. (Modular Laboratory Program in Chemistry Ser.). 12p. (C). 1989. pap. text ed. 1.25x (*0-87540-360-3*) Chem Educ Res.

Colorimetric Determination of Nonmetals. 2nd ed. David F. Boltz. LC 77-12398. (Chemical Analysis Ser.: No. 8). (Illus.). 560p. reprint ed. pap. 160.50 (*0-685-23825-3*, 2056606) Bks Demand.

Coloring Alaska's Cordova. Michael Anderson. (Illus.). 32p. 1986. pap. 4.98 (*0-9607358-5-2*) Fathom Pub.

Coloring & Additives, Surface Finishing & Assembly, Thermoplastics, Vol. II. 213p. 1980. pap. 31.00 (*0-938648-34-9*, 1504) T-C Pubns CA.

Coloring Atlas of Horse Anatomy. Robert A. Kainer & Thomas O. McCracken. (Illus.). 180p. (Orig.). 1994. pap. 16.95 (*0-931866-69-3*) Alpine Pubns.

Coloring Atlas of Human Anatomy. Marvin M. Shrewsbury & Edwin Chin, Jr. 196p. (C). 1982. pap. text ed. 16.00 (*0-15-511800-5*) SCP.

Coloring Atlas of Human Anatomy. 2nd ed. Stephen W. Langjahr & Robert D. Brister. 202p. (C). 1992. spiral bd. 20.50 (*0-8053-4020-3*); write for info. (*0-8053-4021-1*) Benjamin-Cummings.

Coloring Bears. Illus. by Lucinda McQueen. LC 90-83242. (Wee Pudgy Board Bks.). 24p. (J). (ps). 1991. 2.50 (*0-448-40126-6*, G&D) Putnam Pub Group.

Coloring Book for Lowell. Elizabeth D. Hengen & Carole Zellie. (Illus.). 16p. (Orig.). 1982. pap. 1.50 (*0-942472-06-3*) Lowell Museum.

Coloring Book for the Super-Intelligent. Brett Bender. (Illus.). 20p. (Orig.). 1984. pap. write for info. (*0-9615356-0-1*) B Bender.

Coloring Book of Bible Proverbs: KJV. Illus. by Penny Clark. 32p. (J). (ps-5). 1988. ring bd. 2.50 (*0-9618608-2-0*) Lynn's Bookshelf.

Coloring Book of Bible Verses from Proverbs: NIV. Ed. by Barbara Decker. (Illus.). 32p. (Orig.). (J). (ps-8). 1991. ring bd. 2.50 (*0-9618608-6-3*) Lynn's Bookshelf.

Coloring Book of Bible Verses from the Epistles. Ed. by Barbara Decker. (Illus.). 32p. (Orig.). (J). 1989. ring bd. 2.50 (*0-9618608-4-7*) Lynn's Bookshelf.

Coloring Book of Bible Verses from the Epistles. Ed. by Barbara Decker. (Illus.). 32p. (Orig.). (J). (ps-5). 1992. ring bd. 2.50 (*0-9618608-9-8*) Lynn's Bookshelf.

Coloring Book of Embryology. Matsumura & England. (Illus.). 311p. 1992. 19.95 (*0-8151-5726-6*) Mosby Yr Bk.

Coloring Book of Pikes Peak Country: Follow the Pikes Peak Trail & See the Wonders of the Area. Sandy Whelchel. (Illus.). 38p. (Orig.). (J). (gr. k-4). 1989. reprint ed. pap. 3.50 (*1-878406-01-9*) Parker Dstb.

Coloring Book of Stained Glass Windows from the Cathedral of St. John the Divine. A. G. Smith. (Illus.). (J). (gr. 1-6). 1983. pap. 2.95 (*0-915075-00-8*) Cathedral Shop.

Coloring Books on Events of the Jewish Months: Nisan. M. Liebermann. (Learn As You Color Ser.: No. II). (J). (ps-2). 1987. 3.00 (*0-914131-86-9*, D712) Torah Umesorah.

Coloring Books on Events of the Jewish Months: Tishrei, Cheshvan. M. Liebermann. (Learn As You Color Ser.: No. II). (J). (ps-2). 1987. 3.00 (*0-914131-84-2*, D710) Torah Umesorah.

Coloring Books on the Parshas Hashavua: Bereishis. M. Liebermann. (Learn As You Color Ser.: No. I). (J). (ps-2). 1987. 3.00 (*0-914131-79-6*, D700) Torah Umesorah.

Coloring Books on the Parshas Hashavua: Devorim. M. Liebermann. (Learn As You Color Ser.: No. I). (J). (ps-2). 1987. 3.00 (*0-914131-83-4*, D704) Torah Umesorah.

Coloring Books on the Parshas Hashavua: Shemos. M. Liebermann. (Learn As You Color Ser.: No. I). (J). (ps-2). 1987. 3.00 (*0-914131-80-X*, D701) Torah Umesorah.

Coloring Books on the Parshas Hashavua: Vayikrah. M. Liebermann. (Learn As You Color Ser.: No. I). (J). (ps-2). 1987. 3.00 (*0-914131-81-8*, D702) Torah Umesorah.

Coloring Calendar Cookbook for Kids. Aileen Paul. (Illus.). 24p. (Orig.). (J). (gr. 5 up). 1982. pap. 2.95 (*0-913270-90-3*) Sunstone Pr.

***Coloring Charleston.** Sheila P. Rudd. (Coloring the Low Country Ser.). (Illus.). 32p. (J). (gr. 1-8). 1994. pap. text ed. 4.95 (*1-880795-75-2*) MBT Ent P&P.

Coloring Cookbook for Children. Annie Meyer & Mary Lynn Munro. 64p. (Orig.). (J). (gr. 1-6). 1974. pap. 3.95 (*0-89716-061-4*) P B Pubng.

Coloring Guide to Regional Human Anatomy. 2nd ed. T. Alan Twietmeyer & Thomas O. McCracken. (Illus.). 232p. 1992. pap. 18.50 (*0-8121-1526-0*) Williams & Wilkins.

Coloring Mapbook: Countries & Flags. Bo Gramfors. (Coloring Bks.). (Illus.). 39p. (J). (gr. 2-6). 1992. pap. 7.95 (*1-879856-96-4*) Interarts.

Coloring Mapbook: Living Earth & Countries & Flags, 2 bks., Set. Bo Gramfors. (Coloring Bks.). (Illus.). 78p. (J). (gr. 2-6). 1992. pap. 12.95 (*1-879856-97-2*) Interarts.

Coloring Mapbook - Countries & Flags, Bk. I. Bo Gramfors. (Coloring MAPBOOKs Ser.). (Illus.). 39p. (J). (gr. 2-6). 1992. pap. 5.95 (*1-879856-15-8*) Interarts.

Coloring Mapbook - Living EarthFlags: Single Book with Pencils. Bo Gramfors. (Coloring Bks.). (Illus.). 39p. (J). (gr. 2-6). 1992. pap. 7.95 (*1-879856-95-6*) Interarts.

Coloring Mapbook - The Living Earth, Bk. II. Bo Gramfors. (Coloring MAPBOOKs Ser.). (Illus.). 39p. (J). (gr. 2-6). 1992. pap. 5.95 (*1-879856-16-6*) Interarts.

Coloring of Plastics. Thomas G. Webber. LC 79-10922. (Society of Plastics Engineers Monographs). 220p. 1979. text ed. 99.00 (*0-471-92327-3*, Wiley-Interscience) Wiley.

Coloring of Plastics: Cost Effective Color Compounding with Proper Equipment; Regional Technical Conference, October 3-4-5, 1983. Society of Plastics Engineers Staff. 226p. reprint ed. pap. 64.50 (*0-317-28113-5*, 2022510) Bks Demand.

Coloring of Plastics - Now & the Future: Regional Technical Conference, 1984. Society of Plastics Engineers Staff. 149p. reprint ed. pap. 42.50 (*0-317-27168-7*, 2024726) Bks Demand.

Coloring Outside the Lines; Discipleship for the Undisciplined. John F. Westfall. 1991. pap. 10.00 (*0-06-069298-7*) Harper SF.

Coloring Performance Plastics for Automotive: Regional Technical Conference, September 18-20, 1989. Society of Plastics Engineers Staff. (Illus.). 239p. reprint ed. pap. 68.20 (*0-8357-3619-9*, 2036320) Bks Demand.

Coloring Review Guide of Human Anatomy & Physiology. Robert J. Stone & Judith A. Stone. (Illus.). 344p. (C). 1995. spiral bd. write for info. (*0-697-17109-4*) Wm C Brown Pubs.

Coloring Review Guide to Human Anatomy. W. Hogin McMurtrie & James E. Rikel. 448p. (C). 1990. spiral bd. write for info. (*0-697-03150-0*) Wm C Brown Pubs.

***Coloring Review of Neuroscience.** 2nd ed. D. Michael McKeough. LC 94-45666. 1995. 22.95 (*0-316-56209-2*) Little.

Coloring Shadows. Caroline Sniffen & Frances Sniffen. (Illus.). 80p. (J). 1994. pap. 5.95 (*0-8059-3536-3*) Dorrance.

Coloring the Book of the Shadowboxes: A Story of the ABC's. Laura L. Seeley. (Illus.). 64p. (Orig.). (J). (ps-3). 1993. pap. 4.95 (*1-56145-037-5*) Peachtree Pubs.

Coloring the Halls of Ivy: Leadership & Diversity in the Academy. Ed. by Josephine D. Davis. 200p. (C). 1993. text ed. 28.95 (*0-927042-97-6*) Anker Pub.

Coloring the Wind: Using Photos & Words. David P. Young. (Illus.). 120p. (Orig.). 1992. pap. 12.99 (*0-664-25376-8*) Westminster John Knox.

Coloring Theories. S. Fisk. LC 89-27623. 164p. 1989. pap. 37.00 (*0-8218-5109-8*, CONM-103) Am Math.

Coloring Tour of Sharlot Hall Museum: Featuring the Sharlot Hall Kids. Jim Willoughby. (Illus.). 32p. (J). (gr. k-5). 1994. 2.75 (*0-927579-05-7*) Sharlot Hall Mus Pr.

Colorist. Susan Daitch. (Vintage Contemporaries Ser.). (Orig.). 1990. pap. 8.95 (*0-679-72492-3*, Vin) Random.

Colorist. Susan Daitch. 40p. (Orig.). 1985. pap. 3.00 (*0-917061-22-5*) Top Stories.

***Colorless Reality.** Pearl Fisher. 156p. 1995. pap. text ed. 12.95 (*0-9646071-0-7*) Whispering Leaf.

Colormore Travels - Austin, Texas: The Travel Guide for Kids. Susan C. Koch. (Illus.). 32p. (Orig.). (J). (gr. k-4). 1988. pap. 4.50 (*0-945600-00-3*) Colormore Inc.

Colormore Travels - Fort Worth, Texas: The Travel Guide for Kids. Susan C. Koch. (Illus.). (Orig.). (J). (gr. k-4). 1989. pap. 4.50 (*0-945600-02-X*) Colormore Inc.

Colormore Travels - San Antonio, Texas: The Travel Guide for Kids. Susan C. Koch. (Illus.). 32p. (Orig.). (J). (gr. k-4). 1990. pap. 4.50 (*0-945600-05-4*) Colormore Inc.

Colorology: The Study of the Science of Color. Caryl Dennis. (Illus.). 128p. (Orig.). 1990. pap. 12.00 (*0-9627845-0-8*) Rainbows Unltd.

Colors. (Sticker Activity Ser.). 1993. pap. 6.95 (*1-56458-239-6*) Dorling Kindersley.

***Colors.** (Tab Board Bks.). (J). Date not set. bds. 4.95 (*0-7894-0230-0*, 5-70642) Dorling Kindersley.

Colors. Richard L. Allington. LC 79-19116. (Beginning to Learn about Ser.). (Illus.). 32p. (J). (gr. k-3). 1985. lib. bdg. 9.95 (*0-8172-1280-9*); pap. 3.95 (*0-8114-8240-5*) Raintree Steck-V.

Colors. Illus. by Tedd Arnold. (Nursery Rhyme Concept Bks.). 16p. (J). (ps). 1992. pap. 3.95 (*0-671-77825-0*, Litl Simon S&S) S&S Childrens.

Colors. Rowan Barnes-Murphy. (Blackboard Bks.). 16p. (J). (ps). 1992. bds. 3.95 (*0-8249-8530-3*, Ideals Child) Hambleton-Hill.

Colors. Roma Bishop. (Nursery Board Mini Pop Bks.). (J). (ps). 1992. pap. 2.95 (*0-671-79120-6*, Litl Simon S&S) S&S Childrens.

Colors. K. Bryant-Mole. (First Learning Ser.). (Illus.). 24p. (J). (ps-3). 1990. pap. 3.50 (*0-7460-0594-6*, Usborne) EDC.

Colors. Illus. by Jane Conteh-Morgan. (So Tall Board Bks.). 9p. (J). (ps-1). 1993. bds. 4.95 (*0-448-40522-9*, G&D) Putnam Pub Group.

Colors. Illus. by Sue Cony. (Learn-a-Round Ser.). 8p. (J). (ps-00). 1991. bds. 4.95 (*1-56293-148-2*) McClanahan Bk.

Colors. Nancy M. Davis et al. (Davis Teaching Units Ser.: Vol. 2, No. 6). (Illus.). (Orig.). (J). (ps-2). 1986. pap. 4.95 (*0-937103-13-6*) DaNa Pubns.

Colors. Pascale De Bourgoing. (First Discovery Bks.). (Illus.). (J). 1991. pap. 11.95 (*0-590-45236-3*, Cartwheel) Scholastic Inc.

***Colors.** Illus. by Marion H. Ekberg. (1-2-3 Ser.). 160p. (J). 1995. 14.95 (*0-614-06801-0*, WPH 0403) Totline Bks.

Colors. Monique Felix. (Mouse Bks.). (J). 1992. lib. bdg. 10.95 (*0-88682-404-4*) Stewart Tabori & Chang.

Colors. Monique Felix. (J). (ps up). 1993. 7.95 (*1-56846-075-9*) Creative Ed.

Colors. Barbara Gregorich. Ed. by Joan Hoffman. (Get Ready! Bks.). (Illus.). 32p. (J). (ps). 1983. student ed 1.99 (*0-938256-64-5*) Sch Zone Pub Co.

Colors. Shirley Hughes. LC 86-2732. (Illus.). 24p. (J). (ps). 1986. 4.95 (*0-688-04206-6*) Lothrop.

Colors. Illus. by Jonathan Lambert. (Early Learning Board Bks.). 18p. (J). (ps-1). 1992. bds. 1.95 (*0-681-41562-2*) Longmeadow Pr.

Colors. David Moss. (Pull the Tab Bks.). 10p. (J). 1989. 4.99 (*0-517-69421-2*) Random Hse Value.

Colors. Jan Pienkowski. (Nursery Board Bks.). (Illus.). 14p. (J). (ps). 1989. 2.95 (*0-671-68134-6*, Litl Simon S&S) S&S Childrens.

Colors. John J. Reiss. LC 69-13653. (Illus.). 32p. (J). (ps-2). 1982. text ed. 13.95 (*0-02-776130-4*, Bradbury S&S) S&S Childrens.

Colors. Illus. by Tony Tallarico. (Tiny Bks.). 28p. (J). (ps-1). 1988. bds. 2.95 (*0-448-48819-1*, Tuffy) Putnam Pub Group.

Colors. Annette Taulbee. (Be Smart Bks.). (Illus.). 24p. (J). (ps-00). 1986. 3.98 (*0-86734-060-6*, FS-3052) Schaffer Pubns.

Colors. Sian Tucker. (Nursery Board Bks.). (Illus.). 24p. (J). (ps-00). 1992. pap. 2.95 (*0-671-76907-3*, Litl Simon S&S) S&S Childrens.

Colors. Philip Yenawine. (Illus.). (J). (gr. 2-5). 1991. 14.95 (*0-385-30254-1*) Delacorte.

Colors. John J. Reiss. LC 86-22189. (Illus.). 32p. (J). (ps-2). 1987. reprint ed. pap. 4.95 (*0-689-71119-0*, Aladdin Paperbacks) S&S Childrens.

Colors, Vol. 1. Heidi Goennel. (J). (ps-4). 1990. 15.95 (*0-316-31843-4*) Little.

Colors: A Turn-the-Wheel Book. Mavis Smith. (Wheelies Ser.). (Illus.). 12p. (J). 1994. 4.50 (*0-307-17375-5*, Artsts Writrs) Western Pub.

Colors: Active Minds. Photos by George Siede & Donna Preis. (Active Minds-English Ser.). (Illus.). 24p. (J). (ps-3). 1992. lib. bdg. 9.95 (*1-56674-001-0*) Forest Hse.

Colors: Multicultural Inspirations for Growth & Recovery. Deborah Stein. LC 92-72159. 272p. 1991. 8.95 (*0-925190-58-6*) Fairview Press.

Colors: Stories of the Kingdom. John R. Aurelio. LC 93-15750. 216p. (Orig.). 1993. pap. 14.95 (*0-8245-1361-4*) Crossroad NY.

***Colors: The Rainbow Around Us.** Ed. by Brigitta Geltrich. (Thematic Anthologies Ser.). (Illus.). 80p. (Orig.). 1995. pap. text ed. 11.25 (*0-936945-52-4*) Creat with Wds.

***Colors - Gems of the Seven Rays.** unabridged ed. William C. Stuber. Ed. & Pref. by Charlotte Sykes. LC 95-68351. 252p. (Orig.). 1995. pap. text ed. 17.95 (*1-887198-04-0*) Shabda Pub.

***Colors & Chords: The Art of Johnny Otis.** Lee Hildebrand & Mary L. O'Neal. (Illus.). 112p. (Orig.). 1995. pap. 22.95 (*0-87654-359-X*) Pomegranate Calif.

Colors & Markings: F-4D Phantom II, Vol. 4. Bert Kinzey. (Illus.). 40p. 1986. pap. 12.95 (*0-8306-8428-X*, NO. 24528, TAB-Aero) TAB Bks.

Colors & Markings Vol. 5: A-6 Intruder. Bert Kinzey & Ray Leader. (Illus.). 64p. (Orig.). 1987. pap. 12.95 (*0-8306-8529-4*, 24529) TAB Bks.

Colors & Markings Vol. 6: U. S. Navy Adversary Aircraft. Bert Kinzey & Ray Leader. (Illus.). 80p. (Orig.). 1987. pap. 14.95 (*0-8306-8530-8*, 24530) TAB Bks.

Colors & Markings Vol. 7: Special Purpose, C-130 Hercules. Ray Leader. (Illus.). 64p. (Orig.). 1987. pap. 12.95 (*0-8306-8531-6*, 24531) TAB Bks.

Colors & Markings Vol. 9: A-7-E Corsair II; U. S. Navy Atlantic Coast Post-Vietnam Markings. Bert Kinzey. (Illus.). 64p. 1987. pap. 12.95 (*0-8306-8433-6*, 24533) TAB Bks.

Colors & Markings Vol. 10: U. S. Navy CAG Aircraft: Pt. 1: Fighters. Bert Kinzey. (Illus.). 80p. 1988. pap. 14.95 (*0-8306-8534-0*, 24534P) TAB Bks.

Colors & Markings Vol. 11: U.S. Air Force Aggressor Squadrons. Bert Kinzey & Ray Leader. (Illus.). 64p. 1988. pap. 12.95 (*0-8306-8535-9*, 24535) TAB Bks.

Colors & Markings Vol. 12: MIG Kill Markings of the Vietnam War. Bert Kinzey & Ray Leader. (Illus.). 64p. 1989. pap. 14.95 (*0-8306-8536-7*, 24536) TAB Bks.

Colors & Markings, F-106 Delta Dart, Vol. 1. Bert Kinzey. Ed. by Ernest J. Gentle. (Colors & Markings Ser.). (Illus.). 64p. (Orig.). 1984. pap. 12.95 (*0-8168-4525-5*, 24525, TAB-Aero) TAB Bks.

Colors & Markings of the A-10 Warthog. Dana Bell. (Colors & Markings Ser.: Vol. 21). 64p. 1991. pap. 12.95 (*0-8306-3096-1*, 24548) TAB Bks.

Colors & Markings of the F-100 Super Sabre. David W. Menard. (Colors & Markings Ser.: Vol. 23, Pt. 2). 64p. 1992. pap. 12.95 (*0-8306-3947-0*, 24547) TAB Bks.

Colors & Markings of the F-14 Tomcat. Bert Kinzey. Ed. by Ernest J. Gentle. (Colors & Markings Ser.: Vol. 3). (Illus.). 64p. (Orig.). 1986. pap. 9.95 (*0-8168-4526-3*, 24526, TAB-Aero) TAB Bks.

Colors & Markings of the F-15 Eagle. Bert Kinzey & Ray Leader. (Colors & Markings Ser.: Vol. 20). 64p. 1991. pap. 12.95 (*0-8306-2152-0*, 24544) TAB Bks.

Colors & Markings of the F-4C Phantom II, Pt. 1: Post Vietnam Markings, 1974-1984, Vol. 3. Bert Kinzey. (Colors & Markings Ser.). (Illus.). 64p. (Orig.). 1985. pap. 11.95 (*0-8168-4527-1*, 24527, TAB-Aero) TAB Bks.

***Colors & Markings of the Recon Phantoms.** (Colors & Markings: 23). 64p. 1994. pap. 15.95 (*0-89024-221-6*) Kalmbach.

Colors & Markings of the U. S. Navy F-4 Phantoms. Bert Kinzey & Ray Leader. (Colors & Markings Ser.: Vol. 22, Pt. 2). 64p. 1991. pap. 12.95 (*0-8306-2153-9*, 24545) TAB Bks.

Colors & Materials for Oil Painting: A Practical Guide. Jacques Turner. 104p. 1993. pap. 13.95 (*1-55821-267-1*) Lyons & Burford.

Colors & Numbers. Burton Marks. LC 91-17493. (Read-a-Picture Ser.). (Illus.). 24p. (J). (gr. k-2). 1992. lib. bdg. 9.89 (*0-8167-2411-3*); pap. text ed. 2.95 (*0-8167-2412-1*) Troll Assocs.

Colors & Numbers 1994: Your Personal Guide to Positive Vibrations in Daily Life. rev. ed. Louise L. Hay. 64p. 1993. pap. 5.00 (*1-56170-063-0*, 1044) Hay House.

Colors & Numbers '95. Louise L. Hay. 64p. 1994. pap. 5.00 (*1-56170-102-5*, 1045) Hay House.

***Colors & Numbers '96.** 10th ed. Louise L. Hay. Ed. by Jill Kramer. 64p. Date not set. pap. 5.95 (*1-56170-123-8*, 1046) Hay House.

Colors & Opposites. (Let's Have Fun Spanish-English Coloring & Activity Bks.). (Illus.). 32p. (J). (ps-1). 1992. pap. 2.95 (*1-56144-107-4*, Honey Bear Bks) Modern Pub NYC.

Colors Around Me. Vivian Church. LC 75-154209. (Illus.). 28p. (J). (gr. k-3). 1971. 4.95 (*0-910030-15-4*) Afro-Am.

Colors by Lori: Crayons, Colored Pencils, Watercolors - A Coloring Book for the Advanced Colorer. Lori M. Vicento & Michael A. Sward. (Illus.). 44p. (Orig.). 1990. pap. 7.95 (*0-9626094-0-4*) Colors By Lori.

Colors Changing Hue. Yvonne Porcella. Ed. by Harold Nadel & Joyce Lytle. LC 94-13305. (Illus.). 96p. 1994. pap. 21.95 (*0-914881-86-8*, 10103) C & T Pub.

Colors Everywhere. Tana Hoban. LC 93-24847. (Illus.). 32p. (J). (ps up). 1995. 16.00 (*0-688-12762-2*); lib. bdg. 15.93 (*0-688-12763-0*) Greenwillow.

Colors for Brides. Lauren Smith & Kathleen Hughes. 272p. 1990. pap. 12.95 (*0-380-70986-4*) Avon.

Colors for Living: Baths. 128p. 1995. 24.99 (*1-56496-103-6*) Rockport Pubs.

Colors for Living: Bedrooms. 128p. 1996. 24.99 (*1-56496-105-2*) Rockport Pubs.

Colors for Living: Kitchens. 128p. 1995. 24.99 (*1-56496-102-8*) Rockport Pubs.

Colors for Living: Livingrooms. 128p. 1996. 24.99 (*1-56496-104-4*) Rockport Pubs.

Colors for Survival: Mimicry & Camouflage in Nature. Marco Ferrari. LC 93-22184. (Adventures in Nature Ser.). (Illus.). 144p. (ENG.). 1993. 29.95 (*1-56566-048-X*) Thomasson-Grant.

Colors from Nature: Growing, Collecting, & Using Natural Dyes. Bobbi McRae. Ed. by Gwen Steege. LC 92-53808. (Illus.). 168p. 1993. 26.95 (*0-88266-806-4*, Storey Pub); pap. 17.95 (*0-88266-799-8*, Storey Pub) Storey Comm Inc.

Colors from the Zohar. Jerry Winston. LC 75-45790. 1977. pap. 3.95 (*0-685-74778-6*) Barah.

Colors in Cambridge. National Cambridge Society Staff. (Illus.). 128p. 1991. 19.95 (*0-89145-270-2*) Collector Bks.

Colors in God's World. Beverly Beckmann. 1983. 6.99 (*0-570-04082-5*, 56-1437) Concordia.

Colors in Hawaiian. Cassandra Land-Nellist. (Hawaiian Treasures Ser.). (Illus.). 10p. (ENG & HAU.). (J). (ps). 1993. 3.95 (*0-916630-72-2*) Pr Pacifica.

Colors in the Sky. Harry D. Eshleman. (Illus.). 24p. (Orig.). 1993. pap. 5.00 (*0-926935-86-0*) Runaway Spoon.

Colors of a Clown: Selected Poems 1974-1990. A. E. Figueredo. (Poetry Ser.). 50p. (Orig.). 1991. pap. 10.00 (*0-916611-05-1*) Antilles Pr.

Colors of a Different Horse: Rethinking Creative Writing Theory & Pedagogy. Ed. by Wendy Bishop & Hans Ostrom. LC 94-7323. 328p. 1994. pap. 22.95 (*0-8141-0716-8*) NCTE.

Colors of Christmas. H. Michael Nehls. Ed. by Michael L. Sherer. (Orig.). 1986. pap. 4.15 (*0-89536-838-2*, 6862) CSS OH.

Colors of Desire: Poems. David Mura. LC 94-6587. 1995. mass mkt. 10.00 (*0-385-47461-X*, Anchor NY) Doubleday.

Colors of God's Love. Alice G. Rusin. 1994. pap. 10.95 (*0-533-10812-8*) Vantage.

Colors of Haiku. Helen J. Sherry. LC 91-80503. (Illus.). 96p. (Orig.). 1991. pap. write for info. (*0-922273-02-2*) Chocho Bks.

Colors of Heaven: Short Stories from the Pacific Rim. Intro. by Trevor Carolan. LC 91-58058. 1992. 11.00 (*0-679-73885-1*, Vin) Random.

Colors of Infinity. Donald E. Axinn. (Orig.). 1990. 16.95 (*0-929654-96-X*, North Star Line) Blue Moon Bks.

Colors of Infinity. Donald E. Axinn. 1990. pap. 8.95 (*0-929654-92-7*, North Star Line) Blue Moon Bks.

Colors of Ink: Chinese Paintings & Related Ceramics from the Cleveland Museum of Art. Sherman E. Lee. LC 74-27415. (Asia Society Ser.). (Illus.). 1976. reprint ed. lib. bdg. 33.95 (*0-405-06564-7*) Ayer.

Colors of Love. Leon Del Ciervo. LC 91-68364. 64p. (Orig.). 1992. pap. 7.95 (*1-877978-31-0*, STARbks Pr) Woldt.

Colors of Mankind: The Range & Role of Human Pigmentation. Spencer L. Rogers. (Illus.). 68p. (C). 1990. text ed. 21.95x (*0-398-05643-9*) C C Thomas.

Colors of My Rainbow. Joe Wayman. (Illus.). 36p. (J). (gr. k-8). 1988. pap. 7.95 (*0-945799-03-9*) Pieces of Lrning.

Colors of Nature. Bobbie Kalman. (Primary Ecology Ser.). (Illus.). 32p. (Orig.). (J). (gr. 3-6). 1993. lib. bdg. 15.95 (*0-86505-557-2*); pap. 7.95 (*0-86505-583-1*) Crabtree Pub Co.

Colors of Passion. Valeska Lee. 150p. 1996. pap. 3.79 (*0-9634431-1-9*) C Y Pub Grp.

Colors of Poetry: Essays on Classic Japanese Verse. Ooka Makoto. Ed. by Thomas Fitzsimmons. Tr. by Takako Lento & Thomas Lento. (Reflections Ser.: No. 1). 152p. (C). 1991. 19.95 (*0-942668-28-6*); pap. 12.95 (*0-942668-27-8*) Katydid Bks.

An Asterisk (*) at the beginning of an entry indicates that the title is appearing in BIP for the first time.

An Asterisk (*) at the beginning of an entry indicates that the title is appearing in BIP for the first time.

C

Colour Schemes for the Flower Garden. rev. ed. Gertrude Jekyll. LC 82-16348. (Jekyll Garden Bks.). (Illus.). 276p. 1983. reprint ed. 24.95 (*0-88143-000-5*) Ayer.

Colour Schemes for the Flower Garden. rev. ed. Gertrude Jekyll. LC 82-16348. (Jekyll Garden Bks.). (Illus.). 276p. 1984. reprint ed. pap. 10.95 (*0-88143-060-9*) Ayer.

Colour Slide Set of Human Cross-Sectional Anatomy: Atlas of Body Sections & CT Images. Harold Ellis et al. (Illus.). 1993. write for info. (*0-7506-1730-6*) Buttrwrth-Heinemann.

Colour Studies in Paris. Arthur Symons. 1972. 59.95 (*0-87968-351-1*) Gordon Pr.

***Colour Vision: A Study in Cognitive Science & the Philosophy of Perception.** Evan Thompson. LC 94-13588. (Philosophical Issues in Science Ser.). 400p. 1994. 65.00x (*0-415-07717-6*, B4190) Routledge.

Colour Vision: Physiology & Psychophysics. Ed. by John Mollon & L. Ted Sharpe. 1983. text ed. 115.00 (*0-12-504280-9*) Acad Pr.

Colour Vision Deficiencies, IX. Ed. by B. Drum & G. Verriest. (Documents Ophthalmologica Proceedings Ser.). (C). 1988. lib. bdg. 251.50 (*0-89838-403-6*) Kluwer Ac.

Colour Vision Deficiencies: Proceedings of the Seventh Symposium of the International Research Group on Color Vision Deficiencies, Geneva 1983, No. VII. G. Verriest. (Documenta Ophthalmologica Proceedings Ser.). (Illus.). 434p. 1984. lib. bdg. 170.00 (*90-6193-735-3*) Kluwer Ac.

***Colour Vision Deficiencies Five: Proceedings of the Fifth Symposium of the International Research Group on Colour Vision Deficiencies Held at St. Mary's College, Strawberry Hill, London, 26-28 June 1979.** fac. ed. International Research Group on Colour Vision Deficiencies Staff. Ed. by G. Verriest. LC 80-751. (Illus.). 422p. 1980. reprint ed. pap. 120.30 (*0-7837-8016-8*, 2047772) Bks Demand.

Colour Vision Deficiencies Four: Proceedings of the Symposium, Parma, June 1977. International Research Group on Colour Vision Deficiencies Staff. Ed. by E. B. Streiff & G. Verriest. (Modern Problems in Ophthalmology Ser.: Vol. 19). (Illus.). 1978. 158.50 (*3-8055-2800-0*) S Karger.

Colour Vision Deficiencies, No. 11: Proceedings of the Eleventh International Symposium, Sydney, Australia, 21-23 June 1991. Ed. by B. Drum. LC 92-23627. (Documenta Ophthalmologica Proceedings Ser.: Vol. 56). (C). 1993. lib. bdg. 238.00 (*0-7923-1864-1*) Kluwer Ac.

Colour Vision Deficiencies Six. G. Verriest. 1982. lib. bdg. 219.00 (*90-6193-729-9*) Kluwer Ac.

Colour Vision Deficiencies Ten. Ed. by B. Drum et al. (Documenta Ophthalmologica Proceedings Ser.). (C). 1991. lib. bdg. 248.50 (*0-7923-0948-0*) Kluwer Ac.

Colour Vision Deficiencies Three: Proceedings of the Symposium, 3rd. International Research Group on Colour Vision Deficiencies Staff. Ed. by G. Verriest. (Modern Problems in Ophthalmology Ser.: Vol. 17). 300p. 1976. 142.50 (*3-8055-2297-5*) S Karger.

Colour Vision Deficiencies Twelve: Proceedings of the Twelfth Symposium of the International Research Group on Colour Vision Deficiencies, Held in Tubingen, Germany, 18-22 July 1993. Ed. by B. Drum et al. LC 94-13946. (Documents, Ophthalmologica Proceedings Ser.: Vol. 57). 572p. (C). 1995. lib. bdg. 224.00 (*0-7923-2889-2*) Kluwer Ac.

Colour Vision Deficiencies Two: Proceedings of the Symposium, 2nd, Edinburgh, June 1973. International Research Group on Colour Vision Deficiencies Staff. Ed. by G. Verriest. (Modern Problems in Ophthalmology Ser.: Vol. 13). 300p. 1974. 127.25 (*3-8055-1698-3*) S Karger.

Colour Your Garden with Australian Natives. Geoff Rigby & Bev Rigby. (Illus.). 128p. 1993. 29.95 (*0-86417-492-6*, Pub. by Kangaroo Pr AT) Seven Hills Bk.

Coloured Bangles & Other Stories. Saloni Narang. LC 83-50208. 78p. (C). 1984. 17.00 (*0-89410-403-9*); pap. 8.00 (*0-89410-404-7*) Three Continents.

***Coloured Pencil Drawing.** Jenny Rodwell. (Illus.). 96p. 1995. 17.95 (*0-289-80119-2*, Pub. by Studio Vista Bks UK) Sterling.

***Coloured Petri Nets: Basic Concepts, Analysis Methods & Practical Use.** K. Jensen. (Monographs in Theoretical Computer Science. A Series of EATCS). 180p. 1995. 49.00 (*0-387-58276-2*) Spr-Verlag.

Coloured Petri Nets: Basic Concepts, Analysis Methods & Practical Use, Vol. 1. K. Jensen. Ed. by W. Brauer et al. (EATCS Monographs on Theoretical Computer Science). (Illus.). x, 234p. 1992. 69.00 (*0-387-55597-8*) Spr-Verlag.

Coloured Rice--Symbolic Structure in Hindu Family Festivals. Suzanne Hanchett. (C). 1988. 40.00 (*81-7075-006-7*, Pub. by Hindustan IA) S Asia.

Coloured Stars: Oriental Love Poetry. Ed. by Edward P. Mathers. pap. 3.95 (*0-8283-1432-2*, 11) Branden Pub Co.

Coloured, Type & Song Canaries: A Complete Guide to Keeping, Breeding & Showing. G. B. Walker & Dennis Avon. (Illus.). 400p. 1993. pap. 19.95 (*0-7137-2378-5*, Pub. by Blandford Pr UK) Sterling.

Colouring Books: The Saints (2): June-November. Illus. by Judi H. Winkowski. (C). 1992. pap. text ed. 24.95x (*0-85439-294-7*, Pub. by St Paul Pubns UK) St Mut.

Colouring, Bronzing, & Patination of Metals. Richard Hughes & Michael Rowe. (Illus.). 372p. 1991. 65.00 (*0-8230-0762-6*, Whitney Lib) Watsn-Guptill.

***Colours: Their Nature & Representation.** Barry Maund. (Studies in Philosophy). 272p. (C). Date not set. 49.95 (*0-521-47273-3*) Cambridge U Pr.

Colours for Food. 2nd rev. ed. Ed. by Dyestuffs Commission of the Deutsch Forschungsgemeinschaft Staff. 454p. 1989. 220.00 (*0-89573-617-9*) VCH Pubs.

Colours in the Dark. Reaney. (NFS Canada Ser.). 1993. pap. 11.95 (*0-88922-001-8*, Pub. by Talonbooks CN) InBook.

***Colours of Australia.** 95p. 1995. 25.95 (*0-614-04343-3*) Quilters Res.

***Colours of Australia: Director of Quiltmaking.** 1995. 25.95 (*0-9629056-1-5*) Quilters Res.

Colours of India. Barbara Lloyd. LC 88-50595. (Illus.). 160p. 1989. pap. 19.95 (*0-500-27531-9*) Thames Hudson.

Colours of Love. large type ed. Rosalie Henaghan. (Harlequin Ser.). 1994. 18.95 (*0-263-13722-8*, Pub. by Mills & Boon UK) Thorndike Pr.

Colours of Opaque Minerals. Andrew Peckett. (Illus.). 573p. 1992. text ed. 124.95 (*0-442-30808-6*) Chapman & Hall.

Colours of the Arab Fatherland. Angelo Pesce. 144p. (C). 1990. 150.00 (*0-907151-16-7*, Pub. by IMMEL Pubng UK) St Mut.

Colourwash Quilts: A Personal Approach to Design & Technique. Deirdre Amsden. LC 94-119425. 1994. 24.95 (*1-56477-051-6*) That Patchwork.

***Colpopoiesis from the Colon.** M. Kun. 172p. (C). 1975. 33.00x (*963-05-0161-9*) St Mut.

Colporteur Ministry. Ellen G. White. 1953. 11.95 (*0-8163-0110-7*, 03431-4) Pacific Pr Pub Assn.

Colposcopy: A Scientific & Practical Approach to the Cervix, Vagina & Vulva in Health & Disease. 3rd ed. Malcolm Coppleson et al. (Illus.). 624p. (C). 1986. 97.95x (*0-398-05153-4*) C C Thomas.

Colposcopy: Cervical Pathology. 2nd ed. Erich Burghardt. Tr. by Andrew G. Oster. (Illus.). 249p. 1991. 129.00 (*0-86577-348-3*) Thieme Med Pubs.

Colposcopy: Text & Atlas. Louis Burke et al. (Illus.). 228p. 1991. boxed 95.00 (*0-8385-0523-6*, A0523-9) Appleton & Lange.

Colposcopy in Diagnosis & Treatment of Preneoplastic Lesions. Ed. by H. E. Stegner & M. Coppleson. (Illus.). 70p. 1987. pap. 31.50 (*0-387-17947-X*) Spr-Verlag.

Colquhoun & MacBryde. John Byrne. 96p. (Orig.). 1993. pap. 8.95 (*0-571-16959-7*) Faber & Faber.

Colregs Study Guide & Reference. Greg Szczurek. 1994. pap. 19.95 (*0-932889-34-4*) Examco Inc.

Colt. Nancy Springer. 128p. (J). (gr. 5 up). 1994. pap. 3.99 (*0-14-036480-3*) Puffin Bks.

Colt: An American Legend. R. L. Wilson. (Illus.). 368p. 1990. 29.98 (*0-89660-011-4*, Artabras) Abbeville Pr.

Colt: Chief of Scouts, Vol. 3. Don Bendell. 352p. (Orig.). 1994. pap. 4.50 (*0-451-17830-0*, Sig) NAL-Dutton.

Colt: Genealogical Memoirs of the Families of Colt & Coutts. Charles Rogers. 59p. 1992. reprint ed. pap. 12.00 (*0-8328-2647-2*) Higginson Bk Co.

Colt Automatic Pistols. rev. ed. Donald B. Bady. 1973. 25.00 (*0-87505-099-9*) Borden.

***Colt Cavalry & Artillery Revolvers: A Continuing Study - Custer's Seventh Cavalry Colts.** John A. Kopec & H. Sterling Fenn. LC 93-81255. 304p. 1994. 79.95 (*1-882824-09-1*) Graphic Pubs.

Colt Cavalry, Artillery & Militia Revolvers, 1873-1903. Keith Cochran. LC 87-72969. (Illus.). 288p. 1987. 45.00 (*0-936259-07-8*) Cochran Pub.

Colt Cavalry, Artillery & Militia Revolvers, 1873-1903. deluxe limited ed. Keith Cochran. LC 87-72969. (Illus.). 288p. 1987. 175.00 (*0-936259-08-6*) Cochran Pub.

Colt-Challenger-Conquest-Vista, 1971-88: Repair & Tune-Up Guide. Chilton Automotives Editorial Staff. LC 88-43184. (Illus.). 336p. 1989. pap. text ed. 16.95 (*0-8019-7940-4*) Chilton.

Colt Creek. Roy LeBeau. (Buckskin Ser.: No. 4). 240p. (Orig.). 1984. pap. 2.75 (*0-8439-2168-4*) Dorchester Pub Co.

Colt Crossing. Kit Dalton. (Buckskin Ser.: No. 24). 176p. (Orig.). 1989. pap. 2.95 (*0-8439-2728-3*) Dorchester Pub Co.

Colt Crossing - Powder Charge, 2 vols. in 1. Kit Dalton. (Buckskin Double Edition Ser.). 352p. 1993. pap. 4.99 (*0-8439-3409-3*) Dorchester Pub Co.

Colt Firearms. Serven. (World's Great Gun Books Ser.). 1990. 45.00 (*0-935632-95-6*) Wolfe Pub Co.

Colt Flame. large type ed. John Blaze. (Linford Western Library). 288p. 1993. pap. 14.95 (*0-7089-7313-2*, Trailtree Bookshop) Ulverscroft.

Colt for a Railroad. large type ed. Mark Donovan. (Dales Western Ser.). 195p. 1992. pap. 16.95 (*1-85389-315-3*, Medcom-Trainex) Ulverscroft.

***Colt Lightning.** large type ed. Tim Champlin. LC 94-32529. 242p. 1995. lib. bdg. 16.95 (*0-7862-0029-4*) Thorndike Pr.

Colt Peacemaker British Model. Keith Cochran. LC 88-71574. (Illus.). 160p. 1989. 35.00 (*0-317-93279-9*); 35.00 (*0-936259-11-6*) Cochran Pub.

Colt Peacemaker Encyclopedia. Keith Cochran. LC 86-71569. (Illus.). 434p. 1986. 59.95 (*0-936259-03-5*); 300.00 (*0-936259-10-8*); 60.00 (*0-936259-14-0*) Cochran Pub.

Colt Peacemaker Encyclopedia. deluxe limited ed. Keith Cochran. LC 86-71569. (Illus.). 434p. 1986. 150.00 (*0-685-48507-2*) Cochran Pub.

Colt Peacemaker Encyclopedia, Vol. II. Keith Cochran. LC 86-71569. (Illus.). 416p. 1991. 65.00 (*0-936259-15-9*) Cochran Pub.

Colt Peacemaker Ready-Reference Handbook. Keith Cochran. (Illus.). 76p. (Orig.). 1985. pap. 12.95 (*0-936259-02-7*) Cochran Pub.

Colt Peacemaker Yearly Variations. Keith Cochran. LC 87-70487. (Illus.). 96p. 1987. 20.00 (*0-936259-05-1*); pap. 15.00 (*0-936259-04-3*) Cochran Pub.

***Colt Percussion Accoutrements 1834-1873: Including Cartridge Conversions & Their Valves.** Robin J. Rapley. 432p. 1994. pap. 39.95 (*1-882824-08-3*) Graphic Pubs.

***Colt Single Action: Three Generations.** Joe Poyer. (For Collectors Only Ser.). (Illus.). 150p. 1995. pap. 16.95 (*1-882391-06-3*) N Cape Pubns.

Colt Single Action Army. Larry Hacker. 1989. 4.00 (*0-913150-63-0*) Pioneer Pr.

Colt Single Action Army Revolvers & the London Agency. Kenneth Moore. LC 90-60405. (Illus.). 144p. 1990. 35.00 (*0-917218-43-4*) A Mowbray.

Colt Thunder. large type ed. Jim Cleveland. (Dales Mystery Ser.). 201p. 1992. pap. 16.95 (*1-85389-336-6*, Medcom-Trainex) Ulverscroft.

Colt U. S. General Officers' Pistol. Horace Greeley, IV. LC 89-63839. (Illus.). 199p. 1989. 38.00 (*0-917218-41-8*) A Mowbray.

***Colt Wages.** large type ed. D. B. Newton. LC 94-19825. 1994. 18.95 (*0-7927-2132-2*, Curley Lrg Print); pap. 17.95 (*0-7927-2131-4*, Curley Lrg Print) Chivers N Amer.

Colt Whitneyville-Walker Pistol. Robert D. Whittington, III. LC 83-73228. (Illus.). 96p. 1984. 20.00 (*0-9613049-0-1*) Brownlee Books.

Colt Who Had Never Been Ridden. Bill Scott. LC 93-60919. (Illus.). 44p. (J). 1994. 7.95 (*1-55523-648-0*) Winston-Derek.

Colt Woodsman .22 Automatic Pistol: Its Predecessor & Variations. Larry Hacker. 1989. 4.00 (*0-913150-65-7*) Pioneer Pr.

Colt 1911 Automatic Pistol: Its Predecessor & Variations. Larry Hacker. 1989. 4.00 (*0-913150-64-9*) Pioneer Pr.

Colt 45 Service Pistols: Models of 1911 & 1911A1. Charles W. Clawson. LC 92-90443. (Illus.). 448p. 1992. 65.00 (*0-9633971-0-9*) C W Clawson.

Colt 45 Service Pistols: Models of 1911 & 1911A1. rev. ed. Charles W. Clawson. LC 92-90443. (Illus.). 448p. 1993. 65.00 (*0-9633971-9-2*) C W Clawson.

Colt .45 Vengence. Kit Dalton. (Buckskin Ser.: No. 37). 176p. (Orig.). 1993. pap. 3.99 (*0-8439-3533-2*) Dorchester Pub Co.

Colter's Hell. Mattes. 87p. 1962. 2.25 (*0-685-39940-0*) Yellowstone Assn.

Colter's Run. Judith Edwards. (Highlights from American History Ser.). (Illus.). 32p. (Orig.). (J). 1993. pap. 5.95 (*1-56044-178-X*) Falcon Pr MT.

Coltness Collections. Ed. by James Dennistoun. LC 72-1031. (Maitland Club, Glasgow. Publications: No. 58). reprint ed. 45.00 (*0-404-53047-8*) AMS Pr.

Colton Cousins Adventure: Daniel Colton under Fire. Elaine L. Schulte. 144p. 1992. pap. 5.99 (*0-310-54821-7*) Zondervan.

Colton Cousins Adventure: Susannah Strikes Gold. Elaine L. Schulte. 144p. (J). 1992. pap. 5.99 (*0-310-54611-7*) Zondervan.

Colton Cousins Adventure: Suzannah & the Secret Coins. Elaine L. Schulte. 144p. 1992. pap. 5.99 (*0-310-54431-9*) Zondervan.

Colton's Book of Short Stories. David M. Colton. Ed. by Thomson-Shore Inc. Printers Staff. 339p. write for info. (*0-318-63111-3*) D M Colton.

Coltrane. C. O. Simpkins. LC 88-72107. (Illus.). 274p. 1988. reprint ed. pap. 11.95 (*0-933121-20-2*) Black Classic.

***Coltrane: Descendants of David Coltrane & James Frazier of N.C.** Robert H. Frazier. (Illus.). 121p. 1994. reprint ed. lib. bdg. 29.50 (*0-8328-4396-2*); reprint ed. pap. 19.50 (*0-8328-4397-0*) Higginson Bk Co.

Coltrane in a Cadillac. Robbie Coltrane & Graham Stuart. (Illus.). 192p. 1994. pap. 22.95 (*1-85702-120-7*, Pub. by Fourth Estate UK) Trafalgar.

Coltray. David Alexander. 176p. (Orig.). 1990. pap. 2.95 (*0-8439-3007-1*) Dorchester Pub Co.

Colt's SAA Post-War Models. George Garton. 29.95 (*0-88227-027-3*) Gun Room.

Columba. Wild Goose Publications Staff. (C). 1990. 20.00 (*0-947988-11-4*, Pub. by Wild Goose Pubns UK) St Mut.

Columbanus in His Own Words. Tomas. 176p. 1989. pap. 22.00 (*1-85390-190-3*, Pub. by Veritas IE) St Mut.

Columbeis, Bks. 1 & 2: Epos over Columbus' Ontdekking Van Amerika. Julius C. Stella. Tr. by H. Hofmann. xix, 74p. (DUT & LAT.). 1993. pap. 20.00 (*90-6980-062-4*, Pub. by Egbert Forsten NE) Benjamins North Am.

Columbella. Phyllis A. Whitney. 256p. 1982. pap. 5.99 (*0-449-20220-8*, Crest) Fawcett.

Columbia. Stewart Holbrook. 1991. 9.95 (*0-89174-051-1*) Comstock Edns.

Columbia: A General Survey. 2nd ed. W. O. Galbraith. LC 85-21913. (Illus.). xi, 190p. 1985. reprint ed. text ed. 49.75 (*0-313-24980-6*, GALC, Greenwood Pr) Greenwood.

Columbia: Business Risk Overview. Ed. by Lewis B. Sckolnick. 125p. (Orig.). (C). 1994. pap. text ed. 495.00 (*1-57205-569-3*) Rector Pr.

Columbia: From Southern Village to. Alan R. Havig. 1985. 19.95 (*0-89781-138-0*, 5148) Preferred Mktg.

Columbia: Trade, Licensing & Investing Rules & Regulations. Ed. by Lewis B. Sckolnick. (Illus.). 80p. (Orig.). (C). 1994. pap. 225.00 (*1-57205-059-4*) Rector Pr.

Columbia & Plateau: The Roger J. Bounds Foundation, Inc. Collection Exhibition. Ed. by Frank Munns & David Lynx. (Illus.). 8p. (Orig.). (C). 1990. pap. 6.95 (*1-880269-06-6*) D H Sheehan.

Columbia & Richland County: A South Carolina Community, 1740-1990. John H. Moore. LC 92-18919. (Illus.). 534p. 1992. text ed. 29.95 (*0-87249-827-1*) U of SC Pr.

***Columbia Anthology of British Poetry.** Ed. by Carl Woodring & James Shapiro. LC 94-46333. 1995. write for info. (*0-231-10180-5*) Col U Pr.

***Columbia Anthology of Modern Chinese Literature.** Ed. by Joseph S. M. Lau & Howard Goldblatt. LC 94-35304. (Modern Asian Literature Ser.). 726p. (CHI & ENG.). 1995. 39.00 (*0-231-08002-6*) Col U Pr.

Columbia Anthology of Traditional Chinese Literature. Ed. by Victor H. Mair. LC 93-48174. (Translation from the Asian Classics Ser.). 1,350p. 1994. 65.00 (*0-231-07428-X*) Col U Pr.

***Columbia Book of American Poetry.** Ed. by Jay Parini. LC 94-32423. 1995. write for info. (*0-231-08122-7*) Col U Pr.

Columbia Book of Chinese Poetry: From Early Times to the Thirteenth Century. Ed. by Burton Watson. LC 83-26182. (Translations from the Oriental Classics Ser.). 352p. 1986. text ed. 44.00 (*0-231-05682-6*); pap. text ed. 17.00 (*0-231-05683-4*) Col U Pr.

Columbia Book of Later Chinese Poetry: Yuan, Ming, & Ch'ing Dynasties (1279-1911) Ed. & Tr. by Jonathan Chaves. LC 86-2302. (Illus.). 520p. 1988. pap. text ed. 18.50 (*0-231-06149-8*) Col U Pr.

Columbia Book on Civil War Poetry. Ed. by Richard Marius & Keith W. Frome. LC 94-6481. 350p. 1994. 24.95 (*0-231-10002-7*) Col U Pr.

Columbia Business Systems: Blue Book, No. 101. 1987. 295.00 (*0-9604828-0-6*) Columbia Busn Sys.

Columbia Business Systems: Red Book, No. 102. 1981. 15.00 (*0-9604828-1-4*) Columbia Busn Sys.

Columbia Business Systems Inc. No. 300 Pre-Printed Color-Coded General Ledger. 1982. 44.95 (*0-9604828-7-3*) Columbia Busn Sys.

Columbia Checklist: The Feature Films, Serials, Cartoons & Short Subjects of the Columbia Pictures Corporation, 1922-1988. Len D. Martin. LC 90-53507. 647p. 1991. lib. bdg. 72.00x (*0-89950-556-2*) McFarland & Co.

***Columbia Chronicles of American Life, 1910-1992.** Lois Gordon & Alan Gordon. (Illus.). 800p. 1995. 39.95 (*0-231-08100-6*) Col U Pr.

Columbia College Student in the Eighteenth Century: Essays. Daniel Tompkins. (BCL1-PS American Literature Ser.). 67p. 1993. reprint ed. lib. bdg. 59.00 (*0-7812-6940-7*) Rprt Serv.

Columbia Comedy Shorts: Two-Reel Hollywood Film Comedies, 1933-1958. Ted Okuda & Edward Watz. LC 84-43241. (Illus.). 272p. 1986. lib. bdg. 38.50x (*0-89950-181-8*) McFarland & Co.

***Columbia Commercial Law.** 150p. (C). 1994. pap. 295.00 (*0-7605-0099-1*) Rector Pr.

Columbia Conserve Company, Indianapolis, Indiana: An Experiment in Worker's Management & Ownership. William P. Hapgood. LC 74-31437. (American Utopian Adventure Ser.). xi, 187p. 1975. reprint ed. lib. bdg. 29.50 (*0-87991-022-4*) Porcupine Pr.

Columbia County, N. Y. Gravestone Inscriptions, Guide to Interpretation with Comprehensive Family Name Index. A. L. Divine. 210p. 1991. lib. bdg. 39.50 (*1-56012-119-X*) Kinship Rhinebeck.

Columbia County Place Names. Walter M. Brasch. (Illus.). 232p. 1982. 15.00 (*0-88023-028-2*) Columbia County Hist Soc.

Columbia Dictionary of European Political History Since 1914. Ed. by John Stevenson. 448p. 1992. text ed. 69.50 (*0-231-07880-3*) Col U Pr.

Columbia Dictionary of Modern European Literature. 2nd ed. Ed. by Jean-Albert Bede & William Edgerton. LC 80-17082. 800p. 1980. text ed. 163.00 (*0-231-03717-1*) Col U Pr.

***Columbia Dictionary of Modern Literary & Cultural Criticism.** Ed. by Joseph Childers & Gary Hentzi. LC 94-42535. 1995. 49.50 (*0-231-07242-2*) Col U Pr.

***Columbia Dictionary of Modern Literary & Cultural Criticism.** Ed. by Joseph Childers & Gary Hentzi. 362p. 1995. pap. 19.50 (*0-231-07243-0*) Col U Pr.

Columbia Dictionary of Political Biography. Economist Books, Ltd. Staff. 320p. 1991. text ed. 40.00 (*0-231-07586-3*) Col U Pr.

Columbia Dictionary of Quotations. Robert Andrews. 1993. 34.95 (*0-231-07194-9*) Col U Pr.

***Columbia Documents of Architecture & Theory, Vol. 3.** Robin Evans et al. Ed. by Bernard Tschumi et al. (Illus.). 183p. (Orig.). (C). 1993. pap. text ed. 15.00 (*1-883584-00-0*) CUGSA.

Columbia Documents of Architecture & Theory, Vol. 4. Bernard Benjamin et al. Ed. by Bernard Tschum et al. Tr. by Taeg Nishimoto. (Illus.). 150p. (Orig.). (C). 1993. pap. text ed. 15.00 (*1-883584-01-9*) CUGSA.

***Columbia Documents of Architecture & Theory Vol. 5.** Joseph Abram et al. Ed. by Bernard Tschumi et al. (Illus.). 170p. (Orig.). (C). 1995. pap. text ed. 15.00 (*1-883584-04-3*) CUGSA.

Columbia Documents of Architecture & Theory, Vol. 1: D. Peter Rice et al. (Illus.). 150p. (Orig.). 1992. pap. 20.00 (*0-9623829-5-7*) CUGSA.

Columbia Encyclopedia. 5th ed. Columbia University Press. 1993. 125.00 (*0-395-62438-X*) HM.

Columbia Encyclopedia. 5th rev. ed. LC 92-26989. 1993. 125.00 (*0-231-08098-0*) Col U Pr.

Columbia Gorge. (Northwest Mythic Landscape Ser.). (Illus.). 28p. 1992. text ed. 5.95 (*0-912365-59-5*) Sasquatch Bks.

Columbia Gorge Gouged. S. Taylor-Moore. 64p. pap. 10.50 (*0-938758-16-0*) MTM Pub Co.

Columbia Granger's Dictionary of Poetry Quotations. Edith P. Hazen. 1200p. 1992. text ed. 99.00 (*0-231-07546-4*) Col U Pr.

Columbia Granger's Guide to Poetry Anthologies. Ed. by William Katz & Linda S. Katz. 1991. text ed. 45.00 (*0-231-07244-9*) Col U Pr.

Columbia Granger's Guide to Poetry Anthologies. 2nd ed. William Katz & Linda S. Katz. LC 94-6482. 1994. write for info. (*0-231-10104-X*) Col U Pr.

Columbia Granger's Index to Poetry. 9th ed. Edith P. Hazen & Deborah Fryer. 2048p. 1990. text ed. 175.00 (*0-231-07104-3*) Col U Pr.

C

An Asterisk (*) at the beginning of an entry indicates that the title is appearing in BIP for the first time.

An Asterisk (*) at the beginning of an entry indicates that the title is appearing in BIP for the first time.

1395

Columbus Day. Dennis B. Fradin. LC 89-7663. (Best Holiday Books Ser.). (Illus.). 48p. (J). (gr. 1-4). 1990. lib. bdg. 15.95 (*0-89490-233-4*) Enslow Pubs.

Columbus Day. Vicki Liestman. (Holiday on My Own Ser.). (Illus.). 56p. (J). (gr. k-3). 1991. lib. bdg. 15.95 (*0-87614-444-X*, Carolrhoda) Lerner Group.

Columbus Day. Vicki Liestman. (J). (gr. k-3). 1992. pap. 5.95 (*0-87614-559-4*, Carolrhoda) Lerner Group.

Columbus Day. Cass Sandak. LC 89-25399. (Holidays Ser.). (Illus.). 48p. (J). (gr. 5-6). 1990. text ed. 12.95 (*0-89686-498-7*, Crstwood Hse) Silver Burdett Pr.

Columbus' Dictionary. Ed. by A. Caso. 100p. (Orig.). (YA). (gr. 5-10). 1992. pap. 11.95 (*0-8283-1993-6*) Branden Pub Co.

Columbus Dictionary. Foster Provost. 142p. 1991. lib. bdg. 54.00 (*1-55888-158-1*) Omnigraphics Inc.

Columbus Documents: Summaries of Documents in Genoa. Tr. by Luciano F. Farina & Robert W. Tolf. 150p. 1992. lib. bdg. 68.00 (*1-55888-156-5*) Omnigraphics Inc.

Columbus' Egg. Gerardo Sanchez-Ballate. Ed. by Editorial Colon Staff. Tr. by Abrapalabra Staff. (Illus.). 223p. (Orig.). 1992. pap. 15.00 (*0-9631649-1-0*) Edit Colon.

Columbus' Egg: New Latin American Stories on the Conquest. Ed. & Tr. by Nick Caistor. 224p. (Orig.). 1992. pap. 12.95 (*0-571-19799-X*) Faber & Faber.

Columbus: His Enterprise: Exploding the Myth. Hans Koning. (J). (ps-12). 1991. reprint ed. pap. 8.95 (*0-85345-825-1*) Monthly Rev.

Columbus in Black & White. Shawn R. McAllister. (Illus.). 114p. (Orig.). 1993. pap. 5.95 (*0-9637286-0-1*) Remmington Pr.

Columbus in Numismatics. N. Eglit. 1990. reprint ed. pap. 12.00 (*0-942666-43-7*) S J Durst.

Columbus in the Bay of Pigs. John Curl. (Illus.). 72p. (Orig.). 1988. pap. 5.00 (*0-938392-09-3*) Homeward Pr.

Columbus in the Bay of Pigs. 2nd rev. ed. John Curl. 80p. (Orig.). 1991. pap. 6.00 (*0-938392-10-7*) Homeward Pr.

Columbus Indiana: An American Landmark. Balthazar Korab. (Illus.). 168p. 1989. 32.95 (*0-932076-20-3*); pap. 24.95 (*0-932076-21-1*) Documan.

Columbus, Kentucky as the Nation's Capital: Legend or Near Reality? Illus. by Susan L. Tanner. 170p. (Orig.). 1993. pap. 12.95 (*0-9625865-1-X*) River Microstudies.

Columbus Landfall in America & the Hidden Clues in His Journal. Alejandro R. Perez. LC 87-47679. (Illus.). 113p. 1987. 37.50 (*0-88164-684-9*); pap. 29.50 (*0-88164-685-7*) ABBE Pubs Assn.

Columbus Model Book. Watermill Press Staff. (J). (gr. 4-7). 1992. pap. 9.95 (*0-8167-2748-1*) Troll Assocs.

Columbus Names the Flowers: Mr. Cogito's 12th Year Poetry Anthology. John M. Gogol & Robert A. Davies. (Illus.). 104p. (Orig.). (C). 1985. pap. 10.00 (*0-932191-04-5*, PN6101) Mr Cogito Pr.

Columbus of Space. Garrett P. Serviss. LC 73-13265. (Classics of Science Fiction Ser.). (Illus.). 331p. 1986. reprint ed. 22.25 (*0-88355-119-5*); reprint ed. pap. 10.00 (*0-88355-148-9*) Hyperion Conn.

Columbus of the Woods: Daniel Boone & the Typology of Manifest Destiny. J. Gray Sweeney. LC 91-67237. (Illus.). 83p. 1992. pap. 20.00 (*0-936316-14-4*) Wash U Gallery.

Columbus, Ohio: Its History, Resources & Progress. Jacob H. Studer. (Illus.). 582p. 1993. reprint ed. lib. bdg. 59.50 (*0-8328-3471-8*) Higginson Bk Co.

Columbus Option. large type ed. Richard Cox. 544p. 1988. 15.95 (*0-7089-1845-X*) Ulverscroft.

Columbus Papers. Mauricio Obregon. (Illus.). 96p. 1991. text ed. 100.00 (*0-02-591045-0*) Macmillan.

Columbus People: Proceedings of the International Conference on 500 Years of Italian Immigration to the Americas & Australia. Ed. by Lydio F. Tomasi et al. LC 93-21555. 1994. 37.50 (*0-934733-72-4*) Ctr Migration.

Columbus Roberts: Christian Steward Extraordinary. Spright Dowell. LC 83-887. xvi, 171p. 13.95 (*0-86554-071-3*, H67) Mercer Univ Pr.

Columbus' Spain. Ellen Hoffman. LC 91-66621. (Guide Ser.). 150p. (Orig.). 1992. pap. 10.95 (*0-9628576-2-9*) Timetraveler.

Columbus, the Man. Paul H. Chapman. (Illus.). 100p. 1992. 13.95 (*1-880820-04-8*) ISAC Pr.

Columbus Today. Photos by Ed Kreminski. (Urban Portrait Color Ser.). (Illus.). 96p. 1991. 22.50 (*1-878005-07-3*) Northmont Pub.

Columbus Was Never in San Salvador. Alejandro R. Perez. LC 88-47786. (Illus.). 133p. 1988. text ed. 37.50 (*0-88164-876-0*); pap. text ed. 29.50 (*0-88164-877-9*) ABBE Pubs Assn.

***Columbus's Orphan.** Rane Arroyo. 62p. (Orig.). 1993. pap. 7.95 (*1-878116-17-7*) JVC Bks.

Column Base Plates. DeWolf & Ricker. 1990. 16.00 (*1-56424-032-0*, D801) Am Inst Steel Construct.

Column Flotation. J. A. Finch & G. S. Dobby. LC 89-48009. (Illus.). 192p. 1990. 77.00 (*0-08-040186-4*, Pergamon Pr) Elsevier.

Column Flotation: Processes, Designs & Practices. Julius B. Rubinstein. (Process Engineering for the Chemical Ser.). 1995. text ed. 95.00 (*2-88124-917-5*) Gordon & Breach.

Column of Antoninus Pius. Lise Vogel. LC 74-173409. (Loeb Classical Monographs). (Illus.). 236p. 1973. 29.00 (*0-674-14325-6*) HUP.

Column Show: Metaphor & Motif. Susan M. Anderson et al. 28p. 1986. pap. 5.00 (*0-9602974-4-8*) USC Fisher Gallery.

Columns & Catalogues. Peter Schjeldahl. 1994. per. 15.00 (*0-935724-68-0*) Figures.

Columns Left: A Chattanooga Legacy. Jac Chambliss. LC 93-42556. 1993. write for info. (*0-916078-34-5*) Iris Pr.

Colunga. Ronny Cohen. (Illus.). 24p. 1990. 20.00 (*0-925941-02-6*) Dorsky Gallery.

Colusa County (California) Justus H. Rogers. (Illus.). 473p. 1993. reprint ed. lib. bdg. 49.50 (*0-8328-3524-2*) Higginson Bk Co.

Colver - Culver Genealogy, Descendants of Edward Colver of Boston, Dedham & Roxbury, Mass., & New London & Mystic, Connecticut, 1635-1909. F. L. Colver. 271p. 1993. reprint ed. lib. bdg. 50.50 (*0-8328-1374-5*); reprint ed. pap. 40.50 (*0-8328-1375-3*) Higginson Bk Co.

Colver-Culver Family Genealogy. Valerie D. Giorgi. LC 84-72989. (Illus.). 700p. 1985. text ed. 35.00 (*0-9614222-0-3*) Giorgi.

Colver Trading Method for Winning the Commodity Game. Jay Colver. 1983. 50.00 (*0-318-00211-6*) Windsor.

Colville Collection, Bk. 1. Patrick J. Graham. (Illus.). 132p. (Orig.). 1989. pap. text ed. 14.95 (*0-940151-12-X*) Statesman Exam.

Colville for the Defense: A Critique of the Reports of the U. N. Special Rapporteur for Guatemala. Neil Levine. 31p. write for info. (*0-318-62436-2*, Am Watch) Hum Rts Watch.

Colvin in the Adirondacks. Francis Rosevear & Barbara McMartin. 150p. 1992. 22.00 (*0-932052-98-3*) North Country.

Colvins & Their Friends. Edward V. Lucas. (BCL1-PR English Literature Ser.). 365p. 1992. reprint ed. lib. bdg. 89.00 (*0-7812-7505-9*) Rprt Serv.

Colvin's Clinic: Bonanza - DeBonair-Baron Maintenance Simplified. J. Norman Colvin. LC 84-60672. (Illus.). 130p. 1984. write for info. (*0-911978-02-X*) McCormick-Armstrong.

Colvin's Clinic: Bonanza-DeBonair-Baron-Travelair Maintenance Simplified. 2nd rev. ed. J. Norman Colvin. LC 92-61832. (Illus.). 256p. 1992. write for info. (*0-911978-06-2*) McCormick-Armstrong.

Colyer's Variations & Diseases of the Teeth of Animals. 2nd ed. Ed. by A. E. Miles & C. Grigson. (Illus.). 850p. 1990. 390.00 (*0-521-25273-3*) Cambridge U Pr.

Com. Bib. Continente Nueva (New Continent Com) Efesios (Ephesians) R. Yoccou. (SPA.). Date not set. 12.99 (*1-56063-219-4*, 498635); pap. 8.99 (*0-685-74914-2*, 498636) Editorial Unilit.

Com. Bib. Continente Nuevo (New Continent Com) Juan (John), Vol. I. L. Palau. (SPA.). Date not set. 12.99 (*1-56063-089-2*, 498631); pap. 8.99 (*0-685-74915-0*, 498632) Editorial Unilit.

Com. Bib. Continente Nuevo (New Continent Com) Juan (John), Vol. II. L. Palau. (SPA.). Date not set. 12.99 (*1-56063-115-5*, 498633); pap. 8.99 (*0-685-74916-9*, 498634) Editorial Unilit.

Com. Bib. Continente Nuevo (New Continent Com) Marcos (Mark) C. Morris. (SPA.). Date not set. 12.99 (*1-56063-269-0*, 498637); pap. 8.99 (*0-685-74917-7*, 498638) Editorial Unilit.

***Com Descubrir Sus Vidas Anteriores.** Ted Andrews. 160p. 1995. pap. 10.00 (*1-56718-027-2*) Llewellyn Pubns.

Com Licensa! Brazilian Portuguese for Spanish Speakers. Antonio R. Simoes. LC 91-43927. (Institute of Latin American Studies). 339p. 1992. teacher ed write for info. (*0-292-77676-4*); pap. 24.95 (*0-292-71142-5*); audio 39.95 (*0-292-77677-2*) U of Tex Pr.

Com-Packs: Kids' Committees for Integrated Learning. Tamara L. Gerrard. Ed. by Jane Bluestein. 176p. (Orig.). 1987. pap. 10.95 (*0-915817-15-2*) ISS Pubns.

Coma. Robin Cook. 320p. 1977. pap. 5.99 (*0-451-15953-5*, Sig) NAL-Dutton.

Coma. Robin Cook. 1993. pap. 3.99 (*0-451-17621-9*, Sig) NAL-Dutton.

Coma. Robin Cook. 1994. reprint ed. lib. bdg. 29.95 (*1-56849-266-9*) Buccaneer Bks.

***Coma: The Dreambody Near Death.** Arnold Mindell. 144p. 1995. 10.95 (*0-14-019483-5*, Arkana) Viking Penguin.

Coma, Endocranial Pressure, Extended Neural Pathology: Neuroimaging. Daniel F. Hanley et al. (Current Opinion in Neurology Ser.). (Illus.). 1016p. (Orig.). 1993. pap. text ed. 49.95 (*0-685-70435-1*) Current Science.

Coma Work & Palliative Care. Stan Tomandl. 1991. 20.00 (*0-9696200-0-4*, Pub. by White Bear Bks CN) Interact Media.

Comacine Masters: Examination of the Theory That Would Make Them Ancestors of Freemasonry. 1993. pap. 5.95 (*1-55818-205-5*, Sure Fire) Holmes Pub.

Comacines. W. Ravenscroft. 120p. 1992. reprint ed. pap. 12.95 (*1-56459-054-2*) Kessinger Pub.

COMAL from A to Z. Borge Christensen. (Amazing Adventures of Captain COMAL Ser.). (Illus.). 64p. 1984. pap. 6.95 (*0-928411-00-1*) COMAL Users.

COMAL Handbook: Commodore 64 Version (2.00) Len Lindsay. 1986. 38.95 (*0-8359-0785-6*, Reston); 24.95 (*0-8359-0784-8*, Reston) P-H.

COMAL Library of Functions & Procedures. Kevin Quiggle. (Amazing Adventures of Captain COMAL Ser.). (Illus.). 71p. (Orig.). (J). (gr. 6 up). 1984. pap. 14.95 (*0-928411-03-6*) COMAL Users.

COMAL Workbook. Gordon Shigley. (Amazing Adventures of Captain COMAL Ser.). (Illus.). 69p. (Orig.). (J). (gr. 6 up). 1985. pap. text ed. 6.95 (*0-928411-05-2*) COMAL Users.

Comalcalco, Tabasco, Mexico: Maya Art & Architecture. 2nd ed. George F. Andrews. LC 89-92394. (Illus.). 176p. (C). 1990. pap. 40.00 (*0-911437-11-8*) Labyrinthos.

Comaltepec Chinantec Syntax: Studies in Chinantec Languages, No. 3. Judi L. Anderson. Ed. by William R. Merrifield. (Publications in Linguistics: No. 89). xiv, 120p. 1989. pap. 9.00 (*0-88312-104-2*) Summer Instit Ling.

Comaltepec Chinantec Syntax: Studies in Chinantec Languages, 2 fiche, Set. Judi L. Anderson. Ed. by William R. Merrifield. (Publications in Lingustics: No. 89). xiv, 120p. 1989. fiche 8.00 (*0-88312-912-4*) Summer Instit Ling.

***Comanagement in Refractive Surgery.** R. Bruce Grene. 1995. 75.00 (*1-55642-260-1*); pap. 49.00 (*1-55642-259-8*) SLACK Inc.

Comanche. Barron Brown. Bd. with Marching with Custer. (Illus.). 1941. 17.50 (*0-914074-02-4*, J M C & Co); Bd. with Set pap. 12.95 (*0-685-73714-4*, J M C & Co) Amereon Ltd.

Comanche. David Dary. (Public Education Ser.: No. 5). 19p. 1976. pap. 2.00 (*0-89338-003-2*) U of KS Mus Nat Hist.

***Comanche.** Fabio. 416p. (Orig.). 1995. mass mkt. 5.99 (*0-380-77762-2*) Avon.

Comanche. Willard H. Rollings. (Indians of North America Ser.). (Illus.). 112p. (YA). (gr. 5 up). 1989. 17.95 (*1-55546-702-4*); pap. 9.95 (*0-7910-0359-0*) Chelsea Hse.

Comanche Barrier to South Plains Settlement. Rupert N. Richardson. 1993. reprint ed. lib. bdg. 75.00 (*0-7812-5948-7*) Rprt Serv.

Comanche Bondage. Carl C. Rister. LC 89-4943. (Illus.). 211p. 1989. pap. 7.50 (*0-8032-8934-0*, Bison Books) U of Nebr Pr.

Comanche Bride. Emma Merritt. 480p. 1989. pap. 3.95 (*0-8217-2549-1*) Zebra.

Comanche Captive: You Are There. Bryce Milligan. (Illus.). 156p. (YA). (gr. 5 up). 1989. pap. 3.95 (*0-87719-157-3*, Lone Star Bks) Gulf Pub.

Comanche Caress. Cheryl Black. 448p. 1988. pap. 3.95 (*0-8217-2268-9*) Zebra.

***Comanche Code: Cody's Law, Bk. 12.** Hart. 1995. mass mkt. (*0-553-56108-1*) Bantam.

Comanche Cowboy. Georgina Gentry. 512p. 1988. pap. 3.95 (*0-8217-2449-5*) Zebra.

Comanche Days. Albert S. Gilles. LC 74-77543. 144p. reprint ed. pap. 41.10 (*0-317-20112-3*, 2023179) Bks Demand.

Comanche Dictionary & Grammar. Lila W. Robinson & James Armagost. (Publications in Linguistics: No. 93). 1990. pap. 26.00 (*0-88312-715-6*) Summer Instit Ling.

Comanche Dictionary & Grammar, 6 fiche, Set. Lila W. Robinson & James Armagost. (Publications in Linguistics: No. 93). 1990. fiche 24.00 (*0-88312-554-4*) Summer Instit Ling.

Comanche Embrace. Betty Brooks. 320p. 1991. mass mkt. 4.25 (*0-8217-3350-8*) Zebra.

Comanche Flame. Madeline Baker. 448p. 1994. mass mkt., pap. text ed. 4.99 (*0-8439-3242-2*) Dorchester Pub Co.

Comanche Flame. Genell Dellin. 368p. (Orig.). 1994. mass mkt. 4.99 (*0-380-77524-7*) Avon.

Comanche Heart. Catherine Anderson. (Orig.). 1991. mass mkt. 4.99 (*0-06-104068-1*, Harp PBks) HarpC.

Comanche Indians. Martin Mooney. (Junior Library of American Indians). (Illus.). 80p. (J). (gr. 3-7). 1993. lib. bdg. 14.95 (*0-7910-1653-6*) Chelsea Hse.

Comanche Indians: Great Plains. Janet Hubbard-Brown. (Junior Library of American Indians). (Illus.). 80p. (J). (gr. 3-7). 1993. pap. 6.95 (*0-7910-1957-8*) Chelsea Hse.

Comanche Love Song. Cheryl Black. 1989. pap. 3.75 (*0-8217-2697-8*) Zebra.

***Comanche Magic.** Catherine Anderson. 1994. pap. 5.50 (*0-06-108307-0*, Harp PBks) HarpC.

***Comanche Midnight & Other Essays.** Stephen Harrigan. LC 94-23983. 240p. 1995. text ed. 29.95x (*0-292-73088-8*); pap. 14.95x (*0-292-73096-9*) U of Tex Pr.

Comanche Moon. Catherine Anderson. 1991. mass mkt. 4.99 (*0-06-104010-X*, PL) HarpC.

Comanche Moon. Catherine Anderson. 1993. pap. 2.99 (*0-06-108235-X*, Harp PBks) HarpC.

Comanche Moon. Virginia Brown. 432p. 1993. mass mkt. 4.99 (*0-8217-4153-5*) Zebra.

Comanche Moon. William R. Cox. 224p. 1989. pap. 2.95 (*0-380-70830-2*) Avon.

Comanche Moon. Jack Jackson. 128p. (Orig.). (J). pap. 5.95 (*0-89620-079-5*) Rip off.

***Comanche Moon.** Anita Mills. 384p. (Orig.). 1995. mass mkt. 4.99 (*0-451-40553-6*, Topaz) NAL-Dutton.

Comanche Passion. Betty Brooks. 1992. mass mkt. 4.50 (*0-8217-3717-1*) Zebra.

***Comanche Political History: An Ethnohistorical Perspective 1706-1875.** Thomas W. Kavanagh. (Studies in the Anthropology of North American Indians). (Illus.). 500p. 1995. text ed. 45.00 (*0-8032-2730-2*) U of Nebr Pr.

Comanche Raid. Judd Cole. (Cheyenne Ser.: No. 6). 176p. (Orig.). 1993. pap. 3.50 (*0-8439-3478-6*) Dorchester Pub Co.

Comanche Raiders. B. Dugan. (Ranger Ser.: No. 3). 1991. mass mkt. 3.50 (*0-06-100170-8*) HarpC.

***Comanche Rain.** Genell Dellin. 384p. (Orig.). 1995. mass mkt. 4.99 (*0-380-77525-5*) Avon.

Comanche Summer. G. Clifton Wisler. 256p. 1987. pap. 2.95 (*0-8217-2233-6*) Zebra.

Comanche Sunset. F. Rosanne Bittner. 1991. mass mkt. 4.99 (*0-8217-3568-3*) Zebra.

Comanche Treaties: Historical Background. R. J. DeMallie. (Treaty Manuscripts Ser.: No. 14). 20p. 7.50 (*0-944253-36-9*) Inst Dev Indian Law.

Comanche Treaties During the Civil War. R. J. DeMallie. (Treaty Manuscripts Ser.: No. 19). 30p. 10.00 (*0-944253-41-5*) Inst Dev Indian Law.

Comanche Treaties of Eighteen Fifty, Eighteen Fifty-One, & Eighteen Fifty-Three with the U. S. R. J. DeMallie. (Treaty Manuscripts Ser.). 60p. 12.50 (*0-944253-40-7*) Inst Dev Indian Law.

Comanche Treaties with the Republic of Texas. R. J. DeMallie. (Treaty Manuscripts Ser.: No. 15). 21p. 7.50 (*0-944253-38-5*) Inst Dev Indian Law.

Comanche Treaty of Eighteen Forty-Six with the U. S. R. J. DeMallie. (Treaty Manuscripts Ser.: No. 17). 16p. 6.50 (*0-944253-37-7*) Inst Dev Indian Law.

Comanche Treaty of Eighteen Thirty-Five with the United States. R. J. DeMallie. (Treaty Manuscripts Ser.: No. 15). 19p. 7.00 (*0-317-57440-X*) Inst Dev Indian Law.

Comanche Vengeance. Richard Jessup. 1980. pap. 1.75 (*0-449-13910-7*, GM) Fawcett.

***Comanche Warbonnet.** Troxey Kemper. 102p. Date not set. pap. 12.50 (*0-912586-71-0*) Navajo Coll Pr.

Comanche Wind. Genell Dellin. 400p. (Orig.). 1993. mass mkt. 4.50 (*0-380-76717-1*) Avon.

Comanche Woman. Joan Johnston. 1989. pap. 3.95 (*0-318-41511-9*) PB.

Comanchero Blood. Patrick E. Andrews. 256p. 1993. pap. 3.50 (*0-8217-4197-7*) Zebra.

Comanchero Chase. Ed Newsom. (Brannigan Ser.: No 2). (Orig.). 1981. pap. 2.25 (*0-89083-858-5*) Zebra.

Comanchero Frontier: A History of New Mexican-Plains Indian Relations. Charles L. Kenner. LC 94-8100. (Illus.). 250p. 1994. pap. 14.95 (*0-8061-2670-1*) U of Okla Pr.

Comanchero Kill. William Fieldhouse. (Gun Lust Ser.: No. 2). 224p. 1983. pap. 2.50 (*0-8439-2027-0*) Dorchester Pub Co.

Comancheros. Judd Cole. (Cheyenne Ser.: No. 7). 176p. (Orig.). 1993. pap. 3.50 (*0-8439-3496-4*) Dorchester Pub Co.

Comancheros. Jack Slade. (Sundance Ser.: No. 11). 160p. 1981. pap. 1.75 (*0-8439-1049-6*) Dorchester Pub Co.

Comanches. Judy Alter. LC 93-23265. (First Book Ser.). (J). 1994. 13.93 (*0-531-20115-5*) Watts.

Comanches. Judy Alter. LC 93-23265. (First Bks.). (Illus.). 64p. (J). (gr. 4-6). 1994. pap. 5.95 (*0-531-15683-4*) Watts.

Comanches. T. R. Fehrenbach. LC 73-20761. 1974. 35.00 (*0-394-48856-3*) Knopf.

Comanches. F. M. Myers. 1976. 37.50 (*0-934085-00-5*, J M C & Co) Amereon Ltd.

Comanches: Lords of the South Plains. Ernest Wallace & E. Adamson Hoebel. LC 52-11087. (Civilization of the American Indian Ser.: No. 34). (Illus.). 400p. 1987. pap. 13.95 (*0-8061-2040-1*) U of Okla Pr.

Comanches: The Destruction of a People. T. R. Fehrenbach. LC 94-12128. (Illus.). 592p. 1994. reprint ed. pap. 16.95 (*0-306-80586-3*) Da Capo.

Comanches: The Horse People, 1751-1845. Stanley Noyes. (Illus.). 393p. 1994. pap. 19.95 (*0-8263-1548-8*) U of NM Pr.

Comandante Speaks: Memoirs of an El Salvadoran Guerrilla Leader. Ed. by Courtney E. Prisk. 145p. (C). 1991. pap. text ed. 35.50 (*0-8133-1066-0*) Westview.

COMANDOS Distributed Application Platform. Ed. by V. Cahill et al. (Research Reports ESPRIT, Project 2071, COMANDOS, Coed: Commission of the European Communities: Vol. 1). xviii, 312p. 1993. pap. 50.00 (*0-387-56660-0*) Spr-Verlag.

Comatose Kids. Seymour Simckes. LC 75-10747. 114p. 1976. 15.95 (*0-914590-18-9*); pap. 5.95 (*0-914590-19-7*) Fiction Coll.

Comb Making in America. Bernard W. Doyle. (Illus.). 158p. 1993. reprint ed. lib. bdg. 29.50 (*0-8328-3198-0*) Higginson Bk Co.

Comb-Shaped Polymers & Liquid Crystals. N. A. Plate & V. P. Shibaev. Ed. by J. M. Cowie. Tr. by S. L. Schnur. LC 87-18518. (Specialty Polymers Ser.). (Illus.). 428p. 1987. 115.00 (*0-306-42723-0*, Plenum Pr) Plenum.

Combahee River Collective Statement: Black Feminist Organizing in the Seventies & Eighties. Combahee River Collective Staff. (Freedom Organizing Pamphlet Ser.). 28p. (Orig.). 1986. pap. 3.50 (*0-913175-05-6*) Kitchen Table.

Combar: The Commercial Bar Association Directory 1992. Combar Staff. 141p. 1992. pap. text ed. 47.50 (*0-471-93672-3*, Pub. by Wiley Chancery Law UK) Wiley.

***COMBAR: The Commercial Bar Association Directory 1994.** Commercial Bar Association Staff. 1994. pap. text ed. 55.00 (*0-471-94311-8*) Wiley.

Combat: The Civil War. Don Congdon. 570p. 1995. 12.98 (*0-8317-1335-6*) Smithmark.

***Combat Actions in Korea.** (Illus.). 264p. (Orig.). (C). 1994. pap. text ed. 45.00x (*0-7881-1209-0*) Diane Pub.

***Combat Actions in Korea.** (Military History Ser.). 1995. lib. bdg. 252.75 (*0-8490-7424-X*) Gordon Pr.

***Combat Aircraft.** (Jane's Gem Ser.). (Illus.). 256p. (Orig.). 1995. pap. 8.00 (*0-00-470846-6*) HarpC.

Combat Aircraft of World War II, 2 vols. Glenn B. Bavousett. 1989. 14.99 (*0-517-68019-X*) Random Hse Value.

Combat Ammo of the Twenty-First Century. Duncan Long. (Illus.). 216p. 1991. 30.00 (*0-87364-628-2*) Paladin Pr.

Combat Ammunition: Everything You Need to Know. Duncan Long. 1987. pap. 12.95 (*0-8065-1043-9*, Citadel Pr) Carol Pub Group.

Combat & Survival Knives: A User's Guide. Jerry Younkins. LC 91-73862. (Illus.). 120p. (Orig.). 1991. pap. 17.95 (*0-939427-14-1*, 06010) Alpha Pubns OH.

Combat & Survival Weight Fitness. John J. Williams. Ed. by Laurie Williams. (Illus.). 78p. (Orig.). 1987. pap. 29.00 (*0-934274-24-X*) Consumertronics.

Combat Artist in World War II. Edward Reep. LC 86-22380. (Illus.). 224p. 1987. 25.00 (*0-8131-1602-3*) U Pr of Ky.

Combat at the Barrier. John R. Dunbar. (Illus.). 1967. 12.50 (*0-910330-13-1*) Grant Dahlstrom.

***Combat avec l'Ange.** Jean Giraudoux. 300p. 1934. write for info. (*0-7859-5264-0*) Fr & Eur.

An Asterisk (*) at the beginning of an entry indicates that the title is appearing in BIP for the first time.

C

An Asterisk (*) at the beginning of an entry indicates that the title is appearing in BIP for the first time.

1397

Combinatorial Geometries. Ed. by Neil White. (Encyclopedia of Mathematics & Its Applications Ser.: No. 29). (Illus.). 288p. 1987. 59.95 (*0-521-33339-3*) Cambridge U Pr.

***Combinatorial Geometry.** Janos Pach & Pankaj Agarwal. LC 94-48203. (Discrete Mathematics & Optimization Ser.). 1995. write for info. (*0-471-58890-3*) Wiley-Interscience.

Combinatorial Group Testing & Applications. D. Z. Du & F. K. Hwang. LC 93-26812. (Series on Applied Mathematics). 264p. 1993. text ed. 48.00 (*981-02-1293-3*) World Scientific Pub.

Combinatorial Group Theory. Daniel E. Cohen. (London Mathematical Society Student Texts Ser.: No. 14). 250p. (C). 1989. 69.95 (*0-521-34133-7*); pap. 29.95 (*0-521-34936-2*) Cambridge U Pr.

Combinatorial Group Theory & Topology. John R. Stallings. Ed. by S. M. Gersten. LC 85-43283. (Illus.). 640p. 1987. 85.00x (*0-691-08409-2*) Princeton U Pr.

Combinatorial Group Therapy. Ed. by B. Fine et al. (CONM Ser.: Vol. 109). 191p. 1990. pap. text ed. 38.00 (*0-8218-5116-0*, CONM-109) Am Math.

Combinatorial Heuristic Algorithms with FORTRAN. H. T. Lau. (Lecture Notes in Economics & Mathematical Systems Ser.: Vol. 280). vii, 126p. 1986. pap. 29.60 (*0-387-17161-4*) Spr-Verlag.

Combinatorial Homotopy & Four-Dimensional Complexes. Hans J. Baues. (Expositions in Mathematics Ser.: Vol. 2). xxvii, 380p. (C). 1991. lib. bdg. 92.95 (*3-11-012488-2*) De Gruyter.

Combinatorial Integral Geometry: With Applications to Mathematical Stereology. R. V. Ambartzumian. Ed. by Adrian Baddeley. LC 81-14773. (Wiley Series in Probability & Mathematical Statistics). 239p. reprint ed. pap. 68.20 (*0-7837-6362-X*, 2046074) Bks Demand.

Combinatorial Introduction to Topology. Michael Henle. LC 93-50761. (Illus.). 310p. reprint ed. pap. 8.95 (*0-486-67966-7*) Dover.

Combinatorial Mathematics. Herbert J. Ryser. LC 65-12288. (Carus Monograph: No. 14). 154p. 1963. 25.00 (*0-88385-014-1*) Math Assn.

Combinatorial Mathematics: Proceedings of the International Colloquium on Graph Theory & Combinatorics, Marseille-Luminy, June, 1981. Ed. by C. Berge et al. (Mathematics Studies: Vol. 75). 660p. 1983. 159.00 (*0-444-86512-8*, I-419-83, North Holland) Elsevier.

Combinatorial Mathematics X. Ed. by L. R. Casse. (Lecture Notes in Mathematics Ser.: Vol. 1036). xi, 419p. 1983. pap. 44.70 (*0-387-12708-9*) Spr-Verlag.

Combinatorial Matrix Theory. Richard A. Brualdi & H. Ryser. (Encyclopedia of Mathematics & Its Applications Ser.: No. 39). 300p. (C). 1991. 59.95 (*0-521-32265-0*) Cambridge U Pr.

***Combinatorial Methods in Discrete Mathematics.** V. N. Sachkov. (Encyclopedia of Mathematics & Its Applications Ser.: 55). 320p. (C). 1995. write for info. (*0-521-45513-8*) Cambridge U Pr.

Combinatorial Methods in Topology & Algebraic Geometry. Ed. by J. Harper & R. Mandelbaum. LC 85-11244. (Contemporary Mathematics Ser.: Vol. 44). 349p. 1988. reprint ed. pap. text ed. 44.00 (*0-8218-5039-3*, CONM-44) Am Math.

Combinatorial Methods of Discrete Programming. L. B. Kovacs. (Mathematical Methods of Operation Research Ser.: No. 2). 282p. (C). 1980. 75.00x (*963-05-2004-4*, Pub. by Akad Kiado HU) St Mut.

Combinatorial Methods of Discrete Programming. Laszlo B. Kovacs. 284p. 1980. 110.00 (*0-317-89587-7*) St Mut.

***Combinatorial Morphology.** John T. Stonham. LC 94-37958. (Current Issues in Linguistic Theory Ser.: No. 120). xii, 200p. 1994. lib. bdg. 52.00x (*1-55619-574-5*) Benjamins North Am.

Combinatorial Number-Theory: A Treatise on Growth, Based on the Goodstein-Skolem Hierarchy, Including a Critique of Non-Constructive or First-Order Logic. Muhammad A. McBeth. LC 94-13953. 430p. 1994. text ed. 109.95 (*0-7734-9085-X*) E Mellen.

***Combinatorial Optimization.** Ed. by William Cook et al. LC 95-1957. (DIMACS Discrete Mathematics & Theoretical Computer Science Ser.: Vol. 20). 1995. write for info. (*0-8218-0239-9*) Am Math.

Combinatorial Optimization. L. R. Foulds. (Undergraduate Texts in Mathematics Ser.). (Illus.). 280p. 1984. 51.00 (*0-387-90977-X*) Spr-Verlag.

Combinatorial Optimization. Ed. by B. Simeone. (Lecture Notes in Mathematics Ser.: Vol. 1403). v, 312p. 1989. pap. 41.60 (*0-387-51797-9*, 3633) Spr-Verlag.

Combinatorial Optimization. Ed. by Nicos Christofides et al. LC 78-11131. 435p. reprint ed. pap. 124.00 (*0-8357-3396-3*, 2039653) Bks Demand.

Combinatorial Optimization: Annotated Bibliographies. Ed. by M. O'Heigeartaigh et al. LC 84-5081. 212p. reprint ed. pap. 60.50 (*0-7837-6391-3*, 2046104) Bks Demand.

Combinatorial Optimization: New Frontiers in Theory & Practice. Ed. by Mustafa Akgul et al. LC 92-10793. (NATO ASI Series F: Computer & Systems Sciences, Special Programme AET: Vol. 82). xi, 334p. 1992. write for info. (*3-540-55439-4*); 94.00 (*0-387-55439-4*) Spr-Verlag.

Combinatorial Optimization & Empirical Processes. N. Piersma. (Tinbergen Institute Ser.). 138p. 1993. pap. 25.00 (*90-5170-211-6*, Pub. by Thesis Pubs NE) IBD Ltd.

Combinatorial Pattern Matching: Fourth Annual Symposium, CPM 93, Padova, Italy, June 1993, Proceedings. Ed. by A. Apostolico et al. LC 93-28891. (Lecture Notes in Computer Science Ser.: Vol. 684). viii, 265p. 1993. pap. 44.00 (*0-387-56764-X*) Spr-Verlag.

Combinatorial Pattern Matching: Proceedings of the 5th Annual Symposium, CPM '94, Asilomar, CA, U. S. A., June 5-8, 1994. Ed. by Maxime Crochemore & Dan Gusfield. LC 94-20069. (Lecture Notes in Computer Science: Vol. 807). 1994. 45.00 (*0-387-58094-8*) Spr-Verlag.

Combinatorial Pattern Matching: Third Annual Symposium, Tucson, Arizona, U. S. A., April 29-May 1, 1992, Proceedings. A. Apostolico et al. LC 92-31070. 1992. 47.00 (*0-387-56024-6*) Spr-Verlag.

Combinatorial Patterns for Maps of the Interval. Misiurewicz & Nitecki. LC 91-27263. (MEMO Ser.). 112p. 1991. 21.00 (*0-8218-2513-5*, MEMO 94/456) Am Math.

Combinatorial Problems & Exercises. 2nd ed. L. Lovasz. 636p. 1993. 157.25 (*0-444-81504-X*, North Holland) Elsevier.

Combinatorial Programming: Methods & Application, Proceedings of the NATO Advanced Study Institute, Versailles, France, September 2-13, 1974. NATO Advanced Study Institute Staff. Ed. by B. Roy. (NATO Advanced Study Institutes Ser.: No. C19). 386p. 1975. pap. text ed. 42.50 (*90-277-0506-2*) Kluwer Ac.

Combinatorial Rigidity. Jack Graver et al. LC 93-34431. (Graduate Studies in Mathematics: No. 2). 172p. 1993. 41.00 (*0-8218-3801-6*) Am Math.

Combinatorial Search. Martin Aigner. (Teubner Series in Computer Science). 384p. 1988. text ed. 119.00 (*0-471-92142-4*) Wiley.

Combinatorial Structures & Their Applications. Ed. by R. Guy et al. 524p. (C). 1970. text ed. 261.00 (*0-677-13890-3*) Gordon & Breach.

Combinatorial Symmetries of the M-Dimensional Ball. L. Jones. LC 86-17500. (Memoirs of the AMS Ser.: Vol. 62/352). 124p. 1986. pap. text ed. 25.00 (*0-8218-2414-7*, MEMO 62/352) Am Math.

Combinatorial Theory. 2nd ed. Marshall Hall. LC 85-26799. (Discrete Mathematics Ser.). 440p. 1986. text ed. 110.00 (*0-471-09138-3*, Wiley-Interscience) Wiley.

Combinatorial Theory & Statistical Design. Gregory M. Constantine. LC 88-626782. (Probability & Mathematics Ser.). 1987. text ed. 138.00 (*0-471-84097-1*) Wiley.

Combinatorial Theory of Possibility. D. M. Armstrong. (Cambridge Studies in Philosophy). (Illus.). (C). 1989. 54.95 (*0-521-37427-8*); pap. 16.95 (*0-521-37780-3*) Cambridge U Pr.

Combinatorics. Bela Bollobas. 177p. 1986. pap. 19.95 (*0-521-33703-8*) Cambridge U Pr.

Combinatorics. Ed. by A. Hajnal et al. (Colloquia Mathematica Societatis Janos Bolyai Ser.: No. 52). 596p. 1989. 218.00 (*0-444-70345-4*, North Holland) Elsevier.

Combinatorics. Pure Mathematics Symposium Staff. Ed. by T. S. Motzkin. LC 74-153879. (Proceedings of Symposia in Pure Mathematics Ser., Humboldt State University, Arcata, CA, July 29-August 16, 1974: Vol. 19). 255p. 1971. 59.00 (*0-8218-1419-2*, PSPUM-19) Am Math.

Combinatorics: An Invitation. Joseph Straight. LC 92-36178. 1993. text ed. 59.95 (*0-534-19926-7*) Brooks-Cole.

***Combinatorics: Papers of Gian-Carlo Rota.** Ed. by Joseph P. S. Kung. LC 95-2751. (Contemporary Mathematicians Ser.). 1995. 95.00 (*0-8176-3713-3*) Birkhauser.

Combinatorics: Proceedings of the 5th Hungarian Colloquia on Combinatorics, 2 vols., Set. Ed. by A. Hajnal & V. T. Bos. (Colloquia Mathematica Societatis Janos Bolyai Ser.: Vol. 18). 1220p. 1978. 218.00 (*0-444-85095-3*, North Holland) Elsevier.

Combinatorics: Topics, Techniques, Algorithms. Peter J. Cameron. (Illus.). 350p. (C). 1995. 59.95 (*0-521-45133-7*); pap. 24.95 (*0-521-45761-0*) Cambridge U Pr.

Combinatorics & Algebra. Ed. by Curtis Greene. LC 84-18608. (Contemporary Mathematics Ser.: Vol. 34). 318p. 1989. reprint ed. 42.00 (*0-8218-5029-6*, CONM-34) Am Math.

Combinatorics & Graph Theory: Proceedings of the Spring School & International Conference on Combinatorics. T. H. Ku et al. 288p. 1993. text ed. 81.00 (*981-02-1504-5*) World Scientific Pub.

Combinatorics & Ordered Sets. Rival. LC 86-8006. (Contemporary Mathematics Ser.: Vol. 57). 285p. 1986. pap. text ed. 38.00 (*0-8218-5051-2*, CONM-57) Am Math.

Combinatorics & Partially Ordered Sets: Dimension Theory. William T. Trotter. (Mathematical Sciences Ser.). (Illus.). 328p. 1992. text ed. 45.00 (*0-8018-4425-8*) Johns Hopkins.

Combinatorics, Computing & Complexity. Ed. by Du Dingzhu & Hu Guoding. (C). 1989. lib. bdg. 105.50 (*0-7923-0308-3*) Kluwer Ac.

Combinatorics Ninety, Recent Trends & Applications: Proceedings of the Conference on Combinatorics, Gaeta, Italy, 20-27 May 1990. Ed. by A. Barlotti et al. LC 92-19600. (Annals of Discrete Mathematics Ser.: Vol. 52). 1992. write for info. (*0-444-89452-7*, North Holland) Elsevier.

Combinatorics of Experimental Design. Anne P. Street & Deborah J. Street. (Illus.). 414p. 1987. 55.00 (*0-19-853256-3*) OUP.

Combinatorics of Network Reliability. Charles J. Colbourn. (International Series of Monographs on Computer Science: No. 4). 176p. 1987. 29.95 (*0-19-504920-9*) OUP.

Combinatorics of Train Tracks. R. C. Penner & J. L. Harer. (Annals of Mathematics Studies: No. 125). 216p. 1992. text ed. 49.50 (*0-691-08764-4*); pap. text ed. 22.50 (*0-691-02531-2*) Princeton U Pr.

Combinatorics on Traces. V. Diekert. Ed. by G. Goos & J. Hartmanis. (Lecture Notes in Computer Science Ser.: Vol. 454). xii, 165p. 1990. pap. 28.00 (*0-387-53031-2*) Spr-Verlag.

Combinatorics, 1981. A. Barlotti & P. V. Ceccerini. (Mathematical Studies: Vol. 78). 826p. 1983. 131.00 (*0-444-86546-2*, I-465-82, North Holland) Elsevier.

Combinatorics 79, 2 pts., Set. Ed. by M. M. Deza & I. G. Rosenberg. (Annals of Discrete Mathematics Ser.: Vols. 8 & 9). 1991. 223.00 (*0-444-86112-2*) Elsevier.

Combinatorics '84. Ed. by A. Barlotti et al. (North Holland Mathematics Studies: Vol. 123). 388p. 1986. 79.50 (*0-444-87962-5*, North Holland) Elsevier.

***Combinatorics '86: Proceedings of the International Conference on Incidence Geometries & Combinatorial Structures, Passo della Mendola, Trento, Italy, 30 June-5 July 1986.** International Conference on Inference Geometries & Combinatorial Structures Staff. Ed. by A. Barlotti. (Annals of Discrete Mathematics Ser.: Vol. 37). xvi, 502p. 1986. write for info. (*0-444-70369-1*) Elsevier.

Combinators, Lamda-Terms, & Proof Theory. Soren Stenlund. LC 72-83378. (Synthese Library: No. 42). 284p. 1972. lib. bdg. 71.50 (*90-277-0305-1*) Kluwer Ac.

Combinatory Analysis, 2 Vols. in 1. Percy A. MacMahon. LC 59-10267. 49.50 (*0-8284-1137-9*) Chelsea Pub.

***Combinatory Programme.** Ed. by Erwin Engeler. LC 94-36651. (Progress in Theoretical Computer Science Ser.). 1994. 49.50 (*0-8176-3801-6*) Birkhauser.

Combinatory Vocabulary of CAD - CAM in Mechanical Engineering: A French-English Terminology. 95p. (Orig.). (ENG & FRE.). (C). 1994. pap. text ed. 41.95 (*0-7881-0404-7*) Diane Pub.

Combinatory Vocabulary of CAD-CAM in Mechanical Engineering. Ed. by Claude Laine. 145p. (Orig.). 1993. pap. 20.75 (*0-660-58029-2*, Pub. by Canada Commun Grp CN) Accents Pubns.

Combine Harvesting. Ed. by Deere & Company Staff. (Fundamentals of Machine Operation Ser.). (Illus.). 92p. 1991. Student guide. student ed, pap. text ed. 13.25 (*0-86691-162-6*, FMO15604W) Deere & Co. Extensive use of full-color cutaways helps explain how combines work. Gives the complete story on basic functions such as cutting, feeding, & threshing. Explains propulsion systems, hydraulics, electrical systems, controls, cabs, & special equipment. Tells how to adjust for field operation in various crops, & field conditions. Has photos of field problems - down crops, lodged grain, etc., & extensive troubleshooting charts. CONTENTS: New-Rotary combines, types of combines, basic operation, cutting & feeding, threshing, separating, cleaning, handling, power systems, hydraulics, electrical systems, special equipment, operating controls, field adjustments, field operation, crop & field problems, windrowing of grain, preventive maintenance & safety. *Publisher Provided Annotation.*

Combine Harvesting. rev. ed. Ed. by Deere & Company Staff. (Fundamentals of Machine Operation Ser.). (Illus.). 92p. 1991. Instr's. guide & transparency masters. teacher ed, pap. text ed. 33.20 (*0-86691-161-8*, FMO15504T); Slide set. sl. 220.95 (*0-685-73885-X*, FMO15204S) Deere & Co. Extensive use of full-color cutaways helps explain how combines work. Gives the complete story on basic functions such as cutting, feeding, & threshing. Explains propulsion systems, hydraulics, electrical systems, controls, cabs, & special equipment. Tells how to adjust for field operation in various crops, & field conditions. Has photos of field problems - down crops, lodged grain, etc., & extensive troubleshooting charts. CONTENTS: New-Rotary combines, types of combines, basic operation, cutting & feeding, threshing, separating, cleaning, handling, power systems, hydraulics, electrical systems, special equipment, operating controls, field adjustments, field operation, crop & field problems, windrowing of grain, preventive maintenance & safety. *Publisher Provided Annotation.*

Combine Harvesting. 4th rev. ed. Ed. by Deere & Company Staff. (Fundamentals of Machine Operation Ser.). (Illus.). 224p. 1991. pap. 26.95 (*0-86691-132-4*, FMO15104B) Deere & Co. Extensive use of full-color cutaways helps explain how combines work. Gives the complete story on basic functions such as cutting, feeding, & threshing. Explains propulsion systems, hydraulics, electrical systems, controls, cabs, & special equipment. Tells how to adjust for field operation in various crops, & field conditions. Has photos of field problems - down crops, lodged grain, etc., & extensive troubleshooting charts. CONTENTS: New-Rotary combines, types of combines, basic operation, cutting & feeding, threshing, separating, cleaning, handling, power systems, hydraulics, electrical systems, special equipment, operating controls, field adjustments, field operation, crop & field problems, windrowing of grain, preventive maintenance & safety. *Publisher Provided Annotation.*

Combined Action Platoons: The U. S. Marines Other War in Vietnam. Michael E. Peterson. LC 88-34031. 161p. 1989. text ed. 49.95 (*0-275-93258-3*, C3258, Praeger Pubs) Greenwood.

Combined Antimicrobial Therapy. Ed. by William Brumfitt et al. (New Perspectives in Clinical Microbiology Ser.: No. 3). 1980. lib. bdg. 94.00 (*90-247-2280-2*) Kluwer Ac.

Combined Book of Sash, Doors, Blinds, Mouldings, Stair Work, Mantels & All Kinds of Interior & Exterior Finish see Turn-of-the-Century Doors, Windows & Decorative Millwork: The Mulliner Catalog of 1893

Combined Care of the Rheumatic Patient. A. Bird et al. (Illus.). 320p. 1985. pap. 60.00 (*0-387-13557-X*) Spr-Verlag.

Combined Catalog Anglo-American Law Collections University of California Law Libraries Berkeley & Davis with Library of Congress Class K Added, 10 vols. Ed. by Mortimer D. Schwartz & Dan F. Henke. 1979. Supplement. 750.00 (*0-8377-0400-6*) Rothman.

Combined Catalog Anglo-American Law Collections University of California Law Libraries, Berkeley & Davis with Library of Congress Class K Added, Supplement, 9 vols., Set. Ed. by Mortimer D. Schwartz & Dan F. Henke. 4500p. 1979. 750.00 (*0-8377-0423-5*) Rothman.

Combined Census of Lamar & Red River Counties, Texas, 1850. Ed. by Skipper Steely. (Illus.). 160p. 1985. 20.00 (*0-915263-03-3*) Wright Pr.

Combined Chronology for Use with the Mahatma Letters to A. P. Sinnett & the Letters of H. P. Blavatsky to A. P. Sinnett. Margaret Conger. LC 73-92461. 61p. 1973. pap. 3.00 (*0-911500-17-0*) Theos U Pr.

Combined Concordances to the Scriptures. Arthur E. Starks. 1978. 33.00 (*0-8309-0255-4*) Herald Hse.

Combined Cumulative Index to Obstetrics & Gynecology, Vol. 7 (1992) Ed. by Carl W. Hepp. 580p. 1993. 130.00 (*0-88471-070-X*) Numarc Bk Corp.

Combined Cumulative Index to Obstetrics & Gynecology: 1989, Vol. 4. Ed. by Carl W. Hepp. (C). 1990. 120.00 (*0-88471-064-5*) Numarc Bk Corp.

***Combined Cumulative Index to Obstetrics & Gynecology Vol. 9, 1994.** Ed. by Carl W. Hepp. 600p. 1995. 145.00x (*0-88471-074-2*) Numarc Bk Corp.

Combined Cumulative Index to Obstetrics & Gynecology, 1982-1984, Vol. 1. 1985. 110.00 (*0-88471-046-7*, SUB. 267) Numarc Bk Corp.

Combined Cumulative Index to Obstetrics & Gynecology, 1985-1987, Vol. 2. 1988. 110.00 (*0-88471-059-9*, SUB. 267) Numarc Bk Corp.

Combined Cumulative Index to Obstetrics & Gynecology, 1988, Vol. 3. Ed. by Carl W. Hepp. 500p. (C). 1989. 115.00 (*0-88471-062-9*) Numarc Bk Corp.

Combined Cumulative Index to Obstetrics & Gynecology, 1990, Vol. 5. Ed. by Carl W. Hepp. 600p. (C). 1991. 125.00 (*0-88471-066-1*) Numarc Bk Corp.

Combined Cumulative Index to Obstetrics & Gynecology, 1991, Vol. 6. Ed. by Carl W. Hepp. 565p. (C). 1992. 125.00 (*0-88471-068-8*) Numarc Bk Corp.

Combined Cumulative Index to Obstetrics & Gynecology, 1993, Vol. 8. Ed. by Carl W. Hepp. 600p. 1994. 135.00 (*0-88471-072-6*) Numarc Bk Corp.

Combined Cumulative Index to Pediatrics, Vol. 11 (1992) Ed. by Carl W. Hepp. 595p. 1993. 122.50 (*0-88471-069-6*) Numarc Bk Corp.

Combined Cumulative Index to Pediatrics: 1979-1981, Vol. 2. 1982. 75.00 (*0-88471-051-3*, SUB. 274) Numarc Bk Corp.

Combined Cumulative Index to Pediatrics: 1989, Vol. 8. Ed. by Carl W. Hepp. (C). 1990. 102.50 (*0-88471-063-7*) Numarc Bk Corp.

***Combined Cumulative Index to Pediatrics Vol. 13, 1994.** Ed. by Carl W. Hepp. 600p. 1995. 137.50x (*0-88471-073-4*) Numarc Bk Corp.

Combined Cumulative Index to Pediatrics, Vol. 1: 1976-1978. 1979. 75.00 (*0-88471-050-5*, SUB. 274) Numarc Bk Corp.

Combined Cumulative Index to Pediatrics, 1982-1984, Vol. 3. 1985. 75.00 (*0-88471-052-1*, SUB. 274) Numarc Bk Corp.

Combined Cumulative Index to Pediatrics, 1985, Vol. 4. 1986. 85.00 (*0-88471-053-X*, SUB. 274) Numarc Bk Corp.

Combined Cumulative Index to Pediatrics, 1986, Vol. 5. 1987. 85.00 (*0-88471-054-8*, SUB. 274) Numarc Bk Corp.

Combined Cumulative Index to Pediatrics, 1987, Vol. 6. 1988. 92.50 (*0-88471-057-2*, SUB. 274) Numarc Bk Corp.

C

An Asterisk (*) at the beginning of an entry indicates that the title is appearing in BIP for the first time.

C

An Asterisk (*) at the beginning of an entry indicates that the title is appearing in BIP for the first time.

1399

An Asterisk (*) at the beginning of an entry indicates that the title is appearing in BIP for the first time.

Come Mime with Me: A Guide to Preparing Scriptural Dramas for Children. Gail Kelley & Carol Hershberger. LC 86-62621. (Illus.). 104p. (J). (gr. 1 up). 1987. 10.95 (*0-89390-089-3*) Resource Pubns.

Come Nightfall. Gary Amo. 1990. pap. 3.95 (*1-55817-340-4*, Pinnacle NY) Windsor NY.

Come O Breath. James A. Stewart. pap. 2.99 (*1-56632-056-9*) Revival Lit.

come October: Exclusively Woodcock. Gene Hill et al. LC 90-64145. (Illus.). 176p. 1991. 39.00 (*0-924357-18-5*, 11180-A) Countrysport Pr.

Come On. Jim Cirni. LC 89-6269. 224p. 1989. 17.95 (*0-939149-24-9*) Soho Press.

*__Come On.__ Jim Cirni. 216p. 1995. pap. 10.00 (*1-56947-037-5*) Soho Press.

Come On , Rejoice. Ed. by Larry Carlson & Carol Carlson. 180p. 1986. pap. 5.95 (*0-935779-09-4*) Crown Min.

Come on Down? The Politics of Popular Media Culture in Post-War Britain. Ed. by Dominic Strinati & Stephen Wagg. 352p. 1992. 69.95 (*0-415-06326-4*, A7607); pap. 16.95 (*0-415-06327-2*, A7611) Routledge.

Come on Everybody! Let's Go to the Fair. Margret Turner & Alyson Scott. 32p. (J). (ps-00). 1991. pap. write for info. (*0-9630453-0-X*) Lifeworks.

Come on in, It's Awful. Ed. by Joanna Bogle. 1994. pap. 14. 95 (*0-85244-236-X*, Pub. by Gracewing UK) Morehouse Pub.

Come on Strong. Garson Kanin. 1963. pap. 4.75 (*0-8222-0230-1*) Dramatists Play.

Come on Up. Joy Kim. LC 81-2356. (Giant First Start Reader Ser.). (Illus.). 32p. (J). (gr. k-2). 1981. lib. bdg. 11.59 (*0-89375-511-7*); pap. text ed. 2.95 (*0-89375-512-5*) Troll Assocs.

*__Come on, Vera, Let's Go: The Bittersweet Days of an Alzheimer's Wife.__ Vera Woll. 160p. (Orig.). 1992. pap. 9.95 (*1-881576-05-1*) Providence Hse.

Come out & Play. David Korner. LC 86-2811. (Illus.). 56p. (J). (gr. 1-5). 1987. pap. 9.95 (*0-939827-00-X*) Korn Kompany.

Come Out & Play, Little Mouse. Robert Kraus. Ed. by Amy Cohn. LC 85-30198. (Illus.). 32p. (J). (ps up). 1995. reprint ed. pap. 4.95 (*0-688-14026-2*, Mulberry) Morrow.

Come out, Come out Wherever You Are! Sheri C. Sinykin. (Illus.). 32p. (Orig.). (J). (gr. k-5). 1990. pap. 5.00 (*0-89486-694-X*, 5113A) Hazelden.

Come Out into the Sun: Poems New & Selected. Robert Francis. LC 65-26243. 156p. 1968. reprint ed. 20.00 (*0-87023-015-8*) U of Mass Pr.

Come out, Jessie! Harriet Ziefert. LC 90-41880. (Illus.). 32p. (J). (ps-1). 1991. pap. 4.95 (*0-06-107414-4*) HarpC Child Bks.

Come Out, Mouse. Bernice Chardiet. (Illus.). 20p. (J). (ps-1). 1994. pap. 4.99 (*0-14-054997-8*) Puffin Bks.

Come out, Muskrats. Jim Arnosky. LC 88-26611. (Illus.). 40p. (J). (ps-3). 1989. 12.95 (*0-688-05457-9*); lib. bdg. 12.88 (*0-688-05458-7*) Lothrop.

Come Out, Muskrats. Jim Arnosky. LC 88-26611. (Illus.). 32p. (J). (ps up). 1991. reprint ed. pap. 3.95 (*0-688-10490-8*, Mulberry) Morrow.

Come Out of Her, My People: A Study of the Revelation to John. J. E. Leonard. 208p. 1991. pap. 9.75 (*1-884454-00-3*) Laudemont Pr.

Come Phoenix Word. Joan L. Gibbons. 128p. (Orig.). 1989. pap. 8.50 (*0-917479-14-9*) Guild Psy.

Come Play with Me. Margaret Hillert. (Illus.). (J). (ps-00). 1975. lib. bdg. 8.99 (*0-8136-5036-4*, TK2292); pap. 4.79 (*0-8136-5536-6*, TK2293) Modern Curr.

Come Play with Me: Games & Toys for Creative Lovers. Joan E. Lloyd. 272p. (Orig.). 1994. pap. 11.99 (*0-446-39538-2*) Warner Bks.

Come Rain: A Novel. Jai Numbkar. 1993. pap. 8.95 (*0-86311-328-1*, Pub. by Disha Bks II) Apt Bks.

Come Rejoice! Ed. by Michael Perry et al. 107p. (Orig.). 1989. pap. 11.95 (*0-916642-38-0*) Hope Pub.

Come Retribution: The Confederate Secret Service & the Assassination of Lincoln. William A. Tidwell et al. LC 88-5463. (Illus.). 510p. 1988. 40.00 (*0-87805-347-6*); pap. 18.95 (*0-87805-348-4*) U Pr of Miss.

Come Run Away. Anne Frost. (Illus.). 85p. (Orig.). 1977. pap. 9.95 (*0-9614624-0-X*) Frost Pub.

Come Sail with Me. large type ed. Sinclair. 1991. 16.95 (*0-7451-9681-0*, 4978, Atlantic Lrg Print) Chivers N Amer.

Come See. Willya Holmes. 1995. 10.95 (*0-8062-5029-1*) Carlton.

Come See Our Christmas Village. Suzanne L. Kueppers. (Illus.). 32p. 1993. text ed. 15.95 (*0-9635629-0-8*) Gina B Pr.

*__Come See the Lilies.__ Dorothy E. Schemske. 200p. 1994. pap. text ed. 12.50 (*1-885990-00-6*) Ask Services.

Come Set in the Warm: Twenty-or-So-Anecdotes of Rural Vermont. 2nd ed. Leonard A. Mason & Jeanne Masson-Douglas. (Illus.). 88p. 1982. pap. 4.95 (*0-940282-00-3*) Outermost Pr.

Come Sign with Us: Sign Language Activities for Children. Jan C. Hafer & Robert M. Wilson. LC 90-3478. (Illus.). 157p. (J). (gr. 2-6). 1990. pap. text ed. 24.95 (*0-930323-72-6*, Clerc Bks) Gallaudet Univ Pr.

Come, Sing & Celebrate! Mary J. Mulder & Richard Coyle. (Orig.). 1988. pap. 3.65 (*1-55673-074-8*, 8871) CSS OH.

Come Sing, Jimmy Jo. Katherine Paterson. 192p. (J). (gr. 5 up). 1986. mass mkt. 3.99 (*0-380-70052-2*, Flare) Avon.

Come Sing, Jimmy Jo. Katherine Paterson. LC 84-21123. 208p. (J). (gr. 5 up). 1985. 14.99 (*0-525-67167-6*, Lodestar Bks) Dutton Child Bks.

*__Come Sing, Jimmy Jo.__ Katherine Paterson. 208p. (J). 1995. pap. 3.99 (*0-14-037397-7*) Puffin Bks.

Come Sing, Jimmy Jo: A Study Guide. Joan Le Doux. (Novel-Ties Ser.). (gr. 7-10). 1988. student ed, teacher ed 15.95 (*0-88122-109-0*) Lrn Links.

Come Sit with Me: Sermons for Children. Ron Miner. LC 81-10650. (Illus.). 96p. (Orig.). 1981. pap. 8.95 (*0-8298-0469-2*) Pilgrim OH.

Come Sit with Me Again: Sermons for Children. Don-Paul Benjamin & Ron Miner. LC 86-30588. (Illus.). 128p. (Orig.). (J). 1987. pap. 8.95 (*0-8298-0748-9*) Pilgrim OH.

Come Sit with Me Once More: Sermons for Children. Don-Paul Benjamin & Ron Miner. LC 90-36845. (Illus.). 120p. (Orig.). 1990. pap. 8.95 (*0-8298-0871-X*) Pilgrim OH.

Come Slowly, Eden. Norman Rosten. 1967. pap. 4.75 (*0-8222-0228-X*) Dramatists Play.

Come, Solitude, Speak to Me. Somesh Dasgupta. 8.00 (*0-89253-683-7*); 4.80 (*0-89253-684-5*) Ind-US Inc.

Come Songbook. Gary L. Johnson. 32p. 1980. pap. 2.50 (*0-87123-777-6*) Bethany Hse.

Come Spring. Jill M. Landis. 384p. (Orig.). 1992. mass mkt. 5.50 (*0-515-10861-8*) Jove Pubns.

Come Spring. Ben A. Williams. 866p. 1976. lib. bdg. 32.95 (*0-89966-197-1*) Buccaneer Bks.

Come Spring. Ben A. Williams. (Illus.). 874p. 1940. reprint ed. pap. 19.95 (*0-89272-014-X*) Down East.

Come Stains. Teddy M. Haggarty. LC 76-15757. (Illus.). (Orig.). 1976. 7.50 (*0-917196-01-5*); pap. 2.50 (*0-917196-00-7*) Seattle Air.

Come Sunday: The Liturgy of Zion. William B. McClain. 1990. pap. 12.95 (*0-687-08884-4*) Abingdon.

Come Take My Hand: A Poetic Sequel to An Enchanted Childhood at Raven Rocks. Elsa C. Harper. (Illus.). 168p. (Orig.). 1993. pap. 12.00 (*0-9615961-2-0*) Raven Rocks Pr.

Come Tell Me Right Away. Lynn Sanford. (Illus.). 1983. pap. 1.95 (*0-934978-12-3*) Ed-U Pr.

Come the Dawn. Christopher D. Martinez. 386p. 1994. pap. 9.95 (*1-56901-248-2*) NW Pub.

Come the Millennium. American Society of Newspaper Editors. LC 94-7027. 1994. 8.95 (*0-8362-8070-9*) Andrews & McMeel.

Come the Morning. Mark J. Harris. LC 88-24213. 176p. (J). (gr. 5-9). 1989. text ed. 14.95 (*0-02-742750-1*, Bradbury S&S) S&S Childrens.

Come the Night. Christina Skye. 1994. mass mkt. 4.99 (*0-440-21644-3*) Dell.

Come the Sweet By & By. Eleanor Lerman. LC 75-8449. 80p. 1975. 15.00 (*0-87023-194-4*); pap. 9.95 (*0-87023-195-2*) U of Mass Pr.

*__Come the Terrible Tiger.__ Kim Gamble. (J). 1995. 14.95 (*1-86373-236-5*) IPG Chicago.

*__Come the Terrible Tiger.__ Kim Gamble. (J). 1995. pap. 6.95 (*1-86373-473-2*) IPG Chicago.

Come the Winter. large type ed. Elisabeth Arthur. (Linford Romance Library). 1991. pap. 13.95 (*0-7089-7103-2*) Ulverscroft.

Come This Far to Freedom: A History of African Americans. Angela S. Medearis. LC 92-31251. (Illus.). 160p. (J). (gr. 3-7). 1993. text ed. 14.95 (*0-689-31522-8*, Atheneum Bks Young) S&S Childrens.

Come, Thou Almighty King. Ed. by James Pethel. 1986. 8.95 (*0-8341-9237-3*, MB-560) Lillenas.

Come Thou Reign Over Us. James F. Matheny & Marjorie B. Matheny. 167p. (Orig.). (C). 1981. pap. 6.95 (*0-939422-00-X*) Jay & Assocs.

*__Come to Africa & Save Your Marriage & Other Stories.__ Thomas. 1988. pap. text ed. 10.00 (*0-939149-21-4*) Soho Press.

Come to Africa & Save Your Marriage & Other Stories. Maria Thomas. LC 87-9786. 235p. 1987. 14.95 (*0-939149-06-0*) Soho Press.

Come to Africa & Save Your Marriage & Other Stories. Maria Thomas. 235p. 1988. reprint ed. pap. 10.00 (*1-56947-039-1*) Soho Press.

Come to Bethlehem: The Christmas Story. Joe Cothen. LC 75-25503. (Illus.). 64p. (J). (gr. 4 up). 1975. 8.95 (*0-88289-098-0*) Pelican.

Come to Castlemoor. large type ed. Jennifer Wilde. 346p. 1992. 21.95 (*0-7505-0140-5*) Ulverscroft.

Come to Castlemoor. Jennifer Wilde. 1991. reprint ed. 18. 95 (*0-7278-4230-7*) Severn Hse.

Come to Christmas: The Customs of the Advent Season. 16p. (Orig.). 1993. pap. 1.50 (*0-687-08885-2*) Abingdon.

Come to Jesus: Jesus Blesses the Children. Mary M. Simon. (Hear Me Read Ser.). (Illus.). 24p. (Orig.). (J). (ps-1). 1992. pap. 2.49 (*0-570-04707-2*) Concordia.

Come to Laugh: A Study of African Traditional Theatre in Ghana. Kwabena N. Bame. LC 84-6259. (Illus.). 192p. (C). 1985. text ed. 21.50 (*0-936508-07-8*); pap. text ed. 9.50 (*0-936508-08-6*) Barber Pr.

Come to Me! Tom Wells. 128p. (Orig.). 1986. pap. 4.95 (*0-85151-471-5*) Banner of Truth.

Come to Me. Amy Bloom. 224p. 1994. reprint ed. pap. 10. 00 (*0-06-099514-9*, PL) HarpC.

*__Come to Me: Forgiveness, Inner Healing & Deliverance Through Confession.__ Thomas R. Hyatt. 69p. (Orig.). Date not set. pap. 5.00 (*0-9637789-0-0*) T R Hyatt.

Come to Me: Prayers in Times of Illness. Robert M. Hamma. LC 93-71538. 88p. (Orig.). 1993. pap. 2.95 (*0-87793-512-2*) Ave Maria.

Come to Me My Children. Patricia Soto. 50p. 1994. pap. 1.95 (*1-882972-40-6*) Queenship Pub.

Come to My Party. Judith B. Richardson. LC 91-16320. (Illus.). 32p. (J). (ps-1). 1993. text ed. 13.95 (*0-02-776147-9*, Mac Bks Young Read) S&S Childrens.

Come to My Place. Bobbie Kalman. (In My World Ser.). (Illus.). 32p. (J). (gr. k-2). 1985. 15.95 (*0-86505-062-7*); pap. 6.95 (*0-86505-086-4*) Crabtree Pub Co.

Come to My Tea Party: A Cookbook for Children. Nancy C. Akmon. (Illus.). 84p. (J). (gr. 3-6). 1993. 9.95 (*0-926684-09-4*) Eclectic Oregon.

*__Come to My Tomorrowland.__ Jesse Stuart. Ed. by Jerry A. Herndon. (Illus.). 176p. (J). (gr. 4 up). 1995. 17.50 (*0-945084-55-2*); pap. 10.00 (*0-945084-54-4*) J Stuart Found.

Come to Our Salmon Feast. Martha F. McKeown. LC 59-9823. (Illus.). 80p. (J). (gr. 4-9). 1959. 7.95 (*0-8323-0157-4*) Binford Mort.

Come to School. Jacqueline Paschos & Francoise Destang. (Rejoice Ser.). (J). (ps). 1986. pap. 0.35 (*0-8091-6505-8*) Paulist Pr.

Come to School, Dear Dragon. Margaret Hillert. (Illus.). (J). (ps-00). 1985. lib. bdg. 8.99 (*0-8136-5133-6*, TK2966); pap. 4.79 (*0-8136-5633-8*) Modern Curr.

Come to Stay. David H. Richards. 96p. 1986. pap. 4.95 (*0-913152-25-0*) Folder Edns.

Come to the Circus. (Chubby Board Bks.). 16p. (J). (ps-00). 1980. pap. 2.95 (*0-671-41479-8*, Litl Simon S&S) S&S Childrens.

Come to the Cradle. Michael Card. LC 93-10325. 1993. 12. 95 (*0-917143-24-8*) Sparrow TN.

Come to the Desert with Me. Mary C. Reid. LC 91-71036. 32p. (J). 1991. pap. 4.99 (*0-8066-2552-X*, 9-2552) Augsburg Fortress.

Come to the Doctor, Harry. Chalmers. (J). Date not set. 14.95 (*0-06-021160-1*, HarpT); lib. bdg. 14.89 (*0-06-021161-X*, HarpT) HarpC.

Come to the Feast: A Handbook for Christian Women's Groups. Lorraine A. Brown & Wilma C. Buckner. LC 91-77274. 148p. (Orig.). 1992. pap. text ed. 6.99 (*0-89900-409-1*) College Pr Pub.

Come To the Fountain. Marita L. Tabron. (Illus.). 86p. (Orig.). 1991. pap. 6.75 (*0-9630672-2-2*) MLT Prods.

Come To the Fountain. braille ed. Marita L. Tabron. (Illus.). 86p. (Orig.). 1991. 9.95 (*0-9630672-0-6*) MLT Prods.

Come to the Garden: An Invitation to Serenity. JoAnna OKeefe. Ed. by Julie Mitchell. (Illus.). 1992. 6.50 (*0-8378-2502-4*) Gibson.

Come to the Island With Me. Mary C. Reid. LC 92-73012. (Discover Bks.). 32p. (J). 1992. pap. 4.99 (*0-8066-2632-1*, 9-2632) Augsburg Fortress.

Come to the Mountain With Me. Mary C. Reid. LC 92-73011. (Discover Bks.). 32p. (J). 1992. pap. 4.99 (*0-8066-2631-3*, 9-2631) Augsburg Fortress.

Come to the Ocean with Me. Mary C. Reid. LC 91-71035. 32p. (J). 1991. pap. 4.99 (*0-8066-2551-1*) Augsburg Fortress.

Come to the Park. Laura Magni. (Look-Behind-The-Picture Bks.). (Illus.). 16p. (J). (ps up). 1989. 8.95 (*0-8120-5994-8*) Barron.

Come to the Party! Celebrate Jesus. LeRoy Lawson. LC 93-28842. 192p. (Orig.). 1994. pap. 5.99 (*0-7847-0144-X*) Standard Pub.

Come to the Secret Garden: Sufi Tales of Wisdom. M. R. Bawa Muhaiyaddeen. LC 83-49210. (Illus.). 450p. (J). 1985. 20.00 (*0-914390-27-9*) Fellowship Pr PA.

Come to the Water: The First Twelve Years of the East Central Province Daughters of Charity of Saint Vincent de Paul in the United States, 1969-1981. Virginia Kingsbury. LC 88-72172. (Illus.). 543p. 1988. text ed. 20.00 (*0-685-22946-7*) Daughters Charity.

Come to Think of It. Gilbert K. Chesterton. LC 73-142614. (Essay Index Reprint Ser.). 1977. 20.95 (*0-8369-2042-2*) Ayer.

Come to Your Senses. Milan Tytla. (Illus.). 96p. (J). 1993. pap. 9.95 (*1-55037-292-0*, Pub. by Annick CN) Firefly Bks Ltd.

Come Together. Kate Dooley & Maureen Gallagher. 40p. 1986. pap. 5.95 (*0-89505-393-4*) Tabor Pub.

Come Together: John Lennon in His Time. Jon Wiener. 408p. 1991. pap. 13.95 (*0-252-06131-4*) U of Ill Pr.

Come Under the Wings: A Midrash on Ruth. 2nd ed. Grace Goldin. LC 79-91327. 86p. (C). 1980. reprint ed. pap. 7.95 (*0-8276-0171-9*) JPS Phila.

Come unto Christ. Duane S. Crowther. LC 70-173393. (Scripture Guide Ser.). 240p. 1971. pap. 8.98 (*0-88290-007-2*) Horizon Utah.

Come unto Me. Mildred Spires Jacobs. (Illus.). 56p. (Orig.). (J). (gr. 5-6). 1982. pap. 2.95 (*0-9609612-0-8*) Enrich Enter.

Come unto Me. Philip Patterson. (Illus.). (Orig.). Date not set. pap. 8.99 (*0-89900-613-2*) College Pr Pub.

Come unto These Yellow Sands. Angela Carter. 1985. 35.00 (*0-906427-66-5*, Pub. by Bloodaxe Bks UK); pap. 16.95 (*0-906427-67-3*, Pub. by Bloodaxe Bks UK) Dufour.

Come Walk among the Stars. deluxe ed. Winston O. Abbott. LC 66-29141. 1966. 8.95 (*0-918114-00-4*) Inspiration Conn.

Come, Walk in the Woods with Me. Kathlyn G. Hilton. LC 92-72704. (Illus.). 40p. (YA). (gr. 7-9). 1993. 14.95 (*1-880851-04-0*) Greene Bark Pr.

Come Walk in Their Footsteps: The Flat Tops Trail Scenic Byway. Geri Anderson. 58p. 1993. pap. 7.95 (*1-883546-00-1*) Trail Finders.

Come Walk with Me. Mary Akin. (Illus.). 260p. (Orig.). (C). 1993. 19.95 (*1-880047-13-6*); pap. text ed. 12.95 (*1-880047-08-X*) Creative Des.

*__Come, Walk with Me.__ Walter Burnett. 1995. 10.95 (*0-8062-5138-7*) Carlton.

Come, Walk with Me. Ruth R. Flickinger. 1994. pap. 10.00 (*0-533-10884-5*) Vantage.

*__Come Walk with Me.__ Ruth R. Flickinger. Date not set. pap. 10.00 (*0-615-00500-4*) Vantage.

Come, Walk with Me. Elwood McQuaid. LC 89-82580. 1990. pap. 5.95 (*0-915540-47-9*) Frnds Israel.

Come Walk with Me Across the Years. Marjorie L. Sinks. (Illus.). 164p. (Orig.). 1994. pap. 9.95 (*0-9641708-0-9*) Centennial CO.

Come Walk with Me Thru the Needle's Eye. Irma Davis & Celia Lehman. (Illus.). 124p. 1991. 5.95 (*0-936369-43-4*) Son-Rise Pubns.

Come, Watch with Me. Terry Deffenbaugh. 55p. 1991. 8.95 (*1-877871-14-1*, 8420) Ed Ministries.

Come Winter. Douglas C. Jones. LC 91-46802. 432p. 1992. pap. 14.95 (*1-55728-259-5*) U of Ark Pr.

Come with Me. Ashley Wolff. LC 89-34482. (Illus.). 32p. (J). (ps-2). 1990. 12.95 (*0-525-44555-2*, DCB) Dutton Child Bks.

Come with Me from Lebanon: An American Family Odyssey. Ann Z. Kerr & Malcolm H. Kerr. LC 94-9246. (Contemporary Issues in the Middle East Ser.). (Illus.). 384p. 1994. 28.95 (*0-8156-0298-7*) Syracuse U Pr.

Come with Me Through Europe, 6 vols. E. D. Schoonmaker. 1972. 600.00 (*0-87968-910-2*) Gordon Pr.

Come with Me to Africa. Gregory S. Kreikemeier. (J). (gr. 4-7). 1993. 11.95 (*0-307-15660-5*, Golden Pr) Western Pub.

*__Come with Me to GA: Member Book for Younger Girls in Action.__ Kathy Strawn. Ed. by Cindy McClain. (Illus.). 24p. (Orig.). (J). (gr. 1-4). 1994. pap. text ed. 1.95 (*1-56309-128-3*) Womans Mission Union.

Come with Me to Ireland. Philip Ward. (Travel Bks.). (Illus.). 1972. pap. 12.50 (*0-902675-36-2*) Oleander Pr.

Come Worship with Us: Explaining the Mass. Frank Buckley. 48p. 1987. pap. 2.50 (*0-89243-263-2*) Liguori Pubns.

Come Ye Children. C. H. Spurgeon. 1975. pap. 4.95 (*1-56186-321-1*) Pilgrim Pubns.

Come, Ye Faithful Wise Men. Mark E. Moore. 1962. 4.25 (*0-685-68592-6*, MC-206) Lillenas.

Comeback. Dave Dravecky & Tim Stafford. 1991. mass mkt. 4.99 (*0-06-104048-7*) Zondervan.

Comeback. Dave Dravecky & Tim Stafford. 272p. 1992. pap. 9.99 (*0-310-52881-X*) Zondervan.

Comeback. L. L. Enger. Ed. by Dana Isaacson. 256p. (Orig.). 1990. mass mkt. 4.99 (*0-671-70918-6*) PB.

Comeback. Dick Francis. 1993. mass mkt. 5.99 (*0-449-45308-1*, Crest) Fawcett.

*__Comeback.__ Dick Francis. Date not set. pap. 4.98 (*0-8317-5042-1*) Smithmark.

Comeback. A. R. Gurney. 1965. pap. 2.75 (*0-8222-0229-8*) Dramatists Play.

Comeback. Ed. by Ed Vega. LC 83-72579. 250p. 1984. 10. 00 (*0-934770-29-8*) Arte Publico.

Comeback. large type ed. Dick Francis. LC 92-14133. (General Ser.). 1992. lib. bdg. 23.95 (*0-8161-5418-X*) G K Hall.

Comeback. large type ed. Dick Francis. LC 92-14133. (General Ser.). 420p. 1993. pap. 17.95 (*0-8161-5419-8*) G K Hall.

Comeback: An Actor's Direction. James Fox. LC 83-1545. 151p. reprint ed. pap. 43.10 (*0-317-30138-1*, 2025321) Bks Demand.

Comeback! Four True Stories. Jim O'Connor. LC 91-25028. (Step into Reading Bks.). (Illus.). 48p. (Orig.). (J). (gr. 2-4). 1992. pap. 3.50 (*0-679-82666-1*) Random Bks Yng Read.

Comeback: My Race for the America's Cup. Dennis Conner & Bruce Stannard. (Illus.). 256p. 1988. pap. 7.95 (*0-312-01749-9*) St Martin.

*__Comeback: The Fall & Rise of the American Automobile Industry.__ Ingrassia. 1995. pap. 14.00 (*0-684-80437-9*, Touchstone Bks) S&S Trade.

Comeback: The Fall & Rise of the American Automobile Industry. Paul J. Ingrassia & Joseph B. White. (Illus.). 1994. 25.00 (*0-671-79214-8*) S&S Trade.

Comeback! The Inside Story, in Words & Pictures of the 1991 Atlanta Braves' Race for Baseball Glory. I. J. Rosenberg. 192p. 1991. 29.95 (*0-9631594-0-2*) AJ & the AC.

Comeback: The Restoration of American Banking Power in the New World Economy. Roy C. Smith. LC 92-23757. 368p. 1993. 27.95 (*0-87584-326-3*); pap. 16.95 (*0-87584-567-3*) Harvard Busn.

Comeback Champions: The Restoration of American Banking Power. Roy C. Smith. 1993. text ed. 27.95 (*0-07-103384-X*) McGraw.

*__Comeback Congregation: Renewing a Troubled Ministry.__ Randy Frazee & Lyle E. Schaller. (Innovators in Ministry Ser.). 160p. 1995. 15.95 (*0-687-00620-1*) Abingdon.

Comeback Dog. Jane R. Thomas. (Illus.). 64p. (J). (gr. 2-6). 1981. 13.95 (*0-395-29432-0*, Clarion Bks) HM.

Comeback Dog. Jane R. Thomas. (J). (ps-7). 1983. pap. 3.25 (*0-553-15521-0*, Skylark) Bantam.

Comeback Kid: The Life & Career of Bill Clinton. Charles F. Allen & Jonathan Portis. (Illus.). 256p. 1992. 18.95 (*1-55972-154-5*, Birch Ln Pr) Carol Pub Group.

Comeback Kids: A Fan Relives the Amazing Baltimore Orioles 1989 Season. Steve Keplinger. 156p. (Orig.). 1989. pap. 9.95 (*0-939771-06-3*) Pubs Place UT.

Comeback Man. Mark Crain. LC 94-71433. 1994. 21.00 (*0-9641608-8-9*) F E A Laser.

Comebacks. Jay Jennings. (Sports Triumphs Ser.). (Illus.). 64p. (J). (gr. 5-7). 1991. lib. bdg. 11.95 (*0-382-24109-6*); pap. 5.95 (*0-382-24115-0*); pap. 6.71 (*0-685-47014-8*) Silver Burdett Pr.

Comecon: The Rise & Fall of an International Socialist Organization. Jenny Brine. 250p. (C). 1992. 49.95 (*1-56000-080-5*) Transaction Pubs.

COMECON Data, 1981. Ed. by Vienna Institute for Comparative Economic Studies Staff. LC 82-47960. 464p. 1982. text ed. 59.95 (*0-313-23629-1*, VIC/81, Greenwood Pr) Greenwood.

COMECON Data, 1983. Ed. by Vienna Institute for Comparative Economic Studies Staff. (Illus.). 491p. 1984. text ed. 55.00 (*0-313-24536-3*, VIC/83, Greenwood Pr) Greenwood.

C

An Asterisk (*) at the beginning of an entry indicates that the title is appearing in BIP for the first time. 1401

COMECON Data, 1985. Ed. by Vienna Institute for Comparative Economic Studies Staff. 485p. 1986. text ed. 59.95 (*0-313-25600-4*, VIC/85, Greenwood Pr) Greenwood.

COMECON Data, 1987. 5th ed. Ed. by Vienna Institute for Comparative Economic Studies Staff. 175p. 1989. text ed. 65.00 (*0-313-26561-5*, VIC/87, Greenwood Pr) Greenwood.

COMECON Data, 1989. 432p. 1991. text ed. 99.50 (*0-313-27838-5*, VIC89, Greenwood Pr) Greenwood.

COMECON Data, 1990. 432p. 1991. text ed. 105.00 (*0-313-28392-3*, VIC90, Greenwood Pr) Greenwood.

COMECON Foreign Trade Data, 1980. Ed. by Vienna Institute for Comparative Economic Studies Staff. LC 80-28569. (Illus.). 509p. 1981. text ed. 75.00 (*0-313-22988-0*, VIC/, Greenwood Pr) Greenwood.

COMECON Foreign Trade Data, 1982. Vienna Institute for Comparative Economic Studies Staff. LC 80-28569. 518p. 1983. text ed. 59.95 (*0-313-23982-7*, VIC82, Greenwood Pr); lib. bdg. 45.00 (*0-313-23983-5*, VIC82, Greenwood Pr) Greenwood.

COMECON Foreign Trade Data, 1984. Ed. by Vienna Institute for Comparative Economic Studies Staff. LC 80-28569. (Illus.). 553p. 1985. text ed. 55.00 (*0-313-24973-3*, VIC/84, Greenwood Pr) Greenwood.

COMECON Foreign Trade Data, 1986. Ed. by Vienna Institute for Comparative Economic Studies. 500p. 1987. text ed. 65.00 (*0-313-26081-8*, VIC86/, Greenwood Pr) Greenwood.

Comecon Merchant Ships. 3rd ed. Ambrose Greenway. 186p. 1987. 60.00 (*0-85937-327-4*, Pub. by K Mason Pubns Ltd UK) St Mut.

COMECON, Trade & the West. William V. Wallace & Roger A. Clarke. LC 86-17837. 200p. 1986. text ed. 39.95 (*0-312-15104-7*) St Martin.

Comedia: Art & History. William R. Blue. (University of Kansas Humanistic Studies: Vol. 2). 212p. (C). 1989. text ed. 40.30 (*0-8204-0644-9*) P Lang Pubs.

"Comedia" & Points of View. Everett W. Hesse. 175p. (SPA.). 1984. 24.50 (*0-916379-07-8*) Scripta.

Comedia De la Corte: El Caballerizo. Pietro Aretino. Ed. & Tr. by Angel Chiclana. (Nueva Austral Ser.: No. 74). (SPA.). 1991. pap. text ed. 24.95x (*84-239-1874-2*) Elliots Bks.

Comedia Lacrimosa & Spanish Romantic Drama (1773-1865) Joan L. Kosgrove. (Serie A: Monagrafias, LXVII). 148p. (C). 1977. 45.00 (*0-7293-0049-8*, Pub. by Tamesis Bks Ltd UK) Boydell & Brewer.

Comedia Llamada Serafina: An Anonymous Humanistic Comedy of 1521. Ed. by Glen F. Dille. LC 78-18308. 141p. 1979. 7.95 (*0-8093-0866-5*) S Ill U Pr.

Comedia Nueva. El Si de las Ninas. Leandro Fernandez de Moratin. Ed. by Rene Andioc. (Nueva Austral Ser.: Vol. 69). (SPA.). 1991. pap. text ed. 12.95 (*84-239-1869-6*) Elliots Bks.

Comedia Nueva O El Cafe - El Si De Las Ninas. Moratin. 143p. (SPA.). 1979. 9.95 (*0-8288-7061-6*, S9170) Fr & Eur.

Comedia Nueva O El Cafe - La Derrota de Los Pedantes. Moratin. 126p. (SPA.). 1973. 7.95 (*0-8288-7107-8*) Fr & Eur.

Comedia Thebaida: Spanish Text, English Notes. Ed. by G. D. Trotter & Keith Whinnom. (Serie B: Textos, VIII). 270p. (Orig.). (C). 1969. pap. 45.00 (*0-900411-07-4*, Pub. by Tamesis Bks Ltd UK) Boydell & Brewer.

Comedians. Arthur Grace. LC 91-21465. (Illus.). 192p. 1991. 19.98 (*0-934738-80-7*); pap. 12.98 (*0-934738-92-0*) Thomasson-Grant.

Comedians. Graham Greene. 1976. mass mkt. 4.95 (*0-14-002766-1*, Penguin Bks) Viking Penguin.

Comedians. Graham Greene. (Twentieth-Century Classics Ser.). 1991. 9.95 (*0-14-018494-5*, Penguin Bks) Viking Penguin.

Comedians. Trevor Griffiths. 68p. 1987. pap. 8.95 (*0-571-10884-9*) Faber & Faber.

Comedians. Graham Greene. 275p. 1992. reprint ed. lib. bdg. 19.95 (*0-89966-923-9*) Buccaneer Bks.

Comedians' Quote Book: Quick Takes from the Great Comics. Merrit Malloy & Marsha Rose. LC 92-41346. 128p. 1993. pap. 5.95 (*0-8069-0324-4*) Sterling.

Comedias del Siglo de Oro & Shakespeare. Ed. by Susan L. Fischer. LC 88-48038. (Review Ser.: Vol. 33, No. 1). 152p. 1989. 22.00 (*0-8387-5169-5*) Bucknell U Pr.

Comedias Nuevas. Antonio De Zamora. (Textos y Estudios Clasicos De las Literaturas Hispanicas Ser.). 523p. 1975. reprint ed. write for info. (*3-487-05444-2*, Pub. by Georg Olms GW) Lubrecht & Cramer.

Comedias Religiosas. Calderon. 229p. (SPA.). 1970. 15.95 (*0-8288-7180-9*, S8839) Fr & Eur.

Comedic Pathos: Black Humor in Mark Twain's Fiction. Patricia M. Mandia. LC 91-52757. 176p. 1991. lib. bdg. 27.50x (*0-89950-642-9*) McFarland & Co.

Comedie see Comedies et Actes Divers

Comedie see Paroles et Musique

"Comedie-Ballet" von Moliere-Lully. Friedrich Bottger. 269p. 1979. reprint ed. write for info. (*3-487-06689-0*, Pub. by Georg Olms GW) Lubrecht & Cramer.

Comedie De Charleroi. Pierre Drieu La Rochelle. (FRE.). 1982. pap. 10.95 (*0-7859-1955-4*, 2070373665) Fr & Eur.

***Comedie de l'Innocence.** Joanna Neil. (Horizon Ser.). (FRE.). 1994. pap. 3.50 (*0-373-39292-3*, 1-39292-7) Harlequin Bks.

Comedie De Moeurs En France Au Dixneuvieme Siecle. Louis Allard. LC 23-17333. (Harvard Studies in Romance Languages Monographs: Vol. 5). 1923. 45.00 (*0-527-01103-7*) Periodicals Srv.

Comedie Humaine, Vol. 1. deluxe ed. Honore De Balzac. (Pleiade Ser.). 1574p. (FRE.). 1976. 80.95 (*2-07-010851-1*) Schoenhof.

Comedie Humaine, Vol. 2. deluxe ed. Honore De Balzac. (Pleiade Ser.). 1176p. (FRE.). 1971. 74.95 (*2-07-010852-X*) Schoenhof.

Comedie Humaine, Vol. 3. deluxe ed. Honore De Balzac. 1680p. (FRE.). 1976. 79.95 (*2-07-010858-9*) Schoenhof.

Comedie Humaine, Vol. 4. deluxe ed. Honore De Balzac. (Pleiade Ser.). 1072p. (FRE.). 75.95 (*2-07-010862-7*) Schoenhof.

Comedie Humaine, Vol. 5. 5th deluxe ed. Honore De Balzac. (Pleiade Ser.). 1574p. (FRE.). 1977. 71.95 (*2-07-010849-X*) Schoenhof.

Comedie Humaine, Vol. 6. Honore De Balzac. 1577p. (FRE.). 1977. 75.95 (*2-07-010850-3*) Schoenhof.

Comedie Humaine, Vol. 7. deluxe ed. Honore De Balzac. (Pleiade Ser.). (FRE.). 1970. 81.95 (*2-07-010874-0*) Schoenhof.

Comedie Humaine, Vol. 8. deluxe ed. Honore De Balzac. 1852p. (FRE.). 79.95 (*2-07-010866-X*) Schoenhof.

Comedie Humaine, Vol. 9. Honore De Balzac. 1762p. (FRE.). 83.95 (*2-07-010869-4*) Schoenhof.

Comedie Humaine, Vol. 10. deluxe ed. Honore De Balzac. 1856p. (FRE.). 82.95 (*2-07-010868-6*) Schoenhof.

Comedie Humaine, Vol. 11. deluxe ed. Honore De Balzac. (Pleiade Ser.). 1952p. (FRE.). 79.95 (*2-07-010876-7*) Schoenhof.

Comedie Humaine, Vol. 12. deluxe ed. Honore De Balzac. 1984p. (FRE.). 98.95 (*2-07-010877-5*) Schoenhof.

Comedie Humaine: Etudes de Moeurs (Scenes de la Vie Privee-1), Vol. 1. deluxe ed. Honore De Balzac. 1574p. (FRE.). 1976. 110.00 (*0-7859-4750-7*, M2119) Fr & Eur.

Comedie Humaine: Scenes de la Vie de Province-2, Vol. 3. deluxe ed. Honore De Balzac. 1680p. (FRE.). 1976. 115.00 (*0-7859-4752-3*, M2121) Fr & Eur.

Comedie Humaine: Scenes de la Vie Militaire, Scenes de la Vie de Campagne, Vol. 6. deluxe ed. Honore De Balzac. 1577p. (FRE.). 1977. 105.00 (*0-7859-4755-8*, M2124) Fr & Eur.

Comedie Humaine: Scenes de la Vie Parisienne-1, Vol. 4. deluxe ed. Honore De Balzac. 1072p. (FRE.). 1970. 110.00 (*0-7859-4753-1*, M2121) Fr & Eur.

Comedie Humaine: Scenes de la Vie Parisienne-2, Vol. 5. 5th deluxe ed. Honore De Balzac. 1574p. (FRE.). 1977. 110.00 (*0-7859-4754-X*, M2123) Fr & Eur.

Comedie Humaine: Scenes de la Vie Privee-2, Scenes de la Vie de Province-1, Vol. 2. deluxe ed. Honore De Balzac. 1176p. (FRE.). 1971. 110.00 (*0-7859-4751-5*, M2120) Fr & Eur.

***Comedie Humaine Vol. 1.** Honore D. Balzac. 1712p. (FRE.). Date not set. 125.00 (*0-7859-7575-6*) Fr & Eur.

Comedie of Errors. M. H. Publications Staff. 138p. 1990. 95.00 (*1-872680-13-5*, Pub. by M H Pubns UK) St Mut.

Comediens Francais du 17e Siecle Vol. 2: Dictionnaire Biographique. O. Ducrot & T. Todorov. 475p. (FRE.). 1979. pap. 19.95 (*0-7859-4623-3*) Fr & Eur.

Comedies. Menander. (Loeb Classical Library: No. 132). 582p. 1979. text ed. 18.95 (*0-674-99147-8*) HUP.

Comedies. William Shakespeare. Ed. by Stanley Wells et al. (Oxford Shakespeare Ser.). (Illus.). 576p. 1994. pap. 11.95 (*0-19-818273-2*) OUP.

Comedies. Terence & Betty Radice. 1976. pap. 5.95 (*0-685-13420-2*, Penguin Bks) Viking Penguin.

Comedies. William Congreve. (BCL1-PR English Literature Ser.). 441p. 1992. reprint ed. lib. bdg. 99.00 (*0-7812-7334-X*) Rprt Serv.

***Comedies: Shakespeare, Vol. 1.** Shakespeare. 1995. 23.00 (*0-679-44363-0*) Knopf.

Comedies: The Old Bachelor, the Double Dealer, Love for Love, the Way of the World. William Congreve. Ed. by Anthony Henderson. LC 82-1182. (Plays by Renaissance & Restoration Dramatists Ser.). 407p. 1982. 69.95 (*0-521-24747-0*); pap. 21.95 (*0-521-28932-7*) Cambridge U Pr.

Comedies & Errors. Henry Harland. LC 74-169554. (Short Story Index Reprint Ser.). 1977. reprint ed. 23.95 (*0-8369-4016-4*) Ayer.

Comedies & Proverbs. David Sices. Ed. & Tr. by Alfred De Musset. (PAJ Books Ser.). 296p. (ENG.). 1994. 45.00 (*0-8018-4682-X*); pap. 14.95 (*0-8018-4683-8*) Johns Hopkins.

Comedies & Satires. Edgar Allan Poe. 1987. pap. 8.95 (*0-14-039055-3*, 591, Penguin Classics) Viking Penguin.

Comedies & Tragedies. Thomas Killigrew. LC 67-23861. 1972. 30.95 (*0-405-08702-0*) Ayer.

Comedies et Actes Divers. Samuel Beckett. Incl. Comedie. 1966. (*0-318-51954-2*); Va-Et-Vient. 1966. (*0-318-51955-0*); Cascando. 1966. (*0-318-51956-9*); Paroles et Musique. 1966. (*0-318-51957-7*); Dis Joe. 1966. (*0-318-51958-5*); Actes sans Paroles II. 1966. (*0-318-51959-3*); Film. 1966. (*0-318-51960-7*); Souffle. 1966. (*0-318-51961-5*); 1966. Set pap. 16.95 (*0-7859-0925-7*, F85940) Fr & Eur.

Comedies et Actes Divers: Comedie; Va-et-Vient; Cascando; Parole et Musique; Dis. Samuel Beckett. 104p. (FRE.). 1972. pap. 16.95 (*0-7859-1193-6*, F85940) Fr & Eur.

Comedies et Actes Divers: Comedie; Va-et-Vient; Cascando; Parole et Musique; Dis Joe; Acte Sans. 2nd ed. Rene Descartes & Charles Adam. 160p. (FRE.). 1975. 13.95 (*0-7859-1195-2*, 2711601889) Fr & Eur.

Comedies et Proverbes. Alfred Musset. Ed. by Francis Gastinel. 376p. (FRE.). 1957. pap. 28.95 (*0-7859-4694-2*); pap. 28.95 (*0-7859-4695-0*) Fr & Eur.

Comedies et Proverbes, Vol. 1. Alfred Musset. Ed. by Francis Gastinel. 376p. (FRE.). 1957. pap. 28.95 (*0-7859-4696-9*) Fr & Eur.

Comedies et Proverbes: Avec: Le Chandelier, Il ne faut Jurer de Rein, Set. Alfred De Musset. Ed. by Francis Gastinel. 376p. 1957. 51.95 (*0-685-57704-X*, F68941) Fr & Eur.

Comedies et Proverbes: Avec: Louison, On ne Saurait Penser a Tout, Set. Alfred De Musset. Ed. by Francis Gastinel. 376p. 1957. 51.95 (*0-685-57705-8*, F68941) Fr & Eur.

Comedies et Proverbes, Vol. 2: On ne Badine pas avec l'Amour, Lorenzaccio. Alfred Musset. (FRE.). 1985. pap. 8.95 (*0-7859-4699-3*) Fr & Eur.

Comedies et Proverbes, Vol. 3: Le Chandelier, Il ne Faut Jurer de Rein. 2nd ed. Alfred Musset. 127p. (FRE.). 1985. pap. 8.95 (*0-7859-4700-0*) Fr & Eur.

Comedies et Proverbes, Vol. 4: Louison, on ne Saurait Penser a Tout. Alfred Musset. 128p. (FRE.). 1985. pap. 8.95 (*0-7859-4698-5*) Fr & Eur.

Comedies, Histories, & Tragedies of Mr. William Shakespeare As Presented at the Globe & Blackfriars Theatres, Circa 1591-1623: The "Bankside" Edition, 22 vols., Set. William Shakespeare. Ed. by James A. Morgan et al. LC 69-18316. reprint ed. write for info. (*0-404-05960-0*) AMS Pr.

Comedies, Histories, Tragedies, & Poems, 12 Vols, Set. 2nd ed. William Shakespeare. Ed. by Charles Knight. LC 68-59009. reprint ed. 585.00 (*0-404-05900-7*) AMS Pr.

Comedies of Ariosto. Ludovico Ariosto. Ed. by Edmond M. Beame & Leonard G. Sbrocchi. LC 74-5739. 368p. reprint ed. pap. 104.90 (*0-685-15471-8*, 2027209) Bks Demand.

Comedies of Goldoni. Carlo Goldoni. Ed. & Intro. by Helen Zimmern. Incl. Curious Mishap. LC 76-48424. 1986. (*0-318-53502-5*); Beneficant Bear. LC 76-48424. 1986. (*0-318-53503-3*); Fan. LC 76-48424. 1986. (*0-318-53504-1*); Spendthrift Miser. LC 76-48424. 1986. (*0-318-53505-X*); LC 76-48424. (Library of World Literature Ser.). 1986. reprint ed. 25.25 (*0-88355-544-1*) Hyperion Conn.

Comedies of Holberg. Oscar J. Campbell. LC 68-20216. 1972. reprint ed. 24.95 (*0-405-08339-4*, Pub. by Blom Pubns UK) Ayer.

Comedies of Machiavelli: The Woman from Andros, The Mandrake, Clizia. Niccolo Machiavelli. Ed. by David Sices & James B. Atkinson. Tr. by James B. Atkinson. LC 84-40595. 416p. (ENG & ITA.). 1985. pap. 18.00 (*0-87451-330-8*) U Pr of New Eng.

Comedies of Terence. Terence. Tr. by Frank O. Copley. Incl. Brothers. LC 67-20452. 1967. (*0-318-51102-9*); Eunuch. LC 67-20452. 1967. (*0-318-51103-7*); Mother-in-Law. LC 67-20452. 1967. (*0-318-51104-5*); Phormio. LC 67-20452. 1967. (*0-318-51105-3*); Self-Tormenter. LC 67-20452. 1967. (*0-318-51106-1*); Woman of Andros. LC 67-20452. 1967. (*0-318-51107-X*); LC 67-20452. (Orig.). 1967. Set pap. 8.50 (*0-672-60279-2*, LLA90) Macmillan.

Comedies of William Congreve: The Old Bachelor, The Double Dealer, Love for Love, The Way of the World. William Congreve. Ed. by Eric S. Rump. (Classics Ser.). 464p. 1986. pap. 10.95 (*0-14-043231-0*, Penguin Classics) Viking Penguin.

Comedy: An Annotated Bibliography of Theory & Criticism. James E. Evans. LC 87-4748. 419p. 1987. 37.50 (*0-8108-1987-2*) Scarecrow.

Comedy: An Essay on Comedy by George Meredith & Laughter by Henri Bergson. Ed. by Wylie Sypher. LC 79-3701. 288p. 1980. reprint ed. pap. text ed. 13.95 (*0-8018-2327-7*) Johns Hopkins.

Comedy: The Mastery of Discourse. Susan Purdie. LC 92-95214. 186p. 1993. 45.00 (*0-8020-2980-9*); pap. 17.95 (*0-8020-7437-5*) U of Toronto Pr.

Comedy - Cinema - Theory. Ed. by Andrew S. Horton. (Illus.). 256p. 1991. 35.00 (*0-520-06997-8*); pap. 15.00 (*0-520-07040-2*) U CA Pr.

Comedy, American Style. Jessie R. Fauset. LC 76-95401. reprint ed. 29.50 (*0-404-00257-9*) AMS Pr.

***Comedy, American Style, Vol. 4.** Jessie R. Fauset. LC 94-24678. (African-American Women Writers Ser.). 1995. text ed. 25.00 (*0-8161-1628-8*) G K Hall.

Comedy & Culture: England, 1820-1900. Roger B. Henkle. LC 79-3214. 1980. 60.00 (*0-691-06428-8*) Princeton U Pr.

Comedy & Culture: England, 1820-1900. limited ed. Roger B. Henkle. LC 79-3214. 1980. pap. 21.95 (*0-691-10090-X*) Princeton U Pr.

Comedy & Form in the Fiction of Joseph Conrad. Stanton De Voren Hoffman. (Studies in English Literature: No. 49). 1969. 53.10 (*90-279-0477-4*) Mouton.

Comedy & Society from Congreve to Fielding. John Loftis. LC 76-51940. (Stanford University. Stanford Studies in Language & Literature: 19). reprint ed. 21.50 (*0-404-51829-X*) AMS Pr.

Comedy & the Woman Writer: Woolf, Spark, & Feminism. Judy Little. LC 82-19999. xii, 224p. 1983. 25.00x (*0-8032-2859-7*) U of Nebr Pr.

Comedy Explosion: A New Generation. Photos by Ed Edahl. 128p. 1991. 14.95 (*1-56025-017-8*) Thunders Mouth.

Comedy from Shakespeare to Sheridan: Change & Continuity in the English & European Dramatic Tradition. Ed. by A. R. Braumuller & James C. Bulman. LC 84-40464. 288p. 1986. 42.50 (*0-87413-276-2*) U Delaware Pr.

Comedy High. Stephen Manes. 176p. (YA). (gr. 7 up). 1992. 13.95 (*0-590-44436-0*, Scholastic Hardcover) Scholastic Inc.

***Comedy High.** Stephen Manes. (YA). 1994. pap. 3.50 (*0-590-44437-9*) Scholastic Inc.

Comedy High & Low: An Introduction to the Experience of Comedy. Maurice Charney. (Illus.). 203p. 1988. pap. 25.50 (*0-8204-0538-8*) P Lang Pubs.

Comedy Improvisation. Delton T. Horn. Ed. by Theodore O. Zapel. LC 90-28459. 144p. (Orig.). 1991. pap. text ed. 9.95 (*0-916260-69-0*, B175) Meriwether Pub.

Comedy in Action. Elmer H. Blistein. LC 64-22154. 162p. reprint ed. pap. 46.20 (*0-317-20087-9*, 2023368) Bks Demand.

Comedy in Context: Essays on Moli'ere. H. Gaston Hall. LC 83-21729. (Illus.). 286p. reprint ed. pap. 81.60 (*0-8357-4342-X*, 2037145) Bks Demand.

Comedy in Space, Time, & the Imagination. Paul H. Grawe. LC 82-10603. 368p. 1983. text ed. 35.95 (*0-88229-631-0*) Nelson-Hall.

Comedy of Asses see Amphitryon

***Comedy of Boards.** Brian O'Connell. (Nonprofit Sector Ser.). 1995. 22.95 (*0-7879-0179-2*) Jossey-Bass.

Comedy of Charleroi & Other Stories. Pierre Drieu La Rochelle. (Illus.). 236p. 1980. 9.95 (*0-903747-03-0*) Writers & Readers.

Comedy of Desire. Nils Peterson. (Illus.). 70p. (Orig.). 1994. pap. 10.00 (*0-9638722-0-6*) Blue Sofa.

Comedy of Entropy: Humour, Narrative, Reading. Patrick O'Neill. 320p. 1990. text ed. 50.00 (*0-8020-2737-7*) U of Toronto Pr.

Comedy of Errors. Adapt. by Cecil Pickett. (Illus.). 44p. 1986. pap. 2.50 (*0-88680-258-X*) I E Clark.

Comedy of Errors. Shakespeare. (BBC Television Plays Ser.). 1984. pap. 5.95 (*0-563-20183-5*, Pub. by BBC UK) Parkwest Pubns.

Comedy of Errors. William Shakespeare. (Airmont Shakespeare Ser.). (J). (gr. 9 up). 1968. pap. 0.60 (*0-8049-1023-5*, S-23) Airmont.

Comedy of Errors. William Shakespeare. Ed. by Paul A. Jorgensen. (Pelican Shakespeare Ser.). 1964. mass mkt. 5.95 (*0-14-071432-4*, Pelican Bks) Viking Penguin.

Comedy of Errors. William Shakespeare. (Classics Ser.). 1988. 2.95 (*0-553-21291-5*, Bantam Classics) Bantam.

Comedy of Errors. William Shakespeare. Ed. by T. S. Dorsch. (New Cambridge Shakespeare Ser.). (Illus.). 129p. 1988. 39.95 (*0-521-22153-6*); pap. 9.95 (*0-521-29368-5*) Cambridge U Pr.

Comedy of Errors. William Shakespeare. Ed. by Richard Andrews. (Cambridge School Shakespeare Ser.). (Illus.). 128p. (C). 1992. pap. 6.95 (*0-521-39575-5*) Cambridge U Pr.

***Comedy of Errors.** William Shakespeare. 1977. 3.00 (*0-87129-533-4*, C31) Dramatic Pub.

Comedy of Errors. William Shakespeare. Ed. by Harry T. Levin. 1986. pap. 2.95 (*0-451-52163-3*, Sig Classics) NAL-Dutton.

Comedy of Errors. William Shakespeare. Ed. by Louis B. Wright & Virginia LaMar. 208p. 1991. mass mkt. 3.99 (*0-671-73990-5*, WSP) PB.

Comedy of Errors. William Shakespeare. Ed. by Stanley Wells. (New Penguin Shakespeare Ser.). 1981. mass mkt. 5.50 (*0-14-070725-5*, Penguin Classics) Viking Penguin.

Comedy of Errors. large type ed. William Shakespeare. 1992. pap. 24.95 (*0-7089-4512-0*, Trail West Pubs) Ulverscroft.

Comedy of Errors. rev. ed. William Shakespeare. 1986. pap. 3.95 (*0-451-52311-3*, Sig Classics) NAL-Dutton.

Comedy of Errors. 5th rev. ed. William Shakespeare. Ed. by R. A. Foakes. (Arden Shakespeare Ser.). 1968. 49.95 (*0-415-02749-7*, NO.2446); pap. 8.95 (*0-416-10420-7*, NO.2447) Routledge.

***Comedy of Errors: A Play Packet to Accompany Elementary, My Dear Shakespeare.** Barbara Engen & Joy Campbell. (Illus.). 37p. 1992. 8.95 (*0-922947-04-X*) Mkt Masters.

Comedy of Errors: Modern Text with Introduction. Ed. by A. L. Rowse. LC 86-23395. 94p. (Orig.). (C). 1987. pap. text ed. 3.45 (*0-8191-3935-1*) U Pr of Amer.

Comedy of Errors Notes. Denis Calandra. Bd. with Love's Labour's Lost & The Two Gentlemen of Verona Notes. 88p. (Orig.). 1982. Set pap. 3.95 (*0-8220-0010-5*) Cliffs.

Comedy of Evil & Shakespeare's Stage. Charlotte Spivack. LC 77-69. 184p. 1978. 28.50 (*0-8386-2126-0*) Fairleigh Dickinson.

Comedy of Language: Studies in Modern Comic Literature. Fred M. Robinson. LC 80-125. 200p. 1980. lib. bdg. 27.50x (*0-87023-297-5*) U of Mass Pr.

***Comedy of Menander: Convention, Variation, & Originality.** Netta Zagagi. LC 94-30098. 1995. 39.95 (*0-253-36851-0*) Ind U Pr.

Comedy of Murders. George Herman. 448p. 1994. 23.95 (*0-7867-0064-5*) Carroll & Graf.

Comedy of Neil Simon. Neil Simon. 1971. 25.00 (*0-394-47364-7*) Random.

Comedy of Redemption: Christian Faith & Comic Vision in Four American Novelists. Ralph C. Wood. LC 87-40613. 320p. 1988. text ed. 32.95 (*0-268-00767-5*) U of Notre Dame Pr.

Comedy of Redemption: Christian Faith & Comic Vision in Four American Novelists. Ralph C. Wood. LC 87-40613. (C). 1991. pap. text ed. 15.95 (*0-268-00786-1*) U of Notre Dame Pr.

Comedy of Terrors. Michael Innes. 256p. 1987. pap. 3.95 (*0-14-010090-3*, Penguin Bks) Viking Penguin.

Comedy of the Fantastic: Ecological Perspectives on the Fantasy Novel. Don G. Elgin. LC 84-10851. (Contributions to the Study of Science Fiction & Fantasy Ser.: No. 15). 204p. 1985. text ed. 49.95 (*0-313-23283-0*, ELC/, Greenwood Pr) Greenwood.

Comedy Quote Dictionary. Ronald Smith. 1992. 22.50 (*0-385-41691-1*) Doubleday.

Comedy Quotes from the Movies: Over 4000 Bits of Humorous Dialogue from All Film Genres, Topically Arranged & Indexed. Comp. by Larry Langman & Paul Gold. LC 92-56659. 1993. lib. bdg. 42.00 (*0-89950-863-4*) McFarland & Co.

Comedy Songs from Broadway Musicals. 80p. 1989. pap. 9.95 (*0-88188-857-5*, 00359489) H Leonard.

Comedy Techniques for Writers & Performers: The Hearts Theory of Humor Writing. Melvin Helitzer. 304p. 1984. pap. 14.95 (*0-916199-01-0*) Lawhead.

An Asterisk (*) at the beginning of an entry indicates that the title is appearing in BIP for the first time.

Comedy, Tragedy & Ecological Disaster. 1991. lib. bdg. 75. 00 (0-8490-4707-2) Gordon Pr.

Comedy World of Stan Laurel: Centennial Edition. rev. ed. John McCabe. (Vintage Comedy Ser.). 288p. 1990. reprint ed. 19.95 (0-940410-23-0, Moonstone Pr); reprint ed. pap. 14.95 (0-940410-22-2, Moonstone Pr) Past Times.

Comedy Writing Secrets. Melvin Helitzer. 325p. 1992. pap. 16.99 (0-89879-510-9) Writers Digest.

Comedy Writing Step by Step: How to Write & Sell Your Sense of Humor. 2nd ed. Gene Perret. LC 90-2907. 281p. 1990. reprint ed. pap. 11.95 (0-573-60605-6) S French Trade.

Comedy Writing Workbook. Gene Perrett. LC 89-39963. (Illus.). 192p. (Orig.). 1990. pap. 12.95 (0-8069-6554-1) Sterling.

Comedy Writing Workbook. Gene Perret. LC 94-20150. 1994. reprint ed. pap. 17.00 (0-88734-647-2) Players Pr.

Comenius & the Beginnings of Educational Reform. Will S. Monroe. LC 78-135824. (Eastern Europe Collection Ser.). 1971. reprint ed. 16.95 (0-405-02765-6) Ayer.

Comenius in England: The Visit of Jan Amos Komensky Comenius, Czech Philosopher & Educationalist, to London in 1641-1642. Robert F. Young. LC 70-135838. (Eastern Europe Collection Ser.). 1971. reprint ed. 15.95 (0-405-02780-X) Ayer.

Comenius's Pampaedia. A. M. Dobbie & M. A. Litt. 216p. (C). 1988. 160.00 (0-7212-0781-2, Pub. by Regency Press) St Mut.

Coment. Carroll-Cinco: Evangelios, No. One: Carroll's Comment-6: Gospels. B. H. Carroll. (SPA.). 10.95 (84-7645-112-1, 223165, Pub. by Edit Clie SP) TSELF.

Coment. Carroll-Cinco: Evangelios, No. Two: Carroll's Comment-6: Gospels. B. H. Carroll. (SPA.). 10.95 (84-7645-113-X, 223166, Pub. by Edit Clie SP) TSELF.

Coment. Carroll-Dos: Exodo - Levitico: Carroll's Comment-2: Exodus - Leviticus. B. H. Carroll. (SPA.). 10.95 (84-7645-111-3, 223164, Pub. by Edit Clie SP) TSELF.

Coment. Carroll-Siete: Carroll's Comment-7: Facts. B. H. Carroll. (SPA.). 10.95 (84-7645-133-4, 223179, Pub. by Edit Clie SP) TSELF.

Coment. Carroll-Uno: Genesis: Carroll's Comment-1: Genesis. B. H. Carroll. (SPA.). 10.95 (84-7645-110-5, 223163, Pub. by Edit Clie SP) TSELF.

Coment. Matthew Henry: Mateo: Matthew Henry's Commentary: Matthew. Matthew Henry. (SPA.). 21.95 (84-7228-820-X, 222102, Pub. by Edit Clie SP) TSELF.

Comentario a los Salmos: The Book of Psalms. Juan De Valdes. (SPA.). 6.95 (84-7645-174-1, 223214, Pub. by Edit Clie SP) TSELF.

Comentario Al Evangelio De Juan: The Gospel of John. A. B. Simpson. (SPA.). 6.95 (84-7228-979-6, 223052, Pub. by Edit Clie SP) TSELF.

Comentario Al Evangelio De Lucas: The Gospel of Luke. James G. Chastain. (SPA.). 6.95 (84-7645-074-5, 223137, Pub. by Edit Clie SP) TSELF.

Comentario Al Evangelio De Mateo: The Gospel of Matthew. A. B. Simpson. (SPA.). 6.95 (84-7228-980-X, 223053, Pub. by Edit Clie SP) TSELF.

Comentario Ampliado Del N. T. Vol. 1: Commentary to the New Testament. David Burt. (SPA.). 13.95 (84-7645-481-3, 223411, Pub. by Edit Clie SP) TSELF.

Comentario Biblico Efesios. Curtis Vaughan. Orig. Title: Ephesians. 168p. (POR.). 1986. 7.95 (0-8297-1608-4) Life Pubs Intl.

Comentario Biblico Moody: Antiguo Testamento. Ed. by Charles F. Pfeiffer. Orig. Title: Wycliffe Bible Commentary: Old Testament. 912p. (SPA.). 1993. 24.99 (0-8254-1563-2); pap. 19.99 (0-8254-1562-4) Kregel.

Comentario Biblico Moody: Nuevo Testamento. Ed. by Everett F. Harrison. Orig. Title: Wycliffe Bible Commentary: N. T. 576p. (SPA.). 1965. 19.99 (0-8254-1307-9); pap. 14.99 (0-8254-1306-0) Kregel.

Comentario Biblico Mundo Hispano, Tomo 14 - Hispanic World Biblical Commentary, Vol. 14: Mateo - Matthew. James Bartley et al. (Illus.). 384p. (Orig.). (SPA.). 1993. pap. 9.99 (0-311-03114-5) Casa Bautista.

Comentario Cantar De los Cantares: Song of Solomon Commentary. Vila-Pozo. (SPA.). 5.50 (84-7228-686-X, 220226, Pub. by Edit Clie SP) TSELF.

Comentario Carroll-Cinco: Daniel: Carroll's Commentary 5: Daniel. B. H. Carroll. (SPA.). 6.95 (84-7645-216-0, 223262, Pub. by Edit Clie SP) TSELF.

Comentario Carroll-Diez: Tes - Corintios: Carroll's Commentary 10: Corinthians. B. H. Carroll. (SPA.). 8.95 (84-7645-219-5, 223265, Pub. by Edit Clie SP) TSELF.

Comentario Carroll-Doce: Apocalipsis: Carroll's Commentary-12: Apocalypse. B. H. Carroll. (SPA.). 8.95 (84-7645-221-7, 223267, Pub. by Edit Clie SP) TSELF.

Comentario Carroll-Nueve: Col. - Hebreos: Carroll's Commentary 9: Col. - Hebrews. B. H. Carroll. (SPA.). 8.95 (84-7645-218-7, 223264, Pub. by Edit Clie SP) TSELF.

Comentario Carroll-Ocho: Galatas - Filem: Carroll's Commentary 8. B. H. Carroll. (SPA.). 7.50 (84-7645-217-9, 223263, Pub. by Edit Clie SP) TSELF.

Comentario Carroll-Once: Pastorales: Carroll's Commentary 11: Pastoral. B. H. Carroll. (SPA.). 8.95 (84-7645-220-9, 223266, Pub. by Edit Clie SP) TSELF.

Comentario Carroll-Quattro: Carroll's Commentary 4: the Hebrew. B. H. Carroll. (SPA.). 8.95 (84-7645-215-2, 223261, Pub. by Edit Clie SP) TSELF.

Comentario Carroll-Tres: Numeros - Ruth: Carroll's Commentary 3: Numbers - Ruth. B. H. Carroll. (SPA.). 8.95 (84-7645-132-6, 223178, Pub. by Edit Clie SP) TSELF.

Comentario Confesion Fe Westminster: Westminster's Confession. Archibald A. Hodge. (SPA.). 21.95 (84-7645-172-5, 223219, Pub. by Edit Clie SP) TSELF.

Comentario de las Epistolas Generales. Charles Erdman. 194p. (SPA.). 1986. pap. 4.50 (0-939125-31-5) Evangelical Lit.

Comentario Epistola a los Efesios: Paul's Letter to Ephesians. G. H. Lacy. (SPA.). 5.50 (84-7645-077-X, 223139, Pub. by Edit Clie SP) TSELF.

Comentario Epistola a los Galatas: Galatians-A Practical. Enrique Lund. (SPA.). 3.95 (84-7645-028-1, 223097, Pub. by Edit Clie SP) TSELF.

Comentario Exegetico y Explicativo de la Biblia Tomo I. Jamieson-Fausett Brown. 982p. 1986. reprint ed. 23.00 (0-311-03002-5) Casa Bautista.

Comentario Exegetico y Explicativo de la Biblia Tomo II. Jamieson-Fausett Brown. Tr. by Jaime C. Quarles & Lemuel C. Quarles. 382p. 1986. reprint ed. 22.00 (0-311-03004-1) Casa Bautista.

Comentario Historico y Doct. Del: Commentary on Doctrinal & History. Juan Sanchez. (SPA.). 6.95 (84-7645-197-0, 223347, Pub. by Edit Clie SP) TSELF.

Comentario Homiletico de la Biblia: Handfuls on Purpose, Vol. I. James Smith. (SPA.). 15.95 (84-7645-332-9, 223449, Pub. by Edit Clie SP) TSELF.

Comentario Homiletico de la Biblia: Handfuls on Purpose, Vol. II. James Smith. (SPA.). 15.95 (84-7645-333-7, 223460, Pub. by Edit Clie SP) TSELF.

Comentario Homiletico de la Biblia: Handfuls on Purpose, Vol. III. James Smith. (SPA.). 15.95 (84-7645-359-0, 223489, Pub. by Edit Clie SP) TSELF.

Comentario Homiletico de la Biblia: Handfuls on Purpose, Vol. IV. James Smith. (SPA.). 15.95 (84-7645-360-4, 223490, Pub. by Edit Clie SP) TSELF.

Comentario Homiletico de la Biblia: Handfuls on Purpose, Vol. V. James Smith. (SPA.). 15.95 (84-7645-416-3, 223506, Pub. by Edit Clie SP) TSELF.

Comentario Homiletico de la Biblia: Handfuls on Purpose, Vol. VI. James Smith. (SPA.). 15.95 (84-7645-405-8, 223511, Pub. by Edit Clie SP) TSELF.

Comentario Homiletico de la Biblia: Handfuls on Purpose, Vol. VII. James Smith. (SPA.). 15.95 (84-7645-448-1, 223530, Pub. by Edit Clie SP) TSELF.

Comentario Homiletico De la Biblia: Handfuls on Purpose, Vol. IX. James Smith. (SPA.). 15.95 (0-317-04669-1, 223525, Pub. by Edit Clie SP) TSELF.

Comentario Homiletico de la Biblia: Handfuls on Purpose, Vol. X. James Smith. (SPA.). 15.95 (0-317-04295-5, 223410, Pub. by Edit Clie SP) TSELF.

Comentario Homiletico de la Biblia: Handfuls on Purpose, Vol. XIII. James Smith. (SPA.). 15.95 (84-7645-449-X, 223524, Pub. by Edit Clie SP) TSELF.

Comentario Matthew Henry: Dos Corintios: II Corintios. Matthew Henry. (SPA.). 21.95 (84-7645-368-X, 223357, Pub. by Edit Clie SP) TSELF.

Comentario Matthew Henry: Ezeqias: Matthew Henry's Commentary: Ezekial. Matthew Henry. (SPA.). 21.95 (84-7645-457-0, 223528, Pub. by Edit Clie SP) TSELF.

Comentario Matthew Henry: Hechos: Matthew Henry's Commentary of Acts. Matthew Henry. (SPA.). 21.95 (84-7645-348-5, 223358, Pub. by Edit Clie SP) TSELF.

Comentario Matthew Henry: Historicos: Matthew Henry's Commentary, Historical Books, Vol. I. Matthew Henry. (SPA.). 21.95 (84-7645-146-6, 223192, Pub. by Edit Clie SP) TSELF.

Comentario Matthew Henry: Historicos: Matthew Henry's Commentary: Historical Books, Vol. II. Matthew Henry. (SPA.). 21.95 (84-7645-147-4, 223193, Pub. by Edit Clie SP) TSELF.

Comentario Matthew Henry: Isaias A: Matthew Henry's Commentary: Isaiah. Matthew Henry. (SPA.). 21.95 (84-7645-420-1, 223517, Pub. by Edit Clie SP) TSELF.

Comentario Matthew Henry: Juan: Matthew Henry's Commentary: John. Matthew Henry. (SPA.). 21.95 (84-7228-918-4, 222104, Pub. by Edit Clie SP) TSELF.

Comentario Matthew Henry: Marcos y Lucas: Matthew Henry's Commentary: Mark & Luke. Matthew Henry. (SPA.). 21.95 (84-7228-899-4, 222103, Pub. by Edit Clie SP) TSELF.

Comentario Matthew Henry: Pentateuco: Matthew Henry's Commentary: Pentateuch. Matthew Henry. (SPA.). 23. 95 (84-7228-815-3, 222101, Pub. by Edit Clie SP) TSELF.

Comentario Matthew Henry: Poeticos Vol. I: Matthew Henry's Commentary: Matthew Henry. Matthew Henry. (SPA.). 21.95 (84-7645-222-5, 223269, Pub. by Edit Clie SP) TSELF.

Comentario Matthew Henry: Poeticos Vol. II: Matthew Henry's Commentary: Matthew Henry. Matthew Henry. (SPA.). 21.95 (84-7645-265-9, 223286, Pub. by Edit Clie SP) TSELF.

Comentario Matthew Henry: Santiago: Matthew Henry's Commentary. Matthew Henry. (SPA.). 21.95 (84-7645-504-6, 223412, Pub. by Edit Clie SP) TSELF.

Comentario Practico - Epistolas, Vol. III: Practical Comment. III - Epist. C. Rochedieu. (SPA.). 6.95 (84-7228-567-7, 220127, Pub. by Edit Clie SP) TSELF.

Comentario Practico - Hebreos, Vol. IV: Practical Comment. IV - Heb. - Rev. C. Rochedieu. (SPA.). 5.50 (84-7228-568-5, 220128, Pub. by Edit Clie SP) TSELF.

Comentario Practico - Juan, Vol. II: Practical Comment.I - John. C. Rochedieu. (SPA.). 5.50 (84-7228-570-7, 220126, Pub. by Edit Clie SP) TSELF.

Comentario Practico - Sinopticos, Vol. I: Practical Comment. I - Synoptics. C. Rochedieu. (SPA.). 5.95 (84-7228-569-3, 220125, Pub. by Edit Clie SP) TSELF.

Comentario Sobre los Himnos Que Cantamos. Cecil McConnell. 368p. (SPA.). 1985. pap. 8.95 (0-311-32433-9) Casa Bautista.

***Comentarios al Cantar de los Cantares Vol. 1.** Alfonso Galvez. 447p. (SPA.). 1994. text ed. write for info. (0-9641108-4-9) Shoreless Lake.

Comentarios & Epistolas Pastorales. John Calvin. 415p. (SPA.). 1994. pap. 9.00 (0-939125-09-9) Evangelical Lit.

Comentarios de la Guerra de las Galias, No. 121. Julio C. Cesar. 248p. (SPA.). 1964. write for info. (0-8288-8576-1) Fr & Eur.

***Comepnsatory & Punitive Damages under Title VII - a Foreign Perspective.** 2nd ed. Edward E. Potter & Ann E. Reesman. 11p. 1992. pap. 5.00x (0-614-06149-0) EPF.

Comercio, Estabilidad, Tecnologia y Equidad en America Latina. Ed. by Moshe Syrquin & Simon Teitel. 486p. 1984. write for info. (0-940602-18-0) IADB.

Comercio y Mercado en Espanol: (Business & Marketing in Spanish) Conrad J. Schmitt & Protase E. Woodford. (Schaum's Foreign Language Ser.). 288p. (SPA.). 1992. text ed. 10.95 (0-07-056887-3) McGraw.

Comes a Day. Speed Lamkin. 1959. pap. 4.75 (0-8222-0231-X) Dramatists Play.

Comes Now the Interstate Commerce Practitioner. Frank N. Wilner. (Illus.). 268p. 1993. 35.00 (0-9637506-0-7) Assn Transport.

Comes the Blind Fury. John Saul. 384p. (Orig.). (YA). (gr. 9 up). 1990. mass mkt. 5.99 (0-440-11475-6) Dell.

Comes the Rain. Beverly Bird. 512p. (Orig.). 1990. mass mkt. 4.95 (0-380-75525-4) Avon.

Comes the Reckoning. Robert H. Lockhart. LC 72-4672. (International Propaganda & Communications Ser.). 392p. 1972. reprint ed. 23.95 (0-405-04756-8) Ayer.

Comes the Voyager at Last: A Tale of Return to Africa. Kofi N. Awoonor. LC 91-75602. 148p. 1992. 24.95 (0-86543-262-7); pap. 7.95 (0-86543-263-5) Africa World.

Comes the Wraith. John Tigges. 368p. (Orig.). 1990. pap. 3.95 (0-8439-2906-5) Dorchester Pub Co.

Comes to Life Books: Berenstain Bears - Life with Papa; The Boy Who Became a Frog; Where's Waldo; Waldo in Dinoland, 4 bks., Set. Where's Waldo, Inc. Staff et al. (J). (ps-2). 1993. write for info. (1-883366-39-9) YES Ent.

***Comes to Life Frosty the Snowman Book.** Yes Staff. (J). (ps-3). 1994. pap. 6.99 (1-883366-40-2) YES Ent.

Comes to Life Story Player & Berenstain Bears: Mysterious Numbers Book Set. YES! Entertainment Corporation Staff et al. (Comes to Life Bks.). 16p. (J). (ps-2). 1993. write for info. (1-883366-07-0) YES Ent.

Comes to Life Story Player (Phase I) & Berenstain Bears: Mysterious Numbers & Berenstain Bears Eager Beavers Books. YES! Entertainment Corporation Staff et al. (Comes to Life Bks.). 16p. (J). (ps-2). 1993. write for info. (1-883366-29-1) YES Ent.

Comes to Life StoryPlayer & Berenstain Bears: Eager Beavers Book Set. YES! Entertainment Corporation Staff et al. (Comes to Life Bks.). 16p. (J). (ps-2). 1994. write for info. (1-883366-50-X) YES Ent.

***Comes to Life StoryPlayer & Een Clubhuis Voor de Toons: Tiny Toon Adventures.** Carol A. Hanshaw & YES! Entertainment Corporation Staff. Tr. by DigiPro Staff. (Comes to Life Bks.). 16p. (DUT.). (J). (ps-2). 1994. write for info. (1-883366-88-7) YES Ent.

***Comes to Life StoryPlayer & the Berenstain Bears & les Nombres Mysterieux.** Stan Berenstain et al. Tr. by DigiPro Staff. (Comes to Life Bks.). 16p. (FRE.). (J). (ps-2). 1994. write for info. (1-57234-002-9) YES Ent.

***Comes to Life StoryPlayer & Tiny Toon Adventures: A Clubhouse Built for Toons.** Carol A. Hanshaw & Yes! Entertainment Corp. Staff. (Comes to Life Bks.). 16p. (J). (ps-2). 1994. write for info. (1-883366-72-0) YES Ent.

***Comes to Life Storyplayer & Topo Gigio & the Friends of the Forest Book Set: Comes to Life Storyplayer & Topo Gigio e Gli Animaletti del Bosco.** Maria Perego. Tr. by Giochi Preziosi. (Comes to Life Bks.). 16p. (ITA.). (J). (ps-2). 1994. write for info. (1-57234-004-5) YES Ent.

***Comes to Life StoryPlayer & un Pavillon Pour le Club des Toons: Tiny Toon Adventures.** Carol A. Hanshaw & YES! Entertainment Corporation Staff. Tr. by DigiPro Staff. (Comes to Life Bks.). 16p. (FRE.). (J). (ps-2). 1994. write for info. (1-883366-71-2) YES Ent.

***Comes to Life StoryPlayer & Y los Numeros Misteriosos: The Berenstain Bears.** Stan Berenstain et al. Tr. by DigiPro Staff. (Comes to Life Bks.). 16p. (SPA.). (J). (ps-2). 1994. write for info. (1-57234-006-1) YES Ent.

***Comes to Life Storyplayer (Phase 2) & Micky Mouse: The Eagle's Treasure.** Leslie McGuire. (Comes to Life Bks.). 16p. (J). (ps-2). 1995. write for info. (1-57234-054-1) YES Ent.

***Comes to Us All.** James Thomas. 640p. Date not set. pap. 14.95 (1-56901-884-7) NW Pub.

Comet. Carl Sagan & Ann Druyan. (Illus.). 398p. 1991. 7.99 (0-517-68506-X) Random Hse Value.

Comet. Carl Sagan. 1985. 27.50 (0-394-54908-2) Random.

Comet & You. Edwin C. Krupp. LC 84-20152. (Illus.). 48p. (J). (gr. 1-4). 1985. text ed. 13.95 (0-02-751250-9, Mac Bks Young Read) S&S Childrens.

Comet Book. John C. Brandt & Robert D. Chapman. (Illus.). 176p. 1984. pap. 14.95 (0-86720-029-4) Jones & Bartlett.

Comet Called Halley. Ian Ridpath & Terence Murtagh. LC 85-18981. 48p. reprint ed. pap. 25.00 (0-685-16368-7, 2027290) Bks Demand.

Comet Colony. Malcolm C. Baker. 1994. pap. 7.95 (0-533-10936-1) Vantage.

Comet Connection: Escape from Hitler's Europe. George Watt. LC 89-70733. 184p. 1990. 21.00 (0-8131-1720-8) U Pr of Ky.

Comet Connection: The True Story of a Downed American Flyer...the European Resistance...& a Thrilling Escape from Hitler's Europe. George Watt. (Illus.). 192p. 1992. mass mkt. 4.99 (0-446-36167-4) Warner Bks.

Comet Crash. Edward Packard. (Choose Your Own Adventure Ser.: No. 144). (J). (gr. 4-7). 1994. pap. 3.50 (0-553-56009-3) Bantam.

Comet Encounters. Ed. by T. J. Birmingham & A. J. Dessler. 352p. 1988. pap. 35.00 (0-87590-239-1, CR0232391) Am Geophysical.

Comet Halley: Investigations, Results, Interpretation. Mason. 1990. text ed. 120.00 (0-13-171083-4) P-H.

Comet Halley: Investigations, Results, Interpretations, Vol. 1. Mason. 1990. text ed. 130.00 (0-13-171075-3) P-H.

Comet Halley: Once in a Lifetime. Mark Littmann & Donald Yeomans. 190p. 1985. 21.95 (0-8412-0905-7); pap. 14.95 (0-8412-0911-1) Am Chemical.

Comet Halley - Fact & Folly. Donald K. Yeomans. (Illus.). 1985. 30.00 (0-938237-03-9) Gold Stein Pr.

Comet Handbook. Garry Stasiuk & Dwight Gruber. (Illus.). 32p. (Orig.). 1984. pap. 5.00 (0-932421-00-8) Stasiuk Ent.

Comet in Moominland. Tove Jansson. Tr. by Elizabeth Portch. (Illus.). 192p. (J). (gr. 2-5). 1990. 13.95 (0-374-31526-4) FS&G.

Comet in Moominland. Tove Jansson. Tr. by Elizabeth Portch. (Illus.). 192p. (J). (gr. 2-5). 1991. pap. 3.95 (0-374-41331-2, Sunburst Bks) FS&G.

Comet in the City. Minot Davis. (Illus.). 268p. 1992. pap. 11.95 (0-9633840-9-0) LetterPress.

***Comet Luck.** Madge Harrah. 144p. (Orig.). (J). 1994. pap. 3.50 (0-380-77643-X, Camelot) Avon.

Comet of Fifteen Seventy-Seven: Its Place in the History of Astronomy. Doris Hellman. LC 72-110569. (Columbia University. Studies in the Social Sciences: No. 510). reprint ed. 20.00 (0-404-51510-X) AMS Pr.

Comet Strikes the Earth. rev. ed. H. H. Nininger. (Illus.). 1969. pap. 3.00 (0-910096-04-X) Am Meteorite.

Comet Watch: The Return of Halley's Comet. Frank H. Winter. (Space & Aviation Ser.). (Illus.). 64p. (J). (gr. 4 up). 1986. lib. bdg. 13.50 (0-8225-1579-2, Lerner Publctns) Lerner Group.

Cometary & Solar Plasma Physics, 1987. B. Buti. 372p. (C). 1988. pap. 53.00 (9971-5-0448-0) World Scientific Pub.

Cometary Environments: Proceedings of Symposium 5, Workshop IV & Topical Meeting of the Interdisciplinary Scientific Commission (Meeting C2) of COSPAR Plenary Meeting, No. 27. Ed. by Tamas I. Gombosi et al. (Advances in Space Research Ser.: No. 9). Orig. Title: Advances in Space Research, Vol. 9, No. 3. (Illus.). 406p. 1989. pap. 70.00 (0-08-037387-9, Pergamon Pr) Elsevier.

Cometary Phases. Christine Evans. 90p. 1988. pap. 14.95 (1-85411-002-0, Pub. by Poetry Wales Pr UK) Dufour.

Cometary Phases. Christine Evans. LC 89-50999. 106p. 1990. pap. 12.95 (0-685-33069-9, Pub. by Seren Bks UK) Dufour.

Cometary Plasma Processes. Ed. by A. D. Johnstone. (Geophysical Monograph Ser.: Vol. 61). 364p. 1991. 56. 00 (0-87590-027-5, GM0610275) Am Geophysical.

Cometary Theory in Fifteenth-Century Europe. Jane L. Jervis. 1985. lib. bdg. 39.00 (0-318-04126-X) Kluwer Ac.

Cometh up As a Flower: An Autobiography. Rhoda Broughton. LC 93-29083. (Pocket Classic Ser.). 1993. 8.00 (0-7509-0448-8) A Sutton Pub.

Cometh up as a Flower: An Autobiography, 2 vols. in 1. Rhoda Broughton. LC 79-8240. reprint ed. 44.50 (0-404-61794-8) AMS Pr.

Cometh with Clouds, (Memory: Allen Ginsberg) Dick McBride. LC 81-12272. 64p. 1982. 15.00 (0-916156-54-0); pap. 5.00 (0-916156-51-6) Cherry Valley.

Comets. Franklyn M. Branley. LC 83-46161. (Trophy Let's-Read-&-Find-Out Book & Cassette Set). (Illus.). 32p. (J). (ps-3). 1989. pap. 4.50 (0-06-445088-0, Trophy) HarpC Child Bks.

Comets. Christopher O. Irwin. (Illus.). 48p. 1981. 24.00 (0-88014-033-X) Mosaic Pr OH.

Comets. Ed. by Laurel L Wilkening. LC 81-21814. 766p. 1982. 45.00 (0-8165-0769-4) U of Ariz Pr.

Comets. rev. ed. Franklyn M. Branley. LC 83-46161. (Let's-Read-&-Find-Out Science Bk.). (Illus.). 32p. (J). (gr. k-3). 1984. lib. bdg. 14.89 (0-690-04415-1, Crowell Jr Bks) HarpC Child Bks.

Comets: A Chronological History of Observation, Science, Myth & Folklore. Donald K. Yeomans. (Science Editions Ser.). 485p. 1991. text ed. 35.00 (0-471-61011-9) Wiley.

Comets: An Educational Coloring Book. Spizzirri Publishing Co. Staff. Ed. by Linda Spizzirri. (Illus.). 32p. (J). (gr. k-5). 1982. pap. 1.75 (0-86545-071-4) Spizzirri.

Comets: Speculation & Discovery. Nigel Calder. (Illus.). 176p. 1994. reprint ed. pap. text ed. 8.95 (0-486-27879-4) Dover.

Comets & Carnelians: Poems by Mary L. R. Johnson. Mary L. Johnson. 60p. (Orig.). 1989. pap. 9.00 (0-9624537-0-6) Cowardly Lyon.

Comets & Meteors. Lynda Sorensen. LC 93-15690. (Solar System Ser.). (J). (gr. 5 up). 1993. write for info. (0-86593-277-8) Rourke Corp.

Comets & Meteors: Visitors from Space. Jeanne Bendick. (Early Bird Astronomy Ser.). (Illus.). 32p. (J). (gr. k-2). 1991. lib. bdg. 13.90 (1-56294-001-5); pap. 4.95 (1-878841-55-6) Millbrook Pr.

Comets & the Origin of Life. Ed. by Cyril Ponnamperuma. 292p. 1981. lib. bdg. 80.00 (90-277-1318-9) Kluwer Ac.

Comets, Asteroids & Meteorites. Duncan Brewer. LC 90-40813. (Planet Guides Ser.). (Illus.). 64p. (J). (gr. 5-9). 1992. lib. bdg. 15.95 (1-85435-376-4) Marshall Cavendish.

C

An Asterisk (*) at the beginning of an entry indicates that the title is appearing in BIP for the first time.

Comets, Asteroids, & Meteorites. rev. ed. (Voyage Through the Universe Ser.). 144p. 1992. write for info. (*0-8094-9054-4*); lib. bdg. write for info. (*0-8094-9055-2*) Time-Life.

Comets, Asteroids, & Meteors. Dennis B. Fradin. LC 83-23231. (New True Bks.). (Illus.). 48p. (J). (gr. k-4). 1984. lib. bdg. 12.90 (*0-516-01723-3*); pap. 4.95 (*0-516-41723-1*) Childrens.

Comets in the Post-Halley Era, 2 vols., Set. Ed. by R. L. Newburn, Jr. et al. (C). 1991. lib. bdg. 196.00 (*0-7923-1164-7*); pap. text ed. 61.50 (*0-7923-1165-5*) Kluwer Ac.

Comets, Meteors, & Asteroids. Seymour Simon. LC 93-51251. (Illus.). 32p. (J). (gr. k up). 1994. 15.00 (*0-688-12709-6*); lib. bdg. 14.93 (*0-688-12710-X*) Morrow Jr Bks.

***Comet's Nine Lives.** Jan Brett. LC 95-11646. (Illus.). (J). 1996. write for info. (*0-399-22931-0*, Putnam) Putnam Pub Group.

Comets to Cosmology. Ed. by Anita Lawrence. (Lecture Notes in Physics Ser.: Vol. 297). x, 415p. 1988. 53.00 (*0-387-19052-X*) Spr-Verlag.

Comeuppance of Dipsey Dolan. Peter Eliason. (Michael the Archangel Ser.). 162p. (Orig.). (J). (gr. 2-10). 1984. pap. 5.95 (*0-916777-34-0*) W P Allen.

COMEX: The Communication Experience in Human Relations. 2nd ed. Lyle Sussman & Sam Deep. 240p. (C). 1989. pap. 24.95 (*0-538-70026-2*, EH45BA) S-W Pub.

Comex ASVAB-AFCT. Douglas Prybylowski. (Illus.). 360p. 1989. pap. text ed. 14.95x (*1-56030-022-1*) Comex Systs.

***Comfort: A 30-Day.** Wiersbe. 72p. 1995. pap. 2.99 (*1-56476-402-8*, 6-3402, Victor Books) SP Pubns.

Comfort & Care for the Critically Ill. June C. Kolf. 192p. (Orig.). 1993. pap. 8.99 (*0-8010-5257-2*) Baker Bk.

Comfort & Joy. Andrew Kuyvenhoven. LC 88-39763. 317p. (Orig.). 1988. pap. text ed. 14.85 (*0-930265-57-2*) CRC Pubns.

Comfort & Joy. Ann Patrick. 224p. (Orig.). 1993. pap. 2.95 (*1-56597-105-1*, Kismet) Meteor Pub.

Comfort & Protest. Allan A. Boesak. LC 86-28076. 140p. (Orig.). 1987. pap. 8.99 (*0-664-24602-8*, Westminster) Westminster John Knox.

C

Comfort Below Freezing. Robert McQuilkin. LC 79-28741. (Illus.). 176p. (Orig.). 1980. pap. 5.95 (*0-89037-184-9*) Anderson World.

Comfort Cuisine Recipe Collection. Ed. by Jacqueline Heriteau et al. LC 91-77685. (Illus.). 308p. (Orig.). 1992. pap. 15.00 (*0-9631486-0-5*) Box Project.

Comfort Fairy Story. Nick Nichols. 24p. (J). (gr. k-4). 1990. 19.95 (*0-9632531-0-7*) N Squared Ent.

Comfort Food. Holly Garrison. 1988. 16.95 (*1-55611-095-2*) D I Fine.

Comfort for Christians. Arthur W. Pink. (Summit Bks.). 122p. 1976. pap. 4.99 (*0-8010-7109-7*) Baker Bk.

Comfort for Christians. Arthur W. Pink. pap. 3.99 (*0-87377-074-9*) GAM Pubns.

***Comfort for the Losses in Life.** David E. Rosage. 280p. 1995. 9.99 (*0-89283-887-6*, Charis) Servant.

Comfort for the Sorrowing. William Goulooze. 1959. pap. 0.55 (*0-686-23474-X*) Rose Pub MI.

***Comfort for the Wounded Spirit.** Frank Hammond. 70p. (Orig.). 1992. pap. 4.00 (*0-89228-077-8*) Impact Christian.

Comfort for Those Who Mourn. Comp. by O. V. Armstrong. LC 77-17182. reprint ed. pap. 20.00 (*0-8357-9003-7*, 2016353) Bks Demand.

Comfort for Troubled Christians, 10 bks., Set. J. C. Brumfield. (Moody Acorns Ser.). Date not set. pap. 9.99 (*0-8024-1400-1*) Moody.

Comfort Found in Good Old Books. George H. Fitch. LC 76-121466. (Essay Index Reprint Ser.). 1977. 21.95 (*0-8369-1805-3*) Ayer.

Comfort Found in Good Old Books. George H. Fitch. 1977. lib. bdg. 59.95 (*0-8490-1646-0*) Gordon Pr.

Comfort Heating. 3rd ed. Billy C. Langley. (C). 1985. teacher ed. write for info. (*0-8359-0888-7*, Reston); text ed. 65.00 (*0-8359-0887-9*, Reston) P-H.

Comfort Heating. 4th ed. Billy C. Langley. LC 93-8220. 518p. 1994. text ed. 56.00 (*0-13-151879-8*) P-H.

Comfort in Caring: Nursing the Person with HIV Infection. Janice B. Meisenhelder & Christopher L. LaCharite. 300p. (C). 1989. text ed. 29.50 (*0-673-52004-8*) Lippincott.

Comfort Magazine, Eighteen Eighty-Eight to Nineteen Forty-Two: A History & Critical Study. Dorothy S. Sayward. LC 60-62987. 1960. pap. 6.95 (*0-89101-006-8*) U Maine Pr.

Comfort Me with Apples. A. C. Snow. Ed. by Guy Munger. 212p. 1989. 12.95 (*0-935400-16-8*) News & Observer.

Comfort Me with Apples. large type ed. Catrin Morgan. (Magna General Fiction Ser.). 423p. 1992. 21.95 (*0-7505-0268-1*) Ulverscroft.

Comfort Me with Apples: Dining in Literature. deluxe limited ed. Dorsey Alexander. (Illus.). 1993. pap. 12.50 (*0-937686-17-4*) Turtles Quill.

Comfort My People: Prayers for the Sick & Suffering. Dorothy E. Bedics. (Illus.). 120p. (Orig.). 1990. text ed. 7.95 (*0-8294-0638-7*) Loyola Univ Pr.

Comfort of Cats. large type ed. Doreen Tovey. LC 93-789. 1993. 19.95 (*0-7927-1650-7*, Curley Lrg Print); pap. 17.95 (*0-7927-1624-8*, Curley Lrg Print) Chivers N Amer.

***Comfort of Dreams: Photographs.** Pasquella. Date not set. per. 19.95 (*0-85449-140-6*, Pub. by Gay Mens Pr UK) InBook.

Comfort of Strangers. Ian McEwan. 1994. pap. 9.00 (*0-679-74984-5*, Vin) Random.

***Comfort One Another: Reconstructing the Rhetoric & Audience of One Thessalonians.** Abraham Smith. (Literary Currents in Biblical Interpretation Ser.). 160p. (Orig.). 1995. pap. 15.99 (*0-664-25178-1*) Westminster John Knox.

Comfort Properties of Textiles. K. Slater. 91p. 1989. 90.00 (*0-686-63755-0*) St Mut.

Comfort Properties of Textiles, Vol. 9, No. 4. K. Slater. 91p. (C). 1977. pap. text ed. 100.00 (*0-685-36093-8*, Pub. by Textile Institue UK) St Mut.

Comfort Teacher. Charlotte Muse. (Flowering Quince Poetry Ser.: No. 5). (Illus.). 24p. (Orig.). 1985. pap. 7.50 (*0-940592-17-7*) Heyeck Pr.

Comfort Those Who Mourn: How to Preach Personalized Funeral Messages. Kenn Filkins. 195p. (Orig.). Date not set. pap. 9.99 (*0-89900-602-7*) College Pr Pub.

Comfort to the Sick. Brother Aloysius. LC 82-60161. 448p. 1992. pap. 19.95 (*0-87728-525-X*) Weiser.

Comfort Trap: Spiritual Dangers of the Convenience Culture. Tim Bascom. LC 93-27973. 163p. (Orig.). 1993. pap. 8.99 (*0-8308-1658-5*, 1658) InterVarsity.

Comfort Us, Lord. 1985. pap. 2.95 (*1-56123-032-4*) Centering Corp.

***Comfort Women: Japan's Brutal Regime of Enforced Prostitution in the Second World War.** George Hicks. (Illus.). 260p. 1995. 25.00 (*0-393-03807-6*) Norton.

Comfort Ye My People. Leslie W. Pocock. 128p. 1986. 30.00 (*0-7223-2048-5*, Pub. by A H S Ltd UK) St Mut.

Comfort Zones: Leader's Guide. 2nd ed. Clare B. Corbett & Nancy R. Urquhart. Ed. by Phil Gerould. 1990. 29.95 (*0-931961-98-X*) Crisp Pubns.

Comfort Zones: Looseleaf Edition. 2nd ed. Edwood N. Chapman. Ed. by Michael G. Crisp. LC 88-7248. (Illus.). 320p. pap. 14.95 (*1-56052-026-4*) Crisp Pubns.

Comfort Zones: Planning Your Future. 3rd ed. Elwood N. Chapman. LC 92-20417. 325p. 1993. pap. 14.95 (*1-56052-162-7*) Crisp Pubns.

Comfortable House: Lanford Wilson, Marshall W. Mason & the Circle Repertory Theatre. Philip M. Williams. LC 92-50956. 223p. 1993. lib. bdg. 28.50 (*0-89950-836-7*) McFarland & Co.

Comfortably Fixed. Judith M. Darby. LC 90-93015. (Illus.). 176p. 1990. 28.50 (*0-9626261-0-4*) J M Darby.

Comforted of God. Alice I. Cravens. 1990. pap. 4.25 (*0-89137-454-X*) Quality Pubns.

Comforter. C. H. Spurgeon. 1978. pap. 0.50 (*1-56186-335-1*) Pilgrim Pubns.

***Comforter: The Spirit of Joy.** Andrew Apostoli. LC 95-3954. 1995. pap. 7.95 (*0-8189-0734-7*) Alba.

Comforters. Muriel Spark. LC 94-12825. (Revived Modern Classic Ser.). 208p. (Orig.). 1994. reprint ed. pap. 10.95 (*0-8112-1285-8*, NDP796) New Directions.

***Comforting Foods.** Project Open Hand Staff. LC 95-11422. 1995. write for info. (*0-02-566401-8*) Macmillan.

Comforting the Bereaved. Warren W. Wiersbe & David W. Wiersbe. (Orig.). 1985. pap. 7.99 (*0-8024-5293-0*) Moody.

Comforting the Confused: Strategies for Managing Dementia. Stephanie B. Hoffman & Constance A. Platt. 224p. 1991. pap. 23.95 (*0-8261-7850-2*) Springer Pub.

Comforting Those Who Grieve. Doug Manning. LC 84-48226. 80p. 1987. pap. 9.00 (*0-06-065424-4*) Harper SF.

Comforting Whirlwind. Bill McKibben. 112p. (Orig.). (C). 1994. pap. 8.99 (*0-8028-0499-3*) Eerdmans.

Comforts of Home: Prostitution in Colonial Nairobi. Luise White. LC 90-34266. (Illus.). 256p. 1990. pap. text ed. 14.95 (*0-226-89507-6*) U Ch Pr.

Comforts of Home: Prostitution in Colonial Nairobi. Luise White. LC 90-34266. (Illus.). 256p. 1990. lib. bdg. 34.95 (*0-226-89506-8*) U Ch Pr.

***Comforts of Home: Small Inns, Cottages & Bed & Breakfast of Atlantic Canada.** Fawcett. 1994. per. 14.95 (*0-86492-182-9*, Pub. by Goose Ln Edits CN) InBook.

Comforts of Unreason: A Study of the Motives Behind Irrational Thought. Rupert Crawshay-William. LC 71-98217. 206p. 1970. reprint ed. text ed. 55.00 (*0-8371-3398-X*, CRUN, Greenwood Pr) Greenwood.

Comfrey: What It Is, What It Can Do for You. Ben C. Harris. LC 82-80699. 1982. pap. 2.95 (*0-87983-273-8*) Keats.

Comfrey Report. Lawrence D. Hills. Ed. by Bargyla Rateaver & Gylver Rateaver. Bd. with Comfrey, the Herbal Healer. LC 75-23178. LC 75-23178. (Conservation Gardening & Farming Ser.: Ser. C). 1975. Set pap. 8.00 (*0-9600698-9-5*) Rateavers.

Comfrey, the Herbal Healer see Comfrey Report

Comic Adventures of Felix the Cat. LC 82-74029. (Illus.). (J). 1983. pap. 3.95 (*0-915696-62-2*) Determined Prods.

Comic Adventures of Old Mother Hubbard & Her Dog. Tomie De Paola. LC 80-19270. (Illus.). 32p. (J). (ps-3). 1981. 13.95 (*0-15-219541-6*, HB Juv Bks); pap. 3.95 (*0-15-219542-4*, HB Juv Bks) HarBrace.

Comic Agony: Mixed Impressions in the Modern Theater. Albert Bermel. 280p. 1993. 35.00 (*0-8101-1071-7*) Northwestern U Pr.

Comic Angels: And Other Approaches to Greek Drama Through Vase-Paintings. Oliver Taplin. (Illus.). 224p. 1993. 62.00 (*0-19-814797-X*) OUP.

Comic Angels: And Other Approaches to Greek Drama Through Vase-Paintings. Oliver Taplin. (Illus.). 168p. 1994. reprint ed. pap. 19.95 (*0-19-815000-8*) OUP.

Comic Art Collection Catalog: An Author, Artist, Titles, & Subject Catalog of the Comic Art Collection, Special Collections Division, Michigan State University Libraries M - Z. Comp. by Randall W. Scott. (Bibliographies & Indexes in Popular Culture Ser.: No. 2). 1993. write for info. (*0-313-29030-X*, SRC02, Greenwood Pr); write for info. (*0-313-29029-6*, SRC01, Greenwood Pr) Greenwood.

Comic Art Collection Catalog: An Author, Artist, Titles, & Subject Catalog of the Comic Art Collection, Special Collections Division, Michigan State University Libraries M - Z. Ed. by Randall W. Scott. LC 93-7599. (Bibliographies & Indexes in Popular Culture Ser.: No. 2). 1448p. 1993. text ed. 215.00 (*0-313-28325-7*, SRC/, Greenwood Pr) Greenwood.

Comic Art of Barbara Pym. Mason Cooley. LC 87-45807. (Studies in Modern Literature: No. 18). 1988. 42.50 (*0-404-61588-0*) AMS Pr.

Comic Art of Europe: An International, Comprehensive Bibliography. Ed. by John A. Lent. LC 94-14432. (Bibliographies & Indexes in Popular Culture Ser.: No. 5). 688p. 1994. text ed. 95.00 (*0-313-28212-9*, Greenwood Pr) Greenwood.

***Comic Book.** Paul Sassiene. 1994. 29.98 (*1-55521-999-3*) Bk Sales Inc.

Comic Book Artists. Alex G. Malloy. 352p. 1993. pap. 14.95 (*0-87069-707-2*, Wallace-Hmestead) Chilton.

Comic Book Heroes: One Thousand One Trivia Questions about America's Favorite Superheroes, from the Atom to the X-Men. Robert Bly. LC 94-20250. 1994. 9.95 (*0-8065-1571-6*, Citadel Pr) Carol Pub Group.

Comic Book Heroes of the Screen. William Schoell. (Illus.). 256p. 1991. 25.95 (*0-8065-1252-0*, Citadel Pr) Carol Pub Group.

Comic Book in America: An Illustrated History. Mike Benton. LC 89-5077. 208p. 1989. 29.95 (*0-87833-659-1*) Taylor Pub.

Comic Book in America: An Illustrated History. Mike Benton. (Illus.). 208p. 1993. reprint ed. pap. 19.95 (*0-87833-835-7*) Taylor Pub.

Comic Book Makers. Joe Simon & Jim Simon. LC 90-83473. (Illus.). 208p. (Orig.). 1990. pap. 18.95 (*0-9626858-0-1*) Crestwood Two.

Comic Book Reader's Companion: An A-Z Guide to the World's Favorite Art Form. Ron Goulart. LC 92-18795. 256p. 1993. pap. 15.00 (*0-06-273117-3*, Harper Ref) HarpC.

Comic Book Rebels: Conversations with the Creators of the New Comics. Stanley Wiater & Stephen R. Bissette. (Illus.). 320p. (Orig.). 1993. 25.00 (*1-55611-355-2*); pap. 12.95 (*1-55611-354-4*) D I Fine.

Comic Book Superstars: Who's Who in Comics. Ed. by Don Thompson & Maggie Thompson. LC 93-77544. (Illus.). 256p. 1993. pap. 16.95 (*0-87341-256-7*) Krause Pubns.

Comic Books & America, Nineteen Forty-Five to Nineteen Fifty-Four. William W. Savage, Jr. LC 90-50238. (Illus.). 168p. 1990. 18.95 (*0-8061-2305-2*) U of Okla Pr.

Comic Books & Comic Strips in the United States: An International Bibliography. Ed. by John A. Lent. LC 94-10852. (Bibliographies & Indexes in Popular Culture Ser.: No. 4). 624p. 1994. text ed. 85.00 (*0-313-28211-0*, Greenwood Pr) Greenwood.

Comic Books & Strips: An Information Sourcebook. Randall W. Scott. LC 88-22377. 160p. 1988. pap. 32.95 (*0-89774-389-X*) Oryx Pr.

Comic Books As History: The Narrative Art of Jack Jackson, Art Spiegelman, & Harvey Pekar. Joseph Witek. LC 89-16545. (Studies in Popular Culture Ser.). 200p. 1989. 30.00 (*0-87805-405-7*); pap. 15.95 (*0-87805-406-5*) U Pr of Miss.

***Comic Captioned Capers.** Clarence Dawson. (Illus.). 64p. (Orig.). 1995. pap. 8.95 (*0-86534-232-6*) Sunstone Pr.

Comic Character Timepieces: Seven Decades of Memories. Hy Brown & Nancy Thomas. LC 92-60629. (Illus.). 280p. 1992. text ed. 79.95 (*0-88740-426-X*) Schiffer.

Comic Characters. Walter Foster. (How to Draw & Paint Ser.). (Illus.). 32p. (Orig.). 1989. pap. 5.95 (*0-929261-55-0*, HT24) W Foster Pub.

***Comic Collectibles & Their Values.** Alex G. Malloy & Stuart W. Wells. 352p. 1995. pap. 15.95 (*0-87069-724-2*) Chilton.

Comic Cops. Neil Raphael & Ray Raphael. 182p. (Orig.). (J). (gr. 4-8). 1992. pap. 6.95 (*1-881102-13-0*) Real Bks.

Comic Crime. Earl Bargainnier. LC 87-71031. 202p. (Orig.). (C). 1987. 29.95 (*0-87972-383-1*); pap. 14.95 (*0-87972-384-X*) Bowling Green Univ.

Comic Curios. Barbara Haugh. 32p. (Orig.). 1987. pap. 3.00 (*0-9617236-1-0*) B A H Publishing.

Comic Effects: Interdisciplinary Approaches to Humor in Literature. Paul Lewis. LC 88-28227. 179p. 1989. 59.50 (*0-7914-0022-0*); pap. 19.95 (*0-7914-0023-9*) State U NY Pr.

Comic English Grammar. J. Leech. 1903. 12.00 (*0-8196-5097-8*) Biblo.

Comic Faith: The Great Tradition from Austen to Joyce. Robert M. Polhemus. LC 79-24856. x, 398p. (C). 1980. lib. bdg. 30.00 (*0-226-67320-0*) U Ch Pr.

Comic Faith: The Great Tradition from Austen to Joyce. Robert M. Polhemus. LC 79-24856. x, 398p. (C). 1982. pap. text ed. 9.95 (*0-226-67321-9*) U Ch Pr.

***Comic Fun.** Rodgers. 1995. pap. (*0-590-47027-2*) Scholastic Inc.

Comic Genius of Dr. Alexander Hamilton. Robert Micklus. LC 89-22468. 232p. 1990. text ed. 28.00x (*0-87049-633-6*) U of Tenn Pr.

Comic Hero. Robert M. Torrance. LC 77-16316. 362p. reprint ed. pap. 103.20 (*0-7837-1530-7*, 2041807) Bks Demand.

Comic History of England, 2 Vols, Set. Gilbert A. A'Beckett. LC 72-158218. (Illus.). reprint ed. 76.50 (*0-404-00300-1*) AMS Pr.

Comic History of the United States. Livingston Hopkins. LC 77-85686. (American Fiction Reprint Ser.). 1977. 18.95 (*0-8369-7015-2*) Ayer.

Comic Image of the Jew: Explorations of a Pop Culture Phenomenon. Sig Altman. LC 71-146161. 234p. 1975. 29.50 (*0-8386-7869-6*) Fairleigh Dickinson.

***Comic Inferno: The Satirical World of Robert Sheckley.** Gregory Stephenson. Ed. by Roger C. Schlobin. LC 95-5025. (Milford Ser.: Popular Writers of Today: Vol. 66). 1995. lib. bdg. write for info. (*0-916732-60-6*); pap. write for info. (*0-916732-61-4*) Borgo Pr.

Comic Irishman. Maureen Waters. LC 83-4888. 204p. (C). 1984. 59.50 (*0-87395-766-0*); pap. 19.95 (*0-87395-767-9*) State U NY Pr.

Comic Mind: Comedy & the Movies. Gerald Mast. LC 78-68546. (Illus.). 1979. pap. text ed. 16.95 (*0-226-50978-8*, P827) U Ch Pr.

Comic Moments. Fred M. Robinson. LC 91-43694. (Illus.). 208p. 1992. 27.50 (*0-8203-1424-2*) U of Ga Pr.

Comic Novels of Charles Sorel: A Study of Structure, Characterization & Disguise. Andrew G. Suozzo. LC 81-68139. (French Forum Monographs: No. 32). 145p. (Orig.). 1982. pap. 9.95 (*0-917058-31-3*) French Forum.

Comic Persuasion: Moral Structure in British Comedy from Shakespeare to Stoppard. Alice Rayner. LC 86-28281. (Illus.). 181p. reprint ed. pap. 51.60 (*0-7837-4699-7*, 2044446) Bks Demand.

Comic Power in Emily Dickinson. Suzanne Juhasz et al. LC 93-786. 184p. 1993. text ed. 27.50 (*0-292-74029-8*) U of Tex Pr.

Comic Practice: Comic Response. Robert I. Williams. LC 92-50571. 1993. 35.00 (*0-87413-463-3*) U Delaware Pr.

Comic Recitations & Readings. Ed. by Charles W. Brown. LC 72-139756. (Granger Index Reprint Ser.). 1977. 18.95 (*0-8369-6210-9*) Ayer.

Comic Relief: Humor in Contemporary American Literature. Ed. by Sarah B. Cohen. LC 78-16510. 339p. 1978. 29.95 (*0-252-00576-7*) U of Ill Pr.

Comic Relief: Humor in Contemporary American Literature. Ed. by Sarah B. Cohen. LC 91-15723. (Humor in Life & Letters Ser.). 368p. 1991. pap. 18.95 (*0-8143-1915-7*) Wayne St U Pr.

Comic Sense: Reading Robert Couver, Stanley Elkin, Philip Roth. Thomas Pughe. LC 94-6568. (International Cooper Series in English Language & Literature). 1994. 29.50 (*0-8176-5023-7*) Birkhauser.

Comic Songs of Ireland. Ed. by James N. Healy. 1986. pap. 6.95 (*0-85342-771-2*) Dufour.

Comic Spirit, Boccaccio to Thomas Mann: Giovanni Boccaccio, Charles Dickens, Henry Fielding, Israel Zangwill, Thomas Mann. Bernard N. Schilling. LC 65-21652. 259p. reprint ed. pap. 73.90 (*0-7837-3588-X*, 2043452) Bks Demand.

Comic Spirit in George Meredith: An Interpretation. Joseph W. Beach. (BCL1-PR English Literature Ser.). 230p. 1992. reprint ed. lib. bdg. 79.00 (*0-7812-7595-4*) Rprt Serv.

Comic Spirit of Federico Garcia Lorca. Virginia Higginbotham. LC 75-16079. 199p. reprint ed. pap. 56.80 (*0-8357-7744-8*, 2036101) Bks Demand.

Comic Spirit of Wallace Stevens. Daniel Fuchs. LC 63-9008. 211p. reprint ed. pap. 60.20 (*0-317-42195-6*, 2026199) Bks Demand.

Comic Strip Art of Lyonel Feininger. Bill Blackbeard. (Illus.). 56p. (YA). 1994. 24.95 (*0-87816-293-3*) Kitchen Sink.

Comic Strip Art of Lyonel Feininger. Ed. by Bill Blackbeard. (Illus.). 56p. (YA). 1994. pap. 16.95 (*0-87816-294-1*) Kitchen Sink.

***Comic Strip Book.** Foster. 1995. pap. (*0-590-48533-4*) Scholastic Inc.

***Comic Strip Century, 1895-1995.** Ed. & Intro. by Bill Blackbeard. LC 95-3574. 1995. write for info. (*0-87816-355-7*) Kitchen Sink.

Comic Strip Fun. Charlene Brown & Carolyn Davis. (Beginner's Art Ser.). (Illus.). 64p. (Orig.). (J). (gr. k up). 1989. pap. 3.95 (*0-929261-29-1*, BA04) W Foster Pub.

Comic Strips. Roger Armstrong. (How to Draw & Paint Ser.). (Illus.). 32p. (Orig.). 1990. pap. 5.95 (*1-56010-050-8*, HT220) W Foster Pub.

Comic Support: The Second Bananas Who Made the Stars Look Good. Ron Smith. LC 92-37559. 1993. 14.95 (*0-8065-1399-3*) Carol Pub Group.

Comic Tales Anthology, No. 2. 2nd ed. James C. McCoy et al. LC 88-70551. (Illus.). 100p. (Orig.). (YA). (gr. 7-12). 1988. pap. 6.95 (*0-943864-53-4*) Davenport.

Comic Tales of the Middle Ages: An Anthology & Commentary. Marc Wolterbeek. LC 90-47533. (Contributions to the Study of World Literature Ser.: No. 39). 272p. 1991. text ed. 57.95 (*0-313-27737-0*, WKT/, Greenwood Pr) Greenwood.

Comic Theatre: A Comedy in Three Acts. Carlo Goldoni. Tr. by John W. Miller. LC 69-14867. 116p. reprint ed. pap. 33.10 (*0-7837-1894-2*, 2042098) Bks Demand.

Comic Tones in Science Fiction: The Art of Compromise with Nature. Donald M. Hassler. LC 82-928. (Contributions to the Study of Science Fiction & Fantasy Ser.: No. 2). xiv, 143p. 1982. text ed. 45.00 (*0-313-22814-0*, HCT/, Greenwood Pr) Greenwood.

***Comic Toolbox: How to Be Funny Even If You're Not.** John Vorhaus. LC 94-33037. 250p. 1994. pap. text ed. 14.95 (*1-879505-21-5*) Silman James Pr.

Comic Transactions: Literature, Humor, & the Politics of Community in Twentieth-Century Britain. James F. English. 280p. 1994. 39.95 (*0-8014-2953-6*); pap. 15.95 (*0-8014-8166-X*) Cornell U Pr.

Comic Transformations in Shakespeare. Ruth Nevo. 1981. pap. 13.95 (*0-416-73890-7*, NO.6351) Routledge Chapman & Hall.

Comic Visions: Television Comedy & American Culture. David Marc. (Media Studies). 224p. 1989. text ed. 39.95 (*0-04-445284-5*); pap. text ed. 14.95 (*0-04-445285-3*) Routledge Chapman & Hall.

Comic Women, Tragic Men: A Study of Gender & Genre in Shakespeare. Linda Bamber. LC 81-51903. 224p. 1982. 37.50 (*0-8047-1126-7*) Stanford U Pr.

An Asterisk (*) at the beginning of an entry indicates that the title is appearing in BIP for the first time.

An Asterisk (*) at the beginning of an entry indicates that the title is appearing in BIP for the first time.

1405

C

Coming into Being among the Australian Aborigines. Ashley Montagu. LC 75-41195. (Illus.). reprint ed. 55.00 (*0-404-14573-6*) AMS Pr.
Coming into Eighty: Poems. May Sarton. 48p. 1994. 15.95 (*0-393-03689-8*) Norton.
Coming into Harmony. Ilse Klipper. Ed. by Jude Berman. (Illus.). 168p. (Orig.). 1992. pap. 11.95 (*0-9605022-2-X*) Pathwys Pr CA.
Coming into History. Jeanne M. Walker. (CSU Poetry Ser.: No. XXVIII). 82p. (Orig.). 1990. 12.00 (*0-914946-78-1*); pap. 8.00 (*0-914946-79-X*) Cleveland St Univ Poetry Ctr.
Coming into Our Fullness: On Women Turning Forty. Cathleen Rountree. (Illus.). 200p. (Orig.). 1991. pap. 16.95 (*0-89594-517-7*) Crossing Pr.
Coming into the Country. John McPhee. LC 77-12249. 438p. 1977. 22.95 (*0-374-12645-3*) FS&G.
Coming into the Country. John McPhee. 1991. pap. 9.95 (*0-374-52287-1*, Noonday) FS&G.
Coming into the End Zone: A Memoir. Doris Grubmach. 256p. 1993. pap. 9.95 (*0-393-30944-4*) Norton.
Coming into the End Zone: A Memoir. Doris Grumbach. 256p. 1991. 19.95 (*0-393-03009-1*) Norton.
Coming into the Light see Egyptian Magick: Enter the Body of Light & Travel the Magical Universe
Coming into the United Society of Believers. Carole Oles. (Sansfolio Ser.: No. 2). (Illus.). (Orig.). 1978. pap. 1.75 (*0-913282-13-8*) Seven Woods Pr.
Coming into This World. Kristen S. Rembold. 38p. (Orig.). 1992. pap. 3.00 (*1-880575-13-2*) Hot Pepper.
Coming K------: A Set of Idyll Plays see Anti-Maud: By a Poet of the People
Coming Kingdom. C. C. Cribb. LC 77-70213. pap. 2.95 (*0-932046-04-5*) Manhattan Ltd NC.
Coming Kingdom of the Messiah: The Solution to the Riddle of the New Testament. Anthony Buzzard. 104p. (Orig.). (C). 1988. pap. 4.95 (*0-945517-00-9*) Ministry Schl Pubns.
Coming Late to Motherhood: Twenty Women Tell Their Stories. Ed. by Joan Michelson & Sue Gee. LC 86-16801. 284p. 1986. lib. bdg. 27.00x (*0-8095-7016-5*) Borgo Pr.
***Coming Man: 19th Century American Perceptions of the Chinese.** Philip P. Choy et al. (Illus.). 178p. 1995. pap. 24.95 (*0-295-97453-2*) U of Wash Pr.
Coming Messiah!, 3 bks. Richard Honorof. 192p. 1992. Bk. 1, The Son of David. pap. 12.00 (*0-9632375-0-0*); Bk. 2, The Son of Abraham. pap. 12.00 (*0-685-74424-8*); Bk. 3, The Son of Man. pap. 12.00 (*0-685-74425-6*) Feed My Sheep.
Coming New Man. Jan Van Rijckenborgh. 378p. (Orig.). 1986. reprint ed. pap. 28.50 (*90-70196-47-6*) Rosycross Pr.
Coming of Age. 1985. write for info. (*0-9615354-0-7*) Semans Pub.
Coming of Age. Lisa Courtney. LC 78-54786. (Illus.). 1978. 10.95 (*0-932464-01-7*) Trek-CIR.
Coming of Age. Lorri Huett. (Orig.). 1991. pap. 3.95 (*0-87067-364-5*, Melrose Sq) Holloway.
Coming of Age. G. Wayne Miller. LC 94-20307. 1995. 22.00 (*0-679-42326-5*) Random.
Coming of Age. Samuel B. Shapiro. 200p. 1987. 30.00 (*0-88034-007-X*) Am Soc Assn Execs.
Coming of Age. 2nd ed. Duncan Neuhauser. LC 93-81268. 375p. 1994. 25.00 (*1-56793-009-3*, 0519) Health Admin Pr.
Coming of Age: Four Centuries of Connecticut Women & Their Choices. Ruth B. Moynihan. Ed. by Everett C. Wilkie, Jr. (Illus.). 116p. (C). 1987. reprint ed. pap. write for info. (*0-940748-99-1*) Conn Hist Soc.
Coming of Age: Protestantism in Contemporary Latin America. Ed. by Daniel R. Miller. (Calvin College Ser.: Vol. I). 265p. (Orig.). Date not set. lib. bdg. 53.00 (*0-8191-9406-9*); pap. text ed. 22.50 (*0-8191-9407-7*) U Pr of Amer.
Coming of Age: Selected Papers from the 18th International Conference of the Association for Children & Adults with Learning Disabilities. Ed. by William M. Cruickshank & Janet W. Lerner. LC 81-21404. (Best of ACLD Ser.: No. 3). (Illus.). 251p. reprint ed. pap. 71.60 (*0-8357-3986-4*, 2036684) Bks Demand.
Coming of Age: Short Stories about Youth & Adolescence. Bruce Emra. 1994. pap. 19.95 (*0-8442-5076-7*, Natl Textbk) NTC Pub Grp.
Coming of Age: Teachers in Iowa 1954 to 1993. Fred R. Comer. LC 93-78742. (Illus.). 240p. (YA). 1993. 20.00 (*0-9637413-0-6*) Iowa St Educ.
Coming of Age: The African American Male Rites-of-Passage. Paul Hill, Jr. 9.95 (*0-913543-28-4*) African Am Imag.
***Coming of Age: The Art of Growing Up.** LC 94-27347. (Icarus World Issues Ser.). (YA). 1994. lib. bdg. write for info. (*0-8239-1805-X*); pap. write for info. (*0-8239-1806-8*) Rosen Group.
***Coming of Age: The Story of Our Century by Those Who've Lived It.** Studs Terkel. LC 95-3806. 496p. 1995. 25.00 (*1-56584-284-7*) New Press NY.
Coming-of-Age: Traditions & Rituals Around the World. Karen Liptak. LC 93-1414. (Illus.). 128p. (YA). (gr. 7 up). 1994. lib. bdg. 15.90 (*1-56294-243-3*) Millbrook Pr.
Coming of Age: Urban America, Nineteen Fifteen-Nineteen Forty Five. William H. Wilson. LC 74-2033. 233p. reprint ed. pap. 66.50 (*0-317-07769-4*, 2051233) Bks Demand.
Coming of Age: Your Bar or Bat Mitzvah. Benjamin Efron & Alvan D. Rubin. LC 77-78031. (Illus.). 1977. 5.00 (*0-8074-0084-X*, 142530) UAHC.
Coming of Age at the Y: Delores Lovelady's Hilarious Adventures in Nashville's Opryland. William Cobb. 1984. 12.00 (*0-916620-72-7*) Portals Pr.
Coming of Age in America: A Multicultural Anthology. Mary Frosch. 288p. 1994. 22.95 (*1-56584-146-8*) New Press NY.
***Coming of Age in America: A Multicultural Anthology.** Ed. by Mary Frosch. 288p. 1995. pap. 11.95 (*1-56584-147-6*) New Press NY.
Coming of Age in Buffalo: Youth & Authority in the Postwar Era. William Graebner. (Illus.). 168p. (C). 1994. pap. 19.95 (*1-56639-197-0*) Temple U Pr.
Coming of Age in California: Personal Essays. rev. ed. Gerald Haslam. 112p. 1990. pap. 9.95 (*0-915685-07-8*) Devil Mountain Bks.
Coming of Age in Europe: Older People in the European Community. Age Concern England Staff. (C). 1992. 65.00 (*0-86242-114-4*, Pub. by Age Concern Eng UK) St Mut.
Coming of Age in Mississippi. Anne Moody. 384p. (gr. 9 up). 1992. mass mkt. 5.99 (*0-440-31488-7*, LE) Dell.
Coming of Age in New Jersey: College & American Culture. Michael Moffatt. 345p. 1989. text ed. 35.00 (*0-8135-1358-8*); pap. 12.95 (*0-8135-1359-6*) Rutgers U Pr.
Coming of Age in Philosophy. Ed. by Roger Eastman. 567p. (C). 1990. pap. text ed. 25.25 (*0-06-382594-5*) HarpCollege.
Coming of Age in Samoa. Margaret Mead. 22.75 (*0-8446-2571-X*) Peter Smith.
Coming of Age in Samoa. Margaret Mead. 1971. pap. 12.50 (*0-688-30974-7*, Quill) Morrow.
Coming of Age in Soho. Albert Innaurato. 1985. pap. 4.75 (*0-8222-0232-8*) Dramatists Play.
Coming of Age in the Ghetto, a Dilemma of Youth Unemployment: A Report to the Ford Foundation. Garth L. Mangum & Stephen F. Seninger. (PSEW Ser.: No. 33). 1978. text ed. 16.00 (*0-8018-2125-8*) Johns Hopkins.
Coming of Age in the Global Village: The Science & Technology, Politics, Economics, Environment & Ethics Literacy Book. Stephen Cook. LC 90-62089. (Illus.). 400p. (Orig.). 1990. pap. 14.95 (*0-9627349-0-X*) Parthenon Bks.
Coming of Age in the Land of Computers: A Parent's Guide to Computers for Children. Edward Yourdon. (Illus.). 160p. 1985. pap. text ed. 17.95 (*0-13-152125-X*) P-H.
Coming of Age in the Middle East. Trevor Mostyn. 256p. 1987. 35.00 (*0-7103-0208-8*, Pub. by Kegan Paul Intl UK) Routledge Chapman & Hall.
Coming of Age in the Milky Way. Timothy Ferris. 1989. pap. 11.95 (*0-385-26326-0*) Doubleday.
Coming of Age in the Russian Revolution. Elena Skrjabina. 235p. (C). 1985. 39.95x (*0-88738-034-4*) Transaction Pubs.
Coming of Age in the Russian Revolution: The Soviet Union at War, Vol. 4. Elena Skrjabina. Ed. & Frwd. by Norman Luxenburg. 235p. 1987. pap. 21.95x (*0-88738-710-1*) Transaction Pubs.
Coming of Age in Wartime. Phyllis Willmott. LC 88-70885. 160p. 1988. 27.50 (*0-7206-0696-9*, Pub. by P Owen Ltd UK) Dufour.
Coming of Age in Wartime. large type ed. Phyllis Willmott. 1993. 39.95 (*0-7066-1011-3*, Pub. by Remploy Pr CN) St Mut.
Coming of Age of American Art Music: New England's Classical Romanticists. Nicholas E. Tawa. LC 90-22814. (Contributions to the Study of Music & Dance Ser.: No. 22). 248p. 1991. text ed. 49.95 (*0-313-27797-4*, TCB/, Greenwood Pr) Greenwood.
Coming of Age of Political Economy, 1815-1825. Gary F. Langer. LC 86-31802. (Contributions in Economics & Economic History Ser.: No. 72). (Illus.). 236p. 1987. text ed. 55.00 (*0-313-25645-4*, LCA/, Greenwood Pr) Greenwood.
***Coming of Age with Elephants: A Memoir.** Joyce Poole. (Illus.). 336p. 1996. 24.95 (*0-7868-6095-2*) Hyperion.
Coming of Aphrodite. Dennis Mallonee. (Illus.). 32p. (Orig.). 1992. pap. 3.95 (*0-929729-00-5*) Heroic Pub CA.
Coming of Cassidy. Clarence E. Mulford. (Hopalong Cassidy Ser.: No. 1). 1992. mass mkt. 4.99 (*0-8125-2291-5*) Tor Bks.
Coming of Cassidy. Clarence Mulford. (Hopalong Cassidy Ser.). 438p. 1974. reprint ed. lib. bdg. 27.95 (*0-88411-216-0*, Aeonian Pr) Amereon Ltd.
Coming of Christ. Marianne Dorman. 104p. (C). 1989. text ed. 45.00 (*1-872795-82-X*, Pub. by Pentland Pr UK) St Mut.
Coming of Christ. Harold Mackay. 1989. 3.50 (*0-937396-79-6*) Walterick Pubs.
Coming of Christ & the New Earth. Marjorie Sampair. 120p. 1978. pap. 2.50 (*0-685-60620-1*) Graham Hse.
Coming of Christianity to Anglo-Saxon England. 3rd ed. Henry Mayr-Harting. 336p. 1991. 35.00 (*0-271-00806-7*); pap. 14.95 (*0-271-00769-9*) Pa St U Pr.
Coming of Civilization. 2nd ed. Ed. by Trevor Cairns. (Cambridge Introduction to World History Topic Bks.: Bk. 1). (Illus.). 96p. (YA). (gr. 7 up). 1986. pap. 13.25 (*0-521-33711-9*) Cambridge U Pr.
***Coming of Coyote.** Donald J. Boon. (Illus.). 64p. (Orig.). 1994. pap. 9.95 (*1-56167-174-6*) Am Literary Pr.
***Coming of Dawn.** Ed. by Cynthia Stevens. 802p. 1993. 69.95 (*1-56167-045-6*) Nat Lib Poetry.
Coming of French Absolutism: The Struggle for Tax Reform in the Province of Dauphine 1540-1640. Daniel Hickey. 288p. 1986. 40.00 (*0-8020-5676-8*) U of Toronto Pr.
Coming of God. Russell Terra. (C). 1988. 39.00 (*0-85439-135-5*, Pub. by St Paul Pubns UK) St Mut.
Coming of Industrial Order: Town & Factory Life in Rural Massachusetts, 1810-1860. Jonathan Prude. (Illus.). 372p. 1985. pap. 19.95 (*0-521-31396-1*) Cambridge U Pr.
Coming of Jan. Marian W. Erdman. 288p. (Orig.). 1991. pap. 10.95 (*0-9629896-0-6*) Erdman Assocs.
Coming of Locusts. Tony Fitzpatrick. (Illus.). 72p. (Orig.). 1992. pap. 9.95 (*0-9634262-9-X*) Sheba Pub.
Coming of Managerial Capitalism. Alfred D. Chandler, Jr. & Richard S. Tedlow. (C). 1985. text ed. 63.95 (*0-256-03285-8*) Irwin.
Coming of Post-Industrial Society: A Venture in Social Forecasting. Daniel Bell. LC 72-89178. 532p. 1976. pap. text ed. 18.00 (*0-465-09713-8*) Basic.
Coming of Rain. Richard Marius. LC 91-23076. 448p. 1991. reprint ed. pap. 12.95 (*1-55853-142-4*) Rutledge Hill Pr.
Coming of Roses. Patricia Hingle. (Illus.). 128p. (Orig.). 1988. 16.95 (*0-9620595-0-1*); pap. 8.95 (*0-685-21958-5*) Home Plates Ascension Inc.
Coming of Seth. Jane Roberts. (Orig.). 1993. reprint ed. lib. bdg. 21.95 (*1-56849-243-X*) Buccaneer Bks.
***Coming of Tan: Past, Present & Future of Humanity, Extraterrestrial Attention, Environmental Catastrophe.** Riley L. Martin & O-Qua T. Wann. Ed. by Curtis L. Cooperman. (Illus.). 370p. (Orig.). Date not set. pap. 29.95 (*0-9645745-0-0*) Historicity Prodn.
Coming of the Age of Iron. Theodore A. Wertime & James D. Muly. LC 79-26420. 575p. reprint ed. pap. 163.90 (*0-7837-4525-7*, 2080186) Bks Demand.
Coming of the Age of Steel. Theodore A. Wertime. LC 60-14362. 346p. reprint ed. pap. 98.70 (*0-317-10380-6*, 2015765) Bks Demand.
Coming of the American Civil War. 3rd ed. Ed. by Michael Perman. (Problems in American Civilization Ser.). 322p. (C). 1993. pap. text ed. write for info. (*0-669-27106-3*) Heath.
Coming of the Arabic Speaking People to the United States. Adele L. Younis. 360p. 1995. pap. 19.50 (*0-934733-40-6*) Ctr Migration.
Coming of the Book: The Impact of Printing 1450-1800. Lucien Febvre & Henri-Jean Martin. Ed. by Geoffrey Nowell-Smith & David Wootton. Tr. by David Gerard. 378p. 1976. pap. text ed. 17.95 (*0-86091-797-5*, Pub. by Verso UK) Routledge Chapman & Hall.
Coming of the Civil War. 2nd ed. Avery O. Craven. LC 57-8572. 1966. pap. text ed. 14.95 (*0-226-11894-0*, P210) U Ch Pr.
Coming of the Civil War, 1837-1861. John Niven. Ed. by John H. Franklin & A. S. Eisenstadt. (American History Ser.). 192p. (C). 1990. pap. text ed. write for info. (*0-88295-861-5*) Harlan Davidson.
Coming of the Cosmic Christ. Matthew Fox. LC 88-45136. 288p. (Orig.). 1988. pap. 15.00 (*0-06-062915-0*) Harper SF.
Coming of the Cosmic Christ. Matthew Fox. LC 88-45136. 288p. (Orig.). 1991. teacher ed, pap. 4.95 (*0-06-062959-2*) Harper SF.
Coming of the Electrical Age to the United States. Abram J. Foster. Ed. by Stuart Bruchey. LC 78-22680. (Energy in the American Economy Ser.). 1979. lib. bdg. 31.95 (*0-405-11983-6*) Ayer.
Coming of the First World War. Ed. by R. J. Evans & Hartmut P. Von Strandmann. (Illus.). 200p. 1990. reprint ed. pap. 19.95 (*0-19-822841-4*) OUP.
Coming of the French Revolution. Georges Lefebvre. Tr. by Robert R. Palmer. 256p. 1989. 45.00 (*0-691-05112-7*); pap. 9.95 (*0-691-00751-9*) Princeton U Pr.
Coming of the Friars & Other Historic Essays. Augustus Jessopp. (Select Bibliographies Reprint Ser.). 1977. reprint ed. 23.95 (*0-8369-6696-1*) Ayer.
***Coming of the Glory.** 2nd ed. John S. Tilley. 290p. (C). 1995. pap. text ed. 9.95 (*0-931709-04-0*) B Coats.
Coming of the Great Queen: A Narrative of the Acquisition of Burma. Edmond C. Browne. LC 77-87009. reprint ed. 38.50 (*0-404-16798-5*) AMS Pr.
***Coming of the Greeks: Indo-European Conquests in the Aegean & the Near East.** Drews. 1995. pap. (*0-691-02951-2*) Princeton U Pr.
Coming of the Greeks: Indo-European Conquests in the Aegean & the Near East. Robert Drews. (Illus.). 248p. 1988. 42.50 (*0-691-03592-X*) Princeton U Pr.
Coming of the Holy Spirit. Robert Baden. (Arch Bks.). (Illus.). 24p. (Orig.). (J). (ps-4). 1992. pap. 1.99 (*0-570-09029-6*) Concordia.
***Coming of the Hurricane.** Keith Glover. Date not set. text ed. 4.75 (*0-8222-1490-3*) Dramatists Play.
Coming of the Italian-Ethiopian War. George A. Beer. LC 67-14336. 420p. reprint ed. pap. 119.70 (*0-317-11313-5*, 2017258) Bks Demand.
***Coming of the King James Gospels.** Allen. 1995. pap. text ed. 30.00 (*1-55728-345-1*) U of Ark Pr.
***Coming of the King James Gospels: A Collation of the Translators' Work-in-Progress.** Ward S. Allen & Edward C. Jacobs. LC 94-34592. 1995. write for info. (*1-55728-327-3*) U of Ark Pr.
Coming of the Kingdom. Herman N. Ridderbos. LC 62-15429. 1962. pap. 15.99 (*0-87552-408-7*) Presby & Reformed.
Coming of the Lord. Gerald N. Lund. 9.95 (*0-88494-229-5*) Bookcraft Inc.
Coming of the Lord: A Guide to the Sunday Readings for Advent & the Christmas Season. J. D. Crichton. LC 90-62565. 96p. (Orig.). 1990. pap. 5.95 (*0-89622-461-9*) Twenty-Third.
Coming of the New Deal. Arthur M. Schlesinger, Jr. (American Heritage Library). 688p. 1988. pap. 11.95 (*0-395-48905-9*) HM.
Coming of the New York & Harlem Railroad. Louis V. Grogan. (Illus.). 368p. 1989. pap. 43.95 (*0-9621206-5-0*) L V Grogan.
Coming of the Pond Fishes. Ben H. Lampman. 177p. 1946. 20.00 (*0-8323-0341-0*) Binford Mort.
Coming of the Preachers: A Tale of the Rise of Methodism, 1901 see Minder: The Story of the Courtship, Call & Conflicts of John Ledger, Minder & Minister, 1900
Coming of the Russian Mennonites: An Episode in the Settling of the Last Frontier, 1874-1884. Charles H. Smith. 1977. 20.95 (*0-8369-7123-X*, 7957) Ayer.
Coming of the Saints. rev. ed. John W. Taylor. LC 85-71651. (Illus.). 272p. 1985. reprint ed. pap. 10.00 (*0-934666-19-9*) Artisan Sales.
Coming of the Saints: Imaginations & Studies in Early Church History & Tradition. John W. Taylor. 1977. lib. bdg. 250.00 (*0-8490-1647-9*) Gordon Pr.
Coming of the Spanish Civil War: Reform, Reaction & Revolution in the Second Republic. Paul Preston. LC 93-40967. 1994. pap. 19.95 (*0-415-06355-8*, A7864) Routledge.
Coming of the Spanish Civil War: Reform, Reaction & Revolution in the Second Republic. Paul Preston. 1983. pap. 14.95 (*0-416-35720-2*, NO. 3948) Routledge Chapman & Hall.
Coming of the Spanish Civil War: Reform, Reaction & Revolution in the Second Republic. 2nd ed. Paul Preston. LC 93-40967. 360p. 1994. 69.95x (*0-415-06354-X*, A7860) Routledge.
Coming of the Surfman. Peter Collington. LC 92-41844. (Illus.). 32p. (J). (gr. 3 up). 1994. 16.00 (*0-679-84721-9*) Knopf Bks Yng Read.
Coming of the Third Church: An Analysis of the Present & Future of the Church. Walbert Buhlmann. LC 76-23237. 431p. reprint ed. pap. 122.90 (*0-8357-8540-8*, 2034847) Bks Demand.
***Coming of Vertumnus.** Ian Watson. 288p. 1995. 25.95 (*0-575-05766-1*, Pub. by V Gollancz UK) Trafalgar.
***Coming of Vertumnus.** Ian Watson. 288p. 1995. pap. 10.95 (*0-575-05921-4*, Pub. by V Gollancz UK) Trafalgar.
Coming of Wizards. Michael Reynolds. (Illus.). 234p. (Orig.). 1989. pap. 12.95 (*0-9614010-3-6*) High Mesa Pr.
Coming of Yale to New Haven. Williston Walker. 1917. pap. 29.50 (*0-686-83506-9*) Elliots Bks.
Coming Off Tranquilizers & Sleeping Pills: A Withdrawal Plan That Really Works. Shirley Trickett. 1994. pap. 10.00 (*0-7225-2398-X*) Thorsons SF.
Coming on Center: Essays in English Education. 2nd rev. ed. James Moffett. LC 87-27774. 208p. 1988. pap. text ed. 17.00 (*0-86709-219-X*) Boynton Cook Pubs.
***Coming on Strong: Anthology of New Writing from the Royal Court.** Kevin Coyle et al. 384p. (Orig.). 1995. pap. 14.95 (*0-571-17678-X*) Faber & Faber.
Coming on Strong: Gay Politics & Culture. Ed. by Simon Sheperd & Mick Wallis. 240p. 1989. text ed. 44.95 (*0-04-445351-5*); pap. text ed. 15.95 (*0-04-445352-3*) Routledge Chapman & Hall.
***Coming on Strong: Gender & Sexuality in Twentieth-Century Women's Sport.** Susan K. Cahn. (Illus.). 384p. (C). 1995. pap. 14.95 (*0-674-14434-1*) HUP.
Coming on Strong: Gender & Sexuality in Women's Sport. Susan K. Cahn. 300p. 1994. 22.95 (*0-02-905075-8*) Free Pr.
Coming Out: A Documentary Play about Gay Life & Liberation in the U. S. A. Jonathan N. Katz. LC 75-12327. (Homosexuality Ser.). 1980. 19.95 (*0-405-07399-2*) Ayer.
Coming Out: An Anthology of International Gay & Lesbian Writings. Ed. by Stephan Likosky. LC 91-50834. 576p. (Orig.). 1992. pap. 15.00 (*0-679-74054-6*) Pantheon.
Coming Out: Another Fun 'n Games Book for Lesbians. Elizabeth Dean et al. LC 91-32875. (Illus.). 100p. (Orig.). 1991. pap. 8.95 (*0-934678-33-2*) New Victoria Pubs.
Coming Out: Homosexual Politics in Britain from the 19th Century to the Present. Jeffrey Weeks. 7.95 (*0-7043-3175-6*, Pub. by Quartet UK) Charles River Bks.
Coming Out: An Act of Love: An Inspiring Call to Action for Gay Men, Lesbians, & Those Who Care. Rob Eichberg. 304p. 1991. pap. 12.95 (*0-452-26685-8*, Plume) NAL-Dutton.
***Coming Out Conservative.** M. Lieberman. 1994. pap. 4.99 (*0-517-13024-6*) Random.
Coming Out Fighting. Philip Hobsbaum. LC 68-8307. 1969. 13.95 (*0-8023-1182-2*) Dufour.
Coming Out in College: The Struggle for a Queer Identity. Robert A. Rhoads. LC 94-16454. 208p. 1994. text ed. 55.00 (*0-89789-378-6*) Greenwood.
***Coming Out in College: The Struggle for a Queer Identity.** Robert A. Rhoads. LC 94-16454. (Critical Studies in Education & Culture). 208p. 1994. pap. text ed. 15.95 (*0-89789-421-9*, Bergin & Garvey) Greenwood.
Coming Out of Homosexuality: New Freedom for Men & Women. Bob Davies & Lori Rentzel. LC 93-41902. 201p. (Orig.). 1994. pap. 9.99 (*0-8308-1653-4*, 1653) InterVarsity.
Coming Out of the Blue: British Police Officers Talk about Their Lives on the Job As Lesbians, Gays & Bisexuals. Marc E. Burke. 272p. 1993. 55.00 (*0-304-32716-6*); pap. text ed. 14.95 (*0-304-32714-X*) Cassell.
Coming Out of the Class Closet: Lesbians Speak. Ed. by Julia Penelope. LC 94-17401. 400p. 1994. pap. 14.95 (*0-89594-704-8*) Crossing Pr.
Coming Out of the Classroom Closet: Gay & Lesbian Students, Teachers, & Curricula. Ed. by Karen M. Harbeck. LC 91-39814. (Journal of Homosexuality). 269p. 1992. 39.95 (*1-56024-216-7*); pap. text ed. 14.95 (*1-56023-013-4*) Haworth Pr.
***Coming Out of the Dark: Quiet Time Book for Teens.** 128p. (YA). 1994. pap. 6.99 (*1-884553-48-6*) Discipleshp.
Coming Out of the Middle Ages: Comparative Reflections on China & the West. Zhu Weizheng. Ed. & Tr. by Ruth Hayhoe. LC 90-8161. (Chinese Studies on China). 200p. 1990. 51.95 (*0-87332-638-5*) M E Sharpe.
***Coming Out of Your Psychic Closet: How to Unlock Your Naturally Intuitive Self.** Lynn Robinson. 176p. (Orig.). 1994. 20.95 (*0-9626531-7-9*) Factor Pr.

1406

An Asterisk (*) at the beginning of an entry indicates that the title is appearing in BIP for the first time.

C

An Asterisk (*) at the beginning of an entry indicates that the title is appearing in BIP for the first time.

1407

Comitatus, Individual & Honor: Studies in North Germanic Institutional Vocabulary. John Lindow. LC 75-620093. (University of California Publications in Social Welfare: Vol. 83). 193p. reprint ed. pap. 55.10 (*0-317-08268-X*, 2015111) Bks Demand.

Comites Catulli: Structured Vocabulary Lists for Catullus 1-60. David D. Mulroy. LC 86-10984. 112p. (Orig.). (C). 1986. pap. text ed. 17.00 (*0-8191-5449-0*) U Pr of Amer.

Comlete Book of Wedding Music for Alto Saxophone. Paul Mickelson. 1993. 7.95 (*0-685-64581-9*, 94370) Mel Bay.

Comlete Prose of Woody Allen. Woody Allen. 528p. 1991. reprint ed. 11.99 (*0-517-07229-7*) Random Hse Value.

Comm. on Narcotic Drugs & Psychotropic Substances Act, 1985 with Allied State & Central Rules & Noti. 2nd ed. K. Kumar. (C). 1993. 150.00 (*81-7012-511-1*, Pub. by Eastern Book II) St Mut.

Comma. Barbara Gregorich. (Horizons II Ser.). (Illus.). 24p. (J). (gr. 3-4). 1980. student ed 3.50 (*0-89403-595-9*) EDC.

***Comma after Love: Selected Poems of Raeburn Miller.** Raeburn Miller. Ed. by Donald Justice et al. (Akron Series in Poetry). 107p. 1994. 24.95 (*1-884836-03-8*); pap. 12.95 (*1-884836-04-6*) U Akron Pr.

Comma in the Ear. Gene Frumkin. 160p. 1991. pap. 12.95 (*0-945953-03-8*) Living Batch Bks.

Commager on Tocqueville. Henry S. Commager. 144p. (C). 1993. text ed. 24.95 (*0-8262-0897-5*); pap. text ed. 12.95 (*0-8262-0941-6*) U of Mo Pr.

Commanches. Frank M. Meyers. 400p. 1987. reprint ed. 35.00 (*0-942211-95-2*) Olde Soldier Bks.

Command a King's Ship. large type ed. Alexander Kent. 528p. 1987. 23.95 (*0-7089-8440-1*, Trail West Pubs) Ulverscroft.

Command a King's Ship. Alexander Kent. 1993. reprint ed. lib. bdg. 25.95 (*1-56849-028-3*) Buccaneer Bks.

Command & Control for War & Peace. (Illus.). 237p. (Orig.). (C). 1994. pap. text ed. 45.00 (*0-7881-0825-5*) Diane Pub.

Command & Control of Nuclear Forces. Paul Bracken. LC 83-42874. 264p. 1985. reprint ed. pap. 16.00x (*0-300-03398-2*, Y-522) Yale U Pr.

Command & Control of Nuclear Weapons: A Workshop Report of the Aspen Institute for Humanistic Studies. Lori Esposito & James A. Schear. 38p. (C). 1986. reprint ed. pap. 10.50 (*0-8191-5399-0*, Aspen Strategy Group) U Pr of Amer.

Command & Control of Theater Forces: Adequacy. John H. Cushman. LC 85-9077. (Illus.). 272p. (C). 1985. reprint ed. 29.95 (*0-916159-06-X*) AFCEA Intl Pr.

Command & Control Support Systems in the Gulf War: Land Warfare: Brassey's Battlefield Weapons Systems & Technology. M. A. Rice & A. J. Sammes. Vol. 13. 1994. 40.00 (*1-85753-010-1*) Macmillan.

Command & Control Support Systems in the Gulf War: Land Warfare: Brassey's Battlefield Weapons Systems & Technology, Vol. 13. M. A. Rice & A. J. Sammes. 1994. 25.00 (*1-85753-015-2*, Pub. by Brasseys UK) Brasseys Inc.

Command & Leadership in the German Air Force. Richard Suchenwirth. Ed. by Harry Fletcher. (USAF Historical Studies: No. 174). 351p. 1969. pap. text ed. 37.95 (*0-89126-144-3*) MA-AH Pub.

Command & Leadership in the German Air Force. Richard Suchenwirth. LC 71-111598. (German Air Force in World War 2 Ser.). 1970. reprint ed. 24.95 (*0-405-00051-0*) Ayer.

Command at Sea. 4th ed. William P. Mack, Jr. & Albert H. Konetzni. LC 81-85469. (Illus.). 519p. 1982. 22.95 (*0-87021-130-7*) Naval Inst Pr.

Command Book. Stephen M. Silvers. Ed. by James J. Asher. (Illus.). 312p. (Orig.). 1988. pap. text ed. 14.95 (*0-940296-58-6*) Sky Oaks Prodns.

Command, Control & Communication. M. G. Slade & P. A. Ramsdale. (Brassey's Battlefield Weapons Systems & Technology Ser.: Vol. 6). 160p. 1983. text ed. 30.00 (*0-08-028332-2*, Pergamon Pr); pap. text ed. 14.95 (*0-08-028333-0*, Pergamon Pr) Elsevier.

Command, Control, & Communication Systems for Business Applicaiton. Gibson. 1995. text ed. 40.00 (*0-07-023578-3*) McGraw.

Command, Control, & Communications Systems Engineering. Walter R. Beam. (Illus.). 448p. 1989. text ed. 45.00 (*0-07-004249-7*) McGraw.

Command, Control, & the Common Defense. Carl K. Allard. 288p. (C). 1990. 37.50x (*0-300-04360-0*) Yale U Pr.

Command, Control, & the Common Defense. C. Kenneth Allard. 330p. (C). 1992. reprint ed. pap. text ed. 16.00 (*0-300-05229-4*) Yale U Pr.

Command, Control Communications & Management Information Systems. 255p. 1989. pap. 99.00 (*0-85296-380-7*, IC304) Inst Elect Eng.

Command Decision. William W. Haines. 1948. pap. 4.75 (*0-8222-0233-6*) Dramatists Play.

Command Decision & the Presidency: A Study in National Security Policy & Organization. Gordon Hoxie. 500p. 1977. 16.00 (*0-88349-162-1*) Ctr Study Presidency.

Command Decisions. Martin Blumenson et al. Ed. by Kent R. Greenfield. LC 59-60007. (Center for Military History Publication German Report Series, DA Pam: No. 70-7). (Illus.). 575p. 1984. reprint ed. pap. 18.00 (*0-16-001912-5*, 008-029-00071-7) USGPO.

***Command Decisions in World War II.** (Illus.). 575p. (Orig.). (C). 1994. pap. text ed. 49.95x (*0-7881-1202-3*) Diane Pub.

Command in Crisis. Joseph F. Bouchard. 1991. text ed. 47.50 (*0-231-07448-4*) Col U Pr.

Command in War. Martin Van Creveld. LC 84-12934. (Illus.). 352p. 1987. pap. text ed. 14.95 (*0-674-14441-4*) HUP.

Command Language Cookbook for Mainframes, Minicomputers, & PC's: DOS OS 2 Batch Language. Hallette German. 1992. pap. 51.95 (*0-442-00801-5*) Van Nos Reinhold.

Command-Level CICS Programming. Alex Varsegi. (Illus.). 336p. 1991. 39.95 (*0-8306-6705-9*, 3705) TAB Bks.

Command Level CICS Programming. Alex Varsegi. 1991. 39.95 (*0-07-067169-9*) McGraw.

Command Level COBOL Reference Guide. Mark Hanna & Suzan Hanna. (Illus.). (C). 1993. pap. 34.95 (*0-940479-01-X*) M Hanna & Assocs.

Command Missions. Lucian K. Truscott. 1990. 24.95 (*0-89141-364-2*) Presidio Pr.

Command Missions. Lucian K. Truscott, Jr. Ed. by Richard H. Kohn. LC 78-22401. (American Military Experience Ser.). (Illus.). 1980. reprint ed. lib. bdg. 42.95 (*0-405-11877-5*) Ayer.

Command of Observation Aviation: A Study in Control of Tactical Air Power. Robert F. Futrell. (USAF Historical Studies: No. 24). 44p. 1952. reprint ed. pap. text ed. 17.00 (*0-89126-016-1*) MA-AH Pub.

Command of the Air. Giulio Douhet. Tr. by Dino Ferrari. LC 72-4271. (World Affairs Ser.: National & International Viewpoints). 402p. 1979. reprint ed. 33.95 (*0-405-04567-0*) Ayer.

Command of the Air. Giulio Douhet et al. Ed. by Richard H. Kohn & Joseph P. Harahan. (USAF Warrior Studies). (C). 1983. reprint ed. pap. write for info. (*0-912799-10-2*) Off Air Force.

Command of the Howe Brothers During the American Revolution. Troyer S. Anderson. (History - United States Ser.). 368p. 1993. reprint ed. lib. bdg. 89.00 (*0-7812-4876-0*) Rprt Serv.

Command of the Howe Brothers During the American Revolution. Troyer S. Anderson. 1988. reprint ed. lib. bdg. 49.00 (*0-317-90018-8*) Rprt Serv.

Command of the Howe Brothers During the American Revolution. Troyer S. Anderson. LC 77-144861. 1971. reprint ed. 25.00 (*0-403-00816-6*) Scholarly.

Command of the King. large type ed. Mary Lide. (General Ser.). 1993. 21.95 (*0-7089-2554-5*) Ulverscroft.

Command of the Sea: The History & Strategy of Maritime Empires, 2 vols. Clark G. Reynolds. LC 83-6129. 358p. 1983. reprint ed. Vol. 2 358p. text ed. 31.50 (*0-89874-630-2*) Krieger.

Command of the Sea: The History & Strategy of Maritime Empires, No. 2. Clark G. Reynolds. LC 83-6129. 1983. reprint ed. 31.50 (*0-89874-629-9*) Krieger.

Command of the Sea: The History & Strategy of Maritime Empires, 2 vols., Set. Clark G. Reynolds. LC 83-6129. 1983. reprint ed. text ed. 64.50 (*0-89874-646-9*) Krieger.

Command of the Waters: Iron Triangles, Federal Water Development, & Indian Water. Daniel McCool. 321p. 1994. reprint ed. pap. 16.95 (*0-8165-1502-6*) U of Ariz Pr.

Command on the Western Front: The Military Career of Sir Henry Rawlinson, 1914-1918. Robin Prior & Trevor Wilson. 384p. (C). 1991. text ed. 44.95 (*0-631-16683-1*) Blackwell Pubs.

***Command or Control? Command, Training & Tactics in the British & German Armies, 1888-1918.** Martin Samuels. LC 95-7053. 1995. 30.00 (*0-7146-4570-2*, Pub. by F Cass Pubs UK) Intl Spec Bk.

Command Performance. Nora Roberts. (NR Flowers Ser.: No. 37). 1993. mass mkt. 3.59 (*0-373-51037-3*, 1-51037-9) Silhouette.

Command Performance: The Art of Delivering Quality Service. Pref. by John E. Martin. LC 94-16423. (Harvard Business Review Book Ser.). 1994. 27.95 (*0-87584-562-2*) Harvard Busn.

Command Performance: The Neglected Dimension of European Security. Paul B. Stares. 240p. 1991. 31.95 (*0-8157-8112-1*); pap. 12.95 (*0-8157-8111-3*) Brookings.

Command Post. Jim Grubbs. (Illus.). 32p. (Orig.). 1985. pap. 9.95 (*0-931387-23-X*) QSKY Pub.

***Command Reference (A-L) for Intel Processors (SVR4.2 MP)** UNIX Staff. 1024p. (C). 1994. pap. text ed. 65.00 (*0-13-158072-8*) P-H.

***Command Reference (M-Z) for Intel Processors (SVR4.2 MP)** UNIX Staff. (Illus.). 1104p. (C). 1994. pap. text ed. 65.00 (*0-13-158106-6*) P-H.

Command Sergeant Major's Interventions. Bobby Owens. LC 93-73657. (Illus.). 1995. 40.00 (*1-884308-07-4*); pap. text ed. 25.95 (*1-884308-08-2*) Enlisted Ldrship.

***Command Sergeants Major Spouse's Notes.** Dorothy V. Owens. (Illus.). 190p. (Orig.). 1995. pap. text ed. 6.95 (*1-884308-25-2*) Enlisted Ldrship.

***Command Sergeants Major Spouse's Notes.** Dorothy V. Owens. (Illus.). 190p. (Orig.). 1995. 15.95 (*1-884308-24-4*) Enlisted Ldrship.

Command the Morning. Jo A. Mills. 1989. pap. 6.25 (*0-89137-453-1*) Quality Pubns.

Commandant of Solitude: Journals of Captain Collet Barker 1784-1831. Ed. by D. J. Mulvaney. 1992. 44.95 (*0-522-84472-3*) Intl Spec Bk.

***Commanded Blessing: Overtaken by God's Provision for a Life Without Lack, Acts 4:34.** Rod Parsley. 212p. (Orig.). 1994. pap. 8.99 (*1-880244-17-9*) Wrld Harvest Church.

Commanded to Live. Harold Kushner. LC 73-91738. 1973. 10.95 (*0-87677-154-1*) Hartmore.

Commander. Paul Ader. 1985. 20.00 (*0-946270-19-8*, Pub. by Pentland Pr UK); pap. 15.00 (*0-946270-21-X*, Pub. by Pentland Pr UK) St Mut.

Commander. Vladimir Karpov. 245p. 1987. 49.50 (*0-08-036261-3*, Pub. by Brasseys UK) Brasseys Inc.

Commander: An Autobiography. Eddy F. Steele. 1992. 8.95 (*0-533-09429-1*) Vantage.

Commander in Chief - Franklin Delano Roosevelt: His Lieutenants & Their War. Eric Larrabee. 1988. pap. 16.95 (*0-671-66382-8*, Touchstone Bks) S&S Trade.

Commander Mark's New Secret City Adventures. Mark Kistler. (Illus.). 256p. (Orig.). 1993. pap. 14.00 (*0-671-78131-6*, Fireside) S&S Trade.

Commander of Dead Leaves. Stanley Noyes. (Poetry Ser.). 80p. (Orig.). 1985. pap. 6.00 (*0-940510-10-3*) Tooth of Time.

Commander of the Armada: A Life of the Seventh Duke of Medina Sidonia, 1549-1615. Peter Pierson. LC 89-5258. 312p. (C). 1989. 35.00 (*0-300-04408-9*) Yale U Pr.

Commander of the Faithful: The Moroccan Political Elite-a Study in Segmented Politics. John Waterbury. LC 76-108417. (Modern Middle East Ser.: Vol. 2). 386p. reprint ed. 110.10 (*0-8357-9061-4*, 2011661) Bks Demand.

Commander the Gander. David McKelvey. LC 84-72455. (Illus.). 48p. (J). (gr. 4-6). 1984. lib. bdg. 10.95 (*0-931722-31-4*); pap. 3.95 (*0-931722-30-6*) Corona Pub.

Commander Toad & the Big Black Hole. Jane Yolen. LC 82-23524. (Illus.). (J). (gr. 1-4). 1983. pap. 6.95 (*0-698-20594-4*, Coward) Putnam Pub Group.

Commander Toad & the Dis-Asteroid. Jane Yolen. LC 84-1897. (Commander Toad Bks.). (Illus.). 64p. (J). (gr. 4). 1985. pap. 6.95 (*0-698-20620-7*, Coward) Putnam Pub Group.

Commander Toad & the Intergalactic Spy. Jane Yolen. (Commander Toad Bks.). (Illus.). 64p. (J). (ps-4). 1986. pap. 6.95 (*0-698-20623-1*, Coward) Putnam Pub Group.

Commander Toad & the Planet of the Grapes. Jane Yolen. (Break-of-Day Book Ser.). (Illus.). 64p. (J). (gr. 1-4). 1982. pap. 6.95 (*0-698-20540-5*, Coward) Putnam Pub Group.

Commander Toad & the Space Pirates. Jane Yolen. (Illus.). 64p. (J). (gr. 1-4). 1987. pap. 6.95 (*0-698-20633-9*, Coward) Putnam Pub Group.

Commander Toad in Space. Jane Yolen. (Break-of-Day Book Ser.). (Illus.). 64p. (J). (gr. 3-5). 1980. pap. 6.95 (*0-698-20522-7*, Coward) Putnam Pub Group.

Commanders. Bob Woodward. Ed. by Julie Rubenstein. 640p. 1992. reprint ed. mass mkt. 5.99 (*0-671-76960-X*, Pocket Star Bks) PB.

Commanders & Chiefs: A Brief History of Fort McDowell, Arizona (1865-1890), Its Officers & Men & the Indians They Were Ordered to Subdue. Elaine Waterstrat. (Illus.). 116p. (Orig.). 1993. pap. 6.95 (*0-9636649-0-5*) Mt McDowell Pr.

Commander's Handbook for Water Usage in Desert Operations. 1991. lib. bdg. 74.00 (*0-8490-4203-8*) Gordon Pr.

Commanders in Chief: Presidential Leadership in Modern Wars. Ed. by Joseph G. Dawson, III. LC 92-30601. (Modern War Studies). (Illus.). 240p. 1993. 29.95 (*0-7006-0578-9*); pap. 12.95 (*0-7006-0579-7*) U Pr of KS.

Commanders of the Army of the Potomac. Warren W. Hassler, Jr. LC 79-14217. (Illus.). 281p. 1980. reprint ed. text ed. 59.50 (*0-313-21976-1*, HACR, Greenwood Pr) Greenwood.

Commander's Palace New Orleans Cookbook. Ella Brennan & Dick Brennan. (Illus.). 224p. 1984. 19.00 (*0-517-55049-0*, C P Pubs) Crown Pub Group.

***Commanding Generals & Chiefs of Staff 1775-1983: Portraits & Biographical Sketches of the United States Armys Senior Officers.** (Illus.). 1995. lib. bdg. 299.95 (*0-8490-6627-1*) Gordon Pr.

Commanding Generals & Chiefs of Staff, 1775-1987: Portraits & Biographical Sketches of the United States Army's Senior Officer. LC 85-11829. 1987. 20.00 (*0-16-001932-X*, S/N 008-029-001) USGPO.

Commanding Heights & Community Control: New Economics for a New South Africa. Patrick Bond. 92p. (Orig.). (C). 1992. pap. text ed. 11.95 (*0-86975-407-6*, Pub. by Ravan Pr ZA) Ohio U Pr.

Commanding Power. Kenneth Hagin, Jr. 1985. pap. 0.75 (*0-89276-719-7*) Hagin Ministries.

Commanding Self. Idries Shah. 380p. 1994. 27.00 (*0-86304-066-7*, Pub. by Octagon Pr UK) ISHK Bk Service.

Commanding Sentences. 3rd ed. Helen Mills. 378p. 1990. reprint ed. pap. text ed. 22.95 (*0-88133-524-X*) Sheffield WI.

Commanding WordStar Professional Release 4.0. William W. Pitts. (Illus.). 310p. 1988. pap. 16.95 (*0-8306-2983-1*, 2983P) TAB Bks.

Commanding WordStar Release 7.0. 2nd ed. William W. Pitts. (Illus.). 368p. 1992. pap. 29.95 (*0-8306-3970-5*, 4154, Windcrest) TAB Bks.

Commanding WordStar, Release 7.0. 2nd ed. William W. Pitts. 1993. pap. 29.95 (*0-07-050206-4*) McGraw.

Commandment & Community: New Essays in Jewish Legal & Political Philosophy. Ed. by Daniel H. Frank. LC 94-18406. (SUNY Series in Jewish Philosophy). 288p. (C). 1995. text ed. 59.50 (*0-7914-2429-4*); pap. text ed. 19.95 (*0-7914-2430-8*) State U NY Pr.

Commandments & Concerns. Michael Rosenak. 320p. 1987. 37.50 (*0-8276-0279-0*) JPS Phila.

Commandments at Eleven. Gilbert Allen. LC 94-6556. 80p. (Orig.). 1994. pap. write for info. (*0-914061-46-1*) Orchises Pr.

Commandments for Relationships & Marriage. Lance Martin. Ed. by Edythe Cooper. (Illus.). 216p. 19.95 (*0-317-02260-1*) Pleasure Trove.

Commandments of Maimonides, 2 vols. Tr. by C. B. Chavel. 305p. (HEB.). 1967. pap. 25.00 (*0-317-00899-4*) Soncino Pr.

Commando: Memoirs of a Fighting Commando in World War II. John Durnford-Slater. (Illus.). 222p. 1991. 23.95 (*1-55750-125-4*) Naval Inst Pr.

Commando: Morgan's Mercenaries. Lindsay McKenna. (Silhouette Special Edition Ser.). 1993. mass mkt. 3.50 (*0-373-09830-8*, 5-09830-6) Silhouette.

***Commando: Survival of the Fittest.** Robin Eggar. (Illus.). 242p. 1995. 40.00 (*0-7195-5305-9*, Pub. by John Murray UK) Trafalgar.

Commando Attack. Alan Marks. 256p. (Orig.). 1986. reprint ed. pap. 2.95 (*0-8439-2419-5*) Dorchester Pub Co.

***Commando Brigade 3000.** Martin H. Greenberg. Ed. by Charles Waugh. 224p. (Orig.). 1994. pap. text ed. 4.99 (*0-441-00108-4*) Ace Bks.

Commando Crusade, 1943-44. Thomas Churchill. (C). 1986. text ed. 140.00 (*0-685-38781-X*, Pub. by Maritime Bks UK) St Mut.

Commando Dagger: The Complete Illustrated History of the Fairbairn-Sykes Fighting Knife. Leroy Thompson. (Illus.). 176p. 1985. pap. 25.00 (*0-87364-311-9*) Paladin Pr.

Commando Diary. Ed. by Tag Barnes. 144p. (C). 1991. 95.00 (*0-946771-53-7*, Pub. by Spellmount UK) St Mut.

Commando Diary (WW2) Spellmount Ltd. Publishers Staff. (C). 1986. 110.00 (*0-685-60223-0*, Pub. by Spellmount UK) St Mut.

Commando Extraordinary. Charles Foley. (War & Warriors Ser.). (Illus.). 244p. 1988. 14.95 (*0-939482-07-X*) Noontide.

Commando Fighting Techniques. Jim Wilson & Paul Evans. 144p. (Orig.). 1983. pap. 10.95 (*0-86568-103-1*, 632) Unique Pubns.

Commando Fighting Techniques. rev. ed. Jim Wilson & Paul Evans. (Illus.). 156p. (Orig.). 1984. pap. 12.00 (*0-87364-381-X*) Paladin Pr.

Commando Operations. Time-Life Books Staff. (New Face of War Ser.). (Illus.). 160p. 1991. lib. bdg. write for info. (*0-8094-8617-2*) Time-Life.

Commando Windows Programming: Fast & Easy Programming Solutions in C. Al Williams. LC 93-24862. 1993. pap. 27.95 (*0-201-62484-2*) Addison-Wesley.

Commandos. Elliot Arnold. 304p. reprint ed. pap. 2.75 (*0-8439-2009-2*) Dorchester Pub Co.

Commandos: The Making of America's Secret Soldiers, from Training to Desert Storm. Douglas C. Waller. LC 93-27088. 1994. 23.00 (*0-671-78717-9*) S&S Trade.

Commandos & Politicians: Elite Military Units in Modern Democracies. Eliot A. Cohen. 136p. 1984. reprint ed. lib. bdg. 36.00 (*0-8191-4060-0*); reprint ed. pap. text ed. 16.00 (*0-8191-4061-9*) U Pr of Amer.

Commands. Marie-Jose Shaw. (English Sound Filmstrip Kits Ser.). (gr. 3). 1979. teacher ed 34.00 (*0-8209-0466-X*, FCW3E-13) ESP.

Commands Dictionary for Microsoft Word. David Sangard. (Commands Dictionaries Ser.). 111p. 1988. pap. 19.95 (*0-929475-00-3*) Brookes Commands Dictionaries.

Commas Are Our Friends. Joe Devine. 1991. pap. 4.99 (*0-8041-0868-4*) Ivy Books.

Commas Are Our Friends: The Easy, Enjoyable Way to Master Grammar & Punctuation. Joe Devine. Ed. by Rita Hayes. (Illus.). 280p. (Orig.). 1989. pap. 11.95 (*1-882010-07-8*) Green Stone Pubns.

Comme l'Eau Qui Coule, Anna Soror, un Homme Obscur. Marguerite Yourcenar. (FRE.). 1982. 45.00 (*0-7859-0551-0*, 207021706X) Fr & Eur.

Comme par Hasard. Goscinny Sempe. (FRE.). 1989. pap. 10.95 (*0-8288-3781-3*, F123780) Fr & Eur.

Comme Si de Rien n'Etait. Marie Cardinal. (FRE.). 1992. pap. 10.95 (*0-7859-3168-6*, 2253059188) Fr & Eur.

Commedia Dell'Arte. rev. ed. Winifred Smith. LC 64-14715. (Illus.). 1972. 33.95 (*0-405-08984-8*, Pub. by Blom Pubns UK) Ayer.

Commedia dell'Arte: A Documentary History. Kenneth Richards & Laura Richards. (Illus.). 370p. 1989. text ed. 74.95 (*0-631-19590-4*) Blackwell Pubs.

Commedia Dell'Arte: A Scene Study Book. Bari Rolfe. LC 77-73190. (Illus.). 100p. (gr. 9-12). 1977. pap. 7.50 (*0-932456-00-6*) Personabks.

Commedia Dell'arte from the Renaissance to Dario Fo: The Italian Origins of European Theatre VI. Ed. by Christopher Cairns. LC 89-13576. (Illus.). 472p. 1989. lib. bdg. 109.95 (*0-88946-080-9*) E Mellen.

Commedia dell'Arte in the Twentieth Century. John Rudlin. LC 93-13426. 1994. write for info. (*0-415-04769-2*); pap. write for info. (*0-415-04770-6*) Routledge.

Commemoration of the Fortieth Anniversary of the United Nations: Statements & Messages. 380p. 1986. 60.00 (*92-1-100289-3*, 86.I.6) UN.

Commemoration of the Hero 1800-1846: Monuments to the British Victors of the Napoleonic Wars. Alison Yarrington. LC 87-30055. (Outstanding Dissertations in the Fine Arts Ser.). (Illus.). 444p. 1988. 27.00 (*0-8240-0097-8*) Garland.

Commemorations: The Politics of National Identity. Ed. by John R. Gillis. LC 93-15827. 288p. 1994. text ed. 35.00 (*0-691-03200-9*) Princeton U Pr.

Commemorative Biographical Record of Dutchess County, NY. (Illus.). 950p. 1994. reprint ed. lib. bdg. 95.00 (*0-8328-3911-6*) Higginson Bk Co.

Commemorative Biographical Record of Washington County, Pennsylvania. (Illus.). 1486p. 1993. reprint ed. lib. bdg. 149.00 (*0-8328-3114-X*) Higginson Bk Co.

Commemorative Biographical Record of Wayne County, Ohio. (Illus.). 608p. 1993. reprint ed. lib. bdg. 62.00 (*0-8328-3223-5*) Higginson Bk Co.

***Commemorative Biographical Records of the Counties of Harrison & Carroll, Illinois.** (Illus.). 1150p. 1994. lib. bdg. 115.00 (*0-8328-4368-7*) Higginson Bk Co.

Commemorative Coins of the United States: A Complete Encyclopedia. Q. David Bowers. (Illus.). 768p. 1991. 75.00 (*0-943161-36-3*); text ed. 49.95 (*0-943161-35-5*); pap. text ed. 39.95 (*0-943161-34-7*) Bowers & Merena.

Commemorative Coins of the United States: Identification & Price Guide. Anthony Swiatek. 304p. (Orig.). 1993. pap. 16.00 (*0-380-77439-9*, Confident Collect) Avon.

C

An Asterisk (*) at the beginning of an entry indicates that the title is appearing in BIP for the first time.

Commemorative Historical & Biographical Record of Wood County, Ohio. Intro. by C. W. Evers. (Illus.). 1386p. 1993. reprint ed. lib. bdg. 135.00 (*0-8328-3454-8*) Higginson Bk Co.

Commemorative History of the Cambridge Public Library. Edward G. Doyle. LC 89-17441. 120p. (Orig.). 1989. pap. 6.95 (*0-9623982-0-9*) Cambridge Pub Lib.

Commemorative List of the Departed Servants of Orthodoxy in North America. Ed. by Department of History & Archives Staff. LC 92-90727. 88p. 1992. pap. 6.00 (*0-86642-051-7*, C11) Ortho Church Am.

Commemorative Tributes of the Academy, 1905-1941. American Academy of Arts & Letters Staff. LC 68-20286. (Essay Index Reprint Ser.). 1977. 23.95 (*0-8369-0147-9*) Ayer.

Commemorative Volume: 1945-1973. 374p. 1977. 10.00 (*0-318-14749-1*); 6.00 (*0-930282-01-9*) Lepidopterists.

Commemorative Volume in Honour of Prof. Streiff. Ed. by M. J. Roper-Hall et al. (Advances in Ophthalmology Ser.: Vol. 36). (Illus.). (FRE & GER.). 1978. 150.50 (*3-8055-2828-0*) S Karger.

Commencement of Laytime. 2nd ed. Donald Davies. 1992. 90.00 (*1-85044-147-2*) Lloyds London Pr.

Commencement Parts: Valedictories, Salutatories, Orations, Essays, Class Poems, Ivy Orations, Toasts. Ed. by Harry C. Davis. LC 74-152149. (Granger Index Reprint Ser.). 1977. reprint ed. 31.95 (*0-8369-6252-4*) Ayer.

***Commencements d'une Vie.** Francois Mauriac. 1932. 15.95 (*0-7859-5273-X*) Fr & Eur.

Commensurabilities among Lattices in PU (1,n) Pierre Deligne & G. Daniel Mostow. (Annals of Mathematics Studies: No. 132). 176p. 1993. text ed. 49.50 (*0-691-03385-4*); pap. text ed. 19.95 (*0-691-00096-4*) Princeton U Pr.

Commensurate - Incommensurate; Crystallography in the Life Sciences; Corrections: Accelerated Convergence Treatment of R-N Lattice Sums: A Special Issue of the Journal Crystallography Reviews. E. F. Bertaut et al. 62p. 1990. pap. text ed. 40.00 (*2-88124-743-1*) Gordon & Breach.

Commensurate & Incommensurate Phase Transitions. J. Kocinski. (Phase Transition Phenomena Ser.: No. 3). 420p. 1990. write for info. (*0-444-98775-4*) Elsevier.

Comment C'est. Samuel Beckett. 180p. (FRE.). 1961. pap. 19.95 (*0-7859-0593-6*, F86010) Fr & Eur.

Comment Creer une PME aux U. S. A. Laurent R. Martres. (Illus.). 144p. (Orig.). (FRE.). 1984. pap. 9.95 (*0-916189-00-7*) Graphie Intl.

Comment Dieu A-T-Il Pu Permett. Jim Long. 160p. (FRE.). 1991. 4.95 (*0-8297-1496-0*) Life Pubs Intl.

Comment Fais-Tu l'Amour, Cerise? Rene Fallet. 320p. (FRE.). 1982. pap. 11.95 (*0-7859-2310-1*, 2070363813) Fr & Eur.

Comment Immigrer aux U. S. A. Les Affaires en Amerique. Larry J. Behar. 296p. 1993. pap. text ed. 19.95 (*0-9637164-1-7*) L J Behar.

Comment Je Crois. Pierre Teilhard De Chardin. (FRE.). pap. 24.95 (*0-7859-1245-2*, 2020028662) Fr & Eur.

Comment Jouer le Balcon see Oeuvres Completes

Comment Jouer les Bonnes see Oeuvres Completes

Comment Obelix est Tombe dans la Marmite. Rene De Goscinny & A. Uderzo. (FRE.). 1992. 19.95 (*0-7859-1050-6*, 0-340-517727) Fr & Eur.

Comment Peut-On Etre Francais? Virginia Hules & Jane Baier. (FRE.). 1982. pap. text ed. 22.75 (*0-03-058674-7*) HB Coll Pubs.

Comment Presenter Un Texte Philosophique. Louis-Emile Blanchet. 166p. (FRE.). reprint ed. pap. 47.40 (*0-317-08034-2*, 2022666) Bks Demand.

Comment S'Exprimer en Francais. C. Georgin. 12.95 (*0-7859-0630-4*, F134870) Fr & Eur.

Comment une Figue de Paroles et Pourquoi. Francis Ponge. 213p. (FRE.). 1977. pap. 24.95 (*0-7859-1440-4*, 2082120023) Fr & Eur.

Comment Wang-Fo Fut Sauve. Marguerite Yourcenar. 32p. (FRE.). 1979. 10.95 (*0-7859-0552-9*, 207058075X) Fr & Eur.

Comment Wang-Fo Fut Sauve. Marguerite Yourcenar. (Folio - Cadet Rouge Ser.: No. 178). (Illus.). 48p. (FRE.). (J). (gr. 3-7). 1990. pap. 7.95 (*2-07-031178-3*) Schoenhof.

Commentaire D'Alexandre D'Aphrodise aux "Seconds Analytiques" D'Aristote. Paul Moraux. (Peripatoi Ser.). (C). 1979. text ed. 78.50 (*3-11-007805-8*) De Gruyter.

Commentaire des Protocoles Additionnels du 8 Juin 1977 aux Conventions de Geneve du 12 Aout 1949. Ed. by Claude Pilloud et al. 1986. lib. bdg. 297.50 (*90-247-3403-7*) Kluwer Ac.

***Commentaire sur le Manuel d'Epictete: Introduction, Texte Grec et Apparat Critique par I. Hadot.** Simplicius. 753p. (FRE & GRE.). 1994. 171.50 (*90-04-09772-4*) E J Brill.

Commentaires. Monluc. (FRE.). 1964. lib. bdg. 99.50 (*0-8288-3567-5*, F30400) Fr & Eur.

Commentar Zu Kants Kritik der Reinen Vernunft, 2 vols. Hans Vaihinger. Ed. by Lewis W. Beck. Incl. Vol. 1. Stuttgart 1881. LC 75-32048. 1976. (*0-318-52423-6*); Vol. 2. Stuttgart & Berlin 1892. LC 75-32048. 1976. (*0-318-52424-4*); LC 75-32048. (Philosophy of Immanual Kant Ser.: Vol. 8). 1976. reprint ed. Set. Set lib. bdg. 80.00 (*0-8240-2332-3*) Garland.

Commentar Zu Zamachsaris Mufassal, 2 vols. Ibn Jais. 1515p. reprint ed. write for info. (*0-318-71522-8*, Pub. by Georg Olms GW) Lubrecht & Cramer.

Commentaria in Libros Hippocratis. Giovanni Marinelli. 280p. reprint ed. write for info. (*0-318-72047-7*, Pub. by Georg Olms GW) Lubrecht & Cramer.

Commentaries by the Inner Christ Circle. Julia R. Pogue & Eileen M. Jones. 157p. (Orig.). 1989. pap. 7.95 (*0-9622814-0-9*) Anonymous & Assocs.

Commentaries in Plant Science. Ed. by Harry Smith. LC 76-7531. 272p. 1976. 127.00 (*0-08-019759-0*, Pub. by Pergamon Repr UK) Franklin.

Commentaries in Plant Science, Vol. 2. Ed. by Harold Smith. LC 80-41007. (Illus.). 250p. 1981. 117.00 (*0-08-025898-0*, Pub. by Pergamon Repr UK) Franklin.

Commentaries in the Neurosciences. A. D. Smith et al. (Illus.). 702p. 1980. 280.00 (*0-08-025501-9*, Pub. by Pergamon Repr UK) Franklin.

Commentaries of Caesar, Translated into English, 2 vols. C. Julius Caesar. LC 77-161798. (Augustan Translators Ser.). reprint ed. 135.00 (*0-404-54104-6*) AMS Pr.

Commentaries of Proclus on the Timaeus of Plato: A Treasury of Pythagoric & Platonic Physiology, 5 bks., Set. Tr. by Thomas Taylor. 970p. 1993. reprint ed. pap. 75.00 (*1-56459-349-5*) Kessinger Pub.

Commentaries of the Emperor Marcus Antoninus: Containing His Maxims of Science & Rules of Life, Wrote for His Own Use & Address'd to Himself. Marcus Aurelius. LC 77-158297. (Augustan Translators Ser.). reprint ed. 49.50 (*0-404-54103-8*) AMS Pr.

Commentaries of U. P. Nagar Mahapalika Act, 1959. Surendra Malik. 818p. 1985. 345.00 (*0-317-54839-5*) St Mut.

Commentaries on "A Course in Miracles" Tara Singh. LC 91-58161. 304p. 1992. pap. 13.00 (*0-06-250783-4*) Harper SF.

Commentaries on a Creative Encounter: Proceedings of a Conference on the Culture & Literature of Francophone Africa, Held on October 3, 1987, at Buffalo State College. Intro. by Keith E. Baird. (Orig.). (FRE.). (C). 1988. pap. text ed. write for info. (*0-9621537-0-2*) NY AAI.

Commentaries on Administrative Tribunals Act, 1985. K. N. Goyal. (C). 1990. 135.00 (*0-89771-323-0*) St Mut.

Commentaries on American Law, 4 vols. 12th ed. James Kent. Ed. by O. W. Holmes, Jr. 1989. reprint ed. lib. bdg. 295.00 (*0-8377-2338-8*) Rothman.

Commentaries on American Law, 4 Vols, Set. J. Kent. LC 78-75290. (American Constitutional & Legal History Ser). 1971. reprint ed. lib. bdg. 245.00 (*0-306-71293-8*) Da Capo.

Commentaries on American Law, 4 vols., Set. James Kent. (Historical Writings in Jurisprudence & Classical Legal Literature Ser.). 1984. reprint ed. lib. bdg. 275.00 (*0-89941-339-0*, 303430) W S Hein.

Commentaries on Banking Regulation. John D. Hawke. 524p. 1985. write for info. (*0-318-65470-9*, H43643) P-H.

Commentaries on Colonial & Foreign Laws Generally & in Their Conflict with Each Other & with the Law of England, 4 Vols. in 5 Bks. William Burge. Ed. by Alexander W. Renton et al. LC 80-84956. (Historical Writings in Law & Jurisprudence Ser.: No. 17, Bks. 21-25). 1981. reprint ed. Vol. 4, Pt. 1. write for info. (*0-89941-076-6*); reprint ed. Vol. 4, Pt. 2. write for info. (*0-318-56353-3*) W S Hein.

Commentaries on Colonial & Foreign Laws Generally & in Their Conflict with Each Other & with the Law of England, 4 Vols. in 5 Bks., 1. William Burge. Ed. by Alexander W. Renton et al. LC 80-84956. (Historical Writings in Law & Jurisprudence Ser.: No. 17, Bks. 21-25). 1981. reprint ed. write for info. (*0-89941-073-1*) W S Hein.

Commentaries on Colonial & Foreign Laws Generally & in Their Conflict with Each Other & with the Law of England, 4 Vols. in 5 Bks., 2. William Burge. Ed. by Alexander W. Renton et al. LC 80-84956. (Historical Writings in Law & Jurisprudence Ser.: No. 17, Bks. 21-25). 1981. reprint ed. write for info. (*0-89941-074-X*) W S Hein.

Commentaries on Colonial & Foreign Laws Generally & in Their Conflict with Each Other & with the Law of England, 4 Vols. in 5 Bks., 3. William Burge. Ed. by Alexander W. Renton et al. LC 80-84956. (Historical Writings in Law & Jurisprudence Ser.: No. 17, Bks. 21-25). 1981. reprint ed. write for info. (*0-89941-075-8*) W S Hein.

Commentaries on Colonial & Foreign Laws Generally & in Their Conflict with Each Other & with the Law of England, 4 Vols. in 5 Bks., Set. William Burge. Ed. by R. H. Helmholz et al. LC 80-84956. (Historical Writings in Law & Jurisprudence Ser.: No. 17, Bks. 21-25). 1981. reprint ed. lib. bdg. 315.00 (*0-89941-186-X*, 302100) W S Hein.

Commentaries on Contract Labour. K. D. Srivastava. (C). 1992. 250.00 (*0-89771-787-2*, Pub. by Eastern Book II) St Mut.

Commentaries on Contract Labour (Regulation & Abolition) Act, 1970. K. D. Srivastava. 520p. 1982. 210.00 (*0-317-57711-5*) St Mut.

Commentaries on Contract Labour (Regulation & Abolition) Act, 1970. 4th rev. ed. K. D. Srivastava. (C). 1970. 125.00 (*0-685-25162-4*) St Mut.

Commentaries on Contract Labour (Regulation & Abolition) Act, 1970. 4th suppl. ed. G. Saran. (C). 1989. 75.00 (*0-685-38618-X*) St Mut.

Commentaries on Contract Labour (Regulation & Abolition) Act, 1970. 5th ed. K. D. Srivastava. (C). 1992. 125.00 (*81-7012-460-3*, Pub. by Eastern Book II) St Mut.

Commentaries on Contract Labour (Regulation & Abolition) Act, 1970: With Supplement. 4th rev. ed. Ed. by K. D. Srivastava. (C). 1989. 140.00 (*0-685-39761-0*) St Mut.

Commentaries on Corporate Structure & Governance. Ed. by Donald E. Schwartz. 574p. 1979. 20.00 (*0-686-27219-6*, B164) Am Law Inst.

Commentaries on Delhi Apartment Ownership Act, 1986: With Supplement. Ed. by A. S. Rao. (C). 1989. 90.00 (*0-685-47808-4*) St Mut.

Commentaries on Dhammapada. The Mother. 118p. 5.00 (*81-7058-133-8*) Aurobindo Assn.

Commentaries on Dissolution of Muslim Marriage Act. A. A. Qadri. 137p. 1961. 40.00 (*0-317-54678-3*) St Mut.

Commentaries on Dowry Prohibition Act, 1961: Together with Guroodas Banerjee's Tagore Law Lectures on Law of Streedhan, 1988 with Supplement. Ed. by B. P. Beri. (C). 1990. 90.00 (*0-685-39728-9*) St Mut.

Commentaries on Drugs & Cosmetics Act, Rules & Forms. S. N. Saxena. (C). 1990. 125.00 (*0-89771-171-8*) St Mut.

Commentaries on Employees Providence Funds & Miscellaneous Provisions Act, 1952: Together with Schemes & Notifications. 6th rev. ed. K. D. Srivastava. (C). 1989. 175.00 (*0-685-39643-6*) St Mut.

Commentaries on Employees Provident Funds & Miscellaneous Provisions Act. 7th ed. K. D. Srivastava. (C). 1993. 150.00 (*81-7012-501-4*, Pub. by Eastern Book II) St Mut.

Commentaries on Employees Provident Funds & Miscellaneous Provisions Act, 1952. Ed. by K. D. Srivastava. (C). 1991. 240.00 (*0-89771-689-2*) St Mut.

Commentaries on Employees State Insurance Act, with Rules & Regulations, 1948. K. D. Scrivastava. (C). 1990. 160.00 (*0-89771-327-3*) St Mut.

Commentaries on Employees State Insurance Act, 1948. K. D. Srivastava. 1979. 45.00 (*0-317-57710-7*) St Mut.

Commentaries on Employees State Insurance Act, 1948. K. D. Srivastava. (C). 1986. 85.00 (*0-685-38610-4*) St Mut.

Commentaries on Employees State Insurance Act 1948. 3rd ed. K. D. Srivastava. (C). 1990. With supplement 1990. 170.00 (*0-685-36434-8*) St Mut.

Commentaries on Employees State Insurance Act, 1948. 4th ed. K. D. Srivastava. (C). 1991. 95.00 (*0-685-39649-5*) St Mut.

Commentaries on Employees State Insurance Act, 1948: With Rules & Regulations by. Ed. by K. D. Srivastava. (C). 1991. 285.00 (*0-89771-690-6*) St Mut.

Commentaries on Employees State Insurance Act, 1948, with Rules & Regulations. 4th ed. K. D. Srivastava. (C). 1993. 150.00 (*81-7012-437-9*, Pub. by Eastern Book II) St Mut.

Commentaries on Employees State Insurance Act, 1986: With Supplement. 3rd ed. K. D. Srivastava. (C). 1990. reprint ed. 175.00 (*0-685-39720-3*) St Mut.

Commentaries on Equity & Jurisprudence, As Administered in England & America, 2 vols. Joseph Story. LC 78-37987. (American Law Ser.). 1564p. 1972. reprint ed. 96.95 (*0-405-04029-6*) Ayer.

Commentaries on Equity & Jurisprudence, As Administered in England & America, 2 vols., 1. Joseph Story. LC 78-37987. (American Law Ser.). 1564p. 1972. reprint ed. 48.95 (*0-405-04030-X*) Ayer.

Commentaries on Equity & Jurisprudence, As Administered in England & America, 2 vols., 2. Joseph Story. LC 78-37987. (American Law Ser.). 1564p. 1972. reprint ed. 48.95 (*0-405-04031-8*) Ayer.

Commentaries on Equity Jurisprudence As Administered in England & America, 2 vols., Set. 12th ed. Joseph Story. LC 12-38995. (Historical Reprints in Jurisprudence & Classical Legal Literature Ser.). 1984. reprint ed. lib. bdg. 105.00 (*0-89941-341-2*, 303450) W S Hein.

Commentaries on Equity Jurisprudence, As Administered in England & America, 2 vols., Set. 13th ed. Joseph Story. 1988. reprint ed. Vol. 1, cxiii, 689 pgs.; Vol. 2, 947 pgs. lib. bdg. 97.50 (*0-8377-2618-2*) Rothman.

Commentaries on Essential Commodities ACT with Control Orders. D. P. Varshni. (C). 1988. 250.00 (*0-685-36410-0*) St Mut.

Commentaries on Essential Commodities Act, with Control Orders, 1988. D. P. Varshni. (With Supplement Ser.). (C). 1990. 275.00 (*0-685-39715-7*) St Mut.

Commentaries on Essential Commodities Act, with Control Orders, 1988 with Supplement. (C). 1990. text ed. 275.00 (*0-89771-519-5*) St Mut.

Commentaries on Essential Commodities Act, 1955 with Control Order. D. P. Varshni. (C). 1988. 250.00 (*0-685-25673-1*) St Mut.

Commentaries on Evidence Act. 4th ed. V. B. Raju. (C). 1991. 110.00 (*0-685-39711-4*) St Mut.

Commentaries on Factories Act, 1948. K. D. Srivastava. (C). 1990. text ed. 225.00 (*0-89771-512-8*) St Mut.

Commentaries on Factories Act, 1948. K. D. Srivastava. (C). 1992. 275.00 (*0-89771-795-3*, Pub. by Eastern Book II) St Mut.

Commentaries on Factories Act, 1988: With Supplement. 4th ed. K. D. Srivastava. (C). 1990. reprint ed. 225.00 (*0-685-39646-0*) St Mut.

Commentaries on G. I. Gurdjieff's All & Everything. A. R. Orage. Ed. by C. S. Nott. 100p. 1985. 14.95 (*0-89756-015-9*) Two Rivers.

Commentaries on Gambling Acts in India. A. P. Mathur. 513p. 1973. 110.00 (*0-317-54717-8*) St Mut.

Commentaries on Gambling Acts in India, 1973: With Supplement. 2nd rev. ed. Ed. by A. P. Mathur. (C). 1990. 50.00 (*0-685-39695-9*) St Mut.

Commentaries on Indian Easements Act, 1882. P. S. Narayana. (C). 1988. 100.00 (*0-685-36513-1*) St Mut.

Commentaries on Industrial Disputes Act, 1947. K. D. Scivastava. 1590p. 1985. 750.00 (*0-317-57712-3*) St Mut.

Commentaries on Industrial Disputes Act, 1947. 6th ed. K. D. Srivastava. (C). 1985. 125.00 (*0-685-38617-1*); 250.00 (*0-685-39648-7*) St Mut.

Commentaries on Industrial Employment Standing Orders Act, 1946. K. D. Srivastava. (C). 1990. 125.00 (*0-89771-322-2*) St Mut.

Commentaries on Industrial Employment, Standing Orders Act, 1946. Ed. by K. D. Srivastava. (C). 1991. 250.00 (*0-89771-686-8*) St Mut.

Commentaries on Industrial Employment Standing Orders Act, 1946: (Including Model Standing Orders, Recognition of Unions & Unfair Labour Practices) 2nd ed. Ed. by K. D. Srivastava. (C). 1991. 110.00 (*0-685-39647-9*) St Mut.

Commentaries on Industrial Employment Standing Orders Act, 1946 (Including Model Standing Orders Recognition of Unions & Unfair Labour Practices) K. D. Srivastava. 844p. 1982. 285.00 (*0-317-57713-1*) St Mut.

Commentaries on Industrial Employment Standing Orders Act, 1946 (Including Model Standing Orders, Recognition of Unions & Unfair Labour Practices) 3rd ed. K. D. Srivastava. (C). 1991. text ed. 300.00 (*0-89771-513-6*) St Mut.

Commentaries on Juvenile Justice in India Act. No. 53 of 1986: Along with Probation of Offenders Act. No. 20 of 1958. Keshav P. Tiwari. (C). 1988. 65.00 (*0-685-36514-X*) St Mut.

Commentaries on Kshetra U. P. - Samitis & Zila Parishad Adhiniyam, 1978. 2nd ed. R. P. Saxena & P. L. Malik. (C). 1982. 50.00 (*0-685-39517-0*) St Mut.

Commentaries on Living, Ser. 1. Jiddu Krishnamurti. Ed. by D. Rajagopal. LC 67-8405. 354p. 1967. reprint ed. pap. 8.95 (*0-8356-0390-3*, Quest) Theos Pub Hse.

Commentaries on Living, Ser. 2. Jiddu Krishnamurti. Ed. by D. Rajagopal. LC 67-8405. 242p. 1967. reprint ed. pap. 11.00 (*0-8356-0415-2*, Quest) Theos Pub Hse.

Commentaries on Living, Ser. 3. Jiddu Krishnamurti. Ed. by D. Rajagopal. LC 67-8405. 312p. 1967. reprint ed. pap. 8.95 (*0-8356-0402-0*, Quest) Theos Pub Hse.

Commentaries on Mental Health Act, 1987. B. Nath. (C). 1989. 60.00 (*0-685-25671-5*) St Mut.

Commentaries on Mental Health Act, 1987: With Supplement. Bholeshwar Nath. (C). 1991. 70.00 (*0-685-39626-6*) St Mut.

Commentaries on Motor Vehicles Act. 9th ed. A. P. Mathur. (C). 1990. 400.00 (*0-685-37417-3*) St Mut.

Commentaries on Motor Vehicles Act, 2 vols., Set. A. P. Mathur. 2000p. 1982. 720.00 (*0-317-54714-3*) St Mut.

Commentaries on Narcotic Drugs & Psychotropic Substances Act, 1985. K. Kumar. (C). 1987. 55.00 (*0-685-25160-8*) St Mut.

Commentaries on Narcotic Drugs & Psychotropic Substances Act, 1985: With Central & Madhya Pradesh Rules & Notifications. Ed. by K. Kumar. (C). 1987. 60.00 (*0-685-39607-X*) St Mut.

Commentaries on Narcotic Drugs & Psychotropic Substances Act, 1985: With Central & Maharashtra Rules & Notifications. Ed. by K. Kumar. (C). 1987. 60.00 (*0-685-39608-8*) St Mut.

Commentaries on Narcotic Drugs & Psychotropic Substances Act, 1985: With Central & Uttar Pradesh Rules & Notifications. Ed. by K. Kumar. (C). 1988. 60.00 (*0-685-39606-1*) St Mut.

Commentaries on Narcotic Drugs & Psychotropic Substances Act, 1985: With Central & West Bengal Rules & Notifications. Ed. by K. Kumar. (C). 1987. 65.00 (*0-685-39605-3*) St Mut.

Commentaries on Narcotic Drugs & Psychotropic Substances Act, 1985: With Central, Delhi & Haryana Rules & Notifications. Ed. by K. Kumar. (C). 1987. 60.00 (*0-685-39609-6*) St Mut.

Commentaries on Narcotic Drugs & Psychotropic Substances Act, 1985: With Central Rules & Notifications with Supplement. Ed. by K. Kumar. (C). 1988. 60.00 (*0-685-39610-X*) St Mut.

Commentaries on Opium Act, 1878: With U. P. Opium Rules, 1961, U. P. Poppy-Head Rules, 1961 & U. P. Opium Smoking Act & Rules. Ed. by P. L. Malik. (C). 1984. 40.00 (*0-685-39600-2*) St Mut.

Commentaries on Payment of Bonus Act, 1965. K. D. Srivastava. (C). 1988. 140.00 (*0-685-37431-9*) St Mut.

Commentaries on Payment of Bonus Act, 1965. Ed. by K. D. Srivastava. (C). 1991. 225.00 (*0-89771-693-0*) St Mut.

Commentaries on Payment of Gratuity Act, 1972. K. D. Srivastava. 593p. 1982. 270.00 (*0-317-57715-8*) St Mut.

Commentaries on Payment of Gratuity Act, 1972. K. D. Srivastava. (C). 1989. 100.00 (*0-685-38633-3*) St Mut.

Commentaries on Payment of Gratuity Act, 1972. 4th ed. K. D. Srivastava. (C). 1989. 225.00 (*0-685-36436-4*); 180.00 (*0-685-47802-5*) St Mut.

Commentaries on Payment of Wages Act, 1936. K. D. Srivastava. 814p. 1983. 330.00 (*0-317-57718-2*) St Mut.

Commentaries on Payment of Wages Act, 1936. K. D. Srivastava. (C). 1990. 160.00 (*0-685-38635-X*); text ed. 225.00 (*0-89771-514-4*) St Mut.

Commentaries on Payment of Wages Act, 1936. 4th ed. Ed. by K. D. Srivastava. (C). 1990. 225.00 (*0-685-39656-8*) St Mut.

Commentaries on Payment of Wages Act 1936. 4th ed. K. D. Srivastava. (C). 1990. 225.00 (*0-685-36439-9*) St Mut.

Commentaries on Pindar, Vol. I: Olympian Odes 3, 7, 12, 14. W. J. Verdenius. (Mnemosyne Ser.: Supplement 97). xi, 132p. 1987. pap. 31.00 (*90-04-08126-7*) E J Brill.

Commentaries on Pindar, Vol. 2: Olympian Odes 1-10-11 Nemean 2 - Isthmian 2. W. J. Verdenius. LC 87-138334. (Mnemosyne Ser.: Supplement 101). xi, 154p. (Orig.). 1988. pap. 35.50 (*90-04-08535-1*) E J Brill.

Commentaries on Prevention of Corruption Act. Sandeep Mukherjee. (C). 1990. 65.00 (*0-89771-173-4*) St Mut.

Commentaries on Prevention of Corruption Act, 1947. A. P. Mathur. 699p. 1981. 240.00 (*0-317-54712-7*) St Mut.

Commentaries on Prevention of Corruption Act 1947. 3rd ed. Ed. by A. P. Mathur. (C). 1981. 130.00 (*0-685-36422-4*) St Mut.

Commentaries on Prevention of Corruption Act, 1947: With Supplement of New Act. 3rd rev. ed. A. P. Mathur. (C). 1990. 80.00 (*0-685-39755-6*) St Mut.

C

An Asterisk (*) at the beginning of an entry indicates that the title is appearing in BIP for the first time.

Commentaries on Public Premises (Eviction of Unauthorized Occupants) Act, 1986: With Supplement. S. P. Gupta. (C). 1988. reprint ed. 90.00 (*0-685-39576-6*) St Mut.

Commentaries on Romans Fifteen Thirty-Two to Fifteen Forty-Two. T. H. Parker. 240p. 1986. 37.95 (*0-567-09366-2*, Pub. by T & T Clark UK) Bks Intl VA.

Commentaries on Scheduled Castes & Scheduled Tribes (Prevention of Atrocities) Act, 1989. Ed. by P. K. Gupta. (C). 1991. text ed. 75.00 (*0-89771-474-1*) St Mut.

***Commentaries on the Acts of the Magisterium.** Marcel Lefebvre. Ed. by Angelus Press Staff. Tr. by SSPX Staff. 384p. (Orig.). 1995. pap. 8.95 (*0-935952-28-4*) Angelus Pr.

Commentaries on the Causes, Forms, Symptoms & Treatment, Moral & Medical, of Insanity. George M. Burrows. LC 75-16693. (Classics of Psychiatry Ser.). 1976. reprint ed. 59.95 (*0-405-07422-0*) Ayer.

Commentaries on the Conflict of Laws, Foreign & Domestic, in Regard to Contracts, Rights, & Remedies, & Especially in Regard to Marriages, Divorces, Wills, Successions & Judgments. Joseph Story. LC 74-37986. (American Law Ser.: The Formative Years). 586p. 1972. reprint ed. 37.95 (*0-405-04032-6*) Ayer.

Commentaries on the Constitution. Joseph Story. Ed. by John E. Nowak. LC 86-72657. 808p. 1987. reprint ed. pap. 17.50 (*0-89089-316-0*) Carolina Acad Pr.

Commentaries on the Constitution of India. V. B. Raju. 992p. 1973. 120.00 (*0-317-54672-4*) St Mut.

Commentaries on the Constitution of the Empire of Japan. Hirobumi Ito. LC 78-78353. (Studies in Japanese Law & Government). 310p. 1979. reprint ed. text ed. 65.00 (*0-313-27031-7*, U7031, Greenwood Pr) Greenwood.

Commentaries on the Constitution of the United States: With a Preliminary Review of the Constitutional History of the Colonies & States, Before the Adoption of the Constitution, Set. Joseph Story. 1872p. 1991. reprint ed. lib. bdg. 175.00 (*0-8377-2646-8*) Rothman.

Commentaries on the Criminal Law, 2 vols. 7th enl. rev. ed. Joel P. Bishop. LC 87-80149. 1630p. 1987. reprint ed. lib. bdg. 110.00 (*0-89941-547-4*, 305120) W S Hein.

Commentaries on the Criminal Law, 2 vols., Set. Joel P. Bishop. LC 76-156005. (Foundations of Criminal Justice Ser.). reprint ed. 155.00 (*0-404-09105-9*) AMS Pr.

Commentaries on the Historical Plays of Shakspeare, 2 Vols, 1. Thomas P. Courtenay. LC 72-1030. reprint ed. write for info. (*0-404-01782-7*) AMS Pr.

Commentaries on the Historical Plays of Shakspeare, 2 Vols, 2. Thomas P. Courtenay. LC 72-1030. reprint ed. write for info. (*0-404-01783-5*) AMS Pr.

Commentaries on the Historical Plays of Shakspeare, 2 Vols, Set. Thomas P. Courtenay. LC 72-1030. reprint ed. 115.00 (*0-404-01781-9*) AMS Pr.

Commentaries on the Law in Shakespeare. Edward J. White. xviii, 524p. 1987. reprint ed. lib. bdg. 42.00 (*0-89941-572-5*, 305250) W S Hein.

Commentaries on the Law of Bailments, with Illustrations from the Civil & the Foreign Law. 8th ed. Joseph Story. liii, 653p. 1986. reprint ed. 55.00 (*0-8377-1141-X*) Rothman.

Commentaries on the Law of Married Women under the Statutes of the Several States, & at Common Law & in Equity, 2 vols. Joel P. Bishop. LC 87-80147. (Historical Writings in Law & Jurisprudence Ser.: Second Series No. 14). 1475p. 1987. reprint ed. lib. bdg. 105.00 (*0-89941-548-2*, 305130) W S Hein.

Commentaries on the Law of Promissory Notes, & Guaranties of Notes, & Checks on Banks & Bankers. Joseph Story. xxviii, 675p. reprint ed. lib. bdg. 87.50 (*0-8377-2654-9*) Rothman.

Commentaries on the Law of Scotland (1870) Robert Black. 1580p. 1990. U.K. text ed. 210.00 (*0-406-17899-2*, U.K.) Butterworth Legal Pubs.

Commentaries on the Law of Shakespeare with Explanations of the Legal Terms Used in the Plays, Poems & Sonnets & a Considerarion of the Criminal Types Presented: Also a Full Discussion of the Bacon-Shakespeare Controversy. 2nd ed. Edward J. White. xlviii, 524p. 1987. reprint ed. text ed. 47.50 (*0-8377-2739-1*) Rothman.

Commentaries on the Laws of England: A Facsimile of the First Edition of 1765-1769, 4 vols., I. William Blackstone. LC 79-11753. 1979. pap. 19.95 (*0-226-05538-8*) U Ch Pr.

Commentaries on the Laws of England: A Facsimile of the First Edition of 1765-1769, 4 vols., II. William Blackstone. LC 79-11753. 1979. pap. 19.95 (*0-226-05541-8*) U Ch Pr.

Commentaries on the Laws of England: A Facsimile of the First Edition of 1765-1769, 4 vols., III. William Blackstone. LC 79-11753. 1979. pap. 19.95 (*0-226-05543-4*) U Ch Pr.

Commentaries on the Laws of England: A Facsimile of the First Edition of 1765-1769, 4 vols., IV. William Blackstone. LC 79-11753. 1979. pap. 19.95 (*0-226-05545-0*) U Ch Pr.

Commentaries on the Liberty of the Subject & the Laws of England Relating to the Security of the Person, 2 vols., Set. James Paterson. 1010p. 1980. reprint ed. lib. bdg. 75.00 (*0-8377-1005-7*) Rothman.

Commentaries on the Minor Prophets, 5 vols., Set. John Calvin. (Hosea Through Malachi Ser.). 1990. 99.95 (*0-85151-569-X*) Banner of Truth.

Commentaries on the Minor Prophets: Habakkuk, Zephaniah & Haggai, Vol 4. Calvin John. Tr. by John Owen. (Geneva Series of Commentaries). 411p. (C). 1986. reprint ed. 19.95 (*0-85151-477-4*) Banner of Truth.

Commentaries on the Minor Prophets: Hosea, Vol. 1. John Calvin. Tr. by John Owen. (Geneva Series of Commentaries). 530p. (C). 1986. reprint ed. 21.95 (*0-85151-473-1*) Banner of Truth.

Commentaries on the Minor Prophets: Joel, Amos & Obadiah, Vol. 2. John Calvin. Tr. by John Owen. (Geneva Series of Commentaries). 513p. (C). 1986. reprint ed. 21.95 (*0-85151-474-X*) Banner of Truth.

Commentaries on the Minor Prophets: Jonah, Micah & Nahum, Vol. 3. John Calvin. Tr. by John Owen. (Geneva Series of Commentaries). 534p. 1986. reprint ed. 21.95 (*0-85151-475-8*) Banner of Truth.

Commentaries on the Minor Prophets: Zechariah & Malachi, Vol. 5. John Calvin. Tr. by John Owen. (Geneva Series of Commentaries). 668p. 1986. reprint ed. 26.95 (*0-85151-476-6*) Banner of Truth.

Commentaries on the Muslim Women (Protection of Rights on Divorce) Act, 1986-1987, No. 25. J. P. Bhatnagar. (C). 1987. 50.00 (*0-685-36481-X*) St Mut.

Commentaries on the New Media Arts: Fluxus & Conceptual, Artists' Books, MailArt, Correspondence Art, Audio & Video Art. Robert C. Morgan. 64p. (Orig.). 1992. pap. 9.95 (*0-9635042-0-7*) Umbrella Assocs.

Commentaries on the New Testament, 14 vols., Set. Incl. Matthew. H. Leo Boles. 14.95 (*0-89225-001-1*); Mark. C. E. Dorris. 14.95 (*0-89225-002-X*); Luke. H. Leo Boles. 10.95 (*0-89225-003-8*); Acts. H. Leo Boles. 14.99 (*0-89225-005-4*); Romans. David Lipscomb & J. W. Shepherd. 14.99 (*0-89225-006-2*); Corinthians I. David Lipscomb & J. W. Shepard. 14.99 (*0-89225-007-0*); Corinthians II - Galatians. David Lipscomb & J. W. Shepherd. 14.99 (*0-89225-008-9*); Ephesians - Colossians. J. W. Shepherd. 14.99 (*0-89225-009-7*); Thessalonians I, II; Timothy I, II; Titus; Phelomon. J. W. Shepherd. 14.99 (*0-89225-010-0*); Hebrews. Robert Milligan. 14.99 (*0-89225-011-9*); James. Guy N. Woods. 14.99 (*0-89225-012-7*); Peter I, II; John I, II, III; Jude. Guy N. Woods. 14.99 (*0-89225-013-5*); Revelation. John T. Hinds. 14.99 (*0-89225-014-3*); 135.00 (*0-89225-000-3*) Gospel Advocate.

Commentaries on the Opium Act, 1878. P. L. Malik. 175p. 1984. 90.00 (*0-317-54866-2*) St Mut.

Commentaries on the Railways Act, 1989. M. I. Jand. (C). 1990. 150.00 (*0-89771-244-7*) St Mut.

Commentaries on the Scriptures. Thomas Hora. 35p. 1987. pap. 6.00 (*0-913105-10-4*) PAGL Pr.

Commentaries on the Societies Registration Act, 1860. J. P. Bhatnagar. 314p. 1985. 180.00 (*0-317-54773-9*) St Mut.

Commentaries on the Societies Registration Act, 1980. 6th rev. ed. J. P. Bhatnagar. (C). 1991. 95.00 (*0-685-39552-9*) St Mut.

Commentaries on the Tamilnadu Hindu Religious & Charitable Endowment Act, 1959. R. Sengottuvelan. (C). 1990. 88.00 (*0-89771-140-8*) St Mut.

Commentaries on the U. P. Government Servants' Conduct Rules, 1956. B. N. Upadhyaya. 163p. 1983. 75.00 (*0-317-57745-X*) St Mut.

Commentaries on the U. P. Government Servants Conduct Rules, 1956. B. N. Upadhyaya. (C). 1991. text ed. 55.00 (*0-89771-518-7*) St Mut.

Commentaries on the U. P. Government Servants Conduct Rules, 1956. 3rd ed. Ed. by B. N. Upadhyana. (C). 1991. 110.00 (*0-685-39777-7*) St Mut.

Commentaries on the U. P. Government Servants Conduct Rules, 1956. 4th ed. Ed. by B. N. Upadhyaya. (C). 1991. 95.00 (*0-685-39692-4*) St Mut.

Commentaries on the U. P. Urban Buildings (Regulation of Letting, Rent & Eviction Act), 1972 and Narayan Das-Digest of U. P. Urban Buildings (Regulation of Letting, Rent & Eviction) Cases 1972-1980. 4th ed. Shiva Gopal. 680p. 1981. 195.00 (*0-317-54770-4*) St Mut.

Commentaries on U. P. Co-Operative Societies Act, 1965. 5th rev. ed. Ed. by Ejaz Ahmed. (C). 1989. 200.00 (*0-685-39784-X*) St Mut.

Commentaries on U. P. Cooperative Societies Act, 1965. Ejaz Ahmed. 756p. 1984. 330.00 (*0-317-54828-X*) St Mut.

Commentaries on U. P. Imposition of Ceiling on Land Holdings Act, 1960. V. K. Sircar. 304p. 1977. 160.00 (*0-317-57703-4*) St Mut.

Commentaries on U. P. Imposition of Ceiling on Land Holdings Act, 1977: With Supplement. V. K. Sircar. (C). 1985. reprint ed. 35.00 (*0-685-47806-8*) St Mut.

Commentaries on U. P. Kshettra Samitis & Zila Parishad Adhiniyam, 1978. 2nd ed. R. P. Saxena & P. L. Malik. (C). 1982. 85.00 (*0-685-39659-2*) St Mut.

Commentaries on U. P. Kshettra Samitis & Zila Parishads Adhiniyam. 2nd ed. R. P. Saxena & P. L. Malik. 843p. 1978. 150.00 (*0-317-54784-4*) St Mut.

Commentaries on U. P. Municipalities Act, 1916. Surendra Malik. 866p. 1984. 360.00 (*0-317-54838-7*) St Mut.

Commentaries on U. P. Municipalities Act, 1916. Surendra Malik. (C). 1989. 205.00 (*0-685-39616-9*) St Mut.

Commentaries on U. P. Municipalities Act, 1984: With Supplement. Surendra Malik. (C). 1989. reprint ed. 200.00 (*0-685-39621-5*) St Mut.

Commentaries on U. P. Nagar Mahapalika Adhiniyam, 1959. 5th ed. Surendra Malik. (C). 1989. 135.00 (*0-685-39611-8*) St Mut.

Commentaries on U. P. Panchayar Raj Act, 1948. 2nd ed. Surendra Malik. (C). 1991. 100.00 (*0-685-39599-5*) St Mut.

Commentaries on U. P. Panchayat Raj Act, 1947. 5th ed. R. C. Saxena. 491p. 1980. 135.00 (*0-317-54613-9*) St Mut.

Commentaries on U. P. Public Services (Tribunals) A. S. Misra. (C). 1991. 95.00 (*0-685-39561-8*) St Mut.

Commentaries on U. P. Public Services (Tribunals) Act, 1976. A. S. Misra. 277p. 1980. 100.00 (*0-317-54707-0*) St Mut.

Commentaries on U. P. Public Services (Tribunals) Act, 1980. 2nd rev. ed. Ed. by A. S. Misra. (C). 1991. reprint ed. 95.00 (*0-685-39526-X*) St Mut.

Commentaries on Universal Public Law. George Bowyer. 338p. 1985. reprint ed. lib. bdg. 30.00 (*0-8377-0343-3*) Rothman.

Commentaries on Uttar Pradesh Public Premises (Eviction of Unauthorized Occupants) Act, 1972. S. P. Gupta. 154p. 1983. 60.00 (*0-317-54694-5*) St Mut.

Commentaries on Uttar Pradesh Public Premises (Eviction of Unauthorized Occupants) Act, 1972. 3rd ed. S. P. Gupta. (C). 1988. 95.00 (*0-685-39575-8*) St Mut.

Commentaries on Workmen's Compensation Act, 1923. K. D. Srivastava. 692p. 1984. 300.00 (*0-317-57717-4*) St Mut.

Commentaries on Workmen's Compensation Act, 1923: Republished with Addenda of Latest Case Law. 4th rev. ed. K. D. Srivastava. (C). 1989. 210.00 (*0-685-39519-7*) St Mut.

Commentaries on Workmen's Compensation Act, 1923: Republished with Addenda of Latest Case Law, 1989. 4th ed. K. D. Srivastava. (C). 1989. 140.00 (*0-685-38616-3*) St Mut.

Commentaries on Workmen's Compensation Act, 1924. K. D. Srivastava. (C). 1989. 200.00 (*0-685-37428-9*) St Mut.

Commentaries the Constitution of India, Vol. N. Durga D. Basu. (C). 1988. 160.00 (*0-685-27941-3*) St Mut.

Commentaries Upon Martial Law, with Special Reference to Its Regulation & Restraint: With an Introduction, Containing Comments Upon the Charge of the Lord Chief Justice in the Jamaica Case. W. F. Finlason. 287p. 1980. reprint ed. lib. bdg. 28.50 (*0-8377-0536-3*) Rothman.

Commentarii, 2 vols., 1. Julius Caesar. Ed. by R. L. Du Pontet. (Oxford Classical Texts Ser.). 1968. 18.95 (*0-19-814602-7*) OUP.

Commentarii, 2 vols., 2. Julius Caesar. Ed. by R. L. Du Pontet. (Oxford Classical Texts Ser.). 1922. 19.95 (*0-19-814603-5*) OUP.

Commentarii Ad Homeri Iliadem et Odysseam Cum Indice Devarii, 4 vols., Set. Eustathius. Ed. by G. Stallbaum. 1592p. 1970. reprint ed. write for info. (*0-318-70919-8*, Pub. by Georg Olms GW) Lubrecht & Cramer.

Commentarii De Bello Civili. Caesar. Ed. by Friedrich Kraner et al. xvi, 430p. 1968. write for info. (*3-296-11000-3*, Pub. by Georg Olms GW) Lubrecht & Cramer.

Commentarii de Bello Gallico, Bd. 1, Buch 1-4. Caesar. Ed. by Friedrich Kraner et al. vii, 536p. 1980. write for info. (*3-296-11101-8*, Pub. by Georg Olms GW) Lubrecht & Cramer.

Commentarii de Bello Gallico, Bd. 2, Buch 5-7. Caesar. Ed. by Friedrich Kraner et al. iv, 724p. 1986. write for info. (*3-296-11102-6*, Pub. by Georg Olms GW) Lubrecht & Cramer.

Commentarii de Bello Gallico, Bd. 3, Buch 8 und Register. Caesar. Ed. by Friedrich Kraner et al. 240p. 1966. write for info. (*3-296-11103-4*, Pub. by Georg Olms GW) Lubrecht & Cramer.

Commentarii in Libros Metaphysicorum Aristotelis Sstagiritae, 4 vols. in 2, Set. Petrus Fonseca. 833p. 1975. reprint ed. write for info. (*3-487-00600-6*, Pub. by Georg Olms GW) Lubrecht & Cramer.

***Commentariorum in Aratum Reliquiae.** Aratus of Soli. Ed. by Ernestus Maas. 749p. 1958. pap. text ed. 150.00 (*0-614-07363-4*, Pub. by Georg Olms GW) Lubrecht & Cramer.

Commentariorum in Aratum Reliquiae. Ed. by Ernst Maas. lxxi, 750p. 1958. write for info. (*3-296-11900-0*, Pub. by Georg Olms GW) Lubrecht & Cramer.

Commentarius Cantabrigiensis in Epistolas Pauli e Schola Petri Abaelardi, 3 vols. Arthur Landgraf. Incl. Vol. 1. In Epistolam Ad Romanos. 223p. 1937. 17.95 (*0-268-00133-2*); Vol. 2. In Epistolam Ad Corinthios Iam et Iiam, Ad Galatas et Ad Ephesios. 1223p. 1960. 17.95 (*0-268-00134-0*); Vol. 3. In Epistolam ad Philippenses, ad Colossenses, ad Thessalonicenses Primam et Secundam, ad Timotheam Primam et Secundam, ad Titum et Philemonem. 447p. 1944. 17.95 (*0-268-00132-4*); (Mediaeval Studies Ser.: No. 2). write for info. (*0-318-56117-4*) U of Notre Dame Pr.

Commentarius in Aristotelis Metaphysicam. Hermann Bonitz. viii, 596p. 1992. reprint ed. write for info. (*3-487-05376-4*, Pub. by Georg Olms GW) Lubrecht & Cramer.

Commentarius in Platonis Parmenidem. Proclus Diadochus. Ed. by Victor Cousin. 1314p. 1980. reprint ed. write for info. (*3-487-00166-7*, Pub. by Georg Olms GW) Lubrecht & Cramer.

Commentarius in Plauti Comoedias, 2 vols., Set. Johan L. Ussing. xxiv, 1428p. 1972. reprint ed. write for info. (*3-487-04378-5*, Pub. by Georg Olms GW) Lubrecht & Cramer.

Commentary. John Galsworthy. LC 77-134962. (Short Story Index Reprint Ser.). 1977. 18.95 (*0-8369-3692-2*) Ayer.

Commentary & Ideology: Dante in the Renaissance. Deborah Parker. LC 92-12651. (Illus.). 264p. 1992. text ed. 32.95 (*0-8223-1281-6*) Duke.

Commentary & Planning Guide for Go & Make Disciples: A National Plan & Strategy for Catholic Evangelization in the United States. 102p. 1993. pap. 6.95 (*0-918951-02-X*) Paulist Natl Catholic.

Commentary by a Social Servant, 1924-1983. Geraldine Aves. 1984. 40.00 (*0-317-42885-3*, Pub. by Natl Inst Soc Work) St Mut.

Commentary John's Gospel, 2 vols. in 1. Frederic L. Godet. LC 78-59145. (Kregel Reprint Library). 1112p. 1980. reprint ed. lib. bdg. 38.99 (*0-8254-2714-2*) Kregel.

Commentary of Abraham Ibn Ezra on Hosea. Intro. by Abe Lipshitz. 190p. 1988. 19.95 (*0-87203-127-6*) Hermon.

***Commentary of Apollonius Rhodius Argonautica III 1-471.** Malcolm Campbell. LC 94-29384. (Mnemosyne, Bibliotheca Classica Batava Ser.: Vol. 141). 1994. 123.00 (*90-04-10158-6*) E J Brill.

***Commentary of "Condordat of Agreement"** Ed. by James F. Griffiss & Daniel F. Martensen. 160p. (Orig.). 1995. pap. 11.00 (*0-88028-160-X*, 1310) Forward Movement.

Commentary of Conrad of Prussia on de Unitate et Uno of Dominicus Gundissalinus. Tr. by Joseph Bobik. LC 89-12769. (Studies in the History of Philosophy: Vol. 12). 264p. (ENG & LAT.). 1990. lib. bdg. 89.95 (*0-88946-302-6*) E Mellen.

Commentary of David Kimchi on Isaiah. David B. Kimchi. Ed. by Louis Finkelstein. LC 27-4417. (Columbia University. Oriental Studies: No. 19). reprint ed. 24.50 (*0-404-50509-0*) AMS Pr.

Commentary of Father Monserrate, S. J. on His Journey to the Court of Akbar. M. Huc. (C). 1992. reprint ed. 20.00 (*81-206-0807-0*, Pub. by Asian Educ Servs II) S Asia.

Commentary of Five Odes of Pindar. rev. ed. Christopher Carey. Ed. by W. R. Connor. LC 80-2644. (Monographs in Classical Studies). 1981. lib. bdg. 26.00 (*0-405-14032-0*) Ayer.

Commentary of Ibn Ezra on Isaiah. Ibn Ezra. Tr. by Michael Friedlander. LC 66-15771. 1966. 19.95 (*0-87306-013-X*) Feldheim.

Commentary of Jean-Paul Sartre's "Being & Nothingness" Joseph S. Catalano. LC 79-21234. xvi, 240p. 1985. reprint ed. pap. text ed. 17.95 (*0-226-09699-8*) U Ch Pr.

Commentary of Kant's "Critique of Practical Reason" Lewis W. Beck. LC 60-5464. (Midway Reprint Ser.). xiv, 306p. 1984. reprint ed. pap. text ed. 18.95 (*0-226-04076-3*) U Ch Pr.

Commentary of Rabbi David Kimchi on Hosea. David B. Kimchi. Ed. by Harry Cohen. LC 30-27876. (Columbia University. Oriental Studies: No. 20). reprint ed. 17.00 (*0-404-50510-4*) AMS Pr.

Commentary of Rabbi David Kimhi on Psalms 120-150. Ed. by J. Baker & E. W. Nicholson. (University of Cambridge Oriental Publications: No. 22). 1973. 54.95 (*0-521-08670-1*) Cambridge U Pr.

Commentary of the Bible: A Look at Each Book & Its Message. Bob Snyder. 132p. 1994. pap. 5.95 (*1-883624-12-6*) Hope Hurt Minist.

Commentary of the Complete Greek Tragedies: Aeschylus. James C. Hogan. LC 84-2688. 352p. (C). 1985. pap. text ed. 9.95 (*0-226-34843-1*) U Ch Pr.

Commentary of the Complete Greek Tragedies: Aeschylus. James C. Hogan. LC 84-2688. 352p. (C). 1985. lib. bdg. 23.00 (*0-226-34842-3*) U Ch Pr.

Commentary of the Services & Charge of William Lord Grey of Wilton. Arthur G. Grey De Wilton. Ed. by Philip De Malpas Grey Egerton. LC 71-161716. (Camden Society, London. Publications, First Ser.: No. 40). reprint ed. 27.50 (*0-404-50140-0*) AMS Pr.

Commentary on Acts. James B. Coffman. 546p. 1984. 18.95 (*0-915547-07-4*) Abilene Christ U.

Commentary on Acts. Horatio B. Hackett. LC 91-39377. 480p. 1992. pap. 16.99 (*0-8254-2748-7*) Kregel.

Commentary on Acts. Horatio B. Hackett. LC 91-39377. 480p. 1992. lib. bdg. 21.99 (*0-8254-2749-5*) Kregel.

Commentary on Agreements for Engineering Services & Contract Documents. John R. Clark. 98p. 1986. 25.00 (*0-686-48322-7*) Am Consul Eng.

***Commentary on Aristotle's De Anima.** St. Thomas Aquinas Staff. Tr. by Kenelm Foster & Silvester Humphries. (aristotelian Commentary Ser.). xxii, 276p. (C). 1994. pap. 30.00 (*1-883357-11-X*) Dumb Ox Bks.

***Commentary on Aristotle's De Anima.** St. Thomas Aquinas Staff. Tr. by Kenelm Foster & Silvester Humphries. (Aristotelian Commentary Ser.: xxii, 276). 276p. (C). 1994. 70.00 (*1-883357-10-1*) Dumb Ox Bks.

Commentary on Aristotle's Nicomachecys Ethics. St. Thomas Aquinas. (Thomas Aquinas's Aristotelian Commentaries Ser.). 900p. 1993. text ed. 85.00 (*1-883357-50-0*); pap. text ed. 35.00 (*1-883357-51-9*) Dumb Ox Bks.

Commentary on Book I of the Epigrams of Martial. P. Howell. (Illus.). 369p. (C). 1980. text ed. 85.00 (*0-485-11191-8*, Pub. by Athlone Pr UK) Humanities.

Commentary on Building Code Requirements for Reinforced Concrete (ACI 318-63) Report of ACI Committee 318, Standard Building Code. American Concrete Institute Staff. LC 65-6942. (American Concrete Institute Publication Ser.: No. SP-10). 100p. reprint ed. pap. 28.50 (*0-317-09982-5*, 2002351) Bks Demand.

Commentary on Catullus. 2nd ed. Robinson Ellis. lxxii, 516p. 1989. reprint ed. 96.20 (*3-487-07927-5*, Pub. by Georg Olms GW) Lubrecht & Cramer.

Commentary on Customs Act with Rules & Notifications. M. Mukerjee. (C). 1990. 275.00 (*0-89771-224-2*) St Mut.

Commentary on Daniel, Vol. 4. James B. Coffman. LC 88-71656. (Coffman Commentaries Ser.). 320p. 1989. 19.95 (*0-89112-078-5*) Abilene Christ U.

Commentary on Deuteronomy. James B. Coffman. LC 87-72300. 413p. 1988. 19.95 (*0-915547-76-7*) Abilene Christ U.

Commentary on Ecclesiastes, Song of Solomon, Lamentations, Vol. 3: The Wisdom Literature. James B. Coffman. 1993. 19.95 (*0-89112-065-3*) Abilene Christ U.

Commentary on Ephesians. Benny B. Bristow. 1988. pap. 5.50 (*0-89137-571-6*) Quality Pubns.

An Asterisk (*) at the beginning of an entry indicates that the title is appearing in BIP for the first time.

Commentary on Exodus. George Bush. LC 92-39337. 880p. 1993. 25.99 (*0-8254-2182-9*); pap. 19.99 (*0-8254-2181-0*) Kregel.

Commentary on Exodus. James B. Coffman. 1984. 19.95 (*0-915547-49-X*) Abilene Christ U.

Commentary on Exodus. J. P. Hyatt. Ed. by Ronald E. Clements. (New Century Bible Commentary Ser.). 1981. pap. 16.99 (*0-8028-1844-7*) Eerdmans.

Commentary on Ezekiel. James B. Coffman. LC 90-83132. 431p. 1991. 29.95 (*0-89112-077-7*) Abilene Christ U.

Commentary on Ezra-Nehemiah-Esther. Clayton Williams. 1991. pap. 8.95 (*0-89137-128-1*) Quality Pubns.

Commentary on Ezra, Nehemiah, Esther, Vol. 8: The Historical Books. James B. Coffman. 1993. 19.95 (*0-89112-088-2*) Abilene Christ U.

Commentary on First & Second Corinthians. F. F. Bruce. Ed. by Matthew Black. (New Century Bible Commentary Ser.). 224p. 1980. pap. 15.99 (*0-8028-1839-0*) Eerdmans.

Commentary on First & Second Corinthians. James B. Coffman. 1984. 18.95 (*0-915547-02-3*) Abilene Christ U.

Commentary on First & Second Kings. Clyde Miller. LC 88-72271. (Living Word Ser.). 416p. 1992. 27.95 (*0-89112-188-9*) Abilene Christ U.

Commentary on First & Second Thessalonians. Leon Crouch. 1993. pap. 7.50 (*0-89137-138-9*) Quality Pubns.

Commentary on First & Two Thessalonians. Ed. by W. Ward Gasque & Howard Marshall. (New International Greek Testament Commentary Ser.). xxvi, 326p. 1990. 29.99 (*0-8028-2394-7*) Eerdmans.

Commentary on First Corinthians. Bill Jackson. 1991. pap. 7.75 (*0-89137-130-3*) Quality Pubns.

Commentary on First John. Robert S. Candlish. LC 79-14801. 448p. 1992. pap. 18.99 (*0-8254-2333-3*) Kregel.

Commentary on First Peter. Leonhard Goppelt. 1993. 29.99 (*0-8028-3719-0*) Eerdmans.

Commentary on G. M. Hopkins' "The Wreck of the Deutschland" Peter Milward. LC 90-25437. (Studies in British Literature: Vol. 13). 200p. 1992. reprint ed. lib. bdg. 79.95 (*0-88946-584-3*) E Mellen.

***Commentary on Galatians.** John Eadie. 544p. Date not set. lib. bdg. 23.99 (*0-8254-2499-2*) Kregel.

***Commentary on Galatians.** John Eadie. 544p. Date not set. pap. 17.99 (*0-8254-2501-8*) Kregel.

Commentary on Galatians. Martin Luther. LC 78-59151. 408p. 1987. pap. 14.99 (*0-8254-3124-7*) Kregel.

Commentary on Galatians: A Facsimile of the 1617 Edition. William Perkins. LC 89-35504. (Classic Commentaries Ser.). 686p. (C). 1989. lib. bdg. 35.00 (*0-8298-0790-X*); pap. 19.95 (*0-8298-0786-1*) Pilgrim OH.

Commentary on Galatians: Modern-English Edition. Martin Luther. 416p. 1994. 21.99 (*0-8007-1702-3*) Revell.

Commentary on Galatians, Ephesians, Philippians, Colossians. James B. Coffman. 1984. 18.95 (*0-915547-10-4*) Abilene Christ U.

Commentary on Genesis. James B. Coffman. 1984. 19.95 (*0-915547-48-1*) Abilene Christ U.

Commentary on Guru Yoga. 2nd ed. Sermey G. Tharchin. Bd. with Commentary on Offering of the Mandala. 80p. (Orig.). 1988. Set pap. 6.95 (*0-937938-47-5*) Snow Lion Pubns.

Commentary on Hebrews. James B. Coffman. 1984. 18.95 (*0-915547-12-0*) Abilene Christ U.

Commentary on Hebrews. Philip E. Hughes. 1987. 24.99 (*0-8028-0322-9*) Eerdmans.

Commentary on Hebrews Eleven (1609) William Perkins. Ed. by John H. Augustine. LC 90-22542. (Classic Commentaries Ser.). 222p. 1990. reprint ed. 39.95 (*0-8298-0856-6*); reprint ed. pap. 29.95 (*0-8298-0857-4*) Pilgrim OH.

Commentary on Hegel's Logic. J. M. McTaggert. (C). 1986. reprint ed. pap. text ed. 14.00 (*0-935005-50-1*) Lincoln-Rembrandt.

Commentary on Heidegger's Being & Time. rev. ed. Michael Gelven. 1989. text ed. 30.00 (*0-87580-145-5*); pap. text ed. 12.50 (*0-87580-544-2*) N Ill U Pr.

Commentary on Herodotus, Vol. 2: Bks. 5-9 with Introduction & Appendices. Ed. by Walter W. How & Joseph Wells. 458p. 1990. reprint ed. pap. 28.00 (*0-19-872139-0*) OUP.

Commentary on Homer's Odyssey, Vol. II: Bks. IX-XVI. Ed. by Alfred Heubeck & Arie Hoekstra. 312p. 1990. reprint ed. pap. 24.95 (*0-19-872144-7*) OUP.

Commentary on Homer's Odyssey, Vol. III, Bks. XVII-XXIV. Manuel Fernandez-Galiano & Alfred Heubeck. Ed. by Joseph A. Russo et al. 464p. 1992. 110.00 (*0-19-814048-7*) OUP.

Commentary on Homer's Odyssey, Vol. I: Bks. I-VIII & Introduction. Ed. by Alfred Heubeck et al. 408p. 1990. reprint ed. pap. 32.50 (*0-19-814747-3*) OUP.

Commentary on Homer's Odyssey, Vol. 3: Bks. XVII-XXIV. Ed. by Joseph A. Russo et al. (Illus.). 464p. 1993. reprint ed. pap. 26.00 (*0-19-814953-0*) OUP.

Commentary on Isaiah. Harry Bultema. LC 81-11795. 640p. 1991. pap. 18.99 (*0-8254-2261-2*) Kregel.

Commentary on Isaiah. James B. Coffman. LC 89-81143. 647p. 1990. 29.95 (*0-89112-075-0*) Abilene Christ U.

Commentary on Isaiah. Joseph A. Alexander. LC 92-16125. 996p. 1992. reprint ed. 34.99 (*0-8254-2138-1*); reprint ed. pap. 28.99 (*0-8254-2137-3*) Kregel.

Commentary on James: New International Greek Testament Commentary. Peter Davids. 226p. 1982. 22.99 (*0-8028-2388-2*) Eerdmans.

Commentary on James, First & Second Peter, First, Second & Third John, Jude. James B. Coffman. 1984. 18.95 (*0-915547-13-9*) Abilene Christ U.

Commentary on Jean-Paul Sartre's Critique of Dialectical Reason: Theory of Practical Ensembles, Vol. 1. Joseph S. Catalano. LC 86-11323. 352p. 1987. pap. text ed. 15.95 (*0-226-09701-3*) U Ch Pr.

Commentary on Jeremiah. James B. Coffman. LC 90-81193. 571p. 1990. write for info. (*0-89112-076-9*) Abilene Christ U.

Commentary on Jeremiah, Vol. 1. John Calvin. Tr. by John Owens. (Geneva Series Commentary on Jeremiah & Lamentations). 508p. (C). 1989. reprint ed. 22.95 (*0-85151-547-9*) Banner of Truth.

Commentary on Jeremiah, Vol. 2. John Calvin. Tr. by John Owens. (Geneva Series Commentary on Jeremiah & Lamentations). 496p. (C). 1989. reprint ed. 22.95 (*0-85151-548-7*) Banner of Truth.

Commentary on Jeremiah, Vol. 3. John Calvin. Tr. by John Owens. (Geneva Series Commentary on Jeremiah & Lamentations). 480p. (C). 1989. reprint ed. 22.95 (*0-85151-549-5*) Banner of Truth.

Commentary on Jeremiah, Vol. 4. John Calvin. Tr. by John Owens. (Geneva Series Commentary on Jeremiah & Lamentations). 647p. (C). 1989. reprint ed. 22.95 (*0-85151-550-9*) Banner of Truth.

Commentary on Jeremiah & Lamentations. Anthony Ash. LC 86-72834. 500p. 1987. 17.95 (*0-915547-94-5*) Abilene Christ U.

Commentary on Jeremiah & Lamentations, Vol. 5. John Calvin. Tr. by John Owen. (Geneva Series Commentary on Jeremiah & Lamentations). 576p. (C). 1989. reprint ed. 22.95 (*0-85151-551-7*) Banner of Truth.

Commentary on John. Thomas Whitelaw. LC 92-23991. 1993. 25.99 (*0-8254-3984-1*); pap. 19.99 (*0-8254-3979-5*) Kregel.

Commentary on John, Vol. 4. James B. Coffman. 1984. 18.95 (*0-915547-06-6*) Abilene Christ U.

Commentary on Joshua. James B. Coffman. LC 88-71026. 550p. 1988. 17.95 (*0-915547-78-3*) Abilene Christ U.

Commentary on Jude. Thomas Manton. LC 88-12127. 384p. reprint ed. lib. bdg. 20.99 (*0-8254-3240-5*); reprint ed. pap. 14.99 (*0-8254-3239-1*) Kregel.

Commentary on Jude. Thomas Manton. 376p. (C). 1989. reprint ed. 17.95 (*0-85151-553-3*) Banner of Truth.

Commentary on Judges & Ruth, Vol. 2. James B. Coffman. LC 91-78067. 380p. 1992. write for info. (*0-89112-081-5*) Abilene Christ U.

***Commentary on Kings & Chronicles.** Clayton Winters. 1995. pap. 10.95 (*0-89137-147-8*) Quality Pubns.

Commentary on Law Relating to Insecticides in India. M. Narayanaswamy. (C). 1988. 175.00 (*0-685-36519-0*) St Mut.

Commentary on Leviticus & Numbers. James B. Coffman. 580p. 1987. 19.95 (*0-915547-75-9*) Abilene Christ U.

Commentary on Livy, Bks. 31-33. John Briscoe. 400p. 1990. reprint ed. pap. 32.50 (*0-19-814738-4*) OUP.

Commentary on Loureiro's "Flora Cochinchinensis" E. D. Merrill. 1935. pap. 10.00 (*0-934454-24-8*) Lubrecht & Cramer.

Commentary on Luke. J. Norval Geldenhuys. (New International Commentary on the New Testament Ser.). 1951. 27.99 (*0-8028-2184-7*) Eerdmans.

Commentary on Luke, Vol 1. F. L. Godet. 584p. pap. 39.95 (*0-8254-2720-7*, Pub. by T & T Clark UK) Bks Intl VA.

Commentary on Luke, Vol. 3. James B. Coffman. 1984. 18.95 (*0-915547-05-8*) Abilene Christ U.

Commentary on Mark. J. D. Jones. LC 91-37165. 640p. 1992. lib. bdg. 29.99 (*0-8254-2970-6*); pap. 22.99 (*0-8254-2969-2*) Kregel.

Commentary on Mark. Henry B. Swete. LC 77-79193. (Kregel Reprint Library). 554p. 1978. 18.99 (*0-8254-3715-6*) Kregel.

Commentary on Mark, Vol. 2. James B. Coffman. 1984. 18.95 (*0-915547-04-X*) Abilene Christ U.

Commentary on Matthew. John A. Broadus. LC 89-77852. 610p. 1989. pap. 21.99 (*0-8254-2283-3*) Kregel.

Commentary on Matthew. James B. Coffman. 1984. 18.95 (*0-915547-03-1*) Abilene Christ U.

Commentary on Minor Prophets: Hosea, Obadiah & Micah, Vol. II. James B. Coffman. 1984. 13.95 (*0-915547-45-7*) Abilene Christ U.

Commentary on Minor Prophets: Joel, Amos, & Jonah, Vol. I. James B. Coffman. 1984. 13.95 (*0-915547-44-9*) Abilene Christ U.

Commentary on Minor Prophets: Nahum, Habakkuk, Zephaniah & Haggai, Vol. III. James B. Coffman. 1984. 13.95 (*0-915547-46-5*) Abilene Christ U.

Commentary on Minor Prophets: Zechariah & Malachi, Vol. IV. James B. Coffman. 1984. 13.95 (*0-915547-47-3*) Abilene Christ U.

Commentary on Nietzsche's Ecce Homo. Thomas Steinbuch. LC 94-21257. 118p. (C). reprint ed. lib. bdg. 28.50 (*0-8191-9608-8*) U Pr of Amer.

Commentary on Offering of the Mandala see Commentary on Guru Yoga

Commentary on Ovid Metamorphoses Vol. II. J. J. Moore-Blunt. viii, 192p. 1977. pap. 39.00x (*90-256-0638-5*, Pub. by A M Hakkert NE) Benjamins North Am.

Commentary on Ovid Metamorphoses II. J. J. Moore-Blunt. 192p. 1977. pap. 40.00 (*0-685-43581-4*, Pub. by A M Hakkert SP) Coronet Bks.

Commentary on Peter & Jude. Martin Luther. LC 82-4652. 304p. 1982. pap. 10.99 (*0-8254-3147-6*) Kregel.

Commentary on Philippians. Ralph P. Martin. (New Century Bible Commentary Ser.). 192p. 1980. pap. 14.99 (*0-8028-1840-4*) Eerdmans.

***Commentary on Plato's Euthydemus.** fac. ed. R. S. Hawtrey. LC 79-54280. (American Philosophical Society Memoirs Ser.: No. 147). 222p. 1981. reprint ed. pap. 63.30 (*0-7837-8044-3*, 2047797) Bks Demand.

Commentary on Plato's Meno. Jacob Klein. LC 89-34929. viii, 256p. 1989. pap. text ed. 14.95 (*0-226-43959-3*) U Ch Pr.

Commentary on Plato's Meno. Jacob Klein. LC 65-13664. (Illus.). 264p. reprint ed. pap. 75.30 (*0-8357-3858-2*, 2036591) Bks Demand.

Commentary on Plato's Symposium on Love. 2nd rev. ed. Marsilio Ficino. Tr. by Sears Jayne. LC 84-20255. Orig. Title: Marsilio Ficino's Commentary on Plato's Symposium. 213p. (LAT.). 1983. pap. 22.00 (*0-88214-601-7*) Spring Pubns.

Commentary on Plutarch's Pericles. Philip A. Stadter. LC 88-27029. (Illus.). xxxviii, 416p. (C). 1989. 55.00 (*0-8078-1861-5*) U of NC Pr.

Commentary on Plutarch's Table Talks, Vol. 1, Bks. 1-3. Sven-Tage Teodorsson. (Studia Grawca et Latina Gothoburgensis: No. 51). 394p. (Orig.). 1989. pap. 97.50x (*91-7346-219-5*, Pub. by Almqv & Wiksell SW) Coronet Bks.

Commentary on Plutarch's Table Talks, Vol. 2, Bks. 4-6. Sven-Tage Teodorsson. 302p. (Orig.). 1990. pap. 97.50x (*91-7346-227-6*, Pub. by Almqv & Wiksell SW) Coronet Bks.

Commentary on Proverbs, 2 vols. in 1. George Lawson. LC 80-8070. 572p. 1993. pap. 19.99 (*0-8254-3123-9*) Kregel.

Commentary on Proverbs, 2 vols. in 1. deluxe ed. George Lawson. LC 80-8070. 572p. 1993. 26.99 (*0-8254-3149-2*) Kregel.

Commentary on Proverbs, Vol. 2: The Wisdom Literature. James B. Coffman. 1993. 19.95 (*0-89112-064-5*) Abilene Christ U.

Commentary on Psalms, Chapters 1-72, Vol. 1. James B. Coffman. LC 91-73451. 650p. 1992. 29.95 (*0-89112-079-3*) Abilene Christ U.

Commentary on Psalms 73-150, Vol. 2. James Burton Coffman. LC 91-92970. 29.95 (*0-89112-080-7*) Abilene Christ U.

Commentary on Psychic Energy. Torkom Saraydarian. LC 89-192459. 236p. 1989. pap. 14.00 (*0-929874-12-9*) TSG Pub Found.

Commentary on Q. Curtius Rufus' Historiae Alexandri Magni Books 3 & 4. J. E. Atkinson. (London Studies in Classical Philology: Vol. 4). (Illus.). vi, 495p. (Orig.). 1980. pap. 80.00 (*90-70265-61-3*, Pub. by Gieben NE) Benjamins North Am.

Commentary on Revelation. Ethelbert W. Bullinger. LC 83-24917. 764p. 1990. pap. 19.99 (*0-8254-2289-2*) Kregel.

Commentary on Revelation. James B. Coffman. 1984. 18.95 (*0-915547-14-7*) Abilene Christ U.

Commentary on Romans. James B. Coffman. 1984. 18.95 (*0-915547-08-2*) Abilene Christ U.

Commentary on Romans. Ernst Kasemann. Tr. by Geoffrey W. Bromiley. 1980. 27.99 (*0-8028-3499-X*) Eerdmans.

Commentary on Romans. Martin Luther. Tr. by J. Theodore Mueller. LC 76-12077. Orig. Title: Commentary on the Epistle to the Romans. 224p. 1976. pap. 10.99 (*0-8254-3119-0*) Kregel.

Commentary on Romans. G. A. McLaughlin. 1985. pap. 9.99 (*0-88019-167-8*) Schmul Pub Co.

Commentary on Romans. William S. Plumer. LC 73-155251. (Kregel Reprint Library). 646p. 1993. 25.99 (*0-8254-3501-3*); pap. 19.99 (*0-8254-3543-9*) Kregel.

Commentary on Romans. abr. ed. C. E. Cranfield. 320p. 1985. pap. 17.99 (*0-8028-0012-2*) Eerdmans.

Commentary on Romans. Frederic L. Godet. LC 77-79189. 544p. 1991. reprint ed. lib. bdg. 24.99 (*0-8254-2715-0*); reprint ed. pap. 19.99 (*0-8254-2732-0*) Kregel.

Commentary on Romans. Anders Nygren. Tr. by Carl Rasmussen. LC 49-48317. 472p. 1949. reprint ed. pap. 12.00 (*0-8006-1684-7*, 1-1684, Fortress Pr) Augsburg Fortress.

Commentary on Saint Ignatius' Rules for the Discernment of Spirits: A Guide to the Principles & Practice. Jules J. Toner. Ed. by George E. Ganss. LC 79-89606. (Original Studies Composed in English Series III: No. 5). xx, 332p. 1991. 31.95 (*0-912422-43-2*); pap. 21.95 (*0-912422-42-4*) Inst Jesuit.

Commentary on Saint Luke. G. A. McLaughlin. 1974. pap. 9.99 (*0-88019-012-4*) Schmul Pub Co.

Commentary on Saint Mark974. G. A. McLaughlin. pap. 9.99 (*0-88019-011-6*) Schmul Pub Co.

Commentary on Saint Matthew. G. A. McLaughlin. pap. 9.99 (*0-88019-010-8*) Schmul Pub Co.

Commentary on Saint Paul's Epistle to the Philippians & First Thessalonians. St. Thomas Aquinas. LC 66-19306. (Aquinas Scripture Ser.: Vol. 3). 1969. pap. 6.00 (*0-87343-028-X*) Magi Bks.

Commentary on Second Corinthians. Bill Jackson. 1993. pap. 7.75 (*0-89137-135-4*) Quality Pubns.

Commentary on Second Peter. Herman A. Hoyt. 136p. 1983. pap. 7.99 (*0-88469-153-5*) BMH Bks.

Commentary on St. John the Apostle & Evangelist, Homilies, 1-47. John Chrysostom. LC 57-1545. (Fathers of the Church Ser.: Vol. 33). 485p. 1957. 39.95 (*0-8132-0033-4*) Cath U Pr.

Commentary on St. John the Apostle & Evangelist, Homilies, 48-88. St. John Chrysostom. LC 57-1545. (Fathers of the Church Ser.: Vol. 41). 495p. 1960. 34.95 (*0-8132-0041-5*) Cath U Pr.

Commentary on St. Paul's Epistle to the Ephesians, 2. St. Thomas Aquinas. Tr. by M. L. Lamb. LC 66-19307. (Aquinas Scripture Ser.). 1966. 10.00 (*0-87343-022-0*) Magi Bks.

Commentary on St. Paul's Epistle to the Galatians, 1. St. Thomas Aquinas. Tr. by F. R. Larcher. LC 66-19306. (Aquinas Scripture Ser.). 1966. 10.00 (*0-87343-021-2*) Magi Bks.

Commentary on Standard ML. Robin Milner & Mads Tofte. 160p. 1991. 30.00x (*0-262-13271-0*); pap. 19.95x (*0-262-63137-7*) MIT Pr.

Commentary on Tennyson's In Memoriam. Andrew C. Bradley. (BCL1-PR English Literature Ser.). 251p. 1992. reprint ed. lib. bdg. 79.00 (*0-7812-7694-2*) Rprt Serv.

Commentary on the Acts of the Apostles by the Venerable Bede. Tr. & Intro. by Lawrence Martin. 1989. 24.95 (*0-685-28779-3*); pap. 12.95 (*0-685-28780-7*) Cistercian Pubns.

Commentary on the American Prayer Book. Marion J. Hatchett. 608p. 1985. text ed. 40.00 (*0-8164-0206-X*) Harper SF.

Commentary on the Animal Apocalypse of I Enoch. Patrick A. Tiller. LC 92-33809. (Early Judaism & Its Literature Ser.: No. 04). 444p. 1993. 39.95 (*1-55540-780-3*, 063504); pap. 24.95 (*1-55540-781-1*, 063504) Scholars Pr GA.

Commentary on the Aristotelian Athenaion Politeia. P. J. Rhodes. (Illus.). 832p. 1993. reprint ed. pap. 42.00 (*0-19-814942-5*) OUP.

Commentary on the Augsburg Confession. Caspar Schwenckfeld. Tr. by Fred A. Grater. 182p. 1982. pap. 5.00 (*0-935980-02-4*) Schwenkfelder Lib.

***Commentary on the Australian Constitution: With Sixth Cumulative Supplement.** suppl. ed. P. H. Lane. 298p. 1994. pap. 75.00 (*0-455-21278-3*, Pub. by Law Bk Co) W W Gaunt.

Commentary on the Book of Deuteronomy. Peter C. Craigie. (New International Commentary on the Old Testament Ser.). 520p. 1976. 29.99 (*0-8028-2524-9*) Eerdmans.

Commentary on the Book of Exodus. 3rd ed. U. Cassuto. Tr. by I. Abrahams. xvi, 509p. (C). 1967. text ed. 30.00 (*0-685-74251-2*, Pub. by Magnes Press IS) Eisenbrauns.

Commentary on the Book of Genesis. Robert D. Sacks. LC 90-33701. (Ancient Near Eastern Texts & Studies: Vol. 6). 440p. 1990. lib. bdg. 109.95 (*0-88946-090-6*) E Mellen.

Commentary on the Book of Isaiah: Isaiah As Sacred Scripture. Steven J. Scherrer. LC 93-83956. 160p. (Orig.). 1993. pap. write for info. (*1-883411-00-9*) St Jerome Pubns.

Commentary on the Book of Jeremiah 1-25: To Pluck up, to Tear Down. Walter Brueggemann. (International Theological Commentary Ser.). 1988. pap. 14.99 (*0-8028-0367-9*) Eerdmans.

Commentary on the Book of Job, Vol. 1: The Wisdom Literature. James B. Coffman. 1993. 19.95 (*0-89112-063-7*) Abilene Christ U.

Commentary on the Book of Jonah. Haimo of Auxerre. Tr. by Deborah Everhart. LC 93-1925. (TEAMS Commentary Ser.). (C). 1993. pap. 3.00 (*1-879288-36-2*) Medieval Inst.

Commentary on the Book of Mormon, 7 vols. George Reynolds & Janne M. Sjodahl. 388p. Vol. 3, 388p., 1958. 9.95 (*0-87747-041-3*); Vol. 4, 451p., 1959. 9.95 (*0-87747-042-1*); Vol. 6, 246p., 1961. 9.95 (*0-87747-044-8*) Deseret Bk.

C

Commentary on the Book of Revelation of John. George E. Ladd. 1971. pap. 14.99 (*0-8028-1684-3*) Eerdmans.

Commentary on the Catechism of the Catholic Church. Ed. by Michael J. Walsh. LC 93-37440. 512p. 1994. 24.95 (*0-8146-2305-0*) Liturgical Pr.

Commentary on the Chemical Weapons Convention. Walter Krutzsch & Ralf Trapp. LC 94-357. 544p. (C). 1994. lib. bdg. 185.00 (*0-7923-2697-0*) Kluwer Ac.

Commentary on the Cistercian Hymnal. John M. Beers. (Henry Bradshaw Society Publications CII). 1987. 55.00 (*0-9501009-4-3*) Boydell & Brewer.

Commentary on the Collected Plays of W. B. Yeats. A. Norman Jeffares & A. S. Knowland. LC 74-82993. 336p. 1975. 42.50 (*0-8047-0875-4*) Stanford U Pr.

Commentary on the Constitution of India, Vol. A-M. 6th ed. Durga D. Basu. (C). 1988. 1,290.00 (*0-685-27940-5*) St Mut.

Commentary on the Constitution of India, Vol. P: Silver Jubilee Edition. D. D. Basu. (C). 1990. 110.00 (*0-685-50323-2*) St Mut.

Commentary on the Creed of Islam. Mas'Ud Ibn Umar Al-Taftazani. LC 79-52565. (Islam Ser.). 1980. reprint ed. lib. bdg. 23.95 (*0-8369-9268-7*) Ayer.

Commentary on the Criminal Procedure Act. E. Du Toit et al. 1987. ring bd. write for info. (*0-7021-1962-8*, Pub. by Juta SA) W W Gaunt.

Commentary on the Criminal Procedure Act. E. Du Toit et al. 1993. pap. write for info. (*0-7021-3010-9*, Pub. by Juta SA) W W Gaunt.

Commentary on the Czechoslovak Civil Code. T. J. Vondracek. (C). 1988. lib. bdg. 169.00 (*90-247-3669-2*) Kluwer Ac.

Commentary on the Dhammapada, 5 vols. in 4, Set. Dhammapadatthakatha. Ed. by H. C. Norman. LC 78-72423. reprint ed. 155.00 (*0-404-17620-8*) AMS Pr.

Commentary on the Divine Liturgy. Nicholas Cabasilas. Tr. by J. M. Hussey & P. A. McNulty. LC 62-53410. 120p. 1977. pap. 9.95 (*0-913836-37-0*) St Vladimirs.

Commentary on the Dream of Scipio by Macrobius. William H. Stahl. 278p. 1990. text ed. 58.00 (*0-231-01737-5*); pap. text ed. 12.50 (*0-231-09628-3*) Col U Pr.

Commentary on the Dresden Codex. Ernst Forstemann. Orig. Title: Commentary on the Mayan Manuscript in the Royal Public Library of Dresden (1906). (Illus.). 223p. 1992. pap. 24.80 (*0-89412-180-4*) Aegean Park Pr.

Commentary on the EC Treaty & the Single European Act. Ed. by Ami Barav. LC 92-33884. 1000p. 1996. 195.00 (*0-19-825615-9*, Old Oregon Bk Store) OUP.

Commentary on the Epistle of James. James Adamson. (New International Commentary on the New Testament Ser.). 480p. 1976. 22.99 (*0-8028-2377-7*) Eerdmans.

Commentary on the Epistle of James. Rudolf E. Stier. 278p. lib. bdg. 12.99 (*0-8254-5242-2*) Kregel.

Commentary on the Epistle of the Romans. 2nd ed. C. K. Barrett. (Black's New Testament Commentaries Ser.). 270p. 1991. pap. text ed. 37.50 (*0-685-67201-8*, Pub. by A & C Blk UK) Lubrecht & Cramer.

Commentary on the Epistle to the Romans see Commentary on Romans

An Asterisk (*) at the beginning of an entry indicates that the title is appearing in BIP for the first time.

Commentary on the First Alcibiades of Plato. Olympiodorus. 220p. 1987. lib. bdg. 52.50 (*0-317-54447-0*, Pub. by A M Hakkert SP) Coronet Bks.

Commentary on the First Epistle to the Corinthians. Thomas C. Edwards. 492p. lib. bdg. 18.99 (*0-8254-5103-5*) Kregel.

Commentary on the First Six Books of the Aeneid of Vergil Commonly Attributed to Bernardus Silvestris. Ed. by Julian W. Jones & Elizabeth F. Jones. LC 76-17308. xxxiv, 163p. 1977. 30.00 (*0-8032-0898-7*) U of Nebr Pr.

Commentary on the Fourth Pythian Ode of Pindar. Bruce K. Braswell. (Texte und Kommentare Ser.: Vol. 14). 448p. (C). 1988. lib. bdg. 211.55 (*0-89925-529-9*) De Gruyter.

Commentary on the Gospel According to John, Bks. 1-10. Origen. Tr. by Ronald E. Heine. LC 88-20406. (Fathers of the Church Ser.: Vol. 80). 344p. 1989. 34.95 (*0-8132-0080-6*) Cath U Pr.

Commentary on the Gospel According to John, Books 13-32. Origen. Tr. by Ronald Heine. LC 88-20406. (Fathers of the Church Ser.: Vol. 89). 432p. 1993. 34.95 (*0-8132-0089-X*) Cath U Pr.

Commentary on the Gospel of John, 2 vols. E. W. Hengstenberg. 1108p. lib. bdg. 36.99 (*0-8254-5126-4*) Kregel.

Commentary on the Gospel of Mark. Joseph A. Alexander. 470p. lib. bdg. 17.99 (*0-8254-5002-0*) Kregel.

Commentary on the Gospel of Mark. William L. Lane. (New International Commentary on the New Testament Ser.). 1974. 27.99 (*0-8028-2502-8*) Eerdmans.

Commentary on the Gospel of St. John, Pt. 1. St. Thomas Aquinas. Ed. by James A. Weisheipl. Tr. by Fabian R. Larcher. LC 66-19306. (Aquinas Scripture Ser.: Vol. 4). (Illus.). 512p. 1980. 35.00 (*0-87343-031-X*) Magi Bks.

***Commentary on the Gospel of Thomas.** Albert Gani. 298p. 1994. pap. 15.00 (*1-882853-04-0*) A Gani.

Commentary on the Holy Bible, 3 vols. Matthew Poole. 1979. Vol.1, Genesis through Job. 56.95 (*0-85151-054-X*); Vol. 2, Psalms through Malachi. 56.95 (*0-85151-134-1*); Vol. 3, Matthew through Revelation. 56.95 (*0-85151-135-X*) Banner of Truth.

Commentary on the Holy Bible, 3 vols., Set. Matthew Poole. 1979. 159.95 (*0-85151-211-9*) Banner of Truth.

Commentary on the International Sales Law: The Vienna Sales Convention, 1988. Ed. by C. M. Bianca et al. 903p. 125.00 (*88-14-01276-8*) Transnatl Juris Pubns.

Commentary on the Law & True Construction of the Federal Constitution. John King. 496p. 1985. reprint ed. lib. bdg. 40.00 (*0-8377-0746-3*) Rothman.

Commentary on the Lord's Sermon on the Mount with Seventeen Related Sermons. Augustine. Tr. by Denis J. Kavanagh. Bd. with Related Sermons. LC 63-18827. LC 63-18827. (Fathers of the Church Ser.: Vol. 11). 382p. 1951. 39.95 (*0-8132-0011-3*) Cath U Pr.

Commentary on the Maya Manuscript in the Royal Public Library of Dresden. E. Forstemann. (HU PMP Ser.). 1906. 28.00 (*0-527-01202-5*) Periodicals Srv.

Commentary on the Mayan Manuscript in the Royal Public Library of Dresden (1906) see Commentary on the Dresden Codex

Commentary on the Medical Writings of Rudolf Virchow: Based on Schwalbe's Virchow-Bibliographie, 1843-1901. Lelland J. Rather. (Bibliography Ser.: No. 3). (Illus.). 236p. 1990. 125.00 (*0-930405-19-6*) Norman SF.

Commentary on the Mutus Liber. Adam McLean. LC 90-47419. (Magnum Opus Hermetic Sourceworks Ser.: No. 11). (Illus.). 82p. (Orig.). 1991. 27.00 (*0-933999-89-5*); pap. 15.00 (*0-933999-90-9*) Phanes Pr.

Commentary on the Narcotic Drugs & Psychotropic Substances Act - Rules, 1985: With State Rules. S. N. Saxena. (C). 1990. 75.00 (*0-89771-170-X*) St Mut.

Commentary on the New Testament, 15 vols., Set. (ACNT Ser.). 1990. pap. 215.00 (*0-8066-8852-1*, 10-9002) Augsburg Fortress.

Commentary on the New Testament from the Talmud & Hebraica, 4 vols., Set. John Lightfoot. 1664p. 1989. 59.95 (*0-943575-26-5*) Hendrickson MA.

Commentary on the Occasional Services. Philip H. Pfatteicher. LC 82-48542. 336p. 1983. 29.00 (*0-8006-0697-3*, 1-697, Fortress Pr) Augsburg Fortress.

Commentary on the Old Testament, 10 vols., Set. C. F. Keil & Franz Delitzsch. 11744p. 1989. 249.50 (*0-943575-24-9*) Hendrickson MA.

Commentary on the Pearl of Great Price: A Jewel among the Scriptures. Jerald R. Johansen. LC 84-62621. 183p. 1984. 11.98 (*0-88290-269-5*) Horizon Utah.

Commentary on the Poetry of W. H. Auden, C. Day Lewis, Louis MacNeice, & Stephen Spender, Vol. 9. John Whitehead. LC 92-22581. 280p. 1992. text ed. 89.95 (*0-7734-9582-7*) E Mellen.

Commentary on the Psalms, 2 vols. in 1. J. J. Perowne. LC 89-11054. Orig. Title: Book of Psalms. 1144p. 1989. pap. 29.99 (*0-8254-3485-8*) Kregel.

Commentary on the Psalms. Joseph A. Alexander. LC 89-2563. Orig. Title: The Psalms Translated & Explained. 568p. 1991. reprint ed. 24.99 (*0-8254-2141-1*); reprint ed. pap. 18.99 (*0-8254-2140-3*) Kregel.

Commentary on the Psalms from Primitive & Mediaeval Writers, 4 vols. Ed. by John M. Neale. LC 78-130990. 1976. reprint ed. 275.00 (*0-404-04680-0*) AMS Pr.

Commentary on the Psalms of David. Apostolos Makrakis. Ed. by Orthodox Christian Educational Society Staff. Tr. by Denver Cummings. 990p. 1950. 24.95 (*0-938366-19-X*) Orthodox Chr.

Commentary on the Satires of Juvenal. E. Courtney. (Illus.). 650p. (C). 1980. text ed. 110.00 (*0-485-11190-X*, Pub. by Athlone Pr UK) Humanities.

Commentary on the School System. Jeffery M. Bruns. 180p. (Orig.). 1990. pap. write for info. (*1-877758-10-8*) Calgre Pr.

Commentary on the Scientific Writings of Josiah-Willard Gibbs: A Propos de la Publication Des Ses Memories Scientifiques, 3 vols. in 2, 1. Ed. by Frederick G. Donnan et al. LC 79-7963. (Three Centuries of Science in America Ser.). 1980. reprint ed. lib. bdg. 63.95 (*0-405-12611-5*) Ayer.

Commentary on the Scientific Writings of Josiah-Willard Gibbs: A Propos de la Publication Des Ses Memories Scientifiques, 3 vols. in 2, 2. Ed. by Frederick G. Donnan et al. LC 79-7963. (Three Centuries of Science in America Ser.). 1980. reprint ed. lib. bdg. 63.95 (*0-405-12612-3*) Ayer.

Commentary on the Scientific Writings of Josiah-Willard Gibbs: A Propos de la Publication Des Ses Memories Scientifiques, 3 vols. in 2, Set. Ed. by Frederick G. Donnan et al. LC 79-7963. (Three Centuries of Science in America Ser.). 1980. reprint ed. lib. bdg. 126.95 (*0-405-12544-5*) Ayer.

Commentary on the Second Epistle General of Second Peter. Thomas B. Adams. 900p. 1990. reprint ed. 49.95 (*1-877611-24-7*) Soli Deo Gloria.

Commentary on the Second Epistle to the Corinthians. Philip Hughes. (New International Commentary on the New Testament Ser.). 1962. 24.99 (*0-8028-2186-3*) Eerdmans.

Commentary on the Song of Songs by St. Gregory of Nyssa. Comment by Casimir McCambley. (Archbishop Iakovos Library of Ecclesiastical & Historical Sources: No. 12). 300p. 1987. 22.95 (*0-917653-17-3*); pap. 14.95 (*0-917653-18-1*) Hellenic Coll Pr.

Commentary on the Sonnets of G. M. Hopkins. Peter Milward. 200p. 1985. pap. 6.95 (*0-8294-0494-5*) Loyola Univ Pr.

***Commentary on the Tanya.** Adin Steinsaltz. Date not set. text ed. write for info. (*1-56821-390-5*) Aronson.

Commentary on the UNCITRAL Model Law on International Commercial Arbitration. Aron Broches. 240p. 1990. pap. 60.00 (*90-6544-507-2*) Kluwer Law Tax Pubs.

Commentary on the Uniform Securities Act. Louis Loss. 1977. 45.00 (*0-316-53326-2*) Little.

Commentary on the Whole Bible, Vol. 1: Genesis to Deuteronomy. Matthew Henry. (Reference Library Edition). 912p. 1986. reprint ed. text ed. 14.99 (*0-529-06365-4*) World Bible.

Commentary on the Whole Bible, Vol. 2: Joshua to Esther. Matthew Henry. (Reference Library Edition). 1160p. 1986. reprint ed. text ed. 14.99 (*0-529-06366-2*) World Bible.

Commentary on the Whole Bible, Vol. 3: Job to Song of Solomon. Matthew Henry. (Reference Library Edition). 1112p. 1986. reprint ed. text ed. 14.99 (*0-529-06367-0*) World Bible.

Commentary on the Whole Bible, Vol. 4: Isaiah to Malachi. Matthew Henry. (Reference Library Edition). 1520p. 1986. reprint ed. text ed. 14.99 (*0-529-06368-9*) World Bible.

Commentary on the Whole Bible, Vol. 5: Matthew to John. Matthew Henry. (Reference Library Edition). 1248p. 1986. reprint ed. text ed. 14.99 (*0-529-06369-7*) World Bible.

Commentary on the Will & Testament of 'Abdu'l-Baha. rev. ed. David Hofman. 56p. 1982. pap. 4.95 (*0-85398-158-2*) G Ronald Pub.

Commentary on the 15th Edition of the IEE Wiring Regulations. 2nd rev. ed. Brian D. Jenkins. 288p. 1985. pap. 44.00 (*0-86341-040-5*, WR101) Inst Elect Eng.

Commentary on Thermodynamics. W. A. Day. (Tracts in Natural Philosophy Ser.). 110p. 1987. 54.00 (*0-387-96615-3*) Spr-Verlag.

Commentary on Thucydides, Vol. I, Bks. I-III. Simon Hornblower. 560p. 1991. 120.00 (*0-19-814880-1*) OUP.

Commentary on Trade & Merchandise Marks ACT, 1958. 2nd ed. K. Kulshreshthas. (C). 1982. 140.00 (*0-685-36424-0*) St Mut.

Commentary on True & False Religion. Ulrich Zwingli. Ed. by Samuel M. Jackson & Clarence N. Heller. LC 81-8272. 432p. (C). 1981. reprint ed. pap. 15.95 (*0-939464-00-4*) Labyrinth Pr.

***Commentary on Virgil Ecloques.** Virgil Ecloques. Ed. & Comment by Wendell Clausen. 360p. 1995. pap. 29.95 (*0-19-815035-0*) OUP.

Commentary on Zechariah. David Baron. LC 88-9010. 566p. 1988. reprint ed. lib. bdg. 22.99 (*0-8254-2216-7*); reprint ed. pap. 16.99 (*0-8254-2277-9*) Kregel.

Commentary to Bankruptcy. 3rd ed. Robert L. Jordan & William D. Warren. (University Casebook Ser.). 281p. 1993. pap. text ed. write for info. (*1-56662-117-8*) Foundation Pr.

Commentary to Booklets. Secondary School Mathematics Curriculum Improvement Study Staff. (Unified Modern Mathematics Ser.: Course 6). 305p. reprint ed. pap. 87.00 (*0-317-29985-9*, 2051822) Bks Demand.

Commentary to Chapter Twenty-Four, Masonry, of the Uniform Building Code: 1991 Edition. Masonry Society Codes & Standards Committee Staff. Ed. by B. Hogan. (Illus.). 152p. (Orig.). 1992. pap. text ed. 25.00 (*0-9626074-1-X*) Masonry Soc.

Commentary to Kant's Critique of Pure Reason. 2nd ed. Norman Kemp-Smith. LC 91-37141. (Humanities Paperback Library). 724p. (C). 1991. reprint ed. text ed. 65.00 (*0-391-00457-3*) Humanities.

Commentary to Kant's Critique of Pure Reason. Norman Kemp-Smith. LC 91-37141. (Humanities Paperback Library). 724p. (C). 1991. reprint ed. pap. 25.00 (*0-391-03709-9*) Humanities.

Commentary to Mishnah Aboth. Moses Maimonides. Tr. by Arthur David. LC 68-27871. 1968. 9.95 (*0-8197-0154-8*) Bloch.

Commentary to the US-Netherlands Tax Convention. Mary C. Bennett. LC 94-15760. 1994. write for info. (*90-6544-893-4*) Kluwer Law Tax Pubs.

Commentators' Haggadah: Anthology. Yitzchok Semler. 1990. 19.95 (*0-685-48560-9*) Feldheim.

***Commentators of the Holy Quran.** Maulana A. Lahori. 130p. (Orig.). 1995. text ed. 19.95 (*1-56744-506-3*) Kazi Pubns.

Commentator's Seder. Yitzchok Sender. 1992. 19.95 (*0-685-59621-4*) Feldheim.

Commented Bibliography of One Hundred & One Influential Books by & about People of African Descent (1556-1982), A Collector's Choice. Charles L. Blockson. (Illus.). 74p. 1989. text ed. 60.00 (*90-70775-03-4*) Oak Knoll.

Commenting & Commentaries. Charles H. Spurgeon. LC 88-8921. 270p. pap. 9.99 (*0-8254-3749-0*) Kregel.

Comments & Characters. John Buchan. LC 79-104999. (Essay Index Reprint Ser.). 1977. 30.95 (*0-8369-1453-8*) Ayer.

Comments, Cases & Other Materials on Legislation. Arthur Lenhoff. xxxvii, 1046p. 1954. reprint ed. lib. bdg. 40.00 (*0-89941-603-9*, 501960) W S Hein.

Comments on Computer Terminology (Spanish) with English-Spanish Vocabulary. G. Aguado. 431p. (SPA.). 1994. 45.00 (*84-283-2060-8*, Pub. by Paraninfo) IBD Ltd.

Comments on Film. Federico Fellini. Ed. by Giovanni Grazzini. Tr. & Intro. by Joseph Henry. (Illus.). 231p. (Orig.). 1988. pap. 11.95 (*0-912201-15-0*) CSU Pr Fresno.

Comments on Here & Hereafter. Bob Jones, Sr. Ed. by Grace W. Haight. 189p. 1942. pap. 6.95 (*0-89084-006-7*) Bob Jones Univ Pr.

Comments on Jury Management in Santa Barbara, California. National Center for State Courts Staff. 9p. 1986. 1.00 (*0-685-16705-4*, WRO-066) Natl Ctr St Courts.

Comments on Leading the Spiritual Life. Krysta Gibson. 200p. (Orig.). 1991. pap. 14.95 (*1-879375-00-1*) Silver Owl Pubns.

Comments on "Patients First" PSSC Policy Response. 1980. 35.00 (*0-317-05772-3*, Pub. by Natl Inst Soc Work) St Mut.

Comments on the Book of Romans. L. Grant. pap. 3.95 (*0-88172-078-X*) Believers Bkshelf.

Comments on the Last Edition of Shakespeare's Plays. J. M. Mason. LC 73-172851. reprint ed. 52.50 (*0-404-04225-2*) AMS Pr.

Comments on the Several Editions of Shakespeare's Plays, Extended to Those of Malone & Steevens. J. M. Mason. LC 77-172852. reprint ed. 76.50 (*0-404-04226-0*) AMS Pr.

Comments on the Society of the Spectacle. Guy Debord. Tr. by Malcolm Imrie. 128p. 1990. 45.00 (*0-86091-302-3*, A5072, Pub. by Verso UK); pap. 14.95 (*0-86091-520-4*, A5076, Pub. by Verso UK) Routledge Chapman & Hall.

Comments to the Environmental Protection Agency on the Acid Rain Program: Permits, Allowance System, Continuous Emissions Monitoring, & Excess Emissions. 75p. 1992. 35.00 (*0-317-05037-0*) Consumer Energy Coun.

Commentum in Horatium Flaccum. Pomponius Porfyrio. x, 599p. 1967. reprint ed. write for info. (*0-318-71203-2*, Pub. by Georg Olms GW) Lubrecht & Cramer.

Commerce, Accounts, & Finance, 2 vols., Set. Ed. by Paul J. Miranti, Jr. (New Works in Accounting History). 1106p. 1993. reprint ed. 223.00 (*0-8153-1214-8*) Garland.

Commerce & Coalitions: How Trade Affects Domestic Political Alignments. Ronald Rogowski. (Illus.). 224p. (C). 1990. text ed. 35.00 (*0-691-07812-2*); pap. text ed. 13.95 (*0-691-02330-1*) Princeton U Pr.

Commerce & Conquest in the Mediterranean, 1100-1500. David Abulafia. LC 93-18602. (Collected Studies: No. CS 410). 143p. 1993. 95.00 (*0-86078-377-4*, Pub. by Variorum UK) Ashgate Pub Co.

Commerce & Culture: The Maritime Communities of Colonial Massachusetts, 1690-1750. Christine L. Heyrman. 432p. (C). 1986. reprint ed. pap. text ed. 14.95 (*0-393-95518-4*) Norton.

Commerce & Ethnic Differences: The Case of the Mons in Thailand. Brian L. Foster. LC 81-18916. (Papers in International Studies: Southeast Asia Ser.: No. 59). 103p. reprint ed. pap. 29.40 (*0-7837-1323-1*, 2041471) Bks Demand.

Commerce & Industry: A Historical View of the Economic Conditions of the British Empire 1815-1914, 2 Vols in One. Ed. by William Page. LC 67-19709. (Reprints of Economic Classics Ser.). 1968. reprint ed. 65.00 (*0-678-00404-8*) Kelley.

Commerce & Management Education in India. K. V. Sivayya. (C). 1990. 23.00 (*81-7024-315-7*, Pub. by Ashish II) S Asia.

Commerce & Morality: Alternative Essays in Business Ethics. Ed. by Tibor Machan. 264p. 1988. 53.00 (*0-8476-7586-6*); pap. 25.00 (*0-8476-7587-4*) Rowman.

Commerce & Social Standing in Ancient Rome. John H. D'Arms. LC 80-25956. (Illus.). 224p. 1981. 35.00 (*0-674-14475-9*) HUP.

Commerce & Society in Sung China. Shiba Yoshinobu. Tr. by Mark Elvin. (Michigan Abstracts of Chinese & Japanese Works on Chinese History: No. 2). (Illus.). 228p. 1970. pap. 8.00 (*0-89264-902-X*) Ctr Chinese Studies.

Commerce & the Law: English Russian Equivalents. I. G. Fedotova & N. N. Tsygankova. 214p. (C). 1991. text ed. 80.00 (*0-569-14840-5*, Pub. by Collets) St Mut.

Commerce & the Spread of Pests & Disease Vectors. Ed. by Marshall Laird. LC 83-16627. (Illus.). 368p. 1984. text ed. 59.95 (*0-275-91208-6*, C1208, Praeger Pubs) Greenwood.

Commerce Clause of the Federal Constitution. Frederick H. Cooke. xcii, 320p. 1987. reprint ed. lib. bdg. 42.50 (*0-8377-2010-9*) Rothman.

Commerce Clause of the Federal Constitution. E. Parmalee Prentice & John G. Egan. lxxv, 386p. 1981. reprint ed. lib. bdg. 37.50 (*0-8377-2505-4*) Rothman.

Commerce Clause of the United States Constitution. Bernard C. Gavit. LC 77-121284. reprint ed. 67.50 (*0-404-02688-5*) AMS Pr.

Commerce Clause under Marshall, Taney & Waite. Felix Frankfurter. 11.25 (*0-8446-2086-6*) Peter Smith.

Commerce Colonial Atlantique et la Guerre D'Independance Des Etats Unis D'Ameriques: 1778-1783. Patrick Villiers. Ed. by Stuart Bruchey. LC 77-77192. (Dissertations in European Economic History Ser.). (Illus.). 1978. lib. bdg. 51.95 (*0-405-10804-4*) Ayer.

Commerce Department Speaks, 2 vols., Set. Wendell L. Willkie, II. 1412p. 1990. pap. 30.00 (*0-685-69391-0*) PLI.

Commerce Department Speaks on Legal Aspects of International Trade, 2 vols., Set. (Corporate Law & Practice Course Handbook, 1985-86 Ser.). 1412p. 1990. 30.00 (*0-685-69390-2*) PLI.

Commerce Department Speaks 1992: Developments in Import Administration, Export & Investment Abroad. (Corporate Law & Practice Course Handbook, 1985-86 Ser.: Vol. 789). 1050p. 1992. 70.00 (*0-685-65492-3*, B4-7013) PLI.

Commerce des Hommes. J. Poirier. Bd. with Contribution a l'Etude Sociologique des Marches Nago du Bas-Dahomey. R. Bastide et al.; Marches Africains. J. Binet & J. Poirier.; Suprafamilial Authority & Economic Process in Micronesian Atolls. L. Mason & J. Poirier.; Native Traders in Two Polynesian Atolls. A. P. Vayda & J. Poirier.; Essai de Socio-Economie Juridique de la Terre dans les Societes Paysannes Negro-Africaines Traditionelles. J. Poirier. (Economies et Societes Series V: No. 1). 1959. Set pap. (*0-8115-0803-X*) Periodicals Srv.

Commerce des Lumieres: John Oswald & the British in Paris, 1790-1793. David V. Erdman. LC 86-4306. (Illus.). 352p. 1987. text ed. 39.00 (*0-8262-0607-7*) U of Mo Pr.

Commerce du 5e Quartier a Lyon see Complexe Agricole

Commerce et Finance en Mediterranee au Moyen Age. Andre E. Sayous. Ed. by Mark Steele. (Collected Studies: No. CS286). 348p. (FRE.). (C). 1988. reprint ed. lib. bdg. 105.00 (*0-86078-234-4*, Pub. by Variorum UK) Ashgate Pub Co.

Commerce et Marketing en Francais. Conrad J. Schmitt & Katia B. Lutz. (Schaum's Foreign Language Ser.). 288p. (FRE.). (C). 1992. pap. text ed. 10.95 (*0-07-056811-1*) McGraw.

Commerce Mediterraneem et Banquiers Italiens au Moyen Age. Robert-Henri Bautier. Ed. by Elizabeth Lalou. (Collected Studies: No. CS362). 350p. (FRE.). 1992. text ed. 99.50 (*0-86078-311-1*, Pub. by Variorum UK) Ashgate Pub Co.

Commerce of America with Europe: Particularly with France & Great Britain. Jean P. Brissot De Warville & Etienne Claviere. LC 74-11218. 1970. reprint ed. lib. bdg. 49.50 (*0-678-04029-X*) Kelley.

Commerce of Louisiana During the French Regime, 1699-1763. Nancy M. Surrey. LC 71-76702. (Columbia University. Studies in Social Sciences: No. 167). reprint ed. 39.50 (*0-404-51167-8*) AMS Pr.

Commerce of the Prairies. Josiah Gregg. Ed. by Max L. Moorhead. LC 54-10055. (American Exploration & Travel Ser.: Vol. 17). (Illus.). 512p. 1990. reprint ed. pap. 17.95 (*0-8061-1059-7*) U of Okla Pr.

Commerce of the Prairies, 2 vols., Set. Josiah Gregg. 1993. reprint ed. lib. bdg. 150.00 (*0-7812-5882-0*) Rprt Serv.

Commerce of the Sacred: Mediation of the Divine among Jews in the Graeco-Roman Diaspora. Jack N. Lightstone. LC 83-20180. (Brown Judaic Studies). 234p. (C). 1984. pap. 19.75 (*0-89130-664-1*, 14 00 59) Scholars Pr GA.

Commerce Power Versus States Rights. Edward S. Corwin. 1959. 11.75 (*0-8446-1130-1*) Peter Smith.

Commerce, Shipping & Naval Warfare in the Medieval Mediterranean. John H. Pryor. (Collected Studies: No. CS259). (Illus.). 348p. (C). 1987. reprint ed. lib. bdg. 95.95 (*0-86078-207-7*, Pub. by Variorum UK) Ashgate Pub Co.

Commerce Skills. Ed. by R. Barrett & M. Gow. (C). 1988. 65.00 (*0-85950-129-9*, Pub. by S Thornes Pubs UK) St Mut.

Commerce to Curate. Tom Hearn. 68p. (C). 1989. text ed. 40.00 (*1-872795-52-8*, Pub. by Pentland Pr UK) St Mut.

Commerce Township Cemeteries, Oakland County, Michigan. Intro. by Joan Pate. 200p. (Orig.). 1989. pap. 12.00 (*1-879766-11-6*) OCG Society.

Commercial - Industrial Real Estate Guide to SBA Loans. Jack Fox. (Illus.). 250p. (Orig.). 1989. 45.00 (*1-877793-00-0*); pap. 19.95 (*1-877793-03-5*) CFREG.

Commercial Activities. Dolan. 1990. 125.00 (*0-316-18904-9*) Little.

Commercial Agencies & Distributorships: An International Guide. Ed. by Adam Fremantle. 960p. 1992. ring bd. 126.00 (*0-13-061129-8*) Aspen Law.

Commercial Agencies & Distributorships: An International Guide. Ed. by Adam Fremantle. LC 92-19165. 1992. write for info. (*0-13-019803-X*) P-H.

C

An Asterisk (*) at the beginning of an entry indicates that the title is appearing in BIP for the first time.

Commercial Agency & Distribution Agreements: Law & Practice in the Member States of the EC & EFTA. Ed. by Association Internationale des Jeunes Avocats (AIJA) Staff. 520p. (C). 1993. lib. bdg. 160.00 (*1-85333-785-4*, Pub. by Graham & Trotman UK) Kluwer Ac.

Commercial Agency & Distribution Agreements: Law & Practice in the Member States of the European Community. Ed. by Guy-Martial Weijer. (C). 1990. lib. bdg. 170.00 (*1-85333-358-1*, Pub. by Graham & Trotman UK) Kluwer Ac.

Commercial Agreements, Trade Association Practices, & Competition Law in the EEC. Nicholas Green. 416p. 1986. lib. bdg. 213.00 (*0-86010-788-4*) G & T Inc.

Commercial Air Cleaning Systems. Richard K. Miller & Marcia E. Rupnow. LC 90-83895. (Survey on Technology & Markets Ser.: No. 191). 50p. 1991. pap. text ed. 200.00 (*1-55865-215-9*) Future Tech Surveys.

Commercial Air Transportation. 5th ed. John H. Frederick. LC 54-42. 509p. reprint ed. pap. 145.10 (*0-317-09208-1*, 2000127) Bks Demand.

Commercial Alternative Dispute Resolution. Maxwell J. Fulton. xvii, 156p. 1989. pap. 39.50 (*0-455-20953-7*, Pub. by Law Bk Co) W W Gaunt.

Commercial & Advertising Art. Jack Rudman. (Occupational Competency Examination Ser.: OCE-11). 1994. pap. 23.95 (*0-8373-5711-X*) Nat Learn.

Commercial & Consumer Credit - An Introduction. A. L. Diamond. 1982. U.K. pap. 40.00 (*0-406-57405-7*) Butterworth Legal Pubs.

Commercial & Consumer Law from an International Perspective: Papers from the Conference of the International Academy of Commercial & Consumer Law, Castle Hofen, Austria, July 17-22, 1984. Ed. by Donald B. King. xx, 529p. 1986. text ed. 47.50 (*0-8377-0748-X*) Rothman.

Commercial & Consumer Warranties: Drafting, Performing & Litigating, 3 vols. Jullian B. McDonnell & Elizabeth Coleman. 1987. Updates. ring bd. write for info. (*0-8205-1824-7*) Bender.

***Commercial & Debtor-Creditor Law: Selected Statues, 1994.** Theodore Eisenberg et al. (Illus.). 1979p. 1994. pap. text ed. 27.95 (*1-56662-190-9*) Foundation Pr.

Commercial & Debtor-Creditor Law: Selected Statutes. 1993. pap. write for info. (*0-318-72443-X*) Foundation Pr.

Commercial & Debtor-Creditor Law: Selected Statutes: 1993. Douglas G. Baird et al. 1952p. 1993. pap. text ed. 27.95 (*1-56662-095-3*) Foundation Pr.

Commercial & Economic Law. Ed. by J. Stuyck. 1992. ring bd. write for info. (*0-318-68484-5*) Kluwer Law Tax Pubs.

Commercial & Experimental Organic Insecticides. rev. ed. Larry L. Larson et al. 105p. 1985. 23.00 (*0-938522-28-0*) Entomol Soc.

Commercial & Finance Dictionary: Dictionnaire Commercial et Financier. 2nd ed. J. Servotte. 500p. (DUT, ENG, FRE & GER.). 1981. pap. 15.95 (*0-8288-0154-1*, M4762) Fr & Eur.

***Commercial & Financial Dictionary: French-English-Russian.** K. S. Gavrichina & M. A. Sazonov. (Illus.). 792p. (C). 1993. text ed. 89.00 (*5-900455-55-6*) Technip.

Commercial & Financial Services, 11 vols. Intro. by R. C. Michie. LC 93-43743. (Industrial Revolutions Ser.). 1994. 1,200.00 (*0-631-18123-7*) Blackwell Pubs.

Commercial & Industrial Enzymes. Business Communications Co., Inc. Staff. (Illus.). 160p. 1986. pap. 1,950.00 (*0-89336-492-4*, C-067) BCC.

Commercial & Industrial Law. A. R. Ruff. (C). 1984. 100. 00 (*0-685-33729-4*, Pub. by Witherby & Co UK) St Mut.

***Commercial & Institutional Maintenance Management.** Kenneth Petrocelly. LC 94-22856. 1994. write for info. (*0-88173-184-6*) Fairmont Pr.

***Commercial & Investment Law: Uzbekistan.** Lynda L. Maillet. LC 94-30392. 1994. write for info. (*1-56425-045-8*) Transnatl Juris Pubns.

Commercial & Property Law: Australian Studies in Law. Ed. by W. D. Duncan. 216p. 1991. 58.00 (*1-86287-068-3*, Pub. by Federation Pr AU) W W Gaunt.

Commercial & Shopping Center Management. rev. ed. (Orig.). 9.95 (*0-944298-04-4*, 903) Inst Real Estate.

Commercial Applications of Precision Manufacturing at the Submicron Level (Nov 1991, London) L. R. Baker. 1992. write for info. (*0-8194-0703-8*, 1573) SPIE.

Commercial Arbitration. 2nd ed. Lord Mustill & Stewart C. Boyd. 836p. 1989. boxed 220.00 (*0-406-31124-2*, UK) Butterworth Legal Pubs.

Commercial Arbitration: An International Bibliography, 2 vols. Ed. by Vratislav Pechota. LC 92-23736. 1993. 185. 00 (*1-56425-002-4*) Transnatl Juris Pubns.

Commercial Arbitration Handbook. Berthold H. Hoeniger. 1991. ring bd. 95.00 (*1-55943-130-X*) Butterworth Legal Pubs.

Commercial Arbitration Handbook, No. 1. suppl. ed. Berthold H. Hoeniger. 1991. 35.50 (*0-685-66080-X*) Butterworth Legal Pubs.

Commercial Arbitration in Islamic & Middle East, Glasgow. S. H. Amin. (C). 1989. 150.00 (*0-946706-46-8*, Pub. by Royston Ltd) St Mut.

Commercial Arbitration in the Arab Middle East. Samir Saleh. 493p. 1984. lib. bdg. 151.00 (*0-86010-453-2*) G & T Inc.

Commercial Arbitration in the Australian Construction Industry. Ronald Fitch. 255p. 1988. pap. 52.50 (*1-86287-005-5*, Pub. by Federation Pr AU) W W Gaunt.

Commercial Arbitration in the Federal Republic of Germany. O. Glossner. 1984. lib. bdg. 71.00 (*90-6544-185-9*) Kluwer Law Tax Pubs.

Commercial Arbitration Institutions: An International Directory & Guide. 2nd ed. Paul J. Davidson & Ludwik Kos-Rabcewicz-Zubkowski. LC 92-61341. 262p. 1992. pap. text ed. 30.00 (*0-379-20101-1*) Oceana.

Commercial Arbitration Law & Clauses: A Drafter's Guide. Jeffrey Barist. LC 94-18900. 1994. 95.00 (*0-13-312901-2*) Aspen Law.

Commercial Arbitration Law in Asia & the Pacific. Ed. by Kenneth R. Simmonds et al. 1987. 75.00 (*0-379-20792-3*) Oceana.

Commercial Arbitration with Forms. Robert M. Rodman. LC 84-15345. (Handbook Ser.). 767p. 1988. reprint ed. text ed. 80.00 (*0-314-86732-5*) West Pub.

Commercial Arbitration with Forms: 1992 Pocket Parts. Robert M. Rodman. 180p. 1992. pap. text ed. write for info. (*0-318-68976-6*) West Pub.

***Commercial Arbitration with Forms: 1995 Pocket Part.** Robert M. Rodman. Ed. by William Fever. (West's Handbook Ser.). 240p. 1994. write for info. (*0-314-05382-4*) West Pub.

Commercial Area Energy Assistance Program. 65p. 1981. 10.00 (*0-318-17335-2*, DG/81-323) Pub Tech Inc.

Commercial Art Techniques. S. Ralph Maurello. (Illus.). 10. 95 (*0-8148-0612-0*); pap. 7.95 (*0-8148-0056-4*) L Amiel Pub.

Commercial Aspects of Trusts & Fiduciary Obligations. Ed. by Ewan McKendrick. LC 92-15521. 336p. 1992. 79.00 (*0-19-825765-1*, Clarendon Pr) OUP.

Commercial Asset-Based Financing: 1988-1990, 4 vols. annuals suppl. ed. Raymond Nimmer. 500.00 (*0-685-24490-3*) Clark Boardman Callaghan.

***Commercial Atlas & Marketing Guide, 1996.** Ed. by Rand McNally Staff & David Zapenski. (Illus.). 568p. Date not set. 395.00 (*0-528-81602-0*) Rand McNally.

***Commercial Auto Insurance.** Date not set. 240.00 (*1-886813-11-6*) Intl Risk Mgt.

Commercial Aviation Safety. Alexander Wells. 1991. pap. text ed. 34.95 (*0-07-157716-5*) McGraw.

Commercial Aviation Safety. Alexander T. Wells. 336p. 1991. 32.95 (*0-8306-2194-6*, 1511) TAB Bks.

Commercial Bail Bonding: A Comparison of Common Law Alternatives. F. E. Devine. LC 91-8605. 232p. 1991. text ed. 55.00 (*0-275-93732-1*, C3732, Praeger Pubs) Greenwood.

Commercial Bank Activities in Urban Mortgage Financing. Carl F. Behrens. (Financial Research Program IV: Studies in Urban Mortgage Financing: No. 5). 149p. 1952. reprint ed. 38.80 (*0-87014-143-0*) Natl Bur Econ Res.

Commercial Bank Financial Management: In the Financial Service Industry. 4th ed. Joseph F. Sinkey, Jr. (Illus.). 936p. (C). 1992. Other materials avail. text ed. write for info. (*0-02-410595-3*) Macmillan.

Commercial Bank Liquidity Management, Discretionary Reserve Behavior, & the Allocation of Credit, 1863-1913. rev. ed. J. M. Carter. LC 92-22993. (Financial Sector of the American Economy Ser.). 200p. 1992. 53. 00 (*0-8153-0962-7*) Garland.

Commercial Bank Loan & Investment Behaviour. John H. Wood. LC 75-1192. (Wiley Monographs in Applied Econometrics). (Illus.). 163p. reprint ed. pap. 46.50 (*0-8357-3094-8*, 2039351) Bks Demand.

Commercial Bank Management. Frank P. Johnson & Richard D. Johnson. 720p. (C). 1985. text ed. 43.00 (*0-03-063582-9*) Dryden Pr.

Commercial Bank Management. 2nd ed. Peter S. Rose. 800p. (C). 1992. pap. text ed. 66.95 (*0-256-11557-5*) Irwin.

Commercial Bank Management: Text & Readings. John A. Haslem. (C). 1985. text ed. 55.00 (*0-8359-0964-6*, Reston) P-H.

Commercial Bank Management Reader. Ed. by Robert W. Kolb. LC 92-70168. 640p. 1992. pap. text ed. 28.00 (*1-878975-12-9*) Kolb Pub.

Commercial Bank Underwriting of Municipal Revenue Bonds. Paul A. Leonard. LC 82-4753. (Research for Business Decisions Ser.: No. 48). 107p. reprint ed. pap. 30.50 (*0-685-20848-6*, 2070080) Bks Demand.

Commercial Banking. Prem N. Abrol. (C). 1987. 28.00 (*0-8364-2176-0*, Pub. by Ashish II) S Asia.

Commercial Banking, 2 vols., Set. William H. Kniffin, Jr. Ed. by Stuart Bruchey. LC 80-1156. (Rise of Commercial Banking Ser.). 1981. reprint ed. lib. bdg. 77. 95 (*0-405-13662-5*) Ayer.

***Commercial Banking: The Management of Risk.** Donald R. Fraser et al. 800p. 1995. text ed. 63.00 (*0-314-04459-0*) West Pub.

Commercial Banking & Interstate Expansion: Issues, Prospects, & Strategies. Larry A. Frieder et al. LC 84-28109. (Research for Business Decisions Ser.: No. 74). (Illus.). 195p. reprint ed. pap. 55.60 (*0-8357-1621-X*, 2070378) Bks Demand.

Commercial Banking & Regional Development in the United States, 1950-1960. George Macesich. LC 65-64030. (Florida State University Studies: No. 45). 178p. reprint ed. pap. 50.80 (*0-7837-4932-5*, 2044598) Bks Demand.

Commercial Banking & the Stock Market Before 1863. Joseph E. Heges. LC 78-64170. (Johns Hopkins University. Studies in the Social Sciences. Thirtieth Ser. 1912: 1). reprint ed. 24.50 (*0-404-61279-2*) AMS Pr.

Commercial Banking in an Era of Deregulation. 2nd ed. Emmanuel N. Roussakis. LC 89-3862. (Illus.). 448p. 1989. text ed. 65.00 (*0-275-93144-7*, C3144, Praeger Pubs) Greenwood.

Commercial Banking in Mississippi, 1940-1980. Harvey S. Lewis et al. 1983. pap. 5.00 (*0-938004-10-7*) U MS Bus Econ.

Commercial Banking in the Financial Services Industry. Austin Spencer et al. (C). 1985. teacher ed write for info. (*0-8359-0776-7*, Reston); text ed. 52.00 (*0-8359-0772-4*, Reston) P-H.

Commercial Banking in the United States: A History. Benjamin J. Klebaner. LC 74-45. 1974. lib. bdg. 25.00 (*0-678-08079-8*); pap. 14.95 (*0-678-08078-X*) Kelley.

Commercial Banking Reform in the United States. Leonard L. Watkins. Ed. by Stuart Bruchey. LC 80-1175. (Rise of Commercial Banking Ser.). (Illus.). 1981. reprint ed. lib. bdg. 15.95 (*0-405-13682-X*) Ayer.

Commercial Bankruptcy Litigation. Stephen E. Snyder & Lawrence Ponoroff. LC 89-31911. 1989. ring bd. 145.00 (*0-87632-637-8*) Clark Boardman Callaghan.

Commercial Banks & Consumer Installment Credit. John M. Chapman et al. (Financial Research Program II: Studies in Consumer Installment Financing: No. 3). 342p. 1940. reprint ed. 89.00 (*0-87014-462-6*); reprint ed. mic. film 44.50 (*0-685-61209-0*) Natl Bur Econ Res.

Commercial Banks & Rural Development. R. N. Pandey. (C). 1989. 250.00 (*0-685-46468-7*) St Mut.

Commercial Banks & the Creditworthiness of Less Developed Countries. Yoon-Dae Euh. LC 79-22721. (Research for Business Decisions Ser.: No. 11). 116p. reprint ed. pap. 33.10 (*0-685-20861-3*, 2070128) Bks Demand.

Commercial Banks & Their Trust Activities, 2 vols., 1. Banking & Currency Committee. LC 75-81987. 1969. reprint ed. 20.95 (*0-405-00012-X*) Ayer.

Commercial Banks & Their Trust Activities, 2 vols., 2. Banking & Currency Committee. LC 75-81987. 1969. reprint ed. 20.95 (*0-405-00013-8*) Ayer.

Commercial Banks & Their Trust Activities, 2 vols., Set. Banking & Currency Committee. LC 75-81987. 1969. reprint ed. Set. 39.95 (*0-405-00011-1*) Ayer.

Commercial Blanket Bond Annotated. LC 85-72949. 179p. 1985. 39.95 (*0-89707-202-2*, 519-0046) Amer Bar Assn.

Commercial Break. Paul Fericano. 72p. (Orig.). 1982. 10.00 (*0-916296-07-5*); pap. 4.00 (*0-916296-08-3*) Poor Souls Pr.

Commercial Building: An Introduction for Home Builders. Michael S. Milliner & Home Builder Press. 208p. 1989. pap. 30.00 (*0-86718-329-2*) Home Builder.

***Commercial Buildings Characteristics.** 1995. lib. bdg. 299. 99 (*0-8490-6454-6*) Gordon Pr.

***Commercial Buildings Energy Consumption & Expenditures.** 1995. lib. bdg. 499.99 (*0-8490-6455-4*) Gordon Pr.

Commercial Business & Trade Laws, 21 binders. Incl. India. Robert C. Rosen. 1981. 150.00 (*0-379-22401-1*); Nigeria. Ed. by T. A. Aguda. 1981. 150.00 (*0-379-23001-1*); Set. Peoples' Republic of China, 3 binders. Owen D. Nee, Jr. Ed. by Franklin D. Chu. 1983. ring bd. 450.00 (*0-379-23120-4*); Soviet Union & Mongolia. William E. Butler. 1981. 150.00 (*0-379-22501-8*); United Kingdom, 2 binders. Ed. by Kenneth Simmonds. 1981. 300.00 (*0-379-22201-9*); Taiwan. C. V. Chen. 1981. 150.00 (*0-379-22101-2*); Italy. Louis F. DelDuca & Patrick F. DelDuca. 1981. 150.00 (*0-379-22202-7*); Commercial, Business & Trade Laws: Mexico. Michael W. Gordon. 1981. 150.00 (*0-379-22701-0*); Poland. Jerzy Rajski. 1981. 150.00 (*0-379-22504-2*); Thailand. Montri Hongskrailers. 1981. 150.00 (*0-379-22102-0*); German Democratic Republic. Fritz Enderlein. 1981. 150.00 (*0-379-22502-6*); Hong Kong, 2 binders. A. Keesee. 1981. 300.00 (*0-379-23116-6*); Republic of Korea, 2 binders. W. Choi. 1981. 300.00 (*0-685-42464-2*); United States. J. Norton. 1981. ring bd. 150.00 (*0-379-22703-7*); Zimbabwe. A. Aguda. 1981. ring bd. 150.00 (*0-379-23003-8*); 1981. Caribbean. Phillips, Fred. 150.00 (*0-685-55647-6*); Incl. 150.00 (*0-379-22401-1*); 150.00 (*0-379-23001-1*); Set. ring bd. 450.00 (*0-379-23120-4*); 150.00 (*0-379-22501-8*); 300.00 (*0-379-22201-9*); 150.00 (*0-379-22101-2*); 150.00 (*0-379-22202-7*); 150.00 (*0-379-22701-0*); 150.00 (*0-379-22504-2*); 150.00 (*0-379-22102-0*); 150.00 (*0-379-22502-6*); 300.00 (*0-379-23116-6*); 300.00 (*0-685-42464-2*); ring bd. 150. 00 (*0-379-22703-7*); ring bd. 150.00 (*0-379-23003-8*); Complete Set. Set ring bd. 3,150.00 (*0-379-22702-9*) Oceana.

Commercial, Business & Trade Laws: Mexico see Commercial Business & Trade Laws

Commercial Catfish Farming. 3rd ed. Jasper S. Lee. (Illus.). 338p. 1991. text ed. 31.95 (*0-8134-2905-6*); text ed. 23. 95 (*0-685-47576-X*) Interstate.

Commercial Chicken Production. M. North. 1990. text ed. 79.95 (*0-442-31881-2*) Chapman & Hall.

Commercial Cockle Farming in Southern Thailand. Ed. by Edward McCoy. (ICLARM Translations Ser.: No. 7). 13p. 1986. pap. 2.00 (*971-10-2220-6*, Pub. by ICLARM PH) Intl Spec Bk.

Commercial Companies Law of the United Arab Emirates. Tr. by M. Hall. 95p. 1900. pap. text ed. 163.00 (*0-86010-551-2*) G & T Inc.

Commercial Conference Management. Roy Whipps. (Illus.). 200p. 1974. text ed. 25.00 (*0-8464-1288-8*) Beekman Pubs.

Commercial Contracts. Ed. by Will G. Barber. (Texas Court's Charge Ser.: Vol. 4). 240p. 1994. ring bd. 85.00 (*0-409-25681-1*) Michie Butterworth.

Commercial Cookery: Culinary Art Applications. Jerome A. Uberu. LC 88-90405. 1989. 8.99 (*0-9622209-0-6*) Jerrison Enterprises.

Commercial Cool Storage Design Guide. Electric Power Research Institute Staff. 260p. 1987. 89.00 (*0-89116-687-4*) Hemisp Pub.

Commercial Correspondence: For Students of English As a Second Language. 2nd ed. C. Love & Joseph Tinervia. 1980. text ed. 8.97 (*0-07-038785-0*) McGraw.

Commercial Correspondence in English: La Correspondance Commerciale En Anglais. Michael Geoghegan. 247p. (ENG & FRE.). 1988. pap. 39.95 (*0-8288-1541-0*, M504) Fr & Eur.

Commercial Correspondence in German: La Correspondance Commerciale en Allemand. Jurgen Boelcke. (FRE & GER.). 1988. pap. 14.95 (*0-8288-1558-5*, M508) Fr & Eur.

Commercial Crime Coverages. Diane Swiesz. 1991. 39.50 (*1-56461-033-0*, 46060) Rough Notes.

Commercial Crises of the Nineteenth Century. 2nd ed. Henry M. Hyndman. LC 67-19959. (Reprints of Economic Classics Ser.). ix, 274p. 1967. reprint ed. 37. 50 (*0-678-00322-X*) Kelley.

Commercial Crisis Eighteen Forty-Seven to Eighteen Forty-Eight: Being Facts & Figures Illustrative of the Events of That Important Period. 2nd ed. D. Morier Evans. LC 68-20037. (Library of Money & Banking History). 1969. reprint ed. 39.50 (*0-678-00515-X*) Kelley.

Commercial Culture: The Mass Media System & the Public Interest. Leo Bogart. 288p. 1995. 35.00 (*0-19-509098-5*) OUP.

Commercial Damages: A Guide to Remedies in Business Litigation, 3 vols., Set, incl. reporter svc. 1 yr. Charles L. Knapp. 1986. Set, incl. reporter service for 1 year. ring bd. write for info. (*0-8205-1079-3*) Bender.

Commercial Dictionary: Diccionario Comercial en Seis Idiomas. Diana Staff. 636p. (ENG, FRE, GER, ITA, POR & SPA.). 1982. pap. 39.95 (*0-8288-0140-1*, S20108) Fr & Eur.

Commercial Dictionary in Six Languages. ECON Staff. 637p. (ENG, FRE, GER, ITA, POR & SPA.). 1989. 59. 00 (*3-430-19797-X*) IBD Ltd.

***Commercial Dictionary in Six Languages.** ECON Staff. 1989. 59.00 (*0-7859-8967-6*) Fr & Eur.

***Commercial Dispute Resolution: An ADR Practice Guide.** Karl Mackie & David Miles. 1994. boxed 121.00 (*0-406-02011-6*, UK) Butterworth Legal Pubs.

Commercial Distribution in Europe. John A. Dawson. LC 81-2123. 1982. text ed. 32.50 (*0-312-15264-7*) St Martin.

Commercial Diver Training Manual. Ed. by Best Publishing Co. Staff & College of Oceaneering Staff. (Illus.). 362p. (C). 1990. text ed. 53.00 (*0-941332-10-1*) Best Pub Co.

Commercial Diving Manual. Richard Larn & Rex Whistler. (Illus.). 512p. 1993. 39.95 (*0-7153-0100-4*, Pub. by D & C Pub UK) Sterling.

***Commercial Diving Reference & Operations Handbook.** fac. ed. Mark Freitag & Anthony Woods. LC 82-13607. 430p. Date not set. pap. 122.60 (*0-7837-7369-2*, 2047178) Bks Demand.

***Commercial Driver's License: Interpretations & Guidance.** 56p. 1994. reprint ed. pap. 5.95 (*0-88711-263-3*) Am Trucking Assns.

Commercial Electrical Wiring. John E. Traister. (Illus.). 320p. (Orig.). 1994. pap. 27.50 (*0-934041-97-0*) Craftsman.

Commercial Electrical Wiring & Design. Traister. 1986. text ed. 59.00 (*0-13-152687-1*) P-H.

Commercial Electroplating, 2 bks. set. Randell Nyborg. (Illus.). 225p. 1990. pap. 39.00 (*1-877767-11-5*) Univ Publng Hse.

Commercial Electroplating, 2 bks. set, Set. Randell Nyborg. (Illus.). 225p. 1990. 55.00 (*1-877767-12-3*) Univ Publng Hse.

Commercial EMC Standards of the United States. Jeffrey K. Echert. LC 88-81461. (Electromagnetic Interference & Compatibility Ser.: Vol. 9). (Illus.). 520p. 1988. 75.00 (*0-944916-09-0*) D White Consult.

Commercial, Environmental, & International Contracting: An Evolving Focus. Gerald L. Cruce et al. Ed. by Mary Barrientos et al. 328p. (Orig.). 1993. pap. 59.95 (*0-940343-46-0*) Natl Contract Mgmt.

Commercial Estimator for Europe: L'Estimatif Commercial Bauschatzpreise Fur Gewerbliche Bauten. Pascal Lorthioir. 265p. 1993. write for info. (*1-56842-007-2*); disk write for info. (*1-56842-009-9*) Marshall & Swift.

Commercial Exploitation of Intellectual Property. Hilary Pearson & Clifford Miller. 474p. 1990. pap. 48.00 (*1-85431-044-5*, Pub. by Blackstone Pr UK) W W Gaunt.

Commercial Exploitation of Personality. S. K. Murumba. xvii, 184p. 1986. 64.50 (*0-455-20692-9*, Pub. by Law Bk Co) W W Gaunt.

***Commercial Exterior Perspective.** (Illus.). 152p. 1995. pap. 39.95 (*4-7661-0172-3*, Pub. by Graphic Sha JA) Bks Nippan.

Commercial Finance Guide. Joseph J. Norton et al. 1990. write for info. (*0-8205-1395-4*, 395) Bender.

Commercial Financing. Ed. by Monroe R. Lazere. LC 67-30356. 317p. reprint ed. pap. 90.40 (*0-317-28646-3*, 2055107) Bks Demand.

Commercial Fish Reproduction in Fiberglass. Jim Hall. Ed. by Bob Williamson. (Illus.). 18p. (C). 1986. pap. text ed. 6.95 (*0-925245-23-2*) WASCO Manufact.

Commercial Fisherman's Expense Ledger. 48p. 1989. pap. 9.95 (*0-685-28984-2*) Marine Trade.

Commercial Fisherman's Guide to Financial Planning. Ken Horwitz. Ed. by Jay Lane & Sheila Walter. (Horwitz Financial Planning Guides Ser.). (Illus.). 231p. (Orig.). 1991. pap. 12.95 (*0-934363-08-0*) Lance Pubns.

Commercial Fisherman's Guide, 1990, Vol. 1. Ed. by Joseph Kawaky. 400p. 1989. pap. 12.95 (*0-685-28985-0*) Marine Trade.

Commercial Fisherman's Guide, 1990, Vol. 2. Ed. by Joseph Kawaky. 400p. 1989. pap. 9.95 (*0-685-28986-9*) Marine Trade.

Commercial Fisherman's Guide, 1990, Vol. 3. Ed. by Joseph Kawaky. 400p. 1989. pap. 9.95 (*0-685-28987-7*) Marine Trade.

C

An Asterisk (*) at the beginning of an entry indicates that the title is appearing in BIP for the first time. 1413

Commercial Fishing Methods. John C. Sainsbury. 1992. 125.00 (0-685-63396-9) St Mut.

Commercial Fishing Methods. 3rd ed. Sainsbury. 1994. pap. write for info. (0-85238-217-0) Blackwell Sci.

Commercial Flower Forcing. 8th ed. Alex Laurie et al. (Illus.). 1979. text ed. write for info. (0-07-036633-0) McGraw.

Commercial Flowers in India. T. K. Bose & L. P. Yadav. 850p. (C). 1986. 37.50 (81-85109-48-6, Pub. by Naya Prokash IA) S Asia.

Commercial Fluorine Compounds. Business Communications Co., Inc. Staff. 124p. 1989. pap. 1,750. 00 (0-89336-581-5, C087R) BCC.

Commercial Food Equipment Repair & Maintenance Manual. Roland Greaves. (Professional Bks.). (Illus.). 256p. (C). 1987. pap. 44.95 (0-442-22755-8) Van Nos Reinhold.

Commercial Foodservice Cleaning Manual. W. Marvin. 1992. pap. write for info. (0-442-00803-1) Van Nos Reinhold.

Commercial Fords. Loren Sorenson. (Illus.). 224p. 1988. 39. 98 (0-87938-337-2) Motorbooks Intl.

Commercial Fragrance Bottles. Joanne D. Ball & Dorothy H. Torem. (Illus.). 256p. 1993. 79.95 (0-88740-556-8) Schiffer.

Commercial Fruit Processing. 2nd ed. Ed. by Jasper G. Woodroof & Bor S. Luh. 526p. 1986. text ed. 109.95 (0-87055-502-2) AVI.

Commercial Future of Hong Kong. William F. Beazer. LC 76-24343. 176p. 1978. 55.00 (0-275-90284-6, C0284, Praeger Pubs) Greenwood.

Commercial General Liability. 3rd ed. Donald S. Malecki & Arthur L. Flitner. LC 90-62771. 210p. 1990. pap. 30.00 (0-87218-340-8) Natl Underwriter.

Commercial General Liability Coverages. James O'Neal. 1991. 39.50 (1-56461-007-1, 46020) Rough Notes.

Commercial General Liability Rating. Betsy Cormier. Date not set. 39.50 (1-56461-034-9, 46070) Rough Notes.

Commercial Glasses. Ed. by David C. Boyd & John F. MacDowell. LC 86-10723. (Advances in Ceramics Ser.: No. 18). (Illus.). 238p. reprint ed. pap. 67.90 (0-7837-4335-1, 2044046) Bks Demand.

Commercial Goodwill: Its History, Value & Treatment in Accounts. Percy D. Leake. Ed. by Richard P. Brief. LC 80-1507. (Dimensions of Accounting Theory & Practice Ser.). 1980. reprint ed. lib. bdg. 30.95 (0-405-13532-7) Ayer.

Commercial Greenhouse. James W. Boodley. LC 78-74806. (Agriculture Ser.). 568p. (C). 1981. 35.95 (0-8273-1719-0) Delmar.

Commercial Guide to F. I. D. I. C. Conditions of Contract. Brian Meopham. (Waterlow Practitioner's Library). 352p. 1986. 69.00 (0-08-039234-2, K130, Pergamon Pr) Elsevier.

Commercial Guide to GC-Works-1 Conditions of Contract. Brian Meopham. (Waterlow Practitioner's Library). 336p. 1985. 59.00 (0-08-039233-4, Pergamon Pr) Elsevier.

Commercial Guide to Government Packaging, Vol. 1. David K. Eary. 210p. 1985. pap. 55.00 (0-912702-26-5) Global Eng Doc.

Commercial Guide to Government Packaging, Vol. 2. Global Engineering Documents Staff. Ed. by David K. Eary. 635p. 1985. ring bd. 170.00 (0-912702-30-3) Global Eng Doc.

Commercial Guide to I. C. E. Conditions Contract. Brian Meopham. (Waterlow Practitioner's Library). 336p. 1985. 59.00 (0-08-039232-6, Pergamon Pr) Elsevier.

Commercial Guide to the Forest Economic Products of India. R. S. Pearson. 155p. (C). 1980. text ed. 175.00 (0-89771-619-1, Pub. by Intl Bk Distr II) St Mut.

Commercial Guide to the Forest Economic Products of India. R. S. Pearson. (C). 1988. 40.00 (0-685-22371-X, Scientific) St Mut.

Commercial Guide to the Forest Economic Products of India. R. S. Pearson. 155p. (C). 1980. reprint ed. 125.00 (0-685-21861-9, Pub. by Intl Bk Distr II) St Mut.

Commercial Hiring & Leasing. John Adams. 1989. 124.00 (0-406-10114-0, U.K.) Butterworth Legal Pubs.

Commercial Housekeeping & Maintenance. I. Jones & C. Phillips. (C). 1984. 100.00 (0-685-47488-7, Pub. by S Thornes Pubs UK) St Mut.

Commercial Housekeeping & Maintenance. Iris Jones & Cynthia Phillips. (Illus.). 272p. 1984. pap. 37.50 (0-85950-377-1, Pub. by Stanley Thornes UK) Trans-Atl Phila.

Commercial Hydroponics. John Mason. (Illus.). 172p. reprint ed. 24.95 (0-86417-300-8, Pub. by Kangaroo Pr AT) Seven Hills Bk.

Commercial, Industrial, & Institutional Refrigeration: Design, Installation & Troubleshooting. William B. Cooper. (Illus.). 576p. 1986. text ed. 75.00 (0-13-152018-0) P-H.

Commercial Insurance. 2nd ed. Ed. by Bernard L. Webb et al. LC 90-80138. 295p. 1994. 26.00 (0-89462-053-3) IIA.

***Commercial Interior Perspectives.** (Illus.). 152p. 1995. pap. 39.95 (4-7661-0171-5, Pub. by Graphic Sha JA) Bks Nippan.

Commercial-Investment Real Estate: Marketing & Management, Bk. 1. Lee E. Arnold, Jr. Ed. by Dawn M. Gerth. LC 82-62949. (Illus.). 250p. text ed. 24.95 (0-913652-53-9, BK 161); text ed. 19.96 (0-685-06458-1) Realtors Natl.

Commercial Investment Real Estate: Policies & Procedures. 248p. 19.95 (0-317-36759-5, BK 162) Realtors Natl.

Commercial Investment Real Estate: Policies & Procedures, Bk. 2. 2nd ed. Lee E. Arnold, Jr. (Illus.). 248p. 1986. pap. text ed. 32.40 (0-13-152737-1) P-H.

Commercial Investment Real Estate, Bk. 1: Marketing & Brokerage Management. 2nd ed. Lee E. Arnold, Jr. 332p. 1991. text ed. 60.00 (0-13-151440-7) P-H.

Commercial Irrigation Enterprise: The Fear of Water Monopoly & the Genesis of Market Distortion in the Nineteenth Century American West. Richard M. Alston. LC 77-14752. (Dissertations in American Economic History Ser.). 1977. 30.95 (0-405-11025-1) Ayer.

***Commercial Kitchen in Spanish & English.** Kenneth Weeks. (Illus.). 112p. (Orig.). 1994. pap. 9.95 (0-9644811-0-3) Tennyson CA.

Commercial Kitchens. 6th ed. 368p. 1978. 20.00 (0-318-12594-3); pap. 10.00 (0-318-12593-5, R00469) Am Gas Assn.

***Commercial Launch Vehicle International Guide.** (Illus.). 240p. (Orig.). 1994. pap. 495.00 (0-7605-1154-3) Rector Pr.

Commercial Law. (Legal Research Guides Ser.). 486p. 1989. 99.00 (0-8352-2857-6) Bowker.

Commercial Law. Robert Bradgate & Nigel Savaoe. 1991. U.K. pap. 46.00 (0-406-51412-7) Butterworth Legal Pubs.

Commercial Law. Ed. by Ross Cranston. LC 92-36315. (International Library of Essays in Law & Legal Theory: Vol. 16). (C). 1992. 150.00 (0-8147-1472-2) NYU Pr.

Commercial Law. Terence Prime. (C). 1990. 110.00 (1-85431-087-9, Pub. by Blackstone Pr UK) St Mut.

Commercial Law. P. A. Read. 276p. (C). 1990. pap. 40.00 (1-85352-782-3, Pub. by HLT Pubns UK) St Mut.

Commercial Law. Paul Todd. (C). 1991. text ed. 29.00 (1-85431-138-7, Pub. by Blackstone Pr UK) W W Gaunt.

***Commercial Law.** 2nd ed. Robert Bradgate et al. (Legal Practice Course Guides Ser.). 410p. 1995. pap. 34.00 (1-85431-394-0, Pub. by Blackstone Pr UK) W W Gaunt.

Commercial Law. 3rd ed. D. W. Greig. 585p. 1988. pap. 83. 00 (0-409-49248-5, Austral) Butterworth Legal Pubs.

Commercial Law. 3rd ed. Robert L. Jordan & William D. Warren. (University Casebook Ser.). 1200p. 1992. text ed. 46.95 (0-88277-984-2) Foundation Pr.

Commercial Law. 6th ed. Gordon J. Borrie. 392p. 1988. pap. text ed. 38.00 (0-406-55846-9, UK) Butterworth Legal Pubs.

Commercial Law: Adaptable to Courses Utilizing Farnsworth, Honnald, Reitz, Harris & Mooney's Casebook on Commercial Law. Casenotes Publishing Co., Inc. Staff. Ed. by Norman S. Goldenberg et al. (Legal Briefs Ser.). 1993. pap. write for info. (0-87457-019-0, 1311) Casenotes Pub.

Commercial Law: Adaptable to Courses Utilizing Jordan & Warren's Casebook on Commercial Law, Secured Transactions & Commercial Paper. Casenotes Publishing Co., Inc. Staff. Ed. by Norman S. Goldenberg et al. (Legal Briefs Ser.). 1992. pap. write for info. (0-87457-020-4, 1312) Casenotes Pub.

Commercial Law: Adaptable to Courses Utilizing Spiedel, Summers & White's Casebook on Sales & Secured Transactions. Casenotes Publishing Co., Inc. Staff. Ed. by Norman S. Goldenberg et al. (Legal Briefs Ser.). 1993. pap. write for info. (0-87457-021-2, 1310) Casenotes Pub.

Commercial Law: Cases & Materials. 2nd ed. Calvin W. Corman. 856p. 1983. 48.00 (0-316-15746-5) Little.

Commercial Law: Cases & Materials. 2nd ed. Vern Countryman et al. LC 81-81533. 1326p. (C). 1982. 48.00 (0-316-15796-1) Little.

Commercial Law: Cases & Materials. 4th ed. E. Allan Farnsworth & John O. Honnold. LC 84-28603. (University Casebook Ser.). 1168p. 1990. reprint ed. text ed. 34.50 (0-88277-226-0) Foundation Pr.

Commercial Law: Manual for Teachers to Accompany Cases & Materials. E. Allan Farnsworth & John O. Honnold. (University Casebook Ser.). 107p. (C). 1985. pap. text ed. write for info. (0-88277-267-8) Foundation Pr.

Commercial Law: Selected Statutes. 2nd ed. Vern Countryman et al. 1980. pap. 22.00 (0-316-15813-5) Little.

Commercial Law Adaptable to Courses Utilizing Whaley's Casebook on Commercial Law, Secured Transactions & Sale & Lease of Goods. Ed. by Norman Goldenberg & Peter Tenen. (Legal Briefs Ser.). (C). 1993. pap. write for info. (0-87457-197-9, 1313) Casenotes Pub.

Commercial Law & Practice Guide, Vol. 3. B. Zaretsky et al. 1991. write for info. (0-8205-1192-7) Bender.

Commercial Law & Practice Series, 1992-1993, 20 vols., Set. 1993. pap. 1,025.00 (0-685-69392-9) PLI.

Commercial Law, Cases & Materials On. 5th rev. ed. E. Allan Farnsworth et al. LC 93-23774. (University Casebook Ser.). 1200p. 1993. text ed. 46.50 (1-56662-069-4) Foundation Pr.

Commercial Law, Commentary To. 3rd ed. Robert L. Jordan & William D. Warren. (University Casebook Ser.). 502p. (C). 1992. pap. text ed. write for info. (1-56662-042-2) Foundation Pr.

Commercial Law Handbook: Annual Edition. Gould Editorial Staff. 1100p. (C). ring bd. 24.95 (0-87526-312-7) Gould.

Commercial Law in Ireland. Forde. U.K. write for info. (1-85475-123-9) Butterworth Legal Pubs.

Commercial Law in the Gulf States: The Islamic Legal Tradition. Noel Coulson. 128p. 1984. lib. bdg. 79.00 (0-86010-574-1) G & T Inc.

Commercial Law, Manual for Teachers to Accompany Cases, Problems & Materials On. 5th ed. E. Allan Farnsworth et al. Ed. by Charles R. Reitz. (University Casebook Ser.). 222p. 1993. pap. text ed. write for info. (1-56662-131-3) Foundation Pr.

Commercial Law of Iran. S. H. Amin. 1986. 90.00 (0-946706-29-8, Pub. by Royston Ltd) St Mut.

Commercial Law of Russia: A Legal Treatise. William G. Frenkel. 1000p. 1994. ring bd. 285.00 (1-56425-021-0) Transnatl Juris Pubns.

Commercial Law, Problems & Materials. John E. Murray, Jr. 366p. 1986. reprint ed. pap. text ed. 21.00 (0-314-28310-2) West Pub.

Commercial Law, Vol. 1: Sale of Goods, Consumer Credit & Agency. Ed. by P. A. Read. 390p. (C). 1991. 76.00 (1-85352-382-8, Pub. by HLT Pubns UK) St Mut.

Commercial Law, Vol. 2: International Trade. Ed. by Timothy Portwood. 252p. (C). 1991. 72.00 (1-85352-383-6, Pub. by HLT Pubns UK) St Mut.

***Commercial Law Workbook.** Paul Latimer. 350p. 1995. pap. 29.00 (0-455-21290-2, Pub. by Law Bk Co) W W Gaunt.

Commercial Law, 1993-94. Robert Bradgate et al. (Legal Practice Course Guides Ser.). 368p. 1994. pap. 34.00 (1-85431-348-7, Pub. by Blackstone Pr UK) W W Gaunt.

Commercial Laws & Business Regulations of the People's Republic of China, 1949-1983. Ed. by Victor F. Sit. 600p. 1983. text ed. 78.00 (0-932030-16-5) Eurasia Pr NY.

Commercial Laws of Iran: Iran see Commercial Laws of the Middle East

Commercial Laws of the Middle East, 10 vols. Incl. Algeria. Allen P. Keesee & Gamal Badr. 1981. 150.00 (0-379-22901-3); Egypt, Arab Republic of Egypt. Allen P. Keesee & Gamal Badr. 1981. 150.00 (0-379-22903-X); Commercial Laws of Iran: Iran. G. H. Vafai et al. 1982. 150.00 (0-379-22904-8); Kuwait. Allen P. Keesee & Gamal Badr. 1980. 150.00 (0-379-22905-6); Oman. Allen P. Keesee & Gamal Badr. 1982. 150.00 (0-379-22906-4); QATAR. Allen P. Keesee & Gamal Badr. 1990. 150.00 (0-379-00902-1); United Arab Emirates. Allen P. Keesee & Gamal Badr. 1982. 150.00 (0-379-22909-9); Saudi Arabia. Allen P. Keesee & Gamal Badr. 1981. 150.00 (0-379-22907-2); Sudan. Allen P. Keesee & Gamal Badr. 1981. 150.00 (0-379-22908-0); Syrian Arab Republic. Allen P. Keesee & Gamal Badr. 1992. 150.00 (0-379-22912-9); 1980. Set. 1,475.00 (0-379-22900-5) Oceana.

Commercial Lease Guidebook: Learn How to Win the Leasing Game! Thomas G. Mitchell. Ed. by Warren Jessop. LC 92-80954. (Illus.). 224p. (Orig.). 1992. pap. text ed. 19.95 (0-9632982-0-8) Macore Intl.

Commercial Leases. W. D. Duncan. xxxviii, 239p. 1989. 43. 50 (0-455-20918-9, Pub. by Law Bk Co) W W Gaunt.

Commercial Leases. 2nd ed. W. D. Duncan. 1993. 60.00 (0-455-21184-1, Pub. by Law Bk Co) W W Gaunt.

Commercial Leases & Insolvency. Patrick McLoughlin. 200p. 1992. U.K. pap. 60.00 (0-406-00640-7) Butterworth Legal Pubs.

Commercial, Legal & Business Dictionary: Woerterbuch Fuer Wirtschaft, Recht und Handel, Vol. 1: Deutsch-Franzoesisch. 2nd ed. G. Potonnier & B. Potonnier. 1595p. (FRE & GER.). 1982. 175.00 (0-8288-0812-0, M6919) Fr & Eur.

Commercial Lending. 2nd ed. George E. Ruth. Ed. by Rebecca B. Johns. (Illus.). 454p. 1990. text ed. 57.00 (0-89982-363-7) Am Bankers.

Commercial Lending Basics. Edward K. Gill. (C). 1983. text ed. 44.33 (0-8359-0881-X, Reston) P-H.

Commercial Lending to the Small & Middle Market Business. Robert H. Behrens. 315p. 1990. pap. 52.00 (1-55520-131-8) Probus Pub Co.

***Commercial Liability Insurance.** Date not set. 269.00 (1-886813-12-4) Intl Risk Mgt.

Commercial Liability Risk Management & Insurance, 2 Vols. 2nd ed. Donald S. Malecki et al. LC 86-72708. 978p. 1986. text ed. 26.00 (0-89463-049-0) Am Inst FCPCU.

Commercial Liability Risk Management & Insurance for CPCU Four. 2nd rev. ed. R. Robert Rackley. 1985. 155. 00 (0-88171-106-3) Insurance Achiev.

Commercial Liability Underwriting, 2 vols. 3rd ed. Larry D. Gaunt et al. LC 90-80136. 857p. 1990. text ed. 26.00 (0-89462-051-7, AU63) IIA.

***Commercial Lighting.** Date not set. 39.99 (1-56496-169-9) Rockport Pubs.

Commercial Lighting. Richard K. Miller & Marcia E. Rupnow. (Survey on Technology & Markets Ser.: No. 209). 50p. 1993. pap. text ed. 200.00 (1-55865-240-X) Future Tech Surveys.

Commercial Lines Insurance. John Wormell. 84p. 1993. 30. 00 (1-85609-053-1, Pub. by Witherby & Co UK) St Mut.

***Commercial Loan Analysis: Principles & Techniques for Credit Analysts & Lenders.** Kenneth R. Pirok. 150p. 1994. 42.50 (1-55738-716-8) Probus Pub Co.

Commercial Loan & Constant Tables. Financial Publishing Co. Staff. 288p. 1980. 15.00 (0-87600-387-0) Finan Pub.

Commercial Loan Documentation. 3rd ed. Ed. by William C. Hillman. 426p. 1990. text ed. 40.00 (0-87224-008-8, A1-1415) PLI.

Commercial Loan Documentation Guide. Ed. by Joseph A. Norton. 1988. write for info. (0-8205-1376-8) Bender.

Commercial Loan Handbook. Financial Publishing Co. Staff. 928p. 1987. 32.50 (0-87600-358-7) Finan Pub.

Commercial Loan Manual: An Analysis of Oklahoma's Version of the UCC. Thomas E. English. 235p. (Orig.). 1984. pap. 30.00 (0-916737-00-4) OK Bankers.

Commercial Loan Manual: An Analysis of Oklahoma's Version of the UCC. rev. ed. Thomas E. English. (Orig.). 1988. pap. 40.00 (0-318-32923-9) OK Bankers.

Commercial Loan Portfolio Management. Edgar M. Morsman, Jr. Ed. by Joan Behr. LC 93-16711. (Illus.). 136p. 1993. pap. text ed. 58.00 (0-936742-95-X, 31181) Robt Morris Assocs.

Commercial Loan Practices & Operations. Vincent J. Signoriello. 1990. pap. 35.00 (1-55520-134-2) Probus Pub Co.

Commercial Loan Resale Market: A Banker's Guide to Selling Commercial, Industrial & LBO Debt. Ed. by Jess Lederman. 1991. 60.00 (1-55738-158-5) Probus Pub Co.

Commercial Loan Review Procedures. P. Graham Conlin. 1978. 14.00 (0-317-47027-2) Robt Morris Assocs.

Commercial Lobbyists: Politics for Profit in Britain. Grant Jordan. 180p. 1991. pap. text ed. 29.90 (0-08-037984-2, Pub. by Aberdeen U Pr) Macmillan.

Commercial Management Companies in the Agricultural Development of the Pacific Islands. Andrew McGregor et al. LC 92-16884. (Research Report Ser.: No. 15). 56p. 1993. pap. text ed. 6.00 (0-86638-151-1) EW Ctr HI.

Commercial Media & Classroom Teach. J. Gorham. pap. 29.95 (0-8087-6616-3) Burgess MN Intl.

Commercial Microoganisms Industry. Business Communications Co., Inc. Staff. (Illus.). 300p. 1986. pap. 1,950.00 (0-89336-463-0, C-064) BCC.

***Commercial Nuclear Power.** 1995. lib. bdg. 250.00 (0-8490-6464-3) Gordon Pr.

Commercial Observation Satellites & International Security. Ed. by Michael Krepon et al. LC 89-24070. 280p. 1990. text ed. 45.00 (0-312-04035-0) St Martin.

***Commercial Oil-Field Diving.** 2nd enl. rev. ed. Nicholas B. Zinkowski. LC 78-7214. (Illus.). reprint ed. pap. 93.50 (0-7837-9063-5, 2049812) Bks Demand.

Commercial Operations in Europe. Ed. by R. M. Goode & K. R. Simmonds. 475p. 1978. lib. bdg. 91.50 (90-286-0547-9) Kluwer Ac.

Commercial Operations in Space Nineteen Eighty to Two Thousand. Ed. by John L. McLucas & Charles Sheffield. (Science & Technology Ser.: Vol. 51). (Illus.). 214p. 1981. lib. bdg. 30.00 (0-87703-140-1, Pub. by Am Astro Soc); pap. text ed. 20.00 (0-87703-141-X, Pub. by Am Astro Soc) Univelt Inc.

Commercial Operations in Space Nineteen Eighty to Two Thousand. suppl. ed. Ed. by John L. McLucas & Charles Sheffield. (Science & Technology Ser.: Vol. 51). (Illus.). 214p. 1981. fiche 10.00 (0-87703-165-7, Pub. by Am Astro Soc) Univelt Inc.

Commercial Opportunities for Advanced Composites - STP 704. 133p. 1980. 13.50 (0-8031-0302-6, 04-704000-33) ASTM.

Commercial Opportunities in Space. F. Shahrokhi. 1988. 86.95 (0-930403-39-8) AIAA.

Commercial Opportunities in Space, Including Communications Materials, Research. Business Communications Co., Inc. Staff. 173p. 1984. 1,500.00 (0-89336-370-7, GB-075) BCC.

Commercial Organization of Factories: A Handbook. J. Slater Lewis. Ed. by Richard P. Brief. LC 77-87274. (Development of Contemporary Accounting Thought Ser.). 1978. reprint ed. lib. bdg. 60.95 (0-405-10902-4) Ayer.

Commercial Package Policy Guide. 1991. 29.50 (0-942326-64-4, 30060) Rough Notes.

Commercial Paper. Clayton Gillette. (Smith's Review Ser.). 160p. 1990. pap. text ed. 12.95 (1-56542-112-4) E Law Outlines.

Commercial Paper. Hawkland. 1967. text ed. 26.95 (0-88277-505-7) Foundation Pr.

Commercial Paper: Suitable for Use with Farnsworth. Richard G. Bell. (Cambridge Ser.). 136p. 1984. pap. text ed. 14.00 (0-685-54301-3, Chicago Law Bk) Cambridge Law.

Commercial Paper & Alternative Payment Systems. Benfield & Alces. 1987. write for info. (0-8205-0151-4, 276); teacher ed write for info. (0-8205-0152-2) Bender.

Commercial Paper & Check Collection. William H. Lawrence. 650p. 1990. pap. 40.00 (0-88063-740-4) Michie Butterworth.

Commercial Paper & Payment Systems, 2 vols., Set. William H. Lawrence. 880p. 1990. ring bd. 150.00 (0-88063-325-5) Michie Butterworth.

Commercial Paper House in the United States. Albert O. Greef. LC 75-2637. (Wall Street & the Security Market Ser.). 1975. reprint ed. 46.95 (0-405-06962-6) Ayer.

Commercial Paper Market. Nevins D. Baxter. LC 65-29170. 169p. reprint ed. pap. 48.20 (0-8357-9038-X, 2051727) Bks Demand.

Commercial Paper Market. Roy A. Foulke. Ed. by Stuart Bruchey. LC 80-1148. (Rise of Commercial Banking Ser.). (Illus.). 1981. reprint ed. lib. bdg. 26.95 (0-405-13651-X) Ayer.

Commercial Paper under the Uniform Commercial Code, 2 vols. Frederick M. Hart & William F. Willier. (Bender's Uniform Commercial Code Service Ser.). 1972. Updates. ring bd. write for info. (0-8205-1613-9) Bender.

Commercial Paper, 1991 Supplement to Farnsworth - Case & Materials on Third Edition & Commercial Law, 4th Edition, Case & Materials on Farnsworth & Honnold. E. Allan Farnsworth & Cynthia Starnes. (University Casebook Ser.). 32p. (C). 1991. pap. text ed. 3.95 (0-88277-910-9) Foundation Pr.

Commercial Perfume Bottles. rev. ed. Jacquelyne Jones-North. LC 87-61436. (Illus.). 256p. 1987. 69.95 (0-88740-108-2) Schiffer.

Commercial Photography. Jack Rudman. (Occupational Competency Examination Ser.: OCE-12). 1994. pap. 23. 95 (0-8373-5712-8) Nat Learn.

Commercial Pilot: Complete Programmed Course. 3rd ed. Department of Aviation Education. LC 67-8618. (Illus.). 412p. 1969. 4.95 (0-912682-01-9) Aero Products.

Commercial Pilot: Practical Test Standards--ASMEL. rev. ed. Federal Aviation Administration Staff. 93p. 1988. pap. text ed. 4.50 (0-318-42427-4) Flightshops.

Commercial Pilot FAA Written Exam. 5th ed. Irvin N. Gleim. LC 93-80092. 282p. 1994. pap. text ed. 14.95 (0-917539-45-1) Gleim Pubns.

An Asterisk (*) at the beginning of an entry indicates that the title is appearing in BIP for the first time.

***Commercial Pilot Practical Test Prep & Flight Maneuvers.** Irvin N. Gleim. 426p. 1994. pap. text ed. 14.95 (*0-917539-47-8*) Gleim Pubns.

Commercial Pilot Practical Test Standards: Airplane SE & ME Land (FAA S-8081-2, changed) FAA, Department of Transportation Staff. 114p. (Orig.). (C). 1987. pap. text ed. 3.95 (*0-317-58742-0*) Astro Pubs.

***Commercial Pilot Practical Test Standards: For Airplane (Single & Multi-Engine Land)** FAA Staff. (Practical Test Standards Ser.). 1994. pap. 4.95 (*1-56027-201-5*, ASA-8081-12) Av Suppl & Acad.

Commercial Pilot Practical Test Standards: Multi, Single-Engine, Land. FAA Reprint Staff. 102p. (C). 1989. reprint ed. pap. 4.95 (*0-89100-335-5*, EA-FAA-S-8081-2) IAP.

Commercial Pilot Practical Test Standards: Rotorcraft-Helicopter (FAA S-8081-2) Department of Transportation Staff. 54p. (Orig.). 1985. pap. text ed. 3.95 (*0-317-39834-2*) Astro Pubs.

Commercial Pilot Practical Test Standards for Rotorcraft-Helicopters (FAA 5-8081-2, Change 1) FAA, Department of Transportation Staff. 48p. (Orig.). 1987. reprint ed. pap. text ed. 3.00 (*0-317-58707-2*) Astro Pubs.

Commercial Pilot Question Book. Federal Aviation Administration Staff. (Illus.). 236p. (Orig.). 1985. reprint ed. pap. text ed. 6.50 (*0-685-43019-7*) Astro Pubs.

Commercial Pilot Question Book with Answers (FAA T-8080-2A) FAA, Department of Transportation Staff. (Illus.). 158p. (Orig.). (C). 1986. pap. text ed. 8.00 (*0-317-58930-X*) Astro Pubs.

Commercial Pilot Questions Answers Explanations (QAE 8080-2A) John E. Coleman. (Illus.). 312p. (Orig.). 1986. pap. text ed. 15.95 (*0-685-08651-8*) Astro Pubs.

Commercial Pilot Test Guide. rev. ed. ASA Staff. LC 92-29987. (Illus.). 290p. 1993. pap. 14.95 (*1-56027-180-9*, ASA-C020F) Av Suppl & Acad.

Commercial Pilot Test Prep TP-16B. rev. ed. ASA Staff. LC 92-29986. (Illus.). 326p. 1993. pap. 14.95 (*1-56027-183-3*, ASA-TP16B) Av Suppl & Acad.

Commercial Pilot Written Exam Study Guide, 1993-1995. (Pilot Training Ser.). (Illus.). 201p. Date not set. text ed. 14.95 (*0-88487-162-2*) Jeppesen Sanderson.

Commercial Pilot Written Test Book, FAA-T8080-16A. 1994. 13.00 (*0-685-62684-9*) Aviation.

Commercial Pilot Written Test Book, FAA-T8080-16A. (Illus.). 160p. 1990. per., pap. 9.50 (*0-16-019889-5*, S/N 050-007-008) USGPO.

Commercial Pistols. 1991. lib. bdg. 79.95 (*0-8490-4124-4*) Gordon Pr.

Commercial Policy in the French Revolution: A Study of the Career of G. J. A. Ducher. Frederick L. Nussbaum. LC 79-111782. reprint ed. 41.50 (*0-404-04807-2*) AMS Pr.

Commercial Policy of the European Economic Community & the Association Agreements. G. Sundaram. 1983. 22.00 (*0-8364-1018-1*, Pub. by Allied II) S Asia.

Commercial Practice. (Legal Skills for the 1990s Ser.). 1993. pap. 48.00 (*1-85431-245-6*, Pub. by Blackstone Pr UK) W W Gaunt.

***Commercial Practice: Inns of Court School of Law.** 399p. 1995. pap. 48.00 (*1-85431-391-6*) W W Gaunt.

Commercial Printing Industry: Guides to Pollution Prevention. (Illus.). 45p. (Orig.). (C). 1993. pap. text ed. 40.00 (*1-56806-667-8*) Diane Pub.

Commercial Processing of Poultry. G. H. Weiss. LC 76-3399. (Food Technology Review Ser.: No. 31). (Illus.). 254p. 1976. 32.00 (*0-8155-0612-0*) Noyes.

Commercial Production of Monoclonal Antibodies. Seaver. (Bioprocess Technology Ser.: Vol. 2). 352p. 1987. 150.00 (*0-8247-7765-4*) Dekker.

Commercial Products of India. G. Watt. (C). 1988. text ed. 65.00 (*0-685-44236-5*, Scientific) St Mut.

Commercial Products of India. Sir George Watt. 1966. 20.00 (*0-934454-25-6*) Lubrecht & Cramer.

***Commercial Project Manager: Key Commercial, Financial & Legal Skills for Project Managers.** J. Rodney Turner. 1995. write for info. (*0-07-707946-9*) McGraw.

Commercial Property & Multiple-Lines Underwriting. 2nd ed. E. P. Hollingsworth, Jr. & J. J. Launie. LC 84-81101. 591p. 1988. 26.00 (*0-89462-018-5*, AU64) IIA.

Commercial Property Coverages. Virginia Bates. 1991. 39.50 (*1-56461-005-5*, 46010) Rough Notes.

***Commercial Property Insurance.** Date not set. 250.00 (*1-886813-14-0*) Intl Risk Mgt.

***Commercial Property Insurance & Risk Management.** 4th ed. James S. Trieschmann et al. LC 94-71921. 282p. (C). 1994. pap. text ed. 26.00 (*0-89463-068-7*) Am Inst FCPCU.

Commercial Property Rating. Betsy Cormier. 1991. 39.50 (*1-56461-035-7*, 46080) Rough Notes.

Commercial Property Risk Management & Insurance (For CPCU 3) Robert R. Rackley. (CPCU Ser.). 1984. 155.00 (*0-88171-099-7*) Insurance Achiev.

Commercial Property, 1993-94. Peter Luxton & Margaret Wilkie. (Legal Practice Course Guides Ser.). 225p. 1994. pap. 34.00 (*1-85431-351-7*, Pub. by Blackstone Pr UK) W W Gaunt.

Commercial Rabbit Raising. R. B. Casady et al. (Lost Arts Ser.). (Illus.). 69p. reprint ed. pap. 3.95 (*0-8466-6054-7*, U54) Shorey.

Commercial Radio Operator's Question & Answer License Guide, Element 3. Martin Schwartz. LC 63-23778. 1988. pap. 5.95 (*0-912146-05-2*, 9-01) Ameco.

Commercial Real Estate: An Intro to Marketing Investment Properties. Leta McCurry. 304p. 1990. text ed. 51.00 (*0-13-151465-2*) P-H.

***Commercial Real Estate Compendium: Five Years of Insight & Analysis.** Building Owners & Managers Assn. Int. Staff. 140p. (Orig.). 1993. pap. 155.00 (*0-943130-06-9*) Build Own & Man.

Commercial Real Estate Finance. Michael R. Buchanan. (Illus.). 400p. (C). 1993. pap. text ed. 45.00 (*0-89982-320-3*) Am Bankers.

Commercial Real Estate Financing. Stuart M. Saft. LC 93-3970. (Shepard's Real Estate Law Ser.). 1993. text ed. 115.00 (*0-07-172400-1*) Shepards-McGraw.

***Commercial Real Estate Forms.** 2nd rev. ed. Stuart M. Saft. LC 94-28153. 1994. write for info. (*0-07-172588-1*) Shepards-McGraw.

Commercial Real Estate Forms, 4 vols., Set. Stuart M. Saft. 4988p. 1987. text ed. 380.00 (*0-07-022862-0*) Shepards-McGraw.

***Commercial Real Estate Investment: An Executive Guide to the Investment, Management & Finance of Commercial Property in the 90s.** Dowd. Date not set. text ed. 55.00 (*0-471-01637-3*) Wiley.

Commercial Real Estate Leases, 2 vols. 2nd ed. Mark A. Senn. 1017p. 1990. Vol. 2: Forms, 419p. text ed., disk 123.00 (*0-471-51500-0*) Wiley.

Commercial Real Estate Leases, 2 vols., Vol. 2. 2nd ed. Mark A. Senn. 1017p. 1990. Set. text ed. 246.00 (*0-471-51502-7*); Vol. 1: Preparation & Negotiation, 598p. text ed. 123.00 (*0-471-51501-9*) Wiley.

Commercial Real Estate Leases, 1989. (Real Estate Law & Practice Course Handbook Ser.). 980p. 1989. 70.00 (*0-685-69393-7*) PLI.

Commercial Real Estate Leases, 1990. (Real Estate Law & Practice Ser.). 927p. 1990. 17.50 (*0-685-38026-2*, N4-4533) PLI.

Commercial Real Estate Leases, 1992. (Real Estate Law & Practice Course Handbook Ser.). 907p. 1992. pap. 70.00 (*0-685-69394-5*) PLI.

Commercial Real Estate Leases 1993. (Real Estate Law & Practice Course Handbook Ser.: Vol. 388). 907p. 1993. 70.00 (*0-685-69752-5*, N4-4571) PLI.

Commercial Real Estate Leasing. Stuart M. Saft. 500p. 1992. text ed. 115.00 (*0-07-172313-7*) Shepards-McGraw.

Commercial Real Estate Lending. 76p. 1985. 50.00 (*0-929097-04-1*, 17939) Sav & Comm Bank.

Commercial Real Estate Loan Administration. Ed. by Roland Lee. 171p. (Orig.). 1993. pap. 60.00 (*0-945359-20-9*) Mortgage Bankers.

Commercial Real Estate Transactions. Stuart M. Saft. 500p. 1989. text ed. 99.00 (*0-07-172143-6*) Shepards-McGraw.

Commercial Real Estate Transactions Practice Manual & Forms Diskette. Real Estate Section Council Staff. 590p. 1989. ring bd. 90.00 (*0-88726-010-1*); disk 25.00 (*0-88726-011-X*) AZ St Bar.

Commercial Real Estate Workouts. Stuart M. Saft. 450p. 1991. text ed. 110.00 (*0-07-172312-9*) Shepards-McGraw.

Commercial Real Property Lease Practice. Michael A. Dean et al. Ed. by California Continuing Education of the Bar. LC 75-26448. (California Practice Book Ser.: No. 68). (Illus.). xiii, 426p. 1976. 75.00 (*0-88124-044-3*, RE-30330) Cont Ed Bar-CA.

Commercial Real Property Lease Practice. Michael A. Dean et al. Ed. by California Continuing Education of the Bar. LC 75-26448. (California Practice Book Ser.: No. 68). (Illus.). 114p. 1990. Nov. '90 supp. (*0-88124-342-6*, RE-31142) Cont Ed Bar-CA.

Commercial Reciprocity Policy of the United States 1774-1839. Vernon G. Setser. LC 76-90212. (American Scene Ser.). 1969. reprint ed. lib. bdg. 35.00 (*0-306-71819-7*) Da Capo.

Commercial Recreation. Ellis & Norton. (Illus.). 400p. (C). 1988. pap. 34.95 (*0-8016-1494-5*) Mosby Yr Bk.

Commercial Refrigeration. James H. Doolin. 72p. 1982. pap. 15.00 (*0-914626-08-6*) Doolco Inc.

***Commercial Refrigeration.** Andrew Rhinefort. 206p. (C). 1994. 19.54 (*1-56870-156-X*) RonJon Pub.

***Commercial Reimbursement Insurance Monograph.** National Hospice Organization, Commercial Reimbursement Task Force Staff. 10p. Date not set. lp 7.35 (*0-931207-25-8*) Natl Hospice.

Commercial Rent Reviews: Law & Valuation Practice. Ed. by R. T. Whipple. xxvii, 205p. 1986. pap. 37.50 (*0-455-20641-4*, Pub. by Law Bk Co) W W Gaunt.

Commercial Revolution in Nineteenth-Century China: The Rise of Sino-Western Mercantile Capitalism. Yen-P'ing Hao. 1986. 55.00 (*0-520-05344-3*) U CA Pr.

Commercial Revolution of the Middle Ages, 950-1350. Robert S. Lopez. LC 75-35453. (Illus.). 204p. 1976. pap. 16.95 (*0-521-29046-5*) Cambridge U Pr.

Commercial Revolvers-Repairs, Parts & Tools. 1987. lib. bdg. 79.50 (*0-8490-3937-1*) Gordon Pr.

Commercial Securities in New Zealand: An Introduction to the Law. 2nd ed. G. G. Viskovic & S. C. Calderwood. xxxi, 214p. 1986. pap. 40.00 (*0-455-20707-0*, Pub. by Law Bk Co) W W Gaunt.

Commercial Shotguns-Repairs, Parts & Tools. 1987. lib. bdg. 79.00 (*0-8490-3936-3*) Gordon Pr.

Commercial Situations & Techniques: Situations et Techniques Commerciales. O. Girault & D. Nony. 334p. (FRE.). 1987. pap. 45.00 (*0-8288-1555-0*, F27680) Fr & Eur.

***Commercial Spaces: Hotels, Bars & Restaurants.** RotoVision Staff. 1995. pap. text ed. (*0-8230-6439-5*) Watsn-Guptill.

***Commercial Spaces: Office Spaces, Furniture & Lighting.** RotoVision Staff. 1995. pap. text ed. (*0-8230-6440-9*) Watsn-Guptill.

***Commercial Spaces: Shops, Malls & Boutiques.** RotoVision Staff. 1995. pap. text ed. (*0-8230-6438-7*) Watsn-Guptill.

Commercial Square Foot Building Costs, 1992. Ed. by Stanley J. Strychaz. (Illus.). (Orig.). 1992. pap. 49.95 (*0-931708-29-X*) Saylor.

Commercial Square Foot Building Costs 1994. Ed. by Stanley J. Strychaz. (Illus.). 320p. 1994. pap. 49.95 (*0-931708-40-0*) Saylor.

***Commercial Square Foot Building Costs, 1995.** Ed. by Stanley J. Strychaz. (Illus.). 320p. 1995. pap. 49.95 (*0-931708-48-6*) Saylor.

Commercial Stormwater Permitting. Washington U. S. EPA Staff. 1993. 65.00 (*0-87371-960-3*, TD428) Lewis Pubs.

Commercial Television & European Children. Ray Brown & Scott Ward. 300p. 1985. text ed. 68.95 (*0-566-05073-0*) Ashgate Pub Co.

***Commercial Tenancy Law in Australia.** A. J. Bradbrook & C. E. Croft. 488p. 1990. boxed 111.00 (*0-409-30061-6*, Austral) Butterworth Legal Pubs.

Commercial Tenant's Leasing Transactions Guide: Forms & Strategies. Alan D. Sugarman & Joel J. Goldberg. (Business Practice Library). 381p. 1991. text ed. 128.00 (*0-471-63473-5*) Wiley.

Commercial Tenant's Leasing Transactions Guide: Forms & Strategies. suppl. ed. Alan D. Sugarman & Joel J. Goldberg. (Business Practice Library). 96p. 1993. write for info. (*0-471-58679-X*) Wiley.

Commercial Tenant's Leasing Transactions Guide: Forms & Strategies, 1992 Supplement. Alan D. Sugarman & Joel J. Goldberg. 52p. 1992. pap. text ed. 40.00 (*0-471-55883-4*) Wiley.

Commercial Timber of India, Set, Vols. 1 & 2. R. S. Pearson. (C). 1988. Set. 820.00 (*0-685-22370-1*) St Mut.

Commercial Torts. 2nd ed. George J. Alexander. 477p. 1988. 55.00 (*0-87473-350-2*) Michie Butterworth.

Commercial Torts & DTPA. Ed. by Will G. Barber. (Texas Court's Charge Ser.: Vol. 3). 300p. 1994. ring bd. 85.00 (*0-409-25680-3*) Michie Butterworth.

***Commercial Transactions: Cases & Materials.** B. Pentony. 700p. 1991. pap. 90.00 (*0-409-30814-5*, Austral) Butterworth Legal Pubs.

Commercial Transactions: Sales. Lionel H. Frankel et al. (Contemporary Legal Education Ser.). 463p. (C). 1982. pap. text ed. 17.00 (*0-87215-470-X*) Michie Butterworth.

Commercial Transactions: Secured Financing. 2nd ed. Raymond T. Nimmer et al. (Contemporary Legal Education Ser.). 685p. 1992. 37.00 (*0-87215-963-9*); 37.00 (*0-685-62351-3*) Michie Butterworth.

Commercial Transactions: Text, Cases & Problems. Jonathan Eddy & Peter Winship. LC 84-81934. (C). 1985. 48.00 (*0-316-20057-3*) Little.

Commercial Transactions, Principles & Policies. 2nd ed. Alan Schwartz & Robert E. Scott. (University Casebook Ser.). 1234p. 1990. text ed. 43.50 (*0-88277-807-2*) Foundation Pr.

Commercial Transactions Principles & Policies, Teacher's Manual to Accompany. Alan Schwartz & Robert E. Scott. (University Casebook Ser.). 273p. 1988. reprint ed. pap. text ed. write for info. (*0-88277-121-3*) Foundation Pr.

Commercial Transactions under the UCC. 4th ed. King et al. 1987. write for info. (*0-8205-0136-0*, 244); teacher ed write for info. (*0-318-67315-0*) Bender.

Commercial Transactions, Vol. 1: Problems & Materials on Secured Transactions under the Uniform Commercial Code. Louis F. Del Duca et al. 500p. 1992. pap. text ed. write for info. (*0-87084-151-3*) Anderson Pub Co.

Commercial Translations: A Business Like Approach. LC 85-72415. 135p. 1986. 19.95 (*0-935047-01-8*); pap. 16.95 (*0-935047-02-6*) Americas Group.

Commercial Truck Driver's Guide to Driver Licensing. Arco Editorial Board Staff. 512p. 1990. pap. 24.95 (*0-13-152258-2*) P-H.

Commercial Truck Driving Series, 4 bks. 1991. Bk. 2: Mastering Reading: Skills for Success - Commercial Truck Driving. write for info. (*0-8273-4451-1*) Delmar.

Commercial Trucks. Don Wood. 1993. pap. 19.95 (*0-87938-811-0*) Motorbooks Intl.

Commercial Trusts: The Growth & Rights of Aggregated Capital. An Argument Delivered Before the Industrial Commission at Washington, D. C., December 12, 1899. John R. Dos Passos. LC 77-38275. (Evolution of Capitalism Ser.). 152p. 1972. reprint ed. 18.95 (*0-405-04118-7*) Ayer.

Commercial Typewriting. 10th ed. Bettina Croft. 192p. 1993. pap. 24.00 (*0-273-03962-8*, Pub. by Pitman Pub Ltd UK) Trans-Atl Phila.

Commercial Uses of Geothermal Heat. Ed. by Geothermal Resources Council. (Special Report Ser.: No. 9). (Illus.). 143p. 1980. pap. 1.25 (*0-934412-09-X*) Geothermal.

Commercial Utilization of Outer Space: Law & Practice. H. L. Van Traa-Engelman. LC 92-22174. 462p. (C). 1993. lib. bdg. 152.00 (*0-7923-1892-7*) Kluwer Ac.

Commercial Utilization of Space. Ed. by J. R. Gilmer et al. (Advances in the Astronautical Sciences Ser.: Vol. 23). 1968. 60.00 (*0-87703-026-X*, Pub. by Am Astro Soc); fiche 60.00 (*0-87703-216-5*, V. 3 AAS, Pub. by Am Astro Soc) Univelt Inc.

Commercial Utilization of Space: An International Comparison of Framework Conditions. M. Harr & R. Kohli. LC 88-7471. 176p. 1990. 44.50 (*0-935470-46-8*) Battelle.

Commercial Valuation Specialist. (Career Examination Ser.: C-3289). 1994. pap. 29.95 (*0-8373-3289-3*) Nat Learn.

Commercial Vehicle Electronics, Diagnostics, & Service Systems. 1990. 49.00 (*1-56091-088-7*, SP-844) Soc Auto Engineers.

Commercial Vehicle Preventable Accident Manual. S. C. Uzgiris et al. 90p. 1991. 15.00 (*0-9633957-0-X*) Triodyne.

Commercial Vehicle Suspensions, Steering Systems, & Traction. 136p. 1991. pap. 49.00 (*1-56091-195-6*, SP-892) Soc Auto Engineers.

Commercial Winemaking: Processing & Controls. Richard P. Vine. (Illus.). (C). 1981. text ed. 52.95 (*0-87055-376-3*) AVI.

Commercialisation of English Society 1000-1500. R. H. Britnell. 280p. (C). 1992. 59.95 (*0-521-41823-2*) Cambridge U Pr.

Commercialising Economy: England 1086 to c. 1300. Ed. by Richard Britnell & Bruce M. S. Campbell. LC 94-17562. 1995. text ed. write for info. (*0-7190-3994-0*, Pub. by Manchester Univ Pr UK) St Martin.

Commercialism & Frontier: Perspectives on the Early Shenandoah Valley. Robert D. Mitchell. LC 76-26610. (Illus.). 267p. reprint ed. pap. 76.10 (*0-7837-4358-0*, 2044068) Bks Demand.

Commercialization & Agricultural Development in Central & Eastern China: 1870-1937. Loren Brandt. (Illus.). (C). 1990. 49.95 (*0-521-37196-1*) Cambridge U Pr.

Commercialization & Wildlife Management: Dancing with the Devil. Ed. by Alex W. Hawley. 136p. 1993. 16.50 (*0-89464-866-7*) Krieger.

Commercialization & Wildlife Management: Dancing with the Devil. Ed. by Alex W. Hawley. LC 92-30179. 136p. (C). 1993. lib. bdg. 16.50 (*0-89464-795-4*) Krieger.

Commercialization of Accountancy: Flexible Accumulation & the Transformation of the Service Class. Gerard Hanlon. LC 94-16014. 1994. write for info. (*0-312-12291-8*) St Martin.

Commercialization of Agriculture under Population Pressure. Joachim Von Braun et al. 123p. 1991. 10.00 (*0-89629-087-5*) Intl Food Policy.

Commercialization of Fluidized-Bed Combustion Systems in Urban Areas: The Local Government Role. 126p. 1982. 20.00 (*0-318-17328-X*, DG/82-311) Pub Tech Inc.

Commercialization of New Materials for a Global Economy. National Research Council, Commission on Engineering & Technical Systems Staff. 80p. (C). 1993. pap. text ed. 25.00 (*0-309-04734-X*) Natl Acad Pr.

Commercialization of News in the Nineteenth Century. Gerald J. Baldasty. LC 91-10590. 256p. (Orig.). (C). 1992. 60.00 (*0-299-13400-8*); pap. 19.95 (*0-299-13404-0*) U of Wis Pr.

Commercialization of Outer Space: Opportunities & Obstacles for American Business. Jonathan N. Goodrich. LC 88-23665. 240p. 1989. text ed. 65.00 (*0-89930-342-0*, GCZ/, Quorum Bks) Greenwood.

***Commercialization of Postal & Delivery Services: National & International Perspectives.** Ed. by Michael A. Crew & Paul R. Kleindorfer. (Topics in Regulatory Economics Ser.: Vol. 19). 304p. (C). 1994. lib. bdg. 79.95 (*0-7923-9514-X*) Kluwer Ac.

Commercialized Prostitution in New York City. George J. Kneeland. LC 69-14937. (Criminology, Law Enforcement, & Social Problems Ser.: No. 52). 1969. reprint ed. 24.00 (*0-87585-052-9*) Patterson Smith.

Commercializing SDI Technologies. Ed. by Stewart Nozette & Robert L. Kuhn. LC 87-18333. 256p. 1987. text ed. 59.95 (*0-275-92332-0*, C2332, Praeger Pubs) Greenwood.

Commercializing Technology: Linking Research to the Marketplace. James Breagy. Ed. by Jenny Murphy. 60p. (Orig.). 1989. pap. 21.50 (*0-317-04915-1*) Natl Coun Econ Dev.

Commercially Available Chemical Agents for Paper & Board Manufacture. 3rd rev. ed. Technical Association of the Pulp & Paper Industry Staff. Ed. by Walter F. Reynolds. 82p. reprint ed. pap. 25.00 (*0-317-28725-7*, 2020299) Bks Demand.

Commercially Available Chemical Agents for Paper & Board Manufacture. Technical Association of the Pulp & Paper Industry Staff. (Technical Association of the Pulp & Paper Car Ser.: No. 60). 58p. reprint ed. pap. 25.00 (*0-317-29318-4*, 2022348) Bks Demand.

Commercially Available Chemical Agents for Paper & Paperboard Manufacture. 4th ed. Technical Association of the Pulp & Paper Industry Staff. Ed. by John Farewell. LC 90-31125. reprint ed. pap. 24.70 (*0-8357-4121-4*, 2036952) Bks Demand.

***Commercials.** Greg Evason. (Illus.). 36p. (YA). (gr. 7 up). 1990. pap. text ed. 3.95 (*0-929611-09-8*) Plutonium Pr.

Commercials: A One-Act Play. Conrad E. Davidson. (Illus.). 24p. (Orig.). 1990. pap. 3.00 (*0-88680-322-5*) I E Clark.

Commercials, Just My Speed!! Vernee W. Johnson. (Illus.). 193p. (Orig.). 1993. reprint ed. pap. text ed. 15.95 (*0-9639824-1-9*) Wizards Prod Grp.

Commerical Dictionary in Four Languages. 7th ed. J. V. Servotte. 1186p. (DUT, ENG, FRE & GER.). 1982. 91.00 (*90-02-14319-2*) IBD Ltd.

Commerical Oral Exam Guide. Michael D. Hayes. LC 92-36217. 1993. pap. 9.95 (*1-56027-138-8*, ASA-OEG-C) Av Suppl & Acad.

Commerical Paper. Richard Felix. 182p. (Orig.). 1987. 95.00 (*0-318-23271-5*) Thomson Financial.

***Commerical Recreation & Tourism.** Susan A. Weston. 336p. (C). 1995. pap. write for info. (*0-697-21992-5*) Brown & Benchmark.

Commetorum Omnium Aueroys: Super Librum Aristotelis De Physico Auditu Expositor Clarissimus. Averroes, pseud. ix, 558p. reprint ed. write for info. (*0-318-71484-1*, Pub. by Georg Olms GW) Lubrecht & Cramer.

Commie-The Girl Who Married the Butler: A Novella of the 19th Century Australia, 1953-93. Ed. by Dorothy Michell. 184p. (C). 1990. 36.00 (*0-947333-01-0*, Pub. by Pascoe Pub AT) St Mut.

***Commies, Crooks, Gypsies, Spooks, & Poets: Thirteen Books of Prague in the Year of the Great Lice Epidemic.** Jan Novak. 225p. 1995. 22.00 (*1-883642-09-4*) Steerforth Pr.

C

An Asterisk (*) at the beginning of an entry indicates that the title is appearing in BIP for the first time.

***Comminution: Theory & Practice.** Ed. by S. Komar Kawatra. LC 91-67679. (Illus.). reprint ed. pap. 180.00 (*0-7837-9174-7*, 2049873) Bks Demand.

Comminution - Theory & Practice. Ed. by K. Kawatra. LC 91-67679. (Illus.). 693p. 1992. 50.00 (*0-87335-112-6*, 112-6) SMM&E Inc.

Comminution of Wood & Bark. 223p. 1986. pap. 24.00 (*0-935018-25-5*) Forest Prod.

Commiserations. Cathy Guisewite. (Illus.). 64p. 1993. 4.95 (*0-8362-3048-5*) Andrews & McMeel.

Commissaire Dans la Truffiere. Pierre Lagnan. 250p. (FRE.). 1991. pap. 11.95 (*0-7859-4348-X*, 2070383245) Fr & Eur.

Commissar of the Gold Express: An Episode in the Civil War. Vladimir Matveev. LC 74-10088. (Soviet Literature in English Translation Ser.). (Illus.). 212p. 1974. reprint ed. 18.15 (*0-88355-174-8*) Hyperion Conn.

Commissariot Record of Edinburgh: Register of Testaments, Pt. I, Vols. 1-35: 1514-1600. Ed. by Francis J. Grant. (British Record Society Index Library Ser.: Vol. 16). 1972. reprint ed. pap. 30.00 (*0-8115-1461-7*) Periodicals Srv.

***Commissariot Record of Glasgow Register of Testaments, 1547-1800: And Register of Burials in the Chapel Royal or Abbey of Holyroodhouse, 1706-1900.** Scottish Record Society Staff. 547p. 1994. pap. text ed. 33.00 (*0-7884-0009-6*) Heritage Bk.

Commissariot Record of Hamilton & Campsie: Register of the Testaments, 1564-1800 see Commissariot Record of Inverness: Register of Testaments, 1630-1800

Commissariot Record of Inverness: Register of Testaments, 1630-1800. Ed. by Francis J. Grant. Bd. with Commissariot Record of Hamilton & Campsie: Register of the Testaments, 1564-1800. (British Record Society Index Library Ser.: Vol. 20). 1972. reprint ed. Set pap. 19.00 (*0-8115-1465-X*) Periodicals Srv.

Commissars, Commanders, & Civilian Authority: The Structure of Soviet Military Politics. Timothy J. Colton. LC 78-23342. (Russian Research Center Studies: No. 79). (Illus.). 373p. 1979. 38.50 (*0-674-14535-6*) HUP.

Commissary Clerk I. Jack Rudman. (Career Examination Ser.: C-216). 1994. pap. 19.95 (*0-8373-0216-1*) Nat Learn.

Commissary Clerk II. Jack Rudman. (Career Examination Ser.: C-217). 1994. pap. 23.95 (*0-8373-0217-X*) Nat Learn.

Commissary Clerk III. Jack Rudman. (Career Examination Ser.: C-218). 1994. pap. 27.95 (*0-8373-0218-8*) Nat Learn.

Commissary Clerk IV. Jack Rudman. (Career Examination Ser.: C-219). 1994. pap. 27.95 (*0-8373-0219-6*) Nat Learn.

Commission. Richard Barrett. LC 82-72373. (Illus.). 438p. 1982. 25.00 (*0-9609396-0-1*) Barrett.

Commission. Finn Carling. Tr. by Louis A. Muinzer. 176p. 1993. 29.00 (*0-7206-0896-1*, Pub. by P Owen Ltd UK) Dufour.

Commission. Sergei P. Zalygin. Tr. by David G. Wilson. LC 93-7009. 386p. (C). 1993. 35.00 (*0-87580-177-3*); pap. 18.50 (*0-87580-558-2*) N Ill U Pr.

Commission for Climatology: Abridged Final Report of the Eleventh Session, 1993. World Meteorological Organization Staff. (WMO Ser.: No. 791). 1993. pap. 25.00 (*92-63-10791-2*, Pub. by Wrld Meteorological SZ) Am Meteorological.

Commission for Hydrology: Abridged Final Report of the Eighth Session Geneva, 24 October-4 November 1988 WMO-No. 715. O. Starosolsky et al. 118p. 1989. pap. 34.00 (*92-63-10715-7*, Pub. by Wrld Meteorological SZ) Am Meteorological.

Commission for Instruments & Methods of Observation - Abridged Final Report of the Tenth Session: Brussels, 11-22 September, 1989. World Meteorological Organization Staff. (WMO Ser.: No. 727). 125p. 1990. pap. 35.00 (*92-63-10727-0*, Pub. by Wrld Meteorological SZ) Am Meteorological.

Commission for Marine Meteorology: Abridged Final Report of the Tenth Session Paris, 8-17 February 1989 WMO-No. 716. F. Gerard et al. 154p. 1989. pap. 42.00 (*92-63-10716-5*, Pub. by Wrld Meteorological SZ) Am Meteorological.

Commission on Chronic Illness, Vol. 2: Care of the Long-Term Patient, Vol. 2. Commission on Chronic Illness Staff. (Illus.). 620p. 1956. 50.00 (*0-674-09650-9*) HUP.

Commission on Chronic Illness, Vol. 3: Chronic Illness in a Rural Area: The Hunterdon Study, Vol. 3. Commission on Chronic Illness Staff. 454p. 1956. 50.00 (*0-674-12901-6*) HUP.

Commission on Chronic Illness, Vol. 4: Chronic Illness in a Large City: The Baltimore Study, Vol. 4. Commission on Chronic Illness Staff. (Illus.). 642p. 1957. 49.95 (*0-674-12900-8*) HUP.

Commission on Civil Rights. Karen Arrington. (Know Your Government Ser.). (Illus.). (J). (gr. 5 up). 1992. 14.95 (*1-55546-127-1*) Chelsea Hse.

Commission on Graduates of Foreign Nursing Schools Qualifying Examinations (CGFNS) Jack Rudman. (Admission Test Ser.: ATS-90). 1994. 45.95 (*0-8373-5190-1*); pap. 29.95 (*0-8373-5090-5*) Nat Learn.

Commission on Narcotic Drugs - Cumulative Index, 1980-1986. 68p. 1986. 16.00 (*92-1-148077-9*, 89.XI.1) UN.

***Commission on Preservation & Access Working Paper on the Future.** 6p. 1994. pap. 5.00 (*1-887334-30-0*) Comm Preserv & Access.

***Commission on Security & Cooperation in Europe Handbook.** 70p. (Orig.). Date not set. pap. 125.00 (*0-7605-1521-2*) Rector Pr.

Commission on the Organization of the Government for the Conduct of Foreign Policy. U. S. Congress Staff. 1982. reprint ed. Appendices, vol. 1-7, set. lib. bdg. 215.00 (*0-89941-217-3*, 201390) W S Hein.

Commission Politics: The Processing of Racial Crisis in America. Michael Lipsky & David J. Olson. LC 74-20192. 492p. 1977. 39.95x (*0-87855-078-X*) Transaction Pubs.

Commission Politics: The Processing of Racial Crisis in America. Michael Lipsky & David J. Olson. LC 74-20192. 490p. reprint ed. pap. 139.70 (*0-318-34655-9*, 2056584) Bks Demand.

***Commission Possible.** 2nd ed. Tim Howard. Ed. by Cindy G. Spear. 83p. 1995. digital audio, ring bd. 39.95 (*1-57052-028-3*) Chrch Grwth VA.

***Commissioned Papers on Historical, Institutional & Economic Contexts of Drug Treatment.** 1994. lib. bdg. 250.95 (*0-8490-6422-8*) Gordon Pr.

***Commissioned Sea Officers of the Royal Navy, 1660-1815.** 2nd ed. Ed. by David Syrett & R. L. Dinardo. (Publications of the Navy Records Society: No. 13). 508p. (C). 1995. text ed. 127.95 (*1-85928-122-2*, Pub. by Scolar Pr UK) Ashgate Pub Co.

Commissioned Spirits: The Shaping of Social Motion in Dickens, Carlyle, Melville, & Hawthorne. Jonathan Arac. 216p. 1989. text ed. 41.00 (*0-231-07116-7*); pap. text ed. 14.50 (*0-231-07117-5*) Col U Pr.

Commissioned to Communicate. Harrold D. Harrison. (Sunday School Workers Training Course Ser.: No. 2). 1969. pap. 6.95 (*0-89265-003-6*) Randall Hse.

Commissioned to Communicate: Teacher's Guide. Larry D. Hampton. 1978. pap. 1.50 (*0-89265-056-7*) Randall Hse.

Commissioned to Heal & Other Helpful Essays. George Bennett. (C). 1990. pap. 24.00 (*0-85305-212-3*, Pub. by J Arthur Ltd UK) St Mut.

Commissioner. Jack Rudman. (Career Examination Ser.: C-1199). 1994. pap. 39.95 (*0-8373-1199-3*) Nat Learn.

Commissioner. large type ed. Stanley Johnson. 448p. 1988. 15.95 (*0-7089-1821-2*) Ulverscroft.

Commissioner Lin & the Opium War. Hsin-Pao Chang. LC 64-21786. (Harvard East Asian Ser.: No. 18). 333p. reprint ed. pap. 96.10 (*0-7837-2232-X*, 2057322) Bks Demand.

Commissioner of Correction. Jack Rudman. (Career Examination Ser.: C-1203). 1994. pap. 49.95 (*0-8373-1203-5*) Nat Learn.

Commissioner of Deeds. Jack Rudman. (Career Examination Ser.: C-157). 1994. pap. 39.95 (*0-8373-0157-2*) Nat Learn.

Commissioner of General Services. Jack Rudman. (Career Examination Ser.: C-1858). 1994. pap. 49.95 (*0-8373-1858-0*) Nat Learn.

Commissioner of Jurors. Jack Rudman. (Career Examination Ser.: C-1204). 1994. pap. 39.95 (*0-8373-1204-3*) Nat Learn.

Commissioner of Police. Jack Rudman. (Career Examination Ser.: C-1200). 1994. pap. 49.95 (*0-8373-1200-0*) Nat Learn.

Commissioner of Recreation & Community Services. Jack Rudman. (Career Examination Ser.: C-1890). 1994. pap. 49.95 (*0-8373-1890-4*) Nat Learn.

Commissioner of Social Services. Jack Rudman. (Career Examination Ser.: C-1205). 1994. pap. 49.95 (*0-8373-1205-1*) Nat Learn.

Commissioner Roosevelt: The Story of Theodore Roosevlet & the New York City Police, 1895-1897. H. Paul Jeffers. LC 94-18144. 1994. text ed. 27.95 (*0-471-02407-4*) Wiley.

***Commissioners & Commodores: The East India Squadron & American Diplomacy in China.** Curtis T. Henson. LC 81-10359. (Illus.). 239p. 1982. pap. 68.20 (*0-7837-8378-7*, 2059188) Bks Demand.

Commissioner's Little Handbook: A Portable Guide for Local Government Advisory Board Members. Len Wood. 146p. 1992. 24.95 (*0-9634374-0-2*) Trng Shoppe.

Commissioners of Indian Affairs, 1824-1977. Ed. by Robert M. Kvasnicka & Herman J. Viola. LC 79-12336. xviii, 384p. 1979. 35.00 (*0-8032-2700-0*) U of Nebr Pr.

***Commissioners of the FCC: 1927-1994.** Ed. by Gerald V. Flannery. 238p. (C). 1994. lib. bdg. 49.50 (*0-8191-9669-X*) U Pr of Amer.

Commissioners' Reports to the Crown: The Twenty-Seventh Report, 1982-1990. 67p. 1992. 11.00 (*0-11-887533-7*, HM75337, Pub. by HMSO UK) UNIPUB.

Commissioner's Task Force on Parent Involvement in Head Start. 60p. 1987. write for info. (*0-318-62179-7*) US HHS.

Commissioning Building Services: An Annotated Bibliography. Ed. by S. Loyd. (C). 1987. 110.00 (*0-86022-149-0*, Pub. by Build Servs Info Assn UK) St Mut.

Commissioning Hospital Buildings. Graham Millard. (King Edward's Hospital Fund Ser.). 1975. pap. text ed. 19.95 (*0-8464-0260-2*) Beekman Pubs.

Commissioning HVAC Systems: Division of Responsibilities. L. J. Wild. (C). 1988. 70.00 (*0-86022-207-1*, Pub. by Build Servs Info Assn UK) St Mut.

Commissioning of Air Systems in Buildings. C. Parsloe. 1989. 120.00 (*0-86022-231-4*, Pub. by Build Servs Info Assn UK) St Mut.

Commissioning of BEMS Code of Practice. 1992. 90.00 (*0-86022-275-6*, Pub. by Build Servs Info Assn UK) St Mut.

Commissioning of VAV systems in Buildings. 1991. 160.00 (*0-86022-270-5*, Pub. by Build Servs Info Assn UK) St Mut.

Commissioning of Water Systems in Building. C. Parsloe. 1992. 160.00 (*0-86022-230-6*, Pub. by Build Servs Info Assn UK) St Mut.

Commissions, Bonuses & Beyond: Sales & Marketing Management's Guide to Sales Compensation. William Keenan. 1994. 47.50 (*1-55738-593-9*) Probus Pub Co.

Commissions of Inquiry, Practice & Principles. J. Sarma Sarkar. (C). 1990. 50.00 (*0-89771-307-9*) St Mut.

***Commissions, Reports, Reforms, & Educational Policy.** Ed. by Rick Ginsberg & David N. Plank. LC 94-46172. 280p. 1995. text ed. 59.95 (*0-275-94210-4*, Praeger Pubs) Greenwood.

Commit to Quality. Patrick L. Townsend. 1990. pap. text ed. 12.95 (*0-471-52018-7*) Wiley.

Commitment. Frank E. Bird, Jr. & George L. Germain. 1988. pap. text ed. 30.00 (*0-88061-073-5*) Intl Loss Cntrl.

Commitment. Julie Ellis. 1994. 18.95 (*0-8217-4422-4*) Zebra.

Commitment. Julie Ellis. 608p. 1994. mass mkt. 5.99 (*0-8217-4681-2*) Zebra.

Commitment. Robert B. Munger. (Christian Basics Bible Studies). 64p. (Orig.). 1994. pap. 4.99 (*0-8308-2005-1*, 2005) InterVarsity.

***Commitment.** large type ed. Julie Ellis. LC 95-15710. (Large Print Bks.). 1995. pap. 21.95 (*1-56895-218-X*) Wheeler Pub.

Commitment: Key to Christian Maturity. Susan Muto & Adrian Van Kaam. 1989. pap. 8.95 (*0-8091-3069-6*) Paulist Pr.

Commitment: Select Sculptures by Annette S. Friedman. Sandra F. Alpert. (Illus.). 16p. 1994. pap. 5.00 (*1-884931-00-6*) Global Commit.

Commitment: The Dynamic of Strategy. Pankaj Ghemawat. 1991. text ed. 35.00 (*0-02-911575-2*) Free Pr.

Commitment: The Reality of Adoption. Grace Sandness. LC 84-20730. (Illus.). 160p. (Orig.). 1984. pap. 7.95 (*0-931323-00-2*) Mini-World Pubns.

Commitment: There Is Only One Sure Way to Lose Pounds. Harvey Kule. 200p. (Orig.). Date not set. pap. 9.95 (*1-879191-35-0*) Forms Man.

Commitment & Commemoration: Jews, Christians, Muslims in Dialogue. Intro. by Andre LeCocque. LC 93-72787. 151p. 1994. text ed. 25.95 (*0-913552-54-2*) Exploration Pr.

Commitment & Community: Communes & Utopias in Sociological Perspective. Rosabeth M. Kanter. LC 72-76565. 317p. 1972. pap. 15.95 (*0-674-14576-3*) HUP.

Commitment As a Theme in African American Literature: A Study of James Baldwin & Ralph Ellison. R. Jothiprakash. 220p. (Orig.). (C). Date not set. text ed. 39.95 (*1-55605-239-1*); pap. text ed. 29.95 (*1-55605-237-5*) Wyndhall Pr.

Commitment, Educative Action & Adults: Learning Programmes with a Social Purpose. Denis O'Sullivan. 215p. 1993. 59.95 (*1-85628-292-9*, Pub. by Avebury Pub UK) Ashgate Pub Co.

***Commitment in Dialogue: Basic Concepts of Interpersonal Reasoning.** Ed. by Douglas N. Walton & Erik C. Krabbe. LC 94-37799. (Logic & Language Ser.). 160p. (C). 1995. text ed. 54.50x (*0-7914-2585-1*); pap. text ed. 17.95x (*0-7914-2586-X*) State U NY Pr.

Commitment in Reflection: Essays in Literature & Moral Philosophy. Ed. by Leona Toker. LC 93-6402. (Reference Library of the Humanities: Vol. 1763). 328p. 1993. 49.00 (*0-8153-1457-4*) Garland.

Commitment to a Christian Renewal: Conversations with an Indian Sage. Raymond A. Hauserman. LC 88-27199. 64p. (Orig.). 1989. pap. 6.50 (*0-924136-00-6*) Ligate Pubs.

Commitment to an Aging Workforce: Strategies & Models for Helping Older Workers Achieve Full Potential. Ed. by Frances R. Rothstein. 194p. 1988. 15.00 (*0-910883-46-7*, 352) Natl Coun Aging.

Commitment to Campaign: A Sociological Study of CND. John Mattausch. LC 88-32592. 256p. 1989. text ed. 69.95 (*0-7190-2908-2*, Pub. by Manchester Univ Pr UK) St Martin.

Commitment to Care: An Integrated Philosophy of Science, Education, & Religion. Dean Turner. LC 77-78421. 1977. 12.50 (*0-685-01431-2*) Devin.

Commitment to Care: An Integrated Philosophy of Science, Education, & Religion. Dean Turner. LC 77-78421. 431p. 1978. 12.95 (*0-8159-5216-3*) Hope Pub Hse.

Commitment to Critical Thinking. rev. ed. Carl B. Smith. LC 91-71319. 120p. 1991. pap. 9.95 (*0-9628556-0-X*) Grayson Bernard Pubs.

Commitment to Deviance: The Nonprofessional Criminal in the Community. Robert A. Stebbins. LC 75-95504. (Contributions in Sociology Ser.: No. 5). 201p. 1971. text ed. 27.50 (*0-8371-2339-9*, STDPB, Greenwood Pr) Greenwood.

Commitment to Excellence. Ed. by Mac Anderson. 77p. (Orig.). 1986. pap. 7.50 (*1-880461-25-0*) Celebrat Excell.

Commitment to Excellence: Developing a Professional Nursing Staff. SueEllen Pinkerton & Patricia Schroeder. 320p. (C). 1987. 62.00 (*0-87189-882-9*) Aspen Pub.

Commitment to Higher Education. J. Wyatt. 1990. 90.00 (*0-335-09371-X*, Open Univ Pr) Taylor & Francis.

***Commitment to Love.** Deanna McClary & Jerry Jenkins. 220p. 1989. pap. 12.95 (*0-9640666-0-2*) C McClary Evang.

Commitment to Public Service: The History of the Houston Bar Association. Eric L. Fredrickson. 202p. 1992. 24.95 (*0-88415-082-8*) Gulf Pub.

Commitment to Purpose: How Alliance Partnership Won the Cold War. Richard L. Kugler. LC 93-10986. 1993. write for info. (*0-8330-1385-8*, MR-190-FF) Rand Corp.

Commitment to Quality. Ed. by Mac Anderson. (Orig.). 1988. pap. 7.50 (*1-880461-17-X*) Celebrat Excell.

Commitment to Renewal: Baltimore County Public Library Long Range Plan, 1989-1993. Eleanor J. Rodger. (Illus.). 55p. 1988. pap. 20.00 (*0-937076-04-X*) Baltimore Co Pub Lib.

Commitment to Service: The Library's Mission. Ed. by Alphonse F. Trezza. (Professional Librarian Ser.). 130p. 1990. pap. 22.50 (*0-8161-1931-7*, Hall Reference) Macmillan.

Commitment to the Committed. J. T. Feldbrugge. xvi, 276p. 1986. 24.00 (*90-265-0678-3*, Pub. by Swets Pub Serv NE) Taylor & Francis.

Commitment to the Dead: One Woman's Journey Toward Understanding. Helen Waterford. LC 87-20819. (Illus.). 200p. 1987. pap. 11.95 (*0-939650-62-2*) R H Pub.

Commitment to Youth. A. S. Goodheartz. 1967. 19.95 (*0-317-18407-5*) NCUP.

Commitments. Barbara Delinsky. 384p. 1995. mass mkt. 5.99 (*0-446-60215-9*) Warner Bks.

Commitments. Roddy Doyle. (Vintage Contemporaries Ser.). 1989. pap. 9.00 (*0-679-72174-6*, Vin) Random.

Committals for Trial to the Crown Court: The Law & Practice. Clifford E. Chatterton & Philip K. Brown. 305p. (C). 1988. 95.00 (*1-85190-058-6*, Pub. by Fourmat Pub UK) St Mut.

Committed: White Activists in the Civil Rights Movement. Alphonso Pinkney. 1968. 19.95x (*0-8084-0084-3*) NCUP.

Committed Aestheticism: The Poetic Theory & Practice of Gunter Eich. Larry Richardson. LC 83-48707. (American University Studies: Germanic Languages & Literature: Ser. I, Vol. 21). 248p. 1983. pap. text ed. 25.25 (*0-8204-0034-3*) P Lang Pubs.

Committed by Choice. Judith Merkle. 158p. (Orig.). 1993. 9.95 (*0-8146-2072-8*) Liturgical Pr.

Committed Church. Ed. by Laurence Bright & Simon Clements. 1966. 69.50 (*0-317-27423-6*) Elliots Bks.

Committed Communities: Fresh Streams for World Missions. Charles J. Mellis. LC 76-53548. 138p. reprint ed. pap. 6.95 (*0-87808-426-6*, WCL426-6) William Carey Lib.

***Committed Couples: God's Plan for Marriage & the Family.** Jimmy R. Lee. 168p. (Orig.). 1995. pap. 9.99 (*0-8010-5693-4*) Baker Bk.

Committed Eye: Alexander Alland's Photography. Bonnie Yochelson. (Illus.). 52p. (Orig.). 1991. pap. write for info. (*0-910961-02-6*) Mus City NY.

Committed Journalism: An Ethic for the Profession. 2nd ed. Edmund B. Lambeth. LC 91-32569. 256p. 1992. text ed. 35.00 (*0-253-33220-6*); pap. text ed. 12.95 (*0-253-20719-3*, MB-719) Ind U Pr.

Committed Marriage. Elizabeth Achtemeier. LC 76-7611. 224p. 1976. pap. 13.99 (*0-664-24754-7*, Westminster) Westminster John Knox.

***Committed Mercy: You & Your Church Can Serve the Disabled.** Stan Carder. LC 95-15372. 144p. (Orig.). 1995. pap. 10.99 (*0-8010-9004-0*) Baker Bk.

Committed Observer: Raymond Aron Interviews with Jean-Louis Missika & Dominque Wolton. Tr. by James C. McIntosh & Marie McIntosh. LC 82-42902. 1983. 17.00 (*0-89526-624-5*) Regnery Pub.

Committed Organization: How to Develop Companies to Compete Successfully in the 1990s. Graham Saunders. 206p. 1984. text ed. 55.00 (*0-566-02493-4*) Ashgate Pub Co.

Committed to Christ & His Church. Stephen F. Olford. (Olford Biblical Preaching Library). 144p. 1991. pap. 6.99 (*0-8010-6717-0*) Baker Bk.

Committed to Grace. Earl Lee & Hazel Lee. 79p. (Orig.). 1993. pap. 5.95 (*0-8341-1500-X*, 55705) Beacon Hill.

***Committed to Peace: Blue Valley Stake Lectures.** Barbara M. Higdon. LC 94-26140. 1994. pap. text ed. 11.00 (*0-8309-0679-7*) Herald Hse.

Committed To Print: Social & Political Themes in Recent American Printed Art. Deborah Wye. 120p. (Orig.). 1987. pap. 9.95 (*0-87070-299-8*, 0-8109-6022-2) Mus of Modern Art.

Committed to World Missions: A Focus on International Strategy. Ed. by Don Loewen. 129p. (Orig.). 1990. pap. 4.95 (*0-921788-00-2*) Kindred Prods.

Committed Worship, Vol. 1: Adult Conversion. Donald Gelpi. 276p. (Orig.). 1993. 17.95 (*0-8146-5825-3*, M Glazier) Liturgical Pr.

Committed Worship, Vol. 2: The Sacraments of Ongoing Conversion. Donald L. Gelpi. 300p. (Orig.). 1993. 17.95 (*0-8146-5826-1*, M Glazier) Liturgical Pr.

Committee. Hank Braxton. (Orig.). 1979. pap. 2.25 (*0-89083-484-9*) Zebra.

***Committee.** B. G. Killion. 300p. Date not set. pap. 9.95 (*0-7610-0402-5*) NW Pub.

Committee Book. Audrie Stratford. 144p. 1995. pap. 9.95 (*0-572-01473-2*, Pub. by Foulsham UK) Atrium Pubs.

Committee for Inland Fisheries of Africa: Report of the Fourth Session of the Sub-committee for Lake Tanganyika: Rome, Italy, 25-27 April 1988. (Fisheries Reports: No. 403). 25p. 1988. pap. 12.00 (*92-5-002725-7*, F7254) UNIPUB.

Committee Management in Human Services. 2nd ed. John E. Tropman et al. (Social Welfare Ser.). 300p. (C). 1992. pap. text ed. 21.95 (*0-8304-1291-3*) Nelson-Hall.

Committee of One. Patricia M. Holt. 165p. 1991. pap. 12.50 (*0-915597-82-9*) Amana Bks.

Committee of Public Accounts Twenty-Seventh Report: Bus Fuel Grants. 5p. 1989. pap. 9.00 (*0-10-223889-8*, HM5152, Pub. by HMSO UK) UNIPUB.

Committee of Public Accounts Twenty-Sixth Report: Coronary Heart Disease. 37p. 1989. pap. 22.00 (*0-10-224989-X*, HM989X, Pub. by HMSO UK) UNIPUB.

Committee of the States, Vol. 1: Inside the Radical Right. Cheri Seymour. (Illus.). 448p. 1991. boxed 21.95 (*0-9628772-0-4*) Camden Place.

***Committee of Vigilance.** John B. Cooke. 1994. 5.99 (*0-553-56869-8*) Bantam.

***Committee of 300.** 3rd ed. John Coleman. 1994. pap. 20.00 (*0-9634019-2-0*) J Holding.

An Asterisk (*) at the beginning of an entry indicates that the title is appearing in BIP for the first time.

C

An Asterisk (*) at the beginning of an entry indicates that the title is appearing in BIP for the first time.

1417

Common Ailments & Their Natural Remedies. Rudolf Steiner. 1973. lib. bdg. 250.00 (0-87968-557-3) Krishna Pr.

Common Ailments Cured Naturally. Caroline Wheater. (Family Matters Ser.). (Illus.). 96p. 1991. pap. 4.95 (0-7063-6895-9, Pub. by Ward Lock UK) Sterling.

Common American Birds. Harry J. Baerg. 1994. 16.95 (0-87961-234-7); pap. 8.95 (0-87961-235-5) Naturegraph.

Common American Phrases in Everyday Contexts. Richard A. Spears. 224p. 1991. pap. 9.95 (0-8442-5154-2, Natl Textbk) NTC Pub Grp.

Common & Courtly Language: The Stylistics of Social Class in Eighteenth-Century British Literature. Carey McIntosh. LC 85-17857. 168p. 1986. text ed. 29.95 (0-8122-7998-0) U of Pa Pr.

Common & Scientific Names of Aquatic Invertebrates from the United States & Canada: Cnidaria & Ctenophora. S. D. Cairns et al. LC 91-73763. (Special Publication Ser.: No. 22). 86p. 1991. pap. 25.50 (0-913235-74-1) Am Fisheries Soc.

Common & Scientific Names of Aquatic Invertebrates from the United States & Canada: Decapod Crustaceans. A. B. Williams et al. LC 88-70618. (Special Publication Ser.: No. 17). 71p. 1989. pap. 17.50 (0-913235-49-0) Am Fisheries Soc.

Common & Scientific Names of Fishes from the United States & Canada. 5th ed. C. R. Robins et al. LC 90-86052. (Special Publication Ser.: No. 20). 183p. 1991. 32.50 (0-913235-70-9); pap. 24.50 (0-913235-69-5) Am Fisheries Soc.

Common & Uncommon Sense of Social Behavior. Francis C. Dane. LC 87-15833. 182p. (C). 1988. pap. 17.95 (0-534-08406-0) Brooks-Cole.

Common Asphodel. Robert Graves. LC 78-117590. (English Literature Ser.: No. 33). 1970. reprint ed. lib. bdg. 75.00 (0-8383-1023-0) M S G Haskell Hse.

Common Australian Fungi. Tony Young. (Illus.). 157p. 1982. 14.95 (0-86840-082-3, Pub. by New South Wales Univ Pr AT) Intl Spec Bk.

Common Base of Social Work Practice. Harriett M. Bartlett. LC 72-116893. 224p. 1970. pap. 16.95 (0-87101-054-2) Natl Assn Soc Wkrs.

Common Beans: Research for Crop Improvement. Ed. by Aart Van Schoonhoven & O. Voysest. 992p. 1991. text ed. 123.50 (0-85198-679-X) CAB Intl.

C

Common Beliefs about the Rural Elderly: What Do National Data Tell Us? LC 93-3076. (Vital & Health Statistics Ser. 3: Analytical & Epidemiological Studies: No. 28). 1993. write for info. (0-8406-0477-7) Natl Ctr Health Stats.

Common Bible Questions of Our Day. George Rich. (New Life Ser.). 24p. (Orig.). 1991. teacher ed 1.95 (0-87227-164-1); student ed, pap. text ed. 1.95 (0-87227-160-9) Reg Baptist.

Common Bile Duct Exploration. A. Cushieri. (Developments in Surgery Ser.). 1984. lib. bdg. 170.00 (0-89838-639-X) Kluwer Ac.

Common Bird Songs. Donald J. Borror. (Illus.). (Orig.). 1968. lp, pap. 7.95 (0-486-21829-5) Dover.

Common Bird Songs. Donald J. Borror. 64p. (Orig.). 1984. student ed, audio 8.95 (0-486-99911-4) Dover.

Common Birds of Egypt: A Practical Guide. El Din Sherif Baha. 1985. pap. 15.00 (977-424-062-6, Pub. by Am Univ Cairo Pr UA) Col U Pr.

Common Birds of San Salvador Island, Bahamas. Brian White. (Illus.). 57p. (Orig.). (C). 1991. pap. text ed. 8.00 (0-935909-34-6) Bahamian.

Common Birds of Santa Barbara. Edward S. Spaulding. (Illus.). 78p. (Orig.). 1985. pap. 4.50 (0-87461-060-5) McNally & Loftin.

Common Blessings. Arthur L. Clements. LC 87-2639. 64p. (Orig.). 1987. pap. 5.95 (0-9617589-1-0) Lincoln Springs Pr.

Common Blood Tests: Getting Acquainted with Your Lab Results. Ed. by N. L. Gifford. LC 91-75199. 125p. (Orig.). 1992. pap. 10.00 (1-881818-00-4) TBL.

***Common Blood Tests: Getting Acquainted with Your Lab Results.** 2nd ed. Ed. by N. L. Gifford. 209p. 1995. pap. write for info. (1-881818-06-3) TBL.

Common Body of Professional Knowledge for Internal Auditors: A Research Study. M. J. Barrett et al. Ed. by Richard Holman. (Illus.). 145p. 1985. pap. text ed. 25.00 (0-89413-138-9) Inst Inter Aud.

Common Body, Royal Bones. Evelyn Shefner. LC 87-27761. 119p. (Orig.). 1987. pap. 9.95 (0-918273-33-1) Coffee Hse.

Common Bond: Maintaining the Constancy of Purpose Throughout Your Health Care Organization. Francis L. Ulschak. LC 93-33143. (Health-Management Ser.). 360p. 1994. 35.95 (1-55542-614-X) Jossey-Bass.

Common Bond: The Story of Lutheran Brotherhood, 1917-1987. Hakala Associates Staff. 304p. 1989. 20.00 (0-9621237-0-6) Lutheran Brotherhood.

***Common Bonds: Reflections of a Cancer Doctor.** E. Roy Berger & Linda Mittiga. 250p. 1994. write for info. (1-883257-07-7) Hlth Edu Lit.

Common Bonds: Stories by & about Modern Texas Women. Ed. by Suzanne Comer. LC 88-43251. (Southwest Life & Letters Ser.). 320p. 1990. text ed. 22.50 (0-87074-287-6); pap. 10.95 (0-87074-288-4) SMU Press.

Common Book of Consciousness. rev. ed. Diana Saltoon. 1991. pap. 11.95 (0-89087-627-4) Celestial Arts.

Common Boundary-Common Problems: The Environmental Consequences of Energy Production. American Bar Association, Standing Committee on Environmental Law Staff. LC 82-70885. 116p. 1982. pap. 15.00 (0-318-36242-2, 359-0008) Amer Bar Assn.

Common Boundary Graduate Education Guide: Holistic Programs & Resources Integrating Spirituality & Psychology. 2nd ed. Charles H. Simpkinson et al. LC 93-73988. (Illus.). 208p. 1994. pap. 19.95 (0-9638795-0-2) Common Boundary.

Common Branches (1-6), Elementary School. Jack Rudman. (Teachers License Examination Ser.: T-9). 1994. pap. 23.95 (0-8373-8009-X) Nat Learn.

Common Bridge Conventions Flipper. Ron Klinger. 32p. 1994. 5.95 (0-575-05740-8, Pub. by V Gollancz UK) Trafalgar.

Common Bushes Afire with God. Kieran Kay. LC 94-66743. (Illus.). 128p. (Orig.). 1994. pap. 8.95 (1-878718-23-1) Resurrection.

Common But Less Frequent Loon & Other Essays. Keith S. Thomson. (Illus.). 192p. 1993. 22.50 (0-300-05630-3) Yale U Pr.

Common Butterflies of India. Thomas Gay & Isaac Kehimkar. (Nature Guides Ser.). (Illus.). 84p. 1993. 9.95 (0-19-563164-1) OUP.

Common Cagebirds in America. Val Clear. LC 66-16027. 1966. pap. 4.95 (0-672-52270-5, Bobbs) Macmillan.

Common Calling: The Witness of Our Reformation Churches in North America Today, the Report of the Lutheran-Reformed Committee for Theological Conversations, 1988-1992. Ed. by Keith F. Nickle & Timothy F. Lull. LC 92-43096. 64p. 1993. 4.99 (0-8066-2665-8, 9-2665) Augsburg Fortress.

Common Campground Critters of the West. Robert Pollock & Jean Pollock. (J). (gr. 1-6). 1987. reprint ed. pap. 5.95 (0-911797-77-7) R Rinehart.

Common Cause: Lobbying in the Public Interest. Andrew S. McFarland. LC 84-7732. (Chatham House Series on Change in American Politics). (Illus.). 224p. 1984. pap. text ed. 14.95 (0-934540-28-4) Chatham Hse Pubs.

Common Cents. Samuel J. Lucci. 1985. write for info. (0-9613870-0-9) McClain.

***Common Cents.** Timothy J. Penny & Major Garrett. 1995. 21.95 (0-316-69912-8) Little.

Common Cents: The ABC Performance Breakthrough. Peter B. Turney. (Illus.). 393p. (Orig.). 1991. pap. 19.95 (0-9629576-0-7) Cost Tech.

Common Cents: The Complete Money Management Workbook. Judy Lawrence. 84p. (Orig.). 1989. 10.95 (0-9607096-6-5) Lawrence & Co Pubs.

Common Cents Credit: Two Hundred Thirty Sense Wits to Keep You Out of the Red. Chester King. 128p. (YA). 1993. text ed. 14.95 (0-9639263-0-6); pap. text ed. 9.95 (0-9639263-1-4) Che-King Pubng.

***Common Cents Livestock Feeding.** Michael J. Mehren. (Illus.). 156p. (Orig.). (C). 1990. write for info. (0-9626390-0-1) Haywire Pub.

Common Chorus: A Version of Aristophanes "Lysistrata" Tr. by Tony Harrison. 136p. (Orig.). 1992. pap. 8.95 (0-571-14723-2) Faber & Faber.

Common Cold. Mary Kittredge. (Medical Disorders & Their Treatment Ser.). (Illus.). 104p. (YA). (gr. 6-12). 1990. 18.95 (0-7910-0060-5) Chelsea Hse.

Common Cold & Common Sense. Dale Alexander. LC 73-143000. 1971. 14.95 (0-911638-04-0) Witkower.

Common Cold & Flu. Alvin Virginia & Robert Silverstein. LC 93-4685. (Diseases & People Ser.). (Illus.). 128p. (J). (gr. 6 up). 1994. lib. bdg. 17.95 (0-89490-463-9) Enslow Pubs.

Common Cold & Influenza. Nancy Stedman. LC 86-8387. (Understanding Disease Ser.). (Illus.). 72p. (J). (gr. 4-8). 1986. lib. bdg. 11.98 (0-671-60022-2, Julian Messner) Silver Burdett Pr.

Common Cold & the Flu. Nathan Aaseng. LC 92-15137. (Venture Book Ser.). (Illus.). 128p. (YA). (gr. 9-12). 1992. lib. bdg. 14.28 (0-531-12537-8) Watts.

***Common Cold Crusade.** Peter Schwed. 200p. Date not set. pap. 8.95 (0-7610-0356-8) NW Pub.

Common Command Language for On-Line Interactive Information Retrieval, Z39.58, 1992. National Information Standards Organization Staff. 30p. 1993. 35.00 (0-88738-940-6) Transaction Pubs.

Common Command Language for Online Interactive Information Retrieval, Z39.58-1992. National Information Standards Organization Staff. LC 93-40322. (National Information Standards Ser.). 25p. 1994. 48.00 (1-880124-03-3) NISO.

Common Core: Thais & Americans. rev. ed. John P. Fieg. LC 89-2124. 120p. 1989. pap. 12.95 (0-933662-80-7) Intercult Pr.

Common Culture: Symbolic Work at Play in the Everyday Cultures of Youth. Paul Willis. 165p. (C). 1990. pap. text ed. 20.95 (0-8133-1097-0) Westview.

Common Culture & the Great Tradition: The Case for Renewal. Marshall W. Fishwick. LC 81-4232. (Contributions to the Study of Popular Culture Ser.: No. 2). (Illus.). x, 230p. 1982. text ed. 55.00 (0-313-23042-0, FCC/, Greenwood Pr) Greenwood.

Common Cures for Common Ailments: A Doctor's Guide to Nonprescription, Over-the-Counter Medicines & His Recommendations for Their Use. Albert Marchetti. LC 77-16114. 368p. 1981. pap. 8.95 (0-8128-6107-8, Scrbrough Hse) Madison Bks UPA.

Common Death. large type ed. Natasha Cooper. Orig. Title: Festering Lillies. 1991. 21.95 (0-7089-2458-1) Ulverscroft.

Common Decency: Domestic Policies after Reagan. Alvin L. Schorr & James P. Comer. LC 86-1615. 246p. 1986. 30.00 (0-300-03603-5) Yale U Pr.

Common Decency: Domestic Policies after Reagan. Alvin L. Schorr. LC 86-1615. 246p. (C). 1988. reprint ed. 14.00 (0-300-04214-0) Yale U Pr.

Common Defense. Ed Ruggero. Ed. by Paul McCarthy. 432p. 1992. reprint ed. mass mkt. 5.99 (0-671-73009-6) PB.

Common Defense: Strategic Programs in National Politics. Samuel P. Huntington. LC 61-18197. 512p. reprint ed. pap. 146.00 (0-7837-0427-5, 2040750) Bks Demand.

Common Dermatoses Recognition & Therapy. Baden. 1991. 24.95 (0-8151-0435-9, Yr Bk Med Pubs) Mosby Yr Bk.

Common Descent Group in China & Its Functions. Hsien Chin Ho. 204p. 1985. reprint ed. pap. 12.00 (0-89986-376-0) Oriental Bk Store.

Common Destiny: Blacks & American Society. Committee on the Status of Black Americans Staff. Ed. by Gerald D. Jaynes & Robin M. Williams, Jr. 624p. 1990. 35.00 (0-309-03998-3); pap. 22.95 (0-685-74077-3) Natl Acad Pr.

Common Destiny: Japan & the United States in the Global Age. Richard Krooth & Hiroshi Fukurai. LC 89-43691. (Illus.). 335p. 1990. lib. bdg. 29.95 (0-89950-522-8) McFarland & Co.

Common Diagnostic Procedures: Orthopedics & Neurology. Menachem Epstein. 1992. write for info. (0-8205-1039-4) Bender.

Common Diagnostic Tests: Use & Interpretation. 2nd ed. Ed. by Harold C. Sox. (Illus.). 400p. 1990. pap. text ed. 37.00 (0-943126-15-0, CDT89) Amer Coll Phys.

Common Differences: Conflicts in Black & White Feminist Perspectives. 2nd ed. Gloria Joseph & Jill Lewis. LC 86-13864. 306p. 1981. reprint ed. lib. bdg. 35.00 (0-89608-318-7); reprint ed. pap. 14.00 (0-89608-317-9) South End Pr.

Common Dilemmas in Family Medicine. Ed. by J. Fry. 1983. lib. bdg. 35.00 (0-85200-565-2) Kluwer Ac.

Common Diseases: Their Nature, Incidence & Care. 3rd ed. John Fry. 1983. lib. bdg. 29.00 (0-85200-454-0) Kluwer Ac.

Common Diseases: Their Nature, Incidence & Care. 4th ed. John Fry. 1985. lib. bdg. 49.50 (0-85200-918-6) Kluwer Ac.

Common Diseases: Their Nature, Prevalence, & Care. 5th ed. John Fry & Gerald Sandler. LC 93-12605. 448p. (C). 1993. lib. bdg. 57.50 (0-7923-8803-8) Kluwer Ac.

Common Disorders of the Hip. Mary C. Singleton & Eleanor F. Branch. LC 86-3074. (Physical Therapy in Health Care Ser.: Vol. 1, No. 1). 116p. 1986. 29.95 (0-86656-557-4) Haworth Pr.

Common Disorders of the Temporomandibular Joint. 2nd ed. Hugh D. Ogus & Paul A. Toller. (Dental Practitioners' Handbook Ser.: No. 26). (Illus.). 123p. 1986. 37.50 (0-7236-0874-1) Buttrwrth-Heinemann.

***Common Dolphin.** John F. Prevost. LC 95-12363. (Dolphins Ser.). (J). 1995. write for info. (1-56239-496-7) Abdo & Dghtrs.

***Common Doom.** Liliane L. Baker. LC 91-67442. 183p. (Orig.). 1991. pap. text ed. 12.95 (1-878815-01-6) Reflected Images.

Common Dung Beetles in Pastures of Southeast Australia. Marina Tyndale-Biscoe. 1990. pap. 15.00 (0-643-05090-6, Pub. by CSIRO AT) Intl Spec Bk.

Common Edible & Useful Plants of the West. rev. ed. Muriel Sweet. LC 76-58. (Illus.). 64p. (J). (gr. 4 up). 1976. pap. 5.95 (0-87961-046-8) Naturegraph.

Common Elegies. Charles Molesworth. (Illus.). 1977. per. 2.50 (0-912284-85-4) New Rivers Pr.

Common Elements in New Mathematics Programs: Their Origins & Evolution. Helene Sherman. LC 72-75560. (Practical Suggestions for Teaching Ser.). 176p. reprint ed. pap. 50.20 (0-685-12283-2, 2026068) Bks Demand.

***Common Era: Best New Writings on Religion.** Ed. & Pref. by Steven Scholl. (Common Era Annual Anthology Ser.). 232p. (Orig.). 1995. pap. 14.95 (1-883991-12-9) Whte Cloud Pr.

Common Errors: A Short Handbook for Writers. J. M. Ferguson, Jr. & Charles A. Peek. 42p. (C). 1988. pap. text ed. 3.60 (0-9619001-1-3) Prairiend Pr.

Common Errors in English: An ESL Guide. Martin Boyne & Don LePan. 1993. pap. 13.95 (1-55111-008-3) Broadview Pr.

Common Errors in English & How to Avoid Them. Alexander M. Witherspoon. LC 73-11433. (Quality Paperback Ser.: No. 268). 348p. 1976. reprint ed. pap. 11.00 (0-8226-0268-7) Littlefield.

Common Experience: Signposts on the Path to Enlightenment. J. M. Cohen & J. F. Phipps. LC 91-51013. 301p. 1992. pap. 12.95 (0-8356-0679-1, Quest) Theos Pub Hse.

Common Expression From Real Life Chinese Version in Simplified Characters: Contextual Word Groupings Most Commonly Heard in American Daily Life. Dee G. Davis. 65p. (CHI.). 1989. reprint ed. pap. 5.00 (0-929350-54-5) Spoken English Pubns.

Common Expression From Real Life Chinese Version in Traditional Characters: Contextual Word Grouping Most Commonly Heard in American Spoken English of Daily Life. Dee G. Davis. 65p. (CHI.). 1989. reprint ed. pap. 5.00 (0-929350-55-3) Spoken English Pubns.

Common Expressions from Real Life - Japanese Translation. Futsu Hyogen. 48p. pap. 5.00 (0-929350-56-1) Spoken English Pubns.

Common Expressions from Real Life - Spanish Translation. Giros Usuales del Ingles. 32p. pap. 5.00 (0-929350-57-X) Spoken English Pubns.

Common Eye Diseases & Their Management. N. R. Galloway. (Illus.). 290p. 1985. pap. 66.00 (0-387-13659-2) Spr-Verlag.

Common Factors in Psychotherapy. Ed. by A. M. Van Kalmthout et al. xii, 194p. 1985. 18.75 (90-265-0639-2, Pub. by Swets Pub Serv NE) Taylor & Francis.

Common Faith. John Dewey. (Terry Lecture Ser.). 1960. pap. 8.00 (0-300-00069-3, Y18) Yale U Pr.

Common Fate: Endangered Salmon & the People of the Pacific Northwest. Joseph Cone. LC 94-12020. 1995. 25.00 (0-8050-2388-7) H Holt & Co.

Common Fate, Common Bond. Mitter Swasti. (C). 1986. pap. text ed. 17.50 (0-7453-0026-X) Westview.

Common Faults in Writing English. 1991. lib. bdg. 69.00 (0-8490-4162-7) Gordon Pr.

Common Ferns of Luquillo Forest. Angela K. Kepler. LC 72-91603. (Illus.). 125p. 1975. 15.00 (0-913480-06-1); 15.00 (0-913480-07-X); pap. 5.00 (0-913480-08-8); pap. 5.00 (0-913480-09-6) Inter Am U Pr.

Common Fisheries Policy. M. J. Holden. 1994. 82.00 (0-85238-205-7) Blackwell Sci.

Common Florida Angiosperm Families, Pt. II. Wendy B. Zomlefer. (Illus.). 112p. 1986. pap. 11.99 (0-932353-02-9) Bio Illustra.

Common Florida Angiosperm Families, Pt. I. Wendy B. Zomlefer. (Illus.). 107p. (C). 1983. pap. 9.99 (0-932353-01-0) Bio Illustra.

Common Food Intolerances One: Epidemiology of Coeliac Disease. Ed. by S. Auricchio & J. Visakorpi. (Dynamic Nutrition Research Ser.: Vol. 2). (Illus.). x, 192p. 1992. 149.00 (3-8055-5616-0) S Karger.

Common Food Intolerances Two: Milk in Human Nutrition & Adult-Type Hypolactasia. Ed. by S. Auricchio & R. Troncone. (Dynamic Nutrition Research Ser.: Vol. 3). (Illus.). x, 212p. 1993. 157.00 (3-8055-5741-8) S Karger.

***Common Foot Problems.** Whitine. 1996. pap. write for info. (0-7506-2063-3, Focal) Buttrwrth-Heinemann.

Common Foot Problems in Primary Care. Ed. by Michael P. Dellacorte & Patrick J. Grisafi. (Illus.). 182p. 1992. text ed. 45.00 (1-56053-050-2) Hanley & Belfus.

Common Fossils of Missouri. A. G. Unklesbay. LC 56-62812. 100p. 1973. pap. 8.95 (0-8262-0588-7) U of Mo Pr.

Common Foundation Studies in Nursing. Ed. by Neil Kenworthy et al. LC 92-15511. (Illus.). 400p. (Orig.). 1992. pap. text ed. 36.00 (0-443-04401-5) Churchill.

Common Foundations of East Asian Success. Peter Petri. LC 93-32722. (Lessons of East Asia Ser.). 46p. 1993. 6.95 (0-8213-2616-3, 12616) World Bank.

Common Fragrance & Flavor Materials. 2nd ed. Ed. by Kurt Bauer & Dorothea Garbe. 218p. 1990. text ed. 85.00 (0-89573-919-4) VCH Pubs.

Common Fresh & Brackish Water Algal Flora: India & Burma. K. Biswas. 105p. (C). 1980. text ed. 100.00 (0-89771-555-1, Pub. by Intl Bk Distr II) St Mut.

Common Globe or Global Commons: Population Regulation & Income Distribution. John C. Boot. LC 74-79919. (Business Economics & Finance Ser.: No. 1). 155p. reprint ed. pap. 44.20 (0-7837-0857-2, 2041165) Bks Demand.

Common Glory. Paul Green. LC 72-11622. (Illus.). 273p. 1973. reprint ed. text ed. 35.00 (0-8371-7080-X, GRCH, Greenwood Pr) Greenwood.

Common Good & U. S. Capitalism. Ed. by Oliver F. Williams & John W. Houck. 434p. (Orig.). 1987. lib. bdg. 58.50 (0-8191-6364-3, Notre Dame Ctr-EVRB) U Pr of Amer.

Common Grief: Poems by Roberto Sosa. 2nd ed. Roberto Sosa. Tr. by JoAnne Engelbert. 1994. pap. 11.95 (1-880684-23-3) Curbstone.

Common Ground. John Daniel. LC 87-73557. 80p. 1988. pap. 7.95 (0-917652-73-8) Confluence Pr.

Common Ground. Robert Finch. 1994. pap. 10.95 (0-393-31179-1) Norton.

Common Ground. Jeane Gilbert-Lewis. 224p. (Orig.). 1993. pap. 2.95 (1-56597-040-3, Kismet) Meteor Pub.

Common Ground. Adrian Moyes. 98p. (C). 1987. pap. text ed. 21.00 (0-85598-078-8, Pub. by Oxfam Pubns UK) St Mut.

***Common Ground: A Gathering of Poems on Rural Life.** Ed. by Mark Vinz & Thom Tammaro. 1990. per. 7.50 (0-941127-04-4) Dacotah Terr Pr.

***Common Ground: A Natrualist's Cape Cod.** Robert Finch. 1995. 21.00 (0-8446-6856-7) Peter Smith.

Common Ground: A Thematic Reader. Jane Epstein & Laury Magnus. (C). 1982. pap. text ed. 17.75 (0-673-15505-6) HarpCollege.

Common Ground: A Turbulent Decade in the Lives of Three American Families. J. Anthony Lukas. LC 85-127. 672p. 1985. 19.95 (0-394-41150-1) Knopf.

Common Ground: A Turbulent Decade in the Lives of Three American Families. J. Anthony Lukas. LC 86-40132. 784p. 1986. pap. 15.00 (0-394-74616-3, Vin) Random.

Common Ground: An Introduction to Eastern Christianity. J. Bajis. 1991. pap. 16.95 (0-937032-81-6) Light&Life Pub Co MN.

Common Ground: Dialogue, Understanding, & the Teaching of Composition. Kurt Spellmeyer. 312p. 1993. pap. text ed. 25.00 (0-13-157777-8) P-H.

Common Ground: Personal Writing & Public Discourse. Carolyn P. Collette & Richard Johnson. LC 92-26338. (C). 1992. 22.00 (0-06-041369-7) HarpCollege.

Common Ground: Photographs of Rural & Small Town Life. Raymond Bial. Ed. by Linda L. Bial. LC 85-63625. (Illus.). 110p. (Orig.). 1986. pap. 10.00 (0-935153-01-2) Stormline Pr.

***Common Ground: Reading & Writing about America's Cultures.** Laurie G. Kirszner & Stephen R. Mandell. 544p. 1993. pap. text ed. 17.50 (0-312-07586-3) St Martin.

Common Ground: The Arts, Therapy, & Spirituality. (Conference Proceedings Ser.). 168p. (Orig.). 1993. pap. 25.00 (1-882147-21-9) Am Art Therapy.

Common Ground: Whole Language & Phonics Working Together. Priscilla Vail. 88p. (Orig.). 1991. pap. 8.95 (0-935493-27-1) Modern Learn Pr.

Common Ground - Uncommon Vision: The Michael & Julie Hall Collection of American Folk Art. Russell Bowman et al. LC 93-9542. (Illus.). 335p. (Orig.). 1993. 75.00 (0-944110-43-6); pap. 45.00 (0-944110-33-9) Milwauk Art Mus.

An Asterisk (*) at the beginning of an entry indicates that the title is appearing in BIP for the first time.

C

An Asterisk (*) at the beginning of an entry indicates that the title is appearing in BIP for the first time.

1419

Common Plants of the East Bay: A Guide to Common Non-Woody Plants Found in East Bay Communities. Lisa K. Wagner. LC 83-71995. (Illus.). 72p. (Orig.). 1983. pap. 4.95 (*0-9611956-0-6*) Appletree Pr.

***Common Plants of the Inland Pacific, 2 vols., Set.** 1995. lib. bdg. 615.75 (*0-8490-7436-3*) Gordon Pr.

Common Plants of the Mid-Alantic Coast: A Field Guide. Gene M. Silberhorn. (Illus.). 272p. 1982. text ed. 35.00 (*0-8018-2319-6*); pap. 12.95 (*0-8018-2725-6*) Johns Hopkins.

Common Pleas Court Records of Highland County, Ohio 1805-1860. David N. McBride & Jane N. McBride. (Vital Records of Highland County, Ohio Ser.). 306p. 1984. lib. bdg. 32.50 (*0-941000-02-8*) S Ohio Genealog.

Common Poisonous Plants & Mushrooms of North America. 2nd ed. Nancy J. Turner & Adam F. Szczawinski. LC 90-37574. (Illus.). 324p. 1991. 55.00 (*0-88192-179-3*) Timber.

***Common Poisonous Plants & Mushrooms of North America.** 2nd ed. Nancy J. Turner & Adam F. Sczawinski. (Illus.). 324p. 1995. pap. 24.95 (*0-88192-312-5*) Timber.

Common-Practice Harmony. William H. Reynolds & Gerald Warfield. 216p. (C). 1985. pap. 18.00 (*0-02-873170-0*) Schirmer Bks.

Common Prayer. Leunig. 1991. pap. 7.00 (*0-85924-933-6*) Harper SF.

Common Principal Components & Related Multivariate Models. Bernhard Flury. LC 88-10821. (Probability & Mathematical Statistics Ser.). 258p. 1988. text ed. 86.95 (*0-471-63427-1*) Wiley.

Common Principles in the Neuroethology of Acoustic & Electric Communication. Ed. by W. Wilczynski et al. (Journal: Brain, Behavior & Evolution 1986: Vol. 28, NO. 13). (Illus.). 156p. 1987. pap. 92.00 (*3-8055-4462-6*) S Karger.

Common Principles of Psychotherapy. Chris L. Kleinke. LC 93-30265. 1994. text ed. 43.95 (*0-534-19998-4*) Brooks-Cole.

Common Problems - Proper Solutions: Avoiding Error in Quantitative Research. J. Scott Long. (Focus Editions Ser.: Vol. 94). 360p. 1988. 49.95 (*0-8039-2806-8*); pap. 24.95 (*0-8039-2807-6*) Sage.

Common Problems & Ideas of Modern Physics. Ed. by T. Bressani et al. 600p. (C). 1992. text ed. 130.00 (*981-02-0711-5*) World Scientific Pub.

Common Problems & Trends of Modern Physics: Proceedings of the 12th Winter Schedule on Hadronic Physics. T. Bressani et al. 512p. 1993. text ed. 116.00 (*981-02-1203-8*) World Scientific Pub.

Common Problems in Cancer Surgery. Wanebo. 440p. 1989. 65.00 (*0-685-65366-8*, Yr Bk Med Pubs) Mosby Yr Bk.

Common Problems in Critical Care, Vol. 1: Pulmonary. Prough. 1991. write for info. (*0-8151-6783-0*, Yr Bk Med Pubs) Mosby Yr Bk.

Common Problems in Endocrine Surgery. Van Heerdan. 416p. 1988. 69.00 (*0-8151-4243-9*, Yr Bk Med Pubs) Mosby Yr Bk.

Common Problems in Gastrointestinal Radiology. Thompson. 694p. 1989. 95.00 (*0-8151-8799-8*, Yr Bk Med Pubs) Mosby Yr Bk.

Common Problems in Gastrointestional Surgery, Vol. 1. Fischer. 480p. 1988. 69.00 (*0-8151-3237-9*, Yr Bk Med Pubs) Mosby Yr Bk.

Common Problems in Infections & Stones. Drach. 350p. 1991. 65.00 (*0-8151-2909-2*, Yr Bk Med Pubs) Mosby Yr Bk.

Common Problems in Infertility & Impotence. Rajfer. 416p. 1989. 69.00 (*0-8151-6991-4*, Yr Bk Med Pubs) Mosby Yr Bk.

***Common Problems in Obstetric Anesthesia.** 2nd ed. Ed. by Sanjay Datta. LC 94-34612. 1994. write for info. (*0-8151-2348-5*) Mosby Yr Bk.

Common Problems in Otology. Britton. 376p. 1991. 59.00 (*0-8151-1009-X*, Yr Bk Med Pubs) Mosby Yr Bk.

Common Problems in Pediatric Anesthesia. 2nd ed. Ed. by Linda Stehling. LC 92-18735. 523p. 1992. 59.00 (*0-8016-6495-0*) Mosby Yr Bk.

Common Problems in Pediatric, Gastroenterology & Nutrition. John Snyder. 384p. 1989. 59.00 (*0-8151-9139-1*, Yr Bk Med Pubs) Mosby Yr Bk.

Common Problems in Pediatric Otolaryngology. Gerald B. Healy. (Illus.). 352p. 1990. 54.95 (*0-685-34723-0*, Yr Bk Med Pubs) Mosby Yr Bk.

Common Problems in Pediatric Pathology. Vijay V. Joshi. LC 93-38969. 536p. 1994. 125.00 (*0-89640-242-8*) Igaku-Shoin.

Common Problems in Pediatric Sports Medicine. Smith. 400p. 1988. 59.00 (*0-8151-7837-9*, Yr Bk Med Pubs) Mosby Yr Bk.

Common Problems in Pediatric Surgery. Grosfeld. 320p. 1991. 65.00 (*0-8151-3949-7*, Yr Bk Med Pubs) Mosby Yr Bk.

Common Problems in Surgical Oncology. Ed. by Harold J. Wanebo. (Illus.). 400p. 1988. 59.95 (*0-8151-9143-X*, OPW-1, Yr Bk Med Pubs) Mosby Yr Bk.

Common Problems in Trauma. Ed. by James M. Hurst. (Illus.). 400p. 1986. 69.95 (*0-8151-4785-6*, TIC-1, Yr Bk Med Pubs) Mosby Yr Bk.

Common Problems in Vascular Surgery. Brewster. 496p. 1988. 65.00 (*0-8151-1222-X*, Yr Bk Med Pubs) Mosby Yr Bk.

Common Property Economics: A General Theory & Land Use Applications. Glenn G. Stevenson. (Illus.). 300p. (C). 1991. 64.95 (*0-521-38441-9*) Cambridge U Pr.

Common Property Resources: A Missing Dimension of Development Strategies. N. S. Jodha. LC 92-16722. (Discussion Paper Ser.: No. 169). 100p. 1992. 7.95 (*0-8213-2146-3*, 12146) World Bank.

Common Property Resources: Ecology & Community Based Sustainable Development. F. Berkes. 312p. (C). 1991. 65.00 (*81-7089-140-X*, Pub. by Intl Bk Distr II) St Mut.

Common Property Resources: Ecology of Community Based Sustainable Development. Fikret Berkes. 320p. 1989. 59.50 (*1-85293-080-2*, Pub. by Pinter Pubs UK) St Martin.

Common Pursuit. Simon Gray. 1987. pap. 4.75 (*0-8222-0234-4*) Dramatists Play.

Common Questions on Schizophrenia & Their Answers. Abram Hoffer. 220p. (Orig.). 1987. pap. 14.95 (*0-87983-377-7*) Keats.

***Common Re-Entry for Head Injured Adults.** Ylvisaker & Gobble. 40.00 (*0-316-96880-3*) Buttrwrth-Heinemann.

Common Reader. Virginia Woolf. 1984. pap. 8.00 (*0-15-619806-1*) HarBrace.

Common Riparian Plants of California. Phyllis M. Faber & Robert F. Holland. LC 88-92430. (Illus.). 147p. (Orig.). (C). 1988. pap. 18.00 (*0-9607890-1-4*, 1500) Pickleweed.

Common Rocks & Minerals of Missouri. rev. ed. W. D. Keller. LC 67-66173. (Illus.). 80p. 1973. pap. 7.95 (*0-8262-0585-2*) U of Mo Pr.

Common Room. Reynolds Price. 416p. 1989. pap. 11.95 (*0-689-70817-3*, Atheneum S&S) S&S Trade.

Common Room: New & Selected Essays. Reynolds Price. 352p. 1987. text ed. 24.95 (*0-689-11948-8*, Atheneum S&S) S&S Trade.

Common Roots - Diverse Objectives: Risd Alumni in Boston. Fuller Museum of Art Staff. (Illus.). 8p. 1989. 2.00 (*0-934358-25-7*) Fuller Mus Art.

Common Russian Similes. V. Ogoltsev. (Illus.). 174p. (C). 1984. 30.00 (*0-685-39364-X*, Pub. by Collets) St Mut.

***Common Saltwater Fishes of Southwest Florida.** Ralph Allen. (Florida Sea Grant Bulletin Ser.: No. 25). 48p. 1993. write for info. (*0-912747-06-4*) FL Sea Grant Coll.

Common Salvation. David Ward. 120p. (Orig.). (C). 1989. pap. 5.50 (*1-877917-05-2*) Alpha Bible Pubns.

Common Salvation. David Ward. (Orig.). (C). 1989. pap. write for info. (*0-318-65602-7*) D Ward.

Common School & the Negro American. Ed. by W. E. B. Du Bois. (Atlanta Univ. Publ. Ser.: No. 16). (Orig.). 1911. reprint ed. pap. 15.00 (*0-527-03117-8*) Periodicals Srv.

Common-School Grammar of the English Language. Simon Kerl. LC 84-27711. (American Linguistics, 1700-1900 Ser.). 1985. reprint ed. 50.00 (*0-8201-1403-0*) Schol Facsimiles.

Common Scientific Names of Aquatic Invertebrates from the United States & Canada: Mollusks. D. D. Turgeon et al. LC 88-70617. (Special Publication Ser.: No. 16). 277p. 1988. text ed. 35.00 (*0-913235-47-4*); pap. 24.50 (*0-913235-48-2*) Am Fisheries Soc.

Common Scientist in the Seventeenth Century: A Study of the Dublin Philosophical Society, 1683-1708. K. Theodore Hoppen. LC 72-98307. 310p. reprint ed. pap. 88.40 (*0-317-09774-1*, 2010035) Bks Demand.

Common Screening Tests. Ed. by David M. Eddy. 200p. 1991. pap. 37.00 (*0-943126-19-3*, CST91) Amer Coll Phys.

Common Seal. Paul Thompson. 1989. pap. 30.00 (*0-7478-0017-0*, Pub. by Shire UK) St Mut.

Common Seashore Life of Southern California. Joel Hedgpeth. (Illus.). 64p. (J). (gr. 4 up). 1961. pap. 6.95 (*0-911010-62-9*) Naturegraph.

Common Seashore Life of Southern California. Joel Hedgpeth. (Illus.). 64p. (J). (gr. 4 up). 1961. 14.95 (*0-911010-63-7*) Naturegraph.

Common Seashore Life of the Pacific Northwest. Lynwood S. Smith. (Illus.). 66p. (C). 1962. pap. 6.95 (*0-911010-64-5*) Naturegraph.

Common Secret: Sexual Abuse of Children & Adolescents. C. Henry Kempe & Ruth Kempe. 344p. (C). 1995. pap. text ed. write for info. (*0-7167-1625-9*) W H Freeman.

Common Secretarial Mistakes & How to Avoid Them. Prentice-Hall Editorial Staff. (Illus.). 1986. 5.95 (*0-13-152744-4*, Reward) P-H.

Common Security & Nonoffensive Defense: A Neorealist Perspective. Bjorn Moller. LC 91-28864. 285p. 1992. lib. bdg. 40.00 (*1-55587-259-X*) Lynne Rienner.

Common Security Interests of Japan, The United States & NATO. U. Alexis Johnson & George R. Packard. 38p. (C). 1983. pap. 10.95 (*0-87855-873-X*) Transaction Pubs.

***Common Sense.** Mario Cuomo. 1995. 21.00 (*0-684-81517-6*) S&S Trade.

Common Sense. Lynd Forguson. 240p. 1990. 35.00 (*0-415-02302-5*, A3742) Routledge.

Common Sense. Thomas Paine. 16.95 (*0-8488-1088-0*) Amereon Ltd.

Common Sense. Thomas Paine. (American Library). 1982. pap. 6.95 (*0-14-039016-2*, Penguin Classics) Viking Penguin.

***Common Sense.** Thomas Paine. (Great Books in Philosophy Ser.). 67p. (C). 1994. pap. text ed. 5.95 (*0-87975-918-6*) Prometheus Bks.

Common Sense. Thomas Paine. 1986. reprint ed. lib. bdg. 17.95 (*0-89966-542-X*) Buccaneer Bks.

Common Sense: A New Approach to Understanding Scripture. David W. Bercot. LC 92-80133. 180p. (Orig.). 1992. pap. 7.95 (*0-924722-06-1*) Scroll Pub.

Common Sense: America's Roots Revisited. Laurie Efrein. (Illus.). 135p. (Orig.). 1987. pap. 12.00 (*0-917573-06-4*) CAO Times.

Common Sense: Receiving God's Financial Promises. Randy E. Parlor. LC 93-90574. 120p. (Orig.). 1993. student ed 10.00 (*0-9637561-1-7*); pap. 10.00 (*0-9637561-0-9*) Com Sense Christian.

Common Sense: The Foundations for Social Science, Vol VI. Ed. by Frits Van Holthoon & David R. Olson. LC 87-14780. (Sources in Semiotics Ser.). (Illus.). 392p. 1987. lib. bdg. 43.50 (*0-8191-6504-2*, Sources in Semiotics) U Pr of Amer.

Common Sense: What to Write, How to Write it, & Why. Marie Ponsot & Rosemary Deen. LC 85-4126. 166p. (Orig.). (C). 1985. pap. text ed. 15.50 (*0-86709-079-0*) Boynton Cook Pubs.

Common Sense: Why It's No Longer Common & No Longer Even Makes Sense. Lawrence E. Joseph. LC 93-5393. 1993. 19.18 (*0-201-58116-7*) Addison-Wesley.

Common Sense about Abortion. Yuda Molk. 112p. 1992. pap. 9.95 (*0-9633910-5-4*) Comm Sense.

Common Sense about Dyslexia. Anne M. Huston. (Illus.). 300p. (Orig.). (C). 1987. lib. bdg. 24.95 (*0-8191-6323-6*); pap. 16.95 (*0-8191-5666-3*) U Pr of Amer.

Common Sense about Men & Women in the Ministry. Donna Schaper. LC 90-83136. 155p. (Orig.). 1990. pap. 11.95 (*1-56699-039-4*, AL120) Alban Inst.

***Common Sense about Police Review.** Perez. (C). 1995. pap. text ed. 18.95 (*1-56639-336-1*) Temple U Pr.

***Common Sense about Police Review.** Douglas W. Perez. LC 93-11192. 328p. 1994. pap. write for info. (*0-614-03052-8*) Temple U Pr.

Common Sense about Police Review. Douglas W. Perez. LC 93-11192. 328p. 1994. 44.95 (*1-56639-132-6*) Temple U Pr.

Common Sense about Yoga. Swami Pavitrananda. pap. 1.25 (*0-87481-105-8*, Pub. by Advaita Ashrama II) Vedanta Pr.

***Common Sense & a Little Fire: Women & Working-Class Politics in the United States, 1900-1965.** Annalise Orleck. LC 94-24544. (Gender & American Culture Ser.). (Illus.). 410p. 1995. text ed. 39.95x (*0-8078-2199-3*) U of NC Pr.

***Common Sense & a Little Fire: Women & Working-Class Politics in the United States, 1900-1965.** Annalise Orleck. LC 94-24544. (Gender & American Culture Ser.). (Illus.). 410p. 1995. pap. 15.95x (*0-8078-4511-6*) U of NC Pr.

Common Sense & Everyday Ethics. Ivan Hill. 36p. 1980. write for info. (*0-916152-06-5*) Ethics Res Ctr.

Common Sense & the Battle of the Sexes. Marie B. Hall. 1973. pap. 9.00 (*0-938760-02-5*) Veritat Found.

Common Sense & the Rights of Man. Thomas Paine. 1984. mass mkt. 4.95 (*0-452-00712-7*, Plume) NAL-Dutton.

Common Sense Approach to a Healthy Lifestyle. Thom Slagle. LC 93-84106. (Illus.). 86p. (Orig.). 1993. pap. 15.95 (*0-9636421-7-0*) Pacific Word.

Common Sense Approach to Ghosts. Robert L. Gruzdis. 100p. (Orig.). 1986. pap. 7.95 (*0-9616043-4-4*) Knowledge Unltd.

Common Sense Approach to Hazardous Materials. Frank L. Fire. LC 85-81203. 404p. 1986. 45.00 (*0-87814-908-2*); student ed 20.00 (*0-912212-15-2*) Fire Eng.

***Common Sense Approach to Retaining Students of Color.** Steven T. Birdine. 50p. (Orig.). (C). 1994. 25.00 (*0-9644477-0-3*) Creat Diversity.

Common-Sense BASIC: Structured Programming with Microsoft QuickBASIC. Alice M. Dean & Gove W. Effinger. 450p. (C). 1991. disk, pap. text ed. 39.00 (*0-15-512297-5*) Dryden Pr.

Common Sense Bidding. William S. Root. 1986. pap. 14.00 (*0-517-56129-8*, Crown) Crown Pub Group.

***Common Sense Bidding.** William S. Root. 1995. 15.00 (*0-517-88430-5*) Random.

Common Sense Blackjack. 1984. 4.80 (*0-9613193-0-5*) Old Hickory.

Common Sense Book. Harry Miller. 1987. mass mkt. 4.95 (*0-553-27789-8*) Bantam.

Common Sense Book of Kitten & Cat Care. Harry Miller. 144p. (Orig.). 1984. pap. 4.99 (*0-553-26805-8*) Bantam.

Common Sense Business in a Nonsense Economy: The Entrepreneur's Guide to Avoiding Pitfalls & Maximizing Assets - In Good Times & Bad. Steven R. Gottry. LC 94-5601. 288p. 1994. pap. 14.95 (*0-89384-259-1*) Pfeiffer & Co.

Common-Sense C: Advice & Warnings for C & C Plus Plus Programmers. Paul Conte. 100p. (Orig.). 1993. pap. 24.95 (*1-882419-00-6*) Duke Commns Intl.

Common Sense Child Care. Cleta Toomey. 75p. 1993. pap. text ed. 9.95 (*0-9638042-0-0*) C Toomey.

Common Sense Christianity. C. Randolph Ross. LC 88-61552. 266p. 1989. 19.95 (*0-929368-00-2*) Occam Pubs.

Common Sense Composition: A Modern Approach to Improving Written Communication. Isabel L. Hawley. LC 73-83546. 140p. (Orig.). 1977. pap. 19.95 (*0-913636-04-5*) Educ Res MA.

Common Sense Credit. Charles M. Wilson. 1962. 9.95 (*0-8159-5207-4*) Devin.

Common Sense Decision-Making. Gordon C. Fulcher. LC 65-14421. 90p. reprint ed. pap. 25.70 (*0-317-10298-2*, 2010128) Bks Demand.

Common Sense Discipline. Roger Allen & Ron Rose. Ed. by Dave Horton. 240p. 1993. pap. 8.99 (*0-7814-0125-9*, LifeJourney) Chariot Family.

***Common Sense Discipline: Building Self-Esteem in Young Children: Stories from Life.** Grace Mitchell & Lois Dewsnap. LC 95-11901. (Orig.). (J). (ps-4). 1995. pap. 14.95 (*0-910287-11-2*) TelShare Pub Co.

Common Sense Discipline: What to Say & Do When Children Misbehave. Roger B. Allen. (Illus.). 86p. (Orig.). 1984. pap. 4.95 (*0-916979-00-8*) Common Sen Pubns.

Common Sense Dressage: An Illustrated Guide. Sally O'Connor. LC 90-5375. (Illus.). 178p. 1990. 24.95 (*0-939481-21-9*) Half Halt Pr.

Common-Sense Fitting for Machine Knitters. Pat Hampton. (Illus.). 74p. 1975. pap. 9.75 (*0-9614397-0-X*) P K Hampton.

Common Sense for Uncommon Times: The Power of Balance in Work, Family, & Personal Life. Mark Guterman. LC 93-41373. 192p. 1994. pap. 14.95 (*0-89106-065-0*) Consulting Psychol.

Common-Sense Geriatrics. Malloy. 1991. pap. 38.95 (*0-86542-107-2*) Blackwell Sci.

Common Sense Guide to a Happy, Healthy, Long Life. Geoffrey B. Koblick. Tr. by David Koblick. LC 91-91278. (Illus.). 184p. (Orig.). (GER.). 1991. pap. 10.50 (*0-9630938-0-0*) Sig Pub.

Common Sense Guide to American Colleges, 1993-1994. Madison Center for Education Staff. 666p. (Orig.). Date not set. pap. 14.95 (*0-8191-8734-8*) Madison Bks UPA.

Common Sense Guide to Coping with Anger. Melvyn L. Fein. LC 92-46556. 256p. 1993. pap. text ed. 12.95 (*0-275-94244-9*, B4244, Praeger Pubs) Greenwood.

Common Sense Guide to Growth & Nutrition. George S. Sturtz & Susan S. Zabriskie. 147p. 1991. pap. 15.00 (*0-9631089-0-5*) Hojack Pub.

***Common Sense II: Practical Suggestions to Get America Back on Track for the 21st Century.** Kevin J. Shay. 52p. (Orig.). 1995. pap. 7.95 (*0-614-03691-7*); pap. 7.95 (*1-881365-67-0*) Shay Pubns.

Common Sense III: Growlin' for Peace, Moewing for Love. Dennis DeNure. 140p. (Orig.). 1986. 15.00 (*0-915659-05-0*) Video Athlete.

Common Sense in a Complex World: What Every Young Person Should Know. James L. Blake. LC 88-72165. 192p. (Orig.). (YA). (gr. 8-11). 1989. pap. 8.95 (*0-9621230-0-5*) CSI Pub.

Common Sense in Business Writing, Vols. I & II. Richard J. Londo. 480p. (C). 1991. per., pap. text ed. 29.95 (*0-8403-7068-7*) Kendall-Hunt.

Common Sense in Chess. Emanuel Lasker. 1965. pap. 3.95 (*0-486-21440-0*) Dover.

Common Sense in Law. 3rd ed. Paul Vinogradoff & Harold G. Hanbury. LC 86-29430. (Home University Library of Modern Knowledge: No. 83). 192p. 1987. reprint ed. text ed. 69.50 (*0-313-25706-X*, VICS, Greenwood Pr) Greenwood.

Common-Sense in Law. Paul Vinogradoff. LC 74-25793. (European Sociology Ser.). 260p. 1975. reprint ed. 23.95 (*0-405-06545-0*) Ayer.

Common Sense in U. S. - Soviet Trade. Ed. by Carl Marcy et al. 1983. pap. 5.00 (*0-318-00157-8*) Am Comm US Soviet.

Common Sense Leadership: Your Guide to Effective Management. Dahk Knox & Jan Knox. 150p. (C). 1993. pap. text ed. 13.95 (*1-881116-04-2*, 017) Black Forrest Pr.

Common Sense Management. Alfred Fleishman. LC 84-80765. 75p. 1984. 3.33 (*0-918970-33-4*) Intl Gen Semantics.

Common Sense Management. Henry R. Migliore. 108p. (Orig.). 1986. pap. 6.95 (*1-56292-515-6*, HB515) Honor Bks OK.

Common Sense Management. R. Henry Migliore. 100p. (Orig.). 1990. pap. 11.95 (*0-87683-633-3*) GP Pub.

Common Sense Management & Motivation: For the Real World. Roy H. Holmes. 208p. 1993. 16.95 (*0-914984-49-7*) Starburst.

Common Sense Manufacturing: Becoming a Top Value Competitor. James A. Gardner. 225p. 1991. text ed. 45.00 (*1-55623-527-5*) Irwin Prof Pubng.

Common Sense Math for Kindergartners. Yuriko Nichols. 11p. 1993. Kit. pap. 12.00 (*1-880892-68-5*) Fam Lrng Ctr.

Common Sense Medical Guide & Outdoor Reference. 2nd ed. Newell D. Breyfogle. 413p. 1988. pap. text ed. 14.95 (*0-07-007676-6*) Hlth Prof Div.

***Common Sense Medicine.** Francis Lai. 200p. 1996. pap. 8.95 (*0-7610-0472-6*) NW Pub.

Common-Sense Morality & Consequentialism. Michael Slote. (International Library of Philosophy). 160p. 1985. 27.50 (*0-7102-0309-8*, RKP) Routledge.

***Common-Sense Mortgage.** Peter G. Miller. 336p. 1995. pap. 13.00 (*0-06-273332-X*, Harper Ref) HarpC.

Common Sense Not Needed. Corrie Ten Boom. 1993. pap. 3.95 (*0-87508-309-9*) Chr Lit.

Common Sense Occultism. F. G. Richford. 1972. 69.95 (*0-87968-911-0*) Gordon Pr.

Common Sense of Music. Sigmund G. Spaeth. 378p. 1990. reprint ed. lib. bdg. 79.00 (*0-7812-9131-3*) Rprt Serv.

Common Sense of Physical Immortality. Leonard Orr. pap. 5.00 (*0-318-23459-9*) L Orr.

Common Sense of Physical Immortality. rev. ed. Leonard D. Orr. 1988. pap. 5.00 (*0-945793-00-6*) Inspir Univ.

Common Sense of Science. Jacob Bronowski. LC 53-9924. 158p. 1978. pap. text ed. 9.95 (*0-674-14651-4*) HUP.

Common Sense of Teaching Foreign Languages. Caleb Gattegno. (Common Sense of Teaching Ser.). 1976. pap. 9.95 (*0-87825-071-9*) Ed Solutions.

Common Sense of Teaching Mathematics. Caleb Gattegno. (Common Sense of Teaching Ser.). (Illus.). 144p. 1974. pap. 8.95 (*0-87825-024-7*) Ed Solutions.

Common Sense of Teaching Reading & Writing. Caleb Gattegno. (Common Sense of Teaching Ser.). 1985. pap. text ed. 12.95 (*0-87825-181-2*) Ed Solutions.

Common Sense of the Exact Sciences. William K. Clifford. Ed. by Karl Pearson & James R. Newman. LC 72-5510. (Biography Index Reprint Ser.). 1977. reprint ed. 21.95 (*0-8369-8135-9*) Ayer.

***Common Sense Parenting.** Kent Hughes & Barbara Hughes. LC 94-40287. 1995. 16.99 (*0-8423-1707-4*) Tyndale.

Common Sense Parenting: A Practical Approach from Boys Town. Raymond V. Burke & Ronald W. Herron. 137p. (Orig.). 1992. student ed, pap. 14.95 (*0-938510-33-9*, 39-001) Boys Town Pr.

Common Sense Personal Computing: A Handbook for Professionals. Walt Crawford. LC 86-15074. (Common Sense Computing Ser.: No. 1). 1986. pap. 30.00 (*0-87650-218-4*) Pierian.

An Asterisk (*) at the beginning of an entry indicates that the title is appearing in BIP for the first time.

C

An Asterisk (*) at the beginning of an entry indicates that the title is appearing in BIP for the first time.

1421

C

Commonsense Methods for Children with Special Needs: Strategies for the Regular Classroom. 2nd ed. Peter Westwood. LC 92-34904. 192p. 1993. 52.50 (*0-415-08772-4*, A9943); pap. 16.95 (*0-415-08773-2*, A9947) Routledge.

Commonsense of Singing. 2nd rev. ed. Re Koster. 70p. (C). 1990. reprint ed. pap. text ed. 10.95 (*1-878617-01-X*) Leyerle Pubns.

Commonsense Outdoor Medicine & Emergency Companion. 3rd ed. Newell D. Breyfogle. 1993. pap. 14.95 (*0-87742-381-4*, Ragged Mntn) Intl Marine.

***Commonsense Outdoor Survival: How to Survive in the Wilderness for Five Days.** Bob Newman. (Nuts-n-Bolts Ser.). (Illus.). 32p. 1994. pap. 4.95 (*0-89732-166-9*) Menasha Ridge.

Commonsense Paediatrics. M. Pollak & J. Fry. 1986. lib. bdg. 95.00 (*0-85200-945-3*) Kluwer Ac.

Commonsense Psychiatry of Dr. Adolf Meyer: Fifty-Two Selected Papers. Adolf Meyer. Ed. by Alfred Lief. LC 73-2406. (Mental Illness & Social Policy; the American Experience Ser.). 1973. reprint ed. 46.95 (*0-405-05216-2*) Ayer.

Commonsense, Science, & Scepticism: A Historical Introduction to the Theory of Knowledge. Alan E. Musgrave. LC 92-12657. (Illus.). 310p. (C). 1993. 59.95 (*0-521-43040-2*); pap. 18.95 (*0-521-43625-7*) Cambridge U Pr.

Commonsense Speculation. Trader. LC 92-71284. 120p. (C). 1992. reprint ed. pap. 11.00 (*0-87034-103-0*) Fraser Pub Co.

Commonsense Suicide: The Final Right. Doris Portwood. 142p. 1983. pap. 8.00 (*0-9606030-2-6*) Hemlock Soc.

***Commonsense Theology: The Bible, Faith & American Society.** Mark Ellingsen. LC 95-5760. (Studies in American Biblical Hermeneutics: Vol. 9). 1995. write for info. (*0-86554-457-3*) Mercer Univ Pr.

Commonsense Time Management. Roy Alexander. (AMA Worksmart Ser.). 120p. (Orig.). 1992. pap. 10.95 (*0-8144-7791-7*) AMACOM.

Commonsense Use of Medicines. J. Fry et al. (Commonsense Ser.). 208p. (C). 1987. lib. bdg. 67.50 (*0-85200-996-8*) Kluwer Ac.

***Commonsense Vegetable Gardening for the South.** William D. Adams & Thomas LeRoy. LC 94-25304. (Illus.). 1995. 19.95 (*0-87833-876-4*) Taylor Pub.

Commonsense View of All Music: Reflections on Percy Grainger's Contribution to Ethnomusicology & Music Education. John Blacking. 229p. 1987. 54.95 (*0-521-26500-2*) Cambridge U Pr.

Commonware & Brittle Ware: Final Report IV, Part 1, Fascicle 3. Stephen Dyson. LC 43-2669. pap. 15.00 (*0-685-71742-9*) J J Augustin.

Commonwealth. Ed. by Harry Hannam. LC 93-9377. (International Organizations Ser.: Vol. 5). 330p. 1993. text ed. 59.95 (*1-56000-110-0*) Transaction Pubs.

***Commonwealth.** Patrick G. Walker. 408p. 1962. 79.50x (*0-614-01800-5*) Elliots Bks.

Commonwealth: A Study of the Role of Government in the American Economy, Massachusetts, 1774-1861. Oscar Handlin & Mary F. Handlin. LC 69-18032. 314p. 1987. pap. 14.95 (*0-674-14691-3*) Belknap Pr.

***CommonWealth: Self-Sufficiency & Work in American Communities, 1830 to 1993.** Torry D. Dickinson. LC 94-23739. (Illus.). 244p. (C). 1995. lib. bdg. 42.50 (*0-8191-9802-1*) U Pr of Amer.

Commonwealth Administrative Law. D. C. Pearce. 1986. Australia. 74.00 (*0-409-49088-1*); Australia. pap. 72.00 (*0-409-49089-X*) Butterworth Legal Pubs.

Commonwealth & the Nations: Studies in British Commonwealth Relations. N. Mansergh. 229p. 1968. reprint ed. 20.00 (*0-8464-0261-0*) Beekman Pubs.

Commonwealth Caribbean: The Integration Experience. Sidney E. Chernick. LC 77-17246. (World Bank Country Economic Report Ser.). 537p. reprint ed. pap. 153.10 (*0-7837-4212-6*, 2043040) Bks Demand.

Commonwealth Caribbean Legal Studies. Ed. by Gilbert Kodiline & P. K. Menon. 375p. 1992. pap. 67.50 (*0-406-01366-7*) W W Gaunt.

Commonwealth Caribbean Legal Systems: A Study of Small Jurisdictions. Velma Newton. LC 89-46052. xxv, 325p. 1989. reprint ed. 73.00 (*0-912004-76-2*) W W Gaunt.

Commonwealth, Comrades & Friends. Arthur Bottomley. 216p. 1986. 32.00 (*0-8364-1835-2*, Pub. by Somaiya) S Asia.

Commonwealth Criminal Law. Neil Williams & Deborah Sweeney. 300p. 1989. 53.00 (*1-86287-023-3*, Pub. by Federation Pr AU) W W Gaunt.

Commonwealth Economy in Southeast Asia. Thomas H. Silcock. LC 59-7085. (Commonwealth Studies Center: No. 10). 279p. reprint ed. pap. 79.60 (*0-8357-9099-1*, 2017928) Bks Demand.

Commonwealth Elections, 1945-1970: A Bibliography. Valerie Bloomfield. LC 76-24992. 306p. 1977. text ed. 59.95 (*0-8371-9067-3*, BCE/, Greenwood Pr) Greenwood.

Commonwealth Experience, 2 vols. rev. ed. Nicholas Mansergh. Incl. Vol. 1. Durham Report to the Anglo-Irish Treaty. 1982. pap. 12.95 (*0-8020-6515-5*); Vol. 2. From British to Multiracial Commonwealth. 1982. 27.50 (*0-8020-2492-0*); Vol. 2. From British to Multiracial Commonwealth. 1982. pap. 12.95 (*0-8020-6516-3*); 1982. Set. Set pap. 25.00 (*0-8020-6497-3*) U of Toronto Pr.

Commonwealth Experience, 2 vols., Set. rev. ed. Nicholas Mansergh. Incl. Vol. 1. Durham Report to the Anglo-Irish Treaty. 1982. pap. 12.95 (*0-8020-6515-5*); Vol. 2. From British to Multiracial Commonwealth. 1982. 27.50 (*0-8020-2492-0*); Vol. 2. From British to Multiracial Commonwealth. 1982. pap. 12.95 (*0-8020-6516-3*); 1982. 50.00 (*0-8020-2477-7*) U of Toronto Pr.

Commonwealth in Arms: A Guide to Military Sites & Museums in Pennsylvania. John B. Trussell, Jr. (Illus.). 48p. 1987. pap. 3.95 (*0-89271-041-1*) Pa Hist & Mus.

Commonwealth in the World. 3rd ed. J. D. Miller. LC 65-8789. (Illus.). 362p. 1965. 29.00 (*0-674-14700-6*) HUP.

Commonwealth International Law Cases, 17 vols., Set. Ed. by Clive M. Parry & J. A. Hopkins. LC 73-20151. 1974. lib. bdg. 1,054.00 (*0-379-00950-1*) Oceana.

Commonwealth Literature see St. James Reference Guide to English Literature

Commonwealth of Art. Curt Sachs. (Music Ser.). 1990. 42.50 (*0-306-79467-5*) Da Capo.

Commonwealth of Dominica: Consolidated Index of Statutes & Subsidiary Legislation. Ed. by C. J. Hammett. (West Indian Legislation Indexing Project Ser.). vi, 94p. (Orig.). 1991. pap. text ed. 25.00 (*0-317-60538-0*, Pub. by UWI Fac Law BB) W W Gaunt.

Commonwealth of Independent States. Mary J. Clark. LC 92-20745. (Headliners Ser.). (Illus.). 64p. (J). (gr. 5-8). 1992. lib. bdg. 15.90 (*1-56294-081-3*) Millbrook Pr.

Commonwealth of Independent States. Karen Jacobsen. LC 92-12946. (New True Bks.). (Illus.). 48p. (J). (gr. k-4). 1992. lib. bdg. 12.90 (*0-516-02194-X*) Childrens.

Commonwealth of Independent States. Karen Jacobsen. LC 92-12946. (New True Bks.). (Illus.). 48p. (J). (gr. k-4). 1993. pap. 4.95 (*0-516-42194-8*) Childrens.

Commonwealth of Independent States. Abraham Resnick. (Enchantment of the World Ser.). (Illus.). 128p. (J). (gr. 5-9). 1993. lib. bdg. 20.55 (*0-516-02613-5*) Childrens.

Commonwealth of Man: An Inquiry into Power Politics & World Government. Frederick L. Schuman. LC 76-30305. 1977. reprint ed. text ed. 75.00 (*0-8371-9372-9*, SCCO, Greenwood Pr) Greenwood.

Commonwealth of Massachusetts vs. Lizzie A. Borden-The Knowlton Papers-1892-1893: A Collection of Previously Unpublished Letters from the Files of Prosecuting Attorney Hosea Morrill Knowlton. Michael Martins & Dennis A. Binette. (Illus.). 400p. 1994. 49.95 (*0-9641248-3-1*) Fall River Hist Soc.

Commonwealth of Oceana & A System of Politics. James Harrington. Ed. by J. G. Pocock. (Cambridge Texts in the History of Political Thought Ser.). 320p. (C). 1992. 59.95 (*0-521-41189-0*); pap. 18.95 (*0-521-42329-5*) Cambridge U Pr.

Commonwealth of Science: ANZAAS & the Scientific Enterprise in Australasia 1888-1988. Ed. by Roy MacLeod. (Illus.). 400p. 1988. 45.00 (*0-19-554683-0*) OUP.

Commonwealth of the Philippines. George A. Malcolm. Ed. by Philippines Commonwealth Constitution 1972 Staff. 1977. 40.95 (*0-8369-6982-0*, 7860) Ayer.

Commonwealth of Wings: An Ornithological Biography Based on the Life of John James Audubon. Pamela Alexander. LC 90-50908. (Wesleyan Poetry Ser.). 72p. 1991. 22.50 (*0-8195-2191-4*, Wesleyan Univ Pr); pap. 10.95 (*0-8195-1193-5*, Wesleyan Univ Pr) U Pr of New Eng.

Commonwealth Perspectives. Ed. by Nicholas Mansergh. LC 58-11381. (Duke University Commonwealth Studies Center: No. 8). 224p. reprint ed. 63.90 (*0-8357-9100-9*, 2017911) Bks Demand.

Commonwealth Policy in a Global Context. Ed. by Paul Streeten & Hugh Corbet. LC 75-163825. 240p. reprint ed. pap. 68.40 (*0-685-15420-3*, 2026539) Bks Demand.

Commonwealth Secretariat & the Contemporary Commonwealth. Margaret P. Doxey. LC 88-35565. 208p. 1989. text ed. 55.00 (*0-312-03072-X*) St Martin.

Commonwealth Statutes Annotations, 1991. 1372p. 1992. pap. 244.00 (*0-685-65887-2*, Pub. by Law Bk Co) W W Gaunt.

Commonwealth Taxation Board of Review Decisions: Consolidated Index & Tables, 1925-1986. 1988. Australia. text ed. 605.00 (*0-409-48793-7*) Butterworth Legal Pubs.

Commonwealth to Protectorate. Austin Woolrych. (Illus.). 458p. 1986. pap. 29.95 (*0-19-822973-9*) OUP.

Commonwealth Universites Yearbook, 1993, 4 vols., Set. Association of Commonwealth Universities Staff. 3300p. 1993. boxed 265.00 (*1-56159-101-7*, Stockton Pr) Groves Dictionaries.

***Commonwealth Universities Yearbook 1994, 4 vols., Set.** 70th ed. Comp. by Association of Commonwealth Universities Staff. 3300p. 1994. boxed 275.00 (*1-56159-110-6*, Stockton Pr) Groves Dictionaries.

Commonwealth Yearbook, 1993-1994. 558p. 1994. pap. 49.95 (*0-11-591711-X*, HM1711X, Pub. by HMSO UK) UNIPUB.

Commulative Algebra One. O. Zariski & P. Samuel. LC 75-17751. (Graduate Texts in Mathematics Ser.: Vol. 28). 340p. 1986. reprint ed. 59.00 (*0-387-90089-6*) Spr-Verlag.

Communal & Pan-Islamic Trends in Colonial India. Ed. by Mushirul Hasan. 1986. 44.00 (*0-8364-1620-1*, Pub. by Manohar II) S Asia.

Communal Experience: Anarchist & Mystical Communities in Twentieth-Century America. Laurence R. Veysey. LC 78-55045. 1978. pap. text ed. 7.95 (*0-226-85458-2*, P786) U Ch Pr.

Communal Experience of the Kibbutz. Joseph Blasi. 275p. (C). 1986. 39.95 (*0-88738-056-5*); pap. 21.95 (*0-88738-611-3*) Transaction Pubs.

Communal Family Living: Model for Change. Steve Bridge. (Illus.). 108p. (Orig.). 1992. pap. 10.95 (*0-9631099-0-1*) S Bridge.

Communal Labour in the Sudan. Ed. by Leif Manger. (Bergen Studies in Social Anthropology: No. 41). 150p. 1988. pap. 13.95 (*0-936508-71-X*) Barber Pr.

Communal Life: An International Perspective. Ed. by Yosef Gorni et al. 756p. 1987. 59.95 (*0-88738-150-2*) Transaction Pubs.

Communal Love at Oneida: A Perfectionist Vision of Authority, Property & Sexual Order. Richard De Maria. LC 78-60958. (Texts & Studies in Religion: Vol. 2). xiii, 248p. 1978. pap. 69.95 (*0-88946-986-5*) E Mellen.

Communal Love at Oneida: A Perfectionist Vision of Authority, Property & Sexual Order. Richard DeMaria. LC 78-60958. (Texts & Studies in Religion: Vol. 2). 248p. 1983. 89.95 (*0-88946-988-1*) E Mellen.

Communal Pietism Among Early American Moravians. John J. Sessler. LC 70-134387. reprint ed. 42.50 (*0-404-08430-3*) AMS Pr.

Communal Reformation: The Quest for Salvation in Sixteenth-Century Germany. Peter Blickle. Tr. by Thomas J. Dunlap. LC 91-33112. (Studies in German Histories). 286p. (C). 1992. text ed. 49.95 (*0-391-03730-7*) Humanities.

Communal Riots in Bengal, 1905-1947. Suranjan Das. (South Asian Studies). (Illus.). 320p. 1992. 18.95 (*0-19-562840-3*) OUP.

Communal Riots in Bengal, 1905-1947. Suranjan Das. (South Asian Studies Ser.). (Illus.). 328p. 1994. reprint ed. pap. 7.95 (*0-19-563233-8*) OUP.

Communal Riots in India. S. K. Ghosh. (C). 1987. 28.50 (*81-7024-087-5*, Pub. by Ashish II) S Asia.

Communal Riots in Post-Independence India. 2nd ed. 1991. 35.00 (*0-86311-139-4*, Pub. by Orient Longman Ltd II) Apt Bks.

Communal Riots in Post-Independence India. 2nd ed. Ed. by Asghar A. Engineer. 366p. 1991. 35.00 (*0-685-65252-1*, Pub. by Sangam Bks II) Apt Bks.

Communal Road to a Secular Kerala. George Mathew. 1989. 28.50 (*81-7022-282-6*, Pub. by Concept II) S Asia.

Communal Sick-Care in the German Ghetto. Jacob R. Marcus. 335p. 1978. reprint ed. pap. 11.95 (*0-87820-202-1*) Hebrew Union Coll Pr.

Communal Societies in America, 137 titles. reprint ed. write for info. (*0-404-08170-3*) AMS Pr.

Communal Violence. V. V. Singh. 1993. 21.00 (*81-7033-184-6*, Pub. by Rawat II) S Asia.

Communal Violence in India. P. R. Rajgopal. 141p. 1987. 34.95 (*0-318-37208-8*) Asia Bk Corp.

Communal Violence in India. P. R. Rajgopal. (C). 1987. 24.00 (*81-85024-14-6*, Pub. by Uppal Pub Hse II) S Asia.

Communal Violence in Malaysia 1969: The Political Aftermath. Felix V. Gagliano. LC 78-630854. (Papers in International Studies: Southeast Asia Ser.: No. 13). 95p. reprint ed. pap. 27.10 (*0-317-09479-3*, 2005117) Bks Demand.

Communal Webs: Communication & Culture in Contemporary Israel. Tamar Katriel. LC 90-10057. (Anthropology & Judaic Studies & Human Communication Processes Ser.). 226p. 1991. 64.50 (*0-7914-0644-X*); pap. 21.95 (*0-7914-0645-8*) State U NY Pr.

Communalisation of Politics & Tenth Lok Sabha Elections. Ed. by Asghar A. Engineer. 1993. 34.00 (*81-202-0364-X*, Pub. by Ajanta II) S Asia.

Communalism & Constitution. Anirban Kashyap. (C). 1988. 47.50 (*81-7095-007-4*, Pub. by Lancer II) S Asia.

Communalism & Constitution. Ed. by Anirban Kashyap. (C). 1989. 275.00 (*0-685-27922-7*) St Mut.

Communalism in India: Challenge & Response. Ed. by Mehdi Arslan & Janaki Rajan. (C). 1994. text ed. 21.00 (*81-7304-073-7*, Pub. by Manohar II) S Asia.

Communalism in India: History, Politics & Culture. K. N. Panikkar. (C). 1991. 21.50 (*81-85425-51-5*, Pub. by Manohar II) S Asia.

Communalism vs. Communism: A Study of the Socio-Religious Communities & Political Parties in Kerala, 1892-1970. P. M. Mammen. 1981. 18.50 (*0-8364-0041-0*) S Asia.

Communaute Judeo-Arameenne a Elephantine en Egypte aux VI et V Siecles avant Jesus-Christ. A. Van Hoonacker. (British Academy, London, Schweich Lectures on Biblical Archaeology Series, 1930). 1972. reprint ed. pap. 20.00 (*0-8115-1256-8*) Periodicals Srv.

Communautes Syriaques en Iran et Irak des Origines a 1552. Jean M. Fiey. (Collected Studies: No. CS106). 382p. (FRE.). (C). 1979. reprint ed. lib. bdg. 124.95 (*0-86078-051-1*, Pub. by Variorum UK) Ashgate Pub Co.

Commune of Lucca Under Pisan Rule, 1342-1369. Christine E. Meek. LC 78-70245. 1980. 20.00 (*0-910956-69-3*, SAM6); pap. 12.00 (*0-910956-80-4*) Medieval Acad.

Commune Presence. Rene Char. 361p. (FRE.). 1978. pap. 49.95 (*0-7859-4713-2*) Fr & Eur.

Commune with the Angels: A Heavenly Handbook. Jane M. Howard. Ed. by Jon Robertson. (Illus.). 236p. (Orig.). 1992. pap. 11.95 (*0-87604-294-9*, 372) ARE Pr.

Communes of Lombardy from the VI to the X Century. William K. Williams. LC 78-63803. (Johns Hopkins University. Studies in the Social Sciences. Thirtieth Ser. 1912: 5-6). reprint ed. 11.50 (*0-404-61066-8*) AMS Pr.

Communes, Sociology & Society. P. Abrams & A. McCulloch. LC 75-40985. (Themes in the Social Sciences Ser.: No. 3). 200p. 1976. 39.50 (*0-521-21188-3*) Cambridge U Pr.

Communicable & Tropical Diseases: Mainstream Med. Cook. 330p. 1988. pap. 39.95 (*0-433-00029-5*) Buttrwrth-Heinemann.

Communicable Disease Control Plan for School District Employees. MESD School Health Services Staff. 106p. 1992. student ed 25.00 (*1-880118-08-4*) MESD Pr.

Communicable Disease Control Plan for School District Employees - Instructor Manual. MESD School Health Services Staff. 155p. 1992. student ed 50.00 (*1-880118-09-2*) MESD Pr.

Communicable Disease Statistics: 1986 Statistical Tables. (Illus.). 64p. 1988. pap. 17.00 (*0-11-691233-2*, HM4200, Pub. by HMSO UK) UNIPUB.

Communicable Disease Statistics MB2 1990. Office of Population Censuses & Surveys Staff. (Office of Population Censuses & Surveys Reference Series AB: No. 17). 73p. 1992. pap. 19.00 (*0-11-691445-9*, HM14459, Pub. by HMSO UK) UNIPUB.

***Communicable Disease Statistics (OPCS Series MB2) 1992, No. 19.** Office of Population Censuses & Surveys Staff. 66p. 1994. pap. 19.00 (*0-11-691572-2*, HM15722, Pub. by HMSO UK) UNIPUB.

Communicable Disease Statistics, 1991 MB2. Office of Population Censuses & Surveys Staff. (Office of Population Censuses & Surveys Reference Series AB: No. 18). 66p. 1993. pap. 19.00 (*0-11-691531-5*, HM15315, Pub. by HMSO UK) UNIPUB.

Communicable Diseases. Incl. Vol. 16, No. 5. 192p. 1957. pap. 2.80 (*0-686-09215-5*); Vol. 24, No. 1. 127p. 1961. pap. 2.80 (*0-686-09217-1*); Vol. 26, No. 6. 134p. 1962. pap. 3.60 (*0-686-09218-X*); Vol. 30, No. 2. 146p. 1964. pap. 3.60 (*0-686-09219-8*); Vol. 30, No. 5. 130p. 1964. pap. 3.60 (*0-686-09220-1*); Vol. 39, No. 2. 204p. 1968. pap. 3.60 (*0-686-09221-X*); (Bulletin of WHO Ser.). (ENG & FRE.). Set pap. write for info. (*0-318-56474-2*) World Health.

Communicable Diseases. Jacqueline L. Harris. (Bodies in Crisis Ser.). (Illus.). 64p. (J). (gr. 5-8). 1993. lib. bdg. 15.98 (*0-8050-2599-5*) TFC Bks NY.

Communicable Diseases: Medical Subject Analysis & Research Bibliography. Manfred J. Robineault. LC 84-45644. 150p. 1985. 44.50 (*0-88164-194-4*); pap. 39.50 (*0-88164-195-2*) ABBE Pubs Assn.

Communicable Diseases-Policies & Procedures. Marguerite Bouvette. 200p. (C). 1992. ring bd. 23.95 (*1-877735-23-X*, 139) M&H Pub Co TX.

Communicate. Patty Mayo & Pattii Waldo. (Educational Game Activity Ser.). (Orig.). (YA). (gr. 5-12). 1986. 39.00 (*0-930599-04-7*) Thinking Pubns.

Communicate. Stefan Neilson & Shay Thoelke. (Personality Language Ser.). (Illus.). 112p. 1988. text ed., spiral bd. 40.00 (*1-880830-03-5*); pap. 42.00 (*1-880830-24-8*) AEON-Hierophant.

Communicate! 7th ed. Rudolph F. Verderber. 504p. (C). 1993. pap. 31.95 (*0-534-17928-2*) Intl Thomson.

***Communicate!** 8th ed. Rudolph F. Verderber. LC 95-15056. 1996. pap. 30.95 (*0-534-25812-3*) Intl Thomson.

Communicate: A Guide to Basic PR for Christians. Kim Cook. (C). 1989. 25.00 (*0-9510086-7-6*, Pub. by Jay Bks UK) St Mut.

Communicate: A Librarian's Guide to Interpersonal Relations. Anne J. Mathews. LC 83-2557. 88p. reprint ed. pap. 25.10 (*0-7837-5972-X*, 2045774) Bks Demand.

Communicate: A Video Course in English Viewer's Guides 1 & 2. Terrence Carrol et al. (Illus.). (Orig.). 1986. write for info. (*0-318-60903-7*); Viewer Guide 1. pap. text ed. 12.50 (*0-582-90703-9*, 75219); Viewer Guide 2. pap. text ed. 12.50 (*0-582-90704-7*, 75220); pap. text ed. 12.50 (*0-582-90680-6*, 75212) Longman.

Communicate: A Workbook for Interpersonal Communication. 4th ed. Comm. Research (CRA) Staff. 400p. (C). 1994. pap. text ed., spiral bd. 21.95 (*0-8403-9337-7*) Kendall-Hunt.

Communicate: Strategies for International Teaching Assistants. Jan Smith et al. 288p. (C). 1992. pap. text ed. 21.25 (*0-13-137720-5*) P-H.

***Communicate: Workbook.** Communication Research Association Staff. 400p. (C). 1994. pap. text ed., spiral bd. 22.95 (*0-8403-9541-8*) Kendall-Hunt.

***Communicate! A Communication Skills Guide for Health Care Workers.** Burnard. 204p. 1992. pap. 32.00 (*1-56593-519-5*, 0533) Singular Publishing.

Communicate & Use Evaluation-Based Decisions Module, Competency-Based Career Guidance (CBCG) - Category E: Evaluating. National Center for Research in Vocational Education Staff. 1985. 6.95 (*0-317-03861-3*, CG100E02) Ctr Educ Trng Employ.

Communicate Effectively! Arnold Carter. LC 78-9397. 128p. 1978. 14.95 (*0-88289-201-0*) Pelican.

Communicate Effectively Module, Connections: School & Work Transitions - Work Skills-Work Maturity Skills. National Center for Research in Vocational Education Staff. 1987. write for info. (*0-318-67160-3*, SP100CB11) Ctr Educ Trng Employ.

Communicate Expansion Cards. Patty Mayo & Pattii Waldo. (Educational Game Activity Ser.). (YA). (gr. 5-12). 1988. 25.00 (*0-930599-22-5*) Thinking Pubns.

Communicate for Success: How to Manage, Motivate & Lead Your People. Eric W. Skopec. 1990. pap. 20.95 (*0-201-10528-4*) Addison-Wesley.

Communicate in Colloquial Arabic. Raja T. Nasr. 1989. 12.00x (*0-86685-457-6*) Intl Bk Ctr.

Communicate in French: Listening. J. Webb & D. Webb. (C). 1989. 45.00 (*0-7487-0325-X*, Pub. by S Thornes Pubs UK); audio 95.00 (*0-09-170020-5*, Pub. by S Thornes Pubs UK) St Mut.

Communicate in French: Reading. C. Harvey. (C). 1987. 40.00 (*0-7487-0330-6*, Pub. by S Thornes Pubs UK) St Mut.

Communicate in French: Writing. D. Morris. (C). 1989. 40.00 (*0-09-173081-3*, Pub. by S Thornes Pubs UK) St Mut.

Communicate Junior. Patty Mayo et al. (Illus.). 60p. (J). (gr. 1-4). 1991. bds. 35.00 (*0-930599-68-3*) Thinking Pubns.

Communicate What You Mean: Grammar for High Level ESL. Carroll W. Pollock. 224p. (C). 1982. pap. text ed. 20.75 (*0-13-153486-6*) P-H.

Communicate with Confidence. Time-Life Books Editors. LC 93-455. (Mindpower Ser.: Vol. 4). 1993. write for info. (*0-7835-1258-9*) Time-Life.

Communicate with Confidence! How to Say It Right the First Time & Every Time. Dianna Booher. 1994. text ed. 39.95 (*0-07-006455-5*); pap. text ed. 12.95 (*0-07-006606-X*) McGraw.

An Asterisk (*) at the beginning of an entry indicates that the title is appearing in BIP for the first time.

C

An Asterisk (*) at the beginning of an entry indicates that the title is appearing in BIP for the first time.

1423

Communicating the Catholic Vision of Life: Proceedings of the Twelfth Bishops' Workshop, Dallas, Texas. Twelfth Bishops Workshop Staff. Ed. by Russell E. Smith. LC 93-34979. 296p. (Orig.). 1993. pap. 19.95 (*0-935372-36-9*) Pope John Ctr.

Communicating the Contributions of Home Economics Education. Cathleen T. Love & Susan F. Weis. 1985. 4.00 (*0-911365-25-7*, A261-08466) Home Econ Educ.

Communicating the Gospel. William Barclay. 1978. reprint ed. pap. 3.25 (*0-7152-0401-7*) Outlook.

Communicating the Gospel in a Scientific Age. Hugh Montefiore. 76p. (C). 1988. pap. text ed. 24.00 (*0-7152-0631-1*) St Mut.

Communicating the Gospel in a Scientific Age. Ed. by Hugh Montefiore. 76p. (C). 1989. pap. 20.00 (*0-685-60689-9*, Pub. by St Andrew UK) St Mut.

*__Communicating the Horoscope.__ Ed. by Noel Tyl. LC 95-2097. (New World Astrology Ser.). 256p. 1995. pap. 12.00 (*1-56718-866-4*) Llewellyn Pubns.

Communicating the Infinite: The Emergence of the Habad School. Naftali Loewenthal. (Illus.). 368p. 1990. 39.95 (*0-226-49045-9*) U Ch Pr.

Communicating the Joy, Pain & Everything. 2nd ed. Jack H. Majors. 176p. (C). 1976. pap. 6.00 (*0-937104-00-0*) Programs Comm.

Communicating Therapeutic Risks. L. A. Morris. (Recent Research in Psychology Ser.). xii, 186p. 1989. pap. 54.00 (*0-387-97192-0*, 3675) Spr-Verlag.

*__Communicating Through Story Characters.__ Pamela Brooke. (Illus.). 174p. (Orig.). (C). 1995. lib. bdg. 48.00 (*0-8191-9924-9*); pap. text ed. 24.50 (*0-8191-9925-7*) U Pr of Amer.

Communicating Today. Raymond B. Zeuschner. LC 92-40830. 1992. pap. text ed. write for info. (*0-205-14534-5*) Allyn.

*__Communicating, Training, & Developing for Quality Performance.__ Ed. by Saul W. Gellerman. (Management Masters Ser.). (Illus.). 47p. 1995. 15.95 (*1-56327-077-3*) Prod Press.

Communicating University Research. Ed. by Patricia L. Alberger & Virginia Carter Smith. 137p. 1985. pap. 24.00 (*0-89964-238-1*) Coun Adv & Supp Ed.

Communicating Vessels. Andre Breton. Tr. by Mary A. Caws & Geoffrey Harris. LC 90-12123. (French Modernist Library). xxvi, 159p. 1990. 27.50 (*0-8032-1218-6*) U of Nebr Pr.

Communicating When Your Company Is under Siege: Surviving Public Crisis. Marion K. Pinsdorf. LC 85-45473. 192p. 1986. text ed. 27.95 (*0-669-11790-0*) Free Pr.

Communicating with Competency Plus TIME Package. Rosenfeld & Roy M. Berko. (C). 1990. pap. text ed. 24.25 (*0-673-46250-1*) HarpCollege.

Communicating with Consumers: The Information Processing Approach. Ed. by Michael L. Ray & Scott Ward. LC 75-32370. (Sage Contemporary Social Science Issues Ser.: No. 21). 142p. reprint ed. pap. 40.50 (*0-317-09979-5*, 2021943) Bks Demand.

*__Communicating with Customers Around the World: A Quick Guide to Effective Cross-Cultural Business Communication.__ K. C. Chan-Herur. LC 94-94276. (Global Business Ser.). 134p. 1994. pap. 12.95 (*1-885269-18-8*) AuMonde Intl.

Communicating with Employees: Improving Organizational Communication. Frank Corrado. Ed. by Philip Gerould. LC 93-73208. (Fifty-Minute Ser.). (Illus.). 87p. (Orig.). 1994. pap. 9.95 (*1-56052-255-0*) Crisp Pubns.

Communicating with Employees about Pension & Welfare Benefits. Jozetta H. Srb. (Key Issues Ser.: No. 8). 44p. 1971. pap. 2.00 (*0-87546-244-8*) ILR Pr.

Communicating with Friends. Deena Borchers. (Active Bible Curriculum Ser.). (Illus.). 48p. 1992. pap. 9.99 (*1-55945-228-5*) Group Pub.

Communicating with KI: The "Spirit" in Japanese Idioms. Jeff Garrison & Kayoko Kimiya. Ed. by Brase & Suzuki. (Power Japanese Ser.). 128p. 1994. pap. 10.00 (*4-7700-1833-9*) Kodansha.

Communicating with Kids: A Practical Guide to the Forgotten Language. Estes J. Lockhart. 224p. (Orig.). 1990. 21.95 (*0-9623538-2-5*); pap. 16.95 (*0-9623538-0-9*) Undercurrents Pr.

Communicating with Legal Databases: Terms & Abbreviations for the Legal Researcher. Ann L. McDonald. 206p. 1987. pap. 75.00 (*0-918212-95-2*) Neal-Schuman.

Communicating with Medical Patients. Ed. by Moira Stewart & Debra Roter. (Series in Interpersonal Communication: Vol. 9). 264p. (C). 1989. text ed. 49.95 (*0-8039-3216-2*); pap. text ed. 24.00 (*0-8039-3217-0*) Sage.

Communicating with Microcomputers. Ian Cullimore. 1987. 21.95 (*1-85058-055-3*, Pub. by Sigma Pr UK) Bk Clearing Hse.

Communicating with Microcomputers: An Introduction to the Technology of Man-Computer Communication. Ian H. Witten. LC 80-40650. (Computers & People Ser.). 1980. text ed. 68.00 (*0-12-760750-1*); pap. text ed. 46.00 (*0-12-760752-8*) Acad Pr.

Communicating with Myself: A Journal. 2nd ed. Jacqueline B. Carr. 224p. 1991. pap. write for info. (*0-697-11518-6*) Brown & Benchmark.

Communicating with Neurological Patients. Margot Lindsay. 182p. 1990. pap. 25.00 (*1-871364-37-X*) Ishiyaku Euro.

Communicating with Parents of Exceptional Children. 2nd ed. Roger L. Kroth. LC 84-81940. 242p. (C). 1985. pap. text ed. 21.95 (*0-89108-167-4*) Love Pub Co.

Communicating with Patients. Brent D. Ruben. 128p. (C). 1992. pap. text ed. 9.95 (*0-8403-7430-5*) Kendall-Hunt.

Communicating with Patients: Improving Communication, Satisfaction & Compliance. Philip Ley. 240p. 1989. 49.95 (*0-7099-4161-7*); pap. 17.95 (*0-7099-4174-9*) Routledge Chapman & Hall.

Communicating with People: The Supervisor's Introduction to Verbal Communication & Decision-Making. Raymond J. Burby. LC 78-109507. (Supervision Ser.). 1970. pap. 14.95 (*0-201-00735-5*) Addison-Wesley.

Communicating with Quotes: The Igbo Case. Joyce Penfield. LC 82-15626. (Contributions in Intercultural & Comparative Studies: No. 8). (Illus.). xiv, 138p. 1983. text ed. 55.00 (*0-313-23767-0*, PEN/, Greenwood Pr) Greenwood.

Communicating with Sabre. Paula E. Wagner. (C). 1988. pap. 28.95 (*0-538-19240-2*, S24) S-W Pub.

Communicating with Skill. Theresa C. Timmons. 144p. (C). 1991. pap. text ed. write for info. (*0-8403-8503-X*) Kendall-Hunt.

Communicating with Strangers: An Approach to Intercultural Communication. 2nd ed. William B. Gudykunst. 304p. (C). 1992. text ed. write for info. (*0-07-034602-X*) McGraw.

Communicating with Students in Schools: A Workbook for Practitioners & Teachers in Training. Richard R. Burke. 180p. 1984. student ed 14.75 (*0-8191-3878-9*) U Pr of Amer.

*__Communicating with Students in Schools: Exercises in Motivation & School Discipline Through Rapport.__ 3rd ed. Richard R. Burke. 168p. (Orig.). (C). 1994. pap. text ed. 19.95 (*0-8191-9726-2*) U Pr of Amer.

Communicating with the Adopted Child. Miriam Komar. 282p. 1991. 21.95 (*0-8027-1124-3*) Walker & Co.

Communicating with the Adopted Child. Miriam Komar. 1993. pap. 12.95 (*0-8027-7404-0*) Walker & Co.

*__Communicating with the Dead: Reaching Friends & Loved Ones Who Have Passed on to Another Dimension in Life.__ Linda Georgian. 1995. pap. 11.00 (*0-684-81088-3*, Fireside) S&S Trade.

Communicating with the IBM PC Series: Concepts, Hardware, Software, Networking. Gilbert Held. LC 87-29595. 324p. (Orig.). reprint ed. pap. 92.40 (*0-7837-5873-1*, 2045593) Bks Demand.

*__Communicating with the Public about Education Reform.__ 76p. (Orig.). 1994. pap. text ed. 18.00 (*1-55877-225-1*) Natl Governor.

Communicating with the Public about Major Accident Hazards: Proceedings of the European Conference Organized by the Commission of the European Communities, Directorate-General Environment, Consumer Protection & Nuclear Safety (DGXI) in Collaboration with the Joint Research Centre (JRC), Inspra Establishment, & Held at the Palace Hotel, Varese, Italy, 30 May - June 1989. Ed. by H. B. Gow & H. Otway. 640p. 1990. 138.75 (*1-85166-457-2*) Elsevier.

Communicating with the World: U. S. Public Diplomacy Overseas. Hans N. Tuch. (Institute for the Study of Diplomacy Book Ser.). 200p. 1990. text ed. 45.00 (*0-312-04532-8*); pap. 16.95 (*0-312-04809-2*) St Martin.

Communicating with Virtual Worlds. Ed. by Nadia M. Thalmann & Daniel Thalmann. LC 93-10966. (CGS CG International Ser.). (Illus.). ix, 613p. 1993. 269.00 (*0-387-70125-7*) Spr-Verlag.

*__Communicating with Your Doctor: Getting the Most Out of Health Care.__ J. Alfred Jones et al. Ed. by Gerald M. Phillips. (Communication Series). 256p. 1995. text ed. 52.50 (*1-57273-022-6*); pap. text ed. 19.95 (*1-57273-023-4*) Hampton Pr NJ.

Communicating with Your Dog: A Humane Approach to Dog Training. Ted Baer. (Illus.). 1989. pap. 10.95 (*0-8120-4203-4*) Barron.

Communicating...Isn't Just Talking! The Art & the Power of Communications for the Professional & the Individual. Dennis H. Zorn et al. LC 90-91391. 168p. (Orig.). 1990. pap. 11.19 (*0-9626840-9-0*) Trilogy Enterprize.

*__Communication.__ (Life in America 100 Years Ago Ser.). (Illus.). 104p. (YA). (gr. 5 up). 1995. 18.95 (*0-7910-2845-3*) Chelsea Hse.

Communication. Aliki. LC 91-48156. (Illus.). 32p. (J). (gr. k up). 1993. 14.00 (*0-688-10529-7*); lib. bdg. 13.93 (*0-688-11248-X*) Greenwillow.

Communication. Robert Gardner. (Yesterday's Science, Today's Technology Ser.). (Illus.). 96p. (J). (gr. 5-8). 1994. lib. bdg. 16.98 (*0-8050-2854-4*) TFC Bks NY.

*__Communication.__ Concept by L. Ron Hubbard. 56p. 1994. pap. 4.00 (*0-88404-912-4*) Bridge Pubns Inc.

Communication. Denis McQuail. LC 75-11683. (A.O.M.S. Social Processes Ser.). (Illus.). 240p. 1975. pap. text ed. 14.95 (*0-582-29578-5*) Longman.

*__Communication.__ Ting Morris. LC 95-11620. (Craft Topics Ser.). (J). 1995. write for info. (*0-531-14385-6*) Watts.

*__Communication.__ Multimedia Development Services Staff. (Plant Fundamentals Ser.). (Illus.). (Orig.). 1995. student ed 30.00 (*1-57431-002-X*) Tech Trng Systs.

Communication. 6th ed. Larry L. Barker & Deborah A. Barker. LC 92-569. 480p. (C). 1992. pap. text ed. write for info. (*0-13-155946-X*) P-H.

*__Communication, Vol 1, Module 11.__ Multimedia Development Services Staff. (Plant Fundamentals Ser.). (Illus.). (Orig.). 1995. teacher ed 45.00 (*1-57431-042-9*) Tech Trng Systs.

*__Communication: A Common Sense Approach.__ Candace Clanton & Gary Cruice, Jr. 288p. (C). 1994. per., pap. text ed. 32.95 (*0-8403-9856-5*) Kendall-Hunt.

Communication: A Salute to Black Inventors. rev. ed. Ann C. Howell. Ed. by Evelyn L. Ivery. (Black Inventors Activity Bks.). (Illus.). 24p. (J). (gr. 3-7). 1992. reprint ed. pap. text ed. 1.50 (*1-877804-05-3*) Chandler White.

Communication: A Unique Significance for Law Enforcement. Morris M. Womack & Hayden H. Finley. 232p. 1986. 42.95 (*0-398-05269-7*) C C Thomas.

*__Communication: A Unique Significance for Law Enforcement.__ Morris M. Womack & Hayden H. Finley. 232p. 1986. pap. 26.95 (*0-398-06503-9*) C C Thomas.

*__Communication: An Introduction to the Basic Course.__ 3rd ed. William J. Seiler. LC 94-29862. (C). 1995. text ed. 22.00 (*0-673-99375-2*) HarpCollege.

*__Communication: Apprehension, Avoidance, & Effectiveness.__ 4th ed. Virginia P. Richmond & James C. McCroskey. LC 94-21097. 1994. per. 16.00 (*0-89787-354-8*) Gorsuch Scarisbrick.

Communication: Electricity & Electronics. R. Miller. 1976. 10.48 (*0-13-153098-4*); pap. text ed. 10.16 (*0-13-153072-0*) P-H.

*__Communication: Enhancing Your Relationships.__ Group Publishing, Inc. Editors. Ed. by Paul Woods. (Adult Curriculum Ser.). 1995. 9.99 (*1-55945-512-8*) Group Pub.

Communication: Ethical & Moral Issues. Ed. by Lee Thayer. (Current Topics of Contemporary Thought Ser.). 402p. 1973. text ed. 96.00 (*0-677-13360-X*) Gordon & Breach.

Communication: Graphic Arts. D. Carlsen & V. Tryon. 1976. pap. 10.16 (*0-13-153189-1*) P-H.

Communication: Industry & Careers. R. Miller. 1976. 10.16 (*0-685-03796-7*); pap. 10.14 (*0-13-152967-6*) P-H.

*__Communication: International Case Studies in English.__ Drew Rodgers. 176p. (C). 1995. pap. text ed. 19.95 (*0-312-11171-1*) St Martin.

Communication: Key to Effective Nursing. Ernestine Wiedenbach & Caroline E. Falls. LC 78-50063. (Illus.). 128p. 1978. pap. text ed. 9.00 (*0-913292-23-0*) Tiresias Pr.

Communication: Key to Your Marriage. rev. ed. H. Norman Wright. LC 73-88317. 208p. 1979. pap. 7.99 (*0-8307-0726-3*, 5415004) Regal.

Communication: Photography. P. Gerace & S. Mangione. 1976. pap. 10.16 (*0-13-153239-1*) P-H.

Communication: Skills to Inspire Confidence. Barrie Hopson & Mike Scally. Ed. by JoAnn Padgett. LC 92-50990. 84p. 1993. pap. 7.95 (*0-89384-211-7*) Pfeiffer & Co.

Communication: Strategic Action in Context. Beth Haslett. (Dolf Zillman & Jennings Bryant Communication Ser.). 304p. 1987. text ed. 59.95 (*0-89859-871-0*) L Erlbaum Assocs.

Communication: The Bottom Line. 2nd ed. Elizabeth Warner. 480p. 1991. per. 33.95 (*0-8403-6983-2*) Kendall-Hunt.

Communication: The Essence of Science Facilitating Information Exchange among Librarians, Scientists, Engineers, & Students. William D. Garvey. 1979. 140.00 (*0-08-022254-4*, Pub. by Pergamon Repr UK) Franklin.

Communication: The Miracle of Dialogue. George Manning & Kent Curtis. (Human Side of Work Ser.). 303p. (C). 1988. pap. 22.95 (*0-538-21252-7*, U252) S-W Pub.

Communication: The Process of Organizing. Bonnie M. Johnson. 404p. 1981. pap. text ed. 19.95 (*0-89641-089-7*) American Pr.

Communication: The Social Matrix of Psychiatry. Jurgen Ruesch & Gregory Bateson. 1987. 25.00 (*0-393-02377-X*) Norton.

Communication: The Vital Artery. Richard C. Anderson. LC 73-2682. (Illus.). 83p. 7.95 (*0-913842-02-8*) Correlan Pubns.

Communication: The Ways & Means of Spreading Information. Piero Ventura & Max Casalini. LC 94-4521. (J). 1994. 16.95 (*0-395-66789-5*) HM.

Communication Vol. 4: (Incl. 1990-94 Supplements) Ed. by Eleanor C. Goldstein. (Social Issues Resources Ser.). 1995. 95.00 (*0-89777-161-3*) Sirs Inc.

Communication see Time in the Play of "Hamlet"

Communication - Persuasive, Suggestive, Masterminding & Propaganda: Index of New Information with Authors & Subjects. Science & Life Consultants Association Staff. LC 92-54201. 180p. 1992. 49.50 (*1-55914-554-4*); pap. 39.50 (*1-55914-555-2*) ABBE Pubs Assn.

Communication Access for Persons with Hearing Loss: Compliance with the Americans with Disabilities Act. Ed. by Mark Ross. LC 94-2594. (Illus.). 306p. (C). 1994. pap. text ed. 37.50 (*0-912752-35-1*) York Pr.

Communication Activity Guide: Arlie the Alligator. Sandra Warren. (Illus.). 80p. 1993. pap. 8.95 (*0-9623835-9-7*) Pieces of Lrning.

Communication Alert Series. Incl. Non-Parents & Schools: Creating a New Team. (*0-318-59957-0*, 411-13303); School Labor Strife: Rebuilding the Team. (*0-318-59958-9*); New Voices on the Right: Impact on Schools. (*0-318-59959-7*, 415-14403); 29.95 (*0-317-35250-4*); Incl. (*0-318-59957-0*, 411-13303); (*0-318-59958-9*); (*0-318-59959-7*, 415-14403); 10.95 (*0-318-59956-2*) Natl Sch PR.

Communication among Social Bees. Martin Lindauer. LC 61-5579. (Harvard Bks. in Biology: No. 2). (Illus.). 152p. reprint ed. pap. 44.20 (*0-7837-1714-8*, 2057243) Bks Demand.

*__Communication & Adults with Learning Disabilities: New Map of an Old Country.__ Anna van der Gaag & Klara Dormandy. 1993. 49.95 (*1-56593-248-X*, 0428) Singular Publishing.

Communication & Aging. Jon F. Nussbaum et al. 275p. (C). 1990. pap. text ed. 21.00 (*0-06-046684-7*) HarpCollege.

*__Communication & Anger Management.__ Kathleen Middleton. (Comprehensive Health for Middle Grades Ser.). (J). (gr. 6-9). 1996. 24.00 (*1-56071-465-4*, H567) ETR Assocs.

Communication & Assertion Skills for Older Persons. Leilani Doty. (Death Education, Aging & Health Care Ser.). 110p. 1987. 39.00 (*0-89116-400-6*) Hemisp Pub.

Communication & Awareness in a Cancer Ward. Jim McIntosh. LC 76-30331. 1977. 22.50 (*0-88202-109-5*, Prodist) Watson Pub Intl.

Communication & Change: The Last Ten Years. Ed. by Wilbur Schramm & Daniel Lerner. LC 76-18893. (East-West Center Book Ser.). 387p. reprint ed. pap. 110.30 (*0-7837-3983-4*, 2043813) Bks Demand.

Communication & Change in American Religious History. Ed. by Leonard I. Sweet. 400p. (Orig.). (C). 1993. pap. text ed. 24.99 (*0-8028-0682-1*) Eerdmans.

Communication & Channel Systems in Tourism Marketing. Ed. by Daniel R. Fesenmaier. LC 93-30947. (Journal of Travel & Tourism Marketing: Vol. 2, Nos 2-3). (Illus.). 238p. 1993. reprint ed. lib. bdg. 49.95 (*1-56024-580-8*); reprint ed. pap. text ed. 19.95 (*1-56024-581-6*) Haworth Pr.

Communication & Citizenship: Journalism & the Public Sphere in the Media Age. Ed. by Peter Dahlgren & Colin Sparks. (Communication & Society Ser.). 256p. 1991. 69.95 (*0-415-05779-5*, A6054) Routledge.

Communication & Class Struggle: Capitalism, Imperialism, Vol. 1. Ed. by Armand Mattelart & Seth Siegelaub. 445p. (Orig.). 1979. pap. 45.00 (*0-88477-011-7*) Intl General.

Communication & Class Struggle: Liberation, Socialism, Vol. 2. Ed. by Armand Mattelart & Seth Siegelaub. LC 80-110213. (Illus.). 438p. (Orig.). 1983. pap. 45.00 (*0-88477-018-4*) Intl General.

Communication & Class Struggle: New Historical Subjects, Vol. 3. Ed. by Armand Mattelart. (Illus.). 275p. (Orig.). 1995. pap. 30.00 (*0-88477-034-6*) Intl General.

Communication & Cognition in Normal Aging & Dementia. Kathryn A. Bayles et al. LC 90-21692. 400p. (Orig.). (C). 1987. pap. text ed. 34.00 (*0-89079-330-1*, 1606) PRO-ED.

Communication & Community: An Approach to Social Psychology. William M. Berg & Robert Boguslaw. (Illus.). 400p. (C). 1985. text ed. write for info. (*0-13-153818-7*) P-H.

Communication & Computer Networks: Modelling with Discrete-Time Queues. Michael E. Woodward. LC 93-45351. 216p. 1993. write for info. (*0-8186-5171-7*, 5172) IEEE Comp Soc.

Communication & Computer Networks: Modelling with Discrete-Time Queues. Michael E. Woodward. LC 93-45351. 216p. 1993. text ed. 54.00 (*0-8186-5172-5*) IEEE Comp Soc.

Communication & Conflict Management in Church & Christian Organizations. Kenneth O. Gangel & Samuel L. Canine. 1993. 24.99 (*0-8054-3009-1*) Broadman.

*__Communication & Consequences: Laws of Interaction.__ Robert Norton & David Brenders. (LEA's Communication Ser.). 350p. 1995. text ed. 70.00 (*0-8058-2033-7*); pap. 35.00 (*0-8058-2034-5*) L Erlbaum Assocs.

Communication & Control: Networks & the New Economies of Communication. G. J. Mulgan. LC 90-40759. (Guilford Communication Ser.). 302p. 1991. text ed. 36.95 (*0-89862-311-1*) Guilford Pr.

Communication & Control in Society. K. Krippendorff. 544p. 1979. text ed. 135.00 (*0-677-05440-8*) Gordon & Breach.

Communication & Cross-Cultural Adaptation: An Interdisciplinary Theory. Young Yun Kim. (Intercommunication Ser.: No. 1). 1988. 59.00 (*0-905028-83-X*, Pub. by Multilingual Matters UK); pap. 24.95 (*0-905028-82-1*, Pub. by Multilingual Matters UK) Taylor & Francis.

Communication & Culture: A Reading-Writing Text. 4th ed. Joan Y. Gregg. (C). 1993. teacher ed write for info. (*0-8384-5051-2*); pap. 20.95 (*0-8384-5050-4*) Heinle & Heinle.

Communication & Culture: Language, Performance, Technology & Media. Ed. by Sari Thomas & William Evans. LC 89-17536. (Studies in Communication: Vol. 4). 392p. (C). 1990. text ed. 75.00 (*0-89391-497-5*) Ablex Pub.

Communication & Culture in Ancient India & China. Robert T. Oliver. LC 73-151717. 1971. 29.95 (*0-8156-0082-8*) Syracuse U Pr.

Communication & Culture in War & Peace. Ed. by Colleen Roach. (Communication & Human Values Ser.: Vol. 11). (Illus.). 216p. (C). 1993. text ed. 49.95 (*0-8039-5062-4*); pap. text ed. 24.00 (*0-8039-5063-2*) Sage.

Communication & Delivery Systems for Librarians. Roy Adams. 70p. 1990. text ed. 63.95 (*0-566-05750-6*) Ashgate Pub Co.

Communication & Democracy. Slavko Splichal & Janet Wasko. Ed. by Brenda Dervin. (Communication & Information Science Ser.). 288p. (C). 1993. text ed. 55.00 (*0-89391-764-8*); pap. text ed. 29.50 (*0-89391-894-6*) Ablex Pub.

Communication & Development: A Study of Two Indian Villages. Y. V. Rao. LC 66-21940. 152p. reprint ed. pap. 43.40 (*0-317-42280-4*, 2055898) Bks Demand.

Communication & Diplomacy in a Changing World. Tran Van Dinh. LC 87-1834. (Communication & Information Science Ser.). 192p. 1987. text ed. 42.50 (*0-89391-347-2*) Ablex Pub.

Communication & Domination: Essays to Honor of Herbert I. Schiller. Ed. by Jorg Becker et al. (Communication & Information Science Ser.). 288p. 1986. text ed. 55.00 (*0-89391-380-4*) Ablex Pub.

Communication & Education Skills: The Dietician's Guide. 2nd ed. Betsy B. Holli & Richard J. Calabrese. LC 90-20796. (Illus.). 269p. 1991. text ed. 29.50 (*0-8121-1386-1*) Williams & Wilkins.

C

1424

An Asterisk (*) at the beginning of an entry indicates that the title is appearing in BIP for the first time.

Communication & Expression in Hoofed Mammals. Fritz R. Walther. LC 82-49011. (Animal Communication Ser.). (Illus.). 448p. 1984. 45.00 (*0-253-31380-5*) Ind U Pr.

Communication & Handicap: Aspects of Psychological Compensation & Technical Aids. Ed. by E. Hjelmquist & L. G. Nilsson. 286p. 1986. 102.75 (*0-444-70034-X*, North Holland) Elsevier.

Communication & Health: Systems & Applications. Ed. by E. B. Ray & L. Donohew. 224p. 1990. pap. 22.50 (*0-8058-0697-0*) L Erlbaum Assocs.

Communication & Health: Systems & Applications. Ed. by E. B. Ray & L. Donohew. 224p. 1990. 49.95 (*0-8058-0154-5*) L Erlbaum Assocs.

***Communication & Health Outcomes.** Ed. by Gary L. Kreps & Dan O'Hair. (Speech Communication Association Applied Communication Ser.). 256p. 1995. text ed. 52.50 (*1-881303-52-7*) Hampton Pr NJ.

***Communication & Health Outcomes.** Ed. by Gary L. Kreps & Dan O'Hair. (Speech Communication Association Applied Communication Ser.). 256p. 1995. pap. text ed. 21.95 (*1-881303-53-5*) Hampton Pr NJ.

***Communication & High-Speed Management.** Donald P. Cushman & Sarah S. King. (Human Communication Processes Ser.). 288p. 1995. text ed. 59.50x (*0-7914-2535-5*); pap. 19.95x (*0-7914-2536-3*) State U NY Pr.

Communication & Human Behavior. 3rd ed. Brent D. Ruben. 448p. (C). 1992. pap. text ed. write for info. (*0-13-155847-1*) P-H.

Communication & Human Needs in Africa. Ed. by Onuira E. Nwuneli. 99p. 1989. pap. 8.95 (*0-940738-13-9*) Lamplight Edits.

Communication & Image in Nursing: Behaviors That Work. Karen W. Sherman. LC 93-33352. (Real Nursing Ser.). 166p. 1994. pap. text ed. 19.95 (*0-8273-5689-7*) Delmar.

Communication & Image Skills. Susan Gill. 22p. (Orig.). (C). 1991. pap. text ed. 17.00 (*0-935229-11-6*) Am Assoc Med.

Communication & Imperial Control in China: Evolution of the Palace Memorial System, 1693-1735. Silas H. Wu. LC 73-119078. (Harvard East Asian Ser.: No. 51). 212p. reprint ed. pap. 62.70 (*0-7837-1739-3*, 2057269) Bks Demand.

Communication & Indian Agriculture. Ed. by Ronald E. Ostman. 320p. (C). 1989. text ed. 25.00 (*0-8039-9599-7*) Sage.

Communication & Information Economics. Meheroo Jussawalla & Ebenfield. (Information Research & Resource Reports Ser.: Vol. 5). 1984. 56.50 (*0-444-87589-1*) Elsevier.

Communication & Information Technologies. Armand Mattelart & Hector Schmucler. Ed. by Melvin J. Voigt. Tr. by David Buxton. (Communication & Information Science Ser.). 192p. 1985. text ed. 49.50 (*0-89391-214-X*) Ablex Pub.

Communication & Interpersonal Relations: Text & Cases. 6th ed. William V. Haney. 608p. (C). 1991. text ed. 60.95 (*0-256-06974-3*, 11-0283-06) Irwin.

Communication & Knowledge: An Investigation in Rhetorical Epistemology. Richard A. Cherwitz & James W. Hikins. (Studies in Rhetoric-Communication). 192p. 1986. text ed. 34.95 (*0-87249-465-9*) U of SC Pr.

Communication & Law Enforcement. D. F. Gunderson & Robert Hopper. 192p. (C). 1988. reprint ed. pap. text ed. 25.00 (*0-8191-7023-2*) U Pr of Amer.

Communication & Leadership. John W. Gray. LC 73-78227. 72p. reprint ed. pap. 25.00 (*0-8357-4665-8*, 2037610) Bks Demand.

***Communication & Learning Revisited: Making Meaning Through Talk.** Barnes & Todd. LC 95-3111. 250p. 1995. pap. text ed. 19.50 (*0-86709-356-0*) Boynton Cook Pubs.

Communication & Litigation: Case Studies of Famous Trials. Janice Schuetz & Kathryn H. Snedaker. LC 87-35654. 304p. (C). 1988. text ed. 29.95 (*0-8093-1456-8*) S Ill U Pr.

Communication & Lonergan: Common Ground for Forging the New Age. Thomas J. Farrell & Paul A. Soukup. LC 93-37360. (Communication, Culture & Theology Ser.). 416p. (Orig.). 1994. pap. 22.95 (*1-55612-623-9*) Sheed & Ward MO.

Communication & Mass Media: A Guide to the Reference Literature. Eleanor S. Block & James K. Bracken. Ed. by James Rettig. (Humanities Ser.). 198p. 1991. lib. bdg. 40.00 (*0-87287-810-4*) Libs Unl.

Communication & Meaning. Andrew J. Jones. 1983. lib. bdg. 72.00 (*90-277-1543-2*) Kluwer Ac.

Communication & Medical Practice: Social Relations in the Clinic. David Silverman. 288p. (C). 1988. text ed. 45.00 (*0-8039-8108-2*); pap. text ed. 18.95 (*0-8039-8109-0*) Sage.

Communication & Negotiation. Linda L. Putnam & Michael E. Roloff. (Annual Reviews of Communication Research Ser.: Vol. 20). 304p. (C). 1992. text ed. 52.00 (*0-8039-4011-4*); pap. text ed. 24.00 (*0-8039-4012-2*) Sage.

Communication & Networking. 3rd ed. Larry Jordan. 1989. pap. 29.95 (*0-13-153933-7*) P-H.

Communication & Networking for the PC. 5th ed. Larry Jordan & Bruce Churchill. (Illus.). (Orig.). 1994. pap. 29.95 (*1-56686-183-7*) Brady Compu Bks.

Communication & Noncommunication by Cephalopods. Martin Moynihan. LC 84-47821. (Animal Communication Ser.). (Illus.). 154p. 1985. 35.00 (*0-253-31382-1*) Ind U Pr.

Communication & Other Social Behavior in Parus Carolinensis. Susan T. Smith. (Publications of the Nuttall Ornithological Club: No. 11). (Illus.). 125p. 1972. 7.75 (*1-877973-21-1*, 11) Nuttall Ornith.

Communication & Parapsychology: Proceedings of an International Conference Held in Vancouver, Canada; August 9-10, 1979. Ed. by Betty Shapin & Lisette Coly. LC 80-80486. 1980. 17.00 (*0-912328-32-0*) Parapsych Foun.

Communication & Persuasion. G. H. Jamieson. LC 84-23768. (Information Technology Ser.). 170p. 1985. 32.00 (*0-7099-1424-5*, Pub. by Croom Helm UK) Routledge Chapman & Hall.

Communication & Persuasion. R. E. Petty & J. T. Cacioppo. (Social Psychology Ser.). (Illus.). 220p. 1986. 58.00 (*0-387-96344-8*) Spr-Verlag.

Communication & Persuasion: Psychological Studies of Opinion Change. Carl I. Hovland et al. LC 81-20104. xii, 315p. 1982. reprint ed. text ed. 49.75 (*0-313-23348-9*, HOVC, Greenwood Pr) Greenwood.

Communication & Power in Organizations. Dennis K. Mumby. Ed. by Lee Thayer. LC 88-3356. (People, Communication, Organization Ser.). 208p. 1988. text ed. 39.50 (*0-89391-480-0*) Ablex Pub.

Communication & Reference. A. P. Martinich. LC 84-14283. (Foundations of Communication & Cognition Ser.). xiii, 205p. 1984. lib. bdg. 76.15 (*3-11-010067-3*) De Gruyter.

Communication & Relational Maintenance. Ed. by Daniel J. Canary & Laura Stafford. (Illus.). 313p. 1994. text ed. 59.95 (*0-12-158430-5*) Acad Pr.

Communication & Rural Development. J. B. Ambedkar. (C). 1992. 29.00 (*81-7099-358-X*, Pub. by Mittal II) S Asia.

Communication & Rural Development in India: The Changing Perceptions & the Search for a New Public Policy. S. N. Ray. (C). 1992. pap. text ed. 5.00 (*81-7304-030-3*, Pub. by Manohar II) S Asia.

Communication & Rural Women. Seema Rani & Achla Malviya. (Illus.). x, 148p. 1991. 13.00 (*81-85445-15-X*, Pub. by Manak Pubns Pvt Ltd) Nataraj Bks.

Communication & Sex-Role Socialization. Ed. by Cynthia Berryman-Fink et al. LC 92-33993. (Reference Library of Social Science: Vol. 889). 592p. 1993. 75.00 (*0-8153-1256-3*) Garland.

Communication & Simulation: From Two Fields to One Theme. David Crookall & Danny Saunders. 340p. 1989. 99.00 (*0-905028-85-6*, Pub. by Multilingual Matters UK); pap. 39.95 (*0-905028-84-8*, Pub. by Multilingual Matters UK) Taylor & Francis.

***Communication & Social Influence Processes.** Ed. by Charles R. Berger & Michael Burgoon. LC 95-2096. 1995. 24.95 (*0-87013-380-2*) Mich St U Pr.

Communication & Social Order. Hugh D. Duncan. 528p. 1985. pap. 24.95 (*0-87855-971-X*) Transaction Pubs.

Communication & Social Structure: Critical Studies in Mass Media Research. Ed. by Emile G. McAnany et al. 348p. 1981. text ed. 37.95 (*0-275-90679-5*, C0679, Praeger Pubs); pap. write for info. (*0-275-91459-3*, B1459, Praeger Pubs) Greenwood.

Communication & Society in Latin America: Trends in Critical Research 196-1985. Ed. by Rita Atwood & Emile G. McAnany. LC 86-40044. (Studies in Communication & Society). 288p. 1986. text ed. 36.00 (*0-299-10720-5*) U of Wis Pr.

Communication & Student Socialization. Ann Q. Staton-Spicer. LC 89-78253. 240p. (C). 1990. text ed. 42.50 (*0-89391-551-3*); pap. 24.50 (*0-89391-674-9*) Ablex Pub.

***Communication & Swallowing Management of Tracheostomized & Ventilator Dependent Adults.** Karen J. Dikeman & Marta S. Kazandjian. (Illus.). 448p. (Orig.). 1995. pap. 57.50 (*1-56593-601-9*, 1212) Singular Publishing.

***Communication & Swallowing Management of Tracheostomized & Ventilator Dependent Adults.** Karen J. Dikeman & Marta S. Kazandjian. (Illus.). 448p. (Orig.). (C). 1995. pap. text ed. 57.50 (*1-56593-347-8*, 0645) Singular Publishing.

Communication & Technology: Today & Tomorrow. William H. Baker et al. Ed. by Al Williams & Douglas Goings. 236p. (Orig.). (C). 1994. pap. text ed. 14.95 (*0-931874-20-3*) Assn Busn Comm.

Communication & the Culture of Technology. Ed. by Martin J. Medhurst et al. LC 90-12257. xviii, 330p. 1990. pap. 30.00 (*0-87422-068-8*) Wash St U Pr.

Communication & the Evolution of Society. Jurgen Habermas. Tr. by Thomas McCarthy. LC 77-88324. 234p. 1979. pap. 16.00 (*0-8070-1513-X*, BP572) Beacon Pr.

Communication & the Human Condition. W. Barnett Pearce. LC 88-30565. 224p. (C). 1989. text ed. 29.95 (*0-8093-1411-8*); pap. text ed. 19.95 (*0-8093-1412-6*) S Ill U Pr.

Communication & the Schools. C. W. Bending. LC 71-103930. 1970. 137.00 (*0-08-015663-0*, Pub. by Pergamon Repr UK) Franklin.

Communication & the Sexes. Barbara Bate. (Illus.). 258p. (C). 1992. reprint ed. pap. text ed. 13.95 (*0-88133-710-2*) Waveland Pr.

***Communication & the Transformation of Society: A Developing Region's Perspectives.** Ed. by Peter Nwosu et al. LC 95-10746. 1995. Not sold separately (*0-8191-9961-3*) U Pr of Amer.

Communication & Values. Krishan Sondhi. 1986. 22.50 (*0-685-14353-8*, Pub. by Somaiya) S Asia.

Communication & Women's Friendships: Parallels & Intersections in Literature & Life. Janet D. Ward & Joanna S. Mink. LC 93-73079. 201p. 1993. 42.95 (*0-87972-643-1*) Bowling Green Univ.

***Communication & Women's Friendships: Parallels & Intersections in Literature & Life.** Janet D. Ward & Joanna S. Mink. 201p. 1993. pap. 15.95 (*0-87972-644-X*) Bowling Green Univ.

Communication Apprehension & Avoidance. Booth-Butterfield. pap. 29.95 (*0-8087-7389-5*) Burgess MN Intl.

Communication As a Second Language, 5 pts. Amy Maid. Incl. Pt. 1. Language. 1978. pap. 7.95 (*0-916250-28-8*); Pt. 2. Ideas. 1978. pap. 7.95 (*0-916250-29-6*); Pt. 3. Mass Communication. 1978. pap. 7.95 (*0-916250-30-X*); Pt. 4. Print. 1978. pap. 7.95 (*0-916250-31-8*); Pt. 5. Airwaves & Beyond. 1978. pap. 7.95 (*0-916250-32-6*); (Mandala Series in Education). (Illus.). write for info. (*0-318-53705-2*) Irvington.

Communication As Action: An Introduction to Rhetoric & Communication. Phillip K. Tompkins. 253p. (C). 1982. text ed. 29.95 (*0-534-01157-8*) Intl Thomson.

Communication As Culture: Essays on Media & Society. James W. Carey. (Media & Popular Culture Ser.: No. 1). 1988. pap. 16.95 (*0-04-445064-8*) Routledge Chapman & Hall.

Communication As Performance. Ed. by Janet L. Palmer. (Illus.). 171p. (Orig.). (C). 1986. pap. text ed. 25.00 (*0-9620922-0-7*) Comn Excellence.

Communication Assessment & Intervention for Adults with Mental Retardation. Stephen N. Calculator & Jan L. Bedrosian. LC 90-9212. (Illus.). 359p. 1988. pap. text ed. 32.00 (*0-89079-374-3*, 1629) PRO-ED.

Communication Assessment & Intervention Strategies for Adolescents. Vicki L. Larson & Nancy L. McKinley. LC 86-51418. 387p. (YA). (gr. 5-12). 1987. text ed. 39.00 (*0-930599-07-1*) Thinking Pubns.

Communication at a Distance: Exploring the Effect of Print on Sociocultural Organization & Change. David Kaufer & Kathleen Carley. (Communication Ser.). 488p. 1993. text ed. 89.95 (*0-8058-1238-5*); pap. 29.95 (*0-8058-1273-3*) L Erlbaum Assocs.

***Communication at Work.** 3rd ed. Susan K. Gilmore & Patrick W. Fraleigh. (Illus.). 170p. 1993. pap. 12.95 (*0-938070-09-6*) Friendly Oregon.

***Communication at Work.** 5th ed. Adler. 1995. text ed. write for info. (*0-07-000478-1*) McGraw.

Communication at Work: Listening, Speaking, Writing & Reading. Kathleen S. Abrams. (Illus.). 384p. (C). 1985. pap. text ed. write for info. (*0-13-153826-8*) P-H.

Communication Audits. Cal W. Downs. (Management Applications Ser.). (C). 1988. pap. text ed. 20.25 (*0-673-18275-4*) HarpCollege.

Communication-Based Intervention for Problem Behavior: A User's Guide for Producing Positive Change. Edward G. Carr et al. 288p. 1994. pap. 23.00 (*1-55766-159-6*, 1596) P H Brookes.

Communication Basics for Human Service Professionals. Elam Nunnally & Caryl Moy. (Human Services Guides Ser.: Vol. 56). 172p. (C). 1989. pap. text ed. 17.95 (*0-8039-3118-2*) Sage.

Communication Before Speech: Normal Development & Impaired Communication. Ed. by Judith Coupe & Juliet Goldbart. 128p. 1988. text ed. 45.00 (*0-7099-4841-7*) Routledge Chapman & Hall.

Communication Behavior & Aging: A Source Book for Clinicians. Barbara Shadden. 392p. (C). 1988. pap. text ed. 48.00 (*0-683-07723-6*) Williams & Wilkins.

Communication Behaviors & Skills of Children Having Down's Syndrome. (Journal of Childhood Communication Disorders Special Issues Ser.). 1988. 20.00 (*0-685-21933-X*, D404) Coun Exc Child.

Communication Between Cultures. Larry A. Samovar & Richard E. Porter. 330p. (C). 1991. pap. 25.95 (*0-534-15006-3*) Intl Thomson.

***Communication Between Cultures.** 2nd ed. Larry A. Samovar & Richard E. Porter. LC 94-5376. 313p. 1995. pap. 25.95 (*0-534-21582-3*) Intl Thomson.

Communication Between the Sexes: Sex Differences & Sex-Role Stereotypes. 2nd ed. Lea P. Stewart et al. 230p. (C). 1990. pap. text ed. 27.00 (*0-89787-335-1*) Gorsuch Scarisbrick.

Communication Breakdown: Cause & Cure. David W. Shave. LC 73-377. 320p. 1975. 15.70 (*0-87527-125-1*) Green.

Communication Breakthrough: Instruments for Success. Glaser & Associates, Inc. Staff. 96p. 1988. per. 19.95 (*0-8403-4996-3*) Kendall-Hunt.

Communication by Design: A Study in Corporate Identity. Pilditch. 1970. 19.50 (*0-07-094214-5*) McGraw.

***Communication by Engineers: A Literature Review of Engineers' Information Needs, Seeking Processes & Use.** Donald W. King et al. 1994. write for info. (*0-615-00330-3*) Council on Library Resources Inc.

Communication Campaign Management: A Systems Approach. Robert E. Simmons. 237p. (C). 1990. pap. text ed. 43.95 (*0-8013-0404-0*, 78213) Longman.

Communication Campaigns about Drugs: Government, Media & the Public. Ed. by P. J. Shoemaker. (CTS Ser., Bryant Ser.). 144p. 1989. 29.95 (*0-8058-0230-4*) L Erlbaum Assocs.

Communication Careers, 6 vols., Set. 98.00 (*0-685-23046-5*, CG114S) Ready Ref Pr.

Communication Cartoons. Cathy A. Hazelton. (Illus.). 160p. 1989. teacher ed 22.95 (*0-937857-09-2*, 1566) Speech Bin.

Communication Circuits: Analysis & Design. Kenneth K. Clarke & Donald T. Hess. LC 78-125610. (Engineering Ser.). (C). 1971. text ed. 48.76 (*0-201-01040-2*) Addison-Wesley.

Communication Circuits: Analysis & Design. Kenneth T. Clarke & Donald T. Hess. 670p. (C). 1994. reprint ed. lib. bdg. 68.50 (*0-89464-863-2*) Krieger.

Communication, Cognition, & Anxiety. Ed. by Melanie Booth-Butterfield. (Illus.). 232p. 1991. 46.00 (*0-8039-4087-4*); pap. 22.95 (*0-8039-4088-2*) Sage.

***Communication Coloring Book.** Denise Grigas. (Illus.). 48p. (J). (gr. k-5). 1994. pap. text ed. 14.95 (*0-937857-53-X*, 1495) Speech Bin.

Communication Competencies & Contexts. 3rd ed. Nancy Buerkel-Rothfuss & Pamela L. Gray. 544p. 1993. per. 27.95 (*0-8403-8776-8*) Kendall-Hunt.

Communication Competencies for Adults: Capital Letters & Endmarks. Dorothy Williams & Sally Pasley. (Communication Competencies Ser.: Bk. 1). 64p. 1988. pap. text ed. 4.65 (*0-8428-9731-3*) Cambridge Bk.

Communication Competencies for Adults: Messages, Invitations & Letters. Dorothy Williams & Sally Pasley. (Communication Competencies Ser.: Bk. 3). 64p. 1988. pap. text ed. 4.35 (*0-8428-9733-X*) Cambridge Bk.

Communication Competencies for Adults: Punctuation. Dorothy Williams & Sally Pasley. (Communication Competencies Ser.: Bk. 2). 64p. 1988. pap. text ed. 4.65 (*0-8428-9732-1*) Cambridge Bk.

Communication Competencies for Adults: Using the Newspaper. Dorothy Williams & Sally Pasley. (Communication Competencies Ser.: Bk. 6). 1988. pap. text ed. 4.35 (*0-8428-9736-4*) Cambridge Bk.

Communication Complexity: A New Approach to Circuit Depth. Mauricio Karchmer. 100p. 1989. 25.00 (*0-262-11143-8*) MIT Pr.

***Communication, Compromise & Commitment.** Rosemary Menlo & Shirley Haney. 88p. (YA). (gr. 7-12). 1994. pap. write for info. (*1-57515-045-X*) PPI Pubng.

Communication, Conflict & Marriage. Harold L. Raush. LC 73-18506. (Jossey-Bass Behavioral Science Ser.). 264p. reprint ed. pap. 75.30 (*0-317-08634-0*, 2013751) Bks Demand.

Communication, Control, & Signal Processing: Proceedings of the Bilkent International Conference, Ankara, Turkey, 2-5 July 1990, 2 vols., Set. Ed. by E. Arikan. 1860p. 1990. 254.00 (*0-444-88762-8*) Elsevier.

***Communication, Creativity, Collaboration: Current Challenges for School Supervisors & Administrators.** Ed. by Cassandra Peters-Johnson et al. 500p. 1995. pap. text ed. 45.00 (*0-614-06523-2*, 0111964) Am Speech Lang Hearing.

Communication Crisis at Kent State: A Case Study. Phillip K. Tompkins & Elaine V. Anderson. LC 77-161215. (Illus.). 186p. (C). 1971. text ed. 63.00 (*0-677-03970-0*) Gordon & Breach.

Communication Criticism: Approaches & Genres. Karyn C. Rybacki & Donald J. Rybacki. 381p. (C). 1991. text ed. 34.95 (*0-534-14118-8*) Intl Thomson.

Communication, Culture & Hegemony: From Media to Mediations. Jesus Martin-Barbero & Philip Schlesinger. (Communication & Human Values Ser.). (Illus.). 288p. (C). 1993. text ed. 65.00 (*0-8039-8488-X*); pap. text ed. 24.00 (*0-8039-8489-8*) Sage.

Communication, Culture & Organizational Processes. William B. Gudykunst et al. (International & Intercultural Communication Ser.: Vol. 9). 1985. 52.00 (*0-8039-2427-5*) Sage.

Communication, Culture, & the Iranian Revolution. Annabelle Sreberny-Mohammadi & Ali Mohammadi. LC 93-46191. (C). 1994. text ed. 44.95 (*0-8166-2216-7*); pap. text ed. 17.95 (*0-8166-2217-5*) U of Minn Pr.

Communication Curriculum: A Practical Guide for Speech & Language. Linda B. Collins & Carol S. Spangler. 200p. (Orig.). (gr. k-12). 1988. teacher ed 39.95 (*0-937857-06-8*, 1558) Speech Bin.

Communication Development: Foundations, Processes, & Clinical Applications. Ed. by William O. Haynes & Brian B. Shulman. LC 93-727. 1993. text ed. write for info. (*0-13-014143-7*) P-H Gen Ref & Trav.

Communication, Development, & the Third World: The Global Politics of Information. Robert Louis Stevenson. 240p. (C). 1991. reprint ed. pap. text ed. 17.50 (*0-8191-8488-8*) U Pr of Amer.

Communication Development During Infancy. Lauren B. Adamson. 256p. (C). 1994. pap. text ed. write for info. (*0-697-14590-5*) Brown & Benchmark.

Communication Disorders. Ed. by Robert W. Rieber. LC 80-18394. (Applied Psycholinguistics & Communication Disorders Ser.). 366p. 1981. 65.00 (*0-306-40527-X*, Plenum Pr) Plenum.

***Communication Disorders & Interventions in Low Incidence Pediatric Populations.** Lisa Schoenbrodt et al. 256p. (Orig.). (C). 1995. pap. 39.95x (*1-56593-220-X*, 0580) Singular Publishing.

Communication Disorders Following Traumatic Brain Injury: Management of Cognitive, Language, & Motor Impairments. Ed. by David R. Beukelman & Kathryn M. Yorkston. LC 89-14560. (Illus.). 439p. (C). 1991. pap. text ed. 35.00 (*0-89079-295-X*, 1586) PRO-ED.

Communication Disorders in Aging. Ed. by Raymond H. Hull & Kathleen M. Griffin. (Human Services Guides Ser.: Vol. 57). (C). 1989. pap. text ed. 17.95 (*0-8039-3124-7*) Sage.

***Communication Disorders in Aging: Assessment & Management.** fac. ed. Ed. by H. Gustav Mueller & Virgina C. Geoffery. LC 87-21084. (Illus.). 528p. 1994. pap. 150.50 (*0-7837-7687-X*, 2047441) Bks Demand.

Communication Disorders in Children. 5th ed. Jon Eisenson & Mardel Ogilvie. 480p. (C). 1983. text ed. write for info. (*0-02-332100-8*) Macmillan.

Communication Disorders in Infants & Toddlers: Assessment & Intervention. Frances P. Billeaud. 262p. 1992. 32.50 (*1-56372-036-1*) Buttrwrth-Heinemann.

Communication Disorders in Multicultural Populations. Ed. by Dolores E. Battle. 322p. 1992. 39.50 (*1-56372-017-5*) Buttrwrth-Heinemann.

***Communication Disorders in the Classroom.** 2nd ed. William O. Haynes et al. LC 93-80317. 302p. 1994. pap. 39.95 (*0-8403-9073-4*) Kendall-Hunt.

Communication Displays for Engineered Preschool Environments, Bk. I. Carol Goossens et al. (Illus.). 480p. (Orig.). 1994. spiral bd., pap. 69.00 (*1-884135-05-6*) Mayer-Johnson.

C

An Asterisk (*) at the beginning of an entry indicates that the title is appearing in BIP for the first time. 1425

Communication Displays for Engineered Preschool Environments, Bk. II. Carol Goossens et al. (Illus.). 480p. (Orig.). 1994. spiral bd., pap. 69.00 (1-884135-07-2) Mayer-Johnson.

Communication-Education: Effective Communication for the Teacher. Terry M. Thibodeaux. 160p. (C). 1991. pap. text ed. 23.95 (0-8403-6881-X) Kendall-Hunt.

*__Communication Efficiency & Rural Development in Africa: The Case of Cameroon.__ Emmanuel K. Ngwainmbi. (Illus.). 196p. (Orig.). (C). 1994. lib. bdg. 46.50 (0-8191-9734-3); pap. text ed. 27.50 (0-8191-9735-1) U Pr of Amer.

Communication Electrician. (Career Examination Ser.: C-3268). 1994. pap. 23.95 (0-8373-3268-0) Nat Learn.

Communication Electronics. Louis E. Frenzel, Jr. 1989. student ed 19.96 (0-07-058231-9); teacher ed 6.95 (0-07-058232-7) McGraw.

Communication Electronics. Louis E. Frenzel, Jr. 320p. 1989. text ed. 19.95 (0-07-058230-0) McGraw.

Communication Electronics. Louis E. Frenzel. (McGraw-Hill Basic Skills in Electricity Ser.). 1989. text ed. write for info. (0-07-022356-4) McGraw.

Communication Electronics. 2nd ed. Louis E. Frenzel, Jr. LC 93-34935. (Basic Skills in Electricity & Electronics Ser.). 1993. write for info. (0-02-801842-7) Glencoe.

Communication Electronics for Technicians. Lloyd Temes. 400p. (C). 1974. text ed. 44.95 (0-07-063487-4) McGraw.

Communication Engineering: A Guide to the Study of Paper 347 of the CEI Examinations. David P. Howson. (PPL Study Guide Ser.: No. 7). 45p. reprint ed. pap. 25.00 (0-317-08163-2, 2011487) Bks Demand.

Communication Equipment of the German Army: Nineteen Thirty-Three - Nineteen Forty-Five. Charles Barger. (Illus.). 192p. 1989. pap. 30.00 (0-87364-534-0) Paladin Pr.

Communication Ethics: Methods of Analysis. James A. Jaksa & Michael S. Pritchard. 172p. (C). 1988. pap. 17.95 (0-534-09102-4) Intl Thomson.

Communication Ethics: Methods of Analysis. 2nd ed. James A. Jaksa & Michael S. Pritchard. 244p. 1994. pap. 18.95 (0-534-19896-1) Intl Thomson.

Communication Failure in Dialogue & Discourse: Detection & Repair Processes. Ed. by R. G. Reilly. 404p. 1987. 81.50 (0-444-70112-5, North Holland) Elsevier.

Communication Flows: A Census in the United States & Japan. Ithiel De Sola Pool et al. (Information Research & Resource Reports Ser.: Vol. 3). 250p. 1984. 66.75 (0-444-87521-2, I-192-84, North Holland) Elsevier.

Communication for a Livable World: A Curriculum for Grades 4-8. Jory Post & Alan Friedman. 149p. 1988. pap. text ed. 19.95 (0-941816-51-6) ETR Assocs.

*__Communication for Business.__ Elisa Lluesma. 240p. (C). 1994. per., pap. text ed. 26.95 (0-7872-0278-9) Kendall-Hunt.

Communication for Business. Margaret Z. Mergal. 238p. 1974. pap. 2.50 (0-8477-2610-X) U of PR Pr.

Communication for Business & the Professions. 5th ed. Patricia H. Andrews & John E. Baird. 496p. (C). 1992. pap. write for info. (0-697-08628-3) Brown & Benchmark.

Communication for Business & the Professions. 6th ed. Patricia H. Andrews & John E. Baird. 512p. (C). 1995. pap. text ed. write for info. (0-697-20120-1) Brown & Benchmark.

Communication for Child Survival. Mark R. Rasmuson et al. 144p. 1988. pap. 8.00 (0-685-59932-9) Acad Educ Dev.

Communication for Development in the Third World: Theory & Practice from 1950's to 1990's. R. Srimivas Melkote. 252p. (C). 1991. text ed. 29.95 (0-8039-9683-7); pap. text ed. 14.95 (0-8039-9684-5) Sage.

Communication for Emotional Management: The Book. Michael C. Giammatteo. (Orig.). 1985. pap. text ed. 19.95 (0-918428-12-2) Sylvan Inst.

Communication for Everyday Living. Sharon A. Ratliffe & David D. Hudson. 256p. (C). 1988. pap. text ed. write for info. (0-13-154386-5) P-H.

Communication for Health & Behavior Change: A Developing Country Perspective. Judith Graeff. (Health Ser.). 1993. 24.95 (1-55542-585-2) Jossey-Bass.

Communication for Health Professionals: A Relational Perspective. Teresa L. Thompson. 176p. (C). 1988. reprint ed. pap. text ed. 20.00 (0-8191-6994-3) U Pr of Amer.

Communication for Management & Business. 5th ed. Norman B. Sigband & Arthur H. Bell. (C). 1988. text ed. 60.50 (0-673-38322-9) HarpCollege.

Communication for Management & Business: A Function of Principles, Methods, Strategies, Process & Practice. Christine Y. Durham. 236p. 1992. per. 34.95 (0-8403-8094-1) Kendall-Hunt.

Communication for Managers. 6th ed. Norman B. Sigband & Arthur H. Bell. (C). 1994. text ed. 53.95 (0-538-83475-7, EH61FA) S-W Pub.

Communication for New Loyalties: African Soldier's Songs. Anthony Clayton. (Papers in International Studies: Africa Ser.: No. 34). 70p. reprint ed. pap. 25.00 (0-317-09667-2, 2007851) Bks Demand.

Communication for Professional Engineers. Bill Scott. 240p. 1984. 25.00 (0-7277-0187-8, Pub. by T Telford UK) Am Soc Civil Eng.

Communication for Technicians: Reading, Writing & Speaking on the Job. Ann G. Tench & Isabelle Thompson. (Illus.). 448p. (C). 1988. pap. text ed. write for info. (0-13-154246-X) P-H.

*__Communication for the Classroom Teacher.__ 5th ed. Pamela J. Cooper. 356p. 1994. per. 34.00 (0-89787-356-4) Gorsuch Scarisbrick.

Communication for the Speechless. Franklin H. Silverman. 1980. text ed. write for info. (0-13-153361-4) P-H.

*__Communication for the Speechless.__ 3rd ed. Franklin H. Silverman. 1994. write for info. (0-615-00134-3) Allyn.

Communication from an Artificial Intelligence Perspective: Theoretical & Applied Issues. Ed. by Andrew Ortony et al. LC 92-31538. xi, 260p. 1992. write for info. (3-540-55881-0); 77.00 (0-387-55881-0) Spr-Verlag.

Communication from the Secretary of the Treasury. Israel D. Andrews. LC 75-22797. (America in Two Centuries Ser.). 1976. reprint ed. 75.95 (0-405-07668-1) Ayer.

Communication Game: Perspectives on the Development of Speech, Language & Non-Verbal Communication Skills. Ed. by Abigail P. Reilly. (Pediatric Round Table Ser.: No. 4). 98p. 1980. 10.00 (0-931562-05-8) J & J Consumer Prods.

Communication, Gender & Sex Roles in Diverse Interaction Contexts. Ed. by Lea P. Stewart et al. LC 86-17462. (Communication & Information Science Ser.). 272p. 1987. text ed. 55.00 (0-89391-336-7) Ablex Pub.

Communication, Health & the Elderly. Ed. by H. Giles et al. (Fulbright Papers: Proceedings of Colloquia: Vol. 8). 1990. text ed. 59.95 (0-7190-3174-5, Pub. by Manchester Univ Pr UK) St Martin.

Communication Highlights, No. 1452. (Illus.). 48p. 1987. 5.95 (1-878259-05-9) Neibauer Pr.

Communication in Action: Teaching the Language Arts, 4 Vols. 4th ed. Hennings. (C). 1989. text ed. 53.56 (0-395-43212-X) HM.

Communication in Africa: A Search for Boundaries. Leonard W. Doob. LC 78-27557. (Illus.). 406p. 1979. reprint ed. text ed. 37.50 (0-313-20789-5, DOCA, Greenwood Pr) Greenwood.

Communication in Business & Industry. 2nd ed. William M. Schutte & Erwin R. Steinberg. LC 90-28248. 432p. (C). 1991. reprint ed. 47.00 (0-89464-579-X) Krieger.

Communication in Cancer Care. Ivan Lichter. LC 86-20764. (Illus.). 209p. 1987. text ed. 60.00 (0-443-03698-5) Churchill.

*__Communication in Congress: Members, Staff, & the Search for Information.__ David Whiteman. (Studies in Government & Public Policy). 248p. (C). 1996. 35.00x (0-7006-0719-6); pap. 15.95x (0-7006-0720-X) U Pr of KS.

Communication in Development. Fred L. Casmir. Ed. by Brenda Dervin. LC 90-19861. (Communication & Information Science Ser.). 368p. (C). 1991. text ed. 59.50 (0-89391-641-2); pap. text ed. 25.00 (0-89391-770-2) Ablex Pub.

*__Communication in Eastern Europe: The Role of History, Culture & Media in Contemporary Conflicts.__ Ed. by Fred L. Casmir. (Communication Ser.). 300p. 1995. text ed. 45.00 (0-8058-1625-9) L Erlbaum Assocs.

*__Communication in Education.__ Ed. by Richard A. Fiordo. 403p. (Orig.). (C). 1990. 21.95 (1-55059-003-0, Pub. by Detselig CN) Temeron Bks.

Communication in Educational Organizations. McCroskey & Richmond. pap. 29.95 (0-8087-7641-X) Burgess MN Intl.

Communication in English. R. P. Bhatnagar & R. T. Bell. 266p. (C). 1979. pap. text ed. 8.95 (0-86131-097-7, Pub. by Orient Longman Ltd II) Apt Bks.

Communication in Everyday Life: A Social Interpretation. Wendy Leeds-Hurwitz. Ed. by Lee Thayer. LC 89-282. (Communication: The Human Context Ser.: Vol. 3). 224p. (C). 1989. text ed. 42.50 (0-89391-524-6); pap. text ed. 19.95 (0-89391-812-1) Ablex Pub.

Communication in Family Relationships. Patricia Noller & MaryAnn Fitzpatrick. 352p. (C). 1992. pap. text ed. write for info. (0-13-301748-6) P-H.

*__Communication in History: Technology, Culture, & Society.__ 2nd ed. David J. Crowley & Paul Heyer. LC 94-22579. 368p. (C). 1995. pap. text ed. 29.95 (0-8013-1250-7) Longman.

Communication in History: Technology, Culture, Society. Ed. by David Crowley & Paul Heyer. 352p. (Orig.). (C). 1991. pap. text ed. 31.50 (0-8013-0598-5, 78524) Longman.

Communication in International Bargaining. Christer Jonsson. 256p. 1990. text ed. 39.95 (0-312-04181-0) St Martin.

Communication in Interpersonal Relationships. Donald P. Cushman & Dudley D. Cahn. LC 83-24228. (Series in Human Communication Processes). 170p. 1984. 44.50 (0-87395-909-4); pap. 14.95 (0-87395-910-8) State U NY Pr.

Communication in Japan & the United States. Ed. by William B. Gudykunst. LC 92-27134. (SUNY Series, Human Communication Processes). 330p. (C). 1993. 64.50 (0-7914-1603-8); pap. 21.95 (0-7914-1604-6) State U NY Pr.

Communication in Legal Advocacy. Richard D. Rieke & Randall K. Stutman. (Studies in Communication Processes). 255p. 1989. text ed. 29.95 (0-87249-639-2) U of SC Pr.

Communication in Legal Advocacy. Richard D. Rieke & Randall K. Stutman. (Studies in Communication Processes). 255p. (C). 1992. pap. text ed. 21.95 (0-87249-681-3) U of SC Pr.

Communication in Marriage. John C. Hagee. Ed. by Lucretia Hobbs & Connie Reece. 31p. (Orig.). 1991. per., pap. 30.00 (1-56908-005-4) Global Evang.

Communication in Medicine: A Challenge to the Profession. O. K. Harlem. (Illus.). 1977. 14.50 (3-8055-2387-4) S Karger.

Communication in Medicine & Psychology: Reference & Research Guide. Mary R. Bartone. LC 84-45658. 150p. 1986. 39.50 (0-88164-214-2); pap. 34.50 (0-88164-215-0) ABBE Pubs Assn.

Communication in Modern Organizations. George T. Vardaman & Patricia B. Vardaman. LC 82-12694. 534p. 1982. reprint ed. lib. bdg. 49.50 (0-89874-537-3) Krieger.

Communication in Nursing Practice. 2nd ed. Eleanor C. Hein. 280p. 1980. 14.00 (0-316-35453-8) Little.

Communication in-on the "Third World" National Development, Critical International Bibliography, Vol. I. Ed. by Kazem Motamed-Nejad. 450p. Date not set. 35.00 (0-88477-027-3) Intl General.

Communication in Organizations. Everett M. Rogers & Rekha Agarwala-Rogers. LC 75-32368. (Illus.). 1976. pap. 18.95 (0-02-926710-2) Free Pr.

Communication in Organizations. 2nd ed. Dalmar Fisher. Ed. by Fenton. LC 92-41866. 650p. (C). 1993. text ed. 52.75 (0-314-01235-4) West Pub.

Communication in Practice, Vol. 1. Ed. by Theon Wilkinson. 216p. (C). 1981. 102.00 (0-85292-288-4, Pub. by IPM Hse UK) St Mut.

Communication in Quebec: The State of the Art. Jean-Guy Lacroix & Benoit Levesque. 96p. Date not set. pap. 12.00 (0-88477-026-5) Intl General.

Communication in Small Group Discussions: An Integrated Approach. 3rd ed. John F. Cragan & David W. Wright. Ed. by Jucha. 313p. (C). 1991. text ed. 37.00 (0-314-72205-X) West Pub.

*__Communication in Successful Total Quality Management.__ P. M. Prigen. (C). 1994. 150.00x (0-946655-61-8, Pub. by S Thornes Pubs UK) St Mut.

Communication in the Age of Virtual Reality. Ed. by Frank Biocca & Mark R. Levy. (Communication Ser.). 408p. 1995. text ed. 79.95 (0-8058-1549-X); pap. 29.95 (0-8058-1550-3) L Erlbaum Assocs.

Communication in the Chiroptera. M. Brock Fenton. LC 84-47965. (Animal Communication Ser.). (Illus.). 174p. 1985. 35.00 (0-253-31381-3) Ind U Pr.

Communication in the Classroom: The Importance of Good Questioning. Peter Sullivan & David Clarke. 73p. (C). 1991. pap. 51.00 (0-7300-1355-3, ECT403, Pub. by Deakin Univ AT) St Mut.

Communication in the Counseling Relationship. Bonnie J. Headington. LC 78-9026. 1979. 16.50 (0-910328-23-4); pap. 11.00 (0-910328-24-2) Sulzburger & Graham Pub.

Communication in the Education of Deaf Children. Wendy Lynas. 100p. (Orig.). (C). 1994. pap. text ed. 32.50 (1-56593-373-7, 0750) Singular Publishing.

Communication in the Family. 2nd ed. Judy C. Pearson. (C). 1993. 29.50 (0-06-500047-1) HarpCollege.

Communication in the Legal Process. Ronald J. Matlon. LC 87-16852. (Illus.). 400p. (C). 1988. text ed. 34.75 (0-03-062771-0) HB Coll Pubs.

Communication in the Multicultural Classroom. Klopf & Thompson. pap. 29.95 (0-8087-5646-X) Burgess MN Intl.

Communication in the Multinational Organization. Richard L. Wiseman & Robert Shuter. (International & Intercultural Communication Ser.: Vol. 18). 216p. (C). 1994. text ed. 52.00 (0-8039-5538-3); pap. text ed. 24.00 (0-8039-5539-1) Sage.

Communication in the Nursing Context. 3rd ed. Jean C. Bradley & Mark A. Edinberg. (Illus.). 276p. (C). 1990. pap. text ed. 29.95 (0-8385-1327-1, A1327-4) Appleton & Lange.

Communication in the Third World: A Select Bibliography. 1987. 48.50 (0-317-90969-X, Patriot) S Asia.

Communication in the Work Place. Paul Olson & Susan Olson. 200p. 1991. 29.95 (0-913690-16-3) Aloray.

Communication in the Workplace: A Guide to Business & Professional Speaking. Lynne Kelly. (C). 1990. pap. 30.50 (0-06-043628-X) HarpCollege.

Communication in Writing. E. F. Pardoe. 1965. 44.00 (0-08-011136-X, Pub. by Pergamon Repr UK) Franklin.

Communication Incompetencies: A Theory of Training Oral Performance Behavior. Gerald M. Phillips. 360p. (C). 1991. 34.95 (0-8093-1459-2) S Ill U Pr.

*__Communication Intervention: Birth to Three.__ Louis M. Rossetti. 350p. 1995. 34.95 (1-56593-101-7, 0404) Singular Publishing.

Communication, Intimacy & Close Relationships. Valerian J. Derlega. 1984. text ed. 55.00 (0-12-210840-X) Acad Pr.

Communication, Language & Grammar: A Course for Teachers. Gerald P. Delahunty & James J. Garvey. LC 93-39640. 1994. text ed. write for info. (0-07-022911-2) McGraw.

Communication Law. Hemmer. 1993. pap. 19.95 (0-685-65898-8) Burgess MN Intl.

Communication, Learning, & Affects. Richmond & Gorham. pap. 29.95 (0-8087-4699-5) Burgess MN Intl.

Communication Made Easy for Pilots. Dick Doberstein. (Illus.). 98p. 1976. pap. text ed. 8.95 (0-9607866-2-7) Simplified Reg.

Communication Manual for Drug Abuse Prevention Programs. Development Associates, Inc. Staff. 192p. 1991. pap. text ed. 15.00 (1-879839-00-8) Develop Assocs.

Communication, Marital Dispute & Divorce Mediation. William A. Donohue. 256p. (C). 1991. text ed. 49.95 (0-8058-0387-4) L Erlbaum Assocs.

Communication Matters. Randall McCutcheon et al. LC 93-10452. (J). 1993. text ed. 46.50 (0-314-01390-3) West Pub.

Communication, Media & Change. Jack Lyle & Douglas McLeod. LC 92-19127. 264p. (C). 1993. pap. text ed. 25.95 (0-87484-935-7) Mayfield Pub.

Communication Media in Higher Education: A Directory of Academic Programs & Faculty in Radio-Television-Film & Related Media. Ed. by Garland C. Elmore. 530p. 1987. pap. text ed. 18.00 (0-318-40107-X) ACA VA.

Communication Models for the Study of Mass Communications. 2nd ed. Denis McQuail & Sven Windahl. LC 92-28665. (C). 1994. pap. text ed. 21.95 (0-582-03650-X, 79758) Longman.

Communication Networks: Towards a New Paradigm for Research. Everett M. Rogers & D. Lawrence Kincaid. LC 80-65202. (Illus.). 1981. text ed. 29.95 (0-02-926740-4) Free Pr.

Communication Networks for Computers. Donald W. Davies & Derek L. Barber. LC 73-2775. (Wiley Series in Computing). (Illus.). 593p. reprint ed. pap. 169.10 (0-8357-4563-5, 2037465) Bks Demand.

Communication Networks in Health Care: Proceedings of the IFIP-IMIA Working Conference on Communication Networks in Health Care, Ulvsunda Palace, Sweden, 14-18 June, 1982. Ed. by H. E. Peterson & A. J. Isaksson. 366p. 1983. 64.00 (0-444-86513-6, I-495-82, North Holland) Elsevier.

Communication Networks Management. 2nd ed. Kornel Terplan. (Computer Communication Ser.). 656p. 1991. text ed. 78.00 (0-13-156449-8, 270805) P-H.

Communication of Emotion. Ross Buck. LC 83-1613. (Guilford Social Psychology Ser.). 391p. 1986. lib. bdg. 45.00 (0-89862-110-0); pap. text ed. 21.95 (0-89862-915-2) Guilford Pr.

Communication of Ideas. Institute for Religious & Social Studies Staff. Ed. by Lyman Bryson. (Religion & Civilization Series of the Institute for Religious & Social Studies). 1964. reprint ed. 39.50 (0-8154-0035-7) Cooper Sq.

Communication of Important Ideas. Harvey Jackins. 1963. pap. 2.00 (0-911214-09-7) Rational Isl.

Communication of Innovations. 2nd ed. E. Rogers & F. Shoemaker. LC 78-122276. 1971. text ed. 19.95 (0-02-926680-7) Free Pr.

Communication of Language-Impaired Children. H. Van Balkom. 200p. 1991. pap. 43.00 (90-265-1183-3, Pub. by Swets Pub Serv NE) Taylor & Francis.

Communication of Social Support: Messages, Interactions, Relationships, & Community. Ed. by Brant Burleson et al. LC 93-40639. 304p. (C). 1994. text ed. 48.00 (0-8039-4350-4); pap. text ed. 21.50 (0-8039-4351-2) Sage.

Communication, Organization, & Change Within a Feminist Context: A Participant Observation of a Feminist Collective. Lynette J. Eastland. LC 91-31400. 187p. 1991. lib. bdg. 79.95 (0-88946-121-X) E Mellen.

Communication Pedagogy: Approaches to Teaching Undergraduate Courses in Communication. Ed. by Linda C. Lederman & Brenda Dervin. (Communication & Information Science Ser.). 352p. (C). 1992. text ed. 59.50 (0-89391-848-2); pap. text ed. 27.50 (0-89391-893-8) Ablex Pub.

Communication Philosophy & the Technological Age. Ed. by Michael J. Hyde. LC 81-3420. (Illus.). 144p. 1982. 17.50 (0-8173-0077-5) U of Ala Pr.

Communication Planning at the Institutional Level: A Selected Annotated Bibliography. Ronny Adhikarya & John Middleton. ix, 99p. (Orig.). 1979. pap. text ed. 6.00 (0-86638-022-1) EW Ctr HI.

Communication Planning Process in the Philippine Commission on Population. Melina S. Pugne. (East-West Communication Institute Case Studies: No. 6). xii, 136p. (Orig.). 1983. pap. 5.00 (0-86638-005-1) EW Ctr HI.

Communication Policy & Planning in Singapore. Eddie C. Kuo & Peter S. Chen. 120p. (Orig.). 1984. pap. 19.95 (0-7103-0064-6, Pub. by Kegan Paul Intl UK) Routledge Chapman & Hall.

Communication Policy & Planning in the American Cancer Society Public Education Program. Gerald E. Klonglan & Chun-Nan Lo. (Institute of Culture & Communication Case Studies: No. 8). xii, 61p. (Orig.). 1984. pap. text ed. 5.00 (0-86638-044-2) EW Ctr HI.

Communication Power in an Hour. A. D. Jeary. 81p. 1993. write for info. (1-883454-00-X) IBI TX.

Communication Power Tools: Getting to Winning Colors. Stefan Neilson & Shay Thoelke. LC 90-84510. (Personality Language & Winning Colors Ser.). (Illus.). 59p. 1990. student ed, spiral bd. 30.00 (1-880830-04-3) AEON-Hierophant.

Communication Problem Solving: The Language of Effective Management. I. McCall. 1990. text ed. 71.50 (0-471-92026-6) Wiley.

Communication Problems Correlated with College English & Communication. 4th ed. Marie M. Stewart & Kenneth Zimmer. 1982. pap. text ed. 18.75 (0-07-072847-X) McGraw.

Communication Problems in Autism. Ed. by Eric Schopler & Gary B. Mesibov. LC 85-3416. (Current Issues in Autism Ser.). 350p. 1985. 49.50 (0-306-41859-2, Plenum Pr) Plenum.

*__Communication Problems in Childhood.__ Rashmin C. Tamhne et al. 1995. pap. 27.95 (1-85775-098-5) Scovill Paterson.

Communication Problems of Children. Richmond et al. pap. 29.95 (0-8087-7644-4) Burgess MN Intl.

Communication Problems with College English & Communications. 5th ed. Marie M. Stewart et al. 272p. 1986. pap. text ed. 16.95 (0-07-072856-9) McGraw.

Communication Processes: Proceedings of Symposium, Washington, 1963. F. Geldard & M. Bouman. LC 64-24962. (NATO Conference Ser.: Vol. 4). 1965. 132.00 (0-08-010970-5, Pub. by Pergamon Repr UK) Franklin.

Communication Program Planning Book: A Plan Book for Speech-Language Pathologists. Linda B. Collins & Carol S. Spangler. 200p. (J). (gr. k-12). 1989. 19.95 (0-937857-10-6, 1567) Speech Bin.

An Asterisk (*) at the beginning of an entry indicates that the title is appearing in BIP for the first time.

C

An Asterisk (*) at the beginning of an entry indicates that the title is appearing in BIP for the first time.

1427

Communications. Robin Kerrod. LC 93-1913. (Let's Investigate Science Ser.). (Illus.). 64p. (J). (gr. 5 up). 1993. lib. bdg. 16.95 (*1-85435-624-0*) Marshall Cavendish.

Communications. Dan Mackie. (CHP Technology Ser.). (Illus.). 32p. (J). (gr. 4-9). 1987. pap. 5.95 (*0-88625-135-4*) Durkin Hayes Pub.

Communications. Philip Sauvain. LC 93-14869. (Breakthrough Ser.). (Illus.). 48p. (J). (gr. 5-8). 1993. lib. bdg. 22.80 (*0-8114-2333-6*) Raintree Steck-V.

Communications. rev. ed. Time-Life Books Editors. (Understanding Computers Ser.). (Illus.). 128p. 1990. write for info. (*0-8094-7578-2*); lib. bdg. write for info. (*0-8094-7579-0*) Time-Life.

Communications: A Positive Message from You. Trudy Seita. (Volunteer Management Ser.). 1989. 7.00 (*0-911029-17-6*) Heritage Arts.

Communications: Competencies & Contexts. Nancy Buerkel-Rothfuss. 432p. (C). 1944. student ed 8.95 (*0-685-09740-4*) McGraw.

Communications: Problems & Opportunities. Didactic Systems, Inc. Staff & Didactic Systems Staff. (Simulation Game Ser.). 1971. pap. 26.25 (*0-89401-008-5*) Didactic Syst.

Communications: The Transfer of Meaning. Don Fabun. 52p. 1987. pap. text ed. 6.00 (*0-02-477490-1*) Intl Gen Semantics.

Communications: Urban & Rural Survival. CWL. (Security & Survival Ser.). (Illus.). 50p. (Orig.). 1985. pap. 10.00 (*0-939856-49-2*) Tech Group.

Communications Across the Borders: The U. S., the Non-Aligned & the New Information Order. K. P. Lakshmi. (C). 1993. text ed. 16.00 (*81-7027-204-1*, Pub. by Radiant Pubs II) S Asia.

Communications after Two Thousand AD. Ed. by D. E. Davies et al. LC 92-46391. (Technology in the Third Millenium Ser.: Vol. 3). 1993. write for info. (*0-412-49550-3*) Chapman & Hall.

Communications Aide. Jack Rudman. (Career Examination Ser.: C-1201). 1994. pap. 23.95 (*0-8373-1201-9*) Nat Learn.

Communications-An Industry on the Move (Comms 86) Related Conference Proceedings. Ed. by J. E. Flood & C. J. Hughes. (IEE Conference Publications). 139p. 1986. 50.00 (*0-85296-329-7*, IC262) Inst Elect Eng.

C

Communications Analyst. Jack Rudman. (Career Examination Ser.: C-1202). 1994. pap. 27.95 (*0-8373-1202-7*) Nat Learn.

Communications & China's National Integration: An Analysis of People's Daily & Central Daily News on the China Reunification Issue. Shuhua Chang. (Occasional Papers-Reprints Series in Contemporary Asian Studies: No. 5). 120p. (Orig.). (C). 1986. pap. text ed. 8.00 (*0-942182-79-0*) Occasional Papers.

Communications & Cryptography: Two Sides of One Tapestry. Ed. by Richard E. Blahut et al. LC 94-20006. (International Series in Engineering & Computer Science, VLSI, Computer Architecture, & Digital Screen Processing). 504p. (C). 1994. lib. bdg. 89.95 (*0-7923-9469-0*) Kluwer Ac.

Communications & Cultural Analysis: A Religious View. Michael Warren. LC 92-192. 184p. 1992. text ed. 49.95 (*0-89789-288-7*, H288, Bergin & Garvey) Greenwood.

Communications & Education. Jack Rudman. (College Proficiency Examination Ser.: CPEP-20). 1994. pap. 23. 95 (*0-8373-5420-X*) Nat Learn.

Communications & History: Theories of Media, Knowledge, & Civilization. Paul Heyer. LC 87-29554. (Contributions to the Study of Mass Media & Communications Ser.: No. 10). 224p. 1988. text ed. 55. 00 (*0-313-26157-1*, HYC/, Greenwood Pr) Greenwood.

Communications & Information Handling Equipment & Services, 1979. Ed. by Chung I. Park. 244p. 1979. pap. 5.00 (*0-939670-07-0*) Info Digest.

Communications & Information in the Post Cold War Era, No. I-93-2: Forces & Trends. Oswald H. Ganley. 29p. (Orig.). 1993. pap. text ed. write for info. (*1-879716-02-X*) Ctr Info Policy.

Communications & Information Systems for Battlefield Command & Control. M. A. Rice & A. J. Sammes. Ed. by R. G. Lee & Frank Hartley. (Brassey's Battlefield Weapons Systems & Technology Ser.: Vol. 5). 276p. 1989. 40.00 (*0-08-036266-4*, Pub. by Brasseys UK); 25. 00 (*0-08-036267-2*, Pub. by Brasseys UK) Brasseys Inc.

Communications & Motivation Personal Growth Set. Learning Forum Staff. (YA). (gr. 8-12). 1988. 45.00 (*0-945525-14-1*) Supercamp.

Communications & Networking for the IBM PC, PS-2 & Compatibles. 4th ed. Larry Jordan & Bruce Campbell. (Illus.). pap. 29.95 (*0-13-157769-7*) Brady Compu Bks.

***Communications & Networking for the PC.** 5th ed. Lary Jordan & Bruce Churchill. LC 94-26887. (Illus.). 800p. 1994. pap. 35.00 (*1-56205-405-8*) New Riders Pub.

Communications & Networking with the IBM PC: Revised & Enlarged. 2nd ed. Larry Jordan. 352p. (C). 1987. 22. 95 (*0-89303-634-X*) P-H.

Communications & Networks: A Survey of Recent Advances. Ed. by Ian F. Blake & H. V. Poor. (Illus.). x, 433p. 1985. 108.00 (*0-387-96253-0*) Spr-Verlag.

Communications & Networks for the Year Two Thousand: Proceedings of SICON - ICIE '93. IEEE Singapore Section Staff. Ed. by IEEE Staff. 275p. 1993. pap. write for info. (*0-7803-1445-X*, 93TH0588-4); fiche write for info. (*0-7803-1446-8*, 93TH0588-4) Inst Electrical.

Communications & Political Development. Ed. by Lucian W. Pye. (Studies in Political Development: Vol. 1). 1963. 55.00 (*0-691-07504-2*); pap. 17.95 (*0-691-02152-X*) Princeton U Pr.

Communications & Power: Propaganda & the Press in the Indian Nationalist Struggle, 1920-1947. Milton Israel. (South Asian Studies: No. 56). 342p. (C). 1994. 69.95 (*0-521-42037-7*); pap. 24.95 (*0-521-46763-2*) Cambridge U Pr.

Communications & Power in Medieval Europe: The Carolingian & Ottonian Centures. Karl Leyser. Ed. by Timothy Reuter. LC 94-20663. 1994. 60.00 (*1-85285-013-2*) Hambledon Press.

***Communications & Power in Medieval Europe: The Gregorian Revolution & Beyond.** Karl Leyser. Ed. by Timothy Reuter. LC 94-25531. 1994. write for info. (*1-85285-113-9*) Hambledon Press.

Communications & Society: A Bibliography on Communications Technologies & Their Social Impact. Comp. by Benjamin F. Shearer & Marilyn Huxford. LC 83-12659. ix, 242p. 1983. text ed. 59.95 (*0-313-23713-1*, SHE/, Greenwood Pr) Greenwood.

Communications & the Arts see Comprehensive Dissertation Index 1861-1972

Communications & the Future. Ed. by Howard F. Didsbury, Jr. 400p. 1982. 14.50 (*0-930242-16-5*) World Future.

Communications & the 'Third World' Geoffrey W. Reeves. LC 92-13310. (Studies in Culture & Communication). 496p. 1993. 55.00 (*0-415-04761-7*, A7902); pap. 17.95 (*0-415-04762-5*, A7906) Routledge.

Communications & Transport. Mark Lambert & Jane Insley. (World of Science Ser.). (Illus.). 64p. 1985. 15.95 (*0-8160-1073-0*) Facts on File.

Communications Architecture for Distributed Systems. Rudolph J. Cypser. LC 76-52673. (Illus.). 1978. text ed. 52.75 (*0-201-14458-1*) Addison-Wesley.

Communications Architectures & Protocols: Proceedings of the SIGCOMM '88 Symposium on Communications Architectures & Protocols. (Communications Review Ser.: Vol. 18, No. 4). (Illus.). 352p. 1988. pap. text ed. 30.00 (*0-89791-279-9*, 533880) Assn Compu Machinery.

Communications at the Crossroads: The Gender Gap Connection. Ed. by Ramona Rush et al. LC 88-26757. (Communication & Information Science Ser.). 352p. (C). 1989. text ed. 55.00 (*0-89391-481-9*); pap. 19.95 (*0-89391-569-6*) Ablex Pub.

Communications at Work. 2nd ed. Desmond Evans. 250p. 1987. pap. 29.50 (*0-273-02759-X*, Pub. by Pitman Pub Ltd UK) Trans-Atl Phila.

***Communications Catalog No. 90001: One Hundred Fifty Communications Tools & Techniques.** L. F. Hutar. (OnePage Way Ser.). 12p. 1992. pap. 5.00 (*0-918896-94-0*) Hutar.

Communications Challenge: Personnel & PR Perspectives. Theon Wilkinson. 150p. (C). 1989. 95.00 (*0-85292-413-5*, Pub. by IPM Hse UK) St Mut.

Communications Circuits Ready-Reference. John Markus. (Illus.). 160p. 1982. pap. text ed. 22.95 (*0-07-040460-7*) McGraw.

Communications Committee. 154p. 1994. 8.00 (*0-317-01633-4*) NARUC.

Communications Conference, 1990: Electronic Communications in the 1990's - A New Era. Intro. by G. N. Rao. (Illus.). 246p. (Orig.). 1990. pap. 67.25 (*0-85825-507-3*) Accents Pubns.

Communications Electronics: Systems, Circuits, & Devices. Forrest Barker. (Illus.). 688p. 1986. text ed. 65.00 (*0-13-153883-7*) P-H.

Communications Examples for Child Health. Susan M. Thorton. (Johnson & Johnson Pediatric Round Table Ser.). 66p. (Orig.). 1983. pap. text ed. 6.00 (*0-931562-10-4*) J & J Consumer Prods.

Communications Factor in Office Decentralization see Progress in Planning

Communications for Careers. Leila R. Smith & Yolanda Grisolia. LC 93-13569. 1993. pap. text ed. write for info. (*0-13-369000-8*) P-H.

Communications for Community Associations. Janice Phagan. (GAP Report Ser.: Vol. 15). (C). 1991. reprint ed. pap. 14.50 (*0-944715-17-6*) CAI.

***Communications for Community Associations, GAP #15.** 3rd ed. Janice Phagan. (Illus.). 16p. (C). 1995. pap. 14. 50 (*0-944715-36-2*) CAI.

Communications for Cooperating Systems: OSI, SNA, & TCP-IP. Ed. by Rudolph J. Cypser. (Systems Programming Ser.). (Illus.). 736p. (C). 1991. text ed. 51. 75 (*0-201-50775-7*) Addison-Wesley.

Communications for Fire Fighting & Evaluation. Stanley J. Kravontka. 1976. 3.25 (*0-686-17607-3*, TR 76-5) Society Fire Protect.

Communications for Manufacturing: Proceedings of the Open Congress 4-7 September 1990, Stuttgart, Germany, CEC DG XIII: Telecommunications, Information Industries & Innovation. Ed. by S. Withnell & W. Van Puymbroeck. x, 287p. 1990. pap. 84. 00 (*0-387-19642-0*) Spr-Verlag.

Communications for Mobile Society: An Assessment of New Technology. Raymond Bowers. Ed. by Alfred M. Lee. LC 77-28119. 432p. reprint ed. pap. 123.20 (*0-317-09831-4*, 2021873) Bks Demand.

Communications for the Safety Professional. Robert B. Konikow & Frank E. McElroy. LC 75-11315. 528p. reprint ed. pap. 150.50 (*0-317-41990-0*, 2025680) Bks Demand.

Communications for Tomorrow. Ed. by Glen Robinson. 8.95 (*0-686-26005-8*) Aspen Inst Human.

Communications Formulas & Algorithms: For Systems Analysis & Design. C. Britton Rorabaugh. 1990. text ed. 40.00 (*0-07-053644-9*) McGraw.

Communications from Outer Space. 2nd ed. Ruth Norman & Charles Spaegel. (Illus.). 469p. 1991. 24.95 (*0-932642-80-2*) Unarius Acad Sci.

Communications in Girl Scouting. 104p. 1987. pap. 6.50 (*0-88441-455-8*, 26-187) Girl Scouts USA.

Communications in Marketing. Kenneth L. Rowe. (Occupational Manuals & Projects in Marketing Ser.). (Illus.). 1978. text ed. 12.28 (*0-07-054154-X*) McGraw.

Communications in Nursing: Communicating Assertively & Responsibly in Nursing. 2nd ed. Susan Smith. 384p. 1992. pap. 22.95 (*0-8016-6357-1*) Mosby Yr Bk.

***Communications in Small Groups: Theory, Process & Skills.** 4th ed. John F. Cragan & David W. Wright. LC 94-33080. 380p. 1994. pap. text ed. 37.00 (*0-314-04226-1*) West Pub.

Communications in the Family: Seeking Satisfaction in Changing Times. Judy C. Pearson. (C). 1990. pap. 19.50 (*0-06-045114-9*) HarpCollege.

Communications in the Rural Third World: The Role of Information in Development. Ed. by Emile G. McAnany. LC 79-21406. (Praeger Special Studies). 240p. 1980. text ed. 39.95 (*0-275-90519-5*, C0519, Praeger Pubs) Greenwood.

Communications in Transition: Issues & Debates in Current Research. Ed. by Mary S. Mander. LC 83-13985. 352p. 1983. text ed. 42.95 (*0-275-91040-7*, C1040, Praeger Pubs) Greenwood.

Communications Is a "People Process" for School Districts-Schools. 2nd rev. ed. Jean W. Huyler. LC 81-19398. (Illus.). 64p. (C). 1981. pap. 6.95 (*0-941554-01-5*, LC221.H89) EdCom.

Communications Law: Liberties, Restraints, & the Modern Media. John D. Zelezny. 540p. (C). 1993. text ed. 48. 95 (*0-534-13452-1*) Intl Thomson.

Communications Law, 1989, 3 vols., Set. (Patents, Copyrights, Trademarks, & Literary Property Ser.). 2035p. 1989. 35.00 (*0-317-99755-6*, G4-3839) PLI.

Communications Law, 1991, 3 vols., Set. (Patents, Copyrights, Trademarks, & Literary Property Ser.). 2651p. 1991. pap. text ed. 35.00 (*0-685-56905-5*, G4-3868) PLI.

Communications Law, 1992, 3 vols., Set. (Patents, Copyrights, Trademarks, & Literary Property Ser.: Vols. 346, 347-348). 2922p. 1992. 90.00 (*0-685-65512-1*, G4-3890) PLI.

Communications Licensing & Certification Examination: The Complete Tab Reference. Sam Wilson. 1994. pap. text ed. 29.95 (*0-07-070823-1*) McGraw.

Communications Licensing & Certification Examinations: The Complete Tab Reference. Sam Wilson & Joseph A. Risse. 1994. text ed. 44.95 (*0-07-070822-3*) McGraw.

***Communications Media in the Information Society.** Joseph Strubhaar & Robert LaRose. LC 95-6379. 1996. pap. 37.95 (*0-534-21534-3*) Intl Thomson.

***Communications Miracle: The Telecommunication Pioneers from Morse to the Information Superhighway.** John Bray. (Illus.). 350p. 1995. 28.95 (*0-306-45042-9*, Plenum Pr) Plenum.

***Communications Network Security.** Simonds. 1995. pap. text ed. 39.95 (*0-07-057634-3*) McGraw.

Communications Networking in Dense Electromagnetic Environments. Ed. by Wu. 1988. 38.00 (*0-89252-911-3*, 876) SPIE.

Communications Networks: A First Course. Jean Walrand. 480p. (C). 1991. text ed. 63.95 (*0-256-08864-0*, 19-3298-01) Irwin.

Communications Networks for Manufacturing. Juan Pimentel. 1990. text ed. 89.67 (*0-13-154402-0*) P-H.

Communications on Communication. 3rd ed. George M. Naimark. 135p. 1987. 19.95 (*0-911204-03-2*) Rajah.

Communications Operator. Jack Rudman. (Career Examination Ser.: C-2296). 1994. reprint ed. pap. 19.95 (*0-8373-2296-0*) Nat Learn.

Communications Outlook, 1990. OECD Staff. 54p. (Orig.). 1990. pap. 32.00 (*92-64-03336-X*) OECD.

Communications Outlook, 1993. OECD Staff. 164p. (Orig.). 1993. pap. 40.00 (*92-64-13841-2*) OECD.

***Communications Outlook, 1995.** 222p. (Orig.). 1995. pap. 83.00x (*92-64-14330-0*) OECD.

Communications Policy: Issues for the New Administration. Ed. by Claire Blue et al. (International Communications Report Ser.). 91p. (Orig.). 1993. pap. text ed. 30.00 (*0-89206-228-2*) CSI Studies.

Communications Policy & the Political Process. Ed. by John J. Havick. LC 83-1673. (Contributions in Political Science Ser.: No. 101). (Illus.). xi, 223p. 1983. text ed. 55.00 (*0-313-23234-2*, HCM, Greenwood Pr) Greenwood.

Communications Policy in Europe: Proceedings of the 4th Annual Communications Policy Research Conference, Held at Kronberg, FRG, October 25-27, 1989. Ed. by D. Elixmann & K. H. Neumann. (Illus.). xiii, 324p. 1990. pap. 65.00 (*0-387-52875-X*) Spr-Verlag.

Communications, Probability, Information Theory, Coding. Richard E. Blahut. (Illus.). 448p. (C). 1987. text ed. 75. 25 (*0-201-10709-0*, Adv Bk Prog) Addison-Wesley.

***Communications Programming for Windows 95.** Charles A. Mirho & Andre Terrisse. 1995. disk 39.95 (*1-55615-668-5*) Microsoft.

Communications, Reading Level 5: Today & Tomorrow, 6 bks. Carlienne Frisch & Bill Balcziak. (Illus.). 288p. (J). (gr. 4-8). 1989. lib. bdg. 77.70 (*0-86592-055-9*) Rourke Corp.

Communications, Reading Level 5: Today & Tomorrow, 6 bks., Set. Carlienne Frisch & Bill Balcziak. (Illus.). 288p. (J). (gr. 4-8). 1989. lib. bdg. 103.60 (*0-685-54148-7*) Rourke Corp.

Communications Receivers: Principles & Design. U. Rhode & T. T. Bucher. 608p. 1988. text ed. 65.00 (*0-07-053570-1*) McGraw.

Communications Receivers: Principles & Design. U. Rhode & T. Bucher. 1995. text ed. 64.95 (*0-07-053608-2*) McGraw.

Communications Research: Issues & Methods. J. Anderson. (Mass Communications Ser.). 416p. 1987. text ed. write for info. (*0-07-001651-8*) McGraw.

Communications Research: The Challenge of the Information Age. Ed. by Nancy W. Sharp. (Illus.). 240p. (C). 1988. 39.95 (*0-8156-2432-8*); pap. text ed. 19. 95 (*0-8156-2433-6*) Syracuse U Pr.

Communications Research, Nineteen Forty-Eight to Nineteen Forty-Nine. Ed. by Paul F. Lazarsfeld et al. LC 79-7005. (Perennial Works in Sociology Ser.). (Illus.). 1980. reprint ed. lib. bdg. 29.95 (*0-405-12103-2*) Ayer.

Communications Revolution. Frederick Williams. LC 81-18498. (Illus.). 291p. reprint ed. pap. 83.00 (*0-8357-4866-9*, 2037798) Bks Demand.

Communications Revolution & the Education of Americans. George W. Bonham et al. LC 80-66849. 64p. (Orig.). 1980. pap. 19.95 (*0-915390-24-8*, Pub. by Change Mag) Transaction Pubs.

Communications Satellite. Mark Williamson. LC 89-37838. (Illus.). 440p. 1990. 85.00 (*0-85274-192-8*) IOP Pub.

Communications Satellite Developments: Technology. Ed. by Gilbert E. Lavean & William G. Schmidt. LC 75-45243. (PAAS Ser.: Vol. 42). (Illus.). 419p. 1976. 54.95 (*0-915928-06-X*) AIAA.

Communications Satellite Handbook. Walter L. Morgan & Gary D. Gordon. LC 88-6077. 900p. 1989. text ed. 115. 00 (*0-471-31603-2*) Wiley.

Communications Satellite Systems. Ed. by P. L. Bargellini. LC 73-15613. (PAAS Ser.: Vol. 32). (Illus.). 480p. 1974. 54.95 (*0-262-02100-5*) AIAA.

Communications Satellite Systems Engineering. Wilbur L. Pritchard & Joseph A. Sciulli. (Illus.). 352p. (C). 1986. text ed. 42.95 (*0-685-10916-X*) P-H.

Communications Satellite Technology. Ed. by P. L. Bargellini. LC 73-15612. (PAAS Ser.: Vol. 33). (Illus.). 540p. 1974. 64.95 (*0-262-02101-3*) AIAA.

Communications Satellites. 3rd ed. Larry Van Horn. LC 87-82311. (Illus.). 300p. (Orig.). 1987. pap. text ed. 6.00 (*0-944543-01-4*) Grove Enterp.

Communications Services Management Industry Review, 1995. Mitchell B. Wander. 35p. 1992. pap. 203.00 (*0-940919-22-2*, 265) NA Telecomm Assn.

Communications Skills at the Keyboard. Mary Miller & James Miller. 94p. (Orig.). 1986. pap. text ed. 13.95 (*0-273-04236-X*) Trans-Atl Phila.

***Communications Skills for Information Systems.** Tony Warner. 256p. 1995. pap. 44.50 (*0-273-60910-6*, Pub. by Pitman Pub Ltd UK) Trans-Atl Phila.

Communications Skills for the Military Family. Carol B. Richardson. (Family Forum Library). 16p. 1994. 1.95 (*1-56688-167-6*) Bur For At-Risk.

Communications Source Book. McGraw-Hill Editors. (Science Reference Ser.). 352p. 1989. text ed. 49.50 (*0-07-045510-4*) McGraw.

Communications Specialist. (Career Examination Ser.: C-3586). 1994. pap. 27.95 (*0-8373-3586-8*) Nat Learn.

Communications Standard Dictionary. 2nd ed. Martin H. Weik. (Illus.). 1168p. 1989. text ed. 54.95 (*0-442-20556-2*) Van Nos Reinhold.

Communications Systems. 2nd ed. A. B. Carlson. (Electrical & Electronic Engineering Ser.). 1974. text ed. write for info. (*0-07-009957-X*) McGraw.

Communications Systems. 3rd ed. A. B. Carlson. (Electrical Engineering Ser.). 704p. 1985. text ed. write for info. (*0-07-009960-X*) McGraw.

Communications Systems Engineering. John G. Proakis & Masoud Salehi. LC 93-23109. 1993. text ed. 76.00 (*0-13-158932-6*) P-H.

Communications Technician. Jack Rudman. (Career Examination Ser.: C-2186). 1994. pap. 23.95 (*0-8373-2186-7*) Nat Learn.

Communications Technology & Social Policy: Understanding the New "Cultural Revolution" Ed. by George Gerbner & Larry P. Gross. LC 73-7563. 603p. reprint ed. pap. 171.90 (*0-317-09559-5*, 2051292) Bks Demand.

Communications Technology & the Elderly: Issues & Forecasts. Ruth E. Dunkle et al. 256p. 1984. 35.00 (*0-8261-4060-2*) Springer Pub.

Communications Technology in Education & Training. 1982. 20.00 (*0-317-04662-4*) Assn Ed Comm Tech.

Communications (Telephone, Telegraph, Radio, Newpaper) 130p. 1982. 6.95 (*0-916934-05-5*) Shawnee County Hist.

Communications Tomorrow: The Coming of the Post-Industrial Society. Ed. by Howard F. Didsbury, Jr. (Illus.). 160p. (C). 1982. pap. text ed. 16.95 (*0-930242-14-9*) Transaction Pubs.

Communications, Traffic Signals, & Traffic Control Devices, 1991. LC 92-5623. 145p. 1992. 26.00 (*0-309-05170-3*, R1324) Transport Res Bd.

Communications, Transport, Travel. Amos J. Peaslee. (International Governmental Organizations Constitutional Documents Ser.: Pt. 5). 1977. lib. bdg. 281.50 (*90-247-1826-0*) Kluwer Ac.

Communications Wiring & Interconnection. Fred J. Mcclimans. 352p. 1992. text ed. 40.00 (*0-07-044847-7*) McGraw.

Communications with Reality. S. Ramanda. 1993. pap. 12. 95 (*0-533-10354-1*) Vantage.

Communications Workbook: Spelling. Clark & Hashimoto. 119p. (C). 1984. pap. text ed. 12.25 (*0-89702-056-1*) Irwin.

Communications Workbook: Vocabulary. 4th ed. Hodges et al. 54p. (C). 1987. pap. text ed. 9.95 (*0-89702-058-8*) Irwin.

Communications '92: Communications Technology, Services & Systems - Getting It All Together. Intro. by Allan Sangster. (Illus.). 297p. (Orig.). 1992. pap. text ed. 77.00 (*0-85825-559-6*, Pub. by Inst Engrs Aust-EA Bks AT) Accents Pubns.

An Asterisk (*) at the beginning of an entry indicates that the title is appearing in BIP for the first time.

C

An Asterisk (*) at the beginning of an entry indicates that the title is appearing in BIP for the first time.

1429

Communism in Indian Politics. B. S. Gupta. 472p. 1978. 21.95 (0-318-37294-0) Asia Bk Corp.

Communism in Indian Politics. Bhabani Gupta. LC 73-190190. (Studies of the South Asian Institute). 455p. 1972. text ed. 56.00 (0-231-03568-3) Col U Pr.

***Communism in Italy & France.** Ed. by Donald L. Blackmer & Sidney Tarrow. LC 74-25612. reprint ed. pap. 180.00 (0-7837-9299-9, 2060038) Bks Demand.

***Communism in Punjab: A Study of the Movement up to 1967.** Gurharpal Singh. (C). 1994. text ed. 32.00 (81-202-0403-4, Pub. by Ajanta II) S Asia.

Communism in Rumania, 1944-1962. Ghita Ionescu. LC 75-46619. 378p. 1976. reprint ed. text ed. 55.00 (0-8371-8168-2, IOCR, Greenwood Pr) Greenwood.

***Communism in Sub-Saharan Africa: A Reappraisal.** Peter Duignan & L. H. Gann. LC 94-33511. (Essays Ser.: Vol. 8). 1994. pap. write for info. (0-8179-3712-9) Hoover Inst Pr.

Communism in the Bible. Jose P. Miranda. Tr. by Robert R. Barr. LC 81-16936. Orig. Title: Comunismo En la Biblia. 95p. (Orig.). reprint ed. pap. 27.10 (0-7837-5500-7, 2045270) Bks Demand.

Communism in the World Since 1945: An Annotated Bibliography. Susan K. Kinnell. (Clio Bibliography Ser.: No. 25). 450p. 1987. lib. bdg. 99.50 (0-87436-169-9) ABC-CLIO.

Communism in Transition: The End of the Soviet Empire. rev. ed. Amos Yoder. LC 92-37040. Orig. Title: Communist Systems & Challenges. 1993. pap. 27.50 (0-8448-1739-2, Crane Russak); boxed 49.50 (0-8448-1738-4, Crane Russak) Taylor & Francis.

Communism, Islam, & You. Haji Abu Idris. 65p. (Orig.). 1985. pap. 3.00 (1-56744-252-8) Kazi Pubns.

Communism, Revolution, & American Policy. Bernard S. Morris. LC 86-29214. xiv, 200p. 1987. lib. bdg. 37.00 (0-8223-0706-5); pap. 16.95 (0-8223-0760-X) Duke.

Communism Today: American Edition. Douglas Hyde. LC 72-12639. 182p. reprint ed. pap. 51.90 (0-317-29694-9, 2022065) Bks Demand.

Communism Unmasked. Abba Gordin. 1976. lib. bdg. 59.95 (0-8490-1649-5) Gordon Pr.

Communisme. Ed. by Institut Francais d'Histoire Sociale, Paris Staff. 378p. 1989. lib. bdg. 82.00 (3-598-10800-1) K G Saur.

Communism's Collapse, Democracy's Demise? The Cultural Context & Consequences of the East German Revolution. Laurence H. McFalls. LC 94-20535. 1995. 40.00 (0-8147-5521-6) NYU Pr.

***Communist - Socialist Practices in Capitalist U. S. A.** Afrikadzata Deku (Afrikan Culture Institute) Staff. LC 91-72664. (Research Ser.). 250p. 1994. write for info. (1-56454-008-1) Cont Afrikan.

Communist Agriculture: Farming in the Far East & Cuba. Ed. by Karl-Eugen Wadekin. 192p. 1990. 45.00 (0-415-04205-4, A4086) Routledge.

Communist Agriculture: Farming in the Soviet Union & Eastern Europe. Ed. by Karl-Eugen Wadekin. 448p. 1990. 112.00 (0-415-03870-7, A4090) Routledge.

Communist & Co-Operative Colonies. Charles Gide. Tr. by Ernest F. Row. LC 72-2939. reprint ed. 37.50 (0-404-10705-2) AMS Pr.

Communist & Marxist Parties of the World. Charles Hobday. 529p. 1986. lib. bdg. 52.50 (0-87436-476-0) ABC-CLIO.

Communist & Marxist Parties of the World. 2nd ed. 480p. 1990. lib. bdg. 85.00 (1-55862-073-7) St James Pr.

Communist & Postcommunist Political Systems: An Introduction. Stephen White et al. 300p. 1990. text ed. 39.95 (0-312-05019-4); pap. 16.95 (0-312-05020-8) St Martin.

Communist & Socialist Movement in India. Chandrika Singh. 1987. 34.95 (0-318-37205-3) Asia Bk Corp.

Communist & Socialist Movement in India. Chandrika Singh. 231p. (C). 1987. 27.00 (81-7099-031-9, Pub. by Mittal II) S Asia.

Communist Capitalism. Joseph W. Eaton & Yurij Lvov. (Illus.). 148p. (Orig.). 1991. pap. 29.95 (0-9631407-0-1) Micro-Mgmt Res.

Communist Collapse in Indonesia. Arnold C. Brackman. LC 70-77399. 1969. 6.95 (0-393-05377-6) Norton.

Communist Controversy in Washington: From the New Deal to McCarthy. Earl Latham. LC 66-14447. 460p. reprint ed. pap. 131.10 (0-685-09008-6, 2002785) Bks Demand.

Communist Councilman from Harlem. Benjamin J. Davis. LC 90-21426. (Illus.). 248p. 1991. reprint ed. pap. 6.95 (0-7178-0680-4) Intl Pubs Co.

Communist Coup in Czechoslovakia. Morton A. Kaplan. (Research Monograph: Center for International Studies, Woodrow Wilson School of Public & International Affairs: No. 5). 44p. reprint ed. pap. 25.00 (0-317-29732-5, 2015724) Bks Demand.

Communist Front? The Civil Rights Congress, 1946-1956. Gerald Horne. LC 85-45950. 1988. 60.00 (0-8386-3285-8) Fairleigh Dickinson.

Communist Guerilla Warfare. 1982. lib. bdg. 250.00 (0-87700-403-X) Revisionist Pr.

Communist Ideal in Hegel & Marx. David MacGregor. 320p. 1984. 40.00 (0-8020-5616-4); pap. 19.95 (0-8020-6816-2) U of Toronto Pr.

Communist Idealogy in Hungary: Handbook for Basic Research. Ervin Laszlo. (Sovietica Ser.: No. 23). 351p. 1966. lib. bdg. 89.00 (90-277-0056-7) Kluwer Ac.

Communist Ideology, Law & Crime: A Comparative View of the U. S. S. R. & Poland. Maria Los. 320p. 1988. text ed. 39.95 (0-312-15281-7) St Martin.

Communist International: Documents, 3 vols. Ed. by Jane Degras. 1971. Vol. 2: 1923-1928, 584p. 55.00 (0-7146-1555-2, Pub. by F Cass Pubs UK); Vol. 3: 1929-1943, 494p. 55.00 (0-7146-1556-0, Pub. by F Cass Pubs UK) Intl Spec Bk.

Communist League of America Nineteen Thirty-Two to Nineteen Thirty-Four. James P. Cannon. Ed. by Fred Stanton & Michael Taber. LC 85-72188. (James P. Cannon: Writings & Speeches). 480p. (Orig.). 1985. lib. bdg. 60.00 (0-913460-98-2); pap. 22.95 (0-913460-99-0) Pathfinder NY.

***Communist Left in Russia, 1918-1938.** Ian Hebbes. 1996. pap. 15.00 (1-899438-14-9, Pub. by Porcupine Bks UK) Humanities.

Communist Life Revisited. 3rd ed. William F. Settles. 186p. 1982. pap. 3.95 (0-686-36920-3) Settles Bks.

***Communist Logistics in the Korean War.** Charles R. Shrader. LC 95-9753. 1995. text ed. write for info. (0-313-29509-3, Greenwood Pr) Greenwood.

Communist Manifesto. Karl Marx & Friedrich Engels. Ed. by Leo Huberman. Bd. with Principles of Communism. LC 64-21175. LC 64-21175. 1964. 12.00 (0-85345-019-6, CL0196); Bd. with Set pap. 10.00 (0-85345-062-5); Bd. with Set pap. 12.00 (0-685-03407-0, PB0625) Monthly Rev.

Communist Manifesto. Ed. by Frederic L. Bender. (Critical Editions Ser.). (Orig.). (C). 1988. pap. text ed. 7.95 (0-393-95616-4) Norton.

Communist Manifesto. Karl Marx. 1992. pap. 3.95 (0-553-21406-3, Bantam Classics) Bantam.

Communist Manifesto. Karl Marx & Friedrich Engels. 1988. mass mkt. 4.99 (0-671-67881-7, WSP) PB.

Communist Manifesto. Karl Marx & Frederick Engels. 1976. 16.95 (0-89190-549-9, Am Repr) Amereon Ltd.

Communist Manifesto. Karl Marx & Friedrich Engels. Ed. by Samuel H. Beer. LC 55-10808. (Crofts Classics Ser.). 128p. (C). 1955. pap. text ed. write for info. (0-88295-055-X) Harlan Davidson.

Communist Manifesto. Karl Marx & Friedrich Engels. 48p. (C). 1948. pap. text ed. 1.75 (0-7178-0241-8) Intl Pubs Co.

Communist Manifesto. Karl Marx & Friedrich Engels. Ed. by David McLellan. (World's Classics Ser.). 128p. 1992. pap. 5.95 (0-19-282954-8) OUP.

***Communist Manifesto.** Karl Marx & Frederick Engels. (Illus.). 80p. Date not set. pap. write for info. (0-85315-732-4, Pub. by Lawrence & Wishart UK) Humanities.

Communist Manifesto. Karl Marx & Friedrich Engels. Tr. by Samuel Moore. 60p. 1978. reprint ed. pap. 3.95 (0-88286-043-7) C H Kerr.

Communist Manifesto. Karl Marx & Fredrich Engels. 1990. reprint ed. pap. 2.50 (0-87348-140-2) Pathfinder NY.

Communist Manifesto in Cartoon Form. 3rd ed. Jorge Rius. Tr. by Morris Edelson. (Illus.). reprint ed. pap. 1.50 (0-9600306-1-1) Quixote.

Communist Manifesto of Marx & Engels. Karl Marx & Friedrich Engels. 1985. mass mkt. 5.95 (0-14-044478-5, Penguin Classics) Viking Penguin.

Communist Military of the Vietnam War. Darrel R. Lulling. LC 80-83872. (Illus.). 1980. pap. 14.95 (0-912958-10-3); spiral bd. 8.95 (0-912958-09-X) MCN Pr.

Communist Movement in Egypt, 1920-1988. Tareq Y. Ismael & Rifa'at El-Sa'id. LC 90-32961. (Contemporary Issues in the Middle East Ser.). 280p. (C). 1990. text ed. 39.95x (0-8156-2497-2) Syracuse U Pr.

Communist Neo-Traditionalism: Work & Authority in Chinese Industry. Andrew G. Walder. LC 85-27093. 250p. (C). 1986. pap. 14.00 (0-520-06470-4) U CA Pr.

Communist Parties of Eastern Central Europe. Ed. by Stephen Fischer-Galati. LC 79-13016. 1979. text ed. 53.00 (0-231-03591-8) Col U Pr.

Communist Parties of Eastern Europe. Ed. by Stephen A. Fischer-Galati. LC 79-13016. 401p. reprint ed. pap. 114.30 (0-8357-4580-5, 2037489) Bks Demand.

Communist Parties of West Bengal. John Field & Marc Franda. LC 75-904675. (Studies in Electoral Politics in the Indian States Ser.). ix, 158p. 1974. 9.50 (0-88386-410-X) S Asia.

Communist Parties of Western Europe: A Comparative Study. R. Neal Tannahill. LC 77-94750. (Contributions in Political Science Ser.). 299p. 1978. text ed. 38.50 (0-313-20318-0, TCP/, Greenwood Pr) Greenwood.

Communist Party & Soviet Science. Stephen Fortescue. LC 86-10652. 248p. 1987. text ed. 36.00x (0-8018-3401-5) Johns Hopkins.

Communist Party & the Auto Workers' Unions. Roger Keeran. LC 84-15808. 1986. pap. 8.75 (0-7178-0639-1) Intl Pubs Co.

Communist Party in Spain. Victor Alba. Tr. by Vincent G. Smith. LC 82-19339. 475p. 1983. 49.95 (0-87855-464-5) Transaction Pubs.

Communist Party of Bulgaria. Joseph Rothschild. LC 72-174967. reprint ed. 26.00 (0-404-07164-3) AMS Pr.

Communist Party of China: Party Powers & Group Politics from the Third Plenum to the Twelfth Party Congress. Tien Hung-mao. (Occasional Papers-Reprints Series in Contemporary Asian Studies: No. 2-1984). 30p. (Orig.). (C). 1984. pap. 3.00 (0-942182-61-8) Occasional Papers.

Communist Party of China & Marxism, 1921-1985: A Self Portrait. Laszlo Ladany. (Publication Ser.: No. 362). 585p. 1992. pap. text ed. 24.95 (0-8179-8622-7) Hoover Inst Pr.

Communist Party of Poland: An Outline of History. M. K. Dziewanowski. LC 75-18050. (Russian Research Center Studies: No. 32). 431p. reprint ed. pap. 122.90 (0-7837-1690-7, 2057220) Bks Demand.

Communist Party of Poland 1918-1929: A Study in Political Ideology. Gabriele Simoncini. LC 93-35755. 272p. 1993. 89.95 (0-7734-9414-6) E Mellen.

Communist Party of the Soviet Union. Boris Meissner. Ed. by John S. Reshetar, Jr. Tr. by Fred Holling. LC 75-27684. (Foreign Policy Research Institute Ser.: No. 4). 276p. 1976. reprint ed. text ed. 59.75 (0-8371-8461-4, MECP) Greenwood.

Communist Party of the United States from the Depression to World War II. Fraser M. Ottanelli. LC 90-34391. 300p. (C). 1991. text ed. 45.00 (0-8135-1612-9); pap. text ed. 15.00 (0-8135-1613-7) Rutgers U Pr.

Communist Party Power in Kampuchea (Cambodia) Documents & Discussion. Ed. by Timothy M. Carney. LC 76-152199. (Southeast Asia Program, Cornell University, Data Paper Ser.: No. 106). 86p. reprint ed. pap. 25.00 (0-8357-2558-8, 2040249) Bks Demand.

Communist Party States: Comparative & International Studies. Ed. by Jan F. Triska. LC 69-15728. (C). 1969. pap. write for info. (0-672-61254-2, Bobbs) Macmillan.

Communist Party vs. the Cio: A Study in Power Politics. Max M. Kampelman. LC 78-156445. (American Labor Ser., No. 2). 1974. reprint ed. 23.95 (0-405-02929-2) Ayer.

Communist Policies Toward the Intellectual Class. Chalmers A. Johnson. LC 72-10698. 139p. 1973. reprint ed. text ed. 49.75 (0-8371-6613-6, JOCP, Greenwood Pr) Greenwood.

Communist Political Systems: An Introduction. 2nd ed. Stephen White et al. 310p. 1987. pap. 14.95 (0-685-18690-3) St Martin.

Communist Politics under the Knife: Surgery or Autopsy? Ronald J. Hill. 256p. 1990. text ed. write for info. (0-86187-025-5); text ed. write for info. (0-86187-026-3) Col U Pr.

Communist Power System. Ota Sik. LC 80-22011. 192p. 1981. 29.95 (0-03-044106-4, Praeger Pubs) Greenwood.

Communist Reformation: Nationalism, Internationalism, & Change in the World Communist Movement. Ed. by George Urban. LC 79-5326. 1979. text ed. 29.95 (0-312-15280-9) St Martin.

Communist Regimes in Comparative Perspective. Peter Ferdinand. 352p. (C). 1991. text ed. 75.00 (0-389-20975-9) B&N Imports.

Communist Regimes in Eastern Europe. 5th ed. Richard F. Staar. LC 81-84232. (Publication Ser.: No. 381). (Illus.). 369p. 1988. pap. text ed. 11.95 (0-8179-8812-2) Hoover Inst Pr.

Communist Resistance in Nazi Germany. Merson. (C). 1985. pap. 22.50 (0-85315-602-6, Pub. by Lawrence & Wishart UK) Humanities.

Communist Road to Power in Vietnam. William J. Duiker. LC 80-22098. (Special Studies on South & Southeast Asia). 394p. (C). 1982. pap. text ed. 23.50 (0-86531-505-1) Westview.

Communist Road to Power in Vietnam. 2nd ed. William J. Duiker. (C). 1996. pap. text ed. 21.95 (0-8133-8587-3) Westview.

***Communist States in the Era of Detente.** Ed. by Adam Romke & Derry Novak. 360p. 1995. lib. bdg. 33.00 (0-8095-4934-4) Borgo Pr.

Communist Strategies in Asia. Ed. by A. Doak Barnett. LC 75-32454. 293p. 1976. reprint ed. text ed. 38.50 (0-8371-8547-5, BACSA, Greenwood Pr) Greenwood.

Communist Strategy & Tactics in Czechoslovakia, 1918-48. Paul E. Zinner. LC 75-32464. 264p. 1976. reprint ed. text ed. 38.50 (0-8371-8550-5, ZICS, Greenwood Pr) Greenwood.

Communist Subversion of Czechoslovakia, 1938-1948: The Failure of Coexistence. Josef Korbel. LC 59-11080. 270p. reprint ed. pap. 77.00 (0-317-09541-2, 2011474) Bks Demand.

Communist Systems & Challenges see Communism in Transition: The End of the Soviet Empire

Communist Theory of Law. Hans Kelsen. viii, 203p. 1988. reprint ed. lib. bdg. 27.50 (0-8377-2337-X) Rothman.

Communist Tide in Latin America: A Selected Treatment. Robert Alexander et al. Ed. by Donald L. Herman. (Illus.). 215p. 1973. 10.00 (0-87959-072-6) U of Tex H Ransom Ctr.

Communist Uprisings of 1926-1927 in Indonesia: Key Documents. Ed. by Harry J. Benda & Ruth T. McVey. (Translation Ser.: No. 25). 1960. pap. 5.50 (0-87763-024-0) Cornell Mod Indo.

Communist World: Marxist & Non-Marxist Views. Ed. by Harry G. Shaffer. LC 67-21993. (Illus.). 1967. 29.50 (0-89197-093-2) Irvington.

Communistes ont Peur de la Revolution. Jean-Paul Sartre. (Coll. Contro Verses). pap. 6.95 (0-685-36556-5) Fr & Eur.

Communistic Settlements in the Jewish Colonization in Palestine. Yitzhak Elazari-Volkani. LC 75-6430. (Rise of Jewish Nationalism & the Middle East Ser.). 140p. 1975. reprint ed. 16.50 (0-88355-317-1) Hyperion Conn.

Communistic Societies of the United States: From Personal Visit & Observation. Charles Nordhoff. (Illus.). 439p. pap. 9.95 (0-486-21580-6) Dover.

Communistic Societies of the United States from Personal Visit & Observation. Charles Nordhoff. (Illus.). 439p. 1978. reprint ed. 24.00 (0-87928-092-1) Corner Hse.

Communists: The Story of Power & Lost Illusions, 1948-1991. Adam B. Ulam. 528p. 1992. text ed. 27.50 (0-684-19236-5) Macmillan.

Communists & Catholics in France, 1936-1939: The Politics of the Outstretched Hand. Francis J. Murphy. (University of Florida Social Sciences Monographs: No. 76). (Illus.). 168p. 1989. pap. text ed. 17.95 (0-8130-0936-7) U Press Fla.

Communists & Their Law: A Search for the Common Core of the Legal Systems of the Marxian Socialist States. John N. Hazard. LC 75-92770. 576p. reprint ed. pap. 164.20 (0-317-28200-X, 2020078) Bks Demand.

Communists Are Rebels see Leadership

Communists, Cowboys, & Queers: The Politics of Masculinity in the Work of Arthur Miller & Tennessee Williams. David Savran. 256p. (C). 1992. text ed. 39.95 (0-8166-2122-5); pap. 16.95 (0-8166-2123-3) U of Minn Pr.

Communists in Harlem During the Depression. Mark Naison. LC 84-48112. 384p. 1985. pap. 9.95 (0-8021-5183-3) Grove-Atltic.

Communists in Harlem During the Depression. Mark Naison. LC 82-10848. (Blacks in the New World Ser.). 384p. 1983. 34.95 (0-252-00644-5) U of Ill Pr.

Communists Like Us: New Lines of Alliance. Felix Guattari & Toni Negri. Ed. by Thomas Yemm. Tr. by Michael Ryan. (Foreign Agents Ser.). 192p. (Orig.). (C). 1990. pap. 6.00 (0-936756-21-7) Autonomedia.

Communists of Poland: An Historical Outline. rev. ed. Jan B. De Weydenthal. (Publication Ser.: No. 347). 296p. (C). 1987. pap. text ed. 10.95 (0-8179-8472-0) Hoover Inst Pr.

***Communitarian Defence of Liberalism: Emile Durkheim & Contemporary Social Theory.** Mark S. Cladis. 1994. pap. 15.95 (0-8047-2365-6) Stanford U Pr.

Communitarian Defense of Liberalism: Emile Durkheim & Contemporary Social Theory. Mark S. Cladis. LC 92-10125. (Series in Philosophy). 360p. (C). 1993. 45.00 (0-8047-2042-8) Stanford U Pr.

***Communitarian Ideology & Democracy.** Beng-Huat Chua. LC 94-39923. (Politics in Asia Ser.). 208p. 1995. 55.00x (0-415-12054-3, C0093) Routledge.

***Communitarian Moment: The Radical Challenge of the Northampton Association.** Christopher Clark. (Illus.). 280p. 1995. 27.50x (0-8014-2730-4) Cornell U Pr.

Communitarianism: A New Public Ethics. Markate Daly. 353p. (C). 1994. pap. 24.95 (0-534-20088-5) Intl Thomson.

Communitarianism: A Prospectus for Revolution. Lineaus H. Lorette. Ed. by Nancy Scales. 65p. (Orig.). 1990. pap. 10.00 (0-932225-01-2) Comm Pr.

Communitarianism & Individualism. Ed. by Shlomo Avineri & Avner De-Shalit. (Oxford Readings in Politics & Government Ser.). 204p. 1992. 56.00 (0-19-878027-3); pap. 19.95 (0-19-878028-1) OUP.

Communitarianism & Its Critics. Daniel Bell. 304p. (C). 1993. pap. 16.95 (0-19-827922-1) OUP.

Communitarianism, Liberalism, & Social Responsibility. Ed. by Creighton Peden & Yeager Hudson. LC 91-35244. (Studies in Social & Political Theory: Vol. 14). 336p. 1991. lib. bdg. 99.95 (0-7734-9656-4) E Mellen.

Communitas. Paul Goodman & Percival Goodman. (Morningside Bk.). (Illus.). 300p. 1990. text ed. 44.00 (0-231-07298-8); pap. text ed. 14.50 (0-231-07299-6) Col U Pr.

Communities. Gomer Pr. Staff. 388p. (C). 1987. 45.00x (0-86383-223-7, Pub. by Gomer Pr UK) St Mut.

Communities & Caring: The Mixed Economy of Welfare. Marjorie Mayo. LC 93-37356. 1994. text ed. 45.00 (0-312-12027-3) St Martin.

Communities & Conflict in Early Modern Colmar, 1575-1730. Peter G. Wallace. Ed. by Roger Chickering & Thomas A. Brady, Jr. LC 93-6916. (Studies in German Histories). (Illus.). 288p. (C). 1995. text ed. 55.00 (0-391-03822-2) Humanities.

Communities & Crime. Ed. by Albert J. Reiss, Jr. & Michael H. Tonry. LC 80-642217. (Studies in Crime & Justice Ser.: Vol. 8). viii, 421p. (C). 1986. lib. bdg. 27.50 (0-226-80802-5) U Ch Pr.

Communities & Crime. Ed. by Albert J. Reiss, Jr. & Michael H. Tonry. LC 80-642217. (Studies in Crime & Justice Ser.: Vol. 8). viii, 421p. (C). 1987. pap. text ed. 19.95 (0-226-80798-3) U Ch Pr.

***Communities & Electroates.** Dick Kooiman. (Comparative Asian Studies: Vol. 16). 80p. 1995. pap. 13.00 (90-5383-394-3) Paul & Co Pubs.

Communities & Families. Ed. by J. M. Golby. (Studying Family & Community History Ser.: No. 3). 240p. (C). 1994. 59.95 (0-521-46003-4); pap. 19.95 (0-521-46579-6) Cambridge U Pr.

***Communities & Sustainable Forestry in Developing Countries.** William Ascher. LC 94-29702. 1994. pap. 9.95 (1-55815-419-1) ICS Pr.

Communities & Their Development: An Introductory Study with Special Reference to the Tropics. Thomas R. Batten. LC 80-14699. (Illus.). vi, 248p. 1980. reprint ed. text ed. 35.00 (0-313-22447-1, BACD, Greenwood Pr) Greenwood.

Communities at Risk: Collective Responses to Technical Hazards. Stephen R. Couch & J. Stephen Kroll-Smith. LC 89-13557. (Worcester Polytechnic Institute Studies in Science, Technology, & Culture: Vol. 3). 328p. (C). 1991. text ed. 50.95 (0-8204-0712-7) P Lang Pubs.

Communities, Churches, & Children: Italian Immigrants & the Archdiocese of New York, 1880-1950. Mary E. Brown. (Migration & Ethnicity Ser.). (Illus.). 219p. (C). 1995. text ed. 19.50 (0-934733-56-2); pap. text ed. 14.50 (0-934733-57-0) Ctr Migration.

***Communities Directory: A Guide to Cooperative Living.** 2nd ed. Ed. by Fellowship for Intentional Community Staff et al. (Illus.). 440p. 1995. pap. 20.00 (0-9602714-3-0) Fllwshp Intent.

Communities in Action: A Comparative Study. Severyn T. Bruyn, Jr. 1963. pap. 16.95x (0-8084-0086-X) NCUP.

Communities in Britain: Social Life in Town & Country. rev. ed. Ronald Frankenburgh. (Modern Revivals in Sociology Ser.). 340p. (C). 1993. reprint ed. text ed. 59.95 (0-7512-0233-9, Pub. by Gregg Revivals UK) Ashgate Pub Co.

Communities in Conflict: Evangelicals & Jews. David A. Rausch. LC 91-24449. 216p. (Orig.). (C). 1991. pap. 14.95 (1-56338-029-3) TPI PA.

Communities in Economic Crisis: Appalachia & the South. Ed. by John Gaventa et al. (Labor & Social Change Ser.). 360p. (C). 1990. 34.95 (0-87722-649-0); pap. 18.95 (0-87722-650-4) Temple U Pr.

An Asterisk (*) at the beginning of an entry indicates that the title is appearing in BIP for the first time.

C

An Asterisk (*) at the beginning of an entry indicates that the title is appearing in BIP for the first time.

1431

Community Care: Caring for People - A Summary of the White Papers. Ian Vallender. (C). 1989. 30.00 (0-7855-0096-0, Pub. by Natl Inst Soc Work) St Mut.

Community Care: Funding from April 1993 - Report Together with Proceedings of Committee. HMSO Staff. (House of Commons Paper Ser.: No. 309-1). 50p. 1993. pap. 25.00 (0-10-297093-9, HM70939, Pub. by HMSO UK) UNIPUB.

Community Care: New Agendas & Challenges from the U. K. & Overseas. Ed. by David Challis et al. 330p. 1994. 59.95 (1-85742-208-2, Pub. by Arena UK) Ashgate Pub Co.

***Community Care: The Provision of Mental Health Services in North Wales.** Ed. by Charles Crosby & Margaret Barry. 284p. 1995. 54.95 (1-85628-531-6, Pub. by Avebury Pub UK) Ashgate Pub Co.

Community Care - Findings from Department of Health Funded Research, 1988-92. Ed. by Diana Robbins. 300p. 1993. pap. 45.00 (0-11-321567-3, HM15673, Pub. by HMSO UK) UNIPUB.

Community Care & the Future of Mental Health Service Provision. 2nd ed. Simon Goodwin. LC 93-24410. (Studies of Care in the Community). 247p. 1993. 59.95 (1-85628-479-4, Pub. by Avebury Pub UK) Ashgate Pub Co.

***Community Care: Caring for People: A Summary of the White Paper.** Ian Vallender. 1989. pap. 35.00 (0-902789-67-8, Pub. by Natl Inst Soc Work) St Mut.

Community Care for Mentally Handicapped Children: The Origins & Consequences of a Social Policy. Pamela Abbot & Roger Sapsford. (Contemporary Issues in Social Sciences Ser.). 80p. 1987. pap. 20.00 (0-335-15523-5, Open Univ Pr) Taylor & Francis.

***Community Care in Context.** NISW Staff. 1992. 90.00 (0-614-07447-9, Pub. by Natl Inst Soc Work) St Mut.

***Community Care in Practice.** 1995. 29.95 (0-7134-7076-3, Pub. by Batsford UK) Trafalgar.

Community Care in the Next Decade & Beyond. HMSO Staff. 116p. 1990. pap. 19.00 (0-11-321338-7, HM3873) UNIPUB.

***Community Care Practice & the Law.** Michael Mandelstam & Belinda Schwehr. LC 95-5881. 450p. 1995. pap. 32.00 (1-85302-273-X, Pub. by J Kingsley Pubs UK) Taylor & Francis.

Community Carnival: Sports Heroes. 1991. pap. 1.00 (0-8395-4211-9, 34211) BSA.

Community Centers (Physical Education) Jack Rudman. (Teachers License Examination Ser.: T-10). 1994. pap. 23.95 (0-8373-8010-3) Nat Learn.

Community Chest: A Case Study in Philanthropy. John R. Seeley et al. 600p. 1989. lib. bdg. 49.95 (0-88738-251-7) Transaction Pubs.

Community Child Health: An Action Plan for Today. Judith S. Palfrey. LC 94-8641. 328p. 1994. text ed. 55.00 (0-275-94696-7, Praeger Pubs) Greenwood.

Community Child Health & Pediatrics. Ed. by David Harvey et al. LC 94-11861. 1995. 250.00 (0-7506-1323-8) Buttrwrth-Heinemann.

Community Choice Nineteen Ninety-Four Edition: Selecting the Community That's Right for You. 1994. pap. 14.95 (0-9637638-0-6) Enterprise.

Community, Church & Healing. Ed. by R. A. Lambourne. (C). 1990. pap. 30.00 (0-85305-279-4, Pub. by J Arthur Ltd UK) St Mut.

Community Collaborations for Family Literacy Handbook. Shelley Quezada & Ruth S. Nickse. LC 93-21017. 181p. 1993. pap. 35.00 (1-55570-164-7) Neal-Schuman.

Community College Fact Book. American Council on Education Staff. (ACE-Oryx Series on Higher Education). (Illus.). 192p. 1988. 31.95 (0-02-900941-3, ACE-Oryx) Oryx Pr.

Community College Financing 1990: Challenges for a New Decade. David Honeyman et al. 72p. 1991. 20.00 (0-87117-228-3) Am Assn Comm Coll.

Community College Futures: From Rhetoric to Reality. Ed. by Neal A. Norris. 229p. (Orig.). 1989. pap. 16.95 (0-913507-09-1) New Forums.

Community College Libraries: Centers for Lifelong Learning. Ed. by Rosanne Kalick. 208p. 1992. 27.50 (0-8108-2607-0) Scarecrow.

Community College Library. Fritz Veit. LC 72-843. (Contributions in Librarianship & Information Science Ser.: No. 14). (Illus.). 221p. 1975. text ed. 49.95 (0-8371-6412-5, VEJ/, Greenwood Pr) Greenwood.

Community College Presidency. George B. Vaughan. 248p. 1986. text ed. write for info. (0-318-62000-6, ACE) Macmillan.

Community College Presidency. George B. Vaughan. (ACE-Oryx Series on Higher Education). 272p. 1986. 27.95 (0-02-933170-6, ACE-Oryx) Oryx Pr.

Community College Reference Services: A Working Guide for & by Librarians. Ed. by Bill Katz. LC 92-39703. (Illus.). 371p. 1992. 42.50 (0-8108-2615-1) Scarecrow.

Community Colleges: An Economic Development Resource. James Breagy. Ed. by Jenny Murphy. 38p. (Orig.). 1989. pap. 21.50 (0-317-04917-8) Natl Coun Econ Dev.

Community Colleges & Economic Development: Models of Institutional Effectiveness. Stephen G. Katsinas & Vincent A. Lacey. 1989. 18.50 (0-87117-202-X, 1214) Am Assn Comm Coll.

Community Colleges in the Nineteen Nineties. Glen Gabert. LC 91-60201. (Fastback Ser.: No. 318). (Orig.). 1991. pap. 1.25 (0-87367-318-2) Phi Delta Kappa.

Community Colleges, Public Libraries, & the Humanities: A Study of Cooperative Programs. Sandra L. Drake & Mary J. Lynch. LC 78-107550. 48p. reprint ed. pap. 25.00 (0-685-16372-5, 2027293) Bks Demand.

Community Colleges, the Future & SPOD (Staff, Program & Organizational Development) National Council of Staff, Program & Organizational Development Staff. Ed. by Richard J. Brass. LC 84-61248. 162p. (Orig.). 1984. pap. 6.95 (0-913507-01-6) New Forums.

Community Conflict & the Press. Philip J. Tichenor. LC 79-24401. (People & Communication Ser.: No. 8). 240p. reprint ed. pap. 68.40 (0-7837-1118-2, 2041648) Bks Demand.

Community, Conflict, Partition & Nationalism. Ed. by Colin H. Williams & Eleonore Kofman. 272p. 1989. 62.50 (0-415-00450-0) Routledge.

Community Consultation. Patrick I. O'Neill & Edison J. Trickett. LC 82-48062. (Jossey-Bass Social & Behavioral Science Ser.). 307p. reprint ed. pap. 87.50 (0-8357-4914-2, 2037844) Bks Demand.

Community Context. (C). 1989. 40.00 (0-685-52505-8, Pub. by Jordanhill College UK) St Mut.

***Community, Control & Change: Asia-Pacific Experiences in Community Development & Adult Education.** Adele Jones. 148p. (C). 1995. boxed, pap. text ed. 51.95 (1-85972-062-5, Pub. by Avebury Pub UK) Ashgate Pub Co.

Community Cooks. Ed. by Susan Cadogan. (Illus.). 216p. (Orig.). 1990. pap. text ed. write for info. (0-9627566-0-1) Amazon Pubns.

Community Corrections. Marilyn D. McShane & Wesley Krause. (Illus.). 530p. (C). 1993. text ed. write for info. (0-02-379765-7) Macmillan.

Community Corrections: A Community Field Approach. David E. Duffee & Edmund F. McGarrell. LC 89-80505. 352p. (C). 1990. pap. text ed. 21.95 (0-87084-210-2) Anderson Pub Co.

Community Corrections Acts for State & Local Partnerships. Mary K. Shilton. 92p. 1992. pap. 8.00 (0-929310-74-8, 185) Am Correctional.

Community Councils. Comp. by Richard Morris & Ross Zerchykov. (Working Papers). 21p. 1980. pap. 2.50 (0-317-00494-8) Inst Responsive.

Community Counseling. William E. Amos & David E. Williams. LC 71-154110. 244p. 1972. 8.50 (0-87527-092-1) Green.

Community Counseling. Judith A. Lewis & Michael D. Lewis. (Counseling, Human Services Ser.). 300p. (C). 1990. text ed. 38.95 (0-534-10248-4) Brooks-Cole.

Community Counseling Circles: A New Social Invention. Inst. for Social Inventions Staff. 1992. 49.00 (0-948826-00-2, Pub. by Inst Social Invent UK) St Mut.

Community CPR. American Red Cross Staff. LC 92-584. 1993. 6.50 (0-685-61104-3) Mosby Yr Bk.

Community Crime Prevention: An Annotated Bibliography. National Council on Crime & Delinquency Staff. 1983. 4.50 (0-318-02049-1) Natl Coun Crime.

Community Cultural Planning Work Kit, 2 vols. Louise K. Stevens. Ed. by John Fiscella. (Illus.). (Orig.). 1990. Vol. 1: Conducting a Community Cultural Assessment, 56p. pap. 15.00 (0-945464-05-3); Vol. 2: Developing a Strategic Cultural Plan, 58p. pap. 15.00 (0-945464-06-1) Univ MA Arts.

Community Cultural Planning Work Kit, 2 vols., Set. Louise K. Stevens. Ed. by John Fiscella. (Illus.). (Orig.). 1990. pap. 25.00 (0-945464-04-5) Univ MA Arts.

***Community, Culture, & Economic Development: The Social Roots of Local Action.** Meredith Ramsay. (Democracy in American Politics Ser.). 160p. (C). 1995. text ed. 49.50x (0-7914-2749-8); pap. 16.95x (0-7914-2750-1) State U NY Pr.

Community Culture & National Change. Incl. Political Modernization in Three Guatemalan Indian Communities. Roland H. Ebel. (Illus.). 77p. 1969. 5.00 (0-685-19989-4); Change of Officials in Tz'ontahal, Chiapas, Mexico. 1970. 4.00 (0-685-19990-8); Popular Medicine in Puntarenas, Costa Rica: Urban & Societal Features. Miles Richardson & Barbara Bode. 1971. 2.50 (0-685-19991-6); (Publication Ser.: No. 24). 275p. 1971. 25.00 (0-939238-26-8) Tulane MARI.

Community Dental Health. 3rd ed. Jong. 347p. 1993. pap. 33.95 (0-8016-6387-3) Mosby Yr Bk.

Community Design & the Culture of Cities: The Crossroad & the Wall. Eduardo E. Lozano. (Illus.). 300p. (C). 1990. 79.95 (0-521-38067-7); pap. 29.95 (0-521-38979-8) Cambridge U Pr.

Community Design Primer. Randolph T. Hester, Jr. 1990. pap. text ed. 12.00 (0-934203-06-7) Ridge Times Pr.

Community Development: Learning & Action. Hayden Roberts. LC 78-12986. (Canadian University Paperbooks Ser.: No. 224). 219p. reprint ed. pap. 62.50 (0-685-15925-6, 2056125) Bks Demand.

Community Development Administrator. Jack Rudman. (Career Examination Ser.: C-1420). 1994. pap. 39.95 (0-8373-1420-8) Nat Learn.

Community Development & Human Reproductive Behavior. Sawon Hong. 196p. 1979. text ed. 12.00 (0-8248-0685-9, Korea Devel Inst) UH Pr.

Community Development & the Revolutionary Transition in 18th-Century Lancaster County, Pennsylvania. Rodger C. Henderson. (Studies in Historical Demography). 350p. 1990. reprint ed. 25.00 (0-8240-3996-3) Garland.

Community Development As a Process. Ed. by Lee J. Cary. LC 74-130669. 224p. 1983. reprint ed. pap. 14.50 (0-8262-0415-5) U of Mo Pr.

Community Development Assistant. Jack Rudman. (Career Examination Ser.: C-904). 1994. pap. 27.95 (0-8373-0904-2) Nat Learn.

Community Development Block Grant Budgetary & Financial Management. Municipal Finance Officers Association Staff. 134p. 1978. 14.95 (0-686-84366-5) Municipal.

Community Development Corporations. Barbara Block. Ed. by Michael Segel. 13p. (Orig.). 1977. pap. 8.00 (0-317-04853-8) Natl Coun Econ Dev.

Community Development for the City of Norfolk, Nebraska. Jack Ruff. 28p. (Orig.). 1980. pap. 2.50 (1-55719-033-X) U NE CPAR.

Community Development Housing Analyst. Jack Rudman. (Career Examination Ser.: C-905). 1994. pap. 34.95 (0-8373-0905-0) Nat Learn.

Community Development in America. Ed. by James A. Christenson & Jerry W. Robinson. LC 80-11046. 255p. reprint ed. pap. 72.70 (0-317-55360-7, 2029169) Bks Demand.

Community Development in Nepal. Madhav P. Sharma. 171p. 1964. 15.00 (0-318-03451-4) Am-Nepal Ed.

Community Development in Nepal: A Critical Analysis. Madhav P. Sharma. (MA Research Paper Ser.). 162p. 1971. 15.00 (0-317-01484-6) Am-Nepal Ed.

Community Development in Perspective. Ed. by James A. Christenson & Jerry W. Robinson, Jr. LC 88-37954. (Illus.). 412p. (C). 1989. text ed. 38.95 (0-8138-1474-X); pap. text ed. 23.95 (0-8138-1473-1) Iowa St U Pr.

Community Development Initiative: A Story of the Manor Employment Project in Sheffield. Mike Pedler et al. 256p. 1990. text ed. 59.95 (0-566-07124-X) Ashgate Pub Co.

Community Development Needs in Rural Nebraska & Iowa. Thomas C. Moss & Micheal G. O'Connor. 16p. (Orig.). 1975. pap. 1.50 (1-55719-026-7) U NE CPAR.

Community Development Program Analyst. Jack Rudman. (Career Examination Ser.: C-903). 1994. pap. 34.95 (0-8373-0903-4) Nat Learn.

Community Development Program Technician. Jack Rudman. (Career Examination Ser.: C-902). 1994. pap. 29.95 (0-8373-0902-6) Nat Learn.

Community Development Project: National & Local Strategies for Improving the Delivery of Services. Harry Specht. 1976. 25.00 (0-685-08684-4, Pub. by Natl Inst Soc Work) St Mut.

Community Development Project Director. Jack Rudman. (Career Examination Ser.: C-909). 1994. pap. 39.95 (0-8373-0909-3) Nat Learn.

Community Development Project Supervisor. Jack Rudman. (Career Examination Ser.: C-908). 1994. pap. 34.95 (0-8373-0908-5) Nat Learn.

Community Development Research: Concepts, Issues & Strategies. Ed. by Edward Blakely. LC 78-11568. 224p. 1979. 36.95 (0-87705-334-0); pap. 20.95 (0-87705-348-0) Human Sci Pr.

Community Development Specialist. Jack Rudman. (Career Examination Ser.: C-1421). 1994. pap. 29.95 (0-8373-1421-6) Nat Learn.

Community Disaster Education Guide. (Illus.). 97p. (Orig.). (C). 1993. pap. text ed. 35.00 (1-56806-773-9) Diane Pub.

Community Disorders & Policing. Tony Marshall. 300p. 1992. 70.00 (1-871177-25-1, Pub. by Whiting & Birch UK); pap. text ed. 29.95 (1-871177-26-X, Pub. by Whiting & Birch UK) Paul & Co Pubs.

Community, Diversity, & a New World Order: Essays in Honor of Inis L. Claude, Jr. Ed. by Kenneth W. Thompson. LC 94-1354. (Miller Center Series on a New World Order: Vol. 2). 330p. Date not set. lib. bdg. 61.00 (0-8191-9482-4); pap. text ed. 26.50 (0-8191-9483-2) U Pr of Amer.

Community Documentation Centre on Industrial Risk Comparison of Selected, EUR 14636. S. Harris et al. 150p. 1992. pap. 25.00 (92-826-4737-4, CL-NA-14636-EN, Pub. by Europ Com) UNIPUB.

Community Dynamics & Mental Health. D. C. Klein. LC 68-8105. 242p. reprint ed. 69.00 (0-8357-9859-3, 2017408) Bks Demand.

***Community Dynamics of Small Mammals in Mature & Logged Atlantic White Cedar Swamps of the New Jersey Pine Barrens.** Lyda J. Craig & David S. Dobkin. (Bulletin Ser.: No. 487). (Illus.). 32p. 1994. 8.95 (1-55557-229-4) NYS Museum.

Community Ecology. Ed. by A. Hastings. (Lecture Notes in Biomathematics Ser.: Vol. 77). vii, 131p. 1988. pap. 28.00 (0-387-50398-6) Spr-Verlag.

Community Ecology. R. J. Putman. LC 93-33026. 178p. 1993. write for info. (0-412-56690-7, Chap & Hall NY); pap. 29.95 (0-412-54500-4, Chap & Hall NY) Chapman & Hall.

Community Ecology & Salamander Guilds. Nelson G. Hairston, Sr. (Cambridge Studies in Ecology). (Illus.). 320p. 1987. 59.95 (0-521-32578-1) Cambridge U Pr.

Community Ecology of Coral Cay: A Study of One-Tree Island, Great Barrier Reef, Australia. H. Heatwolfe et al. (Monographiae Biologicae: No. 43). 400p. 1981. lib. bdg. 158.00 (90-6193-096-0) Kluwer Ac.

Community Ecology of Neotropical Kingfishers. J. V. Remsen, Jr. LC 90-46525. (Publications in Zoology: Vol. 124). (Illus.). 128p. 1991. pap. 13.00 (0-520-09673-8) U CA Pr.

Community Economic Analysis: A How-to Manual. Ron Hustedde et al. 90p. 1984. pap. text ed. 3.50 (0-685-60769-0) NCRCRD.

Community Economic Analysis: A How-to Manual. Ronald J. Hustedde et al. Ed. by Julie Stewart. 72p. (C). 1993. student ed write for info. (0-936913-06-1, RRD 141) NCRCRD.

Community Economic Base Study. Charles M. Tiebout. LC 62-22333. 216p. 1962. pap. 2.50 (0-87186-216-6) Comm Econ Dev.

Community Economic Development: A Case Study from Austin. Contrib by Robert Wilson. (Policy Research Project Report Ser.: No. 42). 81p. 1980. 5.50 (0-89940-644-0) LBJ Sch Pub Aff.

Community Economic Development: Building Capacity Through Stronger Partnerships. Wayne Welch. Ed. by Jenny Murphy. 26p. (Orig.). 1988. pap. 18.00 (0-317-04849-X) Natl Coun Econ Dev.

Community Economic Development: Policy Formation in the U. S. & U. K. Ed. by David Fasenfest. LC 92-4985. (Policy Studies Organization). 230p. 1993. text ed. 45.00 (0-312-08059-X) St Martin.

Community Economic Development & Employee Ownership: A Resource Guide. Matthew Kumin & Corey Rosen. Ed. by Karen M. Young. 82p. (Orig.). (C). 1988. pap. 25.00 (0-926902-09-1) NCEO.

Community Economic Vitality: Major Trends & Selected Issues. Ed. by Gene F. Summers et al. 85p. 1988. pap. write for info. (0-936913-01-0) NCRCRD.

Community Economics: Economic Structure & Change in Smaller Communities. Ron Shaffer. LC 88-6149. (Illus.). 334p. (C). 1989. text ed. 37.95 (0-8138-0031-5) Iowa St U Pr.

Community Education: Building Learning Communities. Decker, Larry E. & Associates Staff. (Illus.). 24p. (C). 1990. pap. text ed. 2.95 (0-932399-05-3) Natl Comm Ed.

Community Education: Connections & Contradictions. Garth Allen et al. 272p. 1987. 90.00 (0-335-10288-3, Open Univ Pr); pap. 32.00 (0-335-10287-5, Open Univ Pr) Taylor & Francis.

Community Education: Managing for Success. American Association of School Administrators Staff. 9.95 (0-686-36532-1, 021-00202) Am Assn Sch Admin.

Community Education & the Western World. Ed. by Cyril Poster & Angelika Kruger. 288p. 1990. 52.50 (0-415-03140-0, A4320); pap. 18.95 (0-415-04715-3, A4324) Routledge.

Community Education in the Third World. Ed. by Cyril Poster & Jurgen Zimmer. LC 92-4405. 256p. 1992. 69.95 (0-415-04209-7, A5928) Routledge.

Community Efforts to Improve Local Schools: Pt. I, A Case Study of District Planning. Elizabeth Colon. 21p. (Orig.). 1983. pap. 5.00 (0-88156-013-8) Comm Serv Soc NY.

Community Efforts to Improve Local Schools: Pt. II, An Inventory of Programs & Resources in New York City, Pt. 2. Robyn Govan-Kleckley. 23p. (Orig.). 1983. pap. 5.00 (0-88156-014-6) Comm Serv Soc NY.

Community Elite & the Public Library: Uses of Information in Leadership. Pauline Wilson. LC 76-15336. (Contributions in Librarianship & Information Science Ser.: No. 18). 173p. 1977. text ed. 49.95 (0-8371-9031-2, WCE/, Greenwood Pr) Greenwood.

Community Emergency Management: Development & Strategies. Patrick Lavalla et al. (Illus.). 1987. ring bd. 25.00 (0-913724-39-4) Emerg Response Inst.

***Community Empowerment: A Reader in Participation & Development.** Ed. by Gary Craig & Marjorie Mayo. 240p. (C). 1995. text ed. 59.95 (1-85649-337-7, Pub. by Zed Books UK); pap. 25.00 (1-85649-338-5, Pub. by Zed Books UK) Humanities.

Community Energy Strategies. 484p. 1982. 35.00 (0-317-36381-6, 4001); 25.00 (0-317-36382-4) Natl League Cities.

***Community Energy Workbook: A Guide to Building a Sustainable Economy.** Alice Hubbard & Clay Fong. (Illus.). 276p. (Orig.). 1995. pap. 16.95 (1-881071-04-9) Rocky Mtn Inst.

Community Food Webs: Data & Theory. J. E. Cohen et al. Ed. by S. A. Levin et al. (Biomathematics Ser.: Vol. 20). 312p. 1990. 79.00 (0-387-51129-6) Spr-Verlag.

Community for Life. Ulrich Eggers. LC 87-17817. (Illus.). 192p. (Orig.). 1988. pap. 10.95 (0-8361-3451-6) Herald Pr.

Community Full Employment. 76p. 1981. 8.00 (0-317-36374-3, 6001); 4.00 (0-317-36375-1) Natl League Cities.

Community Garden Book. Larry Sommers. 121p. 1980. pap. 8.95 (0-915873-01-X, 1-1022) Natl Gardening Assn.

Community, Gender & Individual Identity: English Writing, 1360-1430. David Aers. 256p. 1989. 49.95 (0-415-01378-X); pap. 15.95 (0-415-01379-8) Routledge.

Community Government in War Relocation Centers see U. S. War Relocation Authority

Community Guide to Money. 3.50 (0-944253-81-4) Inst Dev Indian Law.

Community Guide to Social Impact Assessment. Rabel J. Burdge. 200p. (Orig.). (C). Date not set. pap. text ed. 18.95 (0-941042-17-0) Soc Ecology Pr.

Community Health. 6th ed. Green. (Illus.). 624p. (C). 1989. 38.95 (0-8016-3308-7) Mosby Yr Bk.

Community Health. 7th ed. Green. 624p. 1993. 39.95 (0-8016-7898-6) Mosby Yr Bk.

Community Health Analysis: A Global Awareness at the Local Level. 2nd rev. ed. G. E.Alan Dever. (Health Care Administration Ser.). (Illus.). 416p. (C). 1991. 49.00 (0-8342-0191-7) Aspen Pub.

Community Health & Mental Health Care Delivery for North American Indians. E. Fuller Torrey et al. (Health Problems of N. A. Indians Ser.: Vol. 3). 1975. 19.00 (0-8422-7218-6) Irvington.

***Community Health Care Nursing.** Ed. by David Sines. LC 95-1289. 1995. pap. 13.99 (0-632-03856-X) Blackwell Sci.

Community Health Concepts & Issues. Wigley & Cook. 1975. pap. 33.75 (0-442-21633-5) Jones & Bartlett.

Community Health Education: Settings, Roles & Skills. 3rd ed. Donald J. Breckon et al. 384p. (C). 1989. 47.00 (0-8342-0068-6) Aspen Pub.

Community Health Education: Settings, Roles, & Skills for the 21st Century. 3rd ed. Donald J. Breckon et al. LC 93-42924. 380p. 1994. 47.00 (0-8342-0526-2) Aspen Pub.

Community Health Information Networks: Creating the Health Care Data Highway. Ed. by Ralph T. Wakerly. LC 94-12428. 200p. 1994. 56.00 (1-55648-121-7, 093104) AHPI.

An Asterisk (*) at the beginning of an entry indicates that the title is appearing in BIP for the first time.

An Asterisk (*) at the beginning of an entry indicates that the title is appearing in BIP for the first time.

1433

*Community of Nations. Ed. by Mia Adjali & Deborah Storms. 1995. 7.95 (0-377-00292-5) Friendship Pr.

Community of One: Masculine Autobiography & Autonomy in Nineteenth-Century Britain. Martin A. Danahay. (SUNY Series, The Margins of Literature). 232p. (C). 1993. 64.50 (0-7914-1511-2); pap. 21.95 (0-7914-1512-0) State U NY Pr.

Community of Science in Europe. Mark N. Franklin. 300p. 1989. text ed. 58.95 (0-566-05632-1, Pub. by Dartmth Pub UK) Ashgate Pub Co.

Community of Self. rev. ed. Na'im Akbar. 80p. 1985. pap. 6.00 (0-935257-00-4) Mind Prods Assocs.

Community of Strangers. A. F. Robertson. (C). 1979. pap. text ed. 19.95 (0-85967-715-X, Pub. by Scolar Pr UK) Ashgate Pub Co.

Community of Suffering & Struggle: Women, Men, & the Labor Movement in Minneapolis, 1915-1945. Elizabeth Faue. LC 90-48929. (Gender & American Culture Ser.). (Illus.). xx, 304p. (C). 1991. 42.50 (0-8078-1945-X); pap. 15.95 (0-8078-4307-5) U of NC Pr.

Community of the Abandoned: Stories of Salty Saints. Micheal Elliott. LC 88-43048. 176p. (Orig.). 1989. pap. 8.95 (0-940989-47-6) Meyer Stone Bks.

Community of the Ark. Mark Shepard. (Illus.). 64p. (Orig.). 1993. pap. 8.00 (0-943734-28-2) Ocean Tree Bks.

Community of the Beloved Disciple. Raymond E. Brown. LC 78-65894. 204p. 1979. pap. 9.95 (0-8091-2174-3) Paulist Pr.

Community of the Blind: Applying the Theory of Community Formation. Yoon H. Kim. LC 70-117059. (American Foundation for the Blind Research Ser.: No. 22). 161p. reprint ed. pap. 45.90 (0-7837-0130-6, 2040414) Bks Demand.

Community of the Book: A Directory of Selected Organizations & Programs. Ed. by John Y. Cole. 1987. 29.95x (0-88738-145-6) Transaction Pubs.

Community of the Book: A Directory of Selected Organizations & Programs. 2nd ed. Comp. by Maurvene D. Williams. LC 89-600030. 140p. 1989. 8.95 (0-8444-0635-X) Lib Congress.

Community of the Book: A Directory of Selected Organizations & Programs. 3rd ed. Comp. by Maurvene D. Williams. LC 93-37094. 1993. pap. 8.95 (0-8444-0807-7) Lib Congress.

Community of the Free. Yves R. Simon. Tr. by Willard R. Trask. 196p. 1985. reprint ed. pap. text ed. 17.50 (0-8191-4338-3) U Pr of Amer.

Community of the Future. Emanuel Lasker. 1976. lib. bdg. 59.95 (0-8490-1650-9) Gordon Pr.

Community of the Future & the Future of Community. Arthur E. Morgan. 1957. pap. 2.00 (0-910420-02-5) Comm Serv OH.

Community of the King. Howard A. Snyder. LC 77-6030. (Illus.). 1977. pap. 11.99 (0-87784-752-5, 752) InterVarsity.

Community of the New Age: Studies in Mark's Gospel. Howard C. Kee. LC 83-17416. xii, 225p. 1983. 16.95 (0-86554-100-0, MUP/H92) Mercer Univ Pr.

Community of the Renewed Covenant: The Notre Dame Symposium on the Dead Sea Scrolls. Ed. by Eugene Ulrich & James VanderKam. (C). 1994. text ed. 29.95 (0-268-00802-7) U of Notre Dame Pr.

Community of the Spirit: How the Church Is in the World. C. Norman Kraus. 224p. (Orig.). (C). 1993. pap. 14.95 (0-8361-3619-5) Herald Pr.

Community of the Young. Robert E. Mason. (Occasional Paper: No. 8). 1975. pap. 3.00 (0-933669-11-9) Soc Profs Ed.

Community of Those Who Have Nothing in Common. Alphonso Lingis. LC 93-23955. (Studies in Continental Thought). 1994. 29.95 (0-253-33438-1); pap. 12.95 (0-253-20852-1) Ind U Pr.

Community of Twelve & Drug Demand Comparative Study of Legislation, No. EUR 13447. B. Leroy. 188p. 1991. pap. 19.00 (92-826-0594-9, CD-NA-13447-2A-C) UNIPUB.

Community of Voices: Reading & Writing in the Disciplines. Toby Fulwiler & Arthur W. Biddle. (Illus.). 1008p. (Orig.). (C). 1992. pap. write for info. (0-02-340135-4) Macmillan.

Community of Women & Men in the Church: A Report of the World Council of Churches' Conference, Sheffield, England, 1981. World Council of Churches' Conference Staff. 215p. reprint ed. pap. 61.30 (0-7837-6006-X, 2045816) Bks Demand.

Community of Writers. Peter Elbow & Patricia Belanoff. 400p. (C). 1989. pap. text ed. write for info. (0-07-557219-2) McGraw.

Community of Writers: A Workshop Course in Writing. 2nd ed. Peter Elbow & Patricia Belanoff. 1994. pap. text ed. write for info. (0-07-019693-1) McGraw.

Community of Writers: Teaching Writing in the Junior & Senior High School. Steven Zemelman & Harvey Daniels. LC 88-790. ix, 286p. (Orig.). (C). 1988. pap. text ed. 21.00 (0-435-08463-1, 08463) Heinemann.

Community on the American Frontier: Separate but Not Alone. Robert V. Hine. LC 80-5238. (Illus.). 292p. 1985. 24.95 (0-8061-1678-1); pap. 12.95 (0-8061-1922-5) U of Okla Pr.

Community Orchestra: A Handbook for Conductors, Managers, & Boards. James Van Horn. LC 78-60531. (Illus.). 127p. 1979. text ed. 42.95 (0-313-20562-0, VCO/, Greenwood Pr) Greenwood.

Community Organization: Action & Inaction. Floyd Hunter et al. LC 77-22052. 268p. 1977. reprint ed. text ed. 59. 75 (0-8371-9788-0, HUCOR, Greenwood Pr) Greenwood.

Community Organization: Traditional Principles & Modern Applications. Ed. by Robert B. Patton & William B. Cissell. (Illus.). 372p. (C). 1990. pap. text ed. 36.50 (0-9625490-1-0) Latchpins Pr.

Community Organization & Development. Herb Rubin & Irene Rubin. 480p. (C). 1986. pap. write for info. (0-675-20349-X, Merrill Pub Co) Macmillan.

*Community Organization & Social Administration: Advances, Trends, & Emerging Principles. Ed. by Terry Mizrahi & John Morrison. LC 92-47278. (Illus.). 254p. 1992. pap. 17.95 (1-56024-277-9) Haworth Pr.

Community Organization & Social Administration: Advances, Trends, & Emerging Principles. Ed. by Terry Mizrahi & John Morrison. LC 92-8960. (Illus.). 254p. 1992. lib. bdg. 49.95 (1-56024-257-4) Haworth Pr.

Community Organization Curriculum in Graduate Social Work Education: Report & Recommendations. 1970. 4.00 (0-318-35339-3) Coun Soc Wk Ed.

Community Organization for Urban Social Change: A Historical Perspective. Ed. by Robert M. Fisher & Peter Romanofsky. LC 80-21498. (Illus.). 280p. 1981. text ed. 38.50 (0-313-21427-1, RCO/, Greenwood Pr) Greenwood.

Community Organization Specialist. (Career Examination Ser.: C-3292). 1994. pap. 27.95 (0-8373-3292-3) Nat Learn.

*Community Organization Specialist (Urban Renewal) (Career Examination Ser.: Series 1). Date not set. pap. 29.95 (0-8373-1206-X) Nat Learn.

Community Organization Workbook. 68p. 1976. 2.50 (0-318-15303-3) Natl Coun Alcoholism.

Community Organizations: Studies in Resource Mobilization & Exchange. Ed. by Carl Milofsky. (Yale Studies in Nonprofit Organizations). 320p. 1988. 55.00 (0-19-504680-3) OUP.

*Community Organizations in Latin America. Ed. by Juan C. Navarro. 157p. (Orig.). 1994. 18.50x (0-940602-75-X) IADB.

Community Organizing. 2nd ed. George A. Brager et al. LC 72-8947. 416p. 1987. text ed. 34.50 (0-231-05462-9) Col U Pr.

Community Organizing: Theory & Practice. Douglas P. Biklen. 336p. (C). 1982. text ed. write for info. (0-13-153676-1) P-H.

*Community Organizing in a Diverse Society. 2nd ed. Ed. by Felix G. Rivera & John L. Erlich. LC 94-26040. 1995. pap. text ed. write for info. (0-205-15620-7) Allyn.

Community Oriented Evaluation of the Effectiveness of Child Caring Institutions. George Thomas. 304p. 1975. 5.00 (0-318-16350-0, B18) Regional Inst Social Welfare.

Community-Oriented Primary Care: From Principle to Practice. Ed. by Paul A. Nutting. LC 90-12627. 572p. 1990. reprint ed. pap. text ed. 22.50 (0-8263-1230-6) U of NM Pr.

Community Oriented Primary Care: Training for Urban Practice. Jo I. Boufford & Pat A. Shonubi. LC 85-6495. 187p. 1985. text ed. 45.00 (0-275-91307-4, C1307, Praeger Pubs) Greenwood.

Community Ownership in New Towns & Old Cities. Edward M. Kirshner & James I. Morey. 75p. 1975. pap. text ed. 18.95 (0-87855-778-4) Transaction Pubs.

Community Paleoecology As a Geologic Tool: The Chinese Ashgillian-Eifelian (Latest Ordovician Through Early Middle Devonian As an Example) Wang Yu et al. (Special Paper Ser.: No. 211). (Illus.). 106p. 1987. pap. 3.00 (0-8137-2211-X) Geol Soc.

*Community Participation & Slum Housing: A Study of Bombay. Vandana Desai. LC 94-45235. (Illus.). 220p. 1995. 28.00 (0-8039-9228-9) Sage.

Community Participation in Health: The Politics of Primary Care in Costa Rica. Lynn M. Morgan. LC 92-9575. (Studies in Medical Anthropology). (Illus.). 208p. (C). 1993. 54.95 (0-521-41898-4) Cambridge U Pr.

Community Participation in Research: Proceedings of Colloquium Held in Nairobi, Kenya, September 23-37, 1991. Ed. by S. Baldwin & J. Cervinskas. 120p. 1993. pap. 13.00 (0-88936-677-2, IDRC6772, Pub. by IDRC CN) UNIPUB.

Community Participation in Urban Projects in the Third World. Ed. by Caroline O. Moser. (Progress in Planning Ser.: No. 32). (Illus.). 68p. 1990. pap. 30.00 (0-08-040159-7, Pergamon Pr) Elsevier.

Community Participation, Social Development & the State. James Midgley et al. 200p. 1986. 42.50 (0-416-39820-0, 1014); pap. 15.95 (0-416-39830-8, 1038) Routledge Chapman & Hall.

Community Partnership in Communications for Ministry. Robert L. Litteral. (BGC Monograph Ser.). 139p. (Orig.). 1988. pap. 3.25 (1-879089-01-7) B Graham Ctr.

Community Partnerships in Action. 88p. 1993. pap. text ed. 15.00 (0-929310-97-7) Am Correctional.

Community Piped Water Supply Systems in Developing Countries: A Planning Manual. Daniel Okun & Walter Ernst. (Technical Paper Ser.: No. 60). 262p. 1987. 17.95 (0-8213-0896-3, BK0896) World Bank.

Community Police Administration. Jack L. Kuykendall & Peter C. Unsinger. LC 75-2119. (Justice Administration Ser.). 348p. 1975. 37.95 (0-88229-158-0) Nelson-Hall.

Community Policing: A Contemporary Perspective. Robert Trojanowicz & Bonnie Bucqueroux. LC 89-80504. 450p. (C). 1989. pap. text ed. 24.95 (0-87084-875-5) Anderson Pub Co.

Community Policing: Comparative Perspectives & Prospects. Robert R. Friedmann. LC 92-20809. 1992. text ed. 49.95 (0-312-08672-5); pap. 19.95 (0-312-08673-3) St Martin.

Community Policing: How to Get Started. Robert Trojanowicz & Bonnie Bucqueroux. LC 93-79363. 173p. (C). 1993. pap. text ed. write for info. (0-87084-874-7) Anderson Pub Co.

Community Policing: Rhetoric or Reality. Ed. by Jack R. Greene & Stephen D. Mastrofski. LC 88-15559. (Illus.). 293p. 1988. text ed. 55.00 (0-275-92952-3, C2952, Praeger Pubs) Greenwood.

Community Policing: Rhetoric or Reality. Ed. by Jack R. Greene & Stephen D. Mastrofski. LC 88-15559. 296p. 1991. pap. text ed. 18.95 (0-275-94063-2, B4063, Praeger Pubs) Greenwood.

Community Policing: Theory & Practice. Karen M. Hess & Linda Miller. Ed. by Jucha. LC 93-25941. 650p. (C). 1993. text ed. 54.75 (0-314-02391-7) West Pub.

Community, Policing & Accountability: The Politics of Policing in Manchester in the 1980s. Eugene McLaughlin. 206p. 1994. 51.95 (1-85628-488-3, Pub. by Avebury Pub UK) Ashgate Pub Co.

Community Policing & Crime Prevention in America & England. Robert C. Wadman & Stanley E. Bailey. LC 92-44179. 1993. pap. 9.50 (0-942511-50-6) OICJ.

*Community Policing & Problem Solving: Strategies & Practices. Kenneth J. Peak & Ronald W. Glensor. LC 95-10498. 1996. write for info. (0-13-294687-4) PH School.

*Community Policing in Madison: Quality from the Inside Out: An Evaluation of Implementation & Impact. Mary A. Wycoff & Wesley K. Skogan. (Illus.). 96p. (Orig.). (C). 1994. pap. text ed. 40.00x (0-7881-1411-5) Diane Pub.

Community Policing in New York: The CPOP Research. Jerome E. McElroy et al. (Illus.). 216p. (C). 1992. 44.00 (0-8039-4789-5); pap. 19.95 (0-8039-4790-9) Sage.

Community Politics & Peasant-State Relations in Paraguay. Brian Turner. 336p. (C). 1993. lib. bdg. 42.50 (0-8191-9119-1) U Pr of Amer.

Community Power & Decision-Making. Irving P. Leif & Terry N. Clark. (Current Sociology - la Sociologie Contemporaine Ser.: Vol. 20, No. 2). 138p. 1973. pap. text ed. 19.25 (90-279-7941-3) Mouton.

Community Power in a Postreform City: Politics in New York City. Robert F. Pecorella. 240p. 1993. 46.95 (1-56324-136-6) M E Sharpe.

Community Power Structure: A Study of Decision Makers. Floyd Hunter. LC 79-305. xvii, 297p. 1953. reprint ed. pap. 13.95 (0-8078-4033-5) U of NC Pr.

Community Press in an Urban Setting. 2nd ed. Morris B. Janowitz. LC 67-21391. (Midway Reprint Ser.). 1980. pap. text ed. 12.00 (0-226-39318-6) U Ch Pr.

Community Prevention & Control of Cardiovascular Disease. (Technical Report Ser.: No. 732). 62p. (Orig.). 1986. pap. 5.40 (92-4-120732-9) World Health.

Community Prevention Trials for Alcohol Problems: Methodological Issues. Ed. by Harold D. Holder & Jan M. Howard. LC 92-9804. 336p. 1992. text ed. 55.00 (0-275-94196-5, C4196, Praeger Pubs) Greenwood.

Community Problems & Opportunities in North Carolina. Gibson Gray. 328p. (Orig.). (C). 1989. pap. 20.00 (0-9600320-3-7) Gibson Gray.

Community Problems & Social Work in Southeast Asia: The Hong Kong & Singapore Experience. Ed. by Peter Hodge. 254p. (C). 1980. pap. text ed. 36.00 (962-209-022-2, Pub. by Hong Kong U Pr HK) St Mut.

Community Profiling: Auditing Social Needs. Murray Hawtin et al. LC 93-39909. 160p. 1994. pap. text ed. 27. 50 (0-335-19113-4, Open Univ Pr) Taylor & Francis.

Community Programme of Censuses of Population Comparative Analysis 1990-1991. Eurostat Staff. 70p. 1992. pap. 9.00 (92-826-4418-9, CA-71-91-598-3A-C, Pub. by Europ Com) UNIPUB.

Community Programs for Mental Health: Theory, Practice, Evaluation. Ruth Kotinsky & Helen L. Witmer. LC 55-11030. (Commonwealth Fund Publications). 381p. 1955. 32.00 (0-674-15151-8) HUP.

Community Programs for the Depressed Elderly: A Rehabilitation Approach. Ed. by Ellen D. Taira. LC 86-31956. (Physical & Occupational Therapy in Geriatrics Ser.: Vol. 5, No. 1). 89p. 1987. text ed. 29.95 (0-86656-644-9) Haworth Pr.

Community Programs for the Health- Impaired Elderly. Ed. by Ellen D. Taira. LC 88-2084. (Physical & Occupational Therapy in Geriatrics Ser.: Vol. 6, No. 1). (Illus.). 87p. 1989. text ed. 29.95 (0-86656-760-7) Haworth Pr.

Community Property: Adaptable to Courses Utilizing Bird's Casebook on California Community Property. Casenotes Publishing Co., Inc. Staff. Ed. by Norman S. Goldenberg et al. (Legal Briefs Ser.). 1994. pap. write for info. (0-87457-022-0, 1320) Casenotes Pub.

Community Property in a Nutshell. 2nd ed. Robert L. Mennell & Thomas M. Boykoff. (Nutshell Ser.). 432p. (C). 1993. reprint ed. pap. text ed. 17.50 (0-314-68355-0) West Pub.

Community Property in California: Cases, Statutes & Problems. 2nd ed. William A. Reppy, Jr. (Contemporary Legal Education Ser.). 443p. 1988. 38.00 (0-87473-375-8) Michie Butterworth.

Community Property in the United States. Reppy & Samuel. 422p. (C). 1991. 45.50 (1-879581-00-0) Lupus Pubns.

Community Property in the United States, 1994. Reppy & Samuel. 464p. Date not set. ring bd. 46.50 (1-879581-15-9) Lupus Pubns.

*Community Psychiatric Nursing, Vol. 3. C. Brooker & E. White. 256p. 1995. pap. 38.25 (1-56593-354-0, 0678) Singular Publishing.

Community Psychiatric Nursing: A Research Perspective. Ed. by Charles Brooker. 320p. 1990. 40.50 (0-412-34790-3, A4880) Chapman & Hall.

Community Psychiatry: A Reappraisal. Group for the Advancement of Psychiatry Staff. LC 83-5443. (Group for the Advancement of Psychiatry, Symposium Ser.: Vol. 11, No. 113). 86p. reprint ed. pap. 25.00 (0-7837-2101-3, 2042377) Bks Demand.

*Community Psychiatry in Action: Analysis & Prospects. Ed. by Peter Tyrer & Francis Creed. (Illus.). 150p. (C). 1995. 42.95 (0-521-47427-2) Cambridge U Pr.

*Community Psychology. Karen G. Duffy & Frank Y. Wong. LC 94-42725. 1995. text ed. write for info. (0-205-13696-6) Allyn.

Community Psychology: Perspective & Applications. Murray Levine & David V. Perkins. (Illus.). 384p. 1987. 35.00 (0-19-503946-7) OUP.

Community Psychology: Perspectives in Training & Research. Ed. by Ira Iscoe & Charles D. Spielberger. LC 76-102038. (Century Psychology Ser.). (C). 1970. 29.00 (0-89197-095-9) Irvington.

Community Psychology: Theory & Practice. Jim Orford. 292p. 1992. pap. text ed. 36.95 (0-471-93810-6) Wiley.

Community Psychology: Values, Research, & Action. Julian Rappaport. LC 76-55422. 482p. (C). 1977. text ed. 42.75 (0-03-006441-4) HB Coll Pubs.

Community Psychology & Coordination. Patrick R. Penland & James G. Williams. LC 74-77111. (Communications Science & Technology Ser.: No. 4). 200p. reprint ed. pap. 57.00 (0-7837-0727-4, 2041051) Bks Demand.

Community Psychology & Mental Health. Gibbs. 1992. pap. text ed. 34.95 (0-89876-136-0) Gardner Pr.

Community Re-Entry for Head-Injured Adults. Ed. by Mark Ylvisaker & Eva M. Gobble. LC 90-21329. (Illus.). 444p. (C). 1987. text ed. 40.00 (0-89079-337-9, 1574) PRO-ED.

Community Reconstruction after Earthquake: Dialectical Sociology in Action. Ino Rossi. LC 93-2856. 208p. 1993. text ed. 59.95 (0-275-94602-9, C4602, Praeger Pubs) Greenwood.

Community Reconstructs: The Meaning of Pragmatic Social Thought. James Campbell. 160p. 1992. pap. 12.95 (0-252-06207-8) U of Ill Pr.

Community Recovery from a Major Disaster. Claire B. Rubin et al. (Program on Environment & Behavior Monograph Ser.: No. 41). 295p. (Orig.). (C). 1985. pap. 10.00 (0-685-28115-9) Natural Hazards.

Community Recreation & Persons with Disabilities: Strategies for Integration. Stuart J. Schleien & M. Tipton Ray. LC 87-21300. 288p. (Orig.). (C). 1988. pap. 25.95 (0-933716-95-8, 958) P H Brookes.

Community Recycling: System Design to Management. Nyles V. Reinfeld. 240p. 1992. text ed. 62.00 (0-13-155789-0) P-H.

*Community Rehabilitation Services for People with Disabilities. Karan. 400p. 1995. 45.00 (0-7506-9532-3, Focal) Buttrwrth-Heinemann.

Community Reinvestment Act. 2nd ed. Stevenson. 375p. 1992. 155.00 (1-55738-363-4) Probus Pub Co.

Community Reinvestment Act: Policies & Compliance. 2nd ed. Roland E. Brandel & David E. Teitelbaum. LC 94-12533. 606p. 1994. ring bd. 126.00 (0-13-310962-3) Aspen Law.

Community Reinvestment Act & Economic Development: A Profile of Community Lending in Eight Cities. Lori Gillen. Ed. by Nancy McCrea. 205p. (Orig.). 1990. pap. 21.00 (0-317-05573-9) Natl Coun Econ Dev.

Community Reinvestment Act Bulletin. 152.00 (0-685-69616-2, CRAU) Warren Gorham & Lamont.

Community Reinvestment Performance: Making CRA Work for Banks, Communities & Regulators. Kenneth H. Thomas. 1993. 75.00 (1-55738-379-0) Probus Pub Co.

Community Relations Assistant. Jack Rudman. (Career Examination Ser.: C-1207). 1994. pap. 23.95 (0-8373-1207-8) Nat Learn.

Community Relations Guide. 134p. 1985. 6.50 (0-930713-51-6) Lit Vol Am.

Community Relations Specialist. Jack Rudman. (Career Examination Ser.: No. C-3535). 1994. 27.95 (0-8373-3535-3) Nat Learn.

Community Relations Strategies: A Handbook for Sponsors of Community-Based Programs for the Homeless. Rose Anello & Tillie Shuster. LC 87-401908. 38p. (Orig.). 1985. pap. text ed. 5.00 (0-88156-051-0) Comm Serv Soc NY.

*Community, Religion & Literature: Essays. Cleanth Brooks. LC 94-43049. 336p. 1995. 34.95 (0-8262-0993-9) U of Mo Pr.

Community Research: Methods, Paradigms, & Applications. Ed. by Edwin C. Susskind & Donald C. Klein. LC 84-17921. 540p. 1985. text ed. 65.00 (0-275-90171-8, C0171, Praeger Pubs) Greenwood.

Community Research & Development Programme on Decommissioning of Nuclear Installations: 1989-93 Annual Progress Report 1992, EUR 14498. European Communities Staff. 323p. 1992. pap. 45.00 (92-826-4400-6, CDNA14498ENC, Pub. by Europ Com) UNIPUB.

Community Research & Development Programme on Radioactive Waste Management, EUR 14418. European Communities Staff. 627p. 1992. pap. 80.00 (92-826-4398-0, CD-NA-14418-EN-C, Pub. by Europ Com) UNIPUB.

Community Residence Aide. Jack Rudman. (Career Examination Ser.: C-3135). 1994. pap. 23.95 (0-8373-3135-8) Nat Learn.

Community Resource Management: Lessons from the Zanjera. Robert Y. Siy, Jr. 211p. 1983. text ed. 12.50 (0-8248-0908-4) UH Pr.

Community Resources. Rulon K. Wood. Ed. by James E. Duane. LC 80-20963. (Instructional Media Library: Vol. 2). (Illus.). 96p. 1981. 23.95 (0-87778-162-1) Educ Tech Pubns.

Community Resources Directory: A Guide to U. S. Volunteer Organizations & Other Resource Groups, Services, Training Events & Courses & Local Program Models. 2nd ed. Ed. by Harriet C. Kipps. LC 83-25349. 984p. 1984. 120.00 (0-8103-1794-X) Gale.

An Asterisk (*) at the beginning of an entry indicates that the title is appearing in BIP for the first time.

C

An Asterisk (*) at the beginning of an entry indicates that the title is appearing in BIP for the first time.

1435

C

Commuter Marriage: A Study of Work & Family. Naomi Gerstel & Harriet Gross. LC 84-12829. (Perspectives on Marriage & the Family Ser.). 228p. 1984. lib. bdg. 30.00 (0-89862-076-7) Guilford Pr.

Commuter Marriage: Living Together, Apart. Fairlee E. Winfield. LC 84-17528. (Illus.). 200p. 1985. text ed. 33.50 (0-231-05948-5) Col U Pr.

Commuter Nation: Perspectives on Puerto Rican Migration. William Burgos et al. 1994. pap. 13.75 (0-8477-2498-0) U of PR Pr.

Commuter, Regional, & Rail Transit. (Research Record Ser.: No. 1162). 66p. 1988. 7.00 (0-309-04673-4) Transport Res Bd.

Commuter Trains to Central Terminal. Tom Nelligan. 1986. pap. 7.95 (0-915276-45-3) Quadrant Pr.

***Commuter's Tale.** Jonathan Margolis & Gabrielle Morris. (Illus.). 224p. 1993. pap. 8.95 (1-85592-631-8) Trafalgar.

Commuting Nonselfadjoint Operations in Hilbert Space. M. S. Livsic & L. L. Waksman. (Lecture Notes in Mathematics Ser.: Vol. 1272). iii, 115p. 1987. pap. 28.10 (0-387-18316-7) Spr-Verlag.

Commuting Versus Resident Students: Overcoming the Educational Inequities of Living off Campus. Arthur W. Chickering. LC 74-6737. (Jossey-Bass Higher Education Ser.). 168p. reprint ed. pap. 47.90 (0-685-23493-2, 2052200) Bks Demand.

Comnock's School Speaker: Rhetorical Recitations for Boys & Girls. Comp. by Robert M. Comnock. LC 73-2838. (Granger Index Reprint Ser.). 1977. reprint ed. 23.95 (0-8369-6412-8) Ayer.

Como Acercarse a Dios: How Shall I Go to God. Horatius Bonar. (SPA.). 3.25 (84-7228-851-X, 220215, Pub. by Edit Clie SP) TSELF.

Como Aconsejar en Situaciones de Crisis: Crisis Counseling. Norman Wright. (SPA.). 8.95 (84-7645-447-3, 223352, Pub. by Edit Clie SP) TSELF.

Como Administrar el Ministerio Juvenil - How to Administer a Youth Program. Comp. by David Fajardo. 64p. (SPA.). 1991. pap. 2.50 (0-311-12332-5) Casa Bautista.

Como Adquirir Personalidad Encantadora: How to Have a Winning Personality. Salvador Iserte. (SPA.). 4.25 (84-7645-327-2, 223287, Pub. by Edit Clie SP) TSELF.

Como Agua Para Chocolate. Laura Esquivel. 1993. 19.95 (0-385-47137-8) Doubleday.

Como Agua para Chocolate. Laura Esquivel. 1994. mass mkt. 5.99 (0-385-47148-3, Anchor NY) Doubleday.

Como Alcanzar la Libertad: How to Be Free. Salvador Iserte. (SPA.). 5.50 (84-7645-097-4, 223157, Pub. by Edit Clie SP) TSELF.

Como Alcanzar una Vida Radiante: How to Have a Happy Life. Salvador Iserte. (SPA.). 3.25 (84-7645-090-7, 223145, Pub. by Edit Clie SP) TSELF.

Como Aumentar Ingresos y Triunfar: How to Increase Your Earnings. Johnston-Rank. (SPA.). 3.95 (84-7645-162-8, 223203, Pub. by Edit Clie SP) TSELF.

Como Cambiar Tu Vida. Ernest Holmes. Tr. by Cielo Torrens & Lila Bolvia. 372p. (Orig.). (SPA.). 1990. pap. 12.95 (0-917849-09-4, 0556) Sci of Mind.

Como Celebrar el Culto Familiar: How to Have Family Prayers. Rosalind Rinker. (SPA.). 4.95 (84-7228-488-3, 220163, Pub. by Edit Clie SP) TSELF.

Como Compartir Su Fe. Paul E. Little. 144p. 1988. reprint ed. pap. 4.95 (0-311-13025-9) Casa Bautista.

***Como Complementarse y No Fastidiarse.** Victor Ricardo & Gloria Ricardo. 36p. 1993. pap. 1.00 (1-885630-06-9) HLM Producciones.

Como Conducir un Alma a Cristo: How to Win a Soul to Christ. Robert G. Lee. (SPA.). 2.95 (84-7228-187-6, 220162, Pub. by Edit Clie SP) TSELF.

Como Conocer A Tu Hijo. Ross Campbell. Tr. by Cecilia R. De De Francesco. 144p. (SPA.). (C). 1989. pap. 4.50 (0-88113-044-3) Edit Betania.

Como Conocer la Voluntad De Dios: How to Know the Will of God. William Orr. (SPA.). 2.95 (84-7228-224-4, 220165, Pub. by Edit Clie SP) TSELF.

Como Conocer y Resolver los Problemas Emocionales De Sus Hijos. Maria E. Del Real. (Illus.). 240p. (Orig.). (SPA.). 1990. pap. 3.50 (0-944499-47-3) Editorial Amer.

Como Conseguir Aquello Por Que: How to Get What We Pray For. Bill Austin. (SPA.). 5.50 (84-7645-140-7, 223184, Pub. by Edit Clie SP) TSELF.

Como Conseguir Cosas De Dios: How to Get Things from God. John Zoller. (SPA.). 3.25 (84-7228-032-2, 220167, Pub. by Edit Clie SP) TSELF.

Como Conseguir el Empleo Que Usted Desea. Lynda Mandlowitz. (Careers in Depth Ser.). (Illus.). 128p. 1980. lib. bdg. 7.97 (0-8239-0517-9) Rosen Group.

***Como Conseguir el Trabajo Que Usted Quiere! How to Get the Job You Want.** Scott E. Davis. Ed. & Tr. by Constanza G. Paramo. 36p. (Orig.). (SPA.). 1994. pap. 6.95 (0-9640932-8-6) Simsbury Mgmt.

Como Convertirse En la Esposa Ideal: The Sensitive Woman. Sandra Chandler. (SPA.). 4.25 (84-7228-749-1, 222310, Pub. by Edit Clie SP) TSELF.

***Como Convertirse en Padre Eficaz De Su Adolescente: Guia Para Los Padres.** D. D. Dale & Thomas Baker. Tr. by Gabriel Gonzalez et al. 88p. (SPA.). 1994. pap. 12.00 (1-885903-01-4, TX 3882834) Fam & Rltnship Ctr.

Como Cortar el Cabello: Guia Facil para Cortar el Cabello con Precision Profesional. Martha G. Fernandez. Tr. by Maria V. Vila. LC 89-31804. (Illus.). 176p. (Orig.). 1989. pap. 16.95 (0-944460-10-0) Good Life Prods.

Como Crecen los Perritos: (How Puppies Grow) Millicent E. Selsam. Tr. by Argentina Palacios. (Illus.). 32p. (SPA.). (J). (ps-3). 1990. pap. 3.50 (0-590-43410-1) Scholastic Inc.

***Como Crecer Por el Divorcio.** Jim Smoke. Date not set. pap. 8.99 (0-8254-1673-6) Kregel.

Como Crencen los Gatitos: How Kittens Grow. Millicent E. Selsam. (SPA.). (J). (ps-3). 1993. pap. 2.95 (0-590-45000-X) Scholastic Inc.

Como Criar a los Hijos Con Amor Y: Parenting with Love & Care. Bruce Narramore. (SPA.). 5.50 (84-7228-558-8, 220164, Pub. by Edit Clie SP) TSELF.

Como Criar a los Hijos Para Cristo: How to Raise Children for Christ. Andrew Murray. (SPA.). 6.95 (84-7228-682-7, 220227, Pub. by Edit Clie SP) TSELF.

Como Criar a un Nino Dificil: The Strong-Willed Child. James Dobson. (SPA.). 6.95 (84-7228-456-5, 220168, Pub. by Edit Clie SP) TSELF.

Como Criar Hijos Felices y Obedientes. Roy Lessin. 160p. 1981. 3.50 (0-88113-037-0) Edit Betania.

Como Cuidar Los Grandes Organos: Corazon, Rinones, Higado; Pulmones. Editorial America, S. A. Staff. Ed. by Maria E. Del Real. (Illus.). 296p. (Orig.). (SPA.). 1990. pap. 3.95 (0-944499-46-5) Editorial Amer.

Como Dar A Los Ninos Una Ventaja Emocional: Spanish Translation. Marjon Riekerk. 1989. pap. 2.00 (0-913937-37-1) Rational Isl.

Como Darle una Mano a los Perros y los Gatos: (How to Be a Helping Hand for Dogs & Cats) Charlotte B. Montgomery. (Illus.). 32p. (Orig.). (ENG & SPA.). (J). (gr. k). Date not set. pap. 3.00 (0-941246-07-8) NAHEE.

***Como Defender Sus Cargos Federales: Manual Para Acusados Arrestados Por Los Federales.** 5th ed. Larry Fassler. 100p. (SPA.). 1994. pap. 29.95 (0-9644908-1-7) SW Legal Servs.

Como Desarrollar el Temperamento de Su Hijo. Beverly LaHaye. 182p. 1979. 4.95 (0-88113-036-2) Edit Betania.

Como Desarrollar la Autoestima De Su Hijo (Building Your Child's Self-Esteem) Smalley & Trent. (SPA.). Date not set. 1.79 (1-56063-103-1, 498129) Editorial Unilit.

Como Desatar Su Fe. 2nd ed. Kenneth E. Hagin. (SPA.). 1982. pap. 1.95 (0-89276-107-5) Hagin Ministries.

Como Descobrir E Fazer A Vonta. Gary Friesen. 240p. (POR.). 1991. 9.95 (0-8297-1631-9) Life Pubs Intl.

Como Descubrir los Secretos De: How to Discover the Secrets Of. W. Scroggie. (SPA.). 3.25 (84-7228-742-4, 220171, Pub. by Edit Clie SP) TSELF.

Como Dibujar Personajes Comicos. Watermill Pr. Staff. (J). (ps-3). 1992. pap. 1.95 (0-8167-2646-9) Troll Assocs.

***Como Dirigir un Biblico Estudio por Metodos Indirectos.** Charles Brock. Tr. by Ruby Vargas. 19p. (Orig.). (SPA.). 1985. pap. 1.00 (1-885504-01-2) Church Gwth.

Como Disciplinar a Tus Hijos. Roy Lessin. 96p. 1982. 2.95 (0-88113-032-X) Edit Betania.

Como Disfrutar De los Hijos: I Want to Enjoy My Children. Henry Brandt. (SPA.). 5.50 (84-7228-581-2, 220157, Pub. by Edit Clie SP) TSELF.

Como Distinguir y Refutar las Sectas: Know the Marks of the Cults. David Breese. (SPA.). 3.95 (84-7228-922-2, 222013, Pub. by Edit Clie SP) TSELF.

Como Doblarse Sin Quebrarse (How to Bend Without Breaking) Larry Jones. (SPA.). 1987. 4.99 (0-945792-24-7, 490238) Editorial Unilit.

Como Dominar la Tension Nerviosa. Clyde Narramore & Ruth Narramore. Tr. by Rhode Ward. 216p. (SPA.). pap. 6.25 (0-89922-129-7) Edit Caribe.

Como Echar El Diablo De Su Vida. Robert Tilton. 109p. (SPA.). 1989. pap. write for info. (0-318-64835-0) Abbasons.

Como Educar a Tus Hijos: Train up a Child. Harold Sala. (SPA.). 4.95 (84-7228-728-9, 220175, Pub. by Edit Clie SP) TSELF.

***Como el Aire de Abril.** Arturo Echavarria. 217p. 1994. 12.95 (0-8477-0212-X) U of PR Pr.

Como el Eco de un Silencio. Ignacio Galbis. LC 83-51277. (Senda Poetica Ser.). (Illus.). 111p. (Orig.). (SPA.). 1984. pap. 6.95 (0-918454-41-7) Senda Nueva.

Como Elegir Una Casa Particular Donde Le Cuiden a Su Nino: Manual Para Padres. National Council of Jewish Women Staff. (Illus.). 21p. 1992. 3.00 (0-685-62942-2) NCJW.

Como Empezar y Terminar Bien Su Ministerio - A Glad Beginning - a Gracious Ending. D. L. Lowrie. Tr. by Edgar O. Morales. 112p. (Orig.). (SPA.). 1991. pap. 3.95 (0-311-42088-5) Casa Bautista.

Como Enfrentar la Vida Con Exito: How to Succeed in Life. Salvador Iserte. (SPA.). 3.95 (84-7228-968-0, 223040, Pub. by Edit Clie SP) TSELF.

***Como Enriquecer la Vida: Lucha Contra la Malnutricion por Carencia de Vitaminas y Minerales en los Paises en Desarrollo.** Ed. by International Bank for Reconstruction & Development Staff. LC 94-49155. (El Desarrollo en la Practica Ser.). (SPA.). 1995. write for info. (0-8213-3097-7) World Bank.

Como Ensenar Con Eficacia: How to Teach with Efficience. Martha Berberian. (SPA.). 5.25 (84-7645-296-9, 223365, Pub. by Edit Clie SP) TSELF.

Como Ensenar la Biblia. Lucien E. Coleman, Jr. Tr. by Jorge E. Diaz. Orig. Title: How to Teach the Bible. 265p. (SPA.). 1985. reprint ed. 7.50 (0-311-11039-8) Casa Bautista.

Como Entend. y Explic. los Num. De La: Numbers in Scripture. E. W. Bullinger. (SPA.). 7.95 (84-7645-435-X, 223512, Pub. by Edit Clie SP) TSELF.

Como Entender a Wall Street. Jeffrey B. Little & Lucien Rhodes. 1991. pap. text ed. 10.95 (0-07-104045-5) McGraw.

Como Entender el Antiguo Testamento: How to Understand the Old. Larry Richards. (SPA.). 2.95 (84-7228-591-X, 220158, Pub. by Edit Clie SP) TSELF.

Como Entender Ensen. y Misterios Cruz: How to Understand the Teachings. Jessie Penn-Lewis. (SPA.). 3.25 (84-7228-888-9, 222312, Pub. by Edit Clie SP) TSELF.

Como Escribir Cartas De Amor. Ed. by Maria E. Alvarez del Real. (Illus.). 288p. (Orig.). (SPA.). (YA). 1988. pap. 4.00 (0-944499-38-4) Editorial Amer.

Como Escribir Sin Faltas de Ortografia. Editorial America, S. A. Staff. Ed. by Maria E. Del Real. 256p. (Orig.). (SPA.). 1989. pap. 4.00 (0-944499-25-2) Editorial Amer.

Como Escribir Su Propio Guion Musical: Instrucciones para Anotar Canciones en Papel. Leslyn Tepper. Tr. by Livia Kampe. (Illus.). 62p. (Orig.). (SPA.). 1985. pap. 6.95 (0-930867-01-7) S O S Pubs.

Como Escribirlo - How to Write It. 4th rev. ed. Editorial America, S. A. Staff. Ed. by Maria E. Del Real. 456p. (ENG & SPA.). 1988. pap. 4.50 (0-944499-24-4) Editorial Amer.

Como Escribirlo - How to Write It. 5th rev. ed. Editorial America, S. A. Staff. Ed. by Maria E. Del Real. 456p. (SPA.). 1990. pap. write for info. (0-944499-58-9) Editorial Amer.

Como Estudar A Biblia. James Braga. 152p. (POR.). 1990. 7.95 (0-8297-1707-2) Life Pubs Intl.

Como Estudiar Inteligentemente: How to Study Smart. Waln K. Brown. (Illus.). 20p. 1992. 2.95 (1-56456-064-3, 252S) W Gladden Found.

Como Estudiar la Biblia. W. H. Thomas. 112p. (SPA.). 1989. pap. 3.99 (0-8254-1717-1) Kregel.

Como Estudiar la Biblia: How to Study the Bible. Ruben A. Torrey. (SPA.). 3.95 (84-7228-677-0, 220166, Pub. by Edit Clie SP) TSELF.

Como Estudiar la Biblia por Si Mismo. Tim LaHaye. 192p. 1977. 4.95 (0-88113-042-7) Edit Betania.

Como Evitar As Doencas. Harold P. Adolph & David Bourne. 176p. (POR.). 1991. 4.95 (0-8297-1638-6) Life Pubs Intl.

***Como Evitar el Insomnio Infantil.** Richard Ferber. (ENG & SPA.). 1995. pap. 10.00 (0-684-81330-0) S&S Trade.

Como Excribir y Predicar Con Eficacia: How to Write & Preach With Efficacy. Martha Berberian. (SPA.). 4.95 (84-7645-285-3, 223366, Pub. by Edit Clie SP) TSELF.

***Como Experimentar la Presencia De Dios.** Victor Ricardo & Gloria Ricardo. 35p. 1993. pap. 2.00 (1-885630-08-5) HLM Producciones.

Como Explicar el Credo: The Apostle's Creed Made Easy. Samuel Vila. (SPA.). 3.95 (84-7228-789-0, 222315, Pub. by Edit Clie SP) TSELF.

Como Fomentar la Participacion de Voluntarios: (Spanish - Volunteers) WCCU (World Council of Credit Unions, Inc.) Staff. 160p. (C). 1990. per., pap. text ed. 24.00 (0-8403-5834-2) Kendall-Hunt.

Como Formar Hijos Cristianos en un Mundo No Cristiano: How to Raise Christian Kids in a Non Christian World. Tr. by Josie Smith. 160p. (Orig.). (SPA.). 1990. pap. 5.50 (0-311-46121-2) Casa Bautista.

Como Ganar a Tu Familia Para Cristo. Nathanael Olson. Tr. by Ildefonso Villarello. 182p. 1987. reprint ed. pap. 2.75 (0-311-13801-2) Casa Bautista.

Como Ganar Almas (How to Win Souls for Christ) V. Valencia. (SPA.). Date not set. 2.99 (1-56063-003-5, 490216) Editorial Unilit.

Como Gozar de la Salvacion. Ronald Sprik. (SPA.). 1991. 0.25 (1-55955-108-9) CITE MI.

Como Guiar a los Adultos: How to Guide Adults. Polly Cooper. Tr. by Carol Martinez. 160p. (Orig.). (SPA.). 1990. pap. 4.95 (0-311-11823-2) Casa Bautista.

Como Guiar a Los Escolares: How to Guide Children. Louise Caldwell. Tr. by Nancy Bedford. 160p. (Orig.). (SPA.). (J). (gr. 1-3). 1990. pap. text ed. 4.95 (0-311-11821-6) Casa Bautista.

Como Guiar a los Jovenes: How to Guide Youth. Ann Sullivan. Tr. by Josie Smith. 160p. (Orig.). (SPA.). 1990. pap. 4.95 (0-311-11822-4) Casa Bautista.

Como Guiar a los Preescolares: How to Guide Preschoolers. Tr. by Adelina M. Almanza. (Illus.). 240p. (Orig.). (SPA.). 1990. pap. text ed. 4.95 (0-311-11820-8) Casa Bautista.

Como Hablar Con Su Pareja (How to Talk to Your Mate) H. N. Wright. (SPA.). Date not set. 2.49 (1-56063-002-7, 498049) Editorial Unilit.

Como Hacer Discipulos-Cristo (How to Make Disciples-Christ) V. Gonzalez. (SPA.). Date not set. 1.79 (1-56063-421-9, 498258) Editorial Unilit.

Como Hacer Felices a los Que Te Rodean: How to Make Others Happy. Salvador Iserte. (SPA.). 4.25 (84-7645-082-6, 223138, Pub. by Edit Clie SP) TSELF.

Como Hacer Feliz a la Esposa: How to Keep Your Wife Happy. William Orr. (SPA.). 2.95 (84-7228-668-1, 220211, Pub. by Edit Clie SP) TSELF.

Como Hacer Feliz Al Marido: How to Keep Your Husband Happy. William Orr. (SPA.). 2.95 (84-7228-669-X, 220213, Pub. by Edit Clie SP) TSELF.

Como Hacer un Estudio de Factibilidad: Entrenamiento para Iniciar o Reexaminar una Pequena Empresa. Ed. by Suzanne Kindervatter. LC 87-62631. (Formacion Comercial Apropiada a la Mujer del Tercer Mundo Ser.). 176p. (Orig.). (SPA.). 1988. pap. text ed. 17.00 (0-912917-15-6) UNIFEM.

Como Hacer un Libro Con Microcomputadora. Ramon C. Barrios. 260p. 1992. pap. text ed. 17.95 (968-18-3990-0, Pub. by Limusa MX) Computer & Tech.

Como Hallar la Fe (Finding Faith) A. Knowles. (SPA.). Date not set. 5.99 (0-8423-6187-1, 490200) Editorial Unilit.

Como Incrementar Nuestra Com. Con: How to Improve Our Fellowship. Matthew Henry. (SPA.). 3.95 (84-7228-896-X, 222012, Pub. by Edit Clie SP) TSELF.

Como Iniciar la Vida Cristiana. George Sweeting. Orig. Title: How to Begin the Christian Life. 160p. (SPA.). 1977. pap. 4.50 (0-8254-1697-3) Kregel.

Como Iniciar un Grupo Vecinal (Neigh Bib Study: How to Start Neigh. Bible Study) Kuns & Schell. (SPA.). Date not set. 1.50 (0-945792-52-2, 490450) Editorial Unilit.

Como Interpretar la Biblia Uno Mismo. Richard Mayhue. Orig. Title: How to Interpret the Bible for Yourself. 112p. (SPA.). 1994. pap. 6.99 (0-8254-1471-7) Kregel.

Como Leer a Blas de Otero. Jose A. Arrieta. Date not set. 46.50 (0-685-69532-8) Scripta.

Como Leer a Garcia Marquez: Una Interpretacion Sociologica. Jose L. Mendez. LC 89-5381. 224p. (Orig.). 1992. pap. text ed. 12.50 (0-8477-3640-7) U of PR Pr.

Como Leer a Juan Ramon Jimenez. Isabel P. Almansa. Date not set. 45.50 (0-685-69530-1) Scripta.

Como Leer a Julio Cortazar. Alicia H. Puleo. Date not set. 42.50 (0-685-69533-6) Scripta.

Como Leer a Leandro Fernandez de Moratin. Rosalia F. Cabezon. Date not set. 43.50 (0-685-69531-X) Scripta.

Como Leer el Lazarillo. Francisco G. Perez. Date not set. 43.00 (0-685-69535-2) Scripta.

Como Leer La Celestina. Maria E. Lanz. Date not set. 45.50 (0-685-69534-4) Scripta.

Como Leer y Orar los Evangelios. Marilyn Norquist. Ed. by John McPhee. Tr. by Olimpia Diaz. (Handbook of the Bible Ser.). Orig. Title: Hand. 64p. 1980. pap. 3.95 (0-89243-127-X) Liguori Pubns.

Como Llegar a Ser Vencedor. R. Escandon. 128p. (SPA.). 1982. pap. 2.75 (0-311-46092-5, Edit Mundo) Casa Bautista.

Como Llevar Ninos a Cristo: How to Lead Young Kids to Christ. William Orr. (SPA.). 3.25 (84-7228-707-6, 220218, Pub. by Edit Clie SP) TSELF.

Como Llevarse Bien Con Casi Todo el Mundo (How to Get along with Almost Anyone) Norman Wright. (SPA.). 1993. 6.99 (1-56063-324-7, 490259) Editorial Unilit.

Como Manejar Su Dinero. Larry Burkett. Orig. Title: How to Manage Your Money. (Illus.). 160p. (SPA.). 1993. pap. 6.99 (0-8254-1097-5) Kregel.

Como Mantener Unida Familia Que Ora: How to Keep the Family That Prays. Elva Anson. (SPA.). 6.95 (84-7228-384-4, 220169, Pub. by Edit Clie SP) TSELF.

Como Mejorar el Concepto Que Uno: Improving Your Self Image. Norman Wright. (SPA.). 2.95 (84-7228-725-4, 220161, Pub. by Edit Clie SP) TSELF.

Como Mejorar Sus Relaciores Humanas. R. Lofton Hudson. Tr. by O. S. D. De Lerin. 62p. 1987. reprint ed. 1.95 (0-311-46037-2) Casa Bautista.

***Como Motivar a los Ninos a Aprender.** Illus. by Dave Coverly. 50p. (Orig.). (SPA.). 1995. pap. 9.95 (1-883790-13-1) Grayson Bernard Pubs.

Como Nave de Mercader. Ed. by Loida C. Camacho. 47p. (SPA.). 1974. pap. 2.00 (0-87148-180-4) Pathway Pr.

Como Ninos (Like Little Children) Scandinavia Staff. (SPA.). Date not set. 4.99 (0-685-74918-5, 491395) Editorial Unilit.

Como Nos Guia Dios? E. Stanley Jones. Tr. by Paul Borgeson. 1977. pap. 0.25 (0-8358-0363-5) Upper Room Bks.

Como Obra la Fe. Frederick Price. 111p. 1980. pap. 2.95 (0-89274-157-0) Harrison Hse.

Como Obtener la Plenitud del Poder. R. A. Torrey. Tr. by Jose G. Rivas. Orig. Title: How to Obtain Fullness of Power. 112p. (SPA.). 1986. reprint ed. pap. 3.25 (0-311-46083-6) Casa Bautista.

***Como Obtener la Tarjeta Verde: Maneras Legitimas de Permanecer en los EE.VV.** Loida N. Lewis & Len T. Madlansacay. Tr. by Cambridge Translation Resources Staff. (Illus.). 225p. (SPA.). 1994. pap. 24.95 (0-87337-264-6) Nolo Pr.

Como Orar. R. A. Torrey & J. E. Davis. 96p. 1987. reprint ed. 3.25 (0-311-40001-9) Casa Bautista.

Como Orar: How to Pray. Ruben A. Torrey. (SPA.). 3.00 (84-7228-541-3, 220173, Pub. by Edit Clie SP) TSELF.

Como Orar y Obtener Respuesta: How to Pray & Get the Answer. William Orr. (SPA.). 2.95 (84-7228-711-4, 220220, Pub. by Edit Clie SP) TSELF.

Como Organizar la Escuela Dominical (Sunday School Manual) Burroughs et al. 336p. (Orig.). (SPA.). 1992. pap. 8.95 (84-7645-562-3, 223617, Pub. by Edit Clie SP) TSELF.

Como Organizar una Iglesia: Administration for the Church. Marin Gutierrez. (SPA.). 5.25 (84-7645-375-2, 223503, Pub. by Edit Clie SP) TSELF.

***Como Pasar de Grado: La Lucha de un Adolescente Con ADD.** Roberta N. Parker & Harvey C. Parker. (Illus.). 48p. (Orig.). 1994. pap. 11.00 (0-9621629-7-3) Spec Pr FL.

Como Pescar Marido por Primera, Segunda, y Tercera Vez. Frank Calderon. 112p. (Orig.). (SPA.). 1987. pap. 2.95 (0-939193-16-7) Edit Concepts.

Como Planear una Boda Inolvidable: Planning a Wedding to Remember. Beverly Clark. (SPA.). 1993. pap. 15.95 (0-934081-07-7) Wlshre Pubns.

Como Predicar Expositivamente. Walter Lefield. 192p. (SPA.). 1990. 8.95 (0-8297-1218-6) Life Pubs Intl.

Como Preparar el Examen de la CDL - Examen Para Obtener la Licencia que le Permitira Conducir un Vehiculo Comercial: (How to Prepare for the CDL - Commercial Driver's License Test) Byrnes, Mike & Associates Staff. 486p. (SPA.). 1991. pap. 16.95 (0-8120-4528-9) Barron.

Como Preparar Materiales Sencillos para Lectores Inexpertos. Thomas E. Fountain. (Illus.). 104p. 1974. pap. 7.50 (0-940048-02-7) Austin Bilingual Lang Ed.

Como Preparar Mensajes. James Braga. Orig. Title: How to Prepare Bible Messages. 228p. (POR.). 1986. 8.95 (0-8297-1609-2) Life Pubs Intl.

Como Preparar Mensajes Biblicos. James Braga. Orig. Title: How to Prepare Bible Messages. 320p. (SPA.). 1986. pap. 9.99 (0-8254-1072-X) Kregel.

Como Preparar-Su Hijo-Decir No-Presiones Sexuale (How to Help Your Kids Say No to Sexual Pressure) J. McDowell. (SPA.). Date not set. 4.99 (0-945792-39-5, 498403) Editorial Unilit.

An Asterisk (*) at the beginning of an entry indicates that the title is appearing in BIP for the first time.

Como-Prepararse-Persecucion Que Se Avecina (The Coming Persecution) Larry Poland. (SPA.). 1990. 5.50 (1-56063-439-1, 494029) Editorial Unilit.
Como Preservar Su Matrimonio (How to Preserve Your Marriage) J. Dobson. (SPA.). Date not set. 1.79 (1-56063-053-1, 497415) Editorial Unilit.
Como Prolongar y Transformar La: How to Live Longer Here. Samuel Vila. (SPA.). 3.25 (84-7228-718-1, 220221, Pub. by Edit Clie SP) TSELF.
Como Pueden los Padres Ser Escuchas de Sus Hijas. Tim Jackins. (SPA.). 1993. pap. 4.00 (0-913937-74-6) Rational Isl.
Como Recuperar el Progreso Social en America Latina. Enrique De la Piedra. (Policy Seminar Report Ser.: No. 17). 36p. (SPA.). 1989. 6.95 (0-8213-1248-0, 11248) World Bank.
***Como Recuperar la Autoestima.** Hillman. (SPA.). 1995. pap. 11.00 (0-684-81550-8, Fireside) S&S Trade.
Como Reparar 500 Problemas De la Casa. Ed. by Maria E. Alvarez del Real. (Illus.). 352p. (Orig.). (SPA.). (YA). 1988. pap. 4.50 (0-944499-33-3) Editorial Amer.
Como Resolver los Problemas De Aprendizaje y Estudio De Su Hijos. Editorial America, S. A. Staff. Ed. by Maria E. Del Real. (Illus.). 256p. (Orig.). (SPA.). 1989. pap. 4.00 (0-944499-30-9) Editorial Amer.
Como Retener Su Sanidad. Kenneth E. Hagin. (SPA.). 1983. pap. 0.75 (0-89276-159-8) Hagin Ministries.
***Como Romper la Maldicion De la Pobreza.** Victor Ricardo. 30p. 1992. pap. 1.00 (1-885630-16-6) HLM Producciones.
Como Sabes Que Es Invierno? - How Do You Know It's Winter? LC 91-3129. (Rookie Read-about Science - Spanish Ser.). (Illus.). 32p. (SPA.). (J). (ps-2). 1994. pap. 3.95 (0-516-54915-4) Childrens.
Como Sabes Que Es Invierno? - How Do You Know It's Winter? LC 91-3129. (Rookie Read-about Science - Spanish Ser.). (Illus.). 32p. (SPA.). (J). (ps-2). 1994. lib. bdg. 11.10 (0-516-34915-5) Childrens.
Como Sabes Que Es Otono? How Do You Know It's Fall? Allan Fowler. LC 91-35060. (Rookie Read-about Science Ser.). (Illus.). 32p. (SPA.). (J). (ps-2). 1992. lib. bdg. 11.10 (0-516-34922-8); pap. 3.95 (0-516-54922-7); 23.48 (0-516-59623-3) Childrens.
Como Sabes Que Es Primavera? - How Do You Know It's Spring? Allan Fowler. LC 91-12760. (Rookie Read-about Science - Spanish Ser.). (Illus.). 32p. (SPA.). (J). (ps-2). 1994. lib. bdg. 11.10 (0-516-34914-7); pap. 3.95 (0-516-54914-6) Childrens.
Como Sabes Que Es Verano? How Do You Know It's Summer? Allan Fowler. LC 91-35061. (Rookie Read-about Science Ser.). (Illus.). 32p. (SPA.). (J). (ps-2). 1992. lib. bdg. 11.10 (0-516-34923-6); pap. 3.95 (0-516-54923-5); 23.48 (0-516-59624-1) Childrens.
Como Sacar una A: Getting Straight A's Spanish Language Edition. Gordon W. Green, Jr. 192p. (SPA.). 1992. pap. 8.95 (0-8184-0566-X, L Stuart) Carol Pub Group.
Como Sanar a los Enfermos. rev. ed. 340p. (SPA.). 1988. pap. 6.95 (0-917726-88-X) Hunter Bks.
Como se Dice...? Ana C. Jarvis et al. LC 89-84202. 504p. (SPA.). (C). 1990. Tapescript. 2.00 (0-669-19618-5) Heath.
Como se Dice...? 4th annot. ed. Ana C. Jarvis et al. LC 89-84202. 504p. (SPA.). (C). 1990. Instr.'s annotated ed. teacher ed 29.50 (0-669-19615-0) Heath.
Como se Dice...? 4th ed. Ana C. Jarvis et al. LC 89-84202. 504p. (SPA.). (C). 1990. text ed. 29.50 (0-669-19614-2); Wkbk./Lab. manual. student ed 14.50 (0-669-19616-9); Cassette program. audio 35.00 (0-669-19617-7); Demotape. audio 2.00 (0-669-19619-3) Heath.
***Como Se Dice...?** 5th ed. Ana C. Jarvis et al. 539p. (SPA.). (C). 1994. text ed. write for info. (0-669-29505-1) Heath.
Como se Dice...?, Incl. cass. 4th ed. Ana C. Jarvis et al. LC 89-84202. 504p. (SPA.). (C). 1990. Student text with cassette. student ed, audio 29.50 (0-669-21545-7) Heath.
Como Se Escribe. Ed. by Pagan H. Valdes & Richard V. Teschner. LC 82-10251. 217p. (SPA.). (gr. 10-12). 1982. text ed. 20.25 (0-684-17414-6, Scribners) S&S Trade.
Como Se Hacen: Spanish Take-Home Parent Pack, Set. (Take-Home Parent Packs Ser.). (Illus.). (Orig.). (SPA.). 1993. pap. 11.95 (1-56334-390-8) Hampton-Brown.
Como Se Hacen Las Cosas: Teacher's Theme Guide. (Que Maravilla! Ser.). (Illus.). (Orig.). (SPA.). 1992. pap. 29.95 (1-56334-167-0) Hampton-Brown.
Como Se Ven las Cosas, 10 vols. Ruth Bowdoin. Tr. by Ana Wier. (Metodo Bowdoin Ser.: Vol. VII). (Illus.). 48p. (Orig.). (SPA.). 1978. pap. text ed. write for info. (1-55997-066-9) Websters Intl.
Como Ser Artifice De Tu Propio Destino: How to Be the Guide of Your Future. Salvador Iserte. (SPA.). 3.95 (84-7228-988-5, 223069, Pub. by Edit Clie SP) TSELF.
Como Ser Buenos Padrastros (Successful Stepparenting) D. Juroe & B. Juroe. (SPA.). Date not set. 1.79 (1-56063-255-0, 497436) Editorial Unilit.
Como Ser Cristiano En Iglesia: How to Be a Christian. Fritz Ridenour. (SPA.). 2.95 (84-7228-159-0, 220170, Pub. by Edit Clie SP) TSELF.
Como Ser Cristiano En un Mundo No: How to Be a Christian. Fritz Ridenour. (SPA.). 3.25 (84-7228-147-7, 220172, Pub. by Edit Clie SP) TSELF.
Como Ser Cristiano Sin Ser Religioso (How to Be a Christian Without Being Religious) rev. ed. Fritz Ridenour. (SPA.). 1986. 4.50 (0-685-74919-3, 490231) Editorial Unilit.
Como Ser el Lider Que Debieras Ser: Be the Leader You Were Meant to Be. Leroy Eims. (SPA.). 5.50 (84-7645-240-3, 223313, Pub. by Edit Clie SP) TSELF.
Como Ser Encantadora (Para Alumna) Emily Hunter. Tr. by Wilma Mendoza De Mann & Frederico A. Mariotti. Orig. Title: Christian Charm Notebook. (Illus.). 56p. (SPA.). 1991. teacher ed, pap. 4.50 (0-311-46054-2); student ed, pap. 5.95 (0-311-46055-0) Casa Bautista.
Como Ser Escritor: How to Be a Writer. Martha Berberian. (SPA.). 5.25 (84-7645-394-9, 223504, Pub. by Edit Clie SP) TSELF.
Como Ser Feliz. Richard W. DeHaan. Orig. Title: How to Be Happy. 64p. (SPA.). 1978. pap. 2.75 (0-8254-1156-4) Kregel.
Como Ser Feliz en el Matrimonio. Elam J. Daniels. Orig. Title: How to Be Happily Married. 96p. 1986. reprint ed. pap. 2.95 (0-311-46066-6) Casa Bautista.
Como Ser Feliz en el Trabajo Que a Veces Ya No Soporto: How to Be Happier in the Job You Sometimes Can't Stand. Ross West. Tr. by Hiram Duffer. 128p. (SPA.). 1993. pap. 5.99 (0-311-46136-0) Casa Bautista.
Como Ser Libres Del Egoismo: Freedom from Self. Andrew Murray. (SPA.). 4.95 (84-7228-623-1, 220199, Pub. by Edit Clie SP) TSELF.
Como Ser Pentecostal Sin Hablar En Lenguas (How to Be a Pentecostal Without Speaking in Tongue) T. Campolo. (SPA.). Date not set. 5.99 (1-56063-262-3, 498519) Editorial Unilit.
Como Ser Su Propio Siguiatra. Martin Shepard. Ed. by Editorial Concepts Co. Staff et al. Tr. by Pedro Romanch. 166p. (Orig.). (SPA.). 1987. pap. 4.95 (0-939193-12-4) Edit Concepts.
Como Ser Su Propio Siquiatra. Martin Shepard. 166p. (Orig.). (SPA.). 1990. pap. 4.95 (0-944499-78-3) Editorial Amer.
Como Ser un Joven Ideal (Para Alumno) Wayne Hunter & Emily Hunter. Tr. by Federico A. Mariotti. Orig. Title: Man in Demand. 80p. (SPA.). 1990. student ed, pap. 5.50 (0-311-46074-7); teacher ed, pap. 6.95 (0-311-46075-5) Casa Bautista.
Como Ser un Lider: How to Be a Leader. Anthony D'Souza. (SPA.). 6.50 (84-7645-198-9, 223234, Pub. by Edit Clie SP) TSELF.
***Como Ser un Triunfador Desde Joven: 18 Secretos Que un Joven Tiene Que Conocer Para Triunfar en la Vida.** Rick Jones. LC 94-92412. 256p. (SPA.). (YA). (gr. 7-12). 1995. pap. 8.95 (0-937958-45-X) Chick Pubns.
Como Sobreponerse a la Adversidad (How to Handle Adversity) Charles Stanley. (SPA.). 1992. 5.99 (1-56063-190-2, 498477) Editorial Unilit.
Como Suple Dios Nuestras Necesidades: How God Supplies Our Needs. A. B. Simpson. (SPA.). 3.25 (84-7228-883-8, 220182, Pub. by Edit Clie SP) TSELF.
Como Tener Exito En Relaciones: How to Succeed in Family Living. Clyde Narramore. (SPA.). 3.95 (84-7228-163-9, 220174, Pub. by Edit Clie SP) TSELF.
Como Testificar Con Eficacia: You Can Witness with Confidence. Rosalind Rinker. (SPA.). 4.95 (84-7228-188-4, 220177, Pub. by Edit Clie SP) TSELF.
Como Transformar la Personalidad: You Can Change Your Personality. Andre Bustanoby. (SPA.). 5.50 (84-7228-352-6, 220179, Pub. by Edit Clie SP) TSELF.
Como Transformar Su Vida De Familia: A Family Love Story. Lou Beardsley. (SPA.). 4.25 (84-7228-604-5, 220201, Pub. by Edit Clie SP) TSELF.
Como Transformar Tension Mental: Turning Your Stress into Strength. Robert Schuller. (SPA.). 3.25 (84-7228-615-0, 220200, Pub. by Edit Clie SP) TSELF.
Como Triunfar En la Vida. Don Gosset. 157p. (SPA.). 1992. pap. 4.95 (0-938127-13-6) Gospel Pr FL.
Como Triunfar En los Negocios: How to Succeed in Business. Glen H. Bump. (SPA.). 4.50 (84-7228-047-0, 220180, Pub. by Edit Clie SP) TSELF.
***Como Triunfar Sobre la Ansiedad y Los Problemas.** Guy Finley. LC 94-36466. 240p. 1995. pap. 9.95 (1-56718-277-1) Llewellyn Pubns.
Como Triunfar Vendiendo Por Correo. Alberto Cruz. (Illus.). 172p. (SPA.). (C). 1990. 29.95 (0-685-29083-2) A Cruz.
Como un Grano De Mostaza: Like a Mustard's Seed. Dionisio Byler. (SPA.). 7.00 (84-7645-297-7, 223368, Pub. by Edit Clie SP) TSELF.
Como un Viento Recio. Mel Tari. 208p. 1972. 3.95 (0-88113-041-9) Edit Betania.
Como un Viento Recio: Like a Mighty Wind. C. I. Scofield. (SPA.). 2.95 (84-7228-643-6, 220217, Pub. by Edit Clie SP) TSELF.
Como Us a Microsoft Works. Rebecca B. Altman. 486p. 1993. pap. text ed. 31.95 (968-18-4492-0, Pub. by Limusa MX) Computer & Tech.
Como Usa FoxPro 2. Charles Siegel. 611p. 1992. pap. text ed. 31.95 (968-18-4450-5, Pub. by Limusa MX) Computer & Tech.
***Como Use la Verdad.** rev. ed. Myrtle Fillmore. 115p. (SPA.). 1995. write for info. (0-87159-068-9) Unity Bks.
Como Vencer Al Diablo: How to Win over Satan. Juan A. Monroy. (SPA.). 4.25 (84-7645-372-8, 223491, Pub. by Edit Clie SP) TSELF.
Como Vencer la Soledad (How to Overcome Loneliness) F. Elliott. (SPA.). 1992. 1.79 (1-56063-126-0, 498132) Editorial Unilit.
Como Vencer la Tension Nerviosa. Gilbert Little. Orig. Title: Nervous Christians. 128p. 1987. pap. 3.99 (0-8254-1443-1) Kregel.
Como Vencer las Preocupaciones: How to Win over Worry. William Orr. (SPA.). 3.25 (84-7645-307-8, 223288, Pub. by Edit Clie SP) TSELF.
Como Vivir al Maximo. Edwin Cole. Orig. Title: The Potential Principal. 144p. (SPA.). 1986. 3.95 (0-8297-0566-X) Life Pubs Intl.
Como Vivir Como Reyes (How to Live Like Kings) J. Fernandez. (SPA.). Date not set. 1.99 (1-56063-268-2, 498150) Editorial Unilit.
Como Vivir Con Cancer. 1992. 2.00 (0-914733-13-3) Desert Min.
Como Vivir Con Conyuge Inconverso (Living with an Unsaved Spouse) W. Deal. (SPA.). Date not set. 1.79 (0-685-74920-7, 497406) Editorial Unilit.
Como Vivir en el Mundo de Hoy. T. B. Maston. Tr. by Bob Adams. 110p. (SPA.). 1987. pap. 4.65 (0-311-46084-4) Casa Bautista.
Como Vivir en el Plano Superior. Ruth Paxson. Orig. Title: Life on the Highest Plane. 254p. (SPA.). 1984. pap. 5.99 (0-8254-1551-9) Kregel.
Como Vivir En la Voluntad De Dios: How to Live in the Will of God. Andrew Murray. (SPA.). 5.50 (84-7228-914-1, 222236, Pub. by Edit Clie SP) TSELF.
Como Vivir la Vida Victoriosa: How to Live a Victorious Life. (SPA.). 4.95 (84-7228-630-4, 220208, Pub. by Edit Clie SP) TSELF.
Como Vivir Sobre - Nivel - la Medi. Charles Swindoll. 320p. (SPA.). 1990. 5.95 (0-8297-0427-2) Life Pubs Intl.
Como Vivir Vida Cristiana Abundante: How to Live an Abundant Life. A. B. Simpson. (SPA.). 4.95 (84-7228-889-7, 222311, Pub. by Edit Clie SP) TSELF.
Como Viviren Paz con Tu Conciencia Sin Volverte Loco - How to Live in Peace with Your Conscience Without Going Crazy. Joel A. Freeman. 220p. (SPA.). 1992. pap. 6.95 (84-7645-597-6) TSELF.
Como Yo Te Amo. Rafael Crespo. (Romance Real Ser.). 192p. (SPA.). 1981. pap. 1.50 (0-88025-003-8) Roca Pub.
Comoediae, 2 vols. Plautus. Ed. by Friedrich Leo. 1958. Vol. I, viii, 478p. write for info. (0-318-71198-2, Pub. by Georg Olms GW); Vol. II, iv, 575p. write for info. (0-318-71199-0, Pub. by Georg Olms GW) Lubrecht & Cramer.
Comoediae. 2nd ed. Terence. Ed. by R. Kauer & W. M. Lindsay. (Oxford Classical Texts Ser.). 1926. 24.95 (0-19-814636-1) OUP.
Comoediae, 2 Vols, 1. Plautus. Ed. by W. M. Lindsay. 1922. 39.95 (0-19-814628-0) OUP.
Comoediae, 2 Vols, 2. Plautus. Ed. by W. M. Lindsay. 1922. 39.95 (0-19-814629-9) OUP.
Comoediae, 2 vols., Set. Plautus. Ed. by Friedrich Leo. 1958. write for info. (0-318-71197-4, Pub. by Georg Olms GW) Lubrecht & Cramer.
Comorbidity of Addictive & Psychiatric Disorders. Ed. by Barry Stimmel. LC 93-24682. (Journal of Addictive Diseases: Vol. 12, No. 3). (Illus.). 185p. 1993. lib. bdg. 39.95 (1-56024-457-7) Haworth Pr.
Comorbidity of Mood & Anxiety Disorders. Ed. by Jack Maser & C. Robert Cloninger. LC 89-17681. 800p. 1990. text ed. 67.50 (0-88048-324-5) Am Psychiatric.
Comp Avengers. Dave Rogers. 1989. pap. 13.95 (0-312-03187-4) St Martin.
***Comp Cancer Nursing Review.** 2nd ed. Susan Groenwald et al. (Nursing Ser.). 430p. 1995. pap. 37.50 (0-86720-720-5) Jones & Bartlett.
Comp Checklists - Essentials LT CR. Shirley A. Badash & Doreen Chesbro. 1990. 15.95 (0-8273-4529-1) Delmar.
***Comp City: A Guide to Free Las Vegas Vacations.** Max Rubin. 296p. (Orig.). 1994. 39.95 (0-929712-35-8) Huntington Pr.
Comp Coll Stories. Victor S. Pritchett. 1991. 35.00 (0-679-40215-2) McKay.
Comp-Compilers 1990 Annual. John R. Levine. 700p. (Orig.). (C). 1991. pap. text ed. 50.00 (0-944954-02-2) Ctr Bk Pubs.
Comp Defence to 1d4. 2nd ed. Robert Bellin. 1991. pap. write for info. (0-08-037151-5, Pub. by CHES UK) Macmillan.
Comp Encyclopedia of Photography. Mark Edwards. 192p. 1994. 14.98 (0-8317-1235-X) Smithmark.
Comp HyperCard 2.0 Handbook. 3rd ed. Danny Goodman. 1990. pap. 30.00 (0-679-79026-8) Random.
Comp One: An Introduction Composition Wookbook for Students of ESL. Thomas Sheehan. (Illus.). 256p. (C). 1985. pap. text ed. 16.95 (0-13-154022-X) P-H.
Comp Package for Fundamentals of Nursing. 3rd ed. Potter. 1993. write for info. (0-8016-7299-6) Mosby Yr Bk.
Comp Package of Rawlins Mental Health-Psychiatric. 3rd ed. Rawlins. 1993. write for info. (0-8016-7359-3) Mosby Yr Bk.
Comp Printmaker. rev. ed. John Ross. 1989. text ed. 49.95 (0-02-927371-4) Free Pr.
Comp Recreational Rower & Race. Stephen Kiesling. 1991. pap. 17.95 (0-517-57749-6, Crown) Crown Pub Group.
Comp Review Dental Hygiene. 2nd ed. Darby. 832p. 1990. pap. 38.95 (0-8016-1209-8) Mosby Yr Bk.
***Comp Vienna.** Tseitlin. 1995. pap. 19.95 (0-8050-3909-0) H Holt & Co.
Compact. Maurice Roche. Tr. & Intro. by Mark Polizzatti. LC 88-14194. 160p. 1988. 19.95 (0-916583-29-5) Dalkey Arch.
Compact Atlas of Idaho. Alan A. DeLucia. (Illus.). 117p. (Orig.). 1983. pap. 20.95 (0-940982-02-1) U ID Ctr Busn.
***Compact Bedford Introduction to Literature: Reading, Thinking, & Writing.** 3rd ed. Michael Meyer. 1512p. 1993. pap. text ed. 21.00 (0-312-08620-2) St Martin.
Compact Bible Atlas with Gazetteer. rev. ed. (Illus.). 76p. 1979. pap. 4.95 (0-8010-2432-3) Baker Bk.
Compact Bible Dictionary. T. Alton Bryant. 1972. pap. 7.99 (0-310-22082-3, 6726P) Zondervan.
Compact Blue - Green Lasers. LC 92-62710. (Technical Digest Series, 1993: Vol. 2, 1993). 200p. (Orig.). 1993. Postconference. pap. 75.00 (1-55752-278-2); Conference. pap. 48.00 (1-55752-277-4) Optical Soc.
Compact Blue-Green Lasers. LC 91-80504. (Technical Digest Series, 1992: Vol. 6). 200p. (Orig.). 1992. Postconference. pap. 75.00 (1-55752-226-X); Conference. pap. 48.00 (1-55752-225-1) Optical Soc.
Compact Blue-Green Lasers, 1994. LC 93-97353. (Technical Digest Ser.: Vol. 1). 250p. (Orig.). 1994. pap. 75.00 (1-55752-325-8); pap. text ed. 48.00 (1-55752-324-X) Optical Soc.
***Compact Cameras: How to Get the Best from Your Point-&-Shoot Camera.** John Garrett. (Illus.). 128p. 1995. pap. 19.95 (0-09-178359-3, Pub. by Ebury Pr UK) Trafalgar.
***Compact Classics, Vol. 3.** Compact Classics Staff. 1994. pap. 19.95 (1-880184-25-7) Compact Classics.
Compact Classics: Your Personal Portable Library, Vol. I. (Illus.). 624p. 1991. pap. 19.95 (1-880184-01-X); ring bd. 39.95 (1-880184-00-1) Compact Classics.
***Compact Classics Leather, Vol. 3.** Compact Classics Staff. 1994. 49.95 (1-880184-28-1) Compact Classics.
***Compact Classics Planner Edition, Vol. 3.** Compact Classics Staff. 1994. pap. 39.95 (1-880184-27-3) Compact Classics.
Compact Complex Surfaces. W. P. Barth et al. (Series of Modern Surveys in Mathematics, Band 4: Vol. 4). 320p. 1984. 79.00 (0-387-12172-2) Spr-Verlag.
Compact Convex Sets & Boundary Integrals. E. M. Alfsen. LC 72-136352. (Ergebnisse der Mathematik und Ihrer Grenzgebiete Ser.: Vol. 57). (Illus.). 1971. 65.00 (0-387-05090-6) Spr-Verlag.
Compact Culture: The Japanese Tradition of Smaller is Better. O-Young Lee. Tr. by Robert N. Huey. (Illus.). 192p. 1992. reprint ed. pap. text ed. 6.95 (4-7700-1643-3) Kodansha.
Compact Data for Astronomy & Navigation for the Years 1901-1995. B. D. Yallop & C. Y. Hohenkerk. (Illus.). 100p. (C). 1990. pap. 21.95 (0-521-38731-0) Cambridge U Pr.
Compact Dictionary: French. 1278p. (ENG & FRE.). 1989. 14.95 (0-88729-070-1) Langenscheidt.
Compact Dictionary: German. 1408p. (ENG & GER.). 1993. 14.95 (0-88729-071-X) Langenscheidt.
Compact Dictionary: Spanish. 1104p. (ENG & SPA.). 1989. 14.95 (0-88729-069-8) Langenscheidt.
Compact Dictionary of Doctrinal Words. Terry L. Miethe. LC 88-12161. 224p. (Orig.). 1988. reprint ed. pap. 8.99 (0-87123-678-8, 210678) Bethany Hse.
Compact Dictionary of Exact Science & Technology, Vol. 1. 2nd ed. Antonin Kucera. 1470p. (ENG & GER.). 1989. lib. bdg. 115.00 (0-685-48304-5, M9027) Fr & Eur.
Compact Dictionary of Exact Science & Technology, Vol. 2. Antonin Kucera. 590p. (ENG & GER.). 1981. 115.00 (0-8288-0629-2, M 9090) Fr & Eur.
Compact Dictionary of Exact Science & Technology, Vol. 2. 2nd ed. A. Kundera. 825p. (ENG & GER.). 1989. lib. bdg. 225.00 (3-87097-088-X, M9090) Fr & Eur.
***Compact Dictionary of Exact Science & Technology German-English.** Antonin Kucera. 825p. (ENG & GER.). 1994. 135.00 (0-614-00358-X, M9090) Fr & Eur.
Compact Dictionary of Exact Science & Technology, Vol. 1 Vol. 1: English - German. 2nd ed. Antonin Kucera. 1470p. (ENG & GER.). 1989. lib. bdg. 225.00 (0-8288-4044-X, M9090) Fr & Eur.
Compact Dictionary of Exact Science & Technology, Vol. 2: German - English. 2nd ed. Antonin Kucera. 825p. (ENG & GER.). 1994. lib. bdg. 135.00 (0-8288-4045-8, M9027) Fr & Eur.
Compact Dictionary of Food Technology. Erich Luck. 443p. (ENG & GER.). 1985. 150.00 (0-8288-0843-0, M8221) Fr & Eur.
Compact Dictionary of Science & Technology: German - French. Antonin Kucera. 812p. (FRE & GER.). 1991. lib. bdg. 250.00 (0-8288-3832-1, F99970) Fr & Eur.
Compact Dictionary of Science & Technology, Vol. 2: German-French. Antonin Kucera. 812p. (FRE & GER.). 1991. 195.00 (0-8288-8242-8, 3870971495) Fr & Eur.
***Compact Dictionary of the Social Sciences, 2.** 1995. write for info. (3-598-11281-5) K G Saur.
***Compact Dictionary of the Social Sciences: German-English, English-German, 2.** 1995. write for info. (3-598-11283-1) K G Saur.
***Compact Dictionary of the Social Sciences: German-English, English-German, Vol. 1.** (ENG & GER.). 1995. write for info. (3-598-11282-3) K G Saur.
Compact Disc Book: A Complete Guide to the Digital Sound of the Future. Bryan Brewer & Edd Key. LC 87-17706. (Illus.). 1987. pap. 12.95 (0-15-620050-3, Harvest Bks) HarBrace.
Compact Disc Handbook. 2nd ed. Ken C. Pohlmann. LC 92-13287. (Computer Music & Digital Audio Ser.: Vol. 5). (Illus.). 349p. (C). 1992. 49.95 (0-89579-301-6); pap. 34.95 (0-89579-300-8) A-R Eds.
Compact Disc Player Maintenance & Repair Manual. Gordon McComb & John Cook. 256p. 1987. 19.95 (0-8306-0190-2, 2790H); pap. 15.95 (0-8306-2790-1) TAB Bks.
Compact Disc Player Maintenance & Repair Service Manual. Gordon McComb & J. Cook. 1987. pap. text ed. 17.95 (0-07-157051-9) McGraw.
Compact Disc Technology. H. Nakajima & H. Ogawa. 228p. 1991. 60.00 (90-5199-066-9, Pub. by IOS Pr NE) IOS Press.
Compact Discs & Computers: Converging Technologies. J. Megarry. 1994. pap. 33.00 (0-412-37880-9, Blackie & Son-Chapman NY) Routledge Chapman & Hall.
Compact Dish: The Bread & Breakfast Cookbook. Sally L. Owens. LC 93-71980. (Compact Dish Cookbooks Ser.). 60p. (Orig.). 1993. spiral bd. write for info. (1-883810-06-X) Compact Ckbk.
Compact Dish: The Casual Chic Cookbook. Sally L. Owens. LC 93-71980. (Compact Dish Cookbooks Ser.). 60p. (Orig.). 1993. spiral bd. write for info. (1-883810-02-7) Compact Ckbk.
Compact Dish: The Cuisine with Kids Cookbook. Sally L. Owens. LC 93-71980. (Compact Dish Cookbooks Ser.). 60p. (Orig.). 1993. spiral bd. write for info. (1-883810-04-3) Compact Ckbk.

C

An Asterisk (*) at the beginning of an entry indicates that the title is appearing in BIP for the first time.

Compact Dish: The Double Income, No Kids Cookbook. Sally L. Owens. LC 93-71980. (Compact Dish Cookbooks Ser.). 60p. (Orig.). 1993. spiral bd. write for info. (*1-883810-03-5*) Compact Ckbk.

Compact Dish: The Home on the Range Cookbook. Cary C. Atkins & Sally L. Owens. LC 93-71980. (Compact Dish Cookbooks Ser.). 60p. (Orig.). 1993. spiral bd. write for info. (*1-883810-05-1*) Compact Ckbk.

Compact Dish: The Rush Hour Cookbook. Sally L. Owens. LC 93-71980. (Compact Dish Cookbooks Ser.). 60p. (Orig.). 1993. spiral bd. write for info. (*1-883810-01-9*) Compact Ckbk.

Compact Dish Cookbook Series, 6 vols., Set. Sally L. Owens. LC 93-71980. 360p. (Orig.). 1993. spiral bd. write for info. (*1-883810-00-0*) Compact Ckbk.

Compact Disk Players. Gene B. Williams. (All Thumbs Guide Ser.). (Illus.). 144p. 1992. pap. 9.95 (*0-8306-4179-3*, 4251) TAB Bks.

Compact Edition of the Oxford English Dictionary: A Supplement to the Oxford English Dictionary, Vol. III. Ed. by Robert W. Burchfield. 1987. 125.00 (*0-19-861211-7*) OUP.

Compact Equipment - Engines. Ed. by Deere & Company Staff. (Fundamentals of Service Ser.). (Illus.). 84p. 1992. Student guide. student ed, pap. text ed. 16.95 (*0-86691-176-6*, FCP80303W) Deere & Co.
This text covers basic theory of 2- & 4-cycle engines from chain-saw engines to 40-horsepower diesel engines. It covers the fundamentals of service for all engine systems: fuel, intake & exhaust, lubrication, cooling, & governors. It explains engine diagnosis & testing. For each chapter it provides the reader with a list of skills & knowledge that should be learned. CONTENTS: How It Works: 4 Cycle Engines, types, parts & functions, 2 Cycle Engines, types, parts & functions & fuel systems. Service Repairs, Adjustments: Diagnostic procedures, fuel systems, cooling systems (liquid & air) & lubrication systems. *Publisher Provided Annotation.*

Compact Equipment - Engines. rev. ed. Ed. by Deere & Company Staff. (Fundamentals of Service Ser.). (Illus.). 245p. 1992. Slide set. sl. 245.95 (*0-685-01387-1*, FCP80203S) Deere & Co.
This text covers basic theory of 2- & 4-cycle engines from chain-saw engines to 40-horsepower diesel engines. It covers the fundamentals of service for all engine systems: fuel, intake & exhaust, lubrication, cooling, & governors. It explains engine diagnosis & testing. For each chapter it provides the reader with a list of skills & knowledge that should be learned. CONTENTS: How It Works: 4 Cycle Engines, types, parts & functions, 2 Cycle Engines, types, parts & functions & fuel systems. Service Repairs, Adjustments: Diagnostic procedures, fuel systems, cooling systems (liquid & air) & lubrication systems. *Publisher Provided Annotation.*

Compact Equipment - Engines. 2nd rev. ed. Ed. by Deere & Company Staff. (Fundamentals of Service Ser.). (Illus.). 288p. 1992. pap. text ed. 29.95 (*0-86691-146-4*, FCP80103B) Deere & Co.
This text covers basic theory of 2- & 4-cycle engines from chain-saw engines to 40-horsepower diesel engines. It covers the fundamentals of service for all engine systems: fuel, intake & exhaust, lubrication, cooling, & governors. It explains engine diagnosis & testing. For each chapter it provides the reader with a list of skills & knowledge that should be learned. CONTENTS: How It Works: 4 Cycle Engines, types, parts & functions, 2 Cycle Engines, types, parts & functions & fuel systems. Service Repairs, Adjustments: Diagnostic procedures, fuel systems, cooling systems (liquid & air) & lubrication systems. *Publisher Provided Annotation.*

Compact Equipment - Engines, Instr.'s Kit. Ed. by Deere & Company Staff. (Fundamentals of Service Ser.). (Illus.). 1992. student ed, teacher ed 69.95 (*0-86691-203-7*, FCP80103KIT) Deere & Co.
This text covers basic theory of 2- & 4-cycle engines from chain-saw engines to 40-horsepower diesel engines. It covers the fundamentals of service for all engine systems: fuel, intake & exhaust, lubrication, cooling, & governors. It explains engine diagnosis & testing. For each chapter it provides the reader with a list of skills & knowledge that should be learned. CONTENTS: How It Works: 4 Cycle Engines, types, parts & functions, 2 Cycle Engines, types, parts & functions & fuel systems. Service Repairs, Adjustments: Diagnostic procedures, fuel systems, cooling systems (liquid & air) & lubrication systems. *Publisher Provided Annotation.*

Compact Equipment - Power Trains. rev. ed. Ed. by Deere & Company Staff. (Fundamentals of Service Ser.). (Illus.). 40p. (C). 1991. Student guide. student ed, pap. text ed. 16.95 (*0-86691-156-1*, FCP81302W); Slide set. sl. 150.95 (*0-685-05503-5*, FCP81201S) Deere & Co.
Tells how clutches & transmissions work - gear, friction, & hydrostatic. Gives basics of service & repair of major types of drives, transmission, transaxles, & clutches used in compact equipment. Includes troubleshooting guides. It provides the reader with a list of skills & knowledge that should be learned with each chapter. CONTENTS: Basic principles, clutches, mechanical transmissions, hydrostatic transmissions, belt & chain drives, differentials, final drives, power take-offs, service & maintenance & troubleshooting. *Publisher Provided Annotation.*

Compact Equipment - Power Trains. 2nd rev. ed. Ed. by Deere & Company Staff. (Fundamentals of Service Ser.). (Illus.). 188p. (C). 1991. pap. text ed. 29.95 (*0-86691-136-7*, FCP81102B) Deere & Co.
Tells how clutches & transmissions work - gear, friction, & hydrostatic. Gives basics of service & repair of major types of drives, transmission, transaxles, & clutches used in compact equipment. Includes troubleshooting guides. It provides the reader with a list of skills & knowledge that should be learned with each chapter. CONTENTS: Basic principles, clutches, mechanical transmissions, hydrostatic transmissions, belt & chain drives, differentials, final drives, power take-offs, service & maintenance & troubleshooting. *Publisher Provided Annotation.*

Compact Equipment - Power Trains, Instr.'s Kit. Ed. by Deere & Company Staff. (Fundamentals of Service Ser.). (Illus.). (C). 1991. Instr.'s kit, incl. textbook, instr.'s guide & student guide. student ed, teacher ed 69.95 (*0-86691-204-5*, FCP81102KIT) Deere & Co.
Tells how clutches & transmissions work - gear, friction, & hydrostatic. Gives basics of service & repair of major types of drives, transmission, transaxles, & clutches used in compact equipment. Includes troubleshooting guides. It provides the reader with a list of skills & knowledge that should be learned with each chapter. CONTENTS: Basic principles, clutches, mechanical transmissions, hydrostatic transmissions, belt & chain drives, differentials, final drives, power take-offs, service & maintenance & troubleshooting. *Publisher Provided Annotation.*

Compact Equipment-Electrical Systems. 2nd rev. ed. Ed. by Deere & Company Staff. (Fundamentals of Service Ser.). (Illus.). 312p. 1994. pap. text ed. 29.95 (*0-86691-205-3*, FCP83102B) Deere & Co.
This book discusses electrical theory as it applies to small equipment. It covers how the basic systems work. Explains generators, alternators & electronic ignition systems & how to test typical designs. It provides the reader with a list of skills & knowledge that should be learned with each chapter. CONTENTS: Basic electrical principles, basic electrical circuits, basic electric motor & generator principles, wiring diagrams, special tools, battery & charging circuits, starter circuits, coil ignition systems, magneto ignition systems & diagnostic procedures. *Publisher Provided Annotation.*

***Compact Equipment-Electrical Systems. 2nd rev. ed. Ed. by Deere & Company Staff. (Illus.). 74p. 1994. student ed, pap. text ed. 16.95 (*0-86691-209-6*, FCP83302W); sl. 226.95 (*0-614-03185-0*, FCP83201S) Deere & Co.**
This book discusses electrical theory as it applies to small equipment. It covers how the basic systems work. Explains generators, alternators & electronic ignition systems & how to test typical designs. It provides the reader with a list of skills & knowledge that should be learned with each chapter. CONTENTS: Basic electrical principles, basic electrical circuits, basic electric motor & generator principles, wiring diagrams, special tools, battery & charging circuits, starter circuits, coil ignition systems, magneto ignition systems & diagnostic procedures. *Publisher Provided Annotation.*

Compact Equipment-Electrical Systems, Instr.'s Kit. 2nd rev. ed. Ed. by Deere & Company Staff. (Fundamentals of Service Ser.). (Illus.). 1994. Instr's. kit, incl. textbook, instr's. guide & student guide. student ed, teacher ed 69.95 (*0-86691-201-0*, FCP83102KIT) Deere & Co.
This book discusses electrical theory as it applies to small equipment. It covers how the basic systems work. Explains generators, alternators & electronic ignition systems & how to test typical designs. It provides the reader with a list of skills & knowledge that should be learned with each chapter. CONTENTS: Basic electrical principles, basic electrical circuits, basic electric motor & generator principles, wiring diagrams, special tools, battery & charging circuits, starter circuits, coil ignition systems, magneto ignition systems & diagnostic procedures. *Publisher Provided Annotation.*

***Compact Equipment-Hydraulics. 2nd ed. Ed. by Deere & Company Staff. (Illus.). 42p. 1994. student ed, pap. text ed. 16.95 (*0-86691-197-9*, FCP82302W) Deere & Co.**
Covers hydraulics as normally used on small equipment, such as lawn & garden tractors, small utility tractors & skid steer loaders. It discusses basic principles of hydraulics & then expands into typical systems & components. Gives tips on maintenance & troubleshooting. It provides the reader with a list of skills & knowledge that should be learned with each chapter. CONTENTS: Basic hydraulic theory, basic hydraulic circuits, hydraulic pumps, hydraulic valves, hydraulic cylinders, hydraulic filters, hydraulic oil coolers, hoses, lines & couplers, general maintenance & troubleshooting. *Publisher Provided Annotation.*

Compact Equipment-Hydraulics. 2nd rev. ed. Ed. by Deere & Company Staff. (Fundamentals of Service Ser.). (Illus.). 188p. 1994. pap. text ed. 29.95 (*0-86691-189-8*, FCP82102B) Deere & Co.
Covers hydraulics as normally used on small equipment, such as lawn & garden tractors, small utility tractors & skid steer loaders. It discusses basic principles of hydraulics & then expands into typical systems & components. Gives tips on maintenance & troubleshooting. It provides the reader with a list of skills & knowledge that should be learned with each chapter. CONTENTS: Basic hydraulic theory, basic hydraulic circuits, hydraulic pumps, hydraulic valves, hydraulic cylinders, hydraulic filters, hydraulic oil coolers, hoses, lines & couplers, general maintenance & troubleshooting. *Publisher Provided Annotation.*

***Compact Equipment-Hydraulics. 2nd rev. ed. Ed. by Deere & Company Staff. (Illus.). 193p. 1994. sl. 193.95 (*0-614-03186-9*, FCP82202S) Deere & Co.**
Covers hydraulics as normally used on small equipment, such as lawn & garden tractors, small utility tractors & skid steer loaders. It discusses basic principles of hydraulics & then expands into typical systems & components. Gives tips on maintenance & troubleshooting. It provides the reader with a list of skills & knowledge that should be learned with each chapter. CONTENTS: Basic hydraulic theory, basic hydraulic circuits, hydraulic pumps, hydraulic valves, hydraulic cylinders, hydraulic filters, hydraulic oil coolers, hoses, lines & couplers, general maintenance & troubleshooting. *Publisher Provided Annotation.*

Compact Equipment-Hydraulics, Instr.'s Kit. 2nd rev. ed. Ed. by Deere & Company Staff. (Fundamentals of Service Ser.). (Illus.). 1994. Instr's. kit, incl. textbook, instr's. guide & student guide. student ed, teacher ed 69.95 (*0-86691-202-9*, FCP82102KIT) Deere & Co.
Covers hydraulics as normally used on small equipment, such as lawn & garden tractors, small utility tractors & skid steer loaders. It discusses basic principles of hydraulics & then expands into typical systems & components. Gives tips on maintenance & troubleshooting. It provides the reader with a list of skills & knowledge that should be learned with each chapter. CONTENTS: Basic hydraulic theory, basic hydraulic circuits, hydraulic pumps, hydraulic valves, hydraulic cylinders, hydraulic filters, hydraulic oil coolers, hoses, lines & couplers, general maintenance & troubleshooting. *Publisher Provided Annotation.*

Compact Garden: Discovering the Pleasures of Planting in a Small Place. Brian Fawcett. (Illus.). 128p. (Orig.). 1992. pap. 17.95 (*0-921820-43-7*, Pub. by Camden Hse CN) Firefly Bks Ltd.

Compact German - Italian, Italian - German Dictionary. G. Tomat. 1991. 39.95 (*0-8288-8501-X*) Fr & Eur.

Compact Guide to Colleges. 9th ed. Barron's Editors. 750p. 1994. pap. 7.95 (*0-8120-1886-9*) Barron.

Compact Guide to Korea. 72p. 1987. pap. 3.50 (*0-941009-02-5*) Hollym Corp Pubs.

Compact Guide to Lotus Smartsuite. Sandra E. Eddy. LC 94-65380. 750p. 1994. pap. 29.99 (*0-7821-1484-9*) Sybex.

***Compact Guide to Microsoft Office Professional.** Ron Mansfield. LC 94-68438. 1191p. 1994. pap. 29.99 (*0-7821-1604-3*) Sybex.

***Compact Guide to PerfectOffice.** Alan Simpson et al. 1995. 29.99 (*0-7821-1728-7*) Sybex.

Compact Guide to Property Law: A Civilized Approach to the Law. Jefferson H. Weaver. Ed. by Hannan. 235p. (C). 1992. pap. text ed. 23.25 (*0-314-93388-3*) West Pub.

Compact Guide to the Christian Life. Ed. by Karen Hinckley. LC 89-60511. 240p. (Orig.). 1989. pap. 6.00 (*0-89109-282-X*) NavPress.

Compact Guide to the Microsoft Office. Ron Mansfield. LC 93-87701. 779p. 1994. pap. 29.99 (*0-7821-1483-0*) Sybex.

C

An Asterisk (*) at the beginning of an entry indicates that the title is appearing in BIP for the first time.

An Asterisk (*) at the beginning of an entry indicates that the title is appearing in BIP for the first time.

Companion Studies to the History of Tamil Literature. Kamil V. Zvelebil. LC 91-34907. (Handbuch der Orientalistik. Zweite Abteilung Ser.: No. 5). xxv, 291p. 1991. 80.00 (90-04-09365-6) E J Brill.

Companion Through Darkness: Inner Dialogues on Grief. Stephanie Ericsson. LC 92-53402. 256p. 1993. pap. 13.00 (0-06-096974-1, PL) HarpC.

Companion to a Sand County Almanac: Interpretive & Critical Essays. Ed. by J. Baird Callicott. LC 87-10396. 310p. (C). 1987. text ed. 27.50 (0-299-11230-6); pap. text ed. 14.95 (0-299-11234-9) U of Wis Pr.

Companion to Aesthetics. Ed. by David E. Cooper. LC 92-38691. (Companions to Philosophy Ser.). 480p. 1993. 74.95 (0-631-17801-5) Blackwell Pubs.

Companion to American Thoughts. Ed. by Richard Fox & James Kloppenberg. 1995. text ed. 265.00 (1-55786-268-0) Blackwell Pubs.

Companion to Animal Physiology. Ed. by C. Richard Taylor et al. LC 01-17055. 304p. 1982. 59.95 (0-521-24437-4); pap. 24.95 (0-521-28685-9) Cambridge U Pr.

Companion to Aristotle's Politics: A Critical Reader. Ed. by David Keyt & Fred D. Miller. 380p. (Orig.). (C). 1991. pap. text ed. 27.95 (1-55786-098-X) Blackwell Pubs.

Companion to Baroque Music: A Biographical Dictionary & Guide to National Traditions. Ed. by Julie A. Sadie. 550p. 1991. text ed. 50.00 (0-02-872275-2) Schirmer Bks.

Companion to Baugh & Cable's History of the English Language. 2nd ed. Thomas Cable. LC 93-14419. 1993. pap. text ed. write for info. (0-13-395716-0) P-H.

Companion to Beethoven's Pianoforte Sonatas. Donald F. Tovey. LC 74-24243. reprint ed. 49.50 (0-404-13117-4) AMS Pr.

Companion to Beethoven's Pianoforte Sonatas: Music Book Index. Donald F. Tovey. 301p. 1993. reprint ed. lib. bdg. 89.00 (0-7812-9670-6) Rprt Serv.

Companion to Biochemistry: Selected Topics for Further Study, Vol. 1. Ed. by Alan T. Bull et al. LC 73-89489. 710p. reprint ed. pap. 180.00 (0-685-16380-6, 2027711) Bks Demand.

Companion to Bleak House. Susan Shatto. 336p. 1988. 49.95 (0-04-800047-7) Routledge Chapman & Hall.

Companion to Calculus. Dennis Ebersole et al. LC 94-11340. 1994. pap. 30.95 (0-534-23316-3) Brooks-Cole.

***Companion to Calculus.** rev. ed. Dennis Ebersole. LC 94-42997. 1995. pap. 23.95 (0-534-26592-8) Brooks-Cole.

Companion to California. rev. ed. James S. Hart. LC 86-30903. (Illus.). 576p. 1987. pap. 19.00 (0-520-05544-6) U CA Pr.

Companion to Chaucer Studies. rev. ed. Ed. by Beryl Rowland. 1979. pap. text ed. 18.95 (0-19-502489-3) OUP.

***Companion to Chaucer's Canterbury Tales.** Margaret Hallissy. LC 95-16017. 344p. 1995. text ed. 49.95 (0-313-29189-6, Greenwood Pr) Greenwood.

Companion to Chian. Frances Wood. (Illus.). 256p. 1990. 22.95 (0-312-04283-3) St Martin.

Companion to Chinese History. Hugh B. O'Neill. 416p. 1987. 27.50 (0-87196-841-X) Facts on File.

Companion to Chinese History. Hugh B. O'Neill. 416p. 1988. pap. 14.95 (0-8160-1825-1) Facts on File.

Companion to Classical Texts. F. W. Hall. viii, 363p. 1968. reprint ed. 63.70 (0-685-66473-2, 05101877, Pub. by Georg Olms GW) Lubrecht & Cramer.

Companion to Classical Texts. Frederick W. Hall. LC 72-2568. (Select Bibliographies Reprint Ser.). 1977. reprint ed. 27.95 (0-8369-6855-7) Ayer.

Companion to Clinical Anaesthesia Exams. C. F. Corke & I. J. Jackson. LC 94-1429. 1994. 32.50 (0-443-04962-9) Churchill.

***Companion to Clinical Neurology.** William Pryce-Phillips. LC 94-19605. 1994. 99.95 (0-316-72041-0) Little.

Companion to Concrete Mathematics, Vol. 1: Mathematical Techniques & Various Applications. Z. A. Melzak. LC 72-14171. (Wiley Series in Pure & Applied Mathematics). 284p. reprint ed. pap. 81.00 (0-317-08619-7, 2022492) Bks Demand.

Companion to Concrete Mathematics, Vol. 2: Mathematical Ideas, Modeling & Applications. Z. A. Melzak. LC 72-14171. 432p. reprint ed. pap. 123.20 (0-317-08554-9, 2055165) Bks Demand.

Companion to Contemporary Architectural Thought. Ed. by Ben Farmer et al. LC 92-12839. (Companion Encyclopedia Ser.). (Illus.). 750p. 1993. 145.95 (0-415-01022-5, A7194) Routledge.

Companion to Contemporary Economic Thought. David Greenaway. 1992. 99.95 (0-415-02612-1, Pub. by Tavistock UK) Routledge Chapman & Hall.

Companion to Contemporary Musical Thought, 2 vol. set. John Paynter et al. (Companion Encyclopedia Ser.). 1992. 149.95 (0-415-01990-7, A7201) Routledge.

Companion to Contemporary Political Philosophy. Ed. by Robert E. Goodin & Philip Pettit. LC 92-41450. (Companions to Philosophy Ser.). 640p. 1993. 74.95 (0-631-17993-3) Blackwell Pubs.

Companion to Early Middle English Literature. Ed. by H. Aertsen & N. H. Veldhoen. 104p. 1993. pap. 15.00 (90-6256-632-4, Pub. by VU Univ Pr NE) Paul & Co Pubs.

***Companion to Early Middle English Literature.** 2nd rev. ed. Ed. by N. H. Veldhoen & Aertsen. 144p. 1995. pap. 11.50 (90-5383-349-8) Paul & Co Pubs.

Companion to Epistemology. Ed. by Jonathan Dancy & Ernest Sosa. LC 92-32205. 1992. 79.95 (0-631-17204-1) Blackwell Pubs.

Companion to Epistemology. Ed. by Jonathan Dancy & Ernest Sosa. (Companions to Philosophy Ser.). 560p. 1994. pap. text ed. 26.95 (0-631-19258-1) Blackwell Pubs.

Companion to Ethics. Ed. by Peter Singer. (Companions to Philosophy Ser.). 588p. 1993. 79.95 (0-631-16211-9); pap. 24.95 (0-631-18785-5) Blackwell Pubs.

Companion to General Analysis. Griffiths. (C). Date not set. text ed. write for info. (0-7167-2561-4) W H Freeman.

Companion to Greek Tragedy. John Ferguson. LC 74-38380. 635p. reprint ed. 180.00 (0-8357-9768-6, 2051580) Bks Demand.

Companion to Gynaecology. C. L. Huang & V. G. Daniels. 1985. lib. bdg. 42.00 (0-318-11846-7) Kluwer Ac.

Companion to Henry James Studies. Daniel M. Fogel. LC 92-1129. 568p. 1993. text ed. 79.95 (0-313-25792-2, FCJ/, Greenwood Pr) Greenwood.

Companion to Henslowe's Diary. Neil Carson. 168p. 1988. 64.95 (0-521-23545-6) Cambridge U Pr.

Companion to Hymnbook for Christian Worship. Arthur N. Wake. LC 72-129621. 1970. 8.99 (0-8272-8025-4) Chalice Pr.

Companion to Irish History. Peter R. Newman. 256p. 1991. lib. bdg. 27.95 (0-8160-2572-X) Facts on File.

Companion to Japanese Literature, Culture, & Language. Susanna Cuyler. (Illus.). 93p. (Orig.). 1992. pap. write for info. (0-9612018-5-1) B Rugged.

Companion to John: Readings in Johannine Theology. Ed. by Michael J. Taylor. LC 77-7042. 1977. pap. 6.95 (0-8189-0348-1) Alba.

Companion to Joyce Studies. Ed. by Zack R. Bowen & James F. Carens. LC 83-1479. (Illus.). 832p. 1984. text ed. 105.00 (0-313-22832-9, BJS/, Greenwood Pr) Greenwood.

Companion to Kant's Critique of Pure Reason: Transcendental Aesthetic & Analytic. Karl Aschenbrenner. LC 83-6889. 334p. (Orig.). (C). 1983. pap. text ed. 26.00 (0-8191-3230-6) U Pr of Amer.

Companion to Kimberley Rainforests Australia. M. K. Kenneally & N. L. McKenzie. (C). 1991. text ed. 25.00 (0-949324-41-8, Pub. by Surrey Beatty & Sons AT) St Mut.

***Companion to Language Dictionaries.** Andrew Dalby. 1996. write for info. (1-85739-156-X) Bowker-Saur.

Companion to Literary Myths: Heroes & Archetypes. P. Brunel. 864p. 1993. 99.95 (0-415-06460-0, A7985) Routledge.

Companion to Medical Statistics. Edmond A. Murphy. LC 84-21806. 288p. (C). 1985. text ed. 45.00 (0-8018-2612-8) Johns Hopkins.

Companion to Medieval & Renaissance Music. Ed. by Tess Knighton & David Fallows. (Illus.). 428p. 1992. text ed. 50.00 (0-02-871221-8) Schirmer Bks.

Companion to Melville Studies. Ed. by John Bryant. LC 86-361. 934p. 1986. text ed. 125.00 (0-313-23874-X, BMV/, Greenwood Pr) Greenwood.

Companion to Metaphysics. Ed. by Jaegwon Kim & Ernest Sosa. (Companions to Philosophy Ser.). 1995. 79.95 (0-631-17272-6) Blackwell Pubs.

Companion to Microbiology: Selected Topics for Further Study. Ed. by Alan T. Bull & Pauline M. Meadow. LC 77-13967. (Illus.). 515p. reprint ed. pap. 146.80 (0-8357-6065-0, 2034513) Bks Demand.

Companion to Middle English Romance. Ed. by Henk Aertsen & Alasdair A. MacDonald. 216p. 1991. pap. 34.95 (90-6256-899-8, Pub. by VU Univ Pr NE) Paul & Co Pubs.

Companion to Modal Logic. G. E. Hughes & Maxwell J. Cresswell. 224p. (Orig.). (C). 1985. pap. 15.95 (0-416-37510-3, 9057) Routledge Chapman & Hall.

***Companion to My Tears: Working Through The Process of Bereavement.** Ed. by Margaret A.R. Drucker. LC 94-23550. 96p. (Orig.). 1994. pap. 3.95 (0-8189-0710-X) Alba.

Companion to Narnia. Paul F. Ford. 1987. pap. 14.00 (0-02-084940-0, Collier S&S) S&S Trade.

Companion to Narnia. Paul F. Ford. 512p. 1994. reprint ed. pap. 15.00 (0-06-251136-X) Harper SF.

Companion to Narnia: A Complete, Illustrated Guide to the Themes, Characters, & Events of C. S. Lewis's Imaginary World. Paul F. Ford. LC 80-7734. (Illus.). 512p. 1983. pap. 6.95 (0-06-250341-3, P/5006) Harper SF.

Companion to Neo-Latin Studies, Pt. 1: History & Diffusion of Neo-Latin Literature. Jozef Ijsewijn. 371p. 1990. 54.95 (1-55540-576-2) Scholars Pr GA.

Companion to Neonatal Medicine. Ed. by C. L. Huang & V. G. Daniels. (Companion Ser.). (Illus.). 120p. 1982. lib. bdg. 36.50 (0-85200-380-3) Kluwer Ac.

Companion to Obstetrics. Ed. by C. L. Huang & V. G. Daniels. (Companion Ser.). 1982. lib. bdg. 37.50 (0-85200-379-X) Kluwer Ac.

Companion to Old English Poetry. Ed. by Ed H. Aertsen & Rolf H. Bremmer, Jr. 250p. (Orig.). 1993. pap. text ed. 23.50 (90-5383-116-9, Pub. by VU Univ Pr NE) Paul & Co Pubs.

Companion to Oliver Twist. David Paroissien. (Illus.). 400p. 1991. text ed. 69.00 (0-7486-0272-0, Pub. by Edinburgh U Pr UK) Col U Pr.

Companion to Pharmacology: A Study Guide for Self Assessment & Revision. M. M. Dale & A. H. Dickenson. LC 92-19270. (Illus.). 206p. 1993. pap. text ed. 19.95 (0-443-04178-4) Churchill.

Companion to Pirandello Studies. Ed. by John L. Digaetani. LC 90-43377. 472p. 1991. text ed. 95.00 (0-313-25714-0, DLP/, Greenwood Pr) Greenwood.

Companion to Plato's Republic. Nicholas P. White. LC 78-70043. 284p. (C). 1979. 32.50 (0-915144-56-5); pap. text ed. 9.95 (0-915144-92-1) Hackett Pub.

Companion to Post-War British Theatre. Philip Barnes. 288p. 1986. 58.50 (0-389-20669-5, N8233) B&N Imports.

Companion to Psychiatric Studies. 5th ed. Ed. by R. E. Kendell & A. K. Zealley. LC 92-49324. 1993. write for info. (0-443-04668-9) Churchill.

***Companion to Russian History.** fac. ed. John Paxton. LC 82-5192. (Illus.). 515p. 1983. reprint ed. pap. 146.80 (0-7837-7829-5, 2047585) Bks Demand.

Companion to Russian Studies: An Introduction to Russian History, Vol. 1. Ed. by R. Auty & D. Obolensky. LC 75-10688. 403p. 1981. pap. 29.95 (0-521-28038-9) Cambridge U Pr.

Companion to Samaritan Studies. Ed. by Alan D. Crown et al. 500p. 1993. 137.50 (3-16-145666-1, Pub. by J C B Mohr GW) Coronet Bks.

Companion to Scottish Culture. Ed. by David Daiches. LC 82-986. (Illus.). 441p. 1982. 49.50 (0-8419-0792-7) Holmes & Meier.

Companion to Senya. Senya Darklight et al. Ed. by Marty Campbell. LC 88-92536. (Illus.). 160p. (Orig.). 1989. pap. 9.00 (0-929749-01-4) Mar Crafs.

Companion to Seventh-Day Adventist Hymnal. Wayne W. Hooper & Edward E. White. Ed. by Raymond H. Woolsey. 701p. 1988. 34.95 (0-8280-0425-0) Review & Herald.

Companion to Shakespeare Studies. Harley G. Granville-Barker & George B. Harrison. (Cambridge Companions to Literature Ser.). 1934. 75.00 (0-521-05132-0) Cambridge U Pr.

***Companion to Social Theory.** Ed. & Intro. by Bryan S. Turner. (Illus.). (C). 1996. write for info. (0-631-18399-X); pap. text ed. write for info. (0-631-18401-5) Blackwell Pubs.

Companion to Statistics: Basic Principles & Applications. William Adams et al. 144p. (C). 1994. 18.95 (0-8403-9414-4) Kendall-Hunt.

Companion to the Bible. Ed. by Miriam Ward. LC 85-15817. 419p. (Orig.). 1985. pap. 14.95 (0-8189-0487-9) Alba.

Companion to the Bible. 2nd ed. T. W. Manson. Ed. by H. H. Rowley. 592p. 1963. pap. 31.95 (0-567-02197-1, Pub. by T & T Clark UK) Bks Intl VA.

Companion to the Calendar. Mary E. Hynes. Ed. by Peter Mazar. 287p. (Orig.). 1993. pap. 14.00 (1-56854-011-6) Liturgy Tr Pubns.

Companion to the Cantos of Ezra Pound. Carroll F. Terrell. 1993. pap. 25.00 (0-520-08287-7) U CA Pr.

Companion to the Cantos of Ezra Pound, Vol. II: Cantos 74-120. Carroll F. Terrell. LC 78-54802. 320p. 1984. 52.00 (0-520-04731-1) U CA Pr.

Companion to the Cantos of Ezra Pound, Volume I: Cantos 1-71. Carroll F. Terrell. 800p. 1980. 52.00 (0-520-03687-5) U CA Pr.

Companion to the Catechism of the Catholic Church: A Complete Book of References. 704p. 1993. 39.95 (0-89870-450-2); pap. 29.95 (0-89870-451-0) Ignatius Pr.

Companion to the Clams. Hugh Noonan. (Illus.). 1980. 4.95 (0-8199-0680-8, Frncscn Herld) Franciscan Pr.

Companion to the Concerto. Ed. by Robert Layton. 369p. 1989. text ed. 40.00 (0-02-871961-1) Schirmer Bks.

Companion to The Crying of Lot 49. J. Kerry Grant. LC 93-38157. 176p. 1994. 25.00 (0-8203-1635-0); pap. 12.95 (0-8203-1636-9) U of Ga Pr.

Companion to the English Civil Wars. Peter R. Newman. (Illus.). 256p. 1991. 29.95 (0-8160-2237-2) Facts on File.

Companion to the French Revolution. John Paxton. 256p. 1989. pap. 12.95 (0-8160-1937-1) Facts on File.

Companion to the Grapes of Wrath. Ed. by Warren G. French. LC 77-122056. xi, 243p. 1972. reprint ed. lib. bdg. 35.00 (0-678-03156-8) Kelley.

Companion to the History of Modern Science. Ed. by Robert Olby et al. 992p. 1989. 89.95 (0-415-01988-5, A3891) Routledge.

Companion to the "Iliad" Malcolm M. Willcock. LC 75-20894. 1976. pap. text ed. 9.95 (0-226-89855-5, P677) U Ch Pr.

Companion to the Industrial Revolution. Clifford J. Lines. 256p. 1990. 27.50 (0-8160-2157-0) Facts on File.

Companion to the Medieval Theatre. Ed. by Ronald W. Vince. LC 88-21337. 453p. 1989. text ed. 89.50 (0-313-24647-5, VID/, Greenwood Pr) Greenwood.

Companion to the Philosophy of Mind. Ed. by Samuel Guttenplan. (Companions to Philosophy Ser.). 576p. 1994. text ed. 79.95 (0-631-17953-4) Blackwell Pubs.

Companion to the Physical Sciences. David C. Knight. 192p. 1989. 25.00 (0-415-00901-4) Routledge.

Companion to the Poor. Rev. by Viv Grigg. 205p. 1990. 8.95 (0-912552-69-7) MARC.

***Companion to the Prayer of Christians.** John Burke. 300p. (Orig.). 1995. pap. text ed. 11.95 (0-8146-2097-3, Liturg Pr Bks) Liturgical Pr.

***Companion to the Qur'an.** William M. Watt. 1995. pap. 14.95 (1-85168-036-5) Onewrld Pubns.

Companion to the Songbook: North American Edition. 1991. pap. 10.95 (0-86544-064-6) Salv Army Suppl South.

Companion to the Study of History. Michael Stanford. 320p. (Orig.). (C). 1994. text ed. 59.95 (0-631-18158-X); pap. text ed. 22.95 (0-631-18159-8) Blackwell Pubs.

***Companion to the Study of Virgil.** Nicholas Horsfall. LC 95-15065. (Mnemosyne, Bibliotheca Classica Batava: Supplementum Ser.: No. 151). 336p. 1995. 98.25 (90-04-09559-4) E J Brill.

Companion to the United Methodist Hymnal. Carlton R. Young. LC 93-4115. 1993. 39.95 (0-687-09260-4) Abingdon.

Companion to the United States Constitution & Its Amendments. John R. Vile. LC 92-31847. 240p. 1993. text ed. 57.95 (0-275-94511-1, C4511, Praeger Pubs); pap. text ed. 16.95 (0-275-94512-X, B4512, Praeger Pubs) Greenwood.

Companion to the Worshiping Church. Donald P. Hustad & Richard Stanislaw. (C). 1993. 29.95 (0-916642-53-4) Hope Pub.

***Companion to Theatre in Australia.** Ed. by Philip Parsons. (Illus.). 608p. (C). 1992. write for info. (0-521-34528-6) Cambridge U Pr.

Companion to Twentieth-Century German Literature. Ed. by Raymond Furness & Malcolm Humble. 288p. (C). 1991. text ed. 49.95 (0-415-01987-7, A5148) Routledge.

Companion to Twentieth-Century Music. Norman Lebrecht. (Illus.). 288p. 1993. 30.00 (0-671-66654-1) S&S Trade.

Companion to Twentieth Century Opera. George Martin. 654p. 1992. pap. 24.95 (0-7195-4767-9, Pub. by John Murray UK) Trafalgar.

***Companion to Under the Volcano.** Lawrence J. Clipper. 492p. 1984. 49.95 (0-7748-0199-9) U of Wash Pr.

Companion to Victorian Literature. Thomas M. Parrott. 1988. reprint ed. lib. bdg. 59.00 (0-7812-0070-9) Rprt Serv.

Companion to Victorian Literature. Thomas M. Parrott & Martin Robert. 1981. reprint ed. lib. bdg. 59.00 (0-403-01495-6) Scholarly.

***Companion to Wine.** Frank Prial. 1994. pap. 34.98 (0-8317-4237-2) Smithmark.

Companion to Wittgenstein's Philosophical Investigations. Garth Hallett. LC 76-28014. 800p. 1977. 64.50 (0-8014-0997-7) Cornell U Pr.

Companion to Wittgenstein's Tractatus. Max Black. 466p. 1964. 49.95 (0-8014-0039-2) Cornell U Pr.

Companion to Your Study of the Book of Mormon. Daniel H. Ludlow. LC 76-27139. 396p. 1976. 12.95 (0-87747-610-1) Deseret Bk.

Companion to Your Study of the Doctrine & Covenants, 2 vols. Daniel H. Ludlow. LC 78-64752. 1978. Vol. 2, 390 p. write for info. (0-87747-729-9) Deseret Bk.

Companion to Your Study of the New Testament: The Four Gospels. Daniel H. Ludlow. 454p. 1982. 13.95 (0-87747-945-3) Deseret Bk.

Companion to Your Study of the Old Testament. Daniel H. Ludlow. LC 80-28088. 437p. 1981. 15.95 (0-87747-853-8) Deseret Bk.

Companion Volume see New Cambridge Modern History

Companion Volume to the Songs We Sing. Harry Coopersmith. 1950. 3.50 (0-8381-0210-7) United Syn Bk.

Companion Way: Mentoring Youth in Searching Faith. John Vitek. Ed. by Robert Stamschror. (Illus.). 70p. 1992. spiral bd. 15.95 (0-88489-283-2) St Marys.

Companionable Books Series One. George S. Gordon. LC 68-16935. (Essay Index Reprint Ser.). 1977. 19.95 (0-8369-0485-0) Ayer.

Companionate Marriage. Ben B. Lindsey & Wainwright Evans. LC 73-169393. (Family in America Ser.). 400p. 1977. reprint ed. 21.95 (0-405-03870-4) Ayer.

Companions. Lygia Bojunga-Nunes. 1989. 11.95 (0-374-31465-9) FS&G.

Companions. Tina Daniell. (Dragonlance Meetings Sextet Ser.: Vol. 6). 320p. 1992. pap. 4.95 (1-56076-340-X) TSR Inc.

Companions: Quilts & Miniatures. Darlene Zimmerman. 72p. 1992. 15.95 (1-881588-00-9) E-Z Intl.

Companions along the Way. Ruth Montgomery. 1985. mass mkt. 5.99 (0-449-21221-1) Fawcett.

Companions along the Way. Paul Wilkes. 1990. 14.95 (0-88347-238-4) Thomas More.

***Companions & Other Stories.** Lynn Stearns. 140p. (Orig.). Date not set. pap. 7.95 (0-7610-0371-1) NW Pub.

***Companions for the Soul: A Year Long Journey of Miracles, Prayers, & Epiphanies.** Comp. by R. Hudson & Shelley Townsend-Hudson. 384p. 1995. 17.99 (0-310-49791-4) Zondervan.

Companions in Consciousness: The Bible & the New Age Movement. Ronald Quillo. LC 93-33422. 192p. 1994. 18.95 (0-89243-655-7, Triumph Books) Liguori Pubns.

***Companions in Consciousness: The Bible & the New Age Movement.** Ronald Quillo. 192p. 1995. pap. 12.95 (0-89243-824-X) Liguori Pubns.

Companions in Grace: Spiritual Exercises of St. Ignatius of Loyola. Marian Cowan & John C. Futrell. LC 93-6194. 256p. (Orig.). 1993. pap. 14.95 (1-55612-667-0) Sheed & Ward MO.

***Companions in Spirit.** Laeh M. Garfield & Jack Grant. 187p. (Orig.). 1995. pap. 9.95 (0-89087-753-X) Celestial Arts.

Companions in the Mission of Jesus: Texts for Prayer & Reflection. 107p. (Orig.). 1987. pap. 4.95 (0-87840-450-3) Georgetown U Pr.

Companions of Jesus: The Jesuit Martyrs of El Salvador. Jon Sobrino. LC 90-41772. 1990. pap. 12.95 (0-88344-699-5) Orbis Bks.

Companion's of the Cross. Bob Bedard. 220p. 1994. pap. 8.00 (1-882972-36-8) Queenship Pub.

Companions of the Fire. Ali Wadud. 1980. pap. 2.75 (0-8222-0235-2) Dramatists Play.

Companions of the Heart. Alan Cohen. 887p. 1987. 19.95 (0-910367-38-8) A Cohen.

***Companions of the Military Order of the Loyal Legion of the United States: An Album Containing Portraits of Members of the Military Order of the Loyal Legion of the United States.** (Military Order of the Loyal Legion of the United States Ser.). (Illus.). 337p. 1994. 60.00 (1-56837-249-3) Broadfoot.

***Companions of the Night.** Vivian V. Velde. LC 94-30106. (J). 1995. 17.00 (0-15-200221-9) HarBrace.

Companions of the Trail. Hamlin Garland. (Collected Works of Hamlin Garland). 1988. reprint ed. lib. bdg. 79.00 (0-7812-1253-7) Rprt Serv.

Companions of the Trail see Collected Works of Hamlin Garland

An Asterisk (*) at the beginning of an entry indicates that the title is appearing in BIP for the first time.

C

An Asterisk (*) at the beginning of an entry indicates that the title is appearing in BIP for the first time.

1441

Company-Wide Total Quality Control. Shigeru Mizuno. 313p. 1988. text ed. 32.50 (*92-833-1099-3*, Pub. by APO JA) Qual Resc.

***Company Woman.** Kathleen De Grave. 1995. pap. 10.95 (*1-884365-04-3*) See Sharp Pr.

Company's Coming. 115p. spiral bd. 4.95 (*0-86701-025-8*) U of Tex Inst Tex Culture.

Company's Coming. Heritage House, Inc. Staff. LC 93-71693. (Home Sweet Home Cooking Ser.: Vol. 2). 1993. write for info. (*0-87197-377-4*) Favorite Recipes.

Company's Coming: Foods for Entertaining. 2nd ed. Junior League of Kansas City, MO. Ed. by Janet Thoma. (Illus.). 288p. 1988. spiral bd., pap. 11.95 (*0-929410-00-9*) Cookbook Collection Inc.

Companywide Quality Management. Alberto Galgano. (Illus.). 480p. 1994. 45.00 (*1-56327-038-2*) Prod Press.

***Comparability & Evaluation: Essays on Comparative Law, Private International Law, & International Commercial Arbitration in Honour of Dimitra Kokkini-Iatridou.** Ed. by K. Boele-Woelki et al. LC 94-35315. 432p. (C). 1994. lib. bdg. 135.50 (*0-7923-3157-5*, Pub. by M Nijhoff) Kluwer Ac.

Comparability of Statistics of Causes of Death According to the Fifth & Sixth Revisions of the International List. 1952. pap. 1.20 (*92-4-156007-X*) World Health.

Comparability of the Birth Certificate & the 1988 National Maternal & Infant Health Survey Questionnaire, No. 116. Kenneth C. Schoendorf et al. LC 92-49066. (Vital & Health Statistics Ser. 2: Data Evaluation & Methods Research). 1992. write for info. (*0-8406-0473-4*) Natl Ctr Health Stats.

Comparability of the Death Certificate & the 1986 National Mortality Followback Survey. LC 93-14607. (Vital & Health Statistics Ser. 2: Data Evaluation & Methods Research: No. 118). 1993. write for info. (*0-8406-0484-X*) Natl Ctr Health Stats.

Comparable Worth: A Bibliography. Ed. by Joan Nordquist. (Contemporary Social Issues: A Bibliographic Ser.: No. 2). 1986. pap. 15.00 (*0-937855-03-0*) Ref Rsch Serv.

Comparable Worth: A Case Book ... 1986 Supplement. Alice H. Cook. (Occasional Publication: No. 155). 174p. 1986. 7.00 (*0-318-23506-4*) U Hawaii.

Comparable Worth: A Case Book of Experiences in States & Localities. Alice H. Cook. (Occasional Publication: No. 151). 264p. 1985. 20.00 (*0-318-19011-7*) U Hawaii.

Comparable Worth: An Annotated Bibliography. June L. DeWeese & Jo A. Humphreys. (CompuBibs Ser.: No. 12). 81p. 1985. pap. 15.00 (*0-914791-11-7*) Vantage Info.

Comparable Worth: Is It a Worthy Policy? Elaine Sorensen. LC 93-23874. 189p. 1994. text ed. 29.95 (*0-691-03263-7*) Princeton U Pr.

Comparable Worth: Issues & Alternatives. 2nd ed. Ed. by E. Robert Livernash. LC 84-81267. 299p. 1984. pap. 11.00 (*0-937856-08-8*) Equal Employ.

Comparable Worth: New Directions for Research. National Research Council. 192p. 1985. pap. text ed. 19.95 (*0-309-03534-1*) Natl Acad Pr.

Comparable Worth: The Problem & States' Approaches to Wage Equity. Alice H. Cook. (Occasional Publication: No. 145). 84p. 1983. 3.00 (*0-318-04752-7*) U Hawaii.

Comparable Worth: Theories & Evidence. Paula England. (Social Institutions & Social Change Ser.). 360p. (Orig.). 1992. lib. bdg. 49.95 (*0-202-30348-9*); pap. text ed. 24.95 (*0-202-30349-7*) Aldine de Gruyter.

Comparable Worth & Public Policy: The Case of Pennsylvania. Suzanne M. Perrin. LC 85-51721. (Labor Relations & Public Policy Ser.: No. 29). 136p. reprint ed. pap. 38.80 (*0-8357-3155-3*, 2039418) Bks Demand.

Comparable Worth & Wage Discrimination: Technical Possibilities & Political Realities. Ed. by Helen Remick. (Women in the Political Economy Ser.). 320p. 1985. pap. 22.95 (*0-87722-385-8*) Temple U Pr.

Comparable Worth & Wages: Economic Equity for Women. Helen Remick. (Occasional Publication: No. 149). 14p. 1984. 1.00 (*0-318-04754-3*) U Hawaii.

Comparable Worth Controversy. Henry J. Aaron & Cameran Lougy. LC 85-48206. 57p. 1986. pap. 7.95 (*0-8157-0041-5*) Brookings.

Comparable Worth, Pay Equity, & Public Policy. Ed. by Rita M. Kelly & Jane Bayes. LC 87-17735. (Contributions in Labor Studies: No. 22). 291p. 1988. text ed. 65.00 (*0-313-26014-1*, BYY/, Greenwood Pr) Greenwood.

Comparable Worth Primer. Steven L. Willborn. LC 85-40329. 144p. 1986. text ed. 29.95 (*0-669-11018-3*) Free Pr.

Comparaison Des Poemes d'Homere et De Virgile. Rene Rapin. xvi, 167p. 1973. reprint ed. write for info. (*3-487-04807-8*, Pub. by Georg Olms GW) Lubrecht & Cramer.

Comparation of a Virgin & a Martyr, 1537. Desiderius Erasmus. Tr. by Thomas Paynell. LC 70-101148. 1970. reprint ed. 50.00 (*0-8201-1072-8*) Schol Facsimiles.

Comparative Abdominal & Pelvic Anatomy by Computed Tomography & Ultrasound. Michael M. Raskin. 304p. 1979. 86.95 (*0-8493-5369-6*, RC944, CRC Reprint) Franklin.

Comparative Advantage, Trade Policy & Economic Development. Bela Balassa. 336p. 1989. 65.00 (*0-8147-1129-4*); pap. 20.00 (*0-8147-1167-7*) NYU Pr.

Comparative Advantages of Far Eastern Business. Ed. by Robert Fitzgerald. LC 94-10026. (Studies in Far Eastern Business). 1994. write for info. (*0-7146-4592-3*, Pub. by F Cass Pubs UK) Intl Spec Bk.

Comparative Advertising: What Every Advertising Executive Should Know about Comparative Advertising Lawsuits under S43(a) of the Lanham Act. Barry R. Fischer & Douglas J. Wood. 8p. 1991. pap. 9.95 (*1-56318-000-6*) Assn Natl Advertisers.

Comparative Aesthetics: East & West. Angraj Chaudhary. xvi, 296p. 1991. 27.00 (*0-685-62636-9*, Estrn Bk Linkers) Nataraj Bks.

Comparative African Experiences in Implementing Educational Policies. John Craig. (Discussion Paper Ser.: No. 83). 102p. 1990. 7.95 (*0-8213-1578-1*, 11578) World Bank.

Comparative American Identities: Race, Sex, & Nationality in the Modern Text. Ed. by Hortense J. Spillers. 224p. 1991. 39.95 (*0-415-90349-1*, A4805, Routledge NY); pap. 13.95 (*0-415-90350-5*, A4809, Routledge NY) Routledge.

Comparative Analyses of Ecosystems: Patterns, Mechanisms, & Theories. Ed. by J. Cole et al. (Illus.). 360p. 1991. 87.00 (*0-387-97488-1*) Spr-Verlag.

Comparative Analysis of Amino-Acid Sequences of Key Enzymes of Replication & Expression of Positive-strand Rna Viruses, Vol. 11. A. Gorbalenya & E. Koonin. (Soviet Scientific Reviews Series, Section D: Biology Reviews: Vol. 11, Pt. 3). 1993. pap. text ed. 101.00 (*3-7186-5396-6*) Gordon & Breach.

Comparative Analysis of Complex Organizations. rev. ed. Amitai Etzioni. LC 74-21488. 1975. pap. 19.95 (*0-02-909620-0*) Free Pr.

Comparative Analysis of Economic Reforms in Central & East Europe. Ed. by Carlo Frateschi & Gianni Salvini. 224p. 1992. 59.95 (*1-85521-155-6*, Pub. by Dartmth Pub UK) Ashgate Pub Co.

Comparative Analysis of Evaluation Theory & Practice for the Instructional Component of Bilingual Programs. Amelia C. Medina. Ed. by Francesco Cordasco. LC 77-90549. (Bilingual-Bicultural Education in the U. S. Ser.). 1978. lib. bdg. 33.95 (*0-405-11089-8*) Ayer.

Comparative Analysis of Human Societies: Toward Common Standards for Data Collection & Reporting. Ed. by Emilio F. Moran. LC 94-3601. 202p. 1994. lib. bdg. 40.00 (*1-55587-514-9*) Lynne Rienner.

Comparative Analysis of Quality Assurance Requirements. K. P. Kleinert. 116p. 1992. pap. 12.00 (*92-826-3394-2*, CD-NA-13903-EN-C, Pub. by Europ Com) UNIPUB.

Comparative Analysis of Selected Income Measurement Theories in Financial Accounting, Vol. 12. James A. Anderson. (Studies in Accounting Research). 120p. 1976. 12.00 (*0-86539-024-X*) Am Accounting.

Comparative Analysis of Standardized Achievement Tests with Learning Disabled & Non-Learning Disabled Adolescent Boys. National Center for State Courts Staff. 20p. 1979. 1.20 (*0-685-16962-6*, LDJD-006) Natl Ctr St Courts.

Comparative Analysis of the Gospel Genre: The Synoptic Mode & Its Uniqueness. J. Arthur Baird. LC 91-43164. (Studies in the Bible & Early Christianity: Vol. 24). 180p. 1991. lib. bdg. 79.95 (*0-7734-9460-X*) E Mellen.

Comparative Analysis of the Jajmani System. Thomas O. Beidelman. 2.50 (*0-685-71736-4*) J J Augustin.

Comparative Analysis of Utility- & Non-Utility-Based Energy Service Companies: A Case Study Approach. 91p. 1986. 55.00 (*0-318-23866-7*) Consumer Energy Coun.

Comparative Anatomy of Domestic Animals: A Guide. Bonnie V. Beaver. LC 80-148036. 219p. reprint ed. pap. 62.50 (*0-685-20367-0*, 2029822) Bks Demand.

***Comparative Anatomy of the External & Middle Ear of Palaeognathous Birds.** J. Matthias Starck. LC 95-8260. (Advances in Anatomy, Embryology, & Cell Biology Ser.: Vol. 131). 1995. write for info. (*3-540-58991-0*) Spr-Verlag.

Comparative Anatomy of the Male Genital Tube in Coleoptera. D. Sharp & F. A. Muir. (Illus.). 304p. 1969. 25.00 (*0-686-09300-3*) Entomol Soc.

Comparative Anatomy of the Vertebrates. 7th ed. Kent. (Illus.). 705p. 1991. 55.95 (*0-8016-6237-0*) Mosby Yr Bk.

Comparative Anatomy of the Vertebrates. 7th ed. George Kent. 688p. (C). 1993. text ed. write for info. (*0-697-23486-X*) Wm C Brown Pubs.

Comparative & Critical Study of Ekavali: Contribution of Vidyadhara to Sanskrit Poetics. Savitri Gupta. xx, 316p. 1992. 28.00 (*81-85133-57-3*, Estrn Bk Linkers) Nataraj Bks.

Comparative & Historical Essays in Scots Law. Ed. by David C. Miller & David Meyers. 232p. 1992. U.K. pap. 60.00 (*0-406-00877-9*) Butterworth Legal Pubs.

Comparative & International Librarianship. Ed. by Miles M. Jackson. LC 77-98710. 307p. 1970. text ed. 55.00 (*0-8371-3327-0*, JAL/, Greenwood Pr) Greenwood.

Comparative & International Librarianship. Ed. by P. S. Kawatra. LC 87-80656. (Illus.). xii, 216p. (C). 1987. text ed. 30.00 (*0-938719-22-X*, Envoy Pr) Apt Bks.

Comparative & Multinational Management. Simcha Ronen. LC 85-17971. (International Business Ser.). 636p. (C). 1986. Net. text ed. write for info. (*0-471-86875-2*) Wiley.

Comparative & Veterinary Medicine: A Guide to the Resource Literature. Ann E. Kerker & Henry T. Murphy. LC 72-7989. 324p. reprint ed. pap. 92.40 (*0-8357-6789-2*, 2035466) Bks Demand.

Comparative Animal Biochemistry. Klaus Urich. Tr. by Patrick J. King. LC 94-7808. 1994. write for info. (*3-540-57420-4*) Spr-Verlag.

Comparative Animal Biochemistry. Klaus Urich. Tr. by Patrick J. King. LC 94-7808. 1994. 98.00 (*0-387-57420-4*) Spr-Verlag.

Comparative Animal Physiology. Philip C. Withers. 900p. (C). 1992. text ed. 56.00 (*0-03-012847-1*) SCP.

Comparative Animal Physiology, Pt. A. 4th ed. C. Ladd Prosser. 590p. 1991. text ed. 69.95 (*0-471-85767-X*) Wiley.

Comparative Animal Physiology, 2 vols., Set. 4th ed. Ed. by C. Ladd Prosser. 1376p. 1991. text ed. 97.90 (*0-471-56093-6*) Wiley.

Comparative Animal Physiology: Neural & Integrative Animal Physiology, Vol. 2. 4th ed. Ed. by C. Ladd Prosser. 786p. 1991. text ed. 59.95 (*0-471-56071-5*) Wiley.

***Comparative Approaches in Medical Reasoning.** Ed. by M. E. Cohen & D. L. Hudson. LC 94-48854. (Advances in Fuzzy Systems Ser.: Vol. 3). 328p. 1995. text ed. 86.00 (*981-02-2162-2*) World Scientific Pub.

***Comparative Approaches to Cognitive Science.** Ed. by Herbert L. Roitblat & Jean-Arcady Meyer. (Illus.). 550p. 1995. 50.00 (*0-262-18166-5*) MIT Pr.

Comparative Archeology of Early Mesopotamia. Ann L. Perkins. LC 49-10748. (Studies in Ancient Oriental Civilization: No. 25). (Illus.). xx, 201p. (Orig.). (C). 1949. reprint ed. pap. text ed. 17.00 (*0-226-62396-3*) Orientl Inst Pr IT.

Comparative Asian Politics: Power, Policy & Change. James C. Wang. LC 93-40378. 400p. 1994. pap. text ed. 22.00 (*0-13-155458-1*) P-H.

Comparative Aspects of Mechanoreceptor Systems. Ed. by F. Ito. (Advances in Comparative & Environmental Physiology Ser.: Vol. 10). (Illus.). xiii, 309p. 1992. 139.00 (*0-387-54118-7*) Spr-Verlag.

Comparative Aspects of Neuroendocrine Control of Behavior. Ed. by C. Valverde-Rodriguez & H. Arechiga. (Frontiers of Hormone Research Ser.: Vol. 6). (Illus.). 1980. 78.50 (*3-8055-0571-X*) S Karger.

Comparative Aspects of Neuropeptide Function. Ed. by Ernst Florey & George B. Stefano. LC 92-23207. (Studies in Neuroscience: No. 2). 1992. 130.00 (*0-08-041984-4*, Pergamon Pr) Elsevier.

Comparative Aspects of Nutritional & Metabolic Diseases. Ed. by James C. Woodard & Michael Bruss. 160p. 1983. 85.00 (*0-8493-5697-0*, RC620, CRC Reprint) Franklin.

Comparative Aspects of Sodium Cotransport Systems. Ed. by R. K. Kinne. (Comparative Physiology Ser.: Vol. 7). (Illus.). x, 278p. 1990. 210.50 (*3-8055-5165-7*) S Karger.

Comparative Aspects of Tumor Development. Ed. by Hans E. Kaiser. (Cancer Growth & Progression Ser.). (C). 1988. lib. bdg. 140.00 (*0-89838-994-1*) Kluwer Ac.

Comparative Assessment of the ASEAN Countries see ASEAN Report

***Comparative Austronesian Dictionary: An Introduction to Austronesian Studies.** Ed. by Darrell T. Tryon. (Trends in Linguistics, Documentation Ser.: No. 10). 3558p. (C). 1994. lib. bdg. 938.50 (*3-11-012729-6*, 199-94) Mouton.

Comparative Behavior of the American Avocet & the Black-Necked Stilt (Recurvirostridae) Robert B. Hamilton. 98p. 1975. 7.50 (*0-943610-17-6*) Am Ornithologists.

Comparative Biochemistry: A Comprehensive Treatise, 7 vols. Ed. by Marcel Florkin & Howard S. Mason. Incl. Vol. 1. Sources of Free Energy. LC 67-23158. 1960. 76.50 (*0-12-261001-6*); Vol. 2. Free Energy & Biological Function. LC 67-23158. 1960. 78.00 (*0-12-261002-4*); Vol. 3. Constituents of Life. LC 67-23158. 1962. 95.00 (*0-12-261003-2*); Vol. 4. Constituents of Life. LC 67-23158. 1962. 97.50 (*0-12-261004-0*); Vol. 5. Constituents of Life. LC 67-23158. 1963. 78.00 (*0-12-261005-9*); Vol. 6. Cells & Organisms. LC 67-23158. 1963. 78.00 (*0-12-261006-7*); Vol. 7. Supplementary Volume. LC 67-23158. 1964. 76.50 (*0-12-261007-5*); LC 67-23158. write for info. (*0-318-50249-6*) Acad Pr.

Comparative Biochemistry & Physiology of Enzymatic Digestion. Ed. by Hubertus J. Vonk & Richard H. Western. 1984. text ed. 179.00 (*0-12-727850-8*) Acad Pr.

Comparative Biochemistry, Molecular see Comprehensive Biochemistry, Section 5: Chemical Biology

Comparative Biochemistry of Parasitic Helminths. Ed. by Eva Bennett et al. 256p. 1989. 65.00 (*0-412-32730-9*) Chapman & Hall.

Comparative Biochemistry of Parasitic Helminths. Ed. by Eva Bennett et al. 224p. 1988. lib. bdg. 65.00 (*0-7099-5912-5*, Pub. by Croom Helm UK) Routledge Chapman & Hall.

Comparative Biology of the Meadowlarks (Sturnella) in Wisconsin. Wesley E. Lanyon. (Publications of the Nuttall Ornithological Club: No. 1). (Illus.). 66p. 1957. pap. 4.00 (*1-877973-10-6*) Nuttall Ornith.

Comparative Biology of the Normal Lung. Parent. 1992. 163.95 (*0-8493-8839-2*, RC732) CRC Pr.

Comparative Brain Research in Mammals, Vol. 1: Insectivora. H. Stephan et al. (Illus.). 576p. 1991. 99.00 (*0-387-97505-5*) Spr-Verlag.

Comparative Calendar of the Iranian, Muslim Lunar, & Christian Eras for Three-Thousand Years: 1260 B.H.-2000 A.H. - 639 B.C.-2621 A.D. Ahmad Birashk. (Persian Studies: No. 15). 189p. 1992. lib. bdg. 35.00 (*0-939214-95-4*) Mazda Pubs.

Comparative Carcinogenicity of Ionizing Radiation & Chemicals. (Report Ser.: No. 96). 140p. (Orig.). 1988. pap. text ed. 25.00 (*0-913392-96-0*) NCRP Pubns.

Comparative Cardiovascular Dynamics of Mammals. Li. 1994. write for info. (*0-8493-0169-6*) CRC Pr.

***Comparative Civil (Private) Law: Law Types, Law Groups, the Roads of Legal Development.** G. Eorsi. 652p. (C). 1979. 138.00x (*963-05-2001-X*, Pub. by Akad Kiado HU) St Mut.

Comparative Coachability of Certain Types of Intelligence Tests. Hsuan-Shan Chen. (Columbia University. Teachers College. Contributions to Education Ser.: No. 338). reprint ed. 37.50 (*0-404-55338-9*) AMS Pr.

Comparative Color Vision. Ed. by Gerald Jacobs. LC 81-17654. (Cognition & Perception Ser.). 1981. text ed. 81.00 (*0-12-378520-0*) Acad Pr.

Comparative Commentaries on Private International Law or Conflict of Laws. Arthur K. Kuhn. xi, 381p. 1981. reprint ed. lib. bdg. 32.50 (*0-8377-0737-4*) Rothman.

Comparative Constitutional Engineering. Giovanni Sartori. 200p. 1994. 40.00 (*0-8147-7974-3*); pap. 18.50 (*0-8147-8002-4*) NYU Pr.

Comparative Constitutional Federalism: Europe & America. Ed. by Mark V. Tushnet. LC 90-37838. (Contributions in Legal Studies: No. 61). 184p. 1990. text ed. 49.95 (*0-313-26888-6*, TCA/, Greenwood Pr) Greenwood.

Comparative Constitutional Law. Mahendra Singh. (C). 1989. 250.00 (*0-89771-758-9*, Pub. by Eastern Book II) St Mut.

Comparative Constitutional Law. Mahendra P. Singh. (C). 1989. 250.00 (*0-685-36445-3*) St Mut.

Comparative Constructions in Spanish & French Syntax. Susan Price. 272p. 1990. 75.00 (*0-415-01024-1*, A4910) Routledge.

Comparative Cost Study of Staff Panel & Participating Attorney Panel Prepaid Legal Services Plans. 50p. 1982. pap. 12.50 (*0-685-07149-9*, 455-0001) Amer Bar Assn.

Comparative Costs & Staffing Report for College & University Facilities, 1989-90. 1990. 90.00 (*0-913359-56-4*); 35.00 (*0-685-41109-5*) APPA VA.

Comparative Costs & Staffing Report for College & University Facilities, 1991-1992. (Illus.). 336p. 1993. pap. 90.00 (*0-913359-72-6*); 3.5 hd 150.00 (*0-913359-76-9*); 5.25 hd 150.00 (*0-913359-77-7*) APPA VA.

Comparative Criminal Justice Systems. Erika S. Fairchild. 320p. (C). 1993. pap. 29.95 (*0-534-12996-X*) Intl Thomson.

Comparative Criminal Justice Systems: Topical Approach. Philip L. Reichel. LC 93-4493. 1993. text ed. 45.00 (*0-13-151937-9*) Prentice ESL.

Comparative Criminal Law in the United States. Gerhard O. Mueller. (New York University Criminal Law Education & Research Center Monograph: No. 4). (Illus.). 72p. 1970. pap. text ed. 8.50 (*0-8377-0827-3*) Rothman.

Comparative Criminology: An Annotated Bibliography. Ed. by Joan Hill. LC 91-27306. (Research & Bibliographical Guides in Criminal Justice Ser.: No. 3). 160p. 1991. text ed. 45.00 (*0-313-26572-0*, BVR/, Greenwood Pr) Greenwood.

Comparative Critical Approaches to Renaissance Comedy. Ed. by D. A. Beecher & Massimo Ciavolella. 172p. 1989. pap. 14.00 (*0-919473-55-5*, DH43, Pub. by Dovehouse CN) MRTS.

Comparative Criticism: A Yearbook, Vol. 1. Ed. by E. S. Shaffer. 1979. write for info. (*0-521-22296-6*) Cambridge U Pr.

Comparative Criticism: A Yearbook, Vol. 2. Ed. by E. S. Shaffer. 350p. 1980. write for info. (*0-521-22756-9*) Cambridge U Pr.

Comparative Criticism: A Yearbook, Vol. 3. Ed. by E. S. Shaffer. 320p. 1981. write for info. (*0-521-23276-7*) Cambridge U Pr.

Comparative Criticism: A Yearbook, Vol. 4. Ed. by E. S. Shaffer. (Illus.). 320p. 1982. write for info. (*0-521-24578-8*) Cambridge U Pr.

Comparative Crystal Chemistry: Temperature, Pressure, Composition & the Variation of Crystal Structure. Robert M. Hazen & Larry W. Finger. LC 82-2834. 229p. 1982. text ed. 168.00 (*0-471-10268-7*, Wiley-Interscience) Wiley.

Comparative Data State & Provincial Licensing Systems. rev. ed. U. S. Department of Transportation. 136p. 1986. pap. 4.95 (*0-915179-51-2*) Loompanics.

Comparative Data State & Provincial Licensing Systems in the U. S. & Canada: Guidelines for Motor Vehicle Administrators. 1991. lib. bdg. 79.95 (*0-8490-4773-0*) Gordon Pr.

Comparative Democracy: Policymaking & Governing Coalitions in Europe & Israel. Gregory M. Luebbert. 352p. 1986. text ed. 42.00 (*0-231-06298-2*) Col U Pr.

Comparative Development of Adaptive Skills: Evolutionary Implications. Ed. by Eugene S. Gollin. 288p. 1985. text ed. 49.95 (*0-89859-519-3*) L Erlbaum Assocs.

Comparative Development Studies: In Search of the World View. Masudul A. Choudhury. LC 92-26140. 260p. 1993. text ed. 69.95 (*0-312-08355-6*) St Martin.

Comparative Developmental Investigation of the Gametophyte Generation in the Metzgeriales (Hepatophyta) Karen S. Renzglia. (Bryophytorum Bibliotheca Ser.: Vol. 24). (Illus.). 253p. (Orig.). 1982. text ed. 84.00 (*3-7682-1336-6*) Lubrecht & Cramer.

Comparative Dictionary of Proverbs. Gy. Paczolay. 300p. (C). 1987. 99.00 (*0-685-54133-9*, Pub. by Collets) St Mut.

Comparative Dictionary of the Finno-Ugric Elements in the Hungarian Vocabulary. Jozsef Budenz. LC 66-64927. (Uralic & Altaic Ser.: Vol. 78). viii, 987p. (FIN & HUN.). 1966. pap. text ed. 22.00 (*0-87750-029-0*) Res Inst Inner Asian Studies.

Comparative Dictionary of the Indo-Aryan Languages. Ralph Turner. (C). 1966. text ed. 105.00 (*0-19-713550-1*) OUP.

Comparative Dictionary of the Indo-Aryan Languages: Addenda & Corrigenda. R. L. Turner. Ed. by J. C. Wright. 1985. pap. 16.00 (*0-8364-1394-6*, Pub. by Sch Orient & African Stud UK) S Asia.

Comparative Dictionary of the Tahitian Language: Tahitian-English with an English-Tahitian Finding List. Edmund Andrews & Irene D. Andrews. LC 75-35171. reprint ed. 37.50 (*0-404-14201-X*) AMS Pr.

Comparative Discourse Analysis & the Translation of Psalm 22 in Chichewa, a Bantu Language of South-Central Africa. Ernst R. Wendland. LC 93-17222. (Studies in the Bible & Early Christianity: Vol. 32). 260p. 1993. text ed. 89.95 (*0-7734-9289-5*) E Mellen.

C

An Asterisk (*) at the beginning of an entry indicates that the title is appearing in BIP for the first time.

An Asterisk (*) at the beginning of an entry indicates that the title is appearing in BIP for the first time.

Comparative Kadai: Linguistic Studies Beyond Tai, 7 fiche, Set. Ed. by Jerold A. Edmondson & David B. Solnit. LC 88-63461. (Publications in Linguistics: No. 86). 377p. 1988. fiche 28.00 (*0-88312-437-8*) Summer Instit Ling.

***Comparative Kadai: The Tai Branch.** Ed. by Jerold A. Edmondson & David B. Solnit. (Publications in Linguistics). (Orig.). Date not set. pap. write for info. (*1-55671-005-4*) Summer Inst Ling.

***Comparative Kadai: The Tai Branch.** Ed. by Jerold A. Edmondson & David B. Solnit. (Publications in Linguistics). (Orig.). Date not set. mic. film write for info. (*1-55671-979-5*) Summer Inst Ling.

Comparative Karyology of Primates. Ed. by Brunetto Chiarelli et al. (World Anthropology Ser.). text ed. 44.00 (*90-279-7840-9*) Mouton.

Comparative Karyology of Primates. Ed. by Brunetto Chiarelli et al. (World Anthropology Ser.). (Illus.). xiv, 336p. 1979. 50.80 (*90-279-7850-6*) Mouton.

Comparative Labour Law: Anglo-Soviet Perspectives. William E. Butler & B. A. Hepple. LC 86-25695. 200p. 1987. 55.95 (*0-566-05387-X*) Ashgate Pub Co.

Comparative Labour Law & Industrial Relations. Ed. by Roger Blanpain. 412p. 1982. 26.00 (*90-312-0179-0*) Kluwer Ac.

Comparative Labour Law & Industrial Relations in Industrialised Market Economics: Industrial Relations, Vol. II. 4th rev. ed. Ed. by R. Blanpain. 262p. 1990. pap. 48.00 (*90-6544-495-5*) Kluwer Law Tax Pubs.

Comparative Labour Law & Industrial Relations in Industrialised Market Economics: Labour Law, Vol. I. 4th rev. ed. Ed. by R. Blanpain. 400p. 1990. pap. 64.00 (*90-6544-466-1*) Kluwer Law Tax Pubs.

Comparative Labour Law & Industrial Relations in Industrialised Market Economies. 5th rev. ed. Ed. by R. Blanpain & C. Engels. LC 93-5969. 1993. write for info. (*90-6544-742-3*) Kluwer Law Tax Pubs.

Comparative Law. George E. Glos. xxxv, 787p. 1979. 35.00 (*0-8377-0610-6*) Rothman.

Comparative Law: Adaptable to Courses Utilizing Schlesinger, Baade, Damska & Herzog's Casebook on Comparative Law, Casenote Legal Briefs. Casenotes Publishing Co., Inc. Staff. Ed. by Norman S. Goldenberg et al. (Orig.). (C). 1992. pap. text ed. write for info. (*0-87457-174-X*, 1630) Casenotes Pub.

Comparative Law: Cases-Text-Materials. 5th ed. Rudolf B. Schlesinger et al. (University Casebook Ser.). 926p. 1990. reprint ed. text ed. 41.50 (*0-88277-615-0*) Foundation Pr.

Comparative Law: Western European & Latin American Legal Systems. 2nd ed. John H. Merryman & David S. Clark. (Contemporary Legal Education Ser.). 1993. 25. 00 (*0-685-48590-0*) Michie Butterworth.

Comparative Law & Social Theory. Jerome Hall. LC 63-20406. 175p. reprint ed. pap. 49.90 (*0-317-29876-3*, 2051879) Bks Demand.

Comparative Law, Cases, Text, Materials, 1994 Supplement. 5th ed. Rudolf B. Schlesinger et al. (University Casebook Ser.). 204p. 1993. pap. text ed. 10. 95 (*1-56662-155-0*) Foundation Pr.

Comparative Law of Monopolies. David Raybould. (C). 1988. lib. bdg. 541.00 (*1-85333-074-4*, Pub. by Graham & Trotman UK); pap. text ed. 450.50 (*1-85333-073-6*, Pub. by Graham & Trotman UK) Kluwer Ac.

Comparative Law of Monopolies: Basic Work & Supplement Service, 1990. Ed. by David Raybould. 1990. ring bd. 350.00 (*1-85333-326-3*, Pub. by Graham & Trotman UK) Kluwer Ac.

Comparative Law of Monopolies: 1989 Basic Work & 1989 Supplement Services. David Raybould. (C). 1989. ring bd. 324.00 (*0-86010-941-0*, Pub. by Graham & Trotman UK) Kluwer Ac.

Comparative Law of Monopolies: 1991 Basic Work & 1991 Supplement Service. David Raybould. 400p. 1991. 400. 00 (*1-85333-515-0*, Pub. by Graham & Trotman UK) Kluwer Ac.

Comparative Law of Monopolies Vols. 1-2: 1995 Basic Work, 2 vols., Set. David Raybould. 1000p. 1995. ring bd. 346.00 (*1-85333-826-5*, Pub. by Graham & Trotman UK) Kluwer Ac.

Comparative Law of Monopolies, Vols. 1 & 2: 1992 Basic Work & 1992 Supplement Service. David Raybould. 600p. 1992. ring bd. 332.00 (*1-85333-669-6*, Pub. by Graham & Trotman UK) Kluwer Ac.

Comparative Law Yearbook, Vol. III. D. L. Campbell. 294p. 1980. lib. bdg. 89.00 (*90-286-0340-9*) Kluwer Ac.

Comparative Law Yearbook, Vol. 8. Ed. by Dennis Campbell. 1985. lib. bdg. 134.50 (*90-247-3178-X*) Kluwer Ac.

Comparative Law Yearbook, Vol. 11. Ed. by Dennis Campbell. 248p. (C). 1992. lib. bdg. 129.00 (*0-7923-1701-7*) Kluwer Ac.

Comparative Law Yearbook of International Business Vol. 16, 1994. Ed. by Dennis Campbell. 400p. (C). 1994. lib. bdg. 134.00 (*90-247-3002-3*, Pub. by Graham & Trotman UK) Kluwer Ac.

Comparative Law Yearbook of International Business 1990, Vol. 12. Ed. by Dennis Campbell. (C). 1991. lib. bdg. 142.00 (*1-85333-484-7*, Pub. by Graham & Trotman UK) Kluwer Ac.

Comparative Law Yearbook of International Business, 1991, Vol. 13. Ed. by Dennis Campbell. 320p. 1991. lib. bdg. 150.00 (*1-85333-588-6*) G & T Inc.

Comparative Law 1978: Selected Essays for the Tenth International Congress of Comparative Law. I. Szabo & Z. Peteri. 438p. 1978. 125.00 (*0-569-08458-X*) St Mut.

Comparative Legal Cultures. Ed. by Csaba Varga. (International Library of Essays in Law & Legal Theory). 638p. 1992. text ed. 150.00 (*0-8147-8765-7*) NYU Pr.

Comparative Legal Philosophies Applied to Legal Institutions. Luigi Miraglia. 1977. lib. bdg. 59.95 (*0-8490-1653-3*) Gordon Pr.

Comparative Legal Philosophy Applied to Legal Institutions. Luigi Miraglia. (Modern Legal Philosophy Ser.: Vol. 3). xl, 793p. 1969. reprint ed. 37.50 (*0-8377-2427-9*) Rothman.

Comparative Legal Traditions. 2nd ed. Mary A. Glendon. Ed. by Michael W. Gordon & Christopher Osakwe. (American Casebook Ser.). 768p. 1994. text ed. 45.00 (*0-314-03501-X*) West Pub.

Comparative Legal Traditions: Text, Materials & Cases on the Civil Law, Common Law & Socialist Law Traditions with Special Reference to French, West German, English & Soviet Law. Mary A. Glendon et al. LC 85-11583. (American Casebook Ser.). 1091p. (C). 1991. reprint ed. text ed. 49.00 (*0-314-91764-0*) West Pub.

Comparative Legal Traditions in a Nutshell. Mary A. Glendon et al. LC 82-2022. (Nutshell Ser.). 402p. 1991. reprint ed. pap. text ed. 16.50 (*0-314-65175-6*) West Pub.

Comparative Legislative Behaviour: Frontiers of Research. Ed. by Samuel C. Patterson & John C. Wahlke. LC 72-3387. (Comparative Studies in Behavioral Science). 323p. reprint ed. pap. 92.10 (*0-317-09357-6*, 2055106) Bks Demand.

Comparative Legislative Reforms & Innovations. Ed. by Abdo I. Baaklini & James J. Heaphey. LC 77-4249. 353p. 1977. 39.50 (*0-87395-805-5*) State U NY Pr.

Comparative Leukemia Research, 1969: Proceedings of the International Symposium, 4th, Cherry Hill, New Jersey, 1969. International Symposium on Comparative Leukemia Research Staff. Ed. by R. M. Dutcher. (Bibliotheca Haematologica Ser.: No. 36). 1970. 125.00 (*3-8055-1160-4*) S Karger.

Comparative Leukemia Research 1975: Proceedings of the Symposium, 7th International, Copenhagen, October 1975. Comparative Leukemia Research Symposium Staff. Ed. by J. Clemmesen et al. (Bibliotheca Haematologica Ser.: No. 43). (Illus.). 600p. 1976. 170.50 (*3-8055-2316-5*) S Karger.

***Comparative Literary Study of Daniel & Revelation: Shaping the End.** James H. Sims. LC 94-26154. 168p. 1995. text ed. 79.95 (*0-7734-2361-3*, Mellen Biblical Pr) E Mellen.

Comparative Literary Theory: An Overview: Annual Volume Review of National Literatures. Ed. by Anne Paolucci. 148p. 1987. 23.00 (*0-918680-24-7*) Bagehot Council.

Comparative Literature: A Critical Introduction. Susan Bassnett. LC 92-45856. 192p. 1993. pap. 17.95 (*0-631-16705-6*) Blackwell Pubs.

Comparative Literature as Academic Discipline: A Statement of Principles, Praxis, Standards. Robert J. Clements. LC 77-91123. 366p. reprint ed. pap. 104.40 (*0-8357-7549-6*, 2036271) Bks Demand.

Comparative Literature East & West: Traditions & Trends. Ed. by Cornelia N. Moore & Raymond Moody. (Literary Studies: East & West: Vol. 1). 304p. 1989. pap. text ed. 18.00 (*0-8248-1247-6*, Univ HI Coll Languages) UH Pr.

***Comparative Literature in the Age of Multiculturalism.** Ed. by Charles Bernheimer. LC 94-29219. (Parallax). 232p. 1994. text ed. 37.50x (*0-8018-5004-5*); pap. text ed. 13.95x (*0-8018-5005-3*) Johns Hopkins.

Comparative Literature Today: Methods & Perspectives. Yves Chevrel. Tr. by Farida E. Dahab. LC 93-49337. 128p. (C). 1994. lib. bdg. 32.50 (*0-943549-24-8*) TJU Pr.

Comparative Load Capacity Evaluation of CBN-Finished Gears. Raymond J. Drago. (Fall Technical Meeting Papers 88FTM8). (Illus.). 10p. 1988. pap. text ed. 30.00 (*1-55589-513-1*) AGMA.

Comparative Management: Business Styles in Japan & the United States. Khalid R. Mehtabdin. LC 86-16395. (Mellen Studies in Business: Vol. 1). 140p. 1986. pap. 69.95 (*0-88946-153-8*) E Mellen.

Comparative Management of Firms in Chile. Bernard D. Estafen. LC 78-633856. (International Business Research Institute Ser.: No. 4). 217p. 1972. 6.95 (*0-87925-001-1*) Ind U Busn Res.

Comparative Marine Policy. Center for Ocean Management Studies Staff. 272p. 1981. 39.95 (*0-03-058307-1*, Bergin & Garvey) Greenwood.

Comparative Marine Policy: Perspectives from Europe, Scandinavia, Canada & the United States. Ed. by Center for Ocean Management Studies Staff. LC 80-21455. 336p. 1981. text ed. 59.95 (*0-275-90591-8*, C0591, Praeger Pubs) Greenwood.

Comparative Marketing: Wholesaling in Fifteen Countries. Ed. by Robert Bartels. LC 82-25149. (Illus.). xii, 317p. 1983. text ed. 69.50 (*0-313-23838-3*, BARC, Greenwood Pr) Greenwood.

Comparative Marketing Systems. Ed. by Erdener Kaynak & Ronald Savitt. LC 83-24468. 328p. 1984. text ed. 30. 95 (*0-275-91202-7*, C1202, Praeger Pubs) Greenwood.

Comparative Method: Moving Beyond Qualitative & Quantitative Strategies. Charles C. Ragin. LC 86-30800. 218p. 1987. pap. 13.00 (*0-520-06618-9*) U CA Pr.

Comparative Method: Moving Beyond Qualitative & Quantitative Strategies. Charles C. Ragin. LC 86-30800. 203p. reprint ed. pap. 57.90 (*0-7837-4698-9*, 2044445) Bks Demand.

Comparative Method for the Study of Politics. David E. Apter. (Reprint Series in Social Sciences). (C). 1993. reprint ed. pap. text ed. 1.00 (*0-8290-3379-3*, PS-8) Irvington.

Comparative Method in Evolutionary Biology. Paul H. Harvey & Mark D. Pagel. (Oxford Series in Ecology & Evolution). (Illus.). 248p. 1991. pap. 24.95 (*0-19-854640-8*) OUP.

Comparative Method in Historical Linguistics. A. Meillet. Tr. by G. B. Ford, Jr. 1967. pap. 26.50 (*0-685-00758-8*) Adlers Foreign Bks.

***Comparative Method Reviewed.** Ed. by Mark Durie & Malcolm Ross. (Illus.). 352p. 1995. 65.00 (*0-19-506607-3*) OUP.

Comparative Methodology: Theory & Practice in International Social Research. Else Oyen. (Studies in International Sociology). (Illus.). 224p. (C). 1990. 45.00 (*0-8039-8325-5*); pap. 18.95 (*0-8039-8326-3*) Sage.

Comparative Methods in Psychology. Ed. by Marc H. Bornstein. LC 79-27558. (Crosscurrents in Contemporary Psychology Ser.). (Illus.). 320p. 1980. text ed. 59.95 (*0-89859-037-X*) L Erlbaum Assocs.

Comparative Methods in Sociology: Essays on Trends & Applications. Ed. by Ivan Vallier. LC 76-121194. (Institute of International Studies, UC Berkeley). 1971. pap. 14.00 (*0-520-02488-5*) U CA Pr.

Comparative Midrash: The Plan & Program of Genesis Rabbah & Leviticus Rabbah. Jacob Neusner. (Brown Judaic Studies). (C). 1986. 29.95 (*0-89130-958-6*, 14-01-11); pap. 23.95 (*0-89130-959-4*) Scholars Pr GA.

Comparative Models for Electrical Load Forecasting. Ed. by Derek Bunn & E. D. Farmer. LC 84-20873. 232p. 1985. text ed. 178.00 (*0-471-90635-2*) Wiley.

Comparative Molecular Carcinogenisis: Proceedings of the Fifth International Conference on Carcinogenesis & Risk Assessment Held in Austin, Texas, November 19-22, 1 991. Ed. by Andrew Klein-Szanto et al. LC 92-13722. (Progress in Clinical & Biological Research Ser.: Vol. 376). 404p. 1992. text ed. 179.95 (*0-471-56205-X*, Wiley-Liss) Wiley.

Comparative Molecular Neurobiology. Ed. by Y. Pichon. LC 92-49315. (Experientia Supplementa Ser.: No. 63). ix, 433p. 1992. write for info. (*3-7643-2785-5*); 147.50 (*0-8176-2785-5*) Birkhauser.

Comparative Morphology & Shell History of the Ordovician Strophomenacea (Brachiopoda) see Palaeontographica Americana: No. 2

Comparative Morphology of the Inner Ear in Salamanders: Caudata-Amphibia. R. E. Lombard. (Contributions to Vertebrate Evolution Ser.: Vol. 2). 1977. 60.00 (*3-8055-2408-0*) S Karger.

Comparative Morphology of the Life Stages of Cryptocellus Pelaezi (Arachnida, Ricinulie) Kay Pittard & Robert W. Mitchell. (Graduate Studies: No. 1). (Illus.). 77p. (Orig.). 1972. pap. 4.00 (*0-89672-008-X*) Tex Tech Univ Pr.

Comparative Morphology of the Mammalian Ovary. Harland W. Mossman & Kenneth L. Duke. LC 72-143765. (Illus.). 492p. 1975. pap. 20.00 (*0-299-05934-0*) U of Wis Pr.

Comparative Musicology & Anthropology of Music: Essays in the History of Ethnomusicology. Bruno Nettl & Philip V. Bohlman. (Chicago Studies in Ethnomusicology). (Illus.). 400p. 1991. pap. text ed. 18. 95 (*0-226-57409-1*) U Ch Pr.

Comparative Mythology. Jaan Puhvel. LC 86-20882. (Illus.). 320p. 1989. reprint ed. pap. text ed. 14.95 (*0-8018-3938-6*) Johns Hopkins.

Comparative Mythology: An Essay. rev. ed. Friedrich M. Muller. Ed. by Richard M. Dorson. LC 77-70612. (International Folklore Ser.). 1979. reprint ed. lib. bdg. 24.95 (*0-405-10111-2*) Ayer.

Comparative National Balance Sheets: A Study of Twenty Countries, 1688-1978. Raymond W. Goldsmith. LC 84-16277. (Illus.). 376p. 1985. lib. bdg. 49.00 (*0-226-30153-2*) U Ch Pr.

Comparative National Development: Society & Economy in the New Global Order. Ed. by A. Douglas Kincaid & Alejandro Portes. LC 93-34721. 300p. 1994. lib. bdg. 45. 00 (*0-8078-2142-X*); pap. text ed. 18.95 (*0-8078-4450-0*) U of NC Pr.

Comparative National Policies on Health Care. Milton I. Roemer. (Political Science & Public Administration Ser.: Vol. 2). 264p. 1977. 65.00 (*0-8247-7730-1*) Dekker.

Comparative Nationalism: Definitions, Interpretations, & the Black American & British West African Experience to 1947. 2nd ed. Jacquelyn G. Alston. LC 85-80588. 283p. (Orig.). 1985. pap. 10.95 (*0-9614733-6-3*) Hist Dimensions.

Comparative Negligence, 3 vols. L. Larson et al. 1984. Updates. ring bd. write for info. (*0-8205-1226-5*) Bender.

***Comparative Negligence.** 2nd suppl. ed. Victor E. Schwartz. 516p. 1993. 90.00 (*0-87473-194-1*) Michie Butterworth.

***Comparative Negligence & Contribution in Florida.** 4th ed. Florida Bar Staff. LC 95-60490. 188p. 1995. pap. 45. 00 (*0-945979-72-X*) FL Bar Legal Ed.

Comparative Negligence Manual. John J. Palmer & Stephen Flanagan. LC 85-21297. 1986. ring bd. 135.00 (*0-685-59925-6*) Clark Boardman Callaghan.

Comparative Neurobiology: Problems for a New Decade: 1st Annual Karger Workshop - Journal: Brain, Behavior & Evolution, Vol. 36, Nos. 2 & 3, 1990. Ed. by R. G. Northcutt. 104p. 1990. pap. 120.00 (*3-8055-5319-6*) S Karger.

Comparative Neurology of the Optic Tectum. Ed. by Horacio Vanegas. LC 84-3372. 870p. 1984. 145.00 (*0-306-41236-5*, Plenum Pr) Plenum.

Comparative Neuroscience: Select Works. Bullock. 1991. 70.00 (*0-685-45914-4*) Birkhauser.

Comparative Neuroscience & Neurobiology. Louis N. Irwin. (Readings from the Encyclopedia of Neuroscience Ser.). 144p. 1988. 32.50 (*0-8176-3394-4*) Birkhauser.

Comparative Neuroscience & Neurobiology. Ed. by Louis N. Irwin. (Readings from the Encyclopedia of Neuroscience Ser.). 100p. 1988. pap. 24.50 (*0-318-35449-7*) Spr-Verlag.

Comparative Operating Experience of Consumer Installment Financing Agencies & Commercial Banks, 1929-41. Ernst A. Dauer. (Financial Research Program II: Studies in Consumer Installment Financing: No. 10). 239p. 1944. reprint ed. 62.20 (*0-87014-126-0*) Natl Bur Econ Res.

Comparative Overview of Mammalian Fertilization. Ed. by Bonnie S. Dunbar & M. G. O'Rand. (Illus.). 500p. 1991. 95.00 (*0-306-43841-0*, Plenum Pr) Plenum.

Comparative Pathobiology of Viral Diseases. Ed. by Richard G. Olsen et al. 232p. 1985. Vol. I, 232 p. 156.00 (*0-8493-5945-7*, SF780, CRC Reprint); Vol. II, 232p. 156.00 (*0-8493-5946-5*, SF780, CRC Reprint) Franklin.

Comparative Pathology of the Heart: Proceedings of the Symposium, Boston, Sept. 1973. Comparative Pathology of the Heart Symposium Staff. Ed. by F. Homburger & I. Lucas. (Advances in Cardiology Ser.: Vol. 13). 250p. 1974. 208.00 (*3-8055-1697-5*) S Karger.

Comparative Pathology of Zoo Animals. Ed. by Richard J. Montali & George Migaki. LC 79-24354. (National Zoological Park Symposia for the Public Ser.: No. 6). (Illus.). 684p. 1980. pap. text ed. 29.95 (*0-87474-643-4*, MOCCP) Smithsonian.

Comparative Pathophysiology of Regulatory Reptides. Ed. by A. Rijnberk & Wimersma Greidanus. (Frontiers of Hormone Research Ser.: Vol. 17). (Illus.). viii, 236p. 1987. 170.50 (*3-8055-4621-1*) S Karger.

Comparative Patterns of Economic Development, 1850-1914. Cynthia T. Morris & Irma Adelman. LC 87-45480. (Johns Hopkins Studies in Development). 528p. 1988. text ed. 55.00 (*0-8018-3507-0*) Johns Hopkins.

Comparative Patterns of Foreign Policy & Trade: The Communist Balkans in International Politics. Cal Clark & Robert L. Farlow. LC 76-9078. (Studies in East European & Soviet Planning, Development, & Trade: No. 23). (Illus.). 1976. pap. 6.00 (*0-89249-016-0*) Intl Development.

Comparative Perception, 2 vols., Set. Ed. by Mark A. Berkley & William C. Stebbins. 1990. text ed. 192.50 (*0-471-52428-X*) Wiley.

Comparative Performance of U. S. Econometric Models. Ed. by Lawrence R. Klein. (Illus.). 336p. 1991. 48.00 (*0-19-505772-4*) OUP.

Comparative Performance of U. S. Hospitals: The Sourcebook. 250p. 1993. disk 1,299.00 (*0-685-60057-2*) HCIA.

Comparative Performance of U. S. Hospitals: The Sourcebook. 250p. 1994. 399.00 (*1-880678-41-1*) HCIA.

Comparative Perinatal Carcinogenesis. Ed. by Hildegard M. Schuller. 192p. 1984. 115.00 (*0-8493-5461-7*, RS201, CRC Reprint) Franklin.

Comparative Perspective on Literature: Approaches to Theory & Practice. Ed. by Clayton Koelb & Susan Noakes. LC 87-25062. 392p. 1988. 48.95 (*0-8014-2031-8*); pap. 16.95 (*0-8014-9477-X*) Cornell U Pr.

Comparative Perspective on the U. S. & Japanese Economies. Yasuo Sakakibara. (Occasional Papers, Institute for Education on Japan: Vol. 1, No. 1). 22p. (C). 1989. pap. 5.00 (*0-9619977-1-0*) Earlham College Pr.

Comparative Perspectives of Third World Women: The Impact of Race, Sex, & Class. Ed. by Beverly Lindsay. LC 78-19793. (Praeger Special Studies). 334p. 1980. text ed. 38.50 (*0-275-90514-4*, C0514, Praeger Pubs) Greenwood.

Comparative Perspectives on Indian Literature. Ed. by A. Ramakrishna Rao. 160p. (C). 1992. 25.00 (*81-85218-64-1*, Pub. by Prestige II) Advent Bks Div.

Comparative Perspectives on Manzoni. Olga Ragusa. 38p. 1986. pap. 4.95 (*0-913298-78-6*) S F Vanni.

Comparative Perspectives on Slavery in New World Plantation Societies, Vol. 292. Ed. by Vera Rubin & Arthur Tuden. (Annals Ser.). 1977. 42.00 (*0-89072-038-X*) NY Acad Sci.

Comparative Perspectives on the Development of Memory. Ed. by Robert Kail & Norman E. Spear. 384p. 1984. text ed. 89.95 (*0-89859-317-4*) L Erlbaum Assocs.

Comparative Pharmacology, 2 vols., Set. Ed. by M. J. Michelson. 1008p. (C). 1973. 420.00 (*0-08-016389-0*, Pub. by Pergamon Repr UK) Franklin.

Comparative Pharmacology of Some Psychotropic Drugs. Ed. by E. Jacobsen. (WHO Bulletin Reprint Ser.: Vol. 21, No. 4-5). 1960. pap. 2.00 (*92-4-056001-7*) World Health.

Comparative Philology & the Text of Job: A Study in Methodology. Lester L. Grabbe. LC 77-23489. (Society of Biblical Literature. Dissertation Ser.: No. 34). 224p. reprint ed. pap. 69.60 (*0-7837-5429-9*, 2045194) Bks Demand.

Comparative Philology & the Text of the Old Testament. James Barr. LC 87-15698. ix, 436p. (C). 1987. reprint ed. text ed. 25.00 (*0-931464-33-1*) Eisenbrauns.

Comparative Philosophy: Selected Essays. Intro. by Charlene McDermott. 566p. (Orig.). (C). 1983. pap. text ed. 34.00 (*0-8191-3487-2*) U Pr of Amer.

Comparative Philosophy: Western, Indian & Chinese Philosophies Compared. Archie J. Bahm. LC 76-10406. 112p. 1987. pap. text ed. 6.00 (*0-911714-10-3*, World Bks) Bahm.

Comparative Philosophy & the Philosophy of Scholarship: On the Western Interpretation of Nagarjuna. Andrew P. Tuck. 144p. 1990. 36.00 (*0-19-506156-X*) OUP.

Comparative Phonology & Morphology of the Baltic Languages. J. Endzelins. Tr. by William R. Schmalsteig & Benjamin Jegers. LC 71-144010. (Slavistic Printings & Reprintings Ser.: No. 85). 357p. 1971. text ed. 103.85 (*90-279-1915-1*) Mouton.

1444

An Asterisk (*) at the beginning of an entry indicates that the title is appearing in BIP for the first time.

An Asterisk (*) at the beginning of an entry indicates that the title is appearing in BIP for the first time.

1445

C

Comparative Studies in Sociology: An Annual Compilation of Research, Vol. 1. Ed. by Richard F. Tomasson. 1978. lib. bdg. 73.25 (*0-89232-025-7*) Jai Pr.

Comparative Studies in Special Education. Ed. by Kas Mazurek & Margret A. Winzer. LC 94-212. 504p. 1994. 55.95 (*1-56368-027-0*) Gallaudet Univ Pr.

Comparative Studies of American & African Trypanosomiasis: Proceedings of the WHO Scientific Group, Washington, 1967. WHO Staff. (Technical Report Ser.: No. 411). 1969. pap. 2.00 (*92-4-120411-7*) World Health.

Comparative Studies of Current Practice in Reading with Techniques for the Improvement of Teaching. Laura Zirbes. LC 74-177609. reprint ed. 37.50 (*0-404-55316-8*) AMS Pr.

Comparative Studies of Hearing in Invertebrates. Ed. by A. N. Popper & R. R. Fay. (Proceedings in Life Sciences Ser.). (Illus.). 512p. 1980. 119.00 (*0-387-90460-3*) Spr-Verlag.

Comparative Studies of How People Think: An Introduction. Michael Cole & Barbara Means. 222p. 1986. pap. 12.95 (*0-674-15261-1*) HUP.

***Comparative Studies of Magnetospheric Phenomena.** A. J. Coates. (Advances in Space Research (RJ) Ser.: Vol. 16). 220p. 1995. pap. 94.00 (*0-08-042624-7*, Pergamon Pr) Elsevier.

Comparative Studies of Political Conflict & Change: Cross National Datasets. Ted R. Gurr et al. LC 78-59713. 1978. write for info. (*0-89138-996-2*); fiche write for info. (*0-89138-997-0*) ICPSR.

Comparative Studies of Social Structure: Recent Research on France, the United States & the Federal Republic of Germany. Ed. by Wolfgang Teckenberg. LC 86-33866. 240p. 1987. 51.95 (*0-87332-408-0*) M E Sharpe.

Comparative Studies on Humar. Adaptability of Japanese, Caucasians & Japanese Americans, Vol. 1. Ed. by S. M. Horvath et al. (Japan International Biological Program Synthesis Ser.). 184p. 1975. 34.50 (*0-86008-211-3*, Pub. by U of Tokyo JA) Col U Pr.

***Comparative Study Between Minjung Theology & Reformed Theology from a Missiological Perspective.** Sang-Bok Lee. (Asian Thought & Culture Ser.: Vol. 22). 1995. write for info. (*0-8204-2702-0*) P Lang Pubs.

Comparative Study in the Theology of Atonement in Jonathan Edwards & John McLeod Campbell: Atonement & the Character of God. Michael Jinkins. LC 92-44975. 472p. 1993. text ed. 109.95 (*0-7734-9827-3*, Mellen Univ Pr) E Mellen.

Comparative Study of Chinese & Western Cyclic Myths. Robert S. Chen. LC 91-21217. (Asian Thought & Culture Ser.: Vol. 8). 216p. (C). 1992. text ed. 47.95 (*0-8204-1675-4*) P Lang Pubs.

Comparative Study of Chlorococcum Meneghini & Other Spherical, Zoo Spore-Producing Genera of the Chlorococcales. Richard C. Starr. (Illus.). 111p. 1981. reprint ed. lib. bdg. 45.00 (*3-87429-191-X*) Koeltz Sci Bks.

Comparative Study of Colombian & Costa Rican Emigrants to the United States. Charlotte A. Redden. Ed. by Carlos E. Cortes. LC 79-6218. (Hispanics in the United States Ser.). (Illus.). 1981. lib. bdg. 23.95 (*0-405-13166-6*) Ayer.

Comparative Study of Entrance to Teacher-Training Institutions. Mellicent McNeil. LC 79-177042. (Columbia University. Teachers College. Contributions to Education Ser.: No. 443). reprint ed. 22.50 (*0-404-55443-1*) AMS Pr.

Comparative Study of Firefighting... in Britain, Denmark, Netherlands & Sweden. HMSO Staff. (Home Office Research Study Ser.: No. 127). 67p. 1992. pap. 15.00 (*0-11-341043-3*, HM10433, Pub. by HMSO UK) UNIPUB.

Comparative Study of Gender Assignment to Borrowed Nouns. Shana Poplack & Alicia Pousada. (Illus.). 43p. Date not set. lib. bdg. 3.00 (*1-878483-15-3*) Hunter Coll CEP.

Comparative Study of Islam & Other Religions. Syed Muzaffaruddin. 125p. (Orig.). 1987. pap. 7.50 (*1-56744-254-4*) Kazi Pubns.

Comparative Study of Lake-Iroquoian Accent. Karin Michelson. (C). 1988. lib. bdg. 114.50 (*1-55608-054-9*) Kluwer Ac.

***Comparative Study of Landscape Aesthetics: Landscape Morphology.** Jiahua Wu. LC 94-40516. (Illus.). 480p. 1995. text ed. 109.95 (*0-7734-9131-7*) E Mellen.

Comparative Study of Liability Law & Compensation Schemes in Ten Countries & the United States. Werner Pfennigstorf & Donald G. Gifford. 224p. (C). 1991. text ed. 45.00 (*1-56594-000-8*) Ins Res Coun.

Comparative Study of Low-Grade Metamorphism in the California Coast Ranges & the Outer Metamorphic Belt of Japan. Wallace G. Ernst et al. LC 74-98022. (Geological Society of America, Memoir Ser.: No. 124). 338p. reprint ed. pap. 96.40 (*0-317-28383-9*, 2025464) Bks Demand.

Comparative Study of Multinational Corporation Joint International Business Ventures with Family Firm or Non-Family Firm Partners. William Renforth & Sion Raveed. Ed. by Stuart Bruchey. LC 80-782. (Multinational Corporations Ser.). 1981. lib. bdg. 23.95 (*0-405-13395-2*) Ayer.

Comparative Study of Occupational Stress in African American & White University Faculty. Earl Smith. LC 92-17295. 144p. 1992. lib. bdg. 69.95 (*0-7734-9859-1*) E Mellen.

Comparative Study of Old English Metre. Frank H. Whitman. (McMaster Old English Studies & Texts: No. 6). 176p. 1993. 55.00 (*0-8020-0540-3*) U of Toronto Pr.

Comparative Study of Parallel Programming Languages: The Salishan Problems. Ed. by John T. Feo. LC 92-14602. (Special Topics in Supercomputing Ser.: Vol. 6). 1992. write for info. (*0-444-88135-2*, North Holland) Elsevier.

Comparative Study of Pushkin's "The Bronze Horseman", Nekrasov's "Red-Nosed Frost", & Blok's "The Twelve" The Wild World. A. D. Briggs. LC 90-42249. (Studies in Slavic Language & Literature: Vol. 5). 288p. 1990. lib. bdg. 89.95 (*0-88946-082-5*) E Mellen.

Comparative Study of Religion: A Sufi & a Sanatani (Ramakrishna) Ananda. 1993. 22.00 (*81-202-0373-9*, Pub. by Ajanta II) S Asia.

Comparative Study of Religions. Y. Masih. (C). 1993. 22.00x (*81-208-0743-X*, Pub. by Motilal Banarsidass II) S Asia.

Comparative Study of Responses of Children of Different Nationalities & Environments on Intelligence & Achievement Tests. Adelin Scott. LC 73-177807. (Columbia University. Teachers College. Contributions to Education Ser.: No. 367). reprint ed. 37.50 (*0-404-55367-2*) AMS Pr.

Comparative Study of Rural Relief & Non-Relief Households. Thomas C. McCormick. LC 70-165684. (Research Monograph Ser.: Vol. 2). 1971. reprint ed. lib. bdg. 22.50 (*0-306-70334-3*) Da Capo.

***Comparative Study of Santali & Bengali.** Byomkes Chakrabarti. (C). 1994. 28.50x (*81-7074-128-9*, Pub. by KP Bagchi IA); 28.00x (*0-614-00718-6*, Pub. by KP Bagchi IA) S Asia.

Comparative Study of Selected American Film Critics, 1958-1974. Joseph D. Blades, Jr. Ed. by Garth S. Jowett. LC 75-21429. (Dissertations on Film Ser.). 1976. lib. bdg. 20.95 (*0-405-07532-4*) Ayer.

Comparative Study of Selected Hindustani Ragas on Contemporary Practice. Patrick Moutal. (C). 1991. text ed. 38.00 (*0-685-50093-4*, Pub. by Munshiram Manoharial II) S Asia.

Comparative Study of Social Attitudes of Adolescents in Glasgow & in Taipei. Hwang Chien-Hou. (Asian Folklore & Social Life Monographs: No. 63). 239p. 1974. 20.00 (*0-89986-058-3*) Oriental Bk Store.

Comparative Study of Some of the Leading Music Systems of the Fifteenth, Sixteenth, Seventeenth & Eighteenth Centuries. V. N. Bhatkande. 1990. reprint ed. 9.00 (*81-85395-85-3*, Pub. by Low Price II) S Asia.

Comparative Study of Some Social Communication Patterns in the Pelecaniformes. Gerard F. Van Tets. Ed. by American Ornithologists' Union Staff. 88p. 1965. 3.50 (*0-943610-02-8*) Am Ornithologists.

Comparative Study of Southern Folk Speech. H. H. Kroll. 1973. 35.00 (*0-87968-913-7*) Gordon Pr.

Comparative Study of Teachings of Don Juan & Madhyamaka Buddhism. Mark MacDowell. xv, 116p. (C). 1991. reprint ed. 11.00 (*81-208-0162-8*, Pub. by Motilal Banarsidass II) S Asia.

Comparative Study of the Bantu & Semi-Bantu Languages, 2 vols., Set. Harry H. Johnston. LC 74-15054. reprint ed. 115.00 (*0-404-12092-X*) AMS Pr.

Comparative Study of the Concentration & Regular Plans of Organization in the Senior High School. Hugh H. Stewart. LC 72-177820. (Columbia University. Teachers College. Contributions to Education Ser.: No. 600). reprint ed. 37.50 (*0-404-55600-0*) AMS Pr.

Comparative Study of the Educational Stances of Madeline Hunter & James Britton. Joan N. Steiner. (Concept Paper Ser.: No. 6). 83p. 1993. pap. 6.95 (*0-8141-0791-5*) NCTE.

Comparative Study of the Jaina Theories of Reality & Knowledge. Y. J. Padmarajiah. 432p. 1986. reprint ed. 22.00 (*81-208-0036-2*, Pub. by Motilal Banarsidass II) S Asia.

Comparative Study of the Law of Corporations. Arthur K. Kuhn. LC 72-76705. (Columbia University. Studies in the Social Sciences: No. 123). reprint ed. 31.50 (*0-404-51123-6*) AMS Pr.

Comparative Study of the Literatures of Egypt, Palestine & Mesopotamia. T. E. Peet. (British Academy, London, Schweich Lectures on Biblical Archaeology Series, 1930). 1972. reprint ed. pap. 20.00 (*0-8115-1271-1*) Periodicals Srv.

Comparative Study of the Mayas & the Lacandones. Alfred M. Tozzer. LC 76-43869. (Archaeological Institute of America. Report on the Fellow in American Archaeology Ser.: 1902-1905). reprint ed. 31.00 (*0-404-15728-9*) AMS Pr.

Comparative Study of the Melanesian Island Languages. Sidney H. Ray. LC 75-35151. reprint ed. 87.50 (*0-404-14166-8*) AMS Pr.

Comparative Study of the Organization & Performance of Hospital Emergency Services. Basil S. Georgopoulos & Robert A. Cooke. 512p. (Orig.). 1980. pap. 20.00 (*0-87944-253-0*) Inst Soc Res.

Comparative Study of the Organization & Performance of Hospital Emergency Services: Selected Descriptive Findings & the Research Instruments. Basil S. Georgopoulos & Robert A. Cooke. LC 80-13467. (Institute for Social Research, Research Report Ser.). 510p. reprint ed. pap. 145.40 (*0-7837-5277-6*, 2045015) Bks Demand.

Comparative Study of the Planets. Ed. by A. Coradini & M. Fulchignoni. 1982. lib. bdg. 131.50 (*90-277-1406-1*) Kluwer Ac.

Comparative Study of the Play Activities of Adult Savages & Civilized Children. Lilla E. Appleton. LC 75-35062. (Studies in Play & Games). 1976. reprint ed. 17.95 (*0-405-07913-3*) Ayer.

Comparative Study of Todies (Todidae), with Emphasis on the Puerto Rican Tody, Todus Mexicanus. Angela K. Kepler. (Publications of the Nuttall Ornithological Club: No. 16). (Illus.). 206p. 1977. 11.75 (*1-877973-26-2*, 16) Nuttall Ornith.

Comparative Study of Very Large Data Bases. E. Hill, Jr. (Lecture Notes in Computer Science Ser.: Vol. 59). 1978. pap. 14.00 (*0-387-08653-6*) Spr-Verlag.

Comparative Study of Word Order in Old Spanish & Old French Prose Works. Daniel M. Crabb. LC 78-94189. (Catholic University of America. Studies in Romance Languages & Literatures: No. 51). reprint ed. 37.50 (*0-404-50351-9*) AMS Pr.

Comparative Survey Analysis. Stein Rokkan et al. (Confluence Ser: Vol. 12). 1969. text ed. 28.00 (*90-279-6246-4*) Mouton.

Comparative Survey of Anglo-American & Latin-American Law. Phanor J. Eder. vii, 257p. 1981. reprint ed. lib. bdg. 30.00 (*0-8377-0541-X*) Rothman.

***Comparative Survey of Hindu, Christian, & Jewish Mysticism.** E. M. Abrahams. (C). 1995. 28.00x (*81-7030-406-7*, Pub. by Sri Satguru Pubns II) S Asia.

Comparative Survey of Seven Adult Functional Literacy Programs in Sub-Saharan Africa. Edmun B. Richmond. (Illus.). 122p. (Orig.). (C). 1986. pap. text ed. 17.00 (*0-8191-5521-7*) U Pr of Amer.

Comparative Survey of the Laws on Abortion of Selected Countries. Theresa Papademetriou. 181p. (Orig.). (C). 1993. pap. text ed. 29.95 (*1-56806-214-1*) Diane Pub.

Comparative Tables of Supreme Court Cases, 1950-1985. S. Malik. 1986. 65.00 (*0-317-56721-7*) St Mut.

Comparative Tax Jurisprudence: Germany & Japan. Takeshi Iizuka. LC 92-42207. 1993. 45.00 (*0-8147-3755-2*) NYU Pr.

Comparative Tax Studies: Essays in Honor of Richard Goode. Ed. by S. Cnossen. (Contributions to Economic Analysis Ser.: Vol. 144). 450p. 1983. 102.75 (*0-444-86421-0*, I-339-82, North Holland) Elsevier.

Comparative Technology Choice in Development: The Indian & Japanese Cotton Textile Industries. Keijiro Itsuka et al. LC 86-29666. 350p. 1988. text ed. 49.95 (*0-312-00516-4*) St Martin.

Comparative Theory & Political Experience: Mario Einaudi & the Liberal Tradition. Ed. by Peter J. Katzenstein et al. LC 89-39112. 240p. 1990. 29.95 (*0-8014-2368-6*) Cornell U Pr.

***Comparative Toxicology of Hypolipidaemic Fibrates.** Ed. by Mary J. Tucker & Terry C. Orton. 128p. 1995. 75.00x (*0-7484-0137-7*, Pub. by Tay Francis Ltd UK) Taylor & Francis.

Comparative Union Democracy: Organization & Opposition in British & American Union. J. David Edelstein & Malcolm Warner. LC 77-80874. 388p. 1979. reprint ed. pap. 21.95 (*0-87855-623-0*) Transaction Pubs.

Comparative Urban Design-Rare Engravings: 1830-1843. Melville C. Branch. 108p. 49.50 (*0-686-69145-8*) Ayer.

Comparative Urban Politics: A Performance Approach. Robert C. Fried & Frances F. Rabinovitz. 240p. 1980. pap. text ed. 15.95 (*0-685-03797-5*) P-H.

Comparative Urban Politics: Power & the City in the United States, Canada, Britain & France. Michael Keating. 256p. 1991. text ed. 59.95 (*1-85278-155-6*, Pub. by E Elgar Pub UK) Ashgate Pub Co.

Comparative View of the Huttonian & Neptunian Systems of Geology: In Answer to the Illustrations of the Huttonian Theory of the Earth. John Murray. Ed. by Claude C. Albritton, Jr. LC 77-6533. (History of Geology Ser.). 1978. reprint ed. lib. bdg. 26.95 (*0-405-10453-7*) Ayer.

Comparative View of the Various Institutions for the Assurance of Lives. Charles Babbage. LC 67-18568. (Reprints of Economic Classics Ser.). 1967. reprint ed. 29.50 (*0-678-00335-1*) Kelley.

Comparative Vocabulary of Aubuan Dialects. Hans Wolff. 293p. 1969. 22.00 (*0-89771-003-7*) St Mut.

Comparative Vocabulary of Aubuan Dialects. Hans Wolff. LC 72-93745. 303p. reprint ed. pap. 86.40 (*0-8357-9450-4*, 2015313) Bks Demand.

***Comparative Welfare Systems: The Scandinavian Model in a Period of Change.** Ed. by Bent Greve. LC 95-14911. 1995. write for info. (*0-312-12831-2*) St Martin.

Comparative Women's Rights & Politcal Participation in Europe. Gisbert R. Flanz. (Comparative Women's Rights Ser.). 520p. 1984. pap. 20.00 (*0-941320-23-5*) Transnatl Pubs.

Comparative Women's Rights & Political Participation in Europe. Gisbert H. Flanz. LC 82-19317. (Comparative Women's Rights Ser.). 520p. (C). 1983. lib. bdg. 50.00 (*0-941320-02-2*) Transnatl Pubs.

Comparative Wood Anatomy. S. Carlquist. (Wood Science Ser.). (Illus.). 450p. 1988. 299.00 (*0-387-18827-4*) Spr-Verlag.

Comparative Work Systems: Ideologies & Reality in Eastern Europe. Alexander J. Matejko. LC 85-6354. 256p. 1985. text ed. 59.95 (*0-275-90216-1*, C0216, Praeger Pubs) Greenwood.

Comparative World Atlas. exp. rev. ed. Hammond Incorporated Editors. 88p. (Orig.). 1994. pap. text ed. 9.66 (*0-8437-7111-9*) Hammond Inc.

Comparative World Data: A Statistical Handbook for Social Science. Georg Muller. LC 88-45391. 504p. (C). 1989. text ed. 60.00 (*0-8018-3734-0*); 3.5 hd 95.00 (*0-8018-3805-3*); 5.25 hd 95.00 (*0-8018-3770-7*) Johns Hopkins.

Comparative World Literature: Seven Essays. John B. Alphonso-Karkala. 98p. 1976. lib. bdg. 9.95 (*0-89253-048-0*) Ind-US Inc.

Comparative Worldwide National Computer Policies. Ed. by H. Sackman. 460p. 1986. 87.25 (*0-444-70056-0*, North Holland) Elsevier.

Comparative Youth Culture: The Sociology of Youth Cultures & Youth Subcultures in America, Britain & Canada. Michael Brake. 224p. (Orig.). 1985. pap. 14.95 (*0-7100-9898-7*, RKP) Routledge.

Comparatively Speaking: Communication Scholarship Across Space & Time. Jay G. Blumler et al. (Annual Reviews of Communication Research Ser.: Vol. 19). (Illus.). 320p. 1992. 52.00 (*0-8039-4172-2*); pap. 24.00 (*0-8039-4173-0*) Sage.

Comparator Book: With 49 Projects. Delton T. Horn. (Illus.). 200p. 1990. 23.95 (*0-685-34809-1*, 3312); pap. 15.95 (*0-8306-8312-7*) TAB Bks.

Comparator Book: With 49 Projects. Delton T. Horn. 1990. text ed. 23.95 (*0-07-155348-7*); pap. 15.95 (*0-07-155356-8*) McGraw.

Compare Ultrastructural Path: Selected Tumors in Man & Animals. Hildegard M. Reznick-Schuller. 208p. 1989. 168.00 (*0-8493-5662-8*, RC269) CRC Pr.

Compared to What? An Introduction to the Analysis of Algorithms. Gregory J. Rawlins. LC 91-30850. 536p. (C). 1995. text ed. 50.95 (*0-7167-8243-X*, Computer Sci Pr) W H Freeman.

Comparing Adult Education Worldwide. Alexander N. Charters et al. LC 80-8911. (Jossey-Bass Series in Higher Education). 296p. reprint ed. pap. 84.40 (*0-8357-4936-3*, 2037866) Bks Demand.

Comparing Algorithm Syntheses. Steier. 1989. pap. 31.00 (*0-387-96960-8*, 2634) Spr-Verlag.

Comparing & Assessing Programming Languages: Ada, C & Pascal. Alan R. Feuer & Narain Gehani. (Software Ser.). (Illus.). 256p. 1984. text ed. 25.67 (*0-685-07963-5*) P-H.

Comparing Behavior: Studying Man Studying Animals. D. W. Rajecki. 304p. (C). 1983. 69.95 (*0-89859-259-3*) L Erlbaum Assocs.

Comparing Capitalist Economies: Variations in the Governance of Sectors. Ed. by J. Rogers Hollingsworth. LC 93-6603. 1994. 45.00 (*0-19-507968-X*) OUP.

Comparing Charcoal & Wood-Burning Cookstoves in the Caribbean. Jeffrey Wartluft. 35p. 1984. 8.75 (*0-86619-181-X*) Vols Tech Asst.

***Comparing Constitutions.** Ed. by S. E. Finer et al. 300p. 1995. pap. 19.95 (*0-19-876344-1*) OUP.

***Comparing Constitutions.** Ed. by S. E. Finer et al. 300p. 1995. 39.95 (*0-19-876345-X*) OUP.

***Comparing Cultures: Readings for Writers on Contemporary America & Japan.** Merry I. White & Sylvan Barnet. 576p. 1995. pap. text ed. 23.94 (*0-312-10620-3*) St Martin.

***Comparing Cultures: Readings in a Cross-Disciplinary Perspective.** Ed. by Alex Inkeles & Masamichi Sasaki. LC 94-47519. 1995. pap. text ed. 24.00 (*0-13-297029-5*) P-H.

***Comparing Decisionmaking Arrangements in Four High Schools: Comparing Decision-Making Arrangements in Four High Schools.** Bruce Bimber. LC 94-26055. 1994. write for info. (*0-8330-1561-3*, MR459GGFLE) Rand Corp.

Comparing Economic Systems: A Political-Economic Approach. 2nd ed. Andrew Zimbalist et al. 480p. (C). 1988. text ed. 52.00 (*0-15-512403-X*) Dryden Pr.

Comparing English & Spanish: Patterns in Phonology & Orthography. Rose Nash. (C). 1977. pap. text ed. 10.95 (*0-88345-297-9*, 18448); audio 25.00 (*0-685-79303-6*, 58449) Prentice ESL.

Comparing Housing Systems: Housing Performance & Housing Policy in the U. S. & Britain. Valerie Karn & Harold Wolman. (Illus.). 284p. 1992. 58.00 (*0-19-827372-X*) OUP.

Comparing Languages: English & Its European Relatives. Jim McGurn. (Awareness of Language Ser.). (Illus.). 48p. (C). 1991. pap. 10.95 (*0-521-33638-4*) Cambridge U Pr.

Comparing Legislatures. Gerhard Loewenberg & Samuel C. Patterson. (Illus.). 362p. (C). 1988. reprint ed. pap. text ed. 31.00 (*0-8191-7050-X*) U Pr of Amer.

Comparing Muslim Societies: Knowledge & the State in a World Civilization. Ed. by Juan R. Cole. (Comparative Studies in Society & History). 350p. (C). 1992. text ed. 52.50 (*0-472-09449-1*); pap. text ed. 21.95 (*0-472-06449-5*) U of Mich Pr.

Comparing Nations: Concepts, Strategies, Substance. Mattei Dogan & Ali Jazancigil. (Illus.). 256p. 1994. 59.95 (*0-631-18644-1*); pap. 21.95 (*0-631-18645-X*) Blackwell Pubs.

Comparing Pluralist Democracies: Strains on Legitimacy. Ed. by Mattei Dogan. (New Directions in Comparative & International Politics Ser.). (Illus.). 288p. 1988. text ed. 55.85 (*0-8133-0451-2*) Westview.

Comparing Political Systems: Power & Policy in Three Worlds. 4th ed. Gary K. Bertsch et al. 752p. (C). 1991. write for info. (*0-02-309020-0*) Macmillan.

Comparing Political Thinkers. Ed. by Ross Fitzgerald. 320p. 1980. text ed. 44.00 (*0-08-024800-4*, Pergamon Pr); pap. text ed. 23.00 (*0-08-024799-7*, Pergamon Pr) Elsevier.

Comparing Presidential Behavior: Carter, Reagan & the Macho Presidential Style. John M. Orman. LC 86-19445. (Contributions in Political Science Ser.: No. 163). 200p. 1987. text ed. 49.95 (*0-313-25516-4*, OCP/, Greenwood Pr) Greenwood.

Comparing Psychoanalytic Psychotherapies: Developmental, Self, & Object Relations; Self Psychology; Short-Term Dynamic. James F. Masterson et al. LC 91-8288. 312p. 1991. 39.95 (*0-87630-640-7*) Brunner-Mazel.

***Comparing Public Bureaucracies: Problems of Theory & Method.** B. Guy Peters. LC 87-5077. 240p. 1988. pap. 14.95 (*0-8173-0368-5*) U of Ala Pr.

An Asterisk (*) at the beginning of an entry indicates that the title is appearing in BIP for the first time.

An Asterisk (*) at the beginning of an entry indicates that the title is appearing in BIP for the first time.

1447

*__Compass American Guide to Washington.__ Fodor's Staff. 1995. pap. 17.95 (*1-878867-58-X*, Compass Amrcn) Fodors Travel.

Compass American Guides: Chicago. Jack Schnedler. 1993. 24.95 (*1-878867-29-6*, Compass Amrcn) Fodors Travel.

Compass & Gyroscope: Integrating Science & Politics for the Environment. Kai N. Lee. LC 92-38824. (Illus.). 290p. 1993. 29.95 (*1-55963-197-X*) Island Pr.

*__Compass & Gyroscope: Integrating Science & Politics for the Environment.__ Kai N. Lee. LC 92-38824. 243p. (C). 1994. reprint ed. pap. text ed. 16.95 (*1-55963-198-8*) Island Pr.

Compass for the Sunflower. Liana Badr. Tr. by Catherine Cobham. 160p. 1990. 19.95 (*0-7043-5037-8*, Pub. by Womens Pr UK) Interlink Pub.

Compass in an Armored Car. Bana Witt. (Illus.). 60p. (Orig.). 1988. pap. 4.95 (*0-929730-02-X*) Zeitgeist Pr.

Compass in Your Nose & Other Astonishing Facts about Humans. Marc McCutcheon. (Illus.). 208p. (Orig.). 1989. pap. 8.95 (*0-87477-544-2*) J P Tarcher.

Compass Inside Ourselves: Short Stories. Nancy Lord. 1984. 7.95 (*0-914221-03-5*); pap. 5.95 (*0-914221-01-9*) Fireweed Pr AK.

Compass of the Heart. Robert W. Caswell. 1978. 20.00 (*0-913028-59-2*); pap. 12.00 (*0-913028-52-5*) North Atlantic.

Compass Points: Jan Morris Introduces a Selection from the First Hundred Issues of Planet. Ed. by Janet Davies. 288p. 1994. 35.00 (*0-7083-1220-9*, Pub. by U of Wales UK) Bks Intl VA.

Compass Rose. Ursula K. Le Guin. 1991. mass mkt. 4.50 (*0-06-100181-3*, Harp PBks) HarpC.

Compass Windows of Old Blandford Church: A Tribute in Tiffany Glass. Martha W. Briggs. 16p. 1992. 9.95 (*0-9633240-0-4*) Dory Pr.

Compass-Wise: Or Getting to Know Your Compass. J. Klinkert. (C). 1987. 42.00 (*0-85174-252-1*, Pub. by Brwn Son Ferg) St Mut.

Compass, '91. IEEE Aerospace & Electronic Systems Society Staff. Ed. by IEEE Staff. LC 91-72673. 200p. 1991. lib. bdg. write for info. (*0-7803-0127-7*, 91CH3033-8); pap. text ed. write for info. (*0-7803-0126-9*, 91CH3033-8); fiche write for info. (*0-7803-0128-5*, 91CH3033-8) Inst Electrical.

Compasses in Small Craft. C. A. Lund. (C). 1987. 40.00 (*0-85174-453-2*, Pub. by Brwn Son Ferg) St Mut.

Compasses of God: Science & Human Destiny. Martin E. Luther. 144p. (Orig.). 1991. 14.95 (*0-9615847-1-8*) Marwolf Pub.

Compassion. Alice Margulies. (Illus.). 64p. (YA). (gr. 7-12). 1990. lib. bdg. 14.95 (*0-8239-1108-X*) Rosen Group.

Compassion. Ida Richter. 1973. pap. 2.95 (*0-686-16723-6*) Malcolm Hse.

Compassion: A Reflection on the Christian Life. Don McNeill et al. LC 83-45045. (Illus.). 160p. (C). 1983. mass mkt. 8.00 (*0-385-18957-5*, Image Bks) Doubleday.

*__Compassion: The Little Books of Virtue.__ Ariel Books Staff. (Illus.). 80p. 1995. 4.95 (*0-8362-3124-4*) Andrews & McMeel.

Compassion: Toward A Science of Value. William Eckhardt. 1972. 12.00 (*0-933061-02-1*); pap. 6.00 (*0-933061-03-X*) Lentz Peace Res.

Compassion, a Tibetan Analysis: A Buddhist Monastic Textbook. Tr. by Guy Newland. (Advanced Book - Blue Ser.). 168p. (Orig.). 1984. pap. 12.95 (*0-86171-024-X*) Wisdom MA.

Compassion & Common Sense. Carl E. Ockert. LC 79-92791. (Illus.). 172p. (Orig.). 1980. 6.95 (*0-9603926-0-2*); pap. 4.95 (*0-9603926-1-0*) MCP Bks.

Compassion & Responsibility: Readings in the History of Social Welfare Policy in the United States. Ed. by Frank R. Breul & Steven J. Diner. LC 79-56040. 1985. pap. text ed. 11.95 (*0-226-07413-7*) U Ch Pr.

Compassion & Self Hate: An Alternative to Despair. rev. ed. Theodore I. Rubin. 288p. 1986. pap. 6.00 (*0-02-077750-7*, Collier S&S) S&S Trade.

Compassion Fatigue: Coping with Secondary Traumatic Stress Disorder in Those Who Treat the Traumatized. Ed. by Charles R. Figley. (Psychosocial Stress Ser.: No. 23). 296p. 1995. 35.95 (*0-87630-759-4*) Brunner-Mazel.

Compassion in Action: Setting Out on the Path of Service. Ram Dass & Mirabai Bush. 288p. 1992. pap. 11.00 (*0-517-57635-X*, Bell Tower) Crown Pub Group.

Compassion Manual. William Eckhardt. 1979. pap. 4.00 (*0-933061-01-3*) Lentz Peace Res.

Compassion Protocol. Herve Guibert. Tr. by James Kirkup. 200p. 1994. 20.00 (*0-8076-1352-5*) Braziller.

***Compassion Seeds. Karin Morrison. 101p. (Orig.). 1994. pap. 6.95 (*0-9645283-0-4*) K Morrison.**
COMPASSION SEEDS takes a new approach to reach the toughest man, to melt the hardest heart, to plant seeds that will awaken feelings you never thought you had. COMPASSION SEEDS makes grown men cry. The book reminds mankind that there are more important things than man-made treasures. COMPASSION SEEDS is possibly one of the first books to bring peace to all living creatures. COMPASSION SEEDS message is powerful! It glorifies God, embraces all life & gives strength to all those doubting in God's love & His concern for all creatures. Simple, yet rich in wisdom! To order: Karin Morrison Publishing, 405-229-0400. ***Publisher Provided Annotation.***

Compassion the Ultimate Ethic: An Exploration of Veganism. 3rd ed. Victoria Moran. 112p. 1991. reprint ed. pap. 6.95 (*0-942401-12-3*) Am Vegan Soc.

Compassion Versus Guilt: And Other Essays. Thomas Sowell. LC 87-7906. (Illus.). 254p. (C). 1989. pap. 7.95 (*0-688-08670-5*, Quill) Morrow.

Compassion vs. Guilt, & Other Essays. Thomas Sowell. LC 87-7906. 224p. 1987. 15.95 (*0-688-07114-7*) Morrow.

Compassionate Address to the Christian Negroes in Virginia. Benjamin Fawcett. LC 72-168011. reprint ed. 29.50 (*0-404-00258-7*) AMS Pr.

*__Compassionate & Trusting.__ Ellen Larson. Ed. by Debbie Bible. (Value Builders Ser.). (J). 1995. 7.95 (*0-7814-5095-0*, 10090) Cook.

Compassionate Authority: Democracy & the Representation of Women. Kathleen B. Jones. 272p. 1992. 49.95 (*0-415-90643-1*, A7580, Routledge NY); pap. 14.95 (*0-415-90644-X*, A7584, Routledge NY) Routledge.

Compassionate Beast: The Scientific Inquiry into Human Altruism. Morton Hunt. 1991. pap. 11.00 (*0-385-41859-0*, Anchor NY) Doubleday.

Compassionate Capitalism: People Helping People Help Themselves. Rich DeVos. 320p. 1993. 22.00 (*0-525-93567-3*) NAL-Dutton.

Compassionate Capitalism: People Helping People Help Themselves. Rich DeVos. 352p. 1994. pap. 11.95 (*0-452-27051-0*, Plume) NAL-Dutton.

Compassionate Care, Practical Love for Your Aging Parents. Marilyn Fanning. 196p. 1994. reprint ed. pap. 9.95 (*1-56616-003-0*, 535013) Aglow Communs.

Compassionate Child-Rearing: An In-Depth Approach to Optimal Parenting. R. W. Firestone. (Illus.). 388p. 1989. 23.95 (*0-306-43356-7*, Plenum Insight) Plenum.

Compassionate Cook: Or Please Don't Eat the Animals! A Vegetarian Cookbook. People for the Ethical Treatment of Animals Staff & Ingrid Newkirk. 256p. (Orig.). 1993. pap. 9.99 (*0-446-39492-0*) Warner Bks.

Compassionate Democracy - Next Steps in Self Government: Excerpts from 'Choose Love' Teddy Milne. 40p. 1987. pap. 3.95 (*0-938875-10-8*); student ed. pap. 4.95 (*0-685-67620-X*) Pittenbruach Pr.

Compassionate God. Choan-Seng Song. LC 81-16972. 204p. (Orig.). reprint ed. pap. 58.20 (*0-8357-4054-4*, 2036744) Bks Demand.

Compassionate Healing: Eastern Perspectives. Carol Aronoff. 256p. (C). 1994. per., pap. text ed. 30.00 (*0-8403-9148-X*) Kendall-Hunt.

*__Compassionate Kids: How to Get Your Kids Involved in Mission & Service.__ Jim Hancock. LC 94-44901. 1995. pap. 8.95 (*0-910125-17-1*) Youth Special.

Compassionate Memsahibs: Welfare Activities of British Women in India, 1900-1947. Mary Ann Lind. LC 87-24953. (Contributions in Woman Studies). 144p. 1988. text ed. 45.00 (*0-313-26059-1*, LRJ/, Greenwood Pr) Greenwood.

Compassionate Mind: Theological Dialog with the Educated. Donald L. Deffner. (Scholarship Today Ser.). 192p. (Orig.). 1990. pap. 14.95 (*0-570-04543-6*, 12-3147) Concordia.

Compassionate Ministry. Ed. by Gary L. Sapp. 225p. (Orig.). 1994. pap. 16.95 (*0-89135-090-X*) Religious Educ.

Compassionate Peace: A Future for Israel & the Palestinians. rev. ed. American Friends Service Committee. Ed. by Everett Mendelsohn. 256p. 1989. 19.95 (*0-8090-3576-6*) Hill & Wang.

Compassionate Presence. Stephen R. Schwartz. (Orig.). 1988. 18.00 (*0-936415-19-3*); pap. 12.00 (*0-936415-09-6*) Riverrun Piermont.

Compassionate Samaritan: The Life of Lyndon Baines Johnson. Philip R. Rulon. LC 81-210. 356p. (C). 1981. text ed. 28.95 (*0-88229-306-0*) Nelson-Hall.

Compassionate School: A Practical Guide to Educating Abused & Traumatized Children. Gertrude Morrow. 250p. 1987. text ed. 27.95 (*0-13-154742-9*) P-H.

Compassionate Side of Divorce. C. S. Lovett. 1975. pap. 7.45 (*0-938148-08-7*) Prsnl Christianity.

Compassionate Therapy: Working with Difficult Clients. Jeffrey A. Kottler. LC 91-30554. (Social & Behavioral Sciences Ser.). 272p. 1992. 25.95 (*1-55542-422-8*) Jossey-Bass.

Compassionate Touch: Hands-on Caregiving for the Elderly, the Ill & the Dying. Dawn Nelson. 1993. pap. 13.95 (*0-88268-149-4*) Station Hill Pr.

Compassionate Touch: The Role of Human Touch in Healing & Recovery. Clyde Ford. (Illus.). 288p. (Orig.). 1993. pap. 11.00 (*0-671-75607-9*, Fireside) S&S Trade.

Compassionate Universe. Eknath Easwaran. LC 89-23058. 188p. (Orig.). 1989. 22.00 (*0-915132-59-1*); pap. 12.00 (*0-915132-58-3*) Nilgiri Pr.

Compassionate Visitor: Resources for Ministering to People Who Are Ill. Arthur H. Becker. LC 84-28370. 128p. (Orig.). 1985. pap. 9.99 (*0-8066-2094-3*, 10-1620, Augsburg) Augsburg Fortress.

Compassioning: Basic Counselling Skills for Christian Care-Givers. Margaret Ferris. LC 92-39456. 96p. (Orig.). 1993. pap. 8.95 (*1-55612-567-4*) Sheed & Ward MO.

Compatibility Between Bureaucratic & Democratic Ideologies: A Psycho-Cultural Analysis. Sung-Don Hwang. LC 93-47405. (Major Concepts in Politics & Political Theory Ser.: Vol. 7). 1994. write for info. (*0-8204-2437-4*) P Lang Pubs.

Compatibility of Analog Signals for Electronic Industrial Process Instruments: ANSI-ISA Standard S50.1. 12p. 1992. pap. text ed. 25.00 (*0-87664-389-6*, 1389-6) Instru Soc.

Compatibility of Fish, Wildlife, & Floral Resources with Electric Power Facilities & Lands: An Industry Survey Analysis. Daniel L. Leedy et al. 130p. 1980. write for info. (*0-318-60025-0*) Natl Inst Urban Wildlife.

Compatibility of Interactive Videodisc Systems: Players, Controllers, Overlay Devices, Authoring Programs, Touch Screens, Integrated Systems. Rockley L. Miller. (Monitor Report Ser.). (Illus.). 150p. 1987. pap. 49.95 (*0-938907-03-4*) Future Syst.

Compatibility of Names: A Companion to the Name Book. Pierre Le Rouzic. 1989. pap. 7.95 (*0-9622069-1-1*) Topos Pr.

*__Compatibility, Stability & Sheaves.__ J. L. Bueso et al. LC 94-32079. (Pure & Applied Mathematics Ser.: Vol. 185). 1994. 125.00 (*0-8247-9589-X*) Dekker.

Compatible & Incompatible Relationships. Ed. by W. Ickes. (Social Psychology Ser.). (Illus.). 615p. 1985. 71.00 (*0-387-96024-4*) Spr-Verlag.

Compatible FORTRAN. A. Colin Day. LC 78-2483. 115p. reprint ed. pap. 32.80 (*0-318-34778-4*, 2031639) Bks Demand.

Compatir la Luz de la Fe. (SPA.). 1981. 9.95 (*1-55586-016-8*) US Catholic.

*__COMPCON - 40th IEEE International Computer Conference, Spring '95.__ 512p. 1995. pap. text ed. 100.00 (*0-8186-7029-0*, PR07029) IEEE Comp Soc.

COMPCON Spring '92 (Computer Conference) LC 91-76808. 520p. 1992. 90.00 (*0-8186-2655-0*, 2655) IEEE Comp Soc.

COMPCON Spring '93 (Computer Conference) 616p. 1993. pap. text ed. 100.00 (*0-8186-3400-6*, 3400) IEEE Comp Soc.

*__CompControl: Secrets of Reducing Workers' Compensation Costs.__ Edward J. Priz. Ed. by Camille Akin. LC 95-17314. (Successful Business Library Ser.). 150p. (Orig.). 1995. pap. 19.95 (*1-55571-355-6*); ring bd. 39.95 (*1-55571-356-4*) Oasis Pr OR.

Compelled Compassion: Government Intervention in the Treatment of Critically Ill Newborns. Intro. by Arthur L. Caplan et al. LC 91-44190. (Contemporary Issues in Biomedicine, Ethics, & Society Ser.). 352p. 1992. 44.50 (*0-89603-224-8*) Humana.

Compelled to Control: Why Relationships Break Down & What Makes Them Well. J. Keith Miller. 300p. 1992. 18.95 (*1-55874-212-3*) Health Comm.

Compelling Alliance: Trek Adventure & Romance. Warrick Bourque. LC 94-70205. 265p. 1994. per. write for info. (*0-9640237-0-9*) Also Bks.

Compelling Belief: The Culture of American Schooling. S. Arons. 256p. 1982. text ed. 19.95 (*0-07-002326-3*) McGraw.

Compelling Belief: The Culture of American Schooling. Stephen Arons. LC 85-28818. 240p. 1986. reprint ed. pap. 15.95 (*0-87023-524-9*) U of Mass Pr.

Compelling Case. large type ed. Michael Underwood. 1991. 21.95 (*0-7089-2381-X*) Ulverscroft.

Compelling Case for a Constitutional Amendment to Balance the Budget & Limit Taxes. Alvin Rabushka. 29p. 1984. pap. 2.50 (*0-318-02038-6*) Natl Taxpayers Union Found.

Compelling Christ: Why We Can Be Sure of the Bible, Christ, & Salvation. Floyd C. McElveen. (Illus.). 56p. (Orig.). 1989. pap. 0.95 (*0-9620963-1-8*) Inst Rel Rsch.

Compelling Evidence. Steve Martini. 448p. 1993. mass mkt. 6.99 (*0-515-11039-6*) Jove Pubns.

Compelling Evidence. large type ed. Steve Martini. LC 92-18331. (General Ser.). 608p. 1992. lib. bdg. 23.95 (*0-8161-5548-8*) G K Hall.

Compelling Evidence. large type ed. Steve Martini. LC 92-18331. (General Ser.). 657p. 1993. pap. 16.95 (*0-8161-5549-6*) G K Hall.

Compelling Image: Nature & Style in Seventeenth-Century Chinese Painting. James Cahill. (Charles Eliot Norton Lectures). (Illus.). 262p. 1986. pap. 29.95 (*0-674-15281-6*) HUP.

Compelling Proposals! Sheila Kessler. LC 90-85528. (Illus.). 112p. (Orig.). 1990. pap. 8.95 (*1-879404-12-5*) Cmpetitive Edge.

Compend of the Principles of Homeopathy. William Boericke. 160p. 1971. reprint ed. spiral bd. 7.70 (*0-7873-0114-0*) Mokelumne.

Compendio Biblico Doctrinal: Doctrinal Handbook of the Bible. Armando Dipardo. (SPA.). 7.95 (*84-499-0067-0*, 220184, Pub. by Edit Clie SP) TSELF.

Compendio de Anatomia Descriptiva. J. A. Fort. 546p. (SPA.). pap. 19.95 (*0-7859-0869-2*, S-50272) Fr & Eur.

Compendio de la Historia Cristiana. R. A. Baker. Tr. by Francisco G. Almanza. Orig. Title: A Summary of Christian History. 372p. (SPA.). 1985. reprint ed. pap. 8.95 (*0-311-15032-2*) Casa Bautista.

Compendio De la Historia Del A. T. An Outline of Old Testament. Ira Maurice Price. (SPA.). 5.25 (*84-7645-425-2*, 223331, Pub. by Edit Clie SP) TSELF.

Compendio de la Humana Salud, I-51: Biblioteca Nacional, Madrid. Ed. by Maria T. Herrera. (Medieval Spanish Medical Texts Ser.: No. 9). 4p. (SPA.). 1987. fiche 10.00 (*0-940639-05-X*) Hispanic Seminary.

Compendio de Medicina, Biblioteca Universitaria, Salamanca, 2262. Gomez De Salamanca. Ed. by Maria Jesus Mancho. (Medieval Spanish Medical Texts Ser.: No. 12). 8p. (SPA.). 1987. fiche 10.00 (*0-940639-08-4*) Hispanic Seminary.

Compendio Manual de la Biblia. Henry H. Halley. 768p. (SPA.). 1955. 18.99 (*0-8254-1300-1*); pap. 13.99 (*0-8254-1299-4*) Kregel.

Compendio Manual de la Biblia. Henry H. Halley. Tr. by C. P. Denyer. (Illus.). 768p. (SPA.). 1990. reprint ed. 19.75 (*0-311-03666-X*) Casa Bautista.

*__Compendiolo di Molti Dubbi, Segreti & Sentenze Intorno al Canto Fermo & Figurato.__ Pietro Aaron. (Monuments of Music & Music Literature Ser.). 1974. lib. bdg. 35.00 (*0-8450-2266-0*) Broude.

Compendious German-English Dictionary. A. H. Edgren & W. D. Whitney. (ENG & GER.). 1972. 75.00 (*0-87968-914-5*) Gordon Pr.

Compendious History of the Cotton Manufacture. R. Guest. (Illus.). 74p. 1968. reprint ed. 37.50 (*0-7146-1396-7*, BHA-01396, Pub. by F Cass Pubs UK) Intl Spec Bk.

Compendious Introduccion Unto the Pistle off Paul to the Romayns. William Tyndale. LC 74-28890. (English Experience Ser.: No. 767). 1975. reprint ed. 20.00 (*90-221-0767-1*) Walter J Johnson.

Compendious Syriac Dictionary Founded upon the Thesaurus Syriacus of R. Payne Smith. R. Payne Smith. Ed. by J. Payne Smith. (SYR.). 1922. 165.00 (*0-19-864307-1*) OUP.

Compendious Tamil English Dictionary. G. U. Pope. 100p. 1986. reprint ed. 12.50 (*0-8364-1680-5*, Pub. by Manohar II) S Asia.

Compendious Tamil-English Dictionary; a Handbook of the Tamil Language. 7th ed. G. U. Pope. 98p. (ENG & TAM.). 1992. 25.00 (*0-8288-1724-3*, M 14118) Fr & Eur.

*__Compendium.__ P. A. Matthioulus. 921p. (C). 1992. 810.00x (*963-05-0200-3*, Pub. by Akad Kiado HU) St Mut.

Compendium. C. J. Scheiner (Books). 1978-1988. C. J. Scheiner. 192p. (Orig.). 1989. pap. 15.00 (*0-685-29050-6*) C J Scheiner.

Compendium der Vergleichenden Grammatik der Indogermanischen Sprachen. August Schleicher. (Documenta Semiotica, Series Linguistica). 829p. 1975. reprint ed. write for info. (*3-487-05382-9*, Pub. by Georg Olms GW) Lubrecht & Cramer.

Compendium for the Study of Christian Science: No. 1, Introduction. Max Kappeler. 28p. 1951. pap. 4.50 (*0-85241-055-7*) Kappeler Inst Pub.

Compendium for the Study of Christian Science: No. 10, Love. Max Kappeler. 23p. 1953. pap. 4.50 (*0-85241-064-6*) Kappeler Inst Pub.

Compendium for the Study of Christian Science: No. 2, The Seven Days of Creation. Max Kappeler. 24p. 1951. pap. 4.50 (*0-85241-056-5*) Kappeler Inst Pub.

Compendium for the Study of Christian Science: No. 3, The Commandments, the Beatitudes, the Lord's Prayer. Max Kappeler. 29p. 1951. pap. 4.50 (*0-85241-057-3*) Kappeler Inst Pub.

Compendium for the Study of Christian Science: No. 4, Mind. Max Kappeler. 36p. 1951. pap. 4.50 (*0-85241-058-1*) Kappeler Inst Pub.

Compendium for the Study of Christian Science: No. 5, Spirit. Max Kappeler. 28p. 1951. pap. 4.50 (*0-85241-059-X*) Kappeler Inst Pub.

Compendium for the Study of Christian Science: No. 6, Soul. Max Kappeler. 23p. 1952. pap. 4.50 (*0-85241-060-3*) Kappeler Inst Pub.

Compendium for the Study of Christian Science: No. 7, Principle. Max Kappeler. 25p. 1952. pap. 4.50 (*0-85241-061-1*) Kappeler Inst Pub.

Compendium for the Study of Christian Science: No. 8, Life. Max Kappeler. 23p. 1952. pap. 4.50 (*0-85241-062-X*) Kappeler Inst Pub.

Compendium for the Study of Christian Science: No. 9, Truth. Max Kappeler. 20p. 1953. pap. 4.50 (*0-85241-063-8*) Kappeler Inst Pub.

Compendium in Astronomy. E. Mariolopoulos. 1982. lib. bdg. 112.50 (*90-277-1373-1*) Kluwer Ac.

Compendium of Abnormal Psychology. 2nd ed. Henry H. Reiter. 110p. 1980. pap. text ed. 10.00 (*0-9606044-0-5*) Psychometric.

Compendium of Aeronomy. T. Tohmatsu. (C). 1990. lib. bdg. 222.00 (*0-7923-0748-8*) Kluwer Ac.

Compendium of Alchemical Processes Extracted from the Writings of Glauber, Basil Valentine, & Other Adepts. 173p. 1993. pap. 16.95 (*1-56459-344-4*) Kessinger Pub.

Compendium of Alfalfa Diseases. 2nd ed. Ed. by D. L. Stuteville & D. C. Erwin. LC 90-82462. (Illus.). 104p. (Orig.). 1990. pap. 30.00 (*0-89054-108-6*) Am Phytopathol Soc.

*__Compendium of American Railroad Radio Frequencies.__ 13th ed. Sturm. 200p. 1995. pap. text ed. 16.95 (*0-89024-231-3*, 01064) Kalmbach.

Compendium of Apple & Pear Diseases. Ed. by A. L. Jones & H. S. Aldwinckle. LC 90-81440. (Disease Compendium Ser.). (Illus.). 100p. (Orig.). 1990. pap. 30.00 (*0-89054-109-4*) Am Phytopathol Soc.

Compendium of Approved Projects As of September 30, 1986. (Series A: No.17). 459p. 1987. 15.00 (*92-1-126007-8*, E.87.III.B.2) UN.

Compendium of Approved Projects as of 30 September 1987, No. 16. 479p. 1988. 20.00 (*92-1-126009-4*, E. 88. III.B.2) UN.

Compendium of Armaments & Military Hardware. Christopher Chant. 1987. 99.00 (*0-7102-0720-4*, RKP) Routledge.

Compendium of Astrology. Rose Lineman & Jan Popelka. LC 83-63067. 1984. pap. 14.95 (*0-914918-43-5*, Whitford Pr) Schiffer.

Compendium of Barley Diseases. Ed. by D. E. Mathre. LC 82-72159. 94p. 1982. pap. 30.00 (*0-89054-047-0*) Am Phytopathol Soc.

Compendium of Bean Diseases. Ed. by Robert Hall. LC 91-71728. (Disease Compendium Ser.). (Illus.). 102p. (Orig.). 1991. pap. 30.00 (*0-89054-118-3*) Am Phytopathol Soc.

Compendium of Beet Diseases & Insects. Ed. by E. D. Whitney & J. E. Duffus. LC 86-71222. 107p. 1986. 30.00 (*0-89054-070-5*) Am Phytopathol Soc.

An Asterisk (*) at the beginning of an entry indicates that the title is appearing in BIP for the first time.

Compendium of Biochemical Nomenclature & Related Documents. 2nd ed. Ed. by C. Leibecq. 350p. 1992. pap. 36.00 (*1-85578-005-4*, Pub. by Portland Pr Ltd UK) Ashgate Pub Co.

*__Compendium of Blueberry & Cranberry Diseases.__ Ed. by Frank L. Caruso & Donald C. Ramsdell. (Disease Compendium Ser.). (Illus.). 120p. 1995. pap. 30.00x (*0-89054-173-6*) Am Phytopathol Soc.

*__Compendium of British Club Makers.__ Peter Georgiady. (Illus.). 379p. (Orig.). 1994. pap. 55.00 (*1-886752-00-1*) Airlie Hall Pr.

Compendium of Cartographic Techniques. Ed. by J. P. Curran et al. 114p. 1988. 115.00 (*1-85166-229-4*) Elsevier.

Compendium of Case Law Relating to the European Communities, 1973. Ed. by H. J. Eversen et al. LC 74-23454. 304p. 1975. 113.00 (*0-444-10794-0*, North Holland) Elsevier.

Compendium of Case Law Relating to the European Communities, 1974. Ed. by H. J. Eversen et al. 348p. 1976. 92.50 (*0-444-11047-X*, North Holland) Elsevier.

Compendium of Case Law Relating to the European Communities, 1975. H. Sperl & John A. Usher. Ed. by H. J. Everson et al. 432p. 1977. 107.75 (*0-7204-0579-3*, North Holland) Elsevier.

Compendium of Case Law Relating to the European Communities, 1976. H. J. Eversen et al. 562p. 1978. 97.50 (*0-444-85206-9*, North Holland) Elsevier.

Compendium of Citrus Diseases. Ed. by J. O. Whiteside et al. LC 88-71819. (Disease Compendium Ser.). (Illus.). 105p. (Orig.). 1988. pap. 30.00 (*0-89054-092-6*) Am Phytopathol Soc.

Compendium of Confederate Armies: Mississippi. Stewart Sifakis. 160p. 1995. lib. bdg. 24.95 (*0-8160-2292-5*) Facts on File.

Compendium of Contemporary Weapons. Kevin Siembieda & Maryann Siembieda. Ed. by Alex Marciniszyn et al. (Palladium Books Presents Ser.). (Illus.). 176p. (Orig.). (YA). (gr. 8 up). 1993. pap. 19.95 (*0-916211-65-7*, 415) Palladium Bks.

Compendium of Corn Diseases. 2nd ed. M. C. Shurtleff. LC 80-67517. 117p. 1980. pap. 30.00 (*0-89054-029-2*) Am Phytopathol Soc.

Compendium of Cosmotology & Anesthetics. U. E. Austermann. (C). 1987. 120.00 (*0-85950-660-6*, Pub. by S Thornes Pubs UK) St Mut.

Compendium of Cotton Diseases. Ed. by G. M. Watkins. LC 80-85457. 95p. 1981. pap. 30.00 (*0-89054-031-4*) Am Phytopathol Soc.

Compendium of Drawing & Drawing Instruments. Ed. by G. Lister Sutcliffe. (Modern Carpenter Joiner & Cabinet-Maker Ser.: Vol. 3). (Illus.). 136p. 1990. reprint ed. 19.95 (*0-918678-57-9*) Natl Hist Soc.

Compendium of Early Mohawk Valley Families, 2 vols., Set. Maryly B. Penrose. 1173p. 1990. 75.00 (*0-685-54336-6*, 4558) Genealog Pub.

Compendium of Educational Materials on the Water Environment. Alliance for Environmental Education, Inc. Staff. (Illus.). 200p. 1992. 9.95 (*1-882504-00-3*) All Environ Educ.

Compendium of Elm Diseases. Ed. by R. J. Campana & R. J. Stipes. LC 81-67058. 120p. 1981. pap. 30.00 (*0-89054-042-X*) Am Phytopathol Soc.

*__Compendium of Executive Compensation Surveys, 1994.__ Ed. by James H. Kennedy. 15p. 1994. 24.95 (*0-916654-89-3*) Kennedy Pubns.

Compendium of Fire Safety Data, 6 vols., set. Fire Protection Association Staff. (C). 1989. Set. ring bd. 600.00 (*0-685-33726-X*, Pub. by Witherby & Co UK) St Mut.

Compendium of Foliar Sclerids in Angiosperms: Morphology & Taxonomy. T. Ananda Rao. (C). 1991. 62.00 (*81-224-0067-1*, Pub. by Wiley Eastern II) S Asia.

*__Compendium of Food Consumption Statistics from Household Surveys in Developing Countries: Africa, Latin America & Oceania, Vol. 2.__ FAO Staff. 400p. 1994. pap. 35.00 (*92-5-103568-7*, F35687, Pub. by FAO IT) UNIPUB.

Compendium of Forms, Tables & Charts. Joint Commission on Accreditation of Healthcare Staff. 1991. 30.00 (*0-86688-257-X*) Mosby Yr Bk.

Compendium of General Sociology: Abridged in Italian with Approval of the Author by Giulio Farina from Pareto's Trattato di Sociologia Generale. Vilfredo Pareto. Ed. by Elisabeth Abbott. 517p. LC 79-24899. 517p. reprint ed. pap. 147.40 (*0-7837-2928-6*, 2057526) Bks Demand.

Compendium of Good Practices in Biotechnology. BIOTOL Partners Staff. (BIOTOL Ser.). (Illus.). 300p. 1994. pap. 41.95 (*0-7506-1600-8*) Buttrwrth-Heinemann.

Compendium of Grape Diseases. Ed. by Roger C. Pearson & Austin C. Goheen. LC 88-70733. (Disease Compendium Ser.). (Illus.). 121p. (Orig.). 1988. pap. 30.00 (*0-89054-088-8*) Am Phytopathol Soc.

Compendium of Health Promotion--Related Initiatives for Older Adults. U. S. Dept. of Health & Human Services Editorial Staff. 48p. 1986. write for info. (*0-318-61572-X*) US HHS.

*__Compendium of Historical Sources: The How & Where of American Genealogy.__ 7th rev. ed. Ronald A. Bremer. 914p. 1994. per. 100.00 (*0-614-06928-9*) Progenitor Soc.

Compendium of History & Biography of Central & Northern Minnesota. (Illus.). 828p. 1994. reprint ed. lib. bdg. 85.00 (*0-8328-3842-X*) Higginson Bk Co.

*__Compendium of History & Biography of Central & Northern Minnesota, Containing a History of the State of Minnesota...& a Compendium of Biography.__ (Illus.). 828p. 1995. reprint ed. lib. bdg. 85.00 (*0-8328-4623-6*) Higginson Bk Co.

Compendium of History & Biography of Minneapolis & Hennepin County, Minnesota. Ed. by R. I. Holcombe & William H. Bingham. (Illus.). 584p. 1994. reprint ed. lib. bdg. 59.50 (*0-8328-3844-6*) Higginson Bk Co.

Compendium of History & Biography of North Dakota. (Illus.). 1410p. 1994. reprint ed. lib. bdg. 145.00 (*0-685-71283-4*) Higginson Bk Co.

Compendium of History & Biography of Northern Minnesota. (Illus.). 1039p. 1994. reprint ed. lib. bdg. 105.00 (*0-8328-3833-0*) Higginson Bk Co.

Compendium of HIV-AIDS: Positions, Policies & Documents. rev. ed. 1993. 9.00 (*1-55810-082-2*, PR-08) Am Nurses Pub.

Compendium of Hyde Park History, 3 vols. Nancy Hannan. (Illus.). 600p. 1989. 50.00 (*0-913553-07-7*) Albert Hse Pub.

Compendium of Icebreakers, Energizers & Introductions. Ed. by Andy Kirby. 150p. 1993. 89.95 (*1-85904-044-6*, Pub. by Gower UK) Ashgate Pub Co.

Compendium of Icebreakers, Energizers, & Introductions. Ed. by Andy Kirby. ring bd. 59.95 (*0-87425-197-4*) Human Res Dev Pr.

Compendium of Information on Edible Horticultural Crops. C. Hackett & J. Carolane. LC 81-71777. 1982. text ed. 138.00 (*0-12-312820-X*) Acad Pr.

Compendium of Information Relevant to Manpower Agencies. John C. Erfurt. 1973. pap. 7.00 (*0-87736-330-7*) U of Mich Inst Labor.

Compendium of International AIDS Programs & Policies. George M. Worthington. 310p. (Orig.). (C). 1989. 29.50 (*0-9623474-2-6*); pap. text ed. 15.00 (*0-685-27257-5*); pap. text ed. 15.00 (*0-685-27258-3*) G M Worthington.

Compendium of International Conventions Concerning the Status of Women. 186p. 1989. pap. 20.00 (*92-1-130128-9*, E.88.IV.3) UN.

Compendium of International Ocean Energy Activities: Committee Report. 91p. 1989. 14.00 (*0-87262-682-2*) Am Soc Civil Eng.

Compendium of Kaffir Laws & Customs. Maclean. (Illus.). 171p. 1968. reprint ed. 37.50 (*0-7146-1907-8*, Pub. by F Cass Pubs UK) Intl Spec Bk.

Compendium of Land Trust Documents. Comp. by Herb Goldstein. 1981. reprint ed. pap. 3.00 (*0-686-84741-5*) Comm Serv OH.

Compendium of Landshells: A Full-Color Guide to More Than 2,000 of the World's Terrestrial Shells. R. Tucker Abbott. LC 89-84434. (Illus.). 240p. (C). 1989. 19.95 (*0-915826-23-2*) Am Malacologists.

Compendium of Latin American Debt-Swap Deals: A Guide to Programs & Players. Katalin Holzman. Ed. by Rosemary Werrett. 140p. (Orig.). 1988. pap. 225.00 (*0-923351-00-0*) Latin Am Info.

Compendium of Legislative & Regulatory Issues. (Illus.). 40p. 1992. pap. 10.00 (*1-56318-014-6*) Assn Natl Advertisers.

Compendium of Lottery Statistics 1992. Terri LaFleur. 207p. 1992. pap. 100.00 (*1-883567-50-5*) TLF Pubns.

*__Compendium of Machine Learning I: Symbolic Learning.__ Terry Caelli & Garry Briscoe. (Artificial Intelligence Ser.). 1995. write for info. (*1-56750-178-8*); pap. write for info. (*1-56750-179-6*) Ablex Pub.

*__Compendium of Massachusetts Criminal Law.__ R. Marc Kantrowitz & Massachusetts Continuing Legal Education, Inc. Staff. LC 93-78215. 1993. 50.00 (*0-944490-52-2*) Mass CLE.

Compendium of Massachusetts Family Law. Michael Leshin. LC 90-63089. 300p. 1990. ring bd. 50.00 (*0-944490-28-X*) Mass CLE.

*__Compendium of Massachusetts Family Law.__ Michael Leshin. LC 90-63089. 503p. 1990. ring bd. 50.00 (*0-944490-60-3*) Mass CLE.

Compendium of Mercantile Law. John W. Smith. 320p. 1987. reprint ed. text ed. 37.50 (*0-8377-2612-3*) Rothman.

Compendium of Methods for the Microbiological Examination of Foods. 3rd ed. Ed. by Carl Vanderzant & Don Splittstoesser. 1264p. 1992. 90.00 (*0-87553-173-3*) Am Pub Health. Presents a comprehensive selection of proven methods with an emphasis on accuracy, relevance, & reliability. Contents: General Laboratory Procedures; Microorganisms Involved in the Processing & Spoilage of Foods; Indicator Microorganisms & Pathogens; Microorganisms & Food Safety; Food Borne Illness; Foods & the Microorganisms Involved in Their Safety; Media, Reagents, & Special Procedures. Nonmembers: $90.00 APHA Members: $63.00. ***Publisher Provided Annotation.***

---

*__Compendium of Modern Firearms.__ Kevin Dockery. (Edge of the Sword Ser.). (Illus.). 224p. (Orig.). 1991. pap. 20.00 (*0-937279-23-4*, ES4001) R Talsorian.

Compendium of Modern Instrumental Techniques. Gardner Read. LC 92-17854. 280p. 1993. text ed. 59.95 (*0-313-28512-8*, RCZ, Greenwood Pr) Greenwood.

Compendium of Neuropsychological Tests: Administration, Norms & Commentary. Otfried Spreen & Esther Strauss. (Illus.). 464p. 1991. 47.50 (*0-19-505439-3*) OUP.

Compendium of Neutron Spectra & Detector Responses for Radiation Protection Purposes. (Technical Reports Ser.: No. 318). 274p. 1990. pap. 105.00 (*92-0-125290-0*, STI/DOC/318) UNIPUB.

Compendium of Occult Laws. R. Swinburne Clymer. 311p. 1966. 9.95 (*0-932785-08-5*) Philos Pub.

Compendium of Ongoing Projects: December 1990. 484p. 1991. 25.00 (*92-1-126019-1*, 91.III.B.1) UN.

Compendium of Ongoing Projects as of 31 December 1988. 488p. 20.00 (*92-1-126017-5*, E.89.III.B.8) UN.

Compendium of Ongoing Projects as of 31 December 1989. 500p. 1989. 20.00 (*92-1-126018-3*, 90.III.B.1) UN.

*__Compendium of Onion & Garlic Diseases.__ Ed. by Howard F. Schwartz & S. Krishna Mohan. LC 94-78502. (Disease Compendium Ser.). (Illus.). 90p. (Orig.). 1994. pap. 30.00x (*0-89054-170-1*) Am Phytopathol Soc.

Compendium of Organic Synthetic Methods. Dan T. Harrison & Shuyen Harrison. LC 71-162800. 529p. 1971. Vol. 1, 529p. text ed. 84.95 (*0-471-35550-X*) Wiley.

Compendium of Organic Synthetic Methods, 6 vols., Set. Dan T. Harrison & Shuyen Harrison. LC 71-162800. 1974. Six vol. set, 1988. text ed. 240.00 (*0-471-50135-2*) Wiley.

Compendium of Organic Synthetic Methods, Vol. 2. Dan T. Harrison & Shuyen Harrison. LC 71-162800. 437p. 1974. text ed. 74.95 (*0-471-35551-8*) Wiley.

Compendium of Organic Synthetic Methods, Vol. 3. Louis S. Hegedus & Leroy G. Wade, Jr. LC 71-162800. 495p. 1977. text ed. 79.95 (*0-471-36752-4*, Wiley-Interscience) Wiley.

Compendium of Organic Synthetic Methods, Vol. 4. Leroy G. Wade, Jr. LC 71-162800. (Compendium of Organic Synthetic Methods Ser.). 497p. 1980. text ed. 74.95 (*0-471-04923-9*, Wiley-Interscience) Wiley.

Compendium of Organic Synthetic Methods, Vol. 5. Leroy G. Wade, Jr. (Compendium of Organic Synthetic Methods Ser.: 1-101). 552p. 1984. text ed. 74.95 (*0-471-86728-4*, Wiley-Interscience) Wiley.

Compendium of Organic Synthetic Methods, Vol. 6. Michael B. Smith. 534p. 1988. text ed. 74.95 (*0-471-84896-4*) Wiley.

Compendium of Organic Synthetic Methods, Vol. 7. Michael B. Smith. 568p. 1992. text ed. 79.95 (*0-471-60713-4*) Wiley.

Compendium of Ornamental Foliage Plant Diseases. A. R. Chase. LC 87-70833. (Disease Compendium Ser.). (Illus.). 114p. (Orig.). 1987. 30.00 (*0-89054-077-2*) Am Phytopathol Soc.

Compendium of Patient Safety. 1990. 50.00 (*0-685-45431-2*, OP984089) AMA.

Compendium of Pea Diseases. Ed. by D. J. Hagedorn. LC 84-81532. 73p. 1984. 30.00 (*0-89054-060-8*) Am Phytopathol Soc.

Compendium of Peanut Diseases. Ed. by D. M. Porter et al. LC 84-70853. 93p. 1984. pap. 30.00 (*0-89054-055-1*) Am Phytopathol Soc.

Compendium of Pharmaceuticals & Specialties. 19th ed. Ed. by Carmen M. Krogh. 920p. reprint ed. pap. 180.00 (*0-318-35014-9*, 2030877) Bks Demand.

Compendium of Philosophy. Tr. by S. Z. Aung & C. A. F. Rhys Davids. (C). 1910. 27.50 (*86013-000-2*, Pub. by Pali Text) Wisdom MA.

Compendium of Phonetics in Ancient & Archaic Chinese. Bernhard Karlgren. 1988. reprint ed. 20.00 (*0-89986-364-7*) Oriental Bk Store.

Compendium of Piano Music. Louis M. Gottschalk. Ed. by Eugene List. (Illus.). 64p. 1971. pap. 8.95 (*0-8258-0226-1*, 0-4818) Fischer Inc NY.

Compendium of Post Accident Heat Removal Models for Liquid Metal Cooled Fast Breeder Reactors. B. D. Turland & J. Morgan. 415p. 1985. pap. text ed. 251.00 (*3-7186-0309-8*) Gordon & Breach.

Compendium of Potato Diseases. Ed. by W. J. Hooker. LC 80-85459. 141p. 1981. pap. 30.00 (*0-89054-027-6*) Am Phytopathol Soc.

Compendium of Practical Astronomy, 3 vols. rev. ed. Ed. by Gunter D. Roth. Tr. by Harry J. Augensen & Wulff D. Heintz. LC 93-27023. (Illus.). (ENG & GER.). 1993. Vol. 1: Instrumentation & Reduction Techniques, 560p. pap. 59.00 (*0-387-53596-9*); Vol. 2: Earth & Solar System, 384p. pap. 44.50 (*0-387-54885-8*); Vol. 3: Stars & Stellar Systems, 288p. pap. 44.50 (*0-387-54886-6*) Spr-Verlag.

Compendium of Practical Astronomy, 3 vols., Set. rev. ed. Ed. by Gunter D. Roth. Tr. by Harry J. Augensen & Wulff D. Heintz. LC 93-27023. (Illus.). (ENG & GER.). 1994. pap. 125.00 (*0-387-56273-7*) Spr-Verlag.

Compendium of Pumped Storage Plants in the United States. American Society of Civil Engineers Staff. LC 93-33564. 1993. write for info. (*0-87262-991-0*) Am Soc Civil Eng.

Compendium of Raspberry & Blackberry Diseases & Insects. Ed. by Michael A. Ellis et al. LC 91-76318. (Disease Compendium Ser.). (Illus.). 122p. (Orig.). 1991. pap. 30.00 (*0-89054-121-3*) Am Phytopathol Soc.

Compendium of Regulatory Air Quality Simulation Mode I. D. Szepesi. (Illus.). 516p. (C). 1989. 400.00 (*0-685-46642-6*, Pub. by Collets) St Mut.

Compendium of Rhododendron & Azalea Diseases. Ed. by Duane L. Coyier & Martha K. Roane. LC 86-72873. (Disease Compendium Ser.). (Illus.). 77p. (Orig.). 1986. pap. 30.00 (*0-89054-075-6*) Am Phytopathol Soc.

Compendium of Rice Diseases. Ed. by Robert K. Webster & Pamela S. Gunnell. LC 92-71949. (Disease Compendium Ser.). (Illus.). 86p. (Orig.). 1992. pap. 30.00 (*0-89054-126-4*) Am Phytopathol Soc.

Compendium of Roman Law: Founded on the Institutes of Justinian Together with Examination Questions Set in the University & Bar Examinations (with Solutions) 2nd ed. Gordon Campbell. LC 92-79710. 302p. 1994. reprint ed. 70.00 (*1-56169-068-6*) W W Gaunt.

Compendium of Rose Diseases. R. Kenneth Horst. 64p. 1983. pap. 30.00 (*0-89054-052-7*) Am Phytopathol Soc.

Compendium of Safety Data Sheets for Research & Industrial Chemicals, Pts. 4-6. Lawrence H. Keith & Douglas B. Walters. LC 84-27107. 1696p. 1987. lib. bdg. 325.00 (*0-89573-288-2*) VCH Pubs.

Compendium of Safety Data Sheets for Research & Industrial Chemicals, Set. L. H. Keith & D. B. Walters. LC 84-27107. 1862p. 1985. lib. bdg. 325.00 (*0-89573-313-7*) VCH Pubs.

Compendium of Safety Data Sheets for Research & Industrial Chemicals, Set, Pts. 4-6. Lawrence H. Keith & Douglas B. Walters. LC 84-27107. 1696p. 1987. Set, Pts. 1-6. lib. bdg. 595.00 (*0-89573-289-0*) VCH Pubs.

Compendium of Safety Data Sheets for Research & Industrial Chemicals, Pt. 7: Flavors & Fragrances. Thomas C. Zebovitz. LC 84-27107. 694p. 1989. lib. bdg. 115.00 (*0-89573-764-7*) VCH Pubs.

Compendium of Seashells. rev. ed. R. Tucker Abbott & S. Peter Dance. LC 81-67757. (Illus.). 411p. 1986. reprint ed. 49.95 (*0-915826-17-8*) Am Malacologists.

Compendium of Shakespeare. C. Marydass. 180p. (YA). (gr. 7 up). 1988. text ed. 25.00 (*81-207-0713-3*, Pub. by Sterling Pubs II) Apt Bks.

Compendium of Small Animal Surgery. Robert L. Leighton & Kathy Jones. (Venture Series in Veterinary Medicine). (Illus.). 282p. (C). 1983. pap. text ed. 36.95 (*0-8138-0366-7*) Iowa St U Pr.

Compendium of Social Statistics & Indicators: 1988. 683p. 1991. 75.00 (*92-1-061145-4*, 91.XVII.6) UN.

*__Compendium of Soil Fungi, 2 vols., Set.__ K. H. Domsch et al. (Illus.). 1264p. 1993. reprint ed. lib. bdg. 55.00 (*3-9803083-8-3*, Pub. by IHW GW) Lubrecht & Cramer.

Compendium of Sorghum Diseases. Ed. by R. A. Frederiksen. LC 86-70382. 98p. 1986. pap. 30.00 (*0-89054-069-1*) Am Phytopathol Soc.

Compendium of Soybean Diseases. 3rd ed. Ed. by J. B. Sinclair & P. A. Backman. LC 88-83464. (Disease Compendium Ser.). (Illus.). 116p. 1989. pap. 30.00 (*0-89054-093-4*) Am Phytopathol Soc.

*__Compendium of Spirituality, 2 vols., Set.__ Ed. by Emetrio De Cea. Tr. by Jordan Aumann. (Orig.). 1996. pap. write for info. (*0-8189-0723-1*) Alba.

*__Compendium of Spirituality, Vol. 2.__ Ed. by Emeterio De Cea. Tr. by Jordan Aumann. (Orig.). 1996. pap. write for info. (*0-8189-0725-8*) Alba.

*__Compendium of Spirituality Vol. 1: Doctrinal & Pastoral Teaching.__ Ed. by Emetrio De Cea. Tr. by Jordan Aumann. LC 95-10473. (Orig.). 1995. pap. 12.95 (*0-8189-0724-X*) Alba.

Compendium of Standards, Practices, & Methods Relating to Contamination Control. 53p. 1984. pap. text ed. 50.00 (*0-915414-78-3*) Inst Environ Sci.

Compendium of Standards, Practices, Methods, & Similar Documents Relating to Contamination Control. Ed. by Vinette Kopetz. (Recommended Practice Ser.). 72p. 1993. pap. text ed. 125.00 (*1-877862-29-0*, IES-RD-CC009.2) Inst Environ Sci.

Compendium of State Peer Review Immunity Laws. American Medical Association Staff. 101p. (Orig.). 1988. pap. 39.95 (*0-685-20110-4*, OP097588) AMA.

*__Compendium of State Privacy & Security.__ 155p. (Orig.). (C). 1994. pap. text ed. 25.00x (*0-7881-0784-4*) Diane Pub.

Compendium of State Statutes & International Treaties in Trust & Estate Law: A Reference & Referral Guide for Practicing Attorneys. M. Henner. LC 85-3554. (Illus.). xiii, 352p. 1985. text ed. 75.00 (*0-89930-076-6*, HML/, Quorum Bks) Greenwood.

Compendium of Statistics & Indicators on the Situation of Women in Africa, 1986. 592p. 1988. pap. 65.00 (*92-1-061130-6*, EF.88.XVII.6) UN.

*__Compendium of Stone Fruit Diseases.__ J. M. Ogawa et al. (Disease Compendium Ser.). 128p. 1995. 30.00 (*0-89054-174-4*) Am Phytopathol Soc.

Compendium of Strawberry Diseases. Ed. by John L. Maas. 159p. 1984. pap. 30.00 (*0-89054-054-3*) Am Phytopathol Soc.

Compendium of Swedenborg's Theological Writings. Samuel Warren. LC 73-94196. 816p. 1974. 12.00 (*0-87785-123-9*) Swedenborg.

Compendium of Sweet Potato Diseases. C. A. Clark & J. W. Moyer. LC 88-70995. (Disease Compendium Ser.). (Illus.). 75p. (Orig.). 1988. pap. 30.00 (*0-89054-089-6*) Am Phytopathol Soc.

Compendium of the Confederacy: An Annotated Bibliography: Books - Pamphlets - Serials, 2 vols., Set. John H. Wright. 1326p. 1989. 150.00 (*0-916107-74-4*) Broadfoot.

Compendium of the Confederate Armies: Alabama. Stewart Sifakis. 160p. 1991. 24.95 (*0-8160-2287-9*) Facts on File.

Compendium of the Confederate Armies: Florida & Arkansas. Stewart Sifakis. 160p. 1991. 24.95 (*0-8160-2288-7*) Facts on File.

Compendium of the Confederate Armies: Kentucky, Maryland, Missouri & the Indian Units. Stewart Sifakis. 216p. 1995. lib. bdg. 27.50 (*0-8160-2294-1*) Facts on File.

Compendium of the Confederate Armies: Louisiana. Stewart Sifakis. 160p. 1995. lib. bdg. 24.95 (*0-8160-2291-7*) Facts on File.

Compendium of the Confederate Armies: North Carolina. Stewart Sifakis. 192p. 1991. 24.95 (*0-8160-2289-5*) Facts on File.

C

Compendium of the Confederate Armies: South Carolina & Georgia. Stewart Sifakis. 320p. 1995. lib. bdg. 29.95 (*0-8160-2290-9*) Facts on File.

Compendium of the Confederate Armies: Tennessee. Stewart Sifakis. 208p. 1991. 24.95 (*0-8160-2286-0*) Facts on File.

Compendium of the Confederate Armies: Texas. Stewart Sifakis. 160p. 1995. lib. bdg. 24.95 (*0-8160-2293-3*) Facts on File.

Compendium of the Confederate Armies: Virginia. Stewart Sifakis. 304p. 1991. 29.95 (*0-8160-2284-4*) Facts on File.

Compendium of the Enumeration of the Inhabitants, 1840. U. S. Census Office Staff. LC 75-22850. (America in Two Centuries Ser.). 1976. reprint ed. 35.95 (*0-405-07753-X*) Ayer.

Compendium of the Impending Crisis of the South. Hinton R. Helper. LC 75-83966. (Black Heritage Library Collection). 1977. 19.95 (*0-8369-8595-8*) Ayer.

Compendium of the Ninth Census, Eighteen Seventy. U. S. Census Office Staff. LC 75-24112. (America in Two Centuries Ser.). 1976. reprint ed. 75.95 (*0-405-07720-3*) Ayer.

***Compendium of the North American Symposium on International Child Abduction: How to Handle International Child Abduction Cases.** (Illus.). 928p. (Orig.). (C). 1994. pap. text ed. 75.00x (*0-7881-1346-1*) Diane Pub.

Compendium of the Overland Mail Company on the South Route, 1858-1861 & the Period Surrounding It. G. C. Tompkins. LC 85-193324. (Illus.). 399p. (C). 1990. reprint ed. lib. bdg. 37.00x (*0-8095-6004-6*) Borgo Pr.

Compendium of the Scriptures. Ed. by L. J. Lea. 1951. pap. 13.50 (*0-8309-0253-8*) Herald Hse.

Compendium of the Tenth Census, Eighteen Eighty, 2 vols., 1. U. S. Census Office Staff. LC 75-22854. (America in Two Centuries Ser.). 1976. reprint ed. 72.95 (*0-405-07745-9*) Ayer.

Compendium of the Tenth Census, Eighteen Eighty, 2 vols., 2. U. S. Census Office Staff. LC 75-22854. (America in Two Centuries Ser.). 1976. reprint ed. 72.95 (*0-405-07746-7*) Ayer.

Compendium of the Tenth Census, Eighteen Eighty, 2 vols., Set. U. S. Census Office Staff. LC 75-22854. (America in Two Centuries Ser.). 1976. reprint ed. 145.95 (*0-405-07744-0*) Ayer.

Compendium of the War of the Rebellion. Frederick H. Dyer. 1796p. 1994. 125.00 (*0-89029-046-6*) Morningside Bkshop.

Compendium of the World's Languages, 2 Vols. George L. Campbell. 1400p. 1991. 225.00 (*0-415-02937-6*) Routledge.

Compendium of Thermophysical Property Measurement Methods, Vol. 2. Ed. by Kosta D. Maglic et al. (Illus.). 666p. 1991. 165.00 (*0-306-43854-2*, Plenum Pr) Plenum.

Compendium of Thermophysical Property Measurement Methods, Vol. 1: Survey of Measurement Techniques. Ed. by Kosta D. Maglic. 806p. 1984. 165.00 (*0-306-41424-4*, Plenum Pr) Plenum.

Compendium of Tobacco Diseases. Ed. by H. D. Shew & G. B. Lucas. LC 90-86097. (Disease Compendium Ser.). (Illus.). 90p. (Orig.). 1991. pap. 30.00 (*0-89054-117-5*) Am Phytopathol Soc.

Compendium of Tomato Diseases. Ed. by J. B. Jones et al. LC 91-71246. (Disease Compendium Ser.). 100p. (Orig.). 1991. pap. 30.00 (*0-89054-120-5*) Am Phytopathol Soc.

Compendium of Trends on General Social Survey Questions. Tom W. Smith & Guy J. Rich. (National Opinion Research Center Ser.: No. 129). (Orig.). 1980. pap. text ed. 7.50 (*0-932132-24-3*) NORC.

***Compendium of Trick Plays.** Ishida Yoshio et al. Tr. by Bob J. Terry. 220p. (Orig.). Date not set. pap. 14.95 (*0-9641847-1-0*) Yutopian Ent.

Compendium of Tropical Fruit Diseases. Ed. by R. C. Ploetz et al. LC 94-70664. (Disease Compendium Ser.). (Illus.). viii, 118p. (Orig.). 1994. pap. 30.00 (*0-89054-162-0*) Am Phytopathol Soc.

Compendium of Turfgrass Diseases. 2nd ed. Richard W. Smiley et al. LC 91-77313. (Disease Compendium Ser.). (Illus.). 128p. 1992. pap. 30.00 (*0-89054-124-8*) Am Phytopathol Soc.

Compendium of Utility-Sponsored Energy Efficiency Rebate Programs. 267p. 1987. 75.00 (*0-318-23864-0*) Consumer Energy Coun.

Compendium of Victim-Witness Legislation. 1984. write for info. (*0-318-61008-6*) SEARCH Grp.

Compendium of Weapons, Armor & Castles. Matthew Balent. Ed. by Alex Marciniszyn & Kevin Siembieda. (Illus.). 224p. (Orig.). (YA). (gr. 8 up). 1989. pap. 19.95 (*0-916211-38-X*, 411) Palladium Bks.

Compendium of What Works for Vocational Educators in Dropout Prevention. National Center for Research in Vocational Education Staff. 1988. 11.50 (*0-317-03862-1*, SP700DP03) Ctr Educ Trng Employ.

Compendium of Wheat Diseases. 2nd ed. M. V. Wiese. LC 87-70237. (Disease Compendium Ser.). (Illus.). 124p. (Orig.). 1987. pap. 30.00 (*0-89054-076-4*) Am Phytopathol Soc.

Compendium on Metal Injection Molding. Metal Powder Industries Federation Staff. (Illus.). 137p. reprint ed. pap. 39.10 (*0-7837-5162-1*, 2044891) Bks Demand.

Compendium on Metal Injection Molding II. (Illus.). 302p. 1989. pap. 20.00 (*0-918404-94-0*) Metal Powder.

Compendium, Vol. 1: Thermoplastic Matrices & Composites. 312p. 1991. 38.00 (*0-938994-61-1*) SAMPE.

Compendium, Vol. 2: Composites for Commercial Applications: Technology Transfer Examples. 1992. 48.00 (*0-938994-63-8*) SAMPE.

Compensated Worksharing: An Alternative to Layoffs. (State Legislative Reports: Vol. 16, No. 2). 5p. 1991. 5.00 (*1-55516-301-7*, 7301-1602) Natl Conf State Legis.

Compensating for Missing Survey Data. Graham Kalton. LC 82-12106. (Illus.). 164p. (Orig.). (C). 1983. pap. 14.00 (*0-87944-282-4*) Inst Soc Res.

Compensating Key Personnel in the Health Care Industry. Jay R. Schuster. LC 85-14166. 176p. 1985. text ed. 24.95 (*0-88331-121-6*) Luce.

Compensating Pendulums. J. L. Finn & S. Riefler. (Illus.). 48p. 1993. pap. 5.95 (*0-930163-53-2*) Arlington Bk.

Compensating the Administrative Team. American Association of School Administrators & National School Boards Association. (Administrative Team Career Development Ser.: Bk. 2). 3.50 (*0-87652-016-6*, 021-00844) Am Assn Sch Admin.

Compensating the Administrative Team (Full Report) American Association of School Administrators Staff & National School Boards Association. (Administrative Team Career Development Ser.: Bk. 4). 15.00 (*0-87652-017-4*, 021-00850) Am Assn Sch Admin.

Compensating the Superintendent: Full Report. American Association of School Administrators Staff. 15.00 (*0-87652-018-2*, 021-00825) Am Assn Sch Admin.

Compensating the Superintendent: Summary Report. American Association of School Administrators Staff. (Superintendent Career Development Ser.). 3.50 (*0-87652-019-0*, 021-00819) Am Assn Sch Admin.

Compensating United States Employees Abroad. Charles F. O'Connell. (International Business Portfolios Ser.). 1988. write for info. (*0-8205-1953-7*) Bender.

Compensating Your Sales Force: How to Use Commissions, Draws, Bonuses & Quotas to Keep Revised. W. G. Ryckman & Robert G. Head. 1993. 27.50 (*1-55738-485-1*) Probus Pub Co.

Compensating Your Sales Personnel. 113p. 1991. 100.00 (*0-318-14961-3*, P309) NAPL.

Compensation. BNA's Business & Human Resources Services Staff. (Policy & Practice Ser.). 1952. 562.00 (*0-685-14342-2*) BNA.

Compensation. Harvard Business School Staff. 1991. pap. text ed. 19.95 (*0-07-103327-0*) McGraw.

Compensation. 3rd ed. George T. Milkovich & Jerry M. Newman. 736p. (C). 1990. text ed. 59.95 (*0-256-07671-5*) Irwin.

Compensation. 4th ed. George T. Milkovich & Jerry M. Newman. LC 92-27604. 656p. (C). 1992. text ed. 64.95 (*0-256-10527-8*) Irwin.

***Compensation.** 5th ed. George T. Milkovich et al. LC 95-16253. 656p. (C). 1995. text ed. 64.95 (*0-256-14145-2*) Irwin Prof Pubng.

Compensation. 5th ed. Robert E. Sibson. LC 90-55210. 416p. 1990. 69.95 (*0-8144-5977-3*) AMACOM.

Compensation: Effect Reward Management. Kanango. 1992. 84.95 (*0-409-89778-7*, Pub. by Buttrwrth Can Acad CN) Buttrwrth-Heinemann.

Compensation: Fair Pay for Executives & Employees. Harvard Business Review Staff. (People Management Ser.). 111p. 1991. pap. 19.95 (*0-87584-267-4*) Harvard Busn.

Compensation Administration. 2nd ed. Leonard R. Burgess. 512p. (C). 1989. write for info. (*0-675-20797-5*, Merrill Pub Co) Macmillan.

Compensation & Benefits. (SHRM-BNA Ser.: Vol. 3). 260p. 1989. pap. 25.00 (*0-685-56817-2*, P110) Soc Human Resc Mgmt.

Compensation & Benefits, 3 vols. 1994. 446.00 (*0-7913-1832-X*) Warren Gorham & Lamont.

Compensation & Benefits. Ed. by Luis R. Gomez-Mejia. (SHRM-BNA Ser.: Vol. 3). 306p. 1989. pap. text ed. 25.00 (*0-87179-603-1*, 0603) BNA.

Compensation & Benefits Alerts. 1993. 261.00 (*0-685-67944-6*) Warren Gorham & Lamont.

Compensation & Benefits Alerts. annuals 1993. 275.00 (*0-685-68093-2*) Warren Gorham & Lamont.

***Compensation & Benefits in Consulting Engineering & Land Surveying Firms in California.** 3rd ed. Ed. by Steven Langer. 229p. 1994. pap. 395.00 (*0-614-05745-0*) Abbott Langer Assocs.

***Compensation & Benefits in Consulting Engineering Firms - 1995 National Edition.** Ed. by Steven Langer. 467p. 1995. pap. 495.00 (*0-614-05741-8*) Abbott Langer Assocs.

***Compensation & Benefits in Consulting Engineering Firms in Indiana.** 2nd ed. Ed. by Steven Langer. 208p. 1994. pap. 395.00 (*0-614-05742-6*) Abbott Langer Assocs.

***Compensation & Benefits in Consulting Engineering Firms in New England.** 3rd ed. Ed. by Steven Langer. 225p. 1994. pap. 395.00 (*0-614-05744-2*) Abbott Langer Assocs.

***Compensation & Benefits in Consulting Engineering Firms in Utah.** Ed. by Steven Langer. 202p. 1994. pap. 395.00 (*0-614-05743-4*) Abbott Langer Assocs.

***Compensation & Benefits in Engineering Firms in the Geotechnical Field.** 6th ed. Ed. by Steven Langer. 307p. 1994. pap. 395.00 (*0-614-05746-9*) Abbott Langer Assocs.

Compensation & Benefits Survey, 1992. AEDC Staff. 48p. 1992. pap. text ed. 75.00 (*0-9616567-3-5*) Amer Econ Dev Council.

Compensation & Liability for Product & Process Injuries see Enterprise Responsibility for Personal Injuries: Final Report - Preliminary Draft

Compensation & Motivation: Maximizing Employee Performance with Behavior-Based Incentive Plans. Thomas J. McCoy. 320p. 1992. 65.00 (*0-8144-5029-6*) AMACOM.

Compensation & Restitution to Victims of Crime. 2nd ed. Stephen Schafer. LC 74-108237. (Criminology, Law Enforcement, & Social Problems Ser.: No. 120). 227p. (Orig.). (C). 1970. 18.00 (*0-87585-120-7*); pap. 9.00 (*0-87585-901-1*) Patterson Smith.

Compensation & Utilization of Court Reporters in Ventura County. National Center for State Courts Staff. 167p. 1974. 10.02 (*0-685-16306-7*, MAB-023) Natl Ctr St Courts.

Compensation Claims Auditor. Jack Rudman. (Career Examination Ser.: C-2126). 1994. reprint ed. pap. 29.95 (*0-8373-2126-3*) Nat Learn.

Compensation Claims Clerk. Jack Rudman. (Career Examination Ser.: C-866). 1994. pap. 23.95 (*0-8373-0866-6*) Nat Learn.

Compensation Claims Examiner. Jack Rudman. (Career Examination Ser.: C-2133). 1994. reprint ed. pap. 27.95 (*0-8373-2133-6*) Nat Learn.

Compensation Claims Examiner Trainee. Jack Rudman. (Career Examination Ser.: C-879). 1994. pap. 23.95 (*0-8373-0879-8*) Nat Learn.

Compensation Claims Investigator. Jack Rudman. (Career Examination Ser.: C-949). 1994. pap. 27.95 (*0-8373-0949-2*) Nat Learn.

Compensation Claims Legal Investigator. Jack Rudman. (Career Examination Ser.: C-2100). 1994. pap. 27.95 (*0-8373-2100-X*) Nat Learn.

***Compensation Claims Referee.** (Career Examination Ser.: Series 1). Date not set. pap. 39.95 (*0-8373-3631-7*) Nat Learn.

Compensation Decision Making. Frederick S. Hills. 470p. (C). 1987. text ed. 55.00 (*0-03-063339-7*) Dryden Pr.

Compensation Decision Making. 2nd ed. Frederick S. Hills et al. LC 93-80337. 522p. (C). 1993. text ed. 53.75 (*0-03-033058-0*) Dryden Pr.

Compensation Decision Making: A Computer-Based Approach. Nancy A. Bereman & Mark L. Lengnick-Hall. LC 93-39774. 116p. (C). 1993. 3.5 hd, pap. text ed. 21.50 (*0-03-001869-2*) Dryden Pr.

Compensation for Criminal Injuries. David Miers. 1990. U.K. text ed. 90.00 (*0-406-12324-1*) Butterworth Legal Pubs.

Compensation for Damage: An International Perspective. Sheila McLean. 200p. 1993. 59.95 (*1-85521-169-6*, Pub. by Dartmth Pub UK) Ashgate Pub Co.

Compensation for Dismissal, 1993. Anthony Korn. (Blackstone's Employment Law Library). 1993. pap. 42.00 (*1-85431-211-1*, Pub. by Blackstone Pr UK) W W Gaunt.

Compensation for Industrial Disease. N. J. Wikeley. 238p. 1993. 57.95 (*1-85521-264-1*, Pub. by Dartmth Pub UK) Ashgate Pub Co.

Compensation for Industrial Injuries. Richard Lewis. 1987. U.K. text ed. 65.00 (*0-86205-214-9*) Butterworth Legal Pubs.

Compensation for Personal Injury in Sweden & 17 Other Countries. Ed. by Carl Oldertz & Eva Tidefelt. 408p. 1988. 109.00x (*91-7598-197-1*) Coronet Bks.

***Compensation for Psychological Deficits & Declines: Managing Losses & Promoting Gains.** Ed. by Roger A. Dixon & Lars Backman. 352p. 1995. text ed. 59.95 (*0-8058-1559-7*) L Erlbaum Assocs.

Compensation Handbook: A State-of-the-Art Guide to Compensation Strategy & Design. 3rd ed. Milton L. Rock & Lance A. Berger. 592p. 1991. text ed. 89.50 (*0-07-053352-0*) McGraw.

***Compensation in Food & Beverage Processing.** Ed. by Steven Langer. 1995. pap. 450.00 (*0-614-05751-5*) Abbott Langer Assocs.

Compensation in Manufacturing. 14th ed. Ed. by Steven Langer. 622p. 1994. pap. 450.00 (*0-916506-25-8*) Abbott Langer Assocs.

***Compensation in Medical Equipment Manufacturing.** Ed. by Steven Langer. 198p. 1994. pap. 450.00 (*0-614-05750-7*) Abbott Langer Assocs.

***Compensation in Nonprofit Organizations.** 7th ed. Ed. by Steven Langer. 1233p. 1994. pap. 225.00 (*0-614-05748-5*) Abbott Langer Assocs.

Compensation in Research & Development. 9th ed. Ed. by Steven Langer. 573p. 1995. pap. 650.00 (*0-916506-34-7*) Abbott Langer Assocs.

Compensation in the Accounting-Financial Field. 14th ed. Ed. by Steven Langer. 353p. 1995. pap. 495.00 (*0-317-55984-2*) Abbott Langer Assocs.

Compensation in the Human Resources Field. 16th ed. Ed. by Steven Langer. 1071p. 1994. pap. 500.00 (*0-916506-31-2*) Abbott Langer Assocs.

Compensation in the MIS-dp Field. 12th ed. Ed. by Steven Langer. 687p. 1995. pap. 750.00 (*0-916506-37-1*) Abbott Langer Assocs.

Compensation in the Security-Loss Prevention Field. 8th ed. Ed. by Steven Langer. 367p. 1994. pap. 395.00 (*0-916506-23-1*) Abbott Langer Assocs.

Compensation Investigator. Jack Rudman. (Career Examination Ser.: C-950). 1994. pap. 27.95 (*0-8373-0950-6*) Nat Learn.

Compensation Management. Myers. 832p. 1989. 75.00 (*0-685-67123-2*, 5109) Commerce.

Compensation Management: Rewarding Performance. 6th ed. Richard I. Henderson. LC 93-13934. 1993. text ed. write for info. (*0-13-157728-X*) P-H Gen Ref & Trav.

Compensation Mechanisms for Job Risks: Wages, Workers' Compensation & Product Liability. Michael J. Moore & W. Kip Viscusi. 224p. 1990. text ed. 37.50 (*0-691-04247-0*) Princeton U Pr.

Compensation Ninety-Four: An Annual Report on Local Government Executive Salaries & Fringe Benefits. Ed. by Evelina Moulder. (Illus.). 404p. (Orig.). 1994. pap. text ed. 180.00 (*0-87326-095-3*) Intl City-Cnty Mgt.

Compensation of Credit Executives. (Credit Research Foundation Ser.). 28p. 1987. 40.00 (*0-939050-54-4*) Credit Res NYS.

***Compensation of Credit Executives Study.** Credit Research Foundation Staff. Ed. by Teresa Donohue. 64p. 1994. pap. 69.95 (*0-614-06133-4*) NACM.

Compensation of Industrial Engineers. 12th ed. 217p. 1993. 150.00 (*0-916506-82-7*) Abbott Langer Assocs.

Compensation of Injuries: Civil Jury Verdicts in Cook County. Institute for Civil Justice (U.S.) Staff et al. LC 84-13473. 1984. 7.50 (*0-8330-0590-1*, R-3011-ICJ) Rand Corp.

Compensation of Legal & Related Jobs (Non-Law Firms), 3 vols., Set. 16th ed. 1751p. 1994. 575.00 (*0-685-29543-5*, LAW4 94) Abbott Langer Assocs.

***Compensation of Plant & Facilities Managers & Engineers.** Ed. by Steven Langer. 438p. 1994. pap. 150.00 (*0-614-05752-3*) Abbott Langer Assocs.

***Compensation of Professional Geologists.** Ed. by Steven Langer. 437p. 1994. pap. 150.00 (*0-614-05747-7*) Abbott Langer Assocs.

Compensation, Organizational Strategy & Firm Performance. Luis R. Gomez-Mejia & David B. Balkin. 304p. (C). 1992. text ed. 28.95 (*0-538-80269-3*, GJ63AA) S-W Pub.

Compensation Planning for Executives in a New Environment, 2 vols. (Tax Law & Estate Planning Course Handbook Ser.). 1239p. 1992. pap. 80.00 (*0-685-69395-3*) PLI.

Compensation Plans for Lawyers & Their Staffs: Salaries, Bonuses, & Profit Sharing. LC 85-73458. 90p. 1986. pap. 36.95 (*0-89707-210-3*, 511-0201-01) Amer Bar Assn.

Compensation Report on Management Employees in Hospital & Nursing Home Management Companies. John Zabka R., Associates Inc. Staff. 50p. 1989. 250.00 (*0-939326-58-2*) Hosp Compensation.

Compensation Report on Management Employees in Hospital & Nursing Home Management Companies, 1993. Date not set. 250.00 (*0-939326-74-4*) Hosp Compensation.

Compensation Surveys. Incl. Sales Compensation in the Printing Industries. 155.00 (*0-318-02608-2*); write for info. (*0-318-58051-9*) Print Indus Am.

Compensation Systems for Injury & Disease: The Policy Options. Terence G. Ison. 240p. pap. text ed. 66.00 (*0-409-90719-7*) Butterworth Legal Pubs.

Compensation Tax Guide. Lassila & Kilpatrick. 480p. 1990. pap. 25.00 (*0-685-66965-3*, 5069) Commerce.

Compensation Tax Guide. 2nd ed. Dennis R. Lasilla & Bob G. Kilpatrick. 504p. Date not set. pap. 39.50 (*0-8080-0008-X*) Commerce.

Compensation Theory & Practice. 2nd ed. Marc J. Wallace, Jr. & Charles H. Fay. 330p. (C). 1988. pap. 27.95 (*0-534-87198-4*) Intl Thomson.

Compensation 93: An Annual Report on Local Government Executive Salaries & Fringe Benefits. Ed. by Evelina Moulder. 1993. per. 180.00 (*0-87326-982-9*) Intl City-Cnty Mgt.

***Compensation 95: An Annual Report on Local Government Executive Salaries & Fringe Benefits.** Ed. by Evelina Moulder. (Illus.). 404p. (Orig.). 1995. pap. text ed. 180.00 (*0-87326-098-8*, 41000) Intl City-Cnty Mgt.

Compensatory Adaptations, Reflex Activity & the Brain. E. A. Asratian. 1965. 90.00 (*0-08-010591-2*, Pub. by Pergamon Repr UK) Franklin.

Compensatory Education for Children, Ages 2 to 8, Recent Studies of Educational Intervention: Proceedings. Ed. by Julian C. Stanley. LC 72-12355. (Hyman Blumberg Symposium Ser.). 222p. 1973. 27.50 (*0-8018-1457-X*) Johns Hopkins.

Compensatory Education in the Preschool: A Canadian Approach. Mary Wright. LC 83-12744. 397p. 1983. pap. 15.95 (*0-931114-20-9*) High-Scope.

Compensatory Justice. Ed. by John W. Chapman. (Nomos Ser.: Vol. 33). 352p. 1991. text ed. 45.00 (*0-8147-1453-6*) NYU Pr.

Compere General Soleil. Jacques S. Alexis. (Imaginaire Ser.). 350p. (FRE.). 1985. pap. 15.95 (*2-07-028730-0*) Schoenhof.

Compete: A Dynamic Marketing Simulation. 3rd ed. Anthony J. Faria et al. (C). 1984. text ed. 30.95 (*0-256-03060-X*) Irwin.

Competence, Admissions, & Articulation: Returning to the Basics in Higher Education. Jean L. Preer. Ed. by Jonathan D. Fife. LC 84-160913. (ASHE-ERIC Higher Education Report Ser.: No. 6, 1983). 115p. (Orig.). 1983. pap. 7.50 (*0-913317-05-5*) GWU Schl E&HD.

***Competence & Accountability in Education.** Ed. by Peter McKenzie et al. 165p. 1995. text ed. 42.95 (*1-85742-279-1*, Pub. by Arena UK) Ashgate Pub Co.

Competence & Power in Managerial Decision-Making: A Study of Senior Levels of Organization in Eight Countries. Frank A. Heller et al. LC 80-49978. (Illus.). 256p. reprint ed. pap. 73.00 (*0-685-24172-6*, 2033050) Bks Demand.

***Competence & Responsibility: Proceedings of the Third European Conference of the European Council for High Ability, No. 2.** Ed. by Kurt A. Heller & Ernst A. Hany. (Illus.). 436p. 1994. pap. 69.00 (*0-88937-126-1*) Hogrefe & Huber Pubs.

Competence & Responsibility, Vol. 1: Abstracts of the Third European Conference of the European Council for Higher Ability, Held in Munich, Germany, October 11-14, 1992. Ed. by Ernst A. Hany & Kurt A. Heller. LC 92-36870. (Illus.). 212p. 1992. pap. text ed. 33.00 (*0-88937-111-3*) Hogrefe & Huber Pubs.

Competence at Work: Models for Superior Performance. Lyle Spencer & Signe Spencer. LC 92-31255. 384p. 1993. text ed. 64.95 (*0-471-54809-X*) Wiley.

An Asterisk (*) at the beginning of an entry indicates that the title is appearing in BIP for the first time.

An Asterisk (*) at the beginning of an entry indicates that the title is appearing in BIP for the first time.

C

Competing Video Media: A Market-by-Market Guide, 1993. suppl. ed. Warren Publishing, Inc. Staff. Ed. by Michael Taliaferro. (Television & Cable Factbook Ser.: No. 61). (Illus.). 1993. 95.00 (0-911486-72-0) Warren Pub Inc.

Competing Visions: The Political Conflict over America's Economic Future. Richard B. McKenzie. LC 85-11305. 216p. 1985. 5.00 (0-932790-51-8); pap. 3.00 (0-932790-52-6) Cato Inst.

Competing Visions, Complex Realities: Social Aspects of the Information Society. Ed. by Jorge R. Schement et al. LC 87-14318. (Communication & Information Science Ser.). 176p. 1987. text ed. 35.00 (0-89391-402-9) Ablex Pub.

Competing Visions of Paradise: The Californian Experience of 19th-Century American Sectarianism. John Simmons & Brian Wilson. Ed. by Philip Hammond & Ninian Smart. (Religious Contours of California: Window to the World's Religions: Vol. III). 128p. (Orig.). 1993. pap. 9.95 (1-56474-064-1) Fithian Pr.

Competing with Flexible Lateral Organizations. 2nd ed. Jay R. Galbraith. (Organization Development Ser.). (Illus.). 164p. (C). 1994. pap. text ed. 26.95 (0-201-50836-2) Addison-Wesley.

Competing with Integrity in International Business. Richard T. De George. LC 92-39089. 1993. pap. 17.95 (0-19-508226-5) OUP.

***Competing with the Retail Giants: How to Survive in the New Retail Landscape.** Kenneth E. Stone. (Wiley Small Business Editions Ser.). 1995. text ed. 34.95 (0-471-05440-2); pap. text ed. 17.95 (0-471-05442-9) Wiley.

Competing with the Sylph: The Quest for the Perfect Dance Body. L. M. Vincent. LC 88-84124. 180p. 1989. 19.95 (0-916622-82-7) Princeton Bk Co.

***Competition.** B. B. Calhoun, pseud. LC 95-11468. (Dinosaur Detective Ser.: Vol. 7). (Illus.). (J). 1995. text ed. write for info. (0-7167-6604-3, Sci Am Yng Rdrs) W H Freeman.

***Competition.** B. B. Calhoun, pseud. LC 95-11468. (Dinosaur Detective Ser.: Vol. 7). (Illus.). (J). 1995. pap. text ed. write for info. (0-7167-6605-1, Sci Am Yng Rdrs) W H Freeman.

Competition. Melissa Lowell. (Silver Blades Ser.: No. 3). (J). (gr. 4-7). 1994. pap. 3.50 (0-553-48136-3, Skylark) Bantam.

Competition: A Feminist Taboo? Ed. by Helen E. Longino & Valerie Miner. LC 87-8515. 208p. 1987. text ed. 35.00 (0-935312-75-7); pap. 12.95 (0-935312-74-9) Feminist Pr.

Competition: An Inhuman Activity. Perry Saidman. 1994. pap. 2.00 (0-913937-88-6) Rational Isl.

Competition: Dealing with Japan. Thomas Pepper et al. LC 85-6304. 336p. 1985. text ed. 49.95 (0-275-91754-1, C1754, Praeger Pubs) Greenwood.

Competition Across the Atlantic: The States Face Europe '92. Brandon Roberts. Ed. by Larry Hurley. (Illus.). 48p. 1991. pap. text ed. 15.00 (1-55516-805-1, 3909) Natl Conf State Legis.

Competition Act, the Competition Tribunal Act, Rules & Regulations: An Office Consolidation. 136p. 1991. pap. 19.00 (0-409-89952-6) Butterworth Legal Pubs.

Competition Acts of 1984. 130p. 1985. pap. 25.00 (0-89707-187-5, 539-0047-01) Amer Bar Assn.

***Competition among Institutions.** Ed. by Luder Gerken. LC 94-42269. 1995. write for info. (0-312-12581-X) St Martin.

Competition among Japan, the United States, & Europe over High Definition Television. Ellis S. Krauss. (Pew Case Studies in International Affairs). 50p. (C). 1994. pap. text ed. 2.50 (1-56927-151-8) Geo U Inst Dplmcy.

Competition among States & Local Governments: Efficiency & Equity in American Federalism. Ed. by Daphne A. Kenyon & John Kincaid. LC 91-12344. (Illus.). 302p. (Orig.). 1991. lib. bdg. 61.00 (0-87766-516-8); pap. text ed. 26.50 (0-87766-517-6) Urban Inst.

Competition among the Few: Oligopoly & Similar Market Structures. rev. ed. William J. Fellner. LC 64-17622. (Reprints of Economic Classics Ser.). 1965. reprint ed. 37.50 (0-678-00042-5) Kelley.

Competition & Choice: Telecommunications Policy for the 1990's. HMSO Staff. (Command Paper Ser.: No. 1461). 70p. 1991. pap. 25.00 (0-10-114612-4, HM2614) UNIPUB.

Competition & Choice in the Publishing Industry. Walter Allan & Peter Curwen. 78p. (C). 1991. text ed. write for info. (0-318-69926-5, Pub. by Inst Economic Affairs UK) St Mut.

Competition & Co-Operation in World Banking. Ed. by Institute of Bankers Staff. 1985. 95.00 (0-85297-140-0, Pub. by Inst Bankers UK) St Mut.

Competition & Coercion: Blacks in the American Economy, 1865-1914. Robert Higgs. LC 76-9178. (Hoover Institution Publications: P163). 218p. reprint ed. pap. 62.20 (0-317-26402-8, 2024459) Bks Demand.

***Competition & Collaboration: Parsi Merchants & the English East India Company in the 18th Century India.** David L. White. (C). 1995. 23.00x (81-215-0663-8, Pub. by Munshiram Manoharial II) S Asia.

Competition & Collective Bargaining in the Needle Trades, 1910-1967. Jesse T. Carpenter. LC 79-630987. (Cornell Studies in Industrial & Labor Relations: No. 17). 936p. 1972. 17.50 (0-87546-035-6) ILR Pr.

Competition & Compassion: Conflicting Roles for Public Hospitals. Ed. by Stuart H. Altman et al. LC 88-32066. 220p. 1989. text ed. 36.00 (0-910701-37-7, 0877) Health Admin Pr.

Competition & Competition Policy: A Comparative Analysis. Ed. by Saul Estrin & Martin Cave. LC 93-12901. 143p. 1993. 49.00 (1-85567-125-5, Pub. by Pinter Pubs UK) St Martin.

Competition & Concentration: The Economics of the Carbonated Soft Drink Industry. David P. Kaplan & Richard S. Higgins. 240p. 1990. text ed. 49.95 (0-669-27139-X) Free Pr.

Competition & Control at Work: A New Industrial Sociology. Stephen Hill. (Organization Studies). 288p. 1982. pap. 12.95 (0-262-58053-5) MIT Pr.

Competition & Cooperation: The Emergence of a National Trade Association. Louis Galambos. LC 66-22999. 344p. reprint ed. pap. 98.10 (0-317-41662-6, 2025847) Bks Demand.

***Competition & Cooperation in Japanese Labour Markets.** Carl Mosk. LC 95-4170. (Studies in the Modern Japanese Economy). 1995. write for info. (0-312-12683-2) St Martin.

Competition & Currency: Essays on Free Banking & Money. Lawrence H. White. (Cato Institute Book Ser.). 260p. 1992. pap. text ed. 20.00 (0-8147-9247-2) NYU Pr.

Competition & Diversification in the United States Petroleum Industry. Arabinda Ghosh. LC 84-24932. (Illus.). xiv, 124p. 1985. text ed. 45.00 (0-89930-064-2, GHC/, Quorum Bks) Greenwood.

Competition & Economic Development. OECD Staff. 268p. (Orig.). 1991. pap. 34.00 (92-64-03347-5) OECD.

Competition & Entrepreneurship. Israel M. Kirzner. x, 246p. 1978. pap. text ed. 14.95 (0-226-43776-0, P787) U Ch Pr.

Competition & Innovation in Postal Services. Ed. by Michael A. Crew. (C). 1991. lib. bdg. 65.50 (0-7923-9147-0) Kluwer Ac.

Competition & Monopoly in American Industry. Clair Wilcox. LC 73-158856. reprint ed. 35.00 (0-404-06944-4) AMS Pr.

***Competition & Monopoly in Medical Care.** H. E. Frech, 3rd. 240p. 1995. 37.95 (0-8447-3884-0) Am Enterprise.

***Competition & Planning in the NHS: The Danger of Unplanned Markets.** Paton. 174p. 1992. pap. 57.50 (1-56593-058-4, 0364) Singular Publishing.

Competition & Regulation: The Development of Oligopoly in the Meat Packing Industry, Vol. 2. Mary Yeager. Ed. by Glenn Porter. LC 76-52011. (Industrial Development & the Social Fabric Ser.). 250p. 1981. 73.25 (0-89232-058-3) Jai Pr.

Competition & Regulation in Financial Markets. Albert Verheirstraeten. 1981. text ed. 39.95 (0-312-15501-8) St Martin.

Competition & Service: The Impact of the Local Government Act 1988. Kieron Walsh & Howard Davis. 174p. 1993. pap. 25.00 (0-11-752808-0, HM28080, Pub. by HMSO UK) UNIPUB.

Competition & Service (Utilities) Act 1992: Chapter 43. HMSO Staff. 52p. 1992. pap. 17.00 (0-10-544392-1, HM43921, Pub. by HMSO UK) UNIPUB.

Competition & the Law. Alex Hunter. LC 66-1244. 328p. 1966. 37.50 (0-678-06020-7) Kelley.

Competition & the Role of Technology: An Assessment of the Pharmaceutical Industry. (Research Report Ser.). 144p. 1988. 35.00 (0-87762-606-5) Technomic.

***Competition & Trade.** Ed. by Roger Kosch. (Spicers European Union Policy Briefings Ser.). 228p. 1994. 150.00 (1-56159-081-9, Stockton Pr) Groves Dictionaries.

Competition As a Dynamic Process. John M. Clark. LC 79-26651. xvii, 501p. 1980. reprint ed. text ed. 48.50 (0-313-22300-9, CLCD, Greenwood Pr) Greenwood.

Competition, Automation Create Significant Demand for SCADA Systems: Traditional Hosts Lose Ground to More Flexible, PC-Based Systems. 205p. 1992. 1,695.00 (1-56753-011-7) Frost & Sullivan.

Competition Car Controls. Ian Bamsey. 240p. 1990. 39.95 (0-946132-61-5, Pub. by J H Haynes & Co UK) Motorbooks Intl.

Competition Car Suspension. Allan Staniforth. (Illus.). 39.95 (0-85429-645-X, F645, Pub. by G T Foulis Ltd) Haynes Pubns.

***Competition Car Suspension.** Allan Staniforth. (Illus.). 240p. 1994. 39.95 (0-85429-956-4) Motorbooks Intl.

***Competition, Commitment, & Welfare.** Kotaro Suzumura. (Illus.). 350p. 1995. text ed. 55.00 (0-19-828914-6) OUP.

Competition-Constructive & Destructive. John M. Culbertson. 44p. (Orig.). 1985. pap. 2.95 (0-918357-05-5); pap. text ed. 2.20 (0-918357-06-3) Twen Fir Pr.

Competition, Cooperation, Efficiency & Social Organization. Antonio Jorge. LC 76-20272. 89p. 1978. 19.50 (0-8386-2026-4) Fairleigh Dickinson.

Competition Driving on a Shoestring. Jinny Johnson. 1990. pap. 40.00 (0-85131-512-7, Pub. by J A Allen & Co UK) St Mut.

***Competition, Fair or Foul? Organising EC Competition Law Compliance.** Stanbrook & Hooper. LC 94-24349. 1994. pap. text ed. 135.00 (0-471-95416-0) Wiley.

Competition for California Water: Alternative Resolutions. Ed. by Ernest A. Engelbert. 224p. 1982. 40.00 (0-520-04822-9); pap. 12.00 (0-520-04823-7) U CA Pr.

Competition for Capital: On the Role of Governments in an Integral World Economy. Stefan Sinn. 206p. text ed. 37.50 (0-472-08253-1) U of Mich Pr.

***Competition for Dollars, Scholars & Influence in the Public Policy Research Industry.** James G. McGann. 216p. (C). 1995. lib. bdg. 48.00 (0-8191-9750-5); pap. text ed. 26.50 (0-8191-9751-3) U Pr of Amer.

Competition for Land in the American South: Agriculture, Human Settlement, & the Environment. Robert G. Healy. LC 85-25459. (Illus.). 334p. (Orig.). (C). 1985. pap. 17.50 (0-89164-094-0) World Wildlife Fund.

Competition for Markets in International Telecommunications. Ronald S. Eward. LC 84-45199. 198p. reprint ed. pap. 56.50 (0-7837-5844-8, 2045563) Bks Demand.

Competition for Space & the Structure of Ecological Communities. P. Yoozis. (Lecture Notes in Biomathematics Ser.: Vol. 25). 1978. pap. 20.00 (0-387-08936-5) Spr-Verlag.

Competition for U. S. Banking Markets. Margaret L. Mullally. 320p. 1989. 1,700.00 (0-945235-18-6) Lead Edge Reports.

Competition for Wetlands in the Midwest: An Economic Analysis. Jon H. Goldstein. LC 74-149240. 119p. reprint ed. pap. 34.00 (0-317-26460-5, 2023796) Bks Demand.

Competition Game. Arthur A. Thompson, Jr. (C). 1989. pap. text ed. 42.00 (0-13-155516-2) P-H.

Competition Game: Players Manual. 2nd ed. Arthur A. Thompson, Jr. & Gregory Steppenbach. 100p. (C). 1993. Version 3.5. 3.5 hd 29.95 (0-13-146101-X); Version 5.25. 5.25 hd 29.95 (0-13-146127-3) P-H.

Competition in a Dual Economy. Joseph Bowring. LC 85-43271. 180p. 1986. text ed. 37.50 (0-691-04234-9) Princeton U Pr.

Competition in Defense Procurement. Donald L. Pilling. 80p. 1989. pap. 7.95 (0-8157-7081-2) Brookings.

Competition in Education. John M. Rich & Joseph L. DeVitis. 214p. (C). 1992. text ed. 41.95x (0-398-05819-9) C C Thomas.

***Competition in Education.** John M. Rich & Joseph L. DeVitis. 214p. 1992. pap. 24.95 (0-398-06348-6) C C Thomas.

Competition in Electricity: New Markets and New Structures. Ed. by James L. Plummer. 1990. 65.00 (0-910325-26-X) Public Util.

Competition in Europe: Essays in Honor of Henk W. de Jong. Ed. by Peter De Wolf. 308p. (C). 1990. lib. bdg. 102.50 (0-7923-1050-0) Kluwer Ac.

Competition in Global Industries. Ed. by Michael E. Porter. 1986. text ed. 35.00 (0-07-103262-2) McGraw.

Competition in Government-Financed Services. John C. Hilke. LC 91-36409. 224p. 1992. text ed. 47.95 (0-89930-750-7, HIK, Quorum Bks) Greenwood.

Competition in International Business. Oscar Schachter & Robert Hellawell. LC 81-3856. 448p. 1981. text ed. 64.50 (0-231-05220-0) Col U Pr.

Competition in Religious Life. Jay Newman. (Editions SR Ser.: Vol. 11). 264p. (C). 1989. pap. 28.50 (0-88920-989-8, Pub. by Wilfrid Laurier CN) Humanities.

Competition in the American Tobacco Industry, 1911-1932. Reavis Cox. LC 68-58562. (Columbia University. Studies in the Social Sciences: No. 381). reprint ed. 26.50 (0-404-51381-6) AMS Pr.

Competition in the Cellular Telephone Service Industry. 57p. (Orig.). (C). 1992. pap. text ed. 75.00 (1-56806-031-9) Diane Pub.

Competition in the Health Care Sector: Ten Years Later. Ed. by Warren Greenberg. LC 88-21920. 153p. 1988. lib. bdg. 26.95 (0-8223-0893-2) Duke.

Competition in the History of Economic Thought. Kenneth G. Kennis. Ed. by Stuart Bruchey. LC 77-81827. (Dissertations in European Economic History Ser.). 1978. lib. bdg. 40.95 (0-405-10779-X) Ayer.

Competition in the Investment Banking Industry. Samuel L. Hayes, III et al. (Illus.). 192p. 1983. 33.00 (0-674-15415-0) HUP.

Competition in the Market for an Exhaustible Resource. Ed. by Y. Hossein Farzin. LC 85-23765. (Contemporary Studies in Energy Analysis & Policy: Vol. 6). 209p. 1986. 73.25 (0-89232-604-2) Jai Pr.

Competition in the Marketplace: Health Care in the 1980s, Vol. 1. Ed. by James Gay & Barbara S. Jacobs. (Monographs in Health Care). 128p. 1981. text ed. 14.95 (0-88331-122-4) Luce.

Competition in the Midwestern Coal Industry. Reed Moyer. (Economic Studies: No. 122). (Illus.). 238p. 1964. 16.50 (0-674-15400-2) HUP.

Competition in the Natural Gas Pipeline Industry: An Economic Policy Analysis. Edward C. Gallock. LC 92-14536. 304p. 1993. text ed. 55.00 (0-275-94346-1, C4346, Praeger Pubs) Greenwood.

Competition in the Open Economy: A Model Applied to Canada. Richard E. Caves et al. LC 79-23908. (Economic Studies: No. 150). 452p. 1980. 30.00 (0-674-15425-8) HUP.

Competition in the Pharmaceutical Industry: The Declining Profitability of Drug Innovation. Meir Statman. LC 83-3880. (AEI Studies: No. 374). 95p. reprint ed. pap. 27.10 (0-8357-4451-5, 2037288) Bks Demand.

Competition in the Provision of Local Authority Services - The Commercial Role. Institute of Purchasing & Supply Staff. (C). 1988. 45.00 (0-685-29248-7, Inst Pur & Supply) St Mut.

Competition in the Provision of Local Authority Services-the Commercial Role. Institute of Purchasing & Supply Staff. (C). 1988. 40.00 (0-685-36121-7, Inst Pur & Supply) St Mut.

Competition in the Provisions of Local Authority Services - the Commercial Role. IPS Editors. (C). 1987. 40.00 (0-685-39878-1, Inst Pur & Supply) St Mut.

Competition in the Swiss Plastics Manufacturing Industry: A Group Analysis Based on Micro-Micro Consideration. F. Von Gunten. (Contributions to Management Science Ser.). (Illus.). xii, 408p. 1991. pap. 77.00 (0-387-91403-X) Spr-Verlag.

Competition in Theory & Practice. Terry Burke et al. 270p. 1988. lib. bdg. 69.95 (0-7099-5005-5, Pub. by Croom Helm UK) Routledge Chapman & Hall.

Competition in Transportation: Policy & Legislation in Review. National Transportation Act Review Commission Staff. 474p. (Orig.). Date not set. pap. 55.25 (0-660-14959-1, Pub. by Canada Commun Grp CN) Accents Pubns.

Competition, Instability, & Nonlinear Cycles. Ed. by Willi Semmler. (Lecture Notes in Economics & Mathematical Systems Ser.: Vol. 275). xii, 340p. 1986. pap. 51.80 (0-387-16794-3) Spr-Verlag.

Competition Law. 3rd ed. Whish. 1993. pap. 60.00 (0-406-01155-9, UK) Butterworth Legal Pubs.

Competition Law: A Legal Handbook for Business. Mungovan. 104p. 1990. pap. 25.00 (0-409-89648-9) Butterworth Legal Pubs.

Competition Law & Policy: Cases, Materials & Commentary. Tim Frazer & Michael Waterson. 512p. 1994. pap. 45.00 (0-13-302357-5) P-H.

Competition Law & Policy: The Aviation & Telecommunications Industries. Stephen Corones. 248p. 1992. 83.00 (1-86287-086-1, Pub. by Federation Pr AU) W W Gaunt.

Competition Law & Policy in Australia. Steven G. Corones. xix, 324p. 1990. 75.00 (0-455-20990-1, Pub. by Law Bk Co); pap. 55.00 (0-455-20991-X, Pub. by Law Bk Co) W W Gaunt.

Competition Law & Policy in New Zealand. Rex Ahdar. lxi, 321p. 1991. pap. 70.00 (0-455-21014-4, Pub. by Law Bk Co) W W Gaunt.

***Competition Law in Ireland.** Vincent J. Power. 1995. boxed write for info. (1-85475-065-8, IE) Butterworth Legal Pubs.

***Competition Law in the European Communities (Situation As of 30 June 94) Rules Applicable to Undertakings, Vol. 1A.** European Commission Staff. 550p. 1994. pap. 35.00 (92-826-6759-6, CM-29-93-A01-EC, Pub. by Europ Com) UNIPUB.

Competition Law in the European Community: A Concise Guide for Business. Jack Stewart-Clark & David Jacobs. 152p. (Orig.). 1990. pap. text ed. 41.95 (0-8464-1345-0) Beekman Pubs.

Competition Law in Western Europe & the U. S. A., 17 vols., Set. Ed. by D. J. Gijlstra et al. ring bd. 858.00 (0-686-40940-X, 90P1462005) Kluwer Law Tax Pubs.

Competition Law of Britain & the Common Market. V. Korah. 1982. lib. bdg. 59.00 (0-686-37430-4) Kluwer Ac.

Competition Law of Canada. Julian D. Kalinowski. 1968. write for info. (0-8205-1836-0) Bender.

Competition Law of the EEC. Julian O. Von Kalinowski. 1979. write for info. (0-8205-1846-8) Bender.

Competition Law of the UK. Julian O. Von Kalinowski. 1974. write for info. (0-8205-1865-4) Bender.

Competition Ltd, the Marketing of Gasoline. Fred C. Allvine & James M. Patterson. LC 70-180491. 344p. reprint ed. pap. 98.10 (0-317-28578-5, 2055197) Bks Demand.

Competition Models in Population Biology. Paul Waltman. LC 83-50665. (CBMS-NSF Regional Conference Ser.: No. 45). v, 77p. 1983. pap. text ed. 17.75 (0-89871-188-6) Soc Indus-Appl Math.

Competition Monologues: Forty-Four Contemporary Speeches from the Best Professionally Produced American Plays. Ed. by Roger Ellis. 96p. (Orig.). (C). 1988. lib. bdg. 28.00 (0-8191-6849-1); pap. text ed. 13.50 (0-8191-6850-5) U Pr of Amer.

Competition Monologues II: Forty-Nine Contemporary Speeches for Young Actors from the Best Professionally Produced American Plays. Intro. by Roger Ellis. LC 89-5675. 130p. (Orig.). (C). 1989. lib. bdg. 28.00 (0-8191-7439-4) U Pr of Amer.

Competition, Monopoly, & Differential Profit Rates: On the Relevance of the Classical & Marxian Theories of Production for Modern Industrial & Corporate Pricing. Willi Semmler. LC 84-231168. 240p. 1984. text ed. 53.50 (0-231-05616-8, King's Crown Paperbacks); pap. text ed. 22.50 (0-231-05617-6, King's Crown Paperbacks) Col U Pr.

Competition Obsession: A Philosophy of Non-Competitive Living. Steven H. Homel. 192p. 1981. 20.00 (0-9606868-0-0) ACS Pub.

Competition or Credit Controls? David Llewellyn & Mark Holmes. 103p. (C). 1991. text ed. 70.00 (0-255-36300-1, Pub. by Inst Economic Affairs UK) St Mut.

Competition Policies for a Highly Integrated World Economy. F. M. Scherer. LC 94-11819. (Integrating National Economies: Promise & Pitfalls Ser.). 160p. (C). 1994. 28.95x (0-8157-7798-1); pap. 10.95x (0-8157-7797-3) Brookings.

Competition Policies for Industrializing Countries. Claudio Frischtak et al. (Policy & Research Ser.: No. 7). 38p. 1989. 6.95 (0-685-74578-3, 11362) World Bank.

***Competition Policy: A Game-Theoretic Perspective.** Louis Phlips. (Illus.). 296p. (C). 1995. write for info. (0-521-49521-0); pap. write for info. (0-521-49871-6) Cambridge U Pr.

Competition Policy: European & International Trends & Practices. A. E. Walsh & John Paxton. LC 74-33134. 200p. (C). 1975. text ed. 29.95 (0-312-15540-9) St Martin.

Competition Policy & a Changing Broadcast Industry. Steven Brenner. 300p. (Orig.). 1993. pap. text ed. 50.00 (92-64-13987-7, 24-93-04-1) OECD.

Competition Policy & Intellectual Property Rights. OECD Staff. 122p. (Orig.). 1989. pap. 19.00 (92-64-13242-2) OECD.

Competition Policy & Merger Control in the Single European Market. Ed. by Leon Birttan. 68p. (C). 1991. 60.00 (0-949009-92-X, Pub. by Grotius Pubns UK) St Mut.

Competition Policy & the Deregulation of Road Transport. OECD Staff. 78p. (Orig.). 1990. pap. 16.00 (92-64-13428-X) OECD.

Competition Policy & Vertical Restraints: Franchising Agreements. OECD Staff. 241p. (Orig.). 1994. pap. 42.00 (92-64-14053-0) OECD.

An Asterisk (*) at the beginning of an entry indicates that the title is appearing in BIP for the first time.

An Asterisk (*) at the beginning of an entry indicates that the title is appearing in BIP for the first time.

1453

C

Competitiveness, Convergence & International Specialization. David Dollar & Edward N. Wolff. (Illus.). 232p. 1993. 37.50x (*0-262-04135-9*) MIT Pr.

Competitiveness in Banking. Ed. by N. Blattner et al. (Studies in Contemporary Economics). (Illus.). 315p. 1992. pap. 59.00 (*0-387-91418-8*) Spr-Verlag.

Competitiveness in International Food Market. Maury E. Bredahl. 360p. (C). 1993. pap. text ed. 47.50 (*0-8133-1736-3*) Westview.

Competitiveness Issues: The Business Environment in the U. S., Japan & Germany. (Illus.). 136p. (Orig.). (C). 1993. pap. text ed. 60.00 (*0-7881-0105-6*) Diane Pub.

Competitiveness of European Industry. Ed. by Arthur Francis & Matthew Tharakan. 224p. 1989. 67.50 (*0-415-03123-0*, A3699) Routledge.

***Competitiveness of Financial Institutions & Centers in Europe.** Ed. by Donald E. Fair. LC 94-23317. (Financial & Monetary Policy Sudies: 28). 1994. lib. bdg. 155.00 (*0-7923-3131-1*) Kluwer Ac.

Competitiveness of Industry in Ireland: An International Perspective. D. M. Hitchins & J. E. Birnie. 256p. 1994. 59.95 (*1-85628-643-6*, Pub. by Avebury Pub UK) Ashgate Pub Co.

***Competitiveness of Industry in the Czech Republic & Hungary.** D. M. Hitchens et al. 388p. 1995. 63.95 (*1-85972-042-0*, Pub. by Avebury Pub UK) Ashgate Pub Co.

Competitiveness of Small Firms & the Economies of Scale. Clifford F. Pratten. (Department of Applied Economics, Occasional Papers). (Illus.). 300p. (C). 1991. 54.95 (*0-521-40035-X*) Cambridge U Pr.

Competitiveness of the U. S. Chemical Industry in International Markets. Ed. by Jaromir J. Ulbrecht. LC 90-214. (AIChE Symposium Ser.: Vol. 86, No. 274). 88p. 1990. pap. 40.00 (*0-8169-0486-3*) Am Inst Chem Eng.

Competitiveness of the U. S. Minerals & Metals Industries. National Research Council, Committee on Competitiveness of the U. S. Minerals & Metals Industry Staff. 160p. 1990. text ed. 22.95 (*0-309-04245-3*) Natl Acad Pr.

Competitiveness Strategy for America: Second Report to the President & Congress. (Illus.). 61p. (Orig.). (C). 1993. pap. text ed. 45.00 (*1-56806-985-5*) Diane Pub.

Competitiveness Through Strategic Success. Peter Antoniou. 160p. 1994. text ed. 30.00 (*0-7863-0311-5*) Irwin Prof Pubng.

C

Competitiveness Through Technology: What Business Needs from Government. Ed. by Jerry Dermer. LC 85-45379. (Illus.). 240p. 1986. text ed. 40.00 (*0-669-11604-1*) Free Pr.

Competitiveness Through Total Cycle Time: An Overview for CEOs. P. R. Thomas & Kenneth R. Martin. 1990. text ed. 29.95 (*0-07-064273-7*) McGraw.

Competitor Intelligence: Cassette Version. Leonard M. Flud. (Sound Business Cassette Bks.). 1987. text ed. 15.95 (*0-471-62910-3*) Wiley.

Competitor Intelligence: How to Get It, How to Use It. Leonard M. Fuld. LC 84-19539. 479p. 1985. text ed. 49.95 (*0-471-80967-5*) Wiley.

Competitor Intelligence Manual & Guide: Gathering, Analyzing, & Using Business Intelligence. Kirk W. Tyson. 400p. 1989. 79.95 (*0-13-155292-9*) P-H.

Competitor Intelligence Seminar Binder. Kirk W. Tyson. 450p. 1986. 400.00 (*0-941101-01-0*) Lead Edge IL.

Competitors & Comrades: Culture, Economics & Personality. Robert D. Smither. LC 84-15155. 188p. 1984. text ed. 45.00 (*0-275-91272-8*, C1272, Praeger Pubs) Greenwood.

***Competitors in Alliance: Industry Associations, Global Rivalries & Business.** Andrew A. Procassini. LC 94-39659. 360p. 1995. text ed. 59.95 (*0-89930-962-3*, Quorum Bks) Greenwood.

CompEuro 92: European Computer Conference, 6th. LC 91-78034. 736p. 1992. 96.00 (*0-8186-2760-3*, 2760) IEEE Comp Soc.

CompEuro 93: Computers in Design, Manufacturing & Production. LC 93-77041. 560p. 1993. pap. text ed. 90.00 (*0-8186-4030-8*, 4030) IEEE Comp Soc.

Compilation & Index of Trade Names, Specifications, & Producers of Stainless Alloys & Superalloys. American Society for Testing & Materials Staff. LC 72-91409. (ASTM Data Ser.: DS45A). 57p. reprint ed. pap. 25.00 (*0-317-08287-6*, 2019652) Bks Demand.

Compilation & Review. AICPA Staff. (Technical Information for Practitioners Ser.: No. 3). 104p. (Orig.). 1990. pap. text ed. 26.50 (*0-87051-062-2*) Am Inst CPA.

Compilation & Review Manual. Larry L. Perry. 240p. 1987. ring bd. 95.00 (*0-13-162934-4*, Busn) P-H.

Compilation & Review Manual. O. Ray Whittington & Alan J. Winters. (AICPA Integrated Practice System Ser.). 238p. reprint ed. Vol. 1, 238p. pap. 67.90 (*0-7837-4867-1*, 2044398); reprint ed. Vol. 2, 333p. pap. 95.00 (*0-7837-4868-X*, 2044398) Bks Demand.

Compilation & Review Manual Documentation. Larry L. Perry. 144p. 1987. text ed. 40.00 (*0-13-162942-5*) P-H.

Compilation, Critical Evaluation & Distribution of Stellar Data. Ed. by Carlos Jaschek & George A. Wilkins. (Astrophysics & Space Science Library: No.64). 1977. lib. bdg. 99.00 (*90-277-0792-8*) Kluwer Ac.

***Compilation of American & Canadian Passenger - Emigration Registers.** Diane S. Ptak. 25p. 1993. pap. 15.00 (*1-886905-02-9*) D S Ptak.

***Compilation of American & Canadian Passenger/ Emigration Registers: Supplement.** Diane S. Ptak. (Illus.). 15p. (Orig.). 1995. pap. 10.00 (*1-886905-09-6*) D S Ptak.

Compilation of ASTM Standard Definitions. 7th ed. 560p. pap. text ed. 83.00 (*0-8031-1238-6*, 03-001090-42) ASTM.

***Compilation of ASTM Standard Definitions.** 8th ed. Ed. by ASTM, Committee on Terminology Staff. LC 94-36690. (Def Ser.: Vol. 94). 596p. 1994. 99.00 (*0-8031-1804-X*, 03-001094-42) ASTM.

Compilation of ASTM Standards & Literature References for Composite Materials. 2nd ed. 512p. 1990. pap. 69.00 (*0-8031-1230-0*, 03-430090-33); ring bd. 74.00 (*0-8031-1231-9*, 03-430190-33) ASTM.

Compilation of Chemical Shift Anisotropies. T. Michael Duncan. 180p. 1990. text ed. 39.95 (*0-917903-01-3*); pap. text ed. 19.95 (*0-685-40150-2*) Farragut Pr.

Compilation of Chinese Dictionaries. J. Mathias & Sandra Hixson. (CHI.). 1975. 8.95 (*0-88710-020-1*) Yale Far Eastern Pubns.

Compilation of EPA's Sampling & Analysis Methods. Keith. 1991. 140.95 (*0-87371-433-4*, TD692) Lewis Pubs.

Compilation of Food & Drug Laws (1993) Ed. by Food & Drug Law Institute Staff. 1095p. 1993. pap. 50.00 (*1-885259-05-0*) Food & Drug Law.

Compilation of ISDN Applications. rev. ed. IGI Staff. 1993. 95.00 (*0-918435-99-4*) Info Gatekeepers.

Compilation of Narratives of Explorations in Alaska (1869-1899) Complete with All Folded Maps, Figures & Plates, & indexes to Each Report & a Separate Index of Indian Tribes; with a New Introduction to the AMS Edition by Marvin W. Falk. U. S. Congress. Senate Committee on Military Affairs. LC 89-18203. (Senate Report Ser. (56th Congress, First Session): No. 1023). reprint ed. 765.00 (*0-404-20323-X*) AMS Pr.

Compilation of North American Maize Breeding Germplasm. J. T. Gerdes. Ed. by W. F. Tracy et al. LC 93-26663. 1993. pap. 18.00 (*0-89118-536-4*) Am Soc Agron.

Compilation of Odor & Taste Threshold Values Data. Ed. by William H. Stahl. LC 73-75377. (ASTM Data Ser.: DS 48). (Illus.). 261p. reprint ed. pap. 74.40 (*0-7837-4795-0*, 2044836) Bks Demand.

Compilation of Odor & Taste Threshold Values Data-DS 48A: Compilations Parens. 508p. 1978. 55.00 (*0-8031-0306-9*, 05-048010-36) ASTM.

Compilation of Principles & Practices Board Statements, Nos. 1-13. HFMA P & P Board Staff. 99p. 1991. 15.00 (*0-930228-56-1*) Hlthcare Fin Mgmt.

Compilation of Scripture Passages on Music. Don Thiessen. LC 93-16044. 1993. pap. 4.95 (*0-940895-06-4*) Cornerstone IL.

Compilation of State & Federal Privacy Laws. 1989. write for info. (*0-318-67137-9*) Privacy Journal.

Compilation of State & Federal Privacy Laws. rev. ed. Ed. by Robert E. Smith & James S. Sulanowski. 112p. 1992. pap. text ed. write for info. (*0-930072-08-1*) Privacy Journal.

Compilation of State & Federal Privacy Laws. 4th ed. Robert E. Smith. LC 81-177618. 1978. pap. 14.50 (*0-930072-01-4*) Privacy Journal.

Compilation of State & Federal Privacy Laws, 1988. Robert E. Smith. 100p. 1988. 26.00 (*0-317-65242-7*) Privacy Journal.

Compilation of State & Federal Privacy Laws, 1981. 5th ed. Ed. by Robert E. Smith. 80p. (Orig.). 1981. pap. 19.00 (*0-930072-02-2*) Privacy Journal.

Compilation of State & Federal Privacy Laws, 1984-85. 6th ed. Robert E. Smith. 100p. 1984. 22.00 (*0-930072-04-9*); (*0-318-57616-3*) Privacy Journal.

Compilation of Statistical Data & Results of Survey of Clothing Retailers & Manufacturers Presented at CMA Seminar on September 9, 1986 on Marketing Men's Tailored Clothing. 40p. 1986. 50.00 (*0-318-21998-0*) Clothing Mfrs.

Compilation of Stress Relaxation Data for Engineering Alloys - DS 60: Compilations Parens. 589p. 1982. pap. 49.00 (*0-8031-0808-7*, 05-060000-30) ASTM.

Compilation of Texts: Association of the Overseas Countries & Territories, 1 January-31 December 1989, Vol. 13. 200p. 1991. pap. 10.00 (*92-824-0808-6*, BX-59-90-289-EN-C) UNIPUB.

Compilation of Texts: Association of the Overseas Countries & Territories, 1 January-31 December 1989, Vol. 14. 200p. 1992. pap. 13.00 (*92-824-0923-6*, BX-72-91-940-EN-C, Pub. by Europ Com) UNIPUB.

Compilation of Texts: Cooperation, January 1, 1989 - December 31, 1989. (Cooperation Ser.: Vol. 6). 145p. 1992. pap. 30.00 (*92-824-0842-6*, BX-59-90-209-EN-C, Pub. by Europ Com) UNIPUB.

Compilation of Texts Association EEC Cyprus, Malta, & Turkey. 268p. 1990. pap. 15.00 (*92-824-0651-2*, BX-56-89-013-EN-C) UNIPUB.

Compilation of Texts 5-1 Jan. - Dec. 1988: Cooperation EEC-Algeria, EEC-Egypt, EEC-Israel, EEC-Jordon, EEC-Lebanon, EEC-Morocco, EEC-Syria, EEC-Tunisia, EEC-Yugosl. 714p. 1990. pap. 30.00 (*92-824-0660-1*, BX-56-89-005-EN) UNIPUB.

Compilation of the Poor Laws of the State of Pennsylvania from the Year 1700 to 1788, Inclusive. Guardians of the Poor Staff. LC 76-137168. (Poverty U. S. A. Historical Record Ser.). 1975. reprint ed. 16.95 (*0-405-03106-8*) Ayer.

Compilation of Twenty-Fifth Annual Production - Management Seminars - May 10, 1991: New Directions in Plant Technology & Human Resources. 1991. 50.00 (*0-685-49340-7*) Clothing Mfrs.

Compilation of Twenty-Fourth Annual Production - Management Seminar Presentations - May 11, 1990: Changes Needed in Manufacturing Men's Clothing in the 90's. 1990. audio 75.00 (*0-317-03089-2*) Clothing Mfrs.

Compilation of Twenty-Sixth Annual Manufacturing-Management Seminar Presentations: "How U. S. Clothing Manufacturers Can Increase Market Share" & "Tailoring with Microfibers" 1992. 50.00 (*0-685-62430-7*) Clothing Mfrs.

Compilation of Works Listed in Granger's Index to Poetry 1904-1978. LC 80-65559. 232p. 1980. lib. bdg. 49.95 (*0-89609-201-1*) Roth Pub Inc.

Compilation on Sex. Alice A. Bailey. 1980. pap. 8.00 (*0-85330-136-0*) Lucis.

Compilation Publication of Registers of the Staffordshire, Parishes of Armitage, Blymill & Himley. (C). 1987. 50.00 (*0-317-89855-8*, Pub. by Birmingham Midland Soc UK) St Mut.

Compilations of Litanies & Vesper Hymns. John Aitken. 1954. 25.00 (*0-87556-004-0*) Saifer.

Compiled by see Advances in Powder Metallurgy & Particulate Materials - 1992

Compiled by A. P. Braga. Comp. by Antone P. Braga. LC 81-65344. (Illus.). 146p. 1993. pap. 14.95 (*0-939206-02-1*, Acorn MA) S Station Bks.

Compiler. Ed. by David Gilluly. (Illus.). 56p. (Orig.). (C). 1988. pap. text ed. 45.00 (*0-317-91086-8*) Forest Res Syst.

Compiler Compilers: Proceedings of the International Workshop CC '90 Schwerin, FRG, October 22-24, 1990. Ed. by D. Hammer. (Lecture Notes in Computer Science Ser.: Vol. 477). vi, 227p. 1991. pap. 29.00 (*0-387-53669-8*) Spr-Verlag.

Compiler Compilers & High Speed Compilation. Ed. by D. Hammer. (Lecture Notes in Computer Science Ser.: Vol. 371). vi, 242p. 1989. pap. 34.00 (*0-387-51364-7*, 3197) Spr-Verlag.

Compiler Construction. W. M. Waite & G. Goos. LC 83-14714. (Texts & Monographs in Computer Science). (Illus.). 446p. 1985. 49.00 (*0-387-90821-8*) Spr-Verlag.

Compiler Construction: A Recursive Descent Model. John Elder. LC 93-49801. (Prentice Hall International Series in Computer Science). 456p. 1994. pap. text ed. 44.00 (*0-13-291139-6*) P-H Gen Ref & Trav.

Compiler Construction: Fifth International Conference, CC '94, Edinburgh, U.K., April 7-9, 1994. Ed. by Peter A. Fritzson. LC 94-8474. (Lecture Notes in Computer Science Ser.: Vol. 786). 1994. 58.00 (*0-387-57877-3*) Spr-Verlag.

Compiler Construction: Fourth International Conference CC'92, Paderborn, FRG, October 5-7, 1992 - Proceedings. Ed. by U. Kastens & P. Pfahler. LC 92-30269. (Lecture Notes in Computer Science Ser.: Vol. 641). 1992. 52.00 (*0-387-55984-1*) Spr-Verlag.

Compiler Design in C. Allen I. Holub. 500p. 1990. text ed. 73.33 (*0-13-155045-4*) P-H.

Compiler Design Theory. Philip M. Lewis, 2nd et al. LC 75-9012. (Illus.). 672p. (C). 1976. text ed. write for info. (*0-201-14455-7*) Addison-Wesley.

Compiler Engineering Using Pascal. P. C. Capon & P. J. Jinks. (Computer Science Ser.). (Illus.). 224p. (C). 1988. pap. text ed. 35.00 (*0-333-47155-5*, Pub. by Macmill Press UK) Scholium Intl.

Compiler Generators. M. Tofte. (EATCS Monographs on Theoretical Computer Science: Vol. 19). 152p. 1990. 42.00 (*0-387-51471-6*, 3301) Spr-Verlag.

Compiler Specification & Verification. W. Polak. (Lecture Notes in Computer Science Ser.: Vol. 124). 269p. 1981. pap. 24.00 (*0-387-10886-6*) Spr-Verlag.

Compiler Writer's Toolbox. W. P. Cockshott. 320p. 1992. pap. text ed. 42.00 (*0-13-173790-2*) P-H.

Compiler Writing Made Easy. Charles G. Petersen. 340p. (C). 1988. pap. text ed. 25.00 (*0-9631838-9-3*) P&M Pub Co.

Compilers: Principles, Techniques, & Tools. Alfred V. Aho et al. LC 85-15647. 800p. (C). 1986. text ed. 56.95 (*0-201-10088-6*) Addison-Wesley.

Compiling Functional Languages. Antoni Diller. 289p. 1988. pap. text ed. 57.95 (*0-471-92027-4*) Wiley.

Compiling in Modula 2: A First Introduction to Classical Recursive Descent Compiling. Julian R. Ullmann. LC 93-33826. 500p. 1994. pap. text ed. 53.00 (*0-13-088741-2*) P-H.

Compiling Parallel Loops for High Performance Computers: Partitioning, Data Assignment, & Remapping. David E. Hudak & Santosh G. Abraham. LC 92-30509. (International Series in Engineering & Computer Science, VLSI, Computer Architecture, & Digital Screen Processing: Vol. SECS 200). (C). 1992. lib. bdg. 67.50 (*0-7923-9283-3*) Kluwer Ac.

Compiling Pascal S. Mike Rees & David Robson. (Illus.). 256p. (C). 1988. pap. text ed. 29.25 (*0-201-18487-7*) Addison-Wesley.

Compiling the Annotated Bibliography, a Guide. Michael J. Eula & Janet Madden. 32p. (C). 1993. 9.95 (*0-8403-8900-0*) Kendall-Hunt.

Compiling with Continuations. Andrew W. Appel. (Illus.). 288p. (C). 1991. 39.95 (*0-521-41695-7*) Cambridge U Pr.

Complaining & Commiserating: A Speech Act View of Solidarity in Spoken American English. Diana Boxer. LC 92-35429. (History & Language Ser.: Vol. 2). 223p. (C). 1994. text ed. 49.95 (*0-8204-2021-2*) P Lang Pubs.

Complaint & Answer. Muhammad Iqbal. 50p. (Orig.). 1987. pap. 4.95 (*1-56744-253-6*) Kazi Pubns.

Complaint Behavior: Beyond Obedience to Authority. Ed. by Max Rosenbaum. 254p. 1983. 35.95 (*0-89885-115-7*) Human Sci Pr.

Complaint Investigator. Jack Rudman. (Career Examination Ser.: C-1863). 1994. pap. 27.95 (*0-8373-1863-7*) Nat Learn.

Complaint of Peace. Desiderius Erasmus. Ed. by William J. Hirten. Tr. by Thomas Paynell. LC 46-5043. 180p. 1976. reprint ed. lib. bdg. 50.00 (*0-8201-1211-9*) Schol Facsimiles.

Complaints. Edmund Spenser. (BCL1-PR English Literature Ser.). 273p. 1992. reprint ed. lib. bdg. 79.00 (*0-7812-7224-6*) Rprt Serv.

Complaints. Edmund Spenser. Ed. by W. L. Renwick. LC 72-131837. 1970. reprint ed. 29.00 (*0-403-00724-0*) Scholarly.

Complaints Against God. Andrew M. Greeley. 1989. 10.95 (*0-88347-248-1*) Thomas More.

***Complaints Against the Police: A Sociological View.** 4th rev. ed. Kenneth V. Russell. 152p. 1994. pap. 12.00 (*0-9504906-7-9*) Milltak Ltd.

Complaints Against the Police: The Trend to External Review. Ed. by Andrew Goldsmith. 352p. 1991. 79.00 (*0-19-825257-9*, 9835) OUP.

Complaints & Disorders: The Sexual Politics of Sickness. Barbara Ehrenreich & Deirdre English. LC 73-18356. (Illus.). 96p. 1973. pap. 6.95 (*0-912670-20-7*) Feminist Pr.

Complaints. Containing Sundrie Small Poems of the Worlds Vanitie. Edmund Spenser. LC 74-25577. (English Experience Ser.: No. 278). 88p. 1970. reprint ed. 25.00 (*90-221-0278-5*) Walter J Johnson.

Complaints Is Many & Various, but the Odd Devil Likes It: Nineteenth Century Views of Newfoundland. R. G. Moyles. (Illus.). 187p. 1977. pap. 4.95 (*0-88778-160-8*, Pub. by Stoddart Pubng CN) Genl Dist Srvs.

Complaints of Police Corruption. John C. Meyer, Jr. (Criminal Justice Center Monographs). 1977. pap. text ed. 3.25x (*0-318-37489-7*) John Jay Pr.

Complaints of the Poor People of England. George Dyer. LC 90-36718. 262p. 1990. reprint ed. 48.00 (*1-85477-044-6*, Pub. by Woodstock Bks UK) Cassell.

Complaints Procedure in the Personal Social Services: Discussion Paper. 1976. 45.00 (*0-317-05773-1*, Pub. by Natl Inst Soc Work) St Mut.

Complaisant Lover. Graham Greene. LC 61-7280. 87p. 1961. 16.95 (*0-910278-24-5*) Boulevard.

Complaynt of Scotlande, Pts. 1 & 2. Ed. by J. A. Murray. (EETS, ES Ser.: Nos. 17, 18). 1872. reprint ed. 40.00 (*0-527-00231-3*) Periodicals Srv.

Compleat Academic: A Practical Guide for the Beginning Social Scientist. Society for the Psychological Study of Social Issues. Ed. by Mark P. Zanna & John M. Darley. 1987. pap. text ed. write for info. (*0-07-554907-7*) McGraw.

Compleat Academic: A Practical Guide for the Beginning Social Scientist. Ed. by Mark P. Zanna & John M. Darley. 248p. 1986. 36.00 (*0-8058-0019-0*); pap. text ed. 14.95 (*0-89859-949-0*) L Erlbaum Assocs.

Compleat Alchemist. 2nd ed. Anthony Pryor et al. (Illus.). 72p. 1993. pap. 10.95 (*1-880992-09-4*) Wizards Coast.

Compleat American Candy Containers Handbook. rev. ed. George Eikelberner & Serge Agadjanian. Ed. by Adele L. Bowden. LC 86-70006. (Illus.). 264p. 1986. pap. 24.95 (*0-9616177-0-5*) Bowden Pub.

Compleat Angler. Isaak Walton. 24.95 (*0-8488-0657-3*) Amereon Ltd.

Compleat Angler. Izaak Walton & Charles Cotton. Ed. by John Buxton. (World's Classics Ser.). (Illus.). 1982. pap. 5.95 (*0-19-281511-3*) OUP.

Compleat Angler. large type ed. Izaak Walton. 1988. 23.95 (*0-7089-8507-6*, Trail West Pubs) Ulverscroft.

Compleat Angler. Izaak Walton. (BCL1-PR English Literature Ser.). 631p. 1992. reprint ed. lib. bdg. 109.00 (*0-7812-7418-4*) Rprt Serv.

Compleat Angler: Or, The Contemplative Man's Recreation; Being a Discourse of Fish & Fishing Not Unworthy the Perusal of Most Anglers. deluxe limited ed. Izaak Walton. LC 88-71190. (Illus.). 340p. 1988. 40.00 (*0-929309-00-6*) Birdalone Bks.

***Compleat Angler, or, the Contemplative Man's Recreation: Being a Discourse of Rivers, Fishponds, Fish & Fishing Not Unworthy the Perusal of Most Anglers.** Izaak Walton. LC 94-42170. (Illus.). 1995. 23.00 (*0-88001-406-7*) Ecco Pr.

Compleat Anthology of Lesbian Humour. H. M. Koutoukas. (Illus.). 54p. (Orig.). 1983. pap. 6.09 (*0-931174-05-8*) Beau Rivage.

Compleat Anthology of Lesbian Humour. H. M. Koutoukas. 56p. (Orig.). 1983. pap. text ed. 6.09 (*0-317-02726-3*) Beau Rivage.

Compleat Apple Spreadsheeter. Roger E. Clark & Patricia Johnson-Swersey. 1986. 17.95 (*0-13-155086-1*) S&S Trade.

Compleat Arduin Bk. 2: Resources. rev. ed. David A. Hargrave. Ed. by Mark Schynert. (Illus.). 256p. Date not set. pap. 21.95 (*1-881632-01-6*) Grimoire Games.

Compleat Arduin, Bk. 1: Rules. rev. ed. David A. Hargrave. Ed. by Mark Schynert. (Illus.). 208p. 1993. pap. 19.95 (*1-881632-00-8*) Grimoire Games.

Compleat Baseball Advocate. David Srinivasan et al. 224p. 1993. pap. 12.95 (*0-9635768-0-1*) CBPS Pub.

***Compleat Baseball Advocate, 1995.** Doug Byron et al. 325p. 1995. pap. 15.95 (*0-9635768-2-8*) CBPS Pub.

Compleat Bolo. Keith Laumer. 320p. (Orig.). 1990. mass mkt. 4.99 (*0-671-69879-6*) Baen Bks.

Compleat Chemist or a New Treatise of Chemistry (1677) Teaching by a Short & Easy Method All Its Most Necessary Preparations. Christopher Glaser. 300p. 1993. pap. 19.95 (*1-56459-354-1*) Kessinger Pub.

Compleat Cladist: A Primer of Phylogenetic Procedures. Edward O. Wiley et al. (Special Publication Ser.: No. 19). 168p. 1991. pap. 14.95 (*0-89338-035-0*) U of KS Mus Nat Hist.

Compleat Crow. Brian Lumley. LC 86-81094. (Illus.). 192p. 1987. 21.00 (*0-932445-22-5*); pap. 7.50 (*0-932445-21-7*) Ganley Pub.

Compleat Cruiser: The Art, Practice & Enjoyment of Boating. L. Francis Herreshoff. (Illus.). 382p. 1990. pap. 16.50 (*0-911378-67-7*) Sheridan.

An Asterisk (*) at the beginning of an entry indicates that the title is appearing in BIP for the first time.

***Compleat Day-Trader: Trading Systems, Strategies, Timing Indicators, & Analytical Methods.** Jacob Bernstein. LC 94-41343. 1995. text ed. 39.95 (*0-07-009251-6*) McGraw.

Compleat Drum Reader. Joel Rothman & Gar Whaley. 1976. 30.00 (*0-913952-07-9*) J R Pubns.

Compleat Drum Technique. Joel Rothman. 256p. 1974. 25. 00 (*0-913952-02-8*) J R Pubns.

Compleat Falconer. Frank L. Beebe. (Illus.). 300p. 70.00 (*0-88839-253-2*) Hancock House.

Compleat Freshwater Fisherman. Dick Sternberg. 1992. 19. 98 (*0-88365-799-6*) Galahad Bks.

Compleat Gentleman: Five Centuries of Aristocratic Life. Geoffrey Beard. LC 92-14418. (Illus.). 224p. 1992. 50.00 (*0-8478-1468-8*) Rizzoli Intl.

Compleat Guide to Nassau. Steve Dodge. (Illus.). 116p. (Orig.). 1987. pap. 4.95 (*0-932265-04-9*) White Sound.

Compleat Gunner. Frwd. by Brig. Hogg. (Illus.). 1976. reprint ed. 10.50 (*0-85409-677-9*) Charles River Bks.

Compleat Handbook & Glossary of Soviet Education. George R. Fletcher. 130p. (Orig.). 1992. pap. 40.00 (*0-9631999-0-0*) Globe Lang Srvs.

Compleat I Hate to Cook Book. Peg Bracken. (Illus.). 288p. 1986. 15.95 (*0-15-120480-2*) HarBrace.

Compleat I Hate to Cook Book. Peg Bracken. 1992. 7.98 (*0-88365-794-5*) Galahad Bks.

Compleat IBM Spreadsheeter. Roger E. Clark & Patricia Johnson-Swersey. 1986. 17.95 (*0-13-155102-7*) S&S Trade.

Compleat Journal of the Votes, Speeches & Debates Both of the House of Lords & House of Commons Throughout the Whole Reign of Queen Elizabeth, of Glorious Memory. Comp. by Simonds D'Ewes. LC 74-75952. 1974. reprint ed. 60.00 (*0-8420-1739-9*) Scholarly Res Inc.

Compleat Just Jim. 2nd ed. Jim Carmichel. Ed. by Dave Wolfe. (Illus.). 128p. (C). 1981. text ed. 13.50 (*0-935632-09-3*) Wolfe Pub Co.

Compleat Khash, Vol. I: Never a Backward Glance. Brian Lumley. LC 90-81729. (Illus.). 1991. 25.00 (*0-932445-43-8*); 40.00 (*0-932445-44-6*) Ganley Pub.

Compleat Manager: What Works When. Alan C. Filley. LC 85-70081. 248p. (C). 1985. reprint ed. pap. 15.00 (*0-9614511-0-6*) Green Briar Pr.

Compleat Marriage. rev. ed. Nancy L. Van Pelt. LC 78-20770. (Orion Ser.). 1979. pap. 8.95 (*0-8127-0218-2*) Review & Herald.

Compleat Melancholick. Lewis Turco. LC 82-33742. 1985. 100.00 (*0-931460-12-3*); pap. 6.95 (*0-931460-15-8*) Bieler.

Compleat Mozart: A Guide to the Musical Works of Wolfgang Amadeus Mozart. Neal Zaslaw. 1991. 29.95 (*0-393-02886-0*) Norton.

Compleat Necromancer. Jesper Myrfors. (Pandevelopment Ser.). 72p. 1994. pap. 10.95 (*1-880992-18-3*) Wizards Coast.

Compleat Nevada Industrial Directory. Ed. by David W. Toll. (Illus.). 272p. (Orig.). 1986. pap. 45.00 (*0-940936-03-8*) Gold Hill.

Compleat Nevada Traveler. 4th ed. David W. Toll. (Illus.). 192p. 1985. pap. 7.95 (*0-940936-02-X*) Gold Hill.

Compleat Option Player. Kenneth R. Trester. 320p. 1977. 16.95 (*0-9604914-0-6*) Liberty Pub.

Compleat Option Player. rev. ed. Kenneth R. Trester. (Illus.). 392p. 1993. 16.95 (*0-685-71986-3*) Inst Options.

***Compleat Option Player.** 2nd rev. ed. Kenneth R. Trester. (Illus.). 392p. 1993. pap. 16.95 (*0-89709-200-7*) Inst Options.

Compleat Parent. rev. ed. Nancy L. Van Pelt. Ed. by Richard W. Coffen. 224p. 1985. pap. 8.95 (*0-8280-0283-5*) Review & Herald.

Compleat Politician: Political Strategy in Massachusetts. Murray B. Levin & George Blackwood. LC 62-18204. 1962. 29.50 (*0-672-51133-9*) Irvington.

Compleat Rokkaku Kite Chronicles & Training Manual. Illus. by George Peters. (Best of Kite Lines Ser.). 20p. (Orig.). 1991. reprint ed. pap. 6.95 (*0-937315-00-1*) Aeolus Pr.

Compleat Show Drummer. Joel Rothman. 370p. 1975. 30. 00 (*0-913952-04-4*) J R Pubns.

Compleat Slug. N. S. Nelson. LC 85-61964. (Illus.). 76p. (Orig.). 1986. pap. 6.50 (*0-935195-12-2*) Plaid Pony Pubns.

Compleat Strategyst: Being a Primer on the Theory of Games of Strategy. J. D. Williams. 268p. 1986. reprint ed. pap. 6.95 (*0-486-25101-2*) Dover.

Compleat Surfcaster. C. Boyd Pfeiffer. (Illus.). 192p. 1989. pap. 14.95 (*1-55821-052-0*) Lyons & Burford.

Compleat Taildragger Pilot. Harvey S. Plourde. (Illus.). 263p. (Orig.). 1991. pap. 24.95 (*0-9639137-0-0*) H S Plourde.

***Compleat Tangler.** Norman Thelwell. (Illus.). 96p. 1990. pap. 11.95 (*0-7493-0959-8*, Pub. by Methuen London UK) Trafalgar.

Compleat Teacher's Almanack: A Practical Guide to Every Day of the Year. Dana Newmann. 384p. 1991. 24.95 (*0-87628-243-5*) P-H.

Compleat Theory of Scots Highland Bagpipe: Manuscript of J. MacDonald. J. MacDonald. Ed. by A. MacRaonuill. (Illus.). 117p. 1992. pap. 20.00 (*0-685-59540-4*) A MacRaonuill.

Compleat Therapist. Jeffrey A. Kottler. LC 90-5197. (Social & Behavioral Science Ser.). 240p. 1991. 24.95 (*1-55542-302-7*) Jossey-Bass.

Compleat Tween. Nancy L. Van Pelt. Ed. by Richard W. Coffen. 96p. (Orig.). (J). (gr. 5 up). 1986. pap. 7.50 (*0-8280-0288-6*) Review & Herald.

Compleat University. Ed. by Harry Hermanns et al. 322p. 1983. 24.95 (*0-87073-644-2*); pap. 13.95 (*0-87073-645-0*) Schenkman Bks Inc.

Compleat Werewolf. Anthony Boucher. 1990. pap. 4.50 (*0-88184-557-4*) Carroll & Graf.

Compleat Woman. Jacques Du Bosc. LC 68-54642. (English Experience Ser.: No. 12). 88p. 1968. reprint ed. 35.00 (*90-221-0012-X*) Walter J Johnson.

Complement. Susan K. Law & K. B. Reid. (In Focus Ser.). 82p. 1988. pap. 13.95 (*1-85221-061-3*, IRL Pr) OUP.

Complement. Ed. by H. J. Muller-Eberhard & P. A. Miescher. (Illus.). vi, 480p. 1985. pap. 93.00 (*0-387-15075-7*) Spr-Verlag.

Complement: Clinical Aspects & Relevance to Disease. Paul Morgan. 215p. 1991. text ed. 55.00 (*0-12-506955-3*) Acad Pr.

***Complement: In Focus.** S. K. Law & K. B. Reid. (In Focus Ser.). (Illus.). 88p. 1995. pap. text ed. 17.50 (*0-19-963356-8*, IRL Pr) OUP.

Complement & Infectious Diseases. Ed. by Douglas P. Fine. 176p. 1981. 98.95 (*0-8493-6075-7*, RC112, CRC Reprint) Franklin.

Complement in Health & Disease. Ed. by K. Whaley. (Immunology & Medicine Ser.). 1987. lib. bdg. 129.50 (*0-85200-954-2*) Kluwer Ac.

Complement in Health & Disease. 2nd ed. Ed. by K. Whaley. (Immunology & Medicine Ser.). 400p. (C). 1993. lib. bdg. 105.00 (*0-7923-8823-2*) Kluwer Ac.

Complement in Human Disease, Third European Meeting, Bratislava, Abstracts, September 1990: Journal: Complement & Inflammation, Vol. 7, No. 3. Ed. by Z. Starsia & U. Nydegger. 60p. 1990. pap. 34.50 (*3-8055-5282-3*) S Karger.

Complement in Laboratory Medicine. Ed. by A. P. Dalmasso. (Journal: Complement & Inflammation: Vol. 6, No. 1, 1989). (Illus.). 72p. 1988. pap. 199.25 (*3-8055-4914-8*) S Karger.

Complement System. Ed. by K. Rother & G. O. Till. (Illus.). 540p. 1988. 121.00 (*0-387-18205-5*) Spr-Verlag.

Complement System. D. R. Schultz. (Monographs in Allergy: Vol. 6). 1971. 35.00 (*3-8055-1086-1*) S Karger.

Complement to the Farm Bill: Ending Tax Subsidies for Sodbusting & Swampbusting. Justin Ward. 1987. 2.50 (*0-318-23634-6*) NRDC Newsletter.

Complement Today. Ed. by J. M. Cruse & R. E. Lewis, Jr. (Complement Profiles Ser.: Vol. 1). (Illus.). x, 156p. 1993. 97.75 (*3-8055-5673-X*) S Karger.

Complementarities: Uncollected Essays. Ivor A. Richards. Ed. by John P. Russo. LC 76-19044. (Illus.). 317p. reprint ed. pap. 90.40 (*0-7837-6087-6*, 2059133) Bks Demand.

Complementarity: Anti-Epistemology after Bohr & Derrida. Arkady Plotnitsky. LC 93-29583. 328p. 1994. lib. bdg. 49.95 (*0-8223-1433-9*); pap. text ed. 17.95 (*0-8223-1437-1*) Duke.

Complementarity & Political Science: An Essay on Fundamentals of Political Science Theory & Research Strategy. Erik Rasmussen. 137p. (Orig.). 1987. pap. 37. 50x (*87-7492-628-4*, Pub. by Odense Universitets Forlag DK) Coronet Bks.

***Complementarity in Trade & Production: Intra-South Potentials.** V. R. Panchamukhi et al. LC 94-23401. (Indo-Dutch Studies on Development Alternatives: Vol. 15). 1994. 25.00 (*0-8039-9206-8*) Sage.

Complementarity Problems. George Isac. LC 92-33495. (Lecture Notes in Mathematics Ser.: Vol. 1528). 1992. write for info. (*3-540-56251-6*) Spr-Verlag.

Complementarity Problems. George Isac. Ed. by A. Dold et al. (Lecture Notes in Mathematics Ser.: Vol. 1528). vi, 294p. 1992. pap. 49.00 (*0-387-56251-6*) Spr-Verlag.

Complementary & Fixed Point Problems. Ed. by M. L. Balinski & R. W. Cottle. (Mathematical Programming Studies: Vol. 7). 184p. 1978. pap. 38.50 (*0-444-85123-2*, North Holland) Elsevier.

Complementary Approaches to Double & Multiple Star Research. Ed. by H. McAlister. (ASP Conference Series Publications: Vol. 32). 598p. 1992. 40.00 (*0-937707-51-1*) Astron Soc Pacific.

Complementary Immunoassays. Ed. by W. P. Collins. 304p. 1988. text ed. 212.95 (*0-471-91745-1*) Wiley.

***Complementary Medicine: A Guide to Natural Therapies.** Andrew Stanway. 336p. 1995. pap. 12.95 (*0-14-019482-7*, Arkana) Viking Penguin.

Complementary Medicine: Its Practice in the Health Service. R. Hill. 224p. 1994. pap. 23.95 (*0-632-03439-4*, Pub. by Blckwell Sci Pubns UK) Blackwell Sci.

Complementary Medicine: New Approaches to Good Practice. British Medical Association Staff. 184p. (C). 1993. pap. 13.95 (*0-19-286166-2*, 7314) OUP.

***Complementary Medicine & Disability: Alternatives for People with Disabling Conditions.** Andrew Vickers. 310p. 1994. pap. 44.75 (*1-56593-232-3*) Singular Publishing.

Complementary Medicine & the European Community. Research Council for Complementary Medicine Staff. 160p. (Orig.). Date not set. pap. 23.95 (*0-8464-4198-5*) Beekman Pubs.

Complementary Medicine Today: Practitioners & Patients. Ursula Sharma. 208p. 1991. 69.50 (*0-415-04793-5*, A5930); pap. 18.95 (*0-415-04794-3*, A5934) Routledge.

Complementary Methods for Research in Education. Ed. by Richard M. Jaeger. LC 88-70121. 1988. 45.00 (*0-935302-09-3*); pap. 36.00 (*0-935302-08-5*) Am Educ Res.

Complementary Norms. National Conference of Catholic Bishops Staff. 56p. (Orig.). (C). 1991. pap. 3.95 (*1-55586-433-3*) US Catholic.

***Complementary Triangular Forms for Pairs of Matrices & Operators.** R. Zuidwijk. (Tinbergen Institute Research Ser.: No. 80). 142p. 1994. pap. 25.00 (*90-5170-299-X*, Pub. by Thesis Pubs NE) IBD Ltd.

Complementation: Its Meaning & Forms. Evelyn Ransom. LC 86-3554. (Typological Studies in Language: Vol. 10). xii, 226p. 1986. 59.00x (*0-915027-87-9*); pap. 29.95x (*0-915027-88-7*) Benjamins North Am.

Complementation & Case Grammar: A Syntactic & Semantic Study of Selected Patterns of Complementation in Present-Day English. Juhani Rudanko. LC 88-20983. (Linguistics Ser.). 173p. (C). 1989. 74.50 (*0-88706-931-2*); pap. 24.95 (*0-88706-932-0*) State U NY Pr.

Complementing the Welfare State: The Development of Private Pension, Health Insurance & Other Employee Benefits in the United States. Beth Stevens. (Labour-Management Relations Ser.: No. 65). viii, 73p. (Orig.). 1986. pap. 12.00 (*92-2-105673-2*) Intl Labour Office.

***Complements.** Ed. by Anna Katsavos & Elizabeth Wheeler. LC 94-21171. 1994. write for info. (*0-07-033872-8*) McGraw.

Complements a la "Flore Analytique" R. Kuhner & H. Romagnesi. (Bibliotheca Mycologica Ser.: No. 56). (Illus.). 1977. reprint ed. lib. bdg. 65.00 (*3-7682-1131-2*) Lubrecht & Cramer.

Complements of Discriminants of Smooth Maps: Topology & Applications. Vassiliev. LC 92-8176. 208p. 1992. 164. 00 (*0-8218-4555-1*, MMONO-98) Am Math.

Complements of Discriminents of Smooth Maps: Topology & Applications. rev. ed. V. A. Vassiliev. LC 93-36963. (Translations of Mathematical Monographs: Vol. 98). 1994. pap. 114.00 (*0-8218-4618-3*) Am Math.

Complete "About Acting" Peter Barkworth. 1992. pap. 16.95 (*0-413-66110-5*, A0640, Pub. by Methuen UK) Heinemann.

Complete Academic. Darley Zana. 1987. text ed. write for info. (*0-07-553737-0*) McGraw.

Complete Acrylic Painting Book. Wendon Blake. (Illus.). 160p. 1989. 29.99 (*0-89134-306-7*, 30156) North Light Bks.

Complete Actors' Television Credits, 1948- 1988, Vol. 1: Actors. 2nd ed. James R. Parish & Vincent Terrace. LC 89-10607. (Illus.). 560p. 1989. 62.50 (*0-8108-2204-0*) Scarecrow.

Complete Actors' Television Credits, 1948-1988, Vol. 2: Actresses. 2nd ed. James R. Parish & Vincent Terrace. LC 89-10607. (Illus.). 447p. 1990. 49.50 (*0-8108-2258-X*) Scarecrow.

Complete Advanced Pilot. Bob Gardner. (Complete Pilot Ser.). (Illus.). 425p. (Orig.). 1994. pap. text ed. 22.95 (*1-56027-174-4*, ASA-APT) Av Suppl & Acad.

Complete Adventures of Peter Rabbit. Beatrix Potter. (Illus.). 96p. (J). (ps-3). 1987. 13.00 (*0-7232-2951-1*) Warne.

Complete Adventures of Peter Rabbit. Beatrix Potter. (Picture Puffins Ser.). 80p. (J). (ps-3). 1984. pap. 6.99 (*0-14-050444-3*, Puffin) Puffin Bks.

Complete Adventures of Tom Kitten & His Friends. Beatrix Potter. (Illus.). 80p. (J). (ps-3). 1985. 13.00 (*0-7232-3288-1*) Warne.

Complete Airbrush & Photo-Retouching Manual. Peter Owen & John Sutcliffe. (Illus.). 160p. 1985. 24.95 (*0-89134-170-6*, 7326) North Light Bks.

Complete Airbrush Book. Curtis & C. Hunt. 39.95 (*0-685-19090-0*) Van Nos Reinhold.

Complete Akita. Joan M. Linderman & Virginia B. Funk. LC 83-6180. (Complete Breed Book Ser.). (Illus.). 216p. 1983. 25.95 (*0-87605-006-2*) Howell Bk.

Complete Alabama Fisherman. Mike Bolton & Tom Bailey. (Illus.). 360p. (Orig.). 1990. pap. text ed. 14.95 (*1-878561-00-6*) Seacoast AL.

Complete Alec. Eddie Campbell. (Illus.). 1990. 35.00 (*1-56060-046-2*); pap. 12.95 (*1-56060-047-0*) Eclipse Bks.

Complete Alekhine. Graham Burgess. 256p. 1992. pap. 22. 95 (*0-8050-2425-5*, Pub. by Batsford Chess UK) H Holt & Co.

Complete AMA Guide to Management Development. William J. Rothwell & H. C. Kazanas. 336p. 1993. 65.00 (*0-8144-5079-2*) AMACOM.

***Complete Amateur Boat Building.** 4th ed. Michael Verney. (Illus.). 160p. Date not set. 36.50 (*0-7136-5731-6*) Sheridan.

Complete American Candymaking. D. Pisegna. Date not set. 25.00 (*0-06-016972-9*, HarpT) HarpC.

Complete American Cocker Spaniel. Norman A. Austin & Jean S. Austin. (Illus.). 256p. 1993. 25.95 (*0-87605-129-8*) Howell Bk.

Complete American Eskimo: A Special Kind of Companion. Barbara Beynon. Ed. by Seymour Weiss. 224p. 1990. 25. 95 (*0-87605-013-5*) Howell Bk.

Complete American-Jewish Cookbook. Anne London & Bertha K. Bishov. LC 88-45726. 672p. 1989. reprint ed. pap. 17.00 (*0-06-091590-0*, PL 1590, PL) HarpC.

Complete & Compact Minimal Surfaces. Kichoon Yang. (C). 1989. lib. bdg. 84.50 (*0-7923-0399-7*) Kluwer Ac.

Complete & Easy Guide to Social Security & Medicare: 1995 Edition. rev. ed. Faustin F. Jenk. LC 94-61274. 176p. 1995. pap. 11.95 (*0-930045-13-0*) Fraser-Vance.

***Complete & Easy Guide to Social Security & Medicare, 1994 Edition.** 11th ed. Faustin F. Jehle. 176p. 1995. (*0-614-03125-7*) Williamson Pub Co.

Complete & Painless Guide to the Guitar for Young Beginners. Wayne Erbsen. 64p. (J). 1979. pap. 9.95 (*0-8258-0002-1*, PCB 111) Fischer Inc NY.

Complete & Simplified Spelling Book of Verbs. Raymond E. Laurita. 87p. (Orig.). 1984. pap. 9.95 (*0-914051-02-4*) Leonardo Pr.

Complete & Systematic Concordance of Works of Shakespeare, 9 vols, Set. William Shakespeare. Ed. by Marvin Spevack. 1980. 2,280.00 (*3-487-01817-9*) Adlers Foreign Bks.

Complete & Systematic Concordance to the Works of Shakespeare, 9 vols., Set. Ed. by Marvin Spevack. 11303p. 1980. lib. bdg. 1,485.00 (*0-685-67779-6*, Pub. by Georg Olms GW) Lubrecht & Cramer.

Complete & up-to-Date Fat Book: A Guide to Fat, Calories & Fat Percentages in Your Food. 2nd ed. Karen J. Bellerson. LC 92-20337. 624p. 1993. pap. 5.95 (*0-89529-561-X*) Avery Pub.

Complete & Utter Failure: A Celebration of Also-Rans, Runners-Up, Never-Weres, & Total Flops. Neil Steinberg. LC 94-4908. 1994. 17.50 (*0-385-47291-9*) Doubleday.

***Complete Angel: Angels Through the Ages-All You Need to Know.** James Pruitt. 256p. (Orig.). 1995. mass mkt. 5.50 (*0-380-78045-3*) Avon.

Complete Angler. Isaac Walton. Ed. by Jonquil Bevan. 272p. 1993. pap. 6.95 (*0-460-87281-8*, Everyman's Classic Lib) C E Tuttle.

Complete Annals of Thomas Jefferson. Thomas Jefferson. Ed. by Franklin R. Sawvel. LC 70-75272. (American Public Figures Ser.). 1970. reprint ed. lib. bdg. 37.50 (*0-306-71311-X*) Da Capo.

Complete Answer Book-Lawless. Date not set. 6.95 (*1-56222-252-X*, 94642) Mel Bay.

Complete Anthology of Elementary Classic Guitar Solos. Joseph Castle. (Complete Book Ser.). 1993. 15.00 (*1-56222-281-3*, 94641) Mel Bay.

Complete Anti-Federalist, 7 Vols., Set. Ed. by Herbert J. Storing & Murray Dry. LC 81-10287. 1856p. 1981. lib. bdg. 175.00 (*0-226-77573-9*) U Ch Pr.

***Complete Antique Shop Directory for Eastern Michigan, 1994-95.** Edward Lawrence. (Illus.). 260p. (Orig.). Date not set. pap. 10.95 (*0-9634597-2-4*) Complete Antique.

***Complete Antique Shop Directory for Indiana, 1994.** Edward Lawrence. (Illus.). 272p. (Orig.). 1993. pap. text ed. 5.00 (*0-9634597-1-6*) Complete Antique.

***Complete Antique Shop Directory for Western Michigan, 1993.** Edward Lawrence. (Illus.). 163p. (Orig.). 1992. pap. 5.00 (*0-9634597-0-8*) Complete Antique.

***Complete Antique Shop Directory for Western Michigan, 1995.** rev. ed. Edward Lawrence. (Illus.). 224p. 1994. pap. 10.95 (*0-9634597-3-2*) Complete Antique.

Complete AppleScript Handbook. Danny Goodman. 1993. pap. 35.00 (*0-679-79148-5*) Random.

Complete Appreciation of Oneself. Harvey Jackins. 1964. pap. 2.00 (*0-911214-08-9*) Rational Isl.

Complete Aquarium. Peter Scott. 1991. 39.50 (*0-394-58743-X*) Knopf.

***Complete Aquarium.** Peter Scott. (Illus.). 192p. 1995. pap. 16.95 (*0-7894-0013-8*) Dorling Kindersley.

Complete Aquarium: An Encyclopedia of Tropical Freshwater Fish. J. D. Van Ramshorst. 1992. 19.98 (*1-55521-795-8*) Bk Sales Inc.

Complete Aquarium Logbook. Kevin W. Boyd. 1993. 10.95 (*1-56465-112-6*, 16007) Tetra Pr.

Complete Aquarium Problem Solver. Kevin W. Boyd. (Illus.). 32p. (YA). (gr. 10). 1989. pap. write for info. (*0-318-65747-3*) Boylen.

Complete Aquarium Problem Solver: A Total Trouble-Shooting Guide for Freshwater & Marine Aquariums. Kevin W. Boyd. 1992. 14.95 (*0-9624099-7-9*, 16099) Tetra Pr.

Complete AR-15 - M16 Sourcebook. Duncan Long. (Illus.). 1992. pap. 35.00 (*0-87364-687-8*) Paladin Pr.

Complete Arizona Contractor's Study Guide - Commercial Construction. Ed. & Illus. by James A. Holish. 139p. 1991. student ed 75.00 (*1-879020-05-X*) ACS Assocs Pub.

Complete Arizona Contractors Study Guide - Electrical. James A. Holish. Ed. by Robert J. Petrillo & Richard M. Stewart. (Collection of Eight Ser.). (Illus.). (Orig.). (C). 1990. student ed 75.00 (*1-879020-01-7*) ACS Assocs Pub.

Complete Arizona Contractors Study Guide-Electrical. Robert J. Petrillo. 1990. write for info. (*0-318-68031-9*) ACS Assocs Pub.

Complete Army & Navy Register of the U. S. A. from 1776 to 1887. T. H. Hamersley. 1972. 59.95 (*0-87968-915-3*) Gordon Pr.

Complete Aromatherapy Gift Set: Essential Oils for Radiant Health. LC 90-24305. (Illus.). 240p. 1992. pap. 40.00 (*0-8069-5687-9*) Sterling.

Complete Aromatherapy Handbook: Essential Oils for Radiant Health. Susanne Fischer-Rizzi. LC 90-24305. (Illus.). 240p. 1991. pap. 16.95 (*0-8069-8222-5*) Sterling.

Complete Art of Breaking. Richard Bryne. Ed. by Mike Lee. (Specialties Ser.). 128p. 1984. pap. 12.95 (*0-89750-099-7*, 434) Ohara Pubns.

Complete Art of Firework-Making: The Pyrotechnist's Treasury. rev. ed. Thomas Kentish. (Illus.). 130p. 1994. pap. 13.40 (*0-929931-09-2*) Amer Fireworks.

Complete Art of Witchcraft. Sybil Leek. (Illus.). 208p. 1973. pap. 4.99 (*0-451-16421-0*, Sig) NAL-Dutton.

Complete Art of Witchcraft. Sybil Leek. 1989. pap. 3.95 (*0-451-15344-8*) NAL-Dutton.

***Complete Ascension Manual for the Aquarian Age.** Joshua D. Stone. LC 94-21181. 297p. 1994. 14.95 (*0-929385-55-1*) Light Tech Comns Servs.

***Complete ASQ System.** Bricker et al. 1995. boxed 135.00 (*0-614-02521-4*, SQU) P H Brookes.

***Complete ASQ System - Spanish Version.** 1995. 135.00 (*0-614-06525-9*, SQUS) P H Brookes.

Complete Assembling. Ed. by Richard Kostelanetz et al. (Orig.). 1979. pap. 200.00 (*0-915066-34-3*) Assembling Pr.

Complete Atlas of Polarization Observables in Deuteron Photodisintegration below Pion-Threshold. K. M. Schmitt & H. Arenhovel. (Few-Body Systems Ser.: Suppl. 4). 308p. 1991. 126.00 (*0-387-82320-4*) Spr-Verlag.

C

An Asterisk (*) at the beginning of an entry indicates that the title is appearing in BIP for the first time.

Complete Atlas of the World. Keith Lye. LC 94-19316. (J). 1994. lib. bdg. 31.36 (*0-8114-5804-0*) Raintree Steck-V.

Complete Audio-Visual Guide for Teachers & Media Specialists. Jacquelyn Peake & Carol A. Petersen. 224p. 1989. text ed. 27.95 (*0-13-155441-7*) P-H.

Complete Audio Writing, 9 cass., Set. Richard Kostelanetz. 1985. audio 75.00 (*0-932360-71-8*) Archae Edns.

Complete Australian Cattle Dog. John Holmes & Mary Holmes. (Illus.). 160p. 1993. 29.95 (*0-87605-014-3*) Howell Bk.

***Complete Auto Body Painting.** Scharff. 1994. 34.95 (*0-8273-3582-2*) Delmar.

Complete Auto Mechanics. Hathaway. 1986. pap. 29.32 (*0-02-666080-6*) Macmillan.

Complete Auto Rebuild & Parts Machining SM: Shop Manual. Scharff Associates Staff. 1990. student ed 9.95 (*0-8273-4721-9*) Delmar.

***Complete Auto Welding.** Robert Scharff. 1994. 34.95 (*0-8273-3622-5*) Delmar.

Complete AutoCAD. David S. Cohn. 1990. pap. 34.95 (*0-201-51783-3*) Addison-Wesley.

Complete Autoharp Songbook. Meg Peterson. (Complete Book Ser.). 1993. 15.00 (*0-87166-769-X*, 93694) Mel Bay.

Complete Automobile Mechanics Refresher Course. Bob Leigh et al. (Illus.). 441p. 1981. student ed 79.95 (*0-88098-067-2*, H M Gousha) P-H Gen Ref & Trav.

Complete Automobile Mechanics Refresher Course, 5 cass., Set. rev. ed. Bob Leigh et al. (Illus.). 441p. 1981. audio 70.00 (*0-88098-073-7*, H M Gousha) P-H Gen Ref & Trav.

Complete Automotive Service Library. Chek-Chart Staff. (Automotive Service Ser.). (Illus.). 665p. (C). (gr. 12). 1983. pap. text ed. 52.55 (*0-88098-053-2*, H M Gousha) P-H Gen Ref & Trav.

Complete Aviation - Aerospace Career Guide. Robert Calderone. 1989. pap. 15.95 (*0-07-156462-4*) McGraw.

Complete Aviation-Aerospace Career Guide. Robert Calderone. (Illus.). 176p. (Orig.). 1989. 21.95 (*0-8306-8280-5*, TAB-Aero); pap. 15.95 (*0-8306-8380-1*, TAB-Aero) TAB Bks.

***Complete Baby & Child Care.** Miriam Stoppard. LC 94-26720. (Illus.). 352p. 1995. 29.95 (*1-56458-850-5*) Dorling Kindersley.

Complete Baby Checklist: A Total Organizing System for Parents. Elise Z. Karlin et al. 1992. pap. 10.00 (*0-380-76347-8*) Avon.

Complete Baby Name Book. Consumer Guide Editors. (Illus.). 160p. 1993. spiral bd. 9.98 (*0-88176-814-6*, 4003001) Pubns Intl Ltd.

Complete Baby Name Book. Consumer Guide Editors. 1990. pap. 6.99 (*0-517-03147-7*) Random Hse Value.

Complete Back Issues of Dvorak Developments. Intro. by Randy Cassingham. (Illus.). 106p. 1990. spiral bd. 29.95 (*0-935309-09-8*) Freelance Comm.

***Complete Baja California Guidebook.** Annelise Sorensen. (Mexico Ser.). (Illus.). 152p. 1995. pap. 9.95 (*0-916841-54-5*) Indian Chief.

Complete Baja Guidebook. B. Sangwan. (Mexico Ser.). (Illus.). 152p. 1994. pap. 8.95 (*0-916841-36-7*) Indian Chief.

Complete Ballades, Impromptus & Sonatas: The Paderewski Edition. Frederic Chopin. Ed. by L. Bronarski & J. Turczynski. 240p. 1981. pap. 9.95 (*0-486-24164-5*) Dover.

Complete Banjo Book. Neil Griffin. (Complete Book Ser.). 1993. spiral bd. 15.00 (*0-87166-572-7*, 93723) Mel Bay.

Complete Banjo Repair. Larry Sandberg. (Illus.). 96p. pap. 12.95 (*0-8256-0227-0*, Oak) Music Sales.

Complete Banner Handbook: A Creative Guide for Banner Design & Construction. Janet Litherland. Ed. & Illus. by Michelle Z. Gallardo. LC 87-71778. 122p. (Orig.). 1987. pap. 12.95 (*0-916260-48-8*, B-172) Meriwether Pub.

Complete Bar - Bat Mitzvah Planner: An Indispendable, Money-Saving Workbook for Organizing Every Aspect of the Event - from Temple Services to Reception. Linda S. Sage. LC 93-14857. 160p. (Orig.). 1993. pap. 14.95 (*0-312-09260-1*) St Martin.

Complete Bard's Handbook. Jeff Grubb & TSR Hobbies Staff. 1992. 18.00 (*1-56076-360-4*) TSR Inc.

Complete Bartender. Robyn M. Feller. 1990. mass mkt. 5.99 (*0-425-12687-0*) Berkley Pub.

Complete Baseball Advocate. David Srinivasan. 1994. pap. 12.95 (*0-9635768-1-X*) CBPS Pub.

Complete Baseball Card Book, 1989. Consumer Guide Staff. 1989. 12.99 (*0-517-67428-9*) Random Hse Value.

Complete Baseball Player. Dave Winfield & Eric Swenson. (Illus.). 192p. 1990. pap. 9.95 (*0-380-75830-X*) Avon.

***Complete Baseball Record Book, 1995.** Sporting News Staff. 1995. pap. 17.95 (*0-89204-515-9*) Sporting News.

Complete Basenji. Elspet Ford. (Illus.). 160p. 1993. 25.95 (*0-87605-016-X*) Howell Bk.

Complete BASIC: For the Short Course. James S. Quasney & John Maniotes. (Illus.). 196p. 1985. write for info. (*0-87835-158-2*); pap. text ed. 19.50 (*0-87835-151-5*) Boyd & Fraser.

Complete BASIC Programming. Steven L. Mandell. (Illus.). 349p. 1984. pap. text ed. 28.50 (*0-314-77921-3*) West Pub.

Complete BASIC Programming. 3rd ed. Susan K. Baumann. Ed. by Clyde Perlee. 441p. (C). 1990. pap. text ed. 47.25 (*0-314-75284-6*) West Pub.

Complete Bass Book. Mike Hiland. (Complete Book Ser.). 1993. 15.00 (*1-56222-180-9*, 94552); audio 9.98 (*1-56222-160-4*, 94552) Mel Bay.

Complete Bearded Collie. Joyce Collis & Pat Jones. (Illus.). 160p. 1992. 25.00 (*0-87605-131-X*) Howell Bk.

Complete Beatles, Vol. 1. 448p. (Orig.). 1988. pap. 24.95 (*0-88188-913-X*, 00356240) H Leonard.

Complete Beatles, Vol. 2. 448p. (Orig.). 1988. pap. 24.95 (*0-88188-914-8*, 00356241) H Leonard.

Complete Beatles: 0-7935-1979-9, 2 vols., Set. 1993. pap. 49.90 (*0-685-67458-4*, 00308170) H Leonard.

Complete Beatles Chronicle. Mark Lewisohn. LC 92-19561. (Illus.). 368p. 1992. 14.00 (*0-517-58100-0*, Harmony) Crown Pub Group.

Complete Beatles Lyrics. 183p. 1993. pap. 14.95 (*0-7935-1537-8*, 00308137) H Leonard.

Complete Beginner's Guide to the Atari Portfolio. Barry Thomas & Alan Thomas. 1990. pap. 30.95 (*0-442-30314-9*) Van Nos Reinhold.

Complete Belgian Tervuren. American Belgian Tervuren Club Staff. 256p. 1990. 25.95 (*0-87605-051-8*) Howell Bk.

Complete Bernese Mountain Dog. Jude Simonds. Ed. by Marcy Zingler. 160p. 1990. 25.95 (*0-87605-050-X*) Howell Bk.

Complete Best of the Herman Sourdough Herald. Watland-Johnson. 1990. 12.95 (*0-934860-65-3*) Adventure Pubns.

Complete Beverage Dictionary. Robert A. Lipinski & Kathleen A. Lipinski. 416p. 1992. text ed. 39.95 (*0-442-23987-4*) Van Nos Reinhold.

Complete Bewko Gambit. John Fedorwicz. Ed. by Jeremy Silman. (Illus.). 233p. (Orig.). 1990. pap. 17.95 (*0-685-38733-X*) Summit CA.

Complete Bible Commentary. George Williams. 1058p. 1994. pap. 29.99 (*0-8254-3993-0*) Kregel.

Complete Bible Discussion Guide: New Testament. Mack Thomas. 384p. 1992. 21.99 (*0-945564-55-4*, Multnomah Bks) Questar Pubs.

Complete Bible Discussion Guide: Old Testament. Mack Thomas. 384p. 1993. 21.99 (*0-945564-54-6*, Multnomah Bks) Questar Pubs.

Complete Bible Quiz Book. Dan Carlinsky. 1988. 4.99 (*0-517-23278-2*) Random Hse Value.

Complete Bibliography of Fencing & Duelling. Carl A. Thimm. 600p. 1992. 75.00 (*1-882860-02-0*) J Cummins Bksell.

Complete Bibliography of Fencing & Duelling. Carl A. Thimm. LC 68-17152. (Illus.). 1972. reprint ed. 33.95 (*0-405-09028-5*) Ayer.

***Complete Bibliography of the Works of Seyyed Hossein Nasr: From 1958 Through April 1993.** Q. Mushtaq & A. L. Tan. Ed. by Mehdi Aminrazavi & Zailan Moris. (Orig.). 1995. pap. text ed. 14.95 (*0-934905-60-6*) Kazi Pubns.

Complete Bibliography of the Writings of Eugen Rosenstock-Huessy. Comp. by Lise Van der Molen. LC 89-77129. (Toronto Studies in Theology: Vol. 45). 160p. 1990. lib. bdg. 69.95 (*0-88946-748-X*) E Mellen.

Complete Bichon Frise. Barbara Stubbs. Ed. by Marcy Zingler. 288p. 1990. 25.95 (*0-87605-053-4*) Howell Bk.

Complete Big Island of Hawaii Guidebook. David J. Russ. (Hawaii Ser.). (Illus.). 144p. 1994. pap. 9.95 (*0-916841-39-1*) Indian Chief.

***Complete Big Island of Hawaii Guidebook.** David J. Russ. (Hawaii Ser.). (Illus.). 152p. 1995. pap. 9.95 (*0-916841-63-4*) Indian Chief.

Complete Bio Industry Source Book. Jane Sims. 125p. 1993. pap. 89.95 (*0-9640112-0-4*) Global Design.

Complete Bird Owner's Handbook. 2nd rev. ed. Gary A. Gallerstein. (Illus.). 352p. reprint ed. 27.50 (*0-87605-903-5*) Howell Bk.

Complete Birder: A Guide to Better Birding. LC 87-27217. 288p. 1988. pap. 11.95 (*0-395-46807-8*) HM.

Complete Birdhouse Book, Vol. 1. Donald W. Stokes. 1990. pap. 11.95 (*0-316-81714-7*) Little.

Complete Black Belt Hyung. Hee Il Cho. LC 88-92050. 208p. (Orig.). 1988. pap. 15.95 (*0-929015-08-8*) Chos Taekwon Do Pub Hse.

Complete Black Belt Hyung. Il Cho Hee. 1990. pap. 15.95 (*0-86568-143-0*) Unique Pubns.

Complete Black Powder Handbook. rev. ed. Sam Fadala. LC 79-54268. (Illus.). 320p. (Orig.). 1990. pap. 18.95 (*0-87349-101-7*) DBI.

Complete Blader. Joel Rappelfeld. (Illus.). 144p. (Orig.). 1992. pap. 8.95 (*0-312-06936-7*) St Martin.

Complete Bladesmith: Forging Your Way to Perfection. Jim Hrisoulas. (Illus.). 192p. 1987. text ed. 30.00 (*0-87364-430-1*) Paladin Pr.

***Complete Blankbook.** Mike Baron & Jim Homan. 687p. 1992. pap. text ed. 39.95 (*0-614-04595-9*) Wordbks & Listmats.

Complete Block Book. Eugene F. Provenzo, Jr. & Arlene Brett. (Illus.). 182p. 1983. text ed. 34.95 (*0-8156-2300-3*); pap. 14.95 (*0-8156-0188-3*) Syracuse U Pr.

Complete Bluegrass Banjo Method. Neil Griffin. 1993. 15.00 (*0-87166-879-3*, 93345); audio 9.98 (*1-56222-587-1*, 93345) Mel Bay.

Complete Bluegrass Banjo Player. Wayne D. Goforth. (Illus.). 160p. 1984. pap. 17.95 (*0-8256-0245-9*, OK64329, Oak) Music Sales.

Complete Blues & Ragtime Guitar Player Book. Russ Shipton. (Illus.). 80p. 1986. pap. 15.95 (*0-7119-0907-5*, AM62910) Music Sales.

Complete Blues Guitar Book. Mike Christiansen. (Complete Book Ser.). 1993. 12.95 (*1-56222-311-9*, 94682); audio 9.98 (*1-56222-323-2*, 94682) Mel Bay.

Complete Boating Guide to the Connecticut River. 2nd ed. Ed. by Mark C. Borton et al. (Illus.). 240p. (Orig.). 1990. 11.95 (*0-9616371-1-0*) CT River Watershed.

Complete Body Massage: A Hands-on Manual. Fiona Harrold. LC 92-19415. (Illus.). 160p. 1992. pap. 14.95 (*0-8069-8718-9*) Sterling.

Complete Bond Book: A Guide to All Types of Fixed-Income Securities. David M. Darst. (Illus.). 352p. (Orig.). 1975. text ed. 49.95 (*0-07-017390-7*) McGraw.

***Complete Bone Adventures Vol. 2: Issues 7-12.** Jeff Smith. 144p. 1994. pap. 12.95 (*0-9636609-2-6*) Cartoon Bks.

Complete Bonsai Handbook. Darlene Dunton. 1978. pap. 12.95 (*0-8128-6008-X*, Scrbrough Hse) Madison Bks UPA.

Complete Booger Book. David E. Nordstran. Ed. by Sandra Bascom-Haase. (Illus.). 104p. (Orig.). 1994. pap. 7.95 (*0-9640360-1-0*) Guardian Car.

Complete Book Fashion Illustration. Sharon L. Tate. (C). 1990. text ed. 35.25 (*0-06-046679-0*) HarpCollege.

Complete Book for Artists for Israel. Phillip E. Goble. Ed. by Linda Morel. LC 92-70282. 1251p. 1992. pap. 49.95 (*0-939341-02-6*) AFI Intl Pubs.

Complete Book for Tracing Your Irish Ancestors. 2nd ed. (Illus.). 268p. 1981. text ed. 26.00 (*0-940134-02-0*) Irish Genealog.

Complete Book of Abs. Kurt Brungardt. LC 92-53816. 1993. pap. 20.00 (*0-679-74435-5*, Villard Bks) Random.

Complete Book of Acupuncture. Stephen T. Chang. LC 75-28762. (Illus.). 264p. 1976. pap. 12.95 (*0-89087-124-8*) Celestial Arts.

***Complete Book of Affordable Homes.** Archway Press Inc. Staff. 1994. pap. 8.95 (*1-882697-01-4*) Archway Pr.

Complete Book of All-Bisque Dolls, The. Mildred Seeley. LC 92-82867. 216p. 1992. text ed. 59.95 (*0-916809-59-5*) Scott Pubns MI.

Complete Book of Allergy Control. Stevens. 1983. 14.95 (*0-02-614450-6*) Macmillan.

Complete Book of Alpine Gardening. Richard Bird & John Kelly. (Illus.). 256p. 1992. 29.95 (*0-7063-7023-6*, Pub. by Ward Lock UK) Sterling.

***Complete Book of Alpine Gardening.** Richard Bird & John Kelly. (Illus.). 240p. 1995. pap. 16.95 (*0-7063-7341-3*, Pub. by Ward Lock UK) Sterling.

Complete Book of American Fish & Shellfish. Elizabeth Bjornskov. 1989. 8.99 (*0-517-67955-8*) Random Hse Value.

Complete Book of American Fish & Shellfish Cookery. Elizabeth Bjornskov. 499p. 1984. 18.95 (*0-317-03383-2*) HM.

Complete Book of Amulets & Talismans. Migene G. Gonzalez-Wippler. LC 91-19432. (Sourcebook Ser.). (Illus.). 302p. 1991. pap. 12.95 (*0-87542-287-X*) Llewellyn Pubns.

Complete Book of Anchoring & Mooring. 2nd rev. ed. Earl R. Hinz. (Illus.). 352p. 1994. 24.95 (*0-87033-452-2*) Cornell Maritime.

***Complete Book of Applique & Patchwork.** Lesley Turpin-Delport. (Illus.). 192p. 1995. pap. 19.95 (*1-85368-119-9*, Pub. by New Holland Pubs UK) Sterling.

Complete Book of Aquarium Fish. Ulrich Schliewen. 1992. pap. 13.95 (*0-8120-1350-6*) Barron.

Complete Book of Astrological Geomancy: The Master Divination System of Cornelius Agrippa. Priscilla Schwei & Ralph Pestka. LC 90-6224. (Modern Astrology Library). 444p. (Orig.). 1990. pap. 14.95 (*0-87542-704-9*) Llewellyn Pubns.

Complete Book of Baby & Child Care. rev. ed. Grace H. Ketterman. 560p. 1981. pap. 12.99 (*0-8007-1515-2*) Revell.

Complete Book of Baby Names: Traditional & Modern. Hilary Spence. 368p. (Orig.). 1993. pap. 13.95x (*0-572-01643-3*, Pub. by W Foulsham UK) Trans-Atl Phila.

Complete Book of Baking. 512p. 1993. 25.00 (*0-670-84768-2*, Viking) Viking Penguin.

Complete Book of Bananas. W. O. Lessard. Ed. by Joan Wilbur. (Illus.). 120p. 1992. text ed. 35.00 (*0-9633161-0-9*) W O Lessard.

Complete Book of Baseball Signs. Harold S. Southworth. 336p. (Orig.). 1993. pap. 10.00 (*0-380-76378-8*) Avon.

Complete Book of Bass Chords. Dana Roth. (Complete Book Ser.). 1993. 19.95 (*1-56222-548-0*, 94754) Mel Bay.

Complete Book of Bass Essentials: For 4 & 5 String Bass. Bunny Brunel. (Complete Book Ser.). 1993. 19.95 (*1-56222-367-4*, 94740) Mel Bay.

Complete Book of Bass Tech. Date not set. 19.95 (*1-56222-646-0*, 94523) Mel Bay.

Complete Book of Bathroom Design. Barbara Machowski & Consumer Reports Books Editors. (Illus.). 224p. (Orig.). 1993. pap. 18.95 (*0-89043-590-1*) Consumer Reports.

Complete Book of Beauty. Viktor Blevi & Gretchen Sween. 208p. (Orig.). 1993. pap. 10.00 (*0-380-76188-2*) Avon.

Complete Book of Bedroom Elegance. Caroline Wrey. LC 93-23163. (Illus.). 136p. 1994. 29.95 (*0-87951-509-0*) Overlook Pr.

Complete Book of Beer Drinking Games. rev. ed. Andy Griscom et al. LC 94-22068. (Illus.). 144p. 1994. pap. 8.95 (*0-914457-65-9*) Mustang Pub.

Complete Book of Bible Literacy. Mark D. Taylor. LC 92-22170. 1992. 9.99 (*0-8423-1072-X*) Tyndale.

Complete Book of Bible Promises for Kids. 318p. (J). (gr. 1-6). 1994. pap. 12.99 (*0-8423-0526-2*) Tyndale.

Complete Book of Bible Proverbs for Kids. 320p. (J). (gr. 1-6). 1994. pap. 12.95 (*0-8423-0527-0*) Tyndale.

Complete Book of Bible Puzzles, No. 1. Randy Petersen. 1992. pap. 7.99 (*0-8423-1067-3*) Tyndale.

Complete Book of Bible Puzzles, No. 2. Randy Petersen. 1992. pap. 7.99 (*0-8423-1079-7*) Tyndale.

***Complete Book of Bible Quotations.** Ed. by Mark Levine & Eugene Rachlis. 592p. 1994. 10.95 (*1-56865-103-1*, GuildAmerica) Dblday Bk Music.

Complete Book of Bible Quotations. Mark L. Levine. 1989. pap. 18.00 (*0-671-70551-2*) PB.

Complete Book of Bible Trivia. J. Stephen Lang. 400p. 1988. pap. 11.99 (*0-8423-0421-5*) Tyndale.

Complete Book of Bicycling. 4th ed. Eugene A. Sloane. (Illus.). 736p. 1988. pap. 15.95 (*0-671-65802-6*, Fireside) S&S Trade.

Complete Book of Birdhouse Construction for Woodworkers. Scott D. Campbell. (Crafts Ser.). 48p. (Orig.). 1984. pap. 1.95 (*0-486-24407-5*) Dover.

Complete Book of Birdhouses & Feeders. Monica Russo & Robert Dewire. (Illus.). 128p. 1990. 8.99 (*0-517-69314-3*) Random Hse Value.

Complete Book of Blues Guitar Licks & Phrases. Austin Sicard, Jr. (Complete Book Ser.). 1993. 12.95 (*1-56222-288-0*, 94687); audio 9.98 (*1-56222-296-1*, 94687) Mel Bay.

Complete Book of Boating. 2nd ed. Ernest A. Zadig. LC 76-16006. (Illus.). 1976. 14.95 (*0-13-157503-1*) P-H.

Complete Book of Bonsai: A Practical Guide to Its Art & Cultivation. Harry Tomlinson. (Illus.). 224p. 1991. 30.00 (*1-55859-118-4*) Abbeville Pr.

Complete Book of Braids. (Illus.). 128p. 1993. 9.98 (*0-7853-0282-4*, 3617600) Pubns Intl Ltd.

Complete Book of Braids. Linda S. Ksiazek. (Illus.). 152p. 1991. pap. 7.95 (*0-681-41128-7*) Longmeadow Pr.

Complete Book of Bread Machine Baking. Trillium Health Products Nutritionists Staff & Michael Murray. LC 92-32285. 256p. 1993. pap. 12.95 (*1-55958-283-9*) Prima Pub.

Complete Book of Breastfeeding. rev. ed. Marvin S. Eiger & Sally W. Olds. 224p. 1985. mass mkt. 5.99 (*0-553-26232-7*) Bantam.

Complete Book of Breastfeeding. rev. ed. Marvin S. Eiger & Sally W. Olds. LC 86-40201. (Illus.). 320p. 1986. pap. 7.95 (*0-89480-153-8*, 1153) Workman Pub.

Complete Book of Bridge. 2nd ed. Terence Reese & Albert Dormer. LC 84-28767. 475p. 1985. pap. 13.95 (*0-571-13528-5*) Faber & Faber.

Complete Book of Budgerigars. Stanley Moizer & Barbara Moizer. (Illus.). 144p. 1988. 16.95 (*0-8120-6059-8*) Barron.

Complete Book of Bulbs, Corms, Tubers, & Rhizomes. Brian Mathew & Philip Swindells. LC 93-13775. (Illus.). 240p. 1994. 30.00 (*0-89577-546-8*) RD Assn.

Complete Book of Business Forms. Richard G. Stuart. LC 91-67661. (Successful Business Library). 234p. 1992. pap. 19.95 (*1-55571-107-3*); ring bd. 49.95 (*1-55571-103-0*) Oasis Pr OR.

Complete Book of Business Forms & Agreements. Cliff Roberson. LC 93-24204. 1993. 3.5 hd 79.95 (*0-07-911611-6*) McGraw.

***Complete Book of Business Math: Every Manager's Guide to Analyzing Facts & Figures.** Joel G. Siegel. 1995. text ed. 59.95 (*0-07-057624-6*) McGraw.

Complete Book of Business Plans: Simple Steps to Writing a Powerful Business Plan. Joseph A. Covello & Brian J. Hazelgren. (Small Business Sourcebooks Ser.). (Illus.). 288p. 1994. 29.95 (*0-942061-40-3*, Sourcebooks Trade); pap. 19.95 (*0-942061-41-1*, Sourcebooks Trade) Sourcebks.

***Complete Book of Butt & Legs.** Kurt Brungardt et al. LC 94-29524. 1995. 20.00 (*0-679-75481-4*, Villard Bks) Random.

Complete Book of Cacti & Succulents. Terry Hewitt. LC 93-22107. (Illus.). 176p. 1993. 29.95 (*1-56458-337-6*) Dorling Kindersley.

Complete Book of Cake Decorating with Sugarpaste. Sylvia Coward. 176p. (C). 1988. 110.00 (*1-85368-000-1*, Pub. by New Holland Pubs UK) St Mut.

Complete Book of Cake Decorating with Sugarpaste. Sylvia Coward. (Illus.). 176p. 1994. pap. 19.95 (*1-85368-242-X*, Pub. by New Holland Pubs UK) Sterling.

Complete Book of Calligraphy. Emma M. Butterworth. 1991. pap. 10.95 (*0-7225-0704-6*) Thorsons SF.

***Complete Book of Calligraphy.** C. Young. (Practical Guides Ser.). (Illus.). 80p. (YA). (gr. 5 up). 1995. pap. 9.95 (*0-7460-2146-1*, Usborne) EDC.

Complete Book of Candlewick Embroidery. Sue Millard. (Illus.). 96p. 1994. pap. 14.95 (*1-85368-150-4*, Pub. by New Holland Pubs UK) Sterling.

Complete Book of Car Maintenance & Repair. Jay Hirsch. 1977. 14.95 (*0-684-14900-1*, Scribners) S&S Trade.

Complete Book of Caribbean Cooking. Elisabeth L. Ortiz. 432p. 1986. mass mkt. 5.95 (*0-345-33256-3*) Ballantine.

Complete Book of Caricature. Bob Staake. (Illus.). 134p. 1991. 18.99 (*0-89134-367-9*, 30283) North Light Bks.

Complete Book of Cat Care. Katrin Behrend & Monika Wegler. 144p. 1991. pap. 10.95 (*0-8120-4613-7*) Barron.

***Complete Book of Cat Care.** Jan Olivi. 1994. 14.98 (*0-7858-0133-2*) Bk Sales Inc.

Complete Book of Cats. Yvonne Rees. 1993. 14.99 (*0-517-06593-2*) Random Hse Value.

Complete Book of Chess Stratagems. Fred Reinfeld. 188p. 1972. reprint ed. pap. 5.95 (*0-486-20690-4*) Dover.

Complete Book of Chicken Wings. Joie Warner. LC 85-60363. (Illus.). 112p. (Orig.). 1985. pap. 8.00 (*0-688-05713-6*) Hearst Bks.

Complete Book of Children's Activities. Melanie Rice. LC 92-30859. (J). 1993. pap. 9.95 (*1-85697-907-5*, Kingfisher LKC) LKC.

Complete Book of Children's Everyday Ailments & Emergencies. Martin Edwards. 224p. (Orig.). 1995. pap. 11.95 (*0-572-01837-1*, Pub. by Foulsham UK) Atrium Pubs.

Complete Book of Children's Parties: Themes, Food, Cakes, Games. Clare Beaton. LC 92-53104. (Illus.). 96p. (Orig.). 1992. pap. 9.95 (*1-85697-807-9*, Kingfisher LKC) LKC.

Complete Book of Chinese Health & Healing. Daniel Reid. LC 93-26702. (Illus.). 464p. (Orig.). 1994. 27.50 (*0-87773-929-3*) Shambhala Pubns.

***Complete Book of Chinese Health & Healing: Guarding the Three Treasures.** Daniel Reid. LC 93-26702. 496p. 1994. pap. text ed. 17.00 (*1-57062-071-7*) Shambhala Pubns.

Complete Book of Coaching Youth Soccer. Simon Whitehead. (Illus.). 128p. (Orig.). 1991. pap. 12.95 (*0-8092-4072-6*) Contemp Bks.

***Complete Book of Cocktails & Punches.** Michalski. 1995. 12.98 (*1-56138-477-1*) Courage Bks.

C

An Asterisk (*) at the beginning of an entry indicates that the title is appearing in BIP for the first time.

Complete Book of Collectible Cars: 1930-1980. Consumer Guide Auto Editors. 1985. 14.98 (*0-517-47934-6*) Random Hse Value.

Complete Book of Collection Letters, Telephone Scripts, & Faxes. Cecil J. Bond. LC 93-49991. 1994. text ed. 69.95 (*0-07-006605-1*) McGraw.

Complete Book of Combat Handgunning. Chuck Taylor. (Illus.). 200p. 1982. pap. 16.95 (*0-87364-327-5*) Paladin Pr.

***Complete Book of Companion Gardening.** Bob Flowerdew. (Illus.). 176p. 1995. pap. 22.95 (*1-85626-171-9*, Pub. by C Kyle) Trafalgar.

Complete Book of Comprehensives. Robert Cullinane. (Illus.). 240p. 1990. pap. 34.95 (*0-442-21742-0*) Van Nos Reinhold.

***Complete Book of Conservatory Plants.** William Davidson & Jane Bland. (Illus.). 256p. 1995. pap. 19.95 (*0-7063-7340-5*, Pub. by Ward Lock UK) Sterling.

Complete Book of Container Gardening. Peter McHoy et al. Ed. by Alan Toogood. (Illus.). 192p. 1993. 29.95 (*0-943955-66-1*) Trafalgar.

Complete Book of Contemporary Business Letters. Strategic Communications Staff. Ed. by Stephen P. Elliott. 470p. 1989. pap. 19.95 (*0-929543-07-6*) Round Lake Pub.

Complete Book of Corporate Forms. Ted Nicholas. LC 80-67502. 256p. 1990. 69.95 (*0-913864-54-4*, 5615-06, Enter-Dearbrn) Dearborn Finan.

Complete Book of Corporate Forms. rev. ed. Ted Nicholas. LC 92-19051. 245p. 1992. pap. 19.95 (*0-7931-0488-2*, 561554) Dearborn Finan.

Complete Book of Corporate Legal Forms. Daniel Sitarz. (Legal Self-Help Ser.). 248p. (Orig.). 1993. pap. 18.95 (*0-935755-08-X*) Nova Pub IL.

Complete Book of Covers from the New Yorker 1925-1989. New Yorker Magazine Editors. LC 89-45280. (Illus.). 400p. 1989. 75.00 (*0-394-57841-4*) Knopf.

***Complete Book of Creative Crafts: A Perfect Source of Inspirational Projects & Decorative.** Heather Dillon. 1994. 19.98 (*0-8317-1369-0*) Smithmark.

Complete Book of Curtains & Drapes. Caroline Wrey. (Illus.). 144p. 1991. 29.95 (*0-87951-430-2*) Overlook Pr.

***Complete Book of Decorating Techniques.** Linda Gray & Jocasta Innes. 1995. pap. 19.95 (*0-316-32757-3*) Little.

Complete Book of Decorative Paint Techniques. Annie Sloan & K. Gwynn. 1990. 19.99 (*0-517-02265-6*) Random Hse Value.

Complete Book of Deer Hunting. Byron W. Dalrymple. 256p. pap. 11.95 (*0-88317-050-7*) Stoeger Pub Co.

***Complete Book of Dental Remedies: A Practical Guide to Nutritional & Conventional Dental Care.** Flora Parsa-Stay. 220p. 1995. pap. 12.95 (*0-89529-657-8*) Avery Pub.

Complete Book of Desserts. 1991. 14.99 (*0-517-03388-7*) Random Hse Value.

Complete Book of Disco & Ballroom Dancing. A. T. Kilbride. (Ballroom Dance Ser.). 1986. lib. bdg. 150.00 (*0-8490-3258-X*) Gordon Pr.

Complete Book of Disco & Ballroom Dancing. A. T. Kilbride. (Ballroom Dance Ser.). 1985. lib. bdg. 78.50 (*0-87700-850-7*) Revisionist Pr.

Complete Book of Dog Care. Ulrich Klever. (Illus.). 176p. 1989. pap. 10.95 (*0-8120-4158-5*) Barron.

***Complete Book of Dog Care.** Jan Olivi. 1994. 14.98 (*0-7858-0132-4*) Bk Sales Inc.

Complete Book of Dog Care. rev. ed. Leon F. Whitney & George D. Whitney. LC 84-28763. (Illus.). 480p. 1985. pap. 12.50 (*0-385-15547-6*) Doubleday.

Complete Book of Dog Health. Animal Medical Center Staff et al. Ed. by Sean Frawley. 272p. 1990. pap. 15.00 (*0-87605-455-6*) Howell Bk.

Complete Book of Dog Health: The Animal Medical Center. William J. Kay & Elizabeth Randolph. 253p. 1985. 19.95 (*0-02-600930-7*) Macmillan.

Complete Book of Dog Nutrition. Lauri Amato. (Illus.). 1995. write for info. (*0-87714-148-7*) Denlingers.

Complete Book of Dog Obedience: The Guide for Trainers. 4th ed. Blanche Saunders. LC 77-91206. (Illus.). 288p. 1978. 21.95 (*0-87605-459-9*) Howell Bk.

Complete Book of Dogs. A. J. Barker & H. A. Barker. 192p. 1992. 14.98 (*0-681-41766-8*) Longmeadow Pr.

Complete Book of Dogs. Outlet Staff. 1993. 14.99 (*0-517-06594-0*) Random Hse Value.

Complete Book of Doll Making & Collecting. 2nd rev. ed. Catherine Christopher. LC 76-102176. 1970. reprint ed. pap. 6.50 (*0-486-22066-4*) Dover.

Complete Book of Doll Making & Collecting. 2nd rev. ed. Catherine Christopher. (Illus.). 19.75 (*0-8446-0058-X*) Peter Smith.

Complete Book of Drafting. Madelyn Van der Hoogt. (Illus.). 144p. 1993. pap. 19.95 (*0-916658-51-1*, 92-060840) Shuttle Craft.

Complete Book of Drawing. (Illus.). 128p. (J). (gr. 5 up). 1994. lib. bdg. 21.96 (*0-88110-670-4*, Usborne); pap. 15.95 (*0-7460-1662-X*, Usborne) EDC.

Complete Book of Dreams. Edwin Raphael. 344p. (Orig.). 1995. pap. 11.95 (*0-572-01714-6*, Pub. by Foulsham UK) Atrium Pubs.

Complete Book of Dried Flowers. Malcolm Hillier & Colin Hilton. 1987. 24.95 (*0-671-61939-X*) S&S Trade.

***Complete Book of Duplicate Bridge.** Kay-Silodor. Date not set. 14.95 (*0-910791-92-9*, 4705) Devyn Pr.

Complete Book of Dwarf Cichlids. Hans-Joachim Richter. Tr. by William Charlton. (Illus.). 208p. (C). 1988. lib. bdg. 29.95 (*0-86622-701-6*, TS-121) TFH Pubns.

Complete Book of Edible Landscaping: Home Landscaping with Food-Bearing Plants & Resource-Saving Techniques. Rosalind Creasy. LC 81-14465. (Illus.). 400p. (Orig.). 1982. pap. 22.00 (*0-87156-278-2*) Sierra.

Complete Book of Effective Personal Letters. Robert Tietz & Elaine Tietz. LC 83-15949. 328p. 1986. 29.95 (*0-13-156414-5*, Busn) P-H.

Complete Book of Effective Personal Letters. Robert Tietz. 1989. pap. 9.95 (*0-13-156019-0*) P-H.

Complete Book of Egg Cookery. Ann Seranne. 1983. 14.95 (*0-02-609620-X*) Macmillan.

Complete Book of Elves. Colin McComb. (Advanced Dungeons & Dragons, Second Edition; Al-Qadim Ser.). (Illus.). 1992. 18.00 (*1-56076-376-0*) TSR Inc.

Complete Book of Emigrants: 1751-1776. Peter W. Coldham. 358p. 1993. 29.95 (*0-8063-1376-5*, 1106) Genealog Pub.

Complete Book of Emigrants in Bondage, 1614-1775. Peter W. Coldham. 920p. 1988. 60.00 (*0-8063-1221-1*, 1098) Genealog Pub.

Complete Book of Emigrants, 1607-1660. Peter W. Coldham. LC 87-80832. 600p. 1992. 34.95 (*0-8063-1192-4*) Genealog Pub.

Complete Book of Emigrants, 1661-1699. Peter W. Coldham. 900p. 1990. 49.95 (*0-8063-1282-3*, 1102) Genealog Pub.

Complete Book of Emigrants 1700-1750. Peter W. Coldham. 748p. 1992. 44.95 (*0-8063-1334-X*) Genealog Pub.

Complete Book of Entertaining From the Emily Post Institute. Elizabeth L. Post & Anthony Staffieri. 1982. pap. 8.50 (*0-686-97246-5*, Fireside) S&S Trade.

Complete Book of Erotic Art. Ed. by Eberhard Kronhausen. (Illus.). 1991. 24.99 (*0-517-24893-X*) Random Hse Value.

Complete Book of Essential Oils & Aromatherapy: Over 600 Natural, Non-Toxic & Fragrant Recipes to Create Health, Beauty & a Safe Home Environment. Valerie A. Worwood. LC 91-20111. 448p. 1991. pap. 18.95 (*0-931432-82-0*) New Wrld Lib.

Complete Book of Everlastings. Mark Silber & Terry Silber. 1993. 29.50 (*0-8446-6717-X*) Peter Smith.

Complete Book of Everlastings: Growing, Drying, & Designing with Dried Flowers. Mark Silber & Terry Silber. LC 87-45121. (Illus.). 224p. 1992. pap. 25.00 (*0-394-74370-9*) Knopf.

Complete Book of Fabric Painting. Linda S. Kanzinger. LC 85-73432. (Illus.). 260p. 1986. pap. 24.95 (*0-9616180-0-0*) Alcott Pr OR.

Complete Book of Fabric Painting. enl. rev. ed. Linda S. Kanzinger. LC 85-73432. (Illus.). 190p. 1993. pap. 32.95 (*0-9616180-1-9*) Alcott Pr OR.

Complete Book of Facial Cosmetic Surgery. Dennis P. Cirillo & Mark Rubenstein. write for info. (*0-318-59567-2*) S&S Trade.

Complete Book of Family Aromatherapy. Joan Radford. 192p. Date not set. pap. 11.95 (*0-572-01622-0*, Pub. by W Foulsham UK) Trans-Atl Phila.

***Complete Book of Fashion Illustration.** 3rd ed. Sharon L. Tate & Mona S. Edwards. LC 95-1946. 1995. text ed. 36.00 (*0-13-059222-6*) P-H.

Complete Book of Feature Writing. Leonard Witt. 278p. 1991. 18.95 (*0-89879-470-6*) Writers Digest.

Complete Book of Festive Vegetarian Recipes. Jean Conil. 1994. pap. 11.95 (*0-572-01815-0*, Pub. by W Foulsham UK) Trans-Atl Phila.

***Complete Book of Fighters: An Illustrated Encyclopedia of Every Fighter Aircraft Built & Flown.** Green & Swanborough. (Illus.). 608p. 1995. 59.98 (*0-8317-3939-8*) Smithmark.

Complete Book of Fingermath. Edwin M. Lieberthal. (Illus.). 1979. text ed. 21.96 (*0-07-037680-8*) McGraw.

Complete Book of Fingerpicking. Date not set. 15.99 (*0-7866-0098-5*, 95216); audio 9.98 (*0-7866-0099-3*, 95216C) Mel Bay.

Complete Book of Firearms. Sergio Masini. 1988. 19.99 (*0-517-66947-1*) Random Hse Value.

Complete Book of Flowers. 2nd ed. Denise Diamond. (Illus.). 312p. 1990. pap. 16.95 (*1-55643-079-5*) North Atlantic.

Complete Book of Fly Fishing. 2nd ed. Tom McNally. LC 93-9152. 1993. 29.95 (*0-87742-345-8*, Ragged Mntn) Intl Marine.

Complete Book of Fly Fishing. 2nd ed. Tom McNally. 1993. 29.95 (*0-07-045672-0*) McGraw.

Complete Book of Fly Tying. Eric Leiser. LC 77-74975. 1977. 27.50 (*0-394-40047-X*) Knopf.

Complete Book of Flyfishing. 1990. 19.99 (*0-517-69328-3*) Random Hse Value.

Complete Book of Foaling. Karen E. Hayes. (Illus.). 288p. 1993. 30.00 (*0-87605-951-5*) Howell Bk.

Complete Book of Food Counts. Corinne T. Netzer. 1991. mass mkt. 6.99 (*0-440-21271-5*) Dell.

Complete Book of Forms for Managing the Preschool Program. Kathleen Watkins & Lucius Durant. 256p. 1990. spiral bd. 34.95 (*0-87628-232-X*) Ctr Appl Res.

Complete Book of Forms for Managing the School Library Media Center. Ruth Toor & Hilda K. Weisburg. 256p. 1982. spiral bd. 34.95 (*0-87628-229-X*) Ctr Appl Res.

Complete Book of Forms for the School Health Professional: Ready-to-Use Forms for the School Health Professional. Jerry Newton. 480p. 1987. text ed. 34.95 (*0-13-156498-6*) P-H.

Complete Book of Fortune. 1990. 9.99 (*0-517-02723-2*) Random Hse Value.

Complete Book of Fortune. Christine Carswell. 1989. 14.95 (*0-7011-3380-5*) Random.

Complete Book of Fruit Growing in Australia. Louis Glowinski. (Illus.). 400p. 1995. 55.00 (*0-85091-401-9*, Pub. by Lothian Pub AT) Seven Hills Bk.

***Complete Book of Fund-Raising Writing.** Don Fey. LC 95-76071. 176p. 1995. 39.95 (*0-9645356-0-2*) Morris-Lee Pub.

***Complete Book of Furniture Restoration.** Tristan Salazar. 1994. 15.99 (*0-517-12023-2*) Random Hse Value.

Complete Book of Gambits. Raymond Keene. (Batsford Chess Library). 224p. 1993. pap. 19.95 (*0-8050-2635-5*, Owl) H Holt & Co.

Complete Book of Garden Design, Construction & Planting. David Stevens et al. (Illus.). 256p. 1991. 29.95 (*0-7063-6964-5*, Pub. by Ward Lock UK) Sterling.

Complete Book of Garden Design, Construction & Planting. David Stevens et al. (Illus.). 256p. 1994. pap. 16.95 (*0-7063-7234-4*, Pub. by Ward Lock UK) Sterling.

Complete Book of Gardening. Brian Leverett. (Illus.). (Orig.). 1994. pap. 17.95 (*0-572-01986-6*, Pub. by W Foulsham UK) Trans-Atl Phila.

Complete Book of Gnomes & Halflings. Douglas Niles. (Advanced Dungeons & Dragons, Second Edition; Al-Qadim Ser.). (Illus.). 1993. pap. 15.00 (*1-56076-573-9*) TSR Inc.

Complete Book of Golf Games. Scott Johnston. LC 95-2890. (Illus.). 96p. 1995. pap. 9.95 (*0-914457-55-1*) Mustang Pub.

***Complete Book of Greed: The Strange & Amazing History of Human Excess.** M. Hirsch Goldberg. 1995. 9.70 (*0-688-14231-1*, Quill) Morrow.

Complete Book of Greek Cooking: The Recipe Club of Saint Paul's Church. St. Paul's Greek Orthodox Cathedral, Recipe Club Staff. LC 89-45708. (Illus.). 352p. 1991. reprint ed. pap. 18.00 (*0-06-092129-3*, PL) HarpC.

Complete Book of Greyhounds. Ed. by Julia Barnes. (Illus.). 224p. 1994. 29.95 (*0-87605-189-1*) Howell Bk.

Complete Book of Guitar Chords, Scales & Arpeggios. William Bay. (Complete Book Ser.). 1993. 19.95 (*1-56222-526-X*, 94792); audio 9.95 (*0-685-63907-X*, 94792) Mel Bay.

Complete Book of Guitar Technique. Sal Salvador. (Complete Book Ser.). 1993. 15.00 (*1-56222-557-X*, 94845) Mel Bay.

Complete Book of Hanukah. Kinneret Chiel. (Illus.). (J). (gr. 6-8). pap. 6.95 (*0-87068-367-5*) Ktav.

***Complete Book of Hardanger.** Janny Geldens. (Illus.). 108p. 1995. write for info. (*1-86315-073-0*) Lacis Pubns.

***Complete Book of Hardy Perennials.** Richard Bird. (Illus.). 256p. 1995. pap. 16.95 (*0-7063-7360-X*, Pub. by Ward Lock UK) Sterling.

Complete Book of Harmony. Date not set. 19.95 (*1-56222-994-X*, 95112) Mel Bay.

Complete Book of Herbs. Emma Callery. LC 93-85549. (Illus.). 128p. 1994. 14.98 (*1-56138-351-1*) Courage Bks.

Complete Book of Herbs. Clevely & Richmond. (Illus.). 256p. 1995. 19.98 (*0-8317-1164-7*) Smithmark.

Complete Book of Herbs: A Practical Guide to Growing & Using Herbs. Lesley Bremness. 1988. pap. 30.00 (*0-670-81894-1*, Viking Studio) Studio Bks.

Complete Book of Herbs: A Practical Guide to Growing & Using Herbs. Lesley Bremness. (Illus.). 288p. 1994. 16.95 (*0-14-023802-6*, Viking Studio) Studio Bks.

Complete Book of Herbs & Spices. Sarah Garland. LC 93-1089. (Illus.). 288p. 1993. reprint ed. 35.00 (*0-89577-499-2*) RD Assn.

Complete Book of Herbs, Spices & Condiments. Carol Rinzler. 224p. 1990. 19.95 (*0-8160-2008-6*) Facts on File.

Complete Book of Herbs, Spices, & Condiments: From Garden to Kitchen to Medicine Chest. Carol A. Rinzler. (Illus.). 208p. (Orig.). 1991. pap. 12.00 (*0-8050-1618-X*, Owl) H Holt & Co.

Complete Book of Holograms: How They Work & How to Make Them. Joseph E. Kasper & Steven A. Feller. LC 87-16209. (Science Editions Ser.). (Illus.). 216p. 1987. pap. text ed. 22.95 (*0-471-62941-3*) Wiley.

Complete Book of Home Decorating. Barbara Mayer. 1994. pap. 19.95 (*1-56799-063-0*, Friedman-Fairfax) M Friedman Pub Grp Inc.

Complete Book of Home Decorating: A Step-by-Step Guide. Mike Lawrence. 1994. 19.98 (*0-8317-6508-9*) Smithmark.

Complete Book of Home Design. rev. ed. Mary Gilliatt. 1989. 40.00 (*0-316-31406-4*) Little.

Complete Book of Home Design, Vol. 1. Mary Gilliatt. 1984. 29.95 (*0-316-31371-8*) Little.

Complete Book of Home Details. Outlet Staff. 1993. 29.99 (*0-517-06113-9*) Random Hse Value.

Complete Book of Home Environmental Hazards. Roberta Altman. (Illus.). 304p. 1990. 24.95 (*0-8160-2095-7*) Facts on File.

Complete Book of Home Environmental Hazards. Roberta Altman. (Illus.). 304p. 1991. reprint ed. pap. 12.95 (*0-8160-2419-7*) Facts on File.

Complete Book of Home Inspection. 2nd ed. Norman Becker. (Illus.). 192p. (Orig.). 1992. 19.95 (*0-8306-3786-9*, 4100); pap. 12.95 (*0-8306-3785-0*, 4100) TAB Bks.

Complete Book of Home Inspection for the Buyer or Owner. Norman Becker. 1983. 22.75 (*0-8446-6055-8*) Peter Smith.

Complete Book of Home Welding. John Todd. (Illus.). 352p. 1986. 29.95 (*0-8306-0317-4*, NO. 2717); pap. 21.95 (*0-8306-2717-0*) TAB Bks.

Complete Book of Homeopathy. Michael Weiner & Kathleen Gross. LC 88-38463. 312p. 1989. pap. 9.95 (*0-89529-412-5*) Avery Pub.

Complete Book of Hors-d'Oeuvres. David Rogers. 288p. (Orig.). 1992. pap. 29.95 (*0-273-03779-X*, Pub. by Pitman Pub Ltd UK) Trans-Atl Phila.

Complete Book of Horse Care. Tim Hawcroft. (Illus.). 208p. 1983. 27.50 (*0-947116-77-X*) Howell Bk.

Complete Book of Horses. James Kerswell. 1993. 14.99 (*0-517-06595-9*) Random Hse Value.

***Complete Book of Hot Wheels.** Bob Parker. (Illus.). 160p. (Orig.). 1995. pap. 19.95 (*0-88740-827-3*) Schiffer.

Complete Book of Houseplants. John Evans. (Illus.). 256p. 1994. 27.95 (*0-670-85868-4*, Viking Studio) Studio Bks.

Complete Book of How to Succeed with Women. Victor Wild. (Illus.). 208p. (Orig.). 1981. pap. 11.95 (*0-938444-01-8*) Wildfire Pub.

***Complete Book of Humorous Art.** Bob Staake. (Illus.). 144p. 1995. 24.99 (*0-89134-623-6*) North Light Bks.

Complete Book of Hypertalk Two. Dan Shafer. 1990. pap. 26.95 (*0-201-57082-3*) Addison-Wesley.

Complete Book of Illustrated K-3 Alphabet Games & Activities. Patricia T. Muncy. 1980. 24.95 (*0-87628-230-3*) Ctr Appl Res.

Complete Book of Improvisation - Composition & Funk Techniques: Essentials & Augmentations for the Vital Self-Instrument in Jazz Music - Theory, Practices & Life Parallels. Howard C. Harris, Jr. & William Fielder. (Illus.). 178p. (Orig.). 1982. 21.95 (*0-940026-00-7*) DeMos Music.

Complete Book of Incense, Oils & Brews. rev. ed. Scott Cunningham. LC 89-35510. (Practical Magick Ser.). (Illus.). 288p. 1989. pap. 14.95 (*0-87542-128-8*) Llewellyn Pubns.

Complete Book of Indian Cookery. Premila Lal. 1994. pap. 11.95 (*0-572-01938-6*, Pub. by W Foulsham UK) Trans-Atl Phila.

Complete Book of Inflatable Boats. Don Hubbard. LC 79-27460. (Illus.). 256p. (Orig.). 1980. pap. 5.95 (*0-930030-18-4*) Western Marine Ent.

Complete Book of Insults, Boasts & Riddles. William H. Roylance. 1971. pap. text ed. 9.95 (*0-13-157479-5*, Reward) P-H.

***Complete Book of Insurance: The Consumer's Guide to Insuring Your Life, Health, Property & Income.** rev. ed. Ben G. Baldwin. 275p. 1995. 19.95 (*1-55738-880-6*) Probus Pub Co.

***Complete Book of Interviewing: Everything You Need to Know from Both Sides of the Table.** Arnold B. Kanter. LC 94-27672. 1995. 15.00 (*0-8129-2281-6*, Times Bks) Random.

Complete Book of Irish Family Names. Michael C. O'Laughlin. 311p. 1987. 15.00 (*0-940134-41-1*) Irish Genealog.

Complete Book of Japanese Cooking. Elisabeth L. Ortiz & Mitsuko Endo. LC 76-16008. (Illus.). 264p. 1976. 12.50 (*0-87131-212-3*); pap. 6.95 (*0-87131-321-9*) M Evans.

Complete Book of Japanese Cooking. Elisabeth L. Ortiz. 1994. 8.98 (*0-88365-854-2*) Galahad Bks.

Complete Book of Jewish Observance. Leo Trepp. LC 79-1352. (Illus.). 1979. 25.00 (*0-87441-281-1*) Behrman.

Complete Book of Jewish Observance. Leo Trepp. LC 79-1352. (Behrman House Book Ser.). (Illus.). 370p. 1980. 25.00 (*0-671-41797-5*) Summit Bks.

Complete Book of Jiffy Needle Tatting. Selma Morin & Ed Morin. Ed. by Workbasket Magazine Staff. (Illus.). 156p. (Orig.). 1992. pap. 18.95 (*0-86675-338-9*) KC Pub.

Complete Book of Juicing: Your Delicious Guide to Healthful Living. Michael T. Murray. (Illus.). 250p. (Orig.). 1992. pap. 12.95 (*1-55958-268-5*) Prima Pub.

***Complete Book of Jumps.** Ed Jacoby & Bob Fraley. (Illus.). 160p. (Orig.). 1995. pap. write for info. (*0-87322-673-9*, PJAC0673) Human Kinetics.

Complete Book of Karate Weapons. Theodore Gambordella. (Illus.). 256p. 1981. pap. 20.00 (*0-87364-206-6*) Paladin Pr.

Complete Book of Kitchen Wisdom. Frieda Arkin. 1993. 9.98 (*0-88365-823-2*) Galahad Bks.

Complete Book of Knife Fighting. William Cassidy. (Illus.). 136p. 1993. text ed. 25.00 (*0-87364-029-2*) Paladin Pr.

Complete Book of Les Miserables. Edward Behr. (Illus.). 192p. 1993. pap. 17.95 (*1-55970-156-0*) Arcade Pub Inc.

Complete Book of Locks & Locksmithing. 1991. lib. bdg. 88.95 (*0-8490-5246-7*) Gordon Pr.

Complete Book of Locks & Locksmithing. 3rd ed. C. A. Roper & Bill Phillips. 1991. pap. 19.95 (*0-07-155241-3*) McGraw.

Complete Book of Locks & Locksmithing. 3rd ed. C. A. Roper & Bill Phillips. (Illus.). 360p. 1991. 26.95 (*0-8306-7522-1*, 3522); pap. 19.95 (*0-8306-3522-X*) TAB Bks.

***Complete Book of Locks & Locksmithing.** 4th ed. Phillips. 1995. pap. text ed. 24.95 (*0-07-049866-0*) McGraw.

Complete Book of Long-Distance & Competitive Cycling. Tom Doughty et al. 1983. pap. 10.95 (*0-671-42434-3*) S&S Trade.

Complete Book of Macaws. Rosemary Low. 144p. 1990. 18.95 (*0-8120-6073-3*) Barron.

Complete Book of Machine Embroidery & Applique. Robbie Fanning. LC 86-46715. 304p. 1986. pap. 18.95 (*0-8019-7648-0*) Chilton.

Complete Book of Machine Quilting. 2nd ed. Robbie Fanning. 288p. 1994. pap. 24.95 (*0-8019-8388-6*) Chilton.

Complete Book of Macra-Tack. 4th rev. ed. Rebecca Albertson. (Illus.). 50p. (J). (gr. 3-12). 1983. spiral bd. 9.95 (*0-9611536-0-1*) Macra-Tack Inc.

Complete Book of Magic. C. Evans & I. Keable-Elliott. (Magic Guides Ser.). (Illus.). 64p. (J). 1989. lib. bdg. 13.96 (*0-88110-383-7*); pap. 7.95 (*0-7460-0300-5*) EDC.

***Complete Book of Magic & Magic Tricks.** C. Evans et al. (Magic Guides Ser.). (Illus.). 128p. (J). 1992. 12.95 (*0-7460-1188-1*) EDC.

Complete Book of Magic & Witchcraft. Kathryn Paulsen. 1970. pap. 4.99 (*0-451-16832-1*, E92712, Sig) NAL-Dutton.

***Complete Book of Make-up: Quick Tricks & Simple Secrets for Smart, Confident Beauty.** Lorin Cole. 1995. spiral bd. 7.95 (*0-681-45324-9*) Longmeadow Pr.

Complete Book of Making Miniatures. Thelma R. Newman & Virginia H. Merrill. (Arts & Crafts Ser.). (Illus.). 328p. 1975. pap. 16.95 (*0-517-52460-0*, Crown) Crown Pub Group.

C

An Asterisk (*) at the beginning of an entry indicates that the title is appearing in BIP for the first time. 1457

Complete Book of Marzipan. 2nd rev. ed. E. Storer. (Illus.). 167p. 1984. reprint ed. 36.00 (0-85334-317-9, Pub. by Elsevier Applied Sci UK) Elsevier.

Complete Book of MASH. Suzy Kalter. (Illus.). 240p. 1988. pap. 19.98 (0-8109-8083-5, Abradale Pr) Abrams.

Complete Book of Massage. Hudson C. Maxwell. 1988. pap. 17.00 (0-394-75975-3) Random.

Complete Book of Medical Symptoms in Children. Martin Edwards. 1994. pap. 9.95 (0-572-01922-X, Pub. by W Foulsham UK) Trans-Atl Phila.

*Complete Book of Menopause. Carol Landau et al. 368p. (Orig.). 1995. pap. 15.00 (0-399-51906-8, Perigree Bks) Berkley Pub.

Complete Book of Menopause: Every Woman's Guide to Good Health. Carol Landau et al. LC 93-38651. 352p. 1994. 22.95 (0-399-13946-X, Grosset-Putnam) Putnam Pub Group.

*Complete Book of Men's Health: The Essential Guide for Men & Women. Sarah Brewer. 1995. pap. 16.00 (0-7225-3019-6) Thorsons SF.

Complete Book of Mexican Cooking. Elisabeth Ortiz. 1994. 9.98 (0-88365-860-7) Galahad Bks.

Complete Book of Mexican Cooking. Elisabeth L. Ortiz. 304p. 1985. mass mkt. 5.99 (0-345-32559-1) Ballantine.

Complete Book of Mexican Cooking. Elisabeth L. Ortiz. LC 67-18534. (Illus.). 352p. 1967. 14.95 (0-87131-074-0); pap. 6.95 (0-87131-333-2) M Evans.

Complete Book of Microwave Baking. Marty Klinzman & Shirley Guy. 96p. (C). 1989. 90.00 (1-85368-060-5, Pub. by New Holland Pubs UK) St Mut.

Complete Book of Mixed Drinks: Over One Thousand Alcoholic & Non-Alcoholic Cocktails. Anthony D. Blue. LC 92-54840. 1993. pap. 16.00 (0-06-095007-2, PL) HarpC.

Complete Book of Model Business Letters. Martha W. Cresci. 298p. 1986. 21.95 (0-13-157438-8); 6.95 (0-13-157412-4) P-H.

Complete Book of Money Secrets. 498p. 1989. 35.00 (0-88723-022-9) Boardroom.

Complete Book of Motocross. Frank Melling. 1987. 29.95 (0-85429-473-2, Pub. by G T Foulis Ltd) Haynes Pubns.

Complete Book of Muslim & Parsi Names. Maneka Gandhi. (C). 1994. text ed. 29.00 (81-7223-100-8, Pub. by Indus Pub II) S Asia.

Complete Book of Natural & Medicinal Cures: How to Choose the Most Potent Healing Agents for over 200 Conditions & Diseases. Ed. by Prevention Magazine Health Book Editors. LC 94-4888. 1994. 29.95 (0-87596-190-8) Rodale Pr Inc.

Complete Book of Nature Crafts: How to Make 150 Beautiful Wreaths, Dried Flower Arrangements, Potpourris, Baskets, Dolls, Gifts, Decorative Accessories for the Home & Much More. Dawn Cusick et al. (Illus.). 256p. 1992. 26.95 (0-87596-141-X, 11-770-0) Rodale Pr Inc.

Complete Book of Needlecraft. Ida R. Duncan. LC 61-15020. (Illus.). 1972. pap. 3.95 (0-87140-265-3) Liveright.

Complete Book of Nineteen Ninety-One Baseball Cards. 1991. 15.99 (0-517-05673-9) Random Hse Value.

Complete Book of Opening Leads. Easley Blackwood. 475p. 1991. pap. 14.95 (0-910791-05-8) Devyn Pr.

Complete Book of Origami. Robert J. Lang. 160p. 1989. pap. 6.95 (0-486-25837-8) Dover.

Complete Book of Oscilloscopes. Stan Prentiss. 1992. pap. 16.95 (0-07-157781-5) McGraw.

Complete Book of Oscilloscopes. 2nd ed. Stan Prentiss. 320p. 1991. 26.95 (0-8306-3909-8); pap. 16.95 (0-8306-3908-X) TAB Bks.

*Complete Book of Paint Techniques. Penny Swift & Janek Szymanowski. (Illus.). 96p. 1995. pap. 14.95 (1-85368-306-X, Pub. by New Holland Pubs UK) Sterling.

Complete Book of Palmistry. Joyce Wilson. (Orig.). 1983. mass mkt. 4.99 (0-553-25595-9) Bantam.

Complete Book of PAN: The Card Game You'll Love for the Rest of Your Life! Howard S. Warshaw. (Orig.). (C). 1990. pap. text ed. 19.95 (0-9626724-1-6) Scott W Unltd.

Complete Book of Paper Mask Making. Michael Grater. 144p. 1984. pap. 4.95 (0-486-24712-0) Dover.

Complete Book of Parakeet Care. Annette Wolter & Monika Wegler. LC 93-11625. 1994. pap. 13.95 (0-8120-1688-2) Barron.

Complete Book of Parenting. Robert Mendelson. 1991. 9.99 (0-517-05670-4) Random Hse Value.

Complete Book of Parrots. Rosemary Low. 144p. 1989. 18.95 (0-8120-5971-9) Barron.

*Complete Book of Partner Massage & Aromatherapy. Royston Scott-Green. 1994. pap. 11.95 (0-572-01969-6, Pub. by W Foulsham UK) Trans-Atl Phila.

Complete Book of Pastry: Sweet & Savory. Bernard Clayton, Jr. (Illus.). 416p. 1984. pap. 13.00 (0-671-53074-7, Fireside) S&S Trade.

*Complete Book of Patio & Container Gardening. Robin Williams et al. (Illus.). 256p. 1995. pap. 16.95 (0-7063-7358-8, Pub. by Ward Lock UK) Sterling.

*Complete Book of Perennials. Graham Rice. LC 95-13645. 1996. write for info. (0-89577-825-4) RD Assn.

Complete Book of Personal Finance. Boardroom's Experts & Editors. LC 87-30948. 500p. 1989. 50.00 (0-88723-013-X) Boardroom.

Complete Book of Personal Legal Forms. Daniel Sitarz. (Legal Self-Help Ser.). 248p. (Orig.). 1993. pap. 16.95 (0-935755-10-1) Nova Pub IL.

*Complete Book of Pet Care. Peter Roach. (Illus.). 272p. 1995. 17.95 (0-87605-484-X) Howell Bk.

Complete Book of Pet Names. Renee Cowing. 8.95 (0-9626950-1-7) Fireplug CA.

Complete Book of Pet Names. Renee Cowing. LC 90-81851. 112p. (YA). 1990. 9.95 (0-9626950-2-5) Fireplug CA.

Complete Book of Photographic Lenses: How to Select & Use Optics for Every Format. Joe Meehan. (Illus.). 144p. 1991. pap. 22.50 (0-8174-3697-9, Amphoto) Watsn-Guptill.

Complete Book of Pizza. Louise Love. (Illus.). 100p. (Orig.). 1983. pap. 6.00 (0-930528-03-4) Sassafras Pr.

Complete Book of Plant Propagation. Graham Clarke & Alan Toogood. (Illus.). 256p. 1992. pap. 17.95 (0-7063-7079-1, Pub. by Ward Lock UK) Sterling.

*Complete Book of Pocketknife Repair: A Cotler's Manual. Kelly. 1995. pap. text ed. 10.95 (0-87341-387-3) Krause Pubns.

Complete Book of Pocketknife Repair: A Cutlers Manual. Ben Kelley, Jr. Ed. by J. Bruce Voyles. (Illus.). 129p. (Orig.). 1982. pap. 9.95 (0-911881-01-8) Am Blade Bk Serv.

Complete Book of Portable Power Tools Techniques. R. J. DeChristoforo. LC 87-13342. (Illus.). 388p. (Orig.). 1987. pap. 19.95 (0-8069-6502-9) Sterling.

Complete Book of Potpourri & Perfumery. Denise Greig. (Illus.). 112p. 1993. 24.95 (0-86417-461-6, Pub. by Kangaroo Pr AT) Seven Hills Bk.

Complete Book of Pottery Making. 2nd ed. John B. Kenny. LC 76-302. (Chilton's Creative Crafts Ser). (Illus.). 328p. 1976. pap. 22.95 (0-8019-5933-0) Chilton.

Complete Book of Power: How to Negotiate, Manipulate & Use Common Sense to Achieve Success. Renee Harmon. write for info. (0-318-59675-X) S&S Trade.

Complete Book of Power: Your Guide to the Professional Power Style. Renee Harmon. (Illus.). 208p. 1985. 18.95 (0-13-157611-9); pap. 8.95 (0-13-157603-8) P-H.

Complete Book of Practical Productivity. Leonard R. Sayles. LC 83-2759. 190p. 1983. 50.00 (0-932648-28-2) Boardroom.

Complete Book of Pregnancy & Childbirth. rev. ed. Sheila Kitzinger. LC 89-2260. (Illus.). 400p. 1989. 22.50 (0-394-58011-7) Knopf.

Complete Book of Preserving. Marye Cameron-Smith. LC 76-3976. 1976. 18.95 (0-672-52241-1, Bobbs) Macmillan.

Complete Book of Pruning. Duncan Coombs et al. (Illus.). 256p. 1994. pap. 16.95 (0-7063-7235-2, Pub. by Ward Lock UK) Sterling.

Complete Book of Raising Capital. Lawrence W. Tuller. 1993. 3.5 hd 59.95 (0-07-911697-3) McGraw.

Complete Book of Raising Livestock & Poultry. Ed. by Katie Thear & Alistair Fraser. (Illus.). 224p. (Orig.). 1980. pap. 42.50 (0-330-30158-6, Pub. by Pan Books UK) Trans-Atl Phila.

Complete Book of Ready-to-Finish Furniture. Lou Oates. (Illus.). 1984. 21.95 (0-13-158239-9, Busn); pap. 12.95 (0-13-158221-6, Busn) P-H.

Complete Book of Relaxation Techniques. Jenny Sutcliffe. LC 93-21237. 1994. 24.95 (1-882606-07-8); pap. 14.95 (1-882606-08-6) Peoples Med Soc.

Complete Book of Ribbon Embroidery. Heather Joynes. (Illus.). 128p. 1993. 24.95 (0-86417-482-9, Pub. by Kangaroo Pr AT) Seven Hills Bk.

Complete Book of Roasts, Boasts, & Toasts. Elmer Pasta. LC 82-6296. 375p. 1982. pap. 4.95 (0-13-158329-8, Parker Publishing Co) P-H.

Complete Book of Roses. John Mattock et al. (Illus.). 256p. 1994. 29.95 (0-7063-7163-1, Pub. by Ward Lock UK) Sterling.

*Complete Book of Roses. John Mattock et al. (Illus.). 240p. 1995. pap. 16.95 (0-7063-7359-6, Pub. by Ward Lock UK) Sterling.

Complete Book of Rug Hooking. Joan Moshimer. (Illus.). 176p. 1989. pap. 9.95 (0-486-25945-5) Dover.

Complete Book of Running. James F. Fixx. (Illus.). 1977. 24.00 (0-394-41159-5) Random.

Complete Book of Sauces. Sallie Williams. 256p. 1990. text ed. 21.00 (0-02-629391-9) Macmillan.

Complete Book of Scales, Cadences & Arpeggios. Brimhall & Abrill. (Beginning Skills Ser.). 1990. 5.95 (0-685-32028-6, T386) Hansen Ed Mus.

*Complete Book of Sea Kayaking. 4th ed. Derek C. Hutchinson. LC 94-46774. Orig. Title: Derek C. Hutchinson's Guide to Sea Kayaking. (Illus.). 192p. 1995. pap. 19.95 (1-56440-722-5) Globe Pequot.

Complete Book of Self-Hypnosis. John M. Yates & Elizabeth S. Wallace. LC 83-17430. 208p. 1984. 29.95 (0-8304-1033-3) Nelson-Hall.

Complete Book of Self-Hypnosis. John M. Yates. 1994. mass mkt. 4.95 (0-8041-9817-9) Ivy Books.

Complete Book of Seminole Patchwork. rev. ed. Beverly Rush & Lassie Wittman. Orig. Title: The Complete Book of Seminole Patchwork: From Traditional Methods to Contemporary Uses. (Illus.). 128p. 1993. reprint ed. pap. 7.95 (0-486-27617-1) Dover.

Complete Book of Seminole Patchwork: From Traditional Methods to Contemporary Uses see Complete Book of Seminole Patchwork

*Complete Book of Sewing Shortcuts. Schaeffer. Date not set. (0-8069-5432-9) Sterling.

Complete Book of Sewing Shortcuts. rev. ed. Claire B. Shaeffer. LC 81-8818. (Illus.). 256p. (J). (gr. 6 up). 1992. pap. 14.95 (0-8069-7564-4) Sterling.

Complete Book of Sewing Shortcuts. Claire B. Schaeffer. (Illus.). 256p. (C). 1990. reprint ed. lib. bdg. 37.00x (0-8095-7554-X) Borgo Pr.

Complete Book of Sexual Trivia. Leslee Welch. 128p. 1992. pap. 7.95 (0-8065-1347-0, Citadel Pr) Carol Pub Group.

Complete Book of Shaker Furniture. Timothy D. Rieman & Jean M. Burks. LC 92-47357. 1993. 75.00 (0-8109-3841-3) Abrams.

Complete Book of Shiatsu Therapy: Health & Vitality at Your Fingertips. Toru Namikoshi. LC 79-1963. (Illus.). 256p. 1994. pap. 19.00 (0-87040-461-X) Japan Pubns USA.

Complete Book of Sick Jokes. Max Rezwin. (Illus.). 192p. 1984. pap. 4.95 (0-8065-0761-6, Citadel Pr) Carol Pub Group.

Complete Book of Silk Painting. Diane Tuckman & Jan Janas. (Illus.). 128p. 1992. 24.95 (0-89134-422-5, 30362) North Light Bks.

Complete Book of Silk Screen Printing Production. Jacob I. Biegeleisen. (Illus.). (Orig.). (C). 1963. pap. 5.95 (0-486-21100-2) Dover.

Complete Book of Silk Screen Printing Production. Jacob I. Biegeleisen. (Illus.). (Orig.). 18.25 (0-8446-1677-X) Peter Smith.

Complete Book of Slowpitch Softball. rev. ed. Glen D. Eley. (Illus.). 100p. (Orig.). 1984. pap. 9.95 (0-940934-02-7) GDE Pubns OH.

Complete Book of Small Business Forms & Agreements. Gustav Berle. 1992. 49.95 (0-13-174632-4, Busn) P-H.

Complete Book of Small Business Legal Forms. Daniel Sitarz. (Legal Self-Help Ser.). 248p. (Orig.). 1991. pap. 17.95 (0-935755-03-9) Nova Pub IL.

*Complete Book of Small Business Legal Forms. 2nd ed. Daniel Sitarz. (Small Business Library). 256p. (Orig.). 1995. pap. 17.95 (0-935755-17-9) Nova Pub IL.

Complete Book of Snowboarding. K. C. Althen & Craig Althen. 176p. (Orig.). 1990. pap. 15.95 (0-8048-7035-7) C E Tuttle.

Complete Book of Soft Furnishings: Upholstery - Curtains & Blinds - Cushions & Covers. Dorothy Gates et al. (Illus.). 240p. 1993. pap. 14.95 (0-7063-7178-X, Pub. by Ward Lock UK) Sterling.

Complete Book of Softball: The Loonies' Guide to Playing & Enjoying the Game. Robert G. Meyer. LC 83-80707. (Illus.). 192p. (Orig.). 1984. pap. 14.95 (0-88011-212-3, PMEY0212) Human Kinetics.

Complete Book of Solitaire & Patience Games. Albert H. Morehead. (Illus.). 192p. 1983. mass mkt. 5.50 (0-553-26240-8) Bantam.

Complete Book of Soups & Stews. Bernard Clayton, Jr. (Illus.). 416p. 1987. pap. 13.00 (0-671-43864-6, Fireside) S&S Trade.

Complete Book of Southern African Birds. Ed. by Geoff Mclleron et al. 752p. (C). 1989. 500.00 (1-85368-019-2, Pub. by New Holland Pubs UK) St Mut.

Complete Book of Speech Communication: A Workbook of Ideas & Activities for Students of Speech & Theatre. Carol Marrs. Ed. by Arthur L. Zapel. LC 91-47621. (Illus.). 176p. (Orig.). 1992. pap. text ed. 12.95 (0-916260-87-9, B142) Meriwether Pub.

Complete Book of Spelling Demons. 2nd ed. Carl W. Salser & C. Theo Yerian. 86p. 1983. pap. text ed. 7.95 (0-89420-104-2, 411030); audio 158.95 (0-89420-243-X, 411000) Natl Book.

Complete Book of Spells, Ceremonies & Magic. Migene Gonzalez-Wippler. LC 88-8381. (Sourcebook Ser.). (Illus.). 400p. 1988. pap. 14.95 (0-87542-286-1) Llewellyn Pubns.

Complete Book of Spices: A Practical Guide to Spices & Aromatic Seeds. Jill Norman. LC 90-50371. (Illus.). 160p. 1991. 25.00 (0-670-83437-8, Viking Studio) Studio Bks.

*Complete Book of Spices: A Practical Guide to Spices & Aromatic Seeds. Jill Norman. (Illus.). 160p. 1995. 14.95 (0-14-023804-2, Viking Studio) Studio Bks.

Complete Book of Spices: Their Medical, Nutritional & Cooking Uses. John Heinerman. LC 82-80700. 1983. 15.95 (0-87983-347-5); pap. 12.95 (0-87983-281-9) Keats.

Complete Book of Sportfishing. 1988. 19.99 (0-517-66219-1) Random Hse Value.

Complete Book of Sports Medicine. Dominguez. 1979. 2.95 (0-684-16384-5, Scribners) S&S Trade.

Complete Book of Stationary Power Tool Techniques. Richard DeCristoforo. LC 87-29625. (Popular Science Ser.). (Illus.). 416p. (Orig.). 1988. pap. 19.95 (0-8069-6666-1) Sterling.

Complete Book of Steam Cookery: Tasty & Healthful Dishes from Around the World. Coralie Castle. 256p. 1990. spiral bd., pap. 12.95 (0-87477-366-0) J P Tarcher.

Complete Book of Stencilcraft. JoAnne Day. 224p. 1987. reprint ed. pap. 9.95 (0-486-25372-4) Dover.

Complete Book of Straw Craft & Corn Dollies: Techniques & Projects. Doris Johnson & Alec Coker. 64p. 1987. pap. 4.95 (0-486-25249-3) Dover.

*Complete Book of Stretching. Tony Lycholat. (Illus.). 96p. 1995. pap. 15.95 (1-85223-917-4, Pub. by Crowood Pr UK) Trafalgar.

Complete Book of Swimming. James E. Counsilman. LC 72-82682. (Illus.). 256p. (C). 1979. pap. 10.00 (0-689-70583-2, 246, Atheneum S&S) S&S Trade.

Complete Book of Swimming. Phillip Whitten. LC 92-56805. 416p. 1994. pap. 16.00 (0-679-74667-6) Random.

*Complete Book of Swords, 3 vols. in 1. Fred Saberhagen. 648p. 1985. 12.98 (1-56865-009-4, GuildAmerica) Dblday Bk Music.

Complete Book of Taekwon Do Forms. rev. ed. Keith D. Yates. (Illus.). 192p. 1988. pap. 23.95 (0-87364-492-1) Paladin Pr.

Complete Book of Tanning Skins & Furs. James Churchill. LC 83-9151. 224p. 1983. 18.95 (0-8117-1719-4) Stackpole.

Complete Book of Tarot: A Step-by-Step Guide to Help You Become a Better Reader of the Cards. Juliet Sharman-Burke. 160p. 1987. pap. 10.95 (0-312-00579-2) St Martin.

Complete Book of Tatting. Rebecca Jones. 1989. 20.00 (0-85219-652-0) Robin & Russ.

Complete Book of Tatting. Rebecca Jones. 112p. 1992. reprint ed. 20.00 (0-916896-39-0) Lacis Pubns.

Complete Book of Teddy Bears. 1989. 29.99 (0-517-69526-X) Random Hse Value.

Complete Book of the Cat. Angela Sayer. 1988. 14.99 (0-517-43735-X) Random Hse Value.

Complete Book of the Corvette. Consumer Guide Staff. 1988. 17.99 (0-517-63673-5) Random Hse Value.

Complete Book of the Dog. Robert Leighton. 1992. lib. bdg. 88.00 (0-8490-5225-4) Gordon Pr.

Complete Book of the Dog. Amanda O'Neil. 19.98 (1-55521-492-4) Bk Sales Inc.

Complete Book of the Ford Mustang. Consumer Guide Staff. 1989. 17.99 (0-517-67668-0) Random Hse Value.

Complete Book of the Gnomes. Rien Poorvliet & Wil Huygen. LC 94-4254. 1994. write for info. (0-8109-3195-8) Abrams.

Complete Book of the Great Musicians: A Course in Appreciation for Young Readers, 3 vols. Percy A. Scholes. 1990. reprint ed. lib. bdg. 210.00 (0-7812-9130-5) Rprt Serv.

Complete Book of the Greenhouse. Ian G. Walls. (Illus.). 256p. 1993. 29.95 (0-7063-7186-0, Pub. by Ward Lock UK) Sterling.

Complete Book of the Horse & Rider. 128p. 1992. 9.98 (0-681-41734-X) Longmeadow Pr.

Complete Book of the Water Garden. Philip Swindells & David Mason. (Illus.). 208p. 1990. 29.95 (0-87951-385-3) Overlook Pr.

Complete Book of the Winter Olympics. David Wallechinsky. LC 93-17631. 1993. pap. 8.95 (0-316-92080-0) Little.

Complete Book of Top Gun. Consumer Guide Editors. 1990. 19.99 (0-517-03301-1) Random Hse Value.

Complete Book of Topiary. Barbara Gallup & Deborah Reich. LC 86-40539. (Illus.). 256p. (Orig.). 1988. pap. 12.95 (0-89480-318-2, 1318) Workman Pub.

Complete Book of Traditional Aran Knitting. Shelagh Hollingsworth. (Illus.). 144p. 1983. pap. 14.95 (0-312-15635-9) St Martin.

Complete Book of Trapping. Bob Gilsvik. (Illus.). 172p. (J). (gr. 7). reprint ed. 14.95 (0-936622-29-6) A R Harding Pub.

Complete Book of Trick & Fancy Shooting. Ernie Lind. 1977. pap. 3.95 (0-8065-0588-5, Citadel Pr) Carol Pub Group.

Complete Book of Tricot. Rebecca Jones. (Illus.). 96p. 1991. 21.95 (0-86417-327-X, Pub. by Kangaroo Pr AT) Seven Hills Bk.

Complete Book of Trusts. Martin M. Shenkman. LC 92-12059. 304p. 1992. text ed. 55.00 (0-471-57447-3); pap. text ed. 21.95 (0-471-57448-1) Wiley.

Complete Book of Turkish Cooking. Ayla E. Algar. (Illus.). 336p. 1989. pap. 17.95 (0-7103-0334-3, Pub. by Kegan Paul Intl UK) Routledge Chapman & Hall.

Complete Book of U. S. Presidents. William Degregoria. 1993. 12.99 (0-517-08244-6) Random Hse Value.

Complete Book of U. S. Presidents. 4th ed. William A. DeGregorio. LC 93-13441. pap. 21.00 (0-942637-92-5) Barricade Bks.

Complete Book of U. S. Sniping. Peter R. Senich. (Illus.). 288p. 1988. text ed. 39.95 (0-87364-460-3) Paladin Pr.

*Complete Book of U. S. State Studies. James L. Shoemaker et al. (YA). (gr. 4 up). 1995. student ed 19.95 (1-56500-037-4) Gldn Educ.

Complete Book of Underground Houses: How to Build a Low Cost Home. Rob Roy. LC 94-16840. (Illus.). 148p. 1994. pap. 14.95 (0-8069-0728-2) Sterling.

Complete Book of Unicycling. Jack Wiley. LC 84-50464. (Illus.). 187p. (YA). (gr. 7 up). 1984. pap. 27.95 (0-913999-05-9) Solipaz Pub Co.

*Complete Book of Victims' Rights. Debra J. Wilson. 208p. (Orig.). 1995. pap. 16.95 (0-9637285-1-2) Prose Assocs.

Complete Book of Villains. Rick Swan. (Advanced Dungeons & Dragons 2nd Ed. Accessory Ser.: DMGR6). 1994. pap. 18.00 (1-56076-837-1) TSR Inc.

Complete Book of Vitamins & Minerals. Consumer Guide Editors. 576p. (Orig.). 1994. pap. 6.99 (0-451-18213-8, Sig) NAL-Dutton.

Complete Book of Vitamins & Minerals. Editors of Consumer Guide Staff. 288p. 1989. 7.98 (0-88176-497-3) Pubns Intl Ltd.

Complete Book of Vitamins & Minerals. Prevention Magazine Staff. 1992. 14.99 (0-517-08132-6) Random Hse Value.

Complete Book of Walking. Charles T. Kuntzleman. 1989. mass mkt. 5.99 (0-671-70074-X) PB.

*Complete Book of Water Healing. Dian D. Buchman. 261p. 1995. 29.98 (0-941683-33-8) Instant Improve.

Complete Book of Water Therapy. rev. ed. Dian D. Buchman. LC 93-47004. (Illus.). 1994. 11.95 (0-87983-613-X) Keats.

Complete Book of Wedding Flowers: Stunning Flower Arranging Inspiration for Everyone & Every Location. Shirley Monckton. (Illus.). 96p. 1993. pap. 19.95 (0-304-34201-7, Pub. by Cassell UK) Sterling.

*Complete Book of Wedding Flowers: Stunning Flower Arranging Inspiration for Everyone & Every Location. Shirley Monckton. (Illus.). 96p. 1995. pap. 12.95 (0-304-34565-2, Pub. by Cassell UK) Sterling.

Complete Book of Wedding Music for Clarinet - Tenor Saxophone. Paul Mickelson. 1993. 7.95 (0-685-64604-1, 94372) Mel Bay.

Complete Book of Wedding Music for Flute or Violin. Paul Mickelson. 1993. 7.95 (0-87166-757-6, 94368) Mel Bay.

Complete Book of Wedding Music for Trombone. Paul Mickelson. 1993. 7.95 (0-685-64611-4, 94371) Mel Bay.

Complete Book of Wedding Music for Trumpet. Paul Mickelson. 1993. 7.95 (0-87166-759-2, 94369) Mel Bay.

An Asterisk (*) at the beginning of an entry indicates that the title is appearing in BIP for the first time.

Complete Book of Western Hatches. Dave Hughes & Rick Hafele. (Illus.). 223p. (Orig.). 1981. pap. 24.95 (*0-936608-12-9*) F Amato Pubns.

Complete Book of Wills & Estates. Alexander A. Bove. LC 88-31380. 1991. pap. 10.95 (*0-8050-1464-0*, Owl) H Holt & Co.

Complete Book of Window Treatments & Curtains: Traditional & Innovative Ways to Dress Up Your Windows. Carol Parks. LC 93-39113. 143p. 1990. 24.95 (*0-8069-0612-X*) Sterling.

***Complete Book of Window Treatments & Curtains: Traditional & Innovative Ways to Dress up Your Windows.** Carol Parks. (Illus.). 144p. 1995. pap. 14.95 (*0-8069-0613-8*) Sterling.

Complete Book of Winning Leg Wrestling: Offensive & Defensive Techniques. Michael Stever & Scott Stever. LC 82-22375. 192p. 1983. 17.95 (*0-13-158626-2*, Parker Publishing Co) P-H.

Complete Book of Word Processing & Business Graphics. Walter Sikonowiz. 256p. (Orig.). 1982. pap. 14.95 (*0-942412-03-6*) Micro Text Pubns.

Complete Book of World War II Combat Aircraft. Enzo Angelucci. 1988. 39.99 (*0-517-66475-5*) Random Hse Value.

***Complete Book of Yacht Care.** Michael Verney. (Illus.). 264p. Date not set. 30.00 (*0-7136-3773-0*) Sheridan.

Complete Book of Yoga: Harmony of Body & Mind. Sri Ananda. 175p. 1985. 12.95 (*0-317-12476-5*, Pub. by Vision Books II) Asia Bk Corp.

Complete Book of Youth Ministry. Ed. by Warren Benson & Mark Senter, III. 1987. 26.99 (*0-8024-9849-3*) Moody.

Complete Book of Zingers. Croft M. Pentz. 1990. pap. 9.99 (*0-8423-0467-3*) Tyndale.

Complete Book on Balancing in Contract Bridge. Mike Lawrence. LC 84-223527. 209p. 1981. 14.95 (*0-939460-14-9*); pap. 11.95 (*0-939460-13-0*) Devyn Pr.

Complete Book on Childbirth. Debra Evans. 256p. (Orig.). 1986. 9.99 (*0-8423-0407-X*) Tyndale.

Complete Book on Hand Evaluation in Contract Bridge. Mike Lawrence. LC 84-223827. 194p. 1983. pap. 11.95 (*0-939460-27-0*) Devyn Pr.

Complete Book on Housetraining Rabbits: The Only Rabbit Book You'll Need. S. T. Percan. (Illus.). 37p. (Orig.). 1984. pap. 3.95 (*0-916005-01-1*) Silver Sea.

***Complete Book on Kids: Everything You Need to Know & Then Some; the First Twelve Years.** Jennifer Jones. (Illus.). (Orig.). 1995. pap. 24.95 (*0-9639167-2-6*) Andante Pubng.

Complete Book on Overcalls in Contract Bridge. Mike Lawrence. LC 80-123383. 202p. 1979. 14.95 (*0-939460-08-4*); pap. 11.95 (*0-939460-07-6*) Devyn Pr.

Complete Book on Takeout Doubles. Michael Lawrence. (Doubles Ser.). 256p. 1994. pap. text ed. 12.95 (*0-9637533-1-2*) Magnus Bks.

Complete Book on Taming & Training Your Guinea Pig. Vicki Lasell. (Illus.). 32p. (Orig.). (J). (gr. 5-12). 1987. pap. 3.95 (*0-916005-06-2*) Silver Sea.

Complete Book to Develop Your IQ. Gilles Azzopardi. 320p. (Orig.). 1993. pap. 19.95 (*0-572-01934-3*, Pub. by W Foulsham UK) Trans-Atl Phila.

Complete Books of Charles Fort, 4 vols. in 1. Charles Fort. Incl. Book of the Damned. 1975. reprint ed. (*0-318-51754-X*); New Lands. 1975. reprint ed. (*0-318-51755-8*); Lo! 1975. reprint ed. (*0-318-51756-6*); Wild Talents. 1975. reprint ed. (*0-318-51757-4*); 1975. 29.95 (*0-486-23094-5*) Dover.

Complete Borzoi. Lorraine Groshans. LC 81-4377. (Complete Breed Book Ser.). (Illus.). 288p. 1981. 25.00 (*0-87605-057-7*) Howell Bk.

Complete Bowhunting. Glenn Helgeland. Ed. by Bill Miller. LC 87-62919. (Hunter's Information Ser.). 262p. 1987. 19.95 (*0-914697-08-0*) N Amer Outdoor Grp.

Complete Brand Name Guide to Choosing the Lowest Fat, Calorie, Cholesterol, & Sodium Foods. Denise Webb. 1993. mass mkt. 4.99 (*0-553-29149-1*) Bantam.

Complete Brother Grimm Fairy Tales. Jacob Grimm & Wilhelm K. Grimm. 1993. 12.99 (*0-517-09293-X*) Random Hse Value.

Complete Brothers Grimm Fairy Tale. Jacob Grimm & Wilhelm K. Grimm. (J). 1986. 9.99 (*0-517-45374-6*) Random Hse Value.

Complete Brothers Grimm Fairy Tales. (YA). (gr. 2-6). 6.98 (*0-517-33631-6*) Random Hse Value.

Complete Bugler: Practice & Performance Aid for the Young Bugler. Mark Johnson. (Illus.). 24p. (Orig.). (J). (gr. 4-12). 1993. pap. 2.95 (*1-883988-10-1*); audio, pap. 8.95 (*1-883988-04-7*) RSV Prods.

Complete Builder's Guide: A 1726 Dictionary of Builders Terms & Usage. Richard Neve. 45.00 (*0-89979-004-6*) British Am Bks.

Complete Building Construction. 2nd ed. Ed. by John Phelps & Tom Philbin. LC 82-17789. 1983. text ed. 24.95 (*0-672-23377-0*, Audel) Macmillan.

Complete Building Construction. 4th ed. Eugene Leger. 736p. 1994. pap. 30.00 (*0-02-517882-2*) Macmillan.

Complete Building Equipment Maintenance Desk Book. Ed. by Sheldon J. Fuchs. 450p. 1982. text ed. 54.95 (*0-13-158808-7*) P-H.

Complete Building Equipment Maintenance Desk Book: Supplement 1. 2nd ed. Ed. by Sheldon J. Fuchs. LC 93-20739. 1993. write for info. (*0-13-157553-8*) P-H Gen Ref & Trav.

Complete Building Maintenance Equipment Desk Book. 2nd ed. Sheldon J. Fuchs. 623p. 1992. 69.95 (*0-685-71674-0*, 720) Inst Real Estate.

Complete Business BASIC for the Apple II, II Plus, IIe, & IIc: A Self-Instructional Approach. Kenneth R. Trester et al. LC 84-12439. 368p. 1985. pap. write for info. (*0-201-16281-4*) Addison-Wesley.

***Complete Business Statistics.** 2nd ed. Amir Aczel. 288p. (C). 1992. student ed, text ed. 21.95 (*0-256-09277-X*) Irwin.

Complete Business Statistics. 2nd ed. Amir D. Aczel. 928p. (C). 1992. text ed. 65.95 (*0-256-08613-3*) Irwin Prof Pubng.

Complete Business Writer's Manual: Model Letters, Memos, Reports & Presentations. Arthur H. Bell. 1991. text ed. 39.95 (*0-13-157538-4*, Busn) P-H.

Complete Business Writing Kit: All the Skills You Need in 10 Self-Instructional Lessons. Oliva Stockard & Fredric Margolis. 1989. pap. text ed. 42.50 (*0-471-61282-0*) Wiley.

Complete Butcher's Tales. Rikki Ducornet. LC 93-36127. 163p. 1994. 19.95 (*1-56478-043-0*) Dalkey Arch.

Complete C Language Programming, Vol. 1. Douglas A. Troy. 1986. pap. 24.95 (*0-316-85311-9*) Little.

Complete C Plus Plus Primer. 2nd ed. Keith Weiskamp & Bryan Flamig. 540p. 1993. pap. 34.95 (*0-12-742688-4*, AP Prof) Acad Pr.

Complete C Reference Guide. Anatole Olczak. (Orig.). pap. text ed. 9.95 (*0-935739-08-4*) A System Pubns.

Complete Cable Book. (Entertainment Directory Ser.). 186p. (Orig.). 1994. pap. 39.00 (*0-9637522-3-5*) Homily Pr.

Complete CAD-CIM Multivendor Compatibility & Connectivity Survival Kit. 1988. pap. 79.00 (*0-932007-14-7*) Mgmt Roundtable.

Complete Calligrapher. Emma Callery. 1994. 17.98 (*0-7858-0032-8*) Bk Sales Inc.

Complete Calorie-Slim Cookbook. Christine Wiess & Ann B. Hardwick. (Illus.). 246p. 1982. pap. 12.00 (*0-910347-01-8*) Chatham Comm Inc.

Complete Camper's Cookbook. Alberta Vigil. (Illus.). 105p. 1980. pap. 5.95 (*0-317-67450-1*) Pan-Am Publishing Co.

Complete Campus Companion: The Survival Guide Every Christian Student Needs. Robert M. Kachur. LC 87-29877. (Illus.). 311p. (Orig.). 1987. pap. 12.99 (*0-8308-1212-1*, 1212) InterVarsity.

Complete Canvasworker's Guide: How to Outfit Your Boat Using Natural or Synthetic Cloth. 2nd ed. Jim Grant. 1992. pap. text ed. 19.95 (*0-07-024080-9*) McGraw.

Complete Canvasworker's Guide: How to Outfit Your Boat Using Natural or Synthetic Cloth. 2nd ed. Jim Grant. 224p. 1992. pap. 19.95 (*0-87742-335-0*, 60323) Intl Marine.

Complete Capital Runner's Guide. Kim J. Diffendal & Kasia Johnson. 99p. (Orig.). 1985. pap. 7.95 (*0-9614260-0-4*) Diffendal & Johnson.

***Complete Capitation Handbook: How to Design & Implement at-Risk Contracts for Behavioral Healthcare.** Gayle Zieman. (Managed Behavioral Healthcare Library). 1995. 58.00 (*1-887452-03-6*) CentraLink.

Complete Car Cost Guide, 1990. 359p. 1990. per., pap. 39.00 (*0-941443-09-4*) IntelliChoice.

Complete Car Cost Guide, 1991. Peter Levy. 368p. 1991. per., pap. 39.00 (*0-941443-11-6*) IntelliChoice.

Complete Car Cost Guide, 1992. Peter Levy. 353p. 1992. per., pap. 39.00 (*0-941443-13-2*) IntelliChoice.

Complete Car Cost Guide, 1993. Peter Levy. 379p. 1993. per., pap. 45.00 (*0-941443-15-9*) IntelliChoice.

Complete Car Modeler I. 2nd ed. Gerald A. Wingrove. (Illus.). 136p. 1993. 39.95 (*0-85429-946-7*, Pub. by J H Haynes & Co UK) Motorbooks Intl.

Complete Car Modeler II. 2nd ed. Gerald A. Wingrove. (Illus.). 128p. 1994. 34.95 (*0-85429-857-6*) Haynes Pubns.

Complete Carcassi Guitar Method. Mel Bay & Joseph Castle. (ENG & SPA.). 1993. 8.95 (*0-87166-378-3*, 93611EN/SP) Mel Bay.

Complete Care Plan Manual for Long-Term Care. Connie S. March. LC 91-44365. 143p. (Orig.). 1992. 37.95 (*1-55648-085-7*, 130105) AHPI.

Complete Career Handbook. Dan J. McLaughlin. Ed. by Diane Parker. LC 91-50988. 60p. 1992. pap. 4.95 (*0-88247-914-8*, 914) R & E Pubs.

Complete Caribbean Cookbook. Pamela Lalbachan. (Illus.). 304p. 1994. 34.95 (*0-8048-3038-X*) C E Tuttle.

Complete Carpet Manual. Jerry Levinstein. (Illus.). 376p. 1992. 59.95 (*0-912526-60-2*) Lib Res.

Complete Cat Book. Richard H. Gebhardt. (Illus.). 224p. 1991. 19.95 (*0-87605-841-1*) Howell Bk.

***Complete Cat Book: Expert Advice on Every Phase of Cat Ownership.** Gebhardt. 1995. pap. text ed. 14.95 (*0-87605-919-1*) Howell Bk.

Complete Catalog. 242p. 1993. Published Annually. write for info. (*0-318-62854-6*) Am Math.

Complete Catalog of Ampico Reproducing Piano Rolls. Elaine Obenchain. LC 77-22349. 197p. 1987. reprint ed. 30.00 (*0-911572-62-7*) Vestal.

Complete Catalog of British Cigarette Cards. London Cigarette Co. Staff. 24.95 (*0-906671-48-5*) Viking Penguin.

Complete Catalog of British Cigarette Cards. 2nd ed. London Cigarette Co. Staff. 24.95 (*0-906671-85-X*) Viking Penguin.

Complete Catalogue of Sheet Music & Musical Works. Music Trade Board, U. S. A. Staff. LC 69-1666. 575p. 1973. reprint ed. lib. bdg. 95.00 (*0-306-71401-9*) Da Capo.

Complete Catalogue of the Gemaldegalerie, Berlin. Henning Bock. (Illus.). 560p. 1987. 85.00 (*0-8109-0972-3*) Abrams.

Complete Categorized Greek-English New Testament Vocabulary. David Holly. 141p. (ENG & GRE.). 1978. 12.50 (*0-85150-119-2*) Attic Pr.

Complete Categorized Guide to Statistical Selection & Ranking Procedures. Edward J. Dudewicz & Joo Ok Koo. LC 80-68288. (American Sciences Press Series in Mathematical & Management Sciences: Vol. 6). 1982. text ed. 110.00 (*0-935950-03-6*) Am Sciences Pr.

Complete Caterer: A Practical Guide to the Craft & Business of Catering. rev. ed. Elizabeth Lawrence. 1992. pap. 15.00 (*0-385-23480-5*) Doubleday.

Complete Cavaletti: Basic to Advanced Training of Horse & Rider. Peter Lichtner-Hoyer. 128p. 1992. 22.50 (*0-914327-40-2*) Breakthrgh NY.

Complete CB Dictionary. Ed. by Aero Products Research, Inc., Industries Division Staff. 1977. pap. 2.98 (*0-912682-17-5*) Aero Products.

Complete Chamber Music for Pianoforte & Strings. Franz Schubert. 192p. 1966. pap. 9.95 (*0-486-21527-X*) Dover.

Complete Chamber Music for Strings. Felix Mendelssohn. Ed. by Julius Rietz. 1978. reprint ed. pap. 12.95 (*0-486-23679-X*) Dover.

Complete Chamber Music for Strings. Franz Schubert. Ed. by Eusibius Mandyczewski & Joseph Hellmesberger. reprint ed. pap. 11.95 (*0-486-21463-X*) Dover.

Complete Chamber Music for Strings & Clarinet Quintet. Johannes Brahms. Ed. by Hans Gal. 1968. pap. 10.95 (*0-486-21914-3*) Dover.

Complete Chamber Music for Strings & Clarinet Quintet. Johannes Brahms. Ed. by Hans Gal. 9.00 (*0-8446-1724-5*) Peter Smith.

Complete Chart Hits of 'Ninety's. (Piano-Vocal-Guitar Ser.). 256p. (Orig.). 1991. pap. 14.95 (*0-7935-0408-2*, 00311502) H Leonard.

Complete Chauvinist. Berman. 1982. 11.95 (*0-02-510120-X*) Macmillan.

Complete Checking Operation of Gear Hobs Using a Multi-Coordinate Checking Center. S. Franke et al. (Fall Technical Meeting Papers). (Illus.). 16p. 1986. pap. 30.00 (*1-55589-471-2*, 86FTM7) AGMA.

Complete Checklist of the Birds of the World. 2nd ed. Richard Howard & Alick Moore. (Illus.). 622p. 1991. text ed. 39.50 (*0-12-356910-9*) Acad Pr.

Complete Cheerful Cherub. Rebecca McCann. 514p. 1990. reprint ed. lib. bdg. 35.95 (*0-89966-662-0*) Buccaneer Bks.

Complete Chemical Engineer. Robert B. Barat & Worbent Elliot. 350p. 1993. per., pap. 29.95 (*0-8403-9026-2*) Kendall-Hunt.

Complete Chess Course. Fred Reinfeld. LC 59-13043. 1959. 25.00 (*0-385-00464-8*) Doubleday.

Complete Chessplayer. Fred Reinfeld. 1981. pap. 2.50 (*0-449-14101-2*, GM) Fawcett.

Complete Chet Akins Guitar Method. Ed. by Bobby Caldwell. 1993. 12.95 (*0-87166-939-0*, 93232); audio 9.98 (*1-56222-900-1*, 93232) Mel Bay.

***Complete Chicken Breast Cookbook: Easy & Delicious Everyday Recipes for the Whole Family.** Marge Poore. LC 95-1605. 1995. write for info. (*0-7615-0005-7*) Prima Pub.

Complete Child Care in Body & Mind. I. Newton Kugelmass. 1959. 25.95x (*0-8084-0367-2*) NCUP.

Complete Chinese Materia Medica. Nigel A. Wiseman & Ken Boss. write for info. (*0-912111-30-5*) Paradigm Publns.

Complete Chinese Ornament. Owen Jones. 1990. pap. 14.95 (*0-486-26259-6*) Dover.

Complete Chinese Shar-Pei. Dee Gannon. (Illus.). 288p. 1988. 25.95 (*0-87605-101-8*) Howell Bk.

Complete Cholesterol Counter. Penny Mintz. (Heart Care Titles Ser.). 256p. 1990. mass mkt. 4.95 (*0-345-36321-3*) Ballantine.

Complete Choral Conductor: Gesture & Method. Brian R. Busch. (Illus.). 256p. (Orig.). 1984. spiral bd., pap. 26.00 (*0-02-870340-5*) Schirmer Bks.

Complete Chow Chow. Kip Kopatch. (Illus.). 288p. 1988. 25.95 (*0-87605-102-6*) Howell Bk.

Complete Christmas Music Collection. Ed. by Carol Cuellar. 264p. (Orig.). (YA). 1993. pap. text ed. 16.95 (*0-89898-642-7*) CPP Belwin.

Complete Chromatic Harmonica Method. Phil Duncan. 1993. 9.95 (*0-87166-831-9*, 93890); audio 9.98 (*0-87166-832-7*, 93890) Mel Bay.

Complete Church Clip Art Book. Rick Bundschuh. (Illus.). 240p. 1990. pap. text ed. 16.99 (*0-87403-636-4*, 18-03167) Standard Pub.

Complete Church Newsletter: A Guide to Starting, Strengthening, Renovating, or Resurrecting. Jeffrey D. Dennis. 128p. 1992. pap. 7.99 (*0-8010-3012-9*) Baker Bk.

Complete Circuit Training Guide. Edwin J. C. Sobey. LC 78-66002. (Illus.). 160p. 1980. pap. 5.95 (*0-89037-202-0*) Anderson World.

***Complete City Maps of Michigan.** Dave Daenzer. (Illus.). 574p. 1994. pap. 19.95 (*1-882062-02-7*) CITMAP.

Complete City Maps of Michigan. Intro. by Michael Jenkins. LC 90-84569. 544p. (Orig.). 1991. pap. 11.95 (*1-882062-00-0*) CITMAP.

Complete City Maps of Ohio. Dave Daenzer. LC 90-84568. (Illus.). 480p. (Orig.). 1995. pap. 16.95 (*1-882062-01-9*) CITMAP.

Complete Clarinet Player, Bk. 1. Paul Harvey. (Illus.). 48p. 1986. pap. 8.95 (*0-7119-0877-X*, AM62613) Music Sales.

Complete Clarinet Player, Bk. 2. Paul Harvey. (Illus.). 48p. 1986. pap. 8.95 (*0-7119-0878-8*, AM62621) Music Sales.

Complete Clarinet Player, Bk. 3. Paul Harvey. (Illus.). 48p. 1986. pap. 8.95 (*0-7119-0879-6*, AM62639) Music Sales.

Complete Clarinet Player, Bk. 4. Paul Harvey. (Illus.). 48p. 1986. pap. 8.95 (*0-7119-0880-X*, AM62647) Music Sales.

Complete Clarinet Player: Omnibus Edition, 4 bks. in 1. Paul Harvey. (Illus.). 192p. 1988. pap. 29.95 (*0-7119-1048-0*, AM64585) Music Sales.

Complete Clawhammer Banjo Bk. Date not set. 15.00 (*0-7866-0049-7*, 95153); audio 9.98 (*0-7866-0050-0*, 95153C) Mel Bay.

Complete CNC Training Library, 3 bks., Set. Josef Franz & Hans Frommer. (C). 1985. pap. text ed. 445.50 (*1-56990-115-5*) Hanser-Gardner.

Complete Cocktail Training Guide. 1988. 2.95 (*0-685-44002-8*, 109) Am Bartenders.

Complete Coffee Book. Sarah Perry et al. (Illus.). 96p. (Orig.). 1991. 19.95 (*0-87701-899-5*); pap. 12.95 (*0-87701-820-0*) Chronicle Bks.

Complete Collagraph: The Art & Technique of Printmaking from Collage Plates. Clare Romano & John Ross. (Illus.). 1980. 35.00 (*0-02-926770-6*) Macmillan.

Complete Collected Essays. Victor S. Pritchett. 1992. 34.50 (*0-679-41112-7*) Random.

Complete Collected Poems of Maya Angelou. Maya Angelou. LC 94-14501. 1994. 23.00 (*0-679-42895-X*) Random.

Complete Collected Stories. Victor S. Pritchett. LC 91-5806. 1992. pap. 20.00 (*0-679-73892-4*, Vin) Random.

Complete Collected Stories. Victor S. Pritchett. LC 91-58068. 1992. pap. 20.00 (*0-06-797389-2*, Vin) Random.

Complete Collector's Guide to Shells & Shelling. 2nd ed. Sandra Romashko. LC 81-51067. (Illus.). 112p. (Orig.). 1994. pap. 9.95 (*0-89317-032-1*) Windward Pub.

Complete College Catalog Book. Ronald H. Kacmarczyk & Persis Rickes. 88p. 1984. 24.00 (*0-89964-230-6*) Coun Adv & Supp Ed.

Complete Color Book. Jeri Carroll. (Illus.). 112p. (J). (ps-3). 1991. 10.95 (*0-86653-585-3*, GP1300) Good Apple.

Complete Color Glossary. 1994. pap. 19.95 (*1-56830-096-4*) Hayden.

Complete Color Polly & Her Pals, Vol. 2. Cliff Sterrett. Ed. by Rick Marschall. (Polly & Her Pals Ser.). (Illus.). 96p. 1991. 34.95 (*0-924359-15-3*) Remco Wrldserv Bks.

Complete Color Polly & Her Pals, Vol. I: The Surrealist Period, 1926-1927. Cliff Sterrett. (Illus.). 96p. (YA). 1990. 34.95 (*0-924359-14-5*) Remco Wrldserv Bks.

Complete Color Polly & Her Pals, 1929-30, Vol. III. Cliff Sterrett. Ed. by Richard Marschall. (Illus.). 96p. 1992. 34.95 (*0-924359-16-1*) Remco Wrldserv Bks.

Complete Color Terry & the Pirates by Milton Caniff, 1936, Vol. III. Milton Caniff. Ed. by Richard Marschall. (Illus.). 96p. 1992. 34.95 (*0-924359-21-8*) Remco Wrldserv Bks.

Complete Color Terry & the Pirates, Vol. 1. Milton Caniff. (Illus.). 96p. (YA). (gr. 6 up). 1990. 34.95 (*0-924359-19-6*) Remco Wrldserv Bks.

C

Complete Colored Pencil Book. Bernard Poulin. 185p. 1992. 27.99 (*0-89134-418-7*, 30363) North Light Bks.

Complete Come & Praise: Words & Music Edition. Comp. by Geoffrey Marshall-Taylor. 256p. 1990. pap. 21.95 (*0-563-34581-0*, Pub. by BBC UK) Parkwest Pubns.

Complete Come & Praise: Words Edition. 136p. 1990. pap. 5.95 (*0-563-34580-2*, TD883, Pub. by BBC UK) Parkwest Pubns.

Complete Comedies of Shakespeare. William Shakespeare. 1994. 20.50 (*0-679-60107-4*, Modern Lib) Random.

Complete Comedies of Terence: Modern Verse Translations. Terence. Ed. by Palmer Bovie. LC 74-5264. 419p. reprint ed. pap. 119.50 (*0-8357-7941-6*, 2057014) Bks Demand.

Complete Commercial Driver's License (CDL) Study Program, 2 bks., Set, Bks. 1-2. CDL Institute, Inc., Staff. 1992. Set. 64.95 (*0-8273-4778-2*) Delmar.

Complete Commercial Driver's License Training Program. Carol D. Young & Douglas E. Long. 1991. Resource Binder. 99.95 (*0-8273-4545-3*); Essex Manual. 4.95 (*0-8273-4543-7*) Delmar.

Complete Commercial Driver's License Training Program, Set. Carol D. Young & Douglas E. Long. 1991. 250.00 (*0-8273-4734-0*) Delmar.

Complete Commodity Futures Directory. rev. ed. Ed. by M. C. Marasco. 550p. Date not set. ring bd. 175.00 (*0-685-45274-3*) Christopher Res.

***Complete Communications Handbook.** 2nd ed. Ed Paulson. 1995. pap. 21.95 (*1-55622-476-1*) Wordware Pub.

Complete Communications Manual for Coaches & Athletic Directors. P. Susan Mamchak & Steven R. Mamchak. 328p. 1989. pap. text ed. 34.95 (*0-13-159229-7*, Busn) P-H.

Complete Company Policies & Procedures Manual. Cary Cohen. 1992. 79.95 (*0-13-158981-4*) P-H.

Complete Compleat Enchanter. L. Sprague De Camp & Fletcher Pratt. 544p. (Orig.). 1989. mass mkt. 5.99 (*0-671-69809-5*) Baen Bks.

Complete Computer Career Guide. Judith Norback. 256p. 1987. 19.95 (*0-8306-9554-0*, 2654, Liberty Hall Pr) TAB Bks.

Complete Computer Concepts. Waggoner. (Shelly Cashman Ser.). (Illus.). 400p. (C). 1992. student ed, per. 27.00 (*0-87835-573-1*) Boyd & Fraser.

Complete Computer Concepts & Learning to Use Windows Applications. Gary B. Shelly & Thomas J. Cashman. LC 93-20650. (Shelly Cashman Ser.). (C). 1994. pap. 52.95 (*0-87709-149-8*, BF1498) S-W Pub.

Complete Computer Concepts & Learning to Use Windows Applications: Microsoft Word 2.0 for Windows, Microsoft Excel 4.0 for Windows, Paradox 1.0. Gary B. Shelly & Thomas J. Cashman. LC 93-20648. (Shelly Cashman Ser.). (C). 1994. pap. 50.95 (*0-87709-145-5*, BF1455); pap. 53.95 (*0-87709-146-3*) S-W Pub.

Complete Computer Concepts & Microcomputer Applications: WordPerfect 5.1, Lotus 1-2-3 Release 2.2, dBASE IV Version 1.1. rev. ed. Waggoner et al. (Shelly Cashman Ser.). (Illus.). 1008p. (C). 1992. spiral bd. 35.00 (*0-87835-531-6*); spiral bd. 35.00 (*0-87835-901-X*); per. 33.00 (*0-87835-529-4*); per. 33.00 (*0-87835-900-1*) Boyd & Fraser.

An Asterisk (*) at the beginning of an entry indicates that the title is appearing in BIP for the first time.

Complete Computer Concepts & Programming in Microsoft BASIC. Waggoner & Quasney. (Shelly Cashman Ser.). (Illus.). 450p. (C). 1992. per. 28.00 (*0-87835-784-X*) Boyd & Fraser.

Complete Computer Concepts & Programming in QuickBasic. Gary B. Shelly et al. LC 94-6014. (Shelly Cashman Ser.). 1994. write for info. (*0-87709-655-4*) Boyd & Fraser.

Complete Computer Virus Handbook. Ed. by Price Waterhouse Staff. 192p. (C). 1989. text ed. 170.00 (*0-273-03255-0*, Pub. by Pitman Pubng UK) St Mut.

Complete Concerti Grossi in Full Score. George F. Handel. 20.25 (*0-8446-5890-1*) Peter Smith.

Complete Concerti Grossi in Full Score. George F. Handel. 272p. 1981. reprint ed. pap. 12.95 (*0-486-24187-4*) Dover.

Complete Concerti in Full Score. Johannes Brahms. Orig. Title: Johannes Brahms, Samtliche Werke. 352p. 1981. reprint ed. pap. 14.95 (*0-486-24170-X*) Dover.

Complete Concordance to Gottfried Von Strassburg's "Tristan" Comp. by Clifton D. Hall. LC 92-42222. 632p. 1993. text ed. 129.95 (*0-7734-9203-8*) E Mellen.

Complete Concordance to Shakespeare. rev. ed. Mary C. Clarke. LC 72-1029. reprint ed. lib. bdg. 97.50 (*0-404-01574-3*) AMS Pr.

Complete Concordance to Shakespeare. Ed. by John Bartlett. 1910p. 1969. reprint ed. 95.00 (*0-312-15645-6*) St Martin.

Complete Concordance to the Comedies & Fragments of Aristophanes. 2nd enl. rev. ed. Henry Dunbar. x, 398p. 1985. reprint ed. 128.70 (*3-487-05017-X*, Pub. by Georg Olms GW) Lubrecht & Cramer.

Complete Concordance to the French Poetry & Prose of John Gower. R. F. Yeager & Mark West. (Medieval Texts & Studies: No. 13). 1567p. 1995. 125.00 (*0-937191-41-8*) Colleagues Pr Inc.

Complete Concordance to the Iliad of Homer. enl. rev. ed. Guy L. Prendergast. vii, 427p. 1983. reprint ed. 128.70 (*3-487-04161-8*, Pub. by Georg Olms GW) Lubrecht & Cramer.

Complete Concordance to the Works of Geoffrey Chaucer, 10 vols., Set. 2,587.00 (*0-685-67810-5*, Pub. by Georg Olms GW) Lubrecht & Cramer.

Complete Concordance to the Works of Geoffrey Chaucer, 10 vols., Set. Ed. by Aklo Oizumi. (Alpha-Omega Series C. English Authors: Vol. 1). 9510p. 1992. lib. bdg. 3,400.00 (*3-487-09412-6*, Pub. by Georg Olms GW) Lubrecht & Cramer.

***Complete Concordance to the Works of Geoffrey Chaucer, Vol. 11.** Aklo Oizumi. (Alpha-Omega Series C. English Authors C: Suppl. 1). 555p. 1994. lib. bdg. 340.00 (*3-487-09821-0*, Pub. by Georg Olms GW) Lubrecht & Cramer.

***Complete Concordance to the Works of Geoffrey Chaucer, Vol. 12.** Ed. by Aklo Oizzumi. (Alpha-Omega Series C: Suppl. 2). 767p. 1994. lib. bdg. 340.00 (*3-487-09822-9*, Pub. by Georg Olms GW) Lubrecht & Cramer.

Complete Concordance to Wolfram Von Eschenbach's Parzival: A Complete Concordance. Clifton Hall. LC 90-2854. 800p. 1990. 171.00 (*0-8240-4841-5*, 995) Garland.

Complete Concrete Masonry & Brick Handbook. J. T. Adams. 1983. pap. 33.95 (*0-442-20830-8*) Chapman & Hall.

***Complete Conditioning for Basketball.** Greg Brittenham. LC 95-13033. (Complete Conditioning Ser.). 216p. (Orig.). 1996. pap. 14.95 (*0-87322-881-2*, PBRI 0881) Human Kinetics.

Complete Conductor. Gunther Schuller. LC 93-36065. (C). 1994. write for info. (*0-19-506377-5*) OUP.

Complete Conductor: A Comprehensive Resource for the Professional Conductor of the Twenty-First Century. Robert W. Demaree, Jr. & Don V. Moses. LC 93-48392. 491p. 1994. text ed. 56.00 (*0-13-173014-2*) P-H.

***Complete Confectionery Techniques.** Ildo Nicolello & Rowland Foote. LC 94-45597. 1995. pap. text ed. 29.95 (*0-470-23493-8*) Wiley.

Complete Confined Spaces Handbook. Rekus. 1995. write for info. (*0-87371-487-3*) Lewis Pubs.

Complete Conservatory Method for Trumpet (Cornet) or E-Flat Alto, B-Flat Tenor, Baritone, Euphonium & B-Flat Bass in Treble Clef. Jean B. Arban. Ed. by Edwin F. Goldman & Walter M. Smith. 350p. (Orig.). (J). 1936. pap. 25.95 (*0-8258-0010-2*, 021) Fischer Inc NY.

Complete Constitution of the United States of America. William J. Murray. (Orig.). 1986. pap. 4.95 (*0-940917-01-7*) MFM Publish.

Complete Cookbook of American Fish & Shellfish. John F. Nicolas. 1990. text ed. 44.95 (*0-442-23504-6*) Van Nos Reinhold.

Complete Cookery Manual. Anthony O'Reilly. 608p. (Orig.). 1993. pap. 57.50 (*0-273-03387-5*, Pub. by Pitman Pub Ltd UK) Trans-Atl Phila.

Complete Cookie Jar Book. Mike Schneider. LC 91-65647. (Illus.). 300p. 1991. 59.95 (*0-88740-336-0*) Schiffer.

Complete Cord Classics. Date not set. 9.95 (*1-56222-574-X*, 94810) Mel Bay.

Complete Correspondence of Clara & Robert Schumann Vol. 1. Ed. by Eva Weissweiler. Tr. by Hildegard Fritsch & Ronald Crawford. LC 93-44817. 424p. (C). 1994. text ed. 59.59 (*0-8204-2444-7*) P Lang Pubs.

Complete Correspondence of Sigmund Freud & Ernest Jones, 1908-1939. Ed. by R. Andrew Paskauskas. LC 92-23913. (Illus.). 888p. 1993. 42.50 (*0-674-15423-1*) Belknap Pr.

***Complete Correspondence of Sigmund Freud & Ernest Jones 1908-1939.** Ed. by R. Andrew Paskauskas. 896p. (Orig.). (C). 1995. pap. 24.95 (*0-674-15424-X*) Belknap Pr.

Complete Cost-Keeper: Some Original Systems of Shop Cost-Keeping or Factory Accounting Together with an Exposition of the Advantages of Account Keeping by Means of Cards. Horace L. Arnold, Jr. Ed. by Alfred D. Chandler. LC 79-7530. (History of Management Thought & Practice Ser.). 1980. reprint ed. lib. bdg. 40.95 (*0-405-12313-2*) Ayer.

Complete Country Blues Guitar Book. Mike Christensen. (Complete Book Ser.). 1993. 19.95 (*1-56222-322-4*, 94710); audio 9.98 (*1-56222-327-5*, 94710) Mel Bay.

Complete Country Fiddler. Stacy Phillips. 1993. 15.00 (*1-56222-275-9*, 94696); audio 9.98 (*1-56222-438-7*, 94696) Mel Bay.

Complete Country Guitar Book. Fred Sokolew. (Complete Book Ser.). 1993. 9.95 (*0-87166-867-X*, 93935); audio 9.98 (*1-56222-188-4*, 93935) Mel Bay.

Complete Country Music Collection. Ed. by Carol Cuellar. 288p. (Orig.). (YA). 1992. pap. text ed. 16.95 (*0-89898-584-6*) CPP Belwin.

Complete Country Music Discography: 1922-1942. Tony Russell. Date not set. 30.00 (*0-915608-07-3*) Country Music Found.

Complete Course in Business Mathematics. R. S. Soni. 786p. 1988. pap. 48.00 (*81-209-0005-7*, Pub. by Pitambar Pub II) St Mut.

Complete Course in Canning, Set, Vols. 1, 2 & 3. rev. ed. Anthony Lopez. LC 46-19487. (Illus.). (Orig.). 1987. Set. pap. text ed. 100.00 (*0-930027-10-8*) CTI Pubns.

Complete Course in Canning, Set, Vols. 1, 2 & 3. 12th rev. ed. Anthony Lopez. LC 46-19487. (Illus.). (Orig.). 1987. Set. text ed. 125.00 (*0-930027-06-X*) CTI Pubns.

Complete Course in Canning, Vols. 1, 2 & 3. rev. ed. Anthony Lopez. LC 46-19487. (Illus.). (Orig.). 1987. Bk. I. text ed. 50.00 (*0-930027-07-8*); Bk. II. text ed. 50.00 (*0-930027-08-6*); Bk. III. text ed. 50.00 (*0-930027-09-4*) CTI Pubns.

Complete Course in English Series Book. R. Dixson. 1987. pap. text ed. 9.25 (*0-13-158817-6*) P-H.

Complete Course in ISC Physics. V. P. Bhatnagar. 764p. 1992. 80.00 (*81-209-0202-5*, Pub. by Pitambar Pub II) St Mut.

Complete Course in ISC Physics, Vol. 1. V. P. Bhatnagar. 784p. 1992. 90.00 (*81-209-0385-4*, Pub. by Pitambar Pub II) St Mut.

Complete Course in Predictive Astrology: Self-Taught Version. Bobbye Bratcher-Nelson. Ed. by Carol A. Wiggers. (Illus.). 478p. (Orig.). (C). 1990. student ed 150.00 (*1-878935-08-9*) JustUs & Assocs.

Complete Course in Pretrial Litigation. 2nd ed. Roy D. Simon, Jr. 574p. 1987. 24.95 (*1-55681-136-5*, FBA0136) Natl Inst Trial Ad.

Complete Course in Professional Locksmithing. Robert L. Robinson. LC 73-174584. (Illus.). 414p. 1973. 63.95 (*0-911012-15-X*) Nelson-Hall.

Complete Course in Professional Piano Tuning, Repair & Rebuilding. Floyd A. Stevens. LC 74-173598. (Illus.). 216p. 1972. 54.95 (*0-911012-07-9*) Nelson-Hall.

Complete Course of Lithography. Alois Felder. LC 68-27721. (Quality Paperbacks Ser.). 1977. pap. 7.95 (*0-306-80053-5*) Da Capo.

Complete Court Reporter's Handbook. 2nd ed. Mary H. Knapp. 384p. (C). 1991. pap. text ed. write for info. (*0-13-159369-2*) P-H.

***Complete Credit & Collection Letters Kit.** Michael V. Meerman. Ed. by Teresa Donohue. 140p. 1994. pap. 32.00 (*0-934914-90-7*) NACM.

Complete Credit & Collection Model Letter Book. Harold E. Meyer & Scott A. Sievert. 384p. 1990. 49.95 (*0-13-156126-X*) P-H.

Complete Credit Book: Getting Loans & Credit Cards. 1987. lib. bdg. 72.95 (*0-8490-3922-3*) Gordon Pr.

Complete Credits & Collection Starter Success Kit. 4th ed. James V. Scalo. 150p. 1990. pap. 29.50 (*0-934311-68-4*) Intl Wealth.

Complete Credits & Collection Starter Success Kit. 5th ed. James V. Scalo. 150p. 1992. pap. 29.50 (*1-56150-019-4*) Intl Wealth.

Complete Credits & Collection Starter Success Kit. 6th ed. James V. Scalo. 150p. 1993. pap. 29.50 (*1-56150-069-0*) Intl Wealth.

Complete Credits & Collection Starter Success Kit. 7th ed. James V. Scalo. 150p. 1994. pap. 29.50 (*1-56150-117-4*) Intl Wealth.

Complete Crumb Comics, Vol. 3: Starring Fritz the Cat. Robert Crumb. Ed. by Gary Groth & Robert Fiore. (Illus.). 144p. 1988. 35.00 (*0-930193-76-8*) Fantagraph Bks.

Complete Crumb Comics, Vol. 4: "Mr. Sixties!" Robert Crumb. Ed. by Gary Groth & Robert Fiore. (Illus.). 144p. 1989. 35.00 (*0-930193-80-6*) Fantagraph Bks.

Complete Crumb Comics, Vol. 5: Happy Hippy Comix. Robert Crumb. Ed. by Gary Groth & Robert Boyd. (Illus.). 144p. (Orig.). 1990. 35.00 (*0-930193-91-1*); pap. 16.95 (*0-930193-92-X*) Fantagraph Bks.

Complete Crumb Comics, Vol. 6: On the Crest of a Wave. Robert Crumb. Ed. by Gary Groth & Robert Boyd. (Illus.). 144p. (Orig.). 1991. 35.00 (*1-56097-057-X*); pap. 16.95 (*1-56097-056-1*) Fantagraph Bks.

Complete Crumb Comics, Vol. 7: "Hot 'n' Heavy" Robert Crumb. Ed. by Gary Groth & Robert Boyd. (Illus.). 144p. (Orig.). 1991. 35.00 (*1-56097-062-6*); pap. 16.95 (*1-56097-061-8*) Fantagraph Bks.

Complete Crumb Comics, Vol. 8: The Death of Fritz the Cat. R. Crumb. 148p. 1992. 35.00 (*1-56097-077-4*); pap. 16.95 (*1-56097-076-6*) Fantagraph Bks.

Complete Crumb Comics, Vol. 9: "R. Crumb vs. the Sisterhood" Robert Crumb. Ed. by Gary Groth & Robert Boyd. (Illus.). 144p. (Orig.). 1992. 35.00 (*1-56097-108-8*); pap. 16.95 (*1-56097-107-X*) Fantagraph Bks.

Complete Crystal Guidebook. Uma Silbey. 240p. 1987. pap. 10.95 (*0-553-34499-4*, New Age Bks) Bantam.

Complete Crystal Guidebook: A Practical Path to Self Development, Empowerment & Healing. Uma Silbey. (Illus.). 256p. 1986. pap. 9.95 (*0-938925-00-8*) U-Music.

Complete Custodial Handbook. William R. Griffin. 486p. 1989. text ed. 69.95 (*0-13-162520-9*) P-H.

Complete Customer Service Letter Book, with Disk. Edward W. Werz. 1993. Book only. pap. write for info. (*0-07-069589-X*) McGraw.

Complete Customer Service Letter Book, with Disk. Edward W. Werz. 1995. Book only. pap. text ed. 60.00 (*0-07-069588-1*) McGraw.

Complete Customer Service Letter Book, with Disk, Set. Edward W. Werz. 1993. text ed. 60.00 (*0-07-911618-3*); pap. text ed. 34.95 (*0-07-911619-1*) McGraw.

***Complete Customer Service Model Letter & Memo Book.** Michael Ramundo. LC 94-29915. (C). 1994. text ed. 32.95 (*0-13-335803-8*) P-H.

Complete Cyberspace Reference & Directory: An Addressing & Utilization Guide to the Internet, Electronic Mail Systems, & Bulletin Board Systems. Gilbert Held. LC 94-17569. 784p. 1994. disk, pap. 29.95 (*0-442-01913-0*) Van Nos Reinhold.

***Complete Cymbal Guide: For the Drumset.** Sandy Feldstein. Ed. by Dan Thress & Emily Moorefield. (Illus.). 48p. (Orig.). (YA). 1995. pap. text ed. 9.95 (*0-89724-514-8*) Warner Brothers.

Complete Dalmatian Dog. Milo G. Denlinger. 1991. lib. bdg. 79.95 (*0-8490-5206-8*) Gordon Pr.

***Complete Dan George.** Dan George. 1995. pap. 15.95 (*0-88839-344-X*) Hancock House.

***Complete Database Marketer: Second-Generation Strategies & Techniques for Tapping the Power of Your Customer Database.** Arthur M. Hughes. 550p. 1995. 29.95 (*1-55738-893-8*) Probus Pub Co.

Complete Decorating & Home Improvement Book: A Step-by-Step Guide. Mike Lawrence. 256p. Date not set. 19.98 (*0-8317-2739-X*) Smithmark.

Complete Defence to 1d4: A Study of the Queen's Gambit Accepted. Bernard Cafferty & David Hooper. LC 79-41623. (Chess Ser.). 144p. 1981. 19.50 (*0-08-024103-4*, Pergamon Pr); pap. 13.95 (*0-08-024102-6*, Pergamon Pr) Elsevier.

Complete Defence to 1e4. Bernard Cafferty & David Hooper. (Chess Ser.). 115p. 1986. 29.90 (*0-08-032036-8*, P115, Pergamon Pr); pap. 17.90 (*0-08-032035-X*, Pergamon Pr) Elsevier.

Complete Defensive Bridge Play. Edwin Kantar. 1974. pap. 20.00 (*0-87980-287-1*) Wilshire.

Complete Demographic Reference Guide. (Illus.). 1300p. 1992. 195.00 (*0-9634625-0-4*) Urban Decision.

***Complete Dental Bleaching.** Ronald E. Goldstein & David A. Garber. LC 95-14260. 1995. write for info. (*0-86715-290-7*) Quint Pub Co.

Complete Denture & Overdenture Prosthetics. Ed. by A. H. Geering et al. (Color Atlas of Dental Medicine Ser.). (Illus.). 272p. 1993. text ed. 159.00 (*0-86577-350-5*) Thieme Med Pubs.

Complete Denture Prosthetics. 3rd ed. Neill & Hairn. 151p. 1991. pap. 75.00 (*0-7236-2063-6*, Pub. by John Wright UK) Buttrwrth-Heinemann.

Complete Dentures. John A. Hobkirk. (Dental Practitioners' Handbook Ser.: No. 13). 117p. 1986. 24.95 (*0-7236-0779-6*, Pub. by John Wright UK) Buttrwrth-Heinemann.

Complete Diabetic Cookbook. Mary J. Finsand. LC 79-91382. (Illus.). 192p. 1990. pap. 9.95 (*0-8069-8908-4*) Sterling.

Complete Dickie Dare. Milt Caniff. (Illus.). 160p. (Orig.). 1986. pap. 12.95 (*0-930193-21-0*) Fantagraph Bks.

Complete Dictionary of Astrology. Alan Leo. (Astrologer's Library). 216p. 1989. pap. 12.95 (*0-89281-182-X*) Inner Tradit.

Complete Dictionary of Astrology. James Wilson. 406p. 1971. reprint ed. spiral bd. 13.75 (*0-7873-0973-7*) Mokelumne.

Complete Dictionary of Buying & Merchandising. 138p. (C). pap. 6.00 (*0-87102-014-9*, 45-3483) Natl Ret Merch.

Complete Dictionary of Chinese Medicine. Nigel Wiseman. 850p. (C). 1995. 60.00 (*0-912111-45-3*) Paradigm Publns.

Complete Dictionary of English & Hebrew First Names. Alfred J. Kolatch. 520p. 1984. 25.00 (*0-8246-0295-1*) Jonathan David.

Complete Dictionary of Furniture. rev. ed. John Gloag. LC 90-43798. (Illus.). 832p. 1991. 35.00 (*0-87951-414-0*) Overlook Pr.

Complete Dictionary of Graphic Arts & Desktop Publishing Terminology: With Overview of Industry Growth & Technology. Harvey R. Levenson. (Illus.). 276p. (Orig.). 1994. pap. 19.95 (*0-932423-09-4*) Summa Bks. THE COMPLETE DICTIONARY OF GRAPHIC ARTS & DESKTOP PUBLISHING TERMINOLOGY (WITH OVERVIEW OF INDUSTRY GROWTH, TECHNOLOGY, & SEGMENTS) is a beginner to advanced level dictionary of all aspects of Graphic Arts & Desktop Publishing: Art & Copy Preparation; Color Reproduction; Computer Hardware & Software; Desktop & Electronic Publishing; Digital Photography; Environmental Issues; Finishing; Photography; Image Assembly (Stripping); Ink; Laser Applications; Multimedia; Printing Processes; Proofing; Quality Control; Scanning; Substrates; Telecommunications; Typesetting; Imagesetting; & Typography. Every definition is cross-referenced to its primary area of focus to facilitate usage. Illustrations are provided for the traditional printing processes & for all the non- impact & digital printing processes. Plus complete bibliography & detailed information on all industry associations. Harvey R. Levenson, Ph.D. is currently Department Head, Graphic Communication Department, California Polytechnic State University at San Luis Obispo, California, with a prestigious career in the graphic arts profession & has created an authoritative dictionary for anyone working in these fields. Books can be ordered through a bookstore or directly from the publisher: Summa Books, 560 N. Moorpark Rd., Suite 134, Thousand Oaks, CA 91360. ***Publisher Provided Annotation.***

Complete Dictionary of Media Times. William P. Brown & Kathryn Sederberg. 156p. 1986. pap. 14.95 (*0-913247-01-4*) Commerce Comns.

Complete Dictionary of Music. Jean-Jacques Rousseau. LC 72-1664. reprint ed. 55.00 (*0-404-08335-8*) AMS Pr.

Complete Dictionary of Opera & Operetta. James Anderson. 1993. 12.99 (*0-517-09156-9*) Random Hse Value.

Complete Dictionary of Sexology. enl. ed. Ed. by Robert T. Francoeur et al. 784p. (C). 1995. pap. text ed. 29.95 (*0-8264-0672-6*) Continuum.

Complete Dictionary of Wood. Thomas Corkhill. (Reprints Ser.). (Illus.). 656p. 1989. reprint ed. 24.95 (*0-88029-346-2*); reprint ed. pap. 14.95 (*0-88029-329-2*) Dorset Pr.

Complete Diet Guide: For Runners & Other Athletes. Hal Higdon. LC 77-84521. (Illus.). 232p. 1978. pap. 5.95 (*0-89037-090-7*) Anderson World.

Complete Digest of Supreme Court Cases, 16 vols. Surendra Malik. (C). 1991. Vols. 1-14. 135.00 (*0-318-69177-9*) St Mut.

Complete Digest of Supreme Court Cases, 16 vols., 15. Surendra Malik. (C). 1991. 150.00 (*0-685-54753-1*) St Mut.

Complete Digest of Supreme Court Cases, 16 vols., 16. Surendra Malik. (C). 1991. 175.00 (*0-89771-692-2*) St Mut.

Complete Digest of Supreme Court Cases, 13 vols., Set. Surendra Malik. 9100p. (C). 1987. 1,235.00 (*0-685-25173-X*) St Mut.

Complete Digest of Supreme Court Cases, Vol. XVI. Surendra Malik. (C). 1991. text ed. 175.00 (*0-685-52020-X*) St Mut.

Complete Digest of Supreme Court Cases (Since 1950), Vol. XV. Surendra Malik. (C). 1991. 150.00 (*0-685-39737-8*) St Mut.

Complete Digest of Supreme Court Cases (Since 1950), Vol. XVI. Ed. by Surendra Malik. (C). 1991. 110.00 (*0-685-39736-X*) St Mut.

Complete Digest of Supreme Court Cases (Since 1950), Vols. I-XIV. Ed. by Surendra Malik. (C). 1991. 135.00 (*0-685-74318-7*) St Mut.

Complete Digest of Supreme Court Cases (1950 to Date), 16 vols. S. Malik. (C). 1989. Vol I to XIV published. 2,100.00 (*0-685-27878-6*) St Mut.

Complete Digest of Supreme Court Cases, 1950 to Present, Vol. XIV. Surendra Malik. 700p. 1987. 125.00 (*0-317-54851-4*) St Mut.

Complete Dinosaur Dictionary. Donald F. Glut. (Illus.). 320p. 1992. pap. 17.95 (*0-8065-1335-7*, Citadel Pr) Carol Pub Group.

Complete Direct Mail List Handbook: Everything You Need to Know about Lists & How to Use Them for Greater Profit. Ed Burnett. 736p. 1988. text ed. 59.95 (*0-13-159278-5*, Busn) P-H.

Complete Direct Marketing Sourcebook: A Step-by-Step Guide to Organizing & Managing a Successful Direct Marketing Program. John Kremer. (Small Business Editions Ser.). 309p. 1992. text ed. 59.95 (*0-471-55386-7*); pap. text ed. 19.95 (*0-471-55387-5*) Wiley.

Complete Directory for People with Chronic Illness, 1994. Ed. by Leslie Mackenzie. 600p. 1993. 135.00 (*0-939300-56-7*); pap. 125.00 (*0-939300-55-9*) Grey Hse Pub.

Complete Directory for People with Disabilities. Ed. by Leslie Mackenzie. 800p. 1992. text ed. 125.00 (*0-939300-19-2*); pap. text ed. 99.95 (*0-685-60585-X*) Grey Hse Pub.

Complete Directory for People with Disabilities. 2nd ed. 1993. 125.00 (*0-939300-21-4*, 101590) Grey Hse Pub.

Complete Directory for People with Learning Disabilities, 1993. Ed. by Leslie Mackenzie. 800p. pap. 125.00 (*0-939300-29-X*); boxed write for info. (*0-939300-24-9*) Grey Hse Pub.

C

An Asterisk (*) at the beginning of an entry indicates that the title is appearing in BIP for the first time.

Complete Directory of Large Print Books & Serials 1994. Ed. by Bowker, R. R., Staff. 331p. 1994. 149.95 (*0-8352-3462-2*) Bowker.

Complete Directory of Large Print Books & Serials 1995. Ed. by Bowker, R. R., Staff. 343p. 1995. pap. 154.95 (*0-8352-3592-0*) Bowker.
"...fills an important niche...will prove indispensable to all libraries having visually handicapped patrons."-- ACADEMIC LIBRARY BOOK REVIEW. Bigger than ever, this invaluable guide covers the large-print field like no other resource. Inside you'll discover current, accurate book finding & ordering information on some 9,700 titles, 1,850 new this year, including scores of forthcoming works - with full entries for each in separate Subject (General, Children's & Textbook), Author & Title indexes. Books from British publishers are also listed. Up-to-date subject headings include Mystery & Suspense, Sports & Games, Crossword Puzzles, Humor & Historical Fiction & there's an enlarged Serials Index to some 96 large-print periodicals & newspapers. ***Publisher Provided Annotation.***

***Complete Directory of Large Print Books & Serials 1996.** Ed. by Bowker, R. R., Staff. 1996. write for info. (*0-8352-3750-8*) Bowker.

***Complete Directory to Prime Time Network & Cable TV Shows, 1946-Present.** 6th ed. Tim Brooks & Earle Marsh. 1440p. 1995. pap. 23.00 (*0-345-39736-3*) Ballantine.

Complete Directory to Prime Time Network TV Shows, 1946-Present. 5th ed. Tim Brooks & Earle Marsh. 1216p. 1992. pap. 19.00 (*0-345-37792-3*, Ballantine Trade) Ballantine.

Complete Dirty Laundry Comics. R. Crumb. 1993. pap. 16.95 (*0-86719-379-4*) Last Gasp.

Complete Displaywriter Manual & Guide with 98 Time-Saving Techniques. Betty Hutchinson & Warner A. Hutchinson. LC 86-3267. 378p. 1986. text ed. 34.95 (*0-13-157249-0*) P-H.

Complete Divorce Recovery Handbook: Grief, Stress, Guilt, Children, Co-dependence, Self-esteem, Dating, Remarriage. John P. Splinter. 288p. 1992. pap. 9.99 (*0-310-57391-2*) Zondervan.

Complete Do-It-Yourself Guide to Nitrous-Oxide Injection. David Vizard. 128p. 1987. 16.95 (*0-931472-16-4*, TC-070115) Motorbooks Intl.

Complete Do-It-Yourself Personnel Department: Includes Model Forms, Checklists, & Sample Manuals. Mary E. Cook. 547p. 1991. ring bd. 89.95 (*0-685-71685-6*, 796) Inst Real Estate.

Complete Document Restoration Manual for Laypersons. Hughes. 24p. (Orig.). 1985. reprint ed. 6.95 (*0-910653-04-6*, 80-012, Red River Pr) Archival Servs.

Complete Dog Book. William Bruette. 1992. lib. bdg. 250.00 (*0-8490-5215-7*) Gordon Pr.

Complete Dog Book. 18th ed. American Kennel Club Staff. (Illus.). 832p. 1992. 27.50 (*0-87605-464-5*) Howell Bk.

Complete Dog Buyer's Guide. rev. ed. William A. Bruette & Kerry V. Donnelly. (Illus.). 608p. (Orig.). 1983. 17.95 (*0-86622-026-7*, H-1061) TFH Pubns.

Complete Dolls' House Book. Jean Nisbett. (Illus.). 208p. 1993. pap. 19.95 (*0-946819-44-0*, Pub. by Guild Mstr Craftsman UK) Sterling.

Complete Dracula. Radu Florescu & Raymond McNally. LC 92-28644. 1992. pap. 19.95 (*0-87411-595-7*) Copley Pub.

***Complete Draw-&-Design Kit.** (Let's Draw Dresses! Ser.). (J). (gr. 3-5). 1995. 7.95 (*0-448-40859-7*, G&D) Putnam Pub Group.

Complete Drawing Course: A Comprehensive Learning Guide & Reference Manual. Ian Simpson. LC 93-84163. (Illus.). 224p. 1993. 29.95 (*1-56138-349-X*) Running Pr.

Complete Drawings of Albrecht Durer: A Complete Catalogue Raisonne, 6 vols, Set. Walter L. Strauss. LC 73-80442. (Illus.). 1974. 540.00 (*0-913870-00-5*) Abaris Bks.

Complete Dream Book. rev. ed. Edward F. Allen. 288p. 1985. mass mkt. 5.50 (*0-446-34105-3*) Warner Bks.

Complete Dream Journal. Laynee Wild. (Illus.). 128p. 1992. 17.95 (*1-56640-445-2*) Pomegranate Calif.

Complete Drug Reference: 1995 Edition. United States Pharmacopeia Staff. 1848p. 1994. 39.95 (*0-89043-769-6*) Consumer Reports.

Complete Druid's Handbook. David Pulver. (Advanced Dungeons & Dragons 2nd Ed. Accessory Ser.). 1994. pap. 18.00 (*1-56076-886-X*) TSR Inc.

***Complete DSM-IV Training Program, Set.** Reid. 1995. text ed., sl. 405.00 (*0-87630-771-3*); text ed., trans. 405.00 (*0-87630-772-1*) Brunner-Mazel.

Complete Dublin Diary of Stanislaus Joyce. Ed. by George H. Healey. LC 77-144033. 205p. reprint ed. pap. 58.50 (*0-8357-9076-2*, 2010319) Bks Demand.

Complete Dulcimer Handbook. Mark Biggs. 1993. 12.95 (*0-87166-892-0*, 94047); audio 9.98 (*1-56222-338-0*, 94047) Mel Bay.

Complete Dwarves. TSR Hobbies Staff. (Advanced Dungeons & Dragons Ser.). 128p. 1991. 18.00 (*1-56076-110-5*) TSR Inc.

Complete DX'er. 2nd ed. R. C. Locher, Jr. (Illus.). (Orig.). 1989. pap. 12.00 (*0-9617577-0-1*) Idiom Pr.

Complete DX7. Howard Massey. (Illus.). 288p. 1986. pap. 24.95 (*0-7119-0996-2*, AM63843) Music Sales.

Complete DX7II. Howard Massey. (Illus.). 308p. 1987. pap. 29.95 (*0-8256-1119-9*, AM67109) Music Sales.

Complete E. C. Segar Popeye, Vol. 10. E. C. Segar. Ed. by Richard Marshall. (Illus.). 160p. 1990. 35.00 (*1-56097-014-6*); pap. 16.95 (*1-56097-013-8*) Fantagraph Bks.

Complete E. C. Segar Popeye, Vol. 11. E. C. Segar. Ed. by Richard Marschall. (Illus.). 160p. 1990. 35.00 (*1-56097-016-2*); pap. 16.95 (*1-56097-015-4*) Fantagraph Bks.

Complete E. C. Segar Popeye, Dailies, 1935-37, Vol. 9. E. C. Segar. Ed. by Richard Marschall. (Illus.). 160p. (Orig.). 1989. 30.00 (*0-930193-94-6*); pap. 14.95 (*0-930193-93-8*) Fantagraph Bks.

Complete E. C. Segar Popeye, Vol. 3: Sundays, 1934-36. E. C. Segar. Ed. by Richard Marschall. (Illus.). 120p. (Orig.). 1985. 30.00 (*0-930193-11-3*); pap. 14.95 (*0-930193-10-5*) Fantagraph Bks.

Complete E. C. Segar Popeye, Vol. 4: Sundays, 1936-38. E. C. Segar. Ed. by Richard Marschall. (Illus.). 120p. (Orig.). 1986. 30.00 (*0-930193-20-2*); pap. 14.95 (*0-930193-19-9*) Fantagraph Bks.

Complete E. C. Segar Popeye, Vol. 6: Dailies, 1930-31. E. C. Segar. Ed. by Richard Marschall. (Illus.). 160p. (Orig.). 1987. 30.00 (*0-930193-51-2*); pap. 14.95 (*0-930193-50-4*) Fantagraph Bks.

Complete E. C. Segar Popeye, Vol. 7: Dailies, 1931-32. E. C. Segar. Ed. by Richard Marschall. (Illus.). 160p. (Orig.). 1988. 30.00 (*0-930193-59-8*); pap. 14.95 (*0-930193-58-X*) Fantagraph Bks.

Complete E. C. Segar Popeye, Vol. 8: Dailies, 1933-34. E. C. Segar. Ed. by Richard Marschall. (Illus.). 160p. (Orig.). 1989. 30.00 (*0-930193-87-3*); pap. 14.95 (*0-930193-86-5*) Fantagraph Bks.

Complete Early Childhood Behavior Management Guide. Kathy Watkins & Lucius Durant. 256p. 1992. 27.95 (*0-87628-261-3*) Ctr Appl Res.

Complete Early Childhood Curriculum Resource. Mary A. Sobut & Bonnie N. Bogen. 304p. 1991. pap. text ed. 24.95 (*0-87628-238-9*) P-H.

Complete Electric Bass Player, Bk. 1: The Method. Chuck Rainey. (Illus.). 200p. 1985. pap. 15.95 (*0-8256-2425-8*, AM37250) Music Sales.

Complete Electric Bass Player, Bk. 2: Playing Concepts & Dexterity. Chuck Rainey. (Illus.). 80p. 1985. pap. 9.95 (*0-8256-2426-6*, AM37268) Music Sales.

Complete Electric Bass Player, Bk. 3: Electric Bass Improvisation. Chuck Rainey. (Illus.). 64p. 1985. pap. 9.95 (*0-8256-2427-4*, AM37284) Music Sales.

Complete Electric Bass Player, Bk. 4: Slapping Techniques. Chuck Rainey. (Illus.). 64p. 1985. pap. 9.95 (*0-8256-2428-2*, AM37276) Music Sales.

Complete Electric Bass Player, Bk. 5: Bass Chording. Chuck Rainey. (Illus.). 48p. 1985. pap. 9.95 (*0-8256-2429-0*, AM39405) Music Sales.

Complete Electric Blues Guitar Book. Mike Christansen. (Complete Book Ser.). 1993. 12.95 (*1-56222-556-1*, 94846); audio 9.98 (*1-56222-555-3*, 94846) Mel Bay.

Complete Electronic Percussion Book. David Crombie. (Illus.). 80p. 1987. pap. 11.95 (*0-8256-1092-3*, AM65772) Music Sales.

Complete Electronic, Spring-Summer 1991. 1991. write for info. (*0-8306-0847-8*) TAB Bks.

Complete Electronics Home-Study Course, 2 Vols. 224p. 1989. Vol. 1, 224p. pap. write for info. (*0-933132-09-3*) Command Prods.

Complete Electronics Home-Study Course, 2 Vols., Set. 768p. 1990. pap. 49.95 (*0-933132-10-7*) Command Prods.

Complete Elementary Physical Education Guide. Rosalie Bryant & Eloise M. Oliver. 1974. text ed. 22.95 (*0-13-159939-9*, Parker Publishing Co) P-H.

Complete ElfQuest. limited ed. Wendy Pini & Richard Pini. Ed. by Kay Reynolds. (ElfQuest Ser.). (Illus.). 652p. 1985. 120.00 (*0-89865-453-X*, Starblaze) Donning Co.

Complete Elliott Wave Writings of A. Hamilton Bolton. Robert R. Prechter, Jr. (Illus.). 412p. 1994. 39.00 (*0-932750-22-2*) New Classics Lib.

***Complete Employee Handbook: A Guide for Small & Medium Businesses.** Michael Holzschu. 220p. 1995. 39.95 (*1-55921-135-0*); pap. 29.95 (*1-55921-136-9*) Moyer Bell.

***Complete Employee Handbook Made Easy.** Ed. by Jim Collison. 209p. 1994. 189.00 (*0-9624320-7-5*) Sunburst IA.

Complete Encyclopedia of Aerobics. A. K. Klinger et al. (Illus.). 319p. 1986. pap. 14.95 (*0-317-59361-7*) Mouvement Pubns.

Complete Encyclopedia of Alcoholic Beverages. 1988. 2.00 (*0-685-43999-2*, 103) Am Bartenders.

Complete Encyclopedia of Arms & Weapons. Ed. by L. Tarassuk & C. Blair. (Illus.). 544p. 1987. 41.50 (*0-685-43883-X*) Random Hse Value.

Complete Encyclopedia of Fingering Charts: A Vital Reference for Teachers, Directors & Students. Heritage Music Press Staff. (Illus.). 32p. (Orig.). 1992. pap. 7.95 (*0-89328-105-0*, PP362) Lorenz Corp.

Complete Encyclopedia of Hockey. Zander Hollander. 1992. pap. 22.95 (*0-8103-9419-7*, 089151) Visible Ink Pr.

Complete Encyclopedia of Hockey,, Vol. 4. 4th ed. Ed. by Zander Hollander. 1992. 55.00 (*0-8103-8869-3*, 101514) Gale.

Complete Encyclopedia of Illustration. J. G. Heck. (Illus.). 500p. 1979. 17.95 (*0-517-27889-8*) Random Hse Value.

Complete Encyclopedia of Music. John W. Moore. LC 72-1713. reprint ed. 79.50 (*0-404-09916-5*) AMS Pr.

***Complete Encyclopedia of Stitchery.** Milded G. Ryan. (Illus.). 704p. 1995. pap. 15.95 (*1-55850-474-5*) Adams Pubng.

***Complete Encyclopedia of Stitchery.** Mildred G. Ryan. 704p. 1991. 11.95 (*1-56865-066-3*, GuildAmerica) Dblday Bk Music.

Complete Encyclopedia of Teddy Bears. Jacki Brooks. 191p. 1983. 29.95 (*0-87588-365-6*) Hobby Hse.

Complete Encyclopedia of Wild Game & Fish Cleaning & Cooking, 3 Vols., 1. Pat Billmeyer. LC 83-50091. (Illus.). 96p. 1983. pap. 4.95 (*0-9606262-4-7*) Yesnaby Inc.

Complete Encyclopedia of Wild Game & Fish Cleaning & Cooking, 3 Vols., 2. Pat Billmeyer. LC 83-50091. (Illus.). 96p. 1983. pap. 4.95 (*0-9606262-5-5*) Yesnaby Inc.

Complete Encyclopedia of Wild Game & Fish Cleaning & Cooking, 3 Vols., 3. Pat Billmeyer. LC 83-50091. (Illus.). 96p. 1983. pap. 4.95 (*0-9606262-6-3*) Yesnaby Inc.

Complete Encyclopedia of Wild Game & Fish Cleaning & Cooking, 3 Vols., Set. Pat Billmeyer. LC 83-50091. (Illus.). 96p. 1983. pap. write for info. (*0-9606262-3-9*) Yesnaby Inc.

Complete Encyclopedia to G. I. Joe. Vincent Santelmo. LC 92-74793. (Illus.). 448p. 1993. 24.95 (*0-87341-225-7*) Krause Pubns.

Complete English Cocker Spaniel. Connie Vanacore & Dale Hood. Ed. by Marcy Zingler. (Illus.). 256p. 1990. 25.95 (*0-87605-117-4*) Howell Bk.

Complete English Poems. George Herbert. 496p. 1992. pap. 11.95 (*0-14-042348-6*, Penguin Classics) Viking Penguin.

Complete English Poems. Samuel Johnson. 272p. 1993. 11.95 (*0-14-042296-X*, Penguin Classics) Viking Penguin.

Complete English Poems. annot. ed. John Skelton. 576p. 1992. 12.95 (*0-14-042233-1*, Penguin Classics) Viking Penguin.

Complete English Poems, of Education, Areopagitica. John Milton. Ed. by Gordon Campbell. 412p. 1993. pap. 12.95 (*0-460-87275-3*, Everyman's Classic Lib) C E Tuttle.

Complete English Poems of John Donne. John Donne. Ed. by A. J. Smith. (Poets Ser.). 1977. pap. 11.95 (*0-14-042209-9*, Penguin Classics) Viking Penguin.

Complete Engravings, Etchings, & Dry Points of Albrecht Durer. Albrecht Durer. Ed. by Walter L. Strauss. (Illus.). 240p. (Orig.). 1972. pap. 10.95 (*0-486-22851-7*) Dover.

Complete Enochian Dictionary: A Dictionary of the Angelic Language As Revealed to John Dee & Edward Kelley. Donald C. Laycock. (Illus.). 272p. (Orig.). 1994. pap. 16.95 (*0-87728-817-8*) Weiser.

Complete Entertainment Discography from 1897 to 1942. 2nd ed. Brian Rust & Allen Debus. (Roots of Jazz Ser.). 790p. 1988. reprint ed. lib. bdg. 95.00 (*0-306-76210-2*) Da Capo.

Complete Erotic Reader. (Orig.). 1992. pap. 4.95 (*1-56333-063-6*) Masquerade.

Complete Essays. Michel E. De Montaigne. Tr. & Intro. by M. A. Screech. 1344p. 1993. 22.50 (*0-14-044604-4*, Penguin Classics) Viking Penguin.

Complete Essays, Vol. 1. Zora Neale Hurston. Date not set. 22.50 (*0-06-016730-0*, HarpT); pap. 12.95 (*0-685-69205-1*, PL) HarpC.

Complete Essays, Vol. 2. Zora Neale Hurston. Date not set. pap. 12.95 (*0-06-092174-9*, PL) HarpC.

Complete Essays of Montaigne. Michel De Montaigne. Tr. by Donald M. Frame. xxiii, 883p. 1958. 47.50 (*0-8047-0485-6*); pap. 19.95 (*0-8047-0486-4*) Stanford U Pr.

Complete Estate Planning Guide. rev. ed. Robert Brosterman & Kathleen Adams. 384p. 1994. pap. 6.99 (*0-451-62875-6*, Ment) NAL-Dutton.

Complete Estate Planning Guide: Including the Pros & Cons of Avoiding Probate. rev. ed. Robert Brosterman & Kathleen J. Adams. 1982. pap. 5.99 (*0-451-62830-6*, Ment) NAL-Dutton.

***Complete Etchings of David Hunter 1978-1991.** Chester Smith. (Illus.). 297p. 1995. pap. 9.50 (*0-9633587-1-5*) Seaside Art.

***Complete Etchings of Rembrandt: Reproduced in Original Size.** unabridged ed. Rembrandt Van Rijn. Ed. by Gary Schwartz. LC 94-27405. (Illus.). 224p. 1994. pap. text ed. 17.95 (*0-486-28181-7*) Dover.

Complete Exorcist: Exorcism from Scratch. Nelson White & Anne White. LC 83-50160. (Illus.). 75p. (Orig.). 1983. pap. 18.00 (*0-939856-33-6*) Tech Group.

***Complete Facilitator: A Guide.** Barry J. Roberts & Kevin Upton. (Illus.). 96p. (Orig.). 1994. pap. 29.95 (*0-9646972-0-3*) Howick Assocs.

Complete Fairy Tales of Charles Perrault. Tr. by Neil Philip & Nicoletta Simborowski. LC 92-17781. (Illus.). (J). 1993. 18.95 (*0-395-57002-6*, Clarion Bks) HM.

Complete Fairy Tales of Oscar Wilde. Oscar Wilde. 224p. (J). 1990. pap. 4.95 (*0-451-52435-7*, Sig Classics) NAL-Dutton.

Complete Fairy Tales of the Brothers Grimm, 2 vols. Tr. by Jack D. Zipes. (Classics Ser.). (Illus.). 432p. 1988. Vol. II, 432 pgs. 5.95 (*0-553-21251-6*, Bantam Classics); Vol. I, 480 pgs. mass mkt. 5.50 (*0-553-21238-9*, Bantam Classics) Bantam.

Complete Fairy Tales of the Brothers Grimm. Jack D. Zipes. 1992. pap. 15.95 (*0-553-37101-0*) Bantam.

Complete Family Cookbook. Alex Barker. 160p. 1994. 15.98 (*0-8317-5652-7*) Smithmark.

***Complete Family Guide to College Financial Aid.** Richard W. Black. LC 95-8201. 1995. pap. write for info. (*0-399-52158-5*, Perigree Bks) Berkley Pub.

***Complete Family Guide to Healthy Living.** 1995. 24.95 (*0-7894-0114-2*, 6-70468) Dorling Kindersley.

***Complete Family Guide to Healthy Living.** 1995. pap. 15.95 (*0-7894-0120-7*, 6-70469) Dorling Kindersley.

Complete Family Guide to Jewish Holidays. Dalia H. Renberg. LC 84-11008. (Illus.). (J). (gr. 4 up). 1985. pap. 22.95 (*0-915361-09-4*) Modan-Adama Bks.

Complete Family Health & Medical Guide. Gregg Albers. 608p. 1993. 34.99 (*0-8499-0839-6*) Word Inc.

***Complete Family Medical Adviser.** Martin Edwards. 1994. pap. 11.95 (*0-572-01995-5*, Pub. by W Foulsham UK) Trans-Atl Phila.

***Complete Family Preventive Law Pack.** John F. Goodson. 1991. pap. 44.95 (*0-934141-10-X*) Forms Man.

Complete Fantasy Sports Handbook: Comprehensive Rules & Guidelines for Playing Fantasy Versions of All Four Major Sports. Casey Moore & Bob Alessi. 106p. (Orig.). 1994. pap. write for info. (*0-9641982-0-7*) FSF.

Complete Fantasy-Suites for Three Viols with Organ, Vol. 1: Nine Suites for Treble, Tenor & Bass Viols. John Hingeston. Ed. by John Dornenburg. (Viol Consort Ser.: No. 20). ii, 120p. 1994. 30.00 (*1-56571-080-0*, VC020) PRB Prods.

Complete Fat, Fiber, & Calorie Counter Also Includes Sodium. Darwin Dennison et al. 250p. 1993. pap. write for info. (*0-923713-15-8*) DINE Syst.

***Complete Father Brown.** G. K. Chesterton. 1032p. 1987. 19.98 (*1-56865-098-1*, GuildAmerica) Dblday Bk Music.

Complete Father Brown. Gilbert K. Chesterton. 1987. pap. 13.95 (*0-14-009766-X*, Penguin Bks) Viking Penguin.

Complete Fawlty Towers. John Cleese & Connie Booth. 1989. pap. 16.00 (*0-679-72127-4*) Pantheon.

Complete Federal Taxes Service. write for info. (*0-318-57349-0*) P-H.

***Complete Ferrari.** Roger Hicks. (Illus.). 240p. 1994. 24.98 (*0-87938-961-3*) Motorbooks Intl.

Complete Fiction of Bruno Schulz: The Street of Crocodiles & Sanatorium Under the Sign of the Hourglass. Aft. by Bruno Schulz & Jerzy Ficowski. 320p. 1989. 22.95 (*0-8027-1091-3*) Walker & Co.

Complete Fiddling Book. Craig Duncan et al. (Complete Book Ser.). 1993. 15.00 (*0-87166-837-8*, 94367) Mel Bay.

Complete Field Guide to Kitty Cat Positions. Linda Miles & Betty Wilson. LC 92-40530. 128p. 1993. 6.95 (*0-681-41788-9*) Longmeadow Pr.

Complete Fifty State Guidebook to Kit Cars & Street Rod Registration. LC 85-132042. 160p. 1985. 4.95 (*0-932685-00-5*) News Media Info.

Complete Film Dictionary. Ira Konigsberg. (Illus.). 512p. 1989. pap. 15.95 (*0-452-00980-4*, Mer) NAL-Dutton.

Complete Film Production Handbook. Eve L. Honthaner. LC 93-9433. (Illus.). 1993. pap. 34.95 (*0-943728-41-X*) Lone Eagle Pub.

Complete Films of Alfred Hitchock. Robert A. Harris & Michael Lasky. (Illus.). 256p. 1993. pap. 16.95 (*0-8065-1464-7*, Citadel Pr) Carol Pub Group.

Complete Films of Bela Lugosi. Richard Bojarski. 1992. pap. 15.95 (*0-8065-0808-6*, Citadel Pr) Carol Pub Group.

Complete Films of Bette Davis. Gene Ringgold. 1990. pap. 15.95 (*0-8065-1177-X*, Citadel Pr) Carol Pub Group.

Complete Films of Buster Keaton. Jim Kline. LC 92-37553. 1993. pap. 16.95 (*0-8065-1303-9*) Carol Pub Group.

Complete Films of Cecil B. Demille. Gene Ringgold & DeWitt Bodeen. (Illus.). 386p. 1985. reprint ed. pap. 12.95 (*0-8065-0956-2*, Citadel Pr) Carol Pub Group.

Complete Films of Charlie Chaplin. rev. ed. Gerald D. McDonald et al. (Illus.). 224p. 1988. reprint ed. pap. 15.95 (*0-8065-1095-1*, Citadel Pr) Carol Pub Group.

Complete Films of Clark Gable. Gabe Essoe. (Illus.). 256p. 1986. pap. 16.95 (*0-8065-0985-6*, Citadel Pr) Carol Pub Group.

Complete Films of Corrado Costa. Corrado Costa. Tr. by Paul Vangelisti. LC 83-60077. 64p. (Orig.). 1983. pap. 4.00 (*0-88031-063-4*) Invisible-Red Hill.

Complete Films of Edward G. Robinson. Alvin H. Marill. 1990. pap. 15.95 (*0-8065-1181-8*, Citadel Pr) Carol Pub Group.

Complete Films of Frank Capra. Victor Scherle & William T. Levy. (Illus.). 288p. 1992. pap. 17.95 (*0-8065-1296-2*, Citadel Pr) Carol Pub Group.

Complete Films of Henry Fonda. Tony Thomas. 1990. pap. 15.95 (*0-8065-1189-3*, Citadel Pr) Carol Pub Group.

Complete Films of Humphrey Bogart. Clifford Mccarty. 1985. pap. 16.95 (*0-8065-0955-4*, Citadel Pr) Carol Pub Group.

Complete Films of Ingrid Bergman. Lawrence J. Quirk. 1989. pap. 14.95 (*0-8065-0972-4*, Citadel Pr) Carol Pub Group.

Complete Films of James Cagney. Homer Dickens. (Citadel Film Ser.). 1989. pap. 14.95 (*0-8065-1152-4*, Citadel Pr) Carol Pub Group.

Complete Films of Jeanette MacDonald & Nelson Eddy. Philip Castanza. 1991. 14.95 (*0-685-47900-5*, Citadel Pr) Carol Pub Group.

Complete Films of Joan Crawford. rev. ed. Lawrence J. Quirk. (Illus.). 224p. 1988. pap. 14.95 (*0-8065-1078-1*, Citadel Pr) Carol Pub Group.

Complete Films of John Huston. John McCarty. 1990. pap. 15.95 (*0-8065-1190-7*, Citadel Pr) Carol Pub Group.

Complete Films of John Wayne. Steve Zmijewsky et al. 304p. 1983. 19.95 (*0-8065-0872-8*, Citadel Pr) Carol Pub Group.

Complete Films of Judy Garland. Joe Morella & Edward Z. Epstein. (Illus.). 204p. 1986. reprint ed. pap. 14.95 (*0-8065-1017-X*, Citadel Pr) Carol Pub Group.

Complete Films of Laurence Olivier. Jerry Vermilye. (Illus.). 288p. 1992. pap. 18.95 (*0-8065-1302-0*, Citadel Pr) Carol Pub Group.

Complete Films of Mae West. rev. ed. Jon Tuska. (Classics from the Citadel Film Ser.). (Illus.). 208p. 1992. pap. 15.95 (*0-8065-1359-4*, Citadel Pr) Carol Pub Group.

Complete Films of Marilyn Monroe. Michael Conway & Mark Ricci. (Illus.). 160p. 1986. reprint ed. pap. 14.95 (*0-8065-1016-1*, Citadel Pr) Carol Pub Group.

C

An Asterisk (*) at the beginning of an entry indicates that the title is appearing in BIP for the first time.

Complete Films of Marlene Dietrich. rev. ed. Homer Dickens. LC 92-17767. (Illus.). 256p. 1992. pap. 17.95 (*0-8065-1354-3*, Citadel Pr) Carol Pub Group.

Complete Films of Orson Welles. James Howard. 1991. pap. 16.95 (*0-8065-1241-5*, Citadel Pr) Carol Pub Group.

Complete Films of Rita Hayworth: The Legend & Career of a Love Goddess. Gene Ringgold. (Illus.). 256p. 1992. pap. 15.95 (*0-8065-1260-1*, Citadel Pr) Carol Pub Group.

Complete Films of Spencer Tracy. Donald Deschner. (Illus.). 272p. 1987. reprint ed. pap. 12.95 (*0-8065-1038-2*, Citadel Pr) Carol Pub Group.

Complete Films of the Marx Brothers. Allen Eyles. (Illus.). 256p. 1992. pap. 17.95 (*0-8065-1301-2*, Citadel Pr) Carol Pub Group.

Complete Films of W. C. Fields. Donald Deschner. 1989. pap. 14.95 (*0-8065-1136-2*, Citadel Pr) Carol Pub Group.

Complete Films of William Holden. rev. ed. Lawrence J. Quirk. (Illus.). 288p. 1986. pap. 12.95 (*0-8065-0987-2*, Citadel Pr) Carol Pub Group.

Complete Films of William Powell. Lawrence J. Quirk. (Illus.). 288p. (Orig.). 1986. pap. 15.95 (*0-8065-0998-8*, Citadel Pr) Carol Pub Group.

Complete Financial Guide for Couples. Larry Burkett. 1993. pap. 10.99 (*1-56476-130-4*, Victor Books) SP Pubns.

Complete Financial Guide for Single Parents. Larry Burkett. 1992. pap. 8.99 (*0-89693-094-7*) SP Pubns.

Complete Financial Guide for Young Couples. Larry Burkett. 200p. 1989. 18.99 (*0-89693-634-1*, Victor Books) SP Pubns.

Complete Fingerstyle Guitar Book. Date not set. 15.00 (*0-685-75008-6*, 94561) Mel Bay.

Complete Firefighter Candidate. Arthur R. Couvillon. LC 89-81738. 150p. (Orig.). 1990. pap. 12.95 (*0-938329-58-8*) Info Guides.

Complete Firefighter's Exam Preparation Book. Norman Hall. 272p. 1991. pap. 9.95 (*1-55850-052-9*) Adams Pubng.

***Complete First Kitchen Handbook: A Complete Guide to Setting up Your First Kitchen Including over a Hundred Quick & Easy Recipes for Both the New & More Experienced Cook.** Karen J. Covey. (Illus.). 176p. (Orig.). 1995. pap. write for info. (*0-9646880-0-X*) Fiyah Pubng.

Complete Fish & Shellfish Cookbook. Diana Vowels. 1993. 17.98 (*1-55521-913-6*) Bk Sales Inc.

Complete Fish Cookbook. Dan Morris & Inez Morris. LC 73-161249. 1972. 10.00 (*0-672-51421-4*, Bobbs) Macmillan.

Complete Fish Cookbook. rev. ed. Dan Morris & Inez Morris. 436p. 1989. reprint ed. pap. 16.95 (*0-88317-155-4*) Stoeger Pub Co.

Complete Fish on the Grill: More Than 200 Easy & Delectable Recipes. Barbara Grunes & Phyllis Magida. 320p. 1994. pap. 11.95 (*0-8092-3618-4*) Contemp Bks.

Complete Fishing Guide to Deep Creek Lake: Maryland's Best Kept Secret. T. A. Doolan. (Illus.). 96p. (Orig.). 1992. pap. 8.95 (*0-929915-07-0*) Headline Bks.

Complete Fishkeeper: Everything Aquarium Fishes Need to Stay Happy, Healthy, & Alive. Joseph S. Levine. (Illus.). 288p. 1991. 30.00 (*0-688-10146-1*) Morrow.

***Complete Fishkeeper: Everything Aquarium Fishes Need to Stay Happy, Healthy, & Alive.** Joseph S. Levine. 1995. pap. 15.00 (*0-688-14068-8*, Quill) Morrow.

Complete Flatpicking Guitar Book. Steve Kaufman. (Complete Book Ser.). 1993. 15.00 (*1-56222-161-2*, 94562); audio 9.98 (*1-56222-178-7*, 94562) Mel Bay.

Complete Flower Arranger. Pamela Westland. (Illus.). 256p. 1995. 19.98 (*0-8317-8199-8*) Smithmark.

Complete Flower Arranging Book. Susan Conder. (Illus.). 192p. 1992. 24.95 (*0-89134-454-3*, 30405) North Light Bks.

Complete Flower Craft Book. Susan Conder et al. (Illus.). 144p. 1994. 24.95 (*0-89134-539-6*) North Light Bks.

Complete Flower Paintings & Drawings of Graham Stuart Thomas. Intro. by George Taylor. (Alternate Selection of the Garden Book Club Ser.). (Illus.). 208p. 1987. 45.00 (*0-317-61187-9*) Abrams.

Complete Flower Paintings & Drawings of Graham Stuart Thomas. Graham S. Thomas. (Illus.). 208p. 1987. 45.00 (*0-8109-1666-5*) Sagapr.

Complete Flute Player. John Sands. (Illus.). 48p. 1986. pap. 8.95 (*0-7119-0901-6*, AM62852) Music Sales.

Complete Flute Player, Bk. 2. John Sands. (Illus.). 48p. 1986. pap. 8.95 (*0-7119-0902-4*, AM62860) Music Sales.

Complete Flute Player, Bk. 3. John Sands. (Illus.). 48p. 1986. pap. 8.95 (*0-7119-0903-2*, AM62878) Music Sales.

Complete Flute Player, Bk. 4. John Sands. (Illus.). 48p. 1986. pap. 8.95 (*0-7119-0904-0*, AM62886) Music Sales.

Complete Flute Player: Omnibus Edition, 4 bks. in 1. John Sands. (Illus.). 192p. 1986. pap. 29.95 (*0-7119-0905-9*, AM62894) Music Sales.

Complete Folding Kayaker. Ralph A. Diaz. 1994. pap. text ed. 14.95 (*0-07-016734-6*) McGraw.

Complete Folk Guitar Book. Jerry Silverman. (Complete Book Ser.). 1993. 19.95 (*1-56222-092-6*, 94410); audio 9.98 (*1-56222-162-0*, 94410) Mel Bay.

Complete Foot Book: First Aid for Your Feet. Donald S. Pritt & Morton Walker. LC 91-33326. (Illus.). 176p. (Orig.). 1992. pap. 12.95 (*0-89529-434-6*) Avery Pub.

Complete Footwear Dictionary. William A. Rossi. LC 91-48230. 171p. 1994. lib. bdg. 34.50 (*0-89464-715-6*) Krieger.

***Complete Ford Flathead V8 Engine Manual.** Ron Caridono. (Illus.). 200p. 1995. pap. 19.95 (*1-884089-11-9*) CarTech.

Complete Ford V8 Flathead Engine Manual. Ron Ceridano. (Illus.). 200p. 1994. pap. 19.95 (*1-884089-09-7*) Voyageur Pr.

Complete Foundation & Floor Framing Book. Dan Ramsey. (Illus.). 220p. 1987. pap. 15.95 (*0-8306-2878-9*) TAB Bks.

Complete Fox. Les Stocker. (Illus.). 170p. 1994. pap. 15.95 (*0-7011-3776-2*, Pub. by Chatto & Windus UK) Trafalgar.

Complete Franchise Book: Everything You Need to Know about Buying or Starting Your Own Franchise. 2nd rev. ed. Dennis L. Foster. 275p. (Orig.). 1993. pap. 14.95 (*1-55958-316-9*) Prima Pub.

Complete Franchise Book: What You Must Know & Are Rarely Told about Buying or Starting Your Own Franchise. Dennis L. Foster. 250p. 1989. 17.95 (*0-685-24420-2*); pap. 14.95 (*0-914629-84-0*) Prima Pub.

Complete Frank Miller Batman. Frank Miller. (Deluxe Leatherbound Ser.). (Illus.). 312p. 1989. 29.95 (*0-681-40969-X*) Longmeadow Pr.

Complete Freedom & Other Stories. Tove Ditlevsen. Tr. by Jack Brondum. LC 81-15124. 96p. 1982. pap. 9.95 (*0-915306-24-7*) Curbstone.

Complete French. Lev Psakhis. (Batsford Chess Library). 256p. 1993. pap. 22.95 (*0-8050-2641-X*, Owl) H Holt & Co.

Complete French Poems of Rainer Maria Rilke. Rainer Maria Rilke. Tr. & Pref. by A. Poulin, Jr. LC 86-81786. 383p. (Orig.). 1986. pap. 14.00 (*0-915308-83-5*) Graywolf.

Complete Frog: A Guide for the Very Young Naturalist. Elizabeth A. Lacey. LC 88-9343. (Illus.). 72p. (J). (gr. k-4). 1989. 12.95 (*0-688-08017-0*); lib. bdg. 12.88 (*0-688-08018-9*) Lothrop.

Complete Fuel Systems & Emission Control: Student Technician's Shop Manual. Ed. by Robert Scharff. LC 93-20196. 1993. 45.95 (*0-8273-4769-3*) Delmar.

Complete Funk Bass Book. Mike Hiland. (Complete Book Ser.). 1993. 9.95 (*1-56222-660-6*, 94882); audio 9.98 (*1-56222-812-9*, 94882) Mel Bay.

Complete Funk Drum Book. Date not set. 12.95 (*0-7866-0032-2*, 95164); audio 9.98 (*0-7866-0033-0*, 95164C) Mel Bay.

Complete Galley Slave. Gillian Morgan. 144p. 1987. 40.00 (*0-85937-123-9*, Pub. by K Mason Pubns Ltd UK) St Mut.

Complete Games of Bobby Fischer. Ed. by Robert G. Wade & Kevin J. O'Connell. (Batsford Chess Library). 476p. 1993. pap. 29.00 (*0-8050-2623-1*, Owl) H Holt & Co.

Complete Games Trainers Play: Experiential Learning Exercises. Edward E. Scannell & John W. Newstrom. LC 94-19014. 1994. write for info. (*0-07-046432-4*) McGraw.

Complete Garage Sale Book: How to Organize & Operate a Sure-Fire Money Maker. Marian Hoyle. 60p. (Orig.). 1986. pap. 5.95 (*0-937351-02-4*) Hoyle Bks.

Complete Garage Sale Kit: Everything You Need to Make Money At Your Next Garage Sale. Diana Rix & Monica Rix-Paxson. LC 94-8046. 1994. pap. 7.95 (*1-57071-000-7*) Sourcebks.

Complete Garbo Talks. Garbo. 125p. (Orig.). 1992. pap. 9.95 (*1-881152-03-0*) Big Breakfast.

Complete Garden Guide to Native Perennia. Glenn Keator. 1990. pap. 16.95 (*0-87701-699-2*) Chronicle Bks.

Complete Garden Guide to the Native Shrubs of California. Glenn Keator. 320p. 1994. pap. 16.95 (*0-8118-0402-X*) Chronicle Bks.

Complete Garden Planning Manual. Derek Fell et al. (Illus.). 224p. 1989. 24.95 (*0-89586-658-7*) Price Stern.

Complete Gardener's Almanac: A Month-by-Month Guide to Successful Gardening. Marjorie Willison. (Illus.). 320p. (Orig.). 1993. pap. 24.95 (*1-55109-057-0*, Pub. by Nimbus Publishing Ltd CN) Chelsea Green Pub.

***Complete Gardner.** John Brookes. 1994. 24.99 (*0-517-10287-0*) Random Hse Value.

Complete Garlic Lovers' Cookbook. Gilroy Garlic Festival Committee Staff. LC 87-13865. 376p. 1987. 19.95 (*0-89087-503-0*) Celestial Arts.

Complete GCSE Computer Studies. M. Amor & J. Fairhurst. (C). 1987. 80.00 (*0-85950-244-9*, Pub. by S Thornes Pubs UK) St Mut.

Complete GCSE Computer Studies: Teacher's Guide. Ed. by Stanley Thornes. (C). 1987. 90.00 (*0-85950-548-0*, Pub. by S Thornes Pubs UK) St Mut.

Complete GD AM PK 1986. National Park Foundation Staff. 1986. pap. 7.95 (*0-685-14507-7*) Viking Penguin.

Complete GED Preparation. Steck-Vaughn Staff. 1993. pap. 11.95 (*0-8114-4477-5*) Raintree Steck-V.

***Complete GED Preparation Package.** Steck-Vaughn Staff. (YA). 1994. pap. 15.95 (*0-8114-6195-5*) Raintree Steck-V.

***Complete Geography Project & Activity Book.** Julio. 1995. pap. (*0-590-49473-2*) Scholastic Inc.

Complete George Washington Anniversary Programs for Every School Grade: New Ways to Honor the Father of Our Country. Alma Laird. 1977. 15.95 (*0-8369-6389-X*, 7453) Ayer.

***Complete Gil Hibben Knife Throwing Guide.** Gil Hibben. Ed. by C. Houston Price. (Illus.). 64p. (Orig.). 1994. pap. 7.95 (*1-886950-02-4*) United Cutlery.

Complete Gillette Collector Handbook. Phillip L. Krumholz. (Illus.). 250p. 1992. 23.95 (*0-9620987-2-8*) AdLibs Pub Co.

Complete Ginseng Grower's Manual. rev. ed. David F. Curran. Ed. by Patricia A. Curran. LC 83-70439. (Illus.). 185p. (Orig.). 1993. reprint ed. ring bd. 79.95 (*1-881417-02-6*) D F Curran Prods.

Complete Gladiators Handbook. Colin McComb. (Advanced Dungeons & Dragons, Second Edition; Al-Qadim Ser.). (Illus.). 1993. pap. 15.00 (*1-56076-616-6*) TSR Inc.

Complete Gold Country Guidebook: Discovering California's Gold Rush Region. 4th ed. B. Sangwan. (California Ser.). (Illus.). 168p. 1993. pap. 9.95 (*0-916841-29-4*) Indian Chief.

***Complete Golden Dawn Cipher Manuscript.** Ed. & Pref. by Darcy Kuntz. (Golden Dawn Studies: No. 1). (Illus.). (Orig.). 1995. pap. 19.95 (*1-55818-325-6*) Holmes Pub.

***Complete Golden Dawn Cipher Manuscripts.** Ed. & Pref. by Darcy Kuntz. (Illus.). 1995. 37.50 (*1-55818-321-3*) Holmes Pub.

Complete Golden Dawn System of Magic. Israel Regardie. LC 83-81664. (Illus.). 1200p. 1991. reprint ed. 49.95 (*1-56184-037-8*) New Falcon Pubns.

***Complete Golden Dawn System of Magic: An Interpretation of Aleister Crowley.** Israel Regardie. LC 83-81664. 1983. 49.95 (*0-941404-12-9*) New Falcon Pubns.

Complete Golf Club Fitting Plan. Ralph Maltby. (Illus.). 400p. 1986. pap. 38.50 (*0-9606792-7-8*) R Maltby.

Complete Golfer. 2nd ed. Ed. by Herbert W. Wind & Robert T. Jones. (Illus.). 315p. 1991. reprint ed. 28.00 (*0-940889-31-5*) Classics Golf.

Complete Golfer. Harry Vardon. LC 85-30575. (Illus.). 287p. 1986. reprint ed. 14.95 (*0-914178-90-3*) Golf Digest.

***Complete Golfer Peter Thomson: A Biography.** Peter Mitchell. (Illus.). 287p. 1995. 34.95 (*0-85091-474-4*, Pub. by Lothian Pub AT) Seven Hills Bk.

***Complete Golfer's Almanac, 1995.** James M. Lane. (Orig.). 1995. pap. 13.95 (*0-399-52151-8*, Perigee Bks) Berkley Pub.

Complete Gone with the Wind Sourcebook. Pauline Bartel. LC 92-35649. 184p. 1993. pap. 14.95 (*0-87833-817-9*) Taylor Pub.

Complete Gone with the Wind Trivia Book. Pauline Bartel. LC 89-30442. 208p. 1989. pap. 9.95 (*0-87833-619-2*) Taylor Pub.

***Complete Gospels.** annot. ed. Robert J. Miller. LC 94-34585. 1994. pap. 18.00 (*0-06-065587-9*) Harper SF.

Complete Gospels: Annotated Scholars Version. Ed. by Robert J. Miller. LC 91-35779. 320p. (C). 1991. 29.95 (*0-944344-29-1*) Polebridge Pr.

Complete Gospels: Annotated Scholars Version. 2nd rev. ed. Ed. by Robert J. Miller. LC 91-35779. 320p. (C). 1991. pap. 19.95 (*0-944344-30-5*) Polebridge Pr.

***Complete Gospels: Annotated Scholars Version.** 3rd expanded rev. ed. Ed. by Robert J. Miller. LC 94-34585. 480p. 1995. 28.00 (*0-944344-45-3*); pap. 18.00 (*0-944344-49-6*) Polebridge Pr.

Complete Grants Sourcebook for Higher Education. 2nd ed. American Council on Education Staff & David G. Bauer. 608p. 1985. 85.00 (*0-02-901950-8*, 2019) Macmillan.

Complete Grants Sourcebook for Higher Education. 3rd ed. David G. Bauer. 480p. 1995. 85.00 (*0-89774-821-2*, 2142) Oryx Pr.

Complete Grants Sourcebook for Nursing & Health. David G. Bauer. (ACE-Oryx Series on Higher Education). 320p. (C). 1988. 75.00 (*0-02-925901-0*, ACE-Oryx) Oryx Pr.

Complete Graphic Work of Jack Levine. Jack Levine. (Fine Art Ser.). (Illus.). 112p. (Orig.). 1983. pap. 11.95 (*0-486-24481-4*) Dover.

Complete Graphics of Eyvind Earle & Selected Poems & Writings, 1940-1990. Eyvind Earle. LC 91-70216. (Illus.). 365p. 1991. 150.00 (*0-9622646-0-1*) R Bane Ltd.

Complete Greek Cookbook: The Best from 3000 Years of Greek Cooking. rev. ed. Theresa K. Yianilos. 1986. 15.95 (*0-9621142-0-0*) La Jolla Bk Pub.

Complete Greek Tragedies: Aeschylus II. 2nd ed. Ed. by David Grene & Richmond Lattimore. viii, 180p. 1991. pap. text ed. 7.95 (*0-226-30794-8*) U Ch Pr.

Complete Greek Tragedies: Sophocles I. 2nd ed. Ed. by David Grene & Richmond Lattimore. vi, 206p. 1991. pap. text ed. 7.95 (*0-226-30792-1*) U Ch Pr.

Complete Greek Tragedies, Vol. I: A Centennial Edition. Ed. by David Grene & Richmond Lattimore. 368p. 1992. 27.50 (*0-226-30764-6*) U Ch Pr.

Complete Greek Tragedies, Vol. II: A Centennial Edition. Ed. by David Grene & Richmond Lattimore. 480p. 1992. 32.00 (*0-226-30765-4*) U Ch Pr.

Complete Greek Tragedies, Vol. III: A Centennial Edition. Ed. by David Grene & Richmond Lattimore. 624p. 1992. 40.00 (*0-226-30766-2*) U Ch Pr.

Complete Greek Tragedies, Vol. IV: A Centennial Edition. Ed. by David Grene & Richmond Lattimore. 624p. 1992. 37.50 (*0-226-30767-0*) U Ch Pr.

Complete Greek Tragedies, Vols. 1-4: A Centennial Edition, 4 vols., Set. Ed. by David Grene & Richmond Lattimore. LC 91-45936. 1992. Boxed set. 125.00 (*0-226-30763-8*) U Ch Pr.

Complete Green Letters. Miles J. Stanford. 368p. 1983. pap. 10.99 (*0-310-33051-3*, 9480P) Zondervan.

Complete Grimm's Fairy Tales. Jacob Grimm & Wilhelm K. Grimm. Ed. by James Stern. LC 44-40373. (Illus.). (J). 1976. 17.00 (*0-394-49415-6*); pap. 16.00 (*0-394-70930-6*) Pantheon.

Complete Grunfeld. Alexei Suetin. 304p. 1992. pap. 22.95 (*0-8050-2318-6*, Pub. by Batsford Chess UK) H Holt & Co.

Complete Guide & Descriptive Books of Mexico. R. Campbell. 1976. lib. bdg. 59.95 (*0-8490-1654-1*) Gordon Pr.

Complete Guide & Resource to In-Line Skating. Stephen C. Joyner. (Illus.). 176p. (Orig.). 1993. pap. 12.95 (*1-55870-289-X*) Betterway Bks.

Complete Guide for Building Your New Jewish Community Center. Harry R. Rosen. Ed. by Frank F. Wundohl. LC 83-80776. (Illus.). 217p. 1983. text ed. 225.00 (*0-914820-11-7*) JWB.

Complete Guide for Business Owners. Ed. by John L. Springer. LC 81-85667. 620p. 49.00 (*0-918000-03-3*) TPR Pub Inc.

Complete Guide for Business Owners. rev. ed. Ed. by John L. Springer. LC 88-51934. 600p. 1989. 59.95 (*0-918000-05-X*) TPR Pub Inc.

***Complete Guide for Horse Business Success.** Janet E. English. Ed. & Illus. by Equine Research, Inc. Staff. 304p. (C). 1995. pap. text ed. 46.00 (*0-935842-09-8*) Equine Res.

Complete Guide for Occupational Exploration: An Easy-to-Use Guide to Exploring over 12,000 Job Titles Based on Interests, Experience, Skills, & Other Factors. U. S. Department of Labor, Employment & Training Administration Staff. Ed. by J. Michael Farr. LC 92-39246. 936p. 1993. 47.95 (*1-56370-100-6*, CGOEH); pap. 37.95 (*1-56370-052-2*, CGOE) JIST Works.

Complete Guide for the Development & Implementation of Health Promotion Programs. Werner K. Hoeger. (Illus.). 300p. (C). 1987. pap. text ed. 29.95x (*0-89582-165-6*) Morton Pub.

Complete Guide for the Guitar. Cathy Ellis. (Illus.). 255p. (YA). (gr. 6-12). 1990. teacher ed 34.95 (*1-879542-01-3*); student ed, spiral bd. 29.95 (*1-879542-00-5*) Ellis Family Mus.

Complete Guide for the Guitar: Bass Guitar Edition. rev. ed. 1991. pap. text ed. 32.95 (*1-879542-02-1*) Ellis Family Mus.

Complete Guide for the Manufacturer's Rep: How to Get & Hold Key Accounts. Louis H. Clark. 264p. 1975. text ed. 37.50 (*0-07-011160-X*) McGraw.

Complete Guide of Home Inspection. 2nd ed. Norman Becher. 1992. pap. text ed. 14.95 (*0-07-004535-6*) McGraw.

Complete Guide to a Successful Leveraged Buyout. Allen Michel & Israel Shaked. 300p. 1987. text ed. 72.00 (*0-87094-891-1*) Irwin Prof Pubng.

Complete Guide to Active Filter Design Op Amps & Passive Components. Steve Meiksin. 224p. 1989. pap. text ed. 38.00 (*0-13-159971-2*) P-H.

Complete Guide to Acupressure. Iona M. Teeguarden & Jin Shin Do Acupressure Staff. (Illus.). 364p. (Orig.). 1995. pap. 28.00 (*0-87040-880-1*) Japan Pubns USA.

Complete Guide to Acupuncture: The Five-Volume Reference Library, Set. Ralph A. Dale. (Illus.). 1994. write for info. (*1-877589-09-8*) Dialectic Pubns.

Complete Guide to Acupuncture & Acupressure, 2 vols. in one. Frank Z. Warren & Masaru Toguchi. (Illus.). 528p. 1991. 9.99 (*0-517-47316-X*) Random Hse Value.

Complete Guide to Airbrushing Techniques & Materials. Judy Martin. 1992. 14.98 (*1-55521-527-0*) Bk Sales Inc.

Complete Guide to Airbrushing Techniques & Materials. Judy Martin. 1992. 14.98 (*0-685-60285-0*) Bk Sales Inc.

Complete Guide to Alternative Cancer Therapies: What You Need to Know to Make an Informed Choice. Ron Falcone. LC 94-17473. 1994. pap. 12.95 (*0-8065-1553-8*, Citadel Pr) Carol Pub Group.

Complete Guide to Alternative Medicine see American Holistic Health Association's Complete Guide to Alternative Medicine

Complete Guide to Amateur Radio. Joseph Dubovy. 1986. 7.95 (*0-13-159798-1*, Reward) P-H.

Complete Guide to American Bed & Breakfast. 3rd rev. ed. Rik Barnes & Nancy Barnes. LC 90-27782. (Illus.). 1120p. (Orig.). 1991. pap. 19.95 (*0-88289-770-5*) Pelican.

***Complete Guide to American Bed & Breakfast.** 4th ed. Rik Barnes. (Orig.). 1995. pap. 19.95 (*1-56554-036-0*) Pelican.

Complete Guide to American Film Schools & Cinema & Television Courses. Ernest Pintoff. LC 93-30073. 624p. 1994. pap. 15.95 (*0-14-017226-2*, Penguin Bks) Viking Penguin.

Complete Guide to America's National Parks: The Official & Only Comprehensive Guide to 367 National Parks. National Park Foundation. LC 93-86476. 540p. 1994. pap. 14.95 (*0-679-02676-2*) Fodors Travel.

Complete Guide to America's National Parks, 1994-1995. 6th rev. ed. Intro. by Alan A. Rubin. LC 89-63985. 1990. pap. 14.95 (*0-9603410-6-4*) Natl Pk Found.

Complete Guide to Anti-Aging Nutrients. Sheldon S. Hendler. 352p. 1986. pap. 8.95 (*0-685-11924-6*, Fireside) S&S Trade.

Complete Guide to Asset-Based Lending. Peter S. Clarke. LC 85-9362. 314p. 1985. text ed. 69.95 (*0-13-159831-7*, Busn) P-H.

Complete Guide to Automotive Refinishing. 2nd ed. Harry T. Chudy. (Illus.). 496p. 1987. text ed. 73.00 (*0-13-159807-4*) P-H.

Complete Guide to Aviation Photography. 2nd ed. Peter M. Bowers. (Illus.). 240p. 1988. pap. 16.95 (*0-8306-0924-5*, 2424) TAB Bks.

Complete Guide to Backpacking in Canada. E. Katz. (Illus.). 264p. 1988. pap. 9.95 (*0-385-23147-4*) Firefly Bks Ltd.

***Complete Guide to Backup Management.** Dorian Cougias. (Network Frontiers Field Manual Ser.). 425p. 1994. pap. 59.00 (*1-885871-00-7*) Floating Point.

Complete Guide to Balaton. T. Sebestyen. (Illus.). 194p. (C). 1986. pap. 90.00 (*0-685-37550-1*, Pub. by Collets) St Mut.

Complete Guide to Barber Dimes. David Lawrence. 124p. 1991. 40.95 (*1-880731-02-9*); pap. 23.95 (*1-880731-03-7*) DLRC Pr.

Complete Guide to Barber Halves. David Lawrence. 120p. 1991. 40.95 (*1-880731-04-5*); pap. 24.95 (*1-880731-05-3*) DLRC Pr.

Complete Guide to Barber Quarters. David Lawrence. 101p. 1989. 3.95 (*1-880731-00-2*); pap. 21.95 (*1-880731-01-0*) DLRC Pr.

***Complete Guide to Barber Quarters.** 2nd ed. Harry Laibstain & David Lawrence. LC 94-80033. (Illus.). 176p. 1995. 49.95 (*1-880731-50-9*); pap. 29.95 (*1-880731-24-X*) DLRC Pr.

C

1462

An Asterisk (*) at the beginning of an entry indicates that the title is appearing in BIP for the first time.

Complete Guide to Barrier-Free Housing: Convenient Living for the Elderly & Physically Handicapped. Gary D. Branson. (Illus.). 176p. (Orig.). 1991. pap. 14.95 (*1-55870-188-5*) Betterway Bks.

Complete Guide to Baseball Memorabilia. Mark Larson. LC 92-71451. (Illus.). 464p. 1992. pap. 14.95 (*0-87341-190-0*) Krause Pubns.

Complete Guide to Basic Gardening. Ed. by Michael MacCaskey. LC 85-80863. 240p. pap. 12.95 (*0-89586-325-1*) Price Stern.

***Complete Guide to Becoming a U. S. Citizen.** Eve P. Steinberg. LC 94-32804. 1994. pap. 10.00 (*0-671-89291-6*, Arco Test) P-H Gen Ref & Trav.

Complete Guide to Bed & Breakfasts, Inns & Guesthouses. Pamela Lanier. 1993. pap. 16.95 (*0-89815-530-4*) Ten Speed Pr.

Complete Guide to Bed & Breakfasts, Inns & Guesthouses. 11th ed. Pamela Lanier. 1994. pap. 16.95 (*0-89815-582-7*) Ten Speed Pr.

***Complete Guide to Bed & Breakfasts, Inns & Guesthouses.** 12th ed. Lanier. 1995. pap. text ed. 16.95 (*0-89815-666-1*) Ten Speed Pr.

Complete Guide to Bed & Breakfasts, Inns & Guesthouses: Southern Edition. Pamela Lanier. 1993. pap. 7.95 (*0-89815-532-0*) Ten Speed Pr.

Complete Guide to Bed & Breakfasts, Inns & Guesthouses: Western Edition. Pamela Lanier. 1993. pap. 7.95 (*0-89815-531-2*) Ten Speed Pr.

***Complete Guide to Being an Independent Contractor.** 1995. pap. 24.95 (*0-7931-0889-6*) Upstart Pub.

Complete Guide to Being an Independent Contractor. Herman R. Holtz & Joyce S. Friedman. 304p. 1994. pap. 24.95 (*0-936894-80-6*, 561579-01) Upstart Pub.

Complete Guide to Being Your Own Remodeling Contractor. Kent Lester. LC 94-15295. (Illus.). 288p. (Orig.). 1994. pap. 18.99 (*1-55870-337-3*) Betterway Bks.

Complete Guide to Better Golf. Bob Toski. (Illus.). 1977. 12.95 (*0-689-10722-6*, Atheneum S&S) S&S Trade.

Complete Guide to Bible Versions. Philip W. Comfort. 157p. 1991. mass mkt. 3.99 (*0-8423-1251-X*) Tyndale.

Complete Guide to Bicycling in Canada. Elliot Katz. (Illus.). 320p. 1993. pap. 14.95 (*0-920361-04-8*, Pub. by Great North Bks CN) Firefly Bks Ltd.

Complete Guide to Bird Dog Training. rev. ed. John Falk. (Illus.). 168p. 1994. 22.95 (*1-55821-319-8*) Lyons & Burford.

Complete Guide to Bird Feeding. John V. Dennis. 1975. 25.00 (*0-394-47937-8*) Knopf.

Complete Guide to Bird Feeding. John V. Dennis. 1994. pap. 16.00 (*0-679-75052-5*) Knopf.

***Complete Guide to Bolt-on Street Power.** Jay Storer. 1987. pap. 16.95 (*0-931472-23-7*) Motorbooks Intl.

Complete Guide to Boston's Freedom Trail. 2nd ed. Charles Bahne. (Illus.). 80p. (Orig.). 1993. pap. 4.95 (*0-9615705-1-2*) Newtowne Pub.

Complete Guide to Bowhunting Deer. Chuck Adams. LC 84-70734. (Illus.). 256p. (Orig.). 1984. pap. 16.95 (*0-910676-73-9*) DBI.

Complete Guide to Bowling Principles: The Encyclopedia of Principles. George Allen & Dick Ritger. LC 81-85284. (Encyclopedia of Bowling Instruction Ser.: Vol. 1). (Illus.). 280p. 1982. 17.95 (*0-933554-00-1*); pap. 12.95 (*0-933554-01-X*) Tech Ed Pub.

Complete Guide to Bowling Spares: The Encyclopedia of Spares. Dick Ritger & George Allen. LC 78-68659. (Encyclopedia of Bowling Instruction Ser.: Vol. 3). (Illus.). 240p. (C). 1979. 17.95 (*0-933554-04-4*); pap. 12.95 (*0-933554-05-2*) Tech Ed Pub.

Complete Guide to Bowling Strikes: The Encyclopedia of Strikes. George Allen & Dick Ritger. LC 80-53200. (Encyclopedia of Bowling Instruction Ser.: Vol. 2). (Illus.). 222p. (C). 1981. 17.95 (*0-933554-02-8*); pap. 12.95 (*0-933554-03-6*) Tech Ed Pub.

Complete Guide to Brass: Instruments & Pedagogy. Scott Whitener. 320p. 1990. pap. 35.00 (*0-02-873050-X*); spiral bd. 35.00 (*0-02-872861-0*) Schirmer Bks.

Complete Guide to British Moths. Margaret Brooks. (Illus.). 256p. 1992. 45.00 (*0-224-02195-8*, Pub. by Jonathan Cape UK) Trafalgar.

Complete Guide to Budapest. I. Wellner. (Illus.). 202p. (C). 1980. 85.00 (*0-685-32399-4*, Pub. by Collets) St Mut.

Complete Guide to Budapest. I. Wellner. (Illus.). 202p. (C). 1988. 85.00 (*0-569-19586-1*, Pub. by Collets) St Mut.

Complete Guide to Buffalo Nickels. David W. Lange. 130p. (Orig.). 1993. 44.95 (*1-880731-13-4*); pap. 24.95 (*1-880731-14-2*) DLRC Pr.

Complete Guide to Building a Real Estate Fortune Investing in Older Multiple Dwellings. Richard F. Gabriel. 1975. 69.50 (*0-686-30515-9*) Exec Reports.

Complete Guide to Building & Outfitting an Office in Your Home. Jerry Germer. (Illus.). 176p. (Orig.). 1994. pap. 18.99 (*1-55870-335-7*) Betterway Bks.

Complete Guide to Building & Plant Maintenance. 2nd ed. Thomas F. Sack. LC 71-126828. (Illus.). 672p. 1971. text ed. 49.95 (*0-13-160101-6*) P-H.

Complete Guide to Building Log Homes. Monte Burch. LC 90-39505. (Illus.). 416p. (Orig.). 1990. pap. 19.95 (*0-8069-7486-9*) Sterling.

Complete Guide to Building Taos Pueblo. Louann Jourdan. (Illus.). 32p. 1989. pap. text ed. 12.95 (*0-89013-194-5*) Museum NM Pr.

Complete Guide to Building Your Automobile Deductions - Legally. Irving L. Blackman. LC 84-102959. (Special Report Ser.: No. 6). 78p. 1988. pap. 21.00 (*0-916181-05-7*) Blackman Kallick Bartelstein.

Complete Guide to Building Your Entertainment Deductions - Legally. Irving L. Blackman. LC 84-102962. (Special Report Ser.: No. 7). 44p. 1987. pap. 21.00 (*0-916181-06-5*) Blackman Kallick Bartelstein.

Complete Guide to Building Your Travel Deductions: Legally. Irving L. Blackman. (Special Report Ser.: No. 8). 50p. 1987. pap. 21.00 (*0-916181-07-3*) Blackman Kallick Bartelstein.

Complete Guide to Business Agreements. rev. ed. Ted Nicholas. 333p. 1992. pap. 19.95 (*0-7931-0489-0*, 561553) Dearborn Finan.

Complete Guide to Business & Sales Presentation. Malcolm Bird. 1990. text ed. 13.98 (*0-442-30288-6*) Chapman & Hall.

Complete Guide to Business Writing. Janis Forman. 518p. (C). 1988. text ed. write for info. (*0-394-32372-6*) Random.

Complete Guide to Buying a Business. Richard Snowden. 224p. 1993. 24.95 (*0-8144-5158-6*) AMACOM.

Complete Guide to Buying a Telephone System. Paul Daubitz. LC 86-71825. 160p. reprint ed. pap. 45.60 (*0-7837-5845-6*, 2045564) Bks Demand.

Complete Guide to Buying an Older Existing Home - Buyer Beware - "If Homes Could Only Talk" Complete Exterior & Interior Home Inspection - Well Informed Consumer Most Likely to Buy Wisely. Michael E. Corrieri, Jr. (Illus.). 106p. (Orig.). 1985. pap. 4.95 (*0-9615686-1-5*) M Corrieri.

Complete Guide to Buying & Selling a Business. Arnold S. Goldstein. LC 84-6792. 288p. 1984. pap. 9.95 (*0-452-25622-4*, Plume) NAL-Dutton.

Complete Guide to Buying & Selling Real Estate. Lowell R. Hodgkins. 152p. (Orig.). 1989. pap. 11.95 (*1-55870-118-4*) Betterway Bks.

***Complete Guide to Buying Treasury Bills, Notes & Bonds from the Federal Reserve.** Milton Kahn. LC 95-76905. 200p. (Orig.). 1995. pap. 19.95 (*0-9646555-0-0*) Klondike Publng.

Complete Guide to Buying Your First Home: Road Map to a Successful, Worry-Free Closing. R. Dodge Woodson. (Illus.). 224p. (Orig.). 1992. pap. 16.99 (*1-55870-228-8*) Betterway Bks.

Complete Guide to Cabins & Lodges in America's State & National Parks. George Zimmerman. LC 84-25065. (Illus.). 284p. 1985. 24.45 (*0-316-98808-1*) Little.

Complete Guide to California. 1986. 12.95 (*0-933692-29-3*) A R Collings.

Complete Guide to Calligraphy Techniques & Materials. Judy Martin. 1993. 14.98 (*0-89009-675-9*) Bk Sales Inc.

***Complete Guide to Canadian Universities: How to Select a University & Succeed When You Get There.** 3rd ed. Kevin Paul. (Reference Ser.). 248p. 1994. pap. 14.95 (*0-88908-524-2*) Self-Counsel Pr.

Complete Guide to Car Noises. Jorge Lugo. 64p. (Orig.). 1983. pap. 2.95 (*0-9611794-0-6*) EXPIM Co.

Complete Guide to Children's Dental Care from Prenatal Through Teens. Karen B. Greenberg. 136p. 1993. pap. 14.95 (*0-9635998-0-1*) Hlth Monitor.

Complete Guide to Choosing Child Care. Judy Berezin. 1983. pap. 12.95 (*0-679-73100-8*) Random.

***Complete Guide to Christian Videos.** Anne Zanko. LC 95-60926. 381p. 1995. pap. 16.95 (*0-9646611-0-1*) Venture NJ.

***Complete Guide to Christian Writing & Speaking.** Comp. by Susan T. Osborn. 320p. 1994. pap. 9.95 (*0-939497-35-2*) Promise Pub.

Complete Guide to Citing Government Information Resources: A Manual for Writers & Librarians. Diane L. Garner & Diane H. Smith. LC 93-16059. 1993. write for info. (*0-88692-254-2*) Cong Info.

Complete Guide to Claiming Thoroughbreds: Finding, Fixing & Making Winners. Tom Ivers. 250p. 1992. ring bd. 69.00 (*0-929346-15-7*) R Meerdink Co Ltd.

***Complete Guide to ClarisWorks Vol. I.** ClarisWorks Users Group Staff. (Illus.). 445p. (Orig.). (C). 1995. pap. 39.95 (*0-9620807-6-4*) Natl AppleWrks.

Complete Guide to Classics Illustrated. Dan Malan. (U. S. Ser.: Vol. 1). (Illus.). 112p. 1994. reprint ed. 34.95 (*0-9631135-6-9*); reprint ed. pap. 24.95 (*0-9631135-0-X*) Malan Class.

Complete Guide to Classics Illustrated. Dan Malan. (Foreign Ser.: Vol. 2). (Illus.). 116p. 1994. reprint ed. 34.95 (*0-9631135-7-7*); reprint ed. pap. 24.95 (*0-9631135-1-8*) Malan Class.

Complete Guide to Co-ops & Condominiums. David T. Goldstick & Carolyn Janik. LC 82-22513. 240p. 1983. 7.95 (*0-452-25400-0*, Plume) NAL-Dutton.

Complete Guide to COBOL 370. David S. Kirk. 1993. pap. 39.95 (*0-89435-481-7*) Wiley.

***Complete Guide to Cobra Replicas.** Ed. & Comp. by Curt Scott. (Illus.). 44p. 1994. pap. 15.95 (*0-9614882-7-1*) Crown Pub CA.

***Complete Guide to College Success: What Every Student Needs to Know.** Richard Newman. (Illus.). 320p. 1996. 50.00 (*0-8147-5783-9*); pap. 15.95 (*0-8147-5784-7*) NYU Pr.

Complete Guide to College Visits. Janet Spencer & Sandra Maleson. (Illus.). 544p. 1992. pap. 19.95 (*0-8065-1320-9*, Citadel Pr) Carol Pub Group.

Complete Guide to Colorado Wilderness. John Fielder & Mark Pearson. 280p. 1994. pap. 19.95 (*1-56579-052-9*) Westcliffe Pubs Inc.

Complete Guide to Competency-Based Education: Practical Techniques for Planning, Developing, Implementing, Evaluating Your Program. Leo H. Bradley. 1987. text ed. 29.95 (*0-13-160078-8*, Busn) P-H.

Complete Guide to Computer Camps & Workshops. Mike Benton. LC 83-15578. 208p. 1984. pap. write for info. (*0-672-52796-0*) Macmillan.

Complete Guide to Conjugating 12,000 French Verbs: English Edition. Ed. by Bescherelle. (Hatier Ser.). 174p. 1989. 13.95 (*2-218-06591-6*) Hatier Pub.

Complete Guide to Conservatory Plants. Ann Bonar. (Illus.). 192p. Date not set. pap. 22.95 (*1-85585-120-2*) Trafalgar.

Complete Guide to Conservatory Plants. Ann Bonar. (Illus.). 192p. 1992. 34.95 (*1-85585-084-2*) Trafalgar.

***Complete Guide to Conservatory Plants.** Ann Bonar. LC 95-984. (Illus.). 1996. 29.95 (*0-87951-610-0*) Overlook Pr.

Complete Guide to Consulting Contracts: How to Understand, Draft & Negotiate Contracts & Agreements That Work. Herman Holtz. (Complete Guide Ser.). 224p. (Orig.). 1993. pap. 29.95 (*0-7931-0670-2*, 561409, Enter-Dearbrn) Dearborn Finan.

Complete Guide to Consulting Success. Howard Shenson. 1991. ring bd. 69.95 (*0-942103-02-5*, 5615-40, Enter-Dearbrn) Dearborn Finan.

Complete Guide to Consulting Success. Howard Shenson & Ted Nicholas. 205p. 1992. pap. 29.95 (*0-7931-0492-0*, 561551) Dearborn Finan.

Complete Guide to Contested Auctions. Mike Lawrence. LC 92-90023. 368p. (Orig.). 1992. text ed. 14.95 (*1-877908-04-5*) Lawrence & Leong Pub.

***Complete Guide to Contract Lawyering: What Every Lawyer Needs to Know about Using & Providing Temporary Legal Services.** Deborah Arron & Deborah Guyol. 275p. (Orig.). 1995. pap. 34.95 (*0-940675-45-5*) Niche Pr.

Complete Guide to Contracting Your Home: A Step-by-Step Method for Managing Home Construction. 2nd rev. ed. David L. McGuerty & Kent Lester. (Illus.). 288p. (Orig.). 1992. pap. 18.99 (*1-55870-229-6*) Betterway Bks.

Complete Guide to Convertible Securities Worldwide. Laura A. Zubulake. (Finance Editions Ser.). 300p. 1991. text ed. 55.00 (*0-471-52802-1*) Wiley.

Complete Guide to Corporate Fund Raising. Ed. by Joseph Dermer & Stephen Wertheimer. 1991. pap. 19.95 (*0-914977-12-1*, 600031) Fund Raising.

Complete Guide to Correspondence Chess. Alex Dunne. Ed. by Robert B. Long. (Illus.). 160p. 1991. pap. 14.95 (*0-938650-52-1*) Thinkers Pr.

Complete Guide to Cosmetic Facial Surgery. rev. ed. John A. McCurdy. (Illus.). 288p. 1993. 17.95 (*0-8119-0740-6*); pap. 12.95 (*0-8119-0681-7*) LIFETIME.

Complete Guide to Cost-Effective Employee Benefits Program. Joseph G. Kozlowski & Walter Oleksy. 320p. 1987. text ed. 59.95 (*0-13-160037-0*) P-H.

Complete Guide to Creative Watercolor. Miles G. Batt. LC 87-71439. (Illus.). (C). 1988. 35.00 (*0-9619386-5-X*) Crtive Art Pubns.

Complete Guide to Customer Service. Linda Lash. (Training & Development Ser.). 1989. text ed. 37.50 (*0-471-62428-4*) Wiley.

Complete Guide to dBASE III: A Self-Teaching Guide. Philip Greenberg & Rita Greenberg. LC 85-31746. (IBM Personal Computer Ser.). 378p. 1986. pap. text ed. 22.95 (*0-471-81041-X*) Wiley.

Complete Guide to Decorative Landscaping with Brick & Masonry. Edward J. Heddy & Pete Peterson. (Illus.). 160p. (Orig.). 1990. pap. 11.95 (*1-55870-145-1*) Betterway Bks.

***Complete Guide to Designing Your Own Home.** Scott Ballard. (Illus.). 144p. (Orig.). 1995. pap. 17.99 (*1-55870-334-9*) Betterway Bks.

Complete Guide to Developing & Marketing Your Own Seminar. Allan Mulligan. 164p. 1984. pap. 14.95 (*0-912551-00-3*) Independence House.

Complete Guide to Digital Television Troubleshooting & Repair. John D. Lenk. 240p. 1988. text ed. 46.00 (*0-13-160094-X*) P-H.

Complete Guide to Dog Law. Deidre E. Gannon. (Illus.). 256p. 1994. 25.95 (*0-87605-658-3*) Howell Bk.

Complete Guide to Doing Business in Mexico. Anita Winsor. 336p. 1994. 29.95 (*0-8144-0211-9*) AMACOM.

Complete Guide to Drawing for the Theater. 2nd ed. Harvey Sweet & Deborah M. Dryden. 1994. pap. text ed. 39.95 (*0-205-14882-4*, Longwood Div) Allyn.

Complete Guide to Effective Excuses. Ellis W. Allred. (Illus.). 51p. (Orig.). 1993. pap. 5.00 (*1-885027-01-X*) Willow T Bks.

Complete Guide to Electronics Troubleshooting. James Perozzo. 850p. 1994. text ed. 52.95 (*0-8273-5045-7*) Delmar.

Complete Guide to Electronics Troubleshooting: Instructor's Guide. James Perozzo. 29p. 1994. 15.00 (*0-8273-5046-5*) Delmar.

Complete Guide to Employing Persons With Disabilities. Ed. by Henry McCarthy. LC 84-43093. 1985. 15.00 (*0-318-19037-0*) Human Res Ctr.

Complete Guide to Environmental Careers. CEIP Fund, Inc. Staff. LC 89-1947. (Illus.). 328p. (C). 1989. pap. 14.95 (*0-933280-84-X*) Island Pr.

Complete Guide to Equity Sharing: Everything You Need to Know to Create Profitable Equity Sharing Transactions. Marilyn D. Sullivan. LC 91-65283. 336p. (Orig.). 1992. pap. 19.95 (*0-9629239-0-7*) Venture Two.

Complete Guide to Establishing an Effective Relocation Department. Jan Dickinson. 64p. 1990. 250.00 (*0-934701-08-3*) Wheatherstone Pr.

Complete Guide to Estate Accounting & Taxes. 2nd ed. J. G. Denhardt, Jr. 1978. 39.95 (*0-13-160242-X*) P-H.

Complete Guide to Estate Accounting & Taxes. 4th ed. J. G. Denhardt, Jr. & John D. Grider. 280p. 1988. text ed. 59.95 (*0-13-159872-4*, Busn) P-H.

Complete Guide to Everyday Kanji. Yaeko Habein & Gerald B. Mathias. Ed. by Ichiba. 410p. 1991. pap. 24.95 (*0-87011-793-9*) Kodansha.

Complete Guide to Everything Romantic: Unique & Creative Ideas. Michael Newman. LC 94-20220. 1995. 15.95 (*0-8065-1547-3*, Citadel Pr) Carol Pub Group.

***Complete Guide to Everything Sold in Marine Supply Stores.** Steve Ettlinger. LC 94-34757. 1995. write for info. (*0-688-13300-2*) Morrow.

Complete Guide to Exotic Pets. Chris Mattison. LC 93-85543. (Illus.). 128p. 1994. 15.98 (*1-56138-370-8*) Courage Bks.

***Complete Guide to Experiential Psychotherapy.** Alvin R. Mahrer. LC 95-7302. 1995. text ed. 59.95 (*0-471-12438-9*) Wiley.

Complete Guide to Eyecare, Eyeglasses & Contact Lenses. 3rd rev. ed. Walter Zinn & Herbert Soloman. (Illus.). 336p. 1995. pap. 14.95 (*0-8119-0786-4*) LIFETIME.

Complete Guide to Factory-Made Houses. A. M. Watkins. (Illus.). 184p. 1984. 14.95 (*0-911749-00-4*); pap. 8.95 (*0-911749-01-2*) Building Inst.

Complete Guide to Family Relocation. Jan Dickinson. LC 83-91431. 246p. 1983. pap. 19.95 (*0-9613011-0-4*) Wheatherstone Pr.

Complete Guide to Fashion Illustration. Colin Barnes. (Illus.). 160p. 1988. 32.95 (*0-89134-250-8*, 30074) North Light Bks.

Complete Guide to Federal & State Benefits for Veterans, Their Families & Survivors. 10th ed. Robert L. Berko. 192p. (Orig.). 1987. pap. 9.00 (*0-934873-05-4*) Consumer Ed Res.

Complete Guide to Federal & State Benefits for Veterans, Their Families & Survivors. 11th ed. Robert L. Berko. (Illus.). (Orig.). 1989. write for info. (*0-934873-12-7*) Consumer Ed Res.

Complete Guide to Fertility & Family Planning. Sarah Freeman & Vern L. Bullough. LC 93-10850. 129p. 1992. pap. 15.95 (*0-87975-798-1*) Prometheus Bks.

Complete Guide to Fertility & Family Planning. Sarah Freeman & Vern Bullough. (Illus.). 129p. 1992. 23.95x (*0-87975-785-X*) Prometheus Bks.

Complete Guide to Finesse Bass Fishing. Michael Jones. (Illus.). 128p. (Orig.). 1991. pap. 8.99 (*0-9630200-0-5*) McGrady Media.

Complete Guide to Fishing. Vlad Evanoff. 1981. pap. 2.00 (*0-87980-250-2*) Wilshire.

Complete Guide to Fleet Management. Joel Levitt. 220p. 1989. boxed 39.00 (*0-13-159328-5*) P-H.

Complete Guide to Flight Instruction. Gregory M. Penglis. LC 93-38698. 550p. 1994. pap. 29.95 (*1-56825-012-6*) Rainbow Books.

Complete Guide to Floors, Walls, & Ceilings: A Comprehensive Do-It-Yourself Handbook. Gary D. Branson. (Illus.). 176p. (Orig.). 1992. pap. 14.95 (*1-55870-230-X*) Betterway Bks.

Complete Guide to Florida Foundations. 4th ed. Ed. by Lonna J. Hord. 717p. (Orig.). 1992. 90.00 (*1-879543-03-6*) FL Fund Pubns.

Complete Guide to Florida Foundations: 1993. 5th ed. Ed. by Alice N. Culbreath. 250p. (Orig.). 1992. per. 90.00 (*1-879543-07-9*) FL Fund Pubns.

Complete Guide to Florida Foundations: 1994. 6th ed. Ed. by Alice N. Culbreath. 250p. 1993. pap. 90.00 (*1-879543-10-9*) FL Fund Pubns.

Complete Guide to Florida Foundations, 1995. 7th ed. Ed. by Alice N. Culbreath. 350p. 1994. pap. 90.00 (*1-879543-13-3*) FL Fund Pubns.

Complete Guide to Florida Gardening. rev. ed. Stan DeFreitas. LC 87-5038. 368p. 1987. 21.95 (*0-87833-572-2*) Taylor Pub.

Complete Guide to Flower & Foliage Arrangement. Iris Webb. 256p. 1982. 95.00 (*0-85223-144-X*, Pub. by Ebury Pr UK) Trafalgar.

***Complete Guide to Flower Arranging: A Practical Illustrated Guide to Choosing, Arranging, & Displaying Fresh Dried Flowers.** Jane Packer. LC 94-31858. (Illus.). 192p. 1995. 29.95 (*1-56458-868-8*) Dorling Kindersley.

Complete Guide to Fly Fishing Maine: Where, When, & How to Take Maine's Best Fighting Fish. Bob Newman. LC 94-14256. 144p. 1994. pap. 13.50 (*0-89272-348-3*) Down East.

Complete Guide to Food Allergy & Intolerance. Jonathan Brostoff & Linda Gamlin. (Illus.). 368p. 1992. pap. 15.00 (*0-517-57756-9*, Crown) Crown Pub Group.

Complete Guide to Food & Cooking. Ed. by Better Homes & Gardens Staff. 480p. 1991. 29.95 (*0-696-01911-6*) Meredith Bks.

Complete Guide to Food for Sports Performance: Peak Nutrition for Your Sport. Louise Burke. (Illus.). 293p. (Orig.). 1993. pap. 16.95 (*1-86373-073-7*, Pub. by Allen & Unwin Aust Pty AT) IPG Chicago.

Complete Guide to Food Service Success: What You Need to Know to Plan a Profitable Operation. Fred Schmid. LC 92-16883. (Illus.). 128p. 1992. pap. 12.95 (*1-881443-06-X*) RWI Pub Grp.

Complete Guide to Foot Reflexology. Kevin Kunz & Barbara Kunz. Ed. by Ken Shoemaker. 150p. 1982. 16.95 (*0-686-97525-1*, Spectrum) P-H.

Complete Guide to Foot Reflexology. rev. ed. Kevin Kunz & Barbara Kunz. 168p. 1991. pap. 10.95 (*0-13-155342-9*) P-H.

Complete Guide to Four Season Home Maintenance: How to Prevent Costly Problems Before They Occur. Dave Heberle & Richard M. Scutella. (Illus.). 160p. (Orig.). 1993. pap. 18.95 (*1-55870-278-4*) Betterway Bks.

Complete Guide to Furniture Styles. Louise A. Boger. (Illus.). 688p. 1982. pap. 31.00 (*0-684-17641-6*, Scribners) S&S Trade.

Complete Guide to Game Care & Cookery. 3rd ed. Sam Fadala. LC 81-68258. (Illus.). 320p. (Orig.). 1994. pap. 18.95 (*0-87349-155-6*, GCC3) DBI.

Complete Guide to Game Fish. Byron W. Dalrymple. LC 80-8780. 512p. 1992. 18.95 (*0-8329-0467-8*) New Win Pub.

***Complete Guide to Gardening.** 552p. 1994. 59.95 (*0-696-20389-8*) Meredith Bks.

C

An Asterisk (*) at the beginning of an entry indicates that the title is appearing in BIP for the first time. 1463

Complete Guide to Gentlemen's Entertainment, Vol. 2, Issue 1. William A. Harland & Kinsley D. Jones. 336p. (Orig.). 1993. pap. 16.95 (*0-9636533-2-6*) O S J G.

***Complete Guide to Gentlemen's Entertainment: North American Edition.** 4th ed. William Harland & Kinsley Jones. 399p. (Orig.). 1995. pap. 18.95 (*0-9636533-3-4*) O S J G.

Complete Guide to Getting a Grant: How to Turn Your Ideas into Dollars. Laurie Blum. 256p. 1993. 23.00 (*0-671-77834-X*) S&S Trade.

Complete Guide to Getting & Keeping Your VISA-MasterCard Merchant Status. 4th ed. Larry Schwartz & Pearl Sax. 200p. 1993. 199.95 (*0-914801-09-0*) Nat Assn Credit.

Complete Guide to Golf on Cape Cod, Nantucket & Martha's Vineyard. Paul Harber. (Illus.). 175p. 1994. pap. 9.95 (*1-883684-02-1*) Peninsula MA.

Complete Guide to Graduate School Admission: Psychology & Related Programs. Ed. by P. Keith-Spiegel. 296p. (C). 1990. text ed. 49.95 (*0-8058-0637-7*); pap. 17.95 (*0-8058-0638-5*) L Erlbaum Assocs.

Complete Guide to Greeting Card Design & Illustration. rev. ed. Eva Szela. (Illus.). 144p. 1994. 29.95 (*0-89134-480-2*) North Light Bks.

Complete Guide to Growing Berries & Grapes. Louise Riotte. LC 92-34629. (Illus.). 160p. 1993. reprint ed. pap. 9.95 (*0-87833-825-X*) Taylor Pub.

Complete Guide to Growing Nuts. Louise Riotte. LC 93-3709. (Illus.). 168p. 1993. reprint ed. pap. 9.95 (*0-87833-836-5*) Taylor Pub.

Complete Guide to Guitar & Amp Maintenance: A Practical Manual for Every Guitar Player. Richie Fliegler. (Illus.). 80p. (Orig.). 1994. pap. 14.95 (*0-7935-3490-9*, HL00330117) H Leonard.

Complete Guide to Handloading. Phil Sharpe. (Library Classics Ser.). 230p. 1988. reprint ed. 60.00 (*0-935632-64-6*) Wolfe Pub Co.

Complete Guide to Health Insurance: How to Beat the High Cost of Being Sick. Kathleen Hogue et al. 384p. 1990. mass mkt. 4.95 (*0-380-70785-3*) Avon.

Complete Guide to Health Insurance: How to Beat the High Cost of Being Sick. Kathleen Hogue et al. 336p. 1988. 24.95 (*0-8027-1024-7*) Walker & Co.

Complete Guide to Health Insurance: How to Beat the High Cost of Being Sick. braille ed. Kathleen Hogue et al. 755p. 1991. vinyl bd. 60.40 (*1-56956-214-8*, BR7719) W A T Braille.

C

Complete Guide to Heraldry. A. C. Fox-Davies. 1983. 12.99 (*0-517-26643-1*) Random Hse Value.

Complete Guide to High-End Audio. Robert Harley. (Illus.). 450p. (Orig.). 1994. 39.95 (*0-9640849-1-0*); pap. 29.95 (*0-9640849-0-2*) Acapella Pubng.

Complete Guide to High Yield Power Selling. Richard H. DuBois. LC 93-17861. 192p. 1994. pap. 14.95 (*1-56825-008-8*) Rainbow Books.

***Complete Guide to Hold 'Em Poker.** 2nd ed. Ken Warren. LC 95-68283. (Illus.). 256p. 1995. pap. 14.95 (*0-940685-59-0*) Cardoza Pub.

Complete Guide to Home & Auto Burglar Alarms. Doug Kirkpatrick & Vikki Richards. LC 86-71338. (Illus.). 192p. (Orig.). 1987. pap. 12.95 (*0-913193-02-X*) Baker Pub.

Complete Guide to Home Automation. David A. Wacker. 176p. (Orig.). 1993. pap. 16.95 (*1-55870-301-2*) Betterway Bks.

Complete Guide to Home Canning, 7 guides. (Illus.). 40p. 1988. Guide 1| Priniciples of Home Canning, 40p. pap. 2.75 (*0-16-000078-5*, S/N 001-000-04522-9) USGPO.

Complete Guide to Home Canning, 7 guides, Set. (Illus.). 167p. 1988. per., pap. 11.00 (*0-16-000077-7*, S/N 001-000-045) USGPO.

Complete Guide to Home Canning, Preserving & Freezing. rev. ed. United States Department of Agriculture Staff. (Illus.). 240p. 1994. reprint ed. pap. text ed. 6.95 (*0-486-27888-3*) Dover.

Complete Guide to Home Canning, Preserving & Freezing. U. S. Department of Agriculture Staff. LC 72-92754. (Illus.). 215p. 1973. reprint ed. pap. 5.95 (*0-486-22911-4*) Dover.

Complete Guide to Home Nursing. Diana Hastings. Ed. by Helen L. Maule. 228p. 1986. text ed. 16.95 (*0-8120-5754-6*) Barron.

Complete Guide to Home Plumbing Repair & Replacement: A Practical Handbook to (Almost Always) Doing It Yourself. R. Dodge Woodson. (Illus.). 224p. (Orig.). 1991. pap. 16.95 (*1-55870-248-2*) Betterway Bks.

Complete Guide to Home Roofing Installation & Maintenance: How to Do It Yourself & Avoid the 60 Ways Your Roofer Can Nail You. John W. Chiles, Jr. (Illus.). 176p. (Orig.). 1993. pap. 16.95 (*1-55870-277-6*) Betterway Bks.

Complete Guide to Home Security: How to Protect Your Family & Home from Harm. David A. Wacker. (Illus.). 190p. (Orig.). 1990. pap. 14.95 (*1-55870-163-X*) Betterway Bks.

Complete Guide to Homemade Income. Paul E. Purcell. 128p. (Orig.). 1987. pap. 7.95 (*0-942369-00-9*) P & P Pubns GA.

***Complete Guide to Homeopathy: The Principles & Practice of Treatment with a Comprehensive Range of Self-Help Remedies for Common Ailments.** Andrew Lockie & Nicola Geddes. LC 95-6746. 240p. 1995. 29.95 (*0-7894-0148-7*, 6-70479) Dorling Kindersley.

***Complete Guide to Household Chemicals.** Robert J. Palma, Sr. & Mark Espenscheid. 300p. 1995. 24.95 (*0-87975-983-6*) Prometheus Bks.

***Complete Guide to Immigration: Masters of Wisdom.** John G. Bennett. 224p. 1995. pap. 20.00 (*1-881408-01-9*) Bennett Bks.

***Complete Guide to Immigration & Successful Living in the United States.** Ed. by Access U. S. A., Inc. Staff. (Illus.). 450p. 1994. pap. 59.95 (*0-9639667-2-3*) Access USA.

Complete Guide to Income Property Financing & Loan Packaging. Donald W. Coker. LC 83-22574. 408p. 1984. text ed. 99.50 (*0-87624-099-6*, Inst Busn Plan) P-H.

Complete Guide to Industrial Safety in Manufacturing. S. Z. Mansdorf. LC 93-4986. 1993. 69.95 (*0-13-159633-0*) P-H.

Complete Guide to International Jobs & Careers: Your Passport to a World of Exciting & Exotic Employment. Ron Krannich & Caryl Krannich. 337p. (Orig.). 1990. 24.94 (*0-942710-25-8*); pap. 13.95 (*0-685-40159-6*) Impact VA.

Complete Guide to International Jobs & Careers: Your Passport to a World of Exciting & Exotic Employment. 2nd ed. Ron Krannich. 318p. 1992. 24.95 (*0-942710-83-5*); pap. 13.95 (*0-942710-69-X*) Impact VA.

Complete Guide to Iso Protocols, Vol. 1. S. Thomas. 1989. 39.00 (*0-387-97023-1*) Spr-Verlag.

***Complete Guide to Jazz Improvisation (for All Instruments)** Garree Stephan & Karen Stephan. (Illus.). 86p. (Orig.). 1995. spiral bd., pap. 20.00 (*1-884524-14-1*) Stephan Pubns.

Complete Guide to Job Sharing. Patricia Lee. 192p. 1983. 13.95 (*0-8027-0740-8*); pap. 6.95 (*0-8027-7213-7*) Walker & Co.

Complete Guide to Kansas Museums. Jay Workman. Ed. by Kim Dinell & Phyllis Jacobs. (Illus.). 152p. 1993. pap. 7.95 (*1-880662-30-2*) Wichita Eagle.

***Complete Guide to Kenai Fjords National Park, Alaska.** Jim Pfeiffenberger. (Illus.). 144p. (Orig.). 1995. pap. text ed. 11.95 (*0-936425-26-1*) Greatland Graphics.

Complete Guide to Kentucky Horse Country. William Strode. LC 80-67138. (Orig.). 1980. 4.95 (*0-937222-00-3*) Classic Pub.

Complete Guide to Kitchen Design with Cooking in Mind. Ed. by Donald E. Silvers. (Illus.). 100p. (Orig.). 1994. pap. 24.95 (*0-932767-04-4*) Newmark Mgmt Inst.

***Complete Guide to Knots & How to Tie Them.** rev. ed. Walter B. Gibson. (Illus.). 144p. (YA). (gr. 9 up). 1995. pap. 6.95 (*0-8119-0829-1*) LIFETIME.

Complete Guide to Landscape Design, Renovation, & Maintenance: A Practical Handbook for the Home Landscape Gardener. Cass Turnbull. (Illus.). 192p. (Orig.). 1991. pap. 14.95 (*1-55870-208-3*) Betterway Bks.

***Complete Guide to Learning Through Community Service: Grades K-9.** Lillian S. Stephens. 1995. pap. text ed. 34.95 (*0-205-15132-9*) Allyn.

Complete Guide to Liberty Seated Half Dollars. Bill Bugert & Randy Wiley. (Illus.). 250p. 1993. 59.95 (*1-880731-17-7*) DLRC Pr.

***Complete Guide to Life in Florida.** 3rd ed. Ed LaFreniere & Barbara B. LaFreniere. LC 94-42574. (Illus.). 422p. 1995. pap. 16.95 (*1-56164-066-2*) Pineapple Pr.

Complete Guide to Loan Documentation. Peter Clark. 494p. 1986. text ed. 69.95 (*0-13-160615-8*, Busn) P-H.

Complete Guide to Lock Picking. Eddie Wire. LC 84-80703. (Illus.). 78p. (Orig.). 1981. pap. 14.95 (*0-915179-06-7*) Loompanics.

Complete Guide to Log & Cedar Homes: All about Buying, Building, Decorating, & Furnishing Log, Cedar, & Post & Beam Homes. Gary D. Branson. (Illus.). 168p. (Orig.). 1993. pap. 16.95 (*1-55870-276-8*) Betterway Bks.

Complete Guide to Lumber Yards & Home Centers: A Consumer's Guide to Choosing & Using Building Materials & Tools. Gary D. Branson. (Illus.). 176p. (Orig.). 1990. pap. 14.95 (*1-55870-209-1*) Betterway Bks.

Complete Guide to Magazine Article Writing. John M. Wilson. 304p. 1993. 17.99 (*0-89879-547-8*) Writers Digest.

Complete Guide to Maintaining & Repairing Your Power Tools & Equipment. Mort Schultz. LC 93-29808. 1994. pap. text ed. 17.95 (*0-471-53501-X*) Wiley.

Complete Guide to Maintaining & Repairing Your Power Tools & Equipment. Mort Schultz. LC 93-29808. 1994. text ed. 34.95 (*0-471-53500-1*) Wiley.

Complete Guide to Making the Most of Video in Religious Settings: How to Produce, Find, Use & Distribute Video in the Church & Synagogue. Tom N. Emswiler et al. LC 85-50019. 128p. (Orig.). 1985. pap. 9.95 (*0-9606652-1-8*) Wesley Found.

***Complete Guide to Making Your Home Safe.** David Heberle & Ricard M. Scutella. (Illus.). 240p. 1995. pap. 17.99 (*1-55870-349-7*) Betterway Bks.

Complete Guide to Managing Corporate Real Estate, Vol. IV. B. Alan Whitson. (Corporate Real Estate Ser.). (Illus.). 225p. 1991. lib. bdg. 119.95 (*0-9627392-9-4*); Incls. software. disk, ring bd. 119.95 (*0-9627392-8-6*) B A Whitson.

Complete Guide to Manufactured Housing: The Affordable Alternative to Stick-Built Construction. Gary D. Branson. (Illus.). 160p. (Orig.). 1992. pap. 14.95 (*1-55870-249-0*) Betterway Bks.

Complete Guide to Marketing a Small Business or Product Successfully. Dennis L. Morgan. 269p. (Orig.). 1993. 29.95 (*0-9640823-0-6*) Morgan Mktg.

Complete Guide to Marketing & the Law. Robert J. Posch, Jr. 848p. 1988. text ed. 79.95 (*0-13-160904-1*) P-H.

Complete Guide to Marketing & the Law, 1990 Cumulative Supplement. Robert J. Posch, Jr. 240p. 1990. pap. 40.00 (*0-685-38167-6*) P-H.

Complete Guide to Mechanic's & Materialman's Lien Laws of Texas: 1990-1993. 3rd ed. Sterling W. Steves & Brenda T. Cubbage. 360p. 1994. ring bd. 135.00 (*0-409-25016-3*) Michie Butterworth.

Complete Guide to Mechanic's & Materialman's Lien Laws of Texas: 1990-1993. 3rd suppl. ed. Sterling W. Steves & Brenda T. Cubbage. 360p. 1994. 65.00 (*1-56257-981-9*) Butterworth Legal Pubs.

Complete Guide to Meeting Women. rev. ed. Don Diebel. 208p. 1991. pap. 14.95 (*0-937164-01-1*) Gemini Pub Co.

Complete Guide to Mercury Dimes. David W. Lange. (Illus.). 180p. Date not set. 49.95 (*1-880731-19-3*); pap. 29.95 (*1-880731-77-0*) DLRC Pr.

Complete Guide to Mercury Toxicity from Dental Fillings: How to Find Out If Your Dental Fillings Are Poisoning You & What You Can Do about It. Joyal Taylor. LC 88-90719. (Illus.). 208p. (Orig.). 1988. pap. 14.95 (*0-944796-36-2*) EDA Pubg.

Complete Guide to Microsystem Management. Steven K. Roberts. 192p. (C). 1984. 26.00 (*0-13-160556-9*) P-H.

Complete Guide to Middle Earth: From "the Hobbit" to "the Silmarillion" Robert Foster. LC 77-26825. 1985. mass mkt. 5.95 (*0-345-32436-6*, Del Rey) Ballantine.

Complete Guide to MIDI Software. PASS Staff & Howard Massey. (Illus.). 228p. 1987. pap. 19.95 (*0-8256-1088-5*, AM65715) Music Sales.

Complete Guide to Modern Management, No. 2. Robert Heller. 1991. 40.00 (*1-85251-151-6*, Mercury) Slawson Comm.

Complete Guide to Modern VCR Troubleshooting & Repair. John D. Lenk. (Illus.). 288p. (C). 1985. text ed. 68.00 (*0-13-160359-0*) P-H.

Complete Guide to Modern Warehouse Management. Creed H. Jenkins. 608p. 1990. 69.95 (*0-13-155409-3*) P-H.

Complete Guide to Modular Home Building: Have the House of Your Dreams for Thousands Less! Neil Smith. Ed. by Phyllis Hobe & Merit Books Inc. Staff. (Illus.). (Orig.). (C). 1991. pap. 24.50 (*0-9629509-0-4*) Neilson Assocs.

Complete Guide to Money & Your Business. Robert E. Butler & Donald Rappaport. LC 85-32094. (Illus.). 464p. 1986. text ed. 37.50 (*0-13-160276-4*) NY Inst Finance.

Complete Guide to Money & Your Business. Robert E. Butler & Donald Rappaport. 1986. 37.50 (*0-13-600073-8*) P-H.

Complete Guide to Money-Making Ventures for Nonprofit Organizations. Peter C. Brown. 256p. (Orig.). 1986. pap. 50.00 (*0-914977-30-X*) Taft Group.

Complete Guide to Motorcycle Mechanics. Motorcycle Mechanics Institute Staff. (Illus.). 416p. (C). 1984. text ed. 60.00 (*0-13-160549-6*) P-H.

Complete Guide to Motorcycle Mechanics. 2nd ed. Motorcycle Mechanics Institute Staff. LC 93-14849. 1993. text ed. 57.00 (*0-13-225889-7*) P-H Gen Ref & Trav.

Complete Guide to Mysterious Beings. rev. ed. John A. Keel. LC 93-45544. Orig. Title: Strange Creatures from Time & Space. 1994. reprint ed. 9.95 (*0-385-47094-0*) Doubleday.

Complete Guide to Needlework. Reader's Digest Editors. LC 78-71704. (Illus.). 504p. 1981. 28.00 (*0-89577-059-8*, Random) RD Assn.

Complete Guide to Netware Printing. Dave Doering. 1994. pap. 29.95 (*0-13-511289-3*) P-H.

Complete Guide to NetWare 4.1. James E. Gaskin. 1995. 49.99 (*0-7821-1500-4*) Sybex.

Complete Guide to Newport. Terrence Gavan. (Illus.). 64p. (Orig.). (YA). 1988. pap. 5.95 (*0-929249-00-3*) Pineapple Pubns.

Complete Guide to Nine Star Ki. Sachs. 1992. pap. 13.95 (*1-85230-334-4*) Element MA.

Complete Guide to Nonprofit Corporations. rev. ed. Ted Nicholas. 248p. 1993. pap. 19.95 (*0-7931-0615-X*, 5615-66) Dearborn Finan.

***Complete Guide to Nonprofit Management.** Busklin Smith & Robert H. Wilbur. Ed. by Susan K. Finn & Carolyn M. Freeland. (Nonprofit Law, Finance & Management Ser). 1994. text ed. 45.00 (*0-471-30955-9*); pap. text ed. 16.95 (*0-471-30953-2*) Wiley.

Complete Guide to North American Gardens: The Northeast. William C. Mulligan. 1991. pap. 15.95 (*0-316-58907-1*) Little.

Complete Guide to North American Gardens: The Northeast, Vol. 1. William C. Mulligan. 1991. pap. 15.95 (*0-316-59807-0*) Little.

Complete Guide to North American Gardens: The West Coast. William C. Mulligan. 1991. pap. 15.95 (*0-316-58909-8*) Little.

Complete Guide to Northern California Gardening. Maureen Gilmer. LC 93-33779. 248p. 1994. 29.95 (*0-87833-842-X*) Taylor Pub.

Complete Guide to Operational Auditing. Harry R. Reider. 296p. 1993. text ed. 100.00 (*0-471-59419-9*) Wiley.

Complete Guide to OSHA Compliance. Cohen. 1994. 59.95 (*0-87371-681-7*, TK) Lewis Pubs.

Complete Guide to Owning a Home Based Business. Entrepreneur Magazine Staff. 1990. pap. 13.95 (*0-553-34919-8*) Bantam.

Complete Guide to Painting Your Home. Jack Luts & Pete Peterson. (Illus.). 160p. (Orig.). 1989. pap. 14.95 (*1-55870-119-2*) Betterway Bks.

Complete Guide to Passed Hand Bidding. Mike Lawrence. LC 89-80899. 224p. 1989. pap. 12.95 (*1-877908-01-0*) Lawrence & Leong Pub.

Complete Guide to PATHWORKS: PATHWORKS for VMS & DOS. Kenneth L. Spencer. LC 92-25716. 394p. 1993. pap. 39.00 (*1-878956-22-1*) CBM Bks.

Complete Guide to PC-File: Through Version 5.01. Brugruet L. Young & Robert J. Levine. (Illus.). 800p. (Orig.). 1991. disk, pap. 26.95 (*0-944954-01-4*) Ctr Bk Pubs.

Complete Guide to Pediatric Symptoms, Illness, & Medications. H. Winter Griffith. 1989. pap. 14.95 (*0-89586-816-4*, Body Pr-Perigree) Berkley Pub.

Complete Guide to Pest Control: With & Without Chemicals. 2nd ed. George W. Ware. LC 80-52306. (Illus.). 304p. 1988. pap. 20.50 (*0-913702-09-9*) Thomson Pubns.

***Complete Guide to Photographing Underwater Wonders.** Rick Sammon. LC 94-31816. 1995. 14.95 (*0-89658-252-3*) Voyageur Pr.

Complete Guide to Planned Giving: Everything You Need to Know to Compete Successfully for Major Gifts. 2nd rev. ed. Debra Ashton. (Nonprofit Technical Assistance Ser.: Vol. 2). 440p. 1991. pap. 50.00 (*0-940374-15-3*) JLA Pubns.

Complete Guide to Planning Your Family Reunion. Ed E. Duncan. LC 93-70485. 83p. (Orig.). 1993. pap. 9.95 (*0-9636044-0-6*) Cleve-Coast.

***Complete Guide to Point & Charting Figure.** Carroll D. Aby. LC 92-75231. 286p. (Orig.). 1992. pap. 19.95 (*0-938991-99-X*) Colonial Pr AL.

Complete Guide to Practical Cutting (1853) 2nd enl. rev. ed. Edward Minister. Ed. by R. L. Shep. LC 92-50696. (Illus.). 480p. 1993. pap. 31.95 (*0-914046-17-9*) R L Shep.

Complete Guide to Prescription & Non-Prescription Drugs. H. Winter Griffith. LC 94-14531. 1104p. 1994. pap. 15.95 (*0-399-52145-3*, Body Pr-Perigree) Berkley Pub.

Complete Guide to Prescription & Non-Prescription Drugs, 1994. H. Winter Griffith. 1104p. 1993. pap. 15.95 (*0-399-51835-5*, Body Pr-Perigree) Berkley Pub.

Complete Guide to Pressed Glass. Bob H. Batty. LC 77-19211. (Illus.). 261p. 1978. 24.95 (*0-88289-057-3*) Pelican.

Complete Guide to Preventing Cancer: How You Can Reduce Your Risks. Elizabeth Whelan. 385p. (C). 1994. 26.95 (*0-87975-890-2*) Prometheus Bks.

Complete Guide to Professional Woodworking: Including Projects & Schematics. Ken Calhoun. 368p. 1988. text ed. 46.00 (*0-13-160193-8*) P-H.

Complete Guide to Pruning & Training Plants. David Joyce. (Illus.). 224p. 1992. 30.00 (*0-671-73842-9*) S&S Trade.

Complete Guide to Public Employment. 2nd ed. Ronald L. Krannich & Caryl R. Krannich. 510p. (Orig.). 1990. 29.95 (*0-942710-51-7*); pap. 15.95 (*0-942710-23-1*) Impact VA.

Complete Guide to Public Employment. 3rd ed. Ron Krannich. 1995. pap. 19.95 (*0-942710-94-0*) Impact VA.

Complete Guide to Public Employment: Opportunities & Strategies with Federal, State, & Local Governments; Trade & Professional Associations; Consulting Firms; Nonprofit Organizations; Foundations; Research Organizations; Political Support Groups; & International Institutions. 2nd ed. Ron Krannich & Caryl Krannich. 528p. (Orig.). 1990. 29.95 (*0-942710-26-6*); pap. 15.95 (*0-685-40160-X*) Impact VA.

Complete Guide to Punctuation: A Quick Reference Desk Book. Margaret E. Wye. write for info. (*0-318-58201-5*) P-H.

Complete Guide to Racetrack Betting. David K. Rosenthal. 160p. (Orig.). 1986. pap. 9.95 (*0-89709-144-2*) Liberty Pub.

Complete Guide to Reading Schematic Diagrams. 2nd ed. Douglas A. Young. 1986. 9.95 (*0-13-160424-4*) P-H.

Complete Guide to Reading Schematic Diagrams. 3rd ed. John Douglas-Young. 340p. 1988. text ed. 27.95 (*0-13-160334-5*, Busn) P-H.

Complete Guide to Real Estate Foreclosure Super Bargains in California. rev. ed. John Beck & Ronald Starr. Ed. by Johnathan Albert. 355p. (Orig.). pap. 149.00 (*0-934521-04-2*); spiral bd. 79.00 (*0-934521-03-4*) Unlimited Golden Pr.

***Complete Guide to Refractive Surgery: Nearsightedness, Farsightedness, & Astigmatism. Stanley C. Grandon & Susan Giffin. (Illus.). 175p. (Orig.). 1995. pap. 10.95 (*0-9628886-1-3*) Patton Pub.**
At last, a consumer's guide for anyone afflicted with nearsightedness, farsightedness, & astigmatism. Everything you need to know, from learning the difference between an ophthalmologist & an optician...to diagnosing refractive problems...to deciding which corrective method best suits you & your lifestyle. THE COMPLETE GUIDE TO REFRACTIVE SURGERY offers insights into the developments of RK surgery in the U.S.S.R. (& subsequent refinements in the United States), the development in Mexico of surgical procedures to correct farsightedness & astigmatism, the controversial Excimer laser procedure, & the status of other surgical & non-surgical treatments. Based largely on the surgical practice of author, Dr. Stanley C. Grandon, Director of the Eye Surgery Institute,

An Asterisk (*) at the beginning of an entry indicates that the title is appearing in BIP for the first time.

Dearborn, MI, one of the world's leading refractive surgeons. THE COMPLETE GUIDE TO REFRACTIVE SURGERY replaces GOOD-BYE, GLASSES, written by co-author Susan Giffin (formerly Abbas) & published by Patton Publ. in 1990, as a complete guide to radial keratotomy (RK). THE COMPLETE GUIDE TO REFRACTIVE SURGERY is an interesting, enlightening, & helpful guide to good vision & how you can achieve it. Order from Patton Publishing, P.O. Box 7365, Dearborn, MI 48126; 313-584-7223. ***Publisher Provided Annotation.***

*Complete Guide to Reiki. Jeffery A. Martin. (Illus.). 236p. (Orig.). 1995. pap. 16.95 (*1-57242-578-4*) Integration Pr.

*Complete Guide to Reiki. Jeffery A. Martin. (Illus.). 112p. (Orig.). 1994. spiral bd., pap. 16.95 (*1-57242-592-X*) Integration Pr.

*Complete Guide to Reiki Vol. II: A Master's Toolbox. Jeffery A. Martin et al. (Illus.). 124p. (Orig.). 1995. pap. 16.95 (*1-57242-258-0*) Integration Pr.

Complete Guide to Religious Education Volunteers. Donald Ratcliff & Blake Neff. 280p. (Orig.). 1993. pap. 16.95 (*0-89135-089-6*) Religious Educ.

Complete Guide to Remodeling & Expanding Your Dollhouse. Nola Theiss. LC 92-44443. (Illus.). 128p. (J). 1989. pap. 12.95 (*0-8069-8369-8*) Sterling.

Complete Guide to Remodeling Your Basement: How to Create New Living Space the Professional Way. Gary D. Branson. (Illus.). 176p. (Orig.). 1990. pap. 14.95 (*1-55870-162-1*) Betterway Bks.

*Complete Guide to Repairing & Restoring Aurora Slot Cars. Mike Vitale. Ed. by Mike Lane. (Illus.). 72p. (Orig.). Date not set. pap. text ed. 9.95 (*88-379-6067-0*) What It Is.

Complete Guide to Researching & Writing the English Term Paper. Allan Blonde. LC 78-63036. (Orig.). 1978. pap. text ed. 5.50 (*0-87936-013-5*) Scholium Intl.

Complete Guide to Residential Deck Construction: From the Simplest to the Most Sophisticated. Greg Roy. (Illus.). 176p. (Orig.). 1992. pap. 16.95 (*1-55870-231-8*) Betterway Bks.

Complete Guide to Residential Remodeling. Mortimer Reed. (Illus.). 320p. 1983. 19.95 (*0-13-160663-8*) P-H.

Complete Guide to Restoring & Maintaining Wood Furniture & Cabinets. Brad Hughes. 160p. (Orig.). 1993. pap. 19.95 (*1-55870-302-0*) Betterway Bks.

*Complete Guide to Riki: Master Level Manual. Jeffery A. Martin. (Illus.). 106p. (Orig.). 1995. pap. 14.95 (*1-57242-579-2*) Integration Pr.

Complete Guide to Riverboat Gambling: Its History & How to Play, Win & Have Fun. Scott Faragher. LC 94-18302. 1994. 12.95 (*0-8065-1569-4*, Citadel Pr) Carol Pub Group.

Complete Guide to Root Reflexology. rev. ed. Kevin Kunz & Barbara Kunz. (Illus.). Date not set. pap. 13.95 (*0-9606070-1-3*) Reflex Res Proj.

Complete Guide to "S" Corporations. Ted Nicholas. 175p. 1993. pap. 19.95 (*0-7931-0613-3*, 561565) Dearborn Finan.

Complete Guide to Safe Sex. Ted McIlvenna et al. 200p. (Orig.). 1987. pap. text ed. 6.95 (*0-930846-05-2*) Specific Pr.

Complete Guide to Safe Storage of Silver & Gold. Chris Weber. 124p. (Orig.). 1985. pap. text ed. 68.00 (*0-9615814-0-9*) Rosenthal Assocs.

Complete Guide to Safer Sex: The Institute for Advanced Study of Human Sexuality. Ted McIlvenna. 1992. pap. 6.95 (*0-942637-58-5*) Barricade Bks.

Complete Guide to Sales Force Compensation: How to Plan Salaries, Commissions, Bonuses, Quotas...Everything Needed to Achieve Top Sales Results. James F. Carey. 310p. 1992. 70.00 (*1-55623-696-4*) Irwin Prof Pubng.

Complete Guide to Sales Territory Planning & Management. Charles C. Schlom. 214p. 1990. ring bd. 91.50 (*0-85013-174-X*) Dartnell Corp.

*Complete Guide to Saxophone Playing (for Classical & Jazz Musicians) Karen Stephan. (Illus.). 86p. (Orig.). 1995. spiral bd., pap. 20.00 (*1-884524-30-3*) Stephan Pubns.

*Complete Guide to Scientific & Common Names of Reptiles & Amphibians of the World. Norman Frank & Erica Ramus. 300p. Date not set. pap. write for info. (*0-9641032-3-0*) Reptile & Amphibian.

Complete Guide to Screenprinting. Brad Faine. (Illus.). 144p. 1993. pap. 28.95 (*0-89134-544-2*, 30527) North Light Bks.

Complete Guide to Sea & Sea. Joe Liburdi & Cara Sherman. (Illus.). 256p. (Orig.). 1994. pap. text ed. 10.25 (*0-9621111-2-0*) Orca Pubns.

Complete Guide to Securities Transactions: Controlling Costs & Enhancing Investment Performance. Michael J. Wagner. 1989. text ed. 59.50 (*0-471-61013-5*) Wiley.

Complete Guide to Selected Health & Health-Related Careers. L. Riddick Lynch. Ed. by Urella Chatman et al. (Illus.). (Orig.). 1980. pap. 10.45 (*0-685-04204-9*) R Bernard.

Complete Guide to Self-Publishing: Everything You Need to Know to Write, Publish, Promote, & Sell Your Own Book. 3rd ed. Tom Ross & Marilyn Ross. LC 94-16872. 432p. 1994. pap. 18.99 (*0-89879-646-6*) Writers Digest.

Complete Guide to Selling a Business. Michael Semanik & John Wade. 172p. 1994. 22.95 (*0-8144-0223-2*) AMACOM.

Complete Guide to Selling New Cars. Mike Whitty. Ed. by Irene M. McDonald. LC 89-92422. 248p. 1990. pap. text ed. 12.95 (*0-9625079-9-7*); audio 29.95 (*0-9625079-8-9*) Michael Pub.

Complete Guide to Selling Your Business. Paul S. Sperry & Beatrice Mitchell. 1992. 21.95 (*0-936894-31-8*) Upstart Pub.

*Complete Guide to Semiconductor Devices. Kwok K. Ng. 1994. pap. 62.50 (*0-07-035860-5*) McGraw.

Complete Guide to Sensible Eating: The Egg Project Updated with New & Expanded Chapters on Detoxification, Environmental Medicine, Herbs & Healing. Gary Null. LC 89-71488. (Illus.). 300p. 1990. pap. 14.95 (*0-941423-37-9*) FWEW.

Complete Guide to Sewing. Reader's Digest Editors. LC 75-32106. (Illus.). 528p. 1976. 28.00 (*0-89577-026-1*) RD Assn.

*Complete Guide to Sewing: Step-by-Step Techniques for Making Clothes & Home Furnishings. rev. ed. Reader's Digest Editor. 1995. 30.00 (*0-88850-247-8*) RD Assn.

Complete Guide to Sexual Fulfillment. Philip Cauthery & Andrew Stanway. LC 86-61822. (Illus.). 349p. (Orig.). 1986. pap. 20.95 (*0-87975-356-0*) Prometheus Bks.

Complete Guide to Sharpening. Leonard Lee. 245p. 1995. pap. 34.95 (*1-56158-067-8*) Taunton.

Complete Guide to Sherlock Holmes. Michael Hardwick. (Illus.). 256p. 1992. pap. 10.95 (*0-312-07248-1*) St Martin.

Complete Guide to Shortboard Sailing. Jeremy Evans. (Illus.). 144p. 1987. pap. text ed. 12.95 (*0-87742-245-1*) Intl Marine.

Complete Guide to Silk Painting. Susanne Hahn. (Illus.). 136p. (Orig.). 1992. pap. 22.50 (*0-85532-718-9*, Pub. by Search Pr UK) A Schwartz & Co.

Complete Guide to Single-Engine Cessnas. 3rd ed. Joe Christy. (Illus.). 1979. 9.95 (*0-8306-9800-0*); pap. 10.95 (*0-8306-2268-3*, 2268) TAB Bks.

Complete Guide to Single Engine Cessnas. 4th ed. Joe Christy & Brian J. Dooley. 1993. pap. text ed. 12.95 (*0-07-017766-X*) McGraw.

Complete Guide to Single-Engine Cessnas. 4th rev. ed. Joe Christy & Brian A. Dooley. (Illus.). 144p. 1992. pap. 12.95 (*0-8306-4224-2*, 4274) TAB Bks.

Complete Guide to Skin Care for Men. Zia Wesley-Hosford. 72p. 1987. pap. 6.95 (*0-15-620990-X*, Harvest Bks) HarBrace.

Complete Guide to Snakes of South Africa. Johan Marais. 284p. 1992. 37.50 (*1-86812-439-8*, Pub. by Southern Bk Pubs) Krieger.

Complete Guide to Software Testing. 2nd ed. Bill Hetzel. 1993. text ed. 49.95 (*0-471-56567-9*, GD2423) Wiley.

Complete Guide to Software Testing. 2nd ed. William Hetzel. LC 88-6014. 290p. 1988. 44.95 (*0-89435-242-3*) Wiley.

Complete Guide to Solving Your Bill Problems. Dennis Shears. 117p. (Orig.). 1983. reprint ed. pap. text ed. 12.95 (*0-911539-00-X*) Prime Pr AZ.

*Complete Guide to Southern California Gardening. Maureen Gilmer. LC 94-38093. 1995. 29.95 (*0-87833-875-6*) Taylor Pub.

Complete Guide to Special Event Management: Business Insights, Financial Advice, & Successful Strategies from Ernst & Young, Consultants to the Olympics, the Emmy Awards, & the PGA Tour. Ernst & Young Staff. 320p. 1992. text ed. 24.95 (*0-471-54908-8*) Wiley.

Complete Guide to Special Interest Videos: More Than 7,500 Videos You've Never Seen Before. James R. Spencer. LC 90-92008. (Illus.). 602p. (Orig.). 1991. pap. 14.95 (*0-9627836-0-9*) James-Robert Pub Co.

Complete Guide to Special Interest Videos 1993-1994. James Spencer. 1993. pap. 19.95 (*0-9627836-1-7*) James-Robert Pub Co.

*Complete Guide to Special Interest Videos 1995-1996. James R. Spencer. 1995. pap. 19.95 (*0-9627836-2-5*) James-Robert Pub Co.

Complete Guide to Specialty Cars. 7th rev. ed. Curt Scott. Ed. by Judy Scott. (Illus.). 104p. 1991. pap. 14.95 (*0-9614882-5-5*) Crown Pub CA.

*Complete Guide to Specialty Cars. 8th ed. Ed. & Comp. by Curt Scott. (Illus.). 104p. 1994. pap. 17.95 (*0-9614882-6-3*) Crown Pub CA.

Complete Guide to Sports Injuries: How to Treat Fractures, Bruises, Sprains, Strains, Dislocations, Head Injuries. H. Winter Griffith. 1986. pap. 15.00 (*0-399-51712-X*, Body Pr-Perigree) Berkley Pub.

Complete Guide to Sports Injuries: How to Treat Fractures, Bruises, Sprains, Strains, Dislocations, Head Injuries. H. Winter Griffith. LC 86-70726. 528p. reprint ed. pap. 150.50 (*0-7837-2842-5*, 2057630) Bks Demand.

Complete Guide to Stamp Collecting. rev. ed. Prescott H. Thorp. (Illus.). 198p. 1982. reprint ed. 3.50 (*0-912236-00-0*, Minkus Pubns) Novus Debut.

Complete Guide to Standard Script Formats, Pt. 1: The Screenplay. 7th ed. Hillis R. Cole & Judith H. Haag. 229p. (C). 1994. pap. text ed. 18.95 (*0-929583-00-0*) CMC Pub CA.

Complete Guide to Standard Script Formats, Pt. 2: Taped Formats for Television. Judith H. Haag. 177p. (C). 1994. pap. 18.95 (*0-929583-01-9*) CMC Pub CA.

Complete Guide to Starting a Local Church Counseling Ministry, 3 cass., Set. deluxe ed. Walter Major & David Hoagland. Ed. by Cindy G. Spear & Tamara Johnson. 92p. (Orig.). 1993. audio, ring bd. 79.95 (*0-941005-92-5*) Chrch Grwth VA.

Complete Guide to Starting a Used Bookstore. 2nd ed. Dale L. Gilbert. 208p. 1991. pap. 14.95 (*0-936894-28-8*) Upstart Pub.

Complete Guide to Starting or Evaluating a Children's Ministry. Herb Owen. Ed. by Cindy G. Spear. 156p. 1993. How to Shepherd Children in a World Full of Wolves. pap. text ed. 8.95 (*0-941005-66-6*); Resource pkt. incl. text, planning & teaching instructions & audiotapes. ring bd. 69.95 (*0-941005-67-4*) Chrch Grwth VA.

Complete Guide to Starting or Evaluating a Dynamic Youth Ministry. Larry Maxwell. Ed. by Tamara Johnson & Cindy Spear. 164p. 1993. Resource pkt. incl. 3 audiotapes & 208p. textbk. ring bd. 79.95 (*0-941005-87-9*) Chrch Grwth VA.

Complete Guide to Starting or Evaluating a Singles Ministry, 3 cass., Set. Glen Martin. 172p. 1993. audio, ring bd. 79.95 (*0-941005-93-3*) Chrch Grwth VA.

Complete Guide to Stereo Television (MIS-MCS) Troubleshooting & Repair. John D. Lenk. (Illus.). 160p. (C). 1988. text ed. 44.00 (*0-13-160839-8*) P-H.

Complete Guide to Stress Management. Chandra Patel. (Illus.). 376p. 1991. 23.95 (*0-306-43967-0*, Plenum Pr) Plenum.

Complete Guide to Successful Publishing. Avery Cardoza. (Illus.). 320p. 1995. per., pap. 19.95 (*0-940685-43-4*) Cardoza Pub.

Complete Guide to Successful Small Client Tax Practice. Ralph L. Guyette. LC 81-5235. 392p. 1981. 39.50 (*0-13-160622-0*, Busn) P-H.

Complete Guide to Supervisory Training & Development. Lester R. Bittel. LC 86-22267. 1987. 37.95 (*0-201-12220-0*) Addison-Wesley.

*Complete Guide to Symptoms, Illness, & Surgery. rev. ed. H. Winter Griffith. 1104p. (Orig.). 1995. pap. 15.95 (*0-399-51942-4*, Perigree Bks) Berkley Pub.

Complete Guide to Symptoms, Illness & Surgery. 2nd ed. H. Winter Griffith. (Illus.). 896p. 1989. pap. 15.95 (*0-399-51709-X*, Body Pr-Perigree) Berkley Pub.

Complete Guide to Symptoms, Illness & Surgery for People over Fifty. H. Winter Griffith. (Illus.). 896p. (Orig.). 1992. pap. 19.00 (*0-399-51749-9*, Body Pr-Perigree) Berkley Pub.

Complete Guide to Telemarketing Management. Joel Linchitz. LC 89-46218. 360p. 1990. 59.95 (*0-8144-5885-8*) AMACOM.

Complete Guide to Telemarketing Management. Joel Linchitz. 333p. 1993. pap. 24.95 (*0-8144-7863-8*) AMACOM.

Complete Guide to Tested Telephone Collection Techniques. Arthur Winston. 440p. 1988. text ed. 59.95 (*0-13-160185-7*, Busn) P-H.

Complete Guide to Texas Lawn Care. William Knoop. (Illus.). 160p. 1986. 17.95 (*0-914641-03-4*); pap. 12.95 (*0-914641-04-2*) TX Gardener Pr.

Complete Guide to the Advanced Optics - Electro-Optics Industry, 2 pts., Pts. 1-2. Business Communications Company, Inc. Staff. 1992. Pt. I: Overview of the Optics - Electro-Optics Industry; Pt. II: The Directory. 1,650.00 (*0-685-62469-2*, DOM92) BCC.

Complete Guide to the Alesis HR-16 & MMT-8. Craig Anderton. (Illus.). 192p. 1989. pap. 19.95 (*0-685-65828-7*, AM73008) Music Sales.

*Complete Guide to the Birds of Alaska. 4th ed. Robert H. Armstrong. LC 95-5431. 1995. 24.95 (*0-88240-462-8*) Alaska Northwest.

Complete Guide to the Blue Ridge Parkway, Vol. I. rev. ed. William G. Lord. (Illus.). 160p. 1990. pap. 2.95 (*0-915992-38-8*) Eastern Acorn.

Complete Guide to the Blue Ridge Parkway, Vol. II. rev. ed. William G. Lord. (Illus.). 160p. 1990. pap. 2.95 (*0-915992-39-6*) Eastern Acorn.

*Complete Guide to the Book of Proverbs: King Solomon Reveals the Secrets to Long Life, Riches, & Honor. Cody L. Jones. LC 95-5589. 1995. write for info. (*0-9638944-7-1*); pap. write for info. (*0-9638944-6-3*) Quinten Pubng.

*Complete Guide to the FCC General Radiotelephone Operator License: Exam Questions & Answers with Explanations. Laurence Goldberg. LC 95-92161. 288p. 1995. pap. 29.95 (*1-886176-18-3*) Ctr for F C C.

Complete Guide to the Futures Markets: Fundamental Analysis, Technical Analysis, Trading, Spreads & Options. Jack D. Schwager. LC 84-3705. 741p. 1984. text ed. 85.00 (*0-471-89376-5*) Wiley.

Complete Guide to the Golf Courses of Scotland: With Sections on England & Ireland. Robert F. Kroeger. (Illus.). 258p. (Orig.). 1992. pap. 21.95 (*0-9618291-2-5*) Heritage Conn.

*Complete Guide to the Hazardous Waste Regulations: The Comprehensive Step-by-Step Guide to the Regulation of Hazardous Waste under RORA, TSCA, HMTA, OSHA & Superfund. 2nd ed. Travis P. Wagner. (Illus.). 488p. 1994. pap. 49.95 (*0-442-01931-9*) Van Nos Reinhold.

Complete Guide to the Home Remodeling & Construction Process. J. Hardy LeGwin. 1990. pap. 29.95 (*0-685-47694-4*) J H LeGwin Assocs.

Complete Guide to the Law: Everything You Ever Wanted to Know. Michael L. Gabriel. 480p. 1993. pap. 16.95 (*0-8065-1433-7*, Citadel Pr) Carol Pub Group.

Complete Guide to the Maintenance & Repair of Band Instruments. Kenneth Mueller. 288p. 1982. text ed. 29.95 (*0-13-160499-6*, Parker Publishing Co) P-H.

*Complete Guide to the Music of Bob Marley. Contrib by Ian McCann. (Illus.). (Orig.). 1995. pap. 7.95 (*0-7119-3550-5*, OP 47384, Pub. by Omnibus Press UK) Omnibus NY.

*Complete Guide to the Music of Elvis Presley. John Robertson. (Illus.). (Orig.). 1995. pap. 7.95 (*0-7119-3549-1*, OP47376, Pub. by Omnibus Press UK) Omnibus NY.

*Complete Guide to the Music of Eric Clapton. Marc Roberty. (Illus.). 150p. (Orig.). 1995. pap. 7.95 (*0-7119-4305-2*, OP 47739, Pub. by Omnibus Press UK) Omnibus NY.

*Complete Guide to the Music of Jimi Hendrix. John Robertson. (Illus.). 128p. (Orig.). 1995. pap. 7.95 (*0-7119-4304-4*, OP 47738, Pub. by Omnibus Press UK) Omnibus NY.

*Complete Guide to the Music of Led Zeppelin. Dave Lewis. (Illus.). (Orig.). 1995. pap. 7.95 (*0-7119-3528-9*, OP 47350, Pub. by Omnibus Press UK) Omnibus NY.

*Complete Guide to the Music of Pink Floyd. Andy Mabbett. (Illus.). 150p. (Orig.). 1995. pap. 7.95 (*0-7119-4301-X*, OP 47735, Pub. by Omnibus Press UK) Omnibus NY.

*Complete Guide to the Music of Queen. Peter Hogan. (Illus.). (Orig.). 1995. pap. 7.95 (*0-7119-3526-2*, OP 47334, Pub. by Omnibus Press UK) Omnibus NY.

*Complete Guide to the Music of The Beatles. John Robertson. (Illus.). (Orig.). 1995. pap. 7.95 (*0-7119-3548-3*, OP 47368, Pub. by Omnibus Press UK) Omnibus NY.

*Complete Guide to the Music of The Doors. Peter Hogan. (Illus.). (Orig.). 1995. pap. 7.95 (*0-7119-3527-0*, OP 47342, Pub. by Omnibus Press UK) Omnibus NY.

*Complete Guide to the Music of the Rolling Stones. James Hector. (Complete Guide to the Music of...Ser.). (Illus.). 168p. (Orig.). 1995. pap. 7.95 (*0-7119-4303-6*, OP 47737) Omnibus NY.

*Complete Guide to the Music of The Who. Chris Charlesworth. (Illus.). 136p. (Orig.). 1995. pap. 7.95 (*0-7119-4306-0*, OP 47740, Pub. by Omnibus Press UK) Omnibus NY.

*Complete Guide to the Music of U2. Bill Graham. (Illus.). 118p. (Orig.). 1995. pap. 7.95 (*0-7119-4302-8*, OP 47736, Pub. by Omnibus Press UK) Omnibus NY.

Complete Guide to the NeXTSTEP User Environment. Michael B. Shebanek. LC 93-9064. 472p. 1993. pap. 42.95 (*0-387-97956-5*) Spr-Verlag.

Complete Guide to the Non-Commissioned Officers Evaluation Report. Wilson L. Walker. 1993. pap. 14.95 (*0-942710-98-3*) Impact VA.

Complete Guide to the Soviet Union: New York St. Martin's Press, 1980. V. Louis & J. Louis. (Illus.). 378p. (C). 1980. 115.00 (*0-685-32379-X*) St Mut.

Complete Guide to the Street Drug Game. Scott French. (Illus.). 256p. 1976. 12.00 (*0-8184-0208-3*); pap. 6.95 (*0-8184-0237-7*) Carol Pub Group.

Complete Guide to the Tarot. Eden Gray. 1983. mass mkt. 5.50 (*0-553-27752-9*) Bantam.

Complete Guide to the Tax Reform Act of 1986. Prentice-Hall Editorial Staff. LC 87-110898. write for info. (*0-13-160649-2*) P-H.

*Complete Guide to the Treatment of Premenstrual Problems. Barbara Kass-Annese & Hal Danzer. 96p. 1993. lib. bdg. 23.00 (*0-8095-6347-9*) Borgo Pr.

Complete Guide to the U. S. Advanced Ceramic Industry. Business Communications Company, Inc. Staff. 1990. 1,475.00 (*0-685-62465-X*, DCD90) BCC.

Complete Guide to Thematic Units: Creating the Integrated Curriculum. Anita Meinbach et al. (Illus.). 250p. (Orig.). (C). 1995. pap. text ed. 28.95 (*0-926842-42-0*) CG Pubs Inc.

Complete Guide to TOEFL. Bruce Rogers. 1993. cd-rom 22.00 (*0-8384-5093-8*) Heinle & Heinle.

Complete Guide to TOEFL. Bruce Rogers. 1993. cd-rom, text ed. 23.95 (*0-8384-4225-0*); audio, text ed. 22.95 (*0-8384-4226-9*); pap. 20.95 (*0-8384-3415-0*); teacher ed, pap. 5.95 (*0-8384-4134-3*); audio 21.00 (*0-8384-4133-5*) Heinle & Heinle.

Complete Guide to TOEFL: Intermediate to Advanced. Bruce Rogers. 1993. pap. 28.95 (*0-8384-4227-7*) Heinle & Heinle.

Complete Guide to TOEFL: Practice Tests. Bruce Rogers. (College ESL Ser.). 1994. pap. 15.95 (*0-8384-4279-X*) Heinle & Heinle.

Complete Guide to Touch Dancing. K. Lustgarten. (Ballroom Dance Ser.). 1986. lib. bdg. 79.95 (*0-8490-3315-2*) Gordon Pr.

Complete Guide to Touch Dancing. K. Lustgarten. (Ballroom Dance Ser.). 1985. lib. bdg. 69.95 (*0-87700-818-3*) Revisionist Pr.

Complete Guide to Trading Profits. Alexander P. Paris. LC 75-84640. 196p. 1981. reprint ed. 24.95 (*0-934380-05-8*) Traders Pr.

Complete Guide to Travel Agency Automation. 2nd ed. Nadine Godwin. LC 86-29200. 148p. (C). 1987. text ed. 28.95 (*0-8273-2980-6*) Delmar.

Complete Guide to Truck Lettering, Pinstriping & Graphics. Gary D. Steele. 165p. 1994. pap. 29.95 (*0-944094-02-3*) ST Pubns.

*Complete Guide to Trumpet Playing (for Classical & Jazz Musicians) Garree Stephan. (Illus.). 94p. (Orig.). 1995. spiral bd., pap. 20.00 (*1-884524-22-2*) Stephan Pubns.

Complete Guide to U. S. Civil Service Jobs. 10th ed. Hy Hammer. 240p. 1991. pap. 10.00 (*0-13-932658-8*, Arco Test) P-H Gen Ref & Trav.

Complete Guide to Understanding & Caring for Your Home: A Practical Handbook for Knowledgeable Homeowners. James Madorma. (Illus.). 272p. (Orig.). 1991. pap. 18.95 (*1-55870-210-5*) Betterway Bks.

Complete Guide to Understanding Electronic Diagrams. Edward A. Lacy. 368p. 1989. text ed. 61.00 (*0-13-160920-3*) P-H.

Complete Guide to Underwater Modeling. Tom Mount & Patti Schaeffer. (Illus.). 80p. pap. 10.95 (*0-915539-00-4*) Sea-Mount Pub Co.

Complete Guide to United States Civil Service Jobs. 11th ed. Hammer. Date not set. pap. 10.00 (*0-671-89749-7*, Arco Test) P-H Gen Ref & Trav.

C

An Asterisk (*) at the beginning of an entry indicates that the title is appearing in BIP for the first time.

1465

Complete Guide to Used Cars: 1993 Edition. Consumer Guide Editors. 448p. (Orig.). 1993. pap. 5.99 (*0-451-17610-3*, Sig) NAL-Dutton.

*__Complete Guide to Used Cars: 1995 Edition.__ Consumer Guide Editors. 448p. (Orig.). 1995. mass mkt. 5.99 (*0-451-18354-1*, Sig) NAL-Dutton.

Complete Guide to Using Color in Your Garden: How to Combine Perennials, Annuals, Trees, & Shrubs for a More Beautiful Landscape. David Squire. LC 90-29086. (Illus.). 320p. 1991. 24.95 (*0-87857-968-0*, 01-224-0) Rodale Pr Inc.

Complete Guide to Using Depthfinders. rev. ed. Buck Taylor. LC 84-62198. (Illus.). 272p. (Orig.). 1985. pap. 9.95 (*0-940022-03-6*) Outdoor Skills.

Complete Guide to Vitamins, Minerals & Supplements. H. Winter Griffith. LC 87-25156. 516p. (Orig.). 1988. pap. 14.95 (*1-55561-006-4*) Fisher Bks.

Complete Guide to Walking in Canada: Includes Day-Hiking & Backpacking. Elliott Katz. (Illus.). 300p. 1991. pap. 12.95 (*0-920361-03-X*, Pub. by Great North Bks CN) Firefly Bks Ltd.

Complete Guide to Walking Liberty Half Dollars. Bruce W. Fox. (Illus.). 148p. 1993. 49.95 (*1-880731-15-0*); pap. 29.95 (*1-880731-16-9*) DLRC Pr.

Complete Guide to Wallpapering. David Groff. LC 93-72177. (Illus.). 136p. 1993. pap. 12.95 (*1-880029-24-3*) Creative Homeowner.

Complete Guide to Wallpapering. rev. ed. David M. Groff. (Illus.). 136p. 1989. reprint ed. write for info. (*0-318-64725-7*) Wallpaper Instr.

Complete Guide to Washington Internships, Vol. 1. Jeffrey M. Parness. LC 88-83185. 144p. (Orig.). (C). 1989. pap. text ed. 16.95 (*0-9621953-0-8*) JMP Enter.

Complete Guide to Washington Quarters. 160p. 1994. 29.95 (*1-880731-20-7*); pap. 16.95 (*1-880731-23-1*) DLRC Pr.

Complete Guide to Washington Real Estate Practices. 3rd rev. ed. Alan N. Tonnon. LC 76-58651. 680p. (C). 1988. reprint ed. pap. 22.95 (*0-9614167-0-X*) Wash Prof Pubns.

*__Complete Guide to Weddings: An Interactive Wedding Etiguette & Planning Guide.__ rev. ed. Emily Posts. 1995. 49.95 (*0-06-279018-8*) HarpC.

Complete Guide to West Virginia Bed & Breakfasts & County Inns. 2nd enl. ed. Mary R. Furbee. (Pocket Guide Ser.). (Illus.). 209p. 1993. pap. 10.95 (*0-685-57598-5*) South Wind.

Complete Guide to West Virginia Inns: Bed & Breakfasts, Country Inns, Wilderness Lodges & Historic Hotels in the Mountain State. Mary R. Furbee. (Illus.). 100p. (Orig.). 1991. pap. 6.95 (*0-9630920-0-6*) McClain.

*__Complete Guide to Western Horsemanship.__ J. P. Forget. (Illus.). 256p. 1995. 29.95 (*0-87605-982-5*) Howell Bk.

Complete Guide to Whitewater Rafting Tours: California Edition, 1986. Rena K. Margulis. (Complete Guide to Whitewater Rafting Tours Ser.). (Illus.). 304p. (Orig.). 1986. pap. 11.95 (*0-9616150-0-1*) Aquatic Adv Pubns.

Complete Guide to Whitewater Rafting Tours: Western States Edition. 2nd rev. ed. Rena K. Margulis. (Complete Guide to Whitewater Rafting Tours Ser.). (Illus.). 448p. (Orig.). 1988. pap. 12.95 (*0-9616150-2-8*) Aquatic Adv Pubns.

Complete Guide to Wildlife Photography. Joe McDonald. (Illus.). 160p. 1992. pap. 24.95 (*0-8174-3718-5*, Amphoto) Watsn-Guptill.

Complete Guide to Windsurfing. rev. ed. Jeremy Evans. (Illus.). 192p. 1986. lib. bdg. 21.95 (*0-8160-1527-9*) Facts on File.

*__Complete Guide to Winning Keno.__ David Cowles. LC 95-68285. (Illus.). 60p. 1995. pap. 9.95 (*0-940685-62-0*) Cardoza Pub.

Complete Guide to Winning Poker. Albert H. Morehead. 1973. pap. 8.95 (*0-671-21646-5*, Fireside) S&S Trade.

*__Complete Guide to Women's Health.__ braille rev. ed. Bruce D. Shephard & Carroll A. Shephard. 1749p. 1994. text ed., vinyl bd. 139.92 (*1-56956-538-4*, BR9238) W A T Braille.

Complete Guide to Women's Health. rev. ed. Bruce D. Shepherd & Carroll A. Shepherd. LC 84-29501. 448p. 1985. pap. 13.95 (*0-452-25980-0*, Plume) NAL-Dutton.

Complete Guide to Women's Health. 2nd rev. ed. Bruce Shepard & Carroll Shepard. (Illus.). 480p. 1990. pap. 19.95 (*0-452-26439-1*, Plume) NAL-Dutton.

Complete Guide to Wood Finishes. Derrick Crump. LC 92-20299. (Illus.). 176p. 1993. pap. 18.00 (*0-671-79669-0*, Fireside) S&S Trade.

Complete Guide to Woodcarving. E. J. Tangerman. LC 84-2756. (Illus.). 352p. 1985. 14.95 (*0-8069-5532-5*); pap. 13.95 (*0-8069-7922-4*) Sterling.

Complete Guide to Woodcarving. E. J. Tangerman. (Illus.). 352p. (C). 1989. reprint ed. lib. bdg. 37.00x (*0-8095-7547-7*) Borgo Pr.

Complete Guide to Woodworking. Chris Simpson. (Illus.). 176p. 1994. 24.95 (*1-56138-409-7*) Running Pr.

*__Complete Guide to Writers' Conferences & Workshops.__ William Noble. 129p. (Orig.). Date not set. pap. 16.95 (*0-8397-1840-3*) Eriksson.

*__Complete Guide to Writers' Groups & Workshops: Where to Find Them & How to Get the Most Out of Them.__ Eileen Malone. 304p. 1995. pap. 12.95 (*0-8065-1642-9*, Citadel Pr) Carol Pub Group.

Complete Guide to Writing Biographies. Ted Schwarz. 208p. 1990. 19.95 (*0-89879-407-2*) Writers Digest.

Complete Guide to Writing Fiction. Barnaby Conrad & Santa Barbara Writer's Conference Staff. 312p. 1990. 18.95 (*0-89879-395-5*) Writers Digest.

Complete Guide to Writing Fiction & Nonfiction, & Getting It Published. 2nd ed. Pat Kubis & Bob Howland. 352p. 1990. pap. 16.95 (*0-13-161019-8*) P-H.

Complete Guide to Writing Fiction, Non-Fiction & How to Publish. Pat Kubis & Bob Howland. (C). 1984. 27.67 (*0-8359-0819-4*, Reston) P-H.

*__Complete Guide to Writing Your Memories.__ Robert Gilmartin. 65p. 1990. pap. text ed. 12.00 (*0-9627740-5-7*) Gilmartin Phoenix Grp.

Complete Guide to Yearbook Journalism. Darlene Blakely & Christopher Evans. 263p. (C). 1991. ring bd. 49.95 (*0-9629406-0-7*) Advise Pubns.

Complete Guide to Your Emotions & Your Health: Hundreds of Proven Techniques to Harmonize Mind & Body for Happy, Healthy Living. Ed. by Emrika Padus. 656p. 1992. 26.95 (*0-87596-144-4*, 05-713-2) Rodale Pr Inc.

*__Complete Guide to Youth Fitness Testing.__ Margaret J. Safrit. LC 94-30281. (Illus.). 152p. 1995. pap. text ed. 15.00x (*0-87322-757-3*, BSAF0757) Human Kinetics.

Complete Guidebook to Yosemite National Park. Steven P. Medley. (Illus.). 112p. 1991. 10.95 (*0-939666-55-3*) Yosemite Assn.

Complete Guidebook to Yosemite National Park. rev. ed. Steven P. Medley. LC 94-10712. (Illus.). 112p. 1994. 9.95 (*0-939666-74-X*) Yosemite Assn.

Complete Guitar Player, Bk. 1. Russ Shipton. 1980. pap. 6.95 (*0-8256-2322-7*) Music Sales.

Complete Guitar Player, Bk. 2. Russ Shipton. 1980. pap. 6.95 (*0-8256-2323-5*) Music Sales.

Complete Guitar Player, Bk. 3. Russ Shipton. 1980. pap. 6.95 (*0-8256-2324-3*) Music Sales.

Complete Guitar Player, Bk. 4. Russ Shipton. 1980. pap. 6.95 (*0-8256-2325-1*) Music Sales.

Complete Guitar Player, Songbook 1. Russ Shipton. 1980. pap. 7.95 (*0-8256-2327-8*) Music Sales.

Complete Guitar Player, Songbook 2. Russ Shipton. 1980. pap. 7.95 (*0-8256-2328-6*) Music Sales.

Complete Guitar Player: Blues Songbook. Arthur Dick. (Illus.). 48p. 1992. pap. 9.95 (*0-7119-2620-4*, AM84484) Music Sales.

Complete Guitar Player: Bob Dylan Songbook. Arthu Dick. (Illus.). 48p. 1990. pap. 9.95 (*0-7119-2177-6*, AM78882) Music Sales.

Complete Guitar Player: Cat Stevens Songbook. Arthur Dick. (Illus.). 48p. 1989. pap. 9.95 (*0-7119-1836-8*, AM74741) Music Sales.

Complete Guitar Player: Classical Book. Russ Shipton. (Illus.). 64p. pap. 9.95 (*0-7119-0592-4*, AM38217) Music Sales.

Complete Guitar Player: Omnibus Edition. Russ Shipton. 1980. pap. 17.95 (*0-8256-2326-X*) Music Sales.

Complete Guitar Player: Paul Simon Songbook. Sel. by Arthur Dick. (Illus.). 48p. 1988. pap. 99.95 (*0-7119-1156-8*, PS10875) Music Sales.

Complete Guitar Player: Paul Simon Songbook Two. Arthur Dick. (Illus.). 48p. 1992. pap. 9.95 (*0-7119-2655-7*, PS11220) Music Sales.

Complete Guitar Player: Tablature Book. Russ Shipton. (Illus.). 96p. 1987. pap. 15.95 (*0-7119-0906-7*, AM62902) Music Sales.

*__Complete Guitar Player CD Chordfinder.__ Contrib by Arthur Dick. 1994. 14.95 (*0-7119-3196-8*, AM90134) Omnibus NY.

Complete Guitar Player Chord Book. Russ Shipton. (Illus.). 160p. 1982. pap. 6.95 (*0-7119-0159-7*, AM31717) Music Sales.

Complete Guitar Player Songbook: Omnibus Edition. Russ Shipton. (Illus.). 192p. 1989. pap. 21.95 (*0-8256-2536-X*, AM75797) Music Sales.

Complete Guitar Repair. Hideo Kamimoto. LC 74-76821. (Illus.). 192p. (Orig.). 1975. pap. 15.95 (*0-8256-0156-8*, Oak) Music Sales.

Complete Guitar Scale Dictionary. Mike Christansen. (Complete Book Ser.). 1993. 7.95 (*1-56222-417-4*, 94756) Mel Bay.

Complete Guitarist. Richard Chapman. (Illus.). 192p. 1993. 29.95 (*1-56458-181-0*) Dorling Kindersley.

Complete Guitarist. Richard Chapman. (Illus.). 192p. 1993. pap. 17.95 (*1-56458-711-8*) Dorling Kindersley.

Complete Handbook: How to Pay Yourself More at Retirement by Paying Less Taxes. Daniel A. Van Bogaert. Ed. by Ronald L. Reitenauer. (Illus.). 110p. (Orig.). (C). pap. 7.95 (*0-9614180-0-1*) Planning Retire.

Complete Handbook for College Women: Making the Most of Your College Experience. Carol Weinberg. LC 94-2245. 384p. 1994. 55.00 (*0-8147-9266-9*); pap. 15.95 (*0-8147-9267-7*) NYU Pr.

Complete Handbook for Combating Substance Abuse in the Workplace: Medical Facts, Legal Issues, & Practical Solutions. William F. Banta & Forest Tennant. 528p. 1989. text ed. 74.95 (*0-669-17879-9*) Free Pr.

Complete Handbook for Dental Auxiliaries. Charles A. Reap, Jr. (Illus.). 150p. (C). 1981. pap. text ed. 34.00 (*0-931386-44-6*) Quint Pub Co.

Complete Handbook for Medical Secretaries & Assistants. 2nd ed. Jean M. Doyle & Robert L. Dennis. 1978. pap. text ed. 18.95 (*0-316-18082-3*, Little Med Div) Little.

Complete Handbook of All Purpose Telemarketing Scripts. Barry Z. Masser. 456p. 1990. 59.95 (*0-13-161068-6*) P-H.

Complete Handbook of Amateur Radio. 3rd ed. Clay Laster. 1993. pap. text ed. 21.95 (*0-07-036594-6*) McGraw.

Complete Handbook of Amateur Radio. 3rd ed. Clay Laster. LC 93-1556. 1993. pap. 19.60 (*0-8306-4354-0*) TAB Bks.

Complete Handbook of Athletic Footwear. Melvyn P. Cheskin et al. (Illus.). 350p. 1986. text ed. 25.00 (*0-87005-548-8*) Fairchild.

Complete Handbook of Automobile Hobbies. Ed. by Beverly R. Kimes. LC 81-80931. (Hobby Bks.). (Illus.). 400p. 1981. 24.95 (*0-915038-28-5*, 3-AQ-0032) Auto Quarterly.

Complete Handbook of Baseball: 1993 Edition. Zander Hollander. 1993. pap. 5.99 (*0-451-17533-6*, Sig) NAL-Dutton.

*__Complete Handbook of Baseball: 1995 Edition.__ Zander Hollander. 464p. (Orig.). 1995. pap. 5.99 (*0-451-18389-4*, Sig) NAL-Dutton.

Complete Handbook of Baseball, 1992. Ed. by Zander Hollander. 416p. (Orig.). 1992. pap. 5.99 (*0-451-17201-9*, Sig) NAL-Dutton.

Complete Handbook of Baseball, 1994. Zander Hollander. (Illus.). 400p. (Orig.). 1994. pap. 5.99 (*0-451-17927-7*, Sig) NAL-Dutton.

Complete Handbook of Business English. William Repp. 1982. 29.50 (*0-13-160960-2*, Busn) P-H.

Complete Handbook of Children's Reading Disorders: You Can Prevent or Correct Learning Disorders. 2nd ed. Hilde L. Mosse. (Illus.). 714p. (Orig.). 1987. pap. text ed. 34.95 (*0-942311-00-0*) Riggs Inst Pr.

Complete Handbook of Dog Training. Thomas A. Knott & Dolores O. Cooper. (Illus.). 224p. 1994. 21.95 (*0-87605-555-2*) Howell Bk.

Complete Handbook of Electric Motor Controls. 2nd ed. John Traister & Press Fairmont. 290p. 1994. text ed. 69.00 (*0-13-301334-0*) P-H.

Complete Handbook of Electric Motor Controls. 2nd ed. John E. Traister. LC 93-33784. 1994. write for info. (*0-88173-192-7*) Fairmont Pr.

Complete Handbook of Garden Plants. Michael Wright. (Illus.). 544p. 1984. 24.95 (*0-87196-632-8*) Facts on File.

Complete Handbook of Greek Verbs. N. Marinone & F. Guala. 353p. 1972. 9.95 (*0-87774-001-1*) Schoenhof.

Complete Handbook of Health Tips. rev. ed. R. Emil Neuman. 256p. 1986. pap. 12.95 (*0-9614924-1-4*) United Res CA.

Complete Handbook of Home Brewing. Dave Miller. Ed. by Sarah M. Clarkson. LC 87-46447. 256p. 1988. 19.95 (*0-88266-522-7*, Garden Way Pub); pap. 11.95 (*0-88266-517-0*, Garden Way Pub) Storey Comm Inc.

Complete Handbook of Indoor & Outdoor Games & Activities for Young Children. Jean Feldma. LC 94-15861. (Illus.). 1994. spiral bd. 27.95 (*0-87628-119-6*) Ctr Appl Res.

Complete Handbook of Italian Verbs. (BBC Phrase Books for Teenagers Ser.). 1995. pap. 9.95 (*0-8442-8075-5*, Passport Bks) NTC Pub Grp.

Complete Handbook of Leathercrafting. Jane E. Garnes. LC 85-19751. 352p. 1986. reprint ed. lib. bdg. 35.00 (*0-89874-899-2*) Krieger.

Complete Handbook of Magic. Marvin Kaye. Date not set. pap. 16.95 (*0-8128-8559-7*, Scrbrough Hse) Madison Bks UPA.

Complete Handbook of Magnetic Recording. 3rd ed. Finn Jorgensen. (Illus.). 768p. 1988. 49.95 (*0-8306-1979-8*, 3029) TAB Bks.

*__Complete Handbook of Magnetic Recording.__ 4th ed. Finn Jorgensen. LC 94-36652. 1995. text ed. 65.00 (*0-07-033045-X*) TAB Bks.

Complete Handbook of Music Games & Activities for Early Childhood. Margaret Athey & Gwen Hotchkiss. LC 82-2289. 218p. 1982. text ed. 22.95 (*0-13-161083-X*) P-H.

Complete Handbook of Natural Healing. Marcia Starck. LC 91-14163. (Illus.). 416p. (Orig.). 1991. pap. 12.95 (*0-87542-742-1*) Llewellyn Pubns.

Complete Handbook of Personal Computer Communications. 3rd braille ed. Alfred Glossbrenner. 930p. (Orig.). 1992. Braille. vinyl bd. 74.40 (*1-56956-344-6*, BR8359) W A T Braille.

Complete Handbook of Personal Computer Communications. 3rd ed. Alfred Glossbrenner. 400p. (Orig.). 1989. pap. 18.95 (*0-312-03312-5*) St Martin.

Complete Handbook of Phonetic Vocabulary Building: A Simplified, Sequential Student Guide for Developing Reading Vocabulary & Analysis Skills. John M. Sarian. 93p. (Orig.). 1989. teacher ed 10.00 (*0-685-28350-X*); pap. text ed. 10.00 (*0-9623412-0-7*); audio write for info. (*0-318-65604-3*); Tape 1, Pgs. 1-43. write for info. (*0-9623412-2-3*); Tape 2, Pgs. 44-84. write for info. (*0-9623412-3-1*) J M Sarian.

Complete Handbook of Phonetic Vocabulary Building: A Simplified, Sequential Student Guide for Developing Reading Vocabulary & Analysis Skills, 2 cass., Set. John M. Sarian. 93p. (Orig.). 1989. audio, pap. text ed. write for info. (*0-9623412-1-5*) J M Sarian.

Complete Handbook of Plant Propagation. Wright. 1984. 16.95 (*0-02-631580-7*) Macmillan.

Complete Handbook of Pro Basketball. Zander Hollander. 400p. 1992. pap. 5.99 (*0-451-17382-1*, Sig) NAL-Dutton.

Complete Handbook of Pro Basketball. Zander Hollander. 432p. 1994. pap. 5.99 (*0-451-18173-5*) NAL-Dutton.

Complete Handbook of Pro Basketball: 1994 Edition. 20th ed. Zander Hollander. (Illus.). 384p. 1993. pap. 5.99 (*0-451-17794-0*, Sig) NAL-Dutton.

Complete Handbook of Pro Basketball, 1992. Ed. by Zander Hollander. 384p. (Orig.). 1991. pap. 5.99 (*0-451-17095-4*, Sig) NAL-Dutton.

Complete Handbook of Pro Football. 1,992th ed. Zander Hollander. 368p. 1992. 5.99 (*0-451-17380-5*, Sig) NAL-Dutton.

Complete Handbook of Pro Football: 1994 Edition. Zander Hollander. 480p. (Orig.). 1994. pap. 5.99 (*0-451-18171-9*, Sig) NAL-Dutton.

Complete Handbook of Pro Football, 1991. 17th ed. Zander Hollander. (Illus.). 368p. 1991. pap. 5.99 (*0-451-17024-5*, Sig) NAL-Dutton.

Complete Handbook of Pro Football, 1993. 19th ed. Zander Hollander. 368p. (Orig.). (YA). 1993. pap. 5.99 (*0-451-17765-7*, Sig) NAL-Dutton.

*__Complete Handbook of Pro Football, 1995.__ 21th ed. Ed. by Zander Hollander. 496p. 1995. pap. 6.99 (*0-451-18504-8*, Sig) NAL-Dutton.

Complete Handbook of Profitable Marketing Research Techniques. Robert P. Vichas. 432p. 1982. 59.95 (*0-13-161158-5*, Busn) P-H.

Complete Handbook of Profitable Trade Show Exhibiting. Christine Christman. 448p. 1991. 59.95 (*0-13-155722-X*) P-H.

Complete Handbook of Pruning. B. Halliwell et al. (Illus.). 168p. 1992. pap. 14.95 (*0-7063-6706-5*, Pub. by Ward Lock UK) Sterling.

Complete Handbook of Robotics. Edward L. Safford, Jr. (Illus.). 1978. 15.95 (*0-8306-9872-8*); pap. 14.95 (*0-8306-1071-5*, 1071) TAB Bks.

Complete Handbook of Russian Verbs. L. I. Pirogova. 320p. (Orig.). 1991. pap. 16.95 (*0-8442-4270-5*, Natl Textbk) NTC Pub Grp.

Complete Handbook of Sand Casting. C. W. Ammen. 1979. pap. text ed. 13.95 (*0-07-157204-X*) McGraw.

Complete Handbook of Sand Casting. C. W. Ammen. (Illus.). 1979. pap. 12.95 (*0-8306-1043-X*, 1043) TAB Bks.

Complete Handbook of Science Fair Projects. Julianne B. Bochinski. (J). 1991. pap. text ed. 12.95 (*0-471-52728-9*) Wiley.

Complete Handbook of Science Fair Projects. Julianne B. Bochinski. (Science Editions Ser.). (J). 1991. text ed. 29.95 (*0-471-52729-7*) Wiley.

Complete Handbook of Songwriting: An Insider's Guide to Making It in the Music Industry. Mark Ligget & Cathy Ligget. LC 85-7197. 352p. 1985. pap. 9.95 (*0-452-25687-9*, Plume) NAL-Dutton.

Complete Handbook of Songwriting: An Insider's Guide to Making It in the Music Industry. 2nd ed. Mark Liggett & Cathy Liggett. 272p. 1993. pap. 12.00 (*0-452-27011-1*, Plume) NAL-Dutton.

Complete Handbook of Spanish Verbs. J. Noble & J. Lacasas. (C). 1984. 130.00 (*0-8442-7634-0*, Pub. by S Thornes Pubs UK) St Mut.

Complete Handbook of Spanish Verbs. Judith Noble & Jaime Lacasa. 360p. (SPA.). 1991. 19.95 (*0-8442-7633-2*, Natl Textbk) NTC Pub Grp.

Complete Handbook of Spanish Verbs. Judith Noble & Jaime Lacasa. 360p. (C). 1984. 95.00 (*0-685-33819-3*, Pub. by S Thornes Pubs UK) St Mut.

Complete Handbook of U. S. Government Benefits. rev. ed. R. Emil Neuman. (Illus.). 326p. 1993. pap. 15.95 (*0-685-65181-9*) Kesend Pub Ltd.

Complete Handbook of Videocassette Recorders. 3rd ed. Harry Kybett & Delton T. Horn. (Illus.). 272p. 1986. pap. 14.95 (*0-8306-2731-6*) TAB Bks.

Complete Handloader. John Wootters. 1988. 29.95 (*1-55654-036-1*) Times Mir Mag Bk Div.

Complete Handyman Do-It-Yourself Encyclopedia, 26 vols. LC 74-21375. 1983. 181.48 (*0-87475-725-8*) Stuttman.

Complete Hans Christian Andersen Fairy Tales. (YA). (gr. 2-6). 6.98 (*0-517-33632-4*) Random Hse Value.

Complete Hans Christian Andersen Fairy Tales. Hans Christian Andersen. (J). 1987. 11.99 (*0-517-45375-4*) Random Hse Value.

Complete Hans Christian Andersen Fairy Tales. Hans Christian Andersen. 1993. 12.99 (*0-517-09291-3*) Random Hse Value.

Complete Harmonica Book. Phil Dunccan. (Complete Book Ser.). 1993. 17.95 (*1-56222-280-5*, 94713); audio 9.98 (*1-56222-339-9*, 94713) Mel Bay.

Complete Hedgehog. Les Stocker. (Illus.). 128p. 1994. pap. 19.95 (*0-7011-3272-8*, Pub. by Chatto & Windus UK) Trafalgar.

Complete Herb Book. Maggie Stuckey. 464p. (Orig.). 1994. mass mkt. 5.99 (*0-425-14233-7*) Berkley Pub.

Complete Herbal. Nicholas Culpeper. (Illus.). 1960. 29.95 (*0-685-21926-7*) Wehman.

Complete Herbal Guide to Natural Health & Beauty. Dian D. Buchman & Peter Firebrace. 256p. 1995. pap. 12.95 (*0-87983-637-7*) Keats.

Complete Herbal Handbook for Farm & Stable. Juliette de Bairacli Levy. 384p. (Orig.). 1991. pap. 12.95 (*0-571-16116-2*) Faber & Faber.

Complete Herbal Handbook for the Dog & Cat. Juliette D. Levy. 1991. pap. 12.95 (*0-571-16115-4*) Faber & Faber.

Complete Herbalist. D. Phelps Brown. Ed. by Gina R. Gross. (Illus.). 504p. 1993. reprint ed. pap. 14.95 (*0-87877-184-0*) Newcastle Pub.

Complete Herbalist: The People Their Own Physicians. O. Phelps Brown. 504p. 1992. pap. 35.00 (*0-89540-118-5*, SB-118) Sun Pub.

Complete Herbalist: The People Their Own Physicians. O. Phelps Brown. 504p. 1975. reprint ed. spiral bd. 22.00 (*0-7873-0121-3*) Mokelumne.

Complete Herbalist or, the People Their Own Physicians. O. Phelps Brown. 1991. lib. bdg. 250.00 (*0-8490-4969-5*) Gordon Pr.

Complete Hiring Manual: Policies, Practices & Procedures. Joseph D. Levesque. 700p. 1991. 80.00 (*0-685-52664-X*) P-H.

***Complete Historical & Statistical Reference to the World Hockey Association, 1972-1979. Scott A. Surgent. LC 94-61968. 448p. 1995. pap. 28.95 (*0-9644774-0-8*) Xaler Pr.**
From 1972-1979, the World Hockey Association (WHA) functioned as the only major hockey league to rival the established National Hockey League (NHL) since the NHL's 1917 formation. Not expected to survive its first season, the WHA managed to string together seven controversial yet entertaining seasons, & in the process permanently

An Asterisk (*) at the beginning of an entry indicates that the title is appearing in BIP for the first time.

changed the face of North American major league hockey. It was the league that provided a refreshing career boost for two of hockey's greatest stars, Bobby Hill & Gordie Howe, while giving future stars Wayne Gretzky, Mark Messier & Mike Gartner their first taste of major league action. THE COMPLETE...WORLD HOCKEY ASSOCIATION, 1972-1979 offers the reader a factual historical account of the WHA from its inception through to its demise. Features of the book include histories of each of the teams, chronologies of important events & anecdotal stories. The book also features complete game-by-game results for every game played during the league's duration, including playoffs, all-star games, & international series. Further sections provide complete player, goal tender & coaching statistics, team standings, seasonal statistics, complete player draft charts & much more. (See our Flyer in the February Forthcoming Books). To order: Xaler Press, P.O. Box 26073, Tempe, AZ 85285, USA, Phone: (602) 929-0823, FAX: (602) 829-7432. *Publisher Provided Annotation.*

Complete History Alpena County, Michigan. William Boulton & Fred R. Trelfa. (Local History Reprints Ser.). (Illus.). 1964. reprint ed. pap. 3.25 (*0-916699-01-3*) CMU Clarke Hist Lib.

Complete History of Connecticut, Civil & Ecclesiastical, from the Immigration of Its First Planters, from England, in the Year 1630 to the Year 1764, 2 Vols. in 1, Set. Benjamin Trumbull. LC 79-14096. (Research Library of Colonial Americana). (Illus.). 1972. reprint ed. 94.95 (*0-405-03301-X*) Ayer.

Complete History of Fairfield County, Ohio, 1795-1876. Hervey Scott. 304p. 1994. reprint ed. lib. bdg. 32.50 (*0-8328-3915-9*) Higginson Bk Co.

Complete History of Grand Prix Motor Racing. 1990. 24.99 (*0-517-69709-2*) Random Hse Value.

Complete History of Jack the Ripper. Philip Sugden. 512p. 1994. 26.00 (*0-7867-0124-2*) Carroll & Graf.

***Complete History of the Most Remarkable Transactions at Sea.** Ed. by John B. Hattendorf. 1995. write for info. (*0-8201-1489-8*) Schol Facsimiles.

***Complete History of the Negro Leagues, 1884 to 1955.** Mark Ribowsky. (Illus.). 400p. 1995. 24.95 (*1-55972-283-5*, Birch Ln Pr) Carol Pub Group.

Complete History of the New York & Brooklyn Bridge from Its Conception in 1866 to Its Completion in 1883. Samuel W. Green. 1979. lib. bdg. 59.95 (*0-8490-1655-X*) Gordon Pr.

Complete Hockey Book: 1992-1993 Edition. Ed. by Craig Carter & Mark Shimabukuro. 672p. 1992. pap. 16.95 (*0-89204-438-1*) Sporting News.

Complete Hockey Book, 1994-95. 760p. 1994. pap. 17.95 (*0-89204-498-5*) Sporting News.

***Complete Hockey Book, 1995-96.** 1995. pap. 18.95 (*0-89204-529-9*) Sporting News.

Complete Hockey Instruction: Skills & Strategies for Coaches & Players. Dave Chambers. (Illus.). 224p. 1994. pap. 12.95 (*0-8092-3511-0*) Contemp Bks.

***Complete Holiday Celebration.** 1994. 19.95 (*0-8256-1428-7*, AM91477) Omnibus NY.

Complete Home Business Workbook. Swain Hepler. 155p. (Orig.). 1992. pap. text ed. 12.95 (*0-9632102-0-3*) Triwell Pub.

***Complete Home Buyer's Bible: Everything You Need to Know to Buy a Resale Home, a New Construction Home, a Building Lot.** William J. Molloy. LC 95-17416. 1996. write for info. (*0-471-13110-5*); pap. write for info. (*0-471-13111-3*) Wiley.

***Complete Home Buyers Guide.** American Home Foundation Staff. 150p. 1995. pap. 12.95 (*0-940313-09-X*) Am Home Found.

***Complete Home Buyers Guide: The Only Guide You'll Need to Get the Best Possible Deal & Protect Your Interests.** Bruce N. Hahn. (Illus.). 151p. (Orig.). 1994. pap. 12.95 (*0-940313-10-3*) Am Home Found.

Complete Home Decorating Book. Nicholas Barnard. LC 94-639. (Illus.). 288p. 1994. 29.95 (*1-56458-667-7*) Dorling Kindersley.

***Complete Home Decorator: 1000 Design Ideas for the Home.** Stewart Walton. LC 95-1234. (Illus.). 256p. 1995. 40.00 (*0-8478-1898-5*) Rizzoli Intl.

Complete Home Guide to All the Vitamins see Big Family Guide to All the Vitamins

Complete Home Guide to Aromatherapy: Self-Help with Essential Oils. Erich Keller. Ed. by Nancy Carleton. LC 91-52841. 228p. 1991. pap. 9.95 (*0-915811-36-7*) H J Kramer Inc.

Complete Home Healer: Your Guide to Every Treatment Available for 300 of the Most Common Health Problems. Angela Smyth. LC 93-40025. 560p. 1994. 23.00 (*0-06-250844-X*) Harper SF.

***Complete Home Health Advisor.** Woodland Publishing Staff. 1994. pap. 16.95 (*0-913923-96-6*) Woodland UT.

Complete Home Inspection Kit. William L. Ventolo. 218p. 1990. pap. 15.95 (*0-88462-988-0*, 1913-08) Dearborn Finan.

Complete Home Landscape Designer. Joel M. Lerner. (Illus.). 144p. (Orig.). 1991. pap. 19.95 (*0-312-06937-5*) St Martin.

***Complete Home Office: Planning Your Work Space for Maximum Efficiency.** Alvin Rosenbaum. LC 94-45190. 1995. write for info. (*0-670-85293-7*, Viking Studio) Studio Bks.

Complete Home Organizer: A Guide to Functional Storage Space for All the Rooms in Your Home. Maxine Ordesky. 1993. pap. 19.95 (*0-8021-3340-1*) Grove-Atltic.

Complete Home Renovation Manual. Ed. by Mike Lawrence & Derek Bradford. LC 92-32002. (Illus.). 224p. 1993. 19.98 (*0-8317-1588-X*) Smithmark.

Complete Home Security Guide. Jonathan Erickson. 1994. pap. 14.95 (*0-8306-4412-1*) TAB Bks.

Complete Home Storage. Ed. by Southern Living Staff. (Southern Living Bks.). 248p. 1992. pap. 16.99 (*0-376-09028-6*) Oxmoor Hse.

Complete Home Storage. Sunset Magazine & Book Editors. LC 89-83975. 248p. 1989. pap. 16.99 (*0-376-01767-8*) Sunset Menlo Pk.

Complete Home Video Director: Produce Better Videos Immediately. David Owen. (Illus.). 192p. (Orig.). 1994. pap. 14.95 (*0-572-01784-7*, Pub. by W Foulsham UK) Trans-Atl Phila.

Complete Homeopathy Handbook: Safe & Effective Ways to Treat Fevers, Coughs, Colds & Sore Throats, Childhood Ailments, Food Poisoning, Flu, & a Wide Range of Everyday Complaints. Miranda Castro. (Illus.). 272p. (Orig.). 1991. pap. 14.95 (*0-312-06320-2*) St Martin.

Complete Horoscope Interpretation: Putting Together Your Plantary Profile. Maritha Pottenger. 568p. (Orig.). 1986. pap. 19.95 (*0-917086-81-3*) ACS Pubns.

Complete Horse Book. Ed. by Elwyn H. Edwards & Candida Geddes. (Illus.). 344p. 1991. pap. 22.95 (*0-943955-41-6*, Trafalgar Sq Pub) Trafalgar.

***Complete Horse Care Manual.** Colin Vogel. LC 95-6744. 192p. 1995. 24.95 (*0-7894-0170-3*, 6-70491) Dorling Kindersley.

***Complete Horseshoeing Guide.** 2nd rev. ed. Robert F. Wiseman. LC 72-9279. (Illus.). 312p. 1995. pap. 16.95 (*0-8061-2719-8*) U of Okla Pr.

Complete Hot Tub Planner. Sharon R. Hines. (Illus.). 128p. (Orig.). 1982. ring bd. 16.95 (*0-941904-01-6*) Hot Water Pubs.

Complete House Inspection Book. Don Fredriksson. 1988. pap. 9.95 (*0-449-90263-3*, Columbine) Fawcett.

***Complete Houseplant Book.** Peter McHoy. 256p. 1995. 19.98 (*0-8317-1175-2*) Smithmark.

Complete How to Book: One Hundred One Lessons about Language. Raymond E. Laurita. 400p. (Orig.). (J). (gr. 1-12). 1995. pap. text ed. 21.95 (*0-914051-34-2*) Leonardo Pr.

Complete How-to Book of Indian Craft. B. Hunt. Orig. Title: Ben Hunt's Big Indian Craft Book. (Illus.). 188p. 1973. pap. 12.00 (*0-02-011690-X*, Collier S&S) S&S Trade.

***Complete How to Figure It.** Darrell Huff. (Illus.). 352p. 1995. 27.50 (*0-393-03600-6*) Norton.

Complete Humanoids Handbook. Bill Slavicsek. (Advanced Dungeons & Dragons, Second Edition; Al-Qadim Ser.). (Illus.). 1993. pap. 18.00 (*1-56076-611-5*) TSR Inc.

Complete Hurricane Survival Guide. Lee Shaw. 172p. 1993. 9.95 (*0-9637995-0-9*) Sea Horse Pubns.

Complete Hypercard Handbook. 3rd ed. Danny Goodman. 864p. 1990. 29.95 (*0-317-99843-9*) Bantam.

Complete HyperCard 2.X Handbook. 4th ed. Danny Goodman. 1994. pap. 35.00 (*0-679-79122-1*) Random.

Complete Hypnotism, Mesmerism, Mind Reading & Spiritualism. A. Alpheus. 217p. 1972. reprint ed. spiral bd. 2.75 (*0-7873-0030-6*) Mokelumne.

Complete I Hate to Cook Book. Peg Bracken. 228p. 1988. mass mkt. 5.99 (*0-553-27130-X*) Bantam.

Complete Identification Guide to the Wurlitzer Jukebook. Ricky J. Botts. LC 83-82604. (Illus.). 114p. (Orig.). 1987. pap. 14.00 (*0-912789-01-8*) Jukebox Coll New.

Complete Idiot's Guide to Access. Paul McFedries. 1994. pap. 14.95 (*1-56761-457-4*) Alpha Bks IN.

***Complete Idiot's Guide to America Online.** John Pivovarnick. (Illus.). 350p. (Orig.). 1995. pap. text ed. 19.99 (*1-56761-597-X*) Alpha Bks IN.

Complete Idiot's Guide to Ami Pro. Jennifer Flynn. 1994. pap. 14.95 (*1-56761-453-1*) Alpha Bks IN.

***Complete Idiot's Guide to Buying & Repairing PCs.** 2nd ed. Alpha Development Group Staff. (Illus.). 400p. (Orig.). 1995. pap. 16.99 (*1-56761-583-X*) Alpha Bks IN.

***Complete Idiot's Guide to Buying & Selling a Home.** Shelley O'Hara. 384p. 1994. 16.95 (*1-56761-510-4*) Alpha Bks IN.

***Complete Idiot's Guide to CD-ROM.** 2nd ed. John Pivovarnick. (Illus.). 375p. (Orig.). 1995. pap. 19.99 (*1-56761-606-2*) Alpha Bks IN.

***Complete Idiot's Guide to College Planning.** O'Neal Turner. 368p. 1994. 14.95 (*1-56761-508-2*) Alpha Bks IN.

***Complete Idiot's Guide to CompuServe.** Alpha Development Group Staff. (Illus.). 350p. (Orig.). 1995. pap. 19.99 (*1-56761-607-0*) Alpha Bks IN.

***Complete Idiot's Guide to Computer Terms.** 2nd ed. Joe Kraynak. 350p. 1994. 10.95 (*1-56761-506-6*) Alpha Bks IN.

***Complete Idiot's Guide to Cooking Basics.** Ronnie Fein. 350p. 1995. 14.99 (*1-56761-523-6*) Alpha Bks IN.

Complete Idiot's Guide to CorelDRAW! Jenna Howard & Michael Howard. (Illus.). 350p. (Orig.). 1994. pap. 16.95 (*1-56761-429-9*) Alpha Bks IN.

***Complete Idiot's Guide to Doing Your 1995 Taxes.** Gail Perry. 350p. 1995. 14.99 (*1-56761-586-4*) Alpha Bks IN.

Complete Idiot's Guide to DOS, New Edition. Jennifer Fulton. (Illus.). 400p. (Orig.). 1994. pap. 16.95 (*1-56761-496-5*) Alpha Bks IN.

Complete Idiot's Guide to DOS 6. Jennifer Flynn. 1993. pap. 14.95 (*1-56761-169-9*) Alpha Bks IN.

***Complete Idiot's Guide to Excel for Windows 95.** Alpha Staff. 384p. 1995. 16.99 (*1-56761-604-6*) Alpha Bks IN.

Complete Idiot's Guide to Excel 5. Ricardo Birmele. 1993. pap. 14.95 (*1-56761-318-7*) Alpha Bks IN.

***Complete Idiot's Guide to Getting the Job You Want.** Robert Bly. 350p. 1995. disk 24.99 (*1-56761-608-9*) Alpha Bks IN.

***Complete Idiot's Guide to Internet E-Mail.** Paul McFedries. (Illus.). 325p. (Orig.). 1995. pap. 16.99 (*1-56761-596-1*) Alpha Bks IN.

***Complete Idiot's Guide to Internet Pipeline.** Peter Kent. (Illus.). 325p. (Orig.). 1995. pap. 19.99 (*1-56761-609-7*) Alpha Bks IN.

***Complete Idiot's Guide to Internet Security.** Karen Strauss. (Illus.). 325p. (Orig.). 1995. pap. text ed. 16.99 (*1-56761-593-7*) Alpha Bks IN.

***Complete Idiot's Guide to Making Money on Wall Street.** Christy Heady. 448p. 1994. 16.95 (*1-56761-509-0*) Alpha Bks IN.

***Complete Idiot's Guide to Managing Your Money.** Christy Heady & Robert Heady. 350p. 1995. 16.99 (*1-56761-530-9*) Alpha Bks IN.

***Complete Idiot's Guide to Microsoft Office.** Sherry Kinkoph. 400p. 1995. 19.99 (*1-56761-544-9*) Alpha Bks IN.

Complete Idiot's Guide to Microsoft Works for Windows. Susan. 1994. pap. 14.95 (*1-56761-451-5*) Alpha Bks IN.

***Complete Idiot's Guide to Modems & Online Services.** Sherry Kinkoph. 400p. 1994. 19.95 (*1-56761-526-0*) Alpha Bks IN.

***Complete Idiot's Guide to Mosiac.** Joe Kraynak. (Illus.). 350p. (Orig.). 1995. pap. text ed. 16.99 (*1-56761-588-0*) Alpha Bks IN.

***Complete Idiot's Guide to Multimedia.** Dave Haskin. 384p. 1994. 19.95 (*1-56761-505-8*) Alpha Bks IN.

***Complete Idiot's Guide to Netscape.** John Dupuy. (Illus.). 300p. (Orig.). 1995. pap. 16.99 (*1-56761-612-7*) Alpha Bks IN.

***Complete Idiot's Guide to Networking.** Dan Bobola. (Illus.). 375p. (Orig.). 1995. pap. text ed. 19.99 (*1-56761-590-2*) Alpha Bks IN.

***Complete Idiot's Guide to Online Chat.** Sherry Kinkoph. (Illus.). 325p. (Orig.). 1995. pap. text ed. 16.99 (*1-56761-595-3*) Alpha Bks IN.

***Complete Idiot's Guide to OS-2.** Jennifer Fulton. (Illus.). 375p. (Orig.). 1995. pap. text ed. 16.99 (*1-56761-589-9*) Alpha Bks IN.

***Complete Idiot's Guide to PageMaker.** Ted Alspach. 400p. 1995. 24.99 (*1-56761-617-8*) Alpha Bks IN.

***Complete Idiot's Guide to PC Games.** David Haskin. (Illus.). 350p. (Orig.). 1995. pap. text ed. 19.99 (*1-56761-547-3*) Alpha Bks IN.

***Complete Idiot's Guide to PCs.** 3rd ed. Joe Kraynak. (Illus.). 375p. 1995. pap. 16.99 (*1-56761-584-8*) Alpha Bks IN.

***Complete Idiot's Guide to PhotoShop.** Ted Alspach. 336p. 1994. 24.95 (*1-56761-527-9*) Alpha Bks IN.

***Complete Idiot's Guide to Planning the Perfect Vacation.** Scott Alhsmith. 350p. 1995. 14.95 (*1-56761-531-7*) Alpha Bks IN.

***Complete Idiot's Guide to Preparing Your 1996 Taxes.** Gail Perry. 350p. 1995. 14.99 (*0-614-03572-4*) Alpha Bks IN.

Complete Idiot's Guide to Q Basic. Greg Perry. 300p. 1994. 19.95 (*1-56761-490-6*) Alpha Bks IN.

***Complete Idiot's Guide to QuarkXPress.** Ted Alspach. (Illus.). 384p. (Orig.). 1994. pap. 19.95 (*1-56761-519-8*) Alpha Bks IN.

***Complete Idiot's Guide to Sound Blaster.** David Haskin. (Illus.). 350p. (Orig.). 1995. pap. 19.99 (*1-56761-651-8*) Alpha Bks IN.

***Complete Idiot's Guide to Starting Your Own Business.** Ed Paulson & Marcia Layton. 350p. 1995. 16.99 (*1-56761-529-5*) Alpha Bks IN.

***Complete Idiot's Guide to the Internet.** 2nd ed. Peter Kent. 400p. 1994. 19.95 (*1-56761-535-X*) Alpha Bks IN.

***Complete Idiot's Guide to the Mac.** 2nd ed. John Pivovarnick. 400p. 1994. 16.95 (*1-56761-534-1*) Alpha Bks IN.

***Complete Idiot's Guide to the Perfect Wedding.** Teddy Lenderman. 350p. 1995. 16.99 (*1-56761-532-5*) Alpha Bks IN.

***Complete Idiot's Guide to Unix.** John McMullen. 400p. 1995. 19.99 (*1-56761-511-2*) Alpha Bks IN.

***Complete Idiot's Guide to USENET.** Paul McFedries. (Illus.). 325p. (Orig.). 1995. pap. text ed. 16.95 (*1-56761-592-9*) Alpha Bks IN.

Complete Idiot's Guide to VCRs. 1993. pap. 9.95 (*1-56761-294-6*) Alpha Bks IN.

***Complete Idiot's Guide to Visual Basic.** 2nd ed. Greg Perry. 350p. 1995. 19.99 (*1-56761-520-1*) Alpha Bks IN.

***Complete Idiot's Guide to Windows.** 2nd ed. Paul McFedries. (Illus.). 350p. 1995. pap. text ed. 16.95 (*1-56761-546-5*) Alpha Bks IN.

Complete Idiot's Guide to Windows 95. Paul McFedries. 375p. 1995. 16.99 (*1-56761-495-7*) Alpha Bks IN.

Complete Idiot's Guide to Word for Windows 6.0. Jennifer Flynn. LC 93-72390. 316p. 1993. pap. 14.95 (*1-56761-355-1*) Alpha Bks IN.

***Complete Idiot's Guide to Word for Windows 95.** Jennifer Fulton. 384p. 1995. 16.99 (*1-56761-603-8*) Alpha Bks IN.

Complete Idiot's Guide to WordPerfect. 2nd ed. Paul McFedries. 375p. 1994. 16.95 (*1-56761-499-X*) Alpha Bks IN.

***Complete Idiot's Guide to WordPerfect for Windows 6.1.** 2nd ed. Paul McFedries. (Illus.). 350p. (Orig.). 1994. pap. text ed. 16.95 (*1-56761-543-0*) Alpha Bks IN.

***Complete Idiot's Guide to World Wide Web.** Peter Kent. 380p. 1995. 16.99 (*1-56761-542-2*) Alpha Bks IN.

Complete Idiot's Guide to 1-2-3. Peter Aitken. 1993. pap. 14.95 (*1-56761-285-7*) Alpha Bks IN.

Complete Idiot's Guide to 1-2-3. 2nd ed. Peter Aitken. 380p. 1994. 16.95 (*1-56761-404-3*) Alpha Bks IN.

Complete Idiot's Guide to 1-2-3 for Windows. Peter Aitken. 375p. 1994. 16.95 (*1-56761-485-X*) Alpha Bks IN.

Complete Idiot's Guide to 1-2-3 for Windows 4.1. Peter Aitken. 1993. pap. 14.95 (*1-56761-400-0*) Alpha Bks IN.

***Complete Idiot's Guide to 1-2-3 for Windows 95.** Alpha Staff. 384p. 1995. 16.99 (*1-56761-605-4*) Alpha Bks IN.

***Complete Idiot's Next Step with the Internet.** Peter Kent. 400p. 1994. 19.95 (*1-56761-524-4*) Alpha Bks IN.

***Complete Idiot's Next Step with Windows.** Paul McFedries. 400p. 1994. 19.95 (*1-56761-525-2*) Alpha Bks IN.

***Complete Idiot's Next Step with Windows 95.** Paul McFedries. 400p. 1995. 19.99 (*1-56761-614-3*) Alpha Bks IN.

Complete Idiot's Pocket Guide to Excel 5. Sherry Kinkoph. 1993. pap. 5.99 (*1-56761-370-5*) Alpha Bks IN.

***Complete Idiot's Pocket Guide to MS-DOS 6.2.** Kelly Oliver. 130p. 1993. pap. 5.99 (*1-56761-417-5*) Alpha Bks IN.

Complete Idiot's Pocket Guide to Windows 3.1. 1993. pap. 5.99 (*1-56761-302-0*) Alpha Bks IN.

Complete Idiot's Pocket Guide to Word for Windows 6.0: New Edition. Alpha Books Staff. 1993. pap. 5.99 (*1-56761-368-3*) Alpha Bks IN.

Complete Idiot's Pocket Guide to WordPerfect for Windows. Kelly Oliver. 1993. pap. 5.99 (*1-56761-371-3*) Alpha Bks IN.

Complete Idiot's Pocket Guide to WordPerfect 6. 1993. pap. 5.99 (*1-56761-300-4*) Alpha Bks IN.

***Complete Idiot's Pocket Reference: MS-DOS 6.22.** Jennifer Fulton. (Illus.). 256p. (Orig.). 1994. pap. 8.95 (*1-56761-516-3*) Alpha Bks IN.

***Complete Idiot's Pocket Reference: Windows 95.** Jennifer Fulton. 225p. 1995. 9.99 (*1-56761-517-1*) Alpha Bks IN.

***Complete Idiot's Pocket Reference to the Internet.** Neal Goldman. 224p. 1994. 9.95 (*1-56761-528-7*) Alpha Bks IN.

C

Complete Illustrated Book of the Psychic Sciences. Walter B. Gibson. (Illus.). 1988. 7.99 (*0-517-67152-2*) Random Hse Value.

***Complete Illustrated Book of Yoga.** Swami Vishnu-Devananda. (Illus.). 1995. 16.00 (*0-517-88431-3*) Random.

Complete Illustrated Book of Yoga. Swami Vishnudevananda. (Illus.). 384p. 1988. pap. 14.95 (*0-517-57096-3*, Harmony) Crown Pub Group.

Complete Illustrated Catalogue. Kai Kin Yung. (Illus.). 749p. 1981. pap. 29.50 (*0-904017-38-9*) Antique Collect.

Complete Illustrated Condom Handbook. Tyrone Throb, pseud. (Illus.). 28p. (Orig.). 1987. pap. 4.95 (*0-9619726-0-2*) T G McNeel.

Complete Illustrated Guide to Everything Sold in Garden Centers (Except the Plants) Steve R. Ettlinger. (Illus.). 448p. 1990. text ed. 24.95 (*0-02-536301-8*) Macmillan.

Complete Illustrated Guide to Everything Sold in Hardware Stores. Steve R. Ettlinger. LC 92-29763. (Illus.). 1993. pap. 15.00 (*0-02-043005-1*, Collier S&S) S&S Trade.

Complete, Illustrated Guide to Everything Sold in Hardware Stores. Tom Philbin & Steve R. Ettlinger. (Illus.). 352p. 1988. text ed. 25.95 (*0-02-536310-7*) Macmillan.

Complete Illustrated Shakespeare, 3 vols., Set. William Shakespeare. Ed. by John Gilbert. 1979. 79.95 (*0-405-12410-4*) Ayer.

Complete Illustration Guide for Architects, Designers, Artists & Students. Larry Evans. LC 92-35273. (Illus.). 1993. pap. 39.95 (*0-442-01373-6*) Van Nos Reinhold.

Complete in Christ: Discovering God's View of You. Bob George. 1994. pap. 6.99 (*1-56507-203-0*) Harvest Hse.

Complete Index to C. H. Spurgeon's Sermons, 1855-1917. C. H. Spurgeon. 1980. 9.95 (*1-56186-110-3*) Pilgrim Pubns.

Complete Index to Optical Engineering Journal: 1962-1984, Vols. 1-23. Ed. by E. Cherry. 192p. 1984. 50.00 (*0-89252-587-8*, 552) SPIE.

Complete Index to "Photogrammetric Engineering & Remote Sensing", Vol. I-XLV, 1934-1979. 28p. 1980. pap. 7.00 (*0-937294-16-0*) ASP & RS.

Complete Index to the Names of Persons, Places & Subjects Mentioned in Littell's Laws of Kentucky: A Genealogical & Historical Guide. W. T. Smith. 223p. 1994. reprint ed. pap. 21.00 (*0-685-75099-X*, 9090) Clearfield Co.

Complete Index to the Quilt Keys. Judy Rehmel. LC 84-90562. 60p. (Orig.). 1984. pap. 2.00 (*0-913731-06-4*) J Rehmel.

Complete Indian Cookbook. Diane Voules. 1992. 19.98 (*1-55521-810-5*) Bk Sales Inc.

Complete Indoor Gardner. Ed. by Michael Wright & Dennis G. Brown. (Pan Book Ser.). (Illus.). 1979. 19.95 (*0-394-73813-6*) Random.

***Complete Inflatable Kayaker.** Jeff Bennett. 1995. pap. text ed. 16.95 (*0-07-005428-2*) McGraw.

Complete Information Bank for Entrepreneurs & Small Business Managers. Ron Christy & Billy M. Jones. LC 81-70750. (Illus.). 300p. 1982. pap. 19.50 (*0-941958-00-0*) Wichita Ctr Entrep SBM.

Complete Information Systems Audit Handbook. Thomas J. Zarecki. (Illus.). 76p. 25.00 (*0-936503-03-3*) TJ Enter IL.

An Asterisk (*) at the beginning of an entry indicates that the title is appearing in BIP for the first time. 1467

Complete Inservice Staff Development Program: A Step-by-Step Manual for School Administrators. R. Lloyd Ryan. 256p. 1987. text ed. 39.95 (*0-13-161316-2*) P-H.

Complete Intaglio Print. John Ross & Clare Romano. LC 74-2697. 1974. pap. text ed. 14.95 (*0-02-927400-1*) Free Pr.

Complete Internal Revenue Code: (January 1993 Edition) rev. ed. RIA Staff. 2400p. 1993. pap. text ed. 32.00 (*0-7811-0074-7*) Res Inst Am.

Complete Internal Revenue Code: (Summer 1993 Edition) rev. ed. RIA Staff. 2700p. 1993. pap. text ed. 32.00 (*0-7811-0075-5*) Res Inst Am.

***Complete Internal Revenue Code: January 1995 Edition.** rev. ed. RIA In-House Professional Staff. 2500p. 1995. pap. text ed. 34.50 (*0-7811-0098-4*) Res Inst Am.

Complete Internal Revenue Code January 1994 Edition. rev. ed. RIA In-house Professional Staff. 2500p. 1994. pap. text ed. 33.50 (*0-7811-0084-4*) Res Inst Am.

Complete Internet Directory. Eric Braun. 352p. (Orig.). 1993. pap. 25.00 (*0-449-90898-4*, Columbine) Fawcett.

***Complete Internet Kit for Windows.** John P. Morphet. 352p. 1994. pap. 34.95 (*0-9642539-0-9*) Advnced Systs.

Complete Intersections. Ed. by S. Greco & R. Strano. (Lecture Notes in Mathematics Ser.: Vol. 1092). vii, 299p. 1984. pap. 42.30 (*0-387-13884-6*) Spr-Verlag.

Complete Introduction to Aquarium Plants: Windelov Tropica Catalogue. Holger Windelov. (Illus.). 128p. 1987. pap. 5.95 (*0-86622-289-8*) TFH Pubns.

Complete Introduction to Bettas. Walt Maurus. (Complete Introduction to...Ser.). (Illus.). 128p. 1987. pap. 5.95 (*0-86622-288-X*, CO-005S) TFH Pubns.

Complete Introduction to Budgerigars. Tony David. (Complete Introduction to...Ser.). (Illus.). 128p. (Orig.). 1987. pap. 5.95 (*0-86622-286-3*, CO-008S) TFH Pubns.

Complete Introduction to Cichlids. Robert J. Goldstein. (Illus.). 128p. 1987. pap. 5.95 (*0-86622-279-0*, CO011S) TFH Pubns.

Complete Introduction to Cockatiels. Elaine Radford. (Illus.). 128p. 1987. pap. 5.95 (*0-86622-284-7*, CO012S) TFH Pubns.

Complete Introduction to Cocker Spaniels. Anna K. Nicholas. (Complete Introduction to...Ser.). (Illus.). 128p. (Orig.). 1987. pap. 5.95 (*0-86622-381-9*, CO-036S) TFH Pubns.

C

Complete Introduction to Community Aquariums. Herbert R. Axelrod. (Illus.). 128p. 1987. pap. 5.95 (*0-86622-283-9*, CO013S) TFH Pubns.

Complete Introduction to Corydoras & Related Catfishes. Warren E. Burgess. (Illus.). 128p. 1987. pap. 5.95 (*0-86622-287-1*, CO015S) TFH Pubns.

Complete Introduction to Doberman Pinschers. Anna K. Nicholas. (Complete Introduction to...Ser.). (Illus.). 128p. (Orig.). 1987. pap. 5.95 (*0-86622-376-2*, CO-033S) TFH Pubns.

Complete Introduction to Finches. Jurgen Nicolai. (Complete Introduction to... Ser.). (Illus.). 128p. (Orig.). 1987. pap. 5.95 (*0-86622-293-6*, CO-006S) TFH Pubns.

Complete Introduction to Frogs & Toads. Jay Pyrom. (Complete Introduction to...Ser.). (Illus.). 128p. (Orig.). 1987. pap. 5.95 (*0-86622-395-9*, CO-041S) TFH Pubns.

Complete Introduction to Garden Ponds. Al David. (Complete Introduction to...Ser.). (Illus.). 128p. (Orig.). 1987. pap. 5.95 (*0-86622-298-7*, CO-017S) TFH Pubns.

Complete Introduction to Gerbils. M. Ostrow. (Complete Introduction to...Ser.). (Illus.). 128p. (Orig.). 1987. pap. 5.95 (*0-86622-299-5*, CO-018S) TFH Pubns.

Complete Introduction to Golden Retrievers. Kerry Donnelly. (Complete Introduction to...Ser.). (Illus.). 128p. (Orig.). 1987. pap. 5.95 (*0-86622-377-0*, CO-034S) TFH Pubns.

Complete Introduction to Hamsters. Mervin F. Roberts. (Illus.). 128p. 1987. pap. 5.95 (*0-86622-282-0*) TFH Pubns.

Complete Introduction to Koi & Garden Ponds. Herbert R. Axelrod. (Complete Introduction to...Ser.). (Illus.). 128p. (Orig.). 1987. pap. 5.95 (*0-86622-399-1*, CO-040S) TFH Pubns.

Complete Introduction to Marine Aquariums. Warren E. Burgess. (Complete Introduction to...Ser.). (Illus.). 128p. (Orig.). 1987. pap. 5.95 (*0-86622-351-7*, CO-021S) TFH Pubns.

Complete Introduction to Poodles. Anne K. Nicholas. (Complete Introduction to...Ser.). (Illus.). 128p. (Orig.). 1987. pap. 5.95 (*0-86622-380-0*, CO-032S) TFH Pubns.

Complete Introduction to Setting up an Aquarium. Jim Kelly. (Complete Introduction to...Ser.). (Illus.). 128p. (Orig.). 1987. pap. 5.95 (*0-86622-291-X*, CO-003S) TFH Pubns.

Complete Introduction to Snakes. Mervin F. Roberts. (Complete Introduction to...Ser.). (Illus.). 128p. (Orig.). 1987. pap. 5.95 (*0-86622-352-5*, CO-023S) TFH Pubns.

Complete Introduction to Turtles & Terrapins. Jo Cobb. (Illus.). 128p. 1987. pap. 5.95 (*0-86622-280-4*) TFH Pubns.

Complete Introduction to Zebra Finches. John L. Corbett. (Complete Introduction to...Ser.). (Illus.). 128p. (Orig.). 1987. pap. 5.95 (*0-86622-355-X*, CO-027S) TFH Pubns.

Complete Introductory Course of English for Poles. Irena Dobrzycka. 554p. (C). 1984. 19.95 (*0-88254-904-9*) Hippocrene Bks.

Complete Investor's Guide to Silver Dollar Investing. Dick A. Reed. 1982. 18.95 (*0-911349-00-6*) English Fact.

Complete Irish Tin Whistle Tutor. L. E. McCullough. (Illus.). 80p. 1987. pap. 8.95 (*0-8256-0311-0*, OK64923, Oak) Music Sales.

***Complete Iron Palm.** Hee I. Cho. 1978. pap. 19.95 (*0-86568-031-0*) Unique Pubns.

Complete Iron Palm Training. Brian Gray. LC 88-51060. (Illus.). (Orig.). 1989. pap. 12.95 (*0-86568-131-7*, 415) Unique Pubns.

***Complete Irrigation Workbook: Design, Installation, Maintenance & Water Management.** Larry Keesen. Ed. by Cindy Code. (Illus.). 250p. (C). 1995. pap. 27.00 (*1-883751-01-2*) GIE Pub.

Complete Italian & Spanish Phraseological Dictionary: Dizionario Fraseologico Completo Italiano-Spagnole e Spagnole-Italiano, Vol. 1. S. Carbonell. 840p. (ITA & SPA.). 1987. lib. bdg. 4,200.00 (*0-8288-3361-3*) Fr & Eur.

Complete Italian-Brazilian Portuguese-Italian Dictionary: Dizionario Completo Italiano-Portoghese (Brasiliano)-Italiano. V. Spinelli. (ITA & POR.). 1980. 45.00 (*0-8288-1040-0*, F45890) Fr & Eur.

Complete James Bond Movie Encyclopedia. Steven J. Rubin. 480p. 1991. pap. 18.95 (*0-8092-3966-3*) Contemp Bks.

Complete James Joyce Catalog. State University of New York at Buffalo Editorial Staff. 375p. 1987. lib. bdg. 55.00 (*0-8161-0446-8*) G K Hall.

Complete Japanese Expression Guide. Mizue Sasaki. 336p. 1992. pap. 14.95 (*0-8048-1689-1*) C E Tuttle.

Complete Japanese Verb Guide. Hiroo Japanese Center Staff. LC 89-50024. 352p. (Orig.). 1989. pap. 14.95 (*0-8048-1564-X*) C E Tuttle.

Complete Jazz Guitarist. Date not set. 15.00 (*1-56222-989-3*, 95113); audio 9.98 (*0-685-75009-4*, 95113C) Mel Bay.

Complete Jazz Music Collection. Ed. by Carol Cuellar. 260p. (Orig.). (YA). 1993. pap. text ed. 16.95 (*0-89898-587-0*) CPP Belwin.

Complete Jefferson. Thomas Jefferson. Ed. by Saul K. Padover. LC 78-80623. (Select Bibliographies Reprint Ser.). 1977. 82.95 (*0-8369-5027-5*) Ayer.

Complete Jefferson: Containing His Major Writings, Published & Unpublished, Except His Letters. Thomas Jefferson. (American Biography Ser.). 1322p. 1991. reprint ed. lib. bdg. 169.00 (*0-7812-8217-9*) Rprt Serv.

Complete Jethro Burns Mandolin Book. Jethro Burns & Ken Eidson. (Complete Book Ser.). 1993. 19.95 (*1-56222-663-0*, 94875); audio 9.98 (*1-56222-677-0*, 94875) Mel Bay.

Complete Jewish Wedding Planner. 2nd ed. Wendy C. Hefter. Ed. by David Hefter. (Illus.). 208p. 1993. pap. 17.95 (*0-9635753-0-9*) PSP Pr.

Complete Job & Career Handbook: One Hundred One Ways to Get from Here to There. S. Norman Feingold & Marilyn N. Feingold. LC 92-39716. (Illus.). 179p. (Orig.). (YA). (gr. 9 up). 1993. pap. 15.00 (*1-880774-01-1*) Garrett Pk.

Complete Job Finder's Guide for the 90's: Marketing Yourself in the New Job Market. Scott A. MacDonald. 230p. (Orig.). 1993. pap. 13.95 (*0-942710-84-3*) Impact VA.

***Complete Job-Finding Guide for Secretaries & Administrative Support Staff.** Paul Falcone. 256p. 1995. pap. 16.95 (*0-8144-7885-9*) AMACOM.

Complete Job-Finding Kit. John F. Truitt. 1986. 29.95 (*0-940101-01-7*) Telestar.

Complete Job Interview Handbook. John Marcus. 163p. 7.95 (*0-318-41634-4*, 216) Am Bartenders.

Complete Job Interview Handbook. 3rd ed. John J. Marcus. 192p. 1994. pap. 10.00 (*0-06-273266-8*, Harper Ref) HarpC.

Complete Job-Search Handbook: All the Skills You Need to Get Any Job & Have a Good Time Doing It. rev. ed. Howard Figler. LC 87-26610. 384p. 1988. pap. 12.95 (*0-8050-0537-4*, Owl) H Holt & Co.

***Complete Job Search Organizer.** Jack O'Brien. 1995. 9.95 (*0-938721-41-0*) Kiplinger Bks.

Complete Joel's Journal. Donald Wetzel. 128p. 1994. 7.95 (*0-88009-070-7*, 909) Planet Bks.

Complete Johnny Smith Approach to Guitar. Johnny Smith. 1993. 19.95 (*1-56222-239-2*, 93669) Mel Bay.

Complete Jowett History. Paul Clark & Edmund Mankivell. (Illus.). 224p. 1991. 59.95 (*0-85429-683-2*, Pub. by G T Foulis Ltd) Haynes Pubns.

Complete Joy of Home Brewing. Charlie Papazian. (Illus.). 352p. (Orig.). 1984. pap. 8.95 (*0-380-88369-4*) Avon.

Complete Juggler. rev. ed. Dave Finnigan. LC 91-61138. (Illus.). 576p. (YA). (gr. 9-12). 1991. reprint ed. pap. 14.95 (*0-9615521-0-7*) Jugglebug.

Complete Juggler. 2nd rev. ed. Dave Finnigan. LC 91-61138. (Illus.). 576p. (YA). (gr. 9-12). 1991. reprint ed. lib. bdg. 19.95 (*0-9615521-1-5*) Jugglebug.

Complete K-Six Collection Text & Prints. (Illus.). 126p. 1992. pap. text ed. 275.00 (*0-935493-51-4*) Modern Learn Pr.

Complete Kama Sutra: The First Unabridged Modern Translation of the Classic Indian Text. Tr. by Alain Danielou. 512p. 1993. 29.95 (*0-89281-492-6*) Inner Tradit.

***Complete Kama Sutra: The First Unabridged Modern Translation of the Classic Indian Text.** unabridged ed. Tr. by Alain Danielou. 576p. 1995. pap. 19.95 (*0-89281-525-6*, Park St Pr) Inner Tradit.

Complete Kano Jiu-Jitsu. H. Irving Hancock & Katsukuma Higashi. (Illus.). 1905. pap. 7.95 (*0-486-20639-4*) Dover.

Complete Karate. J. Allen Queen. LC 93-24831. (Illus.). 192p. (YA). (gr. 10-12). 1993. 19.95 (*0-8069-8678-6*) Sterling.

Complete Karate. J. Allen Queen. (Illus.). 192p. 1994. pap. 12.95 (*0-8069-8679-4*) Sterling.

Complete Karting Guide. Jean Genibrel. (Illus.). 80p. (Orig.). Date not set. pap. text ed. 10.95 (*0-936834-40-4*) S S Autosports.

***Complete Kauai Guidebook.** 2nd ed. Indian Chief Travel Guides Staff. 1995. pap. 8.95 (*0-916841-52-9*) Indian Chief.

Complete Kauai Guidebook: Discovering Hawaii's Garden Isle. David J. Russ. (Hawaii Ser.). (Illus.). 152p. (Orig.). 1993. pap. 8.95 (*0-916841-25-1*) Indian Chief.

Complete Keyboard Player, Bk. 1. Kenneth Baker. (Illus.). 48p. 1985. pap. 7.95 (*0-8256-2445-2*, AM38308) Music Sales.

Complete Keyboard Player, Bk. 2. Kenneth Baker. (Illus.). 48p. 1985. pap. 7.95 (*0-8256-2446-0*, AM38316) Music Sales.

Complete Keyboard Player, Bk. 3. Kenneth Baker. (Illus.). 48p. 1985. pap. 7.95 (*0-8256-2447-9*, AM38324) Music Sales.

Complete Keyboard Player: Chord Book. Kenneth Baker. (Illus.). 32p. 1987. pap. 3.95 (*0-7119-1189-4*, AM66507) Music Sales.

Complete Keyboard Player: Classics. Kenneth Baker. (Illus.). 40p. 1987. pap. 7.95 (*0-7119-1288-2*, AM67661) Music Sales.

Complete Keyboard Player: Omnibus Edition, 3 bks., set. Kenneth Baker. (Illus.). 144p. 1985. Set. pap. 17.95 (*0-8256-1063-X*, AM60476) Music Sales.

Complete Keyboard Player: Richard Clayderman. Kenneth Baker. (Illus.). 40p. 1987. pap. 7.95 (*0-8256-1159-8*, AM66002) Music Sales.

Complete Keyboard Player Christmas Songs. Kenneth Baker. (Illus.). 40p. pap. 7.95 (*0-8256-1169-5*, AM65954) Music Sales.

Complete Keyboard Player Picture Chords. (Illus.). 56p. 1993. pap. 7.95 (*0-7119-3041-4*) Music Sales.

Complete Keyboard Player Songbook, No. 1. Sel. by Kenneth Baker. (Illus.). 40p. 1986. pap. 7.95 (*0-8256-1075-3*, AM39116) Music Sales.

Complete Keyboard Player Songbook, No. 2. Sel. by Kenneth Baker. (Illus.). 40p. 1986. pap. 7.95 (*0-8256-1188-1*, AM39124) Music Sales.

Complete Keyboard Player Songbook, No. 3. Sel. by Kenneth Baker. (Illus.). 40p. 1986. pap. 7.95 (*0-8256-1189-X*, AM39132) Music Sales.

Complete Keys to Progress. John McCallum. Ed. by Randall J. Strossen. LC 93-80635. (Orig.). 1993. pap. 17.95 (*0-926888-01-3*) IronMind Enterprises.

Complete King Lear, 1608-1623, Set. William Shakespeare. 325p. (C). 1988. Boxed set. 230.00 (*0-520-05269-2*) U CA Pr.

Complete King's Indian. Raymond Keene & Byron Jacobs. 256p. 1992. pap. 22.95 (*0-8050-2429-8*, Pub. by Batsford Chess UK) H Holt & Co.

Complete Kitten & Cat Book. Norman H. Johnson. 1993. 8.98 (*0-88365-819-4*) Galahad Bks.

Complete Kung Fu Fighting Guide, Vol. 1. Jane Hallander. LC 85-51725. 112p. 1985. pap. 9.95 (*0-86568-065-5*, 221) Unique Pubns.

Complete Kung Fu Fighting Guide, Vol. 2. Jane Hallander. LC 85-51725. 1991. 12.95 (*0-86568-156-2*) Unique Pubns.

Complete Kwanzaa Celebration Book. Linda Robartson. 52p. 1993. pap. 9.95 (*0-9639026-9-5*) Creat Acrylic.

***Complete Kwanzaa Celebration Book.** rev. ed. Linda Robertson. LC 94-92261. (Illus.). 80p. 1994. pap. 9.95 (*0-9639026-8-7*) Creat Acrylic.

Complete Lake Tahoe Guidebook. 5th ed. B. Sangwan. (California Ser.). (Illus.). 136p. 1993. pap. 8.95 (*0-916841-30-8*) Indian Chief.

***Complete Lake Tahoe Guidebook.** 6th ed. B. Sangwan. (California Ser.). (Illus.). 136p. 1995. pap. 8.95 (*0-916841-56-1*) Indian Chief.

Complete LAN Security & Control. Peter T. Davis. 1993. pap. 27.95 (*0-8306-4549-7*, Windcrest) TAB Bks.

Complete Lan Security & Control. Peter T. Davis. 1993. text ed. 39.95 (*0-07-015837-1*); pap. text ed. 27.95 (*0-07-015838-X*) McGraw.

Complete Land Angler. George Junghanns. (Treasure Hunting Ser.). (Illus.). 1977. pap. write for info. (*0-686-21782-9*) Gauntlet Bks.

Complete Landscape Designs & Gardens of Geoffrey Jellicoe. Michael Spens. LC 93-61887. (Illus.). 212p. 1994. 65.00 (*0-500-01596-1*) Thames Hudson.

Complete Law School Companion: How to Excel at America's Most Demanding Post- Graduate Curriculum. 2nd ed. Jeff Deaver. 240p. 1992. pap. text ed. 14.95 (*0-471-55491-X*) Wiley.

Complete Layout Plans. enl. rev. ed. Harold Carstens & William Schopp. (Hobby Bks.: No. C-73). (Illus.). 50p. 1991. pap. 7.95 (*0-911868-73-9*, C73) Carstens Pubns.

***Complete Learning Center Book: An Illustrated Guide to 32 Different Early Childhood Learning Centers.** Rebecca Isbell. LC 95-19106. (Illus.). (Orig.). 1995. pap. 29.95 (*0-87659-174-8*) Gryphon Hse.

Complete Learning Disabilities Handbook: Ready-to-Use Techniques for Teaching Learning Handicapped Students. Joan M. Harwell. 176p. 1989. pap. 29.95 (*0-87628-239-7*) Ctr Appl Res.

Complete Lectures of Ingersoll. 411p. 15.00 (*0-318-16675-5*) Truth Seeker.

Complete Legal Guide to Special Education Services: A Handbook for Administrators, Counselors & Supervisors. Allen G. Osborne, Jr. 264p. 1988. text ed. 34.95 (*0-13-162025-8*) P-H.

Complete Lesson Plan Book. Diane Cherkerzian. (Illus.). 112p. 1993. 9.95 (*0-9627389-5-6*, Crystal Spgs) Soc Dev Educ.

Complete Letter Book. Michele Borba & Dan Ungaro. 112p. (J). (ps-3). 1980. 11.95 (*0-916456-80-3*, GA 182) Good Apple.

***Complete Letter Writer.** Mager. 1991. mass mkt. 5.99 (*0-671-74419-4*) PB.

Complete Letters. Emily E. Dickinson. (Notable American Authors Ser.). 1992. reprint ed. lib. bdg. 75.00 (*0-7812-2635-X*) Rprt Serv.

Complete Letters of Robert Burns: Souvenir Edition. M. Mackay. (C). 1988. 160.00 (*0-907526-32-2*, Alloway Pub) St Mut.

Complete Letters of Sigmund Freud to Wilhelm Fliess: 1887-1904. Sigmund Freud. Tr. by Jeffrey M. Masson. (Illus.). 544p. 1985. 39.95 (*0-674-15420-7*) Belknap Pr.

Complete Letters of Sigmund Freud to Wilhelm Fliess: 1887-1904. Sigmund Freud. Ed. & Tr. by Jeffrey M. Masson. (Illus.). 544p. 1986. pap. text ed. 14.95 (*0-674-15421-5*) Belknap Pr.

Complete Letters of Vincent Van Gogh. Vincent Van Gogh. LC 78-7073. (Illus.). 1979. reprint ed. 125.00 (*0-8212-0735-0*) Bulfinch Pr.

Complete Letters, Vol. 3: 1868-1871. Fyodor Dostoyevsky. Ed. & Tr. by David A. Lowe. 1991. 35.00 (*0-88233-542-1*) Ardis Pubs.

Complete Letters, Vol. 4: 1872-1877. Fyodor Dostoyevsky. Ed. & Tr. by David Lowe. (Illus.). 350p. (C). 1991. 35.00 (*0-88233-543-X*) Ardis Pubs.

Complete Letters, Vol. 5: 1878-1881. Fyodor Dostoyevsky. Ed. & Tr. by David Lowe. (Illus.). 350p. (C). 1991. 35.00 (*0-88233-544-8*) Ardis Pubs.

Complete Letters, 1860-67: Fyodor Dostoevsky, Vol. 2. Fyodor Dostoyevsky. Tr. by David Lowe. 1989. 35.00 (*0-88233-926-5*) Ardis Pubs.

Complete Letterwriter's Almanac. Dianna D. Booher. 1991. 34.95 (*0-13-155904-4*, Busn) P-H.

Complete Library of American Phonograph Recordings, 1959. Jerry Osborne. 256p. 1987. 24.95 (*0-932117-06-6*) Jellyroll Prodns.

Complete Library of American Phonograph Recordings, 1960. Jerry Osborne. 240p. 1987. 24.95 (*0-932117-05-8*) Jellyroll Prodns.

Complete Library of American Phonograph Recordings, 1961. Jerry Osborne. 249p. 1990. 24.95 (*0-932117-16-3*) Jellyroll Prodns.

Complete Library of American Phonograph Recordings, 1962. 1992. pap. 39.95 (*0-932117-18-X*) Jellyroll Prodns.

Complete Library of American Phonograph Recordings, 1963. 1993. pap. 39.95 (*0-932117-19-8*) Jellyroll Prodns.

Complete Library of American Phonograph Recordings, 1964. 1994. pap. 39.95 (*0-932117-20-1*) Jellyroll Prodns.

Complete Library Skills Activities Program: Ready-to-Use Lessons for Grades K-6. Arden Druce. 304p. 1990. pap. 27.95 (*0-87628-240-0*) Ctr Appl Res.

Complete Lieder, 2 vols., Set. Ed. by Clive Brown. LC 87-752507. (Selected Works of Louis Spohr, 1784-1859: Vol. 8). 504p. 1989. 30.00 (*0-8240-1507-X*) Garland.

Complete Life. John Erskine. LC 74-134073. (Essay Index Reprint Ser.). 1977. 23.95 (*0-8369-2153-4*) Ayer.

Complete Life of Christ. John F. Millar. LC 85-51584. (Illus.). 180p. (Orig.). 1986. 16.00 (*0-934943-04-4*); pap. 9.00 (*0-934943-01-X*) Thirteen Colonies Pr.

Complete Life of General George A. Custer, 2 vols. Frederick Whittaker. LC 92-37701. xxiv, 356p. 1993. Vol. 1, xxiv, 356p. 40.00 (*0-8032-4766-4*); Vol. 2, xiv, 314p. 40.00 (*0-8032-4767-2*) U of Nebr Pr.

Complete Life of General George A. Custer, 2 vols., 1. Frederick Whittaker. LC 92-37701. xxiv, 356p. 1993. pap. 12.95 (*0-8032-9742-4*) U of Nebr Pr.

Complete Life of General George A. Custer, 2 vols., 2. Frederick Whittaker. LC 92-37701. xiv, 314p. 1993. pap. 12.95 (*0-8032-9743-2*) U of Nebr Pr.

Complete Life of General George A. Custer, 2 vols., Set. Frederick Whittaker. LC 92-37701. xxiv, 356p. 1993. 80.00 (*0-8032-4768-0*); pap. 25.90 (*0-8032-9744-0*) U of Nebr Pr.

Complete Limerick Book: The Origin, History & Achievements of the Limerick. Langford Reed. (Illus.). 1995. reprint ed. 35.00 (*1-55888-943-4*) Omnigraphics Inc.

Complete Lincoln-Douglas Debates of 1858. Intro. by Paul M. Angle. (Illus.). 468p. 1991. pap. 17.95 (*0-226-02084-3*) U Ch Pr.

***Complete Linux Kit.** Daniel A. Tauber et al. 1995. 29.99 (*0-7821-1669-8*) Sybex.

***Complete Linux Tool Kit (Box)** Tauber et al. 1995. write for info. (*0-7821-1731-7*) Sybex.

Complete LISFAN. Ed. by Flint Mitchell. 100p. 1991. pap. 19.95 (*1-880417-05-7*) Star Tech.

Complete Literary Guide to the Bible. Ed. by Leland Ryken & Tremper Longman, III. 592p. 1993. 29.99 (*0-310-51830-X*) Zondervan.

Complete Literary Rot. Ed. by Bill Henderson. 1991. 25.00 (*0-916366-70-7*) Pushcart Pr.

***Complete Litigator: Reality, Perception & Persuasion in & Out of Court.** Paul M. Lisnek & Eric G. Oliver. LC 94-33504. 1994. 90.00 (*0-9636246-5-2*) Andrews Pubns.

Complete Little Nemo, Vol. 1. Winsor McCay. Ed. by Rick Marschall. (Illus.). 112p. 1989. 35.00 (*0-930193-63-6*) Fantagraph Bks.

Complete Little Nemo, Vol. 2. Winsor McCay. (Illus.). 95p. 1990. 29.95 (*0-930193-64-4*) Fantagraph Bks.

Complete Little Nemo, Vol. 3. Winsor McCay. Ed. by Richard Marschall. (Illus.). 96p. 1990. 35.00 (*1-56097-025-1*) Fantagraph Bks.

Complete Little Nemo, Vol. 4. Winsor McCay. Ed. by Richard Marschall. (Illus.). 96p. 1990. 35.00 (*1-56097-045-6*) Fantagraph Bks.

Complete Little Nemo in Slumberland, Vol. II. Winsor McCay. Ed. & Intro. by Richard Marschall. (Illus.). 96p. (J). (gr. 6 up). 1989. 34.95 (*0-924359-02-1*) Remco Wrldserv Bks.

Complete Little Nemo in Slumberland: In the Land of Wonderful Dreams, Part 2 - 1913-1914, Vol. VI. Winsor McCay. Ed. by Richard Marschall. (Illus.). 96p. (J). (gr. 6 up). 1992. 34.95 (*0-924359-36-6*) Remco Wrldserv Bks.

An Asterisk (*) at the beginning of an entry indicates that the title is appearing in BIP for the first time.

An Asterisk (*) at the beginning of an entry indicates that the title is appearing in BIP for the first time.

1469

Complete Novels of Jane Austen, Vol. 1. LC 92-50209. 1992. 19.00 (*0-679-60025-6*, Modern Lib) Random.

Complete Novels of Jane Austen, Vol. 2. LC 92-50209. 1992. 20.00 (*0-679-60026-4*, Modern Lib) Random.

Complete Nursing Home Guide: Finding Quality Care for Your Loved Ones. Mary B. Forrest et al. LC 92-37175. 304p. 1993. pap. 14.95 (*0-87833-822-5*) Taylor Pub.

Complete Nutrition: How to Live in Total Health. Michael Sharon. 1994. pap. 12.95 (*1-85375-076-X*) Avery Pub.

Complete Nutrition Counter. Lynn Sonberg. 496p. (Orig.). 1993. mass mkt. 5.99 (*0-425-13859-3*) Berkley Pub.

Complete O-Level Chemistry. G. N. Gilmore. (C). 1978. text ed. 70.00 (*0-85950-317-8*, Pub. by S Thornes Pubs UK) St Mut.

Complete Oahu Guidebook. David J. Russ. (Hawaii Ser.). (Illus.). 152p. (Orig.). 1994. pap. 9.95 (*0-916841-26-X*) Indian Chief.

Complete Oarsman. R. C. Lehmann. 1977. lib. bdg. 250.00 (*0-8490-1656-8*) Gordon Pr.

Complete Object-Oriented Design Example. Joseph E. Richardson et al. (Illus.). 355p. (C). 1992. pap. text ed. 50.00 (*1-881974-01-4*) Berard Sftware.

Complete Off-Premise Caterer. Judy S. Lieberman. 1991. text ed. 49.95 (*0-442-31858-8*) Van Nos Reinhold.

Complete Office Handbook. Mary A. De Vries. LC 92-38931. 1993. pap. 7.99 (*0-517-08906-8*, Pub. by Wings Bks) Random Hse Value.

Complete Official Road Guide of the Lincoln Highway. 5th ed. Lincoln Highway Association Staff. (Illus.). 542p. 1993. reprint ed. pap. text ed. 17.95 (*1-880397-05-6*) Patrice Pr.

Complete Oil Painting Book. Wendon Blake. (Illus.). 160p. 1989. 29.95 (*0-89134-293-1*, 30111) North Light Bks.

Complete Old English Sheepdog. Christina Smith. (Illus.). 160p. 1993. 25.95 (*0-87605-223-5*) Howell Bk.

Complete One & Three Step Sparring. Il Cho Hee. 1990. pap. 16.95 (*0-86568-141-4*) Unique Pubns.

Complete One Step & Three Sparring. Hee Il Cho. LC 88-92047. (Orig.). 1988. pap. 16.95 (*0-929015-10-X*) Chos Taekwon Do Pub Hse.

Complete Operas of Mozart. Charles Osborne. LC 82-23639. (Quality Paperbacks Ser.). (Illus.). 349p. 1983. reprint ed. pap. 13.95 (*0-306-80190-6*) Da Capo.

Complete Operas of Puccini. Charles Osborne. LC 83-10142. (Quality Paperbacks Ser.). (Illus.). 282p. 1983. reprint ed. pap. 10.95 (*0-306-80200-7*) Da Capo.

Complete Operas of Richard Strauss. Charles Osborne. (Quality Paperbacks Ser.). (Illus.). 248p. 1991. reprint ed. pap. 13.95 (*0-306-80459-X*) Da Capo.

Complete Operas of Richard Wagner. Charles Osborne. LC 92-34417. (Illus.). 304p. 1992. pap. 13.95 (*0-306-80522-7*) Da Capo.

Complete Operas of Richard Wagner. Charles Osborne. (Illus.). 352p. 1991. 24.95 (*0-943955-33-5*, Trafalgar Sq Pub) Trafalgar.

Complete Operas of Verdi: An Interpretive Study of the Librettos & Music & Their Relation to the Composer's Life. Charles Osborne. LC 77-23409. (Quality Paperbacks Ser.). 1977. pap. 14.95 (*0-306-80072-1*) Da Capo.

Complete Orations & Speeches. Henry W. Grady. (Notable American Authors Ser.). 1992. reprint ed. lib. bdg. 75.00 (*0-7812-2938-3*) Rprt Serv.

Complete Orations & Speeches of Henry W. Grady. Henry W. Grady. Ed. by Edwin Shurter. 1976. lib. bdg. 59.95 (*0-8490-1657-6*) Gordon Pr.

Complete Organ Player: Classical Pieces. Sel. by Kenneth Baker. (Illus.). 48p. 1985. pap. 8.95 (*0-7119-0757-9*, AM60559) Music Sales.

Complete Organ Player: Hymn Book. Kenneth Baker. (Illus.). 48p. 1985. pap. 8.95 (*0-7119-0565-7*, AM37680) Music Sales.

Complete Organ Player: Marches. Kenneth Baker. (Illus.). 48p. 1985. pap. 8.95 (*0-7119-1129-0*, AM65822) Music Sales.

Complete Organ Player: Songbook Three. Ed. by Kenneth Baker. (Illus.). 48p. 1988. pap. 8.95 (*0-8256-1199-7*, AM34083) Music Sales.

Complete Organ Player: Songbook Two. Sel. by Kenneth Baker. (Illus.). 48p. 1988. pap. 8.95 (*0-8256-1198-9*, AM33739) Music Sales.

Complete Organ Player Songbook: Songbook One. Sel. by Kenneth Baker. (Illus.). 48p. 1988. pap. 8.95 (*0-8256-1197-0*, AM33721) Music Sales.

Complete Origami. Eric Kenneway. (Illus.). 192p. 1987. pap. 12.95 (*0-312-00898-8*) St Martin.

***Complete Origami Collection.** Toshie Takahama. (Illus.). 160p. (Orig.). 1996. pap. 17.00 (*0-87040-960-3*) Japan Pubns USA.

Complete Origami Kit. Tuttle Staff. 1993. pap. 14.95 (*0-8048-1816-9*) C E Tuttle.

Complete Origami Kit for Children. (Illus.). 1993. boxed 14.95 (*0-8048-1973-4*) C E Tuttle.

Complete Origami Kit for Holidays. (Illus.). 1993. boxed 14.95 (*0-8048-1972-6*) C E Tuttle.

***Complete Oscar Wilde.** Wilde. 1995. 12.99 (*0-517-12073-9*) Random Hse Value.

Complete Outdoor Building Book: Patios, Decks, Fences, Landscaping, etc. L. Donald Meyers. 352p. 1991. text ed. 40.00 (*0-13-155276-7*) P-H.

Complete Outdoor Cookbook. Yvonne Y. Tarr. LC 72-90453. (Illus.). 320p. 1983. write for info. (*0-8129-0334-X*, Times Bks) Random.

Complete Owl. Michael Leach. (Illus.). 160p. 1993. pap. 22.95 (*0-7011-3786-X*, Pub. by Chatto & Windus UK) Trafalgar.

Complete Package for Maternity & Gynecologic Care, No. 5. Bobak. 1992. write for info. (*0-8016-7286-4*) Mosby Yr Bk.

Complete Painters Handbook: How to Paint Your House Inside & Out-the Right Way. Gregg E. Sandreuter. LC 88-4483. (Illus.). 160p. 1988. pap. 14.95 (*0-87857-756-4*, 14-520-1) Rodale Pr Inc.

Complete Painting Course. Wendon Blake. 1988. 29.99 (*0-517-45692-3*) Random Hse Value.

Complete Painting Course: A Comprehensive Learning Guide & Reference Manual. Ian Simpson. LC 93-84162. (Illus.). 224p. 1993. 29.95 (*1-56138-350-3*) Running Pr.

Complete Paintings of Vermeer. Intro. by John Jacob. (Illus.). 104p. 1987. 10.95 (*0-317-56066-2*, Penguin Bks) Viking Penguin.

Complete Paladin's Handbook. Rick Swan. (Advanced Dungeons & Dragons 2nd Ed. Accessory Ser.: PHBR12). 1994. pap. 18.00 (*1-56076-845-2*) TSR Inc.

Complete Paragraph Workout Book. Carolyn H. Fitzpatrick & Marybeth B. Ruscica. 432p. (C). 1989. pap. text ed. 18.00 (*0-318-40037-5*) Heath.

Complete Paragraph Workout Book. Carolyn H. Fitzpatrick & Marybeth B. Ruscica. 432p. (C). 1993. Instr.'s ed. teacher ed write for info. (*0-669-27451-8*); Test book. write for info. (*0-669-27452-6*) Heath.

Complete Paragraph Workout Book. 2nd ed. Carolyn H. Fitzpatrick & Marybeth B. Ruscica. 432p. (C). 1993. pap. text ed. write for info. (*0-669-27450-X*) Heath.

Complete Parallel Bible with the Apocryphal: Deuterocanonical Books. 1993. 59.95 (*0-19-528318-X*) OUP.

Complete Parallel Bible with the Apocryphal: Deuterocanonical Books. 1994. 100.00 (*0-19-528319-8*) OUP.

***Complete Parrot.** Arthur Freud. LC 95-4031. 1995. 34.95 (*0-87605-905-1*) Howell Bk.

Complete Partner Stunt Book. Rusty McKinley. (Illus.). 208p. (Orig.). 1982. pap. 14.95 (*0-914338-05-6*) Regmar Pub.

Complete Party Book: How to Plan, Host, & Enjoy Your Party from Conception to Cleanup. Don Ernstein & Deborah Sroloff. LC 93-28131. 1994. 24.95 (*0-670-84959-6*, Viking) Viking Penguin.

***Complete Party Book: Hundreds of Things to Do & Make.** La Coccinella. (Illus.). 48p. (J). (ps-3). 1995. 19.95 (*1-56397-488-6*, Wordsong) Boyds Mills Pr.

Complete Passover Cookbook. Frances R. AvRutick. LC 80-39633. 432p. 1981. 17.95 (*0-8246-0262-5*) Jonathan David.

***Complete Pastrywork Techniques.** I. Nicolello. 1993. pap. text ed. 32.95 (*0-470-23348-6*) Halsted Pr.

***Complete Pastrywork Techniques.** I. Nicolello. 1993. pap. text ed. 12.95 (*0-470-23353-2*) Wiley.

Complete Patents. Tesla Nikola. 500p. 35.00 (*0-913022-44-6*) Angriff Pr.

Complete Patient History. 2nd ed. Maurice Kraytman. (Illus.). 656p. 1991. pap. 29.50 (*0-07-035614-9*) Hlth Prof Div.

Complete Patio Book. Ed. by Southern Living Staff. (Southern Living Home Improvement Ser.). 144p. 1992. pap. 13.99 (*0-376-09044-8*) Oxmoor Hse.

Complete Patio Book. Sunset Magazine & Book Editors. LC 89-69850. 144p. 1990. pap. 13.99 (*0-376-01399-0*) Sunset Menlo Pk.

Complete Pattern Book of Soft Dolls. Valerie Janitch. (Illus.). 160p. 1992. 27.95 (*0-7153-9926-8*, Pub. by D & C Pub UK) Sterling.

Complete Payment Book. Michael Sherman. (Illus.). 144p. 1982. reprint ed. pap. 6.95 (*0-8092-5710-6*) Contemp Bks.

***Complete PC Upgrade & Maintenance Guide.** Mark Minasi. 1995. 34.99 (*0-7821-1660-4*) Sybex.

Complete PC Upgrade & Maintenance Guide. 3rd ed. Mark Minasi. LC 93-87698. 807p. 1994. pap. 29.99 (*0-7821-1498-9*) Sybex.

Complete Pec Asia. 3rd ed. Roberts. 1989. 10.95 (*0-316-74991-5*) Little.

Complete Peddler's Pack: Games, Songs, Rymes, & Riddles from Mountain Folkore. May Justus. LC 66-14774. (Illus.). 99p. reprint ed. pap. 28.30 (*0-317-55796-3*, 2029376) Bks Demand.

Complete Peerage of England, Scotland, Ireland, Great Britain, & the United Kingdom: Extant, Extinct or Dormant, 6 vols. Ed. by George E. Cokayne. LC 84-40342. 2830p. 1984. reprint ed. 450.00 (*0-312-15836-X*) St Martin.

Complete Pelican Shakespeare. Ed. by Alfred Harbage. (Pelican Shakespeare Ser.). 1974. pap. 55.00 (*0-14-071449-9*, Pelican Bks) Viking Penguin.

Complete Penguin Guide to Compact Discs & Cassettes. rev. ed. Ivan March et al. 1400p. 1993. pap. 23.50 (*0-14-046918-4*, Penguin Bks) Viking Penguin.

Complete Penguin Stereo Record & Cassette Guide. 3rd ed. Ed. by Edward Greenfield & Robert Layton. 1344p. 1985. pap. 12.95 (*0-14-046682-7*, Penguin Bks) Viking Penguin.

Complete Persian. William Thompson & Eric Wickham-Ruffle. (Illus.). 224p. 1993. 24.95 (*0-87605-798-9*) Howell Bk.

Complete Personal & Business Legal Forms & Agreements Kit. 112p. (Orig.). 1991. pap. 19.95 (*1-878459-02-3*) Total Rsch Pub.

Complete Personal Budgeting Workbook. Richard P. Steinberger & Paul W. Steinberger. 73p. (Orig.). 1991. pap. text ed. 12.95 (*0-9629582-0-4*) Am Assn Ed Con.

Complete Personal Injury Practice Manual. Al J. Cone & Verne Lawyer. LC 83-3166. 318p. 1983. text ed. 44.95 (*0-13-162248-X*) P-H.

Complete PFE Study Reference. Fred A. Anderson. 96p. (Orig.). 1983. pap. 18.95 (*0-939570-01-7*) Skills Improvement.

Complete Phantom of the Opera. George Perry. (Illus.). 176p. 1988. 29.95 (*0-8050-0657-5*) H Holt & Co.

Complete Phantom of the Opera. George Perry. 168p. 1991. pap. 19.95 (*0-8050-1722-4*, Owl) H Holt & Co.

Complete Photographic Work of Jacob A. Riis. Ed. by Robert J. Doherty. (Illus.). 38p. 1981. lib. bdg. 70.00 (*0-8161-1732-2*, Hall Reference) Macmillan.

Complete Photography Careers Handbook. 2nd ed. George Gilbert. 307p. 1992. pap. 19.95 (*0-913069-41-8*) Consultant Pr.

Complete Photography Course. Michael Joseph & Dave Saunders. (Illus.). 288p. 1994. 29.95 (*0-670-85350-X*, Viking) Viking Penguin.

Complete Phraseological Dictionary, Spanish-Italian: Dizionario Fraseologico Completo, Vol. 2. S. Carbonell. 1524p. (ITA & SPA.). 1987. lib. bdg. 5,200.00 (*0-8288-3362-1*) Fr & Eur.

Complete Pianist: Body, Mind, Synthesis. Ruth C. Friedberg. LC 92-39275. (Illus.). 157p. 1992. 22.50 (*0-8108-2630-5*) Scarecrow.

Complete Piano Concertos in Full Score. Ludwig van Beethoven. (Music Ser.). 384p. 1983. reprint ed. pap. 14.95 (*0-486-24563-2*) Dover.

Complete Piano Music. John K. Paine. LC 83-18890. (Earlier American Music Ser.: No. 27). 100p. 1984. reprint ed. lib. bdg. 25.00 (*0-306-77323-6*) Da Capo.

Complete Piano Player, Bk. 1. Kenneth Baker. (Illus.). 48p. 1984. pap. 7.95 (*0-8256-2434-7*, AM34828) Music Sales.

Complete Piano Player, Bk. 2. Kenneth Baker. (Illus.). 48p. 1984. pap. 7.95 (*0-8256-2435-5*, AM34836) Music Sales.

Complete Piano Player, Bk. 3. Kenneth Baker. (Illus.). 48p. 1984. pap. 7.95 (*0-8256-2436-3*, AM34844) Music Sales.

Complete Piano Player, Bk. 4. Kenneth Baker. (Illus.). 48p. 1984. pap. 7.95 (*0-8256-2437-1*, AM34851) Music Sales.

Complete Piano Player, Bk. 5. Kenneth Baker. (Illus.). 48p. 1984. pap. 7.95 (*0-8256-2438-X*, AM34869) Music Sales.

Complete Piano Player, Collection 1. Poldi Zeitlin & David Goldberger. (Illus.). 96p. 1985. pap. 9.95 (*0-8256-0668-3*, AM39603) Music Sales.

Complete Piano Player, Collection 2. Poldi Zeitlin & David Goldberger. (Illus.). 96p. 1985. pap. 9.95 (*0-8256-0669-1*, AM39611) Music Sales.

Complete Piano Player, Collection 3. Poldi Zeitlin & David Goldberger. (Illus.). 96p. 1985. pap. 9.95 (*0-8256-0670-5*, AM39629) Music Sales.

Complete Piano Player, Collection 4. Poldi Zeitlin & David Goldberger. (Illus.). 96p. 1985. pap. 9.95 (*0-8256-0671-3*, AM39637) Music Sales.

Complete Piano Player, Songbook 1. Comp. by Kenneth Baker. (Illus.). 48p. 1986. pap. 7.95 (*0-8256-1059-1*, AM39140) Music Sales.

Complete Piano Player: Children's Pieces. Kenneth Baker. (Illus.). 48p. 1988. pap. 7.95 (*0-7119-1132-0*, AM65855) Music Sales.

Complete Piano Player: Christmas Party Songs. (Illus.). 64p. 1987. pap. 7.95 (*0-8256-1167-9*, AM60534) Music Sales.

Complete Piano Player: Omnibus Edition. Kenneth Baker. (Illus.). 240p. 1984. pap. 21.95 (*0-8256-2439-8*, AM39645) Music Sales.

Complete Piano Player: Style Book. Kenneth Baker. (Illus.). 48p. 1984. pap. 7.95 (*0-8256-2433-9*, AM35338) Music Sales.

Complete Piano Player: Theory Book. Poldi Zeitlin & David Goldberger. (Illus.). 112p. 1986. pap. 9.95 (*0-7119-0667-X*, AM39595) Music Sales.

Complete Piano Rags. Scott Joplin. 208p. 1988. pap. 8.95 (*0-486-25807-6*) Dover.

Complete Piano Sonatas, 2 vols., 1. Ludwig van Beethoven. Ed. by Heinrich Schenker. LC 74-83473. 1975. reprint ed. pap. 11.95 (*0-486-23134-8*) Dover.

Complete Piano Sonatas, 2 vols., 2. Ludwig van Beethoven. Ed. by Heinrich Schenker. LC 74-83473. 1975. reprint ed. pap. 11.95 (*0-486-23135-6*) Dover.

Complete Piano Transcriptions, Cadenzas & Exercises. Johannes Brahms. Ed. by Eusebius Mandyczewski. LC 72-116826. 1970. reprint ed. pap. 8.50 (*0-486-22652-2*) Dover.

Complete Piano Works for Four Hands. Johannes Brahms. Ed. by Eusebius Mandyczewski. LC 75-27674. 224p. 1976. reprint ed. pap. 10.95 (*0-486-23271-9*) Dover.

Complete Picture Chords. Brimhall. (Keyboard Chords Ser.). 1990. 5.95 (*0-685-32021-9*, 77-100) Hansen Ed Mus.

Complete Plain Words. Ernest Gowers. (C). 1987. 40.00 (*0-685-33725-1*, Pub. by Witherby & Co UK) St Mut.

Complete Plain Words. Ernest Gowers. Ed. by Sidney Greenbaum & Janet Whitcut. LC 87-46281. 288p. 1990. reprint ed. 18.95 (*0-87923-733-3*); reprint ed. pap. 12.95 (*0-87923-850-X*) Godine.

Complete Plans for Building Horse Barns Big & Small. 2nd ed. Nancy Ambrosiano & Mary Harcourt. (Illus.). 250p. 1995. 29.95 (*0-914327-28-3*) Breakthrgh NY.

Complete Plant Operations Handbook: A Guide to Cost Reduction Quality Control & On-Time Delivery. Allan I. Young. 400p. 1990. 59.95 (*0-13-161431-2*) P-H.

Complete Playgirl Fantasies. (Orig.). 1993. pap. 4.95 (*1-56333-075-X*) Masquerade.

Complete Playground Book. Arlene Brett et al. LC 92-43598. (Illus.). 129p. (C). 1993. text ed. 34.95 (*0-8156-2576-6*); pap. 16.95 (*0-8156-0271-5*) Syracuse U Pr.

Complete Plays. Ronald Firbank. LC 93-36133. 170p. 1994. 19.95 (*1-56478-047-3*) Dalkey Arch.

Complete Plays. Zora Neale Hurston. Date not set. 25.00 (*0-06-016727-0*, HarpT); pap. 12.95 (*0-06-092169-2*, PL) HarpC.

Complete Plays. Christopher Marlowe. Ed. by J. B. Steane. Incl. Dido Queen of Carthage. 1969. (*0-318-55022-9*); Massacre at Paris. 1969. (*0-318-55023-7*); Tamburlaine, Parts 1 & 2. 1969. (*0-318-55024-5*); Edward Second. 1969. (*0-318-55025-3*); Doctor Faustus. 1969. (*0-318-55026-1*); (English Library). (Orig.). 1969. Set pap. 10.95 (*0-14-043037-7*, Penguin Classics) Viking Penguin.

Complete Plays, 3 vols. Eugene O'Neill. Ed. by Travis Bogard. 1988. Vol. I, 1913-1920. 35.00 (*0-940450-48-8*); Vol. II, 1920-1931. 35.00 (*0-940450-49-6*); Vol. III, 1932-1943. 35.00 (*0-940450-50-X*) Library of America.

Complete Plays. Joe Orton. Incl. Entertaining Mr. Sloane. 1977. (*0-318-52761-8*); Erpingham Camp. 1977. (*0-318-52762-6*); Funeral Games. 1977. (*0-318-52763-4*); Good & Faithful Servant. 1977. (*0-318-52764-2*); Loot. 1977. (*0-318-52765-0*); Ruffian on the Stair. 1977. (*0-318-52766-9*); What the Butler Saw. 1977. (*0-318-52767-7*); 1977. Set pap. 6.95 (*0-394-17001-6*, B400) Grove-Atltic.

Complete Plays. Joe Orton. 448p. 1990. pap. 12.95 (*0-8021-3215-4*) Grove-Atltic.

Complete Plays: The Hostage, The Quare Fellow, Richard's Cork Leg. Brendan Behan. 352p. (Orig.). 1988. pap. 12.95 (*0-8021-3070-4*) Grove-Atltic.

***Complete Plays, Lenz & Other Writings.** Georg Buchner. 1995. 21.00 (*0-8446-6850-8*) Peter Smith.

Complete Plays, Lenz & Other Writings. Georg Buchner. Tr. & Intro. by John Reddick. 368p. 1994. pap. 10.95 (*0-14-044586-2*, Penguin Classics) Viking Penguin.

Complete Plays of Aristophanes. Aristophanes. 1984. pap. 4.95 (*0-553-21343-1*, Bantam Classics) Bantam.

Complete Plays of Gilbert & Sullivan. W. S. Gilbert & Arthur Sullivan. 34.95 (*0-8488-0051-6*, Amereon Hse) Amereon Ltd.

Complete Plays of Gilbert & Sullivan. Jerome Robinson. 711p. 1991. reprint ed. text ed. 119.00 (*0-7812-9326-X*) Rprt Serv.

Complete Plays of Henry James. Henry James. Ed. by Leon Edel. (Illus.). 872p. 1991. 60.00 (*0-19-504379-0*) OUP.

Complete Plays of John Bale I. Ed. by Peter Happe. LC 84-29240. (Tudor Interludes Ser.: No. IV). 167p. 1985. 79.00 (*0-85991-174-8*) Boydell & Brewer.

Complete Plays of John Bale II. Ed. by Peter Happe. (Tudor Interludes Ser.: No. V). 192p. (C). 1986. 79.00 (*0-85991-219-1*) Boydell & Brewer.

Complete Plays of John M. Synge. John Millington Synge. Incl. Playboy of the Western World. 1960. (*0-318-55445-3*); Riders to the Sea. 1960. (*0-318-55446-1*); In the Shadow of the Glen. 1960. (*0-318-55447-X*); Well of the Saints. 1960. (*0-318-55448-8*); Tinker's Wedding. 1960. (*0-318-55449-6*); Deirdre of the Sorrows. 1960. (*0-318-55450-X*); 1960. Set pap. 10.00 (*0-394-70178-X*, Vin) Random.

Complete Plays of Sophocles. Sophocles. 1982. pap. 3.95 (*0-553-21354-7*) Bantam.

Complete Plays of Synge. John Millington Synge. (Methuen World Dramatists Ser.). 311p. 1988. pap. 11.95 (*0-413-48520-X*, A0062, Pub. by Methuen UK) Heinemann.

Complete Plays of the Wakefield Master. Wakefield Master. Ed. by John R. Brown. 1983. pap. 10.95 (*0-87830-584-X*, Theatre Arts Bks) Routledge Chapman & Hall.

Complete Poems. Martin Bell. 1988. 27.50 (*1-85224-042-3*, Pub. by Bloodaxe Bks UK); pap. 18.95 (*1-85224-043-1*, Pub. by Bloodaxe Bks UK) Dufour.

Complete Poems. Emily J. Bronte. 352p. 1993. 10.95 (*0-14-042352-4*, Penguin Classics) Viking Penguin.

Complete Poems. Basil Bunting. Ed. by Richard Caddel. LC 93-48950. (Oxford Poets Ser.). 240p. 1994. pap. 16.95 (*0-19-282282-9*) OUP.

Complete Poems. Guido Cavalcanti. Tr. & Intro. by Marc Cirigliano. LC 92-12123. 200p. (Orig.). 1992. pap. 11.00 (*0-934977-27-5*) Italica Pr.

Complete Poems. Keith Douglas. Ed. by Desmond Graham. 176p. 1988. pap. 11.95 (*0-19-281964-X*) OUP.

Complete Poems. Jean Genet. 1988. pap. 9.95 (*0-686-28714-2*) Man-Root.

Complete Poems. Hardy. 29.95 (*0-02-548150-9*) Macmillan.

Complete Poems. Thomas Hardy. Ed. by James Gibson. 1024p. 1982. pap. 23.00 (*0-02-069600-0*, Collier S&S) S&S Trade.

Complete Poems. Randall Jarrell. LC 68-29469. 507p. 1981. 45.00 (*0-374-12716-6*); pap. 14.95 (*0-374-51305-8*) FS&G.

Complete Poems. Ben Jonson. Ed. by George Parfitt. 640p. 1988. pap. 12.95 (*0-14-042277-3*, Penguin Classics) Viking Penguin.

Complete Poems. Patrick Kavanagh. 400p. 1972. 50.00 (*0-914612-04-2*) Kavanagh.

Complete Poems. John Keats. Ed. by John Barnard. (Poets Ser.). 1977. pap. 10.95 (*0-14-042210-2*, Penguin Classics) Viking Penguin.

Complete Poems. D. H. Lawrence. Ed. & Intro. by F. Warren Roberts. 1088p. 1994. pap. 19.95 (*0-14-018657-3*, Penguin Classics) Viking Penguin.

Complete Poems. Andrew Marvell. Ed. by Elizabeth S. Donno. (Poets Ser.). 1977. pap. 9.95 (*0-14-042213-7*, Penguin Classics) Viking Penguin.

Complete Poems. John Milton. LC 92-52905. 1992. 20.00 (*0-679-40997-1*, Everymans Lib) Knopf.

Complete Poems. Marianne Moore. 320p. 1994. 12.95 (*0-14-018851-7*, Penguin Classics) Viking Penguin.

Complete Poems. William Shakespeare. LC 92-52934. 256p. 1992. 15.00 (*0-679-41741-9*, Everymans Lib) Knopf.

Complete Poems. Robert Louis Stevenson. 1973. 250.00 (*0-87968-101-2*) Gordon Pr.

C

1470

An Asterisk (*) at the beginning of an entry indicates that the title is appearing in BIP for the first time.

C

An Asterisk (*) at the beginning of an entry indicates that the title is appearing in BIP for the first time.

1471

Complete Potter's Companion, Vol. 1. rev. ed. Tony Birks. (Illus.). 192p. 1993. pap. 24.95 (*0-8212-2014-4*) Bulfinch Pr.

Complete Practical Joker. H. Allen Smith. 225p. 1992. reprint ed. lib. bdg. 18.95 (*0-89966-931-X*) Buccaneer Bks.

***Complete Prefaces Vol. II: 1914-1929.** Bernard Shaw. Ed. by Dan H. Laurence & Daniel J. Leary. 640p. 1995. 45.00 (*0-7139-9057-0*) Allen Lane.

Complete Prefaces, Vol. I: 1889-1913. Bernard Shaw. Ed. by Dan H. Laurence & Daniel J. Leary. 656p. 1994. 40.00 (*0-7139-9056-2*, A Lane) Viking Penguin.

Complete Pregnancy & Baby Book. Consumer Guide Editors & Vicki Lansky. (Illus.). 448p. 1993. 14.98 (*0-7853-0230-1*, 3211600) Pubns Intl Ltd.

Complete Pregnancy & Baby Book. Consumer Guide Editors & Vicky Lansky. (Illus.). 448p. 1991. reprint ed. pap. 15.00 (*0-452-26651-3*, Plume) NAL-Dutton.

Complete Pregnancy Exercise Program. Diana Simkin. LC 80-36712. (Illus.). 176p. mass mkt. 5.95 (*0-452-25417-5*, Plume) NAL-Dutton.

Complete Pregnancy Workbook: A Guide for Parents-to-Be. Philip D. Sloane et al. (Illus.). 272p. 1986. pap. text ed. 13.95 (*0-912697-23-7*) Algonquin Bks.

Complete Preludes & Etudes for Pianoforte Solo. Alexander Scriabin. Ed. by K. N. Igumnov & Y. I. Mil'Shteyn. 250p. 1973. pap. 9.95 (*0-486-22919-X*) Dover.

Complete Preludes & Etudes for Solo Piano. Frederic Chopin. Ed. by Ignacy J. Paderewski. 224p. 1980. reprint ed. pap. 8.95 (*0-486-24052-5*) Dover.

Complete Preludes & Fugues for Organ. Johann Sebastian Bach. (Music Scores to Play & Study Ser.). 168p. 1985. reprint ed. pap. 8.95 (*0-486-24816-X*) Dover.

Complete Premarital Contracting: Loving Communication for Today's Couples. Jacqueline Rickard. 1993. 8.95 (*0-87131-739-7*) M Evans.

Complete Prenatal Water Workout Book: Watercise While You Wait. Helga Hughes. LC 88-7441. (Illus.). 120p. (Orig.). 1989. pap. 8.95 (*0-89529-306-4*) Avery Pub.

Complete Preparation: A Guide to Auditioning for Opera. Joan Dornemann & Maria Ciaccia. 156p. (Orig.). (C). 1992. pap. 18.95 (*0-9627226-3-4*) Excalibur Pub.

Complete Preparation for Childbirth: A Self Help Manual for Expectant Parents. Janice Morton. 240p. (C). 1990. pap. text ed. 80.00 (*962-209-220-9*, Pub. by Hong Kong U Pr HK) St Mut.

Complete Preparation for the MCAT. 6th ed. AFTAB Hassan et al. (Illus.). 800p. (C). 1992. pap. 49.50 (*0-941406-29-6*) Betz Pub Co Inc.

Complete Preparation for the SAT. Karl Weber. LC 85-17674. 430p. 1986. pap. 10.95 (*0-15-601224-3*) HarBrace.

Complete Preparation for the SAT. Karl Weber. LC 85-17674. 430p. 1987. teacher ed 3.25 (*0-15-601264-2*) HarBrace.

Complete Preparation for the SAT. Karl Weber. (Harvest Test Preparation Ser.). 1994. pap. 12.95 (*0-15-601221-9*) HarBrace.

Complete Preschool Program. Arlene L. Martin. 143p. 1987. pap. text ed. 19.95 (*1-55691-008-8*) Learning Pubns.

Complete Presidential Press Conferences of Franklin Delano Roosevelt (1933-1945), 12 annual vols., Set. Franklin D. Roosevelt. LC 78-155953. (FDR & the Era of the New Deal Ser.). 7000p. 1973. 495.00 (*0-306-77500-X*) Da Capo.

Complete Price Guide to Cards Worth Collecting. Paul M. Green. 1993. pap. 8.95 (*0-8092-3793-8*) Contemp Bks.

***Complete Price Guide to Watches No. 15.** Cooksey Shugart. 1995. pap. 19.95 (*0-89145-657-0*) Collector Bks.

Complete Primer: Caring for Aging Parents. Virginia Morris. (Illus.). 480p. (Orig.). 1994. pap. 12.95 (*1-56305-435-3*) Workman Pub.

Complete Printmaker. John Ross & Clare Romano. LC 72-77151. (Illus.). 1972. 39.95 (*0-02-927370-6*) Free Pr.

Complete Printmaker: Techniques - Traditions - Innovations. enl. rev. ed. John Ross et al. 352p. 1991. pap. 35.00 (*0-02-927372-2*) Free Pr.

Complete Private Pilot. 7th rev. ed. Bob Gardner. (Complete Pilot Ser.). (Illus.). 325p. 1994. pap. text ed. 18.95 (*1-56027-173-6*, ASA-PPT) Av Suppl & Acad.

Complete Private Pilot Syllabus. 2nd ed. Bob Gardner. (Complete Pilot Ser.). 53p. 1994. pap. 8.95 (*1-56027-121-3*, ASA-PPT-S) Av Suppl & Acad.

Complete Private Pilot Workbook. 2nd ed. Bob Gardner. (Complete Pilot Ser.). (Illus.). 76p. 1994. 8.95 (*1-56027-120-5*, ASA-PPT-W) Av Suppl & Acad.

Complete Probate Kit. Jens C. Appel & F. Bruce Gentry. 1991. text ed. 64.95 (*0-471-53579-6*); pap. text ed. 22.95 (*0-471-53492-7*) Wiley.

Complete Problem Solver. 2nd ed. John R. Hayes. 376p. (gr. 12 up). 1989. 79.95 (*0-89859-782-X*); pap. 34.50 (*0-8058-0309-2*) L Erlbaum Assocs.

Complete Problem Solver: A Total System for Competitive Decision Making. John Arnold. 1992. text ed. 24.95 (*0-471-54198-2*) Wiley.

***Complete Process Color Finder.** Rockport Publishers Staff. 1995. 24.99 (*1-56496-134-6*) Rockport Pubs.

***Complete Prophecies of Nostradamus.** Henry Roberts. 1994. 20.00 (*0-517-59092-1*, Crown) Crown Pub Group.

Complete Prophecies of Nostradamus. Tr. by Henry C. Roberts. (Illus.). 352p. 1983. 15.00 (*0-517-54956-5*, Crown) Crown Pub Group.

Complete Prose Works of John Milton, 8 vols. Incl. Vol. 2. 1643-1648. John Milton. Ed. by Ernest Sirluck. 840p. 1959. 95.00 (*0-300-00956-9*); Set. History of Britain & the Miltonic State Papers, 2 pts. John Milton. Ed. by French Fogle & J. Max Patrick. 928p. 1971. 110.00 (*0-300-01288-8*); Vol. 7. 1659-1660. rev. ed. John Milton. 1980. text ed. 80.00 (*0-300-02015-5*); write for info. (*0-318-56513-7*) Yale U Pr.

Complete Prose Works of Matthew Arnold, 11 vols. Matthew Arnold. Ed. by R. H. Super. Incl. Vol. 1. On the Classical Tradition. LC 60-5018. 282p. 1960. 49.50 (*0-472-11651-7*); Vol. 2. Democratic Education. LC 60-5018. 430p. 1962. 49.50 (*0-472-11652-5*); Vol. 3. Lectures & Essays in Criticism. LC 60-5018. 586p. 1962. 49.50 (*0-472-11653-3*); Vol. 4. Schools & Universities on the Continent. LC 60-5018. 446p. 1964. 49.50 (*0-472-11654-1*); Vol. 5. Culture & Anarchy. LC 60-5018. 580p. 1965. 49.50 (*0-472-11655-X*); Vol. 6. Dissent & Dogma. LC 60-5018. 624p. 1967. 49.50 (*0-472-11656-8*); Vol. 7. God & the Bible. LC 60-5018. 604p. 1970. 49.50 (*0-472-11657-6*); Vol. 8. Essays Religious & Mixed. LC 60-5018. 576p. 1972. 49.50 (*0-472-11658-4*); Vol. 9. English Literature & Irish Politics. LC 60-5018. 1973. 49.50 (*0-472-11659-2*); Vol. 10. Philistinism in England & America. LC 60-5018. 1974. 49.50 (*0-472-11660-6*); Vol. 11. Last Word. LC 60-5018. 1976. 49.50 (*0-472-11661-4*); LC 60-5018. write for info. (*0-318-56091-7*) U of Mich Pr.

Complete Protest Desk Guide. Edward J. Tolchin. 366p. 1992. ring bd. 139.00 (*1-56726-002-0*) Holbrook & Kellogg.

Complete Psionics Handbook. Steve Winter. (Advanced Dungeons & Dragons Ser.). 1991. pap. 15.00 (*1-56076-054-0*) TSR Inc.

Complete Psychological Works: Standard Edition, 24 vols., Set. Sigmund Freud. Ed. & Tr. by James Strachey. (C). 1976. text ed. 895.00 (*0-393-01128-3*) Norton.

***Complete Psychotherapy Treatment Planner: An Options Handbook.** Arthur E. Jongsma et al. (Series in Clinical Personality). 1995. pap. text ed. 29.95 (*0-471-11738-2*) Wiley.

Complete Public Records Guide. 4th ed. Fred D. Knapp. (Illus.). 261p. 1991. pap. 49.95 (*0-9629879-1-3*) REYN.

Complete Public Records Guide: Central & Northern New Jersey. Fred D. Knapp. 180p. 1993. pap. 39.95 (*0-9629879-6-4*) REYN.

Complete Public Records Guide: Real Estate Edition. Fred D. Knapp. (Illus.). 257p. (Orig.). 1991. pap. text ed. 99.00 (*0-9629879-0-5*) REYN.

Complete Public Speaking Handbook for School Administrators. Edward F. Deroche. 1988. text ed. 34.95 (*0-13-162009-6*) P-H.

Complete Published Poems of Nathaniel Tucker, Together with Columbinus: A Mask (1783) Nathaniel Tucker. LC 73-12391. 192p. 1973. lib. bdg. 50.00 (*0-8201-1121-X*) Schol Facsimiles.

***Complete Puccini Libretti, Vol. 1.** Nico Castel. (Illus.). xv, 579p. (Orig.). (C). 1993. pap. text ed. 55.00 (*1-878617-08-7*) Leyerle Pubns.

***Complete Puccini Libretti, Vol. 2.** Nico Castel. (Illus.). xvi, 434p. (Orig.). (C). 1994. pap. text ed. 50.00 (*1-878617-09-5*) Leyerle Pubns.

Complete Pumpkin Cookbook. rev. ed. Helen O. Dandar & Emil B. Dandar. (Illus.). 108p. 1988. pap. text ed. 7.95 (*0-9620818-1-7*) Sterling Specialty.

Complete Pun Book. Art Moger. 256p. 1981. pap. 5.95 (*0-8065-0776-4*, Citadel Pr) Carol Pub Group.

Complete Puppy & Dog Book. Norman H. Johnson. 1993. 10.98 (*0-88365-824-0*) Galahad Bks.

Complete Purim Service. Morris Silverman & Jacob Neusner. pap. 4.95 (*0-87677-064-2*) Prayer Bk.

Complete Puzzle World. Susannah Leigh & Brenda Haw. (Young Puzzles Ser.). (Illus.). 1192p. (J). (gr. 2 up). 1994. pap. 18.95 (*0-7460-1859-2*, Usborne) EDC.

Complete Q & A Job Interview Book. Jeffrey G. Allen. (Orig.). 1988. pap. text ed. 12.95 (*0-471-60135-7*) Wiley.

Complete Q & A Job Interview Book. Jeffrey G. Allen. (Orig.). 1988. text ed. 42.50 (*0-471-60136-5*) Wiley.

Complete Q Modem Toolkit: Everything You Need to Go on-Line. Nick Anis. (Illus.). (Orig.). 1992. pap. 49.95 (*0-13-747544-6*) Brady Compu Bks.

***Complete Q&A Book for the NCLex-CAT-PN.** Patricia A. Hoefler. Ed. by Chellis E. Neal. 384p. (C). Date not set. write for info. (*1-56533-015-3*) M E D S Inc.

Complete Q&A Book for the NCLex-CAT-RN. Patricia A. Hoefler. Ed. by Amy Hummel & Judith Freeman. 409p. (C). Date not set. 29.95 (*1-56533-005-6*) M E D S Inc.

Complete Quality Manual: A Blueprint for Producing Your Own Quality System. Gerry McGoldrick. (Financial Times Management Ser.). 224p. 1994. 62.50x (*0-273-60558-5*, Pub. by Pitman Pub Ltd UK) Trans-Atl Phila.

Complete Queen's Indian. Efim Geller. 296p. 1992. pap. 22.95 (*0-8050-2427-1*, Pub. by Batsford Chess UK) H Holt & Co.

Complete Question & Answer Book of General Nutrition. Gary Null et al. LC 79-187997. (Health Library: Vol. 5). 184p. 1972. 9.95 (*0-8315-0128-6*) Speller.

Complete Question & Answer Book of Natural Therapy. Gary Null et al. LC 75-187996. (Health Library: Vol. 3). 272p. 1972. 9.95 (*0-8315-0127-8*) Speller.

Complete Question & Answer Guide to Hairdressing & Cosmetology. Anthony B. Colletti. 1978. text ed. 16.00 (*0-912126-48-5*, 1258-01); pap. text ed. 15.75 (*0-912126-49-3*, 1258-00) Keystone Pubns.

Complete Ragtime Guitar Book. Stefan Grossman. (Complete Book Ser.). 1993. 12.95 (*1-56222-387-9*, 94640); audio 9.98 (*1-56222-372-0*, 94640) Mel Bay.

Complete Rainbow Guide to OS-9. Dale Puckett & Peter Dibble. Ed. by Lawrence C. Falk & Courtney Noe. (Illus.). 420p. (Orig.). (C). 1985. pap. 19.95 (*0-932471-00-5*) Falsoft.

Complete Rainbow Guide to OS-9 Level II. Dale Puckett & Peter Dibble. Ed. by JoAnne Arnott. (Illus.). (Orig.). 1987. pap. 19.95 (*0-932471-09-9*) Falsoft.

Complete Ranger's Handbook. Rick Swan. (Advanced Dungeons & Dragons, Second Edition; Al-Qadim Ser.). (Illus.). 1993. 18.00 (*1-56076-634-4*) TSR Inc.

Complete Raw Juice Therapy. Thorsons Editorial Board Staff. (Illus.). 128p. 1983. pap. 3.95 (*0-7225-1877-3*) Thorsons SF.

Complete Reading Disabilities Handbook. Wilma H. Miller. 356p. 1993. spiral bd. 29.95 (*0-87628-249-4*) Ctr Appl Res.

Complete Real Estate Investment Handbook. C. F. Sirmans, Jr. & Austin J. Jaffe. write for info. (*0-318-59708-X*) S&S Trade.

Complete Real Estate Math Book. 2nd ed. Margie Sussex & John F. Stapleton. (Illus.). 320p. 1987. pap. text ed. 36.20 (*0-13-162298-6*) P-H.

Complete Records of St. Matthew's Lutheran Church 1844-1932, McVille, Armstrong Co., PA. Peggy C. Cramer. 175p. 1991. pap. text ed. 16.95 (*1-55856-064-5*) Closson Pr.

Complete Recovery Room Book. Anthea Hatfield & Michael Tronson. (Illus.). 400p. 1992. 80.00 (*0-19-262130-0*) OUP.

Complete Recovery Room Book. Anthea Hatfield & Michael Tronson. (Illus.). 400p. 1993. reprint ed. pap. 29.95 (*0-19-262129-7*) OUP.

Complete Reference Guide to United Nations Sales Publications: 1946-1978, 2 vols. E. Birchfield & J. Coolman. 700p. 1982. 115.00 (*0-89111-011-9*) UNIFO Pubs.

Complete Rehabilitation of the Flintlock Rifle. T. B. Tryon. 1987. reprint ed. 5.95 (*0-913150-54-1*) Pioneer Pr.

Complete Reiki Handbook. Walter Lubeck. 256p. (Orig.). 1994. pap. 14.95 (*0-941524-87-6*) Lotus Light.

***Complete Reiki Healing Book: Heal Yourself, Others, & the World Around You.** Brigitte Muller & Horst H. Gunther. LC 94-47299. 1995. 12.95 (*0-940795-16-7*) LifeRhythm.

Complete Relaxation. Steve Kravette. (Illus.). (Orig.). 1979. pap. 10.95 (*0-914918-14-1*, Whitford Pr) Schiffer.

Complete Relaxation Book: A Manual of Eastern & Western Techniques. James Hewitt. 212p. 1992. pap. 17.95 (*0-7126-3096-1*, Pub. by Century UK) Trafalgar.

Complete Report of Mayor La Guardia's Commission on the Harlem Riot of March 19, 1935. Mayor la Guardia's Commission on the Harlem Riot. LC 76-90204. (Mass Violence in America Ser.). 1977. reprint ed. 20.95 (*0-405-01328-0*) Ayer.

Complete Reporter. 6th ed. Julian Harriss et al. (Illus.). 576p. (C). 1992. Other materials avail. pap. write for info. (*0-02-350640-7*) Macmillan.

Complete Research Paper Guide. Dorothy U. Seyler. 1992. pap. text ed. write for info. (*0-07-056351-9*) McGraw.

Complete Restaurateur: A Practical Guide to the Craft & Business of Restaurant Ownership. Elizabeth Lawrence. 240p. (Orig.). 1992. pap. 11.95 (*0-452-26752-8*, Plume) NAL-Dutton.

Complete Resume & Job Search Book for College Students. Bob Adams & Laura Morin. 200p. (Orig.). 1992. pap. 9.95 (*1-55850-188-6*) Adams Pubng.

Complete Resume Book & Job Getter's Guide. Juvenal L. Angel. 1990. mass mkt. 5.99 (*0-671-72564-5*) PB.

Complete Resume Guide. 4th ed. Marian Faux. 192p. (Orig.). 1993. pap. 9.00 (*0-671-84709-0*, Arco Test) P-H Gen Ref & Trav.

***Complete Resume Guide.** 5th ed. Marian Faux. 1995. pap. 8.95 (*0-02-860028-2*) Macmillan.

Complete Retirement Handbook. Forest Bowman. LC 89-22758. 248p. 1989. 25.00 (*0-8131-1710-0*); pap. 15.00 (*0-8131-0192-1*) U Pr of Ky.

Complete Retirement Workshop: Your Guide to Planning a Secure & Rewarding Future. Bureau of Business Practice Editorial Staff. LC 92-37107. 1993. 24.95 (*0-13-501314-3*) Bur Busn Prac.

Complete Review of Radiography. Kathryn M. Marzano & Pauline D. Lyons. LC 86-9117. (Red Bks.). 252p. 1986. pap. text ed. 27.95 (*0-8273-4233-0*) Delmar.

Complete Rhodesian Ridgeback. Peter Nicholson & Janet Parker. (Illus.). 160p. 1991. 25.95 (*0-87605-295-2*) Howell Bk.

Complete Rhyming Dictionary. Clement Wood. 1992. mass mkt. 6.99 (*0-440-21205-7*) Dell.

Complete Rhyming Dictionary. rev. ed. Clement Wood. Ed. by Ronald Bogus & John Duff. 640p. 1991. 25.00 (*0-385-41350-5*) Doubleday.

Complete Richard Allen, Vol. 1. Richard Allen. 288p. (Orig.). 1992. pap. 16.95 (*0-9518497-1-9*, Pub. by S T Pubng UK) AK Pr Dist.

Complete Richard Allen, Vol. 2. Richard Allen. 288p. (Orig.). 1992. pap. 16.95 (*0-9518497-5-1*, Pub. by S T Pubng UK) AK Pr Dist.

Complete Richard Allen, Vol. 3. Richard Allen. 288p. (Orig.). 1992. pap. 16.95 (*0-9518497-7-8*, Pub. by S T Pubng UK) AK Pr Dist.

***Complete Richard Allen, Vol. 4.** Richard Allen. 272p. (Orig.). 1994. pap. 16.95 (*1-898927-15-4*, Pub. by S T Pubng UK) AK Pr Dist.

Complete Roadside Guide to Nebraska. 2nd ed. Alan Boye. (Illus.). 512p. (Orig.). 1993. pap. 18.95 (*0-913473-11-1*) Saltillo Pr.

Complete Robert Bloch: An Illustrated International Bibliography. Randall D. Larson. LC 87-20858. (Illus.). x, 126p. 1987. lib. bdg. 25.00x (*0-8095-6106-9*) Borgo Pr.

Complete Robert Johnson. Woody Mann. (Illus.). 96p. 1991. pap. 12.95 (*0-8256-0314-5*, OK64965, Oak) Music Sales.

Complete Rock & Metal Guitar. Fred Sokolow. Ed. by Aaron Stang. 80p. (Orig.). (YA). 1982. pap. text ed. 16.95 (*0-89898-576-5*) CPP Belwin.

Complete Rock & Pop Keyboard Player. Kenneth Baker. (Illus.). 48p. 1987. pap. 7.95 (*0-8256-1093-1*, AM62696) Music Sales.

Complete Rock Family Trees. Pete Frame. (Illus.). 64p. pap. 25.95 (*0-7119-0465-0*, OP42811) Omnibus NY.

Complete Rock Guitar Book. Mike Christiansen. (Complete Book Ser.). 1993. 15.00 (*1-56222-181-7*, 94560); audio 9.98 (*1-56222-159-0*, 94560) Mel Bay.

Complete Rock Guitar Player, Bk. 1. Steve Tarshis. (Illus.). 32p. 1988. pap. 7.95 (*0-8256-1072-9*, AM63934) Music Sales.

Complete Rock Guitar Player, Bk. 2. (Illus.). 48p. 1988. pap. 7.95 (*0-8256-1073-7*, AM63942) Music Sales.

Complete Rock Guitar Player, Bk. 3. (Illus.). 48p. 1988. pap. 7.95 (*0-8256-1074-5*, AM63959) Music Sales.

Complete Rock Guitar Player, Bk. 4. (Illus.). 48p. 1988. pap. 7.95 (*0-8256-1100-8*, AM63967) Music Sales.

Complete Rock Guitar Player: Chord Book. Len Vogler. (Illus.). 48p. 1989. pap. 6.95 (*0-8256-2546-7*, AM71325) Music Sales.

Complete Rock Guitar Player: Omnibus Edition. (Illus.). 192p. 1988. pap. 17.95 (*0-8256-1168-7*, AM68826) Music Sales.

***Complete Rock 'n' Roll Collection.** Ed. by Carol Cuellar. 256p. (Orig.). (YA). (gr. 9-12). 1994. pap. 16.95 (*0-89898-966-3*) CPP Belwin.

***Complete Rock 'n' Roll Collection.** Warner. 1995. pap. (*0-7604-0084-9*) CPP Belwin.

Complete Romances of Chretien de Troyes. David Staines. LC 90-4060. 576p. 1990. 57.50 (*0-253-35440-4*) Ind U Pr.

Complete Romances of Chretien de Troyes. Ed. & Tr. by David Staines. 1993. pap. 12.95 (*0-253-20787-8*) Ind U Pr.

Complete Roofing. 2nd ed. James E. Brumbaugh. (Illus.). 528p. 1992. text ed. 30.00 (*0-02-517851-2*) Macmillan.

Complete Roommate Handbook: How to Sucessfully Find, Live with & Lose a Roommate. Bruce Brown. (Illus.). 32p. (Orig.). 1982. pap. 5.00 (*0-941256-01-4*) New Lifestyle.

Complete Rottweiler. Muriel Freeman et al. LC 83-22688. (Illus.). 288p. 1984. 25.95 (*0-87605-269-3*) Howell Bk.

Complete Runner. Runner's World Editors. LC 74-83666. (Illus.). 391p. 1974. 7.95 (*0-89037-041-9*) Anderson World.

Complete RV-Auto Buying Guide Series. J. D. Gallant. (Illus.). 448p. 1994. pap. 27.65 (*1-884046-58-4*) Quill Pubng.

***Complete Sailor: Learning the Art of Sailing.** Seidman. 1995. pap. text ed. 15.95 (*0-07-057131-7*) Intl Marine.

Complete Sailor's Log: An All-Purpose Logbook Dedicated to the Prudent Sailor. Lewis R. Hackler. LC 84-91287. (Illus.). 320p. 1985. 19.95 (*0-931595-00-2*) Seascape Enters.

Complete Saki. Intro. by Noel Coward. 960p. 1991. pap. 12.95 (*0-14-018420-1*, Penguin Classics) Viking Penguin.

Complete Salt & Pepper Shaker Book. Mike Schneider. LC 92-63108. (Illus.). 252p. 1993. 49.95 (*0-88740-494-4*) Schiffer.

Complete San Diego Guidebook. B. Sangwan. (California Ser.). (Illus.). 144p. (Orig.). 1994. pap. 8.95 (*0-916841-21-9*) Indian Chief.

Complete San Francisco Bay Area Sightseeing Guide. Rand Richards. LC 94-25847. (Illus.). 224p. (Orig.). 1994. pap. 12.95 (*1-879367-02-5*) Hrtage Hse.

***Complete Sausage Cookbook: How to Make the World's Best Bologna, Salami, Frankfurters, Kielbasa, Bratwurst, Mettwurst, & Chorizo.** Jack Sleight. LC 94-39137. 304p. 1995. 19.95 (*0-8117-0336-3*) Stackpole.

Complete Saxophone Player, Bk. 1. Raphael Ravenscroft. (Illus.). 48p. 1987. pap. 8.95 (*0-7119-0887-7*, AM62712) Music Sales.

Complete Saxophone Player, Bk. 2. Raphael Ravenscroft. (Illus.). 48p. 1987. pap. 8.95 (*0-7119-0888-5*, AM62720) Music Sales.

Complete Saxophone Player, Bk. 3. Raphael Ravenscroft. (Illus.). 48p. 1987. pap. 8.95 (*0-7119-0889-3*, AM62738) Music Sales.

Complete Saxophone Player, Bk. 4. Raphael Ravenscroft. (Illus.). 48p. 1987. pap. 8.95 (*0-7119-0890-7*, AM62746) Music Sales.

Complete Sayings. Hazrat I. Khan. 299p. 1991. reprint ed. pap. 14.95 (*0-930872-39-8*) Omega Pubns NY.

Complete Scales for All Guitarists. Harvey Vinson. 1984. pap. 7.95 (*0-8256-2138-0*) Music Sales.

Complete Scanner Handbook for Desktop Publishing. 2nd ed. David D. Busch. Ed. by Susan Glinert. 425p. (Orig.). 1992. Macintosh ed. 29.00 (*1-55623-576-3*) Irwin Prof Pubng.

Complete Scanner Toolkit: IBM PC with Disk. David D. Busch. 560p. 1991. pap. 44.00 (*1-55623-479-1*) Irwin Prof Pubng.

Complete Scarsdale Medical Diet. Herman Tarnower & Samm S. Baker. 240p. 1982. mass mkt. 6.50 (*0-553-26886-4*) Bantam.

Complete Schipperke. Schipperke Club of America Staff. (Illus.). 256p. 1993. 25.95 (*0-87605-303-7*) Howell Bk.

***Complete School-Age Child Care Resource Kit: Practical Guidelines, Materials, & Activities for Implementing a Quality SACC Program.** Abby B. Bergman et al. LC 94-44935. 1995. spiral bd. 27.95 (*0-87628-268-0*) Ctr Appl Res.

An Asterisk (*) at the beginning of an entry indicates that the title is appearing in BIP for the first time.

C

An Asterisk (*) at the beginning of an entry indicates that the title is appearing in BIP for the first time.

1473

Complete String Quartets. Ludwig van Beethoven. LC 75-104809. 448p. 1970. reprint ed. pap. 14.95 (*0-486-22361-2*) Dover.
Complete String Quartets Transcribed for Four-Hand Piano, 2 series. unabridged ed. Ludwig van Beethoven. 320p. Ser. 1, 320p. pap. 11.95 (*0-486-23974-8*); Ser. 2, 256p. pap. 11.95 (*0-486-23975-6*) Dover.
Complete String Quintets. Wolfgang Amadeus Mozart. 181p. 1978. reprint ed. pap. 8.95 (*0-486-23603-X*) Dover.
Complete Student Assistance Program Handbook: Techniques & Materials for Alcohol-Drug Prevention & Intervention in Grades 7-12. Barbara S. Newsam. LC 92-22749. (Illus.). 302p. 1992. spiral bd. 34.95 (*0-87628-878-6*) Ctr Appl Res.
Complete Student's Handbook. Ed. by Danny Saunders. LC 93-39670. 1994. 17.95 (*0-631-19373-1*) Blackwell Pubs.
Complete Student's Musical. Date not set. 6.95 (*0-685-75010-8*, 95114) Mel Bay.
***Complete Studio Tips for Artists & Graphic Designers.** rev. ed. Bill Gray. (Illus.). 256p. 1996. pap. 20.00 (*0-393-73000-X*, Norton Paperbks) Norton.
Complete Study Editions Library: Collection of 12 Study Guides. 1990. pap. text ed. 59.40 (*1-56271-301-9*) Moonbeam Pubns.
Complete Stylist & Handbook. 3rd ed. Sheridan Baker. 560p. (C). 1989. text ed. 40.50 (*0-06-040442-6*) HarpCollege.
Complete Sun Sign Guide. Bernard Fitzwalter. (Illus.). 512p. (Orig.). 1983. pap. 14.95 (*0-85030-777-5*, Pub. by Aquarian Pr UK) Thorsons SF.
Complete Suntanning Guide. Lex Kuhta. LC 79-64302. (Illus.). 112p. (Orig.). 1980. pap. 4.95 (*0-89037-220-9*) Anderson World.
***Complete Super Bowl Book, 1995.** Sporting News Staff. (Illus.). 1995. pap. 13.95 (*0-89204-523-X*) Sporting News.
Complete Super Bowl Story: Games I-XXIII. Richard J. Brenner. (Great Sports Events Ser.). (Illus.). 112p. (J). (gr. 5 up). 1989. lib. bdg. 15.95 (*0-8225-1503-2*, Lerner Publctns) Lerner Group.
Complete Supreme Court Criminal Digest - Second Cumulative Supplement (July 1987 to Dec. 1990) Surendra Malik. (C). 1991. text ed. 125.00 (*0-89771-494-6*) St Mut.
Complete Supreme Court Criminal Digest, 1950 to June 1987, 7 vols. Ed. by S. Malik. (C). 1989. 660.00 (*0-685-27879-4*) St Mut.
Complete Supreme Court Criminal Digest, 1950 to Present, 8 vols., Set. Surendra Malik. 800p. 1991. 595.00 (*0-317-54849-2*) St Mut.
Complete Supreme Court Criminal Digest, 1950 up to Date, Set, Vols. I, II, III-A, III-B, IV & V. Surendra Malik. (C). 1987. Set. 660.00 (*0-685-37420-3*) St Mut.
Complete Supreme Court Criminal Digest, 1950 up to Date: With Supplement, 1987 Vol., 6 vols., Set, Vols. I, II, III-A, III-B, IV & V. Ed. by Surendra Malik. (C). 1990. Set. 660.00 (*0-685-39731-9*) St Mut.
Complete Supreme Court Criminal Digest, 1950 up to 1990 with 1st & 2nd Supplements, Set. Surendra Malik. (C). 1991. text ed. 950.00 (*0-89771-493-8*) St Mut.
Complete Supreme Court Labour & Services Digest, 4 vols., Set. Surendra Malik. (C). 1987. 360.00 (*0-685-25174-8*) St Mut.
Complete Swimming Pool Reference. Griffiths. 300p. 1994. pap. 39.95 (*0-8016-7182-5*) Mosby Yr Bk.
Complete Sylvie & Bruno: The Mercury House Edition. Lewis Carroll. Ed. by Thomas Christensen. LC 91-9958. (Illus.). 416p. 1991. 30.00 (*1-56279-009-9*) Mercury Hse Inc.
Complete Symphonies in Full Orchestral Score. Johannes Brahms. Ed. by Hans Gal. LC 73-92635. 352p. 1974. reprint ed. pap. 12.95 (*0-486-23053-8*) Dover.
Complete Symphonies in Full Orchestral Score: The Vienna Gesellschaft der Musikfreunde Edition. Johannes Brahms. Ed. by Hans Gal. 16.50 (*0-8446-5010-2*) Peter Smith.
Complete Symphonies in Full Score. Robert Schumann. 1980. reprint ed. pap. 17.95 (*0-486-24013-4*) Dover.
Complete System of Self-Healing: Internal Exercises. Stephen T. Chang. LC 86-1859. (Illus.). 224p. 1986. 21.95 (*0-942196-06-6*) Tao Pub.
Complete Systems Analysis: The Workbook, the Textbook, the Answers, 2 vols. James Robertson & Suzanne Robertson. LC 93-44616. 532p. 1994. 70.00 (*0-932633-25-0*) Dorset Hse Pub Co.
Complete T. Rex: How Stunning New Discoveries Are Changing Our Understanding of the World's Most Famous Dinosaur. John Horner & Don Lessem. 1994. pap. 15.00 (*0-671-89164-2*, Touchstone Bks) S&S Trade.
Complete T. Rex: How Stunning New Discoveries Are Changing Our Understanding of the World's Most Famous Dinosaur. John R. Horner & Don Lessem. LC 93-211. (Illus.). 208p. 1993. 25.00 (*0-671-74185-3*) S&S Trade.
Complete Tae Geuk Hyung. Hee Il Cho. LC 88-92051. 208p. (Orig.). 1988. pap. 15.95 (*0-929015-09-6*) Chos Taekwon Do Pub Hse.
Complete Tae Geuk Hyung. Il Cho Hee. 1990. pap. 15.95 (*0-86568-142-2*) Unique Pubns.
Complete Tae Kwon Do Hyung, 1. Hee Il Cho. LC 88-92053. (Orig.). 1988. 13.95 (*0-929015-04-5*) Chos Taekwon Do Pub Hse.
Complete Tae Kwon Do Hyung, 2. Hee Il Cho. LC 88-92053. (Orig.). 1988. 13.95 (*0-929015-03-7*) Chos Taekwon Do Pub Hse.
Complete Tae Kwon Do Hyung, 3. Hee Il Cho. LC 88-92053. (Orig.). 1988. pap. 13.95 (*0-929015-00-2*) Chos Taekwon Do Pub Hse.
Complete Tae Kwon Do Hyung, Vols. 1-3. Hee Il Cho. (Orig.). 1988. write for info. (*0-318-63114-8*) Chos Taekwon Do Pub Hse.
***Complete Tae Kwon Do Hyung Vol. 1.** Hee I. Cho. 1989. pap. 13.95 (*0-86568-054-X*) Unique Pubns.
***Complete Tae Kwon Do Hyung Vol. 3.** Hee I. Cho. 1989. pap. 12.95 (*0-86568-056-6*) Unique Pubns.
Complete Taekwondo Hyung, 3 vols. Hee I. Cho. (Illus.). 205p. (Orig.). 1984. pap. 13.95 (*0-685-73707-1*); pap. 13.95 (*0-685-73708-X*); pap. 13.95 (*0-685-73709-8*) Unique Pubns.
Complete Tai Chi: The Definitive Guide to Physical & Emotional Self-Improvement. Alfred Huang. (Illus.). 296p. (Orig.). 1992. pap. 19.95 (*0-8048-1897-5*) C E Tuttle.
Complete Tales & Poems (Giant) Edgar Allan Poe. LC 75-9506. 1975. pap. 13.00 (*0-394-71678-7*, Vin) Random.
Complete Tales & Poems of Edgar Allan Poe. Edgar Allan Poe. LC 38-27279. 1977. 15.95 (*0-394-60408-3*, Modern Lib) Random.
Complete Tales & Poems of Edgar Allan Poe. Edgar Allan Poe. LC 92-50231. 1992. 20.00 (*0-679-60007-8*, Modern Lib) Random.
Complete Tales of Beatrix Potter. Beatrix Potter. (Illus.). 384p. (J). (ps-6). 1989. 35.00 (*0-7232-3618-6*) Viking Child Bks.
Complete Tales of Nikolai Gogol: 1923-1985, 2 vols. Nikolai V. Gogol. Ed. by Leonard J. Kent. LC 84-16221. (Illus.). xii, 262p. 1985. reprint ed. Vol. I, xii, 262 p. pap. 11.95 (*0-226-30068-4*); reprint ed. Vol. II, viii, 352 p. pap. 12.95 (*0-226-30069-2*) U Ch Pr.
Complete Tales of Peter Rabbit: And Other Favorite Stories. Beatrix Potter. LC 86-10116. (Illus.). 56p. (J). (gr. k up). 1986. 9.98 (*0-89471-460-0*) Courage Bks.
Complete Tales of Uncle Remus. Joel C. Harris. Ed. by Richard Chase. (Illus.). 832p. (J). (gr. 7 up). 1955. 35.00 (*0-395-06799-5*) HM.
Complete Tales of Voltaire, 3 vols., Set. Voltaire. Tr. by William Walton. LC 89-23768. xx, 988p. 1990. reprint ed. lib. bdg. 95.00 (*0-86527-393-6*) Fertig.
***Complete Talking Machine: A Guide to the Restoration of Antique Phonographs.** Eric L. Reiss. (Illus.). 184p. Date not set. reprint ed. pap. 19.95 (*1-886606-08-0*) Sonoran Pub.
Complete Taste of Life: Better Living Through Better Eating. Julie Stafford. 304p. 1993. 34.95 (*0-8048-1843-6*) C E Tuttle.
Complete Telemarketing Handbook for Recruiting & Retaining Students. Anthony Pappas, Jr. 125p. 1988. pap. 89.00 (*0-912150-16-5*) Magna Pubns.
Complete Tenor Banjo Method. Mel Bay. (Complete Book Ser.). 1993. 9.95 (*1-56222-018-7*, 93236) Mel Bay.
Complete Terry & the Pirates, Vol. 2. Milton Caniff. (Illus.). 96p. 1991. 34.95 (*0-924359-20-X*) Remco Wrldserv Bks.
Complete Testing Program for Fitness & Nutrition: The Winning Combination. 3rd ed. Jane Buch. Ed. by Tate Bard. LC 84-51951. (Illus.). 160p. (YA). (gr. 7-12). 1993. teacher ed, disk 8.66 (*0-914127-48-9*) Univ Class.
Complete Textbook of Lotus 1-2-3. Robin Stark. 320p. (C). 1990. pap. write for info. (*0-675-21103-4*, Merrill Pub Co) Macmillan.
Complete Textbook of Phlebotomy. Lynn B. Hoeltke. LC 93-5846. 216p. 1994. pap. text ed. 24.95 (*0-8273-6231-5*) Delmar.
Complete Thanksgiving Cookbook. Holly Garrison. (Illus.). 320p. 1991. text ed. 22.95 (*0-02-542750-4*) Macmillan.
Complete Theological Works of Herbert Thorndike, 6 Vols. in 10, Set. Herbert Thorndike. LC 76-177454. (Library of Anglo-Catholic Theology: No. 17). reprint ed. 295.00 (*0-404-52150-9*) AMS Pr.
Complete Theories. 2nd rev. ed. A. Robinson. (Studies in Logic & the Foundations of Mathematics: Vol. 46). 130p. 1977. 56.50 (*0-7204-0690-0*, North Holland) Elsevier.
Complete Theory-to-Practice Handbook of Adult Literacy: Curriculum Design & Teaching Approaches. Rena Soifer et al. (Language & Literacy Ser.: No. 1). 224p. (C). 1990. pap. text ed. 18.95 (*0-8077-3028-9*) Tchrs Coll.
Complete Thinking Man's Guide to Handicapping & Training. Katcha Goodwon. 232p. (Orig.). 1983. 19.95 (*0-932896-05-7*) Westcliff Pubns.
Complete Time Traveler. Howard Blumenthal et al. 192p. (Orig.). 1988. 13.95 (*0-89815-284-4*) Ten Speed Pr.
Complete Tomato Cookbook. Mabel Hoffman. 144p. (Orig.). 1994. pap. 9.00 (*1-55788-097-2*, HP Books) Berkley Pub.
Complete Torre Attack. Eric Tangborn. Ed. by Eric Woro. (Illus.). vi, 106p. (Orig.). 1993. pap. 11.95 (*1-879479-14-1*) ICE WA.
Complete Traffic Engineering Handbook. Jerry Nader. 1991. 59.50 (*0-685-61696-7*) Telecom Lib.
Complete Training Course for Altar Guilds. B. Don Taylor. LC 92-40960. (Illus.). 180p. 1993. pap. 19.95 (*0-8192-1593-7*) Morehouse Pub.
Complete Training of Horse & Rider. Alois Podhajsky. 1982. pap. 10.00 (*0-87980-235-9*) Wilshire.
Complete Transcripts of the Clarence Thomas-Anita Hill Hearings: October 11, 12, 13, 1991. Ed. by Anita Miller. 450p. 1994. pap. 19.95 (*0-89733-408-6*) Academy Chi Pubs.
Complete Trapping Guide. Brian Lawler. 1994. pap. 19.95 (*1-56830-098-0*) Hayden.
Complete Travel Marketing Handbook. Andrew Vladimir. 448p. 1989. 59.95 (*0-8442-3156-8*, Passport Bks) NTC Pub Grp.
Complete Treatise on Field Fortification. Dennis H. Mahan. LC 68-54797. 268p. 1969. reprint ed. text ed. 35.00 (*0-8371-0557-9*, MAFF, Greenwood Pr) Greenwood.
Complete Treatise on the Art of Singing, Pt. 1. Manuel Garcia, II. Tr. by Donald V. Paschke. (Music Reprint Ser.). lxi, 221p. 1983. reprint ed. lib. bdg. 42.50 (*0-306-76212-9*) Da Capo.
Complete Treatise on the Art of Singing, Pt. 2. Manuel Garcia, II. Tr. & Pref. by V. Paschke. LC 74-23382. xii, 261p. 1975. reprint ed. lib. bdg. 39.50 (*0-306-70660-1*) Da Capo.
Complete Tree Utilization of Southern Pine. 484p. 1978. 29.00 (*0-935018-01-8*, 610) Forest Prod.
Complete Triad Trainer's Inservice Manual. Joseph S. Renzulli & Sally M. Reis. 140p. 1990. pap. 22.95 (*0-936386-57-6*) Creative Learning.
Complete Triathlon Endurance Training Manual: Swim, Bike, Run, Bragg Bible of Health & Fitness. rev. ed. Patricia Bragg & Bob Johnson. (Illus.). 600p. pap. 16.95 (*0-87790-028-0*) Hlth Sci.
Complete Trip Diary. rev. ed. Marlor Press Editors. (Illus.). 96p. 1994. pap. 8.95 (*0-943400-78-3*) Marlor Pr.
Complete Trumpet Player, Bk. 1. Don Bateman. (Illus.). 48p. 1986. pap. 8.95 (*0-7119-0648-3*, AM39207) Music Sales.
Complete Trumpet Player, Bk. 2. Don Bateman. (Illus.). 48p. 1986. pap. 8.95 (*0-7119-0649-1*, AM39215) Music Sales.
Complete Trumpet Player, Bk. 3. Don Bateman. (Illus.). 48p. 1986. pap. 8.95 (*0-7119-0650-5*, AM39223) Music Sales.
Complete Trumpet Player, Bk. 4. Don Bateman. (Illus.). 48p. 1986. pap. 8.95 (*0-7119-0651-3*, AM39231) Music Sales.
Complete Turbo Programmers Reference: Algorithms. Keith Weiskamp. 1989. text ed. 26.95 (*0-471-61009-7*) Wiley.
***Complete Tutankhamun: The King - The Tomb - The Royal Treasure.** Nicholas Reeves. LC 90-70202. (Illus.). 224p. 1995. pap. 17.95 (*0-500-27810-5*) Thames Hudson.
Complete TV Servicing Handbook. Walter H. Buchsbaum. 464p. 1987. text ed. 32.95 (*0-13-162843-7*) P-H.
Complete "Twenty Thousand Leagues Under the Sea" A New Translation of Jules Verne's Science Fiction Classic. Jules Verne. Tr. & Intro. by Emanuel J. Mickel. (Visions Ser.). (Illus.). 516p. 1992. 29.95 (*0-253-33810-7*) Ind U Pr.
Complete Typing Business Guide: Everything You Need to Know to Start & Successfully Operate a Home Typing Business. Frank Chisenhall. (Illus.). 128p. (Orig.). 1990. pap. 12.95 (*0-9625133-3-4*) Supertext Pub.
Complete Typographer. 224p. 1992. 34.99 (*1-56496-042-0*) Rockport Pubs.
Complete Typographer. Christopher Perfect. 224p. 1992. pap. text ed. 39.20 (*0-13-045667-5*) P-H.
Complete Unabridged Information Manual & Reference Guide to the Oklahoma Non-Coal Mining Industry. Edward W. Rucker. Ed. by Gayle Tommerlin. 198p. 1985. pap. 24.95 (*0-9614352-0-8*) Edw Rucker Ent.
***Complete United States Jewish Travel Guide.** 3rd ed. Oscar Israelowitz. 455p. 1995. 14.95 (*1-878741-23-3*) Israelowitz Pub.
Complete Upholsterer: A Practical Guide to Upholstering Traditional. Carole Thomerson. 1989. pap. 25.00 (*0-679-72599-7*) Knopf.
Complete Vampire Companion: Legend & Lore of the Living Dead. Rosemary E. Guiley & J. B. Macabre. LC 94-10737. 1994. 16.00 (*0-671-85024-5*) Macmillan.
Complete Van Gogh: Paintings, Drawings, Sketches. Jan Hulsker. 500p. 1984. 39.95 (*0-517-44867-X*, Harrison Hse) Random Hse Value.
Complete Vegetable Cookbook. Lorraine Bodger. LC 93-25566. Date not set. 30.00 (*0-517-58671-1*, Harmony) Crown Pub Group.
Complete Vegetarian. Ed. by Sunset Editors. LC 93-84194. 160p. 1993. pap. 14.99 (*0-376-02050-4*) Sunset Menlo Pk.
Complete Vegetarian Campside Cuisine. Carolyn Fortuna. (Illus.). 160p. (Orig.). 1989. pap. 9.95 (*0-929935-07-1*) Countrywomans Pr.
Complete Vegetarian Cookbook. Anne Marshall. (Illus.). 304p. 1993. 34.95 (*0-8048-1974-2*) C E Tuttle.
Complete Vegetarian Cookbook. Charmaine Solomon. (Illus.). 470p. 1991. 35.00 (*0-207-15772-3*, Pub. by Angus & Robertson AT) HarpC.
***Complete Verdi Libretti, Vol. 1.** Nico Castel. (Illus.). xv, 438p. (C). Date not set. text ed. 60.00 (*1-878617-10-9*) Leyerle Pubns.
***Complete Verdi Libretti, Vol. 2.** Nico Castel. (Illus.). (C). 1995. text ed. 60.00 (*1-878617-11-7*) Leyerle Pubns.
***Complete Vermont Outdoor Adventure Guide.** Flip Brown. (Illus.). 248p. (Orig.). 1994. pap. 14.95 (*0-944187-34-X*) N Cartographic.
Complete Video Book. Larry Langman & Paul Spinelli. 1984. pap. 3.95 (*0-685-07892-2*) Zebra.
Complete Video Course. Keith Brookes. 176p. (C). 1990. 60.00 (*1-85283-269-X*, Pub. by Boxtree Ltd UK) St Mut.
***Complete Video Hook-up & Help Guide: A One-on-One, Very Easy-to-Understand Guide on VCR's, Camcorder's, Monitor Receivers, DSS, & Video Editing.** Dan Hale. LC 95-94102. (Illus.). 144p. (Orig.). (C). 1995. lib. bdg. 14.95 (*1-877725-16-1*) Video One Prodns.
Complete View of the Shakespeare Controversy. Clement M. Ingleby. LC 74-170064. reprint ed. 55.00 (*0-404-03484-5*) AMS Pr.
Complete Violin Sonatas. Ludwig Van Beethoven. 1990. pap. 12.95 (*0-486-26277-4*) Dover.
Complete Vitamin Book. Carl Lowe. 320p. (Orig.). 1994. pap. text ed. 5.99 (*0-425-14365-1*) Berkley Pub.
Complete Vizsla. Gay Gottlieb. (Illus.). 160p. 1992. 25.95 (*0-87605-377-0*) Howell Bk.
Complete Waiter & Waitress Training Manual. 3rd ed. Sondra Dahmer & Kurt Kahl. (Illus.). 160p. (C). 1988. pap. 29.95 (*0-442-20484-1*) Van Nos Reinhold.
Complete Walker III. Colin Fletcher. LC 83-48870. (Illus.). 1984. pap. 19.00 (*0-394-72264-7*) Knopf.
Complete Walker III. 3rd ed. Colin Fletcher. LC 83-48870. (Illus.). 1984. 22.95 (*0-394-51962-0*) Knopf.
Complete War Memoirs of Charles de Gaulle: 1940-1946. Charles De Gaulle. Tr. by Richard Howard. (Quality Paperbacks Ser.). 1048p. (C). 1984. reprint ed. pap. 14.95 (*0-306-80227-9*) Da Capo.
Complete Wargames Handbook: How to Play, Design, & Find Them. rev. ed. James F. Dunnigan. (Illus.). 288p. 1992. pap. 12.00 (*0-688-10368-5*, Quill) Morrow.
Complete Warrior: Perspectives of a Karate Sensei, Warrior Within, & Vision of Destiny, 3 vols., Set. Jerry L. Aiello. (Warrior Training Ser.). 1993. pap. text ed. 30.00 (*1-883702-04-6*) Aiello Grp.
***Complete Watercolor Artist.** Sally Harper. 1994. 19.98 (*0-7858-0035-2*) Bk Sales Inc.
Complete Watercolor Book. Wendon Blake. (Illus.). 160p. 1989. 29.95 (*0-89134-315-6*, 30157) North Light Bks.
Complete Waterpower Workout Book: Programs for Fitness, Injury Prevention, & Healing. Lynda Huey & Robert Forster. LC 92-34286. 240p. 1993. pap. 15.95 (*0-679-74554-8*) Random.
Complete Wedding Music Coll. Cpp Belwin Staff. 1993. pap. 16.95 (*0-89898-586-2*) CPP Belwin.
Complete Wedding Organiser & Record. Carol Chapman. 256p. (Orig.). 1993. pap. 19.95 (*0-572-10785-4*, Pub. by W Foulsham UK) Trans-Atl Phila.
Complete Wedding Planner. Edith Gilbert. 256p. 1988. pap. 8.95 (*0-446-38678-2*) Warner Bks.
Complete Wedding Planner. Suzanne Kresse. 160p. (Orig.). 1991. pap. 10.00 (*0-380-76374-5*) Avon.
Complete Wedding Planner. rev. ed. Edith Gilbert. Ed. by Allan Taber. (Illus.). 304p. 1989. 15.95 (*0-8119-0749-X*) LIFETIME.
Complete Wedding Planner: Helpful Choices for the Bride & Groom. Edith Gilbert. LC 93-38936. 1994. 8.99 (*0-517-10156-4*, Pub. by Wings Bks) Random Hse Value.
Complete Wedding Planner: Helpful Choices for the Bride & Groom. rev. ed. Edith Gilbert. 1991. pap. 11.99 (*0-446-39216-2*) Warner Bks.
Complete Wedding Video Organiser. David Owen. 192p. (Orig.). 1993. pap. 19.95 (*0-572-01817-7*, Pub. by W Foulsham UK) Trans-Atl Phila.
Complete Weight Training Book. Bill Reynolds. LC 75-32443. (Illus.). 222p. 1979. pap. 4.95 (*0-89037-149-0*) Anderson World.
Complete Weightloss Workbook: A Self-Help Guide to Permanent Weight Loss Including Food Journal, Weightloss Tips, Low Fat Recipes, Food Values. Debbie Martin. (Illus.). 220p. (Orig.). 1993. pap. 15.95 (*0-9635558-0-4*) Slender Visions.
Complete West Highland White Terrier. 4th ed. John T. Marvin. LC 76-58225. (Complete Breed Book Ser.). (Illus.). 256p. 1977. 25.95 (*0-87605-355-X*) Howell Bk.
Complete White Oxen: Collected Short Fiction. Kenneth Burke. LC 68-17629. 1968. reprint ed. pap. 7.00 (*0-520-00155-9*) U CA Pr.
Complete Whole Grain Cookbook. Carol Gelles. 1991. pap. 14.00 (*1-55611-237-8*, Primus Lib Contemp) D I Fine.
***Complete Who's Who in the Bible.** Ed. by Paul D. Gardner. 496p. 1995. boxed 24.99 (*0-310-49440-0*) Zondervan.
Complete Wicklow Way: A Step-by-Step Guide. rev. ed. J. B. Malone. 127p. 1994. pap. 8.95 (*0-86278-158-2*, Pub. by OBrien Pr IE) Dufour.
Complete Wild Body. Wyndham Lewis. Ed. by Bernard Lafourcade. LC 82-4498. (Illus.). 418p. (Orig.). 1982. 25.00 (*0-87685-552-4*); pap. 15.00 (*0-87685-551-6*) Black Sparrow.
Complete Wilderness Paddler. James W. Davidson & John Rugge. LC 82-40021. 288p. 1982. pap. 12.00 (*0-394-71153-X*, Vin) Random.
Complete Wilderness Training Book. Hugh McManners. LC 93-5686. (Illus.). 192p. 1994. 29.95 (*1-56458-488-7*) Dorling Kindersley.
Complete Will Kit. Jens C. Appel & F. Bruce Gentry. 1990. pap. text ed. 22.95 (*0-471-51295-8*) Wiley.
Complete Wilton Book of Candy. Ed. by Marilynn C. Sullivan & Eugene T. Sullivan. LC 81-11681. (Illus.). 176p. 1981. 12.99 (*0-912696-18-4*) Wilton.
Complete Wine Country Guidebook. 3rd ed. B. Sangwan. (California Ser.). (Illus.). 152p. 1992. pap. 8.95 (*0-916841-28-6*) Indian Chief.
***Complete Wine Country Guidebook.** 4th ed. Indian Chief Travel Guides Staff. 1994. pap. 9.95 (*0-916841-53-7*) Indian Chief.
Complete Wine Country Guidebook. 4th ed. B. Sangwan. (California Ser.). (Illus.). 152p. 1994. pap. 9.95 (*0-916841-38-3*) Indian Chief.
Complete Wok & Stir Fry Cookbook. Angelika Ilies. 1994. 12.98 (*0-7858-0070-0*) Bk Sales Inc.
Complete Wok Cook Book. LC 87-83244. (Illus.). 160p. 1988. 15.99 (*0-376-02049-0*) Sunset Menlo Pk.
***Complete Woman: Being a Whole Person.** Patricia Gundry. 240p. 1995. pap. 11.95 (*1-882169-03-4*) Suitcase Bks.
Complete Woman Runner. Runner's World Editors. LC 78-58048. (Illus.). 440p. 1979. 12.00 (*0-89037-143-1*) Anderson World.
***Complete Woman's Herbal: A Manual of Healing Herbs & Nutrition for Personal Well-Being & Family Care.** Anne McIntyre. LC 94-29291. (Reference Bks.). 1995. pap. 25.00 (*0-8050-3537-0*) H Holt & Co.
Complete Women's Weight Training Guide. Edie Leen. LC 78-64384. (Illus.). 160p. 1980. pap. 6.95 (*0-89037-161-X*) Anderson World.
Complete Woodcuts of Albrecht Durer. Albrecht Durer. Ed. by Willi Kurth. (Illus.). 1963. pap. 10.95 (*0-486-21097-9*) Dover.

An Asterisk (*) at the beginning of an entry indicates that the title is appearing in BIP for the first time.

Complete Woodfinishing. Ian Hosker. (Illus.). 192p. 1993. pap. 14.95 (0-946819-33-5, Pub. by Guild Mstr Craftsman UK) Sterling.

Complete Woodworker. Bernard E. Jones. LC 80-634. (Illus.). 416p. 1980. 16.95 (0-89815-034-5); pap. 9.95 (0-89815-022-1) Ten Speed Pr.

Complete Word & Phrase Concordance to the Poems & Songs of Robert Burns, Incorporating a Glossary of Scotch Words. J. B. Reid. (BCL1-PR English Literature Ser.). 568p. 1992. reprint ed. lib. bdg. 99.00 (0-7812-7468-0) Rprt Serv.

Complete Word Book: The Practical Guide to Anything & Everything You Need to Know about Words & How to Use Them. Mary A. DeVries. 512p. 1991. 29.95 (0-13-161902-0, Busn) P-H.

Complete Word-Indexes to J. van den Vondel's Bespiegelingen van Godt en Godtsdienst & Lucifer: With Ranking Lists of Frequencies, Reverse Indexes & Rhyming Indexes. P. K. King. LC 74-183525. (Literary & Linguistic Computing Center Publications Ser.: Vol. 2). 602p. reprint ed. pap. 171.60 (0-317-09547-1, 2050723) Bks Demand.

Complete Word Study Bible (New Testament) Ed. by Spiros Zodhiates. 1293p. 1992. text ed. 29.99 (0-529-07184-3) World Bible.

Complete Word Study Dictionary. Spiros Zodhiates. 1992. 34.99 (0-529-07310-2); Indexed. 38.99 (0-529-07330-7) World Bible.

Complete Word Study O. T. Ed. by Spiros Zodhiates. 2700p. 1994. 39.99 (0-529-10058-4) World Bible.

Complete Word Study Old Testament. Ed. by AMG Publishers Staff. 1994. 44.99 (0-89957-665-6) AMG Pubs.

***Complete Wordbook.** Mike Baron & Brian Sheppard. 300p. 1994. pap. text ed. 27.50 (0-614-04596-7) Wordbks & Listmats.

Complete Work-at-Home Companion. Herman Holtz. 354p. 1990. pap. 15.95 (1-55958-010-0) Prima Pub.

Complete Work-at-Home Companion: Everything You Need to Know to Prosper as a Home-Based Entrepreneur or Employee. 2nd rev. ed. Herman Holtz. LC 93-17735. 1993. 14.95 (1-55958-347-9) Prima Pub.

Complete Work of Amy Kashiwabara: Pocket Meteors, Vol. II. Amy Kashiwabara. 64p. 1994. pap. text ed. 3.00 (1-879665-18-2) Cyborg Prods.

***Complete Worker's Compensation Guide for Texas Physicians.** Barbara A. Langham. (Illus.). 150p. 1994. student ed 149.00 (0-9640262-3-6) TX Med Assn.

Complete Workplace Violence Prevention Manual. Ed. by Jurg W. Mattman & Steve Kaufer. (Illus.). 400p. 1994. student ed 149.00 (0-9637790-5-2) Inter-Act Assocs.

Complete Works, 10 vols. Helene P. Blavatsky. 1972. 4,000.00 (0-87968-918-8) Gordon Pr.

Complete Works, 12 vols. William C. Brann. 1974. 2,000.00 (0-8490-1658-4) Gordon Pr.

Complete Works, 2 vols. Anthony Holborne. Ed. by Masakata Kanazawa. Incl. Vol. 1. Music for Lute & Bandora. LC 67-14341. (Illus.). 196p. 1967. 26.50 (0-674-15500-9); Vol. 2. Music for Cittern. LC 67-14341. 192p. 1974. 22.00 (0-674-15512-2); LC 67-14341. (Publications in Music Ser.: Nos. 1, 5). write for info. (0-318-53032-5) HUP.

Complete Works, 18 vols. Friedrich Nietzsche. 1974. 300.00 (0-87968-173-X) Gordon Pr.

Complete Works, 4 vols. Harold Pinter. 251p. 1990. Vol. 1, 251p. pap. 10.95 (0-8021-5096-9); Vol. 2, 248p. pap. 10.95 (0-8021-3237-5); Vol. 3, 248p. pap. 10.95 (0-8021-5049-7); Vol. 4, 384p. pap. 10.95 (0-8021-5050-0) Grove-Atltic.

Complete Works. Arthur Rimbaud. Tr. by Paul Schmidt. 1976. pap. 13.00 (0-06-090490-9, CN490, PL) HarpC.

Complete Works. Tacitus. Ed. by Moses Hadas. (Modern Library College Editions). (YA). 1964. pap. text ed. write for info. (0-07-553639-0, T53) McGraw.

Complete Works. John Wilmot. (Illus.). 464p. 1994. 11.95 (0-14-042362-1, Penguin Classics) Viking Penguin.

Complete Works, 12 vols. William Beveridge. LC 72-39437. (Library of Anglo-Catholic Theology: No. 2). reprint ed. write for info. (0-404-52040-5) AMS Pr.

Complete Works. John C. Calhoun. (Works of John Calswell Calhoun Ser.). 1990. reprint ed. lib. bdg. 79.00 (0-7812-2240-0) Rprt Serv.

Complete Works. Benjamin Franklin. (Notable American Authors Ser.). 1992. reprint ed. lib. bdg. 75.00 (0-7812-2895-6) Rprt Serv.

Complete Works. Thomas Reid. Ed. by Sir William Hamiliton. 1986. reprint ed. lib. bdg. 45.00 (0-935005-68-4) Lincoln-Rembrandt.

Complete Works, 4 vols, 1. John Vanbrugh. Ed. by Bonamy Dobree & Geoffrey Webb. LC 28-18054. (Chertsey Worthies' Library). reprint ed. write for info. (0-404-06761-1) AMS Pr.

Complete Works, 4 vols, 2. John Vanbrugh. Ed. by Bonamy Dobree & Geoffrey Webb. LC 28-18054. (Chertsey Worthies' Library). reprint ed. write for info. (0-404-06762-X) AMS Pr.

Complete Works, 4 vols, 3. John Vanbrugh. Ed. by Bonamy Dobree & Geoffrey Webb. LC 28-18054. (Chertsey Worthies' Library). reprint ed. write for info. (0-404-06763-8) AMS Pr.

Complete Works, 4 vols, 4. John Vanbrugh. Ed. by Bonamy Dobree & Geoffrey Webb. LC 28-18054. (Chertsey Worthies' Library). reprint ed. write for info. (0-404-06764-6) AMS Pr.

Complete Works, Set. LC 84-90478. (Orig.). 1985. pap. write for info. (0-930759-04-4) D Lekas.

Complete Works, 11 vols, Set. Lancelot Andrewes. Ed. by J. P. Wilson & J. Bliss. LC 78-158257. (BCL Ser.: No. 1). reprint ed. 907.50 (0-404-52020-0) AMS Pr.

Complete Works, 4 vols., Set. William Congreve. (BCL1-PR English Literature Ser.). 1992. reprint ed. lib. bdg. 300.00 (0-7812-7333-1) Rprt Serv.

Complete Works, 12 Vols, Set. Ralph Waldo Emerson. Ed. by Edward W. Emerson. LC 79-15830. (Centenary Edition Ser.). reprint ed. write for info. (0-404-05480-3) AMS Pr.

Complete Works, 16 vols., Set. Ralph Waldo Emerson. (Notable American Authors Ser.). 1992. reprint ed. lib. bdg. 840.00 (0-7812-2816-6) Rprt Serv.

Complete Works, 2 Vols, Set. George Farquhar. Ed. by Charles Stonehill. LC 67-28475. 888p. 1967. reprint ed. 150.00 (0-87752-032-1) Gordian.

Complete Works, 16 vols., Set. Henry Fielding. (BCL1-PR English Literature Ser.). 1992. reprint ed. lib. bdg. 1,440.00 (0-7812-7350-1) Rprt Serv.

Complete Works, 10 vols., Set. Benjamin Franklin. 1993. reprint ed. lib. bdg. 750.00 (0-7812-5459-0) Rprt Serv.

Complete Works, 2 vols., Set. George Gascoigne. (BCL1-PR English Literature Ser.). 1992. reprint ed. lib. bdg. 150.00 (0-7812-7209-2) Rprt Serv.

Complete Works, 2 vols., Set. George Gascoigne. LC 07-42099. 1968. reprint ed. 39.00 (0-403-00089-0) Scholarly.

Complete Works, 2 vols., Set. George Gascoigne. Ed. by John W. Cunliffe. (Anglistica & Americana Ser.: No. 82). 1974. reprint ed. 161.20 (3-487-05082-X, Pub. by Georg Olms GW) Lubrecht & Cramer.

Complete Works, 10 vols., Set. Henry George. LC 75-168107. (Chertsey Worthies' Library). reprint ed. 675.00 (0-404-02800-4) AMS Pr.

Complete Works, 4 vols., Set. John Gower. (BCL1-PR English Literature Ser.). 1992. reprint ed. lib. bdg. 300.00 (0-7812-7182-7) Rprt Serv.

Complete Works, 16 vols., Set Walter S. Landor. (BCL1-PR English Literature Ser.). 1992. reprint ed. lib. bdg. 1,440.00 (0-7812-7587-3) Rprt Serv.

Complete Works, 3 Vols, Set. Thomas Otway. Ed. by Montague Summers. LC 27-20965. (Chertsey Worthies' Library). reprint ed. 210.00 (0-404-04860-9) AMS Pr.

Complete Works, 10 vols., Set. Percy Bysshe Shelley. (BCL1-PR English Literature Ser.). 1992. reprint ed. lib. bdg. 900.00 (0-7812-7648-9) Rprt Serv.

Complete Works, 7 Vols, Set. Richard Sibbes. Ed. by A. B. Grosart. LC 74-176017. (Chertsey Worthies' Library). reprint ed. 140.00 (0-404-06060-9) AMS Pr.

Complete Works, 4 vols., Set. Sir Philip Sidney. (BCL1-PR English Literature Ser.). 1992. reprint ed. lib. bdg. 375.00 (0-7812-7219-X) Rprt Serv.

Complete Works, 20 vols., Set. Algernon C. Swinburne. (BCL1-PR English Literature Ser.). 1992. reprint ed. lib. bdg. 1,800.00 (0-7812-7674-8) Rprt Serv.

Complete Works, 4 vols, Set. John Vanbrugh. Ed. by Bonamy Dobree & Geoffrey Webb. LC 28-18054. (Chertsey Worthies' Library). reprint ed. 225.00 (0-404-06760-3) AMS Pr.

Complete Works, 7 Vols. in 8, Set. Thomas Wilson. LC 73-178307. (Library of Anglo-Catholic Theology: No. 18). reprint ed. 235.00 (0-404-52170-3) AMS Pr.

Complete Works, 2 vols. in one, Set, Vols. 1 & 2. Jack Wikoff. 472p. 1983. Set. 20.00 (0-685-10189-4) Station Hill Pr.

Complete Works, Vol. 1. Danny Lekas. LC 84-90478. (Orig.). 1984. pap. 2.00 (0-930759-00-1) D Lekas.

Complete Works, Vol. 2. Danny Lekas. LC 84-90478. (Orig.). 1985. pap. 2.00 (0-930759-01-X) D Lekas.

Complete Works, Vol. 3. LC 84-90478. (Orig.). 1985. pap. 2.00 (0-930759-02-8) D Lekas.

Complete Works, Vol. 4. LC 84-90478. (Orig.). 1985. pap. 2.00 (0-930759-03-6) D Lekas.

Complete Works & Letters. Georg Buchner. (German Library: Vol. 28). 320p. 1986. 29.50 (0-8264-0300-X); pap. text ed. 14.95 (0-8264-0301-8) Continuum.

Complete Works & Letters of Burns, 2 vols., Set. M. Mackay. (C). 1988. 290.00 (0-907526-33-0, Alloway Pub) St Mut.

Complete Works & Life of Laurence Sterne, 12 vols. in 6. Laurence Sterne. Ed. by Wilbur L. Cross. reprint ed. 67.50 (0-318-50542-8) AMS Pr.

Complete Works & Life of Laurence Sterne, 12 vols. in 6, Set. Laurence Sterne. Ed. by Wilbur L. Cross. LC 78-118949. reprint ed. 405.00 (0-404-07790-0) AMS Pr.

***Complete Works (And Other Stories)** Augusto Monterroso. Tr. by Edith Grossman. LC 95-14550. (Texas Pan American Ser.). 1995. write for info. (0-292-75183-4); pap. write for info. (0-292-75184-2) U of Tex Pr.

Complete Works, Ed. by F. L. Lucas, 4 vols., Set. John Webster. (BCL1-PR English Literature Ser.). 1992. reprint ed. lib. bdg. 300.00 (0-7812-7314-5) Rprt Serv.

Complete Works for Pianoforte Solo, 2 vols., 1. Felix Mendelssohn. 416p. 1975. pap. 10.95 (0-486-23136-4) Dover.

Complete Works for Pianoforte Solo, 2 vols., 2. Felix Mendelssohn. 416p. 1975. pap. 10.95 (0-486-23137-2) Dover.

Complete Works in Prose & Verse, 3 vols., Set. Francis Quarles. (BCL1-PR English Literature Ser.). 1992. reprint ed. lib. bdg. 225.00 (0-7812-7395-1) Rprt Serv.

Complete Works in Prose & Verse of Francis Quarles see Chertsey Worthies Library

Complete Works in Verse & Prose of Abraham Cowley see Chertsey Worthies Library

Complete Works in Verse & Prose of Andrew Marvell, 4 vols., Set. Andrew Marvell. LC 77-181955. (Fuller Worthies' Library). reprint ed. 345.00 (0-404-04270-8) AMS Pr.

Complete Works in Verse & Prose of Andrew Marvell, 4 vols., Set. Andrew Marvell. (BCL1-PR English Literature Ser.). 1992. reprint ed. lib. bdg. 300.00 (0-7812-7372-2) Rprt Serv.

Complete Works in Verse & Prose of George Herbert, 3 vols., 1. George Herbert. LC 73-21066. (Fuller Worthies' Library). reprint ed. write for info. (0-404-11490-3) AMS Pr.

Complete Works in Verse & Prose of George Herbert, 3 vols., 2. George Herbert. LC 73-21066. (Fuller Worthies' Library). reprint ed. write for info. (0-404-11491-1) AMS Pr.

Complete Works in Verse & Prose of George Herbert, 3 vols., 3. George Herbert. LC 73-21066. (Fuller Worthies' Library). reprint ed. write for info. (0-404-11492-X) AMS Pr.

Complete Works in Verse & Prose of George Herbert, 3 vols., Set. George Herbert. LC 73-21066. (Fuller Worthies' Library). reprint ed. 229.50 (0-404-11489-X) AMS Pr.

Complete Works of Alejandro Tapia y Rivera, 3 vols., Set. Alejandro Tapia & Rivera. (Puerto Rico Ser.). 1979. lib. bdg. 300.00 (0-8490-2887-6) Gordon Pr.

Complete Works of Amy Kashiwabara, Vol. I: BUG. Amy Kashiwabara. 64p. 1994. pap. text ed. 3.00 (1-879665-16-6) Cyborg Prods.

Complete Works of Antonio S. Pedreira, 2 vols., Set. Antonio S. Pedreira. (Puerto Rico Ser.). 1979. lib. bdg. 400.00 (0-8490-2888-4) Gordon Pr.

Complete Works of Aristotle: The Revised Oxford Translation, 2 Vols., Set. Aristotle. Ed. by Jonathan Barnes. LC 82-5317. (Bollingen Ser.: Vol. LXXI, No. 2). 3762p. 1984. 79.00 (0-691-09950-2) Princeton U Pr.

Complete Works of Artemus Ward. Charles F. Browne. 1993. reprint ed. lib. bdg. 89.00 (0-7812-5346-2) Rprt Serv.

Complete Works of Captain John Smith, 1580-1631:, 3 vols. John Smith et al. Ed. by Philip L. Barbour & Thad W. Tate. (Illus.). xi, 513p. 1986. Vol. III, xi, 513p. write for info. (0-318-59863-9); Vol. I, lxxii, 448p. write for info. (0-318-59861-2); Vol. II, xii, 488p. write for info. (0-318-59862-0) U of NC Pr.

Complete Works of Captain John Smith, 1580-1631:, 3 vols., Set. John Smith et al. Ed. by Philip L. Barbour & Thad W. Tate. LC 81-10364. (Institute of Early American History & Culture Ser.). (Illus.). 1986. 195.00 (0-8078-1525-X) U of NC Pr.

Complete Works of Christopher Marlowe: Dr. Faustus, Vol. II. Christopher Marlowe. Ed. by Roma Gill. (Oxford English Texts Ser.). (Illus.). 184p. 1990. 69.00 (0-19-812769-3) OUP.

Complete Works of Christopher Marlowe: Edward II, Vol. III. Christopher Marlowe. LC 94-9290. (English Texts Ser.). (Illus.). 188p. 1995. 59.00 (0-19-812278-0, Clarendon Pr) OUP.

***Complete Works of Christopher Marlowe Vol. IV: The Jew of Malta.** Christopher Marlowe. Ed. by Roma Gill. (Oxford English Texts Ser.). (Illus.). 180p. 1995. 55.00 (0-19-812770-7) OUP.

Complete Works of Chuang Tzu. Chuang Tzu. Tr. by Burton Watson. LC 68-19000. (Translations from the Oriental Classics Ser.). 397p. 1968. text ed. 47.00 (0-231-03147-5) Col U Pr.

Complete Works of Concha Melendez, 5 vols., Set. Concha Melendez. (Puerto Rico Ser.). 1979. lib. bdg. 1,000.00 (0-8490-2889-2) Gordon Pr.

Complete Works of Count Tolstoy, 24 Vols, Set. Leo Tolstoy. Tr. by Leo Wiener. LC 74-149669. reprint ed. 2,100.00 (0-404-06580-5) AMS Pr.

Complete Works of E. M. Bounds on Prayer, 8 Bks. E. M. Bounds. 560p. 1990. 19.99 (0-8010-0985-5) Baker Bk.

Complete Works of Edgar Allan Poe, 17 vols., Set. Edgar Allan Poe. Ed. by James A. Harrison. LC 79-15593. reprint ed. 695.00 (0-404-09400-7) AMS Pr.

Complete Works of Elizabeth Barrett Browning, 6 Vols, Set. Elizabeth Barrett Browning. Ed. by Charlotte Porter & Helen A. Clarke. LC 74-148759. reprint ed. 545.00 (0-404-08840-6) AMS Pr.

***Complete Works of Elizabeth of the Trinity, Vol. 2.** Tr. by Anne E. Nash. LC 84-3748. 400p. (Orig.). 1995. pap. 12.95 (0-935216-54-5) ICS Pubns.

Complete Works of Elizabeth of the Trinity: Major Spiritual Writings, Vol. 1. Tr. by Aletheia Kane. LC 84-3748. (Illus.). 208p. (Orig.). 1984. pap. 6.95 (0-935216-01-4) ICS Pubns.

Complete Works of Enrique Laguerre, 2 vols., Set. Enrique Laguerre. (Puerto Rico Ser.). 1975. 250.00 (0-8490-2890-6) Gordon Pr.

Complete Works of Eugenio Maria De Hostos, 20 vols., Set. Eugenio M. De Hostos. (Puerto Rico Ser.). 1979. lib. bdg. 50.00 (0-8490-2891-4) Gordon Pr.

Complete Works of Francis A. Schaeffer. Francis A. Schaeffer. LC 84-72010. 2250p. 1985. pap. 75.00 (0-89107-331-0) Crossway Bks.

Complete Works of Francois Rabelais. Francois Rabelais. Tr. by Donald M. Frame. 1114p. 1991. 75.00 (0-520-06400-3) U CA Pr.

Complete Works of George Farquhar in Two Volumes, 2 vols., Set. George Farquhar. (BCL1-PR English Literature Ser.). 1992. reprint ed. lib. bdg. 150.00 (0-7812-7349-8) Rprt Serv.

Complete Works of George Savile, First Marquess of Halifax. George S. Halifax. LC 76-105080. (Illus.). 1970. reprint ed. 39.50 (0-678-00605-9) Kelley.

***Complete Works of Goswami Tulsidas Vol. 2: Vinaya Patrika (A Letter of Plaint)** Tr. by S. P. Bahadur. (C). 1995. reprint ed. 29.00x (81-215-0650-6, Pub. by Munshiram Manoharial II) S Asia.

***Complete Works of Goswami Tulsidassa Vol. 1: Ramacharitmanasa.** Tulsidas. Tr. by S. P. Bahadur. (C). 1995. 32.00x (81-215-0635-2, Pub. by Munshiram Manoharial II) S Asia.

***Complete Works of H. Emilie Cady.** H. Emilie Cady. Ed. by Michael Maday. 360p. 1995. pap. 13.95 (0-87159-029-8) Unity Bks.

Complete Works of Hugo Margenat. Hugo Margenat. (Puerto Rico Ser.). 1979. lib. bdg. 600.00 (0-8490-2892-2) Gordon Pr.

Complete Works of James Whitcomb Riley, 6 vols., Set. James W. Riley. LC 74-153347. (Illus.). reprint ed. 435.00 (0-404-05340-8) AMS Pr.

Complete Works of John Cosin, 5 Vols, Set. John Cosin. LC 72-1028. (Library of Anglo-Catholic Theology: No. 5). reprint ed. write for info. (0-404-52080-4) AMS Pr.

Complete Works of John Davies see Chertsey Worthies Library

Complete Works of John Gower, 4 vols., Set. John Gower. Ed. by G. C. Macaulay. LC 01-21828. 1968. reprint ed. 250.00 (0-403-00087-4) Scholarly.

Complete Works of John Keats, 5 Vols. John Keats. Ed. by H. Buxton Forman. reprint ed. 19.50 (0-318-50543-6) AMS Pr.

Complete Works of John Keats, 5 vols., Set. John Keats. Ed. by H. Buxton Forman. LC 76-128980. reprint ed. write for info. (0-404-03650-3) AMS Pr.

Complete Works of John Lyly, 3 vols., Set. John Lyly. (BCL1-PR English Literature Ser.). 1992. reprint ed. lib. bdg. 225.00 (0-7812-7212-2) Rprt Serv.

Complete Works of John Webster, 4 Vols, Set. John Webster. Ed. by F. L. Lucas. LC 66-20023. 1328p. 1966. reprint ed. 250.00 (0-87752-119-0) Gordian.

Complete Works of Jose De Diego, 2 vols., Set. Jose De Diego. (Puerto Rico Ser.). 1979. lib. bdg. 250.00 (0-8490-2893-0) Gordon Pr.

Complete Works of Josephus. Flavius Josephus. Tr. by William Whiston. LC 60-15405. 840p. (C). 1974. 19.99 (0-8254-2951-X); pap. 15.99 (0-8254-2952-8) Kregel.

Complete Works of Josephus, 4 vols, Set. Flavius Josephus. 1993. 59.95 (0-8010-5056-1) Baker Bk.

Complete Works of Joshua Sylvester see Chertsey Worthies Library

Complete Works of Justin Morgan: A Collection of Fuging Tunes, Anthems ... Etc., 4 vols. rev. ed. Intro. by James G. Chapman. (Vermont Harmony Ser.: Vol. 1). 92p. 1990. reprint ed. pap. 7.50 (0-937243-05-1) Chapman Assocs.

Complete Works of Justin Morgan: A Collection of Fuging Tunes, Anthems ... Etc., 4 vols., Set. rev. ed. Intro. by James G. Chapman. (Vermont Harmony Ser.: Vol. 1). 92p. 1990. reprint ed. pap. write for info. (0-937243-00-0) Chapman Assocs.

Complete Works of Kate Chopin. Kate Chopin. Ed. by Per Seyersted. LC 73-80043. (Southern Literary Studies). 1032p. 1969. text ed. 90.00 (0-8071-0849-9) La State U Pr.

Complete Works of Lao Tzu: Tao Teh Ching & Hua Hu Ching. Hua-Ching Ni. LC 79-88745. 212p. 1979. reprint ed. pap. 12.95 (0-937064-00-9) SevenStar Comm.

Complete Works of Lewis Carroll. Lewis Carroll. LC 36-27494. 1293p. 1979. 15.95 (0-394-60485-7, Modern Lib) Random.

Complete Works of Lewis Carroll. Lewis Carroll. 1993. 21.00 (0-679-42575-6) McKay.

Complete Works of Lola Rodriguez De Tio, 3 vols., Set. Lola R. De Tio. (Puerto Rico Ser.). 1979. lib. bdg. 300.00 (0-8490-2894-9) Gordon Pr.

Complete Works of Luis Llorens Torres, 3 vols., Set. Luis L. Torres. (Puerto Rico Ser.). 1979. lib. bdg. 600.00 (0-8490-2895-7) Gordon Pr.

Complete Works of Luis Munoz Rivera, 9 vols., Set. Luis M. Rivera. (Puerto Rico Ser.). 1979. lib. bdg. 1,350.00 (0-8490-2896-5) Gordon Pr.

Complete Works of Manuel Corchado y Juarbe, 2 vols., Set. Manuel Corchado y Juarbe. (Puerto Rico Ser.). 1979. lib. bdg. 250.00 (0-8490-2897-3) Gordon Pr.

Complete Works of Manuel Zeno Gandia, 2 vols., Set. Manual Z. Gandia. (Puerto Rico Ser.). 1979. lib. bdg. 250.00 (0-8490-2898-1) Gordon Pr.

Complete Works of Marcel Duchamp. 3rd rev. ed. Arturo Schwarz. (Illus.). 750p. 1993. 200.00 (0-929445-02-3) D Greenidge Editions.

Complete Works of Marcus Uteris. Larry L. Meyer. LC 87-10325. 176p. 1987. 15.00 (0-942273-03-6) Calafia Pr.

Complete Works of Miguel Melendez Munoz, 3 vols., Set. Miguel M. Munoz. (Puerto Rico Ser.). 1979. lib. bdg. 350.00 (0-8490-2899-X) Gordon Pr.

Complete Works of Montaigne: Essays, Travel Journal, Letters. Michel De Montaigne. Tr. by Donald M. Frame. xxvi, 1094p. 1957. 57.50 (0-8047-0484-8) Stanford U Pr.

Complete Works of Mustapha Al Manfaloute: Al Thagharat, 3 Vols. (ARA.). 1982. 45.00 (0-86685-368-5) Intl Bk Ctr.

Complete Works of Oliver W. Holmes, 13 vols., Set. Oliver W. Holmes. 1987. reprint ed. lib. bdg. 795.00 (0-7812-1360-6) Rprt Serv.

Complete Works of Oliver Wendell Holmes, 13 vols. Oliver W. Holmes. (Illus.). 1972. reprint ed. 39.00 (0-318-68143-9) Scholarly.

Complete Works of Oliver Wendell Holmes, 13 vols., Set. Oliver W. Holmes. LC 73-108494. (Illus.). 1972. reprint ed. 795.00 (0-403-00472-1) Scholarly.

Complete Works of Oscar Wilde. Oscar Wilde. LC 89-45117. 1216p. 1989. pap. 22.00 (0-06-096393-X, PL 6393, PL) HarpC.

Complete Works of Philippe De Monte, Set. Incl. Vol. 30. Missa "Sine nomine" 6 vocum. 1965. pap. 37.50 (0-8450-1530-3); Vol. 31. Missa "Sine nomine" 6 vocum. 1965. pap. 37.50 (0-8450-1531-1); 1966. Set pap. 575.00 (0-685-00888-6) Broude.

Complete Works of Philippe de Monte, Set.

***Complete Works of Plato.** Plato. 1995. 19.00 (0-679-60164-3) Random.

Complete Works of Plotinus with Concordance, 4 vols. Plotinus. Ed. by K. S. Guthrie. 1977. lib. bdg. 1,000.00 (0-8490-1659-2) Gordon Pr.

C

An Asterisk (*) at the beginning of an entry indicates that the title is appearing in BIP for the first time.

1475

Complete Works of Ram Chandra. Ram Chandra. 400p. 1989. 15.00 (*0-945242-08-5*) Shri Ram Chandra.

Complete Works of Ram Chandra, Vol. II. Ram Chandra. 400p. 1991. 15.00 (*0-945242-09-3*) Shri Ram Chandra.

Complete Works of Rather of Verona. Tr. by Peter L. Reid. (Medieval & Renaissance Texts & Studies: Vol. 76). 1991. 40.00 (*0-86698-087-3*, MR76) MRTS.

Complete Works of Richard Crashaw, 2 vols., Set. Richard Crashaw. LC 73-21062. (Fuller Worthies' Library). (Illus.). reprint ed. 153.00 (*0-404-11479-2*) AMS Pr.

Complete Works of Richard Sibbes see Work of Richard Sibbes

Complete Works of Robert & James Adam. David King. (Illus.). 440p. 1992. 130.00 (*0-7506-1286-X*, Butterwrth Archit) Buttrwrth-Heinemann.

Complete Works of Robert Browning: With Variant Readings & Annotations, Vol. V. Robert Browning. Ed. by Roma A. King, Jr. et al. LC 68-18389. (Illus.). xxiv, 395p. 1981. 65.00 (*0-8214-0220-X*, 82-82261) Ohio U Pr.

Complete Works of Robert Browning: With Variant Readings & Annotations, Vol. VII. Ed. by Jack W. Herring. LC 68-18389. (Illus.). 320p. 1985. text ed. 65.00 (*0-8214-0230-7*) Ohio U Pr.

Complete Works of Robert Browning, with Variant Readings & Annotations, 4 vols. Robert Browning. Ed. by Roma A. King, Jr. et al. Incl. Vol. 1. LC 68-18389. xx, 306p. 1969. 65.00 (*0-8214-0049-5*); Vol. 2. LC 68-18389. xx, 422p. 1971. 65.00 (*0-8214-0074-6*); Vol. 3. LC 68-18389. xxviii, 397p. 1972. 65.00 (*0-8214-0084-3*); LC 68-18389. write for info. (*0-318-54772-4*) Ohio U Pr.

***Complete Works of Robert Browning with Variant Readings & Annotations Vol. XIII.** Robert Browning. Ed. by Ashby B. Crowder. (Illus.). 368p. (C). 1995. text ed. 65.00x (*0-8214-1111-X*) Ohio U Pr.

Complete Works of Robert Browning with Variant Readings & Annotations, Vol. IX: The Ring & the Book, Books 9-12. Robert Browning. Ed. by Roma A. King, Jr. & Susan Crowl. (Complete Works of Robert Browning). 384p. 1990. lib. bdg. 65.00 (*0-8214-0381-8*) Ohio U Pr.

Complete Works of Robert Browning with Variant Readings & Annotations, Vol. VIII: The Ring & the Book, Bks. 5-8. Ed. by Susan Crowl & Roma A. King, Jr. 400p. 1988. text ed. 65.00 (*0-8214-0380-X*) Ohio U Pr.

Complete Works of Robert Burns: Presentation Edition. M. Mackay. (C). 1988. 350.00 (*0-907526-29-2*, Alloway Pub) St Mut.

Complete Works of Robert Burns: Souvenir Edition. M. Mackay. (C). 1988. 110.00 (*0-907526-23-3*, Alloway Pub) St Mut.

Complete Works of Robert Burns: Tartan Deluxe Edition. (C). 1988. 195.00 (*0-907526-28-4*, Alloway Pub) St Mut.

Complete Works of Saki. Ed. by H. H. Munro. (Reprints Ser.). 960p. 1989. 19.95 (*0-88029-259-8*) Dorset Pr.

Complete Works of Scott Joplin. Scott Joplin. Ed. by Vera B. Lawrence. LC 80-28215. (American Collection Music Ser.: No. I). (Illus.). xlvi, 327p. 1982. Vol. I, Works for Piano, xlvi, 327 pgs. 40.00 (*0-87104-275-4*); Vol. II, Works for Voice, xlvii, 341 pgs. 40.00 (*0-87104-276-2*) NY Pub Lib.

Complete Works of Scott Joplin, 2 vols., Set. Scott Joplin. Ed. by Vera B. Lawrence. LC 80-28215. (American Collection Music Ser.: No. I). (Illus.). 1982. 75.00 (*0-87104-274-6*) NY Pub Lib.

Complete Works of Shakespeare. 4th ed. Ed. by David Bevington. (C). 1991. text ed. 58.50 (*0-673-38873-5*) HarpCollege.

Complete Works of Shelley, 10 vols., Set. Percy Bysshe Shelley. Ed. by R. Ingpen & W. E. Peck. Incl. Vols. 1-4. Poems: Friendship. LC 65-14696. 1965. (*0-318-52684-0*); Vols. 5-7. Prose. LC 65-14696. 1965. (*0-318-52685-9*); Vols. 8-10. Letters. LC 65-14696. 1965. (*0-318-52686-7*); LC 65-14696. 3984p. 1965. reprint ed. 500.00 (*0-87752-101-8*) Gordian.

Complete Works of Sister Nivedita, 5 vols., Set. Nivedita. Ed. by Margaret Noble. Incl. Vol. 1. Our Master & His Message, the Master As I Saw Him, Kali the Mother, Lectures & Articles. 1967. 8.95 (*0-87481-112-0*); Vol. 2. Web of Indian Life, an Indian Study on Love & Death, Studies from an Eastern Home, Lectures & Articles. 1967. 8.95 (*0-87481-113-9*); Vol. 3. Indian Art, Cradle Tales of Hinduism, Religion & Dharma. 1967. 8.95 (*0-87481-114-7*); Vol. 4. Footfalls of Indian History, Bodh-Gaya, Civic Ideal & Indian Nationality, Hints on National Education in India. 1967. 8.95 (*0-87481-115-5*); Vol. 5. Lectures & Writings. 1967. 8.95 (*0-87481-226-7*); 1967. 65.00 (*0-87481-216-X*) Vedanta Pr.

Complete Works of St. Thomas More: The Debellation of Salem & Bizance, Vol. 10. St. Thomas More. Ed. by John Guy et al. LC 63-7949. 600p. (C). 1988. text ed. 75.00 (*0-300-03376-1*) Yale U Pr.

Complete Works of Swami Vivekananda, 8 vols. Swami Vivekananda. 1922. pap. 55.00 (*0-87481-176-7*) Vedanta Pr.

Complete Works of Swami Vivekananda, 8 Vols. Swami Vivekananda. 1947. 78.00 (*0-87481-092-2*) Vedanta Pr.

Complete Works of Swami Vivekananda. Vivekananda. 1989. pap. 25.00 (*0-87481-237-2*) Vedanta Pr.

Complete Works of Swami Vivekananda, 1. Swami Vivekananda. 1907. pap. 6.95 (*0-87481-177-5*) Vedanta Pr.

Complete Works of Swami Vivekananda, 8 Vols, 1. Swami Vivekananda. 1947. 9.50 (*0-87481-137-6*) Vedanta Pr.

Complete Works of Swami Vivekananda, 2. Swami Vivekananda. 1907. pap. 6.95 (*0-87481-178-3*) Vedanta Pr.

Complete Works of Swami Vivekananda, 8 Vols, 2. Swami Vivekananda. 1947. 9.50 (*0-87481-138-4*) Vedanta Pr.

Complete Works of Swami Vivekananda, 3. Swami Vivekananda. 1907. pap. 6.95 (*0-87481-179-1*) Vedanta Pr.

Complete Works of Swami Vivekananda, 8 Vols, 3. Swami Vivekananda. 1947. 9.50 (*0-87481-139-2*) Vedanta Pr.

Complete Works of Swami Vivekananda, 4. Swami Vivekananda. 1907. pap. 6.95 (*0-87481-180-5*) Vedanta Pr.

Complete Works of Swami Vivekananda, 8 Vols, 4. Swami Vivekananda. 1947. 9.50 (*0-87481-140-6*) Vedanta Pr.

Complete Works of Swami Vivekananda, 5. Swami Vivekananda. 1907. pap. 6.95 (*0-87481-181-3*) Vedanta Pr.

Complete Works of Swami Vivekananda, 8 Vols, 5. Swami Vivekananda. 1947. 9.50 (*0-87481-141-4*) Vedanta Pr.

Complete Works of Swami Vivekananda, 6. Swami Vivekananda. 1907. pap. 6.95 (*0-87481-182-1*) Vedanta Pr.

Complete Works of Swami Vivekananda, 8 Vols, 6. Swami Vivekananda. 1947. 9.50 (*0-87481-142-2*) Vedanta Pr.

Complete Works of Swami Vivekananda, 7. Swami Vivekananda. 1922. pap. 6.95 (*0-87481-183-X*) Vedanta Pr.

Complete Works of Swami Vivekananda, 8 Vols, 7. Swami Vivekananda. 1947. 9.50 (*0-87481-143-0*) Vedanta Pr.

Complete Works of Swami Vivekananda, 8 Vols, 8. Swami Vivekananda. 1947. 9.50 (*0-87481-144-9*) Vedanta Pr.

Complete Works of Swami Vivekananda, 8. Swami Vivekananda. 1951. pap. 6.95 (*0-87481-184-8*) Vedanta Pr.

Complete Works of the Late Rev. Thomas Boston, Ettrick: Including His Memoirs, Written by Himself, 12 vols., Set. Thomas Boston. Ed. by Samuel M'Millan. (Puritan Library). (Illus.). 1980. reprint ed. lib. bdg. 250.00 (*0-940033-00-3*) R O Roberts.

Complete Works of the "Pearl" Poet. Tr. by Casey Finch. 488p. (C). 60.00 (*0-520-06874-2*); pap. 20.00 (*0-520-07871-3*) U CA Pr.

Complete Works of Thomas Boston (1676-1732), 12 vols., Set. Thomas Boston. 7278p. 1980. 250.00 (*0-939464-19-5*) Labyrinth Pr.

Complete Works of Thomas Brooks, 6 Vols. Thomas Brooks. Ed. by Alexander B. Grosart. reprint ed. lib. bdg. write for info. (*0-318-50544-4*) AMS Pr.

Complete Works of Thomas Brooks, 6 Vols, 1. Thomas Brooks. Ed. by Alexander B. Grosart. LC 74-39538. reprint ed. lib. bdg. 67.50 (*0-404-01121-7*) AMS Pr.

Complete Works of Thomas Brooks, 6 Vols, 2. Thomas Brooks. Ed. by Alexander B. Grosart. LC 74-39538. reprint ed. lib. bdg. 67.50 (*0-404-01122-5*) AMS Pr.

Complete Works of Thomas Brooks, 6 Vols, 3. Thomas Brooks. Ed. by Alexander B. Grosart. LC 74-39538. reprint ed. lib. bdg. 67.50 (*0-404-01123-3*) AMS Pr.

Complete Works of Thomas Brooks, 6 Vols, 4. Thomas Brooks. Ed. by Alexander B. Grosart. LC 74-39538. reprint ed. lib. bdg. 67.50 (*0-404-01124-1*) AMS Pr.

Complete Works of Thomas Brooks, 6 Vols, 5. Thomas Brooks. Ed. by Alexander B. Grosart. LC 74-39538. reprint ed. lib. bdg. 67.50 (*0-404-01125-X*) AMS Pr.

Complete Works of Thomas Brooks, 6 Vols, 6. Thomas Brooks. Ed. by Alexander B. Grosart. LC 74-39538. reprint ed. lib. bdg. 67.50 (*0-404-01126-8*) AMS Pr.

Complete Works of Thomas Brooks, 6 Vols, Set. Thomas Brooks. Ed. by Alexander B. Grosart. LC 74-39538. reprint ed. lib. bdg. 405.00 (*0-404-01120-9*) AMS Pr.

Complete Works of Thomas Holley Chivers, Vol. 1. Thomas Holley Chivers. Ed. by Emma L. Chase & Lois F. Parks. LC 57-8677. 336p. reprint ed. pap. 95.80 (*0-317-20638-9*, 2024129) Bks Demand.

Complete Works of Thomas Shadwell, 5 vols., 1. Thomas Shadwell. Ed. by Montague Summers. LC 68-20247. 1972. reprint ed. 36.95 (*0-405-08953-8*) Ayer.

Complete Works of Thomas Shadwell, 5 vols., 2. Thomas Shadwell. Ed. by Montague Summers. LC 68-20247. 1972. reprint ed. 36.95 (*0-405-08954-6*) Ayer.

Complete Works of Thomas Shadwell, 5 vols., 3. Thomas Shadwell. Ed. by Montague Summers. LC 68-20247. 1972. reprint ed. 36.95 (*0-405-08955-4*) Ayer.

Complete Works of Thomas Shadwell, 5 vols., 4. Thomas Shadwell. Ed. by Montague Summers. LC 68-20247. 1972. reprint ed. 36.95 (*0-405-08956-2*) Ayer.

Complete Works of Thomas Shadwell, 5 vols., 5. Thomas Shadwell. Ed. by Montague Summers. LC 68-20247. 1972. reprint ed. 36.95 (*0-405-08957-0*) Ayer.

Complete Works of Thomas Shadwell, 5 vols., Set. Thomas Shadwell. Ed. by Montague Summers. LC 68-20247. 1968. reprint ed. 164.00 (*0-405-08952-X*) Ayer.

Complete Works of Virgilio Davila. Virgilio Davila. (Puerto Rico Ser.). 1979. lib. bdg. 75.00 (*0-8490-2900-7*) Gordon Pr.

Complete Works of Vladimir Kovalevsky: Original Anthology. Ed. by Stephen J. Gould. LC 79-8354. (History of Paleontology Ser.). (Illus.). (ENG, FRE & GER.). 1980. lib. bdg. 75.95 (*0-405-12750-2*) Ayer.

Complete Works of W. H. Auden: Plays & Other Dramatic Writings 1928-1938, Vol. I. W. H. Auden. 544p. 1989. 60.00 (*0-691-06740-6*) Princeton U Pr.

Complete Works of W. H. Auden, Vols. I & II: Libretti & Other Dramatic Writings, 1939-1973, Set. W. H. Auden & Chester Kallman. Ed. by Edward Mendelson. LC 92-18681. 823p. 1993. text ed. 49.50 (*0-691-03301-3*) Princeton U Pr.

Complete Works of W. H. Auden, Vols. III-VI: Essays & Reviews. W. H. Auden. 1988. write for info. (*0-318-62735-3*) Princeton U Pr.

Complete Works of W. H. Auden, Vols. VII-VIII: Complete Poetry. W. H. Auden. 1988. write for info. (*0-318-62736-1*) Princeton U Pr.

Complete Works of William Billings: Volume 2: The Singing Master's Assistant(1778), Music in Miniature (1779) William Billings. Ed. by Hans Nathan et al. LC 76-28587. 362p. 1977. 50.00 (*0-8139-0839-6*) U Pr of Va.

Complete Works of William Billings, Vol. III: The Psalm-Singer's Amusement (1781), The Suffolk Harm (1786) & Independent Publications. William Billings. Ed. by Karl Kroeger & Richard Crawford. (Illus.). 399p. 1986. text ed. 50.00 (*0-8139-1130-3*) U Pr of Va.

Complete Works of William Billings, Vol. 1: The New England Psalm-Singer (1770) William Billings. Ed. by Karl Kroeger & Richard Crawford. LC 80-69464. (Illus.). 383p. 1981. 50.00 (*0-8139-0917-1*) U Pr of Va.

Complete Works of William Billings, Vol. 4: The Continental Harmony, 1794. William Billings. Ed. by Karl Kroeger. (Illus.). 332p. 1990. text ed. 50.00 (*1-878528-01-7*) U Pr of Va.

Complete Works of William Shakespeare. William Shakespeare. (Classics - Bonded Leather Fibers Ser.). 1240p. 1990. 19.95 (*0-681-41003-5*) Longmeadow Pr.

Complete Works of William Shakespeare: Avenel Complete Classics. William Shakespeare. 1988. 14.99 (*0-517-44551-4*) Random Hse Value.

Complete Works of William Shakespeare: Library of Literary Classics. William Shakespeare. 1990. 17.99 (*0-517-05361-6*) Random Hse Value.

Complete Works of Wllm Shkspr (Abridged) Jess Borgenson et al. (Illus.). 192p. 1994. pap. 8.95 (*1-55783-157-2*) Applause Theatre Bk Pubs.

Complete Works on Criminal Jurisprudence: Consisting of Systems of Penal Law for the State of Louisiana & for the United States of America, with Introductory Reports to the Same, 2 vols., Set. Edward Livingston. LC 68-55775. (Criminology, Law Enforcement, & Social Problems Ser.: No. 7). 1968. reprint ed. 45.00 (*0-87585-007-3*) Patterson Smith.

Complete Works with Selected Letters. Arthur Rimbaud. Tr. by Wallace Fowlie. LC 66-13885. 1967. reprint ed. pap. 13.95 (*0-226-71973-1*, P288) U Ch Pr.

Complete World. Lewis Carroll. 1993. 21.00 (*0-679-42475-X*, Modern Lib) Random.

Complete World Bartender Guide. 1988. 5.95 (*0-318-33256-6*, 104) Am Bartenders.

Complete World Bartender Guide: The Standard Reference to More Than 2,000 Drinks. Bob Sennett. 1993. 5.99 (*0-553-29900-X*) Bantam.

Complete World War Two Military Jeep Manual. U. S. Army Staff. 586p. 1991. pap. 39.95 (*1-85520-121-6*) Portrayal.

Complete Writer's Workout Book. Carolyn H. Fitzpatrick & Marybeth B. Ruscica. 332p. (C). 1988. pap. text ed. 18.00 (*0-669-12159-2*); Instr.'s guide. teacher ed 2.00 (*0-669-12160-6*) Heath.

Complete Writing Lessons for the Middle Grades. Marjorie Frank. (Illus.). 128p. (J). (gr. 4-6). 1987. pap. text ed. 9.95 (*0-86530-160-3*, IP 1603) Incentive Pubns.

Complete Writing Lessons for the Primary Grades. Marjorie Frank. (Illus.). 128p. (J). (gr. 1-3). 1987. pap. text ed. 9.95 (*0-86530-163-8*, IP1638) Incentive Pubns.

Complete Writings. Justin Martyr. LC 65-18317. (Fathers of the Church Ser.: Vol. 6). 486p. 1948. 34.95 (*0-8132-0006-7*) Cath U Pr.

Complete Writings. Salvian the Presbyter. (Fathers of the Church Ser.: Vol. 3). 396p. 1947. 34.95 (*0-8132-0003-2*) Cath U Pr.

Complete Writings, 11 vols., Set. Henry Wadsworth Longfellow. (BCL1-PS American Literature Ser.). 1992. reprint ed. lib. bdg. 900.00 (*0-7812-6779-X*) Rprt Serv.

Complete Writings, 16 vols., Set. James Russell Lowell. Ed. by Charles E. Norton. LC 74-181949. reprint ed. write for info. (*0-404-04070-5*) AMS Pr.

Complete Writings, 16 vols., Set. James Russell Lowell. (BCL1-PS American Literature Ser.). 1992. reprint ed. lib. bdg. 1,440.00 (*0-7812-6783-8*) Rprt Serv.

Complete Writings, 10 vols., Set. Walt Whitman. (BCL1-PS American Literature Ser.). 1992. reprint ed. lib. bdg. 900.00 (*0-7812-6896-6*) Rprt Serv.

Complete Writings of Alexander Mack. 1991. 13.95 (*0-936693-12-6*) Brethren Encyclopedia.

***Complete Writings of Alexander Mack.** Ed. by William R. Eberly. 1992. 13.95 (*0-614-06602-6*) Brethren Encyclopedia.

Complete Writings of Menno Simons: Circa 1496-1561. Ed. by John C. Wenger. Tr. by Leonard Verduin. LC 55-9815. 1104p. 1956. 44.95 (*0-8361-1353-5*) Herald Pr.

Complete Writings of Thomas Say on the Entomology of North America, 2 vols., 1. Thomas Say. Ed. by John L. Leconte & Keir B. Sterling. LC 77-81102. (Biologists & Their World Ser.). (Illus.). 1978. reprint ed. lib. bdg. 57.95 (*0-405-10687-4*) Ayer.

Complete Writings of Thomas Say on the Entomology of North America, 2 vols., 2. Thomas Say. Ed. by John L. Leconte & Keir B. Sterling. LC 77-81102. (Biologists & Their World Ser.). (Illus.). 1978. reprint ed. lib. bdg. 57.95 (*0-405-10688-2*) Ayer.

Complete Writings of Thomas Say on the Entomology of North America, 2 vols., Set. Thomas Say. Ed. by John L. Leconte & Keir B. Sterling. LC 77-81102. (Biologists & Their World Ser.). (Illus.). 1978. reprint ed. lib. bdg. 114.95 (*0-405-10686-6*) Ayer.

Complete Writings of William Blake, with Variant Readings. William Blake. Ed. by Geoffrey Keynes. (Oxford Standard Authors Ser.). 1966. pap. 18.95 (*0-19-281050-2*) OUP.

***Complete X86: The Definitive Guide to 386, 486, & Pentium-Class Microprocessors, Set, Vols. I & II.** John Wharton. 1995. spiral bd. 2,695.00 (*1-885330-04-9*) MicroDes Res.

***Complete X86: The Definitive Guide 386, 486, & Pentium-Class Microprocessors, Vols. I & II.** John Wharton. 700p. 1994. 2,695.00 (*1-885330-02-2*) MicroDes Res.

***Complete Yachtmaster: Sailing, Seamanship, & Navigation for the Modern Yacht Skipper.** Tom Cunliffe. (Illus.). 240p. Date not set. 39.00 (*0-7136-3617-3*) Sheridan.

Complete Year-by-Year New York Mets Fan's Almanac. Will Balliett. 1992. 13.00 (*0-517-58669-X*, Crown) Crown Pub Group.

Complete Year-Round Gas Barbecue Cookbook. Jo-Anne Bennett. LC 94-1652. 218p. 1994. 13.95 (*0-88415-165-4*) Gulf Pub.

Complete Yoga Book. James Hewitt. LC 77-15934. (Illus.). 576p. 1989. pap. 16.00 (*0-8052-0969-7*) Schocken.

Complete Yogurt Cookbook. Anne Lanigan. Ed. by Andrew Adler & Roger Adler. (Illus.). 1978. 9.95 (*0-916844-02-1*); pap. text ed. 5.95 (*0-916844-03-X*) Turtle Pr.

Complete Youth Group Checkup: And Other Great Retreats. Ed. by Tom Salsgiver. (Essentials for Christian Youth Ser.). 96p. (Orig.). 1992. pap. 10.95 (*0-687-36171-0*) Abingdon.

***Complete Yucatan Peninsula Guidebook.** Annelise Sorensen. (Mexico Ser.). (Illus.). 152p. 1995. pap. 9.95 (*0-916841-55-3*) Indian Chief.

Complete 35MM Sourcebook. rev. ed. Michael Busselle. (Illus.). 232p. 1992. 32.50 (*0-8174-3704-5*, Amphoto); pap. 24.95 (*0-8174-3701-0*, Amphoto) Watsn-Guptill.

Completed Hickory Dickory Dock. Jim Aylesworth. LC 89-38484. (Illus.). 32p. (J). (ps-2). 1990. text ed. 13.95 (*0-689-31606-2*, Atheneum Bks Young) S&S Childrens.

Completed Hickory Dickory Dock. Jim Aylesworth. LC 94-1226. (Illus.). 32p. (J). (gr. k-3). 1994. pap. 4.95 (*0-689-71862-4*, Aladdin Paperbacks) S&S Childrens.

Completed Research, Vol. 31. 1989. 15.00 (*0-88314-478-6*) AAHPERD.

Completely Cheese. Anita M. Pearl. 365p. 1990. pap. 9.95 (*0-8246-0348-6*) Jonathan David.

***Completely Collapsible Portable Man: Selected Shorter Lyrics.** J. Michael Yates. 128p. 1995. lib. bdg. 27.00 (*0-8095-4534-9*) Borgo Pr.

Completely Cookies. Leslie Weiner. 1991. pap. 5.95 (*0-312-05405-X*) St Martin.

***Completely Diane Warren.** 164p. (Orig.). 1994. pap. 24.95 (*0-89724-361-7*) Warner Brothers.

Completely Mad: A History of the Comic Book & Magazine. Maria Reidelbach. 1991. 50.00 (*0-316-73890-5*) Little.

Completely Mad: A Histroy of the Comic Book & Magazine. Maria Reidelbach. 1992. pap. 24.95 (*0-316-73891-3*) Little.

Completely Morgan: Four-Wheelers from 1968. Ken Hill. (Illus.). 192p. 1994. 39.95 (*1-874105-34-0*, Pub. by Veloce Pub UK) Motorbooks Intl.

Completely Morgan Four Wheelers, 1936-68. Ken Hill. (Illus.). 224p. 1994. 49.95 (*1-874105-33-2*, Pub. by Veloce Pub UK) Motorbooks Intl.

Completely New Look at Interracial Sexuality: Public Opinion & Select Commentaries. Lawrence R. Tenzer. LC 90-63946. (Orig.). 1991. pap. 16.95 (*0-9628348-1-5*) Scholars Pub Hse.

Completely Prime Maximal Ideals & Quantization. William M McGovern. LC 93-48292. (Memoirs of the American Mathematical Society Ser.: Vol. 519). 1994. pap. 29.00 (*0-8218-2580-1*) Am Math.

Completeness: Quality for the 21st Century. Philip B. Crosby. LC 93-20944. 1994. 11.95 (*0-452-27024-3*, Plume) NAL-Dutton.

Completeness of Kant's Table of Judgments. Klaus Reich. Tr. by Jane Kneller & Michael Losonsky. LC 91-38006. (Series in Philosophy). 160p. (C). 1992. 25.00 (*0-8047-1934-9*) Stanford U Pr.

***Completeness of Root Functions of Regular Differential Operators.** Sasun Yakubov. (Pitman Monographs & Surveys in Pure & Applied Mathematics). 1994. text ed. 130.00 (*0-470-23374-5*) Wiley.

Completeness of Scientific Theories: On the Derivation of Empirical Indicators Within a Theoretical Framework: The Case of Physical Geometry. Martin Carrier. LC 93-30527. (University of Western Ontario Series in Philosophy of Science). 292p. (C). 1993. lib. bdg. 112.50 (*0-7923-2475-7*) Kluwer Ac.

Completest Angling Booke That Ever Was Writ. Joseph Crahall. (Illus.). 256p. 1970. boxed 27.50 (*0-88395-007-3*) Freshet Pr.

Completest Fly Tier. Reuben Cross. (Illus.). 224p. 1971. 7.95 (*0-88395-008-1*) Freshet Pr.

Completest Mode. John Needham. 210p. 1982. 22.50 (*0-85224-387-1*, Pub. by Edinburgh U Pr UK) Col U Pr.

Completing a Stewardship: The Malayan Civil Service, 1942-1957. Robert Heussler. LC 83-5543. (Contributions in Comparative Colonial Studies: No. 15). (Illus.). xvii, 240p. 1983. text ed. 69.95 (*0-313-23930-4*, HES/, Greenwood Pr) Greenwood.

Completing Dissertations in the Behavioral Sciences & Education: A Systematic Guide for Graduate Students. Thomas J. Long et al. LC 85-45063. (Higher & Adult Education Ser.). 238p. 1985. 28.95x (*0-87589-658-8*) Jossey-Bass.

***Completing the Circle.** Virginia D. Sneve. LC 94-22777. 1995. 20.00 (*0-8032-4226-3*) U of Nebr Pr.

Completing the Circle: Artists' Books on the Environment. Betty Bright. (Illus.). 35p. 1992. pap. 7.00 (*1-879832-01-1*) MN Ctr Book Arts.

Completing the Food Chain: Strategies for Combating Hunger & Malnutrition. Ed. by Paula M. Hirschoff & Neil G. Kotler. LC 89-6168. (Papers & Proceedings of a Colloquium Organized by the Smithsonian Institution). 140p. (C). 1989. pap. 14.95 (*0-87474-561-6*) Smithsonian.

An Asterisk (*) at the beginning of an entry indicates that the title is appearing in BIP for the first time.

C

An Asterisk (*) at the beginning of an entry indicates that the title is appearing in BIP for the first time.

1477

Complex Analysis. 3rd ed. Serge A. Lang. LC 92-21625. (Graduate Texts in Mathematics Ser.: Vol. 103). (Illus.). 400p. 1995. 59.00 (*0-387-97886-0*) Spr-Verlag.

Complex Analysis: An Introductory Course. Guttalu R. Viswanath. (Illus.). 290p. (Orig.). (C). 1993. pap. text ed. 35.00 (*0-9626723-3-5*) G R Viswanath.

Complex Analysis: Proceedings of the International Workshop, Wuppertal 1990. Ed. by Klas Diederich. (Aspects of Mathematics Ser.: Vol. E 17). x, 341p. 1991. 64.00 (*3-528-06413-7*, Pub. by Vieweg & Sohn GW) Ballen Bkslr.

Complex Analysis: Proceedings of the S.U.N.Y. Brockport Conference. S. U. N. Y. Brockport Conference Staff. Ed. by Sanford Miller. (Lecture Notes in Pure & Applied Mathematics Ser.: Vol. 36). 192p. 1978. 99.75 (*0-8247-6725-X*) Dekker.

Complex Analysis: Selected Topics. Mario O. Gonzalez. (Pure & Applied Mathematics Ser.: Vol. 152). 544p. 1991. 150.00 (*0-8247-8416-2*) Dekker.

Complex Analysis: The Argument Principle in Analysis & Topology. Alan F. Beardon. LC 78-8540. 253p. reprint ed. pap. 72.20 (*0-8357-3393-9*, 2039650) Bks Demand.

Complex Analysis: The Geometric Viewpoint. Steven G. Krantz. (Carus Mathematical Monograph). 210p. 1990. 32.00 (*0-88385-026-5*) Math Assn.

Complex Analysis & Algebraic Geometry. Ed. by H. Grauert. (Lecture Notes in Mathematics Ser.: Vol. 1194). vi, 235p. 1986. pap. 39.30 (*0-387-16490-1*) Spr-Verlag.

Complex Analysis & Applications. Alan Jeffrey. (Illus.). 448p. 1991. 49.95 (*0-8493-8603-9*, QA) CRC Pr.

Complex Analysis & Applications. 2nd ed. William R. Derrick. LC 83-6865. (Mathematics Ser.). 350p. (C). 1984. text ed. 60.95 (*0-534-02853-5*) Brooks-Cole.

***Complex Analysis & Geometry.** Ed. by Ancona et al. (Lecture Notes in Pure & Applied Mathematics Ser.). 1995. write for info. (*0-8247-9672-1*) Dekker.

Complex Analysis & Geometry. Ed. by V. Ancona & A. Silva. (University Series in Mathematics). (Illus.). 370p. (C). 1993. 89.50 (*0-306-44179-9*, Plenum Pr) Plenum.

***Complex Analysis & Its Applications.** Ed. by C Chun Yang et al. (Pitman Research Notes in Mathematics). 1994. pap. text ed. 84.95 (*0-470-23405-9*) Wiley.

***Complex Analysis & Special Topics in Harmonic Analysis.** Carlos A. Berenstein & Roger Gay. LC 94-41894. 528p. 1995. 79.00 (*0-387-94411-7*) Spr-Verlag.

C

Complex Analysis-Fifth Romanian--Finnish Seminar, Pt. I. Ed. by C. A. Cazacu et al. (Lecture Notes in Mathematics Ser.: Vol. 1013). 393p. 1983. pap. 44.70 (*0-387-12682-1*) Spr-Verlag.

Complex Analysis-Fifth Romanian--Finnish Seminar, Pt. II. Ed. by C. A. Cazacu et al. (Lecture Notes in Mathematics Ser.: Vol. 1014). 338p. 1983. 37.00 (*0-387-12683-X*) Spr-Verlag.

Complex Analysis for Mathematics & Engineering. 3rd ed. John Mathews & Russ Howell. 448p. (C). 1995. text ed. write for info. (*0-697-13548-9*) Wm C Brown Pubs.

Complex Analysis, Functional Analysis & Approximation Theory: Proceedings of a Conference on Complex Analysis & Approximation Theory, Univesidade Estadual de Campinas, Brazil, 23-27 July 1984. Ed. by J. Mujica. (North Holland Mathematics Studies: Vol. 125). 298p. 1986. 64.00 (*0-444-87997-8*) Elsevier.

Complex Analysis I. Ed. by C. A. Berenstein. (Lecture Notes in Mathematics Ser.: Vol. 1275). xv, 331p. 1987. pap. text ed. 43.60 (*0-387-18356-6*) Spr-Verlag.

Complex Analysis II. Ed. by C. A. Berenstein. (Lecture Notes in Mathematics Ser.: Vol. 1276). ix, 320p. 1987. pap. 43.60 (*0-387-18357-4*) Spr-Verlag.

Complex Analysis III. Ed. by C. A. Berenstein. (Lecture Notes in Mathematics Ser.: Vol. 1277). x, 350p. 1987. pap. 47.90 (*0-387-18355-8*) Spr-Verlag.

Complex Analysis in Banach Spaces: Holomorphic Functions & Domains of Holomorphy in Finite & Infinite Dimensions. J. Mujica. (Mathematics Studies: Vol. 120). 434p. 1986. 84.75 (*0-444-87886-6*, North Holland) Elsevier.

***Complex Analysis in Number Theory.** Anatoly A. Karatsuba. 208p. 1994. 49.95 (*0-8493-2866-7*, 2866) CRC Pr.

Complex Analysis, Microbial Calculus & Relativistic Quantum Theory. Ed. by D. Iagolnitzer. (Lecture Notes in Physics Ser.: Vol. 126). 502p. 1980. pap. 43.00 (*0-387-09996-4*) Spr-Verlag.

Complex Analysis of One Variable. Raghavan Narasimhan. (C). 1985. text ed. 46.50 (*0-8176-3237-9*) Birkhauser.

Complex Analysis of Several Variables. Ed. by Yum-Tong Siu. LC 83-25734. (Proceedings of Symposia in Pure Mathematics Ser., Humboldt State University, Arcata, CA, July 29-August 16, 1974: Vol. 41). 297p. 1984. 70. 00 (*0-8218-1446-X*, PSPUM/41C) Am Math.

Complex Analysis with Applications. Richard A. Silverman. 274p. 1984. reprint ed. pap. 8.95 (*0-486-64762-5*) Dover.

Complex Analytic Geometry. G. Fischer. (Lecture Notes in Mathematics Ser.: Vol. 538). 1976. 20.00 (*0-387-07857-6*) Spr-Verlag.

***Complex Analytic Methods for Partial Differential Equations: An Introductory Text.** Heinrich G. W. Begehr. LC 94-34414. 250p. 1994. text ed. 44.00 (*981-02-1550-9*) World Scientific Pub.

Complex Analytic Sets. E. M. Chirka. (C). 1989. lib. bdg. 137.00 (*0-7923-0234-6*) Kluwer Ac.

Complex Analytic Singularities. Ed. by T. Suwa & P. Wagreich. 698p. 1987. 177.00 (*0-444-70200-8*, North Holland) Elsevier.

Complex Analytic Theory of Teichmuller Spaces. Subhashis Nag. LC 87-28037. (Canadian Mathematical Society Series of Mnongraphs & Advanced Texts). 427p. 1988. text ed. 132.00 (*0-471-62773-9*) Wiley.

Complex & Simplified Forms of Chinese Characters with Conversion Tables. rev. ed. John Montanaro. (Mirror Ser. C-16: No. C-16). 88p. (CHI.). 1985. 4.95 (*0-88710-142-9*) Yale Far Eastern Pubns.

Complex Approximation, Proceedings, Quebec, Canada. Bernard Aupetit. (Progress in Mathematics Ser.: No. 4). 128p. 1980. pap. 28.50 (*0-8176-3004-X*) Birkhauser.

Complex Archetype Symbol in the Psychology of C. J. Jung. Jolande Jacobi. Tr. by R. Manheim. (Bollingen Ser.: Vol. 57). (Illus.). 248p. 1959. pap. 11.95 (*0-691-01774-3*, 241) Princeton U Pr.

Complex Arrhythmias: Self Assessment. E. K. Chung. (Illus.). xiv, 310p. 1985. 65.75 (*3-8055-3639-9*) S Karger.

***Complex Carbohydrate Therapeutics Market.** 325p. (Orig.). 1995. pap. 24.90 (*0-7605-2327-4*) Rector Pr.

Complex Carbohydrates see Methods in Enzymology

Complex Carbohydrates in Food: The Report of the British Nutrition Foundation's Task Force. Ed. by M. Ashwell. (Illus.). 176p. 1990. pap. 78.95 (*0-442-31288-1*) Chapman & Hall.

Complex Chemistry. Contrib by G. Blasse et al. (Structure & Bonding Ser.: Vol. 76). (Illus.). 208p. 1991. 99.00 (*0-387-53499-7*) Spr-Verlag.

Complex Chemistry. R. D. Ernst et al. (Structure & Bonding Ser.: Vol. 57). (Illus.). 210p. 1984. 75.00 (*0-387-13411-5*) Spr-Verlag.

Complex Cobordism & Stable Homotopy of Spheres. Douglas C. Ravenel. (Pure & Applied Mathematics Ser.). 1986. text ed. 70.00 (*0-12-583430-6*) Acad Pr.

Complex Compounds of Uranium. I. I. Chernyaev. 536p. 1966. text ed. 115.00 (*0-7065-0584-0*, Pub. by Keter Pub IS) Coronet Bks.

Complex Contour Integral Representation of Cardinal Spline Functions: Contemporary Math. Walter Schempp. LC 81-22771. (Contemporary Mathematics Ser.: Vol. 7). 109p. 1982. pap. 18.00 (*0-8218-5006-7*, CONM-7) Am Math.

Complex Craniofacial Problems. Ed. by Craig R. Dufresne et al. (Illus.). 556p. 1992. text ed. 169.95 (*0-443-08624-9*) Churchill.

Complex Derivatives: Understanding & Managing the Risks of Exotic Options Complex Swaps. Erik Banks. 1993. 65.00 (*1-55738-550-5*) Probus Pub Co.

Complex Differential Geometry. Shoshichi Kobayashi & H. H. Wu. (DMV Seminar Ser.: No. 3). 159p. 1980. 29.00 (*0-8176-1494-X*) Birkhauser.

Complex Differential Geometry & Nonlinear Differential Equations. Ed. by Y. Siu. LC 85-28656. (Contemporary Mathematics Ser.: Vol. 49). 184p. 1986. pap. text ed. 29. 00 (*0-8218-5049-0*, CONM-49) Am Math.

Complex Differential Geometry & Supermanifolds in Strings & Fields. Ed. by P. J. Bongaarts & R. Martini. (Lecture Notes in Physics Ser.: Vol. 311). v, 252p. 1988. 41.00 (*0-387-50324-2*) Spr-Verlag.

Complex Dynamical Systems: Selected Papers. Ralph H. Abraham. (Science Frontier Express Ser.). (Illus.). 125p. 1990. pap. 25.00 (*0-942344-07-3*) Aerial Pr.

***Complex Dynamical Systems: The Mathematics Behind the Manderbrot & Julia Sets.** Ed. by Robert L. Devaney. LC 94-24190. (Proceedings of Symposia in Applied Mathematics Ser.: 49). 1994. write for info. (*0-8218-0290-9*) Am Math.

Complex Dynamical Systems & Fractales: Max-Planck-Lecture Series in Mathematics. Ed. by Heinz-Otto Peitgen & Peter H. Richter. 320p. (C). 1990. pap. 31.00 (*3-528-06363-7*, Pub. by Vieweg & Sohn GW) Ballen Bkslr.

Complex Dynamics. L. Carleson & T. Gamelin. LC 92-32457. (Universitext Ser.). 1993. 32.50 (*0-387-97942-5*) Spr-Verlag.

Complex Dynamics. Ed. by R. Livi et al. 320p. (C). 1993. text ed. 97.00 (*1-56072-086-7*) Nova Sci Pubs.

***Complex Dynamics & Renormalization.** LC 94-29390. (Annals of Mathematics Studies: 135). 1994. pap. 22.50 (*0-691-02981-4*) Princeton U Pr.

***Complex Dynamics & Renormalization.** Curtis T. McMullen. LC 94-29390. (Annals of Mathematics Studies: 135). 1994. 49.50 (*0-691-02982-2*) Princeton U Pr.

Complex Ecology. Bernard C. Patten & Sven E. Jorgensen. 737p. 1994. text ed. 99.00 (*0-13-161506-8*) P-H.

Complex Economic Dynamics, Vol. 1: An Introduction to Dynamical Systems & Market Mechanisms. Richard H. Day. LC 93-30291. 340p. 1993. 39.95 (*0-262-04141-3*) MIT Pr.

Complex Fate: Hawthorne, Henry James, & Some American Writers. Marius Bewley. LC 67-28474. 248p. 1967. reprint ed. 30.00 (*0-8752-008-9*) Gordian.

Complex Federal Litigaion: An Attorney's Guide to Management & Trial. Larry S. Kaplan. LC 93-29967. (Trial Practice Ser.). 1993. write for info. (*0-07-172379-X*) Shepards-McGraw.

Complex Fluids. Ed. by D. Weitz et al. (MRS Symposium Proceedings Ser.: Vol. 248). 1992. text ed. 59.00 (*1-55899-142-5*) Materials Res.

Complex Fluids: Proceedings of the Twelfth Sitges Conference, Sitges, Barcelona, Spain, 1-5 June 1992. Ed. by Luis Garrido. LC 92-44027. (Lecture Notes in Physics Ser.: Vol. 415). 1993. 72.00 (*0-387-56396-2*) Spr-Verlag.

Complex Foot Deformities in Children. Sherman S. Coleman. LC 82-15249. 313p. reprint ed. pap. 89.30 (*0-7837-2695-3*, 2043073) Bks Demand.

Complex Forms of the Religious Life: A Durkheimian View of New Religious Movements. Frances Westley. LC 83-4579. (American Academy of Religion Academy Ser.). 210p. (C). 1983. 20.95 (*0-89130-626-9*, 01 01 45) Scholars Pr GA.

Complex Function Theory. A. S. Holland. 304p. 1980. 56. 75 (*0-444-00342-8*, North Holland) Elsevier.

Complex Functions: An Algebraic & Geometric Viewpoint. Gareth A. Jones & David Singerman. (Illus.). 350p. 1987. pap. 29.95 (*0-521-31366-X*) Cambridge U Pr.

***Complex General Relativity.** Giampiero Esposito. LC 94-48071. (Fundamental Theories of Physics Ser.). 214p. (C). 1995. lib. bdg. 96.00 (*0-7923-3340-3*) Kluwer Ac.

Complex Geometry. Ed. by Gen Komatsu & Yusuke Sakane. LC 92-31060. (Lecture Notes in Pure & Applied Mathematics Ser.: Vol. 143). 248p. 1992. 125.00 (*0-8247-8818-4*) Dekker.

Complex Geometry & Analysis. Ed. by V. Villani. (Lecture Notes in Mathematics Ser.: Vol. 1422). v, 109p. 1990. pap. 27.70 (*0-387-52434-7*) Spr-Verlag.

Complex Geometry & Lie Theory. Carlson & Morrison. LC 91-25148. (PSPUM Ser.: No. 53). 348p. 1991. 73.00 (*0-8218-1492-3*, PSPUM-53) Am Math.

Complex Hydrides & Related Reducing Agents in Organic Synthesis. A. Hajos. LC 78-14524. (Studies in Organic Chemistry: Vol. 1). 398p. 1979. 107.75 (*0-444-99791-1*) Elsevier.

Complex Image: Faith & Method in American Autobiography. Joseph Fichtelberg. LC 89-14704. 252p. (C). 1989. text ed. 29.95 (*0-8122-8146-2*) U of Pa Pr.

Complex Information Processing: The Impact of Herbert A. Simon. Ed. by D. Klahr & K. Kotovsky. (Carnegie-Mellon Symposium on Cognition Ser.). 480p. 1989. 79. 95 (*0-8058-0178-2*); pap. 36.00 (*0-8058-0179-0*) L Erlbaum Assocs.

Complex Inheritance: The Idea of Self-Transcendence in the Theology of Henry James, Sr., & the Novels of Henry James. James G. Moseley. LC 75-8955. (American Academy of Religion. Dissertation Ser.: No. 4). 179p. reprint ed. pap. 51.10 (*0-7837-5469-8*, 2045234) Bks Demand.

Complex Interactions in Lake Communities. Ed. by S. R. Carpenter. (Illus.). 320p. 1990. 84.00 (*0-387-96684-6*) Spr-Verlag.

Complex Litigation: Adaptable to Courses Utilizing Marcus & Sherman's Casebook on Complex Litigation. Casenote Publishing Co., Inc. Staff et al. (Legal Briefs Ser.). (Orig.). 1994. pap. text ed. write for info. (*0-87457-202-9*, 1048) Casenotes Pub.

***Complex Litigation: Statutory Recommendations & Analysis.** xxxi, 592p. 1994. 115.00 (*0-614-00756-9*, 5472) Am Law Inst.

***Complex Litigation: Statutory Recommendations & Analysis with Reporter's Study: a Model System for State-to-State Transfer & Consolidation.** xxx, 592p. 1994. 115.00 (*0-8318-5472-3*, 5472) Am Law Inst.

Complex Litigation, Cases & Materials on Advanced Civil Procedure: Teacher's Manual. 2nd ed. Richard L. Marcus & Edward F. Sherman. (American Casebook Ser.). 1026p. (C). 1993. reprint ed. text ed. 51.50 (*0-314-00769-5*); reprint ed. pap. text ed. write for info. (*0-314-01192-7*) West Pub.

Complex Litigation Confronts the Jury System: A Case Study. Arthur D. Austin. LC 84-19500. 120p. 1984. text ed. 55.00 (*0-313-27099-6*, U7099, Greenwood Pr) Greenwood.

Complex Litigation Project: Proposed Final Draft. xxxviii, 716p. 1993. 60.00 (*0-685-70594-3*, 5430) Am Law Inst.

Complex Litigation Project: Tentative Draft No. 1. xviii, 242p. 1989. 35.00 (*0-685-31327-1*, 5976) Am Law Inst.

Complex Litigation Project: Tentative Draft No. 2 & Reporters' Preliminary Memorandum on Chap. 6. xix, 152p. 1988. 25.00 (*0-685-41232-6*, 5986/5989) Am Law Inst.

Complex Litigation Project: Tentative Draft No. 3. xxviii, 390p. 1992. 40.00 (*0-685-70593-5*, 5378) Am Law Inst.

Complex Litigation Project: 1987 Preliminary Study. 1987. 25.00 (*0-685-41233-4*, 5856) Am Law Inst.

Complex Litigation Research Manual. suppl. ed. Terrence F. Kiely. LC 87-23033. (Trial Practice Library). 136p. 1992. 55.00 (*0-471-57162-8*) Wiley.

Complex Managerial Decisions Involving Multiple Objectives. Allan Easton. LC 79-25513. 446p. 1980. reprint ed. lib. bdg. 37.50 (*0-89874-079-7*) Krieger.

Complex Manifolds & Deformation of Complex Structures. K. Kodaira. (Grundlehren der Mathematischen Wissenschaften Ser.: Vol. 283). (Illus.). 480p. 1985. 76. 00 (*0-387-96188-7*) Spr-Verlag.

Complex Manifolds Without Potential Theory. S. S. Chern. (Universitext Ser.). 1979. 25.00 (*0-387-90422-0*) Spr-Verlag.

Complex Ministry of Rural Pastorate. Kenneth Thrasher. 1984. pap. 4.99 (*0-89957-054-2*) AMG Pubs.

Complex Mixtures: Methods for In Vivo Toxicity Testing. National Research Council. 240p. 1988. text ed. 35.00 (*0-309-03778-6*) Natl Acad Pr.

Complex Mixtures & Cancer Risk. Ed. by Harri Vainio et al. (IARC Scientific Publications: No. 104). (Illus.). 466p. 1990. pap. 95.00 (*92-832-2104-4*) OUP.

Complex Movement Behaviour: The Motor-Action Controversy. Ed. by O. G. Meijer & K. Roth. (Advances in Psychology Ser.: Vol.50). 584p. 1988. 115. 50 (*0-444-70389-6*, North Holland) Elsevier.

Complex Multiplications. Serge A. Lang. (Grundlehren der Mathematischen Wissenschaften Ser.: Vol. 255). 192p. 1983. 72.00 (*0-387-90786-6*) Spr-Verlag.

Complex Numbers & Elementary Complex Functions. F. M. Hawkins & J. Q. Hawkins. 154p. 1970. text ed. 134. 00 (*0-677-61110-2*) Gordon & Breach.

Complex Oceanographic Research on the Black Sea. Ed. by V. N. Eremeev. 138p. 1992. 89.50 (*90-6764-144-8*) Coronet Bks.

Complex Operations at Massachusetts General Hospital. Ronald A. Malt et al. (Illus.). 272p. 1983. text ed. 115. 00 (*0-7216-6008-8*) Saunders.

Complex Organismal Functions: Integration & Evolution in Vertebrates. D. B. Wake et al. Ed. by G. Roth. 1989. text ed. 239.95 (*0-471-92375-3*) Wiley.

Complex Organizations. Ed. by Richard H. Hall. LC 94-5610. (History of Management Thought Ser.). 500p. 1995. 112.95 (*1-85521-443-1*, Pub. by Dartmth Pub UK) Ashgate Pub Co.

Complex Organizations. 3rd ed. Charles Perrow. 1986. pap. text ed. write for info. (*0-07-554799-6*) McGraw.

Complex Organometallic Catalysts. N. N. Korneev et al. 192p. 1971. text ed. 49.00 (*0-7065-1110-7*, Pub. by Keter Pub IS) Coronet Bks.

***Complex Potential Theory: Proceedings of the NATO Advanced Study Institute & Seminaire de Mathematiques Superieures, Montreal, Canada, July 26-August 6, 1993.** Ed. by Paul M. Gauthier. (NATO ASI Series C: Mathematical & Physical Sciences). 576p. (C). 1994. lib. bdg. 237.00 (*0-7923-3005-6*) Kluwer Ac.

Complex Predicates in Japanese. Chiharu Uda. LC 93-45593. (Outstanding Dissertations in Linguistics Ser.). 376p. 1994. 72.00 (*0-8153-1698-4*) Garland.

Complex Problem Solving: Principles & Mechanisms. Ed. by R. J. Sternberg & P. Frensch. 424p. (C). 1991. text ed. 79.95 (*0-8058-0650-4*); pap. 34.50 (*0-8058-0651-2*) L Erlbaum Assocs.

***Complex Problem Solving: The European Perspective.** Ed. by Peter A. Frensch & Joachim Funke. 336p. 1995. text ed. 59.95 (*0-8058-1336-5*) L Erlbaum Assocs.

***Complex Problem Solving: The European Perspective.** Ed. by Peter A. Frensch & Joachim Funke. 336p. 1995. pap. 34.50 (*0-8058-1783-2*) L Erlbaum Assocs.

Complex Projective Geometry: Selected Papers. Ed. by G. Ellingsrud et al. (London Mathematical Society Lecture Note Ser.: No. 179). 352p. (C). 1992. pap. 42.95 (*0-521-43352-5*) Cambridge U Pr.

Complex Representations of GL (2,K) for Finite Fields K. Ilya Piatetski-Shapiro. LC 82-24484. (Contemporary Mathematics Ser.: Vol. 16). 71p. 1992. pap. 22.00 (*0-8218-5019-9*, CONM-16) Am Math.

Complex Roles of the Teacher: An Ecological Perspective. Shirley F. Heck & C. Ray Williams. LC 83-17865. 212p. (Orig.). (C). 1984. pap. text ed. 17.95 (*0-8077-2748-2*) Tchrs Coll.

Complex Semisimple Lie Algebras. Jean-Pierre Serre. LC 87-13037. (Illus.). 90p. 1987. 31.00 (*0-387-96569-6*) Spr-Verlag.

Complex Sentence Constructions in Australian Languages. Ed. by Peter Austin. LC 87-29971. (Typological Studies in Language: Vol. 15). vii, 289p. 1987. 71.00x (*1-55619-016-6*); pap. 34.95x (*1-55619-017-4*) Benjamins North Am.

Complex Socket Deformities. Stephen L. Bosniak. 320p. 1992. text ed. 85.00 (*0-07-105383-2*) Hlth Prof Div.

Complex Socket Deformities. Stephen L. Bosniak & Byron C. Smith. (Advances in Ophthalmic Plastic & Reconstructive Surgery Ser.: No. 9). (Illus.). 272p. 1991. 82.50 (*0-08-040293-3*, Pub. by PPI UK) McGraw.

Complex Sorrow: Reflections on Cancer & an Abbreviated Life. Marianne A. Paget. Ed. by Marjorie L. DeVault. LC 92-49403. (Illus.). 176p. 1993. 29.95 (*1-56639-041-9*) Temple U Pr.

Complex Sorrow: Reflections on Cancer & an Abbreviated Life. Marianne A. Paget. Ed. by Marjorie L. DeVault. LC 92-49403. (Illus.). 176p. (C). 1994. pap. 16.95 (*1-56639-192-X*) Temple U Pr.

Complex Stochastic Processes: An Introduction to Theory & Application. Kenneth S. Miller. LC 73-18094. 252p. reprint ed. pap. 71.90 (*0-317-55523-5*, 2056328) Bks Demand.

Complex Stochastic Systems. Ed. by D. R. Cox & D. M. Titterington. (Royal Society Discussion Volumes Ser.). 120p. (C). 1992. pap. 34.95 (*0-521-43614-1*) Cambridge U Pr.

***Complex Stochastic Systems & Engineering.** Ed. by D. M. Titterington. (Institute of Mathematics & Its Applications Monograph: No. 54). (Illus.). 312p. 1995. 80.00 (*0-19-853485-X*) OUP.

Complex Structures in Hinid-Urdu: Explorations in Government & Binding Theory. Guprit S. Bains. LC 94-19019. (Monographs in Linguistics & the Philosophy of Language: Vol. 3). 1995. write for info. (*0-8204-2589-3*) P Lang Pubs.

Complex Study of Ancient India. G. M. Bongard-Levin. 1986. 39.95 (*81-202-0141-8*) Asia Bk Corp.

Complex Sulfides: Processing of Ores, Concentrates & By-Products: Proceedings of a Symposium. Ed. by A. D. Zunkel et al. LC 85-18962. (Illus.). 952p. reprint ed. pap. 180.00 (*0-685-23390-1*, 2032594) Bks Demand.

Complex Systems: From Biology to Computation. Ed. by D. Green & T. Bossomaier. LC 92-55077. 386p. 1993. pap. 98.00 (*90-5199-117-7*, Pub. by IOS Pr NE) IOS Press.

***Complex Systems: Mechanism of Adaptation.** R. Stonier & X. Yu. LC 94-78474. 400p. 1994. pap. 93.00 (*90-5199-186-X*) IOS Press.

Complex Systems: Operational Approaches in Neurobiology, Physics & Computers. H. Haken. (Synergetics Ser.: Vol. 31). (Illus.). 350p. 1985. 78.00 (*0-387-15923-1*) Spr-Verlag.

Complex Systems & Cognitive Processes. R. Serra & G. Zanarini. (Illus.). 240p. 1990. 51.00 (*0-387-51393-0*, 3275) Spr-Verlag.

Complex Treatment for Stutterers. Laszlo Vekassy. 171p. 1993. pap. text ed. 23.00 (*963-05-6603-6*, Pub. by A K HU) Intl Spec Bk.

Complex Variable Boundary Element Method in Engineering Analysis. Theodore V. Hromadka, II & C. Lai. (Illus.). 400p. 1986. 65.00 (*0-387-96400-2*) Spr-Verlag.

Complex Variable Boundary Elements. T. V. Hromadka. 1987. disk, ring bd. 395.00 (*0-931215-15-3*) Computational Mech MA.

An Asterisk (*) at the beginning of an entry indicates that the title is appearing in BIP for the first time.

***Complex Variable Methods in Plane Elasticity.** J. K. Lu. (Series in Pure Mathematics). 300p. 1995. text ed. 61.00 (*981-02-2093-6*) World Scientific Pub.

Complex Variable with Applications. 2nd ed. A. David Wunsch. (Illus.). 500p. (C). 1994. text ed. 63.50 (*0-201-12299-5*) Addison-Wesley.

Complex Variables. H. R. Chillingworth. LC 72-86178. 280p. (C). 1973. 116.00 (*0-08-016938-4*, Pub. by Pergamon Repr UK) Franklin.

Complex Variables. Norman Levinson & Raymond Redheffer. 1988. text ed. write for info. (*0-07-037492-9*); Solutions manual. pap. text ed. write for info. (*0-07-037493-7*) McGraw.

Complex Variables. Murray R. Spiegel. (Orig.). (C). 1964. pap. text ed. 13.95 (*0-07-060230-1*) McGraw.

Complex Variables. 2nd ed. Stephen D. Fisher. LC 89-70694. (Wadsworth & Brooks - Cole Mathematics Ser.). 424p. (C). 1990. text ed. 69.95 (*0-534-13260-X*) Brooks-Cole.

Complex Variables. George Polya et al. LC 73-14882. 343p. reprint ed. pap. 97.80 (*0-317-09340-1*, 2055266) Bks Demand.

Complex Variables: An Introduction. C. A. Berenstein & R. Gay. Ed. by J. H. Ewing et al. (Graduate Texts in Mathematics Ser.: Vol. 125). (Illus.). 664p. 1991. 59.00 (*0-387-97349-4*) Spr-Verlag.

Complex Variables: An Introduction. Fulks. (Pure & Applied Mathematics Ser.: Vol. 176). 408p. 1993. 55.00 (*0-8247-9079-0*) Dekker.

Complex Variables: Harmonic & Analytic Functions. Francis J. Flanigan. (Illus.). 353p. 1983. reprint ed. pap. 7.95 (*0-486-61388-7*) Dover.

Complex Variables & Applications. 5th ed. Ruel V. Churchill & James W. Brown. 1990. text ed. write for info. (*0-07-010905-2*) McGraw.

***Complex Variables & Applications.** 6th ed. James W. Brown & Ruel V. Churchill. LC 95-9898. (Churchill-Brown Ser.: International Series in Pure & Applied Mathematics). 1995. write for info. (*0-07-008496-3*) McGraw.

Complex Variables & the Laplace Transform for Engineers. Wilbur R. LePage. (Illus.). 1980. reprint ed. pap. text ed. 9.95 (*0-486-63926-6*) Dover.

Complex Variables for Math & Engineering. 2nd ed. John Mathews. 368p. (C). 1988. text ed. write for info. (*0-697-06764-5*) Wm C Brown Pubs.

Complex Variables for Scientists & Engineers. 2nd ed. John D. Paliouras & Douglas S. Meadows. (Illus.). 805p. (C). 1990. pap. write for info. (*0-02-390561-1*) Macmillan.

Complex Variables Problem Solver. rev. ed. Research & Education Association Staff. (Illus.). 928p. 1994. pap. text ed. 29.95 (*0-87891-604-0*) Res & Educ.

Complex Variables with Applications. A. David Wunsch. LC 82-16288. 416p. (C). 1983. text ed. 61.25 (*0-201-08885-1*, Adv Bk Prog) Addison-Wesley.

Complex Verb Formation. Gary D. Miller. LC 92-34479. (Current Issues in Linguistic Theory Ser.: No. 95). xix, 381p. 1993. 83.00x (*1-55619-156-1*) Benjamins North Am.

Complex Vision of Philo St. John. 1976. pap. 6.95 (*0-912710-08-X*) Regent Graphic Serv.

Complex Vision of Philo St. John. R. Martin Helick. LC 75-27035. 1976. 10.00 (*0-912710-07-1*) Regent Graphic Serv.

***Complex WKB Method for Nonlinear Equations I.** LC 94-22799. (Progress in Physics Ser.: Vol. 16). 1994. 123.00 (*0-8176-5088-1*) Birkhauser.

Complexation Chromatography. Ed. by Cagniant. 312p. 1991. 125.00 (*0-8247-8577-0*) Dekker.

Complexation of Trace Metals in Natural Waters. Ed. by C. J. Kramer & J. C. Duinker. (Developments in Biogeochemistry Ser.). 1984. lib. bdg. 140.00 (*90-247-2973-4*) Kluwer Ac.

Complexe Agricole. J. R. Boudeville. Bd. with Resolution Mathematique des Problemes d'Economie Regionale en U. R. S. S. Analyse, Planification, Optimation. A. Nowicki.; Commerce du 5e Quartier a Lyon. M. Grawitz.; Structure Economique et Niveau de Revenu des Departements Francais. E. Maurel. (Economies et Societes Series L: No. 12). 1963. Set pap. 11.00 (*0-8115-0737-8*) Periodicals Srv.

Complexe Atomique see Atomic Complex: A Worldwide Political History of Nuclear Energy

Complexe de Broadway. Damon Runyon. 320p. (FRE.). 1982. pap. 11.95 (*0-7859-4169-X*, 2070373886) Fr & Eur.

Complexe de Theophile. Georges Duhamel. 228p. (FRE.). 1958. pap. 16.95 (*0-7859-5412-0*) Fr & Eur.

Complexes in Free-Radical Polymerization. J. Barton & E. Borsig. (Polymer Science Library: Vol. 6). 296p. 1988. 123.00 (*0-444-98930-7*) Elsevier.

Complexes of Partial Differential Operators. Aldo Andreotti. LC 75-8440. (Yale Mathematical Monographs: No. 6). 59p. reprint ed. pap. 25.00 (*0-8357-9106-8*, 2016793) Bks Demand.

Complexes of the Rare Earths. S. Sinha. LC 66-17814. 1966. 92.00 (*0-08-011616-7*, Pub. by Pergamon Repr UK) Franklin.

***Complexification.** John L. Casti. 336p. 1995. pap. 13.00 (*0-06-092587-6*, PL) HarpC.

Complexification: Explaining a Paradoxical World Through the Science of Surprise. John L. Casti. LC 93-36049. (Illus.). 352p. 1994. 25.00 (*0-06-016888-9*, HarpT) HarpC.

Complexing & Hydrothermal Ore Deposition. H. Helgeson & D. Ingerson. LC 63-19782. (International Series of Monographs on Earth Sciences: Vol. 17). 1964. 54.00 (*0-08-010084-8*, Pub. by Pergamon Repr UK) Franklin.

Complexites de l' Alliance. F. Heritier-Auge & E. Copet-Rougier. (Ordres Sociaux Ser.). 1990. pap. text ed. 55.00 (*2-88124-222-7*) Gordon & Breach.

Complexites de l'Alliance: Economie, Politique et Fondements Symboliques (Afrique), Vol. III. F. Heritier-Auge & E. Copet-Rougier. 1993. pap. text ed. 32.00 (*2-88124-891-8*) Gordon & Breach.

Complexities. Photos & Text by Bea Nettles. (Illus.). 48p. (Orig.). 1992. pap. 15.00 (*0-930810-07-4*) Inky Pr.

Complexities & Contraries: Essays of Mild Discontent. Eugene J. McCarthy. LC 81-48016. 192p. 1982. 10.95 (*0-15-121202-3*) HarBrace.

Complexities of Higher Education Administration: Case Studies & Issues. Mary L. Higgerson & Susan S. Rehwaldt. 288p. (C). 1993. text ed. 31.95 (*0-9627042-7-X*) Anker Pub.

Complexities of Women: Integrative Essays in Psychology & Biology. Nancy J. Kenney et al. 416p. 1993. per. 30.95 (*0-8403-8548-X*) Kendall-Hunt.

Complexity. M. Mitchell Waldrop. 1993. pap. 12.00 (*0-671-87234-6*, Touchstone Bks) S&S Trade.

Complexity: Knots, Colourings & Countings. Dominic Welsh. (London Mathematical Society Lecture Note Ser.: No. 186). (Illus.). 200p. (C). 1993. pap. 37.95 (*0-521-45740-8*) Cambridge U Pr.

Complexity: Life at the Edge of Chaos. Roger Lewin. LC 93-21652. (Illus.). 224p. 1994. pap. 10.00 (*0-02-014795-3*, Collier S&S) S&S Trade.

Complexity: Life on the Edge of Chaos. Roger Lewin. (Illus.). 256p. 1992. text ed. 22.00 (*0-02-570485-0*) Macmillan.

***Complexity: Metaphors, Models & Reality.** George A. Cowan et al. 752p. (C). 1994. 55.95 (*0-201-62605-5*) Addison-Wesley.

***Complexity: Metaphors, Models & Reality.** George W. Cowan et al. 752p. (C). 1994. pap. 31.95 (*0-201-62606-3*) Addison-Wesley.

Complexity & Contradiction in Modern Architecture. Robert Venturi. (Illus.). 144p. 1977. pap. 12.95 (*0-87070-282-3*, 0-8109-6023-0) Mus of Modern Art.

Complexity, Chaos & Biological Evolution. Ed. by E. Mosekilde & L. Mosekilde. (NATO ASI Series B, Physics: Vol. 270). (Illus.). 424p. 1991. 110.00 (*0-306-44026-1*, Plenum Pr) Plenum.

Complexity, Entropy & the Physics of Information. Wojciech H. Zurek. 544p. (Orig.). (C). 1990. pap. 31.95 (*0-201-51506-7*, Adv Bk Prog) Addison-Wesley.

Complexity, Entropy & the Physics of Information. Ed. by Wojiech H. Zurek. (Santa Fe Institute Ser.). 544p. (Orig.). (C). 1990. 47.95 (*0-201-51509-1*, 130J90, Adv Bk Prog) Addison-Wesley.

Complexity in Information Theory. Ed. by Y. S. Abu-Mostafa. (Illus.). 150p. 1990. 30.00 (*0-387-96600-5*) Spr-Verlag.

Complexity in Numerical Optimization. Panos M. Pardalos. LC 93-4827. 400p. 1993. text ed. 121.00 (*981-02-1415-4*) World Scientific Pub.

Complexity in Physics & Technology. M. S. Garrido & R. V. Mendes. 300p. 1993. text ed. 95.00 (*981-02-1016-7*) World Scientific Pub.

***Complexity in Urban Crisis Management: Amsterdam's Response to the Bijlmer Disaster.** R. Uriel & Crisis Research Centre Staff. (Illus.). 176p. 1994. 60.00 (*1-873936-34-6*, Pub. by J & J Sci Pubs UK) Bks Intl VA.

Complexity, Language, & Life: Mathematical Approaches. Ed. by John L. Casti & Anders Karlqvist. (Biomathematics Ser.: Vol. 16). x, 284p. 1986. 64.00 (*0-387-16180-5*) Spr-Verlag.

Complexity of Boolean Functions. Ingo Wegener. LC 87-10388. (Teubner Series in Computer Science). 450p. 1987. text ed. 139.00 (*0-471-91555-6*) Wiley.

Complexity of Boolean Networks. Paul E. Dunne. (APIC Studies). 400p. 1988. text ed. 66.00 (*0-12-224460-5*) Acad Pr.

Complexity of Computation: Proceedings of the SIAM-AMS Symposia, New York, April, 1973. Society for Industrial & Applied Mathematics Staff & American Mathematical Society Staff. Ed. by R. M. Karp. LC 74-22062. (SIAMS-AMS Proceedings Ser.: Vol 7). 166p. 1974. 47.00 (*0-8218-1327-7*, SIAMS-7) Am Math.

Complexity of Computing. John E. Savage. LC 84-27818. 408p. 1987. reprint ed. lib. bdg. 44.95 (*0-89874-833-X*) Krieger.

Complexity of Interdependence. John A. Kroll. (CISA Working Paper Ser.: No. 72). 36p. (Orig.). Date not set. pap. 10.00 (*0-86682-090-6*) Ctr Intl Relations.

Complexity of Proofs & Their Transformations in Axiomatic Theories. V. P. Orevkov. Ed. by David Louvish. Tr. by Alexander Bochman. LC 93-11139. (ENG.). 1993. write for info. (*0-8218-4576-4*) Am Math.

Complexity of Robot Motion Planning, 1987. John F. Canny. (ACM Doctoral Dissertation Award Ser.). 150p. 1988. 29.95 (*0-262-03136-1*) MIT Pr.

Complexity of the Self: Developmental Approach to Psychopathology & Therapy. Vittorio F. Guidano. LC 87-350. (Guilford Clinical Psychology & Psychotherapy Ser.). 248p. 1987. lib. bdg. 30.00 (*0-89862-012-0*) Guilford Pr.

Complexity Security Guide for Executives: How to Protect Yourself, Employees, & Corporate... Neil C. Livingstone. 1991. pap. 18.95 (*0-669-27667-7*) Free Pr.

Complexity Theory: Current Research. Ed. by Klaus Ambos-Spies et al. 255p. (C). 1993. 29.95 (*0-521-44220-6*) Cambridge U Pr.

Complexity Theory of Real Functions. K. I. Ko. (Progress in Theoretical Computer Science Ser.). 315p. 1991. 49.50 (*0-8176-3586-6*) Spr-Verlag.

Complexity Theory Retrospective: In Honor of Juris Hartmanis on the Occasion of His Sixtieth Birthday, July 5, 1988. Ed. by A. L. Selman. (Illus.). x, 234p. 1990. 69.00 (*0-387-97350-8*) Spr-Verlag.

***Compliance.** N. Whallen. (Orig.). 1995. pap. text ed. 5.95 (*1-56333-356-2*) Masquerade.

Compliance: The Dilemma of the Chronically Ill. Kenneth E. Gerber & Alexis M. Nehemkis. 256p. 1986. 26.95 (*0-8261-4580-9*) Springer Pub.

Compliance & Public Authority: A Theory with International Applications. Oran R. Young. LC 79-2193. (Resources for the Future Ser.). 1979. 17.95 (*0-8018-2279-3*) Johns Hopkins.

***Compliance Auditing Applicable to Governmental Entities & Other Recipients of Governmental Financial Assistance.** fac. ed. American Institute of Certified Public Accountants Staff. (Statement on Auditing Standards Ser.: No. 63). 73p. 1989. reprint ed. pap. 25.00 (*0-7837-8251-9*, 2049019) Bks Demand.

Compliance Auditing for Pharmaceutical Manufacturers: A Practical Guide to In-Depth Systems Auditing. Karen Ginsbury & Gil Bismuth. 402p. 1994. ring bd. 235.00 (*0-935184-60-0*) Interpharm.

Compliance Auditing in Georgia Counties & Municipalities: A Practical Guide to State Laws for Auditors & Local Government Officials. Paul T. Hardy et al. LC 93-14769. 152p. (C). 1995. 14.95 (*0-89854-165-4*) U of GA Inst Govt.

Compliance Examinations Update. Virginia J. Thomas. 1985. 278.00 (*0-88712-291-4*) Warren Gorham & Lamont.

***Compliance Guide for Administrators.** AMS Distributors Staff & CTTS Safety Products Staff. 176p. 1994. per., pap. text ed. 29.95 (*0-7872-0327-0*) Kendall-Hunt.

Compliance Guide to Electronic Health Records. Jonathan P. Tomes. 200p. 1994. pap. 149.95 (*1-881393-23-2*) Faulkner & Gray.

Compliance Guide to Electronic Healthcare Payments. Jonathan P. Tomes. 200p. 1994. pap. 149.95 (*1-881393-24-0*) Faulkner & Gray.

***Compliance Guide to the Americans with Disabilities Act.** G. John Tysse et al. 110p. 1991. 50.00 (*0-916559-34-3*, 2004-MO-4035) EPF.

***Compliance Guide to the Federal Family & Medical Leave Act.** Human Resources Policy Dept. Staff. 1993. ring bd. 89.00 (*0-88711-254-4*) Am Trucking Assns.

Compliance Ideologies: Rethinking Political Culture. Richard W. Wilson. (Illus.). 208p. (C). 1992. 49.95 (*0-521-41581-0*) Cambridge U Pr.

Compliance in Epilepsy: Epilepsy Research Supplement - One. Ed. by D. A. Schmidt & Ilo E. Leppik. 196p. 1988. 87.25 (*0-444-81006-4*) Elsevier.

Compliance in Health Care. Ed. by R. Brian Haynes et al. LC 78-20527. 534p. reprint ed. pap. 152.20 (*0-8357-8078-3*, 2034148) Bks Demand.

Compliance Investigator. Jack Rudman. (Career Examination Ser.: C-2421). 1994. pap. 27.95 (*0-8373-2421-1*) Nat Learn.

Compliance Manual: A Guide to the Rules & Regulations of P.L. 94-142. James C. Chalfant & Margaret Van Dusen Pysh. LC 79-90320. (Illus.). 100p. (Orig.). 1980. pap. 9.95 (*0-933922-01-9*, P501) GA-CH.

Compliance Manual for OSHA's Bloodborne Pathogens Standard 29 CFR 1910.1030. James Testo. Ed. by Failsafe Risk Management Alternatives Staff. (Illus.). 370p. (Orig.). 1993. ring bd. 99.00 (*0-931690-47-1*) Genium Pub.

Compliance Manual for OSHA's Hazard Communication Standard. 222p. 1992. pap. text ed. 99.00 (*0-931690-43-9*) Genium Pub.

Compliance Manuals for the New Antitrust Era. 500p. 1990. pap. 95.00 (*0-685-47174-8*, 503-0085) Amer Bar Assn.

***Compliance or Alliance?** Alan Pearson & Helen Baker. (Case Study on Introducing Research Papers: No. 9). 1992. pap. text ed. 21.00 (*0-614-04014-0*, Pub. by Deakin Univ AT) St Mut.

Compliance Programs & the Corporate Sentencing Guidelines: Preventing Criminal & Civil Liability. Jeffrey M. Kaplan et al. 1993. 145.00 (*0-318-72273-9*) Clark Boardman Callaghan.

***Compliance Review Tool Kit: An Internal Control System for Auditing & Monitoring.** 4th ed. Barefoot. 1995. 225.00 (*1-55738-783-4*) Probus Pub Co.

***Compliance Review Toolkit: An Internal Control System for Auditing & Monitoring Consumer Regulatory Compliance.** rev. ed. Barefoot, Marrinan & Associates, Inc. Staff. 225p. 1995. 225.00 (*1-55738-741-9*) Probus Pub Co.

Compliance Supplement for Single Audits of State & Local Governments. rev. ed. 268p. (Orig.). 1985. pap. 13.00 (*0-16-004325-5*, S/N 041-001-00294-4) USGPO.

***Compliance Training Service.** Regulatory Compliance Assocs., Inc. Staff. 500p. 1995. 295.00 (*1-55738-712-5*) Probus Pub Co.

Compliance with Federal Election Campaign Requirements: A Guide for Candidates. 4th ed. American Institute of Certified Public Accountants Staff. LC 83-208707. (Illus.). 224p. reprint ed. pap. 63.90 (*0-8357-4116-8*, 2036897) Bks Demand.

Compliance with Federal Election Campaign Requirements: A Guide for Candidates. 5th ed. American Institute of Certified Public Accountants Staff & Federal Election Campaign Guide Task Force Staff. LC 83-208707. 216p. 1990. 44.25 (*0-87051-073-8*) Am Inst CPA.

***Compliance with International Law.** Edith B. Weiss. 300p. 1995. 65.00 (*1-57105-000-0*) Transnatl Pubs.

Compliance with the Safe Drinking Water Act. (State Legislative Reports: Vol. 15, No. 7). 10p. 1990. 5.00 (*1-55516-263-0*, 7302-1507) Natl Conf State Legis.

Compliant Offshore Structures. Minoo H. Patel & Joel A. Witz. 416p. 1991. 170.00 (*0-7506-1070-0*) Buttrwrth-Heinemann.

***Compilation of 28th Annual CMA Seminar on "How NAFTA, GATT Will Affect Men's Tailored Clothing Manufacturers.** 1994. 35.00 (*0-614-05676-4*) Clothing Mfrs.

***Complicated Choices, Unacceptable Contracts: The 1992 Referendum in Quebec.** Robert L. Dion. (MacArthur Scholar Ser.). 89p. (Orig.). 1995. pap. 4.50 (*1-881157-31-8*) In Ctr Global.

Complicated Medical Patient: New Approaches to Psychomedical Syndromes. John I. Walker et al. LC 86-20808. 290p. 1987. 45.95 (*0-89885-331-1*) Human Sci Pr.

Complicated War: The Harrowing of Mozambique. William Finnegan. 325p. 1992. 28.00 (*0-520-07804-7*) U CA Pr.

Complicated War: The Harrowing of Mozambique. William Finnegan. 1993. pap. 14.00 (*0-520-08266-4*) U CA Pr.

Complicated Watches & Their Repair. Donald De Carle. (Illus.). 174p. 1978. 34.50 (*0-7198-0090-0*, Pub. by NAG Press UK) Antique Collect.

Complications & Quality Assurance in Anesthesia. Brown & Caplan. (Illus.). 750p. 1991. 89.00 (*0-8016-0263-7*) Mosby Yr Bk.

Complications & Sequelae of Head Injury. Ed. by Daniel L. Barrow. (Neurosurgical Topics Ser.). (Illus.). 200p. 1991. text ed. 90.00 (*1-879284-00-6*) Am Assn Neuro.

Complications from Standing in a Circle. Mark Wallace. 72p. (Orig.). (C). 1993. pap. 6.95 (*0-922668-10-8*) SUNYB Poetry Rare Bks.

Complications in Arthroscopy. Norman F. Sprague, III. 252p. 1989. 135.50 (*0-88167-523-7*) Raven.

Complications in Cardiopulmonary Surgery. G. H. Smith. (Illus.). 240p. 1984. text ed. 70.50 (*0-7216-0967-8*) Saunders.

Complications in Cardiothoracic Surgery. Waldhausen & Orringer. 480p. 1990. 119.00 (*0-8151-9175-8*, Yr Bk Med Pubs) Mosby Yr Bk.

***Complications in Colon & Rectal Surgery.** Terry Hicks et al. 1995. 125.00 (*0-942219-78-3*) Quality Med Pub.

Complications in Critical Care Medicine. Ed. by Philip D. Lumb. (Illus.). 576p. 1987. 75.00 (*0-8151-5652-9*, ZGD-1, Yr Bk Med Pubs) Mosby Yr Bk.

Complications in Foot & Ankle Surgery: Prevention & Management. 3rd ed. Jeffrey M. Carrel & Howard M. Sokoloff. (Illus.). 486p. 1993. 80.00 (*0-683-01465-X*) Williams & Wilkins.

Complications in Foot Surgery: Prevention & Management. American College of Foot Surgeons Staff. LC 75-28130. 253p. reprint ed. pap. 72.20 (*0-317-30007-5*, 2051867) Bks Demand.

Complications in Gynecologic Surgery: Prevention, Recognition & Management. James W. Orr, Jr. et al. Ed. by J. Marion Sims. LC 93-41475. (Illus.). 360p. 1994. pap. 69.50 (*0-397-51269-4*, Lippincott Medical) Lippincott.

Complications in Hand Surgery. John Boswick, Jr. (Illus.). 401p. 1986. text ed. 132.50 (*0-7216-1877-4*) Saunders.

Complications in Head & Neck Surgery. Ed. by David W. Eisele. LC 92-49964. 827p. 1992. 149.00 (*1-55664-367-5*) Mosby Yr Bk.

Complications in Head & Neck Surgery. Yosef P. Krespi & Robert H. Ossoff. (Illus.). 600p. 1992. text ed. 93.50 (*0-7216-2980-6*) Saunders.

Complications in Laparoscopic Surgery. Robert W. Bailey & John L. Flowers. LC 94-32028. 1994. 135.00 (*0-942219-47-3*) Quality Med Pub.

Complications in Modern Ophthalmic Surgery. Ed. by Ilse Strempel. (Developments in Ophthalmology Ser.: Vol. 13). (Illus.). xii, 160p. 1987. 102.50 (*3-8055-4413-8*) S Karger.

Complications in Neurosurgery I. Ed. by A. M. Landolt. (Progress in Neurological Surgery Ser.: Vol. 11). (Illus.). x, 174p. 1984. 78.50 (*3-8055-3691-7*) S Karger.

Complications in Ophthalmic Surgery. Judie Charlton & George Weinstein. (Illus.). 500p. 1994. 87.50 (*0-397-51295-3*) Lippincott.

Complications in Orthopaedic Surgery, 2 vols., Set. 3rd ed. Ed. by Charles H. Epps, Jr. LC 93-40983. 1350p. 1994. 240.00 (*0-397-51216-3*) Lippincott.

Complications in Otolaryngology - Head & Neck Surgery, Vol. II. rev. ed. Johns. 322p. (C). 1992. 55.00 (*0-941158-63-2*) Mosby Yr Bk.

Complications in Pediatric Ophthalmology. Charles H. Epps, Jr. 1993. 125.00 (*0-397-51217-1*) Lippincott.

Complications in PTCA: Workshop "Complications in PTCA" German Heart Institute Berlin, June 17th, 1989. Ed. by E. Fleck & E. Frantz. x, 152p. 1991. 47.00 (*0-387-91371-8*) Spr-Verlag.

Complications in Spinal Surgery. Richard A. Balderston & An. (Illus.). 208p. 1990. text ed. 60.95 (*0-7216-3522-9*) Saunders.

Complications in Surgery & Trauma. 2nd ed. Greenfield. (Illus.). 1064p. 1989. text ed. 140.00 (*0-397-50904-9*) Lippincott.

Complications in Surgery in General. J. A. Smith. (Illus.). 240p. 1984. text ed. 58.95 (*0-7020-0983-0*) Saunders.

Complications in the Management of Breast Disease. R. W. Blamey. (Complications in Surgery Ser.). (Illus.). 272p. 1987. text ed. 48.50 (*0-7020-1131-2*, Bailliere-Tindall) Saunders.

Complications in Vascular Surgery. 2nd ed. Ed. by Victor M. Bernhard & Jonathon B. Towne. LC 79-574. 832p. 1985. text ed. 159.00 (*0-8089-1747-1*, Grune) Saunders.

Complications of Cancer: Diagnosis & Management. Ed. by Martin D. Abeloff. LC 79-7563. 1980. text ed. 70.00x (*0-8018-2254-8*) Johns Hopkins.

Complications of Cancer Management. Ed. by P. N. Plowman et al. 528p. 1991. text ed. 295.00 (*0-7506-1341-6*) Buttrwrth-Heinemann.

C

An Asterisk (*) at the beginning of an entry indicates that the title is appearing in BIP for the first time. 1479

Complications of Cardiac Catheterization & Angiography: Prevention & Management. Ed. by Jack Kron & Mark J. Morton. (Illus.). 408p. 1989. 55.00 (*0-87993-338-0*) Futura Pub.

Complications of Chronic Liver Disease. Rector. 383p. 1991. 69.00 (*0-8151-7236-2*, Yr Bk Med Pubs) Mosby Yr Bk.

Complications of Colon & Rectal Surgery: Prevention & Management. Bernard T. Ferrari et al. (Illus.). 450p. 1985. text ed. 90.50 (*0-7216-3622-5*) Saunders.

Complications of Contact Lens Wear. Ed. by Alan Tomlinson. LC 92-16488. 283p. 1992. 77.95 (*0-8016-6309-1*) Mosby Yr Bk.

Complications of Coronary Angioplasty. Ed. by Alexander J. Black. (Fundamental & Clinical Cardiology Ser.: Vol. 3). 280p. 1991. 110.00 (*0-8247-8440-5*) Dekker.

Complications of Dermatologic Surgery: Prevention & Treatment. Ed. by Marwali Harahap. LC 92-48955. 1992. 99.00 (*0-387-55337-1*) Spr-Verlag.

Complications of Diabetes: Prevention & Treatment. Reinout Van Schilfgaarde. 400p. 1987. text ed. 105.00 (*0-8089-1853-2*, 794691, Grune) Saunders.

Complications of Foot & Ankle Surgery. Jeffrey E. Johnson et al. 350p. 1994. write for info. (*0-683-04461-3*) Williams & Wilkins.

Complications of Fractures & Dislocations. Segelov. 1990. 89.00 (*0-8016-4483-6*, Yr Bk Med Pubs) Mosby Yr Bk.

Complications of Gastric Surgery. David Fromm. LC 77-9313. (Illus.). 172p. reprint ed. pap. 49.10 (*0-7837-3442-5*, 2057765) Bks Demand.

Complications of Glaucoma Therapy. Mark B. Sherwood & George L. Spaeth. LC 85-5237. 390p. 1990. 85.00 (*1-55642-174-5*) SLACK Inc.

Complications of Gynecologic & Obstetric Management. Michael Newton & Edward R. Newton. (Illus.). 544p. 1988. text ed. 79.50 (*0-7216-6769-4*) Saunders.

***Complications of Head & Neck Surgery.** Mark Weissler & Harold Pillsbury. (Illus.). 544p. 1995. 99.00 (*0-86577-529-X*) Thieme Med Pubs.

***Complications of Laparoscopy & Flexible Endoscopy: Postgraduate Course of the Annual Meeting of the Society of American Gastrointenstinal Endoscopic Surgeons (SAGES) 1994.** Ed. by Medical Support Systems Staff. 1994. 125.00 (*0-387-14219-3*) Spr-Verlag.

Complications of Laparoscopy & Hysteroscopy. R. S. Corfman et al. (Illus.). 304p. 1993. 75.00 (*0-86542-201-X*) Blackwell Sci.

Complications of Minor Surgery. C. J. Stoddard & J. A. Smith. (Illus.). 250p. 1984. text ed. 58.95 (*0-7020-0985-7*, Bailliere-Tindall) Saunders.

Complications of Nervous System Trauma. Ed. by Richard A. Thompson & John R. Green. LC 78-52425. (Advances in Neurology Ser.: Vol. 22). 345p. 1979. text ed. 92.50 (*0-89004-295-0*) Raven.

Complications of Organ Transplantation: Medical & Surgical Complications. Toledo-Pereyra. (Immunology Ser.: Vol. 32). 464p. 1987. 165.00 (*0-8247-7639-9*) Dekker.

Complications of Orthopedic Surgery, Set. 2nd ed. Charles H. Epps, Jr. et al. (Illus.). 1584p. 1986. text ed. 175.00 (*0-397-50638-4*, Lippincott Medical) Lippincott.

Complications of Plastic Surgery. Morris et al. 504p. 1989. text ed. 121.00 (*0-7020-1360-9*) Saunders.

Complications of Pregnancy: Medical, Surgical, Gynecologic, Psychosocial & Perinatal. 4th ed. Sheldon H. Cherry et al. (Illus.). 1352p. 1991. 155.00 (*0-683-01672-5*) Williams & Wilkins.

Complications of Shoulder Surgery. Louis U. Bigliani. LC 92-49883. (Illus.). 296p. 1993. 99.00 (*0-683-00751-3*) Williams & Wilkins.

Complications of Spinal Surgery. Ed. by Edward Tarlov. (Neurosurgical Topics Ser.). (Illus.). 145p. 1991. 90.00 (*0-9624246-8-4*) Am Assn Neuro.

Complications of Spine Surgery. Steven R. Garfin. (Illus.). 500p. 1989. 80.00 (*0-683-03435-9*) Williams & Wilkins.

Complications of Surgery of the Upper Gastrointestinal Tract. Robert W. Kirk & C. J. Stoddard. 1986. text ed. 76.50 (*0-7020-1138-X*, Bailliere-Tindall) Saunders.

Complications of Thoracic Surgery. Wolfe. 319p. 1991. 89.00 (*1-55664-175-3*) Mosby Yr Bk.

Complications of Total Hip Arthroplasty. Richard H. Rothman & Hozak. 256p. 1988. text ed. 98.50 (*0-7216-2447-2*) Saunders.

Complications of Trauma. Ed. by Kenneth L. Mattox. (Illus.). 616p. 1993. text ed. 139.95 (*0-443-08851-9*) Churchill.

Complications of Urologic Surgery: Prevention & Management. 2nd ed. Robert B. Smith & Erlich. 544p. 1990. text ed. 115.00 (*0-7216-8414-9*) Saunders.

Complications of Viral & Mycoplasmal Infections in Rodents to Toxicology Research & Testing. Ed. by Thomas E. Hamm, Jr. LC 84-12789. (Chemical Industry Institute of Toxicology Ser.). (Illus.). 300p. 1986. 79.00 (*0-89116-388-3*) Hemisp Pub.

Complications Requiring Reoperation, Vol. 5. Ronald J. Stoney & David J. Effeny. (Illus.). 224p. 1991. text ed. 99.50 (*0-397-50971-5*) Lippincott.

Complicit Fictions: The Subject in the Modern Japanese Prose Narrative. James A. Fujii. (Twentieth-Century Japan: The Emergence of a World Power Ser.: No. 2). (C). 1992. pap. 15.00 (*0-520-07770-9*) U CA Pr.

Complicit Fictions: The Subject in the Modern Japanese Prose Narrative. James A. Fujii. (Twentieth-Century Japan: The Emergence of a World Power Ser.: No. 2). (C). 1992. 40.00 (*0-520-07757-1*) U CA Pr.

Complicite. Francis Iles. 256p. (FRE.). 1972. pap. 10.95 (*0-7859-2288-1*, 2070362396) Fr & Eur.

Complicity. Iain Banks. LC 94-13820. 299p. 1995. 22.50 (*0-385-47540-3*, N A Talese) Doubleday.

Complicity. Elizabeth Cooke. 288p. 1988. 16.95 (*0-316-15507-1*) Little.

Complicity & Conviction: Steps Toward an Architecture of Convention. William Q. Hubbard. (Illus.). 1980. pap. 12.50x (*0-262-58057-8*) MIT Pr.

***Complier Design.** Renhard Wilhelm. (C). 1995. text ed. 56.95 (*0-201-42290-5*) Addison-Wesley.

Complier Design in C. 2nd ed. Allen I. Holub. 1994. 63.00 (*0-13-175936-1*) P-H.

Complimentarity in Mathematics. Willem Kuyk. LC 77-8838. (Mathematics & Its Applications Ser.: No. 1). 1977. lib. bdg. 44.50 (*90-277-0814-2*) Kluwer Ac.

Compliments: A Treasury of Tributes to Friends & Lovers, Relatives, & Rivals. Ed. by Gertrude Buckman. LC 80-678. (Illus.). 88p. 1980. 9.95 (*0-672-52650-6*, Bobbs) Macmillan.

Compliments of the Chef. 2nd enl. rev. ed. Ruth Dorman & Lois Marcus. 1989. pap. 12.45 (*0-201-19626-3*) Addison-Wesley.

Compliments of the Chef: One Hundred Great Recipes from the Innovative Restaurants & Cafes of Berkeley, California. Temple Beth El Sisterhood Staff & Paul Johnston. LC 84-24378. (Illus.). 160p. (Orig.). 1985. pap. 9.95 (*0-943186-20-X*) Aris Bks.

Complot Para Destruir las Fuerzas Armadas de Ibero-America. Gretchen Small & Dennis Small. Ed. by Executive Intelligence Review Staff. 500p. (Orig.). (SPA.). 1993. pap. 25.00 (*0-943235-10-3*) Exec Intel Review.

Complutenses Discalceati - Collegii Complutensis Disputationes in Aristotelis Dialecticam Et Philosophiam Naturalem. Ed. by W. Risse. vii, 338p. 1977. reprint ed. write for info. (*3-487-06240-2*, Pub. by Georg Olms GW) Lubrecht & Cramer.

***Complying with Clean Air Act Regulations: Issues & Techniques.** 175p. 1995. pap. 55.00 (*0-444-10001-6*) Elsevier.

Complying with FDA Good Manufacturing Requirements: How to Develop Your GMP - QA Manual. John Riordan & William Cotliar. 252p. 1991. 175.00 (*0-910275-53-X*, GMP1-113); student ed. disk 275.00 (*0-685-59181-6*, GMP3-113); disk 175.00 (*0-685-59180-8*, GMP2-113) Assn Adv Med Instrn.

Complying with Federal Law: A Manual for College Decision Makers. Kent M. Weeks. 161p. (C). 1992. text ed. write for info. (*1-881434-00-1*) Coll Legal Info.

Complying with Federal Law: A Manual for College Decision Makers. Kent M. Weeks. 158p. (C). 1992. text ed. write for info. (*1-881434-03-6*) Coll Legal Info.

Complying with FIRPTA: A Manual of Forms. LC 88-84138. 156p. 1989. pap. 34.95 (*0-89707-418-1*, 543-0097-01) Amer Bar Assn.

Complying with Government Regulations Module, PACE: A Program for Acquiring Competence in Entrepreneurship, 3 levels. rev. ed. National Center for Research in Vocational Education Staff. 1983. 2.50 (*0-317-06032-5*); Level 1. 2.50 (*0-317-06033-3*, RD240AB10); Level 2. 2.50 (*0-317-06034-1*, RD240BB10); Level 3. 2.50 (*0-317-06035-X*, RD240CB10) Ctr Educ Trng Employ.

***Complying with OBRA: Managing Restraint Reduction Programs in Nursing Home & Healthcare Centers.** Joseph K. Egbebike. Ed. by Jeff Gollin. (Illus.). 98p. (Orig.). Date not set. pap. write for info. (*0-9639841-0-1*) PTS Pubng.

Complying with the ADA: A Small Business Guide to Hiring & Employing the Disabled. Jeffrey G. Allen. (Small Business Editions Ser.). 224p. 1993. text ed. 42.50 (*0-471-59049-5*); pap. text ed. 17.95 (*0-471-59051-7*) Wiley.

Complying with the Americans with Disabilities Act: A Guide for Employers. (ADA Practice Ser.). 54p. 1994. pap. 21.00 (*0-934753-89-X*) LRP Pubns.

Complying with the Americans with Disabilities Act: A Guide for Union Representatives. (ADA Practice Ser.). 74p. 1994. pap. 24.00 (*0-934753-94-6*) LRP Pubns.

Complying with the Americans with Disabilities Act: A Guidebook for Management & People with Disabilities. Don Fersh & Peter W. Thomas. LC 92-28478. 280p. 1993. text ed. 52.95 (*0-89930-714-0*, FNE/, Quorum Bks) Greenwood.

Complying with the Americans with Disabilities Act, ADA: A Guide for Health Care Facilities. Nancy C. Aldrich et al. (Illus.). 560p. (Orig.). 1992. pap. 60.00 (*0-87258-591-3*, 055980) Am Hospital.

***Complying with the Bank Secrecy Act.** rev. ed. Robert E. Powis. 22p. 1994. 22.00 (*1-55738-399-5*) Probus Pub Co.

Complying with the Bloodborne Pathogen Standard: A Step-by-Step Guide. Jane M. Whitehead. 102p. 1992. pap. 45.00 (*0-86587-327-5*) Gov Insts.

***Complying with the CFC Prohibitions.** Jack Dale Associates, Inc. Staff. 196p. (Orig.). 1994. pap. text ed. 75.00 (*0-86587-423-9*) Gov Insts.

Complying with the Family & Medical Leave Act: A Detailed Guide. John Thurman & Frank Palmieri. 200p. 1993. disk, ring bd. 179.00 (*0-86587-354-2*) Gov Insts.

Complying with the New Nondiscrimination & Minimum Coverage Regulations. (Tax Law & Estate Planning Ser.). 198p. 1992. pap. text ed. 5.50 (*0-685-56934-9*, J4-3656) PLI.

Complying with Trihalomethane Reduction Requirements in Water Treatment Facilities. Philip C. Singer. LC 89-8666. (Pollution Technology Review Ser.: No. 167). (Illus.). 285p. 1990. 39.00 (*0-8155-1207-4*) Noyes.

Compo Dolls: Cute & Collectible, Vol. II. Rhoda Shoemaker. 1973. spiral bd. 10.95 (*0-685-30846-4*) R Shoemaker.

Compo Dolls-Cute & Collectible, Vol. III. 1979. spiral bd. 12.95 (*0-317-40451-2*) R Shoemaker.

Compo Dolls, 1909-1928 Vol. II: Identification & Price Guide. Polly Judd. 1994. 25.00 (*0-87588-418-0*) Hobby Hse.

Component & Correspondence Analysis. Ed. by J. L. Van Rijckevorsel. LC 87-33981. (Probability & Mathematical Statistics Ser.). 200p. 1988. text ed. 89.95 (*0-471-91847-4*) Wiley.

Component Failure: A Tribology Handbook. M. J. Neale. (Authored (Royalty) Ser.). 1994. 39.00 (*1-56091-451-3*, R-137) Soc Auto Engineers.

***Component Failures. Maintenance & Repair.** Ed. by Neale M. J. LC 94-32562. (Tribology Handbook). 1995. write for info. (*0-615-00175-0*) Buttrwrth-Heinemann.

Component Failures, Maintenance & Repair. Michael J. Neale. (Tribology Handbooks Ser.). (Illus.). 144p. 1995. pap. 4,795.00 (*0-7506-0980-X*) Buttrwrth-Heinemann.

Component Locator Manual 1989-91. 432p. 1992. pap. 60.00 (*0-8019-8280-4*) Chilton.

Component Locator Manual 1991-93. Ed. by Chilton Staff. 736p. 1994. pap. 60.00 (*0-8019-8545-5*) Chilton.

Component Parts - Stevens-Rifles-Shotguns-Pistols. reprint ed. White cover. pap. 2.50 (*1-877704-09-1*) Pioneer Pr.

Component Parts Price List of Marlin Rifle - Shotguns. reprint ed. 2.50 (*1-877704-07-5*) Pioneer Pr.

Component Repair, Replacement & Failure Prevention in Light Water Reactors: Proceedings of the 4th International Seminar on Assuring Structural Integrity of Steel Reactor Pressure Boundary Components, Held at the CEC Joint Research. International Seminar on Assuring Structural Integrity of Steel Reactor Pressure Boundary Components Staff. Ed. by K. E. Stahlkopf & L. E. Steele. 494p. 1986. reprint ed. 169.25 (*1-85166-025-9*, Pub. by Elsevier Applied Sci UK) Elsevier.

Component Support Snubbers: Design, Application, & Testing: Presented at the Pressure Vessels & Piping Conference, ASME Century 2--Emerging Technology Conferences, San Francisco, California, August 12-15, 1980. Pressure Vessels & Piping Conference Staff. Ed. by D. D. Reiff. LC 80-66043. (PVP Ser.: No. 42). (Illus.). 75p. reprint ed. pap. 25.00 (*0-8357-2818-8*, 2039057) Bks Demand.

Component Units of Federal States & International Agreement. Luigi Di Marzo. LC 80-83265. 272p. 1981. lib. bdg. 84.00 (*90-286-0330-1*) Kluwer Ac.

Componentes de un Sistema de Practica Docente Renovada. Pura Quesada de Rodriguez. LC 78-3641. 119p. 1978. pap. 3.20 (*0-8477-2742-4*) U of PR Pr.

Componential Analysis of Lushai Phonology. Alfons Weidert. (Current Issues in Linguistic Theory Ser.: No. 2). xiv, 139p. 1975. pap. 38.00x (*90-272-0903-0*) Benjamins North Am.

Components. 1976. 39.00 (*0-317-43781-X*) St Mut.

Components & Instruments for Distributed Computer Control Systems: Proceedings of the IFAC Symposium, Paris, France, Dec. 1982. IFAC Symposium Staff. Ed. by Z. Binder & R. Perret. LC 83-11448. (IFAC Proceedings Ser.). 178p. 1983. 106.00 (*0-08-029991-1*, Pub. by Pergamon Repr UK) Franklin.

Components for Fiber Optic Applications, No. II. Ed. by Tekippe. 1987. 45.00 (*0-89252-874-5*, 839) SPIE.

Components for Fiber Optic Applications & Coherent Lightwave Communications, Vol. 988. Ed. by P. M. Kopera & H. R. Sunak. 1988. 59.00 (*0-8194-0023-8*) SPIE.

Components for Fiber Optic Applications IV. Ed. by Paul M. Kopera. 215p. 1990. 53.00 (*0-8194-0212-5*, VOL. 1176) SPIE.

Components for Fiber Optic Applications V, Vol. 1365. P. M. Kopera. 1991. 53.00 (*0-8194-0426-8*) SPIE.

Components for High Purity Water Treatment Systems, Including Mobile Systems. 1992. 1,550.00 (*0-89336-943-8*, GB-147A) BCC.

Components for Pneumatic Control Instruments: Static & Dynamic Character of Pneumatic Resistance Capacitances. L. Zalmanzon & R. Hardbottle. LC 64-24301. 1965. 144.00 (*0-08-010519-X*, Pub. by Pergamon Repr UK) Franklin.

Components of a Trial: Final Arguments. Philip H. Corboy. 126p. 1989. 32.00 (*0-941916-54-5*) ATLA Pr.

Components of a Trial: Opening Statements. Peter Perlman. 100p. 23.00 (*0-941916-57-X*) ATLA Pr.

Components of Dress: Design, Marketing & Image. Juliet Ash & Lee Wright. (Illus.). 144p. 1988. lib. bdg. 45.00 (*0-415-00647-3*); pap. 15.95 (*0-415-00648-1*) Routledge.

Components of Fiber Optic LANs. rev. ed. IGI Staff. (Fiber Optic Reprint Ser.: Vol. 5). (Illus.). 200p. 1994. pap. 75.00 (*1-56851-054-3*) Info Gatekeepers.

Components of Productivity of Mediterranean-Climate Regions: Basic & Applied Aspects. Ed. by N. S. Margaris & Harold A. Mooney. (Tasks for Vegetation Science Ser.: No. 4). viii, 280p. 1981. lib. bdg. 107.50 (*90-6193-944-5*) Kluwer Ac.

Components of Technical Writing. Susan Feinberg. (Illus.). 528p. (C). 1989. pap. 26.00 (*0-03-071576-8*) HB Coll Pubs.

Components of the Content Structure of the Word. N. G. Komlev. LC 74-80542. (Janua Linguarum, Series Minor: No. 138). 227p. 1976. pap. text ed. 49.25 (*90-279-3364-2*) Mouton.

Components of the Future. Ed. by Jeffrey B. Friedman. 397p. 1985. pap. text ed. 35.00 (*0-940690-10-1*) Soc Motion Pic & TV Engrs.

***Components of Understanding.** Concept by L. Ron Hubbard. 30p. 1994. pap. 4.00 (*0-88404-910-8*) Bridge Pubns Inc.

Components Quality & Reliability, 1991-1992 Edition. 1991. pap. text ed. 23.95 (*0-07-031248-6*) McGraw.

Components Quality-Reliability. Intel Staff. 336p. (Orig.). 1991. pap. 23.95 (*1-55512-132-2*) Intel Corp.

Components Technology & Standardization Manual, 3 vols. General Electric Company Staff. (Illus.). 2200p. 1981. 295.00 (*0-931690-03-X*) Genium Pub.

Componimenti Musicali see Monuments of Music & Music Literature in Facsimile: Series One

Comportement: Moteur de l'Evolution. Jean Piaget. (FRE.). 1976. pap. 10.95 (*0-7859-2846-4*) Fr & Eur.

Composed on the Tongue. Allen Ginsberg. Ed. by Donald Allen. LC 79-21115. 160p. 1980. pap. 9.95 (*0-912516-29-1*) Grey Fox.

***Composer: Perspective in Music for Christian School.** Karen Kuehmann. Ed. by Keith Skaggs. 122p. (Orig.). 1994. pap. 10.60 (*0-89084-738-X*) Bob Jones Univ Pr.

Composer & Critic: Two Hundred Years of Musical Criticism. Max Graf. LC 81-6376. 331p. 1981. reprint ed. text ed. 59.75 (*0-313-23110-9*, GRCR, Greenwood Pr) Greenwood.

Composer & His Art. Gordon Jacob. LC 85-27091. 127p. 1986. reprint ed. text ed. 49.75 (*0-313-25050-2*, JACA, Greenwood Pr) Greenwood.

Composer & Nation. rev. ed. Sidney Finkelstein. LC 88-23190. 348p. (C). 1989. pap. 8.95 (*0-7178-0671-5*) Intl Pubs Co.

Composer in Hollywood. Christopher Palmer. (Illus.). 320p. 1990. 35.00 (*0-7145-2885-4*) M Boyars Pubs.

Composer in Hollywood. Christopher Palmer. 1992. 19.95 (*0-7145-2950-8*) M Boyars Pubs.

Composer Michelangelo Rossi: A "Diligent Fantasy Maker" in Seventeenth-Century Rome. Catherine Moore. LC 93-13018. (Outstanding Dissertations in Music from British Universities Ser.). (Illus.). 312p. 1993. 69.00 (*0-8153-0954-6*) Garland.

Composer to Composer: Conversations about Contemporary Music. Andrew Ford. 1994. pap. 16.95 (*1-86373-443-0*, Pub. by Allen & Unwin Aust Pty AT) IPG Chicago.

Composers & the Computer. Illus. by I. Xenakis. LC 84-23323. (Computer Music & Digital Audio Ser.: Vol. 2). 201p. 1985. 27.95 (*0-86576-085-3*, 085-3) A-R Eds.

Composers Clothed & Disclosed. Harry Hewitt. Ed. by Elizabeth Hewitt. 54p. (Orig.). 1991. pap. 8.00 (*0-9627244-1-6*, PSP1) Penn Sounds.

***Composers Clothed & Disclosed.** rev. ed. Harry D. Hewitt. Ed. by Elizabeth R. Hewitt. 52p. 1993. pap. text ed. 10.00 (*0-9627244-3-2*) Penn Sounds.

***Composer's Dream.** Mark O'Hara. 32p. 1995. pap. 5.50 (*0-9647127-2-5*) Coreopsis Bks.

Composers Eleven. Neville Cardus. (Essay Index Reprint Ser.). (Illus.). 1958. 23.95 (*0-8369-1554-2*) Ayer.

Composer's Gallery: Biographical Sketches of Contemporary Composers. Donald Brook. LC 76-136641. (Biography Index Reprint Ser.). 1977. 20.95 (*0-8369-8036-0*) Ayer.

Composers' Gallery; Biographical Sketches of Contemporary Composers: Music Book Index. Donald Brook. 218p. 1993. reprint ed. lib. bdg. 79.00 (*0-7812-9569-6*) Rprt Serv.

Composers in America. Claire R. Reis. LC 77-4158. (Music Reprint Ser.: 1977). 1977. reprint ed. lib. bdg. 42.50 (*0-306-70893-0*) Da Capo.

***Composers' Letters.** Jan Fielden. 216p. 1995. 22.95 (*1-874572-75-5*, Pub. by Marginalia Pr UK); pap. 13.95 (*1-874572-85-2*, Pub. by Marginalia Pr UK) Trafalgar.

Composers of Operetta. Gervase Hughes. LC 74-9604. (Illus.). 283p. 1974. reprint ed. text ed. 59.75 (*0-8371-7612-3*, HUCO, Greenwood Pr) Greenwood.

Composers of the Americas: Biographical Data & Catalog of Their Works, 18 vols. Incl. Vol. 1. 100p. 1979. 7.00 (*0-8270-4485-2*); Vol. 2. 155p. 1956. 7.00 (*0-8270-4435-6*); Vol. 3. 122p. 1957. 7.00 (*0-8270-4430-5*); Vol. 4. 164p. 1958. 7.00 (*0-8270-4490-9*); Vol. 5. 107p. 1959. 7.00 (*0-8270-4495-X*); Vol. 6. 116p. 1979. 7.00 (*0-8270-4500-X*); Vol. 11. 144p. 1965. 7.00 (*0-8270-4505-0*); Vol. 12. 172p. 1966. 7.00 (*0-8270-4395-3*); Vol. 15. 180p. 1969. 7.00 (*0-8270-4425-9*); Vol. 16. 173p. 1970. 7.00 (*0-8270-4510-7*); Vol. 17. 120p. 1971. 7.00 (*0-8270-4515-8*); Vol. 18. 126p. 1972. 7.00 (*0-8270-4440-2*); Vol. 7. 104p. reprint ed. (*0-8270-4410-0*); Vol. 10. 123p. reprint ed. (*0-8270-1087-7*); Vol. 13. 136p. reprint ed. (*0-318-54733-3*); Vol. 14. 172p. reprint ed. (*0-318-54734-1*); (ENG & SPA.). write for info. (*0-318-54729-5*) OAS.

Composers of the Americas: Biographical Data & Catalog of Their Works, Vols. 7-10 & 13-14. Incl. Vol. 1. 100p. 1979. 7.00 (*0-8270-4485-2*); Vol. 2. 155p. 1956. 7.00 (*0-8270-4435-6*); Vol. 3. 122p. 1957. 7.00 (*0-8270-4430-5*); Vol. 4. 164p. 1958. 7.00 (*0-8270-4490-9*); Vol. 5. 107p. 1959. 7.00 (*0-8270-4495-X*); Vol. 6. 116p. 1979. 7.00 (*0-8270-4500-X*); Vol. 11. 144p. 1965. 7.00 (*0-8270-4505-0*); Vol. 12. 172p. 1966. 7.00 (*0-8270-4395-3*); Vol. 15. 180p. 1969. 7.00 (*0-8270-4425-9*); Vol. 16. 173p. 1970. 7.00 (*0-8270-4510-7*); Vol. 17. 120p. 1971. 7.00 (*0-8270-4515-8*); Vol. 18. 126p. 1972. 7.00 (*0-8270-4440-2*); Vol. 7. 104p. reprint ed. (*0-8270-4410-0*); Vol. 10. 123p. reprint ed. (*0-8270-1087-7*); Vol. 13. 136p. reprint ed. (*0-318-54733-3*); Vol. 14. 172p. reprint ed. (*0-318-54734-1*); 1980. write for info. (*0-318-54730-9*) OAS.

Composers of the Low Countries. Willem Elders. Tr. by Graham Dixon. (Illus.). 208p. 1991. 55.00 (*0-19-816147-6*) OUP.

Composers of Tomorrow's Music: A Non-Technical Introduction to the Musical Avant-Garde Movement. David Ewen. LC 79-18514. (Illus.). 1980. reprint ed. lib. bdg. 24.75 (*0-313-22107-3*, EWCT, Greenwood Pr) Greenwood.

Composers of Yesterday. David Ewen. (Music Book Index Ser.). 488p. 1992. reprint ed. lib. bdg. 99.00 (*0-7812-9475-4*) Rprt Serv.

C

An Asterisk (*) at the beginning of an entry indicates that the title is appearing in BIP for the first time.

An Asterisk (*) at the beginning of an entry indicates that the title is appearing in BIP for the first time.

1481

Composites in Pressure Vessels & Piping: Presented at the Energy Technology Conference, Houston, Texas, September 18-23, 1977: Sponsored by the Pressure Vessels & Piping Division, ASME. Energy Technology Conference (1977: Houston, TX) Staff. Ed. by S. V. Kulkarni & C. H. Zweben. LC 77-82211. 188p. reprint ed. pap. 53.60 (0-317-55583-9, 2056370) Bks Demand.

Composites Materials Glossary. Ed. by C. M. Bower. 68p. 1991. reprint ed. 18.00 (0-938648-22-5) T-C Pubns CA.

Composition. Sarah Kent. LC 94-31839. (Eyewitness Art Ser.). (Illus.). 64p. 1995. 16.95 (1-56458-612-X) Dorling Kindersley.

Composition: Guided-Free. Ed. by Gerald Dykstra et al. LC 73-76064. 1974. teacher ed 3.95 (0-8077-2383-5); Program 1, Grades 1-3. pap. text ed. 3.95 (0-8077-2384-3); Program 2, Grades 2-4. pap. text ed. 3.95 (0-8077-2385-1); Program 3, Grades 3-5. pap. text ed. 3.95 (0-8077-2386-X); Program 4, Grades 4-6. pap. text ed. 3.95 (0-8077-2387-8) Tchrs Coll.

Composition: Guided Free Manual, Programs 5-8. Gerald Dykstra et al. 1978. pap. text ed. 3.95 (0-8077-2388-6) Tchrs Coll.

Composition: Guided Free Program 5, Grades 5-7. Gerald Dykstra et al. 1978. pap. text ed. 3.95 (0-8077-2389-4) Tchrs Coll.

Composition: Guided Free Program 7, Grades 7-9. Gerald Dykstra et al. 1978. pap. text ed. 3.95 (0-8077-2391-6) Tchrs Coll.

Composition: Guided Free Program 8, Grades 8-10. Gerald Dykstra et al. 1978. pap. text ed. 3.95 (0-8077-2392-4) Tchrs Coll.

Composition: Proceso y Sintesis. 2nd ed. Guadalupe Valdes et al. 256p. (C). 1989. write for info. (0-318-72110-4); pap. text ed. write for info. (0-07-557360-1) McGraw.

Composition & Analysis of Heavy Petroleum Fractions. Ed. by Altgelt & Boduszynski. (Chemical Industries Ser.: Vol. 54). 512p. 1994. 175.00 (0-8247-8946-6) Dekker.

Composition & Creative Writing for the Middle Grades. Imogene Forte & Joy MacKenzie. (Illus.). 80p. (Orig.). (J). (gr. 5-8). 1991. pap. text ed. 7.95 (0-86530-176-X, IP 192-1) Incentive Pubns.

Composition & Date of Acts. C. C. Torrey. (Harvard Theological Studies: Vol. 1). 1916. pap. 15.00 (0-527-01001-4) Periodicals Srv.

Composition & Facts about Foods & Their Relationship to the Human Body. Ford Heritage. 121p. 1968. reprint ed. spiral bd. 8.80 (0-7873-0407-7) Mokelumne.

Composition & Literature: Bridging the Gap. Winifred B. Horner. LC 83-3558. 208p. (C). 1987. pap. text ed. 8.95 (0-226-35340-0) U Ch Pr.

Composition & Literature: Exploring Human Experience. Jesse Jones et al. 924p. (C). 1987. pap. text ed. 26.75 (0-15-512625-3); pap. text ed. 1.50 (0-15-512626-1) HB Coll Pubs.

Composition & Origin of Cosmic Rays. Ed. by Maurice M. Shapiro. 1983. lib. bdg. 126.50 (90-277-1609-9) Kluwer Ac.

Composition & Physiological Properties of Human Milk. Ed. by J. Schaub. 334p. 1986. 105.75 (0-444-80748-9) Elsevier.

Composition & Properties of Concrete. 2nd ed. George E. Troxell et al. LC 68-13104. (Series in Civil Engineering). 1968. text ed. write for info. (0-07-065286-4) McGraw.

Composition & Properties of Drilling & Completion Fluids. 5th ed. H. C. Darley & George Gray. (Illus.). 644p. 1988. 79.00 (0-87201-147-X) Gulf Pub.

Composition & Resistance. Ed. by C. Mark Hurlbert & Michael Blitz. 178p. 1991. pap. text ed. 20.00 (0-86709-281-5, 0281) Boynton Cook Pubs.

Composition & the Academy: A Study of Writing Program Administration. Carol P. Hartzog. LC 86-16278. xviii, 167p. 1986. 37.50 (0-87352-377-6); pap. 19.75 (0-87352-378-4) Modern Lang.

Composition & Tradition in the Book of Hosea. Gale A. Yee. LC 87-9715. (Society of Biblical Literature Dissertation Ser.). 440p. 1987. pap. 15.95 (1-55540-091-4) Scholars Pr GA.

Composition As a Cultural Practice. Alan W. France. LC 93-48970. (Language & Ideology Ser.). 192p. 1994. text ed. 49.95 (0-89789-403-0, Praeger Pubs) Greenwood.

Composition As a Human Science: Contributions to the Self-Understanding of a Discipline. Louise W. Phelps. (Illus.). 288p. 1991. pap. 16.95 (0-19-506782-7) OUP.

Composition as Communication. Candace G. Montoya & Joan M. Roxberg. 496p. (C). 1994. pap. write for info. (0-02-382431-X) Macmillan.

Composition Chemicals & Climate of the Atmosphere. H. Singh. 1995. text ed. 79.95 (0-442-01264-0) Van Nos Reinhold.

Composition Companion. 2nd ed. Marieanna Pape. 80p. (Orig.). 1993. pap. text ed. 13.95 (0-940139-28-6) Consortium RI.

Composition Dolls Vol. 1: 1928-1955, Vol. I. Polly Judd & Pam Judd. (Illus.). 208p. 1994. 25.00 (0-87588-389-3) Hobby Hse.

Composition Five: Skills for Writing. 2nd ed. J. Kenneth Sieben & Lillian S. Anthony. (C). 1984. pap. text ed. 18.50 (0-673-18003-4) HarpCollege.

Composition for Personal Growth: A Teacher's Handbook of Meaningful Student Writing Experiences. Robert C. Hawley et al. 184p. (Orig.). 1983. pap. 14.95 (0-913636-15-0) Educ Res MA.

*Composition, Geochemistry & Conversion of Oil Shales: Proceedings of the NATO ASI, Akcay, Turkey, 18-31 July 1993. Ed. by Colin Snape. LC 94-48069. (NATO Advanced Science Institutes Series: C: Vol. 455). 516p. (C). 1995. lib. bdg. 224.00 (0-7923-3343-8) Kluwer Ac.

Composition Handbook. 3rd ed. William E. Merriss & David H. Griswold. 1985. pap. text ed. 8.50 (0-88334-084-4) Longman.

Composition Handbook. 3rd ed. William E. Merriss & David H. Griswold. (J). 1985. teacher ed 10.84 (0-8013-0074-6, 75738); pap. text ed. 17.28 (0-88334-186-7, 76152) Longman.

Composition in Art. Henry R. Poore. (Illus.). 1976. reprint ed. pap. 5.95 (0-486-23358-8) Dover.

*Composition in Black & White: The Life of Philippa Schuyler. Kathryn Talalay. (Illus.). 368p. 1995. 25.00 (0-19-509608-8) OUP.

Composition in Context: Essays in Honor of Donald C. Stewart. Ed. by W. Ross Winterowd & Vincent Gillespie. LC 93-15739. 304p. (C). 1994. pap. 34.95x (0-8093-1862-8) S Ill U Pr.

Composition in Portraiture. Sadakichi Hartmann, pseud. LC 72-9205. (Literature of Photography Ser.). 1979. reprint ed. 12.95 (0-405-04914-5) Ayer.

Composition in Retrospect. John Cage. 1993. pap. 13.95 (1-878972-11-1) Exact Change.

*Composition in the 21st Century: Crisis & Change. Ed. by Lynn Z. Bloom et al. LC 95-1147. 360p. (C). 1995. 39.95x (0-8093-1878-4) S Ill U Pr.

Composition Made Easy. William Palluth. (How to Draw & Paint Ser.). (Illus.). 32p. (Orig.). 1989. pap. 5.95 (0-929261-43-7, HT194) W Foster Pub.

Composition Musicale et Composition Litteraire a Propos du Chant Gregorien. Antoine Dechevrens. viii, 366p. 1981. reprint ed. lib. bdg. 54.60 (3-487-06974-1, Pub. by Georg Olms GW) Lubrecht & Cramer.

Composition of Aristotle's Athenaion Politeia: Observation & Explanation. John J. Keaney. 192p. 1992. 45.00 (0-19-507032-1) OUP.

Composition of Cosmic Radiation. K. M. Apparao. 96p. 1975. text ed. 105.00 (0-677-03770-8) Gordon & Breach.

Composition of Foods. 1994. lib. bdg. 250.00 (0-8490-8563-2) Gordon Pr.

Composition of Foods: Baked Products - Raw, Processed, Prepared. (Illus.). 200p. (Orig.). (C). 1994. pap. text ed. 75.00 (0-7881-0522-1) Diane Pub.

Composition of Glass. Phillip Foss. (Lost Roads Ser.: No. 34). 88p. (Orig.). 1988. pap. 7.95 (0-918786-38-X) Lost Roads.

Composition of Governing Boards, 1985: A Survey of College & University Boards. Association of Governing Boards & Higher Education Panel of the American Council on Education The. 43p. 1986. 12.00 (0-318-21459-8) Assn Gov Bds.

Composition of Gross Farm Income since the Civil War. Frederick Strauss. (NBER Bulletin Ser.: No. 78). 1940. reprint ed. 20.00 (0-685-61214-7) Natl Bur Econ Res.

Composition of Mutanabbi's Panegyrics to Sayf al-Dawla. Andras Hamori. LC 90-25142. (Studies in Arabic Literature: Vol. 14). viii, 127p. 1992. 40.00 (90-04-09366-4) E J Brill.

*Composition of "Ourselves" Marcia Curtis. 240p. (C). 1994. per., pap. text ed. 29.95 (0-8403-9767-4) Kendall-Hunt.

Composition of Outdoor Painting. 4th rev. ed. Edgar A. Payne. Ed. by J. B. Hatcher. LC 84-90701. (Illus.). 155p. 1985. reprint ed. 35.00 (0-939370-03-4) DeRu's Fine Art.

Composition of Pascal's Apologia. Anthony R. Pugh. (Romance Ser.: No.49). 656p. 1984. 75.00 (0-8020-5611-3) U of Toronto Pr.

Composition of Scientific Words. Roland W. Brown. 882p. (C). 1991. reprint ed. text ed. 40.00 (0-87474-286-2) Smithsonian.

Composition of Shakespeare's Plays. Albert Feuillerat. LC 76-128885. (Select Bibliographies Reprint Ser.). 1977. 23.95 (0-8369-5505-6) Ayer.

Composition of the Book of Isaiah in the Light of History & Archaeology. R. H. Kennett. (British Academy, London, Schweich Lectures on Biblical Archaeology Series, 1930). 1972. reprint ed. pap. 20.00 (0-8115-1251-7) Periodicals Srv.

Composition of the Deuteronommistic History. Brian Peckham. (Harvard Semitic Museum Monographs). (C). 1985. 15.95 (0-89130-909-8, 04-00-35) Scholars Pr GA.

Composition of the Organ. Ernest M. Skinner & Richmond H. Skinner. Ed. & Intro. by Leslie A. Olsen. (Illus.). 330p. (Orig.). 1981. pap. 29.95 (0-318-20046-5) M J Light.

Composition of The Rainbow & Women in Love: A History. Charles L. Ross. LC 79-1422. (Illus.). 168p. 1979. 25.00 (0-8139-0704-7) U Pr of Va.

Composition Operators & Classical Function Theory. Joel H. Shapiro. Ed. by P. R. Halmos et al. LC 93-26147. (Universitext Tracts in Mathematics Ser.). (Illus.). 223p. 1993. pap. 37.50 (0-387-94067-7) Spr-Verlag.

Composition Operators on Function Spaces. R. K. Singh & J. S. Manhas. LC 93-28741. (Mathematics Studies: Vol. 179). 1993. write for info. (0-444-81593-7, North Holland) Elsevier.

*Composition Operators on Spaces of Analytic Functions. Carl C. Cowen, Jr. & Barbara I. MacCluer. 288p. 1995. 59.95 (0-8493-8492-3, 8492) CRC Pr.

Composition Practice, Bk. 4. 2nd ed. Linda L. Blanton. LC 92-41832. 1993. pap. 17.95 (0-8384-4075-4) Heinle & Heinle.

Composition Practice, Bks. 1 & 2. 2nd ed. Linda L. Blanton. 1988. Bk. 2. pap. 17.95 (0-8384-2942-4) Heinle & Heinle.

Composition Practice, Bks. 1 & 2. 2nd ed. Linda L. Blanton. 1993. Bk. 1. pap. 17.95 (0-8384-2943-2) Heinle & Heinle.

Composition Practice Bk. 3: A Text for English Language Learners. 2nd ed. Linda L. Blanton. LC 92-31028. 1993. pap. 17.95 (0-8384-4076-2, Newbury) Heinle & Heinle.

Composition Research: Empirical Designs. Janice M. Lauer & J. William Asher. (Illus.). 336p. 1988. pap. 19.95 (0-19-504171-2); pap. text ed. 21.00 (0-19-504172-0) OUP.

Composition-Rhetoric: A Synthesis. W. Ross Winterowd. LC 85-2073. 373p. (Orig.). (C). 1986. pap. text ed. 16.95 (0-8093-1238-7) S Ill U Pr.

Composition Skills Activities Kit: Ready-to-Use Lessons & Exercises for Grades 7-12. Phil Schlemmer & Dori Schlemmer. 256p. 1990. pap. 27.95 (0-87628-244-3) Ctr Appl Res.

Composition, Structure & Dynamics of the Lithosphere-Asthenosphere System. K. Fuchs & C. Froidevaux. (Geodynamics Ser.: Vol. 16). 340p. 33.00 (0-87590-518-8) Am Geophysical.

Composition, Structure, & Properties of Mineral Matter: Concepts, Results, & Problems. A. S. Marfunin. (Advanced Mineralogy Ser.: Vol. 1). (Illus.). 562p. 1994. 133.00 (0-387-57254-6) Spr-Verlag.

Composition Structure & Reactivity of Proteins. P. Alexander & R. Block. (Lab Manual Analytical Methods of Protein Chemistry Ser.: Vol. 2). 1960. 220.00 (0-08-009425-2, Pub. by Pergamon Repr UK) Franklin.

Composition Theory for the Postmodern Classroom. Ed. by Gary A. Olson & Sidney I. Dobrin. 360p. (C). 1994. text ed. 59.50 (0-7914-2305-0); pap. text ed. 19.95 (0-7914-2306-9) State U NY Pr.

Composition Variations of Incragrind for Large Sections. Michigan Technological University Staff. 60p. 1970. 9.00 (0-317-34501-X, 78) Intl Copper.

Composition with Pitch-Classes: A Theory of Compositional Design. Robert D. Morris. 416p. 1987. text ed. 47.50 (0-300-03684-1) Yale U Pr.

Composition with Twelve Notes Related Only to One Another. rev. ed. Joseph Rufer. LC 78-9838. (Illus.). 186p. 1979. reprint ed. text ed. 35.00 (0-313-21236-8, RUCT, Greenwood Pr) Greenwood.

Composition Workshop Basic Education Skills Text & Manual. John H. Snyder & Richard A. Alden. 269p. (C). 1988. pap. text ed. 27.30 (0-943437-39-3) CT Pub.

Compositional Analysis by Thermogravimetry, STP 997. Ed. by Charles M. Earnest. LC 88-22183. (Special Technical Publication (STP) Ser.). (Illus.). 300p. 1988. text ed. 59.00 (0-8031-1177-0, 04-997000-40) ASTM.

Compositional Data Objects: The IMC-IMCL Reference Manual. Reiner Durchholz & Gernot Richter. LC 92-25262. 187p. 1992. text ed. 75.95 (0-471-93470-4) Wiley.

Compositional Language in the Oratorio the Second Act: The Composer As Analyst. Harvey J. Stokes. LC 92-23544. (Studies in the History & Interpretation of Music: Vol. 37). 292p. 1992. text ed. 89.95 (0-7734-9166-X) E Mellen.

Compositional Matrix. Allen Forte. LC 73-4337. 1974. reprint ed. lib. bdg. 22.50 (0-306-70577-X) Da Capo.

Compositional Methods for Communication Protocol Design: A Petri Net Approach. N. A. Anisimov. (Series in Computer Science). 200p. 1995. text ed. 53.00 (981-02-1674-2) World Scientific Pub.

Compositional Process of J. S. Bach: A Study of the Autograph Scores of the Vocal Works, 2 vols. Robert L. Marshall. LC 76-113005. (Princeton Studies in Music: No. 4). (Illus.). 287p. reprint ed. Vol. 1, 287 p. pap. 81.80 (0-8357-4037-4, 2036729); reprint ed. Vol. 2, 195 p. pap. 55.60 (0-8357-4038-2, 2036729) Bks Demand.

Compositional Techniques of the Russian Oral Epic, the Bylina. Patricia Arabt. LC 90-36860. (Harvard Dissertations in Folklore & Oral Literature Ser.). 214p. 1990. reprint ed. lib. bdg. 53.00 (0-8240-2962-3) Garland.

Compositional Theory in the Eighteenth Century. Joel Lester. (Illus.). 355p. 1993. text ed. 49.95 (0-674-15522-X) HUP.

Compositional Theory in the Eignteenth Century. Joel Lester. 355p. 1994. pap. 26.50 (0-674-15523-8) HUP.

Compositional Translation. M. T. Rosetta. LC 94-20091. (International Series in Engineering & Computer Science, VLSI, Computer Architecture, & Digital Screen Processing: Vol. 273). 496p. (C). 1994. lib. bdg. 88.00 (0-7923-9462-3) Kluwer Ac.

Compositionality, Concurrency & Partial Correctness. J. Zwiers. (Lecture Notes in Computer Science Ser.: Vol. 321). vi, 272p. 1989. pap. 37.00 (0-387-50845-7) Spr-Verlag.

*Compositions in Two Languages. Kita Antonia. (Illus.). 142p. (Orig.). 1993. pap. 12.00 (1-887116-01-X) Saxon West Pubns.

Compositor (Job) Jack Rudman. (Career Examination Ser.: C-2649). 1994. pap. 23.95 (0-8373-2649-4) Nat Learn.

Compositors Work in Printing. 3rd ed. H. W. Larken. 382p. 1969. 30.00 (0-905418-08-5, Pub. by Gresham Bks) St Mut.

*Compost: From Garbage to Gardens. Linda Glaser. LC 95-10421. (Illus.). (J). 1996. lib. bdg. write for info. (1-56294-659-5) Millbrook Pr.

Compost: What It Is, How It's Made. Koepf. 18p. 1980. pap. 1.50 (0-938250-10-8) Bio-Dynamic Farm.

*Compost & Plant Health: Compost Teas for Natural Fungus Control. Andreas Trankner. Ed. & Tr. by William F. Brinton, Jr. (Illus.). 155p. (C). 1995. pap. text ed. 39.95 (0-9603554-8-0) Woods End.

Compost Critters. Bianca Lavies. LC 92-35651. (Illus.). 32p. (J). (gr. 2-6). 1993. 14.99 (0-525-44763-6, DCB) Dutton Child Bks.

Compost Makes the Strawberries Grow: A Mother's Celebration of Parenting - Its Challenges, Humor & Rewards. Lolita L. Jardeleza. LC 90-85458. 1991. pap. 5.95 (0-87029-232-3) Abbey.

Compost This Book! The Art of Composting for Your Yard, Your Community & the Planet. Tom Christopher & Marty Asher. LC 93-25659. (Illus.). 258p. (Orig.). 1994. pap. 12.00 (0-87156-596-X) Sierra.

Composting. Kevin Handreck. 19p. 1981. pap. 7.00 (0-643-02168-X, Pub. by CSIRO AT) Intl Spec Bk.

Composting: Sanitary Disposal & Reclamation of Organic Wastes. H. B. Gotaas. (Monograph Ser.: No. 31). (Illus.). 205p. (ENG & FRE.). 1956. 14.00 (92-4-140031-5) World Health.

Composting: Solutions for Waste Management. (Special Report Ser.). 75p. 1992. pap. 28.00 (0-87326-088-0) Intl City-Cnty Mgt.

Composting & Compost Quality Assurance. Ed. by D. V. Jackson & J. M. 117 et al Merillot. (EUR Ser.: No. 14254). 441p. 1992. 65.00 (92-826-4163-5, CG-NA-14254-EN-C, Pub. by Europ Com) UNIPUB.

Composting & Recycling Municipal Solid Waste. Diaz. 1993. 59.95 (0-87371-563-2, TD796) Lewis Pubs.

Composting Fish By-Products. William F. Brinton, Jr. & Milton D. Seekins. 55p. (Orig.). 1988. pap. text ed. 25.00 (0-9603554-4-8) Woods End.

Composting Municipal Sludge: A Technology Evaluation. Arthur H. Benedict et al. LC 87-34746. (Pollution Technology Review Ser.: No. 152). (Illus.). 178p. 1988. 36.00 (0-8155-1162-0) Noyes.

Composting of Agricultural & Other Wastes: Proceedings of a Seminar Organized by the Commission of the European Communities, Oxford, England, 19-22, March, 1984. J. K. Gasser. (Illus.). x, 320p. 1985. 90.00 (0-85334-357-8, Pub. by Elsevier Applied Sci UK) Elsevier.

Composting of Municipal & Industrial Sludges. LC 82-83481. 164p. 1982. 20.00 (0-944989-28-4, 040082) Hazardous Mat Control.

Composting Potato Culls & Potato Processing Wastes: A Feasibility Study. William F. Brinton, Jr. (Illus.). 45p. (Orig.). (C). 1991. pap. text ed. 15.00 (0-9603554-6-4) Woods End.

Compotum Magistri Fabrice Pontis Dunkeldensis, MDXIII-MDXVI see Vitae Dunkeldensis Ecclesiae Episcoporum, a Prima Sedis Foundatione, Ad Annum MDXV Ab Alexandro Myln, Eiusdem Ecclesiae Canonica Conscriptae

Compound Adjectives in English & the Ideal Speaker-Listener. W. J. Meys. (Linguistic Ser.: Vol. 18). 226p. 1975. pap. 38.50 (0-444-10780-0, North Holland) Elsevier.

Compound & Josephson High-Speed Devices. Ed. by T. Misugi & A. Shibatomi. (Microdevices: Physics & Fabrication Technologies Ser.). (Illus.). 340p. (C). 1993. 69.50 (0-306-44384-8, Plenum Pr) Plenum.

Compound Cinema: The Film Writings of Harry Alan Potamkin. Harry A. Potamkin. Ed. by Lewis Jacobs. LC 76-55401. (Studies in Culture & Communication). 703p. reprint ed. pap. 180.00 (0-317-41931-5, 2026026) Bks Demand.

Compound Interest. Norris E. Sheppard & D. C. Baillie. 245p. reprint ed. pap. 69.90 (0-317-09367-3, 2016086) Bks Demand.

Compound Interest & Annuity Tables. Jack C. Estes. 240p. (Orig.). (C). 1976. pap. text ed. 6.95 (0-07-019683-4) McGraw.

Compound Interest & Annuity Tables No. 376. 6th ed. Ed. by Financial Publishing Company Staff. 2114p. 1980. 65.00 (0-87600-376-5) Finan Pub.

Compound Interest & Annuity Tables, Supplement. Ed. by Financial Publishing Co. Staff. 296p. 1986. pap. 25.00 (0-87600-377-3) Finan Pub.

Compound Interest Tables. Donald G. Newnan. 30p. (Orig.). 1991. pap. text ed. 2.50x (0-910554-08-0, 08-0) Engineering.

Compound Interest Tables. Michael Sherman. 128p. 1982. pap. 6.95 (0-8092-5704-1) Contemp Bks.

Compound of Alchemy. George Ripley. 87p. 1992. reprint ed. pap. 9.95 (1-56459-077-1) Kessinger Pub.

Compound of Alchymy. George Ripley. LC 77-7423. (English Experience Ser.: No. 887). 1977. reprint ed. lib. bdg. 35.00 (90-221-0887-2) Walter J Johnson.

Compound of Excelsior. Susan Rice. (Illus.). 93p. (Orig.). 1992. pap. 10.95 (0-938501-14-3) Gasogene Pr.

Compound of the Five Cubes. Gerald Jenkins & Magdalen Bear. (Tarquin Polyhedra Ser.). (Illus.). 24p. (Orig.). (J). (gr. 5-9). 1986. pap. 4.95 (0-906212-47-2, Pub. by Tarquin UK) Parkwest Pubns.

Compound Plastic Deformation of Layers of Different Metals. G. E. Arkulis. 204p. 1965. text ed. 61.00 (0-7065-0558-1, Pub. by Keter Pub IS) Coronet Bks.

Compound Semiconductor Bulk Materials & Characterizations. Osamu Oda. 250p. 1995. text ed. 59.00 (981-02-1728-5) World Scientific Pub.

Compound Semiconductor Device Modeling. Ed. by C. M. Snowden & R. E. Miles. LC 93-3820. 1993. 129.00 (0-387-19827-X) Spr-Verlag.

Compound Semiconductor Device Physics. Sandip Tiwari. (Illus.). 828p. 1991. text ed. 94.00 (0-12-691740-X) Acad Pr.

Compound Semiconductor Epitaxy: Materials Research Society Symposium Proceedings, Vol. 340. Ed. by C. W. Tu et al. 1994. text ed. 57.00 (1-55899-240-5) Materials Res.

Compound Semiconductor Strained-Layer Superlattices. Ed. by R. M. Biefeld. 320p. 1989. text ed. 70.00 (0-87849-587-8, Pub. by Trans Tech GW) LPS Dist Ctr.

Compound Semiconductor Technology. David J. Colliver. LC 75-31377. (Illus.). 301p. reprint ed. pap. 85.80 (0-8357-4183-4, 2036961) Bks Demand.

Compound Semiconductor Transistors: Physics & Technology. Intro. by Sandip Tiwari. LC 92-46775. (Illus.). 336p. (C). 1993. text ed. 69.95 (0-7803-0417-9, PC03137) Inst Electrical.

C

An Asterisk (*) at the beginning of an entry indicates that the title is appearing in BIP for the first time.

C

An Asterisk (*) at the beginning of an entry indicates that the title is appearing in BIP for the first time.

1483

An Asterisk (*) at the beginning of an entry indicates that the title is appearing in BIP for the first time.

C

Comprehensive Dissertation Index 1861-1972, 37 vols. Incl. 1973. Vol. 1, Chemistry A-C. (*0-8357-0080-1*); 1973. Vol. 2, Chemistry D-K. (*0-8357-0081-X*); 1973. Vol. 3, Chemistry L-Q. (*0-8357-0082-8*); 1973. Vol. 4, Chemistry R-Z. (*0-8357-0083-6*); 5. Mathematics & Statistics. 1973. (*0-8357-0084-4*); Astronomy & Physics. 1973. Vol. 6. A-L. (*0-8357-0085-2*); Astronomy & Physics. 1973. Vol. 7, M-Z. (*0-8357-0086-0*); 8. Engineering-General & Aeronautical. 1973. (*0-8357-0087-9*); 9. Engineering-Chemical, Mechanical, & Metallurgical. 1973. (*0-8357-0088-7*); 10. Engineering-Civil, Electrical, & Industrial. 1973. (*0-8357-0089-5*); 11. Biological Sciences-Biology & Zoology. 1973. (*0-8357-0090-9*); 12. Biological Sciences-Anatomy, Physiology & Genetics. 1973. (*0-8357-0091-7*); 13. Biological Sciences-Botany, Microbiology, & Bacteriology. 1973. (*0-8357-0092-5*); 14. Health & Environmental Sciences. 1973. (*0-8357-0093-3*); 15. Agriculture. (*0-8357-0094-1*); 16. Geography & Geology. 1973. (*0-8357-0095-X*); 17. Social Sciences. 1973. (*0-8357-0096-8*); Psychology. 1973. Vol. 18, A-L. (*0-8357-0097-6*); Psychology. 1973. Vol. 19, M-Z. (*0-8357-0098-4*); Education. 1973. Vol. 20, A-C. (*0-8357-0099-2*); Education. 1973. Vol. 21, D-H. (*0-318-56301-0*); Education. 1973. Vol. 22, I-Q. (*0-8357-0101-8*); Education. 1973. Vol. 23, P-Se. (*0-8357-0103-4*); Business & Economics. 1973. Vol. 25, A-I. (*0-8357-0104-2*); Business & Economics. 1973. Vol. 26. J-Z. (*0-8357-0105-0*); 27. Law & Political Science. 1973. (*0-8357-0106-9*); 28. History. 1973. (*0-8357-0107-7*); Language & Literature. 1973. Vol. 29, A-L. (*0-8357-0108-5*); Language & Literature. 1973. Vol. 30, M-Z. (*0-8357-0109-3*); 31. Communications & the Arts. 1973. (*0-8357-0110-7*); 32. Philosophy & Religion. 1973. (*0-8357-0111-5*); Author Index. Vol. 33., A-D. (*0-8357-0112-3*); Author Index. Vol. 34, D-HI. (*0-8357-0113-1*); Author Index. Vol. 35, HJ-mC. (*0-8357-0114-X*); Author Index. Vol. 36, M_d-Sc. (*0-8357-0115-8*); Author Index. Vol. 37, SD-Z. (*0-8357-0116-6*); 1973. write for info. (*0-318-56300-2*, Dissertations) Univ Microfilms.

Comprehensive Dissertation Index, 1974: Supplement, 1975, 5 vols. Incl. Sciences, 2 pts. Vol. 1, (Pt. 1). (*0-8357-0070-4*); Sciences, 2 pts. Vol. 2 (Pt. 2). (*0-8357-0071-2*); Social Sciences & Humanities, 2 pts. Vol. 3, (Pt. 1). (*0-8357-0072-0*); Social Sciences & Humanities, 2 pts. Vol. 4, (Pt. 2). (*0-8357-0073-9*); 5. Author Index. (*0-8357-0074-7*); write for info. (*0-318-56302-9*, Dissertations) Univ Microfilms.

Comprehensive Dissertation Index, 1988: Supplement, 5 vols. Incl. Sciences, 2 pts. Vol. 1, Pt. 1. (*0-8357-0854-3*); Sciences, 2 pts. Vol. 2, Pt. 2. (*0-8357-0855-1*); Social Sciences & Humanities, 2 pts. Vol. 3, Pt. 1. (*0-8357-0856-X*); 1989. Vol. 4, Pt. 2. (*0-8357-0857-8*); 5. Author Index. (*0-8357-0858-6*); 1989. write for info. (*0-318-64946-2*, Dissertations) Univ Microfilms.

Comprehensive Dissertation Index, 1989: Supplement, 5 vols. 1990. write for info. (*0-318-69088-8*, Dissertations) Univ Microfilms.

Comprehensive Dissertation Index, 1989: Supplement, 5 vols. Incl. Sciences, 2 pts. Vol. 1, Pt. 1. (*0-8357-0859-4*, Dissertations); Sciences, 2 pts. Vol. 2, Pt. 2. (*0-8357-0860-8*, Dissertations); Social Sciences & Humanities, 2 pts. Vol. 3, Pt. 1. (*0-8357-0861-6*, Dissertations); Social Sciences & Humanities, 2 pts. Vol. 4, Pt. 2. (*0-8357-0862-4*, Dissertations); Vol. 5. Author Index. (*0-8357-0863-2*); 1990. write for info. (*0-318-66997-8*, Dissertations) Univ Microfilms.

Comprehensive Dissertation Index, 1990: Supplement, 5 vols. 1991. write for info. (*0-318-69089-6*, Dissertations) Univ Microfilms.

Comprehensive Dissertation Index, 1991: Supplement, 5 vols. 1992. Author Index: Vol. 5. write for info. (*0-318-69090-X*, Dissertations); Sciences: Vol. 1, Pt. 1. write for info. (*0-8357-0869-1*, Dissertations); Sciences: Vol. 2, Pt. 2. write for info. (*0-318-69091-8*, Dissertations); Social Sciences & Humanities: Vol. 3, Pt. 1. write for info. (*0-318-69092-6*, Dissertations); Social Sciences & Humanities: Vol. 4, Pt. 2. write for info. (*0-318-69093-4*, Dissertations) Univ Microfilms.

Comprehensive, Eco-Botanical Survey of Monocotyledons, Pt. V. Ed. by A. B. Chaudhari. 1985. 25.00 (*81-7089-077-2*, Pub. by Intl Bk Distr II) St Mut.

Comprehensive Ecological Botanical Survey of the (Grasses) & Sedges (Cyperaceae), Pt. IV. A. B. Chaudhari. 66p. 1985. 70.00 (*81-7089-076-4*, Pub. by Intl Bk Distr II) St Mut.

Comprehensive Electrocardiology: Theory & Practice in Health & Disease, 3 vols., Set. Ed. by Peter W. Macfarlane & T. D. Lawrie. LC 88-17891. (Illus.). 1900p. 1988. 715.00 (*0-08-035568-4*, Pergamon Pr) Elsevier.

Comprehensive Emergency Management: Evacuating Threatened Populations. Ronald W. Perry. LC 84-12616. (Contemporary Studies in Applied Behavioral Science: Vol. 3). 1985. 73.25 (*0-89232-436-8*) Jai Pr.

Comprehensive Employment & Training Act (CETA) Trainee. Jack Rudman. (Career Examination Ser.: C-2505). 1994. pap. 27.95 (*0-8373-2505-6*) Nat Learn.

Comprehensive Encyclopedia of United States Seated Liberty Quarters. Larry Briggs. Ed. by Harry Smith. (Illus.). 264p. (Orig.). (C). 1992. text ed. 49.95 (*0-9631667-1-9*); pap. 39.95 (*0-9631667-0-0*) L Briggs Rare Coins.

*__Comprehensive Engagement Manual Vol. 1.__ fac. ed. George Marthinuss & Larry L. Perry. (AICPA Integrated Practice System Ser.). 241p. 1992. pap. 68.70 (*0-7837-8242-X*, 2049009) Bks Demand.

*__Comprehensive Engagement Manual Vol. 2.__ fac. ed. George Marthinuss & Larry L. Perry. (AiCPA Integrated Practice Systems Ser.). 264p. 1992. pap. 75.30 (*0-7837-8243-8*, 2049009) Bks Demand.

*__Comprehensive Engagement Manual Vol. 4.__ fac. ed. George Marthinuss & Larry L. Perry. (AiCPA Integrated Practice Systems Ser.). 256p. 1992. pap. 73.00 (*0-7837-8244-6*, 2049009); pap. 67.90 (*0-7837-8245-4*, 2049009) Bks Demand.

Comprehensive Engagement Manual Vol. 4, 4 vols. George Marthinuss & Larry L. Perry. (AICPA Integrated Practice System Ser.). 265p. reprint ed. Vol. 1, 265p. pap. 75.60 (*0-7837-4872-8*, 2044400); reprint ed. Vol. 2, 318p. pap. 90.70 (*0-7837-4873-6*, 2044400); reprint ed. Vol. 3, 358p. pap. 102.10 (*0-7837-4874-4*); reprint ed. Vol. 4, 237p. pap. 67.60 (*0-7837-4875-2*, 2044400) Bks Demand.

Comprehensive English & Oriya Dictionary. Pike & N. Wilkins. 688p. 1988. 49.95 (*0-8288-8472-2*) Fr & Eur.

Comprehensive English-Arabic Dictionary. Libr Du Liban. 1983. 18.00x (*0-86685-356-1*) Intl Bk Ctr.

*__Comprehensive English-Esperanto Dictionary.__ Peter J. Benson. LC 94-61165. 607p. 1995. text ed. 26.95 (*0-939785-02-1*); pap. 19.95 (*0-939785-03-X*) Esperanto League North Am.

Comprehensive English Oriya Dictionary. Pike & Wilkins. 1988. reprint ed. 30.00 (*81-206-0383-4*, Pub. by Asian Educ Servs II) S Asia.

Comprehensive English-Persian Dictionary. F. Steingass. 1539p. (ENG & PER.). 1980. 125.00 (*0-8288-0547-4*, M8207) Fr & Eur.

Comprehensive English-Russian Scientific & Technical Dictionary. D. E. Stoliarov. 1420p. (C). 1991. text ed. 195.00 (*0-569-09310-4*, Pub. by Collets) St Mut.

*__Comprehensive English-Russian Scientific & Technical Dictionary, 2 vols.__ D. E. Stoliarov & Iu.A. Kuz'min. 1420p. (ENG & RUS.). 1991. 225.00 (*0-7859-7157-2*) Fr & Eur.

Comprehensive English-Russian Scientific & Technical Dictionary, 2 vols., Set. Tomax. 1421p. (ENG & RUS.). 1991. 150.00 (*0-7859-1094-8*, 5200011677) Fr & Eur.

Comprehensive Epileptology. Mogens Dam & Lennart Gram. 864p. 1991. 174.50 (*0-88167-646-2*) Raven.

Comprehensive Etymological Dictionary of the English Language. Ernest Klein. 844p. 1971. reprint ed. 131.00 (*0-444-40930-0*) Elsevier.

Comprehensive Etymological Dictionary of the Hebrew Language. Ernest Klein. 600p. 1988. lib. bdg. 100.00 (*0-02-917431-7*) Macmillan.

Comprehensive Evaluation of Disorders of Sexual Desire. Ed. by Helen S. Kaplan. LC 84-18625. (Clinical Insights Ser.). 84p. reprint ed. pap. 25.00 (*0-8357-7825-8*, 2036198) Bks Demand.

*__Comprehensive Exit Examination for Undergraduate (B. Sc) Degree Program in Health Care Administration.__ Edward Khiwa. 5p. (C). 1994. student ed, text ed. 25.95 (*0-9643899-2-4*) E K Kiwuwa.

Comprehensive Experiment: A Comparison of the Selective & Non-Selective School Organization. Ed. by David Reynolds et al. (Education Policy Perspectives Ser.: Vol. 4). 188p. 1987. 55.00 (*1-85000-210-X*, Falmer Pr); pap. 33.00 (*1-85000-211-8*, Falmer Pr) Taylor & Francis.

Comprehensive Family & Community Health. 4th ed. Clemen & Stone. 1994. 43.95 (*0-8016-7940-0*) Mosby Yr Bk.

Comprehensive Family & Community Health Nursing. Clemen & Stone. (Illus.). 928p. 1991. 43.95 (*0-8016-6068-8*) Mosby Yr Bk.

Comprehensive Family & Community Health Nursing. S. A. Clemen-Stone et al. (Illus.). 544p. 1981. text ed. 36.95 (*0-07-011324-6*) McGraw.

Comprehensive Family & Community Health Nursing. 2nd ed. S. A. Clemen-Stone et al. 896p. (C). 1986. text ed. 39.95 (*0-07-011325-4*) McGraw.

Comprehensive Family Therapy: An Integration of Systemic & Psychodynamic Treatment Models. Diana A. Kirschner & Sam Kirschner. LC 85-18607. 282p. 1986. 35.95 (*0-87630-403-X*) Brunner-Mazel.

Comprehensive Fertility Awareness & Natural Family Planning see Couple's Guide to Fertility: The Complete Sympto-Thermal Method

Comprehensive Food Sanitation Database. William C. Haines. 1995. write for info. (*0-87371-812-7*) Lewis Pubs.

Comprehensive French Grammar. 4th ed. Glanville Byrne. 608p. 1993. 54.95 (*0-631-18164-4*) Blackwell Pubs.

Comprehensive French Grammar. 4th ed. Glanville Price. 608p. 1993. pap. 22.95 (*0-631-18165-2*) Blackwell Pubs.

Comprehensive French-Hungarian Dictionary: Dictionnaire Comprehensif Francais-Hongrois. 8th rev. ed. S. Eckhardt. 856p. (FRE & HUN.). 1985. 49.95 (*0-8288-1059-1*, M8570) Fr & Eur.

Comprehensive General Liability Policies 1993: Insurance Claims & Coverage Litigation. (Commercial Law & Practice Course Handbook Ser.: Vol. 658). 224p. 1993. 70.00 (*0-685-69705-3*, A4-4415) PLI.

Comprehensive General Liability Policy: A Critique of Selected Provisions. American Bar Association Staff. LC 85-72655. 120p. 1985. pap. 29.95 (*0-89707-195-6*, 519-0044) Amer Bar Assn.

Comprehensive General Liability Policy: The Insuring Intent. Sanderson. 256p. 1990. 76.00 (*0-409-89275-0*) Butterworth Legal Pubs.

Comprehensive Geography of the Chinese Empire & Dependencies. L. Richard. Tr. by M. Kennelly. 1978. reprint ed. 40.00 (*0-89986-339-6*) Oriental Bk Store.

Comprehensive Geography of West Africa. Reuben K. Udo. LC 78-2295. (Illus.). 304p. (C). 1978. 49.50 (*0-8419-0379-4*, Africana); pap. 24.50 (*0-8419-0380-8*, Africana) Holmes & Meier.

Comprehensive Glossary of Psychiatry & Psychology. Harold Kaplan & Benjamin Sadock. 224p. 1991. 16.95 (*0-683-04527-X*) Williams & Wilkins.

Comprehensive Glossary of Weather Terms for Storm Spotters. Michael L. Branick. (Monograph Ser.: No. 1-93). 25p. (C). 1993. pap. text ed. 9.00 (*1-883563-09-7*) Natl Weather.

Comprehensive Grammar of Sinhalese. A. M. Gunasekara. 516p. 1986. 23.00 (*0-88431-190-2*) IBD Ltd.

Comprehensive Grammar of Sinhalese Language. A. M. Gunasekara. 532p. 1986. 59.95 (*0-8288-8446-3*) Fr & Eur.

Comprehensive Grammar of the English Language. Randolph Quirk et al. 1779p. (C). 1985. 139.75 (*0-582-51734-6*, 73723) Longman.

Comprehensive Graphic Arts. Ervin A. Dennis & John D. Jenkins. LC 72-92620. 1974. 24.95 (*0-672-97607-2*, Bobbs) Macmillan.

Comprehensive Graphic Arts. Ervin A. Dennis & John D. Jenkins. LC 72-92620. 1975. teacher ed 6.67 (*0-672-97609-9*, Bobbs) Macmillan.

Comprehensive Graphic Arts. Ervin A. Dennis & John D. Jenkins. LC 72-92620. 1976. student ed 11.50 (*0-672-97608-0*, Bobbs) Macmillan.

Comprehensive Graphic Arts. 2nd ed. Ervin A. Dennis & John D. Jenkins. (Illus.). 576p. (C). 1983. teacher ed write for info. (*0-672-97682-X*); student ed write for info. (*0-672-98447-4*); text ed. write for info. (*0-672-97681-1*) Macmillan.

Comprehensive Group Psychotherapy. 3rd ed. Ed. by Harold I. Kaplan & Benjamin J. Sadock. LC 93-16409. 728p. 1993. 65.00 (*0-683-04534-2*) Williams & Wilkins.

Comprehensive Guidance Programs That Work. Norman C. Gysbers. 200p. 1990. pap. 18.95 (*1-56109-001-8*) ERIC Clearinghouse.

Comprehensive Guide & Directory of Schools - Orleans Parish, 2 vols. Naomi C. Brown. LC 89-80766. 125p. (Orig.). 1989. Vol. 1: Private & Parochial, 125p. pap. 10.00 (*0-9623619-1-7*); Vol. 2: Public Schools, 190p. pap. 10.00 (*0-9623619-2-5*) Guide To Schls.

Comprehensive Guide & Directory of Schools - Orleans Parish, 2 vols., Set. Naomi C. Brown. LC 89-80766. (Orig.). 1989. pap. 18.00 (*0-9623619-0-9*) Guide To Schls.

Comprehensive Guide for Doing Business in the U. S. S. R. 1991. Ed. by Valentin Kozitsyn & William W. Johnson. (Illus.). 300p. (Orig.). 1991. 250.00 (*1-879879-20-4*); lib. bdg. 95.00 (*1-879879-00-X*); pap. 195.00 (*1-879879-44-1*); 50.00 (*1-879879-45-X*) TAG Intl.

Comprehensive Guide for Least-Cost Energy Decisions. 1990. lib. bdg. 79.95 (*0-8490-4052-3*) Gordon Pr.

Comprehensive Guide for Pronouncing American English. Dorothy M. Taguchi & Judith L. O'Dea. (Illus.). 210p. (C). 1988. 40.00 (*0-945826-00-1*) Effective Language.

Comprehensive Guide for Third Class Mailers. Ed. by Daniel J. Minnick. 162p. 1992. 80.00 (*0-933505-16-7*) Graph Comm Assn.

Comprehensive Guide to American Colonial Coinage. Sanford J. Durst. LC 75-32796. (Illus.). 1976. lib. bdg. 25.00 (*0-915262-02-9*) S J Durst.

Comprehensive Guide to Arthritis. 3rd ed. James F. Fries. 1990. pap. 12.45 (*0-201-52402-3*) Addison-Wesley.

Comprehensive Guide to Attention Deficit Disorder in Adults: Research, Diagnosis, & Treatment. Ed. by Kathleen G. Nadeau. 426p. 1995. 38.95 (*0-87630-760-8*) Brunner-Mazel.

Comprehensive Guide to Bar Admission Requirements, 1993-94. 55p. 1993. pap. 2.00 (*0-685-60840-9*, 529-0056) Amer Bar Assn.

*__Comprehensive Guide to Business Incubation.__ Ed. by Sally Hayhow. 250p. Date not set. pap. text ed. 85.00 (*1-887183-36-1*) NBIA.

Comprehensive Guide to Careers. Domino Books Ltd Staff. 350p. (C). 1988. 150.00 (*1-85122-046-1*, Pub. by Domino Bks Ltd UK); pap. 125.00 (*1-85122-041-0*, Pub. by Domino Bks Ltd UK) St Mut.

Comprehensive Guide to Child Psychotherapy. Christianne Brems. LC 92-24692. 438p. 1993. text ed. 60.00 (*0-205-14708-9*) Allyn.

Comprehensive Guide to Chinese Herbal Medicine. Zi-lin Chen. 1993. 29.95 (*0-941942-38-4*) Orient Heal Arts.

Comprehensive Guide to Cosmetic Sources. Theodora Myllymaki & James Akerson. 225p. 1992. pap. text ed. 24.95 (*1-56253-102-6*) Milady Pub.

Comprehensive Guide to Educational Equipment & Resources. Domino Books Ltd Staff. 280p. (C). 1988. 125.00 (*1-85122-044-5*, Pub. by Domino Bks Ltd UK); pap. 75.00 (*0-317-91158-9*, Pub. by Domino Bks Ltd UK) St Mut.

Comprehensive Guide to Financing & Pricing at Water & Wastewater Treatment Plants. 2nd ed. George A. Raftelis. 1992. 65.00 (*0-87371-904-2*, HD4456) Lewis Pubs.

Comprehensive Guide to Land Navigation with GPS. Noel J. Hotchkiss. (Illus.). 197p. (Orig.). 1994. pap. 29.95 (*0-9641273-2-6*) Alexis Pubng.

Comprehensive Guide to Medical Halachah. Abraham S. Abraham. Orig. Title: Medical Halacha for Everyone. 1991. 22.95 (*0-87306-529-8*) Feldheim.

Comprehensive Guide to Modern Real Estate Law, Practice & Brokerage. Kaplan. 864p. 1990. 65.00 (*0-685-66966-1*, 5446) Commerce.

*__Comprehensive Guide to Prehospital Skills: Comprehensive Guide to Pre-Hospital Skills.__ A. M. Butman et al. (Illus.). 904p. (Orig.). (C). 1995. pap. text ed. 34.50 (*0-940432-09-9*, ET-2475, Emerg Training Inst) Educ Direction.

Comprehensive Guide to Quality Child Care for Administrators & Teachers. Ellen S. Cromwell. (Practitioner Guidebook Ser.). 474p. 1994. 38.95 (*0-205-15322-4*) Allyn.

Comprehensive Guide to Real Estate Finance. Elias Seminars, Jeff Staff. 384p. (C). 1994. pap. text ed. 69.95 (*0-8403-9497-7*) Kendall-Hunt.

*__Comprehensive Guide to Social Security & Medicare.__ Ken Stern. 192p. (Orig.). 1995. pap. 11.99 (*1-56414-172-1*) Career Pr Inc.

Comprehensive Guide to the Cannabis Literature. Comp. by Ernest L. Abel. LC 78-20014. 699p. 1979. text ed. 105.00 (*0-313-20721-6*, ACG/, Greenwood Pr) Greenwood.

Comprehensive Guide to the Hazardous Properties of Chemical Substances. Pradyot Patnaik. 800p. 1992. text ed. 99.95 (*0-442-00191-6*) Van Nos Reinhold.

Comprehensive Guide to the Therapeutic Use of Aminoglutethimide. 2nd rev. ed. Ed. by R. J. Santen & I. C. Henderson. (Pharmanual Ser.: Vol. 2). (Illus.). vi, 162p. 1981. pap. 34.50 (*3-8055-3452-3*) S Karger.

Comprehensive Guide to the Therapeutic Use of Cefsulodin. Ed. by L. D. Sabath & M. Finland. (Pharmanual Ser.: Vol. 1). (Illus.). vi, 94p. 1980. pap. 19.25 (*3-8055-1042-X*) S Karger.

Comprehensive Guide to the Therapeutic Use of Trasicor. Ed. by J. Stevo. (Pharmanual Ser.: Vol. 4). (Illus.). viii, 116p. 1984. pap. 30.50 (*3-8055-3836-7*) S Karger.

Comprehensive Guide to United States Air Force Pocket-Shoulder Insignia Mottos. Jerome Polder. LC 85-60227. 258p. 1985. pap. 23.00 (*0-9615456-3-1*) Aeroemblem Pubns.

Comprehensive Guide to Western Gamefish. Ed Lusch. (Illus.). 125p. 1985. pap. 14.95 (*0-936608-38-2*) F Amato Pubns.

Comprehensive Guide to Work Injury Management. Isernhagen. 350p. 1994. 75.00 (*0-8342-0558-0*, 20558) Aspen Pub.

*__Comprehensive Guitar Method St.__ Cpp Belwin Staff. 1993. pap. 10.00 (*0-89898-701-6*) CPP Belwin.

Comprehensive GYN Review Package. Herbst & Holzman. 1992. 99.00 (*0-8016-6862-X*) Mosby Yr Bk.

Comprehensive Gynecology. 2nd ed. Herbsts et al. 1344p. 1991. 91.00 (*0-8016-6244-3*) Mosby Yr Bk.

Comprehensive Gynecology Review. 2nd ed. Holzman et al. (Illus.). 298p. 1992. pap. 24.95 (*0-8016-2279-4*) Mosby Yr Bk.

Comprehensive Handbook for the Practitioner. K. Majumdar. (C). 1984. 30.00 (*0-89771-354-0*, Current Dist) St Mut.

Comprehensive Handbook of Cognitive Therapy. Ed. by Arthur Freeman et al. (Illus.). 640p. 1989. 90.00 (*0-306-43052-5*, Plenum Pr) Plenum.

Comprehensive Handbook of Drug & Alcohol Addiction. Ed. by Norman S. Miller. 1360p. 1991. 99.75 (*0-8247-8474-X*) Dekker.

Comprehensive Handbook of Hazardous Materials Regulations, Handling, Monitoring, & Safety. Hildegarde L. Sacarello. (Illus.). 1990. 79.95 (*0-87371-247-1*, TD) Lewis Pubs.

Comprehensive Handbook of Psychopathology. 2nd ed. Ed. by P. B. Sutker & H. E. Adams. (Illus.). 930p. (C). 1993. 95.00 (*0-306-44169-1*, Plenum Pr) Plenum.

Comprehensive Handbook of Psychotherapy Integration. Ed. by George Stricker & J. R. Gold. (Illus.). 650p. (C). 1993. 75.00 (*0-306-44280-9*, Plenum Pr) Plenum.

*__Comprehensive Harmony of the Gospels.__ Duane R. Crowther. 48p. 1995. pap. 5.98 (*0-614-07214-X*, 1053) Horizon Utah.

*__Comprehensive Health Care for Everyone: A Guide for Body, Mind & Spirit.__ Thomas Collins. (Illus.). 320p. (Orig.). 1995. pap. 19.95 (*0-931892-97-X*) B Dolphin Pub.

Comprehensive Heterocyclic Chemistry: Five-Membered Rings with Two or More Nitrogen Atoms, Vol. 5. Ed. by Alan R. Katritzky et al. LC 83-4264. 994p. 1984. 550.00 (*0-08-030705-1*, Pergamon Pr); 2,200.00 (*0-685-43851-1*, Pergamon Pr) Elsevier.

Comprehensive Heterocyclic Chemistry: Five-Membered Rings with Two or More Oxygen, Sulfur or Nitrogen Atoms, Vol. 6. Ed. by Alan R. Katritzky et al. LC 83-4264. 1171p. 1984. 430.00 (*0-317-63487-9*, Pergamon Pr); 2,200.00 (*0-685-19002-1*, Pergamon Pr) Elsevier.

Comprehensive Heterocyclic Chemistry: Indexes, Vol. 8. Ed. by Alan R. Katritzky et al. LC 83-4264. (Illus.). 1111p. 1984. 615.00 (*0-08-030708-6*, Pergamon Pr); 2,200.00 (*0-685-19006-4*, Pergamon Pr) Elsevier.

Comprehensive Heterocyclic Chemistry: Introduction, Nomenclature, Review Literature, Biological Aspects, Industrial Uses, Less-Common Heteroatoms. Ed. by Alan R. Katritzky & C. W. Rees. LC 83-4262. (Illus.). 731p. 1984. 405.00 (*0-08-030701-9*, Pergamon Pr); Incl. 8 vols. 2,200.00 (*0-317-63023-7*, Pergamon Pr) Elsevier.

Comprehensive Heterocyclic Chemistry: Six-Membered Rings with One Nitrogen Atom. Ed. by Alan R. Katritzky & C. W. Rees. LC 83-4264. (Illus.). 689p. 1984. 395.00 (*0-08-030702-7*, Pergamon Pr); Incl. 8 vols. 2,200.00 (*0-317-63024-5*, Pergamon Pr) Elsevier.

Comprehensive Heterocyclic Chemistry: Six-Membered Rings with Oxygen, Sulfur or Two or More Nitrogen Atoms, Vol. 3. Ed. by Alan R. Katritzky & C. W. Rees. LC 83-4264. (Illus.). 1210p. 1984. 675.00 (*0-08-030703-5*, Pergamon Pr); Incl. 8 vols. 2,200.00 (*0-317-63025-3*, Pergamon Pr) Elsevier.

Comprehensive Heterocyclic Chemistry: Small & Large Rings. Ed. by Alan R. Katritzky et al. LC 83-4264. (Illus.). 867p. 1984. 480.00 (*0-08-030707-8*, Pergamon Pr); 2,200.00 (*0-317-63494-1*, Pergamon Pr) Elsevier.

Comprehensive Heterocyclic Chemistry: The Structure, Reactions, Synthesis & Uses of Heterocyclic Compounds, 8 Vols. Ed. by Alan R. Katritzky & C. W. Rees. (Illus.). 8000p. 1984. 4,145.00 (*0-08-026200-7*, Pergamon Pr); 675.00 (*0-08-030704-3*, Pergamon Pr) Elsevier.

C

An Asterisk (*) at the beginning of an entry indicates that the title is appearing in BIP for the first time. 1485

Comprehensive High School. Franklin J. Keller. LC 75-98234. 302p. 1970. reprint ed. text ed. 35.00 (*0-8371-2876-5*, KECH, Greenwood Pr) Greenwood.

Comprehensive High School Reading Methods. 3rd ed. David L. Shepherd. LC 81-86087. 412p. reprint ed. pap. 117.50 (*0-317-58109-0*, AU00345) Bks Demand.

Comprehensive History of Jainism. Asim K. Chatterjee. 1978. 20.00 (*0-8364-0225-1*) S Asia.

Comprehensive History of Jainism, 1000 AD to 1600 AD, Vol. II. Asim K. Chatterjee. 1984. 28.50 (*0-8364-1123-4*, Pub. by Mukhopadhyaya II) S Asia.

Comprehensive History of Minnehaha County History, South Dakota. Charles A. Smith. (Illus.). 504p. 1994. reprint ed. lib. bdg. 52.50 (*0-8328-3862-4*) Higginson Bk Co.

Comprehensive History of Psychology. Arun K. Singh. (C). 1991. 34.00 (*81-208-0804-5*, Pub. by Motilal Banarsidass II) S Asia.

Comprehensive History of Texas, 2 vols., Set. Dudley Wooten. 1993. reprint ed. lib. bdg. 150.00 (*0-7812-5911-8*) Rprt Serv.

Comprehensive History of the Far East. L. L. Ahmad. 1981. text ed. 36.50 (*0-685-14104-7*) Coronet Bks.

Comprehensive History of the Far East. L. L. Ahmed. 808p. 1988. 50.00 (*0-317-52135-7*, Pub. by S Chand II) St Mut.

Comprehensive History of the London Church & Parish of St. Mary, The Virgin, Aldermanbury: The Phoenix of Aldermanbury. Christian E. Hauer, Jr. & William A. Young. LC 93-36433. (Illus.). 456p. 1993. text ed. 109.95 (*0-7734-9390-5*) E Mellen.

Comprehensive History of the Woollen & the Worsted Manufacturers, 2 vols. J. Bischoff. (Illus.). 1968. reprint ed. 75.00 (*0-7146-1387-8*, Pub. by F Cass Pubs UK) Intl Spec Bk.

***Comprehensive Hungarian-English Dictionary.** 9th ed. L. Orszagh. 1991. 87.00 (*0-7859-8943-9*) Fr & Eur.

Comprehensive Hungarian-French Dictionary: Dictionnaire Comprehensif Hongrois-Francais. 6th ed. S. Eckhardt. 1104p. (FRE & HUN.). 1985. 59.95 (*0-8288-1060-5*, M9324) Fr & Eur.

Comprehensive Illustrated Catalog of Chinese Paintings. Ed. by Kei Suzuki. 460p. 1982. Vol. I, United States & Canada. 145.00 (*0-86008-308-X*, Pub. by U of Tokyo JA); Vol. II, Southeast Asia & Europe. 145.00 (*0-86008-309-8*, Pub. by U of Tokyo JA); Vol. III, Japan, Pt.I: Museums. 145.00 (*0-86008-310-1*, Pub. by U of Tokyo JA); Vol. IV, Japan, Pt. II: Temples, Shrines, & Individuals. 145.00 (*0-86008-311-X*, Pub. by U of Tokyo JA) Col U Pr.

Comprehensive Illustrated Catalog of Chinese Paintings, V. Ed. by Kei Suzuki. 460p. 1982. 145.00 (*0-86008-312-8*, Pub. by U of Tokyo JA) Col U Pr.

Comprehensive Illustrated Guide to United States Air Force Insignia of the Persian Gulf. Jerome Polder. (Illustrated Guide Series to Air Force Pocket-Shoulder Insignia). (Illus.). 68p. 1994. pap. 15.00 (*0-9615456-8-2*) Aeroemblem Pubns.

Comprehensive Illustrated Guide to United States Air Force Pocket-Shoulder Insignia, Vol. 1. Jerome Polder. LC 85-72269. (Illus.). 235p. 1985. pap. 23.00 (*0-9615456-0-7*) Aeroemblem Pubns.

Comprehensive Illustrated Guide to United States Air Force Pocket-Shoulder Insignia, Vol. 2. Jerome Polder. LC 85-72269. (Illus.). 235p. 1986. pap. 23.00 (*0-9615456-1-5*) Aeroemblem Pubns.

Comprehensive Illustrated Guide to United States Air Force Pocket-Shoulder Insignia, Vol. 3. Jerome Polder. LC 85-72269. (Illus.). 235p. 1986. pap. 23.00 (*0-9615456-2-3*) Aeroemblem Pubns.

Comprehensive Illustrated Guide to United States Air Force Pocket-Shoulder Insignia, Vol. 4. Jerome Polder. LC 85-72269. (Illus.). 235p. 1987. pap. 23.00 (*0-9615456-4-X*) Aeroemblem Pubns.

Comprehensive Illustrated Guide to United States Air Force Pocket-Shoulder Insignia, Vol. 5. Jerome Polder. LC 85-72269. (Illus.). 238p. 1988. pap. 23.00 (*0-9615456-5-8*) Aeroemblem Pubns.

Comprehensive Illustrated Guide to United State's Air Force Pocket Shoulder Insignia, Vol. 6. Jerome Polder. LC 85-72269. (Illus.). 169p. 1989. pap. 23.00 (*0-9615456-6-6*) Aeroemblem Pubns.

Comprehensive Illustrated Guide to USAF Pocket - Shoulder Insignia, Vol. 7. Jerome Polder. (Illus.). 240p. (Orig.). 1992. pap. 23.00 (*0-9615456-7-4*) Aeroemblem Pubns.

Comprehensive Immortalist Primer. Ed. by A. S. Otto. 1975. 24.95 (*0-912132-06-X*) Dominion Pr.

Comprehensive Index: California Administration Code 1986. Ed. by Daniel G. Kielczewski. 989p. 1986. 370.00 (*0-8357-0711-3*) Univ Microfilms.

Comprehensive Index of Group Psychotherapy Writings. Bernard Lubin. (American Group Psychotherapy Association Monographs: No. 2). (C). 1987. text ed. 70.00 (*0-8236-1045-4*) Intl Univs Pr.

***Comprehensive Index of Publications of the American Association of Petroleum Geologists 1971-1975.** June McFarland & Peggy Rice. 906p. 1979. 33.00 (*0-89181-501-5*) AAPG.

***Comprehensive Index of Publications of the American Association of Petroleum Geologists 1976-1980.** June McFarland & Ronald L. Hart. 334p. 1984. 36.00 (*0-89181-502-3*) AAPG.

***Comprehensive Index of Publications of the American Association of Petroleum Geologists 1981-1985.** June McFarland & Victor V. Van Beuren. 360p. 1986. 42.00 (*0-89181-503-1*) AAPG.

Comprehensive Index of Publications of the American Association of Petroleum Geologists, 1986-1990: Comprehensive Index. Ed. by American Association of Petroleum Geologists Staff. 482p. 1991. 43.00 (*0-89181-504-X*) AAPG.

***Comprehensive Index of the Publications of the American Association of Petroleum Geologists 1956-1965.** June McFarland & Mary E. Gieselman. 792p. 1967. 27.00 (*0-89181-498-1*) AAPG.

Comprehensive Index to A. T. Andreas Illustrated Historical Atlas of Minnesota 1874. Mary H. Bakeman. LC 92-1361. (Illus.). 332p. 1992. 29.50 (*0-915709-01-5*) Pk Geneal Bk.

***Comprehensive Index to ASM Handbooks.** 1000p. 1994. 147.00 (*0-87170-383-1*, 6502U); cd-rom 225.00 (*0-614-03403-5*, 6514U); cd-rom 140.00 (*0-614-03402-7*, 6508U) ASM Intl.

Comprehensive Index to Biblical Archaeologist, Vol. 36-45. Comp. by D. Bruce Makay. 225p. 1986. pap. 11.95 (*0-89757-008-1*, Eisenbrauns) Am Sch Orient Res.

Comprehensive Index to Black Mask, 1920-1951. E. R. Hagemann. 236p. 1982. 16.95 (*0-87972-201-0*); pap. 9.95 (*0-87972-202-9*) Bowling Green Univ.

Comprehensive Index to CPL Exchange Bibliographies, No. 1-1565: A Numerical Index. Jane Colokathis. (CPL Bibliographies Ser.: No. 3). 89p. 1979. pap. 9.00 (*0-86602-003-9*) CPL Biblios.

Comprehensive Index to CPL Exchange Bibliographies, No. 1-1565: A Subject Index. Jane Colokathis. (CPL Bibliographies Ser.: No. 1). 119p. 1979. pap. 12.00 (*0-317-00021-7*, Z5942) CPL Biblios.

Comprehensive Index to CPL Exchange Bibliographies, No. 1-1565: An Author Index. Jane Colokathis. (CPL Bibliographies Ser.: No. 2). 100p. 1979. pap. 10.00 (*0-86602-002-0*) CPL Biblios.

Comprehensive Index to CPL Exchange Bibliographies No. 1-1565, 1958-July 1978. 321p. 1982. reprint ed. lib. bdg. 50.00 (*0-89941-269-6*, 302810) W S Hein.

Comprehensive Index to English-Language Little Magazines, 1890-1970, 8 vols., Set. Ed. by Marion Sader. LC 74-11742. 1976. 695.00 (*0-527-00370-0*) Kraus Intl.

Comprehensive Index to Exchange Bibliographies, Set. Incl. Subject Index. 119p. 1979. 12.00 (*0-318-13847-6*); Author Index. 100p. 10.00 (*0-318-13848-4*); Numerical Index. 89p. 1979. 9.00 (*0-318-13849-2*); (CPL Bibliographies Ser.: Nos. 1-3). 100p. 1979. 25.00 (*0-685-43346-3*) Coun Plan Librarians.

***Comprehensive Index to Oregon Statutes 1994.** 1200p. 1994. pap. 100.50 (*0-614-05794-9*) Michie Butterworth.

Comprehensive Index to Oregon Trail Diaries Published by Webb Research Group for the Convenience of Genealogists & Scholars. Bert Webber. LC 91-375. (Illus.). 64p. (Orig.). 1991. pap. 7.50 (*0-936738-54-5*) Webb Research.

Comprehensive Index to Publications 1875-1930. Louise Barry. 515p. 1959. 9.95 (*0-87726-011-7*) Kansas St Hist.

Comprehensive Index to the Journal of Forensic Sciences, 1972-1986. Ed. by Abel M. Dominguez. LC 87-17453. 1987. 69.00 (*0-8031-0984-9*, 13-020000-42) ASTM.

Comprehensive Inorganic Chemistry, 5 vols., Set. Ed. by J. C. Bailar et al. Incl. Vol. 1. H, Noble Gases, Group 1A, Group 11A, Group 111B, C, & Si. 1973. 654.00 (*0-08-016987-2*); Ge, Sn, Pb, Group VB, Group VIB, Group VIIB, Vol. 2. 1973. 564.00 (*0-08-016988-0*); Lanthanides, Transition Metal Compounds, Vol. 3. 1973. 416.00 (*0-08-016989-9*); Actinides, Master Index, Vol. 4. 1973. 294.00 (*0-08-016990-2*); (C). 1973. 2,534.00 (*0-08-017275-X*, Pub. by Pergamon Repr UK) Franklin.

Comprehensive Inorganic Chemistry in Five Volumes, Vol. I: H - Noble Gases Group IA, IIA, IIIB, C & SI. J. C. Bailar & H. J. Emeleus. LC 77-189736. 1973. 607.00 (*0-08-015655-X*, Pub. by Pergamon Repr UK) Franklin.

Comprehensive Insect Physiology, Biochemistry & Pharmacology, 13 vols., Set. Ed. by G. A. Kerkut. (Illus.). 8536p. 1985. 4,160.00 (*0-08-026850-1*, Pergamon Pr) Elsevier.

Comprehensive Insect Physiology, Biochemistry & Pharmacology: Behaviour, Vol. 9. Ed. by G. A. Kerkut. LC 83-25743. 734p. 1985. 455.00 (*0-08-030810-4*, Pub. by PPL UK) Elsevier.

Comprehensive Insect Physiology, Biochemistry & Pharmacology: Biochemistry, Vol. 10. G. A. Kerkut. LC 83-25743. 715p. 1985. 455.00 (*0-08-030811-2*, Pub. by PPL UK) Elsevier.

Comprehensive Insect Physiology, Biochemistry & Pharmacology: Cumulative Indexes, Vol. 13. Ed. by G. A. Kerkut. LC 83-25743. 400p. 1985. 270.00 (*0-08-030814-7*, Pub. by PPL UK) Elsevier.

Comprehensive Insect Physiology, Biochemistry & Pharmacology: Embryogenesis & Reproduction, Vol. 1. G. A. Kerkut. LC 83-25743. 487p. 1985. 310.00 (*0-08-030802-3*, Pub. by PPL UK) Elsevier.

Comprehensive Insect Physiology, Biochemistry & Pharmacology: Endocrinology I, Vol. 7. Ed. by G. A. Kerkut & L. I. Gilbert. LC 83-25743. 565p. 1985. 365.00 (*0-08-030808-2*, Pub. by PPL UK) Elsevier.

Comprehensive Insect Physiology, Biochemistry & Pharmacology: Endocrinology II, Vol. 8. Ed. by G. A. Kerkut. LC 83-25743. 595p. 1985. 365.00 (*0-08-030809-0*, Pub. by PPL UK) Elsevier.

Comprehensive Insect Physiology, Biochemistry & Pharmacology: Insect Control, Vol. 12. Ed. by G. A. Kerkut. 849p. 1985. 540.00 (*0-08-030813-9*, Pub. by PPL UK) Elsevier.

Comprehensive Insect Physiology, Biochemistry & Pharmacology: Integument, Respiration & Circulation, Vol. 3. Ed. by G. A. Kerkut & L. I. Gilbert. LC 83-25743. 625p. 1985. 405.00 (*0-08-030804-X*, Pub. by PPL UK) Elsevier.

Comprehensive Insect Physiology, Biochemistry & Pharmacology: Nervous System: Sensory, Vol. 6. G. A. Kerkut. LC 83-25743. 711p. 1985. 455.00 (*0-08-030807-4*, Pub. by PPL UK) Elsevier.

Comprehensive Insect Physiology, Biochemistry & Pharmacology: Nervous System: Structure & Motor Function, Vol. 5. Ed. by G. A. Kerkut. LC 83-25743. 646p. 1985. 405.00 (*0-08-030806-6*, Pub. by PPL UK) Elsevier.

Comprehensive Insect Physiology, Biochemistry & Pharmacology: Pharmacology, Vol. 11. L. I. Gilbert. Ed. by G. A. Kerkut. LC 83-25743. 741p. 1985. 455.00 (*0-08-030812-0*, Pub. by PPL UK) Elsevier.

Comprehensive Insect Physiology, Biochemistry & Pharmacology: Postembryonic Development, Vol. 2. Ed. by G. A. Kerkut & L. I. Gilbert. LC 83-25743. 505p. 1985. 310.00 (*0-08-030803-1*, Pub. by PPL UK) Elsevier.

Comprehensive Insect Physiology, Biochemistry & Pharmacology: Regulation: Digestion, Nutrition, Excretion, Vol. 4. Ed. by G. A. Kerkut. LC 83-25743. 743p. 1985. 405.00 (*0-08-030805-8*, Pub. by PPL UK) Elsevier.

Comprehensive Intra-Aortic Balloon Pumping. Quaal. 432p. 1983. pap. 31.95 (*0-8016-4090-3*) Mosby Yr Bk.

Comprehensive Intraaortic Balloon Counterpulsation. 2nd ed. Susan J. Quaal. LC 92-48411. 576p. 1993. pap. 32.95 (*0-8016-6656-2*) Mosby Yr Bk.

Comprehensive Introduction to Differential Geometry, Vol. 1. 2nd ed. Michael Spivak. LC 78-71771. 1979. 30.00 (*0-914098-84-5*) Publish or Perish.

Comprehensive Introduction to Differential Geometry, Vol. 2. Michael Spivak. 1979. text ed. 25.00 (*0-914098-85-3*) Publish or Perish.

Comprehensive Introduction to Differential Geometry, Vol. 3. 2nd ed. Michael Spivak. 1979. text ed. 30.00 (*0-914098-86-1*) Publish or Perish.

Comprehensive Introduction to Differential Geometry, Vol. 4. 2nd ed. Michael Spivak. 1979. text ed. 35.00 (*0-914098-87-X*) Publish or Perish.

Comprehensive Introduction to Differential Geometry, Vol. 5. Michael Spivak. 1979. text ed. 40.00 (*0-914098-88-8*) Publish or Perish.

Comprehensive Introduction to Membrane Biochemistry. Dipak B. Datta. (Illus.). 625p. (Orig.). 1987. write for info. (*0-938057-00-6*); pap. text ed. write for info. (*0-938057-01-4*) Floral Pub.

Comprehensive Introduction to Park Management. 2nd ed. Grant Sharpe et al. 400p. 1993. 37.95 (*0-915611-58-9*) Sagamore Pub.

Comprehensive Land Use Planning Certification Preparation Database, 6 disks, Set. Datachem Software Staff. 1991. 3.5 hd, 5.25 hd 325.00 (*0-87371-514-4*, TK) Lewis Pubs.

Comprehensive Machine Transcription Course, Bk. 1. John Visaggi & Loretta Kmech. 207p. 1978. 8.50 (*0-936862-23-8*, TK-1); pap. 6.50 (*0-936862-90-4*, TTK-1) DDC Pub.

Comprehensive Machine Transcription Course, Bk. 2. John Visaggi & Loretta Kmech. 130p. 1978. 8.50 (*0-936862-24-6*, TK-2) DDC Pub.

***Comprehensive Management of Parkinson's Disease.** Ed. by Andrea M. Cohen & William J. Weiner. LC 94-26984. (Comprehension Neurologic Rehabilitation: 8). 1995. 59.95 (*0-939957-74-4*) Demos Vermande.

Comprehensive Management of Parkinson's Disease. Ed. by Matthew B. Stern & Howard I. Hurtig. (Illus.). 300p. 1988. 45.00 (*0-89335-311-6*); pap. 27.50 (*0-89335-316-7*) PMA Pub Corp.

Comprehensive Management of Spina Bifida. Ed. by Rekate. 1990. 99.95 (*0-8493-0151-3*, RJ496) CRC Pr.

Comprehensive Management of Spinal Cord Injury. Lorraine Buchanan. 288p. 1987. 45.00 (*0-683-01128-6*) Williams & Wilkins.

Comprehensive Management of the Menopause. Ed. by Jacques Lorrain et al. LC 93-3255. (Clinical Perspectives in Obstetrics & Gynecology Ser.). 1993. 79.00 (*0-387-97972-7*) Spr-Verlag.

Comprehensive Management of the Upper Limb Amputee. Ed. by D. J. Atkins & R. H. Meier, III. (Illus.). 280p. 1988. 98.00 (*0-387-96779-6*) Spr-Verlag.

Comprehensive Manual of Foundations & Physical Education Activities for Men & Women. George B. Dintiman et al. (Orig.). 1979. pap. text ed. write for info. (*0-8087-0486-9*) Burgess MN Intl.

Comprehensive Maternity Nursing. 2nd ed. Martha Auvenshine & Martha Enriquez. 1000p. 1989. boxed 58.75 (*0-86720-421-4*) Jones & Bartlett.

Comprehensive Medical Assisting: Competencies for Administrative & Clinical Practice. 3rd ed. Mary A. Frew et al. (Illus.). 930p. (C). 1994. text ed. 39.95 (*0-8036-3871-X*) Davis Co.

Comprehensive Medical Handbook. M. Majumdar. (C). 1984. 45.00 (*0-685-36199-3*, Current Dist) St Mut.

Comprehensive Medicinal Chemistry, 6 vols. Ed. by Corwin Hansch. (Rational Design, Mechanistic Study & Therapeutic Application of Chemical Compounds Ser.). (Illus.). 6000p. 1990. 1,750.00 (*0-08-030700-0*, Pergamon Pr) Elsevier.

Comprehensive Mental Health: The Challenge of Evaluation. Ed. by Leigh M. Roberts et al. (Illus.). 350p. 1968. 30.00 (*0-299-05000-9*) U of Wis Pr.

Comprehensive Mental Health: The Challenge of Evaluation Proceedings. Symposium on Comprehensive Mental Health Staff. Ed. by Leigh M. Roberts et al. LC 68-9022. 349p. reprint ed. pap. 99.50 (*0-7837-6663-7*, 2046275) Bks Demand.

Comprehensive Mortgage Payment Tables. Financial Publishing Co. Staff. 224p. 1978. pap. 8.00 (*0-87600-492-3*) Finan Pub.

Comprehensive Mortgage Payment Tables. Financial Publishing Co. Staff. 224p. 1981. pap. 8.00 (*0-87600-592-X*) Finan Pub.

Comprehensive Multicultural Education: Theory & Practice. 3rd ed. Christine I. Bennett. LC 94-20512. 1994. pap. text ed. 40.00 (*0-205-15024-1*) Allyn.

Comprehensive Musical Analysis. John D. White. LC 93-28520. (Illus.). 315p. 1994. 35.00 (*0-8108-2681-X*) Scarecrow.

***Comprehensive NCLex-CAT-PN Review.** Patricia A. Hoefler. Ed. by Amelia R. Hummel. 274p. (C). Date not set. write for info. (*1-56533-012-9*) M E D S Inc.

Comprehensive NCLex-CAT-RN Review. 7th ed. Patricia A. Hoefler. Ed. by Sandra N. Becker. 306p. (C). Date not set. 29.95 (*1-56533-011-0*) M E D S Inc.

Comprehensive NCLEX-PN Review Book. Patricia A. Hoefler. 190p. (C). Date not set. 25.95 (*1-56533-007-2*) M E D S Inc.

Comprehensive Neonatal Nursing: A Physiologic Perspective. Carole Kenner et al. (Illus.). 1248p. 1993. text ed. 99.50 (*0-7216-2992-X*) Saunders.

Comprehensive Nephrology Nursing. Cleo J. Richard. (C). 1986. text ed. 27.75 (*0-673-39368-2*) HarpCollege.

***Comprehensive Networking Glossary & Acronym Guide.** Gary Malkin. 200p. 1994. pap. text ed. 19.93 (*0-13-319955-X*) P-H.

Comprehensive Networking Glossary & Acronym Guide. Gary S. Malkin. (Illus.). 200p. 1994. pap. 19.95 (*1-884777-02-3*) Manning Pubns.

Comprehensive Neurology. Roger N. Rosenberg. 944p. 1991. 243.50 (*0-88167-717-5*) Raven.

Comprehensive One Tenth & Quarter Mortgage Payment Tables. Ed. by Financial Publishing Co. Staff. (Illus.). 112p. 1981. pap. text ed. 7.55 (*0-87600-753-1*) Finan Pub.

Comprehensive Organic Chemistry, 6 vol. set. Ed. by Derek H. Barton & W. D. Ollis. 8034p. 1979. 2,910.00 (*0-08-030732-9*, Pergamon Pr); pap. 800.00 (*0-08-022066-5*, Pergamon Pr) Elsevier.

Comprehensive Organic Chemistry, 1-3. Derek H. Barton et al. Incl. Vol. 1. Stereochemistry, Hydrocarbons, Halo Compounds & Oxygen Compounds. 1979. 495.00 (*0-08-021313-8*); Vol. 2. Nitrogen Compounds, Carboxylic Acids & Phosphorous Compounds. 1979. 495.00 (*0-08-021314-6*); Vol. 3. Sulphur, Selenium, Boron, & Organometallic Compounds. 1979. 495.00 (*0-08-021315-4*); Vol. 4. Heterocyclic Compounds. 1979. 495.00 (*0-08-021316-2*); Vol. 5. Biological Compounds. 1979. 495.00 (*0-08-021317-0*); Formula, Subject, Author, Reaction & Reagent Indexes, Vol. 6. 1979. 495.00 (*0-08-022931-X*); Vols. 1-3. 1979. 687.50 (*0-685-07575-3*); Vols. 4-6. 1979. 687.50 (*0-685-07576-1*); Vol. 4. Heterocyclic Compounds. 1979. 495.00 (*0-08-021316-2*); Vol. 5. Biological Compounds. 1979. 495.00 (*0-08-021317-0*); Vol. 3. Sulphur, Selenium, Boron, & Organometallic Compounds. 1979. 495.00 (*0-08-021315-4*); Vol. 2. Nitrogen Compounds, Carboxylic Acids & Phosphorous Compounds. 1979. 495.00 (*0-08-021314-6*); Vol. 1. Stereochemistry, Hydrocarbons, Halo Compounds & Oxygen Compounds. 1979. 495.00 (*0-08-021313-8*); 1979. 687.50 (*0-08-021319-7*) Elsevier.

Comprehensive Organic Chemistry, Half Set. Derek H. Barton et al. Incl. Vol. 1. Stereochemistry, Hydrocarbons, Halo Compounds & Oxygen Compounds. 1979. 495.00 (*0-08-021313-8*); Vol. 2. Nitrogen Compounds, Carboxylic Acids & Phosphorous Compounds. 1979. 495.00 (*0-08-021314-6*); Vol. 3. Sulphur, Selenium, Boron, & Organometallic Compounds. 1979. 495.00 (*0-08-021315-4*); Vol. 4. Heterocyclic Compounds. 1979. 495.00 (*0-08-021316-2*); Vol. 5. Biological Compounds. 1979. 495.00 (*0-08-021317-0*); Formula, Subject, Author, Reaction & Reagent Indexes, Vol. 6. 1979. 495.00 (*0-08-022931-X*); Vols. 1-3. 1979. 687.50 (*0-685-07575-3*); Vols. 4-6. 1979. 687.50 (*0-685-07576-1*); Vol. 4. Heterocyclic Compounds. 1979. 495.00 (*0-08-021316-2*); Vol. 5. Biological Compounds. 1979. 495.00 (*0-08-021317-0*); Vol. 3. Sulphur, Selenium, Boron, & Organometallic Compounds. 1979. 495.00 (*0-08-021315-4*); Vol. 2. Nitrogen Compounds, Carboxylic Acids & Phosphorous Compounds. 1979. 495.00 (*0-08-021314-6*); Vol. 1. Stereochemistry, Hydrocarbons, Halo Compounds & Oxygen Compounds. 1979. 495.00 (*0-08-021313-8*); 1979. 687.50 (*0-08-023815-7*) Elsevier.

Comprehensive Organic Synthesis, 9 vols., Set. Ed. by Barry M. Trost et al. 7000p. 1991. 3,510.00 (*0-08-035929-9*, Pergamon Pr) Elsevier.

Comprehensive Organic Transformations: A Guide to Functional Group Preparations. Richard C. Larock. LC 89-30333. 1160p. 1989. lib. bdg. 60.00 (*0-89573-710-8*) VCH Pubs.

Comprehensive Organomentallic Chemistry: Indexes, Vol. 9. Ed. by Geoffrey Wilkinson et al. 1982. 690.00 (*0-08-030724-8*, Pergamon Pr) Elsevier.

Comprehensive Organometallic Analysis. T. R. Crompton. LC 87-13988. (Illus.). 910p. 1988. 185.00 (*0-306-42593-9*, Plenum Pr) Plenum.

Comprehensive Organometallic Chemistry: Cobalt, Rhodium & Iridium, Vol. 5. Ed. by Wilkinson et al. 1982. 285.00 (*0-08-030720-5*, Pergamon Pr) Elsevier.

Comprehensive Organometallic Chemistry: Groups IVB, VB, IB & IIB Environmental Aspects, Vol. 2. Ed. by Geoffrey Wilkinson et al. 1982. 455.00 (*0-08-030717-5*, Pergamon Pr) Elsevier.

Comprehensive Organometallic Chemistry: Groups VIIA; Iron, Ruthenium & Osium, Vol. 4. Ed. by Geoffrey Wilkinson et al. 1982. 470.00 (*0-08-030719-1*, Pergamon Pr) Elsevier.

C

An Asterisk (*) at the beginning of an entry indicates that the title is appearing in BIP for the first time.

Comprehensive Organometallic Chemistry: Main Group Bonding, Groups IA IIA & IIIB, Vol. 14. Ed. by Geoffrey Wilkinson et al. 1982. 340.00 (*0-08-030716-7*, Pergamon Pr) Elsevier.

Comprehensive Organometallic Chemistry: Main Group Compounds Organic Synthesis, Vol. 7. Ed. by Geffrey Wilkerson et al. (Illus.). 730p. 1982. 310.00 (*0-08-030722-1*, Pergamon Pr) Elsevier.

Comprehensive Organometallic Chemistry: Nickel, Palladium & Platinum; Heteronuclear Compounds, Vol. 6. Ed. by Geoffrey Wilkinson et al. 1982. 480.00 (*0-08-030721-3*, Pergamon Pr) Elsevier.

Comprehensive Organometallic Chemistry: The Synthesis, Reactions & Structures of Organometallic Compounds. Geoffrey Wilkinson. Ed. by F. Gordon Stone et al. LC 82-7595. 9000p. 1982. 4,055.00 (*0-08-025269-9*, Pergamon Pr) Elsevier.

Comprehensive Organometallic Chemistry: Transition Metal Bonding; Non-rigidity; Groups IIA, IVA, VA & VIA, Vol. 3. Ed. by Geoffrey Wilkinson et al. 1984. 90.00 (*0-317-66817-X*, Pergamon Pr) Elsevier.

Comprehensive Organometallic Chemistry: Transition Metal Compounds in Organic Synthesis & Catalysis, Vol. 8. Ed. by Geoffrey Wilkinson et al. (Illus.). 1106p. 1982. 480.00 (*0-08-030723-X*, Pergamon Pr) Elsevier.

***Comprehensive Organometallic Chemistry II 14VS: A Review of the Literature 1982-1994, 14 vols.** 2nd ed. Ed. by F. Gordon Stone et al. LC 95-7030. (Illus.). 8750p. 1995. 4,470.00 (*0-08-040608-4*, Pergamon Pr) Elsevier.

Comprehensive Outline of Microbiological Diseases. Perry Haalman. 376p. (C). 1994. pap. text ed. 32.95 (*0-8403-9169-2*) Kendall-Hunt.

Comprehensive Peace Education: Educating for Global Responsibility. Betty Reardon. 136p. 1988. text ed. 25.95 (*0-8077-2886-1*); pap. text ed. 13.95 (*0-8077-2885-3*) Tchrs Coll.

Comprehensive Pediatric Nursing. 3rd ed. Gladys M. Scipien et al. 1472p. 1985. text ed. 52.95 (*0-07-055554-0*) McGraw.

Comprehensive Pediatrics. Summitt. (Illus.). 1312p. 1989. 63.95 (*0-8016-5187-5*) Mosby Yr Bk.

Comprehensive Perinatal & Pediatric Respiratory Care. Kent Whitaker. 1992. student ed 16.00 (*0-8273-3855-4*); text ed. 36.95 (*0-8273-3850-3*) Delmar.

***Comprehensive Perioperative Nursing, 2 vols., Set.** Barbara Gruendemann & Billie Fernsebner. (Nursing Ser.). 1995. 64.95 (*0-86720-731-0*) Jones & Bartlett.

Comprehensive Perioperative Nursing, Vol. 1. Barbara J. Gruendemann & Billie Fernsebner. (Illus.). 850p. 1995. text ed. 45.00 (*0-86720-647-0*) Jones & Bartlett.

***Comprehensive Perioperative Nursing, Vol. 2.** Barbara Gruendemann & Billie Fernsebner. (Nursing Ser.). 624p. 1995. 39.95 (*0-86720-719-1*) Jones & Bartlett.

Comprehensive Perioperative Nursing Review. Susan Fairchild. (Illus.). 350p. 1993. pap. text ed. 34.95 (*0-86720-644-6*) Jones & Bartlett.

Comprehensive Persian-English Dictionary. F. Steingass. 1540p. (ENG & PER.). 1975. 85.00 (*0-86685-130-5*) Intl Bk Ctr.

Comprehensive Persian-English Dictionary: Including the Arabic Words & Phrases to Be Met with in Persian Literature. F. Steingass. (ENG & PER.). 1977. 80.00 (*0-7100-2152-6*, RKP) Routledge.

Comprehensive Perspective on Civil & Criminal RICO Legislation & Litigation. 331p. 1985. pap. 39.50 (*0-685-18951-1*, 509-0020-01) Amer Bar Assn.

Comprehensive Pharmacy Review. 2nd ed. Shargel. (National Medical Series for Independent Study). 1993. 30.00 (*0-683-06253-0*) Williams & Wilkins.

Comprehensive Pharmacy Review Practice Exams. 2nd rev. ed. Ed. by Alan H. Mutnick et al. LC 93-47687. 1994. 19.95 (*0-683-06255-7*) Williams & Wilkins.

Comprehensive Plan for Covington, Kentucky & Environs. Covington, Kentucky City & Zoning Commission. LC 73-2904. (Metropolitan America Ser.). 144p. 1974. reprint ed. 27.95 (*0-405-05393-2*) Ayer.

Comprehensive Planning & the Environment: A Manual for Planners. John S. Wilson et al. 294p. 1984. reprint ed. lib. bdg. 52.50 (*0-8191-4085-6*) U Pr of Amer.

Comprehensive Planning for School Administrators. Hildreth McAshan. (Orig.). (C). 1983. pap. text ed. 11.95 (*0-89894-000-1*) Advocate Pub Group.

Comprehensive Polymer Science: The Synthesis, Characterization, Reactions & Applications of Polymers, 7 vols., Set. Geoffrey Allen & J. C. Bevington. (Illus.). 6000p. 1988. 3,120.00 (*0-08-032515-7*, Pergamon Pr) Elsevier.

Comprehensive Polymer Science, Vol. 3: Chain Polymerization I. Ed. by Geoffrey Allen & J. C. Bevington. (Illus.). 897p. 1990. 585.00 (*0-08-036207-9*, Pergamon Pr) Elsevier.

Comprehensive Polymer Science, Vol. 4: Chain Polymerization II. Ed. by Geoffrey Allen & J. C. Bevington. (Illus.). 602p. 1990. 375.00 (*0-08-036208-7*, Pergamon Pr) Elsevier.

Comprehensive Polymer Science, Vol. 5: Step Polymerization. Ed. by Geoffrey Allen & J. C. Bevington. (Illus.). 753p. 1990. 480.00 (*0-08-036209-5*, Pergamon Pr) Elsevier.

Comprehensive Polymer Science, Vol. 6: Polymer Reactions. Ed. by Geoffrey Allen & J. C. Bevington. (Illus.). 664p. 1990. 440.00 (*0-08-036210-9*, Pergamon Pr) Elsevier.

Comprehensive Polymer Science, Vol. 7: Speciality Polymers & Polymer Processing. Ed. by Geoffrey Allen & J. C. Bevington. (Illus.). 685p. 1990. 440.00 (*0-08-036211-7*, Pergamon Pr) Elsevier.

Comprehensive Programming: Handbook for Planning, Developing, Evaluating Educational Programs for Specially-Gifted. Cox. 1989. pap. 9.99 (*0-89824-506-0*) Trillium Pr.

Comprehensive Project Management: Integrating Optimization Models, Management Practices, & Computers. Adedeji B. Badiru & P. Simin Pulat. LC 94-8035. 576p. 1994. text ed. 60.00 (*0-13-030925-7*) P-H.

Comprehensive Psychiatric Nursing. Judith Haber. 844p. 1991. 43.95 (*0-8016-6040-8*) Mosby Yr Bk.

Comprehensive Psychiatric Nursing. 2nd ed. Judith Haber et al. (Illus.). 1216p. (C). 1982. text ed. 47.95 (*0-07-025411-7*) McGraw.

Comprehensive Psychiatric Nursing. 3rd ed. Judith Haber et al. 1296p. 1987. text ed. 49.95 (*0-07-025415-X*) McGraw.

Comprehensive Psychotherapy, 3. Paul Olsen. 183p. 1984. pap. 79.00 (*0-677-16369-X*) Gordon & Breach.

Comprehensive Psychotherapy, Vol. 1. Ed. by Paul Olsen. viii, 176p. 1980. 63.00 (*0-685-37404-1*) Gordon & Breach.

Comprehensive Psychotherapy, Vol. 2. Ed. by Paul Olsen. vi, 122p. 1981. pap. 75.00 (*0-685-01948-9*) Gordon & Breach.

Comprehensive Psychotherapy, Vol. 4. Paul Olsen. 183p. 1984. pap. text ed. 117.00 (*0-677-16539-0*) Gordon & Breach.

Comprehensive Radiographic Pathology. Eisenberg & Dennis. (Illus.). 400p. 1990. 41.95 (*0-8016-6142-0*) Mosby Yr Bk.

Comprehensive Reference Guide to Airfoil Sections for Light Aircraft. Aviation Publications Staff. (Illus.). 168p. 1982. pap. 21.95 (*0-87994-038-7*) Aviat Pub.

Comprehensive Reference Manual for Signers & Interpreters. 4th ed. Cheryl M. Hoffman. LC 94-16469. 314p. (C). 1994. spiral bd., pap. 41.95 (*0-398-05919-5*) C C Thomas.

Comprehensive Rehabilitation Nursing. Leonide L. Martin et al. (Illus.). 816p. 1981. text ed. 44.95 (*0-07-040611-1*) McGraw.

***Comprehensive Respiratory Care.** David R. Dantzker et al. (Illus.). 1104p. 1995. text ed. 59.00 (*0-7216-2844-3*) Saunders.

Comprehensive Respiratory Care. 2nd ed. Eubanks et al. (Illus.). 1040p. 1990. 55.95 (*0-8016-2932-2*) Mosby Yr Bk.

***Comprehensive Review: DOD (Dept. of Defense) Counterdrug Program.** (Illus.). 111p. (Orig.). (C). 1994. pap. text ed. 45.00x (*0-7881-1423-9*) Diane Pub.

Comprehensive Review in Respiratory Care. Vijay M. Deshpande et al. (Illus.). 398p. (C). 1988. pap. text ed. 43.50 (*0-8385-1295-X*, A1295-3) Appleton & Lange.

Comprehensive Review in Toxicology. 2nd ed. Peter D. Bryson. 714p. (C). 1994. 105.00 (*0-87189-777-6*) Raven.

Comprehensive Review Manual for the Adult Nurse Practitioner. 2nd ed. Susan F. Connor et al. (Illus.). 569p. (C). 1989. text ed. 37.50 (*0-673-39860-9*) Lippincott.

Comprehensive Review of Dental Assisting. Jacqueline W. Sapp. LC 81-1381. 240p. 1981. pap. 16.50 (*0-471-05728-2*) Wiley.

Comprehensive Review of Geriatric Psychiatry. Ed. by Joel Sadavoy et al. LC 90-1203. 600p. 1991. 65.00 (*0-88048-362-8*, FVJA8362) Am Psychiatric.

Comprehensive Review of Practical Nursing. 11th ed. Yannes. 576p. 1993. pap. 25.95 (*0-8016-7006-3*) Mosby Yr Bk.

Comprehensive Review of Respiratory Care. 2nd ed. William Wojciechowski. 640p. 1987. pap. text ed. 36.95 (*0-8273-4395-7*) Delmar.

Comprehensive Rock Engineering: Principles, Practice, & Projects. Ed. by John A. Hudson. LC 92-18616. 1993. 2,475.00 (*0-08-035931-0*, Pergamon Pr) Elsevier.

Comprehensive Russian-English Agricultural Dictionary. B. N. Ussovsky & W. Linnard. (ENG & RUS.). 1967. 195.00 (*0-08-010898-9*, Pub. by Pergamon Repr UK) Franklin.

Comprehensive Russian Grammar. Terence Wade. 500p. 1991. pap. 24.95 (*0-631-17502-4*) Blackwell Pubs.

Comprehensive School: Guidelines for Reorganization of Secondary Education. E. Halsall. LC 72-10107. (Commonwealth & International Library). 1973. 104.00 (*0-08-017068-4*, Pub. by Pergamon Repr UK) Franklin.

Comprehensive School Health Challenge: Promoting Health Through Education. Ed. by Peter Cortese & Kathleen Middleton. LC 93-24711. 1993. write for info. (*1-56071-344-5*) ETR Assocs.

Comprehensive School Health Education: Totally Awesome Strategies for Teaching Health. Linda Meeks & Philip Heit. 100p. (C). 1992. teacher ed, pap. text ed. write for info. (*0-9630009-1-8*) Meeks Heit.

***Comprehensive School Health Education: Totally Awesome Strategies for Teaching Health.** 2nd ed. Linda Meeks et al. Ed. by Julie DeVillers & Ann Turpie. (Illus.). 650p. (C). Date not set. pap. text ed. 50.00 (*1-886693-09-9*) Meeks Heit.

Comprehensive School Health Education: Totally Awesome Strategies for Teaching Health. 2nd ed. Linda Meeks et al. (Illus.). 600p. (C). 1992. pap. text ed. 50.00 (*0-9630009-0-X*) Meeks Heit.

Comprehensive Security & Western Prosperity. Leonard Sullivan, Jr. et al. LC 87-29529. (Illus.). 246p. (Orig.). (C). 1988. lib. bdg. 41.00 (*0-8191-6741-X*); pap. 22.00 (*0-8191-6742-8*) Atl Coun US.

Comprehensive Security for the Baltic: An Environmental Approach. Ed. by Arthur H. Westing. (Illus.). 160p. (C). 1989. text ed. 45.00 (*0-8039-8218-6*) Sage.

Comprehensive Self-Defense. Jose G. Paman & Rod Goodwin. LC 93-70988. (Illus.). (Orig.). 1993. pap. 14.00 (*0-9636286-8-2*) Eghty-Three Brixton.

Comprehensive Set: Purposeful Relaxation, Problem Solutions, Value Considerations & Communication, Set-A. Russell E. Mason. 1975. Incl.: 18 Train-Ascendance C60 cassettes; Notes; Clinical Applications, rev. ed., 1979: Brief Outli. pap. 150.00 (*0-89533-021-0*) F I Comm.

Comprehensive Signed English Dictionary. Ed. by Harry Bornstein et al. LC 82-82830. (Illus.). x, 464p. (J). 1983. 29.95 (*0-913580-81-3*, Clerc Bks) Gallaudet Univ Pr.

***Comprehensive Spanish Grammar.** Jacques De Bruyne & Christopher J. Pountain. (Reference Grammars Ser.). 640p. (C). 1995. write for info. (*0-631-16803-6*); pap. write for info. (*0-631-19087-2*) Blackwell Pubs.

Comprehensive Split Dollar. 3rd ed. Ronald G. Floridis. LC 92-64218. 384p. (Orig.). 1992. pap. 35.00 (*0-87218-102-2*) Natl Underwriter.

Comprehensive Split Dollar Kit. Walter S. Bristow, III. (Illus.). 100p. (Orig.). 1989. pap. 20.00 (*0-317-93893-2*) Hayden Bridge.

***Comprehensive Strategy for Serious, Violent, & Chronic Juvenile Offenders.** 52p. (Orig.). (C). 1994. pap. text ed. 40.00x (*0-7881-1148-5*) Diane Pub.

***Comprehensive Stress Management.** Jerrold S. Greenberg. 416p. (C). 1995. pap. write for info. (*0-697-22306-X*) Brown & Benchmark.

Comprehensive Stress Management. 4th ed. Jerrold S. Greenberg. 480p. (C). 1993. pap. text ed. write for info. (*0-697-12632-3*) Brown & Benchmark.

Comprehensive Structured COBOL. James Bradley. 1990. teacher ed 15.95 (*0-07-007079-2*); pap. text ed. write for info. (*0-07-007078-4*) McGraw.

***Comprehensive Structured Cobol.** 2nd ed. L. Wayne Horn. 1992. pap. 35.00 (*0-87835-857-9*) Boyd & Fraser.

***Comprehensive Structured COBOL.** 3rd ed. Lister W. Horn & Gary M. Gleason. LC 94-23198. 1994. 36.00 (*0-87709-621-X*) Boyd & Fraser.

Comprehensive Structured COBOL. 4th ed. Gary S. Popkin. LC 92-32568. 784p. 1993. pap. 52.95 (*0-534-93270-3*) PWS Pubs.

***Comprehensive Study Guide for Wheelock's Latin.** Dale A. Grote. 318p. (Orig.). (C). 1994. pap. text ed. 38.00 (*0-8191-9762-9*) U Pr of Amer.

Comprehensive Study of Egyptian Arabic: A Reference Grammar of Egyptian Arabic: Grammatical & Linguistic Terms in Dictionary Form, Vol. III. Ernest T. Abdel-Massih et al. LC 76-24957. (C). 1979. pap. text ed. 20.00 (*0-932098-13-4*) UM Ctr MENAS.

Comprehensive Study of Egyptian Arabic: Conversation, Texts, Folk Literature, Cultural, Ethnological & Socio-Linguistic Notes, Vol. 1. Ernest T. Abdel-Massih et al. LC 76-24957. (C). 1978. pap. text ed. 20.00 (*0-932098-11-8*) UM Ctr MENAS.

Comprehensive Study of Egyptian Arabic: Lexicon, Vol. IV. Incl. Pt. I. Egyptian Arabic - English: 34 Cultural Categories. Ernest T. Abdel-Massih et al. LC 76-24957. 1979. (*0-318-51583-0*); Pt. II. English - Arabic: 34 Cultural Categories. Ernest T. Abdel-Massih et al. LC 76-24957. 1979. (*0-318-51584-9*); LC 76-24957. (C). 1979. Set pap. text ed. 20.00 (*0-932098-14-2*) UM Ctr MENAS.

Comprehensive Study of Egyptian Arabic: Proverbs & Metaphoric Phrases, Vol. II. Ernest T. Abdel-Massih et al. LC 76-24957. (C). 1978. pap. text ed. 20.00 (*0-932098-12-6*) UM Ctr MENAS.

Comprehensive Study Questions for the EMI-A: Basic Life Support. Jim Murray. (C). 1982. pap. text ed. 22.00 (*0-8359-0895-X*, Reston) P-H.

Comprehensive Study Questions for the EMT-A: Basic Life Support. Jimm Murray. 151p. 1982. pap. 13.95 (*0-317-58940-7*) P-H.

Comprehensive Subject Index to Universal Prose Fiction. Zella A. Dixson. 1972. 59.95 (*0-87968-920-X*) Gordon Pr.

Comprehensive Support for Families: Final Report of the Family Partnership Program. A Demonstration to Assist Families with Developmentally Disabled Children. Kathleen McKaig et al. LC 90-197879. 140p. (Orig.). 1989. pap. 15.00 (*0-88156-102-9*) Comm Serv Soc NY.

Comprehensive Survey of Epiphytes, Pt. II. A. B. Chaudhari. 1985. 30.00 (*81-7089-074-8*, Pub. by Intl Bk Distr II) St Mut.

Comprehensive Survey of Tropical & Mangrove Forests of Sundarbans & Andaman, Pt. 1. A. B. Chaudhari. (C). 1985. text ed. 110.00 (*0-89771-583-7*, Pub. by Intl Bk Distr II) St Mut.

Comprehensive Systems Design: A New Educational Technology. Ed. by Charles M. Reigeluth et al. (NATO ASI Series F: Computer & Systems Sciences, Special Programme AET: Vol. 95). ix, 437p. 1993. write for info. (*3-540-56677-5*) Spr-Verlag.

Comprehensive Systems Design: A New Educational Technology. Ed. by Charles M. Reigeluth et al. LC 93-11329. (NATO ASI Series F, Computer & Systems Sciences: Vol. 95). 1993. 98.00 (*0-387-56677-5*) Spr-Verlag.

Comprehensive Tamil English Dictionary. Winslow. 990p. 1986. reprint ed. 46.00 (*0-8364-1685-6*, Pub. by Manohar II) S Asia.

Comprehensive Tax Reference & Record Keeping Guide for Day Care Providers, 1992. Laurie Kerridge. 89p. 1991. pap. 15.20 (*0-9632081-0-1*) Cornerstn CA.

***Comprehensive Tax Reform: The Colombian Experience.** Ed. by Parthasarathi Shome. LC 95-6823. (Occasional Papers: Vol. 123). 1995. write for info. (*1-55775-430-6*) Intl Monetary.

Comprehensive Technical Dictionary English-Portuguese. L. L. Sell. 1168p. (ENG & POR.). 1981. 95.00 (*0-8288-0653-5*, M 9629) Fr & Eur.

Comprehensive Textbook of Foot Surgery, Set, Vols. 1 & 2. 2nd ed. E. Dalton McGlamry et al. (Illus.). 1840p. 1992. Set. text ed. 325.00 (*0-683-05857-6*) Williams & Wilkins.

***Comprehensive Textbook of Genitourinary Oncology.** Ed. by Nicholas J. Vogelzang & Brian J. Miles. LC 95-1162. 1995. write for info. (*0-683-08599-9*) Williams & Wilkins.

Comprehensive Textbook of Hallux Valgus Reconstruction. David E. Marcinko. 304p. 1992. 91.00 (*0-8016-3171-8*) Mosby Yr Bk.

Comprehensive Textbook of Oncology, 2 vols. 2nd ed. A. R. Moossa et al. 1918p. 1991. 199.00 (*0-683-06147-X*) Williams & Wilkins.

Comprehensive Textbook of Psychiatry, 2 vols. 5th ed. Harold I. Kaplan & Benjamin Sadock. (Illus.). 2360p. 1989. 229.00 (*0-683-04517-2*) Williams & Wilkins.

Comprehensive Textbook of Psychiatry. 6th ed. Harold I. Kaplan & Benjamin Sadock. (Illus.). 2304p. 1995. 200.00 (*0-683-04532-6*) Williams & Wilkins.

***Comprehensive Textbook of Thoracic Oncology.** Ed. by Joseph Aisner et al. LC 95-2030. 1995. write for info. (*0-683-00062-4*) Williams & Wilkins.

Comprehensive Topical & Textual Lesson Commentary Index: 1922-1982. 4th ed. Ernest A. Clevenger, Jr. & Glenda W. Clevenger. 114p. 1981. pap. text ed. 8.95 (*0-88428-019-5*) Parchment Pr.

Comprehensive Treatise of Electrochemistry, Vol. 9. Ed. by Ernest Yeager et al. 468p. 1984. 130.00 (*0-306-41570-4*, Plenum Pr) Plenum.

Comprehensive Treatise of Electrochemistry, Vol. 1: The Double Layer. Ed. by John O. Bockris et al. LC 80-21493. 472p. 1980. 130.00 (*0-306-40275-0*, Plenum Pr) Plenum.

Comprehensive Treatise of Electrochemistry, Vol. 10: Bioelectrochemistry. Ed. by Supramanian Srinivasin et al. 566p. 1985. 125.00 (*0-306-41541-0*, Plenum Pr) Plenum.

Comprehensive Treatise of Electrochemistry, Vol. 2: Electrochemical Processing. Ed. by John O. Bockris et al. LC 80-24836. 638p. 1981. 139.50 (*0-306-40503-2*, Plenum Pr) Plenum.

Comprehensive Treatise of Electrochemistry, Vol. 3: Electrochemical Energy Conversion & Storage. Ed. by John O. Bockris et al. LC 81-2175. 562p. 1981. 125.00 (*0-306-40590-3*, Plenum Pr) Plenum.

Comprehensive Treatise of Electrochemistry, Vol. 4: Electrochemical Materials Science. Ed. by John O. Bockris et al. LC 81-4780. 586p. 1981. 125.00 (*0-306-40614-4*, Plenum Pr) Plenum.

Comprehensive Treatise of Electrochemistry, Vol. 5: Thermodynamics & Transport Properties of Aqueous & Molten Electrolytes. Ed. by Brian F. Conway et al. LC 82-22372. 490p. 1983. 125.00 (*0-306-40866-X*, Plenum Pr) Plenum.

Comprehensive Treatise of Electrochemistry, Vol. 6: Electrodics-Transport. Ed. by John O. Bockris et al. LC 82-13144. 546p. 1982. 125.00 (*0-306-40942-9*, Plenum Pr) Plenum.

Comprehensive Treatise of Electrochemistry, Vol. 7: Kinetics & Mechanisms of Electrode Processes. Ed. by John O. Bockris et al. LC 83-17831. (Illus.). 806p. 1983. 145.00 (*0-306-41152-0*, Plenum Pr) Plenum.

Comprehensive Treatise of Electrochemistry, Vol. 8: Experimental Methods in Electrochemistry. Ed. by Ralph E. White et al. 638p. 1984. 135.00 (*0-306-41448-1*, Plenum Pr) Plenum.

Comprehensive Treatise on Inorganic & Theoretical Chemistry, Vols. 2-6, 8-9, 14-16. Incl. Vol. 2. LC 22-7753. pap. 160.00 (*0-317-10323-7*); Vol. 3. LC 22-7753. pap. 160.00 (*0-317-10324-5*); Vol. 4. LC 22-7753. pap. 160.00 (*0-317-10325-3*); Vol. 5, Pt. 1. LC 22-7753. pap. 160.00 (*0-317-10326-1*); Vol. 6, Pt. 2. LC 22-7753. pap. 160.00 (*0-317-10327-X*); Vol. 8. LC 22-7753. pap. 160.00 (*0-317-10328-8*); Vol. 9. LC 22-7753. pap. 160.00 (*0-317-10329-6*); Vol. 14. LC 22-7753. pap. 160.00 (*0-317-10330-X*); Vol. 15. LC 22-7753. pap. 160.00 (*0-317-10331-8*); Vol. 16. LC 22-7753. pap. 160.00 (*0-317-10332-6*); LC 22-7753. reprint ed. write for info. (*0-318-58060-8*, 2004548) Bks Demand.

Comprehensive U. S. Silver Dollar Encyclopedia. John W. Highfill & Walter H Breen. LC 91-65854. (Illus.). 1200p. (C). 1992. write for info. (*0-9629900-0-0*); lib. bdg. write for info. (*0-9629900-1-9*) Highfill Pr.

Comprehensive Units in Learning Typewriting see On the Melodic Relativity of Tones

Comprehensive Vet Dictionary. Baillieres. 1990. pap. text ed. 34.95 (*0-7020-1395-1*) Saunders.

Comprehensive View of Freemasonry. Henry W. Coil. (Illus.). xiv, 256p. 1985. reprint ed. text ed. 14.50 (*0-88053-053-7*, M 314) Macoy Pub.

Comprehensive Virology, Vol. 17: Methods Used in the Study of Viruses. Ed. by Heinz Fraenkel-Conrat & Robert R. Wagner. LC 80-21841. 480p. 1981. 89.50 (*0-306-40418-4*, Plenum Pr) Plenum.

Comprehensive Virology, Vol. 18: Virus-Host Interactions: Receptors, Persistence, & Neurological Diseases. Ed. by Heinz Fraenkel-Conrat & Robert R. Wagner. LC 82-2389. 214p. 1983. 69.50 (*0-306-41158-X*, Plenum Pr) Plenum.

Comprehensive Virology, Vol. 19: Viral Cytopathology: Cellular Macromolecular Synthesis & Cytocidal Viruses. Ed. by Heinz Fraenkel-Conrat & Robert R. Wagner. LC 84-16081. 556p. 1984. 110.00 (*0-306-41698-0*, Plenum Pr) Plenum.

Comprehensive Vocabulary Program, Vol. 1. Joseph P. Gutkoska. 96p. (Orig.). (gr. 4-6). 1980. pap. 5.95 (*0-930723-02-3*) Nutshell Enterprises.

Comprehensive Vocabulary Program, Vol. 2. Joseph P. Gutkoska. 94p. (Orig.). (gr. 7-8). 1980. pap. 5.95 (*0-930723-03-1*) Nutshell Enterprises.

C

An Asterisk (*) at the beginning of an entry indicates that the title is appearing in BIP for the first time. 1487

Comprehensive Vocabulary Program, Vol. 3. Joseph P. Gutkoska. 94p. (Orig.). (gr. 9-10). 1980. pap. 5.95 (*0-930723-04-X*) Nutshell Enterprises.

Comprehensive Vocabulary Program, Vol. 4. Joseph P. Gutkoska. 94p. (Orig.). (gr. 11-12). 1981. pap. 5.95 (*0-930723-05-8*) Nutshell Enterprises.

Comprehensive Welsh Grammar. David Thorne. LC 92-39657. 384p. 1993. 59.95 (*0-631-16407-3*); pap. 24.95 (*0-631-16408-1*) Blackwell Pubs.

Comprehensive World Wide Stamp Ablum. rev. ed. (Illus.). 650p. 1990. 49.95 (*0-912236-27-2*, Minkus Pubns) Novus Debut.

Comprehensive World Wide Stamp Album: 1990-1992 Supplement. Ed. by Glenn Hinceman. (Illus.). 50p. 1992. ring bd. 15.95 (*0-912236-03-5*, Minkus Pubns) Novus Debut.

Comprehensive World Wide Stamp Kit. (Illus.). 1990. boxed 63.95 (*0-912236-28-0*, Minkus Pubns) Novus Debut.

Comprendamos al Adulto de Hoy - Understanding Today's Adults. Lucien E. Coleman, Jr. Tr. by Victor A. Quezada. 144p. (Orig.). (SPA.). 1992. text ed. 5.70 (*0-311-11904-2*) Casa Bautista.

Comprendamos al Escolar de Hoy. Max B. Price. Tr. by Nancy A. Bedford. 160p. (Orig.). (SPA.). 1992. pap. 5.70 (*0-311-11902-6*) Casa Bautista.

Comprendamos Al Joven de Hoy - Understanding Today's Youth. Daniel O. Aleshire. Ed. by Orquidea Rivas De Jara. Tr. by Orquidea Rivas de Jara. 160p. (Orig.). (SPA.). 1993. pap. 5.70 (*0-311-11903-4*) Casa Bautista.

Comprendamos Al Preescolar De Hoy: Understanding Today's Preschoolers. C. Sybil Waldrop. Tr. by Priscila Patacsil. (Illus.). 160p. (Orig.). (SPA.). 1992. pap. 5.70 (*0-311-11901-8*) Casa Bautista.

Comprende Usted? Heather Leigh. 1991. pap. text ed. 10.00 (*0-582-22344-X*) Longman.

Comprender y Aconsejar. James E. Taulman. Tr. by Nelly S. De Gonzalez. 96p. (Orig.). (SPA.). 1988. pap. 3.75 (*0-311-11052-5*) Casa Bautista.

Comprendiendo el SIDA. Ethan A. Lerner. (Coping with Modern Problems Ser.). (Illus.). 64p. (SPA.). (J). (gr. 4 up). 1988. 17.50 (*0-8225-2000-1*, Lerner Publctns) Lerner Group.

Comprendiendo Personalidad-Hijo (Understanding Your Child's Personality) J. Dobson. (SPA.). Date not set. 1.79 (*1-56063-058-2*, 497419) Editorial Unilit.

Comprendre l'Anglais Scientifique et Technique. Sally Bosworth-Gerome et al. 381p. (ENG & FRE.). 1992. 79.95 (*0-7859-1007-7*, 2729892206) Fr & Eur.

Comprension y Expresion: Increase Your Word Power Reading. Cristina Sokoluk. (SPA.). 5.25 (*84-7228-573-1*, 220188, Pub. by Edit Clie SP) TSELF.

Compressed Air. 1985. pap. 8.95 (*0-917914-37-6*) Lindsay Pubns.

Compressed Air & Gas. 5th ed. Ed. by John P. Rollins. 384p. 1988. reprint ed. text ed. 130.00 (*0-13-162611-6*) P-H.

Compressed Air Systems: A Guidebook on Energy & Cost Savings. 2nd ed. Fairmont Press Staff & E. M. Talbott. 1993. text ed. 68.00 (*0-13-175852-7*) P-H.

Compressed Air Systems: A Guidebook on Energy & Cost Savings. 2nd ed. E. M. Talbott. LC 92-29641. 1992. write for info. (*0-88173-145-5*) Fairmont Pr.

***Compressed Gases: Compressed Hazards.** George Whitmyre. LC 95-7323. 1995. write for info. (*0-8412-3087-0*) Am Chemical.

***Compressed Gases: Safe Handling Procedures.** George Whitmyre. LC 95-1828. 1995. write for info. (*0-8412-3083-8*) Am Chemical.

Compressed Natural Gas (CNG) Vehicular Fuel Systems. National Fire Protection Association Staff. 25p. 1992. 20.25 (*0-685-18969-4*, 52-92) Natl Fire Prot.

Compressed Russian: Russian-English Dictionary of Acronyms, Semiacronyms & Other Abbreviations Used in Contemporary Standard Russian, with Pronunciation. H. K. Zalucky. 920p. (ENG & RUS.). 1991. 295.00 (*0-8288-9307-1*) Fr & Eur.

Compresseur-Dessin see Grande Encyclopedie

Compressibility of Sandstones, No. 29: Developments in Petroleum Science. R. W. Zimmerman. 174p. 1991. 100.00 (*0-444-88325-8*) Elsevier.

Compressible Flow. Stefan Schreier. LC 80-20607. (Wiley-Interscience Publication Ser.). 593p. reprint ed. pap. 169.10 (*0-7837-2407-1*, 2040092) Bks Demand.

Compressible Flow Tables for Engineers: With Appropriate Computer Programs for Estimating Property Changes Caused by Friction, Heat Transfer &, or Shock Waves. James Palmer et al. (Illus.). 95p. (Orig.). (C). 1987. pap. text ed. 21.50 (*0-333-44764-6*, Pub. by Macmill Press UK) Scholium Intl.

***Compressible Fluid Dynamics with Personal Computer Applications.** B. K. Hodge & Keith Koenig. LC 94-46332. 1995. text ed. 71.00 (*0-13-308552-X*) P-H.

Compressible Fluid Flow. 2nd ed. Michel A. Saad. 608p. 1992. text ed. 77.00 (*0-13-161373-1*) P-H.

Compressible Fluid Flow & Systems of Conservation Laws in Several Space Variables. A. J. Majda. (Applied Mathematical Sciences Ser.: Vol. 53). 160p. 1984. pap. 36.00 (*0-387-96037-6*) Spr-Verlag.

Compressing the Product Development Cycle: From Research to Marketplace. Bernard N. Slade. LC 92-27375. 208p. 1992. 27.95 (*0-8144-5006-7*) AMACOM.

***Compression Anastomosis by Biofragmentable Rings: Proceedings of the Second European Workshop.** Ed. by R. Engemann & A. Thiede. LC 94-33288. (Illus.). 184p. 1994. 107.00 (*0-387-58418-8*) Spr-Verlag.

***Compression Anastomosis by Biofragmentable Rings: Proceedings of the Second European Workshop.** Ed. by R. Engemann & A. Thiede. LC 94-33288. (Illus.). 184p. 1994. 107.00 (*3-540-58418-8*) Spr-Verlag.

Compression Planning. Jerry McNellis & Jack Nettles. (Illus.). (Orig.). 1990. write for info. (*0-318-66540-9*) Braintrain.

***Compression Response of Composite Structures STP 1185.** Ed. by Scott E. Groves & Alton L. Highsmith. LC 94-3606. (Special Technical Publications: No. 1185). (Illus.). 375p. 1994. text ed. 105.00 (*0-8031-1499-0*, 04-011850-33) ASTM.

Compression Testing of Homogeneous Materials & Composites - STP 808. Ed. by Chait Richard & Ralph Papirno. LC 82-73768. 294p. 1983. text ed. 40.00 (*0-8031-0248-8*, 04-808000-23) ASTM.

Compression Wood in Gymnosperms, 3 vols., Set. T. E. Timell. (Illus.). 2210p. 1986. 689.00 (*0-387-15715-8*) Spr-Verlag.

Compressional & Extensional Structural Styles in the Northern Basin & Range. Ed. by Larry J. Garside & David R. Shaddrick. 1989. pap. text ed. 12.00 (*1-881308-01-4*) NV Petroleum.

Compressor Aerodynamics. N. A. Cumpsty. 1990. text ed. 204.00 (*0-470-21334-5*) Halsted Pr.

Compressor Application Engineering, Vol. 1: Compression Equipment. Pierre Pichot. LC 86-7587. (Illus.). 250p. 1986. 49.00 (*0-87201-705-2*) Gulf Pub.

Compressor Application Engineering, Vol. 2: Drivers for Rotating Equipment. Pierre Pichot. LC 86-7587. (Illus.). 230p. 1986. 49.00 (*0-87201-706-0*) Gulf Pub.

Compressor Performance: Selection, Operation, & Testing of Axial & Centrifugal Compressors. M. Theodore Gresh. 192p. 1990. text ed. 62.95 (*0-409-90237-3*) Buttrwrth-Heinemann.

Compressor Station Operations. American Gas Association Operating Section Compressor Committee. Ed. by Robert L. Parker. LC 85-70460. (Gas Engineering & Operating Practices Ser.). (Illus.). 304p. (C). 1985. 25.00 (*0-87257-000-2*, XY0185) Am Gas Assn.

Compressor Surge & Stall. Ronald C. Pampreen. LC 92-70348. 600p. 1993. text ed. 125.00 (*0-933283-05-9*) Concepts ETI.

Compressors. Center for Occupational Research & Development Staff. (EUTEC Power Plant Operator Curriculum Ser.). (Illus.). 48p. (C). 1985. pap. text ed. write for info. (*1-55502-221-9*) CORD Commns.

***Compressors Vol. IV, Module II.** Multimedia Development Services Staff. (Plant Fundamentals Ser.). (Illus.). (Orig.). 1995. teacher ed 45.00 (*1-57431-053-4*); student ed 30.00 (*1-57431-013-5*) Tech Trng Systs.

Compressors & Expanders: Selection & Application for the Process Industry. Bloch. (Chemical Industries Ser.: Vol. 8). (Illus.). 344p. 1982. 135.00 (*0-8247-1854-2*) Dekker.

Compressors & Fans, Vol. 2: Process & Pollution Control Equipment. Paul N. Cheremisinoff. 1992. text ed. 78.00 (*0-13-159740-X*) P-H.

***Compressors & Pumps Market.** 600p. (Orig.). 1994. pap. 1,495.00 (*1-57205-919-2*) Rector Pr.

Comprising the Series of Original Paintings of Charles Bodmer to Illustrate Maximilian, Prince of Wieds Travels in the Interior of North America, 1832-34 see Early Western Travels, 1748-1846

Compro. American Association for Medical Transcription Staff. 6p. 1987. teacher ed 3.00 (*0-935229-06-X*) Am Assoc Med.

Comprobacion Para Sumario De Doctrina Cristiana. Paul Bergsma. (SPA.). 1983. 1.60 (*1-55955-056-2*) CITE MI.

Comprogram: Hospital Space Allocation, 2 vols. Ed. by Clifford D. Stewart et al. LC 73-158290. 1973. 58.00 (*0-915250-02-0*) Environ Design.

Compromis Austro-Hongrois de 1867: Etude Sur le Dualisme. L. Eisenmann. (Central & East European Ser.: Vol. 1). 1904. 75.00 (*0-87569-018-1*) Academic Intl.

Compromise. Sergei Dovlatov. Tr. by Anne Frydman. 148p. 1990. reprint ed. pap. 7.95 (*0-89733-353-5*) Academy Chi Pubs.

Compromise & Political Action: Political Morality in Liberal & Democratic Life. J. Patrick Dobel. LC 88-25953. 224p. (C). 1990. lib. bdg. 46.00 (*0-8476-7604-8*) Rowman.

Compromise & Political Action: Political Morality in Liberal & Democratic Life. J. Patrick Dobel. 1992. pap. 21.95 (*0-8476-7765-6*) Rowman.

Compromise Formations: Current Directions in Psychoanalytic Criticism. Ed. by Vera J. Camden. LC 88-28464. 272p. 1989. 21.00 (*0-87338-380-X*); pap. 12.50 (*0-87338-381-8*) Kent St U Pr.

Compromise in Imperial China. Kung-Chuan Hsiao. (Parerga Ser.: No. 6). 68p. 1979. pap. 7.50 (*0-295-95726-3*) U of Wash Pr.

Compromised: Clinton, Bush, & the CIA. Terry Reed & John Cummings. 1993. 23.95 (*1-56171-249-3*) Sure Sellers.

***Compromised: Clinton, Bush & the CIA How the Presidency Was Co-Opted by the CIA.** Terry Reed & John Cummings. (Illus.). 704p. 1995. pap. 17.95 (*1-883955-02-5*) Penmarin Bks.

Compromised Campus: The Collaboration of Universities with the Intelligence Community, 1945-1955. Sigmund Diamond. 384p. 1992. 30.00 (*0-19-505382-6*) OUP.

Compromised Compliance: Implementation of the 1965 Voting Rights Act. Howard Ball et al. LC 81-6342. (Contributions in Political Science Ser.: No. 66). (Illus.). xi, 300p. 1982. text ed. 59.95 (*0-313-22037-9*, BCM/, Greenwood Pr) Greenwood.

Compromised Hearts. Hannah Howell. 448p. 1989. pap. 3.95 (*0-8439-2860-3*) Dorchester Pub Co.

Compromised Scientist: William James in the Development of American Psychology. Daniel W. Bjork. LC 82-14690. (Illus.). 224p. 1983. text ed. 47.50 (*0-231-05500-5*); pap. text ed. 18.00 (*0-231-05501-3*) Col U Pr.

***Compromises.** Joan Hohl. 448p. 1995. mass mkt. 4.99 (*0-8217-4894-7*) Zebra.

Compromises. Agnes Repplier. LC 78-98626. reprint ed. 27.50 (*0-404-05259-2*) AMS Pr.

Compromises. Agnes Repplier. (BCL1-PS American Literature Ser.). 277p. 1992. reprint ed. lib. bdg. 79.00 (*0-7812-6840-0*) Rprt Serv.

Compromises. Agnes Repplier. 1971. reprint ed. 8.00 (*0-403-00701-1*) Scholarly.

Compromises of Life & Other Lectures & Addresses. Henry Watterson. LC 68-8504. (Essay Index Reprint Ser.). 1977. 30.95 (*0-8369-1936-X*) Ayer.

Compromising Positions. Susan Isaacs. 352p. (Orig.). 1985. mass mkt. 6.99 (*0-515-09302-5*) Jove Pubns.

Compromising Redemption: Relating Characters in the Book of Ruth. Danna N. Fewell & David M. Gunn. (Literary Currents in Biblical Interpretation Ser.). 128p. (Orig.). 1990. pap. 11.99 (*0-664-25135-8*) Westminster John Knox.

COMPSAC '92 (Conference on Software Applications), 16th. LC 83-640060. 408p. 1992. 80.00 (*0-8186-3000-0*, 3000) IEEE Comp Soc.

COMPSAC '93 (Conference on Software Applications), 17th. 400p. 1993. pap. text ed. 80.00 (*0-8186-4440-0*, 4440) IEEE Comp Soc.

***COMPSAC '94 - 18th Computer Software & Applications Conference.** LC 83-640060. 496p. 1994. pap. text ed. 100.00 (*0-8186-6705-2*, PR06705) IEEE Comp Soc.

***COMPSENSE: California's Workers' Compensation Step by Step Usage Guide.** Beverly Dixon & Suzanne Guyan. 125p. 1994. pap. write for info. (*0-9644331-0-9*) Comp Sense.

***Compsognathus.** Janet Riehecky. (Dinosaur Bks.). (Illus.). 32p. (ENG & SPA.). (J). (ps-2). 1990. lib. bdg. 21.36 (*1-56766-133-5*) Childs World.

Compsognathus. Janet Riehecky. (Dinosaur Bks.). (Illus.). 32p. (ENG & SPA.). (J). (ps-2). 1990. lib. bdg. 21.36 (*0-89565-624-8*) Childs World.

Compsognathus: The Smallest Dinosaur. Elizabeth Sandell. Ed. by Marjorie Oelerich & Harlan S. Hansen. LC 88-39801. (Dinosaur Discovery Era Ser.). (Illus.). 32p. (J). (gr. k-5). 1989. lib. bdg. 12.95 (*0-944280-14-5*); pap. text ed. 5.95 (*0-944280-20-X*) Bancroft-Sage.

COMPSTAT 1986: Proceedings in Computational Statistics. Ed. by F. De Antoni et al. (Illus.). xv, 512p. 1986. pap. 84.00 (*0-387-91286-X*) Spr-Verlag.

***COMPSTAT 1994: Proceedings in Computational Statistics.** R. Dutter & W. Grossmann. 576p. 1994. pap. text ed. 129.00 (*3-7908-0793-1*) Spr-Verlag.

***Comptabilite Financiere.** 2nd ed. Kermit Larson et al. 448p. (FRE.). (C). 1992. text ed. 30.95 (*0-256-10853-6*) Irwin.

***Comptabilite Financiere Tome, Vol. 2.** Kermit Larson et al. 528p. (C). 1988. text ed. 32.95 (*0-256-06629-9*) Irwin.

Compte de Gabalis: Discourses on the Secret Sciences & Mysteries in Accordance with the Principles of the Ancient Magi & the Wisdom of the Kabalistic Philosophers. Abbe N. De Montfaucon De Villars. 352p. 1992. pap. 27.00 (*1-56459-201-4*) Kessinger Pub.

***Compte Rendu De la Troisieme Rencontre Assyriologique Internationale Organisee a Leiden Du 28 Juin Au 4 Juillet 1952: Par le Nederlandsch Instituut Voor Het Nabije Oosten.** Ed. by A. A. Kampman & J. P. Van der Ploeg. vi, 164p. 1954. pap. text ed. 17.50 (*0-614-03998-3*, Pub. by Netherlands Inst NE) Eisenbrauns.

***Compte Rendu l'Onzieme Rencontre Assyriologique Internationale Organisee a Leiden Du 23 Au 29 Juin 1962: Par le Nederlands Instituut Voor Het Nabije Oosten.** Ed. by A. A. Kampman & J. P. Van der Ploeg. viii, 116p. 1964. pap. text ed. 17.50 (*0-614-03999-1*, Pub. by Netherlands Inst NE) Eisenbrauns.

Comptes Rendus, 2 pts. Ed. by M. Williams. Incl. Part A (Madrid) 1975. 1976. pap. 69.00 (*0-08-021155-0*); Part B (Madrid) 1975. 1977. pap. 186.00 (*0-08-021357-X*); 1977. Set pap. 155.00 (*0-08-021361-8*, Pub. by Pergamon Repr UK) Franklin.

Compton Gamma-Ray Observatory. Gehrels. (AIP Conference Proceedings Ser.: No. 280). (Illus.). 1248p. 1993. text ed. 205.00 (*1-56396-104-0*, AIP Pr) Am Inst Physics.

Compton's Encyclopedia, 26 vols., Set. (J). (gr. 5-10). 1992. 569.00 (*0-85229-554-5*) Ency Brit Ed.

Compton's Precyclopaedia, 16 vols., Set. (J). (gr. 1-4). 1988. 269.00 (*0-85229-479-4*) Ency Brit Ed.

***CompuCat.** Elaine Mays & Jon Midgley. 85p. Date not set. pap. text ed. 7.95 (*0-9640463-1-8*) Compucat Ptrns.

CompuHelp Inc. An Office Simulation. Olive Church. (C). 1991. teacher ed 5.25 (*1-56118-032-7*) Paradigm MN.

Compulsion. Robin Blake & Eleanors Stephens. 160p. 1988. 40.00 (*1-85283-208-8*, Pub. by Boxtree Ltd UK) St Mut.

Compulsion. Michael Stewart. LC 93-30908. 384p. 1994. 23.00 (*0-06-017767-5*, HarpT) HarpC.

***Compulsion.** Michael Stewart. 1994. pap. 5.50 (*0-06-109167-7*, Harp PBks) HarpC.

Compulsion & Doubt, 2 Vols. rev. ed. Wilhelm Stekel. Ed. by Emil A. Guthiel. (C). 1949. text ed. 14.95 (*0-87140-845-7*) Liveright.

Compulsion in the Criminal Law. Stanley Yeo. xxiv, 300p. 1990. 69.50 (*0-455-20994-4*, Pub. by Law Bk Co) W W Gaunt.

Compulsion of the Spirit: A Roland Allen Reader. Roland Allen. Ed. by David Paton & Charles H. Long. LC 83-14006. 158p. reprint ed. pap. 45.10 (*0-317-30156-X*, 2025338) Bks Demand.

Compulsion to Create: A Psychoanalytic Study of Women Artists. Susan Kavaler-Adler. LC 92-41916. 1993. 55.00 (*0-415-90710-1*, A9795, Routledge NY); pap. 17.95 (*0-415-90711-X*, A9799, Routledge NY) Routledge.

Compulsion to Kill. Time-Life Books Editors. Ed. by Laura Foreman. LC 93-17273. (True Crime Ser.). (Illus.). 192p. 1993. 12.99 (*0-7835-0016-5*); lib. bdg. 17.45 (*0-7835-0017-3*) Time-Life.

Compulsions to Confess: On the Psycho Analysis of Crime & Punishment. Theodor Reik. LC 72-1146. (Essay Index Reprint Ser.). 1977. reprint ed. 36.95 (*0-8369-2856-3*) Ayer.

Compulsive Beauty. Hal Foster. (Illus.). 226p. 1993. pap. 35.00 (*0-262-06160-0*, October Bk) MIT Pr.

***Compulsive Beauty.** Hal Foster. (October Ser.). (Illus.). 338p. 1995. pap. 16.95 (*0-262-56081-X*) MIT Pr.

Compulsive Behavior. Ed. by Dale C. Garell & Solomon H. Snyder. (Psychological Disorders & Their Treatment Ser.). (Illus.). 112p. (YA). (gr. 7-12). 1993. 18.95 (*0-7910-0044-3*); pap. write for info. (*0-7910-0510-0*) Chelsea Hse.

Compulsive Consumption. Judy Hamlin. 64p. (Orig.). 1993. pap. 1.00 (*1-56476-196-7*, Victor Books) SP Pubns.

Compulsive Exercise & the Eating Disorders: Toward an Integrated Theory of Activity. Alayne Yates. LC 90-15153. 272p. 1991. 35.95 (*0-87630-630-X*) Brunner-Mazel.

Compulsive Gambling: Theory, Research, & Practice. Ed. by Howard J. Shaffer et al. 368p. 1989. text ed. 49.95 (*0-669-20715-2*) Free Pr.

Compulsive Gambling: An Examination of Relevant Models: A Special Issue of Journal of Gambling Behavior. Ed. by Julian I. Taber. 82p. 1987. pap. 14.95 (*0-89885-392-3*) Human Sci Pr.

Compulsive Overeater. Bill B. LC 80-70095. 320p. 1981. 18.95 (*0-89638-046-7*) Hazelden.

***Compulsive Overeater.** Bill B. LC 80-70095. 320p. 1981. 18.95 (*1-56838-062-3*) Hazelden.

Compulsive Woman. Sandra S. LeSourd. LC 90-38108. 317p. 1987. pap. 9.99 (*0-8007-9171-1*) Chosen Bks.

Compulsory Admissions to Mental Hospitals. Philip Bean. LC 79-41786. 290p. reprint ed. pap. 82.70 (*0-685-20694-7*, 2030483) Bks Demand.

Compulsory Figures: Essays on Recent American Poets. Henry Taylor. LC 92-5464. 328p. (C). 1992. 32.50 (*0-8071-1755-2*) La State U Pr.

Compulsory Happiness. Norman Manea. Tr. by Linda Coverdale. LC 92-38608. (FRE & ROM.). 1993. 22.00 (*0-374-12785-9*) FS&G.

Compulsory Happiness. Norman Manea. Tr. by Linda Coverdale. LC 94-17021. (Writings from an Unbound Europe Ser.). 264p. 1994. pap. 13.95 (*0-8101-1190-X*) Northwestern U Pr.

Compulsory Health Insurance: The Continuing American Debate. Ed. by Ronald L. Numbers. LC 82-6145. (Contributions in Medical History Ser.: No. 11). xv, 172p. 1982. text ed. 49.95 (*0-313-23436-1*, NHI/, Greenwood Pr) Greenwood.

Compulsory Hospitalization or Freedom of Choice in Childbirth, 3 vols., 3. David Stewart & Lee Stewart. LC 77-92613. 1978. 7.75 (*0-917314-15-8*) NAPSAC.

Compulsory Hospitalization or Freedom of Choice in Childbirth, 3 vols., Set. David Stewart & Lee Stewart. LC 77-92613. 1978. pap. 19.50 (*0-917314-12-3*) NAPSAC.

Compulsory Improvement of Dwellings. Shaw & Sons Ltd. Staff. (Shaway Guides Ser.). (C). 1988. 40.00 (*0-685-44523-2*, Scientific) St Mut.

Compulsory Jurisdiction of the International Court of Justice. Renata Szafarz. LC 92-32722. (Legal Aspects of International Organizations Ser.). (C). 1993. lib. bdg. 82.00 (*0-7923-1989-3*) Kluwer Ac.

***Compulsory Land Acquisition: Singapore & Malaysia.** 2nd ed. N. Khuball. 360p. 1994. write for info. (*0-409-99691-2*) Butterworth Legal Pubs.

Compulsory Military Training. K. N. Kini. 1980. lib. bdg. 59.95 (*0-8490-3081-1*) Gordon Pr.

Compulsory Pension Insurance: Comparative Analysis of National Laws & Statistics, (I. L. O., Studies & Reports) (Series M: No. 10, Vol. 48). 1972. reprint ed. 65.00 (*0-8115-3280-1*) Periodicals Srv.

***Compulsory Purchase & Compensation Vol. 1.** Clive Brand & Jeremy Rowan-Robinson. 1994. 88.00 (*0-421-46540-9*, Pub. by Sweet & Maxwll) W W Gaunt.

***Compulsory Purchase & Compensation in Ireland: Law & Practice.** Sean McDermott & Richard Woulfe. 1992. boxed 104.00 (*1-85475-102-6*, IE) Butterworth Legal Pubs.

Compulsory School Attendance & Child Labor. Forest C. Ensign. LC 72-89176. (American Education: Its Men, Institutions & Ideas, Ser.). 1970. reprint ed. 23.95 (*0-405-01414-7*) Ayer.

***Compulsory Schooling & Human Learning: The Moral Failure of Public Education in American & Japan.** Ed. by Dayle M. Bethel. LC 94-29522. 1994. pap. 17.95 (*1-880192-13-6*) Caddo Gap Pr.

Compulsory Sickness Insurance, (I. L. O.) Studies & Reports. (Series M: No. 6, Vol. 46). 1972. reprint ed. 65.00 (*0-8115-3278-X*) Periodicals Srv.

Compulsory Treatment of Drug Abuse: Research & Clinical Practice. 1991. lib. bdg. 75.00 (*0-8490-4347-6*) Gordon Pr.

Compulsory Treatment of Drug Abuse: Research & Clinical Practice. Ed. by Carl Leukefeld & Frank M. Tims. (DHHS Publication ADM Series National Institute on Drug Abuse Research Monograph, Ser. 86: No. 88-1578). (Illus.). 264p. 1988. pap. 7.50 (*0-16-002486-2*, S/N 017-024-01352-8) USGPO.

Compunctious Poet: Cultural Ambiguity & Hebrew Poetry in Muslim Spain. Ross Brann. LC 90-4788. (Jewish Studies). 220p. 1991. text ed. 38.00 (*0-8018-4073-2*) Johns Hopkins.

An Asterisk (*) at the beginning of an entry indicates that the title is appearing in BIP for the first time.

An Asterisk (*) at the beginning of an entry indicates that the title is appearing in BIP for the first time.

1489

C

Computational Aspects of the Study of Biolgical Macrom. Ed. by J. C. Hoch. (NATO ASI Series A, Life Sciences: Vol. 255). (Illus.). 464p. (C). 1992. 120.00 (0-306-44114-4, Plenum Pr) Plenum.

Computational Aspects of VLSI Design with an Emphasis on Semiconductor Device Simulation Bank. R. Bank. 190p. 1990. 58.00 (0-8218-1132-0, LAM-25) Am Math.

Computational Biomedicine. Ed. by K. D. Held et al. LC 93-71017. (BIOMED Ser.: Vol. 2). 360p. 1993. 145.00 (1-56252-162-4) Computational Mech MA.

Computational Biomedicine III: Proceedings of the Third International Conference. Ed. by C. A. Brebbia & H. Power. (BIOMED Ser.: Vol. 3). 600p. 1995. 223.00 (1-56252-245-0) Computational Mech MA.

Computational Brain. Patricia S. Churchland & Terrence J. Sejnowski. (Illus.). 576p. 1992. 47.50 (0-262-03188-4, Bradford Bks) MIT Pr.

Computational Brain. Patricia S. Churchland & Terence J. Seynowski. (Computational Neuroscience Ser.). (Illus.). 576p. 1993. pap. 19.95x (0-262-53120-8, Bradford Bks) MIT Pr.

Computational Chemical Graph Theory. Ed. by D. H. Rouvray. 329p. (C). 1990. text ed. 115.00 (0-941743-84-5) Nova Sci Pubs.

Computational Chemical Graph Theory: Characterization, Enumeration & Generation of Chemical Structures by Computer Methods. N. Trinajstic et al. 350p. 1991. text ed. write for info. (0-13-151739-2) P-H.

*__Computational Chemistry.__ Guy H. Grant & W. Graham Richards. (Oxford Chemistry Primers Ser.: No. 29). (Illus.). 96p. (C). 1995. pap. text ed. 9.95 (0-19-855740-X) OUP.

Computational Chemistry: An Introduction to Numerical Methods. Anthony C. Norris. LC 80-41691. 468p. reprint ed. pap. 133.40 (0-7837-4767-5, 2044521) Bks Demand.

*__Computational Chemistry: F.E.C.S. Conference.__ Ed. by Francesco Bernardi & Jean-Louis Rivail. (AIP Conference Proceedings Ser.: No. 330). (Illus.). 900p. 1995. text ed. 165.00 (1-56396-457-0) Am Inst Physics.

Computational Chemistry Using the PC. Donald W. Rogers. LC 90-12309. 224p. 1990. lib. bdg. 59.50 (0-89573-770-1) VCH Pubs.

C

Computational Chemistry, Vols. 1 & 2: Structure, Interactions, & Reactivity, 1. Ed. by S. Fraga. LC 92-11596. (Studies in Physical & Theoretical Chemistry: Vol. 77). 1992. write for info. (0-444-89601-5) Elsevier.

Computational Chemistry, Vols. 1 & 2: Structure, Interactions, & Reactivity, 2. Ed. by S. Fraga. LC 92-11596. (Studies in Physical & Theoretical Chemistry: Vol. 77). 1992. write for info. (0-444-89602-3) Elsevier.

Computational Complexity. Christos H. Papadimitriou. LC 93-5662. 1993. write for info. (0-02-015308-2) Addison-Wesley.

Computational Complexity. Christos H. Papadimitriou. (Illus.). 528p. (C). 1994. text ed. 45.25 (0-201-53082-1) Addison-Wesley.

Computational Complexity & Natural Language. G. Edward Barton et al. (Computational Models of Cognition & Perception Ser.). 320p. 1987. 40.00x (0-262-02266-4, Bradford Bks) MIT Pr.

Computational Complexity of Algebraic & Numeric Problems. Allan Borodin & I. Munro. LC 74-21786. (Elsevier Computer Science Library, Theory of Computation Ser.: No. 1). 184p. reprint ed. pap. 52.50 (0-685-15491-2, 2026273) Bks Demand.

Computational Complexity of Bilinear Forms. H. Krishna. (Lecture Notes in Control & Information Sciences Ser.: Vol. 94). xvii, 166p. 1987. pap. 34.00 (0-387-17661-6) Spr-Verlag.

Computational Complexity of Differential & Integral Equations: An Information-Based Approach. Arthur G. Werschulz. (Oxford Mathematical Monographs). 343p. 1991. 55.00 (0-19-853589-9) OUP.

Computational Complexity of Machine Learning. Michael J. Kearns. (ACM Distinguished Dissertation, 1989 Ser.). 175p. 1990. 27.50 (0-262-11152-7) MIT Pr.

Computational Complexity of Sequential & Parallel Algorithms. Lydia Kronsjo. (Computing Ser.). 224p. 1986. text ed. 79.95 (0-471-90814-2) Wiley.

Computational Complexity Theory. Ed. by Hartmanis. LC 89-6857. (PSAPM Ser.: Vol. 38). 128p. 1990. 42.00 (0-8218-0131-7, PSAPM-38) Am Math.

*__Computational Display of Joshua: A Computer-Assisted Analysis & Textual Interpretation.__ Nicolai Winther-Neilsen & Eep Talstra. (Applicatio Ser.: Vol. 13). 136p. 1995. pap. 20.00 (90-5383-390-0) Paul & Co Pubs.

Computational Dynamics. A. A. Shabana. LC 93-44579. 1994. text ed. 69.95 (0-471-30551-0) Wiley.

*__Computational Dynamics in Multibody Systems.__ Ed. by Manuel F. O. S. Pereira & Jorge A. C. Ambrosio. LC 94-45512. (Diverse Ser.). 324p. (C). 1995. lib. bdg. 144.00 (0-7923-3304-7) Kluwer Ac.

Computational Economics. Gerald Thompson & Sten Thore. 352p. 1992. Incl. 5 1/4" diskette. text ed., disk 52.50 (0-89426-200-9); Incl. 3 1/2" diskette. text ed., disk 52.50 (0-89426-201-7) Boyd & Fraser.

Computational Economics & Econometrics. Ed. by Hans M. Amman et al. (Advanced Studies in Theoretical & Applied Econometrics). 192p. (C). 1992. lib. bdg. 93.00 (0-7923-1287-2) Kluwer Ac.

*__Computational Electrodynamics: The Finite-Difference Time-Domain Method.__ Allen Taflove. LC 95-15008. 1995. write for info. (0-89006-792-9) Artech Hse.

Computational Electromagnetics. Konada Umashankar & Allen Taflove. LC 93-12355. (Antennas & Propagation Ser.). 620p. 1993. text ed. 88.00 (0-89006-599-3) Artech Hse.

Computational Electromagnetics: Frequency - Domain Method of Moments. Ed. by Edmund K. Miller et al. LC 91-12159. (Illus.). 528p. (C). 1992. 69.95 (0-87942-276-9, PC02709) Inst Electrical.

Computational Electromagnetics: Proceedings of the IMACS International Symposium, Pittsburgh, PA, December 12-13, 1984. Ed. by Z. J. Cendes. 280p. 1986. 69.25 (0-444-70010-2) Elsevier.

*__Computational Electromagnetics Using Boundary Elements: Advances in Modelling Eddy Currents.__ Jinxing Shen. LC 94-69713. (Topics in Engineering Ser.: Vol. 24). 241p. 1994. 114.00 (1-56252-298-1) Computational Mech MA.

Computational Electronics: Semiconductor Transport & Device Simulation. Ed. by K. Hess et al. (C). 1990. lib. bdg. 87.00 (0-7923-9088-1) Kluwer Ac.

Computational Engineering: Proceedings of the First Pan-Pacific Conference on Computational Engineering-PCCE '93, Seoul, Korea, 1-5 November, 1993. Ed. by Byung Man Kwak & Masataka Tanaka. LC 93-6453. 1993. 303.25 (0-444-81671-2) Elsevier.

Computational Engineering with Boundary Elements, 2 vols., Set. Ed. by S. Grilli et al. LC 90-82733. (BETECH Ser.: Vol. 5). 772p. 1990. 169.00 (0-945824-88-2) Computational Mech MA.

Computational Engineering with Boundary Elements Vol. 1: Fluid & Potential Problems. Ed. by S. Grilli et al. LC 90-82733. (BETECH Ser.: Vol. 5). 363p. 1990. 89.00 (0-945824-64-5) Computational Mech MA.

Computational Engineering with Boundary Elements Vol. 2: Solid & Computational Problems. Ed. by S. Grilli et al. LC 90-82733. (BETECH Ser.: Vol. 5). 409p. 1990. 99.00 (0-945824-65-3) Computational Mech MA.

Computational Experiments in Grammatical Classification. H. T. Carvell & J. Svartvik. LC 68-23805. (Janua Linguarum, Ser. Minor: No. 61). (Orig.). 1969. pap. text ed. 72.35 (90-279-0682-3) Mouton.

Computational Fluid Dynamics: An Introduction for Engineers. Michale B. Abbott & David R. Basco. 1990. text ed. 115.00 (0-470-21316-7) Halsted Pr.

Computational Fluid Dynamics. H. B. Keller et al. LC 78-9700. (SIAMS-AMS Proceedings Ser.: Vol. 11). 177p. 1978. 38.00 (0-8218-1331-5, SIAMS-11) Am Math.

Computational Fluid Dynamics. rev. ed. Patrick J. Roache. vii, 446p. 1976. 26.50 (0-913478-05-9) Hermosa.

Computational Fluid Dynamics: An Introduction. Ed. by J. Von Wendt. (Illus.). 312p. 1992. 89.00 (0-387-53460-1) Spr-Verlag.

Computational Fluid Dynamics: Proceedings of the International Symposium, Sydney, Australia, Aug. 1987. Ed. by Graham De Vahl Davis & C. A. Fletcher. 810p. 1988. 128.25 (0-444-70430-2, North Holland) Elsevier.

*__Computational Fluid Dynamics: Selected Topics.__ Ed. by D. Leutloff & R. C. Srivastava. LC 94-48557. 1995. 98.00 (3-540-58757-8) Spr-Verlag.

Computational Fluid Dynamics: The Basics with Applications. John D. Anderson, Jr. LC 94-21237. (Series in Mathematical Engineering). 1995. text ed. 52.50 (0-07-001685-2) McGraw.

Computational Fluid Dynamics & Reacting Gas Flows. Ed. by B. Engquist et al. (IMA Volumes in Mathematics & Its Applications Ser.: Vol. 12). (Illus.). xi, 346p. 1988. 43.00 (0-387-96732-X) Spr-Verlag.

Computational Fluid Dynamics for Engineers, Vol. I. 2nd ed. Klaus A. Hoffmann & Steve T. Chiang. LC 93-90310. (Illus.). 470p. (C). 1993. pap. text ed. 39.00 (0-9623731-7-6) Engr Educ Syst.

Computational Fluid Dynamics for Engineers, Vol. II. abr. ed. Klaus A. Hoffmann & Steve T. Chiang. LC 93-90311. (Illus.). 370p. (C). 1993. pap. text ed. 39.00 (0-9623731-8-4) Engr Educ Syst.

Computational Fluid Dynamics for the Petrochemical Process Industry. Ed. by R. V. Oliemans. 242p. (C). 1991. lib. bdg. 115.50 (0-7923-1360-7) Kluwer Ac.

Computational Fluid Dynamics '92: Proceedings of the First European Computational Fluid Dynamics Conference, 7-11 September 1992, Brussels, Belgium. Ed. by Charles Hirsch et al. LC 92-23463. 1992. write for info. (0-444-89793-3) Elsevier.

*__Computational Fluid Dynamics '94: Proceedings of the Second European Conference, Stuttgart, Germany.__ Ed. by S. Wagner et al. 1995. text ed. 295.00 (0-471-95063-7) Wiley.

Computational Fluid Mechanics & Heat Transfer. Anderson. 599p. 1984. 59.50 (0-89116-471-5) Hemisp Pub.

Computational Fracture Mechanics: Presented at the Second National Congress on Pressure Vessels & Piping, San Francisco, CA, June 23-27 1975. Ed. by Edmund F. Rybicki & Steven E. Benzley. LC 75-149. 222p. reprint ed. pap. 63.30 (0-317-08124-1, 2016859) Bks Demand.

Computational Frameworks for the Fast Fourier Transform. C. Van Loan. (Frontiers in Applied Mathematics Ser.: No. 10). xiii, 273p. 1992. pap. text ed. 29.75 (0-89871-285-8) Soc Indus-Appl Math.

Computational Galerkin Methods. C. A. Fletcher. (Computational Physics Ser.). (Illus.). 335p. 1983. 70.00 (0-387-12633-3) Spr-Verlag.

*__Computational Geomechanics.__ Arnold Verruijt. LC 95-7182. (Theory & Applications of Transport in Porous Media Ser.). 392p. (C). 1995. lib. bdg. 147.00 (0-7923-3407-8) Kluwer Ac.

Computational Geometry. Ed. by Su Bu-ging & Liu Ding-yuan. 295p. 1989. text ed. 68.00 (0-12-675610-4) Acad Pr.

Computational Geometry: Proceedings of the Workshop. A. Conte et al. 264p. 1993. text ed. 95.00 (981-02-1229-1) World Scientific Pub.

Computational Geometry: Proceedings of the 5th Annual Symposium on Computational Geometry. (Illus.). 401p. 1989. pap. text ed. 30.00 (0-89791-318-3, 429890) Assn Compu Machinery.

Computational Geometry - Methods, Algorithms & Applications: International Workshop on Computational Geometry CG '91 Bern, Switzerland, March 1991 Proceedings. Ed. by H. Bieri & H. Noltemeier. (Lecture Notes in Computer Science Ser.: Vol. 553). viii, 320p. 1991. pap. 43.00 (0-387-54891-2) Spr-Verlag.

Computational Geometry: An Introduction. Franco P. Preparata & M. I. Shamos. (Texts & Monographs in Computer Science). (Illus.). xii, 390p. 1993. 49.50 (0-387-96131-3) Spr-Verlag.

Computational Geometry & Its Applications. Ed. by H. Noltemeir. (Lecture Notes in Computer Science Ser.: Vol. 333). vi, 252p. 1988. pap. 36.00 (0-387-50335-8) Spr-Verlag.

*__Computational Geometry for Ships.__ Ed. by H. Nowacki et al. LC 94-46516. 252p. 1995. text ed. 53.00 (981-02-2139-8) World Scientific Pub.

Computational Geometry in C. Joseph O'Rourke. (Illus.). 320p. (C). 1994. 59.95 (0-521-44034-3); pap. 24.95 (0-521-44592-2) Cambridge U Pr.

Computational Geometry, Second Symposium. (Illus.). 336p. 1986. pap. text ed. 28.00 (0-89791-195-4, 429860) Assn Compu Machinery.

Computational Grammar: An Artificial Intelligence Approach to Linguistic Description. Graeme D. Ritchie. (Harvester Studies in Cognitive Science Ser.: No. 15). 254p. 1980. 42.00 (0-389-20048-4, N6819) B&N Imports.

Computational Graph Theory. Ed. by G. Tinhofer et al. (Computing Ser.: Suppl. 7). (Illus.). 304p. 1990. pap. 96.00 (0-387-82177-5) Spr-Verlag.

Computational Group Therapy. Ed. by Michael Atkinson. 1984. text ed. 141.00 (0-12-066270-1) Acad Pr.

Computational Handbook of Statistics. 3rd ed. James L. Bruning & B. L. Kintz. (C). 1990. pap. text ed. 38.00 (0-673-18407-2) HarpCollege.

Computational Heat Transfer. Yogesh Jaluria & Kenneth E. Torrance. (Illus.). 366p. 1986. 63.00 (0-89116-286-0) Hemisp Pub.

Computational Hydraulics. Ed. by D. Ouazar et al. (Computer Methods & Water Resources Ser.: Vol. 2). 470p. 1988. 119.00 (0-387-18854-1) Spr-Verlag.

Computational Hydraulics: Elements of the Theory of Free Surface Flows. M. B. Abbot. 344p. 1992. 69.95 (1-85742-064-0, Pub. by Ashgate UK) Ashgate Pub Co.

Computational Hydraulics for Civil Engineers. T. V. Hromadka, II et al. LC 86-81847. (Illus.). 146p. (Orig.). 1986. pap. text ed. 19.50 (0-914055-04-6) Lighthouse Pubns.

Computational Hydraulics for Civil Engineers. Ed. by T. V. Hromadka et al. 130p. 1986. pap. 46.00 (0-931215-62-5) Computational Mech MA.

Computational Hydraulics in Irregular Channels. T. V. Hromadka, II et al. LC 88-81083. (Illus.). 274p. 1988. pap. 30.00 (0-914055-07-0) Lighthouse Pubns.

Computational Hydrology in Flood Control Design & Planning. T. V. Hromadka et al. LC 87-80497. (Illus.). 523p. 1987. text ed. 48.00 (0-914055-05-4) Lighthouse Pubns.

Computational Hydrology '87: Proceedings of the First International Conference, Anaheim, CA, U.S.A., July 1987. Ed. by R. H. McCuen & T. V. Hromadka. LC 87-81446. (Illus.). 268p. (Orig.). 1987. pap. text ed. 24.00 (0-914055-06-2) Lighthouse Pubns.

Computational Infant: Looking for Developmental Cognitive Science. Julie Rutkrowska. 288p. 1994. pap. text ed. 44.00 (0-13-302134-3) P-H.

Computational Intelligence, Vol. 3. N. J. Cercone et al. 1991. 105.75 (0-444-89118-8) Elsevier.

Computational Intelligence: Imitating Life. Ed. by Jack Zurada et al. LC 94-19065. 448p. 1994. 49.95 (0-7803-1104-3, PC04580) Inst Electrical.

Computational Intelligence: Proceedings of the International Conference, Milan Italy, 26-30 Sept., 1988, Vol. I. Ed. by A. Martelli & G. Valle. 284p. 1989. 77.00 (0-444-87340-6, North Holland) Elsevier.

Computational Intelligence, Vol II: Proceedings of the International Symposium "Computational Intelligence '89," Milan, Italy, 25-27 Sept., 1989. Ed. by F. Gardin et al. 240p. 1990. 77.00 (0-444-88648-6, North Holland) Elsevier.

Computational Kinematics. Ed. by Jorge Angeles. (Solid Mechanics & Its Applications Ser.). 320p. (C). 1993. lib. bdg. 119.00 (0-7923-2585-0) Kluwer Ac.

Computational Learning & Cognition: Proceedings of the 3rd NEC Research Symposium. Baum. (Proceedings in Applied Mathematics Ser.: No. 64). xi, 276p. 1993. 42.50 (0-89871-311-0) Soc Indus-Appl Math.

Computational Learning Theory. M. H. Anthony & Norman L. Biggs. (Cambridge Tracts in Theoretical Computer Science Ser.: No. 30). (Illus.). 200p. (C). 1992. 39.95 (0-521-41603-5) Cambridge U Pr.

*__Computational Learning Theory: EuroCOLT '93.__ Ed. by John Shawe-Taylor & Martin Anthony. (The Institute of Mathematics & Its Applications Conference Ser.: No. 53). (Illus.). 256p. 1994. text ed. 98.00 (0-19-853492-2) OUP.

Computational Learning Theory: Proceedings of the Third Annual Workshop, Colt 90. Ed. by Mark Fulk & John Case. 1990. 19.95 (1-55860-146-5) Morgan Kaufmann.

*__Computational Learning Theory & Natural Learning Systems Vol. 1: Constrains & Prospects.__ Ed. by Stephen J. Hanson et al. LC 93-34468. 565p. 1994. pap. 49.95 (0-262-58126-4) MIT Pr.

*__Computational Learning Theory & Natural Learning Systems Vol. III: Selecting Good Models.__ Ed. by Thomas Petsche. 405p. 1995. 45.00 (0-262-66096-2, Bradford Bks) MIT Pr.

Computational Learning Theory & Natural Learning Systems, Vol. II: Intersections Between Theory & Experiment. Ed. by Stephen J. Hanson et al. LC 93-34468. (Illus.). 592p. 1994. pap. 42.50 (0-262-58133-7, Bradford Bks) MIT Pr.

Computational Learning Theory Proceedings of the 2nd Annual Workshop: Proceedings. Ed. by Ronald Rivest et al. 450p. (Orig.). (C). 1989. pap. 19.95 (1-55860-086-8) Morgan Kaufmann.

Computational Learning Theory Proceedings of the 4th Annual Workshop. Ed. by Manfred K. Warmuth & Leslie G. Valiant. 1991. pap. text ed. 19.95 (1-55860-213-5) Morgan Kaufmann.

Computational Lexical Semantics. Ed. by Patrick Saint-Dizier & Evelyn Viegas. (Studies in Natural Language Processing). (Illus.). 400p. (C). 1995. 69.95 (0-521-44410-1) Cambridge U Pr.

Computational Limitations for Small Depth Circuits. Johan T. Hastad. (ACM Doctoral Dissertation Award Ser.). (Illus.). 75p. 1987. 21.00x (0-262-08167-9) MIT Pr.

Computational Linguistics. Ed. by N. J. Cercone. (International Series in Modern Applied Mathematics & Computer Science: Vol. 5). (Illus.). 200p. 1983. pap. 45.00 (0-08-030253-X, Pergamon Pr) Elsevier.

Computational Linguistics: A Handbook & Toolbox for Natural Language Processing. A. M. McEnery. 270p. (Orig.). 1992. pap. 52.50 (1-85058-177-0, Pub. by Sigma Press UK) Coronet Bks.

Computational Linguistics: An Introduction. Ralph Grishman. (Studies in Natural Language Processing). (Illus.). 225p. 1986. pap. 21.95 (0-521-31038-5) Cambridge U Pr.

Computational Linguistics - Computerlinguistik: An International Handbook on Computer Oriented Language Research - Ein Internationales Handbuch zur Computergestutzten Sprachforschung und Ihrer Anwendungen. Ed. by Istvan S. Batori et al. (Handbooks of Linguistics & Communication Science Ser.: Vol. - Band 4). xxxiv, 933p. (C). 1989. lib. bdg. 470.00 (0-89925-562-0) De Gruyter.

*__Computational Linguistics - Computerlinguistik: An International Handbook on Computer Oriented Language Research - Ein Internationales Handbuch zur Computergestutzten Sprachforschung und Ihrer Anwendungen.__ Ed. by Istvan S. Batori et al. (Handbooks of Linguistics & Communication Science: Vol. - Band 4). xxxiv, 933p. (C). 1989. lib. bdg. 588.50 (3-11-009792-3) De Gruyter.

Computational Linguistics & Formal Semantics. Ed. by Michael Rosner & Roderick Johnson. (Studies in Natural Language Processing). 250p. (C). 1992. 79.95 (0-521-41959-X); pap. 27.95 (0-521-42988-9) Cambridge U Pr.

Computational Linguistics in Medicine: Proceedings of the IFIP Working Conference on Computational Linguistics in Medicine. Ed. by W. Schneider & A. L. Sagvall Hein. 182p. 1978. 56.50 (0-444-85040-6, North Holland) Elsevier.

Computational Logic: Essays in Honor of Alan Robinson. Ed. by Jean-Louis Lassez & Gordon Plotkin. (Illus.). 752p. 1991. 75.00 (0-262-12156-5) MIT Pr.

Computational Logic: Symposium Proceedings, Brussels, November 13-14, 1990. Ed. by J. W. Lloyd. (ESPRIT Basic Research Ser.). (Illus.). xi, 211p. 1990. 34.95 (0-387-53437-7) Spr-Verlag.

Computational Logic & Proof Theory: Third Kurt Godel Colloquium, KGC'93, Brno Czech Republic, August 1993, Proceedings. Ed. by Georg Gottlob et al. LC 93-5923. (Lecture Notes in Computer Science Ser.: Vol. 713). 1993. 54.00 (0-387-57184-1) Spr-Verlag.

Computational Logic Handbook. Robert S. Boyer & J. Strother Moore. 408p. 1988. text ed. 60.00 (0-12-122952-1) Acad Pr.

*__Computational Material Modeling: 1994 International Mechanical Engineering Congress & Exposition, Chicago, Illinois - November 6-11, 1994.__ Ed. by A. K. Noor & A. Needleman. (AD - PVP Ser.: Vol. 42, Vol. 294). 320p. 1994. 90.00 (0-7918-1444-0, G00939) ASME.

Computational Mathematical Programming. A. J. Hoffman. (Mathematical Programming Studies: Vol. 31). 1987. pap. 59.00 (0-444-70309-8) Elsevier.

Computational Mathematical Programming. Ed. by K. Schittkowski. (NATO Asi Series F: Vol. 15). x, 451p. 1985. 98.00 (0-387-15180-X) Spr-Verlag.

Computational Mathematics. Ed. by A. W. McLnnes. 300p. (C). 1995. text ed. 48.00 (981-02-0203-2) World Scientific Pub.

Computational Mathematics: An Introduction to Numerical Approximation. Terence R. Nonweiler. LC 83-12224. (Mathematics & Its Applications Ser.: I-176). 431p. 1984. pap. 29.95 (0-470-20260-2) P-H.

Computational Mathematics in China. Ed. by Zhong-Ci Shi & Chung-Chun Yang. LC 93-45006. 1994. pap. 44.00 (0-8218-5163-2) Am Math.

Computational Mechanics: Proceedings of the Asian Pacific Conference on, Hong Kong, 11-13 December 1991, 2 vols., Set. Ed. by Y. K. Cheung et al. (Illus.). 1700p. (C). 1991. text ed. 195.00 (90-5410-029-X, Pub. by A A Balkema NE) Ashgate Pub Co.

Computational Mechanics & Computer-Aided Engineering. Ed. by Folker H. Wittmann. (Structural Mechanics in Reactor Technology Ser.: Vol. B). 638p. 1987. 130.00 (90-6191-763-8, Pub. by A A Balkema NE) Ashgate Pub Co.

1490

An Asterisk (*) at the beginning of an entry indicates that the title is appearing in BIP for the first time.

Computational Nuclear Physics 2. Ed. by K. Langanke et al. LC 92-37450. 216p. 1993. 79.00 (0-387-97954-9) Spr-Verlag.

Computational Number Theory: Proceedings of the Colloquium on Computational Number Theory. Ed. by Attila Petho et al. xiii, 342p. (C). 1991. lib. bdg. 98.95 (3-11-012394-0) De Gruyter.

Computational Number Theory & Digital Signal Processing: Fast Algorithms & Error Control Techniques. H. Krishna et al. 352p. 1994. 59.95 (0-8493-7177-5, 7177) CRC Pr.

Computational Optimal Control. Ed. by R. Bulirsch. LC 94-2473. (International Series of Numerical Mathematics: Vol. 115). 1994. 94.00 (0-8176-5015-6, Pub. by Birkhauser Vlg SZ) Birkhauser.

Computational Ordinary Differential Equations: Based on the Proceedings of a Conference on Computational Ordinary Differential Equations Held at Imperial College of Science & Technology, University of London, in July 1989. Ed. by J. R. Cash & I. Gladwell. LC 92-22635. (Institute of Mathematics & Its Applications Conference Series, New Ser.: New Series 39). 1992. 89.95 (0-19-853659-3, Clarendon Pr) OUP.

Computational Organization Theory. Ed. by Kathleen M. Carley & Michael J. Prietula. 336p. 1994. text ed. 69.95 (0-8058-1406-X) L Erlbaum Assocs.

Computational Philosophy of Science. Paul R. Thagard. 224p. 1988. 35.00 (0-262-20068-6, Bradford Bks) MIT Pr.

Computational Philosophy of Science. Paul R. Thagard. (Illus.). 256p. 1993. pap. 14.95x (0-262-70048-4, Bradford Bks) MIT Pr.

***Computational Phonology: A Constraint-Based Approach.** Steven Bird. (Studies in Natural Language Processing). 217p. (C). 1995. 44.95 (0-521-47496-5) Cambridge U Pr.

Computational Physics. Marvin DeJong. 288p. (C). 1991. pap. text ed. 23.75 (0-201-51387-0) Addison-Wesley.

Computational Physics. Ed. by R. D. Kenway & G. S. Pawley. (Scottish Universities Summer School in Physics, a NATO Advanced Study Institute Ser.: No. 32). (Illus.). 484p. 1987. 108.00 (0-905945-15-8) IOP Pub.

Computational Physics. Steven E. Koonin. (Illus.). 413p. (C). 1986. disk 45.95 (0-201-15044-1, Adv Bk Prog) Addison-Wesley.

Computational Physics. Ed. by A. Tenner. 576p. (C). 1991. text ed. 137.00 (981-02-0487-6); pap. 44.00 (981-02-0488-4) World Scientific Pub.

Computational Physics. David E. Potter. LC 72-8613. (Wiley-Interscience Publication Ser.). 316p. reprint ed. pap. 90.10 (0-317-26325-0, 2025203) Bks Demand.

***Computational Physics: An Introduction.** Franz J. Vesely. 280p. 1995. 59.50 (0-306-44903-X, Plenum Pr) Plenum.

Computational Physics: Proceedings of the Computational Physica 1992 Europhysics Conference. J. Nadrchal & Roy A. De Groot. 540p. 1993. text ed. 121.00 (981-02-1245-3) World Scientific Pub.

Computational Physics: Proceedings of the 2nd IMACS Conference. Ed. by J. Potvin. 272p. 1994. text ed. 99.00 (981-02-1747-1) World Scientific Pub.

Computational Physics, Fortran Version. Steven E. Koonin & Dawn Meredith. 656p. (C). 1990. 49.95 (0-201-12779-2, Adv Bk Prog) Addison-Wesley.

Computational Physics, II: Granada Lectures. P. L. Garrido & J. Marro. 388p. 1993. text ed. 105.00 (981-02-1163-5) World Scientific Pub.

Computational Plasticity. Ed. by T. Inoue et al. (Current Japanese Materials Research Ser.: Vol. 7). 250p. 1991. 100.00 (1-85166-506-4) Elsevier.

Computational Problems in Abstract Algebra. J. Leech. 1970. 172.00 (0-08-012975-7, Pub. by Pergamon Repr UK) Franklin.

Computational Processes & Systems. Marchuk. 1994. 59.95 (0-8493-8947-X, QA297) CRC Pr.

Computational Processes in Human Vision: An Interdisciplinary Perspective. Ed. by Zenon W. Pylyshyn. (CIAR Series in Artificial Intelligence & Robotics: Vol. 1). 512p. (C). 1988. text ed. 65.00 (0-89391-460-6) Ablex Pub.

Computational Quantum Chemistry. M. W. Evans & F. Farahi. (Series in Contemporary Chemical Physics). 368p. 1994. text ed. 99.00 (981-02-1664-5) World Scientific Pub.

Computational Quantum Chemistry. Alan Hinchcliffe. LC 88-14405. 150p. 1988. text ed. 64.95 (0-471-91716-8) Wiley.

Computational Quantum Physics. A. S. Umar et al. (Conference Proceeding Ser.: No. 260). 332p. 1992. 95.00 (0-88318-933-X) Am Inst Physics.

Computational Recreations in Mathematica. Ilan Vardi. 208p. (C). 1991. pap. text ed. 31.25 (0-201-52989-0, Adv Bk Prog) Addison-Wesley.

Computational Recreations in Mathematica. Ilan Vardi. (Advanced Book Program Ser.). (Illus.). 304p. (C). 1991. pap. text ed. 29.95 (0-685-47941-2) Addison-Wesley.

Computational Reflection. Ed. by Pattie Maes. (C). 1990. pap. text ed. 180.00 (0-273-08823-8, Pub. by Pitman Pubng UK) St Mut.

Computational Semantics. Eugene Charniak & Y. Wilks. (Fundamental Studies in Computer Science: Vol. 4). 294p. 1976. 51.50 (0-7204-0469-X, North Holland) Elsevier.

Computational Skills with Applications. K. W. Bell & R. G. Parrish. 448p. (C). 1975. teacher ed 2.00 (0-669-93237-X); pap. text ed. 23.00 (0-669-91082-1) Heath.

Computational Solution of Nonlinear Operator Equations. Louis B. Rall. LC 78-2378. 236p. (Orig.). 1979. reprint ed. 17.50 (0-88275-667-2) Krieger.

Computational Solution of Nonlinear Systems of Equations. Ed. by Allgower & Georg. LC 90-27. (LAM Ser.: Vol. 26). 762p. 1990. 235.00 (0-8218-1131-2, LAM-26) Am Math.

Computational Spherical Astronomy. Laurence G. Taff. LC 90-35394. 246p. (C). 1991. reprint ed. lib. bdg. 52.95 (0-89464-478-5) Krieger.

Computational Statistical Mechanics. W. G. Hoover. (Studies in Modern Thermodynamics: No. 11). 310p. 1991. 154.50 (0-444-88192-1) Elsevier.

Computational Statistics. Ed. by Herbert Buning & Peter Naeve. 348p. 1981. text ed. 89.25 (3-11-008419-8) De Gruyter.

Computational Statistics. Ed. by C. R. Rao. LC 93-7155. (Handbook of Statistics Ser.: Vol. 9). 1045p. 1993. 190.00 (0-444-88096-8, North Holland) Elsevier.

***Computational Statistics: Papers Collected on the Occasion of the 25th Conference on Statistical Computing at Schlob Reisensburg.** Ed. by P. Dirschedl & R. Ostermann. (Contributions to Statistics Ser.). (Illus.). viii, 553p. 1995. 129.00 (3-7908-0813-X) Spr-Verlag.

Computational Statistics: Proceedings of the 10th Symposium on Computational Statistics, COMPSTAT, Neuchatel, Switzerland, August 1992. Ed. by Yadolah Dodge & J. Whittaker. (Illus.). xvi, 578p. 1992. Vol. 1, xvi, 578p. 138.00 (0-387-91429-3); Vol. 2, x, 440p. 98.00 (0-387-91430-7) Spr-Verlag.

Computational Stochastic Mechanics. Ed. by A. Chang & C. Y. Yang. LC 93-72437. (Computational Engineering Ser.). 668p. 1993. text ed. 276.00 (1-56252-174-8) Computational Mech MA.

Computational Stochastic Mechanics. Ed. by A. H. Cheng & C. Y. Yang. 1993. 256.00 (1-85861-023-0, Pub. by Elsevier Applied Sci UK) Elsevier.

Computational Stochastic Mechanics. Ed. by P. D. Spanos & C. A. Brebbia. LC 91-75141. 914p. 1991. 275.00 (1-56252-074-1) Computational Mech MA.

Computational Stochastic Mechanics. P. O. Spanos & Carlos A. Brebbia. 1991. 255.00 (1-85166-698-2) Elsevier.

***Computational Stochastic Mechanics: Proceedings of the Second International Conference, Athens, Greece, 12-15 June 1994.** Ed. by P. D. Spanos. (Illus.). 800p. 1995. 130.00 (90-5410-527-5) Balkema RSA.

Computational Structural Mechanics & Fluid Dynamics: Advances & Trends - Papers Presented at the Symposium Held in Washington DC, U. S. A., 17-19 October 1988. Ed. by A. K. Noor & D. L. Dwoyer. (Computers & Structures Ser.). 466p. 1988. 125.00 (0-08-037197-3, Pergamon Pr) Elsevier.

***Computational Structures Technology.** Ed. by A. K. Noor & S. Venneri. (Flight-Vehicle Materials, Structures, & Dynamics Ser.: Vol. 6). 196p. 1995. 100.00 (0-7918-0664-2, 100327) ASME.

Computational Studies of the Most Frequent Chinese Words & Sounds. C. Y. Suen. (Series in Computer Science: Vol. 3). 352p. 1986. text ed. 98.00 (9971-5-0022-1) World Scientific Pub.

Computational Support for Discrete Mathematics: DIMACS Workshop, March 12-14, 1992. Nathaniel Dean & Gregory E. Shannon. LC 94-10076. (DIMACS Series in Discrete Mathematics & Theoretical Computer Science: Vol. 15). 1994. 77.00 (0-8218-6605-2) Am Math.

Computational Synthetic Geometry. B. Strurmfels. (Lecture Notes in Mathematics Ser.: Vol. 1355). v, 126p. 1989. pap. 29.20 (0-387-50478-8, 2480) Spr-Verlag.

Computational Systems Analysis: Topics & Trends. Ed. by Achim Sydow. LC 92-10331. 1992. write for info. (0-444-89190-0) Elsevier.

Computational Systems Analysis, 1992: Proceedings of the 4th International Symposium, August 25-28, 1992, Berlin, Germany. Ed. by Achim Sydow. LC 92-25595. 1992. write for info. (0-444-89780-1) Elsevier.

Computational Systems-Natural & Artificial. Ed. by H. Haken. (Synergetics Ser.: Vol. 38). (Illus.). 220p. 1987. 61.00 (0-387-18477-5) Spr-Verlag.

Computational Techniques & Applications. H. Gardner et al. 552p. 1994. text ed. 121.00 (981-02-1494-4) World Scientific Pub.

Computational Techniques & Applications. Ed. by W. L. Hogarth & B. J. Noye. (Proceedings of the Computational Techniques & Applications Conference Ser.). 776p. 1990. 123.00 (1-56032-047-8) Hemisp Pub.

Computational Techniques & Applications, CTAC - '87: Proceedings of the 1987 International Conference, Sydney, Australia, 24-27 Aug., 1987. Ed. by J. Noye & C. A. Fletcher. 700p. 1988. 179.50 (0-444-70400-0, North Holland) Elsevier.

Computational Techniques & Applications CTAC-85: Proceedings of the Conference, University of Melbourne, Australia, August 25-28, 1985. Ed. by J. Noye & R. May. 810p. 1986. 187.25 (0-444-87995-1) Elsevier.

Computational Techniques for Chemical Engineers. J. Rosenbrock & C. Storey. LC 65-14227. (International Series Mono in Chemical Engineering: Vol. 7). 1966. 144.00 (0-08-010889-X, Pub. by Pergamon Repr UK) Franklin.

Computational Techniques for Differential Equations. B. J. Noye. (Mathematical Studies: Vol. 83). 1984. pap. 115.50 (0-444-86783-X, I-446-83, North Holland) Elsevier.

Computational Techniques for Differential Equations. B. J. Noye. (North-Holland Mathematical Studies: Vol. 83). 1991. 134.50 (0-685-50935-4) Elsevier.

Computational Techniques for Econometrics & Economic Analysis. Ed. by David A. Belsley. LC 93-17956. (Advances in Computational Economics Ser.). 248p. (C). 1993. lib. bdg. 92.00 (0-7923-2356-4) Kluwer Ac.

Computational Techniques for Fluid Dynamics. C. A. Fletcher. (Computational Physics Ser.: Vol. 1). (Illus.). 420p. 1990. 59.50 (0-387-18151-2) Spr-Verlag.

Computational Techniques for Fluid Dynamics: A Solutions Manual. K. Srinivas & C. A. Fletcher. Ed. by R. Glowinski et al. (Computational Physics Ser.). (Illus.). vii, 256p. 1994. pap. 39.95 (0-387-54304-X) Spr-Verlag.

Computational Techniques for Fluid Dynamics: Fundamental & General Techniques, Vol. 1. 2nd ed. C. A. Fletcher. Ed. by R. Glowinski et al. (Computational Physics Ser.). (Illus.). 424p. 1992. pap. text ed. 49.00 (0-387-53058-4) Spr-Verlag.

Computational Techniques for Fluid Dynamics: Specific Techniques for Differential Flow Categories, Vol. 2. 2nd ed. C. A. Fletcher. (Computational Physics Ser.). (Illus.). xiii, 493p. 1994. pap. 59.50 (0-387-53601-9) Spr-Verlag.

Computational Techniques for Fluid Dynamics Two. C. A. Fletcher. (Computational Physics Ser.: Vol. 2). (Illus.). 495p. 1990. 71.50 (0-387-18759-6) Spr-Verlag.

Computational Techniques for Interface Problems: Presented at the Winter Annual Meeting of the American Society of Mechanical Engineers, San Francisco, California, December 10-15, 1978. American Society of Mechanical Engineers Staff. Ed. by K. C. Park & D. K. Gartling. LC 78-59883. (AMD Ser.: Vol. 30). (Illus.). 189p. reprint ed. pap. 53.90 (0-8357-2871-4, 2039107) Bks Demand.

Computational Techniques for Ordinary Differential Equations. Ed. by R. Gladwell & D. K. Sayers. LC 79-42626. (IMA & ITS Applications Conference Ser.). 1980. text ed. 88.00 (0-12-285780-1) Acad Pr.

Computational Techniques in Identification & Control of Flexible Flight Structures: Proceedings of the NASA-UCLA Workshop, Lake Arrowhead, CA, Nov. 2-4, 1989. Intro. by A. V. Balakrishnan. LC 90-44391. 304p. (Orig.). 1990. pap. text ed. 99.00 (0-911575-59-6) Optimization Soft.

Computational Techniques in Operations Research. A. M. Andrew. (Cybernetics & Systems Ser., Abacus Bks.). 1985. text ed. 87.00 (0-85626-425-3) Gordon & Breach.

Computational Techniques in Physics. P. K. MacKeown & D. J. Newman. (Illus.). 240p. 1987. pap. 33.00 (0-85274-548-6); disk 52.00 (0-85274-429-3) IOP Pub.

Computational Techniques in Quantum Chemistry & Molecular Physics: Proceedings of the NATO Advanced Study Institute, C15, Ramsau, Germany, 1974. NATO Advanced Study Institute Staff. Ed. by G. H. Diercksen. LC 75-9913. 568p. 1975. lib. bdg. 136.50 (90-277-0588-7) Kluwer Ac.

Computational Transport Phenomena. Ed. by D. Ouazar & C. A. Brebbia. (Computer Methods & Water Resources Ser.: Vol. 5). 270p. 1988. 66.00 (0-387-18857-6) Spr-Verlag.

Computational Vision. Harry Wechsler. (Computer Science & Scientific Computing Ser.). 558p. 1990. text ed. 74.95 (0-12-741245-X) Acad Pr.

Computational Water Resources. Ed. by D. Bensari et al. LC 91-76271. (CMWR Computational Ser.). 330p. 1991. pap. 82.00 (1-56252-086-5) Computational Mech MA.

Computational Wind Engineering One: Proceedings of the 1st International Symposium on Computational Wind Engineering (CWE92), Tokyo, Japan, August 21-23, 1992. Ed. by S. Murakami. LC 93-31564. 1993. 468.75 (0-444-81688-7) Elsevier.

Computations for the Nano-Scale: Proceedings of the NATO Advanced Research Workshop, Aspet, France October 12-16, 1992. Ed. by P. E. Blochl et al. LC 93-8335. (NATO Advanced Science Institutes Series C: Mathematical & Physical Sciences). 304p. (C). 1993. lib. bdg. 138.00 (0-7923-2360-2) Kluwer Ac.

***Computations, Glassy Materials & Non-Destructive Testing: Proceedings of a Symposia of the Third International Conference on Advanced Materials, Sunshine City, Ikebukuro, Tokyo, Japan, August 31-September 4, 1993.** Ed. by T. Matsumoto et al. LC 95-3190. 1995. write for info. (0-444-81993-2) Elsevier.

Computations of Surface Layer Air Parcel Trajectories, & Weather, in the Oceanic Tropics. Adrian H. Gordon & Ronald C. Taylor. LC 72-92065. (International Indian Ocean Expedition. Meteorological Monographs: No. 7). 118p. reprint ed. pap. 33.70 (0-7837-3989-3, 2043820) Bks Demand.

Computax, 1994. 1993. pap. write for info. (0-318-71658-5, 4384) Commerce.

Compute a Design: Decimals. Patricia Wright. Ed. by Russell Jacobs. 50p. (Orig.). (J). (gr. 5-9). 1985. pap. text ed. 11.95 (0-918272-13-0) Jacobs.

Compute a Design: Whole Numbers. Patricia Wright. Ed. by Russell Jacobs. 50p. (J). (gr. 5-9). 1985. pap. text ed. 11.95 (0-918272-12-2) Jacobs.

Compute a Design - Fractions. Patricia Wright. Ed. by Russell Jacobs. 50p. (Orig.). (J). (gr. 5-9). 1987. pap. text ed. 11.95 (0-918272-14-9) Jacobs.

Compute a Design - Percent. Patricia Wright. Ed. by Russell Jacobs. 50p. (Orig.). (J). (gr. 5-9). 1987. pap. 11.95 (0-918272-15-7) Jacobs.

Compute Arabia. 2nd ed. Yousif Al-Gallaf. 1990. pap. write for info. (0-318-63376-0) Meghan-Kiffer.

Compute Arabia: An Illustrated Guide for Professionals in Government & Business. Peter Fingar. (Illus.). 1988. pap. write for info. (0-318-63375-2) Meghan-Kiffer.

***Compute in Comfort: Practical Simple Exercises & Techniques for Preventing Physical & Mental.** Linden. 1995. pap. text ed. 18.95 (0-13-309915-6) P-H.

Computed Body Tomography: With MRI Correlation. 2nd ed. Ed. by Joseph K. Lee et al. (Illus.). 1184p. 1989. 194.50 (0-88167-331-5) Raven.

Computed Digital Radiography in Clinical Practice. R. Greene & J. W. Oestmann. (Illus.). 224p. 1991. text ed. 83.00 (0-86577-351-3) Thieme Med Pubs.

Computed Tomography of the Lung. S. Galluzzi et al. 194p. 1988. text ed. 30.00 (1-57235-033-4) Piccin NY.

Computed Tomography of the Trunk: Normal & Pathological Anatomy. J. Hureau & J. Pradel. 488p. 1990. text ed. 120.00 (1-57235-034-2) Piccin NY.

Computed Tomographic Angiography of the Mediastinum. Lee Chiu et al. (Illus.). 224p. (C). 1986. 57.50 (0-87527-363-7) Green.

Computed Tomographic Atlas of the Head & Neck. Wilma Maue-Dickson et al. 453p. 1983. 145.00 (0-316-55081-7) Little.

Computed Tomography. Ed. by Lawrence A. Shepp. LC 82-18508. (Proceedings of Symposia in Applied Mathematics Ser.: Vol. 27). 86p. 1986. reprint ed. pap. 23.00 (0-8218-0033-7, PSAPM-27) Am Math.

Computed Tomography: An Atlas for Ophthalmologists. Jonathan D. Wirtschafter & Saul Taylor. 75p. 1982. 25.00 (0-317-94080-5) Am Acad Ophthal.

Computed Tomography: Physical Principles, Clinical Applications, & Quality Control. Euclid Seeram. LC 94-2598. (Illus.). 352p. 1994. text ed. 47.50 (0-7216-6710-4) Saunders.

***Computed Tomography & Cerebral Infarctions: With an Introduction to Practice & Principles of CT Scan Reading.** fac. ed. J. Valk. LC 80-6166. 190p. Date not set. pap. 54.20 (0-7837-7527-X, 2046978) Bks Demand.

Computed Tomography & Magnetic Resonance Imaging. 3rd ed. Haaga et al. 2016p. 1994. 275.00 (0-8016-7057-8) Mosby Yr Bk.

Computed Tomography & Magnetic Resonance Imaging of Head & Neck Tumors: Methods, Guidelines, Differential Diagnoses, & Clinical Results. Martin Lenz. Tr. by Clifford Bergman. LC 93-28314. 206p. 1993. 105.00 (0-86577-504-4) Thieme Med Pubs.

Computed Tomography & Magnetic Resonance Imaging of the Head & Neck. 2nd ed. Anthony Mancuso et al. (Illus.). 504p. 1985. 99.95 (0-683-05476-7) Williams & Wilkins.

Computed Tomography & Magnetic Resonance of the Thorax. 2nd ed. David P. Naidich et al. (Illus.). 624p. 1991. 142.00 (0-88167-567-9) Raven.

Computed Tomography & Magnetic Resonance Tomography of Intracranial Tumors. 2nd ed. Ed. by E. Kazner et al. (Illus.). 720p. 1989. 484.00 (0-387-50576-8, 1954) Spr-Verlag.

Computed Tomography for Radiographers. Malcolm Brooker. 1986. lib. bdg. 67.50 (0-85200-920-8) Kluwer Ac.

Computed Tomography in Intracranial Tumors: Differential Diagnosis & Clinical Aspects. Ed. by E. Kazner et al. Tr. by F. C. Dougherty. (Illus.). 548p. 1982. 267.00 (0-387-10815-7) Spr-Verlag.

Computed Tomography in Radiation Therapy. Ed. by C. Clifton Ling et al. (Illus.). 284p. 1983. text ed. 104.00 (0-89004-831-2) Raven.

Computed Tomography in Trauma. Barry D. Toombs & Carl Sandler. (Illus.). 240p. 1987. text ed. 72.50 (0-7216-8889-6) Saunders.

Computed Tomography in Urology. Ed. by Hans H. Schild et al. Tr. by Claus G. Roehrborn. LC 92-446. 1992. write for info. (3-13-775501-8); 99.00 (0-86577-429-3) Thieme Med Pubs.

Computed Tomography of Abdominal Abnormalities. 2nd ed. Haaga. Date not set. 55.00 (0-8016-2015-5) Mosby Yr Bk.

Computed Tomography of CNS Disease. 2nd ed. Yock. 448p. 1990. 93.00 (0-8151-9778-0, Yr Bk Med Pubs) Mosby Yr Bk.

Computed Tomography of Congenital Brain Malformations. Mohammad Sarwar. (Illus.). 184p. 1984. 45.00 (0-87527-231-2) Green.

Computed Tomography of the Brain & Spine: An Atlas. Robert G. Peyster. 1990. 85.00 (0-8151-6676-1, Yr Bk Med Pubs) Mosby Yr Bk.

Computed Tomography of the Cranial Skeleton: Face & Skull. M. Megret. Tr. by M. T. Wackenheim. (Exercises in Radiological Diagnosis Ser.). (Illus.). 190p. 1986. pap. 32.00 (0-387-15389-6) Spr-Verlag.

Computed Tomography of the Eye & Orbit. Steven B. Hammerschlag et al. (Illus.). 267p. 1983. boxed 115.00 (0-8385-1194-5, A1194-8) Appleton & Lange.

Computed Tomography of the Gastrointestinal Tract. Ed. by Elliot K. Fishman & Bronwyn Jones. (Contemporary Issues in Computed Tomography Ser.: Vol. 9). (Illus.). 298p. 1988. text ed. 69.00 (0-443-08512-9) Churchill.

Computed Tomography of the Gastrointestinal Tract. Ed. by M. A. Meyers. (Illus.). xiv, 279p. 1986. 149.00 (0-387-96232-8) Spr-Verlag.

***Computed Tomography of the Gastrointestinal Tract.** fac. ed. Ed. by Elliot K. Fishman & Bronwyn Jones. LC 87-24907. (Contemporary Issues in Computed Tomography Ser.: No. 9). (Illus.). 310p. 1988. reprint ed. pap. 88.40 (0-7837-7894-5, 2047650) Bks Demand.

Computed Tomography of the Head & Neck. Ed. by Thomas H. Newton et al. (Modern Neuroradiology Ser.: Vol. 3). (Illus.). 480p. 1988. text ed. 160.50 (0-88167-392-7) Raven.

Computed Tomography of the Head & Neck. Ed. by Barbara L. Carter. LC 84-17565. (Contemporary Issues in Computed Tomography Ser.: No. 5). (Illus.). 351p. reprint ed. pap. 100.10 (0-7837-6252-6, 2045964) Bks Demand.

Computed Tomography of the Head, Neck & Spine. Ed. by Richard E. Latchaw. (Illus.). 500p. 1984. 195.00 (0-8151-5329-5, Yr Bk Med Pubs) Mosby Yr Bk.

Computed Tomography of the Musculoskeletal System. Ed. by William W. Scott, Jr. et al. (Contemporary Issues in Computed Tomography Ser.: Vol. 8). (Illus.). 269p. 1987. text ed. 48.00 (0-443-08497-1) Churchill.

An Asterisk (*) at the beginning of an entry indicates that the title is appearing in BIP for the first time.

Computed Tomography of the Pancreas, Liver & Biliary Tract: A Teaching File. Stephens & Johnson. 1990. 55.00 (*0-8151-7943-X*, Yr Bk Med Pubs) Mosby Yr Bk.

Computed Tomography of the Pelvis. Ed. by James W. Walsh. (Contemporary Issues in Computed Tomography Ser.: Vol. 6). (Illus.). 267p. 1985. text ed. 49.95 (*0-443-08386-X*) Churchill.

Computed Tomography of the Pituitary Gland. J. F. Bonneville et al. (Illus.). 256p. 1986. 194.00 (*0-387-15324-1*) Spr-Verlag.

Computed Tomography of the Retroperitoneum. M. A. Feldberg. (Radiology Ser.). 1983. lib. bdg. 136.50 (*0-89838-573-3*) Kluwer Ac.

Computed Tomography of the Spine. Ed. by Victor M. Haughton. LC 83-2080. (Contemporary Issues in Computed Tomography Ser.: No. 2). (Illus.). 233p. pap. 66.50 (*0-8357-6577-6*, 2035963) Bks Demand.

Computed Tomography of the Whole Body. 2nd ed. Haaga & Alfidi. (Illus.). 1544p. 1988. 199.00 (*0-8016-1954-8*) Mosby Yr Bk.

Computer: A Challenge for Business Administration. August-Wilhelm Scheer. 272p. 1985. 29.00 (*0-387-15514-7*) Spr-Verlag.

Computer: A Tool for the Teacher, Incl. disk. Edward B. Wright & Richard C. Forcier. 320p. (C). 1985. disk, pap. 42.95 (*0-534-04782-3*) Boyd & Fraser.

Computer: An Everyday Machine. 2nd ed. E. Squire. 1977. write for info. (*0-201-07158-4*) Addison-Wesley.

Computer: Bit Slices from a Life. Herb Grosch. (Illus.). 342p. 1989. 24.95 (*0-88733-085-1*); 50.00 (*0-88733-084-3*) Underwood-Miller.

Computer: History, Working, Uses, & Limitations. Judith L. Gersting & Michael Gemignani. (Illus.). 542p. (Orig.). (C). 1988. write for info. (*0-912675-21-7*); pap. 38.95x (*0-912675-20-9*) Ardsley.

Computer - Mediated Communication & the Online Classroom, Vol. 3: Distance Education. Zane Berge & Mauri Collins. Ed. by Gerald M. Phillips. (Communication Series: Communication Pedagogy & Practice Subseries). 272p. (C). 1995. text ed. 49.50 (*1-881303-12-8*); pap. text ed. 19.95 (*1-881303-13-6*) Hampton Pr NJ.

Computer - My Life. Konrad Zuse. (Illus.). xvi, 245p. 1993. 49.00 (*0-387-56453-5*) Spr-Verlag.

*__Computer - Neue Fluegel des Geistes? Die Evolution Computergestuetzter Techik, Wissenschaft, Kultur & Philosophie.__ Klaus Mainzer. (Philosophie & Wissenschaft - Transdisziplinaere Studien Ser.: Bd. 9). xii, 882p. (Orig.). (GER.). (C). 1995. pap. text ed. 60.00 (*3-11-014808-0*) De Gruyter.

Computer - Neue Fluegel des Geistes? Die Evolution Computergestuetzter Technick, Wissenschaft, Kultur & Philosophie. Klaus Mainzer. (Illus.). xii, 882p. (GER.). (C). 1994. lib. bdg. 344.65 (*3-11-014004-7*) De Gruyter.

Computer, a Challenge for Business Administration see Principles of Efficient Information Management

Computer: A Child's Play. Dharma Rajaraman. 120p. (J). 1989. reprint ed. pap. text ed. 12.95 (*0-9615336-9-2*) Silicon Pr.

Computer Accounting Applications, Using Lotus 1-2-3 Release 2.2 or Later: A Workbook to Be Used with Financial - Managerial or Accounting Principles Courses. Roger A. Gee. LC 92-23700. 288p. (C). 1993. pap. text ed. write for info. (*0-13-096132-9*) P-H.

Computer Accounting Applications, Using Microsoft Excel with a Mouse: A Workbook to Be Used with Financial - Managerial or Accounting Principles Courses. Roger A. Gee. LC 92-23920. 288p. (C). 1993. pap. text ed. write for info. (*0-13-096157-4*) P-H.

*__Computer Accounting for Microsoft Windows.__ Carol Yacht & Jack Terry. 350p. (C). 1994. pap. 35.95 (*0-256-15462-7*) Irwin.

Computer Addiction: Study of Computer Dependency. Margaret Shotton. 240p. 1989. 95.00 (*0-85066-795-X*); pap. 38.00 (*0-85066-796-8*) Taylor & Francis.

Computer Advancements in the Health Sciences: Index of New Information with Authors & Subjects. Richard L. Hasborough. LC 92-54220. 180p. 1992. 49.50 (*1-55914-592-7*); pap. 39.50 (*1-55914-001-1*) ABBE Pubs Assn.

Computer Adventure Games Secrets. Rick Barba. 1994. pap. 19.95 (*1-55958-456-4*) Prima Pub.

Computer Age. (Understanding Science & Nature Ser.). (YA). 1992. 18.95 (*0-8094-9670-4*) Time-Life.

Computer Age: A Twenty-Year View. Ed. by Michael L. Dertouzos & Joel Moses. 1979. pap. 15.95x (*0-262-54036-3*) MIT Pr.

Computer Aid in Gastroenterology. Ed. by P. Rozen & F. T. De Dombal. (Frontiers of Gastrointestinal Research Ser.: Vol. 7). (Illus.). viii, 196p. 1984. 65.75 (*3-8055-3770-0*) S Karger.

Computer Aid to Drug Therapy & to Drug Monitoring. Ed. by H. Ducrot et al. 444p. 1978. 74.50 (*0-444-85188-7*, North Holland) Elsevier.

Computer Aide. Jack Rudman. (Career Examination Ser.: C-1208). 1994. pap. 23.95 (*0-8373-1208-6*) Nat Learn.

Computer-Aided Acquisition & Logistic Support. Robert A. Cheney. 316p. 1989. 39.95 (*0-9624643-0-9*) EMCA.

Computer-Aided Analysis & Design of Electromagnetic Devices. S. R. Hoole. 490p. 1989. 42.75 (*0-444-01327-X*) P-H.

Computer-Aided Analysis & Design of Electronic Circuits. J. B. Grimbleby. 208p. (C). 1990. pap. text ed. 140.00 (*0-273-03148-1*, Pub. by Pitman Pubng UK) St Mut.

Computer-Aided Analysis & Design of Linear Systems. Mohammad Jamshidi et al. 384p. 1992. text ed. 79.00 (*0-13-161472-X*) P-H.

Computer-Aided Analysis & Design of Switch-Mode Power Suppies. Lee. (Electrical Engineering & Electronics Ser.: Vol. 81). 648p. 1993. 140.00 (*0-8247-8803-6*) Dekker.

Computer-Aided Analysis of Active Circuits. Ioinovici. (Electrical Engineering & Electronics Ser.: Vol. 67). 616p. 1990. 150.00 (*0-8247-8126-0*) Dekker.

Computer-Aided Analysis of Amorite. Ignace J. Gelb. LC 79-84839. (Assyriological Studies: No. 21). 1980. pap. 42.00 (*0-918986-21-4*) Orientl Inst Pr IT.

*__Computer-Aided Analysis of Difference Schemes for Partial Differential Equations.__ V. G. Ghanza & E. V. Vorozhstov. LC 95-10879. 1996. write for info. (*0-471-12946-1*) Wiley-Interscience.

Computer-aided Analysis of Electric Machines: A Mathematical Approach. Vlado Ostovic. LC 93-23664. 400p. 1994. pap. text ed. 73.00 (*0-13-068859-2*, P-H Intl) P-H.

Computer-Aided Analysis of Electrical Networks. Thomas W. Davis et al. LC 72-80234. (Illus.). 446p. reprint ed. pap. 127.20 (*0-317-09130-1*, 2015044) Bks Demand.

Computer-Aided Analysis of Power Electronic Systems. Rajagopalan. (Electrical Engineering & Electronics Ser.: Vol. 40). 552p. 1987. 165.00 (*0-8247-7706-9*) Dekker.

Computer-Aided Analysis of Rigid & Flexible Mechanical Systems: Proceedings of the NATO Advanced Study Institute, Troia, Portugal, June 27 - July 9, 1993. Ed. by Manuel F. Pereira. (NATO Advanced Study Institutes Series E: Applied Sciences Ser.). 640p. (C). 1994. lib. bdg. 262.00 (*0-7923-2839-6*) Kluwer Ac.

Computer-Aided Analysis of the Stress-Strain Response of High Polymers. C. R. Hwang et al. 80p. 1989. disk 89.00 (*0-87762-647-2*) Technomic.

Computer Aided Analysis of the Stress-Strain Response of High Polymers. 2nd ed. C. Robin Hwang. Ed. by Harold H. Hopfe. 98p. 1993. disk, spiral bd. 495.00 (*1-56676-039-9*, 760399); disk 89.00 (*0-685-70212-X*, 626472) Technomic.

Computer-Aided & Workout Exercises on Insurance Law. Robert E. Keeton. 255p. 1989. pap. text ed. 17.00 (*0-314-71662-9*) West Pub.

Computer Aided Architectural Design: 16 ARK-2 Articles. Kaiman Lee. LC 74-160961. 1973. 30.00 (*0-915250-04-7*) Environ Design.

Computer-Aided Architectural Graphics. Ryan. 432p. 1983. 65.00 (*0-8247-1901-8*) Dekker.

Computer Aided Architecture & Design. Frederic H. Jones. LC 92-18044. 1992. 21.95 (*1-56052-163-5*) Crisp Pubns.

*__Computer Aided Architecture & Design.__ Frederic H. Jones. (Illus.). 220p. 1995. pap. 21.95 (*0-614-07002-3*) Crisp Pubns.

Computer-Aided Assemble Planning. A. Delchambre. LC 92-25973. 1992. write for info. (*0-442-31593-7*) Chapman & Hall.

Computer Aided Assessment & Control of Localized Damage, 3 vols., Set. Ed. by M. H. Aliabadi et al. LC 90-61549. (Localized Damage Ser.: Vol. 1). 1990. 350.00 (*0-945824-53-X*) Computational Mech MA.

Computer Aided Assessment & Control of Localized Damage Vol. 1: Fatigue & Fracture Mechanics. Ed. by M. H. Aliabadi et al. LC 90-61549. (Localized Damage Ser.: Vol. 1). 428p. 1990. 130.00 (*0-945824-49-1*) Computational Mech MA.

Computer Aided Assessment & Control of Localized Damage Vol. 2: Non-Linear Behavior, Dynamics, Composite Materials & Industry. Ed. by M. H. Aliabadi et al. LC 90-61549. (Localized Damage Ser.: Vol. 1). 381p. 1990. 130.00 (*0-945824-51-3*) Computational Mech MA.

Computer Aided Assessment & Control of Localized Damage Vol. 3: Advanced Computational Methods. Ed. by M. H. Aliabadi et al. LC 90-61549. (CAACOLD Ser.: Vol. 1). 528p. 1990. 130.00 (*0-945824-52-1*) Computational Mech MA.

Computer-Aided Building Code Checking: A Demonstration. 2nd ed. Kaiman Lee. LC 74-308127. 34p. 1974. 12.00 (*0-915250-08-X*) Environ Design.

Computer-Aided Circuit Analysis Using PSpice. 2nd ed. Walter Banzhaf. 320p. 1992. pap. text ed. 39.60 (*0-13-159534-2*) P-H.

Computer Aided Civil Drafting. Jeff Allen et al. 185p. (C). 1991. student ed 19.96 (*1-56870-007-5*) RonJon Pub.

Computer Aided Control System: Methods, Tools. M. A. Brdys & K. Malinowski. 560p. 1994. text ed. 105.00 (*981-02-1391-3*) World Scientific Pub.

Computer-Aided Control System Design Using Matlab. Bahram Shahian & Michael Hassul. 300p. 1993. pap. text ed. 42.00 (*0-13-174061-X*) P-H.

Computer-Aided Control System Design Using Matrix X. Bahram Shahian & Michael Hassul. 300p. 1992. text ed. 48.00 (*0-13-174095-4*) P-H.

Computer-Aided Control Systems Engineering. Ed. by Mohammad Jamshidi & C. J. Herget. LC 85-10138. 406p. 1985. 100.00 (*0-444-87779-7*, North Holland) Elsevier.

Computer-Aided Cooperative Product Development: MIT-JSME Workshop, MIT, Cambridge, U. S. A. November 20-21, 1989 Proceedings. Ed. by Duvvuru Sriram et al. (Lecture Notes in Computer Science Ser.: Vol. 492). vii, 630p. 1991. pap. 57.00 (*0-387-54008-3*) Spr-Verlag.

Computer-Aided Creativity: For New Product Design & Development. Ben-Zion Sandler. LC 93-29285. (Illus.). 1994. text ed. 49.95 (*0-442-01406-6*) Van Nos Reinhold.

Computer-Aided Data Analysis: A Practical Guide. William R. Green. 288p. (C). 1985. lib. bdg. 39.95 (*0-471-80928-4*) Krieger.

Computer-Aided Database Design: The DATAID Project. Ed. by A. Albano et al. 222p. 1985. 66.75 (*0-444-87735-5*, North Holland) Elsevier.

Computer-Aided Decision Analysis: Theory & Applications. Ed. by Stuart S. Nagel. LC 92-38003. 304p. 1993. text ed. 79.50 (*0-89930-771-X*, NCK/, Quorum Bks) Greenwood.

Computer-Aided Design. Ed. by Becker & Pereira. 640p. 1993. 195.00 (*0-8247-9003-0*) Dekker.

Computer Aided Design. Jurgen Meyer. 1994. pap. 19.95 (*1-55755-243-6*) Abacus MI.

Computer Aided Design. Dean L. Taylor. (Mechanical Engineering Ser.). (Illus.). 480p. (C). 1992. text ed. 64.50 (*0-201-16891-X*) Addison-Wesley.

Computer-Aided Design: An Integrated Approach. T. R. Hsu & Dependra Sinha. Ed. by Michael Slaughter. 487p. (C). 1992. text ed. 65.75 (*0-314-80781-0*) West Pub.

Computer Aided Design: Fundamentals & System Architectures. J. L. Encarnacao & E. G. Schlechtendahl. (Symbolic Computation Ser.). (Illus.). 350p. 1985. 49.00 (*0-387-11526-9*) Spr-Verlag.

Computer Aided Design: Fundamentals & System Architectures. 2nd rev. ed. Ed. by J. L. Encarnacao et al. (Symbolic Computation - Computer Graphics Ser.). 480p. 1990. 96.00 (*0-387-52047-3*) Spr-Verlag.

Computer-Aided Design: Nineteen Eighty-Four Seminar Notes. Technical Association of the Pulp & Paper Industry Staff. 68p. reprint ed. pap. 25.00 (*0-317-20568-4*, 2022796) Bks Demand.

Computer Aided Design: Software & Analytical Tools. C. S. Krishnamoorthy & S. Rajeev. (Illus.). 455p. 1992. 98.00 (*0-387-54442-9*) Spr-Verlag.

Computer Aided Design - CAD '84: Proceedings, IASTED Symposium, Nice, France, June 19-21, 1984. Ed. by M. H. Hamza. 99p. 1984. 40.00 (*0-88986-065-3*, 072) Acta Pr.

Computer Aided Design, Analysis, & Simulation of Off-Highway Equipment. 128p. 1991. pap. 19.00 (*1-56091-176-X*, SP-884) Soc Auto Engineers.

Computer Aided Design & Analysis. 1988. 52.95 (*0-632-02058-X*) Buttrwrth-Heinemann.

Computer Aided Design & Applications - CAD '85: Proceedings, IASTED Symposium, Paris, France, June 18, 1985. Ed. by M. H. Hamza. 219p. 1985. 80.00 (*0-88986-078-5*, 087) Acta Pr.

Computer-Aided Design & Drafting. Martin Zandi. LC 84-23808. 352p. (C). 1985. teacher ed 20.00 (*0-8273-2305-0*) Delmar.

Computer-Aided Design & Manufacturing. Farid M. Amirouche. LC 92-27575. 528p. 1992. text ed. 77.00 (*0-13-472341-4*) P-H.

Computer-Aided Design & Manufacturing. 2nd rev. ed. Ed. by Ulrich Rembold & R. Dillman. (Symbolic Computation Ser.). (Illus.). 510p. 1986. 126.00 (*0-387-16321-2*) Spr-Verlag.

Computer Aided Design & VLSI Device Development. Kit M. Cham et al. 1985. lib. bdg. 65.50 (*0-89838-204-1*) Kluwer Ac.

Computer-Aided Design & VLSI Device Development. 2nd ed. Kit Man Cham et al. (C). 1988. lib. bdg. 94.00 (*0-89838-277-7*) Kluwer Ac.

Computer Aided Design (CAD) of Chemical Process Equipment. Ed. by B. C. Bhattacharyya. (C). 1989. 75.00 (*0-89771-384-2*, Current Dist) St Mut.

Computer Aided Design Directory. Flora. 1991. write for info. (*0-8306-5465-8*) TAB Bks.

Computer Aided Design Explained. Casimir Rakauski. (Series 860). 1981. student ed, pap. 5.00 (*0-8064-0345-4*, 860); audio 179.00 (*0-8064-0346-2*) Bergwall.

Computer-Aided Design for Autocad Users. Daniel L. Ryan. 368p. 1989. pap. text ed. 55.00 (*0-13-162678-7*) P-H.

Computer Aided Design in Civil Engineering. Ed. by Celal N. Kostem & Mark S. Shephard. 138p. 1984. 21.00 (*0-87262-417-X*) Am Soc Civil Eng.

Computer Aided Design in Composite Material Technology. Ed. by Carlos A. Brebbia et al. 600p. 1988. 161.00 (*0-387-19024-4*) Spr-Verlag.

Computer Aided Design in Composite Material Technology III: Proceedings of the Third International Conference on Computer Aided Design in Composite Material Technology (CADCOMP III) Held in Newark, USA, May 1992. Ed. by S. G. Advani et al. LC 91-77814. (CADCOMP Ser.: Vol. 3). 648p. 1992. 275.00 (*1-56252-094-6*) Computational Mech MA.

Computer Aided Design in Composite Material Technology IV: Proceedings of the Third International Conference. Ed. by W. R. Blain & W. P. De Wilde. LC 94-70405. (CADCOMP Ser.: Vol. 4). 440p. 1994. 147.00 (*1-56252-187-X*) Computational Mech MA.

Computer Aided Design in Electronic Packaging. Ed. by A. Agonafer & R. E. Fulton. (DSC Ser.: Vol. 3). 92p. 1992. 30.00 (*0-7918-1127-1*, G00771) ASME.

Computer Aided Design in Magnetics. David A. Lowther & Peter P. Silvester. (Illus.). 324p. 1985. 99.50 (*0-387-15756-5*) Spr-Verlag.

Computer-Aided Design, International Conference on (ICCAD '92) LC 92-71926. 664p. 1992. 100.00 (*0-8186-3010-8*, 3010) IEEE Comp Soc.

Computer-Aided Design, International Conference on (ICCAD '93) 816p. 1993. pap. text ed. 114.00 (*0-8186-4490-7*, 4490) IEEE Comp Soc.

*__Computer-Aided Design, International Conference on (ICCAD '94)__ 808p. 1994. pap. text ed. 160.00 (*0-8186-6415-0*, PR06415) IEEE Comp Soc.

Computer Aided Design, Manufacture & Operation in the Marine & Offshore Industries. Ed. by T. K. Murthy & G. A. Keramidas. (CADMO Ser.). 657p. 1986. 130.00 (*0-931215-34-X*) Computational Mech MA.

Computer Aided Design, Modelling & Simulation - CAD '86: Proceedings, IASTED Symposium, Vancouver, Canada, June 4-6, 1986. Ed. by M. H. Hamza. 189p. 1986. 50.00 (*0-88986-091-2*, 100) Acta Pr.

Computer-Aided Design of Analog Networks, Selected Papers On. J. Singhal Vlach. 136p. 1987. pap. 24.95 (*0-87942-216-5*, PP02097) Inst Electrical.

Computer-Aided Design of Bearings & Seals: Presented at the Winter Annual Meeting of ASME, New York, NY, December 5-10, 1976 (Sponsored by the Lubrication Division) Ed. by Francis E. Kennedy & Herbert S. Cheng. LC 76-28853. 121p. reprint ed. pap. 34.50 (*0-317-11235-X*, 2016884) Bks Demand.

Computer Aided Design of Control Systems: Proceedings of the IFAC Symposium, Zurich,Switzerland, Aug. 29-31, 1979. IFAC Symposium, Zurich, Switzerland, 29-31 Aug. 1979. Ed. by M. A. Cuenod. LC 79-42655. (IFAC Proceedings Ser.). (Illus.). 702p. 1980. 285.00 (*0-08-024488-2*, Pub. by Pergamon Repr UK) Franklin.

Computer-Aided Design of Digital Electronic Circuits & Systems: Proceedings of the Symposium, Brussels, Nov. 1978. Symposium, Brussels Staff. Ed. by G. Musgrave. 326p. 1979. 92.50 (*0-444-85374-X*, North Holland) Elsevier.

Computer Aided Design of Digital Systems: A Bibliography, 4 vols. W. M. Van Cleemput. LC 75-40004. 1991. Vol. II, 1975-76. pap. 35.00 (*0-914894-59-5*, Computer Sci Pr); Vol. III, 1976-77. pap. 35.00 (*0-914894-60-9*, Computer Sci Pr); Vol. IV, 1977-79. pap. 35.00 (*0-914894-61-7*, Computer Sci Pr) W H Freeman.

Computer Aided Design of Digital Systems: A Bibliography, 4 vols., Set. W. M. Van Cleemput. 1991. pap. write for info. (*0-318-57719-4*, Computer Sci Pr) W H Freeman.

Computer Aided Design of Language Processors. Shangin. 1991. 86.95 (*0-8493-7537-1*, QA76) CRC Pr.

Computer Aided Design of Microelectric Circuits & Systems, Vol. 2: Digital-Circuit Aspects & State of the Art. Ed. by A. F. Schwarz. 772p. 1987. text ed. 223.00 (*0-12-632432-8*) Acad Pr.

Computer Aided Design of Microelectronic Circuits & Systems: General Introduction & Analog-Circuit Aspects, Vol. 1. A. F. Schwarz. 736p. 1987. text ed. 223.00 (*0-12-632431-X*) Acad Pr.

Computer-Aided Design of Microwave Circuits. K. C. Gupta et al. LC 82-465904. (Illus.). 676p. reprint ed. pap. 180.00 (*0-8357-4234-2*, 2037021) Bks Demand.

Computer Aided Design of Multivariate Technological Systems: Proceedings of the IFAC Symposium, 2nd, Indiana, USA, Sept., 1982. IFAC Symposium Staff & G. G. Leininger. (IFAC Proceedings Ser.). 632p. 1983. 288.00 (*0-08-029357-3*, Pub. by Pergamon Repr UK) Franklin.

Computer Aided Design of Plasticating Screws: Programs in Fortran & Basic. Natti S. Rao. 134p. (C). 1986. text ed. 47.50 (*1-56990-082-5*) Hanser-Gardner.

*__Computer-Aided Design of Polymer-Matrix Composite Structures.__ Hoa. (Mechanical Engineering Series of Reference Books & Textbooks). 333p. 1995. write for info. (*0-8247-9558-X*) Dekker.

Computer Aided Design of Printed Circuits: The Guide for Evaluating, Purchasing & Using Computer Aided Design Systems. Charles J. Simon. LC 87-72268. (Illus.). 357p. (C). 1987. 55.00 (*0-944365-01-9*) Abbot Foster.

Computer-Aided Design of Surface Acoustic Wave Devices, Vol. 2. J. H. Collins & L. Masotti. 308p. 1976. 92.50 (*0-444-41476-2*) Elsevier.

Computer-Aided Design of Very Large Scale Integrated Circuits, Selected Papers On. A. L. Sangiovanni-Vincentelli. 168p. 1987. pap. 24.95 (*0-87942-227-0*, PP02246) Inst Electrical.

Computer-Aided Design, Selection & Evaluation of Robots. Bartholomew O. Nnaji. (Manufacturing Research & Technology Ser.: No. 2). 292p. 1986. 107.75 (*0-444-42614-0*) Elsevier.

Computer-Aided Drafting & Design. Louis G. Lamit & Vernon Paige. 482p. (C). 1987. write for info. (*0-675-20475-5*, Merrill Pub Co) Macmillan.

Computer-Aided Drafting & Design: Concepts & Applications. Donald D. Voisinet. 384p. 1986. text ed. 24.95 (*0-07-067565-1*) McGraw.

Computer-Aided Drafting & Design Using Autocad. Jackie Potts. 412p. (C). 1988. pap. text ed. 37.25 (*0-15-512629-6*) SCP.

Computer-Aided Drafting, Fundamentals & Applications. Brian L. Duelm. 367p. 1992. 31.96 (*0-87006-893-8*) Goodheart.

Computer Aided Drafting on the Bausch & Lomb Producer Drafting System (Beginning Level) H. L. Murvin. (Illus.). 84p. 1983. pap. 11.95 (*0-9608498-1-5*) H L Murvin.

Computer-Aided Drafting with AutoCAD: Versions 2-5 & 2-6 with Release 9. David L. Goetsch & Rickman. 416p. (C). 1990. pap. write for info. (*0-675-20915-3*, Merrill Pub Co) Macmillan.

Computer Aided Drafting with Computervision. James V. Valentino. 448p. (C). 1987. pap. text ed. 40.00 (*0-03-000922-7*) SCP.

Computer-Aided Drug Design: Methods & Applications. Perun & Propst. 516p. 1989. 140.00 (*0-8247-8037-X*) Dekker.

Computer-Aided Electromyography. Ed. by J. E. Desmedt. (Progress in Clinical Neurophysiology Ser.: Vol. 10). (Illus.). x, 334p. 1983. 132.00 (*3-8055-3748-4*) S Karger.

Computer Aided Electromyography & Expert Systems. J. E. Desmedt. (Clinical Neurophysiology Updates Ser.: Vol. 2). 1989. 161.75 (*0-444-81106-0*) Elsevier.

*__Computer-Aided Electronic Circuit Board Design & Fabrication: Busing OrCAD/SDT & OrCAD/PCB Software Tools.__ Akram Hossain. LC 95-7610. 1995. pap. text ed. 46.00 (*0-13-032095-1*) P-H.

Computer Aided Engineering: Advanced Structural Analysis. Rafaat M. Hussein. LC 88-50838. 388p. 1988. disk, pap. 49.00 (*0-87762-577-8*) Technomic.

Computer-aided Engineering Drawing. Cecil H. Jensen. 1989. 29.95 (*0-07-067568-6*) McGraw.

An Asterisk (*) at the beginning of an entry indicates that the title is appearing in BIP for the first time.

Computer-Aided Engineering Drawing & Graphics for Design. B. L. Davies et al. 328p. 1991. pap. 34.95 (*0-442-31291-1*) Chapman & Hall.

*__Computer-Aided Engineering Drawing Using AutoCAD.__ Cecil Jensen et al. LC 94-46760. 1995. write for info. (*0-02-801797-8*); teacher ed, pap. write for info. (*0-02-801873-7*) Glencoe.

Computer-Aided Engineering for Manufacture. D. Milner & V. Vasiliou. 256p. 1987. text ed. 45.00 (*0-07-042427-6*) McGraw.

Computer-Aided Engineering for Mechanical Engineers. Robert Edney. 450p. 1991. pap. text ed. 58.00 (*0-13-161787-7*) P-H.

Computer Aided Engineering Handbook, 1. Ed. by J. Puig-Pey & C. A. Brebbia. LC 87-70842. 350p. 1987. 87.00 (*0-931215-25-0*) Computational Mech MA.

Computer Aided Engineering Handbook, 2. Ed. by J. Puig-Pey & C. A. Brebbia. LC 87-70842. 350p. 1987. 75.00 (*0-685-67616-1*) Computational Mech MA.

Computer Aided Engineering Of. Bernhard. 1985. 46.95 (*0-02-948590-8*) Macmillan.

Computer Aided Engineering Systems Handbook. J. Puig-Pey. (Illus.). 650p. 1987. 231.00 (*0-387-17936-4*) Spr-Verlag.

Computer-Aided Environmental Education. Ed. by W. J. Rohwedder. (Monograph Ser.: Vol. 8). (Illus.). 250p. (Orig.). 1990. pap. 17.00 (*1-884008-02-X*) NAAEE.

Computer-Aided Ergonomics. Ed. by Waldemar Karwowski. 592p. 1990. 190.00 (*0-85066-753-4*, Pub. by Tay Francis Ltd UK) Taylor & Francis.

Computer-Aided Estimating. Gerald A. Silver. LC 85-82064. 152p. reprint ed. pap. 43.40 (*0-7837-0360-0*, 2040682) Bks Demand.

Computer-Aided Exercises on Civil Procedure. 3rd ed. Roger Park & Douglas D. McFarland. 210p. 1993. reprint ed. pap. text ed. 19.50 (*0-314-86711-2*) West Pub.

*__Computer-Aided Exercises on Civil Procedure.__ 4th ed. Roger C. Park & Douglas D. McFarland. LC 95-16454. 239p. (C). 1995. pap. text ed. 21.00 (*0-314-06194-0*) West Pub.

Computer-Aided Facilities Planning. Hales. (Industrial Engineering Ser.: Vol. 9). 344p. 1984. 110.00 (*0-8247-8143-0*) Dekker.

Computer-Aided Facility Management. Eric Teicholz. 1992. text ed. 37.00 (*0-07-063405-X*) McGraw.

Computer: Aided Financial Analysis. Ross M. Miller. (Illus.). 480p. (C). 1990. text ed. 43.25 (*0-201-12337-1*) Addison-Wesley.

Computer Aided Formulation: A Manual for Implementation. Ed. by Alan H. Bohl. 298p. 1990. lib. bdg. 70.00 (*1-56081-042-4*) VCH Pubs.

Computer Aided Geometric Design: Proceedings of a Conference. Ed. by Robert E. Barnhill & Richard F. Riesenfeld. 1974. text ed. 92.00 (*0-12-079050-5*) Acad Pr.

Computer-Aided Graphics & Design. 3rd expanded rev. ed. Daniel L. Ryan. LC 93-46012. (Computer Aided Engineering Ser.: Vol. 4). 272p. 1994. 59.75 (*0-8247-9164-9*) Dekker.

Computer Aided Innovation of New Material, No. Two: Proceedings of the Second International Conference & Exhibition on Computer Applications to Materials & Molecular Science & Engineering - CAMSE '92, Pacifico Yokohama, Yokohama, Japan, September 22-25, 1992. Ed. by Maseo Doyama et al. LC 92-45915. 1993. write for info. (*0-444-89778-X*, North Holland) Elsevier.

Computer Aided Innovation of New Materials. M. Doyama et al. 1991. 283.00 (*0-444-88864-0*) Elsevier.

Computer-Aided Instruction: A Guide for Authors. Robert V. Price. 464p. (C). 1991. pap. 38.95 (*0-534-13710-5*) Boyd & Fraser.

Computer-Aided Instruction in the Humanities. Ed. by Solveig Olsen. LC 85-13740. (Technology & the Humanities Ser.: No. 2). xviii, 266p. 1985. pap. text ed. 19.75 (*0-87352-553-1*) Modern Lang.

Computer-Aided Judicial Analysis: Predicting, Prescribing, & Administering. Stuart S. Nagel. LC 91-33090. 392p. 1992. text ed. 79.50 (*0-89930-670-5*, NJP/, Quorum Bks) Greenwood.

Computer-Aided Kinematics & Dynamics of Mechanical Systems, Vol. I: Basic Methods. Edward J. Haug. 512p. 1988. text ed. 78.00 (*0-205-11669-8*, H16694) P-H.

Computer-Aided Kinematics & Dynamics of Mechanical Systems, Vol. I: Basic Methods. Edward J. Haug. 512p. 1989. teacher ed 4.00 (*0-685-44215-2*, H22346) P-H.

Computer-Aided Kinetics for Machine Design. Ryan. (Mechanical Engineering Ser.: Vol. 7). 288p. 1981. 65.00 (*0-8247-1421-0*) Dekker.

Computer Aided Logical Design with Emphasis on VLSI. 4th ed. Frederick J. Hill & Gerald R. Peterson. 534p. (C). 1993. Net. text ed. write for info. (*0-471-57527-5*) Wiley.

Computer-Aided Machine Design. Andrew D. Dimarogonas. 432p. 1988. reprint ed. text ed. 78.00 (*0-13-166497-2*) P-H.

Computer-Aided Management. Norman Sanders. 288p. 1985. 32.50 (*0-89397-221-5*) Nichols Pub.

Computer-Aided Manufacturing. Tien-Chien Chang et al. 688p. 1990. text ed. 76.00 (*0-13-161571-8*) P-H.

Computer-Aided Manufacturing: An International Comparison. Hiroyuki Yoshikawa et al. 85p. reprint ed. pap. 25.00 (*0-8357-7709-X*, 2036065) Bks Demand.

Computer-Aided Manufacturing & Women's Employment: The Clothing Industry in Four EC Countries. Ed. by S. Mitter & K. S. Gill. (Artificial Intelligence & Society Ser.). (Illus.). 192p. 1991. pap. 70.00 (*0-387-19656-0*) Spr-Verlag.

Computer Aided Manufacturing Design. Flora. 1991. write for info. (*0-8306-5466-6*) TAB Bks.

Computer Aided Marketing & Selling. Robert Shaw. 160p. 1991. 33.95 (*0-7506-0070-5*) Buttrwrth-Heinemann.

Computer Aided Marketing & Selling. Robert Shaw. (Marketing Practitioner Ser.). 240p. 1993. pap. 19.95 (*0-7506-1707-1*) Buttrwrth-Heinemann.

Computer-Aided Mechanical Assembly Planning. Ed. by Luiz S. Homen De Mello & Sukhan Lee. 464p. (C). 1991. lib. bdg. 96.00 (*0-7923-9205-1*) Kluwer Ac.

Computer-Aided Modelling & Simulation. Jan A. Spriet & G. C. Vansteenkiste. 1982. text ed. 101.00 (*0-12-659050-8*) Acad Pr.

Computer-Aided Molecular Design. Ed. by W. Graham Richards. (Illus.). 284p. 1989. text ed. 115.00 (*0-89573-738-8*) VCH Pubs.

*__Computer-Aided Molecular Design: Applications in Agrochemicals, Materials, & Pharmaceuticals.__ Ed. by Charles H. Reynolds et al. LC 95-2511. (Symposium Ser.: No. 589). (Illus.). 448p. 1995. 109.95 (*0-8412-3160-5*) Am Chemical.

*__Computer-Aided Molecular Design: Theory & Applications.__ J. P. Doucet & J. Weber. (Illus.). 408p. 1995. boxed write for info. (*0-12-221285-1*) Acad Pr.

Computer Aided Optimal Design: Structural & Mechanical Systems. Ed. by Carlos A. Mota Soares. (NATO Asi Series F: Vol. 27). 1045p. 1987. 171.00 (*0-387-17598-9*) Spr-Verlag.

Computer Aided Optimum Design of Structure, 2 vols., Set. Ed. by Carlos A. Brebbia & S. Hernandez. 800p. 1989. 220.00 (*0-387-51266-7*, 3201) Spr-Verlag.

Computer Aided Optimum Design of Structures, 2 vols., Vol. 1: Recent Advances. Ed. by C. A. Brebbia & S. Hernandez. LC 86-61075. (OPTI Ser.: Vol. 1). 377p. 1989. 91.00 (*0-945824-09-2*) Computational Mech MA.

Computer Aided Optimum Design of Structures, 2 vols., Vol. 2: Applications. Ed. by C. A. Brebbia & S. Hernandez. LC 86-61075. (OPTI Ser.: Vol. 1). 354p. 1989. 83.00 (*0-945824-19-X*) Computational Mech MA.

Computer Aided Optimum Design of Structures IV: Proceedings of the Fourth International Conference. Ed. by S. Hernandez et al. (OPTI Ser.: Vol. 4). 700p. 1995. 270.00 (*1-56252-249-3*) Computational Mech MA.

Computer Aided Optimum Design of Structures, Vol. 1: Recent Advances. Ed. by Carlos A. Brebbia & S. Hernandez. 400p. 1989. 123.00 (*0-387-51263-2*, 3199) Spr-Verlag.

Computer Aided Optimum Design of Structures, Vol. 2: Applications. Ed. by Carlos A. Brebbia & S. Hernandez. 400p. 1989. 123.00 (*0-387-51265-9*, 3200) Spr-Verlag.

Computer-Aided Problem Solving for Scientists & Engineers. Sundaresan Jayaraman. 1991. text ed. write for info. (*0-07-032353-4*) McGraw.

Computer-Aided Process Oprations: Proceedings of the 1st International Conference, Park City, UT, July 5-10, 1987. Ed. by G. V. Reklaitis & H. D. Spriggs. 720p. 1988. 218.00 (*0-444-98925-0*) Elsevier.

Computer-Aided Process Planning. H. P. Wang & J. K. Li. (Advances in Industrial Engineering Ser.: No. 13). 400p. 1991. 134.50 (*0-444-88631-1*) Elsevier.

Computer-Aided Process Plant Design. Ed. by Michael E. Leesley. LC 81-20335. 1400p. 1982. 50.00 (*0-87201-130-5*) Gulf Pub.

Computer Aided Production Engineering: Proc. of the 7th Internat. Conf., Cookeville, TN, 13-14 Aug., 1991. V. C. Venkatesh & J. A. McGeough. 600p. 1991. 166.75 (*0-444-89214-1*) Elsevier.

Computer-Aided Production Management. Ed. by A. Rolstadaas. (IFIP State-of-the-Art Reports). (Illus.). 415p. 1988. 113.00 (*0-387-18748-0*) Spr-Verlag.

Computer-Aided Project Management: A Visual Scheduling & Management System. Spiro N. Pollalis. xx, 242p. 1993. 56.00 (*3-528-05347-X*, Pub. by Vieweg & Sohn GW) Ballen Bkslr.

Computer Aided Proofs in Analysis. Ed. by K. R. Meyer et al. (IMA Volumes in Mathematics & Its Applications Ser.: Vol. 28). (Illus.). 264p. 1990. 39.00 (*0-387-97426-1*) Spr-Verlag.

*__Computer-Aided Qualitative Data Analysis: Theory, Methods & Practice.__ Ed. by Udo Kelle. 272p. (C). 1995. 69.95 (*0-8039-7760-3*); pap. 25.95 (*0-8039-7761-1*) Sage.

Computer-Aided Sculpture: Of Arbitrary & Analytical Surfaces. J. P. Duncan & K. K. Law. (Illus.). 160p. 1989. 39.95 (*0-521-36303-9*) Cambridge U Pr.

Computer-Aided Simulation in Railway Dynamics. Dukkipati & Amyot. (Mechanical Engineering Ser.: Vol. 61). 448p. 1988. 140.00 (*0-8247-7787-5*) Dekker.

Computer Aided Simulation of Fluid-Structure Interaction Problems. Ed. by Joseph W. Tedesco. 80p. 1987. 12.00 (*0-87262-583-4*) Am Soc Civil Eng.

Computer Aided Software Engineering. Chris Gane. 1988. 49.95 (*0-07-022759-4*) McGraw.

Computer-Aided Software Engineering. Richard K. Miller & Terri C. Walker. LC 88-81631. (Survey on Technology & Markets Ser.: No. 40). 50p. 1989. pap. text ed. 200.00 (*1-55865-039-3*) Future Tech Surveys.

Computer-Aided Software Engineering: Issues & Trends for the 1990s & Beyond. Ed. by Thomas Bergin. LC 91-76951. 650p. 1993. text ed. 55.95 (*1-878289-15-2*) Idea Group Pub.

Computer Aided Software Engineering: The Olduvai Imperative: A Case Statement. Peter Degrace & Leslie D. Stahl. LC 92-44795. 320p. 1993. pap. text ed. 42.00 (*0-13-161100-3*, Yourdon) P-H.

Computer-Aided Software Engineering (CASE) 2nd ed. Elliott J. Chikofsky. LC 92-41057. 184p. 1993. pap. 35.00 (*0-8186-3590-8*, 3590) IEEE Comp Soc.

Computer-Aided Software Engineering, 5th International Workshop (CASE '92) LC 92-71723. 360p. 1992. 80.00 (*0-8186-2960-6*, 2960) IEEE Comp Soc.

Computer-Aided Software Engineering, 6th International Workshop (CASE '93) 440p. 1993. pap. text ed. 84.00 (*0-8186-3480-4*, 3480) IEEE Comp Soc.

*__Computer-Aided Software Engineering, 8th International Workshop on (CASE '95) (7-95)__ 448p. 1995. pap. text ed. 90.00 (*0-8186-7078-9*, PR07078) IEEE Comp Soc.

*__Computer Aided Software Hardware Engineering.__ Ed. by Jerzy Rozenblit & Klaus Buchenrieder. LC 94-22820. 1994. write for info. (*0-7803-1049-7*) Inst Electrical.

Computer Aided Space Planning. Kaiman Lee. LC 76-366704. 1976. 30.00 (*0-915250-20-9*) Environ Design.

Computer-Aided Specification Techniques. J. Demetrovics et al. (Computer Science Ser.: Vol. 1). 128p. 1986. text ed. 55.00 (*9971-978-53-9*); pap. text ed. 26.00 (*9971-5-0095-7*) World Scientific Pub.

Computer-Aided Statistical Physics. Chin-Kun Hu. (Conference Proceeding Ser.: No. 248). 288p. 1992. 90.00 (*0-88318-942-9*) Am Inst Physics.

Computer-Aided Surface Geometry & Design. Ed. by Adrian Bowyer. (Institute of Mathematics & Its Applications Conference Series, New Ser.: No. 48). (Illus.). 484p. 1994. 98.00 (*0-19-853648-8*) OUP.

Computer Aided Systems Theory - EUROCAST '93: A Selection of Papers from the Third International Workshop on Computer Aided Systems Theory, Las Palmas, Spain, February 1993: Proceedings. Ed. by F. Picler & R. Moreno Diaz. LC 93-44606. (Lecture Notes in Computer Science Ser.: Vol. 763). 1994. 58.00 (*0-387-57601-0*) Spr-Verlag.

Computer Aided Systems Theory, EUROCAST '91: A Selection of Papers from the Second International Workshop on Computer Aided Systems Theory, Krems, Austria, April 15-19, 1991: Proceedings. Ed. by Franz R. Pichler & R. Moreno Diaz. LC 92-9634. (Lecture Notes in Computer Science Ser.: Vol. 585). x, 761p. 1992. pap. 99.00 (*0-387-55354-1*) Spr-Verlag.

Computer-Aided Techniques in Food Technology. Saguy. (Food Science & Technology Ser.: Vol. 8). 512p. 1983. 185.00 (*0-8247-1383-4*) Dekker.

Computer-Aided Tolerancing. 2nd ed. Ed. by Oyvind Bjorke. 220p. 1989. 44.00 (*0-7918-0010-5*, 800105) ASME Pr.

Computer Aided Tolerancing Analysis (CATA) Manual. Samuel J. Levy. 175p. 1986. ring bd. 34.00 (*1-883467-02-0*) Intl Geometric.

Computer Aided Tomography & Ultrasonics in Medicine. Ed. by J. Raviv et al. 320p. 1979. 56.50 (*0-444-85299-9*, North Holland) Elsevier.

Computer Aided Transcription: Current Technology & Court Applications. William E. Hewitt & Jill B. Levy. LC 94-9572. 1994. pap. write for info. (*0-89656-132-1*) Natl Ctr St Courts.

Computer Aided Transcription: Scoping & Editing. Jean Gonzalez & Margaret Cline. (Advanced Court Reporting Technology Ser.). (Illus.). 242p. (C). 1992. pap. text ed. 22.00 (*1-881086-09-7*) Middle Wasley.

Computer-Aided Transcription in the Courts. Richard W. Delaplain et al. (Illus.). 272p. (Orig.). 1981. pap. write for info. (*0-89656-051-1*, R-057) Natl Ctr St Courts.

Computer-Aided Transcription in the Courts: Executive Summary. National Center for State Courts Staff. 67p. 1981. pap. write for info. (*0-89656-052-X*, R-058) Natl Ctr St Courts.

Computer-Aided Transit Scheduling: Proceedings of the Fifth International Workshop on Computer-Aided Scheduling of Public Transport Held in Montreal, Canada, August 19-23, 1990. Ed. by M. Desrochers et al. LC 92-20795. (Lecture Notes in Economics & Mathematical Systems Ser.: Vol. 386). (Illus.). xiv, 432p. 1992. pap. 72.00 (*0-387-55634-6*) Spr-Verlag.

Computer-Aided Verification. Ed. by Robert P. Kurshan. LC 92-33318. 148p. (C). 1992. lib. bdg. 109.00 (*0-7923-9285-X*) Kluwer Ac.

Computer Aided Verification. Ed. by K. G. Larsen & A. Skou. (Lecture Notes in Computer Science Ser.: Vol. 575). 487p. 1992. pap. 61.00 (*0-387-55179-4*) Spr-Verlag.

Computer Aided Verification: Fourth International Workshop, CAC 92, Montreal, Canada, 1992. Ed. by G. V. Bochmann & D. K. Probst. LC 93-9405. (Lecture Notes in Computer Science Ser.: Vol. 663). 1993. 60.00 (*0-387-56496-9*) Spr-Verlag.

*__Computer Aided Verification: Proceedings of the Sixth International Conference, CAV '94, Stanford, California, U.S.A., June 21-23, 1994.__ CAV '94 Staff. Ed. by David L. Dill. LC 94-21760. (Lecture Notes in Computer Science Ser.: Vol. 818). 1994. 62.00 (*0-387-58179-0*) Spr-Verlag.

Computer Aided Verification: Proceedings of the 5th International Conference, CAV 93, Elounda, Crete, Greece, June 28-Jttly 1, 1993. Ed. by C. Courcoubetis. (Lecture Notes in Computer Science Ser.: Vol. 697). ix, 504p. 1993. pap. 72.00 (*0-387-56922-7*) Spr-Verlag.

Computer-Aided Verification: 2nd International Conference, CAV '91 New Brunswick, NJ, June 18-21, 1990 Proceedings. Ed. by E. M. Clarke et al. (Lecture Notes in Computer Science Ser.: Vol. 531). xiii, 372p. 1991. pap. 37.00 (*0-387-54477-1*) Spr-Verlag.

*__Computer-Aided Verification of Coordinating Processes: The Automata-Theoretic Approach.__ Robert P. Kurshan. LC 94-42672. 1995. write for info. (*0-691-03436-2*) Princeton U Pr.

Computer-Aided Verification '90. Clarke & Kurshan. (DIMACS Ser.: Vol. 3). 628p. 1991. 100.00 (*0-8218-6594-3*, DIMACS-3) Am Math.

*__Computer-Aided 3-D Modeling & Animation.__ Issac Kerlow. (Design & Graphic Design Ser.: 1). 224p. 1995. pap. 34.95 (*0-442-01896-7*) Van Nos Reinhold.

Computer Aids for VLSI Design. Steven M. Rubin. LC 86-26571. (VLSI Systems Ser.). (Illus.). 458p. (C). 1987. text ed. 49.50 (*0-201-05824-3*) Addison-Wesley.

Computer Aids to Clinical Decisions, 2 Vols. Ed. by Ben T. Williams. 168p. 1982. Vol. I, 168p. 124.95 (*0-8493-5575-3*, R858, CRC Reprint); Vol. II, 216p. 124.95 (*0-8493-5576-1*, R858, CRC Reprint) Franklin.

Computer Algebra. Ed. by B. Buchberger et al. (Illus.). 283p. 1985. pap. 45.00 (*0-387-81776-X*) Spr-Verlag.

Computer Algebra. Chudnovsky & Jenks. (Lecture Notes in Pure & Applied Mathematics Ser.: Vol. 113). 256p. 1989. 99.75 (*0-8247-8038-8*) Dekker.

Computer Algebra: EUROCAM 82, Marseille, France 1982. Ed. by J. Calmet. (Lecture Notes in Computer Science Ser.: Vol. 144). 301p. 1982. pap. 31.00 (*0-387-11607-9*) Spr-Verlag.

Computer Algebra: Systems & Algorithms for Algebraic Computation. 2nd ed. J. H. Davenport et al. (Illus.). 296p. 1993. text ed. 45.00 (*0-12-204232-8*) Acad Pr.

Computer Algebra & Differential Equations. Ed. by E. Tournier. (London Mathematical Society Lecture Note Ser.: No. 193). (Illus.). 300p. (C). 1994. pap. 39.95 (*0-521-44757-7*) Cambridge U Pr.

Computer Algebra & Differential Equations. Ed. by Evelyne Tournier. (Computational Mathematics & Applications Ser.). 220p. 1990. text ed. 49.00 (*0-12-696260-X*) Acad Pr.

Computer Algebra & Its Applications to Mechanics. Ed. by V. G. Ganzha et al. (International Conference Proceedings Ser.). 210p. 1993. lib. bdg. 93.00 (*1-56072-103-0*) Nova Sci Pubs.

Computer Algebra & Parallelism. Ed. by Jean Della Dora & John Fitch. (Computational Mathematics & Applications Ser.). 250p. 1989. text ed. 52.00 (*0-12-209042-X*) Acad Pr.

Computer Algebra & Parallelism: Proceedings, Second International Workshop, Ithaca, USA, May 9-11, 1990. Ed. by R. E. Zippel. (Lecture Notes in Computer Science Ser.: Vol. 584). ix, 114p. 1992. pap. 30.00 (*0-387-55328-2*) Spr-Verlag.

*__Computer Algebra in Industry 2: Problem Solving in Practice.__ Ed. by Arjeh M. Cohen et al. LC 94-42862. 1995. text ed. 54.95 (*0-471-95529-9*) Wiley.

Computer Algebra in Physical Research. Ed. by D. V. Shirkov et al. 450p. (C). 1991. text ed. 118.00 (*981-02-0687-9*) World Scientific Pub.

Computer Algebra with LISP & REDUCE: An Introduction to Computer-Aided Pure Mathematics. F. Brackx & D. Constales. 304p. 1991. lib. bdg. 103.00 (*0-7923-1441-7*) Kluwer Ac.

Computer Algorithms: Introduction to Design & Analysis. Sara Baase. LC 77-81197. 1978. text ed. write for info. (*0-201-00327-9*) Addison-Wesley.

Computer Algorithms: Introduction to Design & Analysis. 2nd ed. Sara Baase. LC 87-9205. (Illus.). 600p. (C). 1988. text ed. 55.95 (*0-201-06035-3*) Addison-Wesley.

Computer Algorithms: Key Search Strategies. Jun-ichi Aoe. LC 90-27443. 254p. 1991. pap. 30.00 (*0-8186-2123-0*, 2123) IEEE Comp Soc.

Computer Algorithms: String Pattern Matching Strategies. Ed. by Jun-ichi Aoe. LC 93-40355. 296p. 1994. 56.00 (*0-8186-5461-9*, 5462); pap. write for info. (*0-8186-5460-0*) IEEE Comp Soc.

Computer Algorithms for Solving Linear Algebraic Equations: The State of the Art. Ed. by E. Spedicato. (NATO ASI Series F: Computer & Systems Sciences, Special Programme AET: Vol. 77). viii, 352p. 1991. 89.00 (*0-387-54187-X*) Spr-Verlag.

Computer Algorithms in Mining Mineral Reserve Estimation. Marvin W. Barnes. (Illus.). 200p. (C). 1989. write for info. (*0-318-65492-X*) M Barnes & Assocs.

Computer Always Shoots Twice. 96p. 10.00 (*0-87431-087-3*, 12007) West End Games.

Computer Analyses for Juror Utilization Operation Manual. National Center for State Courts Staff. 42p. 1984. 3.00 (*0-685-16706-2*, CJS-007) Natl Ctr St Courts.

*__Computer Analysis & Design of Earthquake Resistant Structures.__ Ed. by D. E. Beskos & S. A. Anagnostopoulos. 1996. 180.00 (*1-85312-374-9*) Computational Mech MA.

Computer Analysis & Perception: Auditory Signals, Vol. II. Ed. by Ching Y. Suen & Renato DeMori. 176p. 1982. 144.00 (*0-8493-6306-3*, TA1650, CRC Reprint) Franklin.

Computer Analysis & Perception: Visual Signals, Vol. I. Ed. by Ching Y. Suen & Renato DeMori. 176p. 1982. 144.00 (*0-8493-6305-5*, TA1650, CRC Reprint) Franklin.

Computer Analysis of Cardiovascular Signals. M. Di Rienzo et al. LC 94-75419. (Studies in Health Technology & Informatics: Vol. 13). 350p. 1994. 104.00 (*90-5199-158-4*) IOS Press.

Computer Analysis of Electrophysiological Signals. John Dempster. (Biological Techniques Ser.). (Illus.). 228p. 1993. 65.00 (*0-12-208940-5*) Acad Pr.

Computer Analysis of Genetic Macromolecules: Structure, Function & Evolution. N. A. Kolchanov & H. A. Lim. 580p. 1994. text ed. 116.00 (*981-02-1378-6*) World Scientific Pub.

Computer Analysis of Images & Patterns: Fifth International Conference, CAIP '93 Budapest, Hungary, September 13-15, 1993 Proceedings. Ed. by D. Chetverikov & W. G. Kropatsch. (Lecture Notes in Computer Science Ser.: Vol. 719). 857p. 1993. pap. 100.00 (*0-387-57233-3*) Spr-Verlag.

Computer Analysis of Images & Patterns: Proceedings of the 3rd International Conference CAIP'89 on Automatic Image Processing, Leipzig, GDR, September 8-10, 1989. Ed. by K. Voss et al. (Frontiers in Artificial Intelligence & Applications Ser.). 288p. 1989. pap. 79.00 (*90-5199-019-7*, Pub. by IOS Pr NE) IOS Press.

An Asterisk (*) at the beginning of an entry indicates that the title is appearing in BIP for the first time.

An Asterisk (*) at the beginning of an entry indicates that the title is appearing in BIP for the first time.

1495

Computer Applications in Language Learning. Ed. by Theo Bongaerts et al. viii, 172p. (Orig.). (C). 1988. pap. 48.60 (*90-6765-400-0*) Mouton.

Computer Applications in Large Scale Power Systems: Proceedings of the IFAC Symposium, New Delhi, India, Aug., 1979, 3 vols., Set. IFAC Symposium Staff. Ed. by B. R. Subramanyam. (Illus.). 1100p. 1982. 438.00 (*0-08-024450-5*, Pub. by Pergamon Repr UK) Franklin.

Computer Applications in Libraries. Anne Clyde. 1993. pap. 30.00 (*1-875589-33-3*) D W Thorpe.

Computer Applications in Manufacturing Systems: Planning, Control, & Robots: Papers Presented at the Winter Annual Meeting of the American Society of Mechanical Engineers, Chicago, Illinois, November 16-21, 1980. American Society of Mechanical Engineers Staff. Ed. by W. R. DeVries. (PED Ser.: Vol. 2). 106p. reprint ed. pap. 30.30 (*0-317-55589-8*, 2056371) Bks Demand.

Computer Applications in Music: A Bibliography, Supplement 1. Deta S. Davis. (Computer Music & Digital Audio Ser.: Vol. 10). 600p. (C). 1993. 79.95 (*0-89579-267-2*) A-R Eds.

Computer Applications in Nursing Education & Practice. Ed. by J. Arnold & G. Pearson. 400p. (C). 1992. 35.95 (*0-88737-522-7*) Natl League Nurse.

Computer Applications in Nutrition & Dietetics: An Annotated Bibliography. John Orta. LC 87-30450. (Reference Library of Social Science). 256p. 1988. lib. bdg. 43.00 (*0-8240-6621-9*) Garland.

Computer Applications in Plasma Science & Engineering. Ed. by A. T. Drobot. (Illus.). x, 457p. 1990. 65.00 (*0-387-97455-5*) Spr-Verlag.

Computer Applications in Production & Engineering. Ernest A. Warman. 1983. 123.00 (*0-444-86614-0*, I-406-83) Elsevier.

Computer Applications in Production & Engineering: Proc. of the 3rd Internat. IFIP Conf. (CAPE '89), Tokyo, Japan. 2-5 Oct., 1989. Ed. by F. Kimura & A. Rolstadas. 826p. 1989. 133.50 (*0-444-88089-5*, North Holland) Elsevier.

Computer Applications in Production & Engineering: Cape '86: Proceedings of the IFIP TCS International Conference, Copenhagen, Denmark, May 20-30, 1986. IFIP TCS International Conference Staff. Ed. by Ketil Bo et al. 950p. 1987. 151.50 (*0-444-70142-7*, North Holland) Elsevier.

Computer Applications in Psychiatry. Jonathan D. Lieff. LC 86-17240. 384p. 1987. boxed 40.00 (*0-88048-031-9*, 48-031-9) Am Psychiatric.

Computer Applications in Psychiatry & Psychology: A Clinicians' Guide. Ed. by David Baskin. LC 93-12563. (Einstein Clinical & Experimental Psychiatry Monograph Ser.: No. 2). 192p. 1990. 29.95 (*0-87630-539-7*) Brunner-Mazel.

Computer Applications in Psychology. Lyle R. Creamer. (C). 1984. spiral bd. 17.50 (*0-318-02994-4*) L R Creamer.

Computer Applications in Resource Exploration: Prediction & Assessment for Metals & Petroleum. Ed. by G. Gaal & Daniel F. Merriam. (Computers & Geology Ser.). (Illus.). 472p. 1991. 170.00 (*0-08-037245-7*, Pergamon Pr) Elsevier.

Computer Applications in Shaping & Forming of Materials. Ed. by M. Y. Demeri. (Illus.). 313p. 1993. 64.00 (*0-87339-220-5*, 460) Minerals Metals.

Computer Applications in Softwood Lumber Production. 63p. 1986. 18.00 (*0-935018-30-1*) Forest Prod.

Computer Applications in Spacecraft Design & Operation. Ed. by T. K. Murthy & R. Munch. 198p. 1987. 51.00 (*0-931215-75-7*) Computational Mech MA.

Computer Applications in Structural Engineering. Ed. by David R. Jenkins. 668p. 1987. 60.00 (*0-87262-614-8*) Am Soc Civil Eng.

Computer Applications in the Automation of Shipyard Operation & Ship Design, Vol. IV. Ed. by D. F. Rogers. (Computer Applications in Shipping & Shipbuilding Ser.: Vol. IX). 356p. 1982. 72.00 (*0-444-86408-3*, I-300-82, North Holland) Elsevier.

Computer Applications in the Automation of Shipyard Operation & Ship Design: Proceedings of the IFIP WG5.6 Sixth International Conference, Shanghai, People's Republic of China, 15-16 Sept., 1988, Vol. VI. Ed. by D. Lin et al. 370p. 1989. 95.00 (*0-444-87343-0*, North Holland) Elsevier.

Computer Applications in the Automation of Shipyard Operation & Ship Design, No. 7: Proceedings of the Seventh International Conference on Computer Applications in the Automation of Shipyard Operation & Ship Design, Rio de Janeiro, Brazil, 10-13 September 1991. Ed. by Claudio B. Vieira et al. LC 92-21617. (IFIP Transactions B: Applications in Technology Ser.: Vol. B-5). 1992. write for info. (*0-444-89728-3*, North Holland) Elsevier.

Computer Applications in the Automation of Shipyard Operation & Ship Design, V: Proceedings of the IFIP, IFAC Fifth International Conference Trieste, Italy, 16-20 September 1985. Ed. by P. Banda et al. (Computer Applications in Shipping & Shipbuilding Ser.: Vol. 11). 522p. 1986. 92.50 (*0-444-87820-3*) Elsevier.

Computer Applications in the Polymer Laboratory. Ed. by Theodore Provder. LC 86-10831. (ACS Symposium Ser.: No. 313). (Illus.). 321p. 1986. 76.95 (*0-8412-0977-4*) Am Chemical.

Computer Applications in the Private Security Business. Anne-Marie Sapse et al. LC 80-36754. 154p. 1980. text ed. 45.00 (*0-275-91694-4*, C1694, Praeger Pubs) Greenwood.

Computer Applications in the Social Sciences. Edward E. Brent, Jr. & Ronald E. Anderson. 384p. (C). 1990. 44.95 (*0-87722-666-0*) Temple U Pr.

Computer Applications in Water Industry Operation & Design. 44p. 1985. pap. 12.50 (*0-89867-338-0*, 20191) Am Water Wks Assn.

Computer Applications in Water Resources. Ed. by Harry C. Torno. 1448p. 1985. 121.00 (*0-87262-467-6*) Am Soc Civil Eng.

Computer Applications in Water Supply, Vol. 1: Systems Analysis & Simulation. Ed. by Bryan Coulbeck & Chun-Hou Orr. (Mechanical Engineering Dynamics Ser.). 445p. 1988. text ed. 275.00 (*0-471-91783-4*) Wiley.

Computer Applications in Water Supply, Vol. 2: Systems Optimization & Control, Vol. 2. Ed. by Bryan Coulbeck & Chun-Hou Orr. (Mechanical Engineering Dynamics Ser.). 438p. 1988. text ed. 295.00 (*0-471-91784-2*) Wiley.

Computer Applications Mental Health, 1991: Education & Evaluation. Intro. by Marvin J. Miller. LC 92-1541. (Computers in Human Services Ser.: Vol. 8, Nos. 3-4). (Illus.). 200p. 1992. text ed. 39.95 (*1-56024-279-5*); pap. text ed. 19.95 (*1-56024-353-8*) Haworth Pr.

Computer Applications of Numerical Methods. Shan S. Kuo. LC 78-164654. (C). 1972. text ed. write for info. (*0-201-03956-7*) Addison-Wesley.

Computer Applications: Programming with SeeLogo: Course Code 194-6. Dan Novak & Paula Weinberger. Ed. by Catherine Doheny & Bonnie Schroeder. (Illus.). 36p. (gr. 8). 1989. reprint ed. pap. text ed. 5.95 (*0-917531-58-2*) CES Compu-Tech.

Computer Applications: Programming with SeeLogo Teacher Edition: Course Code S94-4, Grade 8. Irene Danziger & Paula Weinberger. Ed. by Catherine Doheny & Bonnie Schroeder. (Illus.). 50p. 1989. reprint ed. 19.95 (*0-917531-82-5*) CES Compu-Tech.

Computer Applications Software Workbook. Gerald A. Silver & Myrna L. Silver. LC 91-92962. (Illus.). 96p. (C). 1991. pap. 21.50 (*1-880472-02-3*) Edit Enter.

Computer Applications, Tele Communications Teacher Edition: Course Code 194-6, Grade 8. Paual Weinberger & Dan Novak. Ed. by Catherine Doheny & Bonnie Schroeder. (Illus.). 51p. 1989. reprint ed. 14.95 (*0-917531-81-7*) CES Compu-Tech.

Computer Applications: Telecommunications: Course Code S94-4. Irene Danziger & Paula Weinberger. Ed. by Catherine Doheny & Bonnie Schroeder. (Illus.). 42p. (gr. 7). 1989. reprint ed. pap. text ed. 5.95 (*0-917531-57-4*) CES Compu-Tech.

Computer Applications to Chemical Engineering Process Design & Simulation. Ed. by Robert G. Squires & G. V. Reklaitis. LC 79-27719. (ACS Symposium Ser.: No. 124). 1980. 54.95 (*0-8412-0549-3*) Am Chemical.

Computer Applications to X-Ray Powder Diffraction Analysis of Clay Minerals. Ed. by R. C. Reynolds, Jr. & J. R. Walker. (CMS Workshop Lectures: Vol. 5). (Illus.). 171p. (Orig.). (C). 1993. pap. text ed. 15.00 (*1-881208-06-0*) Clay Minerals.

Computer Applications: Word Processing Teacher Edition: Course Code S94-1. Vickie Forker. Ed. by Bonnie Schroeder. (Illus.). 92p. 1989. reprint ed. 19.95 (*0-917531-78-7*) CES Compu-Tech.

Computer Approximations. John F. Hart et al. LC 77-16187. 352p. 1978. reprint ed. lib. bdg. 38.50 (*0-88275-642-7*) Krieger.

Computer Aptitude Test (CAT) Jack Rudman. (Career Examination Ser.: C-180). 1994. pap. 23.95 (*0-8373-0180-7*) Nat Learn.

Computer Archaeology. Gary Lock & John Wilcock. 1989. pap. 25.00 (*0-85263-877-9*, Pub. by Shire UK) St Mut.

Computer Architecture. Ed. by G. Boulaye & Douglas Lewin. (NATO Advanced Study Institutes Series C, Mathematical & Physical Sciences: No. 32). (Illus.). 1977. lib. bdg. 80.00 (*90-277-0803-7*) Kluwer Ac.

***Computer Architecture.** Mario De Blasi. (C). 1990. pap. text ed. 39.75 (*0-201-41603-4*) Addison-Wesley.

Computer Architecture. D. D. Gajski et al. LC 86-45874. 593p. 1987. pap. 7.95 (*0-8186-0704-1*, 704) IEEE Comp Soc.

Computer Architecture: A Computer Zoo, Vol. II. Gerrit A. Blaauw & Frederick P. Brooks, Jr. (Computer Science Ser.). (Illus.). 512p. (C). 1996. text ed. write for info. (*0-201-10558-6*) Addison-Wesley.

Computer Architecture: A Designer's Text Based on a Generic RISC. James M. Feldman. 1994. text ed. write for info. (*0-07-020453-5*) McGraw.

Computer Architecture: A Quantitative Approach. John L. Hennessy & David A. Patterson. 750p. (C). 1990. text ed. 69.95 (*1-55860-069-8*) Morgan Kaufmann.

***Computer Architecture: A Quantitative Approach.** 2nd ed. John Hennessy & Dave Patterson. 1995. 69.95 (*1-55860-329-8*) Morgan Kaufmann.

Computer Architecture: A Structured Approach. R. W. Doran. (APIC Studies in Data Processing). 1979. text ed. 124.00 (*0-12-220850-1*) Acad Pr.

Computer Architecture: Case Studies. Robert J. Baron & Lee Higbie. (Electrical & Computer Engineering Ser.). (Illus.). 320p. (C). 1992. pap. text ed. 46.25 (*0-201-55804-1*) Addison-Wesley.

Computer Architecture: Concepts & Systems. Ed. by V. M. Milutinovic. 600p. 1988. 61.75 (*0-444-01019-X*) Elsevier.

Computer Architecture: Design & Performance. Barry Wilkinson. 600p. 1991. text ed. 61.00 (*0-13-173899-2*) P-H.

Computer Architecture: Hardware & Software, Vol. II. Richard Y. Kain. 608p. 1989. boxed 56.00 (*0-13-166778-5*) P-H.

Computer Architecture: Pipeline. Flynn. (Computer Science-Math Ser.). (C). 1995. boxed 62.50 (*0-86720-204-1*) Jones & Bartlett.

Computer Architecture: Proceedings of the Sixteenth Annual Symposium on Computer Architecture. (Computer Architecture News Ser.: Vol. 17, No. 3). (Illus.). 426p. 1989. pap. text ed. 90.00 (*0-89791-319-1*, 415890) Assn Compu Machinery.

Computer Architecture: Seventeenth Annual International Symposium on Computer Architecture, Held May 28-31, 1990 in Seattle, WA. Contrib by IEEE Computer Society Staff & ACM SIGARCH Staff. (Illus.). xv, 378p. 1990. pap. text ed. 80.00 (*0-89791-366-3*, 415900) Assn Compu Machinery.

Computer Architecture & Communications. Neil Willis. (Illus.). 288p. 1987. 24.95 (*0-8306-7870-0*, 2870) TAB Bks.

Computer Architecture & Communications. 2nd ed. N. Willis. (Computer Studies Ser.). 320p. 1993. pap. 25.00 (*0-632-03075-5*) Blackwell Sci.

Computer Architecture & Design. A. J. Van de Goor. (Electronic Systems Engineering Ser.). (Illus.). 450p. (C). 1989. pap. text ed. 43.25 (*0-201-18241-6*) Addison-Wesley.

Computer Architecture & Logic Design. Thomas C. Bartee. 640p. 1991. text ed. write for info. (*0-07-003909-7*) McGraw.

Computer Architecture & Organization. 2nd ed. John P. Hayes. 720p. 1988. text ed. write for info. (*0-07-027366-9*) McGraw.

Computer Architecture & Parallel Processing. Kai Hwang & Faye A. Brigts. (Computer Science Ser.). 1984. pap. text ed. write for info. (*0-07-031557-4*) McGraw.

Computer Architecture & Parallel Processing. Kai Hwang & Faye A. Briggs. 848p. 1984. text ed. write for info. (*0-07-031556-6*) McGraw.

Computer Architecture & VAX Assembly Language Programming. Richard Spillman & James Brink. 572p. 1987. teacher ed 10.75 (*0-8053-8921-0*) Benjamin-Cummings.

Computer Architecture & VAX Assembly Language Programming. Richard Spillman & James Brink. 572p. (C). 1987. text ed. 51.75 (*0-8053-8920-2*) Benjamin-Cummings.

Computer Architecture, Vol. I: Design Decisions. Gerrit A. Blaauw & Frederick P. Brooks, Jr. (Computer Science Ser.). (Illus.). 640p. (C). 1996. text ed. write for info. (*0-201-10557-8*) Addison-Wesley.

Computer Architecture, 20th International Symposium. LC 85-642899. 376p. 1993. 80.00 (*0-8186-3810-9*, 3810) IEEE Comp Soc.

Computer Architecture, 21st International Symposium on (ISCA '94) 408p. 1994. text ed. 80.00 (*0-8186-5510-0*, 5510) IEEE Comp Soc.

***Computer Architecture, 22nd International Symposium on (ISCA '95)** 400p. 1995. 80.00 (*0-8186-7077-0*, PR07077) IEEE Comp Soc.

Computer Architectures of Machine Perception, 1993. Ed. by Magdy A. Bayoumi. LC 93-80369. 455p. 1993. pap. text ed. 80.00 (*0-8186-5420-1*) IEEE Comp Soc.

Computer Arithmetic Algorithms. Israel Koren. 208p. 1993. text ed. 65.00 (*0-13-151952-2*) P-H.

Computer Arithmetic & Enclosure Methods: Proceedings of the Third International IMACS-GAMM Symposium on Computer Arithmetic & Scientific Computing (SCAN-91), Oldenburg, Germany, 1-4 October 1991. Ed. by Lidiya Atanassova & Jurgen Herzberger. LC 92-31961. x, 504p. 1992. write for info. (*0-444-89834-4*) Elsevier.

Computer Arithmetic & Self-Validating Numerical Methods. Ed. by Christian Ullrich. (Notes & Reports in Mathematics in Science & Engineering: Vol. 7). 302p. 1990. text ed. 61.00 (*0-12-708245-X*) Acad Pr.

Computer Arithmetic II. Earl E. Swartzlander, Jr. LC 90-80908. 412p. 1990. 55.00 (*0-8186-8945-5*, 1945) IEEE Comp Soc.

Computer Arithmetic in Theory & Practice. Ulrich W. Kulisch & Willard L. Miranker. LC 80-765. (Computer Science & Applied Mathematics Ser.). 1981. text ed. 75.00 (*0-12-428650-X*) Acad Pr.

Computer Arithmetic Systems: Algorithms, Architecture, & Implementation. Amos R. Omondi. LC 93-46281. (Prentice-Hall International Series in Computer Science). 520p. 1994. 52.00 (*0-13-334301-4*) P-H Intl.

***Computer Arithmetic, Twelfth Symposium on, July 1995.** LC 88-647423. 250p. 1995. text ed. 50.00 (*0-8186-7089-4*, PR07089) IEEE Comp Soc.

Computer Arithmetic, 11th Symposium, 1993. LC 88-641433. 304p. 1993. text ed. 74.00 (*0-8186-3862-1*, 3862) IEEE Comp Soc.

Computer Art: A Book of Posters. Donald D. Spencer & Susan L. Spencer. (Illus.). 48p. 1987. pap. 6.95 (*0-89218-112-5*, NO. 3008) Camelot Pub.

Computer Art & Animation for the TRS-80. David L. Heiserman. (Illus.). 288p. 1983. pap. text ed. 30.00 (*0-13-164749-0*) P-H.

Computer Artist's Handbook. Lillian F. Schwartz. 1992. 55.00 (*0-393-02795-3*) Norton.

Computer As a Paintbrush: Creative Uses for the Personal Computer in the Preschool Classroom. Janice J. Beaty & Hugh Tucker. 200p. (C). 1987. pap. write for info. (*0-675-20523-9*, Merrill Pub Co) Macmillan.

Computer As an Architectural Design Tool: An Exploration into Certain Multi-Story Building Plan Layouts. Kaiman Lee. 190p. 1979. 25.00 (*0-915250-00-4*) Environ Design.

Computer As an Educational Tool. Henry F. Olds. LC 86-3132. (Computers in the Schools Ser.: Vol. 3, No. 1). 99p. 1986. text ed. 29.95 (*0-86656-559-0*) Haworth Pr.

Computer As Medium. Ed. by P. B. Andersen et al. (Learning in Doing: Social, Cognitive & Computational Perspectives Ser.). (Illus.). 400p. (C). 1994. 54.95 (*0-521-41995-6*) Cambridge U Pr.

Computer Assisted: The Computer in Contemporary Art. David S. Rubin. LC 87-82883. (Illus.). 24p. (Orig.). 1987. pap. text ed. 4.00 (*0-941972-06-2*) Freedman.

Computer Assisted Analyses of Cell Locomotion & Chemotaxis. P. B. Noble & M. D. Levine. 152p. 1986. 132.00 (*0-8493-6342-X*, QH647, CRC Reprint) Franklin.

Computer-Assisted Analysis System for Mathematical Programming Models & Solutions: A User's Guide for ANALYZE. Harvey J. Greenberg. LC 92-43505. (Operations Research - Computer Science Interface Ser.). 1993. lib. bdg. 105.00 (*0-7923-9322-8*) Kluwer Ac.

Computer Assisted Analytical Review System. Kenney et al. (Accounting Education Ser.: Vol. 7). 76p. 1986. 12.00 (*0-86539-056-8*) Am Accounting.

Computer-Assisted Apprasial & Assessment Systems. Robert C. Denne. (Bibliographic Ser.: No.2). 88p. 1977. pap. 15.00 (*0-88329-046-4*) IAAO.

Computer-Assisted Audit Techniques. (American Institute of CPAs Audit Guides Ser.). 102p. 1979. pap. 26.00 (*0-686-70227-1*) Am Inst CPA.

Computer-Assisted Bacterial Systematics. Ed. by Michael Goodfellow et al. (Society for General Microbiology Special Publications: No. 15). 1985. text ed. 129.00 (*0-12-289665-3*) Acad Pr.

Computer-Assisted Cardiac Nuclear Medicine. B. Leonard Holman & J. Anthony Parker. 546p. 1981. 64.00 (*0-316-37054-1*) Little.

Computer Assisted Composition. Noel Williams. 128p. (Orig.). 1990. pap. text ed. 22.95 (*1-871516-21-8*, Pub. by Intellect Bks UK) Cromland.

Computer Assisted Decision Making: Expert Systems, Decision Analysis, Mathematical Programming. Ed. by G. Mitra. 282p. 1986. 87.25 (*0-444-87887-4*, North Holland) Elsevier.

Computer-Assisted Diagnosis & Medical Services: Subject Analysis with Bibliography. Lee B. Neiderhaus. LC 83-45292. 168p. 1984. 39.50 (*0-88164-072-7*); pap. 34.50 (*0-88164-073-5*) ABBE Pubs Assn.

Computer-Assisted Drug Design. Ed. by Ralph E. Christoffersen & Edward C. Olson. LC 79-21038. (ACS Symposium Ser.: No. 112). 1979. 65.95 (*0-8412-0521-3*) Am Chemical.

Computer Assisted Education: A Communication Approach. Doreen R. Steg et al. (C). 1993. pap. text ed. 26.00 (*0-9637504-6-1*) U PA Grad Schl.

Computer-Assisted Eye Examination. Elwyn Marg. (Illus.). 1980. 15.00 (*0-911302-40-9*) San Francisco Pr.

Computer-Assisted Flood Plain Hydrology & Hydraulics. Dan Hoggan. 416p. (C). 1989. text ed. 66.00 (*0-07-029350-3*) McGraw.

Computer Assisted Flow Visualization: Second Generation Technology. Wen-Jei Yhang. 320p. 1993. 95.00 (*0-8493-9937-8*, TA357) CRC Pr.

Computer-Assisted Ground Control Management System. David P. Conover et al. 1994. write for info. (*0-318-72692-0*) US Interior.

Computer-Assisted Image Analysis Cytology. Ed. by S. D. Greenberg. (Monographs in Clinical Cytology: Vol. 9). (Illus.). x, 202p. 1984. 78.50 (*3-8055-3902-9*) S Karger.

Computer-Assisted Instruction: A Summary of Research in Selected Areas. Albert E. Hickey. 1975. pap. text ed. 20.00 (*0-87567-067-9*) Entelek.

Computer-Assisted Instruction: A Synthesis of Theory, Practice, & Technology. E. R. Steinberg. 232p. (C). 1990. pap. 19.95 (*0-8058-0865-5*) L Erlbaum Assocs.

Computer-Assisted Instruction & Compensatory Education: The ETS-Los Angeles Unified School District Study. Marjorie Ragosta et al. 35.00 (*0-317-67869-8*) Educ Testing Serv.

Computer-Assisted Instruction & Education: Medical Applications & Subject Analysis with Bibliography. Mary R. Bartone. LC 83-71672. 146p. 1984. 39.50 (*0-88164-056-5*); pap. 34.50 (*0-88164-057-3*) ABBE Pubs Assn.

Computer-Assisted Instruction & Intelligent Tutoring Systems: Establishing Communication & Collaboration. Ed. by Jill Larkin et al. 288p. (C). 1991. text ed. 59.95 (*0-8058-0232-0*); pap. 32.50 (*0-8058-0233-9*) L Erlbaum Assocs.

Computer Assisted Instruction (CAI) Review. Literacy Volunteers Computer Task Force Staff. Ed. by Chip Carlin & V. K. Lawson. 1986. pap. text ed. 3.00 (*0-318-41221-7*) Lit Vol Am.

***Computer-Assisted Instruction in Chemistry Part A: General Approach.** James S. Mattson. LC 73-89669. (Computers in Chemistry & Instrumentation Ser.: No. 4). 287p. 1974. reprint ed. pap. 81.80 (*0-7837-8641-7*, 2041000) Bks Demand.

Computer-Assisted Instruction in Chemistry, Pt. B: Applications. Ed. by James S. Mattson et al. LC 73-89669. (Computers in Chemistry & Instrumentation Ser.: No. 4). (Illus.). 1974. reprint ed. pap. 75.10 (*0-7837-0664-2*, 2041000) Bks Demand.

Computer Assisted Instruction in Geology: Proceedings of the 4th Geochautauqua, Syracuse University, 1975. Ed. by Daniel F. Merriam. 1976. pap. 50.00 (*0-08-021040-6*, Pergamon Pr) Elsevier.

Computer Assisted Instruction in the Health Sciences: Index of New Information with Authors & Subjects. Mary R. Bartone. LC 92-54230. 180p. 1992. 44.50 (*1-55914-608-7*); pap. 39.50 (*1-55914-609-5*) ABBE Pubs Assn.

Computer-Assisted Instruction Using BASIC. John F. Huntington. LC 79-539. (Illus.). 240p. 1979. 34.95 (*0-87778-135-4*) Educ Tech Pubns.

Computer-Assisted Instructions. Four Selected Articles & a Cross Referenced, Annotated Bibliography. Ed. by Isadore Newman. 141p. 1975. pap. text ed. 4.00 (*0-917180-03-8*) I Newman.

C

An Asterisk (*) at the beginning of an entry indicates that the title is appearing in BIP for the first time.

An Asterisk (*) at the beginning of an entry indicates that the title is appearing in BIP for the first time.

Computer Buyer's Handbook: How to Select & Buy Personal Computers for Your Home or Business. 2nd braille ed. Wayne R. Parker. 652p. (Orig.). 1993. vinyl bd. 52.16 (*1-56956-410-8*, BR9070) W A T Braille.

Computer Buying Guide. Consumer Guide Editors. (Illus.). 160p. (Orig.). 1993. pap. 9.99 (*0-451-82263-3*, 4017100, Sig) NAL-Dutton.

Computer Buying Guide. Consumer Guide Editors. 160p. (Orig.). 1994. pap. 9.99 (*0-451-82275-7*, Sig) NAL-Dutton.

***Computer Buying Guide.** Consumer Guide Editors. 160p. (Orig.). 1995. pap. 9.99 (*0-451-82293-5*, Sig) NAL-Dutton.

***Computer Buying Guide, 1995.** A. M. Gates. 24p. 1994. pap. 1.95 (*1-882185-25-0*) Crnrstone Pub.

Computer Calculator. Barbara Muncaster & Susan Prescott. LC 93-4198. 1994. pap. 8.95 (*0-538-62332-2*) S-W Pub.

Computer Capacity Planning: Theory & Practice. Shui F. Lam & K. Hung Chan. 214p. 1987. text ed. 54.00 (*0-12-434430-5*) Acad Pr.

Computer Care Speciality Producers. Thomas Zarecki. (Illus.). 14p. 1986. 2.00 (*0-685-14601-4*) TJ Enter IL.

Computer Cartoon Visual Masters. Donald D. Spencer. 96p. 1987. pap. 15.95 (*0-89218-106-0*, NO. 3005) Camelot Pub.

Computer Catalogs & Publications. Barry Klein. 250p. (Orig.). 1995. pap. 35.00 (*0-915344-49-1*) Todd Pubns.

Computer Center Construction: A Guide to Effective Planning, Construction, & Furnishing. Ted Farrell. LC 84-70742. 1000p. 1984. 79.50 (*0-9613766-0-0*) BEK Pr.

Computer Chemistry. Mario Marsili. 192p. 1989. 144.00 (*0-8493-4554-5*, QD39) CRC Pr.

Computer Chemistry. Ed. by I. Ugi. (Topics in Current Chemistry Ser.: Vol. 166). (Illus.). 226p. 1992. 129.00 (*0-387-55902-7*) Spr-Verlag.

Computer Chess Compendium. Ed. by David N. Levy. 450p. 1989. 53.00 (*0-387-91331-9*) Spr-Verlag.

Computer Chips & Paper Clips: Technology & Women's Employment, Vol I. National Research Council. Ed. by Heidi I. Hartman et al. 216p. 1986. pap. text ed. 19.95 (*0-309-03688-7*) Natl Acad Pr.

Computer Chips & Paper Clips, Vol. 2: Technology & Women's Employment. National Research Council. Ed. by Heidi I. Hartmann et al. (Case Studies & Policy Perspectives). 456p. 1987. pap. 34.95 (*0-309-03727-1*) Natl Acad Pr.

C

Computer Choice: A Manual for the Practitioner. R. J. McQuaker. 178p. 1979. 59.00 (*0-444-85250-6*, North Holland) Elsevier.

***Computer Circuits Electrical Design.** Ron K. Poon. LC 94-34252. 408p. 1995. text ed. 60.00 (*0-13-213471-3*) P-H.

Computer Club! Debra Schepp & Brad Schepp. 1993. pap. text ed. 19.95 (*0-07-056945-2*) McGraw.

Computer Club: Includes the Editor, Animated Memory, Strudle, Instant Recall. (J). 1993. disk, pap. text ed. 19.95 (*0-8306-4249-8*, Windcrest) TAB Bks.

Computer Codes: A Bibliography, Supplement 1. DOE Technical Information Center Staff. 924p. 1985. pap. 98.00 (*0-87079-560-0*, DOE/TIC-3386, SUPPLEMENT 1); fiche 9.00 (*0-87079-561-9*, DOE/TIC-3386, SUPPLEMENT 1) DOE.

Computer Color, Ten Thousand Computer-generated Process Colors. Michael Rogondino. 1990. pap. 24.95 (*0-87701-739-5*) Chronicle Bks.

Computer Coloring Book: It's Not Just a Coloring Book. Alan Freedman et al. 80p. 1983. pap. 12.95 (*0-13-164632-X*) P-H.

Computer Comes of Age: The People, the Hardware, & the Software. Rene Moreau. 225p. 1984. reprint ed. pap. 9.95x (*0-262-63103-2*) MIT Pr.

Computer Comics. Ed. by Sebstain Orfali. (Illus.). 96p. (Orig.). 1984. pap. 5.95 (*0-914171-03-8*) Ronin Pub.

Computer Communication Networks in Science & Medicine: Index of New Information. Shoog D. Sewell. 150p. 1994. 44.50 (*0-7883-0132-2*); pap. 39.50 (*0-7883-0133-0*) ABBE Pubs Assn.

Computer Communication Technologies for the Nineties: Proceedings of the Ninth International ICCC Conference on Computer Communication, Tel Aviv, Israel, 30 October to 3 November, 1988. Ed. by J. Raviv. 606p. 1989. 123.00 (*0-444-70539-2*, North Holland) Elsevier.

Computer Communications. Ed. by B. Gopinath. LC 84-24556. (Proceedings of Symposia in Applied Mathematics Ser.: Vol. 31). 124p. 1985. text ed. 31.00 (*0-8218-0082-5*, PSAPM-31) Am Math.

Computer Communications. 2nd ed. R. Cole. 1987. pap. 37.00 (*0-387-91306-8*) Spr-Verlag.

Computer Communications: A Business Perspective. Keith Bearpark & Peter J. Beevor. LC 92-44974. 1993. text ed. 34.00 (*0-07-707794-6*) McGraw.

Computer Communications: Architectures, Protocols, & Standards. 3rd ed. William Stallings. LC 92-6850. (Illus.). 360p. (Orig.). (C). 1992. text ed. 55.00 (*0-8186-2712-3*, 2712) IEEE Comp Soc.

Computer Communications: Towards a New World. Ed. by R. Parodi. 750p. 1992. 140.00 (*90-5199-110-X*, Pub. by IOS Pr NE) IOS Press.

Computer Communications Africom '84: Proceedings of the IFIP TC 6 First African Conference on Computer Communications, Tunis, Tunisia, 21-23 May 1984. Ed. by F. Kamoun. 400p. 1985. 72.00 (*0-444-87830-0*, North Holland) Elsevier.

Computer Communications & Networks. J. R. Freer. LC 88-42815. (Applications of Communications Theory Ser.). (Illus.). 432p. 1988. 95.00 (*0-306-42974-8*, Plenum Pr) Plenum.

Computer Communications & Networks. John Freer. 448p. (C). 1988. pap. text ed. 240.00 (*0-273-02789-1*, Pub. by Pitman Pubng UK) St Mut.

Computer Communications & Networks (IC3N) Ed. by E. K. Park & K. Chae. (Conference Proceedings Ser.). 327p. 1992. write for info. (*1-880843-01-3*) Int Soc Comp App.

Computer Communications Security: Principles, Standard Protocols & Techniques. Warwick Ford. 1993. text ed. 65.00 (*0-13-799453-2*) P-H.

Computer Communications Systems, 2 vols. Henri Nussbaumer. 171p. 1990. Vol. 1: Data Circuits, Error Detection, Data Links, 171p. text ed. 84.95 (*0-471-92379-6*) Wiley.

Computer Communications Systems, 2 vols., Vol. 2. Henri Nussbaumer. 259p. 1990. text ed. 95.00 (*0-471-92495-4*) Wiley.

Computer Communications Systems: Proceedings of the IFIP TC6 First Iberian Conference on Data Communications, IBERICOM '87, Lisbon, Portugal, 19-21 May, 1987. Ed. by A. G. Cerveira. 306p. 1987. 74.50 (*0-444-70334-9*) Elsevier.

Computer Companion: A User Friendly Guide to WordPerfect 5.1, Lotus 1- 2-3 2.3, Paradox 3.5, MSDOS 5.0. Resnick & Laura Chavez. 368p. (C). 1992. pap. text ed. 22.95 (*0-8403-7947-1*) Kendall-Hunt.

***Computer Companion: System & Software Tracker.** M. Ryan Vogt. LC 94-78601. 64p. (Orig.). 1995. pap. 6.95 (*1-885459-01-7*) Jumping Mouse.

Computer Companion for the Commodore 64. Robert P. Haviland. 144p. (Orig.). 1985. pap. 11.95 (*0-8306-1913-5*) TAB Bks.

Computer-Compatible Machine Shorthand for Expanding Careers: Basic Theory, Vol. I. Beverly L. Ritter. (Computer-Compatible Machine Shorthand for Expanding Careers Ser.). 204p. (C). 1986. student ed 5.00 (*0-938643-05-3*); teacher ed 20.00 (*0-938643-00-2*) Stenotype Educ.

Computer-Compatible Machine Shorthand for Expanding Careers: Basic Theory, Vol. I. rev. ed. Beverly L. Ritter. (Computer-Compatible Machine Shorthand for Expanding Careers Ser.). 204p. (C). 1986. pap. text ed. 24.00 (*0-938643-01-0*) Stenotype Educ.

Computer-Compatible Machine Shorthand for Expanding Careers: Student Dictionary. rev. ed. Ed. by Beverly L. Ritter. 216p. (C). 1986. pap. text ed. 16.00 (*0-938643-02-9*) Stenotype Educ.

Computer-Compatible Stenograph Theory, Vol. I. Mae Glassbrenner & G. Allen Sonntag. (Illus.). ix, 286p. (Orig.). (C). 1990. teacher ed 36.95 (*0-937112-02-X*); pap. 36.95 (*0-937112-01-1*); write for info. (*0-685-31716-1*) Stenograph Corp.

Computer-Compatible Stenograph Theory, Vol. II. Mae Glassbrenner & G. Allen Sonntag. (Orig.). (C). 1987. teacher ed 36.95 (*0-685-31721-8*); pap. 36.95 (*0-685-31719-6*); pap. text ed. 29.95 (*0-685-31720-X*) Stenograph Corp.

Computer-Compatible Stenograph Theory: Dictionary-Reference Guide. Mae Glassbrenner & G. Allen Sonntag. (Orig.). (C). 1989. pap. 42.95 (*0-685-31724-2*); pap. text ed. 32.95 (*0-685-31725-0*) Stenograph Corp.

Computer-Compatible Stenograph Theory, Vol. I: Teacher's Manual. Mae Glassbrenner & G. Allen Sonntag. (Orig.). (C). 1987. teacher ed 29.95 (*0-685-31718-8*); pap. 36.95 (*0-685-31717-X*) Stenograph Corp.

Computer-Compatible Stenograph Theory, Vol. II: Teacher's Manual. Mae Glassbrenner & G. Allen Sonntag. (Orig.). (C). 1989. pap. text ed. 29.95 (*0-685-31722-6*); teacher ed, boxed 36.95 (*0-685-31723-4*) Stenograph Corp.

Computer Compilation of Molecular Weights & Percentage Compositions for Organic Compounds. M. J. Dewar & R. Jones. 1969. 203.00 (*0-08-012707-X*, Pub. by Pergamon Repr UK) Franklin.

Computer Compilers Annual, 1991. Ed. by John R. Levine. 900p. (Orig.). 1992. pap. text ed. 70.00 (*0-944954-03-0*) Ctr Bk Pubs.

Computer Composer's Toolbox. Phil Winsor. 1991. 24.95 (*0-8306-5450-X*) TAB Bks.

Computer Composer's Toolbox (5.25) Phil Winsor. 1991. 24.95 (*0-8306-6698-2*) TAB Bks.

Computer Concepts. Shelly et al. 384p. 1990. 27.50 (*0-87835-356-9*) Boyd & Fraser.

Computer Concepts. Gary B. Shelly et al. (C). 1989. pap. text ed. write for info. (*0-318-65186-6*, BF3569) S-W Pub.

Computer Concepts. Ric Williams & Jean Gonzalez. (Advanced Court Reporting Technology Ser.). 175p. 1991. teacher ed write for info. (*1-881086-04-6*); pap. text ed. 29.99 (*1-881086-00-3*); trans. write for info. (*1-881086-10-0*); trans. 84.00 (*1-881086-05-4*) Middle Wasley.

Computer Concepts, 2 vols. Incl. 1. 3rd ed. pap. text ed. 20.51 (*0-672-96021-4*); 3rd ed. (*0-672-96023-0*); Set pap. text ed. write for info. (*0-685-00786-3*) Macmillan.

Computer Concepts, 5 instr's. manuals, Set. Ric Williams & Jean Gonzalez. 175p. 1991. teacher ed, trans. write for info. (*0-318-69210-4*) Middle Wasley.

Computer Concepts: Screen by Screen. Jon Huhtala & George Novotny. Ed. by Michelle Baxter. (Illus.). 204p. (Orig.). (C). 1991. spiral bd. 23.75 (*0-8053-2823-8*) Benjamin-Cummings.

Computer Concepts & Applications. 2nd ed. Timothy N. Trainor & Diane Krasnewich. LC 86-62012. (Illus.). 350p. (J). (gr. 7-8). 1987. pap. text ed. 26.50 (*0-394-39052-0*) Mitchell Pub.

Computer Concepts & Applications. 3rd ed. James A. O'Brien. 640p. (C). 1988. pap. text ed. 42.95 (*0-256-07001-6*) Irwin.

Computer Concepts & Applications for the Medical Office. Kathy Bonewit-West. 296p. 1993. pap. text ed. 29.50 (*0-7216-4945-9*) Saunders.

Computer Concepts for Managers. Gordon G. Schulmeyer. 344p. 1985. text ed. 55.95 (*0-442-28063-7*) Van Nos Reinhold.

Computer Concepts Today. Dennis Curtin. 1993. pap. text ed. 10.00 (*0-13-288655-3*) P-H.

Computer Concepts with BASIC. Shelly et al. 450p. 1990. 29.00 (*0-87835-373-9*) Boyd & Fraser.

Computer Concepts with Microcomputer Applications: Lotus Version. Gary B. Shelly & Thomas J. Cashman. (C). 1989. pap. text ed. write for info. (*0-538-91132-8*, BF3593) S-W Pub.

Computer Concepts with Microcomputer Applications: VP-Planner Plus Version. Gary B. Shelly & Thomas J. Cashman. (C). 1989. pap. text ed. write for info. (*0-538-91104-2*, BF3410) S-W Pub.

Computer Concepts with Microcomputer Applications: WordPerfect 5.0-5.1, Lotus 1-2-3, dBASE III PLUS. Shelly et al. 1008p. 1991. 33.00 (*0-87835-672-X*) Boyd & Fraser.

Computer Concepts with Microcomputer Applications: WordPerfect 5.0-5.1, Lotus 1-2-3 Release 2.2, dBASE IV. Shelly et al. 1088p. 1991. 33.00 (*0-87835-776-9*); 33.00 (*0-87835-739-4*) Boyd & Fraser.

Computer Concepts with Microcomputer Applications - VP-Planner Plus Version. Shelly et al. 976p. 1990. 33.00 (*0-87835-341-0*) Boyd & Fraser.

Computer Concepts with Microcomputer Applications, Lotus Version. Shelly et al. 972p. 1990. 33.00 (*0-87835-359-3*) Boyd & Fraser.

Computer Concepts with QuickBASIC. Shelly et al. (Shelly Cashman Ser.). (Illus.). 448p. 1991. 31.50 (*0-87835-764-5*) Boyd & Fraser.

Computer Conference Software Directory 1986: For Communication Sciences Disorders. Ed. by Arthur H. Schwartz. 186p. 1986. pap. text ed. 15.00 (*0-910329-35-4*) Am Speech Lang Hearing.

Computer Confidence: A Human Approch to Computers. B. D. Sanders. (Books on Professional Computing). (Illus.). 130p. 1983. pap. 25.00 (*0-387-90917-6*) Spr-Verlag.

Computer Confusion. Beth Cruise. (Saved by the Bell Ser.: No. 12). 144p. (Orig.). (YA). (gr. 5 up). 1994. pap. 2.95 (*0-02-042784-0*, Collier Bks Young) S&S Childrens.

Computer Connection: General Ledger & Practice Sets for Introductory Accounting, IBM PC Version. John W. Wanlass. 88p. (C). 1988. pap. text ed. 3.00 (*0-15-512632-6*) HB Coll Pubs.

Computer Consultant's Guide: Real-Life Strategies for Building a Successful Consulting Career. Janet L. Ruhl. LC 93-30876. 304p. 1994. text ed. 45.00 (*0-471-59662-0*); pap. text ed. 19.95 (*0-471-59661-2*) Wiley.

***Computer Consultant's Workbook.** Janet Ruhl. 288p. 1996. pap. 39.95 (*0-9647116-0-5*) Technion Bks.

Computer Consulting on Your Home-Based PC. Herman Holtz. 1994. pap. text ed. 14.95 (*0-07-029669-3*) McGraw.

Computer Consulting on Your Home-Based PC. Herman Holtz. 1994. text ed. 24.95 (*0-07-029668-5*) McGraw.

Computer Consulting on Your Home-Based PC. Herman R. Holtz. 1993. 24.95 (*0-8306-4448-2*, Windcrest); pap. 14.95 (*0-8306-4449-0*, Windcrest) TAB Bks.

***Computer Consulting 101: A Beginner's How-To Guide to Becoming a Computer Consultant.** Lloyd R. Mumford, Jr. Ed. by Gale Kaplan. (Illus.). 104p. (C). 1995. write for info. (*0-9644847-2-2*) Lloyds Bridges.

Computer Contracts, 4 vols. Robert Bigelow. 1987. Updates. ring bd. write for info. (*0-8205-1508-6*) Bender.

***Computer Contracts.** M. Michele Rennie. 1994. disk, ring bd. 160.00 (*0-421-49050-0*) W W Gaunt.

Computer Contracts: An International Guide to Agreements & Software Protection. Hilary E. Pearson. 312p. 1984. 70.50 (*90-6544-198-0*) Kluwer Ac.

Computer Contracts: Principles & Precedents. Gordon Hughes & Anna Sharpe. xxxi, 615p. 1987. 93.50 (*0-455-20736-4*, Pub. by Law Bk Co) W W Gaunt.

Computer Contracts: Principles & Precedents. 2nd ed. Gordon Hughes & Anna Sharpe. 1992. ring bd. 275.00 (*0-685-65889-9*, Pub. by Law Bk Co) W W Gaunt.

***Computer Contradictionary.** 2nd ed. Stan Kelly-Bootle. (Illus.). 260p. 1995. 30.00 (*0-262-11202-7*); pap. 14.95 (*0-262-61112-0*) MIT Pr.

Computer Control & Audit. William C. Mair et al. (Illus.). 1977. text ed. 35.25 (*0-89413-063-3*) Inst Inter Aud.

Computer Control & Audit: A Total Systems Approach. John G. Burch & Joseph L. Sardinas. LC 78-9093. (Illus.). 508p. reprint ed. pap. 144.80 (*0-685-20434-0*, 2056442) Bks Demand.

Computer Control in Process Metallurgy: A Short Course Sponsored by TMS-AIME Held in Las Vegas, Nevada, February 20-21, 1976. Metallurgical Society of AIME Staff. 147p. reprint ed. pap. 41.90 (*0-317-10708-9*, 2004308) Bks Demand.

Computer Control in the Process Industries. Brian Roffel & Patrick Chin. (Illus.). 257p. (C). 1987. text ed. 95.00 (*0-87371-122-X*, TS156, CRC Reprint) Franklin.

Computer Control of BATCH Processes. William T. Shaw. Ed. by James F. McMenamin. LC 82-82986. (Illus.). 400p. 1982. 49.50 (*0-9609256-0-0*) EMC Controls.

Computer Control of Fermentation Processes. Ed. by Daniel R. Omstead. 320p. 1989. 216.00 (*0-8493-5496-X*, TP156) CRC Pr.

Computer Control of Machines & Processes. John G. Bollinger & Neil A. Duffie. LC 87-14019. (Mechanical Engineering Ser.). (Illus.). 576p. (C). 1988. text ed. 72.25 (*0-201-10645-0*) Addison-Wesley.

Computer Control of Manufacturing Systems. Yoram Koren. (Illus.). 352p. 1983. text ed. write for info. (*0-07-035341-7*) McGraw.

Computer Control of Real-Time Processes. Bennett. 1990. 92.00 (*0-86341-220-3*, CE041) Inst Elect Eng.

Computer Control Pioneers: A History of the Innovators & Their Work. ISA Ad Hoc Committee Staff. 124p. 1992. pap. 20.00 (*1-55617-370-9*) Instru Soc.

Computer Control Strategies for the Fluid Process Industries. A. A. Gunkler & J. W. Bernard. 325p. 1990. 60.00 (*1-55617-258-3*) Instru Soc.

Computer Control Supervisor. Jack Rudman. (Career Examination Ser.: C-3001). 1994. pap. 34.95 (*0-8373-3001-7*) Nat Learn.

Computer Control Systems for Log Processing & Lumber Manufacturing. Ed M. Williston. LC 85-62602. (Illus.). 416p. (C). 1985. 58.50 (*0-87930-163-5*) Miller Freeman.

Computer Controlled Interactive Video: Multi-Media Systems. Unicom Seminars, Ltd. Staff. (UNICOM Report Ser.: Vol. 4). 240p. 1987. text ed. 95.50 (*0-291-39722-0*, Pub. by Avebury Pub UK) Ashgate Pub Co.

Computer Controlled Systems: Theory & Applications. George A. Perdikaris. 496p. (C). 1991. lib. bdg. 142.00 (*0-7923-1422-0*) Kluwer Ac.

Computer-Controlled Systems: Theory & Design. 2nd ed. Karl J. Astrom & Bjorn Wittenmark. 464p. 1989. text ed. 76.00 (*0-13-168600-3*) P-H.

Computer Crafts for Kids. Margy Kuntz & Ann Kuntz. 1994. pap. 14.95 (*1-56276-186-2*) Ziff-Davis.

***Computer Crime.** David Icove et al. Ed. by Deborah Russell. (Illus.). (Orig.). 1995. pap. write for info. (*1-56592-086-4*) OReilly & Assocs.

***Computer Crime: A Crime-Fighters Handbook.** David Icove. 1995. pap. 24.95 (*1-56592-106-2*) OReilly & Assocs.

Computer Crime: Criminal Justice Resource Manual. 2nd ed. 241p. (C). 1993. pap. text ed. 60.00 (*0-7881-0053-X*) Diane Pub.

Computer Crime: Phreaks, Spies, & Salami Slicers. Karen Judson. LC 93-41198. (Issues in Focus Ser.). (Illus.). 128p. (J). (gr. 6 up). 1994. lib. bdg. 17.95 (*0-89490-491-4*) Enslow Pubs.

Computer Crime & Business Information: A Practical Guide for Managers. J. A. Schweitzer. 196p. 1985. 38.50 (*0-444-00972-8*) Elsevier.

Computer Crime, Computer Security, Computer Ethics. Ed. by Jay BloomBecker. 32p. (Orig.). 1986. pap. 28.00 (*0-933561-02-4*) Natl Ctr Computer Crime.

Computer Crime Investigation. 52p. (Orig.). (C). 1993. pap. text ed. 20.00 (*1-56806-850-6*) Diane Pub.

Computer Crime Law, 1 vol. Jay J. BloomBecker. 1993. ring bd. 125.00 (*0-685-68849-6*) Clark Boardman Callaghan.

Computer Crime Units. 55p. (Orig.). (C). 1993. pap. text ed. 20.00 (*1-56806-849-2*) Diane Pub.

Computer Crimes & Capers. Ed. by Isaac Asimov et al. 242p. 1983. pap. 10.00 (*0-89733-087-0*) Academy Chi Pubs.

Computer Cryptology: Beyond Decoder Rings & Computer Games. Karl Anderson. (Illus.). 272p. 1987. 22.50 (*0-13-166133-7*) P-H.

Computer Culture: A Symposium to Explore the Computer's Impact on Society. Ed. by Denis Donnelly. LC 83-49215. (Illus.). 176p. 1985. 27.50 (*0-8386-3220-3*) Fairleigh Dickinson.

Computer Culture: The Scientific, Intellectual, & Social Impact of the Computer. Pref. by Heinz R. Pagels. (Annals Ser.: Vol. 426). 228p. 1984. lib. bdg. 66.00 (*0-89766-244-X*); pap. 66.00 (*0-89766-245-8*) NY Acad Sci.

Computer Currents. George Beekman. 432p. 1994. Tchr.'s ed. teacher ed, pap. text ed. 36.75 (*0-8053-2454-2*); Instr.'s manual. teacher ed 10.75 (*0-8053-2452-6*); Acetate transparencies. trans. 80.75 (*0-8053-2449-6*); Test bank. write for info. (*0-8053-2457-7*) Benjamin-Cummings.

Computer Currents. George Beekman. 432p. (C). 1994. text ed. 37.75 (*0-8053-2448-8*) Benjamin-Cummings.

Computer Data Handling in the Primary School. Ed. by John Lodge. (Roehampton Teaching Studies Ser.). 128p. 1991. pap. 27.00 (*1-85346-178-4*, Pub. by D Fulton UK) Taylor & Francis.

Computer Data Security: A Legal & Practical Guide to Liability, Loss Prevention, & Criminal & Civil Remedies. LC 89-70786. (Special Report Ser.). 1990. 95.00 (*1-55871-149-X*, BSP 120) BNA.

Computer Dealers (Eastern Region), 1995. American Business Directories Staff. 1995. spiral bd., pap. 1,295.00 (*1-56105-604-9*) Am Busn Direct.

Computer Dealers (Two Regions), 1995. American Business Directories Staff. 1995. spiral bd., pap. 1,715.00 (*1-56105-603-0*) Am Busn Direct.

Computer Dealers (Western Region), 1995. American Business Directories Staff. 1995. spiral bd., pap. 935.00 (*1-56105-605-7*) Am Busn Direct.

Computer Decisions for Board Members: Getting the Most from What Your District Selects. Stanley Pogrow. LC 85-50953. 250p. (Orig.). 1985. pap. text ed. 18.95 (*0-931028-70-1*) Teach-em.

Computer Design. Glen G. Langdon, Jr. LC 81-71785. (Illus.). 577p. (C). 1982. 39.00 (*0-9607864-0-6*) Computeach.

***Computer Design: VLSI in Computers & Processors.** 664p. 1994. pap. text ed. 100.00 (*0-8186-6565-3*) IEEE Comp Soc.

Computer Design: VLSI in Computers & Processors (ICCD '91) LC 88-647423. 672p. 1991. 100.00 (*0-8186-2270-9*) IEEE Comp Soc.

Computer Design: VLSI in Computers & Processors (ICCD '92) LC 88-647423. 624p. 1992. 100.00 (*0-8186-3110-4*, 3110) IEEE Comp Soc.

Computer Design: VLSI in Computers & Processors (ICCD '93) 640p. 1993. pap. text ed. 100.00 (*0-8186-4230-0*, 4230) IEEE Comp Soc.

Computer Design & Architecture. 2nd ed. Sajjan G. Shiva. (C). 1990. text ed. 74.00 (*0-673-39683-5*) HarpCollege.

An Asterisk (*) at the beginning of an entry indicates that the title is appearing in BIP for the first time.

C

An Asterisk (*) at the beginning of an entry indicates that the title is appearing in BIP for the first time.

1499

Computer Graphics for the IBM Personal Computer. D. Donald Hearn & M. Pauline Baker. (Illus.). 320p. 1983. pap. 22.50 (*0-13-164327-4*) P-H.

Computer Graphics Fundamentals. James L. Pomeroy. (Illus.). 158p. 1993. pap. text ed. 48.00 (*0-9625017-7-8*) Palms & Rhodes Pub.

Computer Graphics Handbook. Michael E. Mortenson. (Illus.). 288p. 1990. 26.95 (*0-8311-1002-3*) Indus Pr.

Computer Graphics Hardware: Image Generation & Display. H. Reghbati & A. Y. Lee. LC 88-70221. 375p. 1988. pap. 50.00 (*0-8186-0753-X*, 753) IEEE Comp Soc.

Computer Graphics: How it Works, What it Does. Larry Kettelkamp. LC 88-38924. (Illus.). 144p. (YA). (gr. 7 up). 1989. 12.95 (*0-688-07504-5*) Morrow Jr Bks.

Computer Graphics in Archaeology: Statistical Cartographic Applications to Spatial Analysis in Archaeological Contexts. Ed. by S. Upham. (Anthropological Research Papers: No. 15). (Illus.). vi, 156p. 1979. 15.00 (*0-685-73901-5*) AZ Univ ARP.

Computer Graphics in Engineering Education. Ed. by D. F. Rogers. 136p. 1982. 54.00 (*0-08-028949-5*, Pub. by Pergamon Repr UK) Franklin.

Computer Graphics Mapping Specialist. Jack Rudman. (Career Examination Ser.: C-3231). 1994. pap. 29.95 (*0-8373-3231-1*) Nat Learn.

Computer Graphics Programming. 2nd enl. rev. ed. G. Enderle et al. (Symbolic Computation - Computer Graphics Ser.). (Illus.). xxii, 630p. (C). 1987. 104.00 (*0-387-16317-4*) Spr-Verlag.

Computer Graphics Project for Design & Descriptive Geometry. Eugene G. Pare & Micheal Shook. 149p. (C). 1986. pap. write for info. (*0-02-390980-3*) Macmillan.

Computer Graphics Secrets & Solutions. John Corrigan. LC 94-65379. 338p. 1994. pap. 19.99 (*0-7821-1354-0*) Sybex.

Computer Graphics Simulations Comparing Productivity with Computer-Assisted Mining Equipment: Shuttle Cars versus Continuous Haulage Systems. Dean H. Ambrose. 1994. write for info. (*0-318-72807-9*) US Interior.

Computer Graphics Software Construction. John R. Rankin. (Illus.). 448p. (C). 1988. text ed. 49.20 (*0-13-162793-7*) P-H.

Computer Graphics Techniques: Theory & Practice. Ed. by D. F. Rogers & R. A. Earnshaw. (Illus.). v, 542p. 1990. 89.00 (*0-387-97237-4*) Spr-Verlag.

Computer Graphics Using C Plus Plus. Cornel Pokorny. LC 94-2872. 1994. write for info. (*0-938661-55-8*) Franklin Beedle.

Computer Graphics Using Object-Oriented Programming. Nancy K. Knolle-Craighill et al. 320p. 1992. pap. text ed. 52.00 (*0-471-54199-0*) Wiley.

Computer Graphics Visual Masters. Donald D. Spencer. 160p. 1987. pap. 15.95 (*0-89218-105-2*, NO. 3004) Camelot Pub.

Computer Graphics with Mathematica. Tom Wickham-Jones. 1994. 49.95 (*0-387-94047-2*) Spr-Verlag.

Computer Graphics 1987. Ed. by T. L. Kunii. (Illus.). 491p. 1987. 131.00 (*0-387-70022-6*) Spr-Verlag.

Computer Graphics 2. 160p. 1994. pap. 29.99 (*1-56496-090-0*) Rockport Pubs.

Computer Graphics 82. 392p. 1982. 116.00 (*0-903796-92-9*, Online) Taylor & Francis.

Computer Graphing Experiments, 3 vols., Set. Charles Lund & Edwin D. Andersen. 1982. write for info. (*0-201-23480-7*) Addison-Wesley.

Computer Graphing Experiments, 4 vols., Vol. 1. Charles Lund & Edwin D. Andersen. 1982. write for info. (*0-201-23465-3*) Addison-Wesley.

Computer Graphing Experiments, 4 vols., Vol. 2. Charles Lund & Edwin D. Andersen. 1982. write for info. (*0-201-23470-X*) Addison-Wesley.

Computer Graphing Experiments, 4 vols., Vol. 3. Charles Lund & Edwin D. Andersen. 1982. write for info. (*0-201-23475-0*) Addison-Wesley.

Computer Guide for Pilots. Larry Reithmaier. LC 78-94966. (Pilot Guides Ser.). pap. 1.00 (*0-8168-7200-7*, 27200, TAB-Aero) TAB Bks.

Computer Handbook: Amstrad PCW 8256 & PCW 8512. David Hawgood. (C). 1986. pap. text ed. 50.00 (*0-685-40852-3*, Pub. by Pitman Pubng UK) St Mut.

Computer Handbook: Amstrad PC1512. Ed. by Peter Gosling. (C). 1987. pap. text ed. 60.00 (*0-273-02819-7*, Pub. by Pitman Pubng UK) St Mut.

Computer Handbook: Amstrad 464, 664, & 6128. Boris Allan. (C). 1985. pap. text ed. 65.00 (*0-273-02390-X*, Pub. by Pitman Pubng UK) St Mut.

Computer Handbook: Assembly Languages for the 80286. Robert Erskine. (C). 1985. pap. text ed. 40.00 (*0-273-02391-8*, Pub. by Pitman Pubng UK) St Mut.

Computer Handbook: C Language. Friedman Wagner-Dobler. (C). 1985. pap. text ed. 40.00 (*0-273-02246-6*, Pub. by Pitman Pubng UK) St Mut.

Computer Handbook: dBase III. Peter Gosling. (C). 1985. pap. text ed. 75.00 (*0-273-02359-4*, Pub. by Pitman Pubng UK) St Mut.

Computer Handbook: Framework & Framework II. Peter Gosling. (C). 1985. pap. text ed. 45.00 (*0-273-02497-3*, Pub. by Pitman Pubng UK) St Mut.

Computer Handbook: Introduction to Prolog. Brian Walsh. (C). 1986. pap. text ed. 65.00 (*0-273-02694-1*, Pub. by Pitman Pubng UK) St Mut.

Computer Handbook: Lisp. Sheila Hughes. (C). 1986. pap. text ed. 40.00 (*0-273-02392-6*, Pub. by Pitman Pubng UK) St Mut.

Computer Handbook: Lotus Symphony. Ed. by Dick Waller. (C). 1986. pap. text ed. 40.00 (*0-273-02529-5*, Pub. by Pitman Pubng UK) St Mut.

Computer Handbook: Lotus 1-2-3. Dick Waller. (C). 1985. pap. text ed. 40.00 (*0-273-02358-6*, Pub. by Pitman Pubng UK) St Mut.

Computer Handbook: Multi Plan. Peter Gosling. (C). 1986. pap. text ed. 40.00 (*0-273-02582-1*, Pub. by Pitman Pubng UK) St Mut.

Computer Handbook: Multimate. Colin Townely. (C). 1987. pap. text ed. 50.00 (*0-273-02831-6*, Pub. by Pitman Pubng UK) St Mut.

Computer Handbook: Structured Programming. Ray Welland. (C). 1986. pap. text ed. 40.00 (*0-273-02249-0*, Pub. by Pitman Pubng UK) St Mut.

Computer Handbook: SuperCalc & SuperCalc 2. Peter Gosling. (C). 1985. pap. text ed. 40.00 (*0-273-02425-6*, Pub. by Pitman Pubng UK) St Mut.

Computer Handbook: The Apricot. Peter Gosling. (C). 1985. pap. text ed. 45.00 (*0-273-02317-9*, Pub. by Pitman Pubng UK) St Mut.

Computer Handbook: The Sinclair QL. Ed. by Guy Langdon & David Hecklingbottom. (C). 1985. pap. text ed. 40.00 (*0-273-02244-X*, Pub. by Pitman Pubng UK) St Mut.

Computer Handbook: UCSD P-System. Ed. by Robin Hunter. (C). 1986. pap. text ed. 40.00 (*0-273-02196-6*, Pub. by Pitman Pubng UK) St Mut.

Computer Handbook: Visi Calc. Ed. by Peter Gosling. (C). 1985. pap. text ed. 40.00 (*0-273-02248-2*, Pub. by Pitman Pubng UK) St Mut.

Computer Handbook: Wordperfect. Ed. by Joanna Gosling. (C). 1987. pap. text ed. 50.00 (*0-273-02832-4*, Pub. by Pitman Pubng UK) St Mut.

Computer Handbook: Wordstar. Maddie Labinger et al. (C). 1985. pap. text ed. 50.00 (*0-273-02496-5*, Pub. by Pitman Pubng UK) St Mut.

Computer Handbook: Wordwise & Wordwise Plus. Wendy Chuter. (C). 1985. pap. text ed. 60.00 (*0-273-02300-4*, Pub. by Pitman Pubng UK) St Mut.

Computer Handling & Dissemination of Data: Proceedings of the 10th International CODATA Conference, Ottawa, Canada, 14-17, July, 1986. Ed. by P. S. Glaeser. 424p. 1987. 118.00 (*0-444-70221-0*, North Holland) Elsevier.

Computer Hardware: Module 2. Robert C. Nickerson. LC 92-37221. (C). 1992. write for info. (*0-06-501698-X*, HarpT) HarpC.

Computer Hardware Description Langauge & Their Applications: Proceedings of the IFIP WG10.2 International Conference, Ottowa, Canada, April 1993. D. Agnew et al. (IFIP Transactions A: Computer Science & Technology Ser.: Vol. A-32). 618p. 1993. pap. 165.75 (*0-444-81641-0*, North Holland) Elsevier.

Computer Hardware Description Languages - & Their Applications: Proc. of the IFIP WG10.2 Ninth Internat. Symp., Washington, DC, 19-21 June 1989. Ed. by J. A. Darringer & F. J. Rammig. 362p. 1990. 89.75 (*0-444-88411-4*, North Holland) Elsevier.

Computer Hardware Description Languages & Their Applications. Ed. by C. J. Koomen & T. Moto-Oka. 506p. 1986. 95.00 (*0-444-87826-2*, North Holland) Elsevier.

Computer Hardware Description Languages & Their Applications: Proceedings of the IFIP WG10.2 Eighth International Conference, Amsterdam, the Netherlands, 27-29 April, 1987. Ed. by M. R. Barbacci & C. J. Koomen. 406p. 1987. 100.00 (*0-444-70235-0*, North Holland) Elsevier.

***Computer Hardware Diagnostics for Engineers.** Ronald E. Howland. 1995. text ed. 55.00 (*0-07-030561-7*) McGraw.

Computer Health Hazards. Marija M. Hughes. LC 90-93371. 67p. 1990. 39.95 (*0-912560-05-3*) Hughes Pr.

Computer Health Hazards, Vol. 2. Marija M. Hughes. LC 90-93371. (Illus.). 132p. 1993. pap. 58.00 (*0-912560-00-2*) Hughes Pr.

Computer History Visual Masters. Donald D. Spencer. 96p. 1987. pap. 15.95 (*0-89218-109-5*, NO. 3001) Camelot Pub.

Computer Humor. 2nd ed. Donald D. Spencer. (Illus.). 96p. 1993. pap. 9.95 (*0-89218-236-9*) Camelot Pub.

Computer Illiterates' Guide: A Lighthearted & Informative Guide for the Computer Beginner. Marjorie Scott. 1989. pap. 8.95 (*0-926623-28-1*) Tools Better Lrn Pubns.

Computer Illusion in Film & TV. Christopher Baker. 196p. 1994. 20.00 (*1-56761-422-1*) Alpha Bks IN.

Computer Image: Applications of Computer Graphics. D. Greenberg et al. 1982. 27.95 (*0-201-06192-9*) Addison-Wesley.

Computer Image Generation. Ed. by Bruce J. Schachter. 256p. (C). 1983. lib. bdg. 46.95 (*0-471-87287-3*) Krieger.

Computer Image Processing in Traffic Engineering. N. Hoose. (Research Studies Press - Traffic Engineering). 220p. 1991. text ed. 145.00 (*0-471-92974-3*) Wiley.

Computer Images. rev. ed. (Understanding Computers Ser.). (Illus.). 128p. 1991. 19.93 (*0-8094-7558-8*); lib. bdg. 25.93 (*0-8094-7559-6*) Time-Life.

Computer Images, 1988. Donald D. Spencer. 1988. pap. 24.95 (*0-89218-181-8*) Camelot Pub.

Computer Images, 1989. Donald D. Spencer. 1989. pap. 24.95 (*0-89218-182-6*) Camelot Pub.

Computer Images, 1990. Donald D. Spencer. 144p. 1990. 24.95 (*0-89218-183-4*) Camelot Pub.

Computer Images, 1991. Donald D. Spencer. 144p. 1991. 24.95 (*0-89218-184-2*) Camelot Pub.

Computer Images, 1992. Donald D. Spencer. 144p. 1992. 24.95 (*0-89218-185-0*) Camelot Pub.

Computer Images, 1993. Donald D. Spencer. 144p. 1993. 24.95 (*0-89218-186-9*) Camelot Pub.

Computer Images, 1994. Donald D. Spencer. 144p. 1994. 24.95 (*0-89218-187-7*) Camelot Pub.

Computer Imaging in Dentistry. Ronald Goldstein et al. (Illus.). 1996. text ed. write for info. (*0-86715-238-9*) Quint Pub Co.

Computer Imaging Recipes in C. Harley R. Myler & Arthur R. Weeks. LC 92-23501. 304p. 1992. boxed, disk 56.00 (*0-13-189879-5*) P-H.

Computer Implementation of Entropy Minimax. R. Christensen. LC 81-202346. (Entropy Minimax Sourcebook Ser.: Vol. III). x, 254p. 1980. 32.95 (*0-938876-05-8*) Entropy Ltd.

Computer in Clinical Dentistry: Proceedings of the First International Conference, Houston, Texas, September 26-29, 1991. Ed. by Jack D. Preston. LC 92-49188. 1993. pap. text ed. 48.00 (*0-86715-229-X*) Quint Pub Co.

Computer in Contemporary Cartography. Ed. by D. Fraser Taylor. LC 79-42727. (Progress in Contemporary Cartography Ser.: Vol. 1). 268p. reprint ed. pap. 76.40 (*0-317-30327-9*, 2024806) Bks Demand.

Computer in Court. Alistair Kelman & Richard Sizer. 112p. 1982. text ed. 42.00 (*0-566-03419-0*) Ashgate Pub Co.

Computer in der Medizin. Dimitris N. Chorafas. (IS-Informations-Systeme Ser.). (Illus.). 127p. (C). 1973. 43.10x (*3-11-004031-X*) De Gruyter.

Computer in Education: A Critical Perspective. Ed. by Douglas Sloan. LC 85-4679. 135p. reprint ed. pap. 38.50 (*0-7837-6482-0*, 2046509) Bks Demand.

Computer in Education: A Critical Perspective. Ed. by Douglas Sloan. 136p. (C). 1985. reprint ed. pap. text ed. 15.95 (*0-8077-2782-2*) Tchrs Coll.

Computer in Experimental Psychology. R. Bird. LC 80-41610. (Computers & People Ser.). 256p. 1981. text ed. 126.00 (*0-12-099760-6*) Acad Pr.

Computer in Graphic Design: From Technology to Style. Ronald Labuz. LC 92-9981. 1993. text ed. 49.95 (*0-442-00971-2*) Van Nos Reinhold.

Computer in Measurement & Evaluation in Physical Education & Sport. Charles F. Cicciarella. 74p. (Orig.). 1987. pap. text ed. 7.95 (*0-926152-55-6*) Persimmon Soft.

Computer in Obstetrics & Gynaecology. Ed. by K. J. Dalton & R. D. Fawdry. 244p. 1987. pap. 60.00 (*1-85221-010-9*, IRL Pr) OUP.

Computer in Reading & Language Arts. Ed. by Jay Blanchard et al. LC 87-8704. (Computers in the Schools Ser.: Vol. 4, No. 1). 132p. 1987. text ed. 39.95 (*0-86656-667-8*) Haworth Pr.

Computer in Small Business: Friend or Foe? Benedict Kruse. LC 90-81914. (Illus.). 160p. (Orig.). 1990. pap. 18.95 (*0-89600-015-X*) IE Pasadena.

Computer in the Classroom. 2nd ed. Edward Vockell & Eileen Schwartz. 1992. pap. text ed. write for info. (*0-07-067535-X*) McGraw.

Computer in the English Curriculum. Edward Vockell & Eileen Schwartz. (Computer in the Curriculum Ser.). 160p. (C). 1989. pap. text ed. write for info. (*0-07-557917-0*) McGraw.

Computer in the Foreign Language Curriculum. Edward Vockell & Paul LaRear. 160p. (C). 1988. text ed. 12.95 (*0-394-39417-8*) Knopf.

Computer in the Home: Its Challenge to Education. Ed. by Bernard Levrat & E. D. Tagg. 152p. 1987. 38.50 (*0-444-70213-X*, North Holland) Elsevier.

Computer in the Library & Media Sciences. Edward Vockell & John Billard. 1991. pap. text ed. write for info. (*0-07-067534-1*) McGraw.

Computer in the Mathematic Curriculum. Edward Vockell et al. (Computer in the Classroom Ser.). 160p. (C). 1988. text ed. 12.95 (*0-394-39419-4*) Knopf.

Computer in the Reading Curriculum. Edward Vockell & Eileen Schwartz. Ed. by Barbara Whitaker. (Computer in the Classroom Ser.). 160p. (C). 1988. text ed. write for info. (*0-394-39415-1*) Knopf.

Computer in the Reading Curriculum. Edward Vockell et al. 1990. pap. text ed. write for info. (*0-07-557916-2*) McGraw.

Computer in the School: Tutor, Tutee, Tool. Ed. by Robert Taylor. LC 80-36803. 280p. (Orig.). 1980. pap. text ed. 18.95 (*0-8077-2611-7*) Tchrs Coll.

Computer in the Science Curriculum. Edward Vockell et al. 1991. pap. text ed. write for info. (*0-07-067533-3*) McGraw.

Computer in the United States: From Laboratory to Market, 1930 to 1960. James W. Cortada. LC 93-4184. (Illus.). 208p. 1993. text ed. 46.95 (*1-56324-234-6*); pap. text ed. 20.95 (*1-56324-235-4*) M E Sharpe.

Computer in Training & Development. David Drumm. LC 84-6707. (Illus.). 155p. 1985. pap. 15.00 (*0-934634-77-7*) Intl Human Res.

Computer Industry: Profiles & Outlooks. 1986. lib. bdg. 200.00 (*0-8490-3756-5*) Gordon Pr.

Computer Industry Advertising & Marketing Forecast, 1989-90. Ed. by Daniel McCarthy. 135p. 1989. ring bd. 1,095.00 (*0-88709-019-2*) Simba Info Inc.

Computer Industry Advertising & Marketing Forecast, 1990-91. Daniel McCarthy. 194p. 1990. ring bd. 1,395.00 (*0-88709-023-0*) Simba Info Inc.

Computer Industry Advertising & Marketing Forecast, 1991-92. Daniel McCarthy. 206p. 1991. ring bd. 1,495.00 (*0-88709-051-6*) Simba Info Inc.

Computer Industry Advertising & Marketing Forecast, 1992-93. Daniel McCarthy. 250p. ring bd. 295.00 (*0-88709-053-2*) Simba Info Inc.

Computer Industry Almanac. Egil Juliussen et al. 780p. 1987. 49.95 (*0-942107-00-4*); pap. 29.95 (*0-942107-01-2*) Computer Indus Al.

Computer Industry Almanac, 1992. Egil Juliussen & Karen Juliussen. 816p. 1992. pap. 45.00 (*0-942107-02-0*) Computer Indus Al.

Computer Industry Almanac, 1993. 6th ed. Karen Juliussen & Egil Juliussen. (Illus.). 816p. 1993. 55.00 (*0-942107-04-7*); pap. 45.00 (*0-942107-03-9*) Computer Indus Al.

Computer Industry Almanac, 1994. Egil Juliussen. 1994. 59.95 (*0-942107-06-3*); pap. 50.00 (*0-942107-05-5*) Computer Indus Al.

***Computer Industry Almanac, 1994-95.** annuals 7th ed. Eqil Juliussen & Karen Petska-Juliussen. Date not set. cd-rom 60.00 (*0-942107-09-8*) Peer-to-Peer Communications.

***Computer Industry Almanac, 1995-96.** 8th ed. 1995. pap. text ed. 63.00 (*0-942107-07-1*) Computer Indus Al.

***Computer Industry Almanac, 1995-96.** 8th ed. 1995. text ed. 63.00 (*0-942107-08-X*) Computer Indus Al.

***Computer Industry Almanac, 1995-96.** 8th ed. 1995. cd-rom 63.00 (*0-942107-10-1*) Computer Indus Al.

Computer Industry Directory. Ed. by Kenneth R. Churilla. 392p. (Orig.). 1991. pap. 49.95 (*0-9629446-0-2*) Mentor Market.

Computer Information Systems. Jerome S. Burstein & Edward G. Martin. (Illus.). 672p. (C). 1989. text ed. 43.00 (*0-03-026672-6*) Dryden Pr.

Computer Information Systems. Steven C. Lawlor. 316p. (C). 1990. pap. text ed. 37.25 (*0-15-512653-9*) HB Coll Pubs.

Computer Information Systems. 2nd ed. Steven C. Lawlor. 500p. (C). 1992. pap. text ed. 37.25 (*0-15-512679-2*) Dryden Pr.

Computer Information Systems. 3rd ed. Steven C. Lawlor. LC 93-72826. 508p. (C). 1993. pap. text ed. 37.75 (*0-03-098191-3*) Dryden Pr.

***Computer Information Systems.** 3rd ed. Steven C. Lawlor. LC 93-72826. (C). 1994. disk 21.50 (*0-03-098197-2*); disk 21.50 (*0-03-098199-9*) Dryden Pr.

Computer Information Systems: Study Guide to Accompany Lawlor. 3rd ed. Kirk P. Arnett & Ronald L. Weir. 287p. (C). 1994. pap. text ed. 20.50 (*0-03-098193-X*) Dryden Pr.

Computer Information Systems for Business. V. Thomas Dock. 614p. (C). 1988. text ed. 56.50 (*0-314-93173-2*) West Pub.

Computer Information Systems with BASIC. Jerome S. Burstein & Edward G. Martin. (Illus.). 752p. (C). 1989. text ed. 45.25 (*0-03-029379-0*) Dryden Pr.

Computer Information Systems 102 Course Supplement. Henry Ford Community College, Department of Computer Science Staff. (C). 1993. student ed 10.00 (*1-881592-48-0*) Hayden-McNeil.

Computer Insectiary: A Field Guide to Viruses, Bugs, Worms, Trojan Horses, & Other Stuff That Will Eat Your Programs & Rot Your Brain. Roger Ebert & John Kratz. LC 93-46524. 1994. pap. 6.95 (*0-8362-8049-0*) Andrews & McMeel.

Computer Inside You. 2nd ed. Kurt Johmann. LC 93-61833. 136p. 1994. pap. 12.95 (*0-9637227-2-7*) Vantex Pub.

Computer-Integrated Agriculture. Ed. by Donald A. Holt. 200p. (Orig.). (C). 1989. pap. text ed. 25.00 (*0-944919-03-0*) Agri Research Inst.

Computer Integrated Construction: Proceedings of the Second IB W78 & W74 Joint Seminar, Tokyo, Japan, 17-19 September, 1990. Ed. by Harry Wagter. LC 92-11730. 1992. write for info. (*0-444-89262-1*) Elsevier.

Computer Integrated Design & Manufacturing. David D. Bedworth et al. 672p. 1991. text ed. write for info. (*0-07-004204-7*) McGraw.

Computer Integrated Experimentation. E. B. Magrab. (Environmental & Energetics Ser.). (Illus.). 272p. 1991. 65.00 (*0-387-53291-9*) Spr-Verlag.

Computer Integrated Instruction Inservice Notebook: Elementary School. Dave Moursund. 222p. 1989. teacher ed, disk 40.00 (*0-924667-57-5*) Intl Society Tech Educ.

Computer Integrated Instruction Inservice Notebook: Secondary School Mathematics. David Moursund. 300p. 1988. teacher ed 40.00 (*0-924667-51-6*) Intl Society Tech Educ.

Computer Integrated Instruction Inservice Notebook: Secondary School Science. Dave Moursund. 290p. 1989. teacher ed, disk 40.00 (*0-924667-67-2*) Intl Society Tech Educ.

Computer Integrated Instruction Inservice Notebook: Secondary School Social Studies. Dave Moursund. 314p. 1989. teacher ed, disk 40.00 (*0-924667-68-0*) Intl Society Tech Educ.

Computer Integrated Manufacturing. Ed. by M. R. Martinez & M. C. Lev. (PED Ser.: Vol. 8). 148p. 1983. pap. text ed. 30.00 (*0-317-02557-0*, H00288) ASME.

Computer Integrated Manufacturing. Richard K. Miller & Terri C. Walker. LC 88-72187. (Survey on Technology & Markets Ser.: No. 34). 50p. 1989. pap. text ed. 200.00 (*1-55865-099-7*) Future Tech Surveys.

Computer Integrated Manufacturing. Ed. by K. Rathmill & P. A. Macconaill. (Illus.). 280p. 1988. 123.00 (*0-387-18758-8*) Spr-Verlag.

Computer Integrated Manufacturing. Roweena Rees & Mike Ward. (Andersen Consulting Management Guides Ser.: No. 1). (Illus.). 176p. 1991. pap. write for info. (*0-434-91754-0*) Buttrwrth-Heinemann.

Computer Integrated Manufacturing. James A. Rehg. 460p. 1994. text ed. 52.00 (*0-13-463886-7*) P-H.

Computer Integrated Manufacturing. Ed. by I. B. Turksen. (NATO Asi Series F: Vol. 49). 580p. 1988. 119.00 (*0-387-50220-3*) Spr-Verlag.

Computer Integrated Manufacturing. Joseph Harrington, Jr. LC 78-31268. 336p. 1979. reprint ed. lib. bdg. 28.50 (*0-88275-856-X*) Krieger.

Computer Integrated Manufacturing: A Competitive Strategy. 2nd ed. Alan Weatherall. (Illus.). 323p. 1992. text ed. 49.95 (*0-7506-0811-0*) Buttrwrth-Heinemann.

An Asterisk (*) at the beginning of an entry indicates that the title is appearing in BIP for the first time.

An Asterisk (*) at the beginning of an entry indicates that the title is appearing in BIP for the first time.

***Computer Methods & Advances in Geomechanics: Proceedings of the Eighth International Conference, Morgantown, West Virginia, May 1994, 4 vols.** H. J. Siriwardane & M. M. Zaman. (Illus.). 3200p. (C). 1994. text ed. 450.00 (*90-5410-380-9*, Pub. by A A Balkema NE) Ashgate Pub Co.

Computer Methods & Advances in Geomechanics: Proceedings of the Seventh International Conference, Cairns, 6-10 May 1991, 3 vols., Set. Ed. by G. Beer et al. 2000p. (C). 1991. text ed. 300.00 (*90-6191-189-3*, Pub. by A A Balkema NE) Ashgate Pub Co.

Computer Methods & Borel Summability Applied to Feigenbaum's Equation. J. P. Eckmann & P. Wittwer. (Lecture Notes in Physics Ser.: Vol. 227). xiv, 297p. 1985. pap. 29.00 (*0-387-15215-6*) Spr-Verlag.

Computer Methods & Experimental Measurements for Surface Treatment Effects. Ed. by M. H. Aliabadi & C. A. Brebbia. LC 92-75799. (Surface Treatment Ser.: Vol. 1). 400p. 1993. 145.00 (*1-56252-150-0*) Computational Mech MA.

Computer Methods & Experimental Measurements for Surface Treatment Effects II: Proceedings of the Second International Conference. Ed. by M. H. Aliabadi et al. (Surface Treatment Ser.: Vol. 2). 400p. 1995. 150.00 (*1-56252-242-6*) Computational Mech MA.

***Computer Methods & Inverse Problems in Nondestructive Testing.** (Illus.). 600p. 1995. text ed. 148.00 (*1-56252-340-6*) Computational Mech MA.

Computer Methods & Water Resources, Vol. 1: Groundwater & Aquifer Modelling. Ed. by D. Ouazar & C. A. Brebbia. LC 87-73387. 210p. 1988. 51.00 (*0-931215-89-7*) Computational Mech MA.

Computer Methods & Water Resources, Vol. 2: Computational Hydraulics. Ed. by D. Ouazar et al. LC 87-73387. 500p. 1988. 108.00 (*0-931215-90-0*) Computational Mech MA.

Computer Methods & Water Resources, Vol. 3: Computational Hydrology. Ed. by D. Ouazar et al. LC 87-73387. 300p. 1988. 71.50 (*0-931215-91-9*) Computational Mech MA.

Computer Methods & Water Resources, Vol. 4: Computer Aided Engineering in Water Resources. Ed. by D. Ouazar & C. A. Brebbia. LC 87-73387. 500p. 1988. 108.00 (*0-931215-92-7*) Computational Mech MA.

Computer Methods & Water Resources, Vol. 5: Computational Transport Phenomena. Ed. by D. Ouazar & C. A. Brebbia. LC 87-73387. 250p. 1988. 60.00 (*0-931215-93-5*) Computational Mech MA.

Computer Methods & Water Resources, Vol. 6: Water Quality, Planning Management. Ed. by D. Ouazar et al. LC 87-73387. 300p. 1988. 71.50 (*0-931215-94-3*) Computational Mech MA.

Computer Methods for Circuit Analysis & Design. Jiri Vlach & Kishore Singhal. (Illus.). 624p. 1983. text ed. 79.95 (*0-442-28108-0*) Van Nos Reinhold.

Computer Methods for Circuit Analysis & Design. 2nd ed. Jiri Vlach & Kishore Singhal. LC 92-35817. 1993. text ed. 69.95 (*0-442-01194-6*) Van Nos Reinhold.

Computer Methods for Nonlinear Solids & Structural Mechanics. Applied Mechanics, Bioengineering & Fluids Engineering Conference Staff. Ed. by Satya N. Atluri & Nicholas Perrone. LC 83-71307. (AMD Ser.: Vol. 54). (Illus.). 269p. reprint ed. pap. 77.00 (*0-8357-6068-5*, 2056812) Bks Demand.

Computer Methods for Ship Surface Design. Chengi Kuo. LC 73-584131. (Illus.). 234p. reprint ed. pap. 66.70 (*0-317-08222-1*, 2010061) Bks Demand.

Computer Methods for the Eighties, in the Mineral Industry. Ed. by Alfred Weiss. LC 79-52274. (Illus.). 975p. 1979. text ed. 55.00 (*0-89520-257-3*) SMM&E Inc.

***Computer Methods for the 80's in the Mineral Industry.** fac. ed. Ed. by Alfred Weiss. LC 79-52274. (Illus.). 1001p. 1979. reprint ed. pap. 180.00 (*0-7837-7852-X*, 2047611) Bks Demand.

Computer Methods in Environmental & Water Resources Engineering. T. V. Hronmadka et al. (Illus.). 458p. 1992. 49.95 (*0-914055-11-9*) Lighthouse Pubns.

Computer Methods in Geology. T. V. Loudon. 1979. text ed. 131.00 (*0-12-456950-1*) Acad Pr.

Computer Methods in Marine & Offshore Engineering. Ed. by T. K. Murthy. LC 90-85217. (CADMO Ser.: Vol. 3). 432p. 1991. 169.00 (*1-56252-054-7*) Computational Mech MA.

Computer Methods in Preliminary Ship Design. L. K. Kupras. 229p. (Orig.). 1982. pap. text ed. 36.50 (*90-6275-106-7*, Pub. by Delft U Pr NE) Coronet Bks.

Computer Methods in Structural Analysis. J. L. Meek. (Illus.). 512p. 1991. write for info. (*0-419-15440-X*, E & FN Spon) Routledge Chapman & Hall.

Computer Methods in Tolerance Design. R. Wilhelm & S. C. Lu. 160p. 1992. text ed. 48.00 (*981-02-1058-2*) World Scientific Pub.

Computer Methods in Urban Watershed Hydraulics. T. V. Hromadka, II et al. Ed. by Laura Hromadka. LC 83-82787. (Illus.). 296p. (Orig.). (C). 1984. pap. text ed. 38.50 (*0-914055-02-X*) Lighthouse Pubns.

Computer Methods in Water Resources. T. V. Hromadka, II et al. Ed. by Laura Hromadka. LC 83-82824. (Illus.). 318p. (Orig.). (C). 1984. pap. text ed. 37.50 (*0-914055-01-1*) Lighthouse Pubns.

Computer Methods in Water Resources II, Vol. 3: Computer Aided Engineering in Water Resources. Ed. by C. A. Brebbia et al. LC 90-85862. 347p. 1991. 89.00 (*1-56252-061-X*) Computational Mech MA.

***Computer Methods in Water Resources III.** 250p. Date not set. text ed. 125.00 (*1-56252-342-2*) Computational Mech MA.

Computer Methods in Water Resources, No. Two: Proceedings of the 2nd International Conference on Computer Methods & Water Resources, 3 vols. Ed. by D. Ben-Sari et al. 390p. 1991. Vol. 1: Ground Water Modelling & Pressure Flow, 390p. 132.00 (*0-387-53645-0*); Vol. 2: Computational Hydraulics & Hydrology, 590p. 198.00 (*0-387-53647-7*); Vol. 3: Computer Aided Engineering in Water Resources, 350p. 119.00 (*0-387-53646-9*) Spr-Verlag.

Computer Methods in Water Resources, No. Two: Proceedings of the 2nd International Conference on Computer Methods & Water Resources, 3 vols., Set. Ed. by D. Ben-Sari et al. 1991. 398.00 (*0-685-48734-2*) Spr-Verlag.

Computer MIDI Desktop Publishing Dictionary. Albert De Vito. LC 91-72194. (Illus.). viii, 228p. 1991. 17.95 (*0-934286-67-1*) Kenyon.

Computer Model of a Growth Company. Claude Burrill & Leon Quinto. LC 79-162628. (Illus.). x, 224p. 1972. text ed. 124.00 (*0-677-00410-9*) Gordon & Breach.

Computer Model of Transformational Grammar. Joyce Friedman et al. LC 71-127770. (Mathematical Linguistics & Automatic Language Processing Ser.: No. 9). 176p. reprint ed. pap. 50.20 (*0-685-15438-6*, 2026266) Bks Demand.

Computer Modeling for Design Using Silverscreen. Bolluyt et al. 1993. pap. 74.95 (*0-534-92872-2*) PWS Pubs.

Computer Modeling for Extrusion & Other Continuous Polymer Processes. Keith T. O'Brien. 552p. (C). 1992. text ed. 125.00 (*1-56990-068-X*) Hanser-Gardner.

Computer Modeling in Agriculture. N. R. Brockington. (Illus.). 1979. 45.00 (*0-19-854523-1*) OUP.

Computer Modeling in Corrosion. Ed. by Raymond S. Munn. LC 92-12525. (Special Technical Publication Ser.: Vol. 1154). (Illus.). 300p. 1992. 86.00 (*0-8031-1473-7*, 04-011540-27) ASTM.

Computer Modeling of Carbohydrate Molecules. Ed. by Alfred D. French & John W. Brady. LC 90-37664. (ACS Symposium Ser.: No. 430). (Illus.). 410p. 1990. 84.95 (*0-8412-1805-6*) Am Chemical.

Computer Modeling of Chemical Reactions in Enzymes & Solutions. Arieh Warshel. 248p. 1991. text ed. 108.00 (*0-471-53395-5*) Wiley.

Computer Modeling of Complex Biological Systems. Ed. by S. Sitharama Iyengar. 152p. 1984. 144.00 (*0-8493-5208-8*, QH323) CRC Pr.

Computer Modeling of Complex Biological Systems. 2nd ed. Ed. by S. Sitharama Ivengar. 1995. write for info. (*0-8493-7962-8*) CRC Pr.

Computer Modeling of Electrical Power Systems. J. Arrillaga et al. LC 82-2664. 423p. 1983. text ed. 350.00 (*0-471-10406-X*, Wiley-Interscience) Wiley.

Computer Modeling of Free-Surface & Pressurized Flows: Proceedings of NATO Advanced Study Institute. Ed. by M. Hanif Chaudhry & Larry W. Mays. LC 94-21770. (NATO ASI Ser. E, Applied Sciences: Vol. 274). 1994. lib. bdg. 292.00 (*0-7923-2946-5*) Kluwer Ac.

Computer Modeling of Geologic Surfaces & Volumes. Ed. by David E. Hamilton & Thomas A. Jones. (Computer Applications in Geology Ser.: No. 1). (Illus.). x, 297p. 1992. 66.00 (*0-89181-700-X*) AAPG.

Computer Modeling of Mathematical Reasoning. Alan Bundy. 1984. pap. text ed. 49.00 (*0-12-141252-0*) Acad Pr.

Computer Modeling of Matter. Ed. by Peter Lykos. LC 78-25828. (ACS Symposium Ser.: No. 86). 1978. 32.95 (*0-8412-0463-2*) Am Chemical.

Computer Modeling of Microstrip Interconnects in Millimeter Waves. Linda P. Katehi. (University of Michigan Report Ser.: No. 024601-2-T). 129p. reprint ed. pap. 36.80 (*0-8357-2934-6*, 2039176) Bks Demand.

Computer Modeling of Phase Diagrams: Proceedings of a Symposium Held at the Fall Meeting of the Metallurgical Society in Toronto, Canada, October 13-17, 1985. Metallurgical Society of AIME Staff. Ed. by L. H. Bennett. LC 86-19174. 427p. reprint ed. pap. 121.70 (*0-8357-2599-5*, 2052379) Bks Demand.

Computer Modeling of Sheet Metal Forming Process: Theory, Verification, & Application, Proceedings of Symposium Sponsored by the Metallurgical Society & the TMS Detroit Section, Held at 12th Automotive Materials Symposium at Ann Arbor, Michigan, April 29-30, 1985. Metallurgical Society of AIME Staff. Ed. by N. M. Wang & S. C. Tang. LC 85-26015. 302p. reprint ed. pap. 86.10 (*0-7837-1442-4*, 2052416) Bks Demand.

Computer Modelling & Expert Systems in Marketing. Luiz Moutinho et al. LC 94-7100. 224p. 1994. 65.00x (*0-415-08983-2*, B4539) Routledge.

Computer Modelling for Discrete Simulation. Ed. by Michael Pidd. 274p. 1989. text ed. 94.95 (*0-471-92282-X*) Wiley.

Computer Modelling in Electrostatics. D. McAllister et al. LC 85-14479. (Electrostatics & Electrostatic Applications Ser.). 130p. 1985. text ed. 125.00 (*0-471-90882-7*) Wiley.

Computer Modelling in Ocean Engineering: Problems & Solutions in Coastal & Offshore Systems: Proceedings of the International Conference, Venice, 19-21 September, 1988. Ed. by B. A. Schrefler & O. C. Zienkiewics. 750p. (C). 1988. text ed. 120.00 (*90-6191-836-7*, Pub. by A A Balkema NE) Ashgate Pub Co.

Computer Modelling in Ocean Engineering 91: Proceedings of the Second International Conference, Barcelona, 30 September-4 October 1991. Ed. by A. S. Arcilla et al. (Illus.). 580p. (C). 1991. text ed. 105.00 (*90-5410-024-9*, Pub. by A A Balkema NE) Ashgate Pub Co.

Computer Modelling in the Environmental Sciences. Ed. by D. G. Farmer & M. J. Rycroft. (Institute of Mathematics & Its Applications Conference Series, New Ser.: New Series 28). (Illus.). 400p. 1991. 95.00 (*0-19-853394-2*) OUP.

Computer Modelling of Biomolecular Processes. J. M. Goodfellow & D. S. Moss. 240p. 1991. write for info. (*0-13-161944-6*) P-H.

Computer Modelling of Combustion Processes. Weicheng Fan. (International Academic Publishers Ser.). 170p. 1992. 91.00 (*0-08-037203-1*, Pergamon Pr) Elsevier.

Computer Modelling of Fluids Polymers & Solids: Proceedings of the NATO Advanced Study Institute Held in Bath, United Kingdom, September 4-17, 1988. Ed. by C. R. Catlow et al. (C). 1989. lib. bdg. 186.50 (*0-7923-0549-3*) Kluwer Ac.

Computer Modelling of New Materials: A Special Issue of the Journal Molecular Simulation. Ed. by M. Allen. 208p. 1989. pap. text ed. 217.00 (*2-88124-728-8*) Gordon & Breach.

Computer Modelling of Seas & Coastal Regions: Proceedings of the International Conference on Computer Modelling of Seas & Coastal Regions Held in Southampton, UK, April 1992. Ed. by P. W. Partridge. LC 91-77632. 534p. 1992. 204.00 (*1-56252-092-X*) Computational Mech MA.

Computer Models: Statistical Methods: Games & Songs, Incl. manipulatives. Turkan Kumbaraci & George H. Gardenier. LC 89-90944. (Gardenier Math-Stat Ser.). (Illus.). 19p. (J). (gr. 1-8). 1989. 20.00 (*0-685-29040-9*, 0004) Teka Trends.

Computer Models & Technology in Media Research. Ed. by R. A. Zwaan & D. Meutsch. Orig. Title: Poetics, Special Issue, Vol. 19, Nos. 1-2. 228p. 1990. reprint ed. 89.75 (*0-444-88204-9*, North Holland) Elsevier.

Computer Models for Management Science. 2nd ed. Warren J. Erikson & Owen P. Hall, Jr. LC 85-9154. (Illus.). 288p. (C). 1985. pap. text ed. write for info. (*0-201-10979-4*) Addison-Wesley.

Computer Models for Management Science, 2 disks, Set. 2nd ed. Warren J. Erikson & Owen P. Hall, Jr. LC 85-9154. (Illus.). 288p. (C). 1985. student ed, disk write for info. (*0-201-10980-8*) Addison-Wesley.

Computer Models for Operations Management. P. Owen Hall & John G. Carlson. (Illus.). (C). 1989. pap. text ed. 47.50 (*0-201-17050-7*) Addison-Wesley.

Computer Models for Operations Management. 2nd ed. James A. Freeman. (Illus.). 352p. (C). 1993. Incl. 5.25" diskette, Ver. 2.0. text ed. 37.75 (*0-201-56639-7*); Incl. 3.5" diskette, Ver. 3.5. text ed. 37.75 (*0-201-53406-1*) Addison-Wesley.

Computer Models for Production & Inventory Control. Bekiroglu. 148p. 1984. 36.00 (*0-685-66799-5*, SS12-2) Soc Computer Sim.

Computer Models in Environmental Planning. Steven I. Gordon. (Illus.). 240p. 1985. text ed. 54.95 (*0-442-22974-7*) Chapman & Hall.

Computer Models in Finance. Lawrence E. McLean. (Illus.). 176p. (Orig.). (C). 1993. pap. write for info. (*0-02-379391-0*) Macmillan.

Computer Models in Operations Management: A Computer-Augmented System. 2nd ed. Roy D. Harris & Michael J. Maggard. (C). 1977. 30.00 (*0-06-042665-9*) HarpCollege.

Computer Models of American Speech. M. Margaret Withgott & Francine R. Chen. (Center for the Study of Language & Information-Lecture Notes Ser.: No. 32). 116p. 1992. 39.95 (*0-937073-97-0*); pap. 15.95 (*0-937073-98-9*) U Ch Pr.

Computer Models of Mind: Computational Approaches in Theoretical Psychology. Margaret A. Boden. (Problems in the Behavioral Sciences Ser.: 6). (Illus.). 310p. 1988. pap. 21.95 (*0-521-27033-2*) Cambridge U Pr.

Computer Models of Speech Using Fuzzy Algorithms. Renato De Mori. LC 83-11082. (Advanced Applications in Pattern Recognition Ser.). 508p. 1983. 115.00 (*0-306-41381-7*, Plenum Pr) Plenum.

Computer Modern Typefaces, Vol. E. Donald E. Knuth. LC 86-1235. 608p. (C). 1986. text ed. 46.25 (*0-201-13446-2*) Addison-Wesley.

Computer Munched My Homework. Dianne Woo. 128p. (Orig.). (YA). 1992. mass mkt. 3.99 (*0-8125-2050-5*) Tor Bks.

***Computer Museum Guide to the Best Software for Kids.** Cathy Miranker & Alison Elliot. 1995. pap. 15.00 (*0-06-273376-1*) HarpC.

Computer Music. Charles Dodge & Thomas A. Jerse. 384p. 1985. 42.00 (*0-02-873100-X*) Schirmer Bks.

Computer Music in C. Phil Winsor. 1990. pap. 24.95 (*0-8306-3637-4*, Windcrest) TAB Bks.

Computer Music in C (3.5) Phil Winsor & G. Delisa. 1991. 24.95 (*0-8306-6756-3*) TAB Bks.

Computer Music in C (5.25) Phil Winsor & G. Delisa. 1991. 24.95 (*0-8306-6755-5*) TAB Bks.

Computer Music Tutorial. Curtis Roads et al. LC 94-19027. 1995. 60.00x (*0-262-18158-4*); pap. 39.95x (*0-262-68082-3*) MIT Pr.

Computer Musicians Source Book, Vol. 1. Ronald A. Wallace. (Illus.). (C). 1987. ring bd. 75.00 (*0-945505-00-0*) Creative IL.

Computer Network & Simulations. S. Schoemaker. 256p. 1978. 64.00 (*0-444-85208-5*, North Holland) Elsevier.

Computer Network Architectures. Anton Meijer & Paul Peeters. 350p. (C). 1982. pap. text ed. 225.00 (*0-273-02845-6*, Pub. by Pitman Pubng UK) St Mut.

Computer Network Architectures. Anton Meijer & Paul Peeters. LC 82-22165. (Electrical Engineering, Telecommunications, & Signal Processing Ser.). 396p. (C). 1995. text ed. write for info. (*0-7167-8075-5*, Computer Sci Pr) W H Freeman.

Computer Network Architectures & Protocols. 2nd ed. Ed. by C. A. Sunshine. (Applications of Communications Theory Ser.). (Illus.). 558p. 1989. 85.00 (*0-306-43189-0*, Plenum Pr) Plenum.

Computer Network Experiments in Teaching Law. Russell Burris. 65p. 1980. 10.00 (*0-318-14010-1*) EDUCOM.

Computer Network Performance Symposium. LC 53-6820. (Performance Evaluation Review Ser.: Vol. 11, No. 1). (Illus.). 184p. 1982. pap. text ed. 23.00 (*0-89791-069-9*) Assn Compu Machinery.

Computer Network Standards Map & Top. Adriano Valenzano. (C). 1991. text ed. 46.25 (*0-201-41665-4*) Addison-Wesley.

Computer Network Usage: Recent Experiences. Ed. by L. Csaba et al. 832p. 1986. 169.25 (*0-444-87982-X*, North Holland) Elsevier.

Computer Networking: Proceedings of the IFIP TC6 Conference (COMNET '90), Budapest, Hungary, 8-10 May, 1990. Ed. by L. Csaba et al. 508p. 1990. 113.00 (*0-444-88872-1*, North Holland) Elsevier.

Computer Networking & Performance Evaluation. Ed. by T. Hasegawa et al. 514p. 1986. 92.50 (*0-444-87960-9*, North Holland) Elsevier.

***Computer Networking & Scholarly Communication in Twenty-First-Century.** Ed. by Teresa M. Harrison & Timothy D. Stephen. (SUNY Series in Computer-Mediated Communication). 368p. (C). 1996. text ed. 59.50x (*0-7914-2853-2*); pap. text ed. 19.95x (*0-7914-2854-0*) State U NY Pr.

Computer Networking Conference, Vol. 5. 1986. pap. 6.00 (*0-87259-033-X*) Am Radio.

Computer Networking Conferences, Vol. 1-4. 1986. pap. 6.00 (*0-87259-022-4*) Am Radio.

Computer Networking for Educators. Ted D. McCain & Mark Ekelund. (Illus.). 244p. 1993. pap. text ed. 28.95 (*1-56484-039-5*) Intl Society Tech Educ.

Computer Networking for System Programmers. Gerald D. Cole. (Data Communications & Networking for Computers Ser.). 242p. 1990. pap. text ed. 42.95 (*0-471-51057-2*) Wiley.

Computer Networking in the University: Success & Potential: Proceedings. 332p. 12.00 (*0-318-14012-8*) EDUCOM.

Computer Networks. 2nd ed. Uyless D. Black. 450p. 1993. text ed. 56.00 (*0-13-175605-2*) P-H.

Computer Networks. 2nd ed. Andrew S. Tanenbaum. 628p. (C). 1988. text ed. 86.00 (*0-13-162959-X*) P-H.

Computer Networks & Computer Systems: Queueing Theory & Performance Evaluation. T. G. Robertazzi. Ed. by M. Gerla et al. (Telecommunications Networks & Computer Systems Ser.). (Illus.). 328p. 1990. text ed. 49.50 (*0-387-97393-1*) Spr-Verlag.

Computer Networks & Simulation II. Ed. by S. Schoemaker. 326p. 1982. 72.00 (*0-444-86438-5*, North Holland) Elsevier.

Computer Networks & Simulation III. Ed. by S. Schoemaker. 420p. 1986. 87.25 (*0-444-70053-6*, North Holland) Elsevier.

Computer Networks & Systems: Queuing Theory & Performance Evaluation. 2nd ed. Thomas G. Robertazzi. LC 93-36469. 1994. 54.00 (*0-387-94170-3*) Spr-Verlag.

Computer Networks, Architecture & Applications: Proceedings, India, October 1992. Ed. by S. V. Raghavan et al. LC 93-15617. (IFIP Transactions C: Communications Systems Ser.: Vol. C-13). x, 298p. 1993. pap. 100.00 (*0-444-89968-5*, North Holland) Elsevier.

Computer Networks Terminology. J. Maronski & M. Rupinska. 73p. 1980. pap. 7.50 (*83-01-01179-3*, M-9061) Fr & Eur.

Computer Notions. Lee D. Rossi et al. (Illus.). 176p. (C). 1985. pap. text ed. 15.50 (*0-13-163932-3*) P-H.

Computer Numerical Control. Herman W. Pollock & Terrance Robinson. 256p. 1990. text ed. 54.00 (*0-13-168378-0*) P-H.

Computer Numerical Control: Concepts & Programming. 3rd ed. Warren Seames. LC 94-10130. (Illus.). 528p. 1994. text ed. 38.95 (*0-8273-6498-9*) Delmar.

Computer Numerical Control: Essentials in Programming & Networking. Su-Chen J. Lin. 1994. text ed. 49.95 (*0-8273-4715-4*) Delmar.

Computer Numerical Control Accessory Devices. Michael Lynch. LC 93-8902. 1993. text ed. 53.00 (*0-07-039226-9*) McGraw.

Computer Numerical Control Advanced Techniques. Michael Lynch. 1992. text ed., disk 75.00 (*0-07-039224-2*) McGraw.

Computer Numerical Control (CNC) Machine. P. Radhakrishnan. (C). 1989. 75.00 (*0-89771-389-3*, Current Dist) St Mut.

Computer Numerical Control from Programming to Networking. S. C. Lin. 106p. 1994. teacher ed 12.00 (*0-8273-4716-2*) Delmar.

Computer Numerical Control of Machine Tools. 2nd ed. G. E. Thyer. LC 93-282. 1993. 32.95 (*0-8311-3048-2*) Indus Pr.

Computer Numerical Control Programming. Michael Sava & Joseph Pusztai. 320p. 1990. text ed. 49.00 (*0-13-156084-0*) P-H.

Computer Numerical Control Programming of Machines. Larry Horath. LC 92-29570. 288p. (C). 1993. write for info. (*0-02-357201-9*, Merrill Pub Co) Macmillan.

Computer Numerical Controls for Machining. Michael Lynch. 416p. 1992. text ed. 60.00 (*0-07-039223-4*) McGraw.

Computer Nut. Betsy C. Byars. (Novels Ser.). (Illus.). 144p. (J). (gr. 3-7). 1986. pap. 3.99 (*0-14-032086-5*, Puffin) Puffin Bks.

An Asterisk (*) at the beginning of an entry indicates that the title is appearing in BIP for the first time.

An Asterisk (*) at the beginning of an entry indicates that the title is appearing in BIP for the first time.

1503

***Computer Science: A Breadth-First Approach with C.** John Impagliazzo & Paul Nagin. LC 94-33250. 1995. pap. text ed. write for info. (*0-471-58552-1*) Wiley.

***Computer Science: A Breadth-First Approach with Pascal.** Paul Nagin & John Impagliazzo. 1995. pap. text ed. write for info. (*0-471-31198-7*) Wiley.

Computer Science: A Modern Introduction. 2nd ed. Goldschlager & Timothy R. Lister. (International Series in Computer Science). 323p. 1988. reprint ed. pap. text ed. 43.00 (*0-13-165945-6*) P-H.

Computer Science: An Overview. 4th ed. J. Glenn Brookshear. (C). 1994. pap. text ed. 39.75 (*0-8053-4627-9*) Benjamin-Cummings.

Computer Science: Japanese Research on ERATO, Parallel Processing, Fuzzy Theory & High Energy Physics. 79p. (Orig.). (C). 1993. pap. text ed. 40.00 (*1-56806-300-8*) Diane Pub.

Computer Science: Quality Management for IT Services. (IT Infrastructure Library Ser.). 200p. 1991. pap. 70.00 (*0-11-330555-9*, Pub. by HMSO UK) UNIPUB.

Computer Science: Research & Applications. Ed. by Ricardo A. Baeza-Yates & U. Manber. (Illus.). 432p. (C). 1992. 110.00 (*0-306-44223-X*, Plenum Pr) Plenum.

Computer Science: The Beginning. Barry Burd. (Illus.). 500p. (C). 1995. pap. text ed. write for info. (*0-201-60263-6*) Addison-Wesley.

Computer Science & Informatics in Medicine: Index of New Information with Authors & Subjects. rev. ed. Sam B. Goodrich. 180p. 1993. 44.50 (*1-55914-990-6*); pap. 39.50 (*1-55914-991-4*) ABBE Pubs Assn.

Computer Science & Multiple Valued Logic: Theory & Applications. rev. ed. Ed. by D. C. Rine. 642p. 1984. 100.00 (*0-444-86882-8*, North Holland) Elsevier.

Computer Science & Operations Research: New Developments in Their Interfaces. Ed. by Osman Balci et al. LC 92-10675. 1992. 145.00 (*0-08-040806-0*, Pergamon Pr) Elsevier.

Computer Science & Statistics: Proceedings. Ed. by W. Eddy. (Illus.). 378p. 1981. pap. 65.00 (*0-387-90633-9*) Spr-Verlag.

Computer Science & Statistics: Proceedings of the Seventeenth Symposium on the Interface, Lexington, KY, March 1985. Ed. by D. M. Allen. 350p. 1986. pap. 75.00 (*0-444-70018-8*) Elsevier.

Computer Science & Statistics: Proceedings of the Symposium on the Interface, 16th, Atlanta, Georgia, March 1984. Ed. by E. Billard. 296p. 1985. pap. 75.00 (*0-444-87725-8*, North Holland) Elsevier.

Computer Science & Statistics: Proceedings of the 14th Symposium on the Interface. Ed. by K. W. Heiner et al. (Illus.). 313p. 1983. pap. 58.00 (*0-387-90835-8*) Spr-Verlag.

Computer Science & Technologies. T. Kitagawa. (Japan Annual Reviews in Electronic Computers & Telecommunications Ser.: Vol. 18). 1988. 141.00 (*0-444-70169-9*) Elsevier.

Computer Science & Technologies 1982 see Japan Annual Reviews in Electronics, Computers & Telecommunications, 1982

Computer Science & Technologies, 1984. Ed. by T. Kitagawa. (Japan Annual Reviews in Electronics, Computers & Telecommunications Ser.: Vol. 12). 360p. 1984. 136.00 (*0-444-87547-6*, North Holland) Elsevier.

Computer Science Education: Proceedings of the Twentieth SIGCSE Technical Symposium on Computer Science Education. Ed. by Robert A. Barrett & Maynard J. Mansfield. (SIGCSE Bulletin Ser.: Vol. 21, No. 1). (Illus.). 350p. 1989. pap. text ed. 25.00 (*0-685-28134-5*, 457890) Assn Compu Machinery.

Computer Science in Asia. (Illus.). 47p. (Orig.). (C). 1993. pap. text ed. 35.00 (*1-56806-795-X*) Diane Pub.

Computer Science in Health Sciences: Index of Information with Authors, Subjects & References. Anna R. Goodrich. 150p. 1994. 49.50 (*1-55914-524-2*); pap. 39.50 (*1-55914-525-0*) ABBE Pubs Assn.

Computer Science in Social & Behavioral Science Education. Ed. by Daniel E. Bailey. LC 77-25087. (Illus.). 520p. 1978. 39.95 (*0-87778-101-X*) Educ Tech Pubns.

Computer Science Logic: Fifth Workshop, CSL '91, Berne, Switzerland, October 1991: Proceedings. Ed. by E. Borger et al. LC 92-23683. (Lecture Notes in Computer Science Ser.: Vol. 626). viii, 428p. 1992. pap. 63.00 (*0-387-55789-X*) Spr-Verlag.

Computer Science Logic: Fourth Workshop, CSL '90 Heidelberg, Germany, October 1-5, 1990 Proceedings. Ed. by E. Borger et al. (Lecture Notes in Computer Science Ser.: Vol. 533). viii, 399p. 1991. pap. 41.00 (*0-387-54487-9*) Spr-Verlag.

Computer Science Logic: Selected Papers of the 6th Workshop, CSL 92, San Miniato, Italy, September 28-October 2, 1992. Ed. by E. Borger et al. (Lecture Notes in Computer Science Ser.: Vol. 702). viii, 439p. 1993. pap. 60.00 (*0-387-56992-8*) Spr-Verlag.

***Computer Science Logic: Seventh Workshop, CSL '93, Swansea, United Kingdom, September 13-17, 1993, Selected Papers.** Ed. by Egon Borger et al. LC 94-28234. (Lecture Notes in Computer Science Ser.: Vol. 832). 1994. 47.00 (*0-387-58277-0*) Spr-Verlag.

Computer Science LOGO Style: Introduction to Programming, Vol. 1 & 2. Brian Harvey. (Illus.). 260p. (Orig.). 1985. Vol. 2, Projects, Styles, & Techniques. pap. 21.95x (*0-262-58080-2*) MIT Pr.

Computer Science Mathematics. Donald D. Spencer. (Mathematics Ser.). 320p. (C). 1976. write for info. (*0-675-08650-7*, Merrill Pub Co) Macmillan.

Computer Science on Your HP-41, Using the Advantage Module. Edward M. Keefe. 192p. (Orig.). 1987. pap. 15.00 (*0-931011-10-8*) Grapevine Pubns.

Computer Science Problem Solver. rev. ed. Research & Education Association Staff. LC 81-50900. (Illus.). 864p. (Orig.). (C). 1994. pap. text ed. 29.95 (*0-87891-525-7*) Res & Educ.

Computer Science Reader. Ed. by E. A. Weiss. (Illus.). 447p. 1987. 50.00 (*0-387-96544-0*) Spr-Verlag.

Computer Science Research Activities in Asia. 54p. (Orig.). (C). 1993. pap. text ed. 60.00 (*0-7881-0011-4*) Diane Pub.

Computer Science Research Activities in Asia: AI & Expert Systems, Computer Architecture, Industrial Automation, Networking, Programming Languages, Parallel Processing & Supercomputing. David K. Kahaner. Ed. by Irene Barron. (Illus.). 98p. (Orig.). (C). 1994. pap. text ed. 45.00 (*0-7881-0459-4*) Diane Pub.

Computer Science Research Activities in Asia: Software Technology & Patents, CIM, Scientific Computation & Differential Equations, Computer & Mathematical Modelling & System Simulation. David K. Kahaner. Ed. by Irene Barron. (Illus.). 67p. (Orig.). (C). 1994. pap. text ed. 45.00 (*0-7881-0457-8*) Diane Pub.

Computer Science Resources: A Guide to Professional Literature. Darlene Myers. LC 81-559. 346p. 1981. pap. 59.50 (*0-313-25774-4*, Greenwood Pr) Greenwood.

Computer Science Source Book. (Science Reference Ser.). (Illus.). 368p. 1989. text ed. 49.50 (*0-07-045507-4*) McGraw.

Computer Science Technical Reports: Selected Holdings at Stanford University. LC 92-27736. 1160p. 1992. 198.00 (*0-8218-0009-4*) Am Math.

Computer Science with Mathematica: Theory & Practice for Science, Mathematics & Engineering. Roman E. Maeder. (Illus.). 384p. (C). 1995. text ed. write for info. (*0-201-56940-X*) Addison-Wesley.

***Computer Science 110.** USAF Academy Computer Science Staff. 556p. (C). 1994. ring bd. 25.25 (*0-7872-0429-3*) Kendall-Hunt.

Computer Science 2: Principles of Software Engineering, Data Types, & Algorithms. Henry M. Walker. (C). 1989. pap. text ed. 49.00 (*0-673-39829-3*) HarpCollege.

Computer Science 2: Research & Applications. Ed. by R. Baeza-Yates. (Illus.). 610p. (C). 1994. 135.00 (*0-306-44730-4*, Plenum Pr) Plenum.

Computer Sciences Education: (Proceedings of the) Twenty-First Technical Symposium on Computer Science Education, Held in Washington, DC, February 22-23, 1990. Ed. by Daniel T. Joyce. (SIGCSE Bulletin Ser.: Vol. 22, No. 1). (Illus.). xviii, 270p. 1990. pap. text ed. 28.00 (*0-89791-346-9*, 457900) Assn Compu Machinery.

Computer Security. Summers. 1995. text ed. 49.95 (*0-07-069419-2*) McGraw.

Computer Security. rev. ed. Time-Life Books Editors. (Understanding Computers Ser.). (Illus.). 128p. 1990. write for info. (*0-8094-7566-9*); lib. bdg. write for info. (*0-8094-7567-7*) Time-Life.

Computer Security. 2nd ed. John M. Carroll. (Illus.). 480p. 1987. text ed. 45.00 (*0-7506-9225-1*) Buttrwrth-Heinemann.

Computer Security: A Comprehensive Controls Checklist. Charles C. Wood et al. 214p. 1987. text ed. 74.95 (*0-471-84795-X*) Wiley.

Computer Security: A Global Challenge. Ed. by J. H. Finch & E. G. Dougall. 1985. 95.00 (*0-444-87618-9*, North Holland) Elsevier.

Computer Security: A Management Audit Approach. Norman L. Enger & Paul W. Howerton. LC 80-65874. 272p. reprint ed. pap. 77.60 (*0-317-27070-2*, 2023536) Bks Demand.

Computer Security: A Source Guide. 1991. lib. bdg. 75.00 (*0-8490-4881-8*) Gordon Pr.

Computer Security: An Integrated Approach. Stephen Marsh. 240p. (C). 1990. pap. text ed. 200.00 (*0-273-03133-3*, Pub. by Pitman Pubng UK) St Mut.

***Computer Security: ESORICS 94.** Ed. by D. Gollmann. (Lecture Notes in Computer Science: Vol. 875). 469p. 1994. 62.00 (*3-540-58618-0*) Spr-Verlag.

***Computer Security: ESORICS 94 : Proceedings of the Third European Symposium on Research in Computer Security, Brighton, United Kingdom, November 7-9, 1994.** Third European Symposium on Research in Computer Security Staff. Ed. by Dieter Gollmann. (Lecture Notes in Computer Science: Vol. 875). 1994. write for info. (*0-387-58618-0*) Spr-Verlag.

Computer Security: Proceedings of the IFIP TC11 Ninth International Conference on Information Security, Toronto, Canada, 12-14 May, 1993. IFIP TC11 Ninth International Conference on Information Security. Ed. by E. Graham Dougall. LC 93-34965. (IFIP Transactions A: Computer Science & Technology Ser.: Vol. A-37). 1993. write for info. (*0-444-81748-4*, North Holland) Elsevier.

Computer Security: Readings from "Security Management Magazine" Shari Gallery. (Illus.). 300p. 1986. pap. text ed. 15.00 (*0-409-90084-2*) Buttrwrth-Heinemann.

Computer Security: The Practical Issues in a Troubled World. Ed. by J. B. Grimson & Hans J. Kugler. 440p. 1986. 79.50 (*0-444-87801-7*, North Holland) Elsevier.

Computer Security - ESORICS '92: Second European Symposium on Research in Computer Security, Toulouse, France, November 23-25, 1992 Proceedings. Ed. by Y. Deswarte et al. (Lecture Notes in Computer Science Ser.: Vol. 648). xi, 451p. 1992. pap. 67.00 (*0-387-56246-X*) Spr-Verlag.

Computer Security & Industrial Cryptography: State of the Art & Evolution: ESAT Course, Leuven, Belgium, May 21-23, 1991. Ed. by Bart Preneel et al. LC 93-32467. (Lecture Notes in Computer Science Ser.: Vol. 741). 1993. 44.00 (*0-387-57341-0*) Spr-Verlag.

Computer Security & Information Integrity: Proceedings of the IFIP TC11 Sixth International Conference, Helsinki, Finland, 23-25 May, 1990. Ed. by K. R. Dittrich et al. 422p. 1991. 117.00 (*0-444-88859-4*, North Holland) Elsevier.

Computer Security & Privacy: An Information Sourcebook. Mark W. Greenia. (Illus.). (C). 1994. 35.00 (*0-944601-55-3*) Lexikon Servs.

Computer Security & Resulting Goods & Services. Business Communications Co., Inc. Staff. 83p. 1986. pap. 1,750.00 (*0-89336-389-8*, G-083) BCC.

***Computer Security Applications, 10th Annual Conference.** 328p. 1994. pap. text ed. 60.00 (*0-8186-6795-8*, PR06795) IEEE Comp Soc.

Computer Security Applications, 8th Annual Conference. 264p. 1992. 70.00 (*0-8186-3115-5*, 3115) IEEE Comp Soc.

Computer Security Applications, 9th Annual Conference. 264p. 1993. pap. text ed. 70.00 (*0-8186-4330-7*, 4330) IEEE Comp Soc.

Computer Security, Auditing & Controls: A Bibliography. Javier F. Kuong. 31p. 1973. 7.50 (*0-940706-04-0*, MAP-1) Management Advisory Pubns.

Computer Security, Auditing & Controls, Text & Readings. Javier F. Kuong. Incl. EDP Security, Auditing & Controls Text. 1974. (*0-318-54281-1*); Selected Readings. 1974. (*0-318-54282-X*); 400p. 1974. 25.00 (*0-940706-05-9*, MAP-3) Management Advisory Pubns.

Computer Security Basics. Deborah F. Russell & G. T. Gangemi, Sr. (Nutshell Handbook Ser.). 464p. (Orig.). 1991. pap. 29.95 (*0-937175-71-4*) OReilly & Assocs.

Computer Security for Small Business. Ed. by D. J. Scherer. 12p. 1991. pap. 4.95 (*0-918734-37-1*) Reymont.

Computer Security Foundations Workshop V. LC 92-70737. 200p. 1992. 60.00 (*0-8186-2850-2*, 2850) IEEE Comp Soc.

Computer Security Foundations Workshop VI. 224p. 1993. 60.00 (*0-8186-3950-4*, 3950) IEEE Comp Soc.

Computer Security Foundations Workshop VII. 225p. 1994. pap. text ed. 44.00 (*0-8186-6230-1*, 6230) IEEE Comp Soc.

***Computer Security Foundations Workshop VIII (6-95)** 224p. 1995. pap. text ed. 50.00 (*0-8186-7033-9*, PR07033) IEEE Comp Soc.

Computer Security Handbook. Richard H. Baker. LC 85-20580. (Illus.). 288p. 1985. 32.95 (*0-8306-0308-5*, 2608H) TAB Bks.

Computer Security Handbook. Ed. by Douglas Hoyt. LC 73-6207. 1973. 25.00 (*0-02-469100-3*) Macmillan Info.

Computer Security Handbook. 2nd ed. Richard H. Baker. (Illus.). 310p. 1991. 34.95 (*0-8306-7592-2*, 3592, TAB/TPR); pap. 24.95 (*0-8306-3592-0*, TAB/TPR) TAB Bks.

***Computer Security Handbook.** 3rd ed. Ed. by Arthur E. Hutt et al. Date not set. text ed. 125.00 (*0-471-01907-0*) Wiley.

***Computer Security Handbook.** 3rd ed. Ed. by Arthur E. Hutt et al. Date not set. pap. text ed. 59.95 (*0-471-11854-0*) Wiley.

Computer Security Handbook: Strategies & Techniques for Preventing Data Loss or Theft. Rolf T. Moulton. LC 85-19124. 246p. 1986. text ed. 39.95 (*0-13-165804-2*, Busn) P-H.

Computer Security in Government Departments. 25p. 1987. pap. 9.00 (*0-11-211188-2*, HM1725, Pub. by HMSO UK) UNIPUB.

Computer Security in The Age of Information: Proc. of the 5th IFIP Internat. Conf. (IFIP - Sec '88), Gold Coast, Queensland, Australia, 19-21 May, 1988. Ed. by William J. Caelli. 500p. 1989. 102.75 (*0-444-88324-X*, North Holland) Elsevier.

Computer Security Management. Karen A. Forcht. LC 94-698. 486p. 1994. 52.75 (*0-87835-881-1*) Boyd & Fraser.

Computer Security Product Buyers Guide. David Stang. (National Computer Security Association Monograph: No. 5). 200p. (Orig.). 1991. pap. 75.00 (*0-941375-28-5*) Diane Pub.

Computer Security Reference Book. Jackson. 1992. 195.00 (*0-8493-7712-9*, QA76) CRC Pr.

Computer Security Requirements. (Orig.). 1986. lib. bdg. 200.00 (*0-8490-3740-9*) Gordon Pr.

Computer Security Requirements. (Guidance for Applying the Department of Defense Trusted Computer System Evaluation Criteria in Specific Environments (CSC-STD-003-85) Ser.). 17p. (Orig.). 1985. pap. 1.00 (*0-16-001478-6*, S/N 008-000-00442-1) USGPO.

Computer Security Risk Management. Ian Palmer. 1990. text ed. 72.95 (*0-442-30290-8*) Van Nos Reinhold.

Computer Security Solutions. Hruska. 1990. 51.95 (*0-8493-7706-4*, Q) CRC Pr.

Computer Security Subsystem Interpretation of the Trusted Computer System Evaluation Criteria. 36p. (Orig.). (C). 1993. pap. text ed. 25.00 (*1-56806-486-1*) Diane Pub.

Computer Security Subsystem Interpretation of the Trusted Computer System Evaluation Criteria. Michael W. Hale & Terry Mayfield. 43p. 1989. pap. 2.25 (*0-16-001503-0*, S/N 008-000-00510-9) USGPO.

Computer Security Techniques. 1986. lib. bdg. 79.95 (*0-8490-3735-2*) Gordon Pr.

Computer Security Training Guidelines. 1990. lib. bdg. 75.00 (*0-8490-4022-1*) Gordon Pr.

Computer Security Training Guidelines. Mary A. Todd & Constance Guitian. LC 89-600771. (NIST Special Publication Ser.: No. 500-172). (Illus.). 38p. 1989. pap. 2.50 (*0-16-000300-8*, 003-003-02975-1) USGPO.

***Computer Security Within Organizations.** Adrian R. Warman. (Macmillan Information Systems Ser.). (Illus.). 151p. (C). 1993. pap. text ed. 35.00 (*0-333-57727-2*, Pub. by Macmill Press UK) Scholium Intl.

Computer Service Bureau: How to Set up Your Own. 1987. lib. bdg. 79.00 (*0-8490-3930-4*) Gordon Pr.

Computer Shorthand: Dictionary. Carmel Montes. 151p. (C). 1987. pap. 13.99 (*0-9618340-0-5*) Prof Educ Dist.

Computer Shorthand: Skill Building & Transcription. 2nd ed. Carolee Freer. 400p. (C). 1990. pap. text ed. write for info. (*0-13-173410-5*) P-H.

Computer Shorthand: Speed Building & Transcription. 2nd ed. Carolee Freer. 400p. (C). 1990. pap. text ed. write for info. (*0-13-173402-4*) P-H.

Computer Shorthand: The Professional Reporter. Carolee Freer. (Orig.). (C). 1987. teacher ed 16.00 (*0-685-31732-3*); pap. 32.00 (*0-685-31730-7*); pap. text ed. 26.00 (*0-685-31731-5*) Stenograph Corp.

Computer Shorthand: Theory Reinforcement Exercises. Carolyn Clymer. (Computer Shorthand Ser.). (C). 1992. text ed. 17.99 (*1-881086-12-7*) Middle Wasley.

Computer Shorthand for Everyone, Testimony. Alton B. Smith. (Orig.). 1991. 59.91 (*0-937112-21-6*) Stenograph Corp.

Computer Shorthand for Everyone, Theory. Alton B. Smith. (Orig.). 1990. 59.95 (*0-937112-20-8*) Stenograph Corp.

Computer Shorthand Theory & Transcription. 2nd ed. Alan Roberts et al. 368p. (C). 1990. pap. text ed. write for info. (*0-13-173105-X*) P-H.

Computer Shorthand Theory Dictionary: Conflict Resolution. 2nd ed. Jean Gonzalez. (Computer Shorthand Ser.). 180p. 1991. pap. text ed. 29.95 (*1-881086-01-1*) Middle Wasley.

Computer Simulation. 2nd ed. George Watson. 512p. 1989. Net. text ed. write for info. (*0-471-88287-9*) Wiley.

Computer Simulation: A Practical Perspective. Roger McHaney. (Illus.). 276p. 1991. text ed. 49.95 (*0-12-484140-6*) Acad Pr.

Computer Simulation & Computer Algebra. Dietrich Stauffer et al. (Illus.). xi, 155p. 1989. pap. 25.00 (*0-387-51141-5*) Spr-Verlag.

Computer Simulation & Computer Algebra: Lectures for Beginners. 3rd enl. ed. Dietrich Stauffer et al. LC 93-14007. (Illus.). 287p. 1993. pap. 29.95 (*0-387-56530-2*) Spr-Verlag.

Computer Simulation & Modeling: An Introduction. Richard S. Lehman. 424p. (C). 1977. text ed. 89.95 (*0-89859-133-3*) L Erlbaum Assocs.

Computer Simulation & Modelling. Francis Neelamkavil. 400p. 1987. text ed. 70.50 (*0-471-91129-1*) Wiley.

Computer Simulation & the Statistical Mechanics of Adsorption. D. Nicholson & N. G. Parsonage. 1983. text ed. 156.00 (*0-12-518060-8*) Acad Pr.

Computer Simulation Applications: An Introduction. Marcia L. Whicker & Lee Sigelman. (Applied Social Research Methods Ser.: Vol. 25). (Illus.). 160p. 1991. 37.00 (*0-8039-3245-6*); pap. 16.95 (*0-8039-3246-4*) Sage.

Computer Simulation for Fluid Flow, Heat & Mass Transfer, & Combustion in Reciprocating Engines: Proceedings of the International Center for Heat & Mass Transfer. Ed. by N. C. Markatos. 500p. 1989. 184.00 (*0-89116-392-1*) Hemisp Pub.

Computer Simulation in Biology: A BASIC Introduction. 2nd ed. Robert E. Keen & James D. Spain. 516p. 1991. pap. text ed. 49.95 (*0-471-50971-X*, Wiley-Liss) Wiley.

Computer Simulation in Biology, Ecology, & Medicine 1992: (8th Prague Symposium) Kotva. 162p. 1992. pap. 60.00 (*1-56555-017-X*, B/E/M92) Soc Computer Sim.

Computer Simulation in Brain Science. Ed. by Rodney M. Cotterill. (Illus.). 450p. 1989. 105.00 (*0-521-34179-5*) Cambridge U Pr.

Computer Simulation in Business Decision Making: A Guide for Managers, Planners, & MIS Professionals. Roy L. Nersesian. LC 88-32390. 268p. 1989. text ed. 65.00 (*0-89930-408-7*, NCR/, Quorum Bks) Greenwood.

Computer Simulation in Financial Risk Management: A Guide for Business Planners & Strategists. Roy L. Nersesian. LC 90-45146. 240p. 1991. text ed. 59.95 (*0-89930-578-4*, NCD, Quorum Bks) Greenwood.

Computer Simulation in Genetics. Jack L. Crosby. LC 72-5715. 489p. reprint ed. pap. 139.40 (*0-317-28345-6*, 2016182) Bks Demand.

Computer Simulation in Industrial Engineering: 1992 Symposium (Mexico City) Ed. by Raczynski. 124p. 1992. pap. 40.00 (*0-685-67785-0*, MEX92) Soc Computer Sim.

Computer Simulation in Management Science. 3rd ed. Michael Pidd. 351p. 1992. pap. text ed. 36.95 (*0-471-93462-3*) Wiley.

Computer Simulation in Materials Science: Interatomic Potentials, Simulation Techniques & Applications. Ed. by Madeleine Meyer & Vassilis Pontikis. 560p. (C). 1991. lib. bdg. 174.00 (*0-7923-1455-7*) Kluwer Ac.

Computer Simulation in Physical Geography. 2nd ed. M. J. Kirkby et al. LC 92-44454. 180p. 1993. pap. text ed. 49.95 (*0-471-93546-8*) Wiley.

Computer Simulation in Physical Metallurgy. Ed. by Gianni Jacucci. (ISPRA Cources on Materials, Engineering & Mechanical Science Ser.). 1986. lib. bdg. 104.50 (*90-277-2192-0*) Kluwer Ac.

Computer Simulation in Sociology: A Special Issue of the Journal Mathematical Sociology. Ed. by N. P. Hummon. 98p. 1990. pap. text ed. 127.00 (*2-88124-446-7*) Gordon & Breach.

Computer Simulation Methods. D. W. Heermann. (Illus.). ix, 148p. (C). 1986. 33.00 (*0-387-16966-0*) Spr-Verlag.

Computer Simulation Methods in Theoretical Physics. 2nd ed. D. W. Heermann. (Illus.). xi, 145p. 1990. pap. text ed. 26.00 (*0-387-52210-7*) Spr-Verlag.

Computer Simulation Models. John Smith. 112p. 1968. pap. text ed. 17.95 (*0-85264-100-1*) Lubrecht & Cramer.

Computer Simulation of Carcinogenic Processes. Ed. by B. D. Silverman. (Cancer Researchers & Biomedical Engineers Ser.). 208p. 1987. 110.00 (*0-8493-6539-2*, RC268, CRC Reprint) Franklin.

An Asterisk (*) at the beginning of an entry indicates that the title is appearing in BIP for the first time.

Computer Systems Validation for the Pharmaceutical & Medical Device Industries. R. L. Chamberlain. 216p. 1994. 235.00 (*0-9631489-0-7*) Alaren Pr. This book presents the topic of computer systems validation in a regulated environment in a manner that the layman can understand. It explains the relationship of validation to the implementation of computer systems. A step-by-step plan for implementing validation procedures in almost any environment is given. The chapters cover preparing validation protocols, writing & implementing Standard Operating Procedures, testing systems, managing files, preparing documentation, conducting audits & inspections, & operating in a validated environment. One of the appendices to the book includes 16 draft Standard Operating Procedures. The book comes with two floppy disks (3.5 & 5.25 inch) each containing the draft Standard Operating Procedures & the forms introduced in the book in both ASCII & WordPerfect formats. The book is essential for management, quality assurance, scientists, & information management personnel in both of these industries. *Publisher Provided Annotation.*

Computer Systems Validation for the Pharmaceutical & Medical Device Industries, Incl. disks. 2nd ed. R. L. Chamberlain. 350p. 1994. Incl. 3.5" disk & 5.25" disk. disk 247.00 (*0-9631489-5-8*) Alaren Pr. This book presents the topic of computer systems validation in a regulation environment in a manner that the layman can understand. It explains the relationship of validation to the implementation of computer systems. A step-by-step plan for implementing validation procedures in almost any environment is given. The chapters

An Asterisk (*) at the beginning of an entry indicates that the title is appearing in BIP for the first time.

1505

cover preparing validation protocols, writing & implementing Standard Operating Procedures, testing systems, managing files, preparing documentation, conducting audits & inspections, operating in a validated environment & the ISO-9000 regulations. The book includes 26 draft Standard Operating Procedures as well as many sample forms. It comes with two floppy disks (3.5 & 5.25 inch), each containing the draft Standard Operating Procedures & forms introduced in the book in both ASCII & WordPerfect 6.0 for DOS formats. The book is essential for management, quality assurance, scientists & information management personnel in both of these industries.
Publisher Provided Annotation.

*Computer Takeover. Packard. (Choose Your Own Adventure Ser.: No. 160). (J). 1995. mass mkt. 3.50 (*0-553-56402-1*) Bantam.

Computer Tales of Fact & Fantasy: or How We Learned to Stop Worrying & Love the Computer. Ed. by Iris Forrest. LC 92-75554. 160p. 1993. pap. 9.95 (*0-9635177-0-8*) Ageless Pr.

Computer Talk Made Easy. Clancy Wells. LC 92-93892. (Illus.). (Orig.). 1993. pap. 10.95 (*0-9633901-0-4*); audio 10.95 (*0-9633901-1-2*) Wells Intl.

Computer Technical Assistant. Jack Rudman. (Career Examination Ser.: C-1210). 1994. pap. 27.95 (*0-8373-1210-8*) Nat Learn.

Computer Technician. Jack Rudman. (Career Examination Ser.: C-952). 1994. pap. 29.95 (*0-8373-0952-2*) Nat Learn.

Computer Technician. Jack Rudman. (Teachers License Examination Ser.: T-67). 1994. pap. 23.95 (*0-8373-8067-7*) Nat Learn.

Computer Technician' Handbook. 3rd ed. Art Margolis. 1989. pap. text ed. 26.95 (*0-07-157547-2*) McGraw.

Computer Technician's Handbook. 2nd ed. Art Margolis. (Illus.). 490p. pap. 19.95 (*0-8306-1939-9*) TAB Bks.

Computer Technician's Handbook. 3rd ed. Art Margolis. (Illus.). 512p. 1989. 32.95 (*0-8306-9279-7*); pap. 24.95 (*0-8306-3279-4*) TAB Bks.

Computer Techniques for Electromagnetics. Ed. by R. A. Mittra. 416p. (C). 1973. 175.00 (*0-08-016888-4*, Pub. by Pergamon Repr UK) Franklin.

Computer Techniques For Electromagnetics. Ed. by Raj Mittra. (Summa Bks.). 403p. 1973. reprint ed. 172.00 (*0-89116-748-X*); reprint ed. pap. 67.00 (*0-89116-820-6*) Hemisp Pub.

Computer Techniques for Image Processing in Electron Microscopy: Supplement 10 to Advances in Electronics & Electron Physics. Cavendish Laboratory, Electron Microscopy Section Staff & W. D. Saxton. 1978. text ed. 151.00 (*0-12-014570-7*) Acad Pr.

Computer Techniques in Cardiology. Ed. by Lee D. Cady, Jr. LC 78-9860. (Biomedical Engineering & Instrumentation Ser.: No. 4). (Illus.). 478p. reprint ed. pap. 136.30 (*0-7837-3366-6*, 2043324) Bks Demand.

Computer Techniques in Environmental Studies. Ed. by P. Zannetti. LC 88-71665. (ENVIROSOFT Ser.: Vol. 2). 790p. 1988. 151.00 (*0-945824-04-1*) Computational Mech MA.

Computer Techniques in Environmental Studies. Ed. by P. Zannetti. (ENVIROSOFT Ser.: Vol. 1). 817p. 1986. 130.00 (*0-931215-35-8*) Computational Mech MA.

Computer Techniques in Environmental Studies. Ed. by Paolo Zannetti. 700p. 1988. 185.00 (*0-387-50141-X*) Spr-Verlag.

Computer Techniques in Environmental Studies IV: Proceedings of the Fourth International Conference on the Development & Application of Computer Techniques to Environmental Studies (Envirosoft 92) Held in Southampton, England, September 1-3, 1992. Ed. by Paolo Zannetti. LC 92-81590. (ENVIROSOFT Ser.: Vol. 4). 896p. 1992. 360.00 (*1-56252-106-3*) Computational Mech MA.

Computer Techniques in Environmental Studies Three: Proceedings of the Third International Conference on Development & Application of Computer Techniques to Environmental Studies Montreal, September 11-13, 1990. Ed. by Paolo Zannetti. 704p. 1990. 180.00 (*0-387-53045-2*) Spr-Verlag.

***Computer Techniques in Environmental Studies V: Environmental Systems, Vol. II: Environmental Systems.** Ed. by Paolo Zannetti. LC 94-79238. (ENVIROSOFT Ser.: Vol. 5). 416p. 1994. 148.00 (*1-56252-295-7*) Computational Mech MA.

***Computer Techniques in Environmental Studies V: Pollution Modeling, Vol. I: Pollution Modeling.** Ed. by Paolo Zannetti. LC 94-79238. (ENVIROSOFT Ser.: Vol. 5). 320p. 1994. 115.00 (*1-56252-294-9*) Computational Mech MA.

Computer Techniques in Environmental Studies V: Proceedings of the Fifth International Conference, 2 vols., Set. Ed. by P. Zannetti. LC 94-79238. (ENVIROSOFT Ser.: Vol. 5). 736p. 1994. 237.00 (*1-56252-196-9*) Computational Mech MA.

Computer Techniques in Neuroanatomy. J. J. Capowski. (Illus.). 502p. 1989. 79.50 (*0-306-43263-3*, Plenum Pr) Plenum.

Computer Technology & Employment. Stephen G. Peitchinis. LC 83-3401. 260p. 1984. text ed. 39.95 (*0-312-15875-0*) St Martin.

Computer Technology & Music Education: The Australian Beginning. Ed. by Robin S. Stevens. 86p. (C). 1987. 23.00 (*0-7300-0249-7*, Pub. by Deakin Univ AT) St Mut.

Computer Technology & Persons with Disabilities: Proceedings. California State University at Northridge, Office of Disabled Student Services Staff. Ed. by Harry J. Murphy & J. A. Dunnigan. 327p. (Orig.). 1986. pap. 12.95 (*0-937475-00-9*) CSUN Disabled.

***Computer Technology & Social Issues.** G. David Garson. LC 94-78932. 475p. (C). 1995. text ed. 59.95 (*1-878289-28-4*) Idea Group Pub.

Computer Technology & the Aged: Implications & Applications for Activity Programs. Ed. by Francis A. McGuire. LC 85-21999. (Activities, Adaptation & Aging Ser.: Vol. 8, No. 1). 119p. 1986. text ed. 29.95 (*0-86656-481-0*) Haworth Pr.

Computer Technology & the Disabled. J. O'Rourke. 1992. text ed. write for info. (*0-442-00507-5*) Van Nos Reinhold.

Computer Technology & the Law. John T. Soma. (Commercial Law Publications). 486p. 1983. text ed. 95.00 (*0-07-059642-5*) Shepards-McGraw.

Computer Technology for Special Education & Rehabilitation: Proceedings from Closing the Gap's 1986 Conference. Ed. by Michael Gergen. LC 86-73087. 348p. (Orig.). 1987. pap. text ed. 21.95 (*0-932719-02-3*) Closing Gap.

Computer Technology for the Handicapped: Proceedings from the 1984 Closing the Gap Conference. Michael Gergen & Dolores Hagen. LC 84-73240. (Illus.). 253p. (Orig.). 1985. pap. text ed. 19.95 (*0-932719-00-7*) Closing Gap.

Computer Technology Impact on Management. G. A. Champine. 292p. 1978. 54.00 (*0-444-85179-8*, North Holland) Elsevier.

Computer Technology in Construction. (Conference Proceedings Ser.). 308p. 1985. 42.00 (*0-7277-0234-3*, Pub. by T Telford UK) Am Soc Civil Eng.

Computer Technology in Fusion Energy Research: Presented at the Winter Annual Meeting of the American Society of Mechanical Engineers, San Francisco, California, December 10-15, 1978. American Society of Mechanical Engineers Staff. Ed. by John E. Akin & W. Harvey Gray. LC 78-59895. (PVP Ser.: No. 031). (Illus.). 123p. reprint ed. pap. 35.10 (*0-8357-2873-0*, 2039109) Bks Demand.

Computer Technology Resource Guide. Michael P. Jones. (Illus.). 40p. (Orig.). 1985. pap. 7.00 (*0-89904-134-5*); pap. text ed. 9.00 (*0-89904-133-7*) Crumb Elbow Pub.

***Computer-Telecom Integration: The SCAI Solution.** Arkady Grinberg. LC 94-35052. (Computer Communications Ser.). 1994. 50.00 (*0-07-024842-7*) McGraw.

Computer Telephone Integration. Rob Walters. LC 93-22174. 352p. 1993. text ed. 69.00 (*0-89006-660-4*) Artech Hse.

Computer Terminology: Terminologie de l'Informatique. 335p. (ENG & FRE.). 1983. 19.95 (*0-8288-1349-3*, M8311) Fr & Eur.

Computer Terminology for Librarians. Florencio O. Garcia. 114p. (Orig.). 1993. pap. text ed. 13.00 (*0-929928-16-4*) Fog Pubns.

Computer Terms: Quick Reference Guide. Susan Sherwin. 1993. pap. 8.95 (*1-56243-093-9*) DDC Pub.

***Computer Terms Handbook.** 200p. (Orig.). 1995. pap. 95.00 (*0-7605-1604-9*) Rector Pr.

Computer Test Bank for Foundations of Electronics. Russell L. Meade. 1991. 69.95 (*0-8273-4588-7*) Delmar.

***Computer Test Bank for Human Sexuality.** Bryan Strong & Christine DeVault. (C). 1993. disk write for info. (*0-614-02711-X*) Mayfield Pub.

***Computer Testbank for Classical Mythology: Images & Insights, Testbank.** Stephen L. Harris & Gloria Platzner. LC 94-13224. 1995. teacher ed, disk write for info. (*1-55934-423-7*) Mayfield Pub.

Computer, the Writer & the Learner. N. Williams. (Illus.). 256p. 1991. pap. 39.00 (*0-387-19572-6*) Spr-Verlag.

Computer Tomographic Imaging & Anatomic Correlation of the Human Brain. C. Plets et al. (Series in Radiology). 1987. lib. bdg. 121.50 (*0-89838-811-2*) Kluwer Ac.

Computer Tomography of Trauma. Martin Heller & Jend Hans-Holger. (Illus.). 144p. 1986. text ed. 65.00 (*0-86577-222-3*) Thieme Med Pubs.

Computer Tomography with the General Purpose Scanner. 2nd ed. L. Kreel. 1977. sl. 532.00 (*90-219-3043-9*, Excerpta Medica) Elsevier.

Computer Tools & Problem Solving in Mathematics. James Wiebe. LC 92-3375. 224p. 1992. pap. 19.95 (*0-938661-36-1*) Franklin Beedle.

Computer Tools, Models, & Techniques for Project Management. Adedeji B. Badiru & Gary E. Whitehouse. (Illus.). 320p. 1989. 32.95 (*0-8306-3200-X*, TAB/TPR) TAB Bks.

Computer Tools, Models & Techniques for Project Management. Adedeji B. Badiru & Gary E. Whitehouse. 1990. text ed. 32.95 (*0-07-156704-6*) McGraw.

Computer Training Handbook: How to Teach People to Use Computers. Elliott Masie & Rebekah Wolman. Ed. by David J. Morris. 296p. 1989. text ed. 39.00 (*0-913393-26-6*) Tools Trg.

Computer Training Handbook: How to Teach People to Use Computers. Elliott Masie & Rebekah Wolman. 264p. 1988. 39.00 (*0-913393-25-8*) Tools Trg.

Computer Training Manuals; a Researchers Workbook: A Reference. rev. ed. Training Manuals, Research Division Staff. 1993. ring bd. 24.95 (*0-318-04429-3*, Training Manuals) Prosperity & Profits.

Computer Transformation of Digital Images & Patterns. Ed. by Z. C. Li et al. 276p. (C). 1989. text ed. 68.00 (*9971-5-0951-2*) World Scientific Pub.

***Computer Treatment of Large Air Pollution Models.** Zahari Zlatev. LC 94-45303. (Environmental Science & Technology Ser.: Vol. 2). 372p. (C). 1995. lib. bdg. 154.00 (*0-7923-3328-4*) Kluwer Ac.

***Computer Triangle: Hardware, Software & People.** Robert L. Oakman. LC 94-35441. 336p. 1995. pap. text ed. 40.95 (*0-471-53561-3*) Wiley.

***Computer Troubles: Troubleshoot Them First.** Trace Naylor. (Illus.). 86p. 1995. pap. 24.00 (*1-886793-05-0*) CompuTutor.

Computer Troubleshooting & Maintenance. Walter J. McBride. 306p. (C). 1988. pap. text ed. 2.25 (*0-15-512664-4*) SCP.

Computer Troubleshooting & Maintenance. Walter J. McBride. 306p. (C). 1988. text ed. 37.25 (*0-15-512663-6*) SCP.

Computer Tutor 1.0: Your Complete Guide to Self Computer Training. Mary E. Pagel. (Illus.). 106p. (Orig.). (C). 1989. teacher ed write for info. (*0-318-64482-7*); pap. text ed. 14.95 (*0-9621823-0-3*) Comput Tutor.

***Computer Type.** M. Rogondino. Date not set. pap. 12.99 (*0-517-13021-1*) Random.

Computer Typesetting. John Negru. (Illus.). 208p. 1988. pap. 49.95 (*0-442-26696-0*) Van Nos Reinhold.

Computer Usability Testing & Evaluation. Richard H. Spencer. (Illus.). 256p. (C). 1985. pap. text ed. 44.00 (*0-13-164088-7*) P-H.

Computer Usage in Materials Education: Proceedings of a Symposium. Metallurgical Society of AIME Staff. LC 85-18907. (Illus.). 149p. reprint ed. pap. 42.50 (*0-8357-4686-0*, 2052341) Bks Demand.

Computer Use for Statistical Analysis of Concrete Test Data. 146p. 1987. pap. 58.50 (*0-318-35479-9*, SP101) ACI.

Computer Use for the Legal Assistant. Juliane K. Ghazi. Ed. by Hannan. LC 94-336. 340p. (C). 1994. pap. text ed. 39.75 (*0-314-02843-9*) West Pub.

Computer Use in Human Services: A Guide to Information Management. Dick J. Schoech. LC 81-6407. 312p. 1982. 45.95 (*0-87705-502-5*) Human Sci Pr.

Computer Use in Psychology: A Directory of Software. 3rd ed. Ed. by Michael L. Stoloff & James V. Couch. (Illus.). 373p. 1992. pap. 29.95 (*1-55798-173-6*) Am Psychol.

Computer User As Toolsmith. Saul Greenberg. LC 92-24677. (Human-Computer Interaction Ser.: No. 5). (C). 1993. 47.95 (*0-521-40430-4*) Cambridge U Pr.

Computer User As Toolsmith: The Use, Reuse & Organization of Computer-Based Tools. Saul Greenberg. (Cambridge Series in Human-Computer Interaction: No. 6). (Illus.). 160p. (C). 1993. text ed. 44.95 (*0-685-70867-5*) Cambridge U Pr.

Computer User's Guide to the Protection of Information Resources. 1990. lib. bdg. 79.95 (*0-8490-4037-X*) Gordon Pr.

Computer User's Guide to the Protection of Information Resources. Cheryl Helsing et al. LC 89-600764. (NIST Special Publication Ser.: No. 500-171). 17p. 1989. pap. 1.00 (*0-16-000295-8*, 003-003-02970-0) USGPO.

***Computer User's Survival Guide: Staying Healthy in a High Tech World.** Stigliani. 1995. pap. (*1-56592-030-9*) OReilly & Assocs.

Computer Utility: Implications for Higher Education. Ed. by Michael A. Duggan et al. LC 75-12104. 1969. 36.00 (*0-89197-708-2*) Irvington.

Computer Utilization in Structural Engineering. Ed. by James K. Nelson, Jr. LC 89-6774. 574p. 1989. pap. text ed. 53.00 (*0-87262-698-9*, 698) Am Soc Civil Eng.

Computer Validation Compliance: A Quality Assurance Perspective. Mary E. Double & Maryann McKendry. 205p. 1993. 187.00 (*0-935184-48-1*) Interpharm.

Computer Virus Crisis. 2nd enl. ed. Philip E. Fites et al. (Illus.). 432p. 1992. pap. 34.95 (*0-442-00649-7*) Van Nos Reinhold.

Computer Virus Desk Reference, 1992. Christopher V. Feudo. 500p. 1992. 38.00 (*1-55623-755-3*) Irwin Prof Pubng.

Computer Virus Handbook. Richard Levin. 1990. text ed. 24.95 (*0-07-881647-5*) Osborne-McGraw.

Computer Virus Prevention Policy. 16p. (Orig.). (C). 1993. pap. text ed. 9.95 (*1-56806-252-4*) Diane Pub.

Computer Virus Survival Guide. Ed. by David Stang. (Illus.). 75p. (Orig.). 1991. pap. 11.95 (*0-941375-36-6*) Diane Pub.

Computer Virus Training Package. (Illus.). 200p. (Orig.). (C). 1993. pap. text ed. 595.00 (*1-56806-255-9*) Diane Pub.

Computer Viruses. F. Cohen. (Orig.). (C). 1985. pap. 48.00 (*1-878109-02-2*) ASP PA.

Computer Viruses. David J. Stang. (Illus.). 254p. (Orig.). 1991. pap. 75.00 (*0-941375-24-2*) Diane Pub.

***Computer Viruses: Detection & Extermination.** Rune Skardhamar. (Illus.). 304p. 1995. pap. text ed. 34.95 (*0-12-647690-X*) Acad Pr.

Computer Viruses: Realities, Myths & Safeguards. MASP Staff. (Illus.). 200p. 1990. 59.00 (*0-940706-24-5*) Management Advisory Pubns.

Computer Viruses & Anti-Virus Warfare. Jan Hruska. 1990. pap. text ed. 54.00 (*0-13-171067-2*) P-H.

Computer Viruses & Anti-Virus Warfare. 2nd rev. ed. Jan Hruska. LC 92-30472. 1992. 35.95 (*0-13-036377-4*, Tavistock-E Horwood) Routledge Chapman & Hall.

Computer Viruses & Related Threats: A Management Guide. 55p. (C). 1993. pap. text ed. 20.00 (*1-56806-852-2*) Diane Pub.

Computer Viruses & Related Threats: A Management Guide. 1992. lib. bdg. 248.95 (*0-8490-8833-X*) Gordon Pr.

Computer Viruses, Artificial Life & Evolution. Mark Ludwig. 384p. 1993. pap. 22.95 (*0-929408-07-1*) Amer Eagle Pubns Inc.

Computer Viruses, Worms, Data Diddlers, Killer Programs, & Other Threats to Your System: What They Are, How They Work, & How to Defend Your PC or Mainframe. John McAfee & Colin Haynes. 240p. 1989. pap. 16.95 (*0-312-02889-X*) St Martin.

Computer Viruses, Worms, Data Diddlers, Killer Programs, & Other Threats to Your System: What They Are, How They Work, & How to Defend Your PC or Mainframe. enl. rev. ed. John McAfee & Colin Haynes. 265p. 1992. pap. 18.95 (*0-312-08164-2*) St Martin.

Computer Vision. Dana H. Ballard & Christopher M. Brown. (Illus.). 544p. (C). 1982. text ed. 95.00 (*0-13-165316-4*) P-H.

Computer Vision. Ed. by Michael Brady. (Journal of Artificial Intelligence Ser.: Vol. 17). vi, 508p. 1982. 89.75 (*0-444-86343-5*, North Holland) Elsevier.

Computer Vision. Ed. by Michael Brady. (Journal: Artifical Intelligence Ser.: Vol. 17). 1984. reprint ed. pap. 46.25 (*0-444-87511-5*) Elsevier.

Computer Vision: A Unified, Biologically-Inspired Approach. I. Overington. 350p. 1991. 95.00 (*0-444-88972-8*, North Holland) Elsevier.

Computer Vision: Advances & Applications. R. Kasturi & R. Jain. 720p. 1991. 85.00 (*0-8186-9103-4*, 2103) IEEE Comp Soc.

Computer Vision: Craft, Engineering, & Science Workshop Proceedings, Killarney, Ireland, September 9-10, 1991. Ed. by D. Vernon. LC 93-43341. (ESPRIT Basic Research Ser.). xiii, 96p. 1994. 44.00 (*0-387-57211-2*) Spr-Verlag.

Computer Vision: Principles. R. Kasturi & R. Jain. 728p. 1991. 85.00 (*0-8186-9102-6*, 2102) IEEE Comp Soc.

Computer Vision: Systems, Theory, & Applications. A. Basu & X. B. Li. (Computer Science Ser.). 268p. 1993. text ed. 109.00 (*981-02-1392-1*) World Scientific Pub.

Computer Vision: Theory & Industrial Applications. Ed. by C. Torras. (Illus.). 464p. 1992. 109.00 (*0-387-52036-8*) Spr-Verlag.

Computer Vision - ECCV, 1992: Second European Conference on Computer Vision, Santa Margherita Ligure, Italy, May 1992, Proceedings. Ed. by G. Sandini et al. LC 92-15347. (Lecture Notes in Computer Science Ser.: Vol. 588). xv, 909p. 1992. pap. 122.00 (*0-387-55426-2*) Spr-Verlag.

Computer Vision - ECCV 90: First European Conference on Computer Vision Antibes, France, April 23-27, 1990 Proceedings. Ed. by D. Faugeras et al. (Lecture Notes in Computer Science Ser.: Vol. 427). xii, 619p. 1990. pap. 57.90 (*0-387-52522-X*) Spr-Verlag.

Computer Vision & Pattern Recognition (CVPR '92) LC 92-71519. 888p. 1992. 130.00 (*0-8186-2855-3*, 2855) IEEE Comp Soc.

Computer Vision & Pattern Recognition (CVPR '93) 824p. 1993. 120.00 (*0-8186-3880-X*, 3880) IEEE Comp Soc.

Computer Vision & Pattern Recognition, 1994 Conference on (CVPR '94) 900p. 1994. pap. text ed. 120.00 (*0-8186-5825-8*, 5825) IEEE Comp Soc.

Computer Vision & Shape Recognition. Ed. by A. Krzyzak et al. 464p. (C). 1989. text ed. 93.00 (*9971-5-0862-1*) World Scientific Pub.

Computer Vision, ECCV '94: Third European Conference on Computer Vision, Stockholm, Sweden, May 1994, Proceedings, Vol. 1. Ed. by Jan-Olof Eklundh. LC 94-14141. (Lecture Notes in Computer Science Ser.: Vol. 801-802). 1994. 77.00 (*0-387-57956-7*) Spr-Verlag.

Computer Vision, ECCV '94: Third European Conference on Computer Vision, Stockholm, Sweden, May 1994, Proceedings, Vol. 2. Ed. by Jan-Olof Eklundh. LC 94-14141. (Lecture Notes in Computer Science Ser.: Vol. 801-802). 1994. 58.00 (*0-387-57957-5*) Spr-Verlag.

Computer Vision for Electronics Manufacturing. Louis F. Pau. LC 89-22910. (Advances in Computer Vision & Machine Intelligence Ser.). (Illus.). 340p. 1990. 65.00 (*0-306-43182-3*, Plenum Pr) Plenum.

Computer Vision, Models & Inspection. A. D. Marshall & R. R. Martin. (Series in Robotics & Automated Systems: Vol. 4). 300p. (C). 1992. text ed. 53.00 (*981-02-0772-7*) World Scientific Pub.

Computer Vision Products Database. Ed. by Philip C. Flora. 1988. 49.00 (*0-929076-02-8*); 5.25 hd 124.00 (*0-929076-03-6*) TecSpec.

Computer Vision Systems. Ed. by Allen R. Hanson & Edward M. Riseman. 1978. text ed. 121.00 (*0-12-323550-2*) Acad Pr.

***Computer Vision, Virtual Reality, & Robotics in Medicine: First International Conference, CVRMed '95, Nice, France, April 3-6, 1995, Proceedings.** Ed. by Nicholas Ayache. LC 95-7442. (Lecture Notes in Computer Sciences Ser.: Vol. 905). 1995. write for info. (*0-387-59120-6*) Spr-Verlag.

Computer Vision, 4th International Conference on (ICCV '93) LC 92-77713. 760p. 1993. 100.00 (*0-8186-3870-2*, 3870) IEEE Comp Soc.

***Computer Vision, 5th International Conference on (ICCV '95) (6-95)** 950p. 1995. pap. text ed. 190.00 (*0-8186-7042-8*, PR07042) IEEE Comp Soc.

Computer Visualization: Graphics Techniques for Engineering & Scientific Analysis. Ed. by Richard S. Gallagher. 352p. 1994. 69.95 (*0-8493-9050-8*, 9050) CRC Pr.

Computer Wars. Charles H. Ferguson. 1993. 23.00 (*0-8129-2156-9*, Times Bks) Random.

Computer Wars: The Fall of IBM & the Future of Global Technology. Charles H. Ferguson. 1993. pap. 12.00 (*0-8129-2300-6*, Times Bks) Random.

Computer Weekly Annual Guide to Resources, 1990. 412p. 1990. pap. 99.95 (*1-85384-017-3*) Buttrwrth-Heinemann.

Computer Weekly Book of Puzzlers. Howson. 1988. pap. 19.95 (*1-85384-002-5*) Buttrwrth-Heinemann.

An Asterisk (*) at the beginning of an entry indicates that the title is appearing in BIP for the first time.

An Asterisk (*) at the beginning of an entry indicates that the title is appearing in BIP for the first time.

C

Computerized Tomography of the Lung: Normal Anatomy & Most Common Diseases. Miriam Sperber. 200p. 1984. 32.50 (*0-87993-209-0*) Futura Pub.

Computerized Tomography of the Orbit & Sella Turcica. Lawrence Jacobs et al. 376p. 1980. text ed. 171.50 (*0-89004-175-X*) Raven.

Computerized Two & Three Dimensional Finite Existents Analysis. Ilija Poplasen. 64p. 1982. 20.00 (*0-935352-09-0*) MIR PA.

Computerized Two & Three Dimensional Finite Existents Analysis. 2nd ed. Ilija Poplasen. (Illus.). reprint ed. 20.00 (*0-935352-01-5*) MIR PA.

Computerizing a Small Business. Patrick D. O'Hara. LC 92-14972. 272p. 1993. pap. text ed. 19.95 (*0-471-57869-X*) Wiley.

Computerizing a Small Business. Patrick D. O'Hara. LC 92-14972. 272p. 1993. text ed. 59.95 (*0-471-57870-3*) Wiley.

Computerizing for Personal Productivity: A Guide for the High Performance Lawyer. Brooks. 216p. 1989. 63.00 (*0-409-80906-3*) Butterworth Legal Pubs.

***Computerizing Healthcare Records: Developing Electronic Patient & Medical Records.** Michael W. Davis. 200p. 1994. 60.00 (*1-55738-609-9*) Probus Pub Co.

Computerizing Personnel Systems: A Basic Guide. Alastair Evans. 160p. (C). 1986. 63.00 (*0-85292-361-9*) St Mut.

Computerizing the Corporation: The Intimate Link Between People & Machines. Mcconnell. 1990. text ed. 39.95 (*0-442-31877-4*) Van Nos Reinhold.

Computerizing the Personnel System: A Practical Guide. 2nd ed. Ed. by Alastair Evans. 160p. (C). 1991. pap. text ed. 80.00 (*0-85292-463-1*, Pub. by IPM Hse UK) St Mut.

Computerizing Warehouse Operations. Raymond A. Nelson. 250p. 1985. text ed. 39.95 (*0-13-163924-2*, Busn) P-H.

Computerizing Your Agency's Information System. Denise F. Bronson et al. (Human Services Guides Ser.: Vol. 54). (Illus.). 160p. (C). 1988. pap. text ed. 17.95 (*0-8039-2653-7*) Sage.

Computerizing Your Medical Office. 2nd ed. Dot Sellars. 256p. 1989. boxed 45.00 (*0-87489-480-8*) Med Economics.

Computerizing Your Real Estate Office. Robert Irwin. 192p. 1985. text ed. 24.95 (*0-07-032116-7*) McGraw.

Computerizing Your Small Business. Bryan Pfaffenberger. 350p. 1991. 19.95 (*0-88022-691-9*) Que.

Computerland Guide to Local Area Networks. Alan Rinzler. 1991. pap. 18.95 (*0-9627212-0-4*) Computer CA.

ComputerLand Guide to Local Area Networks. 2nd ed. Ed. by Alan Rinzler & David Gancher. (Illus.). 177p. (Orig.). 1992. pap. 18.95 (*0-9627212-2-0*) Computer CA.

ComputerMoney: Making Serious Dollars in High-Tech Consulting. A. N. Canton. LC 93-71430. 320p. 1993. pap. 29.95 (*1-883422-01-9*) Adams-Blake.

Computers. Ken Chaffin. (Science Fair Projects Ser.). (Illus.). 48p. (J). (gr. 3-6). Date not set. lib. bdg. 12.95 (*1-56065-115-6*) Capstone Pr.

***Computers.** Marjorie Eberts & Margaret Gisler. LC 94-42629. (Career Portraits Ser.). (J). 1995. write for info. (*0-8442-4366-3*, VGM Career Bks) NTC Pub Grp.

Computers. H. Kavet. 64p. 1993. 8.95 (*0-88032-351-5*) Ivory Tower Pub.

Computers. Peter Lear. (E. G. Let's Look At Ser.). (Illus.). 32p. (J). (gr. 1-5). 1985. pap. 4.95 (*0-88625-083-8*) Durkin Hayes Pub.

Computers. Francene Sabin. LC 84-2708. (Illus.). 32p. (J). (gr. 3-6). 1985. lib. bdg. 9.49 (*0-8167-0314-0*); pap. text ed. 2.95 (*0-8167-0315-9*) Troll Assocs.

Computers. Time Life Staff. (How Things Work Ser.). 1990. lib. bdg. 25.93 (*0-8094-7859-5*) Time-Life.

Computers. Timothy N. Trainor. 544p. (C). 1987. student ed 10.50 (*0-685-14451-8*) McGraw.

Computers. L. Watts & L. Inglis. (Young Scientist Ser.). (Illus.). 32p. (J). (gr. 3-9). 1993. lib. bdg. 13.96 (*0-88110-595-3*); pap. 6.95 (*0-7460-1055-9*) EDC.

***Computers.** David Wright. (Inventors & Inventions Ser.). 64p. (J). (gr. 3-5). 1995. lib. bdg. write for info. (*0-7614-0064-8*, Benchmark NY) Marshall Cavendish.

Computers. 3rd ed. Larry Long & Nancy Long. 704p. 1992. pap. text ed. write for info. (*0-13-156241-X*) P-H.

Computers. 4th ed. Timothy Trainor & Diane Krasnewich. 1994. pap. text ed. write for info. (*0-07-065248-1*) McGraw.

Computers: A Guide to Choosing & Using. Andrew Willis & Thomas Stewart. (Practical Guides for General Practice Ser.: No. 7). (Illus.). 146p. 1989. pap. 14.95 (*0-19-261754-0*) OUP.

Computers: A Visual Encyclopedia. Sherry Kinkoph. 400p. 1994. pap. 25.00 (*1-56761-464-7*) Alpha Bks IN.

Computers: An Introduction. David M. Kroenke & Randolph P. Johnston. LC 83-22130. (Illus.). 720p. 1985. student ed 8.50 (*0-938188-14-3*); student ed 5.95 (*0-685-08310-1*); pap. text ed. 23.95 (*0-938188-13-5*); disk write for info. (*0-318-57718-6*) Mitchell Pub.

Computers: An Introduction. Donald D. Spencer. 384p. (C). 1986. pap. write for info. (*0-675-20559-X*, Merrill Pub Co); pap. write for info. (*0-675-20629-4*, Merrill Pub Co) Macmillan.

Computers: An Introduction to Hardware & Software Design. Larry L. Wear. 1991. text ed. write for info. (*0-07-068674-2*) McGraw.

Computers: Appreciation, Applications, Implications: An Introduction. J. Mack Adams & Douglas H. Haden. LC 73-1688. 600p. reprint ed. pap. 171.00 (*0-317-42268-5*, 2012504) Bks Demand.

Computers: Community Access. Pryor Bryan. 1995. 40.00 (*1-885522-02-9*) Telecommunity Pr.

Computers: Concepts & Application. 2nd ed. Robert C. Nickerson. (C). 1993. 51.00 (*0-673-46790-2*) HarpCollege.

Computers: Concepts & Applications. 4th ed. David Feinstein et al. 560p. (C). 1990. pap. write for info. (*0-697-08183-4*); write for info. (*0-697-00317-5*) Wm C Brown Pubs.

Computers: Concepts & Applications for Users. Robert C. Nickerson. (C). 1989. pap. text ed. 31.75 (*0-673-39828-5*) HarpCollege.

Computers: Concepts & Applications for Users. 2nd ed. Robert C. Nickerson. (C). 1992. text ed. 47.00 (*0-673-46554-3*) HarpCollege.

Computers: Concepts & Applications for Users with BASIC. Robert C. Nickerson. (C). 1990. pap. text ed. 32.75 (*0-673-46016-9*) HarpCollege.

Computers: Concepts & Applications with BASIC. 2nd ed. Robert C. Nickerson. (C). 1992. write for info. (*0-673-46690-6*); text ed. 51.50 (*0-673-46553-5*) HarpCollege.

***Computers: Concepts & Implications.** Fritz Erickson & John Vonk. 256p. (C). 1995. pap. write for info. (*0-697-27798-4*) Bus & Educ Tech.

Computers: Concepts, Implications, & Applications with Microsoft Works 3.0, DOS. Fritz Erickson & John Vonk. 640p. (C). 1995. pap. write for info. (*0-697-23989-6*) Bus & Educ Tech.

Computers: Concepts, Implications, & Applications with Microsoft Works 3.0, DOS. Fritz Erickson & John Vonk. 640p. 1997. pap. text ed. write for info. (*0-697-23988-8*) Bus & Educ Tech.

Computers: Concepts, Implications & Applications with Windows 3.1, Word, Excel, & Paradox. Fritz Erickson & John Vonk. 752p. (C). 1995. pap. write for info. (*0-697-23974-8*) Bus & Educ Tech.

***Computers: Concepts, Implications & Applications with Windows 3.1, Wordperfect 6.0, Quattro Pro 5.0 & Paradox 4.5 for Windows.** Fritz Erickson & John Vonk. 928p. (C). 1994. pap. write for info. (*0-697-23975-6*) Bus & Educ Tech.

Computers: Crimes, Clues & Controls, a Management Guide. (Illus.). 48p. 1986. pap. 3.25 (*0-16-001482-4*, S/N 008-000-00460-9) USGPO.

Computers: Forty-Nine Science Fair Projects. Robert L. Bonnet & G. Daniel Keen. (Science Fair Project Ser.). 1990. pap. text ed. 10.95 (*0-07-155261-8*) McGraw.

Computers: Forty-Nine Science Fair Projects. Robert L. Bonnet. (Illus.). 160p. (J). (gr. 4-7). 1990. 16.95 (*0-8306-7524-8*, 3524); pap. 9.95 (*0-8306-3524-6*) TAB Bks.

Computers: Inside & Out. Kurt F. Lauckner & Mildred D. Lintner. (Illus.). 400p. (C). 1991. pap. 31.95 (*0-9624073-9-9*) Pippin Publishing.

Computers: Instructor's Edition. 3rd annot. ed. Larry Long & Nancy Long. LC 92-32920. 1993. write for info. (*0-13-156258-4*) P-H.

Computers: Manager's Guide. Paul Richardson. (Primary Health Care Management Advancement Programme (PHC MAP) Modules Ser.). 76p. 1993. pap. text ed. write for info. (*1-882839-20-X*) Aga Khan Fnd.

Computers: Mechanical Minds. Don Nardo. LC 90-6648. (Encyclopedia of Discovery & Invention Ser.). (Illus.). 96p. (J). (gr. 5-8). 1990. lib. bdg. 17.95 (*1-56006-206-1*) Lucent Bks.

Computers: New Opportunities for Personalized Ministry. Kenneth Bedell & Parker Rossman. 128p. 1984. pap. 7.00 (*0-8170-1039-4*) Judson.

Computers: New Opportunities for the Disabled. Harold Remmes. LC 84-1058. 31p. (Orig.). 1984. pap. 3.50 (*0-87576-114-3*) Pilot Bks.

Computers: Planning for People. Enid Mumford & T. B. Ward. (Modern Management Ser.). (Illus.). 176p. (C). 1968. text ed. 25.00 (*0-8464-1177-6*) Beekman Pubs.

Computers: The User Perspective. 3rd ed. Sarah E. Hutchinson & Stacey C. Sawyer. 888p. (C). 1991. text ed. 41.95 (*0-256-09372-5*) Irwin.

Computers: Those Amazing Machines. Ed. by Donald J. Crump. (Books for World Explorers Series 7: No. 2). (Illus.). 104p. 1986. 8.95 (*0-87044-574-X*); lib. bdg. 12.50 (*0-87044-579-0*) Natl Geog.

Computers: Tools for an Information Age. H. L. Capron. 1987. 32.95 (*0-8053-2248-5*) Benjamin-Cummings.

Computers: Tools for an Information Age. H. L. Capron. (C). 1987. pap. text ed. 35.50 (*0-8053-2249-3*) Benjamin-Cummings.

Computers: Tools for Knowledge Workers. Jack B. Rochester. LC 92-16801. 640p. (C). 1993. pap. text ed. 39.95 (*0-256-11015-8*) Irwin.

***Computers: User Perspective with Software Laboratories.** 3rd ed. Sarah Hutchinson & Stacey Sawyer. 112p. (C). 1992. student ed, text ed. 16.95 (*0-256-11728-4*) Irwin.

***Computers: User Prespective - Concepts Version.** 3rd ed. Sarah Hutchinson & Stacey Sawyer. 112p. (C). 1992. student ed, text ed. 17.50 (*0-256-11727-6*) Irwin.

Computers - Crimes, Clues & Controls: A Management Guide. (Illus.). 52p. (Orig.). (C). 1993. pap. text ed. 25.00 (*1-56806-524-8*) Diane Pub.

Computers - How to Break into the Field. 2nd ed. L. Peter Carron, Jr. 160p. 1983. pap. 6.95 (*0-89709-034-9*, 30034, Liberty Hse) TAB Bks.

Computers & Accounting. Thomas W. McRae. LC 75-6793. 179p. reprint ed. pap. 51.10 (*0-8357-2590-1*, 2052370) Bks Demand.

Computers & Applications: An Introduction to Data Processing. 2nd ed. Daniel L. Slotnick et al. LC 88-82326. 631p. (C). 1989. pap. text ed. 28.00 (*0-669-19938-9*); Study guide. student ed 13.00 (*0-669-19939-7*); Instr.'s guide with transparency masters. teacher ed, trans. 2.00 (*0-669-19940-0*); Transparencies. trans. 50.00 (*0-669-19942-7*); Test item file. 2.00 (*0-669-19941-9*) Heath.

Computers & Applications Software. 2nd ed. R. Szymanski et al. 576p. (C). 1991. pap. write for info. (*0-675-21269-3*, Merrill Pub Co) Macmillan.

Computers & Applications with BASIC: An Introduction to Data Processing. 2nd ed. Daniel L. Slotnick et al. LC 89-82242. 863p. (C). 1990. BASIC test item file. teacher ed 2.00 (*0-669-21756-5*); Study guide. student ed 13.00 (*0-669-21754-9*); pap. text ed. 29.00 (*0-669-21753-0*); Instr.'s guide with transparency masters. student ed, teacher ed 2.00 (*0-669-21755-7*); BASIC with transparencies. trans. write for info. (*0-669-21757-3*) Heath.

Computers & Astrology: Your Universal User's Guide & Reference. Patricia Foreman. LC 92-82652. (Illus.). 304p. (Orig.). 1992. pap. 19.95 (*0-9624648-1-3*) Good Earth Pubns.

Computers & Business Information Processing. William S. Davis. LC 80-10946. 448p. (C). 1981. pap. text ed. write for info. (*0-201-03161-2*); write for info. (*0-201-03713-0*) Addison-Wesley.

Computers & Business Tasks. deluxe ed. Douglas D. Downing. (Barron's Business Library). 320p. 1991. 14.95 (*0-8120-4543-2*) Barron.

***Computers & Children Bk. I.** Helen P. Singletary. 1994. pap. text ed. write for info. (*1-880850-05-2*) Comp Trng Clinic.

***Computers & Children Bk. II.** Helen P. Singletary et al. (Illus.). 218p. 1991. pap. text ed. 75.00 (*1-880850-06-0*) Comp Trng Clinic.

***Computers & Classroom Culture.** Janet W. Schofield. 200p. (C). 1995. write for info. (*0-521-47368-3*); pap. write for info. (*0-521-47924-X*) Cambridge U Pr.

***Computers & Communications, 1995 IEEE Symposium on (ISCC '95) (6-95)** 300p. 1995. pap. text ed. 60.00 (*0-8186-7075-4*, PR07075) IEEE Comp Soc.

Computers & Community: Teaching Composition in the Twenty-First Century. Ed. by Carolyn Handa. 197p. 1990. pap. text ed. 18.50 (*0-86709-257-2*, 0257) Boynton Cook Pubs.

Computers & Composing: How the New Technologies Are Changing Writing. Jeanne W. Halpern & Sarah Liggett. LC 83-9300. 152p. 1984. 12.95 (*0-8093-1146-1*) S Ill U Pr.

Computers & Computer Applications. Neville Ford et al. (Computers & Their Applications Ser.). 256p. 1991. boxed 33.00 (*0-13-161886-5*, 250301) P-H.

Computers & Computer Languages. G. Silverman & D. B. Turkiew. 592p. (C). 1988. text ed. 33.95 (*0-07-057523-1*) McGraw.

Computers & Computing. J. M. Rushforth & J. L. Morris. LC 72-8616. (Introductory Mathematics for Scientists & Engineers Ser.). 269p. reprint ed. pap. 76.70 (*0-317-08336-8*, 2022104) Bks Demand.

Computers & Computing in Heat Transfer Science & Engineering. Ed. by Wataru Nakayama & Kwang-Tzu Yang. LC 92-38379. 1992. 188.95 (*0-8493-9935-1*, TJ260) CRC Pr.

Computers & Computing Information Research Directory. 2nd ed. 1995. 195.00 (*0-8103-2743-0*) Gale.

Computers & Computing Information Research Directory. 3rd ed. 1997. 195.00 (*0-8103-5466-7*) Gale.

Computers & Computing Information Resources Directory: Supplement. Ed. by Martin Connors. 1987. 100.00 (*0-8103-2138-6*) Gale.

Computers & Control in Clinical Medicine. Ed. by Ewart R. Carson & D. G. Cramp. 272p. 1985. 69.50 (*0-306-41892-4*, Plenum Pr) Plenum.

Computers & Conversation. Ed. by Paul Luff et al. (Computers & People Ser.). 284p. 1990. text ed. 61.00 (*0-12-459560-X*) Acad Pr.

***Computers & Creativity.** Derek Partridge. 192p. (Orig.). 1994. write for info. (*1-56750-170-2*) Ablex Pub.

Computers & Creativity. Derek Partridge & Jon Rowe. 224p. (Orig.). 1994. pap. text ed. 22.95 (*1-871516-51-X*, Pub. by Intellect Bks UK) Cromland.

Computers & Cultural Diversity: Restructuring for School Success. Robert A. DeVillar & Christian J. Faltis. LC 90-9668. (Computers in Education Ser.). 171p. 1991. 59.50 (*0-7914-0524-9*); pap. 19.95 (*0-7914-0525-7*) State U NY Pr.

Computers & Curriculum-Training Program Development. John J. Carroll. 200p. 1992. 39.95 (*0-938639-00-5*); (*0-318-61535-5*) Special Resc Pubns.

Computers & Cybernetics. B. H. Rudall. (Cybernetics & Systems Ser., Abacus Bks.). x, 188p. 1981. text ed. 84.00 (*0-85626-173-4*) Gordon & Breach.

Computers & Data Processing. Jack Rudman. (College Level Examination Ser.: CLEP-8). 1994. pap. 23.95 (*0-8373-5308-4*) Nat Learn.

Computers & Data Processing: Concepts & Applications. 3rd ed. Steven L. Mandell. (Illus.). 512p. (C). 1984. text ed. 33.00 (*0-314-85262-X*) West Pub.

Computers & Data Processing: Concepts & Applications with BASIC. 3rd ed. Steven L. Mandell. (Illus.). 292p. (C). 1984. text ed. 35.00 (*0-314-87560-3*) West Pub.

Computers & Data Processing Today. Steven L. Mandell. (Illus.). 161p. (C). 1983. student ed 10.75 (*0-314-71106-6*); pap. text ed. 28.50 (*0-314-69663-6*) West Pub.

Computers & Data Processing Today with BASIC. Steven L. Mandell. (Illus.). 510p. (C). pap. text ed. 29.50 (*0-314-70646-1*) West Pub.

Computers & Data Processing Today with BASIC. 2nd ed. Steven L. Mandell. (Illus.). 472p. (C). 1985. pap. text ed. 35.50 (*0-314-96079-1*) West Pub.

Computers & Data Processing Today with Pascal. Steven L. Mandell. (Illus.). 332p. (C). 1983. pap. text ed. 29.50 (*0-314-70647-X*) West Pub.

Computers & Data Processing Today with Pascal. 2nd ed. Steven L. Mandell. (Illus.). 472p. (C). 1986. pap. text ed. 50.75 (*0-314-96080-5*) West Pub.

Computers & DNA. Ed. by George I. Bell & Thomas G. Marr. (Santa Fe Institute Ser.). (Illus.). 304p. (C). 1990. pap. 29.95 (*0-201-51561-X*, Adv Bk Prog) Addison-Wesley.

Computers & Economic Planning, the Soviet Experience. Martin Cave. LC 79-7659. (Soviet & East European Studies). 236p. reprint ed. pap. 67.30 (*0-685-20630-0*, 2030585) Bks Demand.

Computers & Education. Charles S. White & Guy Hubbard. 316p. (C). 1988. pap. write for info. (*0-02-427090-3*) Macmillan.

Computers & Education see Educational Technology Reviews Ser.

Computers & Education in the Soviet Union. Bryce F. Zender. LC 75-19470. 184p. 1975. 32.95 (*0-87778-082-X*) Educ Tech Pubns.

Computers & Electronics Dictionary: Dizionario di Informatica e Degli Elaboratori Elettronici. 3rd ed. M. Morelli. 231p. (ENG & ITA.). 1982. pap. 24.95 (*0-8288-0904-6*, M7821) Fr & Eur.

Computers & Electronics Market Reports, Studies & Surveys. Ed. by Joan Verniero & Susan De Gange. 250p. (Orig.). 1985. pap. 115.00 (*0-931634-06-7*) FIND-SVP.

Computers & Embryos: Models in Developmental Biology. Robert J. Ransom. LC 81-197475. 224p. reprint ed. pap. 63.90 (*0-318-34727-X*, 2031941) Bks Demand.

Computers & End-User Software. 3rd ed. Thomas H. Athey et al. (C). 1991. text ed. 50.00 (*0-673-46269-2*) HarpCollege.

Computers & End-User Software: Study Guide. 3rd ed. Thomas H. Athey et al. (C). 1991. 19.00 (*0-673-46429-6*) HarpCollege.

Computers & ESL. David H. Wyatt. (Language in Education Ser.: No. 56). 132p. 1986. pap. text ed. 11.00 (*0-13-165499-3*) P-H.

Computers & Ethics: A Sourcebook for Discussions. Ed. by Jane Robinett & Ramon Barquin. 46p. (Orig.). (C). 1989. pap. text ed. write for info. (*0-918902-25-8*) Polytechnic Pr.

Computers & Exceptional Individuals. 2nd ed. Ed. by Jimmy D. Lindsey. LC 91-48182. 416p. 1993. pap. text ed. 29.00 (*0-89079-547-9*, 6548) PRO-ED.

Computers & Family Therapy. Ed. by Charles R. Figley. LC 85-956. (Journal of Psychotherapy & the Family: Vol. 1, Nos. 1-2). 200p. 1985. text ed. 49.95 (*0-86656-375-X*); pap. text ed. 19.95 (*0-86656-408-X*) Haworth Pr.

Computers & Graph Theory. Ramachandran Bharath. 150p. 1991. pap. text ed. write for info. (*0-13-161605-6*) P-H.

Computers & Human Language. George W. Smith. (Illus.). 496p. (C). 1991. 49.95 (*0-19-506281-7*); pap. text ed. 18.95 (*0-19-506282-5*) OUP.

Computers & Information Processing. Floyd Fuller & William Manning. LC 93-46579. 1994. write for info. (*0-87709-484-5*) Boyd & Fraser.

Computers & Information Processing. Gerald A. Silver & Myrna Silver. LC 92-53289. (College Outline Ser.). 320p. (C). 1993. pap. 13.00 (*0-06-467176-3*, Harper Ref) HarpC.

Computers & Information Processing. Donald D. Spencer. 608p. (C). 1985. write for info. (*0-675-20290-6*, Merrill Pub Co); pap. write for info. (*0-675-20367-8*, Merrill Pub Co) Macmillan.

Computers & Information Processing. 2nd ed. William M. Fuori & Lawrence J. Aufiero. 784p. (C). 1988. boxed write for info. (*0-13-165514-0*) P-H.

Computers & Information Processing. 3rd ed. William M. Fuori & Louis V. Gioia. 640p. (C). 1991. text ed. write for info. (*0-13-173329-X*) P-H.

Computers & Information Processing. 4th ed. William M. Fuori & Louis V. Gioia. LC 93-25638. 1993. pap. text ed. write for info. (*0-13-235722-4*) P-H Gen Ref & Trav.

Computers & Information Processing: Application Software Edition. Floyd Fuller & William Manning. LC 93-43779. 896p. 1994. pap. 39.50 (*0-87709-487-X*) Boyd & Fraser.

Computers & Information Processing: Concepts & Applications. 6th ed. Steven L. Mandell. Ed. by Clyde Perlee. 512p. (C). 1992. text ed. 50.75 (*0-314-92964-9*) West Pub.

Computers & Information Processing: Concepts & Applications with BASIC. Steven L. Mandell. Ed. by Clyde Perlee. (Illus.). 174p. (C). 1987. pap. text ed. 15.00 (*0-314-35299-6*) West Pub.

Computers & Information Processing: Concepts & Applications with BASIC. 6th ed. Steven L. Mandell. Ed. by Clyde Perlee. 512p. (C). 1992. text ed. 54.75 (*0-314-89569-8*) West Pub.

Computers & Information Processing: Microsoft Works Edition. Floyd Fuller & William Manning. LC 93-40585. 512p. 1994. pap. 53.50 (*0-87709-486-1*) Boyd & Fraser.

Computers & Information Processing: QuickBASIC Edition. Floyd Fuller & William Manning. LC 93-44532. 660p. 1994. pap. 39.50 (*0-87709-485-3*) Boyd & Fraser.

Computers & Information Processing Today with BASIC. 3rd ed. Robert H. Dunikoski. Ed. by Clyde Perlee. 401p. (C). 1989. pap. text ed. 58.00 (*0-314-64976-X*) West Pub.

Computers & Information Processing Today Without BASIC. 3rd ed. Robert H. Dunikoski. Ed. by Clyde Perlee. 401p. (C). 1988. pap. text ed. 56.00 (*0-314-64975-1*) West Pub.

***Computers & Information Systems.** Ed. by Jill Muehrcke. (Leadership Ser.). 106p. 1993. spiral bd. 20.00 (*0-614-07093-7*) Soc Nonprofit Org.

Computers & Information Systems. Robert A. Szymanski et al. LC 94-16833. 1994. pap. text ed. 49.00 (*0-02-418767-4*) P-H.

C

An Asterisk (*) at the beginning of an entry indicates that the title is appearing in BIP for the first time.

C

***Computers for Handicapped Persons: Proceedings of the 4th International Conference, ICCHP '94, Vienna, Austria, September 14-16, 1994.** Ed. by Wolfgang L. Zagler et al. LC 94-35139. (Lecture Notes in Computer Science: Vol. 860). 1994. write for info. (*3-540-58476-5*) Spr-Verlag.

***Computers for Handicapped Persons: Proceedings of the 4th International Conference, ICCHP '94, Vienna, Austria, September 14-16, 1994.** Ed. by Wolfgang L. Zagler et al. LC 94-35139. (Lecture Notes in Computer Science: Vol. 860). 1994. 82.00 (*0-387-58476-5*) Spr-Verlag.

Computers for Kids. Taylor R. Taylor. (LogicNotes Ser.). (Illus.). (Orig.). 1990. pap. text ed., vhs write for info. (*0-929978-55-2*) M-USA Busn Systs.

Computers for Kids over Sixty: Keeping up with the Computer Generation. Greg P. Kearsley & Mary Furlong. 128p. 1984. pap. write for info. (*0-201-05155-9*) Addison-Wesley.

Computers for Lawyers. Paul Bernstein. 297p. 1992. pap. 50.00 (*0-941916-64-2*) ATLA Pr.

***Computers for Lawyers Vol. II: Comprehensive Guide to Automating Your Law Firm.** Paul Bernstein. Ed. by Cathy Kruvant. (Orig.). 1995. pap. write for info. (*0-941916-71-5*) ATLA Pr.

Computers for Libraries. 3rd ed. Jennifer Rowley. 250p. 1993. 60.00 (*1-85604-013-5*, LAP0135, Pub. by Lib Assn Pub UK) UNIPUB.

Computers for Managing Information Tests. Marly K. Bergerud et al. 1988. write for info. (*0-471-60228-0*); student ed 12.95 (*0-471-84439-X*) P-H.

Computers for Neighborhoods. 2nd ed. Amalio Madueno. 53p. (C). 1987. pap. 7.50 (*0-317-93050-8*) CIE Inc.

Computers for Non-Profit Organizations. Elliott Masie & Dan Margulies. 80p. (Orig.). 1985. pap. 8.95 (*0-913393-17-7*) Tools Trg.

Computers for Nonprofits. Public Management Institute Staff & Kenneth Gilman. LC 81-80946. 1981. ring bd. 49.00 (*0-916664-32-5*) Datarex Corp.

Computers for People. 2nd ed. Jack B. Rochester & Jon Rochester. LC 93-3703. 280p. (C). 1993. pap. text ed. 26.95 (*0-256-10777-7*) Irwin.

***Computers for People: Basic Programming.** Jack Rochester & Jon Rochester. 88p. (C). 1991. text ed. 11.00 (*0-256-10214-7*) Irwin.

Computers for People: Concepts & Applications. Jack B. Rochester & Jon Rochester. (Illus.). 512p. (C). 1991. pap. text ed. 23.95 (*0-256-06680-9*, 14-2710-01) Irwin.

***Computers for People & Using Microsoft Works Package.** Jack Rochester et al. (C). 1991. text ed. 43.95 (*0-256-10735-1*) Irwin.

Computers for Professional Practice. Ellis J. Neiburger. LC 83-72626. (Illus.). 281p. 1984. pap. 14.95 (*0-914555-00-6*) Andent Inc.

Computers for Social Change & Community Organizing. John Downing et al. (Computers in Human Services Ser.: Vol. 8, No. 1). 136p. 1991. text ed. 29.95 (*0-86656-865-4*) Haworth Pr.

Computers for Technicians. Abraham Marcus & John D. Lenk. (Illus.). 400p. 1973. text ed. 40.00 (*0-13-166181-7*) P-H.

Computers for the Arts. Dick Higgins. 1970. pap. 0.90 (*0-911856-03-X*) Abyss.

Computers, Graphics, & Learning. Lloyd Rieber. 304p. 1994. pap. write for info. (*0-697-14894-7*) Brown & Benchmark.

Computers Illustrated. Nat Gertler. 1994. pap. 24.95 (*1-56529-676-1*) Que.

Computers in Accountants' Offices. Gordon E. Louvau & Marjorie E. Jackson. (Accounting Ser.). (Illus.). 132p. 1982. text ed. 44.95 (*0-534-97967-X*) Van Nos Reinhold.

Computers in Accounting Buyers Guide, No. 2772. 150p. 1991. per. 39.95 (*0-685-45987-X*) Warren Gorham & Lamont.

Computers in Activation Analysis & Gamma-Ray Spectroscopy: Proceedings. Ed. by B. Stephen Carpenter et al. LC 79-19600. (DOE Symposium Ser.). 905p. 1979. pap. 30.50 (*0-87079-117-6*, CONF-780421); fiche 9.00 (*0-87079-169-9*, CONF-780421) DOE.

Computers in Aerodynamics: Proceedings of the Symposium, Polytechnic Institute of New York, Aerodynamics Laboratories, 1979. Computers in Aerodynamics Symposium Staff. Ed. by S. G. Rubin & M. H. Bloom. 130p. 1980. pap. 46.00 (*0-08-025426-8*, Pergamon Pr) Elsevier.

Computers in Agricultural Extension Programs: Internatinal Conference Proceedings, 4th, January 1992. 806p. pap. 58.00 (*0-929355-24-5*, P0192) Am Soc Ag Eng.

Computers in Agriculture. LC 93-74815. 918p. 1994. 58.00 (*0-929355-46-6*, P0394) Am Soc Ag Eng.

Computers in Algebra & Number Theory: Proceedings of the SIAM-AMS Seminar, New York, March, 1971. Society for Industrial & Applied Mathematics Staff & American Mathematical Society Staff. Ed. by Garrett Birkhoff & Marshall Hall, Jr. LC 76-167685. (SIAM-AMS Proceedings Ser.: Vol. 4). 200p. 1980. reprint ed. pap. 27.00 (*0-8218-1323-4*, SIAMS-4) Am Math.

Computers in Applied Linguistics: An International Perspective. Ed. by Martha C. Pennington & Vance Stevens. (Multilingual Matters Ser.: No. 75). 300p. 1991. 99.00 (*1-85359-120-3*, Pub. by Multilingual Matters UK); pap. 39.95 (*1-85359-119-X*, Pub. by Multilingual Matters UK) Taylor & Francis.

Computers in Art, Design & Animation. Ed. by J. Lansdown & R. A. Earnshaw. (Illus.). xvii, 305p. 1989. 89.00 (*0-387-96896-2*, 2321) Spr-Verlag.

Computers in Battle: Will They Work? Gary Chapman. Ed. by David Bellin. 1987. 14.95 (*0-15-121232-5*) HarBrace.

Computers in Biology. J. A. Nelder & R. D. Kime. (Wykeham Science Ser.: No. 32). 168p. (C). 1974. 14.00 (*0-8448-1159-9*, Crane Russak) Taylor & Francis.

Computers in Biology: An Introduction. Robert Ransom & Ray Matela. 160p. 1985. pap. 40.00 (*0-335-15018-7*, Open Univ Pr) Taylor & Francis.

Computers in Biomedicine. Ed. by K. D. Held et al. LC 91-75140. (BIOMED Ser.: Vol. 1). 456p. 1991. 148.00 (*1-56252-075-X*) Computational Mech MA.

Computers in Business. Martin Chamberlain et al. (Illus.). 448p. (C). 1987. Study guide & lab manual. student ed, pap. text ed. write for info. (*0-13-164048-8*) P-H.

Computers in Business. 4th ed. Donald H. Sanders. (Illus.). 1979. text ed. write for info. (*0-07-054645-2*) McGraw.

Computers in Business: Information Processing. Richard D. Jones et al. LC 89-70528. (Illus.). xviii, 476p. 1991. text ed. 48.00 (*0-314-69562-1*) West Pub.

Computers in Business Blueprint. Christopher Barnatt. 224p. (Orig.). 1994. pap. 29.95 (*0-631-19303-0*) Blackwell Pubs.

***Computers in Cardiology.** 1994. 120.00 (*0-8186-670X-6*) IEEE Comp Soc.

Computers in Cardiology, 1991. LC 80-641097. 784p. 1992. 100.00 (*0-8186-2485-X*, 2485) IEEE Comp Soc.

Computers in Cardiology, 1992. LC 80-641097. 752p. 1993. pap. 100.00 (*0-8186-3550-9*, 3550) IEEE Comp Soc.

Computers in Cardiology, 1993. LC 80-641097. 911p. 1993. pap. text ed. 120.00 (*0-8186-5470-8*) IEEE Comp Soc.

***Computers in Cardiology, 1994: Proceedings of the National Institutes of Health.** 848p. 1994. pap. text ed. 120.00 (*0-8186-6570-X*) IEEE Comp Soc.

***Computers in Clinical Practice: Managing Patients, Information & Communication.** Ed. by Jerome A. Osheroff. LC 95-7875. (Information Technology Ser.). 1995. 46.00 (*0-943126-33-9*) Amer Coll Phys.

Computers in Company Training. David Hawkridge et al. 256p. 1988. pap. text ed. 28.50 (*0-415-00755-0*) Routledge.

Computers in Concrete Design. 85p. 1991. 55.50 (*0-685-62946-5*, C-14) ACI.

Computers in Congress: The Politics of Information. Stephen E. Frantzich. LC 82-3285. (Managing Information Ser.: No. 4). (Illus.). 287p. reprint ed. pap. 81.80 (*0-8357-4791-3*, 2037728) Bks Demand.

Computers in Context: The Philosophy & Practice of Systems Design. Bo Dahlbom & Lars Mathiassen. LC 93-6779. (Illus.). 256p. 1993. 49.95 (*1-55786-430-6*); pap. 19.95 (*1-55786-405-5*) Blackwell Pubs.

Computers in Corrosion Control. Ed. by J. Fu et al. LC 86-61980. (Illus.). 380p. 1986. 10.00 (*0-915567-24-5*) NACE Intl.

***Computers in Corrosion Control.** Ed. by P. R. Roberge et al. (Illus.). 128p. 1994. 60.00 (*1-877914-72-X*) NACE Intl.

Computers in Corrosion Control, Vol. II. Ed. by Al Van Orden et al. (Illus.). 350p. (Orig.). 1991. pap. text ed. 10.00 (*1-877914-30-4*) NACE Intl.

Computers in Corrosion Control, Vol. 3: Expert Systems for Corrosion Control. Ed. by Ann C. Van Orden & T. Hakkarainen. (Illus.). 250p. 1992. pap. text ed. 60.00 (*1-877914-41-X*) NACE Intl.

Computers in Criminal Justice: An Introduction to Small Computers. Joseph A. Waldron. 73p. 1983. pap. 8.95 (*0-932930-58-1*) Pilgrimage Inc.

Computers in Criminal Justice: Issues & Applications. Contrib by Frank Schmalleger. LC 90-50553. (Illus.). iv, 278p. (C). 1991. text ed. 39.95 (*1-55605-176-X*); pap. text ed. 29.95 (*0-685-49368-7*) Wyndhall Pr.

Computers in Criminal Justice Administration & Management. 2nd ed. Archambeault & Archambeault Staff. 260p. 1989. pap. 19.95 (*0-932930-83-2*) Anderson Pub Co.

Computers in Design. Patrick Whitney. 250p. (C). 1985. text ed. 12.00 (*0-394-34305-0*) Random.

Computers in Design, Construction & Operation of Automobiles. Ed. by T. K. Murthy & C. A. Brebbia. 1987. 72.00 (*0-931215-69-2*) Computational Mech MA.

Computers in Diagnostic Radiology: A Book of Selected Readings. Euclid Seeram. (Illus.). 402p. (C). 1989. text ed. 73.95 (*0-398-05559-9*) C C Thomas.

Computers in Early & Primary Education. Douglas H. Clements. (Illus.). 352p. (C). 1984. pap. text ed. 47.00 (*0-13-164013-5*) P-H.

Computers in Education. Ed. by Ann Jones & Peter Scrimshaw. 320p. 1987. 65.00 (*0-317-89468-4*, EH803, Open Univ Pr); pap. 26.00 (*0-317-89469-2*, Open Univ Pr) Taylor & Francis.

Computers in Education. Valdemar Setzer. 78p. 1990. pap. 8.95 (*0-86315-084-5*, 1341, Pub. by Floris Books UK) Anthroposophic.

Computers in Education. 2nd ed. Paul F. Merrill et al. 384p. (C). 1991. pap. text ed. 42.00 (*0-205-13391-6*) Allyn.

Computers in Education: A Guide for Educators. Bobbie K. Hentrel & Linda Harper. LC 84-28094. 110p. reprint ed. pap. 33.70 (*0-7837-4715-2*, 2059067) Bks Demand.

Computers in Education: Legal Liabilities & Ethical Issues Concerning Their Use & Misuse. Patricia A. Hollander. LC 86-2610. (Higher Education Administration Ser.). 120p. 1994. pap. 16.95 (*0-912557-03-6*) Coll Admin Pubns.

Computers in Education: Proceedings of a Conference on Computing Laboratory in Technical College May, 1960. J. Hall & Nicholas Metropolis. LC 92-19032. (International Tracts Computer Science & Technology & Their Application Ser.: No. 10). 1962. 61.00 (*0-08-009688-3*, Pub. by Pergamon Repr UK) Franklin.

Computers in Education: Proceedings of the IFIP TC3 Fifth World Conference, Sydney, Australia 9-13 July, 1990, 2 vols., Set. Ed. by A. McDougall & C. Dowling. 1140p. 1990. 151.50 (*0-444-88750-4*, North Holland) Elsevier.

Computers in Education: Proceedings of the IFIP TC3 Fourth World Conference on Computers in Education WCCE '85 Norfolk, Va, July 29-August 2, 1985. Ed. by K. Duncan & D. Harris. 1060p. 1985. 161.75 (*0-444-87797-5*, North Holland) Elsevier.

Computers in Education: Proceedings of the IFIP TC3 1st European Conf., Lausanne, Switzerland, 24-29 July 1988. Ed. by F. B. Lovis & E. D. Tagg. 690p. 1988. 115.50 (*0-444-70483-3*, North Holland) Elsevier.

Computers in Education: Social, Political & Historical Perspectives. Robert Muffoletto & Nancy N. Knupfer. (Media, Education, Culture, Technology Ser.). 272p. 1993. text ed. 45.00 (*1-881303-59-4*); pap. text ed. 19.95 (*1-881303-60-8*) Hampton Pr NJ.

Computers in Education: What's Happening? What's Possible? (On Line Ser.). (Illus.). 48p. (Orig.). 1988. pap. text ed. 12.00 (*0-88364-164-X*) Natl Sch Boards.

Computers in Education Today. Gary G. Bitter. 384p. (C). 1989. text ed. write for info. (*0-394-39474-7*) Knopf.

Computers in Education 5-13. Ed. by Ann Jones & Peter Scrimshaw. 320p. 1988. 90.00 (*0-335-15549-9*, Open Univ Pr); pap. 32.00 (*0-335-15543-X*, Open Univ Pr) Taylor & Francis.

Computers in Educational Administration. J. Ray & L. Davis. 1991. pap. text ed. write for info. (*0-07-051257-4*) McGraw.

Computers in Elementary Language Arts. Dublin & Pressman. (C). 1994. text ed. 13.00 (*0-06-501672-6*) HarpCollege.

Computers in Elementary Math. Dublin & Pressman. (C). 1994. text ed. 13.00 (*0-06-501670-X*) HarpCollege.

Computers in Elementary Science. Dublin & Pressman. (C). 1994. text ed. 13.00 (*0-06-501674-2*) HarpCollege.

Computers in Engineering: Papers Of the International Conference, 1983, 3 Vols. Incl. Vol. 1. Computer-Aided Design, Manufacturing, & Simulation, 55 papers. Ed. by T. J. Cokonis. 357p. 1983. 70.00 (*0-685-08458-2*, GOO230); Vol. 2. Robotics Theory & Applications; Computers in Education, 47 papers. Ed. by C. F. Ruoff & T. E. Shoup. 320p. 1983. 70.00 (*0-685-08459-0*, GOO231); Vol. 3. Computer Software & Applications, 44 papers. Ed. by D. E. Dietrich. 263p. 1983. 70.00 (*0-685-08460-4*, GOO232); 1983. Set. 180.00 (*0-685-08457-4*, GOO233) ASME.

Computers in Engineering Windows Manual. William F. Beckwith. 48p. (C). 1993. pap. text ed., spiral bd. 6.95 (*0-8403-9173-0*) Kendall-Hunt.

Computers in Engineering, 1982, 4 Vols. Incl. Vol. 1. Computer-Aided Design, Manufacturing, & Simulation. 351p. 1982. 60.00 (*0-318-57978-2*, G00215); Vol. 2. Robots & Robotics. 261p. 1982. 60.00 (*0-318-57979-0*, G00216); Vol. 3. Mesh Generation, Finite Elements, Computers in Structural Optimization, Computers in the Engineering Workplace, Computers in Energy Systems, Personal Computing. 273p. 1982. 60.00 (*0-318-57980-4*, G00217); Process Control, State-of-the-Art Printing Technology, Software Engineering & Management, Statistical Modeling & Reliability Techniques, Computers in Education. 305p. 1982. 60.00 (*0-318-57981-2*, G00218); 1982. Set. 200.00 (*0-317-07007-X*, G00219) ASME.

Computers in Engineering, 1982: Proceedings of the Second International Computer Engineering Conference, August 15-19, 1982, San Diego, California, 4 vols. International Computer Engineering Conference Staff. LC 82-72306. (Illus.). 359p. reprint ed. Vol. 1, 359p. pap. 102.40 (*0-8357-2819-6*, 2039058); reprint ed. Vol. 2, 269p. pap. 76.70 (*0-8357-2820-X*, 2039058); reprint ed. Vol. 3, 283p. pap. 80.70 (*0-8357-2821-8*, 2039058); reprint ed. Vol. 4, 315p. pap. 89.80 (*0-8357-2822-6*, 2039058) Bks Demand.

***Computers in Engineering 1994: Proceedings of the 1994 ASME International Computers in Engineering Conference & Exhibition, Minneapolis, MN.** Ed. by Kosuke Ishii. 955p. 1994. pap. 200.00 (*0-7918-1380-0*) ASME.

Computers in English-Language Arts. Sharon Sorenson. (Teaching Resources in the ERIC Database (TRIED) Ser.). (Illus.). 1990. pap. 14.95 (*0-927516-15-2*) ERIC-REC.

Computers in English Language Teaching & Research. Ed. by Geoffrey N. Leech & Christopher N. Candlin. (Applied Linguistics & Language Study Ser.). 320p. (Orig.). (C). 1986. pap. text ed. 27.95 (*0-582-55069-6*, 74300) Longman.

Computers in Family History. (C). 1987. 35.00 (*0-317-89825-6*, Pub. by Birmingham Midland Soc UK) St Mut.

Computers in Fermentation Technology: Progress in Industrial Microbiology, 25 1988. Ed. by M. E. Bushell. 198p. 1988. 72.00 (*0-444-42979-4*) Elsevier.

Computers in Flavor & Fragrance Research. Ed. by Craig B. Warren & John P. Walradt. LC 84-14607. (Symposium Ser.: No. 261). 176p. 1984. lib. bdg. 32.95 (*0-8412-0861-1*) Am Chemical.

Computers in Flow Predictions & Fluid Dynamics Experiments. American Society of Mechanical Engineers Staff. Ed. by K. N. Ghia et al. LC 81-69010. 242p. reprint ed. pap. 69.00 (*0-317-19851-3*, 2023147) Bks Demand.

Computers in Forestry: Selecting a Computer to Meet Your Needs. Dudley R. Hartel & Timothy M. Cooney. 42p. (Orig.). 1984. pap. text ed. 10.00 (*0-9615391-0-0*) Forest Res Syst.

Computers in Forestry: Use of Spreadsheets. Roy Lorrain-Smith. LC 93-3425. (Forestry Ser.: Vol. 1). 192p. 1993. text ed. 59.95 (*0-471-93961-7*) Wiley.

Computers in Geography. David J. Maguire. 248p. 1989. pap. text ed. 52.95 (*0-470-21194-6*) Halsted Pr.

Computers in Geology: 25 Years of Progress. Ed. by John C. Davis & Ute C. Herzfeld. (International Association for Mathematical Geology: Studies in Mathematical Geology: No. 5). (Illus.). 316p. 1993. 45.00 (*0-19-508593-0*) OUP.

Computers in Health & Safety. Ed. by Greg Rawls. 255p. 1990. 40.00 (*0-932627-39-0*) Am Indus Hygiene.

Computers in Health Care: Introduction to Health. Covvey et al. Date not set. disk, pap. write for info. (*0-8016-3197-1*) Mosby Yr Bk.

Computers in Human Services: An Overview for Clinical & Welfare Services. Ed. by J. T. Pardech & J. W. Murphy. x, 150p. 1990. text ed. 52.00 (*3-7186-5009-6*); pap. text ed. 26.00 (*3-7186-5005-3*) Gordon & Breach.

Computers in Insurance. 3rd ed. Alan J. Turner & James Gatza. LC 89-82257. 167p. 1990. pap. 10.00 (*0-685-37873-X*) Am Inst FCPCU.

Computers in Language Research. Ed. by Walter A. Sedelow, Jr. & Sally Y. Sedelow. (Trends in Linguistic Ser.). 1979. pap. text ed. 45.50 (*90-279-7846-8*) Mouton.

Computers in Language Research 2. 2nd ed. Ed. by Walter A. Sedelow, Jr. & Sally Y. Sedelow. LC 83-11476. (Trends in Linguistics, Studies & Monographs: No. 19). viii, 301p. 1983. 89.35 (*90-279-3009-0*) Mouton.

Computers in Manufacturing. Ed. by Ulrich Rembold et al. (Manufacturing Engineering & Materials Processing Ser.: No. 1). (Illus.). 592p. 1977. 175.00 (*0-8247-1821-6*) Dekker.

Computers in Manufacturing. David A. Turbide. (Illus.). 224p. 1991. 36.95 (*0-8311-3033-4*) Indus Pr.

Computers in Materials Technology: Proceedings of the Conference Held in Linkoping, June 1980. Ed. by T. Ericsson. 200p. 1981. 98.00 (*0-08-027570-2*, Pub. by Pergamon Repr UK) Franklin.

Computers in Mathematical Research. Ed. by N. M. Stephens & M. P. Thorne. (Institute of Mathematics & Its Applications Conference Series, New Ser.: New Series 14). (Illus.). 264p. 1988. 57.50 (*0-19-853620-8*) OUP.

Computers in Mathematics. Chudnovsky & Jenks. (Lecture Notes in Pure & Applied Mathematics Ser.: Vol. 125). 432p. 1990. 125.00 (*0-8247-8341-7*) Dekker.

Computers in Mathematics Education: 1984 Yearbook. Ed. by Viggo P. Hansen. LC 84-2037. (Illus.). 244p. 1984. 20.00 (*0-87353-210-4*) NCTM.

Computers in Medical Physics. Ed. by A. R. Benedetto et al. (American Association of Physicists in Medicine Symposium Ser.: No. 17). 417p. 1990. 75.00 (*0-88318-802-3*) Am Inst Physics.

Computers in Medicine: An Introduction. Derek Enlander. 120p. 1984. 15.00 (*0-685-08621-6*) Med Software.

Computers in Medicine: Applications & Possibilities. Jonathan Javitt. (Illus.). 317p. 1986. pap. text ed. 23.00 (*0-7216-1578-3*) Saunders.

Computers in Medicine: Current Medical Subject Analysis & Research Directory with Bibliography. J. C. Bartone. LC 81-71809. 162p. 1983. 44.50 (*0-941864-32-4*); pap. 39.50 (*0-941864-33-2*) ABBE Pubs Assn.

Computers in Microbiology. Ed. by T. N. Bryant & J. W. Wimpenny. (Practical Approach Ser.). (Illus.). 264p. 1989. 62.00 (*0-19-963014-3*, IRL Pr); pap. 40.00 (*0-19-963015-1*, IRL Pr) OUP.

Computers in Middle & Secondary English. Dublin & Pressman. (C). 1994. text ed. 13.00 (*0-06-501676-9*) HarpCollege.

Computers in Middle & Secondary Math. Dublin & Pressman. (C). 1994. text ed. 13.00 (*0-06-501678-5*) HarpCollege.

Computers in Middle & Secondary Science Classrooms. Dublin & Pressman. (C). 1994. text ed. 13.00 (*0-06-501680-7*) HarpCollege.

***Computers in Mineral Industry.** R. V. Ramani et al. (Illus.). 366p. (C). 1994. text ed. 55.00 (*90-5410-242-X*) Ashgate Pub Co.

Computers in Modern Society. Ralph J. Kochenburger & Carolyn J. Turcio. LC 73-21685. 282p. reprint ed. 80.40 (*0-8357-9862-3*, 2015187) Bks Demand.

Computers in Neurobiology & Behavior. Branko Souicek & Albert D. Carlson. LC 75-25677. 340p. reprint ed. 96.90 (*0-8357-9863-1*, 2055105) Bks Demand.

Computers in Newspaper Publishing: User-Oriented Systems. Dineh Moghdam. LC 77-17887. (Books in Library & Information Science: No. 22). (Illus.). 221p. reprint ed. pap. 63.00 (*0-7837-3387-9*, 2043345) Bks Demand.

Computers in Nuclear Medicine: A Practical Approach. Kai Lee. LC 91-4859. (Illus.). 290p. (Orig.). 1991. pap. text ed. 45.00 (*0-932004-36-9*) Soc Nuclear Med.

Computers in Nursing: Hospital & Clinical Applications. Maureen P. Mikuleky & Cathleen Ledford. 280p. (C). 1988. pap. text ed. 32.25 (*0-201-15908-2*) Addison-Wesley.

Computers in Nursing Management. Virginia K. Saba et al. 1994. pap. 11.95 (*1-55810-099-7*, NP87) Am Nurses Pub.

Computers in Nursing Research: A Theoretical Perspective. American Nurses Association Staff. 52p. 1992. pap. 11.95 (*1-55810-072-5*, NS-34) Am Nurses Pub.

Computers in Nutrition. Chalda Maloff & Russell W. Zears. LC 79-4339. (Illus.). 368p. reprint ed. pap. 104.90 (*0-8357-5587-8*, 2035218) Bks Demand.

Computers in Nutrition Education. 117p. 1984. pap. 12.00 (*0-910869-21-9*) Soc Nutrition Ed.

Computers in Personnel: Papers of the Tenth National Conference, June 1991. 240p. (C). 1989. 165.00 (*0-685-60722-4*, Pub. by IPM Hse UK) St Mut.

Computers in Physics Instruction: Abstracts of Contributed Papers. Ed. by John S. Risley & Edward F. Redisch. 237p. (Orig.). (C). 1988. pap. text ed. 25.00 (*0-317-90354-3*) NCSU Physics.

C

An Asterisk (*) at the beginning of an entry indicates that the title is appearing in BIP for the first time.

Computers in Polymer Sciences. Ed. by James S. Mattson et al. LC 75-40603. (Computers in Chemistry & Instrumentation Ser.: No. 6). (Illus.). 390p. reprint ed. pap. 111.20 (*0-7837-0732-0*, 2041056) Bks Demand.

Computers in Private Practice Management. B. B. Oberst & J. L. Long. (Illus.). 290p. 1987. 79.00 (*0-387-96502-5*) Spr-Verlag.

Computers in Psychology: Application in Education, Research & Psychodiagnostics. Ed. by L. J. Mulder et al. 240p. 1991. 48.00 (*90-265-1170-1*, Pub. by Swets Pub Serv NE) Taylor & Francis.

***Computers in Psychology: Applications, Methods & Instrumentation.** Ed. by F. J. Maarse et al. (Computers in Psychology Ser.: Vol. 5). 286p. 1995. 73.00 (*90-265-1415-8*, Pub. by Swets Pub Serv NE) Taylor & Francis.

Computers in Psychology: Methods, Instrumentation, & Psychodiagnostics. F. J. Maarse et al. 220p. 1988. pap. 44.00 (*90-265-0896-4*, Pub. by Swets Pub Serv NE) Taylor & Francis.

Computers in Psychology: Tools for Experimental & Applied Psychology. Ed. by F. J. Maarse et al. LC 92-49200. 260p. 1992. 57.00 (*90-265-1268-6*, Pub. by Swets Pub Serv NE) Taylor & Francis.

Computers in Public Administration: An International Perspective. Ed. by Samuel J. Bernstein. 450p. 1976. 203.00 (*0-08-017869-3*, Pub. by Pergamon Repr UK) Franklin.

Computers in Radiology: Proceedings. International Meeting on the Use of Computers in Radiology, Brussels, 1969. Ed. by A. Wambersie & R. De Haene. 1970. 94.50 (*3-8055-0805-0*) S Karger.

Computers in Radiotherapy & Oncology: Proceedings of the Workshop on the Use of Computers in Data Handling in Radiotherapy & Oncology in Europe Held at the Headquarters of the World Health Organization, Geneva, 26-28 March 1984. Workshop on the Use of Computers in Data Handling in Radiotherapy & Oncology in Europe (1984: World Health Organization) Staff. Ed. by R. F. Mould. LC 84-24245. 264p. 1984. reprint ed. pap. 75.30 (*0-7837-4503-6*, 2044280) Bks Demand.

Computers in Radiotherapy Planning. Raymond G. Wood. LC 82-108915. (Medical Computing Ser.: No. 5). (Illus.). 183p. reprint ed. pap. 52.20 (*0-8357-6069-3*, 2034244) Bks Demand.

Computers in Railway Installations, Track, & Signalling. Ed. by T. K. Murthy & F. E. Young. LC 87-70872. (COMPRAIL Ser.: Vol. 1). 324p. 1987. 79.00 (*0-931215-78-1*) Computational Mech MA.

Computers in Railway Installations, Track, & Signalling. Ed. by T. K. Murthy et al. 480p. 1987. 119.00 (*0-387-17933-X*) Spr-Verlag.

Computers in Railway Management. Ed. by T. K. Murthy et al. LC 87-70871. (COMPRAIL Ser.: Vol. 1). 254p. 1987. 66.00 (*0-931215-58-7*) Computational Mech MA.

Computers in Railway Management & Technology: Proceedings of the Third International Conference on Computer Aided Design, Manufacture & Operation in Railway & Other Advanced Mass Transit Systems Held in Washington, DC, August 18-20, 1992, 2 vols., Set. Ed. by T. K. Murthy et al. LC 91-81589. (COMPRAIL Ser.: Vol. 3). 1992. 378.00 (*1-56252-105-5*) Computational Mech MA.

Computers in Railway Management & Technology: Proceedings of the Third International Conference on Computer Aided Design, Manufacture & Operation in Railway & Other Advanced Mass Transit Systems, Vol. 1: Management. Ed. by T. K. Murthy et al. LC 91-81589. (COMPRAIL Ser.: Vol. 3). 632p. 1992. 235.00 (*1-56252-132-2*) Computational Mech MA.

Computers in Railway Operations. Ed. by T. K. Murthy et al. LC 87-70870. (COMPRAIL Ser.: Vol. 1). 344p. 1987. 84.00 (*0-931215-79-X*) Computational Mech MA.

Computers in Railways III: Proceedings of the Third International Conference on Computer Aided Design, Manufacture & Operation in Railway & Other Advanced Mass Transit Systems, Vol. 2: Technology. Ed. by T. K. Murthy et al. LC 91-81589. (COMPRAIL Ser.: Vol. 3). 498p. 1992. 186.00 (*1-56252-133-0*) Computational Mech MA.

Computers in Railways IV: Proceedings of the Fourth International Conference, 2 vols., Set. Ed. by T. K. Marthy et al. LC 94-72459. (Comprail Ser.: Vol. 4). 1074p. 1994. 379.00 (*1-56252-190-X*) Computational Mech MA.

***Computers in Railways IV Vol. 1: Railway Design & Management.** Ed. by B. Mellitt et al. LC 94-72459. (Comprail Ser.: Vol. 4). 1994. 226.00 (*1-56252-282-5*) Computational Mech MA.

***Computers in Railways IV Vol. 2: Railway Operations.** Ed. by B. Mellitt et al. LC 94-72459. (Comprail Ser.: Vol. 4). 1994. 193.00 (*1-56252-283-3*) Computational Mech MA.

Computers in School. M. Bramble. 1985. text ed. write for info. (*0-07-007151-9*) McGraw.

Computers in Small Business. Russell W. Rumberger & Henry M. Levin. 50p. (Orig.). 1986. pap. text ed. 6.00 (*0-940791-04-8*) NFIB Found.

Computers in Small Bytes: The Computer Workbook. I. Joos et al. (Illus.). 272p. (C). 1992. pap. text ed. 22.95 (*0-88737-562-6*, 14-2496) Natl League Nurse.

Computers in Society. Nancy B. Stern & Robert A. Stern. (Illus.). 624p. (C). 1982. pap. text ed. write for info. (*0-13-165282-6*) P-H.

Computers in Space. James Tomayko. 1994. pap. 20.00 (*1-56761-463-9*) Alpha Bks IN.

Computers in Stereotactic Neurosurgery. Ed. by P. J. Kelly & B. Kall. (Contemporary Issues in Neurological Surgery Ser.). (Illus.). 384p. 1992. 120.00 (*0-86542-145-5*) Blackwell Sci.

Computers in Teaching: A Complete Training Manual for Teachers to Use Computers in Their Classrooms. Walter Wager et al. 229p. 1989. disk, pap. 34.95 (*0-914797-53-0*) Brookline Bks.

Computers in Teaching Mathematics. John Burton et al. (Computers in Education Ser.). 192p. 1983. text ed. 22.90 (*0-201-10565-9*) Addison-Wesley.

Computers in Textiles - A Buyer's Guide to European Products & Services. Peter J. Allen. 106p. (C). 1989. pap. text ed. 175.00 (*1-870812-16-6*, Pub. by Textile Institue UK) St Mut.

Computers in the Artroom. Deborah Greh. (Illus.). 128p. 1990. spiral bd. 26.95 (*0-87192-221-5*) Davis Mass.

Computers in the Classroom. Johnson & Sasser. 160p. (C). 1992. pap. text ed. 12.95 (*0-8403-7915-3*) Kendall-Hunt.

Computers in the Classroom. Edward Vockell et al. 1988. pap. text ed. write for info. (*0-07-554190-4*) McGraw.

Computers in the Classroom. 2nd ed. Ed. by Henry S. Kepner, Jr. 160p. 1986. 10.95 (*0-8106-1829-X*) NEA.

***Computers in the Classroom: Mindtools for Critical Thinking.** David H. Jonassen. LC 94-43081. 1995. write for info. (*0-02-361191-X*, Merrill Pub Co) Macmillan.

Computers in the Clinical Laboratory: An Introduction. E. Clifford Toren & Arthur A. Eggert. LC 78-6055. (Clinical & Biochemical Analysis Ser.: No. 8). 174p. reprint ed. pap. 49.60 (*0-685-16021-1*, 2027084) Bks Demand.

Computers in the Dental Office: How to Evaluate, Select & Get the Most Out of Your System. Frank J. Sapienza. LC 92-80574. 128p. 1992. ring bd. 39.95 (*0-9632212-6-4*) Mare Pub Dist.

Computers in the Doctor's Office. Stephen Radin & Harold Greenberg. LC 84-8378. 160p. 1984. text ed. 45.00 (*0-275-91245-0*, C1245, Praeger Pubs) Greenwood.

Computers in the Elementary Classroom. abr. ed. Mindy S. Pollock. 130p. 1995. pap. 6.95 (*1-56901-336-5*) NW Pub.

Computers in the English Classroom: Promises & Pitfalls. Ed. by Charles R. Chew. 148p. 1984. pap. text ed. 7.00 (*0-930348-11-7*) NY St Eng Coun.

Computers in the Fashion Industry. Patrick Taylor. 215p. 1990. pap. 29.95 (*0-434-91916-0*) Buttrwrth-Heinemann.

Computers in the Human Context: Information Theory, Productivity, & People. Ed. by Tom Forester. 528p. (Orig.). 1989. 42.00 (*0-262-06124-4*); pap. 20.00 (*0-262-56050-X*) MIT Pr.

Computers in the Laboratory: Current Practice & Future Trends. Ed. by Joseph G. Liscouski. LC 84-18518. (Symposium Ser.: No. 265). 136p. 1984. lib. bdg. 43.95 (*0-8412-0867-0*) Am Chemical.

Computers in the Language Classroom. R. Hertz. 1987. text ed. 18.75 (*0-201-20574-2*) Addison-Wesley.

Computers in the Medical Office: Using MediSoft. Ed. by Claire Baptist et al. LC 94-20025. 1995. write for info. (*0-02-803042-7*) Glencoe.

Computers in the Office. McGill. 1989. pap. 15.95 (*0-8384-3325-1*) Heinle & Heinle.

***Computers in the Primary Care Office.** 3rd ed. American Academy of Pediatrics Staff. 248p. 1995. pap. 54.95 (*0-910761-70-1*) Am Acad Pediat.

***Computers in the Primary School.** Jon Griffin & Leslie Bash. LC 94-45160. (Education Ser.). (Illus.). 144p. 1995. 60.00 (*0-304-32997-5*); pap. 20.00 (*0-304-32991-6*) Cassell.

***Computers in the Professional Practice of Design.** Karen M. Brown & Curtis B. Charles. LC 94-25997. 1994. write for info. (*0-07-011075-1*) McGraw.

Computers in the Schools: A Guide to Planning & Administration. Anthony G. Picciano. 320p. (C). 1993. text ed. write for info. (*0-02-395281-4*, Merrill Pub Co) Macmillan.

Computers in the Schools: The New Frontier. Anne McKay. LC 85-106180. 66p. (Orig.). 1984. pap. 6.00 (*0-88156-027-8*) Comm Serv Soc NY.

Computers in the Service of Society. Ed. by Robert L. Chartrand. LC 73-112401. 256p. 1972. 89.00 (*0-08-016332-7*, Pub. by Pergamon Repr UK) Franklin.

Computers in the Special Education Classroom. Ed. by D. La Mont Johnson et al. LC 86-22834. (Computers in the Schools Ser.: Vol. 3, No. 3-4). 194p. 1987. text ed. 39.95 (*0-86656-257-5*) Haworth Pr.

Computers in the Water Environment. 1993. pap. 150.00 (*1-881369-26-9*) Water Environ.

Computers in the World of Textiles. Textile Institute Staff. 718p. (C). 1984. pap. text ed. 150.00 (*0-900739-69-X*, Pub. by Textile Institue UK) St Mut.

Computers in the 1980's. Rein Turn. LC 74-1488. 224p. 1974. text ed. 52.00 (*0-231-03844-5*) Col U Pr.

Computers in Third World Schools: Examples, Experience & Issues. David Hawkridge et al. LC 90-49501. 352p. 1991. text ed. 49.95 (*0-312-05777-6*) St Martin.

Computers in Translation: A Practical Appraisal. John Newton. 224p. 1992. write for info. (*0-415-05432-X*, A6955) Routledge.

Computers in Transport Planning & Operation. A. Wren. 152p. 1971. text ed. 116.00 (*0-677-65370-0*) Gordon & Breach.

Computers in Transportation. Ed. by Cargo Systems Staff. 1987. 195.00 (*0-317-89777-2*, Pub. by Cargo Systs UK) St Mut.

Computers in Ultrasonic Diagnostics. Peter Wells & John P. Woodcock. LC 77-1571. (Medical Computing Ser.: No. 1). (Illus.). 108p. reprint ed. pap. 30.80 (*0-8357-6070-7*, 2034243) Bks Demand.

Computers in Welfare: The MIS-Match. David Dery. LC 81-2240. (Managing Information Ser.: No. 3). 260p. reprint ed. pap. 74.10 (*0-8357-8455-X*, 2034719) Bks Demand.

Computers, Inc. Japan's Challenge to IBM. Marie Anchordoguy. (East Asian Monographs: No. 144). 300p. 1989. 32.00 (*0-674-15630-7*) HUP.

Computers, Information, Awareness: A Practical Course. P. Ayre & A. W. Payne. 120p. (C). 1984. pap. text ed. 60.00 (*0-273-01996-1*, Pub. by Pitman Pubng UK) St Mut.

Computers, Jobs, & Skills: The Industrial Relations of Technological Change. C. Baldry. LC 88-23384. (Approaches to Information Technology Ser.). (Illus.). 212p. 1988. pap. 42.50 (*0-306-42963-2*, Plenum Pr) Plenum.

Computers, Language Reform & Lexicography in China: A Report by the CETA Delegation. Ed. by Jim Mathias & Thomas L. Kennedy. LC 81-112015. 84p. reprint ed. pap. 25.00 (*0-685-24155-6*, 2033029) Bks Demand.

Computers: Literacy & Learning: A Primer for Administrators. George E. Marsh, II. Ed. by Jerry J. Herman & Janice L. Herman. (Road Maps to Success Ser.). 72p. 1993. 15.00 (*0-8039-6073-5*) Corwin Pr.

Computers Made Easy. Don Cassel. 1984. text ed. 34.00 (*0-8359-0859-3*, Reston); pap. text ed. 30.00 (*0-8359-0858-5*, Reston) P-H.

***Computers Made Really Easy for Beginners.** Norma L. Leone. LC 95-2941. 120p. (Orig.). 1995. pap. 8.95 (*0-936635-08-8*) Lion Pr & Vid.

Computers, Minds & Robots. William S. Robinson. 350p. (C). 1992. 44.95 (*0-87722-915-5*) Temple U Pr.

Computers, Minds, & Robots. William S. Robinson. 230p. 1993. pap. 19.95 (*1-56639-082-6*) Temple U Pr.

Computers, My First Book. Nada J. Green. 86p. 1992. pap. 9.95 (*0-9635023-1-X*) N J Classics.

Computers, Nomads & Other Things. Chris Bigum. 79p. (C). 1988. 35.00 (*0-7300-0603-4*, Pub. by Deakin Univ AT) St Mut.

***Computers of the Future: Intelligent Machines & Virtual Reality.** David Darling. LC 95-14212. (Beyond 2000 Ser.). (J). 1995. lib. bdg. write for info. (*0-87518-617-3*, Dillon Silver Burdett); pap. write for info. (*0-382-39169-1*, Dillon Silver Burdett) Silver Burdett Pr.

Computers on the Battlefield: The Automated Battlefield, Computer Design and Maintenance in War. 1986. lib. bdg. 79.95 (*0-8490-3738-7*) Gordon Pr.

Computers on the Farm: Farm Uses for Computers-How to Select Software, Hardware & Online Information Sources In Agriculture. 1986. lib. bdg. 69.95 (*0-8490-3759-X*) Gordon Pr.

Computers, Pattern, Chaos & Beauty: Graphics from an Unseen World. Clifford A. Pickover. LC 89-70068. (Illus.). 415p. 1991. pap. 19.95 (*0-312-06179-X*) St Martin.

Computers, People & Productivity. Ed. by Lee W. Frederiksen & Anne W. Riley. LC 84-25281. (Journal of Organizational Behavior Management: Vol. 6, Nos. 3 & 4). 183p. 1985. text ed. 49.95 (*0-86656-339-3*) Haworth Pr.

***Computers, Peripherals, & Computer Components: Industry & Trade Summary.** Julie Throne. (Illus.). 51p. (Orig.). (C). 1994. pap. text ed. 45.00x (*0-7881-1540-5*) Diane Pub.

Computers, Self & Society. Michael G. Wessells. 288p. (C). 1989. pap. text ed. write for info. (*0-13-171273-X*) P-H.

Computers Service & Repair, 1995. American Business Directories Staff. 1995. spiral bd., pap. 1,105.00 (*1-56105-607-3*) Am Busn Direct.

***Computers Simplified.** Richard Maran Graphics Staff. 1994. pap. 14.99 (*1-56884-651-7*) IDG Bks.

***Computers Simplified.** 2nd ed. Maran Graphics Staff. 1995. pap. 19.99 (*1-56884-676-2*) IDG Bks.

Computers Simplified: MaranGraphics Simplified Computer Guide. Richard Maran & Eric Feistmantl. LC 93-12260. 160p. (J). 1993. Academic edition. pap. text ed. 16.80 (*0-13-095324-5*) P-H Gen Ref & Trav.

Computers Simplified & Illustrated, Bk. 1: Learn the Easy Way. Gary L. Lesperance & John J. Purvins. (Illus.). 80p. (Orig.). (C). 1985. pap. 5.95 (*0-932285-00-7*) Rockway Hse.

Computers Simplified-Expanded Edition. MaranGraphics Staff. 1994. pap. 19.95 (*0-13-304080-1*) P-H.

Computers: The Non-Technological (Human) Factors: A Recommended Reading List on Computer Ergonomics & User Friendly Design. Ed. by John L. Burch. LC 84-60013. 101p. 1984. pap. 17.50 (*0-916313-00-X*) Ergosyst Assocs.

Computers the Plain English Guide: Almost Everything You Need to Know about Computers, Even If You Don't Know Anything about Computers. 3rd ed. Phillip A. Covington. LC 88-92376. (Illus.). 295p. 1991. pap. 19.95 (*0-942059-01-8*) QNS Pub.

Computers Today! Everett E. Murdock. 160p. (C). 1995. write for info. (*0-697-20403-0*) Bus & Educ Tech.

Computers Today & International Educations Lab Manual: Using Wordperfect 4.2, VP Planner & dBase III. 3rd ed. Intentional Educations Staff & Donald H. Sanders. 1988. student ed 45.95 (*0-318-32781-3*) McGraw.

Computers under Attack: Intruders, Worms & Viruses. Ed. by Peter J. Denning. (ACM Press Ser.). (Illus.). 160p. (C). 1990. pap. text ed. 25.75 (*0-201-53067-8*) Addison-Wesley.

Computers, Video Games & Your Child's Development. Hector Robertin & Joseph C. Bratton. LC 83-62878. (Illus.). 120p. 1984. pap. 9.95 (*0-912921-02-1*) Pau Hana Pr.

***Computers Visual Pocket Guide.** Maran Graphics Staff. 1995. pap. 14.99 (*1-56884-675-4*) IDG Bks.

Computers! We'll Assume You Know Nothing. 2nd ed. Yvonne B. Hannah. LC 90-93508. (Illus.). 143p. (Orig.). 1991. pap. 12.95 (*1-878044-07-9*) Mayhaven Pub.

Computers Wholesale & Manufacturers, 1995. American Business Directories Staff. 1995. spiral bd., pap. 350.00 (*1-56105-608-1*) Am Busn Direct.

Computers, Work & Health. Trevor A. Williams. 250p. 1989. 85.00 (*0-85066-453-5*) Taylor & Francis.

ComputerSleuths: Adventure Mystery for Kids Ages 8-12. Wayne Geehan. (BePuzzled Junior Ser.). (Illus.). (J). (gr. 2-6). 1993. 14.00 (*0-922242-45-3*) Lombard Mktg.

***Computicon: German-English-German PC Version.** Diebel. 600p. (ENG & GER.). 1992. 150.00 (*0-7859-7542-X*, 3893622004) Fr & Eur.

Computing. Ed. by E. G. Coffman, Jr. et al. LC 92-16696. (Handbooks in Operations Research & Management Science Ser.: Vol. 3). 1992. write for info. (*0-444-88097-6*, North Holland) Elsevier.

***Computing.** Larry Long & Nancy Long. LC 94-32975. 1994. pap. text ed. write for info. (*0-13-309956-3*) P-H.

Computing: A Human Activity. Peter Naur. (Illus.). 640p. (C). 1992. pap. text ed. 29.25 (*0-201-58069-1*) Addison-Wesley.

Computing: An Introduction to Structured Problem Solving Using Pascal. V. A. Dyck et al. (C). 1981. write for info. (*0-8359-0903-4*, Reston); text ed. write for info. (*0-8359-0902-6*, Reston) P-H.

Computing: Concepts for End Users. Nancy B. Stern & Robert A. Stern. 1990. Net. pap. text ed. write for info. (*0-471-53218-5*) Wiley.

***Computing: The Technology of Information.** Tony Dodd. (New Encyclopedia of Science Ser.). (Illus.). 160p. 1995. 35.00 (*0-19-521139-1*) OUP.

Computing Across America: The Bicycle Odyssey of a High-Tech Nomad. Steven K. Roberts. (Illus.). 368p. 1988. 14.95 (*0-938734-25-3*); pap. 9.95 (*0-938734-18-0*) Learned Info.

Computing Across the Curriculum. William H. Graves. (Educom Strategies Ser.). (Illus.). (C). 1991. text ed. 43.25 (*0-201-50642-4*) Addison-Wesley.

***Computing Against the Odds: The Beginner's Guide to Sports Handicapping with a Personal Computer.** Randall J. Rutecki. (Orig.). 1995. pap. 29.95 (*0-9646727-0-7*) Cybersource.

Computing & Change on Campus. Ed. by Sara B. Kiesler & Lee S. Sproull. (Illus.). 225p. 1987. 34.95 (*0-521-34431-X*) Cambridge U Pr.

Computing & Education: The Second Frontier. Ed. by Robert McClintock. (Special Issues for the Teachers College Record Ser.). 128p. 1988. reprint ed. pap. text ed. 15.95 (*0-8077-2943-4*) Tchrs Coll.

Computing & Graphics in Statistics. Ed. by A. Buja et al. (IMA Volumes in Mathematics & Its Applications Ser.: Vol. 35). (Illus.). xiv, 279p. 1991. 39.50 (*0-387-97633-7*) Spr-Verlag.

Computing & Information: Proceedings of the International Conference (ICCI '89), Toronto, Canada, 23-27 May 1989. Ed. by R. Janicki & W. W. Koczkodaj. 540p. 1989. 102.75 (*0-444-88055-0*, North Holland) Elsevier.

***Computing & Information Systems.** Fritz Erickson & John Vonk. 320p. (C). 1995. pap. write for info. (*0-697-25642-1*) Bus & Educ Tech.

Computing & Information, 4th International Conference on (ICCI '92) LC 92-52645. 520p. 1992. 98.00 (*0-8186-2812-X*, 2812) IEEE Comp Soc.

Computing & Information, 5th International Conference on (ICCI '93) 520p. 1993. text ed. 110.00 (*0-8186-4212-2*, 4212) IEEE Comp Soc.

Computing & Logic: Mathematics & Language. G. Satty et al. (Introductiones Ser.). 223p. (C). 1988. pap. text ed. 23.00 (*3-88405-071-0*) Philosophia Pr.

Computing & Mathematics: The Impact on Secondary School Curricula. Ed. by James T. Fey. LC 84-2091. (Illus.). 100p. (Orig.). 1984. pap. 8.50 (*0-87353-212-0*) NCTM.

Computing & Monitoring Anesthesia & Intensive Care: Recent Technological Advances. Ed. by K. Ikeda et al. (Illus.). xxvi, 518p. 1992. 139.00 (*0-387-70101-X*) Spr-Verlag.

Computing & Software Career Directory. Ed. by Bradley J. Morgan & Joseph M. Palmisano. (Career Advisor Ser.). 300p. 1993. 39.00 (*0-8103-9152-X*, 101797) Gale.

Computing & Software Career Directory. Ed. by Bradley J. Morgan & Joseph M. Palmisano. (Career Advisor Ser.). 300p. 1993. pap. 17.95 (*0-8103-9448-0*, 089162) Visible Ink Pr.

Computing Before Computers. Ed. by William Aspray, Jr. (Illus.). 276p. 1990. 27.95 (*0-8138-0047-1*) Iowa St U Pr.

Computing Boolean Statistical Models. Paulo M. De Oliveria. 140p. (C). 1991. text ed. 40.00 (*981-02-0238-5*) World Scientific Pub.

Computing Catastrophes. Robert L. Glass. 1983. 10.00 (*0-686-35783-3*) Computing Trends.

Computing Concepts. Tim Duffy. 293p. (C). 1992. pap. 22.95 (*0-534-17538-4*) Boyd & Fraser.

***Computing Concepts.** 2nd ed. Tim Duffy & Traci Berchelmann. 372p. 1994. pap. text ed. 24.95 (*0-534-21912-8*) Boyd & Fraser.

Computing Concepts for End-Users & Getting Started with Structured BASIC. Nancy B. Stern & Robert A. Stern. (C). 1990. Net. pap. text ed. write for info. (*0-471-53309-2*) Wiley.

Computing Concepts Plus Four Software Tools. 2nd ed. Tim Duffy. 746p. (C). 1992. pap. 42.95 (*0-534-16200-2*) Boyd & Fraser.

Computing Developments in Experimental & Numerical Stress Analysis. Ed. by Philip E. Stanley. (Illus.). x, 239p. 1976. 63.00 (*0-85334-680-1*, Pub. by Elsevier Applied Sci UK) Elsevier.

Computing Diagrams for the Tetrachoric Correlation Coefficient. Leone Chesire et al. 58p. 1968. pap. text ed. 10.00 (*0-317-11974-5*, William James) Psychometric.

Computing Electric Filters with a PC. 2nd ed. C. Y. Chang. Ed. by Harold F. John. (Illus.). 220p. (Orig.). 1994. pap. text ed. 19.95 (*0-9607806-8-8*) Li Kung Shaw.

C

C

An Asterisk (*) at the beginning of an entry indicates that the title is appearing in BIP for the first time.

An Asterisk (*) at the beginning of an entry indicates that the title is appearing in BIP for the first time.

1513

C

Conan the Defender. Robert Jordan. 1991. pap. 3.95 (*0-8125-1394-0*) Tor Bks.

Conan the Defiant. Steve Perry. 256p. 1987. pap. 6.95 (*0-8125-4264-9*) Tor Bks.

Conan the Destroyer. Robert Jordan. 1993. mass mkt. 4.50 (*0-8125-3136-1*) Tor Bks.

***Conan the Formidable.** Perry. 1990. pap. text ed. 7.95 (*0-8125-0998-6*) Tor Bks.

Conan the Formidable. Steve Perry. 1991. mass mkt. 3.99 (*0-8125-1377-0*) Tor Bks.

Conan the Free Lance. Steve Perry. 1990. pap. 3.95 (*0-8125-0690-1*) Tor Bks.

Conan the Gladiator. Leonard Carpenter. 288p. 1995. mass mkt. 4.99 (*0-8125-2492-6*) Tor Bks.

Conan the Great. Leonard Carpenter. 1990. pap. 3.95 (*0-8125-0714-2*) Tor Bks.

Conan the Guardian. Roland J. Green. 1991. pap. 3.95 (*0-8125-0961-7*) Tor Bks.

Conan the Hunter. Sean A. Moore. 256p. 1994. mass mkt. 4.99 (*0-8125-3531-6*) Tor Bks.

Conan the Indomitable. Steve Perry. 1989. pap. 7.95 (*0-8125-0295-7*) Tor Bks.

Conan the Indomitable. Steve Perry. 1990. pap. 3.95 (*0-8125-0860-2*) Tor Bks.

Conan the Invincible. Robert Jordan. 1990. pap. 3.95 (*0-8125-0997-8*) Tor Bks.

Conan the Outcast. Larry Carpenter. 1991. pap. 3.95 (*0-8125-0928-5*) Tor Bks.

Conan the Relentless. Roland J. Green. 1992. mass mkt. 3.99 (*0-8125-0962-5*) Tor Bks.

Conan the Rogue. John Buscema & Roy Thomas. 64p. 1991. 9.95 (*0-87135-842-5*) Marvel Entmnt.

Conan the Savage. Leonard Carpenter. 288p. 1992. pap. 7.99 (*0-8125-2238-9*) Tor Bks.

Conan the Savage. Leonard Carpenter. 288p. 1993. mass mkt. 4.50 (*0-8125-1412-2*) Tor Bks.

Conan the Triumphant. Robert Jordan. 1991. pap. 3.95 (*0-8125-1398-3*) Tor Bks.

Conan the Unconquered. Robert Jordan. 288p. (Orig.). 1991. mass mkt. 3.99 (*0-8125-1400-9*) Tor Bks.

Conan the Valiant. Roland Green. 288p. 1988. pap. 6.95 (*0-8125-4270-3*) Tor Bks.

Conan the Victorious. Robert Jordan. (Orig.). 1991. pap. 3.95 (*0-8125-1399-1*) Tor Bks.

Conan the Warlord. Leonard Carpenter. 288p. 1988. pap. 3.50 (*0-8125-4268-1*) Tor Bks.

***Conan TK 4.** 1995. pap. 7.99 (*0-614-03871-5*) Tor Bks.

Conan's World & Robert E. Howard. Darrell Schweitzer. LC 78-14569. (Milford Series: Popular Writers of Today: Popular Writers of Today: Vol. 17). 64p. 1978. lib. bdg. 20.00 (*0-89370-123-8*); pap. 10.00 (*0-89370-223-4*) Borgo Pr.

C

Conapack: Program for Canonical Analysis of Classification Tables. L. Orloci. 126p. 1991. pap. 30.00 (*90-5103-063-0*, Pub. by SPB Acad Pub NE) Koeltz Sci Bks.

Conartist: Thirty Years with the Los Angeles Times. Paul Conrad. 1993. 35.00 (*0-9619095-5-2*) LA Times.

Conations: On Striving, Willing & Wishing & Their Relationships with Cognition, Emotions, & Motives. Henrik Poulsen. 151p. (Orig.). 1991. pap. 37.50 (*87-7288-358-8*, Pub. by Aarhus Univ Pr DK) Coronet Bks.

Conative Connection. Kathy Kolbe. 1990. 16.95 (*0-685-26630-3*) Addison-Wesley.

Conative Connection: Uncovering the Link Between Who You Are & How You Perform. Kathy Kolbe. 1991. pap. 8.61 (*0-201-57095-5*) Addison-Wesley.

Concanavalin A as a Tool. Ed. by H. Bittiger & H. P. Schnebli. LC 75-37841. (Wiley-Interscience Publication Ser.). 659p. reprint ed. pap. 180.00 (*0-317-26200-9*, 2052066) Bks Demand.

Concatenation: Enoch's Prophecy Fulfilling! Hebrew-Christian Metaphysics Supported by Modern Science. Evolyn B. Feiring. LC 72-96989. 5.00 (*0-9603386-0-8*); pap. 2.00 (*0-9603386-1-6*) Rocky Mtn Bks.

Concave Mirror. Marguerite Iknayan. (Stanford French & Italian Studies: Vol. 30). 240p. 1983. pap. 46.50 (*0-915838-07-9*) Anma Libri.

Concealed Essence of the Havajra Tantra. G. W. Farrow. (C). 1992. text ed. 28.50 (*81-208-0911-4*) S Asia.

Concealed Wisdom in World Mythology. Geoffrey Hodson. 1983. 19.95 (*81-7059-132-5*) Theos Pub Hse.

Concealments in Hemingway's Works. Gerry Brenner. LC 83-6283. 301p. 1983. 42.50 (*0-8142-0338-8*) Ohio St U Pr.

Conceited News of Sir Thomas Overbury & His Friends: With Sir Thomas Overbury His Wife. Thomas Overbury. Ed. by James E. Savage. LC 68-29084. 1968. 60.00 (*0-8201-1039-6*) Schol Facsimiles.

Conceived by Liberty: Maternal Figures & Nineteenth-Century American Literature. Stephanie A. Smith. (Reading Women Writing Ser.). (Illus.). 264p. 1994. 39.95 (*0-8014-2924-2*); pap. 15.95 (*0-8014-8150-3*) Cornell U Pr.

Conceived in Liberty, 4 vols. Murray N. Rothbard. 1672p. (C). 1988. reprint ed. pap. text ed. 49.95 (*0-685-21085-5*) Independent Inst.

Conceived in Liberty: The Rise & Transformation of Modern Conservatism. Kenneth Murphy. 350p. 1994. text ed. 22.95 (*0-02-922317-2*) Free Pr.

Conceived Presences: Literary Genealogy in Renaissance England. Raphael Falco. LC 94-14812. (Massachusetts Studies in Early Modern Culture). 248p. (C). 1994. lib. bdg. 32.50 (*0-87023-935-X*) U of Mass Pr.

Conceived with Malice: Literature as Revenge. Louise DeSalvo. LC 94-9927. 1994. 24.95 (*0-525-93899-0*, Dutton) NAL-Dutton.

***Conceived with Malice: Literature as Revenge in the Lives & Works of Virginia & Leonard Woolf, D. H. Lawrence, Djuna Barnes & Henry Miller.** Louise DeSalvo. 448p. 1995. 13.95 (*0-452-27323-4*, Plume) NAL-Dutton.

Conceiving Sexuality: Approaches to Sex Research in a Postmodern World. Ed. by Richard Parker & John H. Gagnon. LC 94-17761. 320p. 1994. pap. 18.95 (*0-415-90928-7*, B3848, Routledge NY) Routledge.

Conceiving Sexuality: Approaches to Sex Research in a Postmodern World. Ed. by Richard Parker & John Gagnon. LC 94-17761. 320p. 1994. 59.95 (*0-415-90927-9*, B3844, Routledge NY) Routledge.

***Conceiving the New World Order: The Global Politics of Reproduction.** Ed. by Faye D. Ginsburg & Rayna Rapp. LC 94-29011. 1995. 45.00 (*0-520-08913-8*); pap. text ed. 18.00 (*0-520-08914-6*) U CA Pr.

Conceiving the Self. Morris Rosenberg. LC 86-7431. 336p. 1986. reprint ed. text ed. 36.50 (*0-89874-961-1*) Krieger.

Concentrated & Dried Dairy Products. Marijana Caric. LC 93-37115. 249p. 1994. 110.00 (*1-56081-531-0*) VCH Pubs.

Concentrated Course in Traditional Harmony, Bk. 1. Paul Hindemith. 1943. pap. 17.95 (*0-901938-42-4*, STAP036) Eur-Am Music.

Concentrated Course in Traditional Harmony: Bk. 2, Exercises for Advanced Students. Paul Hindemith. 1953. pap. 17.95 (*0-901938-43-2*, STAP068) Eur-Am Music.

Concentrated Youth-Restoring Foods. William H. Lee & Lynn Lee. LC 93-50191. 315p. 1994. 29.98 (*0-941683-10-9*) Instant Improve.

Concentration. Sam Horn. Ed. by Michael G. Crisp. LC 90-83476. (Fifty-Minute Ser.). (Illus.). 92p. (Orig.). 1991. pap. 9.95 (*1-56052-073-6*) Crisp Pubns.

Concentration. Annie R. Militz. 84p. 1972. reprint ed. spiral bd. 2.20 (*0-7873-0614-2*) Mokelumne.

Concentration: A Guide to Mental Mastery. M. Sadhu. 1980. pap. 7.00 (*0-87980-023-2*) Wilshire.

Concentration: An Approach to Meditation. Ernest Wood. LC 67-2874. 1985. pap. 5.95 (*0-8356-0176-5*, Quest) Theos Pub Hse.

Concentration: Focus Your Mind, Power Your Game. Marie Dalloway. 62p. (Orig.). 1993. pap. text ed. 14.95 (*0-9634933-1-0*) Optimal Perf.

Concentration: Strategies for Attaining Focus. Becky Patterson. 128p. (C). 1993. per., pap. text ed. 16.95 (*0-8403-8685-0*) Kendall-Hunt.

Concentration: The Secret of Success. Julia S. Sears. 20p. 1993. reprint ed. spiral bd. 3.30 (*0-7873-0759-9*) Mokelumne.

Concentration & Control: A Solution of the Trust Problem in the United States. Charles R. Van Hise. LC 73-2538. (Big Business; Economic Power in a Free Society Ser.). 1973. reprint ed. 23.95 (*0-405-05116-6*) Ayer.

Concentration & Drying of Foods: Proceedings of the Kellog Foundation Second International Food Research Symposium, University College, Cork, Republic of Ireland, 16-18 September 1985. Ed. by D. MacCarthy. 320p. 1986. 72.00 (*0-85334-442-6*) Elsevier.

Concentration & Meditation. Christmas Humphreys. 1993. pap. 15.95 (*1-85230-008-6*, COMEDP) Element MA.

Concentration & Meditation. Christmas Humphreys. 343p. 1981. pap. 25.00 (*0-89540-068-5*, SB-068) Sun Pub.

Concentration & Meditation. Swami Jyotir Maya Nanda. (Illus.). 1971. 14.95 (*0-934664-03-X*) Yoga Res Foun.

Concentration & Meditation. 8th ed. Swami Paramananda. 1974. pap. 3.95 (*0-911564-07-1*) Vedanta Ctr.

Concentration & Price. Ed. by Leonard W. Weiss. 304p. 1989. 39.95 (*0-262-23143-3*) MIT Pr.

Concentration & Profit Rates: New Evidence on an Old Issue. Michael Gort & Rao Singamsetti. (Explorations in Economic Research Three Ser.: No. 1). 20p. 1976. reprint ed. 35.00 (*0-685-61395-X*) Natl Bur Econ Res.

Concentration & the Acquirement of Personal Magnetism. O. H. Hara. 1992. lib. bdg. 88.95 (*0-8490-8748-1*) Gordon Pr.

Concentration & the Acquirement of Personal Magnetism. 5th ed. O. Hashnu Hara. 118p. 1969. reprint ed. spiral bd. 3.85 (*0-7873-0372-0*) Mokelumne.

Concentration & the Rate of Change of Wages in the United States, 1950-1962. Peter A. Prosper, Jr. Ed. by Stuart Bruchey. LC 76-4511. (Nineteen Seventy-Seven Dissertations Ser.). (Illus.). 1977. lib. bdg. 23.95 (*0-405-09922-3*) Ayer.

Concentration & Will Power: Correspondence Course - 12 Lessons. F. W. Sears. 199p. 1976. reprint ed. spiral bd. 8.25 (*0-7873-0760-2*) Mokelumne.

Concentration Camps: North American Japanese in the United States & Canada During World War II. Roger Daniels. 262p. 1993. 19.50 (*0-89464-819-5*) Krieger.

Concentration Camps: North American Japanese in the United States & Canada During World War II. rev. ed. Roger Daniels. LC 80-19813. 260p. 1981. text ed. 16.50 (*0-89874-025-8*) Krieger.

Concentration Can: When Does Human Life Begin? An Eminent Geneticist Testifies. Jerome Lejeune. LC 91-77302. 228p. (Orig.). 1992. pap. 13.95 (*0-89870-394-8*) Ignatius Pr.

Concentration Control in the European Economic Community. Ed. by P. V. Bos et al. 304p. 1992. lib. bdg. 125.00 (*1-85333-570-3*, Pub. by Graham & Trotman UK) Kluwer Ac.

Concentration in Canadian Manufacturing Industries. Gideon Rosenbluth. (General Ser.: No. 61). 168p. 1957. reprint ed. 43.70 (*0-87014-060-4*); reprint ed. mic. film 21.90 (*0-685-61309-7*) Natl Bur Econ Res.

Concentration, Mergers & Public Policy. Yale Brozen. (Illus.). 496p. 1982. text ed. 40.00 (*0-02-904270-4*) Free Pr.

Concentration of Economic Power & Monopolies in India. V. K. Agarwal. (C). 1989. 235.00 (*0-685-36512-3*) St Mut.

Concentration, Relaxation & Academic Success: A Guide for Students. M. S. Prokop. 1990. 9.95 (*0-933879-35-0*) Alegra Hse Pubs.

Concentrations of Cadmium in Air & Urine in an Alkaline Battery Works: A Case Study. Peter Dewell. 1994. 75.00 (*0-948237-20-1*, Pub. by H&H Sci Cnslts UK) St Mut.

Concentrations of Toxic Substances in Industry: Held in Prague Czechoslovakia 4-59. IUPAC Staff & Permanent Commission & International Association Staff. (International Union of Pure & Applied Chemistry Ser.). 1961. 160.00 (*0-08-021160-7*, Pub. by Pergamon Repr UK) Franklin.

Concentric Circles of Concern. W. Oscar Thompson, Jr. & Carolyn Thompson. LC 81-67488. 1981. 11.99 (*0-8054-6233-3*) Broadman.

Concentric Circles of Concern Study Guide. Carolyn T. Ritzmann. LC 88-36738. (Orig.). 1989. pap. 3.99 (*0-8054-6260-0*) Broadman.

***Concentric Imagination: Mandala Literary Theory.** Charu S. Singh. (C). 1994. 22.00 (*81-7018-776-1*, Pub. by BR Pub II) S Asia.

Concentric Perspective. Eric Butterworth. LC 88-51451. 120p. 1989. 10.95 (*0-87159-022-0*) Unity Bks.

Concepcion Cristiana de Dios y el Mundo (Christian View of God & the World) James Orr. 598p. (SPA.). 1992. 16.95 (*84-7645-550-X*, 223486, Pub. by Edit Clie SP) TSELF.

Concept. (Illus.). 82p. 1969. pap. 3.00 (*0-89192-033-1*) Interbk Inc.

Concept: An Anthology of Contemporary Writing. Ed. by Cameron Northouse. (Orig.). 1979. pap. 9.95 (*0-89683-014-4*) New London Pr.

Concept & Case Studies Nursing: A Life Cycle Approach. Gertrude T. Redmond & Frances Ouellette. 1983. pap. write for info. (*0-201-06207-0*, Health Sci) Addison-Wesley.

Concept & Design in Music: A Comprehensive Approach to Theory. Robert W. Sherman. 502p. (C). 1988. pap. text ed. 38.75 (*0-15-512835-3*); student ed, pap. text ed. 23.00 (*0-15-512836-1*) HB Coll Pubs.

Concept & Dynamics of Culture. Ed. by Bernardo Bernardi. (World Anthropology Ser.). xii, 630p. 1977. 78.50 (*90-279-7939-1*) Mouton.

Concept & Logic of Classical Thermodynamics As a Theory of Heat Engines. Rigorously Constructed Upon Foundations Laid by S. Carnot & F. Reech. Clifford A. Truesdell & S. Bharatha. LC 76-48115. (Texts & Monographs in Physics). (Illus.). 1989. 51.00 (*0-387-07971-8*) Spr-Verlag.

Concept & Measurement of Poverty. Aroon Sharma. 1990. 21.00 (*81-7041-287-0*, Pub. by Anmol II) S Asia.

Concept & Measurement of Quality of Life in the Frail Elderly. Ed. by James E. Birren et al. (Illus.). 385p. 1991. text ed. 55.00 (*0-12-101275-1*) Acad Pr.

Concept & Method of Cultural Ecology. Julian H. Steward. (Reprint Series in Social Sciences). (C). 1993. reprint ed. pap. text ed. 1.00 (*0-8290-2923-0*, S-516) Irvington.

Concept & Object: The Unity of the Proposition in Logic & Psychology. Anthony Palmer. (Studies in Philosophical Psychology). 176p. 1988. text ed. 32.50 (*0-415-00172-2*) Routledge.

Concept & Practice of International Law During the Period of the Warring States: 403-221 B.C. Joseph D. Lowe. LC 88-91011. (Illus.). xi, 42p. 1994. 16.00 (*0-930325-04-4*) Lowe Pub.

Concept & Present Status of the International Protection of Human Rights. B. G. Ramcharan. (C). 1989. lib. bdg. 207.50 (*90-247-3759-1*) Kluwer Ac.

Concept Approach to Spanish. 4th ed. DaSilva. 1987. text ed. 48.95 (*0-8384-3501-7*); pap. 28.95 (*0-8384-3504-1*) Heinle & Heinle.

Concept Cookery. Kathy Faggella. Ed. by Lisa L. Durkin. (Illus.). 105p. 1985. pap. 10.95 (*0-9615005-1-4*) First Teacher.

Concept de Sous-Developpement. 5th ed. Jacques Freyssinet. (Series Economies du Developpement: No. 1). 1980. pap. 32.35 (*90-279-7973-1*) Mouton.

Concept Decoratif Anti-Formalist Art of the Seventies. Robert C. Morgan. (Illus.). 28p. (Orig.). 1990. pap. 10.00 (*0-9624615-5-5*) Nahan Contemporary.

Concept Development & the Development of Word Meaning. Ed. by T. B. Seiler. (Language & Communication Ser.: Vol. 12). (Illus.). 370p. 1983. 50.00 (*0-387-12251-6*) Spr-Verlag.

Concept Development for Visually Handicapped Children: A Resource Guide for Teachers & Other Professionals Working in Educational Settings. rev. ed. William T. Lydon & M. Loretta McGraw. 80p. 1973. pap. 12.95 (*0-89128-018-9*) Am Foun Blind.

Concept Development in Nursing: Foundations, Techniques, & Applications. Beth L. Rodgers & Kathleen A. Knafl. (Illus.). 256p. 1993. pap. text ed. 36.95 (*0-7216-3674-8*) Saunders.

Concept Development in the Primary School. Peter Langford. 144p. 1987. lib. bdg. 45.00 (*0-7099-4162-5*, Pub. by Croom Helm UK) Routledge Chapman & Hall.

Concept Development in the Secondary School. Peter Langford. 192p. 1987. lib. bdg. 42.50 (*0-7099-4163-3*, Pub. by Croom Helm UK) Routledge Chapman & Hall.

Concept d'Homme de Lettres, en France, A L'Epoque de L'Encyclopedie. Michel Gaulin. LC 91-3046. (Harvard Romance Languages Ser.). 208p. 1991. reprint ed. 50.00 (*0-8240-0481-7*) Garland.

Concept Dictionary of English with Computer Programs for Content Analysis. Julius Laffal. LC 89-81593. (Orig.). 1990. disk, pap. 150.00 (*0-913622-06-0*) Gallery Pr.

Concept Formation: Knowledge & Experience in Unsupervised Learning. Ed. by Douglas H. Fisher, Jr. et al. (Representation & Reasoning Ser.). 1991. pap. text ed. 42.95 (*1-55860-201-1*) Morgan Kaufmann.

***Concept Formation & Knowledge Revision.** Stefan Wrobel. LC 94-32968. 256p. (C). 1994. lib. bdg. 79.95 (*0-7923-9500-X*) Kluwer Ac.

Concept Formation in the Humanities & the Social Sciences. Tadeusz Pawlowski. (Synthese Library: No. 144). 233p. 1980. lib. bdg. 74.50 (*90-277-1096-1*) Kluwer Ac.

Concept, Image, & Symbol: The Cognitive Basis of Grammar. Ronald W. Langacker. 1990. 105.75 (*3-11-012599-4*) Mouton.

Concept, Image & Symbol: The Cognitive Basis of Grammar. Ronald W. Langacker. (Cognitive Linguistics Research Ser.: No. 1). (Illus.). x, 395p. (Orig.). (C). 1991. pap. text ed. 29.95 (*3-11-012863-2*, 152-91) Mouton.

Concept Invention Catalog. (Illus.). 215p. (Orig.). (C). 1993. pap. text ed. 75.00 (*1-56806-695-3*) Diane Pub.

Concept of a Blood-Brain Barrier. Michael W. Bradbury. LC 78-16764. (Wiley-Interscience Publication Ser.). 471p. reprint ed. pap. 134.30 (*0-7837-3217-1*, 2043235) Bks Demand.

Concept of a Legal System: An Introduction to the Theory of a Legal System. 2nd ed. Joseph Raz. 1980. pap. 29.95 (*0-19-825363-X*) OUP.

Concept of a University. Kenneth R. Minogue. LC 72-95301. 239p. reprint ed. pap. 68.20 (*0-685-23494-0*, 2029054) Bks Demand.

Concept of Academic Freedom: (Papers) Conference on the Concept of Academic Freedom Staff. Ed. by Edmund L. Pincoffs. LC 74-20852. 296p. reprint ed. pap. 84.40 (*0-8357-7755-3*, 2036113) Bks Demand.

Concept of Action: An Analytical Study. Saroj K. Mohanty. (C). 1992. 18.00 (*81-85182-67-1*, Pub. by Indus Pub II) S Asia.

Concept of Activity in Soviet Psychology. James V. Wertsch. LC 80-5453. 452p. reprint ed. pap. 128.90 (*0-685-16258-3*, 2056251) Bks Demand.

Concept of an Atom from Democritus to John Dalton. John J. McDonnell. LC 91-40434. 144p. 1992. lib. bdg. 69.95 (*0-7734-9649-1*) E Mellen.

Concept of an Indian Literature: Six Essays by P. Lal. P. Lal. 49p. 1973. 10.00 (*0-88253-303-7*) Ind-US Inc.

Concept of an Islamic State: An Analysis of the Ideological Controversy in Pakistan. Ishtiaq Ahmed. 266p. (Orig.). 1985. pap. text ed. 65.00x (*91-7146-458-1*, Pub. by Almqv & Wiksell SW) Coronet Bks.

Concept of an Islamic State: An Analysis of the Ideological Controversy in Pakistan. Ishtiaq Ahmed. LC 86-33847. 250p. (Orig.). 1987. text ed. 39.95 (*0-312-00791-4*) St Martin.

Concept of Anxiety. Soren Kierkegaard. Ed. by Howard V. Hong & Edna H. Hong. Tr. by Reider Thomte. LC 79-3217. (Kierkegaard's Writings: VIII). 304p. 1980. 45.00 (*0-691-07244-2*); pap. 12.95 (*0-691-02011-6*) Princeton U Pr.

Concept of Anxiety: A Commentary. Ed. by Robert L. Perkins. LC 85-11571. (International Kierkegaard Commentary Ser.: Vol. 8). xii, 203p. 1985. 18.95 (*0-86554-142-6*, MUP/H133) Mercer Univ Pr.

Concept of Apokatastasis in Acts: A Study in Primitive Christian Theology. James Parker. 140p. 1981. pap. text ed. 5.95 (*0-931016-01-0*) Schola Pr TX.

Concept of Being Human. Royal Purcell. 173p. (Orig.). 1985. pap. 9.95 (*0-933189-00-1*) Purcell Pub.

Concept of Belief in Islamic Theology. Toshihiko Izutsu. LC 79-52553. (Islam Ser.). 1980. reprint ed. lib. bdg. 27.95 (*0-8369-9261-X*) Ayer.

Concept of Buddhism. Law Bimla Churn. 142p. 1986. 22.95 (*0-318-37011-5*) Asia Bk Corp.

Concept of Business Organisation. J. P. Bose. 1985. 75.00 (*0-317-38756-1*, Current Dist) St Mut.

Concept of Church: A Methodological Inquiry into the Use of Metaphors in Ecclesiology. Herwi Rikhof. LC 80-84751. xvi, 304p. 1981. 35.00 (*0-915762-11-0*) Patmos Pr.

Concept of Class: An Historical Introduction. Peter Calvert. LC 82-10617. 1985. pap. 12.95 (*0-312-15919-6*) St Martin.

Concept of Consciousness. Edwin B. Holt. LC 73-2969. (Classics in Psychology Ser.). 1977. reprint ed. 25.95 (*0-405-05141-7*) Ayer.

Concept of Consciousness: A Survey. David B. Klein. LC 83-5851. x, 250p. 1984. 30.00 (*0-8032-2707-8*) U of Nebr Pr.

Concept of Correlation: Paul Tillich & the Possibility of a Mediating Theology. John P. Clayton. (Theologische Bibliothek Toepelmann Ser.: Vol. 37). 427p. (C). 1979. text ed. 80.80 (*3-11-007914-3*) De Gruyter.

Concept of Cultural Systems: A Key to Understanding Tribes & Nations. Leslie A. White. LC 75-33003. 206p. reprint ed. pap. 58.80 (*0-8357-7781-2*, 2036141) Bks Demand.

Concept of Dance Education. Graham McFee. LC 93-9997. 1994. write for info. (*0-415-08376-1*) Routledge.

Concept of Defense Mechanisms in Contemporary Psychology: Theoretical, Research, & Clinical Perspectives. Ed. by Uwe Hentschel et al. LC 92-48254. 1993. 69.00 (*0-387-94003-0*) Spr-Verlag.

Concept of Development Vol. 15: The Minnesota Symposium on Child Psychology. Ed. by W. Andrew Collins. (Minnesota Symposium on Child Psychology Ser.). 192p. 1982. 49.95 (*0-89859-159-7*) L Erlbaum Assocs.

Concept of Dwelling. Christian Norberg-Schulz. (Illus.). 150p. 1985. pap. 27.50 (*0-8478-0590-5*) Rizzoli Intl.

An Asterisk (*) at the beginning of an entry indicates that the title is appearing in BIP for the first time.

C

An Asterisk (*) at the beginning of an entry indicates that the title is appearing in BIP for the first time.

1515

Conceptos Linguisticos: Linguistic Concepts. Kenneth L. Pike. Tr. by Thomas Hemingway & Katherine Langan. LC 94-65901. 190p. (SPA.). Date not set. pap. write for info. (*0-88312-710-5*); fiche write for info. (*1-55671-990-6*) Summer Instit Ling.

Concepts: Six Contemporary Asian Artists. (Illus.). 100p. 1976. pap. 2.95 (*0-685-66762-6*) Pacific Asia.

Concepts: Their Nature & Significance for Metaphysics & Epistemology. Lennart Norreklit. (Odense Studies in Philosophy: No. 2). 226p. (Orig.). 1973. pap. 23.50 (*87-7492-079-0*, Pub. by Odense Universitets Forlag DK) Coronet Bks.

Concepts - Strategic Management. 3rd ed. Byars. (C). 1991. text ed. 37.00 (*0-06-500673-9*) HarpCollege.

Concepts & Applications of Finited Element Analysis. 3rd ed. Robert D. Cook et al. 630p. 1989. Net. text ed. write for info. (*0-471-84788-7*) Wiley.

Concepts & Applications of Molecular Similarity. Ed. by Mark A. Johnson & Gerald M. Maggiora. 1990. text ed. 99.95 (*0-471-62175-7*) Wiley.

***Concepts & Bases of Art: Gallery Guide.** Jenny Grenfell. 1993. pap. 33.00 (*0-7300-1579-3*, AAP205, Pub. by Deakin Univ AT) St Mut.

Concepts & Calculations in Analytical Chemistry. Freiser. 1992. 29.95 (*0-8493-4717-3*, QD75) CRC Pr.

Concepts & Case Analysis in the Law of Contracts. 2nd ed. Marvin A. Chirelstein. (University Textbook Ser.). 185p. 1993. pap. text ed. 14.95 (*1-56662-065-1*) Foundation Pr.

Concepts & Cases in Fashion Buying & Merchandising. Sidney Packard & Nathan Axelrod. LC 76-50439. (C). 1977. text ed. 16.50 (*0-87005-182-2*) Fairchild.

Concepts & Cases in Nursing Ethics. Michael Yeo. 280p. 1991. pap. text ed. 17.95 (*0-921149-82-4*) Broadview Pr.

Concepts & Categories: Philosophical Essays. Isaiah Berlin. Ed. by Henry Hardy. 1981. pap. 8.95 (*0-14-005805-2*, Penguin Bks) Viking Penguin.

Concepts & Comments. Patricia Ackert. 240p. (C). 1986. pap. text ed. 19.50 (*0-03-071841-4*) HB Coll Pubs.

***Concepts & Cultures: A Reader for Writers.** Ed. by Martin Itzkowitz. LC 94-28818. (C). 1994. pap. text ed. 18.75 (*0-205-15279-1*) Allyn.

Concepts & Design of Chemical Reactors: Concepts & Design. Ed. by Stephen Whitaker & Alberto E. Cassano. (Chemical Engineering: Concepts & Reviews Ser.: Vol. 3). x, 572p. 1986. text ed. 304.00 (*2-88124-118-2*) Gordon & Breach.

Concepts & Experiences in Elementary School Science. Peter C. Gega. (C). 1990. pap. write for info. (*0-02-413405-8*) Macmillan.

Concepts & Experiences in Elementary School Science. 2nd ed. Peter C. Gega. LC 92-43307. (Illus.). 544p. (C). 1994. pap. write for info. (*0-02-341331-X*) Macmillan.

Concepts & Formalisations in the Control of Breathing. Ed. by G. Benchetrit & J. Demongeot. 250p. 1988. text ed. 69.95 (*0-7190-2322-X*, Pub. by Manchester Univ Pr UK) St Martin.

Concepts & Images: Visual Mathematics. Arthur L. Loeb. (Design Science Collections). (Illus.). xi, 228p. 1992. 49.50 (*0-8176-3620-X*) Birkhauser.

Concepts & Influences: Towards a Regionalized International Architecture. Rifat Chadirji. (Illus.). 192p. 1986. 87.50 (*0-7103-0180-4*, 01804) Routledge Chapman & Hall.

Concepts & Issues in Nursing Practice. 2nd ed. Barbara Kozier et al. 672p. (C). 1992. pap. text ed. 40.95 (*0-8053-3520-X*) Addison-Wesley.

Concepts & Issues in Nursing Practice. 4th ed. Barbara Kozier. (C). 1993. pap. text ed. 49.50 (*0-8053-5950-8*) Benjamin-Cummings.

***Concepts & Issues in School Choice.** Ed. by Margaret D. Tannenbaum. LC 94-40515. 520p. 1995. text ed. 119.95 (*0-7734-9129-5*) E Mellen.

Concepts & Language: An Essay in Generative Semantics & the Philosophy of Language. Philip L. Peterson. 1973. pap. 40.00 (*90-279-2442-2*) Mouton.

Concepts & Measurement of Quality of Life in Health Care. Ed. by Lennart Nordenfelt. LC 94-14441. (Philosophy & Medicine Ser.: Vol. 47). 292p. (C). 1994. lib. bdg. 87.00 (*0-7923-2824-8*) Kluwer Ac.

Concepts & Methods for Integrating Social & Economic Statistics on Health, Education & Housing: A Technical Report. (Studies in Methods, Series F: No. 40). 67p. 1986. pap. 8.50 (*92-1-161275-6*, E.86.XVII.23) UN.

Concepts & Methods in Energy Statistics with Special Reference to Energy Accounts & Balances. 176p. 1982. 16.50 (*92-1-161203-9*, E.82.XVII.13) UN.

***Concepts & Methods in Evolutionary Biology.** Robert N. Brandon. (Cambridge Studies in Philosophy & Biology). (Illus.). 240p. (C). 1995. write for info. (*0-521-49545-8*); pap. write for info. (*0-521-49888-0*) Cambridge U Pr.

Concepts & Methods of Constitutional Law. William Kaplin. LC 92-71954. (Illus.). 230p. (C). 1992. pap. text ed. 17.50 (*0-89089-427-2*) Carolina Acad Pr.

Concepts & Methods of Environment Statistics: Human Settlements Statements - A Technical Report. 80p. 1989. pap. 8.50 (*92-1-161300-0*, E.88.XVII.14) UN.

Concepts & Models of Biomathematics: Simulation Techniques & Methods. Ed. by Ferdinand Heinmets. LC 73-78832. (Biomathematics Ser.: No. 1). (Illus.). 301p. reprint ed. pap. 85.80 (*0-7837-0934-X*, 2041239) Bks Demand.

Concepts & Models of Dolomitization. Ed. by Donald H. Zenger et al. (Special Publications Ser.: No. 28). 320p. 1980. 29.50 (*0-918985-08-0*, 28) SEPM.

Concepts & Models of Inorganic Chemistry. 3rd ed. Bodio E. Douglas et al. LC 93-38708. 1994. text ed. write for info. (*0-471-62978-2*) Wiley.

Concepts & Practice of Architectural Daylighting. Fuller Moore. LC 84-29929. (Illus.). 304p. 1991. pap. 34.95 (*0-442-00679-9*) Van Nos Reinhold.

Concepts & Procedures in Indian Census. Anand Mahatme. (C). 1988. 21.00 (*0-8364-2455-7*) S Asia.

Concepts & Responses: International Architectural Design Competition for the Indira Gandhi National Center for the Arts, New Delhi. Kapila Vatsyayan et al. LC 89-84642. (Illus.). 184p. 1993. 60.00 (*0-944142-18-4*, Pub. by Grantha India) U of Wash Pr.

Concepts & Strategies for Lifetime Fitness. Norris & Fanning. 298p. 1989. pap. text ed. 21.95 (*0-88725-115-3*) Hunter Textbks.

Concepts & Strategies in New Drug Development, Vol.4. Ed. by Peter Nwangu. LC 83-19248. (Clinical Pharmacology & Therapeutics Ser.). 282p. 1983. text ed. 59.95 (*0-275-91406-2*, C1406, Praeger Pubs) Greenwood.

Concepts & Structures of Maya Calendrical Arithmetics. Linton Satterthwaite. LC 57-3294. (Museum of the University of Pennsylvania, The Philadelphia Anthropological Society Ser.). 176p. reprint ed. pap. 50.20 (*0-317-26205-X*, 2052125) Bks Demand.

Concepts & Techniques in Oil & Gas Exploration. Ed. by K. C. Jain & R. J. DeFigueiredo. LC 82-50079. 289p. 1982. 19.00 (*0-931830-22-2*, 525) Soc Expl Geophys.

Concepts & Techniques of Machine Safeguarding. (Illus.). 89p. (C). 1992. pap. text ed. 29.95 (*1-56806-126-9*) Diane Pub.

Concepts & Themes in the Regional Geography of Canada. Robinson. (NFS Canada Ser.). 1993. pap. 17.95 (*0-88922-264-9*, Pub. by Talonbooks CN) InBook.

Concepts & Theories in Carcinogenesis: Proceedings of the 4th Annual Symposium on the European Organization for Cooperation in Cancer Prevention Studies, (ECP), Brugge, Belgium, June 11-13, 1986. Ed. by A. P. Maskens et al. (International Congress Ser.: No. 732). 332p. 1987. 106.25 (*0-444-80869-8*) Elsevier.

Concepts & Theories of Human Development. Richard M. Lerner. LC 75-12098. (Illus.). (C). 1976. text ed. 22.00 (*0-394-34773-0*) Random.

Concepts & Theories of Human Development. 2nd ed. Richard A. Lerner. 512p. 1985. text ed. 29.95 (*0-89859-886-9*) L Erlbaum Assocs.

Concepts & Theories of Human Development. 2nd ed. Richard M. Lerner. 512p. 1986. text ed. write for info. (*0-07-554899-2*) McGraw.

Concepts & Theories of Modern Democracy. Anthony H. Birch. LC 92-33977. 272p. 1993. 59.95 (*0-415-09107-1*, B0404, Routledge NY); pap. 17.95 (*0-415-09108-X*, B0408, Routledge NY) Routledge.

Concepts & Theories of Parapsychology: Proceedings of the International Conference, Dec. 6, 1980. International Conference, New York Staff. Ed. by Betty Shapin & Lisette Coly. LC 81-83135. 112p. (C). 1981. 16.00 (*0-912328-35-5*) Parapsych Foun.

Concepts & Trends in Particle Physics. Ed. by H. Latal & H. Mitter. (Illus.). 340p. 1987. 59.00 (*0-387-17372-2*) Spr-Verlag.

Concepts Basic to Nursing. 3rd ed. P. Mitchell. (Illus.). 720p. 1981. text ed. 36.95 (*0-07-042582-5*) McGraw.

***Concepts Biology Lab Manual.** Roger Davis. 208p. (C). 1995. pap. text ed., spiral bd. 20.00 (*0-7872-1122-2*) Kendall-Hunt.

Concepts, Clinical Developments, & Therapeutic Advances in Cancer Chemotherapy. Ed. by Franco M. Muggia. (Cancer Treatment & Research Ser.). (C). 1987. lib. bdg. 75.00 (*0-89838-875-9*) Kluwer Ac.

Concepts, Design & Performance Analysis of a Parallel Prolog Machine. J Beer. (Lecture Notes in Computer Science Ser.: Vol. 404). vi, 128p. 1989. pap. 27.00 (*0-387-52053-8*, 3833) Spr-Verlag.

Concepts for a Musical Foundation. Richard J. Colwell & Ruth Colwell. LC 73-7749. (Illus.). 320p. (C). 1974. pap. text ed. 23.95 (*0-685-03800-9*) P-H.

Concepts for Communication & Development in Bilingual - Bicultural Communities Ser. Ed. by Florencio Sanchez-Camara & Felipe Ayala. (World Anthropology Ser.). (Illus.). x, 208p. 1979. text ed. 32.35 (*90-279-7860-3*) Mouton.

Concepts for Compositions. (C). 1976. pap. text ed. 2.00 (*0-393-09158-9*) Norton.

***Concepts for End-Users: With Exploring DOS, WordPerfect 5.1, Lotus 2.2, & dBASE III+** Nancy Stern & Robert A. Stern. 1992. disk, pap. text ed. write for info. (*0-471-55571-1*) Wiley.

Concepts for Learning. Julie A. Blonigen. (Illus.). 172p. (ps-2). 1989. teacher ed 22.95 (*0-937857-08-4*, 1565) Speech Bin.

Concepts for Operations Management. Ray Wild. LC 77-7232. (Illus.). 191p. reprint ed. pap. 54.50 (*0-8357-7548-8*, 2036270) Bks Demand.

Concepts for R & R Studies. Larry B. Barrentine. (Illus.). 48p. 1991. pap. 21.95 (*0-87389-107-4*) ASQC Qual Pr.

Concepts for the Ideal Diabetes Clinic. Ed. by C. E. Mogensen & E. Standl. LC 92-49365. xiv, 402p. (C). 1993. pap. text ed. 113.85 (*3-11-013231-1*) De Gruyter.

Concepts for Today. Smith. 1994. pap. 19.95 (*0-8384-3436-3*) Heinle & Heinle.

***Concepts in Algebra: A Technological Approach.** James T. Fey et al. LC 94-26696. (Illus.). 536p. 1995. text ed. 39.95 (*0-939765-73-X*, G-174) Janson Pubns.

***Concepts in Algebra: A Technological Approach, Instructor's Guide.** 1995. teacher ed. pap. 19.95 (*0-939765-78-0*) Janson Pubns.

Concepts in American History. Asher. (C). 1994. pap. text ed. 5.50 (*0-06-501483-9*) HarpCollege.

***Concepts in Artificial Intelligence: Mechatronics Designing.** Johnson & Pictor. 312p. 1995. pap. 34.95 (*0-7506-2403-5*, Focal) Buttrwrth-Heinemann.

Concepts in Biochemistry. 3rd ed. William K. Stephenson. LC 87-34619. 229p. 1988. Net. text ed. write for info. (*0-471-63716-5*) Wiley.

Concepts in Biological Oceanography: An Interdisciplinary Primer. Peter A. Jumars. LC 92-39069. 1993. 49.95 (*0-19-506732-0*) OUP.

Concepts in Biology. 6th ed. Eldon Enger et al. 560p. (C). 1990. pap. write for info. (*0-697-13746-5*) Wm C Brown Pubs.

Concepts in Biology. 6th ed. Eldon Enger et al. 560p. (C). 1991. text ed. write for info. (*0-697-13794-5*); write for info. (*0-697-09889-3*) Wm C Brown Pubs.

Concepts in Biology. 7th ed. Eldon Enger et al. (Illus.). 480p. (C). 1993. Lab manual. student ed write for info. (*0-697-13647-7*) Wm C Brown Pubs.

Concepts in Biology. 7th ed. Eldon Enger et al. (Illus.). 480p. (C). 1993. text ed. write for info. (*0-697-13644-2*); pap. text ed. 42.00 (*0-697-13645-0*) Wm C Brown Pubs.

Concepts in Biology. 7th ed. Eldon Enger et al. (Illus.). 480p. (C). 1993. Study guide. student ed write for info. (*0-697-17456-5*) Wm C Brown Pubs.

Concepts in Building Firesafety. M. David Egan. LC 86-7501. 288p. 1986. reprint ed. text ed. 46.50 (*0-89874-956-5*) Krieger.

Concepts in Cancer Care: A Practical Explanation of Radiotherapy & Chemotherapy for Primary Care Physicians. Jay S. Cooper & Donald J. Pizzarello. LC 80-10334. (Illus.). 285p. reprint ed. pap. 81.30 (*0-8357-7642-5*, 2056967) Bks Demand.

Concepts in Chemistry, Bk. 9. H. T. Taylor. Ed. by L. G. Bill & K. Yandall. 84p. (C). 1989. 60.00 (*0-85973-037-9*, Pub. by S Thornes Pubs UK) St Mut.

Concepts in Climatology. Percy R. Crowe. LC 72-176213. (Geographies for Advanced Study Ser.). 609p. reprint ed. pap. 173.60 (*0-317-08860-2*, 2019601) Bks Demand.

Concepts in Clinical Pharmacokinetics. Joseph T. DiPiro et al. (Orig.). 1991. pap. text ed. 69.00 (*0-930530-86-1*) Am Soc Hlth-Syst.

Concepts in Clothing. Judy Graef & J. Strom. (C). 1976. text ed. 29.88 (*0-07-023889-8*) McGraw.

Concepts in Computer Art. MIS Press Staff. (Welcome to... Ser.). (Illus.). 1993. pap. 19.95 (*1-55828-240-8*) MIS Press.

Concepts in Computer Design. Dawn Erdos. 1993. pap. 34.95 (*1-55828-297-1*) MIS Press.

Concepts in Construction: 1910-1980. Irving Sandler. LC 82-83655. (Illus.). 96p. 1982. 10.00 (*0-916365-03-4*) Ind Curators.

Concepts in Data Structures & Software Development: A Text for the Second Course in Computer Science. G. Michael Schneider & Steven Bruell. Ed. by Westby. 526p. (C). 1991. text ed. 58.25 (*0-314-77460-2*) West Pub.

Concepts in Discrete Mathematics. Sartaj Sahni. 436p. (C). 1981. text ed. 40.00 (*0-942450-00-0*) Camelot Pub FL.

Concepts in Drug Metabolism, Pt. A. Jenner & Testa. (Drugs & Pharmaceutical Sciences Ser.: Vol. 10). 424p. 1980. 140.00 (*0-8247-6906-6*) Dekker.

***Concepts in Drug Metabolism Pt. B.** fac. ed. Ed. by Peter Jenner & Bernard Testa. LC 80-12792. (Drugs & the Pharmaceutical Sciences Ser.: No. 10). 641p. Date not set. pap. 180.00 (*0-7837-7398-6*, 2047192) Bks Demand.

Concepts in Ethology: Animal & Human Behavior. Michael W. Fox. LC 73-93834. (Wesley W. Spink Lectures on Comparative Medicine: No. 2). 156p. reprint ed. pap. 44.50 (*0-7837-2964-2*, 2057490) Bks Demand.

Concepts in Federal Taxation: 1995 Edition. Kevin E. Murphy. Ed. by Leyh. LC 93-40131. 450p. (C). 1994. text ed. 61.50 (*0-314-02595-2*) West Pub.

Concepts in Federal Taxation: 1995 Edition. Kevin E. Murphy. LC 93-47062. 766p. 1994. text ed. 63.00 (*0-314-03653-9*) West Pub.

Concepts in Fetal Movement Research. Intro. by Joyce W. Sparling. LC 92-48442. (Physical & Occupational Therapy in Pediatrics Ser.: Vol. 12, Nos. 2 & 3). (Illus.). 207p. 1993. lib. bdg. 39.95 (*1-56024-449-6*) Haworth Pr.

Concepts in Film Theory. Dudley Andrew. LC 83-17365. 1984. pap. 10.95 (*0-19-503428-7*) OUP.

Concepts in General Chemistry: Laboratory Manual. 4th ed. Solomon et al. 160p. 1993. spiral bd. 15.95 (*0-8403-8364-9*) Kendall-Hunt.

Concepts in Hand Rehabilitation. Barbara G. Stanley & Susan M. Tribuzi. (Contemporary Perspectives in Rehabilitation Ser.: Vol. 9). (Illus.). 582p. 1992. text ed. 42.00 (*0-8036-8092-9*) Davis Co.

Concepts in Immunology & Immunotherapeutics. 2nd rev. ed. Ed. by Jim Koeller & Joseph Tanci. (Illus.). 500p. (C). 1992. reprint ed. pap. text ed. write for info. (*1-879907-06-2*) Am Soc Hlth-Syst.

Concepts in Information Retrieval. Miranda L. Pao. 285p. 1989. lib. bdg. 35.00 (*0-87287-405-2*) Libs Unl.

Concepts in Inhalation Toxicology. Roger O. McClellan & Rogene F. Henderson. 506p. 1988. 121.00 (*0-89116-805-2*) Hemisp Pub.

***Concepts in Inhalation Toxicology.** 2nd ed. Ed. by Roger O. McClellan & Rogene F. Henderson. LC 95-13914. 1995. write for info. (*1-56032-368-X*) Taylor & Francis.

Concepts in Intramedullary Nailing. Ed. by David Seligson. 368p. 1985. text ed. 110.00 (*0-8089-1706-4*, 793987, Grune) Saunders.

Concepts in Judgement & Decision Research: Definitions, Sources, Interrelations, Comments. Barry F. Anderson et al. LC 81-7345. 320p. 1981. text ed. 65.00 (*0-275-90577-2*, C0577, Praeger Pubs) Greenwood.

Concepts in Learning Disabilities: Selected Writings, Vol. 2. William M. Cruickshank. LC 80-29024. 296p. 1981. text ed. 39.95x (*0-8156-2239-2*) Syracuse U Pr.

Concepts in Lighting for Architecture. M. David Egan. LC 82-20832. (Illus.). 272p. 1983. text ed. write for info. (*0-07-019054-2*) McGraw.

Concepts in Manipulation of Groundwater Colloids for Environmental Restoration. Ed. by John F. McCarthy et al. 1993. 79.95 (*0-87371-828-3*, TD426) Lewis Pubs.

Concepts in Marine Pollution Measurements. Ed. by Harris H. White. 24.95 (*0-943676-18-5*) MD Sea Grant Col.

Concepts in Nematode Systematics. Ed. by A. R. Stone et al. (Systematics Association Special Ser.: Vol. 22). 1983. text ed. 139.00 (*0-12-672680-9*) Acad Pr.

***Concepts in Nutrition.** Kathleen O'Dell. (RN NCLEX Ser.). 300p. (Orig.). (C). 1995. pap. text ed. 18.95 (*1-56930-017-8*) Skidmore Roth Pub.

Concepts in Oncology Therapeutics. Ed. by Rebecca S. Finley. (Illus.). 500p. (Orig.). (C). 1991. pap. text ed. write for info. (*1-879907-08-9*) Am Soc Hlth-Syst.

Concepts in Pediatric Neurosurgery. P. H. Chapman. (Concepts in Pediatric Neurosurgery Ser.: Vol. 6). (Illus.). xii, 244p. 1985. 139.25 (*3-8055-4136-8*) S Karger.

Concepts in Pediatric Neurosurgery. Ed. by R. P. Humphreys. (Concepts in Pediatric Neurosurgery Ser.: No. 4). (Illus.). xiv, 394p. 1983. 185.75 (*3-8055-3734-4*) S Karger.

Concepts in Pediatric Neurosurgery. Ed. by A. E. Marlin. (Concepts in Pediatric Neurosurgery Ser.: Vol. 9). (Illus.). viii, 236p. 1989. 169.75 (*3-8055-4835-4*) S Karger.

Concepts in Pediatric Neurosurgery, No. 2. Ed. by American Society of Pediatric Neurosurgery. (Illus.). x, 222p. 1982. 152.00 (*3-8055-3454-X*) S Karger.

Concepts in Pediatric Neurosurgery, No. 3. Ed. by A. J. Raimondi. (Illus.). xxii, 226p. 1983. 158.50 (*3-8055-3580-5*) S Karger.

Concepts in Pediatric Neurosurgery, Vol. 5. Ed. by Robin P. Humphreys. (Illus.). xii, 244p. 1985. 131.25 (*3-8055-3915-0*) S Karger.

Concepts in Pediatric Neurosurgery, Vol. 7. Ed. by A. E. Marlin. (Illus.). viii, 240p. 1987. 168.00 (*3-8055-4396-4*) S Karger.

Concepts in Pediatric Neurosurgery, Vol. 8. Ed. by A. E. Marlin. (Illus.). viii, 224p. 1988. 149.00 (*3-8055-4622-X*) S Karger.

Concepts in Pediatric Neurosurgery, Vol. 11. Ed. by A. E. Marlin. (Illus.). viii, 164p. 1991. 172.00 (*3-8055-5328-5*) S Karger.

Concepts in Pediatric Neurosurgery, No. 1. Ed. by American Society of Pediatric Neurosurgery. (Illus.). x, 238p. 1981. 152.00 (*3-8055-2904-X*) S Karger.

Concepts in Pediatric Neurosurgery Series, Vol. 10. Ed. by A. E. Marlin. (Illus.). 262p. 1990. 202.50 (*3-8055-5022-7*) S Karger.

Concepts in Physical Fitness: A Self-Paced Program to Improved Health Fitness. Russell & Grant. 208p. (C). 1991. spiral bd. 20.95 (*0-8403-6588-8*) Kendall-Hunt.

***Concepts in Probability & Stochastic Modeling.** James J. Higgins & Sallie Keller-McNulty. LC 94-3497. 420p. 1995. text ed. 52.95 (*0-534-23136-5*) Intl Thomson.

***Concepts in Protein Engineering & Design: An Introduction.** Ed. by Paul Wrede & Gisbert Schneider. LC 94-30261. 396p. 1994. lib. bdg. 78.95 (*3-11-012975-2*) De Gruyter.

Concepts in Solids. P. W. Anderson. (Advanced Book Program Ser.). (Illus.). 208p. (C). 1992. 36.95 (*0-201-53355-3*) Addison-Wesley.

Concepts in Solids: Lectures on the Theory of Solids. P. W. Anderson. (Frontiers in Physics Ser.: No. 10). 188p. (C). 1963. pap. 34.95 (*0-8053-0229-8*, Adv Bk Prog) Addison-Wesley.

Concepts in Special Education Vol. 1: Selected Writings. William M. Cruickshank. LC 80-29024. 392p. 1981. text ed. 39.95 (*0-8156-2238-4*) Syracuse U Pr.

Concepts in Statistical Mechanics. Arthur Hobson. xii, 172p. 1971. text ed. 160.00 (*0-677-21870-2*) Gordon & Breach.

Concepts in String Playing: Reflections by Artist-Teachers at the Indiana University School of Music. Ed. by Murray Grodner. LC 78-13811. (Illus.). 190p. reprint ed. pap. 54.20 (*0-317-09952-3*, 2055499) Bks Demand.

Concepts in Submarine Design. rev. ed. Roy Burcher & Louis Rydill. (Cambridge Ocean Technology Ser.: No. 2). (Illus.). 320p. (C). 1994. 79.95 (*0-521-41681-7*) Cambridge U Pr.

Concepts in Surface Physics. M. C. Desjonqueres & D. Spanjaard. LC 93-18561. (Surface Sciences Ser.: Vol. 30). (Illus.). 624p. 1993. 98.00 (*0-387-56506-X*) Spr-Verlag.

Concepts in Use. Ed. by H. G. Widdowson. (Reading & Thinking in English Ser.). (Illus.). 1980. teacher ed 11.95 (*0-19-451352-1*); pap. text ed. 10.75 (*0-19-451351-3*) OUP.

Concepts in User Interfaces. Ed. by D. Beech. (Lecture Notes in Computer Science Ser.: Vol. 234). x, 116p. 1986. pap. 26.00 (*0-387-16791-9*) Spr-Verlag.

Concepts in Vehicle Dynamics & Simulation: SAE International Congress & Exposition 1994, 12 papers. (Special Publications). 1994. pap. 36.00 (*1-56091-468-8*, SP-1016) Soc Auto Engineers.

Concepts in Veterinary Dentistry. Mark A. Tholen. LC 82-51310. (Illus.). 164p. 1983. 20.00 (*0-935078-23-1*) Veterinary Med.

Concepts in Viral Pathogenesis. Ed. by A. L. Notkins & M. B. Oldstone. (Illus.). 390p. 1984. 79.00 (*0-387-90982-6*) Spr-Verlag.

Concepts in Viral Pathogenesis II. Ed. by A. L. Notkins & M. B. Oldstone. (Illus.). 450p. 1986. 85.00 (*0-387-96322-7*) Spr-Verlag.

Concepts in Viral Pathogenesis III. Ed. by A. L. Notkinds & M. B. Oldstone. 415p. 1989. 109.00 (*0-387-96974-8*, 2692) Spr-Verlag.

Concepts in Zoology. Harris. (C). 1991. text ed. 74.00 (*0-06-042659-4*) HarpCollege.

Concepts in Zoology. Harris. (C). 1992. 34.50 (*0-06-500422-1*) HarpCollege.

An Asterisk (*) at the beginning of an entry indicates that the title is appearing in BIP for the first time.

An Asterisk (*) at the beginning of an entry indicates that the title is appearing in BIP for the first time.

1517

Conceptual Commentary on Midrash Leviticus Rabbah. Max Kadushin. LC 87-20506. (Brown Judaic Studies). 265p. 1987. 38.95 (*1-55540-175-9*, 14-01-26) Scholars Pr GA.

Conceptual Cost Estimating Manual. John S. Page. LC 83-22601. 332p. 1984. spiral bd. 55.00 (*0-87201-134-8*) Gulf Pub.

Conceptual Database Design: An Entity Relationship Approach. Carol Batini et al. (C). 1992. text ed. 47.50 (*0-8053-0244-1*) Benjamin-Cummings.

Conceptual Design Analysis Applied to Offshore Control Systems. Bill G. Tompkins. LC 92-25533. (Independent Learning Module from the Instrument Society of America Ser.). 304p. 1992. 65.00 (*1-55617-392-X*) Instru Soc.

Conceptual Design for Engineers. 2nd ed. M. French. (Illus.). 240p. 1985. 47.00 (*0-387-15175-3*) Spr-Verlag.

Conceptual Design Guideline for Optical Disk Document Management Systems. James J. Fruscione. 67p. 1988. pap. 30.00 (*0-89258-133-6*, L020) Assn Inform & Image Mgmt.

Conceptual Design of Chemical Processes. James M. Douglas. 512p. (C). 1988. text ed. write for info. (*0-07-017762-7*) McGraw.

Conceptual Design of Multichip Modules & Systems. Peter A. Sandborn. LC 93-32222. (International Series in Electrical Engineering & Computer Science). 280p. (C). 1993. lib. bdg. 88.00 (*0-7923-9395-3*) Kluwer Ac.

Conceptual Development of Quantum Mechanics. Max Jammer. (History of Modern Physics & Astronomy Ser.: No. 12). (Illus.). 448p. 1989. 90.00 (*0-88318-617-9*) Am Inst Physics.

Conceptual Encyclopaedia of Guru Granth Sahib. S. S. Kohli. (C). 1992. 32.00 (*81-7304-006-0*, Pub. by Manohar II) S Asia.

***Conceptual Foundations for Multidisciplinary Thinking.** Stephen J. Kline. LC 94-44008. 352p. 1995. 45.00x (*0-8047-2409-1*) Stanford U Pr.

Conceptual Foundations of Behavioral Assessment. Ed. by Rosemary O. Nelson & Steven C. Hayes. LC 85-27363. (Guilford Behavioral Assessment Ser.). 544p. 1986. lib. bdg. 65.00 (*0-89862-142-9*) Guilford Pr.

Conceptual Foundations of Descriptive Cataloging. Ed. by Elaine Svenonius. (Library & Information Science Ser.). 380p. 1989. text ed. 66.00 (*0-12-678210-5*) Acad Pr.

Conceptual Foundations of Management Accounting. Ahmed R. Belkaoui. LC 80-16086. (A-W Paperback Series in Accounting). 125p. 1980. pap. write for info. (*0-201-00097-0*) Addison-Wesley.

Conceptual Foundations of Modern Particle Physics. R. E. Marshak. 704p. 1993. text ed. 99.00 (*981-02-1098-1*); pap. text ed. 53.00 (*981-02-1106-6*) World Scientific Pub.

Conceptual Foundations of Occupational Therapy. Gary Kielhofner. (Illus.). 303p. (C). 1992. text ed. 36.00 (*0-8036-5318-2*) Davis Co.

Conceptual Foundations of Professional Nursing Practice, No. 1. Creasia. (Illus.). 704p. 1991. 31.95 (*0-8016-6148-X*) Mosby Yr Bk.

Conceptual Framework for the Study of Clientism. Luigi Graziano. (Western Societies Papers). 56p. 1975. pap. 11.95 (*0-8014-9626-8*) Cornell U Pr.

Conceptual Frameworks for Bibliographic Education: Theory into Practice. Ed. by Mary Reichel & Mary A. Ramey. 208p. 1987. lib. bdg. 27.50 (*0-87287-552-0*) Libs Unl.

Conceptual Graphs for Knowledge Representation: Proceedings of the First International Conference on Conceptual Structures, ICCS 93, Quebec, Canada, August 4-7, 1993. Ed. by G. W. Mineau et al. (Lecture Notes in Artificial Intelligence Ser.: Vol. 699). ix, 451p. 1993. 65.00 (*0-387-56979-0*) Spr-Verlag.

Conceptual History of Modern Embryology. Ed. by Scott F. Gilbert. LC 93-31904. 288p. 1994. pap. text ed. 24.95 (*0-8018-4737-0*) Johns Hopkins.

Conceptual Information Processing. Roger C. Schank. LC 74-84874. (Fundamental Studies in Computer Science: Vol. 3). 374p. 1975. 87.25 (*0-444-10773-8*, North Holland) Elsevier.

Conceptual Information Retrieval: A Case Study in Adaptive Partial Parsing. Michael L. Mauldin. 240p. (C). 1991. lib. bdg. 68.00 (*0-7923-9214-0*) Kluwer Ac.

Conceptual Issues in Alcoholism & Substance Abuse. Ed. by Joyce H. Lowinson & Barry Stimmel. LC 84-3762. (Advances in Alcohol & Substance Abuse Ser.: Vol. 3, No. 3). 102p. 1984. text ed. 39.95 (*0-86656-316-4*) Haworth Pr.

Conceptual Issues in Ecology. Esa Saarinen. 1982. pap. text ed. 44.50 (*90-277-1391-X*) Kluwer Ac.

Conceptual Issues in Environmental Archaeology. John L. Blintiff et al. 300p. 1988. 60.00 (*0-85224-545-9*, Pub. by Edinburgh U Pr UK) Col U Pr.

Conceptual Issues in Environmental Archaeology. John L. Blintiff et al. 300p. 1990. pap. 22.50 (*0-85224-546-7*, Pub. by Edinburgh U Pr UK) Col U Pr.

Conceptual Issues in Environmental Education. Ed. by Uri Zoller & Shoshana Keiny. LC 90-35970. (American University Studies: Education: Ser. XIV, Vol. 26). 311p. (C). 1991. text ed. 46.00 (*0-8204-1188-4*) P Lang Pubs.

Conceptual Issues in Evolutionary Biology. 2nd ed. Elliott Sober. (Illus.). 795p. (C). 1993. 55.00 (*0-262-19336-1*, Bradford Bks); pap. 28.50 (*0-262-69162-0*, Bradford Bks) MIT Pr.

Conceptual Issues in Operant Psychology. Peter Harzem & T. R. Miles. LC 77-21280. 146p. reprint ed. pap. 41.70 (*0-685-20718-8*, 2030506) Bks Demand.

Conceptual Issues in Psychoanalysis: Essays in History & Method. John E. Gedo. 255p. 1986. text ed. 29.95 (*0-88163-050-0*) Analytic Pr.

Conceptual Issues in Psychological Medicine: Collected Papers of Michael Shepherd. Michael Shepherd. 320p. 1990. 45.00 (*0-415-03727-1*, A4017) Routledge.

Conceptual Issues in Psychology. 2nd ed. Elizabeth Valentine. (Illus.). 208p. 1991. 69.50 (*0-415-03924-X*, A6695); pap. 16.95 (*0-415-03925-8*, A6699) Routledge.

Conceptual Learning: From Mollusks to Adult Education. Robert A. Carlson. LC 73-72. (Occasional Papers: No. 35). 1973. pap. 2.00 (*0-87060-058-3*, OCP 35) Syracuse U Cont Ed.

Conceptual Mathematics: A First Introduction to Categories. rev. ed. F. William Lawvere & Stephen Schanuel. (Illus.). 353p. 1993. pap. text ed. 28.00 (*0-9631805-1-7*) Buffalo Wksp.

Conceptual Modeling, Databases, & CASE: An Integrated View of Information Systems Development. Peri Loucopoulos & Roberto Zicari. 576p. 1992. text ed. 65.00 (*0-471-55462-6*) Wiley.

Conceptual Models & the Cuban Missile Crisis. Graham T. Allison. (Reprint Series in Political Science). (C). 1991. reprint ed. pap. text ed. 2.30 (*0-8290-2617-7*, P-422) Irvington.

Conceptual Models for Nursing Practice. 3rd ed. Joan P. Riehl-Sisca. 502p. (C). 1988. pap. text ed. 34.95 (*0-8385-1210-0*, A1210-2) Appleton & Lange.

Conceptual Models of Nursing: Analysis & Application. 2nd ed. Joyce J. Fitzpatrick & Ann L. Whall. (Illus.). 456p. (C). 1989. pap. text ed. 36.95 (*0-8385-1217-8*, A1217-7) Appleton & Lange.

Conceptual Nervous System. Henry A. Buchtel. LC 82-16509. (Foundations & Philosophy of Science & Technology Ser.). (Illus.). 196p. 1982. 85.00 (*0-08-027418-8*, Pub. by Pergamon Repr UK) Franklin.

Conceptual People Photography 6: Portrait, Lifestyle, Fashion & Beauty. New York Gold Staff. (Illus.). 128p. 1994. 22.95 (*0-8230-6317-8*, Watsn-Guptill) Watsn-Guptill.

***Conceptual People Photography 7: Portrait, Lifestyle, Fashion & Beauty.** 1994. pap. text ed. (*0-8230-6070-5*) Watsn-Guptill.

Conceptual Physical Science. Paul G. Hewitt et al. LC 93-4561. (C). 1993. 58.50 (*0-673-46379-6*); Lab. manual. student ed 22.50 (*0-673-46381-8*); Study guide wkbk. student ed 13.50 (*0-673-46380-X*) HarpCollege.

Conceptual Physics. Geoffrey F. Hewitt. (C). 1992. pap. text ed. 9.50 (*0-673-52319-5*) HarpCollege.

Conceptual Physics. Tillery. 1995. 48.95 (*0-8016-7720-3*) Mosby Yr Bk.

Conceptual Physics. 7th ed. Geoffrey F. Hewitt. (C). 1992. pap. text ed. 24.50 (*0-673-52252-0*) HarpCollege.

Conceptual Physics. 7th ed. Paul G. Hewitt. LC 92-14180. 733p. (C). 1992. 47.25 (*0-673-52185-0*) HarpCollege.

Conceptual Practices of Power: A Feminist Sociology of Knowledge. Dorothy E. Smith. (Northeastern Series in Feminist Theory). 224p. 1990. text ed. 32.50 (*1-55553-072-9*) NE U Pr.

Conceptual Practices of Power: A Feminist Sociology of Knowledge. Dorothy E. Smith. (Northeastern Series in Feminist Theory). 235p. 1991. pap. text ed. 12.95 (*1-55553-080-X*) NE U Pr.

Conceptual Problem Solving. Gerald Nadler & Shozo Hibino. LC 94-19879. 1994. pap. text ed. write for info. (*1-55958-567-6*) Prima Pub.

Conceptual Problems in Quantum Gravity. A. Ashtekar & J. J. Stachel. 1991. 105.00 (*0-8176-3443-6*) Birkhauser.

Conceptual Problems of Quantum Gravity. Ed. by A. Ashtekar & J. J. Stachel. (Einstein Studies: Vol. 2). 600p. 1991. 98.00 (*0-685-48719-9*) Spr-Verlag.

Conceptual Relevance. Joseph Grunfeld. 248p. (Orig.). 1989. pap. 41.00 (*90-6032-013-1*, Pub. by B R Gruener NE) Benjamins North Am.

Conceptual Revolutions. Paul Thagard. (Illus.). 344p. 1992. text ed. 45.00 (*0-691-08745-8*) Princeton U Pr.

Conceptual Revolutions. Paul Thagard. 301p. 1993. pap. text ed. 16.95 (*0-691-02490-1*) Princeton U Pr.

Conceptual Selling. R. B. Miller & S. E. Heiman. (C). 1987. 190.00 (*0-685-33724-3*, Pub. by Witherby & Co UK) St Mut.

Conceptual Selling. Robert B. Miller et al. 320p. 1989. pap. 13.99 (*0-446-38906-4*) Warner Bks.

Conceptual Statistics for Beginners. 2nd ed. Isadore Newman & Carole Newman. 298p. (C). 1994. pap. text ed. 28.50 (*0-8191-9420-4*) U Pr of Amer.

Conceptual Still Life Photography Six: General Still Life, Food & Interiors. New York Gold Staff. (Illus.). 128p. 1994. 22.95 (*0-8230-6318-6*) Watsn-Guptill.

***Conceptual Still Life Photography 7: General Still LIfe, Food & Interiors.** 1994. pap. text ed. (*0-8230-6071-3*) Watsn-Guptill.

***Conceptual Structures: Current Practices, 835.** Ed. by W. M. Tepfenhart et al. (Lecture Notes in Artificial Intelligence: Vol. 835). 331p. 1994. pap. text ed. 47.00 (*0-387-58328-9*) Spr-Verlag.

Conceptual Structures: Current Research & Practice. Tim Nagle et al. LC 92-18180. (Ellis Horwood Workshop Ser.). 500p. 1992. 63.00 (*0-13-175878-0*, Tavistock-E Horwood) Routledge Chapman & Hall.

Conceptual Structures: Information Processing in Mind & Machine. John F. Sowa. LC 82-20720. (Systems Programming Ser.). 300p. 1984. text ed. 40.95 (*0-201-14472-7*) Addison-Wesley.

Conceptual Structures - Theory & Implementation: Proceedings of the Seventh Annual Workshop, Las Cruces, New Mexico, U. S. A., July 1992. Ed. by Timothy E. Nagle & Heather D. Pfeiffer. LC 93-39736. (Lecture Notes in Computer Science, Lecture Notes in Artificial Intelligence Ser.: Vol. 754). 1993. 50.00 (*0-387-57454-9*) Spr-Verlag.

Conceptual Toolmaking: Expert Systems of the Mind. Jerry Rhodes. (Developmental Management Ser.). 206p. (Orig.). 1994. 39.95 (*0-631-17489-3*); pap. 19.95 (*0-631-19321-9*) Blackwell Pubs.

Conceptual Tools for Understanding Nature: Proceedings of the International Symposium. G. Costa et al. 260p. 1993. text ed. 67.00 (*981-02-1564-9*) World Scientific Pub.

Conceptual Trends in Quantum Chemistry. Ed. by E. S. Kryachko & J. L. Calais. LC 93-38823. 264p. (C). 1994. lib. bdg. 99.50 (*0-7923-2621-0*) Kluwer Ac.

Conceptualising Reflection in Teacher Development. Ed. by James Calderhead & Peter Gates. LC 92-2724. 192p. 1993. 80.00 (*0-7507-0123-4*, Falmer Pr); pap. 29.00 (*0-7507-0124-2*, Falmer Pr) Taylor & Francis.

Conceptualising Religion: Immanent Anthropologists, Transcendent Natives, & Unbounded Categories. Benson Saler. LC 92-31879. (Numen Supplements Ser.: Vol. 56). 292p. 1993. 80.00 (*90-04-09585-3*) E J Brill.

Conceptualising Society. Ed. by Adam Kuper. LC 91-43623. (European Association of Social Anthropologists Ser.). 224p. 1992. 69.95 (*0-415-06124-5*, A7470); pap. 19.95 (*0-415-06125-3*, A7474) Routledge.

Conceptualising Territorial Mobility in Low-Income Countries. Guy Standing. iv, 50p. (Orig.). 1982. pap. 8.00 (*92-2-102929-8*) Intl Labour Office.

Conceptualization & Measurement of Organism-Environment Interaction. Ed. by Theodore D. Wachs & Robert Plomin. 203p. 1991. text ed. 40.00 (*1-55798-126-4*) Am Psychol.

***Conceptualization & Measurement of Organism-Environment Interaction.** Ed. by Theodore D. Wachs & Robert Plomin. 203p. 1991. pap. text ed. 19.95 (*1-55798-264-3*) Am Psychol.

Conceptualization & Mental Processing in Language: Including a Selection of Papers from the First International Cognitive Linguistics Conference, Duisburg, Germany, March-April 1989. Ed. by Richard A. Geiger & Brygida Rudzka-Ostyn. LC 93-19401. (Cognitive Linguistics Research Ser.: Vol. 3). (Illus.). xiv, 825p. (C). 1993. lib. bdg. 198.50 (*3-11-012714-8*) Mouton.

Conceptualization in Psychotherapy: The Models Approach. Frederic M. Levine & Evelyn Sandeen. 232p. (C). 1985. text ed. 49.95 (*0-89859-549-5*) L Erlbaum Assocs.

Conceptualizing Global History. Ed. by Bruce Mazlish & Ralph Buultjens. LC 93-25123. (Global History Ser.). 253p. 1993. text ed. 63.00 (*0-8133-1683-9*) Westview.

Conceptualizing Global History. Ed. by Bruce Mazlish & Ralph Buultjens. LC 93-25123. (Global History Ser.). 253p. (C). 1993. pap. text ed. 14.85 (*0-8133-1684-7*) Westview.

Conceptualizing Sexual Harrassment as Discursive Practice. Ed. by Shereen G. Bingham. LC 93-37025. 224p. 1994. text ed. 55.00 (*0-275-94593-6*, Praeger Pubs) Greenwood.

Conceptualizing the Evaluation of Clinical Counseling. William D. Eldridge. LC 93-2284. 544p. (C). 1993. reprint ed. pap. text ed. 45.00 (*0-8191-9192-2*) U Pr of Amer.

***Conceptualizing the State: Innovation & Dispute in British Political Thought, 1880-1914.** James Meadowcroft. (Oxford Historical Monographs). 310p. 1995. 55.00 (*0-19-820601-1*) OUP.

Conceptualizing Two Thousand: Proactive Planning. Ed. by Dan Angel & Mike DeVault. 153p. (C). 1991. text ed. 35.00 (*0-87117-226-7*) Am Assn Comm Coll.

***Concern & Reverence.** Ellen Larson. Ed. by Debbie Bible. (Value Builders Ser.). (J). 1995. 7.95 (*0-7814-5094-2*, 10082) Cook.

Concern for Others: A New Psychology of Conscience & Morality. Tom Kitwood. 240p. 1990. 49.95 (*0-415-02338-6*, A4146); pap. 14.95 (*0-415-04377-8*, A4150) Routledge.

Concern for the Church see Theological Investigations

Concern for the Living. 1990. 14.95 (*0-944070-60-4*) Feldheim.

Concern, No. 3: Harmony & Contrast. Antoine A. Raphael. 216p. (Orig.). 1992. text ed. 11.99 (*0-9631764-0-4*); pap. text ed. 9.99 (*0-9631764-1-2*) A A Raphael.

Concerned about the Planet: The Reporter Magazine & American Liberalism, 1949-1968. Martin K. Doudna. LC 77-10048. (Contributions in American Studies: No. 32). 197p. 1977. text ed. 49.95 (*0-8371-9698-1*, DCA/, Greenwood Pr) Greenwood.

Concerned Citizen's Introduction to National Security. Natlie J. Goldring. 25p. (Orig.). (C). 1987. pap. 2.50 (*0-9619615-0-3*) MEND.

Concerned Intervention: When Your Loved One Won't Quit Alcohol or Drugs. 2nd ed. John O'Neill & Pat O'Neill. (Illus.). 190p. (Orig.). (C). 1993. text ed. 24.95 (*1-879237-37-7*); pap. text ed. 11.95 (*1-879237-36-9*) New Harbinger.

Concerned Parents Guide to L. A. County Schools. Lynda Bensky & Wendy Shawn. 212p. 1990. pap. text ed. 13.95 (*0-9626059-0-5*) Castbusters.

Concerned Parent's Guide to LA County Schools. Lynda B. Small & Wendy Shawn. 200p. (Orig.). 1989. pap. write for info. (*0-318-66798-3*) Paris Pub LA.

Concerning a New Federal Financial Statement. Morris A. Copeland. (Technical Papers: No. 5). 71p. 1947. reprint ed. 20.00 (*0-87014-450-2*); reprint ed. mic. film 20.00 (*0-685-61271-6*) Natl Bur Econ Res.

***Concerning Angels.** Rafael Alberti. Tr. by Christopher Sawyer-Lauoanno. 200p. (Orig.). 1995. pap. 12.95 (*0-87286-297-5*) City Lights.

Concerning Belinda. Eleanor Brainerd. LC 78-86138. (Short Story Index Reprint Ser.). (Illus.). 1977. 19.95 (*0-8369-3042-8*) Ayer.

Concerning Carpenters & Childhood Saints. Glenn Swetman. 1980. boxed 10.00 (*0-931757-07-X*); 20.00 (*0-931757-08-8*) Pterodactyl Pr.

Concerning Commonness & Other Conceptual Dysfunctions. Kenneth Gaburo. (Illus.). 64p. Date not set. 8.75 (*0-939044-29-3*) Lingua Pr.

Concerning Death: A Practical Guide for the Living. Ed. by Earl A. Grollman. LC 73-17117. 384p. 1974. pap. 16.00 (*0-8070-2765-0*, BP484) Beacon Pr.

Concerning English Administrative Law. Cecil T. Carr. LC 70-38958. reprint ed. 20.00 (*0-404-01395-3*) AMS Pr.

Concerning H. P. Blavatsky. G. R. Mead. 1992. pap. 9.00 (*1-56459-252-9*) Kessinger Pub.

Concerning Handel: His Life & Works. William C. Smith. LC 78-59044. (Encore Music Editions Ser.). (Illus.). 1979. reprint ed. 27.50 (*0-88355-716-9*) Hyperion Conn.

Concerning Handel, His Life & Works; Essays: Music Book Index. William C. Smith. 299p. 1993. reprint ed. lib. bdg. 79.00 (*0-7812-9602-1*) Rprt Serv.

Concerning Home Telematics: Proceedings of the IFIP TC9 Conference, Amsterdam, the Netherlands, 24-27 June, 1987. Ed. by F. Van Rijn & R. A. Williams. 462p. 1988. 107.75 (*0-444-70406-X*, North Holland) Elsevier.

Concerning Inner Life. Evelyn Underhill. (Mystical Classics of the World Ser.). 96p. 1992. reprint ed. pap. 6.95 (*1-85168-054-3*) Onewrld Pubns.

Concerning Music. Wilhelm Furtwangler. Tr. by Lawrence L. J. LC 76-57174. (Illus.). 96p. 1977. reprint ed. text ed. 35.00 (*0-8371-8665-X*, FUCM, Greenwood Pr) Greenwood.

Concerning Our Duties to God. Apostolos Makrakis. Ed. by Orthodox Christian Educational Society Staff. 170p. 1958. pap. text ed. 5.95 (*0-938366-13-0*) Orthodox Chr.

Concerning Our Girls & What They Tell Us: A Study of Some Phases of the Confidential Relationship of Mothers & Adolescent Daughters. Eugenie Leonard. LC 75-176986. (Columbia University. Teachers College. Contributions to Education Ser.: No. 430). reprint ed. 37.50 (*0-404-55430-X*) AMS Pr.

Concerning Psychology: Psychology Applied to Social Issues. Dennis Howitt. 192p. 1991. 90.00 (*0-335-09373-6*, Open Univ Pr); pap. 32.00 (*0-335-09372-8*, Open Univ Pr) Taylor & Francis.

Concerning Scandals. John Calvin. Tr. by John W. Fraser. LC 78-8675. 131p. reprint ed. 37.40 (*0-8357-9126-2*, 2012802) Bks Demand.

Concerning Some of the Ancestors & Descendants of Royal Denison Belden & Olive Cadwell Belden. Jessie P. Belden. (Illus.). 248p. 1988. reprint ed. lib. bdg. 47.00 (*0-8328-0228-X*); reprint ed. pap. 37.00 (*0-8328-0229-8*) Higginson Bk Co.

Concerning Spiritual Gifts. rev. ed. Donald Gee. LC 80-83784. 144p. 1980. reprint ed. pap. 2.95 (*0-88243-486-1*, 02-0486) Gospel Pub.

Concerning Spiritual Gifts. 2nd ed. Kenneth E. Hagin. 1982. pap. 3.95 (*0-89276-072-9*) Hagin Ministries.

Concerning Spiritualism. Gerard Massey. 130p. 1993. reprint ed. pap. 14.95 (*1-56459-395-9*) Kessinger Pub.

Concerning Sulphur. Michael Sendivogius. reprint ed. pap. 2.95 (*1-55818-135-0*, Sure Fire) Holmes Pub.

Concerning the Beautiful, Plotinus see Hymns of Orpheus

Concerning the Bible. Bill Freeman. 17p. (Orig.). 1991. pap. 0.75 (*0-914271-15-6*) Mnstry Wrd.

Concerning the Biosynthesis of Vitamin B12. A. I. Scott. 1976. pap. 15.50 (*0-08-020478-3*, Pergamon Pr) Elsevier.

Concerning the Careers. Ed. by J. A. Lunn & H. A. Waldron. 155p. 1991. pap. text ed. 39.95 (*0-7506-0022-5*) Buttrwrth-Heinemann.

Concerning the Deep Structures of Spanish Reflexive Verbs. Jan Schroten. (Janua Linguarum, Ser. Practica: No. 173). 122p. (Orig.). 1972. pap. text ed. 42.70 (*90-279-0000-0*) Mouton.

Concerning the Degrees, Grades & Compositions of Alchemy. Paracelsus. 1990. reprint ed. pap. 4.95 (*1-55818-126-1*) Holmes Pub.

Concerning the Education of a Prince: Correspondence of the Princess of Nassau-Saarbruck 13 June - 15 November 1758. Ed. by J. M. Allison. 1941. 49.50 (*0-686-51358-4*) Elliots Bks.

Concerning the Force & Effect of Manual Weapons of Fire. Humphrey Barwick. LC 74-80163. (English Experience Ser.: No. 643). 86p. 1974. reprint ed. 20.00 (*90-221-0643-8*) Walter J Johnson.

Concerning the Fourth Estate. 2nd ed. John E. Drewry. LC 42-18567. 181p. reprint ed. pap. 51.60 (*0-317-29264-1*, 2055537) Bks Demand.

Concerning the Gods & the Universe: With Peolegomena & Translation. Serenus Sallustius. Ed. & Tr. by Arthur D. Nock. cxxiii, 47p. (ENG & GRE.). 1988. reprint ed. pap. text ed. 29.85 (*3-487-01413-0*) Lubrecht & Cramer.

Concerning the Jews. Mark Twain. 30p. 1991. reprint ed. lib. bdg. 9.95 (*0-89966-826-7*) Buccaneer Bks.

Concerning the League: The Iroquois League Tradition. Ed. by Hanni Woodbury. 850p. (C). 1993. pap. text ed. 80.00 (*0-921064-09-8*) Syracuse U Pr.

Concerning the Lord's Table. Bill Freeman. 40p. (Orig.). 1992. pap. 1.00 (*0-914271-30-X*) Mnstry Wrd.

Concerning the More Certain Fundamentals of Astrology. Johann Kepler. 1987. pap. 4.95 (*0-916411-68-0*, Sure Fire) Holmes Pub.

Concerning the Mysteries. Ambrosius. 1977. pap. 1.25 (*0-89981-013-6*) Eastern Orthodox.

Concerning the Person of Christ. Bill Freeman. 22p. (Orig.). 1991. pap. 0.75 (*0-914271-17-2*) Mnstry Wrd.

Concerning the Principles of Morals see Enquiries Concerning the Human Understanding

***Concerning the Rites of Psychoanalysis: or The Villa of the Mysteries.** Bice Benvenuto. 261p. 1995. 59.00 (*0-415-91255-5*, B7261, Routledge NY); pap. 16.95x (*0-415-91256-3*, B7265, Routledge NY) Routledge.

An Asterisk (*) at the beginning of an entry indicates that the title is appearing in BIP for the first time.

C

An Asterisk (*) at the beginning of an entry indicates that the title is appearing in BIP for the first time.

1519

Concise Catechism for Catholics: A Simple Exposition of Catholic Doctrine. James Tolhurst. 80p. (Orig.). 1993. pap. 4.99 (*0-8028-0122-6*) Eerdmans.

***Concise Catholic Dictionary.** R. Reynolds & Rosemary Ekstrom. LC 94-60980. 208p. 1994. pap. 9.95 (*0-89622-622-0*) Twenty-Third.

Concise Chemical & Technical Dictionary. 4th ed. H. Bennett. 1986. 125.00 (*0-8206-0310-4*) Chem Pub.

Concise Chinese - English Dictionary Romanized. James C. Quo. LC 60-14372. 226p. (CHI & ENG.). 1961. pap. 7.95 (*0-8048-0116-9*) C E Tuttle.

Concise Chinese-English Dictionary. James C. Quo. 225p. (CHI & ENG.). 1980. pap. 9.95 (*0-8288-1607-7*, M14144) Fr & Eur.

Concise Chronicle of the Events of the Great War, 1914-1920. R. P. Rowe. 1976. lib. bdg. 69.95 (*0-8490-1660-6*) Gordon Pr.

Concise Chronology of English Literature. Philip Smallwood. LC 85-22865. 224p. 1986. 50.00 (*0-389-20597-4*, N8155) B&N Imports.

***Concise Chronology of Typesetting Developments 1886-1986.** L. W. Wallis. (Illus.). 96p. 1988. pap. 35.00 (*1-874084-00-9*, Pub. by Lund Humphries UK) Antique Collect.

Concise Church History: St. Joseph Edition. Lawrence G. Lovasik. (Orig.). 1989. pap. 5.95 (*0-89942-262-4*) Catholic Bk Pub.

Concise Code of Jewish Law: A Guide to Prayer & Religious Observance on the Sabbath, Vol. 2. Gersion Appel. 1989. 22.50 (*0-88125-314-6*); pap. 16.95 (*0-88125-324-3*) Ktav.

Concise Code of Jewish Law: Daily Prayers & Religious Observances in the Life-Cycle of the Jew, Vol. 1. G. Appel. 14.95 (*0-87068-298-9*) Ktav.

Concise Columbia Dictionary of Quotations. Robert Andrews. 343p. 1989. 19.95 (*0-231-06990-1*) Col U Pr.

Concise Columbia Dictionary of Quotations. Robert Andrews. 352p. 1990. reprint ed. pap. 9.95 (*0-380-70932-5*) Avon.

Concise Columbia Dictionary of Quotations in Large Print. large type ed. Robert Andrews. LC 92-14134. (Reference Bks.). 700p. 1992. text ed. 34.95 (*0-8161-5568-2*) G K Hall.

Concise Columbia Encyclopedia. Columbia University Press Editors. (Illus.). 960p. 1983. pap. 14.95 (*0-380-63396-5*) Avon.

Concise Columbia Encyclopedia. large type ed. Judith S. Levey. 1985. text ed. 368.00 (*0-231-06026-2*) Col U Pr.

Concise Columbia Encyclopedia. 2nd ed. Columbia University Press Staff. 944p. 1989. 39.95 (*0-231-06938-3*) Col U Pr.

Concise Columbia Encyclopedia. 3rd ed. LC 94-16721. 1994. 49.95 (*0-395-62439-8*) HM.

Concise Companion & Commentary for the New Catechism. James Tolhurst. LC 93-74852. (Catechism Resource Library). 250p. (Orig.). 1994. pap. 18.95 (*0-87061-203-4*, 6937) Chr Classics.

***Concise Compendium of the World's Languages.** George Campbell. 640p. (Orig.). 1995. 75.00 (*0-415-11392-X*, B4069) Routledge.

Concise Concordance Bible to the New Revised Standard Version. 1993. 12.95 (*0-19-528410-0*) OUP.

Concise Contract Law. Peter Gillies. 1988. pap. 43.00 (*1-86287-001-2*, Pub. by Federation Pr AU) W W Gaunt.

***Concise Corporations Law.** Julie Cassidy. 350p. 1995. pap. 39.00 (*1-86287-166-3*, Pub. by Federation Pr AU) W W Gaunt.

***Concise Course in A-Level Statistics.** 3rd ed. J. Crawshaw & J. Chambers. 752p. (C). 1994. 59.00x (*0-7487-1757-9*, Pub. by S Thornes Pubs UK) St Mut.

Concise Course in A-Level Statistics with Worked Examples. J. Crawsha & J. Chambers. (C). 1987. text ed. 40.00 (*0-85950-709-2*, Pub. by S Thornes Pubs UK) St Mut.

Concise Course in Electromagnetism for Electrical Engineering. Ta-Peng Tsao. 372p. 1994. text ed. 61.00 (*981-02-1773-0*) World Scientific Pub.

Concise Czech-English, English-Czech Dictionary. 3rd rev. ed. Nina Trnka. (Concise Dictionaries Ser.). 594p. (Orig.). 1993. pap. 11.95 (*0-87052-981-1*) Hippocrene Bks.

Concise Defining Dictionary of Russian. V. Rozanova. 256p. (C). 1989. 75.00 (*0-685-46851-8*, Pub. by Collets) St Mut.

Concise Defining Dictionary of Russian for Foreigners. V. Rozanova. 227p. (RUS.). (C). 1978. 70.00 (*0-685-46850-X*, Pub. by Collets) St Mut.

Concise Dental Anatomy & Morphology. 2nd ed. James L. Fuller & Gerald E. Denehy. (Illus.). 293p. 1984. 39.95 (*0-8151-3298-0*, FU-2, Yr Bk Med Pubs) Mosby Yr Bk.

Concise Desk Book of Business Finance. 2nd ed. Donald W. Moffat. 385p. 1984. text ed. 44.95 (*0-13-166851-X*, Busn) P-H.

Concise Dictionary & Handbook of Economics, Finance & Statistics for Healthcare. Les Seplaki. 380p. 1991. pap. text ed. write for info. (*0-9618644-2-7*) Prof Homzons Pr.

Concise Dictionary for Automobile & Transportation Engineering: English-Japanese. Interpress Staff. 652p. (ENG & JPN.). 1988. 125.00 (*0-8288-7223-6*, F126678) Fr & Eur.

Concise Dictionary for Building Engineering Terms. Interpress Staff. 828p. (ENG & JPN.). 1990. 225.00 (*0-8288-7221-X*, 4871982157) Fr & Eur.

Concise Dictionary for Chemistry & Chemical Engineering: English-Japanese. Interpress Staff. 472p. (ENG & JPN.). 1988. 125.00 (*0-8288-7222-8*, 4871981142) Fr & Eur.

Concise Dictionary for Electric & Electronics Terms. Interpress Staff. 868p. (ENG & JPN.). 1991. reprint ed. 195.00 (*0-8288-7219-8*, F117810) Fr & Eur.

Concise Dictionary for Mechanical Engineering Terms. Interpress Staff. 1144p. (ENG & JPN.). 1990. reprint ed. 225.00 (*0-8288-0639-X*, M606) Fr & Eur.

Concise Dictionary for Science: English-Japanese. Interpress Staff. 722p. (ENG & JPN.). 1988. 125.00 (*0-8288-7224-4*, 4871981134) Fr & Eur.

Concise Dictionary of Acronyms & Initialisms. Stuart W. Miller. 192p. 1988. 24.95 (*0-8160-1577-5*) Facts on File.

Concise Dictionary of American Biography. 3rd ed. Ed. by American Council of Learned Societies Staff. LC 80-13892. 1980. lib. bdg. 90.00 (*0-684-16631-3*, Scribners) S&S Trade.

Concise Dictionary of American Biography: Complete to 1970. 4th ed. LC 90-8951. 1536p. 1990. text ed. 150.00 (*0-684-19188-1*, Scribners) S&S Trade.

Concise Dictionary of American History. LC 82-43721. 1140p. 1983. text ed. 95.00 (*0-684-17321-2*, Scribners) S&S Trade.

Concise Dictionary of American Jewish Biography. Ed. by Jacob R. Marcus & Judith M. Daniels. LC 94-20231. 750p. 1994. 200.00 (*0-926019-74-0*) Carlson Pub.

Concise Dictionary of American Literary Biography, 6 vols. Ed. by Mary Bruccoli & Richard Layman. 1987. 380.00 (*0-8103-1818-0*) Gale.

Concise Dictionary of American Literary Biography: Broadening Views, 1968-1988. Ed. by Matthew J. Bruccoli & Richard Layman. LC 86-33657. (Illus.). 408p. 1989. text ed. 70.00 (*0-8103-1823-7*, 007182) Gale.

Concise Dictionary of American Literary Biography: The Twenties, 1917-1929. Mary Bruccoli. 1989. 70.00 (*0-8103-1824-5*) Gale.

Concise Dictionary of American Literary Biography (DALB), Vol. V: The Age of Maturity, 1929-1941. Mary Bruccoli. 1989. 70.00 (*0-8103-1820-2*) Gale.

Concise Dictionary of American Literary Biography, Realism, Naturalism, & Local Color, 1865-1917. Matthew J. Bruccoli & Richard Layman. (Dictionary of Literary Biography Ser.). 400p. 1988. 70.00 (*0-8103-1821-0*) Gale.

Concise Dictionary of Architectural & Design History. Frederic H. Jones. Ed. by Michael G. Crisp. LC 91-70350. (Concise Dictionary Ser.). 150p. (Orig.). 1991. pap. 13.95 (*1-56052-069-8*) Crisp Pubns.

Concise Dictionary of Architecture. Frederic H. Jones. Ed. by Michael G. Crisp. LC 91-19372. (Concise Dictionary Ser.). 150p. 1991. pap. 13.95 (*1-56052-066-3*) Crisp Pubns.

Concise Dictionary of Astronomy. Ed. by Jacqueline Mitton. 284p. 1992. 24.95 (*0-19-853967-3*) OUP.

Concise Dictionary of Australian Artists. Gwenda Robb & Elaine Smith. Ed. by Robert Smith. 288p. (Orig.). 1993. pap. 24.95 (*0-522-84478-2*) Intl Spec Bk.

Concise Dictionary of Biology: New Edition. (Oxford Paperback Reference Ser.). (Illus.). 288p. 1990. pap. 10.95 (*0-19-286109-3*) OUP.

Concise Dictionary of British Literary Biography, Vol. 2: Writers of the Restoration & 18th Century, 1660-1789. 580p. 1992. 65.00 (*0-8103-7982-1*, PR19) Gale.

Concise Dictionary of British Literary Biography, Vol. 4: Victorian Writers, 1832-1890. 516p. 1991. 65.00 (*0-8103-7984-8*, PR19) Gale.

Concise Dictionary of Business. 504p. 1992. reprint ed. pap. 10.95 (*0-19-285231-0*, 12212) OUP.

Concise Dictionary of Chemistry: New Edition. (Oxford Paperback Reference Ser.). (Illus.). 336p. 1990. pap. 10.95 (*0-19-286110-7*) OUP.

Concise Dictionary of Chemistry & Chemical Technology. 128p. 1975. 40.00 (*0-686-44771-9*, Pub. by Collets UK) St Mut.

Concise Dictionary of Christian Theology. Millard J. Erickson. 187p. 1994. reprint ed. pap. 8.99 (*0-8010-3029-3*) Baker Bk.

Concise Dictionary of Christianity in America. abr. ed. Ed. by Daniel G. Reid et al. 350p. 1995. pap. 16.99 (*0-8308-1446-9*) InterVarsity. Now thousands of facts related to the 500-year history of Christianity in America are right at your fingertips. BASED ON THE CRITICALLY ACCLAIMED DICTIONARY OF CHRISTIANITY IN AMERICA, THIS CONCISE DICTIONARY INCLUDES HUNDREDS OF BRIEF, UP-TO-DATE & INFORMATIVE ENTRIES on denominations & traditions; missionaries & evangelists; beliefs & practices; colleges & seminaries; women & ethnic groups; theologians, educators & writers; lay & denominational leaders; mission societies & social welfare organizations; & historical events, movements & struggles. Praise for the DICTIONARY OF CHRISTIANITY IN AMERICA: "The single most important volume on religion in the U.S. during 1990... Warmly, wholeheartedly, & enthusiastically recommended."--ADRIS NEWSLETTER. Editors include DANIEL G. REID, reference book editor at InterVarsity Press; ROBERT D. LINDER, professor of history at Kansas State University; BRUCE L. SHELLEY, professor of church history at Denver Seminary; & HARRY S. STOUT, professor of American religious history at Yale University. The work was condensed by freelance editor CRAIG A. NOLL. To order contact: Baker & Taylor, Riverside, Spring Arbor, Ingram or write InterVarsity Press, P.O. Box 1400 Downers Grove, IL 60515. Phone: 800-843-7225, FAX: 708-887-2520.** ***Publisher Provided Annotation.

Concise Dictionary of Classical Mythology. Pierre Grimal. Ed. by Stephen Kershaw. Tr. by A. R. Maxwell-Hyslop. 350p. 1990. 34.95 (*0-631-16696-3*) Blackwell Pubs.

Concise Dictionary of Confusables: All Those Impossible Words You Never Get Right. B. A. Phythian. 198p. 1990. pap. text ed. 10.95 (*0-471-52880-3*) Wiley.

Concise Dictionary of Construction. Frederic H. Jones. Ed. by Michael G. Crisp. LC 91-70349. (Concise Dictionary Ser.). 150p. (Orig.). 1991. pap. 13.95 (*1-56052-068-X*) Crisp Pubns.

Concise Dictionary of Correct English. Ed. by B. A. Phythian. (Quality Paperback Ser.: No. 349). 166p. 1979. pap. 6.95 (*0-8226-0349-7*) Littlefield.

Concise Dictionary of Correct English. Ed. by B. A. Phythian. 166p. 1979. 17.75 (*0-8476-6212-8*) Rowman.

Concise Dictionary of Cults & Religions. William Watson. 1991. pap. 12.99 (*0-8024-1726-4*) Moody.

Concise Dictionary of Data Processing & Computer Terms. A. Anderson. 1990. 29.00 (*0-7121-0442-9*, Pub. by Northcote UK) St Mut.

Concise Dictionary of Data Processing & Computer Terms. 2nd ed. R. G. Anderson. 149p. 1984. pap. 24.00 (*0-7121-0435-6*) Trans-Atl Phila.

Concise Dictionary of Economical Mathematics. Science Press Staff. 494p. (CHI.). 1985. 49.95 (*0-8288-6991-X*) Fr & Eur.

Concise Dictionary of Egyptian Archaeology. M. Broderick & A. A. Morton. vii, 193p. 1979. reprint ed. pap. 15.00 (*0-89005-303-0*) Ares.

Concise Dictionary of First Names. Patrick Hanks & Flavia Hodges. 224p. 1993. 14.95 (*0-19-866188-6*); pap. 8.95 (*0-19-866190-8*) OUP.

Concise Dictionary of Fishing. V. I. Kozlov. 160p. (RUS.). 1982. 12.95 (*0-8288-1426-0*, M15332) Fr & Eur.

Concise Dictionary of Indian Philosophy: Sanskrit Terms Defined in English. John Grimes. LC 88-36717. 440p. (C). 1989. 49.50 (*0-7914-0100-6*); pap. 16.95 (*0-7914-0101-4*) State U NY Pr.

Concise Dictionary of Indian Tribes of North American. 2nd rev. ed. Barbara Leitch et al. Ed. by Keith Irvine. write for info. (*0-917256-48-4*) Ref Pubns.

Concise Dictionary of Interior Design. Frederic H. Jones. Ed. by Michael G. Crisp. LC 91-70348. (Concise Dictionary Ser.). 150p. (Orig.). 1991. pap. 13.95 (*1-56052-067-1*) Crisp Pubns.

Concise Dictionary of Islamic Terms. pap. 6.95 (*0-935782-60-5*) Kazi Pubns.

Concise Dictionary of Islamic Terms: English-Arabic. M. A. Qazi. 1979. 8.50 (*0-86685-276-X*) Intl Bk Ctr.

Concise Dictionary of Judaism. Ed. by Dagobert D. Runes. LC 77-88933. 124p. 1982. reprint ed. text ed. 75.00 (*0-8371-2109-4*, AERUDJ, Greenwood Pr) Greenwood.

Concise Dictionary of Library & Information Science. Stella Keenan. 350p. 1995. lib. bdg. 50.00 (*1-85739-022-9*) Bowker-Saur.

Concise Dictionary of Literary Terms. Harry Shaw. (McGraw-Hill Paperbacks Ser.). Orig. Title: Dictionary of Literary Terms. 224p. 1976. pap. text ed. 6.95 (*0-07-056483-3*) McGraw.

Concise Dictionary of Management. David A. Statt. 192p. 1991. 49.95 (*0-415-05568-7*, A5936); pap. 14.95 (*0-415-05569-5*, A5884) Routledge.

Concise Dictionary of Middle Egyptian. Faulkner. 1962. 45.00 (*0-900416-32-7*, Pub. by Aris & Phillips UK) David Brown.

Concise Dictionary of Military Biography. Martin Windrow & Francis K. Mason. 337p. 1991. text ed. 29.95 (*0-471-53441-2*) Wiley.

Concise Dictionary of Military Biography. Martin Windrow & Francis K. Mason. 352p. 1992. pap. text ed. 15.95 (*0-471-55181-3*) Wiley.

***Concise Dictionary of Minnesota Ojibwe.** expanded rev. ed. John D. Nichols & Earl Nyholm. LC 94-35219. Orig. Title: Ojebwewi-Ikodowinan. (ENG & OJI.). 1995. 19.95 (*0-8166-2427-5*); pap. 9.95 (*0-8166-2428-3*) U of Minn Pr.

Concise Dictionary of Modern Japanese History. Janet E. Hunter. LC 82-17456. (Illus.). 464p. (C). 1984. 55.00 (*0-520-04390-1*); pap. 17.00 (*0-520-04557-2*) U CA Pr.

Concise Dictionary of National Biography: From Earliest Times to 1985, 3 vols., Set. 1992. 195.00 (*0-19-865305-0*) OUP.

Concise Dictionary of National Biography, Pt. 2: 1901-1970, 2 pts. 750p. 1982. 39.95 (*0-19-865303-4*) OUP.

Concise Dictionary of Old Icelandic. Geir T. Zoega. (ICE.). 1922. 79.00 (*0-19-863108-1*) OUP.

Concise Dictionary of Phrase & Fable. Passport Books Staff. 1993. pap. 11.95 (*0-8442-3901-1*, Teach Yourslf) NTC Pub Grp.

Concise Dictionary of Physics: New Edition. (Oxford Paperback Reference Ser.). (Illus.). 320p. 1990. pap. 10.95 (*0-19-286111-5*) OUP.

Concise Dictionary of Physics & Related Subjects. 2nd ed. J. Thewlis. LC 79-40209. 1979. 195.00 (*0-08-023048-2*, Pergamon Pr) Elsevier.

***Concise Dictionary of Plant Names.** Richard J. Pankhurst. 512p. 1995. 25.00 (*0-19-866189-4*) OUP.

Concise Dictionary of Proper Names & Notable Matters in the Works of Dante. Paget Toynbee. LC 68-15695. 568p. 1968. reprint ed. 75.00 (*0-87753-040-8*) Phaeton.

Concise Dictionary of Psychology. David A. Statt. 1990. pap. 9.95 (*0-415-02662-8*) Routledge.

Concise Dictionary of Religion. Irving Hexham. LC 93-18089. 252p. (Orig.). (C). 1993. pap. 15.99 (*0-8308-1404-3*, 1404) InterVarsity.

Concise Dictionary of Scientific Biography. Ed. by American Council of Learned Societies Staff. 784p. 1981. text ed. 95.00 (*0-684-16650-X*, Scribners) S&S Trade.

Concise Dictionary of Soviet Terminology, Institutions & Abbreviations. B. Crowe. LC 69-10545. 1969. 85.00 (*0-08-012989-7*, Pub. by Pergamon Repr UK) Franklin.

Concise Dictionary of Spoken Chinese. Chao Yuen-Ren & Lien-Sheng Yang. LC 47-5464. (Harvard-Yenching Institute Publications). 330p. 1947. 22.50 (*0-674-15800-8*) HUP.

Concise Dictionary of the Assyrian Languages, 2 vols., Set. William Muss-Arnolt. LC 78-72752. (Ancient Mesopotamian Texts & Studies). (AKK.). reprint ed. 97.50 (*0-404-18195-3*) AMS Pr.

Concise Dictionary of the Early Christianity. Joseph F. Kelly. 224p. (Orig.). 1992. pap. text ed. 24.95 (*0-8146-5527-0*) Liturgical Pr.

Concise Dictionary of the System of Psychological Understanding. 2nd ed. K. K. Platanov. 174p. (RUS.). 1984. 12.95 (*0-8288-2212-3*, M15380) Fr & Eur.

Concise Dictionary of Theology. Gerald O'Collins & Edward G. Farrugia. LC 91-7187. 272p. 1991. pap. 14.95 (*0-8091-3235-4*) Paulist Pr.

Concise Economic History of Britain, from the Earliest Times to 1750. John H. Clapham. LC 75-41059. (BCL Ser.: No. II). 1976. reprint ed. 34.50 (*0-404-14654-6*) AMS Pr.

Concise Economic History of the World: From Paleolithic Times to the Present. Rondo Cameron. (Illus.). 464p. (C). 1993. pap. text ed. 22.00 (*0-19-507446-7*) OUP.

Concise Economic History of the World: From Paleolithic Times to the Present. 2nd ed. Rondo Cameron. (Illus.). 464p. (C). 1993. text ed. 49.95 (*0-19-507445-9*) OUP.

Concise Electronics Dictionary, Vol. 1. 5th ed. George Moellerke. 174p. (ENG & GER.). 0198. pap. 29.95 (*0-8288-4407-0*, M15120) Fr & Eur.

Concise Electronics Dictionary, Vol. 2: German-English. 2nd ed. George Moellerke. 160p. (ENG & GER.). 1985. pap. 29.95 (*0-8288-0291-2*, M15119) Fr & Eur.

Concise Encyclopaedia of Information Technology. 2nd ed. Adrian Stokes. 288p. 1985. text ed. 55.95 (*0-566-02531-0*) Ashgate Pub Co.

Concise Encyclopaedia of Participation & Co-Management. Ed. by Gyorgy Szell. LC 92-21593. (Studies in Organization: No. 38). xiv, 1047p. (C). 1992. lib. bdg. 138.00 (*3-11-012173-5*) De Gruyter.

Concise Encyclopaedia of the Home. I. Terekhov. 640p. (C). 1988. 175.00 (*0-685-46824-0*, Pub. by Collets) St Mut.

Concise Encyclopaedic Dictionary of Astronautics. J. Nayler. 1964. 20.50 (*0-444-99986-8*) Elsevier.

Concise Encyclopedia Chemistry. Tr. by Mary Eagleson. vii, 1203p. (C). 1994. lib. bdg. 69.95 (*3-11-011451-8*, 12-94) De Gruyter.

Concise Encyclopedia of Advanced Ceramic Materials. Ed. by Richard J. Brook. 400p. 1990. 150.00 (*0-262-02304-0*) MIT Pr.

Concise Encyclopedia of Aeronautics & Space Systems. Ed. by Marc Pelegrin & Walter M. Hollister. LC 93-10616. (Advances in Systems Control, & Information Engineering Ser.). 1993. 310.00 (*0-08-037049-7*, Pergamon Pr) Elsevier.

Concise Encyclopedia of Biochemistry. 2nd expanded rev. ed. Ed. by Thomas Scott & Mary Eagleson. 649p. 1988. lib. bdg. 89.90x (*3-11-011625-1*) De Gruyter.

***Concise Encyclopedia of Biochemistry.** 2nd expanded rev. ed. Ed. by Thomas Scott & Mary Eagleson. 649p. (C). 1988. lib. bdg. 89.90 (*0-89925-457-8*) De Gruyter.

Concise Encyclopedia of Biological & Biomedical Measurement Systems. Peter A. Payne. (Advances in Systems Control & Information Engineering Ser.: No. 3). 512p. 1991. 290.00 (*0-08-036188-9*, Pergamon Pr) Elsevier.

Concise Encyclopedia of Building & Construction Materials. Ed. by Fred Moavenzadeh. (Advances in Materials Science & Engineering Ser.: No. 4). (Illus.). 650p. 1990. 230.00 (*0-08-034728-2*, Pergamon Pr) Elsevier.

Concise Encyclopedia of Building & Construction Materials. Ed. by Fred Moavenzadeh. (Advances in Materials Science & Engineering Ser.). 562p. 1990. 175.00 (*0-262-13248-6*) MIT Pr.

Concise Encyclopedia of Chemical Technology. 2nd ed. 1989. pap. text ed. 99.95 (*0-471-51700-3*) Wiley.

Concise Encyclopedia of Composite Materials. Ed. by Anthony Kelly. (Advances in Materials Science & Engineering Ser.: No. 3). (Illus.). 350p. 1989. 168.00 (*0-08-034718-5*, Ed Skills Dallas) Elsevier.

Concise Encyclopedia of Composite Materials. Ed. by Anthony Kelly. (Advances in Materials Science & Engineering Ser.). 336p. 1990. 135.00 (*0-262-11145-4*) MIT Pr.

Concise Encyclopedia of Composite Materials. rev. ed. Ed. by Anthony Kelly et al. LC 93-48542. (Advances in Materials Science & Engineering Ser.). 1994. pap. 63.00 (*0-08-042300-0*, Ed Skills Dallas) Elsevier.

Concise Encyclopedia of Early Buddhist Philosophy: Based on the Study of the Abhidhammatthasangahasarupa. Chandra B. Varma. (C). 1992. 27.00 (*81-85133-59-X*, Estrn Bk Linkers) Nataraj Bks.

An Asterisk (*) at the beginning of an entry indicates that the title is appearing in BIP for the first time.

Concise Encyclopedia of Early Buddhist Philosophy: Based on the Study of the Abhidhammatthasangahasarupa. Chandra B. Varma. xviii, 133p. 1992. 27.00 (*0-685-62642-3*, Estrn Bk Linkers) Nataraj Bks.
Concise Encyclopedia of Environmental Systems. Ed. by Peter C. Young. LC 93-10618. (Advances in Systems Control, & Information Engineering Ser.). 769p. 1993. 340.00 (*0-08-036198-6*) Elsevier.
Concise Encyclopedia of Garden Flowers. David Papworth. 1987. 12.99 (*0-517-63953-X*) Random Hse Value.
Concise Encyclopedia of Gastronomy. Andre L. Simon. LC 81-47413. (Illus.). 816p. 1983. pap. 14.95 (*0-87951-180-X*) Overlook Pr.
Concise Encyclopedia of Heat Transfer. S. Kutateladz & V. Borishanskii. LC 63-10056. 1966. 204.00 (*0-08-010120-8*, Pub. by Pergamon Repr UK) Franklin.
Concise Encyclopedia of Houseplants. P. Chapman. 1987. 12.99 (*0-517-63368-X*) Random Hse Value.
Concise Encyclopedia of Information Processing in Systems & Organizations. Ed. by A. P. Sage. (Advances in Systems Control & Information Engineering Ser.: No. ASCI 2). (Illus.). 510p. 1990. 300.00 (*0-08-035954-X*, Pergamon Pr) Elsevier.
Concise Encyclopedia of Interior Design. Allen Dizik. 320p. 1988. text ed. 24.95 (*0-442-22109-6*) Van Nos Reinhold.
Concise Encyclopedia of Islam. Cyril Glasse. LC 91-55138. (Illus.). 472p. 1991. reprint ed. pap. 24.95 (*0-06-063126-0*) Harper SF.
Concise Encyclopedia of Magnetic & Superconducting Materials. Ed. by J. E. Evetts. (Advances in Materials Science & Engineering Ser.: No. 7). 600p. 1992. 290.00 (*0-08-034722-3*, Pergamon Pr) Elsevier.
Concise Encyclopedia of Materials Characterization. Ed. by Robert W. Cahn & Eric Lifshin. LC 92-10673. (Advances in Materials Science & Engineering Ser.). 1992. 330.00 (*0-08-040603-3*, Pergamon Pr) Elsevier.
Concise Encyclopedia of Materials Economics, Policy & Management. Ed. by Michael B. Bever & Robert W. Cahns. LC 92-27943. (Advances in Materials Science & Engineering Ser.). 1992. 265.00 (*0-08-037056-X*, Pergamon Pr) Elsevier.
Concise Encyclopedia of Measurement & Instrumentation. Ed. by L. Finkelstein & K. T. Grattan. LC 93-10617. (Advances in Systems Control, & Information Engineering Ser.). 1993. Alk. paper. 310.00 (*0-08-036212-5*, Pergamon Pr) Elsevier.
Concise Encyclopedia of Medical & Dental Materials. Ed. by David F. Williams. (Advances in Materials Science & Engineering Ser.: No. 5). 400p. 1990. 210.00 (*0-08-036194-3*, Pergamon Pr) Elsevier.
Concise Encyclopedia of Mineral Resources. Ed. by Donald D. Carr & Norman Herz. (Advances in Materials Science & Engineering Ser.: No. 2). (Illus.). 470p. 1989. 195.00 (*0-08-034734-7*, Pergamon Pr) Elsevier.
Concise Encyclopedia of Mineral Resources. Ed. by Donald D. Carr & Norman Herz. (Advances in Materials Science Ser.). 440p. 1989. 145.00 (*0-262-03155-8*) MIT Pr.
Concise Encyclopedia of Modelling & Simulation. Ed. by Derek P. Atherton & Pierre Borne. (Advances in Systems Control & Information Engineering Ser.: No. 5). 554p. 1991. 290.00 (*0-08-036201-X*, Pergamon Pr) Elsevier.
Concise Encyclopedia of Polymer Processing & Applications. Ed. by P. J. Corish. (Advances in Materials Science & Engineering Ser.: No. 10). (Illus.). 800p. 1991. 290.00 (*0-08-037064-0*, Pergamon Pr) Elsevier.
Concise Encyclopedia of Polymer Science & Engineering. Herman F. Mark. 1341p. 1990. text ed. 199.00 (*0-471-51253-2*) Wiley.
***Concise Encyclopedia of Preaching.** Ed. by William H. Willimon & Richard Lischer. LC 94-3469. 544p. 1995. 39.00 (*0-664-21942-X*) Westminster John Knox.
Concise Encyclopedia of Psychology. Ed. by Raymond J. Corsini. 1264p. 1987. text ed. 135.00 (*0-471-01068-5*) Wiley.
Concise Encyclopedia of Semiconducting Materials & Related Technologies. S. Mahajan & L. C. Kimerling. (Advances in Materials Science & Engineering Ser.: No. 8). 600p. 1992. 270.00 (*0-08-034724-X*, Pergamon Pr) Elsevier.
Concise Encyclopedia of Software Engineering. Ed. by D. Morris & B. Tamm. LC 92-27942. (Advances in Systems Control, & Information Engineering Ser.). 1992. 345.00 (*0-08-036214-1*, Pergamon Pr) Elsevier.
Concise Encyclopedia of Solid State Physics. Ed. by Rita G. Lerner & George L. Trigg. 300p. (C). 1983. text ed. 55.95 (*0-201-14204-X*, Adv Bk Prog); pap. text ed. 40. 95 (*0-201-14205-8*, Adv Bk Prog) Addison-Wesley.
Concise Encyclopedia of Special Education. Cecil R. Reynolds & Elaine Fletcher-Janzen. 1215p. 1990. text ed. 135.00 (*0-471-51527-2*) Wiley.
Concise Encyclopedia of the American Indian. Bruce Grant. (Illus.). 352p. (J). 1989. 8.99 (*0-517-69310-0*) Random Hse Value.
***Concise Encyclopedia of the Human Body.** 160p. (J). 1995. 19.95 (*0-7894-0204-1*, 5-70617) Dorling Kindersley.
Concise Encyclopedia of Traffic & Transportation Systems. M. Papageorgiou. (Advances in Systems Control & Information Engineering Ser.: No. 6). (Illus.). 700p. 1991. 425.00 (*0-08-036203-6*, Pergamon Pr) Elsevier.
***Concise Encyclopedia of Western Philosophy & Philosophers.** J. Urmson. 1993. pap. 16.95 (*0-415-07883-0*) Routledge Chapman & Hall.
Concise Encyclopedia of Western Philosophy & Philosophers. Ed. by J. O. Urmson & Jonathan Ree. 256p. 1990. pap. 16.95 (*0-04-445342-6*) Routledge Chapman & Hall.
Concise Encyclopedia of Western Philosophy & Philosophers. 3rd ed. Jonathan Ree. Ed. by J. O. Urmson. 256p. (C). 1990. text ed. 44.95 (*0-685-46018-5*); pap. text ed. 16.95 (*0-685-46019-3*) Routledge Chapman & Hall.
Concise Encyclopedia of Wood & Wood-Based Materials. Ed. by Arno P. Schniewind. (Advances in Materials Science & Engineering Ser.: No. 1). (Illus.). 360p. 1989. 175.00 (*0-08-034726-6*, Pergamon Pr) Elsevier.
Concise Encyclopedia of Wood & Wood-Based Materials. Ed. by Arno P. Schniewind. (Advances in Materials Science & Engineering Ser.). 346p. 1989. 125.00 (*0-262-19289-6*) MIT Pr.
Concise Enclypedia of Advanced Ceramic Materials. Ed. by R. J. Brook. (Advances in Materials Science & Engineering Ser.: No. 6). 600p. 1991. 230.00 (*0-08-034720-7*, Pergamon Pr) Elsevier.
Concise English & Arabic Dictionary of Data Processing & Computer Terms. E. W. Haddad. 187p. (ARA & ENG.). 1984. 35.00 (*0-8288-1343-4*, F51550) Fr & Eur.
Concise English Assamese Dictionary. Kiran. (ASM & ENG.). 1992. reprint ed. 19.95 (*0-8288-8452-8*) Fr & Eur.
Concise English-Chinese Chinese-English Dictionary. Ed. by A. P. Cowie & A. Evison. 1100p. (CHI & ENG.). 1994. reprint ed. pap. 11.95 (*0-19-584097-6*) OUP.
Concise English-Chinese Dictionary. Commercial Press Staff. 1211p. (CHI & ENG.). 1972. 19.95 (*0-8288-6803-4*, M-9563) Fr & Eur.
Concise English-Chinese Dictionary. rev. ed. Shau W. Chan. xviii, 390p. 1955. reprint ed. pap. 12.95 (*0-8047-0384-1*) Stanford U Pr.
Concise English-Chinese Dictionary Romanized. James C. Quo. LC 55-11585. 324p. (CHI & ENG.). 1960. pap. 7.95 (*0-8048-0117-7*) C E Tuttle.
Concise English-Gujarati Dictionary. P. G. Deshpande. 468p. 1987. 16.95 (*0-19-561827-0*) OUP.
Concise English Handbook. 2nd annot. ed. James W. Kirkland & Collett B. Dilworth, Jr. LC 89-84586. 479p. (C). 1990. Instr.'s annotated ed. teacher ed 13.00 (*0-669-17850-0*) Heath.
Concise English Handbook. 2nd ed. James W. Kirkland & Collett B. Dilworth, Jr. LC 89-84586. 479p. (C). 1990. pap. text ed. 13.00 (*0-669-17849-7*); Wkbk. student ed 11.50 (*0-669-17851-9*) Heath.
Concise English Hindi Dictionary. R. C. Pathak. (ENG & HIN.). 1979. 6.00 (*0-89744-972-X*) Auromere.
Concise English-Hungarian Dictionary. Ed. by T. Maqay & Laszlo Orszagh. 1056p. 1990. 39.95 (*0-19-864170-2*) OUP.
***Concise English-Hungarian Dictionary.** L. Orszagh & T. Magay. 1052p. (C). 1992. 54.00x (*963-05-6338-X*, Pub. by Akad Kiado HU) St Mut.
Concise English-Hungarian Dictionary. V. Orszagh. 1091p. (ENG & HUN.). 1981. 99.00 (*0-569-00407-1*, Pub. by Collets UK) St Mut.
Concise English-Interlingua Dictionary. Ed. by F. P. Gospill. 1987. pap. 9.00 (*0-917848-01-2*) Interlingua Inst.
Concise English-Japanese-English Dictionary. Oreste Vaccari. 500p. (ENG & JPN.). 1980. 39.95 (*0-8288-0469-9*, F48270) Fr & Eur.
Concise English-Korean Dictionary Romanized. Joan V. Underwood. LC 55-5891. 320p. (ENG & KOR.). 1960. pap. 7.95 (*0-8048-0118-5*) C E Tuttle.
Concise English-Korean Dictionary Romanized. 31th ed. J. V. Underwood. 320p. (ENG & KOR.). 1980. pap. 9.95 (*0-8288-1615-8*, M9547) Fr & Eur.
Concise English-Mongolian Dictionary. John G. Hangin. (Uralic & Altaic Ser.: Vol. 89). 287p. (ENG & MON.). 1970. pap. text ed. 34.90 (*0-87750-079-7*) Res Inst Inner Asian Studies.
Concise English-Persian Dictionary. rev. ed. Abbas A. Kashani & Manoocheher A. Kashani. (Illus.). 1322p. (ENG & PER.). 1986. reprint ed. lib. bdg. 45.00 (*0-939214-19-9*) Mazda Pubs.
Concise English-Russian & Russian-English Dictionary. S. Zaimovskii. 464p. (ENG & RUS.). (C). 1987. 40.00 (*0-569-09283-3*, Pub. by Collets) St Mut.
Concise English-Russian, Russian-English Dictionary. 27th ed. S. G. Zaimovskii. 464p. (ENG & RUS.). 1988. 60.00 (*0-569-06089-3*, Pub. by Collets) St Mut.
Concise English-Russian Technical Dictionary. Kurz'min Iu. 416p. (C). 1992. text ed. 75.00 (*0-569-08310-9*, Pub. by Collets) St Mut.
Concise English-Russian Technical Dictionary. Kusmin. 416p. (ENG & RUS.). 1992. 49.95 (*0-7859-1085-9*, 5823400020) Fr & Eur.
Concise English-Swedish Glossary of Legal Terms. A. Bruzelius et al. 200p. (ENG & SWE.). 1980. 89.95 (*0-8288-0408-7*, M9477) Fr & Eur.
Concise English-Tagalog Dictionary. J. Villa Panganiban. LC 69-13501. 170p. (ENG & TAG.). 1969. bds. 14.95 (*0-8048-0119-3*) C E Tuttle.
Concise Etymological Dictionary of Chemistry. Stanley C. Bevan et al. ix, 140p. 1976. 38.00 (*0-85334-653-4*, Pub. by Elsevier Applied Sci UK) Elsevier.
Concise Etymological Dictionary of the Czech Language. Holub. 536p. (CZE & ENG.). 1982. write for info. (*0-8288-1695-6*, F1680) Fr & Eur.
Concise Evangelical Dictionary of Theology. Ed. by Walter A. Elwell. LC 91-26424. 620p. 1991. text ed. 19.99 (*0-8010-3210-5*) Baker Bk.
Concise Exegetical Grammar of New Testament Greek. 5th rev. ed. J. Harold Greenlee. 88p. (Orig.). 1986. pap. text ed. 9.99 (*0-8028-0173-0*) Eerdmans.
Concise Family Seder. Alfred J. Kolatch. 1987. pap. 1.95 (*0-8246-0318-4*) Jonathan David.
Concise Flowers of the Himalaya. Oleg Polunin & Adam Stainton. (Illus.). 426p. 1987. 39.95 (*0-19-561832-7*) OUP.
Concise French-American Dictionary of Figurative & Idiomatic Language. Perreau & Langford. (ENG & FRE.). 17.95 (*0-685-36686-3*) Fr & Eur.
Concise Glossary of Architectural Terms. John H. Parker. 1989. 6.99 (*0-517-68134-X*) Random Hse Value.
***Concise Glossary of Contemporary Literary Theory.** 2nd ed. Jeremy Hawthorn. 240p. 1994. pap. 16.95 (*0-340-60187-6*, Pub. by E Arnld UK) St Martin.
Concise Grammar of Contemporary English. Randolph Quirk & Sidney Greenbaum. 484p. (C). 1973. text ed. 37.25 (*0-15-512930-9*) HB Coll Pubs.
Concise Guide for Writers. 6th ed. Louis E. Glorfeld et al. LC 83-22828. 240p. (C). 1984. pap. text ed. 18.00 (*0-03-062628-5*) HB Coll Pubs.
Concise Guide for Writing Research Papers, 1984 MLA System. Eleanor M. Robinson. LC 84-90682. 54p. 1984. pap. 5.00 (*0-932587-00-3*) E M Robinson.
***Concise Guide to American Aircraft of WW II.** David Mondey. 1994. 10.98 (*0-7858-0147-2*) Bk Sales Inc.
Concise Guide to Assessment & Management of Violent Patients. Kenneth Tardiff. LC 88-36585. (American Psychiatric Press Concise Guides Ser.). 125p. 1989. pap. text ed. 19.50 (*0-88048-124-2*, 8326) Am Psychiatric.
Concise Guide to Auditing Standards & Guidelines. R. Dodge. 224p. 1990. pap. text ed. 20.95 (*0-412-02671-6*, A4464, Chap & Hall NY) Chapman & Hall.
***Concise Guide to British Aircraft of WW II.** David Mondey. 1994. 10.98 (*0-7858-0146-4*) Bk Sales Inc.
Concise Guide to British Clocks. Brian Loomes. (Illus.). 192p. 1992. pap. 22.95 (*0-7126-5187-X*, Pub. by Barrie & Jenkins) Trafalgar.
Concise Guide to British Pottery & Porcelain. Geoffrey Godden. (Illus.). 192p. 1990. pap. 19.95 (*0-7126-3600-5*, Pub. by Barrie & Jenkins) Trafalgar.
Concise Guide to Child & Adolescent Psychiatry. Mina K. Dulcan & Charles W. Popper. LC 90-908. 240p. 1991. pap. text ed. 21.00 (*0-88048-332-6*) Am Psychiatric.
Concise Guide to Clinical Psychiatry. Steven L. Dubovsky. LC 88-3385. (American Psychiatric Press Concise Guides Ser.). 198p. 1988. pap. 19.50 (*0-88048-331-8*) Am Psychiatric.
Concise Guide to Clinical Psychiatry & the Law. Robert I. Simon. LC 87-35164. (American Psychiatric Press, Concise Guides Ser.). 177p. reprint ed. pap. 50.50 (*0-7837-2089-0*, 2042365) Bks Demand.
Concise Guide to Community Planning. Kenneth B. Hall. 1994. text ed. 40.00 (*0-07-025591-1*) McGraw.
Concise Guide to Consultation Psychiatry. 2nd ed. Michael G. Wise & James R. Rundell. LC 93-6911. 192p. 1993. pap. text ed. 19.50 (*0-88048-342-3*) Am Psychiatric.
Concise Guide to Customs of Ethnic Minority Religions. David Collins et al. 70p. 1993. pap. 9.95 (*1-85742-120-5*, Pub. by Arena UK) Ashgate Pub Co.
Concise Guide to Evaluation & Management of Sleep Disorders. Martin Reite et al. LC 89-15117. (American Psychiatric Press Concise Guides Ser.). 175p. 1990. pap. text ed. 19.50 (*0-88048-334-2*) Am Psychiatric.
Concise Guide to Executive Etiquette. Linda Phillips. 1990. mass mkt. 9.95 (*0-385-24766-4*) Doubleday.
Concise Guide to Geriatric Psychiatry. J. Edward Spar & Asenath LaRue. LC 89-18625. (American Psychiatric Press Concise Guides Ser.). 175p. 1990. pap. text ed. 19. 50 (*0-88048-335-0*) Am Psychiatric.
Concise Guide to Group Psychotherapy. Ed. by Sophia Vinogradov & Irvin D. Yalom. LC 88-38281. (American Psychiatric Press Concise Guides Ser.). 169p. (Orig.). 1989. pap. text ed. 19.50 (*0-88048-327-X*) Am Psychiatric.
Concise Guide to Homeopathy: An Introduction to the Understanding & Use of Homeopathy. Nigel Garion-Hutchings & Susan Garion-Hutchings. 1993. pap. 10.95 (*1-85230-384-0*) Element MA.
Concise Guide to Interpreting Accounts. J. D. Blake. 176p. 1990. pap. 22.95 (*0-412-02631-7*, A4432, Chap & Hall NY) Chapman & Hall.
Concise Guide to Jazz. Mark C. Gridley. 240p. 1991. pap. text ed. 31.60 (*0-13-175092-5*) P-H.
Concise Guide to Judaism: History, Practice, Faith. Roy A. Rosenberg. 160p. 1994. pap. 10.95 (*0-452-01136-1*, Mer) NAL-Dutton.
Concise Guide to Laboratory & Diagnostic Testing in Psychiatry. Richard Rosse et al. LC 89-3. (American Psychiatric Press Concise Guides Ser.). 175p. 1989. pap. text ed. 19.50 (*0-88048-333-4*) Am Psychiatric.
Concise Guide to Microsoft Windows 3.1. Kris Jamsa. (Concise Guides Ser.). 208p. (Orig.). 1992. pap. 12.95 (*1-55615-470-4*) Microsoft.
Concise Guide to MS-DOS Batch Files. rev. ed. Kris Jamsa. LC 93-38176. 1993. pap. 12.95 (*1-55615-638-3*) Microsoft.
***Concise Guide to Neuropsychiatry & Behavioral Neurology.** Jeffrey L. Cummings & Michael R. Trimble. (Concise Guide Ser.). 368p. 1995. pap. text ed. 21.00 (*0-88048-493-4*, 8493) Am Psychiatric.
Concise Guide to Newspaper Feature Writing. E. J. Friedlander. LC 81-40648. 56p. (Orig.). 1982. pap. text ed. 14.50 (*0-8191-2115-0*) U Pr of Amer.
Concise Guide to Parenteral Medications. James C. King & Mary W. Macmillan. LC 88-92512. (Orig.). (C). 1988. pap. text ed. 19.50 (*0-685-23254-9*) Pacemarq.
Concise Guide to Plastics. 2nd ed. Herbert R. Simonds & J. M. Church. LC 74-32300. 404p. 1975. reprint ed. 39.50 (*0-88275-269-3*) Krieger.
Concise Guide to Psychiatry & the Law. Robert I. Simon. LC 91-33323. (Concise Guides Ser.). 225p. 1992. pap. text ed. 21.00 (*0-88048-341-5*) Am Psychiatric.
Concise Guide to Psychodynamic Psychiatry. Robert J. Ursano et al. LC 90-1206. 176p. 1991. pap. 19.50 (*0-88048-337-7*, FUJA8337) Am Psychiatric.
Concise Guide to Psychopharmacology & Electroconvulsive Therapy. 2nd ed. Laurence B. Guttmacher. LC 93-5676. (Concise Guides Ser.). 224p. 1994. pap. text ed. 21.00 (*0-88048-340-7*) Am Psychiatric.
Concise Guide to Semigroups & Evolution Equations. Aldo Belleni-Morante. LC 94-7754. (Series on Advances in Mathematics for Applied Sciences). 180p. 1994. text ed. 46.00 (*981-02-1294-1*) World Scientific Pub.
Concise Guide to Standard English Usage. Gordon J. Loberger. 384p. (C). 1993. per., pap. text ed. 34.95 (*0-8403-8573-0*) Kendall-Hunt.
Concise Guide to Successful Employment Practices. Thorne. 208p. 1990. pap. 30.00 (*0-685-67124-0*, 4988) Commerce.
***Concise Guide to the IDEFO Technique: A Practical Approach to Business Process Reengineering.** Steven C. Hill & Lee A. Robinson. LC 94-61921. 304p. (C). 1994. pap. text ed. 39.95 (*1-886717-00-1*) Enter Tech Concepts.
Concise Guide to the JCT Insurance Clauses, 1986. P. Madge. (C). 1987. 110.00 (*0-685-33723-5*, Pub. by Witherby & Co UK) St Mut.
Concise Guide to Tracing Your Ancestry. Brian Loomes. 192p. 1993. pap. 22.95 (*0-7126-9877-9*, Pub. by Barrie & Jenkins) Trafalgar.
Concise Guide to Treatment of Alcoholism & Addictions. Richard J. Frances & John E. Franklin, Jr. LC 89-413. (American Psychiatric Press Concise Guides Ser.). 176p. 1989. pap. text ed. 19.50 (*0-88048-326-1*) Am Psychiatric.
Concise Guide to Type Identification. Vincent Apicella et al. (Illus.). 176p. 1990. pap. 24.95 (*0-8306-3449-5*, 3449) TAB Bks.
Concise Guide to Upholstery Fabrics. 1985. 60.00 (*0-317-43702-X*) St Mut.
Concise Guide to Windows. 2nd ed. Chris Jamsa. 224p. 1994. write for info. (*1-55615-666-9*) Microsoft.
Concise Guide to Writing. Rise B. Axelrod & Charles R. Cooper. LC 92-83763. (Illus.). 237p. (C). 1993. pap. text ed. 11.00 (*0-312-09156-7*) St Martin.
Concise Handbook in Physics & Mathematics. 1994. write for info. (*0-8493-7745-5*, NP7745) CRC Pr.
Concise Handbook of Futures Markets: Money Management, Forecasting & the Markets. Ed. by Perry J. Kaufman. LC 86-13336. 864p. 1986. pap. text ed. 34. 95 (*0-471-85088-8*) Wiley.
Concise Handbook of Respiratory Diseases. 3rd ed. Sattar Farzan. (Illus.). 433p. (C). 1992. text ed. 42.95 (*0-8385-1225-9*, A1225-0) Appleton & Lange.
Concise Hebrew & Aramaic Lexicon of the Old Testament. William L. Holladay. (ARC & HEB.). 1972. 34.99 (*0-8028-3413-2*) Eerdmans.
Concise Hindi-English Dictionary. R. C. Pathak. (ENG & HIN.). 1979. 6.00 (*0-89744-971-1*) Auromere.
Concise Historical Atlas of Pennsylvania. Ed. by Edward K. Muller. 1989. pap. 29.95 (*0-87722-672-5*) Temple U Pr.
Concise Histories of American Popular Culture. Ed. by M. Thomas Inge. LC 82-6115. (Contributions to the Study of Popular Culture Ser.: No. 4). viii, 504p. (C). 1982. pap. text ed. 10.95 (*0-313-23302-0*, IPCPB, Greenwood Pr) Greenwood.
***Concise History of Africa.** Robert Garfield. (Illus.). 78p. 1995. pap. 11.95 (*0-87411-751-8*) Copley Pub.
Concise History of America & Its People. James K. Martin et al. LC 94-20138. (C). 1995. 30.00 (*0-673-46780-5*, HarpT) HarpC.
***Concise History of America & Its People.** James K. Martin et al. 960p. 1995. reprint ed. pap. 30.00 (*1-886746-00-1*) Talman Pub.
***Concise History of America & Its People, Vol. 1.** Chiaro. (C). 1995. student ed, text ed. 11.25 (*0-673-99233-0*) HarpCollege.
***Concise History of America & Its People, Vol. 2.** Chiaro. (C). 1995. student ed, text ed. 9.50 (*0-673-99234-9*) HarpCollege.
Concise History of American Architecture. Leland M. Roth. LC 78-2169. (Icon Editions Ser.). (Illus.). 1980. pap. 25.00 (*0-06-430086-2*, IN-86, Icon Edns) HarpC.
Concise History of American Painting & Sculpture. Matthew Baigell. LC 84-47555. (Illus.). 432p. 1984. pap. text ed. 22.50 (*0-06-430085-4*, IN-85, Icon Edns) HarpC.
Concise History of Ancient India, 3 vols., Set. Asoke K. Majumdar. 1931p. 1983. text ed. 100.00 (*0-685-13637-X*) Coronet Bks.
Concise History of Australia. Russel Ward. (Orig.). 1992. pap. 19.95 (*0-7022-2386-7*, Pub. by Univ Queensland Pr AT) Intl Spec Bk.
***Concise History of Australian Wine.** John Beeston. 1995. pap. 17.95 (*1-86373-621-2*) IPG Chicago.

Concise History of Buddhism. Andrew Skilton. 263p. (Orig.). (C). 1995. pap. 19.95 (*0-904766-66-7*, Pub. by Windhorse UK) Windhorse Pubns. BUDDHISM presents a bewildering array of forms, both doctrinal & practical, to the modern student. How are we to make sense of them all? Why & when did the many schools & sub-sects of Buddhism emerge? This book draws on the most recent historical & literary research to present an overview of the development of Buddhist thought & practice that is helpful to both the student & the practitioner. The author traces this development from the earliest times through to the most

C

An Asterisk (*) at the beginning of an entry indicates that the title is appearing in BIP for the first time.

1521

recent developments in the various forms of Asian Buddhism. He explains the views of all the major schools & explains how they are related to each other. This book will be very useful as a text book, & for the practicing Buddhist who wants to understand the broader dimensions of the tradition. An extensive bibliography provides the basis for further investigation. WINDHORSE PUBLICATIONS is based in the UK & has been publishing books on Buddhism for the last twenty years. These titles are now available in the Unites States through Windhorse Publications, 14 Heartwood Circle, Newmarket, NH 03857; Tel. (603) 659-2279 or (800) 303-5728. CALL, OR WRITE FOR OUR LATEST CATALOG. *Publisher Provided Annotation.*

Concise History of Canadian Architecture. Hal Kalman. (Illus.). 448p. 1996. pap. 29.95 (0-19-540700-8) OUP.
Concise History of China. Po-Tsan Chien. 1976. lib. bdg. 59.95 (0-8490-1661-4) Gordon Pr.
Concise History of Christianity. R. Dean Peterson. 334p. (C). 1993. pap. 25.95 (0-534-13278-2) Intl Thomson.
Concise History of Classical Sanskrit Literature. Shastri Gaurinath. 220p. (C). 1978. 7.50 (0-685-19273-3, Pub. by Motilal Banarsidass II) S Asia.
Concise History of Education to Nineteen Hundred A. D. E. H. Gwynne-Thomas. LC 81-40315. 325p. (Orig.). 1981. pap. text ed. 23.50 (0-8191-1660-2) U Pr of Amer.
Concise History of England: From Stonehenge to the Atomic Age. F. E. Halliday. (Illus.). 240p. 1980. pap. 15.95 (0-500-27182-8) Thames Hudson.
Concise History of France. Roger Price. (Cambridge Concise Histories Ser.). (Illus.). 375p. (C). 1993. 44.95 (0-521-36239-3); pap. 14.95 (0-521-36809-X) Cambridge U Pr.
***Concise History of Freemasonry.** Robert F. Gould. (Illus.). 390p. 1994. pap. 24.95 (1-56459-470-X) Kessinger Pub.
Concise History of German Literature to 1900. Ed. by Kim Vivian. LC 92-17763. (Studies in German Literature, Linguistics & Culture). 380p. 1992. 59.95 (1-879751-29-1); pap. 26.95 (1-879751-30-5) Camden Hse.
Concise History of Germany. Mary Fulbrook. (Concise Histories Ser.). (Illus.). 250p. (C). 1991. 49.95 (0-521-36283-0); pap. 12.95 (0-521-36836-7) Cambridge U Pr.
Concise History of Glass Represented in the Chrysler Museum Glass Collection. Nancy O. Merrill. LC 89-63529. (Illus.). 227p. 1989. pap. 45.00 (0-940744-58-9) Chrysler Museum.
Concise History of Greece. Richard Clogg. (Concise Histories Ser.). (Illus.). 248p. (C). 1992. 44.95 (0-521-37228-3) Cambridge U Pr.
Concise History of Greece. Richard Clogg. (Concise Histories Ser.). (Illus.). 248p. (C). 1992. pap. 12.95 (0-521-37830-3) Cambridge U Pr.
Concise History of Hungarian Music. Bence Szabolcsi. Tr. by Sara Karig et al. (Illus.). 256p. 1989. reprint ed. 17.95 (0-912483-25-3) Pro-Am Music.
Concise History of India. Francis Watson. (Illus.). 1979. pap. 15.95 (0-500-27164-X) Thames Hudson.
Concise History of Ireland. 3rd rev. ed. Conor C. O'Brien & Maire O'Brien. (Illus.). 1985. pap. 15.95 (0-500-27379-0) Thames Hudson.
Concise History of Islam & the Origin of Its Empires. Gregory C. Kozlowski. 97p. 1991. pap. text ed. 7.95 (0-87411-489-6) Copley Pub.
Concise History of Italy. Christopher Duggan. (Concise Histories Ser.). (Illus.). 320p. (C). 1994. 44.95 (0-521-40285-9); pap. 12.95 (0-521-40848-2) Cambridge U Pr.
Concise History of Italy from Prehistoric Times to Our Own Day. Luigi Salvatorelli. Tr. by Bernard Miall. LC 75-41239. reprint ed. 36.00 (0-404-14596-5) AMS Pr.
Concise History of Japanese Art. Peter C. Swann. LC 78-71254. (Illus.). 332p. 1979. 19.95 (0-87011-377-1) Kodansha.
Concise History of Kongo & Angola see Strange Adventures of Andrew Battell of Leigh in Angola & the Adjoining Regions
Concise History of Mathematics. 4th rev. ed. Dirk J. Struik. (Illus.). (YA). (gr. 7-12). 1987. pap. text ed. 7.95 (0-486-60255-9) Dover.
Concise History of Mexico from Hidalgo to Cardenas 1805-1940. J. Bazant. (Illus.). 1977. pap. 18.95 (0-521-29173-9) Cambridge U Pr.
Concise History of Modern Britain, 1707-1975. W. A. Speck. LC 92-20187. (Concise Histories Ser.). (Illus.). 200p. (C). 1993. 44.95 (0-521-36400-0); pap. 12.95 (0-521-36702-6) Cambridge U Pr.
Concise History of Modern Painting. Herbert E. Read. LC 84-51313. (World of Art Ser.). (Illus.). 396p. 1985. pap. 14.95 (0-500-20141-2) Thames Hudson.
Concise History of Modern Rajasthan. M. S. Jain. (C). 1993. text ed. 22.00 (81-7328-010-X, Pub. by Wiley Eastern II) S Asia.
Concise History of Orange County. rev. ed. A. E. Corning. (Illus.). 130p. 1993. reprint ed. pap. 13.95 (0-910746-30-3, TCH01) Hope Farm.
Concise History of Photography. 3rd rev. ed. Helmut Gernsheim. 314p. 1986. reprint ed. pap. 13.95 (0-486-25128-4) Dover.
Concise History of Portugal. David Birmingham. LC 92-33824. (Cambridge Concise Histories Ser.). (Illus.). 240p. (C). 1993. 44.95 (0-521-43308-8); pap. 12.95 (0-521-43880-2) Cambridge U Pr.
Concise History of Preaching. Paul S. Wilson. LC 92-16294. 160p. (Orig.). 1992. pap. 10.95 (0-687-09342-2) Abingdon.
Concise History of Sport in Canada. Don Morrow et al. (Illus.). 400p. 1990. pap. 19.95 (0-19-540693-1) OUP.
Concise History of Texas. Mike Kingston. 240p. 1991. pap. 11.95 (0-88415-007-0) Gulf Pub.
Concise History of Texas: From the Texas Almanac. Mike Kingston. 160p. (Orig.). 1988. pap. 7.95 (0-914511-08-4) Dallas Morning.
Concise History of the American People. Arthur S. Link et al. LC 83-23184. (Illus.). 622p. (C). 1984. pap. text ed. write for info. (0-88295-817-8); teacher ed. pap. text ed. write for info. (0-88295-821-6) Harlan Davidson.
Concise History of the American People, Vol. 1. Arthur S. Link et al. LC 83-23184. (Illus.). 622p. (C). 1984. student ed, pap. text ed. write for info. (0-88295-822-4) Harlan Davidson.
Concise History of the American People, Vol. 1: To 1877. Arthur S. Link et al. LC 83-23184. (Illus.). 622p. (C). 1984. pap. text ed. write for info. (0-88295-818-6) Harlan Davidson.
Concise History of the American People, Vol. 2. Arthur S. Link et al. LC 83-23184. (Illus.). 622p. (C). 1984. student ed, pap. text ed. write for info. (0-88295-823-2) Harlan Davidson.
Concise History of the American People, Vol. 2: Since 1865. Arthur S. Link et al. LC 83-23184. (Illus.). 622p. (C). 1984. pap. text ed. write for info. (0-88295-819-4) Harlan Davidson.
Concise History of the American Republic, 2 vols. in 1. Samuel E. Morison et al. LC 82-3621. (Illus.). 1983. pap. 31.00 (0-19-503180-6) OUP.
Concise History of the American Republic, 2 vols. in 1, 1. Samuel E. Morison et al. LC 82-3621. (Illus.). 1983. pap. 23.00 (0-19-503181-4) OUP.
Concise History of the American Republic, 2 vols. in 1, 2. Samuel E. Morison et al. LC 82-3621. (Illus.). 1983. pap. 23.00 (0-19-503182-2) OUP.
***Concise History of the Arab-Israeli Conflict.** 2nd ed. Ian J. Bickerton & Carla L. Klausner. LC 94-25823. 320p. 1994. pap. text ed. 21.33 (0-13-292038-7) P-H.
Concise History of the British House. Edmund Gray. (Illus.). 192p. 1992. pap. 22.95 (0-7126-4589-6, Pub. by Barrie & Jenkins) Trafalgar.
Concise History of the Catholic Church. Thomas Bokenkotter. 1990. 12.50 (0-385-41147-2) Doubleday.
Concise History of the Christian World Mission. 2nd ed. J. Herbert Kane. 1978. pap. 9.99 (0-8010-5395-1) Baker Bk.
***Concise History of the Civil War.** William Davis. (Civil War Ser.). 60p. (Orig.). 1994. pap. 3.95 (0-915992-64-7) Eastern Acorn.
Concise History of the Civil War, 1861-1865. (Illus.). text ed. 17.95 (0-8488-0041-9, J M C & Co) Amereon Ltd.
Concise History of the Common Law. 5th ed. Theodore F. Plucknett. 802p. 1912. 45.00 (0-316-71083-0) Little.
***Concise History of the Early Church, Vol. 1.** Norbert Brox. 192p. 1995. 18.95 (0-8264-0792-7) Continuum.
Concise History of the Great Trial of the Chicago Anarchists in 1886. Dyer D. Lum. LC 75-90181. (Mass Violence in America Ser.). 1973. reprint ed. 24.95 (0-405-01324-8) Ayer.
Concise History of the Italian Theatre. Vincent Luciani. (C). 1961. pap. 5.95 (0-913298-10-7) S F Vanni.
Concise History of the Kehukee Bapist Association from Its Original Rise to the Present Time. rev. ed. Lemuel Burkitt & Jesse Read. Ed. by Edwin S. Gaustad. LC 79-52591. (Baptist Tradition Ser.). 1980. reprint ed. lib. bdg. 31.95 (0-405-12458-9) Ayer.
***Concise History of the Medieval Church.** Isnard W. Frank. LC 95-10867. 192p. 1995. 18.95 (0-8264-0828-1) Continuum.
Concise History of the Middle East. 4th rev. ed. Arthur Goldschmidt, Jr. 465p. (C). 1991. pap. text ed. 24.95 (0-8133-1118-7) Westview.
Concise History of the Modern World: 1500 to the Present. William Woodruff. 307p. 1993. pap. 18.95 (0-312-09962-2) St Martin.
Concise History of the Rabbinate. Simon Schwarzfuchs. LC 92-42506. 264p. 1993. 49.95 (0-631-16132-5) Blackwell Pubs.
***Concise History of the Russian Revolution.** Richard Pipes. LC 95-3127. 1995. 27.50 (0-679-42277-3) Knopf.
***Concise History of the U. S.** House et al. 106p. (C). 1994. pap. text ed. 17.50 (0-9646019-0-7) T L I Assocs.
Concise History of the U. S. Airborne Army, Corps, Divisions & Brigades. Geoffrey T. Barker. (U. S. Army Concise History Ser.: Vol. II). (Illus.). 175p. (Orig.). (C). 1989. pap. text ed. 15.00 (0-922004-01-3) Anglo-Am Pub.
Concise History of the U. S. Army Airborne Infantry. Geoffrey T. Barker. (Concise History Ser.: Vol. III). (Illus.). 168p. 1990. pap. 20.00 (0-922004-02-1) Anglo-Am Pub.
Concise History of the United States Marine Corps, 1775 to 1969. William D. Parker. LC 80-29554. (Illus.). x, 143p. 1981. reprint ed. text ed. 35.00 (0-313-22854-X, PACO, Greenwood Pr) Greenwood.
***Concise History of the World.** J. M. Roberts. (Illus.). 616p. 1995. 30.00 (0-19-521151-0) OUP.
Concise History of U. S. Army Special Operations Forces. rev. ed. Geoffrey T. Barker. (Concise History Ser.: Vol. I). (Illus.). 218p. (Orig.). (C). 1988. pap. 25.00 (0-922004-00-5) Anglo-Am Pub.
Concise History of U. S. Army Special Operations Forces, Vol. 1. 2nd ed. 258p. 1993. write for info. (0-922004-09-9) Anglo-Am Pub.
Concise History of Western Architecture. Robert F. Jordan. 359p. (C). 1969. pap. text ed. 21.50 (0-15-512950-3) HB Coll Pubs.
Concise Hopi & English Lexicon. Comp. by Roy Albert & David L. Shaul. LC 84-9197. vi, 204p. 1985. 46.00 (90-272-2015-8); pap. 17.95 (90-272-2026-3) Benjamins North Am.
Concise Human Physiology. M. Y. Sukkar et al. (Illus.). 528p. 1993. pap. 32.95 (0-632-03383-5) Blackwell Sci.
Concise Hungarian-English Dictionary. V. Orszagh. 1180p. (ENG & HUN.). 1987. 95.00 (0-569-00343-1, Pub. by Collets) St Mut.
***Concise Hungarian-English Dictionary.** 3rd rev. ed. T. Magay & L. Orszagh. 1152p. (C). 1993. 54.00x (963-05-6547-1, Pub. by Akad Kiado HU) St Mut.
Concise Illustrated Dental Dictionary. F. J. Harty & R. Ogston. 291p. 1987. 29.95 (0-7236-0788-5, Pub. by John Wright UK) Buttrwrth-Heinemann.
Concise Illustrated Dictionary of Science & Technology. Stan Gibilisco. (Illus.). 496p. 1992. 36.95 (0-8306-4152-1, 3715); pap. 24.95 (0-8306-4153-X, 3715) TAB Bks.
Concise Illustrated Dictionary of Science & Technology. Stan Gibilisco. 1992. text ed. 36.95 (0-07-023509-0); pap. text ed. 24.95 (0-07-023510-4) McGraw.
Concise Illustrated Russian-English Dictionary of Mechanical Engineering. V. V. Shvarts. (Illus.). 224p. (ENG & RUS.). 1981. pap. 98.00 (0-08-027574-5, Pub. by Pergamon Repr UK) Franklin.
Concise Illustrated Russian-English Dictionary of Mechanical Engineering. Vladimir Shvarts. 224p. (ENG & RUS.). 1980. 35.00 (0-686-44774-3, Pub. by Collets UK) St Mut.
Concise Illustrated Russian-English Dictionary of Mechanical Engineering. 2nd ed. V. V. Shvarts. (Illus.). (ENG & RUS.). 1983. 75.00 (0-8288-3963-8, M15458) Fr & Eur.
Concise Inorganic Chemistry. 4th enl. rev. ed. John D. Lee. (Illus.). 950p. 1991. pap. 39.95 (0-412-40290-4, A5898) Chapman & Hall.
Concise Inorganic Chemistry U. K. 3rd ed. Lee. pap. 28.95 (0-685-19092-7) Chapman & Hall.
Concise Interlingua-English Dictionary. Ed. by F. P. Gopsill. 1980. pap. 9.00 (0-685-60085-8) Interlingua Inst.
Concise International Encyclopedia of Robotics. Ed. by Richard C. Dorf & Shimon Y. Nof. 1190p. 1990. text ed. 175.00 (0-471-51698-8) Wiley.
***Concise Intro Logic.** Daniel Rothbart. 150p. (C). 1995. student ed, pap. text ed. 19.95 (0-7872-0958-9) Kendall-Hunt.
***Concise Introduction to Calculus.** Wu-Yi Hsiang. 120p. (C). (gr. 13). 1995. text ed. 39.00 (981-02-1900-8) World Scientific Pub.
***Concise Introduction to Calculus.** Wu-Yi Hsiang. 120p. (C). (gr. 13). 1995. pap. text ed. 21.00 (981-02-1901-6) World Scientific Pub.
Concise Introduction to Ceramics. George Phillips. (Illus.). 200p. 1991. text ed. 49.95 (0-442-00890-2) Van Nos Reinhold.
Concise Introduction to Engineering Economics. P. Cassimatis. 288p. 1988. text ed. 60.00 (0-04-445038-9); pap. text ed. 29.95 (0-04-445047-8) Routledge Chapman & Hall.
Concise Introduction to Logic. 4th ed. Patrick J. Hurley. 596p. (C). 1991. text ed. 40.95 (0-534-14514-0) Intl Thomson.
Concise Introduction to Logic. 5th ed. Patrick J. Hurley. 624p. 1994. text ed. 42.95 (0-534-21174-7) Intl Thomson.
Concise Introduction to Philosophy. 4th ed. William H. Halverson. 493p. (C). 1981. text ed. write for info. (0-07-554307-9) McGraw.
Concise Introduction to Syntactic Theory: The Government-Binding Approach. Elizabeth A. Cowper. 240p. 1992. pap. text ed. 15.95 (0-226-11646-8) U Ch Pr.
Concise Introduction to the Philosophy of Nicholas of Cusa. 3rd ed. Jasper Hopkins. LC 85-72432. xii, 194p. (C). 1986. text ed. 20.00 (0-938060-32-5) Banning Pr.
Concise Introduction to the Theory of Integration. Daniel W. Stroock. (Series in Pure Mathematics: Vol. 12). 160p. (C). 1990. text ed. 21.00 (981-02-0145-1) World Scientific Pub.
Concise Introduction to the Theory of Integration. 2nd ed. Daniel W. Stroock. LC 94-6246. 184p. 1994. 24.50 (0-8176-3759-1) Birkhauser.
Concise Irish Grammar with Pieces for Reading. Ernst W. Windisch. Tr. by N. Moore. LC 78-72659. reprint ed. 16.50 (0-404-17615-1) AMS Pr.
Concise Italian Dictionary. 1088p. 1990. pap. 16.95 (0-13-383415-8, Harraps); vinyl bd. 15.00 (0-13-383381-X, Harraps) P-H Gen Ref & Trav.
Concise Jewish Bible. large type ed. Tr. by Philip Birnbaum. (Large Print Jewish Classics Ser.). 1991. reprint ed. pap. 16.95 (0-8027-2644-5) Walker & Co.
Concise Jurisprudence. Sandra Berns. (Concise Ser.). 180p. 1993. pap. 30.00 (1-86287-109-4, Pub. by Federation Pr AU) W W Gaunt.
Concise Korner Coding Book for General Surgery & Urology. 2nd ed. Comp. by R. Earlam. 112p. 1991. pap. 23.95 (0-412-43230-7) Chapman & Hall.
Concise Law Dictionary of Words, Phrases, & Maxims with an Explanatory List of Abbreviations Used in Law Books. rev. ed. Frederic J. Stimson & Harvey C. Voorhees. 346p. 1987. reprint ed. lib. bdg. 35.00 (0-8377-2611-5) Rothman.
Concise Law on Solicitors. P. M. Bird & J. B. Weir. (Waterlow Practitioner's Library). (Illus.). 352p. 1989. 63.00 (0-685-24819-4, Waterlow) Macmillan.
Concise Legal Research. Robert Watt. 246p. 1993. pap. 29.00 (1-86287-106-X, Pub. by Federation Pr AU) W W Gaunt.
***Concise Legal Research.** 2nd ed. Robert Watt. 270p. 1995. pap. 29.00 (1-86287-165-5, Pub. by Federation Pr AU) W W Gaunt.
Concise Lexicon of the Occult. Gerina Dunwich. 1990. pap. 7.95 (0-8065-1191-5, Citadel Pr) Carol Pub Group.
Concise Logic. William H. Halverson. 512p. (C). 1984. pap. text ed. write for info. (0-07-554352-4) McGraw.
Concise Manual of Chemical & Environmental Safety in Schools & Colleges, Vol. 3: Chemical Incompatibilities. George Thompson. 198p. Date not set. pap. text ed. write for info. (1-882851-00-5) Chem Comp Systs.
Concise Manual on the Theory of Music. Sharon A. Dombrowski. (Illus.). 64p. (Orig.). (C). 1983. 10.00 (0-9610658-0-X) Blue Note.
Concise Marine Almanac. Gerard J. Mangone. 1990. 58.00 (0-8448-1674-4) Taylor & Francis.
Concise Medical Physiology. C. Chaudhuri. (C). 1988. 140.00 (0-685-46428-8, Current Dist) St Mut.
Concise Medical Physiology. S. Chowdhury. (C). 1989. 190.00 (0-89771-376-1, Current Dist) St Mut.
Concise Neurosurgery. E. Pasztor. (Illus.). 292p. 1980. 75.25 (3-8055-1431-X) S Karger.
Concise Nuclear Isobar Charts: Nuclear Ground States & Low Lying Energy Levels. Ed. by Jans Bucka. (Illus.). (C). 1986. pap. text ed. 161.55 (0-89925-197-8) De Gruyter.
***Concise Nuclear Isobar Charts: Nuclear Ground States & Low Lying Energy Levels.** Ed. by Jans Bucka. (Illus.). (C). 1986. pap. text ed. 161.55 (3-11-008404-X) De Gruyter.
Concise Object Sermons for Children. Robert S. Coombs. (Object Lesson Ser.). 128p. (Orig.). 1989. pap. 5.99 (0-8010-2541-9) Baker Bk.
Concise Old Irish Grammar & Reader, 2 vols., Set. Julius Pokorny. LC 78-72643. (Celtic Language & Literature Ser.: Goidelic & Brythonic). 240p. reprint ed. 57.50 (0-404-17576-7) AMS Pr.
Concise OSI Acronym Dictionary. Wendy E. Brown. 1992. text ed. 32.50 (0-07-057600-9); pap. text ed. 19.95 (0-07-057601-7) McGraw.
Concise Overview of Foreign Policy (1945-1985) Kenneth L. Hill. LC 86-10254. 174p. (C). 1986. pap. text ed. 10.50 (0-89874-849-6) Krieger.
Concise Oxford Companion to American Literature. abr. ed. James D. Hart. 512p. 1986. 35.00 (0-19-503982-3) OUP.
Concise Oxford Companion to American Literature. James D. Hart. (Oxford Paperback Reference Ser.). 510p. 1988. reprint ed. pap. 15.95 (0-19-504771-0) OUP.
Concise Oxford Companion to American Theatre. Gerald Bordman. (Oxford Paperback Reference Ser.). 462p. 1990. reprint ed. pap. 13.95 (0-19-506327-9) OUP.
Concise Oxford Companion to Classical Literature. Margaret Howatson & Ian Chilvers. LC 92-18585. (Oxford Reference Ser.). 1993. 18.95 (0-19-211687-8); pap. 14.95 (0-19-282708-1) OUP.
Concise Oxford Companion to English Literature. Ed. by Margaret Drabble & Jenny Stringer. (Illus.). 640p. 1987. 24.95 (0-19-866140-1) OUP.
Concise Oxford Companion to English Literature. Margaret Drabble. 1990. pap. 12.95 (0-19-282667-0) OUP.
Concise Oxford Companion to the Theatre. 2nd ed. Ed. by Phyllis Hartnoll & Peter Found. 624p. 1992. 40.00 (0-19-866136-3) OUP.
Concise Oxford Companion to the Theatre. Ed. by Phyllis Hartnoll & Peter Found. 576p. 1993. reprint ed. pap. 14.95 (0-19-282574-7) OUP.
Concise Oxford Dictionary of Art & Artists. Ed. by Ian Chilvers. (Oxford Paperback Reference Ser.). 528p. 1990. pap. 10.95 (0-19-282676-X) OUP.
***Concise Oxford Dictionary of Australian History.** Ed. by Jan Bassett. (Oxford Paperback Reference Ser.). 341p. 1995. pap. 29.95 (0-19-553664-9) OUP.
Concise Oxford Dictionary of Botany. Ed. by Michael Allaby. 448p. 1992. pap. 12.95 (0-19-286094-1) OUP.
***Concise Oxford Dictionary of Current English.** Ed. by Della Thompson. 1664p. 1995. 29.95 (0-19-861320-2) OUP.
Concise Oxford Dictionary of Current English. 8th ed. Ed. by Richard E. Allen. 1504p. 1990. 27.50 (0-19-861200-1) OUP.
***Concise Oxford Dictionary of Current English.** 9th ed. Ed. by Della Thompson. 1664p. 1995. pap. 27.50 (0-19-861319-9) OUP.
Concise Oxford Dictionary of Earth Sciences. Ed. by Ailsa Allaby & Michael Allaby. (Oxford Paperback Reference Ser.). 432p. 1991. reprint ed. pap. 10.95 (0-19-286125-5) OUP.
Concise Oxford Dictionary of Ecology. Ed. by Michael Allaby. (Oxford Reference Shelf Ser.). 1994. 12.95 (0-19-286160-3) OUP.
Concise Oxford Dictionary of English Etymology. Ed. by T. F. Hoad. LC 85-31970. 750p. 1986. 29.95 (0-19-861182-X) OUP.
Concise Oxford Dictionary of English Etymology. Ed. by T. F. Hoad. LC 92-41178. (Oxford Paperback Reference Ser.). 576p. (C). 1993. reprint ed. pap. 14.95 (0-19-283098-8, 14269) OUP.
Concise Oxford Dictionary of English Place-Names. 4th ed. Eilert Ekwall. 1960. 49.95 (0-19-869103-3) OUP.
Concise Oxford Dictionary of Geography. Susan Mayhew & Anne Penny. 256p. 1992. pap. 8.95 (0-19-282565-8) OUP.
Concise Oxford Dictionary of Literary Terms. Chris Baldick. 256p. 1990. 24.00 (0-19-811733-7) OUP.

An Asterisk (*) at the beginning of an entry indicates that the title is appearing in BIP for the first time.

C

An Asterisk (*) at the beginning of an entry indicates that the title is appearing in BIP for the first time.

1523

Concordance to Henry James's Turn of the Screw. Todd K. Bender. LC 87-32834. (Reference Library of the Humanities: Vol. 3). 264p. 1988. lib. bdg. 25.00 (*0-8240-4147-X*, 828) Garland.

Concordance to Herman Melville's Mardi: And a Voyage Thither, 2 vols., Set. Larry E. Wegener. LC 91-8008. 1991. 300.00 (*0-8240-6694-4*, H1116) Garland.

Concordance to James Joyce's Dubliners with a Reverse Index, a Frequency List, & a Conversion Table. Ed. by Wilhelm Fuger. 892p. 1980. lib. bdg. 122.20 (*3-487-06950-4*, Pub. by Georg Olms GW) Lubrecht & Cramer.

Concordance to John Gower's Confessio Amantis. John Gower. Ed. by J. D. Pickles. 1987. 199.00 (*0-85991-245-0*) Boydell & Brewer.

Concordance to Juan Ruiz's "Libro De Buen Amor" Rigo Mignani et al. (State University of New York Press Ser.: Vol. SU4). 328p. 1977. 18.00 (*0-87395-322-3*) MRTS.

Concordance to Livy, 4 Vols, Set. David W. Packard. LC 68-29181. 5395p. 1968. 340.00 (*0-674-15890-3*) HUP.

Concordance to Pascal's "Pensees" Blaise Pascal. Ed. by Hugh M. Davidson & Pierre H. Dube. LC 75-16808. (Cornell Concordances Ser.). 1488p. 1975. 97.50 (*0-8014-0972-1*) Cornell U Pr.

Concordance to Personae: Concordance to the Poems of Ezra Pound. Gary Lane. LC 72-6462. (Reference Ser.: No. 44). (C). 1972. lib. bdg. 75.00 (*0-8383-1613-1*) M S G Haskell Hse.

Concordance to Poems of John Keats. L. N. Broughton & D. C. Baldwin. 1972. 59.95 (*0-87968-922-6*) Gordon Pr.

Concordance to Proust. Frances Stern. 134p. (C). Date not set. text ed. 42.50 (*0-389-20990-2*) B&N Imports.

Concordance to Q. Richard A. Edwards. LC 75-6768. (Society of Biblical Literature. Sources for Biblical Study Ser.: No. 7). 194p. reprint ed. 55.30 (*0-8357-9568-3*, 2017677) Bks Demand.

Concordance to Shakespeare. Andrew Becket. LC 77-134319. reprint ed. 74.50 (*0-404-00698-1*) AMS Pr.

Concordance to Shakespeare's Poems. Helen K. Furness. LC 71-168078. reprint ed. 47.50 (*0-404-02645-1*) AMS Pr.

Concordance to Shakespeare's Poems: An Index to Every Word Therein Contained. Horace H. Furness. LC 75-109647. (Select Bibliographies Reprint Ser.). 1977. 35.95 (*0-8369-5256-1*) Ayer.

Concordance to Technical Manuals: Dictionary for Technical Writing Japanese-Engliah. K. Kobayashi. 966p. (ENG & JPN.). 1989. 350.00 (*0-8288-7215-5*, M12264) Fr & Eur.

Concordance to Technical Manulas: Dictionary for Technical Writing English-Japanese. K. Kobayashi. 1122p. (ENG & JPN.). 1989. 350.00 (*0-8288-7216-3*, 487198222X) Fr & Eur.

Concordance to Tennyson. D. B. Brightwell. LC 72-124396. (Studies in Tennyson: No. 27). 1970. reprint ed. lib. bdg. 75.00 (*0-8383-1099-0*) M S G Haskell Hse.

Concordance to the "Ancrene Wisse" Ed. by Jocelyn Wogan-Browne et al. 1280p. (C). 1993. text ed. 216.00 (*0-85991-395-3*, DS Brewer) Boydell & Brewer.

Concordance to the Anonymous Constitution of Athens. Dana F. Sutton. LC 81-66741. (Illus.). 160p. 1981. text ed. 30.00 (*0-86516-004-X*) Bolchazy-Carducci.

Concordance to the Celestina. Lloyd Kasten & Jean Anderson. 1977. 12.50 (*0-87535-124-7*) Hispanic Soc.

Concordance to the Celestina (1499) Ed. by Lloyd Kasten & Jean Anderson. (Spanish Ser.: No. 1). 338p. 1976. 12. 50 (*0-942260-10-4*) Hispanic Seminary.

Concordance to the Child Ballads. Cathy L. Preston. 1000p. Date not set. 158.00 (*0-8240-8983-9*, H484) Garland.

Concordance to the Collected Poems of Sylvia Plath. Richard M. Matovich. LC 85-45126. 623p. 43.00 (*0-8240-8664-3*, H618) Garland.

***Concordance to "The Complete Poems & Plays of T. S. Eliot"** Ed. by J. L. Dawson et al. (Cornell Concordances Ser.). 1264p. 1995. 85.00x (*0-8014-1561-6*) Cornell U Pr.

Concordance to the Complete Poems of E E Cummings. E. E. Cummings. Ed. by Kate McBride. LC 88-47749. 984p. 1989. 67.50 (*0-8014-2239-6*) Cornell U Pr.

Concordance to the Complete Poems of John Skelton. John Skelton. Ed. by Alistair Fox & Gregory Waite. LC 87-47552. (Cornell Concordances Ser.). 1056p. (C). 1987. 65.00 (*0-8014-1944-1*) Cornell U Pr.

Concordance to the Complete Poems of John Wilmot, Earl of Rochester. John F. Moehlmann. LC 78-69872. 1979. 20.00 (*0-87875-164-5*) Whitston Pub.

Concordance to the Complete Writings of George Herbert. George Herbert. Ed. by Mario A. Di Cesare & Rigo Mignani. LC 76-56642. (Cornell Concordances Ser.). 1344p. 1977. 95.00 (*0-8014-1106-8*) Cornell U Pr.

Concordance to the Correlated Greek & Hebrew Text of Ruth, Part II: The Greek & Hebrew Syntactical Concordance. Raymond Martin & Sylvio Scorza. Ed. by J. Arthur Baird & David N. Freedman. (Computer Bible Ser.: Vol. XXX-B). 209p. (Orig.). 1990. pap. 45.00 (*0-935106-30-8*) Biblical Res Assocs.

Concordance to the English Poems of George Herbert. Cameron Mann. 277p. reprint ed. lib. bdg. 79.00 (*0-7812-0251-5*) Rprt Serv.

Concordance to the English Poems of George Herbert. Cameron Mann. 1971. reprint ed. 49.00 (*0-403-01089-6*) Scholarly.

Concordance to the English Poems of John Donne. H. C. Combs & Z. R. Sullens. LC 74-92960. (Studies in Poetry: No. 38). 1970. reprint ed. lib. bdg. 75.00 (*0-8383-0969-0*) M S G Haskell Hse.

Concordance to the English Poems of Thomas Gray. Albert S. Cook. 16.50 (*0-8446-1124-7*) Peter Smith.

Concordance to the English Poems of Thomas Gray. Albert S. Cook. (BCL1-PR English Literature Ser.). 160p. 1992. reprint ed. lib. bdg. 69.00 (*0-7812-7362-5*) Rprt Serv.

Concordance to the English Poetry of Richard Crashaw. Robert M. Cooper. LC 80-51219. 536p. 1980. 35.00 (*0-87875-188-2*) Whitston Pub.

Concordance to the Essays of Francis Bacon. Ed. by David W. Davies & Elizabeth S. Wrigley. LC 73-8947. 408p. 1973. 90.00 (*0-8103-1004-X*) Gale.

Concordance to the Fables & Tales of Jean de la Fontaine. Jean De la Fontaine. Ed. by J. Allen Tyler & Stephen M. Parrish. LC 73-8388. (Cornell Concordances Ser.). 1104p. 1974. 91.50 (*0-8014-0811-3*) Cornell U Pr.

Concordance to the Gospel of Sri Ramakrishna. rev. ed. Katharine Whitmarsh. Ed. by Mary Dresser. LC 89-50672. 500p. 1990. pap. 24.95 (*0-87481-046-9*) Vedanta Pr.

Concordance to the Greek Testament. 5th ed. Ed. by W. F. Moulton et al. 1120p. (GRE.). 1978. 59.95 (*0-567-01021-X*, Pub. by T & T Clark UK) Bks Intl VA.

Concordance to the Hidden Words of Baha'u'llah. Jalil Mahmoudi. LC 80-21346. (Orig.). 1980. pap. 0.95 (*0-87743-148-5*, 368-052) Bahai.

Concordance to the Inscriptions of Palenque, Chiapas, 2 vols. William M. Ringle & Thomas C. Smith-Stark. (Publication Ser.: No. 62). Date not set. write for info. (*0-939238-92-6*) Tulane MARI.

Concordance to the Inscriptions of Palenque, Chiapas, Maxico. William M. Ringle & Thomas C. Smith-Stark. LC 92-12571. 1994. write for info. (*0-939238-93-4*) Tulane MARI.

Concordance to the Minor Poetry of Edward Taylor (1642? - 1729) American Colonial Poet, 2 vols. Ed. by Raymond A. Craig. LC 92-3910. 596p. 1992. Vol. 1, 596p. lib. bdg. 119.95 (*0-7734-9632-7*); Vol. 2, 616p. lib. bdg. 109.95 (*0-7734-9633-5*) E Mellen.

Concordance to the New Testament Greek. C. H. Bruder. xlii, 885p. (C). 1978. text ed. 50.00 (*0-89005-031-7*) Ares.

Concordance to the Novels of John Lyly. Ed. by Harald Mittermann & Herbert Schendl. (Elizabethan Concordance Ser.: Vol. 2). 904p. 1984. lib. bdg. 245.70 (*3-487-07564-4*, Pub. by Georg Olms GW) Lubrecht & Cramer.

Concordance to the Novum Testamentum Graece of Nestle-Aland, 26th Edition, & to the Greek N. T. 3rd ed. Ed. by H. Bachmanj & W. A. Slaby. 1016p. (C). 1987. lib. bdg. 89.90 (*0-89925-438-1*) De Gruyter.

***Concordance to the Novum Testamentum Graece of Nestle-Aland, 26th Edition, & to the Greek N. T.** 3rd ed. Ed. by H. Bachmanj & W. A. Slaby. 1016p. (C). 1987. lib. bdg. 89.90 (*3-11-011570-0*) De Gruyter.

Concordance to the Peshitta Version of the Aramaic New Testament. Ed. by Way International Research Team Staff. LC 85-51248. 494p. 1985. 19.95 (*0-910068-61-5*) Am Christian.

Concordance to the Plays & Poems of Federico Garcia Lorca. Federico G. Lorca. Ed. by Philip H. Smith & Alice M. Pollin. LC 73-20817. (Cornell Concordances Ser.). 1216p. 1975. 95.00 (*0-8014-0808-3*) Cornell U Pr.

Concordance to the Plays & Poems of Sir George Etherege. Comp. by David D. Mann. LC 84-27917. xi, 445p. 1985. text ed. 125.00 (*0-313-20976-6*, MPO/, Greenwood Pr) Greenwood.

Concordance to the Plays of Shakespeare. W. Adams. 1973. 250.00 (*0-8490-1662-2*) Gordon Pr.

Concordance to the Plays of the Towneley Manuscript. Gerald Kinneavy. LC 89-48682. 722p. 1990. 75.00 (*0-8240-8392-X*, 750) Garland.

Concordance to the Plays of W. B. Yeats, 2 vols., Set. William Butler Yeats. Ed. by Eric Domville. LC 71-162547. (Cornell Concordances Ser.). 2330p. 1972. 105. 00 (*0-8014-0663-3*) Cornell U Pr.

Concordance to the Plays of William Congreve. William Congreve. Ed. by David D. Mann. LC 72-13384. (Cornell Concordances Ser.). 888p. 1973. 88.50x (*0-8014-0767-2*) Cornell U Pr.

Concordance to the Plays, Poems, & Translations of Christopher Marlowe. Christopher Marlowe. Ed. by Robert J. Fehrenbach et al. LC 81-67175. (Cornell Concordances Ser.). 1710p. 1982. 99.50 (*0-8014-1420-2*) Cornell U Pr.

Concordance to the Poems & Plays of Robert Browning, 7 vols. Ed. by Thomas J. Collins. LC 93-4051. (AMS Studies in the Nineteenth Century: No. 14). 1993. 1,440. 00 (*0-404-61494-9*) AMS Pr.

Concordance to the Poems of Ben Jonson. Ben Jonson. Ed. by Mario A. Di Cesare & Ephim Fogel. LC 78-59630. (Cornell Concordances Ser.). 904p. 1978. 88.50 (*0-8014-1217-X*) Cornell U Pr.

Concordance to the Poems of Edmund Spenser. Charles G. Osgood. 42.00 (*0-8446-1332-0*) Peter Smith.

Concordance to the Poems of Emily Dickinson. Emily Dickinson. Ed. by Stanford P. Rosenbaum. LC 64-25335. (Cornell Concordances Ser.). 921p. 1964. 135.00 (*0-8014-0362-6*) Cornell U Pr.

Concordance to the Poems of Hart Crane. Hilton Landry et al. LC 72-10663. (Concordances Ser.: No. 4). 1973. 20. 00 (*0-8108-0564-2*) Scarecrow.

Concordance to the Poems of Hart Crane. Gary Lane. LC 72-1872. (Reference Ser.: No. 44). 356p. (C). 1972. lib. bdg. 75.00 (*0-8383-1437-6*) M S G Haskell Hse.

Concordance to the Poems of Jonathan Swift. Jonathan Swift. Ed. by Michael Shinagel. LC 72-4870. (Cornell Concordances Ser.). 1008p. 1972. 89.50 (*0-8014-0747-8*) Cornell U Pr.

Concordance to the Poems of Marianne Moore. Gary Lane. LC 72-6438. (Reference Ser.: No. 44). 1972. lib. bdg. 75. 00 (*0-8383-1588-7*) M S G Haskell Hse.

Concordance to the Poems of Robert Browning, 2 vols., Set. Leslie N. Broughton. (BCL1-PR English Literature Ser.). 1992. reprint ed. lib. bdg. 150.00 (*0-7812-7461-3*) Rprt Serv.

Concordance to the Poems of Robert Browning 1924-1925, 4 Vols. Leslie N. Broughton & Benjamin F. Stelter. LC 77-92950. (Studies in Browning: No. 4). 1970. reprint ed. lib. bdg. 325.00 (*0-8383-1101-6*) M S G Haskell Hse.

Concordance to the Poems of Robert Herrick. Malcolm L. Macleod. LC 76-92974. (Studies in Poetry: No. 38). 1970. reprint ed. lib. bdg. 75.00 (*0-8383-0991-7*) M S G Haskell Hse.

Concordance to the Poems of Samuel Johnson. Samuel Johnson. Ed. by Helen H. Naugle. LC 72-13383. (Cornell Concordances Ser.). 578p. 1973. 65.00 (*0-8014-0769-9*) Cornell U Pr.

Concordance to the Poems of Sidney Lanier. Philip Graham. (BCL1-PS American Literature Ser.). 447p. 1993. reprint ed. lib. bdg. 99.00 (*0-7812-6982-2*) Rprt Serv.

Concordance to the Poems of Sir Philip Sidney. Philip Sidney. Ed. by Herbert S. Donow. LC 73-20816. (Cornell Concordances Ser.). 637p. 1975. 72.50 (*0-8014-0805-9*) Cornell U Pr.

Concordance to the Poems of William Wordsworth. Lane Cooper. (BCL1-PR English Literature Ser.). 1136p. 1992. reprint ed. lib. bdg. 119.00 (*0-7812-7654-3*) Rprt Serv.

Concordance to the Poetical & Dramatic Works of Alfred Lord Tennyson. Arthur E. Baker. (BCL1-PR English Literature Ser.). 1212p. 1992. reprint ed. lib. bdg. 119.00 (*0-7812-7691-8*) Rprt Serv.

Concordance to the Poetical Works of John Milton. John Bradshaw. (BCL1-PR English Literature Ser.). 412p. 1992. reprint ed. lib. bdg. 99.00 (*0-7812-7379-X*) Rprt Serv.

Concordance to the Poetical Works of William Cowper. J. Neve. LC 68-26363. (Studies in Poetry: No. 38). 1969. reprint ed. lib. bdg. 69.95 (*0-8383-0289-0*) M S G Haskell Hse.

Concordance to the Poetical Works of William Cowper. John Neve. (BCL1-PR English Literature Ser.). 504p. 1992. reprint ed. lib. bdg. 99.00 (*0-7812-7340-4*) Rprt Serv.

Concordance to the Poetry of Anna Akhmatova. Comp. by Tatiana Patera. LC 94-7867. 353p. 1995. 60.00 (*0-87501-111-X*) Ardis Pubs.

Concordance to the Poetry of Byron, 4 vols., Set. Ed. by Ione D. Young. LC 66-674. 1965. reprint ed. 32.00 (*0-9605660-0-7*) I Young.

Concordance to the Poetry of D. H. Lawrence. Ed. by Reloy Garcia & James Karabatsos. LC 70-120277. xvi, 523p. 1970. 50.00 (*0-8032-0768-9*) U of Nebr Pr.

Concordance to the Poetry of Edgar Allan Poe. Elizabeth Wiley. LC 87-43350. 752p. 1989. 95.00 (*0-941664-96-1*) Susquehanna U Pr.

Concordance to the Poetry of Robert Frost. rev. ed. Ed. by Edward C. Lathem. 640p. 1994. 65.00 (*0-88432-742-6*) Audio-Forum.

Concordance to the Poetry of Thomas Traherne. George R. Guffey. LC 73-76112. 1974. 75.00 (*0-520-02449-4*) U CA Pr.

Concordance to the Poets of the "Dolce Stil Novo", 5 vols. Walter J. Centuori. LC 77-294. 1977. Vol. 1: vi, 566p.; Vols. 2-5: iv, 568p. ea. 185.00 (*0-8032-0929-0*) U of Nebr Pr.

Concordance to the Russian Poetry of Fedor I. Tiutchev. Borys Bilokur. LC 75-9419. 357p. reprint ed. pap. 101. 80 (*0-685-15992-2*, 2008978) Bks Demand.

***Concordance to the Science of Being.** Craig Shaw. 71p. Date not set. 5.00 (*0-923569-15-4*) Maharishi Intl U Pr.

Concordance to the Science of Mind. Martha A. Stewart & Albert G. Lowe. 312p. 1980. pap. 18.95 (*0-911336-82-6*) Sci of Mind.

***Concordance to the Septuagint & Other Greek Versions of the Old Testament (Including the Apocryphal Books), 2 vols.** E. Hatch & H. A. Redpath. Incl. Vol. I. Concordance to the Septuagint & Other Greek Versions of the Old Testament. 1504p. (C). 1977. text ed. (*0-89005-029-5*); Vol. II. Concordance to the Septuagint & Other Greek Versions of the Old Testament. (GRE & HEB.). 272p. (C). 1977. text ed. (*0-89005-030-9*); 125.00 (*0-685-60579-5*) Ares.

Concordance to the Septuagint & Other Greek Versions of the Old Testament (Including the Apocryphal Books), 3 vols. in 2, Set. Edwin Hatch & Henry A. Redpath. 1088p. 1983. reprint ed. 95.00 (*0-8010-4270-4*) Baker Bk.

***Concordance to the Septuagint & the Other Greek Versions of the Old Testament (Including the Apocryphal Books)** E. Hatch & H. A. Redpath. (C). 1977. text ed. 125.00 (*0-614-00202-8*) Ares.

Concordance to the Sermons of Gerard Manley Hopkins. William Foltz & Todd K. Bender. LC 89-31442. 362p. 1989. 85.00 (*0-8240-5699-X*, H1235) Garland.

Concordance to the Shakespeare Apocrypha, 3 vols., Set. Ed. by Louis Ule. (Elizabethan Concordance Ser.: Vol. 3). 1491p. 1987. lib. bdg. 444.95 (*3-487-07844-9*) Lubrecht & Cramer.

Concordance to the Short Fiction of D. H. Lawrence. Ed. by Reloy Garcia & James Karabatsos. LC 72-77195. xx, 474p. 1972. 50.00 (*0-8032-0807-3*) U of Nebr Pr.

Concordance to the Standard Edition of the Complete Works of Sigmund Freud, 6 vols., 1. Samuel A. Guttman et al. LC 83-22874. lxiii, 5512p. 1984. write for info. (*0-8236-1071-3*) Intl Univs Pr.

Concordance to the Standard Edition of the Complete Works of Sigmund Freud, 6 vols., 2. Samuel A. Guttman et al. LC 83-22874. lxiii, 5512p. 1984. write for info. (*0-8236-1072-1*) Intl Univs Pr.

Concordance to the Standard Edition of the Complete Works of Sigmund Freud, 6 vols., 3. Samuel A. Guttman et al. LC 83-22874. lxiii, 5512p. 1984. write for info. (*0-8236-1073-X*) Intl Univs Pr.

Concordance to the Standard Edition of the Complete Works of Sigmund Freud, 6 vols., 4. Samuel A. Guttman et al. lxiii, 5512p. 1984. write for info. (*0-318-58328-3*) Intl Univs Pr.

Concordance to the Standard Edition of the Complete Works of Sigmund Freud, 6 vols., 5. Samuel A. Guttman et al. lxiii, 5512p. 1984. write for info. (*0-318-58329-1*) Intl Univs Pr.

Concordance to the Standard Edition of the Complete Works of Sigmund Freud, 6 vols., 6. Samuel A. Guttman et al. LC 83-22874. lxiii, 5512p. 1984. write for info. (*0-8236-1076-4*) Intl Univs Pr.

Concordance to the Standard Edition of the Complete Works of Sigmund Freud, 6 vols., Set. Samuel A. Guttman et al. LC 83-22874. lxiii, 5512p. 1984. text ed. 800.00 (*0-8236-1075-6*) Intl Univs Pr.

Concordance to the Targum of Isaiah. J. B. Van Zijl. LC 78-25832. (Society of Biblical Literature. Aramaic Studies: No. 3). 215p. reprint ed. 61.30 (*0-8357-9569-1*, 2017542) Bks Demand.

Concordance to the Utopia of St. Thomas More & a Frequency Word List. Thomas More. Ed. by Ladislaus J. Bolchazy et al. (Alpha-Omega, Reihe B Ser.: Bd. II). vii, 332p. (GER.). 1978. lib. bdg. 63.70 (*3-487-06514-2*, Pub. by Georg Olms GW) Lubrecht & Cramer.

Concordance to the Works of Jorge Luis Borges, Argentine Author, 1899-1986. Ed. by Peter Standish. LC 91-45038. 452p. 1992. lib. bdg. 109.95 (*0-7734-9628-9*) E Mellen.

Concordance to the Works of Thomas Nashe, 2 vols., Set. Thomas Nashe. Ed. by Louis Ule. (Elizabethan Concordance Ser.). 1000p. write for info. (*3-487-09704-4*, Pub. by Georg Olms GW) Lubrecht & Cramer.

Concordance to the York Plays. Gerald B. Kinneavy. LC 85-4513. 976p. 1986. 75.00 (*0-8240-8656-2*, H626) Garland.

Concordance to What Maisie Knew. Erika Hulpke & Todd K. Bender. LC 89-11983. (Concordances to the Works of Henry James). 544p. 1989. 75.00 (*0-8240-4348-0*, 915) Garland.

Concordances d'Armance. Stendhal. Ed. by Jean-Jacques Hamm & Gregory Lessard. (Alpha-Omega, Reihe E, Franzoisische Autoren Ser.: No. 1). vi, 576p. 1991. write for info. (*3-487-09477-0*, Pub. by Georg Olms GW) Lubrecht & Cramer.

Concordances to Montaigne's Journal de Voyage en Italie, Lettres, & Ephemerides. Ian Winter. 8p. 1981. fiche 10. 00 (*0-942260-16-3*) Hispanic Seminary.

Concordancia Alfabetica de la Biblia. W. H. Sloan & Alfredo Lerin. 1024p. 1988. reprint ed. pap. 23.50 (*0-311-42054-0*) Casa Bautista.

Concordancia Analitica: Greek-Spanish Analytical Concor. A. Tuggy. (SPA.). 26.95 (*84-7228-991-5*, 223058, Pub. by Edit Clie SP) TSELF.

Concordancia Breve de la Biblia. 280p. 1985. reprint ed. pap. 5.95 (*0-311-42055-9*, Edit Mundo) Casa Bautista.

Concordancia Completa Santa Biblia: Complete Concordance of the Bible. William H. Sloan. (SPA.). 21.95 (*84-7228-262-7*, 220186, Pub. by Edit Clie SP) TSELF.

Concordancia de las Sagradas Escrituras. Carlos Denyer. LC 74-21722. 936p. (SPA.). 1969. 28.95 (*0-89922-004-5*); pap. 21.95 (*0-89922-121-1*) Edit Caribe.

Concordancia Greco-Espanola N. T. Greek-Spanish Concordance. Hugo Petter. (SPA.). 18.95 (*84-7228-263-5*, 220189, Pub. by Edit Clie SP) TSELF.

Concordancia Preposiciones Griegas: Concordance of Greek Prepositions. Alfred Tuggy. (SPA.). 41.95 (*84-7228-928-1*, 222235, Pub. by Edit Clie SP) TSELF.

Concordancia Tematica De la Biblia. Tr. by Carlos Branbsby. 199p. 1990. reprint ed. pap. 6.20 (*0-311-42043-5*) Casa Bautista.

Concordant Commentary on the New Testament. rev. ed. A. E. Knoch. 407p. 1968. 12.00 (*0-910424-48-9*) Concordant.

Concordant Greek Text. deluxe ed. Comp. by A E. Knoch. 735p. 1975. 30.00 (*0-910424-32-2*) Concordant.

Concordant Greek Text. rev. ed. Comp. by A E. Knoch. 735p. 1975. 15.00 (*0-910424-31-4*) Concordant.

Concordant Literal New Testament. Comp. by A. E. Knoch. 624p. 1978. pap. text ed. 8.00 (*0-910424-09-8*) Concordant.

Concordant Literal New Testament with Keyword Concordance. Comp. by A. E. Knoch. 992p. 1983. text ed. 15.00 (*0-910424-14-4*) Concordant.

Concordant Studies in the Book of Daniel. rev. ed. A. E. Knoch. 1968. pap. 6.00 (*0-910424-53-5*) Concordant.

Concordant Studies in the Book of Daniel. rev. ed. A. E. Knoch. 464p. 1968. 9.00 (*0-910424-52-7*) Concordant.

Concordant Version of the Old Testament. Comp. by A. E. Knoch. Incl. Isaiah. 128p. 1978. pap. 2.50 (*0-910424-22-5*); Daniel. 128p. 1968. pap. 1.50 (*0-910424-23-3*); Genesis. 122p. 1978. pap. 2.50 (*0-910424-21-7*); Minor Prophets. 141p. 1979. pap. 2.50 (*0-910424-25-X*); Leviticus & Numbers. 167p. 1983. pap. 3.00 (*0-910424-27-6*); Deuteronomy. 86p. 1984. pap. 2.00 (*0-910424-28-4*); Exodus. 104p. 1982. pap. 2.50 (*0-910424-26-8*); Set pap. write for info. (*0-318-51423-0*) Concordant.

Concordantia in Apulei Apologiam Et Florides. Apuleius. Ed. by P. Fleury & M. Zuinghedau. Bd. LXVI. 350p. Date not set. write for info. (*0-318-71065-X*, Pub. by Georg Olms GW) Lubrecht & Cramer.

1524

An Asterisk (*) at the beginning of an entry indicates that the title is appearing in BIP for the first time.

Concordantia in Flavii Corippi Ioannida. Corippus. Ed. by Jean U. Andres. (Alpha-Omega, Reihe A Ser.: Vol. 134). 614p. (GER.). 1993. lib. bdg. 186.00 (*3-487-09714-1*, Pub. by Georg Olms GW) Lubrecht & Cramer.

Concordantia in Iuvenci Evangeliorum Libros. Ed. by Manfred Wacht. Bd. CVII. vii, 379p. (GER.). 1990. write for info. (*0-318-70464-1*, Pub. by Georg Olms GW) Lubrecht & Cramer.

Concordantia in Libros XIII Confessionum, 2 vols., Set. S. Aurelii Augustini. (Alpha-Omega, Reihe A Ser.: Bd. CXXIV). 1191p. (GER.). 1991. write for info. (*3-487-09402-9*, Pub. by Georg Olms GW) Lubrecht & Cramer.

Concordantia in Patres Apostolicos, Vol. 1: Concordantia in Epistulam Ad Diognetum. Patres Apostolici. Ed. by Angel Urban. (Alpha-Omega, Reihe A Ser.: Bd. CXXXV). 212p. (GER.). 1993. write for info. (*3-487-09726-5*, Pub. by Georg Olms GW) Lubrecht & Cramer.

Concordantia in Publium Papinium Statium. Statius. Ed. by Joseph Klecka. (Alpha-Omega, Reihe A Ser.: Bd. LVII). vi, 606p. (GER.). 1983. write for info. (*3-487-07230-0*, Pub. by Georg Olms GW) Lubrecht & Cramer.

Concordantia in Sidonii Apollinaris Carmina. Sidonius Apollinaris. Ed. by Peder G. Christiansen & James E. Holland. (Alpha-Omega, Reihe A Ser.: Bd. CXII). 256p. (GER.). 1993. write for info. (*3-487-09684-6*, Pub. by Georg Olms GW) Lubrecht & Cramer.

Concordantia in Statium. Statius. Ed. by Manfred Wacht. Bd. CXXVI. Date not set. write for info. (*0-318-71226-1*, Pub. by Georg Olms GW) Lubrecht & Cramer.

Concordantia in Terentianum Maurum. Terentianus Maurus. Ed. by Jan-Wilhelm Beck. (Alpha-Omega, Reihe A Ser.: Bd. CXXXVI). 268p. (GER.). 1993. write for info. (*3-487-09723-0*, Pub. by Georg Olms GW) Lubrecht & Cramer.

Concordantia in Velleium Paterculum. Velleius Paterculus. Ed. by Maria Elefante. (Alpha-Omega, Reihe A Ser.: Bd. LXXVI). vi, 524p. (GER.). 1992. write for info. (*3-487-09506-8*, Pub. by Georg Olms GW) Lubrecht & Cramer.

Concordantiae Bibliorum Sacrorum Vulgatae Editionis. xxiii, 1484p. 1986. reprint ed. write for info. (*3-487-05839-1*, Pub. by Georg Olms GW) Lubrecht & Cramer.

Concordantiae in Libanium, Pars Tertia: Declamationes Et Progymnasmata. Libanius. Date not set. write for info. (*0-318-70964-3*, Pub. by Georg Olms GW) Lubrecht & Cramer.

Concordantiae in Platonis Opera Omnia. Plato. Ed. by Mauro Siviero. Bd. CX. (GER.). Date not set. write for info. (*0-318-70541-9*, Pub. by Georg Olms GW) Lubrecht & Cramer.

Concordantiae in Platonis Opera Omnia, Pt. I: Euthyphro. Platon. Ed. by Mauro Siviero. (Alpha-Omega, Reihe A Ser.: Bd. CX). 180p. (GER.). 1990. write for info. (*3-487-09360-X*, Pub. by Georg Olms GW) Lubrecht & Cramer.

Concordantiae Senecanae: Auspicioauctoritate Societatis Linguae Latinae Historice Investigandiae ab Italico Consilio Studiisprovehendisconstitutae, 2 vols., Set. Lucius A. Seneca. Ed. by Antonio Busa & Roberto Zampolli. (Alpha-Omega Reihe A Ser.: Vol. 21). 1647p. (LAT.). 1975. lib. bdg. 336.00 (*3-487-05671-2*) Lubrecht & Cramer.

Concordanza Dei Carmina Latina Epigraphica: Compresi Nella Silloge Di J. W. Zarker. Maria R. Mastidoro. (Classical & Byzantine Monographs: No. xxi). xxxi, 259p. (ITA.). 1991. pap. 46.00 (*90-256-1007-2*, Pub. by A M Hakkert SP) Benjamins North Am.

Concordanza Delle 'Stanze' Di Poliziano. Angelo A. Poliziano. Ed. by Diego Rossi. (Alpha-Omega, Series F, Italienische Autoren). xvi, 406p. 1983. write for info. (*3-487-06997-0*, Pub. by Georg Olms GW) Lubrecht & Cramer.

Concordanze Diacroniche Delle 'Operette Morali' Di Giacomo Leopardi. Giacomo Leopardi. (Alpha-Omega, Series F, Italienische Autoren). xiii, 775p. 1988. write for info. (*3-487-07757-4*, Pub. by Georg Olms GW) Lubrecht & Cramer.

*__Concordat of Agreement: Supporting Essays.__ Ed. by Daniel F. Martensen. LC 94-44791. 1995. pap. 15.00 (*0-8066-2667-4*, Augsburg) Augsburg Fortress.

*__Concordat of Agreement--Supporting Essays.__ Ed. by James F. Griffiss. 240p. (Orig.). 1995. pap. 15.00 (*0-88028-161-8*, 1311) Forward Movement.

Concordat of 1801. Henry H. Walsh. LC 34-12835. (Columbia University. Studies in the Social Sciences: No. 387). reprint ed. 21.00 (*0-404-51387-5*) AMS Pr.

Concordat Proviso Ascendant. deluxe ed. Christopher Dewdney. 1991. per. 20.00 (*0-935724-42-7*) Figures.

Concorde: The Full Story of the Anglo-French SST. Richard K. Schrader. LC 89-60233. (Illus.). 90p. (Orig.). 1989. pap. text ed. 9.95 (*0-929521-16-1*) Pictorial Hist.

Concorde Affair. large type ed. Melinda Wright. 416p. 1985. 15.95 (*0-7089-1277-X*) Ulverscroft.

Concorde & Dissent: Explaining High Technology Project Failures in Britain & France. Elliot J. Feldman. (Illus.). 192p. 1985. 54.95 (*0-521-30519-5*) Cambridge U Pr.

*__Concorde Story.__ Christopher Orlebar. (Illus.). 144p. 1994. 17.95 (*0-600-58515-8*, Pub. by Osprey Pubng Ltd UK) Motorbooks Intl.

Concordex of the URANTIA Book. 3rd rev. ed. Clyde Bedell. LC 85-18502. 512p. 1986. 17.95 (*0-916014-75-4*) BASIC Bedell.

Concordia Primary Religion Ser. 1968. teacher ed 7.35 (*0-570-01520-0*, 22-1206) Concordia.

Concordia Self-Study Bible. LC 86-14727. 1990. 39.95 (*0-570-00505-1*, 01-1781) Concordia.

Concordia Self-Study Commentary. Roehrs & Franzmann. LC 15-2721. 1979. 28.99 (*0-570-03277-6*) Concordia.

*__Concordially Yours: Cobbercasts of the 1930s, 1940s & 1960s.__ G. L. Schoberg. Ed. & Narr. by Borghild S. Jacobson. 216p. 1994. pap. 24.95 (*0-9641036-0-5*) Saga Pubs.

Concrete. Thomas Bernhard. Tr. by David McLintock. LC 86-1285. vi, 156p. 1986. pap. 10.95 (*0-226-04398-3*) U Ch Pr.

Concrete. Sidney Mindess & J. Francis Young. (Civil Engineering & Engineering Mechanics Ser.). 4488p. 1981. text ed. 87.00 (*0-13-167106-5*) P-H.

Concrete: A Homeowner's Illustrated Guide. David H. Jacobs, Jr. (Illus.). 1992. pap. 14.95 (*0-07-157803-X*) McGraw.

Concrete: A Homeowner's Illustrated Guide. David H. Jacobs, Jr. 320p. 1992. 22.95 (*0-8306-3910-1*); pap. 14.95 (*0-8306-3913-6*) TAB Bks.

Concrete: A Homeowner's Illustrated Guide. deluxe ed. David H. Jacobs, Jr. 1992. 22.95 (*0-07-157798-X*) McGraw.

Concrete: Complete Short Stories, 1986-1989. Paul Chadwick. Ed. by Randy Stradley. (Illus.). 128p. 1990. pap. 12.95 (*1-878574-17-5*) Dark Horse Comics.

Concrete: Complete Short Stories 1986-1989. deluxe limited ed. Paul Chadwick. Ed. by Randy Stradley. (Illus.). 128p. 39.95 (*1-56971-012-0*) Dark Horse Comics.

*__Concrete: Fragile.__ Paul Chadwick. (Illus.). 164p. 1994. pap. 15.95 (*1-56971-022-8*) Dark Horse Comics.

*__Concrete: Killer Smile.__ Paul Chadwick. (Illus.). 1995. pap. write for info. (*1-56971-080-5*) Dark Horse Comics.

Concrete: Materials Technology. J. F. Troy. 31p. 1982. pap. 9.00 (*0-7277-0139-8*, Pub. by T Telford UK) Am Soc Civil Eng.

Concrete: Structure, Properties, & Materials. P. Kumar Mehta. (Illus.). 416p. (C). 1986. text ed. 43.95 (*0-685-10931-3*) P-H.

Concrete: Structure, Properties, & Materials. 2nd ed. P. Kumar Mehta & Paulo Monteiro. LC 92-15278. 576p. 1993. text ed. 81.00 (*0-13-175621-4*) P-H.

*__Concrete: Surface Preparation, Coating & Lining, & Inspection.__ Ed. by J. Steve Poncio et al. (Illus.). 124p. 1991. ring bd. 52.00 (*1-877914-22-3*) NACE Intl.

Concrete - Ready Mixed, 1995. American Business Directories Staff. 1995. spiral bd., pap. 590.00 (*1-56105-609-X*) Am Busn Direct.

Concrete Admixtures. Dodson. 1990. text ed. 46.95 (*0-442-00149-5*) Chapman & Hall.

Concrete AlkLi-Aggregate Reactions. Ed. by Patrick E. Grattan-Bellow. LC 87-24759. (Illus.). 509p. 1988. 64.00 (*0-8155-1142-6*) Noyes.

Concrete & Abstract Voronoi Diagrams. R. Klein. (Lecture Notes in Computer Science Ser.: Vol. 400). ix, 167p. 1990. pap. 27.40 (*0-387-52055-4*, 3871) Spr-Verlag.

Concrete & Concrete Construction. (Research Record Ser.: No. 1110). 137p. 1987. 18.00 (*0-309-04460-X*) Transport Res Bd.

Concrete & Concrete Masonry. rev. ed. Donald L. Ahrens et al. (Illus.). 128p. 1988. pap. text ed. 10.00x (*0-913163-22-8*, 176) Hobar Pubns.

Concrete & Concrete Structures. Ed. by Folker H. Wittmann. (Structural Mechanics in Reactor Technology Ser.: Vol. H). 640p. (C). 1987. text ed. 130.00 (*90-6191-769-7*, Pub. by A A Balkema NE) Ashgate Pub Co.

Concrete & Concrete Structures: Numerical Modelling Applications Ser. Y. Bangash. 660p. 1990. 234.00 (*1-85166-294-4*) Elsevier.

Concrete & Construction: New Developments & Management. (Transportation Research Record Ser.: No. 1234). 93p. 1989. 13.00 (*0-309-04950-4*) Transport Res Bd.

Concrete & Cryogenics. F. H. Turner. (Viewpoint Publication Ser.). (Illus.). 125p. 1979. pap. text ed. 60.00 (*0-7210-1124-1*, Pub. by C & CA UK) Scholium Intl.

Concrete & Its Chemical Behavior. Ed. by M. S. Eglinton. 152p. 1987. 35.00 (*0-7277-0372-2*, Pub. by T Telford UK) Am Soc Civil Eng.

*__Concrete & Masonry Cost Data, 1995.__ 13th ed. 1994. pap. 77.95 (*0-87629-370-4*) R S Means.

Concrete & Masonry Problem Clinic, Vol. 1. (Illus.). 208p. (Orig.). 1990. pap. 20.00 (*0-924659-39-4*, 4060) Aberdeen Group.

Concrete & Statistics. J. D. McIntosh. (Illus.). 139p. 1963. 36.00 (*0-85334-038-2*, Pub. by Elsevier Applied Sci UK) Elsevier.

Concrete & Structures: Progress & Products Update. (SHRP Publication Ser.: No. 89CONC). 54p. 1989. 5.00 (*0-685-41014-5*) Transport Res Bd.

Concrete Approach to Abstract Algebra. W. W. Sawyer. 1978. reprint ed. pap. text ed. 6.95 (*0-486-63647-X*) Dover.

Concrete Approach to Mathematical Modelling. Michael Mesterton-Gibbons. (Illus.). 624p. (C). 1989. 49.95 (*0-201-12910-8*, Adv Bk Prog); 14.95 (*0-201-09099-6*, Adv Bk Prog) Addison-Wesley.

*__Concrete Approach to Mathematical Modelling.__ 2nd ed. Micahel Mesterton-Gibbons. LC 94-35535. 1995. text ed. 64.95 (*0-471-10960-6*) Wiley.

Concrete Atlantis: U. S. Industrial Building & European Modern Architecture. Reyner Banham. (Illus.). 280p. 1986. reprint ed. pap. 18.50 (*0-262-52124-5*) MIT Pr.

Concrete Battleship: Fort Drum, El Fraile Island, Manila Bay. Francis J. Allen. LC 88-90957. (Illus.). 60p. (Orig.). (C). 1989. pap. 8.95 (*0-929521-06-4*) Pictorial Hist.

Concrete Block Construction. 3rd ed. Robert E. Putnam & John Burnett. LC 73-75302. (Illus.). 232p. reprint ed. pap. 66.20 (*0-317-10862-X*, 2011567) Bks Demand.

Concrete Blonde. Michael Connelly. LC 93-11802. 1994. 21.95 (*0-316-15383-4*) Little.

*__Concrete Blonde.__ Michael Connelly. 397p. 1995. mass mkt. 5.99 (*0-312-95500-6*) St Martin.

*__Concrete Blonde.__ large type ed. Michael Connelly. LC 94-31287. 1995. 22.95 (*0-7862-0342-0*) Thorndike Pr.

Concrete Blonde- Bloodletting. Ed. by Milton Okun. pap. 12.05 (*0-89524-624-4*) Cherry Lane.

Concrete Box Girder Bridges. Oris H. Degenkolb. (Monograph: No. 10). 1977. 59.95 (*0-685-85763-8*) ACI.

Concrete Box Girder Bridges. Oris H. Degenkolb. LC 76-43388. (American Concrete Institute Monograph Ser.: No. 10). (Illus.). 106p. 1977. text ed. 18.50 (*0-8138-1815-X*) Iowa St U Pr.

Concrete Bridge Design. R. E. Rowe. (Illus.). 372p. 1966. 86.50 (*0-85334-110-9*, Pub. by Elsevier Applied Sci UK) Elsevier.

Concrete Bridge Design: Papers Presented to the First International Symposium on Concrete Bridge Design, Toronto, 1967. American Concrete Institute Staff. LC 68-54701. (American Concrete Institute Publication Ser.: SP-23). (Illus.). 831p. reprint ed. pap. 180.00 (*0-317-10038-6*, 2003079) Bks Demand.

Concrete Bridge Designer's Manual. Ernest Pennells. (Viewpoint Publication Ser.). (Illus.). 1978. text ed. 80.00 (*0-7210-1083-0*, Pub. by C & CA UK) Scholium Intl.

Concrete Bridge Engineering: Performance & Advances. R. J. Cope. 1988. 110.00 (*1-85166-110-7*) Elsevier.

Concrete Bridges: Design & Construction. A. C. Liebenberg. LC 92-5592. (Concrete Design & Construction Ser.). 280p. 1993. text ed. 145.00 (*0-470-21865-7*) Halsted Pr.

*__Concrete Bridges in Aggressive Environments.__ 296p. 1994. pap. 36.25 (*0-614-02512-5*, SP151) ACI.

Concrete Buildings: Analysis for Safe Construction. W. F. Chen & K. H. Mosallan. 1991. 85.00 (*0-8493-4213-9*, TA683) CRC Pr.

*__Concrete Complete Short Stories 1986-1989, Bk. 1.__ 2nd ed. Paul Chadwick. (Illus.). 144p. 1995. pap. 15.95 (*1-56971-114-3*) Dark Horse Comics.

Concrete Construction & Estimating. Portland Cement Association Staff. Ed. by Craig Avery. LC 80-12349. (Illus.). 576p. 1980. reprint ed. pap. 20.50 (*0-910460-75-2*) Craftsman.

Concrete Construction Handbook. 3rd ed. Ed. by Joseph J. Waddell & Joseph A. Dobrowolski. LC 92-35397. 1993. text ed. 94.50 (*0-07-067666-6*) McGraw.

Concrete Construction in Hot Weather. (FIP Guide to Good Practice Ser.). 16p. 1986. 22.00 (*0-7277-0257-2*, Pub. by T Telford UK) Am Soc Civil Eng.

Concrete Culverts & Conduits. (Hydraulic Structures Reference Ser). (Illus.). 73p. 1975. pap. 10.50 (*0-89312-012-X*, EB061W) Portland Cement.

Concrete Dam Instrumentation Manual. USDI Staff. (C). 1992. text ed. 175.00 (*81-7233-039-1*, Pub. by Scientific Pubs II) St Mut.

Concrete Design: United States & European Practices. American Concrete Institute Staff. LC 78-72044. (American Concrete Institute Publication Ser.: No. SP-59). (Illus.). 352p. reprint ed. pap. 100.40 (*0-317-10026-2*, 2022762) Bks Demand.

Concrete Design Based on Fracture Mechanics. 176p. 1992. 62.50 (*0-685-62945-7*, SP-134) ACI.

Concrete Detail Design. Concrete Society. 1986. 49.95 (*0-85139-795-6*, Butterwrth Archit) Buttrwrth-Heinemann.

Concrete Dome Roofs. Charles B. Wilby. LC 93-3886. 313p. 1994. text ed. 159.00 (*0-470-22149-6*) Halsted Pr.

Concrete Durability: Corrosion Protection. 64p. 1993. 30.95 (*0-685-72299-6*, C-25) ACI.

Concrete Durability: Katharine & Bryant Mather International Conference, 2 vols., Set. 2179p. 1987. pap. 111.95 (*0-318-35478-0*, SP100) ACI.

*__Concrete Durability Vol. 1: Katharine & Bryant Mather International Conference.__ Katharine & Bryant Mather International Conference Staff. Ed. by John M. Scanlon. LC 86-73182. (American Concrete Institute Ser.: Vol. Sp-100). (Illus.). 1079p. Date not set. reprint ed. pap. 180.00 (*0-7837-9125-9*, 2049926) Bks Demand.

*__Concrete Evidence.__ Rose. 1995. mass mkt. 3.50 (*0-590-20358-4*) Scholastic Inc.

Concrete Face Rockfill Dams: Design, Construction, & Performance. Ed. by J. Barry Cooke & James L. Sherard. 645p. 1985. 55.00 (*0-87262-503-6*) Am Soc Civil Eng.

Concrete Fit for People. Paul Ritter. LC 79-40711. 1981. 57.00 (*0-08-024671-0*, Pub. by Pergamon Repr UK) Franklin.

Concrete Floors. Philip H. Perkins. (Illus.). 144p. 1993. 59.95 (*0-7506-0770-X*) Buttrwrth-Heinemann.

Concrete Floors: Design & Construction. rev. ed. 60p. 1974. pap. 11.00 (*0-924659-01-7*, 1300) Aberdeen Group.

*__Concrete Floors: Finishes & External Paving.__ Philip H. Perkins. 184p. 1995. pap. 28.95 (*0-7506-2334-9*, Butterwrth Archit) Buttrwrth-Heinemann.

Concrete for Nuclear Reactors, 3 vols., 1. American Concrete Institute Staff. LC 72-81007. (American Concrete Institute Publication Ser.: No. SP-34). (Illus.). reprint ed. pap. 160.00 (*0-317-10390-3*, 2012301) Bks Demand.

Concrete for Nuclear Reactors, 3 vols., 2. American Concrete Institute Staff. LC 72-81007. (American Concrete Institute Publication Ser.: No. SP-34). (Illus.). reprint ed. pap. 135.30 (*0-317-10391-1*) Bks Demand.

Concrete for Nuclear Reactors, 3 vols., 3. American Concrete Institute Staff. LC 72-81007. (American Concrete Institute Publication Ser.: No. SP-34). (Illus.). reprint ed. pap. 142.30 (*0-317-10392-X*) Bks Demand.

Concrete Form Construction. Cairl E. Moore. 1977. pap. text ed. 21.95 (*0-8273-1094-3*); 6.00 (*0-8273-1093-5*) Delmar.

Concrete Formwork. L. Koel. (Illus.). 282p. 1988. pap. 26.96 (*0-8269-0704-0*) Am Technical.

Concrete Foundations. 68p. 1992. 34.25 (*0-685-72535-9*, C-19) ACI.

Concrete Framed Structures: Stability & Strength. Ed. by R. Narayanan. 290p. 1986. 81.00 (*1-85166-014-3*, Pub. by Elsevier Applied Sci UK) Elsevier.

Concrete Garden. Geoffrey F. Dutton. 64p. (Orig.). 1991. pap. 14.95 (*1-85224-141-1*, Pub. by Bloodaxe Bks UK) Dufour.

Concrete Hero. Rob Kantner. 1994. mass mkt. 4.99 (*0-06-104129-7*, Harp PBks) HarpC.

Concrete in Hot Environments. I. Soroka. LC 92-31292. (Modern Concrete Technology Ser.). 1993. write for info. (*1-85166-894-2*) Elsevier.

Concrete in Residential Construction. 28p. 1976. pap. 11.00 (*0-924659-05-X*, 3590) Aberdeen Group.

Concrete in the Middle East, Pt. I. P. J. Fookes et al. 1982. reprint ed. pap. 15.00 (*0-86310-001-5*, Pub. by Palladian) Scholium Intl.

Concrete in the Middle East, Pt. II. P. J. Fookes et al. 1982. pap. 15.00 (*0-86310-007-4*, Pub. by Palladian) Scholium Intl.

Concrete in Transportation. 938p. 1986. 110.25 (*0-317-53450-5*, SP-93) ACI.

Concrete Inquisition. Joseph Flynn. 352p. (Orig.). 1993. pap. 4.99 (*0-451-17605-7*, Sig) NAL-Dutton.

Concrete Inspection. 32p. 1976. pap. 8.00 (*0-924659-06-8*, 2370) Aberdeen Group.

Concrete Introduction to Higher Algebra. L. N. Childs. LC 78-21870. (Undergraduate Texts in Mathematics Ser.). (Illus.). 340p. 1993. 49.00 (*0-387-90333-X*) Spr-Verlag.

*__Concrete Introduction to Higher Algebra.__ 2nd ed. Lindsay N. Childs. LC 95-5934. (Undergraduate Texts in Mathematics Ser.). (Illus.). 500p. 1995. 49.95 (*0-387-94484-2*) Spr-Verlag.

Concrete Island. J. G. Ballard. 1994. pap. 12.00 (*0-374-52413-0*, Noonday) FS&G.

Concrete Liquid Retaining Structures. J. Keith Green & Philip H. Perkins. (Illus.). 355p. 1979. 93.75 (*0-85334-856-1*, Pub. by Elsevier Applied Sci UK) Elsevier.

Concrete Manual. 8th ed. USDI Staff. 627p. 1983. text ed. 75.00 (*0-471-80012-0*, 1698, Wiley-Interscience) Wiley.

Concrete Manual: A Manual for the Control of Concrete Construction. (C). 1990. 400.00 (*81-85046-90-5*, Scientific) St Mut.

Concrete Manual: A Manual for the Control of Concrete Construction. 8th rev. ed. (Illus.). 1988. reprint ed. pap. 18.00 (*0-16-003371-3*, S/N 024-003-00141-4) USGPO.

Concrete Manual: 1991 Edition. 46.85 (*1-884590-05-5*, 228H91) Intl Conf Bldg Off.

*__Concrete Manure Storages Handbook.__ J. H. Pedersen & J. A. Runestad. Ed. by C. J. Huffman. LC 91-26955. (Illus.). 80p. (Orig.). 1994. pap. 20.00 (*0-89373-082-3*, MWPS-36) MidWest Plan Serv.

Concrete, Masonry & Brickwork. 1993. lib. bdg. 259.95 (*0-8490-9009-1*) Gordon Pr.

Concrete, Masonry & Brickwork: A Practical Handbook for the Homeowner & Small Builder. U. S. Army Staff. LC 75-12130. (Illus.). 204p. 1975. reprint ed. pap. 7.95 (*0-486-23203-4*) Dover.

Concrete Masonry Design Tables. 650p. (Orig.). 1993. pap. 50.00 (*1-881384-00-4*, TR-121) Nat Concrete Mason.

Concrete Masonry Designer's Handbook. J. J. Roberts et al. (Viewpoint Ser.). (Illus.). 1983. 90.00 (*0-86310-013-9*, Pub. by Palladian); pap. 75.00 (*0-86310-008-2*, Pub. by Palladian) Scholium Intl.

Concrete Masonry Handbook for Architects, Engineers, Builders. 5th rev. ed. W. C. Panarese et al. LC 90-6460. (Illus.). 264p. (C). 1991. pap. 33.00 (*0-89312-093-6*, EB008M) Portland Cement.

Concrete Materials: Properties, Specifications & Testing. 2nd ed. Sandor Popovics. LC 92-8953. (Illus.). 645p. 1992. 86.00 (*0-8155-1308-9*) Noyes.

Concrete Materials & Practice. 6th ed. L. J. Murdock et al. (Illus.). 480p. 1991. 95.00 (*0-7131-3653-7*, A7294, Pub. by E Arnold UK) Routledge Chapman & Hall.

Concrete Materials & Structures: A University Civil Engineering Text. Charles B. Wilby. (Illus.). 375p. (C). 1991. 89.95 (*0-521-37334-4*); pap. 37.95 (*0-521-37706-4*) Cambridge U Pr.

Concrete Mathematics: A Foundation for Computer Science. 2nd ed. Ronald L. Graham et al. LC 93-40325. (Illus.). 650p. (C). 1994. text ed. 51.75 (*0-201-55802-5*) Addison-Wesley.

Concrete Microstructure. D. M. Roy & G. M. Idorn. 179p. (Orig.). (C). 1993. pap. text ed. 15.00 (*0-309-05254-8*, SHRP-C-340) SHRP.

Concrete Microstructure: Recommended Revisions to Test Methods. D. M. Roy et al. 107p. (Orig.). (C). 1993. pap. text ed. 15.00 (*0-309-05601-2*, SHRP-C-339) SHRP.

Concrete Mix Design. 2nd ed. F. D. Lydon. (Illus.). xii, 196p. 1983. 63.00 (*0-85334-162-1*, I-358-82, Pub. by Elsevier Applied Sci UK) Elsevier.

Concrete Mixtures. 64p. 1990. 19.50 (*0-685-62948-1*, C-12) ACI.

Concrete Music. F. D. Reeve. 88p. 1992. 18.00 (*1-881119-56-4*); pap. 11.00 (*1-881119-72-6*) Pyncheon Hse.

Concrete Music & Other Poems. limited ed. F. D. Reeve. 96p. 1993. 75.00 (*1-881119-84-X*) Pyncheon Hse.

Concrete Pavements. Ed. by A. F. Stock. 430p. 1988. 129.75 (*1-85166-168-9*) Elsevier.

C

An Asterisk (*) at the beginning of an entry indicates that the title is appearing in BIP for the first time.

Concrete Pavements: Harold Halm International Symposium on Concrete Pavement Construction & PIARC 18th World Congress. (Transportation Research Record Ser.: No. 1182). 61p. 1988. 10.50 (*0-685-47697-9*) Transport Res Bd.

***Concrete Pillow.** Ronald Tierney. LC 94-46273. 1995. 21.00 (*0-312-11762-0*) St Martin.

Concrete Pipe & the Soil Structure System - STP 630. 148p. 1977. pap. 14.00 (*0-8031-0311-5*, 04-630000-07) ASTM.

Concrete Poetry: An Annotated International Bibliography, with an Index of Poets & Poems. Kathleen McCullough. LC 87-50085. 1100p. 1989. 90.00 (*0-87875-332-X*) Whitston Pub.

Concrete Poetry from East & West Germany: The Language of Exemplarism & Experimentalism. Liselotte Gumpel. LC 75-43317. (Yale Germanic Studies: No. 6). 284p. reprint ed. pap. 81.00 (*0-8357-3747-0*, 2036473) Bks Demand.

Concrete Pressure Pipe, No. M9. 128p. 1979. pap. 24.00 (*0-89867-067-5*, 30009) Am Water Wks Assn.

Concrete Primer. 4th ed. F. R. McMillan & Lewis H. Tuthill. 28.25 (*0-685-72804-8*, SP-1) ACI.

Concrete Properties & Manufacture. T. Akroyd. LC 61-11155. 1962. 144.00 (*0-08-009595-X*, Pub. by Pergamon Repr UK) Franklin.

Concrete Pumping & Spraying. Cooke. 1990. text ed. 57.95 (*0-442-30352-1*) Chapman & Hall.

***Concrete (Ready Mixed) Market.** 300p. (Orig.). 1994. pap. 1,295.00 (*1-57205-910-9*) Rector Pr.

***Concrete Rehabilitation - Users Manual.** Tom Yu et al. (SHRP Ser.: C-412). (Illus.). 207p. (Orig.). (C). 1994. pap. text ed. 75.00 (*0-309-05816-3*) Natl Res Coun.

Concrete Reinforcing Steel Institute Handbook. 6th ed. 1024p. 1984. 53.00 (*0-318-13727-5*) Concrete Reinforcing.

Concrete Repair, Vol. 1. 54p. 1982. pap. 11.00 (*0-924659-15-7*, 1290) Aberdeen Group.

Concrete Repair, Vol. 2. 56p. 1992. pap. 11.00 (*0-924659-55-6*, 1040) Aberdeen Group.

Concrete Repair, Vol. 3. Concrete Construction Magazine Editors. (Illus.). 48p. 1988. pap. 11.00 (*0-924659-30-0*, 1320) Aberdeen Group.

Concrete Repair & Maintenance, Illustrated. Peter Emmons. (Illus.). 200p. 1992. 64.95 (*0-87629-286-4*, 67146) R S Means.

Concrete River. Luis J. Rodriguez. LC 90-56217. 128p. (Orig.). 1991. pap. 9.95 (*0-915306-42-5*) Curbstone.

Concrete Sealers for Protection of Bridge Structures. (National Cooperative Highway Research Program Report Ser.: No. 244). 138p. 1981. 10.00 (*0-309-03409-4*) Transport Res Bd.

Concrete Shell Buckling. Ed. by Egor P. Popov & Stefan J. Medwadowski. LC 80-69968. (SP-67 Ser.). 240p. (Orig.). 1981. pap. 38.50 (*0-686-95244-8*) ACI.

Concrete Site Work. Graham Taylor. 64p. 1984. 9.00 (*0-7277-0215-7*, Pub. by T Telford UK) Am Soc Civil Eng.

Concrete Slabs: Analysis & Design. Ed. by R. J. Cope & L. A. Clark. (Illus.). 512p. 1984. 110.00 (*0-85334-254-7*, I-216-84, Pub. by Elsevier Applied Sci UK) Elsevier.

***Concrete Spirit: The Architecture of Ralph Allen.** 128p. 1995. 39.99 (*1-56496-219-9*) Rockport Pubs.

Concrete Strength & Strains. Constantin Avram et al. (Developments in Civil Engineering Ser.: Vol. 3). 558p. 1982. 143.75 (*0-444-99733-4*) Elsevier.

Concrete Structures: Materials, Maintenance & Repair. Denison Campbell-Allen & Harold Roper. (Concrete Design & Construction Ser.). 1991. text ed. 187.00 (*0-470-21727-8*) Halsted Pr.

Concrete Structures for Marginal Field Development. Arnt Knudsen. 1989. 160.00 (*90-6314-583-7*, Pub. by Lorne & MacLean Marine) St Mut.

Concrete Structures in Earthquake Regions: Design & Analysis. Ed. by Edmund Booth. LC 93-40447. (Concrete Design & Construction Ser.). 1994. text ed. 195.00 (*0-470-23377-X*) Halsted Pr.

Concrete Technology. LC 92-19392. (Transportation Research Record Ser.: No. 1335). 80p. 1992. 20.00 (*0-309-05173-8*) Transport Res Bd.

Concrete Technology. Adam Neville et al. 438p. 1987. pap. text ed. 67.95 (*0-470-20716-7*) Wiley.

Concrete Technology. 3rd ed. George R. White. 1991. teacher ed 9.00 (*0-8273-3636-5*); text ed. 22.95 (*0-8273-3635-7*) Delmar.

Concrete Technology: Past, Present, & Future. 683p. 1994. 52.95 (*0-685-72649-5*, SP-144) ACI.

***Concrete Technology: Past, Present, & Future.** 683p. 1994. pap. 52.95 (*0-614-02518-4*, SP144) ACI.

Concrete Technology: Properties & Testing of Aggregates. 3rd ed. D. F. Orchard. (Concrete Technology Ser.: Vol. 3). 1976. 65.00 (*0-85334-654-2*, Pub. by Elsevier Applied Sci UK) Elsevier.

Concrete Testing. 40p. 1983. pap. 11.00 (*0-924659-16-5*, 3980) Aberdeen Group.

Concrete Thin Shells. Symposium on Concrete Thin Shells (1970: New York) Staff. Ed. by S. J. Medwadowski. LC 70-158717. (Illus.). 432p. reprint ed. pap. 123.20 (*0-685-23495-9*, 2027959) Bks Demand.

Concrete Under My Chin: Portraits of the City. Jeanne Ave. 1986. 1.50 (*0-932593-04-6*) Black Bear.

Concrete Watertight Structures & Hazardous Liquid Containment. Robert T. Hengst. LC 93-42990. 1994. write for info. (*0-87262-791-8*, ASCE Press) Am Soc Civil Eng.

Concrete Work Simplified. rev. ed. Donald R. Brann. LC 66-24876. 1974. lib. bdg. 5.95 (*0-87733-017-4*) Easi-Bild.

Concrete Work Simplified. Donald R. Brann. LC 66-24876. 1980. reprint ed. pap. 9.95 (*0-87733-617-2*) Easi-Bild.

Concreteridge Proteciton, Repair & Rehabilitation Relative to Reinforcement Corrosion: A Methods Application Manual. Richard E. Weyers et al. 268p. (Orig.). (C). 1993. pap. text ed. 15.00 (*0-309-05616-0*, SHRP-S-360) SHRP.

***Concreting Deep Lifts & Large Volume Pours.** P. B. Bamforth & W. F. Price. (CIRIA Report Ser.: No. 135). 84p. 1995. pap. 57.60 (*0-7277-2025-2*, Pub. by T Telford UK) Am Soc Civil Eng.

Concretions. Arlene Zekowski. LC 62-7480. (Illus.). 92p. 1962. pap. 100.00 (*0-913844-16-0*) Am Canadian.

Concubine. Elechi Amadi. (African Writers Ser.). 222p. (C). 1966. pap. 9.95 (*0-435-90556-2*) Heinemann.

Concubines & Bond Servants: The Social History of a Chinese Custom. Maria Jaschok. LC 88-29347. 192p. (C). 1988. text ed. 49.95 (*0-86232-782-2*, Pub. by Zed Books UK); pap. 15.00 (*0-86232-783-0*, Pub. by Zed Books UK) Humanities.

***Concubine's Children: The Story of a Chinese Family Living on Both Sides of the Globe.** Denise Chong. LC 94-28442. (Illus.). 288p. 1995. 21.95 (*0-670-82961-7*, Viking) Viking Penguin.

Concur '90: Theories of Concurrency: Unification & Extension, Amsterdam, the Netherlands, August 27-30, 1990 Proceedings. Ed. by J. C. Baeten et al. (Lecture Notes in Computer Science Ser.: Vol. 458). vii, 537p. 1990. pap. 50.00 (*0-387-53048-7*) Spr-Verlag.

Concur '91: 2nd International Conference on Concurrency Theory Amsterdam, The Netherlands, August 26-29, 1991 Proceedings. Ed. by J. C. Baeten et al. (Lecture Notes in Computer Science Ser.: Vol. 527). viii, 541p. 1991. pap. 48.00 (*0-387-54430-5*) Spr-Verlag.

***CONCUR '94: Concurrency Theory.** Ed. by B. Jonsson et al. (Lecture Notes in Computer Science: Vol. 836). 529p. 1994. pap. text ed. 69.00 (*0-387-58329-7*) Spr-Verlag.

Concurrences Between Dio Chrysostom's First Discourse & the New Testament. Arthur F. Hallam. 91p. (Orig.). 1985. pap. 9.95 (*0-938770-04-7*) Capitalist Pr OH.

Concurrency & Nets. Ed. by K. Voss et al. xvi, 622p. 1987. 63.00 (*0-387-18057-5*) Spr-Verlag.

Concurrency Control & Recovery in Database Systems. Philip Bernstein et al. LC 86-14127. (C). 1987. text ed. 35.50 (*0-201-10715-5*) Addison-Wesley.

Concurrency Control in Distributed Database Systems. W. Cellary et al. (Studies in Computer Science & Artificial Intelligence: Vol. 3). 350p. 1988. 113.00 (*0-444-70409-4*, North Holland) Elsevier.

Concurrency Control Problem for Database Systems. M. A. Casanova. (Lecture Notes in Computer Science Ser.: Vol. 116). 175p. 1981. pap. 23.00 (*0-387-10845-9*) Spr-Verlag.

Concurrency Eighty-Eight. Ed. by F. H. Vogt. (Lecture Notes in Computer Science Ser.: Vol. 335). vi, 401p. 1988. pap. 45.00 (*0-387-50403-6*) Spr-Verlag.

***Concurrency in Ada.** Alan Burns & Andy Wellings. (Illus.). 384p. (C). 1992. 39.95 (*0-521-41471-7*) Cambridge U Pr.

Concurrency in Programming & Database Systems. Lewis Bernstein. (Computer Science-Math Ser.). 1992. boxed 50.00 (*0-86720-205-X*) Jones & Bartlett.

Concurrency Theory--CONCUR '93: Proceedings of the 4th International Conference on Concurrency Theory, Hildesheim, Germany, August 1993. Ed. by Eike Best. LC 93-30066. (Lecture Notes in Computer Science Ser.: Vol. 715). 1993. 72.00 (*0-387-57208-2*) Spr-Verlag.

Concurrency: Theory, Language & Architecture: UK - Japan Workshop on Concurrency Oxford, UK, September 25-27, 1989 Proceedings. Ed. by A. Yonezawa & T. Ito. (Lecture Notes in Computer Science Ser.: Vol. 491). viii, 339p. 1991. pap. 36.00 (*0-387-53932-8*) Spr-Verlag.

Concurrent Aggregates: Supporting Modularity in Massively Parallel Programs. Andrew A. Chien. LC 92-29676. (Illus.). 205p. 1993. 30.00 (*0-262-03206-6*) MIT Pr.

Concurrent & Comparative Discrete Event Simulation. Ernst G. Ulrich et al. LC 93-39705. 208p. (C). 1993. lib. bdg. 69.95 (*0-7923-9411-9*) Kluwer Ac.

Concurrent C. Narain Gehani & William D. Roome. 320p. (Orig.). 1989. pap. text ed. 31.95 (*0-929306-00-7*) Silicon Pr.

Concurrent Computations: Algorithms, Architecture, & Technology. Ed. by Stuart K. Tewksbury et al. LC 88-17660. (Illus.). 738p. 1988. 135.00 (*0-306-42939-X*, Plenum Pr) Plenum.

Concurrent Computer Integrated Building Design. Steven Fenves et al. 325p. 1994. text ed. 69.00 (*0-13-175753-9*) P-H.

Concurrent Constraint Programming. Vijay A. Saraswat. Ed. by Ehud Y. Shapior. (Logic Programming Ser.). 500p. 1992. pap. 50.00 (*0-262-19297-7*) MIT Pr.

Concurrent Engineering. Jon Turino. (Illus.). 147p. 1991. 150.00 (*0-912253-09-6*) Logical Solns Tech.

Concurrent Engineering: Automation, Tools & Techniques. Andrew Kusiak. 624p. 1992. text ed. 89.95 (*0-471-55492-8*) Wiley.

Concurrent Engineering: Contemporary Issues & Modern Design Tools. Ed. by H. R. Parsaei & W. G. Sullivan. LC 93-14639. 1993. write for info. (*0-412-46510-8*, Chap & Hall NY) Chapman & Hall.

Concurrent Engineering: Methodology & Applications. Ed. by Peihua Gu & Andrew Kusiak. LC 93-29032. (Advances in Industrial Engineering Ser.: Vol. 19). 1993. 157.25 (*0-444-81475-2*) Elsevier.

***Concurrent Engineering: Research & Applications Conference Proceedings 1994.** Ed. by Anand J. Paul & Michael Sobolewski. 800p. 1994. pap. 40.00 (*0-9642449-0-X*) Concurrent Tech.

Concurrent Engineering: Shortening Lead Times, Raising Quality & Lowering Costs. John R. Hartley. LC 91-29936. (Illus.). 330p. 1992. 60.00 (*1-56327-006-4*, CONC) Prod Press.

Concurrent Engineering: The Product Development Environment for the 1990s. Donald E. Carter & Barbara S. Baker. (Illus.). 208p. (C). 1992. 39.95 (*0-201-56349-5*) Addison-Wesley.

Concurrent Engineering: Tools & Technologies for Mechanical System Design. Ed. by Edward J. Haug. LC 93-1624. (NATO ASO Ser.). 1993. 205.00 (*0-387-56532-9*) Spr-Verlag.

Concurrent Engineering - 1992. Ed. by D. Dutta et al. (PED Ser.: Vol. 59). 472p. 1992. 72.50 (*0-7918-1090-9*, G00734) ASME.

Concurrent Engineering & Design for Manufacture of Electronics Products. Sammy G. Shina. (Illus.). 400p. 1991. text ed. 64.95 (*0-442-00616-0*) Van Nos Reinhold.

Concurrent Engineering Approach to Materials Processing. Ed. by S. N. Dwivedi et al. (Illus.). 359p. 1993. 66.00 (*0-87339-194-2*, 461) Minerals Metals.

Concurrent Engineering Design: Integrating Best Practices for Process Improvement. L. Miller. LC 92-85526. 319p. 1993. 60.00 (*0-87263-433-7*) SME.

Concurrent Engineering Seminar. Jon Turino. (Illus.). 486p. 1990. 295.00 (*0-912253-06-1*) Logical Solns Tech.

Concurrent Euclid, Unix & Tunis. Richard C. Holt. (C). 1983. pap. text ed. 24.76 (*0-201-10694-9*) Addison-Wesley.

Concurrent Hardware: The Theory & Practice of Self-Timed Design. M. Kishinevsky et al. LC 93-29284. 1994. text ed. 64.95 (*0-471-93536-0*) Wiley.

***Concurrent Information Processing: A Real Time Neurocomputing Approach.** Robert J. Jannarone. 1994. text ed. 64.95 (*0-442-01884-3*) Van Nos Reinhold.

Concurrent Jurisdiction of the Federal & State Courts. George C. Holt. xxvi, 237p. 1980. reprint ed. lib. bdg. 24.00 (*0-8377-0630-0*) Rothman.

Concurrent Languages in Distributed Systems-Hardware Supported Implementation: Proceedings of the WG 10.3 Workshop Held in Bristol, U. K., March 26-28, 1984. Ed. by G. L. Reijns & E. L. Dagless. 164p. 1985. 48.75 (*0-444-87635-9*, North Holland) Elsevier.

***Concurrent Marketing: Integrating Product, Sales, & Service.** Frank V. Cespedes. LC 95-4325. 1995. write for info. (*0-87584-444-8*) Harvard Busn.

Concurrent Pascal Compiler for Minicomputers. A. C. Hartmann. Ed. by G. Goos & J. Hartmanis. (Lecture Notes in Computer Science Ser.: Vol. 50). 1983. pap. 30.00 (*0-387-08240-9*) Spr-Verlag.

***Concurrent Product Design: 1994 International Mechanical Engineering Congress & Exposition, Chicago, Illinois - November 6-11, 1994.** (Design Engineering Ser.: Vol. 74). 204p. 1994. 74.00 (*0-7918-1399-1*, G00894) ASME.

Concurrent Program Verification. Leslie Lamport. (Computer Science Ser.). (Illus.). 400p. (C). 1996. text ed. write for info. (*0-201-50421-9*) Addison-Wesley.

Concurrent Programming. Alan Burns & Geoff Davies. LC 93-14713. (International Computer Science Ser.). (C). 1993. pap. text ed. 32.25 (*0-201-54417-2*) Addison-Wesley.

Concurrent Programming. Narain Gehani & Andrew D. McGettrick. (Illus.). 621p. (C). 1988. text ed. 43.25 (*0-201-17435-9*) Addison-Wesley.

Concurrent Programming. Andre Schiper. 1989. text ed. 56.95 (*0-470-21346-9*) Halsted Pr.

Concurrent Programming. C. R. Snow. (Computer Science Texts Ser.: No. 23). (C). 1992. 74.95 (*0-521-32796-2*); pap. 32.95 (*0-521-33993-6*) Cambridge U Pr.

Concurrent Programming: Fundamental Techniques for Real-Time & Parallel Programming. T. Axford. 1989. pap. text ed. 40.95 (*0-471-92303-6*) Wiley.

Concurrent Programming: Principles & Practices. Gregory R. Andrews. Ed. by Sally Elliott. 637p. (C). 1991. text ed. 54.95 (*0-8053-0086-4*) Benjamin-Cummings.

Concurrent Programming in ADA. Alan Burns. (Ada Companion Ser.). 250p. 1986. 54.95 (*0-521-30033-9*) Cambridge U Pr.

***Concurrent Programming in ML.** John H. Reppy. 280p. (C). 1995. write for info. (*0-521-48089-2*) Cambridge U Pr.

Concurrent Programming with SR. Gregory R. Andrews & Ron Olsson. LC 92-25056. 350p. (C). 1993. pap. text ed. 35.50 (*0-8053-0088-0*) Benjamin-Cummings.

Concurrent Prolog: Collected Papers, 1. Ed. by Ehud Y. Shapiro. (Logic Programming Ser.). 275p. (C). 1987. 45.00 (*0-262-19266-7*) MIT Pr.

Concurrent Prolog: Collected Papers, 2. Ed. by Ehud Y. Shapiro. (Logic Programming Ser.). 275p. (C). 1987. 45.00 (*0-262-19267-5*) MIT Pr.

Concurrent Prolog: Collected Papers, Set. Ed. by Ehud Y. Shapiro. (Logic Programming Ser.). 275p. (C). 1987. 85.00x (*0-262-19255-1*) MIT Pr.

Concurrent Scientific Computing: With Forty-One Figures. Eric F. Van De Welde. LC 93-43289. (Texts in Applied Mathematics Ser.: No. 16). 1994. 39.95 (*0-387-94195-9*) Spr-Verlag.

Concurrent Systems: An Integrated Approach to Operating Systems, Database & Distributed Systems. Jean Bacon. LC 92-34364. (International Computer Science Ser.). (C). 1993. pap. text ed. 47.50 (*0-201-41677-8*) Addison-Wesley.

***Concurrent Systems: Formal Development in CSP.** Michael G. Hinchey & Stephen A. Jarvis. LC 94-39116. (International Series in Software Engineering). 1995. write for info. (*0-07-707649-4*) McGraw.

Condado de Belken-Klail City. Rolando Hinojosa. LC 93-29599. (Clasicos Chicanos - Chicano Classics Ser.: No. 8). 168p. 1994. 24.00 (*0-927534-33-9*); pap. 14.00 (*0-927534-34-7*) Biling Rev-Pr.

Condamne a Mort see Oeuvres Completes

Conde Centennial Conde, South Dakota 1986. 260p. 1986. write for info. (*0-87970-165-X*) Conde Cent Bk Comm.

Conde Lucanor. Don Juan Manuel. Ed. by Maria J. Lacarra. (Nueva Austral Ser.: Vol. 21). (SPA.). 1991. pap. text ed. 24.95x (*84-239-1821-1*) Elliots Bks.

Conde Lucanor. Don J. Manuel. (SPA.). 9.95 (*84-241-5615-3*) E Torres & Sons.

Conde Nast Traveler Caribbean Resort & Cruise Ship Finder: The World's Smartest Travelers Recommend Their Favorite Hotels, Cruises & Islands in the Caribbean, Bermuda, & the Bahamas. Fodor's Travel Staff. (Illus.). 1994. pap. 14.00 (*0-679-02850-1*) Fodors Travel.

Condell Collection of Oriental Art. Frances S. Ridgely. (Handbook of Collections: No. 1). (Illus.). 64p. 1963. pap. 1.25 (*0-89792-025-2*) Ill St Museum.

Condemnation Law: Strategies & Procedures for Winning Just Compensation. Theodore Novak & Brian W. Blaesser. (Real Estate Practice Library). 408p. 1994. text ed. 128.00 (*0-471-57403-1*) Wiley.

Condemnation of Heroism in the Tragedy of Beowulf: A Study in the Characterization of the Epic. Fidel Fajardo-Acosta. LC 88-7926. (Studies in Epic & Romance Literature: Vol. 2). 215p. 1989. lib. bdg. 89.95 (*0-88946-110-4*) E Mellen.

Condemnation Practice in California. California Continuing Education of the Bar et al. LC 72-619711. (California Practice Book Ser.: No. 59). (Illus.). xiii, 466p. 1973. 85.00 (*0-88124-027-3*, RE-30680) Cont Ed Bar-CA.

Condemnation Procedures & Techniques-Forms, 6 vols. Patrick J. Rohan & Melvin A. Reskin. (Real Estate Transactions Ser.). 1968. ring bd. write for info. (*0-8205-1243-5*) Bender.

Condemned. Paul Kuttner. LC 83-1872. 296p. 1983. 10.95 (*0-911025-02-2*) Dawnwood Pr.

Condemned at Stanley. John-Smith. 40p. (C). 1987. pap. 30.00 (*0-948251-11-5*, Pub. by Picton UK) St Mut.

Condemned Building: An Architect's Pretext. Douglas Darden. LC 92-29548. (Illus.). 160p. (Orig.). 1993. pap. 24.95 (*0-910413-63-0*) Princeton Arch.

Condemned Forever! Eryl Davies. 1987. pap. 3.99 (*0-85234-241-1*, Pub. by Evangel Pr UK) Presby & Reformed.

Condemned Judge. Janko Ferk. Tr. & Aft. by Lowell A. Bangerter. LC 92-14029. (Studies in Austrian Literature, Culture & Thought). 160p. 1993. pap. 12.95 (*0-929497-58-9*) Ariadne CA.

Condemned to Co-Exist: Road Maps to the Future. Bohdan Hawrylyshyn. (Illus.). 200p. 1980. pap. text ed. 24.00 (*0-08-026114-0*, Pergamon Pr) Elsevier.

Condemned to Die: Life under Sentence of Death. Robert Johnson. 190p. (C). 1989. reprint ed. pap. text ed. 11.50x (*0-88133-427-8*) Waveland Pr.

Condemned to Repetition: The United States & Nicaragua. Robert A. Pastor. LC 87-45531. 352p. 1988. text ed. 55.00 (*0-691-07752-5*); pap. 15.95 (*0-691-02291-7*) Princeton U Pr.

Condemned Without Judgment: The Three Lives of a Holocaust Survivor. Bert Linder. 1994. 19.95 (*1-56171-340-6*) Sure Sellers.

Condemning the Use of Force in the Gulf Crisis. Farhad Malekian. 116p. (Orig.). 1992. pap. 78.00x (*91-630-1251-0*, Pub. by Almqv & Wiksell SW) Coronet Bks.

Condenado Por Desconfiado. Tirso de Molina. Ed. by Angel R. Fernandez. (Nueva Austral Ser.: Vol. 139). (SPA.). 1991. pap. text ed. 24.95x (*84-239-1939-0*) Elliots Bks.

Condensate & Feedwater Systems. Center for Occupational Research & Development Staff. (EUTEC Power Plant Operator Curriculum Ser.). (Illus.). 26p. (C). 1987. pap. text ed. write for info. (*1-55502-236-7*) CORD Commns.

Condensation & Condenser Design. Ed. by J. Taborek et al. 620p. 1993. 95.00 (*0-7918-0693-6*, I00356) ASME.

Condensation & Evaporation: Nucleation & Growth Kinetics. J. Hirth & G. Pound. LC 49-50107. (Progress in Materials Science Ser.: Vol. 11). 1963. 86.00 (*0-08-010033-3*, Pub. by Pergamon Repr UK) Franklin.

Condensation & Evaporation of Solids. Ed. by Emile Rutner et al. 708p. 1964. text ed. 551.00 (*0-677-00740-X*) Gordon & Breach.

Condensation Heat Transfer: Presented at the 18th National Heat Transfer Conference, San Diego, CA, August 6-8, 1979. National Heat Transfer Conference Staff. Ed. by P. J. Marto & P. G. Kroeger. LC 79-53410. 124p. reprint ed. pap. 35.40 (*0-318-35019-X*, 2030887) Bks Demand.

Condensation in Containers. ICHCA Staff. (C). 1988. 120.00 (*0-685-46512-8*, Pub. by ICHCA UK) St Mut.

Condensation in Containers: An Interim Report. ICHCA Staff. (C). 1974. 100.00 (*0-685-37343-6*, Pub. by ICHCA UK) St Mut.

Condensation in Containers: An Update of the 1974 Interim Report. ICHCA Staff. (C). 1986. 120.00 (*0-906297-54-0*, Pub. by ICHCA UK) St Mut.

Condensation in High-Speed Flows: Presented at the 1977 Joint Applied Mechanics, Fluids Engineering & Bioengineering, Yale University. Joint Applied Mechanics, Fluids Engineering & Bioengineering Conference Staff. Ed. by A. A. Pouring. LC 77-77423. 102p. reprint ed. pap. 29.10 (*0-317-27653-0*, 2013874) Bks Demand.

Condensation of Metal Vapor in a Supersonic Carrier Gas. P. M. Sherman et al. LC 76-132894. 256p. 1969. 34.50 (*0-403-04538-X*) Scholarly.

Condensed Alphabets: One Hundred Complete Fonts. Dan X. Solo. 104p. 1986. pap. 5.95 (*0-486-25194-2*) Dover.

Condensed Analysis of the Ninth Air Force in the European Theater of Operations. William B. Reed et al. Ed. by Richard H. Kohn & Joseph P. Harahan. (USAF Warrior Studies). (Illus.). 148p. (C). 1984. reprint ed. write for info. (*0-912799-13-7*) Off Air Force.

An Asterisk (*) at the beginning of an entry indicates that the title is appearing in BIP for the first time.

*__Condensed Chaos: An Introduction to Chaos Magic.__ Phil Hine. (Illus.). 192p. (Orig.). 1994. pap. 12.95 (1-56184-117-X) New Falcon Pubns.

Condensed Collections of Thermodynamic Formulas for One-Component & Binary Systems of Unit & Variable Mass. George Tunell. LC 85-71416. 315p. (Orig.). 1985. pap. 16.00 (0-87279-955-7, 408B) Carnegie Inst.

Condensed Encyclopedia of Surfactants. Ed. by Michael Ash & Irene Ash. 678p. 1989. 125.00 (0-8206-0337-6) Chem Pub.

Condensed Geography & History of the Western States or the Mississippi Valley 1828, 2 Vols. Timothy Flint. LC 70-119865. 1970. reprint ed. 150.00 (0-8201-1076-0) Schol Facsimiles.

Condensed Gospel of Sri Ramakrishna. M, pseud. 1979. pap. 5.95 (0-87481-489-8) Vedanta Pr.

Condensed History of the U. S. A. in Rhyme. Frederick Howe. 1972. 59.95 (0-87968-924-2) Gordon Pr.

Condensed Master Index to Poetry. 2nd ed. 417p. 1991. pap. 29.95 (0-89609-308-5) Roth Pub Inc.

*__Condensed Matter-Disordered Solids.__ S. K. Srivastava & N. H. March. 450p. 1995. text ed. 106.00 (981-02-1924-5) World Scientific Pub.

Condensed Matter Physics. Akira Isihara. (Illus.). 376p. 1991. 59.95 (0-19-506286-8) OUP.

Condensed-Matter Physics. National Research Council. (Physics Through the 1990's Ser.). 328p. 1986. pap. text ed. 31.50 (0-309-03577-5) Natl Acad Pr.

Condensed Matter Physics. Ed. by R. L. Orbach. (Illus.). 210p. 1987. 66.00 (0-387-96528-9) Spr-Verlag.

Condensed Matter Physics Aspects of Electrochemistry. Ed. by Mario P. Tosi & A. A. Kornyshev. 536p. (C). 1991. text ed. 118.00 (981-02-0560-0) World Scientific Pub.

Condensed Matter Studies by Nuclear Methods. Ed. by J. Stanek. 350p. (C). 1991. text ed. 104.00 (981-02-0681-X) World Scientific Pub.

Condensed Matter Theories, No. 8. Ed. by L. Blum & F. B. Malik. (Illus.). 674p. (C). 1993. 149.50 (0-306-44405-4, Plenum Pr) Plenum.

Condensed Matter Theories, Vol. 1. Ed. by F. B. Malik. LC 86-9400. 354p. 1986. 125.00 (0-306-42284-0, Plenum Pr) Plenum.

Condensed Matter Theories, Vol. 2. Ed. by P. Vashishta et al. LC 87-65691. (Illus.). 420p. 1987. 125.00 (0-306-42671-4, Plenum Pr) Plenum.

Condensed Matter Theories, Vol. 3. Ed. by J. S. Arponen et al. LC 87-656591. (Illus.). 414p. 1988. 125.00 (0-306-42829-6, Plenum Pr) Plenum.

Condensed Matter Theories, Vol. 4. Ed. by J. Keller. (Illus.). 442p. 1989. 125.00 (0-306-43214-5, Plenum Pr) Plenum.

Condensed Matter Theories, Vol. 5. Ed. by V. C. Aguilera-Navarro. LC 87-656591. (Illus.). 406p. 1990. 125.00 (0-306-43509-8, Plenum Pr) Plenum.

Condensed Matter Theories, Vol. 6. Ed. by S. Fantoni & S. Rosati. (Illus.). 444p. 1991. 125.00 (0-306-43839-9, Plenum Pr) Plenum.

Condensed Matter Theories, Vol. 7. Ed. by A. N. Proto & J. L. Aliaga. (Illus.). 432p. (C). 1992. 125.00 (0-306-44201-9, Plenum Pr) Plenum.

Condensed Matter Theories, Vol. 9. Ed. by John W. Clark et al. (Illus.). 495p. (C). 1994. lib. bdg. 98.00 (1-56072-181-2) Nova Sci Pubs.

*__Condensed Matter Theories Vol. 10.__ Ed. by M. Casas et al. (Illus.). 551p. (C). 1995. lib. bdg. 145.00 (1-56072-223-1) Nova Sci Pubs.

Condensed Muret-Sanders Dictionary: English-German. H. Willman & H. Messinger. 1200p. 1986. 99.00 (0-88729-006-X) Langenscheidt.

Condensed Muret-Sanders German-English Dictionary. 1296p. 1982. 99.00 (0-88729-007-8) Langenscheidt.

Condensed Novels. Bret Harte. LC 71-122715. (Short Story Index Reprint Ser.). (Illus.). 1977. 18.95 (0-8369-3548-9) Ayer.

Condensed Novels & Stories. Bret Harte. LC 75-122716. (Short Story Index Reprint Ser.). 1977. 24.95 (0-8369-3549-7) Ayer.

Condensed Novels, Second Series: New Burlesques. Bret Harte. LC 74-110197. (Short Story Index Reprint Ser.). 1977. 20.95 (0-8369-3348-6) Ayer.

Condensed Parliamentary Procedure: How to Conduct a Board or Committee Meeting. 5th rev. ed. Ed. by William R. Conrad, Jr. & Angele M. Wexler. (Illus.). 11p. reprint ed. 3.50 (0-945571-00-3, 203) Voluntary Mgmt Pr.

Condensed Pascal. Doug Cooper. 550p. (Orig.). (C). 1987. pap. text ed. 43.95 (0-393-95540-0) Norton.

Condensed Silica Fume in Concrete. V. M. Malhotra et al. 256p. 1987. 217.00 (0-8493-5657-1, TP884) CRC Pr.

Condensed Systems of Low Dimensionality. Ed. by J. L. Beeby et al. (NATO ASI Series B, Physics: Vol. 253). (Illus.). 844p. 1991. 159.50 (0-306-43887-9, Plenum Pr) Plenum.

Condensed Weekly, Monthly, Quarterly: Economic Models of the U. S. Economy, Vol. 2. Richard G. Zambell. LC 84-3727. (Illus.). 160p. (C). 1984. 24.95 (0-9613048-4-7) M D Weiss Pub.

Condenser Cooling-Water Systems. Center for Occupational Research & Development Staff. (EUTEC Power Plant Operator Curriculum Ser.). (Illus.). 32p. (C). 1986. pap. text ed. write for info. (1-55502-237-5) CORD Commns.

Condensers. Center for Occupational Research & Development Staff. (EUTEC Power Plant Operator Curriculum Ser.). (Illus.). 26p. (C). 1985. pap. text ed. write for info. (1-55502-217-0) CORD Commns.

Condensing Boilers. B. Peat. (C). 1986. 105.00 (0-86022-158-X, Pub. by Build Servs Info Assn UK) St Mut.

Condensing Boilers, Pt. 1: An Introduction to More Efficient Boiler Houses in the 90s. 1990. 30.00 (0-685-72008-X, Pub. by Build Servs Info Assn UK) St Mut.

Condensing Boilers, Pt. 2: Selection Procedure. 1990. 30.00 (0-685-72007-1, Pub. by Build Servs Info Assn UK) St Mut.

Condensing Boilers, Pt. 3: Condensing Circuit Selection. 1990. 39.00 (0-86022-303-5, Pub. by Build Servs Info Assn UK) St Mut.

Condescend to Evil. Jimmy A. Harris. Ed. by James B. Van Treese. 208p. 1993. pap. 7.95 (1-56901-108-7) NW Pub.

*__Condiment, Sauce & Dressing Market.__ 400p. (Orig.). 1994. pap. 1,295.00 (1-57205-958-3) Rector Pr.

*__Condiments Market.__ 750p. (Orig.). 1995. pap. 2,195.00 (0-7605-2226-X) Rector Pr.

Condition Black. Gerald Seymour. 1992. mass mkt. 5.50 (0-06-100435-9, Harp PBks) HarpC.

Condition Black. large type ed. Gerald Seymour. (Adventure Suspense Ser.). 496p. 1992. 23.95 (0-7089-8636-6) Ulverscroft.

Condition Black: A Novel. Gerald Seymour. 336p. 1991. 20.00 (0-688-10631-5) Morrow.

Condition Critical: America's Fight for Survival! Ronald Wright & Bonnie Wright. Ed. by Mary V. Mullins et al. 176p. (Orig.). 1992. pap. 9.95 (0-9616309-2-2) Mountain Pubs.

Condition Critical: The Story of A Nurse Continued. Echo Heron. LC 93-49058. 384p. 1994. 22.00 (0-449-90782-1, Columbine) Fawcett.

*__Condition Critical: The Story of a Nurse Continues.__ Echo Heron. 1995. mass mkt. 6.99 (0-8041-1335-1) Ivy Books.

Condition, Elevation, Emigration & Destiny of the Colored People of the U. S. Politically Considered. Martin R. Delany. LC 68-28993. (American Negro: His History & Literature, Ser. No. 1). 1968. reprint ed. 22.95 (0-405-01812-6) Ayer.

Condition, Elevation, Emigration, & Destiny of the Colored People of the United States of America. Martin R. Delaney. 215p. 1994. reprint ed. pap. 11.95 (0-933121-42-3) Black Classic.

Condition Evaluation & Maintenance of Tanker Structures. Witherby & Co., Ltd. Staff. (C). 1992. 150.00 (1-85609-039-6, Pub. by Witherby & Co UK) St Mut.

Condition Humaine. Andre Malraux. (Folio Ser.: No. 1). (FRE.). 1933. 9.95 (2-07-036001-6) Schoenhof.

Condition Humaine. Andre Malraux. (FRE.). 1972. pap. 11.95 (0-8288-3710-4, F110891) Fr & Eur.

Condition Humaine see Oeuvres Completes

Condition Humaine see Romans

Condition Humaine de Malraux. Alain Meyer. 254p. (FRE.). 1991. pap. 15.95 (0-7859-4530-X, 207038442X) Fr & Eur.

Condition Monitoring, Vol. 3. Ed. by J. R. McEwan. 284p. 1992. 79.00 (0-87201-224-7) Gulf Pub.

Condition Monitoring: An Introduction to Its Application in Building Services. J. Armstrong. (C). 1986. 105.00 (0-86022-108-3, Pub. by Build Servs Info Assn UK) St Mut.

Condition Monitoring of Electrical Machine. Peter J. Tavner & James Penman. 1987. text ed. 185.00 (0-471-91753-2) Wiley.

Condition of Affairs in Georgia. Nelson Tift. LC 73-164397. (Black Heritage Library Collection). 1977. reprint ed. 24.95 (0-8369-8856-6) Ayer.

Condition of Affairs in Indian Territory & California. Charles C. Painter. LC 74-15121. reprint ed. 29.50 (0-404-11981-6) AMS Pr.

*__Condition of Britain: Essays to Mark the Centenary of the Death of Frederick Engels.__ Pilling. Ed. by Lea. (C). 1996. text ed. 59.00 (0-7453-0962-3, Pub. by Pluto Pr UK) Westview.

Condition of Citizenship. Ed. by Bart Van Steenbergen. (Theory, Culture & Society Ser.). 192p. (C). 1994. text ed. 65.00 (0-8039-8881-8); pap. text ed. 21.95 (0-8039-8882-6) Sage.

Condition of Creatures: Suffering & Action in Chaucer & Spenser. Georgia R. Crampton. LC 73-93281. 218p. reprint ed. pap. 62.20 (0-317-09682-6, 2021992) Bks Demand.

*__Condition of Education.__ 1994. pap. 30.00 (0-614-06320-5) Claitors.

Condition of Education, 2 vols., Set. 1994. lib. bdg. 450.00 (0-8490-5738-8) Gordon Pr.

*__Condition of Education in Rural Schools.__ Ed. by Joyce D. Stern. (Illus.). 140p. (Orig.). (C). 1994. pap. text ed. 45.00 (0-7881-1388-7) Diane Pub.

Condition of Education, 1990, Vol. 1: Elementary & Secondary Education. Laurence T. Ogle & Nabeel Alsalam. 250p. 1990. per., pap. 9.00 (0-16-022853-0, S/N 065-000-00403-5) USGPO.

Condition of Education, 1990, Vol. 2: Postsecondary Education. Nabeel Alsalam & Gayle T. Rogers. (Illus.). 251p. 1990. per., pap. 9.50 (0-16-022854-9, S/N 065-000-003) USGPO.

*__Condition of Education (1993)__ (Illus.). 250p. (Orig.). (C). 1994. pap. text ed. 60.00x (0-7881-1156-6) Diane Pub.

Condition of India: Report of the Delegation Sent to India 1932. 1989. reprint ed. 74.50 (81-7041-180-7, Pub. by Anmol II) S Asia.

*__Condition of Jewish Belief.__ Commentary Magazine Editors. LC 88-33345. 280p. 1995. reprint ed. pap. text ed. 24.95 (1-56821-408-1) Aronson.

*__Condition of Major Aquatic Habitats Theme 1: Proceedings of the World Fisheries Congress.__ Ed. by N. B. Armantrout. 1995. text ed. write for info. (1-886106-12-6) Science Pubs.

Condition of Man. Lewis Mumford. LC 72-91160. (Illus.). 467p. 1973. reprint ed. pap. 9.95 (0-15-621550-0, Harvest Bks) HarBrace.

Condition of Poetry in the Modern World: A Stoogist Manifesto. Paul Fericano. (Orig.). 1980. 5.00 (0-916296-05-9) Poor Souls Pr.

Condition of Postmodernity. David Harvey. (Illus.). 320p. 1989. text ed. 49.95 (0-631-16292-5); pap. text ed. 21.95 (0-631-16294-1) Blackwell Pubs.

Condition of Retention see Iowa University Studies in Psychology

Condition of States. Ed. by Cornelia Navari. 256p. 1991. 90.00 (0-335-09668-9, Open Univ Pr); pap. 36.00 (0-335-09667-0, Open Univ Pr) Taylor & Francis.

Condition of Teaching: A State by State Analysis, 1985. C. Emily Feistritzer. LC 85-26898. 175p. reprint ed. pap. 49.90 (0-8357-3046-8, 2039301) Bks Demand.

Condition of Teaching: A State-by-State Analysis, 1988. Carnegie Foundation for the Advancement of Teaching Staff. LC 85-26898. 106p. 1988. pap. 10.50 (0-931050-35-9) Carnegie Fnd Advan Teach.

Condition of Teaching: A State-by-State Analysis, 1990. Carnegie Foundation Staff. (Illus.). 330p. (Orig.). 1990. pap. 12.00 (0-931050-39-1) Carnegie Fnd Advan Teach.

Condition of the Banking & Thrift Industries & Their Insurance Funds. 1994. lib. bdg. 255.95 (0-8490-5695-0) Gordon Pr.

Condition of the Christian Philosopher. Roger Mehl. Tr. by Eva Kushner. 221p. 1963. 9.00 (0-227-67654-8) Attic Pr.

Condition of the Labouring Classes of Society. John Barton. 1979. 15.95 (0-405-10579-7) Ayer.

Condition of the Professoriate: Attitudes & Trends, 1989. Carnegie Foundation Staff. LC 89-28921. (Illus.). 148p. (Orig.). 1989. pap. 12.00 (0-931050-37-5) Carnegie Fnd Advan Teach.

*__Condition of the Working Class in England.__ Frederick Engels. 307p. Date not set. lib. bdg. 17.95 (0-614-04214-3) Pathfinder NY.

Condition of the Working Class in England. Friedrich Engels. LC 92-18294. (World's Classics Ser.). (Illus.). 320p. 1993. 7.95 (0-19-282955-6) OUP.

Condition of the Working Class in England. Friedrich Engels. Tr. by W. O. Henderson & W. H. Chaloner. (Illus.). xxix, 386p. 1958. 47.50 (0-8047-0633-6); pap. 15.95 (0-8047-0634-4) Stanford U Pr.

Condition of the Working Class in England. Victor G. Kiernan & Friedrich Engels. Ed. by Victor Kierman. 304p. 1987. pap. 10.95 (0-14-044486-6, Penguin Classics) Viking Penguin.

Condition of the Working Class in England: From Personal Observation & Authentic Sources. Frederick Engels. (Illus.). 336p. reprint ed. pap. 12.00 (0-89733-137-0) Academy Chi Pubs.

Condition of Woman in the United States: A Traveller's Notes. Marie T. De Solms, pseud. Tr. by Abby L. Alger. LC 72-2590. (American Women Ser.: Images & Realities). (Illus.). 292p. 1974. reprint ed. 21.95 (0-405-04447-X) Ayer.

Condition of Women in France: 1945 to the Present - A Documentary Anthology. Ed. by Claire Laubier. (Illus.). 144p. 1991. pap. 29.95 (0-415-03091-9, A4635) Routledge.

Condition Purple. braille ed. Peter Turnbull. 321p. 1991. vinyl bd. 25.68 (1-56956-215-6, BR8093) W A T Braille.

Condition Purple. large type ed. Peter Turnbull. 1991. 21.95 (0-7089-2380-1) Ulverscroft.

Condition Surveys of Concrete Bridge Components-User's Manual. (National Cooperative Highway Research Program Report Ser.: No. 312). 84p. 1988. 11.00 (0-309-04609-2) Transport Res Bd.

*__Condition the NBA Way: Pro Basketball Insiders' Strengthening Secrets.__ NBA Conditioning Coaches Staff. 208p. 1994. 19.95 (1-56977-886-8) Cadell & Davies.

Condition Zero. Norman Loftis. LC 91-17805. (American University Studies: Philosophy: Ser. V, Vol. 123). 148p. (C). 1993. text ed. 34.95 (0-8204-1698-3) P Lang Pubs.

Conditional & Typed Rewriting Systems: Second International CTRS Workshop, Montreal, Canada, June 11-14, 1990 Proceedings. Ed. by S. Kaplan et al. (Lecture Notes in Computer Science Ser.: Vol. 516). x, 461p. 1991. pap. 64.00 (0-387-54317-1) Spr-Verlag.

Conditional Eyelid Reaction to a Light Stimulus. Ernest R. Hilgard. Bd. with Influence of Training on Changes in Variability in Achievement. H. B. Reed.; Judging Emotions from Facial Expressions. Leo Kanner.; No. 14. Iowa University Studies in Psychology. Ed. by C. A. Ruckwick. (Psychology Monographs General & Applied: Vol. 41). 1972. reprint ed. Set pap. 35.00 (0-8115-1440-4) Periodicals Srv.

Conditional Inference & Logic for Intelligent Systems: A Theory of Measure-Free Conditioning. I. R. Goodman et al. 1991. 103.00 (0-444-88685-0) Elsevier.

Conditional Logic in Expert Systems. I. R. Goodman et al. 1991. 111.50 (0-444-88819-5) Elsevier.

Conditional Love. 1988. write for info. (0-318-68228-1) Crushed Grapes.

Conditional Love: Parents' Attitudes Toward Handicapped Children. Meira Weiss. LC 92-39123. 296p. 1994. text ed. 49.95 (0-89789-324-7, H324, Bergin & Garvey) Greenwood.

Conditional Markov Processes & Their Application to the Theory of Optimal Control. R. L. Stratonovich. LC 67-28450. (Modern Analytic & Computational Methods in Science & Mathematics Ser.: Vol. 7). 368p. reprint ed. pap. 104.90 (0-317-08621-9, 2007767) Bks Demand.

Conditional Measures & Applications. Rao. (Pure & Applied Mathematics Ser.: Vol. 177). 424p. 1993. 150.00 (0-8247-8884-2) Dekker.

Conditional Relations, 2 vols., 1. Tr. by Ven U. Narada. (C). 1981. 55.00 (0-86013-028-2, Pub. by Pali Text) Wisdom MA.

Conditional Relations, 2 vols., 2. Tr. by Ven U. Narada. (C). 1981. 66.00 (0-86013-264-1, Pub. by Pali Text) Wisdom MA.

Conditional Relations, 2 vols., Set. Tr. by Ven U. Narada. (C). 1981. 115.00 (0-86013-257-9, Pub. by Pali Text) Wisdom MA.

Conditional Security. David Anderson. 1985. pap. 5.99 (0-88019-171-6) Schmul Pub Co.

Conditional Stability & Real Analytic Pseudo-Anosov Maps. M. Gerber. LC 84-29008. (Memoirs of the AMS Ser.: No. 54/321). 116p. 1986. reprint ed. pap. text ed. 21.00 (0-8218-2320-5, MEMO 54/321) Am Math.

Conditional Term Rewriting Systems: Third International Workshop, CTRS-92, Pont-a-Mousson, France, July 8-10, 1992, Proceedings. Ed. by Michael Rusinowitch & J. L. Remy. LC 92-44413. (Lecture Notes in Computer Science Ser.: Vol. 656). 1993. 70.00 (0-387-56393-8) Spr-Verlag.

Conditionality As Bargaining Process: Structural-Adjustment Lending. Paul Mosley. LC 87-25806. (Essays in International Finance Ser.: No. 168). 1987. pap. text ed. 8.00 (0-88165-075-7) Princeton U Int Finan Econ.

Conditionally Specified Distributions. Barry C. Arnold et al. Ed. by J. O. Berger et al. (Lecture Notes in Statistics Ser.: Vol. 73). 160p. 1992. pap. 33.00 (0-387-97794-5) Spr-Verlag.

Conditionally Well-Posed Problems. Ed. by M. M. Lavrent'sev et al. 366p. 1994. 210.00x (90-6764-160-X) Coronet Bks.

Conditionals. Frank Jackson. 256p. 1987. text ed. 51.95 (0-631-14621-0) Blackwell Pubs.

Conditionals. Ed. by Frank Jackson. (Oxford Readings in Philosophy Ser.). 248p. 1991. 39.95 (0-19-875096-X); pap. 15.95 (0-19-875095-1) OUP.

*__Conditionals: From Philosophy to Computer Science.__ G. Crocco et al. (Studies in Logic & Computation: No. 5). 400p. 1995. 79.00 (0-19-853861-8) OUP.

Conditioned Reflex. Curtis Zahn. LC 90-53081. (Orig.). (C). 1991. pap. 5.00 (0-88734-315-5) Players Pr.

Conditioned Reflexes: An Investigation of the Physiological Activity of the Cerebral Cortex. Ivan P. Pavlov. Ed. by G. V. Anrep. 1927. pap. text ed. 9.95 (0-486-60614-7) Dover.

Conditioners, Emollients, & Lubricants. Ed. by Michael Ash & Irene Ash. (What Every Chemical Technologist Wants to Know About...Ser.: Vol. IV). 400p. 1990. text ed. 60.00 (0-8206-0330-9) Chem Pub.

Conditioning. Dewayne J. Johnson et al. (Illus.). 77p. 1982. pap. text ed. 5.95x (0-89641-090-0) American Pr.

Conditioning: An Image Approach. Donald King. 502p. 1979. 39.95 (0-89876-067-4) Gardner Pr.

Conditioning & Enuresis. S. Lovibond. LC 63-22192. 1964. 94.00 (0-08-010449-5, Pub. by Pergamon Repr UK) Franklin.

Conditioning & Learning: Student Booklet. American Psychological Association Staff. (Human Behavior Curriculum Project Ser.). 64p. (gr. 9-12). 1981. pap. text ed. 3.95 (0-8077-2623-0) Tchrs Coll.

Conditioning & Learning: Teachers Handbook & Duplication Masters. American Psychological Association. (Human Behavior Curriculum Project Ser.). (gr. 9-12). 1981. 9.95 (0-8077-2624-9) Tchrs Coll.

Conditioning & Storage of Spent Fuel Element Hulls on Radioactive Waste. Ed. by W. Hebel & G. Cottone. 350p. 1982. text ed. 171.00 (3-7186-0149-4) Gordon & Breach.

Conditioning, Cognition & Methodology: Contemporary Issues in Experimental Psychology. Ed. by Joseph B. Sidowski. 286p. 1989. 45.00 (0-8191-7496-3) U Pr of Amer.

Conditioning Cut Flowers & Foliage. Bernie Knight. (Illus.). 20p. 1992. 5.00 (0-944266-14-2) Maecenas Pr.

Conditioning Diagnostics: Collinearity & Weak Data in Regression. David A. Belsley. 1991. text ed. 97.95 (0-471-52889-7) Wiley.

Conditioning for Basketball. Mark Brzycki & Shaun Brown. LC 93-15176. (Illus.). 160p. (Orig.). 1993. pap. 12.95 (0-940279-56-8) Masters Pr IN.

Conditioning for Football. Tom Zupancic. LC 94-20601. (Illus.). 160p. 1993. pap. 12.95 (0-940279-77-0) Masters Pr IN.

Conditioning for Football: The University of Washington Way. Don James & Rich Huegli. LC 80-82967. (Illus.). 144p. (Orig.). 1982. pap. text ed. 10.95 (0-88011-016-3, PJAM0016) Human Kinetics.

Conditioning for Football: The Oklahoma State Way. Bert Jacobson. LC 80-84216. (Illus.). 136p. (Orig.). (C). 1981. pap. 10.95 (0-918438-71-3, PJAC0071) Human Kinetics.

Conditioning for Sport. N. Whitehead. (EP Sports Ser.). (Illus.). 1975. 6.95 (0-7158-0593-2) Charles River Bks.

Conditioning Monitoring & Diagnostic Engineering Management 91: Proceedings from the 3rd International Congress, Southampton, 2-4 July 1991. Ed. by Raj B. Rao & A. D. Hope. (Illus.). 560p. 1991. 174.00 (0-7503-0154-6) IOP Pub.

Conditioning of Alpha Bearing Wastes. IAEA Staff. (Technical Reports Ser.: No. 326). 102p. 1991. pap. 40.00 (92-0-125591-8, STI/DOC/326) UNIPUB.

*__Conditioning Skills for Alpine Skiing.__ Ellen P. Foster. 108p. 1993. pap. 11.95 (0-9647390-0-3) Turning Pt Ski Found.

Conditioning to Win. Equine Research, Inc. Research Staff. Ed. by Don Wagoner. (Illus.). 312p. (C). 1974. text ed. 33.00 (0-935842-02-0) Equine Res.

Conditioning with Physical Disabilities. Kevin F. Lockette & Ann M. Keyes. LC 93-47606. 288p. 1994. pap. 22.95 (0-87322-614-3, PLOC0614) Human Kinetics.

C

An Asterisk (*) at the beginning of an entry indicates that the title is appearing in BIP for the first time.

Conditions & Conditionals: An Investigation of Ancient Greek. Gerry Wakker. (Amsterdam Studies in Classical Philology Ser.: No. 3). xii, 450p. 1994. 96.00 (*90-5063-196-7*, Pub. by Gieben NE) Benjamins North Am.

***Conditions & Weight Training.** Charles Smith & Don Jones. 80p. (C). 1994. pap. text ed., spiral bd. 9.26 (*0-8403-9636-8*) Kendall-Hunt.

Conditions de Croissance des Economies Regionales en Etat de Suremploi: Le Cas de Liege. L. E. Davin. Bd. with Destin Europeen de la Meuse. (Economies et Societes Series L: No. 5). 1959. Set pap. (*0-8115-0730-0*) Periodicals Srv.

Conditions for Answered Prayer see Lay Counseling Series

Conditions for Business Cooperation: Current Status, January 1992. 82p. 1992. pap. 25.00 (*92-826-3583-X*, CO-62-91-003-EN-C, Pub. by Europ Com) UNIPUB.

Conditions for Business Cooperation Current Status 1 January 1993. EC Staff. 82p. 1993. pap. 30.00 (*92-826-5277-7*, CO-10-93-003-EN-C, Pub. by Europ Com) UNIPUB.

Conditions for Chile's Plebiscite on Pinochet. Washington Office on Latin America Staff. 21p. 1988. pap. 4.00 (*0-929513-05-3*) WOLA.

Conditions for Criticism: Authority, Knowledge, & Literature in the Late Nineteenth Century. Ian Small. (Illus.). 168p. 1991. 49.95 (*0-19-812241-1*) OUP.

Conditions for Partnership in International Economic Management. C. Fred Bergsten et al. (Triangle Papers: No. 32). 1986. pap. 6.00 (*0-930503-01-5*) Trilateral Comm.

Conditions for Second Language Learning: Introduction to a General Theory. Bernard Spolsky. (Language Education Ser.). 284p. 1989. pap. text ed. 16.25 (*0-19-437063-1*) OUP.

Conditions Handsome & Unhandsome: The Constitution of Emersonian Perfectionism. Stanley Cavell. LC 89-49128. (Paul Carus Lecture Ser.). (C). 1991. 49.95 (*0-8126-9149-0*) Open Court.

Conditions Handsome & Unhandsome: The Constitution of Emersonian Perfectionism: The Carus Lectures. Stanley Cavell. 192p. 1991. pap. 11.95 (*0-226-09821-4*) U Ch Pr.

Conditions in Occupational Therapy: Effect on Occupational Performance. Ruth Hansen & Ben Atchison. (Illus.). 386p. 1993. pap. 35.00 (*0-683-03878-8*) Williams & Wilkins.

Conditions Not of Their Choosing: The Guaymi Indians & Mining Multinationals in Panama. Chris Gjording. LC 90-45490. (Ethnographic Inquiry Ser.). 424p. (C). 1991. 42.50 (*0-87474-472-5*) Smithsonian.

Conditions of Agricultural Growth: The Economics of Agrarian Change under Population Pressure. Ester Boserup. 128p. 1992. 17.00 (*1-85383-159-X*, Pub. by Erthscan Pubns UK) Island Pr.

Conditions of Awareness: Subjective Factors in the Social Adaptations of Man & Other Primates. Anthony Shafton. LC 76-26201. 1976. pap. 20.00 (*0-9601130-1-0*) Riverstone.

Conditions of Contract for Ground Investigation. 40p. 1983. 9.00 (*0-7277-0178-9*, Pub. by T Telford UK) Am Soc Civil Eng.

Conditions of Discretion: Autonomy, Community, Bureaucracy. Joel F. Handler. LC 85-62808. 450p. (C). 1986. text ed. 39.95 (*0-87154-349-4*) Russell Sage.

Conditions of Freedom. John Macmurray. LC 93-9222. 108p. (C). 1993. reprint ed. pap. 15.00 (*0-391-03714-5*) Humanities.

Conditions of Freedom: Essays in Political Philosophy. Harry V. Jaffa. LC 74-24389. 293p. reprint ed. pap. 83.60 (*0-685-20479-0*, 2029911) Bks Demand.

Conditions of Happiness. Ruut Veenhoven. 1984. lib. bdg. 119.00 (*90-277-1792-3*) Kluwer Ac.

Conditions of Happiness, Set. Ruut Veenhoven. 1987. lib. bdg. 185.00 (*90-277-1794-X*) Kluwer Ac.

Conditions of Human Growth. Jane Pearce & Saul Newton. 1969. reprint ed. 6.95 (*0-685-08130-3*, Citadel Pr) Carol Pub Group.

Conditions of Identity: A Study in Identity & Survival. Andrew Brennan. (Illus.). 384p. 1988. 79.00 (*0-19-824974-8*) OUP.

Conditions of Labor in American Industries. William J. Lauck & Edgar Sydenstricker. LC 70-89746. (American Labor, from Conspiracy to Collective Bargaining Ser., No. 1). 404p. 1971. reprint ed. 26.95 (*0-405-02134-8*) Ayer.

Conditions of Labour in Indian Agriculture. Marabendu Chattopadhyay. 1985. 17.50 (*0-8364-1399-7*, Pub. by KP Bagchi IA) S Asia.

Conditions of Learning & Theory of Instruction. 4th ed. Robert M. Gagne. 352p. (C). 1985. text ed. 41.25 (*0-03-063688-4*) HB Coll Pubs.

Conditions of Liberty. Ernest Gellner. 1994. 27.95 (*0-7139-9114-3*) Allen Lane.

Conditions of Life in the Sea: Short Account of Quantitative Marine Biological Research. James Johnstone. Ed. by Frank N. Egerton, 3rd. LC 77-74232. (History of Ecology Ser.). (Illus.). 1978. reprint ed. lib. bdg. 30.95 (*0-405-10401-4*) Ayer.

Conditions of Music. Alan Durant. LC 84-16408. 256p. 1985. 59.50 (*0-88706-015-3*); pap. 19.95 (*0-88706-017-X*) State U NY Pr.

Conditions of Peace. Julia Sweig. 1991. pap. 15.95 (*0-936391-40-5*) Expro Pr.

Conditions of Peace: An Inquiry. Ed. by Michael Shuman & Julia Sweig. 254p. (Orig.). (C). 1991. pap. 15.95 (*0-685-60302-4*) Inst Policy Stud.

Conditions of Progress in Democratic Government. Charles E. Hughes. LC 73-19154. (Politics & People Ser.). 130p. 1974. reprint ed. 13.95 (*0-405-05876-4*) Ayer.

***Conditions of Reciprocal Understanding: A Centennial Conference at International House, the University of Chicago, September 12-17, 1992.** Ed. by James W. Fernandez & Milton B. Singer. 463p. (Orig.). Date not set. pap. write for info. (*0-9645072-0-X*) Ctr Internat Stud.

Conditions of Ships Flying the Panama Flag see Freedom of Association & Conditions of Work in Venezuela

Conditions of Success: How the Modern Artist Rises to Fame. Alan Bowness. (Illus.). 1990. 12.95 (*0-500-55021-2*) Thames Hudson.

Conditions of Successful Degradation Ceremonies. Harold Garfinkel. (Reprint Series in Sociology). (C). 1993. reprint ed. pap. text ed. 1.00 (*0-8290-2795-5*, S-92) Irvington.

Conditions of Trust. Sierra Leone. 256p. (Orig.). 1995. pap. 3.95 (*1-877606-00-6*) R Romance.

Conditions of Validity & Cognition in Modern Legal Thought: Proceedings of the 11th World Congress on Philosophy of Law & Social Philosophy Helsinki. Ed. by Neil MacCormick et al. 214p. (Orig.). 1985. pap. 44.00 (*3-515-04460-4*) Coronet Bks.

Conditions of War. Lierre Keith. 163p. 1993. pap. 10.95 (*0-9632660-1-2*) Fighting Wds.

Conditions of Work & Employment in Water, Gas & Electricity Supply Services. 62p. (Orig.). 1982. pap. 12.00 (*92-2-102912-3*) Intl Labour Office.

Conditions of Work & Living: The Reawakening of the English Conscience, 1838-1844. LC 72-2520. (British Labour Struggles Before 1850 Ser.). 1974. reprint ed. 23.95 (*0-405-04413-5*) Ayer.

Conditions of Work & Quality of Working Life: A Directory of Institutions. 2nd rev. ed. Ed. by Linda Stoddart. xxi, 306p. 1986. pap. 32.00 (*92-2-105328-8*) Intl Labour Office.

Conditions on Phonological Government. Monik Charette. (Cambridge Studies in Linguistics: No. 58). 256p. (C). 1991. 59.95 (*0-521-39246-2*) Cambridge U Pr.

Conditions on Rules. Ger De Haan. 248p. 1981. pap. 75.40 (*90-70176-08-4*) Mouton.

Conditions to Be Observed by British Undertakers of the Escheated Lands in Ulster. LC 74-38139. (English Experience Ser.: No. 490). 1972. reprint ed. 5.00 (*90-221-0490-7*) Walter J Johnson.

Conditions Uncertain & Likely to Pass Away: Tales. Frank Stanford. 136p. 1990. pap. 10.95 (*0-918786-42-8*) Lost Roads.

Condo & Villa Vacations Rated: Caribbean, Mexico, & Hawaii. Clinton Burr. 1993. pap. 17.00 (*0-671-87005-X*, P-H Travel) P-H Gen Ref & Trav.

Condo & Villa Vacations Rated: U. S. A. & Canada. Clinton Burr. 1993. pap. 17.00 (*0-671-86987-6*, P-H Travel) P-H Gen Ref & Trav.

Condo, Co-Op, & Apartment Dweller's Guide to Repairs & Improvements. Bernard Gladstone. LC 92-34107. 1993. 25.00 (*0-671-55670-3*) S&S Trade.

Condo Kill. Richard Barth. (Margaret Binton Mystery Ser.). 160p. 1991. pap. 3.95 (*0-449-21812-0*, Crest) Fawcett.

Condo Vacations: The Complete Guide. 4th ed. Pamela Lanier. 496p. 1992. pap. 14.95 (*0-89815-461-8*) Ten Speed Pr.

Condo Vacations: The Complete Guide. 5th ed. Pamela Lanier. 1993. pap. 14.95 (*0-89815-551-7*) Ten Speed Pr.

Condom: Increasing Utilization in the U. S. Ed. by M. H. Redford et al. (Illus.). 1974. 10.00 (*0-911302-25-5*); pap. 7.50 (*0-317-58587-8*) San Francisco Pr.

Condom: Increasing Utilization in United States. (AIDS & Venereal Disease Ser.). 1985. lib. bdg. 90.00 (*0-8490-3960-6*) Gordon Pr.

Condom Chronicle, Vol. I. John C. Bangert. (Illus.). (Orig.). 1988. pap. 6.95 (*0-317-91071-X*) Occasion Thing.

Condom Encyclopedia. 2nd rev. ed. Gary Griffin. (Illus.). 128p. 1993. pap. 9.95 (*1-879967-14-6*) Added Dimensns.

Condom Industry in the United States. James S. Murphy. LC 90-52637. (Illus.). 174p. 1990. lib. bdg. 32.50x (*0-89950-533-3*) McFarland & Co.

Condominium. John D. MacDonald. 1985. mass mkt. 5.99 (*0-449-20737-4*, Crest) Fawcett.

Condominium & Co-op Closings. 295p. (Orig.). 1987. pap. text ed. 10.00 (*0-317-66042-X*, Q1-3001) PLI.

Condominium & Homeowner Association Practice: Community Association Law. Wayne S. Hyatt. LC 81-69439. 397p. 1981. pap. 10.00 (*0-317-30761-4*, B254) Am Law Inst.

Condominium & Homeowner Association Practice: Community Association Law. 2nd ed. Wayne S. Hyatt. LC 88-71903. 540p. 1988. text ed. 99.00 (*0-8318-0526-9*, B526) Am Law Inst.

Condominium & Homeowner Associations That Work: On Paper & in Action. David B. Wolfe. LC 78-67831. (Illus.). 144p. reprint ed. pap. 41.10 (*0-8357-3187-1*, 2039457) Bks Demand.

Condominium & Sudanese Nationalism. Peter Woodward. LC 79-53234. (Illus.). 221p. 1980. text ed. 44.00 (*0-06-497863-X*, N 6746) B&N Imports.

Condominium Bluebook: Arizona. Branden E. Bickel. 1993. pap. 6.95 (*1-882889-03-7*) B&B Pubns.

Condominium Bluebook: California. Branden E. Bickel. 260p. 1993. pap. 6.95 (*1-882889-01-0*) B&B Pubns.

***Condominium Bluebook: California.** Ed. by Branden E. Bickel. 1995. pap. 9.95 (*1-882889-09-6*) B&B Pubns.

Condominium Bluebook: Hawaii. Branden E. Bickel. 1993. pap. 6.95 (*1-882889-02-9*) B&B Pubns.

Condominium Book: California. Branden E. Bickel. Ed. by Marge Williams. 269p. 1994. pap. 7.50 (*1-882880-05-6*) G Autry Wstrn.

Condominium Buying Guide: Basic Information to Protect Your Condominium Purchase. Ed. by D. J. Scherer. 20p. (Orig.). 1990. pap. 3.95 (*0-918734-35-5*) Reymont.

***Condominium Concept: A Practical Guide for Officers, Owners & Directors.** 5th ed. Peter M. Dunbar. 352p. 1994. pap. 18.95 (*0-937569-14-3*) Suncoast Prof Pub.

Condominium Concept: A Practical Guide for Officers, Owners & Directors of Florida Condominiums. 4th ed. Peter M. Dunbar. 344p. 1992. pap. text ed. 18.95 (*0-937569-11-9*) Suncoast Prof Pub.

Condominium Development: Forms with Commentary, 2 vols. Gurdon H. Buck. (Real Property-Zoning Ser.). 1990. disk, ring bd. 225.00 (*0-685-34492-4*) Clark Boardman Callaghan.

Condominium Development Guide. 2nd ed. Keith B. Romney & Brad Romney. 1000p. 1990. boxed 98.00 (*0-88262-908-5*) Warren Gorham & Lamont.

Condominium Development Guide, No. 1. 2nd suppl. ed. Keith B. Romney & Brad Romney. 1000p. 1990. 59.50 (*0-7913-0699-2*) Warren Gorham & Lamont.

Condominium, Homeowner & Cooperative Community Associations-Information Resource. Lester J. Giese. 40p. (Orig.). 1984. pap. text ed. 13.95 (*0-910049-03-3*) Lateral Thinkers.

Condominium Law & Practice-Forms, 8 vols. Patrick J. Rohan & Melvin A. Reskin. (Real Estate Transactions Ser.). 1965. Updates. ring bd. write for info. (*0-8205-1235-4*) Bender.

Condominium Living: How to Purchase, Live In and Manadge Condominiums. John Summersett. LC 91-90010. (Illus.). 168p. (Orig.). 1991. pap. 9.95 (*0-9628325-0-2*) Sagamon Pr.

Condominium Management Agreement: The Best Protection Money Can Buy. 28p. 1989. 17.95 (*0-685-71694-5*, 988); 49.95 (*0-685-71695-3*, 98810) Inst Real Estate.

Condominium Owner's & Director's Almanac. Lester J. Giese et al. 100p. (Orig.). 1989. pap. text ed. 29.95 (*0-910049-04-1*) Lateral Thinkers.

Condominium Ownership: A Buyer's Guide. Andrew Ludy. LC 83-102592. (Illus.). 128p. (Orig.). 1982. pap. 7.95 (*0-943912-00-8*) Landing Pr.

Condominium Property Law of the Federal Republic of Germany of 15 March 1951. Tr. by Simon L. Goren. LC 93-46351. vii, 23p. 1995. 15.00x (*0-8377-0652-1*) Rothman.

Condominium Reserve Builder. Lester J. Giese. 1983. pap. text ed. 32.50 (*0-910049-02-5*) Lateral Thinkers.

Condominium Specialist. P. J. Thompson. LC 88-13591. (Illus.). 200p. (Orig.). 1989. pap. 15.95 (*0-918785-04-9*) Kricket.

Condominium Trap. Hugo Paul. LC 79-65558. 1985. 8.95 (*0-916620-36-0*) Portals Pr.

Condominiums: The Effects of Conversion on a Community. John R. Dinkelspiel et al. LC 80-39894. 203p. 1981. text ed. 49.95 (*0-86569-059-6*, Auburn Hse) Greenwood.

Condominiums: The Professional's Complete Manual & Guide. John R. Wade. LC 82-21581. 320p. 1983. 39.95 (*0-13-167130-8*) P-H.

Condominiums: What You Should Know - Before You Buy, When You Buy, After You Buy. Arnold Higgins. LC 81-68939. (Illus.). 112p. 1981. pap. 12.00 (*0-9605082-0-1*) Allied Ent.

Condominiums & Cooperatives: Appraisal & Assessment. (Bibliographic Ser.). 4p. 1981. pap. text ed. 5.00 (*0-88329-119-3*) IAAO.

Condominiums & Cooperatives: State & Local Conversion Regulations. 1986. lib. bdg. 79.95 (*0-8490-3533-3*) Gordon Pr.

Condominiums & Home Owner Associations: A Guide to the Development Process. Wayne S. Hyatt. 509p. 1985. text ed. 115.00 (*0-07-016723-0*) Shepards-McGraw.

Condominiums in the 1970s: A Selected Bibliography. Jean E. Koch. 1977. 6.00 (*0-686-19110-2*, 1252) CPL Biblios.

Condoms & Sexually Transmitted Diseases Including AIDS. 1991. lib. bdg. 75.00 (*0-8490-5147-9*) Gordon Pr.

Condoms in the Schools. Ed. by Mark Smith & Sarah Samuels. (Kaiser Forums Ser.). 135p. (Orig.). 1993. pap. 5.00 (*0-944525-13-X*) H J Kaiser.

Condon Notetaking & Transcription Skills: Advanced Course. Gregg Condon. 256p. (C). 1991. teacher ed 5.45 (*1-56118-043-2*); pap. text ed. 18.95 (*1-56118-353-9*); student ed 6.00 (*1-56118-356-3*); audio 142.00 (*1-56118-355-5*); 12.00 (*1-56118-045-9*) Paradigm MN.

Condoning the Killing: Ten Years of Massacres in El Salvador. Ed. by Ecumenical Program on Central America & the Caribbean Staff. (Illus.). 81p. 1990. pap. 5.95 (*0-918346-10-X*) EPICA.

Condor. Westberg Peters. LC 89-28270. (Wildlife Ser.). (Illus.). 48p. (J). (gr. 5). 1990. text ed. 12.95 (*0-89686-515-0*, Crstwood Hse) Silver Burdett Pr.

Condor & Other Stories. Sabine R. Ulibarri. LC 88-14648. 1989. pap. 9.50 (*0-934770-92-1*) Arte Publico.

Condor Conspiracy. Charlotte Yarborough. (Orig.). 1980. pap. 1.75 (*0-8439-0739-8*) Dorchester Pub Co.

Condor Dreams & Other Fictions. Gerald W. Haslam. LC 93-33531. (Western Literature Ser.). 216p. 1994. 24.95 (*0-87417-227-6*); pap. 13.95 (*0-87417-232-2*) U of Nev Pr.

Condorcet: Foundations of Social Choice & Political Theory. Ed. by Iain McLean & Fiona Hewitt. Tr. by Fiona Hewitt. LC 93-50634. 1994. 89.95 (*1-85898-068-2*, Pub. by E Elgar Pub UK) Ashgate Pub Co.

Condorcet: From Natural Philosophy to Social Mathematics. Keith M. Baker. LC 74-5725. 538p. (C). 1982. pap. text ed. 17.00 (*0-226-03533-6*) U Ch Pr.

Condorcet: Selected Writings. Ed. by Keith M. Baker. LC 75-38680. (Library of Liberal Arts: No. 159). 1976. pap. 12.81 (*0-672-60381-0*, Bobbs) Macmillan.

Condorcet Studies II. Ed. by David Williams. 183p. (C). 1988. text ed. 39.95 (*0-8204-0261-3*) P Lang Pubs.

***Condors: A Novel.** Ray Rosenbaum. LC 94-32681. 1995. 21.95 (*0-89141-478-9*, Lyford Bks) Presidio Pr.

Condor's Egg. Jonathan London. LC 93-31001. (Illus.). 32p. (J). 1994. 13.95 (*0-8118-0260-4*) Chronicle Bks.

***Condottieri.** Nicolo D'Alessandro. (Fine Editions Ser.). 1986. pap. 15.00 (*0-89304-651-5*) Cross-Cultrl NY.

Condrau, Gion, Festschrift: Depression - Medizinische, Kulturelle und Anthropologische Aspekte, Zuerich, 10.-11. Juni 1988. Ed. by A. Hicklin. (Journal: Daseinsanalyse, 1989: Vol. 6, No. 1-2). 148p. 1989. pap. 40.00 (*3-8055-4964-4*) S Karger.

Conduct a National Radio Talk Show Tour Without Leaving Your Home or Office...Without Paying a Cent for Air Time. Sheila Ring Danzig. Ed. by William Danzig. (How to Make People Buy Whatever You're Selling Whether They Know They Need It or Not Ser.). 11p. (Orig.). 1989. 49.00 (*0-9624333-5-7*); spiral bd. 39.95 (*0-9624333-6-5*) Natl Success.

Conduct & Character: Readings in Moral Theory. Mark Timmons. 245p. (C). 1990. pap. 20.95 (*0-534-12126-8*) Intl Thomson.

Conduct & Character: Readings in Moral Theory. 2nd ed. Mark Timmons. LC 94-541. 263p. 1995. pap. 21.95 (*0-534-23191-8*) Intl Thomson.

Conduct & the Weather see Problems in the Psychology of Reading

Conduct at the Bar & the Unwritten Laws of the Legal Profession. C. A. Oputa. LC 81-85780. xiv, 69p. 1982. reprint ed. lib. bdg. 28.00 (*0-912004-20-7*) W W Gaunt.

Conduct Better Job Interviews. Robert F. Wilson. (Business Success Ser.). 96p. 1991. pap. 4.95 (*0-8120-4580-7*) Barron.

Conduct Computerized Guidance Module, Competency-Based Career Guidance (CBCG) - Category C: Implementing. National Center for Research in Vocational Education Staff. 1985. 6.95 (*0-317-03864-8*, CG100C03) Ctr Educ Trng Employ.

Conduct Demonstrations. (EUITS Ser.: No. D-2). 54p. 1991. spiral bd. write for info. (*0-87683-508-6*) GP Pub.

Conduct Disorders & Social Maladjustments: Policies, Politics, & Programming. Frank H. Wood et al. 27p. 1991. 8.00 (*0-86586-197-8*, P338) Coun Exc Child.

Conduct Disorders in Childhood & Adolescence. Alan E. Kazdin. (Developmental Clinical Psychology & Psychiatry Ser.: Vol. 9). 160p. (Orig.). 1986. text ed. 37.00 (*0-8039-2750-9*); pap. text ed. 16.95 (*0-8039-2751-7*) Sage.

***Conduct Disorders in Childhood & Adolescence, Vol. 9.** 2nd ed. Alan E. Kazdin. LC 95-5295. (Developmental Clinical Psychology & Psychiatry Ser.: No. 9). (Illus.). 160p. 1995. 37.00 (*0-8039-7180-X*); pap. 16.95 (*0-8039-7181-8*) Sage.

***Conduct Disorders in Children & Adolescents: Etiology, Assessment, & Treatment.** Ed. by G. Pirooz Sholevar. LC 94-26150. 1994. boxed 49.95 (*0-88048-517-5*) Am Psychiatric.

Conduct Disorders of Childhood: Psychodynamics & Psychotherapy. Richard A. Gardner. LC 94-6855. 550p. 1994. pap. 40.00 (*0-933812-32-9*) Creative Therapeutics.

Conduct Expected: The Unwritten Rules for a Successful Business Career. William Lareau. 198p. 1986. pap. 12.95 (*0-8329-0443-0*) New Win Pub.

Conduct Independent Instruction. (EUITS Ser.: No. D-8). 56p. 1991. spiral bd. write for info. (*0-87683-514-0*) GP Pub.

Conduct Job - Shop Exercises. (EUITS Ser.: No. D-3). 86p. 1991. spiral bd. write for info. (*0-87683-509-4*) GP Pub.

Conduct Job & Task Analysis. (EUITS Ser.: No. A-2). 108p. 1991. spiral bd. 69.50 (*0-87683-502-7*) GP Pub.

Conduct Mock-up Training. (EUITS Ser.: No. D-5). 60p. 1991. spiral bd. write for info. (*0-87683-511-6*) GP Pub.

Conduct of a Just & Limited War. William V. O'Brien. LC 81-11883. 512p. 1981. text ed. 50.95 (*0-275-90693-0*, C0693, Praeger Pubs) Greenwood.

Conduct of American Foreign Policy. Herbert S. Levine. 1990. pap. text ed. write for info. (*0-07-037489-9*) McGraw.

Conduct of American Foreign Policy since World War II. Amos Yoder. (Government & Politics Ser.). (Illus.). 304p. 1985. text ed. 60.00 (*0-08-032773-7*, Pergamon Pr); pap. text ed. 19.95 (*0-08-032772-9*, Pergamon Pr) Elsevier.

Conduct of an Action. Williston & Rolls. 216p. 1982. 73.00 (*0-409-87710-7*) Butterworth Legal Pubs.

***Conduct of an Appeal.** John Sopinka & Mark Gelowitz. 296p. 1993. boxed 80.00 (*0-409-91172-0*, CN) Butterworth Legal Pubs.

Conduct of Industrial Relations. Peter D. Antony. 336p. (C). 1977. 60.00 (*0-85292-157-8*) St Mut.

Conduct of Lawsuits Out of & in Court: Practically Teaching, & Copiously Illustrating, the Preparation & Forensic Management of Litigated Cases of All Kinds. John C. Reed. LC 94-17732. xxvii, 434p. 1994. reprint ed. lib. bdg. 52.50 (*0-8377-2576-3*) Rothman.

Conduct of Life. Benedetto Croce. Tr. by A. Livingston. LC 67-30204. (Essay Index Reprint Ser.). 1977. 20.95 (*0-8369-0351-X*) Ayer.

Conduct of Life. Lewis Mumford. LC 51-12387. 342p. 1960. pap. 7.95 (*0-15-621600-0*, Harvest Bks) HarBrace.

Conduct of Life. Ralph Waldo Emerson. (Notable American Authors Ser.). 1992. reprint ed. lib. bdg. 75.00 (*0-7812-2812-3*) Rprt Serv.

Conduct of Life see Essays & Lectures

Conduct of Life, & Other Addresses. Richard B. Haldane. LC 68-16936. (Essay Index Reprint Ser.). 1977. 17.95 (*0-8369-0507-5*) Ayer.

Conduct of Life; or, the Universal Order of Confucius. Chung Yung Staff. 1972. lib. bdg. 79.95 (*0-87968-497-6*) Krishna Pr.

C

An Asterisk (*) at the beginning of an entry indicates that the title is appearing in BIP for the first time.

An Asterisk (*) at the beginning of an entry indicates that the title is appearing in BIP for the first time.

1529

Confabulations: Creating False Memories, Destroying Families. Eleanor Goldstein. Ed. by Kevin Farmer. 348p. (Orig.). (C). 1992. pap. 14.95 (*0-89777-144-3*, Upton Bks) Sirs Inc.

*__Confectionary International Market.__ 250p. (Orig.). 1995. pap. 3,195.00 (*0-7605-2215-4*) Rector Pr.

*__Confectionary Market International Handbook, 2 vols., Set.__ (Illus.). 525p. (Orig.). 1994. pap. 8,900.00 (*0-7605-0943-3*) Rector Pr.

Confectioner's Art. (Illus.). 92p. 1988. 16.00 (*0-88321-058-4*) Am Craft.

Confectionery Manufacturers. Ed. by ICC Information Group Staff. 1987. 595.00 (*1-85319-034-9*, Pub. by ICC Info Group Ltd UK) St Mut.

Confederacion Latinoamericana: Edificacion de un Proyecto Para il Futuro. Aline Frambes-Buxeda. (Libros Homines Ser.). (Illus.). 224p. (SPA.). (C). 1990. pap. text ed. 15.00 (*0-9623590-1-7*) Libros-Ediciones.

Confederacy. Charles P. Roland. LC 60-12573. (Chicago History of American Civilization Ser.). (Illus.). 1962. pap. text ed. 11.95 (*0-226-72451-4*, CHAC18) U Ch Pr.

Confederacy: Guide to the Archives of the Confederate States of America. Henry P. Beers. LC 86-8362. 536p. 1986. reprint ed. text ed. 25.00 (*0-911333-18-5*, 100010) National Archives & Recs.

Confederacy As a Revolutionary Experience. Emory M. Thomas. LC 91-10406. 170p. 1991. reprint ed. pap. 9.95 (*0-87249-780-1*) U of SC Pr.

Confederacy Is on Her Way up the Spout: Letters to South Carolina, 1861-1864. Ed. by J. Roderick Heller, III & Carolynn A. Heller. LC 91-36585. (Illus.). 168p. 1992. 19.95 (*0-8203-1434-X*) U of Ga Pr.

Confederacy of Dunces. John K. Toole. 416p. 1987. pap. 11.95 (*0-8021-3020-8*) Grove-Atltic.

Confederacy of Dunces. John K. Toole. LC 79-20190. 352p. 1980. 22.95 (*0-8071-0657-7*) La State U Pr.

Confederacy of Dunces. John K. Toole. 19.95 (*0-8488-1207-7*) Amereon Ltd.

*__Confederacy of Dunces.__ John K. Toole. LC 94-30317. 1994. 9.99 (*0-517-12270-7*) Random Hse Value.

*__Confederacy of the Dead.__ Ed. by Richard Gilliam et al. 464p. (Orig.). 1995. mass mkt. 5.99 (*0-451-45477-4*, ROC) NAL-Dutton.

Confederacy of the Dead. Ed. by Martin H. Greenberg et al. 480p. (Orig.). 1993. pap. 12.00 (*0-451-45249-6*, ROC) NAL-Dutton.

Confederacy's Fighting Chaplain: Father John B. Bannon. Phillip T. Tucker. LC 91-24815. (Illus.). 272p. (C). 1992. 32.95 (*0-8173-0573-4*) U of Ala Pr.

Confederacy's Last Hurrah: Spring Hill, Franklin, & Nashville. Wiley Sword. (Modern War Studies). Orig. Title: Embrace an Angry Wind. 528p. (C). 1993. reprint ed. pap. 14.95 (*0-7006-0650-5*) U Pr of KS.

*__Confederados: Old South Immigrants in Brazil.__ Ed. by Cyrus B. Dawsey & James M. Dawsey. (Illus.). 296p. 1995. text ed. 34.95 (*0-614-01953-2*) U of Ala Pr.

Confederate. Jerry Ahern. 1983. pap. 3.25 (*0-8217-1285-3*) Zebra.

Confederate Air Force Ghost Squadron. (Illus.). 48p. 1989. pap. 5.00 (*0-685-24811-9*) Confederate Air.

Confederate & Southern States Bonds. Crover Criswell, Jr. (Illus.). 400p. 1995. 40.00 (*0-931960-37-1*) BNR Pr.

Confederate & Southern States Currency. 3rd ed. Grover C. Criswell, Jr. (Illus.). 320p. 1992. 40.00 (*0-931960-20-7*) BNR Pr.

Confederate & Union Buttons of the Gulf Coast 1861-1865. Dan Jenkins. (Illus.). 58p. 1983. pap. 6.00 (*0-914334-08-5*) Museum Mobile.

Confederate Arkansas: The People & Policies of a Frontier State in Wartime. Michael B. Dougan. LC 76-40053. 176p. 1991. pap. 14.50 (*0-8173-0522-X*) U of Ala Pr.

Confederate Arms. William A. Albaugh, III & Edward N. Simmons. (William Albaugh Collection Ser.). (Illus.). 278p. 1993. reprint ed. 30.00 (*1-56837-264-7*) Broadfoot.

Confederate Battle Stories: The Civil War in Stories by Thomas Wolfe, F. Scott Fitzgerald, Owen Wister, & Other Writers. Ed. by Martin Greenberg et al. 196p. 1992. 18.95 (*0-87483-192-X*); pap. 9.95 (*0-87483-191-1*) August Hse.

Confederate Belles - Lettres. R. B. Harwell. 1974. 250.00 (*0-87968-468-2*) Gordon Pr.

Confederate Blockade Running Through Bermuda, 1861-1865: Letters & Cargo Manifests. Frank E. Vandiver. (History - United States Ser.). 155p. 1993. reprint ed. lib. bdg. 69.00 (*0-7812-4902-3*) Rprt Serv.

Confederate Brass-Framed Colt & Whitney. William A. Albaugh, III. (William Albaugh Collection Ser.). (Illus.). 105p. 1993. reprint ed. 25.00 (*1-56837-265-5*) Broadfoot.

Confederate Broadside Poems: An Annotated Descriptive Bibliography. William Moss. (Illus.). 225p. 1988. text ed. 55.00 (*0-313-27704-4*) Greenwood.

Confederate Calendar, Vol. 8. Lawrence T. Jones, III. (Illus.). (Orig.). 1982. pap. 5.95 (*0-943030-00-5*) Confed Calendar.

Confederate Camp Cooking. rev. ed. Patricia B. Mitchell. 1991. pap. 4.00 (*0-925117-46-3*) Mitchells.

Confederate Cannon Foundries. Larry J. Daniel & Riley W. Gunter. Ed. by Pioneer Press. LC 76-62878. 1977. 12.95 (*0-913150-38-X*) Pioneer Pr.

Confederate Carbines & Musketoons. John M. Murphy. (Illus.). 224p. 1986. 45.00 (*0-9616425-0-5*); 125.00 (*0-9616425-1-3*) J M Murphy.

*__Confederate Carpetbaggers.__ fac. ed. Daniel E. Sutherland. LC 87-29945. 378p. 1988. reprint ed. pap. 107.80 (*0-7837-7745-0*, 2047501) Bks Demand.

Confederate Cavalry West of the River. Stephen B. Oates. LC 61-10044. (Illus.). 262p. 1992. reprint ed. pap. 12.95 (*0-292-71152-2*) U of Tex Pr.

Confederate Challenge: One Thousand One Questions & Answers about the War of the Rebellion. John M. Hightower. (Illus.). 160p. (Orig.). 1992. pap. 10.00 (*0-9623572-6-X*) Rockbridge Pub.

*__Confederate Chaplain William Edward Wiatt: An Annotated Diary.__ Alex L. Wiatt. (Virginia Civil War Battles & Leaders Ser.). (Illus.). 255p. 1994. 25.00 (*1-56190-064-8*) H E Howard.

Confederate Charleston: An Illustrated History of the City & the People During the Civil War. Robert N. Rosen. LC 94-13751. 1994. write for info. (*0-87249-991-X*) U of SC Pr.

Confederate Cherokees: John Drew's Regiment of Mounted Rifles. W. Craig Gaines. LC 88-31358. (Illus.). 200p. 1989. 22.95 (*0-8071-1488-X*) La State U Pr.

Confederate Chronicle of Capt. Croft's Flying Artillery Battery, Columbus, Georgia. William A. Forbes. 1994. 24.95 (*0-89029-319-8*) Morningside Bkshop.

Confederate Colonel & Cherokee Chief: The Life of William Holland Thomas. E. Stanly Godbold, Jr. & Mattie U. Russell. LC 90-32971. 224p. 1990. 24.95 (*0-87049-664-6*) U of Tenn Pr.

Confederate Commissary General: Lucius Bellinger Northrop & the Subsistence Bureau of the Southern Army. Jerold N. Moore. (Illus.). 256p. (C). 1995. text ed. 24.95 (*0-942597-75-3*) White Mane Pub.

Confederate Constitution of 1861: An Inquiry into American Constitutionalism. Marshall L. DeRosa. 192p. (Orig.). (C). 1991. text ed. 32.50 (*0-8262-0806-1*); pap. 16.95 (*0-8262-0812-6*) U of Mo Pr.

Confederate Constitutions. Charles R. Lee, Jr. LC 73-16628. 225p. 1974. reprint ed. text ed. 52.50 (*0-8371-7201-2*, LECC, Greenwood Pr) Greenwood.

Confederate Cookbook. 1990. reprint ed. 2.50 (*0-913150-09-6*) Pioneer Pr.

Confederate Death Roster at Gettysburg. Krick. 1993. 22.50 (*0-89029-056-3*) Morningside Bkshop.

Confederate Echoes. Albert Goodloe. 1983. reprint ed. 24.95 (*0-89201-105-X*) Zenger Pub.

*__Confederate Edged Weapons.__ William A. Albaugh, III. 198p. 1993. 30.00 (*1-884849-05-9*) R&R Bks.

Confederate Edged Weapons. William S. Albaugh, III. (William Albaugh Collection Ser.). (Illus.). 224p. 1993. reprint ed. 30.00 (*1-56837-267-1*) Broadfoot.

Confederate Faces: Photographs of Confederates. William A. Albaugh, III. (William Albaugh Collection Ser.). (Illus.). 229p. 1993. reprint ed. 40.00 (*1-56837-260-4*) Broadfoot.

Confederate Field Manual with Photographic Supplement: The Field Manual for the Use of Officers on Ordnance Duty. C. S. Ordnance Bureau Staff. (Illus.). 176p. (C). 1984. reprint ed. 14.95 (*0-939631-02-4*) Thomas Publications.

Confederate First & Second Missouri Brigades & from Wakarusa to Appomattox. Robert S. Bevier. (Illus.). 500p. 1985. reprint ed. 24.50 (*0-940435-00-4*) Inland Print Ltd.

Confederate Florida: The Road to Olustee. William H. Nulty. 1990. pap. 19.95 (*0-8173-0748-6*) U of Ala Pr.

Confederate General Service Accoutrement Plates. Lon W. Keim et al. Ed. by Stephen W. Sylvia & Michael J. O'Donnell. (Illus.). 250p. 1987. 34.95 (*0-317-56465-X*) Moss Pubns VA.

Confederate General, Vol. 2: Cobb, Thomas-Goggin James. Ed. by Julie Hoffman. (Confederate General Ser.). 240p. 1991. 29.95 (*0-918678-64-1*) Natl Hist Soc.

Confederate General, Vol. 3: Gordon, George - Jordan, Thomas. Ed. by William C. Davis & Julie Hoffman. 221p. 1991. 29.95 (*0-918678-65-X*) Natl Hist Soc.

Confederate General, Vol. 4: Kelly, J. H. - Payne, W. H. F. Ed. by William C. Davis & Julie Hoffman. 225p. 1991. 29.95 (*0-918678-67-6*) Natl Hist Soc.

Confederate General, Vol. 6: Steuart, G. H. - Zollicoffer, F. K. Ed. by William C. Davis & Julie Hoffman. 250p. 1992. 29.95 (*0-918678-68-4*) Natl Hist Soc.

*__Confederate Generals of Georgia & Their Burial Sites.__ Robert H. Kerlin. (Illus.). 200p. 1994. 23.50 (*1-881454-04-5*) Amer Hist Bks.

Confederate Gestures: Search for Method in Indian Literature Studies. Ed. by Charu S. Singh. 1993. 30.00 (*81-7045-082-9*, Pub. by Associated Pub Hse II) Advent Bks Div.

Confederate Ghosts. Susan Crites. 48p. 1994. pap. 5.00 (*1-881562-05-0*) Butternut Pubns.

Confederate Goliath: The Battle of Fort Fisher. Rod Gragg. LC 90-38095. (Illus.). 400p. 1994. pap. 14.95 (*0-8071-1917-2*) La State U Pr.

Confederate Governors. Ed. by W. Buck Yearns. LC 84-154. 296p. 1985. 27.50 (*0-8203-0719-X*) U of Ga Pr.

Confederate Guns of Navarro County. John Spencer. 152p. 1986. 20.00 (*0-942211-48-0*) Olde Soldier Bks.

Confederate Handguns. William A. Albaugh, III et al. (William Albaugh Collection Ser.). (Illus.). 250p. 1993. reprint ed. 30.00 (*1-56837-261-2*) Broadfoot.

Confederate History. Ed. by Clement A. Evans. (Confederate Military History Extended Edition Ser.: Vol. I). 737p. 1987. reprint ed. 50.00 (*1-56837-020-2*) Broadfoot.

Confederate Home Cooking. rev. ed. Patricia B. Mitchell. 1991. pap. 4.00 (*0-925117-45-5*) Mitchells.

Confederate Hospitals on the Move: Samuel H. Stout & the Army of Tennessee. Glenna R. Schroeder-Lein. LC 93-25612. 226p. 1993. 29.95 (*0-87249-964-2*) U of SC Pr.

Confederate Image: Prints of the Lost Cause. Mark E. Neely, Jr. et al. LC 86-30797. (Illus.). xiv, 258p. 1987. 39.95 (*0-8078-1742-2*) U of NC Pr.

Confederate Imprints: A Bibliography of Southern Publications from Secession to Surrender. T. Michael Parrish & Robert M. Willingham. (Illus.). 1133p. 1987. 95.00 (*0-318-37956-2*, PA-999-2) Jenkins.

Confederate Imprints: A Reel Index to the Microfilm Collection. 14p. 1974. 25.00 (*0-89235-051-2*) Res Pubns CT.

Confederate Infantryman 1861-65. Ian Drury. (Warrior Ser.). (Illus.). 64p. 1993. pap. 12.95 (*1-85532-401-6*, 9605, Pub. by Osprey UK) Stackpole.

Confederate Invasion of New Mexico & Arizona 1861-1862. Robert L. Kerby. LC 58-14001. (Illus.). 24.95 (*0-87026-055-3*) Westernlore.

Confederate Lady Comes of Age: The Journal of Pauline DeCaradeuc Heyward, 1863-1888. Pauline D. Heyward. Ed. by Mary D. Robertson. (Women's Diaries & Letters of the Nineteenth-Century South Ser.). (Illus.). 181p. 1992. text ed. 29.95 (*0-87249-782-8*) U of SC Pr.

Confederate Letters & Diaries, 1861-1865. Ed. by Walbrook D. Swank. (Illus.). 198p. (C). 1992. pap. 17.95 (*0-942597-25-7*, Burd St Pr) White Mane Pub.

Confederate Mail Carrier: From Missouri to Arkansas Through Mississippi, Alabama, Georgia, & Tennessee. An Unwritten Leaf of the Civil War. James Bradley. (Illus.). 318p. 1990. reprint ed. pap. 21.50 (*1-55613-349-9*) Heritage Bk.

Confederate Military History: Cumulative Index, 2 vols. Ed. by Robert S. Bridgers. 1159p. 1987. Vol. II, I-Z. write for info. (*1-56837-003-2*) Broadfoot.

Confederate Military History Extended Edition, 19 vols., Set. Ed. by Clement A. Evans. (Illus.). 1988. reprint ed. 750.00 (*0-916107-62-0*) Broadfoot.

Confederate Mobile. Arthur W. Bergeron, Jr. LC 91-15776. 304p. 1991. 29.50 (*0-87805-512-6*) U Pr of Miss.

*__Confederate Monuments at Gettysburg.__ Martin. 1995. pap. text ed. 14.95 (*0-938289-48-9*) Combined Bks.

Confederate Monuments at Gettysburg: The Gettysburg Battle Monuments, Vol. 1. David G. Martin. LC 85-82570. (Illus.). 295p. (C). 1986. 25.00 (*0-944413-01-3*) Longstreet Hse.

Confederate Morale & Church Propaganda. James W. Silver. 11.25 (*0-8446-1407-6*) Peter Smith.

Confederate Nation Eighteen Sixty-One to Eighteen Sixty-Five. Emory M. Thomas. Ed. by Richard B. Morris & Henry S. Commager. LC 76-26255. (New American Nation Ser.). (Illus.). 416p. 1981. pap. text ed. 13.00 (*0-06-131965-1*, TB 1965, Torch) HarpC.

Confederate Nation Series. John McGlone & Archie McDonald. 1992. 23.00 (*0-9631963-9-1*) So Herit Pr.

Confederate Navy: A Pictorial History. Philip V. Stern. (Illus.). 256p. 1992. reprint ed. pap. 16.95 (*0-306-80488-3*) Da Capo.

Confederate Negro: Virginia's Craftsmen & Military Laborers, 1861-1865. James H. Brewer. LC 75-86479. 234p. reprint ed. pap. 66.70 (*0-685-12282-4*, 2026191) Bks Demand.

Confederate, No. 2: Ride Beyond Glory. Forrest A. Randolph. pap. 2.50 (*0-8217-1357-4*) Zebra.

Confederate Nurse: The Diary of Ada W. Bacot 1860-1863. Ed. by Jean V. Berlin. LC 93-30098. 144p. 1993. 29.95 (*0-87249-970-7*) U of SC Pr.

Confederate Operations in Canada & New York. Headley. LC 84-2677. (Collector's Library of the Civil War). (gr. 7 up). 1984. lib. bdg. 26.60 (*0-8094-4283-3*) Time-Life.

Confederate Ordeal. (Civil War Ser.). (Illus.). 176p. 1984. 19.93 (*0-8094-4728-2*); lib. bdg. 25.93 (*0-8094-4729-0*) Time-Life.

Confederate Order of Battle: The Army of Northern Virginia. F. Ray Sibley, Jr. (Illus.). 400p. (C). 1995. text ed. 80.00 (*0-942597-73-7*) White Mane Pub.

Confederate Portraits. Gamaliel Bradford. LC 68-29193. (Essay Index Reprint Ser.). 1977. 31.95 (*0-8369-0241-6*) Ayer.

Confederate Portraits. Gamaliel Bradford. (History - United States Ser.). 291p. 1992. reprint ed. lib. bdg. 79.00 (*0-7812-6173-2*) Rprt Serv.

Confederate Privateers. William M. Robinson. 1994. pap. 15.95 (*1-57003-005-7*) U of SC Pr.

Confederate Propaganda in Europe, 1861-1865. Charles P. Cullop. LC 69-12937. 1969. 10.95 (*0-87024-106-0*) U of Miami Pr.

Confederate Purchasing Operations Aboard. Samuel B. Thompson. 11.75 (*0-8446-4055-7*) Peter Smith.

Confederate Raider: Raphael Semmes of the "Alabama" John M. Taylor. (Illus.). 336p. 1994. 24.95 (*0-02-881086-4*) Brasseys Inc.

*__Confederate Raider: Raphael Semmes of the "Alabama"__ John M. Taylor. (Illus.). 336p. 1996. pap. 17.95 (*1-57488-027-6*) Brasseys Inc.

*__Confederate Raider in the North Pacific: The Saga of the C.S.S. "Shenandoah," 1864-65.__ Murray Morgan. (Illus.). 352p. Date not set. reprint ed. pap. 19.95 (*0-87422-123-4*) Wash St U Pr.

Confederate Reader. Richard Harwell. 1992. 19.95 (*0-88029-757-3*) Marboro Bks.

Confederate Reader. Ed. by Richard B. Harwell. 1989. pap. 9.95 (*0-486-25980-3*) Dover.

Confederate Receipt Book. 1,863th ed. 12.95 (*0-8488-0007-9*) Amereon Ltd.

Confederate Receipt Book: A Compilation of Over One Hundred Receipts, Adapted to the Times. Ed. by E. Merton Coulter. LC 60-9896. 38p. 1960. pap. 3.95 (*0-8203-0561-8*) U of Ga Pr.

Confederate Records of the State of Georgia, 1860-1868, 6 vols., Set. Georgia General Assembly Staff. Ed. by Allen D. Candler. LC 78-155622. reprint ed. 625.00 (*0-404-07290-9*) AMS Pr.

Confederate Regular Army. Richard P. Weinert, Jr. (Illus.). 131p. 1991. 24.95 (*0-942597-21-4*) White Mane Pub.

Confederate Regular Army. deluxe ed. Richard P. Weinert, Jr. LC 91-2216. (First Edition Library). (Illus.). 131p. (C). 1991. 39.95 (*0-942597-27-3*) White Mane Pub.

Confederate Republic: A Revolution Against Politics. George C. Rable. LC 93-36491. (Civil War America Ser.). (Illus.). xii, 428p. (C). 1994. 34.95 (*0-8078-2144-6*) U of NC Pr.

Confederate Research Sources: A Guide to Archive Collections. James C. Neagles. LC 86-72004. (Illus.). 286p. (Orig.). 1986. pap. 14.95 (*0-916489-16-7*) Ancestry.

Confederate Rifles & Muskets. John M. Murphy & Howard M. Madaus. LC 92-75534. 700p. Date not set. 99.95 (*1-882824-01-6*) Graphic Pubs.

Confederate Roll of Honor. John M. Carroll. 1976. 19.95 (*0-8488-0049-4*); pap. 12.95 (*0-8488-0048-6*) Amereon Ltd.

Confederate Roll of Honor: Missouri. Intro. by Leslie Anders. (Illus.). 180p. 1989. lib. bdg. 29.00 (*0-9624743-0-4*) WCMGS&L.

Confederate Sheet-Music Imprints. Frank W. Hoogerwerf. LC 84-80735. (I.S.A.M. Monographs: No. 21). (Illus.). 170p. (Orig.). 1984. pap. 12.00 (*0-914678-23-X*) Inst Am Music.

Confederate Shipbuilding. William N. Still, Jr. LC 68-54090. 122p. reprint ed. pap. 34.80 (*0-317-08226-4*, 2005201) Bks Demand.

Confederate Soldier Artists & Their Art of the Civil. Lauralee Stevenson. (Illus.). 136p. (C). 1996. text ed. 40.00 (*0-942597-79-6*) White Mane Pub.

Confederate Son. Hugh D. McCormick. 260p. 1993. 17.95 (*0-9636351-0-7*) Shenandoah Univ.

Confederate Staff Officers 1861-1865. Joseph H. Crute, Jr. 267p. 1984. 25.00 (*0-942211-33-2*) Olde Soldier Bks.

Confederate States Lithographs Issues, Set. Brian M. Green. (Illus.). 66p. 1978. 6.40 (*0-911989-06-4*) Philatelic Found.

Confederate States Marine Corps: The Rebel Leathernecks. rev. ed. Ralph W. Donnelly. LC 89-24824. (Illus.). 340p. (C). 1990. 24.95 (*0-942597-13-3*) White Mane Pub.

Confederate States Medical & Surgical Journal. Samuel P. Moore. (American Civil War Medical Ser.: No. 12). 272p. 1992. reprint ed. 95.00 (*0-930405-40-4*) Norman SF.

Confederate States of America. John C. Schwab. 1972. 59.95 (*0-7968-9269-5*) Gordon Pr.

Confederate States of America Currency, 1861-1865, No. 5: Handbook. Douglas B. Ball. 35p. 1986. 6.00 (*0-685-72027-6*); boxed, sl. 20.00 (*0-685-72028-4*) Am Numismatic.

Confederate States of America, Markings & Postal History of Richmond, Virginia. Peter W. Powell. Ed. by Leonard H. Hartmann. LC 87-32110. (Illus.). 188p. 1987. 50.00 (*0-917528-09-3*) L H Hartmann.

Confederate States of America Philatelic Subject Index & Bibliography, 1862-1984. Richard H. Byne. Ed. by Leonard H. Hartmann. LC 85-70099. (Illus.). 352p. 1986. 45.00 (*0-917528-08-5*) L H Hartmann.

Confederate States of America Two Cent Red Jack Intaglio Stamp. Brian M. Green. (Illus.). 62p. 1983. pap. 5.50 (*0-911989-12-9*) Philatelic Found.

Confederate States Paper Money. 8th ed. Arlie Slabaugh. LC 91-72196. (Illus.). 128p. 1993. pap. 12.95 (*0-87341-242-7*) Krause Pubns.

Confederate States Paper Money. A. Slabaugh. LC 89-91827. (Illus.). 1990. reprint ed. pap. 10.00 (*0-685-36399-6*) S J Durst.

Confederate States Typographs Issues. Brian M. Green. 40p. 1981. 5.00 (*0-911989-05-6*) Philatelic Found.

Confederate Strategy from Shiloh to Vicksburg. Archer Jones. LC 61-7085. 258p. (C). 1991. pap. 9.95 (*0-8071-1716-1*) La State U Pr.

Confederate Supply. Richard D. Goff. LC 68-57274. (Duke Historical Publications). 287p. reprint ed. pap. 81.80 (*0-317-08166-7*, 2017904) Bks Demand.

Confederate Surgeon. (Illus.). 152p. 1985. 25.00 (*0-9619508-1-1*) W R Scaife.

Confederate Surgeon: The Personal Recollections of E. A. Craighill. Peter W. Houck. (Virginia Civil War Battles & Leaders Ser.). (Illus.). 106p. 1989. 19.95 (*0-930919-91-2*) H E Howard.

*__Confederate Surrender & Parole, Jacksonport & Wittsburg, Arkansas, May & June, 1865.__ Jerry Ponder & Victor Ponder. (Orig.). (C). Date not set. pap. text ed. 15.00 (*0-9623922-4-3*) Ponder Bks.

*__Confederate Underwater Warfare: An Illustrated History.__ Lewis S. Schafer. 224p. 1995. lib. bdg. 28.50 (*0-7864-0114-1*) McFarland & Co.

Confederate Upper Battery Site, Grand Gulf, Mississippi: Excavations, 1982. William C. Wright. LC 84-62001. (Mississippi Department of Archives & History Archaeological Reports: No. 13). (Illus.). (Orig.). 1984. pap. 5.00 (*0-938896-38-5*) Mississippi Archives.

Confederate Veteran, 40 vols. Ed. by S. A. Cunningham. (Illus.). 20000p. 1990. reprint ed. 1,200.00 (*0-916107-14-0*) Broadfoot.

Confederate Veteran Index, 3 vols, Set. Ed. by Louis Manarin. 1990. 300.00 (*0-916107-15-9*) Broadfoot.

Confederate Veteran Magazine, Vol. Eight: January 1900-December 1900. Ed. by S. A. Cunningham. (Illus.). 560p. 1988. reprint ed. 40.00 (*1-56837-059-8*) Broadfoot.

Confederate Veteran Magazine, Vol. Eighteen: January 1910-December 1910. Ed. by S. A. Cunningham. (Illus.). 592p. 1989. reprint ed. 40.00 (*1-56837-069-5*) Broadfoot.

Confederate Veteran Magazine, Vol. Fifteen: January 1907-December 1907. Ed. by S. A. Cunningham. (Illus.). 576p. 1988. reprint ed. 40.00 (*1-56837-066-0*) Broadfoot.

Confederate Veteran Magazine, Vol. Five: January 1897-December 1897. Ed. by S. A. Cunningham. (Illus.). 642p. 1988. reprint ed. 40.00 (*1-56837-056-3*) Broadfoot.

C

1530

An Asterisk (*) at the beginning of an entry indicates that the title is appearing in BIP for the first time.

Confederate Veteran Magazine, Vol. Four: January 1896-December 1896. Ed. by S. A. Cunningham. (Illus.). 452p. 1988. reprint ed. 40.00 (*1-56837-055-5*) Broadfoot.

Confederate Veteran Magazine, Vol. Nine: January 1901-December 1901. Ed. by S. A. Cunningham. (Illus.). 574p. 1988. reprint ed. 40.00 (*1-56837-060-1*) Broadfoot.

Confederate Veteran Magazine, Vol. Nineteen: January 1911-December 1911. Ed. by S. A. Cunningham. (Illus.). 600p. 1989. reprint ed. 40.00 (*1-56837-070-9*) Broadfoot.

Confederate Veteran Magazine, Vol. One: January 1893-December 1893. Ed. by S. A. Cunningham. (Illus.). 386p. 1988. reprint ed. 40.00 (*1-56837-052-0*) Broadfoot.

Confederate Veteran Magazine, Vol. Seven: January 1899-December 1899. Ed. by S. A. Cunningham. (Illus.). 576p. 1988. reprint ed. 40.00 (*1-56837-058-X*) Broadfoot.

Confederate Veteran Magazine, Vol. Seventeen: January 1909-December 1909. Ed. by S. A. Cunningham. (Illus.). 624p. 1989. reprint ed. 40.00 (*1-56837-068-7*) Broadfoot.

Confederate Veteran Magazine, Vol. Six: January 1898-December 1898. Ed. by S. A. Cunningham. (Illus.). 594p. 1988. reprint ed. 40.00 (*1-56837-057-1*) Broadfoot.

Confederate Veteran Magazine, Vol. Sixteen: January 1908-December 1908. Ed. by S. A. Cunningham. (Illus.). 672p. 1988. reprint ed. 40.00 (*1-56837-067-9*) Broadfoot.

Confederate Veteran Magazine, Vol. Ten: January 1902-December 1902. Ed. by S. A. Cunningham. (Illus.). 575p. 1988. reprint ed. 40.00 (*1-56837-061-X*) Broadfoot.

Confederate Veteran Magazine, Vol. Three: January 1895-December 1895. Ed. by S. A. Cunningham. (Illus.). 402p. 1988. reprint ed. 40.00 (*1-56837-054-7*) Broadfoot.

Confederate Veteran Magazine, Vol. Twenty: January 1912-December 1912. Ed. by S. A. Cunningham. (Illus.). 592p. 1989. reprint ed. 40.00 (*1-56837-071-7*) Broadfoot.

Confederate Veteran Magazine, Vol. Twenty-One: January 1913-December 1913. Ed. by S. A. Cunningham. (Illus.). 608p. 1989. reprint ed. 40.00 (*1-56837-072-5*) Broadfoot.

Confederate Veteran Magazine, Vol. Twenty Three: January 1915-December 1915. Ed. by S. A. Cunningham. (Illus.). 576p. 1989. reprint ed. 40.00 (*1-56837-074-1*) Broadfoot.

Confederate Veteran Magazine, Vol. Twenty Two: January 1914-December 1914. Ed. by S. A. Cunningham. (Illus.). 576p. 1989. reprint ed. 40.00 (*1-56837-073-3*) Broadfoot.

Confederate Veteran Magazine, Vol. Two: January 1894-December 1894. Ed. by S. A. Cunningham. (Illus.). 386p. 1988. reprint ed. 40.00 (*1-56837-053-9*) Broadfoot.

Confederate Veteran Magazine, Vol. 24: January 1916-December 1916. Ed. by S. A. Cunningham. (Illus.). 576p. 1989. reprint ed. 40.00 (*1-56837-075-X*) Broadfoot.

Confederate Veteran Magazine, Vol. 25: January 1917-December 1917. Ed. by S. A. Cunningham. (Illus.). 580p. 1989. reprint ed. 40.00 (*1-56837-076-8*) Broadfoot.

Confederate Veteran Magazine, Vol. 26: January 1918-December 1918. Ed. by S. A. Cunningham. (Illus.). 544p. 1989. reprint ed. 40.00 (*1-56837-077-6*) Broadfoot.

Confederate Veteran Magazine, Vol. 27: January 1919-December 1919. Ed. by S. A. Cunningham. (Illus.). 480p. 1989. reprint ed. 40.00 (*1-56837-078-4*) Broadfoot.

Confederate Veteran Magazine, Vol. 28: January 1920-December 1920. Ed. by S. A. Cunningham. (Illus.). 480p. 1989. reprint ed. 40.00 (*1-56837-079-2*) Broadfoot.

Confederate Veteran Magazine, Vol. 29: January 1921-December 1921. Ed. by S. A. Cunningham. (Illus.). 448p. 1989. reprint ed. 40.00 (*1-56837-080-6*) Broadfoot.

Confederate Veteran Magazine, Vol. 30: January 1922-December 1922. Ed. by S. A. Cunningham. (Illus.). 480p. 1989. reprint ed. 40.00 (*1-56837-081-4*) Broadfoot.

Confederate Veteran Magazine, Vol. 31: January 1923-December 1923. Ed. by S. A. Cunningham. (Illus.). 480p. 1989. reprint ed. 40.00 (*1-56837-082-2*) Broadfoot.

Confederate Veteran Magazine, Vol. 32: January 1924-December 1924. Ed. by S. A. Cunningham. (Illus.). 488p. 1989. reprint ed. 40.00 (*1-56837-083-0*) Broadfoot.

Confederate Veteran Magazine, Vol. 33: January 1925-December 1925. Ed. by S. A. Cunningham. (Illus.). 480p. 1989. reprint ed. 40.00 (*1-56837-084-9*) Broadfoot.

Confederate Veteran Magazine, Vol. 34: January 1926-December 1926. Ed. by S. A. Cunningham. (Illus.). 480p. 1989. reprint ed. 40.00 (*1-56837-085-7*) Broadfoot.

Confederate Veteran Magazine, Vol. 35: January 1927-December 1927. Ed. by S. A. Cunningham. (Illus.). 480p. 1989. reprint ed. 40.00 (*1-56837-086-5*) Broadfoot.

Confederate Veteran Magazine, Vol. 36: January 1928-December 1928. Ed. by S. A. Cunningham. (Illus.). 480p. 1989. reprint ed. 40.00 (*1-56837-087-3*) Broadfoot.

Confederate Veteran Magazine, Vol. 37: January 1929-December 1929. Ed. by S. A. Cunningham. (Illus.). 480p. 1989. reprint ed. 40.00 (*1-56837-088-1*) Broadfoot.

Confederate Veteran Magazine, Vol. 38: January 1930-December 1930. Ed. by S. A. Cunningham. (Illus.). 488p. 1989. reprint ed. 40.00 (*1-56837-089-X*) Broadfoot.

Confederate Veteran Magazine, Vol. 39: January 1931-December 1931. Ed. by S. A. Cunningham. (Illus.). 480p. 1990. reprint ed. 40.00 (*1-56837-090-3*) Broadfoot.

Confederate Veteran Magazine, Vol. 40: January 1932-December 1932. Ed. by S. A. Cunningham. (Illus.). 448p. 1990. reprint ed. 40.00 (*1-56837-091-1*) Broadfoot.

Confederate Vixen. Teresa Howard. 432p. 1993. mass mkt. 4.50 (*0-8217-4342-2*) Zebra.

Confederate War Journal, 2 vols., Set. Marcus J. Wright. Ed. by Phillip A. Sperry & Joe R. Goss. (Illus.). 420p. 1993. reprint ed. 139.95 (*1-56869-033-9*) Oldbuck Pr.

Confederate War Poems. 6th ed. Walter B. Jones. 77p. 1951. reprint ed. 3.95 (*0-931709-00-8*) B Coats.

Confederate War Stories 1861, 1865. 2nd ed. Walbrook D. Swank. LC 91-91145. (Civil War Heritage Ser.: Vol. I). (Illus.). 109p. (C). 1993. pap. 12.00 (*0-942597-54-0*, Burd St Pr) White Mane Pub.

Confederate Wizards of the Saddle: Being Reminiscences & Observations of One Who Rode with Morgan. Bennett H. Young. (American Biography Ser.). 633p. 1991. reprint ed. lib. bdg. 109.00 (*0-7812-8433-3*) Rprt Serv.

Confederate Woman of New River Border Country. Patricia G. Johnson. (Illus.). 80p. (Orig.). (YA). 1993. pap. 12.00 (*1-878188-03-8*) Walpa Pub.

Confederate Women. Bell I. Wiley. LC 74-5995. (Contributions in American History Ser.: No. 38). (Illus.). xiv, 204p. 1975. text ed. 49.95 (*0-8371-7534-8*, WCW/, Greenwood Pr) Greenwood.

***Confederate Women of Arkansas: Memorial Reminiscences.** Date not set. 20.00 (*0-943099-09-9*) M&M Pr.

Confederates. Thomas Keneally. LC 80-7606. 448p. 1987. reprint ed. pap. 12.00 (*0-06-091446-7*, PL/1446, PL) HarpC.

Confederates Downeast. Mason P. Smith. LC 86-30288. (Illus.). 240p. (Orig.). 1987. pap. 11.50 (*0-931675-09-X*) Prov Pr Maine.

***Confederates on the Caney: An Illustrated Account of the Civil War on the Texas Gulf Coast.** Bobby J. McKinney. LC 94-79109. (Illus.). 145p. (Orig.). (C). 1994. pap. write for info. (*0-9643351-0-7*) B J McKinney.

Confederation. Ed. by Ramsay Cook. LC 23-16213. (Canadian Historical Readings Ser.: No. 3). 1967. pap. 9.95 (*0-8020-1456-9*) U of Toronto Pr.

Confederation & the Constitution: The Critical Issues. Gordon S. Wood. LC 79-66423. 1979. reprint ed. pap. text ed. 16.50 (*0-8191-0821-9*) U Pr of Amer.

Confederation, Constitution, & Early National Period, 1781-1815. E. James Ferguson. LC 74-76969. (Goldentree Bibliographies Series in American History). (C). 1975. pap. text ed. write for info. (*0-88295-534-9*) Harlan Davidson.

Confederation of European Computer User Associations Model Conditions of Contract for the Purchase of Computer Equipment. Institute of Purchasing & Supply Staff. (C). 1989. 100.00 (*0-685-39906-0*, Inst Pur & Supply) St Mut.

Conference About the Next Succession to the Crown of England. Robert Parsons. LC 70-38217. (English Experience Ser.: No. 481). 1972. reprint ed. 32.50 (*90-221-0481-8*) Walter J Johnson.

***Conference Abstracts & Resources 1995.** American Occupational Therapy Association Staff. 332p. (C). 1995. pap. write for info. (*1-56900-024-7*) Am Occup Therapy.

Conference Approach. (C). 1989. 45.00 (*0-903915-77-4*, Pub. by Jordanhill College UK) St Mut.

Conference Book. Leonard Nadler & Zeace Nadler. LC 76-52238. 266p. 1977. 19.00 (*0-87201-140-2*) Gulf Pub.

Conference Centres & Lecture Theatres. 1990. 36.00 (*0-86022-267-5*, Pub. by Build Servs Info Assn UK) St Mut.

Conference Diplomacy. Johan Kaufman. 1988. lib. bdg. 71.50 (*90-247-3682-X*) Kluwer Ac.

Conference Diplomacy: An Introductory Analysis. 208p. 40.00 (*90-247-3631-5*, E.88.III.K/PS.11) UN.

Conference Diplomacy-A Case Study: The World Food Conference, Rome, 1974. Edwin M. Martin. LC 79-91018. 58p. (Orig.). 1979. pap. 5.00 (*0-934742-01-4*) Geo U Inst Dplmcy.

Conference Diplomacy, A Case Study: The World Food Conference Rome, 1974. Edwin M. Martin. 72p. (C). 1985. reprint ed. pap. text ed. 12.50 (*0-8191-5054-1*, Inst Study Diplomacy) U Pr of Amer.

Conference Diplomacy II-A Case Study: The U. N. Conference on Science & Technology for Development, Vienna, 1979. Jean M. Wilkowski. LC 82-12103. 56p. (Orig.). 1982. pap. 5.00 (*0-934742-20-0*) Geo U Inst Dplmcy.

Conference Diplomacy II, A Case Study: The U. N. Conference on Science & Technology for Development, Vienna, 1979. Jean M. Wilkowski. LC 85-22468. 56p. (C). 1985. reprint ed. pap. text ed. 14.00 (*0-8191-5055-X*, Inst Study Diplomacy) U Pr of Amer.

Conference in Distributed Simulation, 1985. Reynolds. (Simulations Series of Bks.). 112p. 1985. 40.00 (*0-685-66815-0*, SS15-2) Soc Computer Sim.

Conference in Pilgrimage: The Story of the Southern District Conference & Its Churches. Orlando Harms. (Illus.). 319p. 1992. pap. write for info. (*1-877941-03-4*) Ctr Mennonite Brethren Studies.

Conference Leadership: A Manual to Assist in the Development of Conference Leaders. rev. ed. Ed. by Ernest C. Miller. LC 72-86426. (Illus.). 124p. reprint ed. pap. 35.40 (*0-317-09780-6*, 2050344) Bks Demand.

Conference of Aims & Methods of Legal Research. Ed. by Alfred F. Conard. (Michigan Legal Publications). x, 199p. 1986. reprint ed. lib. bdg. 37.50 (*0-89941-487-7*, 304140) W S Hein.

Conference of Educational Administrators Serving the Deaf: A History. Richard G. Brill. LC 86-9868. 189p. reprint ed. pap. 53.90 (*0-7837-1851-9*, 2042051) Bks Demand.

Conference of Golden Spawn. Cosmo Trelawny. (Orig.). 1993. pap. 5.95 (*1-55818-247-0*) Holmes Pub.

Conference of the Birds. 79p. 1982. pap. 5.45 (*0-87129-106-1*, C55) Dramatic Pub.

Conference of the Birds. Farid ud-Din Attar. Tr. by Afkham Darbandi & Dick Davis. (Classics Ser.). 240p. 1984. pap. 9.95 (*0-14-044434-3*, Penguin Classics) Viking Penguin.

Conference of the Birds: A Sufi Fable. 2nd ed. Farid Ud-Din Attar. Tr. by C. S. Nott. LC 92-56447. (Illus.). 160p. 1993. pap. 11.00 (*0-87773-031-8*) Shambhala Pubns.

Conference of the Birds: The Story of Peter Brook in Africa. John Heilpern. 327p. (Orig.). 1989. pap. 14.95 (*0-413-61400-X*, A0375, Pub. by Methuen UK) Heinemann.

Conference of Victims see Son

Conference on Acoustical Factors Affecting Hearing Aid Measurement & Performance. 2nd ed. Ed. by Gerald A. Studebaker & Irving Hochbert. LC 92-20408. 464p. 1992. write for info. (*0-205-13778-4*) Allyn.

Conference on Acquisitions, Budgets, & Collections. Ed. by David C. Genaway. (Acquisitions '90 Ser.). 435p. (Orig.). 1990. pap. 39.95 (*0-943970-06-7*) Genaway.

Conference on Acquisitions, Budgets, & Collections. Ed. by David C. Genaway. (Acquisitions '91 Ser.). 357p. (Orig.). 1991. pap. 35.95 (*0-943970-07-5*) Genaway.

Conference on Advanced Research in VLSI: Proceedings - January 23-25, 1984, Massachusetts Institute of Technology, Cambridge, MA. Conference on Advanced Research in VLSI (1984: MIT). Ed. by Paul Penfield, Jr. LC 83-73683. 235p. reprint ed. pap. 67.00 (*0-317-42050-X*, 2025958) Bks Demand.

Conference on Advanced Research in VLSI: Proceedings, January 25-27, 1982, Massachusetts Institute of Technology, Cambridge, MA, USA. Massachusetts Institute of Technology, Conference on Advanced Research in VLSI Staff. Ed. by Paul Penfield, Jr. LC 81-71335. (Illus.). 219p. reprint ed. pap. 62.50 (*0-8357-4191-5*, 2036969) Bks Demand.

Conference on Algebraic Topology in Honor of Peter Hilton. Ed. by R. Piccinini & D. Sjerve. LC 84-24518. (Contemporary Mathematics Ser.: Vol. 37). 161p. 1985. pap. text ed. 30.00 (*0-8218-5036-9*, CONM-37) Am Math.

Conference on Antiviral Substances, Third, Vol. 284. Ed. by Ernest C. Herrmann, Jr. (Annals Ser.). 720p. 1977. 58.00 (*0-89072-030-4*) NY Acad Sci.

Conference on Applied Defense, 1992. Ed. by Peter Rizik. 166p. 1992. 60.00 (*1-56555-005-6*) Soc Computer Sim.

Conference on Automated Deduction, 7th International: Proceedings, Napa, California, May 14-16, 1984. Ed. by R. E. Shostak. (Lecture Notes in Computer Science Ser.: Vol. 170). iv, 508p. 1984. pap. 51.00 (*0-387-96022-8*) Spr-Verlag.

Conference on Business & Management, 1991. Ed. by Jay Weinroth & Joe E. Hilber. (Simulation Ser.: Vol. 23, No. 2). 160p. 1991. 48.00 (*0-685-59044-5*, SS23-2) Soc Computer Sim.

Conference on Business Cycles. Universities-National Bureau Staff. (Conference Ser.: No. 2). 445p. 1951. reprint ed. 115.70 (*0-87014-193-7*); reprint ed. mic. film 59.70 (*0-685-61287-2*) Natl Bur Econ Res.

Conference on Clearance & Settlement Systems: London, 14th March 1990. Study Group Staff. 75p. 1990. pap. write for info. (*0-318-69212-0*) Grp of Thirty.

Conference on Coherent Laser Radar, 5th, Munich, June 1989: Technology & Applications. Ed. by J. W. Bilbro & C. Werner. 333p. 1989. 62.00 (*0-685-48542-0*, VOL. 1181) SPIE.

Conference on Computers, Freedom & Privacy, 1st. LC 91-75772. 248p. 1991. 39.00 (*0-8186-2565-1*) IEEE Comp Soc.

Conference on Computers in Physics Instruction Proceedings. Edward W. Redish & John S. Risley. (Illus.). 608p. (C). 1990. 49.95 (*0-201-16306-3*, Adv Bk Prog) Addison-Wesley.

Conference on Control Engineering, Fourth, 1990: Control Technology for Australian Industry. Intro. by Robert B. Newell. (Illus.). 238p. (Orig.). 1990. pap. 72.00 (*0-85825-502-2*) Accents Pubns.

Conference on Cooperation & Regional Development Between Chejudo & Hawaii, Second: Proceedings. Ed. by Center for Korean Studies Staff. (Illus.). 186p. (Orig.). 1988. pap. text ed. 10.00 (*0-917536-16-9*) UH Manoa CKS.

Conference on Creative Arts Therapies, June 28-30, 1979. Conference on Creative Arts Therapies Staff. 86p. pap. 25.00 (*0-8357-7798-7*, 2036162) Bks Demand.

Conference on Crime Countermeasures & Security, 1983: Proceedings. Ed. by R. William De Vore & J. S. Jackson. LC 82-64615. (Illus.). 118p. 1983. pap. 22.50 (*0-89779-055-3*, UKY BU 130) OES Pubns.

Conference on Design Criteria & Equipment for Transmission at 400 KV & High Voltages: Contributions, Pt. 1. Conference on Design Criteria & Equipment for Transmission at 400 KV & High Voltages(1965: London). LC 66-1977. (Institution of Electrical Engineers Conference Report Ser.: No. 15). 234p. reprint ed. pap. 66.70 (*0-317-10161-7*, 2007389) Bks Demand.

Conference on Design Methods: Conference on Systematic & Intuitive Methods in Engineering, Industrial Design, Architecture & Communications, London, October, 1962. C. Jones & D. Thornley. LC 63-18671. 1963. 96.00 (*0-08-010281-6*, Pub. by Pergamon Repr UK) Franklin.

Conference on Differential Geometric Methods in Theoretical Physics: Proceedings of June 30-July 3, 1981 Conference, Trieste, Italy. Ed. by G. DeNardo & H. D. Doebner. 300p. 1983. 52.00 (*9971-950-58-8*) World Scientific Pub.

Conference on Display Devices & Systems, 1974. (Illus.). 163p. 30.00 (*0-318-16520-1*); 20.00 (*0-318-16521-X*) SID.

Conference on Editorial Problems: Papers Given at the Annual Conference on Editorial Problems, University of Toronto 1978-1993, Vols. 1-27. Ed. by A. F. Johnston et al. 29.50 (*0-685-73894-9*) AMS Pr.

Conference on Editorial Problems: University of Toronto, No. 1-27. LC 86-47860. 29.50 (*0-685-73871-X*) AMS Pr.

Conference on Editorial Problems: University of Toronto, Set, Nos. 1-27. LC 86-47860. Set. 37.50 (*0-404-63650-0*) AMS Pr.

Conference on Education for Business & Management & MIS, 1992. Ed. by Joseph Hilber. 124p. 1992. 50.00 (*0-685-59091-7*, MC92-1) Soc Computer Sim.

Conference on Energy & Environment in European Economies in Transition: Priorities & Opportunities for Cooperation & Integration. OECD Staff. 256p. (Orig.). 1992. pap. 53.00 (*92-64-13813-7*) OECD.

Conference on Engineering in Agriculture, 1992: Quality Soils, Quality Food, Quality Environment. Ed. by Ian Gould et al. (Illus.). 410p. (Orig.). 1992. pap. text ed. 81.75 (*0-85825-558-8*, Pub. by Inst Engrs Aust-EA Bks AT) Accents Pubns.

Conference on Frequency Generation & Control for Radio Systems. Conference on Frequency Generation & Control for Radio Systems(1967: London). LC 67-112020. (Institution of Electrical Engineers Conference Report Ser.: No. 31). 199p. reprint ed. pap. 56.80 (*0-317-10119-6*, 2007383) Bks Demand.

Conference on Harmonic Analysis in Honor of Antoni Zygmund, Set. Calderon et al. Ed. by Alberto P. Calderon & Robert Fefferman. LC 82-11172. (Mathematics Ser.: Vols. I & II). 880p. (C). 1982. text ed. 99.95 (*0-534-98043-0*) Chapman & Hall.

Conference on Hydraulics in Civil Engineering, 1990. Intro. by James E. Ball. (Illus.). 224p. (Orig.). 1990. pap. 62.50 (*0-85825-500-6*, Pub. by Inst Engrs Aust-EA Bks AT) Accents Pubns.

Conference on Informational Theory, Statistical Decision Functions, Random Processes: Transactions of the Ninth Prague Conference, Prague, from June 28th to July 2nd, 1982, A. Jaroslav Kozesnik. 1983. lib. bdg. 117.00 (*90-277-1499-1*) Kluwer Ac.

Conference on Informational Theory, Statistical Decision Functions, Random Processes: Transactions of the Ninth Prague Conference, Prague, from June 28th to July 2nd, 1982, B. Jaroslav Kozesnik. 1983. lib. bdg. 117.00 (*90-277-1500-9*) Kluwer Ac.

Conference on Intellectual Trends in Latin America, University of Texas, 1945. LC 69-19001. reprint ed. lib. bdg. 16.25 (*0-8371-1037-8*, TLIT, Greenwood Pr) Greenwood.

Conference on Intelligence Legislation. 138p. 1980. pap. write for info. (*0-318-66100-4*, 700-0041-01) Amer Bar Assn.

Conference on Interference Problems Associated with the Operation of Microwave Communication Systems, 23rd-24th April, 1968. Conference on Interference Problems Associated with the Operation of Microwave Communication Systems(1968: London). LC 71-586382. (Institution of Electrical Engineers Conference Report Ser.: No. 39). 208p. reprint ed. pap. 59.30 (*0-317-10149-8*, 2007388) Bks Demand.

Conference on International Operations of North American Insurers, 1991. Ed. by Bernard B. Goodman. 350p. 1991. write for info. (*1-56423-002-3*) Ntl Ctr Tax Ed.

Conference on International Operations of North American Insurers, 1992. Ed. by Bernard B. Goodman. 250p. 1992. ring bd. 125.00 (*1-56423-012-0*) Ntl Ctr Tax Ed.

Conference on International Trade, Finance, & Economic Development of Pacific Basin Countries, December 6-7, 1974. (Explorations in Economic Research Three Ser.: No. 2). 144p. 1976. reprint ed. 35.00 (*0-685-61399-2*) Natl Bur Econ Res.

Conference on Inverse Scattering: Theory & Application. Ed. by J. B. Bednar et al. LC 85-51381. (Proceedings in Applied Mathematics Ser.: No. 11). x, 290p. 1983. 36.00 (*0-89871-190-8*) Soc Indus-Appl Math.

Conference on Key Factor Analysis: A Logic Leading to Social Accountability. Ed. by Irwin M. Jarett & Patricia A. Brady. LC 76-20624. 450p. 1976. 10.00 (*0-8093-0793-6*); pap. 4.95 (*0-8093-0795-2*) S Ill U Pr.

Conference on Lasers & Electro-Optics. LC 87-60493. (Technical Digest Series, 1987: Vol. 14). 458p. (Orig.). 1987. lib. bdg. 92.00 (*0-936659-69-6*); pap. 60.00 (*0-936659-49-1*) Optical Soc.

Conference on Lasers & Electro-Optics. LC 87-62777. (Technical Digest Series, 1988: Vol. 7). 534p. (Orig.). 1988. lib. bdg. 92.00 (*1-55752-034-8*); pap. 60.00 (*1-55752-033-X*) Optical Soc.

Conference on Lasers & Electro-Optics. (Technical Digest Series, 1989: Vol. 11). 400p. (Orig.). 1989. Postconference ed. lib. bdg. 92.00 (*1-55752-087-9*); Conference ed. pap. 60.00 (*1-55752-086-0*) Optical Soc.

Conference on Lasers & Electro-Optics. LC 89-64035. (Technical Digest Series, 1990: Vol. 7). 550p. (Orig.). 1990. lib. bdg. 92.00 (*1-55752-132-8*); pap. 60.00 (*1-55752-131-X*) Optical Soc.

Conference on Lasers & Electro-Optics. LC 90-63174. (Technical Digest Series, 1991: Vol. 10). 350p. (Orig.). 1991. lib. bdg. 92.00 (*1-55752-189-1*); pap. 60.00 (*1-55752-188-3*) Optical Soc.

Conference on Lasers & Electro-Optics. LC 94-65353. (Technical Digest Series, 1992). 400p. (Orig.). 1992. Conference. pap. 60.00 (*1-55752-237-5*) Optical Soc.

Conference on Lasers & Electro-Optics. LC 92-80621. (Technical Digest Series, 1992: Vol. 12). 400p. (Orig.). 1992. Postconference. pap. 92.00 (*1-55752-238-3*) Optical Soc.

Conference on Lasers & Electro-Optics. LC 92-62917. (Technical Digest Series, 1993: Vol. 11). 500p. (Orig.). 1993. pap. 92.00 (*1-55752-300-2*); pap. text ed. 60.00 (*1-55752-299-5*) Optical Soc.

C

An Asterisk (*) at the beginning of an entry indicates that the title is appearing in BIP for the first time. 1531

Conference on Lasers & Electro-Optics. LC 94-65353. (Nineteen Ninety-Four Technical Digest Ser.: Vol. 8). 400p. (Orig.). 1994. pap. 92.00 (*1-55752-341-X*); pap. text ed. 60.00 (*1-55752-340-1*) Optical Soc.

Conference on Lasers & Electro-Optics. IEEE, Lasers & Electro-Optics Society Staff. Ed. by IEEE Staff. LC 92-80621. 576p. 1992. lib. bdg. write for info. (*0-7803-0664-3*, 92CH3154-2); fiche write for info. (*0-7803-0665-1*) Inst Electrical.

Conference on Lasers & Electro Optics Europe 1994. IEEE, Lasers & Electro Optics Society Staff. Ed. by IEEE, Institute of Electrical & Electronics Engineers, Inc. Staff. LC 93-80952. 600p. 1994. pap. write for info. (*0-7803-1789-0*, 94TH0614-8); fiche write for info. (*0-7803-1790-4*) Inst Electrical.

Conference on Lasers & Electro-Optics, 1991. IEEE Lasers & Electro-Optics Society Staff. Ed. by IEEE Staff. LC 90-63175. 600p. 1991. lib. bdg. write for info. (*0-87942-606-3*, 91 CH2945-4); fiche write for info. (*0-87942-607-1*, 91CH2945-4) Inst Electrical.

Conference on Lasers & Electro-Optics, 1994. IEEE Laser & Electro-Optics Society Staff. Ed. by IEEE Staff. 464p. 1994. lib. bdg. write for info. (*0-7803-1971-0*, 94CH3463-7); fiche write for info. (*0-7803-1972-9*) Inst Electrical.

Conference on Malaria in Africa - Proceedings: Practical Considerations on Malaria Vaccines & Clinical Trials. Intro. by Alfred A. Buck. 328p. (Orig.). 1988. pap. write for info. (*0-936829-02-8*) Am Inst Bio Sci.

Conference on Measurement & Modeling of Computer Systems, 1990: Conference Record, Held in Boulder, CO, May 22-15, 1990. (Performance Evaluation Review Ser.: Vol. 18, No. 1). (Illus.). ix, 273p. 1990. pap. text ed. 26.00 (*0-89791-359-0*, 488900) Assn Compu Machinery.

Conference on Modern Analysis & Probability. Ed. by Richard Beals et al. LC 84-484. (Contemporary Mathematics Ser.: No. 26). 432p. 1991. pap. 47.00 (*0-8218-5030-X*, CONM-26) Am Math.

Conference on Molecular Spectroscopy: Proceedings of the Institute of Petro Hydrocarbon Research Group, London, February, 1958. E. Thornton & H. Thompson. LC 58-12668. 1959. 153.00 (*0-08-009153-9*, Pub. by Pergamon Repr UK) Franklin.

Conference on Nepal at Claremont. 46p. 1974. 8.50 (*0-318-23192-1*) Am-Nepal Ed.

Conference on Object Oriented Simulation, 1991. Ed. by Raimund K. Ege. 212p. 1991. 60.00 (*0-911801-81-2*, SS23-3) Soc Computer Sim.

Conference on Object-Oriented Simulation, 1993. Beaumariage & Roberts. 190p. 1993. pap. 60.00 (*1-56555-022-6*, MC93-1) Soc Computer Sim.

Conference on Office Information Systems, No. 3. (SIGOIS Bulletin Ser.: Vol. 7, Nos. 2-3). (Illus.). 132p. 1986. pap. text ed. 15.00 (*0-89791-210-1*) Assn Compu Machinery.

Conference on Optical - Hybrid Access Networks, 5th, 1993. IEEE (Communications Society & Region 7) Staff. Ed. by IEEE (Institute of Electrical & Electronics Engineers, Inc.) Staff. LC 93-77593. 250p. 1993. pap. write for info. (*0-7803-1249-X*, 93TH0542-1); fiche write for info. (*0-7803-1250-3*) Inst Electrical.

Conference on Optimisation Techniques in Circuit & Control Applications, 29-30 June 1970. Conference on Optimisation Techniques in Circuit & Control Applications(1970: London). LC 71-595801. (Institution of Electrical Engineers Conference Report Ser.: No. 66). 82p. reprint ed. pap. 25.00 (*0-317-10170-6*, 2050329) Bks Demand.

Conference on Peru, June 19-21, 1987. Washington Office on Latin America Staff. 31p. 1988. pap. 3.00 (*0-929513-04-5*) WOLA.

Conference on Physics & Technology of Semiconductor Devices & Integrated Circuits (Feb 1991, Madras, India) V. Krishnan. 1992. write for info. (*0-8194-0651-1*, 1523) SPIE.

Conference on Pioneers & Peers, 1988. McLeod. 70p. 1988. pap. 20.00 (*0-911801-37-5*) Soc Computer Sim.

Conference on Power Applications of Controllable Semi-Conductor Devices: Contributions. Conference on Power Applications of Controllable Semi-Conductor Devices(1965: London). LC 66-9749. (Institution of Electrical Engineers Conference Report Ser.: No. 17). 64p. reprint ed. pap. 25.00 (*0-317-10168-4*, 2050327) Bks Demand.

Conference on Precision Electromagnetic Measurements Digest, 1994. IEEE (Instrumentation & Measurement Society) Staff. LC 94-76263. 550p. 1994. lib. bdg. write for info. (*0-7803-1985-0*, 94CH3449-6); pap. text ed. write for info. (*0-7803-1984-2*); fiche write for info. (*0-7803-1986-9*) Inst Electrical.

Conference on Propagation of Radio Waves at Frequencies above 10 GHz, 10-13 April, 1973. Conference on Propagation of Radio Waves at Frequencies above 10 GHz(1973: London). (Institution of Electrical Engineers Conference Report Ser.: NO. 98). 270p. reprint ed. pap. 77.00 (*0-317-10088-2*, 2012132) Bks Demand.

Conference on Quantum Electronics, 1992. IEEE, Lasers & Electro-Optics Society Staff. Ed. by IEEE Staff. LC 91-80623. 250p. 1992. lib. bdg. write for info. (*0-7803-0662-7*, 92CH3153-4); pap. write for info. (*0-7803-0663-5*); fiche write for info. (*0-318-69222-8*) Inst Electrical.

Conference on Quantum Electronics, 1994. IEEE Lasers & Electro-Optics Society Staff. Ed. by IEEE Staff. 272p. 1994. lib. bdg. write for info. (*0-7803-1973-7*, 94CH3462-9); fiche write for info. (*0-7803-1974-5*) Inst Electrical.

Conference on Railway Engineering, 1993: Contracting Railways-Safety, Standards & the Surroundings. Intro. by Steve Maxwell & Bruce Hall. (National Conference Publication Ser.: No. 93-12). (Illus.). 288p. (Orig.). 1993. pap. text ed. 54.00 (*0-85825-582-0*, Pub. by Inst Engrs Aust-EA Bks AT) Accents Pubns.

Conference on Real-Time Computer Applications in Nuclear, Particle & Plasma Physics, 8th. IEEE (Nuclear & Plasma Sciences Society) Staff. Ed. by IEEE (Institute of Electrical & Electronics Engineers, Inc.) Staff. LC 93-77595. 500p. 1993. pap. write for info. (*0-7803-1215-5*, 93TH0543-9); fiche write for info. (*0-7803-1216-3*) Inst Electrical.

Conference on Recent Advances in Magnesium Technology: Proceedings. 1987. 50.00 (*0-317-59829-5*, NF8601) Am Foundrymen.

Conference on Research in Business Finance. Universities-National Bureau Staff. (Conference Ser.: No. 3). 361p. 1952. reprint ed. 93.90 (*0-87014-194-5*) Natl Bur Econ Res.

Conference on Secular Inflation: Supplement to "Journal of Money, Credit & Banking 5, No. 1, Pt. 2. Universities-National Bureau Staff. Ed. by Karl Brunner. No. 25. 356p. 1973. reprint ed. write for info. (*0-318-69579-0*); reprint ed. mic. film 14.40 (*0-685-61363-1*) Natl Bur Econ Res.

Conference on Security & Cooperation in Europe: Analysis & Basic Documents, 1972-1993. Ed. by Arie Bloed. LC 93-41128. (Europa Institute, University of Utrecht Ser.). 1368p. (C). 1993. lib. bdg. 360.00 (*0-7923-2593-1*) Kluwer Ac.

Conference on Security & Cooperation in Europe Follow-up Meeting in Vienna, November, 1986: Soviet Violations in the Implementation of the Final Act in Occupied Latvia. World Federation of Free Latvians Staff. 191p. 1986. 10.00 (*0-317-61421-5*) World Fed Free Latvians.

Conference on Security, Disarmament & Development in Africa: Meeting of Experts, Lome, Togo, August 11-12, 1985. 122p. 1986. 11.00 (*92-1-142120-9*, E.86.IX.6) UN.

Conference on Simulation at the Frontiers of Science. Young et al. 165p. 1986. 28.00 (*0-911801-09-X*, ESC86-1) Soc Computer Sim.

Conference on Simulation in Engineering Education, 1989. Cynar. 128p. 1989. pap. 30.00 (*0-911801-46-4*, SEE89-1) Soc Computer Sim.

Conference on Simulation in Engineering Education, 1992. Ed. by Hamid Vakilzadian. 366p. 1992. 66.00 (*1-56555-001-3*, SS24-2) Soc Computer Sim.

Conference on Simulation Technology (SIMTEC '92) Including Second Neural Nets Workshop. 724p. 1992. pap. 80.00 (*1-56555-024-2*, SIMTEC92) Soc Computer Sim.

Conference on Simulation Work & Progress, 1991. Sahinkaya. 124p. 1991. pap. 32.00 (*0-911801-87-1*, MC91-1) Soc Computer Sim.

Conference on Software Engineering for Telecommunication Switching Systems. Conference on Software Engineering for Telecommunication Switching Systems (1973: University of Essex). (Institution of Electrical Engineers Conference Report Ser.: No. 97). 346p. reprint ed. pap. 98.70 (*0-317-10093-9*, 2012131) Bks Demand.

Conference on Some Economic Aspects of Postwar Inter-American Relations - University of Texas, 1946. LC 69-19002. reprint ed. lib. bdg. 15.00 (*0-8371-1038-6*, TLEP, Greenwood Pr) Greenwood.

Conference on Space Science & Space Law: Proceedings. Ed. by Mortimer D. Schwartz. (Illus.). x, 176p. 1964. pap. text ed. 6.75 (*0-8377-1100-2*) Rothman.

Conference on Space Simulation, 11th, 1980: Proceedings. 426p. 55.00 (*0-317-36275-5*) Inst Environ Sci.

Conference on Space Simulation, 6th, 1972: Proceedings. 1071p. 45.00 (*0-317-36281-X*) Inst Environ Sci.

Conference on Space Simulation, 8th 1975: Proceedings. 859p. 55.00 (*0-317-36283-6*) Inst Environ Sci.

Conference on Space Simulation, 9th, 1977: Proceedings. 456p. 55.00 (*0-317-36277-1*) Inst Environ Sci.

Conference on Spetsnaz: Soviet Special Purpose Forces. Ed. by Hale Foundation Staff. (Orig.). 1987. pap. write for info. (*0-935067-13-2*) Nathan Hale Inst.

Conference on System Dynamics, 1989. Spenser & Richardson. 104p. 1989. pap. 20.00 (*0-911801-47-2*, MC89-1) Soc Computer Sim.

Conference on Tax Planning for the Charitable Sector, New York University: Biennial Conference, 1953-1987, 20 vols. mic. film write for info. (*0-318-57427-6*) Rothman.

Conference on Tax Planning for the Charitable Sector, New York University: Biennial Conference, 1953-1987, 20 vols., Set. 1,260.00 (*0-8377-9121-9*) Rothman.

Conference on Telecommunication Transmission, September 9-11, 1975. Conference on Telecommunication Transmission (1975: London). LC 76-371266. (Institution of Electrical Engineers Conference Report Ser.: No. 131). 206p. reprint ed. pap. 58.80 (*0-317-10159-5*, 2012128) Bks Demand.

Conference on the Application of Large Industrial Drives. suppl. ed. Conference on the Application of Large Industrial Drives(1965: London). LC 67-2581. (Institution of Electrical Engineers Conference Report Ser.: No. 10). reprint ed. pap. 20.00 (*0-317-11159-0*) Bks Demand.

Conference on the Application of Large Industrial Drives. Conference on the Application of Large Industrial Drives(1965: London). LC 67-2581. (Institution of Electrical Engineers Conference Report Ser.: No. 10). reprint ed. pap. 68.80 (*0-317-11158-2*, 2050326) Bks Demand.

Conference on the Care of Dependent Children: Proceedings. LC 79-137182. (Poverty U. S. A. Historical Record Ser.). 1976. reprint ed. 23.95 (*0-405-03120-3*) Ayer.

Conference on the Establishment of an International Compensation Fund for Oil Pollution Damage, 1971. International Maritime Organization Staff. 1972. 35.00 (*0-685-61553-7*, Pub. by Intl Maritime Org UK); Bilingual. 50.00 (*0-685-61554-5*, Pub. by Intl Maritime Org UK) St Mut.

Conference on the Global Responsibility of Law Librarians Proceedings: October 18-21, 1989, the University of Texas School of Law, Austin, Texas. Ed. by David R. Burch & Stephen E. Young. LC 90-38909. xiii, 256p. 1991. 42.50 (*0-8377-0359-X*) Rothman.

Conference on the History of Medical Informatics. 206p. 1987. pap. text ed. 20.00 (*0-89791-248-9*, 554872) Assn Compu Machinery.

Conference on the History of Scientific & Numeric Computation. (Illus.). 250p. 1987. pap. text ed. 17.00 (*0-89791-229-2*, 701870) Assn Compu Machinery.

Conference on the Laser, Third, Vol. 267. Leon Goldman. (Annals Ser.). 481p. 1976. 57.00 (*0-89072-021-5*) NY Acad Sci.

Conference on the Simulation Profession, 1985. Edwards. 88p. 1985. pap. 10.00 (*0-911801-06-5*, EMC85-1) Soc Computer Sim.

Conference on the Tax Consequences of American Investments in Israel: Proceedings. Nov. 12-14, 1972. Ed. by Yaakov Neeman. x, 337p. (Orig.). 1974. 20.00 (*0-8377-0902-4*) Rothman.

Conference on Theoretical Aspects of Reasoning about Knowledge, 2nd: Proceedings. Ed. by Moshe Vardi. 402p. (Orig.). (C). 1988. pap. text ed. 29.95 (*0-934613-66-4*) Morgan Kaufmann.

Conference on Tools for the Simulationist, 1990. Nilsen. 36p. 1990. 10.00 (*0-685-66845-2*, MC90-1) Soc Computer Sim.

Conference on Toward Understanding Our Environment 1991. McLeod. 108p. 1991. pap. 40.00 (*0-911801-93-6*, MC91-3) Soc Computer Sim.

Conference Papers: Proceedings of Selected Sessions of the 1991 AACRAO Annual Meeting. AACRAO Staff. Ed. by Henrianne Wakefield & Jennifer M. Harrison. 300p. 1991. pap. text ed. 30.00 (*0-929851-07-2*) Am Assn Coll Registrars.

Conference Proceedings: First & Second Annual Women's Policy Research Conferences, 2 vols. Pref. by Heidi Hartmann. LC 91-75395. (C). 1991. pap. text ed. 50.00 (*1-878428-06-3*) Inst Womens Policy Rsch.

Conference Proceedings: First Annual Women's Policy Research Conference. 195p. 1989. pap. 20.00 (*1-878428-01-2*) Inst Womens Policy Rsch.

Conference Proceedings, Vol. II: Second Annual Women's Policy Research Conference. Pref. by Teresa Odendahl. LC 91-75395. 325p. (Orig.). (C). 1991. pap. text ed. 30. 00 (*1-878428-04-7*) Inst Womens Policy Rsch.

***Conference Proceedings 1995 Power Industry Computer Application Conference.** IEEE, Power Engineering Society Staff. Ed. by Institute of Electrical & Electronics Engineers, Inc. Staff. 450p. 1995. lib. bdg. write for info. (*0-7803-2664-4*, 95CH35798); pap. text ed. write for info. (*0-7803-2663-6*, 95CH35798); fiche write for info. (*0-7803-2665-2*) Inst Electrical.

Conference Record of Annual Pulp & Paper Industry Technical Conference, 1994. IEEE (Industry Applications Society) Staff. Ed. by IEEE Staff. LC 74-136000. 224p. 1994. lib. bdg. write for info. (*0-7803-2029-8*, 94CH3470-2); pap. text ed. write for info. (*0-7803-2028-X*); fiche write for info. (*0-7803-2030-1*) Inst Electrical.

Conference Record of LISP Conference, 1980. (Illus.). 247p. 1980. pap. text ed. 24.00 (*0-685-32253-X*) Assn Compu Machinery.

Conference Record of the IEEE Industry Applications Society Annual Meeting, 1994. IEEE, Industry Applications Society Staff. Ed. by Institute of Electrical & Electronics Engineers, Inc. Staff. LC 80-640527. 2128p. 1994. lib. bdg. write for info. (*0-7803-1994-X*, 94CH3452-0); pap. text ed. write for info. (*0-7803-1993-1*, 94CH3452-0); fiche write for info. (*0-7803-1995-8*) Inst Electrical.

Conference Report on the Deficit Reduction Act of 1984 (Tax Provisions) To Accompany H. R. 4170, House Report 98-861, June 23, 1984. United States Congress Staff. write for info. (*0-318-59323-8*) P-H.

Conference Terminology. Buntrock. 181p. (ENG, FRE, GER & RUS.). 1989. 29.95 (*0-8288-7635-5*) Fr & Eur.

Conference Terminology. H. Fronsdal. 333p. (ENG, GER & NOR.). 1988. pap. 95.00 (*0-8288-7752-1*) Fr & Eur.

Conference Terminology. 2nd rev. ed. J. Herbert. 208p. (ENG, FRE, GER, HUN, ITA, RUS & SPA.). 1980. 195.00 (*0-8288-9305-5*, M7766) Fr & Eur.

Conference Terminology in English, Spanish, Russian, Italian, German & Hungarian. 2nd rev. ed. J. Herbert. 208p. 1976. 79.50 (*0-444-41354-5*) Elsevier.

Conference under the Tamarind Tree: Three Essays in Burmese History. Paul J. Bennett. LC 77-137999. (Monograph Ser.: No. 15). viii, 153p. 1971. 8.25 (*0-938692-14-3*) Yale U SE Asia.

***Conferences & Their Literature: A Question of Value.** Robert Oseman. LC 90-121875. reprint ed. pap. 45.60 (*0-7837-9263-8*, 2060002) Bks Demand.

Conferences de Litterature Francaise: XVIe Siecle. 1984. 15.00 (*0-686-83919-6*) C de Bussy.

Conferences de Litterature Francaise: XVIIIe Siecle. Carvel De Bussy. LC 78-66098. (FRE.). (C). 1979. pap. text ed. 15.00 (*0-9602260-0-1*) C de Bussy.

Conferences for Franciscan Religious. Philotheus Boehner. (Spirit & Life Ser.). 1966. 2.00 (*0-686-11571-6*) Franciscan Inst.

Conferences of John Cassian, No. 1. John Cassian. Tr. by Boniface Ramsey. (Cistercian Studies). 300p. 1992. write for info. (*0-87907-337-3*); pap. write for info. (*0-87907-537-6*) Cistercian Pubns.

Conferences of John Cassian, No. 2. John Cassian. Tr. by Boniface Ramsey. 300p. 1992. write for info. (*0-318-69181-7*) Cistercian Pubns.

Conferences of John Cassian, No. 3. John Cassian. Tr. by Boniface Ramsey. (Cistercian Studies). 300p. 1992. write for info. (*0-87907-338-1*); pap. write for info. (*0-87907-538-4*) Cistercian Pubns.

Conferences of the Inter-Parliamentary Union on European Cooperation & Security 1973-1991. Victor Yves-Ghebali. 190p. 1993. 39.95 (*1-85521-445-8*, Pub. by Dartmth Pub UK) Ashgate Pub Co.

Conferences on Cellular Dynamics: Proceedings of the 5th Interdisciplinary Conference, 5 vols. Interdisciplinary Conference Staff. Ed. by L. D. Peachey. 446p. 1969. Vols. 1 & 2, 446. 173.00 (*0-677-65010-8*); Vols. 3 & 4, 310. 113.00 (*0-677-65020-5*); Vol. 5, xiv, 552p. 198.00 (*0-677-13300-6*) Gordon & Breach.

Conferences on the Chief Decrees of the Jesuit General Congregation XXXII: A Symposium by Some of Its Members. J. Y. Calvez et al. LC 76-2977. (Studies on Jesuit Topics Series IV: No. 4). xii, 161p. 1976. pap. 3.50 (*0-912422-13-0*) Inst Jesuit.

Conferences on the Our Father. John F. Marshall. (Spirit & Life Ser.). 1967. 2.00 (*0-686-11573-2*) Franciscan Inst.

Conferences to Revise the Unit of Account Provisions of the CLC 1969, Fund 1971 & Pal 1974 Conventions, 1976. International Maritime Organization Staff. 1983. text ed. 30.00 (*0-89771-941-7*, Pub. by Intl Maritime Org UK) St Mut.

Conferencing Parents of Exceptional Children. 2nd ed. Richard Simpson. LC 80-39434. 439p. 1990. text ed. 39. 00 (*0-89079-210-0*, 1489) PRO-ED.

Conferrate High Command - Themes in Honor of T. Harry Williams: The 1988 Deep Delta Civil War Symposium. Roman J. Heleniak & Lawrence L. Hewitt. LC 90-37958. (Illus.). 260p. (C). 1990. 29.95 (*0-942597-17-6*); pap. 18.95 (*0-942597-23-0*) White Mane Pub.

Conferring Church. M. Richard Troeh & Marjorie Troeh. 1987. pap. 5.00 (*0-8309-0465-4*) Herald Hse.

Confesion de Fe de Westminster y Catecismo Menor. 117p. (SPA.). 1990. spiral bd. 6.95 (*0-85151-563-0*) Banner of Truth.

Confesion y Perdon: Confession & Forgiveness. Andrew Murray. (SPA.). 4.95 (*84-7228-536-7*, 220187, Pub. by Edit Clie SP) TSELF.

Confesiones De un Pequeno Filosofo. Azorin. Ed. by Jose M. Martinez Cachero. (Nueva Austral Ser.: No. 136). (SPA.). 1991. pap. text ed. 11.95x (*84-239-1936-6*) Elliots Bks.

Confesiones Pequeno Filosofo. 6th ed. Azorin. 144p. (SPA.). 1990. pap. 12.95 (*0-7859-5177-6*, S362) Fr & Eur.

Confess, Fletch. Gregory McDonald. 272p. 1976. mass mkt. 4.99 (*0-380-00814-9*) Avon.

Confessing Christ. 3rd rev. ed. Calvin K. Cummings. (Orig.). 1977. pap. 1.45 (*0-934688-04-4*) Great Comm Pubns.

Confessing Christ & Doing Politics. Mark Hatfield et al. Ed. by James Skillen. LC 80-71233. 100p. (Orig.). 1982. pap. 3.95 (*0-936456-02-7*) Ctr Pub Justice.

Confessing Church, Conservative Elites, & the Nazi State. Shelley Baranowski. LC 86-12575. (Texts & Studies in Religion: Vol. 28). 200p. 1986. lib. bdg. 79.95 (*0-88946-816-8*) E Mellen.

Confessing Conscience: Churched Women on Abortion. Ed. by Phyllis Tickle. LC 90-30080. 160p. 1990. pap. 9.95 (*0-687-09388-0*) Abingdon.

Confessing Excess: Women & the Politics of Body Reduction. Carole Spitzack. LC 89-36513. (Gender & Society Ser.). 200p. 1990. 59.50 (*0-7914-0271-1*); pap. 19.95 (*0-7914-0272-X*) State U NY Pr.

Confessing Our Faith: An Interpretation of the Statement of Faith of the United Church of Christ. Roger L. Shinn. LC 90-35445. 132p. (Orig.). 1990. pap. 9.95 (*0-8298-0866-3*) Pilgrim OH.

Confessing the Faith: Reformers Define the Church 1530-1580. Robert Kolb. (Scholarship Today Ser.). 192p. (Orig.). 1991. pap. 14.95 (*0-570-04556-8*) Concordia.

Confessio Amantis. John Gower. Ed. by Russell A. Peck. (Medieval Academy Reprints for Teaching Ser.). 570p. 1981. pap. 14.95 (*0-8020-6438-8*) U of Toronto Pr.

Confession. John Grazer. Ed. by James B. Van Treese. 170p. 1993. pap. 8.95 (*1-56901-027-7*) NW Pub.

Confession. Lori Herter. 288p. (Orig.). 1992. mass mkt. 4.99 (*0-425-13358-3*) Berkley Pub.

Confession. Antony Khrapovitsky. Tr. by Christopher Birchall. LC 74-29537. 100p. (Orig.). 1975. pap. 3.00 (*0-88465-005-7*) Holy Trinity.

Confession. Nancy Pickard. 1994. 20.00 (*0-671-78261-4*) PB.

Confession. Adrienne Von Speyr. Tr. by Douglas W. Stott. LC 84-80757. 262p. (Orig.). 1985. pap. 12.95 (*0-89870-040-X*) Ignatius Pr.

Confession. Leo Tolstoy. Tr. by David Patterson. LC 83-42640. 96p. 1984. reprint ed. pap. 5.95 (*0-393-30192-3*) Norton.

***Confession: A Jenny Cain Mystery.** large type ed. Nancy Pickard. LC 94-37389. 1995. write for info. (*0-7862-0344-7*) Thorndike Pr.

Confession: A Little Book for the Reluctant. Louis G. De Segur. LC 89-51366. 68p. 1989. reprint ed. pap. 1.50 (*0-89555-385-6*) TAN Bks Pubs.

Confession: An Athonite guide. 1994. pap. 0.50 (*0-89981-152-3*) Eastern Orthodox.

An Asterisk (*) at the beginning of an entry indicates that the title is appearing in BIP for the first time.

C

An Asterisk (*) at the beginning of an entry indicates that the title is appearing in BIP for the first time.

1533

Confessions of a Puzzled Parson, & Other Pleas for Reality. Charles Fiske. LC 68-54345. (Essay Index Reprint Ser.). 1977. reprint ed. 20.95 (*0-8369-0442-7*) Ayer.

Confessions of a Rational Mystic: Anselm's Early Writings. Gregory Schufreider. LC 92-26252. (History of Philosophy Ser.). 408p. (C). 1994. 39.95 (*1-55753-035-1*); pap. 15.95 (*1-55753-036-X*) Purdue U Pr.

Confessions of a Raving, Unconfined Nut. Krassner. 1994. pap. 12.00 (*0-671-89843-4*, Fireside) S&S Trade.

Confessions of a Reformer. Frederic C Howe. LC 87-31111. 376p. 1988. reprint ed. pap. 12.50x (*0-87338-361-3*) Kent St U Pr.

Confessions of a Reluctant Elf. Page McBrier. LC 94-68006. 144p. (J). (gr. 3-7). 1995. pap. 3.95 (*0-7868-1010-6*) Hyprn Ppbks.

Confessions of a Rock 'n Roll Groupie. Connie Hamzy. 336p. 1994. pap. 5.99 (*1-56171-257-4*, S P I Bks) Sure Sellers.

Confessions of a School Master. William A. Alcott. LC 77-89145. (American Education: Its Men, Institutions & Ideas, Ser.). 1974. reprint ed. 19.95 (*0-405-01381-7*) Ayer.

Confessions of a Scientist. Raymond L. Ditmars. LC 75-121463. (Essay Index Reprint Ser.). 1977. 23.95 (*0-8369-1800-2*) Ayer.

Confessions of a Sex Crazed Money Man: Alternatives to Twelve-Step Groups, Poverty & the American Way. rev. ed. Alex S. Gabor. 208p. (Orig.). (C). 1992. pap. 9.95 (*1-880983-89-3*) Excalibur Pr.

Confessions of a Sex Kitten. Eartha Kitt. LC 91-19299. 1991. 20.00 (*0-942637-33-X*) Barricade Bks.

Confessions of a Skewed Romantic. Ann Darr. 70p. (Orig.). Date not set. pap. text ed. write for info. (*0-938572-04-0*) Bunny Crocodile.

Confessions of a Special Eddie: Reflections in Appreciation of Human Difference. T. Mark Costello. 190p. (Orig.). 1994. pap. write for info. (*1-881135-04-7*) Wizard Pr.

Confessions of a Sportswriter. Don Bloom. 1988. 16.95 (*0-533-07266-2*) Vantage.

Confessions of a Stockbroker: You, Too Can Find Tomorrow's Blue Chips Before Wall Street Finds Them. Andrew A. Lanyi. LC 92-25479. 1992. 19.95 (*0-13-175746-6*) P-H.

Confessions of a Struggling Christian. Jim Toombs. 175p. 1993. pap. 8.99 (*0-88070-559-0*, Multnomah Bks) Questar Pubs.

Confessions of a Taoist on Wall Street. David Payne. 864p. 1985. mass mkt. 5.99 (*0-345-32696-2*) Ballantine.

***Confessions of a Technophile.** Lewis Branscomb. LC 94-5330. (AIP Masters of Modern Physics Ser.). 250p. (C). 1994. 29.95 (*1-56396-118-0*, AIP Pr) Am Inst Physics.

Confessions of a Teenage Baboon. Paul Zindel. (gr. 9 up). 1984. mass mkt. 3.99 (*0-553-27190-3*) Bantam.

Confessions of a Thug. Taylor Meadows. 1986. 22.00 (*0-8364-1737-2*, Pub. by Manohar II) S Asia.

Confessions of a Thug. Taylor Meadows. 1988. reprint ed. 17.50 (*81-206-0330-3*, Pub. by Asian Educ Servs II) S Asia.

Confessions of a Transplant. Peggy B. Russell. (Illus.). 50p. 1990. reprint ed. pap. 6.95 (*0-9625237-0-4*) Transplant Pubns.

***Confessions of a Trolley Dodger from Brooklyn.** Stan Fischler. (Illus.). 136p. 1995. 24.95 (*1-882608-10-0*) H & M Prods.

***Confessions of a True Diva.** LaRita Shelby. 110p. 1995. pap. 8.95 (*0-9636952-8-2*) Pines One.

Confessions of a Union Buster. Martin J. Levitt. LC 93-14736. 1993. 25.00 (*0-517-58330-5*, Crown) Crown Pub Group.

***Confessions of a Used Program Salesman: Institutionalizing Software Reuse.** Will Tracz. 224p. 1995. pap. 17.95x (*0-201-63369-8*) Addison-Wesley.

Confessions of a Waldorf Parent. Margaret Gorman. 1991. 2.50 (*0-945803-06-0*) R Steiner Col Pubns.

Confessions of a Woodpecker. deluxe ed. George Mackley. 1981. 250.00 (*0-905418-92-1*, Pub. by Gresham Bks UK) St Mut.

***Confessions of a Yakuza.** Junichi Saga. Tr. by John Bester. Orig. Title: The Gambler's Tale. 264p. 1995. pap. 10.00 (*4-7700-1948-3*) Kodansha.

Confessions of a Young Man. George Moore. (BCL1-PR English Literature Ser.). 301p. 1992. reprint ed. lib. bdg. 89.00 (*0-7812-7601-2*) Rprt Serv.

Confessions of a Young Man. George Moore. LC 70-145188. (Literature Ser.). (Illus.). 314p. 1972. reprint ed. 29.00 (*0-403-01113-2*) Scholarly.

Confessions of al-Ghazali. Muhammad Al-Ghazali. Tr. by Claude Field. 70p. (Orig.). 1987. pap. 4.95 (*1-56744-256-0*) Kazi Pubns.

Confessions of Aleister Crowley. Ed. by John Symonds & Kenneth Grant. (Illus.). 1989. 19.95 (*0-685-30421-3*) Viking Penguin.

Confessions of Aleister Crowley: An Autobiography. Aleister Crowley. Ed. by John Symonds & Kenneth Grant. (Illus.). 984p. 1989. pap. 21.95 (*0-14-019189-5*, Penguin Bks) Viking Penguin.

Confessions of an Abusive Husband. Robert Robertson. 1993. pap. 10.95 (*0-9631739-0-1*) Heritage Pk Pub.

Confessions of an Actor. John Barrymore. LC 70-84506. (Illus.). 1980. 20.95 (*0-405-08240-1*, Pub. by Blom Pubns UK) Ayer.

Confessions of an Advertising Man. David Ogilvy. 172p. 1987. 11.00 (*0-8442-3711-6*, NTC Busn Bks) NTC Pub Grp.

Confessions of an Advertising Man. 2nd ed. David Ogilvy. 180p. 1989. pap. 11.00 (*0-689-70800-9*, Atheneum S&S) S&S Trade.

***Confessions of an Agnostic Clergyman.** Edwin Hodgin. (American Autobiography Ser.). 235p. 1995. reprint ed. lib. bdg. 79.00 (*0-7812-8557-7*) Rprt Serv.

Confessions of an Alaska Bootlegger. Ralph Soberg. (Illus.). 64p. (Orig.). 1990. pap. 6.95 (*0-9625429-1-1*) Hardscratch Pr.

Confessions of an Also-Ran. Peter Ashley. (Illus.). 160p. 1987. 6.95 (*0-85236-168-8*, Pub. by Farming Pr UK) Diamond Farm Bk.

Confessions of an American Poetaster, a Selection of Poetry by John Edward Westburg. John E. Westburg. LC 89-90229. (Illus.). 366p. 1989. pap. 16.50 (*0-87423-057-8*) Westburg.

Confessions of an American Scholar. Simon O'Toole. LC 71-123152. 117p. reprint ed. pap. 33.40 (*0-317-29453-9*, 2055895) Bks Demand.

Confessions of an Apostate. Mary A. Sadlier. 1978. 23.95 (*0-405-10850-8*, 11853) Ayer.

Confessions of an Eco-Warrior. Dave Foreman. 1991. 20.00 (*0-517-58123-X*, Harmony) Crown Pub Group.

Confessions of an Eco-Warrior. Dave Foreman. 1993. 12.00 (*0-517-88058-X*, Crown) Crown Pub Group.

Confessions of an Eighty Year Old Boy: A Blue-Print for True Happiness & Fulfillment. Stan Hill. 352p. (Orig.). 1994. pap. write for info. (*0-318-72893-1*) Red Oak MN.

Confessions of an English Maid. 224p. 1984. pap. 4.50 (*0-88184-044-0*) Carroll & Graf.

***Confessions of an English Maid & Other Delights.** 384p. 1995. mass mkt. 5.95 (*0-7867-0234-6*) Carroll & Graf.

Confessions of an English Opium Eater. Thomas De Quincey. Tr. by Aileen Ward. 336p. 1985. pap. 4.95 (*0-88184-130-7*) Carroll & Graf.

Confessions of an English Opium Eater. Thomas De Quincey. Ed. by Alethea Hayter. (English Library). 1971. pap. 8.95 (*0-14-043061-X*, EL61, Penguin Classics) Viking Penguin.

Confessions of an English Opium-Eater. Thomas De Quincey. 1976. 23.95 (*0-8488-1280-8*) Amereon Ltd.

Confessions of an English Opium-Eater. Thomas De Quincey. LC 89-206175. 220p. 1989. reprint ed. 40.00 (*1-85477-020-9*, Pub. by Woodstock Bks UK) Cassell.

Confessions of an English Opium-Eater & Other Writings. Thomas De Quincey. Ed. by Grevel Lindop. (World's Classics Paperback Ser.). 1985. pap. 8.95 (*0-19-281675-6*) OUP.

Confessions of an English Opium-Eater & Other Writings. Thomas De Quincey. 256p. 1987. reprint ed. lib. bdg. 24.95 (*0-89966-609-4*) Buccaneer Bks.

Confessions of an Ex-Secret Service Agent. Marty Venker & George Rush. LC 87-81421. 320p. 1988. 17.95 (*1-55611-054-5*) D I Fine.

Confessions of an Immigrant's Daughter. Laura G. Salverson. (Social History of Canada Ser.). 400p. 1981. pap. 18.95 (*0-8020-6434-5*) U of Toronto Pr.

Confessions of an Immigrant's Daughter. Laura G. Salverson. LC 81-197144. (Social History of Canada Ser.: No. 34). 433p. reprint ed. pap. 123.50 (*0-685-23496-7*, 2026442) Bks Demand.

***Confessions of an Opium Eater.** DeQuincy. (Thrift Editions Ser.). 1995. pap. 1.00 (*0-486-28742-4*) Dover.

Confessions of an Organized Homemaker. rev. ed. Deniece Schofield. 224p. 1994. pap. 10.99 (*1-55870-361-6*) Betterway Bks.

Confessions of an S. O. B. Al Neuharth. 432p. 1992. pap. 5.99 (*0-451-17272-8*, Sig) NAL-Dutton.

Confessions of Arsene Lupin. Maurice LeBlanc. 327p. 1980. reprint ed. lib. bdg. 15.50 (*0-89968-202-2*, Lghtyr Pr) Buccaneer Bks.

Confessions of Augustine. Augustine. Ed. by W. R. Connor et al. LC 78-67139. (Latin Texts & Commentaries Ser.). (ENG & LAT.). 1979. reprint ed. lib. bdg. 40.95 (*0-405-11604-7*) Ayer.

Confessions of Blessed Alonso de Orozco. Alonso De Orozco. Ed. by John E. Rotelle. Tr. by Matthew J. O'Connell. LC 91-70265. (Augustinian Ser.: Vol. 23). (Illus.). 212p. (Orig.). 1991. 14.95 (*0-941491-46-3*, 6526); pap. text ed. 7.95 (*0-941491-26-9*, 6525) Augustinian Pr.

Confessions of Brother Haluin. Ellis Peters. 1989. mass mkt. 5.50 (*0-445-40855-3*, Mysterious Paperbk) Warner Bks.

Confessions of Brother Haluin. Ellis Peters. 1989. 15.95 (*0-89296-349-2*) Mysterious Pr.

Confessions of Charles Dickens: A Very Factual Fiction. Alan S. Watts. LC 91-21166. (Dickens' Universe Ser.: Vol. 1). 179p. (C). 1992. text ed. 37.95 (*0-8204-1533-2*) P Lang Pubs.

Confessions of Dan Yack. Blaise Cendrars. Tr. by Nina Rootes. 120p. 1990. 30.00 (*0-7206-0766-3*, Pub. by Peter Owen Ltd UK) Dufour.

Confessions of Empowering Organizations: Who's Doing It & How. Ray Redburn et al. LC 91-77165. (Illus.). 224p. (Orig.). 1992. pap. 19.95 (*0-9631461-0-6*) Assn Qual & Part.

Confessions of Eveline. 206p. 1987. pap. 3.95 (*0-88184-308-3*) Carroll & Graf.

Confessions of Felix Krull. Thomas Mann. 1993. 21.00 (*0-8446-6715-3*) Peter Smith.

Confessions of Felix Krull Con. Thomas Mann. 1992. pap. 11.00 (*0-679-73904-1*, Vin) Random.

Confessions of Felix Krull, Confidence Man. Thomas Mann. 382p. 1969. pap. 9.00 (*0-394-70496-7*, Vin) Random.

Confessions of Henry Lee Lucas. Mike Cox. Ed. by Leslie Wells. 310p. (Orig.). 1991. mass mkt. 4.95 (*0-671-70665-9*, Pocket Star Bks) PB.

Confessions of Jacob Boehme. Intro. by Evelyn Underhill. 188p. 1992. pap. 19.95 (*1-56459-214-6*) Kessinger Pub.

Confessions of Jeremiah: Their Interpretation & Their Role in Chapters 1-25. Kathleen O'Connor. LC 86-29803. (Society of Biblical Literature Ser.). 199p. 1988. pap. 11.95 (*1-55540-001-9*, 06 01 94) Scholars Pr GA.

Confessions of Julius Antoine, Vol. 1: Lea, Le Tendre & Rossi. Tr. by Dick Hansom. (Illus.). 48p. 1989. reprint ed. 9.95 (*1-870084-30-6*) Fantagraph Bks.

"Confessions" of Kurt Gerstein. Henri Roques. Tr. by Ronald Percival. 297p. (Orig.). 1989. pap. 11.00 (*0-939484-27-7*) Inst Hist Rev.

Confessions of Lady Nijo. Tr. by Karen Brazell. 320p. 1973. 39.50 (*0-8047-0929-7*); pap. 13.95 (*0-8047-0930-0*) Stanford U Pr.

Confessions of Lord Byron. George Gordon Byron. Ed. by W. A. Bettany. LC 72-3739. (Studies in Byron: No. 5). 1972. reprint ed. lib. bdg. 75.00 (*0-8383-1578-X*) M S G Haskell Hse.

Confessions of Love. Uno Chiyo. Tr. by Phyllis Birnbaum. LC 88-39612. 176p. 1989. lib. bdg. 27.00 (*0-8248-1170-4*); pap. 12.95 (*0-8248-1176-3*) UH Pr.

Confessions of Madame Psyche. Dorothy Bryant. LC 86-71677. (Illus.). 376p. (Orig.). 1986. pap. 13.95 (*0-931688-14-0*) Ata Bks.

Confessions of Nat Turner. William Styron. 1994. 15.50 (*0-679-60101-5*, Modern Lib) Random Bks Yng Read.

Confessions of Nat Turner. William Styron. 1994. 15.50 (*0-685-70622-2*, Modern Lib) Random.

Confessions of Nat Turner. William Styron. LC 91-50738. 1993. write for info. (*0-679-73663-8*) Vintage NY.

Confessions of Nat Turner. William Styron. 1994. reprint ed. lib. bdg. 29.95 (*1-56849-344-4*) Buccaneer Bks.

Confessions of Nat Turner, Leader of the Late Insurrection in Southampton, Va., As Fully and Voluntarily Made to Thos. C. Gray. Nat Turner. LC 70-79011. (Black Heritage Library Collection). 1861. 7.00 (*0-8369-8672-5*) Ayer.

Confessions of Rock Groups. Bob Andrews. 1993. pap. 5.99 (*1-56171-039-3*) Sure Sellers.

Confessions of Saint Augustine. St. Augustine. (Airmont Classics Ser.). (J). (gr. 11 up). 1968. pap. 1.95 (*0-8049-0190-2*, CL-190) Airmont.

Confessions of Saint Augustine. St. Augustine. Tr. by Rex Warner. 1963. pap. 5.99 (*0-451-62474-2*, Ment) NAL-Dutton.

Confessions of Saint Augustine. St. Augustine. Tr. by Edward B. Pusey. 256p. 1961. pap. 5.00 (*0-02-064230-X*, Collier S&S) S&S Trade.

Confessions of Saint Augustine. St. Augustine. LC 60-13725. 1960. mass mkt. 6.95 (*0-385-02955-1*, Image Bks) Doubleday.

Confessions of Some Lonely Housewives: A Book on Marriage Problems. Earl V. Campbell. 106p. 1973. 4.95 (*0-686-02488-5*) Dade Variety Pr.

Confessions of Son of Sam. David Abrahamsen. LC 84-21487. 256p. 1985. text ed. 37.50 (*0-231-05760-1*) Col U Pr.

Confessions of St. Augustine. 7.99 (*0-916441-07-5*, Christian Lib) Barbour & Co.

Confessions of St. Augustine. abr. ed. Augustine. (Summit Bks.). 1977. reprint ed. pap. 5.99 (*0-8010-0118-8*) Baker Bk.

Confessions of St. Augustine. Campbell & McGuire. 1984. reprint ed. pap. 14.00x (*0-86516-058-9*) Bolchazy-Carducci.

Confessions of St. Augustine: Modern English Version. Ed. by Hal Helms. 330p. 1986. pap. 9.95 (*0-941478-55-6*) Paraclete MA.

Confessions of T. E. Lawrence: The Romantic Hero's Presentation of Self. Thomas J. O'Donnell. LC 77-92257. x, 196p. 1979. 18.95 (*0-8214-0370-2*) Ohio U Pr.

Confessions of the Barbarian. Edward Abbey. Bd. with Edward Abbey. LC 85-26939.; Red Knife Valley. Jack Curtis & Edward Abbey. LC 85-26939.; Edward Abbey. LC 85-26939. LC 85-26939. (Back-to-Back Bks.: Vol. VII). 162p. (Orig.). 1986. Set pap. 7.50 (*0-88496-244-X*) Capra Pr.

***Confessions of the Guerrilla Girls.** Whitney Chadwick. (Illus.). 96p. 1995. pap. 18.00 (*0-06-095088-9*, PL) HarpC.

Confessions of the Nun of St. Omer: A Tale, 2 Vols, Set. Charlotte Dacre. LC 76-131314. (Gothic Novels Ser.). 1972. reprint ed. 46.95 (*0-405-00803-1*) Ayer.

Confessions of the Power Trust: A Summary of the Testimony Given in the Hearings of the Federal Trade Commission on Utility Corporations. Carl D. Thompson. LC 75-40022. (Getting & Spending: the Consumer's Dilemma Ser.). 1976. reprint ed. 56.95 (*0-405-08050-6*) Ayer.

Confessions of Two Brothers. John C. Powys & Lewellyn Powys. LC 70-131804. 1971. reprint ed. 29.00 (*0-403-00691-0*) Scholarly.

Confessions of Wanda Von Sacher Masoch. 2nd ed. Wanda Von Sacher-Masoch. Tr. by Marian Phillips et al. (Illus.). 162p. 1991. pap. 13.99 (*0-940642-23-9*) Re Search Pubns.

Confessions of Zeno. Italo Svevo. Tr. by Beryl De Zoete. (International Ser.). 1989. pap. 12.00 (*0-679-72234-3*, Vin) Random.

Confessions, Truth, & the Law. Joseph D. Grano. 476p. (C). 1993. text ed. 49.50 (*0-472-10168-4*) U of Mich Pr.

Confessions, Vol. I: Text & Prolegomena. St. Augustine. Ed. by James J. O'Donnell. (Illus.). 208p. 1992. 85.00 (*0-19-814378-8*) OUP.

Confessions, Vol. II, Bks. 1-7: Commentary. St. Augustine. Ed. by James J. O'Donnell. 376p. 1992. 115.00 (*0-19-814074-6*) OUP.

Confessions, Vol. III, Bks. 8-13: Commentary. St. Augustine. Ed. by James J. O'Donnell. 352p. 1992. 110.00 (*0-19-814075-4*) OUP.

***Confessor.** John Gardner. 560p. 1995. 23.00 (*1-883402-25-5*) S&S Trade.

***Confessor Between East & West: A Portrait of Ukrainian Cardinal Josyf Slipyj.** fac. ed. Jaroslav J. Pelikan. LC 89-27536. (Illus.). 262p. 1990. reprint ed. pap. 74.70 (*0-7837-7970-4*, 2047726) Bks Demand.

Confessyon of the Fayth of the Germaynes in the Councell, 2 pts., Set. Melanchthon. LC 76-57351. (English Experience Ser.: No. 771). 1977. reprint ed. lib. bdg. 39.00 (*90-221-0771-X*) Walter J Johnson.

Confetti. Barbara Hauk. LC 92-75962. 104p. (Orig.). 1993. pap. 10.95 (*1-880391-05-8*) Event Horizon.

Confetti. Merrily T. Karr. 1980. 7.95 (*0-87212-142-9*) Libra.

***Confetti.** Pat Mora. LC 95-2038. 1995. 14.95 (*1-880000-25-3*) Lee & Low Bks.

Confidante in Henry James: Evolution & Moral Value of a Fictive Character. Corona Sharp. LC 63-19326. 336p. reprint ed. pap. 95.80 (*0-317-29693-0*, 2022066) Bks Demand.

Confidence. Warren W. Wiersbe. LC 94-8536. (Thirty-Day Devotionals Ser.). 72p. (Orig.). 1994. pap. 2.99 (*1-56476-262-9*, Victor Books) SP Pubns.

Confidence: A Child's First Weapon. Larry Tatum. 189p. 1984. pap. 8.95 (*0-318-18525-3*) L Tatum.

***Confidence: Finding It & Living It.** Barbara De Angelis. Ed. by Jill Kramer. 128p. 1995. 12.95 (*1-56170-318-4*, 177) Hay House.

Confidence: How to Succeed at Being Yourself. Alan L. McGinnis. LC 87-1470. 192p. (Orig.). 1987. pap. 5.99 (*0-8066-2262-8*, 10-1639, Augsburg) Augsburg Fortress.

Confidence: The Missing Substance of Faith. Creflo A. Dollar, Jr. 22p. (Orig.). 1993. pap. 1.99 (*0-9634781-6-8*, 004CX) Wrld Chang Minist.

Confidence see Novels, 1871-1880

Confidence- & Security-Building Measures in Europe: The Stockholm Conference. Carl C. Krehbiel. LC 89-30294. 399p. 1989. text ed. 75.00 (*0-275-93240-0*, C3240, Praeger Pubs) Greenwood.

Confidence Africaine. Roger Martin du Gard. 67p. (FRE.). 1991. pap. 19.95 (*0-7859-1583-4*, 29035344458) Fr & Eur.

Confidence Africaine. Roger Martin Du Gard. Tr. by Austryn Wainhouse. LC 83-60469. 48p. 1983. pap. 5.25 (*0-910395-08-X*) Marlboro Pr.

Confidence Amid Chaos. Mark Finley. 62p. 1992. pap. 1.95 (*0-8163-1131-5*) Pacific Pr Pub Assn.

***Confidence & Mathematics: The Effects of Gender.** Sue Fullarton. 1993. pap. 45.00 (*0-7300-0815-0*, Pub. by Deakin Univ AT) St Mut.

Confidence & Security-Building Measures from Europe to Other Regions. (Topical Papers Ser.: No. 7). 186p. 1991. 13.50 (*92-1-142180-2*, 91.IX.17) UN.

Confidence & Security-Building Measures in Asia. (Topical Paper Ser.: No. 1). 1991. 13.50 (*92-1-142158-6*, 90.IX.7) UN.

Confidence Book: Building Trust in the Language Classroom. Paul Davis & Mario Rinvolucri. (Pilgrims Resource Bks.). 85p. 1990. pap. text ed. 17.95 (*0-582-03766-2*, 78670) Longman.

***Confidence-Building & Verification: Prospects in the Middle East.** Ed. by Shai Feldman. (JCSS Study Ser.). 255p. (C). 1994. pap. text ed. 38.50 (*0-8133-2223-5*) Westview.

Confidence-Building Measures & International Security - The Political & Military Aspects: A Soviet Approach. 178p. 1991. 28.00 (*92-9045-052-5*, GV.91.0.7) UN.

Confidence-Building Measures in Africa. 16p. 1988. pap. 10.00 (*92-9045-019-3*, GV.E.87.0.5) UN.

Confidence Building Measures in the Asia-Pacific Region. (Disarmament Topical Papers: No. 6). 181p. 1991. 13.50 (*92-1-142179-9*, 91.IX.16) UN.

***Confidence Building Measures in the Middle East.** Ed. by Gabriel Ben-Dor & David B. DeWitt. LC 94-26211. (C). 1994. text ed. 59.95 (*0-8133-2293-6*) Westview.

Confidence-Building Measures within the CSCE Process: Paragraph-by-Paragraph Analysis of the Helsinki & Stockholm Regimes. 110p. 23.00 (*92-9045-035-5*, E. GV.89.0.5) UN.

***Confidence, Credibility & Macroeconomic Policy: Past, Present, Future.** Richard C. Burdekin & Farrokh K. Langdana. LC 94-33820. 208p. 1995. 65.00x (*0-415-10278-2*, C0295) Routledge.

Confidence Crisis: An Analysis of University Departments. Paul L. Dressel et al. LC 70-110642. (Jossey-Bass Higher Education Ser.). 286p. reprint ed. 81.60 (*0-8357-9309-5*, 2013948) Bks Demand.

Confidence De Maigret. Georges Simenon. 192p. (FRE.). 1992. pap. 11.95 (*0-7859-1605-9*, 226604978X) Fr & Eur.

Confidence Factor: How Self-Esteem Can Change Your Life. Judith Briles. 1990. 18.95 (*0-942361-15-6*) MasterMedia Ltd.

Confidence Factor: How Self-Esteem Can Change Your Life. Judith Briles. 1991. pap. 9.95 (*0-942361-26-1*) MasterMedia Ltd.

***Confidence Game: How Unelected Central Bankers Are Governing the Changed Global Economy.** Steven Solomon. LC 94-45734. 1995. 30.00 (*0-684-80182-5*) S&S Trade.

Confidence Game in American Literature. Warwick Wadlington. LC 75-3480. 389p. 1975. 52.50 (*0-691-06294-3*) Princeton U Pr.

***Confidence Game in American Literature.** Warwick Wadlington. LC 75-3480. Date not set. reprint ed. pap. 98.10 (*0-7837-9470-3*, 2060212) Bks Demand.

Confidence Gap: Business, Labor & Government in the Public Mind. rev. ed. Seymour M. Lipset & William Schneider. LC 86-27416. 480p. 1987. pap. text ed. 14.95 (*0-8018-3044-3*) Johns Hopkins.

Confidence in God in Times of Danger. Alex Carson. pap. 5.99 (*0-87377-035-8*) GAM Pubns.

C

An Asterisk (*) at the beginning of an entry indicates that the title is appearing in BIP for the first time.

***Confidence in Public Speaking.** Paul E. Nelson & Judy Pearson. 304p. (C). 1995. pap. write for info. (*0-697-24635-3*) Brown & Benchmark.

Confidence in Public Speaking. 5th ed. Paul E. Nelson & Judy Pearson. 368p. (C). 1993. pap. text ed. write for info. (*0-697-12934-9*) Brown & Benchmark.

Confidence in Writing: A Basic Text. 2nd ed. Ed Reynolds & Marcia Mixdorf. 350p. (C). 1990. pap. text ed. 20.00 (*0-15-512987-2*) HB Coll Pubs.

Confidence Intervals on Variance Components. Ed. by Burdick & Graybill. (Statistics: Vol. 127). 224p. 1992. 110.00 (*0-8247-8644-0*) Dekker.

Confidence Man. Herman Melville. (Airmont Classics Ser.). (J). (gr. 11 up). 1966. pap. 1.95 (*0-8049-0121-X*, CL-121) Airmont.

Confidence Man. Herman Melville. (C). 1971. pap. text ed. 9.95 (*0-393-09968-7*) Norton.

Confidence Man. Herman Melville. 24.95 (*0-89190-890-0*, Am Repr) Amereon Ltd.

Confidence Man. Herman Melville. 1964. mass mkt. 4.95 (*0-452-00894-8*, Mer) NAL-Dutton.

Confidence-Man. Herman Melville. Ed. by Harrison Hayford et al. (Northwestern-Newberry Edition of the Writings of Herman Melville: Vol. 10). 518p. 1984. 49.95 (*0-8101-0324-9*); pap. 18.95 (*0-8101-0325-7*) Northwestern U Pr.

Confidence-Man. Herman Melville. Ed. by Tony Tanner & John Dugdale. (World's Classics Ser.). (Illus.). 408p. 1989. pap. 7.95 (*0-19-281824-4*) OUP.

Confidence-Man. Herman Melville. 400p. 1991. mass mkt. 8.95 (*0-14-044547-1*, Penguin Classics) Viking Penguin.

Confidence Man. annot. ed. Herman Melville. Ed. by Elizabeth S. Foster. (Complete Works of Herman Melville Ser.). 1979. 29.95 (*0-87532-009-0*) Hendricks House.

Confidence-Man. Herman Melville. 260p. 1990. reprint ed. lib. bdg. 21.95 (*0-89966-714-7*) Buccaneer Bks.

Confidence-Man: His Masquerade. Herman Melville. Ed. by H. Bruce Franklin. LC 66-30445. 1967. pap. 6.95 (*0-672-60986-X*, LL13, Bobbs) Macmillan.

Confidence-Man see Pierre, Israel Potter, the Confidence-Man, Tales & Billy Budd

Confidence Men & Painted Women: A Study of Middle-Class Culture in America, 1830-1870. Karen Halttunen. LC 82-8336. (Historical Publications, Miscellany Ser.: No. 129). 280p. 1986. text ed. 14.00 (*0-300-03788-0*) Yale U Pr.

***Confidence of the Heart.** David Schweidel. LC 94-33644. (Orig.). 1995. pap. 12.95 (*1-57131-004-5*) Milkweed Ed.

Confidence Regained: Economics, Mrs. Thatcher, & the British Voter. Helmut Norpoth. 250p. (C). 1992. text ed. 42.50 (*0-472-10333-4*) U of Mich Pr.

Confidence Without Conceit see Prime-Time Principles for Success

Confidence, 1880. Henry James. Ed. by Herbert Ruhm. LC 76-39775. 238p. 1977. reprint ed. text ed. 38.50 (*0-8371-9296-X*, JACO, Greenwood Pr) Greenwood.

Confidences. Marcel Pagnol. (FRE.). 1990. pap. 13.95 (*0-7859-3329-8*, 2877060691) Fr & Eur.

Confidences de Nicolas. Gerard de Nerval. 236p. 1945. 50.00 (*0-686-54813-2*) Fr & Eur.

Confident & Competent: A Challenge for the Lay Church. William L. Droel & Gregory F. Pierce. 110p. (Orig.). 1987. reprint ed. pap. 4.95 (*0-914070-80-0*, 112) ACTA Pubns.

Confident Childbirth: Your Guide Through Pregnancy, Labor, Birth & Early Parenthood. Mary J. Smith. (Illus.). 100p. (Orig.). 1991. pap. 12.95 (*0-9630874-0-1*) A P P L E Fam.

Confident Collector Posters Identification & Price Guide. 2nd ed. Tony Fusco. LC 93-42431. (Illus.). 520p. (Orig.). 1994. pap. 17.00 (*0-380-77010-5*) Avon.

***Confident Consumer.** Sally R. Campbell. LC 94-30365. (Illus.). 386p. 1995. text ed. 39.96 (*1-56637-088-4*) Goodheart.

Confident Decision Maker: How to Make the Right Business & Personal Decisions Every Time. Roger Dawson. LC 92-21364. 1993. 20.00 (*0-688-11564-0*) Morrow.

***Confident Decision Maker: How to Make the Right Business & Personal Decisions Every Time.** Roger Dawson. 1995. 11.50 (*0-688-14228-1*, Quill) Morrow.

Confident Kids: Helping Your Child Cope with Fear. Janet Hall. 120p. (Orig.). 1995. pap. 12.95 (*0-85091-577-5*, Pub. by Lothian Pub AT) Seven Hills Bk.

Confident Leader: Management Strategies That Work in the Local Church. Arlo Grenz. LC 93-26960. (Orig.). 1994. pap. 15.99 (*0-8054-6061-6*) Broadman.

Confident Learner: Help Your Child Succeed in School. Marjorie R. Simic et al. Ed. by Carl B. Smith. LC 91-77793. (Successful Learner Ser.). (Illus.). 156p. (Orig.). 1992. pap. 9.95 (*0-9628556-4-2*) Grayson Bernard Pubs.

Confident Living: Practical Psychology & the Christian Faith. Chris Schriner & Sue I. Mauck. (Illus.). 101p. (Orig.). (C). 1982. pap. text ed. 6.00 (*0-914527-17-7*) C-Four Res.

Confident Music Performance. Barbara Schneiderman. LC 91-29298. 160p. (Orig.). 1992. pap. 14.95 (*0-918812-70-4*, SE0170) MMB Music.

Confident Parenting. Mel Silberman. 144p. (Orig.). 1988. mass mkt. 6.95 (*0-446-38670-7*) Warner Bks.

***Confident Parents, Confident Children: Policy & Practice in Parent Education & Support.** Gillian Pugh et al. 288p. 1995. 25.50 (*1-874579-37-7*, Pub. by Natl Childrens Bur UK) Paul & Co Pubs.

Confident Pastoral Leadership. 2nd ed. Howard F. Sugden & Warren W. Wiersbe. LC 92-42722. 192p. (Orig.). 1993. pap. 9.99 (*0-8010-8351-6*) Baker Bk.

Confident Speaker: How to Master Fear & Persuade an Audience. Ray Harlan. LC 92-62046. 274p. 1993. 24.95 (*1-881117-01-4*) McGuinn & McGuire.

Confident Student. Carol Kanar. (C). 1991. write for info. (*0-395-54003-8*) HM Soft Schl Col Div.

Confident Traveler: A Complete Travel Guide for the Business Woman. Illus. by Dolores L. Popp. LC 88-60723. 128p. (Orig.). 1988. pap. 12.95 (*0-945565-00-3*) Shiro Pubs.

Confident Woman. Anabel Gillham. LC 93-19. 1993. pap. 8.99 (*1-56507-071-2*) Harvest Hse.

***Confident Woman.** Trobisch. 1995. pap. 10.00 (*0-06-067595-0*) Harper SF.

Confident Woman. Joanne Wallace. 168p. (Orig.). 1991. pap. text ed. 12.95 (*1-880527-00-6*) J Wallace Sem.

Confident Woman: Finding Quiet Strength in a Turbulent World. Ingrid Trobisch. LC 92-56741. 1993. 14.00 (*0-06-068552-2*) Harper SF.

Confident Writer: A Norton Handbook. Constance Gefvert. (C). 1987. Instr's. manual. teacher ed, pap. text ed. write for info. (*0-393-95622-9*); student ed, pap. text ed. 16.95 (*0-393-95620-2*) Norton.

Confident Writer: A Norton Handbook. Constance Gefvert. (C). 1988. Diagnostic tests. student ed, pap. text ed. write for info. (*0-393-95624-5*) Norton.

Confident Writer: A Norton Handbook. 2nd ed. Constance Gefvert. (C). 1987. text ed. 25.95 (*0-393-95618-0*) Norton.

Confident You: A Guide to Eternal Beauty. Barbara B. Jones & Kris Mackay. LC 91-47723. xvi, 158p. (Orig.). 1992. pap. 10.95 (*0-87579-604-4*) Deseret Bk.

Confidential Attendant. Jack Rudman. (Career Examination Ser.: C-1211). 1994. pap. 23.95 (*0-8373-1211-6*) Nat Learn.

Confidential Clerk. T. S. Eliot. LC 54-5253. 160p. 1901. pap. 6.95 (*0-15-622015-6*, Harvest Bks) HarBrace.

Confidential Correspondence of Gustavus Vasa Fox, 2 vols, Set. Ed. by Robert M. Thompson & Richard Wainwright. LC 77-39710. (Select Bibliographies Reprint Ser.). 1977. reprint ed. 50.95 (*0-8369-9946-0*) Ayer.

Confidential Correspondence of Gustavus Vasa Fox, Assistant Secretary of the Navy, 1861-1865, 2 vols. Gustavus V. Fox. (American Biography Ser.). 1991. reprint ed. lib. bdg. write for info. (*0-7812-8136-9*) Rprt Serv.

Confidential Dispatches: Analyses of America by the British Ambassador, 1939-1945. Ed. by Thomas E. Hachey. 335p. 1974. 19.95x (*0-89044-019-0*) Transaction Pubs.

Confidential Frequency List. 7th ed. Halligey. LC 88-80150. 376p. 1988. pap. 19.95 (*0-914542-20-6*) Gilfer.

Confidential Information Sources Public & Private. 2nd ed. John M. Carroll. 416p. 1991. text ed. 52.95 (*0-7506-9018-6*) Buttrwrth-Heinemann.

Confidential Investigator. Jack Rudman. (Career Examination Ser.: C-2806). 1994. pap. 27.95 (*0-8373-2806-3*) Nat Learn.

Confidential Loophole! A Little Known Business That Has Been Kept Secret for the Past Twenty-Five Years! rev. ed. Scott T. Hagen. (Illus.). 122p. 1988. pap. text ed. 10.00 (*0-915451-13-1*) New Start Pubns.

Confidential Matter: The Letters of Richard Strauss & Stefan Zweig, 1931-1935. Richard Strauss. Tr. by Max Knight. LC 75-13162. 154p. reprint ed. pap. 43.90 (*0-685-23497-5*, 2029064) Bks Demand.

Confidential Proxy Voting. Patrick S. McGurn. 118p. 1989. pap. 50.00 (*0-931035-73-2*) IRRC Inc DC.

Confidential Reporter. Jack Rudman. (Career Examination Ser.: C-1212). 1994. pap. 23.95 (*0-8373-1212-4*) Nat Learn.

Confidential Secretary. Jack Rudman. (Career Examination Ser.: C-3023). 1994. pap. 23.95 (*0-8373-3023-8*) Nat Learn.

Confidentiality & Clergy: Churches, Ethics & the Law. William W. Rankin. LC 90-37966. 176p. (Orig.). 1990. pap. 8.95 (*0-8192-1530-9*) Morehouse Pub.

Confidentiality & the Law. Linda Clarke. 1990. 100.00 (*1-85044-323-8*) Lloyds London Pr.

Confidentiality & the Law. B. C. Reid. (Waterlow Practitioner's Library). 224p. 1986. 49.00 (*0-08-039236-9*, Pergamon Pr) Elsevier.

Confidentiality, Due Process & the Business of Central Registries: Legal & Policy Considerations. 56p. 1988. 3.00 (*0-685-24113-0*, NCSC-061) Natl Ctr St Courts.

Confidentiality in Libraries: An Intellectual Freedom Modular Education Program. Anne Penway. LC 92-38348. 140p. 1993. 12.50 (*0-8389-3425-0*); 12.50 (*0-8389-3422-6*); 12.50 (*0-8389-3423-4*); 12.50 (*0-8389-3424-2*); 12.50 (*0-8389-3421-8*); teacher ed, pap. text ed. 99.00 (*0-8389-3420-X*) ALA.

Confidentiality in Mediation: A Practitioner's Guide. Lawrence Freedman et al. LC 86-128698. v, 320p. 1985. pap. 20.00 (*0-89707-173-5*, 474-0021-01) Amer Bar Assn.

Confidentiality in Social Work. Joseph T. Alves. LC 84-721. xvi, 268p. (C). 1984. reprint ed. text ed. 59.75 (*0-313-24459-6*, ALCO, Greenwood Pr) Greenwood.

Confidentiality in Social Work: Issues & Principles. Suanna J. Wilson. LC 77-18475. 1980. pap. 15.95 (*0-02-934850-1*) Free Pr.

Confidentiality in the United States: A Legal & Canonical Study. Ed. by Donna K. Ioppolo et al. 167p. (Orig.). 1989. pap. 20.00 (*0-943616-43-3*) Canon Law Soc.

Confidentiality of Health Records: The Meeting of Law, Ethics, & Clinical Issues. Herman Schuchman et al. LC 82-990. 1982. text ed. 30.00 (*0-89876-024-0*) Gardner Pr.

Confidentiality Orders. Francis H. Hare, Jr. et al. LC 87-28807. (Trial Practice Library). 349p. 1988. text ed. 125.00 (*0-471-62461-6*) Wiley.

Confidentiality Versus the Duty to Protect: Foreseeable Harm in the Practice of Psychiatry. Ed. by James C. Beck. LC 90-13. 192p. 1990. 27.50 (*0-88048-170-6*, FTFA8170) Am Psychiatric.

Confidently Committed: A Look at the Baptist Heritage. Virgil W. Bopp. LC 87-23404. 244p. (Orig.). 1987. pap. 10.95 (*0-87227-119-6*) Reg Baptist.

Confiding. Susan Baur. 320p. 1994. 23.00 (*0-06-018238-5*, HarpT) HarpC.

***Confiding.** Susan Baur. 1995. pap. 12.00 (*0-06-092633-3*, PL) HarpC.

Confieso Que He Vivido. Pablo Neruda. 464p. (SPA.). 1984. pap. 10.95 (*0-7859-5004-4*) Fr & Eur.

Configural Polysampling: A Route to Practical Robustness. Ed. by S. Morgenthaler & John W. Tukey. (Series in Probability & Mathematics). 228p. 1991. text ed. 69.95 (*0-471-52372-0*) Wiley.

***Configuration & Capacity Planning for Solaris Servers.** Wong. 1995. pap. text ed. 38.00 (*0-13-349952-9*) P-H.

Configuration Management. W. F. Tichey. 1995. pap. text ed. 34.95 (*0-471-94245-6*) Wiley.

Configuration Management Deskbook. Thomas T. Samaras. Ed. by Marilyn J. Humm. (Illus.). 1988. 48.00 (*0-934321-09-4*, 602-1) Adv Appl Consul.

Configuration Management Deskbook Instruction Supplement. Thomas T. Samaras. Ed. by Marilyn J. Humm. 1988. 12.00 (*0-934321-10-8*, 602-2) Adv Appl Consul.

Configuration Management for Software. Stephen B. Compton & Guy Connor. (Illus.). 256p. 1994. pap. 39.95 (*0-442-01746-4*) Van Nos Reinhold.

Configuration Management Procedures. Powers Management Consultants Staff. Ed. by J. H. Leiblich. 121p. 1984. pap. 35.00 (*0-912702-25-7*) Global Eng Doc.

Configurationality: The Typology of Asymmetries. Ed. by Laszlo K. Maracz & Pieter Muysken. (Studies in Generative Grammar). vi, 236p. (Orig.). (C). 1989. pap. 64.30 (*90-6765-405-1*) Mouton.

Configurationality in Hungarian. Katalin E. Kiss. (C). 1987. pap. text ed. 45.50 (*90-277-2456-3*) Kluwer Ac.

Configurations. Octavio Paz. LC 78-145932. (ENG & SPA.). 1971. pap. (*0-8112-0150-3*, NDP303) New Directions.

Configurations: Number Puzzles & Patterns for All Ages. Harold L. Dorwart. 1972. 10.00 (*0-911624-32-5*) Wffn Proof.

Configurations at Midnight. Ralph Gustafson. 80p. (C). 1992. pap. 12.00 (*1-55022-173-6*, Pub. by ECW Press CN) Genl Dist Srvs.

Configurations of Faust: Three Studies in the Gothic (1798-1820) Joseph A. Soldati. Ed. by Devendra P. Varma. LC 79-8482. (Gothic Studies & Dissertations). 1980. lib. bdg. 23.95 (*0-405-12662-X*) Ayer.

Configurations of Masculinity: A Feminist Perspective on Modern Political Theory. Christine Di Stefano. LC 90-55730. 256p. 1991. 34.50 (*0-8014-2534-4*); pap. 13.95 (*0-8014-9765-5*) Cornell U Pr.

Configurations of Power: Holistic Anthropology in Theory & Practice. Ed. by John S. Henderson & Patricia J. Netherly. LC 92-52759. 360p. 1993. 46.00 (*0-8014-2487-9*) Cornell U Pr.

Configuring a Customized Engineering Workstation. Harley Bjelland. LC 94-12266. 1995. pap. text ed. 29.95 (*0-07-005927-6*, Windcrest) TAB Bks.

***Configuring Topic & Focus in Russian.** Tracy H. King. (Dissertations in Linguistics Ser.). 1995. text ed. 45.00 (*1-881526-63-1*); pap. text ed. 22.95 (*1-881526-62-3*) Ctr Study Language.

***Confined Electrons & Photons: New Physics & Applications: Proceedings of a NATO ASI Held in Erice, Italy, July 13-26, 1993.** Ed. by Elias Burstein & Claude Weisbuch. (NATO ASI Series B: Vol. 340). 925p. 1995. 195.00 (*0-306-44990-0*) Plenum.

Confined Space Compliance Manual: OSHA (CFR 1910.146) James Testo. Ed. by Failsafe Risk Management Alternative Staff. 350p. 1993. ring bd. 99.00 (*0-931690-61-7*) Genium Pub.

Confined Space Entry: A Special Publication. Task Force on Confined Space Entry. LC 94-13098. 1994. 20.00 (*1-881369-39-0*) Water Environ.

***Confined Space Entry: Complying with the Standard.** James E. Roughton. 190p. (Orig.). 1994. per., pap. text ed. 75.00 (*0-86587-406-9*) Gov Insts.

Confined Space Pocket Guide. John Conforti & Christine Gorman. (Illus.). 80p. (Orig.). 1993. pap. 41.80 (*0-931690-41-2*) Genium Pub.

Confined Space Safety & Rescue. R. Schroll. 1988. text ed. write for info. (*0-442-00250-5*) Van Nos Reinhold.

Confined Space Safety & Rescue. R. Craig Schroll. (Illus.). 1990. pap. text ed. 25.00 (*0-945492-02-2*) Firecon.

***Confined Space Safety Manual.** R. Craig Schroll. (Illus.). 1995. pap. text ed. 35.00 (*0-945492-03-0*) Firecon.

Confirm or Deny. large type ed. Graham Ison. 1993. 39.95 (*0-7066-1032-6*, Pub. by Remploy Pr CN) St Mut.

***Confirmation.** John Barnie. 129p. 1992. pap. 24.00 (*0-86383-671-2*, Pub. by Gomer Pr UK) St Mut.

Confirmation. John Barnie. 129p. (C). 1992. pap. 40.00 (*0-685-60032-7*, Pub. by Gomer Pr UK) St Mut.

***Confirmation.** K. Peters. 1994. pap. 6.95 (*1-55713-154-6*) Sun & Moon CA.

Confirmation. Karl Rahner. 1979. pap. 4.95 (*0-87193-123-0*) Dimension Bks.

Confirmation. 2nd ed. Allan D. Coleman. (Illus.). 48p. 1982. pap. 4.00 (*0-9608870-0-8*) ADCO Enterp.

Confirmation: A Parish Celebration. Timothy Fitzgerald. (Font & Table Ser.). (Illus.). 62p. 1983. pap. 4.50 (*0-930467-22-1*) Liturgy Tr Pubns.

Confirmation: A Workbook Based on the Book of Common Prayer 1979. Comp. by Steven L. Cunningham. (Orig.). 1984. pap. 2.75 (*0-8192-4106-7*) Morehouse Pub.

Confirmation: Origins & Reform. Aidan Kavanagh. 137p. 1992. pap. 12.95 (*0-8146-6088-6*, Pueblo Bks) Liturgical Pr.

Confirmation: The Baby in Solomon's Court. Paul Turner. LC 92-32094. 208p. 1993. pap. 11.95 (*0-8091-3370-9*) Paulist Pr.

Confirmation in the Church Today. Philip E. Hughes. 56p. reprint ed. pap. 25.00 (*0-317-08439-9*, 2012949) Bks Demand.

Confirmation Learning Theory. Raymond E. Hartley & Carl D. Williams. (American University Studies: Psychology: Ser. VIII). 419p. (C). 1989. text ed. 50.50 (*0-8204-0713-5*) P Lang Pubs.

Confirmation Mess: Cleaning up the Federal Appointments Process. Stephen L. Carter. LC 93-40377. 208p. 1994. 21.00 (*0-465-01364-3*) Basic.

***Confirmation Mess: Cleaning up the Federal Appointments Process.** Stephen L. Carter. 272p. 1995. pap. 12.00 (*0-465-01365-1*) Basic.

Confirmation of Accounts Receivable. (Auditing Procedure Studies). 53p. 1984. 25.00 (*0-317-37156-8*) Am Inst CPA.

Confirmatory Factor Analysis. J. Scott Long. (Quantitative Applications in the Social Sciences Ser.: Vol. 33). 88p. 1983. pap. text ed. 9.95 (*0-8039-2044-X*) Sage.

Confirmed As Children, Affirmed As Teens. Ed. by James A. Wilde. (Font & Table Ser.). 98p. (Orig.). 1990. pap. 5.95 (*0-929650-27-1*) Liturgy Tr Pubns.

Confirmed in Christ. Roy C. Gesch. (YA). (gr. 7 up). 1983. pap. 2.99 (*0-570-03911-8*, 12-2852) Concordia.

Confirmed in Love. B. Bres. (C). 1988. 30.00 (*0-85439-125-8*, Pub. by St Paul Pubns UK) St Mut.

***Confirmed in the Spirit: Prayer Services for Confirmation Classes & Retreats.** M. Valerie Schneider. LC 95-60518. 224p. (Orig.). 1995. pap. 12.95 (*0-89622-655-7*) Twenty-Third.

Confirmed Kill: Direct Hit, No. 3. 176p. (Orig.). 1993. pap. 4.50 (*1-55773-815-7*) Diamond.

Confirmed Kill, No. 4: Point Blank. Mike Morris. 208p. (Orig.). 1993. pap. 4.50 (*1-55773-898-X*) Diamond.

***Confirming Faith: A Faith Development Program for High School Students Preparing to Celebrate the Sacrament of Confirmation with the Support of the Entire Faith Community.** Kieran Sawyer & Mike Amodei. LC 94-73211. (Illus.). 32p. (YA). (gr. 10-12). 1995. pap. text ed. 1.95 (*0-87793-550-5*) Ave Maria.

***Confirming Faith: A Faith Development Program for High School Students Preparing to Celebrate the Sacrament of Confirmation with the Support of the Entire Faith Community.** Kieran Sawyer & Mike Amodei. LC 94-73211. (Illus.). 232p. (YA). (gr. 10-12). 1995. teacher ed, spiral bd. 14.95 (*0-87793-548-3*) Ave Maria.

***Confirming Faith: A Faith Development Program for High School Students Preparing to Celebrate the Sacrament of Confirmation with the Support of the Entire Faith Community.** rev. ed. Kieran Sawyer & Mike Amodei. LC 94-73211. (Illus.). 152p. (YA). (gr. 11-12). 1995. pap. text ed. 4.95 (*0-87793-549-1*) Ave Maria.

Conflatio. John Byrum. 26p. (Orig.). 1991. pap. 3.00 (*0-926935-40-2*) Runaway Spoon.

Conflict. Poul Anderson. 288p. (Orig.). 1985. pap. 2.95 (*0-8125-3088-8*) Tor Bks.

Conflict. David C. Phillips. (Collected Works of David G. Phillips). 1988. reprint ed. lib. bdg. 79.00 (*0-7812-1341-X*) Rprt Serv.

Conflict. David G. Phillips. (American Author Ser.). 1981. reprint ed. lib. bdg. 49.00 (*0-686-71911-5*) Scholarly.

Conflict: Human Needs Theory. Ed. by John Burton. 375p. 1993. pap. 24.95 (*0-312-10618-1*) St Martin.

Conflict: Resolution & Ethnicity. Mohamed Rabie. LC 94-6381. 240p. 1994. text ed. 55.00 (*0-275-94598-7*, Praeger Pubs) Greenwood.

Conflict: Resolution & Prevention. John Burton. LC 89-10747. 270p. 1990. pap. 19.95 (*0-312-03748-1*) St Martin.

Conflict: Resolution & Public Policy. Ed. by Miriam K. Mills. LC 90-36780. (Contributions in Political Science Ser.: No. 262). 232p. 1990. text ed. 55.00 (*0-313-27519-X*, MRG, Greenwood Pr) Greenwood.

Conflict! The World, the Flesh & the Devil. G. W. Steidl. 98p. pap. 3.95 (*0-88172-173-5*) Believers Bkshelf.

Conflict - From Theory to Action. Roxane S. Lulofs. LC 93-32038. 1993. pap. text ed. 30.00 (*0-89787-352-1*) Gorsuch Scarisbrick.

Conflict Across the Strait: A Battery Commander's Story of Kent's Defences 1939-1945. B. E. Arnold. 174p. 1984. 39.00 (*0-906124-06-9*, Pub. by Regency Press) St Mut.

Conflict, Action & Suspense. Bill Noble. (Elements of Fiction Ser.). 176p. 1994. 14.99 (*0-89879-634-2*) Writers Digest.

Conflict After the Cold War: Arguments on Causes of War & Peace. Ed. by Richard K. Betts. LC 93-10550. 528p. (C). 1994. pap. write for info. (*0-02-309191-6*) Macmillan.

Conflict among Nations: Bargaining, Decision Making & System Structure in International Crises. Glenn H. Snyder & Paul Diesing. LC 77-72135. 1977. pap. 26.95 (*0-691-10057-8*) Princeton U Pr.

***Conflict among Nations: Bargaining, Decision Making, & System Structure in International Crises.** Glenn H. Snyder & Paul Diesing. LC 77-72135. reprint ed. pap. 169.60 (*0-7837-9284-0*, 2060023) Bks Demand.

Conflict among Nations: Trade Policies in the 1990s. Ed. by Thomas R. Howell et al. 633p. (C). 1992. pap. text ed. 49.85 (*0-8133-1255-8*) Westview.

Conflict Analysis: Models & Resolutions. Ed. by N. M. Fraser & K. W. Hipel. (Series in System Science & Engineering: Vol. 11). 1984. 50.50 (*0-444-00921-3*) Elsevier.

C

An Asterisk (*) at the beginning of an entry indicates that the title is appearing in BIP for the first time. 1535

Conflict Analysis & Practical Conflict Management Procedures: For Regional Scientists (or Regional Science Students) Walter Isard & Christine Smith. (Regional Science Reprint Ser.: No. 5). (Illus.). 500p. (C). 1985. pap. text ed. 7.50 (*0-943019-04-4*) Cornell CRPP.

Conflict Analysis-The Formal Theory of Behavior: A Theory & Its Experimental Validation. Albert J. Levis. LC 88-90914. (Illus.). 500p. (C). 1989. 50.00 (*0-929642-00-7*) Normative Pubns.

Conflict Analysis Training: A Program of Emotional Education. Albert J. Levis. LC 88-90913. (Illus.). 160p. (Orig.). (C). 1989. pap. 25.00 (*0-929642-01-5*) Normative Pubns.

Conflict & Accommodation: Coal Miners, Steel Workers & Socialism, 1890 to 1920. Michael H. Nash. LC 81-6691. (Contributions in Labor History Ser.: No. 11). (Illus.). xiv, 197p. 1982. text ed. 49.95 (*0-313-22838-8*, NCO/, Greenwood Pr) Greenwood.

Conflict & Accommodation Between Jews in Israel: Religious & Secular. Ed. by Charles S. Liebman. 8.95 (*0-88125-374-X*) Ktav.

Conflict & Accommodation in Early Modern East Asia: Essays in Honour of Erik Zurcher. Ed. by Leonard Blusse & Harriet T. Zurndorfer. LC 92-46561. 1993. 91.50 (*90-04-09775-9*) E J Brill.

Conflict & Accommodation in Western Kenya: The Gusii & the British, 1907-1963. Robert M. Maxon. LC 88-45734. (Illus.). 216p. 1989. 37.50 (*0-8386-3350-1*) Fairleigh Dickinson.

Conflict & Acculturation: Manuel Alvarez's 1842 Memorial. Ed. by Tom Chavez. (Illus.). 98p. 1989. text ed. 15.95 (*0-89013-191-0*) Museum NM Pr.

Conflict & Amity in East Asia: Essays in Honor of Ian Nish. Ed. by T. G. Fraser & Peter Lowe. 196p. (C). 1992. text ed. 69.95 (*0-333-54539-7*) St Martin.

Conflict & Bargaining. Ed. by Sanjaya Lall. 1976. pap. 19.75 (*0-08-021060-0*, Pergamon Pr) Elsevier.

Conflict & Bargaining in the Middle East: An Israeli Perspective. Shlomo Aronson. LC 77-10967. 1978. text ed. 68.00x (*0-8018-2046-4*) Johns Hopkins.

Conflict & Change in Cuba. Ed. by Enrique A. Baloyra & James A. Morris. LC 93-2426. 366p. 1993. pap. 20.95 (*0-8263-1465-1*) U of NM Pr.

Conflict & Change in Cuba. Ed. by Enrique A. Baloyra & James A. Morris. LC 93-2426. 366p. 1993. 45.00x (*0-8263-1464-3*) U of NM Pr.

Conflict & Change in Mexican Economic Strategy: Implications for Mexico & for Latin America. John Sheahan. (Monograph Ser.: No. 34). (Orig.). 1991. pap. 10.95 (*1-878367-05-6*, MN-34) UCSD Ctr US-Mex.

Conflict & Change in the Catholic Church. John Seidler & Katherine Meyer. LC 88-21758. 224p. (C). 1989. text ed. 40.00 (*0-8135-1384-7*); pap. text ed. 13.00 (*0-8135-1385-5*) Rutgers U Pr.

Conflict & Change, 1650-1800. Fiona Reynoldson. LC 92-20460. (Illustrated History of the World Ser.). (Illus.). 80p. (J). (gr. 2-6). 1993. 17.95 (*0-8160-2790-0*) Facts on File.

***Conflict & Chaos in Eastern Europe Vol. 1.** Dennis P. Hupchick. LC 94-38207. 1995. 29.95 (*0-312-12116-4*) St Martin.

Conflict & Christianity in Northern Ireland. Brian Mawhinney & Ronald Wells. LC 75-8948. (Illus.). 126p. reprint ed. pap. 36.00 (*0-317-09250-2*, 2012891) Bks Demand.

Conflict & Class: Scottish Workers, 1700-1838. W. Hamish Fraser. 212p. (C). 1989. 80.00 (*0-85976-207-6*, Pub. by J Donald) St Mut.

Conflict & Coexistence in Belgium: The Dynamics of a Culturally Divided Society. Ed. by Arend Lijphart. LC 81-7200. (Research Ser.: No. 46). (Illus.). ix, 171p. 1981. pap. 10.50 (*0-87725-146-0*) U of Cal IAS.

Conflict & Cohesion in Socialist Yugoslavia: Political Decision Making since 1966. Steven L. Burg. LC 82-61358. 456p. 1983. 57.50 (*0-691-07651-0*) Princeton U Pr.

***Conflict & Cohesion in Socialist Yugoslavia: Political Decision Making since 1966.** Steven L. Burg. LC 82-61358. reprint ed. pap. 108.10 (*0-7837-9309-X*, 2060049) Bks Demand.

Conflict & Collaboration: The Kingdoms of Western Uganda, 1890-1907. Edward I. Steinhart. LC 77-722136. 1977. 47.50 (*0-691-03114-2*) Princeton U Pr.

***Conflict & Collaboration: The Kingdoms of Western Uganda, 1890-1907.** Edward I. Steinhart. LC 77-72136. Date not set. reprint ed. pap. 91.80 (*0-7837-9453-3*, 2060195) Bks Demand.

Conflict & Community: New Studies in Thomistic Thought. Michael B. Lukens. LC 89-34167. 204p. (C). 1992. text ed. 39.95 (*0-8204-1204-X*) P Lang Pubs.

Conflict & Community in Corinth: A Socio-Rhetorical Commentary on First & Second Corinthians. Ben Witherington, III. 600p. (C). 1994. pap. text ed. 34.99 (*0-8028-0144-7*) Eerdmans.

Conflict & Community in Southern England. Ed. by Barry Stapleton. (Illus.). 192p. (C). 1992. text ed. 70.00 (*0-7509-0161-6*) A Sutton Pub.

Conflict & Community in Southern England: Essays in the Social History of Rural & Urban Labour from Medieval to Modern Times. Ed. by Barry Stapleton. LC 92-18693. 1992. text ed. 59.95 (*0-312-08611-3*) St Martin.

Conflict & Competition: The Latin American Church in a Changing Environment. Ed. by Edward L. Cleary & Hannah Stewart-Gambino. LC 91-44237. 234p. 1992. lib. bdg. 40.00 (*1-55587-251-4*); pap. text ed. 17.95 (*1-55587-332-4*) Lynne Rienner.

Conflict & Compliance: Class Consciousness among Swedish Workers. Mona Rosendahl. 214p. (Orig.). 1985. pap. text ed. 54.00x (*91-85284-24-6*) Coronet Bks.

Conflict & Compromise: An Introduction to Politics. Herbert R. Winter & Thomas J. Bellows. (C). 1991. text ed. 54.00 (*0-673-38807-7*) HarpCollege.

***Conflict & Compromise: How Congress Makes the Law.** Ronald D. Elving. LC 95-5572. 1995. 25.00 (*0-684-80195-7*) S&S Trade.

Conflict & Compromise: International Law & World Order in a Revolutionary Age. Edward McWhinney. LC 80-29045. 152p. (C). 1981. 29.50 (*0-8419-0694-7*); pap. 16.95 (*0-8419-0696-3*) Holmes & Meier.

Conflict & Compromise: The Political Economy of Slavery, Emancipation, & the American Civil War. Roger L. Ransom. (Illus.). (C). 1989. 59.95 (*0-521-32343-6*); pap. 17.95 (*0-521-31167-5*) Cambridge U Pr.

Conflict & Compromise: Therapeutic Implications. Ed. by Scott Dowling. LC 91-30989. (Workshop Series of the American Psychoanalytic Association: Monograph 7). 248p. (C). 1991. text ed. 32.50 (*0-8236-3435-3*) Intl Univs Pr.

Conflict & Compromise in Multilingual Societies, Vol. 2: Belgium. K. McRae. (Politics of Cultural Diversity Ser.: No. V. 1-2). 384p. (C). 1986. pap. 19.95 (*0-88920-195-1*, Pub. by Wilfrid Laurier CN) Humanities.

Conflict & Compromise in Multilingual Societies, Vol. 2: Belgium. 3rd ed. K. McRae. (Politics of Cultural Diversity Ser.: No. V. 1-2). 384p. (C). 1986. text ed. 49.95 (*0-88920-163-3*, Pub. by Wilfrid Laurier CN) Humanities.

Conflict & Conciliation in Ireland 1890-1910: Parnellites & Radical Agrarians. Paul Bew. LC 86-28578. (Illus.). 240p. 1987. 49.95 (*0-19-822758-2*) OUP.

Conflict & Conflict Resolution: A Sociological Introduction with Updated Bibliography & Theory Section. Jack N. Porter & Ruth Taplin. LC 87-8215. 114p. (Orig.). (C). 1987. lib. bdg. 42.00 (*0-8191-6368-6*) U Pr of Amer.

Conflict & Confrontation: A Training Program. Peter Muniz & Robert Chasnoff. 26p. (C). 1981. pap. text ed. 7.00 (*0-943300-01-0*) LABS.

Conflict & Consensus. Ed. by Allen F. Davis & Harold D. Woodman. 556p. (C). 1992. In Modern American History, 556 p. pap. text ed. write for info. (*0-669-26908-5*) Heath.

Conflict & Consensus. 8th ed. Ed. by Allen F. Davis & Harold D. Woodman. 454p. (C). 1992. In Early American History, 454 p. pap. text ed. write for info. (*0-669-24990-4*) Heath.

Conflict & Consensus: A Festchrift in Honor of Lewis A. Coser. Ed. by Walter W. Powell & Richard Robbins. LC 83-48642. 464p. (C). 1984. text ed. 35.00 (*0-02-925400-0*) Free Pr.

Conflict & Consensus: A General Theory of Collective Decisions. Serge Moscovici & Willem Doise. 240p. 1994. 69.95 (*0-8039-8456-1*); pap. 21.95 (*0-8039-8457-X*) Sage.

Conflict & Consensus in American History, 2 vols. 6th ed. Allen F. Davis & Harold D. Woodman. (C). 1983. pap. text ed. write for info. (*0-318-57819-0*) Heath.

Conflict & Consensus in American History, 2 vols., 1. 6th ed. Allen F. Davis & Harold D. Woodman. (C). 1983. pap. text ed. 16.00 (*0-669-06751-2*) Heath.

Conflict & Consensus in American History, 2 vols., 2. 6th ed. Allen F. Davis & Harold D. Woodman. (C). 1983. pap. text ed. write for info. (*0-669-06750-4*) Heath.

Conflict & Consensus in American History, 2 vols., I. 7th ed. Allen F. Davis & Harold D. Woodman. LC 87-81344. 1988. pap. text ed. 16.00 (*0-669-12802-3*) Heath.

Conflict & Consensus in American History, 2 vols., II. 7th ed. Allen F. Davis & Harold D. Woodman. LC 87-81344. 1988. pap. text ed. 16.00 (*0-685-19350-0*) Heath.

Conflict & Consensus in France. Ed. by Vincent Wright. 1979. 35.00 (*0-7146-3119-1*, Pub. by F Cass Pubs UK) Intl Spec Bk.

Conflict & Consensus in Labour's Foreign Policy, 1914-1965. Michael R. Gordon. xviii, 333p. 1969. 42.50 (*0-8047-0686-7*) Stanford U Pr.

Conflict & Consensus in South-North Security. Ed. by Caroline Thomas & Paikiasothy Saravanamuttu. (Illus.). (C). 1989. 59.95 (*0-521-37268-2*) Cambridge U Pr.

Conflict & Continuity: A History of Ideas in Social Equality & Human Development. Ed. by John R. Snarey et al. LC 80-83476. (Reprint Ser.: No. 15). 471p. 1981. 16.95 (*0-916690-17-2*) Harvard Educ Rev.

Conflict & Control in Late Imperial China. Ed. by Frederic E. Wakeman & Carolyn Grant. LC 73-87247. (Publication - The Center for Chinese Studies, University of California). 350p. reprint ed. pap. 99.80 (*0-685-23498-3*, 2029068) Bks Demand.

Conflict & Control in Welfare Policy: The Swedish Experience. Arthur Gould. LC 88-4560. 199p. reprint ed. pap. 56.80 (*0-7837-5178-8*, 2044908) Bks Demand.

Conflict & Cooperation in Job Interviews: A Study of Talk, Tasks, & Ideas. Martha L. Komter. LC 91-4906. (Pragmatics & Beyond New Ser.: No. 15). viii, 252p. 1991. 89.00 (*1-55619-281-9*) Benjamins North Am.

Conflict & Crises: A Foreign Service Story. Roy M. Melbourne. LC 92-23345. 300p. (C). 1993. lib. bdg. 38.50 (*0-8191-8874-3*) U Pr of Amer.

Conflict & Crisis: Romanian Political Development, 1861-1871. Paul E. Michelson. Ed. by William H. McNeill & Charles Jelavich. (Modern European History Ser.). 300p. 1987. lib. bdg. 15.00 (*0-8240-8029-7*) Garland.

Conflict & Crisis in Rural America. Larry W. Waterfield. LC 85-19366. (Illus.). 240p. 1986. text ed. 49.95 (*0-275-92071-2*, C2071, Praeger Pubs) Greenwood.

Conflict & Decision Making in Elementary Schools: Contemporary Vignettes & Cases for School Administrators. Dennis C. Zuelke & Marvin Willerman. 192p. (Orig.). (C). 1992. pap. text ed. write for info. (*0-697-14002-4*) Brown & Benchmark.

Conflict & Decision-Making in Soviet Russia: A Case Study of Agricultural Policy, 1953-1963. Sidney L. Ploss. (Center of International Studies Ser.). 1965. 47.50 (*0-691-08706-7*); pap. 14.95 (*0-691-02503-7*) Princeton U Pr.

Conflict & Defense: A General Theory. Kenneth E. Boulding. 362p. (C). 1988. reprint ed. pap. text ed. 31.00 (*0-8191-7112-3*) U Pr of Amer.

Conflict & Effective Demand in Economic Growth. Peter Skott. (Illus.). (C). 1990. 47.95 (*0-521-36596-1*) Cambridge U Pr.

Conflict & Gender. Anita Taylor & Judi B. Miller. (Communication Series: Interpersonal Communication Subseries). 344p. 1994. text ed. 65.00 (*1-881303-80-2*); pap. text ed. 26.50 (*1-881303-81-0*) Hampton Pr NJ.

Conflict & Harmony: A Source-Book of Man in His Environment. Ed. by Grace E. King. 450p. 1972. 25.00 (*0-8464-0274-2*) Beekman Pubs.

Conflict & Harmony in Education in Tropical Africa. Godfrey N. Brown & Mervyn Hiskett. 496p. 45.00 (*0-8386-1938-X*) Fairleigh Dickinson.

Conflict & Human Relations Training. R. Hacon. LC 65-19843. 1965. 52.00 (*0-08-011158-0*, Pub. by Pergamon Repr UK) Franklin.

***Conflict & Integration in Indo-Pakistan Relations.** Sarbjit Johal. LC 89-83322. (Monograph Ser.: No. 30). 266p. (Orig.). 1989. pap. text ed. 16.00 (*0-944613-16-0*) UC Berkeley Ctrs SE Asia.

***Conflict & Invention: Literary, Rhetorical, & Social Studies on the Sayings Gospel Q.** Ed. by John S. Kloppenborg. 224p. (Orig.). (C). 1995. pap. text ed. 16.00 (*1-56338-123-0*) TPI PA.

Conflict & Language Planning in Quebec. Ed. by Richard Y. Bourhis. 304p. 1984. 99.00 (*0-905028-16-3*); pap. 39.95 (*0-905028-25-2*) Taylor & Francis.

Conflict & Order: The Police & Labour Disputes in England & Wales 1900-1939. Jane Morgan. (Illus.). 320p. 1988. 69.00 (*0-19-820128-1*) OUP.

Conflict & Peace in the Horn of Africa. Ed. by Peter Woodward & Murray Forsyth. LC 94-11913. 1994. 57.95 (*1-85521-486-5*, Pub. by Dartmth Pub UK) Ashgate Pub Co.

Conflict & Peace in the Modern International System: A Study of the Principles of International Order. Evan Luard. LC 87-27977. 318p. (C). 1988. 64.50 (*0-88706-696-8*); pap. 21.95 (*0-88706-697-6*) State U NY Pr.

Conflict & Peacemaking in Multiethnic Societies. Ed. by Joseph V. Montville. 554p. 1989. text ed. 29.95 (*0-669-21453-1*) Free Pr.

Conflict & Political Change in Venezuela. Daniel H. Levine. LC 75-39790. 328p. 1973. 47.50x (*0-691-07547-6*) Princeton U Pr.

Conflict & Political Change in Venezuela. Daniel H. Levine. LC 75-39790. 299p. reprint ed. pap. 85.30 (*0-8357-3401-3*, 2039658) Bks Demand.

Conflict & Power in Marriage: Expecting the First Child. Ralph LaRossa. LC 77-8566. (Sage Library of Social Research: No. 50). 176p. reprint ed. pap. 50.20 (*0-8357-8445-2*, 2034709) Bks Demand.

Conflict & Resolution in US-EC Trade Relations at the Opening of the Uruguay Round. Ed. by Seymour J. Rubin & Mark L. Jones. LC 88-62364. 531p. 1989. lib. bdg. 60.00 (*0-379-20967-5*) Oceana.

Conflict & Rhetoric in French Policymaking. Frank R. Baumgartner. LC 89-4742. (Series in Policy & Institutional Studies). 303p. 1989. 49.95 (*0-8229-3616-X*) U of Pittsburgh Pr.

Conflict & Schism in Nez Perce Acculturation: A Study of Religion & Politics. Deward E. Walker, Jr. 171p. 1985. pap. 10.95 (*0-89301-105-3*) U of Idaho Pr.

Conflict & Schism in Nez Perce Acculturation: A Study of Religion & Politics. Deward E. Walker, Jr. LC 68-3945. (Illus.). 185p. reprint ed. pap. 52.80 (*0-685-24152-1*, 2033025) Bks Demand.

Conflict & Social Psychology. Ed. by Knud S. Larsen. 272p. (C). 1993. text ed. 65.00 (*0-8039-8745-5*) Sage.

Conflict & Stress: A Management Workbook for the Recovering Chemically Dependent. Paul K. Shields. 1993. student ed 14.95 (*0-9638325-0-6*) P K Shields.

Conflict & Tension in the Far East: Key Documents, 1894-1960. John M. Maki. LC 61-17709. 254p. 1961. 20.00 (*0-295-73751-4*) U of Wash Pr.

***Conflict & Tension in Tribal Society.** S. P. Sinha. (C). 1993. 49.00x (*81-7022-493-4*, Pub. by Concept II) S Asia.

Conflict & the Web of Group Affiliations. Georg Simmel. LC 54-10671. 1964. 18.95 (*0-02-928830-4*); pap. 12.95 (*0-02-928840-1*) Free Pr.

Conflict & Transcendence: African-American Art in South Carolina. Theresa Singeltary et al. Ed. by Joy Pierce-Johnson & Lisa K. Clarkson. (Illus.). 40p. (Orig.). 1992. 8.00 (*0-685-61563-4*) Columbia Mus Art.

Conflict & Triumph: Over Fifty Years with Missions. Jewell Conningham. Ed. by Florence Biros & Melva Libb. (Illus.). 320p. (Orig.). 1988. pap. 6.95 (*0-936369-12-4*) Son-Rise Pubns.

Conflict & War in the Middle East, 1967-1991: Regional Dynamic & the Superpowers. rev. ed. Bassam Tibi. Tr. by Clare Krojzlova. LC 92-12771. 1992. text ed. 39.95 (*0-312-08405-6*) St Martin.

Conflict, Antithesis & the Ancient Historian. Ed. by June W. Allison. 145p. 1990. 39.50 (*0-8142-0508-9*) Ohio St U Pr.

Conflict at the Border: True Tales of a U. S. Customs Border Officer. Charles S. Park. LC 89-1923. (Illus.). 160p. (Orig.). 1989. pap. 5.00 (*0-914846-41-8*) Golden West Pub.

Conflict Between Atomism & Conservation Theory 1644-1860. Wilson L. Scott. LC 72-101423. 1970. lib. bdg. 35.00 (*0-685-52433-7*) Watson Pub Intl.

Conflict Between Communities: American County Seat Wars. James A. Schellenberg. LC 86-22716. 130p. 1987. 22.95 (*0-943852-23-4*) Prof World Peace.

Conflict Between Equilibrium & Disequilibrium Theories: The Case of the U. S. Labor Market. Richard E. Quandt & Harvey S. Rosen. LC 88-10618. 125p. 1988. text ed. 20.00 (*0-88099-061-9*); pap. text ed. 10.00 (*0-88099-060-0*) W E Upjohn.

Conflict Between Flesh & Spirit. Bill Freeman. (Illus.). 14p. (Orig.). 1984. pap. 0.50 (*0-914271-04-0*) Mnstry Wrd.

Conflict Between Individualism & Collectivism in a Democracy, Three Lectures. Charles W. Eliot. LC 67-22060. (Essay Index Reprint Ser.). 1977. 15.95 (*0-8369-0411-7*) Ayer.

Conflict Between Liberty & Equality. Arthur T. Hadley. LC 79-84310. (Essay Index Reprint Ser.). 1977. 19.95 (*0-8369-1083-4*) Ayer.

Conflict Between Liberty & Equality. Arthur T. Hadley. LC 79-84310. (Essay Index Reprint Ser.). 135p. 1982. reprint ed. lib. bdg. 14.00 (*0-8290-0472-6*) Irvington.

Conflict Between People & Groups: Causes, Processes, & Resolutions. Ed. by Stephen Worchel & Jeffry A. Simpson. 300p. 1993. pap. text ed. 19.95 (*0-8304-1307-3*) Nelson-Hall.

Conflict Between the California Indian & White Civilization, 4 vols. in 1. Sherburne F. Cook. LC 76-43678. (Ibero-Americana Ser.: Nos. 21-24). reprint ed. 27.50 (*0-404-15512-X*) AMS Pr.

Conflict Between the Civil Power & the Clergy: Historical & Legal Essay. Emilio Portes Gil. 1976. lib. bdg. 59.95 (*0-87968-928-5*) Gordon Pr.

***Conflict Center's Conflict Management Middle School Curriculum.** Elizabeth Loescher. 64p. (J). (gr. 6-8). 1990. teacher ed 20.00 (*1-887249-01-X*) Conflict Ctr.

Conflict, Competition, or Cooperation? Dilemmas of State Education Policymaking. Douglas M. Abrams. (SUNY Series, Education & Culture: Critical Factors in the Formation of Character & Community in American Life). 227p. (C). 1993. 57.50 (*0-7914-1677-1*); pap. 18.95 (*0-7914-1678-X*) State U NY Pr.

***Conflict, Cooperation, & Justice: Essays Inspired by the Work of Morton Deutsch.** Barbara B. Buker & Jeffrey Z. Rubin. LC 94-46743. (Conflict Resolution Ser.). 384p. 1995. 35.95 (*0-7879-0069-9*) Jossey-Bass.

***Conflict, Culture & History: Regional Dimensions.** 1995. lib. bdg. 255.95 (*0-8490-7518-1*) Gordon Pr.

Conflict, Decision, & Dissonance. Leon Festinger. vii, 163p. 1964. 22.50 (*0-8047-0205-5*) Stanford U Pr.

Conflict Helix: Principles & Practices of Interpersonal, Social & International Conflict & Cooperation. R. J. Rummel. 297p. (C). 1990. 39.95 (*0-88738-389-0*) Transaction Pubs.

Conflict, Holiness & Politics in the Teachings of Jesus. Marcus J. Borg. LC 84-9029. (Studies in the Bible & Early Christianity: Vol. 5). 397p. 1984. lib. bdg. 99.95 (*0-88946-603-3*) E Mellen.

Conflict in a Voluntary Association: A Case Study of a Classic Suburban Church Fight. Ed. by Perry D. LeFevre. LC 75-12388. (Studies in Ministry & Parish Life). 1975. pap. 9.95 (*0-913552-09-7*) Exploration Pr.

Conflict in Afghanistan. J. Griffiths. (Flashpoints Ser.). (Illus.). 80p. (J). (gr. 7 up). 1988. lib. bdg. 18.60 (*0-86592-039-7*) Rourke Corp.

Conflict in Africa. Ed. by O. W. Furley. 256p. 1995. text ed. 59.50 (*1-85043-690-8*, Pub. by I B Tauris UK) St Martin.

Conflict in Africa: Concepts & Realities. limited ed. Adda B. Bozeman. LC 75-30187. 1976. text ed. 69.50 (*0-691-03104-5*) Princeton U Pr.

Conflict in Africa: Concepts & Realities. Adda B. Bozeman. LC 75-30187. 444p. reprint ed. pap. 126.60 (*0-8357-3419-6*, 2039676) Bks Demand.

Conflict in Catalonia: Images of an Urban Society. Ed. by Gary McDonogh. LC 86-956. (University of Florida Social Sciences Monographs: No. 71). 112p. (Orig.). 1985. pap. 19.95 (*0-8130-0821-2*) U Press Fla.

Conflict in Central America. Ed. by Helen Schooley. 1987. 45.00 (*0-582-90274-6*) St James Pr.

Conflict in Central America: Approaches to Peace & Security. Ed. by Jack Child. 208p. 1986. 27.50 (*1-85065-015-2*) Intl Peace.

Conflict in Central America: Approaches to Peace & Security. Ed. by Jack Child. LC 85-27916. 230p. 1986. text ed. 35.00 (*0-312-16230-8*) St Martin.

Conflict in Child & Adolescent Development. Ed. by Carolyn U. Shantz & Willard W. Hartup. (Studies in Social & Emotional Development). (Illus.). 512p. (C). 1992. 64.95 (*0-521-40416-9*) Cambridge U Pr.

***Conflict in Child & Adolescent Development.** Ed. by Carolyn U. Shantz & Willard W. Hartup. (Studies in Social & Emotional Development). (Illus.). 463p. (C). 1995. pap. 24.95 (*0-521-48377-8*) Cambridge U Pr.

Conflict in Culture: Permissions Versus Controls & Alcohol Use in American Society. John E. Tropman. 118p. (Orig.). 1986. lib. bdg. 39.00 (*0-8191-5246-3*); pap. text ed. 16.00 (*0-8191-5247-1*) U Pr of Amer.

Conflict in Early Stuart England: Studies in Religion & Politics, 1603-1642. Ed. by Richard Cust & Ann Hughes. 279p. (Orig.). (C). 1989. pap. text ed. 25.95 (*0-582-30173-4*) Longman.

Conflict in Eastern Europe. Bernard Harbor. LC 93-3035. (Conflicts Ser.). (Illus.). 48p. (YA). (gr. 6 up). 1993. text ed. 13.95 (*0-02-742626-2*, New Dscvry Bks) Silver Burdett Pr.

Conflict in Economics. Ed. by Yanis Varoufakis & David G. Young. LC 90-37551. 191p. 1990. text ed. 49.95 (*0-312-05218-9*) St Martin.

Conflict in Education in a Democratic Society. Robert M. Hutchins. LC 77-138117. 112p. 1972. reprint ed. text ed. 38.50 (*0-8371-5693-9*, HUED, Greenwood Pr) Greenwood.

C

1536 An Asterisk (*) at the beginning of an entry indicates that the title is appearing in BIP for the first time.

An Asterisk (*) at the beginning of an entry indicates that the title is appearing in BIP for the first time.

*Conflict Resolution: Making It Work in the Medical Group. Andrea Molberg. 32p. (Orig.). 1993. student ed 165.00 (1-56829-002-0) Med Group Mgmt.

Conflict Resolution: The Analytic Hierarchy Process. Thomas L. Saaty & Joyce M. Alexander. LC 88-35466. 262p. 1989. text ed. 59.95 (0-275-93229-X, C3229, Praeger Pubs) Greenwood.

Conflict Resolution & Democratization in Panama. Ed. by Eva Loser. (Significant Issues Ser.). 1992. pap. text ed. 9.95 (0-89206-183-9) CSI Studies.

Conflict, Resolution & Diversity. Ellen J. DeBenedetti. 1993. student ed write for info. (0-318-72424-3) EduPRESS PA.

Conflict Resolution & Mediation for Peer Helpers. Don L. Sorenson. LC 92-70818. (Illus.). 128p. (Orig.). (YA). (gr. 8-12). 1992. pap. text ed. 8.95 (0-932796-42-7) Ed Media Corp.

Conflict Resolution & the Structure of the State System: An Analysis of Arbitrative Settlements. Gregory A. Raymond. LC 79-53702. (Illus.). 122p. 1980. text ed. 41.00 (0-916672-12-3) Rowman.

Conflict Resolution Drill & Practice: Variable Speeds. David Kennedy & Jean Gonzalez. (Advanced Court Reporting Technology Ser.). (Illus.). (C). 1992. pap. text ed. write for info. (1-881086-11-9) Middle Wasley.

*Conflict Resolution for Kids: A Group Facilitator's Guide. Pamela S. Lane. 80p. 1995. spiral bd. 12.95x (1-56032-387-6) Accel Devel.

Conflict Resolution in Africa. Ed. by Francis M. Deng & I. William Zartman. 410p. 1991. 36.95 (0-8157-1798-9); pap. 18.95 (0-8157-1797-0) Brookings.

Conflict Resolution in the Middle East: Simulating a Diplomatic Negotiation Between Israel & Syria. J. Lewis Rasmussen & Robert B. Oakley. LC 92-30410. (Orig.). 1992. pap. 6.95 (1-878379-19-4) US Inst Peace.

Conflict Resolution in Uganda. Ed. by Kumar Rupesinghe. LC 89-30799. 320p. 1989. text ed. 29.95 (0-8214-0929-8) Ohio U Pr.

*Conflict Resolution Skills for Teens. David Cowan et al. (Illus.). 181p. (Orig.). (YA). (gr. 7-12). Date not set. pap. text ed. 19.95 (1-56499-023-0) Innerchoice Pub.

Conflict Resolution Theory & Practice: Integration & Application. Ed. by Dennis J. Sandole & Hugo Van der Merwe. LC 92-2493. 1993. text ed. 79.95 (0-7190-3747-6, Pub. by Manchester Univ Pr UK); text ed. 24.95 (0-7190-3748-4, Pub. by Manchester Univ Pr UK) St Martin.

C

Conflict Talk: Sociolinguistic Investigations of Arguments in Conversations. Ed. by Allen D. Grimshaw. (Illus.). (C). 1990. 74.95 (0-521-33544-2); pap. 24.95 (0-521-33550-7) Cambridge U Pr.

Conflict Termination in Europe: Games Against War. Stephen J. Cimbala. LC 89-77107. 288p. 1990. text ed. 59.95 (0-275-93592-2, C3592, Praeger Pubs) Greenwood.

*Conflict Transformation. Ed. by Kumar Rupesinghe. LC 94-34691. 1995. text ed. write for info. (0-312-12487-2) St Martin.

Conflict under the Microscope: An Inter-Disciplinary Diagnosis. Roderick C. Ogley. 750p. 1991. text ed. 68.95 (1-85628-023-3, Pub. by Avebury Pub UK) Ashgate Pub Co.

Conflict with Israel in Arab Politics & Society. Ed. by Ian S. Lustick. LC 93-50083. (Arab-Israeli Relations Ser.: Vol. 8). 408p. 1994. reprint ed. 64.00 (0-8153-1588-0) Garland.

Conflict with the Arabs in Israeli Politics & Society. Ed. by Ian Lustick. LC 93-51015. (Arab-Israeli Relations Ser.: Vol. 7). 384p. 1994. 62.00 (0-8153-1587-2) Garland.

Conflict Within the AFL. James O. Morris. LC 73-22506. (Cornell Studies in Industrial & Labor Relations: Vol. 10). 319p. 1974. reprint ed. text ed. 75.00 (0-8371-6371-4, MOCA, Greenwood Pr) Greenwood.

Conflicting Agendas: Personal Morality in Institutional Settings. D. Don Welch. LC 94-6912. 208p. 1994. 19.95 (0-8298-1001-3) Pilgrim OH.

Conflicting Images: India & the United States. Ed Sulochana et al. LC 89-51129. 250p. 1990. 45.00 (0-913215-47-3) Riverdale Co.

Conflicting Interests: Corporate-Governance Controversies. Intro. by Fred D. Baldwin & Roberta S. Karmel. LC 83-48400. 224p. 1984. text ed. 26.00 (0-669-07123-4) Pennon Pr.

Conflicting Interests: The Public Lives of Women in Scotland, 1880-1945. Ed. by Esther Breitenbach & Eleanor Gordon. 272p. 1992. pap. text ed. 22.00 (0-7486-0372-7, Pub. by Edinburgh U Pr UK) Col U Pr.

Conflicting Interpretations of the Rise of Capitalism: Marx & Weber. N. Birnbaum. (Reprint Series in Social Sciences). (C). 1993. reprint ed. pap. text ed. 1.90 (0-8290-3702-0, S-26) Irvington.

Conflicting Loyalties: Law & Politics in the Attorney General's Office, 1789-1990. Nancy V. Baker. LC 91-42344. viii, 250p. 1992. 25.00 (0-7006-0530-4) U Pr of KS.

Conflicting Paradigms in the Economics of Developing Nations. Wilfred L. David. LC 86-16906. 236p. 1986. text ed. 55.00 (0-275-92108-5, C2108, Praeger Pubs) Greenwood.

*Conflicting Paths: Growing up in America. Harvey J. Graff. 442p. 1995. text ed. 39.95 (0-674-16066-5, GRACON) HUP.

Conflicting Readings: Variety & Validity in Interpretation. Paul B. Armstrong. LC 89-37186. xvi, 192p. 1990. 29.95 (0-8078-1895-X); pap. 14.95 (0-8078-4279-6) U of NC Pr.

Conflicting Realities: Four Readings of a Chapter by Perez Galdos (Fortunata Y Jacinta), Pt. III, Chapter IV. Ed. by Peter B. Goldman. (Serie A: Monografias, XC). 145p. (C). 1980. 35.00 (0-7293-0158-3, Pub. by Tamesis Bks Ltd UK) Boydell & Brewer.

Conflicting Stories: American Women Writers at the Turn into the Twentieth Century. Elizabeth Ammons. 234p. 1992. reprint ed. pap. 16.95 (0-19-508038-6) OUP.

Conflicting Tides. large type ed. D. Y. Cameron. 320p. 1989. 17.95 (0-7089-2005-5) Ulverscroft.

Conflicting Visions: Spiritual Possibilities of Modern Israel. David Hartman. LC 89-43305. 320p. 1990. 24.95 (0-8052-4060-8) Schocken.

*Conflicting Visions of Reform: German Lay Propaganda Pamphlets, 1519-1530. Miriam U. Chrisman. (Studies in German Histories Ser.). 336p. (C). 1995. text ed. 60.00 (0-391-03892-3) Humanities.

Conflicting Ways of Interpreting the Bible. Ed. by Hans Kung & Jurgen Moltmann. (Concilium Ser.: Vol. 138). 128p. 1980. pap. 5.95 (0-8164-2280-X) Harper SF.

Conflicting Ways of Interpreting the Bible, Concilium 138. Ed. by Hans Kung & Jurgen Moltmann. (New Concilium 1980 Ser.). 128p. 1981. pap. 5.95 (0-8245-4771-3) Harper SF.

Conflicting Worlds of Working Mothers. K. Chakrabortty. 305p. 1978. 17.95 (0-318-37050-6) Asia Bk Corp.

Conflicto de Baja Intensidad. Tom Barry. 60p. (SPA.). 1987. 5.95 (0-911213-13-9) Interhemisp Res Ctr.

Conflictos de Clase y Politica en PR. Angel G. Quintero. (Cuadernos CEREP Ser.). 168p. 1981. pap. 6.75 (0-940238-09-8) Ediciones Huracan.

Conflicts. Burton Goodman et al. 160p. (J). (gr. 8). 1993. pap. 9.50 (0-89061-717-1) Jamestown Pubs.

Conflicts. Lewis B. Namier. LC 73-90667. (Essay Index Reprint Ser.). 1977. 20.95 (0-8369-1230-6) Ayer.

Conflicts: A Better Way to Resolve Them. Edward De Bono. 1990. 25.00 (0-317-90564-3) Intl Ctr Creat Think.

Conflicts: Adaptable to Courses Utilizing Cramton, Currie, Kay & Kramer's Casebook on Conflict of Laws. Casenotes Publishing Co., Inc. Staff. Ed. by Norman S. Goldenberg et al. (Legal Briefs Ser.). 1993. pap. write for info. (0-87457-023-9, 1071) Casenotes Pub.

Conflicts: Adaptable to Courses Utilizing Reese, Rosenberg & Hay Casebook on Conflict of Laws. Casenotes Publishing Co., Inc. Staff. Ed. by Norman S. Goldenberg et al. (Legal Briefs Ser.). 1990. pap. write for info. (0-87457-024-7, 1070) Casenotes Pub.

Conflicts: The Breakup of the Soviet Union. Bernard Harbor. LC 92-19917. (Conflicts Ser.). (Illus.). 48p. (YA). (gr. 6 up). 1993. text ed. 13.95 (0-02-742625-4, Mac Bks Young Read) S&S Childrens.

Conflicts Adaptable to Courses Utilizing Brilmayer & Martin's Casebook on Conflict of Law. Ed. by Norman Goldenberg & Peter Tenen. (Legal Briefs Ser.). (C). 1993. pap. write for info. (0-87457-193-6, 1072) Casenotes Pub.

Conflicts & Conspiracies: Brazil & Portugal, 1750-1808. Kenneth R. Maxwell. LC 72-89813. (Cambridge Latin American Studies: No. 16). 301p. reprint ed. pap. 85.80 (0-685-44043-5, 2030608) Bks Demand.

Conflicts & Contradiction: Work Psychologists in Europe. Charles J. De Wolff et al. (Organizational & Occupational Psychology Ser.). 1981. text ed. 88.00 (0-12-214650-6) Acad Pr.

Conflicts & Contradictions. Meron Benvenisti. LC 85-40705. 221p. 1986. 15.95 (0-394-53647-9, Villard Bks) Random.

Conflicts & Contradictions: Israel, the Arabs & the West Bank. Meron Benvenisti. 1990. pap. 9.95 (0-935437-27-4) Sure Sellers.

Conflicts & Cooperation in Managing Environmental Resources. Ed. by R. Pethig et al. (Microeconomic Studies). (Illus.). xii, 338p. 1992. 98.00 (0-387-54968-4) Spr-Verlag.

Conflicts & New Departures in World Society. Ed. by Volker Bornschier & Peter Lengyel. (World Society Studies: Vol. 3). 409p. (C). 1994. text ed. 49.95 (1-56000-129-1) Transaction Pubs.

Conflicts Between Labor & Environmentalism in the Federal Republic of Germany & the United States. Heinrich Siegmann. LC 85-10004. 212p. 1985. text ed. 32.50 (0-312-16236-7) St Martin.

Conflicts Between Labor Legislation & Bankruptcy Law. Thomas R. Haggard & Mark S. Pulliam. LC 86-83223. (Labor Relations & Public Policy Ser.). (Orig.). 1987. pap. 27.50 (0-89546-064-5) U PA Wharton Ctr Human Resc.

Conflicts Between Multinational Corporations & Less Developed Countries: The Case of Bauxite Mining in the Caribbean with Special Reference to Guyana. Thakoor Persaud. Ed. by Stuart Bruchey. LC 80-587. (Multinational Corporations Ser.). 1981. lib. bdg. 31.95 (0-405-13378-2) Ayer.

Conflicts Between Staff & Line Managerial Officers. Melville Dalton. (Reprint Series in Sociology). (C). 1993. reprint ed. pap. text ed. 1.00 (0-8290-3704-7, S-59) Irvington.

Conflicts in a Nutshell. 2nd ed. David D. Siegel. (Nutshell Ser.). 409p. 1993. pap. text ed. 17.00 (0-314-02952-4) West Pub.

Conflicts in a Nutshell. David D. Siegel. LC 81-21893. (Nutshell Ser.). 470p. (C). 1992. reprint ed. pap. text ed. 16.00 (0-314-64260-9) West Pub.

Conflicts in & Around Russia: Nation-Building in Difficult Times. Victor A. Kremenyuk. LC 93-11848. (Contributions in Political Science Ser.: No. 341). 176p. 1994. text ed. 49.95 (0-313-28943-3, Greenwood Pr) Greenwood.

Conflicts in Feminism. Ed. by Marianne Hirsch & Evelyn F. Keller. 397p. 1990. 49.50 (0-415-90177-4, A3573, Routledge NY); pap. 15.95 (0-415-90178-2, A3577, Routledge NY) Routledge.

*Conflicts in Nature. Robert E. Coleman. LC 93-92777. 128p. (Orig.). 1994. pap. 8.00 (1-56002-380-5) Aegina Pr.

Conflicts in Reference Services. Ed. by Bill Katz & Ruth A. Fraley. LC 84-25147. (Reference Librarian Ser.: No. 12). 236p. 1985. text ed. 49.95 (0-86656-385-7) Haworth Pr.

Conflicts in the National Health Service. Ed. by Keith Barnard & Kenneth Lee. LC 76-57740. 1977. 22.50 (0-88202-114-1, Prodist) Watson Pub Intl.

Conflicts in Tudor & Stuart England. Ed. by Ivan Roots. LC 68-97374. (Selections from History Today Ser.: No. 5). (Illus.). 1969. pap. 8.95 (0-05-001536-2) Dufour.

Conflicts in Urban Development: A Comparison Between East & West Europe. Ed. by Arie Dekker et al. 170p. 1992. 68.95 (1-85742-040-3, Pub. by Ashgate UK) Ashgate Pub Co.

*Conflicts Issues in Family & Succession Law. Tan Yock Lin. 680p. 1993. 185.00 (0-409-99641-6, SI) Butterworth Legal Pubs.

*Conflicts of All Types: Variety Pack. David W. Felder. 98p. 1995. 19.95 (0-614-04825-7, B&G 23H); teacher ed 39.95 (0-910959-43-9, B&G 23T) Felder Bks.

*Conflicts of Divided Nations: The Cases of China & Korea. Weiqun Gu. LC 94-42818. 272p. 1995. text ed. 59.95 (0-275-95112-X, Praeger Pubs) Greenwood.

*Conflicts of Interest. John Martel. LC 94-45781. 464p. 1995. 23.00 (0-671-89094-8) PB.

*Conflicts of Interest in Clinical Practice & Research. Ed. by Roy G. Spece et al. 416p. 1995. text ed. 49.95 (0-19-508024-6) OUP.

Conflicts of Interest in Engineering. Illinois Institute of Technology Staff. 80p. 1986. 7.75 (0-8403-3944-5) Kendall-Hunt.

Conflicts of Interest in Land Use Management Decisions. David W. Owens. 105p. (Orig.). (C). 1991. pap. text ed. 9.00 (1-56011-175-5) Institute Government.

Conflicts of Interest in the Changing Financial World. Ed. by R. M. Goode. 1986. 150.00 (0-85297-167-2, Pub. by Inst Bankers UK) St Mut.

Conflicts of Law & European Community Law. I. F. Fletcher. 396p. 1982. 105.25 (0-444-86376-1, I-190-82, North Holland) Elsevier.

Conflicts of Law & Morality. Kent Greenawalt. LC 86-8335. (Clarendon Law Ser.). 400p. 1987. reprint ed. 49.95 (0-19-504110-0) OUP.

Conflicts of Law & Morality. Kent Greenawalt. LC 86-8335. (Clarendon Law Ser.). 400p. 1989. reprint ed. pap. 19.95 (0-19-505824-0) OUP.

Conflicts of National Laws with International Business Activity: Issues of Extraterritoriality. A. H. Hermann. (British-North American Committee Ser.: No. 30). 104p. 1982. pap. 6.00 (0-902594-41-9, BN30-NPA195) Natl Planning.

Conflicts of Power in Modern Culture. Conference On Science - Philosophy And Religion - 7th Symposium. Ed. by L. Bryson et al. 703p. 1964. reprint ed. 45.00 (0-8154-0037-3) Cooper Sq.

Conflicts over Coca Fields in 16th-Century Peru. Maria R. De Diez Canseco. Ed. by Joyce Marcus. Tr. by Jorge E. Silva. (Memoirs Ser.: No. 21). xii, 316p. 1988. pap. 19.50 (0-915703-13-0) U Mich Mus Anthro.

Conflicts over Land & the Crisis of Nationalism in Mauritania. Thomas K. Park et al. (LTC Research Paper Ser.: No. 142). 55p. 1991. pap. 7.00 (0-685-49240-0) U of Wis Land.

Conflicts over Resource Ownership: The Use of Public Policy by Private Interests. Albert M. Church. LC 82-47942. 255p. reprint ed. pap. 72.70 (0-7837-5749-2, 2045411) Bks Demand.

Conflicts Unending: The United States & Regional Disputes. Richard N. Haass. LC 89-38200. 184p. (C). 1990. 27.00 (0-300-04555-7) Yale U Pr.

Conflicts Unending: The United States & Regional Disputes. Richard Haass. 190p. (C). 1992. reprint ed. pap. text ed. 12.00 (0-300-05129-8) Yale U Pr.

Conflicts with Modernism or the Absence of Kurt Schwitters. Rudi Fuchs. 50p. 1991. pap. 12.50 (3-906127-34-6, Pub. by Gachnang & Springer SZ) Dist Art Pubs.

Confluence: Historico-Comparative & Other Literary Studies. Abhay Maurya. 160p. 1988. text ed. 27.50 (81-207-0781-8, Pub. by Sterling Pubs II) Apt Bks.

Confluence: Linguistics, L2 Acquisition & Speech Pathology. Ed. by Fred R. Eckman. LC 92-36058. (Language Acquisition & Language Disorders (LALD) Ser.: No. 4). xvi, 260p. 1993. 69.00 (1-55619-237-1) Benjamins North Am.

Confluence: Selected Poems. Peter Jensen et al. (Illus.). 128p. (Orig.). 1992. pap. 10.00 (0-9615387-1-6) Walking Bird OR.

Confluence of Colors: The First Anthology of Wisconsin Minority Poets, Vol. I. Ed. by Angela Lobo-Cobb. 79p. (C). 1984. pap. text ed. 5.00 (0-916783-04-9) Blue Reed.

*Confluence of Cultures: French Contributions to Indo-Persian Studies. Ed. by Francoise N. Delvoye. (C). 1994. text ed. 28.00 (81-7304-092-3, Pub. by Manohar II) S Asia.

Confluence of Opposites or Scientific Comparative Study of Religions. C. R. Jain. 432p. 1975. reprint ed. 16.00 (0-685-04533-1, Messers Today & Tomorrow) Scholarly Pubns.

Confluent Education: Attitudinal & Behavioral Consequences of Confluent Teacher Training. John M. Shiflett & George I. Brown. LC 78-60626. (Illus.). (C). 1978. reprint ed. pap. 10.00 (0-930626-02-8) Psych & Consul Assocs.

Confluent Hypergeometric Functions. Lucy J. Slater. LC 60-4198. 259p. reprint ed. pap. 73.90 (0-317-08557-3, 2051427) Bks Demand.

Confluent String Rewriting. M. Jantzen. (EATCS Monographs on Theoretical Computer Science: Vol. 14). 120p. 1988. 49.50 (0-387-13715-7) Spr-Verlag.

*Confocal Laser Scanning Microscopy. C. Sheppard & D. Shotton. (Microscopy Handbooks Ser.: No. 34). 150p. 1995. pap. 42.50 (1-872748-72-4, Pub. by Bios Scientific UK) Coronet Bks.

Confocal Microscopy. Ed. by T. Wilson. (Illus.). 426p. 1990. text ed. 83.00 (0-12-757270-8) Acad Pr.

*Conformable Wife. large type ed. Alice C. Ley. 1994. 21.95 (0-7089-3150-2) Ulverscroft.

Conformal Coatings. BCC Staff. 123p. 1990. 2,750.00 (0-89336-728-1, GB-131) BCC.

Conformal Coatings in the Global Electronics Industry, No. GB-131R. 2,750.00 (1-56965-211-2) BCC.

Conformal Field Theory. S. V. Katov. 500p. 1995. text ed. 86.00 (981-02-1608-4) World Scientific Pub.

Conformal Field Theory & Critical Phenomena in Two-Dimensional Systems, Vol. 10. A. B. Zamolodchikov & Al B. Zamolodchikov. (Physics Reviews Ser.: SSR Sec. A, Vol. 10, Pt. 4). iv, 166p. 1989. pap. text ed. 107.00 (3-7186-4863-6) Gordon & Breach.

Conformal Field Theory & Solvable Lattice Models. Ed. by Michio Jimbo et al. (Advanced Studies in Pure Mathematics: Vol. 16). 426p. 1988. text ed. 140.00 (0-12-385340-0) Acad Pr.

Conformal Field Theory Anomalies & Superstrings: Proceedings. Ed. by B. E. Baaquie et al. 576p. (C). 1988. pap. 52.00 (9971-5-0446-4) World Scientific Pub.

Conformal Geometry & Quasiregular Mappings. Matti Vuorinen. (Lecture Notes in Mathematics Ser.: Vol. 1319). 209p. 1988. pap. 36.20 (0-387-19342-1) Spr-Verlag.

Conformal Groups & Related Symmetries - Physical Results & Mathematical Background. Ed. by Asim O. Barut & H. D. Doebner. (Lecture Notes in Physics Ser.: Vol. 261). vi, 443p. 1986. 58.00 (0-387-17163-0) Spr-Verlag.

Conformal Invariance & Applications to Statistical Mechanics. Claude Itzykson et al. 992p. 1988. text ed. 108.00 (9971-5-0605-X); pap. text ed. 61.00 (9971-5-0606-8) World Scientific Pub.

Conformal Invariance & String Theory. Ed. by Petre Dita & Vladimir Georgesca. (Perspectives in Physics Ser.). 557p. 1989. text ed. 96.00 (0-12-218100-X) Acad Pr.

Conformal Mapping. Ludwig Bieberbach. LC 53-7209. 1986. 12.00 (0-8284-0090-3) Chelsea Pub.

Conformal Mapping. Zeev Nehari. LC 74-27513. (Illus.). 416p. 1975. reprint ed. pap. text ed. 7.95 (0-486-61137-X) Dover.

Conformal Mapping: Methods & Applications. R. Schinzinger & P. A. Laura. 604p. 1991. 160.00 (0-444-88806-3) Elsevier.

Conformal Mapping & Boundary Value Problems. Guo-Chun Wen. LC 92-14225. (Translations of Mathematical Monographs: Vol. 106). 303p. 1992. 99.00 (0-8218-4562-4) Am Math.

Conformal Mapping on Riemann Surfaces. Harvey Cohn. (Illus.). 352p. 1980. pap. text ed. 8.95 (0-486-64025-6) Dover.

Conformal Mapping Technique for Infinitely Connected Regions. Maynard G. Arsove & Guy Johnson, Jr. LC 52-42839. (Memoirs Ser.: No. 1/91). 56p. 1970. pap. 16.00 (0-8218-1291-2, MEMO 1/91) Am Math.

Conformal Quantum Field Theory in D Dimensions: Lecture Notes. E. S. Fradkin & M. Ya Palchik. 300p. 1995. text ed. 48.00 (981-02-1097-3) World Scientific Pub.

Conformally Invariant Quantum Field Theories in Two Dimensions. W. Nahm. (Advanced Series in Mathematical Physics: Vol. 6). 250p. 1995. text ed. 61.00 (9971-5-0649-1); pap. text ed. 40.00 (9971-5-0650-5) World Scientific Pub.

Conformance Test Methodology for IEEE Standards for Local & Metropolitan Area Networks: Supplement to Carrier Sense Multiple Access with Collision Detection (CSMA-CD) Access Method & Physical Layer Specifications: Type 10Base-T Medium Attachment Unit (MAU) Conformance Test Methodology (Section 6), IEEE Std 1802.3d-1993. Institute of Electrical & Electronics Engineers, Inc. Staff. (Illus.). 96p. (Orig.). 1994. pap. 45.00 (1-55937-419-5, SH17251) IEEE Standards.

Conformance Testing & Certification in Information Technology & Telecommunications. Ed. by Cen-Cenelec & Etsi Staff. LC 90-84753. 399p. 1991. 130.00 (90-5199-038-3, Pub. by IOS Pr NE) IOS Press.

Conformance Testing Methodologies & Architecture for OSI Protocols. Ed. by Richard J. Linn & M. Umit Uyar. LC 93-45664. 512p. 1994. text ed. 60.00 (0-8186-5352-3, 5352) IEEE Comp Soc.

Conformation. Pegotty Henriques. (Threshold Picture Guides Ser.). (Illus.). 24p. (Orig.). 1991. pap. 10.00 (1-872082-22-X, Pub. by Threshhold Bks UK) Half Halt Pr.

Conformation Guide. Larry Smith, Jr. Tr. by Thompson Day Graphics. (Illus.). 82p. (Orig.). 1984. pap. 150.00 (0-931741-01-7) L Smith Assoc.

Conformation in Biology. Ed. by R. H. Sarma & R. Srinivasan. (Illus.). 500p. 1983. lib. bdg. 107.00 (0-940030-05-5) Adenine Pr.

Conformational Analysis. Ed. by Ernest L. Eliel et al. LC 81-1083. 1965. 24.95 (0-8412-0653-8) Am Chemical.

Conformational Analysis of Cyclohexenes, Cyclohexadienes, & Related Hydroaromatic Compounds. Ed. by Peter W. Rabideau. LC 88-33970. (Methods in Stereochemical Analysis Ser.). 323p. 1989. lib. bdg. 100.00 (0-89573-702-7) VCH Pubs.

An Asterisk (*) at the beginning of an entry indicates that the title is appearing in BIP for the first time.

C

An Asterisk (*) at the beginning of an entry indicates that the title is appearing in BIP for the first time.

Confronting the Victim Role: Healing from an Abusive Childhood. Barry McCarthy & Emily McCarthy. 224p. 1993. pap. 11.95 (*0-7867-0011-4*) Carroll & Graf.

Confronting Urban Malnutrition: The Design of Nutrition Programs. James E. Austin. LC 79-3705. (World Bank Staff Occasional Paper Ser.: No. 28). 132p. reprint ed. pap. 37.70 (*0-7837-4253-3*, 2043943) Bks Demand.

Confronting Values in Policy Analysis: The Politics of Criteria. Ed. by Frank Fischer & John Forester. LC 86-6647. (Sage Yearbooks in Politics & Public Policy Ser.: No. 14). 296p. (Orig.). reprint ed. pap. 84.40 (*0-7837-4571-0*, 2044100) Bks Demand.

Confronting War: An Examination of Humanity's Most Pressing Problem. 3rd ed. Ronald J. Glossop. 447p. (C). 1994. lib. bdg. 28.50 (*0-89950-980-0*) McFarland & Co.

***Confronting Without Guilt Or Conflict: How to Prepare & Deliver a Confrontation in a Way That Minimizes Risk, Conflict & Guilt.** Robert F. Weyant. LC 94-96630. 144p. 1995. pap. 14.95 (*0-9642576-5-3*) Brassy Pubng.

***Confronting Your Bottom Line: Financial Guide for Child Care Centers.** Keith Stephens. (Illus.). 48p. (Orig.). (C). 1991. pap. 15.00 (*0-942702-09-3*) Child Care.

Confronting Youth Crime: Report of the Twentieth Century Fund Task Force on Sentencing Policy Toward Young Offenders. Twentieth Century Fund Staff. LC 78-3612. (Illus.). 120p. 1978. text ed. 14.50 (*0-8419-0381-6*) Holmes & Meier.

Confucian Analects. W. Jennings. 1972. 59.95 (*0-87968-929-3*) Gordon Pr.

Confucian China & Its Modern Fate: A Trilogy. Joseph R. Levenson. 1968. reprint ed. 52.00 (*0-520-00736-0*); reprint ed. pap. 20.00 (*0-520-00737-9*) U CA Pr.

Confucian-Christian Encounters in Historical & Contemporary Perspective. Ed. by Peter K. Lee. LC 91-40387. (Religions in Dialogue Ser.: Vol. 5). 500p. 1992. lib. bdg. 109.95 (*0-88946-521-5*) E Mellen.

Confucian Continuum: Educational Modernization in Taiwan. Ed. by Douglas C. Smith. LC 90-31136. 480p. 1991. text ed. 69.95 (*0-275-93517-5*, C3517, Greenwood Pr) Greenwood.

Confucian Creation of Heaven: Philosophy & the Defense of Ritual Mastery. Robert Eno. LC 89-31194. (Chinese Philosophy & Culture Ser.). (Illus.). 349p. 1990. 64.50 (*0-7914-0190-1*); pap. 21.95 (*0-7914-0191-X*) State U NY Pr.

Confucian Discourse & Chu Hsi's Ascendancy. Hoyt C. Tillman. (C). 1992. text ed. 38.00 (*0-8248-1416-9*) UH Pr.

Confucian Ethics of the Axial Age: A Reconstruction under the Aspect of the Breakthrough Toward Postconventional Thinking. Heiner Roetz. (Chinese Philosophy & Culture Ser.). 373p. (C). 1993. 59.50 (*0-7914-1649-6*); pap. 19.95 (*0-7914-1650-X*) State U NY Pr.

Confucian Moral Self Cultivation. Philip J. Ivanhoe. LC 93-24085. (Rockwell Lecture Ser.: Vol. 3). 116p. 1994. 35.95 (*0-8204-2200-2*) P Lang Pubs.

Confucian Notebook. Edward H. Kenney. LC 79-2828. 89p. 1986. reprint ed. 16.00 (*0-8305-0008-1*) Hyperion Conn.

Confucian Odes of Ezra Pound: A Critical Appraisal. I. S. Dembo. 111p. 1963. 20.00 (*0-910278-74-1*) Boulevard.

Confucian Personalities. Ed. by Arthur F. Wright & Denis C. Twitchett. LC 62-16950. (Illus.). x, 411p. 1962. 49.50 (*0-8047-0044-3*) Stanford U Pr.

Confucian Persuasion. Ed. by Arthur F. Wright. LC 60-8561. x, 390p. 1960. 47.50 (*0-8047-0018-4*) Stanford U Pr.

Confucian Renaissance. Ed. by Reg Little & Warren Reed. 110p. (C). 1990. text ed. 20.00 (*1-86287-007-1*, Pub. by Federation Pr AU) W W Gaunt.

Confucian Rituals in Korea. Spencer J. Palmer. LC 84-256844. (Religions of Asia Ser.: No. 3). 274p. pap. 78.10 (*0-8357-4423-X*, 2037253) Bks Demand.

Confucian Thought: Selfhood as Creative Transformation. Wei-ming Tu. LC 84-16263. (SUNY Series in Philosophy). 165p. 1985. 57.50 (*0-88706-005-6*); pap. 18.95 (*0-88706-006-4*) State U NY Pr.

Confucian Transformation of Korea: A Study of Society & Ideology. Martina Deuchler. LC 92-18507. (Harvard-Yenching Institute Monograph: No. 36). 439p. 1993. text ed. 35.00 (*0-674-16088-6*) HUP.

***Confucian Transformation of Korea: A Study of Society & Ideology.** Martina Deuchler. (Harvard-Yenching Institute Monograph Ser.: No. 36). (Illus.). 439p. 1995. pap. 19.00 (*0-674-16089-4*, DEUCOX) HUP.

Confucian Values & Popular Zen: Sekimon Shingaku in Eighteenth-Century Japan. Janine A. Sawada. LC 92-45047. (Illus.). 264p. (C). 1993. text ed. 30.00 (*0-8248-1414-2*) UH Pr.

Confucian Way: A New & Systematic Study of the Four Books. Liu F. Chen. Tr. by Shih S. Liu. 620p. 1986. text ed. 47.50 (*0-7103-0171-5*); pap. 9.95 (*0-7103-0250-9*) Routledge Chapman & Hall.

Confucian Way of Contemplation: Okada Takehiko & the Tradition of Quiet Sitting. Rodney L. Taylor. Ed. by Frederick Denny. (Studies in Comparative Religion). 230p. 1988. text ed. 34.95 (*0-87249-532-9*) U of SC Pr.

Confucian World Observed: A Contemporary Discussion of Confucian Humanism in East Asia. Weiming Tu et al. Ed. by Milan G. Hjemanek & Alan Wachman. 144p. (C). 1992. pap. text ed. 12.95 (*0-8248-1451-7*) UH Pr.

***Confucianism.** Chai. (YA). 1977. pap. 7.95 (*0-8120-0303-9*) Barron.

Confucianism. Francis X. Clooney. (World Religions Ser.). (Illus.). 128p. (YA). (gr. 7-12). 1992. bds. 17.95 (*0-8160-2445-6*) Facts on File.

Confucianism: The Dynamics of Tradition. Irene Eber. 264p. 1986. text ed. 27.50 (*0-02-908780-5*) Macmillan.

Confucianism & Autocracy: Professional Elites in the Founding of the Ming Dynasty. John W. Dardess. LC 82-4822. 400p. (C). 1983. pap. 17.00 (*0-520-04733-8*) U CA Pr.

Confucianism & Chinese Civilization. Ed. by Arthur F. Wright. LC 75-6317. xvi, 368p. 1964. 47.50 (*0-8047-0890-8*); pap. 15.95 (*0-8047-0891-6*) Stanford U Pr.

Confucianism & Christianity: Their First Encounter. John D. Young. 196p. 1983. 39.50x (*962-209-037-0*, Pub. by Hong Kong Univ Pr HK) Coronet Bks.

Confucianism & Economic Development: An Oriental Alternative? Ed. by Hung-Chao Tai. LC 89-5483. 224p. 1989. 22.95 (*0-88702-048-8*) Washington Inst Pr.

Confucianism & Family Rituals in Imperial China: A Social History of Writing about Rites. Patricia B. Ebrey. 277p. 1991. text ed. 29.95 (*0-691-03150-9*) Princeton U Pr.

Confucianism & Its Rivals. H. A. Giles. 1972. lib. bdg. 79.95 (*0-87968-520-4*) Krishna Pr.

Confucianism & Its Rivals. Herbert A. Giles. LC 77-27155. (Hibbert Lectures: 1914). reprint ed. 39.00 (*0-404-60416-1*) AMS Pr.

Confucianism & Modern China. Reginald F. Johnston. LC 79-2830. (Illus.). 272p. 1986. reprint ed. 24.50 (*0-8305-0007-3*) Hyperion Conn.

Confucianism & Taoism. R. Douglas. 1973. 59.95 (*0-87968-930-7*) Gordon Pr.

Confucianism & Tokugawa Culture. Ed. by Peter Nosco. LC 83-43086. 360p. (C). 1989. pap. text ed. 18.95 (*0-691-00839-6*) Princeton U Pr.

***Confucianism & Tokugawa Culture.** Ed. by Peter Nosco. LC 83-43086. 301p. 1984. reprint ed. pap. 85.80 (*0-7837-8595-X*, 2049410) Bks Demand.

Confucianism, Buddhism, Daoism, Christianity & Chinese Culture. Tang Yi-jie. (Cultural Heritage & Contemporary Change Series VI: Foundations of Moral Education,: Vol. III, No. 3). 186p. (Orig.). 1991. 45.00 (*1-56518-035-6*, B5231.T36); pap. 14.00 (*1-56518-034-8*) Coun Res Values.

Confucianism in Action. Ed. by David S. Nivison & Arthur F. Wright. LC 59-7433. xiv, 390p. 1959. 47.50 (*0-8047-0554-2*) Stanford U Pr.

Confucian's Progress: Autobiographical Writings in Traditional China. Pei-Yi Wu. 297p. 1992. text ed. 45.00 (*0-691-06788-0*); pap. text ed. 16.95 (*0-691-01524-4*) Princeton U Pr.

Confucion Analects. Ezra L. Pound. 136p. 1980. 30.00 (*0-7206-1850-9*, Pub. by P Owen Ltd UK) Dufour.

***Confucius.** rev. ed. Betty Kelen. 160p. 1983. reprint ed. pap. 6.95 (*9971-947-48-X*) Heian Intl.

Confucius: A Novel. Yasushi Inoue. Tr. by Roger K. Thomas. (Illus.). 168p. 1993. 30.00 (*0-7206-0836-8*, Pub. by P Owen Ltd UK) Dufour.

Confucius: The Analects (Lun yu) 2nd ed. Tr. by D. C. Lau. 288p. 1992. 67.50x (*962-201-527-1*, Pub. by Chinese Univ HK) Coronet Bks.

Confucius: The Great Digest, the Unwobbling Pivot, the Analects. Tr. by Ezra Pound. LC 74-87911. 1969. pap. 11.95 (*0-8112-0154-6*, NDP285) New Directions.

Confucius: The Secular As Sacred. Herbert Fingarette. 160p. 1972. pap. text ed. 12.00 (*0-06-131682-2*, TB1682, Torch) HarpC.

***Confucius: The Wisdom.** Ed. by Peg Streep. Tr. by James Legge. LC 94-41432. (Illus.). 1995. 12.95 (*0-8212-2161-2*) Bulfinch Pr.

***Confucius As a Teacher: Philosophy of Confucius with Special Reference to Its Educational Implications.** Chen Jingpan. 522p. 1995. pap. text ed. 7.95 (*983-9808-19-2*, Pub. by Delta Edits II) Weatherhill.

Confucius, Christ, & Co-Partnership: Competing Liturgies for the Soul of Korean American Women. Hwain Chang Lee. LC 93-14548. 116p. (Orig.). (C). 1993. lib. bdg. 29.50 (*0-8191-9223-6*) U Pr of Amer.

Confucius, His Life & Time. Liu Wu-Chi. LC 73-138159. 189p. (C). 1972. reprint ed. text ed. 35.00 (*0-8371-5616-5*, LICO, Greenwood Pr) Greenwood.

Confucius, the Buddha, & Christ: A History of the Gospel in Chinese. Ralph R. Covell. LC 86-8615. (American Society of Missiology Ser.). 304p. (Orig.). 1986. pap. 19.95 (*0-88344-267-1*, CIP) Orbis Bks.

Confucius to Cummings: An Anthology of Poetry. Ed. by Ezra Pound & Marcella Spann. LC 62-17274. (C). 1964. 14.95 (*0-8112-0352-2*); pap. 12.95 (*0-8112-0155-4*, NDP126) New Directions.

Confused Epiphanies: L'Abbe Prevost & the Romance Tradition. Carol M. Lazzaro-Weis. LC 90-24446. (American University Studies: Romance Languages & Literature: Ser. II, Vol. 161). 195p. (C). 1991. text ed. 34.95 (*0-8204-1459-X*) P Lang Pubs.

Confused Minds, Burdened Families: Finding Help for People with Alzheimer's & Other Dementia. (Illus.). 421p. 1990. per., pap. 18.00 (*0-16-024304-1*, S/N 052-003-011) USGPO.

Confused Quarterbacks, Jumpy Gymnasts, & Other Sports Jokes. Stephanie Johnson. (Orig.). (YA). 1994. mass mkt. 3.50 (*0-8125-2052-1*) Tor Bks.

Confused Roaring: Evelyn Waugh & the Modernist Tradition. George McCartney. LC 86-46166. 206p. (C). 1987. 25.00 (*0-253-31411-9*) Ind U Pr.

Confusing Realities: A Study on Child Abuse & Psychiatric Symptoms. Bernadine J. Ensink. 254p. (Orig.). 1992. pap. text ed. 35.50 (*90-5383-085-5*, Pub. by VU Univ Pr NE) Paul & Co Pubs.

***Confusing World of Benny Hinn.** G. Richard Fisher et al. 190p. (Orig.). 1995. pap. write for info. (*1-885591-94-2*) Morris Pubng.

***Confusion.** Elizabeth J. Howard. Ed. by Bill Grose. 448p. 1995. pap. 12.00 (*0-671-52796-7*) PB.

***Confusion.** large type ed. Elizabeth J. Howard. LC 94-26348. (Cazalet Chronicle Ser.: Vol. 3). 596p. 1994. 22.95 (*0-8161-7475-X*) Hall.

Confusion: By Cupid. Janet Lambert. 18.95 (*0-8488-0127-X*, Amereon Hse) Amereon Ltd.

Confusion Beyond Imagination. William B. Sinclair. LC 86-9155. (Ten Books Planned Ser.: Bk. 3). (Illus.). 198p. (Orig.). 1988. 24.00 (*0-937577-04-9*); pap. text ed. 16.00 (*0-937577-05-7*) J F Whitley.

Confusion Beyond Imagination, Bk. 1. William B. Sinclair. (Illus.). 345p. (Orig.). 1986. 24.95 (*0-937577-00-6*); pap. text ed. 16.95 (*0-937577-01-4*) J F Whitley.

Confusion Beyond Imagination, Bk. 2. William B. Sinclair. (Illus.). 320p. (Orig.). 1987. 25.50 (*0-937577-02-2*); pap. 17.50 (*0-937577-03-0*) J F Whitley.

Confusion Beyond Imagination, Bk. 4. William B. Sinclair. (Illus.). 333p. (Orig.). 1988. 26.00 (*0-937577-06-5*); pap. 18.00 (*0-937577-07-3*) J F Whitley.

Confusion Beyond Imagination: Several Sides of CBI Life. William B. Sinclair. (More Aspects of CBI Life Ser.). (Illus.). 280p. (Orig.). 1990. write for info. (*0-937577-16-2*); pap. write for info. (*0-937577-17-0*) J F Whitley.

Confusion Beyond Imagination: That Old Happy Morale, Bk. 8. William B. Sinclair. (Illus.). 330p. (Orig.). 1990. 26.00 (*0-937577-14-6*); pap. 18.00 (*0-937577-15-4*) J F Whitley.

Confusion Beyond Imagination, Bk. 5: Medics & Nurses. William B. Sinclair. (Illus.). 243p. (Orig.). 1989. 25.00 (*0-937577-08-1*); pap. 17.00 (*0-937577-09-X*) J F Whitley.

Confusion Beyond Imagination, Bk. 6: Police, Pleaders & Prisoners Too Few for Too Many. William B. Sinclair. (Illus.). 211p. (Orig.). 1989. 24.50 (*0-937577-10-3*); pap. 16.50 (*0-937577-11-1*) J F Whitley.

Confusion Beyond Imagination, Bk. 7: Under Wraps for Eyes Alone. William B. Sinclair. (Illus.). 382p. (Orig.). 1989. 20.50 (*0-937577-12-X*); pap. 20.50 (*0-937577-13-8*) J F Whitley.

Confusion by Any Other Name: Essays Exploring the Negative Impact of the Blackman's Guide to Understanding the Blackwoman. Ed. by Haki R. Madhubuti. 1992. 3.95 (*0-88378-148-4*) Third World.

***Confusion Is a State of Grace: Humor & Wisdom for Families in Recovery.** Barbara F. LC 95-15680. 1995. write for info. (*1-56838-089-5*) Hazelden.

Confusion Is Next: The Sonic Yough Story. Alec Foege. LC 94-12768. 1994. pap. 13.95 (*0-312-11369-2*) St Martin.

Confusion of Tongues. Paul R. Frothingham. LC 68-22913. (Essay Index Reprint Ser.). 1977. 19.95 (*0-8369-0462-1*) Ayer.

Confusion Reigns: A Quick-&-Easy Guide to the Most Easily Mixed-Up Words. Jim Harrison. 128p. 1987. pap. 6.95 (*0-312-00582-2*) St Martin.

Confusion to Confidence: Informed Parenting. F. Barry Roberts. (Illus.). 210p. 1988. 16.95 (*0-9620695-0-7*) F B Roberts.

***Confusional States in Older People.** E. J. Byrne. 112p. 1994. 37.99 (*1-56593-401-6*, 0806) Singular Publishing.

Confusions. Alan Ayckbourn. (Methuen Student Editions Ser.). (Illus.). 63p. (J). 1988. pap. 9.95 (*0-413-53270-4*, A0063, Pub. by Methuen UK) Heinemann.

***Confusions in Christian Social Ethics: Problems for Geneva & Rome.** Ronald H. Preston. 202p. 1995. pap. 16.99 (*0-8028-4125-2*) Eerdmans.

Confutation of Certaine Articles Delivered by H. Niklaes, Unto the Familye of Love. William Wilkinson. LC 72-238. (English Experience Ser.: No. 279). 200p. 1970. reprint ed. 22.00 (*90-221-0279-3*) Walter J Johnson.

Confutation of That Treatise Which One John Standish Made Agaynst the Protestacion of D. Barnes. Myles Coverdale. LC 79-84096. (English Experience Ser.: No. 917). 212p. 1979. reprint ed. lib. bdg. 30.00 (*90-221-0917-8*) Walter J Johnson.

Confutation of the Rhemists Translation, Glosses & Annotations on the New Testament. Thomas Cartwright. LC 71-171737. (English Experience Ser.: No. 364). 830p. 1971. reprint ed. 120.00 (*90-221-0364-1*) Walter J Johnson.

Conga Crocodile. Nicole Rubel. LC 92-31856. (J). 1993. 14.95 (*0-395-58773-5*) HM.

***Conga Drumming: A Beginner's Guide to Playing with Time.** Alan Dworsky & Betsy Sansby. (Illus.). 160p. (Orig.). 1994. pap. text ed. 24.95 (*0-9638801-0-1*) Dancing Hands.

Conga Drumming: Disco, Soul, Reggae, Rock with Conga Drumming: the Demonstration Recording. Jerry R. Daraca. LC 79-19350. (Illus.). 72p. 1980. audio, spiral bd. 15.00 (*0-918628-21-0*); audio 10.00 (*0-918628-06-7*) Congeros Pubns.

Conga Drumming: Instructor's Edition. Jerry R. Daraca. Ed. by Marian Haldeman. LC 79-19350. (Illus.). 83p. (C). 1982. audio, ring bd. 25.00 (*0-918628-23-7*, C311-1) Congeros Pubns.

Congal: A Poem in Five Books. Samuel Ferguson. LC 75-28812. reprint ed. 29.50 (*0-404-13805-5*) AMS Pr.

Congenial Spirits: The Selected Letters of Virginia Woolf. Joanne T. Banks. LC 89-19769. 472p. 1990. 24.95 (*0-15-122100-6*) HarBrace.

Congenial Spirits: The Selected Letters of Virginia Woolf. Virginia Woolf. 1991. pap. 14.95 (*0-15-622030-X*, Harvest Bks) HarBrace.

Congenital Abnormalities of the Optic Nerve & Related Forebrain. Thomas E. Acers. LC 82-24962. (Illus.). 85p. reprint ed. pap. 25.00 (*0-8357-7638-7*, 2056961) Bks Demand.

Congenital Adrenal Hyperplasia. Ed. by Maria I. New. (Annals Ser.: Vol. 458). 290p. 1985. text ed. 66.00 (*0-89766-311-X*); pap. text ed. 66.00 (*0-89766-312-8*) NY Acad Sci.

Congenital Cataracts. Cotlier. (Medical Intelligence Unit Ser.). 1994. 89.95 (*1-57059-159-8*) R G Landes.

Congenital Chromosome Aberations. G. Fekete. (Illus.). 161p. (C). 1990. text ed. 24.00 (*963-05-5753-3*, Pub. by A K HU) Intl Spec Bk.

Congenital Deafness: A New Approach to Early Detection of Deafness Through a High Risk Register. Franklin O. Black et al. LC 76-135285. (Illus.). 84p. reprint ed. pap. 25.00 (*0-8357-5513-4*, 2035129) Bks Demand.

Congenital Diaphragmatic Hernia. Ed. by P. Puri. (Modern Problems in Pediatrics Ser.: Vol. 24). (Illus.). 164p. 1989. 96.00 (*3-8055-4807-9*) S Karger.

Congenital Disorders of Erythropoiesis. Ciba Foundation Staff. (Ciba Foundation Symposium: New Ser.: No. 37). 416p. reprint ed. pap. 118.60 (*0-317-29170-X*, 2022165) Bks Demand.

Congenital Displacement of the Hip Joint. J. A. Wilkinson. (Illus.). 172p. 1985. 215.00 (*0-387-13947-8*) Spr-Verlag.

Congenital Dysplasia & Dislocation of the Hip in Children & Adults. D. Tonis. Tr. by Terry C. Telger. (Illus.). 520p. 1987. 248.00 (*0-387-16286-0*) Spr-Verlag.

Congenital External & Middle Ear Malformations: Management. Ed. by B. Ars. LC 92-49672. (Illus.). 80p. 1992. 30.00 (*90-6299-086-X*, Pub. by Kugler NE) Kugler Pubns.

Congenital Heart Disease. Burton W. Fink. (Illus.). 183p. 1975. pap. 29.95 (*0-8151-3222-0*, Yr Bk Med Pubs) Mosby Yr Bk.

Congenital Heart Disease. Ed. by F. J. Macartney. (Current Status of Clinical Cardiology Ser.). 1985. lib. bdg. 103.50 (*0-85200-719-1*) Kluwer Ac.

Congenital Heart Disease. abr. ed. Mary Kleinman. Ed. by James B. Van Treese. Tr. by Ingram. 300p. 1993. 9.95 (*1-880416-82-4*) NW Pub.

Congenital Heart Disease. 3rd ed. Burton W. Fink. 208p. 1990. pap. 31.00 (*0-8151-3387-1*, Yr Bk Med Pubs) Mosby Yr Bk.

Congenital Heart Disease: A Diagrammatic Atlas. Charles E. Mullins & David C. Mayer. (Illus.). 1991. pap. text ed. 99.95 (*0-471-58817-2*, Wiley-Liss) Wiley.

Congenital Heart Disease: Echocardiography & Magnetic Resonance Imaging. Charles B. Higgins et al. 416p. 1990. 149.50 (*0-88167-604-7*) Raven.

Congenital Heart Disease in Adolescents & Adults. Ed. by John Hess & George R. Sutherland. LC 92-49625. (Developments in Cardiovascular Medicine Ser.: Vol. 136). 216p. (C). 1992. lib. bdg. 128.50 (*0-7923-1862-5*) Kluwer Ac.

Congenital Heart Disease in Adults. Joseph K. Perloff & Child. (Illus.). 352p. 1990. text ed. 91.95 (*0-7216-7192-6*) Saunders.

Congenital Heart Disease with Cyanosis Symposium, Amsterdam 1968. Congenital Heart Disease with Cyanosis Symposium Staff. Ed. by A. C. Klinkhammer. (Radiologia Clinica et Biologica Ser.: Vol. 39, No. 2). 1970. reprint ed. pap. 25.75 (*3-8055-0802-6*) S Karger.

Congenital Heart Surgery: Current Techniques & Controversies. Ed. by Anthony L. Moulton. LC 83-21342. (Illus.). 347p. 1984. text ed. 97.50 (*0-941022-00-5*) Appleton Davies.

Congenital Hypothyroidism. Ed. by Jean H. Dussault & Peter Walker. LC 83-15331. (Basic & Clinical Endocrinology Ser.: No. 2). (Illus.). 496p. reprint ed. pap. 141.40 (*0-7837-4319-X*, 2044005) Bks Demand.

Congenital Limb Deficiencies in Hungary Genetic & Teratologic Epidemiological Studies. A. Czeizel et al. 420p. Date not set. 54.00 (*963-05-6631-1*, Pub. by A K HU) Intl Spec Bk.

Congenital Lower Limb Deficiencies. Ed. by A. Kalamchi. (Illus.). xii, 258p. 1989. 115.00 (*0-387-96968-3*, 2656) Spr-Verlag.

Congenital Malformations: Antenatal Diagnosis, Perinatal Management, & Counseling. John W. Seeds & Richard G. Azizkhan. 390p. 1990. 79.00 (*0-8342-0140-2*) Raven.

Congenital Malformations: Notes & Comments. Josef Warkany. LC 76-152353. 1349p. reprint ed. pap. 180.00 (*0-318-34980-9*, 2030793) Bks Demand.

Congenital Malformations in Laboratory & Farm Animals. Ed. by Kalman T. Szabo. 1000p. 1989. text ed. 97.00 (*0-12-680130-4*) Acad Pr.

Congenital Malformations in Singletons: Epidemiologic Survey. Ed. by Daniel Bergsma. LC 74-79906. (March of Dimes Ser.: Vol. 10, No. 11). 1976. 12.50 (*0-686-14567-4*) March of Dimes.

***Congenital Malformations of the Brain: Pathological, Embryological, Clinical, Radiological, & Genetic Aspects.** Margaret G. Norman et al. (Illus.). 432p. 1995. 95.00 (*0-19-506245-0*) OUP.

Congenital Malformations of the Brain & Skull see Handbook of Clinical Neurology

Congenital Malformations of the Female Reproductive Tract & Their Treatment. Barry S. Verkauf. (Illus.). 240p. 1993. text ed. 65.00 (*0-8385-1377-8*, A1377-9) Appleton & Lange.

Congenital Malformations of the Heart, 2 vols. 2nd ed. Helen B. Taussig. Incl. Vol. 1. General Considerations. 2nd ed. 232p. 1960. 25.50 (*0-674-16150-5*); Vol. 2. Specific Malformations. 2nd ed. 1059p. 1961. 65.00 (*0-674-16151-3*); (Commonwealth Fund Publications). 1960. write for info. (*0-318-53033-3*) HUP.

Congenital Malformations of the Spine see Handbook of Clinical Neurology

Congenital Malformations of the Urinary Tract. F. Douglas Stephens. LC 83-11207. (Illus.). 592p. 1983. text ed. 53.95 (*0-275-91414-3*, C1414, Praeger Pubs) Greenwood.

Congenital Malformations of the Urinary Tract. F. Douglas Stephens. LC 83-11207. reprint ed. pap. 159.60 (*0-7837-0004-0*, AU000417) Bks Demand.

C

 An Asterisk (*) at the beginning of an entry indicates that the title is appearing in BIP for the first time.

An Asterisk (*) at the beginning of an entry indicates that the title is appearing in BIP for the first time.

1541

Congress & the Nation VII. Congressional Quarterly, Inc. Staff. Incl. Vol. 2. 1965 to 1968. LC 65-22351. 1120p. 1969. 205.00 (*0-87187-004-5*); Vol. 3. 1969 to 1972. LC 65-22351. 1178p. 1973. 205.00 (*0-87187-055-X*); Vol. 4. 1973 to 1976. LC 65-22351. 1217p. 1977. 205.00 (*0-87187-112-2*); Vol. 2. 1965 to 1968. LC 65-22351. 1120p. 1969. 205.00 (*0-87187-004-5*); Vol. 3. 1969 to 1972. LC 65-22351. 1178p. 1973. 205.00 (*0-87187-055-X*); Vol. 4. 1973 to 1976. LC 65-22351. 1217p. 1977. 205.00 (*0-87187-112-2*); Congress & the Nation VIII, 1989-1992: A Review of Government & Politics. LC 65-22351. 1308p. 1993. 205.00 (*0-87187-789-9*); LC 65-22351. write for info. (*0-318-51426-5*) Congr Quarterly.

Congress & the Nation VIII, 1989-1992: A Review of Government & Politics. Congressional Quarterly, Inc. Staff. LC 65-22351. (Congress & the Nation VII). 1308p. 1993. 205.00 (*0-87187-789-9*) Congr Quarterly.

Congress & the Nuclear Freeze: An Inside Look at the Politics of a Mass Movement. Douglas C. Waller. LC 86-19336. 368p. 1987. lib. bdg. 37.50x (*0-87023-559-1*); pap. 18.95x (*0-87023-560-5*) U of Mass Pr.

Congress & the Politics of U. S. Foreign Economic Policy, 1929 to 1976. Robert A. Pastor. LC 79-63552. (Studies in International Political Economy: Vol. 5). 416p. 1980. pap. 14.00 (*0-520-04645-5*) U CA Pr.

Congress & the Politics of U. S. Foreign Policy. James M. Lindsay. LC 94-1246. 228p. 1994. text ed. 42.50x (*0-8018-4881-4*); pap. text ed. 13.95x (*0-8018-4882-2*) Johns Hopkins.

Congress & the Presidency: Invitation to Struggle. Ed. by Roger H. Davidson. (Annals Ser.: Vol. 499). 1988. 26.00 (*0-8039-3105-0*); pap. 17.00 (*0-8039-3106-9*) Sage.

Congress & the President: The Policy Connection. Lance T. LeLoup & Steven A. Shull. 274p. (C). 1993. pap. 19.95 (*0-534-15876-5*) Intl Thomson.

Congress & the Separation of Powers. John L. FitzGerald. LC 85-12187. 175p. 1985. text ed. 49.95 (*0-275-90034-7*, C0034, Praeger Pubs) Greenwood.

***Congress & U. S. Military Aid to Britain: Interdependence & Dependence, 1949-56.** Helen Leigh-Phippard. LC 94-35564. 1995. write for info. (*0-312-12516-X*) St Martin.

Congress & United States Foreign Policy: Controlling the Use of Force in the Nuclear Age. Ed. by Michael Barnhart. LC 86-23057. 196p. 1987. 64.50 (*0-88706-465-5*); pap. 21.95 (*0-88706-466-3*) State U NY Pr.

C

Congress & Water Resources. Arthur A. Mass. (Reprint Series in Social Sciences). (C). 1993. reprint ed. pap. text ed. 1.00 (*0-8290-2735-1*, PS-176) Irvington.

***Congress As Public Enemy: Public Attitudes Toward American Political Institutions.** John R. Hibbing & Elizabeth Theiss-Morse. (Cambridge Studies in Political Psychology & Public Opinion). (Illus.). 208p. (C). 1995. write for info. (*0-521-48299-2*); pap. write for info. (*0-521-48336-0*) Cambridge U Pr.

Congress As Santa Claus. C. Warren. LC 77-74970. (American Federalism-the Urban Dimension Ser.). 1978. reprint ed. lib. bdg. 19.95 (*0-405-10512-6*) Ayer.

Congress at Princeton: Being the Letters of Charles Thomson to Hanna Thomson, June-October, 1783. Ed. by Eugene R. Sheridan & John M. Murrin. (Illus.). 146p. 1985. 20.00 (*0-87811-025-9*) Princeton Lib.

***Congress at Your Fingertips: Condensed Edition.** Ed. by John E. Hansan. 96p. 1995. pap. 5.95 (*1-879617-19-6*) Capitol Advantage.

***Congress at Your Fingertips, Alpha Edition: A Guide to the 104th Congress.** Ed. by John E. Hansan. 236p. 1995. pap. text ed., spiral bd. 10.95 (*1-879617-18-8*) Capitol Advantage.

***Congress at Your Fingertips, Standard Edition: A Guide to the 104th Congress.** Ed. by John E. Hansan. 192p. 1995. pap. text ed., spiral bd. 8.95 (*1-879617-16-1*) Capitol Advantage.

***Congress at Your Fingertips, Standard Edition: A Guide to the 104th Congress.** Ed. by John E. Hansan. 192p. 1995. per., pap. 8.95 (*1-879617-17-X*) Capitol Advantage.

Congress Book, 1990. Ed. by Barbara R. Mueller. LC 40-2870. (Illus.). 198p. 1990. text ed. 25.00 (*0-929333-16-0*) Am Philat Congr.

Congress, Courts, & Criminals: The Development of Federal Criminal Law, 1801-1829. Dwight F. Henderson. LC 84-28960. (Contributions in American History Ser.: No. 113). x, 259p. 1985. text ed. 59.95 (*0-313-24600-9*, HEG/, Greenwood Pr) Greenwood.

Congress Declares War: Rhetoric, Leadership, & Partisanship in the Early Republic. Ronald L. Hatzenbuehler & Robert L. Ivie. LC 83-8996. (Illus.). 184p. reprint ed. pap. 52.50 (*0-7837-0500-X*, 2040824) Bks Demand.

***Congress Dictionary: The Ways & Meanings of Capitol Hill.** Paul Dickson & Paul Clancy. 1995. pap. text ed. 19.95 (*0-471-11988-1*) Wiley.

Congress Hall: Capitol of the U. S. 1790-1800. National Park Service Staff. LC 90-13556. (Handbook Ser.: No. 147). (Illus.). 49p. (Orig.). 1991. pap. 1.50 (*0-912627-42-5*, 024-005-01074-2) Natl Park Serv.

Congress, Human Nature, & the Federal Debt: Essays on the Political Psychology of Deficit Spending. Cole S. Brembeck. LC 90-28077. 192p. 1991. text ed. 49.95 (*0-275-93674-0*, C3674, Praeger Pubs) Greenwood.

Congress in Indian Politics: A Centenary Perspective. Ed. by Ram Joshi & R. K. Hebsur. LC 88-60171. 299p. (C). 1988. 32.00 (*0-913215-34-1*) Riverdale Co.

Congress in Indian Politics: A Centenary Perspective. Ram Joshi & R. K. Hensur. 299p. (C). 1987. 42.00 (*0-86132-142-1*, Pub. by Popular Prakashan II) S Asia.

Congress in Tamiland: Nationalist Politics in South India, Nineteen Nineteen to Nineteen Thirty-Seven. David Arnold. 1977. 12.00 (*0-88386-958-6*) S Asia.

Congress in the American System. Carl P. Chelf. LC 77-1084. 272p. 1978. text ed. 28.95 (*0-88229-210-2*) Nelson-Hall.

Congress Makes a Law: The Story Behind the Employment Act of 1946. Stephen K. Bailey. LC 80-12550. xii, 282p. 1980. reprint ed. text ed. 38.50 (*0-313-22407-2*, BACK, Greenwood Pr) Greenwood.

Congress of Arras, Fourteen Thirty-Five. Joycelyne G. Dickinson. 1973. reprint ed. 25.00 (*0-8196-0281-7*) Biblo.

Congress of Arts & Science. Ed. by Howard J. Rogers. LC 73-14177. (Perspectives in Social Inquiry Ser.). 342p. 1974. reprint ed. 24.95 (*0-405-05520-X*) Ayer.

Congress of Berlin & After. William N. Medlicott. 442p. 1963. 34.00 (*0-7146-1501-3*, Pub. by F Cass Pubs UK) Intl Spec Bk.

Congress of Nations: Addresses at the International Peace Congresses at Brussels (1848), Paris (1849), & Frankfort (1850) see Learned Blacksmith: The Letters & Journals of Elihu Burritt

Congress of Neurological Surgeons, Vol. 38. CNS Clinical Neurosurgery Staff & Warren Selman. (Illus.). 736p. 1992. 67.00 (*0-683-02035-8*) Williams & Wilkins.

Congress of Neurological Surgeons, Vol. 41. CNS Clinical Neurosurgery Staff & Warren Selman. (Illus.). write for info. (*0-683-02038-2*) Williams & Wilkins.

Congress of the International Council of the Aeronautical Sciences, 15th, London, England, 7-12 September, 1986: Proceedings, 2 vols., Set. International Council of Aeronautical Sciences Staff. 1200p. 1987. pap. 89.50 (*0-930403-16-9*) AIAA.

Congress of the International Society for Rock Mechanics, 5th: Proceedings Melbourne, 1983, 3 vols., Set. 2060p. (C). 1987. text ed. 695.00 (*90-6191-236-9*, Pub. by A A Balkema NE) Ashgate Pub Co.

Congress of the United States: Its Origins & Early Development. Pref. by Joel Silbey. LC 90-28960. (Congress of the United States, 1789-1989 Ser.: Vol. 1). 483p. 1991. 100.00 (*0-926019-28-7*) Carlson Pub.

Congress of the United States: Patterns of Recruitment, Leadership, & Internal Structure, 1789-1989, 2 vols., Set. Ed. by Joel Silbey. LC 90-28968. (Congress of the United States, 1789-1989 Ser.: Vol. 2). 646p. 1995. 150.00 (*0-926019-29-5*) Carlson Pub.

Congress of Vienna: A Study of Allied Unity 1812-1822. Harold Nicolson. LC 46-7614. 312p. 1970. reprint ed. pap. 10.95 (*0-15-622061-X*, Harvest Bks) HarBrace.

Congress of Women, Held in the Woman's Building, World's Columbian Exposition, Chicago, U. S. A., 1893. Ed. by Mary D. Eagle. LC 74-3944. (Women in America Ser.). (Illus.). 840p. 1974. reprint ed. 64.95 (*0-405-06090-4*) Ayer.

Congress on Electrocardiology, 1st, Wiesbaden, Oct. 1974. Congress on Electrocardiology, 1st, Wiesbaden, Oct. 1974. Ed. by H. Abel. (Advances in Cardiology Ser.: Vol. 16). 1976. 102.50 (*3-8055-2197-9*) S Karger.

Congress on Trial: The Legislative Process & the Administrative State. James M. Burns. LC 66-29462. 224p. 1966. reprint ed. 45.00 (*0-87752-013-5*) Gordian.

Congress Overseas the United States Intelligence Community: 1947-1994. 2nd ed. Frank J. Smist, Jr. 380p. (C). 1994. pap. text ed. 24.95 (*0-87049-841-X*) U of Tenn Pr.

Congress Oversees the Bureaucracy: Studies in Legislative Supervision. Morris S. Ogul. LC 75-33546. 250p. (C). 1976. pap. 15.95 (*0-8229-5288-2*) U of Pittsburgh Pr.

Congress, Parliament & Defence: The Impact of Legislative Reform on Defence Accountability in Britain & America. Andrew Cox & Stephen Kirby. LC 86-3812. 246p. 1986. text ed. 39.95 (*0-312-16243-X*) St Martin.

Congress Party. Meenakshi Jain. 1990. text ed. 25.00 (*0-7069-5319-3*, Pub. by Vikas II) S Asia.

Congress Party in India. Ed. by N. S. Gehlot. 1991. 45.00 (*81-7100-306-0*, Pub. by Deep) S Asia.

Congress Party in Transition. D. Suran Naidu. (C). 1991. 22.50 (*81-85135-64-9*, Pub. by Natl Bk Org II) S Asia.

Congress Party in West Bengal: A Study of Factionalism, 1947-86. Prasanta S. Gupta. (C). 1988. 20.00 (*81-85195-12-9*, Pub. by Minerva II) S Asia.

Congress Party of India: The Dynamics of a One-Party Democracy. Stanley A. Kochanek. LC 68-10393. 1968. 75.00 (*0-691-03013-8*) Princeton U Pr.

Congress Party of India: The Dynamics of One-Party Democracy. Stanley A. Kochanek. LC 68-10393. 542p. reprint ed. pap. 154.50 (*0-7837-1416-5*, 2041770) Bks Demand.

Congress' Permanent Minority? The Republicans in the U. S. House. William F. Connelly, Jr. & John J. Pitney, Jr. 160p. (C). 1994. lib. bdg. 44.50 (*0-8476-7923-3*); pap. text ed. 14.95 (*0-8226-3032-X*) Rowman.

Congress Reconsidered. 5th ed. Ed. by Lawrence C. Dodd & Bruce I. Oppenheimer. 480p. 1993. pap. text ed. 26.95 (*0-87187-712-0*) Congr Quarterly.

Congress Resurgent: Foreign & Domestic Policy on Capitol Hill. Ed. by Randall B. Ripley & James M. Lindsay. LC 93-16033. (Mershon Center Series on International Security & Foreign Policy). 350p. (C). 1993. text ed. 54.50 (*0-472-09533-1*); pap. text ed. 18.95 (*0-472-06533-5*) U of Mich Pr.

Congress Terminology. IAPCO Staff CEC. 172p. (ENG, FRE, GER, ITA & SPA.). 1987. pap. 75.00 (*0-8288-7642-8*) Fr & Eur.

Congress, the Bureaucracy, & Public Policy. 5th ed. Randall B. Ripley & Grace A. Franklin. LC 90-2022. 264p. (C). 1991. pap. 23.95 (*0-534-14454-3*) Intl Thomson.

Congress, the Executive Branch, & Special Interests: The American Response to the Arab Boycott of Israel. Kennan L. Teslik. LC 81-20338. (Contributions in Political Science Ser.: No. 80). x, 280p. 1982. text ed. 55.00 (*0-313-23120-6*, TCE/) Greenwood.

Congress, the Presidency, & the Taiwan Relation Act. Louis W. Koenig et al. LC 84-26305. 208p. 1985. text ed. 49.95 (*0-275-90129-7*, C0129, Praeger Pubs) Greenwood.

Congress, the President, & Foreign Policy. American Bar Association, Standing Commission on Law & National Security. 1984. pap. 7.50 (*0-89707-163-8*) Amer Bar Assn.

Congress, the President, & Policymaking: A Historical Analysis. Jean R. Schroedel. (American Political Institutions & Public Policy Ser.). (Illus.). 224p. 1994. text ed. 55.00 (*1-56324-176-5*); pap. text ed. 22.95 (*1-56324-177-3*) M E Sharpe.

Congress, the Press, & the Public. Thomas E. Mann & Norman J. Ornstein. 212p. (C). 1994. 36.95 (*0-8157-5462-0*); pap. 16.95 (*0-8157-5461-2*) Brookings.

Congress Today. Edward V. Schneier & Bertram M. Gross. LC 92-50019. (Illus.). 560p. (C). 1993. pap. text ed. 23.50 (*0-312-05193-X*) St Martin.

Congress Versus the Supreme Court, Nineteen Fifty-Seven to Nineteen Sixty. C. Herman Pritchett. LC 73-249. (American Constitutional & Legal History Ser). 182p. 1973. reprint ed. lib. bdg. 25.00 (*0-306-70568-0*) Da Capo.

Congress Volume: Leuven, 1989. Ed. by J. A. Emerton. LC 91-7207. (Supplements to Vetus Testamentum Ser.: Vol. 43). vi, 398p. (ENG & GER.). 1991. 97.25 (*90-04-09398-2*) E J Brill.

***Congress Volume: Paris, 1992.** Ed. by J. A. Emerton. LC 95-3906. (Supplements to Vetus Testamentum Ser.: Vol. 61). 1995. write for info. (*90-04-10259-0*) E J Brill.

Congress vs. the Supreme Court. Raoul Berger. LC 75-75426. 440p. 1969. 35.00 (*0-674-16210-2*) HUP.

***Congressional Action Pts. I & II: A Documentary History.** Ed. by Neal Devins & Wendy L. Watson. LC 94-49562. (Federal Abortion Politics Ser.: Vol. 1). 792p. 1995. 135.00 (*0-8153-1906-1*) Garland.

Congressional Action Contact Network Handbook. Roger P. Kingsley & Suzanne Wandersman. (Illus.). 1988. write for info. (*0-910329-42-7*) Am Speech Lang Hearing.

Congressional Action in R&D in the FY 1992 Budget. Albert H. Teich et al. 56p. 1992. 8.50 (*0-87168-435-7*, 91-44S) AAAS.

Congressional Action on Research & Development in the Fiscal Year 1991 Budget. Albert H. Teich et al. 54p. 1990. pap. 8.50 (*0-87168-387-3*, 90-33S) AAAS.

Congressional Almanac. Paul Dickson, Jr. & Paul Clancy. Ed. by S. Ross. 416p. 1993. text ed. 29.95 (*0-471-58064-3*) Wiley.

Congressional & Gubernatorial Primaries, 1991-1992: A Handbook of Election Statistics. Alice V. McGillivray. 265p. 1993. 129.00 (*0-87187-906-9*) Congr Quarterly.

***Congressional & Gubernatorial Primaries 1993-1994: A Handbook of Election Statistics.** Alice V. McGillivray. LC 93-11872. 450p. 1995. 134.00 (*0-87187-899-2*) Congr Quarterly.

Congressional Anecdotes. Paul F. Boller, Jr. 368p. 1992. pap. 10.95 (*0-19-507706-7*) OUP.

Congressional Apportionment. Laurence F. Schmeckebier. LC 74-4731. (Studies in Administration Ser.: No. 40). 233p. 1976. reprint ed. text ed. 59.75 (*0-8371-7486-4*, SCCA, Greenwood Pr) Greenwood.

Congressional Attitudes Toward Science & Scientists: A Study of Legislative Reactions to Atomic Energy & the Political Participation of Scientists. Harry S. Hall. Ed. by Stuart Bruchey. LC 78-22687. (Energy in the American Economy Ser.). 1979. lib. bdg. 35.95 (*0-405-11990-9*) Ayer.

Congressional Black Caucus in the One Hundred Third Congress. David A. Bositis. 180p. (C). 1994. lib. bdg. 54.00 (*0-8191-9560-X*); pap. text ed. 23.50 (*0-8191-9561-8*) U Pr of Amer.

Congressional Budget Process After Five Years. Ed. by Rudolph G. Penner. LC 81-8000. (AEI Symposia Ser.: No. 81H). 216p. reprint ed. pap. 61.60 (*0-8357-4453-1*, 2037291) Bks Demand.

Congressional Budgeting: Politics, Process & Power. Ed. by W. Thomas Wander et al. LC 84-47943. (C). 1984. text ed. 38.50x (*0-8018-2392-7*); pap. text ed. 13.95 (*0-8018-2396-X*) Johns Hopkins.

Congressional Campaign Finances. 200p. 1992. pap. 31.95 (*0-87187-626-4*) Congr Quarterly.

Congressional Careers: Contours of Life in the U. S. House of Representatives. John R. Hibbing. LC 91-182. xvi, 214p. (C). 1991. 32.50 (*0-8078-1984-0*); pap. 13.95 (*0-8078-4340-7*) U of NC Pr.

Congressional Chronicles: Amusing & Amazing Anecdotes of the U. S. Congress & Its Members. Anthony S. Pitch. LC 90-91538. (Illus.). 200p. (Orig.). 1990. pap. 12.95 (*0-931719-07-0*) Mino Pubns.

Congressional Committee Chairmen: Three Who Made an Evolution. Andree E. Reeves. LC 92-34812. (Illus.). 280p. 1993. text ed. 39.00 (*0-8131-1816-6*) U Pr of Ky.

Congressional Committee Politics: Continuity & Change. Joseph K. Unekis & Leroy N. Rieselbach. LC 84-2141. 320p. 1984. text ed. 55.00 (*0-275-91285-X*, C1285, Praeger Pubs) Greenwood.

***Congressional Committees.** Cass Sandak. (Inside Government Ser.). (Illus.). 96p. (J). (gr. 5-8). 1995. lib. bdg. 14.98 (*0-8050-3425-0*) TFC Bks NY.

Congressional Committees, Seventeen Eighty-Nine to Nineteen Eighty-Two: A Checklist. Ed. by Walter Stubbs. LC 85-10007. (Bibliographies & Indexes in Law & Political Science Ser.: No. 6). xv, 210p. 1985. text ed. 55.00 (*0-313-24539-8*, STG/) Greenwood.

Congressional Conference Committee. Ada C. McCown. LC 76-181952. (Columbia University. Studies in the Social Sciences: No. 290). reprint ed. 16.50 (*0-404-51290-9*) AMS Pr.

Congressional Conservatism & the New Deal: The Growth of the Conservative Coalition in Congress, 1933 to 1939. James T. Patterson. LC 81-4195. (Illus.). ix, 369p. 1981. reprint ed. text ed. 59.75 (*0-313-22676-8*, PACC, Greenwood Pr) Greenwood.

Congressional Control of Administration. Joseph P. Harris. LC 80-55. xi, 306p. 1980. reprint ed. text ed. 59.75 (*0-313-22304-1*, HACG, Greenwood Pr) Greenwood.

Congressional Decision Making for National Security. Committee for Economic Development. LC 74-12944. 1974. lib. bdg. 3.50 (*0-87186-755-9*); pap. 2.00 (*0-87186-055-4*) Comm Econ Dev.

Congressional Directory, 104th Congress. 296p. 1995. 13.95 (*0-685-65178-9*) Heritage Found.

Congressional Directory 1987-1988. (Illus.). 1625p. 1987. 20.00 (*0-685-43877-5*, S/N 052-070-06239-8) USGPO.

Congressional Directory 1987-1988. (Illus.). 1625p. 1987. pap. 15.00 (*0-685-43878-3*, 052-070-06239-8) USGPO.

Congressional Directory 1993-1994: 103rd Congress. Joint Committee on Printing of the United States Congress Staff. (Illus.). 1320p. 1993. reprint ed. lib. bdg. 30.00 (*0-89059-017-6*); reprint ed. pap. 19.95 (*0-89059-018-4*) Bernan Pr.

Congressional District Atlas: One Hundredth Congress of the United States. LC 72-600344. (Illus.). 696p. 1987. pap. 33.00 (*0-16-000489-6*, S/N 003-024-06234-8) USGPO.

Congressional Districting: The Issue of Equal Representation. Andrew Hacker. LC 86-18312. 155p. 1986. reprint ed. text ed. 52.50 (*0-313-25277-7*, HCON, Greenwood Pr) Greenwood.

Congressional Districts in the 1990's. Congressional Quarterly Staff. 1016p. 1993. 189.00 (*0-87187-722-8*) Congr Quarterly.

Congressional Dynamics: Structure, Coordination, & Choice in the First American Congress, 1774-1789. Calvin Jillson & Rick K. Wilson. LC 93-36655. (Series in the New Political History). 1994. 45.00 (*0-8047-2293-5*) Stanford U Pr.

***Congressional Elections: Campaigning at Home & in Washington.** Paul S. Herrnson. 291p. 1994. 32.95 (*0-87187-973-5*) Congr Quarterly.

Congressional Elections, Eighteen Ninety-Six to Nineteen Forty-Four. Cortez A. Ewing. LC 84-19825. xiii, 110p. 1984. reprint ed. text ed. 55.00 (*0-313-24681-5*, EWCE, Greenwood Pr) Greenwood.

Congressional Endorsement for a Jewish Commonwealth. Aaron Klieman. LC 90-45878. (American Zionism Ser.). 528p. 1991. reprint ed. 150.00 (*0-8240-7358-4*) Garland.

Congressional Ethics. 200p. 1992. pap. 31.95 (*0-87187-624-8*) Congr Quarterly.

Congressional Experience: A View from the Hill. David E. Price. LC 92-13949. (Transforming American Politics Ser.). 194p. (C). 1992. pap. text ed. 17.95 (*0-8133-1156-X*) Westview.

Congressional Experience: A View from the Hill. David E. Price. LC 92-13949. (Transforming American Politics Ser.). 194p. 1992. text ed. 61.00 (*0-8133-1157-8*) Westview.

Congressional Government. Woodrow Wilson. 1958. 25.25 (*0-8446-3187-6*) Peter Smith.

Congressional Grants of Land in Aid of Railways. John B. Sanborn. Ed. by Stuart Bruchey. LC 80-1343. (Railroads Ser.). 1981. reprint ed. lib. bdg. 18.95 (*0-405-13814-8*) Ayer.

Congressional Hearings Calendar 99th-101st Congress, 2 vols. Dora R. Bertram, Jr. & Kimberly A. Martin. (AALL Legal Research Ser.: NO. 1). 1987. lib. bdg. 110.00 (*0-89941-558-X*, 305160); lib. bdg. 115.00 (*0-685-73946-5*) W S Hein.

Congressional Hearings on American Defense Policy, 1947-1971: An Annotated Bibliography. Ed. by Richard Burt & Geoffrey Kemp. LC 73-11321. xvi, 380p. (Orig.). (C). 1974. pap. 9.95 (*0-7006-0109-0*) U Pr of KS.

Congressional History of Railways in the United States, 2 vols. in 1. Lewis H. Haney. LC 67-30858. (Library of Early American Business & Industry: No. 25). 1968. reprint ed. 65.00 (*0-678-00426-9*) Kelley.

Congressional Insurgents & the Party System, Nineteen Nine to Nineteen Sixteen. James Holt. LC 67-22866. (Historical Monographs: No. 60). 196p. 1967. 14.00 (*0-674-16250-1*) HUP.

Congressional Intent. Thomas B. Curtis & Donald L. Westerfield. LC 92-9567. 192p. 1992. text ed. 42.95 (*0-275-94197-3*, Praeger Pubs) Greenwood.

Congressional Investigating Committees. Marshall E. Dimock. LC 72-155626. reprint ed. 12.50 (*0-404-02134-4*) AMS Pr.

Congressional Investigations: Law & Practice. John C. Grabow. 488p. 1988. ring bd. 95.00 (*0-13-526466-9*) Aspen Law.

Congressional Journals of the United States: James Madison, 11th-14th Congresses, 1809-1817, 10 vols., Set. LC 77-76813. 1977. 550.00 (*0-89453-050-X*, 30518G); 605.00 (*0-685-59108-5*, 30615G) Scholarly Res Inc.

Congressional Journals of the United States: John Adams, 5th-6th Congresses, 1797-1801, 10 vols. LC 77-76813. 1977. 275.00 (*0-685-72511-1*) Scholarly Res Inc.

Congressional Journals of the United States: John Adams, 5th-6th Congresses, 1797-1801, 5 vols. 1977. Senate. write for info. (*0-318-68895-6*, 30232G); House of Representatives. write for info. (*0-318-68896-4*, 30283G) Scholarly Res Inc.

Congressional Journals of the United States: Thomas Jefferson, 7th-10th Congresses, 1801-1809, 16 vols. LC 77-76813. 1977. 440.00 (*0-89453-033-X*, 30348G); 440.00 (*0-318-68897-2*, 30429G) Scholarly Res Inc.

An Asterisk (*) at the beginning of an entry indicates that the title is appearing in BIP for the first time.

C

An Asterisk (*) at the beginning of an entry indicates that the title is appearing in BIP for the first time.

Congressman's Civil War. Allan G. Bogue. (Interdisciplinary Perspectives on Modern History Ser.). 224p. (C). 1989. 54.95 (*0-521-35405-6*); pap. 15.95 (*0-521-35705-5*) Cambridge U Pr.

Congressman's Daughter. Patricia M. Markum. 144p. (J). (gr. 5-8). 1994. pap. 2.99 (*0-87406-674-3*) Willowisp Pr.

Congressmen & Their Constituencies. Lewis A. Froman, Jr. LC 74-15553. 127p. 1974. reprint ed. text ed. 55.00 (*0-8371-7820-7*, FRCO, Greenwood Pr) Greenwood.

Congressmen, Constituents, & Contributors: An Analysis of Determinants of Roll-Call Voting in the House of Representatives. James B. Kau & Paul H. Rubin. (Studies in Public Choice). 144p. 1981. lib. bdg. 40.50 (*0-89838-070-7*) Kluwer Ac.

Congressmen's Voting Decisions. 3rd ed. John W. Kingdon. 250p. 1989. pap. 16.95 (*0-472-06401-0*) U of Mich Pr.

Congressperson. Louis Sabin. LC 84-2651. (Illus.). 32p. (J). (gr. 3-6). 1985. lib. bdg. 9.49 (*0-8167-0266-7*); pap. text ed. 2.95 (*0-8167-0267-5*) Troll Assocs.

Congreve: The Critical Heritage. Ed. by Alexander D. Lindsay & Howard Erskine-Hall. 496p. 1989. 112.00 (*0-415-02535-4*) Routledge.

Congreve, the Drama, & the Printed Word. Julie S. Peters. LC 89-26167. (Illus.). 302p. 1991. 35.00 (*0-8047-1751-6*) Stanford U Pr.

Congruence of People & Organizations: Healing Dysfunction from the Inside Out. Lloyd C. Williams. LC 92-23978. 216p. 1993. text ed. 47.95 (*0-89930-800-7*, WBS, Quorum Bks) Greenwood.

Congruence of Sets, & Other Monographs, 4 vols. in 1. Incl. On the Congruence of Sets. Waclaw Sierpinski. LC 67-17000. (*0-318-51330-7*); Mathematical Theory of the Top. Felix Klein. LC 67-17000. (*0-318-51331-5*); Graphical Methods. Carl Runge. LC 67-17000. (*0-318-51332-3*); Algebraic Equations. Leonard E. Dickson. LC 67-17000. (*0-318-51333-1*); LC 67-17000. 19.95 (*0-8284-0209-4*) Chelsea Pub.

Congruity & Innovation in Indian Agriculture. P. O. Ingle. 133p. 1987. text ed. 15.95 (*81-7027-112-6*, Pub. by Radiant Pubs II) S Asia.

Conhecimento Espiritual. Watchman Nee. Orig. Title: Spiritual Knowledge. 144p. (POR.). 1986. 3.95 (*0-8297-0781-6*) Life Pubs Intl.

Conic Sections. 6th ed. George Salmon. LC 55-3390. 19.50 (*0-8284-0099-7*) Chelsea Pub.

Conical Double-Crown Telescopic Periodontic Prosthesis. Haruhiko Shiba. (Illus.). 56p. 1992. pap. 20.00 (*1-56386-002-3*) Ishiyaku Euro.

Conical Refraction & Higher Microlocalization. Otto Liess. (Lecture Notes in Mathematics Ser.: Vol. 1555). x, 389p. 1993. pap. write for info. (*3-540-57105-1*) Spr-Verlag.

Conical Refraction & Higher Microlocalization. Otto Liess. LC 93-26024. (Lecture Notes in Mathematics Ser.: Vol. 1555). 1993. pap. 56.00 (*0-387-57105-1*) Spr-Verlag.

Conifer Manual, Vol. 1. Humphrey J. Welch. (Forestry Sciences Ser.). 448p. 1991. lib. bdg. 188.50 (*0-7923-0616-3*) Kluwer Ac.

Coniferen Im Westlichen: Malayischen Archipel. Norbert Stein. (Biogeographica Ser.: No. 11). 1978. lib. bdg. 65.50 (*90-6193-212-2*) Kluwer Ac.

Coniferous Forest Ecology, from an International Perspective. Ed. by N. Nakagoshi & F. B. Golley. (Illus.). 182p. 1991. pap. 45.00 (*90-5103-065-7*, Pub. by SPB Acad Pub NE) Koeltz Sci Bks.

Coniferous Trees. George Zauner. (Mini Fact Finders Ser.). 64p. 1991. spiral bd. 4.95 (*0-8120-4451-7*) Barron.

***Conifers.** fac. ed. Keith Rushforth. LC 87-28965. (Illus.). 240p. 1987. reprint ed. pap. 68.40 (*0-7837-8153-9*, 2047858) Bks Demand.

Conifers. 2nd ed. D. M. Van Gelderen & J. R. Van Hoey Smith. (Illus.). 373p. 1989. 69.95 (*0-88192-153-X*) Timber.

Conifers: Morphology & Variation. Mirko Vidakovic. (Illus.). 754p. 1992. text ed. 123.50 (*0-85198-807-5*) CAB Intl.

Conifers for Your Garden. Adrian Bloom. 1972. 21.95 (*0-903001-01-2*, Pub. by Burall Floraprint UK) J Markham & Assocs.

Conimbricenses - Commentarii Collegii Conimbricensis. 818p. 1984. reprint ed. write for info. (*3-487-07469-9*, Pub. by Georg Olms GW) Lubrecht & Cramer.

Conimbricenses - Commentarii Collegii Conimbricensis...in Universam Dialecticam Aristotelis, 2 vols. in 1. Ed. by W. Risse. 38p. 1976. reprint ed. write for info. (*3-487-05906-1*, Pub. by Georg Olms GW) Lubrecht & Cramer.

Conimicut Hurricane: The Exciting Adventure Novel of Two Lonely Kids...Trapped by Deadly Hurricane Glenna. Don Vieweg. (Illus.). 210p. (Orig.). 1994. pap. 14.95 (*1-884487-05-X*) Bellman Pubng.

Coningsby. Benjamin Disraeli. 1979. lib. bdg. 69.95 (*0-87700-296-7*) Revisionist Pr.

Coningsby. Benjamin Disraeli. 1989. reprint ed. lib. bdg. 35.95 (*0-89966-637-X*) Buccaneer Bks.

Coningsby, or The New Generation. Benjamin Disraeli. Ed. by Thom Braun. (English Library). 528p. 1983. 7.95 (*0-14-043192-6*, Penguin Classics) Viking Penguin.

Coningsby: Or, the New Generation & Selected Speeches see Works of Benjamin Disraeli, Earl of Beaconsfield

Coniston. Winston Churchill. LC 72-96877. (Illus.). 543p. reprint ed. lib. bdg. 29.00 (*0-8398-0264-1*) Irvington.

Conjectures de Stark sur les Fonctions L d'Artin en s Equals 0, Vol. 47. John Tate. (Progress in Mathematics Ser.). 152p. (FRE.). 1984. 34.50 (*0-8176-3188-7*) Birkhauser.

Conjectures in Arithmetic Algebraic Geometry: A Survey. 2nd rev. ed. Wilfried W. Hulsbergen. (Aspects of Mathematics Ser.: Vol. E18). viii, 246p. 1994. 48.00 (*3-528-16433-6*, Pub. by Vieweg & Sohn GW) Ballen Bkslr.

Conjectures of a Guilty Bystander. Thomas Merton. LC 66-24311. 1968. pap. 12.00 (*0-385-01018-4*, Image Bks) Doubleday.

Conjoining an Input-Output Model & a Policy Analysis Model: A Case Study of the Regional Effects of Expanding a Port Facility. B. H. Stevens et al. (Discussion Paper Ser.: No. 117). 1980. pap. 10.00 (*1-55869-017-4*) Regional Sci Res Inst.

Conjoint Family Therapy. 3rd rev. ed. Virginia M. Satir. LC 82-61781. 1982. pap. 15.95 (*0-8314-0063-3*) Sci & Behavior.

Conjoint Marital Therapy. R. V. Fitzgerald. LC 73-81208. 256p. 1990. reprint ed. 30.00x (*0-87668-091-0*) Aronson.

Conjuctions & Disjunctions. Octavio Paz. 1991. pap. 8.95 (*1-55970-137-4*) Arcade Pub Inc.

***Conjugaison Dictionnaire de Douze Milles Verbes.** rev. ed. Louis-Michel Becherelle. 175p. (FRE.). 1990. 17.95 (*0-7859-7783-X*, 2218016605) Fr & Eur.

Conjugal Bliss: A Comedy of Marital Arts. John Nichols. LC 93-1245. 320p. 1994. 22.50 (*0-8050-2803-X*) H Holt & Co.

***Conjugal Bliss: A Comedy of the Marital Arts.** John Nichols. 1995. pap. 5.99 (*0-345-38790-2*) Ballantine.

Conjugal Contraries & Quart. John Wieners. 64p. (Orig.). 1987. pap. 5.95 (*0-937815-12-8*) Hanuman Bks.

Conjugal Lewdness, or Matrimonial Whoredom. Daniel Defoe & Maximillian E. Novak. LC 67-10178. 1967. reprint ed. 50.00 (*0-8201-1013-2*) Schol Facsimiles.

Conjugal Love. Emanuel Swedenborg. Tr. by S. M. Warren. 636p. 1914. 15.00 (*0-87785-045-3*) Swedenborg.

***Conjugal Love: Delights of Wisdom Relating to Conjugal Love Followed by Pleasures of Insanity Relating to Licentious Love.** Emanuel Swedenborg. Tr. by N. Bruce Rogers. 618p. 1995. write for info. (*0-945003-04-8*) General Church.

***Conjugal Love: Delights of Wisdom Relating to Conjugal Love Followed by Pleasures of Insanity Relating to Licentious Love, The Word Edition.** Emanuel Swedenborg. Tr. by N. Bruce Rogers. 618p. 1995. write for info. (*0-945003-05-6*) General Church.

Conjugal Sins Against the Laws of Life & Health: Their Effects Upon the Father, Mother & Child. Augustus K. Gardner. LC 73-20624. (Sex, Marriage & Society Ser.). 244p. 1974. reprint ed. 23.95 (*0-405-05800-4*) Ayer.

Conjugal Spirituality: The Primacy of Mutual Love in Christian Tradition. Mary A. Oliver. 176p. (Orig.). (C). 1994. pap. 12.95 (*1-55612-312-4*) Sheed & Ward MO.

Conjugal Terrorism: A Psychological & Community Treatment Model of Wife Abuse. Steven M. Morgan. Ed. by R. Reed. LC 81-83615. (Illus.). 125p. (C). 1982. pap. 12.00 (*0-88247-623-8*) R & E Pubs.

Conjugate Addition Reactions in Organic Synthesis. P. Perlmutter. (Organic Chemistry Ser.: No. 9). 373p. 1992. text ed. 125.00 (*0-08-037066-7*, Pergamon Pr); pap. text ed. 53.00 (*0-08-037067-5*, Pergamon Pr) Elsevier.

Conjugate Direction Methods in Optimization. M. Hestenes. (Applications of Mathematics Ser.: Vol. 12). (Illus.). 325p. 1980. 79.00 (*0-387-90455-7*) Spr-Verlag.

Conjugate Duality & Optimization. R. Tyrrell Rockafellar. (CBMS-NSF Regional Conference Ser.: No. 16). vi, 74p. (Orig.). 1974. pap. text ed. 16.50 (*0-89871-013-8*) Soc Indus-Appl Math.

Conjugate Duality & the Exponential Fourier Spectrum. W. Britton. (Lecture Notes in Statistics Ser.: Vol. 18). (Illus.). 226p. 1983. pap. 39.00 (*0-387-90826-9*) Spr-Verlag.

***Conjugate Gradient Type Methods for Ill-Posed Problems.** M. Hanke. LC 95-6873. (Pitman Research Notes in Mathematics Ser.). 1995. write for info. (*0-615-00668-X*) Longman.

Conjugate Vaccines. Ed. by J. M. Cruse & R. F. Lewis, Jr. (Contributions to Microbiology & Immunology Ser.: Vol. 10). (Illus.). vi, 198p. 1989. 132.00 (*3-8055-4932-6*) S Karger.

Conjugated Conducting Polymers. Ed. by H. Kiess et al. (Solid-State Sciences Ser.: Vol. 102). (Illus.). 336p. (C). 1992. text ed. 69.00 (*0-387-53594-2*) Spr-Verlag.

Conjugated Polymeric Materials: Opportunities in Electronics, Optoelectronics & Molecular Electronics. Ed. by J. L. Bredas & R. R. Chance. (C). 1990. lib. bdg. 191.50 (*0-7923-0751-8*) Kluwer Ac.

Conjugated Polymers: The Novel Science & Technology of Highly Conducting & Nonlinear Optically Active Materials. Ed. by J. L. Bredas & R. Silbey. 648p. (C). 1991. lib. bdg. 190.00 (*0-7923-1403-4*) Kluwer Ac.

Conjugated Polymers & Related Materials: The Interconnection of Chemical & Electronic Structure: Proceedings of the Eighty-First Nobel Symposium. Ed. by R. Salaneck et al. LC 92-35008. 1993. 98.00 (*0-19-855729-9*) OUP.

Conjugation-Deconjugation Reactions in Drug Metabolism & Toxicity. Ed. by Frederick C. Kauffman. LC 93-43134. (Handbook of Experimental Pharmacology Ser.: Vol. 112). (Illus.). 576p. 1994. 329.00 (*0-387-57122-1*) Spr-Verlag.

Conjugation of Russian Verbs. L. Pirogova. 319p. 1988. text ed. 10.95 (*0-8285-4944-3*) Firebird NY.

Conjugation of Russian Verbs. L. Pirogova. 320p. (C). 1988. 60.00 (*0-685-39369-0*, Pub. by Collets) St Mut.

Conjugation Reactions in Drug Metabolism: An Integral Approach. Ed. by Gerard J. Mulder. 300p. 1990. 135.00 (*0-85066-738-0*) Taylor & Francis.

Conjunction: Bi-Annual Volumes of New Writing, Vol. 16. Ed. by Bradford Morrow. 350p. 1991. pap. 10.00 (*0-679-73541-0*) Conjunctions.

Conjunction, Contiguity, Contingency: Essays on the Verbal System in Egyptian & Coptic. Leo Depuydt. LC 92-29818. 1993. 65.00 (*0-19-508092-0*) OUP.

Conjunction of Interests: Business, Politics, & Tariffs 1825-1879. Ben Forster. (State & Economic Life Ser.). 297p. 1986. 40.00 (*0-8020-5680-6*) U of Toronto Pr.

Conjunctions, No. 22. Bradford Morrow. 1994. pap. 10.00 (*0-679-75581-0*) Random.

Conjunctions: Bi-Annual Volumes of New Writing, Vol. 8. Ed. by Bradford Morrow. (Illus.). 262p. 1985. 25.00 (*0-941964-18-3*); pap. 10.00 (*0-941964-17-5*) Conjunctions.

Conjunctions: Bi-Annual Volumes of New Writing, Vol. 9. Ed. by Bradford Morrow. (Illus.). 289p. 1986. 25.00 (*0-941964-16-7*); pap. 10.00 (*0-941964-15-9*) Conjunctions.

Conjunctions: Bi-Annual Volumes of New Writing, Vol. 10. Ed. by Bradford Morrow et al. (Conjunctions--Bi-Annual Volumes of New Writing Ser.). (Illus.). 304p. 1987. 25.00 (*0-941964-22-1*); pap. 10.00 (*0-941964-21-3*) Conjunctions.

Conjunctions: Bi-Annual Volumes of New Writing, Vol. 11. Ed. by Bradford Morrow. (Illus.). 288p. 1988. 25.00 (*0-941964-24-8*); pap. 10.00 (*0-941964-23-X*) Conjunctions.

Conjunctions: Bi-Annual Volumes of New Writing, Vol. 12. Ed. by Bradford Morrow. 312p. 1988. 25.00 (*0-684-58712-2*); pap. 10.00 (*0-02-035281-6*) Conjunctions.

Conjunctions: Bi-Annual Volumes of New Writing, Vol. 13. Ed. by Bradford Morrow. 275p. 1989. pap. 10.00 (*0-02-035282-4*) Conjunctions.

Conjunctions: Bi-Annual Volumes of New Writing, Vol. 14. Ed. by Bradford Morrow. 287p. 1989. 25.00 (*0-684-19149-0*); pap. 10.00 (*0-02-035290-5*) Conjunctions.

Conjunctions: Bi-Annual Volumes of New Writing, Vol. 15. Ed. by Bradford Morrow. 415p. 1990. pap. 10.00 (*0-679-73515-1*) Conjunctions.

Conjunctions: Bi-Annual Volumes of New Writing, Vol. 17. Ed. by Bradford Morrow. 414p. 1991. pap. 10.00 (*0-679-73774-X*) Conjunctions.

Conjunctions: Bi-Annual Volumes of New Writing, Vol. 18. Ed. by Bradford Morrow. 370p. 1992. pap. 10.00 (*0-679-74051-1*) Conjunctions.

Conjunctions: Bi-Annual Volumes of New Writing, Vol. 19. Ed. by Bradford Morrow. 324p. 1992. pap. 10.00 (*0-679-74399-5*) Conjunctions.

Conjunctions: Bi-Annual Volumes of New Writing, Vol. 20. Ed. by Bradford Morrow. 341p. 1993. pap. 10.00 (*0-679-74710-9*) Conjunctions.

Conjunctions: Bi-Annual Volumes of New Writing, Vol. 21. Ed. by Bradford Morrow. 360p. 1994. pap. text ed. 10.00 (*0-679-75112-2*) Conjunctions.

Conjunctions: 1. Ed. by Bradford Morrow. (Bi-Annual Volumes of New Writing Ser.). (Illus.). 312p. 1981. pap. 9.00 (*0-941964-01-9*) Conjunctions.

Conjunctions: 2. Ed. by Bradford Morrow. (Bi-Annual Volumes of New Writing Ser.). (Illus.). 240p. 1982. 22.50 (*0-941964-04-3*); pap. 7.50 (*0-941964-03-5*) Conjunctions.

Conjunctions: 3. Ed. by Bradford Morrow. (Bi-Annual Volumes of New Writing Ser.). (Illus.). 240p. 1982. 22.50 (*0-941964-06-X*); pap. 7.50 (*0-941964-05-1*) Conjunctions.

Conjunctions: 4. Ed. by Bradford Morrow. (Bi-Annual Volumes of New Writing Ser.). (Illus.). 240p. 1983. 22.50 (*0-941964-08-6*); pap. 7.50 (*0-941964-07-8*) Conjunctions.

Conjunctions: 5. Ed. by Bradford Morrow. (Bi-Annual Volumes of New Writing Ser.). (Illus.). 248p. (C). 1983. 22.50 (*0-941964-10-8*); pap. 7.50 (*0-941964-09-4*) Conjunctions.

Conjunctions: 6. Ed. by Bradford Morrow. (Bi-Annual Volumes of New Writing Ser.). (Illus.). 316p. 1984. 22.50 (*0-941964-12-4*); pap. 7.50 (*0-941964-11-6*) Conjunctions.

Conjunctions: 7. Ed. by Bradford Morrow. (Bi-Annual Volumes of New Writing Ser.). (Illus.). 282p. 1985. 20.00 (*0-941964-14-0*); pap. 8.95 (*0-941964-13-2*) Conjunctions.

Conjunctions & Interjections. Marie-Jose Shaw. (English Sound Filmstrip Kits Ser.). (gr. 6). 1980. teacher ed 34.00 (*0-8209-0520-8*, FCW6E-7) ESP.

Conjunctions & Prepositions. Marie-Jose Shaw. (English Sound Filmstrip Kits Ser.). (gr. 5). 1980. teacher ed 34.00 (*0-8209-0501-1*, FCW5E-8) ESP.

Conjunctions Fifteen: Biannual Volumes of New Writing. Ed. by Bradford Morron. (Illus.). 415p. (Orig.). (C). 1991. pap. 9.95 (*0-685-49112-9*) Random.

Conjunctions Through Pictures. Harris Winitz. (Language Through Pictures Ser.). (Illus.). 57p. (gr. 2-12). 1982. pap. 4.95 (*0-939990-36-9*) Intl Linguistics.

***Conjunctions 12.** Ed. by Bradford Morrow. Date not set. pap. 12.00 (*0-941964-26-4*) Conjunctions.

***Conjunctions 13.** Ed. by Bradford Morrow. Date not set. pap. 12.00 (*0-941964-30-2*) Conjunctions.

***Conjunctions 14: The New Gothic.** Ed. by Bradford Morrow. Date not set. pap. 12.00 (*0-941964-31-0*) Conjunctions.

***Conjunctions 15: The Poetry Issue.** Ed. by Bradford Morrow. Date not set. pap. 12.00 (*0-941964-32-9*) Conjunctions.

***Conjunctions 16: The Music Issue.** Ed. by Bradford Morrow. Date not set. pap. 12.00 (*0-941964-33-7*) Conjunctions.

***Conjunctions 17: Tenth Anniversary Issue.** Ed. by Bradford Morrow. Date not set. pap. 12.00 (*0-941964-34-5*) Conjunctions.

***Conjunctions 18: Fables, Yarns, Fairy Tales.** Ed. by Bradford Morrow. Date not set. pap. 12.00 (*0-941964-35-3*) Conjunctions.

***Conjunctions 19: Other Worlds.** Ed. by Bradford Morrow. Date not set. pap. 12.00 (*0-941964-36-1*) Conjunctions.

***Conjunctions 20: Unfinished Business: Novels-in-Progress.** Ed. by Bradford Morrow. Date not set. pap. 12.00 (*0-941964-37-X*) Conjunctions.

***Conjunctions 21: The Credos Issue.** Ed. by Bradford Morrow. Date not set. pap. 12.00 (*0-941964-38-8*) Conjunctions.

***Conjunctions 22: The Novellas Issue.** Ed. by Bradford Morrow. Date not set. pap. 12.00 (*0-941964-39-6*) Conjunctions.

***Conjunctions 23: New World Writing.** Bradford Morrow. 1994. 10.00 (*0-679-75820-8*) Random.

***Conjunctions 23: New World Writing.** Ed. by Bradford Morrow. Date not set. pap. 12.00 (*0-941964-40-X*) Conjunctions.

***Conjunctions 24: Critical Mass.** Ed. by Bradford Morrow. 1995. pap. 12.00 (*0-941964-29-9*) Conjunctions.

Conjunctiv Bei Hartmann Von Aue. Starr W. Cutting. LC 76-173037. (Chicago. University. Germanic Studies: No. 1). reprint ed. 29.50 (*0-404-50271-7*) AMS Pr.

Conjunctive Mood in English As a Problem in General Linguistics. Irina B. Khlebnikova. (Janua Linguarum, Ser.: No. 212). 139p. (Orig.). 1976. pap. text ed. 38.50 (*90-279-3404-5*) Mouton.

Conjunctivitis of the Newborn: Prevention & Treatment at the Primary Health Care Level. (Illus.). 35p. 1986. pap. 7.80 (*92-4-156088-6*) World Health.

Conjuncture of Body & Garden. Claude Esteban. Tr. by James Phillips. LC 87-17028. (Modern Poets in Translation Ser.: Vol. IV). ix, 79p. (Orig.). 1988. 17.00 (*0-916426-11-4*); pap. 6.95 (*0-916426-12-2*) KOSMOS.

Conjuration of the Four. Eliphas Levi. Tr. by Abner Doubleday. 1991. pap. 3.95 (*1-55818-140-7*, Sure Fire) Holmes Pub.

Conjurations: The Poems of Sarah Kirsch. Sarah Kirsch. Ed. by Wayne Kvam. LC 84-7592. xviii, 197p. 1985. text ed. 25.95 (*0-8214-0787-2*) Ohio U Pr.

Conjure-Man Dies. Rudolph Fisher. LC 78-140605. 320p. reprint ed. 9.00 (*0-405-02800-8*) Ayer.

Conjure-Man Dies: A Mystery Tale of Dark Harlem. Rudolph Fisher. LC 91-44256. (Ann Arbor Paperbacks Ser.). 300p. (C). 1992. reprint ed. text ed. 37.50 (*0-472-09492-0*, Ann Arbor Bks); reprint ed. pap. text ed. 13.95 (*0-472-06492-4*, Ann Arbor Bks) U of Mich Pr.

Conjure Wife. Fritz Leiber. 1993. reprint ed. lib. bdg. 18.95x (*0-89968-435-1*, Lghtyr Pr) Buccaneer Bks.

Conjure Wife & Our Lady of Darkness. Fritz Leiber. 352p. 1991. mass mkt. 4.99 (*0-8125-1296-0*) Tor Bks.

Conjure Woman. Charles W. Chesnutt. 1969. pap. 13.95 (*0-472-06156-9*, 156, Ann Arbor Bks) U of Mich Pr.

Conjure Woman. Charles W. Chesnutt. 1988. reprint ed. lib. bdg. 59.00 (*0-7812-0047-4*) Rprt Serv.

Conjure Woman. Charles W. Chesnutt. reprint ed. 45.00 (*0-403-07386-3*) Scholarly.

Conjure Woman & Other Conjure Tales. Charles W. Chesnutt. LC 93-4215. 216p. 1993. lib. bdg. 34.95 (*0-8223-1378-2*); pap. 12.95 (*0-8223-1387-1*) Duke.

Conjurians' Discoveries. John Booth. LC 92-60082. (Illus.). 287p. 1992. 38.00 (*0-943230-06-3*) Ridgeway Pr.

Conjuring. James Randi. (Illus.). 336p. 1993. pap. 19.95 (*0-312-09771-9*) St Martin.

Conjuring: Black Women, Fiction, & Literary Tradition. Ed. by Marjorie Pryse & Hortense J. Spillers. LC 84-43171. (Illus.). 274p. 1985. 29.95 (*0-253-31407-0*); pap. 10.95 (*0-253-20360-0*, MB-360) Ind U Pr.

Conjuring a Counter-Culture. Walt Shepperd. 80p. 1973. pap. 2.50 (*0-913218-18-9*) Dustbooks.

Conjuring Culture: Biblical Formations of Black America. Theophus H. Smith. (Religion in America Ser.). 288p. 1994. 35.00 (*0-19-506740-1*) OUP.

***Conjuring Culture: Biblical Formations of Black America.** Theophus H. Smith. (Religion in America Ser.). 288p. 1995. reprint ed. pap. 15.95 (*0-19-510281-9*) OUP.

Conjuring Tricks: Revealing the Mysteries of the Magic Arts. Anness Publishing Staff. (Illus.). 96p. 1992. 8.95 (*0-8212-1969-3*) Bulfinch Pr.

Conjurors. Julian Orde. (C). 1990. 35.00 (*0-906887-25-9*, Pub. by Greville Pr UK) St Mut.

Conklin's Atlas. Frank A. Chadwick. (Space: Eighteen Eighty-Nine Ser.). (Illus.). 80p. (Orig.). (YA). 1989. pap. 10.00 (*1-55878-024-6*) Game Designers.

Conklin's Guide, Maritime Auction Annual, July 4, 1988 - July 4, 1989. Sara Conklin-Halaj. 460p. (Orig.). 1989. pap. 100.00 (*0-9623625-4-9*) Leeward Shore.

Conklin's Guide, Maritime Auction Annual, July 4, 1989-May 12, 1990. Sara Conklin-Halaj. 400p. 1990. 115.00 (*0-9623625-5-7*) Leeward Shore.

Conklin's Guide Maritime Auction Annual, July 5, 1989 to May 12, 1990. Sara Conklin-Halaj. 400p. (Orig.). 1990. pap. 110.00 (*0-685-45319-7*) Leeward Shore.

Conklin's Vest-Pocket Argument Settler: 1914 Edition. George Conklin. 1981. 4.95 (*0-8065-0788-8*, Citadel Pr) Carol Pub Group.

CONLAN Report. R. Piloty et al. (Lecture Notes in Computer Science Ser.: Vol. 151). 174p. 1983. pap. 24.00 (*0-387-12275-3*) Spr-Verlag.

Conley Family in America. Julia V. Conley. LC 90-63788. (Illus.). 242p. (Orig.). 1991. pap. 15.95 (*0-917012-95-X*) RI Pubns Soc.

***Conmigo Dia Tras Dia: Prayers & Devotions: 365 Daily Meditations.** Pope John Paul II. 1994. 15.95 (*0-670-86199-5*, Viking) Viking Penguin.

Connaissance Cybernetique de L'Economie et l'Information Statistique see Quelques Notions de Base pour l'Economie

Connaissance de l'est. Paul Claudel. (Poesie Ser.). (FRE.). pap. 9.95 (*2-07-032133-9*) Schoenhof.

Connaissance de l'Est, l'Oiseau Noir. Paul Claudel. (FRE.). 1974. pap. 10.95 (*0-8288-3851-8*, F93980) Fr & Eur.

Connaissance de l'Islam dans l'Occident Medievale. Marie-Therese D'Alverny & Charles Burnett. (Collected Studies: No. CS 445). 342p. 1994. 99.50 (*0-86078-440-1*, Pub. by Variorum UK) Ashgate Pub Co.

C

An Asterisk (*) at the beginning of an entry indicates that the title is appearing in BIP for the first time.

An Asterisk (*) at the beginning of an entry indicates that the title is appearing in BIP for the first time.

1545

C

Connecticut Kid's Cookbook: Recipes, How-to, History, Lore & More! Carole Marsh. (Carole Marsh Connecticut Bks.). (Illus.). (YA). (gr. 3-12). 1994. lib. bdg. 24.95 (*0-7933-0226-9*); pap. 14.95 (*0-7933-0225-0*); disk 29.95 (*0-7933-0227-7*) Gallopade Pub Group.

***Connecticut Land Surveying Law: Questions & Answers.** John E. Keen. 51p. (C). 1995. pap. text ed. 20.00 (*1-56569-019-2*) Land Survey.

Connecticut Land Use Regulation. Terry J. Tondro. LC 79-68712. 356p. (Orig.). 1979. pap. text ed. 21.50 (*0-939328-02-X*) U CT Law Sch Found.

Connecticut Land Use Regulation. 2nd ed. Terry J. Tondro. 820p. (Orig.). 1992. text ed. 150.00 (*1-878698-15-X*) Atlantic Law.

Connecticut Land Use Regulation: Supplement. Terry J. Tondro. 236p. 1983. pap. text ed. 10.00 (*0-939328-06-2*) U CT Law Sch Found.

Connecticut Law Enforcement Handbook. Gould Editorial Staff. 260p. 1989. ring bd. 7.95 (*0-87526-353-4*) Gould.

Connecticut Law of Check Fraud. Timothy S. Fisher. 136p. (Orig.). 1991. pap. 50.00 (*1-878698-12-5*) Atlantic Law.

Connecticut Law of Torts, 1992: Supplement. 3rd ed. Douglass B. Wright et al. 67p. 1992. pap. 50.00 (*1-878698-14-1*) Atlantic Law.

Connecticut Law of Uninsured & Underinsured Motorist Coverage. Jon Berk & Michael C. Jainchill. 437p. 1993. text ed. 145.00 (*1-878698-22-2*) Atlantic Law.

Connecticut Law Reports. Ephraim Kirby. LC 86-10242. 1986. reprint ed. 50.00 (*0-8201-1414-6*) Schol Facsimiles.

Connecticut Law Review: 1968-1988, 25 vols., Set. 1,172.50 (*0-8377-9042-5*) Rothman.

Connecticut Legal Forms, 5 vols., 1A. Douglass B. Wright. (Connecticut Law Ser.). 1987. 75.00 (*0-685-17463-8*) Atlantic Law.

Connecticut Legal Forms, 5 vols., Set. Douglass B. Wright. (Connecticut Law Ser.). 1987. 300.00 (*0-318-21421-0*) Atlantic Law.

Connecticut Library Book: A Surprising Guide to the Unusual Special Collections in Libraries Across Our State for Students, Teachers, Writers & Publishers - Includes Reproducible Mailing Labels Plus Activities for Young People! Carole Marsh. (Carole Marsh Connecticut Bks.). (Illus.). 1994. lib. bdg. 24.95 (*0-7933-3158-7*); pap. 14.95 (*0-7933-3159-5*); disk 29.95 (*0-7933-3160-9*) Gallopade Pub Group.

Connecticut Life Correspondence Course. James Smith. 1991. 32.00 (*1-877723-83-5*, 26200) Rough Notes.

Connecticut Life Insurance Licensing Course. James J. Smith. 1991. ring bd. 32.00 (*1-877723-00-2*, 26302) Rough Notes.

***Connecticut Limited Liability Company Forms & Practice Manual.** Richard G. Convincer & Louis B. Schatz. 496p. 1995. ring bd. 149.95 (*1-57400-001-2*) Data Trace Legal.

Connecticut Living Trust: Cornerstone of Modern Estate Planning. Gayle B. Wilhelm. 173p. (Orig.). 1993. pap. text ed. 14.95 (*0-9637764-1-X*) Chase Pubng.

Connecticut Media Book: A Surprising Guide to the Amazing Print, Broadcast & Online Media of Our State for Students, Teachers, Writers & Publishers - Includes Reproducible Mailing Labels Plus Activities for Young People! Carole Marsh. (Carole Marsh Connecticut Bks.). (Illus.). 1994. lib. bdg. 24.95 (*0-7933-3179-X*); pap. 14.95 (*0-7933-3180-3*); disk 29.95 (*0-7933-3181-1*) Gallopade Pub Group.

Connecticut Militia General: Gold Selleck Silliman. Katherine H. Cummin. LC 79-57128. (Connecticut Bicentennial Ser.: Vol. XXXV). 1980. write for info. (*0-918676-21-5*) Conn Hist Com.

Connecticut Motor Vehicles & Traffic Law: Annual Edition. Ed. by Gould Editorial Staff. 250p. 1990. ring bd. 9.95 (*0-87526-391-7*) Gould.

Connecticut Motor Vehicles Law, Title 14. 275p. 1994. ring bd. 10.95 (*0-930137-69-8*) Looseleaf Law.

Connecticut Mutual Life Report on American Values in the '80s: The Impact of Belief. Ed. by John C. Pollock & Peter Finn. (Illus.). 346p. 1984. reprint ed. pap. text ed. 36.00 (*0-8191-4020-1*) U Pr of Amer.

Connecticut Mystery Van Takes Off! Book 1: Handicapped Connecticut Kids Sneak Off on a Big Adventure. Carole Marsh. (Carole Marsh Connecticut Bks.). (Illus.). (J). (gr. 3-12). 1994. 24.95 (*0-7933-4982-6*); pap. 14.95 (*0-7933-4983-4*); disk 29.95 (*0-7933-4984-2*) Gallopade Pub Group.

Connecticut Naturally, 1990: A Resource Directory for Natural Living in the Tri-State Area, Including New York & New Jersey. Ed. by Jerome Rubin & Stephen Donaldson. (Orig.). 1990. pap. 4.95 (*0-9622953-3-7*) City Spirit Pubns.

Connecticut Notary Law Primer. National Notary Magazine Editors. LC 87-62621. 1988. pap. 10.95 (*0-933134-24-X*) Natl Notary.

***Connecticut: Off the Beaten Path: A Guide to Unique Places.** 2nd ed. David Ritchie & Deborah Ritchie. LC 94-22267. (Voyager Ser.). 160p. 1995. 9.95 (*1-56440-519-2*) Globe Pequot.

Connecticut Office for Appeals Procedures Manual. National Center for State Courts Staff. 53p. 1986. 3.00 (*0-685-16861-1*, NERO-181) Natl Ctr St Courts.

Connecticut Outdoor Activity Guide. Kelley Roark. LC 93-47044. (Outdoor Activity Guide Ser.). (Illus.). 120p. (Orig.). 1994. pap. 9.95 (*1-56626-046-9*) Country Rds.

Connecticut PC Correspondence Course. James J. Smith. 1991. 32.00 (*1-877723-90-8*, 26953) Rough Notes.

Connecticut PC Course. James J. Smith. 1991. 50.00 (*1-877723-89-4*, 26864) Rough Notes.

Connecticut Pewter & Pewterers. John C. Thomas. (Illus.). 194p. 1976. 15.00 (*0-940748-05-3*) Conn Hist Soc.

Connecticut Politics at the Crossroads. Gary L. Rose. LC 92-16636. 122p. (Orig.). (C). 1992. lib. bdg. 38.50 (*0-8191-8755-0*) U Pr of Amer.

Connecticut Politics at the Crossroads. Gary L. Rose. LC 92-16636. 122p. (Orig.). (C). 1992. pap. text ed. 14.50 (*0-8191-8756-9*) U Pr of Amer.

Connecticut Practice Book Annotated - Supreme Court & Appellate Court Rules & Forms. Moller & Horton. 336p. 1985. pap. 28.50 (*0-317-52100-4*) West Pub.

Connecticut Probate Deskbook. Gayle B. Wilhelm et al. LC 88-81924. 1988. ring bd. 110.00 (*0-317-02928-2*) Lawyers Cooperative.

Connecticut Quiz Bowl Crash Course! Carole Marsh. (Carole Marsh Connecticut Bks.). (Illus.). (YA). (gr. 3-12). 1994. lib. bdg. 24.95 (*1-55609-545-7*); pap. 14.95 (*1-55609-544-9*); disk 29.95 (*0-7933-1432-1*) Gallopade Pub Group.

Connecticut Railroads: An Illustrated History. Gregg M. Turner & Melancthon W. Jacobus. Ed. by Oliver Jensen. (Illus.). 317p. 1989. 29.95 (*0-940748-96-7*) Conn Hist Soc.

***Connecticut Real Estate Law Journal.** Ed. by Robin M. Pearson. 1983. ring bd. 105.00 (*0-88063-018-3*) Michie Butterworth.

Connecticut Real Property Law. Robert H. Anderson et al. Ed. by Richard E. Burke. 543p. 1984. text ed. 95.00 (*1-878698-00-1*) Atlantic Law.

Connecticut Real Property Statutes, 1991-1992. 2nd ed. Butterworths Staff. 720p. 1991. Latest suppl. 2/92. 35.00 (*1-56257-266-0*) Butterworth Legal Pubs.

Connecticut Real Property Statutes, 1991-1992. 2nd ed. Butterworths Staff. 720p. 1992. ring bd. 55.00 (*0-88063-008-6*) Michie Butterworth.

Connecticut Researchers Handbook. Ed. by Thomas J. Kemp. (Genealogy & Local History Ser.: Vol. 12). 776p. (C). 1982. 68.00 (*0-8103-1488-6*) Gale.

Connecticut Revolutionary: Eliphalet Dyer see Connecticut Revolutionary Series

Connecticut Revolutionary Series, 35 vols. Incl. Vol. 1. Connecticut Joins the Revolution. Thomas C. Barrow. 1978. 2.50 (*0-87106-123-6*); Vol. 2. Connecticut in the Continental Congress. Christopher Collier. 1978. 2.50 (*0-87106-121-X*); Vol. 3. Connecticut's Revolutionary War Leaders. North Callahan. 1978. 2.50 (*0-87106-120-1*); Vol. 4. Connecticut's Black Soldiers, 1775-1783. David O. White. 1978. 2.50 (*0-87106-119-8*); Vol. 5. Connecticut: The Provisions State. Chester M. Destler. 1978. 2.50 (*0-87106-122-8*); Vol. 10. Connecticut Attacked: A British Viewpoint, Tryon's Raid on Danbury. Robert McDevitt. 1978. 2.50 (*0-87106-050-7*); Vol. 11. Connecticut's First Family: William Pitkin & His Connections. Bruce C. Daniels. 1978. 2.50 (*0-87106-060-4*); Vol. 12. Connecticut Signer: William Williams. Bruce P. Stark. 1978. 2.50 (*0-87106-061-2*); Vol. 13. Connecticut's Revolutionary Cavalry: Sheldon's Horse. John T. Hayes. 1978. 2.50 (*0-87106-062-0*); Vol. 14. Connecticut's Revolutionary Press. Charles L. Cutler. 1978. 2.50 (*0-87106-063-9*); Vol. 15. Connecticut Women in the Revolutionary Era. Catherine Fennelly. 1978. 2.50 (*0-87106-064-7*); Vol. 16. Connecticut Art & Architecture: Looking Backwards Two Hundred Years. William L. Warren. 1978. 2.50 (*0-918676-06-1*); Vol. 17. Connecticut's Loyalist Gadfly: the Reverend Samuel Andrew Peters. Sheldon S. Cohen. 1978. 2.50 (*0-918676-02-9*); Vol. 18. Connecticut's Colonial & Continental Money. Wyman W. Parker. 1978. 2.50 (*0-918676-05-3*); Vol. 19. Connecticut Revolutionary: Eliphalet Dyer. William F. Willingham. 1978. 2.50 (*0-918676-03-7*); Vol. 20. Connecticut Congressman: Samuel Huntington, 1731-1796. Larry R. Gerlach. 1978. 2.50 (*0-918676-04-5*); Vol. 25. Connecticut's Nationalist Revolutionary: Jonathan Trumbull, Jr. John Ifkovic. 1978. 2.50 (*0-918676-11-8*); Vol. 28. Connecticut Anglicans in the Revolutionary Era: A Study in Communal Tensions. Bruce E. Steiner. 1978. 2.50 (*0-918676-14-2*); Vol. 29. Connecticut Industry & the Revolution. James P. Walsh. 1978. 2.50 (*0-918676-15-0*); 1978. write for info. (*0-318-51582-2*) Conn Hist Com.

Connecticut River & Other Poems. Reuel Denney. LC 79-144745. (Yale Series of Younger Poets: No. 38). reprint ed. 18.00 (*0-404-53838-X*) AMS Pr.

Connecticut River Ecological Study: The Impact of a Nuclear Power Plant. Ed. by D. Merriman & L. M. Thorpe. LC 76-11293. (AFS Monograph Ser.: No. 1). 252p. 1976. pap. 10.50 (*0-913235-12-1*) Am Fisheries Soc.

Connecticut Rollercoasters! Carole Marsh. (Carole Marsh Connecticut Bks.). (Illus.). (YA). (gr. 3-12). 1994. lib. bdg. 24.95 (*0-7933-5242-8*); pap. 14.95 (*0-7933-5243-6*); disk 29.95 (*0-7933-5244-4*) Gallopade Pub Group.

Connecticut School Trivia: An Amazing & Fascinating Look at Our State's Teachers, Schools & Students! Carole Marsh. (Carole Marsh Connecticut Bks.). (Illus.). (YA). (gr. 3-12). 1994. lib. bdg. 24.95 (*0-7933-0223-4*); pap. 14.95 (*0-7933-0222-6*); disk 29.95 (*0-7933-0224-2*) Gallopade Pub Group.

Connecticut (Second Part) Fitz-Greene Halleck. (Notable American Authors Ser.). 1992. reprint ed. lib. bdg. 75.00 (*0-7812-2992-8*) Rprt Serv.

Connecticut Service Directory, 1992-1993. George D. Hall Co. Staff. 1992. pap. 64.00 (*1-56803-001-0*) G D Hall Co.

Connecticut Signer: William Williams see Connecticut Revolutionary Series

Connecticut Silly Basketball Sportsmysteries, Vol. I. Carole Marsh. (Carole Marsh Connecticut Bks.). (Illus.). (YA). (gr. 3-12). 1994. lib. bdg. 24.95 (*0-7933-0220-X*); pap. 14.95 (*0-7933-0219-6*); disk 29.95 (*0-7933-0221-8*) Gallopade Pub Group.

Connecticut Silly Basketball Sportsmysteries, Vol. II. Carole Marsh. (Carole Marsh Connecticut Bks.). (Illus.). (YA). (gr. 3-12). 1994. lib. bdg. 24.95 (*0-7933-1580-8*); pap. 14.95 (*0-7933-1581-6*); disk 29.95 (*0-685-45929-2*) Gallopade Pub Group.

Connecticut Silly Football Sportsmysteries, Vol. I. Carole Marsh. (Carole Marsh Connecticut Bks.). (Illus.). (YA). (gr. 3-12). 1994. lib. bdg. 24.95 (*1-55609-541-4*); pap. 14.95 (*1-55609-540-6*); disk 29.95 (*0-7933-1425-9*) Gallopade Pub Group.

Connecticut Silly Football Sportsmysteries, Vol. II. Carole Marsh. (Carole Marsh Connecticut Bks.). (Illus.). (YA). (gr. 3-12). 1994. lib. bdg. 24.95 (*0-7933-1426-7*); pap. 14.95 (*0-7933-1427-5*); disk 29.95 (*0-7933-1428-3*) Gallopade Pub Group.

Connecticut Silly Trivia! Carole Marsh. (Carole Marsh Connecticut Bks.). (Illus.). (YA). (gr. 3-12). 1994. lib. bdg. 24.95 (*1-55609-536-8*); pap. 14.95 (*1-55609-535-X*); disk 29.95 (*0-7933-1422-4*) Gallopade Pub Group.

Connecticut State Constitution: A Reference Guide. Wesley W. Horton. LC 92-42672. (Reference Guides to the State Constitutions of the United States Ser.: No. 17). 193p. 1993. text ed. 65.00 (*0-313-28565-9*, HTB, Greenwood Pr) Greenwood.

Connecticut State Industrial Directory, 1992. 568p. 1992. 145.00 (*0-317-04928-3*) Manufacturers.

Connecticut Study Manual for Life & Accident & Health Insurance. Dearborn Financial Publishing, Inc. Staff. 56p. 1991. pap. text ed. 7.95 (*0-7931-0401-7*, 5310-12) Dearborn Finan.

Connecticut Summary Process Manual. Paul J. Marzinotto. 259p. 1986. ring bd. 115.00 (*0-910051-04-6*) CT Law Trib.

Connecticut Summary Process Manual - Second Supplement. Paul J. Marzinotto. 1991. ring bd. 15.00 (*0-910051-14-3*) CT Law Trib.

Connecticut Superior Court Clerks' Manual, Geographical Area. National Center for State Courts Staff. 276p. 1986. 17.00 (*0-685-15221-9*, NERO-179) Natl Ctr St Courts.

Connecticut Superior Court Clerks' Manual, Judicial District. National Center for State Courts Staff. 286p. 1985. 17.00 (*0-685-15224-3*, NERO-168) Natl Ctr St Courts.

Connecticut Superior Court Clerks' Manual, Juvenile Matters. 255p. 1986. 16.00 (*0-685-18274-6*, NERO-202) Natl Ctr St Courts.

Connecticut Superior Court Reports, Vol. VI, 1991. 1000p. 1991. ring bd. 310.50 (*0-910051-13-5*); ring bd. 270.00 (*0-685-40700-4*) Amer Law Media.

Connecticut Superior Court, Support Enforcement Division, Child Support Enforcement Manual. Lorraine Adams. 413p. 1990. 25.00 (*0-685-50606-1*, NERO-245) Natl Ctr St Courts.

***Connecticut Supplement for Modern Real Estate Practice.** 6th ed. Katherine A. Pancak. LC 94-46598. 1995. pap. 12.95 (*0-7931-1327-X*) Dearborn Finan.

Connecticut Survival. Betty L. Hall & Louis K. Weinstein. 160p. (Orig.). (gr. 10-12). 1984. pap. text ed. 5.84 (*0-03-051186-0*) Westwood Pr.

Connecticut, Tastefully Done! An Exceptional Collection of Recipes from Famous Celebrities & Chefs. Susan M. Strickland. 162p. Date not set. 24.95 (*0-9641598-0-5*) Coastal Design.

Connecticut Tax Handbook. Ernst & Young Staff & Whinney. 256p. 1988. pap. 17.00 (*0-13-167868-X*) P-H.

Connecticut: The Provisions State see Connecticut Revolutionary Series

Connecticut Time Limitations, 1991. 2nd ed. Butterworths Staff. 390p. 1994. Latest suppl. 2/92. 56.00 (*1-56257-265-2*) Butterworth Legal Pubs.

Connecticut Time Limitations, 1991. 2nd ed. Butterworths Staff. 390p. 1994. ring bd. 65.00 (*0-88063-002-7*) Michie Butterworth.

Connecticut Timeline: A Chronology of Connecticut History, Mystery, Trivia, Legend, Lore & More. Carole Marsh. (Carole Marsh Connecticut Bks.). (Illus.). (J). (gr. 3-12). 1994. lib. bdg. 24.95 (*0-7933-5893-0*); pap. 14.95 (*0-7933-5894-9*); disk 29.95 (*0-7933-5895-7*) Gallopade Pub Group.

Connecticut Towns & Counties. Ed. by Michael J. Denis. (New England Towns & Counties Ser.). 45p. (Orig.). 1985. pap. 7.00 (*0-935207-01-5*) Danbury Hse Bks.

Connecticut Trial Court Delay Reduction: Assistance to Judicial Department Staff Serving the Committee to Study the Rules of Civil Practice & Procedure. National Center for State Courts Staff. 207p. 1985. 13.00 (*0-685-15493-9*, NERO-178) Natl Ctr St Courts.

Connecticut Trial Evidence Handbook. Dale P. Faulkner & Carolyn R. Spencer. 1993. 90.00 (*1-56257-212-1*) Butterworth Legal Pubs.

Connecticut Wait List Law for Nursing Homes. 1988. pap. 2.75 (*0-685-30142-7*, 40,912) NCLS Inc.

Connecticut Walk Book. 16th ed. Intro. by John S. Burlew. (Illus.). 1990. 15.96 (*0-9619052-1-2*) CT Forest & Pk Assn.

Connecticut-Western Mass. Publicity Guide. Ed. by Harriet B. Seder. 328p. 1989. 67.25 (*0-317-93659-X*) Seder Media.

Connecticut-Western Massachusetts Publicity Guide, 1991. 376p. 1991. pap. 60.25 (*0-9622552-0-3*) Seder Media.

Connecticut Wits. Leon Howard. reprint ed. 40.00 (*0-404-20125-3*) AMS Pr.

Connecticut Wits, & Other Essays. Henry A. Beers. LC 70-153303. reprint ed. 24.50 (*0-404-04643-6*) AMS Pr.

Connecticut Wits & Other Essays. Henry A. Beers. (BCL1-PR English Literature Ser.). 26p. 1992. reprint ed. lib. bdg. 79.00 (*0-7812-7006-5*) Rprt Serv.

Connecticut Women in the Revolutionary Era see Connecticut Revolutionary Series

***Connecticut Woodlands: A Century's Story of the Connecticut Forest & Park Association.** George M. Milne. (Illus.). 160p. 1995. 30.00x (*0-914659-73-1*) Phoenix Pub.

***Connecticut Woodlands: A Century's Story of the Connecticut Forest & Park Association.** George McLean Milne. LC 95-3080. 1995. 30.00 (*0-9619052-3-9*) CT Forest & Pk Assn.

Connecticut Workers' Compensation after Reforms. Angelo P. Sevarino. 551p. 1994. text ed. 135.00 (*1-878698-24-9*) Atlantic Law.

Connecticut Workers' Compensation Practice Manual. suppl. ed. John T. Asselin. 354p. 1989. 110.00 (*0-910051-03-8*) CT Law Trib.

Connecticut Workers' Compensation Review Opinions, 8 vols. Clifford Davis. 200p. 1979. ring bd. 80.00 (*0-88063-004-3*) Michie Butterworth.

Connecticut Yankee. Mark Twain. 22.95 (*0-8488-0649-2*) Amereon Ltd.

Connecticut Yankee see Prince & the Pauper

Connecticut Yankee Cooks New England Favorites. Patricia G. Wagner. LC 91-75564. 160p. 1992. spiral bd., pap. 15.95 (*1-880620-00-6*) CT Yankee Ckbk.

Connecticut Yankee in King Arthur's Court. Samuel Clemens. (Illustrated Classics Collection 3). 64p. 1994. pap. 3.60 (*1-56103-525-4*) Lake Pub Co.

Connecticut Yankee in King Arthur's Court. Mark Twain. LC 83-9162. (Airmont Classics Ser.). (J). (gr. 5 up). 1964. pap. 3.25 (*0-8049-0029-9*, CL-29) Airmont.

Connecticut Yankee in King Arthur's Court. Mark Twain. 334p. 1963. pap. 2.25 (*0-451-52353-9*, Sig Classics) NAL-Dutton.

Connecticut Yankee in King Arthur's Court. Mark Twain. 1991. pap. 2.50 (*0-8125-0436-4*) Tor Bks.

Connecticut Yankee in King Arthur's Court. Mark Twain. pap. 2.95 (*0-89375-411-0*) Troll Assocs.

Connecticut Yankee in King Arthur's Court. Mark Twain. 208p. (Orig.). 1983. pap. 3.95 (*0-553-21143-9*, Bantam Classics) Bantam.

Connecticut Yankee in King Arthur's Court. Mark Twain. LC 87-62879. (Books of Wonder). (Illus.). 384p. (Orig.). (J). (gr. 5 up). 1988. 20.00 (*0-688-06346-2*) Morrow Jr Bks.

Connecticut Yankee in King Arthur's Court. Mark Twain. LC 83-47881. (Mark Twain Library: No. 4). (Illus.). 482p. (Orig.). (C). 1983. 30.00 (*0-520-05089-4*); pap. 12.00 (*0-520-05109-2*) U CA Pr.

Connecticut Yankee in King Arthur's Court. Mark Twain, pseud. Ed. by Allison E. Ensor. (Critical Editions Ser.). (Illus.). 450p. (C). 1982. pap. text ed. 11.95 (*0-393-95137-5*) Norton.

Connecticut Yankee in King Arthur's Court. Mark Twain, pseud. (English Library). 1972. mass mkt. 4.95 (*0-14-043064-4*, Penguin Classics) Viking Penguin.

Connecticut Yankee in King Arthur's Court. Mark Twain, pseud. Ed. by Bernard L. Stein. (Iowa-California Edition of the Works of Mark Twain: No. 9). (Illus.). 1979. 50.00 (*0-520-03621-2*) U CA Pr.

Connecticut Yankee in King Arthur's Court. abr. ed. Mark Twain. Ed. by John N. Fago. LC 83-9162. (Now Age Illustrated III Ser.). (Illus.). (Orig.). (J). (gr. 4-12). 1977. pap. text ed. 2.95 (*0-88301-263-4*) Pendulum Pr.

Connecticut Yankee in King Arthur's Court. deluxe limited ed. Mark Twain. LC 87-62879. (Books of Wonder). (Illus.). 384p. (Orig.). (J). (gr. 5 up). 1988. 100.00 (*0-688-08258-0*) Morrow Jr Bks.

Connecticut Yankee in King Arthur's Court. Samuel L. Clemens. (Works of Mark Twain). 1988. reprint ed. lib. bdg. 79.00 (*0-7812-1121-2*) Rprt Serv.

Connecticut Yankee in King Arthur's Court. Mark Twain. (Orig.). 1982. reprint ed. lib. bdg. 19.95 (*0-89966-381-8*) Buccaneer Bks.

Connecticut Yankee in King Arthur's Court: Student Activity Book. Marcia Sohl & Gerald Dackerman. (Now Age Illustrated Ser.). (Illus.). (gr. 4-12). 1976. 1.25 (*0-88301-287-1*) Pendulum Pr.

Connecticut Yankee in King Arthur's Court Notes. L. David Allen & James L. Roberts. 64p. (Orig.). (gr. 9-12). 1982. pap. 3.95 (*0-8220-0324-4*) Cliffs.

Connecticut Yankee in King Arthur's Court Readalong. Samuel Clemens. (Illustrated Classics Collection 3). 64p. 1994. audio, pap. 13.50 (*1-56103-527-0*) Lake Pub Co.

Connecticut Yankee in Penn's Woods: The Life & Times of Thomas Bennet. Charles E. Myers. LC 93-60796. (Illus.). 220p. (Orig.). Date not set. pap. 14.95 (*0-912975-03-2*) Upshur Pr.

Connecticut Yankee in the Frontier Ozarks: The Writings of Theodore Pease Russell. Ed. by James F. Keefe & Lynn Morrow. LC 87-19155. (Illus.). 376p. 1988. text ed. 28.00 (*0-8262-0655-7*) U of Mo Pr.

Connecticut Yankee in the Twentieth Century: Travel to the Past in Science Fiction. Bud Foote. LC 90-38418. (Contributions to the Study of Science Fiction & Fantasy Ser.: No. 43). 216p. 1990. text ed. 49.95 (*0-313-24327-1*, FOC, Greenwood Pr) Greenwood.

Connecticut Yankee in the 8th Gurkha Rifles: A Burma Memoir. Scott Gilmore & Patrick Davis. (WWII Commemorative Ser.). (Illus.). 310p. 1995. 24.95 (*0-02-881106-2*) Brasseys Inc.

Connecticut Yankees at Gettysburg. Charles P. Hamblen. Ed. by Walter L. Powell. LC 92-34747. (Illus.). 200p. (Orig.). 1993. pap. 12.00 (*0-87338-478-4*) Kent St U Pr.

Connecticut's Bass Fishing: Guides to the Best Bass Lakes & Ponds. Jim Mattingly et al. 60p. 1992. pap. 3.95 (*1-881514-00-5*) Red Bk Atlas.

Connecticut's Best Dining & Wining, 1995. Patricia Brooks. 208p. (Orig.). 1994. pap. 9.95 (*0-9626946-7-3*) De Gustibus Pr.

Connecticut's Black Soldiers, 1775-1783 see Connecticut Revolutionary Series

An Asterisk (*) at the beginning of an entry indicates that the title is appearing in BIP for the first time.

An Asterisk (*) at the beginning of an entry indicates that the title is appearing in BIP for the first time.

1547

C

Connections: Using Personality Types to Draw Parents & Kids Closer. Jim Brawner & Duncan Jaenicke. 1991. text ed. 14.99 (*0-8024-1542-3*) Moody.

Connections: Writing, Reading, & Thinking. Robert Di Yanni. LC 84-16825. 320p. (Orig.). 1985. pap. text ed. 15.00 (*0-86709-049-9*) Boynton Cook Pubs.

Connections - Literacy & Cultural Heritage: Lessons from Iceland. Darlene E. Weingand. (Illus.). 220p. 1992. 29. 50 (*0-8108-2602-X*) Scarecrow.

Connections among Particle Physics, Nuclear Physics, Statistical Physics & Condensed Matter: Proceedings, ELAF 1987. Ed. by J. Giambiagi et al. 628p. (C). 1988. pap. 48.00 (*9971-5-0405-7*) World Scientific Pub.

***Connections & Partings: Abstracts of Marriage, Divorce, Death, & Legal Notices Regarding Clarke County, Virginia, 1857-1884 (Derived from Local & Regional Newspapers)** Mary T. Morris. 210p. 1990. lib. bdg. 37. 00 (*0-8095-8186-8*); pap. 15.00 (*0-8095-8549-9*) Borgo Pr.

Connections & Symbols. Ed. by Steven Pinker & Jacques Mehler. (Cognition Special Issue Ser.). 272p. (Orig.). 1988. pap. 18.50x (*0-262-66064-4*, Bradford Bks) MIT Pr.

Connections Between Sex & Aggression. Dolf Zillmann. LC 83-20633. 272p. 1984. 29.95 (*0-89859-333-6*) L Erlbaum Assocs.

Connections, Curvature, & Cohomology, 3 vols. Incl. Vol. 1. De Rham Cohomology of Manifold & Vector Bundles. Werner Greub et al. 1972. text ed. 121.00 (*0-12-302701-2*); Vol. 2. Lie Groups, Principal Bundles & Characteristic Classes. Werner Greub et al. 1973. text ed. 143.00 (*0-12-302702-0*); (Pure & Applied Mathematics Ser.). write for info. (*0-318-50250-X*) Acad Pr.

Connections, Definite Forms, & Four-Manifolds. Ted Petrie & John Randall. (Oxford Mathematical Monographs). 144p. 1991. 45.00 (*0-19-853599-6*) OUP.

Connections for Health. Kathleen D. Mullen et al. (C). 1990. student ed write for info. (*0-697-07611-3*) Brown & Benchmark.

Connections for Health. 3rd ed. Kathleen D. Mullen et al. 624p. (C). 1993. student ed write for info. (*0-697-10129-0*); pap. write for info. (*0-697-20948-2*); pap. text ed. write for info. (*0-697-10127-4*); write for info. (*0-697-17345-3*) Brown & Benchmark.

Connections for Precast Prestressed Concrete Buildings Including Earthquake Resistance. 297p. 1982. ring bd. 30.00 (*0-937040-20-7*, TR2-82) P-PCI.

Connections for Tilt-Up Wall Construction. Portland Cement Association Staff. 43p. (Orig.). (C). 1987. pap. text ed. 10.00 (*0-89312-086-3*, EB110T) Portland Cement.

***Connections in Classical & Quantum Field Theory.** Y. N. Obukhov & G. A. Sardanashvily. 400p. 1995. text ed. 86.00 (*981-02-2013-8*) World Scientific Pub.

Connections in Electronic Assemblies. Bilotta. (Manufacturing Engineering & Materials Processing Ser.: Vol. 17). 288p. 1985. 99.75 (*0-8247-7319-5*) Dekker.

Connections in Precast Concrete Structures: Strength of Corbels. (PCI Journal Reprints Ser.). 45p. 1965. pap. 8.00 (*0-685-06887-0*, JR31) P-PCI.

Connections in Steel Structures: Behaviour, Strength, & Design. Ed. by Reidar Bjorhovde et al. 398p. 1988. 83. 00 (*1-85166-177-8*) Elsevier.

Connective Networks in Ergonomics: General Methodological Considerations. E. Franus. (Advances in Human Factors-Ergonomics Ser.: No. 16). 288p. 1991. 105.75 (*0-444-87436-4*) Elsevier.

Connective Planning. Morris Verger. 256p. 1993. text ed. 35.00 (*0-07-067403-5*) McGraw.

Connective Tissue: Biological & Clinical Aspects. Ed. by K. Kuehn & T. Krieg. (Rheumatology Ser.: Vol. 10). (Illus.). x, 490p. 1986. 280.00 (*3-8055-4225-9*) S Karger.

Connective Tissue & Its Disorders: Molecular, Genetic, & Medical Aspects. Ed. by Peter M. Royce & Beat Steinmann. LC 92-49777. 800p. 1992. text ed. 269.95 (*0-471-58819-9*, Wiley-Liss) Wiley.

Connective Tissue Disease: Molecular Pathology of the Extracellular Matrix. Uitto & Perejda. (Biochemistry of Disease Ser.: Vol. 12). 568p. 1987. 195.00 (*0-8247-7533-3*) Dekker.

Connective Tissue Diseases. Tuffanelli. 1991. write for info. (*0-8151-8862-5*, Yr Bk Med Pubs) Mosby Yr Bk.

Connective Tissue Diseases. 4th ed. Graham R. V. Hughes. LC 93-38328. (Illus.). 328p. 1994. 70.00 (*0-632-03752-0*) Blackwell Sci.

Connective Tissue Diseases of the Skin. Ed. by Lapiere & Krieg. (Basic & Clinical Dermatology Ser.: Vol. 9). 408p. 1993. 165.00 (*0-8247-9133-9*) Dekker.

Connective Tissue in Health & Disease. Ed. by Marcos Rojkind. 224p. 1989. 144.00 (*0-8493-4161-2*, RC924) CRC Pr.

Connective Tissue in Meat & Meat Products. A. J. Bailey. 350p. 1989. 130.00 (*1-85166-284-7*) Elsevier.

Connective Tissue Manipulations. Maria Ebner. LC 84-9636. 288p. (C). 1985. lib. bdg. 25.50 (*0-89874-763-5*) Krieger.

Connective Tissue Matrix. Hukins. 1990. 83.95 (*0-8493-7116-3*, QH) CRC Pr.

Connective Tissues in Arterial & Pulmonary Disease. T. F. McDonald. Ed. by A. B. Chandler. (Illus.). 355p. 1981. pap. 79.00 (*0-387-90623-1*) Spr-Verlag.

Connectivity. 1993. pap. 19.95 (*1-55512-202-7*) Intel Corp.

Connectivity. Intel Staff. 1600p. 1993. pap. 26.95 (*1-55512-174-8*, 231658-009) Intel Corp.

Connectivity, Vol. 2. Intel Staff. 1993. write for info. (*1-55512-175-6*, 231658-009) Intel Corp.

Connectivity Symposium Proceedings: Spring & Fall, 1988. 1988. 250.00 (*0-318-41121-0*) Digit Consult MA.

Connector's Guide, Connections: School & Work Transitions. National Center for Research in Vocational Education Staff. 1987. 39.95 (*0-317-03867-2*, SP100AA) Ctr Educ Trng Employ.

***Connemara Champion.** Ann Henning. 184p. (J). (gr. 4-7). 1995. pap. 8.95 (*1-85371-335-X*) Dufour.

Connemara Stallion. Ann Henning. 224p. (Orig.). (YA). (gr. 7-10). 1991. pap. 9.95 (*1-85371-158-6*, Pub. by Poolbeg Pr IE) Dufour.

Connemara Whirlwind. Ann Henning. 201p. (Orig.). (YA). (gr. 10-12). 1990. pap. 8.95 (*1-85371-079-2*, Pub. by Poolbeg Pr IE) Dufour.

Conner Prairie Cookbook. Ed. by Margaret A. Hoffman. 140p. 1990. reprint ed. 12.00 (*0-9614736-0-6*) Guild Pr IN.

Conners of Conner Prairie. Janet Hale. Ed. by Nancy N. Baxter. LC 89-80212. (Hoosier Heritage Ser.). (Illus.). 120p. (J). (gr. 4-6). 1989. 13.95 (*0-9617367-5-5*) Guild Pr IN.

***Connersville: A Pictorial History.** Harry S. Smith. (Indiana Pictorial History Ser.). (Illus.). 1993. write for info. (*0-943963-27-3*) G Bradley.

***Connexions Guide to North Carolina.** 1994. write for info. (*0-9644182-0-7*) Connexions.

Connexity & Coherence: Analysis of Text & Discourse. Ed. by W. Heyrich et al. (Research in Text Theory Ser.: Vol. 12). xii, 404p. (C). 1989. lib. bdg. 161.55x (*0-89925-302-4*) De Gruyter.

***Connexity & Coherence: Analysis of Text & Discourse.** Ed. by W. Heyrich et al. (Research in Text Theory Ser.: Vol. 12). xii, 404p. (C). 1989. lib. bdg. 161.55x (*3-11-011102-0*) De Gruyter.

Connie. Frank Godwin. Ed. by Bill Blackbeard. LC 76-53041. 1977. 17.50 (*0-88355-637-5*) Hyperion Conn.

Connie & Bonnie's Birthday Blastoff. Ray Nelson & Douglas Kelly. (Illus.). 48p. (J). (gr. 1-5). 1994. 12.95 (*1-883772-02-8*) Flying Rhino.

***Connie & Bonnie's Birthday Blastoff.** Ray Nelson & Douglas Kelly. (Illus.). 48p. (J). (gr. k-6). 1994. 14.95 (*1-56977-403-X*) Flying Rhino.

Connie Chung: Broadcast Journalist. Mary Malone. LC 91-25396. (Contemporary Women Ser.). (Illus.). 128p. (J). (gr. 6 up). 1992. lib. bdg. 17.95 (*0-89490-332-2*) Enslow Pubs.

Connie Hagar: The Life History of a Texas Birdwatcher. Karen H. McCracken. LC 85-40748. 312p. 1986. pap. 11.95 (*0-89096-406-8*) Tex A&M Univ Pr.

Connie Mack's Baseball Book. Connie Mack. 1976. 21.95 (*0-8488-1591-2*) Amereon Ltd.

Connie Morgan Hits the Trail. James B. Hendryx. 1976. reprint ed. lib. bdg. 19.95 (*0-88411-833-9*, Aeonian Pr) Amereon Ltd.

Connie Morgan with the Mounted. James B. Hendryx. 1976. reprint ed. lib. bdg. 21.95 (*0-88411-834-7*, Aeonian Pr) Amereon Ltd.

Connie Zehr: Flash Back, 1970-1985: An Installation Using Mnemonic Fragments. Fidel Danieli. LC 84-52883. (Illus.). 31p. (Orig.). 1985. pap. text ed. 5.00 (*0-936429-03-8*, 84-052883) LA Municipal Art.

***Connie's Daughter.** Claire Lorrimer. 1995. lib. bdg. 22.00 (*0-7278-4731-7*) Severn Hse.

Conning, the Cunning of Being: Being a Kierkegaardian Demonstration of the Postmodern Implosion of Metaphysical Sense in Aristotle & the Early Heidegger. Pat Bigelow. 264p. 1990. lib. bdg. 29.95 (*0-8130-0952-9*) U Press Fla.

Conning Tower Book. New York World Staff. 1972. 59.95 (*0-87968-931-5*) Gordon Pr.

Connoisseur Illustrated Guide: Furniture. Edward Joy. (Illus.). 1975. mass mkt. 6.45 (*0-380-01112-3*, 26716-0) Avon.

Connoisseur's Case. large type ed. Michael Innes. 1980. 12. 00 (*0-7089-0421-1*) Ulverscroft.

Connoisseur's Guide to Contemporary Horror Film: The Best of the Beasts & Blood. rev. ed. (Illus.). 64p. (YA). 1993. pap. 7.95 (*0-938782-27-4*) Fantaco.

Connoisseur's Handbook of Antique Collecting. rev. ed. Ed. by Ebury Press Staff. 320p. 1981. 85.00 (*0-900305-19-3*, Pub. by Ebury Pr UK) Trafalgar.

Connoisseurs' Handbook of California Wines. 3rd ed. Charles E. Olken et al. LC 84-47864. (Illus.). 256p. 1984. pap. 6.95 (*0-685-08624-0*) Knopf.

Connoisseurs of Chaos: Ideas of Order in Modern American Poetry. Denis Donoghue. LC 83-20935. 1984. text ed. 43.00 (*0-231-05734-2*); pap. text ed. 17.00 (*0-231-05735-0*) Col U Pr.

Connoisseurship of Chinese Furniture: Ming & Early Qing Dynasties, 2 vols. Wang Shixiang. (Illus.). 226p. 1990. Vol. 1, 226p. (text). 450.00 (*1-878529-00-5*); Vol. 2, 190p. (plates). write for info. (*0-318-68004-1*) Art Media Resources.

Connoisseurship of Chinese Furniture: Ming & Early Qing Dynasties, 2 vols., Set. Wang Shixiang. (Illus.). 1990. 150.00 (*1-878529-01-3*) Art Media Resources.

Connolly Report: An Irish-American Republican Reader. Robert E. Connolly. 160p. 1988. 20.00 (*0-9614659-2-1*); pap. 7.50 (*0-9614659-1-3*) Cuchullain Pubns.

Connolly Tarot. Eileen Connolly. 24p. 1990. 12.95 (*0-88079-437-2*) US Games Syst.

Connolly's Book of Numbers: A New Path to Ancient Wisdom. Eileen Connolly. 1988. pap. 12.95 (*0-87877-135-2*) Newcastle Pub.

Connolly's Book of Numbers: The Fundamentals, Vol. I. Eileen Connolly. 1988. pap. 12.95 (*0-87877-129-8*) Newcastle Pub.

***Connor Quinn: Living on the Edge Case One.** T. G. Miller. LC 93-92785. 96p. (Orig.). 1994. pap. 7.00 (*1-56002-372-4*, Univ Edtns) Aegina Pr.

Connotation & Meaning. Beatriz Garza-Cuaron. (Approaches to Semiotics Ser.: No. 99). (Illus.). x, 286p. (C). 1991. lib. bdg. 106.15 (*0-89925-757-7*) Mouton.

Connotational Theory of Program Structure. J. S. Royer. (Lecture Notes in Computer Science Ser.: Vol. 273). v, 186p. 1987. pap. 30.00 (*0-387-18253-5*) Spr-Verlag.

***Conn's Current Therapy, 1995.** Robert E. Rakel. 1312p. 1994. text ed. 55.00 (*0-7216-4052-4*) Saunders.

Connubial Bliss. Willard Manus. 1989. pap. 9.95 (*0-915572-82-6*) Panjandrum.

Conny the Clown. Nicholas Augustine & Victoria C. Augustine. (Illus.). 32p. (Orig.). (J). 1991. pap. write for info. (*1-879783-00-2*) Staccato Prodns.

Cono Sur: Dinamica y Dimensiones de Su Literatura. Rose S. Mino. 243p. (Orig.). 1985. pap. 12.00 (*0-933559-00-3*) Montclair State.

Conoce a Jesus. Sylvia Mandeville & Lance Pierson. Tr. by Edna L. Gutierrez. (Pointing Out Bks.). 24p. 1980. pap. 7.50 (*0-311-38531-1*, Edit Mundo) Casa Bautista.

Conocer el Mundo, Encyclopedia Salvat De Todos los Paises, 15 vols., Set. Salvat Staff. 4500p. (SPA.). 1975. 750.00 (*0-8288-5794-6*, S50563) Fr & Eur.

Conocernos! Long & Macian. 1992. pap. 29.95 (*0-8384-2344-2*); audio write for info. (*0-318-69351-8*) Heinle & Heinle.

***Conociendo a Dios: Dios Se Revela a Traves de Sus Nombres.** Victor Ricardo & Gloria Ricardo. 64p. 1994. pap. text ed. 4.00 (*1-885630-31-X*) HLM Producciones.

Conociendo a Dios: Knowing God. J. I. Packer. (SPA.). 6.95 (*84-7645-014-1*, 223083, Pub. by Edit Clie SP) TSELF.

Conociendome a Mi Mismo. Jo Evans & Jo E. Moore. Tr. by Liz Wolfe & Dora Ficklin. (Illus.). 24p. (SPA.). (J). (gr. 1-3). 1992. pap. text ed. 4.95 (*1-55799-182-0*) Evan-Moor Corp.

Conocimiento Basico De la Fe. W. V. Gritter & Abraham Marcus. (SPA.). 1992. 2.50 (*1-55955-034-1*) CITE MI.

***Conoco Collector's Bible.** Todd P. Heims. LC 95-5802. (Illus.). 112p. (Orig.). 1995. pap. 24.95 (*0-88740-837-0*) Schiffer.

Conodont Biofacies & Provincialism. Ed. by David L. Clark. (Special Paper Ser.: No. 196). (Illus.). 346p. 1985. pap. 5.00 (*0-8137-2196-2*) Geol Soc.

Conodont Paleoecology: The Proceedings of an International Symposium Organized by the Geological Association of Canada & the Pander Society & Held at the University of Waterloo, Waterloo, Ontario, May 15-17, 1975. Ed. by Christopher R. Barnes. LC 77-369660. (Geological Association of Canada. Special Paper Ser.: No. 15). 330p. reprint ed. pap. 94.10 (*0-685-17099-3*, 2027844) Bks Demand.

Conodonta: Morphology, Taxonomy, Paleoecology, & Evolutionary History of a Long-Extinct Animal Phylum. Walter C. Sweet. (Oxford Monographs on Geology & Geophysics: No. 10). (Illus.). 224p. 1988. 75. 00 (*0-19-504352-9*) OUP.

Conor: A Biography of Conor Cruise O'Brien. Donald H. Akenson. (Illus.). 576p. 1994. 35.00 (*0-8014-3086-0*) Cornell U Pr.

Conor: An Anthology. Conor C. O'Brien. 350p. 1994. 39.95 (*0-8014-3087-9*) Cornell U Pr.

***Conor Vol. I: A Biography of Conor Cruise O'Brien.** Donald H. Akenson. 599p. 1994. 34.95 (*0-7735-1255-1*, Pub. by McGill CN) U of Toronto Pr.

***Conor Vol. II: A Biography of Conor Cruise O'Brien.** Donald H. Akenson. 350p. 1994. 39.95 (*0-7735-1256-X*, Pub. by McGill CN) U of Toronto Pr.

Conor Cruise O'Brien: An Appraisal. E. Young-Bruehl. (Chapbooks Ser.). 1973. pap. 2.50 (*0-912262-33-8*) Proscenium.

Conover Pioneers & Pilgrims. Elizabeth C. Kelley. (Illus.). 454p. 24.50 (*0-686-44801-4*) Harlo Press.

Conozca a Carbon Copy Plus. Marvin Bryan. 157p. 1992. pap. text ed. 17.95 (*968-18-4259-6*, Pub. by Limusa MX) Computer & Tech.

Conozca a Dr DOS 5.0. Joerg Schieb. 195p. 1992. pap. text ed. 22.95 (*968-18-4379-7*, Pub. by Limusa MX) Computer & Tech.

Conozca a Harvard Graphics. Rebeca Bridges. 194p. 1992. pap. text ed. 24.95 (*968-18-4284-7*, Pub. by Limusa MX) Computer & Tech.

***Conozca a Su Conciencia.** Warren W. Wiersbe. 80p. (SPA.). 1995. mass mkt., pap. 3.50 (*0-8254-1859-3*) Kregel.

Conozca las Leyes de Immigracion. 2nd ed. Nancy-Jo Merritt. Tr. by Maria C. Castro. (Layman's Law Guides Ser.). 128p. 1994. pap. 8.95 (*1-56414-090-3*) Career Pr Inc.

Conozca Quienes Son. Adolfo Robleto. 112p. (SPA.). 1986. pap. 3.75 (*0-311-05764-0*) Casa Bautista.

Conozca Su Horoscopo, 1990. 12th ed. Maria E. Alvarez del Real. (Illus.). 144p. (SPA.). 1990. pap. 2.95 (*0-944499-75-9*) Editorial Amer.

Conozca Su Horoscopo, 1992. 14th ed. Editorial America, S. A. Staff. Ed. by Maria E. Alvarez del Real. (Illus.). 144p. (Orig.). (SPA.). 1991. pap. 2.95 (*1-56259-004-9*) Editorial Amer.

Conozca Su Horoscopo, 1993. 15th ed. Editorial America, S. A. Staff. Ed. by Maria E. Alvarez del Real. (Illus.). 144p. (Orig.). (SPA.). 1992. pap. 2.95 (*1-56259-025-1*) Editorial Amer.

Conozca Su Horoscopo 1994. Ed. by Nahyr Acosta. (Illus.). 144p. (SPA.). 1993. pap. 2.95 (*1-56259-030-8*) Editorial Amer.

Conozca Su Iglesia. Arie C. Leder. (SPA.). 1984. 4.50 (*1-55955-057-0*) CITE MI.

***Conozca Sus Derechos!** Richard M. Alderman. Tr. by Arturo Sanchez. 230p. (Orig.). 1992. pap. text ed. 10.95 (*0-88415-060-7*) Gulf Pub.

Conozca Sus Suenos. Ed. by Maria E. Alvarez del Real. (Illus.). 340p. (Orig.). (SPA.). 1987. pap. 4.00 (*0-944499-21-X*) Editorial Amer.

Conozca Sus Suenos. 2nd rev. ed. Editorial America, S. A. Staff. Ed. by Maria E. Del Real. (Illus.). 348p. (SPA.). 1989. pap. 5.00 (*0-944499-60-0*) Editorial Amer.

Conozcamos al Alumno. C. H. Benson. Tr. by Fernando P. Villalobos. (Curso para Maestros Cristianos Ser.: No. 4). 128p. (SPA.). 1972. pap. 4.50 (*0-89922-014-2*) Edit Caribe.

***Conozco: Las Banderas.** Rand. 1995. pap. (*0-528-83739-7*) Rand McNally.

Conozea a Pagemaker para Macintosh. Craig Dauuloff. 1992. pap. text ed. 19.95 (*968-18-4413-0*, Pub. by Limusa MX) Computer & Tech.

CONPAR Eighty-One Conference on Analysing Problem Classes & Programming for Parallel Computing: Proceedings. Ed. by W. Haendler. (Lecture Notes in Computer Science Ser.: Vol. 111). (Illus.). 508p. 1981. pap. 41.00 (*0-387-10827-0*) Spr-Verlag.

CONPAR 86. Ed. by W. Handler et al. (Lecture Notes in Computer Science Ser.: Vol. 237). x, 418p. 1986. pap. 45.00 (*0-387-16811-7*) Spr-Verlag.

Conquer Anxiety & Frustration. Vernon Howard. 1981. pap. 1.50 (*0-911203-07-9*) New Life.

Conquer Candida: And Restore Your Immune System. Jack Tips. 163p. 1988. pap. 9.95 (*0-929167-00-7*) Apple-a-Day.

Conquer Constipation-The Father & Mother of All Diseases: Confidential Report. Edwin Flatto. pap. 8.95 (*0-935540-00-8*) Plymouth Pr.

Conquer Harmful Anger One Hundred Ways. Vernon Howard. 1982. pap. 2.50 (*0-911203-15-X*) New Life.

Conquer Interview Objections. Robert F. Wilson & Erik H. Rambusch. LC 93-29358. 1994. text ed. 37.50 (*0-471-58981-0*); pap. text ed. 10.95 (*0-471-58982-9*) Wiley.

Conquer Resume Objections. Robert F. Wilson & Erik H. Rambusch. LC 93-33090. 1994. text ed. 37.50 (*0-471-58984-5*); pap. text ed. 10.95 (*0-471-58983-7*) Wiley.

Conquer That Cube. Czes Kosniowski. 32p. 1981. pap. 2.95 (*0-521-28814-2*) Cambridge U Pr.

Conquer the Cost - Service Compromise: A Five-Step Program to Improve Performance & Reduce Costs. Rupert Booth. 200p. 1994. text ed. 50.00 (*0-7863-0210-0*) Irwin Prof Pubng.

Conquer the Darkness. E. Florans. 1991. 14.95 (*0-89906-134-6*); pap. 10.95 (*0-89906-135-4*) Mesorah Pubns.

***Conquer the Night.** Selina MacPherson. 384p. (Orig.). 1995. mass mkt. 4.99 (*0-380-77252-3*) Avon.

***Conquer the Seven Deadly Money Mistakes: The No-Math, No-Hassle, Values-Based Way to Reach Your Financial Dreams.** J. Grady Cash & Kathy K. Cash. (Illus.). 224p. Date not set. pap. 16.95 (*1-884121-21-7*) Ctr Fin Well-Being.

Conquer Your Fears: Go Where You Want to Go, Do What You Want to Do--With Comfort & Confidence. E. Wayne Hart. LC 94-400. 448p. 1994. 34.95 (*1-55959-061-0*) Accel Devel.

Conquer Your Headaches: How to Get Rid of Your Headaches & on with Your Life. Robert G. Ford & Kay T. Ford. LC 94-75614. 100p. 1994. pap. 15.95 (*0-9636292-5-5*) Intl Headache.

Conquerants. Andre Malraux. 256p. (FRE.). 1954. 10.95 (*0-8288-9844-8*, F110901); 3.95 (*0-686-56321-2*) Fr & Eur.

Conquerants see Oeuvres Completes

Conquerants see Romans

Conquered Banner & Selected Poems of the Confederate Priest-Poet. Abram Ryan. Ed. by Robert J. Liederbach. (Illus.). 50p. 1988. pap. 8.50 (*0-934906-05-X*) R J Liederbach.

Conquered by His Kiss. Donna Valentino. 1993. mass mkt. 4.50 (*0-06-108159-0*, Harp PBks) HarpC.

Conquered City. Victor Serge. 208p. 1981. pap. 3.95 (*0-904613-51-8*) Writers & Readers.

Conquered Peoples in America. 4th ed. Jose Hernandez. 304p. (C). 1992. pap. text ed. 28.95 (*0-8403-8170-0*) Kendall-Hunt.

***Conquered Peoples in America.** 5th ed. Jose Hernandez. 320p. (C). 1994. per., pap. text ed. 32.95 (*0-8403-9695-3*) Kendall-Hunt.

Conquering Adventure Games. Carl Townsend. (Illus.). 256p. 1984. pap. 15.95 (*0-88056-350-8*) Weber Systems.

Conquering AIDS Now! With Natural Treatment, A Non-Drug Approach. Scott J. Gregory & Bianca Leonardo. 1987. pap. 12.95 (*0-446-38733-9*) Warner Bks.

Conquering Asthma. Miller. Date not set. 14.95 (*1-55664-139-7*) Mosby Yr Bk.

Conquering Athletic Injuries. Ed. by Paul M. Taylor & Diane K. Taylor. LC 87-33905. (Illus.). 344p. (Orig.). 1988. pap. text ed. 22.95 (*0-88011-305-7*, PTAY0305) Human Kinetics.

Conquering Bad Dreams & Nightmares: A Guide to Understanding, Interpretation & Cure. Barry Krakow & Joseph Neidhart. 320p. (Orig.). 1992. pap. 8.95 (*0-425-13211-0*) Berkley Pub.

Conquering C Plus Plus Pointers. Robert J. Traister, Sr. (Illus.). 179p. 1994. disk, pap. 34.95 (*0-12-697420-9*, AP Prof) Acad Pr.

Conquering Cancer: An Invitation to Hope. Paul Johnson. 256p. 1991. pap. 9.99 (*0-310-53781-9*) Zondervan.

***Conquering Carpal Tunnel Syndrome & Other Repetitive Strain Injuries: A Self-Care Program.** Sharon J. Butler. (Illus.). 176p. (Orig.). 1995. pap. 18.95 (*1-886867-02-X*) Advan Pr.

Conquering Christ Is Coming. Clara J. Jones. 110p. (Orig.). 1988. pap. 5.75 (*0-9621462-0-X*) C J Jones.

Conquering College: The Most Fun You Can Have Learning the Things You Need to Know. Howard Scott Warshaw. Ed. by Karen Kellerman. (Illus.). 150p. (Orig.). 1992. pap. 12.95 (*0-9635111-0-6*) EduQuest CA.

Conquering Corporate Co-Dependence: Lifeskills for Making it Within or Without the Corporation. Carolyn Corbin. 1993. 21.95 (*0-13-145848-5*) P-H.

An Asterisk (*) at the beginning of an entry indicates that the title is appearing in BIP for the first time.

TITLE INDEX CONQUEST OF THE CAVES & UNDERGROUND

Conquering Corps Badge, & Other Stories of the Philippines. Charles King. LC 72-122726. (Short Story Index Reprint Ser.). (Illus.). 1977. 23.95 (*0-8369-3559-4*) Ayer.

Conquering Corruption in New York City Education. Carolyn J. Siino. LC 94-76742. 130p. 1994. pap. 16.75 (*0-9611860-1-1*, B001) Lucky Lit.

Conquering Disaster: Family Recovery & Long Term Consequences. Thomas E. Drabek & William H. Key. 485p. 1985. text ed. 49.50 (*0-8290-1000-9*); pap. text ed. 29.50 (*0-8290-1536-1*) Irvington.

Conquering Family. Thomas B. Costain. 1994. reprint ed. lib. bdg. 37.95 (*1-56849-372-X*) Buccaneer Bks.

***Conquering Fear.** Jack Hartman. 125p. 1989. pap. 6.95 (*0-915445-20-4*) Lamplight FL.

Conquering Fear. Karen Randau. 164p. 1991. pap. 9.99 (*0-945276-22-2*) Rapha Pub.

Conquering Frontiers: A History of the Brethren Church. Homer A. Kent, Sr. pap. 6.99 (*0-88469-017-2*) BMH Bks.

Conquering Goliath: Cesar Chavez at the Beginning. Fred Ross. 145p. 1992. reprint ed. pap. 14.95 (*0-9625298-0-X*) Wayne St U Pr.

Conquering Grad School: What You Need to Know. James R. Barner. LC 94-17851. (Illus.). 208p. (Orig.). 1995. pap. 19.95 (*0-9641365-3-8*) Wishbone Pub.

***Conquering Headache.** 1995. 12.95 (*0-9697781-6-3*) Login Pubs Consort.

Conquering Heart Disease: New Ways to Live Well without Drugs or Surgery. Harvey B. Simon. LC 94-10367. 1994. 24.95 (*0-316-79157-1*) Little.

Conquering Heroes. Peter Gent. LC 93-72580. 336p. 1994. 21.95 (*1-55611-384-6*) D I Fine.

***Conquering Heroes.** Peter Gent. 400p. 1995. mass mkt. 5.50 (*0-8439-3743-2*) Dorchester Pub Co.

Conquering Horse. Frederick Manfred. 352p. 1959. pap. 4.50 (*0-451-08739-9*, W8739, Sig) NAL-Dutton.

Conquering Horse. Frederick Manfred. LC 83-5826. xvi, 355p. 1983. reprint ed. pap. 11.95 (*0-8032-8119-6*, Bison Books) U of Nebr Pr.

***Conquering Hypertension.** 1995. 12.95 (*0-9697781-2-0*) Login Pubs Consort.

***Conquering Kashmir-A Pakistani Obsession.** K. K. Nanda. (C). 1995. 36.00x (*81-7095-045-7*, Pub. by Lancers Bks II) S Asia.

Conquering Math Anxiety: A Self-Help Workbook. Cynthia Arem. LC 92-18880. 1992. pap. 10.95 (*0-534-18876-1*) Brooks-Cole.

Conquering Math Phobia: A Painless Primer. Calvin C. Clawson. 314p. 1991. pap. text ed. 14.95 (*0-471-52898-6*) Wiley.

Conquering Mathematics: From Arithmetic to Calculus. Ed. by Lloyd Motz & Jefferson H. Weaver. LC 91-9329. (Illus.). 292p. 1991. 23.50 (*0-306-43768-6*, Plenum Pr) Plenum.

Conquering New Worlds. Sangharakshita. 62p. (Orig.). 1986. pap. 7.95 (*0-904766-26-8*, Pub. by Windhorse UK) Windhorse Pubns.

***Conquering Psoriasis.** 1995. 12.95 (*0-9697781-5-5*) Login Pubs Consort.

Conquering Resources: The Growth & Decline of the PLA's Science & Technology Commission for National Defense. Benjamin C. Ostrov. LC 90-26809. (Studies on Contemporary China). 176p. (C). 1991. 57.95 (*0-87332-654-7*) M E Sharpe.

Conquering Senility. Arthur C. Walsh. 96p. (Orig.). 1985. pap. 5.95 (*0-939332-15-9*) J Pohl Assocs.

Conquering Setbacks. Marilyn Hickey. 34p. (Orig.). pap. write for info. (*1-56441-150-8*) M Hickey Min.

Conquering Stress. Krs Edstrom. LC 92-26960. (Business Success Ser.). 112p. 1993. pap. 4.95 (*0-8120-4837-7*) Barron.

***Conquering Test Anxiety.** Margie Sherman. (Illus.). 8p. 1994. pap. 2.50 (*1-884241-26-3*) Energeia Pub.

Conquering the Corporate Career. Stanley Herz. Ed. by Nina Bouis. LC 85-81788. 304p. 1986. text ed. 19.95 (*0-9615913-2-3*) Kimberly Pr.

***Conquering the Dragon Within: God's Provision for Assurance & Victory in the End Time.** Marvin Moore. LC 94-39860. 1995. 13.95 (*0-8163-1252-4*) Pacific Pr Pub Assn.

Conquering the Fear of Death. 2nd ed. Spiros Zodhiates. 869p. 1982. reprint ed. pap. 12.99 (*0-89957-500-5*) AMG Pubs.

Conquering the Great American Desert: Nebraska. Everett Dick. LC 74-17591. (Nebraska State Historical Publications Ser.: Vol. 27). 456p. 1975. 10.95 (*0-686-18150-6*) Nebraska Hist.

Conquering the Paper Pile Up. Stephanie Culp. 176p. (Orig.). 1990. pap. 11.95 (*0-89879-410-2*) Writers Digest.

Conquering the Past: Austrian Nazism Yesterday & Today. F. Parkinson. LC 88-31328. 348p. 1989. 39.95 (*0-8143-2054-6*); pap. 18.95 (*0-8143-2055-4*) Wayne St U Pr.

***Conquering the Reign of Femeny: Gender & Genre in Chaucer's Romance.** Angela J. Weisl. (Chaucer Studies: Vol. XXII). 192p. (C). 1995. text ed. 53.00 (*0-85991-460-7*) Boydell & Brewer.

Conquering the Wind. rev. ed. Amy B. Toepfer et al. LC 82-72800. (Illus.). 180p. 1982. reprint ed. 14.00 (*0-914222-08-2*) Am Hist Soc Ger.

Conquering Your Child's Allergies. M. Eric Gershwin & Edwin L. Kingelhofer. 1989. 18.22 (*0-201-12967-1*) Addison-Wesley.

***Conquering Your Own Goliaths.** Steven Cramer. 106p. 1988. pap. 9.95 (*1-55517-122-2*) CFI Dist.

Conqueror. Gertrude Atherton. 30.95 (*0-88411-588-7*, Aeonian Pr) Amereon Ltd.

***Conqueror.** Joe McCormack. 1995. 14.95 (*0-8062-5289-8*) Carlton.

Conqueror: A Hero Battles Downsizing. Randall G. Buerkle. 175p. (Orig.). (C). 1995. pap. 9.95 (*1-885397-01-1*) Flagship Pubns.

Don't think for a minute that this story about struggles in the workplace is another theoretical textbook. In contrast, THE CONQUEROR is the working person's suspense novel! When the North American Free Trade Agreement (NAFTA) throws a small company into turmoil, the story's hero is led on a roller coaster ride as he faces downsizing, terrorism, & spiritual challenges. As a consultant to several Fortune 500 companies, Author Randall Buerkle is no stranger to the enigma of the workplace. THE CONQUEROR, as he notes, "poses many concerns about the current state of corporate life. For instance, how do some companies make the decisions they do? Is the organization of more value than its employees? & how can an individual in these times retain a sense of self worth?" As the story unfolds, divine intervention ultimately provides serenity to the main character's turbulent world. $6.99 PLUS 6.5% OHIO TAX PER BOOK. SEND CHECKS OR MONEY ORDERS TO FLAGSHIP PUBLICATIONS, 720 CHELSEA LANE, TIPP CITY, OH 45371. CALL RANDALL BUERKLE 513- 335-0797 FOR QUANTITY DISCOUNT INFORMATION. ***Publisher Provided Annotation.***

Conqueror: Dramatized Biography of Alexander Hamilton. Gertrude Atherton. (BCL1-PS American Literature Ser.). 536p. 1993. reprint ed. lib. bdg. 99.00 (*0-7812-6946-6*) Rprt Serv.

Conquerors. Allan W. Eckert. (Winning of America Ser.). 1971. 29.95 (*0-316-20865-5*) Little.

Conquerors. Andre Malraux. Tr. by Stephen Becker. LC 72-91594. 210p. 1991. pap. 10.95 (*0-226-50290-2*) U Ch Pr.

Conquerors, Vol. 3. Allan W. Eckert. 928p. 1984. mass mkt. 6.99 (*0-553-25820-6*) Bantam.

***Conquerors: Historical Sketches of the American Settlement of the Oregon Country.** A. Atwood. (Illus.). 326p. (Orig.). 1994. pap. text ed. 24.00 (*0-7884-0057-6*) Heritage Bk.

Conquerors & Chroniclers of Early Medieval Spain. Tr. & Intro. by Kenneth B. Wolf. (Translated Texts for Historians Ser.). 222p. (Orig.). 1991. reprint ed. pap. text ed. 16.95 (*0-85323-047-1*, Pub. by Liverpool Univ Pr UK) U of Pa Pr.

Conquerors & Conquered in Medieval Wales. Ralph A. Griffiths. (Illus.). 352p. 1994. 70.00 (*0-7509-0515-8*) A Sutton Pub.

Conqueror's Kiss. Hannah Howell. 384p. (Orig.). 1991. mass mkt. 4.50 (*0-380-76503-9*) Avon.

***Conquerors of the New Kingdom of Granada.** Jose I. Avellaneda. 288p. 1995. text ed. 50.00 (*0-8263-1612-3*) U of NM Pr.

Conquerors of the New World & Their Bondsmen, 2 Vols, Set. Arthur Helps. LC 77-83945. (Black Heritage Library Collection). 1977. 29.95 (*0-8369-8597-4*) Ayer.

Conquerors of the World: Peoples & Races of Europe. G. T. Bettany. 1977. lib. bdg. 59.95 (*0-8490-1664-9*) Gordon Pr.

Conqueror's Pride. Timothy Zahn. 1994. mass mkt. 5.99 (*0-553-56892-2*) Bantam.

Conquest. Jude Deveraux. Ed. by Linda Marrow. 320p. (Orig.). 1991. mass mkt. 5.99 (*0-671-64447-5*, Pocket Star Bks) PB.

***Conquest.** Hugh Thomas. 1995. pap. 16.00 (*0-671-51104-1*, Touchstone Bks) S&S Trade.

Conquest. large type ed. Jude Deveraux. (General Ser.). 408p. 1991. text ed. 20.95 (*0-8161-5231-4*, Large Print Bks); pap. 15.95 (*0-8161-5230-6*, Large Print Bks) Hall.

Conquest: Montezuma, Cortes, & the Fall of Old Mexico. Hugh Thomas. 1994. 30.00 (*0-671-70518-0*) S&S Trade.

Conquest: The Story of a Negro Pioneer. Oscar Micheaux. LC 75-89391. (Black Heritage Library Collection). 1977. 30.95 (*0-8369-8632-6*) Ayer.

Conquest: The Story of a Negro Pioneer. Oscar Micheaux. 15.00 (*1-56675-019-9*) Mnemosyne.

Conquest: The Story of a Negro Pioneer. Oscar Micheaux. (Illus.). xxi, 332p. 1994. pap. 9.95 (*0-8032-8209-5*, Bison Books) U of Nebr Pr.

Conquest, Anarchy & Lordship: Yorkshire, 1066-1154. Paul Dalton. (Studies in Medieval Life & Thought, Fourth Ser.: No. 27). (Illus.). 328p. (C). 1994. 69.95 (*0-521-45098-5*) Cambridge U Pr.

Conquest & Agrarian Change. Robert G. Keith. (Historical Studies: No. 93). 151p. 1971. 20.00 (*0-674-16293-5*) HUP.

Conquest & Capitalism 1492-1992. Steve Brouwer. (Illus.). 120p. (Orig.). (C). 1992. pap. 10.00 (*0-9622152-3-6*) Big Picture Bks.

Conquest & Coalescence: The Shaping of the State in Early Modern Europe. Ed. by Mark Greengrass. 256p. 1991. pap. 16.95 (*0-7131-6563-4*, A5511, Pub. by E Arnold UK) Routledge Chapman & Hall.

Conquest & Colonisation: The Normans in Britain, 1066-1100. Brian Golding. LC 93-47458. (British History in Perspective Ser.). 1994. write for info. (*0-312-12127-X*) St Martin.

Conquest & Crisis: Studies in Joshua, Judges & Ruth. John J. Davis. (Illus.). pap. 8.99 (*0-88469-052-0*) BMH Bks.

Conquest & Empire: The Reign of Alexander the Great. A. B. Bosworth. (Canto Book Ser.). (Illus.). 344p. (C). 1993. pap. 11.95 (*0-521-40679-X*) Cambridge U Pr.

Conquest & Glory: True Tales from the Land of the Taj. Leoda Buckwalter. Ed. by Helen Johns. LC 92-74955. (Illus.). 171p. (Orig.). (YA). 1992. pap. 7.95 (*0-916035-56-5*) Evangel Indiana.

Conquest & Resistance to Colonialism in Africa. Ed. by Gregory Maddox. LC 93-19790. (Articles on Colonialism & Nationalism in Africa Ser.: Vol. 1). 384p. 1993. 62.00 (*0-8153-1388-8*) Garland.

Conquest & Self-Conquest. Maria J. McIntosh. LC 74-76928. (American Fiction Reprint Ser.). 1977. 16.95 (*0-8369-7007-1*) Ayer.

Conquest & Survival in Colonial Guatemala: A Historical Geography of the Cuchumatan Highlands, 1500-1821. rev. ed. W. George Lovell. (Illus.). 312p. 1992. pap. 22.95 (*0-7735-0903-8*, Pub. by McGill CN) U of Toronto Pr.

***Conquest & Union: Fashioning a British State, 1485-1725.** Steven G. Ellis & Sarah Barber. LC 94-32380. (C). 1995. text ed. 47.95 (*0-582-20964-1*) Longman.

***Conquest & Union: Fashioning a British State, 1485-1725.** Steven G. Ellis & Sarah Barber. LC 94-32380. (C). 1996. pap. text ed. 17.95 (*0-582-20963-3*) Longman.

Conquest, Coexistence, & Change: Wales, 1063-1415. R. R. Davies. (Oxford History of Wales Ser.: Vol. II). (Illus.). 552p. 1991. reprint ed. pap. 19.95 (*0-19-820198-2*) OUP.

Conquest Continued: Disregard for Human & Indigenous Rights in the Mexican State of Chiapas. Minnesota Advocates for Human Rights Staff. 93p. 1992. pap. 10.00 (*0-929293-13-4*) MN Advocates.

Conquest of a Continent. Madison Grant. 1984. lib. bdg. 79.95 (*0-87700-583-4*) Revisionist Pr.

Conquest of a Continent: Of the Expansion of Races in America. Madison Grant. LC 76-40680. (Anti-Movements in America Ser.). 1977. reprint ed. lib. bdg. 35.95 (*0-405-09953-3*) Ayer.

Conquest of America. Hans Koning. (Cornerstone Bks.). (Illus.). 144p. (Orig.). (J). (ps-12). 1993. text ed. 22.00 (*0-85345-877-4*); pap. text ed. 10.00 (*0-85345-876-6*) Monthly Rev.

Conquest of America. Tzvetan Todorov. LC 84-47545. (Illus.). 288p. 1985. pap. 12.00 (*0-06-091214-6*, CN1214, PL) HarpC.

***Conquest of America.** Tzvetan Todorov. 1995. 21.50 (*0-8446-6866-4*) Peter Smith.

Conquest of America & Leadership of World Zionist Organization see Letters & Papers of Chaim Weizmann

Conquest of Apacheria. Dan L. Thrapp. (Illus.). 1967. pap. 18.95 (*0-8061-1286-7*) U of Okla Pr.

Conquest of Bacteria, from Salvarsan to Sulphapyridine. Frank S. Taylor. LC 78-142705. (Essay Index Reprint Ser.). 1977. reprint ed. 19.95 (*0-8369-2375-8*) Ayer.

Conquest of Brazil. Roy Nash. LC 67-29550. 1926. 25.00 (*0-8196-0207-8*) Biblo.

Conquest of Bread. Peter Kropotkin. LC 68-56520. 1972. reprint ed. 24.95 (*0-405-08717-9*, Pub. by Blom Pubns UK) Ayer.

***Conquest of Bread & Other Writings.** Pter Kropotkin. Ed. by Marshall S. Shatz. (Cambridge Texts in the History of Political Thought Ser.). 288p. (C). 1995. 59.95 (*0-521-45398-4*); pap. 18.95 (*0-521-45990-7*) Cambridge U Pr.

Conquest of Canaan. Jessie Penn-Lewis. 1992. pap. 4.95 (*0-87508-943-7*) Chr Lit.

Conquest of Canaan. Timothy Dwight. LC 78-129380. reprint ed. 29.50 (*0-404-02226-X*) AMS Pr.

Conquest of Canaan. Timothy Dwight. (Notable American Authors Ser.). 1992. reprint ed. lib. bdg. 75.00 (*0-7812-2736-4*) Rprt Serv.

Conquest of Canaan. Booth Tarkington. LC 73-104574. reprint ed. lib. bdg. 19.50 (*0-8398-1950-1*) Irvington.

Conquest of Canaan: A Poem. Timothy Dwight. 1788. 11.00 (*0-403-00414-4*) Scholarly.

Conquest of Canaan: A Poem. Timothy Dwight. 1988. reprint ed. lib. bdg. 75.00 (*0-7812-0475-5*) Rprt Serv.

Conquest of Cancer: Vaccines & Diet. Virginia Livingston-Wheeler & Edmond G. Addeo. 1993. pap. 9.95 (*0-9627145-1-8*, Cyrus Pr) Waterside Prodns.

Conquest of Death. Edmond B. Szekely. 68p. 1973. pap. 3.50 (*0-89564-043-0*) IBS Intl.

Conquest of Deficiency Diseases: Achievements & Prospects. W. R. Aykroyd. (Freedom from Hunger Campaign Basic Study Ser: No. 24). 98p. 1970. pap. 4.80 (*92-4-156018-5*, 410) World Health.

Conquest of Eden: 1493-1515: Other Voyages of Columbus. Michael Paiewonsky. (Illus.). 176p. 1990. 34.95 (*0-926330-03-9*) Mapes Monde.

Conquest of Eden: 1493-1515: 1493-1515 Other Voyages of Columbus. Michael Paiewonsky. (Illus.). 176p. 1993. reprint ed. pap. 23.95 (*0-926330-04-7*) Mapes Monde.

Conquest of Epidemic Disease: A Chapter in the History of Ideas. Charles-Edward A. Winslow. LC 79-48055. 424p. 1980. reprint ed. 29.50 (*0-299-08240-7*); reprint ed. pap. 15.95 (*0-299-08244-X*) U of Wis Pr.

Conquest of Fear. Basil King. 276p. 1990. reprint ed. lib. bdg. 21.95 (*0-89966-659-0*) Buccaneer Bks.

Conquest of Florida under Hernando De Soto, 1. Theodore Irving. LC 73-78181. 1974. reprint ed. 25.00 (*0-87208-017-X*) Island Pr Pubs.

Conquest of Gaul. Julius Caesar. 1976. 21.95 (*0-8488-0439-2*) Amereon Ltd.

Conquest of Gaul. rev. ed. Julius Caesar. Tr. by S. A. Handford. 1983. pap. 8.95 (*0-14-044433-5*, Penguin Classics) Viking Penguin.

Conquest of Happiness. Bertrand Russell. 1971. pap. 9.95 (*0-87140-244-0*) Liveright.

***Conquest of Happiness.** Bertrand Russell. 256p. 1995. pap. 11.00 (*0-87140-162-2*) Liveright.

Conquest of Java. William Thorn. (Illus.). 460p. 1993. 59.95 (*0-945971-86-9*) Periplus.

Conquest of Kansas, by Missouri & Her Allies. William R. Phillips. LC 76-161271. (Black Heritage Library Collection). 1977. reprint ed. 31.95 (*0-8369-8830-2*) Ayer.

Conquest of Lines & Symmetry: Aerobatics. Duane Cole. 1970. pap. 14.95 (*0-911721-41-X*) Aviation.

Conquest of Mental Retardation. Burton Blatt. LC 86-15129. (Illus.). 408p. 1987. text ed. 38.00 (*0-89079-140-6*, 1410) PRO-ED.

Conquest of Mexico. William H. Prescott. Bd. with Conquest of Peru. LC 36-27495. LC 36-27495. 1979. 22.00 (*0-394-60471-7*, Modern Lib) Random.

Conquest of Mexico: A Modern Rendering of William H. Prescott's History. Ed. by Beatrice Berler. LC 88-70846. (Illus.). 145p. 1988. lib. bdg. 14.95 (*0-931722-80-2*); pap. text ed. 8.95 (*0-931722-70-5*) Corona Pub.

Conquest of Mexico: The Incorporation of Indian Societies into the Western World, 16th-18th Centuries. Serge Gruzinski. Tr. by Eileen Corrigan. (Illus.). 300p. 1993. text ed. 49.95 (*0-7456-0873-6*); pap. text ed. 19.95 (*0-7456-1226-1*) Blackwell Pubs.

Conquest of Mexico see Florentine Codex, General History of the Things of New Spain

Conquest of Mexico by Hernan Cortez, 1518-1521: Selected Translations & a Portfolio of Etchings. Robert E. Lyons. (Illus.). 16p. (Orig.). 1987. 785.00 (*0-943435-00-5*) Cartographer Ink.

Conquest of Michoacan: The Spanish Domination of the Tarascan Kingdom in Western Mexico, 1521-1530. J. Benedict Warren. LC 84-40280. (Illus.). 400p. 1985. 42.95 (*0-8061-1858-X*) U of Okla Pr.

Conquest of Mind. Eknath Easwaran. LC 88-26575. 184p. (Orig.). 1989. 22.00 (*0-915132-51-6*); pap. 12.95 (*0-915132-50-8*) Nilgiri Pr.

Conquest of Morocco. Douglas Porch. LC 82-47804. 1983. 16.95 (*0-394-51158-1*) Knopf.

Conquest of New France: A Chronicle of the Colonial Wars. George M. Wrong. (BCL1 - U. S. History Ser.). 246p. 1991. reprint ed. lib. bdg. 79.00 (*0-7812-6101-5*) Rprt Serv.

Conquest of New Granada: Being the Life of Gonzalo Jimenez De Quesada. R. Cunninghame Graham. LC 66-30734. reprint ed. 66.50 (*0-8154-0086-1*) Cooper Sq.

Conquest of New Mexico & California: An Historical & Personal Narrative. Philip S. Cooke. 1977. reprint ed. lib. bdg. 59.00 (*0-403-07682-X*) Scholarly.

Conquest of New Mexico & California: An Historical & Personal Narrative. Philip St George Cooke. Ed. by Carlos E. Cortes. LC 76-1244. (Chicano Heritage Ser.). 1977. reprint ed. 26.95 (*0-405-09497-3*) Ayer.

Conquest of New Mexico & California: An Historical & Personal Narrative. Phillip St. G. Cooke. 1988. reprint ed. lib. bdg. 59.00 (*0-7812-5049-8*) Rprt Serv.

Conquest of New Spain. Del Castillo Bernal-Diaz. Tr. by John M. Cohen. (Orig.). (YA). (gr. 9 up). 1963. pap. 9.95 (*0-14-044123-9*) Viking Child Bks.

Conquest of New Spain, Fifteen Eighty-Five Revision: Reproductions of the Boston Public Library Manuscript & the Carlos Maria de Bustamante 1840 Edition. Fray B. De Sahagun. Ed. by S. L. Cline. Tr. by Howard F. Cline. LC 88-20700. 592p. (C). 1989. text ed. 50.00 (*0-87480-311-X*) U of Utah Pr.

Conquest of Northern Nigeria. Richard H. Dusgate. 316p. 1985. 45.00 (*0-7146-3227-9*, Pub. by F Cass Pubs UK) Intl Spec Bk.

Conquest of Paradise: Christopher Columbus & the Columbian Legacy. Kirkpatrick Sale. 464p. 1991. pap. 14.00 (*0-452-26669-6*, Plume) NAL-Dutton.

Conquest of Peru see Conquest of Mexico

Conquest of Politics: Liberal Philosophy in Democratic Times. Benjamin R. Barber. 192p. (Orig.). 1990. text ed. 39.50 (*0-691-07764-9*); pap. text ed. 12.95 (*0-691-02323-9*) Princeton U Pr.

Conquest of Pollution. Morris Goran. LC 81-184272. 281p. (C). 1982. 30.00 (*0-915250-37-3*) Environ Design.

Conquest of Poverty. H. Wilmans. 1991. lib. bdg. 75.00 (*0-87700-934-1*) Revisionist Pr.

***Conquest of Poverty.** Henry Hazlitt. 240p. 1994. reprint ed. pap. 19.95 (*1-57246-006-7*) Foun Econ Ed.

Conquest of Poverty. Helen Wilmans. 186p. 1969. reprint ed. spiral bd. 7.70 (*0-7873-0972-9*) Mokelumne.

Conquest of Poverty: A Challenge to the Money Power Bankers. Gerald G. McGeer. 1979. lib. bdg. 59.95 (*0-8490-2901-5*) Gordon Pr.

Conquest of Poverty: The Calvinist Revolt in Sixteenth-Century France. H. Heller. (Studies in Medieval & Reformation Thought: No. 35). xiv, 281p. 1986. 56.00 (*90-04-07598-4*) E J Brill.

Conquest of Rome. Mathilde Serao. Ed. by Ann Caesar. (Women's Classics Ser.). 250p. 1992. text ed. 55.00x (*0-8147-7955-7*); pap. 18.95 (*0-8147-7964-6*) NYU Pr.

Conquest of the Balkans. Ed. by Time-Life Books Editors. (Third Reich Ser.). 1990. 22.60 (*0-8094-6979-0*); lib. bdg. 28.60 (*0-8094-6980-4*) Time-Life.

Conquest of the Caves & Underground Rivers of Czechoslovakia's Macocha Abyss: A Historical & Technical Study of Their Exploration. Karel B. Absolon. (Illus.). 112p. (Orig.). 1987. pap. 39.50 (*0-930329-21-X*) KABEL Pubs.

C

An Asterisk (*) at the beginning of an entry indicates that the title is appearing in BIP for the first time.

Conquest of the Country Northwest of the River Ohio, 1778-1783, 2 vols. in 1. William H. English. Bd. with Life of General George Rogers Clark. LC 70-146394. LC 70-146394. (First American Frontier Ser.). (Illus.). 1194p. 1971. reprint ed. 72.95 (*0-405-02847-4*) Ayer.

Conquest of the Country Northwest of the River Ohio, 1778-1783: And Life of Gen. George Rogers Clark. William H. English. (Illus.). 1186p. 1991. reprint ed. pap. 60.00 (*1-55613-430-4*) Heritage Bk.

Conquest of the Illinois. George R. Clark. (BCL1 - U. S. History Ser.). 190p. 1991. reprint ed. lib. bdg. 69.00 (*0-7812-6115-5*) Rprt Serv.

Conquest of the Incas. John Hemming. LC 73-4616. (Illus.). 641p. 1973. reprint ed. pap. 18.95 (*0-15-622300-7*, Harvest Bks) HarBrace.

Conquest of the Material World. John U. Nef. LC 64-15804. 1964. lib. bdg. 25.00 (*0-226-57121-1*) U Ch Pr.

Conquest of the Microchip. Hans Queisser. LC 87-2440. (Illus.). 272p. 1988. 34.50 (*0-674-16296-X*) HUP.

Conquest of the Microchip. Hans Queisser. 272p. 1990. pap. text ed. 9.95 (*0-674-16297-8*) HUP.

Conquest of the Mind. 1982. 4.50 (*0-89858-037-4*) Fill the Gap.

Conquest of the Moon: A Story of the Bayouda. P. Grousset. LC 74-16504. (Science Fiction Ser.). (Illus.). 340p. 1975. reprint ed. 28.95 (*0-405-06302-4*) Ayer.

Conquest of the New Word: Experimental Fiction & Translation in the Americas. Johnny Payne. LC 93-6537. (Texas Pan American Ser.). 304p. (C). 1993. text ed. 35.00 (*0-292-76546-0*) U of Tex Pr.

Conquest of the North Atlantic. G. J. Marcus. (Illus.). 1981. 29.95 (*0-19-520252-X*) OUP.

Conquest of the Philippines by the United States, 1898-1925. Moorfield Storey & Marcial P. Lichauco. LC 70-37355. (Select Bibliographies Reprint Ser.). 1977. reprint ed. 20.95 (*0-8369-6702-X*) Ayer.

***Conquest of the Reich: D-Day to VE Day-A Soldiers' History.** Robin Neillands. (Illus.). 304p. 1995. 24.95 (*0-8147-5781-2*) NYU Pr.

Conquest of the Sahara. Douglas Porch. LC 86-12092. 332p. 1986. reprint ed. pap. 11.95 (*0-88064-061-8*) Fromm Intl Pub.

Conquest of the Sierra: Spaniards & Indians in Colonial Oaxaca. John K. Chance. LC 89-40213. (Illus.). 240p. 1989. 39.95 (*0-8061-2222-6*) U of Okla Pr.

Conquest of the South Pole & Man to Man. Manfred Karge. Tr. by Tinch Minter & Anthony Vivis. (Royal Court Writers Ser.). 48p. (Orig.). (C). 1988. pap. 8.95 (*0-413-61200-7*, A0364, Pub. by Methuen UK) Heinemann.

Conquest of the Tropics: The Story of the Creative Enterprises Conducted by the United Fruit Company. Frederick U. Adams. Ed. by Stuart Bruchey & Eleanor Bruchey. LC 76-4766. (American Business Abroad Ser.). (Illus.). 1976. reprint ed. 40.95 (*0-405-09263-6*) Ayer.

Conquest of the West: A Sourcebook on the American West. Ed. by Carter Smith. LC 91-31130. (American Albums from the Collections of the Library of Congress). (Illus.). 96p. (YA). (gr. 5-8). 1992. lib. bdg. 18.90 (*1-56294-129-1*) Millbrook Pr.

Conquest of the West India. Francisco Lopez De Gomara. 1940. reprint ed. 60.00 (*0-8201-1193-7*) Schol Facsimiles.

Conquest of Tibet. Sven A. Hedin. LC 74-11786. (Illus.). 400p. 1974. reprint ed. text ed. 65.00 (*0-8371-7695-6*, HECT, Greenwood Pr) Greenwood.

***Conquest of Time.** H. G. Wells. (Great Minds Ser.). 125p. (C). 1994. pap. 7.95 (*0-87975-920-8*) Prometheus Bks.

Conquest of Violence: The Gandhian Philosophy of Conflict. Joan V. Bondurant. 296p. 1988. reprint ed. pap. text ed. 12.95 (*0-691-02281-X*) Princeton U Pr.

Conquest of Viral Diseases: Perspectives in Medical Virology, Vol. 1. John S. Oxford & B. Oberg. 740p. 1985. 260.50 (*0-444-80566-4*) Elsevier.

Conquest of War: Alternative Strategies for Global Security. Harry B. Hollins et al. 224p. (C). 1989. pap. text ed. 19.95 (*0-8133-0787-2*) Westview.

Conquest of Water: The Advent of Health in the Industrial Age. Jean-Pierre Goubert. Tr. by Andrew Wilson. 1989. 39.50 (*0-691-08544-7*) Princeton U Pr.

Conquest of Yucatan. F. Blom. 1976. lib. bdg. 59.95 (*0-8490-1665-7*) Gordon Pr.

Conquest Through Prayer. Denzil Holman. LC 88-23213. (Illus.). 320p. (Orig.). 1988. pap. 6.99 (*0-932581-39-0*) Word Aflame.

Conqueste de Constantinople. Geoffroi De Villehardouin. Ed. by Julian E. White, Jr. LC 68-16196. (Medieval French Literature Ser.). (Orig.). (FRE.). 1968. pap. text ed. 6.95 (*0-89197-102-5*) Irvington.

***Conquests & Historical Identities in California, 1769-1936.** Lisabeth Haas. (Illus.). 272p. 1995. 35.00 (*0-520-08380-6*) U CA Pr.

Conquete de l'Angleterre par les normands. Andre Maurois. (Coll. Le Memorial des Siecles). (FRE.). 19.95 (*0-8288-9873-1*, F113500) Fr & Eur.

Conquete de Plassans. Emile Zola. (FRE.). 1990. pap. 14.95 (*0-7859-1380-7*) Fr & Eur.

Conquete Du Courage. Stephen Crane. (FRE.). 1982. pap. 10.95 (*0-7859-1950-3*, 2070373517) Fr & Eur.

Conquista de la Felicidad. Bertrand Russell. (Nueva Austral Ser.: Vol. 189). (SPA.). 1991. pap. text ed. 24.95x (*84-239-1989-7*) Elliots Bks.

Conquista De la Vida: How to Succeed in Life. Salvador Iserte. (SPA.). 10.95 (*84-7228-939-7*, 222014, Pub. by Edit Clie SP) TSELF.

Conquista Divina: The Divine Conquest. A. W. Tozer. (SPA.). 3.95 (*84-7645-387-6*, 223514, Pub. by Edit Clie SP) TSELF.

Conquista y Cambio Cultural: La Sierra de Los Cuchumatanes De Guatemala, 1500-1821. W. George Lovell. LC 90-82409. (Monograph Ser.: No. 6). (Illus.). 288p. (SPA.). 1990. pap. 16.50 (*0-910443-08-4*) CIRMA.

Conquistador. Ed. by Fred Rendell. (C). 1989. 30.00 (*1-85098-074-8*, Pub. by Jordanhill College UK) St Mut.

Conquistador Without Sword: The Life of Roque Gonzalez S.J. C. J. McNaspy. 1984. 12.95 (*0-8294-0455-4*) Loyola Univ Pr.

***Conquistadora: The Autobiography of an Ancient Statue.** Fray A. Chavez. (Illus.). Date not set. pap. 6.95 (*0-913270-43-1*) Sunstone Pr.

Conquistadora: The Autobiography of an Ancient Statue. rev. ed. Angelico Chauez. LC 81-14473. 96p. 1984. pap. 6.95 (*0-86534-041-2*) Sunstone Pr.

Conquistadores. Terence Wise. (Men-at-Arms Ser.: No. 101). (Illus.). 48p. pap. 11.95 (*0-85045-357-7*, 9034, Pub. by Osprey UK) Stackpole.

Conquistadores. large type ed. Bob Langley. 448p. 1987. 16.95 (*0-7089-1627-9*) Ulverscroft.

Conquistadors. Jean Descola. Tr. by Malcolm Barnes. LC 72-122060. (Illus.). vi, 404p. 1970. reprint ed. lib. bdg. 45.00 (*0-678-03151-7*) Kelley.

Conquistadors: First-Person Accounts of the Conquest of Mexico. Patricia De Fuentes. LC 93-13383. (C). 1993. pap. 17.95 (*0-8061-2562-4*) U of Okla Pr.

Conquistador's Lady. Anita McAndrews. LC 90-30127. 240p. (Orig.). 1990. pap. 10.95 (*0-931832-48-9*) Fithian Pr.

***Conrad.** Ernesto Burden. 300p. 1995. pap. 8.95 (*1-56901-549-X*) NW Pub.

Conrad. Jim Reilly. (Life & Works: Set II). (Illus.). 112p. (YA). (gr. 7 up). 1990. lib. bdg. 19.94 (*0-86593-021-X*); lib. bdg. 14.95 (*0-685-36351-1*) Rourke Corp.

Conrad. Norman Sherry. LC 87-51300. (Literary Lives Ser.). (Illus.). 144p. 1988. pap. 9.95 (*0-500-26028-1*) Thames Hudson.

Conrad: "Almayer's Folly" to "Under Western Eyes" Daniel R. Schwarz. LC 79-48012. 230p. 1980. 35.00 (*0-8014-1311-7*) Cornell U Pr.

Conrad: "Nostromo" Ian Watt. (Landmarks of World Literature Ser.). 128p. 1988. 29.95 (*0-521-32821-7*); pap. 10.95 (*0-521-31365-1*) Cambridge U Pr.

CONRAD: A Maximum Likelihood Program for Estimation of Non-Linear Simultaneous Equations Models. Erik Mellander & Leif Jansson. 94p. (Orig.). 1987. pap. 55.00x (*91-7204-283-4*, Pub. by Industriens SW) Coronet Bks.

Conrad: Heart of Darkness. Richard Adams. (Critical Studies). 144p. 1991. mass mkt. 6.00 (*0-14-077134-4*, Penguin Bks) Viking Penguin.

Conrad Aiken. Frederick J. Hoffman. (Twayne's United States Authors Ser.). 1962. pap. 13.95x (*0-8084-0090-8*, T17) NCUP.

Conrad Aiken. Reuel Denney. LC 64-64445. (University of Minnesota Pamphlets on American Writers Ser.: No. 38). 48p. (Orig.). reprint ed. pap. 25.00 (*0-7837-2891-3*, 2057564) Bks Demand.

Conrad Aiken: A Bibliography. F. C. Bonnell & F. W. Bonnell. LC 82-9241. 291p. 1983. 20.97 (*0-87328-118-7*) Huntington Lib.

Conrad Aiken: Poet of White Horse Vale. Edward Butscher. LC 84-16275. (Illus.). 512p. 1988. 34.95 (*0-8203-0760-2*) U of Ga Pr.

Conrad & Eudora. Thomas H. Chivers. LC 78-18338. 1978. reprint ed. 50.00 (*0-8201-1315-8*) Schol Facsimiles.

Conrad & Eudora: Or the Death of Alonzo. Thomas H. Chivers. (Works of Thomas Holley Chivers Ser.). 1990. reprint ed. lib. bdg. 79.00 (*0-7812-2282-6*) Rprt Serv.

Conrad & His Contemporaries. J. Retinger. 1972. 59.95 (*0-87968-932-3*) Gordon Pr.

Conrad & His Contemporaries. Joseph Retinger. LC 72-6504. (Studies in Conrad: No. 8). 156p. 1972. reprint ed. lib. bdg. 39.95 (*0-8383-1621-2*) M S G Haskell Hse.

Conrad & Me: Childhood Tales of Adventure During the Great Depression. Lillian Claunch. LC 92-61930. (Illus.). 118p. (Orig.). 1992. pap. 9.95 (*1-880222-10-8*) Red-Apple Pub.

Conrad & Religion. John A. Lester. LC 87-14377. 240p. 1988. text ed. 39.95 (*0-312-00979-8*) St Martin.

Conrad Chronology. Owen Knowles. (Reference Guides to Literature Ser.). 160p. 1990. text ed. 38.50 (*0-8161-1839-6*, Hall Reference) Macmillan.

Conrad Clan: Family of John Stephen Conrad, Sr., & Allied Lines. Floyd W. Coffman. (Illus.). 355p. 1993. reprint ed. lib. bdg. 62.50 (*0-8328-3105-0*); reprint ed. pap. 52.50 (*0-8328-3106-9*) Higginson Bk Co.

Conrad Felixmuller: The Complete Graphic Work, 1912-1977. Gerhard Sohn. (Illus.). 280p. (GER.). 1975. 225.00 (*0-915346-44-3*) A Wofsy Fine Arts.

Conrad Ferdinand Meyer & Freud: The Beginnings of Applied Psychoanalysis. Alexander Grinstein. 420p. (C). 1992. text ed. 49.50 (*0-8236-1046-2*) Intl Univs Pr.

Conrad Ferdinand Meyer und Sein Werk. Harry Maync. LC 76-100522. (GER.). reprint ed. 49.50 (*0-404-00597-7*) AMS Pr.

Conrad Grebel, Fourteen Ninety Eight to Fifteen Twenty-Six: The Founder of the Swiss Brethren Sometimes Called Anabaptists. Harold S. Bender. (Studies in Anabaptist & Mennonite History: No. 6). 343p. reprint ed. pap. 97.80 (*0-317-28810-5*, 2020335) Bks Demand.

Conrad Grebel, Son of Zurich: Commissioned by Conrad Grebel College, Waterloo, Ontario, in Observance of the 450th Anniversary of the Mennonites. John L. Ruth. LC 75-8829. (Illus.). 160p. reprint ed. pap. 45.60 (*0-7837-5112-5*, 2044811) Bks Demand.

Conrad in the Nineteenth Century. Ian Watt. 1979. pap. 13.00 (*0-520-04405-3*) U CA Pr.

Conrad Revisited: Essays for the Eighties. Ed. by Ross C. Murfin. LC 83-17937. 200p. 1985. 22.50 (*0-8173-0205-0*) U of Ala Pr.

Conrad Richter. Edwin W. Gaston, Jr. (United States Authors Ser.: No. 81). 140p. (C). 1989. text ed. 20.95 (*0-8057-7530-7*, TUSAS 81, Twayne) Macmillan.

Conrad Richter. Edwin W. Gaston, Jr. (Twayne's United States Authors Ser.). 1965. pap. 13.95x (*0-8084-0091-6*, T81) NCUP.

Conrad the Novelist. Albert J. Guerard. LC 58-8995. 336p. reprint ed. pap. 96.40 (*0-7837-1703-2*, 2057232) Bks Demand.

***Conrad to Cinema: The Art of Adaptation.** Gene D. Phillips. LC 94-30263. (Ars Interpretandi Ser.: Vol. 4). 1995. write for info. (*0-8204-2669-5*) P Lang Pubs.

Conrad under Familial Eyes. Joseph Conrad et al. Ed. by Najder Zdzislaw. Tr. by Halina Carroll-Najder. LC 83-5187. 282p. 1984. 69.95 (*0-521-25082-X*) Cambridge U Pr.

Conrad Veidt: From Caligari to Casablanca. J. C. Allen. (Illus.). 253p. 1987. pap. 12.50 (*0-940168-04-9*) Boxwood.

Conrad Veidt: From Caligari to Casablanca. 2nd ed. Jerry C. Allen. LC 92-39569. 362p. 1993. 18.50 (*0-940168-27-8*) Boxwood.

Conrad Weiser & the Indian Policy of Colonial Pennsylvania. Joseph S. Walton. LC 71-146425. (First American Frontier Ser.). (Illus.). 1971. reprint ed. 38.95 (*0-405-02895-4*) Ayer.

Conrad Weiser & the Indian Policy of Colonial Pennsylvania. Joseph S. Walton. 1993. reprint ed. lib. bdg. 89.00 (*0-7812-5852-9*) Rprt Serv.

Conrade Webb of Hampstead. William T. Hastings. LC 58-7622. 126p. reprint ed. 36.00 (*0-685-15673-7*, 2027508) Bks Demand.

Conradin Kreutzer's Fruhlingslieder & Wanderlieder. Luise E. Peake. LC 85-754791. 200p. 1990. lib. bdg. 64.00 (*0-918728-58-4*) Pendragon NY.

Conrad's Colonialism. Robert F. Lee. LC 68-30868. (Studies in English Literature: No. 54). 1969. text ed. 52.35 (*3-11-000273-6*) Mouton.

Conrad's Dilemma. Geraldine M. Bennett. (J). (gr. 5 up). Date not set. pap. write for info. (*1-882786-06-8*) New Dawn NY.

Conrad's Dilemma: A Helpful Dream. Geraldine M. Bennett. (Illus.). 34p. (Orig.). (J). (gr. 2-8). Date not set. pap. 7.98 (*1-882786-15-7*) New Dawn NY.

Conrad's Early Sea Fiction: The Novelist As Navigator. Paul Bruss. LC 77-74402. 185p. 1979. 29.50 (*0-8387-2133-8*) Bucknell U Pr.

Conrad's Endings: A Study of the Five Major Novels. Arnold E. Davidson. Ed. by A. Walton Litz. LC 84-8508. (Studies in Modern Literature: No. 39). 134p. reprint ed. 38.20 (*0-8357-1587-6*, 2070442) Bks Demand.

Conrad's Existentialism. Otto Bohlmann. LC 90-20663. 256p. 1991. text ed. 45.00 (*0-312-05789-X*) St Martin.

Conrad's Fiction As Critical Discourse. Richard O. Ambrosini. 256p. (C). 1991. 64.95 (*0-521-40349-9*) Cambridge U Pr.

Conrad's Fossil Shells of the Tertiary Formations of North America: 1832-35. G. D. Harris. (Illus.). 121p. 1971. reprint ed. 6.00 (*0-87710-362-3*) Paleo Res.

Conrad's Lingard Trilogy: Empire, Race & Women in the Malay Novels. Hellena Krenn. LC 90-31443. (Origins of Modernism: Studies in British Literature). 192p. 1990. 27.00 (*0-8240-5798-8*, H1284) Garland.

Conrad's Measure of Man. Paul L. Wiley. LC 66-19089. 1966. reprint ed. 45.00 (*0-87752-122-0*) Gordian.

Conrad's Models of Mind. Bruce Johnson. LC 73-150125. 241p. reprint ed. pap. 68.70 (*0-318-39677-7*, 2033260) Bks Demand.

Conrad's Mythology. Robert B. Wilson. LC 86-50942. 200p. 1987. 22.50 (*0-87875-316-8*) Whitston Pub.

Conrad's Narrative Method. Jakob Lothe. (Illus.). 328p. 1991. pap. 22.00 (*0-19-812255-1*) OUP.

Conrad's Prefaces to His Works. Joseph Conrad. LC 70-163112. (English Literature Ser.: No. 33). 1971. lib. bdg. 75.00 (*0-8383-1304-3*) M S G Haskell Hse.

Conrad's Prefaces to His Works. Joseph Conrad. LC 72-160963. (Select Bibliographies Reprint Ser.). 1977. reprint ed. 18.95 (*0-8369-5831-4*) Ayer.

Conrad's Rebels: The Psychology of Revolution in the Novels from Nostromo to Victory. Helen F. Rieselbach. LC 84-23917. (Studies in Modern Literature: No. 42). 162p. reprint ed. pap. 46.20 (*0-8357-1600-7*, 2070572) Bks Demand.

Conrad's Romanticism. David Thorburn. LC 73-86919. 217p. reprint ed. pap. 61.90 (*0-8357-8081-3*, 2033904) Bks Demand.

Conrad's the Secret Agent & the Critics: 1965-1980. Jan Verleun & Jetty De Vries. xv, 320p. (Orig.). 1984. pap. 45.50 (*90-6088-090-0*, Pub. by Boumas Boekhuis NE) Benjamins North Am.

Conrail Commodities. Jeremy Taylor. (Illus.). 168p. 1994. 49.95 (*0-9640425-0-9*) Silver Brook Junct.

Conran Design Gold Kitchen Utensils. Sir T. Conran. 1990. pap. 7.98 (*0-442-30294-0*) Chapman & Hall.

Conran Design Gold Lamps & Light. Sir T. Conran. 1990. pap. 7.98 (*0-442-30302-5*) Chapman & Hall.

Conran Design Gold Tableware. Sir T. Conran. 1990. pap. 7.98 (*0-442-30293-2*) Chapman & Hall.

Conran Design Guides: Home Office. Sir T. Conran. 1990. pap. 7.98 (*0-442-30292-4*) Chapman & Hall.

Conran's Basic Book of Home Gardening: A Complete Guide for the First-Time Gardener. Stefan Buczacki. (Illus.). 192p. 1991. 14.99 (*0-517-02632-5*) Random Hse Value.

Conran's Do-It-Yourself Home Design. Blake Innes. 1991. 14.99 (*0-517-05071-4*) Random Hse Value.

Conran's Living in Small Spaces. Lorrie Mack. 1988. 29.95 (*0-316-54383-7*) Little.

Conran's Stylish Interiors. Andrea Spencer & Elizabeth Wilhide. 1986. 19.95 (*0-316-15264-1*) Little.

Conrey Placer Mining Company: A Pioneer Gold-Dredging Enterprise in Montana, 1897-1922. Clark C. Spence. LC 89-39452. (Illus.). x, 161p. (C). 1989. 12.95 (*0-917298-18-7*) MT Hist Soc.

Cons. Timothy Watts. LC 92-31224. 231p. 1993. 19.95 (*0-939149-70-2*) Soho Press.

***Cons.** Timothy Watts. 232p. 1995. pap. 10.00 (*1-56947-034-0*) Soho Press.

Cons & Scams. John J. Williams. Ed. by Laurie Williams. 50p. 1992. pap. 39.00 (*0-934274-40-1*) Consumertronics.

Con's Fabulous Journey to the Land of Gobel O'Glug. rev. ed. Peter O'Shaughnessy. (Illus.). 104p. (J). (gr. 6-10). 1992. reprint ed. pap. 5.95 (*0-947962-68-9*, Pub. by Anvil Bks Ltd IE) Irish Bks Media.

Consagracion Total: Absolute Surrender. Andrew Murray. (SPA.). 4.25 (*84-7228-633-9*, 220210, Pub. by Edit Clie SP) TSELF.

Consanguineous Marriages in the American Population. George B. Arner. LC 74-77992. (Columbia University. Studies in the Social Sciences: No. 83). reprint ed. 37.50 (*0-404-51083-3*) AMS Pr.

Consat: A System for Constraint Satisfaction. Hans Gusgen. (Research Notes in Artificial Intelligence Ser.). 1989. 29.95 (*1-55860-093-0*) Morgan Kaufmann.

Consat: A System for Constraint Satisfaction. Ed. by Hans W. Gusgen. 152p. (C). 1989. pap. text ed. 160.00 (*0-273-08813-0*, Pub. by Pitman Pubng UK) St Mut.

Conscience. Wilhelm Mensching. LC 61-16821. (Orig.). 1961. pap. 3.00 (*0-87574-117-7*) Pendle Hill.

Conscience. Spiros Zodhiates. LC 82-71843. 1982. pap. 5.99 (*0-89957-555-2*) AMG Pubs.

Conscience: A Structural Theory. M. Kroy. 244p. 1974. text ed. 61.00 (*0-7065-1462-9*, Pub. by Keter Pub IS) Coronet Bks.

Conscience: A Structural Theory. Michael Kroy. 244p. 1974. 28.95 (*0-87855-202-2*) Transaction Pubs.

Conscience: Its Freedom & Limitations. Institute of Pastoral Psychology Staff. Ed. by William C. Bier. LC 79-125029. (Pastoral Psychology Ser.: No. 6). 411p. reprint ed. pap. 117.20 (*0-7837-0438-0*, 2040761) Bks Demand.

Conscience: The Scales of Eternal Justice. Lester Sumrall. 64p. (Orig.). 1985. pap. text ed. 1.95 (*0-937580-42-2*) LeSEA Pub Co.

Conscience: Une Biologie du Moi. exp. ed. Israel Rosenfield. 1991. write for info. (*0-318-68136-6*) Knopf.

Conscience & Captivity: Religion in Eastern Europe. Janice Broun. LC 88-30942. (Illus.). 390p. (Orig.). (C). 1989. lib. bdg. 44.75 (*0-89633-129-6*); pap. text ed. 24.75 (*0-89633-130-X*) Ethics & Public Policy.

Conscience & Caring. Geoffrey Peterson. LC 82-7401. (Creative Pastoral Care & Counseling Ser.). 96p. reprint ed. pap. 27.40 (*0-685-23499-1*, 2029096) Bks Demand.

Conscience & Casuistry in Early Modern Europe. Ed. by Edmund Leites. (Ideas in Context Ser.). 270p. 1988. 59.95 (*0-521-30113-0*) Cambridge U Pr.

Conscience & Catholic Faith: Love & Fidelity. Anthony Marinelli. 1991. pap. 4.95 (*0-8091-3263-X*) Paulist Pr.

Conscience & Command: A Motive Theory of Law. Dale Segrest. Ed. by Harry W. Gilmer. LC 94-12526. (Scholars Press Studies in the Humanities: Vol. 18). 1994. pap. 24.95 (*1-55540-971-7*, 000118) Scholars Pr GA.

Conscience & Command: A Motive Theory of Law. Dale Segrest. LC 94-12526. (Studies in the Humanities: Vol. 18). 318p. 1994. 39.95 (*1-55540-970-9*, 000118) Scholars Pr GA.

Conscience & Conflict: A Trilogy of One-Actor Plays: Thomas Merton, Pope John XXIII, Martin Luther. Anthony T. Padovano. 128p. 1988. pap. 7.95 (*0-8091-3001-7*) Paulist Pr.

Conscience & Convenience: The Asylum & Its Alternatives in Progressive America. David J. Rothman. (C). 1987. pap. text ed. 19.75 (*0-673-39350-X*) HarpCollege.

Conscience & Courage. Baker. Date not set. 29.95 (*0-06-016808-0*, HarpT) HarpC.

***Conscience & Courage: Rescuers of Jews During the Holocaust.** Eva Fogelman. 1995. pap. 14.00 (*0-385-42028-5*, Anchor NY) Doubleday.

Conscience & Courage: The Rescuers of the Jews During the Holocaust. Eva Fogelman. LC 93-34021. 1994. pap. 23.95 (*0-385-42027-7*, Anchor NY) Doubleday.

Conscience & Its Recovery: From the Frankfurt School to Feminism. Guyton B. Hammond. LC 93-9223. (Studies in Religion & Culture). 190p. 1993. 32.50 (*0-8139-1446-9*) U Pr of Va.

Conscience & Memory: Meditations in a Museum of the Holocaust. Harold M. Kaplan. LC 93-15485. 1994. 24.95 (*0-226-42416-2*) U Ch Pr.

Conscience & Slavery: The Evangelistic Calvinist Domestic Missions, 1837-1861. Victor B. Howard. LC 90-34051. 280p. 1990. 27.50 (*0-87338-411-3*) Kent St U Pr.

Conscience & the Constitution: History, Theory, & the Law of the Reconstruction Amendments. David A. Richards. LC 92-42895. 248p. (C). 1993. text ed. 35.00 (*0-691-03231-9*) Princeton U Pr.

Conscience & the Constitution: With Remarks on the Recent Speech of the Hon. Daniel Webster in the Senate of the United States on the Subject of Slavery. M. Stuart. LC 72-83951. (Black Heritage Library Collection). 1977. 17.95 (*0-8369-8661-X*) Ayer.

Conscience & the King: A Study of Hamlet. Bertram L. Joseph. reprint ed. 29.00 (*0-403-08615-9*) Somerset Pub.

Conscience & the Reality of God: An Essay on the Experiential Foundations of Religious Knowledge. John C. Staten. (Religion & Reason Ser.: No. 36). xviii, 162p. (C). 1989. lib. bdg. 70.80 (*0-89925-435-7*) Mouton.

1550

An Asterisk (*) at the beginning of an entry indicates that the title is appearing in BIP for the first time.

An Asterisk (*) at the beginning of an entry indicates that the title is appearing in BIP for the first time.

1551

Consciousness of D. H. Lawrence: An Intellectual Biography. Daniel J. Schneider. LC 85-29415. xvi, 208p. 1986. 25.00 (*0-7006-0285-2*); pap. 12.95 (*0-7006-0452-9*) U Pr of KS.

Consciousness of Deserving. Burkes. 1992. pap. 14.95 (*0-9609888-7-4*) Red Rose Pr.

Consciousness of Earth. George Richter. 195p. (Orig.). 1989. pap. 10.00 (*0-9622662-0-5*) Gaia Pr.

Consciousness of Soul. John-Roger. LC 77-81388. 1976. pap. 5.00 (*0-914829-05-X*) Mandeville LA.

Consciousness of the Atom. Alice A. Bailey. LC 65-1061. 1922. 16.00 (*0-85330-001-1*) Lucis.

Consciousness of the Atom. Alice A. Bailey. LC 65-1061. 1973. pap. 8.00 (*0-85330-101-8*) Lucis.

Consciousness or Entropy? A Guide Toward a Fresh Understanding of Man's Purpose & Required Response. Klaus Heinemann. (Illus.). 176p. (Orig.). 1991. pap. 14.95 (*0-9630502-0-6*) Eloret.

***Consciousness-Raising: A Primer for Multicultural Counseling.** Woodrow M. Parker. 170p. 1988. pap. 19.95 (*0-398-06314-1*) C C Thomas.

Consciousness-Raising: A Primer for Multicultural Counseling. Woodrow M. Parker. 170p. (C). 1988. text ed. 35.95x (*0-398-05416-9*) C C Thomas.

Consciousness Reconsidered. Owen Flanagan. (Illus.). 256p. 1994. pap. 12.95 (*0-262-56077-1*, Bradford Bks) MIT Pr.

Consciousness Research: Theories & Insights. William P. Frost. 282p. (C). 1994. pap. text ed. 27.90 (*1-881003-01-9*) College Pr. Major studies are integrated. E.G., ANIMAL MINDS, (Griffin); THE BRAIN HAS A MIND OF ITS OWN (Restak); THE EVOLUTION OF CONSCIOUSNESS (Ornstein); THE REDISCOVERY OF THE MIND (Searle); BRIGHT AIR, BRILLIANT FIRE (Edelman); CONSCIOUSNESS EXPLAINED (Dennett); NATURE'S MIND (Gazzniga); FIRE IN THE BRAIN (Siegel); ELEMENTAL MIND (Herbert); THE OMEGA PROJECT (Ring); "Making up the Mind" (Sacks); THE CREATIVE LOOP (Hart); QUANTUM CONSCIOUSNESS (Penrose); SHAMANIC CONSCIOUSNESS & neurology. (pp. 282) $27.90 (Shipping included). College Press, P. O. Box 922, Dayton, OH 45409-0922.** ***Publisher Provided Annotation.

Consciousness Speaks: Conversations with Ramesh S. Balsekar. Ramesh S. Balsekar. Ed. by Wayne Liquorman. LC 92-74534. 392p. (Orig.). 1993. pap. 15.95 (*0-929448-14-6*) Advaita Pr CA.

Consciousness Unfolding. Joel Goldsmith. 1978. pap. 6.95 (*0-8065-0626-1*, Citadel Pr) Carol Pub Group.

***Conscoius State of Matter.** E. Ramon Milliner. (Illus.). 1995. pap. 29.95 (*0-615-00499-7*) Vantage.

Conscripted City. Marvin Schlegel. 1991. pap. 12.95 (*1-878901-36-2*) Hampton Roads Pub Co.

Conscription & the Attlee Governments: The Politics & Policy of National Service 1945-1951. L. V. Scott. (Oxford Historical Monographs). 320p. 1993. 53.00 (*0-19-820421-3*) OUP.

Conscription Controversy in Great Britain, 1900-18. R. J. Adams & Philip P. Poirier. LC 86-16181. 288p. 1987. 46.50 (*0-8142-0430-9*) Ohio St U Pr.

Conscription of a People. Katherine Atholl. LC 73-161703. reprint ed. 20.00 (*0-404-00414-8*) AMS Pr.

Conscription of Fashion: Utility Cloth, Clothing & Footwear, 1941-1952. Christopher Sladen. 150p. 1995. 51.95 (*1-85928-007-2*, Pub. by Scolar Pr UK) Ashgate Pub Co.

***Conscription Society: Administered Mass Organizations.** Gregory J. Kasza. LC 94-41148. 1995. write for info. (*0-300-06242-7*) Yale U Pr.

Conscripts & Deserters: The Army & French Society During the Revolution & Empire. Alan Forrest. (Illus.). 304p. 1989. 55.00 (*0-19-505937-9*) OUP.

Conscripts & Volunteers: Military Requirements, Social Values, & the All-Volunteer Force. Ed. by Robert K. Fullinwider. 1983. 56.00 (*0-317-05221-7*) IPPP.

Conscript's Mother. Robert Herrick. (Collected Works of Robert Herrick). 1988. reprint ed. lib. bdg. 79.00 (*0-7812-1276-6*) Rprt Serv.

Conscript's Mother see Collected Works of Robert Herrick

Conscripts of Conscience. Alfred Hassler. Bd. with Help Wanted!: The Experience of Some Quaker Conscientious Objectors. LC 70-147644. LC 70-147644. (Library of War & Peace; Conscrip. & Cons. Object.). 1972. Set lib. bdg. 46.00 (*0-8240-0414-0*) Garland.

Consecrated Cross-Eyed Bear: Stories from the Less-Solemn Side of Church. Charles Allbright. 160p. 1991. pap. 8.95 (*0-87483-159-8*) August Hse.

***Consecrated Life: Crossroads & Directions.** Marcello Azevedo. Tr. by Guillermo Cook. 196p. (Orig.). 1995. pap. 16.95 (*1-57075-003-3*) Orbis Bks.

***Consecrated Life Today.** St. Paul Publications Staff. 284p. 1993. pap. 35.00 (*0-85439-482-6*, Pub. by St Paul Pubns UK) St Mut.

Consecrated Way: The Consecrated Way to Christian Perfection. Alonzo T. Jones. 96p. (YA). (gr. 9-12). 1988. reprint ed. pap. 3.95 (*0-945460-02-3*) Upward Way.

Consecratio Medici & Other Papers. Harvey W. Cushing. LC 70-99688. (Essay Index Reprint Ser.). 1977. 23.95 (*0-8369-1565-8*) Ayer.

Consecration & the Spirit of Carmel. Mother Immaculata. LC 82-72203. (Living Meditation & Prayerbook Ser.). (Illus.). 270p. (Orig.). 1985. pap. text ed. 6.00 (*0-932406-08-4*) AFC.

Consecration of Idols. Malyala Pandurangarao. (Illus.). 32p. (Orig.). 1984. pap. 4.00 (*0-938924-21-4*) Sri Shirdi Sai.

Consecration of Learning: Lectures on Newman's Idea of a University. Fergal McGrath. LC 62-22015. 351p. reprint ed. pap. 100.10 (*0-7837-0454-2*, 2040777) Bks Demand.

Consecration to the Immaculate Heart of Mary: According to the Spirit of St. Louis De-Montfort's True Devotion to Mary. N. A. Norman. LC 88-50839. 68p. 1988. reprint ed. pap. 1.50 (*0-89555-342-2*) TAN Bks Pubs.

Conseil d'Egypte. Leonardo Sciascia. (FRE.). 1983. pap. 10.95 (*0-7859-4196-7*) Fr & Eur.

Conseil International de la Langue Francaise, Dictionnaire Francophone des Organizations Panafricaines: French Speaker's Dictionary of Pan-African Organizations. Conseil International de la Langue Francaise Staff & M. T. Zezeze-Kalonji. 291p. 1992. write for info. (*0-8288-6167-6*, 2853192385) Fr & Eur.

Conseil Prive & the Parlements in the Age of Louis XIV: A Study in French Absolutism. Albert Hamscher. LC 86-72879. (Transactions Ser.: Vol. 77, Pt. 2). 1987. pap. 25.00 (*0-87169-772-6*, T772-HAA) Am Philos.

Consejeria Cristiana Efectiva. Gary Collins. 208p. (SPA.). 1992. pap. 7.99 (*0-8254-1126-2*) Kregel.

Consejo Para los Recien Casados (Advice to Newlyweds) N. Wright. (SPA.). Date not set. 1.79 (*1-56063-133-3*, 497401) Editorial Unilit.

Consejos a la Familia: Advice for the Family. Fidel Molina. (SPA.). 3.95 (*84-7645-384-1*, 223495, Pub. by Edit Clie SP) TSELF.

Consejos a la Juventud. T. B. Maston. Tr. by H. F. Duffer, Jr. Orig. Title: Advice to Youth. 60p. (SPA.). 1990. reprint ed. pap. 2.25 (*0-311-46005-4*) Casa Bautista.

Consejos a los Ganadores De Almas: Words to Winners of Souls. Horatius Bonar. (SPA.). 2.95 (*84-7228-693-2*, 220224, Pub. by Edit Clie SP) TSELF.

Consejos Padre-Madre No Casados (Advice to Single Parents) S. V. Watts. (SPA.). Date not set. 1.79 (*0-685-74921-5*, 497410) Editorial Unilit.

Consejos-Padres De Ninos-Preescolar (Advice to Parents of Preschoolers) P. Meier. (SPA.). Date not set. 1.79 (*1-56063-334-4*, 497427) Editorial Unilit.

Consejos para Jovenes Predicadores. Ernesto Trenchard. 96p. (SPA.). 1957. pap. 3.99 (*0-8254-1726-0*) Kregel.

Consejos Para una Vida Santa: Thoughts for a Holy Life. Watchman Nee. (SPA.). 4.95 (*84-7645-234-9*, 223259, Pub. by Edit Clie SP) TSELF.

Consejos, Pensamientos y Notas de Lydia E. Pinban: (Copiados por P. Guayaba para la Benemerita America Villiarbinbin) Lydia Cabrera. Ed. by Isabel Castellanos. LC 92-74928. (Coleccion Chichereku Ser.). (Illus.). 95p. (Orig.). (SPA.). 1993. pap. 9.95 (*0-89729-654-0*) Ediciones.

Consejos Practicos a los Evangelistas: Quiet Talks on Soul Winning. S. D. Gordon. (SPA.). 4.95 (*84-7228-741-6*, 220246, Pub. by Edit Clie SP) TSELF.

Consejos Practicos Como Seguir a Cristo: Quiet Talks on Following Christ. S. D. Gordon. (SPA.). 4.95 (*84-7228-765-3*, 222240, Pub. by Edit Clie SP) TSELF.

Consejos Practicos Problemas Personales: Quiet Talks on Personal Problems. S. D. Gordon. (SPA.). 4.95 (*84-7228-737-8*, 220247, Pub. by Edit Clie SP) TSELF.

Consejos Practicos Servicio Cristiano: Quiet Talks about Christ's Service. S. D. Gordon. (SPA.). 4.95 (*84-7228-744-0*, 220251, Pub. by Edit Clie SP) TSELF.

Consejos Practicos Sobre el Hogar: Quiet Talks on the Home. S. D. Gordon. (SPA.). 5.50 (*84-7228-836-6*, 222241, Pub. by Edit Clie SP) TSELF.

Consejos Practicos Sobre el Poder: Quiet Talks on Power. S. D. Gordon. (SPA.). 4.95 (*84-7228-840-4*, 222242, Pub. by Edit Clie SP) TSELF.

Consejos Practicos Sobre la Oracion: Quiet Talks on Prayer. S. D. Gordon. (SPA.). 4.95 (*84-7228-756-4*, 220252, Pub. by Edit Clie SP) TSELF.

Consejos Sobre la Vida Cristiana: Thoughts on Christian Living. Watchman Nee. (SPA.). 5.95 (*84-7645-233-0*, 223260, Pub. by Edit Clie SP) TSELF.

***Consensus: A Liberal Looks at His Party.** Roy McLaren. 128p. 1995. lib. bdg. 20.00 (*0-8095-4927-1*) Borgo Pr.

Consensus: Issues & Problems. Ed. by Michael J. Smith & Kenneth W. Thompson. LC 85-17835. (Credibility of Institutions, Policies & Leadership Ser.: Vol. 12). 136p. 1986. pap. text ed. 15.00 (*0-8191-4862-8*) U Pr of Amer.

Consensus & Bibliography of Irish Seaweeds. M. D. Guiry. (Bibliotheca Phycologica Ser.: No. 44). 1979. pap. text ed. 36.00 (*3-7682-1209-2*) Lubrecht & Cramer.

Consensus & Conflict in African Societies: An Introduction to Sociology. Margaret Peil. LC 78-312566. (Illus.). 412p. reprint ed. pap. 117.50 (*0-8357-6073-1*, 2034492) Bks Demand.

Consensus & Conflict in Political Sociology. Seymour M. Lipset. (Illus.). 275p. 1985. 39.95 (*0-88738-051-4*); pap. 21.95 (*0-88738-608-3*) Transaction Pubs.

Consensus & Continuity, Seventeen Seventy-Six to Seventeen Eighty-Seven. Benjamin F. Wright. LC 84-19120. 60p. 1984. reprint ed. text ed. 39.75 (*0-313-22951-1*, WRC0C, Greenwood Pr) Greenwood.

Consensus & Ideology in American Politics. Herbert McClosky. (Reprint Series in Social Sciences). (C). 1993. reprint ed. pap. text ed. 1.00 (*0-8290-3149-9*, P-403) Irvington.

Consensus & the American Mission: The Credibility of Institutions, Policies, & Leadership, Vol. 14. Brian Klunk. Ed. & Intro. by Kenneth W. Thompson. LC 85-28971. 190p. (Orig.). 1986. lib. bdg. 44.50 (*0-8191-4867-9*, Pub. by White Miller Center); pap. text ed. 19.50 (*0-8191-4868-7*) U Pr of Amer.

Consensus, Conflict, & American Historians. Bernard Sternsher. LC 73-16531. 441p. reprint ed. pap. 125.70 (*0-317-27865-7*, 2056060) Bks Demand.

Consensus-Conflict Debate: Form & Content in Social Theories. Thomas Bernard. LC 83-2032. 264p. 1983. text ed. 49.00 (*0-231-05670-2*); pap. text ed. 19.50 (*0-231-05671-0*) Col U Pr.

Consensus Development at the NIH: Improving the Program. Institute of Medicine Staff. 96p. (C). 1990. pap. text ed. 15.00 (*0-309-04242-9*) Natl Acad Pr.

Consensus Diet. Thomas B. Stephens. 168p. 1994. pap. text ed. 9.95 (*0-9639624-0-X*) Pegasus Calif.

Consensus in Clinical Nutrition. Richard V. Heatley et al. LC 93-42563. (Illus.). 560p. (C). 1994. 110.00 (*0-521-44134-X*) Cambridge U Pr.

Consensus in Ireland: Approaches & Recessions. Ed. by Charles Townshend. (Illus.). 220p. 1988. 49.95 (*0-19-827545-5*) OUP.

Consensus on Hyperthermia for the 1990's: Clinical Practice in Cancer Treatment. Ed. by H. I. Bicher et al. LC 90-7312. (Advances in Experimental Medicine & Biology Ser.: Vol. 267). (Illus.). 556p. 1990. 129.50 (*0-306-43533-0*, Plenum Pr) Plenum.

Consensus Politics: From Attlee to Major. 2nd ed. Dennis Kavanagh & Peter Morris. (Making Contemporary Britain Ser.). 176p. 1994. reprint ed. pap. 17.95 (*0-631-19228-X*) Blackwell Pubs.

Consensus Politics from Attlee to Thatcher. Dennis A. Kavanagh & Peter Morris. Ed. by Anthony Seldon. (Making Contemporary Britain Ser.). 128p. 1989. pap. text ed. 18.95 (*0-631-16566-5*) Blackwell Pubs.

Consent: Concept, Capacity, Conditions, & Constraints. Ed. by Lyman T. Sargent. 240p. (Orig.). 1979. pap. 44.50 (*3-515-03213-4*) Coronet Bks.

Consent: The Means to an Active Faith According to St. Thomas Aquinas. Judith Barad. LC 91-27565. (American University Studies: Philosophy: Ser. V, Vol. 126). 126p. (C). 1992. text ed. 35.95 (*0-8204-1596-0*) P Lang Pubs.

Consent & Coercion to Sex & Marriage in Ancient & Medieval Societies. Ed. by Angeliki E. Laiou. LC 93-3070. 308p. 1993. 28.00 (*0-88402-213-7*, Dumbarton Rsch Lib) Dumbarton Oaks.

Consent & Confidentiality in the Health Care of Children & Adolescents: A Legal Guide. James M. Morrissey et al. 304p. 1986. text ed. 49.95 (*0-02-921800-4*) Free Pr.

Consent & the Incompetent Patient: Ethics, Law & Medicine, Proceedings of a Meeting Held at the Royal Society of Medicine, 9 December 1986. Ed. by Steven R. Hirsch & John Harris. LC 89-16557. (Gaskell Psychiatry Ser.). 111p. reprint ed. pap. 31.70 (*0-7837-3158-2*, 2042826) Bks Demand.

Consent, Coercion, & Limit: The Medieval Origins of Parliamentary Democracy. Arthur P. Monahan. xxi, 345p. 1987. 64.75 (*90-04-08304-9*) E J Brill.

Consent, Coercion, & Limit: The Medieval Origins of Parliamentary Democracy. Arthur P. Monahan. 1987. 49.95 (*0-7735-1012-5*, Pub. by McGill CN) U of Toronto Pr.

Consent of Voluntary Hospitalization: Report of the American Psychiatric Task Force on Consent to Voluntary Hospitalization. Francine Cournose et al. LC 93-10490. 1993. write for info. (*0-89042-245-1*) Am Psychiatric.

Consent Set. 2nd ed. Fay A. Rozovsky. 1990. 125.00 (*0-316-76059-5*) Little.

Consent Theory of Political Obligation. Ed. by Preston King. (International Series in Social & Political Thought). 176p. 1987. lib. bdg. 39.95 (*0-7099-5077-2*, Pub. by Croom Helm UK) Routledge Chapman & Hall.

Consent to Treatment. Nancy M. King. (Hospital Law in North Carolina Ser.: Chap. 14). 67p. (C). 1990. ring bd. 10.50 (*1-56011-178-X*, 85.03N) Institute Government.

Consent to Treatment: A Practical Guide. Fay A. Rozovsky. LC 83-81948. 669p. 1984. 80.00 (*0-316-76073-0*) Little.

Consent to Treatment: A Practical Guide. 2nd ed. Fay A. Rozovsky. 750p. 1989. 125.00 (*0-316-76057-9*) Little.

Consenting Hearts. Garda Parker. 512p. 1994. mass mkt. 4.99 (*0-8217-4690-1*) Zebra.

***Consequence.** Colbert Kearney. 324p. 1994. pap. 19.95 (*0-85640-506-X*, Pub. by Blackstaff Pr IE) Dufour.

Consequence of Error & Other Language Essays. Sterling Eisiminger. LC 90-23283. (American University Studies: Linguistics: Ser. XIII, Vol. 20). 274p. (C). 1991. text ed. 37.95 (*0-8204-1472-7*) P Lang Pubs.

Consequences. Sheila Bishop. 224p. 1981. pap. 1.50 (*0-449-50208-2*, Coventry) Fawcett.

Consequences. Douglas A. Powell et al. Ed. by Edward Mycue. (Took Modern Poetry in English Ser.: No. 35). (Illus.). 32p. (Orig.). 1993. pap. 4.50 (*1-879457-37-7*) Norton Coker Pr.

Consequences. Cynthia Victor. 320p. 1989. mass mkt. 5.50 (*0-671-66886-2*) PB.

***Consequences: A Murder Mystery.** Mary W. Syreen. LC 95-90091. 352p. (Orig.). 1995. pap. 7.95 (*0-9645798-9-8*) Lakesde Pr.

Consequences English Discussion Guidelines. DSR Inc. Staff. (Illus.). 4p. 1991. write for info. (*0-936731-09-5*) Devel Self Rel.

Consequences Ndebele Discussion Guidelines. DSR Inc. Staff. (Illus.). 4p. 1991. write for info. (*0-936731-12-5*) Devel Self Rel.

Consequences of Being Single. Douglas R. Austrom. LC 83-49354. (American University Studies: Anthropology & Science: Ser. XI, Vol. 6). 190p. (Orig.). (C). 1984. pap. text ed. 24.70 (*0-8204-0095-5*) P Lang Pubs.

Consequences of Child Abuse. M. Lynch & J. C. Roberts. 1982. text ed. 84.00 (*0-12-460570-2*) Acad Pr.

Consequences of Chromosome Imbalance: Principles, Mechanisms, & Models. Charles J. Epstein. (Developmental & Cell Biology Ser.: No. 18). (Illus.). 450p. 1986. 94.95 (*0-521-25464-7*) Cambridge U Pr.

Consequences of Cuts: The Effects of the Reagan Domestic Program on State & Local Governments. Richard P. Nathan et al. LC 83-60542. (Illus.). 221p. (Orig.). 1983. pap. 7.95 (*0-938882-06-6*) Woodrow Wilson Schl.

Consequences of Desire: Stories by Dennis Hathaway. Dennis Hathaway. LC 92-8947. (Flannery O'Connor Award for Short Fiction Ser.). 264p. 1992. 19.95 (*0-8203-1475-7*) U of Ga Pr.

Consequences of Determinism: A Theory of Determinism, Vol. 2. Ted Honderich. 272p. 1990. pap. 18.95 (*0-19-824283-2*) OUP.

Consequences of Divorce: Economic & Custodial Impact on Children & Adults. Ed. by Craig A. Everett. LC 91-32427. (Journal of Divorce & Remarriage). 350p. 1991. lib. bdg. 39.95 (*1-56024-187-X*); pap. text ed. 19.95 (*1-56024-188-8*) Haworth Pr.

Consequences of Economic Rhetoric. Ed. by Arjo Klamer et al. (Illus.). 325p. 1989. 64.95 (*0-521-34286-4*) Cambridge U Pr.

Consequences of Failure. William R. Corson. 1974. 7.95 (*0-393-05492-6*) Norton.

Consequences of Hermeneutics. Gianni Vattimo. (Philosophy & Literary Theory Ser.). (C). 1996. text ed. write for info. (*0-391-03762-5*) Humanities.

Consequences of Martin's Axiom. D. H. Fremlin. (Cambridge Tracts in Mathematics Ser.: No. 84). 352p. 1984. 79.95 (*0-521-25091-9*) Cambridge U Pr.

Consequences of Modernity. Anthony Giddens. LC 89-62426. 200p. 1990. 32.50 (*0-8047-1762-1*); pap. 10.95 (*0-8047-1891-1*) Stanford U Pr.

Consequences of Mortality Trends & Differentials. 204p. 1985. 21.00 (*92-1-151149-6*) UN.

Consequences of Nuclear & Chemical Disasters. V. C. Marshall. (Chemical Engineering Ser.). 350p. 1995. text ed. 115.95 (*0-13-170770-1*, 520805) P-H.

Consequences of Party Reform. Nelson W. Polsby. (Illus.). 1983. pap. 9.95 (*0-19-503315-9*) OUP.

Consequences of Peace: The New Internationalism & American Foreign Policy - A Twentieth Century Fund Book. James Chace. 208p. 1992. 25.00 (*0-19-507411-4*) OUP.

Consequences of Permanent Lay-off from the Civil Service: Results from a Survey of Retrenched Workers in Ghana. CFNPP Staff et al. (Working Paper Ser.). (C). 1993. pap. 7.00 (*1-56401-135-6*) Cornell Food.

Consequences of Phenomenology. Don Ihde. LC 85-9818. 210p. 1986. 59.50 (*0-88706-141-9*); pap. 19.95 (*0-88706-142-7*) State U NY Pr.

Consequences of Political Violence. Christopher Hewitt. (Illus.). 156p. 1993. 57.95 (*1-85521-399-0*, Pub. by Dartmth Pub UK) Ashgate Pub Co.

Consequences of Pragmatism: Essays 1972-1980. Richard Rorty. LC 82-2597. 239p. (C). 1992. pap. text ed. 14.95x (*0-8166-1064-9*) U of Minn Pr.

Consequences of "Pre-Publication Review" A Case Study of CIA Censorship of 'The CIA & the Cult of Intelligence' (Report: No.109). 67p. 1983. 3.00 (*0-86577-031-X*) Ctr Natl Security.

Consequences of Rapid Population Growth in Developing Countries. Institut National d'etudes Demographiques. 600p. 1991. 52.00 (*0-8448-1566-7*) Taylor & Francis.

Consequences of School Desegregation. Ed. by Christine H. Rossell & Willis D. Hawley. LC 83-6755. 221p. 1983. 34.95 (*0-87722-320-3*) Temple U Pr.

Consequences of the Clinton Victory. Ed. by Peter W. Schramm. 110p. 1994. pap. text ed. 6.00 (*1-878802-18-6*) J M Ashbrook Ctr Pub Affairs.

Consequences of the Peace: The New Internationalism & American Foreign Policy. James Chace. (Twentieth Century Fund Book Ser.). 240p. (C). 1993. reprint ed. pap. 10.95 (*0-19-508354-7*, 6262) OUP.

Consequences of the War to Great Britain. Francis W. Hirst. (Economic & Social History of the World War Ser.). 1934. 125.00 (*0-317-27424-4*) Elliots Bks.

Consequences of Theory. Ed. by Jonathan Arac & Barbara Johnson. LC 90-32670. (Selected Papers from the English Institute; 1982-83, New Ser.: No. 14). 256p. 1990. pap. text ed. 13.95x (*0-8018-4045-7*) Johns Hopkins.

Consequences of Writing: Enhancing Learning in the Disciplines. Robert P. Parker & Vera Goodkin. LC 86-14712. 183p. (Orig.). (C). 1987. pap. text ed. 17.50 (*0-86709-117-7*) Boynton Cook Pubs.

Consequences Shona Discussion Guidelines. DSR Inc. Staff. (Illus.). 4p. 1991. write for info. (*0-936731-11-7*) Devel Self Rel.

Consequential Damages in Comparative Context: From Breach of Promise to Monetary Remedy in the American, Scandinavian & International Law of Contracts & Sales. Joseph M. Lookofsky. 300p. 1989. pap. 137.50x (*87-574-5510-4*, Pub. by Almqv & Wiksell SW) Coronet Bks.

Consequential Light: Poems. Judy Vernon. 40p. (Orig.). 1987. pap. 4.95 (*0-9617776-1-3*) J Vernon.

Consequentialism. Philip Pettit. LC 92-36095. (International Research Library of Philosophy). 512p. 1993. 139.95 (*1-85521-304-4*, Pub. by Dartmth Pub UK) Ashgate Pub Co.

Consequentialism & Its Critics. Ed. by Samuel Scheffler. (Oxford Readings in Philosophy Ser.). 304p. 1988. pap. 16.95 (*0-19-875073-0*) OUP.

An Asterisk (*) at the beginning of an entry indicates that the title is appearing in BIP for the first time.

C

An Asterisk (*) at the beginning of an entry indicates that the title is appearing in BIP for the first time.

1553

Conservation of New World Parrots: Proceedings of the ICBP Parrot Working Group Meeting, St. Lucia, 1980. Ed. by Roger F. Pasquier. 486p. 1981. text ed. 22.50 (*0-87474-745-7*, PANPP) Smithsonian.

Conservation of Nonhuman Primates in Nineteen Seventy. Barbara Harrisson. (Primates in Medicine Ser.: Vol. 5). 1971. 22.50 (*3-8055-1243-0*) S Karger.

Conservation of Oil & Gas: A Legal History, 1948. Ed. by Blakely M. Murphy. LC 72-2858. (Use & Abuse of America's Natural Resources Ser.). 776p. 1972. reprint ed. 57.95 (*0-405-04522-0*) Ayer.

Conservation of Our Natural Resources. Carol Greenwald. (Science Ser.). 24p. (gr. 5 up). 1979. student ed 5.00 (*0-8209-0149-0*, S-11) ESP.

Conservation of Photographs (F-40) Eastman Kodak Co. Staff. LC 84-80244. (Illus.). 156p. (Orig.). 1985. pap. 29. 95 (*0-87985-352-2*) Saunders Photo.

***Conservation of Plant Biodiversity.** Otto H. Frankel et al. (Illus.). 320p. (C). 1995. write for info. (*0-521-46165-0*); pap. write for info. (*0-521-46731-4*) Cambridge U Pr.

Conservation of Plant Genes: DNA Banking & In Vitro Biotechnology. Ed. by Robert P. Adams & Janice E. Adams. (Illus.). 345p. 1991. text ed. 61.00 (*0-12-044140-3*) Acad Pr.

Conservation of Plant Genes, II: Utilization of Ancient & Modern DNA. Ed. by Marshall R. Crosby. (Monographs in Systematic Botany from the Missouri Botanical Garden: No. 48). (Illus.). 276p. 1994. 25.00 (*0-915279-20-7*) Miss Botan.

***Conservation of Stained Glass in America: A Manual for Studios & Caretakers.** Julie L. Sloan. LC 94-79618. 256p. (Orig.). 1995. pap. text ed. 24.95 (*1-884966-01-2*) Art Archit.

Conservation of Strangeness. Dennis Ross. LC 80-22044. 1980. pap. 3.95 (*0-914974-18-1*) Holmgangers.

Conservation of Tapestries & Embroideries: Proceedings of Meetings at the Institut Royal du Patrimoine Artistique Brussels, Belgium. Getty Conservation Institute Staff. LC 89-2058. (Illus.). 133p. 1989. pap. 35. 00 (*0-89236-154-9*) J P Getty Trust.

Conservation of the Orpheus Mosaic at Paphos, Cyprus. LC 91-19192. (Illus.). 88p. 1991. pap. 25.00 (*0-89236-188-3*) J P Getty Trust.

Conservation of the Sea. LC 93-19872. (Junior Library of Ecology). (Illus.). 32p. (J). (gr. 4 up). 1994. lib. bdg. 14. 95 (*0-7910-2102-5*) Chelsea Hse.

Conservation of Vegetation in Africa South of the Sahara. Inga Hedberg & Olov Hedberg. 322p. (Orig.). 1968. pap. text ed. 45.00x (*0-685-13602-7*) Coronet Bks.

Conservation of Wall Paintings. L. Mora et al. Tr. by H. J. Plenderleith & E. Schwartzbaum. (Conservation in the Arts, Archaeology, & Architecture Ser.). 656p. 1984. text ed. 155.00 (*0-408-10812-6*) Buttrwrth-Heinemann.

Conservation of Wall Paintings. Ed. by David Park. LC 91-19192. 130p. 1991. pap. 42.50 (*0-89236-162-X*) J P Getty Trust.

Conservation of Water & Related Land Resources. 2nd ed. Peter E. Black. 352p. (C). 1988. 60.50 (*0-8476-7567-X*) Rowman.

Conservation of West & Central African Rainforests: Conservation de la Foret Dense en Afrique Centrale et de l'Ouest. Ed. by Mohan Munasinghe et al. LC 92-26870. (Technical Paper, 1253-7494 Environment Ser.: No. 1). 366p. (ENG & FRE.). 1992. 21.95 (*0-8213-2256-7*, 12256) World Bank.

Conservation of Wild Plants in Glasgow. Ed. by J. H. Dickson. (Aberdeen University Press Bks.). (Illus.). 144p. 1991. 25.45 (*0-08-041200-9*, Pub. by Aberdeen U Pr) Macmillan.

Conservation Operations Supervisor. (Career Examination Ser.: C-3591). 1994. 34.95 (*0-8373-3591-4*, C-3591) Nat Learn.

Conservation Options: A Landowner's Guide. LC 93-11109. 1993. 7.50 (*0-943915-10-4*) Land Trust DC.

Conservation Pieces. Humphrey Mackworth-Praed. 220p. (C). 1991. pap. text ed. 110.00 (*1-85341-046-2*, Pub. by Surrey Beatty & Sons AT) St Mut.

Conservation Policies for Sustainable Hillslope Farming. Ed. by Istiqlal Amien et al. (Illus.). 368p. (C). 1992. text ed. 35.00 (*0-935734-28-7*) Soil & Water Conserv.

Conservation Policies in the Asia-Pacific Region: A Survey. Saicheue Supavud. (Research Materials Ser.: RM-83-5). 354p. reprint ed. pap. 100.90 (*0-685-15237-5*, 2027142) Bks Demand.

Conservation Politics: The Senate Career of Clinton P. Anderson. Richard A. Baker. LC 85-8748. 352p. reprint ed. pap. 100.40 (*0-7837-5865-0*, 2045584) Bks Demand.

Conservation Practices for Slide & Photograph Collections. Christine L. Sundt. 1989. 15.00 (*0-685-54077-4*) Visual Resources Assn.

Conservation Problems in Antarctica. Ed. by Bruce C. Parker. LC 72-85836. (Illus.). 356p. 1972. 30.00 (*0-8139-0840-X*) U Pr of Va.

***Conservation Research.** National Gallery of Art Staff. 1992. 35.00 (*0-89468-178-8*) Natl Gallery Art.

***Conservation Research 1995.** (Studies in the History of Art: No. 51). (Illus.). 160p. 1995. pap. 30.00 (*0-89468-208-3*) U Pr of New Eng.

Conservation Science in the U. K. Norman H. Tennent. (Illus.). 128p. (Orig.). (C). 1993. 29.50 (*1-873936-22-2*, Pub. by J & J Sci Pubs UK) Bks Intl VA.

Conservation Study Guide. 2nd ed. Douglas D. Piirto. 352p. 1991. per. 24.95 (*0-8403-7066-0*) Kendall-Hunt.

Conservation Surgery & Radiation Therapy in the Treatment of Operable Breast Cancer. J. M. Vaeth. (Frontiers of Radiation Therapy & Oncology Ser.: Vol. 17). (Illus.). viii, 156p. 1982. 113.75 (*3-8055-3560-0*) S Karger.

Conservation Techniques in Botanic Gardens: Proceedings of the International Conference, Cordoba, May 10-14, 1987. Ed. by J. E. Hernandez-Bermejo et al. 205p. 1990. pap. 75.50 (*1-878762-17-6*, 043409) Koeltz Sci Bks.

***Conservation Tillage - Bibliography: January 1991-December 1993.** Jane P. Gates. 91p. (Orig.). (C). 1994. pap. text ed. 40.00x (*0-7881-1445-X*) Diane Pub.

Conservation Tillage in Temperate Agroecosystems: Development & Adaptation to Soil, Climatic, & Biological Constraints. M. R. Carter. 1993. 89.95 (*0-87371-571-3*, S604) Lewis Pubs.

Conservation Tillage Systems & Management. Midwest Plan Service Engineers Staff. LC 92-37291. (Illus.). (Orig.). 1992. pap. 15.00 (*0-89373-088-2*, MWPS-45) MidWest Plan Serv.

Conservation Today. David Pearce. 256p. 1989. 49.95 (*0-415-00778-X*, A3718); pap. 16.95 (*0-415-03914-2*, A3722) Routledge.

Conservation Treatment Procedures: A Manual of Step-by-Step Procedures for the Maintenance & Repair of Library Materials. 2nd ed. Carolyn C. Morrow & Carole Dyal. LC 86-20948. 225p. 1986. lib. bdg. 32.00 (*0-87287-437-0*) Libs Unl.

Conservation under FDR. A. L. Owen. LC 83-3966. 288p. 1983. text ed. 49.95 (*0-275-91055-5*, C1055, Praeger Pubs) Greenwood.

Conservation with Equity: Strategies for Sustainable Development. Peter Jacobs & David Munro. (International Union for the Conservation of Nature & Natural Resources: A Belhaven Press Book Ser.). 466p. 1987. pap. 33.50 (*2-88032-926-4*, Pub. by Pinter Pubs UK) St Martin.

Conservationist. Nadine Gordimer. 1983. pap. 10.00 (*0-14-004716-6*, Penguin Bks) Viking Penguin.

Conservation's Communicator. Henry E. Clepper & Elwood R. Maunder. (Illus.). 1976. fiche write for info. (*0-318-51909-7*) Forest Hist Soc.

Conservations with Richard Wright. Ed. by Keneth Kinnamon & Michel Fabre. LC 93-13938. (Literary Conversations Ser.). 288p. 1993. text ed. 32.50 (*0-87805-632-7*); pap. 14.95 (*0-87805-633-5*) U Pr of Miss.

Conservationworks Book: Practical Conservation Tips for the Home & Outdoors. Lisa Capone & Cady Goldfield. LC 92-6836. (Illus.). 96p. 1992. pap. 7.95 (*1-878239-11-2*) AMC Books.

Conservatism: A Contribution to the Sociology of Knowledge. Karl Mannheim. Ed. by David Kettler et al. Tr. by Elizabeth King. (International Library of Sociology). 256p. (C). 1986. text ed. 49.95 (*0-7102-0338-1*, RKP) Routledge.

Conservatism: Dream & Reality. Robert Nisbet. LC 86-1375. (Concepts in Social Thought Ser.). 128p. (Orig.). 1986. pap. text ed. 12.95 (*0-8166-1526-8*) U of Minn Pr.

Conservatism: From John Adams to Churchill. Peter R. Viereck. LC 78-827. 191p. 1978. reprint ed. text ed. 35. 00 (*0-313-20263-X*, VICO, Greenwood Pr) Greenwood.

Conservatism among the Iroquois at the Six Nations Reserve. Annemarie A. Shimony. (Iroquois & Their Neighbors Ser.). 344p. reprint ed. pap. text ed. 18.95 (*0-8156-2630-4*) Syracuse U Pr.

Conservatism & Collectivism, Eighteen Eighty-Six to Nineteen Fourteen. Matthew Fforde. 1990. text ed. 42. 00 (*0-685-47276-0*, Pub. by Edinburgh U Pr UK) Col U Pr.

Conservatism & Collectivism 1886-1914. Matthew Fforde. 232p. 1990. 42.00 (*0-7486-0139-2*, Pub. by Edinburgh U Pr UK) Col U Pr.

Conservatism & Collectivism, 1886-1914. Matthew Fforde. 232p. 1991. pap. text ed. 29.00 (*0-7486-0152-X*, Pub. by Edinburgh U Pr UK) Col U Pr.

Conservatism & the Conservative Party in 19th-Century Britain. B. I. Coleman. 192p. (C). 1988. pap. text ed. 13.95 (*0-7131-6496-4*, Pub. by E Arnold UK) Routledge Chapman & Hall.

Conservatism As an Ideology. Samuel P. Huntington. (Reprint Series in Political Science). (C). 1993. reprint ed. pap. text ed. 1.00 (*0-8290-2625-8*, P-136) Irvington.

Conservatism for Our Time. Torbjorn Tannsjo. (Illus.). 183p. 1990. 55.00 (*0-415-04700-5*, A4524) Routledge.

Conservatism in America. Clinton Rossiter. 320p. 1982. pap. 13.95 (*0-674-16510-1*) HUP.

Conservatism in America: The Thankless Persuasion. 2nd rev. ed. Clinton L. Rossiter. LC 80-27937. xii, 306p. 1981. reprint ed. text ed. 35.00 (*0-313-22720-9*, ROCN, Greenwood Pr) Greenwood.

Conservatism in Britain & America: Rhetoric & Reality. Ed. by Ralph Miliband et al. (Socialist Register Ser.). 528p. (C). 1987. pap. 12.00 (*0-85345-730-1*, Pub. by Merlin UK) Monthly Rev.

Conservatism in England. F. J. Hearnshaw. LC 67-24582. 1968. reprint ed. 48.00 (*0-86527-031-7*) Fertig.

Conservatism Revisited: With the Addition of "The New Conservatism-What Went Wrong" enl. rev. ed. Peter R. Viereck. LC 78-831. 192p. 1978. reprint ed. text ed. 49. 75 (*0-313-20299-0*, VICR, Greenwood Pr) Greenwood.

Conservative - Moderate - Liberal: The Biblical Authority Debate. Ed. by Charles R. Blaisdell. 160p. (Orig.). 1991. pap. 14.99 (*0-8272-0455-8*) Chalice Pr.

Conservative Against Hitler: Ulrich von Hassell: Diplomat in Imperial Germany, the Weimar Republic & the Third Reich, 1881-1944. Gregor Schollgen. Tr. by Louise Willmot. LC 90-48824. 190p. 1991. text ed. 45.00 (*0-312-05784-9*) St Martin.

Conservative Agenda for Black Americans. 2nd ed. Ed. by Joseph Perkins. 80p. 1987. pap. 8.00 (*0-89195-041-9*) Heritage Found.

Conservative, American & Jewish-I Wouldn't Have It Any Other Way. Jacob Neusner. LC 93-78463. 240p. 1993. pap. 9.99 (*1-56384-048-0*) Huntington Hse.

Conservative American Revolution. Samuel E. Morison. (George Rogers Clark Lecture April 22, 1975 Ser.: Inaugural). (Illus.). 48p. 1985. reprint ed. lib. bdg. 22.50 (*0-8191-4875-X*) U Pr of Amer.

Conservative Capitalism in Britain & the United States: A Critical Appraisal. Kenneth Hoover & Raymond Plant. 368p. 1988. text ed. 45.00 (*0-415-01583-9*); pap. text ed. 16.95 (*0-415-01584-7*) Routledge.

Conservative Care of Low Back Pain. Arthur H. White & Robert Anderson. (Illus.). 472p. 1991. 70.00 (*0-683-09007-0*) Williams & Wilkins.

Conservative Century: The Conservative Party since 1900. Ed. by Anthony Seldon & Stuart Ball. (Illus.). 800p. 1994. 29.95 (*0-19-820238-5*) OUP.

Conservative Constraints: North Carolina & the New Deal. Carl Abrams. LC 91-48025. (Twentieth-Century America Ser.). 312p. 1992. 39.95 (*0-87805-559-2*) U Pr of Miss.

Conservative Crack-Up. R. Emmett Tyrrell, Jr. 320p. 1992. 23.00 (*0-671-66038-1*) Summit Bks.

Conservative Crisis & the Rule of Law: Attitudes of Bar & Bench 1887-1895. Arnold M. Paul. 18.50 (*0-8446-0839-4*) Peter Smith.

Conservative Dentistry: An Integrated Approach. Ed. by P. H. Jacobsen. (Illus.). 224p. 1990. pap. text ed. 47.00 (*0-443-03958-5*) Churchill.

Conservative Echoes in Fin-de-Siecle Parisian Art Criticism. Michael Marlais. (Illus.). 272p. 1992. text ed. 35.00 (*0-271-00773-7*) Pa St U Pr.

***Conservative Futurist.** (Mr. Never Too Late Ser.: No. 3). 20p. 1995. pap. 1.50 (*0-9641448-8-3*) N Late Pub.

***Conservative Futurist.** (Mr. Never Too Late Ser.: No. 4). 20p. 1995. pap. 1.50 (*0-9641448-1-6*) N Late Pub.

***Conservative Futurist.** (Mr. Never Too Late Ser.: No. 5). 20p. 1995. pap. 1.50 (*0-9641448-4-0*) N Late Pub.

***Conservative Futurist.** (Mr. Never Too Late Ser.: No. 6). 20p. 1995. pap. 1.50 (*0-9641448-5-9*) N Late Pub.

***Conservative Futurist.** (Mr. Never Too Late Ser.: No. 1). 20p. 1995. pap. 1.50 (*0-9641448-2-4*) N Late Pub.

***Conservative Futurist.** (Mr. Never Too Late Ser.: No. 2). 20p. 1995. pap. 1.50 (*0-9641448-0-8*) N Late Pub.

Conservative Government & the End of the British Empire, 1951-1957, Pt. 1. Ed. by David Goldsworthy. (British Documents on the End of the Empire: Vol. 1). 471p. 1994. pap. 115.00 (*0-11-290535-8*, HM05358, Pub. by HMSO UK) UNIPUB.

Conservative Government & the End of the Empire, 1951-1957, Pt. 2. Ed. by David Goldsworthy. (British Documents on the End of the Empire: Vol. 2). 437p. 1994. pap. 115.00 (*0-11-290536-6*, HM05366, Pub. by HMSO UK) UNIPUB.

Conservative Government & the End of the Empire, 1951-1957, Pt. 3. Ed. by David Goldsworthy. (British Documents on the End of the Empire: Vol. 3). 450p. 1994. pap. 115.00 (*0-11-290537-4*, HM05374, Pub. by HMSO UK) UNIPUB.

Conservative Hindu of Colonial India: Raja Radhakan'a Deb & His Milieu 1784-1867. Syamalendu Sengupta. 1990. 22.50 (*0-685-48708-3*, Pub. by Navrang) S Asia.

Conservative Imagination: From Edmund Burke to Tom Stoppard. Philip Thody. LC 93-20259. 192p. 1993. text ed. 39.95 (*0-312-09707-7*) St Martin.

Conservative Investor's Guide to Trading Options. LeRoy Gross. 1989. 21.95 (*0-317-03941-5*) NY Inst Finance.

Conservative Investor's Guide to Trading Options. LeRoy Gross. 1989. 21.95 (*0-13-168121-4*) P-H.

Conservative Investors Sleep Well. Philip A. Fisher. (Wall Street Wizard Ser.). 180p. 1975. 21.95 (*0-931133-05-X*, Busn Class) Pac Pub Grp.

Conservative Judaism: Our Ancestors to Our Descendants. 7.95 (*0-686-96053-X*); teacher ed 3.00 (*0-686-99690-9*); pap. 5.00 (*0-686-99689-5*) United Syn Bk.

Conservative Judaism: The New Century. Neil Gillman. LC 93-14637. 1993. 18.00 (*0-87441-547-0*) Behrman.

Conservative Judaism & Jewish Law. Ed. by S. Siegel. 20. 00 (*0-87068-428-0*); pap. 11.95 (*0-685-02911-5*) Ktav.

Conservative Judaism in America: A Biographical Dictionary & Sourcebook. Pamela S. Nadell. LC 87-31782. (Jewish Denominations in America Ser.). 436p. 1988. text ed. 79.50 (*0-313-24205-4*, NCJ, Greenwood Pr) Greenwood.

Conservative Management of Sports Injuries. Robert H. Hazel, Jr. 800p. 1994. write for info. (*0-683-03944-X*) Williams & Wilkins.

Conservative Management of Squint. W. Aust. Tr. by C. H. Bedwell & H. Obstfeld. (Illus.). 152p. 1970. 22.50 (*3-8055-0752-6*) S Karger.

Conservative Manifesto. William T. Hennessy. 104p. (Orig.). 1993. pap. text ed. 10.00 (*0-9638816-0-4*) Right Press.

Conservative Millenarians: The Romantic Experience in Bavaria. Paul Gottfried. LC 74-20028. 184p. reprint ed. pap. 52.50 (*0-7837-5601-1*, 2045507) Bks Demand.

***Conservative Mind: From Burke to Eliot.** Russell Kirk. 544p. 1995. pap. 17.95 (*0-89526-724-1*) Regnery Pub.

Conservative Mind: From Burke to Eliot. 7th rev. ed. Russell Kirk. LC 86-42909. 1986. 25.00 (*0-89526-670-9*) Regnery Pub.

Conservative Minds in America. Ronald Lora. Ed. by David D. Van Tassel. LC 79-14219. 274p. 1980. reprint ed. text ed. 35.00 (*0-313-21468-9*, LOCM, Greenwood Pr) Greenwood.

***Conservative Modernity.** Ed. by Cora Kaplan & David Glover. (New Formations Twenty-Seven Ser.). 192p. (C). 1996. pap. 19.95 (*0-85315-814-2*, Pub. by Lawrence & Wishart UK) Humanities.

Conservative Movement. Paul Gottfried & Thomas Fleming. (Social Movements Past & Present Ser.). 152p. 1988. lib. bdg. 23.95 (*0-8057-9723-8*, Twayne); pap. 11. 95 (*0-8057-9724-6*, Twayne) Macmillan.

Conservative Movement. rev. ed. Paul Gottfried. (Social Movements Past & Present Ser.). 250p. 1992. text ed. 26.95 (*0-8057-9749-1*, Twayne); pap. 14.95 (*0-8057-3850-9*, Twayne) Macmillan.

Conservative Mythology & Public Policy in America. Arnold Vedlitz. LC 88-17961. (Illus.). 184p. 1988. text ed. 49.95 (*0-275-92641-9*, C2641, Praeger Pubs) Greenwood.

Conservative Papers. Intro. by M. R. Laird. LC 74-117774. (Essay Index Reprint Ser.). 1977. 21.95 (*0-8369-1748-0*) Ayer.

***Conservative Party & British Politics, 1902-1951.** Stuart Ball. LC 94-31525. (Seminar Studies in History). (C). 1900. pap. text ed. 11.95 (*0-582-08002-9*, Pub. by Longman UK) Longman.

***Conservative Party & the Trade Unions.** Peter Dorey. LC 95-12516. 1995. write for info. (*0-415-06487-2*) Routledge.

Conservative Party Conferences: The Hidden System. Richard N. Kelly. LC 88-25014. 224p. 1989. text ed. 59. 95 (*0-7190-2955-4*, Pub. by Manchester Univ Pr UK) St Martin.

Conservative Political Tradition in Britain & the United States. Arthur Aughey et al. LC 91-42201. 180p. 1992. 39.50 (*0-8386-3500-8*) Fairleigh Dickinson.

Conservative Politics in Western Europe. Ed. by Zig Layton-Henry. LC 81-710. 320p. 1982. text ed. 32.50 (*0-312-16418-1*) St Martin.

***Conservative Radicalism: A Sociology of Conservative Party Youth Structures & Libertarianism 1970-1992.** Timothy Evans. (Illus.). 192p. 1995. 39.95 (*1-57181-872-3*) Berghahn Bks.

Conservative Regime: South Carolina, 1877-1890. William J. Cooper, Jr. LC 91-17958. 239p. 1991. pap. text ed. 11.95 (*0-8071-1718-8*) La State U Pr.

Conservative Regime: South Carolina, 1877-1890. William J. Cooper. LC 67-26859. (Johns Hopkins University Studies in Historical & Political Science). (Illus.). 239p. reprint ed. pap. 68.20 (*0-317-42318-5*, 2025810) Bks Demand.

Conservative Revolution? The Thatcher-Reagan Decade in Perspective. Ed. by Andrew Adonis & Tim Hames. 200p. 1994. text ed. 69.95 (*0-7190-3668-2*, Pub. by Manchester Univ Pr UK); text ed. 29.95 (*0-7190-3669-0*, Pub. by Manchester Univ Pr UK) St Martin.

Conservative Revolution in America. Guy Sorman. Tr. by Jane Kaplan. LC 85-1798. 256p. 1985. pap. 9.95 (*0-89526-818-3*) Regnery Pub.

Conservative Texts: An Anthology. Ed. by Roger Scruton. LC 90-44031. 320p. 1991. text ed. 45.00 (*0-312-05332-0*); pap. 16.95 (*0-312-05598-6*) St Martin.

Conservative Thought in Latin America: The Ideas of Laureano Gomez. James D. Henderson. (Monographs in International Studies, Latin America Ser.: No.13). 150p. (Orig.). 1988. pap. text ed. 16.00 (*0-89680-148-9*) Ohio U Pr.

Conservatively Speaking. Rene Wormser. (Illus.). 1979. 10. 00 (*0-9603250-0-X*) Dorland Pub Co.

Conservatives & the Union. James Mitchell. 224p. 1989. 45. 00 (*0-7486-0123-6*, Pub. by Edinburgh U Pr UK) Col U Pr.

Conservatives & the Union: A Study of Conservative Party Attitudes to Scotland. James Mitchell. 192p. 1991. pap. text ed. 29.00 (*0-7486-0176-7*, Pub. by Edinburgh U Pr UK) Col U Pr.

Conservatives in an Age of Change: The Nixon & Ford Administrations. A. James Reichley. LC 81-1672. 482p. 1981. 38.95 (*0-8157-7380-3*); pap. 16.95 (*0-8157-7379-X*) Brookings.

Conservatives in Court. Lee Epstein. LC 84-15287. 216p. (C). 1985. text ed. 33.00x (*0-87049-449-X*); pap. 17.00x (*0-87049-567-4*) U of Tenn Pr.

Conservatives in Power: A Study in Frustration. Edwin L. Dale, Jr. LC 60-5921. 214p. reprint ed. pap. 61.00 (*0-317-29959-X*, 2051723) Bks Demand.

Conservatives in Power: The Task of Governing. Terry Eastland. 1992. 24.95 (*0-02-908681-7*) Free Pr.

Conservatives in the Progressive Era: The Taft Republicans of 1912. Norman M. Wilensky. LC 65-63875. (University of Florida Monographs: Social Sciences: No. 25). 84p. reprint ed. pap. 25.00 (*0-7837-4998-8*, 2044665) Bks Demand.

Conservatives Stalk the House. Edwin Feulner, Jr. LC 83-1684. 206p. 1983. 14.95 (*0-89803-112-5*) Green Hill.

Conservators of Hope: The Horace M. Albright Conservation Lectures. Intro. by D. Teeguarden. LC 88-27653. 568p. 1989. lib. bdg. 14.95 (*0-89301-111-8*) U of Idaho Pr.

Conservator's Song. William C. Bowie. LC 92-29036. 88p. 1993. 17.50 (*1-55728-275-7*); pap. 9.95 (*1-55728-276-5*) U of Ark Pr.

Conservatorship Book: California. 2nd ed. Lisa Goldoftas & Carolyn Farren. (Illus.). 350p. 1994. pap. 29.95 (*0-87337-272-7*) Nolo Pr.

***Conserve Nineteen Ninety-Three: The New Water Agenda, 2 vols., Set.** (Illus.). 2034p. 1993. pap. 85.00 (*0-89867-722-X*) Am Water Resources.

Conserve Ninety Proceedings. NWWA Staff. 1310p. 1990. 87.50 (*1-56034-086-X*) Natl Water Well.

Conserve Tuvs, Eh? M. Mark Orkin & Isaac Bickerstaff. (Illus.). 96p. 1986. pap. 9.95 (*0-7737-5077-0*, Pub. by Stoddart Pubng CN) Genl Dist Srvs.

Conserver Society. Ed. by Karl E. Henion, II & Thomas C. Kinnear. LC 79-17463. (American Marketing Association, Proceedings Ser.). 221p. reprint ed. pap. 63. 00 (*0-317-42263-4*, 2023358) Bks Demand.

***Conserver Society: Alternatives for Sustainability.** Ted Trainer. (Illus.). 256p. (C). 1995. text ed. 55.00 (*1-85649-275-3*, Pub. by Zed Books UK); pap. 19.95 (*1-85649-276-1*, Pub. by Zed Books UK) Humanities.

An Asterisk (*) at the beginning of an entry indicates that the title is appearing in BIP for the first time.

An Asterisk (*) at the beginning of an entry indicates that the title is appearing in BIP for the first time.

1555

Consolation; a Poem Addressed to Lady Brydges. Edward Quillinan. Bd. with Monthermer; a Poem. LC 75-31249.; Sacrifice of Isabel. A Poem. LC 75-31249.; Elegiac Verses, Addressed to a Lady. LC 75-31249.; Woodcuts & Verses. LC 75-31249.; Carmina Brigensiana. Domestic Poems. LC 75-31249. LC 75-31249. (Romantic Context: Poetry 1789-1830 Ser.: Vol. 98). 1978. reprint ed. Set lib. bdg. 57.00 (*0-8240-2197-5*) Garland.

Consolation for Our Grammar Schools. John Brinsley. LC 71-177. (English Experience Ser.: No. 203). 84p. 1969. reprint ed. 40.00 (*90-221-0203-3*) Walter J Johnson.

Consolation of Boethius: An Analytical Inquiry into His Intellectual Processes & Goals. Stephen Varvis. LC 91-39930. 240p. 1991. lib. bdg. 89.95 (*0-7734-9976-8*) E Mellen.

Consolation of Philosophy. Axel Boethius. (Classics Ser.). 192p. 1976. mass mkt. 9.95 (*0-14-044208-1*, Penguin Classics) Viking Penguin.

***Consolation of Philosophy.** Gerson. (Janus Ser.: TTL). Date not set. 25.00 (*0-614-04116-3*) Abaris Bks.

Consolation of Philosophy: Boethius. Richard H. Green. 160p. (C). 1962. pap. write for info. (*0-02-346450-X*) Macmillan.

Consolation of Philosophy see Theological Tractates

Consolation of Rhetoric: John Henry Newman & the Realism of Personalist Thought. David M. Whalen. 350p. 1994. 64.95 (*1-883255-10-4*, Cath Scholar Pr); pap. 44.95 (*1-883255-03-1*, Cath Scholar Pr) Intl Scholars.

Consolation of the Blessed. Elizabeth Petroff. (Illus.). 224p. (C). 1980. 12.95 (*0-686-32835-3*) Alta Gaia Bks.

Consolations of Philosophy: Hobbes's Secret; Spinoza's Way. Henry M. Rosenthal. LC 88-24927. 248p. (C). 1989. 29.95 (*0-87722-610-5*) Temple U Pr.

Consolations of Space: The Place of Romance in Hawthorne, Melville, & James. Pamela Schirmeister. LC 89-48085. 240p. 1990. 32.50 (*0-8047-1793-1*) Stanford U Pr.

Consolatory Rhetoric: Grief, Symbol, & Ritual in the Greco-Roman Era. Donovan J. Ochs. LC 93-16393. (Studies in Rhetoric-Communication). (C). 1993. 29.95 (*0-87249-885-9*) U of SC Pr.

Console & Classify: The French Psychiatric Profession in the Nineteenth Century. Jan Goldstein. (Illus.). 512p. (C). 1990. pap. 24.95 (*0-521-39555-0*) Cambridge U Pr.

Console One Another: A Guide to Christian Funerals. Terence P. Curley. LC 93-3540. 104p. (Orig.). 1993. pap. 8.95 (*1-55612-600-X*) Sheed & Ward MO.

Console One Another: The Order of Christian Funerals - A Commentary. William Cieslak. 128p. (Orig.). 1990. pap. 9.95 (*0-912405-68-6*) Pastoral Pr.

Consolidated Agreements of the Motor Industry. Ed. by National Industrial Council Staff & B. G. Du Preez. 1989. ring bd. write for info. (*0-7021-2263-7*, Pub. by Juta SA) W W Gaunt.

Consolidated Agreements of the National Industrial Council for the Iron, Steel, Engineering & Metallurgical Industry. Ed. by National Industrial Council Staff & David Levy. 1987. ring bd. write for info. (*0-7021-1920-2*, Pub. by Juta SA) W W Gaunt.

Consolidated Approach to Activated Sludge Process Design. S. H. Jenkins. 1975. pap. write for info. (*0-08-019835-X*, Pergamon Pr) Elsevier.

***Consolidated Assistance Program: Reforming Welfare by Synchronizing Public Assistance Benefits.** Oren M. Levin-Waldman. (Orig.). 1995. pap. 3.00 (*0-941276-10-4*, J Levy Econ Inst) Bard Coll Pubns.

Consolidated Balance Sheets. George H. Newlove. LC 82-48380. (Accountancy in Transition Ser.). 309p. 1982. lib. bdg. 15.00 (*0-8240-5325-7*) Garland.

Consolidated Bargaining in California Construction: An Appraisal of Twenty-Five Years' Experience. Gordon W. Bertram. (Monograph & Research Ser.: No. 12). 259p. 1966. 6.00 (*0-89215-013-0*) U Cal LA Indus Rel.

Consolidated Cape Provincial Ordinances - Gekonsolideerde Kaapse Provinsiale Ordonnansies, 3 vols., Set. Ed. by Adv J. Cavvadas. (AFR & ENG.). 288.00 (*0-7021-0122-2*, Pub. by Juta SA) W W Gaunt.

Consolidated Catalog of League of Nations Publications Offered for Sale. Mary E. Birchfield. LC 75-17970. 477p. 1976. 60.00 (*0-379-00328-7*) Oceana.

Consolidated Catalog to the Index of American Design. Ed. by Sandra S. Tinkham. (Index of American Design Ser.). 1979. 100.00 (*0-914146-95-5*) Chadwyck-Healey.

***Consolidated Chief Register of Deeds' Circulars & Conference Resolutions.** G. H. Scott. Date not set. ring bd. write for info. (*0-409-03428-2*, SA) Butterworth Legal Pubs.

Consolidated Financial Statements: Concepts, Issues & Techniques. Paul Taylor. (C). 1988. pap. 50.00 (*0-06-318372-2*, Pub. by P Chapman Pub UK); 50.00 (*1-85396-005-5*, Pub. by P Chapman Pub UK) St Mut.

Consolidated Fund & National Loans Fund Accounts, 1987-88: Supplementary Statements. 51p. 1988. pap. 18.00 (*0-10-205989-6*, HM9896, Pub. by HMSO UK) UNIPUB.

Consolidated Gas Dynamics Tables: Data for Isentropic, Rayleigh, & Fanno Flow, & Normal Shock Waves. Michael R. Lindeburg. (Engineering Reference Manual Ser.). 88p. (C). 1989. pap. text ed. 18.95 (*0-932276-96-2*) Prof Pubns CA.

Consolidated Gold Fields: A Centenary Portrait. Paul Johnson. LC 86-31307. (Illus.). 253p. 1987. text ed. 35.00 (*0-312-00549-0*) St Martin.

Consolidated Index: Consolidated Index 1994. Michie Butterworth Staff. (New Hampshire Practice Ser.). 450p. 1992. pap. 47.00 (*1-56257-269-5*) Michie Butterworth.

Consolidated Index to the Oxford History of England. Comp. by Richard Raper. (Oxford History of England Ser.: Vol. 16). 632p. 1991. 56.00 (*0-19-821786-2*) OUP.

Consolidated Index to Units I-V of Bender's UCC Service, 2 vols. rev. ed. Bender's Editorial Staff. 1981. reprint ed. Updates. ring bd. write for info. (*0-8205-1745-3*) Bender.

Consolidated List of Products Whose Consumption &-or Sale Have Been Banned, Withdrawn, Severely Restricted or Not Approved by Governments. 655p. 1987. 60.00 (*92-1-130120-3*) UN.

***Consolidated List of Products Whose Consumption &-or Sale Have Been Banned, Withdrawn, Severely Restricted or Not Approved by Governments.** 5th ed. Department for Policy Coordination & Sustainable Development Staff. 935p. 1994. pap. 100.00 (*92-1-130160-2*) UN.

Consolidated Standards for Dairy Plants. 1988. pap. 10.00 (*0-685-59608-7*) Am Inst Baking.

Consolidated Standards for Food Distribution Centers. 1985. 10.00 (*0-317-01526-5*); pap. 10.00 (*0-685-59607-9*) Am Inst Baking.

Consolidated Standards for Food Safety. (SPA.). 1992. pap. 10.00 (*0-685-59606-0*) Am Inst Baking.

Consolidated Standards for Food Safety. rev. ed. 1990. pap. 10.00 (*0-317-61016-3*) Am Inst Baking.

Consolidated Standards for Packaging Facitilies. 1991. pap. 10.00 (*0-685-59609-5*) Am Inst Baking.

Consolidated Standards Manual, 1989. 300p. 1988. pap. 40.00 (*0-86688-175-1*) Joint Comm Hlthcare.

Consolidated Statements: History & Analysis. R. G. Walker. Ed. by Richard P. Brief. LC 77-87307. (Development of Contemporary Accounting Thought Ser.). 1978. lib. bdg. 37.95 (*0-405-10946-6*) Ayer.

Consolidated Statistics of All International Arrivals & Departures: A Technical Report. 45p. 1985. 6.00 (*92-1-161218-7*, 85.XVII.8) UN.

***Consolidated Tax Return.** Jach Crestel et al. 1056p. 1992. 190.00 (*0-7913-1629-7*) Warren Gorham & Lamont.

Consolidated Tax Return. 4th ed. Jack Crestol et al. 1990. Supplemented semi-annually. ring bd. 175.00 (*0-7913-0083-8*) Warren Gorham & Lamont.

Consolidated Tax Return, No. 1. 4th suppl. ed. Jack Crestol et al. 1991. 65.00 (*0-7913-0894-4*) Warren Gorham & Lamont.

Consolidated Tax Return, No. 2. 4th suppl. ed. Jack Crestol et al. 1991. 68.00 (*0-685-32300-5*) Warren Gorham & Lamont.

Consolidated Tax Return: Principles, Practice, Planning. 4th ed. Jack Crestol et al. 1988. text ed. 175.00 (*0-685-69542-5*, CTR) Warren Gorham & Lamont.

Consolidated Tax Returns: A Treatise on the Law of Consolidated Federal Income Tax Returns, 2 vols., Set. 3rd ed. Fred W. Peel et al. LC 84-23688. 1990. 245.00 (*0-317-14545-2*) Clark Boardman Callaghan.

Consolidated Treaties & International Agreements: United States Current Document Service. Ed. by Erwin C. Surrency. 1990. pap. text ed. 125.00 (*0-379-01108-5*) Oceana.

Consolidated Treaty Series, 1648-1920, 243 vols., Set. annot. ed. Ed. by Clive M. Parry. LC 70-76750. 1977. write for info. (*0-379-13000-9*) Oceana.

Consolidated Wagster's Unexpurgated Dictionary of Humor & Wit. Ed. by H. Gordon Havens. LC 90-61138. (Illus.). 64p. 1990. 7.99 (*0-88088-666-8*) Peter Pauper.

Consolidating Clerical Services in Ventura County. National Center for State Courts Staff. 45p. 1975. 2.70 (*0-685-15225-1*, MAB-025) Natl Ctr St Courts.

Consolidating Credit & Receivables Data. 14p. 1985. 40.00 (*0-939050-09-9*) Credit Res NYS.

Consolidating Democracy: Politicalization & Partisanship in India. John O. Field. 1981. 22.50 (*0-8364-0707-5*, Pub. by Manohar II) S Asia.

Consolidating Police Functions in Metropolitan Areas. Max A. Pock. LC 62-64274. (Michigan Legal Publications). v, 51p. 1985. reprint ed. lib. bdg. 34.00 (*0-89941-384-6*, 303540) W S Hein.

Consolidation, Liquidation & Recapitalization: Banks & Thrifts Face the 90's. (Commercial Law & Practice Course Handbook Ser.). 1007p. 1992. pap. 70.00 (*0-685-69398-8*) PLI.

Consolidation of Concrete. 258p. 1987. pap. 70.50 (*0-318-35474-8*, SP96) ACI.

Consolidation of Concrete for Pavements, Bridge Decks & Overlays. (National Cooperative Highway Research Program Report Ser.). 61p. 1977. 4.80 (*0-309-02546-X*) Transport Res Bd.

***Consolidation of Democracy in Latin America.** Ed. by Joseph S. Tulchin & Bernice Romero. (Woodrow Wilson Center Current Studies on Latin America). 140p. 1995. pap. text ed. 10.95 (*1-55587-607-2*) Lynne Rienner.

Consolidation of Jury Management Services: California Court Services Project. National Center for State Courts Staff. 91p. 1975. 5.46 (*0-685-16708-9*, MAB-026) Natl Ctr St Courts.

Consolidation of Metal Powders. Ed. by H. H. Hausner et al. LC 66-22786. (New Perspectives in Powder Metallurgy Ser.: Vol. 1). 1967. 24.00 (*0-685-24604-3*, Plenum Pr) Plenum.

Consolidation of Professional Services & Witnesses: California Court Services Project. National Center for State Courts Staff. 54p. 1974. 3.24 (*0-685-16752-6*, MAB-027) Natl Ctr St Courts.

Consolidation of Soils: Testing & Evaluation STP 892. Ed. by R. N. Yong & F. C. Townsend. LC 86-1126. (Special Technical Publication Ser.). (Illus.). 735p. 1986. text ed. 79.00 (*0-8031-0446-4*, 04-892000-38) ASTM.

***Consolidation of the Bourgeois State, 1800-1850.** John Saville. LC 94-32945. (Socialist History of Britain Ser.). (C). 1994. text ed. 34.95 (*0-7453-0898-8*, Pub. by Pluto Pr UK) Westview.

Consolidation of the Roman Catholic Church in Ireland, 1860-1870. Emmet Larkin. LC 86-25059. xxii, 714p. 1987. 65.00 (*0-8078-1725-2*) U of NC Pr.

Consolidation of the South China Frontier. George Moselev. LC 73-170719. (Center for Chinese Studies Publications). 260p. 1973. reprint ed. pap. 58.80 (*0-318-34921-3*, 2031442) Bks Demand.

***Consolidators: Air Travel's Bargain Basement.** Kelly Monaghan. 80p. 1995. pap. 6.95 (*0-614-06305-1*) Intrepid Trvlr.

Consoling Heliodorus: A Commentary on Jerome, Letter 60. J. H. Scourfield. (Oxford Classical Monographs). 320p. 1993. 65.00 (*0-19-814722-8*) OUP.

Consonance & Continuity in Poetry: Detroit Black Writers. Ed. by Daphne W. Ntiri. 146p. (Orig.). 1988. pap. text ed. 7.00 (*0-911557-01-6*) Bedford Publishers.

***Consonance & Dissonance in Music.** Theodore Lipps. 142p. 1995. 21.95 (*0-940459-18-3*) Everett Bks.

Consonant, Pt. 1. Virginia Grant. pap. 2.49 (*0-87377-131-1*) GAM Pubns.

Consonant, Pt. 2. Virginia Grant. pap. 2.49 (*0-87377-132-X*) GAM Pubns.

Consonant Quantity & Phonological Units in Estonian. Ilse Lehiste. LC 66-63013. (Uralic & Altaic Ser.: Vol. 65). 73p. 1966. pap. text ed. 8.00 (*0-87750-022-3*) Res Inst Inner Asian Studies.

Consonant Variations of American English. Lorna D. Sikorski. (Mastering Effective English Communication Ser.). 132p. 1989. student ed 22.00 (*1-883574-04-8*, 3603); student ed, audio 70.00 (*1-883574-08-0*, 5311) L D Sikorski.

Consonants see Let's Learn Set

Consonants in Context, Bk. 1: Rapid Review of Vowel & Prosodic Contexts. Joan Morley. 76p. (C). 1992. pap. text ed. 9.95 (*0-472-08127-6*) U of Mich Pr.

Consonants in Context, Bk. 2: Intensive Consonant Pronunciation Practice. Joan Morley. 350p. (C). 1992. pap. text ed. 17.95 (*0-472-08128-4*) U of Mich Pr.

Consonants in Context, Bk. 3: Extempore Speaking Practice. Joan Morley. 200p. 1992. pap. text ed. 13.95 (*0-472-08129-2*) U of Mich Pr.

Consonants Sound Easy! Phonics. Sharron Bassano. (Illus.). 31p. 1981. pap. text ed. 5.50 (*0-13-171091-5*) Alemany Pr.

Consort of Music: A Study of Interpretation & Ensemble. John A. Fuller-Maitland. LC 72-83279. 1972. reprint ed. 21.95 (*0-405-08541-9*, Pub. by Blom Pubns UK) Ayer.

Consortia & Interinstitutional Cooperation. Ed. by Donn C. Neal. (ACE-Oryx Series on Higher Education). 224p. (C). 1988. 27.95 (*0-02-922510-8*, ACE-Oryx) Oryx Pr.

Consorting with Saints: Prayer for the Dead in Early Medieval France. Megan McLaughlin. LC 93-34803. (Illus.). 300p. 1994. 32.50 (*0-8014-2648-0*) Cornell U Pr.

Consortium. David H. Stone. LC 92-37581. 247p. 1995. 18.95 (*0-944957-40-4*) Rivercross Pub.

Consortium for Longitudinal Studies: As the Twig Is Bent: Lasting Effects of Preschool Programs. 512p. (C). 1983. A volume in the Child Psychology Series. text ed. 89.95 (*0-89859-271-2*) L Erlbaum Assocs.

Consortium of Schools for the Future. 178p. 1990. pap. text ed. 25.00 (*0-943397-14-6*) Assn Calif Sch Admin.

Consortium on Revolutionary Europe, 1750-1850: 1972 Proceedings. Consortium on Revolutionary Europe Staff. Ed. by Lee Kennett & Claude C. Sturgill. LC 73-15970. 137p. reprint ed. pap. 39.10 (*0-8357-6724-8*, 2035362) Bks Demand.

Consortium on Revolutionary Europe, 1750-1850: 1973 Proceedings. Consortium on Revolutionary Europe Staff. Ed. by Claude C. Sturgill. 206p. 1975. reprint ed. pap. 58.80 (*0-8357-6725-6*, 2035363) Bks Demand.

Consortium on Revolutionary Europe, 1750-1850: 1974 Proceedings. Consortium on Revolutionary Europe Staff. Ed. by Donald D. Horward & Claude C. Sturgill. 202p. reprint ed. pap. 57.60 (*0-8357-6729-9*, 2035370) Bks Demand.

Conspectus Bryophytorum Orientalum et Arabicum. Annotated Catalogue of the Bryophytes of Southwest Asia, 1991. W. Frey & H. Kuerschner. (Bryophytorum Bibliotheca Ser.: Vol. 39). 184p. 1991. pap. text ed. 56.00 (*3-443-62011-6*, Pub. by Cramer-Borntraeger GW) Lubrecht & Cramer.

Conspectus Florae Graecae & Supplementum Prim, 4 vols. in 3, Set. E. De Halacsy. 1969. 360.00 (*3-7682-7192-7*) Lubrecht & Cramer.

Conspectus of Bryological Taxonomic Literature: Index to Monographs & Regional Reviews, Pt. 1. S. W. Greene & A. J. Harrington. (Bryophytorum Bibliotheca Ser.: Vol. 35). 272p. 1988. pap. text ed. 85.00 (*3-443-62007-8*) Lubrecht & Cramer.

Conspectus of Bryological Taxonomic Literature, Pt. 2: Guide to National & Regional Literature. S. W. Greene & A. J. Harrington. (Bryophytorum Bibliotheca Ser.: Vol. 37). 322p. 1989. pap. 78.00 (*3-443-62009-4*, Pub. by Cramer GW) Lubrecht & Cramer.

Conspectus of the Genera of Polytrichaceae. G. L. Smith. (Memoirs Ser.: Vol. 21 (3)). (Illus.). 83p. 1971. 8.00 (*0-89327-072-5*) NY Botanical.

Conspicuous Destruction: War, Famine & the Reform Process in Mozambique. Ed. by Human Rights Watch Staff. 216p. (Orig.). 1992. pap. 15.00 (*1-56432-079-0*) Hum Rts Watch.

Conspicuous Production: Automobiles & Elites in Detroit, 1899-1933. Donald F. Davis. LC 87-26745. (Technology & Urban Growth Ser.). (Illus.). 320p. (C). 1988. 37.95 (*0-87722-549-4*) Temple U Pr.

Conspiracy. Paul Nizan. Tr. by Quintin Hoare. 256p. 1988. 18.95 (*0-86091-224-8*, Pub. by Verso UK) Routledge Chapman & Hall.

Conspiracy. Summers. 1994. pap. 14.95 (*1-56924-943-1*) Marlowe & Co.

Conspiracy: Essays on Prevention of Learning. Ken Curtis. 114p. (Orig.). 1991. pap. 8.50 (*0-934426-34-1*) NAPSAC Reprods.

Conspiracy: Who Killed JFK? James R. Duffy. 630p. 1992. 5.99 (*1-56171-190-X*, S P I Bks) Sure Sellers.

Conspiracy Against Freedom. 1986. write for info. (*0-935036-11-3*); pap. write for info. (*0-935036-10-5*) Liberty Lobby.

Conspiracy Against Hitler in the Twilight War. Harold C. Deutsch. LC 68-22365. 406p. reprint ed. pap. 115.80 (*0-685-15901-9*, 2056199) Bks Demand.

Conspiracy Against the Tsar: A Portrait of the Decembrists. Ed. by N. Eidelman. 294p. (C). 1985. 50.00 (*0-685-31479-0*) St Mut.

Conspiracy & Romance: Studies in Brockden Brown, Cooper, Hawthorne & Melville. Robert Levine. (Cambridge Studies in American Literature & Culture: No. 33). 317p. (C). 1989. 59.95 (*0-521-36654-2*) Cambridge U Pr.

Conspiracy at Meerut. Lester Hutchinson. LC 78-39303. (Conspiracy: Historical Perspectives Ser.). 1972. reprint ed. 17.95 (*0-405-04154-3*) Ayer.

Conspiracy at Mukden: The Rise of the Japanese Military. Takehiko Yoshihashi. LC 80-13747. (Yale Studies in Political Science: No. 9). (Illus.). xvi, 274p. 1980. reprint ed. text ed. 59.75 (*0-313-22443-9*, YOCO, Greenwood Pr) Greenwood.

Conspiracy for World War III. 1992. lib. bdg. 79.95 (*0-8490-5426-5*) Gordon Pr.

Conspiracy in American Politics Seventeen Eighty-Seven to Eighteen Fifteen. Wendell J. Knox. LC 78-39303. (Conspiracy Ser.). 1976. reprint ed. 26.95 (*0-405-04155-1*) Ayer.

Conspiracy in Athens. large type ed. Marian Hipwell. (Linford Romance Library). 288p. 1993. pap. 14.95 (*0-7089-7323-X*, Trailtree Bookshop) Ulverscroft.

Conspiracy in Jerusalem: The Hidden Origins of Jesus. Kamal S. Salibi. 208p. 1990. text ed. 39.50 (*1-85043-117-5*, Pub. by I B Tauris UK) St Martin.

Conspiracy in Wilmington see Spy in the King's Colony; A Thief on Morgan's Plantation; An Art Bandit on Sugar Hill; A Conspiracy in Washington

Conspiracy Novel: Structure & Metaphor in Balzac's Comedie Humaine. James W. Mileham. LC 81-68004. (French Forum Monographs: No. 31). 142p. (Orig.). 1982. pap. 9.95 (*0-917058-30-5*) French Forum.

Conspiracy of Arnold & Sir Henry Clinton Against the United States & Against General Washington. Ed. by Phyllis O. Flug & Michael J. Miller. LC 77-39299. (Conspiracy: Historical Perspectives Ser.). 1972. reprint ed. 21.95 (*0-405-04152-7*) Ayer.

Conspiracy of Assassins. Gene Garofalo. 1989. pap. 3.95 (*0-8217-2652-8*) Zebra.

Conspiracy of Catiline & the War of Jugurtha. Crispus C. Sallustius. Tr. by Thomas Heywood. LC 25-8759. (Tudor Translations, Second Ser.: No. 1). reprint ed. 57.50 (*0-404-51855-9*) AMS Pr.

Conspiracy of Catline see Jugurthine War

Conspiracy of Cells: The Basic Science of Cancer. R. Grant Steen. 405p. 1993. 29.95 (*0-306-44506-9*, Plenum Pr) Plenum.

Conspiracy of Industrialism, Technology, Art, Time, Language, Time, Work: The Psychopathology of Modern Times. 1991. lib. bdg. 79.95 (*0-8490-4705-6*) Gordon Pr.

Conspiracy of Kindness. Steve Sjogren. 236p. (Orig.). 1993. pap. 8.99 (*0-89283-832-9*, Vine Bks) Servant.

Conspiracy of Mirrors. David Milton. 1992. mass mkt. 4.99 (*1-55817-564-4*, Pinnacle NY) Windsor NY.

Conspiracy of One: The Definite Book on the Kennedy Assassination. Jim Moore. 1991. pap. 11.95 (*0-9626219-6-X*) Summit TX.

Conspiracy of One: The Definitive Book on the Kennedy Assassination. Jim Moore. (Illus.). 217p. 1990. 24.95 (*0-9626219-2-7*) Summit TX.

Conspiracy of One: The Definitive Book on the Kennedy Assassination. Jim Moore. Ed. by Don Turner. 217p. (C). 1990. 24.95 (*0-9626219-5-1*) Summit TX.

Conspiracy of Optimism: Management of the National Forests since World War II. Paul W. Hirt. LC 94-3858. (Our Sustainable Future Ser.: Vol . 6). (Illus.). 464p. 1994. 40.00 (*0-8032-2375-7*) U of Nebr Pr.

Conspiracy of Pontiac: From the Spring of 1763 to the Death of Pontiac, Vol. 2. Francis Parkman. 1994. pap. 12.50 (*0-8032-8737-2*, Bison Books) U of Nebr Pr.

Conspiracy of Pontiac: To the Massacre at Michillimackinac, Vol. 1. Francis Parkman. (Illus.). 387p. 1994. pap. 12.50 (*0-8032-8733-X*, Bison Books) U of Nebr Pr.

Conspiracy of Silence. Mel Silverstein & Karen Silverstein. 1981. pap. 2.95 (*0-89083-850-X*) Zebra.

Conspiracy of Silence: The Secret Life of Anthony Blunt. Barrie Penrose & Simon Freeman. 1988. pap. 10.95 (*0-679-72044-8*, Vin) Random.

Conspiracy of Silence: The Trauma of Incest. Sandra Butler. 208p. 1978. 12.00 (*0-318-17075-2*) Kempe Nat Ctr.

Conspiracy of Silence: The Trauma of Incest. Sandra Butler. LC 78-1975. 215p. 1985. pap. 12.95 (*0-912078-73-1*) Volcano Pr.

Conspiracy of Silence - Alcoholism. Leo P. Hennigan. (Illus.). 170p. 1991. pap. 17.95 (*0-9626382-2-6*) Gannel Pubns.

***Conspiracy of the Secret Nine.** Celia Bland. (Mysteries in Time Ser.). (Illus.). 80p. (J). (gr. 4-6). 1995. lib. bdg. 12.95 (*1-881889-67-X*) Silver Moon.

Conspiracy of the Text: The Place of the Narrative in the Development of Thought. Jeff Adams. 160p. 1987. 35.00 (*0-7102-0799-9*, 07999, RKP) Routledge.

Conspiracy of Thirty: Their Misuse of Music from Aristotle to Onassis. Virginia D. Edwards. (Illus.). 578p. 1995. 50.00 (*0-9628372-0-2*) Conspiracy

An Asterisk (*) at the beginning of an entry indicates that the title is appearing in BIP for the first time.

Pr.
A secret club of 30 power groups has existed for thousands of years. They have used music for centuries to control nations & people. This book exposes the mother of all conspiracies: the real Hidden Hand, the real Christ Killers. The Council of 30's corporate immortality is traced to before 1,000 B.C. Egypt & King Solomon. They founded Greece & Rome & kept the mobs in servitude with loud public music. They were implicated in Jesus' death with "30 Pieces of Silver". They took over the Roman Catholic Church & invented Islam. They are the Beast, the 666 of Saint John's Revelation. With rock music, the 30 have caused rioting, drug use, & possibly Crib Death. Their talented agents--kings, popes, presidents, directors of industry, & the Gnomes of Zurich--have created wars, resulting in migrations of cheap labor to areas for mining & economic development. The Council's 20th century failure to exploit Virginia's Blue Ridge minerals in eastern USA brought on "Watergate", the Irish & Middle Eastern troubles, South Africa's race riots, Korea, Vietnam, & the 1991 Gulf War over oil. Revisionist history, easy print, popular, non-technical. Documented. Topical index, bibliography, footnotes, 22 maps, 90 illustrations. For information send SAE to Conspiracy Press, P.O. Box 87, Waynesboro, VA 22980. Phone: 703-943-0091, FAX: 703-943-5192. ***Publisher Provided Annotation.***

Conspiracy or Degeneracy. Revilo P. Oliver. 1984. lib. bdg. 79.95 (*0-87700-590-7*) Revisionist Pr.

Conspiracy So Immense: The World of Joe McCarthy. David M. Oshinsky. (Illus.). 1985. 24.95 (*0-02-923490-5*); pap. 16.95 (*0-02-923760-2*) Free Pr.

Conspiracy Theory: A Reader. (Studies in Ideology). 1992. lib. bdg. 75.00 (*0-8490-5447-8*) Gordon Pr.

Conspiracy to Destroy All Governments & Religions. William G. Carr. 1982. lib. bdg. 250.00 (*0-87700-358-0*) Revisionist Pr.

Conspiracy Trial for the Murder of the President: And the Attempt to Overthrow the Government by the Assassination of Its Principal Officers, 1. Ed. by Phyllis O. Flug & Michael J. Miller. LC 70-39301. (Conspiracy: Historical Perspectives Ser.). 1972. reprint ed. 44.95 (*0-405-04158-6*) Ayer.

Conspiracy Trial for the Murder of the President: And the Attempt to Overthrow the Government by the Assassination of Its Principal Officers, 2. Ed. by Phyllis O. Flug & Michael J. Miller. LC 70-39301. (Conspiracy: Historical Perspectives Ser.). 1972. reprint ed. 44.95 (*0-405-04159-4*) Ayer.

Conspiracy Trial for the Murder of the President: And the Attempt to Overthrow the Government by the Assassination of Its Principal Officers, 3. Ed. by Phyllis O. Flug & Michael J. Miller. LC 70-39301. (Conspiracy: Historical Perspectives Ser.). 1972. reprint ed. 44.95 (*0-405-04160-8*) Ayer.

Conspiracy Trial for the Murder of the President: And the Attempt to Overthrow the Government by the Assassination of Its Principal Officers, Set. Ed. by Phyllis O. Flug & Michael J. Miller. LC 70-39301. (Conspiracy: Historical Perspectives Ser.). 1972. reprint ed. 132.95 (*0-405-04153-5*) Ayer.

Conspiration. Paul Nizan. (FRE.). 1973. pap. 11.95 (*0-7859-4023-5*) Fr & Eur.

Conspirator's Hierarchy: The Committee of Three Hundred. John Coleman. (Illus.). 267p. (Orig.). (C). 1992. pap. text ed. 16.95 (*0-922356-57-2*) Amer West Pubs.

Conspirators' Hierarchy: The Committee of Three Hundred. 2nd ed. John Coleman. 304p. 1992. pap. 20.00 (*0-9634019-0-4*) J Holding.

Conspiring with Forms: Life in Academic Texts. Terry Caesar. LC 91-5028. 224p. 1992. 30.00 (*0-8203-1421-8*); pap. 15.00 (*0-8203-1494-3*) U of Ga Pr.

Constab Ballads. Claude McKay. 1977. lib. bdg. 59.95 (*0-8490-1666-5*) Gordon Pr.

Constable. (Masterworks Ser.). 1991. 19.99 (*0-517-05375-6*) Random Hse Value.

Constable. Leslie Parris. 1993. 95.00 (*1-55859-636-4*) Abbeville Pr.

Constable. Michael Rosenthal. LC 86-50221. (World of Art Ser.). (Illus.). 168p. 1987. pap. 11.95 (*0-500-20211-7*) Thames Hudson.

Constable. Peter D. Smith. (CAL Art Ser.). (Illus.). 96p. 1988. 14.95 (*0-517-54428-8*, Crown) Crown Pub Group.

Constable. John Walker. (Library of Great Painters). (Illus.). 1978. 49.50 (*0-8109-0752-6*) Abrams.

Constable. John Walker. 1991. 22.95 (*0-8109-3171-0*) Abrams.

***Constable.** (Color Library). (Illus.). 128p. (C). 1994. reprint ed. 19.95 (*0-7148-3209-X*, Pub. by Phaidon Press UK) Chronicle Bks.

Constable. Mary S. Henderson. LC 70-165641. (Select Bibliographies Reprint Ser.). 1977. reprint ed. 24.95 (*0-8369-5950-7*) Ayer.

Constable. John Sunderland. (Color Library). (Illus.). 128p. (C). 1994. reprint ed. pap. 14.95 (*0-7148-2754-1*, Pub. by Phaidon Press UK) Chronicle Bks.

Constable: The Natural Painter. Graham Reynolds. (Illus.). 144p. 1977. reprint ed. pap. 5.95 (*0-586-04401-9*) Academy Chi Pubs.

Constable: The Painter & His Landscape. Michael Rosenthal. LC 82-48908. (Illus.). 264p. 1983. 50.00x (*0-300-03014-2*) Yale U Pr.

Constable: The Painter & His Landscape. Michael Rosenthal. LC 82-48908. (Illus.). 264p. 1986. text ed. 30.00 (*0-300-03753-8*) Yale U Pr.

Constable & His Drawings. Ian Fleming-Williams. (Illus.). 328p. 1991. 80.00 (*0-85667-380-3*); pap. 39.00 (*0-85667-388-9*) Sothebys Pubns.

Constable & the Critics: 1802-1837. Judy C. Ivy. (Illus.). 320p. (C). 1991. text ed. 59.00 (*0-85115-293-7*) Boydell & Brewer.

Constable (John) 1927. Andre Fontinas. 1991. pap. 25.00 (*0-87556-802-5*) Saifer.

***Constable on Call.** large type ed. Nicholas Rhea. (Magna Large Print Ser.). 1994. 26.95 (*0-7505-0693-8*, Pub. by Magna Print Bks) Ulverscroft.

Constables: First Family of the Adirondacks. Edith Pilcher. LC 92-8393. 1992. 32.50 (*0-925168-05-X*); pap. 24.95 (*0-925168-04-1*) North Country.

Constacia & Other Stories for Virgins. Carlos Fuentes. LC 90-56103. 352p. 1991. pap. 13.00 (*0-06-097387-0*, PL) HarpC.

Constance. Patricia Clapp. LC 85-43127. 256p. (J). (gr. 7 up). 1991. reprint ed. pap. 3.95 (*0-688-10976-4*, Pub. by Beech Tree Bks) Morrow.

Constance: A Story of Early Plymouth. Patricia Clapp. (J). (gr. 5-9). 1993. 17.50 (*0-8446-6647-5*) Peter Smith.

Constance: Poems. Jane Kenyon. LC 93-242. 80p. 1993. 18.00 (*1-55597-195-4*); pap. 11.00 (*1-55597-196-2*) Graywolf.

Constance Bennett. M. M. McBride. 1976. lib. bdg. 59.95 (*0-8490-1667-3*) Gordon Pr.

Constance Eberhart: A Musical Career in the Age of Cadman. Arlouine Wu. Ed. by Leland Fox. (Monograph Ser.: No. 4). 200p. (Orig.). 1983. pap. 20.00 (*0-938178-04-0*) Natl Opera Assn.

Constance F. Woolson. Rayburn S. Moore. (Twayne's United States Authors Ser.). 1963. pap. 13.95x (*0-8084-0092-4*, T34) NCUP.

Constance Fenimore Woolson. Rayburn S. Moore. LC 62-19478. (Twayne's United States Authors Ser.). 1963. lib. bdg. 8.95 (*0-89197-710-4*); pap. text ed. 4.95 (*0-8290-0008-9*) Irvington.

***Constance Fenimore Woolson: Homeward Bound.** Sharon L. Dean. LC 95-4332. 1995. write for info. (*0-87049-898-3*) U of Tenn Pr.

Constance Fenimore Woolson: The Grief of Artistry. Cheryl B. Torsney. LC 88-17399. (Illus.). 200p. 1989. 25.00 (*0-8203-1101-4*) U of Ga Pr.

Constance Markievicz: Irish Revolutionary. rev. ed. Anne Haverty. 1988. pap. 15.00 (*0-86358-161-7*, Pub. by Pandora Pr UK) Harper SF.

Constance Ring. Amalie Skram. Tr. by Judith Messick & Katherine Hanson. LC 88-1953. (Women in Translation Ser.). 307p. (Orig.). 1988. 18.95 (*0-931188-61-X*); pap. 10.95 (*0-931188-60-1*) Seal Pr Feminist.

Constance Rourke & American Culture. Joan S. Rubin. LC 79-9272. (Illus.). xv, 244p. 1980. 29.95 (*0-8078-1402-4*) U of NC Pr.

Constance Stumbles. Patricia McKissack & Fredrick McKissack. (Rookie Reader Ser.). (Illus.). 32p. (J). (ps-2). 1988. lib. bdg. 10.35 (*0-516-02086-2*); pap. 2.95 (*0-516-42086-0*) Childrens.

Constancia & Other Stories for Virgins. Carlos Fuentes. Tr. by Thomas Christensen. 204p. 1990. 19.95 (*0-374-12886-3*) FS&G.

Constancy & Change: Moral & Religious Values in the Australian Legal System. Keith Mason. 154p. 1990. pap. 33.00 (*0-685-51046-8*, Pub. by Federation Pr AU) W W Gaunt.

Constancy & Change in Architecture. Ed. by Malcolm Quantrill & Bruce J. Webb. LC 90-23669. (Studies in Architecture & Culture: No. 1). (Illus.). 184p. 1991. 50.00 (*0-89096-472-6*) Tex A&M Univ Pr.

Constancy & Change in Human Development. Ed. by Orville G. Brim, Jr. & Jerome Kagan. (Illus.). 760p. 1980. 50.00 (*0-674-16625-6*) HUP.

Constancy of Objects. Kathleen McCracken. 96p. 1988. 9.95 (*0-920806-98-8*, Pub. by Penumbra Pr CN) U of Toronto Pr.

Constancy of Purpose: An Account of the Foundation & History of the Hong Kong College of Medicine & the Faculty of Medicine of the University of Hong Kong, 1887-1987. Comp. by Dafydd E. Evans. 304p. (C). 1987. text ed. 69.00 (*962-209-194-6*, Pub. by Hong Kong U Pr HK) St Mut.

Constant: Adolphe: "Adolphe" Dennis Wood. (Landmarks of World Literature Ser.). 1987. pap. 10.95 (*0-521-31656-1*) Cambridge U Pr.

Constant Companion. Marion Chesney. 224p. 1980. pap. 1.75 (*0-449-50114-0*, Coventry) Fawcett.

Constant Companion. Marion Chesney. 1987. pap. 2.50 (*0-449-21324-2*) Fawcett.

Constant Companion: Inspiration for Daily Living from the Thousand Names of the Lord. Eknath Easwaran. LC 89-29641. Orig. Title: Thousand Names of Vishnu. 328p. 1990. 22.00 (*0-915132-61-3*); pap. 12.00 (*0-915132-60-5*) Nilgiri Pr.

Constant Companions: An Exhibition of Mythological Animals, Demons, & Monsters. Intro. by Dominique De Menil. (Illus.). 1964. pap. 6.00 (*0-914412-19-1*) Inst for the Arts.

Constant Companions: An Exhibition of Mythological Animals, Demons & Monsters, Phantasmal Creatures, & Various Anatomical Assemblages. (Illus.). 90p. 1986. pap. 3.50 (*0-318-22673-1*) Menil Collect.

Constant Couple. George Farquhar. (Swan Theatre Plays Ser.). (Illus.). 47p. (Orig.). (C). 1988. pap. 9.95 (*0-413-19050-1*, A0330, Pub. by Methuen UK) Heinemann.

***Constant Craving: What Your Food Cravings Mean & How to Overcome Them.** Doreen Virtue. Ed. by Jill Kramer. (Orig.). 1995. pap. 12.95 (*1-56170-124-6*, 166) Hay House.

Constant Defender. James Tate. (American Poetry Ser.: No. 28). 120p. (Orig.). 1983. 13.50 (*0-88001-028-2*); pap. 7.95 (*0-88001-041-X*) Ecco Pr.

Constant Ferment: A History of the Thyroid Clinic & Laboratory at the Massachusetts General Hospital: 1913-1990. John B. Stanbury. (Illus.). 238p. 1991. 20.00 (*0-938864-14-9*) Ipswich Pr.

Constant Flame. Patricia Phillips. 448p. (Orig.). 1993. pap. 4.99 (*0-8439-3454-9*) Dorchester Pub Co.

Constant Flux: A Study of Class Mobility in Industrial Societies. Robert Erikson & John H. Goldthorpe. (Illus.). 412p. 1992. 84.00 (*0-19-827383-5*) OUP.

Constant Flux: A Study of Class Mobility in Industrial Societies. Robert Erikson & John H. Goldthorpe. (Illus.). 448p. (C). 1993. reprint ed. pap. 19.95 (*0-19-827908-6*, 1982) OUP.

Constant Friends: The Victorian Scrapbook of Ophelia B. Clise. Michele D. Clise. (Illus.). 64p. 1992. 13.00 (*0-670-83265-0*, Viking Studio) Studio Bks.

Constant God. Henry Chapin. LC 78-10965. 1979. pap. 8.95 (*0-87233-046-X*) Bauhan.

Constant Heart. large type ed. Judith Ansell. 1994. 17.95 (*0-263-13845-3*, Pub. by Mills & Boon Ltd UK) Chivers N Amer.

Constant Heart. large type ed. Eleanor Farnes. 1974. 12.00 (*0-85456-277-X*) Ulverscroft.

Constant Journey: The Fiction of Monique Wittig. Erika Ostrovsky. LC 89-49482. 208p. (C). 1991. 24.95 (*0-8093-1642-0*) S Ill U Pr.

Constant Lover. Paul Rosenblatt. 175p. 1990. 17.50 (*0-922820-11-2*) Watermark Pr.

Constant Mean Curvature Immersions of Enneper Type. Henry C. Wente. (Memoirs of the American Mathematical Society Ser.: No. 478). 77p. 1992. 24.00 (*0-8218-2536-4*) Am Math.

Constant Processes. Ted S. Davis. (Illus.). 1978. 29.50 (*0-685-19863-4*) Constant Soc.

Constant Reminder. Isaac Charchat. LC 84-51586. 460p. 1984. 20.00 (*0-88400-109-1*) Shengold.

Constantes Selectionnees Pouvoir Rotatoire Naturel: Steroides. Jean P. Mathieu & A. Petit. (Tables of Constants & Numerical Data Ser.: Vol. 6). 1956. 210.00 (*0-08-009716-2*, Pub. by Pergamon Repr UK) Franklin.

Constantin Brancusi. Eric Shanes. (Modern Masters Ser.). (Illus.). 128p. 1989. 32.95 (*0-89659-924-8*); pap. 22.95 (*1-55859-246-6*) Abbeville Pr.

Constantin Caratheodory: An International Tribute, 2 Vols. T. M. Rassias. 1468p. 1991. text ed. 301.00 (*981-02-0544-9*) World Scientific Pub.

Constantin Caratheodory: An International Tribute, 2 vols. Ed. by T. M. Rassias. 1468p. (C). 1991. text ed. 230.00 (*0-685-58547-6*) World Scientific Pub.

Constantin Caratheodory: An International Tribute, 2 vols., Set. Ed. by T. M. Rassias. 1468p. (C). 1991. text ed. 238.00 (*0-685-58546-8*) World Scientific Pub.

Constantin Frantz: Romantik und Realismus im Werk eines Politischen Aussenseiters. P. F. Lauxtermann. (Historische Studies: Bk. XXXV). vi, 217p. (Orig.). 1978. pap. 21.00 (*90-01-39021-8*) Benjamins North Am.

Constantine. Ramsay MacMullen. (Classical Lives Ser.). 272p. 1987. pap. 14.95 (*0-7099-4685-6*, Pub. by Croom Helm UK) Routledge Chapman & Hall.

Constantine. Nancy Z. Walworth. (World Leaders - Past & Present Ser.). (Illus.). 112p. (YA). (gr. 5 up). 1990. 17.95 (*1-55546-805-5*) Chelsea Hse.

Constantine: A Great Christian Monarch & Apostle. Paul Keresztes. 218p. (C). 1981. pap. 38.00 (*90-70265-03-6*, Pub. by Gieben NE) Benjamins North Am.

Constantine & Eusebius. Timothy D. Barnes. 464p. 1964. pap. 22.00 (*0-674-16531-4*) HUP.

Constantine & Eusebius. Timothy D. Barnes. LC 81-4248. (Illus.). 464p. (C). 1981. 47.50 (*0-674-16530-6*) HUP.

Constantine & the Conversion of Europe. A. H. Jones. (Medieval Academy Reprints for Teaching Ser.). 1979. reprint ed. pap. 9.95 (*0-8020-6369-1*) U of Toronto Pr.

Constantine Eleventh Dragas Palaeologus: A Biography of the Last Greek Emperor. Marios Philippides. (Hellenism: Ancient, Mediaeval, Modern Ser.: No. 17). 600p. (C). 1993. text ed. 85.00 (*0-89241-522-3*) Caratzas.

Constantine Nabokov: Letters of a Russian Diplomat to an American Friend, 1906-1922. Ed. by John F. Melby & W. W. Straka. LC 88-11770. (Slavic Studies: Vol. 1). 430p. 1988. lib. bdg. 109.95 (*0-88946-014-0*) E Mellen.

Constantine of Pisa: The Book of the Secrets of Alchemy. Barbara Obrist. LC 90-37150. (Collection de Travaux de l'Academie Internationale d'Histoire des Sciences: Vol. 34). x, 339p. (ENG & LAT.). 1990. 85.75 (*90-04-09288-9*) E J Brill.

***Constantine on Peopleware.** Larry L. Constantine. LC 94-41384. 1995. write for info. (*0-13-221978-6*, Yourdon) P-H.

***Constantine on Peopleware: Practical Insights into the Human Side of Software Development.** Constantine. 1995. pap. text ed. 19.95 (*0-13-331976-8*) P-H.

Constantine Porphyrogenitus, De Administrando Imperio. Ed. by Gyula Moravcsik. Tr. by R. J. Jenkins. LC 85-6950. (Dumbarton Oaks Texts: Vol. 1). 356p. (ENG & GRE.). 1985. reprint ed. 15.00 (*0-88402-021-5*) Dumbarton Oaks.

***Constantine the African & Ali ibn al-Abbas al-Magusi: The Pantegni & Related Texts.** Ed. by Charles Burnett & Danielle Jacquart. (Studies in Ancient Medicine, 925-1421: Vol. 10). 1994. 85.75 (*90-04-10014-8*) E J Brill.

Constantine the Great. Michael Grant. (Illus.). 288p. 1994. text ed. 27.50 (*0-684-19520-8*, Scribners) S&S Trade.

Constantine the Great. Frieda Upson. 1987. pap. 4.95 (*0-917651-11-1*) Holy Cross Orthodox.

Constantine the Great: The Reorganization of the Empire & the Triumph of the Church. John B. Firth. LC 77-152983. (Select Bibliographies Reprint Ser.). 1977. reprint ed. 30.95 (*0-8369-5735-0*) Ayer.

Constantine the Great & Christianity. Christopher B. Coleman. LC 70-155636. (Columbia University. Studies in the Social Sciences: No. 146). reprint ed. 37.50 (*0-404-51146-5*) AMS Pr.

Constantine the Great & the Christian Church. Norman H. Baynes. 1974. lib. bdg. 59.95 (*0-87968-934-X*) Gordon Pr.

Constantine the Great & the Christian Church. Norman H. Baynes. LC 74-34500. (World History Ser.: No. 48). (C). 1972. reprint ed. lib. bdg. 75.00 (*0-8383-0131-2*) M S G Haskell Hse.

Constantine's Triumph: A Tale of the Era of the Martyrs. W. H. Spears, Jr. LC 63-19710. 1964. 3.95 (*0-9600106-1-0*) Spears.

Constantinople. Clara E. Clement. 1977. lib. bdg. 59.95 (*0-8490-1668-1*) Gordon Pr.

Constantinople. Francis M. Crawford. (Works of Francis Marion Crawford Ser.). 1990. reprint ed. lib. bdg. 79.00 (*0-7812-2563-9*) Rprt Serv.

***Constantinople & Its Hinterland: Papers from the Twenty-Seventh Spring Symposium of Byzantine Studies, Oxford, April 1993.** Ed. by Mango Cyril & Geoffrey Greatrex. (Society for the Promotion of Byzantine Studies: No. 3). (Illus.). 368p. 1995. 69.50 (*0-86078-487-8*, Pub. by Variorum UK) Ashgate Pub Co.

Constantinople & the Latins: The Foreign Policy of Andronicus the 2nd, 1282-1328. Angeliki E. Laiou. LC 78-176042. (Historical Studies: No. 88). 400p. 1972. 27.50 (*0-674-16535-7*) HUP.

Constantinople & the West: Essays on the Late Byzantine (Palaeologan) & Italian Renaissances & the Byzantine & Roman Churches. Deno J. Geanakoplos. LC 88-40434. (Illus.). 288p. (Orig.). (C). 1989. text ed. 40.00 (*0-299-11880-0*); pap. text ed. 17.75 (*0-299-11884-3*) U of Wis Pr.

Constantinople in the Age of Justinian. Glanville Downey. (Dorset Classic Reprints Ser.). 196p. 1991. 19.95 (*0-88029-620-8*) Marboro Bks.

Constantinople Today: Or, the Pathfinder Survey of Constantinople, a Study in Oriental Social Life. Ed. by Clarence R. Johnson. LC 77-87631. reprint ed. 34.50 (*0-404-16456-0*) AMS Pr.

Constantly Risking Absurdity: Essays on the Writings of Lawrence Ferlinghetti. Michael Skau. LC 87-50835. 103p. 1989. 15.00 (*0-87875-353-2*) Whitston Pub.

Constants in Some Inequalities of Analysis. Solomon G. Mikhlin. LC 84-13108. 107p. 1986. text ed. 59.95 (*0-471-90559-3*) Wiley.

Constanze, Formerly Widow of Mozart: Her Unwritten Memoir. Klemens Diez, pseud. Tr. by Joseph T. Malloy. LC 90-5760. 272p. 1991. lib. bdg. 89.95 (*0-88946-579-7*) E Mellen.

Constanze Mozart: After the Requiem. Heinz Gaertner. Tr. by Reinhard G. Pauly. LC 91-4377. (Illus.). 238p. 1991. 24.95 (*0-931340-39-X*, Amadeus Pr) Timber.

Constellation see Signe Ascendant

***Constellation of Genius.** John Astolat. 46p. 1982. lib. bdg. 5.00 (*0-902507-02-8*) Greenfriar Pr.

Constellation Question. Howard I. Chapelle & Leon D. Polland. LC 77-609565. (Smithsonian Studies in History & Technology: No. 5). (Illus.). 169p. reprint ed. pap. 48.20 (*0-317-09469-6*, 2004204) Bks Demand.

***Constellational Astrology.** Deluce. Date not set. 35.00 (*0-614-02478-1*) ASI Pubs Inc.

Constellations. James F. Boylan. LC 94-10180. 1994. 22.00 (*0-679-43021-0*) Random.

Constellations. Ed. by Running Press Staff. LC 92-50806. (Miniature Editions Ser.). (Illus.). 160p. 1993. 4.95 (*1-56138-247-7*) Running Pr.

Constellations: A Contextual Reader for Writers. Schilb et al. (C). 1991. text ed. 28.50 (*0-673-46427-X*) HarpCollege.

***Constellations: A Contextual Reader for Writers.** 2nd ed. Schilb et al. (C). 1995. text ed. write for info. (*0-06-502540-7*) HarpCollege.

***Constellations: A Contextual Reader for Writers.** 2nd ed. Ed. by John L. Schilb et al. LC 94-31745. 804p. (C). 1995. pap. 20.00 (*0-673-99036-2*) HarpCollege.

Constellations: How They Came to Be. rev. ed. Roy A. Gallant. LC 84-28755. (Illus.). 224p. (YA). (gr. 7 up). 1991. text ed. 15.95 (*0-02-735776-7*, Four Winds Pr) S&S Childrens.

Constellations & Conjectures. N. R. Hanson & W. C. Humphreys, Jr. LC 70-159654. (Synthese Library: No. 48). (Illus.). 282p. 1973. lib. bdg. 84.00 (*90-277-0192-X*) Kluwer Ac.

Constellations of the Inner Eye. Sonya Hess. Ed. by Constance Hunting. 77p. (Orig.). 1991. pap. 8.95 (*0-913006-47-5*) Puckerbrush.

***Constellations of the Northern Skies.** Gary Mechler. LC 94-34032. (National Audubon Society Pocket Guides Ser.). 1995. 7.99 (*0-679-77998-1*) Knopf.

C

An Asterisk (*) at the beginning of an entry indicates that the title is appearing in BIP for the first time. 1557

Constipation. Ed. by Michael A. Kamm & John E. Lennard-Jones. 560p. 1994. 160.00 (*1-871816-24-6*, Pub. by Wrightson Biomed UK) Taylor & Francis.

Constipation. Raymond W. Bernard. 51p. 1956. reprint ed. spiral bd. 3.30 (*0-7873-1217-7*) Mokelumne.

Constipation: A New Reading on the Subject. J. H. Tilden. 64p. 1960. reprint ed. spiral bd. 4.40 (*0-7873-0873-0*) Mokelumne.

***Constipation: Aetiology, Evaluation & Management.** Ed. by Steven D. Wexner & David C. Bartolo. LC 94-27778. 272p. 1995. 145.00 (*0-7506-0776-9*) Buttrwrth-Heinemann.

Constipation & Civilization: A Study of Eating Habits & the Decline of Civilization. James C. Thomson. 1974. lib. bdg. 69.95 (*0-685-51379-3*) Revisionist Pr.

Constipation & Fecal Incontinence & Mobility Disturbances of the Gut. Ed. by J. Yokoyama & T. A. Angerpointner. (Progress in Pediatric Surgery Ser.: Vol. 24). (Illus.). x, 235p. 1989. 142.00 (*0-387-50813-9*, 3096) Spr-Verlag.

Constipation & Indigestion: Prevention & Cure. L. Ramachandran. 284p. 1985. 14.95 (*0-318-36360-7*) Asia Bk Corp.

Constipation in Childhood. Graham Clayden & Ulfur Agnaarsson. (Illus.). 128p. 1991. 45.00 (*0-19-262044-4*) OUP.

Constitucion: (The Constitution) Warren Colman. LC 86-30968. (New True Bks.). 48p. (SPA.). (J). (gr. k-4). 1989. lib. bdg. 13.28 (*0-516-31231-6*); pap. 5.50 (*0-516-51231-5*) Childrens.

Constitucion de los Estados Unidos: Preparacion para el Examen de Ciudadania. Maria Viramontes de Marin & Reymundo Marin. (Illus.). 156p. (Orig.). (SPA.). (C). 1988. pap. 14.00 (*0-927065-00-2*) Marin Chula Vista.

Constitucion de Puerto Rico. Jose Trias Monge. LC 87-26053. 1988. pap. write for info. (*0-8477-3029-8*) U of PR Pr.

Constituencies & Leaders in Congress: Their Effects on Senate Voting Behavior. John Jackson. LC 73-93372. (Political Studies). 224p. 1974. 25.00 (*0-674-16540-3*) HUP.

Constituency Influence in Congress. Warren E. Miller & Donald E. Stokes. (Reprint Series in Social Sciences). (C). 1993. reprint ed. pap. text ed. 1.00 (*0-8290-3691-1*, PS-404) Irvington.

C

Constituent Order in Functional Grammar: Synchronic & Diachronic Perspectives. John H. Conolly. LC 91-30409. (Functional Grammar Ser.: No. 14). x, 206p. (C). 1991. lib. bdg. 75.40 (*3-11-013389-X*) Mouton.

Constituent Questions. Elisabet Engdahl. 1985. lib. bdg. 117.00 (*90-277-1954-3*) Kluwer Ac.

Constituting Americans: Cultural Anxiety & Narrative Form. Priscilla Wald. (New Americanists Ser.). 368p. 1995. lib. bdg. 56.95 (*0-8223-1550-5*); pap. text ed. 17.95 (*0-8223-1547-5*) Duke.

Constituting Critique: Kant's Writing As Critical Praxis. Willi Goetschel. Tr. by Eric J. Schwab. (Post-Contemporary Interventions Ser.). 256p. 1994. lib. bdg. 49.95 (*0-8223-1534-3*); pap. text ed. 16.95 (*0-8223-1543-2*) Duke.

Constituting the Minangkabau: Peasants, Culture, & Modernity in Colonial Indonesia. Joel S. Kahn. LC 92-5750. 272p. 1993. 54.95 (*0-85496-316-2*) Berg Pubs.

Constitution. 176p. 1993. 3.00 (*0-318-23107-7*) Newspaper Guild.

Constitution. Warren Colman. LC 86-30968. (New True Bks.). (Illus.). 48p. (J). (gr. k-4). 1987. lib. bdg. 13.50 (*0-516-01231-2*); pap. 5.50 (*0-516-41231-0*) Childrens.

Constitution. Max Farrand. 1974. lib. bdg. 59.95 (*0-87968-935-8*) Gordon Pr.

Constitution. Sam Fink. (Illus.). 1985. 25.00 (*0-394-54304-1*) Random.

Constitution. Sam Fink. 1987. pap. 15.95 (*0-394-75336-4*) Random.

Constitution. George Jenkins. (American Government Ser.). (Illus.). 96p. (YA). (gr. 7 up). 1990. lib. bdg. 18.60 (*0-86593-085-6*); lib. bdg. 13.95 (*0-685-46456-3*) Rourke Corp.

***Constitution.** Marilyn Prolman. LC 94-35657. (Cornerstones of Freedom Ser.). (Illus.). 32p. (J). (gr. 3-6). 1995. lib. bdg. 12.30 (*0-516-06692-7*) Childrens.

***Constitution.** rev. ed. (Becoming Informed Citizens Ser.: Vol. I). 204p. (YA). (gr. 8-12). 1995. spiral bd. 19.50 (*0-941690-62-8*) Regina Bks.

Constitution. rev. ed. Richard B. Morris. (American History Topic Bks.). (Illus.). 72p. (YA). (gr. 5 up). 1985. lib. bdg. 13.50 (*0-8225-1702-7*, Lerner Publctns) Lerner Group.

Constitution: A Documentary & Narrative History. Page Smith. LC 78-17225. 1980. pap. 16.45 (*0-688-08349-8*, Quill) Morrow.

Constitution: A History of Its Framing & Ratification. Ed. by Leonard W. Levy & Dennis J. Mahoney. 352p. 1987. 23.99 (*0-02-918790-7*) Macmillan.

Constitution: Group Material. Donald Kuspit et al. (Illus.). 60p. (Orig.). 1987. pap. 20.00 (*0-939351-03-X*) Temple U Tyler Gal.

Constitution: Hanging by a Thread. Joseph Stumph. Tr. by Ingram. 1992. pap. 6.95 (*1-880416-09-3*) NW Pub.

Constitution: Our Written Legacy. Joseph A. Melusky. LC 89-18963. 338p. (Orig.). 1991. 27.50 (*0-89464-334-7*); pap. 21.50 (*0-89464-550-1*) Krieger.

Constitution: That Delicate Balance. Fred W. Friendly & Martha H. Elliott. 352p. (C). 1984. text ed. write for info. (*0-318-57864-6*); pap. text ed. write for info. (*0-07-554612-4*) McGraw.

Constitution: What It Says It Is. Charles Stanke. 96p. (Orig.). 1994. pap. write for info. (*1-56167-138-X*) Am Literary Pr.

Constitution & American Life. Ed. by David Thelen. LC 87-47973. 392p. 1988. 45.00 (*0-8014-2185-3*); pap. 16.95 (*0-8014-9512-1*) Cornell U Pr.

Constitution & American Political Development: An Institutional Perspective. Ed. by Peter F. Nardulli. 344p. 1992. 39.95 (*0-252-01787-0*); pap. 14.95 (*0-252-06174-8*) U of Ill Pr.

Constitution & American Public Education. Arval A. Morris. LC 89-62026. 652p. 1989. lib. bdg. 37.50 (*0-89089-348-9*) Carolina Acad Pr.

Constitution & Bylaws & General Procedures of the National Youth Convention of the Apostolic Faith Churches of God, Inc. Ed. by E. Myron Noble. LC 89-14602. 56p. (Orig.). 1989. pap. 3.95 (*0-9616056-8-5*) Mid Atl Reg Pr.

Constitution & Bylaws, Rules of Procedure of the House of Delegates. 90p. 1991. pap. write for info. (*0-318-66091-1*, 149-0014) Amer Bar Assn.

Constitution & Constitutional Law of India. B. K. Chakraborty. (C). 1989. 35.00 (*0-89771-458-X*, Current Dist) St Mut.

Constitution & Curriculum: Hermeneutical Semiotics of Cases & Controversies in Education, Law & Social Sciences. Ed. by James A. Whitson. (Education Policy Perspectives Ser.). 314p. 1991. 90.00 (*1-85000-332-7*, Falmer Pr); pap. 38.00 (*1-85000-337-8*, Falmer Pr) Taylor & Francis.

Constitution & Economic Change. Jonathan Lurie. LC 88-71596. (Bicentennial Essays on the Constitution Ser.). 52p. 1988. pap. 7.00 (*0-87229-041-7*) Am Hist Assn.

Constitution & Erosion of a Monetary Economy: Problems of India's Development since Independence, Vol. 3. Waltraud Schelkle. LC 94-17159. (GDI Book Ser.). 1994. pap. 35.00 (*0-7146-4138-3*, Pub. by F Cass Pubs UK) Intl Spec Bk.

Constitution & Government of Kenya. H. B. Gicheru & Kabuya Miano. 640p. 1988. text ed. 60.00 (*81-207-0682-X*, Pub. by Sterling Pubs II) Apt Bks.

Constitution & Laws of the Choctaw Nation, 3 vols., 13. LC 75-3680. (Constitutions & Laws of the American Indian Tribes Ser. 2). 1975. reprint ed. 12.00 (*0-8420-1846-8*) Scholarly Res Inc.

Constitution & Laws of the Choctaw Nation, 3 vols., 14. LC 75-3680. (Constitutions & Laws of the American Indian Tribes Ser. 2). 1975. reprint ed. 12.00 (*0-8420-1847-6*) Scholarly Res Inc.

Constitution & Laws of the Choctaw Nation, 3 vols., 15. LC 75-3680. (Constitutions & Laws of the American Indian Tribes Ser. 2). 1975. reprint ed. 13.00 (*0-8420-1848-4*) Scholarly Res Inc.

Constitution & Laws of the Muskogee Nation. LC 75-3694. (Constitutions & Laws of the American Indian Tribes Ser. 2: Vol. 27). 1975. reprint ed. 15.00 (*0-8420-1885-9*) Scholarly Res Inc.

Constitution & Laws of the Muskogee Nation, As Compiled & Codified by A.P. McKellop, Under Act of October 15, 1892. LC 73-88772. (Constitutions & Laws of the American Indian Tribes Ser.: Vol. 18). 1973. reprint ed. 25.00 (*0-8420-1720-8*) Scholarly Res Inc.

Constitution & Laws of the Muskogee Nation, As Compiled by L. C. Perryman, March 1st of 1890. LC 73-3695. (Constitutions & Laws of the American Indian Tribes Ser. 2: Vol. 28). 1975. reprint ed. 20.00 (*0-8420-1886-7*) Scholarly Res Inc.

Constitution & Laws of the Osage Nation: Passed at Pawhuska, Osage Nation, in the Years 1881 & 1882. Bd. with Constitution & Laws of the Sac & Fox Nation: Indian Territory. LC 75-3699. LC 75-3699. (Constitutions & Laws of the American Indian Tribes Ser. 2: Vol. 31). 1975. reprint ed. 11.00 (*0-8420-1891-3*) Scholarly Res Inc.

Constitution & Laws of the Sac & Fox Nation: Indian Territory see Constitution & Laws of the Osage Nation: Passed at Pawhuska, Osage Nation, in the Years 1881 & 1882

Constitution & National Security: A Bicentennial View. Howard E. Shuman & Walter R. Thomas. LC 89-13412. 412p. 1990. per., pap. 12.00 (*0-16-001734-3*, S/N 008-020-011) USGPO.

Constitution & Properties of Ceramic Materials. R. Pampuch. (Materials Science Monographs: No. 58). 460p. 1990. 151.25 (*0-444-98794-0*) Elsevier.

Constitution & Properties of Steels, Vol. 7: A Comprehensive Treatment. Ed. by Cahn et al. (Materials Science & Technology Ser.). 824p. 1992. lib. bdg. 325.00 (*0-89573-695-0*) VCH Pubs.

Constitution & Properties of Steels, Vol. 7: A Comprehensive Treatment, Set. Ed. by Cahn et al. (Materials Science & Technology Ser.). 824p. 1992. 270.00 (*1-56081-190-0*) VCH Pubs.

Constitution & Race. Donald E. Lively. LC 91-30280. 208p. 1992. text ed. 55.00 (*0-275-93914-6*, C3914, Praeger Pubs); pap. text ed. 17.95 (*0-275-94228-7*, B4228, Praeger Pubs) Greenwood.

Constitution & Records of the Claim Association of Johnson County, Iowa. Benjamin F. Shambaugh. Ed. by Stuart Bruchey. LC 78-53565. (Development of Public Land Law in the U. S. Ser.). 1979. reprint ed. lib. bdg. 19.95 (*0-405-11384-6*) Ayer.

Constitution & Socio-Economic Change. Henry Rottschaefer. LC 77-173667. (American Constitutional & Legal History Ser). 253p. 1971. reprint ed. lib. bdg. 35.00 (*0-306-70410-2*) Da Capo.

Constitution & Socio-Economic Change. Henry Rottschaefer. LC 49-2548. (Michigan Legal Publications). xiii, 253p. 1986. reprint ed. lib. bdg. 42.00 (*0-89941-542-3*, 304710) W S Hein.

Constitution & Supplementary Laws & Documents of the Republic of China. LC 76-11419. (Studies in Chinese Government & Law). 198p. 1976. reprint ed. text ed. 55.00 (*0-313-27020-1*, U7020, Greenwood Pr) Greenwood.

Constitution & the American Presidency. Ed. by Martin L. Fausold & Alan Shank. LC 90-9460. (Presidency: Contemporary Issues Ser.). 280p. (C). 1991. 57.50 (*0-7914-0467-6*); pap. 18.95 (*0-7914-0468-4*) State U NY Pr.

Constitution & the Economy: Objective Theory & Critical Commentary. Michael Conant. LC 91-13536. 432p. 1991. 42.95 (*0-8061-2363-X*) U of Okla Pr.

Constitution & the Flag, Vols. 1 & 2. Ed. by Michael K. Curtis. LC 92-39286. (Controversies in Constitutional Law Ser.). 1993. Vol. 1, The Flag Salute Cases. 65.00 (*0-8153-1267-9*); Vol. 2, Flag Burning Cases. 99.00 (*0-8153-1268-7*) Garland.

Constitution & the Government of the U. S. Jack Abromowitz & Kenneth Uva. (YA). (gr. 7-12). 1987. pap. text ed. 3.50 (*0-89525-747-5*) Ed Activities.

Constitution & the Regulation of Society. Ed. by Gary C. Bryner & Dennis L. Thompson. LC 88-457. 258p. 1988. 39.50 (*0-88706-851-0*); pap. 12.95 (*0-88706-852-9*) State U NY Pr.

Constitution & the States: The Role of the Original Thirteen in the Framing & Adoption of the Federal Constitution. Ed. by Patrick T. Conley & John P. Kaminski. LC 88-9028. (Illus.). 352p. 1988. 34.95 (*0-945612-02-8*); pap. 18.95 (*0-945612-30-3*) Madison Hse.

Constitution & World Organization. Edward S. Corwin. LC 73-117869. (Select Bibliographies Reprint Ser.). 1977. 16.95 (*0-8369-5322-3*) Ayer.

Constitution As an Institution. K. N. Llewellyn. (Reprint Series in Social Sciences). (C). 1993. reprint ed. pap. text ed. 1.00 (*0-8290-2737-8*, PS-171) Irvington.

Constitution As Political Structure. Martin H. Redish. LC 93-42364. 224p. 1995. 39.95 (*0-19-507060-7*) OUP.

Constitution Besieged: The Rise & Demise of Lochner Era Police Powers Jurisprudence. Howard Gillman. LC 92-15814. 328p. (C). 1993. text ed. 34.95 (*0-8223-1283-2*) Duke.

***Constitution Besieged: The Rise & Demise of Lochner Era Police Powers Jurisprudence.** Howard Gillman. LC 92-15814. 328p. 1995. pap. 15.95 (*0-8223-1642-0*) Duke.

Constitution Bicentennial Coloring Book. (Illus.). 32p. (J). 1987. pap. 1.75 (*0-16-001664-9*, S/N 008-020-01113-4) USGPO.

***Constitution Conspiracy.** Kenneth C. Hill & Bill Uselton. 27p. (Orig.). 1994. pap. 2.50 (*1-879366-69-X*) Hearthstone OK.

Constitution Explained. Harry Atwood. 5.00 (*0-685-08800-6*) Destiny.

Constitution Faces Technology: The Relationship of the National Government to the Telegraph, 1866-1884. Lester G. Lindley. LC 75-2586. (Dissertations in American Economic History Ser.). 1975. 28.95 (*0-405-07206-6*) Ayer.

***Constitution: Fact or Fiction: The Story of the Nation's Descent from a Constitutional Republic Through a Constitutional Dictatorship to an Unconstitutional Dictatorship.** Eugene Schroder. LC 94-79634. 264p. (Orig.). 1995. pap. 14.95 (*1-885534-06-X*) Buffalo Creek.

***Constitution in Conflict.** Robert A. Burt. 462p. 1992. pap. text ed. 16.95 (*0-674-16537-3*, BURCOX) Belknap Pr.

Constitution in Conflict. Robert A. Burt. (Illus.). 462p. (C). 1992. text ed. 29.95 (*0-674-16536-5*) Belknap Pr.

***Constitution in Crisis.** Kenneth C. Hill et al. 100p. (Orig.). 1994. pap. 8.95 (*1-879366-82-7*); vhs 19.95 (*1-879366-88-6*) Hearthstone OK.

***Constitution in Danger! What You Don't Know CAN Hurt You!** Nita Scoggan. LC 95-68743. 80p. (Orig.). (YA). (gr. 10-12). 1995. pap. text ed. 5.00 (*0-910487-34-0*) Royalty Pub.

Constitution in State Politics. Steven Boyd. LC 90-3722. (Distinguished Studies in American Legal & Constitutional History: Vol. 3). 320p. 1990. reprint ed. 67.00 (*0-8240-0017-X*) Garland.

Constitution in the Courts: Law or Politics? Michael J. Perry. LC 93-18539. 1994. Acid-free paper. 35.00 (*0-19-508347-4*) OUP.

Constitution in the Supreme Court: The First Hundred Years, 1789-1888. David P. Currie. LC 85-1205. xiv, 506p. 1986. 55.00 (*0-226-13108-4*) U Ch Pr.

Constitution in the Supreme Court: The First Hundred Years, 1789-1888. David P. Currie. xiv, 506p. 1992. pap. text ed. 24.95 (*0-226-13109-2*) U Ch Pr.

Constitution in the Supreme Court: The Second Century, 1888-1986. David P. Currie. (C). 1993. pap. text ed. 29.95 (*0-226-13112-2*) U Ch Pr.

Constitution in the Twentieth Century. Paul L. Murphy. LC 86-70475. (Bicentennial Essays on the Constitution Ser.). 70p. 1985. pap. 7.00 (*0-87229-036-0*) Am Hist Assn.

***Constitution Interpretation.** Carter. (Political Pampheleteer Ser.). (C). 1994. text ed. 3.00 (*0-673-99784-7*) HarpCollege.

Constitution, Jefferson's Manual & Rules of the House of Representatives of the U. S., 4 vols., Set. 1994. lib. bdg. 1,200.00 (*0-8490-5722-1*) Gordon Pr.

Constitution, Law, & American Life: Critical Aspects of the Nineteenth-Century Experience. Ed. by Donald G. Nieman. LC 91-21385. 232p. 1992. 35.00 (*0-8203-1403-X*) U of Ga Pr.

Constitution, Laws, & Treaties of the Chickasaws. LC 75-3676. (Constitutions & Laws of the American Indian Tribes Ser. 2: Vol. 9). 1975. reprint ed. 17.00 (*0-8420-1842-5*) Scholarly Res Inc.

Constitution, Laws, & Treaties of the Chickasaws, by Authority. LC 75-3675. (Constitutions & Laws of the American Indian Tribes Ser. 2: Vol. 8). 1975. reprint ed. 17.00 (*0-8420-1841-7*) Scholarly Res Inc.

Constitution Made Easier: Reading Level 6. 1993. 4.95 (*0-88336-484-0*); 28.00 (*0-88336-485-9*) Peoples Rochelle Park.

Constitution Makers on Constitution Making: The Experience of Eight Nations. Ed. by Robert A. Goldwin & Art Kaufman. LC 88-15533. (AEI Studies: No. 479). 475p. (Orig.). (C). 1988. 37.50 (*0-8447-3667-8*); pap. text ed. 19.50 (*0-8447-3666-X*) Am Enterprise.

Constitution Making: Conflict & Consensus in the Federal Convention of 1787. Calvin Jillson. LC 87-28946. (Illus.). 256p. (Orig.). 1988. 36.00 (*0-87586-081-8*); pap. 18.00 (*0-87586-082-6*) Agathon.

Constitution-Making: Principles, Process, Practices. Edward McWhinney. 240p. 1981. 30.00 (*0-8020-5553-2*) U of Toronto Pr.

Constitution Making in Eastern Europe. Ed. by A. E. Howard. (Woodrow Wilson Center Press Ser.). 200p. (Orig.). 1993. pap. text ed. 14.95 (*0-943875-48-X*) Johns Hopkins.

Constitution Making in Illinois, 1818-1970. rev. ed. Janet Cornelius. LC 72-76864. (Studies in Illinois Constitution Making Ser). 191p. reprint ed. pap. 54.50 (*0-8357-3291-6*, 2039514) Bks Demand.

***Constitution Making in Indiana, 4 vols., Set.** Date not set. 32.00 (*0-614-04983-0*) IN Hist Bureau.

***Constitution Making in Indiana, Vol. I.** Charles Kettleborough. 550p. 1971. 7.50 (*1-885323-00-X*) IN Hist Bureau.

***Constitution Making in Indiana, Vol. II.** Charles Kettleborough. 693p. 1971. 7.50 (*1-885323-01-8*) IN Hist Bureau.

***Constitution Making in Indiana, Vol. III.** Charles Kettleborough. 411p. 1977. 7.50 (*1-885323-02-6*) IN Hist Bureau.

***Constitution Making in Indiana, Vol. IV.** John Bremer. 343p. 1994. pap. 15.00 (*1-885323-03-4*) IN Hist Bureau.

Constitution-Making in the New South Africa. Ed. by Alexander Johnston et al. LC 93-14854. (Studies in Federalism). 256p. 1993. 55.00 (*0-7185-1476-9*, Pub. by Leicester Univ Pr) St Martin.

Constitution of Athens & Related Texts. Aristotle. 1974. pap. 9.95 (*0-317-30525-5*) Free Pr.

Constitution of Athens & Related Texts. Aristotle. (Library of Classics: No. 13). 256p. 1970. pap. 11.95 (*0-02-840420-3*) Hafner.

Constitution of Belgium & the Belgian Civil Code. John H. Crabb. 448p. 106.50 (*90-6544-062-3*) Kluwer Ac.

Constitution of Belgium & the Belgian Civil Code As Amended to September 1 , 1982 in the Moniteur Belge. Tr. by John H. Crabb. LC 82-18059. ix, 428p. 1982. text ed. 65.00 (*0-8377-0438-3*) Rothman.

Constitution of Binary Alloys. 2nd ed. Ed. by Max Hansen & Kurt Anderko. (Illus.). 1305p. reprint ed. pap. 150.00 (*0-931690-18-8*) Genium Pub.

Constitution of Binary Alloys: First Supplement. Ed. by Rodney P. Elliott. (Illus.). 896p. reprint ed. 135.00 (*0-931690-19-6*) Genium Pub.

Constitution of Binary Alloys: Second Supplement. Ed. by Francis A. Shunk. 846p. reprint ed. pap. 135.00 (*0-931690-20-X*) Genium Pub.

Constitution of England & les Idees Politiques De J.L. De Lolme: 1741-1806, 2 vols. in one. J. L. De Lolme & Jean-Pierre Machelon. Ed. by J. P. Mayer. LC 78-67366. (European Political Thought Ser.). (ENG & FRE.). 1980. reprint ed. lib. bdg. 55.95 (*0-405-11714-0*) Ayer.

Constitution of Glasses: A Dynamic Interpretation. Woldemar A. Weyl. LC 62-19684. reprint ed. Vol. 2, Pt. 1. pap. 121.20 (*0-317-10915-4*); reprint ed. Vol. 2, Pt. 2. pap. 160.00 (*0-317-10916-2*) Bks Demand.

Constitution of Glasses: A Dynamic Interpretation, 1. Woldemar A. Weyl. LC 62-19684. reprint ed. pap. 111.80 (*0-317-10914-6*, 2055162) Bks Demand.

Constitution of India. P. M. Bakshi. (C). 1990. 40.00 (*0-89771-210-2*) St Mut.

Constitution of India. M. C. Jain & M. C. Kagzi. (C). 1988. 350.00 (*0-685-25713-4*) St Mut.

Constitution of India. Raizada Saxena. (C). 1990. 300.00 (*0-89771-199-8*) St Mut.

Constitution of India. V. N. Shukla. (C). 1990. 100.00 (*0-685-38636-8*) St Mut.

Constitution of India. Mahendra P. Singh. (C). 1990. 100.00 (*0-89771-330-3*) St Mut.

Constitution of India. Mahendra P. Singh. 1994. 90.00 (*81-7012-518-9*) St Mut.

Constitution of India. 7th ed. V. N. Shukla. 871p. 1982. 270.00 (*0-317-54758-5*) St Mut.

Constitution of India. 8th ed. V. N. Shukla. (C). 1991. text ed. 200.00 (*0-89771-509-8*) St Mut.

Constitution of India. 8th ed. M. P. Singh. (C). 1990. 180.00 (*0-685-37451-3*) St Mut.

Constitution of India. 8th rev. ed. V. N. Shukla. (C). 1990. 200.00 (*0-685-39771-8*) St Mut.

Constitution of India, 2 vols., Set. 5th ed. M. C. Kagzi. (C). 1989. 450.00 (*0-685-36531-X*) St Mut.

Constitution of India for the Younger Reader. (YA). 1971. pap. 1.75 (*0-88253-410-6*) Ind-US Inc.

Constitution of Japan & Criminal Statutes. Japan, Military of Justice Staff. LC 78-78386. (Studies in Japanese Law & Government). 349p. 1979. reprint ed. text ed. 85.00 (*0-313-26986-6*, U6986, Greenwood Pr) Greenwood.

Constitution of Judicial Power. Sotirios A. Barber. LC 93-20096. (Constitutional Thought Ser.). 304p. (C). 1993. 25.95 (*0-8018-4587-4*) Johns Hopkins.

Constitution of Liberty. Friedrich A. Hayek. LC 59-11618. 1978. pap. text ed. 19.95 (*0-226-32084-7*, P796) U Ch Pr.

Constitution of Malaysia. 4th ed. L. A. Sheridan & Harry E. Groves. 649p. 1987. 75.00 (*0-685-47111-X*); pap. 54.00 (*9971-70-055-7*) Butterworth Legal Pubs.

Constitution of Man Considered in Relation to External Objects. 2nd ed. George Combe. LC 74-16109. (History of Psychology Ser.). 313p. 1974. reprint ed. 50.00 (*0-8201-1136-8*) Schol Facsimiles.

1558

An Asterisk (*) at the beginning of an entry indicates that the title is appearing in BIP for the first time.

Constitution of Poverty: Toward a Genealogy of Liberal Governance. Mitchell Dean. 224p. 1991. 75.00 (*0-415-04355-7*, A5056); pap. 17.95 (*0-415-04356-5*, A5060) Routledge.

Constitution of Rights: Human Dignity & American Values. Ed. by Michael J. Meyer & William A. Parent. LC 91-55535. (Start to Read! Library Edition Ser.). 256p. 1992. 35.00 (*0-8014-2650-2*); pap. 14.95 (*0-8014-9950-X*) Cornell U Pr.

Constitution of Seventeen Eighty-Seven: A Commentary. George Anastaplo. LC 88-45395. 320p. (C). 1989. pap. text ed. 14.95x (*0-8018-3606-9*) Johns Hopkins.

Constitution of Silence: Essays on Generational Themes. Marvin Rintala. LC 78-20018. (Contributions in Political Science Ser.: No. 25). 95p. 1979. text ed. 49.95 (*0-313-20723-2*, RCS/, Greenwood Pr) Greenwood.

Constitution of Society. Edward Shils. LC 81-16413. (Heritage of Sociology Ser.). 1982. pap. text ed. 13.95 (*0-226-75329-8*) U Ch Pr.

Constitution of Society: Outline of the Theory of Structuration. Anthony Giddens. LC 84-40290. 417p. 1985. pap. 16.00 (*0-520-05728-7*) U CA Pr.

Constitution of South Carolina: The Journey Toward Local Self-Government, Vol. II. James L. Underwood. 314p. 1989. text ed. 49.95 (*0-87249-636-8*) U of SC Pr.

Constitution of South Carolina, Vol. IV: The Struggle for Political Equality. James L. Underwood. 444p. 1993. 49.95 (*0-87249-978-2*) U of SC Pr.

Constitution of South Carolina, Vol. 3: Church & State, Morality & Free Expression. James L. Underwood. LC 86-1709. 441p. 1992. text ed. 49.95 (*0-87249-833-6*) U of SC Pr.

Constitution of the Arab Empire. S. A. Husaini. 14.95 (*0-935782-62-1*) Kazi Pubns.

Constitution of the Athenians: A Philological-Historical Analysis of Pseudo-Xenofon's Treatise De Re Publica Atheniensium. Hartvig Frisch. LC 75-13267. (History of Ideas in Ancient Greece Ser.). 1976. reprint ed. 34.95 (*0-405-07308-9*) Ayer.

Constitution of the Buddhist Sangha. Kanai L. Hazra. (C). 1988. 22.50 (*81-7018-537-8*) S Asia.

Constitution of the Commonwealth of Australia Annotated. 4th ed. R. D. Lumb. 1986. Australia. 85.00 (*0-409-49128-4*); Australia. pap. 69.00 (*0-409-49129-2*) Butterworth Legal Pubs.

Constitution of the Confederate States of America with the Inaugural Address of President Jefferson Davis. Confederate States of America - Constitutional Convention. Ed. by Jefferson Davis. pap. 2.95 (*0-89979-005-4*) British Am Bks.

Constitution of the Earth's Interior. J. Leliwa-Kopystynski & R. Teisseyre. (Physics & Evolution of the Earth's Interior Ser.: Vol. 1). 1984. 113.00 (*0-444-99646-X*, I-344-83) Elsevier.

Constitution of the Federal Republic of Germany. David P. Currie. 392p. 1994. 35.00 (*0-226-13113-0*) U Ch Pr.

Constitution of the Federal Republic of Germany. Ed. by Ulrich Karpen. 314p. 1988. pap. 46.00 (*3-7890-1530-X*, Pub. by Nomos Verlags GW) Intl Bk Import.

Constitution of the Five Nations. A. C. Parker. 158p. 1993. reprint ed. lib. bdg. 69.00 (*0-7812-5161-3*) Rprt Serv.

***Constitution of the Hutterian Brethren Church International.** Hutterian Brethren Church International Staff. LC 95-13448. 1995. write for info. (*0-87486-067-9*) Plough.

Constitution of the Islamic Republic of Iran. Tr. by Hamid Algar. LC 80-19896. 94p. 1980. 9.95 (*0-933782-07-1*); pap. 3.95 (*0-933782-02-0*) Mizan Pr.

Constitution of the Kingdom of Nepal: 2047 & Electoral Laws. L. R. A. Staff. (C). 1991. text ed. 40.00 (*0-7855-0131-2*, Pub. by Ratna Pustak Bhandar) St Mut.

Constitution of the People: Reflections on Citizens & Civil Society. Ed. by Robert E. Calvert. LC 90-48987. xii, 172p. 1991. 27.50 (*0-7006-0476-6*) U Pr of KS.

Constitution of the People: Reflections on Citizens & Civil Society. Ed. by Robert E. Calvert. LC 90-48987. xii, 172p. 1991. pap. 12.95 (*0-7006-0478-2*) U Pr of KS.

Constitution of the Russian Federation: With Commentaries & Interpretations. Ed. by Vladimir V. Belyakov & Walter J. Raymond. LC 94-4723. 1994. 35.00 (*1-55618-143-4*); pap. 12.00 (*1-55618-142-6*) Brunswick Pub.

Constitution of the School of Spiritual Science. 2nd ed. Rudolf Steiner. Tr. by George Adams et al. 78p. 1980. pap. 7.95 (*0-88010-039-7*, Anthroposophic) Anthroposophic.

Constitution of the Socialist Federal Republic of Yugoslavia. Ed. by Michael S. Poulton et al. LC 76-13392. (Constitutions of the World Ser.: Vol. 1). 1976. 30.00 (*0-89304-020-7*, CCC104); pap. 15.00 (*0-89304-006-1*) Cross-Cultrl NY.

Constitution of the State of Louisiana. 1974. pap. 4.00 (*0-87511-076-2*) Claitors.

Constitution of the State of Sequoyah, 3 vols. in 1. Indian Territory Staff. Bd. with Memorial to the Congress of the United States on Behalf of the State of Sequoyah. LC 74-15118.; Proposed State of Sequoyah. LC 74-15118. LC 74-15118. reprint ed. 18.00 (*0-404-11978-6*) AMS Pr.

Constitution of the U. S. A Guide & Bibliography to Current Scholarly Research. Bernard D. Reams, Jr. & Stuart D. Yoak. 545p. 1987. 65.00 (*0-379-20858-X*) Oceana.

Constitution of the U. S. In Some of Its Fundamental Aspects. Gaspar G. Bacon. LC 79-37328. (Select Bibliographies Reprint Ser.). 1977. reprint ed. 22.95 (*0-8369-6673-2*) Ayer.

***Constitution of the U. S. A.** (Illus.). 89p. (Orig.). (C). 1994. pap. text ed. 19.95x (*0-7881-1250-3*) Diane Pub.

Constitution of the U. S. & Explanation of the Veritat Foundation. Marie B. Hall. (Illus.). 110p. 1988. write for info. (*0-318-68054-8*) Veritat Found.

***Constitution of the United States.** Karen Judson. LC 95-12522. (American Government in Action Ser.). (J). 1995. write for info. (*0-89490-586-4*) Enslow Pubs.

Constitution of the United States. Mary M. Slappey. 17p. (J). (gr. 1 up). 1987. pap. 5.00 (*0-930061-20-9*) Interspace Bks.

Constitution of the United States. 13th ed. Harold J. Spaeth & Edward C. Smith. LC 90-56021. (HarperCollins College Outline Ser.). 320p. (Orig.). 1991. pap. 13.00 (*0-06-467105-4*, Harper Ref) HarpC.

Constitution of the United States. Edward Dumbauld. LC 64-11324. (Illus.). 521p. reprint ed. 148.50 (*0-8357-9722-8*, 2016211) Bks Demand.

Constitution of the United States: A Critical Discussion of Its Genesis, Development & Interpretation, 2 vols., Set. John R. Tucker. Ed. by Henry S. Tucker. 1981. reprint ed. 75.00 (*0-8377-1206-8*) Rothman.

Constitution of the United States: A Primer for the People. David P. Currie. x, 150p. 1988. lib. bdg. 25.00 (*0-226-13106-8*); pap. text ed. 7.95 (*0-226-13107-6*) U Ch Pr.

Constitution of the United States: An Introduction. Floyd G. Cullop. 160p. 1969. pap. 4.99 (*0-451-62724-5*, Ment) NAL-Dutton.

Constitution of the United States: Its Sources & Application. 1987. write for info. (*0-935036-13-X*) Liberty Lobby.

Constitution of the United States: La Constitucion de los Estados Unidos. Ed. by Nilda Aldridge. Tr. by Minerva Figueroa. 130p. (SPA.). 1992. 29.95 (*0-929853-12-1*) Condor Pubns Inc.

Constitution of the United States: La Constitucion de los Estados Unidos. Ed. by MariAnn Ping. 130p. 1992. 29.95 (*0-929853-11-3*) Condor Pubns Inc.

Constitution of the United States: La Constitucion de los Estados Unidos. Ed. by MariAnn Ping & Nilda Aldridge. Tr. by Minerva Figueroa. (Illus.). 85p. 1992. teacher ed 29.95 (*0-929853-10-5*); student ed, text ed. 11.95 (*0-929853-07-5*) Condor Pubns Inc.

Constitution of the United States: Published for the Bicentennial of Its Adoption in 1787. Library of Congress Staff & Arion Press Staff. LC 87-600111. 63p. 1987. 2.50 (*0-8444-0560-4*, 030-000-00190-7) Lib Congress.

Constitution of the United States: Published for the Bicentinnial of Its Adoption in 1787. LC 87-60111. 64p. 1987. pap. 2.50 (*0-16-003993-2*, S/N 030-000-00190-7) USGPO.

Constitution of the United States & Related Documents. Ed. by Martin Shapiro. (Crofts Classics Ser.). 128p. 1966. pap. text ed. write for info. (*0-88295-025-8*) Harlan Davidson.

Constitution of the United States at the End of the First Century. George S. Boutwell. xviii, 412p. 1987. reprint ed. text ed. 47.50 (*0-8377-1943-7*) Rothman.

Constitution of the United States of America. Sam Fink. 1987. 25.00 (*0-317-45946-5*); pap. 15.95 (*0-394-75273-2*) Random.

***Constitution of the United States of America.** Morris Staff. 32p. 1995. pap. text ed. 8.95 (*1-55709-105-6*) Applewood.

Constitution of the United States of America: Bicentennial Edition. 28p. (Orig.). 1987. pap. 1.49 (*0-940917-00-9*) MFM Publish.

Constitution of the United States of America: The Definitive Edition. Ed. by Michael J. Mendenhall. 44p. (Orig.). (C). 1991. pap. 2.00 (*0-9625954-0-3*) Inst Cons Res.

Constitution of the United States of America, As Amended, Unratified Amendments, Analytical Index. 96p. 1987. pap. 2.75 (*0-16-006386-8*, S/N 052-071-00758-0) USGPO.

Constitution of the U.S. With Notes of Decisions of the Supreme Court Thereon, from the Organization of the Court till October, 1900. Edwin E. Bryant. xlii, 422p. 1986. reprint ed. lib. bdg. 47.50 (*0-89941-477-X*, 304050) W S Hein.

Constitution of the World Health Organization. 18p. 1985. pap. 1.20 (*92-4-160251-1*) World Health.

Constitution of the World Health Organization: Proceedings of the World Health Assembly, 20th, 1975. WHO Staff & World Health Assembly, 1975, 20th. 1976. pap. 0.80 (*92-4-156032-0*) World Health.

Constitution of Tyranny: Regimes of Exception in Spanish America. Brian Loveman. (Latin American Ser.). 496p. 1994. pap. 19.95 (*0-8229-5536-9*) U of Pittsburgh Pr.

Constitution of Tyranny: Regimes of Exception in Spanish America. Brian Loveman. (Latin American Ser.). 496p. (C). 1994. text ed. 49.95 (*0-8229-3766-2*) U of Pittsburgh Pr.

Constitution on the Sacred Liturgy: December 4, 1963. Second Vatican Council Staff. 60p. 4.95 (*1-55586-303-5*) US Catholic.

Constitution, the Courts, & Human Rights: An Inquiry into the Legitimacy of Constitutional Policymaking by the Judiciary. Michael J. Perry. LC 82-40164. 242p. 1984. reprint ed. pap. 14.00 (*0-300-03238-2*, Y-497) Yale U Pr.

Constitution, the Courts, & the Quest for Justice. Ed. by Robert A. Goldwin & William A. Schambra. LC 86-17659. (American Enterprise Institute Constitutional Studies). 135p. (Orig.). (C). 1988. pap. text ed. 10.75 (*0-8447-3692-9*) Am Enterprise.

Constitution, the Law, & Freedom of Expression: 1787-1987. Ed. by James B. Stewart. LC 87-13106. 131p. 1988. text ed. 15.95 (*0-8093-1428-2*) S Ill U Pr.

Constitution, Treaties & Laws of the Chickasaw Nation. LC 75-3677. (Constitutions & Laws of the American Indian Tribes Ser. 2: Vol. 10). 1975. reprint ed. 22.00 (*0-8420-1843-3*) Scholarly Res Inc.

Constitution, Treaties & Laws of the Choctaw Nation: Made & Enacted by the Choctaw Legislature 1887. LC 75-3686. (Constitutions & Laws of the American Indian Tribes Ser. 2: Vol. 19). 1975. reprint ed. 17.00 (*0-8420-1877-8*) Scholarly Res Inc.

Constitution Two Hundred: A Bicentennial Collection of Essays. Ed. by Mary A. Hepburn. 180p. (Orig.). 1988. pap. 5.95 (*0-89854-126-3*) U of GA Inst Govt.

Constitution under Pressure: A Time for a Change. Marsha L. Whicker et al. LC 87-13178. 235p. 1987. text ed. 55.00 (*0-275-92703-2*, C2703, Praeger Pubs); pap. text ed. 14.95 (*0-275-92704-0*, B2704, Praeger Pubs) Greenwood.

***Constitutional Adjudication in European Community & National Law.** Deirdre Curtin & David O'Keefe. 1992. boxed 69.00 (*1-85475-001-1*, IE) Butterworth Legal Pubs.

Constitutional Amending Process in American Political Thought. John R. Vile. LC 91-43441. 224p. 1992. text ed. 55.00 (*0-275-94280-5*, C4280, Praeger Pubs) Greenwood.

Constitutional Amendment to Require a Balanced Federal Budget. Scott Mackey. (State Legislative Reports: Vol. 17, No. 11). 8p. 1992. pap. text ed. 5.00 (*1-55516-283-5*, 7302-1711) Natl Conf State Legis.

Constitutional Amendments in India, 1950-1989. Sunder Raman. (C). 1990. 85.00 (*0-89771-198-X*) St Mut.

Constitutional Amendments Nineteen Fifty to Nineteen Eighty-Eight. S. Sathe. (C). 1989. 150.00 (*0-685-36528-X*) St Mut.

Constitutional Amendments, 1950-1988. S. P. Sathe. (C). 1990. 75.00 (*0-89771-197-1*) St Mut.

Constitutional Analysis in a Nutshell. Jerre S. Williams. LC 78-23987. (Nutshell Ser.). 388p. 1987. reprint ed. pap. text ed. 15.00 (*0-8299-2022-6*) West Pub.

Constitutional & Administrative Law. L. J. Boulle et al. 403p. 1989. pap. 40.00 (*0-7021-2316-1*, Pub. by Juta SA) W W Gaunt.

Constitutional & Administrative Law. Ed. by R. Hughes & S. Migdal. 196p. (C). 1990. pap. 60.00 (*1-85352-750-5*, Pub. by HLT Pubns UK) St Mut.

Constitutional & Administrative Law. Ed. by Michael T. Molan. 235p. (C). 1991. 60.00 (*1-85352-693-2*, Pub. by HLT Pubns UK); 60.00 (*1-85352-352-6*, Pub. by HLT Pubns UK); pap. 60.00 (*1-85352-822-6*, Pub. by HLT Pubns UK) St Mut.

Constitutional & Administrative Law - Text & Materials. David Pollard & David J. Hughes. 1990. U.K. pap. 44.00 (*0-406-50600-0*) Butterworth Legal Pubs.

Constitutional & Administrative Law in New Zealand. 952p. 1993. 150.00 (*0-455-21091-8*, Pub. by Law Bk Co); pap. 100.00 (*0-455-21092-6*, Pub. by Law Bk Co) W W Gaunt.

Constitutional & Legal History of England. M. M. Knappen. x, 607p. 1987. reprint ed. lib. bdg. 62.50 (*0-8377-2335-3*) Rothman.

Constitutional & Legal History of England. Goldwin Smith. (Dorset Press Reprints Ser.). (Illus.). 565p. 1990. reprint ed. 24.95 (*0-88029-474-4*) Dorset Pr.

Constitutional Aspects of Watergate: Documents & Materials, 1976-1986, Vols. 1-6. Ed. by A. Stephen Boyan, Jr. LC 75-45440. 1986. 275.00 (*0-685-57762-7*) Oceana.

***Constitutional Authority for & Limitations on Texas State Government Finance, Appropriations, & Spending.** Glen H. Cope & Thomas M. Keel. (Working Paper Ser.: No. 73). 170p. 1993. 6.00 (*0-614-01226-0*) LBJ Sch Pub Aff.

Constitutional Bases of Political & Social Change in the United States. Ed. by Shlomo Slonim. LC 89-16215. 388p. 1990. text ed. 65.00 (*0-275-93071-8*, C3071, Praeger Pubs) Greenwood.

Constitutional Beginnings of North Carolina (1653-1729) John S. Bassett. LC 78-63829. (Johns Hopkins University. Studies in the Social Sciences. Thirtieth Ser. 1912: 3). reprint ed. 37.50 (*0-404-61089-7*) AMS Pr.

Constitutional Bricolage. Gerald Garvey. LC 73-141503. 1971. 26.95x (*0-691-07539-5*) Princeton U Pr.

Constitutional Brinksmanship: Amending the Constitution by National Convention. Russell L. Caplan. 264p. 1988. 39.95 (*0-19-505573-X*) OUP.

Constitutional Case Law of Japan: Selected Supreme Court Decisions, 1961-70. Hiroshi Itoh & Lawrence W. Beer. LC 77-24669. (Asian Law Ser.: No. 6). 288p. 1978. 45.00 (*0-295-95571-6*) U of Wash Pr.

Constitutional Change in the Commonwealth. Leslie Zines. 96p. (C). 1991. 34.95 (*0-521-40039-2*) Cambridge U Pr.

Constitutional Change in the United States: A Comparative Study of the Role of Constitutional Amendments, Judicial Interpretations, & Legislative & Executive Actions. John R. Vile. LC 94-1140. 168p. 1994. text ed. 49.95 (*0-275-94918-4*, Praeger Pubs) Greenwood.

Constitutional Choices. Laurence H. Tribe. 480p. 1985. 40.00 (*0-674-16538-1*) HUP.

Constitutional Choices. Laurence H. Tribe. 480p. 1986. pap. 17.95 (*0-674-16539-X*) HUP.

Constitutional Code, Vol. 1. Jeremy Gentham. Ed. by Frederick S. Rosen & J. H. Burns. (Collected Works of Jeremy Bentham Ser.). 1983. 140.00 (*0-19-822608-X*) OUP.

Constitutional Conflicts Between Congress & the President. rev. ed. Louis Fisher. LC 91-2240. xvi, 328p. 1991. pap. 14.95 (*0-7006-0491-X*) U Pr of KS.

***Constitutional Conflicts in Contemporary Malaysia.** H. P. Lee. 200p. 1995. 45.00 (*967-65-3095-6*) OUP.

Constitutional Confrontation in Hong Kong: Issues & Implications of the Basic Law. Michael C. Davis. LC 89-24264. 204p. 1990. text ed. 59.95 (*0-312-04074-1*) St Martin.

Constitutional Construction. Chester J. Antieau. LC 82-1250. 255p. 1982. lib. bdg. 40.00 (*0-379-20682-X*) Oceana.

Constitutional Convention. Martin McPhillips. LC 85-40169. (Turning Points in American History Ser.). (Illus.). 64p. (J). (gr. 5 up). 1985. lib. bdg. 14.95 (*0-382-06827-0*) Silver Burdett Pr.

Constitutional Convention: Threat or Challenge? Wilbur Edel. LC 80-27573. 160p. 1981. text ed. 45.00 (*0-275-90607-8*, C0607, Praeger Pubs) Greenwood.

Constitutional Convention & the Formation of the Union. 2nd ed. Ed. by Winton U. Solberg. 544p. 1990. 39.95 (*0-252-01727-7*); pap. 15.95 (*0-252-06124-1*) U of Ill Pr.

Constitutional Convention As an Amending Device. Ed. by Harold M. Hyman & Leon V. Sigal. (Project Ser.: No. 87). (Orig.). 1981. pap. text ed. 6.50 (*0-685-46202-1*) Am Political.

Constitutional Convention of Seventeen Eighty-Seven: The Evolution of the Constitution of the U. S. William P. Haas. 64p. (Orig.). (YA). (gr. 7-12). 1987. pap. 2.00 (*0-940527-08-1*) Savant Pub.

Constitutional Conventions: The Rules & Forms of Political Accountability. Geoffrey Marshall. 259p. 1987. pap. 19.95 (*0-19-876202-X*) OUP.

Constitutional Conventions & Political Practice in Canada: The Transformation of the Formal Constitution. Andrew Heard. 256p. 1991. pap. 24.00 (*0-19-540719-9*) OUP.

Constitutional Conventions, Their Nature, Powers, & Limitations. Roger S. Hoar. 240p. 1987. reprint ed. lib. bdg. 30.00 (*0-8377-2239-X*) Rothman.

Constitutional Counterrevolution. Richard Funston. 380p. 1977. 22.95 (*0-470-99022-8*) Schenkman Bks Inc.

Constitutional Courts of the U. S. The Formal & Informal Relationships Between U. S. District Courts, Courts of Appeals & Supreme Court of the U. S. Stephen T. Early, Jr. LC 76-44501. (Quality Paperback Ser.: No. 320). 184p. 1977. pap. 5.95 (*0-8226-0320-9*) Littlefield.

Constitutional Criminal Procedure: An Examination of the Fourth, Fifth, & Sixth Amendments, & Related Areas. Ronald Allen & Richard Kuhns. LC 84-80836. (C). 1985. 39.00 (*0-316-03415-0*) Little.

Constitutional Crisis. Intro. by D. Alford. 3.00 (*0-8315-0072-7*) Speller.

Constitutional Cultures: The Mentality & Consequences of Judicial Review. Robert F. Nagel. 1989. pap. 13.00 (*0-520-08278-8*) U CA Pr.

Constitutional Debate in Action: Civil Rights & Liberties. H. L. Pohlman. LC 94-19167. 325p. (C). 1994. 23.00 (*0-06-500513-9*) HarpCollege.

Constitutional Debate in Action: Criminal Justice. H. L. Pohlman. LC 94-19168. (C). 1994. 23.00 (*0-06-500512-0*) HarpCollege.

Constitutional Debate in Action: Governmental Powers. H. L. Pohlman. LC 94-19166. 320p. (C). 1994. text ed. 23.00 (*0-06-500514-7*) HarpCollege.

Constitutional Debates of 1847. Ed. by Arthur C. Cole. LC 20-21984. (Illinois Historical Collections: Vol. 14). 1919. 10.00 (*0-912154-25-X*) Ill St Hist Lib.

Constitutional Decisions of John Marshall, 2 Vols, Set. Ed. by Joseph P. Cotton. LC 67-25445. (Law, Politics & History Ser.). 1969. reprint ed. lib. bdg. 75.00 (*0-306-70947-3*) Da Capo.

***Constitutional Democracy.** Dennis Mueller. 384p. 1995. 55.00 (*0-19-509588-X*) OUP.

Constitutional Democracy in America. Charles W. Dunn. (C). 1987. pap. text ed. 31.00 (*0-673-18380-7*) HarpCollege.

Constitutional Democracy in America: A Reappraisal. Charles W. Dunn. LC 86-17802. (Illus.). 487p. reprint ed. pap. 138.80 (*0-7837-4749-7*, 2044558) Bks Demand.

Constitutional Design & Power-Sharing in the Post-Modern Epoch. Ed. by Daniel J. Elazar. 268p. (C). 1991. lib. bdg. 42.00 (*0-8191-8095-5*) U Pr of Amer.

Constitutional Development in a Modernizing Society: The United States, 1803 to 1917. William M. Wiecek. LC 84-73236. (Bicentennial Essays on the Constitution Ser.). 90p. 1985. pap. 7.00 (*0-87229-027-1*) Am Hist Assn.

Constitutional Development in Alabama, 1798-1901: A Study in Politics, the Negro, & Sectionalism. Malcolm C. McMillan. LC 78-2258. 1978. reprint ed. 25.00 (*0-87152-258-6*) Reprint.

Constitutional Development in Bangladesh - Stresses & Strains. Dilara Choudhury. 240p. 1995. 26.00 (*0-19-577507-4*) OUP.

Constitutional Development in the South Atlantic States, 1776-1860. Fletcher Green. LC 71-158485. (Civil Liberties in American History Ser.). 1971. reprint ed. lib. bdg. 42.50 (*0-306-70189-8*) Da Capo.

Constitutional Development of Japan. Toyokichi Iyenaga. LC 78-63805. (Johns Hopkins University. Studies in the Social Sciences. Thirtieth Ser. 1912: 9). reprint ed. 11.50 (*0-404-61068-4*) AMS Pr.

Constitutional Developments in the Post-Colonial State of Sierra-Leone 1961-1984. Sheikh B. Daramy. LC 93-14707. (African Studies: Vol. 30). (Illus.). 328p. 1993. text ed. 99.95 (*0-7734-9290-9*) E Mellen.

Constitutional Dialogues: Interpretation As Political Process. Louis Fisher. 272p. 1988. 47.50 (*0-691-07780-0*); pap. 15.95 (*0-691-02287-9*) Princeton U Pr.

Constitutional Dimensions of an Inmate's Right to Health Care. Susan L. Kay. 32p. (Orig.). 1991. pap. 15.00 (*0-929561-00-7*) NCCHC.

C

Constitutional Diplomacy. Michael J. Glennon. 377p. 1991. text ed. 49.50 (*0-691-07842-4*); pap. text ed. 15.95 (*0-691-02305-0*) Princeton U Pr.

Constitutional Doctrines of Justice Harlan. Floyd B. Clark. LC 78-63945. (Johns Hopkins University. Studies in the Social Sciences. Thirtieth Ser. 1912: 4). reprint ed. 14.50 (*0-404-61202-4*) AMS Pr.

Constitutional Doctrines of Justice Harlan. Floyd B. Clark. LC 74-87560. (Law, Politics & History Ser.). 1969. reprint ed. lib. bdg. 29.50 (*0-306-71391-8*) Da Capo.

Constitutional Doctrines of Justice Oliver Wendell Holmes. Dorsey Richardson. LC 78-64115. (Johns Hopkins University. Studies in the Social Sciences. Thirtieth Ser. 1912: 3). reprint ed. 15.00 (*0-404-61230-X*) AMS Pr.

***Constitutional Domains: Democracy, Community, Management.** Robert C. Post. LC 94-29882. 475p. 1995. text ed. 45.00x (*0-674-16545-4*, POSCON) HUP.

Constitutional Economics. James M. Buchanan. (IEA Masters of Modern Economics Ser.). (Illus.). 208p. 1990. text ed. 44.95 (*0-631-17108-8*) Blackwell Pubs.

Constitutional Environments & Economic Growth. Gerald W. Scully. (Illus.). 242p. 1992. text ed. 42.50 (*0-691-04261-6*) Princeton U Pr.

Constitutional Faith. Sanford Levinson. 216p. (Orig.). 1990. text ed. 42.50 (*0-691-07769-X*); pap. text ed. 13.95 (*0-691-02321-2*) Princeton U Pr.

Constitutional Faiths: Felix Frankfurter, Hugo Black, & the Process of Judicial Decision Making. Mark Silverstein. LC 83-45946. 234p. 1984. 32.95 (*0-8014-1650-7*) Cornell U Pr.

Constitutional Fate: Theory of the Constitution. Philip Bobbitt. 1984. pap. 15.95 (*0-19-503422-8*) OUP.

Constitutional Federalism in a Nutshell. 2nd ed. David E. Engdahl. (Nutshell Ser.). 411p. (C). 1987. pap. text ed. 16.50 (*0-314-38329-8*) West Pub.

Constitutional Foundations of World Peace. Ed. by Richard A. Falk et al. LC 92-3839. (SUNY Series, Global Conflict & Peace Education). 388p. (C). 1993. 74.50 (*0-7914-1343-8*); pap. 24.95 (*0-7914-1344-6*) State U NY Pr.

Constitutional Free Speech Defined & Defended. Theodore A. Schroeder. LC 72-106497. (Civil Liberties in American History Ser.). 1970. reprint ed. lib. bdg. 55.00 (*0-306-71872-3*) Da Capo.

Constitutional Glossary. Ed. by Cyrille Goulet. 1993. pap. 23.35 (*0-660-58852-8*, Pub. by Canada Commun Grp CN) Accents Pubns.

***Constitutional Government: The American Experience.** James Curry et al. 608p. (C). 1994. per., pap. text ed. 31.16 (*0-8403-9593-0*) Kendall-Hunt.

Constitutional Government in China: Present Conditions & Prospects. Westel W. Willoughby. 1977. 11.95 (*0-8369-7174-4*, 8006) Ayer.

Constitutional Heads & Political Crises: Commonwealth Episodes, 1945-85. Ed. by D. A. Low. LC 88-10116. 550p. 1988. text ed. 65.00 (*0-312-02113-5*) St Martin.

Constitutional History of England. D. D. Stubbs. viii, 692p. 1987. reprint ed. lib. bdg. 135.00 (*0-89941-559-8*, 305170) W S Hein.

Constitutional History of England: A Course of Lectures Delivered. F. W. Maitland. LC 92-75950. 578p. 1993. reprint ed. 110.00 (*1-56169-026-0*) W W Gaunt.

Constitutional History of England from the Accesion of Henry VII to the Death of George II, 2 vols. Henry Hallam. LC 89-80598. 1384p. 1989. reprint ed. lib. bdg. 160.00 (*0-89941-677-2*, 305890) W S Hein.

Constitutional History of England since the Accession of George Third 1760-1860, 2 vols., Set. Thomas E. May. 1080p. 1986. reprint ed. lib. bdg. 75.00 (*0-8377-2429-5*) Rothman.

Constitutional History of Habeas Corpus. William F. Duker. LC 79-6834. (Contributions in Legal Studies: No. 13). 349p. 1980. text ed. 49.95 (*0-313-22264-9*, DHC/, Greenwood Pr) Greenwood.

Constitutional History of Hawaii. Henry E. Chambers. LC 78-63846. (Johns Hopkins University. Studies in the Social Sciences. Thirtieth Ser. 1912: 1). reprint ed. 11.50 (*0-404-61103-6*) AMS Pr.

Constitutional History of India, 2 Pts. rev. ed. Mahajan Vidyadhar. 794p. (Orig.). (C). 1982. lib. bdg. 11.95 (*0-940500-99-X*, Pub. by S Chand India) Asia Bk Corp.

Constitutional History of India, Vol. I. Anil C. Banerjee. 586p. 1987. 44.95 (*0-318-36619-3*) Asia Bk Corp.

Constitutional History of Modern Britain since 1485. David L. Keir. (C). 1967. pap. text ed. 9.95 (*0-393-00405-8*) Norton.

Constitutional History of New York, 5 vols., Set. C. Z. Lincoln. 1993. reprint ed. lib. bdg. 375.00 (*0-7812-5189-3*) Rprt Serv.

Constitutional History of the American People, 1776-1850, 2 vols. Francis N. Thorpe. 1994. reprint ed. lib. bdg. 97.50 (*0-8377-2675-1*) Rothman.

***Constitutional History of the American Revolution.** John P. Reid. LC 94-39045. 176p. 1995. text ed. 29.95 (*0-299-14660-X*) U of Wis Pr.

***Constitutional History of the American Revolution.** abr. ed. John P. Reid. LC 94-39045. 176p. 1995. pap. text ed. 14.95 (*0-299-14664-2*) U of Wis Pr.

Constitutional History of the American Revolution, Vol. 1: The Authority of Rights. John Philip Reid. LC 86-40058. 1987. text ed. 27.50 (*0-299-10870-8*) U of Wis Pr.

Constitutional History of the American Revolution, Vol. 2: The Authority to Tax. John P. Reid. LC 87-8256. 384p. (C). 1987. text ed. 27.50 (*0-299-11290-X*) U of Wis Pr.

Constitutional History of the American Revolution, Vol. 3: The Authority to Legislate. John P. Reid. LC 91-50326. 508p. (C). 1991. 35.00 (*0-299-13070-3*) U of Wis Pr.

Constitutional History of the American Revolution, Vol. 4: The Authority of Law. John P. Reid. LC 86-40058. 288p. (C). 1993. 35.00 (*0-299-13980-8*) U of Wis Pr.

Constitutional History of the Louisiana Purchase, 1803-1812. Everett S. Brown. LC 68-55492. 1972. reprint ed. 37.50 (*0-678-00742-X*) Kelley.

Constitutional History of the Military Draft. John R. Graham. 1971. 6.95 (*0-87018-065-7*); pap. 2.95 (*0-87018-070-3*) Ross.

Constitutional History of the United States. Andrew C. McLaughlin. 1989. reprint ed. 56.50 (*0-89197-103-3*); reprint ed. pap. text ed. 29.95 (*0-89197-104-1*) Irvington.

Constitutional History of the United States, 3 Vols, Set. Francis N. Thorpe. LC 76-124906. (American Constitutional & Legal History Ser). 1970. reprint ed. lib. bdg. 195.00 (*0-306-71998-3*) Da Capo.

Constitutional History of the United States: From Their Declaration of Independence to the Close of Their Civil War, 2 vols., Set. George T. Curtis. (American Constitution & Legal History Ser.). 1100p. 1974. reprint ed. lib. bdg. 145.00 (*0-306-70611-3*) Da Capo.

Constitutional History of the United States As Seen in the Development of American Law: A Course of Lectures Before the Political Science Association of the University of Michigan. Thomas M. Cooley et al. 296p. 1993. reprint ed. 37.50 (*0-8377-2022-2*) Rothman.

Constitutional Inequality: The Political Fortunes of the Equal Rights Amendment. Gilbert Y. Steiner. LC 84-45854. 113p. 1985. 22.95 (*0-8157-8128-8*); pap. 8.95 (*0-8157-8127-X*) Brookings.

Constitutional Interpretation. Philip Bobbitt. 1991. pap. 18.95 (*0-631-16485-5*) Blackwell Pubs.

Constitutional Interpretation. 5th ed. Craig R. Ducat & Harold W. Chase. Ed. by Hannan. 1503p. (C). 1992. text ed. 65.25 (*0-314-93366-2*) West Pub.

Constitutional Interpretation: Powers of Government. 5th ed. Craig R. Ducat & Harold W. Chase. Ed. by Hannan. 900p. (C). 1992. pap. text ed. 33.25 (*0-314-93455-3*) West Pub.

Constitutional Interpretation: Rights of Individuals. 5th ed. Craig R. Ducat & Harold W. Chase. Ed. by Hannan. 900p. (C). 1992. pap. text ed. 42.50 (*0-314-93456-1*) West Pub.

***Constitutional Interpretation: 1994 Supplement.** 5th ed. Craig R. Ducat. Ed. by Hannan. 200p. 1995. pap. text ed. 23.25 (*0-314-04343-8*) West Pub.

Constitutional Interpretation, 1992 Supplement to. 5th ed. Craig R. Ducat. 100p. (C). 1992. pap. text ed. 18.25 (*0-314-01136-6*) West Pub.

Constitutional Issues in the Case of Rev. Moon: Amicus Briefs Presented to the United States Supreme Court. Ed. by Herbert Richardson. (Studies in Religion & Society: Vol. 10). 450p. 1989. 109.95 (*0-88946-873-7*) E Mellen.

Constitutional Journal. St. John. 1989. pap. 8.95 (*0-915463-55-5*) Green Hill.

Constitutional Journal. Jeffrey St. John. 300p. 1987. 24.95 (*0-915463-42-3*, Jameson Bks) Green Hill.

Constitutional Jurisprudence of the Federal Republic of Germany. Donald P. Kommers. 640p. 1989. pap. text ed. 35.00 (*0-8223-0971-8*) Duke.

Constitutional Language: An Interpretation of Judicial Decision. John Brigham. LC 78-4020. (Contributions in Political Science Ser.: No. 17). 182p. 1978. text ed. 49.95 (*0-313-20420-9*, BCO/, Greenwood Pr) Greenwood.

Constitutional Law. Ed. by Andre Alen. (International Encyclopedia of Laws Ser.). 1991. ring bd. 115.00 (*0-685-58993-5*) Kluwer Law Tax Pubs.

Constitutional Law. Ed. by Andre Alen. (International Encyclopedia of Laws Ser.). 1992. ring bd. 117.00 (*90-6544-944-2*) Kluwer Law Tax Pubs.

Constitutional Law. Ed. by Jane Blessley. 200p. (C). 1990. pap. 75.00 (*1-85352-508-1*, Pub. by HLT Pubns UK) St Mut.

***Constitutional Law.** Katherine Delsack. (Education Ser.). 250p. (C). 1992. pap. text ed. 10.95 (*0-9623338-8-3*) Lawprep Pr.

Constitutional Law. Steven Emanuel. 710p. 1994. pap. text ed. 22.95 (*1-56542-036-5*) E Law Outlines.

Constitutional Law. Jerry Goldman. (C). 1990. text ed. 70.00 (*0-06-042396-X*) HarpCollege.

Constitutional Law. Gary S. Goodpaster. Ed. by Robert J. Switzer. (Law Outlines Ser.). 320p. (Orig.). 1993. pap. text ed. 18.95 (*0-87457-180-4*, 5080) Casenotes Pub.

Constitutional Law. A. Hamid. (C). 1989. 270.00 (*0-685-36532-8*) St Mut.

Constitutional Law. Ronald D. Rotunda. LC 86-26555. 609p. 1987. text ed. 65.25 (*0-314-31127-0*); teacher ed, pap. text ed. write for info. (*0-314-66077-1*) West Pub.

Constitutional Law. Geoffrey R. Stone et al. 1560p. (C). 1986. 44.00 (*0-316-81759-7*) Little.

Constitutional Law. Ed. by Mark V. Tushnet. (International Library of Essays in Law & Legal Theory). 550p. 1992. text ed. 150.00 (*0-8147-8195-0*) NYU Pr.

Constitutional Law. 2nd ed. Malcolm M. Feeley & Samuel Krislov. (C). 1990. text ed. 47.50 (*0-673-39690-8*) HarpCollege.

Constitutional Law. 2nd ed. Geoffrey R. Stone. 1991. 55.00 (*0-316-81776-7*) Little.

Constitutional Law. 3rd ed. Jerome A. Barron & C. Thomas Dienes. (Black Letter Ser.). 440p. 1991. reprint ed. pap. text ed. 24.50 (*0-314-80211-8*) West Pub.

***Constitutional Law.** 4th ed. Jerome A. Barron & C. Thomas Dienes. (Black Letter Ser.). 430p. (C). 1995. pap. text ed. write for info. (*0-314-06209-2*) West Pub.

Constitutional Law. 4th ed. Ronald D. Rotunda & John E. Nowak. (Hornbook Ser.). 1357p. 1993. reprint ed. text ed. 41.50 (*0-314-84217-9*) West Pub.

Constitutional Law. 6th rev. suppl. ed. John C. Klotter & Jacqueline R. Kanovitz. LC 90-81067. (Justice Administration Legal Ser.). 980p. (C). 1992. text ed. 42.95 (*0-87084-496-2*) Anderson Pub Co.

***Constitutional Law.** 7th ed. John C. Klotter & Jacqueline R. Kanovitz. LC 94-70781. (Justice Administration Legal Ser.). 932p. (C). 1994. text ed. write for info. (*0-87084-529-2*) Anderson Pub Co.

Constitutional Law. 12th ed. Gerald Gunther. (University Casebook Ser.). 1675p. 1991. text ed. 48.95 (*0-88277-890-0*) Foundation Pr.

Constitutional Law: Adaptable to Courses Utilizing Brest & Levinson's Casebook on Processes of Constitutional Decision-Making. Casenotes Publishing Co., Inc. Staff. Ed. by Norman S. Goldenberg et al. (Legal Briefs Ser.). 1992. pap. write for info. (*0-87457-026-3*, 1086) Casenotes Pub.

Constitutional Law: Adaptable to Courses Utilizing Cohen & Varat's Casebook on Constitutional Law. Casenotes Publishing Co., Inc. Staff. Ed. by Norman S. Goldenberg et al. (Legal Briefs Ser.). 1993. pap. write for info. (*0-87457-025-5*, 1082) Casenotes Pub.

Constitutional Law: Adaptable to Courses Utilizing Gunther's Casebook on Constitutional Law. Casenotes Publishing Co., Inc. Staff. Ed. by Norman S. Goldenberg et al. (Legal Briefs Ser.). 1991. pap. write for info. (*0-87457-028-X*, 1080) Casenotes Pub.

Constitutional Law: Adaptable to Courses Utilizing Lockhart, Kamisar Choper & Shiffrin's Casebook on Constitutional Law. Casenotes Publishing Co., Inc. Staff. Ed. by Norman S. Goldenberg et al. (Legal Briefs Ser.). 1991. pap. write for info. (*0-87457-030-1*, 1081) Casenotes Pub.

Constitutional Law: Adaptable to Courses Utilizing Materials by Gunther. Gary D. Allison. LC 87-115705. (Legalines Ser.). 397p. 14.50 (*0-685-18647-4*) HarBrace.

Constitutional Law: Adaptable to Courses Utilizing Rotunda's Casebook on Modern Constitutional Law. Casenotes Publishing Co., Inc. Staff. Ed. by Norman S. Goldenberg et al. (Legal Briefs Ser.). 1993. pap. write for info. (*0-87457-031-X*, 1085) Casenotes Pub.

Constitutional Law: Adaptable to Courses Utilizing Stone, Seidman, Sunstein & Tushnet's Casebook on Constitutional Law. Casenotes Publishing Co., Inc. Staff. Ed. by Norman S. Goldenberg et al. (Legal Briefs Ser.). (Orig.). 1991. pap. text ed. write for info. (*0-87457-147-2*, 1087) Casenotes Pub.

Constitutional Law: Cases & Materials. 5th ed. Paul G. Kauper & Francis X. Beytagh. 1980. 55.00 (*0-316-48354-0*) Little.

Constitutional Law: Cases in Context. Susan M. Leeson & James C. Foster. LC 90-63560. 912p. (C). 1992. pap. text ed. 41.00 (*0-312-02512-2*) St Martin.

Constitutional Law: Principles & Policy, Cases & Materials. 4th ed. Jerome A. Barron et al. (Contemporary Legal Education Ser.). 1495p. 1992. 47.00 (*0-87473-888-1*); 47.00 (*0-685-62352-1*) Michie Butterworth.

Constitutional Law: Structure & Rights in Our Federal System. Braveman & Banks. 1991. teacher ed write for info. (*0-8205-0336-3*); Supplement 1991. write for info. (*0-8205-0337-1*) Bender.

Constitutional Law: Structure & Rights in Our Federal System. 2nd ed. Braveman & Banks. 1991. write for info. (*0-8205-0335-5*, 604) Bender.

Constitutional Law: 1986 Case Supplement to 11th Edition. Gerald Gunther & Frederick F. Schauer. Bd. with Individual Rights in Constitutional Law: 1986 Supplement 4th Edition. (University Casebook Ser.). 185p. 1986. Set pap. text ed. 7.95 (*0-88277-524-3*) Foundation Pr.

Constitutional Law - The American Constitution - Constitutional Rights & Liberties. 7th suppl. ed. William B. Lockhart et al. (American Casebook Ser.). 226p. 1993. pap. text ed. 12.50 (*0-314-02543-X*) West Pub.

***Constitutional Law - the American Constitution - Constitutional Rights & Liberties, 1994: Cases - Comments.** suppl. ed. William B. Lockhart et al. (American Casebook Ser.). 265p. 1994. pap. text ed. 14.00 (*0-314-04417-5*) West Pub.

Constitutional Law, a Miscellany. Ed. by S. P. Makkar & Abdul Hamid. (C). 1990. 150.00 (*0-89771-203-X*) St Mut.

Constitutional Law & Its Interpretation. Ed. by Jules L. Coleman. LC 93-32690. (Philosophy of Law Ser.: Vol. 3). 592p. 1994. 83.00 (*0-8153-1399-3*) Garland.

Constitutional Law & Judicial Activism. B. R. Sharma. (C). 1990. 29.00 (*81-7024-353-X*, Pub. by Ashish II) S Asia.

Constitutional Law & Judicial Activism. B. R. Sharma. (C). 1990. 100.00 (*0-89771-196-3*) St Mut.

Constitutional Law & Liability for Agents, Deputies & Police Officers. Dan Murrell & William Dwyer. LC 92-73633. 1992. pap. 15.00 (*0-89089-521-X*) Carolina Acad Pr.

Constitutional Law & Liability for Park Law Enforcement Officers. 3rd ed. Dan S. Murrell & William O. Dwyer. 192p. (C). 1991. pap. text ed. 15.00 (*0-89089-474-4*) Carolina Acad Pr.

Constitutional Law & Liability for Public-Sector Police. Dan Murrell & William Dwyer. 1992. pap. 15.00 (*0-89089-502-3*) Carolina Acad Pr.

Constitutional Law & Minorities. Lewis B. Sckolnick. (Civil Rights Reporter Ser.). (Illus.). 60p. (Orig.). (C). 1994. pap. 45.00 (*1-57205-155-8*) Rector Pr.

***Constitutional Law & Politics Vol. 1: Struggles for Power & Governemtal Accountability.** 2nd ed. David M. O'Brien. LC 94-29012. (C). 1994. pap. text ed. 36.95 (*0-393-96610-0*) Norton.

***Constitutional Law & Politics Vol. 2: Civil Rights & Civil Liberties.** David M. O'Brien. LC 94-29012. (C). 1994. pap. text ed. 36.95x (*0-393-96611-9*) Norton.

Constitutional Law & Practice in the International Labour Organization. E. Osieke. 1985. lib. bdg. 129.50 (*90-247-2985-8*) Kluwer Ac.

Constitutional Law Anthology. Ed. by Michael J. Glennon. LC 92-18888. 1992. write for info. (*0-87084-174-2*) Anderson Pub Co.

Constitutional Law as Fiction: Narrative in the Rhetoric of Authority. L. H. LaRue. LC 94-15750. 176p. 1995. 28.50 (*0-271-01406-7*); pap. 13.95 (*0-271-01407-5*) Pa St U Pr.

Constitutional Law, Cases & Materials. 9th ed. William A. Cohen. Ed. by Jonathan D. Varat. (University Casebook Ser.). (C). 1993. text ed. 48.95 (*1-56662-058-9*) Foundation Pr.

Constitutional Law, Cases-Comments-Questions. 7th ed. William B. Lockart et al. (American Casebook Ser.). 1643p. 1991. text ed. 56.50 (*0-314-86319-2*) West Pub.

Constitutional Law Cases from Malaysia & Singapore. Jayakumar. 1976. pap. 39.00 (*0-685-60630-9*) Butterworth Legal Pubs.

Constitutional Law, Civil Liberty & Individual Rights. 2nd ed. William A. Cohen & John Kaplan. LC 82-5186. (University Casebook Ser.). 924p. 1990. reprint ed. text ed. 28.00 (*0-88277-062-4*) Foundation Pr.

Constitutional Law, Civil Liberty & Individual Rights. 3rd ed. William Cohen & David J. Danelski. LC 93-32111. 1138p. 1994. text ed. 46.50 (*1-56662-089-9*) Foundation Pr.

Constitutional Law, Civil Liberty & Individual Rights, 1992. 2nd suppl. ed. William A. Cohen & John Kaplan. (University Casebook Ser.). 250p. (C). 1992. pap. text ed. 11.95 (*0-88277-996-6*) Foundation Pr.

Constitutional Law Deskbook. Ralph C. Chandler et al. LC 87-80244. 1991. 97.50 (*0-317-01499-4*); Suppl. 1993. write for info. (*0-317-03310-7*) Lawyers Cooperative.

Constitutional Law Dictionary Suppl. 3. Ralph C. Chandler. 200p. 1995. Supplement 3. lib. bdg. 50.00 (*0-87436-758-1*) ABC-CLIO.

Constitutional Law Dictionary Supplement 1: Individual Rights, Vol. 1. Ralph C. Chandler et al. 138p. 1987. lib. bdg. 50.00 (*0-87436-484-1*) ABC-CLIO.

Constitutional Law Dictionary Supplement 2: Individual Rights, Vol. 1. Ralph C. Chandler et al. 251p. 1991. lib. bdg. 50.00 (*0-87436-598-8*) ABC-CLIO.

Constitutional Law Dictionary, Vol. 1: Individual Rights. Ralph C. Chandler et al. LC 84-12320. (Clio Dictionaries in Political Science Ser.: No. 8). 507p. (C). 1985. lib. bdg. 55.00 (*0-87436-031-5*) ABC-CLIO.

Constitutional Law Dictionary, Vol. 2: Governmental Powers. Ralph C. Chandler et al. (Clio Dictionaries in Political Science Ser.: No. 13). 715p. 1987. lib. bdg. 55.00 (*0-87436-440-X*) ABC-CLIO.

Constitutional Law, Eleventh Edition, & Individual Rights in Constitutional Law, 1990. 4th suppl. ed. Gerald Gunther. (University Casebook Ser.). 621p. 1991. pap. text ed. 13.95 (*0-88277-830-7*) Foundation Pr.

Constitutional Law, for a Changing America: Institutional Powers & Constraints. Epstein. 1992. 29.95 (*0-87187-612-4*) Congr Quarterly.

***Constitutional Law for a Changing America: Institutional Powers & Constraints.** 2nd ed. Lee Epstein & Thomas G. Walker. 570p. 1995. pap. 33.95 (*0-87187-829-1*) Congr Quarterly.

Constitutional Law, for a Changing America: Rights, Liberties, & Justice. Epstein. 1991. 29.95 (*0-87187-613-2*) Congr Quarterly.

Constitutional Law for Criminal Justice Professionals. 2nd ed. Irving J. Klein. Ed. by Marta Klein. LC 86-71450. 122p. 1986. teacher ed write for info. (*0-938993-01-1*) Coral Gables Pub.

***Constitutional Law for Criminal Justice Professionals.** 2nd ed. Irving J. Klein. 191p. (C). 1991. pap. 7.95 (*0-938993-11-9*) Coral Gables Pub.

Constitutional Law for Criminal Justice Professionals. annuals 2nd suppl. ed. Irving J. Klein. Ed. by Marta Klein. LC 86-71450. 750p. 1986. 3.95 (*0-938993-02-X*) Coral Gables Pub.

Constitutional Law for Criminal Justice Professionals. 3rd ed. Irving J. Klein. 830p. (C). 1992. 45.00 (*0-938993-12-7*) Coral Gables Pub.

***Constitutional Law for Criminal Justice Professionals.** 3rd ed. Irving J. Klein. 36p. (C). 1993. pap. 7.95 (*0-938993-15-1*) Coral Gables Pub.

Constitutional Law for Criminal Justice Professionals, Incl. annual supplement. 2nd ed. Irving J. Klein. Ed. by Marta Klein. LC 86-71450. 750p. 1986. text ed. 34.90 (*0-938993-00-3*) Coral Gables Pub.

Constitutional Law for Young Adults: A Handbook on the Bill of Rights & the Fourteenth Amendment. Peter G. Renstrom. 413p. 1992. lib. bdg. 35.00 (*0-87436-483-3*) ABC-CLIO.

Constitutional Law in a Nutshell. 2nd ed. Jerome A. Barron & C. Thomas Dienes. (Nutshell Ser.). 483p. 1993. reprint ed. pap. text ed. 17.00 (*0-314-80710-1*) West Pub.

***Constitutional Law in a Nutshell.** 3rd ed. Jerome A. Barron & C. Thomas Dienes. (Nutshell Ser.). 504p. (C). 1995. pap. text ed. write for info. (*0-314-06379-X*) West Pub.

***Constitutional Law in Australia.** P. J. Hanks. 1991. pap. 75.00 (*0-409-49575-1*, Austral); boxed 91.00 (*0-409-49574-3*, Austral) Butterworth Legal Pubs.

Constitutional Law in Malaysia & Singapore. Tan et al. 1991. pap. 54.00 (*0-409-99611-4*) Butterworth Legal Pubs.

Constitutional Law in the United States: A Systematic Inquiry into the Change & Relevance of Supreme Court Decisions. Randall W. Bland. LC 92-32142. 382p. 1992. 59.95 (*1-880921-08-1*); pap. 44.95 (*1-880921-07-3*) Austin & Winfield.

***Constitutional Law in Theory & Practice.** Beatty. 1995. pap. text ed. (*0-8020-7650-5*) U of Toronto Pr.

1560

An Asterisk (*) at the beginning of an entry indicates that the title is appearing in BIP for the first time.

*__Constitutional Law in Theory & Practice.__ David M. Beatty. 240p. 1995. 50.00 (*0-8020-0701-5*); pap. 18.95 (*0-614-03707-7*) U of Toronto Pr.

Constitutional Law of Algeria: Texts & Contents. Ahmed Aqued. (C). 1987. 95.00 (*0-685-49139-0*, Pub. by Royston Ltd) St Mut.

Constitutional Law of Algeria: Texts & Contents. Ed. by Ahmed Aqued. (C). 1987. 175.00 (*0-685-61454-9*, Pub. by Royston Ltd) St Mut.

Constitutional Law of Ghana. Francis A. Bennion. LC 63-3133. (Butterworth's African Law Ser.: No. 5). 563p. reprint ed. pap. 160.50 (*0-317-28446-0*, 2051259) Bks Demand.

Constitutional Law of India. Duga D. Basu. LC 83-903490. xi, 488p. write for info. (*0-87692-024-5*) P-H.

Constitutional Law of India. V. D. Mahajan. 600p. 1984. 160.00 (*0-317-54584-1*) St Mut.

Constitutional Law of India. V. D. Mahajan. (C). 1991. text ed. 125.00 (*0-89771-486-5*) St Mut.

Constitutional Law of India. T. K. Tope. 816p. 1988. 225.00 (*0-317-57736-0*) St Mut.

Constitutional Law of India. T. K. Tope. (C). 1992. 400.00 (*0-89771-770-8*, Pub. by Eastern Book II) St Mut.

Constitutional Law of India. 2nd ed. T. K. Tope. (C). 1992. 200.00 (*81-7012-480-8*, Pub. by Eastern Book II) St Mut.

Constitutional Law of India. 7th ed. Ed. by V. D. Mahajan. (C). 1991. 125.00 (*0-685-39772-6*) St Mut.

Constitutional Law of India, Vol. 1. M. Hidayatullah. 1002p. 1985. 60.00 (*0-932639-00-3*) Indian Bk Ctr.

Constitutional Law of India: Critical Commentary (Supplement) H. M. Seervai. (C). 1988. 300.00 (*0-685-27923-5*) St Mut.

Constitutional Law of India, Nineteen Eighty-Two: W-S, 1988. T. K. Tope. (C). 1988. 95.00 (*0-685-46466-0*) St Mut.

Constitutional Law of India, 1982: With Supplement. T. K. Tope. (C). 1990. 95.00 (*0-685-39768-8*) St Mut.

Constitutional Law of Iran: Text & Comments. S. H. Amin. (C). 1987. 195.00 (*0-685-61453-0*, Pub. by Royston Ltd) St Mut.

Constitutional Law of Iran: Texts & Comments. S. H. Amin. (C). 1987. 95.00 (*0-685-49140-4*, Pub. by Royston Ltd) St Mut.

Constitutional Law of the United States of America. H. Von Holst. Tr. by Alfred B. Mason. v, 369p. 1988. reprint ed. lib. bdg. 37.50 (*0-8377-1238-6*) Rothman.

Constitutional Law, Themes for the Constitution's Third Century: Cases & Materials. Daniel A. Farber, Jr. & William N. Eskridge. Ed. by Philip P. Frickey. (American Casebook Ser.). 213p. (C). 1993. teacher ed, pap. text ed. write for info. (*0-314-02517-0*) West Pub.

*__Constitutional Law Themes for the Constitution's Third Century, 1994: Cases & Materials.__ suppl. ed. Daniel A. Farber et al. (American Casebook Ser.). 148p. 1994. pap. text ed. write for info. (*0-314-04419-1*) West Pub.

Constitutional Law, Twelfth Edition, & Individual Rights in Constitutional Law, Fifth Edition, 1993 Supplement. Gerald Gunther & Fred Schauer. (University Casebook Ser.). 250p. 1993. pap. text ed. 10.95 (*1-56662-099-6*) Foundation Pr.

Constitutional Law, 1992 Supplement. 6th ed. John C. Klotter & Jacqueline R. Kanovitz. LC 91-76956. (Justice Administration Legal Ser.). 43p. (C). 1991. text ed. 7.00 (*0-87084-528-4*) Anderson Pub Co.

*__Constitutional Law, 1994: Cases & Materials.__ 9th suppl. ed. William Cohen & Jonathan D. Varat. (University Casebook Ser.). 150p. 1994. pap. text ed. write for info. (*1-56662-217-4*) Foundation Pr.

Constitutional Limitations on Criminal Procedure. Richard B. McNamara. (Federal Publications). 419p. 1982. text ed. 95.00 (*0-07-045674-7*) Shepards-McGraw.

Constitutional Limits to Union Power. Philip D. Bradley. (JSPES Monograph: No. 4). 1976. pap. 15.00 (*0-930690-06-0*) Coun Soc Econ.

Constitutional Literacy: A Core Curriculum for a Multicultural Nation. Toni M. Massaro. LC 93-10861. (Constitutional Conflicts Ser.). 208p. 1993. 24.95 (*0-8223-1364-2*) Duke.

Constitutional Litigation. Kenneth F. Ripple. (Contemporary Litigation Ser.). 696p. 1984. 50.00 (*0-87215-754-7*) Michie Butterworth.

Constitutional Logic of Affirmative Action. Ronald J. Fiscus. Ed. by Stephen L. Wasby. LC 91-33695. 170p. 1992. text ed. 19.95 (*0-8223-1206-9*) Duke.

Constitutional Miscellany. V. R. Iyer. (C). 1986. 90.00 (*0-685-39773-4*) St Mut.

Constitutional Miscellany. V. R. Iyer. (C). 1989. 80.00 (*0-89771-751-1*, Pub. by Eastern Book II) St Mut.

Constitutional Models of Socialist Organisation. O Bihari. 372p. 1979. 100.00 (*0-685-17097-7*) St Mut.

*__Constitutional Models of Socialist State Organization.__ O. Bihari. 372p. (C). 1979. 90.00x (*963-05-2077-X*, Pub. by Akad Kiado HU) St Mut.

Constitutional Odyssey: Can Canadians Be a Sovereign People? 2nd ed. Peter H. Russell. 250p. 1993. pap. 18.95 (*0-8020-6997-5*) U of Toronto Pr.

Constitutional Opinions: Aspects of the Bill of Rights. Leonard W. Levy. 288p. 1989. reprint ed. pap. 18.95 (*0-19-505945-X*) OUP.

Constitutional Options for A Democratic South Africa: A Comparative Perspective. Ziyad Motala. LC 94-6680. 1994. 39.95 (*0-88258-187-2*); pap. 19.95 (*0-88258-180-5*) Howard U Pr.

Constitutional Pluralism: Conflicting Interpretations of the Founders' Intentions. Michael Kammen. LC 87-71560. 40p. 1987. pap. 7.50 (*0-87495-093-7*) Am Jewish Comm.

*__Constitutional Policy & Change in Europe.__ Ed. by Joachim J. Hesse & Nevil Johnson. (Nuffield European Studies). (Illus.). 375p. 1995. text ed. 55.00 (*0-19-827991-4*) OUP.

*__Constitutional Policy in Unified Germany.__ Ed. by Klaus H. Goetz & Peter J. Cullen. LC 94-23943. 1995. write for info. (*0-7146-4631-8*, Pub. by F Cass Pubs UK) Intl Spec Bk.

Constitutional Politics in the Progressive Era: Child Labor & the Law. Stephen B. Wood. LC 67-25525. 336p. reprint ed. pap. 95.80 (*0-317-28196-8*, 2020182) Bks Demand.

Constitutional Powers of the General Conference: With a Special Application to the Subject of Slave Holding. William L. Harris. LC 74-146265. (Black Heritage Library Collection). 1977. 15.95 (*0-8369-8740-3*) Ayer.

*__Constitutional Practice.__ 2nd ed. Rodney Brazier. 325p. 1995. 55.00 (*0-19-876359-X*) OUP.

Constitutional Predicament: Canada after the Referendum of 1992. Ed. by Curtis Cook. 320p. (C). 1994. 49.95 (*0-7735-1192-X*, Pub. by McGill CN); pap. text ed. 17.95 (*0-7735-1202-0*, Pub. by McGill CN) U of Toronto Pr.

Constitutional Principles of Thomas Jefferson. Caleb P. Patterson. LC 77-157352. (Select Bibliographies Reprint Ser.). 1977. reprint ed. 24.95 (*0-8369-5813-6*) Ayer.

Constitutional Problems in Church-State Relations: A Symposium. D. T. Mitzner et al. LC 75-155825. (Symposia on Law & Society Ser.). 1971. reprint ed. lib. bdg. 19.50 (*0-306-70131-6*) Da Capo.

Constitutional Problems in Pakistan. William I. Jennings. LC 72-8240. 378p. 1973. reprint ed. text ed. 69.50 (*0-8371-6540-7*, JECP, Greenwood Pr) Greenwood.

Constitutional Problems of Federal India. H. Haksar. (C). 1988. 160.00 (*0-685-27920-0*) St Mut.

Constitutional Reason of State: The Survival of the Constitutional Order. Carl J. Friedrich. LC 57-10150. (Colver Lectures in Brown University: No. 1956). 143p. reprint ed. pap. 40.80 (*0-685-20543-6*, 2030022) Bks Demand.

Constitutional Reform: Re-Shaping the British Political System. Rodney Brazier. 184p. 1991. 39.95 (*0-19-876257-7*) OUP.

Constitutional Reform & Effective Government. James L. Sundquist. LC 85-26918. 262p. 1986. 31.95 (*0-8157-8228-4*); pap. 12.95 (*0-8157-8227-6*) Brookings.

Constitutional Reform & Effective Government. rev. ed. James L. Sundquist. 344p. (C). 1992. 36.95 (*0-8157-8230-6*); pap. 16.95 (*0-8157-8229-2*) Brookings.

Constitutional Reform & the Future of the Republic of China. Ed. by Harvey J. Feldman. LC 91-16193. (Taiwan in the Modern World Ser.). 200p. 1991. 48.95 (*0-87332-880-9*) M E Sharpe.

Constitutional Resistance to Infection. C. M. Verduin. Ed. by D. A. Watson et al. (Medical Intelligence Unit Ser.). 179p. 1995. write for info. (*1-57059-170-9*) R G Landes.

Constitutional Restrictions Against State Debt. A. James Heins. LC 63-9062. 164p. reprint ed. pap. 46.80 (*0-317-09640-0*, 2021135) Bks Demand.

Constitutional Review & Legislation: An International Comparison. Ed. by Christine Landfried. 266p. 1988. 69.50 (*3-7890-1640-3*, Pub. by Nomos Verlags GW) Intl Bk Import.

Constitutional Revision Comment in Gubernatorial Messages & Party Platforms. W. O. Farber. 1969. 1.00 (*1-55614-026-6*) U of SD Gov Res Bur.

Constitutional Revision in South Dakota. W. H. Cape. 1957. 5.00 (*1-55614-028-2*) U of SD Gov Res Bur.

Constitutional Revision in South Dakota: Ballot Issues in 1972. W. O. Farber. 1972. 1.00 (*1-55614-027-4*) U of SD Gov Res Bur.

*__Constitutional Revolution: The Link Between Constitutionalism & Progress.__ Ulrich K. Preuss. Tr. by Deborah L. Schneider. LC 94-37939. 136p. (C). 1995. text ed. 45.00 (*0-391-03853-2*); pap. 15.00 (*0-391-03854-0*) Humanities.

Constitutional Revolution, Ltd. Edward S. Corwin. LC 77-805. ix, 121p. 1977. reprint ed. lib. bdg. 22.50 (*0-8371-9498-9*, Greenwood Pr) Greenwood.

Constitutional Right of Association. David Fellman. LC 63-9728. 120p. reprint ed. pap. 34.20 (*0-317-07956-5*, 2015755) Bks Demand.

Constitutional Right to a Speedy & Fair Criminal Trial. Warren Freedman. 189p. 1989. 39.95 (*0-318-36033-0*, FCE/, Quorum Bks); text ed. 65.00 (*0-89930-331-5*, FCE/, Greenwood Pr) Greenwood.

Constitutional Right to Suicide: A Legal & Philosophical Examination. G. Steven Neeley. LC 92-32235. (American University Studies, V, Philosophy: Vol. 146). 240p. (C). 1994. text ed. 41.95 (*0-8204-2032-8*) P Lang Pubs.

Constitutional Rights & Liberties, Cases - Comments - Questions. 7th ed. William B. Lockhart et al. (American Casebook Ser.). 1333p. (C). 1991. text ed. 50.00 (*0-314-88940-X*) West Pub.

Constitutional Rights in the Investigative Process. Finkelstein. 240p. 1991. 74.00 (*0-409-81171-8*) Butterworth Legal Pubs.

Constitutional Rights of Prisoners. 4th rev. ed. John W. Palmer. LC 90-82311. 874p. (C). 1990. text ed. 37.95 (*0-87084-692-2*) Anderson Pub Co.

Constitutional Rights of the Accused, 3 vols., Set. 2nd ed. Joseph R. Cook. LC 85-51443. 1985. 345.00 (*0-685-59838-1*) Clark Boardman Callaghan.

Constitutional Rights of Women: Cases in Law & Social Change. Leslie F. Goldstein. LC 87-40361. 656p. (C). 1988. text ed. 39.50 (*0-299-11240-3*); pap. text ed. 17.50 (*0-299-11244-6*) U of Wis Pr.

Constitutional Royalism & the Search for Settlement, c. 1640-1649. David L. Smith. LC 93-34969. (Cambridge Studies in Early Modern British History). 300p. (C). 1994. 64.95 (*0-521-41056-8*) Cambridge U Pr.

Constitutional Sampler: In Order to Form a More Perfect Lesson Plan... 2nd ed. SPICE II Teachers. LC 87-72136. 274p. 1991. 12.00 (*1-879953-01-3*) CRD Law-Related.

*__Constitutional Schemes & Political Development in India Towards Transfer of Power.__ Ed. by Verinder Grover & Ranjana Arora. (C). 1995. 72.00x (*81-7100-539-X*) S Asia.

Constitutional Significance of Trevett vs. Weeden (1786) Patrick T. Conley. (Illus.). 10p. 1976. pap. 1.25 (*0-917012-43-7*) RI Pubns Soc.

Constitutional Status & Government of Alaska. George W. Spicer. LC 78-64125. (Johns Hopkins University. Studies in the Social Sciences. Thirtieth Ser. 1912: 4). reprint ed. 16.00 (*0-404-61239-3*) AMS Pr.

Constitutional Status of Academic Freedom. Ed. by Walter P. Metzger. LC 76-55211. (Academic Profession Ser.). 1978. reprint ed. lib. bdg. 51.95 (*0-405-10038-8*) Ayer.

Constitutional Status of Academic Tenure: An Original Anthology. Ed. by Walter P. Metzger. LC 76-52627. (Academic Profession Ser.). 1979. reprint ed. lib. bdg. 34.95 (*0-405-09982-7*) Ayer.

Constitutional Structure of Modern China. Wen-Yen Tsao. LC 73-900. (China Studies: from Confucius to Mao Ser.). (Illus.). xvii, 304p. 1973. reprint ed. 23.50 (*0-88355-094-6*) Hyperion Conn.

Constitutional Structure of the Commonwealth. Kenneth C. Wheare. LC 82-11866. 201p. 1982. reprint ed. text ed. 55.00 (*0-313-23624-0*, WHCO, Greenwood Pr) Greenwood.

Constitutional Studies: Contemporary Issues & Controversies. Ed. by Robert Blackburn. 224p. 1992. text ed. 80.00 (*0-7201-2125-6*, Mansell Pub) Cassell.

Constitutional Studies: State & Federal. J. Schouler. LC 76-124894. (American Constitutional & Legal History Ser). 1971. reprint ed. lib. bdg. 32.50 (*0-306-71993-2*) Da Capo.

Constitutional System: The Group Character of the Elected Institutions. Henry J. Merry. LC 86-15162. 225p. 1986. text ed. 49.95 (*0-275-92185-9*, C2185, Praeger Pubs) Greenwood.

Constitutional Systems in Late Twentieth-Century Asia. Ed. by Lawrence W. Beer. LC 91-5165. (Asian Law Ser.: No. 12). 752p. 1992. 75.00 (*0-295-97174-6*) U of Wash Pr.

Constitutional Texts: Materials on Government & the Constitution. Rodney Brazier. 648p. 1990. 79.00 (*0-19-876246-1*) OUP.

Constitutional Thought of Thomas Jefferson. David N. Mayer. LC 93-29649. 1994. 39.50 (*0-8139-1484-1*) U Pr of Va.

Constitutional Thought of Thomas Jefferson. David N. Mayer. LC 93-29649. 416p. (C). 1995. pap. text ed. 18.50 (*0-8139-1485-X*) U Pr of Va.

Constitutional Torts: 1984. Kenneth C. Davis. xiv, 338p. 1984. reprint ed. 37.00 (*0-943626-07-2*) K C Davis Pub.

*__Constitutional Torts Casebook.__ Sheldon H. Nahmod et al. LC 94-43425. 1995. text ed. write for info. (*0-87084-903-4*) Anderson Pub Co.

Constitutional Values in the Private Sector Workplace. Joseph R. Grodin. (Benjamin Aaron Annual Lecture Ser.). 40p. 1993. 7.00 (*0-685-70074-7*) U Cal LA Indus Rel.

Constitutionalism: Founding & Future. Ed. by Kenneth W. Thompson. LC 88-27707. (Miller Center Bicentennial Series on Constitutionalism: Vol. I). 132p. (Orig.). (C). 1989. lib. bdg. 31.00 (*0-8191-7217-0*, Pub. by White Miller Center); pap. text ed. 15.00 (*0-8191-7218-9*, Pub. by White Miller Center) U Pr of Amer.

Constitutionalism: The Israeli & American Experiences. Ed. by Daniel J. Elazar. 280p. (C). 1990. pap. text ed. 31.50 (*0-8191-7798-9*) U Pr of Amer.

Constitutionalism: The Israeli & American Experiences. Ed. by Daniel J. Elazar. 280p. (C). 1990. lib. bdg. 51.00 (*0-8191-7797-0*) U Pr of Amer.

Constitutionalism: The Philosophical Dimension. Ed. by Alan S. Rosenbaum. LC 88-5634. (Contributions in Legal Studies: No. 46). 288p. 1988. text ed. 59.95 (*0-313-25671-3*, RCU/, Greenwood Pr) Greenwood.

Constitutionalism & Democracy. Ed. by Jon Elster & Rune Slagstad. (Studies in Rationality & Social Change). 240p. 1988. 64.95 (*0-521-34530-8*) Cambridge U Pr.

Constitutionalism & Democracy. Ed. by Jon Elster & Rune Slagstad. (Studies in Rationality & Social Change). 360p. (C). 1993. pap. 18.95 (*0-521-45721-1*) Cambridge U Pr.

Constitutionalism & Democracy: Transitions in the Contemporary World. Ed. by Douglas Greenberg et al. LC 92-22633. (American Council of Learned Societies Comparative Constitutionalism Papers). 1993. 55.00 (*0-19-507107-7*) OUP.

Constitutionalism & Human Rights: America, Poland & France. Ed. by Kenneth W. Thompson & Rett R. Ludwikowski. (Miller Center Bicentennial Series on Constitutionalism: Vol. VI). 202p. (C). 1991. lib. bdg. 38.00 (*0-8191-8151-X*); pap. text ed. 21.50 (*0-8191-8152-8*) U Pr of Amer.

Constitutionalism & Nationalism in Lower Canada: Essays. Fernand Ouellet et al. LC 75-431747. (Canadian Historical Readings Ser.: No. 5). 106p. reprint ed. pap. 30.30 (*0-8357-6377-3*, 2035731) Bks Demand.

Constitutionalism & Rights. Gary C. Bryner & Noel B. Reynolds. LC 86-23272. (Brigham Young University Bks.). 163p. 1987. 44.50 (*0-88706-657-7*); pap. 14.95 (*0-88706-806-5*) State U NY Pr.

Constitutionalism & the Changing World: Collected Papers. Charles H. McIlwain. LC 75-103801. (Cambridge University Press Library Editions). 320p. reprint ed. pap. 91.20 (*0-685-16092-0*, 2027246) Bks Demand.

Constitutionalism, Democracy, & Foreign Affairs. Louis Henkin. 125p. 1992. text ed. 25.00 (*0-231-07228-7*); pap. 12.95 (*0-231-07229-5*) Col U Pr.

Constitutionalism, Identity, Difference & Legitimacy: Theoretical Perspectives. Ed. by Michel Rosenfeld. LC 94-15777. 448p. 1994. lib. bdg. 49.95 (*0-8223-1505-X*); pap. text ed. 19.95 (*0-8223-1516-5*) Duke.

Constitutionalism in America: E. Pluribus Unum: Constitutional Principles & the Institutions of Government, Vol. 2. Ed. by Sarah B. Thurow. LC 87-31723. 300p. (Orig.). (C). 1988. lib. bdg. 50.00 (*0-8191-6778-9*); pap. text ed. 27.00 (*0-8191-6779-7*) U Pr of Amer.

Constitutionalism in America: To Secure the Blessings of Liberty: First Principles of the Constitution, Vol. 1. Ed. by Sarah B. Thurow. LC 87-31721. 344p. (Orig.). (C). 1988. lib. bdg. 50.00 (*0-8191-6776-2*) U Pr of Amer.

Constitutionalism in America, Vol. III: Constitutionalism in Perspective. Ed. by Sarah B. Thurow. LC 87-31722. (United States Constitution in Twentieth Century Politics Ser.). 320p. (Orig.). (C). 1988. lib. bdg. 50.00 (*0-8191-7158-1*) U Pr of Amer.

Constitutionalism in the Emergent States. B. O. Nwabueze. LC 72-14221. 320p. 1973. 39.50 (*0-8386-1365-9*) Fairleigh Dickinson.

Constitutionalist: Notes on the First Amendment. George Anastaplo. LC 72-165793. 840p. reprint ed. pap. 180.00 (*0-685-15321-5*, 2026233) Bks Demand.

Constitutionalist Years see Mexican Revolution

Constitutionality of Drunk Driver Roadblocks. FBI Staff. 8p. 1994. pap. 10.00 (*0-930179-33-1*) Johns Enter.

Constitutions & Constitutionalism in the Slaveholding South. Don E. Fehrenbacher. LC 88-27680. (Mercer University Lamar Memorial Lecture Ser.: No. 31). 128p. 1989. 20.00 (*0-8203-1119-7*) U of Ga Pr.

Constitutions and Laws of the American Indian Tribes Ser. 2, 33 vols., Set. 1975. reprint ed. 460.00 (*0-8420-2101-9*) Scholarly Res Inc.

Constitutions, Electoral Laws, Treaties of States in the Near & Middle East. Ed. by Helen C. Davis. LC 79-99886. reprint ed. 34.50 (*0-404-01995-1*) AMS Pr.

Constitutions in Crisis: Political Violence & the Rule of Law. John E. Finn. 288p. 1990. 45.00 (*0-19-505738-4*) OUP.

Constitutions in Democratic Politics. Vernon Bogdanor. 395p. 1988. text ed. 58.95 (*0-566-05575-9*, Pub. by Dartmth Pub UK) Ashgate Pub Co.

Constitutions of American Denominations, 3 vols., Set. Ed. by Robert L. Schenck. LC 83-82907. 1983. ring bd. 185.00 (*0-89941-311-0*, 302960) W S Hein.

Constitutions of Canada, Federal & Provincial, 4 bdrs. looseleaf. Christian L. Wiktor & G. Tanguay. LC 78-62326. (ENG & FRE.). 1979. 350.00 (*0-379-20303-0*) Oceana.

Constitutions of Dependencies & Special Sovereignties, 8 binders, Set. Ed. by Albert P. Blaustein & Eric B. Blaustein. LC 75-21651. 1975. ring bd. 895.00 (*0-379-00278-7*) Oceana.

Constitutions of Nations. Incl. No. 2. Asia, Australia, & Oceania, 2 pts. Amos G. Peeslee. 1974. lib. bdg. 257.50 (*90-247-0444-8*); No. 3. Europe, 2 pts. 1974. lib. bdg. 257.50 (*90-247-0447-2*); (Constitutions of Nations Ser). write for info. (*0-318-53996-9*) Kluwer Ac.

Constitutions of Nations. Amos J. Peaslee. 1986. lib. bdg. 464.00 (*90-247-2905-X*) Kluwer Ac.

Constitutions of the Australian States. 5th rev. ed. R. D. Lumb. 1991. pap. 29.95 (*0-7022-2218-6*, Pub. by Univ Queensland Pr AT) Intl Spec Bk.

Constitutions of the Communist World. William B. Simons. 640p. 1980. lib. bdg. 249.00 (*90-286-0070-1*) Kluwer Ac.

Constitutions of the Countries of the World: A Series of Updated Texts, Constitutional Chronologies, & Annotated Bibliographies, 21 vols. Ed. by Albert P. Blaustein & Gisbert H. Flanz. LC 76-141327. 1971. Incl. suppl. historical bdr. approx. 5-6 rel. per year. ring bd. 2,500.00 (*0-379-00467-4*) Oceana.

Constitutions of the Marian Clerics under the Title of the Immaculate Conception of the Most Blessed Virgin Mary. Intro. by Victor Rimselis. 121p. 1991. pap. write for info. (*0-933820-07-0*) Marian Fathers.

Constitutions of the Northwest States. John D. Hicks. LC 89-84956. (Historical Writings in Law & Jurisprudence Ser.: No. 15). 168p. 1990. reprint ed. lib. bdg. 37.50 (*0-89941-713-2*, 306110) W S Hein.

Constitutions of the Order of the Pious Schools. Piarist Fathers Staff. Ed. & Tr. by Salvidor Cudinach. LC 85-60915. 110p. write for info. (*0-9614908-0-2*) Piarist Father.

Constitutions of the Society of Jesus. St. Ignatius of Loyola. Tr. & Comment by George E. Ganss. LC 72-108258. (Jesuit Primary Sources in English Translation Series I: No. 1). xiv, 420p. 1970. pap. 12.00 (*0-912422-20-3*) Inst Jesuit.

Constitutions of the U. S. National & State, 1974: National & State, 1974, 7 bdrs. looseleaf incl. index. 2nd ed. Columbia University, Legislative Drafting Research Fund Staff. Ed. by Frank Grad & Martha O'Connor. 1974. 750.00 (*0-379-00186-1*) Oceana.

Constitutions of the U. S. National & State, 1974: National & State, 1974, 7 bdrs. looseleaf incl. index. 2nd ed. Ed. by Frank Grad & Martha O'Connor. 1974. Approx. 3 releases per yr. write for info. (*0-318-54750-3*) Oceana.

Constitutions of the U.S.S.R. & the Union Republics: Analysis, Texts, Reports, 1979. Ferdinand J. Feldbrugge. 381p. 1979. lib. bdg. 154.50 (*90-286-0489-8*) Kluwer Ac.

Constitutions of the World. Albert P. Blaustein. LC 92-39039. xi, 86p. 1993. pap. 22.50 (*0-8377-0362-X*) Rothman.

*__Constitutions of the World.__ Robert L. Maddex, Jr. 360p. 1995. 69.95 (*0-87187-992-1*) Congr Quarterly.

*__Constitutions of the World.__ Robert L. Maddex. LC 95-11374. 1995. write for info. (*0-87187-922-0*) Congr Quarterly.

C

An Asterisk (*) at the beginning of an entry indicates that the title is appearing in BIP for the first time. 1561

Constitutions, Taxation & Land Policy, 2 vols., Vol. 1. Michael M. Bernard. LC 78-24792. 176p. reprint ed. pap. 50.20 (*0-7837-5715-8*, 2045424) Bks Demand.

Constitutions, Taxation & Land Policy, 2 vols., Vol. 2. Michael M. Bernard. LC 78-24792. 141p. reprint ed. pap. 40.20 (*0-7837-5716-6*, 2045424) Bks Demand.

Constitutive Behavior of High-Temperature Composites. Ed. by B. S. Majumdar et al. (MD Ser.: Vol. 40). 184p. 1992. 50.00 (*0-7918-1117-4*, G00761) ASME.

Constitutive Equations for Anisotropic & Isotropic Materials. Gerald F. Smith. LC 93-42037. (Mechanics & Physics of Discrete Systems Ser.: Vol. 3). 1994. 185. 75 (*0-444-88405-X*, North Holland) Elsevier.

Constitutive Equations for Engineering Materials, 2 vols. Wai-Fah Chen & Atef F. Saleeb. LC 94-9081. (Studies in Applied Mechanics: Vol. 37A-B). 1994. 328.50 (*0-444-88408-4*) Elsevier.

Constitutive Equations for Granular Non-Cohesive Soils. Ed. by Adel S. Saada. (Proceedings of International Workshop Cleveland, Ohio, 22-24 July 1987 Ser.). 400p. (C). 1989. text ed. 170.00 (*90-6191-789-1*, Pub. by A A Balkema NE) Ashgate Pub Co.

Constitutive Equations for Polymer Melts & Solutions. Ronald Larson. (Illus.). 384p. 1988. text ed. 59.95 (*0-409-90119-9*) Buttrwrth-Heinemann.

Constitutive Equations in Viscoplasticity: Phenomenological & Physical Aspects. American Society of Mechanical Engineers Staff. Ed. by K. C. Valanis. (AMD Ser.: Vol. 21). 86p. reprint ed. pap. 25.00 (*0-8357-2887-0*, 2039123) Bks Demand.

Constitutive Equations of Nonlinear Electromagnetic-Elastic Crystals. A. Kiral & A. C. Erigen. (Illus.). 275p. 1990. 79.00 (*0-387-97120-3*) Spr-Verlag.

Constitutive Immunity. S. N. Rumyantsev. (Medical Intelligence Unit Ser.). write for info. (*1-57059-104-0*) R G Landes.

Constitutive Laws & Microstructure. Ed. by D. R. Axelrad & W. Muschik. (Illus.). ix, 206p. 1988. 53.00 (*0-387-18654-9*) Spr-Verlag.

Constitutive Laws for Engineering Materials. Ed. by C. S. Qesai et al. 957p. 1991. 200.00 (*0-7918-0024-5*, 800245) ASME Pr.

Constitutive Laws of Plastic Deformation & Fracture. Ed. by A. S. Krausz. (C). 1990. lib. bdg. 123.00 (*0-7923-0639-2*) Kluwer Ac.

C

Constitutive Models of Deformation. Jagdish Chandra & Ram Srivastav. LC 87-60608. (Proceedings in Applied Mathematics Ser.: No. 28). (Illus.). x, 182p. 1987. text ed. 40.75 (*0-89871-217-3*) Soc Indus-Appl Math.

Constitutive Relations for Finite Deformation of Polycrystalline Metals: Proceedings of the IUTAM Symposium, Held in Beijing, China, July 22-25, 1991. Ed. by Ren Wang & Daniel C. Drucker. LC 92-15215. (International Union of Theoretical & Applied Mechanics Symposia Ser.). (Illus.). 350p. 1992. 125.00 (*0-387-55128-X*) Spr-Verlag.

Constitutive Relations for Soils: Results of an International Workshop, Grenoble, 6-8 September 1982. Ed. by G. Gudehus et al. 512p. (C). 1984. text ed. 185.00 (*90-6191-549-X*, Pub. by A A Balkema NE) Ashgate Pub Co.

Constrained Attitudes. Frank M. Colby. LC 68-8449. (Essay Index Reprint Ser.). 1977. reprint ed. 19.95 (*0-8369-0322-6*) Ayer.

Constrained Mechanics & Lie Theory. Robert Hermann. LC 92-41422. 1992. 95.00 (*0-915692-43-0*) Math Sci Pr.

Constrained Optimization in the Calculus of Variations & Optimal Control Theory. John Gregory & Cantian Lin. (Illus.). 275p. 1992. text ed. 49.95 (*0-442-00722-1*) Chapman & Hall.

Constraint & Variety in American Education. David Riesman. LC 56-13482. (Landmark Edition Ser.). 175p. reprint ed. pap. 49.90 (*0-8357-2945-1*, 2039201) Bks Demand.

Constraint-Based Grammar Formalisms: Parsing & Type Inference for Natural & Computer Languages. Stuart M. Shieber. (Illus.). 200p. 1992. 27.00 (*0-262-19324-8*) MIT Pr.

Constraint-Based Reasoning. Ed. by Eugene C. Freuder & Alan K. Mackworth. LC 93-21600. (Special Issues in Artificial Intelligence Ser.). 408p. 1994. pap. 34.95 (*0-262-56075-5*, Bradford Bks) MIT Pr.

Constraint-Based Searching: Algorithms & Architectures. Jun Gu. (Illus.). 275p. (C). 1994. write for info. (*0-521-41013-4*) Cambridge U Pr.

Constraint-Directed Search: A Case Study of Job-Shop Scheduling. Mark Fox. (Research Notes in Artificial Intelligence Ser.). (Illus.). 184p. (Orig.). 1987. pap. text ed. 29.95 (*0-934613-56-7*) Morgan Kaufmann.

Constraint-Directed Search: A Case Study of Job-Shop Scheduling. Ed. by Mark S. Fox. 200p. (Orig.). (C). 1987. pap. text ed. 100.00 (*0-273-08770-3*, Pub. by Pitman Pubng UK) St Mut.

Constraint Effects in Fracture. Ed. by E. M. Hackett et al. LC 92-42112. (Special Technical Publication Ser.: No. STP 1171). (Illus.). 525p. 1993. 111.00 (*0-8031-1481-8*, 04-011710-30) ASTM.

***Constraint Grammar: A Language-Independent System for Parsing Unrestricted Text.** Ed. by Fred Karlsson et al. LC 94-13182. (Natural Language Processing Ser.: No. 4). 438p. (C). 1994. lib. bdg. 206.15 (*3-11-014179-5*) Mouton.

Constraint Logic Programming: Selected Research. Ed. by Frederic Benhamou & Alan Colmerauer. LC 92-38061. (Logic Programming Ser.). (Illus.). 486p. 1993. 50.00 (*0-262-02353-9*) MIT Pr.

Constraint Model of Space Planning. Ki B. Yoon. LC 92-72945. (Topics in Engineering Ser.: Vol. 9). 240p. 1992. 45.00 (*1-56252-007-5*) Computational Mech MA.

Constraint of Empire: The United States & Caribbean Interventions. Whitney T. Perkins. LC 80-27269. (Contributions in Comparative Colonial Studies: No. 8). 320p. 1981. text ed. 69.50 (*0-313-22266-5*, PCE/, Greenwood Pr) Greenwood.

Constraint Programming. Ed. by B. Mayoh et al. (NATO ASI, Series F, Computer & Systems Sciences: Vol. 131). vii, 452p. 1994. 98.00 (*0-387-57859-5*) Spr-Verlag.

***Constraint Programming: Basics & Trends: 1994 Chatillon Spring School, Chantillon-sur-Seine, France, May 16-20, 1994: Selected Papers.** Ed. by Andreas Podelski. LC 95-10074. (Lecture Notes in Computer Science: No. 910). 1995. write for info. (*0-387-59155-9*) Spr-Verlag.

Constraint Programming Languages: Their Specification & Generation. William Leler. LC 87-1236. (Computer Science Ser.). 145p. (C). 1988. pap. text ed. 31.25 (*0-201-06243-7*) Addison-Wesley.

Constraint Satisfaction in Logic Programming. Pascal Van Hentenryck. (Logic Programming Ser.). 240p. 1989. 40. 00x (*0-262-08181-4*) MIT Pr.

Constraint Theory: An Approach to Policy-Level Modeling. Laurence D. Richards. (Illus.). 424p. (C). 1984. lib. bdg. 63.00 (*0-8191-3512-7*); pap. text ed. 33.00 (*0-8191-3513-5*) U Pr of Amer.

Constraint Theory & Quantization Methods- from Relativistic Particles to Field Theory & General Relativity. F. Colomo et al. 460p. 1994. text ed. 99.00 (*981-02-1582-7*) World Scientific Pub.

Constraints & Compromise: Trade Policy in a Democracy. Orit Frenkel. LC 90-2998. (Foreign Economic Policy of the United States Ser.). 232p. 1990. reprint ed. 20.00 (*0-8240-7464-5*) Garland.

Constraints & Impacts of Privatization. Ed. by V. V. Ramanadham. LC 93-9827. 1993. write for info. (*0-415-09826-2*) Routledge.

Constraints in Bengal Politics, Nineteen Twenty-One to Nineteen Forty-One: Gandhian Leadership. Gitasree Bandyopadhyay. 1985. 20.00 (*0-8364-1448-9*, Pub. by Sarat) S Asia.

***Constraints in Computational Logics: Proceedings of the First International Conference, CCL '94, Munich, Germany, September 7-9, 1994.** Ed. by J. P. Jouannaud. (Lecture Notes in Computer Science: Vol. 845). 367p. 1994. pap. 52.00 (*3-540-58403-X*) Spr-Verlag.

Constraints, Language & Computation. Ed. by M. Rossner et al. (Cognitive Science Ser.). 391p. 1994. text ed. 69.95 (*0-12-597930-4*) Acad Pr.

Constraints of Desire: The Anthropology of Sex & Gender in Ancient Greece. John J. Winkler. 288p. 1989. 47.50 (*0-415-90122-7*, A3201, Routledge NY); pap. 14.95 (*0-415-90123-5*, A3205, Routledge NY) Routledge.

Constraints on Error Variables in Grammar: Bilingual Misspelling Orthographies. Philip Luelsdorff. LC 85-30823. vii, 442p. 1986. 118.00x (*0-915027-73-9*); pap. 27.95x (*0-915027-74-7*) Benjamins North Am.

Constraints on Language Acquisition: Studies of Atypical Children. Ed. by Helen Tager-Flusberg. 248p. 1993. text ed. 49.95 (*0-8058-0667-9*) L Erlbaum Assocs.

Constraints on Rice Production in Madagascar: The Farmer's Perspective. CFNPP Staff et al. (Working Paper Ser.). (C). 1993. pap. 7.00 (*1-56401-134-8*) Cornell Food.

Constraints on U. S. Strategy in Third World Conflicts. Stephen T. Hosmer. LC 87-6492. 150p. 1987. 42.00 (*0-8448-1513-6*, Crane Russak); pap. 21.00 (*0-8448-1514-4*, Crane Russak) Taylor & Francis.

Constronic '84. Ed. by Collet's Holdings, Ltd. Staff. 405p. 1984. 280.00 (*0-317-46595-3*) St Mut.

Construccion de las Americas: Memorias del VI Congreso de Antropologia en Colombia. Ed. by Carlos A. Tobon. (Memorias del VI Congreso de Antropologia en Colombia Ser.). (Illus.). 288p. (SPA.). 1993. pap. 15.00 (*958-95572-3-6*) UPLAAP.

Construccion de Lo Visual. Damian C. Bayon & Juan Fresan. LC 76-10371. (Illus.). 221p. (SPA.). 1981. reprint ed. pap. 4.00 (*0-8477-2108-6*) U of PR Pr.

Construccion de Terrazas - Building Decks: Black & Decker. Cy De Cosse Incorporated Staff. 1993. 14.95 (*0-86573-725-8*) Cy De Cosse.

Construcciones. Frank Rivera. LC 79-92418. (Senda Poetica Ser.). 55p. (Orig.). (SPA.). 1979. pap. 3.95 (*0-918454-19-0*) Senda Nueva.

Construct Lesson Plan: Improving Group Instruction. Danny G. Langdon. LC 77-25406. (Instructional Design Library). (Illus.). 96p. 1978. 23.95 (*0-87778-111-7*) Educ Tech Pubns.

Construct of Language Proficiency: Applications of Psychological Models to Language Assessment. Ed. by Ludo T. Verhoeven & John H. De Jong. LC 92-23643. viii, 212p. 1992. 53.00x (*1-55619-461-7*) Benjamins North Am.

Constructability Concepts File. 104p. 1989. pap. text ed. 25.00 (*0-685-31773-0*) Constr Ind Pr.

Constructed Civil Infrastructre Systems R&D: A European Perspective. LC 94-7939. 1994. write for info. (*0-7844-0001-6*) Am Soc Civil Eng.

Constructed Environment with Man as the Measure: Proceedings of the Engineering Foundation Conference, Nov., 1974. Engineering Foundation Conference Staff. 322p. pap. 24.00 (*0-87262-157-X*) Am Soc Civil Eng.

***Constructed Realities: The Art of Staged Photography.** Micheal Kohler et al. (Illus.). 160p. Date not set. 45.00 (*3-905514-54-0*) Dist Art Pubs.

Constructed View: The Architectural Photography of Julius Shulman. Joseph Rosa. LC 93-39735. (Illus.). 224p. 1994. 50.00 (*0-8478-1777-6*) Rizzoli Intl.

***Constructed Wastelands for Animal Waste Management: Proceedings of Workshop, 4-6 April 1994, Lafayette, Indiana.** Ed. by Paul J. DuBowy & Richard P. Reeves. LC 94-26888. 1994. 10.00 (*0-931682-46-0*) Purdue U Pubns.

Constructed Wetlands for Treatment-Acid Mine Drainage. Wieder. 1995. write for info. (*0-87371-628-0*) Lewis Pubs.

Constructed Wetlands for Wastewater Treatment. Ed. by Donald A. Hammer. (Illus.). 831p. 1989. 79.95 (*0-87371-184-X*, TD756) Lewis Pubs.

Constructed Wetlands for Water Quality Improvement. Gerald A. Moshiri. 1993. 79.95 (*0-87371-550-0*, TD756) Lewis Pubs.

Constructibility. K. J. Devlin. (Perspectives in Mathematical Logic Ser.). (Illus.). 425p. 1984. 89.00 (*0-387-13258-9*) Spr-Verlag.

Constructibility & Mathematical Existence. Charles S. Chihara. (Illus.). 304p. 1990. 49.95 (*0-19-824817-2*) OUP.

Constructibility & Mathematical Existence. Charles S. Chihara. (Illus.). 304p. 1991. reprint ed. pap. 24.95 (*0-19-823975-0*) OUP.

Constructing a Bluegrass Mandolin: A Complete Technical Guide. Roger H. Siminoff. (Illus.). 56p. (Orig.). 1985. pap. 16.95 (*0-88188-141-4*, 00699400) H Leonard.

***Constructing a Collective Memory of the Holocaust: A Life History of Two Brothers' Survival.** Ronald J. Berger. (Illus.). 160p. 1995. 19.95 (*0-87081-368-4*) Univ Pr Colo.

***Constructing a Competitive Order: The Hidden History of British Anti-Trust Policies.** Helen Mercer. (Illus.). 288p. (C). 1995. 59.95 (*0-521-41292-7*) Cambridge U Pr.

Constructing a Five-String Banjo: A Complete Technical Guide. Roger H. Siminoff. (Illus.). 64p. (Orig.). 1985. pap. 16.95 (*0-88188-373-5*, 00183154) H Leonard.

Constructing a Good On-Going Weight Loss Diet Plan: The Continuing Plan. S. Mikielle Chatman. (Fat Chance Series Book Group: No. 12). 45p. 1992. pap. 3.99 (*1-881146-12-X*) Fat Chance.

Constructing a Life Philosophy: Opposing Viewpoints. Ed. by David L. Bender. (Opposing Viewpoints Ser.). (Illus.). 264p. (YA). (gr. 10 up). 1993. lib. bdg. 19.95 (*0-89908-198-3*); pap. text ed. 11.55 (*0-89908-173-8*) Greenhaven.

Constructing a Patient's Drug Therapy Problem List. Leslie A. Shimp & Nancy A. Mason. (Clinical Skills Program: Advancing Pharmaceutical Care Ser.). 126p. 1993. ring bd. 50.00 (*1-879907-36-4*) Am Soc Hlth-Syst.

***Constructing a Productive Other: Discourse Theory & the Convention Refugee Hearing.** Robert F. Barsky. LC 94-33456. (Pragmatics & Beyond New Ser.: No. 29). 271p. 1994. lib. bdg. 64.00x (*1-55619-297-5*) Benjamins North Am.

Constructing a Public Theology: The Church in a Pluralistic Culture. Ronald F. Thiemann. 160p. (Orig.). 1991. pap. 14.99 (*0-664-25130-7*) Westminster John Knox.

Constructing a Social Science for Postwar America: The Cybernetics Group, 1946-1953. Steve J. Heims. LC 92-34901. (Illus.). 352p. 1993. pap. 15.95 (*0-262-58123-X*) MIT Pr.

Constructing a Sociology of the Arts. Vera L. Zolberg. (Contemporary Sociology Ser.). (Illus.). 272p. (C). 1990. pap. 16.95 (*0-521-35959-7*) Cambridge U Pr.

Constructing a Solid Body Guitar: A Complete Technical Guide. Roger H. Siminoff. (Illus.). 64p. 1986. pap. 19.95 (*0-88188-451-0*, 00183152) H Leonard.

Constructing Alternative World Futures: Reordering the Planet. Louis R. Beres & Harry R. Targ. 264p. 1977. 22.95 (*0-87073-566-7*); pap. 13.95 (*0-87073-567-5*) Schenkman Bks Inc.

***Constructing & Calculating Bond Indices: A Guide to the Effas Standard Rules.** Patrick J. Brown. 1994. 65.00 (*1-55738-814-8*) Probus Pub Co.

Constructing & Maintaining Your Well & Septic System. Charlotte Alth & Max Alth. (Illus.). 240p. 1984. 19.95 (*0-8306-0654-8*, 1654); pap. 13.95 (*0-8306-1654-3*) TAB Bks.

Constructing & Reconstructing Childhood: New Directions in the Sociological Study of Childhood. Ed. by Allison James & Alan Prout. 240p. 1990. 75.00 (*1-85000-749-7*, Falmer Pr); pap. 33.00 (*1-85000-750-0*, Falmer Pr) Taylor & Francis.

Constructing & Reconstructing Gender: The Links among Communication, Language, & Gender. Ed. by Linda A. Perry et al. LC 91-29718. (SUNY Series in Feminist Criticism & Theory). 320p. (C). 1992. 59.50 (*0-7914-1009-9*); pap. 19.95 (*0-7914-1010-2*) State U NY Pr.

Constructing & Using Achievement Tests in the Classroom: A Competency Based Text. Fred M. Smith. LC 83-49413. (American University Studies: Education: Ser. XIV, Vol. 1). 172p. (Orig.). (C). 1984. pap. text ed. 18. 10 (*0-8204-0100-5*) P Lang Pubs.

Constructing Brotherhood: Class, Gender, & Fraternalism. Mary A. Clawson. (Illus.). 256p. (C). 1989. text ed. 35. 00 (*0-691-09447-0*) Princeton U Pr.

Constructing Building, Bridges, & Minds: Building an Integrated Curriculum Through Social Studies. Kathy Young. LC 93-28835. 162p. 1994. pap. text ed. 17.50 (*0-435-08796-7*, 08796) Heinemann.

Constructing Buildings, Bridges, & Minds: Building an Integrated Curriculum Through Social Studies. Katherine Young. (Illus.). 1993. pap. write for info. (*0-435-86796-2*, 86796) Routledge.

Constructing Capitalism: The Reemergence of Civil Society & Liberal Economy in the Post-Communist World. Ed. by Kazimierz A. Poznanski. 230p. (C). 1992. pap. text ed. 19.95 (*0-8133-1482-8*) Westview.

Constructing Chicago. Daniel Bluestone. (Illus.). 288p. (C). 1991. 45.00 (*0-300-04848-3*) Yale U Pr.

Constructing Chicago. Daniel Bluestone. (Illus.). 235p. (C). 1993. pap. 27.50 (*0-300-05750-4*) Yale U Pr.

Constructing Civilizations. Carl J. Couch. (Contemporary Studies in Sociology: Vol. 5). 401p. 1984. 73.25 (*0-89232-438-4*) Jai Pr.

***Constructing Community: Moral Pluralism & Tragic Conflicts.** Moon. 1995. pap. (*0-691-02550-9*) Princeton U Pr.

Constructing Community: Moral Pluralism & Tragic Conflicts. J. Donald Moon. LC 93-12930. 256p. 1993. text ed. 29.95 (*0-691-08642-7*) Princeton U Pr.

Constructing Correctional Facilities: Is There a Role for the Private Sector? Ed. by Warren I. Cikins & James R. Sevick. (Dialogues on Public Policy Ser.). 60p. 1987. pap. 10.95 (*0-8157-1415-7*) Brookings.

Constructing Cross-Country Obstacles. Bill Thomson. 1978. 17.50 (*0-87556-615-4*) Saifer.

Constructing Cross Country Obstacles. Bill Thomson. 103p. 1990. pap. 30.00 (*0-85131-350-7*, Pub. by J A Allen & Co UK) St Mut.

Constructing Culture & Power in Latin America. Ed. by Daniel H. Levine. (Comparative Studies in Society & History). 350p. 1993. text ed. 55.00 (*0-472-09456-4*); pap. text ed. 22.50 (*0-472-06456-8*) U of Mich Pr.

***Constructing Curriculum for the Primary Grades.** Diane T. Dodge et al. LC 94-60859. (Illus.). (Orig.). (C). 1994. pap. text ed. 39.95 (*1-879537-12-5*) Tchng Strtgs.

Constructing Gay Theology: Proceedings of the Gay Men's Issues in Religion Consultation of the American Academy of Religion; Fall 1989. J. Michael Clark et al. LC 90-24987. 78p. (Orig.). 1991. pap. 7.00 (*0-930383-19-2*) Monument Pr.

***Constructing Girlhood: Magazine Representations of Adolescent Girlhood & Feminity, 1920-1950.** Penny Tinkler. 224p. 1995. text ed. 75.00 (*0-7484-0285-3*); pap. text ed. 24.95 (*0-7484-0286-1*) Taylor & Francis.

Constructing Inequality: The Fabrication of a Hierarchy of Virtue among the Etoro. Raymond C. Kelly. (Illus.). 600p. 1993. text ed. 69.50 (*0-472-09528-5*); pap. text ed. 24.95 (*0-472-06528-9*) U of Mich Pr.

Constructing Knowledge: Authority & Critique in Social Science. Ed. by Lorraine Nencel & Peter Pels. (Inquiries in Social Construction Ser.). 256p. (C). 1991. text ed. 55.00 (*0-8039-8401-4*); pap. text ed. 22.50 (*0-8039-8402-2*) Sage.

***Constructing Knowledge in the History of Science.** Ed. by Arnold Thackray. 300p. 1994. pap. text ed. 25.00 (*0-226-79378-8*) U Ch Pr.

***Constructing Knowledge in the History of Science.** Ed. by Arnold Thackray. 300p. 1995. lib. bdg. 39.00 (*0-226-79376-1*) U Ch Pr.

Constructing Knowledge Together: Classrooms As Centers of Inquiry & Literacy. Gordon Wells & Ling Chang-Wells. LC 92-11630. 192p. 1992. pap. text ed. 19.50 (*0-435-08731-2*, 08731) Heinemann.

Constructing Language Processors for Little Languages. Randy M. Kaplan. LC 94-6674. 1994. disk, pap. 49.95 (*0-471-59754-6*); pap. text ed. 39.95 (*0-471-59753-8*) Wiley.

Constructing Local Solutions: Affordable Housing. (Capitols & Communities Ser.). 16p. 1991. 15.00 (*1-55516-802-7*, 3903) Natl Conf State Legis.

Constructing Local Theologies. Robert J. Schreiter. LC 84-14797. 240p. (Orig.). 1985. pap. 16.95 (*0-88344-108-X*) Orbis Bks.

Constructing Logic Programs. J. M. Jacquet. 275p. 1993. pap. text ed. 54.95 (*0-471-93789-4*) Wiley.

***Constructing Masculinity.** Ed. by Maurice Berger et al. 320p. 1995. 65.00x (*0-415-91052-8*, B4487, Routledge NY) Routledge.

***Constructing Masculinity.** Ed. by Maurice Berger et al. 320p. 1995. pap. 19.95 (*0-415-91053-6*, B4491, Routledge NY) Routledge.

***Constructing Mathematical Knowledge: Epistemology & Mathematics Education.** Ed. by Paul Ernest. LC 94-31141. (Studies in Mathematics Education: Vol. 4). 282p. 1994. 65.00x (*0-7507-0354-7*, Falmer Pr) Taylor & Francis.

Constructing Nonhomeomorphic Stochastic Flows. R. R. Darling. LC 87-19528. (MEMO Ser.: Vol. 70/376). 97p. 1987. pap. text ed. 18.00 (*0-8218-2439-2*, MEMO 70/376) Am Math.

***Constructing Panic: The Discourse of Agoraphobia.** Lisa Capps & Elinor Ochs. 224p. (C). 1995. text ed. 29.95 (*0-674-16548-9*) HUP.

Constructing Policy: Dialogues with Social Scientists in the National Political Arena. Ed. by Irving L. Horowitz. LC 78-26113. 256p. 1979. text ed. 55.00 (*0-275-90366-4*, C0366, Praeger Pubs) Greenwood.

Constructing Postmodernism. Brian McHale. 256p. 1992. 49.95 (*0-415-06013-3*, A6014); pap. 15.95 (*0-415-06014-1*, A6018) Routledge.

Constructing Predictable Real Time Systems. Wolfgang A. Halang & Alexander D. Stoyenko. (C). 1991. lib. bdg. 82.00 (*0-7923-9202-7*) Kluwer Ac.

***Constructing Professional Knowledge in Teaching: A Narrative of Change & Development.** Mary Beattie. 192p. (C). 1994. text ed. 34.00x (*0-8077-3396-2*); pap. text ed. 16.95x (*0-8077-3395-4*) Tchrs Coll.

Constructing Quality Software: Proceedings of the IFIP Working Conference on Constructing Quality Software, Novosibirsk, U. S. S. R., May, 1977. Ed. by P. G. Hibbard & S. A. Schuman. 520p. 1978. 84.75 (*0-444-85106-2*, North Holland) Elsevier.

Constructing Quarks: A Sociological History of Particle Physics. Andrew Pickering. LC 84-235. xii, 468p. 1984. lib. bdg. 42.50 (*0-226-66798-7*) U Ch Pr.

Constructing Quarks: A Sociological History of Particle Physics. Andrew Pickering. LC 84-235. xii, 468p. 1986. pap. text ed. 19.95 (*0-226-66799-5*) U Ch Pr.

An Asterisk (*) at the beginning of an entry indicates that the title is appearing in BIP for the first time.

C

An Asterisk (*) at the beginning of an entry indicates that the title is appearing in BIP for the first time.

Construction Delays: Documenting Causes, Winning Claims, & Recovering Costs. Theodore H. Trauner & William D. Mahoney. (Illus.). 200p. 1990. 64.95 (*0-87629-174-4*, 67278) R S Means.

Construction Details. 50.00 (*0-685-71324-5*, COLLECTION C1) M Tecton Pub.

Construction Details from Architectural Graphic Standards. 8th ed. Ed. by Charles G. Ramsey et al. (Ramsey-Sleeper Architectural Graphic Standards Ser.: No. 1955). 408p. 1991. text ed. 115.00 (*0-471-54899-5*) Wiley.

Construction Dewatering: New Methods & Applications. 2nd ed. J. Patrick Powers. (Series of Practical Construction Guides: No. 1344). 528p. 1992. text ed. 74.95 (*0-471-60185-3*) Wiley.

Construction Disasters: Design Failures, Causes & Prevention. Steven S. Ross. 1984. 59.00 (*0-07-053865-4*) McGraw.

Construction Disputes: Liability & the Expert Witness. Andrea Burns. 240p. 1989. boxed 96.00 (*0-406-11101-4*, UK) Butterworth Legal Pubs.

Construction Documentation. 2nd ed. John A. Ricchini. (Construction Law Library). 280p. 1991. pap. text ed. 85.00 (*0-471-55334-4*) Wiley.

***Construction Documentation.** 3rd ed. James J. O'Brien. LC 95-1088. (Construction Law Library). 1995. text ed. 110. 00 (*0-471-11041-8*) Wiley.

***Construction Drafting.** 1995. lib. bdg. 255.99 (*0-8490-6631-X*) Gordon Pr.

Construction Drawing for Technicians, Level 1. R. Boxall. (Longman Technician Series, Construction & Civil Engineering). (Illus.). 208p. reprint ed. pap. 59.30 (*0-8357-2980-X*, 2039242) Bks Demand.

Construction Electrical Contracting. 2nd ed. John E. Traister & Paul Rosenberg. (Practical Construction Guides Ser.). 1989. text ed. 64.95 (*0-471-63014-4*) Wiley.

Construction Electrical Contracting. John E. Traister. LC 78-1344. (Wiley Series of Practical Construction Guides). 311p. reprint ed. pap. 88.70 (*0-685-16634-1*, 2027883) Bks Demand.

Construction Employment Guide in the National & International Field. 7th ed. LC 86-50537. 133p. 1990. pap. 16.50 (*0-8360-0035-8*) World Trade.

Construction Engineering Evidence. suppl. ed. Loren W. Peters. 152p. 1993. pap. 55.00 (*0-471-59149-1*) Wiley.

Construction Engineering in Underground Coal Mines. Scott G. Britton. LC 82-71994. (Illus.). 312p. 1983. 48. 00 (*0-89520-403-7*) SMM&E Inc.

Construction Engineer's Complete Handbook of Forms. Edward R. Fisk. LC 92-13839. 1992. text ed. 84.00 (*0-13-175415-7*) P-H.

Construction Engineers Complete Handbook of Forms. Edward R. Fisk. 400p. 1992. pap. text ed. 84.00 (*0-13-092784-8*) P-H.

Construction Equipment & Techniques for the Eighties. C. J. Schexnayder. LC 81-71797. 401p. 1982. pap. 33.00 (*0-87262-293-2*) Am Soc Civil Eng.

Construction Equipment Distribution Has the Career You're Looking For. Associated Equipment Distributors Staff. 1.00 (*0-318-19189-X*) Assn Equip Distrs.

Construction Equipment Guide. 2nd ed. David A. Day. (Series of Practical Construction Guides). 437p. 1991. text ed. 74.95 (*0-471-88840-0*) Wiley.

Construction Equipment Lubrication Recommendations, Nineteen Ninety. 640p. 1989. 550.00 (*0-13-129768-6*, H M Gousha) P-H Gen Ref & Trav.

***Construction Equipment Market.** 400p. (Orig.). 1994. pap. 2,295.00 (*1-57205-987-7*) Rector Pr.

Construction Equipment Mechanic. (Career Examination Ser.: C-3435). 1994. pap. 27.95 (*0-8373-3435-7*) Nat Learn.

Construction Equipment Repair Production Coordinator. (Career Examination Ser.: C-3436). 1994. pap. 34.95 (*0-8373-3436-5*) Nat Learn.

Construction Equities, Evaluation & Trading. Fred Wellings. 192p. 1993. 150.00 (*1-85573-109-6*, Pub. by Woodhead Pubng UK) St Mut.

***Construction Estimates from Take-Off to Bid.** 3rd ed. Norman Foster et al. LC 94-22328. 1994. write for info. (*0-07-021651-7*) McGraw.

Construction Estimating. James J. Adrian. (C). 1982. teacher ed write for info. (*0-8359-0926-3*, Reston); text ed. 49.00 (*0-8359-0925-5*, Reston) P-H.

Construction Estimating. Raymond P. Jones. 152p. (C). 1967. 26.95 (*0-8273-0108-1*) Delmar.

Construction Estimating. R. Petri. 1979. text ed. 74.00 (*0-87909-152-5*, Reston) P-H.

Construction Estimating. 2nd ed. James J. Adrian. 536p. (C). 1919. text ed. 54.80 (*0-87563-439-7*) Stipes.

Construction Estimating for General Contractors. Leo Diamant. LC 87-28032. (Practical Construction Guides Ser.). 139p. 1988. text ed. 64.95 (*0-471-81665-5*) Wiley.

***Construction Estimating IG.** Pratt. 56p. 1995. teacher ed 14.00 (*0-8273-6137-8*) Delmar.

Construction Estimating Reference Data. Ed Sarviel & Scott Sloan. LC 93-16627. (Orig.). 1993. disk 39.50 (*0-934041-84-9*) Craftsman.

Construction Estimating System. J. Hardy LeGwin. Ed. by Susan J. Bicknell. 1991. ring bd. 24.95 (*1-878088-16-5*) J H LeGwin Assocs.

Construction Financing to Build Your Own Home. Jerry L. Nowlin. LC 90-92261. 70p. (Orig.). 1990. pap. 19.95 (*0-9628643-0-7*) J L Nowlin.

Construction Forms & Contracts. Craig Savage & Karen Jones-Mitchell. 432p. (Orig.). 1994. disk, pap. 39.75 (*0-934041-85-7*) Craftsman.

Construction Funding: Where the Money Comes From. 2nd ed. Courtland A. Collier & Don A. Halperin. LC 83-21753. (Practical Construction Guides Ser.: 1-344). 294p. 1984. text ed. 64.95 (*0-471-89065-0*, Wiley-Interscience) Wiley.

Construction Glossary: An Encyclopedic Reference & Manual. 2nd ed. J. Stewart Stein. LC 92-443. (Series in Psychiatry). 1056p. 1993. text ed. 115.00 (*0-471-56933-X*) Wiley.

Construction Guide for Soils & Foundations. 2nd ed. Richard G. Ahlvin & Vernon A. Smoots. LC 87-34639. (Practical Construction Guides Ser.). 276p. 1988. text ed. 69.95 (*0-471-80486-X*) Wiley.

***Construction Handbook for Bridge Temporary Works.** (Bridges Ser.). (C). Date not set. pap. text ed. write for info. (*1-56051-035-8*) AASHTO.

Construction in Cold Regions: A Guide for Planners, Engineers, Contractors & Managers. Terry T. McFadden & F. Lawrence Bennett. LC 09-110317. (Series of Practical Construction Guides: No. 1344). 640p. 1991. text ed. 89.95 (*0-471-52503-0*) Wiley.

Construction Industry & Building Mechanization Dictionary in Four Languages. Ed. by V. Zoltanka & G. Sebestyen. 456p. (ENG, GER, HUN & RUS.). 1986. 28. 00 (*963-05-3539-4*, Pub. by Akade Kiado HU) IBD Ltd.

Construction Industry & the European Community. N. F. Chapman & Christian Grandjean. (Illus.). 296p. 1991. pap. 45.95 (*0-632-03121-2*) Blackwell Sci.

Construction Industry Contracts: Legal Citator & Case Digest. Wiley Law Publications Editorial Staff. (Construction Law Library). 608p. 1988. text ed. 128.00 (*0-471-61577-3*) Wiley.

Construction Industry Contracts: Legal Citator & Case Digest. suppl. ed. Wiley Law Publications Editorial Staff. (Construction Law Library). 336p. 1993. 65.00 (*0-685-67699-4*) Wiley.

Construction Industry Digest. 1992. lib. bdg. 254.95 (*0-8490-5607-1*) Gordon Pr.

***Construction Industry Digest.** 1995. lib. bdg. 250.00 (*0-8490-5864-3*) Gordon Pr.

Construction Industry Formbook. 2nd ed. James Acret. (Environmental Publications). 500p. 1990. text ed. 100. 00 (*0-07-172276-9*) Shepards-McGraw.

Construction Industry Forms, Vol. 1. Ed. by Robert F. Cushman & George L. Blick. LC 88-66. (Construction Law Library). 463p. 1988. text ed. 112.50 (*0-471-61321-5*) Wiley.

Construction Industry Forms, Vols. 1 & 2. Ed. by Robert F. Cushman & George L. Blick. 960p. 1988. text ed. 225.00 (*0-471-63263-5*) Wiley.

Construction Industry Forms, Vols. 1 & 2. suppl. ed. Ed. by Robert F. Cushman & George L. Blick. 472p. 1992. 75. 00 (*0-471-58713-3*) Wiley.

***Construction Industry I Vol. 37: Actions & Requirements.** Gy Sebestyen. 168p. 1976. 30.00x (*963-05-0857-5*, Pub. by Akad Kiado HU) St Mut.

Construction Industry Insurance Handbook. Deutsch et al. (Construction Law Library). 416p. 1991. text ed. 123.00 (*0-471-52714-9*) Wiley.

Construction Industry Insurance Handbook. suppl. ed. Deutsch et al. (Construction Law Library). 136p. 1993. 55.00 (*0-471-59636-1*) Wiley.

Construction Industry Joint Venture Formbook. Mitchell Becker & Robert F. Cushman. (Construction Law Library). 392p. 1992. text ed. 123.00 (*0-471-55638-6*) Wiley.

Construction Industry of Great Britain. Roger C. Harvey & Allan Ashworth. (Illus.). 208p. 1993. pap. 29.95 (*0-7506-0350-X*) Buttrwrth-Heinemann.

***Construction Industry V Vol. 41: Interior Ulities Engineering.** I. Fekete & Fy. Sebestyen. 212p. 1975. 30. 00x (*963-05-0560-6*, Pub. by Akad Kiado HU) St Mut.

***Construction Industry 1V Vol. 40: Building Construction.** Gy Sebestyen. 288p. 1983. 30.00x (*963-05-2955-6*, Pub. by Akad Kiado HU) St Mut.

***Construction Industry 11 Vol. 38: Building Construction.** Gy Sebestyen. 182p. 1977. 30.00x (*963-05-1191-6*, Pub. by Akad Kiado HU) St Mut.

Construction Innovation: Demands, Successes, & Lessons. Ed. by C. B. Tatum. (Sessions Proceedings Ser.). 46p. 1986. 11.00 (*0-87262-522-2*) Am Soc Civil Eng.

Construction Insolvency. Richard Davis. 427p. 1992. text ed. 135.00 (*0-471-93660-X*, Pub. by Wiley Chancery Law UK) Wiley.

***Construction Inspection Checklist.** J. Hardy LeGwin. 20p. 1994. pap. 15.00 (*1-878088-03-3*) J H LeGwin Assocs.

Construction Inspection Manual. 6th ed. 1995. pap. 34.95 (*1-55701-102-8*) BNI Pubns.

Construction Inspector. Jack Rudman. (Career Examination Ser.: C-164). 1994. pap. 29.95 (*0-8373-0164-5*) Nat Learn.

Construction Inspector I. (Career Examination Ser.: C-3441). 1994. pap. 29.95 (*0-8373-3441-1*) Nat Learn.

Construction Inspector II. Jack Rudman. (Career Examination Ser.: C-3042). 1994. pap. 34.95 (*0-8373-3042-4*) Nat Learn.

Construction Inspector III. (Career Examination Ser.: C-3443). 1994. pap. 34.95 (*0-8373-3443-8*) Nat Learn.

Construction Inspector Trainee. Jack Rudman. (Career Examination Ser.: C-3167). 1994. pap. 27.95 (*0-8373-3167-6*) Nat Learn.

Construction Insurance. N. G. Bunni. 334p. 1986. 106.25 (*0-85334-438-8*, Pub. by Elsevier Applied Sci UK) Elsevier.

Construction Insurance. Nael G. Bunni. (C). 1986. 560.00 (*0-685-33722-7*, Pub. by Witherby & Co UK) St Mut.

Construction Insurance. Ed. by John D. Wright. 127p. (C). 1991. 69.00 (*1-85609-022-1*, Pub. by Witherby & Co UK) St Mut.

***Construction Insurance: Coverages & Disputes.** Owen J. Shean & Douglas L. Patin. 562p. 1994. 95.00 (*0-614-05797-3*) Michie Butterworth.

Construction Insurance in the Arab Gulf Area: An Analysis of Cover & Contracts. Rajai K. Sweis. (C). 1991. lib. bdg. 150.00 (*1-85333-372-7*, Pub. by Graham & Trotman UK) Kluwer Ac.

Construction Insurance Management & Claims. R. J. Hickson. (C). 1987. 225.00 (*0-685-33721-9*, Pub. by Witherby & Co UK) St Mut.

Construction into Design: The Influence of New Methods of Construction on Architectural Design 1690-1990. J. Strike. (Illus.). 200p. 1991. pap. 52.95 (*0-7506-1229-0*) Buttrwrth-Heinemann.

***Construction Job Directory-Worldwide.** 135p. (C). 1994. pap. 125.00 (*1-57205-742-4*) Rector Pr.

Construction Joint Ventures in Singapore. Chow K. Fong. 332p. 1985. 74.00 (*0-409-99502-9*) Butterworth Legal Pubs.

Construction Labor & Employment Law. Charles R. Schrader. (Construction Law Library). 438p. 1991. text ed. 125.00 (*0-471-55332-8*) Wiley.

Construction Labor Relations. Smith, Jr. 480p. 1984. 40.00 (*0-685-67125-9*, 4830) Commerce.

Construction Labor Report. BNA's Business & Human Resources Services Staff. 1955. 784.00 (*0-685-07317-3*) BNA.

***Construction Law.** Brian M. Samuels. LC 94-44263. 1995. text ed. 43.33 (*0-13-325192-6*) P-H.

Construction Law, 5 vols. Steven G. Stein. 1986. Updates available. ring bd. write for info. (*0-8205-1109-9*) Bender.

Construction Law, 2 vols., Set. Ed. by Richard E. Alexander & Steven R. Schell. 1100p. 1991. write for info. (*0-318-68350-4*) OR Bar CLE.

Construction Law: Claims & Liability. Michael S. Simon. 1989. text ed. 128.00 (*0-471-50207-3*) Wiley.

Construction Law: Principles & Practice. Bruce M. Jervis & Paul Levin. 352p. 1988. text ed. write for info. (*0-07-037442-2*) McGraw.

Construction Law Briefs. Albert B. Wolf. LC 88-62451. 220p. (C). 1988. student ed 90.00 (*0-932446-02-7*) Jacqueline Enter.

Construction Law Claims: Liability - A Current Treatise. Michael Simon. 900p. 1982. 239.00 (*0-317-67960-0*) Ascot Pub.

Construction Law Digests. James Acret. 2196p. 1991. text ed., ring bd. 220.00 (*0-07-172260-2*) Shepards-McGraw.

Construction Law for Paralegals. Dianne D. Zalewski & Cheryl D. Evans. (Paralegal Law Library). 472p. 1993. text ed. 98.00 (*0-471-58958-6*) Wiley.

Construction Law in Australia. Ian H. Bailey. xviii, 318p. 1981. pap. 47.50 (*0-455-20260-5*, Pub. by Law Bk Co) W W Gaunt.

Construction Law in Contractor's Language. 2nd ed. McNeill Stokes. 1990. text ed. 43.00 (*0-07-061636-1*) McGraw.

Construction Law Reports, 25 vols., Set. Ed. by M. P. Furmston & V. Powell-Smith. 2,240.00 (*0-406-55500-1*) Butterworth Legal Pubs.

***Construction Law Update 1995.** Neal J. Sweeney & Overton A. Currie. (Construction Law Library). 1995. pap. text ed. 115.00 (*0-471-10724-7*) Wiley.

***Construction Law Yearbook, 1994.** Ed. by John Uff & Stephen Furst. 1994. text ed. 95.00 (*0-471-93923-4*) Wiley.

***Construction Layout: A Step-by-Step Field Engineering Methods Manual.** Wesley G. Crawford. Ed. by Sharyn L. Switzer & Bonnie Crawford. (Illus.). 700p. (C). 1994. text ed. 65.00 (*0-9624124-3-0*) POB Pub Co.

Construction Litigation. 2nd ed. Ed. by Kenneth M. Cushman et al. 750p. 1992. 125.00 (*0-685-69400-3*) PLI.

***Construction Litigation: Practice Guide With Forms, Vol. 1.** Thomas J. Kelleher, Jr. & Brian G. Corgan. LC 94-21823. (Construction Law Library). 1994. write for info. (*0-471-01353-6*) Wiley.

***Construction Litigation: Practice Guide With Forms, Vol. 2.** Thomas G. Kelleher, Jr. & Brian G. Corgan. LC 94-21823. (Construction Law Library). 1994. write for info. (*0-471-01362-5*) Wiley.

Construction Litigation: Representing the Contractor. 2nd ed. John D. Carter et al. (Construction Law Library). 800p. 1992. text ed. 138.00 (*0-471-53586-9*) Wiley.

Construction Litigation: Representing the Contractor. 2nd suppl. ed. John D. Carter et al. (Construction Law Library). 96p. 1993. 45.00 (*0-471-59142-4*) Wiley.

Construction Litigation: Representing the Owner. 2nd ed. Ed. by Robert F. Cushman et al. LC 08-936304. (Construction Law Library). 541p. 1990. text ed. 138.00 (*0-471-61914-0*) Wiley.

Construction Litigation: Strategies & Techniques 1993 Cumulative Supplement. Barry B. Bramble & Albert E. Phillips. 152p. 1993. pap. 55.00 (*0-471-58856-3*) Wiley.

Construction Litigation Handbook. James Acret. 477p. 1986. text ed. 110.00 (*0-07-000229-0*) Shepards-McGraw.

Construction Loads on Supporting Floors. 1991. 75.00 (*0-685-48566-8*, CRC Reprint) Franklin.

Construction Machinery. 330p. 1989. 895.00 (*0-318-03907-9*) Busn Trend.

Construction Machinery Puzzle Book. (Illus.). 12p. (J). (ps). Date not set. 4.95 (*1-56828-069-6*) Red Jacket Pr.

Construction Management. I. Atkinson. 150p. 1971. 39.75 (*0-85334-616-X*, Pub. by Elsevier Applied Sci UK) Elsevier.

Construction Management. Daniel W. Halpin & Ronald W. Woodhead. LC 80-11540. 483p. (C). 1980. Net. text ed. write for info. (*0-471-34566-0*) Wiley.

Construction Management: A State-of-the-Art Update. Ed. by C. Edwin Haltenhoff. (Sessions Proceedings Ser.). 144p. 1986. 19.00 (*0-87262-560-5*) Am Soc Civil Eng.

***Construction Management: Law & Practice.** Jon M. Wickwire et al. Date not set. text ed. 123.00 (*0-471-00659-9*) Wiley.

Construction Management & the Chartered Quantity Surveyor. John Bennett. (C). 1986. 39.00 (*0-85406-299-8*, Pub. by Surveyors Pubns) St Mut.

Construction Management in Developing Countries. R. K. Loraine. 171p. 1992. text ed. 78.00 (*0-7277-1651-4*) Am Soc Civil Eng.

Construction Manager. Jack Rudman. (Career Examination Ser.: C-1789). 1994. pap. 39.95 (*0-8373-1789-4*) Nat Learn.

Construction Manager - Nineteen Eighty-Nine. Andrew M. Civitello, Jr. 448p. 1989. text ed. 32.50 (*0-13-168154-0*) P-H.

Construction Manager - Nineteen Ninety-One. Andrew M. Civitello, Jr. 448p. 1991. text ed. 32.50 (*0-13-173535-7*) P-H.

Construction Manager, 1988. Andrew M. Civitello, Jr. 448p. 1988. text ed. 32.50 (*0-13-169525-8*, Busn) P-H.

Construction Manager, 1990. Andrew M. Civitello, Jr. 448p. 1990. text ed. 32.50 (*0-13-171281-0*) P-H.

Construction Manager, 1992. Andrew M. Civitello, Jr. 1991. 34.95 (*0-13-174897-1*, Busn) P-H.

Construction Manual: Concrete & Formwork. T. W. Love. (Illus.). 178p. 1973. pap. 17.75 (*0-910460-03-5*) Craftsman.

Construction Manual: Finish Carpentry. T. W. Love. LC 74-12339. (Illus.). 1974. pap. 15.25 (*0-910460-08-6*) Craftsman.

Construction Manual for Highway Bridges & Incidental Structures, 1973. 66p. 1973. pap. 3.00 (*0-686-40564-1*) AASHTO.

Construction Manual for Highway Construction. rev. ed. AASHTO Staff. (Construction & Right-of-Way Ser.). (Illus.). 236p. (C). 1990. text ed. 25.00 (*1-56051-002-1*) AASHTO.

Construction Manual of Electronic Eavesdropping. 1987. lib. bdg. 79.25 (*0-8490-3954-1*) Gordon Pr.

Construction Marketing: A Professional Approach. Paul Pearce. 138p. 1992. text ed. 54.00 (*0-7277-1652-2*, Pub. by T Telford UK) Am Soc Civil Eng.

Construction Materials: Their Nature & Behaviour. 2nd ed. John M. Illston. LC 93-12011. 1993. write for info. (*0-419-15470-1*, Chap & Hall NY) Chapman & Hall.

Construction Materials: Types, Uses & Applications. 2nd ed. Caleb Hornbostel. 1991. text ed. 145.00 (*0-471-85145-0*) Wiley.

Construction Materials & Processes. 2nd ed. Donald A. Watson. LC 77-612. (Illus.). 1978. text ed. 39.95 (*0-07-068471-5*) McGraw.

Construction Materials & Processes. 3rd ed. Donald Watson. 1986. text ed. write for info. (*0-07-068477-4*) McGraw.

Construction Materials & Processes. 3rd ed. Donald A. Watson. 526p. 1985. text ed. 41.50 (*0-07-068476-6*) McGraw.

Construction Materials for Civil Engineering Projects. Ed. by William T. Johnson, Jr. 58p. 1986. 12.00 (*0-87262-534-6*) Am Soc Civil Eng.

Construction Materials for Interior Design. William Rupp & Arnold Friedmann. (Illus.). 192p. 1989. pap. 24.95 (*0-8230-0930-0*, Whitney Lib) Watsn-Guptill.

Construction Materials I. Resource Systems International Staff. 1982. pap. text ed. 15.00 (*0-8359-0940-9*, Reston) P-H.

***Construction Materials Management.** George Stukhart. LC 95-3755. (Cost Engineering Ser.: Vol. 21). 1995. write for info. (*0-8247-9360-9*) Dekker.

Construction Materials Reference Book. Ed. by D. K. Doran. (Illus.). 992p. 1992. 205.00 (*0-7506-1004-2*) Buttrwrth-Heinemann.

***Construction Materials Reference Book.** D. K. Doran. (Illus.). 920p. 1994. pap. 69.95 (*0-7506-1963-5*) Buttrwrth-Heinemann.

Construction Mathematics, 2 vols., 1. M. K. Jones. LC 76-9870. (Longman Technician Ser.). reprint ed. pap. 59.80 (*0-317-27791-X*, 2025241) Bks Demand.

Construction Mathematics, 2 vols., 2. M. K. Jones. LC 76-9870. (Longman Technician Ser.). reprint ed. pap. 48.80 (*0-317-27792-8*) Bks Demand.

Construction Measurements. 2nd ed. B. Austin Barry. (Practical Construction Guides Ser.). 346p. 1988. text ed. 69.95 (*0-471-83663-X*) Wiley.

Construction Methods & Management. 3rd ed. Stephens W. Nunnally. 496p. 1992. text ed. 70.00 (*0-13-175274-X*) P-H.

Construction Methods & Planning. J. R. Illingworth. LC 92-42121. 1993. write for info. (*0-419-17450-8*, E & FN Spon) Routledge Chapman & Hall.

***Construction of a 150 kw Wind Turbine with a Rotor Diameter of 20 Metres ES-EN - Final Report.** European Communities Staff. 144p. 1994. pap. 25.00 (*92-826-6956-4*, CSNA14857-2SC, Pub. by Europ Com) UNIPUB.

Construction of American Furniture Treasures. Lester Margon. (Illus.). 168p. 1975. reprint ed. pap. 7.95 (*0-486-23056-2*) Dover.

Construction of American Indianness. (Philosophy of History & Culture Ser.: No. 12). 200p. 1995. 57.25 (*90-04-09686-8*, NLG100) E J Brill.

Construction of & on Compacted Fills. Edward J. Monahan. LC 85-29644. (Practical Construction Guides Ser.). 200p. 1986. text ed. 64.95 (*0-471-87463-9*) Wiley.

Construction of Authorship: Textual Appropriation in Law & Literature. Ed. by Martha Woodmansee & Peter Jaszi. LC 93-32347. (Post-Contemporary Interventions Ser.). 480p. 1993. lib. bdg. 45.00 (*0-8223-1382-0*); pap. text ed. 18.95 (*0-8223-1412-6*) Duke.

Construction of Buildings. 5th rev. ed. R. Barry. LC 93-29392. 1993. write for info. (*0-632-02615-4*) Blackwell Sci.

1564

An Asterisk (*) at the beginning of an entry indicates that the title is appearing in BIP for the first time.

C

Constructions of Personality. rev. ed. Sarah E. Hampson. (Introductions to Modern Psychology Ser.). 320p. 1988. text ed. 49.95 (*0-415-00255-9*); pap. text ed. 15.95 (*0-415-00256-7*) Routledge.

Constructions of Race, Place, & Nation. Ed. by Peter Jackson & Jan Penrose. LC 93-34344. 1994. text ed. 49. 95 (*0-8166-2504-2*); pap. text ed. 17.95 (*0-8166-2505-0*) U of Minn Pr.

Constructions of Reason: Explorations of Kant's Practical Philosophy. Onora O'Neill. 300p. (C). 1990. 64.95 (*0-521-38121-5*); pap. 19.95 (*0-521-38816-3*) Cambridge U Pr.

Constructions of "the Jew" in English Literature & Society: Racial Representations, 1875-1945. Bryan Cheyette. LC 93-19911. 240p. (C). 1994. 54.95 (*0-521-44355-5*) Cambridge U Pr.

***Constructions of "the Jew" in English Literature & Society: Racial Representations, 1875-1945.** Bryan Cheyette. 328p. (C). 1995. pap. write for info. (*0-521-55877-8*) Cambridge U Pr.

Constructions of the Self. Ed. by George Levine. LC 91-27274. (Illus.). 325p. 1992. text ed. 45.00 (*0-8135-1772-9*); pap. text ed. 18.00 (*0-8135-1773-7*) Rutgers U Pr.

Constructive Anatomy. George B. Bridgman. (Illus.). 160p. (C). 1973. reprint ed. pap. 4.95 (*0-486-21104-5*) Dover.

Constructive Approaches to the Foreign Debt Dilemma. Ed. by Mark Hulbert & Eric Meltzer. 78p. (Orig.). 1983. pap. 4.00 (*0-911415-04-1*) Natl Taxpayers Union Found.

Constructive Approximation. Ronald A. DeVore & George G. Lorentz. (Grundlehren der Mathematischen Wissenschaften Ser.: Vol. 303). (Illus.). vii, 534p. 1993. write for info. (*3-540-50627-6*) Spr-Verlag.

Constructive Approximation: Polynomials & Splines Approximation. Ronald A. DeVore & George G. Lorentz. LC 93-18420. (Grundlehren der Mathematischen Wissenschaften Ser.: Vol. 303). 1993. 109.00 (*0-387-50627-6*) Spr-Verlag.

Constructive Change in Latin America. Ed. by Stewart C. Blasier. LC 68-12724. 269p. reprint ed. pap. 76.70 (*0-318-34705-9*, 2031900) Bks Demand.

Constructive Classroom Management: Strategies for Creative Positive Learning Environments. Betty C. Epanchin et al. LC 94-4309. 1994. pap. 32.95 (*0-534-22254-4*) Brooks-Cole.

Constructive Combinatorics. D. W. Stanton & D. E. White. (Undergraduate Texts in Mathematics Ser.). (Illus.). 83p. 1986. text ed. 25.00 (*0-387-96347-2*) Spr-Verlag.

Constructive Concepts: A History of Constructive Art from Cubism to the Present. rev. ed. Willy Rotzler. LC 77-89937. (Illus.). 332p. 1989. reprint ed. 50.00 (*0-8478-1024-0*) Rizzoli Intl.

Constructive Conflict. Elaine Yarbrough. (Volunteer Management Ser.). 1988. 7.00 (*0-911029-12-5*) Heritage Arts.

Constructive Conflict Management: Managing to Make a Difference. John Crawley. LC 93-36224. 355p. 1993. pap. 14.95 (*0-89384-239-7*) Pfeiffer & Co.

Constructive Continuity. Mark Mandelkern. LC 82-24358. (Memoirs of the American Mathematical Society Ser.: No. 42/277). 117p. 1983. pap. 17.00 (*0-8218-2277-2*, MEMO 42/277) Am Math.

Constructive Criticism: A Handbook. Gracie Lyons. (Illus.). 72p. (Orig.). 1988. reprint ed. pap. 6.95 (*0-914728-62-8*) Wingbow Pr.

***Constructive Criticism: The Human Sciences in the Age of Theory.** Ed. by Martin Kreiswirth & Thomas Carmichael. (Theory - Culture Ser.). (Illus.). 208p. 1995. 45.00 (*0-8020-0675-2*) U of Toronto Pr.

***Constructive Criticism: The Human Sciences in the Age of Theory.** Ed. by Martin Kreiswirth & Thomas Carmichael. (Theory - Culture Ser.). (Illus.). 208p. 1995. pap. 17.95 (*0-8020-7630-0*) U of Toronto Pr.

Constructive Discipline. 2nd ed. Didactic Systems Staff. (Simulation Game Ser.). 1978. Two Or More Sets. write for info. (*0-685-08735-2*); pap. 26.25 (*0-89401-123-5*) Didactic Syst.

Constructive Drinking: Perspectives on Drink from Anthropology. Ed. by Mary Douglas. (Illus.). 304p. (C). 1991. pap. 22.95 (*0-521-40644-7*) Cambridge U Pr.

Constructive Evaluation of Literate Activity. Peter H. Johnston. 448p. (Orig.). (C). 1992. pap. text ed. 40.95 (*0-8013-0911-5*, 79172) Longman.

Constructive Evolution: Origins & Development of Piaget's Thought. Michael Chapman. 500p. 1988. pap. 34.95 (*0-521-36712-3*) Cambridge U Pr.

Constructive Experience. Charles Bazerman. LC 93-22839. 267p. (C). 1994. 34.95x (*0-8093-1906-3*) S Ill U Pr.

Constructive Feedback: Learning the Art. Brent Kilbourne. 135p. (Orig.). 1990. pap. text ed. 21.95 (*0-914797-78-6*) Brookline Bks.

Constructive Guidance & Discipline: Preschool & Primary Education. Marjorie Fields & Cindy Boesser. LC 93-14777. 320p. (C). 1994. pap. write for info. (*0-02-337285-0*, Merrill Pub Co) Macmillan.

Constructive Interpretation of Predicative Mathematics. Charles Parsons. (Harvard Dissertations in Philosophy Ser.). 350p. 1990. reprint ed. 30.00 (*0-8240-5091-6*) Garland.

Constructive Living. David K. Reynolds. 128p. 1984. pap. 9.50 (*0-8248-0871-1*) UH Pr.

Constructive Measure Theory. Errett Bishop & Henry Cheng. LC 52-42839. (Memoirs Ser.: No. 1/116). 85p. 1972. pap. 16.00 (*0-8218-1816-3*, MEMO 1/116) Am Math.

Constructive Methods for Nonlinear Boundary Value Problems & Nonlinear Oscillations. Ed. by Lothar Collatz et al. (International Series of Numerical Mathematics: Vol. 48). 192p. 1980. pap. 46.00 (*0-8176-1098-7*) Birkhauser.

Constructive Methods for the Practical Treatment of Integral Equations. Gunther Hammerlin & K. H. Hoffman. (International Series of Numerical Mathematics: No. 73). 284p. 1985. lib. bdg. 71.50 (*0-8176-1685-3*) Birkhauser.

Constructive Methods in Computing Science. Ed. by Manfred Broy. (NATO Asi Series F: Vol. 55). (Illus.). viii, 478p. 1989. 104.00 (*0-387-51369-8*, 3249) Spr-Verlag.

Constructive Methods of Wiener-Hopf Factorization. I. Gohberg & M. A. Kaashoek. (Operator Theory Ser.: Vol. 21). 424p. 1986. 116.00 (*0-8176-1826-0*) Birkhauser.

Constructive Philosophy. Paul Lorenzen. Tr. by Karl R. Pavlovic. LC 86-25003. 304p. 1987. lib. bdg. 32.50 (*0-87023-564-8*) U of Mass Pr.

***Constructive Physics: Results in Field Theory, Statistical Mechanics & Condensed Matter Physics: Proceedings of the Conference Held at Palaiseau, France 25-27 July 1994.** Ed. by Vincent Rivasseau. LC 95-12155. (Lecture Notes in Physics Ser.: Vol. 446). 1995. write for info. (*3-540-59190-7*) Spr-Verlag.

Constructive Postmodern Perspective on Self & Community: From Atomism to Holism. Hoyt L. Edge. LC 94-16376. 1994. text ed. 79.95 (*0-7734-9075-2*) E Mellen.

Constructive Program. M. K. Gandhi. 40p. (Orig.). 1982. pap. 1.00 (*0-934676-59-3*) Greenlf Bks.

Constructive Programmes of Mahatma Gandhi. Radhey S. Singh. (C). 1991. 22.50 (*81-7169-160-9*, Pub. by Commonwealth II) S Asia.

Constructive Psychology, or the Building of Character by Personal Effort. J. D. Buck. 207p. 1992. pap. 16.95 (*1-56459-206-5*) Kessinger Pub.

Constructive Quantum Field Theory. Ed. by G. Velo & Arthur S. Wightman. (Lecture Notes in Physics Ser.: Vol. 25). (Illus.). 331p. 1973. pap. 21.00 (*0-387-06608-X*) Spr-Verlag.

Constructive Quantum Field Theory II. Ed. by F. Velo & Arthur S. Wightman. LC 90-7902. (NATO ASI Series B, Physics: Vol. 234). (Illus.). 380p. 1990. 92.50 (*0-306-43674-4*, Plenum Pr) Plenum.

Constructive Reading: Teaching Beyond Communication. Deanne Bogdan & Stanley B. Straw. LC 93-2295. 222p. (C). 1993. pap. text ed. 23.50 (*0-86709-329-3*, 0329) Boynton Cook Pubs.

Constructive Real Numbers & Function Spaces. Nikolai A. Sanin. Tr. by E. Mendelson. LC 68-19437. (Translations of Mathematical Monographs: Vol. 21). 325p. 1968. 58. 00 (*0-8218-1571-7*, MMONO-21) Am Math.

Constructive Revolutionary: John Calvin & His Socio-Economic Impact. W. Fred Graham. 251p. (C). 1987. reprint ed. pap. 12.95 (*0-87013-249-0*) Mich St U Pr.

Constructive Sociological Theory: The Forgotten Legacy of Thomas G. Masaryk. Thomas G. Masaryk. Ed. by Jonathan B. Imber. LC 93-45995. 347p. (C). 1994. 49.95 (*1-56000-164-X*) Transaction Pubs.

Constructive Sociological Theory: The Forgotten Legacy of Thomas G. Masarykj. Werner J. Cahnman & Jonathan B. Imber. Ed. by Alan Woolfolk. 350p. (C). 1994. text ed. 39.95 (*1-56000-134-8*) Transaction Pubs.

Constructive Theory of Functions. Ed. by Collet's Holdings, Ltd. Staff. 940p. 1984. 105.00 (*0-317-46597-X*) St Mut.

Constructive Therapies. Ed. by Michael F. Hoyt. LC 94-14220. 340p. 1994. lib. bdg. 35.00 (*0-89862-094-5*) Guilford Pr.

Constructive Type Theory. Roland Backhouse. 1989. text ed. 54.80 (*0-13-168196-6*) P-H.

Constructive Typology & Social Theory. John C. McKinney. LC 66-25454. (Century Sociology Ser.). 1966. 27.50 (*0-89197-105-X*) Irvington.

Constructive Uses of Atomic Energy. Ed. by S. Charles Rothmann. LC 73-128304. (Essay Index Reprint Ser.). 1977. 23.95 (*0-8369-2129-1*) Ayer.

Constructive Years: The U. S. Economy under Eisenhower. Raymond J. Saulnier. 266p. (Orig.). (C). 1991. lib. bdg. 51.00 (*0-8191-8367-9*); pap. text ed. 25.00 (*0-8191-8368-7*) U Pr of Amer.

Constructivism. (Architectural Design Profiles Ser.). (Illus.). 88p. 1990. pap. 21.95 (*0-312-03989-1*) St Martin.

***Constructivism: Its Foundations & Applications: A Selected Bibliography.** Eleanor R. Lehman & Barbara L. Grabowski. LC 95-3903. (Selected Bibliography Ser.: Vol. 14). 1995. 19.95 (*1-87778-288-1*) Educ Tech Pubns.

***Constructivism: Origins & Evolution.** rev. ed. George Rickey. (Illus.). 306p. 1995. 25.00 (*0-8076-1381-9*) Braziller.

Constructivism & Science. Ed. by Robert E. Butts & James R. Brown. (C). 1989. lib. bdg. 130.00 (*0-7923-0251-6*) Kluwer Ac.

Constructivism & the Technology of Instruction: A Conversation. Ed. by Thomas M. Duffy & David Jonassen. 232p. 1993. pap. 24.95 (*0-8058-1272-5*) L Erlbaum Assocs.

Constructivism in Education. Ed. by Leslie P. Steffe & Jerry Gale. 584p. 1994. text ed. 95.00 (*0-8058-1095-1*); pap. 39.95 (*0-8058-1096-X*) L Erlbaum Assocs.

Constructivism in Film: The Man with the Movie Camera. Vlada Petric. (Studies in Film). (Illus.). 352p. (C). 1993. pap. 19.95 (*0-521-44387-3*) Cambridge U Pr.

Constructivism in Mathematics: An Introduction, Vol. 1. A. S. Troelstra & D. Van Dalen. (Studies in Logic & the Foundations of Mathematics: No. 121). 342p. 1988. 84. 75 (*0-444-70266-0*); pap. 32.00 (*0-444-70506-6*) Elsevier.

Constructivism in Mathematics: An Introduction, Vol. 2. A. S. Troelstra & D. Van Dalen. (Studies in Logic & the Foundations of Mathematics: No. 123). 534p. 1988. 84. 75 (*0-444-70358-6*, North Holland) Elsevier.

***Constructivism in Psychotherapy.** Ed. by Robert A. Neimeyer & Michael J. Mahoney. 480p. 1995. text ed. 49.95 (*1-55798-279-1*) Am Psychol.

Constructivism in the Computer Age. Ed. by George Forman & Peter Pufall. (Jean Piaget Society Ser.). 280p. 1988. text ed. 49.95 (*0-8058-0101-4*) L Erlbaum Assocs.

Constructivist Architecture in the U. S. S. R. Anatole Kopp. (Academy Architecture Bks.). (Illus.). 160p. 1986. 50.00 (*0-312-16599-4*) St Martin.

Constructivist Architecture in the U. S. S. R. T. Kopp. (C). 1990. 300.00 (*0-685-34371-5*, Pub. by Collets) St Mut.

Constructivist Assessment: A Casebook. Greg J. Neimeyer. (Counseling Psychologist Casebook Ser.: Vol. 2). (Illus.). 248p. (C). 1992. 39.95 (*0-8039-4830-1*); pap. 18.95 (*0-8039-4831-X*) Sage.

Constructivist Early Education: Overview & Comparison with Other Programs. Rheta DeVries & Lawrence Kohlberg. LC 90-60618. 423p. 1987. pap. text ed. 10.00 (*0-935989-33-1*, NAEYC#235) Natl Assn Child Ed.

***Constructivist Leader.** Lambert. 240p. (C). 1995. text ed. 44.00x (*0-8077-3463-2*); pap. text ed. 21.95x (*0-8077-3462-4*) Tchrs Coll.

Constructivist Perspectives on Developmental Psychopathology & Atypical Development. Ed. by D. Keating & H. Rosen. 280p. (C). 1990. text ed. 49.95 (*0-8058-0437-4*) L Erlbaum Assocs.

Constructivist Views on the Teaching & Learning of Mathematics. Ed. by Robert B. Davis et al. LC 90-45001. (Journal for Research in Mathematics Education Monograph Ser.: No. 4). 210p. (Orig.). 1990. pap. 10.50 (*0-87353-300-3*) NCTM.

Constructivity in Computer Science: Summer Symposium, San Antonio, TX, June 19-22, 1991, Proceedings. Ed. by J. P. Myers, Jr. et al. LC 92-19519. (Lecture Notes in Computer Science Ser.: Vol. 613). x, 247p. 1992. 47.00 (*0-387-55631-1*); pap. 43.00 (*3-540-55631-1*) Spr-Verlag.

Constructo: A Heuristic Game for Construction Management. Daniel W. Halpin & Ronald W. Woodhead. LC 73-76342. 203p. reprint ed. pap. 57.90 (*0-8357-3292-4*, 2039515) Bks Demand.

Constructs. Richard Kostelanetz. 112p. 1991. pap. 10.00 (*0-685-50710-6*) Archae Edns.

Constructs. deluxe limited ed. Richard Kostelanetz. 112p. 1991. student ed. 75.00 (*0-685-50709-2*) Archae Edns.

Constructs Five: Stories. deluxe limited ed. Richard Kostelanetz. 167p. (Orig.). 1991. pap. 100.00 (*0-932360-96-3*) Archae Edns.

Constructs for Understanding Japan. Ed. by Ross E. Mouer & Yoshio Sugimoto. 250p. 1989. text ed. 69.50 (*0-7103-0209-6*) Routledge Chapman & Hall.

Constructs Four: Stories. deluxe limited ed. Richard Kostelanetz. 176p. (Orig.). 1991. pap. 100.00 (*0-932360-95-5*) Archae Edns.

Constructs Six: Stories. deluxe limited ed. Richard Kostelanetz. 180p. (Orig.). 1991. pap. 100.00 (*0-932360-97-1*) Archae Edns.

Constructs Three: Stories. deluxe limited ed. Richard Kostelanetz. 186p. (Orig.). 1991. pap. 100.00 (*0-932360-91-2*) Archae Edns.

Constructs Two. Richard Kostelanetz. 1978. pap. 5.00 (*0-87924-041-5*) Membrane Pr.

Constructual Marital Therapy: Theory & Practice. Marshall Jung. LC 92-34219. 256p. (C). 1993. pap. text ed. 24.95 (*0-89876-191-3*) Gardner Pr.

Construing Person. Jack R. Adams-Webber. Ed. by James C. Mancuso. LC 81-12101. 320p. 1982. text ed. 40.95 (*0-275-90853-4*, C0853, Praeger Pubs) Greenwood.

Construya en Ingles. (BBC Phrase Books for Teenagers Ser.). 1994. pap. 7.95 (*0-8442-7123-3*, Passport Bks) NTC Pub Grp.

Consuelo: A Romance of Venice. George Sand. LC 79-15632. (Quality Paperbacks Ser.). 799p. 1979. pap. 8.95 (*0-306-80102-7*) Da Capo.

Consuelo Hoy-Esperanza Manana (Comfort Today-Hope Tomorrow) (SPA.). Date not set. 1.00 (*0-8423-6462-5*, 490268) Editorial Unilit.

Consuelo Kanaga: An American Photographer. Barbara H. Millstein & Sarah M. Lowe. LC 91-35933. (Illus.). 224p. 1992. pap. 35.00 (*0-295-97228-9*) U of Wash Pr.

Consuetudo, Vel Lex Mercatoria, or the Ancient Law-Merchant. Gerard De Malynes. LC 79-84121. (English Experience Ser.: No. 940). 524p. 1979. reprint ed. lib. bdg. 78.00 (*90-221-0940-2*) Walter J Johnson.

Consul. 2nd rev. ed. Walter W. Orebaugh & Carol Jose. LC 94-70993. (Illus.). 336p. 1994. pap. 9.95 (*1-878398-08-3*) Blue Note Pubns.

Consul General's Daughter. Erin Pizzey. 1991. mass mkt. 5.50 (*0-06-100151-1*, Harp PBks) HarpC.

Consul, Zephyr, Zodiac, Executive. Michael Allen. (Illus.). 200p. 1990. 49.95 (*0-947981-42-X*, Pub. by Motor Racing UK) Motorbooks Intl.

Consular Dimension of Diplomacy: A Symposium. Ed. by Martin F. Herz. LC 83-332. 88p. (Orig.). 1983. pap. 9.75 (*0-934742-22-7*) Geo U Inst Dplmcy.

Consular Dimension of Diplomacy: A Symposium. Ed. by Martin F. Herz. LC 85-22467. 88p. (Orig.). (C). 1986. reprint ed. pap. text ed. 9.75 (*0-8191-5069-X*, Inst Study Diplomacy) U Pr of Amer.

Consular Law & Practice. 2nd ed. Luke T. Lee. 776p. 1991. 165.00 (*0-19-825601-9*) OUP.

Consular Letters, 1853-1855. Nathaniel Hawthorne. Ed. by Bill Ellis. (Centenary Edition of the Works of Nathaniel Hawthorne: Vol. 19). 480p. 1988. 65.00 (*0-8142-0384-1*) Ohio St U Pr.

Consular Letters, 1856-1857. Nathaniel Hawthorne. Ed. by Bill Ellis. (Centenary Edition of the Works of Nathaniel Hawthorne: Vol. 20). 385p. 1988. text ed. 82.50 (*0-8142-0462-7*) Ohio St U Pr.

Consular Posts Handbook. 5th ed. Ed. by Seymour Rosenburg. 150p. (Orig.). Date not set. pap. text ed. 24. 00 (*1-878677-49-7*) Amer Immi Law Assn.

Consular Privileges & Immunities. Irvin Stewart. LC 68-57583. (Columbia University. Studies in Social Sciences: No. 281). reprint ed. 21.00 (*0-404-51281-X*) AMS Pr.

Consulate & Empire, 2 Vols. Louis Madelin. No. 7. reprint ed. write for info. (*0-318-50547-9*) AMS Pr.

Consulate & Empire, 2 Vols, 1. Louis Madelin. LC 34-10700. (National History of France Ser.: No. 7). reprint ed. 45.00 (*0-404-50808-1*) AMS Pr.

Consulate & Empire, 2 Vols, 2. Louis Madelin. LC 34-10700. (National History of France Ser.: No. 7). reprint ed. 45.00 (*0-404-50809-X*) AMS Pr.

Consulate & Empire, 2 Vols, Set. Louis Madelin. LC 34-10700. (National History of France Ser.: No. 7). reprint ed. 90.00 (*0-404-50810-3*) AMS Pr.

***Consul's Daughter.** large type ed. Jane Jackson. (Dales Large Print Ser.). 1994. pap. 16.95 (*1-85389-506-7*, Pub. by Magna Print Bks) Ulverscroft.

Consuls of the Later Roman Empire. Roger Bagnall et al. LC 86-31452. (American Philological Association Philological Monographs). 769p. 1987. 53.00 (*1-55540-099-X*, 40-00-36) Scholars Pr GA.

Consultamation, Inc. Word Processing Practice & Applications. Lloyd D. Brooks. 192p. 1983. text ed. 18. 50 (*0-07-008081-X*) McGraw.

Consultancy on Strategic Information Planning. Ed. by Zdravka Pejova & Forest W. Horton. 214p. 1993. pap. 30.00 (*92-9038-140-X*, Pub. by Intl Ctr Pub Ent XV) Kumarian Pr.

Consultant. Jack Rudman. (Career Examination Ser.: C-953). 1994. pap. 34.95 (*0-8373-0953-0*) Nat Learn.

Consultant As Communicator. Bagley & Lavin. 1990. pap. 9.99 (*0-89824-202-9*) Trillium Pr.

Consultant Dietitian: Developing Marketable Skills in Health Care. Carolyn Breeding et al. LC 90-48599. (Illus.). 304p. 1991. text ed. 44.95 (*0-442-31884-7*) Van Nos Reinhold.

Consultant (Early Childhood Education) Jack Rudman. (Career Examination Ser.: C-954). 1994. pap. 34.95 (*0-8373-0954-9*) Nat Learn.

Consultant in Audiology. Jack Rudman. (Career Examination Ser.: C-1213). 1994. pap. 34.95 (*0-8373-1213-2*) Nat Learn.

Consultants & Consulting: Sources & Resources. Donald Levitan. (Organizations & Interest Groups Ser.: Vol. 2). 120p. 20.00 (*0-8240-5173-4*, SS656) Garland.

Consultants & Consulting Organizations Directory Supplement 15. 15th ed. McLean & Karin Koek. 1995. 410.00 (*0-8103-8064-1*) Gale.

Consultants & Consulting Organizations Directory, Vol. 1: List. 14th ed. McLean & Karin Koek. 1993. write for info. (*0-8103-8046-3*) Gale.

Consultant's Calling: Bringing Who You Are to What You Do. Geoffrey M. Bellman. LC 90-53092. (Management Ser.). 264p. 1990. 32.95 (*1-55542-253-5*) Jossey-Bass.

Consultant's Calling: Bringing Who You Are to What You Do. Geoffrey M. Bellman. LC 90-53092. (Management Ser.). 264p. 1992. reprint ed. pap. 19.00 (*1-55542-411-2*) Jossey-Bass.

***Consultant's Craft: Improving Organizational Communication.** Sue DeWine. 432p. 1993. pap. text ed. 22.00 (*0-312-06151-X*) St Martin.

Consultants Directory. 3rd ed. 30p. (Orig.). 1989. pap. text ed. write for info. (*0-318-64546-7*) SLA LMD Consult.

Consultants Directory for Business & Industry. 1989. 99.00 (*0-8103-2230-7*) Gale.

Consultant's Guide to Hidden Profits: The 101 Most Overlooked Strategies for Increased Earnings & Growth. Herman R. Holtz. 240p. 1992. text ed. 27.95 (*0-471-55496-0*) Wiley.

Consultant's Guide to Litigation Services: How to Be an Expert Witness. Thomas H. Veitch. LC 92-14945. 240p. 1992. text ed. 64.95 (*0-471-55406-5*) Wiley.

Consultant's Guide to Proposal Writing: How to Satisfy Your Clients & Double Your Income. 2nd ed. Herman R. Holtz. LC 08-922663. 1990. text ed. 34.95 (*0-471-51569-8*) Wiley.

Consultant's Guide to Seminar Presentations: An Insider's Guide to Developing & Marketing Seminars As a Marketing Tool & Independent Profit Center. Herman R. Holtz. LC 87-14231. 240p. 1987. text ed. 32.50 (*0-471-85899-4*) Wiley.

Consultant's Guide to Winning Clients. Herman R. Holtz. LC 87-24945. 1988. text ed. 29.95 (*0-471-62759-3*) Wiley.

Consultant's Handbook: How to Start & Develop Your Own Practice. Stephan Schiffman. 252p. 1988. pap. 12.95 (*0-937860-93-X*) Adams Pubng.

Consultant's Handbook of Database Design. Frank Sweet. (Illus.). 80p. (Orig.). 1988. pap. 6.50 (*0-939479-03-6*) Boxes & Arrows.

Consultants in Japanese Philanthropy: 56 Firms That Counsel the Donors. Corporate Philanthropy Report Editors. 58p. 1991. pap. 60.00 (*1-881065-01-4*) Corp Philan.

***Consultant's Journey: A Dance of Work & Spirit.** Roger Harrison. (Management Ser.). 208p. 1995. 29.95 (*0-7879-0070-2*) Jossey-Bass.

Consultant's Kit: Establishing & Operating Your Successful Consulting Business. 3rd ed. 365p. 1992. 35.00 (*0-940374-22-6*) JLA Pubns.

Consultant's Kit: Operating Your Own Successful Consulting Business. 1987. lib. bdg. 69.50 (*0-8490-3877-4*) Gordon Pr.

Consultant's Manual: A Complete Guide to Building a Successful Consulting Practice. Thomas L. Greenbaum. 228p. 1990. text ed. 70.00 (*0-471-50119-0*) Wiley.

Consultant's Manual: A Complete Guide to Building a Successful Consulting Practice. Thomas L. Greenbaum. 1994. pap. text ed. 19.95 (*0-471-00879-6*) Wiley.

Consultant's Proposal, Fee, & Contract Problem-Solver. Ronald Tepper. 256p. 1993. pap. text ed. 19.95 (*0-471-58213-1*) Wiley.

An Asterisk (*) at the beginning of an entry indicates that the title is appearing in BIP for the first time.

An Asterisk (*) at the beginning of an entry indicates that the title is appearing in BIP for the first time.

1567

C

Consumer Behavior Models for Non-Statisticians: The River of Time. Jerome Greene. LC 82-9076. 192p. 1982. text ed. 45.00 (0-275-90811-9, C0811, Praeger Pubs) Greenwood.

***Consumer Behaviour.** 3rd ed. Peter M. Chisnall. LC 94-31098. 1994. write for info. (0-07-707616-8) McGraw.

Consumer Behaviour in China: Consumer Satisfaction & Cultural Values. Oliver H. Yau. (Consumer Research & Policy Ser.). 240p. 1992. 75.00 (0-415-00436-5, A7305) Routledge.

Consumer-Buyer & the Market. Jessie V. Coles. Ed. by Henry Assael. LC 78-265. (Century of Marketing Ser.). (Illus.). 1979. lib. bdg. 51.95 (0-405-11168-1) Ayer.

Consumer Buying. Boy Scouts of America. (Illus.). 64p. (J). (gr. 6-12). 1975. pap. 1.85 (0-8395-3387-X, 33387) BSA.

Consumer Buying Guide, 1994. Consumer Guide Editors. 448p. (Orig.). 1994. pap. 5.99 (0-451-17910-2, Sig) NAL-Dutton.

***Consumer Buying Guide, 1995.** Consumer Guide Editors Staff. 448p. (Orig.). 1995. pap. 5.99 (0-451-18361-4, Sig) NAL-Dutton.

Consumer Buying Intentions & Purchase Probability: An Experiment in Survey Design. F. Thomas Juster. (Occasional Papers: No. 99). 68p. 1966. reprint ed. 20.00 (0-87014-413-8) Natl Bur Econ Res.

Consumer Buying Patterns 1979-81. 1982. 175.00 (0-317-43750-X) St Mut.

***Consumer Car Care for the Wise, the Poor & the Helpless.** John C. Bartone. LC 95-15996. 1995. write for info. (0-7883-0722-3); pap. write for info. (0-7883-0723-1) ABBE Pubs Assn.

***Consumer Car Care for the Wise, the Poor & the Helpless.** 2nd rev. ed. John C. Bartone, II. LC 90-56237. 190p. 1994. 34.50 (0-7883-0430-5); pap. 29.50 (0-7883-0431-3) ABBE Pubs Assn.

Consumer Cause: A Short Account of Its Organization, Development, Power, & Importance. Ronald Wraith. 80p. (C). 1976. 35.00 (0-686-96573-6) St Mut.

Consumer Chemistry Projects for Young Scientists. David E. Newton. LC 90-48499. (Illus.). 128p. (YA). (gr. 9-12). 1991. lib. bdg. 14.77 (0-531-11011-7) Watts.

***Consumer China 1994.** 171p. 1994. 590.00 (0-86338-551-6, Pub. by Euromonitor Pubns UK) Gale.

Consumer Choice Guide to Restaurants in Ireland. Consumers' Association of Ireland Staff. LC 89-85264. (Illus.). 174p. (Orig.). 1989. pap. 9.95 (0-86278-184-1, Pub. by OBrien Pr IE) Dufour.

Consumer Choice in Historical Archaeology. Ed. by Suzanne M. Spencer-Wood. LC 87-2569. (Illus.). 436p. 1987. 59.50 (0-306-42318-9, Plenum Pr) Plenum.

Consumer Class Action Materials. 221p. 1985. 17.50 (0-317-02666-6, 37,092) NCLS Inc.

Consumer Class Actions: A Practical Litigation Guide. 2nd ed. Yvonne W. Rosmarin & Daniel A. Edelman. LC 90-6335. (Consumer Credit & Sales Legal Practice Ser.). 237p. (Orig.). 1990. pap. 60.00 (0-943116-79-1) Nat Consumer Law.

Consumer Classics. (American Book Ser.). (Illus.). 1980. 3.00 (0-911410-50-3) Applied Arts.

Consumer Clothing: Reproducible Master. (YA). (gr. 7-12). 1989. Package of 10. 15.95 (1-877844-00-4, 2121M) Meridian Educ.

Consumer Complaints & Small Claims Court Actions, N. Y.S. A Comprehensive Guide. 75p. 1994. ring bd. 7.95 (0-930137-64-7) Looseleaf Law.

***Consumer Compliance Handbook: 1995 Edition.** Price Waterhouse Staff. 225p. 1995. 60.00 (1-55738-762-1) Probus Pub Co.

Consumer Cooperation in France: The Politics of Consumption, 1834-1930. Ellen Furlough. LC 90-55726. (Illus.). 320p. 1991. 41.50 (0-8014-2512-3) Cornell U Pr.

Consumer Cost Guide to Car Repair. Larry Conroy & Paul O'Connell. (Illus.). 144p. 1983. pap. 11.00 (0-13-168864-2); pap. text ed. 17.00 (0-13-168872-3) P-H.

Consumer Credit. Ed. by R. M. Goode. 508p. 1978. lib. bdg. 112.50 (90-286-0928-8) Kluwer Ac.

***Consumer Credit & Consumer Hire.** Geoff Harding. 1994. 64.00 (0-421-48340-7, Pub. by Sweet & Maxwll) W W Gaunt.

Consumer Credit & Sales Legal Practice Series, 12 vols. 1995. 672.00 (0-943116-10-4) Nat Consumer Law.

Consumer Credit & the Law. Dee Pridgen. LC 90-37060. 1990. ring bd. 135.00 (0-87632-742-0) Clark Boardman Callaghan.

Consumer Credit & Truth-in-Lending Compliance Report. 168.00 (0-685-69621-9, CCTL) Warren Gorham & Lamont.

Consumer Credit Compliance Manual. 2nd ed. John R. Fonseca. LC 84-81909. 1984. 135.00 (0-685-59828-4) Clark Boardman Callaghan.

Consumer Credit Cost, Nineteen Forty-Nine to Nineteen Fifty-Nine. P. F. Smith. (National Bureau of Economic Research Financial Research Program Ser.). 1964. 35.00x (0-691-04116-4) Princeton U Pr.

Consumer Credit Finance Charges: Rate Information & Quotation. Walter P. Mors. (Financial Research Program II: Studies in Consumer Installment Financing: No. 12). 150p. 1965. 39.30 (0-87014-128-7) Natl Bur Econ Res.

Consumer Credit Handbook. 1990. lib. bdg. 250.00 (0-87700-907-4) Revisionist Pr.

Consumer Credit Law. R. M. Goode. 1989. 180.00 (0-406-12101-X, U.K.) Butterworth Legal Pubs.

Consumer Credit Law: Transaction & Forms, 3 vols. Kenneth M. Lapine. 1984. Update. write for info. (0-8205-1084-X) Bender.

Consumer Credit Law in Australia. S. W. Cavanaugh & S. Barnes. 1988. Australia. 55.00 (0-409-49449-6) Butterworth Legal Pubs.

Consumer Credit Legislation, 2 vols. R. M. Goode et al. 1977. ring bd. 420.00 (0-406-21161-2, U.K.) Butterworth Legal Pubs.

Consumer Credit Regulations. 2nd ed. Dan L. Nicewander. (Business Practice Library). 380p. 1991. 135.00 (0-471-55305-0) Wiley.

Consumer Credit Regulations. 2nd suppl. ed. Dan L. Nicewander. (Business Practice Library). 168p. 1992. 55.00 (0-471-57729-4) Wiley.

Consumer Credit Regulations: 1991 Supplement. 2nd ed. Dan L. Nicewander. 80p. 1991. ring bd. 45.00 (0-471-55806-0) Wiley.

Consumer Credit Terms & Math. H. Clyde Farrell. 37p. pap. 4.00 (0-685-23160-7, 41,575CC) NCLS Inc.

Consumer Credit 1993. (Commercial Law & Practice Course Handbook Ser.: Vol. 663). 517p. 1993. 70.00 (0-685-69713-4, A4-4432) PLI.

Consumer Culture & Postmodernism. Mike Featherstone. (Theory, Culture & Society Ser.). (Illus.). 192p. 1991. 45.00 (0-8039-8414-6); pap. 18.95 (0-8039-8415-4) Sage.

Consumer Culture & the American Home, 1890-1930. Harvey Green et al. 80p. (Orig.). 1990. pap. 10.00 (0-317-93849-5) McFaddin-Ward.

***Consumer Culture & TV Programming.** Andersen. (Critical Studies in Communications). 1995. text ed. 69.95 (0-8133-1541-7) Westview.

***Consumer Culture & TV Programming.** Andersen. (Critical Studies in Communications). (C). 1995. pap. text ed. 19.95 (0-8133-1542-5) Westview.

Consumer Culture Reborn: The Cultural Politics of Consumption. Martyn J. Lee. LC 92-34903. 208p. 1993. 59.95 (0-415-08413-X, B2272); pap. 16.95 (0-415-08414-8, B2276) Routledge.

Consumer Debts. Rich Tomlinson. 27p. pap. 2.75 (0-685-23161-5, 41,575CD) NCLS Inc.

Consumer Demand: A New Approach. Kelvin Lancaster. LC 76-164502. (Columbia Studies in Economics: No. 5). 177p. 1971. text ed. 39.50 (0-231-03357-5) Col U Pr.

Consumer Durable Choice & the Demand for Electricity: Contributions to Economic Analysis, Vol. 155. J. A. Dubin. 284p. 1985. 75.00 (0-444-87766-5, North Holland) Elsevier.

Consumer Eastern Europe. 1992. 550.00 (0-86338-423-4, 073170, Pub. by Europa UK) Gale.

***Consumer Eastern Europe 1994.** 2nd ed. 392p. 1994. 590.00 (0-86338-553-2, Pub. by Euromonitor Pubns UK) Gale.

Consumer Economic Issues in America. E. Thomas Garman. (C). 1991. write for info. (0-395-56791-2) HM Soft Schl Col Div.

Consumer Economics: The Consumer in Our Society. 11th ed. Mel J. Zelenak. LC 93-597. 1993. pap. 44.00 (0-942280-61-X) Pub Horizons.

Consumer Economics after Keynes: Theory & Evidence of the Consumption Function. George Hadjimatheou. 224p. 1987. text ed. 39.95 (0-312-00478-8) St Martin.

Consumer Economics & Personal Finance: Syllabus. Martha C. Bagby. 1974. pap. text ed. 8.95 (0-89420-063-1, 100030); audio 224.55 (0-89420-136-0, 100000) Natl Book.

Consumer Economics & Personal Money Management. 2nd ed. Francis M. Albin. (Illus.). 496p. (C). 1988. Casebound. text ed. write for info. (0-13-168048-X) P-H.

Consumer Education. Wilmer O. Maedke et al. LC 77-73301. 528p. (gr. 11-12). 1984. teacher ed 10.67 (0-02-475740-3); text ed. 27.96 (0-02-475720-9); student ed 7.72 (0-02-475730-6) Glencoe.

Consumer Education Programming in Continuing Education. Margaret Charters. LC 72-13366. (Occasional Papers: No. 34). 36p. (Orig.). 1973. pap. 2.00 (0-87060-057-5, OCP 34) Syracuse U Cont Ed.

Consumer Electronics Industry & the Future of American Manufacturing: How the U. S. Lost the Lead & Why We Must Get Back in the Game. Susan W. Sanderson. LC 89-85121. (Illus.). 52p. 1990. 12.00 (0-944826-12-1) Economic Policy Inst.

Consumer Emancipation & Economic Development. Ed. by Hans B. Thorelli & Gerald D. Sentell. (Contemporary Studies in Economic & Financial Analysis: Vol. 37). 376p. 1982. 73.25 (0-89232-237-3) Jai Pr.

Consumer Engineering: A New Technique for Prosperity. Roy Sheldon & Egmont Arens. LC 75-39274. (Getting & Spending: the Consumer's Dilemma Ser.). 1976. reprint ed. 23.95 (0-405-08046-8) Ayer.

Consumer Europe. 736p. 1985. 750.00 (0-903706-48-2, Pub. by Euromonitor Pubns UK) St Mut.

Consumer Expectations, Plans, & Purchases: A Progress Report. Francis T. Juster. 8.00 (0-405-18757-2, 16476) Ayer.

Consumer Expectations, Plans, & Purchases: A Progress Report. F. Thomas Juster. (Occasional Papers: No. 70). 194p. 1959. reprint ed. 50.50 (0-87014-384-0) Natl Bur Econ Res.

Consumer Expenditure Function. Michael R. Darby. (Explorations in Economic Research Four Ser.: No. 5). 30p. 1978. reprint ed. 35.00 (0-685-61419-0) Natl Bur Econ Res.

Consumer Expenditure Patterns: A Survey of St. Thomas, U. S. V. I., 1975-1976. Jerome L. McElroy & Joseph E. Caines. LC 79-22424. 118p. reprint ed. pap. 33.70 (0-7837-5062-5, 2044752) Bks Demand.

Consumer Expenditure Survey. 1994. lib. bdg. 250.00 (0-8490-5770-1) Gordon Pr.

Consumer Expenditure Survey, 1987. 159p. 1990. per., pap. 8.00 (0-16-024188-X, S/N 029-001-030) USGPO.

***Consumer Expenditures: New Measures & Old Motives.** Stanley Lebergott. LC 95-2852. 1995. write for info. (0-691-04321-3) Princeton U Pr.

Consumer Finance: The Consumer Experience. David J. Ward & Robert M. Niendorf. LC 77-85803. 505p. reprint ed. pap. 144.00 (0-317-27983-1, 2055815) Bks Demand.

Consumer Finance Industry: Its Costs & Regulations. Ed. by John M. Chapman & Robert P. Shay. LC 67-21693. (Illus.). reprint ed. pap. 38.60 (0-317-09347-9, 2015323) Bks Demand.

Consumer Finance Law. Rasor. 1985. write for info. (0-8205-0121-2, 212); teacher ed write for info. (0-8205-0122-0) Bender.

Consumer-Financial Institution Relationship in Electronic Funds Transfer Legislation. Fred M. Greguras & Ann Wright. LC 79-55491. (Computer Law Monograph Ser.). 160p. (Orig.). 1979. 20.00 (0-935200-00-2) Ctr Comp Law.

Consumer Food Selection & Nutrition Information. Fredrica Rudell. LC 79-10149. (Praeger Special Studies). 188p. 1979. text ed. 45.00 (0-275-90415-6, C0415, Praeger Pubs) Greenwood.

Consumer Frauds Representative. Jack Rudman. (Career Examination Ser.: C-876). 1994. pap. 23.95 (0-8373-0876-3) Nat Learn.

Consumer Guide - "Coin World" Guide to U. S. Coins, Prices & Value Trends, 1989. Consumer Guide Staff. 1989. pap. 4.50 (0-317-02796-4) NAL-Dutton.

Consumer Guide Book of Annuals. Consumer Guide Book Editors. 1990. 12.99 (0-517-68643-0) Random Hse Value.

Consumer Guide Book of Perennials. Consumer Guide Book Editors. 1990. 10.99 (0-517-68644-9) Random Hse Value.

Consumer Guide to College Funding: Everything You Need to Know to Get College Money. Marcia Castaneda. 1992. pap. 7.95 (0-929230-12-4) United Res Bks.

Consumer Guide to Divorce in New York: A Complete Manual with Forms. Blisse Alexandra & David Singiser. LC 91-67997. 149p. (Orig.). 1992. pap. 19.95 (0-9631707-0-8) Peoples Leg Guides.

Consumer Guide to Fighting Back. Timothy Scott. 100p. (Orig.). (C). 1989. pap. text ed. write for info. (0-318-65210-2) T Scott Pub.

Consumer Guide to Home Energy Savings: Listing of the Most Efficient Products You Can Buy...& Much More. Alex Wilson & John Morrill. (Consumer Ser.). (Illus.). 275p. 1995. pap. 7.95 (0-918249-21-X) Am Coun Energy.

Consumer Guide to Modern Cataract Surgery. Maloney et al. LC 85-80392. (Illus.). 1986. pap. 12.95 (0-918916-05-4) Lasenda.

Consumer Guide to Solar Energy: Easy & Inexpensive Applications for Solar Energy. Scott Sklar & Kenneth Sheinkopf. 181p. (Orig.). 1991. pap. 9.95 (0-929387-23-6) Bonus Books.

Consumer Guide to the Stock Market: Everything You Need to Know to Invest & Make Money. Marsha Bertrand. 1993. pap. 7.95 (0-929230-13-2) United Res Bks.

Consumer Guide to Veteran's Benefits: Everything You Need to Know to Make the Most of Veteran's. United Resource Press Staff. 1992. pap. 7.95 (0-929230-14-0) United Res Bks.

***Consumer Guidebook to Law & Leading Attorneys - Minnesota Edition: Minnesota Consumer Guidebook to Law & Leading Attorneys.** American Research Corporation Staff. Ed. by Joseph P. Mitzel. (Guidebooks to Law & Leading Attorneys Ser.). 287p. (Orig.). 1994. pap. 12.95 (1-885573-00-6) Am Research.

Consumer Handbook. Ann M. Rees. (Illus.). 160p. 1992. pap. 20.95 (0-632-00692-7) Blackwell Sci.

Consumer Handbook to an Educated Home Purchase: A Complete Self-Analysis Guide for Locating the Home, Community, & Mortgage Plan Best-Suited for You. Richard A. Chana. (Illus.). 414p. (Orig.). 1994. pap. 39.95 (0-9640247-3-X); pap. text ed. 39.95 (0-9640247-4-8) Consumer Housing.

***Consumer Health.** Jon W. Hisgen. (Comprehensive Health for Middle Grades Ser.). (J). (gr. 6-9). 1996. 24.00 (1-56071-466-2, H568) ETR Assocs.

Consumer Health: A Guide to Intelligent Decisions. 5th ed. Harold J. Cornacchia. LC 92-26457. 640p. 1992. pap. 35.95 (0-8016-6747-X) Mosby Yr Bk.

Consumer Health: Products & Services. Jessie H. Haag. LC 74-6033. 284p. reprint ed. pap. 81.00 (0-685-15866-7, 2056186) Bks Demand.

***Consumer Health & Safety.** Tony Askham. 400p. 1994. pap. text ed. 193.00 (0-406-04525-9, UK) Butterworth Legal Pubs.

Consumer Health & Safety Activities. Patricia R. Toner. LC 93-8219. (Just for the Health of It Ser.: Unit 1). 1993. pap. text ed. 18.95 (0-87628-263-X) Ctr Appl Res.

***Consumer Health Decisions.** Ray Petersen. (Health Science Ser.). 512p. 1996. pap. 37.50 (0-86720-936-4) Jones & Bartlett.

Consumer Health Information: Managing Hospital-Based Centers. Salvinija G. Kernaghan & Barbara E. Giloth. 99p. (Orig.). 1991. pap. 8.00 (0-87258-605-7, 070200) Am Hospital.

Consumer Health Information Service, 1985-1987 Index. Ed. by Alan M. Rees. 120p. 1987. pap. 25.00 (0-8357-0721-0) Univ Microfilms.

Consumer Health Information Service, 1987-1989 Index. Ed. by Alan M. Rees. 143p. 1989. pap. 25.00 (0-8357-0808-X) Univ Microfilms.

Consumer Health Information Source Book. 4th ed. Ed. by Alan M. Rees. LC 94-26854. 240p. 1994. pap. 44.50 (0-89774-796-8) Oryx Pr.

Consumer Health Issues: Making Decisions in Today's Society. Janell R. Campbell. 224p. (C). 1992. pap. text ed. 26.95 (0-8403-7507-7) Kendall-Hunt.

***Consumer Health USA.** Ed. by Alan M. Rees. LC 94-37594. 504p. 1994. boxed 59.40 (0-89774-889-1) Oryx Pr.

Consumer Incomes in the United States. United States National Resources Committee. LC 75-174476. (FDR & the Era of the New Deal Ser.). 104p. 1972. reprint ed. lib. bdg. 22.50 (0-306-70386-6) Da Capo.

Consumer Initiatives: For Public Health, Worker Safety & Product Quality. Sheila Harty. 55p. (C). 1983. pap. 10.00 (0-318-00978-1) Copesthetic.

Consumer Insight Workbook see Hitting the Sweet Spot: How Consumer Insights Can Inspire Better Marketing & Advertising

Consumer Installment Credit & Public Policy. Paul W. McCracken et al. LC 65-4634. (Michigan Business Studies: Vol. 17, No. 1). 260p. reprint ed. pap. 74.10 (0-317-28350-2, 2022083) Bks Demand.

Consumer Instalment Credit & Economic Fluctuations. Gottfried Haberler. (Financial Research Program II: Studies in Consumer Installment Financing: No. 9). 262p. 1942. reprint ed. 68.20 (0-87014-125-2) Natl Bur Econ Res.

Consumer Interest. J. D. Forbes. 352p. 1987. lib. bdg. 63.00 (0-7099-1063-0, Pub. by Croom Helm UK) Routledge Chapman & Hall.

Consumer Interest: A Study in Consumer Economics. Persia Campbell. LC 75-17213. (Social Problems & Social Policy Ser.). 1976. reprint ed. 54.95 (0-405-07485-9) Ayer.

***Consumer International 1995.** 279p. 1994. 900.00 (0-86338-550-8, Pub. by Euromonitor Pubns UK) Gale.

Consumer Involvement: Concepts & Research. Pirjo Laaksonen. LC 93-45989. 224p. 1994. 65.00x (0-415-09760-6, B3912, Routledge NY) Routledge.

Consumer Japan. 2nd ed. 1993. 550.00 (0-86338-508-7, 101273, Pub. by Euromonitor Pubns UK) Gale.

Consumer Karate: A Guide to Economic Survival. Eric Reisfeld. 5.95 (0-686-18908-6) Meridian Ed.

Consumer Know-How. Ed. by J. Long. 64p. (Orig.). 1988. pap. text ed. write for info. (0-8428-7408-9) Cambridge Bk.

***Consumer Latin America 1994.** 352p. 1995. 750.00 (0-86338-573-7, Pub. by Euromonitor Pubns UK) Gale.

Consumer Law. 7.25 (0-317-03732-3, 37,357C) NCLS Inc.

***Consumer Law.** Vivienne Kendall. (European Practice Library). 1994. 135.00 (0-471-94253-7) Wiley.

Consumer Law. D. J. McQuoid-Mason et al. (Human Rights for All Ser.: Bk. 3). 108p. 1988. student ed, pap. write for info. (0-7021-2469-9, Pub. by Juta SA) W W Gaunt.

Consumer Law. D. J. McQuoid-Mason et al. (Human Rights for All Ser.: Bk. 3). 91p. 1991. teacher ed, pap. write for info. (0-7021-2470-2, Pub. by Juta SA) W W Gaunt.

Consumer Law. Ed. by Iain Ramsay. (International Library of Essays in Law & Legal Theory). 500p. 1992. text ed. 150.00 (0-8147-7423-7) NYU Pr.

Consumer Law: Cases & Materials. 2nd ed. John A. Spanogle, Jr. et al. (American Casebook Ser.). 916p. (C). 1990. text ed. 47.50 (0-314-78651-1) West Pub.

Consumer Law: Desk Manual. 219p. 1984. 15.00 (0-317-03749-8, 37,526) NCLS Inc.

Consumer Law: Text, Cases & Materials. David W. Oughton. xxxii, 436p. (C). 1991. pap. 54.00 (1-85431-173-5, Pub. by Blackstone Pr UK) W W Gaunt.

Consumer Law - A Selected Bibliography of Articles, 1969-1980. Comp. by J. Ray Ferguson. LC 82-202672. (Washington University Law Library Bibliography Ser.: No. 1). vi, 88p. (Orig.). 1982. pap. text ed. 7.50 (0-318-01098-4) Wash U Law Lib.

Consumer Law & Practice. L. Lowe & W. Woodroffe. 425p. (C). 1985. 180.00 (0-685-39831-5, Inst Pur & Supply) St Mut.

Consumer Law & Practice in South Carolina, Vol. II. W. Lewis Burke, Jr. 1990. ring bd. 60.00 (0-943856-18-3, 441) SC Bar CLE.

Consumer Law, Competencies in Law & Citizenship. National Street Law Institute Staff et al. 107p. (C). 1982. pap. text ed. 24.50 (0-314-65089-X) West Pub.

Consumer Law for the Motor Trade. 3rd ed. Anthea Worsdall. 250p. 1991. pap. 39.00 (0-406-00087-5, U.K.) Butterworth Legal Pubs.

Consumer Law in a Nutshell. 2nd ed. David G. Epstein & Steve H. Nickles. LC 80-27848. (Nutshell Ser.). 418p. 1991. reprint ed. pap. text ed. 15.00 (0-8299-2130-3) West Pub.

***Consumer Law Pleadings, No. 1.** Ed. by Jonathan Sheldon. (Consumer Credit & Sales Legal Practice Ser.). 368p. 1994. pap. 90.00 (1-881793-30-3) Nat Consumer Law.

Consumer Law Sales Practices & Credit Regulation 1993 Pocket Parts: to accompany the bound volume, 2 vols., 1. Howard J. Alperin & Roland F. Chase. 270p. 1993. write for info. (0-314-01870-0) West Pub.

Consumer Law Sales Practices & Credit Regulation 1993 Pocket Parts: to accompany the bound volume, 2 vols., 2. Howard J. Alperin & Roland F. Chase. 270p. 1993. write for info. (0-314-01871-9) West Pub.

Consumer Law Training Manual & Repossession Materials. National Consumer Law Center Staff. 262p. 1986. 18.50 (0-685-23172-0, 41,264) NCLS Inc.

Consumer Law Training Materials. Joel Stein. 124p. 10.00 (0-685-47138-1, 39,833) NCLS Inc.

Consumer Law Training Materials, I. 1985. 35.00 (0-317-03750-1, 40,125A) NCLS Inc.

Consumer Law Training Materials, II. 1985. 32.50 (0-685-54049-9, 40,125B) NCLS Inc.

An Asterisk (*) at the beginning of an entry indicates that the title is appearing in BIP for the first time.

C

An Asterisk (*) at the beginning of an entry indicates that the title is appearing in BIP for the first time.

1569

Consumer's Guide & Crime Picture Book of People Wanted by the F. B. I. - Guide for Identification, Capture & Possible Reward: Murder & Attempted Murder. American Health Research Institute Staff. LC 92-54218. (Illus.). 80p. 1992. 14.95 (*1-55914-586-2*); pap. 11.95 (*1-55914-587-0*) ABBE Pubs Assn.

Consumer's Guide for Aluminum Products, Their Effects on Humans, Animals, & Plants with Alternatives & Commentary. Elinor L. Brown. (Illus.). 144p. (Orig.). 1987. pap. write for info. (*0-918798-04-3*) Midwest Pub NE.

Consumer's Guide to Aging. David H. Solomon et al. (Illus.). 1992. text ed. 45.00 (*0-8018-4301-4*); pap. 25.95 (*0-8018-4302-2*) Johns Hopkins.

Consumer's Guide to Alternative Medicine: A Close Look at Homeopathy, Acupuncture, Faith-Healing & Other Unconventional Treatments. Kurt Butler. 299p. (Orig.). (C). 1992. pap. 17.95 (*0-87975-733-7*) Prometheus Bks.

Consumer's Guide to Art Therapy: For Prospective Employers, Clients & Students. Susan R. Makin. 112p. (C). 1994. 29.95 (*0-398-05917-9*) C C Thomas.

***Consumer's Guide to Art Therapy: For Prospective Employers, Clients & Students.** Susan R. Makin. 112p. (C). 1994. pap. 15.95 (*0-398-06511-X*) C C Thomas.

Consumer's Guide to Buying a Cellular Telephone. Chris Stevens. 13p. (Orig.). 1993. pap. text ed. 5.00 (*0-943927-07-2*) S K Brown Pub.

Consumer's Guide to Buying a Condominium. 4p. write for info. (*0-318-72634-3*, 894); 14.50 (*0-685-71696-1*); 27.50 (*0-685-71697-X*); 45.00 (*0-685-71698-8*) Inst Real Estate.

Consumer's Guide to Child Support Enforcement. Ed. by D. J. Scherer. 20p. 1992. pap. 3.95 (*0-918734-41-X*) Reymont.

Consumer's Guide to Common Illnesses. Ruth Lever. LC 92-18688. (Illus.). 560p. (Orig.). 1992. pap. 13.00 (*0-671-74716-9*, Fireside) S&S Trade.

***Consumer's Guide to Credit Reporting: The Next Person to Read Your Credit Report...Should Be You.** Thomas Conwell, 3rd. 55p. (Orig.). 1995. pap. 3.95 (*0-9643168-0-3*) T Patrick.

Consumer's Guide to Death, Dying & Bereavement. Roger R. Shipley. LC 81-9825. (Illus.). 256p. 1982. 19.95 (*0-88280-085-X*) ETC Pubns.

Consumer's Guide to Doctoral Degree Programs in Nursing. Ed. by Judith C. Allen. 165p. 1990. 15.95 (*0-88737-455-7*) Natl League Nurse.

Consumer's Guide to Drug Interactions. Jeffrey Schein & Philip D. Hansten. LC 92-41050. 432p. 1993. pap. 15.00 (*0-02-028865-4*, Collier S&S) S&S Trade.

Consumer's Guide to Emergency Medical Services. Greg H. Williams. LC 83-62132. (Illus.). 129p. (Orig.). 1983. pap. 6.95 (*0-911223-00-2*) Star Valley.

Consumer's Guide to Environmental Myths & Realities. Lynn Scarlett. 1991. pap. 10.00 (*0-943802-68-7*, 165) Natl Ctr Pol.

Consumer's Guide to Free Medical Information by Phone & by Mail. Ruth Winter & Arthur Winter. LC 92-24402. 1993. 24.95 (*0-13-096199-X*); pap. 14.95 (*0-13-333535-6*) P-H.

Consumer's Guide to Handguns, Defensive Shotguns & Rifles. Doug Briggs. (Illus.). 224p. 1993. 14.95 (*1-881287-05-X*) Beverly Bk.

Consumer's Guide to Health Care Services. Stephen J. Williams & Sandra J. Guerra. LC 84-10669. 225p. 1985. 18.95 (*0-13-169145-7*, Busn) P-H.

Consumer's Guide to Home Buying & Mortgage Financing. Peter J. Anderson. LC 91-70986. (Illus.). 128p. 1991. pap. 16.95 (*0-9628794-0-1*) Anderson Saginaw.

***Consumer's Guide to Home Improvement, Renovation & Repair.** Enterprise Foundation Staff et al. 1995. pap. text ed. 19.95 (*0-471-11872-9*) Wiley.

Consumer's Guide to Home Repair Grants & Loans. Robert L. Berko & Monroe Spiegel. LC 86-70756. 1986. 6.00 (*0-685-18142-1*) Consumer Ed Res.

Consumer's Guide to Home Repair Grants & Subsidized Loans. rev. ed. Robert L. Berxo. Ed. by Monroe Spiegel. (Illus.). 236p. 1988. text ed. 18.00 (*0-934873-08-9*); pap. 12.00 (*0-934873-07-0*) Consumer Ed Res.

Consumer's Guide to Hope: Where to Find It & How to Keep It. Ruth O'Lill. 199p. 1994. pap. 11.95 (*0-87604-313-9*, 384) ARE Pr.

Consumers' Guide to Hospitals. Consumers' Checkbook Magazine Editors. 221p. (Orig.). 1992. pap. 12.00 (*0-9611432-5-8*) Ctr Study Serv.

Consumers' Guide to Hospitals. Consumers' Checkbook Magazine Editors. 224p. (Orig.). 1994. pap. 12.00 (*0-9611432-6-6*) Ctr Study Serv.

Consumer's Guide to Household Chemicals. Robert J. Palma, Sr. & Mark Espenscheid. 175p. (C). 1992. 22.95 (*0-87975-794-9*) Prometheus Bks.

***Consumer's Guide to Intelligence.** (Illus.). 75p. (Orig.). (C). 1995. pap. text ed. 25.00 (*0-7881-1640-1*) Diane Pub.

Consumers' Guide to Long Term Health Care Facilities, 3 vols., Set. 2nd ed. BGA Staff & Bryan Doyle. (Illus.). 200p. 1994. pap. 25.00 (*0-9641280-0-4*) Better Government.

Consumer's Guide to Medical Lingo. Charles B. Inlander. 1992. pap. 5.95 (*0-9627334-4-X*) Peoples Med Soc.

***Consumer's Guide to Medicines in Food: Nutraceuticals That Prevent & Treat Physical & Emotional Disorders.** Ruth Winter. LC 94-31427. 1995. 16.00 (*0-517-88349-X*, Crown) Crown Pub Group.

Consumer's Guide to Mobile Home Living. J. Buchanan. 1982. pap. 3.95 (*0-918734-32-0*) Reymont.

Consumers' Guide to Non-Prescription Drugs, 1991. 1991. 11.95 (*0-87489-721-1*) Med Economics.

Consumer's Guide to One Hundred Sixty-One Jug Wines. California Wine List Panel Staff. Ed. by David Holzgang. (California Wine List Ser.). 60p. (Orig.). 1981. pap. 4.95 (*0-932664-18-0*) Wine Appreciation.

Consumer's Guide to Organic Wine. Robert Johnson. 1993. pap. 12.95 (*0-8226-3029-X*) Littlefield.

Consumer's Guide to Organic Wine. Robert Johnson & Richard Pasichnyk. 172p. (C). 1992. 19.95 (*0-8476-7759-1*) Rowman.

Consumer's Guide to Product Grades & Terms: From Grade A to VSOP -- Definitions of 8,000 Terms Desribing Food Housewares & Other Everyday Items. Ed. by Susan B. Gall & Timothy L. Gall. LC 92-40255. 700p. 1992. 69.00 (*0-8103-8898-7*, 101552) Gale.

Consumer's Guide to Psychiatric Diagnosis. Mark A. Gould. 178p. (Orig.). 1989. pap. 7.95 (*0-929162-08-0*) PIA Pr.

Consumer's Guide to Resort & Urban Timesharing. 1985. 2.00 (*0-318-19149-0*) ARDA.

Consumer's Guide to School-Based Sexuality Education Curricula. Roberta J. Ogletree et al. LC 93-46042. 1994. write for info. (*1-56071-354-2*) ETR Assocs.

Consumer's Guide to School Improvement. Geoffrey E. Mills. (Trends & Issues Ser.). vi, 25p. (Orig.). 1990. 7.00 (*0-86552-101-8*) U of Oreg ERIC.

Consumer's Guide to Schools of Choice. Evans Clinchy. 162p. 1987. pap. text ed. 14.00 (*0-917754-32-8*) Inst Responsive.

Consumer's Guide to Social Research. William T. Markham. 128p. 1994. per., pap. text ed. 17.45 (*0-8403-6500-4*) Kendall-Hunt.

Consumers Guide to Social Security Benefits: How to Get Everything You Are Entitled to under the Latest Laws. Robert L. Berko. LC 86-23933. 144p. 1987. 9.00 (*0-934873-04-6*) Consumer Ed Res.

Consumers Guide to Southwestern Indian Arts & Crafts. Mark Bahti. (Illus.). 32p. 1995. 3.00 (*0-918080-26-6*, 20964) Treas Chest Bks.

Consumer's Guide to Successful Car Shopping: How to Drive Away Your Best Deal. Peter Sessler. (Illus.). 128p. 1986. 15.95 (*0-8306-0217-8*, 2117) TAB Bks.

Consumer's Guide to Tests in Print. 2nd ed. Donald D. Hammill et al. LC 92-3041. 204p. 1992. pap. text ed. 29.00 (*0-89079-548-7*, 1461) PRO-ED.

Consumer's Guide to the Current Bibliography of Historical Literature: Antiquity, the Middle Ages, Modern Western Europe, North America, & Latin America (Consumer's Guides to Reference Works in History, No. 1) Bibliography & Indexes Committee History Section Staff. Ed. by American Library Association, Reference & Adult Services Division Staff. (RASD Occasional Papers: No. 2). 53p. (Orig.). 1988. pap. 17.00 (*0-8389-7240-3*) ALA.

Consumer's Guide to Understanding & Using the Law. Daniel Johnson. 288p. (Orig.). 1994. pap. 14.99 (*1-55870-332-2*) Betterway Bks.

Consumer's Guide to Variable-Rate Mortgages. Harvey Koch. 160p. 1982. 9.95 (*0-312-16628-1*) St Martin.

Consumers' Handbook for Reducing Solid Waste. (Illus.). 52p. (Orig.). (C). 1993. pap. text ed. 14.95 (*1-56806-226-5*) Diane Pub.

Consumers in Politics: A History & General Review of the Co-operative Party. Thomas F. Carbery. LC 68-56547. 1969. 35.00 (*0-678-06754-6*) Kelley.

Consumers Index to Product Evaluations & Information Sources: 1973 Annual. LC 74-25361. 1974. 98.00 (*0-87650-057-2*) Pierian.

Consumers Index to Product Evaluations & Information Sources: 1974 Annual. LC 74-25361. 1975. 98.00 (*0-87650-064-5*) Pierian.

Consumers Index to Product Evaluations & Information Sources: 1975 Annual. LC 74-25361. 1976. 98.00 (*0-87650-069-6*) Pierian.

Consumers Index to Product Evaluations & Information Sources: 1976 Annual. LC 74-25361. 1977. 98.00 (*0-87650-080-7*) Pierian.

Consumer's Index to Product Evaluations & Information Sources: 1977 Annual. LC 74-25361. 1978. 98.00 (*0-87650-094-7*) Pierian.

Consumers Index to Product Evaluations & Information Sources: 1978 Annual. LC 74-25361. 1979. 98.00 (*0-87650-100-5*) Pierian.

Consumers Index to Product Evaluations & Information Sources: 1979 Annual. LC 74-25361. 1980. 98.00 (*0-87650-126-9*) Pierian.

Consumers Index to Product Evaluations & Information Sources: 1980 Annual. LC 74-25361. 1981. 98.00 (*0-87650-133-1*) Pierian.

Consumers Index to Product Evaluations & Information Sources: 1981 Annual. LC 74-25361. 1982. 98.00 (*0-87650-146-3*) Pierian.

Consumers Index to Product Evaluations & Information Sources: 1982 Annual. LC 74-25361. 1983. 98.00 (*0-87650-166-8*) Pierian.

Consumers Index to Product Evaluations & Information Sources: 1983 Annual. LC 74-25361. 1984. 98.00 (*0-87650-187-0*) Pierian.

Consumers Index to Product Evaluations & Information Sources: 1984 Annual. LC 74-25361. 1985. 98.00 (*0-87650-196-X*) Pierian.

***Consumers Index to Product Evaluations & Information Sources: 1993 Annual.** 696p. 1994. 129.00 (*0-87650-311-3*) Pierian.

***Consumers Index to Product Evaluations & Information Sources: 1994 Annual.** 680p. 1995. 129.00 (*0-87650-314-8*) Pierian.

***Consumers Index to Product Evaluations & Information Sources: 1995 Annual.** 1996. 129.00 (*0-87650-320-2*) Pierian.

Consumers Index to Product Evaluations & Information Sources Annual, 1992. LC 74-25361. 1993. 129.00 (*0-87650-286-9*) Pierian.

Consumers Index to Product Evaluations & Information Sources: 1985 Annual. LC 74-25361. 1987. 129.00 (*0-87650-223-0*) Pierian.

Consumer's Index to Product Evaluations & Information Sources: 1986 Annual. LC 74-25361. 1987. 129.00 (*0-87650-226-5*) Pierian.

Consumer's Index to Product Evaluations & Information Sources: 1987 Annual. LC 74-25361. 1988. 129.00 (*0-87650-227-3*) Pierian.

Consumers Index to Product Evaluations & Information Sources: 1988 Annual. LC 74-25361. 1989. 129.00 (*0-87650-228-1*) Pierian.

Consumer's Index to Product Evaluations & Information Sources: 1989 Annual. LC 74-25361. 1990. 129.00 (*0-87650-229-X*) Pierian.

Consumers Index to Product Evaluations & Information Sources: 1990 Annual. LC 74-25361. 1991. 129.00 (*0-87650-275-3*) Pierian.

Consumers Index to Product Evaluations & Information Sources: 1991 Annual. LC 74-25361. 1992. 129.00 (*0-87650-276-1*) Pierian.

Consumer's Legal Guide to Today's Health Care: Your Medical Rights & How to Assert Them. Stephen L. Isaacs & Ava C. Swartz. 320p. 1992. pap. 12.95 (*0-395-63277-3*) HM.

Consumer's Medical Desk Reference: Information Your Doctor Can't Or Won't Tell You-Everything You Need to Know for the Best in Health Care. People's Medical Society Staff & Charles B. Inlander. 672p. 1995. 24.95 (*0-7868-6056-1*) Hyperion.

Consumers, Product Safety Standards & International Trade. 73p. 1991. 16.00 (*92-64-13479-4*) OECD.

Consumers' Reference & Index of What's Going on in Life, Health & Stress Research. Thelma F. Harrison. 150p. 1994. 49.50 (*1-55914-528-5*); pap. 39.50 (*1-55914-529-3*) ABBE Pubs Assn.

Consumers' Reference Book & Index about Abortion in Today's World. John C. Bartone. 90p. 1994. pap. 19.50 (*0-7883-0313-9*) ABBE Pubs Assn.

Consumers' Reference Book & Index about Adolescent Behavior. John C. Bartone. 90p. 1994. pap. 19.50 (*0-7883-0341-4*) ABBE Pubs Assn.

Consumers' Reference Book & Index about Automobile Accidents. John C. Bartone. 90p. 1994. pap. 19.50 (*0-7883-0333-3*) ABBE Pubs Assn.

Consumers' Reference Book & Index about Civil Rights. John C. Bartone. 90p. 1994. pap. 19.50 (*0-7883-0337-6*) ABBE Pubs Assn.

Consumers' Reference Book & Index about Cosmetics Good & Bad. John C. Bartone. 90p. 1994. pap. 19.50 (*0-7883-0326-0*) ABBE Pubs Assn.

Consumers' Reference Book & Index about Crime Prevention. John C. Bartone. 90p. 1994. pap. 19.50 (*0-7883-0323-6*) ABBE Pubs Assn.

Consumers' Reference Book & Index about Crime Today in the U. S. A. John C. Bartone. 90p. 1994. pap. 19.50 (*0-7883-0321-X*) ABBE Pubs Assn.

Consumers' Reference Book & Index about Exercise. John C. Bartone. 90p. 1994. pap. 19.50 (*0-7883-0319-8*) ABBE Pubs Assn.

Consumers' Reference Book & Index about Food, Diet & Cancer. John C. Bartone. 90p. 1994. pap. 19.50 (*0-7883-0279-5*) ABBE Pubs Assn.

Consumers' Reference Book & Index about Human Rights. John C. Bartone. 90p. 1994. pap. 19.50 (*0-7883-0335-X*) ABBE Pubs Assn.

Consumers' Reference Book & Index about Hypnosis. John C. Bartone. 90p. 1994. pap. 19.50 (*0-7883-0295-7*) ABBE Pubs Assn.

Consumers' Reference Book & Index about Illness and Diseases Caused by Jobs & Occupations. John C. Bartone. 90p. 1994. pap. 19.50 (*0-7883-0297-3*) ABBE Pubs Assn.

Consumers' Reference Book & Index about Juvenile Delinquency. John C. Bartone. 90p. 1994. pap. 19.50 (*0-7883-0287-6*) ABBE Pubs Assn.

Consumers' Reference Book & Index about Love & Libido. John C. Bartone. 90p. 1994. pap. 19.50 (*0-7883-0305-8*) ABBE Pubs Assn.

Consumers' Reference Book & Index about Magic & Superstitions. John C. Bartone. 90p. 1994. pap. 19.50 (*0-7883-0291-4*) ABBE Pubs Assn.

Consumers' Reference Book & Index about Marriage. John C. Bartone. 90p. 1994. pap. 19.50 (*0-7883-0307-4*) ABBE Pubs Assn.

Consumers' Reference Book & Index about Massage. John C. Bartone. 90p. 1994. pap. 19.50 (*0-7883-0293-0*) ABBE Pubs Assn.

Consumers' Reference Book & Index about Nutrition. John C. Bartone. 90p. 1994. pap. 19.50 (*0-7883-0329-5*) ABBE Pubs Assn.

Consumers' Reference Book & Index about Relaxation & Its Methods. John C. Bartone. 90p. 1994. pap. 19.50 (*0-7883-0309-0*) ABBE Pubs Assn.

Consumers' Reference Book & Index about Rights to Medical Treatment. John C. Bartone. 90p. 1994. pap. 19.50 (*0-7883-0311-2*) ABBE Pubs Assn.

Consumers' Reference Book & Index about Sex & Bisexuality. John C. Bartone. 90p. 1994. pap. 19.50 (*0-7883-0331-7*) ABBE Pubs Assn.

Consumers' Reference Book & Index about Sex Counseling & Diseases. John C. Bartone. 90p. 1994. pap. 19.50 (*0-7883-0339-2*) ABBE Pubs Assn.

Consumers' Reference Book & Index about Sports. John C. Bartone. 90p. 1994. pap. 19.50 (*0-7883-0317-1*) ABBE Pubs Assn.

Consumers' Reference Book & Index about Stress & Distress Including Treatments. John C. Bartone. 90p. 1994. pap. 19.50 (*0-7883-0289-2*) ABBE Pubs Assn.

Consumers' Reference Book & Index about the Health Benefits of Garlic. John C. Bartone. 90p. 1994. pap. 19.50 (*0-7883-0315-5*) ABBE Pubs Assn.

Consumers' Reference Book & Index about...Death. John C. Bartone. 90p. 1994. pap. 19.50 (*0-7883-0327-9*) ABBE Pubs Assn.

Consumers' Reference Book & Index Concerning Diagnostic Errors in Medicine. John C. Bartone. 90p. 1994. pap. 19.50 (*0-7883-0303-1*) ABBE Pubs Assn.

Consumers' Reference Book & Index Concerning Medical Malpractice. John C. Bartone. 90p. 1994. pap. 19.50 (*0-7883-0301-5*) ABBE Pubs Assn.

Consumer's, Researcher's, & Student's Guide to Government Publications. Betsy McIlvaine. LC 83-3621. 115p. 1983. pap. 18.00 (*0-8242-0690-8*) Wilson.

Consumer's Resource Handbook. 97p. (Orig.). (C). 1993. pap. text ed. 20.00 (*0-7881-0010-6*) Diane Pub.

Consumers Rights & Remedies. 9.95 (*0-9630356-4-9*) Makai.

Consumers' Rights As Armed Citizens for Protection of Home & Family Against Rape, Robbery & Violent Intruders: True Stories of Life in the U. S. A. Stanley H. Smythe. LC 92-54216. 90p. 1992. 10.95 (*1-55914-584-6*); pap. 8.95 (*1-55914-585-4*) ABBE Pubs Assn.

Consumer's Rights under Warranties. 3.50 (*0-944253-76-8*) Inst Dev Indian Law.

***Consumers' Spatial Choice Behavior.** A. Eymann. Ed. by J. Vosgerau. (International Economics & Institutions Ser.). 192p. 1995. pap. 61.00 (*3-7908-0852-0*) Spr-Verlag.

***Consumer's Survival Guide - Florida Edition.** Patrick Comer. LC 94-41814. (Orig.). 1995. pap. 12.95 (*1-56164-067-0*) Pineapple Pr.

Consumer's View of Family Therapy. David Howe. 1989. text ed. 55.95 (*0-566-05793-X*, Pub. by Avebury Pub UK) Ashgate Pub Co.

Consumer's World: Economic Issues & Money Management. 2nd ed. E. Thomas Garman & Sidney W. Eckert. (Illus.). 1979. text ed. 36.40 (*0-07-022878-7*) McGraw.

Consuming Angels: Advertising & Victorian Women. Lori A. Loeb. LC 93-46094. (Illus.). 256p. 1994. 29.95 (*0-19-508596-5*) OUP.

***Consuming Body.** Pasi Falk. (Theory, Culture & Society Ser.: Vol. 30). 256p. 1994. 55.00 (*0-8039-8973-3*); pap. 21.95 (*0-8039-8974-1*) Sage.

Consuming Culture. Jeremy MacClancy. 256p. 1993. 23.00 (*0-8050-2578-2*) H Holt & Co.

***Consuming Culture: Why You Eat What You Eat.** Jeremy MacClancy. 1995. pap. 13.95 (*0-8050-3587-7*) H Holt & Co.

Consuming Desire: Sexual Science & the Emergence of a Culture of Abundance, 1871-1914. Lawrence Birken. LC 88-47719. 168p. 1988. 28.50 (*0-8014-2058-X*) Cornell U Pr.

Consuming Faith: The Social Gospel & Modern American Culture. Susan Curtis. LC 90-28696. (New Studies in American Intellectual & Cultural History). (Illus.). 320p. 1991. text ed. 42.50x (*0-8018-4167-4*) Johns Hopkins.

Consuming Fiction. Terry Lovell. (Questions for Feminism Ser.). 188p. 1987. text ed. 44.95 (*0-86091-173-X*, Pub. by Verso UK); pap. text ed. 14.95 (*0-86091-885-8*, Pub. by Verso UK) Routledge Chapman & Hall.

Consuming Fictions: Gender, Class, & Hunger in Dicken's Novels. Gail T. Houston. LC 93-44723. 256p. (C). 1994. 29.95x (*0-8093-1953-5*) S Ill U Pr.

Consuming Fire: A Christian Introduction to the Old Testament. Michael Duggan. LC 91-72272. 691p. (Orig.). 1991. pap. 29.95 (*0-89870-376-X*) Ignatius Pr.

***Consuming Habits: Drugs in History & Anthropology.** Ed. by Jordan Goodman et al. LC 94-42752. 272p. 1995. 49.95 (*0-415-09039-3*, C0104) Routledge.

***Consuming Modernity: Public Culture in a South Asian World.** Ed. by Carol A. Breckenridge. LC 94-46772. 1995. text ed. 44.95 (*0-8166-2305-8*); pap. text ed. 17.95 (*0-8166-2306-6*) U of Minn Pr.

Consuming Myth: The Work of James Merrill. Stephen Yenser. LC 86-14886. (Illus.). 384p. 1986. 37.50 (*0-674-16615-9*) HUP.

Consuming Passions. Linda Burggraf. 1984. pap. 3.50 (*0-318-04452-8*) Pudding Hse Pubns.

Consuming Passions: Feminist Approaches to Eating Disorders & Weight Preoccupations. Ed. by Catrina Brown & Karin Jasper. 250p. (Orig.). 1993. pap. 16.95 (*0-929005-42-2*, Pub. by Second Story Pr CN) InBook.

Consuming Passions: Finding Real Love When Nothing Else Works. Robert F. Forman. 180p. (Orig.). 1994. pap. 9.95 (*1-55874-298-0*, 2980) Health Comm.

Consuming Passions: Help for Compulsive Shoppers. Ellen M. Catalano & Nina Sonenberg. 190p. (Orig.). (C). 1993. text ed. 24.95 (*1-879237-39-3*); pap. text ed. 11.95 (*1-879237-38-5*) New Harbinger.

Consuming Passions: The Dynamics of Popular Culture. Judith Williamson. (Illus.). 240p. 1986. pap. 12.95 (*0-7145-2851-X*) M Boyars Pubs.

***Consuming Places.** John Urry. LC 94-28911. (International Library of Sociology). 240p. 1995. 55.00x (*0-415-11310-5*, C0381); pap. 17.95 (*0-415-11311-3*, C0382) Routledge.

Consuming Public Services. Nicholas Deakin & Anthony Wright. 240p. 1990. 55.00 (*0-415-03208-3*, A4028) Routledge.

***Consuming Technologies.** Ed. by Roger Silverstone & Eric Hirsch. 240p. 1994. pap. 17.95 (*0-415-11712-7*, B4540) Routledge.

An Asterisk (*) at the beginning of an entry indicates that the title is appearing in BIP for the first time.

Consuming Technologies: Media & Information in Domestic Spaces. Ed. by Roger Silverstone & Eric Hirsch. LC 91-43743. 208p. 1992. 75.00 (*0-415-06990-4*, A7513) Routledge.

Consuming Visions: Accumulation & Display of Goods in America, 1800-1920. Ed. by Simon J. Bronner. (C). 1991. pap. text ed. 16.95 (*0-393-96002-1*) Norton.

Consummate Eveline. 384p. 1992. pap. 4.95 (*0-88184-896-4*) Carroll & Graf.

***Consummate Warrior: The Warrior Training Manual, Zensho, the Warrior Legacy, 3 bks., Set.** Jerry L. Aiello. Ed. by Dina Baganz. (Three Book Ser.). 931p. (Orig.). (C). 1995. pap. text ed. 85.00 (*1-883702-09-7*) Aiello Grp.

Consummation of Human History (4) Ed. by Chung Hwan Rev. Kwak. (Home Study Course Ser.). 40p. (C). 1980. pap. 4.00 (*0-910621-13-6*) HSA Pubns.

Consumo de Alcohol Por Menores de Edad: Underage Drinking. Waln K. Brown. 20p. 1992. 2.95 (*1-56456-061-9*, 217S) W Gladden Found.

Consumption. Robert Bocock. LC 93-3444. (Key Ideas Ser.). 1993. write for info. (*0-415-06962-9*) Routledge.

Consumption & Business Fluctuations: A Case Study of the Shoe, Leather, Hide Sequence. Ruth P. Mack. (Studies in Business Cycles: No. 7). 318p. 1956. reprint ed. 82.70 (*0-87014-090-6*); reprint ed. mic. film 41.40 (*0-685-61304-6*) Natl Bur Econ Res.

Consumption & Class: Divisions & Change. Ed. by Roger Burrows & Catherine Marsh. 258p. 1992. text ed. 49.95 (*0-312-06867-0*) St Martin.

Consumption & Development. Jeffrey James. LC 92-12886. 1993. text ed. 69.95 (*0-312-08526-5*) St Martin.

***Consumption & Marketing: Macro Dimensions.** Ed. by Russell W. Belk et al. LC 95-13608. 1996. text ed. 30.95 (*0-538-85050-7*) S-W Pub.

Consumption & Price, with Special Regard to the Theories & Practice in the Socialist Countries. R. Hoch. 408p. 1981. lib. bdg. 97.50 (*90-286-0048-5*) Kluwer Ac.

Consumption & Standards of Living. Carle C. Zimmerman. LC 75-39283. (Getting & Spending: the Consumer's Dilemma Ser.). (Illus.). 1976. reprint ed. 50.95 (*0-405-08058-1*) Ayer.

Consumption & the World of Goods. Ed. by John Brewer & Roy Porter. (Illus.). 592p. 1993. 59.95 (*0-415-03712-3*, B0607) Routledge.

***Consumption & the World of Goods.** Ed. by John Brewer & Roy Porter. (Illus.). 592p. 1994. pap. 29.95 (*0-415-11478-0*, B4802) Routledge.

Consumption Behavior & the Effects of Government Fiscal Policies. Randall P. Mariger. (Economic Studies: No. 158). (Illus.). 312p. 1986. 32.00 (*0-674-16635-3*) HUP.

Consumption Coagulpathies. Ed. by A. Larcan et al. 176p. 1987. 73.50 (*2-225-80981-X*, MA981, Yr Bk Med Pubs) Mosby Yr Bk.

Consumption Function in Macroeconomic Models: A Comparative Study. E. P. Davis. (Bank of England Technical Series. Discussion Papers: No. 1). 78p. reprint ed. pap. 25.00 (*0-317-27738-3*, 2019470) Bks Demand.

Consumption, Identity & Style. Ed. by Alan Tomlinson. (Illus.). 272p. 1990. 45.00 (*0-415-01150-7*, A3959); pap. 14.95 (*0-415-01151-5*, A3963) Routledge.

Consumption in a Finite World. Joni Keating. 60p. 1988. teacher ed, pap. 9.99 (*0-89824-181-2*) Trillium Pr.

Consumption in New England: Locality, One of Its Chief Causes & Is Consumption Contagious, or Communicated by One Person to Another in Any Manner?, 2 vols. in 1. Henry I. Bowditch. Ed. by Barbara G. Rosenkrantz. LC 76-25653. (Public Health in America Ser.). (Illus.). 1977. reprint ed. lib. bdg. 17.95 (*0-405-09806-5*) Ayer.

***Consumption of Culture, 1600-1800: Image, Object, Text.** Ed. by Ann Bermingham & John Brewer. (Consumption & Culture in 17th & 18th Centuries: 3). 1995. write for info. (*0-415-12135-3*) Routledge.

***Consumption of Energy.** 1995. lib. bdg. 250.00 (*0-8490-6461-9*) Gordon Pr.

Consumption of Wealth. Elizabeth E. Hoyt. LC 75-39249. (Getting & Spending: the Consumer's Dilemma Ser.). (Illus.). 1976. reprint ed. 29.95 (*0-405-08023-9*) Ayer.

Consumption Patterns in Eastern & Western Europe. Vera Cao-Pinna & Stanislav S. Shatalin. 1979. 88.00 (*0-08-021808-3*, Pub. by Pergamon Repr UK) Franklin.

Consumption Patterns in Industry. D. B. Gupta. 1974. text ed. 4.95 (*0-07-096430-0*, Prof & Ref Bk Div) McGraw.

Consumption, Rational Expectations & Liquidity: Theory & Evidence. Alan E. Speight. LC 89-70185. 220p. 1990. text ed. 45.00 (*0-312-04244-2*) St Martin.

Consumption Taxes: Promises & Problems. Michael A. Schuyler. 132p. (Orig.). 1984. pap. 10.95 (*0-922623-01-5*, TX 161581) IRET.

***Contact: A Directory of Ethnic Organizations in Washington State.** 3rd ed. Intro. by Jens Lund. (Illus.). 1995. pap. 20.00 (*0-9627942-1-X*) Ethnic Herit.

Contact: Customer Service in the Hospitality & Tourism Industry. Donald M. Davidoff. LC 93-31853. 1993. pap. text ed. 32.40 (*0-13-808916-7*) P-H.

Contact: The First Four Minutes. Leonard Zunin & Natalie Zunin. 1986. mass mkt. 5.99 (*0-345-33692-5*) Ballantine.

Contact! The Story of the Early Birds. Henry S. Villard. LC 87-600170. (Illus.). 278p. (C). 1987. reprint ed. pap. 27.50 (*0-87474-947-6*) Smithsonian.

Contact: Theory. Ed. by Ralph Gibson et al. LC 80-7809. (Illus.). 176p. 1982. 35.00 (*0-912810-30-0*); pap. 17.95 (*0-912810-31-9*) Lustrum Pr.

Contact Allergy Predictive Test in Guinea Pigs. Ed. by K. E. Andersen & H. I. Maibach. (Current Problems in Dermatology Ser.: Vol. 14). (Illus.). viii, 300p. 1985. 129.75 (*3-8055-4053-1*) S Karger.

***Contact & Conflict: Indian-European Relations in British-Columbia, 1774-1890.** 2nd ed. Robin Fisher. 282p. 1992. pap. 21.95 (*0-7748-0400-9*) U of Wash Pr.

***Contact & Cover: Two-Officer Suspect Control.** Steven Albrecht & John Morrison. 164p. 1992. pap. 19.95 (*0-398-06003-7*) C C Thomas.

Contact & Cover: Two-Officer Suspect Control. Steven Albrecht & John Morrison. 164p. (C). 1992. text ed. 34.95x (*0-398-05773-7*) C C Thomas.

***Contact & Discontinuity: Some Conventions of Speech & Action on the Greek Tragic Stage.** Donald J. Mastronarde. LC 78-62877. (University of California Publications: No. 21). 153p. 1979. pap. 43.70 (*0-7837-7491-5*, 2049213) Bks Demand.

Contact & Occupational Dermatology. James G. Marks & Deleo. 346p. 1992. 69.00 (*0-8016-3123-8*) Mosby Yr Bk.

Contact & Photocontact Allergens: A Manual of Predictive Test Methods. Thomas Maurer. (Dermatology Ser.: Vol. 3). (Illus.). 192p. 1983. 99.75 (*0-8247-7013-7*) Dekker.

Contact Angle, Wettability & Adhesion: In Honor of Professor Robert J. Good. Ed. by K. L. Mittal. xxiv, 972p. 1993. 247.50 (*90-6764-157-X*) Coronet Bks.

Contact Conditioning. Franklin W. Poley. (Illus.). 256p. 1991. text ed. 39.95 (*0-89876-182-4*) Gardner Pr.

Contact Cosmogram. Reinhold Ebertin. 152p. 1974. 9.00 (*0-86690-088-8*, E1090-024) Am Fed Astrologers.

Contact Geometry & Linear Differential Equations. Vladimir E. Nazaikinskii et al. LC 92-24930. (Expositions in Mathematics Ser.: No. 6). vii, 216p. (C). 1992. lib. bdg. 82.95 (*3-11-013381-4*) De Gruyter.

Contact Highs: Selected Poems, 1957-1987. Alan Ansen. LC 89-7768. 240p. 1989. pap. 11.95 (*0-916583-45-7*) Dalkey Arch.

Contact Hypersensitivity in Experimental Animals. Ed. by D. Parker & J. L. Turk. (Monographs in Allergy: Vol. 8). (Illus.). 182p. 1974. 67.25 (*3-8055-1666-5*) S Karger.

Contact Illustrators. 10th ed. Elfande Ltd. Staff. (Illus.). 368p. 1994. 55.00 (*1-870458-85-0*, Pub. by Elfande Art Pub UK) Bks Nippan.

Contact Juggling. James Ernest. 1991. spiral bd. 14.95 (*0-9634054-0-3*) Ernest Graphics Pr.

Contact Lens & Lens Care Products Markets. (Market Research Reports: No. 342). 154p. 1993. 795.00 (*0-317-05456-2*) Theta Corp.

Contact Lens Correction. Norman Bier & Gerald Lowther. (Illus.). 1977. 95.00 (*0-407-00101-8*) Buttrwrth-Heinemann.

***Contact Lens Correction.** 2nd ed. Bier. 672p. 1995. write for info. (*0-7506-9083-6*, Focal) Buttrwrth-Heinemann.

Contact Lens Handbook. James R. Lee. (Illus.). 161p. 1986. text ed. 30.50 (*0-7216-1585-6*) Saunders.

Contact Lens Manual: A Practical Fitting Guide. Andrew Gasson & Judith Morris. (Illus.). 208p. 1992. pap. 50.00 (*0-7506-1059-X*) Buttrwrth-Heinemann.

***Contact Lens Market.** 154p. (Orig.). 1995. pap. 1,295.00 (*0-7605-2042-9*) Rector Pr.

Contact Lens Optics. W. A. Douthwaite. 219p. 1987. text ed. 45.00 (*0-407-01330-X*) Buttrwrth-Heinemann.

***Contact Lens Optics.** 2nd ed. Douthwaite. 1995. pap. write for info. (*0-7506-1818-3*, Focal) Buttrwrth-Heinemann.

Contact Lens Practice. 4th ed. Robert B. Mandell. (Illus.). 1040p. (C). 1988. text ed. 86.95x (*0-398-05509-2*) C C Thomas.

Contact Lens Practice: Clinical & Scientific Aspects. M. Guillon. Ed. by Montague Ruben. (Illus.). 800p. 1994. 195.00 (*0-412-35120-X*) Chapman & Hall.

Contact Lens Primer: A Manual. Barry A. Weissman. LC 84-851. (Illus.). 152p. reprint ed. pap. 43.40 (*0-7837-1501-3*, 2057197) Bks Demand.

Contact Lens Solutions: Report on Supply Within U. K. of Contact Lens Solutions Monopolies & Mergers Commission. (Command Paper Ser.: No. 2242). 293p. 1993. pap. 45.00 (*0-10-122422-2*, HM24222, Pub. by HMSO UK) UNIPUB.

Contact Lenses. Phyllis L. Rakow. LC 87-42948. (Ophthalmic Technical Skills Ser.: Vol. I). 156p. 1988. pap. 40.00 (*1-55642-024-2*) SLACK Inc.

Contact Lenses: A Guide to Successful Wear & Care. Hikaru Hamano & Montague Ruben. 1985. 12.95 (*0-685-43061-8*) S&S Trade.

Contact Lenses: A Textbook for Practitioner & Student. 3rd ed. A. J. Phillips & J. Stone. (Illus.). 1017p. 1989. text ed. 195.00 (*0-407-93275-5*) Buttrwrth-Heinemann.

Contact Lenses: Procedures & Techniques. 2nd ed. Gerald E. Lowther & Christopher Snyder. 432p. 1992. 65.00 (*0-7506-9187-5*) Buttrwrth-Heinemann.

***Contact Lenses: The Clao Guide to Basic Science & Clinical Practice, Value Pak, Set, Vols. I-IV.** CLAO (Massare) Staff. Set. 944p. 1994. 99.99 (*0-8403-9385-7*) Kendall-Hunt.

Contact Lenses: What You Need to Know. Judy A. Kody. (Illus.). 60p. (Orig.). 1986. pap. 6.95 (*0-317-01374-2*) Quinn Pubns.

Contact Lenses in Ophthalmology. M. S. Wilson & E. A. Millis. (Illus.). 168p. 1989. text ed. 85.00 (*0-407-01440-3*) Buttrwrth-Heinemann.

Contact Loading & Local Effects in Thin-Walled Plated & Shell Structures: Proceedings of the IUTAM Symposium Held in Prague, September 4-7, 1990. Ed. by V. Krupka & M. Drdacky. 400p. 1992. 115.00 (*0-387-53551-9*) Spr-Verlag.

Contact Mechanics. K. L. Johnson. 464p. 1987. pap. 39.95 (*0-521-34796-3*) Cambridge U Pr.

Contact Mechanics: Computational Techniques. Ed. by C. A. Brebbia & M. H. Aliabadi. LC 93-71028. (Contact Mechanics Ser.: Vol. 1). 536p. 1993. 157.00 (*1-56252-163-2*) Computational Mech MA.

Contact Mechanics II '95: Proceedings of the Second International Conference. Ed. by M. H. Aliabadi & C. Alexxandri. (Contact Mechanics Ser.: Vol. 2). 400p. 1995. 149.00 (*1-56252-250-7*) Computational Mech MA.

Contact Mechanics Using Boundary Elements. K. W. Man. LC 94-72216. (Topics in Engineering Ser.: Vol. 22). 200p. 1994. 86.00 (*1-56252-258-2*) Computational Mech MA.

Contact Metamorphism. Ed. by D. M. Kerrick. (Reviews in Mineralogy Ser.: Vol. 26). 800p. 1991. per. 28.00 (*0-939950-31-6*) Mineralogical Soc.

***Contact Mr. Delgado.** large type ed. James Pattinson. 1994. 20.95 (*0-7089-3155-3*) Ulverscroft.

Contact or Isolation? Soviet-Western Relations in the Interwar Period. Ed. by John Hiden & Aleksander Loit. (Studia Baltica Stockholmiensia: No. 8). 442p. (Orig.). 1991. pap. 66.00x (*91-22-01441-1*, Pub. by Almqv & Wiksell SW) Coronet Bks.

Contact Person Report. 300p. (C). 1992. 75.00 (*0-89382-219-1*) Nat Assn Insu Comm.

Contact Person Report. 298p. 1993. ring bd. 75.00 (*0-89382-244-2*) Nat Assn Insu Comm.

Contact Person Report. 332p. 1993. ring bd. 75.00 (*0-89382-255-8*) Nat Assn Insu Comm.

***Contact Person Report.** annuals 396p. (C). 1994. ring bd. 75.00 (*0-89382-275-2*) Nat Assn Insu Comm.

***Contact Person Report.** 411p. (C). 1995. ring bd. 75.00 (*0-89382-317-1*) Nat Assn Insu Comm.

Contact Person Report: Report on Multistate Delinquencies. 116p. (C). 1991. 40.00 (*0-89382-183-7*) Nat Assn Insu Comm.

Contact Person Report: Semi-Annual Edition. 193p. (Orig.). (C). 1992. 40.00 (*0-89382-197-7*) Nat Assn Insu Comm.

Contact Photographers. 10th ed. Elfande Ltd. Staff. (Illus.). 432p. 1994. 55.00 (*1-870458-80-X*, Pub. by Elfande Art Pub UK) Bks Nippan.

Contact Problems & Surface Interactions in Manufacturing & Tribological Systems. Ed. by M. H. Attia & R. Komanduri. LC 93-74185. 353p. 1993. pap. 75.00 (*0-7918-1263-4*) ASME.

Contact Problems in Elasticity: A Study of Variational Inequalities & Finite Element Methods. N. Kikuchi & J. T. Oden. LC 86-61596. (Studies in Applied Mathematics: No. 8). xiii, 495p. 1988. 87.50 (*0-89871-202-5*) Soc Indus-Appl Math.

Contact Problems in the Theory of Plates & Shells. E. Grigolyuk & V. Tolkachev. 424p. (C). 1987. 90.00 (*0-685-36872-6*, Pub. by Collets) St Mut.

Contact Spanish. Wolfgang Halm et al. (Illus.). 240p. 1988. student ed, pap. 17.95 (*0-521-26937-7*); pap. 11.95 (*0-521-26936-9*); pap. 51.50 (*0-521-26332-8*) Cambridge U Pr.

Contact Therapy: You Don't Have to Be Afraid to Talk to Me! Robert L. Dotson. LC 86-61285. 209p. 1986. pap. 7.95 (*0-318-32731-7*) Contact Therapy.

Contact Unit Three Facilitator's Guide: Holy Spirit! Our Redemptive Force. Ed. by Judy Edwards. (Orig.). 1993. pap. text ed. 8.95 (*1-56309-065-1*, New Hope) Womans Mission Union.

Contact Unit Three Notebook: Holy Spirit! Our Redemptive Force. Ed. by Judy Edwards. (Orig.). 1993. pap. text ed. 21.95 (*1-56309-064-3*, New Hope) Womans Mission Union.

Contact Unit Two Facilitator's Guide: The Son! His Redemptive Plan. Carol Causey & Trudy Johnson. Ed. by Cindy McClain. 14p. 1991. pap. text ed. 8.95 (*1-56309-044-9*, New Hope) Womans Mission Union.

Contact Unit Two Learners Notebook: The Son! His Redemptive Plan. Carol Causey. Ed. by Cindy McClain. 218p. 1993. pap. text ed. 21.95 (*1-56309-043-0*, New Hope) Womans Mission Union.

CONTACT, Unit 1: The Father: His Redemptive Plan. Mary Ann Appling et al. Ed. by Cindy McClain. 240p. (Orig.). 1991. pap. text ed. 21.95 (*0-936625-97-X*, New Hope AL) Womans Mission Union.

CONTACT, Unit 1: The Father! His Redemptive Plan. Carol Causey. Ed. by Cindy McClain. 16p. 1991. pap. text ed. 8.95 (*0-936625-98-8*, New Hope AL) Womans Mission Union.

Contact USA. 2nd ed. Paul Abraham & Daphne Mackey. 256p. (C). 1989. pap. text ed. 15.95 (*0-13-169616-5*) P-H.

Contact Utricaria Syndrome. Lahti. 1995. write for info. (*0-8493-7352-2*) CRC Pr.

Contact with a Lord of Karma. George King. LC 89-80234. (Illus.). 95p. 1989. pap. 13.55 (*0-937249-13-0*) Aetherius Soc.

Contact with God: Retreat Conferences. rev. ed. Anthony De Mello. LC 91-30524. 224p. 1991. pap. 10.95 (*0-8294-0726-X*) Loyola Univ Pr.

Contactees Die Young. Antoinette Azolakov. 160p. (Orig.). 1989. pap. 8.95 (*0-934411-18-2*, Banned Bks) Edward-William Austin.

Contactics: The Daily Drama of Human Contact. Anoop Chandola. 152p. (Orig.). (C). 1992. lib. bdg. 39.50 (*0-8191-8772-0*); pap. text ed. 18.50 (*0-8191-8773-9*) U Pr of Amer.

Contacto, 4 Vols. 4th ed. Pablo Valencia et al. (C). 1991. text ed. 50.36 (*0-395-47240-7*) HM.

Contacto Directo con el Mas Alla: Guia Para Desarrollar Su Percepcion Extra-Sensorial. Malvin Kristus. 96p. (Orig.). (SPA.). 1985. pap. 2.95 (*0-939193-03-5*) Edit Concepts.

Contacto en el Espiritu. Ralph Neighbour. Ed. by Jose L. Martinez. Tr. by Guillermo Kratzig. 120p. (SPA.). 1983. pap. 4.25 (*0-311-09098-2*) Casa Bautista.

Contacts: Langue et Culture Francaises. 4th annot. ed. Rebecca M. Valette & Jean-Paul Valette. LC 88-81365. (FRE.). 1989. Instr.'s annotated ed. teacher ed 40.26 (*0-318-36903-6*) HM.

Contacts: Langue et Culture Francaises. 4th ed. Rebecca M. Valette & Jean-Paul Valette. (FRE.). 1989. Wkbk./Lab. manual/Test bank. write for info. (*0-318-63339-6*) HM.

Contacts: Langue et Culture Francaises, 4 Vols. 4th ed. Rebecca M. Valette & Jean-Paul Valette. LC 88-81365. (FRE.). (C). 1989. text ed. 49.96 (*0-395-36949-5*) HM.

Contacts Between Cultures, Vol. 1: West Asia & North Africa. Ed. by A. Harrak. LC 92-39880. 508p. 1993. text ed. 119.95 (*0-7734-9200-3*) E Mellen.

Contacts de Civilisations en Martinique et en Guadeloupe. Michel Leiris. 191p. (Orig.). (FRE.). 1986. pap. text ed. 16.00 (*92-3-200422-4*, UFP17) UNIPUB.

Contacts et Circumstances. Paul Claudel. 268p. (FRE.). 1940. pap. 10.95 (*0-7859-1116-2*, 2070215067) Fr & Eur.

Contacts for Kuwait Contracting. (Kuwait Business Guides Ser.: No. III). 1991. 145.00 (*0-915797-04-6*) Intl Exec Reports.

***Contacts in Business U. S. A.** 400p. (C). 1994. 395.00 (*0-7605-0517-9*) Rector Pr.

Contacts to Semiconductors: Fundamentals & Technology. Ed. by Leonard J. Brillson. LC 93-26692. (Illus.). 680p. 1993. 96.00 (*0-8155-1336-4*) Noyes.

Contacts with Burma, 1935-1949: A Personal Account. John F. Cady. LC 81-22544. (Papers in International Studies: Southeast Asia Ser.: No. 61). 130p. reprint ed. pap. 37.10 (*0-7837-6476-6*, 2046481) Bks Demand.

Contacts with the Opposition: A Symposium. Ed. by Martin F. Herz. LC 79-91020. 72p. (Orig.). 1979. pap. 8.00 (*0-934742-03-0*) Geo U Inst Dplmcy.

***Contactus Interuptus: A Science-Fiction Story.** Nelson H. White. 120p. (Orig.). Date not set. pap. 25.00 (*1-877884-15-4*) Tech Group.

Contadora: The Limits of Negotiations. Bruce M. Bagely & Juan G. Tokatlian. (Pew Case Studies in International Affairs). 69p. (C). 1989. pap. text ed. 2.50 (*1-56927-309-X*) Geo U Inst Dplmcy.

Contadora: The Limits of Negotiations. Bruce M. Bagley & Juan G. Tokatlian. 84p. (Orig.). (C). 1987. pap. text ed. 11.75 (*0-941700-12-7*) JH FPI SAIS.

Contagion of Courage: The Untold Story of the People Who Brought Marcos Down. Bryan Johnson. 300p. 1987. text ed. 24.95 (*0-02-916571-7*) Free Pr.

Contagion of War the Way the War Was Fought (1965-1967) Boston Publishing Company Editors et al. (Vietnam Experience Ser.). 192p. 1983. 16.30 (*0-201-15858-2*) Addison-Wesley.

Contagion of War, Vol. 5. Terrence Maitland & Peter McInerney. Ed. by Robert Manning. LC 83-70671. (Vietnam Experience Ser.). (Illus.). 192p. 1983. 16.95 (*0-939526-05-0*) Boston Pub Co.

C

***Contagious & Non-Contagious Infectious Diseases Sourcebook.** Ed. by Karen Bellenir & Peter D. Dresser. 1995. lib. bdg. 80.00x (*0-7808-0075-3*) Omnigraphics Inc.

***Contagious Christianity.** Charles Swindoll. 1993. pap. 4.99 (*0-8499-8481-5*) Word Inc.

Contagious Emotions. Ronald M. Podell. Ed. by Claire Zion. 1993. reprint ed. pap. 10.00 (*0-671-70240-8*) PB.

***Contained Garden.** Susan Berry & Steve Bradley. (Illus.). 160p. 1995. 25.00 (*0-614-02561-3*, Garden Way Pub) Storey Comm Inc.

Contained Garden. rev. ed. Kenneth A. Beckett et al. LC 92-50356. (Illus.). 168p. 1993. 30.00 (*0-670-84729-1*, Viking); pap. 17.50 (*0-14-046940-0*, Penguin Bks) Viking Penguin.

Contained Garden: A Complete Illustrated Guide to Growing Plants, Flowers, Fruits, & Vegetables Outdoors in Pots. David Stevens et al. (Illus.). 168p. 1983. pap. 13.95 (*0-670-23961-5*) Viking Penguin.

***Contained Gardens: Creative Designs & Projects.** Susan Berry & Steve Bradley. LC 94-45673. (Illus.). 160p. 1995. 25.00 (*0-88266-899-4*, Garden Way Pub) Storey Comm Inc.

Container Efficiency & Shipping. Cargo Systems Staff. 1985. 195.00 (*0-907499-51-1*, Pub. by Cargo Systs UK) St Mut.

***Container Expert.** D. G. Hessayon. (Expert Ser.). (Illus.). 128p. 1995. pap. 10.95 (*0-903505-43-6*, Pub. by Expert Bks UK) Sterling.

Container Garden. Nigel Colborn. 1990. 29.95 (*0-316-15045-2*) Little.

***Container Garden.** Nigel Colborn. LC 94-28034. 1995. 15.99 (*0-517-12114-X*) Random Hse Value.

Container Garden: A Practical Guide to Planning & Planting: Wayside Gardens Collection. Thomasina Tarling. LC 94-16478. (Illus.). 128p. 1994. 19.95 (*0-8069-0843-2*) Sterling.

***Container Garden Month-by-Month.** Jackie Bennett. (Illus.). 144p. 1995. 24.95 (*0-7153-0153-5*, Pub. by D & C Pub UK) Sterling.

***Container Gardener.** Rupert Golby. (Illus.). 160p. 1995. 35.00 (*0-88045-129-7*) Stemmer Hse.

Container Gardening. Sam Cotner. 124p. (Orig.). 1987. pap. 12.95 (*0-914641-07-7*) TX Gardener Pr.

Container Gardening. Ed. by George Taloumis. (Plants & Gardens Ser.). (Illus.). 1989. ring bd. 3.95 (*0-945352-23-9*, Sterling) Bklyn Botanic.

Container Gardening. 4th ed. Sunset Magazine & Book Editors. LC 84-80608. (Illus.). 112p. 1984. pap. 8.99 (*0-376-03206-5*) Sunset Menlo Pk.

Container Gardening: All Year Round. Yvonne Rees & David Palliser. (Crowood Gardening Guides Ser.). (Illus.). 128p. 1991. pap. 16.95 (*1-85223-303-6*, Pub. by Crowood Pr UK) Trafalgar.

Container Gardening: The Northern Gardener's Library. Linden Hills Press Staff. 1992. pap. 9.95 (*0-9628378-3-0*) Linden Hills Pr.

Container Gardening for the Handicapped, Vol. 1. Frank J. Schweller. LC 89-83255. (Illus.). 64p. (Orig.). 1990. pap. 8.95 (*0-9624720-0-X*) Hand-D-Cap Publishing.

Container Handling & Transport. Ed. by Cargo Systems International Staff. 244p. (C). 1990. 160.00 (*0-907499-32-5*, Pub. by Cargo Systs UK) St Mut.

Container Handling & Transport. Cargo Systems Staff. 1983. 195.00 (0-907499-31-7, Pub. by Cargo Systs UK) St Mut.

***Container Molecules & Their Guests: Monographs in Supramolecular Chemistry.** Ed. by Donald J. Cram & Jane M. Cram. (Monographs in Supramolecular Chemistry). 223p. 1994. 95.00 (0-85186-972-6, R6972) CRC Pr.

Container Operations, 92. ICHCA-Cargo Systems Editors. (C). 1992. text ed. 210.00 (0-907499-78-3, Pub. by Cargo Systs UK) St Mut.

Container Plants. Halina Heitz. (Illus.). 240p. 1992. 19.95 (0-8120-6278-7) Barron.

Container Repair, Vol. II. Ed. by Cargo Systems Staff. 1983. 395.00 (0-907499-38-4, Pub. by Cargo Systs UK) St Mut.

Container Repair, Vol. III. Cargo Systems Staff. 1985. 195. 00 (0-907499-50-3, Pub. by Cargo Systs UK) St Mut.

Container Repair & Depot Conference, 4th. Ed. by Cargo Systems International Staff. (C). 1988. 150.00 (0-685-55019-2, Pub. by Cargo Systs UK) St Mut.

Container Shipping, Vol. II. Ed. by Cargo Systems Staff. 1981. 195.00 (0-907499-20-1, Pub. by Cargo Systs UK) St Mut.

Container Systems. Eric Rath. LC 72-13139. (Materials Handling & Packaging Ser.). 595p. 1973. reprint ed. pap. 169.60 (0-7837-3464-6, 2057792) Bks Demand.

Container Technology, Vol. IV. Ed. by Cargo Systems Staff. 1982. 300.00 (0-907499-30-9, Pub. by Cargo Systs UK) St Mut.

Container Technology, Vol. V. Cargo Systems Staff. 1985. 195.00 (0-317-89776-4, Pub. by Cargo Systs UK) St Mut.

Container Technology, Vol. VI. Ed. by Cargo Systems Staff. 1986. 225.00 (0-907499-55-4, Pub. by Cargo Systs UK) St Mut.

Container Technology Conference, 7th. Ed. by Cargo Systems International Staff. (C). 1988. 150.00 (0-907499-61-9, Pub. by Cargo Systs UK) St Mut.

Container Top Safety. Mike Compton. 64p. (C). 1989. 350. 00 (1-85330-075-6, Pub. by ICHCA UK) St Mut.

Container Top Safety. ICHCA Staff. (C). 1988. 40.00 (0-685-46520-9, Pub. by ICHCA UK) St Mut.

Container Top Safety: An Overview. Richard Swatton. (C). 1980. 30.00 (0-906297-08-7, Pub. by ICHCA UK) St Mut.

C

Container Tree Nursery Manual: The Biological Components, Nursery Pests & Mycorrhizae, Vol. 5. (Illus.). 177p. 1990. per., pap. 30.00 (0-16-000110-2, S/N 001-001-006) USGPO.

Container Tree Nursery Manual, Vol. 4: Seedling Nutrition & Irrigation. Thomas D. Landis & Rebecca G. Nisley. (Agriculture Handbook Ser.: No. 674). (Illus.). 125p. 1989. per., pap. 15.00 (0-16-000112-9, S/N 001-001-006) USGPO.

Containerisation Asia. Ed. by Cargo Systems Staff. 1990. 395.00 (0-907499-40-6, Pub. by Cargo Systs UK) St Mut.

Containerisation in the Eighties. M. G. Graham & D. O. Hughes. 236p. 1985. pap. 165.00 (1-85044-068-9) Lloyds London Pr.

Containerisation International Yearbook. Ed. by Ebury Press Staff. 630p. 1994. 795.00 (0-317-93736-7, Pub. by Ebury Pr UK) Trafalgar.

Containerless Processing: Techniques & Applications. W. H. Hofmeister & R. Schiffman. LC 93-39340. 147p. 40. 00 (0-87339-202-7) Minerals Metals.

Containers: The Lease-Buy Decision. ICHCA Staff. (C). 1988. 150.00 (0-685-46517-9, Pub. by ICHCA UK) St Mut.

Containers: The Lease-Buy Decision. Jin O. Tan. 78p. (C). 1983. 96.00 (0-906297-36-2, Pub. by ICHCA UK) St Mut.

Containers - Towards a New Generation of Inland & Maritime Loading Units. 207p. 1990. 60.00 (92-1-100352-0, GV.90.0.5) UN.

Containers & Baskets for Year Round Colour. Peter McHoy. (Illus.). 128p. 1994. pap. 14.95 (0-7063-7237-9, Pub. by Ward Lock UK) Sterling.

***Containers Attached to Mobile Gas Fired Equipment Pt. 1.** William Culross & Son Ltd. Staff. (C). 1991. 95.00x (0-900323-49-3, Pub. by W Culross & Son Ltd UK) St Mut.

***Containers (Beverage & Food) Market.** 500p. (Orig.). 1994. pap. 1,395.00 (1-57205-883-8) Rector Pr.

***Containers-Condition Law & Practice of Carriage & Use, 2 vols., Set.** Ed. by Mark D. Booker. 1993. 395.00 (0-907591-04-3, Pub. by Witherby & Co UK) St Mut.

Containers in Small Ports. ICHCA Staff. (C). 1987. 125.00 (0-906297-98-2, Pub. by ICHCA UK) St Mut.

Containing Anxiety in Institutions: Selected Essays, Vol. 1. Isabel M. Lyth. 269p. 1988. pap. 27.00 (1-85343-001-3) Col U Pr.

Containing Beauty: Japanese Bamboo Flower Baskets. Text by Toshiko M. McCallum. LC 88-50730. (Illus.). 96p. 1988. 35.00 (0-930741-15-3); pap. 21.00 (0-930741-16-1) UCLA Fowler Mus.

Containing Costs & Improving Productivity in Higher Education. Ed. by Carol S. Hollins. LC 85-645339. (New Directions for Institutional Research Ser.: No. IR 75). 124p. 1992. 16.95 (1-55542-736-7) Jossey-Bass.

Containing Crime: Community Based Approaches. Ed. by John McNeill & Bryan Williams. (Aberdeen University Press Bks.). 200p. 1991. pap. text ed. 29.00 (0-08-040911-3, Pub. by Aberdeen U Pr) Macmillan.

Containing Crisis: A Guide to Managing School Emergencies. Robert Watson et al. Ed. by Ronald D. Stephens. 113p. (Orig.). 1990. pap. 19.95 (1-879639-06-8) Natl Educ Serv.

Containing Health Benefit Costs: The Self-Insurance Option. Ed. by R. H. Egdahl & Diana C. Walsh. (Springer Series in Industry & Health Care: Vol. 6). (Illus.). 1979. pap. 38.00 (0-387-90385-2) Spr-Verlag.

Containing the Atom: Nuclear Regulation in a Changing Environment, 1963-1971. J. Samuel Walker. (C). 1992. 50.00 (0-520-07913-2) U CA Pr.

Containing the Cost of Social Security: The International Context. 70p. 1993. pap. 25.00 (0-11-762093-9, HM20939, Pub. by HMSO UK) UNIPUB.

Containing the Health Care Cost Spiral. Mary F. Callan. 1991. text ed. 29.95 (0-07-009704-6) McGraw.

***Containing the Patient's Rage, Terror & Despair: An Object Relations Approach to Psychotherapy.** Jeffrey Seinfeld. 1996. 35.00 (1-56821-578-9) Aronson.

Containing the Rising Cost of Health Services! An Examination of the Problems with Expanding Governmental Controls, Vol. 13. Kenneth L. Shellhammer et al. 84p. 1976. 4.95 (0-318-13498-5) Assn U Busn & Econ Res.

Containment: Documents on American Policy & Strategy 1945-1950. Thomas Etzold & John L. Gaddis. LC 77-20024. 449p. 1978. pap. text ed. 21.00 (0-231-04399-6) Col U Pr.

Containment, Soviet Behavior, & Grand Strategy. Robert E. Osgood. LC 81-82418. (Policy Papers in International Affairs Ser.: No. 16). viii, 86p. 1981. pap. 5.50 (0-87725-516-4) U of Cal IAS.

***Containment Systems Design: Chemical Storage, Mixing, & Recycling.** Fredric R. Haskett. (Illus.). 75p. 1995. pap. 74.95 (0-929870-33-6) Advanstar Commns.

Contaminant Effects Fisheries. Ed. by Victor W. Cairns et al. LC 84-7488. (Advances in Environmental Science & Technology Ser.: Vol.16). 333p. 1984. text ed. 190.00 (0-471-88014-0) Wiley.

Contaminant Hydrogeology. Charles W. Fetter, Jr. (Illus.). 480p. (C). 1993. text ed. write for info. (0-02-337135-8) Macmillan.

Contaminant Problems & Management of Living Chesapeake Bay Resources. Ed. by Shyamal K. Majumdar et al. LC 87-62940. xii, 573p. (C). 1987. 40. 00 (0-9606670-7-5) Penn Science.

Contaminant Problems & Strategies in Wastepaper Recycling Seminar, 1989: The Concourse Hotel, Madison WI, April 24-26. Technical Association of the Pulp & Paper Industry Staff. (TAPPI Notes Ser.). (Illus.). 161p. pap. 45.90 (0-8357-6322-6, 2035596) Bks Demand.

Contaminant Problems & Strategies in Wastepaper Recycling Seminar, 1992: Omni Netherland Plaza Hotel, Cincinnati, OH, April 28-30. Technical Association of the Pulp & Paper Industry Staff. (TAPPI Notes Ser.). reprint ed. pap. 66.70 (0-7837-2439-X, 2042591) Bks Demand.

Contaminant Removal from Public Water Systems. Daniel C. Houck et al. LC 84-22748. (Pollution Technology Review Ser.: No. 120). (Illus.). 524p. 1985. 52.00 (0-8155-1022-5) Noyes.

Contaminant Transport in Groundwater: Proceedings of an International Symposium, Stuttgart, 4-6 April 1989. Ed. by H. E. Kobus & W. Kinzelbach. 500p. (C). 1989. text ed. 130.00 (90-6191-879-0, Pub. by A A Balkema NE) Ashgate Pub Co.

Contaminants in the Environment: A Multidisciplinary Assessment of Risks to Man & Other Organisms. Fossi. Ed. by Aristeo Renzoni. LC 93-45760. 1994. write for info. (0-87371-853-4) Lewis Pubs.

Contaminants in the Subsurface Environment: Proceedings of the International Symposium on Processes Governing the Movement & Fate of Contaminants in the Subsurface Environment, Held at Stanford University, California, U. S. A., 23-26 July 1989. Ed. by Perry L. McCarty & P. V. Roberts. (Water Science & Technology Ser.: Vol. 22). (Illus.). 120p. 1990. pap. 86. 00 (0-08-040768-4, Pergamon Pr) Elsevier.

Contaminants Near the Sediment-Water Interface. Joseph V. DePinto. 1993. 69.95 (0-87371-887-9, TD423) Lewis Pubs.

Contaminants of Terrestrial Environments. O. Franzle. (Physical Environment Ser.: Vol. 13). (Illus.). 450p. 1993. 149.00 (0-387-55277-4) Spr-Verlag.

Contaminated Aquatic Sediments: Proceedings of the First International Specialized Conference on Contiminated Aquatic Sediments: Historic Records, Environmental Impact & Remediation, Held in Milwaukee, WI, 14-16 June, 1993, Vol. 28/8-9. E. R. Christensen et al. (Water Science & Technology Ser.: No. 28/8-9). 424p. 1994. pap. 170.00 (0-08-042492-9, Pergamon Pr) Elsevier.

Contaminated Communities: The Social & Psychological Impacts of Residential Toxic Exposure. Michael R. Edelstein. (Social Impact Assessment Ser.: No. 17). 217p. (C). 1989. pap. text ed. 20.95 (0-8133-7657-2) Westview.

Contaminated Dredged Material: Control, Treatment & Disposal Practices. M. John Cullinane et al. LC 89-70988. (Pollution Technology Review Ser.: No. 179). (Illus.). 772p. 1990. 85.00 (0-8155-1229-5) Noyes.

Contaminated Groundwater Control, Set. 1987. 40.00 (0-944989-50-0, 108703-1); 40.00 (0-944989-51-9, 108703-2); 40.00 (0-944989-52-7, 108703-3) Hazardous Mat Control.

Contaminated Groundwater Control, Vol. 1. 1987. 36.00 (0-685-31038-8) Hazardous Mat Control.

Contaminated Groundwater Control, Vol. 2. 1987. 36.00 (0-685-31039-6) Hazardous Mat Control.

Contaminated Groundwater Control, Vol. 3. 1987. 36.00 (0-685-31040-X) Hazardous Mat Control.

***Contaminated Land: Assessment & Redevelopment.** Richard A. Failey & Amanda J. Scrivens. (Business & the Environment Practitioner Ser.). (C). 1994. 150.00x (0-946655-86-3, Pub. by S Thornes Pubs UK) St Mut.

***Contaminated Land: Investigation, Assessment & Remediation.** Mary Harris & Sue Herbert. 88p. 1994. pap. 24.00 (0-7277-2016-3) Am Soc Civil Eng.

Contaminated Land: Problems & Solutions. Ed. by T. Cairney & W. A. Fairhurst. 1992. 103.95 (0-87371-870-4, TD) Lewis Pubs.

Contaminated Land: Reclamation & Treatment. M. A. Smith. LC 85-3562. (NATO - Challenges of Modern Society Ser.: Vol. 8). 456p. 1985. 95.00 (0-306-41928-9, Plenum Pr) Plenum.

Contaminated Land Treatment Technologies. Ed. by John F. Rees. LC 92-28321. 1992. write for info. (1-85166-943-4, Pub. by Elsevier Applied Sci UK) Elsevier.

Contaminated Marine Sediments: Assessment & Remediation. 508p. 1989. pap. text ed. 35.00 (0-309-04095-7) Natl Acad Pr.

Contaminated Soil Treatment Practices. 1987. 14.95 (0-944989-53-5, 108704) Hazardous Mat Control.

Contaminated Soil '93: Fourth International KfK-TNO Conference on Contaminated Soil, 3-7 May 1993, Berlin, Germany, 2 vols., Set. Ed. by F. Arendt. (Soil & Environment Ser.). (C). 1993. lib. bdg. 535.00 (0-7923-2328-9) Kluwer Ac.

Contaminated Surface Soils In-Place Treatment Techniques. Ronald Sims et al. LC 86-5162. (Pollution Technology Review Ser.: No. 132). (Illus.). 536p. 1986. 62.00 (0-8155-1085-3) Noyes.

Contamination. John Vornholt. Ed. by David Stern. (Star Trek: The Next Generation Ser.: No. 16). 288p. (Orig.). 1991. mass mkt. 5.50 (0-671-70561-X) PB.

Contamination Control. Alvin Liebermann. (Illus.). 182p. (C). 1990. 100.00 (0-918247-09-8) Tustin Tech.

Contamination Control: Proceedings of the International Symposium, 3rd, Copenhagen, Denmark, 1976, Vol. 2: Sectional Meetings. International Symposium on Contamination Control Staff. reprint ed. pap. 58.50 (0-317-20111-5, 2023178) Bks Demand.

Contamination Control & Cleanrooms: Problems, Engineering Solutions, & Applications. Alvin Lieberman. (Illus.). 384p. 1992. text ed. 59.95 (0-442-00574-1) Chapman & Hall.

Contamination Control in Trace Element Analysis. Morris Zief & James W. Mitchell. LC 76-16837. (Wiley-Interscience Publication Ser.). (Illus.). 278p. 1976. reprint ed. pap. 79.30 (0-7837-3486-7, 2057819) Bks Demand.

Contamination Control, 1981 Proceedings, Vol. III. LC 62-38584. 85p. 1981. pap. 50.00 (0-915414-64-3) Inst Environ Sci.

Contamination Effects on Electronic Products. Carl J. Tautscher. (Electrical Engineering & Electronics Ser.: Vol. 69). 624p. 1991. 160.00 (0-8247-8423-5) Dekker.

Contamination in Large Lakes, 4 vols. Schmidtke. 1988. 75. 00 (0-685-72489-1) Lewis Pubs.

Contamination in Large Lakes, 4 vols., I. Schmidtke. 1988. write for info. (0-87371-089-4, QH545) Lewis Pubs.

Contamination in Large Lakes, 4 vols., II. Schmidtke. 1988. write for info. (0-87371-090-8) Lewis Pubs.

Contamination in Large Lakes, 4 vols., III. Schmidtke. 1988. write for info. (0-87371-091-6, QH545) Lewis Pubs.

Contamination in Large Lakes, 4 vols., IV. Schmidtke. 1988. write for info. (0-87371-092-4) Lewis Pubs.

Contamination of Ground Water: Prevention, Assessment, Restoration. Michael Barcelona et al. LC 90-31404. (Pollution Technology Review Ser.: No. 184). (Illus.). 213p. 1990. 45.00 (0-8155-1243-0, 900124) Noyes.

Contamination of Groundwater & Groundwater Treatment: Part of the Proceedings of the Specialized Conference of the IWSA Held in Berlin, FRG, 22-28 April 1985. Ed. by R. Urbistondo. LC 83-13344. (Illus.). 234p. 1985. pap. 73.00 (0-08-033230-7, Pub. by PPL UK) Elsevier.

Contando Calorias-Del Fogon al Microondas. Miriam M. Hernandez. (Illus.). 192p. (Orig.). 1986. pap. 9.95 (0-939937-15-8) Microwave Cook Ctr.

Contarini Fleming: A Psychological Romance, etc. see Works of Benjamin Disraeli, Earl of Beaconsfield

***Contatti: A First Course in Italian.** Mariolina Freeth & Guiliana Checketts. LC 94-28952. (ITA.). 1995. write for info. (0-8120-8236-2); write for info. (0-8120-9092-6); student ed, pap. text ed. write for info. (0-8120-9093-4); audio write for info. (0-8120-9094-2); audio write for info. (0-8120-9095-0) Barron.

***Contax Camera Repair.** Edward H. Romney. 44p. 1992. pap. text ed. 18.00 (1-886996-65-2) Hillcrst Pub.

Contax Plan. LC 70-16315. 1970. 4.95 (0-912400-11-0); pap. 2.00 (0-912400-12-9) Western Res Pr.

Contax S Camera Family. Peter Dechert. (Illus.). 40p. 1991. 12.95 (1-879561-10-7) Hist Camera Pubns.

Contax S Family Camera. Peter Dechert. (Illus.). 50p. 1991. pap. 14.00 (1-879561-01-8) Hist Camera Pubns.

Conte Bleu, le Premier Soir: Malefice. Marguerite Yourcenar. 136p. (FRE.). 1992. pap. 34.95 (0-7859-1069-7, 207073062X) Fr & Eur.

Conte De Deux Villes. Charles Dickens. 416p. (FRE.). 1989. pap. 16.95 (0-7859-2128-1, 2070381951) Fr & Eur.

Conte De Fees New-Yorkais. J. P. Donleavy. 464p. (FRE.). 1988. pap. 13.95 (0-7859-2098-6, 2070380645) Fr & Eur.

Conte..., 1: Contes Numero 1 (Pour Enfants de Moins de Trois Ans) Eugene Ionesco. (Illus.). 32p. (FRE.). (J). 1983. 9.95 (0-7859-4602-0) Fr & Eur.

Conte..., 2: Contes Numero 2 (Pour Enfants de Moins de Trois Ans) Eugene Ionesco. (Illus.). 32p. (FRE.). (J). 1983. 9.95 (0-7859-4601-2) Fr & Eur.

Conte..., 3: Contes Numero 3 (Pour Enfants de Moins de Trois Ans) Eugene Ionesco. (Illus.). 32p. (FRE.). (J). 1985. pap. 9.95 (0-685-73256-8) Fr & Eur.

Conte..., 4: Contes Numero 4 (Pour Enfants de Moins de Trois Ans) Eugene Ionesco. (Illus.). 32p. (FRE.). (J). 1985. pap. 9.95 (0-7859-4604-7) Fr & Eur.

***Contemplating Courts.** Lee Epstein. 400p. 1995. 42.95 (0-87187-983-2); pap. 28.95 (0-87187-982-4) Congr Quarterly.

Contemplating Evolution & Doing Politics: Historical Scholars & Students in Sweden & Hungary Facing Historical Change, 1840-1920. Ed. by Ragnar Bjork. (Royal Academy of Letters, Konferenser Ser.: No. 27). 133p. (Orig.). 1993. pap. 45.00x (91-7402-233-4, Pub. by Almqv & Wiksell SW) Coronet Bks.

Contemplating Life's Great Questions. M. Rohani. 96p. (Orig.). 1991. pap. 7.95 (1-85168-024-1) Onewrld Pubns.

***Contemplating Marriage.** Gloria B. Thomas. (Orig.). 1995. pap. write for info. (1-55612-774-X) Sheed & Ward MO.

Contemplating Minds: A Forum for Artificial Intelligence. Ed. by William J. Clancey et al. LC 93-35759. (Artificial Intelligence Ser.). 1994. pap. 35.00 (0-262-53119-4) MIT Pr.

Contemplating Music: Challenges to Musicology. Joseph Kerman. 256p. 1985. 25.00 (0-674-16677-9) HUP.

Contemplating Music: Challenges to Musicology. Joseph Kerman. 256p. 1986. pap. text ed. 14.95 (0-674-16678-7) HUP.

Contemplating Music: Source Readings in the Aesthetics: Community of Discourse. Ruth Katz & Carl Dahlhaus. LC 85-28416. (Aesthetics in Music Ser.: No. 5, Vol. IV). (Illus.). 300p. 1993. lib. bdg. 73.00 (0-945193-16-5) Pendragon NY.

Contemplating Music: Source Readings in the Aesthetics of Music: Import, Vol. II. Ed. by Ruth Katz & Carl Dahlhaus. LC 85-28916. (Aesthetics in Music Ser.). 750p. 1990. lib. bdg. 73.00 (0-918728-68-1) Pendragon NY.

Contemplating Music: Source Readings in the Aesthetics of Music, Vol. III: Essence. Ruth Katz & Carl Dahlhaus. LC 85-28416. (Aesthetics in Music Ser.: No. 5, Vol. 3). (Illus.). 820p. 1992. lib. bdg. 73.00 (0-945193-04-1) Pendragon NY.

Contemplating Now. Monica Furlong. LC 83-70991. 128p. 1983. reprint ed. pap. 9.95 (0-936384-13-1) Cowley Pubns.

***Contemplating Suicide: The Language of Ethics & Self-Harm.** LC 94-21094. (Social Ethics & Policy Ser.). 208p. 1995. 49.95x (0-415-10605-2, C0293) Routledge.

***Contemplating Suicide: The Language of Ethics & Self-Harm.** Gavin Fairbairn. LC 94-21094. (Social Ethics & Policy Ser.). 208p. 1995. pap. 16.95 (0-415-10606-0, C0294) Routledge.

Contemplating the Ancients: Aesthetic & Social Issues in Early Chinese Portraiture. Audrey G. Spiro. (Illus.). 300p. 1990. 40.00 (0-520-06567-0, SPICON) U CA Pr.

Contemplatio Mortis et Immortalitatis. Henry Montagu. LC 72-218. (English Experience Ser.: No. 337). 148p. 1971. reprint ed. 20.00 (90-221-0337-4) Walter J Johnson.

Contemplation. Francis K. Nemeck & Marie T. Coombs. (Way of the Christian Mystics Ser.). 151p. 1982. pap. 9.95 (0-8146-5283-2) Liturgical Pr.

Contemplation: A Christian Path. Willigis Jager. 128p. (Orig.). 1994. pap. 9.95 (0-89243-690-5, Triumph Books) Liguori Pubns.

***Contemplation & Action.** Nasir Al-Din Tusi. Tr. & Intro. by Seyyed H. Badakhchani. 160p. 1995. text ed. 49.50 (1-85043-908-7) St Martin.

***Contemplation & Action: The Other Monasticism.** Roberta Gilchrist. LC 95-8209. 1995. write for info. (0-7185-1730-X, Pub. by Leicester Univ Pr) St Martin.

Contemplation & Action, 1902-1914. Russell Editorial Project Group, Mc Master University Staff. (Collected Papers of Bertrand Russell: Vol. 12). 654p. 1988. text ed. 191.50 (0-04-920078-X, A9420) Routledge Chapman & Hall.

Contemplation & Leisure. rev. ed. Douglas V. Steere. LC 74-30803. 32p. 1975. reprint ed. pap. 3.00 (0-87574-199-1) Pendle Hill.

Contemplation of Otherness. Richard E. Wentz. LC 84-1066. viii, 134p. 1984. 13.90 (0-86554-135-3, MUP-H126) Mercer Univ Pr.

Contemplation of Sinners. LC 75-315474. (English Experience Ser.: No. 645). 200p. 1974. reprint ed. 17.50 (90-221-0645-4) Walter J Johnson.

Contemplations. Victor Hugo. (Class. Garnier Ser.). (FRE.). 1965. pap. 7.95 (0-7859-0005-5, F64284) Fr & Eur.

Contemplations. Victor Hugo. (Poesie Ser.). (FRE.). 1965. pap. 14.95 (2-07-032050-2, 1444) Schoenhof.

***Contemplations... A Collection of Poems for & about Children.** Emory H. Jennings. (Collection of Poems for & about Children). 68p. (J). (gr. k-6). 1994. pap. 7.95 (1-885754-03-5) E H Jennings.

Contemplations: Being Studies in Christian Mysticism. W. L. Wilmshurst. 320p. 1994. reprint ed. pap. 24.95 (1-56459-425-4) Kessinger Pub.

Contemplations of Created Things: Science in Paradise Lost. Harinder S. Marjara. 408p. 1992. 50.00 (0-8020-2750-4) U of Toronto Pr.

***Contemplations of Judas Iscariot.** Touma Al-Khouri. (Trilogy for Christ Ser.: Pt. 3). 300p. 1995. per. 14.95 (1-879038-24-2) Oakwood Pubns.

Contemplations of the Dread & Love of God. LC 90-42799. 84p. 1990. reprint ed. 50.00 (0-8201-1445-6) Schol Facsimiles.

Contemplations of the Dread & Love of God. Ed. by Margaret Connolly. (Early English Text Society, Original Ser.: Vol. 303). (Illus.). 184p. 1994. reprint ed. 47.50 (0-19-722305-2) OUP.

Contemplations of Victor Hugo: An Allegory of the Creative Process. Suzanne Nash. LC 76-3273. 239p. reprint ed. pap. 68.20 (0-8357-6188-6, 2034297) Bks Demand.

 An Asterisk (*) at the beginning of an entry indicates that the title is appearing in BIP for the first time.

An Asterisk (*) at the beginning of an entry indicates that the title is appearing in BIP for the first time.

1573

Contemporary Approaches to Interest Measurement. Ed. by Donald G. Zytowski. LC 73-76895. 263p. reprint ed. pap. 75.00 (*0-317-29463-6*, 2055926) Bks Demand.

Contemporary Approaches to Moral Education: An Analysis of Alternative Theories. Barry Chazan. 176p. (C). 1985. pap. text ed. 16.95 (*0-8077-2765-2*) Tchrs Coll.

Contemporary Approaches to Philosophy. Paul Moser & Dwayne Mulder. (Illus.). 450p. (Orig.). (C). 1994. pap. write for info. (*0-02-384171-0*) Macmillan.

Contemporary Approaches to Psychological Assessment. Ed. by Scott Wetzler & Martin Katz. LC 89-7137. (Einstein Clinical & Experimental Psychiatry Monograph Ser.: No. 1). 368p. 1989. 45.95 (*0-87630-517-6*) Brunner-Mazel.

Contemporary Approaches to Psychotherapy & Counseling: The Self-Regulation & Maturity Model. Joseph F. Burke. LC 88-39587. 427p. (C). 1989. text ed. 44.95 (*0-534-10146-1*) Brooks-Cole.

Contemporary Approaches to State Constitutional Revision. Ed. by Alan L. Clem. 1970. 7.50 (*1-55614-029-0*) U of SD Gov Res Bur.

Contemporary Arabic Readers: Essays in 2 Parts, Vol. 2. McCarus et al. 1976. 18.00 (*0-86685-363-4*) Intl Bk Ctr.

Contemporary Arabic Readers: Formal Arabic in 2 Parts, Vol. 3. McCarus et al. 1987. pap. 19.95 (*0-86685-364-2*) Intl Bk Ctr.

Contemporary Arabic Readers: Modern Arabic Poetry, 2 Pts., Vol. 5. McCarus et al. 1987. 19.95 (*0-86685-366-9*) Intl Bk Ctr.

Contemporary Arabic Readers: Newspaper Arabic, Vol. 1. McCarus et al. 1967. pap. 15.00 (*0-86685-362-6*) Intl Bk Ctr.

Contemporary Arabic Readers: Short Stories in 2 Parts, Vol. 4. McCarus et al. 1992. pap. 19.95 (*0-86685-365-0*) Intl Bk Ctr.

Contemporary Archaeology: A Guide to Theory & Contributions. Ed. by Mark P. Leone. LC 79-156779. (Illus.). 476p. 1972. pap. 19.95 (*0-8093-0534-8*) S Ill U Pr.

Contemporary Architects. 2nd ed. Ed. by Ann L. Morgan. 1987. 145.00 (*0-912289-26-0*) St James Pr.

***Contemporary Architects.** 3rd ed. Ed. by Muriel Emanuel et al. LC 94-5310. (Contemorary Arts Ser.). (Illus.). 1125p. 1994. 149.00 (*1-55862-182-2*) St James Pr.

Contemporary Architectural Art Glass Studios: Glass by Fischer. Ed. by Oliver Loo. (Illus.). 60p. (Orig.). 1994. pap. write for info. (*0-9641371-0-0*) C&R Loo.

Contemporary Architectural Drawings: Donations to the Avery Library Centennial Drawings Archive. Ed. by Janet Parks. LC 91-4216. (Illus.). 143p. 1991. 35.00 (*0-87654-767-6*); pap. 24.95 (*0-87654-766-8*) Pomegranate Calif.

Contemporary Architecture. (Architectural Design Profiles Ser.). (Illus.). 80p. 1989. pap. 21.95 (*0-312-02709-5*) St Martin.

***Contemporary Architecture in Washington, D. C.** Claudia D. Kousoulas & George W. Kousoulas. LC 94-32132. 1995. pap. 24.95 (*0-89133-258-8*) Preservation Pr.

***Contemporary Argentina.** David Keeling. (C). 1995. text ed. 49.00 (*0-8133-8680-2*) Westview.

Contemporary Argentine Cinema. David W. Foster. (Illus.). 208p. 1992. text ed. 29.95 (*0-8262-0860-6*) U of Mo Pr.

Contemporary Arranger. rev. ed. Don Sebesky. 260p. (C). 1984. pap. 39.95 (*0-88284-485-7*, 1479) Alfred Pub.

Contemporary Art & Artists: An Index to Reproductions. Comp. by Pamela J. Parry. LC 78-57763. 327p. 1978. text ed. 59.95 (*0-313-20544-2*, PCO/, Greenwood Pr) Greenwood.

Contemporary Art & Its Philosophical Problems. Ingrid Stadler. LC 86-25279. 152p. 1987. 28.95x (*0-87975-383-8*) Prometheus Bks.

Contemporary Art Documentation & Fine Arts Libraries. Sydney S. Keaveney. LC 85-22234. 1986. 20.00 (*0-8108-1859-0*) Scarecrow.

Contemporary Art from Chile. Fatima Bercht et al. Tr. by Geoffrey Fox et al. (Illus.). 64p. (Orig.). 1991. 12.00 (*1-879128-02-0*) Americas Soc.

Contemporary Art from the Islamic World. Ed. by Wijdan Ali & S. Bisharat. (Illus.). 288p. 1990. pap. 24.95 (*0-905906-80-2*, Pub. by Scorpion Pub UK) Interlink Pub.

***Contemporary Art in Multicultural Education.** Ed. by Susan Cahan & Zoya Kocur. LC 95-10979. 1995. write for info. (*0-415-91189-3*); pap. write for info. (*0-415-91190-7*) Routledge.

Contemporary Art in Rhode Island. Ed. by Judith A. Singsen. LC 94-75216. (Illus.). 112p. 1994. 15.00 (*0-911517-62-6*) Mus of Art RI.

***Contemporary Art of Africa.** Ed. by Andre Magnin & Jacques Soulillou. LC 94-42674. 1995. write for info. (*0-8109-4032-9*) Abrams.

Contemporary Art Periodicals by Artists: Documentation & Index for the Decade of the Seventies. Darlene Tong. (Contemporary Documents Ser.). (Illus.). 400p. pap. write for info. (*0-931818-03-6*) Contemporary Arts.

Contemporary Art Trends, Nineteen Sixty to Nineteen Eighty: A Guide to Sources. Doris L. Bell. LC 81-5668. 183p. 1981. 20.00 (*0-8108-1445-5*) Scarecrow.

Contemporary Art 1965-1900. Bruce D. Kurtz. 256p. 1991. pap. text ed. 49.33 (*0-13-173022-3*) P-H.

Contemporary Artist Dolls: A Collector's Guide. Susanna Oroyan & Carol-Lynn R. Waugh. (Illus.). 224p. 1986. 19.95 (*0-87588-271-4*, 3259) Hobby Hse.

***Contemporary Artist Dolls from Germany.** Ann Bahar. 192p. 1995. 39.95 (*0-87588-430-X*, 4812) Hobby Hse.

Contemporary Artists. (Illus.). 1977. 75.00 (*0-312-16642-7*) St Martin.

Contemporary Artists. 2nd ed. Ed. by Muriel Emanuel et al. LC 82-25048. (Illus.). 1041p. 1983. 75.00 (*0-312-16643-5*) St Martin.

Contemporary Artists. 3rd ed. Ed. by Colin Naylor. 1989. 145.00 (*0-912289-96-1*) St James Pr.

***Contemporary Artists.** 4th ed. Ed. by Amanda Hopkinson. LC 94-34315. (Contemporary Arts Ser.). (Illus.). 1100p. 1995. 149.00 (*1-55862-183-0*) St James Pr.

Contemporary Artists & Craftsmen of the Eastern Band of Cherokee Indians. (Illus.). 152p. 1988. 10.00 (*0-9619549-0-6*) Qualla Arts & Crafts.

Contemporary Artists of South Carolina. Photos by Robert Smeltzer. LC 70-94681. 238p. 1970. pap. 12.00 (*0-910326-07-X*) Carolina Art.

Contemporary Arts & Crafts. 1978. 3.00 (*0-911410-46-5*) Applied Arts.

Contemporary Ascetics of Mount Athos, Vol. 1. Archimandrite C. Karambelas. Tr. by St. Xenia Skete. LC 91-68395. (Illus.). 363p. (Orig.). 1992. pap. 15.00 (*0-938635-55-7*) St Herman AK.

Contemporary Ascetics of Mount Athos, Vol. 2. Archimandrite C. Karambelas & Archimandrite Ioannicius. Tr. by St. Xenia Skete. LC 91-68395. (Illus.). 366p. (Orig.). 1992. 30.00 (*0-938635-57-3*); pap. 15.00 (*0-938635-56-5*) St Herman AK.

Contemporary Aspects of Economic Thinking in Islam. Muslim Students' Association Staff. 1976. pap. 2.75 (*0-89259-003-3*) Am Trust Pubns.

Contemporary Astronomy. 4th ed. Jay M. Pasachoff. (Illus.). 579p. (C). 1989. pap. text ed. 40.00 (*0-03-023247-3*) SCP.

Contemporary Atlas of the United States. Catherine Mattson & Mark T. Mattson. (Illus.). 160p. 1990. text ed. 95.00 (*0-02-897281-3*) Macmillan.

Contemporary Attitudes Toward Mental Illness. Guido M. Crocetti et al. LC 73-80071. (Contemporary Community Health Ser.). 262p. reprint ed. pap. 74.70 (*0-8357-9752-X*, 2017864) Bks Demand.

Contemporary Auditing: Issues & Cases. Michael C. Knapp. Ed. by Leyh. LC 92-20805. 350p. (C). 1993. pap. text ed. 37.75 (*0-314-00861-6*) West Pub.

Contemporary Australia. A. R. Griffiths. LC 76-62534. 1977. text ed. 29.95 (*0-312-16651-6*) St Martin.

Contemporary Australia: Studies in History, Politics & Economics. Geoffrey Serle et al. Ed. by Richard Preston. LC 69-20424. (Duke University, Commonwealth-Studies Center, Publication Ser.: No. 35). 615p. reprint ed. pap. 175.30 (*0-317-20429-7*, 2023436) Bks Demand.

Contemporary Australian Collage & Its Origins. A. McIntyre. (Illus.). 224p. 1990. text ed. 65.00 (*0-947131-31-0*) Gordon & Breach.

Contemporary Australian Drama. Peter Holloway. (C). 1990. 45.00 (*0-86819-108-6*, Pub. by Currency Pr AT) St Mut.

Contemporary Australian Issues. Comp. by Deidre Morris. 140p. 1993. pap. 25.00 (*1-875589-29-5*) D W Thorpe.

Contemporary Australian Poetry: Dual English-Greek (translated from English into Greek) Tr. by Dimitris Tsaloumas. LC 85-20268. 265p. 1987. text ed. 29.95 (*0-7022-1947-9*, Pub. by Univ Queensland Pr AT) Intl Spec Bk.

***Contemporary Australian Printmaking: An Interpretative History.** Sasha Grishin. 1995. 60.00 (*976-8097-76-0*) IPG Chicago.

***Contemporary Australian Society.** Ed. by Gordon Forth. Tr. by Shuming Zhao. 182p. (C). 1994. 70.00x (*0-949823-36-8*, Pub. by Deakin Univ AT) St Mut.

***Contemporary Australian Society.** Ed. by Gordon Forth. Tr. by Shuming Zhao. 350p. 1993. 105.00 (*0-909131-67-8*, Pub. by Deakin Univ AT) St Mut.

***Contemporary Australian Society.** Ed. by Gordon Forth. Tr. by Shuming Zhao. 350p. (CHI.). 1993. 105.00 (*7-305-02375-2*, Pub. by Deakin Univ AT) St Mut.

Contemporary Australian Television. Stuart Cunningham et al. 240p. 1994. pap. 24.95 (*0-86840-397-0*, Pub. by New South Wales Univ Pr AT) Intl Spec Bk.

Contemporary Austrian Poetry. Ed. & Tr. by Beth Bjorklund. LC 84-46116. Orig. Title: Ger. 328p. 1986. 48.50 (*0-8386-3178-9*) Fairleigh Dickinson.

Contemporary Authors, 13 vols. Ed. by Ann Evory. Incl. Vol. 1. LC 81-640179. 744p. 1980. 122.00 (*0-8103-1930-6*); Vol. 2. LC 81-640179. 704p. 1981. 122.00 (*0-8103-1931-4*); Vol. 3. LC 81-640179. 637p. 1981. 122.00 (*0-8103-1932-2*); Vol. 4. LC 81-640179. 616p. 1981. 122.00 (*0-8103-1933-0*); Vol. 5. LC 81-640179. 584p. 1982. 122.00 (*0-8103-1934-9*); Vol. 6. LC 81-640179. 576p. 1982. 122.00 (*0-8103-1935-7*); Vol. 7. LC 81-640179. 552p. 1982. 122.00 (*0-8103-1936-5*); Vol. 8. LC 81-640179. 544p. 1983. 122.00 (*0-8103-1937-3*); Vol. 9. LC 81-640179. 552p. 1983. 122.00 (*0-8103-1938-1*); Vol. 10. LC 81-640179. 552p. 1983. 122.00 (*0-8103-1939-X*); Vol. 11. LC 81-640179. 552p. 1984. 122.00 (*0-8103-1940-3*); Vol. 12. LC 81-640179. 528p. 1984. 122.00 (*0-8103-1941-1*); Vol. 13. LC 81-640179. 536p. 1984. 122.00 (*0-8103-1942-X*); LC 81-640179. (New Revision Ser.). write for info. (*0-318-59215-0*) Gale.

Contemporary Authors, Vol. 1. Ed. by Dedria Bryfonski. (Autobiography Ser.). 432p. 1984. 122.00 (*0-8103-4500-5*) Gale.

Contemporary Authors, Vol. 6. Ed. by Adele Sarkissian. (Autobiography Ser.). 464p. 1987. 122.00 (*0-8103-4505-6*) Gale.

Contemporary Authors, Vol. 7. Ed. by Adele Sarkissian. (Autobiography Ser.). (Illus.). 1988. 122.00 (*0-8103-4506-4*) Gale.

Contemporary Authors, Vol. 8. Ed. by Mark Zadrozny. (Autobiography Ser.). 1988. 122.00 (*0-8103-4507-2*) Gale.

Contemporary Authors, Vol. 9. Ed. by Mark Zadrozny. (Autobiography Ser.). 1989. 122.00 (*0-8103-4508-0*) Gale.

Contemporary Authors, Vol. 10. Ed. by Mark Zadrozny. (Autobiography Ser.). 400p. 1989. 122.00 (*0-8103-4509-9*) Gale.

Contemporary Authors, Vol. 11. Ed. by Mark Zadrozny. (Autobiography Ser.). 1990. lib. bdg. 122.00 (*0-8103-4510-2*) Gale.

Contemporary Authors, Vol. 12. Ed. by Joyce Nakamura. LC 84-647879. (Autobiography Ser.). (Illus.). 400p. 1990. text ed. 122.00 (*0-8103-4511-0*) Gale.

Contemporary Authors, Vol. 13. (Autobiography Ser.). 1991. 122.00 (*0-8103-4512-9*) Gale.

Contemporary Authors, Vol. 14. (Autobiography Ser.). 1991. 122.00 (*0-8103-4513-7*) Gale.

Contemporary Authors, Vol. 14. Ed. by Linda Metzger. LC 81-640179. (New Revision Ser.). 528p. 1985. 122.00 (*0-8103-1943-8*) Gale.

Contemporary Authors, Vol. 15. (Autobiography Ser.). 1992. 122.00 (*0-8103-5348-2*) Gale.

Contemporary Authors, Vol. 15. Ed. by Linda Metzger. LC 81-640179. (New Revision Ser.). 450p. 1985. 122.00 (*0-8103-1944-6*) Gale.

Contemporary Authors, Vol. 16. (Autobiography Ser.). 1992. 122.00 (*0-8103-5349-0*) Gale.

Contemporary Authors, Vol. 16. rev. ed. Linda Metzger & Deborah A. Straub. LC 81-640179. (New Revision Ser.). 483p. 1985. 122.00 (*0-8103-1945-4*) Gale.

Contemporary Authors, Vol. 17. (Autobiography Ser.). 1993. 122.00 (*0-8103-4514-5*) Gale.

Contemporary Authors, Vol. 17. rev. ed. Ed. by Linda Metzger & Deborah A. Straub. (New Revision Ser.). 600p. 1986. 115.00 (*0-8103-1946-2*) Gale.

Contemporary Authors, Vol. 18. (Autobiography Ser.). 1993. 122.00 (*0-8103-4515-3*) Gale.

Contemporary Authors, Vol. 18. Ed. by Linda Metzger. (New Revision Ser.: Vol. 18). 1986. 122.00 (*0-8103-1947-0*) Gale.

Contemporary Authors, Vol. 19. Ed. by Linda Metzger & Deborah A. Straub. (New Revision Ser.: Vol. 19). 600p. 1986. 122.00 (*0-8103-1948-9*) Gale.

Contemporary Authors, Vol. 19. Joyce Nakamura. (Autobiography Ser.). 1994. 122.00 (*0-8103-4516-1*, 002902) Gale.

Contemporary Authors, Vol. 20. Ed. by Linda Metzger & Deborah A. Straub. (New Revision Ser.: Vol. 20). 499p. 1987. 122.00 (*0-8103-1949-7*) Gale.

Contemporary Authors, Vol. 20. Joyce Nakamura. (Autobiography Ser.). 1994. 122.00 (*0-8103-4517-X*, 002903) Gale.

Contemporary Authors, Vol. 21. Ed. by Linda Metzger & Deborah A. Straub. (New Revision Ser.: Vol. 21). 507p. 1987. 122.00 (*0-8103-1975-6*) Gale.

Contemporary Authors, Vol. 23. Ed. by Deborah A. Straub. LC 81-640179. (New Revision Ser.). 550p. 1988. 122.00 (*0-8103-1977-2*) Gale.

Contemporary Authors, Vol. 24. Ed. by Deborah A. Straub. (New Revision Ser.: Vol. 24). 600p. 1988. 122.00 (*0-8103-1978-0*) Gale.

Contemporary Authors, Vol. 26. Gale Research Inc. Staff. Ed. by Hal May & James Lesniak. (New Revision Ser.). 1989. 122.00 (*0-8103-1980-2*) Gale.

Contemporary Authors, Vol. 27. Ed. by Hal May & James Lesniak. (New Revision Ser.). 1989. 122.00 (*0-8103-1981-0*) Gale.

Contemporary Authors, Vol. 28. Ed. by Hal May & James Lesniak. (New Revision Ser.). 510p. 1989. 122.00 (*0-8103-1982-9*) Gale.

Contemporary Authors, Vol. 29. Ed. by Hal May & James Lesniak. (New Revision Ser.). 1990. 122.00 (*0-8103-1983-7*) Gale.

Contemporary Authors, Vol. 31. Ed. by James Lesniak. (New Revision Ser.). 500p. 1990. text ed. 122.00 (*0-8103-1985-3*) Gale.

Contemporary Authors, Vol. 32. (New Revision Ser.). 1991. 122.00 (*0-8103-1986-1*) Gale.

Contemporary Authors, Vol. 33. (New Revision Ser.). 1991. write for info. (*0-8103-1987-X*) Gale.

Contemporary Authors, Vol. 34. (New Revision Ser.). 1991. 122.00 (*0-8103-1988-8*) Gale.

Contemporary Authors, Vol. 39. (New Revision Ser.). 1993. write for info. (*0-8103-1993-4*) Gale.

Contemporary Authors, Vol. 40. (New Revision Ser.). 1993. 122.00 (*0-8103-1994-2*) Gale.

Contemporary Authors, Vol. 41. (New Revision Ser.). 1993. write for info. (*0-8103-1972-1*) Gale.

***Contemporary Authors, Vol. 46.** rev. ed. Ed. by Pamela S. Dear. 500p. 1995. 122.00 (*0-8103-5699-6*) Gale.

Contemporary Authors, Vol. 108. Ed. by Hal May & Ann Evory. 824p. 1983. 122.00 (*0-8103-1908-X*) Gale.

Contemporary Authors, Vol. 109. Ed. by Ed May. 552p. 1983. 122.00 (*0-8103-1909-8*) Gale.

Contemporary Authors, Vol. 110. Ed. by Hal May & Ann Evory. LC 62-52046. 833p. 1984. 122.00 (*0-8103-1910-1*) Gale.

Contemporary Authors, Vol. 111. Ed. by Hal May & Ann Evory. LC 62-52046. 528p. 1984. 122.00 (*0-8103-1911-X*) Gale.

Contemporary Authors, Vol. 112. Ed. by Hal May & Ann Evory. LC 62-52046. 528p. 1984. 122.00 (*0-8103-1912-8*) Gale.

Contemporary Authors, Vol. 113. Ed. by Hal May & Ann Evory. LC 65-52046. 536p. 1985. 122.00 (*0-8103-1913-6*) Gale.

Contemporary Authors, Vol. 114. Ed. by Hal May & Ann Evory. 792p. 1985. 122.00 (*0-8103-1914-4*) Gale.

Contemporary Authors, Vol. 115. Ed. by Hal May & Ann Evory. LC 62-52046. 492p. 1985. 122.00 (*0-8103-1915-2*) Gale.

Contemporary Authors, Vol. 116. Ed. by Hal May & Ann Evory. 600p. 1986. 122.00 (*0-8103-1916-0*) Gale.

Contemporary Authors, Vol. 117. Ed. by Hal May & Ann Evory. 800p. 1986. 122.00 (*0-8103-1917-9*) Gale.

Contemporary Authors, Vol. 118. Ed. by Hal May & Ann Evory. 500p. 1986. 122.00 (*0-8103-1918-7*) Gale.

Contemporary Authors, Vol. 119. Ed. by Hal May. 600p. 1986. 122.00 (*0-8103-1919-5*) Gale.

Contemporary Authors, Vol. 120. Ed. by Hal May. 760p. 1987. 122.00 (*0-8103-1920-9*) Gale.

Contemporary Authors, Vol. 121. Ed. by Hal May. 475p. 1987. 122.00 (*0-8103-1921-7*) Gale.

Contemporary Authors, Vol. 122. Ed. by Hal May. 500p. 1987. 122.00 (*0-8103-1922-5*) Gale.

Contemporary Authors, Vol. 123. Ed. by Hal May & Susan M. Trosky. 488p. 1988. 122.00 (*0-8103-1923-3*) Gale.

Contemporary Authors, Vol. 124. Hal May & Susan M. Trosky. 1988. 122.00 (*0-8103-1924-1*) Gale.

Contemporary Authors, Vol. 125. Ed. by Hal May & Susan M. Trosky. 1988. 122.00 (*0-8103-1950-0*) Gale.

Contemporary Authors, Vol. 126. Gale Research Inc. Staff. Ed. by Susan M. Trosky. 1989. 122.00 (*0-8103-1951-9*) Gale.

Contemporary Authors, Vol. 127. Ed. by Susan M. Trosky. 500p. 1989. 122.00 (*0-8103-1952-7*) Gale.

Contemporary Authors, Vol. 128. 1990. 122.00 (*0-8103-7770-5*, 001143-M99406) Gale.

Contemporary Authors, Vol. 129. Ed. by Susan M. Trosky. 503p. 1990. 122.00 (*0-8103-1954-3*) Gale.

Contemporary Authors, Vol. 130. Ed. by Susan M. Trosky. LC 62-52046. 507p. 1990. 122.00 (*0-8103-1955-1*) Gale.

Contemporary Authors, Vol. 131. 1990. 122.00 (*0-8103-1956-X*) Gale.

Contemporary Authors, Vol. 132. 1991. 122.00 (*0-8103-1957-8*) Gale.

Contemporary Authors, Vol. 132. Susan M. Trosky. 1991. write for info. (*0-8103-1964-0*) Gale.

Contemporary Authors, Vol. 133. Susan M. Trosky. 1991. 122.00 (*0-8103-1958-6*) Gale.

Contemporary Authors, Vol. 134. 1991. 122.00 (*0-8103-1959-4*) Gale.

Contemporary Authors, Vol. 134. Susan M. Trosky. 1991. write for info. (*0-8103-1965-9*) Gale.

Contemporary Authors, Vol. 135. Susan M. Trosky. 1992. 122.00 (*0-8103-1960-8*) Gale.

Contemporary Authors, Vol. 136. 1992. write for info. (*0-8103-1966-7*) Gale.

Contemporary Authors, Vol. 136. Susan M. Trosky. 1992. 122.00 (*0-8103-1961-6*) Gale.

Contemporary Authors, Vol. 137. Susan M. Trosky. 1992. 122.00 (*0-8103-1962-4*) Gale.

Contemporary Authors, Vol. 138. 1992. write for info. (*0-8103-1968-3*); 122.00 (*0-8103-1967-5*) Gale.

Contemporary Authors, Vol. 139. 1993. 122.00 (*0-8103-1969-1*) Gale.

Contemporary Authors, Vol. 140. 1993. write for info. (*0-8103-1971-3*); 122.00 (*0-8103-1970-5*) Gale.

Contemporary Authors, Vol. 141. Susan M. Trosky. 1993. 122.00 (*0-8103-5551-5*, 001156) Gale.

Contemporary Authors, Vol. 142. Susan M. Trosky & James Lesniak. 1994. 122.00 (*0-8103-5553-1*, 001157) Gale.

Contemporary Authors, Vol. 142 & Index. Susan M. Trosky & James Lesniak. 1994. write for info. (*0-8103-5552-3*, 101355) Gale.

Contemporary Authors, Vol. 143. Susan M. Trosky. 1994. 122.00 (*0-8103-5554-X*, 001158) Gale.

Contemporary Authors, Vols. 2-5. Ed. by Adele Sarkissian. Incl. Vol. 2. 514p. 1985. 122.00 (*0-8103-4501-3*); Vol. 3. 450p. 1986. 122.00 (*0-8103-4502-1*); Vol. 4. 460p. 1986. 122.00 (*0-8103-4503-X*); Vol. 5. 491p. 1987. 122.00 (*0-8103-4504-8*); (Autobiography Ser.). 99.00 (*0-685-73773-X*); Incl. Vol. 2. 122.00 (*0-8103-4501-3*); Vol. 3. 122.00 (*0-8103-4502-1*); Vol. 4. 122.00 (*0-8103-4503-X*); Vol. 5. 122.00 (*0-8103-4504-8*); 99.00 (*0-685-73774-8*); Incl. Vol. 2. 122.00 (*0-8103-4501-3*); Vol. 3. 122.00 (*0-8103-4502-1*); Vol. 4. 122.00 (*0-8103-4503-X*); Vol. 5. 122.00 (*0-8103-4504-8*); 99.00 (*0-685-73775-6*); Incl. Vol. 2. 122.00 (*0-8103-4501-3*); Vol. 3. 122.00 (*0-8103-4502-1*); Vol. 4. 122.00 (*0-8103-4503-X*); Vol. 5. 122.00 (*0-8103-4504-8*); 99.00 (*0-685-73776-4*) Gale.

Contemporary Authors: A Bibliographical Guide to Current Writers in Fiction, General Nonfiction, Poetry, Journalism, Drama, Motion Pictures, Television, & Other Fields.

Contemporary Authors: Permanent Series. A Bio-Bibliographical Guide to Current Authors & Their Works, 2 vols. LC 75-13539. 1260p. 1975. Vol. 1 1975. 122.00 (*0-8103-0036-2*) Gale.

Contemporary Authors: Permanent Series. A Bio-Bibliographical Guide to Current Authors & Their Works, 2 vols., Vol. 2. LC 75-13539. 1260p. 1978. 122.00 (*0-8103-0037-0*) Gale.

***Contemporary Authors Autobiography Series, Vol. 21.** Ed. by Joyce Nakamura. 400p. 1995. 122.00 (*0-8103-4518-8*) Gale.

Contemporary Authors New Revision, Vol. 44. James Lesniak. Ed. by James P. Draper & Susan M. Trosky. (Contemporary Authors Revised Ser.). 491p. 1994. 122.00 (*0-8103-1929-2*, 000084) Gale.

Contemporary Authors New Revision Series, Vol. 4. James Lesniak. 1994. write for info. (*0-8103-1928-4*, 101354) Gale.

Contemporary Authors New Revision Series, Vol. 30. Ed. by James Lesniak. 500p. 1990. 115.00 (*0-8103-1984-5*) Gale.

Contemporary Authors New Revision Series, Vol. 42. James Lesniak. (Contemporary Authors Revised Ser.). 1993. 115.00 (*0-8103-1973-X*, 000082) Gale.

Contemporary Authors New Revision Series & Contemporary Authors Index, Vol. 43. James Lesniak. 1994. 119.00 (*0-8103-1974-8*, 000083) Gale.

C

1574

An Asterisk (*) at the beginning of an entry indicates that the title is appearing in BIP for the first time.

An Asterisk (*) at the beginning of an entry indicates that the title is appearing in BIP for the first time.

1575

C

Contemporary Christian. John R. Stott. LC 92-9541. 432p. 1992. 19.99 (*0-8308-1316-0*, 1316) InterVarsity.

Contemporary Christian Music Debate: Worldly Compromise or Agent of Renewal? Steve Miller. LC 92-30629. 1993. 8.99 (*0-685-62282-7*) Tyndale.

Contemporary Christian Options of the World's End: The Eschatology of Lewis Sperry Chafer. Jeffrey J. Richards. LC 93-33936. (Illus.). 256p. 1993. text ed. 89.95 (*0-7734-9391-3*) E Mellen.

Contemporary Christian Religious Responses to the Shoah. Ed. by Steven L. Jacobs. LC 92-46070. (Studies in the Shoah: No. 6). 1993. 51.00 (*0-8191-8984-7*) U Pr of Amer.

Contemporary Christian Today. Ed. by Milton Okun. pap. 14.95 (*0-89524-793-3*) Cherry Lane.

Contemporary Christmas Plays. Evelyn Stenbock. 1980. 4.25 (*0-8341-9150-4*, MC-254) Lillenas.

Contemporary Church History. Orazio M. Premoli. 1977. lib. bdg. 59.95 (*0-8490-1669-X*) Gordon Pr.

Contemporary City Ecology. C. S. Yadav. 1987. 49.00 (*0-317-90506-6*, Pub. by Concept II) S Asia.

Contemporary Clarinet Repertoire for Clarinet & Electronics. 2nd ed. F. Gerard Errante. 47p. 1993. pap. text ed. 9.50 (*0-933251-10-6*) Mill Creek Pubns.

Contemporary Class Guitar, Bks. 1 & 2. Will Schmid. 96p. 1993. Bk. 1, 96p. pap. 9.95 (*0-7935-2498-9*, 00699225); Bk. 2, 96p. pap. 9.95 (*0-7935-2499-7*, 00699226) H Leonard.

Contemporary Class Piano. 3rd ed. Elyse Mach. 320p. (Orig.). (C). 1988. pap. text ed. 26.75 (*0-15-513481-7*, MACH3) HB Coll Pubs.

Contemporary Class Piano, Vol. 1. 4th ed. Elyse Mach. 400p. (Orig.). (C). 1992. pap. text ed. 28.00 (*0-15-513483-3*) HB Coll Pubs.

Contemporary Classical. Kolar & Ramal. (Keyboard Beginning Ser.). 1990. 5.95 (*0-685-31451-0*, T717) Hansen Ed Mus.

Contemporary Classics. Comp. by Ken Bible. 1987. ring bd. 16.95 (*0-8341-9166-0*, MB-512) Lillenas.

Contemporary Classics: Furniture of the Masters. Charles D. Gandy. (Illus.). 176p. 1990. pap. 16.95 (*0-8230-0931-9*, Whitney Lib) Watsn-Guptill.

Contemporary Classics in Philosophy of Religion. Ed. by Ann Loades & Loyal D. Rue. 616p. (C). 1991. 50.00 (*0-8126-9168-7*); pap. 21.00 (*0-8126-9169-5*) Open Court.

Contemporary Climatology. A. Henderson-Sellers & P. J. Robinson. LC 85-11293. 439p. 1986. pap. text ed. 49.95 (*0-470-20664-0*) Halsted Pr.

Contemporary Clinical Neurophysiology. W. A. Cobb & H. Van Duyn. (Electroencephalography & Clinical Neurophysiology Ser.: Vol. 34, Suppl.). 578p. 1978. 146.25 (*0-444-80056-5*) Elsevier.

Contemporary Clothing. Dorothy S. Lyle & Jeanne Brinkley. 1983. text ed. 19.60 (*0-02-663140-7*) Bennett IL.

Contemporary Collage: Extensions. Melinda Lorenz. (Illus.). 32p. 1983. 4.00 (*0-915478-47-1*) Galleries Coll.

Contemporary Collection. Goldstein et al. 48p. (gr. 3-12). 1974. pap. text ed. 7.95 (*0-87487-627-3*) Summy-Birchard.

Contemporary Collection on Loan from the Rothschild Bank AG, Zurich. Robert McDonald. LC 82-84588. (Illus.). 72p. 1983. 13.50 (*0-934418-16-0*) Mus Contemp Art.

***Contemporary Collective Bargaining in the Private Sector.** Ed. by Paula B. Voos. 462p. 1995. 29.95 (*0-913447-60-9*) Indus Relations Res.

Contemporary College Physics. 2nd ed. Edwin R. Jones & Richard L. Childers. LC 92-26814. (C). 1993. text ed. 43.25 (*0-201-55721-5*) Addison-Wesley.

Contemporary College Reader. 3rd ed. Joyce S. Steward. LC 84-13955. 511p. reprint ed. pap. 145.70 (*0-7837-3014-4*, 2042926) Bks Demand.

Contemporary Communication Research Methods. Mary J. Smith. 382p. (C). 1988. text ed. 47.95 (*0-534-08610-1*) Intl Thomson.

Contemporary Community Corrections. Ed. by Thomas Ellsworth. 473p. (Orig.). (C). 1992. pap. text ed. 20.95x (*0-88133-667-X*) Waveland Pr.

Contemporary Composers. Ed. by Brian Morton & Pamela Collins. 1000p. 1992. 125.00 (*1-55862-085-0*, 200105) St James Pr.

Contemporary Composers. Daniel G. Mason. LC 72-1726. reprint ed. 21.45 (*0-404-08327-7*) AMS Pr.

Contemporary Composers on Contemporary Music. Ed. by Elliot Schwartz & Barney Childs. LC 78-1962. (Music Reprint Ser.: 1978). 1978. reprint ed. lib. bdg. 45.00 (*0-306-77587-5*) Da Capo.

Contemporary Conceptions of Social Philosophy: Proceedings of the 12th World Congress on Philosophy of Law. Ed. by Stavros Panou et al. 237p. (Orig.). 1988. pap. 67.50 (*3-515-04983-5*) Coronet Bks.

Contemporary Concerns of Youth. Shirley P. Schwarzrock. (Illus.). 183p. 1979. 29.95 (*0-88671-047-2*, 1801) Am Guidance.

Contemporary Concert Music by Women: A Directory of the Composers & Their Works. Comp. by Judith L. Zaimont & Karen Famera. LC 80-39572. (Illus.). 320p. 1981. text ed. 65.00 (*0-313-22921-X*, ZCM/, Greenwood Pr) Greenwood.

Contemporary Conducting Techniques. Mario F. Oneglia. LC 79-66924. (Illus.). (Orig.). 1979. spiral bd. 15.00 (*0-9603470-0-3*) Tritone Music.

Contemporary Conservative Care for Painful Spinal Disorders. Tom G. Mayer et al. LC 91-9298. (Illus.). 588p. 1991. text ed. 99.00 (*0-8121-1344-6*) Williams & Wilkins.

Contemporary Constitutional Lawmaking: The Supreme Court & the Art of Politics. Lief H. Carter. (Government & Politics Ser.). (Illus.). 256p. 1985. text ed. 55.00 (*0-08-030970-4*, Pergamon Pr); pap. text ed. 19.95 (*0-08-030969-0*, Pergamon Pr) Elsevier.

Contemporary Constructions of the Child: Essays in Honor of William Kessen. F. Kessel et al. 344p. (C). 1991. text ed. 69.95 (*0-8058-0607-5*) L Erlbaum Assocs.

Contemporary Contact Lens Practice. Hartstein. (Illus.). 225p. 1990. pap. 39.95 (*0-8016-2106-2*) Mosby Yr Bk.

Contemporary Continental Philosophy. Bernd Magnus. (Dimensions of Philosophy Ser.). 256p. 1997. 34.50 (*0-8133-0627-2*); pap. 16.95 (*0-8133-0628-0*) Westview.

Contemporary Contrabass. 2nd rev. ed. Bertram Turetzky. (New Instrumentation Ser.: Vol. 7). 128p. (C). 1988. pap. 38.00 (*0-520-06381-3*) U CA Pr.

Contemporary Controversies: An American Government Reader. Ed. by Robert J. Bresler. LC 92-29833. (C). 1992. 20.00 (*0-06-501020-5*) HarpCollege.

Contemporary Cookery. V. Ceserani et al. 323p. 1993. text ed. 37.95 (*0-470-23350-8*) Halsted Pr.

Contemporary Cookery. Victor Ceserani et al. (Illus.). 336p. (C). 1988. text ed. 17.95 (*0-7131-7752-7*, Pub. by E Arnold UK) Routledge Chapman & Hall.

***Contemporary Coptic Nuns.** Pieternella Van Doorn-Harder. LC 94-18770. (Studies in Comparative Religion). 1995. write for info. (*1-57003-034-0*) U of SC Pr.

***Contemporary Corporation Forms.** expanded ed. Ed. by J. Robert Brown, Jr. & Jonathan R. Macy. 5330p. 1993. 395.00 (*0-13-296790-1*, 40149) Aspen Law.

Contemporary Cost Management. Takeo Yoshikawa et al. LC 92-30646. 1992. write for info. (*0-412-45210-3*, Chap & Hall NY) Chapman & Hall.

Contemporary Costume: Strictly Handwoven. Harriet Tidball. LC 76-24014. (Guild Monographs: No. 24). (Illus.). 44p. 1968. pap. 2.95 (*0-916658-24-4*) Shuttle Craft.

Contemporary Counseling: Services, Applications, Issues. Ed. by Charles W. Humes. LC 86-71218. 400p. 1987. text ed. 12.95 (*0-915202-62-X*) Accel Devel.

Contemporary Counterfeits. John J. Davis. 1979. pap. 1.50 (*0-88469-003-2*) BMH Bks.

Contemporary Crafts & the Saxe Collection. Davira S. Taragin et al. LC 93-17546. (Illus.). 216p. 1993. 60.00 (*1-55595-073-6*) Hudson Hills.

Contemporary Crafts for the Home. Bill Kraus. Ed. by Toni F. Sikes. 160p. 1990. 29.99 (*0-935603-18-2*, 30134) Rockport Pubs.

Contemporary Crazy Quilt Project Book see Quick-&-Easy Quilt Patchwork with Fourteen Projects

Contemporary Criminal Justice in America: An Overview. Harry M. Humphreys. 80p. (Orig.). (C). 1980. pap. 6.95 (*0-9608776-0-6*) Public Insights.

Contemporary Criminal Procedure: Annual Edition. Larry E. Holtz. 700p. (C). ring bd. 39.95 (*0-87526-365-8*) Gould.

Contemporary Criminological Theory. Ed. by Francis T. Cullen & Velmer S. Burton, Jr. LC 93-25713. (International Library of Essays in Law & Legal Theory: Vol. 11). 1993. 150.00 (*0-8147-1501-X*) NYU Pr.

Contemporary Crisis: Political Hostage-Taking & the Experience of Western Europe. Clive C. Aston. LC 82-6165. (Contributions in Political Science Ser.: No. 84). xiv, 217p. 1982. text ed. 49.95 (*0-313-23289-X*, ASP/, Greenwood Pr) Greenwood.

***Contemporary Crisis of the Nation State.** John M. Dunn. 224p. Date not set. pap. text ed. 19.95 (*0-631-19263-8*) Blackwell Pubs.

Contemporary Critical Theory. Dan Latimer. 669p. (C). 1988. pap. text ed. 29.50 (*0-15-513494-9*) HB Coll Pubs.

Contemporary Critical Theory: A Selective Bibliography. Donald G. Marshall. LC 92-33515. 260p. 1993. text ed. 32.00 (*0-87352-963-4*, T126C); pap. text ed. 15.50 (*0-87352-964-2*, T126P) Modern Lang.

Contemporary Criticism in Literature. Orlo Williams. LC 73-155148. (English Literature Ser.: No. 33). 1971. 39.95 (*0-8383-1248-9*) M S G Haskell Hse.

Contemporary Criticisms of Dr. Samuel Johnson, His Works, & His Biographers. John K. Spittal. 1977. 19.95 (*0-8369-6955-3*, 7836) Ayer.

Contemporary Critique of Historical Materialism. Anthony Giddens. 250p. 1981. pap. 16.00 (*0-520-04490-8*) U CA Pr.

***Contemporary Critique of Historical Materialism.** 2nd ed. Anthony Giddens. 320p. 1995. 45.00x (*0-8047-2518-7*); pap. 17.95 (*0-8047-2519-5*) Stanford U Pr.

Contemporary Cryptology: The Science of Information Integrity. Ed. by Gustavus J. Simmons. LC 91-19684. (Illus.). 656p. (C). 1992. text ed. 79.95 (*0-87942-277-7*, PC0271-7) Inst Electrical.

***Contemporary Cuban Photography Issue 140: Aperture 141.** (Illus.). 80p. 1995. 14.95 (*0-89381-611-6*) FS&G.

Contemporary Cultural Anthropology. 3rd ed. Michael C. Howard. (C). 1988. pap. text ed. 28.50 (*0-673-39909-5*) HarpCollege.

Contemporary Cultural Anthropology. 4th ed. Michael C. Howard. LC 92-19291. (C). 1992. text ed. 32.50 (*0-673-52255-5*) HarpCollege.

Contemporary Cultural Theory: An Introduction, Nos. 1-4. Andrew Milner. 192p. 1991. pap. 19.95 (*0-04-442292-X*, Pub. by Allen & Unwin Aust Pty AT) Paul & Co Pubs.

***Contemporary Culture of the Cahita Indians.** Ralph L. Beals. (Bureau of American Ethnology Bulletins Ser.). 244p. 1995. lib. bdg. 89.00 (*0-7812-4142-1*) Rprt Serv.

Contemporary Cultures & Societies of Latin America: A Reader in the Social Anthropology of Middle & South America. 2nd ed. Ed. by Dwight B. Heath. 572p. (C). 1988. reprint ed. pap. text ed. 22.95 (*0-88133-359-X*) Waveland Pr.

Contemporary Curriculum K-Eight. George S. Morrison. LC 92-35298. 1993. text ed. write for info. (*0-205-14523-X*) Allyn.

Contemporary Czech. rev. ed. Michael Heim. (UCLA Slavic Studies: Vol. 3). 271p. (Orig.). (C). 1982. pap. text ed. 17.95 (*0-89357-098-2*) Slavica.

Contemporary Czech Cinematography: Jiri Menzel & the History of the "Closely Watched Trains" Josef Skvorecky. (East European Monographs: No. 118). 99p. 1982. text ed. 41.00 (*0-88033-011-2*) East Eur Quarterly.

Contemporary Danish Composers Against the Background of Danish Musical Life... Vagn Kappel. 1988. reprint ed. lib. bdg. 49.00 (*0-7812-0028-8*) Rprt Serv.

Contemporary Danish Composers Against the Background of Danish Musical Life & History. Vagn Kappel. LC 70-181195. 1948. reprint ed. 49.00 (*0-403-01602-9*) Scholarly.

Contemporary Danish Cross-Stitch Design. Danish Handcraft Guild. (Illus.). 96p. 1982. 17.95 (*0-8038-1278-7*) Hastings.

Contemporary Danish Plays. LC 75-132134. (Play Anthology Reprint Ser.). 1977. 23.95 (*0-8369-8211-8*) Ayer.

Contemporary Data Communications: A Practical Approach. Al Schroeder & Emilio Ramos. LC 93-1505. (Illus.). 570p. (C). 1994. text ed. write for info. (*0-02-408021-7*) Macmillan.

Contemporary Democracies: Participation, Stability & Violence. G. Bingham Powell, Jr. 296p. 1984. pap. 14.95 (*0-674-16687-6*) HUP.

Contemporary Dental Assisting. Novak. 1994. 42.95 (*0-8016-7732-7*) Mosby Yr Bk.

Contemporary Dental Assisting: Text & Study Guide. Novak. 1994. write for info. (*0-8016-7733-5*) Mosby Yr Bk.

Contemporary Dental Hygiene Practice, Vol. 1. Phagan-Schostok & Maloney. (Illus.). 221p. 1988. Incl. lab manual. student ed, pap. text ed. 68.00 (*0-86715-169-2*) Quint Pub Co.

Contemporary Dental Hygiene Practice, Vol. 2. Phagan-Schostok & Maloney. (Illus.). 120p. 1989. pap. text ed. 34.00 (*0-86715-170-6*) Quint Pub Co.

Contemporary Design Theory: A Collection of Surveys. Jeffrey H. Dinitz & Douglas R. Stinson. (Interscience Series in Discrete Mathematics). 656p. 1992. text ed. 110.00 (*0-471-53141-3*) Wiley.

Contemporary Designers. 2nd ed. Ed. by Colin Naylor. (Illus.). 641p. 1990. lib. bdg. 145.00 (*0-912289-69-4*) St James Pr.

Contemporary Details: A Visual Sourcebook of Architectural Features, Fittings, & Decorative Finishes for 20th-Century Homes. Nonie Niesewand. (Illus.). 192p. 1993. 35.00 (*0-671-74958-7*) S&S Trade.

Contemporary Developments in Financial Institutions & Markets. 2nd rev. ed. Thomas M. Havrilesky & Robert Schweitzer. LC 86-19965. 574p. (C). 1987. pap. text ed. write for info. (*0-88295-415-6*) Harlan Davidson.

Contemporary Developments in Social Work Research Methodology. National Association of Social Workers. 61p. reprint ed. pap. 25.00 (*0-7837-6546-0*, 2045683) Bks Demand.

Contemporary Devil's Dictionary. I. Q. Anonymous. 128p. 1987. 4.95 (*1-55601-012-5*) Great Sky.

Contemporary Diagnosis & Management of Pituitary Adenomas. Ed. by Paul R. Cooper. (Neurosurgical Topics Ser.). (Illus.). 176p. 1991. 90.00 (*0-9624246-7-6*) Am Assn Neuro.

***Contemporary Diagnosis & Management of the Patient with Epilepsy.** 2nd ed. Ilo E. Leppik. LC 93-79282. 1995. write for info. (*1-884065-02-3*) Assocs in Med.

***Contemporary Diagnosis & Management of Ulcerative Colitis & Proctitis.** Mark A. Peppercorn. LC 94-74425. 1995. write for info. (*1-884065-08-2*) Assocs in Med.

Contemporary Dictionary & Handbook of Economics, Finance & Statistics. Les Seplaki. 350p. 1992. pap. text ed. write for info. (*0-9618644-3-5*) Prof Homzons Pr.

***Contemporary Diesel Spotter's Guide.** 2nd ed. Marre. 352p. 1995. pap. text ed. 19.95 (*0-89024-257-1*, 01068) Kalmbach.

Contemporary Directions in Human Resource Management: A Sourcebook for Human Service Organizations. 300p. 1990. pap. 19.50 (*1-883066-01-8*) Natl Comm Mental.

Contemporary Directions in Psychopathology: Toward the DSM-IV. Ed. by Theodore Millon & Gerald L. Klerman. LC 85-30549. 737p. 1986. lib. bdg. 79.95 (*0-89862-659-5*) Guilford Pr.

Contemporary Director. Harold Chapman et al. 1986. pap. 14.00 (*0-88817-012-2*) NCBA.

Contemporary Doll Stars: Forty Years of the Best. A. Glenn Mandeville. (Illus.). 192p. 1992. pap. 14.95 (*0-87588-385-0*) Hobby Hse.

Contemporary Drama: Eleven Plays. Ed. by Bradlee E. Watson & Benfield Pressey. 341p. 1950. pap. write for info. (*0-02-424620-4*, Scribners) S&S Trade.

Contemporary Drama: Fifteen Plays. Bradlee E. Watson & Benfield Pressey. 577p. (C). 1950. pap. write for info. (*0-02-424630-1*, Scribners) S&S Trade.

Contemporary Drama of Russia. Leo Wiener. LC 71-149679. reprint ed. 39.50 (*0-404-06943-6*) AMS Pr.

Contemporary Dramatists. 4th ed. Ed. by D. L. Kirkpatrick. 785p. 1991. 130.00 (*0-912289-62-7*, 200029-M99019) St James Pr.

Contemporary Dramatists. 5th ed. Ed. by Kate Berney. 843p. 1993. lib. bdg. 135.00 (*1-55862-185-7*) St James Pr.

Contemporary Dramatists, Vol. 2. 6th ed. 1994. write for info. (*0-8103-9867-2*) Gale.

***Contemporary Dutch Linguistics.** fac. ed. Ed. by Flor Aarts & Theo Van Els. LC 89-28805. 169p. 1990. reprint ed. pap. 48.20 (*0-7837-7798-1*, 2047554) Bks Demand.

Contemporary East European Marxism, Vol. 1. Edward D'Angelo et al. (Praxis Ser.: Vol. 6). xii, 302p. 1980. pap. 35.00 (*90-6032-189-8*, Pub. by B R Gruener NE) Benjamins North Am.

Contemporary East European Marxism, Vol. 2. Edward D'Angelo et al. (Praxis Ser.: Vol. 7). vi, 283p. 1982. pap. 35.00 (*90-6032-217-7*, Pub. by B R Gruener NE) Benjamins North Am.

Contemporary East European Poetry: An Anthology. Ed. by Emery George. 544p. (C). 1994. 30.00 (*0-19-508635-X*, 982); pap. 16.95 (*0-19-508636-8*) OUP.

Contemporary Ecology of Arroyo Hondo, New Mexico. N. Edmund Kelley. LC 79-21351. (Arroyo Hondo Archaeological Ser.: Vol. 1). (Illus.). 159p. (Orig.). 1980. pap. 10.00 (*0-933452-01-2*) Schol Am Res.

Contemporary Economic Problems & Issues. 9th ed. Thomas J. Hailstones. (C). 1991. text ed. 23.95 (*0-538-80948-5*, HZ731A) S-W Pub.

Contemporary Economic Problems, 1978. American Enterprise Institute for Public Policy Research Staff. LC 78-14962. 368p. reprint ed. pap. 104.90 (*0-8357-4456-6*, 2037294) Bks Demand.

Contemporary Economic Problems, 1979. American Enterprise Institute for Public Policy Research Staff. 448p. reprint ed. pap. 127.70 (*0-8357-4457-4*, 2037295) Bks Demand.

Contemporary Economic Problems, 1980. American Enterprise Institute for Public Policy Research Staff. (Illus.). 352p. reprint ed. pap. 100.40 (*0-8357-4458-2*, 2037296) Bks Demand.

Contemporary Economic Systems: A Regional & Country Approach. Nicholas V. Gianaris. LC 92-23063. 224p. 1993. text ed. 55.00 (*0-275-94478-6*, C4478, Praeger Pubs) Greenwood.

Contemporary Economic Thought. Paul T. Homan. LC 68-20310. (Essay Index Reprint Ser.). 1977. 23.95 (*0-8369-0546-6*) Ayer.

Contemporary Economic Thought: The Contribution of Neo-Institutional Economics. Allan G. Gruchy. LC 79-184664. iv, 360p. 1972. 37.50 (*0-678-00898-1*) Kelley.

Contemporary Economics. 8th ed. Milton Spencer. 897p. 1993. 59.95x (*0-87901-614-0*); student ed, pap. 14.95 (*0-87901-636-1*) Worth.

Contemporary Economics: A Unifying Approach. David Z. Rich. LC 85-16762. 208p. 1985. text ed. 55.00 (*0-275-92033-X*, C2033, Praeger Pubs) Greenwood.

Contemporary Economists in Perspective, 2 vol. set. Ed. by William Briet & Kenneth G. Elzinga. (Political Economy & Public Policy Ser.: Vol. 1). 1983. 105.00 (*0-89232-347-7*) Jai Pr.

Contemporary Education in Perspective. Charles Gifford et al. 176p. (Orig.). 1989. pap. text ed. 16.95 (*0-8134-2841-6*) Interstate.

Contemporary Educational Psychology. 5th ed. Thomas L. Good & Jere E. Brophy. LC 93-50862. 1995. teacher ed write for info. (*0-8013-1268-X*, 79905) Longman.

Contemporary Educational Psychology. 5th rev. ed. Thomas L. Good & Jere Brophy. LC 93-50862. 784p. (C). 1995. pap. text ed. 47.50 (*0-8013-0775-9*, 78804) Longman.

Contemporary Educational Psychology: Concepts, Issues, Applications. Robert C. Craig et al. LC 74-13462. (Illus.). 570p. reprint ed. pap. 162.50 (*0-7837-3436-0*, 2057758) Bks Demand.

Contemporary Egypt - Through Egyptian Eyes: Essays in Honour of Professor P. J. Vatikiotis. Ed. by Charles R. Tripp. LC 92-13471. 160p. 1993. 59.95 (*0-415-06103-2*, A9594) Routledge.

Contemporary Electroanalytical Chemistry. Ed. by A. Ivaska et al. LC 90-27542. (Illus.). 468p. 1991. 120.00 (*0-306-43818-6*, Plenum Pr) Plenum.

Contemporary Electronic Communication. McGraw-Hill Continuing Education Center Staff. 368p. 1989. pap. text ed. 29.95 (*0-07-045078-1*) McGraw.

Contemporary Electronics Circuits Deskbook. Harry L. Helms. 272p. 1986. text ed. 45.00 (*0-07-027980-2*) McGraw.

Contemporary Embroidery: Exciting & Innovative Textile Art. Anne Morrell. (Illus.). 160p. 1994. 29.95 (*0-289-80105-2*, Pub. by Studio Vista Bks UK) Sterling.

Contemporary Endocrinology, Vol. 2. Ed. by Sidney Ingbar. LC 80-640369. 485p. 1985. 110.00 (*0-306-41746-4*, Plenum Med Bk) Plenum.

Contemporary Engineering Economics. Chan S. Park. (Illus.). 850p. (C). 1993. text ed. write for info. (*0-201-14508-1*); pap. text ed. 22.75 (*0-201-53277-8*) Addison-Wesley.

Contemporary English Crafts. Ed. & Intro. by Charles Harley. (Illus.). 59p. (Orig.). (C). 1991. pap. 9.95 (*1-880269-07-4*) D H Sheehan.

Contemporary English Drama. Ed. by Malcolm Bradbury et al. LC 81-81341. (Stratford-upon-Avon Studies: No. 19). 192p. (C). 1981. pap. 17.50 (*0-8419-0717-X*) Holmes & Meier.

Contemporary English Novel. Ed. by Malcolm Bradbury & David Palmer. LC 79-20447. (Stratford-upon-Avon Studies: No. 18). 214p. (C). 1979. pap. 19.50 (*0-8419-0571-1*) Holmes & Meier.

Contemporary English Poetry: An Introduction. Ed. by Anthony Thwaite. (Orig.). 1968. 9.95 (*0-435-18885-2*) Dufour.

Contemporary Entrepreneurs. Ed. by Craig E. Aronoff & John L. Ward. 450p. 1992. lib. bdg. 95.00 (*1-55888-315-0*) Omnigraphics Inc.

An Asterisk (*) at the beginning of an entry indicates that the title is appearing in BIP for the first time.

An Asterisk (*) at the beginning of an entry indicates that the title is appearing in BIP for the first time.

1577

An Asterisk (*) at the beginning of an entry indicates that the title is appearing in BIP for the first time.

C

An Asterisk (*) at the beginning of an entry indicates that the title is appearing in BIP for the first time.

1579

Contemporary Literary Criticism: Literary & Cultural Studies. 3rd ed. Davis & Schleifer. 704p. (C). 1994. text ed. 44.50 (*0-8013-1113-6*, 79572) Longman.

Contemporary Literary Criticism & Index, Vol. 57. Ed. by Roger Matuz. 1990. 122.00 (*0-8103-4449-1*) Gale.

Contemporary Literary Criticism & Index, Vol. 68. Roger Matuz. 1992. 122.00 (*0-8103-4445-9*) Gale.

Contemporary Literary Criticism Cumulative Index, Vol. 1-68. Ed. by Roger Matuz. 1992. write for info. (*0-8103-4444-0*) Gale.

Contemporary Literary Criticism, Vol. 33, Vol. 33. Ed. by Daniel G. Marowski & Jean Stine. 680p. 1985. 122.00 (*0-8103-4407-6*) Gale.

Contemporary Literary Criticism, Vol. 34, Vol. 34. Ed. by Sharon K. Hall. LC 76-38938. 822p. 1985. 122.00 (*0-8103-4408-4*) Gale.

Contemporary Literary Criticism, Vol. 48, Vol. 48. Ed. by Daniel G. Marowski & Roger Matuz. (Contemporary Literary Criticism Ser.). 600p. 1988. 122.00 (*0-8103-4422-X*) Gale.

Contemporary Literary Criticism, Vol. 49, Vol. 49. Daniel G. Marowski & Roger Matuz. 1988. 122.00 (*0-8103-4423-8*) Gale.

Contemporary Literary Criticism, Vol. 60, Vol. 60. Ed. by Roger Matuz. (Illus.). 525p. 1990. text ed. 122.00 (*0-8103-4434-3*) Gale.

Contemporary Literary Criticism, Vol. 61, Vol. 61. Ed. by Roger Matuz. (Illus.). 525p. 1990. text ed. 122.00 (*0-8103-4435-1*) Gale.

Contemporary Literary Criticism, Vol. 63: In, Vol. 63. Roger Matuz. 1991. 122.00 (*0-8103-4437-8*) Gale.

Contemporary Literary Criticism, Vol. 81: Yb 93, Vol. 81. 8th ed. Roger Matuz. 1994. 122.00 (*0-8103-4989-2*) Gale.

Contemporary Literary Criticism: Yearbook 1989, Vol. 59: The Year in Fiction, Poetry, Drama & World Literature & the Year's New Authors, Prizewinners, Obituaries, & Outstanding Literary Events, Vol. 59. Ed. by Roger Manuz. (Illus.). 525p. 1990. text ed. 122.00 (*0-8103-4433-5*) Gale.

***Contemporary Literary Criticism Yearbook, 1994: The Year in Fiction, Poetry, Drama, & World Literature, & the Year's New Authors, Prizewinners, Obituraries, & Outstanding Literary Events, Vol. 86.** Christopher Giroux. 500p. 1995. 122.00 (*0-8103-4996-5*) Gale.

Contemporary Literary Critics. 2nd ed. Ed. by Elmer Borklund. 600p. 1982. 80.00 (*0-912289-33-3*, 072025) St James Pr.

Contemporary Literary Scholarship: A Critical Review. Ed. by Lewis Leary. LC 58-6939. 1958. 49.50 (*0-89197-107-6*) Irvington.

Contemporary Literary Theory. Ed. by G. Douglas Atkins & Laura Morrow. LC 88-14692. 272p. (Orig.). (C). 1989. lib. bdg. 40.00 (*0-87023-641-5*); pap. 16.95 (*0-87023-642-3*) U of Mass Pr.

***Contemporary Literary Theory: A Christian Appraisal.** fac. ed. Ed. by Clarence Walhout & Leland Ryken. LC 91-36869. 316p. 1991. reprint ed. pap. 90.10 (*0-7837-7976-3*, 2047732) Bks Demand.

Contemporary Literary Theory: A Glossary. Jeremy Hawthorn. 224p. 1992. pap. 15.95 (*0-340-53911-9*, A7302, Pub. by E Arnold UK) Routledge Chapman & Hall.

Contemporary Literature & Social Revolution. R. D. Charques. LC 68-2035. (Studies in Comparative Literature: No. 35). 1969. reprint ed. lib. bdg. 75.00 (*0-8383-0654-3*) M S G Haskell Hse.

Contemporary Literature in Birmingham: An Anthology. Steven F. Brown. LC 82-60123. (Anthology Ser.). (Illus.). 240p. (Orig.). 12.00 (*0-918644-28-3*); pap. 7.00 (*0-918644-27-5*) Ford-Brown.

***Contemporary Living.** rev. ed. Verdene Ryder & Majorie B. Harter. (Illus.). 416p. 1995. 41.28 (*1-56637-099-X*) Goodheart.

***Contemporary Lodging Security.** Beaudry. 1995. write for info. (*0-7506-9574-9*, Focal) Buttrwrth-Heinemann.

Contemporary Logistics. 4th ed. James C. Johnson & Donald F. Wood. 698p. (C). 1990. write for info. (*0-02-360841-2*) Macmillan.

Contemporary Logistics. 5th ed. James C. Johnson & Donald F. Wood. LC 92-21954. 592p. (C). 1993. write for info. (*0-02-360851-X*) Macmillan.

Contemporary Logo Papers. Ed. by Deakin University Press Staff. 68p. (C). 1986. 40.00 (*0-7300-0444-9*, Pub. by Deakin Univ AT) St Mut.

Contemporary Look at the Formula of Concord. Ed. by R. Preus & W. Rosin. 304p. 1987. 15.95 (*0-570-03271-7*, 15HH2716) Concordia.

Contemporary Loomed Beadwork. Therese Spears. (Illus.). 24p. 1987. pap. text ed. 5.95 (*0-932255-02-7*) Promenade Pub.

Contemporary Louisiana & French-Speaking Canada: 1673-1989. Alfred O. Hero, Jr. (Tulane University Series in Political Science). 350p. (C). 1994. lib. bdg. 61.00 (*0-8191-9630-4*); pap. text ed. 26.50 (*0-8191-9631-2*) U Pr of Amer.

Contemporary Low Voice. Comp. by Ken Bible. 1990. 16.95 (*0-8341-9089-3*, MB-616) Lillenas.

Contemporary Macedonian Poetry. Ed. & Tr. by Ewald Osers. (Illus.). 223p. (Orig.). 1992. pap. 21.00 (*0-948259-67-1*, Pub. by Forest Bks UK) Dufour.

Contemporary Macroeconomics. 8th ed. Milton Spencer. 529p. 1993. 42.95 (*0-87901-615-9*); student ed, pap. 10.95 (*0-87901-637-X*) Worth.

***Contemporary Mainstream Religion: Studies from Humberside & Lincolnshire.** Ed. by Peter Forster. 169p. 1995. 51.95 (*1-85628-919-2*, Pub. by Avebury Pub UK) Ashgate Pub Co.

Contemporary Management. C. B. Gupta. (C). 1992. 32.00 (*81-7024-438-2*, Pub. by Ashish II) S Asia.

Contemporary Management. 2nd ed. David D. Van Fleet. (C). 1991. write for info. (*0-395-47223-7*) HM Soft Schl Col Div.

Contemporary Management of Impotence & Infertility. Emil A. Tanagho et al. (Illus.). 400p. 1988. 92.00 (*0-683-08101-2*) Williams & Wilkins.

Contemporary Management of Motor Control Problems: Proceedings of the II Step Conference. 279p. 1991. 39.95 (*0-9628807-0-1*) FPT VA.

***Contemporary Management of Spinal Cord Injury.** Ed. by Edward Benzel & Charles Tator. 275p. 1995. 90.00 (*1-879284-30-8*) Am Assn Neuro.

Contemporary Management of Ventricular Arrhythmias. Ed. by Arnold J. Greenspon & Harvey L. Waxman. LC 70-6558. (Cardiovascular Clinics Ser.: Vol. 22, No. 1). 368p. 1992. text ed. 75.00 (*0-8036-4343-8*) Davis Co.

***Contemporary Manufacturing Processes.** J. Barry DuVall. (Illus.). 350p. (C). 1995. pap. text ed. 38.00 (*1-56637-158-9*) Goodheart.

Contemporary Marathi Literature. Vishwas R. Kanadey. (C). 1990. text ed. 22.50 (*0-685-39105-1*, Pub. by BR Pub II) S Asia.

Contemporary Marathi Literature. Vishwas R. Kanadey. (C). 1991. 16.00 (*81-7018-628-5*, Pub. by BR Pub II) S Asia.

Contemporary Marketing. Gordon Wills. 1971. 24.95 (*0-8464-0279-3*) Beekman Pubs.

Contemporary Marketing. 6th ed. Louis E. Boone & David L. Kurtz. LC 87-38143. (Illus.). 768p. (C). 1989. text ed. 53.00 (*0-03-022814-X*) Dryden Pr.

Contemporary Marketing. 7th ed. Louis E. Boone & David L. Kurtz. 700p. (C). 1992. text ed. 57.25 (*0-03-054018-6*) Dryden Pr.

***Contemporary Marketing & Consumer Behavior: An Anthropological Sourcebook.** John F. Sherry, Jr. LC 95-3257. 440p. 1995. 59.95 (*0-8039-5752-1*); pap. 27.95 (*0-8039-5753-X*) Sage.

Contemporary Marketing Research. 2nd ed. Carl McDaniel, Jr. & Roger H. Gates. Ed. by Leyh. LC 92-17896. 750p. (C). 1993. text ed. 64.00 (*0-314-01026-2*) West Pub.

Contemporary Marriage: Comparative Perspectives on a Changing Institution. Ed. by Kingsley Davis & Amyra Grossbard-Shechtman. LC 85-62452. 360p. (C). 1986. 20.00 (*0-87154-221-8*) Russell Sage.

Contemporary Marx. Mihailo Markovic. 224p. 1986. 40.00 (*0-685-12447-9*, Bertrand Russell Soc) St Mut.

Contemporary Marxist Literary Criticism. Francis Mulhern. 280p. (C). 1993. pap. text ed. 18.50 (*0-582-05976-3*, 79363) Longman.

Contemporary Masters. World Print Council Staff. 60p. 1983. 10.00 (*0-9602496-4-8*); 8.00 (*0-685-08941-X*) World Print Coun.

***Contemporary Masters in Criminology.** Ed. by Joan McCord & John H. Laub. (Plenum Series in Crime & Justice). 410p. 1995. 65.00 (*0-306-44960-9*) Plenum.

Contemporary Masterworks. Ed. by Colin Naylor. (Illus.). 933p. 1992. lib. bdg. 139.00 (*1-55862-083-4*, 200104) St James Pr.

***Contemporary Materialism: A Reader.** Ed. by Paul K. Moser & J. D. Trout. LC 94-32686. 400p. 1995. 65.00x (*0-415-10863-2*, B7037); pap. 22.95 (*0-415-10864-0*, B7041, Routledge NY) Routledge.

Contemporary Mathematics. 4th ed. Bruce E. Meserve et al. (Illus.). 720p. 1986. text ed. write for info. (*0-13-170127-4*) P-H.

Contemporary Medical Office Procedures. Doris Humphrey. 576p. (C). 1990. pap. 33.95 (*0-538-70015-7*, RL43AB) S-W Pub.

***Contemporary Medical Office Procedures.** 2nd ed. Doris D. Humphrey. LC 95-6199. 1995. write for info. (*0-8273-7420-8*) Delmar.

Contemporary Medical Physiology. Robert L. Vick. 1056p. 1984. write for info. (*0-201-08095-8*) Addison-Wesley.

Contemporary Mediterranean World. Ed. by Carl F. Pinkele & Adamantia Pollis. LC 82-16658. 394p. 1983. text ed. 59.95 (*0-275-91058-X*, C1058, Praeger Pubs) Greenwood.

Contemporary Memoirs of Russia from the Year 1727 to 1744. Christof H. Von Mastein. (Russia Through European Eyes Ser.). 1968. reprint ed. lib. bdg. 49.50 (*0-306-77027-X*) Da Capo.

Contemporary Metabolism, Vol. 2. Ed. by Norbert Freinkel. LC 79-643531. (Illus.). 564p. 1982. 95.00 (*0-306-40954-2*, Plenum Med Bk) Plenum.

Contemporary Mexican-American Women Novelists: Toward a Feminist Identity. Maria Gonzalez. LC 93-50801. (Worlds of Change Ser.: Vol. 3). 1994. write for info. (*0-8204-2415-3*) P Lang Pubs.

Contemporary Mexican Artists. Chavez A. Velazquez. LC 77-88034. (Essay Index Reprint Ser.). 1977. 22.95 (*0-8369-1159-8*) Ayer.

***Contemporary Mexican Drama in Translation: Azcarate, Rascon, Urtusastegui, Vol. I.** Leonor Azcarate et al. Ed. & Tr. by Myra S. Gann. LC 94-69405. (Illus.). 144p. (Orig.). 1994. per., pap. text ed. 15.00 (*0-9643288-0-1*) Danzon Pr.

***Contemporary Mexican Drama in Translation: Azcarate, Rascon, Urtusastegui, Vol. 1.** Ed. & Tr. by Myra S. Gann. LC 94-27836. 1994. write for info. (*0-8191-9660-6*); pap. write for info. (*0-8191-9661-4*) U Pr of Amer.

***Contemporary Mexican Painting in a Time of Change.** Shifra M. Goldman. LC 94-44853. (Illus.). 256p. 1995. pap. 29.95 (*0-8263-1562-3*) U of NM Pr.

Contemporary Michigan Poetry: Poems from The Third Coast. Ed. by Conrad Hilberry et al. LC 88-133. (Great Lakes Bks.). (Illus.). 362p. 1988. 34.95 (*0-8143-1923-8*); pap. 15.95 (*0-8143-1924-6*) Wayne St U Pr.

Contemporary Microbial Ecology. Ed. by D. C. Ellwood et al. 1980. text ed. 157.00 (*0-12-236550-X*) Acad Pr.

Contemporary Microcomputer Tools. Baker et al. 720p. (C). 1991. pap. text ed. 32.00 (*0-87835-544-8*, J34) Boyd & Fraser.

Contemporary Microeconomics. 8th ed. Milton Spencer. 561p. 1993. pap. 42.95x (*0-87901-616-7*); student ed, pap. 10.95x (*0-87901-638-8*) Worth.

Contemporary Modal Improvisation. Date not set. 9.95 (*0-7866-0072-1*, 95241); audio 9.98 (*0-7866-0073-X*, 95241C) Mel Bay.

Contemporary Monetary Economics Theory & Policy. Chaman L. Jain. LC 79-55682. (Illus.). 266p. (Orig.). 1981. text ed. 29.50 (*0-932126-02-2*); pap. text ed. 17.50 (*0-932126-03-0*) Graceway.

Contemporary Monetary Theory. Raymond J. Saulnier. LC 70-12744. (Columbia University. Studies in the Social Sciences: No. 443). reprint ed. 27.50 (*0-404-51443-X*) AMS Pr.

***Contemporary Money Banking & Financial Institutions: Theory & Practice.** Michael Hadjimichalakis & Karma Hadjimichalakis. 784p. (C). 1995. text ed. 62.95 (*0-256-06069-X*) Irwin.

Contemporary Moral Controversies in Business. Ed. by A. Pablo Iannone. (Illus.). 608p. (C). 1989. pap. text ed. 23.00 (*0-19-505679-5*) OUP.

Contemporary Moral Controversies in Technology. Ed. by A. Pablo Iannone. 351p. (C). 1987. 52.00 (*0-19-504124-0*); pap. text ed. 16.95 (*0-19-504125-9*) OUP.

Contemporary Moral Issues Facing the Orthodox Christian. S. S. Harakas. 1982. pap. 8.95 (*0-937032-24-7*) Light&Life Pub Co MN.

Contemporary Moral Problems. 3rd ed. James E. White. Ed. by Baxter. 477p. (C). 1991. pap. text ed. 37.25 (*0-314-77301-0*) West Pub.

Contemporary Moral Problems. 4th ed. Ed. by James E. White & Baxter. LC 93-25928. 550p. (C). 1994. pap. text ed. 41.50 (*0-314-02738-6*) West Pub.

Contemporary Mormonism: Social Science Perspectives. Ed. by Marie Cornwall et al. LC 93-6438. (Illus.). 368p. 1994. 32.50 (*0-252-02076-6*) U of Ill Pr.

Contemporary Morphology. Ed. by Dressler et al. (Trends in Linguistics, Studies & Monographs: No. 49). ix, 317p. (C). 1990. lib. bdg. 106.15 (*3-11-012349-5*) Mouton.

Contemporary Motivated Mathematics, Bk. 1. Stanley Bezuszka et al. (Contemporary Motivated Mathematics Ser.). 97p. (Orig.). (gr. 5-8). 1972. pap. text ed. 2.50 (*0-917916-02-6*) Boston Coll Math.

Contemporary Motivated Mathematics, Bk. 2. Stanley Bezuszka et al. (Contemporary Motivated Mathematics Ser.). 97p. (Orig.). (gr. 6-9). 1973. pap. text ed. 2.50 (*0-917916-03-4*) Boston Coll Math.

Contemporary Motivated Mathematics, Bk. 3. Stanley Bezuszka et al. (Contemporary Motivated Mathematics Ser.). 97p. (Orig.). (gr. 7-10). 1972. pap. text ed. 2.50 (*0-917916-04-2*) Boston Coll Math.

***Contemporary Movements & Ideologies.** Roberta Garner. LC 95-16727. 1995. write for info. (*0-07-022900-7*) McGraw.

Contemporary Movements in European Literature. Ed. by William Rose & Jacob Isaacs. (Essay Index Reprint Ser.). 1977. 20.95 (*0-8369-0833-3*) Ayer.

Contemporary Movie Hits. (Piano-Vocal-Guitar Ser.). 128p. (Orig.). 1991. pap. 10.95 (*0-7935-1110-0*, 00311541) H Leonard.

Contemporary Movie Monologues: A Sourcebook for Actors. Jocelyn A. Beard. 1991. pap. 8.95 (*0-449-90354-0*) Fawcett.

Contemporary Music Education. 2nd ed. Michael L. Mark. 368p. (C). 1985. text ed. 29.00 (*0-02-871220-X*) Schirmer Bks.

Contemporary Music Education. 2nd rev. ed. Clifford K. Madsen & Terry L. Kuhn. LC 77-90672. 186p. (C). 1994. pap. text ed. 17.95x (*0-89892-119-8*) Contemp Pub Co of Raleigh.

Contemporary Music Review. J. Kondo et al. 1988. pap. text ed. 9.00 (*3-7186-4846-6*) Gordon & Breach.

Contemporary Music Review: Listening. 2nd ed. J. Kondo et al. 66p. 1988. 17.00 (*0-318-39919-9*) Gordon & Breach.

Contemporary Musicians, Vol. 1. Michael L. LaBlanc. 1989. 65.00 (*0-8103-2211-0*) Gale.

Contemporary Musicians, Vol. 3. Ed. by Michael L. LaBlanc. 300p. 1990. 65.00 (*0-8103-2213-7*) Gale.

Contemporary Musicians, Vol. 4. 1990. 65.00 (*0-8103-2214-5*) Gale.

Contemporary Musicians, Vol. 5. 1991. 65.00 (*0-8103-2215-3*) Gale.

Contemporary Musicians, Vol. 6. 1991. 65.00 (*0-8103-2216-1*) Gale.

Contemporary Musicians, Vol. 7. 1992. 65.00 (*0-8103-5402-0*) Gale.

Contemporary Musicians, Vol. 8. 1992. 65.00 (*0-8103-5403-9*) Gale.

Contemporary Musicians, Vol. 9. 1993. 65.00 (*0-8103-2217-X*) Gale.

Contemporary Musicians, Vol. 10. 1993. 65.00 (*0-8103-2218-8*) Gale.

Contemporary Musicians, Vol. 11. La Blanc. 1994. 65.00 (*0-8103-8552-X*, 004903) Gale.

Contemporary Musicians, Vol. 12. La Blanc. 1994. 65.00 (*0-8103-8553-8*, 004904) Gale.

***Contemporary Musicians: Profiles of the People in Music, Vol. 13.** Ed. by Suzanne M. Bourgoin. 322p. 1994. 63.00 (*0-8103-5737-2*) Gale.

Contemporary Musicians, Vol. 2: Profiles of the People in Music, Vol. 2. Michael L. LaBlanc. 350p. 1989. 65.00 (*0-8103-2212-9*) Gale.

Contemporary Muslim Movement in the Philippines. Cesar A. Majul. LC 85-21519. 158p. (Orig.). (C). 1985. 15.95 (*0-933782-16-0*); pap. 8.95 (*0-933782-17-9*) Mizan Pr.

Contemporary Muslim World: Notes on Current Muslim World. A. Iqbal. 27.50 (*0-935782-63-X*) Kazi Pubns.

***Contemporary Mystery Writers.** Ed. by Harold Bloom. (Writers of English: Lives & Works Ser.). 200p. Date not set. 24.95 (*0-7910-2216-1*) Chelsea Hse.

***Contemporary Mystery Writers.** Ed. by Harold Bloom. (Writers of English: Lives & Works Ser.). 200p. Date not set. pap. 12.95 (*0-7910-2241-2*) Chelsea Hse.

Contemporary Narrative of the Proceedings Against Dame Alice Kyteler. Alice Kyteler. Ed. by Thomas Wright. LC 38-36518. (Camden Society, London. Publications Ser.: No. 24). (LAT.). reprint ed. 35.00 (*0-404-50124-9*) AMS Pr.

Contemporary Nationalism in East Central Europe: Unfinished Business. Ed. by Paul Latawski. LC 94-16291. 1994. write for info. (*0-312-12276-4*) St Martin.

Contemporary Nationalisms: Intensity & Persistence. Louis L. Snyder. LC 91-14474. (Anvil Ser.). 234p. 1992. pap. 13.50 (*0-89464-570-6*) Krieger.

Contemporary Native American Literature: A Selected & Partially Annotated Bibliography. Angeline Jacobson. LC 77-5614. 1977. lib. bdg. 25.00 (*0-8108-1031-X*) Scarecrow.

Contemporary Navajo Affairs. Norman Eck. 244p. 1982. 24.00 (*0-936008-05-9*) Rough Rock Pr.

Contemporary Navajo Weaving: Thoughts That Count. Ann L. Hedlund. (Plateau Ser.: Vol. 65, No. 1). 32p. 1994. pap. 6.95 (*0-89734-118-X*) Mus Northern Ariz.

Contemporary Neon: Architecture-Graphics-Products-Sculpture. Rudi Stern. (Illus.). 192p. 1990. 49.95 (*0-934590-37-0*) Retail Report.

Contemporary Nephrology, Vol. 1. Ed. by Saulo Klahr & Shaul G. Massry. 736p. 1981. 125.00 (*0-306-40664-0*, Plenum Med Bk) Plenum.

Contemporary Nephrology, Vol. 2. Ed. by Saulo Klahr & Shaul G. Massry. 818p. 1983. 125.00 (*0-306-41303-5*, Plenum Med Bk) Plenum.

Contemporary Nephrology, Vol. 3. Ed. by Saulo Klahr & Shaul G. Massry. 792p. 1985. 125.00 (*0-306-41984-X*, Plenum Med Bk) Plenum.

Contemporary Nephrology, Vol. 4. Ed. by Saulo Klahr & Shaul G. Massry. (Illus.). 774p. 1987. 125.00 (*0-306-42531-9*, Plenum Med Bk) Plenum.

Contemporary Neuropsychology & the Legacy of Luria. E. Goldberg. 304p. (C). 1990. text ed. 69.95 (*0-8058-0334-3*) L Erlbaum Assocs.

Contemporary New Communities Movement in the United States. Ed. by Gideon Golany & Daniel Walden. LC 74-13861. (Illus.). 168p. reprint ed. pap. 47.90 (*0-8357-6077-4*, 2034432) Bks Demand.

Contemporary New England Stories. Ed. by C. Michael Curtis. LC 92-26894. 320p. 1993. 19.95 (*1-56440-067-0*); pap. 16.95 (*1-56440-246-0*) Globe Pequot.

Contemporary New Mexico, 1940-1990. Ed. by Richard W. Etulain. LC 93-32426. 219p. 1994. pap. 19.95 (*0-8263-1486-4*) U of NM Pr.

Contemporary News Reporting. Douglas A. Anderson & Bruce D. Itule. 352p. 1984. pap. 15.00 (*0-394-32891-4*) Random.

Contemporary Newsmakers, 1985: Cumulation. Ed. by Ann Evory & Peter M. Gareffa. 1986. 89.00 (*0-8103-2201-3*) Gale.

Contemporary Newsmakers, 1986: Cumulation. Ed. by Peter M. Gareffa. 1987. 89.00 (*0-8103-2202-1*) Gale.

Contemporary Newsmakers, 1987: Cumulation. Ed. by Peter M. Gareffa. 440p. 1988. 89.00 (*0-8103-2203-X*) Gale.

Contemporary Newspaper Design: A Structural Approach. 3rd ed. Mario R. Garcia. LC 92-25405. 304p. 1992. text ed. write for info. (*0-13-174871-8*); pap. text ed. write for info. (*0-13-174905-6*) P-H.

Contemporary Newtonian Research. Zav Bechler. 1982. lib. bdg. 89.00 (*90-277-1303-0*) Kluwer Ac.

Contemporary Nonlinear Optics. Ed. by Govind P. Agrawal & Robert W. Boyd. (Quantum Electronics Ser.). (Illus.). 478p. 1992. text ed. 85.00 (*0-12-045135-2*) Acad Pr.

Contemporary Northwest Writing: A Collection of Poetry & Fiction. Ed. by Roy Carlson. 208p. 1979. text ed. 24.95 (*0-87071-324-8*); pap. text ed. 15.95 (*0-87071-323-X*) Oreg St U Pr.

***Contemporary Novel in France.** Ed. by William Thompson. 408p. 1995. lib. bdg. 49.95 (*0-8130-1409-3*) U Press Fla.

Contemporary Novelists. 5th ed. Ed. by Lesley Henderson. 1053p. 1992. lib. bdg. 120.00 (*1-55862-036-2*, 200031) St James Pr.

Contemporary Nutrition: Issues & Insights. Wardlaw et al. 768p. 1993. pap. 43.95 (*0-8016-7760-2*) Mosby Yr Bk.

Contemporary Nutrition: Issues & Insights. Gordon M. Wardlaw et al. 768p. 1991. pap. 43.95 (*0-8016-2348-0*) Mosby Yr Bk.

Contemporary Nutrition, Diet Analysis Quick Reference. Wardlaw & Insel. 61p. 1992. spiral bd. 8.95 (*0-8016-7166-3*) Mosby Yr Bk.

Contemporary Nutrition Student Study Guide. Wardlaw et al. 320p. 1991. pap. 15.95 (*0-8016-2340-5*) Mosby Yr Bk.

Contemporary Nutrition Text. Wardlaw et al. 1992. 3.5 hd 44.95 (*0-8016-6873-5*); 5.25 hd 44.95 (*0-8016-6874-3*) Mosby Yr Bk.

Contemporary Object Lessons for Children's Church. Lois Edstrom. (Object Lesson Ser.). 112p. 1986. pap. 5.99 (*0-8010-3432-9*) Baker Bk.

Contemporary Obstetrics. Ed. by Geoffrey Chamberlain. (Illus.). 304p. (Orig.). 1984. pap. text ed. 45.00 (*0-407-00291-X*) Buttrwrth-Heinemann.

Contemporary Obstetrics & Gynecology. Geoffrey Chamberlain. 434p. 1988. pap. text ed. 110.00 (*0-407-01580-9*) Buttrwrth-Heinemann.

An Asterisk (*) at the beginning of an entry indicates that the title is appearing in BIP for the first time.

C

An Asterisk (*) at the beginning of an entry indicates that the title is appearing in BIP for the first time.

1581

Contemporary Psychiatry: Selected Reviews from the British Journal of Hospital Medicine. Ed. by Trevor Silverstone & Brian Barraclough. LC 75-325901. (British Journal of Psychiatry. Special Publication Ser.: No. 9). 488p. reprint ed. pap. 139.10 (0-318-34927-2, 2031464) Bks Demand.

Contemporary Psychoanalysis & Eastern Thought. John R. Suler. LC 92-30817. (SUNY Series, Alternatives in Psychology). 292p. (C). 1993. 59.50 (0-7914-1577-5); pap. 19.95 (0-7914-1578-3) State U NY Pr.

Contemporary Psychological Approaches to Depression: Theory, Research, & Treatment. Ed. by R. E. Ingram. LC 90-43004. (Illus.). 210p. 1990. 59.50 (0-306-43690-6, Plenum Pr) Plenum.

***Contemporary Psychology: An Introduction.** Ed. by Clive R. Hollin. LC 95-1198. (Contemporary Psychology Ser.). 272p. 1995. 75.00 (0-7484-0191-1); pap. 24.95 (0-7484-0192-X) Taylor & Francis.

Contemporary Psychology: Biological Processes & Theoretical Issues see International Congress of Psychology of the International Union of Psychological Science, XXIII, Acapulco, Mexico, 2-7 September 1984: Proceedings

Contemporary Psychology Plus Discovery Journal. 7th ed. Charles Morris & James C. Coleman. (C). 1990. text ed. 53.00 (0-673-46051-7) HarpCollege.

Contemporary Public Administration. Dennis J. Palumbo & Steven W. Maynard-Moody. 385p. (C). 1991. text ed. 47.95 (0-8013-0033-9, 75698) Longman.

Contemporary Public Administration. Ed. by David H. Rosenbloom et al. LC 93-47904. 1994. write for info. (0-07-053939-1) P-H Gen Ref & Trav.

Contemporary Public Administration. Ed. by Thomas Vocino & Jack Rabin. 490p. (C). 1981. text ed. 37.25 (0-15-513682-8) HB Coll Pubs.

Contemporary Public Finance. Nicholas V. Gianaris. LC 88-25186. 285p. 1989. text ed. 59.95 (0-275-93044-0, C3044, Praeger Pubs) Greenwood.

Contemporary Public Opinion: Issues & the News. Maxwell McCombs et al. (Communication Textbook Series, Journalism Subseries). 128p. 1991. text ed. 29.95 (0-8058-0537-0); pap. 14.95 (0-8058-1102-8) L Erlbaum Assocs.

Contemporary Public Policy Analysis. Stuart S. Nagel. 192p. 1984. pap. 10.50 (0-8173-0163-1) U of Ala Pr.

Contemporary Public Policy Perspectives & Black Americans: Issues in an Era of Retrenchment Politics. Ed. by Mitchell F. Rice & Woodrow Jones, Jr. LC 84-717. (Contributions in Afro-American & African Studies: No. 77). (Illus.). xiii, 213p. 1984. text ed. 55.00 (0-313-23711-5, RIP/) Greenwood.

Contemporary Public Sculpture: Tradition, Transformation, & Controversy. Harriet F. Senie. (Illus.). 272p. 1992. 35.00 (0-19-507318-5) OUP.

***Contemporary Public Speaking: Principles for Success.** Donald Simmons. (C). 1994. write for info. (0-8403-9439-X) Kendall-Hunt.

***Contemporary Public Speaking: Principles for Success.** Donald Simmons. (C). 1994. vhs write for info. (0-8403-9623-6) Kendall-Hunt.

***Contemporary Public Speaking: Principles for Success, Value Pak.** Donald Simmons. 432p. (C). 1994. 54.95 (0-8403-9624-4) Kendall-Hunt.

Contemporary Quantitive Ecology & Related Ecometrics. Ed. by G. P. Patil & M. L. Rosenzweig. (Statistical Ecology Ser.: Vol. 12). 1979. 60.00 (0-89974-009-X) Intl Co-Op.

Contemporary Quebec & the United States, 1960-1985. Alfred O. Hero, Jr. & Louis Balthazar. LC 87-35996. 548p. (Orig.). (C). 1988. lib. bdg. 48.00 (0-8191-6876-9, Ctr Intl Affairs Harvard); pap. text ed. 29.50 (0-8191-6877-7, Ctr Intl Affairs Harvard) U Pr of Amer.

Contemporary Quebec Criticism. Tr. by Larry Shouldice. 1979. pap. 9.95 (0-8020-6376-4) U of Toronto Pr.

Contemporary Queen Rearing. Harry H. Laidlaw. LC 79-50568. (Illus.). (C). 1979. 11.40 (0-915698-05-6) Dadant & Sons.

Contemporary Questions Surrounding the Constitutional Amending Process. John R. Vile. LC 92-41606. 200p. 1993. text ed. 52.95 (0-275-94541-3, C4541, Praeger Pubs) Greenwood.

Contemporary Quilting Techniques: A Modular Approach. Patricia Cairns. LC 91-53042. (Illus.). 160p. 1991. pap. 18.95 (0-8019-8125-5) Chilton.

Contemporary Quilts: A Stunning Collection from International Designers. Barbara Hallas. (Illus.). 64p. 1994. pap. 16.95 (0-85532-774-X, Pub. by Search Pr UK) A Schwartz & Co.

Contemporary Quilts: Spirit of the 90's. Kalamazoo Institute of Arts Staff. (KIA Bulletin Ser.: No. 83). 12p. (Orig.). 1992. write for info. (0-933742-22-3) Kalamazoo Inst Arts.

***Contemporary Racial & Ethnic Relations.** Charles Jaret. LC 94-25051. (C). 1995. 50.00 (0-673-38769-0) HarpCollege.

Contemporary Radio Programming Strategies. David T. MacFarland. (CTS Broadcasting Ser.). 224p. 1990. pap. text ed. 22.50 (0-8058-0665-2) L Erlbaum Assocs.

Contemporary Radio Programming Strategies. Ed. by David T. MacFarland. 244p. (C). 1990. text ed. 49.95 (0-8058-0664-4) L Erlbaum Assocs.

Contemporary Ragtime Guitar. Stefan Grossman. (Illus.). 112p. pap. 12.95 (0-8256-0130-4, OK62547, Oak) Music Sales.

Contemporary Reader. Ed. by Gary Goshgarian. LC 92-18333. (C). 1992. teacher ed 7.20 (0-673-52222-9) HarpCollege.

Contemporary Reader. 3rd ed. Gary Goshgarian. (C). 1989. pap. text ed. 17.50 (0-673-52001-3) HarpCollege.

Contemporary Reader. 4th ed. Gary Goshgarian. (C). 1992. 25.00 (0-673-52221-0) HarpCollege.

***Contemporary Reader, Bk. 2.** Contemporary Books Staff. LC 94-32588. 1994. pap. 5.95 (0-8092-3462-9) Contemp Bks.

Contemporary Reader for Creative Writing. Ed. by Robert DeMaria & Ellen H. Meyer. 320p. (Orig.). (C). 1993. pap. text ed. 18.75 (0-15-500727-0) HB Coll Pubs.

Contemporary Readings in Articulation Disorders. Bennett et al. 400p. (C). 1982. per. 36.95 (0-8403-2656-4) Kendall-Hunt.

Contemporary Readings in Epistemology. Michael F. Goodman & Robert A. Snyder. LC 92-30053. 416p. 1992. pap. text ed. write for info. (0-13-174541-7) P-H.

Contemporary Readings in Family & Human Development. Ed. by Jackie Mize & Connie Salts. 200p. (C). 1988. pap. text ed. 15.95 (0-89892-075-2) Contemp Pub Co of Raleigh.

Contemporary Readings in Social & Political Ethics. Ed. by Garry Brodsky et al. LC 84-42957. 435p. (Orig.). (C). 1984. pap. text ed. 25.95x (0-87975-265-3) Prometheus Bks.

Contemporary Readings in Social Psychology. Ed. by David A. Schroeder et al. LC 84-19027. 450p. (C). 1984. pap. text ed. 24.95 (0-8304-1093-7) Nelson-Hall.

Contemporary Readings of Medieval Literature. Ed. by Guy Mermier. LC 81-50963. (Michigan Romance Studies: Vol. 8). 226p. (Orig.). 1989. pap. 9.00 (0-939730-07-3) Mich Romance.

Contemporary Realism. Ed. by Joseph Hildreth & Georgia Coopersmith. (Illus.). 68p. 1982. pap. 7.95 (0-942746-00-7) SUNYP R Gibson.

Contemporary Reception of Classical Rhetoric: Appropriations of Ancient Discourse. Kathleen E. Welch. (Communication Ser.). 200p. 1990. 45.00 (0-8058-0131-6); pap. 19.95 (0-8058-1126-5) L Erlbaum Assocs.

Contemporary Reefs. B. V. Preobrazhensky. Tr. by R. Chakravarty. (Russian Translation Ser.: No. 100). (Illus.). 326p. (ENG.). 1993. text ed. 110.00 (90-6191-945-2, Pub. by A A Balkema NE) Ashgate Pub Co.

Contemporary Reflections on the Medieval Christian Tradition: Essays in Honor of Ray C. Petry. George H. Shriver. LC 73-77639. 285p. reprint ed. pap. 81.30 (0-317-20414-9, 2023448) Bks Demand.

Contemporary Reform Response. Solomon B. Freehof. LC 74-23748. 319p. reprint ed. pap. 91.00 (0-8357-8082-1, 2034160) Bks Demand.

Contemporary Relevance of History: A Study in Approaches & Methods. Salo W. Baron. LC 86-2244. 192p. 1986. text ed. 42.50 (0-231-06336-9) Col U Pr.

Contemporary Religions: A World Guide. 600p. 1993. 175.00 (0-582-08695-7, 072470, Pub. by Longman Grp UK) Gale.

Contemporary Religious Ideas: Bibliographic Essays. Ed. by Edward Lundin & Anne H. Lundin. (Illus.). 250p. 1995. lib. bdg. 37.50 (0-87287-679-9) Libs Unl.

Contemporary Religious Poetry. Ed. by Paul Ramsey. 224p. 1987. pap. 9.95 (0-8091-2883-7) Paulist Pr.

Contemporary Republic of China: The Taiwan Experience, 1950-1980. Ed. by James C. Hsiung. LC 81-11993. 540p. 1981. text ed. 75.00 (0-275-90649-3, C0649, Praeger Pubs) Greenwood.

Contemporary Research in Philosophical Logic & Linguistic Semantics. Ed. by Donald Hockney et al. LC 74-34079. (Western Ontario Ser.: No. 4). 330p. (Orig.). 1975. lib. bdg. 112.50 (90-277-0511-9); pap. text ed. 65.50 (90-277-0512-7) Kluwer Ac.

Contemporary Research in Population Geography: A Comparison of the United Kingdom and the Netherlands. Ed. by John C. Stillwell & Henk J. Scholten. (C). 1989. lib. bdg. 112.50 (0-7923-0431-4) Kluwer Ac.

***Contemporary Research in Romance Linguistics: Papers from the 22nd Linguistics Symposium on Romance Languages, El Paso-Cd. Juarez, February 1992.** Linguistic Symposium on Romance Languages Staff. Ed. by Jon Amastae et al. LC 95-15320. (Current Issues in Linguistic Theory Ser.: No. 123). 400p. 1995. lib. bdg. 95.00x (1-55619-577-X) Benjamins North Am.

Contemporary Research in the Foundations & Philosophy of Quantum Theory. Ed. by Clifford A. Hooker. LC 72-83377. (Western Ontario Ser.: No. 2). (Illus.). 385p. 1973. lib. bdg. 112.50 (90-277-0271-3); pap. text ed. 64.50 (90-277-0338-8) Kluwer Ac.

Contemporary Research on Renal Cell Carcinoma: Basic & Clinical Developments. Ed. by G. Staehler & S. Pomer. LC 93-23588. 1994. 88.00 (0-387-57375-5) Spr-Verlag.

Contemporary Research on Terrorism. Ed. by P. Wilkinson & A. M. Stewart. 654p. 1989. text ed. 90.00 (0-08-035068-2, Pub. by Aberdeen U Pr); pap. text ed. 39.00 (0-08-036600-7, Pub. by Aberdeen U Pr) Macmillan.

Contemporary Retailing. 2nd ed. John L. Beisel. (Illus.). 720p. (C). 1993. teacher ed write for info. (0-318-69281-3); text ed. write for info. (0-02-307866-9) Macmillan.

Contemporary Reviews in Neuropsychology. Ed. by H. A. Whitaker. (Neuropsychology Ser.). (Illus.). 200p. 1988. 54.00 (0-387-96606-4) Spr-Verlag.

Contemporary Reviews of Romantic Poetry. Ed. by John Wain. LC 75-76920. (Essay Index Reprint Ser.). 1977. 20.95 (0-8369-0033-2) Ayer.

Contemporary Rhetoric: Conceptual Background with Readings. Ed. by W. Ross Winterowd. 380p. (C). 1975. pap. text ed. 25.50 (0-15-513715-8) HB Coll Pubs.

Contemporary Rhythm & Dynamics: Ten Contemporary EZ Duets. Yoon-Il Auh. (Auh School of Violin Ser.). 20p. (J). (gr. 4-12). 1986. student ed 10.00 (1-882858-40-9) Yoon-il Auh.

Contemporary Rhythm & Dynamics, Bk. I. Yoon-Il Auh. (Auh School of Violin Ser.). 20p. (J). (gr. 1-12). 1986. student ed 10.00 (1-882858-43-3) Yoon-il Auh.

Contemporary Rhythm & Dynamics, Bk. II. Yoon-Il Auh. (Auh School of Violin Ser.). 20p. (J). (gr. 1-12). 1986. student ed 10.00 (1-882858-44-1) Yoon-il Auh.

Contemporary Roumania & Her Problems: A Study in Modern Nationalism. Joseph S. Roucek. LC 74-135831. (Eastern Europe Collection Ser.). 1971. reprint ed. 30.95 (0-405-02773-7) Ayer.

Contemporary Rural Iran. Abdolali Lahsaeizadeh. 366p. 1993. 68.95 (1-85628-417-4, Pub. by Avebury Pub UK) Ashgate Pub Co.

Contemporary Rural Systems in Transition, Vol. 1: Agriculture & Environment. Ed. by I. R. Bowler et al. 250p. 1992. 66.50 (0-85198-811-3) CAB Intl.

Contemporary Rural Systems in Transition, Vol. 2: Ecology & Society. Ed. by I. R. Bowler et al. 250p. 1992. 76.00 (0-85198-812-1) CAB Intl.

Contemporary Rural Systems in Transition, Vol. 2: Ecology & Society, 2 vols., Set. Ed. by I. R. Bowler et al. 250p. 1992. 133.00 (0-85198-813-X) CAB Intl.

Contemporary Russian Art. S. Cullerne Bown. (C). 1990. 250.00 (0-685-34370-7, Pub. by Collets) St Mut.

Contemporary Russian Composers. Montagu Montagu-Nathan. LC 72-109795. 329p. 1970. reprint ed. text ed. 65.00 (0-8371-4285-7, MORC, Greenwood Pr) Greenwood.

Contemporary Russian Composers. Montagu Montagu-Nathan. 329p. 1990. reprint ed. lib. bdg. 79.00 (0-7812-9041-4) Rprt Serv.

Contemporary Russian Drama. Ed. by Franklin D. Reeve. LC 68-20138. 1968. 39.00 (0-672-53521-1); pap. text ed. 14.95 (0-8290-2101-9) Irvington.

Contemporary Russian Novelists. Serge M. Persky. Tr. by Frederick Eisemann. LC 68-26468. (Essay Index Reprint Ser.). 1977. 20.95 (0-8369-0784-1) Ayer.

Contemporary Russian Poetry: A Bilingual Anthology. Tr. & Intro. by Gerald S. Smith. LC 92-17482. 416p. 1993. 39.95 (0-253-35333-5); pap. 17.50 (0-253-20769-X, MB-769) Ind U Pr.

***Contemporary Russian Satire: A Genre Study.** Karen L. Ryan-Hayes. (Cambridge Studies in Russian Literature). 270p. (C). 1995. write for info. (0-521-47515-5) Cambridge U Pr.

Contemporary Sages: The Great Chasidic Masters of the Twentieth Century. Avraham Y. Finkel. LC 94-3078. 248p. 1994. 45.00 (1-56821-155-4) Aronson.

Contemporary Saxophone. John Laughter. 56p. 1992. pap. text ed. 15.95 (0-931759-58-7) Centerstream Pub.

Contemporary Scenes for Student Actors. Ed. by Michael Schulman & Eva Mekler. (Orig.). 1980. pap. 10.95 (0-14-048153-2, Penguin Bks) Viking Penguin.

Contemporary School Administration: An Introduction. Theodore J. Kowalski & Ulrich C. Reitzug. LC 92-27033. 368p. (C). 1993. text ed. 47.95 (0-8013-0832-1, 78899) Longman.

Contemporary School Psychology. 2nd ed. William G. Herron et al. LC 83-15325. 405p. 1984. 29.50 (0-910328-17-X); pap. 19.50 (0-910328-16-1) Sulzburger & Graham Pub.

Contemporary Science & Natural Explanations: Commonsense Conceptions of Causality. Ed. by Denis J. Hilton. 288p. 1988. 55.00 (0-8147-3443-X) NYU Pr.

Contemporary Science Fiction Authors. R. Reginald. LC 74-16517. (Science Fiction Ser.). (Illus.). 358p. 1976. reprint ed. 26.95 (0-405-06332-6) Ayer.

Contemporary Science Fiction, Fantasy, & Horror Poetry: A Resource Guide & Biographical Directory. Scott E. Green. LC 89-16966. 234p. 1989. text ed. 45.00 (0-313-26324-8, GCF/, Greenwood Pr) Greenwood.

***Contemporary Science Fiction Writers.** Ed. by Harold Bloom. (Writers of English: Lives & Works Ser.). 200p. Date not set. 24.95 (0-7910-2217-X) Chelsea Hse.

***Contemporary Science Fiction Writers.** Ed. by Harold Bloom. (Writers of English: Lives & Works Ser.). 200p. Date not set. pap. 12.95 (0-7910-2242-0) Chelsea Hse.

Contemporary Scottish Verse. George B. Douglas. LC 70-144504. (Canterbury Poets Ser.). reprint ed. 49.50 (0-404-08633-0) AMS Pr.

Contemporary Secrets to Finding Love. Richard H. Price. 172p. 1994. pap. 12.95 (1-885280-09-2) Golf Supplies.

Contemporary Serbian Literature. Ante Kadic. 1964. pap. text ed. 19.25 (0-279-1006-5) Mouton.

Contemporary Sexual Mores. Ed. by Leonore Teifer & Gene Brown. (Great Contemporary Issues Ser.). 38.95 (0-405-13939-X) Ayer.

Contemporary Shakespeare: Volume VII-King Henry VI, Part One, King Henry VI, Part Two, King Henry VI, Part Three, King John, Pericles, Titus Andronicus. Ed. by A. L. Rowse. LC 84-5105. (Modern Text with Introduction Ser.). 724p. (C). 1987. lib. bdg. 27.50 (0-8191-3947-5) U Pr of Amer.

Contemporary Shakespeare Series, Vol. I: Macbeth, All's Well That Ends Well, Henry V, King Richard, III & The Taming of the Shrew. A. L. Rowse. LC 84-5105. 650p. (C). 1985. lib. bdg. 27.50 (0-8191-3908-4) U Pr of Amer.

Contemporary Shakespeare Series, Vol. III: Hamlet, Julius Caesar, Merchant of Venice, A Midsummer Night's Dream, Romeo & Juliet, The Tempest. Ed. by A. L. Rowse. LC 84-5105. 690p. (C). 1984. lib. bdg. 27.50 (0-8191-3922-X) U Pr of Amer.

Contemporary Shakespeare Series, Vol. IV: King Henry IV, Pt. I, King Henry IV, Pt. II, Love's Labour's Lost, Othello, The Winter's Tale: Modern Text. William Shakespeare. Ed. & Intro. by A. L. Rowse. LC 84-5105. 650p. 1985. lib. bdg. 27.50 (0-8191-3928-9) U Pr of Amer.

Contemporary Short Stories & Representive Selections, Vol. 2. Ed. by Maurice Baudin, Jr. 1954. pap. 4.35 (0-672-60017-X, AHS13, Bobbs) Macmillan.

Contemporary Short Stories from Central America. Ed. by Enrique J. Levi & Leland H. Chambers. (Institute of Latin American Studies). 320p. (Orig.). (C). 1994. text ed. 37.50 (0-292-74030-1); pap. 15.95 (0-292-74034-4) U of Tex Pr.

Contemporary Slide Guitar. Arvid Smith, Jr. & Barbara Koehler. 1993. 5.95 (0-87166-660-X, 93373); audio 15.95 (0-87166-662-6, 93373); audio 10.98 (0-87166-661-8, 93373) Mel Bay.

***Contemporary Social & Political Philosophy.** James P. Sterba. LC 94-35331. 136p. 1995. pap. 17.95 (0-534-23970-6) Intl Thomson.

Contemporary Social Dance. Skippy Blair. (Ballroom Dance Ser.). 1986. lib. bdg. 71.20 (0-8490-3270-9) Gordon Pr.

Contemporary Social Dance. Skippy Blair. (Ballroom Dance Ser.). 1985. lib. bdg. 70.00 (0-87700-860-4) Revisionist Pr.

Contemporary Social Issues: A Reader. Ed. by Rose Giallombardo. LC 74-32306. (Illus.). 623p. reprint ed. pap. 177.60 (0-317-09399-1, 2055104) Bks Demand.

Contemporary Social Philosophy. Gordon Graham. 224p. 1988. pap. text ed. 21.95 (0-631-15986-X) Blackwell Pubs.

Contemporary Social Problems. 2nd ed. Vincent N. Parrillo et al. 660p. (C). 1989. write for info. (0-02-391731-8) Macmillan.

Contemporary Social Problems. 4th ed. Ed. by Robert K. Merton & Robert A. Nisbet. 782p. (C). 1976. text ed. 40.00 (0-15-513793-X); International ed. write for info. (0-318-52965-3) HB Coll Pubs.

Contemporary Social Spirituality. Ed. by Francis X. Meehan. LC 82-2253. 133p. (Orig.). 1982. pap. 14.95 (0-88344-022-9) Orbis Bks.

Contemporary Social Welfare. 2nd ed. Winifred Bell. vii, 524p. (C). 1987. text ed. write for info. (0-02-307941-X) Macmillan.

Contemporary Socialist Thought: A Critical Study. Vinay K. Malhotra. 1990. 54.00 (81-7041-235-8, Pub. by Anmol II) S Asia.

Contemporary Societies: Problems & Prospects. Ed. by Daniel J. Curran & Claire M. Renzetti. LC 93-3837. 1993. pap. text ed. write for info. (0-13-177031-4) P-H.

Contemporary Society. 7th ed. Perry. (C). 1993. text ed. 32.25 (0-673-99034-6) HarpCollege.

Contemporary Society. 7th ed. Perry. (C). 1993. Study guide. student ed 14.50 (0-673-99038-9) HarpCollege.

Contemporary Sociolinguistics: Theory, Problems, Methods. Aleksandr D. Svejcer. LC 86-3555. (Linguistic & Literary Studies in Eastern Europe: No. 15). vii, 193p. 1985. 91.00x (90-272-1519-7) Benjamins North Am.

Contemporary Sociological Theory. Warren H. Handel. 240p. 1993. text ed. write for info. (0-13-175423-8) P-H.

Contemporary Sociological Theory. Ruth A. Wallace & Alison Wolf. LC 79-13971. (Sociology Ser.). (Illus.). 1980. text ed. 26.95 (0-685-03804-1) P-H.

Contemporary Sociological Theory. 3rd ed. George Ritzer. 1992. text ed. write for info. (0-07-052973-6) McGraw.

***Contemporary Sociological Theory: Continuing the Classical Tradition.** 4th ed. Ruth A. Wallace & Alison Wolf. LC 94-43559. 448p. 1995. text ed. write for info. (0-13-036245-X) P-H.

Contemporary Songs in English. Ed. by Bernard Taylor. (Illus.). 80p. 1961. pap. 10.95 (0-8258-0155-9, 0-3819) Fischer Inc NY.

Contemporary Source for the Siege of Constantinople 1453: The Sphrantzes Chronicle. Georgios Sphrantzes. Tr. & Intro. by M. Carrol. 198p. 1985. text ed. 52.00 (0-317-57958-4, Pub. by A M Hakkert SP) Coronet Bks.

Contemporary Southern Political Attitudes & Behavior: Studies & Essays. Ed. by Laurence W. Moreland et al. LC 81-15694. 314p. 1982. text ed. 55.00 (0-275-90864-X, C0864, Praeger Pubs) Greenwood.

***Contemporary Southern Women Fiction Writers.** Rosemary M. Reisman & Christopher J. Canfield. 237p. 1994. 32.50 (0-8108-2832-4) Scarecrow.

***Contemporary Southwest: The Cafe Terra Cotta Cookbook.** Donna Nordin. LC 94-37365. (Illus.). 168p. 1995. 26.95 (0-9627345-8-6, Astolat Bks) Harlow & Ratner.

Contemporary Southwest Art. Ed. by M. Robert Rich et al. 52p. 1988. 5.00 (0-942746-14-7) SUNYP R Gibson.

Contemporary Southwestern Quilts. Mary E. Dillon. LC 89-42850. (Illus.). 192p. 1989. pap. text ed. 14.95 (0-8019-7977-3) Chilton.

Contemporary Soviet City. Ed. by Henry W. Morton & Robert C. Stuart. LC 83-8543. 288p. 1984. pap. 44.95 (0-87332-254-1) M E Sharpe.

Contemporary Soviet Economics: A Collection of Readings from Soviet Sources, Vol. 1. Murray Yanowitch. LC 68-14426. 202p. reprint ed. pap. 57.60 (0-317-29616-7, 2021864) Bks Demand.

Contemporary Soviet Education: A Collection of Readings from Soviet Journals. Ed. by Fred Ablin. LC 68-14428. 309p. reprint ed. pap. 88.10 (0-317-41930-7, 2026141) Bks Demand.

Contemporary Soviet Interviews. G. Scanlan. 44p. (C). 1985. 35.00 (0-317-92470-2, Pub. by Collets UK) Pro-Am Music.

Contemporary Soviet Military Affairs: The Legacy of World War II. Jonathan R. Adelman & Cristann L. Gibson. 256p. 1989. 55.00 (0-04-445031-1) Routledge Chapman & Hall.

Contemporary Soviet Politics. 4th ed. Donald D. Barry & Carol Barner-Barry. 400p. (C). 1990. pap. text ed. write for info. (0-13-170424-9) P-H.

An Asterisk (*) at the beginning of an entry indicates that the title is appearing in BIP for the first time.

An Asterisk (*) at the beginning of an entry indicates that the title is appearing in BIP for the first time.

1583

Contemporary Women Writers: Hong Kong & Taiwan. Ed. by Eva Hung. (Illus.). xii, 130p. 1992. reprint ed. pap. 10.50 (962-7255-08-4, Pub. by Renditions Papbk HK) SPD-Small Pr Dist.
Contemporary Women Writers in Italy: A Modern Renaissance. Ed. by Santo L. Arico. LC 89-28436. 248p. (C). 1990. lib. bdg. 30.00x (0-87023-710-1) U of Mass Pr.
Contemporary Women Writers of Spain. Janet Perez & Paul W. Horn. (World Authors Ser.: No. 798). 256p. 1988. text ed. 26.95 (0-8057-8229-X, Twayne) Macmillan.
Contemporary Women's Fiction: Narrative Practice & Feminist Theory. Paulina Palmer. 232p. 1989. 32.50 (0-87805-396-4) U Pr of Miss.
Contemporary World: Conflict or Co-Operation? 2nd ed. Jim Cannon et al. (Illus.). 128p. (Orig.). (YA). (gr. 9-12). 1979. pap. text ed. 23.76 (0-05-003734-X, 70092) Longman.
Contemporary World Gold Coins: Comprehensive Catalog. Sanford J. Durst. (Illus.). 128p. 1975. 10.00 (0-915262-01-0) S J Durst.
Contemporary World History, Nineteen Seventeen to Nineteen Forty-Five. V. Alexandrov. 718p. (C). 1986. 78.00 (0-685-31478-2, Pub. by Collets UK) Pro-Am Music.
Contemporary World Issues. Light & Lan-Ying. 1989. pap. 20.95 (0-8384-3328-6) Heinle & Heinle.
Contemporary World Theology. Harvie M. Conn. LC 72-97711. 1974. pap. 5.99 (0-87552-149-5) Presby & Reformed.
Contemporary World Writers. 2nd ed. Ed. by Tracy Chevalier. 686p. 1993. lib. bdg. 135.00 (1-55862-200-4) St James Pr.
***Contemporary Worship for the 21st Century: Worship or Evangelism?** LC 94-68463. 128p. 1994. pap. 14.95 (0-88177-138-4, DR138) Discipleship Res.
Contemporary Worship Services. James L. Christensen. LC 75-137445. 256p. reprint ed. pap. 73.00 (0-8357-9517-9, 2011444) Bks Demand.
Contemporary Writer: A Practical Rhetoric. 3rd ed. W. Ross Winterowd & John S. Nixon. 516p. (C). 1989. pap. text ed. 24.00 (0-15-513728-X); pap. text ed. 2.00 (0-15-513729-8) HB Coll Pubs.
Contemporary Writer: Interviews with Sixteen Novelists & Poets. Ed. by L. S. Dembo & Cyrena N. Pondrom. LC 71-176410. 318p. 1972. pap. 12.95 (0-299-06144-2) U of Wis Pr.
Contemporary Writers. Virginia Woolf. Ed. by Leonard Woolf. LC 76-15984. 1976. pap. 2.45 (0-15-621450-4) HarBrace.
***Contemporary Writing Curriculum: Rehearsing, Composing, & Valuing.** fac. ed. Roland Huff & Charles R. Kline. LC 87-14315. 243p. 1987. reprint ed. pap. 69.30 (0-7837-8207-1, 2047965) Bks Demand.
Contemporary Writing from the Continents: Retrospective. Ed. by Rainer Schulte. 450p. 1981. pap. 20.00 (0-939378-01-9) Mundus Artium.
Contemporary Yugoslav Literature: Sociopolitical Approach. Sveta Lukic. Ed. by Gertrude J. Robinson. Tr. by Pola Triandis. LC 77-166116. 296p. reprint ed. pap. 84.40 (0-317-09655-9, 2020864) Bks Demand.
Contemporary Yugoslav Poetry. Ed. by Vasa D. Mihailovich. LC 77-22865. (Iowa Translations Ser.). 290p. reprint ed. pap. 82.70 (0-317-42148-4, 2025936) Bks Demand.
Contemporary Zoroastrians: An Unstructured Nation. Rashna Writer. 292p. (C). 1993. lib. bdg. 42.50 (0-8191-9142-6) U Pr of Amer.
Contemporary's Foundations Writing. Pamela Bliss & Virginia Lowe. Ed. by Pat Fiene. LC 93-16325. (Contemporary's Foundations Ser.). 1993. pap. 10.33 (0-8092-3829-2) Contemp Bks.
Contemporary's GED: How to Prepare for the High School Equivalency Examination. 816p. 1994. pap. 11.95 (0-8092-3777-6) Contemp Bks.
Contempory Logic Design. Randy Katz. 699p. (C). 1994. text ed. 68.95 (0-8053-2703-7) Benjamin-Cummings.
Contempory Minority Nationalism. Ed. by Michael Watson. 288p. 1990. 74.50 (0-415-00065-3, A4702) Routledge.
***Contempt for Acting.** Uta Hagen-Dasz. 144p. 1994. pap. 6.95 (1-56850-045-9) Chicago Plays.
Contempt of Congress: A Study of the Prosecutions Initiated by the Committee on Un-American Activities, 1945-1957. Carl Beck. LC 75-166090. (American Constitutional & Legal History Ser.). 264p. 1974. reprint ed. lib. bdg. 32.50 (0-306-70229-0) Da Capo.
Contempt of Court. V. G. Ramachandran. (C). 1992. 170.00 (81-7012-483-2, Pub. by Eastern Book II) St Mut.
Contempt of Court. Fred West. LC 90-80882. 210p. 1990. pap. 13.95 (0-89420-267-7, 341240) Natl Book.
Contempt of Court. 2nd ed. C. J. Miller. (Illus.). 552p. 1991. reprint ed. pap. 45.00 (0-19-825684-1) OUP.
Contempt of Court. 5th ed. V. G. Ramachandran & Gopalan. 1146p. 1983. 420.00 (0-317-54659-7) St Mut.
Contempt of Court. 6th ed. V. G. Ramachandran & Gopalan. (C). 1991. 110.00 (0-685-39766-1) St Mut.
Contempt of Court in Labor Injunction Cases. Cleon O. Swayzee. LC 68-58627. (Columbia University. Studies in the Social Sciences: No. 409). reprint ed. 21.00 (0-404-51409-X) AMS Pr.
Contempt of Freedom: The Russian Experiment & After. Michael Polanyi. LC 74-29384. (History, Philosophy & Sociology of Science Ser.). 1979. reprint ed. 18.95 (0-405-06643-0) Ayer.
Contempt Power. Ronald L. Goldfarb. LC 63-20342. 366p. 1963. text ed. 51.00 (0-231-02654-4) Col U Pr.
Contempts by Publication: The Law of Trial by Newspaper. 3rd ed. Harold W. Sullivan. xiv, 230p. 1980. reprint ed. lib. bdg. 24.00 (0-8377-1114-2) Rothman.
Contender. Robert Lipsyte. LC 67-19623. 190p. (YA). (gr. 7-9). 1967. lib. bdg. 14.89 (0-06-023920-4) HarpC Child Bks.
Contender. Robert Lipsyte. LC 67-19623. (Trophy Keypoint Bk.). 176p. (YA). (gr. 7 up). 1987. pap. 3.95 (0-06-447039-3, Trophy) HarpC Child Bks.
***Contender.** Charles White. 1995. 10.95 (0-8062-5296-0) Carlton.
Contender: A Study Guide. Dorothy Collaci. (Novel-Ties Ser.). (J). 1989. student ed, teacher ed 15.95 (0-88122-059-0) Lrn Links.
***Contenders.** White Wolf Staff. (Streetfighter Ser.). 128p. 1995. per., pap. 12.95 (1-56504-551-3, 04551) White Wolf.
Contenders. Terence Winch. 151p. (Orig.). 1989. pap. 11.95 (0-934257-23-X) Story Line.
Contending Approaches to the Political Economy of Taiwan. Ed. by Edwin A. Winckler & Susan M. Greenhalgh. LC 87-16413. (Taiwan in the Modern World Ser.). 334p. 1988. text ed. 62.95 (0-87332-440-4); pap. text ed. 25.95 (0-87332-771-3) M E Sharpe.
Contending Dramas: A Cognitive Approach to International Organization. Ed. by Martha L. Cottam & Chih yu Shih. LC 91-30947. 280p. 1992. text ed. 59.95 (0-275-93526-4, C3526, Praeger Pubs) Greenwood.
Contending for the Authentic. James W. Hayford, Sr. 192p. (Orig.). 1992. pap. write for info. (0-9634445-3-0) Servant Minist.
***Contending for the Faith.** David R. Barnhart. 214p. (Orig.). 1994. pap. 9.95 (0-9617377-2-7) Abiding Word Pubns.
Contending for the Faith. J. Jacqueline Phelps. 1994. 8.75 (0-8062-4930-7) Carlton.
Contending for the Faith. D. L. Welch. LC 87-31730. (Illus.). 288p. (Orig.). 1988. pap. 7.99 (0-932581-26-9) Word Aflame.
***Contending for the Faith Study Guide.** David R. Barnhart. 120p. (Orig.). 1994. pap. 5.00 (0-9617377-3-5) Abiding Word Pubns.
Contending Forces: A Romance Illustrative of Negro Life in the North & South. Pauline E. Hopkins. (Schomburg Library of Nineteenth-Century Black Women Writers). 450p. 1988. 29.95 (0-19-505258-7) OUP.
Contending Forces: A Romance Illustrative of Negro Life in the North & South. Pauline E. Hopkins. (Schomburg Library of Nineteenth-Century Black Women Writers). (Illus.). 464p. 1991. reprint ed. pap. 13.95 (0-19-506785-1) OUP.
Contending Forces: A Romance Illustrative of Negro Life North & South. Pauline E. Hopkins. LC 78-144639. (Illus.). reprint ed. 29.50 (0-404-00173-4) AMS Pr.
Contending Forces: Romances Illustrative of Negro Life, North & South. Pauline E. Hopkins. LC 72-83909. (Black Heritage Library Collection). 1977. 32.95 (0-8369-8602-4) Ayer.
Contending Ideologies in South Africa. Ed. by James Leatt et al. LC 86-531. 328p. (Orig.). reprint ed. pap. 93.50 (0-685-23458-4, 2032736) Bks Demand.
Contending Kingdoms: Historical, Psychological, & Feminist Approaches to the Literature of Sixteenth-Century England & France. Ed. by Marie-Rose Logan & Peter L. Rudnytsky. LC 90-12798. 373p. (C). 1991. text ed. 44.95 (0-8143-2149-6); pap. text ed. 24.95 (0-8143-2150-X) Wayne St U Pr.
Contending Rhetorics: Writing in Academic Disciplines. George L. Dillon. LC 90-25572. (Illus.). 196p. 1991. 27.50 (0-253-31743-6) Ind U Pr.
Contending Sovereignties: Redefining Political Community. Ed. by R. B. Walker & Saul H. Mendlovitz. LC 90-8109. 190p. 1990. lib. bdg. 35.00 (1-55587-186-0) Lynne Rienner.
Contending Theories of Development in the Contemporary International Order - Disorder: Lessons from Kenya & Tanzania. Mulugeta Agonafer. 254p. (Orig.). (C). 1994. lib. bdg. 34.50 (0-8191-9621-5) U Pr of Amer.
Contending Theories of International Relations: A Comprehensive Survey. 3rd ed. James E. Dougherty & Robert L. Pfaltzgraff, Jr. 624p. (C). 1990. pap. text ed. 43.00 (0-06-041706-4) HarpCollege.
Contending to Be the Dream. David Curry. (Illus.). 1978. pap. 3.00 (0-912284-99-4) New Rivers Pr.
Contending with Hitler: Varieties of German Resistance in the Third Reich. Ed. by David C. Large. (Publications of the German Historical Institute, Washington, D.C.). 208p. (C). 1992. 42.95 (0-521-41459-8) Cambridge U Pr.
Contending with Hitler: Varieties of German Resistance in the Third Reich. Ed. by David C. Large. (Publications of the German Historical Institute, Washington, D.C.). 205p. (C). 1994. pap. 13.95 (0-521-46668-7) Cambridge U Pr.
Contending with Kennan: Toward a Philosophy of American Power. Barton D. Gellman. LC 08-4553. 192p. 1984. text ed. 49.95 (0-275-91737-1, C1737, Praeger Pubs) Greenwood.
Contending with Kennan: Toward a Philosophy of American Power. Barton D. Gellman. LC 08-4553. 192p. 1985. pap. text ed. 11.95 (0-275-91805-X, B1805, Praeger Pubs) Greenwood.
***Contending with Modernity: Catholic Higher Education in Twentieth Century America.** Philip Gleason. 496p. 1995. 35.00 (0-19-509828-5) OUP.
Contending with the Dark & Against That Time. Jeffrey Schwartz & Ron Schreiber. LC 77-93269. 88p. 1978. pap. 9.95 (0-914086-22-7) Alicejamesbooks.
Contending with Words: Composition & Rhetoric in a Postmodern Age. Ed. by Patricia Harkin & John Schilb. LC 91-13016. 242p. 1991. text ed. 37.50 (0-87352-387-3, J309C); pap. text ed. 19.75 (0-87352-388-1, J309P) Modern Lang.
Content-Addressable Memories. 2nd ed. T. Kohonen. (Information Sciences Ser.: Vol. 1). 400p. 1989. pap. 50.00 (0-387-17625-X, 542) Spr-Verlag.
Content Analysis: An Introduction to Its Methodology. Klaus Krippendorff. LC 80-19166. (CommText Ser.: Vol. 5). (Illus.). 191p. 1980. 37.00 (0-8039-1497-0); pap. 16.95 (0-8039-1498-9) Sage.
Content Analysis of Verbal Behavior Based on the Gottschalk-Glaser Method: New Findings & Clinical Applications. Louis A. Gottschalk. 232p. 1994. text ed. 49.95 (0-8058-1558-9) L Erlbaum Assocs.
***Content & Communication.** Ed. by Martin Greenberger. (Technologies for the Twenty-First Century Ser.: Vol. 5). 404p. (Orig.). 1994. pap. 29.95 (1-886313-94-6) Coun For Tech.
Content & Consciousness. Daniel C. Dennett. (International Library of Philosophy). 208p. 1986. pap. 16.95 (0-415-10431-9, 08464) Routledge.
Content & Consciousness. 2nd ed. D. C. Dennett. (International Library of Philosophy). 208p. (C). 1986. pap. text ed. 13.95 (0-7102-0846-4, RKP) Routledge.
Content & Context: Essays on College Education. Ed. by Carl Kaysen. LC 73-8858. (Carnegie Commission on Higher Education Ser.). 587p. reprint ed. pap. 167.30 (0-317-55383-6, 2029490) Bks Demand.
Content & Context of the Visual Arts in the Islamic World. Ed. by Priscilla P. Soucek. LC 85-43605. (College Art Association Monographs on the Fine Arts: No. XLIV). (Illus.). 288p. 1988. lib. bdg. 42.50 (0-271-00614-5) Pa St U Pr.
Content & Context of Zulu Folk-Narratives. Brian M. Du Toit. LC 76-28522. (University of Florida Monographs: Social Sciences: No. 58). 104p. reprint ed. pap. 29.70 (0-7837-4908-2, 2044573) Bks Demand.
Content & Process Specificity in the Effects of Prior Experiences. Ed. by T. K. Srull & Robert S. Wyer. (Advances in Social Cognition Ser.: Vol. III). 208p. (C). 1990. 39.95 (0-8058-0700-4); pap. 22.50 (0-8058-0714-4) L Erlbaum Assocs.
Content & Taste: Religion & Myth. Ed. by Peter Davison et al. LC 77-90615. (Literary Taste, Culture & Mass Communication Ser.: Vol. 7). 338p. 1978. lib. bdg. 100.00 (0-85964-042-6) Chadwyck-Healey.
Content Area ESL: Social Studies. Dennis Terdy. Ed. by Linda Mrowicki. (Illus.). 169p. (J). (gr. 5-12). 1986. pap. 8.95 (0-916591-06-9) Linmore Pub.
Content Area Reading. 3rd ed. Richard T. Vacca & JoAnne L. Vacca. (C). 1989. text ed. 35.50 (0-673-39820-X) HarpCollege.
Content Area Reading. 4th ed. Richard T. Vacca. (C). 1993. 54.50 (0-673-52215-6) HarpCollege.
Content Area Reading: A Heuristic Approach. Manzo. 528p. (C). 1990. text ed. write for info. (0-675-20652-9, Merrill Pub Co) Macmillan.
Content Area Reading: An Integrated Approach. 3rd ed. John E. Readence et al. 384p. 1992. per. 32.95 (0-8403-6735-X) Kendall-Hunt.
Content Area Reading Skills-Competency Canada: Main Idea. Stuart Paltrowitz & Donna Paltrowitz. (Illus.). (J). (gr. 4). 1987. pap. text ed. 3.25 (0-89525-853-6) Ed Activities.
Content Area Reading Skills-Competency Mexico: Locating Details. Stuart Paltrowitz & Donna Paltrowitz. (Illus.). (J). (gr. 4). 1987. pap. text ed. 3.25 (0-89525-854-4) Ed Activities.
Content Area Reading Skills-Competency U. S. History: Detecting Sequence. Stuart Paltrowitz & Donna Paltrowitz. (Illus.). (J). (gr. 4). 1987. pap. text ed. 3.25 (0-89525-856-0) Ed Activities.
Content Area Reading Skills Electricity & Magnetism. Johanna P. Pomeroy. (Illus.). (J). (gr. 4). 1987. pap. text ed. 3.25 (0-89525-859-5) Ed Activities.
Content Area Reading Skills Geology: Detecting Sequence. Johanna P. Pomeroy. (Illus.). (J). (gr. 4). 1987. pap. text ed. 3.25 (1-55737-085-0) Ed Activities.
Content Area Reading Skills Light: Main Idea. Johanna P. Pomeroy. (Illus.). (J). (gr. 3). 1989. pap. text ed. 3.25 (1-55737-687-5) Ed Activities.
Content Area Reading Skills Machines: Detecting Sequence. Johanna P. Pomeroy. (Illus.). (J). (gr. 3). 1989. pap. text ed. 3.25 (1-55737-690-5) Ed Activities.
Content Area Reading Skills Matter: Locating Details. Johanna P. Pomeroy. (Illus.). (J). (gr. 4). 1988. pap. text ed. 3.25 (1-55737-086-9) Ed Activities.
Content Area Reading Skills Mechanics: Cause & Effect. Johanna P. Pomeroy. (Illus.). (J). (gr. 4). 1988. pap. text ed. 3.25 (1-55737-088-5) Ed Activities.
Content Area Reading Skills Oceans: Main Idea. Johanna P. Pomeroy. (Illus.). (J). (gr. 4). 1987. pap. text ed. 3.25 (0-89525-857-9) Ed Activities.
Content Area Reading Skills Our Earth: Locating Details. Johanna P. Pomeroy. (Illus.). (J). (gr. 3). 1989. pap. text ed. 3.25 (1-55737-688-3) Ed Activities.
Content Area Reading skills Reproduction & Heredity: Main Idea. Johanna P. Pomeroy. (Illus.). (J). (gr. 4). 1988. pap. text ed. 3.25 (1-55737-087-7) Ed Activities.
Content Area Reading Skills Solar System: Locating Details. Johanna P. Pomeroy. (Illus.). (J). (gr. 4). 1987. pap. text ed. 3.25 (0-89525-858-7) Ed Activities.
Content Area Reading Skills Sound & Hearing: Detecting Sequence. Johanna P. Pomeroy. (Illus.). 1987. pap. text ed. 3.25 (0-89525-860-9) Ed Activities.
Content Area Reading Skills U. S. Geography: Cause & Effect. Stuart Paltrowitz & Donna Paltrowitz. (Illus.). (J). (gr. 4). 1987. pap. text ed. 3.25 (0-89525-855-2) Ed Activities.
Content Area Reading Skills Weather: Cause & Effect. Johanna P. Pomeroy. (Illus.). (J). (gr. 3). 1989. pap. text ed. 3.25 (1-55737-689-1) Ed Activities.
Content Areas. Mary F. Pecci. (Super Seatwork Ser.). (Illus.). 168p. 1984. 11.95 (0-943220-01-7) Pecci Educ Pubs.
Content-Based Second Language Instruction. Donna M. Brinton & Snow. 1990. pap. 21.95 (0-8384-2677-8) Heinle & Heinle.
Content Connection: How to Integrate Thinking & Writing in the Content Areas, Grades 4-8. Hilarie N. Staton. 1991. pap. 13.95 (0-673-46083-5) GdYrBks.
Content Core, Vol. I: A Guide for Curriculum Designers. rev. ed. 160p. 1993. pap. text ed. 16.95 (0-87355-107-9) Natl Sci Tchrs.
Content Family Collection of Ancient Cameos. Martin Henig. (Illus.). 220p. (C). 1990. 88.50 (0-935681-01-9) D J Content.
***Content Literacy.** Gordon. 1994. pap. write for info. (0-409-90545-3, Focal) Buttrwrth-Heinemann.
Content of Culture: Constants & Variants. Ed. by Ralph Bolton. LC 87-80184. (Anthology Ser.). 567p. 1989. 45.00 (0-87536-118-8) HRAFP.
Content of Faith: The Best of Karl Rahner's Theological Writings. Karl Rahner. Ed. by Karl Lehmann et al. 600p. 1993. 42.50 (0-8245-1221-9) Crossroad NY.
Content of Motion Pictures. Edgar Dale. LC 77-124026. (Literature of Cinema Ser.). 1970. reprint ed. 19.95 (0-405-01644-1) Ayer.
Content of Our Character: A New Vision of Race in America. Shelby Steele. LC 90-56430. 192p. 1991. reprint ed. pap. 12.00 (0-06-097415-X, PL) HarpC.
Content of Product Specification Sheets for Microform Readers & Reader-Printers: AIIM TR16-1988. Association for Information & Image Management Staff. 1988. pap. 30.00 (0-318-42059-7, TR16) Assn Inform & Image Mgmt.
Content of Religious Instruction: A Social Science Approach. James M. Lee. LC 84-18255. 815p. (Orig.). 1985. pap. 15.95 (0-89135-050-0) Religious Educ.
Content of Science: A Constructive Approach to Its Teaching & Learning. Ed. by Peter J. Fensham et al. LC 93-32464. 274p. 1994. 85.00 (0-7507-0220-6, Falmer Pr); pap. 30.00 (0-7507-0221-4, Falmer Pr) Taylor & Francis.
Content of Social Explanation. Susan James. 200p. 1985. 59.95 (0-521-26667-X) Cambridge U Pr.
Content of the Curriculum (1988 ASCD Yearbook) Ronald S. Brandt et al. LC 87-72734. 207p. 1988. pap. text ed. 14.95 (0-87120-150-X, 610-88008) Assn Supervision.
Content of the Form: Narrative Discourse & Historical Representation. Hayden White. LC 86-21404. 288p. 1987. text ed. 38.50x (0-8018-2937-2) Johns Hopkins.
Content of the Form: Narrative Discourse & Historical Representation. Hayden White. 264p. 1990. reprint ed. pap. text ed. 13.95x (0-8018-4115-1) Johns Hopkins.
Content Points Advanced Level. J. Johnston & M. Johnston. (Turning Points Ser.). (Illus.). 64p. 1989. pap. text ed. 25.95 (0-201-52193-8) Addison-Wesley.
Content Points High Beginner Level. J. Johnston & M. Johnston. (Turning Points Ser.). (Illus.). 64p. 1989. pap. text ed. 25.95 (0-201-52179-2) Addison-Wesley.
Content Points Intermediate Level. J. Johnston & M. Johnston. (Turning Points Ser.). (Illus.). 64p. 1989. pap. text ed. 25.95 (0-201-52173-3) Addison-Wesley.
Content Reading & Literacy: Succeeding in Today's Diverse Classrooms. Donna E. Alvermann & Stephen F. Phelps. LC 93-26372. 1993. text ed. write for info. (0-205-15164-7) Allyn.
***Content Reading Instruction: A Communication Approach.** 2nd ed. Mark W. Conley. 1995. pap. text ed. write for info. (0-07-012496-5) McGraw.
Content, Structure, & Operation of Thought Systems. Ed. by Robert S. Wyer & Thomas Srull. (Advances in Social Cognition Ser.: Vol. 4). 296p. 1991. text ed. 59.95 (0-8058-0741-1); pap. 29.95 (0-8058-0742-X) L Erlbaum Assocs.
Content Valid Testing for Supervisory & Management Jobs: A Practical - Common Sense Approach see IPMA Assessment Council Monograph Series
***Contented Among Strangers: Rural German-Speaking Women & Their Families in the Nineteenth-Century Midwest.** Linda S. Pickle. Ed. by Roger Daniels et al. LC 95-9849. (Statue of Liberty-Ellis Island Centennial Ser.). (Illus.). 360p. (C). 1995. 49.95 (0-252-02182-7); pap. 14.95 (0-252-06472-0) U of Ill Pr.
Contented Botanist: Letters of W. H. Harvey (1811-1866) Ed. by Sophie C. Ducker. 1988. 69.95 (0-522-84341-7) Intl Spec Bk.
Contented Cat. Nobuo Honda. (Illus.). 90p. (Orig.). 1991. pap. 9.95 (0-8118-0014-8) Chronicle Bks.
Contented Countryman: The Best of C. Henry Warren. Geoffrey Warren. 176p. 1991. 26.00 (0-86299-945-6) A Sutton Pub.
Contented Man. Ken Hollingsworth. (Illus.). 376p. 1993. 19.95 (0-8059-3288-7) Dorrance.
Contention & Shakespeare's 2 Henry V. Charles T. Prouty. 1954. 59.50 (0-685-69852-1) Elliots Bks.
Contention Between Liberality & Prodigality. (Tudor Facsimile Texts. Old English Plays Ser.: No. 98). reprint ed. 49.50 (0-404-53398-1) AMS Pr.
Contentious Alliance: Trade Unions & the Labour Party. Lewis Minkin. 752p. 1991. text ed. 95.00 (0-7486-0301-8, Pub. by Edinburgh U Pr UK) Col U Pr.
Contentious Alliance: Trade Unions & the Labour Party. Lewis Minkin. 704p. 1993. pap. text ed. 30.00 (0-7486-0404-9, Pub. by Edinburgh U Pr UK) Col U Pr.
Contentious French. Charles Tilly. (Illus.). 472p. 1986. 37.50 (0-674-16695-7) HUP.
Contentious French: Four Centuries of Popular Struggle. Charles Tilly. (Illus.). 472p. 1989. pap. 17.95 (0-674-16696-5) Belknap Pr.

1584 An Asterisk (*) at the beginning of an entry indicates that the title is appearing in BIP for the first time.

C

An Asterisk (*) at the beginning of an entry indicates that the title is appearing in BIP for the first time.

1585

Contesting Colonial Hegemony: Gramsci & Imperialism. Ed. by Shula Marks & Dagmar Engels. 240p. 1994. text ed. 59.50 (1-85043-733-5, Pub. by I B Tauris UK) St Martin.

Contesting Confirmation: A Creditor's Perspective. Robert L. Ordin. 524p. 1993. 110.00 (0-13-296955-6) Aspen Law.

Contesting Confirmation: A Creditor's Perspective. Robert L. Ordin. LC 93-7740. 1993. 150.00 (0-13-359183-2) P-H Gen Ref & Trav.

Contesting Cultural Authority: Essays in Victorian Intellectual Life. Frank M. Turner. LC 92-20887. 300p. (C). 1993. 69.95 (0-521-37257-7) Cambridge U Pr.

***Contesting Cultural Rhetorics: Public Discourse & Education 1890-1900.** Margaret J. Marshall. (Illus.). 288p. 1995. text ed. 39.50x (0-472-10536-1) U of Mich Pr.

Contesting Earth's Future: Radical Ecology & Postmodernity. Michael E. Zimmerman. LC 93-21431. 1994. 30.00 (0-520-08477-2) U CA Pr.

Contesting Images: Photography & the World's Columbian Exposition. Julie K. Brown. LC 93-19891. (Illus.). 215p. (Orig.). 1994. lib. bdg. 60.00 (0-8165-1382-1); pap. 27.50 (0-8165-1410-0) U of Ariz Pr.

Contesting Markets: The Anthropology of Ideology, Discourse, & Practice. Ed. by Roy Dilley. 336p. 1992. text ed. 79.00 (0-7486-0371-9, Pub. by Edinburgh U Pr UK) Col U Pr.

Contesting New York State Tax Assessments. 2nd ed. E. Parker Brown, II et al. LC 89-61582. 117p. 1989. 35.00 (0-942954-24-6) NYS Bar.

Contesting Power: Everyday Resistance in South Asian Society & History. Ed. by Douglas Haynes & Gyan Prakash. (C). 1992. 40.00 (0-520-07585-4) U CA Pr.

Contesting the Boundaries of Liberal & Professional Education: The Syracuse Experiment. Ed. by Peter Marsh. (Illus.). 280p. (C). 1988. text ed. 39.95 (0-8156-2428-X) Syracuse U Pr.

***Contesting the Household Estate: Southern Brazilian Peasant & Modern Agriculture.** Frans Papma. (CEDLA Latin America Studies (CLAS): No. 67). 286p. 1992. pap. 27.00 (90-70280-84-1, Pub. by Thesis Pubs NE) IBD Ltd.

Contesting the Sacred: The Anthropology of Christian Pilgrimage. Ed. by John Eade & Michael J. Sallnow. (Illus.). 250p. 1991. 49.95 (0-415-04360-3, A5149); pap. 16.95 (0-415-04361-1, A5153) Routledge.

Contesting the Subject: Essays in the Postmodern Theory & Practice of Biography & Biographical Criticism. Ed. by William H. Epstein. LC 91-17637. (Theory & Practice of Biography & Biographical Criticism Ser.). 280p. 1991. 30.50 (1-55753-018-1) Purdue U Pr.

Contests: Cosmos 6. Ed. by Andrew Duff-Cooper. (Illus.). 200p. 1990. pap. 25.00 (0-7486-0199-6, Pub. by Edinburgh U Pr UK) Col U Pr.

Contests & Legends Eighteen Ninety-Five. Alma J. Mullins. LC 92-91195. 72p. (Orig.). 1994. pap. 9.00 (1-56002-287-6, Univ Edtns) Aegina Pr.

Contests for Corporate Control. Dennis J. Block & Harvey L. Pitt. 1432p. 1991. pap. text ed. 35.00 (0-685-49911-1, B4-6954) PLI.

Contests For Students. 2nd ed. 1996. 34.00 (0-8103-8226-1) Gale.

Contests for Students: All You Need to Know to Enter & Win 600 Contests. Ed. by Mary E. Snodgrass. 350p. 1990. pap. text ed. 40.00 (0-8103-7731-4) Gale.

Contex, Meaning, & Power in Southeast Asia. Ed. by Mark Hobart & Robert H. Taylor. LC 87-109736. (Studies on Southeast Asia). 156p. reprint ed. pap. 44.50 (0-7837-1767-9, 2041961) Bks Demand.

Context & Beyond: Reframing the Theory & Practice of Education. Terri Seddon. LC 93-45397. 230p. 1994. 75.00 (0-7507-0181-1, Falmer Pr) Taylor & Francis.

Context & Cognition. Ed. by Paul Light & George Butterworth. 192p. 1993. text ed. 39.95 (0-8058-1392-6); pap. 19.95 (0-8058-1393-4) L Erlbaum Assocs.

Context & Complexity: Cultivating Contextual Understanding. Ed. by M. Maruyama & S. Reniker. (Illus.). xii, 145p. 1991. 32.00 (0-387-97542-X) Spr-Verlag.

***Context & Consciousness: Activity Theory & Human-Computer Interaction.** Bonnie A. Nardi. (Illus.). 376p. (C). 1995. 40.00x (0-262-14058-6) MIT Pr.

Context & Development. Ed. by Robert Cohen & Alexander Siegel. 336p. (C). 1991. text ed. 69.95 (0-8058-0481-1) L Erlbaum Assocs.

Context & Dynamics in Clinical Knowledge. Howard F. Stein & Maurice Apprey. LC 85-3170. (Ethnicity, Medicine, & Psychoanalysis Ser.: Vol. I). xvi, 276p. 1985. 30.00 (0-8139-1056-0) U Pr of Va.

Context & Learning. Ed. by Peter Balsam & Arthur Tomie. 432p. (C). 1984. text ed. 79.95 (0-89859-442-1) L Erlbaum Assocs.

Context & Meaning in Proverbs 25-27. Raymond Van Leeuwen. LC 86-29830. (Society of Biblical Literature Ser.). 184p. 1988. pap. 11.95 (1-55540-005-1, 06 01 96) Scholars Pr GA.

Context & Presupposition. R. A. Van der Sandt. 224p. 1988. lib. bdg. 67.50 (0-7099-2625-1, Pub. by Croom Helm UK) Routledge Chapman & Hall.

Context & Text: Method in Liturgical Theology. Kevin Irwin. 408p. (Orig.). 1994. pap. text ed. 24.95 (0-8146-6125-4, Pueblo Bks) Liturgical Pr.

Context & the Child's Orientation to Meaning: A Study of the Child's Way of Organizing the Surrounding World in Relation to Public, Institutionalized Socialization. Gunilla Dahlberg. 228p. (Orig.). 1985. pap. text ed. 40.00x (91-40-05120-X) Coronet Bks.

Context & Understanding: An Inquiry into Socialization Theory. William M. Wentworth. LC 80-11424. 183p. 1981. text ed. 25.00 (0-444-99073-9, WCO/) Greenwood.

***Context-Based Vision, 1995 Workshop on (6-95)** 150p. 1995. pap. text ed. 40.00 (0-8186-7023-1, PR07023) IEEE Comp Soc.

Context Clues. Barbara Gregorich. (Horizons II Ser.). (Illus.). 24p. (J). (gr. 3-4). 1980. student ed 3.50 (0-89403-602-5) EDC.

Context Effects in Social & Psychological Research. Ed. by N. Schwarz & Seymour Sudman. (Illus.). 376p. 1991. 54.00 (0-387-97705-8) Spr-Verlag.

Context for Soviet Education Today. Ed. by Gaylen R. Wallace. LC 74-7300. 1974. pap. 14.95 (0-8422-0399-0) Irvington.

Context-Free Grammars: Covers, Normal Forms, & Parsing. A. Nijholt. (Lecture Notes in Computer Science Ser.: Vol. 93). 253p. 1980. pap. 28.00 (0-387-10245-0) Spr-Verlag.

Context North America: Canadian - U. S. Literary Relations. Ed. by Camille R. La Bossiere. 168p. 1994. pap. 22.00 (0-7766-0360-4, Pub. by Univ Ottawa Pr CN) Paul & Co Pubs.

Context of a Late Neanderthal: Implications of Multidisciplinary Research for the Transition to Upper Paleolithic Adaptations at Saint-Cesaire, Charente-Maritime, France. Ed. by Francois Leveque et al. LC 93-14145. (Monographs in World Archaeology: No. 16). (Illus.). 143p. 1993. pap. 25.00 (1-881094-05-7) Prehistory Pr.

***Context of Ancient Drama.** Eric Csapo & William J. Slater. (Illus.). 370p. 1995. text ed. 44.50x (0-472-10545-0) U of Mich Pr.

***Context of Casuistry.** Ed. by James F. Keenan & Thomas A. Shannon. LC 95-7775. (Moral Traditions & Moral Arguments Ser.). 256p. 1995. 55.00 (0-87840-585-2) Georgetown U Pr.

***Context of Casuistry.** Ed. by James F. Keenan & Thomas A. Shannon. LC 95-7775. (Moral Traditions & Moral Arguments Ser.). 1995. pap. 24.95 (0-87840-586-0) Georgetown U Pr.

Context of English Literature 1900-1930. Ed. by Michael Bell. LC 80-7792. (Context of English Literature Ser.). 250p. 1980. 34.50 (0-8419-0423-5); pap. 19.75 (0-8419-0424-3) Holmes & Meier.

Context of Environmental Politics: Unfinished Business for America's Third Century. Harold H. Sprout & Margaret Sprout. LC 77-84066. (Essays for the Third Century Ser.). 224p. reprint ed. pap. 63.90 (0-7837-5788-3, 2045454) Bks Demand.

Context of Explanation. Martin Bunzl. LC 92-47382. 172p. (C). 1993. lib. bdg. 80.50 (0-7923-2153-7) Kluwer Ac.

Context of Human Discourse: A Configurational Criticism of Rhetoric. Eugene E. White. Ed. by Thomas W. Benson. LC 91-39718. (Studies in Rhetoric-Communication). (Illus.). 310p. 1992. text ed. 34.95 (0-87249-817-4) U of SC Pr.

Context of Language Teaching. Jack C. Richards. (Cambridge Language Teaching Library). 228p. 1985. 39.95 (0-521-26565-7); pap. 16.95 (0-521-31952-8) Cambridge U Pr.

Context of Medicines in Developing Countries. Ed. by Sjaak Van der Geest & Susan R. Whyte. (C). 1988. lib. bdg. 114.50 (1-55608-059-X) Kluwer Ac.

Context of Self: A Phenomenological Inquiry Using Medicine As a Clue. Richard M. Zaner. LC 80-18500. (Series in Continental Thought: Vol. 1). (Illus.). xiv, 282p. 1981. 24.95x (0-8214-0443-1) Ohio U Pr.

Context over Foundation. Ed. by William J. Gavin. (C). 1988. lib. bdg. 93.00 (90-277-2670-1) Kluwer Ac.

Contexte. Leonardo Sciascia. (FRE.). 1979. pap. 10.95 (0-7859-4109-6) Fr & Eur.

Contextes. Barbara Freed & Knuts. 1988. student ed, pap. 25.95 (0-8384-3677-3); audio 5.00 (0-8384-3678-1) Heinle & Heinle.

Contextes: A French College Reader. Jean Carduner & Sylvia Carduner. (C). 1975. pap. text ed. 14.50 (0-669-73627-9) Heath.

Contexto Dramatico De la Lozana Andaluza. Louis Imperiale. LC 91-4087. (Scripta Humanistica Ser.: No. 84). 1991. 49.50 (0-916379-90-6) Scripta.

Contextos. Barbara Freed & Knuts. 1972. audio 5.00 (0-685-59482-3) Heinle & Heinle.

Contextos: Literarios Hispanoamericanos. Teresa Mendez-Faith. 228p. (C). 1986. pap. text ed. 25.50 (0-03-063844-5) HB Coll Pubs.

Contextos: Literatura y Sociedad Latino-Americanas del Siglio 19. Ed. by Evelyn P. Garfield & Ivan A. Schulman. 120p. 1991. 34.95 (0-252-01766-8) U of Ill Pr.

***Contextos: Poemas: Anthology of Four Poets.** Juvenal Acosta et al. (Chicano Latino Chapbooks Ser.). (Illus.). 20p. (Orig.). (ENG & SPA.). 1994. pap. 3.50 (0-939952-18-1) Moving Parts.

Contexts: A Celebration of the Augustana College Library. Ed. by Lawrence Falbe. (Illus.). 112p. (Orig.). 1991. pap. 6.00 (1-878326-02-3) East Hall Pr.

Contexts: A Thematic Reader. Linda Simon. LC 90-62715. 576p. (Orig.). (C). 1991. pap. text ed. 17.00 (0-312-02706-0); pap. text ed. 0.48 (0-312-02705-2) St Martin.

Contexts: Writing & Reading. 2nd annot. ed. Jeanette Harris & Ann Moseley. LC 88-81334. 1988. Annotated ed. & resource guide. teacher ed 23.56 (0-318-36892-7) HM.

Contexts & Communities: Rhetorical Perspectives on Writing. Greenberg. 822p. (C). 1994. pap. write for info. (0-02-346645-6) Macmillan.

Contexts & Comparisons: A Student Guide to the Great Works Courses. Baruch College Staff. 336p. (C). 1991. pap. text ed. 21.95 (0-8403-6141-6) Kendall-Hunt.

Contexts for Amos. M. D. Carroll. (JSOT Supplement Ser.: No. 132). 380p. (C). 1992. 35.00 (1-85075-297-4, Pub. by Sheffield Acad UK) CUP Services.

Contexts for Criticism. 2nd ed. Ed. by Donald Keesey. LC 93-22774. 566p. (C). 1994. pap. 33.95 (1-55934-180-7) Mayfield Pub.

Contexts for Early English Drama. Ed. by Marianne G. Briscoe & John C. Coldewey. LC 88-45099. 272p. 1989. 29.95 (0-253-31413-5) Ind U Pr.

Contexts for Hawthorne: The Marble Faun & the Politics of Openness & Closure in American Literature. Milton R. Stern. 216p. 1991. 34.95 (0-252-01819-2) U of Ill Pr.

Contexts for Learning: Sociocultural Dynamics in Children's Development. Ed. by Ellice A. Forman et al. (Illus.). 448p. 1993. 45.00 (0-19-506715-0) OUP.

Contexts for Learning to Write. Arthur Applebee. Ed. by Marcia Farr. LC 84-6428. (Writing Research Ser.: Vol. 1). 240p. 1984. text ed. 42.50 (0-89391-225-5); pap. text ed. 27.50 (0-89391-283-2) Ablex Pub.

Contexts for Prehistoric Exchange. Ed. by Jonathan E. Ericson & Timothy K. Earle. (Studies in Archaeology). 1982. text ed. 53.00 (0-12-241580-9) Acad Pr.

***Contexts in the College Curriculum: A Reading Skills Text to Build Your Information Base.** Judith Pokras. LC 95-12562. 1996. pap. 22.95 (0-534-24211-1) Intl Thomson.

Contexts of Acadian History, 1686-1784. Naomi E. Griffiths. (Illus.). 168p. 1992. 39.95 (0-7735-0883-X, Pub. by McGill CN); pap. 17.95 (0-7735-0886-4, Pub. by McGill CN) U of Toronto Pr.

Contexts of Accommodation: Developments in Applied Sociolinguistics. Ed. by Howard Giles et al. (Studies in Emotion & Social Interaction). (Illus.). 300p. (C). 1991. 59.95 (0-521-36151-6) Cambridge U Pr.

Contexts of Achievement: A Study of American, Chinese, & Japanese Children. Harold W. Stevenson. (Monographs of the Society for Research in Child Development). 1990. pap. text ed. 14.50 (0-226-77400-7) U Ch Pr.

Contexts of Being: The Intersubjective Foundations of Psychological Life. Robert D. Stolorow & George E. Atwood. (Psychoanalytic Inquiry Book Ser.: Vol. 12). 152p. 1992. pap. text ed. 26.95 (0-88163-152-3) Analytic Pr.

Contexts of Communication. Jean M. Civikly. LC 80-19274. 333p. (C). 1981. pap. text ed. 24.75 (0-03-053536-0) HB Coll Pubs.

Contexts of Competence: Social & Cultural Considerations in Communicative Language Teaching. M. Berns. (Topics in Language & Linguistics Ser.). (Illus.). 196p. 1990. pap. 37.50 (0-306-43469-5, Plenum Pr) Plenum.

Contexts of International Politics. Gary Goertz. LC 93-48756. (Cambridge Studies in International Relations: No. 36). (Illus.). 260p. (C). 1995. 59.95 (0-521-44070-X); pap. 21.95 (0-521-46972-4) Cambridge U Pr.

***Contexts of Pre-Novel Narrative: The European Tradition.** Ed. by Roy Eriksen. (Approaches to Semiotics Ser.: No. 114). x, 397p. (C). 1994. lib. bdg. 121.30 (3-11-013883-2) Mouton.

Contexts of Reading. Ed. by Carolyn Hedley et al. LC 85-13432. (Advances in Discourse Processes Ser.: Vol. 18). 224p. (C). 1985. text ed. 75.00 (0-89391-294-8); pap. 39.50 (0-89391-364-2) Ablex Pub.

Contexts of Teaching in Secondary Schools: Teachers' Realities. Ed. by Milbrey W. McLaughlin et al. (Series on School Reform). 296p. (C). 1990. text ed. 42.95 (0-8077-3027-0); pap. text ed. 22.95 (0-8077-3026-2) Tchrs Coll.

Contexts of the Bill of Rights. Ed. by Stephen L. Schechter & Richard B. Bernstein. 180p. (Orig.). (C). 1989. pap. text ed. 13.95 (0-945660-04-9, NYSC BUSC) Madison Hse.

Contexts of Understanding, Vol 1. Herman Parret. (Pragmatics & Beyond Ser.: Vol. 1, No. 6). viii, 109p. 1980. pap. 29.00x (90-272-2509-5) Benjamins North Am.

Contexts: Style & Values in Medieval Art & Literature: Yale French Studies, Special Issue. Yale French Studies Staff. Ed. by Daniel Poirion & Nancy F. Regalado. (French Studies). 304p. (C). 1991. pap. text ed. 20.00 (0-300-05034-8) Yale U Pr.

Contextual Analysis. Gudmund R. Iversen. (Quantitative Applications in the Social Sciences Ser.: Vol. 81). 96p. (C). 1991. pap. text ed. 9.95 (0-8039-4272-9) Sage.

Contextual Authority & Aesthetic Truth. James S. Hans. LC 91-12724. (SUNY Series in Aesthetics & the Philosophy of Art & SUNY Series, The Margins of Literature). 354p. 1992. 59.50 (0-7914-0917-1); pap. 19.95 (0-7914-0918-X) State U NY Pr.

Contextual English-French Dictionary of Chromatography: Dictionnaire Contextuel Anglais-Francais de la Chromatographie. R. Serre. 106p. (ENG & FRE.). 1981. pap. 24.95 (0-8288-0164-9, F39303) Fr & Eur.

Contextual English-French Dictionary of Solar Energy: Dictionnaire Contextuel Anglais-Francais de l'Energie Solaire. R. Serre. 67p. (ENG & FRE.). 1979. pap. 14.95 (0-8288-4792-4, M9032) Fr & Eur.

Contextual Family Therapy: Assessment & Intervention Procedures. Peter Goldenthal. LC 93-10551. (Practitioner's Resource Ser.). 90p. 1993. pap. text ed. 14.70 (0-943158-79-6, CFTBP, Prof Resc Pr) Pro Resource.

***Contextual Media: Multimedia & Interpretation.** Ed. by Edward Barrett & Marie Redmond. 300p. 1995. 35.00x (0-262-02383-0) MIT Pr.

***Contextual Memory Test.** Joan Toglia. (Illus.). 138p. 1993. pap. text ed. 79.00 (0-88450-659-2, 4750) Commun Skill.

***Contextual Perspective to Female Nursing in Victoria, 1850-1914 - (DINROO)** Angela Cushing. (Research Monograph Ser.: No. 7). 1993. pap. 35.00 (0-7300-2028-2, Pub. by Deakin Univ AT) St Mut.

Contextual Reality: A New Approach to Study Mathematics & Physics Paradoxes. Tower Chen. 90p. (C). 1993. text ed. write for info. (0-9630276-1-1) Jern Charng.

***Contextualising Caste: Post-Dumontian Approaches.** Ed. by Mary Searle-Chatterjee & Ursula M. Sharma. (Sociological Review Monographs). (Illus.). 184p. (Orig.). (C). 1995. pap. text ed. 24.95 (0-631-19283-2) Blackwell Pubs.

Contextualism & Understanding in Behavioral Science: Implications for Research & Theory. Ed. by Ralph L. Rosnow & Marianthi Georgoudi. 392p. 1986. text ed. 69.50 (0-275-92121-2, C2121, Praeger Pubs) Greenwood.

Contextualization: Meanings, Methods & Models. David J. Hesselgrave & Edward Rommen. LC 89-7022. 1989. pap. 14.99 (0-8010-4338-7) Baker Bk.

Contextualization of Language. Ed. by Peter Auer & Aldo Di Luzio. LC 91-43673. (Pragmatics & Beyond New Ser.: No. 22). vi, 402p. 1992. 89.00x (1-55619-290-8) Benjamins North Am.

Contexture of Feminism: Marie Cardinal & Multicultural Literacy. Carolyn A. Durham. 312p. 1991. 34.95 (0-252-01811-7); pap. 13.95 (0-252-06184-5) U of Ill Pr.

Contigent Valuation: A Critical Assessment. Ed. by Jerry A. Hausman. LC 93-14109. (Contributions to Economic Analysis Ser.: Vol. 220). 1993. write for info. (0-444-81469-8, North Holland) Elsevier.

Contigo: Essentials of Spanish. Oscar Ozete & Sergio D. Guillen. 384p. (C). 1987. pap. text ed. 40.00 (0-03-001828-5) HB Coll Pubs.

Contigo: Essentials of Spanish. 2nd ed. Ocsar Ozete & Sergio D. Guillen. (Illus.). 368p. (C). 1991. pap. text ed. write for info. (0-03-029979-9) HB Coll Pubs.

Contigo (Poesias) Betty Alexandria, pseud. LC 83-82881. (Coleccion Espejo de Paciencia Ser.). 63p. (Orig.). (SPA.). 1984. pap. 6.95 (0-89729-346-0) Ediciones.

Contiguity & the Statistical Invariance Principle. A. N. Shiryayev & P. E. Greenwood. (Stochastics Monographs). 244p. 1985. text ed. 69.00 (2-88124-013-5) Gordon & Breach.

Continence Promotion in General Practice. Nigel Smith & Maggie Clamp. (Practical Guides for General Practice Ser.: No. 13). (Illus.). 80p. 1991. pap. 14.95 (0-19-262043-6) OUP.

Continence with Biofeedback: New Treatment for Fecal Incontinence. Susan Trunnell. LC 91-75791. 173p. 1991. pap. 24.95 (0-9630339-5-6) Avantage.

Continent Apart: The United States & Canada in World Politics. William T. Fox. 208p. 1985. 12.95 (0-8020-6575-9) U of Toronto Pr.

***Continent Creations.** Elaine Hopkins. 9p. (J). 1995. pap. 5.99 (1-887291-00-8) Sun Sales.

Continent Lost - a Civilization Won: Indian Land Tenure in America. J. P. Kinney. Ed. by Dan C. McCurry & Richard E. Rubenstein. LC 74-30639. (American Farmers & the Rise of Agribusiness Ser.). (Illus.). 1975. reprint ed. 40.95 (0-405-06807-7) Ayer.

Continent Maps & Studies. Randy L. Womack. (Illus.). 64p. (gr. 4 up). 1991. student ed 7.95 (1-56500-017-X) Gldn Educ.

Continent of Islands: Searching for the Caribbean Destiny. Mark Kurlansky. (Illus.). 288p. 1992. 22.07 (0-201-52396-5) Addison-Wesley.

Continent of Islands: Searching for the Caribbean Destiny. Mark Kurlansky. (Illus.). 1993. pap. 12.45 (0-201-62231-9) Addison-Wesley.

Continent Revealed: The European Geotraverse. Ed. by D. J. Blundell et al. (Illus.). 250p. (C). 1992. pap. 37.95 (0-521-42948-X) Cambridge U Pr.

Continent Revealed: The European Geotraverse. Ed. by D. J. Blundell et al. (Illus.). 250p. (C). 1993. 79.95 (0-521-41923-9) Cambridge U Pr.

***Continent Transformed: Human Impact on the Natural Vegetation of Australia.** Jamie Kirkpatrick. (Meridian). (Illus.). 176p. 1995. pap. 22.95 (0-19-553473-5) OUP.

Continent Urinary Diversion. Ed. by R. Wammack & R. Hohenfellner. LC 92-49838. (Societe Internationale D'Urologie Reports). (Illus.). 304p. 1993. text ed. 95.00 (0-443-04645-X) Churchill.

Continental Actress: European Film Stars of the Postwar Era; Biographies, Criticism, Filmographies, Bibliographies. Kerry Segrave & Linda Martin. LC 89-13878. (Illus.). 320p. 1990. lib. bdg. 43.50x (0-89950-510-4) McFarland & Co.

***Continental Afrikan History Recovered: Afrika: From Two Hundred Million Seasons to the Present.** LC 91-72692. 100p. 1995. write for info. (1-56454-030-8) Cont Afrikan.

***Continental Afrikan Manifesto.** Afrikadzata Deku (Afrikan Culture Institute) Staff. LC 91-72668. (Essay Ser.). 250p. 1994. write for info. (1-56454-006-5) Cont Afrikan.

***Continental Afrikan Power Now.** Afrikadzata Deku (Afrikan Culture Institute) Staff. LC 91-72692. (Research Work Ser.). 250p. 1994. write for info. (1-56454-003-0) Cont Afrikan.

Continental Air Defense: A Neglected Dimension of Strategic Defense. Arthur Charo. (Occasional Papers: No. 7). (Illus.). 164p. (C). 1990. lib. bdg. 40.00 (0-8191-7781-4); pap. text ed. 21.00 (0-8191-7782-2) U Pr of Amer.

Continental & American Skeleton Clocks. Derek Roberts. LC 89-62600. (Illus.). 288p. 1989. 79.95 (0-88740-182-1) Schiffer.

C

1586

An Asterisk (*) at the beginning of an entry indicates that the title is appearing in BIP for the first time.

Continental & Ocean Rifts. Ed. by G. Palmason. (Geodynamics Ser.: Vol. 8). 309p. 1982. 26.00 (*0-87590-504-8*) Am Geophysical.

Continental Army. Robert K. Wright, Jr. LC 82-16472. (Army Lineage Ser.). (Illus.). 468p. 1983. pap. 15.00 (*0-16-001931-1*, S/N 008-029-00122-5) USGPO.

Continental Britons: German Jewish Refugees from Nazi Germany. Marion Berghahn. 1988. pap. 14.95 (*0-85496-157-7*, Berg Pubs) St Martin.

Continental Britons: German-Jewish Refugees from Nazi Germany. Marion Berghahn. 304p. 1988. pap. 19.95 (*0-85496-212-3*) Berg Pubs.

Continental Carbonate Sedimentation & Pedogenesis: Late Cretaceous & Early Tertiary of Southern France. P. Freytet & J. Plaziat. (Contributions to Sedimentology Ser.: No. 12). (Illus.). 213p. 1982. pap. text ed. 86.95 (*3-510-57012-X*) Lubrecht & Cramer.

Continental Commitment: The Dilemma of British Defence Policy in the Era of the Two World Wars. Michael C. Howard. LC 89-6811. 176p. (C). 1989. pap. 19.95 (*0-948660-07-4*, Pub. by Ashfield Pr UK) Humanities.

Continental Contract. Don Pendleton. (Executioner Ser.: No. 5). 1988. pap. 3.50 (*1-55817-028-6*, Pinnacle NY) Windsor NY.

Continental Crust: A Geophysical Approach. Rolf Meissner. (International Geophysics Ser.). 1986. text ed. 121.00 (*0-12-488950-6*); pap. text ed. 63.00 (*0-12-488951-4*) Acad Pr.

Continental Crust: Its Composition & Evolution. S. Taylor & S. McLennan. 1985. pap. 52.95 (*0-632-01148-3*) Blackwell Sci.

Continental Crust & Its Mineral Deposits: The Proceedings of a Symposium Held in Honour of J. Tuzo Wilson, Held at Toronto, May 1979. Ed. by David W. Strangway. LC 81-160755. (Geological Association of Canada Special Paper Ser.: No. 20). (Illus.). 813p. reprint ed. pap. 180.00 (*0-8357-6735-3*, 2035391) Bks Demand.

Continental Currency of 1776 & Fugio Cent Varieties. E. Newman. (Illus.). 1982. reprint ed. pap. 6.00 (*0-915262-90-8*) S J Durst.

Continental Deformation. Paul L. Hancock. LC 93-7258. 1994. text ed. 135.00 (*0-08-037931-1*, Pergamon Pr); pap. text ed. 49.50 (*0-08-037930-3*, Pergamon Pr) Elsevier.

Continental Divide. Oliver Hailey. 1973. pap. 4.75 (*0-8222-0237-9*) Dramatists Play.

Continental Divide: The Values & Institutions of the United States & Canada. Seymour M. Lipset. 1990. 29.95 (*0-415-90309-2*, A4356, Routledge NY) Routledge.

Continental Divide: The Values & Institutions of the United States & Canada. Seymour M. Lipset. 337p. 1990. pap. 15.95 (*0-415-90385-8*, A5389, Routledge NY) Routledge.

***Continental Drift.** Russell Banks. 1994. pap. 12.00 (*0-06-092574-4*, HarpT) HarpC.

Continental Drift: Proceedings of the I.A.U. Symposium, No. 32, Stresa, Italy, 1967. International Astronomical Union Staff. Ed. by William Markowitz & B. Guinot. (Proceedings of the International Astronomical Union Symposia Ser.). 107p. 1970. lib. bdg. 43.00 (*90-277-0129-6*) Kluwer Ac.

Continental Drifter: Dispatches from the Uttermost Parts of the Earth. Michael J. McRae. 256p. 1993. 21.95 (*1-55821-243-4*) Lyons & Burford.

Continental Europe. Insight Guides Staff. 384p. 1985. pap. 16.95 (*0-13-291832-3*) P-H.

Continental Eye: The Art & Architecture of Arthur Rotch. Harry L. Katz. LC 85-72502. (Illus.). 72p. (Orig.). 1985. pap. 14.95 (*0-934552-45-2*) Boston Athenaeum.

Continental Film Review Anthology, 1953-55, 2 vols. Ed. by G. Gordon. 1976. lib. bdg. 200.00 (*0-8490-1670-3*) Gordon Pr.

Continental Harmony. Michael Gizzi. (Roof Bks.). 84p. (Orig.). 1991. pap. text ed. 8.95 (*0-937804-41-X*) Segue NYC.

Continental Humanist Poetics: Studies in Erasmus, Castiglione, Marguerite de Navarre, Rabelais, & Cervantes. Arthur F. Kinney. LC 88-24992. 392p. 1989. 40.00x (*0-87023-665-2*) U of Mass Pr.

Continental Intervest's the Latin American Securities & Security Dealers: 1993-94 Edition. 1993. 485.00 (*0-9636475-0-4*) Cont Intervest.

Continental, Latin-American & Francophone Women Writers: Selected Papers from the Wichita State University Conference on Foreign Literature, 1984-1985. Ed. by Eunice Myers & Ginette Adamson. (Illus.). 224p. (C). 1987. lib. bdg. 42.50 (*0-8191-6290-6*) U Pr of Amer.

Continental, Latin-American & Francophone Women Writers, Vol. 2: Selected Papers from the Wichita State University Conference on Foreign Literature, 1986-1987. Ed. by Ginette Adamson & Eunice Myers. LC 87-8105. 212p. (C). 1990. lib. bdg. 48.00 (*0-8191-7593-5*) U Pr of Amer.

Continental Lithosphere: Deep Seismic Reflections. Ed. by R. Meissner et al. (Geodynamics Ser.: Vol. 22). 452p. 1991. 55.00 (*0-87590-522-6*, GD0225226) Am Geophysical.

Continental Lower Crust. Ed. by David M. Fountain et al. LC 92-27225. (Developments in Geotectonics Ser.: Vol. 23). 1992. write for info. (*0-444-88294-4*) Elsevier.

Continental Method of Scene Painting. Vladimir Polunin. Ed. by Cyril W. Beaumont. LC 77-19083. (Series in Dance). (Illus.). 1979. reprint ed. lib. bdg. 29.50 (*0-306-77578-6*) Da Capo.

Continental Method of Scene Painting. Vladimir Polunin. Ed. by Cyril W. Beaumont. (Illus.). xiii, 85p. (C). 1980. reprint ed. 29.95 (*0-903102-57-9*, Pub. by Dance Bks UK) Princeton Bk Co.

Continental Novel: A Checklist of Criticism in English 1967-1980. Louise S. Fitzgerald & Elizabeth I. Kearney. LC 82-20454. 510p. 1983. 35.00 (*0-8108-1598-2*) Scarecrow.

Continental Op. Dashiell Hammett. LC 75-11735. (Vintage Crime Ser.). 1989. pap. 12.00 (*0-679-72258-0*, Vin) Random.

Continental Op. Dashiell Hammett. 1992. pap. 10.00 (*0-394-23902-4*, Vin); pap. 10.00 (*0-679-74095-3*) Random.

Continental Opinion Regarding a Proposed Middle European Tariff-Union. George M. Fisk. LC 78-63892. (Johns Hopkins University. Studies in the Social Sciences. Thirtieth Ser. 1912: 11-12). 64p. 1983. reprint ed. 37.50 (*0-404-61146-X*) AMS Pr.

Continental Permian in West, Central, & South Europe. Ed. by Horst Falke. (NATO Advanced Study Institutes Series C, Mathematical & Physical Sciences: No. 22). 1976. lib. bdg. 112.50 (*90-277-0664-6*) Kluwer Ac.

Continental Philosophy & the Arts. Ed. by Laurence E. Winters et al. LC 83-6854. (Current Continental Research Ser.). (Illus.). 302p. (Orig.). 1984. lib. bdg. 52.50 (*0-8191-3259-4*, U CO Busn Res Div); pap. text ed. 26.00 (*0-8191-3260-8*, U CO Busn Res Div) U Pr of Amer.

Continental Philosophy in America. Ed. by Hugh Silverman et al. LC 83-1628. 272p. 1984. pap. 22.50x (*0-8207-0160-2*) Duquesne.

***Continental Philosophy Reader.** Ed. by Richard Kearney & Mara Rainwater. LC 95-14745. 1995. write for info. (*0-415-09525-5*, Routledge NY); pap. write for info. (*0-415-09526-3*, Routledge NY) Routledge.

Continental Philosophy since 1750: The Rise & Fall of the Self. Robert C. Solomon. (History of Western Philosophy Ser.: No. 7). 222p. (C). 1988. pap. text ed. 14.95 (*0-19-289202-9*) OUP.

Continental Prophecies. William Blake. Ed. by David Worrall & Detlef W. Dorrbecker. LC 93-43943. (Illuminated Manuscripts of William Blake Ser.: Vol. 4). 1995. 75.00 (*0-691-03674-8*) Princeton U Pr.

Continental Radioecology: Soil & Freshwater Ecosystems. N. V. Kulikov & I. V. Molchanova. Tr. by V. P. Pavlov. LC 80-65074. 174p. 1981. 59.50 (*0-306-40494-X*, Plenum Pr) Plenum.

Continental Red Beds. P. Turner. (Developments in Sedimentology Ser.: Vol. 29). 562p. 1980. 107.75 (*0-444-41908-X*) Elsevier.

Continental Rift Formation & Its Prehistory. A. V. Razvalyaev. Ed. by R. Chakraverty. (Russian Translation Ser.: No. 87). (Illus.). 208p. (C). 1991. text ed. 70.00 (*90-6191-991-6*, Pub. by A A Balkema NE) Ashgate Pub Co.

Continental Rift Formation & Its Prehistory. Av Razvayaev. (C). 1991. 38.00 (*81-204-0601-X*, Pub. by Oxford IBH II) S Asia.

***Continental Shelf: Books Across Europe from Ptolemy to Don Quixote.** (Illus.). 140p. 1995. pap. 50.00 (*1-85124-037-3*, 0373, Pub. by Bodleian Lib UK) A Schwartz & Co.

Continental Shelf & the Exclusive Economic Zone - Le Plateau Continental et la Zone Economique Exclusive: Delimitation & Legal Regime - Delimitation et Regime Juridique. Ed. by Donat Pharand & Umberto Leanza. LC 92-37816. (Publications on Ocean Development Ser.: Vol. 19). (ENG & FRE.). 1993. lib. bdg. 154.50 (*0-7923-2056-5*) Kluwer Ac.

Continental Shelves. Ed. by H. Postma & J. J. Zijlstra. (Ecosystems of the World Ser.: No. 27). 406p. 1988. 228.00 (*0-444-42609-4*) Elsevier.

Continental Shift: Free Trade & the New North America. William A. Orme, Jr. 235p. (C). 1993. pap. 49.95 (*0-9625971-2-0*) Washington Post.

Continental Short Stories. Ed. by Edward Mitchell & Rainer Schulte. (C). 1969. pap. text ed. 13.95 (*0-393-09797-8*) Norton.

Continental Stagecraft. Kenneth MacGowan & Robert E. Jones. LC 64-14711. (Illus.). 1972. 20.95 (*0-405-08765-9*, Pub. by Blom Pubns UK) Ayer.

Continental Systems. Eli F. Heckscher. 1964. 13.25 (*0-8446-1230-8*) Peter Smith.

Continental Trading Blocs: The Growth of Regionalism in the World Economy. Ed. by Richard Gibb & Wieslaw Michalik. LC 93-47089. 1994. text ed. 54.95 (*0-471-94909-4*) Wiley.

Continental Waltz. (Ballroom Dance Ser.). 1986. lib. bdg. 79.95 (*0-8490-3336-5*) Gordon Pr.

Continental Waltz. (Ballroom Dance Ser.). 1985. lib. bdg. 67.00 (*0-87700-731-4*) Revisionist Pr.

Continental Water Marketing. Ed. by Terry L. Anderson. LC 94-6028. 1994. write for info. (*0-936488-80-8*) PRIPP.

Continental Wrench - Tectonics & Hydrocarbon Habitat. 2nd rev. ed. Greg Zolnai. (Continuing Education Course Note Ser.: No. 30). (Illus.). 304p. 1991. pap. 27.00 (*0-89181-182-6*) AAPG.

Continents. Dennis Fradin. LC 86-9580. (New True Bks.). (Illus.). 48p. (J). (gr. k-4). 1986. lib. bdg. 13.50 (*0-516-01291-6*); pap. 5.50 (*0-516-41291-4*) Childrens.

Continents. Richard Grossinger. LC 73-10015. 200p. (Orig.). 1973. pap. 4.50 (*0-87685-161-8*) Black Sparrow.

Continents. Tom Mariner. LC 89-17285. (Earth in Action Ser.). (Illus.). 32p. (J). (gr. 3-8). 1990. lib. bdg. 9.95 (*1-85435-195-8*) Marshall Cavendish.

Continents: Puzzles for Learning World Geography. Jeanne Cheyney & Arnold Cheyney. (Illus.). 184p. (J). (gr. 4-6). 1994. pap. 11.95 (*0-673-36072-5*) GdYrBks.

Continents in Collision: The Impact of Europe on the North American Indian Societies. Robert A. Hecht. LC 80-1381. 337p. 1980. pap. text ed. 27.00 (*0-8191-1200-3*) U Pr of Amer.

Continents in Motion. 2nd ed. Walter Sullivan. (Illus.). 425p. 1990. 50.00 (*0-88318-703-5*); pap. 25.00 (*0-88318-704-3*) Am Inst Physics.

Contingencies & Other Essays. Cecil Gray. LC 75-134084. (Essay Index Reprint Ser.). 1977. 19.95 (*0-8369-2159-3*) Ayer.

Contingencies of Value: Alternative Perspectives for Critical Theory. Barbara H. Smith. LC 88-887. 272p. 1988. 32.00x (*0-674-16785-6*) HUP.

Contingencies of Value: Alternative Perspectives for Critical Theory. Barbara H. Smith. 248p. 1991. pap. 17.50x (*0-674-16786-4*, SMICOX) HUP.

Contingency & Freedom: John Duns Scotus Lectura 139. John D. Scotus. Ed. by A. Vos Jaczn et al. LC 94-318. (New Synthese Historical Library: Vol. 42). 216p. (ENG & LAT.). (C). 1994. lib. bdg. 97.00 (*0-7923-2707-1*) Kluwer Ac.

Contingency, Irony, & Solidarity. Richard Rorty. 208p. (C). 1989. 54.95 (*0-521-35381-5*); pap. 15.95 (*0-521-36781-6*) Cambridge U Pr.

Contingency Management in Education & Other Equally Exciting Places. 2nd ed. Richard Malott. (Illus.). 260p. 1972. reprint ed. teacher ed write for info. (*0-318-51874-0*); reprint ed. pap. text ed. 10.00 (*0-917472-07-1*) F Fournies.

Contingency of Theory: Pragmatism, Expressivism, & Deconstruction. Gary Wihl. LC 93-36108. 256p. 1994. 27.50 (*0-300-05798-9*) Yale U Pr.

Contingency Planning & Crew Response Guide for Gas Carrier Damage at Sea & in Port Approaches. ICS Staff et al. (C). 1989. 120.00 (*0-948691-89-1*, Pub. by Witherby & Co UK) St Mut.

Contingency Planning & Disaster Recovery Strategies. Computer Technology Research Corp. (Illus.). 160p. (Orig.). 1994. 210.00 (*1-56607-031-7*) Comput Tech Res.

Contingency Planning for Industrial Emergencies. Piero Armenante. (Illus.). 368p. 1991. text ed. 59.95 (*0-442-20996-7*) Van Nos Reinhold.

***Contingency Planning for Industrial Hazardous Spills & Releases.** Dan McGaskill. (Environmental Management Guides Ser.). 17p. 1994. pap. text ed. 17.50 (*0-86587-433-6*) Gov Insts.

Contingency Table Analysis for Road Safety Studies. G. A. Fleischer. (NATO Advanced Study Institutes Series C, Mathematical & Physical Sciences: No. 42). 300p. 1981. lib. bdg. 62.00 (*90-286-0960-1*) Kluwer Ac.

Contingency Table Analysis in Geographic Research: A Bibliographic Essay, No. 898. Donald E. Altman. 1975. 6.00 (*0-686-20371-2*) CPL Biblios.

Contingency Theory. Ed. by Lex Donaldson. LC 93-47245. (History of Management Thought Ser.: Vol. 9). 500p. (C). 1994. lib. bdg. 112.95 (*1-85521-436-9*, Pub. by Dartmth Pub UK) Ashgate Pub Co.

***Contingent Creatures: A Reward Event Theory of Motivation.** Carolyn R. Morillo. 206p. (C). 1995. text ed. 59.50 (*0-8226-3040-0*); pap. text ed. 22.95 (*0-8226-3041-9*) Littlefield.

Contingent Immaterialism: Meaning, Freedom, Time & Mind. Ben Mijuskovic. 214p. (Orig.). 1984. pap. 30.00 (*90-6032-254-1*, Pub. by B R Gruener NE) Benjamins North Am.

Contingent Meanings: Postmodern Fiction, Mimesis, & the Reader. Jerry A. Varsava. 233p. 1990. lib. bdg. 25.95 (*0-8130-1004-7*, Florida State U Inst) U Press Fla.

***Contingent Valuation, Transport Safety & the Value of Life.** Ed. by Nathalie G. Christe. (Studies in Risk & Uncertainty). 208p. (C). 1995. lib. bdg. 79.95 (*0-7923-9578-6*) Kluwer Ac.

Contingent Work: A Chart Book on Part-Time & Temporary Employment. Polly Callaghan & Heidi Hartmann. 1992. 10.00 (*0-944826-45-8*) Economic Policy Inst.

***Continua: With the Houston Problem Book.** Ed. by Howard Cook. LC 95-4002. (Lecture Notes in Pure & Applied Mathematics: Vol. 170). 1995. pap. write for info. (*0-8247-9650-0*) Dekker.

Continua with Microstructure. G. Capriz. (Tracts in Natural Philosophy Ser.: Vol. 35). 105p. 1989. 54.00 (*0-387-96886-5*) Spr-Verlag.

Continual Feast: A Cookbook to Celebrate the Joys of Family & Faith Throughout the Christian Year. Evelyn B. Vitz. LC 91-73634. (Illus.). 304p. 1991. reprint ed. 21.95 (*0-89870-383-2*); reprint ed. pap. 15.95 (*0-89870-384-0*) Ignatius Pr.

Continual Interest in the Sun & Sea & Inland Missing the Sea. Keith Gunderson. (Illus.). 154p. 1977. pap. 1.00 (*5-555-50075-0*) Nodin Pr.

Continual Lessons: The Journals of Glenway Wescott, 1937-1955. Glenway Wescott. Ed. by Robert Phelps & Jerry Rosco. 1991. 27.95 (*0-374-12889-8*) FS&G.

Continual Means & Boundary Value Problems in Function Spaces. E. M. Polishchuk. (Operator Theory Ser.: No. 31). 180p. 1989. 64.00 (*0-8176-2217-9*) Birkhauser.

Continual Permutations of Action. Anselm L. Strauss. LC 93-4075. (Communication & Social Order Ser.). 295p. 1993. 46.95 (*0-202-30471-X*); pap. text ed. 22.95 (*0-202-30472-8*) Aldine de Gruyter.

Continuance in the Struggle. rev. ed. Anthony L. Ackee. 1989. lib. bdg. write for info. (*0-9626355-0-2*) Kemetic Images.

Continuances in Civil Cases at the Franklin County Court of Common Pleas in Columbus, Ohio. National Center for State Courts Staff. 94p. 1981. 5.64 (*0-685-15497-1*, NERO-087) Natl Ctr St Courts.

Continuation & Bifurcations: Numerical Techniques & Applications. Ed. by Dirk Roose et al. (C). 1990. lib. bdg. 150.00 (*0-7923-0855-7*) Kluwer Ac.

***Continuation Education in California Public Schools.** 36p. 1994. pap. 7.25 (*0-8011-1179-X*) Calif Education.

Continuation of Sir Philip Sidney's Arcadia. Anne Weamys. Ed. by Patrick Cullen. (Women Writers in English Ser.). (Illus.). 128p. 1994. 39.95 (*0-19-507884-5*); pap. 17.95 (*0-19-508719-4*) OUP.

Continuation of the History of Passive Obedience Since the Reformation. Abednego Seller. LC 74-32586. reprint ed. 15.00 (*0-404-13200-6*) AMS Pr.

Continuation Techniques & Bifurcation Problems. Ed. by Hans D. Mittlemann & Dirk Roose. (International Series of Numerical Mathematics: No. 92). 225p. 1990. 64.00 (*0-8176-2397-3*) Birkhauser.

Continuations. Zulma Gonzalez-Parker. (Orig.). 1990. pap. 5.00 (*1-878255-04-5*) Heartfelt Pr.

Continuations: Essays on Medieval French Literature in Honor of John L. Grigsby. Ed. by Gloria Torrini-Roblin. LC 89-62174. 349p. 1989. lib. bdg. 35.95 (*0-917786-74-2*) Summa Pubns.

Continuations of the Old French Perceval of Chretien de Troyes, 5 vols. Incl. Vol. 1. First Continuation: Redaction of Manuscripts T V D. Ed. by William Roach. 1949. 12.00 (*0-87169-999-0*, AP10-ROW); Vol. 2. First Continuation: Redaction of Manuscripts E M Q U. Ed. by Robert H. Ivy, Jr. & William Roach. 1950. 12.00 (*0-87169-998-2*, AP20-ROW); Vol. 3, Pt. 1. First Continuation: Redaction of Manuscripts A L P R S. Ed. by William Roach. 1952. 12.00 (*0-87169-997-4*, AP3A-ROW); Vol. 3, Pt. 2. First Continuation. Ed. by Lucien Foulet & William Roach. 1955. 8.00 (*0-87169-996-6*, AP3B-ROW); Vol. 4. Second Continuation. Ed. by William Roach. 1971. 15.00 (*0-87169-995-8*, AP40-ROW); Vol. 5. Third Continuation. Ed. by William Roach. 1983. 40.00 (*0-87169-994-X*, AP50-ROW); write for info. (*0-318-50513-4*) Am Philos.

***Continue Laughing: A Novel.** Carl Reiner. LC 94-44308. 288p. 1995. 19.95 (*1-55972-273-8*, Birch Ln Pr) Carol Pub Group.

Continue Thine Forever. Henry A. Zinser. LC 84-60538. 98p. 1984. reprint ed. pap. 6.95 (*0-8192-1345-4*) Morehouse Pub.

Continued Fractions. Carl D. Olds. LC 61-12185. (New Mathematical Library: No. 9). 162p. 1963. pap. 12.00 (*0-88385-609-3*) Math Assn.

Continued Fractions. A. M. Rockett & P. Szusz. 200p. 1992. text ed. 55.00 (*981-02-1047-7*); pap. text ed. 25.00 (*981-02-1052-3*) World Scientific Pub.

Continued Fractions. Aleksandr J. Khinchin. Ed. by Herbert Eagle. LC 64-15819. 112p. reprint ed. pap. 32.00 (*0-317-09464-5*, 2016988) Bks Demand.

Continued Fractions: Analytic Theory & Application. William B. Jones & W. J. Thron. (Encyclopedia of Mathematics & Its Applications Ser.: No. 11). 1984. 79.95 (*0-521-30231-5*) Cambridge U Pr.

Continued Fractions & Orthogonal Functions: Theory & Applications. Ed. by S. Clement Cooper & W. J. Thron. LC 93-33234. (Lecture Notes in Pure & Applied Mathematics Ser.: Vol. 154). 400p. 1994. pap. 160.00 (*0-8247-9071-5*) Dekker.

Continued Fractions & Pade Approximants. Ed. by C. Brezinski. 332p. 1991. 97.00 (*0-444-88169-7*, North Holland) Elsevier.

Continued Fractions Found in the Unorganized Portions of Ramanujan's Notebooks. Andrews et al. (Memoirs Ser.: No. 477). 71p. 1992. 23.00 (*0-8218-2538-0*) Am Math.

Continued Fractions in Statistical Applications. Bowman & Shenton. (Statistics: Vol. 103). 352p. 1989. 125.00 (*0-8247-8120-1*) Dekker.

Continued Fractions with Applications. Lisa Lorentzen & Haakon Waadeland. LC 92-8592. (Studies in Computational Mathematics: Vol. 3). 1992. write for info. (*0-444-89265-6*, North Holland) Elsevier.

Continuemos! 3rd ed. Ana C. Jarvis et al. LC 86-82196. 352p. (SPA.). (C). 1987. pap. text ed. 20.50 (*0-669-10142-7*); Wkbk./Lab. manual. student ed 13.50 (*0-669-10143-5*); Bus. & econ. wkbk. 13.50 (*0-669-10144-3*); Nuestro mundo (cultural reader). 15.00 (*0-669-10145-1*) Heath.

Continuemos. 4th ed. Ana C. Jarvis et al. LC 90-80597. 354p. (SPA.). (C). 1991. pap. text ed. write for info. (*0-669-20886-8*); Wkbk./Lab. manual. student ed write for info. (*0-669-20887-6*); Instr.'s ed. teacher ed write for info. (*0-669-24490-2*); Cassettes. audio write for info. (*0-669-20889-2*); Demotape. write for info. (*0-669-20892-2*); Tapescript/Testing program. write for info. (*0-669-20888-4*) Heath.

***Continuemos!** 5th ed. Ana C. Jarvis et al. 404p. (SPA.). (C). 1995. pap. text ed. write for info. (*0-669-33762-5*) Heath.

Continuing Appeal of Nationalism. Fredy Perlman. 58p. 1985. pap. 1.50 (*0-934868-27-1*) Black & Red.

Continuing Care: For the Dying Patient, Family & Staff. Ed. by Robert Debellis et al. LC 85-19165. (Foundation of Thanatology Ser.: Vol. 5). 190p. 1985. text ed. 59.95 (*0-275-91334-1*, C1334, Praeger Pubs) Greenwood.

Continuing Care: The Management of Chronic Disease. 2nd ed. Ed. by John Hasler & Theo Schofield. (Oxford General Practice Ser.: No. 19). (Illus.). 364p. 1990. pap. 42.50 (*0-19-261742-7*) OUP.

Continuing Care in a Community Hospital. Harold N. Willard & Stanislav V. Kasl. LC 75-186676. (Commonwealth Fund Publications). (Illus.). 208p. 1972. 24.00 (*0-674-16775-9*) HUP.

Continuing Care of Terminal Cancer Patients: Proceedings of an International Seminar on Continuing Care of Terminal Cancer Patients, 19-20 October 1979, Milan, Italy. R. G. Twycross & V. Ventafridda. 300p. 1980. 120.00 (*0-08-024943-4*, Pub. by Pergamon Repr UK) Franklin.

Continuing Care Retirement Communities: Political, Social & Financial Issues. Ian A. Morrison et al. LC 85-8669. (Journal of Housing for the Elderly: Vol. 3, No. 1-2). 188p. 1986. text ed. 39.95 (*0-86656-384-9*) Haworth Pr.

C

Continuing Care Retirement Community: A Guidebook for Consumers. LC 84-70076. 31p. 1984. 6.95 (0-943774-16-0) Am Assn Homes.

Continuing Care Retirement Community: A Significant Option for Long-Term Care in the United States. Anne R. Somers & Nancy L. Spears. LC 91-4897. 232p. 1992. 37.95 (0-8261-7830-8) Springer Pub.

Continuing Challenge: The Past & the Future of Brown vs. Board of Education (A Symposium) LC 75-1552. 1975. 3.00 (0-912008-09-1) Equity & Excel.

***Continuing Challenge of Tuberculosis.** 1995. lib. bdg. 250.75 (0-8490-7569-6) Gordon Pr.

***Continuing Child Protection Emergency: A Challenge to the Nation.** 236p. (Orig.). (C). 1994. pap. text ed. 45.00x (0-7881-0893-X) Diane Pub.

Continuing Child Protection Emergency: A Challenge to the Nation. 1994. lib. bdg. 250.95 (0-8490-8506-3) Gordon Pr.

Continuing Chord Piano. Robert Laughlin. (Illus.). (C). 1991. student ed, audio 75.00 (0-929983-16-5) New Schl Am Music.

Continuing City: Urban Morphology in Western Civilization. James E. Vance, Jr. LC 89-37341. 432p. 1990. text ed. 65.00 (0-8018-3801-0); pap. text ed. 25.95x (0-8018-3802-9) Johns Hopkins.

***Continuing Conclusions: New Poems & Translations.** fac. ed. Richmond A. Lattimore. LC 83-727. 71p. 1983. reprint ed. pap. 25.00 (0-7837-7743-4, 2047499) Bks Demand.

Continuing Crackdown in Inner Mongolia. Ed. by Human Rights Watch Staff. 38p. (Orig.). 1992. pap. 5.00 (1-56432-059-6) Hum Rts Watch.

Continuing Crisis: U. S. Policy in Central America & the Caribbean. Ed. by Mark Falcoff & Robert Royal. 500p. (Orig.). (C). 1986. text ed. 37.50 (0-89633-105-9); pap. text ed. 19.50 (0-89633-106-7) Ethics & Public Policy.

Continuing Debate over Depreciation, Capital & Income. Richard Brief. LC 93-9762. (New Works in Accounting History). 320p. 1993. reprint ed. 54.00 (0-8153-1213-X) Garland.

Continuing Development in Advanced Revelation Training Manual. Revelation Technologies Staff. 200p. 1988. 50.00 (0-923387-20-X) Rev Tech Inc.

Continuing Dialogue: Men & Issues in Early American History. rev. ed. Ed. by Richard D. Burns et al. LC 63-23420. (Orig.). (C). 1964. pap. text ed. 8.50 (0-87015-141-X) Pacific Bks.

Continuing Education. Finla G. Crawford. 1958. 2.50 (0-87060-087-7, PUC 7) Syracuse U Cont Ed.

Continuing Education. D. Weil. 1980. pap. 2.25 (0-449-24319-2) Fawcett.

Continuing Education: Version I. 500p. (Orig.). (C). 1991. pap. text ed. 79.50 (1-878025-14-7) Western Schls.

Continuing Education: Version II. 500p. (Orig.). 1991. pap. text ed. 79.50 (1-878025-29-5) Western Schls.

Continuing Education Alternatives. rev. ed. Frieda Carroll. LC 80-68549. 1992. 49.95 (0-939476-14-2, Biblio Pr); ring bd. 39.95 (0-939476-15-0, Biblio Pr) Prosperity & Profits.

Continuing Education Alternatives Workbook. rev. ed. Frieda Carrol. 75p. 1983. student ed 21.95 (0-939476-85-1) Prosperity & Profits.

Continuing Education & Training Counselling Services in a Regional. 125p. 1993. pap. 11.00 (92-826-5887-2, HX-79-93-130-EN-C, Pub. by Europ Com) UNIPUB.

Continuing Education & Training of the Long Term Umemployed in Ten Member States of the European Community Summary Report. CEDEFOP Staff. 181p. 1992. pap. 11.00 (92-826-4325-5, HX-74-92-944-EN, Pub. by Europ Com) UNIPUB.

Continuing Education for Educators of Adults: The Roles of Research. A. Charters. (MS Ser.). 1977. 4.00 (0-686-52213-3, MSS 6) Syracuse U Cont Ed.

Continuing Education for Gerontological Careers. Roberta R. Greene. 315p. 1988. 7.50 (0-87293-020-3) Coun Soc Wk Ed.

Continuing Education for Physicians: Proceedings of the WHO Expert Committee, Geneva, 1973. WHO Staff. (Technical Report Ser.: No. 534). 1973. pap. 1.60 (92-4-120534-2) World Health.

Continuing Education for RE Practitioners. 2nd ed. Clarke R. Marquis & Daniel P. Sarrett. 1994. pap. 14.95 (0-7931-1124-2, 152001-02, Real Estate Ed) Dearborn Finan.

Continuing Education for the Health Professions: Developing, Managing, & Evaluating Programs for Maximum Impact on Patient Care. Ed. by Joseph S. Green et al. LC 83-49261. (Jossey-Bass Higher Education Ser.). 468p. reprint ed. pap. 133.40 (0-7837-2514-0, 2042673) Bks Demand.

Continuing Education for the Library Information Professions. William G. Asp et al. LC 85-18204. 352p. (Orig.). 1985. 41.00 (0-208-01897-2, Lib Prof Pubns); pap. 30.00 (0-208-01898-0, Lib Prof Pubns) Shoe String.

Continuing Education for the Post-Industrial Society. Ed. by Neil Costello & Michael Richardson. 160p. 1982. pap. 29.00 (0-335-10186-0, Open Univ Pr) Taylor & Francis.

Continuing Education Guide: The CEU & Other Professional Development Criteria. Louis Phillips. 144p. (C). 1994. per., pap. text ed. 24.95 (0-8403-9351-2) Kendall-Hunt.

Continuing Education in British Universities. C. Durucan. (C). 1986. 60.00 (1-85041-005-4, Pub. by Univ Nottingham UK) St Mut.

Continuing Education in Landscape Architecture. Council of Educators in Landscape Architecture Staff. Ed. by M. Burkart et al. LC 80-621598. (Illus.). 103p. reprint ed. pap. 29.40 (0-8357-3043-3, 2039298) Bks Demand.

Continuing Education in Management for Health Care Personnel. Donald K. White. LC 75-27158. 1975. 10.00 (0-87914-028-3, 567152) Hosp Res & Educ.

Continuing Education in Pharmacy. Ed. by Jack R. Arndt & Stephen J. Coons. LC 87-71365. (Illus.). 374p. (C). 1987. text ed. 40.00 (0-937526-13-4) AACP Alexandria.

Continuing Education in Polytechnics & Colleges: Perceptions & Policies in the Provision of Continuing Education in Non-University Institutions of Higher Education in England & Wales. D. Wood. 38p. (C). 1982. text ed. 35.00 (0-685-22154-7, Pub. by Univ Nottingham UK) St Mut.

Continuing Education in Polytechnics & Colleges: Perceptions & Policies in the Provision of Continuing Education in Non-University Institutions of Higher Education in England & Wales. David Wood. (C). 1982. 25.00 (0-902031-80-5, Pub. by Univ Nottingham UK) St Mut.

Continuing Education in the Later Years. Southern Conference on Gerontology Staff. Ed. by J. C. Dixon. LC 72-190331. (Institute of Gerontology Ser.: No. 12). 134p. reprint ed. pap. 38.20 (0-7837-4979-1, 2044645) Bks Demand.

Continuing Education in the Year 2000. Ed. by Ralph G. Brockett. LC 85-644750. (New Directions for Continuing Education Ser.: No. 36). 1987. 16.95 (1-55542-950-5) Jossey-Bass.

Continuing Education of Adults in Colonial America. Huey B. Long. LC 75-38925. (Occasional Papers: No. 45). 75p. 1976. pap. text ed. 2.75 (0-87060-070-2, OCP 45) Syracuse U Cont Ed.

Continuing Education of College Professors. Ed. by Ayers Bagley. (Occasional Paper: No. 2). 1974. pap. 3.00 (0-933669-05-4) Soc Profs Ed.

Continuing Education of College Professors, Pts. I & II. Ed. by Ayers Bagley. (Occasional Paper: No. 6). 1974. pap. 3.00 (0-933669-09-7) Soc Profs Ed.

***Continuing Education of Engineers.** National Research Council (U. S.), Panel on Alternative Policies Affecting the Prevention of Alcohol Abuse & Alcoholism Staff. LC 85-62019. (Engineering Education & Practice in the United States Ser.). 102p. 1985. pap. 29.10 (0-7837-7451-6, 2049173) Bks Demand.

Continuing Education of Reference Librarians. Bill Katz. LC 90-4302. (Reference Librarian Ser.: No. 30 & 31). 273p. 1990. text ed. 49.95 (1-56024-020-2) Haworth Pr.

Continuing Education of William Carr: An Autobiography. William G. Carr. LC 78-9918. 452p. reprint ed. pap. 128.90 (0-317-55481-6, 2029529) Bks Demand.

Continuing Education Unit: Criteria & Guidelines. 5th ed. AECET Staff & Grover Andrews. 48p. 1993. 9.00 (0-8403-8745-8) Kendall-Hunt.

Continuing Formation of Priests (Growing in Wisdom, Age & Grace) 34p. 1984. pap. 2.50 (1-55586-954-8) US Catholic.

Continuing Heritage: The Story of the Civil Trust Awards. Lionel Esher. 144p. 1982. 65.00 (0-900382-42-2) St Mut.

Continuing Higher Education: The Coming Wave. Allan W. Lerner & B. Kay King. 176p. (C). 1992. text ed. 31.00 (0-8077-3197-8) Tchrs Coll.

Continuing Human Rights Violations in Irian Jaya. 1991. pap. 3.00 (0-685-53235-6) Amnesty Intl USA.

Continuing Incorporation: Workbook 4. Robert D. Noble. (Welcome in Ser.). 88p. (Orig.). 1987. 10.00 (0-944687-04-0) Gather Family Inst.

Continuing Issues in Early Childhood Education. Carol Seefeldt. 352p. (C). 1990. pap. write for info. (0-675-20935-8, Merrill Pub Co) Macmillan.

Continuing Judicial Education for Alabama Appellate Judges. National Center for State Courts Staff. 50p. 1975. 3.00 (0-685-15086-0, MAB-028) Natl Ctr St Courts.

Continuing Learning in the Professions. Cyril O. Houle. LC 79-92462. (Higher & Adult Education Ser.). 407p. 1980. 39.95x (0-87589-449-6) Jossey-Bass.

Continuing Legal Education for Professional Competence & Responsibility since Arden House II. ALI-ABA Committee on Continuing Professional Education. LC 84-70380. 322p. 1984. pap. 37.00 (0-8318-0427-0, B427) Am Law Inst.

Continuing Liberal Education. David B. House. (ACE-Oryx Series on Higher Education). 224p. 1991. 29.95 (0-02-897181-7, ACE-Oryx) Oryx Pr.

Continuing Medical Education: A Primer. 2nd ed. Ed. by Adrienne B. Rosof & William C. Felch. LC 91-24229. 256p. 1992. text ed. 59.95 (0-275-94009-8, C4009, Praeger Pubs); pap. text ed. 15.95 (0-275-94010-1, B4010, Praeger Pubs) Greenwood.

Continuing Medical Education in the Community Hospital. James J. Bergin & Geraldine C. Holmes. LC 79-55326. (Illus.). 112p. 1979. text ed. 22.00 (0-935466-00-2); pap. text ed. 16.00 (0-935466-01-0) Pierson Pubs.

Continuing Medical Education Syllabus & Scientific Proceedings in Summary Form: The One Hundred & Fortieth Annual Meeting of the American Psychiatric Association, Chicago, IL, May 9-14, 1987. American Psychiatric Association Staff. 327p. reprint ed. pap. 93.20 (0-8357-7795-2, 2036156) Bks Demand.

Continuing Medical Education Syllabus & Scientific Proceedings in Summary Form: The One Hundred & Thirty-Fifth Annual Meeting of the American Psychiatric Association, Toronto, Canada, May 15-21, 1982. American Psychiatric Association Staff. 351p. reprint ed. pap. 100.10 (0-8357-3036-0, 2039284) Bks Demand.

Continuing Medical Education Syllabus & Scientific Proceedings in Summary Form: The One Hundred & Thirty-Ninth Annual Meeting of the American Psychiatric Association, Washington, DC, May 10-16, 1986. American Psychiatric Association Staff. 321p. reprint ed. pap. 91.50 (0-8357-7794-4, 2036155) Bks Demand.

Continuing on Four & One-Half. Mary E. Hopkins. (Illus.). (C). 1991. pap. text ed. 12.00 (0-929950-11-9) ME Pubns.

Continuing Plan. S. Mikielle Chatman. (Series XII Book Group). 70p. 1992. pap. 8.00 (1-881146-03-0) Fat Chance.

Continuing Presence of Walt Whitman: The Life after the Life. Ed. by Robert K. Martin. LC 91-44249. (Illus.). 282p. 1992. 28.95x (0-87745-366-7) U of Iowa Pr.

***Continuing Professional Education.** (IFLA Publications: Vol. 55). 159p. 1991. 55.00 (3-598-21784-6) K G Saur.

Continuing Professional Education. Barrie Brennan. (C). 1992. 60.00 (0-86431-056-0, Pub. by Aust Council Educ Res AT) St Mut.

***Continuing Professionalism - Education & IFLA: Past, Present & a Vision for the Future: Papers from the IFLA CPERT Second World Conference on Continuing Professional Education for the Library & Information Science Professions.** Ed. by Blanche Woolls. (IFLA Publications: Vol. 66-67). 365p. 1994. 110.00 (3-598-21794-3) K G Saur.

Continuing Quest: Introductory Readings in Philosophy. William E. O'Meara et al. 232p. (C). 1994. per., pap. text ed. 22.95 (0-8403-3121-5) Kendall-Hunt.

Continuing Religious Repression in China. Ed. by Human Rights Watch Staff. 60p. (Orig.). 1993. pap. 7.00 (1-56432-102-9) Hum Rts Watch.

Continuing Revolution: A History of Lowell, Massachusetts. Intro. by Robert Weible. (Illus.). 440p. (Orig.). 1991. pap. 19.95 (0-9631604-0-0) Lowell Hist Soc.

Continuing Search for the Lost Dutchman's Gold Mine. Mitchell Waite. (Illus.). 150p. (Orig.). 1993. pap. text ed. 9.95 (1-881260-06-2) Southwest Pubns.

Continuing Struggle: Autobiography of a Labor Activist. C. H. Mayer. LC 89-62399. 187p. 1989. pap. 11.95 (0-938875-20-5) Pittenbrauch Pr.

Continuing Tax Rebellion: What Millions of Americans Are Doing to Restore Constitutional Government. rev. ed. Martin A. Larson. LC 79-89020. 1979. pap. 12.95 (0-8159-5220-1) Devin.

Continuing Terror. Americas Watch Staff. 156p. 1985. 10.00 (0-938579-02-9, Fund Free Exp) Hum Rts Watch.

Continuing the Education Debate. Ed. by Michael Williams & Richard Daugherty. 176p. 1993. pap. text ed. 19.95 (0-304-32614-3) Cassell.

Continuing the Journey: Parishes in Transition. Ed. by Maureen Gallagher. LC 88-62606. 68p. (Orig.). 1988. teacher ed, pap. 4.95 (1-55612-240-3); student ed, pap. 5.95 (1-55612-238-1) Sheed & Ward MO.

Continuing the Nuclear Dialogue: Selected Essays. Weinberg. 224p. 1985. pap. 25.00 (0-89448-552-0, 690009) Am Nuclear Soc.

Continuing the Reformation: Essays on Modern Religious Thought. B. A. Gerrish. LC 93-1796. 288p. 1993. lib. bdg. 49.00 (0-226-28870-6); pap. text ed. 19.95 (0-226-28871-4) U Ch Pr.

Continuing the Revolution: The Political Thought of Mao. John B. Starr. LC 78-63597. 1979. pap. 15.95x (0-691-02189-9) Princeton U Pr.

Continuing to Think: The British Asian Girl. Barrie Wade & Pamela Souter. (Multilingual Matters Ser.: No. 81). 94p. 1992. 59.00 (1-85359-139-4, Pub. by Multilingual Matters UK); pap. 19.95 (1-85359-138-6, Pub. by Multilingual Matters UK) Taylor & Francis.

Continuing Trial of Treatment. Ed. by Stephen Frankel & Gilbert Lewis. (C). 1988. lib. bdg. 117.50 (1-55608-076-X); pap. text ed. 43.00 (0-7923-0078-5) Kluwer Ac.

Continuing Voice of Jesus: Christian Prophecy & the Gospel Tradition. rev. ed. M. Eugene Boring. 288p. 1991. pap. 18.99 (0-664-25184-6) Westminster John Knox.

Continuing with Russian. Charles E. Townsend. xxi, 426p. (C). 1981. reprint ed. pap. text ed. 19.95 (0-89357-085-0) Slavica.

Continuing Your Genealogical Research in Minnesota. Marilyn Lind. LC 85-80942. (Illus.). 161p. 1986. pap. text ed. 14.50 (0-937463-09-4) Linden Tree.

Continuities & Discontinuities: The Political Economy of Social Welfare & Labour Market Policy in Canada. Ed. by Andrew F. Johnson et al. 640p. (C). 1994. 45.00 (0-8020-2916-7); pap. 18.95 (0-8020-7421-9) U of Toronto Pr.

Continuities & Discontinuities in Cultural Conditioning. Ruth Benedict. (Reprint Series in Social Sciences). (C). 1993. reprint ed. pap. text ed. 1.00 (0-8290-3844-2, S-18) Irvington.

Continuities & Discontinuities in Development. Ed. by Robert N. Emde & Robert J. Harmon. LC 84-8225. (Topics in Developmental Psychobiology Ser.). 438p. 1984. 59.50 (0-306-41563-1, Plenum Pr) Plenum.

Continuities in Highland Maya Social Organization: Ethnohistory in Sacapulas, Guatemala. Robert M. Hill, II & John Monaghan. LC 87-15856. (Ethnohistory Ser.). (Illus.). 192p. 1987. text ed. 37.95x (0-8122-8070-9) U of Pa Pr.

Continuities in Political Action: A Longitudinal Study of Political Orientations in Three Western Democracies. Ed. by M. Kent Jennings et al. (Studies on North America: No. 5). vi, 432p. (C). 1990. lib. bdg. 96.95 (3-11-012024-0); pap. text ed. 27.95 (3-11-012410-6) De Gruyter.

Continuities in Popular Culture: The Present in the Past & the Past in the Present & Future. Ed. by Ray B. Browne & Ronald J. Ambrosetti. LC 93-70931. 268p. 1993. 39.95 (0-87972-592-3); pap. 14.95 (0-87972-593-1) Bowling Green Univ.

Continuities in Social Research: Studies in the Scope & Method of the American Soldier. Ed. by Robert K. Merton & Paul F. Lazarsfeld. LC 73-14168. (Perspectives in Social Inquiry Ser.). 260p. 1978. reprint ed. 18.95 (0-405-05514-5) Ayer.

Continuities of Deprivation? The Newcastle 1000 Family Study. I. Kolvin et al. (Illus.). 400p. 1990. text ed. 68.95 (0-566-05799-9) Ashgate Pub Co.

Continuities of Hopi Culture Change. Richard O. Clemmer. 1978. pap. 15.95 (0-916552-15-2) Acoma Bks.

Continuity. Liz Howell. (Illus.). 404p. 1993. 35.00 (0-943120-07-1) Dragonsbreath.

Continuity & Change: Festival of India in Great Britain. 110p. 1982. 14.95 (0-318-36314-3) Asia Bk Corp.

Continuity & Change: London Calvinistic Baptists & the Evangelical Revival, 1760-1820. R. Phillip Roberts. 282p. 1989. lib. bdg. 30.00 (0-940033-30-5) R O Roberts.

Continuity & Change: Political Institutions & Literary Monuments in the Middle Ages. Ed. by Elisabeth Vestergaard. 134p. (Orig.). 1986. pap. 38.50 (87-7492-606-3, Pub. by Odense Universitets Forlag DK) Coronet Bks.

***Continuity & Change: President Constantine Curris' Annual Address to the Faculty, 1983-1993.** Constantine Curris. Ed. by Grace A. Hovet & Darrel Davis. (Northern Iowa Texts Ser.: No. 2). 80p. (C). 1994. pap. text ed. 5.95 (0-9641511-1-1) Assn Text Study.

Continuity & Change among Canadian Mennonite Brethren. Peter M. Hamm. (Religion & Identity: Social Scientific Studies in Religion). 296p. (C). 1987. pap. 32.50 (0-88920-189-7, Pub. by Wilfrid Laurier CN) Humanities.

Continuity & Change among the Old Order Amish of Illinois. Judith A. Nagata. LC 87-45783. (Immigrant Communities & Ethnic Minorities in the U. S. & Canada Ser.: No. 18). 1988. 59.50 (0-404-19428-1) AMS Pr.

Continuity & Change in Art: The Development of Modes of Representation. Sidney J. Blatt & Ethal S. Blatt. 432p. (C). 1984. text ed. 79.95 (0-89859-342-5) L Erlbaum Assocs.

Continuity & Change in Austrian Socialism: The Eternal Quest for the Third Way. Melanie A. Sully. (East European Monographs: No. 114). 288p. 1982. text ed. 47.50 (0-88033-008-2) East Eur Quarterly.

Continuity & Change in Brazil & the Southern Cone: Research Trends & Library Collections for the Year 2000: Continuidade e Mudancas No Brasil e No Cone Sul: Tendencias de Pesquisa e Acervos Bibliograficos Para o Ano 2000. Ed. by Ann Hartness. xi, 361p. (Orig.). (ENG, POR & SPA.). 1992. pap. 52.50 (0-917617-30-4) SALALM.

Continuity & Change in China's Rural Development: Collective & Reform Eras in Perspective. Louis Putterman. (Illus.). 384p. 1993. 49.95 (0-19-507872-1) OUP.

Continuity & Change in Communication Systems: A Cross-Cultural Perspective. Ed. by Georgette Wang et al. LC 84-2969. (Communication & Information Science Ser.). 288p. 1985. text ed. 55.00 (0-89391-150-X) Ablex Pub.

***Continuity & Change in Contemporary Korea.** Ed. by Christopher J. Sigur. (Illus.). 71p. 1994. pap. write for info. (0-87641-124-3) Carnegie Ethics & Intl Affairs.

Continuity & Change in Electoral Politics, 1893-1928. Paul Kleppner. LC 86-14987. (Contributions in American History Ser.: No. 120). (Illus.). 278p. 1987. text ed. 55.00 (0-313-24069-8, KLE/, Greenwood Pr) Greenwood.

Continuity & Change in Latin America. Ed. by John J. Johnson. xiii, 282p. 1964. 39.50 (0-8047-0184-9); pap. 12.95 (0-8047-0185-7) Stanford U Pr.

Continuity & Change in Medieval Persia. Ann K. Lambton. 1988. 45.00 (0-88706-133-8) Mazda Pubs.

Continuity & Change in Pacific Foodways. Miriam Kahn & Lorraine Sexton. 180p. 1988. pap. text ed. 56.00 (3-7186-0477-9) Gordon & Breach.

Continuity & Change in Poland: Conservatism in Polish Political Thought. Rett R. Ludwikowski. LC 90-25001. 313p. 1991. text ed. 39.95 (0-8132-0743-6) Cath U Pr.

Continuity & Change in Psychoanalysis: Letters from Milan. Luciana Nissim-Momigliano. 184p. 1992. pap. 29.95 (1-85575-009-0, Pub. by Karnac Bks UK) Brunner-Mazel.

Continuity & Change in Rural West Bengal. G. K. Lieten. 1993. 38.00 (0-8039-9449-4) Sage.

Continuity & Change in Southeast Asia: Collected Journal Articles of Harry J.Benda. Harry J. Benda. LC 72-84083. (Yale University Southeast Asia Studies: Monographs: No. 18). 319p. reprint ed. pap. 91.00 (0-317-09326-6, 2007479) Bks Demand.

Continuity & Change in Southern Africa. Gwendolyn M. Carter. 117p. 1985. 9.95 (0-918456-57-6, Crossroads) African Studies Assn.

Continuity & Change in the Development of Russell's Philosophy. Paul J. Hager. LC 93-44873. (Nijhoff International Philosophy Ser.). 204p. (C). 1994. lib. bdg. 99.75 (0-7923-2688-1) Kluwer Ac.

Continuity & Change in the Rhetoric of the Moral Majority. David Snowball. LC 90-45196. (Praeger Series in Political Communication). 200p. 1991. text ed. 45.00 (0-275-93689-9, C3689, Praeger Pubs) Greenwood.

Continuity & Change in World Politics: The Clash of Perspectives. 2nd ed. Barry B. Hughes. LC 92-42226. 1993. pap. text ed. write for info. (0-13-227000-5) P-H.

An Asterisk (*) at the beginning of an entry indicates that the title is appearing in BIP for the first time.

C

An Asterisk (*) at the beginning of an entry indicates that the title is appearing in BIP for the first time.

1589

Continuous Quality Improvement in Nursing. American Nurses Association Staff. Ed. & Intro. by Jacqueline Dienemann. LC 92-17870. 144p. (Orig.). (C). 1992. pap. 12.00 (*1-55810-075-X*, NP-80, Am Nurses Fnd) Am Nurses Pub.

Continuous Quantum Measurements & Path Integrals. M. B. Mensky. (Illus.). 188p. 1993. 95.00 (*0-7503-0228-3*) IOP Pub.

Continuous Revival. Norman P. Grubb. 1993. pap. 2.50 (*0-87508-210-6*) Chr Lit.

Continuous Selections for Metric Projections & Interpolating Subspaces. Wu Li. Ed. by B. Brosowski et al. (Approximation & Optimization Ser.: Vol. 1). ii, 114p. 1991. pap. 37.80 (*3-631-43521-5*) P Lang Pubs.

Continuous Surface Mining: Equipment, Operation & Design. Ed. by Tibor G. Rozgonyi & Tad S. Golosinski. (Proceedings of the 2nd International Symposium on Continuous Surface Mining, Austin Texas, October 2-5, 1988 Ser.). (Illus.). x, 225p. 1988. lib. bdg. 120.00 (*90-6191-858-8*, Pub. by A A Balkema NE) Ashgate Pub Co.

Continuous Surface Mining: Proceedings of an International Symposium Edmonton, Canada September 29 - October 1, 1986. (Series on Mining Engineering: Vol. 7). 750p. 1987. text ed. 128.00 (*0-87849-074-4*, Pub. by Trans Tech GW) LPS Dist Ctr.

Continuous System Modeling. F. E. Cellier. (Illus.). xxviii, 775p. 1991. 79.50 (*0-387-97502-0*) Spr-Verlag.

Continuous Time Econometric Modelling. A. R. Bergstrom. (Recent Advances in Econometrics Ser.). (Illus.). 336p. 1990. 89.00 (*0-19-828340-7*); pap. 35.00 (*0-19-828367-9*) OUP.

Continuous-Time Econometrics: Theory & Applications. Ed. by Giancarlo Gandolfo. LC 92-38094. (International Studies in Economic Modelling). 1992. write for info. (*0-412-45020-8*) Chapman & Hall.

Continuous-Time Finance. Robert C. Merton. (Macroeconomics & Finance Ser.). (C). 1992. 29.95 (*0-631-18508-9*) Blackwell Pubs.

Continuous Time Markov Chains: An Applications-Oriented Approach. W. J. Anderson. Ed. by J. Gani & C. C. Heyde. (Series in Statistics-Subseries: Probability & Its Applications). (Illus.). 368p. 1992. 69.00 (*0-387-97369-9*) Spr-Verlag.

C

Continuous-Time Self-Tuning Control: Design, Pt. 1. P. J. Gawthrop. (Mechanical Engineering Dynamics Ser.). 250p. 1987. text ed. 195.00 (*0-471-91417-7*) Wiley.

Continuous-Time Self-Tuning Control: Implementation, Vol. 2. P. J. Gawthrop. (Mechanical Engineering Research Studies Ser.). 322p. 1990. text ed. 195.00 (*0-471-92429-6*) Wiley.

Continuous Transcutaneous Blood Gas Monitoring. Huch. (Reproductive Medicine Ser.: Vol. 5). 840p. 1983. 195. 00 (*0-8247-1794-5*) Dekker.

Continuous Transcutaneous Blood Gas Monitoring. Ed. by Albert Huch et al. LC 79-2586. (Alan R. Liss Ser.: Vol. 15, No. 4). 1979. 82.00 (*0-685-03282-5*) March of Dimes.

Continuous Transcutaneous Monitoring. R. Huch & G. Rooth. Ed. by A. Huch. LC 87-15358. (Advances in Experimental Medicine & Biology Ser.: Vol. 220). (Illus.). 342p. 1987. 69.50 (*0-306-42661-7*, Plenum Pr) Plenum.

Continuous Transitions in Open Waveguides. Viktor V. Shevchenko. Tr. by Petr Beckmann. LC 72-145593. (Electromagnetics Ser.: Vol. 5). (Illus.). 1971. 25.00 (*0-911762-08-6*) Golem.

Continuous Univariate Distributions. 2nd ed. Norman L. Johnson et al. LC 93-45348. (Probability & Mathematical Statistics Ser.). 1994. text ed. 84.95 (*0-471-58495-9*, Wiley-Interscience) Wiley.

***Continuous Univariate Distributions, Vol. 2.** 2nd ed. Norman L. Johnson et al. (Series in Probability & Mathematics: Vol. 2). 1995. text ed. 89.95 (*0-471-58494-0*) Wiley.

Continuous Univariate Distributions: Distributions in Statistics, 2 vols. Norman L. Johnson & Samuel I. Kotz. (Probability & Mathematical Statistics Ser.). 306p. 1971. Vol. 2, 306pp. text ed. 79.95 (*0-471-44627-0*) Wiley.

Continuous Univariate Distributions: Distributions in Statistics, 2 vols., 1. Norman L. Johnson & Samuel I. Kotz. (Probability & Mathematical Statistics Ser.). 306p. 1971. text ed. 79.95 (*0-471-44626-2*) Wiley.

Continuous Wave: Technology & American Radio, 1900-1932. Hugh G. Aitken. LC 84-22265. (Illus.). 607p. reprint ed. pap. 173.00 (*0-7837-4330-0*, 2044034) Bks Demand.

Continuously Improving Self. Jeffrey E. Lickson. Ed. by Michael G. Crisp. LC 91-77764. (Fifty-Minute Ser.). (Illus.). 100p. (Orig.). 1992. pap. 9.95 (*1-56052-151-1*) Crisp Pubns.

Continuously Variable Transmissions for Passenger Cars. 1987. 29.00 (*0-89883-118-0*, PT30) Soc Auto Engineers.

Continuum. Newton Miner. 64p. 1986. 6.95 (*0-317-42525-0*) Harlo Press.

Continuum: A Critical Examination of the Foundation of Analysis. Hermann Weyl. 130p. reprint ed. pap. 5.95 (*0-486-67982-9*) Dover.

Continuum: A Critical Examination of the Foundations of Analysis. Hermann Weyl. Tr. by Stephen Pollard & Thomas Bole. 158p. 1987. lib. bdg. 30.00 (*0-943549-01-9*) TJU Pr.

Continuum: An Autobiography at Thirty. Carol Stetser. LC 78-70872. (Illus.). 1979. pap. 19.95 (*0-917960-03-3*) Padma.

Continuum: Problems in French Literature from the Renaissance to the Early Enlightenment, 5 vols. Ed. by David L. Rubin. LC 87-45806. 1989. Vol. 1: Rethinking Classicism: Overviews. 57.50 (*0-685-73895-7*); Rethinking Classicism: Textual Explorations. 57.50 (*0-404-63751-5*); Vol. 3: Poetics of Exposition & Libertinage & the Art of Writing, Vol. 1. 57.50 (*0-685-73896-5*); Vol. 4: Libertinage & the Art of Writing, Vol. 2. 57.50 (*0-404-63754-X*); Literature & the Other Arts. 57.50 (*0-404-63755-8*) AMS Pr.

Continuum: Problems in French Literature from the Renaissance to the Early Enlightenment, 5 vols., Set. Ed. by David L. Rubin. LC 87-45806. 1989. write for info. (*0-404-63750-7*) AMS Pr.

Continuum Concept. Jean Liedloff. 256p. 1985. pap. 11.54 (*0-201-05071-4*) Addison-Wesley.

Continuum Concept. Jean Liedloff. 21.25 (*0-8446-6267-4*) Peter Smith.

Continuum Damage Mechanics: Theory & Applications. Ed. by D. Krajcinovic & Jean P. Lemaitre. (CISM Ser.: Vol. 295). (Illus.). v, 294p. 1988. pap. 45.00 (*0-387-82011-6*) Spr-Verlag.

Continuum Dictionary of Religion. Ed. by Michael Pye. LC 93-36623. 352p. 1994. 34.95 (*0-8264-0639-4*) Continuum.

Continuum Encyclopedia of Symbols. Ed. by Udo Becker. Tr. by Lance W. Garmer. (Illus.). 500p. 1994. 39.50 (*0-8264-0644-0*) Continuum.

Continuum: Listening & Speaking see Language Learning: The Intermediate Phase

***Continuum Mechanics.** Gy Beda et al. 330p. 1994. 150.00 (*963-05-6758-X*, Pub. by Akad Kiado HU) St Mut.

Continuum Mechanics. D. S. Chandrasekharaiah & Lokenath Debnath. LC 93-41278. (Illus.). 595p. (C). 1994. text ed. 69.95 (*0-12-167880-6*) Acad Pr.

Continuum Mechanics. G. E. Mase. (Schaum's Outline Ser.). 1969. pap. text ed. 12.95 (*0-07-040663-4*) McGraw.

***Continuum Mechanics.** Patrick H. McDonald. LC 94-23728. 1996. text ed. 68.95 (*0-534-93984-8*) PWS Pubs.

Continuum Mechanics. A. J. Spencer. (Longman Mathematical Text Ser.). 192p. 1986. pap. text ed. 46.95 (*0-470-20399-4*) Halsted Pr.

Continuum Mechanics, 4 vols. Ed. by C. Truesdell. Incl. Vol. 1. Mechanical Foundations of Elasticity. xvi, 218p. 1966. text ed. 145.00 (*0-677-00820-1*); Vol. 2. Rational Mechanics of Materials. 446p. 1966. text ed. 152.00 (*0-677-00830-9*); Vol. 3. Foundations of Elasticity Theory. 320p. 1966. text ed. 152.00 (*0-677-00840-6*); Vol. 4. Problems of Nonlinear Elasticity. 276p. 1966. text ed. 145.00 (*0-677-00850-3*); (International Science Review Ser.). (Illus.). 1965. write for info. (*0-318-52698-0*) Gordon & Breach.

Continuum Mechanics & Its Applications. G. A. Graham & S. K. Malik. 650p. 1989. 205.00 (*0-89116-889-3*) Hemisp Pub.

Continuum Mechanics Aspects of Geodynamics & Rock Fracture Mechanics: Proceedings of the NATO Study Institute, Reykjavik, Iceland, August 11-20, 1974. NATO Study Institute Staff & P. Thoft-Christensen. LC 74-34161. (NATO Advanced Study Institutes Ser.: No. C12). 273p. 1974. lib. bdg. 70.00 (*90-277-0504-6*) Kluwer Ac.

Continuum Mechanics for Engineers. George E. Mase & G. Thomas Mase. (Illus.). 176p. 1991. 59.95 (*0-8493-8830-9*, QA808) CRC Pr.

Continuum Mechanics in Environmental Sciences & Geophysics. Ed. by Kolumban Hutter. (CISM International Centre for Mechanical Sciences Ser.: No. 337). xiii, 552p. 1993. pap. 99.00 (*0-387-82449-9*) Spr-Verlag.

Continuum Mechanics of Electromagnetics Solids. Gerard A. Maugin. (Applied Mathematical & Mechanics Ser.: Vol. 33). 598p. 1988. 179.50 (*0-444-70399-3*, North Holland) Elsevier.

Continuum Models of Discrete Systems: Proceedings. Ed. by A. J. Spenser. 248p. (C). 1987. text ed. 140.00 (*90-6191-682-8*, Pub. by A A Balkema NE) Ashgate Pub Co.

***Continuum Models of Discrete Systems: Proceedings of the 7th International Symposium, Paderborn, Germany 1992.** Seventh International Symposium on Continuum Models of Discrete Systems Staff. Ed. by K. H. Anthony & H. J. Wagner. (Materials Science Forum Ser.: Vols. 123-125). 850p. 1993. text ed. 210.00 (*0-87849-657-2*) LPS Dist Ctr.

***Continuum of Long-Term Care: An Integrated Systems Approach.** Ed. by Connie J. Evashwick. LC 94-48856. (Health Services Administration Ser.). 1995. write for info. (*0-8273-6151-3*) Delmar.

Continuum of Services. ALMACA Staff. pap. 12.50 (*0-318-22971-4*) ALMACA.

Continuum Spectra of Heavy-Ion Reactions. Ed. by T. Tamura et al. (Nuclear Science Research Conference Ser.: Vol. 2). 490p. 1980. 190.00 (*3-7186-0028-5*) Gordon & Breach.

Continuum Theories in Solid Earth Physics: Physics & Evolution of the Earth's Interior, No. 3. Ed. by R. Teisseyre. 587p. 1986. 159.00 (*0-444-99569-2*) Elsevier.

Continuum Theory: An Introduction. Ed. by Nadler. (Pure & Applied Mathematics Ser.: Vol. 158). 352p. 1992. 140. 00 (*0-8247-8659-9*) Dekker.

Continuum Theory & Dynamical Systems. M. Brown. (CONM Ser.: Vol. 117). 182p. 1991. 66.00 (*0-8218-5123-3*) Am Math.

Continuum Theory & Dynamical Systems. Ed. by Thelma West. LC 93-14090. (Lecture Notes in Pure & Applied Mathematics Ser.: Vol. 149). 304p. 1993. 125.00 (*0-8247-9072-3*) Dekker.

Continuum Theory of Plasticity. Akhtar S. Khan & Sujian Huang. LC 94-13851. 1995. text ed. 69.95 (*0-471-31043-3*) Wiley.

Continuum Theory of Rock Mechanics. Cs. Assonyi & R. Richter. Tr. by B. Balkay. (Rock & Soil Mechanics Ser.). (Illus.). (C). 1979. 58.00 (*0-87849-027-2*, Pub. by Trans Tech GW) LPS Dist Ctr.

Continuum Theory of the Mechanics of Fibre-Reinforced Composites. Ed. by A. J. Spencer. (CISM International Centre for Mechanical Sciences Ser.: Vol. 282). (Illus.). viii, 284p. 1985. pap. 54.00 (*0-387-81842-1*) Spr-Verlag.

Continuum 1994 Annual of Hermeneutics & Social Concern. Justus G. Lawler. 324p. 1994. pap. text ed. 19.95 (*0-8264-4605-1*) Continuum.

Contorno: Literary Engagement in Post-Peronist Argentina. William H. Katra. LC 86-46407. 176p. 1988. 29.50 (*0-8386-3316-1*) Fairleigh Dickinson.

Contos do Brasil. Ed. by D. Lee Hamilton & Ned C. Fahs. LC 44-4280. (POR.). 1955. pap. text ed. 19.95 (*0-89197-108-4*) Irvington.

Contos Tristes. 2nd ed. Luis Canales. (Illus.). 60p. 1988. pap. 3.95 (*0-933704-64-X*) Dawn Pr.

Contour in Time: The Plays of Eugene O'Neill. rev. ed. Travis Bogard. (Illus.). 528p. 1988. pap. 12.95 (*0-19-504548-3*) OUP.

Contour-Oriented Approach to Digital Shape. Van Otterloo. 380p. 1991. text ed. 54.00 (*0-13-173840-2*) P-H.

Contouring: A Guide to the Analysis & Display of Spatial Data. David F. Watson. LC 92-26607. (Computer Methods in the Geosciences Ser.). 1992. 130.00 (*0-08-040286-0*, Pergamon Pr) Elsevier.

Contouring Geologic Surfaces with the Computer. Thomas A. Jones et al. (Computer Methods in the Geosciences Ser.). (Illus.). 320p. (C). 1986. text ed. 54.95 (*0-442-24437-1*) Chapman & Hall.

Contours for Piano. Harold Zabrack. 1979. 7.50 (*0-934286-03-5*) Kenyon.

Contours for Ritual. Poems. Martha McFerren. LC 87-12486. 64p. 1987. text ed. 13.95 (*0-8071-1421-9*); pap. 6.95 (*0-8071-1422-7*) La State U Pr.

***Contours of a Cause: Theological Vision of the Church of God Movement (Anderson, Indiana)** Barry L. Callen. (Illus.). 230p. 1995. pap. text ed. 4.00 (*0-9646682-0-3*) Anderson Univ.

Contours of American History. William A. Williams. 1989. pap. 12.95 (*0-393-30561-9*) Norton.

Contours of Canadian Thought. A. B. McKillop. 163p. 1987. 14.95 (*0-8020-6652-6*); 30.00 (*0-8020-5740-3*) U of Toronto Pr.

Contours of Christian Education. Jeff Astley & David Day. 416p. (C). 1988. 59.00 (*0-85597-495-8*, Pub. by McCrimmon Pub) St Mut.

Contours of Christian Philosophy, 4 bks., Set. 1991. pap. text ed. 45.99 (*0-87784-339-2*, 339) InterVarsity.

Contours of Christian Theology, 4 vols., Set. Ed. by Gerald Bray. (Orig.). 1994. pap. 56.99 (*0-8308-1530-9*, 1530) InterVarsity.

Contours of Church & State in the Thought of John Paul II. George H. Williams. LC 83-171724. (Institute of Church-State Studies). 90p. (C). 1983. pap. text ed. 5.95 (*0-918954-41-X*) Baylor Univ Pr.

***Contours of Continuity & Change: The Story of the Bonda Highlanders.** Bikram N. Nanda & Jamia M. Islamia. LC 94-31771. 200p. 1995. text ed. 24.95 (*0-8039-9193-2*) Sage.

Contours of Darkness. Marco Vassi. 282p. 1993. pap. 16.95 (*0-933256-90-6*) Second Chance.

Contours of Discovery: Printed Maps Delineating the Texas & Southwestern Chapters in the Cartographic History of North America, 1513-1930. Robert S. Martin & James C. Martin. LC 82-83547. 1982. 39.95 (*0-87611-058-8*) Tex St Hist Assn.

***Contours of European Romanticism.** Lilian R. Furst. LC 79-15141. 174p. 1979. reprint ed. pap. 49.60 (*0-7837-8865-7*, 2049576) Bks Demand.

Contours of Justice: Communities & Their Courts. James Eisenstein et al. (C). 1987. pap. text ed. 21.00 (*0-673-39716-5*) HarpCollege.

Contours of Justice: Communities & Their Courts. James Eisenstein et al. write for info. (*0-316-22550-9*) Little.

Contours of Masculine Desire: Romanticism & the Rise of Women's Poetry. Marlon B. Ross. 360p. 1990. 49.95 (*0-19-505791-0*) OUP.

Contours of the Fantastic: Selected Essays from the Eighth International Conference on the Fantastic in the Arts. Ed. by Michele K. Langford. LC 89-23308. (Contributions to the Study of Science Fiction & Fantasy Ser.: No. 41). 256p. 1990. text ed. 55.00 (*0-313-26647-6*, LCN/) Greenwood.

Contours of the West European Left. Ed. by Perry Anderson & Patrick Camiller. 256p. 1994. 50.00 (*0-86091-213-2*, A2702) Routledge Chapman & Hall.

Contours of the West European Left. Ed. by Patrick Camiller. 256p. 1994. pap. 17.95 (*0-86091-927-7*, A2706, Pub. by Verso UK) Routledge Chapman & Hall.

Contra Amatores Mundi of Richard Rolle of Hampole. Richard Rolle. Ed. by Paul F. Theiner. LC 68-64641. 196p. 1983. reprint ed. lib. bdg. 33.00x (*0-89370-791-0*) Borgo Pr.

Contra Costa & Solano 1994 McCormack's Guides. 1994. pap. 6.95 (*0-931299-40-3*) McCormacks Guides.

Contra Costa County Commerce & Industry Directory, 1994. 24th ed. 312p. 1994. disk write for info. (*0-318-72189-9*) Database Pub Co.

Contra Costa County Commerce & Industry Directory, 1994. 24th ed. 312p. 1995. pap. 75.00 (*0-929695-70-4*) Database Pub Co.

Contra Costa County Street Guide & Directory: 1994 Edition. (Illus.). 136p. 1994. pap. 12.95 (*0-88130-626-6*) Thomas Bros Maps.

***Contra Costa County Street Guide & Directory: 1995 Edition.** Thomas Bros. Maps Staff. (Illus.). 136p. 1994. pap. 12.95 (*0-88130-689-4*) Thomas Bros Maps.

Contra Costa County Street Guide & Directory, 1991. Thomas Bros. Maps Staff. (Illus.). 136p. 1990. pap. 12.95 (*0-88130-463-8*) Thomas Bros Maps.

***Contra Costa County Under the Vitascope.** William L. Metcalfe. Ed. by Robert D. Tatam. (Illus.). 120p. 1994. pap. 14.99 (*0-9637954-1-4*) Highlnd Pubs.

***Contra Costa-Solano 1995: McCormack's Guides.** 1995. pap. 8.95 (*0-931299-47-0*) McCormacks Guides.

***Contra Costa-Solano 1996: McCormack's Guides.** 1995. pap. 8.95 (*0-931299-55-1*) McCormacks Guides.

***Contra Dance Choreography: A Reflection of Social Change.** rev. ed. Mary M. Dart. LC 94-49557. (Garland Studies in American Popular History & Culture). (Illus.). 296p. 1995. 72.00 (*0-8153-1984-3*) Garland.

Contra el Pensamiento Mao Zedong!, No. 5. Marxist-Leninist Party, U. S. A. Staff. Ed. by National Executive Committee of the MLP, U. S. A. 65p. (SPA.). 1981. pap. 1.00 (*0-86714-017-8*) Marxist-Leninist.

Contra el Pensamiento Mao Zedong, No.1. Marxist-Leninist Party, U. S. A. Staff. Ed. by National Executive Committee of the MLP, U. S. A. (Contra el Pensamiento Mao Zedong Ser.). (Illus.). 49p. (Orig.) (SPA.). 1981. pap. 1.00 (*0-86714-013-5*) Marxist-Leninist.

Contra el Pensamiento Mao Zedong!, Nos. 2 & 3. Marxist-Leninist Party, U. S. A. Staff. Ed. by National Executive Committee of the MLP, U. S. A. 61p. (SPA.). 1981. pap. 1.00 (*0-86714-014-3*) Marxist-Leninist.

Contra el Viento: Una Vida De Wohay Amor. Juan Suarez. 470p. 1991. pap. 19.95 (*0-9632334-3-2*) J Suarez.

***Contra Keynes & Cambridge: Essays, Correspondence, 9.** F. A. Hayek. Ed. by Bruce Caldwell. 266p. 1995. 35.00 (*0-226-32065-0*) U Ch Pr.

Contra Technologiam: The Crisis of Value in a Technological Age. Theodore J. Rivers. 128p. (C). 1993. lib. bdg. 29.50 (*0-8191-9090-X*) U Pr of Amer.

Contra Terror In Nicaragua: Report of a Fact-Finding Mission: September 1984-January 1985. Reed Brody. 200p. (Orig.). 1985. 30.00 (*0-89608-313-6*); pap. 8.50 (*0-89608-312-8*) South End Pr.

Contraband, A Romance of the North Atlantic. Randall Parrish. 1976. lib. bdg. 18.25 (*0-89968-085-2*, Lghtyr Pr) Buccaneer Bks.

Contraband of War. Matthew P. Shiel. LC 68-23727. (Americans in Fiction Ser.). (Illus.). 258p. reprint ed. lib. bdg. 19.00 (*0-8398-1857-2*); reprint ed. pap. text ed. 6.95 (*0-89197-713-9*) Irvington.

Contrabandista De Dios (God's Smuggler) Hermano Andres. (SPA.). 1990. 4.50 (*0-945792-89-1*, 498522) Editorial Unilit.

Contraception. Ed. by S. S. Ratnam et al. (Advances in Ferility & Sterility Ser.: Vol. 6). 196p. 1987. 55.00 (*1-85070-156-3*) Prthnon Pub.

Contraception. Ed. by Donna Shoupe. LC 92-48671. (Clinical Perspectives in Obstetrics & Gynecology Ser.). 256p. 1993. 65.00 (*0-387-97859-3*); write for info. (*3-540-97859-3*) Spr-Verlag.

Contraception: A Guide to Birth Control Methods. Vern L. Bullough & Bonnie Bullough. (Illus.). 177p. (Orig.). 1990. pap. 17.95 (*0-87975-589-X*) Prometheus Bks.

Contraception: A History of Its Treatment by the Catholic Theologians & Canonists. John T. Noonan, Jr. 592p. 1986. 45.00 (*0-674-16853-4*) HUP.

Contraception: A User's Handbook. Anne Szarewski & John Guillebaud. LC 93-36749. (C). 1994. 10.00 (*0-19-286164-6*) OUP.

Contraception: Newer Pharmacological Agents, Devices, & Delivery Systems. Ed. by Regine Sitruk-Ware & C. Wayne Bardin. LC 92-22111. 240p. 1992. 110.00 (*0-8247-8700-5*) Dekker.

Contraception: Science & Practice. Marchs Filshie & John Guillebaud. (Illus.). 376p. 1989. text ed. 135.00 (*0-7506-1186-3*) Buttrwrth-Heinemann.

Contraception: The Chemical Control of Fertility. Ed. by Daniel Lednicer. LC 79-99957. (Illus.). 285p. reprint ed. pap. 81.30 (*0-7837-0957-9*, 2041262) Bks Demand.

Contraception: The Facts. 2nd ed. Peter Bromwich & Tony Parsons. (Facts Ser.). (Illus.). 224p. 1990. 21.95 (*0-19-261921-7*) OUP.

Contraception: Your Questions Answered. 2nd ed. John Guillebaud. (Illus.). 372p. (Orig.). 1993. pap. text ed. 21. 95 (*0-443-04070-2*) Churchill.

Contraception & Abortion from the Ancient World to the Renaissance. John . Riddle. 1994. pap. 16.95 (*0-674-16876-3*) HUP.

Contraception & Abortion from the Ancient World to the Renaissance. John M. Riddle. (Illus.). 245p. (C). 1992. 45.00 (*0-674-16875-5*) HUP.

Contraception & Abortion in Nineteenth-Century America. Janet F. Brodie. LC 93-30515. (Illus.). 392p. 1994. 33.95 (*0-8014-2849-1*) Cornell U Pr.

Contraception & Chronic Illness: A Clinician's Sourcebook. Lawrence S. Neinstein & Barbara Katz. LC 86-70099. 98p. 1986. pap. 24.95 (*0-9603332-5-8*) Am Health Consults.

Contraception & Family Planning: A Medical Subject Analysis with Reference Bibliography. Jacob L. Liehaus. LC 85-48080. 150p. 1987. 44.50 (*0-88164-432-3*); pap. 39.50 (*0-88164-433-1*) ABBE Pubs Assn.

Contraception & Fertility in the Southern Appalachians. Gilbert W. Beebe. LC 79-169373. (Family in America Ser.). (Illus.). 396p. 1972. reprint ed. 20.95 (*0-405-03849-6*) Ayer.

Contraception & Reproduction: Health Consequences for Women & Children in the Developing World. 120p. 1989. pap. text ed. 15.00 (*0-309-04094-9*) Natl Acad Pr.

Contraception Explained. C. Wood. 1975. pap. 1.60 (*92-4-156047-9*) World Health.

An Asterisk (*) at the beginning of an entry indicates that the title is appearing in BIP for the first time.

---

*Contract Costs. Linda Bruggeman et al. Ed. by Regina M. Bova. (National Contract Management Association National Education Seminar Ser.). 408p. (Orig.). 1995. pap. 59.95 (0-940343-67-3) Natl Contract Mgmt.
Concerned about cost management? This text examines contract costs from a variety of angles. From basic cost principles to cost accounting standards, there is valuable information for all experience levels. The book explores the difference between cost of goods sold & business expenses. It also looks at different kinds of capital expenditures. Specifically addressing government contracts, the book covers traditional topics such as proposal-related costs, price analysis versus cost analysis, progress payments, contract changes, government audits, cost of fraud, & legal & other professional costs. In its coverage of cost accounting standards (CAS), the book presents the statutory origins of the CAS, the current CAS Board administration, CAS applicability, "full" versus "modified" coverage, & disclosure statements. It also discusses each of the CAS & many of the cost principles in detail. In addition, it covers current topics such as environmental costs & the Federal Acquisition Streamlining Act. This book provides the tools necessary to maximize your understanding of contract costs, & it is particularly useful for those interested in government contracting. To order: **National Contract Management Associations, 1912 Woodford Rd., Vienna, VA 22182. Phone 1-800-344-8096** *Publisher Provided Annotation.*

An Asterisk (*) at the beginning of an entry indicates that the title is appearing in BIP for the first time.

1591

Contract on America: The Mafia Murder of President John F. Kennedy. David E. Scheim. 496p. 19.95 (0-933503-30-X) Sure Sellers.

Contract Perspective on Accounting Valuation, Vol. 20. John S. Hughes. (Studies in Accounting Research). 92p. 1984. 12.00 (0-86539-048-7) Am Accounting.

Contract Plans & Public Enterprise Performance: Les Contrats de Plan et Leur Role Dans l'Amelioration de la Performance des Enterprises Publiques. John Nellis. (Discussion Paper Ser.: No. 48). 100p. 1989. English, 100 pp. 7.95 (0-8213-1188-3, 20048) World Bank.

Contract Practice for Quantity Surveyors. 2nd ed. J. W. Ramus. 224p. 1989. pap. 39.95 (0-434-91677-3) Buttrwrth-Heinemann.

Contract Programming for DP. Lee. 1987. pap. 19.95 (0-9611810-8-7) CCD Online Syst.

Contract Railroad Rates. Bob J. Davis & C. K. Walter. Ed. by Richard E. Hattwick. 175p. 1984. pap. 25.00 (0-931497-01-9) WIU CBER.

Contract Remedies in a Nutshell. Jane M. Friedman. LC 81-11614. (Nutshell Ser.). 323p. (C). 1988. reprint ed. pap. text ed. 15.50 (0-314-60373-5) West Pub.

Contract Research. Ed. by W. E. Duckworth. 144p. 1991. lib. bdg. 64.00 (0-7923-1449-2) Kluwer Ac.

Contract Research Business in the United Kingdom - European Dimension, No. EUR 14578. European Communities Staff. 69p. 1992. pap. 11.00 (92-826-4610-6, CG-NA-14578-EN-C, Pub. by Europ Com) UNIPUB.

Contract Services for Higher Education. 800p. (Orig.). 1995. pap. 89.95 (1-56079-442-9) Petersons Guides.

Contract Specialist. Jack Rudman. (Career Examination Ser.: C-955). 1994. pap. 27.95 (0-8373-0955-7) Nat Learn.

***Contract State: Public Management & the Kennett Government.** John Afford & Deirdre O'Neill. 192p. (C). 1994. 40.00x (0-7300-2111-4, Pub. by Deakin Univ AT) St Mut.

Contract Surety, 2 vols. John W. Welch et al. LC 92-72109. (C). 1992. pap. 26.00 (0-89462-072-X) IIA.

Contract Suretyship. Richard C. Lewis. 1991. 49.50 (1-56461-037-3, 46100) Rough Notes.

Contract Time Determination. (National Cooperative Highway Research Program Report Ser.: No. 79). 45p. 1981. 7.20 (0-309-03166-4) Transport Res Bd.

Contract to Love. Kate Proctor. 1994. mass mkt. 2.99 (0-373-11661-6, 1-11661-5) Harlequin Bks.

***Contract with America: The Bold Plan by Rep. Newt Gingrich, Rep. Dick Armey, & the House Republicans to Change the Nation.** Newt Gingrich et al. 1994. pap. 10.00 (0-8129-2586-6, Times Bks) Random.

***Contract with America's Youth: Toward a National Youth Development System.** Ed. by Samuel Halperin et al. 64p. 1995. pap. write for info. (1-887031-52-9) Am Youth Policy.

Contract with God. Will Eisner. (Illus.). 136p. 1985. pap. 8.95 (0-87816-018-3) Kitchen Sink.

Contract with the World. Jane Rule. 352p. 1990. 9.95 (0-941483-79-7) Naiad Pr.

Contractarian Liberal Ethics & the Theory of Rational Choice. Jung S. Park. LC 91-18282. (American University Studies: Philosophy: Ser. V, Vol. 122). 291p. (C). 1992. text ed. 49.95 (0-8204-1566-9) P Lang Pubs.

Contractarianism & Rational Choice: Essays on David Gauthier's Morals by Agreement. Ed. by Peter Vallentyne. 352p. (C). 1991. pap. 29.95 (0-521-39815-0) Cambridge U Pr.

Contractarianism & Rational Choice: Essays on David Gauthier's Morals by Agreement. Ed. by Peter Vallentyne. 352p. (C). 1991. 79.95 (0-521-39134-2) Cambridge U Pr.

***Contractarianism vs. Holism: Reinterpreting Locke's Two Treatises of Government.** Zbigniew Rau. LC 95-6234. 1995. write for info. (0-8191-9929-X); pap. write for info. (0-8191-9930-3) U Pr of Amer.

***Contracted Marriage.** large type ed. Joan Norton. 1994. 20.95 (0-7089-3154-5) Ulverscroft.

Contractile Proteins & Muscle. Ed. by Koloman Laki. LC 72-134784. (Illus.). 622p. reprint ed. pap. 177.30 (0-7837-0949-8, 2041254) Bks Demand.

Contractile Proteins in Muscle & Non-Muscle Cell Systems: Biochemistry, Physiology & Pathology. Ed. by Emanuele E. Alia et al. LC 85-12294. 752p. 1985. text ed. 125.00 (0-275-91329-5, C1329, Praeger Pubs) Greenwood.

Contracting & Subcontracting for Overseas Projects. Richard M. Hadley & Edgar O. Herzfeld. 1988. lib. bdg. 56.50 (1-85333-025-6, Pub. by Graham & Trotman UK) Kluwer Ac.

Contracting & Volunteerism in Local Government. Lydia Manchester & Geoffrey S. Bogart. (Special Report Ser.). 224p. (Orig.). 1988. pap. text ed. 30.00 (0-87326-933-0) Intl City-Cnty Mgt.

Contracting Colonialism: Translation & Christian Conversion in Tagalog Society under Early Spanish Rule. Vicente L. Rafael. LC 87-23937. 248p. 1988. 32.50 (0-8014-2065-2) Cornell U Pr.

Contracting Colonialism: Translation & Christian Conversion in Tagalog Society under Early Spanish Rule. Vicente L. Rafael. LC 92-32739. (Illus.). 256p. 1993. pap. text ed. 15.95 (0-8223-1341-3) Duke.

Contracting for Atoms. Harold Orlans. LC 80-58. (Illus.). xvii, 242p. 1980. reprint ed. text ed. 69.50 (0-313-22287-8, ORCA, Greenwood Pr) Greenwood.

***Contracting for Cadd Work: A Guide for Design Professionals.** Michael Ingardia & John Hill. 112p. 1994. per., pap. text ed. 24.95 (0-8403-9839-5) Kendall-Hunt.

Contracting for Commercial Products & Services. 220p. 1989. pap. 35.00 (0-89707-505-6, 539-0089) Amer Bar Assn.

Contracting for Computer Systems Integration. Richard A. Beutel. 672p. 1991. 95.00 (0-87473-750-8) Michie Butterworth.

Contracting for Computing: A Checklist of Terms & Clauses for Use in Contracting with Vendors for Computing Resources, Vol. I. Harry Rowell & Carolyn P. Landis. 156p. 1973. 16.00 (0-318-14016-0); 9.00 (0-318-14017-9) EDUCOM.

Contracting for Computing: A Checklist of Terms & Clauses for Use in Contracting with Vendors for Software Packages & Custom Software, Vol. II. James Poage & Carolyn P. Landis. 148p. 1975. 16.00 (0-318-14014-4); 9.00 (0-318-14015-2) EDUCOM.

Contracting for Engineering & Construction Projects. P. D. Marsh. 315p. (C). 1988. 156.00 (0-685-29258-4, Inst Pur & Supply); 395.00 (0-685-39919-2, Inst Pur & Supply) St Mut.

Contracting for Engineering & Construction Projects. P. D. Marsh. 315p. (C). 1989. 375.00 (0-685-36153-5, Inst Pur & Supply) St Mut.

Contracting for Engineering & Construction Projects. 3rd ed. Peter Marsh. 315p. 1989. text ed. 58.95 (0-566-02792-5, Pub. by Gower UK) Ashgate Pub Co.

***Contracting for Engineering & Construction Projects.** 4th ed. Peter D. Marsh. 350p. 1995. 84.95 (0-566-07628-4) Ashgate Pub Co.

Contracting for Goods & Services. A. D. Allwright & O. Oliver. 194p. (C). 1986. 110.00 (0-685-39922-2, Inst Pur & Supply) St Mut.

Contracting for Goods & Services. A. D. Allwright & R. W. Oliver. 194p. (C). 1988. 60.00 (0-685-29260-6, Inst Pur & Supply) St Mut.

Contracting for Goods & Services. A. D. Allwright & R. W. Oliver. 194p. (C). 1989. 90.00 (0-685-36157-8, Inst Pur & Supply) St Mut.

Contracting for Property Rights. Gary D. Libecap. (Political Economy of Institutions & Decisions Ser.). (Illus.). 100p. (C). 1990. 54.95 (0-521-36620-8) Cambridge U Pr.

Contracting for Property Rights. Gary D. Libecap. (Political Economy of Institutions & Decisions Ser.). (Illus.). 100p. (C). 1994. pap. 15.95 (0-521-44904-9) Cambridge U Pr.

Contracting for Services in Alternative Practice Settings. Beverly Entwistle & Bonnie Bruerd. 30.00 (0-318-22825-4) Am Dental Hygienists.

Contracting Maintenance Services. Hilary Green & Rita E. Knorr. (Special Report Ser.: No. 58). 31p. (Orig.). 1990. pap. text ed. 45.00 (0-917084-08-X) Am Public Works.

Contracting-Out. 100p. 15.00 (0-318-14037-3); 7.00 (0-318-14038-1) Elec Ind Assn.

Contracting Out for Human Services: Economic, Political, & Organizational Perspectives. Ruth H. De Hoog. LC 83-24292. (SUNY Series in Urban Public Policy). 186p. 1985. 69.50 (0-87395-893-4); pap. 24.95 (0-87395-894-2) State U NY Pr.

Contracting out in Government: A Guide to Working with Outside Contractors to Supply Public Services. John A. Rehfuss. LC 88-30702. (Public Administration Ser.). 304p. 1989. 36.95 (1-55542-137-7) Jossey-Bass.

Contracting Selected State Government Functions: Issues & Next Steps. Contrib by Terrell Blodgett & Jerome Chapman. (Policy Research Project Report Ser.: No. 75). 216p. 1987. 10.00 (0-89940-677-7) LBJ Sch Pub Aff.

Contracting Selected State Government Functions: Legislation & Implementation. Contrib by Terrell Blodgett. (Policy Research Project Report Ser.: No. 81). 213p. 1986. 12.00 (0-89940-685-8) LBJ Sch Pub Aff.

Contracting State. Ian Harden. (Studies in Law & Politics Ser.). 96p. 1992. pap. 20.00 (0-335-09634-4, Open Univ Pr) Taylor & Francis.

Contracting to Build Your Home. Herschel G. Nance. Ed. by James C. Smith, Jr. LC 91-32694. 160p. (Orig.). 1992. pap. 12.95 (0-86534-160-5) Sunstone Pr.

***Contracting with Architects: A School District's Perspective.** Michael Levin et al. 40p. (Orig.). 1991. pap. 25.00 (0-614-03399-3) Natl Sch Boards.

Contracting with the Federal Government. 3rd ed. Frank M. Alston et al. 600p. 1992. text ed. 115.00 (0-471-55344-1) Wiley.

Contracting with the Federal Government. 3rd suppl. ed. Frank M. Alston et al. 64p. 1993. Suppl. 1993, 64p. 45.00 (0-471-59211-0) Wiley.

Contracting with the RTC & FDIC. Thomas P. Vartanian et al. 3258p. 1991. ring bd. 260.00 (0-13-297672-2, 22221) Aspen Law.

Contractions. Barbara Lipschutz. 1974. pap. 2.50 (0-912786-28-0) Know Inc.

Contractive Projections in C(Sub P) J. Arazy & Y. Friedman. LC 91-36296. (MEMO Ser.: No. 95/459). 134p. 1992. 26.00 (0-8218-2515-1, MEMO 95/459) Am Math.

Contractive Projections in C1 & Coo. Jonathan Arazy & Yaakov Friedman. LC 77-28610. (American Mathematical Society, Memoirs Ser.: No. 200). 180p. reprint ed. pap. 51.30 (0-7837-4420-X, 2044165) Bks Demand.

Contractor or Manipulator? A Guide to Construction Financing from Beginning of Construction to Completion. rev. ed. Andrew Sokol, Jr. LC 68-9511. (Illus.). 1968. 10.95 (0-87024-091-9) U of Miami Pr.

Contractors' All Risks & Public Liability Insurance. L. J. Piper. 80p. 1981. pap. 75.00 (0-948691-03-4, Pub. by Witherby & Co UK) St Mut.

Contractor's Analysis. Richard Lewis. Date not set. write for info. (1-56461-136-1) Rough Notes.

Contractors & Contractor Direction Theory & Applications: A New Approach to Solving Equations. Altman. (Lecture Notes in Pure & Applied Mathematics Ser.: Vol. 32). 304p. 1977. 125.00 (0-8247-6672-5) Dekker.

Contractors' Business Handbook: Accounting, Tax Management, Finance, Cost Control. Michael Milliner. (Illus.). 300p. 1988. 59.95 (0-87629-105-1, 67255) R S Means.

Contractor's Computer System Evaluator. Larry True. 12.50 (0-317-59583-0) Constr Ind Pr.

Contractor's Computer System Specifier. Larry True. 12.50 (0-317-59582-2) Constr Ind Pr.

***Contractor's Dictionary of Equipment, Tools, & Techniques.** Ed. & Comp. by Len F. Webster. LC 94-24421. 1995. text ed. 69.95 (0-471-11523-1) Wiley.

Contractor's Exam Book. 3rd ed. John Gladstone et al. 250p. 1985. pap. 29.00 (0-930644-07-7) Engineers Pr.

Contractor's Exam Book. 3rd ed. John Gladstone et al. LC 85-80734. (Illus.). 250p. 1989. pap. text ed. 29.00 (0-930644-12-3) Engineers Pr.

Contractor's Growth & Profit Guide. Michael C. Thomsett. 300p. (Orig.). 1988. pap. 19.00 (0-934041-34-2) Craftsman.

Contractor's Guide to Change Orders: The Art of Finding, Pricing, & Getting Paid for Contract Changes & the Damages They Cause. Andrew M. Civitello, Jr. 400p. 1987. text ed. 59.95 (0-13-171588-7) P-H.

Contractor's Guide to Quality Concrete Construction. 107p. 1992. 43.25 (0-685-62949-X, ACI/ASCC.1) ACI.

Contractor's Guide to the Building Code, 1992-93. rev. ed. Jack M. Hageman. 544p. 1992. pap. 28.00 (0-934041-67-9) Craftsman.

Contractor's Information "Sourcebook" The Building Code Simplified. David Rochester, Jr. Ed. by Wendy Rene. (Illus.). 170p. (Orig.). (C). 1988. text ed. 45.00 (0-685-19927-4); pap. 35.00 (0-685-19928-2) CIS Pub.

Contractors of Chartres, 2 vols., Set. John James. 1989. 110.00 (0-9596005-3-1) Boydell & Brewer.

***Contractors Pricing Guide: Framing & Rough Carpentry 1995.** 2nd ed. 1994. pap. 34.95 (0-87629-380-1) R S Means.

***Contractors Pricing Guide: Residential Detail Costs 1995.** 2nd ed. 1994. pap. 36.95 (0-87629-382-8) R S Means.

***Contractors Pricing Guide: Residential Square Foot Costs 1995.** 2nd ed. 1994. pap. 39.95 (0-87629-381-X) R S Means.

Contractor's Project Guide. Edward R. Fisk & James R. Negele. LC 87-10455. 354p. 1988. text ed. 40.95 (0-471-88873-7) P-H.

Contractor's Survival Manual. William D. Mitchell. LC 86-16620. 160p. (Orig.). 1986. pap. 16.75 (0-910460-42-6) Craftsman.

***Contractor's Year-Round Tax Guide.** rev. ed. Michael C. Thomsett. (Illus.). 208p. (Orig.). 1995. pap. 26.50 (1-57218-006-4) Craftsman.

Contracts. Olga Aikin. 128p. (C). 1992. write for info. (0-318-69502-2, Pub. by IPM Hse UK) St Mut.

Contracts. Olga Aikin. 176p. (C). 1992. pap. text ed. 95.00 (0-85292-486-0, Pub. by IPM Hse UK) St Mut.

Contracts. Marvin A. Chirelstein. (University Textbook Ser.). 175p. 1990. pap. text ed. 11.95 (0-88277-803-X) Foundation Pr.

Contracts. Steven Emanuel. 507p. 1993. pap. text ed. 16.95 (1-56542-021-7) E Law Outlines.

Contracts. E. Allan Farnsworth. LC 81-84829. (C). 1982. 29.50 (0-316-27461-5) Little.

Contracts. Daniel W. Fessler. Ed. by Robert J. Switzer et al. (Law Outlines Ser.). 328p. (Orig.). 1989. pap. text ed. 16.95 (0-87457-176-6) Casenotes Pub.

Contracts. Ed. by Jacques Herbots. 1992. ring bd. write for info. (0-318-68486-1) Kluwer Law Tax Pubs.

Contracts. 2nd ed. John D. Calamari & Joseph M. Perillo. (Black Letter Ser.). 462p. 1993. reprint ed. pap. text ed. 24.50 (0-314-73305-1) West Pub.

Contracts. 2nd ed. E. Allan Farnsworth. 1990. 38.95 (0-316-27462-3) Little.

Contracts. 3rd ed. John D. Calamari & Joseph M. Perillo. (Hornbook Ser.). 1049p. (C). 1992. reprint ed. text ed. 34.00 (0-314-34698-8) West Pub.

Contracts. Arthur L. Corbin. (Text Ser.). 1224p. 1992. reprint ed. student ed, text ed. 34.00 (0-314-28433-8) West Pub.

Contracts, 3 vols., 1. E. Allan Farnsworth. 1990. 150.00 (0-316-27463-1) Little.

Contracts, 3 vols., 2. E. Allan Farnsworth. 1990. 150.00 (0-316-27467-4) Little.

Contracts, 3 vols., 3. E. Allan Farnsworth. 1990. 150.00 (0-316-27466-6) Little.

Contracts, 3 vols., Set. E. Allan Farnsworth. 1990. 395.00 (0-316-27468-2) Little.

Contracts: A Legal Handbook for Business. Mungovan. 104p. 1990. pap. 25.00 (0-409-89659-4) Butterworth Legal Pubs.

Contracts: Adaptable to Courses Utilizing Calamari, Perillo, & Bender's Casebook on Contracts, Cases & Problems. Casenotes Publishing Co., Inc. Staff. Ed. by Norman S. Goldenberg et al. (Legal Briefs Ser.). 1989. pap. write for info. (0-87457-033-6, 1017) Casenotes Pub.

Contracts: Adaptable to Courses Utilizing Dawson, Harvey & Henderson's Casebook on Contracts. Casenotes Publishing Co., Inc. Staff. Ed. by Norman S. Goldenberg et al. (Legal Briefs Ser.). 1993. pap. write for info. (0-87457-034-4, 1014) Casenotes Pub.

Contracts: Adaptable to Courses Utilizing Farnsworth & Young's Casebook on Contracts. Casenotes Publishing Co., Inc. Staff. Ed. by Norman S. Goldenberg et al. (Legal Briefs Ser.). 1993. pap. write for info. (0-87457-035-2, 1010) Casenotes Pub.

Contracts: Adaptable to Courses Utilizing Fuller & Eisenberg's Casebook on Contracts. Casenotes Publishing Co., Inc. Staff. Ed. by Norman S. Goldenberg et al. (Legal Briefs Ser.). 1990. pap. write for info. (0-87457-036-0, 1011) Casenotes Pub.

Contracts: Adaptable to Courses Utilizing Hamilton, Rau & Weintraub's Casebook on Contracts. Casenotes Publishing Co., Inc. Staff et al. LC 85-206453. 118p. 1993. write for info. (0-87457-039-5, 1100) Casenotes Pub.

Contracts: Adaptable to Courses Utilizing Kessler, Gilmore & Kronman's Casebook on Contracts. Casenotes Publishing Co., Inc. Staff. Ed. by Norman S. Goldenberg et al. (Legal Briefs Ser.). 1986. pap. write for info. (0-87457-037-9, 1013) Casenotes Pub.

Contracts: Adaptable to Courses Utilizing Knapp & Crystal's Casebook on Problems in Contract Law. Casenotes Publishing Co., Inc. Staff. Ed. by Norman S. Goldenberg et al. (Legal Briefs Ser.). 1993. pap. write for info. (0-87457-038-7, 1016) Casenotes Pub.

Contracts: Adaptable to Courses Utilizing Murphy & Speidel's Casebook on Contract Law. Casenotes Publishing Co., Inc. Staff. Ed. by Norman S. Goldenberg et al. (Legal Briefs Ser.). 1991. pap. write for info. (0-87457-041-7, 1012) Casenotes Pub.

Contracts: Adaptable to Courses Utilizing Murray's Casebook on Contracts. Ed. by Norman S. Goldenberg et al. (Legal Briefs Ser.). 1991. pap. write for info. (0-87457-042-5, 1018) Casenotes Pub.

Contracts: Adaptable to Courses Utilizing Rosett's Casebook on Contracts Law & Its Application. Casenotes Publishing Co., Inc. Staff. Ed. by Norman S. Goldenberg et al. (Legal Briefs Ser.). 1994. pap. write for info. (0-87457-040-9, 1015) Casenotes Pub.

Contracts: Adaptable to Courses Utilizing Vernon's Casebook on Contracts: Theory & Practice. Casenotes Publishing Co., Inc. Staff. Ed. by Norman S. Goldenberg et al. (Legal Briefs Ser.). 1981. pap. write for info. (0-87457-043-3, 1019) Casenotes Pub.

Contracts: Analytical Briefs of Cases Suitable for Use with Crandall, & W, 1987 Edition. (Cambridge Ser.). 160p. 1987. pap. text ed. 14.00 (0-685-54305-6, Chicago Law Bk) Cambridge Law.

Contracts: Analytical Briefs of Cases Suitable for Use with Summers & H. 1987 Edition. James J. Jurinski. (Cambridge Ser.). 212p. 1987. pap. text ed. 14.00 (0-685-54294-7, Chicago Law Bk) Cambridge Law.

Contracts: Cases & Materials. 3rd ed. Friedrich Kessler et al. 1986. 53.00 (0-316-49018-0) Little.

Contracts: Cases & Materials. 4th ed. John E. Murray, Jr. 1037p. 1991. 44.00 (0-87473-801-6) Michie Butterworth.

***Contracts: Cases & Materials.** 5th ed. E. Allen Farnsworth & William F. Young. (Illus.). 1995. text ed. 47.95 (1-56662-242-5) Foundation Pr.

Contracts: Exchange Transactions & Relations, Cases & Materials. 2nd ed. Ian R. MacNeil. (University Casebook Ser.). 1320p. 1989. reprint ed. text ed. 39.00 (0-88277-432-8) Foundation Pr.

Contracts: Morality, Economics & the Market Place Cases & Materials. Daniel W. Fessler & Pierre R. Loiseaux. LC 82-10927. (American Casebook Ser.). 837p. 1982. text ed. 41.50 (0-314-66852-7); Tchr's. manual. teacher ed, pap. text ed. write for info. (0-314-71323-9) West Pub.

Contracts: Theory & Practice. 2nd ed. Vernon. 1991. write for info. (0-8205-0103-4, 209) Bender.

Contracts - Adaptable to Courses Utilizing Crandall & Whaley's Casebook on Contracts. Casenotes Publishing Co., Inc. Staff. Ed. by Goldenberg, Tenen & Switzer Staff. (Legal Briefs Ser.). 1993. pap. write for info. (0-87457-166-9, 1101) Casenotes Pub.

Contracts & Agreements. PMA, Ltd. Staff. 156p. 1991. pap. text ed. 65.00 (0-8403-6728-7) Kendall-Hunt.

Contracts & Conveyances of Real Property. Milton R. Friedman. 1437p. 1991. text ed. 195.00 (0-87224-033-9, N6-1367) PLI.

Contracts & Conveyances of Real Property: 1990 Supplement. Milton R. Friedman. 1990. 50.00 (0-685-69401-1) PLI.

Contracts & Liability for Builders & Remodelers. National Association of Home Builders, Legal Department Staff. (Illus.). 119p. 1993. pap. 25.00 (0-86718-376-4) Home Builder.

Contracts & Sales: Cases & Problems. McGovern & Lawrence. 1986. write for info. (0-8205-0106-9, 206); teacher ed write for info. (0-8205-0107-7) Bender.

Contracts & Specifications for Public Works Projects. Edward R. Fisk & Julius C. Calhoun. 352p. 1992. text ed. 89.95 (0-471-55928-8) Wiley.

***Contracts & Terms & Conditions of Employment.** Income Data Services Staff. 208p. (C). 1994. pap. 75.00x (0-85292-559-X, Pub. by IPM Hse UK) St Mut.

Contracts & the Legal Environment for Engineers & Architects. 5th ed. Joseph T. Bockrath. 1994. text ed. write for info. (0-07-018239-6) McGraw.

Contracts & You. 3.50 (0-944253-75-X) Inst Dev Indian Law.

Contracts Anthology. Peter Linzer. 459p. 1989. pap. 24.00 (0-87084-417-2) Anderson Pub Co.

Contracts at Work. Erich Suter. 288p. (C). 1982. 90.00 (0-85292-297-3, Pub. by IPM Hse UK) St Mut.

***Contracts: Building & Engineering: Their Planning & Administration.** C. W. Turner. 168p. 1983. pap. 27.00 (0-409-70127-0, NZ) Butterworth Legal Pubs.

Contracts, Cases & Comment On. 6th ed. John P. Dawson et al. LC 92-45699. (University Casebook Ser.). 1068p. (C). 1993. text ed. 43.95 (1-56662-053-8) Foundation Pr.

Contracts, Cases & Comments. 5th ed. John P. Dawson et al. (University Casebook Ser.). 1021p. 1988. reprint ed. text ed. 36.50 (0-88277-552-9) Foundation Pr.

Contracts, Cases & Materials. 2nd ed. Robert W. Hamilton et al. (American Casebook Ser.). 899p. 1992. text ed. 47.50 (0-314-00360-6) West Pub.

C

An Asterisk (*) at the beginning of an entry indicates that the title is appearing in BIP for the first time.

An Asterisk (*) at the beginning of an entry indicates that the title is appearing in BIP for the first time.

1593

Contributed Papers & Abstracts for the Conference on Water, Laws & Management: September 17-22, 1989, Tampa, Florida. Ed. by Frederick E. Davis. (AWRA Special Publication Ser.: No. 89-4). (Illus.). 872p. reprint ed. pap. 180.00 (*0-7837-1092-5*, 2041624) Bks Demand.

Contributed Papers in Fluids Engineering. Ed. by F. M. White. (FED Ser.: Vol. 139). 76p. 1992. 27.50 (*0-7918-1087-9*, G00731) ASME.

Contributed Papers in Fluids Engineering 1993. Ed. by F. M. White. LC 93-73723. 81p. Date not set. pap. 35.00 (*0-7918-1013-5*) ASME.

***Contributed Papers in Fluids Engineering 1994.** Ed. by F. M White. LC 93-73723. (Fluid Engineering Division Conference Ser.: Vol. 182). 1994. pap. 30.00 (*0-7918-1365-7*) ASME.

Contributing. rev. ed. Russ Korth et al. (Love One Another Bible Study Ser.). 1990. reprint ed. student ed, pap. text ed. 4.50 (*0-934396-51-5*) Churches Alive.

Contributing: Helping Others Fulfill Their Potential. Churches Alive Staff. (Love One Another Ser.). 64p. (Orig.). 1993. pap. 5.00 (*0-89109-784-8*, NavPr) NavPress.

Contributing to Educational Change: Perspectives on Research & Practice. Ed. by Philip Jackson. LC 88-60447. (NSSE Series on Contemporary Educational Issues). 214p. 1988. 29.00 (*0-8211-0911-1*); text ed. 26.25 (*0-685-45509-2*) McCutchan.

Contribution a la Connaissance des Cololejeunnoideae. P. Tixier. (Bryophytorum Bibliotheca Ser.: No. 27). (Illus.). 440p. 1985. lib. bdg. 90.00 (*3-7682-1418-4*) Lubrecht & Cramer.

Contribution a la Lexicographie Francaise Selon D'anciens Textes D'origies Juive. Raphael Levy. (FRE.). 1960. 75.00 (*0-89366-103-1*) Ultramarine Pub.

Contribution a l'Etude Biosystematique des Representants d'Aracees de la Cote d'Ivoire. Marianne Knecht. (Illus.). 314p. 1983. lib. bdg. 60.00 (*3-7682-1372-2*) Lubrecht & Cramer.

Contribution a L'etude De la Force D'articulation En Francais. A. Malecot. 1977. 21.15 (*90-279-3176-3*) Mouton.

Contribution a L'Etude des Algues de L'Eau Douce de la Guyane Francaise, a L'Exclusion des Ditaomees. Y. Therezien. (Bibliotheca Phycologica Ser.: No. 72). (Illus.). 276p. 1984. text ed. 65.00 (*3-7682-1417-6*) Lubrecht & Cramer.

Contribution a l'Etude du Genre Colo-Lejeuna. Les Colclejeuniceas de Nouvelles Caledonie. P. Tixier. (Illus.). 1979. pap. text ed. 18.00 (*3-7682-1230-0*) Lubrecht & Cramer.

Contribution a l'Etude Sociologique des Marches Nago du Bas-Dahomey see Commerce des Hommes

Contribution a l'histoire de la "querelle des Bouffons" Louisette Reichenburg. LC 76-43938. (Music & Theatre in France in the 17th & 18th Centuries Ser.). reprint ed. 32.50 (*0-404-60188-X*) AMS Pr.

Contribution a l'Histoire des Idees Scientifiques dans l'Islam, 2 vols., Set. Jabir Ibn Hayyan. (Memoires de l'Institute d'Egypt Ser.: Vols. 44, 45). lxxx, 620p. 1989. reprint ed. write for info. (*3-487-09113-5*, Pub. by Georg Olms GW) Lubrecht & Cramer.

Contribution & Claim Reduction in Antitrust Litigation. LC 86-70589. vii, 71p. 1986. 20.00 (*0-89707-226-X*, 503-0064) Amer Bar Assn.

Contribution au Debat Post-Saussurien Sur le Signe Linguistique: Introduction Generale et Bibliographie Annotee. E. F. Koerner. (Approaches to Semiotics Ser.: No. 2). 103p. (Orig.). (FRE.). 1972. pap. text ed. 49.25 (*90-279-2301-9*) Mouton.

***Contribution of Amenities to Rural Development.** OECD Staff. 91p. (Orig.). 1994. pap. 18.00x (*92-64-14164-2*) OECD.

Contribution of Aptitude Tests. S. K. Bali et al. viii, 100p. 1984. 16.00 (*90-265-0525-6*, Pub. by Swets Pub Serv NE) Taylor & Francis.

Contribution of Belgium to the Catholic Church in America (1523-1857) Joseph A. Griffin. LC 73-3568. (Catholic University of America. Studies in Romance Languages & Literatures: No. 13). reprint ed. 40.00 (*0-404-57763-6*) AMS Pr.

Contribution of British Writers Between 1560 & 1830 to the Interpretation of Revelation 13. 16-18. David Brady. 341p. 1983. lib. bdg. 77.50 (*3-16-144497-3*, Pub. by J C B Mohr GW) Coronet Bks.

Contribution of Carl Michalson to Modern Theology: Studies in Interpretation & Application. Ed. by Henry O. Thompson. LC 91-10208. (Toronto Studies in Theology: Vol. 54). 264p. 1991. lib. bdg. 89.95 (*0-88946-788-9*) E Mellen.

Contribution of Chemistry to Food Supplies: Proceedings of a Symposium, Hamburg, 1973. Ed. by I. Morton & D. N. Rhodes. 448p. 1974. 188.00 (*0-08-020748-0*, Pub. by Pergamon Repr UK) Franklin.

Contribution of Clusters Physics to Materials Science & Technology. Ed. by J. Davenas & P. M. Rabette. (NATO Advanced Science Institutes Series C: Mathematical & Physical Sciences). 1986. lib. bdg. 100.00 (*0-318-18929-1*) Kluwer Ac.

Contribution of Generalization to the Learning of Additional Facts. Carl L. Thiele. LC 74-177720. (Columbia University. Teachers College. Contributions to Education Ser.: No. 763). reprint ed. 37.50 (*0-404-55763-5*) AMS Pr.

Contribution of Grazyna Bacewicz (1909-69) to Polish Music. Sharon G. Shafer. LC 92-3058. 98p. 1992. 59.95 (*0-7734-9471-5*) E Mellen.

Contribution of Indian Ethnobotany. S. K. Jain. (C). 1991. text ed. 138.00 (*0-7855-0099-5*, Pub. by Scientific Pubs II); text ed. 150.00 (*81-7233-001-4*, Pub. by Scientific Pubs II) St Mut.

Contribution of International Educational Exchange to the International Education of Americans: Projections for the Year 2000. Barbara B. Burn. (Occasional Papers on International Educational Exchange: No. 26). (Orig.). 1990. pap. 5.00 (*1-882036-06-9*) Coun Intl Ed.

Contribution of Irrigation & Drainage to the World Food Supply. Comp. by American Society of Civil Engineers Staff. 430p. 1975. pap. 24.00 (*0-87262-114-6*) Am Soc Civil Eng.

Contribution of Laboratory Animal Science to the Welfare of Man & Animals. Ed. by J. A. Archibald et al. 522p. 1985. pap. 110.00 (*0-89574-203-9*, Pub. by Gustav Fischer Verlag) VCH Pubs.

Contribution of Long-Term Follow-up to the Prediction of Coronary Heart Disease. Ed. by M. Kornitzer & R. Goldberg. (Journal: Cardiology: Vol. 82, Nos. 2-3, 1993). (Illus.). 148p. 1993. pap. 41.75 (*3-8055-5790-6*) S Karger.

Contribution of Methodism to Atlantic Canada. Ed. by Charles H. Scobie & John W. Grant. 296p. 1992. 39.95 (*0-7735-0885-6*, Pub. by McGill CN) U of Toronto Pr.

Contribution of Nutrition to Human & Animal Health. Ed. by Elsie M. Widdowson & John C. Mathers. (Illus.). 360p. (C). 1992. 115.00 (*0-521-42064-4*) Cambridge U Pr.

***Contribution of People's Participation: Evidence from 121 Rural Water Supply Projects.** Deepa Narayan. LC 94-34109. (Environmentally Sustainable Development Occasional Papers: No. 1). 1994. write for info. (*0-8213-3043-8*) World Bank.

Contribution of Religion to Social Work. Reinhold Niebuhr. LC 74-172444. reprint ed. 20.00 (*0-404-04708-4*) AMS Pr.

Contribution of Space Geodesy to Geodynamics: Earth Dynamics. Ed. by David E. Smith & Donald L. Turcotte. LC 93-41649. (Geodynamics Ser.: Vol. 24). 1993. 38.00 (*0-87590-524-2*) Am Geophysical.

Contribution of Space Observations to Global Food Information Systems: Proceedings of the W. Nordberg Memorial Symposium of the 10th Plenary Meeting of COSPAR, Tel Aviv, Israel, June 1977. Ed. by E. A. Godby & J. Otterman. LC 77-30706. (Advances in Space Exploration COSPAR Symposium Ser.: No. 2). (Illus.). 208p. 1978. 93.00 (*0-08-022418-0*, Pub. by Pergamon Repr UK) Franklin.

Contribution of the Arabs to Education. Khalil A. Totah. LC 72-177697. (Columbia University. Teachers College. Contributions to Education Ser.: No. 231). reprint ed. 37.50 (*0-404-55231-5*) AMS Pr.

Contribution of the Japanese National Committee for IBP in 1964-1972, Vol. 20. Ed. by H. Tamiya. (Japan International Biological Program Synthesis Ser.). 234p. 1978. pap. 57.50 (*0-86008-230-X*, Pub. by U of Tokyo JA) Col U Pr.

Contribution to a Bibliography of Antarctic & Subantarctic Algae Together with a Checklist of Freshwater Taxa Reported to 1977. Gerald W. Prescott. (Bibliotheca Phycologica Ser.: No. 45). 1979. lib. bdg. 48.00 (*3-7682-1216-5*) Lubrecht & Cramer.

Contribution to a Union Catalogue of Sixteenth Century Imprints in Certain New England Libraries. Brown University Library Staff. LC 54-1641. 475p. reprint ed. pap. 135.40 (*0-317-41786-X*, 2025644) Bks Demand.

Contribution to African-American History: My Autobiography. Ola Thomas. 1994. 10.95 (*0-533-10948-5*) Vantage.

Contribution to Biblical Lexicography. Israel Eitan. (Columbia University. Contributions to Oriental History & Philology Ser.: No. 10). reprint ed. 12.50 (*0-404-50540-6*) AMS Pr.

Contribution to Indo-English Poetry: Collected & Recollected Poems 1930-1990. Vinayak K. Gokak. (New World Literature Ser.: No. 53). (C). 1992. 15.00 (*81-7018-708-7*, Pub. by BR Pub II) S Asia.

Contribution to Literature of Orcadian Writer George Mackay Brown: An Introduction & a Bibliography. Osamu Yamada et al. LC 91-33423. (Studies in British Literature: Vol. 16). (Illus.). 120p. 1992. lib. bdg. 59.95 (*0-7734-9651-3*) E Mellen.

Contribution to Neuropsychological Assessment: A Clinical Manual. 2nd ed. Arthur L. Benton et al. (Illus.). 160p. 1994. pap. 24.95 (*0-19-509179-5*) OUP.

Contribution to Our Knowledge of the Higher Fungi in China. Shu-Chun Teng. 614p. 1988. reprint ed. text ed. 85.00 (*0-945345-23-2*) Lubrecht & Cramer.

Contribution to the Analysis of the Hydrological Cycle & of the Water Consumption Cycle. J. Riha. 112p. 1982. 49.00 (*0-317-89618-0*, Pub. by Collets UK) Pro-Am Music.

Contribution to the Bibliography of the Bank of England. Thomas A. Stephens. LC 68-19358. (Reprints of Economic Classics Ser.). 1968. reprint ed. 35.00 (*0-678-00385-8*) Kelley.

Contribution to the Broyological Flora of N. W. Himalaya. V. F. Brotherus. (C). 1988. 35.00 (*0-685-22316-7*, Scientific) St Mut.

Contribution to the Broyological Flora of Southern India. V. F. Brotherus. (C). 1988. 35.00 (*0-685-22317-5*, Scientific) St Mut.

Contribution to the Critique of Political Economy. Karl Marx. Ed. by Maurice Dobb. LC 69-20357. 264p. 1989. pap. text ed. 5.95 (*0-7178-0041-5*) Intl Pubs Co.

Contribution to the Critique of Political Economy. Karl Marx. 264p. (C). 1972. text ed. 19.95 (*0-8464-1287-X*) Beekman Pubs.

***Contribution to the Early Isin Craft Archive.** G. T. Ferwerda. ix, 63p. 1985. pap. text ed. 26.25 (*90-6258-127-7*, Pub. by Netherlands Inst NE); pap. text ed. 26.25 (*0-614-06073-7*, Pub. by Netherlands Inst NE) Eisenbrauns.

Contribution to the Flora of Calcutta & Its Neighbourhood. N. M. Dutta. Ed. by A. K. Ganguy. 1985. 79.00 (*0-317-38758-8*, Current Dist) St Mut.

Contribution to the General Theory of Comparative Linguistics. Radoslav Katicic. LC 77-110956. (Janua Linguarum, Ser. Minor: No. 83). (Orig.). 1970. pap. text ed. 24.65 (*90-279-0708-0*) Mouton.

Contribution to the History of English Commonwealth Drama. Hyder Rollins. (Studies in Drama: No. 39). (C). 1970. reprint ed. pap. 39.95 (*0-8383-0065-0*) M S G Haskell Hse.

***Contribution to the History of Geological Mapping: Proceedings of the Xth INHIGEO Symposium 16-22 August 1982, Budapest, Hungary.** Ed. by E. Dudich. 441p. (C). 1984. 102.00x (*963-05-3616-1*, Pub. by Akad Kiado HU) St Mut.

Contribution to the History of Statistics. Harald L. Westergaard. LC 70-85736. (Reprints of Economic Classics Ser.). 1969. reprint ed. 35.00 (*0-678-00521-4*) Kelley.

Contribution to the Life History of Black Drum & Analysis of the Commercial Fishery in Baffin Bay, Vol. 11. Stephen Cornelius. LC 83-71622. 75p. 1984. pap. 5.00 (*0-912229-07-1*) CK Wildlife Res.

Contribution to the Limnology of Arid Regions, Primarily Founded on Observations Made in the Lahontan Basin. George E. Hutchinson. (Connecticut Academy of Arts & Sciences Ser., Trans.: Vol. 33). 1937. pap. 69.50 (*0-685-22914-9*) Elliots Bks.

Contribution to the Marine Algae of Libya Dictyotales. Mohammed Nizamuddin. (Bibliotheca Phycologica Ser.: No. 54). (Illus.). 120p. 1982. pap. text ed. 24.00 (*3-7682-1305-6*) Lubrecht & Cramer.

Contribution to the Orchidology of India. John Lindley. 100p. (C). 1982. 30.00 (*0-685-22346-9*, Scientific) St Mut.

Contribution to the Pure Theory of Taxation. Roger Guesnerie. (Econometric Society Monographs: No. 25). (Illus.). 304p. (C). 1992. 54.95 (*0-521-23689-4*) Cambridge U Pr.

Contribution to the Study of New Zealand Diatoms. V. Cassie. (Bibliotheca Diatomologica Ser.: Vol. 17). (Illus.). 266p. 1989. spiral bd. 91.00 (*3-443-57008-9*, Pub. by Cramer GW) Lubrecht & Cramer.

Contribution to the Taxonomy of the Genus Phanerochaete (Corticiaceae, Aphyllophorales) Harold H. Burdsall, Jr. (Mycologia Memoirs Ser.: No. 10). (Illus.). 170p. 1985. lib. bdg. 39.00 (*3-7682-1392-7*) Lubrecht & Cramer.

Contribution to the Taxonomy of the Genus Tomentella. Michael J. Larsen. (Mycologia Memoirs Ser.: No. 4). (Illus.). 145p. 1974. pap. text ed. 12.50 (*0-945345-40-2*) Lubrecht & Cramer.

Contribution to the Theory of Weak & Strong Interactions of Elementary Particles. Ed. by V. B. Berestetskii. 176p. 1965. text ed. 49.50 (*0-7065-0402-X*, Pub. by Keter Pub IS) Coronet Bks.

Contribution Toward a Bibliography of Ohio Zoology. David J. Gerrick. (Bulletin New Ser.: Vol. 2, No. 4). 1968. 5.00 (*0-86727-055-1*) Ohio Bio Survey.

Contribution Toward a Monograph of North American Species of Suillus. A. H. Smith & H. D. Thiers. (Illus.). 1964. pap. 10.00 (*0-934454-26-4*) Lubrecht & Cramer.

Contribution Towards a Bibliography Dealing with Crime & Cognate Subjects. 3rd ed. John Cumming. LC 71-108220. (Criminology, Law Enforcement, & Social Problems Ser.: No. 103). 1970. reprint ed. 20.00 (*0-87585-103-7*) Patterson Smith.

Contributiones Selectae ad Floram & Vegetationem Orientis: Proceedings of the Third Plant Life of Southwest Asia Symposium, Berlin, 1990. Ed. by T. Engel et al. (Flora et Vegetatio Mundi Ser.: Vol. 9). 324p. 1991. lib. bdg. 104.00 (*3-443-66001-0*, Pub. by Gebrueder Borntraeger GW) Lubrecht & Cramer.

Contributions. Jeremiah Moon. LC 90-71357. 51p. 1991. pap. 5.95 (*1-55523-386-4*) Winston-Derek.

Contributions: Three Short Plays. Ted Shine. 1970. pap. 4.75 (*0-8222-0238-7*) Dramatists Play.

Contributions by W. E. B. Du Bois in Government Publications & Proceedings. Ed. by Herbert Aptheker. LC 80-13063. (Complete Published Works of W. E. B. Du Bois). 1981. lib. bdg. 70.00 (*0-527-25292-1*) Kraus Intl.

Contributions from Breeding Forage & Turf Grasses. D. A. Sleper et al. 140p. 1989. 15.00 (*0-89118-526-7*) Am Soc Agron.

Contributions in Mammalogy in Honor of Robert L. Packard. Ed. by R. E. Martin & B. R. Chapman. (Special Publications: No. 22). 234p. 1984. 50.00 (*0-89672-124-8*); pap. 25.00 (*0-89672-123-X*) Tex Tech Univ Pr.

Contributions in Numerical Mathematics. Ed. by Ravi P. Agarwal. Vol. 2. 1993. text ed. 109.00 (*981-02-1437-5*) World Scientific Pub.

Contributions in Petroleum: Hydrocarbon Phase Behavior, Vol. 7. Tarek Ahmed. 418p. 1989. 75.00 (*0-87201-589-0*) Gulf Pub.

Contributions in Petroleum Geology & Engineering, Vol. 3: Underground Storage of Natural Gas. M. R. Tek. (Illus.). 390p. 1987. 67.00 (*0-87201-913-6*) Gulf Pub.

Contributions in Petroleum Geology & Engineering, Vol. 9: Horizontal Drilling, Completion, & Production. Roberto Aguilera. 352p. 1991. 75.00 (*0-87201-573-4*) Gulf Pub.

Contributions in Phycology. Bruce C. Parker & R. Malcolm Brown. LC 72-170365. (Illus.). 196p. 1971. 25.00 (*0-8139-0841-8*) U Pr of Va.

Contributions in Quaternary Vertebrate Paleontology: A Volume in Memorial to John E. Guilday. Ed. by Hugh H. Genoways & Mary R. Dawson. LC 84-70729. (Special Publication CMNH Ser.: No. 8). (Illus.). 544p. (Orig.). 1984. 58.50 (*0-935868-07-0*) Carnegie Mus.

Contributions of a Cumulative Personnel Records to a Teacher-Education Program As Evidenced by Their Use at the State Teachers College at Towson, Md. Rebecca C. Tansil. LC 79-177724. (Columbia University. Teachers College. Contributions to Education Ser.: No. 764). reprint ed. 37.50 (*0-404-55764-3*) AMS Pr.

Contributions of a Venerable Native to the Ancient History of the Hawaiian Islands. M. Jules Remy. Tr. by W. D. Alexander & William T. Brigham. (Illus.). 1979. pap. 3.95 (*0-89646-056-8*) Vistabooks.

***Contributions of Black Women to America.** Ed. by Marianna W. Davis. LC 94-25944. 1995. write for info. (*0-8204-2411-0*); pap. write for info. (*0-8204-2641-5*) P Lang Pubs.

Contributions of Buddhism to World Civilization & Culture. Ed. by P. N. Chopra. 408p. 1987. 50.00 (*0-317-52136-5*, Pub. by S Chand II) St Mut.

Contributions of Business Cycle Surveys to Empirical Economics: Proceedings of the CIRET Conference, 18th, Zurich, 1987. Karl H. Oppenlander & Gunter Poser. 692p. 1988. text ed. 102.95 (*0-566-05629-1*, Pub. by Avebury Pub UK) Ashgate Pub Co.

Contributions of DOE (Dept. of Energy) Weapons Labs & NIST to Semiconductor Technology. (Illus.). 87p. (Orig.). (C). 1994. pap. text ed. 45.00 (*0-7881-0447-0*) Diane Pub.

Contributions of Faraday & Maxwell to Electrical Science. R. A. Tricker. 1966. write for info. (*0-08-011977-8*, Pub. by Pergamon Repr UK) Franklin.

Contributions of G. Natta & His School to Polymer Chemistry, 2 vols., Set. G. Natta & F. Danusso. LC 63-10026. (Stereoregular Polymers & Stereospecific Polymerizations Ser.). 1967. 379.00 (*0-08-010156-9*, Pub. by Pergamon Repr UK) Franklin.

***Contributions of Harry Stack Sullivan.** Ed. by Patrick Mullahy. 242p. 1995. pap. 30.00 (*1-56821-560-6*) Aronson.

Contributions of Infrastructure to Economic Development: A Review of Experience & Policy Implications. Christine Kessides. LC 93-32012. (Discussion Paper Ser.: No. 213). 62p. 1993. 6.95 (*0-8213-2628-7*, 12628) World Bank.

Contributions of Joseph Ives to Connecticut Clock Technology, 1810-1862. 2nd rev. ed. Kenneth D. Roberts. (Illus.). 388p. 1988. 40.00 (*0-913602-65-5*) K Roberts.

Contributions of Limperg & Schmidt to the Replacement Cost Debate in the 1920s. Frank L. Clarke & Graeme Dean. LC 90-27264. (New Works in Accounting History: Vol. 3). 360p. 1991. reprint ed. 53.00 (*0-8153-0007-7*) Garland.

Contributions of Research to Business Education, 1971. (Yearbook Ser.). 374p. 5.00 (*0-933964-08-0*) Natl Busn Ed Assoc.

Contributions of Sanskrit Description to Lexicography. S. P. Tewari. 1987. 28.50 (*0-8364-2267-8*, Pub. by Agam Kala Prakashan) S Asia.

Contributions of Science to Religion. Shailer Mathews et al. LC 79-117822. (Essay Index Reprint Ser.). 1977. 30.95 (*0-8369-1763-4*) Ayer.

Contributions of Science to the Development of the Textile Industry. Textile Institute Staff. (C). 1975. pap. text ed. 70.00 (*0-900739-22-3*, Pub. by Textile Institue UK) St Mut.

Contributions of Science to the Development of the Textile Industry: The Present Situation & Future Prospects. P. W. Harrison & M. Cordelier. 199p. 1975. 40.00 (*0-686-63756-9*) St Mut.

Contributions of Space Geodesy to Geodynamics: Crystal Dynamics. Ed. by David E. Smith & Donald L. Turcotte. LC 93-41670. (Geodynamics Ser.: Vol. 23). 1993. 56.00 (*0-87590-523-4*) Am Geophysical.

Contributions of Space Geodesy to Geodynamics: Technology. Ed. by David E. Smith & Donald L. Turcotte. LC 93-41653. (Geodynamics Ser.: Vol. 25). 1993. 39.00 (*0-87590-526-9*) Am Geophysical.

Contributions of the Quakers. Elizabeth J. Gray. (C). 1947. pap. 9.00 (*0-87574-034-0*) Pendle Hill.

Contributions of the Social Sciences to Educational Policy & Practice: 1965-1985. Ed. by Jane Hannaway & Marlaine E. Lockheed. LC 85-63433. 252p. 1986. 30.75 (*0-8211-0771-2*); text ed. 27.75 (*0-685-13934-4*) McCutchan.

Contributions of Theology to Medical Ethics. James M. Gustafson. (Pere Marquette Lectures). 1975. 10.00 (*0-87462-507-6*) Marquette.

***Contributions of Walter J. Ong to the Study of Rhetoric: History & Metaphor.** Betty R. Youngkin. LC 94-41557. 156p. 1995. text ed. 69.95 (*0-7734-2277-3*, Mellen Univ Pr) E Mellen.

***Contributions on Entomology, International.** 1995. write for info. (*0-614-05496-6*) Assoc Pubs FL.

Contributions on the Biology of the Gulf of Mexico. Ed. by Fenner A. Chace. LC 71-135998. (Texas A & M University Oceanographic Studies: No. 1). (Illus.). 288p. reprint ed. pap. 82.10 (*0-685-23790-7*, 2032881) Bks Demand.

Contributions on the Geological & Geophysical Oceanography of the Gulf of Mexico. Ed. by Richard Rezak & Vernon J. Henry. LC 72-170029. (Texas A & M University Oceanographic Studies: No. 3). (Illus.). 319p. reprint ed. pap. 91.00 (*0-685-23793-1*, 2032890) Bks Demand.

Contributions on the Physical Oceanography of the Gulf of Mexico. Ed. by Luis R. Capurro & Joseph L. Reid. LC 72-170030. (Texas A & M University Oceanographic Studies: No. 2). (Illus.). 308p. reprint ed. pap. 87.80 (*0-685-23792-3*, 2032889) Bks Demand.

Contributions on the Religion & History of Tibet. Sarat C. Das. 1988. 35.00 (*0-7855-0309-9*, Pub. by Ratna Pustak Bhandar) St Mut.

An Asterisk (*) at the beginning of an entry indicates that the title is appearing in BIP for the first time.

C

An Asterisk (*) at the beginning of an entry indicates that the title is appearing in BIP for the first time.

1595

Contributions to the Geography of Baffin Land & Melville Peninsula. Therkel Mathiassen. LC 76-21640. (Thule Expedition, 5th, 1921-1924 Ser.: Vol. 1, No. 3). reprint ed. 32.00 (*0-404-58303-2*) AMS Pr.

Contributions to the Geology of the Bering Sea Basin & Adjacent Regions: Selected Papers from the Symposium on the Geology & Geophysics of the Bering Region, on the Occasion of the Inauguration of the C. T. Elvery Building. Ed. by Robert B. Forbes. LC 73-87232. (Geological Society of America, Special Paper Ser.: No. 151). 230p. reprint ed. pap. 65.60 (*0-317-51970-0*, 2027372) Bks Demand.

Contributions to the History & Theory of Art. Ed. by R. Zeitler. (Illus.). 190p. (Orig.). 1967. pap. text ed. 36.00x (*0-685-13627-2*) Coronet Bks.

Contributions to the History of American Natural History. LC 73-17809. (Natural Sciences of America Ser.). (Illus.). 876p. 1974. reprint ed. 72.95 (*0-405-05726-1*) Ayer.

Contributions to the History of American Ornithology. LC 73-17810. (Natural Sciences in America Ser.). 382p. 1974. reprint ed. 28.95 (*0-405-05727-X*) Ayer.

Contributions to the History of Geological Mapping. E. Dudich. 442p. 1984. 140.00 (*0-569-08805-4*, Pub. by Collets UK) Pro-Am Music.

Contributions to the History of Herpetology. Adler. LC 89-50341. 1989. write for info. (*0-916984-19-2*) SSAR.

Contributions to the Knowledge of Microalgae Particularly Diatoms: Special Volume in Honour of Grethe R. Hasle on Her 70th Birthday. Ed. by U. Geissler et al. (Beiheft zur Nova Hedwigia Ser.: No. 100). (Illus.). 300p. 1990. pap. 135.00 (*3-443-51022-1*, Pub. by Cramer-Borntraeger GW) Lubrecht & Cramer.

Contributions to the Metallurgy of Steel, 3 vols., Set. 1991. pap. 43.00 (*0-685-53332-8*, 29-000390-02) ASTM.

Contributions to the Monetary History of Serbia, Montenegro & Yugoslavia. F. Weiser. 1975. 5.00 (*0-685-51550-8*) S J Durst.

Contributions to the Natural History of the United States of America, 4 Vols. in 2, 1. Jean L. Agassiz. Ed. by Keir B. Sterling. LC 77-81094. (Biologists & Their World Ser.). (Illus.). 1978. reprint ed. 66.95 (*0-405-10676-9*) Ayer.

Contributions to the Natural History of the United States of America, 4 Vols. in 2, 2. Jean L. Agassiz. Ed. by Keir B. Sterling. LC 77-81094. (Biologists & Their World Ser.). (Illus.). 1978. reprint ed. 66.95 (*0-405-10677-7*) Ayer.

Contributions to the Natural History of the United States of America, 4 Vols. in 2, Set. Jean L. Agassiz. Ed. by Keir B. Sterling. LC 77-81094. (Biologists & Their World Ser.). (Illus.). 1978. reprint ed. lib. bdg. 132.95 (*0-405-10675-0*) Ayer.

***Contributions to the Neogene Paleobotany of Central California.** Daniel I. Axelrod. LC 80-15355. (University of California Publications in Geological Sciences: No. 121). 224p. 1980. pap. 63.90 (*0-7837-7465-6*, 2049187) Bks Demand.

Contributions to the Palaeography of Latin Inscriptions. Joyce Gordon & Arthur E. Gordon. LC 57-9881. (University of California Publications in Social Welfare: Vol. 3, No. 3). 190p. reprint ed. pap. 54.20 (*0-317-29114-9*, 2021333) Bks Demand.

Contributions to the Physical Anthropology of Central Asia & the Caucasus. M. G. Abdushelishvili et al. Ed. by Henry Field. Tr. by Barbara Heath. LC 79-158217. (Harvard University, Peabody Museum of Archaeology & Ethnology, Russian Translation Ser.: Vol. 3, No. 2). 1968. lib. bdg. 115.00 (*0-404-52645-4*) AMS Pr.

Contributions to the Physical Anthropology of the Soviet Union. Viktor V. Bunak et al. Tr. by William W. Howells. LC 60-1045. (Harvard University. Peabody Museum of Archaeology & Ethnology. Antiquities of the New World Ser.: Vol. 1, No. 2). reprint ed. lib. bdg. 47.50 (*0-404-52642-X*) AMS Pr.

Contributions to the Physiography of Southampton Island. Therkel Mathiassen. LC 76-21639. (Thule Expedition, 5th, 1921-1924 Ser.: Vol. 1, No. 2). reprint ed. 20.00 (*0-404-58302-4*) AMS Pr.

Contributions to the Prehistory of Nubia. Fred Wendorf. LC 65-5730. (Southern Methodist University Contributions in Anthropology Ser.: Vol. 1). 211p. reprint ed. pap. 60.20 (*0-8357-8851-2*, 2033448) Bks Demand.

Contributions to the Psychology of Addiction. Ed. by Gerard M. Schippers et al. 160p. 1992. 39.00 (*90-265-1217-1*, Pub. by Swets Pub Serv NE) Taylor & Francis.

Contributions to the Racial Anthropology of the Near East. Carl C. Seltzer. (HU PMP Ser.). 1940. pap. 16.00 (*0-527-01237-8*) Periodicals Srv.

Contributions to the Sociology of the Indian Tribes of Ecuador: Three Essays. Rafael Karsten. LC 76-44742. 1977. reprint ed. 34.50 (*0-404-15941-9*) AMS Pr.

Contributions to the Sociology of Work & Organizations. Ed. by Jaspal Singh. (C). 1993. 24.00 (*81-85135-69-X*, National Bk Ctr) S Asia.

Contributions to the Stratigraphy of New England. Ed. by Lincoln R. Page. LC 76-9220. (Memoir Ser.: No. 148). (Illus.). 451p. 1976. 7.50 (*0-8137-1148-7*) Geol Soc.

Contributions to the Study of the Behavior of Lower Organisms see Last Words on Evolution

Contributions to the Tectonics & Geophysics of Mountain Chains. Ed. by Robert D. Hatcher, Jr. et al. (Memoir Ser.: No. 158). (Illus.). 228p. 1983. 17.00 (*0-8137-1158-4*) Geol Soc.

Contributions to the Textual Criticism of Aristotle's Nicomachean Ethics. Ingram Bywater. LC 72-9285. (Philosophy of Plate & Aristotle Ser.). 1974. reprint ed. 23.95 (*0-405-04835-1*) Ayer.

Contributions to the Theory & Application of Statistics: A Volume in Honor of Herbert Solomon. Ed. by Alan E. Gelfand. 576p. 1987. text ed. 92.00 (*0-12-279450-8*) Acad Pr.

***Contributions to the Theory of Capitalist Money, Business Fluctuations & Crises.** P. Erdos. 466p. (C). 1971. 69.00x (*963-05-1111-8*, Pub. by Akad Kiado HU) St Mut.

Contributions to the Theory of Natural Selection. Alfred R. Wallace. LC 72-1670. reprint ed. 55.00 (*0-404-08181-9*) AMS Pr.

Contributions to the Theory of Nonlinear Oscillations, Vols. 1, 1950. Solomon Lefschetz. (Annals of Mathematics Studies). 1972. Vol. 1, No. 20,. 26.00 (*0-527-02736-7*); Vol. 2, No. 29 of Annals,. 15.00 (*0-527-02745-6*); Vol. 3, No. 36 of Annals, 1956. 23.00 (*0-527-02753-7*); Vol. 5, No. 45 of Annals, 1960. 23.00 (*0-527-02761-8*) Periodicals Srv.

Contributions to the Theory of Partial Differential Equations. L. Bers et al. (Annals of Mathematics Studies: No. 33). 1972. reprint ed. 23.00 (*0-527-02749-9*) Periodicals Srv.

Contributions to the Theory of Transcendental Numbers. G. V. Chudnovsky. LC 83-15728. (Mathematical Surveys & Monographs: No. 19). 450p. 1984. 109.00 (*0-8218-1500-8*, SURV-19) Am Math.

Contributions to Thermal Physiology: Proceedings of a Satellite Symposium of the 28th International Congress of Physiological Sciences, Budapest, 1980. Z Szelenyi & M. Szekely. LC 80-41854. (Advances in Physiological Sciences Ser.: Vol. 32). (Illus.). 560p. 1981. 237.00 (*0-08-027354-8*, Pub. by Pergamon Repr UK) Franklin.

Contributions to Thought. 140p. Date not set. lib. bdg. 16.00 (*1-878977-13-X*) Latitude Pr.

Contributions Toward a Bibliography of Epictetus: A Supplement. William A. Oldfather. Ed. by Marion Harman. LC 28-2296. 197p. reprint ed. pap. 56.20 (*0-317-10227-3*, 2020870) Bks Demand.

Contributions Toward a Classification of Rhododendron. Ed. by James L. Luteyn & Mary E. O'Brien. LC 79-27378. (Illus.). 330p. 1980. pap. 22.00 (*0-89327-221-3*) NY Botanical.

Contributions Toward a Mycobiota of Indonesia: Hypocreales, Synnematous Hyphomycetes, Aphyllophorales, Phragmobasidiomycetes, & Myxomycetes. Gary J. Samuels et al. LC 90-5963. (Memoirs Ser.: No. 59). (Illus.). 173p. 1990. pap. text ed. 36.25 (*0-89327-354-6*) NY Botanical.

Contributions Toward a Rational Arrangement of the Clthraceae. D. M. Dring. (Illus.). 96p. 1979. reprint ed. pap. 15.00 (*0-318-11896-3*) Lubrecht & Cramer.

Contributions Towards the History of Early English Porcelain from Contemporary Sources. J. E. Nightengale. 1976. reprint ed. 12.50 (*0-85409-839-9*) Charles River Bks.

Contributors & Contributions to the Southern Literary Messenger 1834-1864. D. K. Jackson. 1973. 59.95 (*0-87968-941-2*) Gordon Pr.

Contributors' Index to the Dictionary of National Biography, 1885-1901. Gillian Fenwick. LC 89-50389. 413p. 1989. lib. bdg. 48.00 (*0-906795-73-7*) Oak Knoll.

Contrived Competition: Regulation & Deregulation in America. Richard H. Vietor. LC 93-28975. 447p. 1994. 37.50x (*0-674-16962-X*) HUP.

Control. Jack Anderson. 1990. mass mkt. 4.95 (*1-55817-312-9*, Pinnacle NY) Windsor NY.

Control. Jack Anderson. 1988. write for info. (*0-8217-2428-2*) Zebra.

***Control.** Shirley Greenslade. 144p. 1985. pap. write for info. (*1-886799-04-0*) Agape Word.

Control: Sociology's Central Notion. Jack P. Gibbs. LC 88-26192. 520p. 1989. pap. 16.95 (*0-252-06046-6*) U of Ill Pr.

Control & Ability: Towards a Biocybernetics of Language. Waltraud Brennenstuhl. (Pragmatics & Beyond Ser.: III: 4). vi, 122p. (Orig.). 1982. pap. 41.00x (*90-272-2522-2*) Benjamins North Am.

Control & Analysis of Noisy Processes. David M. Koenig. 384p. 1990. text ed. 99.00 (*0-13-033366-2*) P-H.

Control & Assurance of Quality, Reliability & Safety. 2nd ed. C. L. Carter, Jr. 375p. 1991. 45.00 (*1-879519-10-0*) C L Carter.

Control & Audit in Management Accounting. 2nd ed. Jeff Coates et al. 1993. pap. 42.50 (*0-7506-0995-8*) Buttrwrth-Heinemann.

Control & Audit of Minicomputer Systems. British Computer Society Staff. 58p. reprint ed. pap. 25.00 (*0-685-44433-3*, 2032673) Bks Demand.

***Control & Automation in Anesthesia.** Ed. by H. Schwilden & H. Stoeckel. LC 95-1211. 1995. write for info. (*0-387-58968-6*) Spr-Verlag.

***Control & Censorship of Caroline Drama: The Records of Sir Henry Herbert, Master of the Revels, 1623-73.** Ed. by N. W. Bawcutt. 320p. 1995. 75.00 (*0-19-812246-2*) OUP.

Control & Charisma in Rajneeshpuram: The Role of Shared Values in the Creation of a Community. Lewis F. Carter. (ASA Rose Monograph Ser.). (Illus.). 448p. (C). 1990. 64.95 (*0-521-38554-7*) Cambridge U Pr.

Control & Communication in Programs. Loretta G. Reid. LC 82-6893. (Computer Science: Systems Programming Ser.: No. 13). 175p. reprint ed. pap. 49.90 (*0-685-20830-3*, 2070046) Bks Demand.

Control & Crisis in Colonial Kenya: The Dialectic of Domination. Bruce J. Berman. LC 89-72154. (Eastern African Studies). 495p. 1990. text ed. 44.95 (*0-8214-0965-4*) Ohio U Pr.

Control & Discipline in Schools: Perspectives & Approaches. 2nd ed. J. W. Docking. 272p. (C). 1987. pap. 50.00 (*0-06-318374-9*, Pub. by P Chapman Pub UK) St Mut.

Control & Distribution of Production. C. H. Douglas. 1972. 59.95 (*0-87968-942-0*) Gordon Pr.

Control & Dynamic Systems, Vol. 23. Ed. by Cornelius T. Leondes. (Serial Publication Ser.). 336p. 1986. text ed. 112.00 (*0-12-012723-7*) Acad Pr.

Control & Dynamic Systems, Vol. 24. Ed. by Cornelius T. Leondes. (Serial Publication Ser.). 384p. 1986. text ed. 112.00 (*0-12-012724-5*) Acad Pr.

Control & Dynamic Systems, Vol. 26. Ed. by Cornelius T. Leondes. (Serial Publication Ser.). 339p. 1987. text ed. 112.00 (*0-12-012726-1*) Acad Pr.

Control & Dynamic Systems, Vol. 30. Ed. by Cornelius T. Leondes. (Serial Publication Ser.). 257p. 1989. text ed. 104.00 (*0-12-012730-X*) Acad Pr.

Control & Dynamic Systems: Advances in Aerospace Systems Dynamics & Control Systems, Vol. 31. Ed. by Cornelius T. Leondes. (Advances in Theory & Applications Ser.). 264p. 1989. text ed. 126.00 (*0-12-012731-8*) Acad Pr.

Control & Dynamic Systems: Advances in Aerospace Systems Dynamics & Control Systems, Vol. 33. Ed. by Cornelius T. Leondes. (Advances in Theory & Applications Ser.). 305p. 1990. text ed. 132.00 (*0-12-012733-4*) Acad Pr.

Control & Dynamic Systems: Advances in Aerospace Systems Dynamics & Control Systems; Advances in Theory & Applications, Vol. 32. Ed. by Cornelius T. Leondes. 280p. 1990. text ed. 126.00 (*0-12-012732-6*) Acad Pr.

Control & Dynamic Systems: Advances in Algorithm & Computational Techniques in Dynamic Systems Control, Vol. 29. Ed. by Cornelius T. Leondes. (Advances in Theory & Applications Ser.). 393p. 1988. text ed. 112.00 (*0-12-012729-6*) Acad Pr.

Control & Dynamic Systems: Advances in Control Mechanics, Vol. 34. Ed. by Cornelius T. Leondes. 333p. 1990. text ed. 92.00 (*0-12-012734-2*) Acad Pr.

Control & Dynamic Systems: Advances in Theory & Applications, Set. Vol. 20. Ed. by Cornelius T. Leondes. 1983. Pt. 2. write for info. (*0-318-56829-2*) Acad Pr.

Control & Dynamic Systems: Advances in Theory & Applications, Vol. 20. Ed. by Cornelius T. Leondes. (Serial Publication Ser.). 1983. text ed. 112.00 (*0-12-012720-2*) Acad Pr.

Control & Dynamic Systems: Advances in Theory & Applications, Vol. 21. Cornelius T. Leondes. (Serial Publication Ser.). 1984. text ed. 112.00 (*0-12-012721-0*) Acad Pr.

Control & Dynamic Systems: Advances in Theory & Applications, Vol. 22. Ed. by Cornelius T. Leondes. (Serial Publication Ser.). 1985. text ed. 112.00 (*0-12-012722-9*) Acad Pr.

Control & Dynamic Systems: Advances in Theory & Applications, Vol. 25. Ed. by Cornelius T. Leondes. (Serial Publication Ser.). 258p. 1987. text ed. 112.00 (*0-12-012725-3*) Acad Pr.

Control & Dynamic Systems: Advances in Theory & Applications, 3 pts., Vol. 27. Ed. by Cornelius T. Leondes. (System Identification & Adaptive Control Ser.: Pt. 3). 377p. 1988. text ed. 112.00 (*0-12-012727-X*) Acad Pr.

Control & Dynamic Systems: Robust Control System Techniques & Applications, Pt. 2, Vol. 50. Ed. by Cornelius T. Leondes. (Illus.). 467p. 1992. text ed. 85.00 (*0-12-012750-4*) Acad Pr.

Control & Dynamic Systems: Robust Control System Techniques & Applications, Pt. 2, Vol. 51. Ed. by Cornelius T. Leondes. (Illus.). 478p. 1992. text ed. 85.00 (*0-12-012751-2*) Acad Pr.

Control & Dynamic Systems Vol. 66: Discrete-Time Dynamic & Control System Techniques. Ed. by Cornelius T. Leondes. (Illus.). 366p. 1994. text ed. 99.00 (*0-12-012766-0*) Acad Pr.

***Control & Dynamic Systems Vol. 68: Digital Signal Processing Systems Implementation Techniques.** Ed. by Cornelius T. Leondes. (Illus.). 424p. 1995. text ed. 99.00 (*0-12-012768-7*) Acad Pr.

***Control & Dynamic Systems Vol. 70: Digital Control Systems Implementation Techniques.** Ed. by Cornelius T. Leondes. (Illus.). 376p. 1995. boxed write for info. (*0-12-012770-9*) Acad Pr.

***Control & Dynamic Systems Vol. 71: Discrete-Time Control System Analysis & Design.** Ed. by Cornelius T. Leondes. (Illus.). 344p. 1995. boxed write for info. (*0-12-012771-7*) Acad Pr.

***Control & Dynamic Systems Vol. 72: Discrete-Time Control System Implementation Techniques.** Ed. by Cornelius T. Leondes. (Illus.). 346p. 1995. boxed write for info. (*0-12-012772-5*) Acad Pr.

Control & Dynamic Systems, Vol. 35: Advances in Control Mechanics. Ed. by Cornelius T. Leondes. 318p. 1990. text ed. 92.00 (*0-12-012735-0*) Acad Pr.

Control & Dynamic Systems, Vol. 36: Advances in Large Scale Systems Dynamics. Cornelius T. Leondes. 410p. 1990. text ed. 99.00 (*0-12-012736-9*) Acad Pr.

Control & Dynamic Systems, Vol. 37: Advances in Industrial Systems. Ed. by Cornelius T. Leondes. 425p. 1990. text ed. 99.00 (*0-12-012737-7*) Acad Pr.

Control & Dynamic Systems, Vol. 38: Advances in Aeronautical Systems. Ed. by Cornelius T. Leondes. (Illus.). 407p. 1990. text ed. 99.00 (*0-12-012738-5*) Acad Pr.

Control & Dynamic Systems, Vol. 39: Advances in Robotic Systems, Pt. 1. Ed. by Cornelius T. Leondes. (Illus.). 472p. 1991. text ed. 105.00 (*0-12-012739-3*) Acad Pr.

Control & Dynamic Systems, Vol. 40: Advances in Robotic Systems, Pt. 2. Ed. by Cornelius T. Leondes. (Illus.). 419p. 1991. text ed. 94.00 (*0-12-012740-7*) Acad Pr.

Control & Dynamic Systems, Vol. 41: Analysis & Control System Techniques for Electric Power Systems, Pt. 1 of 4. Ed. by Cornelius T. Leondes. (Illus.). 478p. 1991. text ed. 94.00 (*0-12-012741-5*) Acad Pr.

Control & Dynamic Systems, Vol. 42: Analysis & Control System Techniques for Electric Power Systems, Pt. 2 of 4. Ed. by Cornelius T. Leondes. (Illus.). 488p. 1991. text ed. 94.00 (*0-12-012742-3*) Acad Pr.

Control & Dynamic Systems, Vol. 43: Analysis & Control System Techniques for Electric Power Systems, Pt. 3 of 4. Ed. by Cornelius T. Leondes. (Illus.). 468p. 1991. text ed. 94.00 (*0-12-012743-1*) Acad Pr.

Control & Dynamic Systems, Vol. 44: Analysis & Control System Techniques for Electric Power Systems, Pt. 4 of 4. Ed. by Cornelius T. Leondes. (Illus.). 497p. 1991. text ed. 94.00 (*0-12-012744-X*) Acad Pr.

Control & Dynamic Systems, Vol. 45: Advances in Manufacturing & Automation Systems. Ed. by Cornelius T. Leondes. (Illus.). 353p. 1992. text ed. 79.00 (*0-12-012745-8*) Acad Pr.

Control & Dynamic Systems, Vol. 46: Manufacturing & Automation Systems, Pt. 2. Ed. by Cornelius T. Leondes. (Illus.). 421p. 1991. text ed. 94.00 (*0-12-012746-6*) Acad Pr.

Control & Dynamic Systems, Vol. 47: Manufacturing & Automation Systems, Pt. 3. Ed. by Cornelius T. Leondes. (Illus.). 431p. 1991. text ed. 94.00 (*0-12-012747-4*) Acad Pr.

Control & Dynamic Systems, Vol. 48: Manufacturing & Automation Systems, Pt. 4. Ed. by Cornelius T. Leondes. (Illus.). 447p. 1991. text ed. 94.00 (*0-12-012748-2*) Acad Pr.

Control & Dynamic Systems, Vol. 49: Manufacturing & Automation Systems, Pt. 5. Ed. by Cornelius T. Leondes. (Illus.). 424p. 1991. text ed. 94.00 (*0-12-012749-0*) Acad Pr.

Control & Dynamic Systems, Vol. 52: Integrated Technology Methods & Applications in Aerospace Systems Design. Ed. by Cornelius T. Leondes. (Illus.). 550p. 1992. text ed. 85.00 (*0-12-012752-0*) Acad Pr.

Control & Dynamic Systems, Vol. 53: High Performance Systems Techniques & Applications. Ed. by Cornelius T. Leondes. (Illus.). 527p. 1992. text ed. 95.00 (*0-12-012753-9*) Acad Pr.

Control & Dynamic Systems, Vol. 54: System Performance Improvement & Optimization Techniques & Their Applications in Aerospace Systems. Ed. by Cornelius T. Leondes. (Illus.). 521p. 1993. text ed. 99.00 (*0-12-012754-7*) Acad Pr.

Control & Dynamic Systems, Vol. 55: Digital & Numeric Techniques & Their Applications in Control Systems, Pt. 1. Ed. by Cornelius T. Leondes. (Illus.). 521p. 1993. text ed. 99.00 (*0-12-012755-5*) Acad Pr.

Control & Dynamic Systems, Vol. 56: Digital & Numeric Techniques & Their Applications in Control Systems, Pt. 2. Ed. by Cornelius T. Leondes. (Illus.). 574p. 1993. text ed. 99.00 (*0-12-012756-3*) Acad Pr.

Control & Dynamic Systems, Vol. 57: Multidisciplinary Engineering Systems: Design & Optimization Techniques & Their Application. Ed. by Cornelius T. Leondes. (Illus.). 493p. 1993. text ed. 99.00 (*0-12-012757-1*) Acad Pr.

Control & Dynamic Systems, Vol. 58: Computer Aided Design-Engineering (CAD-CAE), Part 1 of 2, Techniques & Their Application. Ed. by Cornelius T. Leondes. (Illus.). 349p. 1993. text ed. 99.00 (*0-12-012758-X*) Acad Pr.

Control & Dynamic Systems, Vol. 59: Computer Aided Design-Engineering (CAD-CAE), Part 2 of 2, Techniques & Their Application. Ed. by Cornelius T. Leondes. (Illus.). 329p. 1993. text ed. 99.00 (*0-12-012759-8*) Acad Pr.

Control & Dynamic Systems, Vol. 60: CAM - CTM: Computer-Aided Manufacturing - Computer-Integrated Manufacturing, Pt. 1 of 2. Ed. by Cornelius T. Leondes. (Illus.). 460p. 1993. text ed. 99.00 (*0-12-012760-1*) Acad Pr.

Control & Dynamic Systems, Vol. 61: CAM - CTM: Computer-Aided Manufacturing - Computer-Integrated Manufacturing, Pt. 2 of 2. Ed. by Cornelius T. Leondes. (Illus.). 414p. 1994. text ed. 99.00 (*0-12-012761-X*) Acad Pr.

Control & Dynamic Systems, Vol. 62: Concurrent Engineering Techniques & Applications. Ed. by Cornelius T. Leondes. (Illus.). 462p. 1994. text ed. 99.00 (*0-12-012762-8*) Acad Pr.

Control & Dynamic Systems, Vol. 63: Analysis & Synthesis Techniques in Control & Dynamic Systems. Ed. by Cornelius T. Leondes. (Illus.). 419p. 1994. text ed. 99.00 (*0-12-012763-6*) Acad Pr.

Control & Dynamic Systems, Vol. 64, Pt. 1: Stochastic Techniques in Digital Processing Systems. Ed. by Cornelius T. Leondes. (Illus.). 424p. 1994. text ed. 99.00 (*0-12-012764-4*) Acad Pr.

Control & Dynamic Systems, Vol. 65, Pt. 2: Stochastic Techniques in Digital Processing Systems. Ed. by Cornelius T. Leondes. (Illus.). 406p. 1994. text ed. 99.00 (*0-12-012765-2*) Acad Pr.

Control & Dynamic Systems, Vol. 67: Digital Image Processing: Techniques & Applications. Ed. by Cornelius T. Leondes. (Illus.). 386p. 1994. text ed. 99.00 (*0-12-012767-9*) Acad Pr.

Control & Dynamic Sytems: Advances in Theory & Applications, 3 pts., Vol. 28. Ed. by Cornelius T. Leondes. (Advances in Algorithms & Computational Techniques in Dynamic Systems Control Ser.: Pt. I). 278p. 1988. text ed. 112.00 (*0-12-012728-8*) Acad Pr.

Control & Estimation of Distributed Parameter Systems. Ed. by H. T. Banks. LC 92-27712. (Frontiers in Applied Mathematics Ser.: Vol. 11). xii, 227p. 1992. 59.75 (*0-89871-297-1*) Soc Indus-Appl Math.

An Asterisk (*) at the beginning of an entry indicates that the title is appearing in BIP for the first time.

An Asterisk (*) at the beginning of an entry indicates that the title is appearing in BIP for the first time.

1597

C

Control of Foreign Policy in Western Democracies: A Comparative Study of Parliamentary Foreign Affairs Committees, 3 vols. Antonio Cassese. 381p. 1983. Vol. 1; Parliamentary Foreign Affairs Committees: The National Setting, 381 pgs. lib. bdg. 20.00 (*0-685-73559-1*); Vol. 2, The European Parliament & Its Foreign Affairs Committee, 161pgs. lib. bdg. 20.00 (*0-379-20041-4*); Vol. 3; The Impact of Foreign Affairs Committee on Foreign Policy 142 pgs. lib. bdg. 20.00 (*0-379-20042-2*) Oceana.

Control of Foreign Policy in Western Democracies: A Comparative Study of Parliamentary Foreign Affairs Committees, 3 vols., Set. Antonio Cassese. 1983. lib. bdg. 60.00 (*0-379-20040-6*) Oceana.

Control of Formation Pressure. (Well Servicing & Workover Ser.: Lesson 9). (Illus.). 35p. (Orig.). 1971. pap. text ed. 12.00 (*0-88698-065-8*, 3.70910) PETEX.

Control of Gas Hazards on Vessels to Be Repaired. (Three Hundred Ser.). 1993. pap. 16.75 (*0-685-58057-1*, 306-93) Natl Fire Prot.

Control of Groundwater. D. W. Quinion & G. R. Quinion. 50p. 1987. 10.00 (*0-7277-0362-5*, Pub. by T Telford UK) Am Soc Civil Eng.

Control of Growth & Differentiation in Plants see Growth & Differentiation in Plants

Control of Growth Factors & Prevention of Cancer. Ed. by Michael B. Sporn. (ESO Monographs). (Illus.). 88p. 1992. 59.00 (*0-387-55301-0*) Spr-Verlag.

Control of Growth Processes by Chemical Agents: Proceedings of the 3rd International Pharmacological Meeting, Sao Paulo, July 1966, Vol. 5. A. Welch. LC 67-19416. 1968. 49.00 (*0-08-012371-6*, Pub. by Pergamon Repr UK) Franklin.

Control of Hazardous Material Spills. 1976. 30.00 (*0-944989-03-9*, 060076) Hazardous Mat Control.

Control of Hazardous Material Spills. 1978. 30.00 (*0-944989-12-8*, 060178) Hazardous Mat Control.

Control of Hazardous Materials Spills. LC 80-51356. 500p. 1980. pap. 30.00 (*0-686-39197-7*) Hazardous Mat Control.

Control of Head Movement. Ed. by Barry W. Peterson & Frances J. Richmond. (Illus.). 336p. 1988. 55.00 (*0-19-504499-1*) OUP.

Control of Hospital Infection. 3rd ed. E. J. Lowbury. 1992. 99.95 (*0-442-31669-0*) Chapman & Hall.

Control of Human Movement. Mark L. Latash. LC 92-36991. (Illus.). 392p. 1993. text ed. 47.00x (*0-87322-455-8*, BLAT0455) Human Kinetics.

Control of Human Retrovirus Gene Expression. Ed. by B. Robert Franza, Jr. et al. LC 88-12289. (Illus.). 480p. 1988. text ed. 55.00 (*0-87969-315-0*) Cold Spring Harbor.

Control of Immigration Statistics (Annual) 1991. 72p. 1992. pap. 40.00 (*0-10-120632-1*, HM06321, Pub. by HMSO UK) UNIPUB.

Control of Immigration Statistics 1992. 129p. 1993. pap. 45.00 (*0-10-123682-4*, HM36824, Pub. by HMSO UK) UNIPUB.

Control of Immunogenesis by the Nervous System. Ed. by A. N. Gordienko. 192p. 1960. text ed. 49.00 (*0-7065-0101-2*, Pub. by Keter Pub IS) Coronet Bks.

Control of Indoor Climate. T. C. Angus. 1968. 54.00 (*0-08-012729-0*, Pub. by Pergamon Repr UK) Franklin.

Control of Industrial Chemical Hazards, 2 vols., Vol. 2. Phillip Carson & Clive Mumford. 1089p. 1989. Set. text ed. 230.00 (*0-470-20886-4*) Halsted Pr.

Control of Information. 1973. 2.00 (*0-686-09553-7*) Network Project.

Control of Information in the United States: An Annotated Bibliography of Books. James R. Bennett. 900p. 1987. text ed. 79.50 (*0-313-28097-5*, BIU/, Greenwood Pr) Greenwood.

Control of Interfaces in Metal & Ceramics Composites. Ed. by Ray Y. Lin & Steven G. Fishman. LC 93-80902. 1994. 84.00 (*0-87339-259-0*) Minerals Metals.

Control of Japanese Foreign Policy. Yale C. Maxon. LC 72-12330. 286p. 1973. reprint ed. text ed. 59.75 (*0-8371-6728-0*, MACJ, Greenwood Pr) Greenwood.

Control of Large Flexible Space Structures. S. M. Joshi. (Lecture Notes in Control & Information Sciences Ser.: Vol. 131). (Illus.). x, 196p. 1989. pap. 42.00 (*0-387-51467-8*, 3342) Spr-Verlag.

Control of Late Ancient & Medieval Population. Josiah C. Russell. LC 83-71298. (Memoirs of the American Philosophical Society Ser.: Vol. 160). 288p. reprint ed. pap. 82.10 (*0-7837-0543-3*, 2040871) Bks Demand.

Control of Light. Brian Fitt & Joe Thornley. LC 92-17942. (Illus.). 184p. 1993. pap. 17.50 (*0-240-51346-0*, Focal) Buttrwrth-Heinemann.

Control of Liquid-Liquid Extraction Columns. Kaddour Najim. Ed. by R. Hughes. (Topics in Chemical Engineering Ser.: Vol. 5). 259p. 1988. text ed. 105.00 (*2-88124-703-2*) Gordon & Breach.

Control of Livestock Diseases. C. A. Kirkbride. (Illus.). 160p. (C). 1986. pap. 27.95x (*0-398-05181-X*) C C Thomas.

Control of Long-Term International Capital Movement. Alexander Cairncross. LC 73-12634. (Brookings Institution Staff Paper Ser.). 118p. reprint ed. pap. 33.70 (*0-317-20780-6*, 2025367) Bks Demand.

Control of Machines with Friction. Brian Armstrong-Helouvry. (C). 1991. lib. bdg. 65.50 (*0-7923-9133-0*) Kluwer Ac.

Control of Mammal Pests. Ed. by C. G. Richards. 250p. 1986. 125.00 (*0-85066-371-7*) Taylor & Francis.

Control of Manufacturing Processes & Robotic Systems. Ed. by D. E. Hardt & W. J. Book. 144p. 1983. 30.00 (*0-317-06646-3*, H00278) ASME.

Control of Manufacturing Processes & Robotic Systems: Presented at the Winter Annual Meeting of ASME, Boston, MA, November 13-18, 1983. American Society of Mechanical Engineers Staff. Ed. by David E. Hardt & Wayne J. Book. LC 83-72724. (Illus.). 290p. reprint ed. pap. 82.70 (*0-685-20617-3*, 2030559) Bks Demand.

Control of Mechanical Systems with Constraints: Complaint Control of Constrained Robot Manipulators. F. M. Salam et al. 200p. (C). 1996. text ed. 43.00 (*981-02-0633-X*) World Scientific Pub.

Control of Membrane Function: Short-Term & Long-Term. Ed. by J. M. Ritchie et al. (Progress in Cell Research Ser.). 340p. 1990. 143.75 (*0-444-81125-7*) Elsevier.

Control of Messenger RHA Stability. Ed. by Joel Belasco & George Brawerman. (Illus.). 517p. 1993. text ed. 79.95 (*0-12-084782-5*) Acad Pr.

Control of Metabolic Processes. Ed. by A. Cornish-Bowden & M. L. Cardenas. LC 90-7160. (NATO ASI Series A, Life Sciences: Vol. 190). (Illus.). 470p. 1990. 129.50 (*0-306-43582-9*, Plenum Pr) Plenum.

Control of Microstructure & Properties in Steel Arc Welds. Lars-Erik Svensson. 1993. 89.95 (*0-8493-8221-1*, TS227) CRC Pr.

Control of Migraine. John B. Brainard. 1979. pap. 7.95 (*0-393-00933-5*) Norton.

Control of Municipal Budgets: Toward the Effective Design of Tax & Expenditure Limitations. David Merriman. LC 87-2495. 180p. 1987. text ed. 55.00 (*0-89930-217-3*, MTM/, Quorum Bks) Greenwood.

Control of Mycotoxins: Proceedings of a Symposium, Goteborg, Sweden, 1972. Ed. by Palle Krogh. 116p. 1973. 54.00 (*0-08-020749-9*, Pub. by Pergamon Repr UK) Franklin.

Control of NATO Forces in Europe. Marco Carnovale. 302p. (C). 1993. pap. text ed. 50.00 (*0-8133-8001-4*) Westview.

Control of Nature. J. McPhee. Date not set. write for info. (*0-7126-5030-X*) Random.

Control of Nature. John McPhee. (Illus.). 288p. 1989. 17.95 (*0-374-12890-1*) FS&G.

Control of Nature. John McPhee. 1990. pap. 10.00 (*0-374-52259-6*, Noonday) FS&G.

Control of Naval Armaments: Prospects & Possibilities. Barry M. Blechman. LC 75-5153. (Brookings Institution Studies in Defense Policy). 110p. reprint ed. pap. 31.40 (*0-317-30180-2*, 2025362) Bks Demand.

***Control of Neoplasia by Modulation of the Immune System.** fac. ed. Ed. by Michael A. Chirigos. LC 76-5665. (Progress in Cancer Research & Therapy Ser.: No. 2). (Illus.). 619p. Date not set. pap. 176.50 (*0-7837-7206-8*, 2047093) Bks Demand.

Control of Nonlinear Mechanical Systems. J. M. Skowronski. (Applied Information Technology Ser.). (Illus.). 456p. 1991. 89.50 (*0-306-43827-5*, Plenum Pr) Plenum.

Control of Nutritional Anaemia with Special Reference to Iron Deficiency: Proceedings of the IAEA-USAID-WHO Joint Meeting, Geneva, 1974. IAEA-USAID-WHO Joint Meeting Staff. (Technical Report Ser.: No. 580). 1975. pap. 2.80 (*92-4-120580-6*) World Health.

Control of Organelle Development. Society for Experimental Biology (Great Britain). LC 74-12179. (Symposia of the Society for Experimental Biology Ser.: No. 24). 571p. reprint ed. pap. 162.80 (*0-685-15258-8*, 2014673) Bks Demand.

Control of Organic Compounds with Powdered Activated Carbon. 222p. 1991. pap. 32.50 (*0-89867-528-6*, 90581) Am Water Wks Assn.

Control of Organic Material by Coagulation & Floc-Separation Processes. Ed. by K. J. Ives & H. Bernhardt. (Water Science & Technology Ser.: Vol. 27). 1993. pap. 110.00 (*0-08-042340-X*, Pergamon Pr) Elsevier.

Control of Organic Substances in Water & Wastewater. Ed. by Bernard B. Berger. LC 86-31141. (Pollution Technology Review Ser.: No. 140). (Illus.). 459p. 1987. 45.00 (*0-8155-1118-3*) Noyes.

Control of Pain & Other Symptoms in Cancer Patients. Tor I. Tonnessen. Ed. by Jan V. Johannessen. Tr. by Allison Olsen. (Cancer Ser.). 1989. 57.00 (*0-89116-868-0*) Hemisp Pub.

Control of Pain in Arthritis in the Knee. Paul Notrik, pseud. LC 84-61283. 32p. (Orig.). 1984. pap. 4.50 (*0-931150-14-0*) Rheumatoid.

Control of Partial Differential Equations. Ed. by Da Prato & Tubaro. (Lecture Notes in Pure & Applied Mathematics Ser.: Vol. 165). 304p. 1994. 125.00 (*0-8247-9240-8*) Dekker.

Control of Partially-Known Dynamical Systems. A. A. Bahnasawi & M. S. Mahmoud. (Lecture Notes in Control & Information Sciences Ser.: Vol. 124). (Illus.). xi, 228p. 1989. pap. 42.00 (*0-387-51144-X*, 2950) Spr-Verlag.

Control of Pesticides: A Survey of Existing Legislation. (International Digest of Health Legislation Ser: Vol. 20, No. 4). 150p. 1969. pap. 5.60 (*92-4-169204-9*, 1020) World Health.

Control of Pipeline Corrosion. LC 76-27507. (Illus.). 190p. 1967. 40.00 (*0-915567-95-4*) NACE Intl.

Control of Plant Gene Expression. Verma. 1992. 149.95 (*0-8493-8866-X*, QK981) CRC Pr.

Control of Polymerization Reactors. F. Joseph Schork et al. LC 92-44695. 376p. 1993. 160.00 (*0-8247-9043-X*) Dekker.

Control of Power Analysis & Design. 2nd rev. ed. Donaldson McCloy & H. R. Martin. 1988. pap. text ed. 52.95 (*0-470-21091-5*) Wiley.

Control of Power Plants & Power Systems: Selected Papers from the IFAC Symposium, Munich, Germany, 9-11 March 1992. Ed. by E. Welfonder et al. LC 92-37412. 1993. 170.00 (*0-08-041709-4*, Pergamon Pr) Elsevier.

Control of Proliferation in Animal Cells. Ed. by Bayard Clarkson & Renato Baserga. LC 73-88195. (Cold Spring Harbor Conferences on Cell Proliferation Ser.: No. 1). 1043p. reprint ed. pap. 180.00 (*0-7837-2007-6*, 2042281) Bks Demand.

Control of Public Expenditure. Ed. by Anthony Harrison. 325p. 1989. 39.95x (*0-946967-26-1*); pap. 21.95x (*0-946967-33-4*) Transaction Pubs.

Control of Quantum-Mechanical Processes & Systems. Anatoliy G. Butkovskiy & Y. I. Samoilenko. (C). 1990. lib. bdg. 120.00 (*0-7923-0689-9*) Kluwer Ac.

Control of Radon in Houses. Intro. by W. K. Sinclair. (Report Ser.: No. 103). 110p. (Orig.). 1989. pap. text ed. 25.00 (*0-929600-07-X*) NCRP Pubns.

Control of Reproductive Functions in Domestic Animals. Wolfgang Jochle & Ross Lamond. (Current Topics in Veterinary Medicine & Animal Science Ser.: No. 7). (Illus.). 1981. lib. bdg. 80.00 (*90-247-2400-7*) Kluwer Ac.

Control of Resources. Partha Dasgupta. (Illus.). 240p. 1983. 32.00 (*0-674-16980-8*) HUP.

Control of Restrictive Practices from 1956. C. Brock. 1969. text ed. 6.95 (*0-07-094038-X*) McGraw.

Control of Robot Manipulators. Frank L. Lewis et al. LC 92-17922. (Illus.). 448p. (C). 1993. write for info. (*0-02-370501-9*) Macmillan.

Control of Scale & Corrosion in Building Water Systems. Russell W. Lane. LC 92-35156. 1993. text ed. 47.00 (*0-07-036217-3*) McGraw.

Control of Schistosomiasis. (Technical Report Ser.: No. 728). 113p. 1986. pap. 6.00 (*92-4-120728-0*) World Health.

Control of Sea Resources by Semi-Autonomous States. Thomas M. Franck. LC 78-69499. 1978. pap. 1.75 (*0-87003-032-9*) Carnegie Endow.

***Control of Semiconductor Interfaces: Proceedings of the First International Symposium, Karuizawa, Japan, 8-12 November 1993.** First International Symposium Staff. Ed. by I. Ohdomari et al. (C). 185.75p. 1994. text ed. 185.75 (*0-444-81889-8*) Elsevier.

Control of Ships & Discharges. International Maritime Organization Staff. 1986. text ed. 50.00 (*0-89771-967-0*, Pub. by Intl Maritime Org UK) St Mut.

Control of Silkworm Reproduction, Development & Sex. V. A. Strunnikov. 280p. 1983. 35.00 (*0-569-08849-6*, Pub. by Collets UK) Pro-Am Music.

Control of Sources of Ionising Radiation. Donald Hughes. 1993. 95.00 (*0-948237-17-1*, Pub. by H&H Sci Cnslts UK) St Mut.

Control of Spacecraft & Aircraft. Arthur E. Bryson, Jr. LC 92-29102. (Illus.). (C). 1993. text ed. 55.00 (*0-691-08782-2*) Princeton U Pr.

Control of Structures. Horst Leipholz & M. Abdel-Rohman. 1986. lib. bdg. 173.00 (*90-247-3321-9*) Kluwer Ac.

Control of Subsidiaries in the Developing Countries: The Case of Swedish Multinationals. Manoocher Kavoosi. 146p. (Orig.). 1992. pap. 65.00x (*91-7246-098-9*, Pub. by Almqv & Wiksell SW) Coronet Bks.

Control of Surface Quality. James A. Broadston & Donald A. Broadston. (Illus.). 1986. pap. 30.00 (*0-685-14197-7*) Surf Chek.

Control of Technology. D. J. Elliott & R. Elliott. (Wykeham Science Ser.: No. 39). 260p. (C). 1976. 18.00 (*0-8448-1166-1*, Crane Russak) Taylor & Francis.

Control of the Campus: A Report on the Governance of Higher Education. Carnegie Foundation for the Advancement of Teaching Staff. LC 82-19772. 126p. 1982. pap. text ed. 6.50 (*0-931050-21-9*) Carnegie Fnd Advan Teach.

Control of the Hypothalamo-Pituitary-Andrenocortical Axis. Ed. by F. Clifford Rose. 470p. 1989. 65.00 (*0-8236-1070-5*) Intl Univs Pr.

Control of the Imaginary: Reason & Imagination in Modern Times. Luiz Costa Lima. LC 88-19154. (Theory & History of Literature Ser.: Vol. 50). xxiii, 250p. 1989. text ed. 39.95 (*0-8166-1562-4*); pap. text ed. 15.95 (*0-8166-1563-2*) U of Minn Pr.

Control of the Media in the United States: An Annotated Bibliography. James R. Bennett. LC 91-26064. 849p. 1992. 125.00 (*0-8240-4438-X*, SS458) Garland.

Control of the Middle East Arms Race. Geoffrey Kemp & Shelley A. Stahl. LC 91-61775. 232p. 1991. pap. 11.95 (*0-87003-046-9*, JX1974) Carnegie Endow.

Control of the Plant Environment: Proceedings. Easter School in Agricultural Science (4th: 1957: University of Nottingham) Staff. Ed. by J. P. Hudson. 270p. reprint ed. pap. 77.00 (*0-317-41733-9*, 2025733) Bks Demand.

Control of the Reactivity of Solids. Ed. by V. V. Boldyrev et al. (Studies in Surface Science & Catalysts: Vol. 2). 226p. 1979. 107.75 (*0-444-41800-8*) Elsevier.

Control of the Thyroid Gland: Regulation of Its Normal Function & Growth. R. Ekholm et al. (Advances in Experimental Medicine & Biology Ser.: Vol. 261). (Illus.). 412p. 1989. 115.00 (*0-306-43380-X*, Plenum Pr) Plenum.

Control of Time-Delay Systems. J. E. Marshall. (IEE Control Engineering Ser.: No. 10). 237p. 1979. boxed 69.00 (*0-906048-12-5*, CE010) Inst Elect Eng.

Control of Tissue Damage. Ed. by A. M. Glauert. (Research Monographs in Cell & Tissue Physiology: Vol. 15). 326p. 1988. 141.00 (*0-444-80924-4*) Elsevier.

Control of Trusts. enl. ed. John B. Clark & John M. Clark. LC 70-108000. (Reprints of Economic Classics Ser.). xi, 202p. 1971. reprint ed. lib. bdg. 29.50 (*0-678-00606-7*) Kelley.

Control of Tumour Growth & Its Biological Bases. Ed. by W. Davis et al. (Developments in Oncology Ser.). 1984. lib. bdg. 170.00 (*0-89838-603-9*) Kluwer Ac.

Control of Uncertain Dynamic Systems. S. P. Bhattacharyya. 1991. 105.00 (*0-8493-0195-5*, TJ210) CRC Pr.

Control of Uncertain Systems. Diederich Hinrichsen & Bent Martensson. (Progress in Systems & Control Theory Ser.: Vol. 6). 344p. 1990. 63.50 (*0-8176-3495-9*) Birkhauser.

Control of Uncertain Systems: A Linear Programming Approach. Munther A. Dahleh & Ignacio J. Diaz-Bobillo. LC 94-10824. 1994. text ed. 72.00 (*0-13-280645-2*) P-H.

Control of Urban Schools: Perspective on the Power of Educational Reformers. Joseph M. Cronin. LC 72-78608. 288p. 1973. 18.95 (*0-02-906910-6*) Free Pr.

Control of Uterine Contractility. Robert E. Garfield. 1993. 210.00 (*0-8493-6812-X*, QP262) CRC Pr.

Control of Variable Structure Networks. V. V. Ivanishchev & A. D. Krasnoshchekov. Ed. by A. V. Balakrishnan. LC 87-24820. (Translations Series in Mathematics & Engineering). 156p. 1987. text ed. 64.00 (*0-911575-05-7*) Optimization Soft.

Control of Virus Diseases. Ed. by N. J. Dimmock et al. (Society for General Microbiology Symposium Ser.: No. 45). 300p. (C). 1990. 99.95 (*0-521-38562-8*) Cambridge U Pr.

Control of Virus Diseases. 2nd expanded rev. ed. Ed. by Edouard Kurstak. LC 92-49728. 456p. 1992. 175.00 (*0-8247-8683-1*) Dekker.

Control of Virus Diseases. Ed. by Edouard Kurstak & Raymond G. Marusyk. LC 83-25226. (Illus.). 608p. reprint ed. pap. 173.30 (*0-7837-0977-3*, 2041283) Bks Demand.

***Control of Volatile Organic Compound Emissions from Reactor Processes & Distillation Operations Processes in the Synthetic Organic Chemical Manufacturing Industry.** (Illus.). 275p. (Orig.). (C). 1994. pap. text ed. 65.00 (*0-7881-0872-7*) Diane Pub.

Control of Wages. Walton H. Hamilton & Stacy May. LC 68-27847. (Reprints of Economic Classics Ser.). vii, 185p. 1968. reprint ed. 29.50 (*0-678-00443-9*) Kelley.

Control Options & Strategies. Ed. by H. S. Stubbs. (Orig.). (C). 1988. 9.95 (*0-935577-20-3*) Acid Rain Found.

Control over Compliance with International Obligations. Ed. by William E. Butler. 216p. (C). 1991. lib. bdg. 106.50 (*0-7923-1025-X*) Kluwer Ac.

Control over Intoxicant Use: Pharmacological, Psychological & Social Considerations: Special Issue of Journal of Drug Issues. Ed. by Norman E. Zinberg & Wayne Harding. LC 81-2333. 207p. 1982. 35.95 (*0-89885-064-9*) Human Sci Pr.

Control Panels. Center for Occupational Research & Development Staff. (EUTEC Power Plant Operator Curriculum Ser.). (Illus.). 22p. (C). 1985. pap. text ed. write for info. (*1-55502-249-9*) CORD Commns.

Control Points in School Business Management. Prod. by Management Techniques Research Committee Staff. 24p. 1979. 6.00 (*0-910170-10-X*, 2805) Assn Sch Busn.

Control Policies of the Reichsbank, 1924-1933. Mildred B. Northrop. LC 68-58613. (Columbia University. Studies in the Social Sciences: No. 436). reprint ed. 27.50 (*0-404-51436-7*) AMS Pr.

Control Problems & Devices in Manufacturing Technology: Proceedings of the IFAC-IFIP Symposium, 3rd, MANUFACONT'80, Budapest, Hungary, Oct., 1980. IFAC-IFIP Symposium Staff. Ed. by T. M. Ellis. (IFAC Proceedings Ser.). 375p. 1981. 162.00 (*0-08-026720-3*, Pub. by Pergamon Repr UK) Franklin.

Control Problems for Systems Described by Partial Differential Equation & Applications. Ed. by I. Lasiecka & R. Triggiani. (Lecture Notes in Control & Information Sciences Ser.: Vol. 97). 400p. 1987. pap. 73.00 (*0-387-18054-0*) Spr-Verlag.

Control Process in Modified Handwriting. June E. Downey. Bd. with No. 5. Iowa University Studies in Psychology. Ed. by C. E. Seashore. (*0-8115-1408-0*); Combination Tones & Other Related Auditory Phenomena. Joseph Peterson. (Psychological Monographs General & Applied: Vol. 9). 1972. reprint ed. 35.00 (*0-685-09929-6*) Periodicals Srv.

Control Products Database. Ed. by Philip C. Flora. 1988. 49.00 (*0-929076-06-0*); 5.25 hd 124.00 (*0-929076-07-9*) TecSpec.

***Control Program API.** Marc A. Stock. 1995. pap. text ed. 29.95 (*0-471-03887-3*) Wiley.

Control Programs of Nonlinear Programming: Proceedings of the IFAC Symposium, Denver, Colorado, June 1979. IFAC Symposium Staff. Ed. by H. E. Rauch. (IFAC Proceedings Ser.). 130p. 1980. 62.00 (*0-08-024491-2*, Pub. by Pergamon Repr UK) Franklin.

Control Revolution: Technological & Economic Origins of the Information Society. James R. Beniger. 512p. 1989. reprint ed. pap. 16.95 (*0-674-16986-7*) HUP.

Control Room Supervisor. Jack Rudman. (Career Examination Ser.: Series 1). 1991. pap. 34.95 (*0-8373-3705-4*) Nat Learn.

Control Science & Technology for the Progress of Society: Proceedings, 7 Vols., 1. H. Akashi. LC 81-23491. (IFAC Proceedings Ser.). 3800p. 1982. 314.00 (*0-08-028713-1*, Pub. by Pergamon Repr UK) Franklin.

Control Science & Technology for the Progress of Society: Proceedings, 7 Vols., 2. H. Akashi. LC 81-23491. (IFAC Proceedings Ser.). 3800p. 1982. 360.00 (*0-08-028714-X*, Pub. by Pergamon Repr UK) Franklin.

Control Science & Technology for the Progress of Society: Proceedings, 7 Vols., 3. H. Akashi. LC 81-23491. (IFAC Proceedings Ser.). 3800p. 1982. 182.00 (*0-08-028715-8*, Pub. by Pergamon Repr UK) Franklin.

Control Science & Technology for the Progress of Society: Proceedings, 7 Vols., 4. H. Akashi. LC 81-23491. (IFAC Proceedings Ser.). 3800p. 1982. 196.00 (*0-08-028716-6*, Pub. by Pergamon Repr UK) Franklin.

An Asterisk (*) at the beginning of an entry indicates that the title is appearing in BIP for the first time.

Control Science & Technology for the Progress of Society: Proceedings, 7 Vols., 5. H. Akashi. LC 81-23491. (IFAC Proceedings Ser.). 3800p. 1982. 210.00 (*0-08-028717-4*, Pub. by Pergamon Repr UK) Franklin.
Control Science & Technology for the Progress of Society: Proceedings, 7 Vols., 6. H. Akashi. LC 81-23491. (IFAC Proceedings Ser.). 3800p. 1982. 180.00 (*0-08-028718-2*, Pub. by Pergamon Repr UK) Franklin.
Control Science & Technology for the Progress of Society: Proceedings, 7 Vols., Set. H. Akashi. LC 81-23491. (IFAC Proceedings Ser.). 3800p. 1982. 1,704.00 (*0-08-027580-X*, Pub. by Pergamon Repr UK) Franklin.
Control Strategies for Photochemical Oxidants Across Europe. OECD Staff. 116p. (Orig.). 1990. pap. 26.00 (*92-64-13401-8*) OECD.
Control System Design: An Introduction to State-Space Methods. B. Friedland. (Electrical Engineering Ser.). 512p. (C). 1986. text ed. write for info. (*0-07-022441-2*) McGraw.
Control System Design Guide: Using Your Computer to Develop & Diagnose Feedback Controllers. Ed. by George Ellis. (Illus.). 248p. 1991. text ed. 59.95 (*0-12-237470-3*) Acad Pr.
Control System Documentation: Applied Instrumentation Symbols & Identification. Raymond Mulley. LC 93-30757. 232p. 1994. 65.00 (*1-55617-490-X*) Instru Soc.
***Control System Dynamics.** Robert N. Clark. (Illus.). 603p. (C). Date not set. write for info. (*0-521-47239-3*) Cambridge U Pr.
Control System Engineering. Mohamed E. El-Hawary. 1984. text ed. 32.95 (*0-685-09872-9*, Reston); write for info. (*0-8359-1016-4*, Reston) P-H.
Control System Interfaces: Design & Implementation Using PCS. Michael F. Hordeski. 352p. 1991. text ed. 57.00 (*0-13-456823-0*, 420701) P-H.
Control System Synthesis: A Factorization Approach. M. Vidyasagar. LC 84-14411. (Series in Signal Processing, Optimization & Control Ser.). (Illus.). 300p. 1985. 57.50 (*0-262-20021-X*) MIT Pr.
Control Systems. Nise. Ed. by Sally Elliott. 844p. (C). 1992. text ed. 69.95 (*0-8053-5420-4*) Benjamin-Cummings.
Control Systems. Naresh K. Sinha. 544p. (C). 1986. text ed. 64.00 (*0-03-069357-8*); Solutions manual. write for info. (*0-03-069358-6*) SCP.
***Control Systems.** 2nd ed. N. K. Sinha. LC 95-7851. 1995. text ed. 39.95 (*0-470-23516-0*) Wiley.
Control Systems: A "How to" Guide for Control Installations in R-C Model Aircraft. Jim Newman. (Illus.). 23p. 1985. pap. 6.95 (*0-911295-01-1*) Air Age.
Control Systems: An Introduction. Kevin Warwick. 500p. 1989. text ed. 68.00 (*0-13-171604-2*) P-H.
Control Systems: Continuous & Discrete. Victor J. Bucek. 320p. 1989. boxed 77.00 (*0-13-171752-9*) P-H.
Control Systems Engineering. William J. Palm. LC 85-26590. 695p. (C). 1986. Net. text ed. write for info. (*0-471-81086-X*) Wiley.
Control Systems Engineering. 2nd ed. Norman Nise. 800p. (C). 1995. text ed. 70.95 (*0-8053-5424-7*) Benjamin-Cummings.
Control Systems Engineering Study Guide for the Professional Engineering Registration Exam. 2nd ed. Instrument Society of America Staff. LC 92-28150. 130p. 1993. pap. 40.00 (*1-55617-476-4*) Instru Soc.
Control Systems for Air Conditioning & Refrigeration. Billy C. Langley. (Illus.). 192p. (C). 1985. text ed. 63.00 (*0-13-171679-4*) P-H.
Control Systems for Heating, Ventilating, & Air Conditioning. Roger W. Haines & Douglas C. Hittle. LC 92-33461. 1993. text ed. 54.95 (*0-442-00837-6*) Chapman & Hall.
Control Systems for Live Entertainment. John Huntington. (Illus.). 288p. 1994. pap. 39.95 (*0-240-80177-6*, Focal) Buttrwrth-Heinemann.
Control Systems I. Center for Occupational Research & Development Staff. (EUTEC Instrumentation & Control Technology Ser.). (Illus.). 210p. 1985. pap. text ed. 25.00 (*1-55502-398-3*) CORD Commns.
Control Systems I. Center for Occupational Research & Development Staff. (EUTEC Instrumentation & Control Curriculum Ser.). (Illus.). 210p. (C). 1985. pap. text ed. write for info. (*1-55502-186-7*) CORD Commns.
Control Systems I, Course 33. Center for Occupational Research & Development Staff. (Nuclear Technology Ser.). (Illus.). 232p. (C). 1984. pap. text ed. 25.00 (*1-55502-122-0*) CORD Commns.
Control Systems II. Center for Occupational Research & Development Staff. (EUTEC Instrumentation & Control Technology Ser.). (Illus.). 210p. 1985. pap. text ed. 28.00 (*1-55502-399-1*) CORD Commns.
Control Systems II. Center for Occupational Research & Development Staff. (EUTEC Instrumentation & Control Curriculum Ser.). (Illus.). 228p. (C). 1985. pap. text ed. write for info. (*1-55502-187-5*) CORD Commns.
Control Systems II, Course 34. Center for Occupational Research & Development Staff. (Nuclear Technology Ser.). (Illus.). 294p. (C). 1984. pap. text ed. 28.00 (*1-55502-123-9*) CORD Commns.
Control Systems Laboratory. Stephen Yurkovich. 92p. 1991. spiral bd. 10.95 (*0-8403-6944-1*) Kendall-Hunt.
Control Systems That Save Energy. F. Greg Shinskey. Ed. by Elias P. Gyftopoulos & Karen C. Cohen. (Industrial Energy-Conservation Manuals Ser.: No. 2). (Illus.). 64p. 1982. ring bd. 20.00 (*0-262-19202-0*) MIT Pr.
***Control Techniques for VOC Emissions from Stationary Sources.** U.S. Environmental Protection Agency, office of Solid Waste & Emergency Response Staff. 474p. (Orig.). 1994. per., pap. text ed. 85.00 (*0-86587-378-X*) Gov Insts.
Control Technologies for Air Pollution. Ed. by M. Miller. (C). 1991. text ed. 350.00 (*0-89771-590-X*, Pub. by Intl Bk Distr II) St Mut.
Control Technologies for Hazardous Air Pollutants. EPA Staff. 260p. (Orig.). 1992. pap. text ed. 69.00 (*0-86587-301-1*) Gov Insts.
Control Technologies for Hazardous Air Pollutants: A Handbook. Michael K. Sink. (Illus.). 250p. (Orig.). (C). 1994. pap. text ed. 65.00 (*0-7881-0643-0*) Diane Pub.
Control Technology & Personal Computers: System Design & Implementation. Michael F. Hordeski. (Illus.). 416p. 1992. text ed. 64.95 (*0-442-00568-7*) Van Nos Reinhold.
***Control Technology Assessment of Enzyme Formation Processes.** 1995. lib. bdg. 251.95 (*0-8490-6682-4*) Gordon Pr.
Control Technology in Elementary Education. Ed. by Brigitte Denis. LC 93-31096. (NATO ASI Series F: Computer & Systems Sciences, Special Programme AET: Vol. 116). ix, 312p. 1993. 69.00 (*0-387-56710-0*) Spr-Verlag.
Control the World with HPIL. Gary Friedman. (Illus.). 340p. (Orig.). (C). 1987. pap. text ed. 24.95 (*0-9612174-9-9*, 490) EduCALC Pubns.
Control Theory. William Glasser. LC 84-47574. 288p. 1985. pap. 12.00 (*0-06-091292-8*, PL 1292, PL) HarpC.
Control Theory: A Guided Tour. J. R. Leigh. (Control Engineering Ser.: No. 45). xii, 186p. 1992. 72.00 (*0-86341-241-6*, Pub. by Peregrinus UK); pap. 37.00 (*0-86341-284-X*, Pub. by Peregrinus UK) Inst Elect Eng.
***Control Theory: A New Exploration of How We Control Our Lives.** William Glasser. 254p. 1994. lib. bdg. 31.00 (*0-8095-9156-1*) Borgo Pr.
Control Theory & Dynamic Games in Economic Policy Analysis. Maria L. Petit. (Illus.). 250p. (C). 1991. 59.95 (*0-521-38523-7*) Cambridge U Pr.
Control Theory & Mathematical Economics Pt. B: Proceedings of the Third Kingston Conference. Liu & Sutinen. (Lecture Notes in Pure & Applied Mathematics Ser.: Vol. 47). 256p. 1979. 115.00 (*0-8247-6852-3*) Dekker.
Control Theory in the Classroom. William Glasser. LC 86-45106. 160p. (Orig.). 1986. pap. 10.00 (*0-06-096085-X*, PL6085, PL) HarpC.
Control Theory in the Plane. O. Hajek. (Lecture Notes in Control & Information Sciences Ser.: Vol. 153). (Illus.). xi, 258p. 1991. pap. 46.00 (*0-387-53553-5*) Spr-Verlag.
Control Theory in the Practice of Reality Therapy: Case Studies. Ed. by Naomi Glasser. LC 89-45092. 288p. (Orig.). 1989. pap. 13.00 (*0-06-096400-6*, PL 6400) HarpC.
Control Theory Manager. William Glasser. LC 93-14546. 128p. 1994. 16.00 (*0-88730-673-X*) Harper Busn.
***Control Theory Manager.** William Glasser. 1994. pap. 10.00 (*0-88730-719-1*) Harper Busn.
Control Theory of Distributed Parameter Systems & Applications: Proceedings of the IFIP WG 7.2 Working Conference, Shanghai, China, May 6-9, 1990. Ed. by X. Li & J. M. Yong. (Lecture Notes in Control & Information Sciences Ser.: Vol. 159). (Illus.). 227p. 1991. pap. 44.00 (*0-387-53894-1*) Spr-Verlag.
Control Theory of Robotic Systems. Ed. by J. M. Skowronski. (Computer Science Ser.: Vol. 11). 364p. (C). 1989. text ed. 66.00 (*9971-5-0624-6*) World Scientific Pub.
Control Theory, Stochastic Analysis & Applications: Proceedings of Symposium on Sys. Sciences & Control Theory. S. P. Chen & J. M. Yong. 300p. 1992. text ed. 95.00 (*981-02-0942-8*) World Scientific Pub.
Control Through Communication: The Rise of System in American Management. JoAnne Yates. LC 88-13745. (Studies in Industry & Society). (Illus.). 352p. 1989. text ed. 45.00 (*0-8018-3757-X*) Johns Hopkins.
Control Through Communication: The Rise of System in American Management. JoAnne Yates. (Studies in Industry & Society). (Illus.). 368p. 1993. reprint ed. pap. text ed. 15.95 (*0-8018-4613-7*) Johns Hopkins.
Control Through Planned Budgeting: An Alternative Approach to Inventory Control & Ordering Procedures in the Christian Bookstore. Mike Phillips. 1978. pap. 12.95 (*0-940652-01-3*) Sunrise Bks.
Control Trap. Barbara Sullivan. 192p. 1991. pap. 7.99 (*1-55661-169-2*) Bethany Hse.
***Control under the Lack of Information.** LC 94-26447. 1994. write for info. (*3-7643-3698-6*) Birkhauser.
***Control under the Lack of Information.** A. N. Krasovski. LC 94-26447. (Systems & Control). 1994. 94.50 (*0-8176-3698-6*) Birkhauser.
Control Valve Aerodynamic Noise Prediction. 1991. pap. 25.00 (*1-55617-207-9*, S75.17) Instru Soc.
Control Valve Capacity Test Procedure. rev. ed. 1988. reprint ed. pap. 25.00 (*1-55617-120-X*, S75.02) Instru Soc.
***Control Valve Primer: A User's Guide.** fac. ed. Hans D. Baumann. LC 91-28927. (Illus.). 145p. 1994. pap. 41.40 (*0-7837-7634-9*, 2047387) Bks Demand.
Control Valve Primer: A User's Guide. 2nd ed. Hans D. Baumann. LC 94-6002. 155p. 1994. text ed. 60.00 (*1-55617-508-6*) Instru Soc.
Control Valve Selection & Sizing. Leslie R. Driskell. LC 82-48157. (Independent Learning Module Ser.). 508p. 1983. text ed. 60.00 (*0-87664-628-3*, 1628-3) Instru Soc.
***Control Valve Sizing.** Les Driskell. (Instrument Society of America Ser.). (Illus.). reprint ed. student ed, pap. 58.80 (*0-7837-9041-4*, 2049792) Bks Demand.
Control Valve Sizing: Instructor's Guide. Les Driskell. (Instructional Resource Package Ser.). (Illus.). 53p. reprint ed. pap. 25.00 (*0-7837-5150-8*, 2044879) Bks Demand.
Control Valve Stability. 1989. pap. 25.00 (*1-55617-205-2*, RP75.18) Instru Soc.
Control Valve Terminology: ANSI-ISA Standard S75.05. 33p. 1986. pap. text ed. 40.00 (*0-87664-753-0*, 1753-0) Instru Soc.
Control Valves for the Chemical Process Industries. Bill Fitzgerald. 1995. pap. text ed. 60.00 (*0-07-021176-0*) McGraw.
Control with a Building Energy Management System. G. J. Levermore. (C). 1988. 140.00 (*0-86022-204-7*, Pub. by Build Servs Info Assn UK) St Mut.
Control Without Confusion: Trouble Shooting Screen-Printed Process Color. Joe Clarke. LC 86-21936. (Orig.). (C). 1987. pap. 29.95 (*0-911380-73-6*) ST Pubns.
Control Your Depression. Peter Lewinsohn et al. 1978. 12.95 (*0-13-171702-2*, Spectrum Bks) P-H.
Control Your Destiny or Someone Else Will: How Jack Welch Is Making General Electric the World's Most Competitive Company. Noel M. Tichy & Stratford Sherman. 400p. 1994. reprint ed. pap. 13.00 (*0-88730-670-5*) Harper Busn.
Control Your Destiny or Someone Else Will: How Jack Welch Is Turning General Electric into the World's Most Competitive Corporation. Noel M. Tichy & Stratford Sherman. LC 92-25822. 384p. 1993. 27.00 (*0-385-24883-0*) Doubleday.
Control Your Dreams. Jayne Gackenbach. 1994. mass mkt. 5.50 (*0-06-109244-4*, Harp PBks) HarpC.
Control Your Overheads: A Practical Programme to Improve Performance & Reduce Costs. Rupert Booth. (Financial Times Management Ser.). 272p. 1994. 75.00x (*0-273-03859-1*, Pub. by Pitman Pubng UK) St Mut.
***Control '84: Mineral Metallurgical Processing.** fac. ed. Intl. Symposium on Automatic Control in Mineral Processing & Process Metallurgy Staff. LC 83-73511. (Illus.). 455p. 1984. reprint ed. pap. 129.70 (*0-7837-7853-8*, 2047612) Bks Demand.
***Controle de l'Alimentation des Plantes Cultives, 2 vols., Set.** P. Kozma. 1624p. (C). 1975. 180.00x (*963-05-0562-2*, Pub. by Akad Kiado HU) St Mut.
Controle Rabietas De Su Hijo (Temper Your Child's Tantrums) J. Dobson. (SPA.). Date not set. 2.49 (*0-8423-6514-1*, 498041) Editorial Unilit.
Controling the Ascent. Susan Takata et al. 386p. 1987. 17.00 (*0-317-33288-0*) Am Sociological.
Controllability of Dynamical Systems. Jerzy Klamka. (C). 1991. lib. bdg. 125.50 (*0-7923-0822-0*) Kluwer Ac.
Controlled Air Incineration. Frank L. Cross & Howard E. Hesketh. LC 85-51123. 128p. 1985. 29.00 (*0-87762-396-1*) Technomic.
Controlled & Conditioned Invariants in Linear System Theory. Giuseppe Basile & Giovanni Marro. 480p. 1991. text ed. 72.00 (*0-13-172974-8*) P-H.
Controlled & Modified Atmosphere Packing, No. GA-067. Business Communications Co., Inc. Staff. 215p. 1991. 2,450.00 (*0-89336-821-0*) BCC.
Controlled Atmosphere & Fumigation in Grain Storages: Proceedings of an International Symposium Held from 11-12 April, 1983, in Perth, Western Australia. Ed. by B. E. Ripp. (Developments in Agricultural Engineering Ser.: No. 5). 798p. 1984. 161.75 (*0-444-42417-2*) Elsevier.
Controlled Atmosphere Storage of Fruits. Ed. by L. V. Metlitskii et al. Tr. by A. K. Dhote. 209p. (C). 1983. text ed. 46.00 (*90-6191-413-2*, Pub. by A A Balkema NE) Ashgate Pub Co.
Controlled Atmosphere Storage of Grains. J. Shejbal. (Developments in Agricultural Engineering Ser.: Vol. 1). 608p. 1981. 133.50 (*0-444-41939-X*) Elsevier.
Controlled Atmospheres for Heat Treatment. R. Nemenyi. (Illus.). 225p. 1984. 108.00 (*0-08-019883-X*, Pub. by Pergamon Repr UK) Franklin.
Controlled Brinkmanship. Bernard M. Bane. 8p. 1968. pap. 0.35 (*0-9600164-1-4*) BMB Pub Co.
Controlled Clinical Trial: An Analysis. Harris L. Coulter. LC 91-8016. 176p. (Orig.). 1991. pap. 11.95 (*0-916386-04-X*) Ctr Emp Med.
Controlled Clinical Trials in Neurological Disease. Ed. by Roger J. Porter & Bruce S. Schoenberg. 464p. 1990. lib. bdg. 156.00 (*0-7923-0613-9*) Kluwer Ac.
Controlled Clinical Trials in Urologic Oncology. Ed. by Louis Denis et al. (European Organization for Research on Treatment of Cancer (EORTC) Monograph Ser.: Vol. 13). 350p. 1984. text ed. 108.00 (*0-89004-152-0*) Raven.
Controlled Delay Devices. S. Doganovski & V. Ivanov. LC 63-10118. (International Series of Monographs on Electronics & Instrumentation: Vol. 19). 1963. 36.00 (*0-08-010045-7*, Pub. by Pergamon Repr UK) Franklin.
Controlled Delivery of Crop Protection Agents. Ed. by R. M. Wilkins. 300p. 1990. 120.00 (*0-85066-739-9*) Taylor & Francis.
Controlled Diffusion Processes. N. V. Krylov. (Applications of Mathematics Ser.: Vol. 14). 448p. 1980. 99.00 (*0-387-90461-1*) Spr-Verlag.
Controlled Directional Drilling. 3rd rev. ed. Ed. by Nancy J. Janicek. (Rotary Drilling Ser.: Unit III, Lesson 1). (Illus.). 46p. (C). 1984. pap. text ed. 14.00 (*0-88698-099-2*, 2.30130) PETEX.
Controlled Drinking. Nick H. Heather & Ian Robertson. 350p. 1984. pap. 16.95 (*0-416-36460-8*, NO. 3949) Routledge Chapman & Hall.
Controlled Drug Delivery, 2 vols. Ed. by Stephen D. Bruck. LC 82-12921. 528p. 1983. Vol. I: Basic Concepts. 110.00 (*0-8493-5181-2*, RS201, CRC Reprint); Vol. II: Clinical Applications. 156.00 (*0-8493-5182-0*, RS201, CRC Reprint) Franklin.
Controlled Drug Delivery: Fundamentals & Applications. 2nd ed. Robinson & Lee. (Drugs & the Pharmaceutical Sciences Ser.: Vol. 29). 744p. 1988. 250.00 (*0-8247-7588-0*) Dekker.
Controlled Drug Rrelease of Oral Dosage Forms. Jean Vergnaud. 500p. 1993. text ed. 83.00 (*0-13-174954-4*) P-H.
Controlled Environment Guidelines for Plant Research. Ed. by T. Tibbitts & T. K. Kozlowski. LC 79-23521. 1980. text ed. 81.00 (*0-12-690950-4*) Acad Pr.
Controlled Environments for Plant Research. Robert J. Downs. LC 74-20878. (Illus.). 175p. 1975. text ed. 43.00 (*0-231-03561-6*) Col U Pr.
Controlled Eye Movements Versus Practice Exercises in Reading. Frederick L. Westover. LC 70-177648. (Columbia University. Teachers College. Contributions to Education Ser.: No. 917). reprint ed. 37.50 (*0-404-55917-4*) AMS Pr.
Controlled Fusion & Plasma Physics: Invited Papers from the Eleventh European Conference of the European Physical Society Plasma Physics Division, 5-9 September 1983, Aachen, Federal Republic of Germany. Ed. by A. Gibson. 276p. 1984. pap. 26.00 (*0-08-030286-6*, Pergamon Pr) Elsevier.
Controlled Impedance Analysis Program. James C. Blankenhorn. (C). 1992. disk 695.00 (*1-882812-11-5*) SMT Plus.
Controlled Information Sharing in a Computer Utility. Dean H. Vanderbilt. LC 72-127836. 173p. 1969. 19.00 (*0-403-04542-8*) Scholarly.
***Controlled Low-Strength Materials.** 119p. 1994. pap. 31.75 (*0-614-02513-3*, SP150) ACI.
Controlled Markov Processes & Viscosity Solutions. Wendall H. Fleming & H. Mete Soner. Ed. by A. V. Balakrishnan et al. LC 92-31619. (Applications of Mathematics Ser.: Vol. 25). 448p. 1992. 49.95 (*0-387-97927-1*) Spr-Verlag.
Controlled-Modified Atmosphere-Vacuum Packaging of Foods. Ed. by Aaron L. Brody. 190p. 1989. 51.00 (*0-917678-24-9*) Technomic.
Controlled Nuclear Chain Reaction: The First Fifty Years. LC 92-34150. 1992. 25.00 (*0-89448-557-1*) Am Nuclear Soc.
Controlled Nuclear Fusion: Fundamentals of Its Utilization for Energy Supply. Jurgen Raeder et al. LC 85-12384. (Wiley-Interscience Publication Ser.). 328p. reprint ed. pap. 93.50 (*0-7837-4519-2*, 2044298) Bks Demand.
Controlled Open Economies: A Neoclassical Approach to Structuralism. David Bevan et al. (Illus.). 384p. (C). 1994. reprint ed. pap. 24.95 (*0-19-828783-6*, 14332) OUP.
Controlled Particle, Droplet, & Bubble Formation. David J. Wedlock. LC 93-32069. (Colloid & Surface Engineering Ser.). 368p. 1993. 89.95 (*0-7506-1494-3*) Buttrwrth-Heinemann.
Controlled-Potential Analysis. G. Rechnitz & R. Belcher. LC 63-19612. (International Series of Monographs on Analytical Chemistry: Vol. 13). 1963. 42.00 (*0-08-013135-2*, Pub. by Pergamon Repr UK) Franklin.
***Controlled Queueing Systems.** Mikhail Y. Kitaev & Vladimir V. Rykov. 270p. 1995. write for info. (*0-8493-2862-4*, 2862) CRC Pr.
Controlled Release, Biochemical Effects of Pesticides, Inhibition of Plant Pathogenic Fungi. (Chemistry of Plant Protection Ser.: Vol. 6). (Illus.). 292p. 1990. 102.00 (*0-387-51316-7*, 3288) Spr-Verlag.
Controlled Release Nitroglycerin in Buccal & Oral Form. Ed. by W. D. Bussmann et al. (Advances in Pharmacotherapy Ser.: Vol. 1). (Illus.). xii, 220p. 1982. 93.00 (*3-8055-3507-4*) S Karger.
Controlled Release of Biological Active Agents. Richard E. Baker. LC 86-22422. 279p. 1987. text ed. 144.00 (*0-471-83724-5*) Wiley.
Controlled Release of Drugs: Polymers & Aggregate Systems. Ed. by Morton Rosoff. LC 88-19177. 315p. 1989. lib. bdg. 80.00 (*0-89573-321-8*) VCH Pubs.
Controlled Release Pesticides. Ed. by Herbert B. Scher. LC 77-22339. (ACS Symposium Ser.: No. 53). 1977. 32.95 (*0-8412-0382-2*) Am Chemical.
Controlled Release Pesticides Formulations. Nate F. Cardarelli. (Uniscience Ser.). 224p. 1976. 124.95 (*0-8493-5114-6*, SB951) CRC Pr.
Controlled Release Polymeric Formulations: Symposium, Jointly Sponsored by the Division of Organic Coatings & Plastics Chemistry & the Division of Polymer Chemistry at the 171st Meeting of the American Chemical Society, New York, N.Y., April 7-9, 1976. Ed. by Donald R. Paul & F. W. Harris. LC 76-29016. (ACS Symposium Ser.: No. 33). 327p. reprint ed. pap. 93.20 (*0-7837-1450-5*, 2052426) Bks Demand.
Controlled Release Systems: Fabrication Technology. Ed. by Dean S. Hsieh. 1988. write for info. (*0-318-62928-3*) CRC Pr.
Controlled Release Systems: Fabrication Technology. Ed. by Dean S. Hsieh. 240p. 1988. Vol. I, 240 pgs. 115.00 (*0-8493-6013-7*, RS201, CRC Reprint); Vol. II, 224 pgs. 115.00 (*0-8493-6014-5*, RS201, CRC Reprint) Franklin.
Controlled-Release Technology: Pharmaceutical Applications. Ping I. Lee & William R. Good. LC 87-17447. (ACS Symposium Ser.: No. 348). (Illus.). 376p. 1987. 76.95 (*0-8412-1413-1*) Am Chemical.
Controlled Release Using Polymers: Characterization of Solid Drugs & Excipients (Seminar Notes - Mar. 1992) ring bd. 150.00 (*0-87762-941-2*) Technomic.
Controlled Released Delivery Systems. Roseman & Mansdorf. 424p. 1983. 140.00 (*0-8247-1728-7*) Dekker.
Controlled Simple Homotopy Theory & Applications. T. A. Chapman. (Lecture Notes in Mathematics Ser.: Vol. 1009). 94p. 1983. pap. 22.00 (*0-387-12338-5*) Spr-Verlag.
Controlled Stochastic Processes. I. I. Giehman & A. V. Skorohod. LC 79-4107. 1979. 95.00 (*0-387-90410-7*) Spr-Verlag.
***Controlled Substance Abuse.** AMS Distributors Staff & CTTS Safety Products Staff. 112p. 1994. per., pap. text ed. 24.95 (*0-7872-0326-2*) Kendall-Hunt.

C

An Asterisk (*) at the beginning of an entry indicates that the title is appearing in BIP for the first time.

Controlled Substance Act: A Complete Reference for Lawyers, Criminologists & Scientists & Resource Manual. (Narcotics Ser.). 1991. lib. bdg. 95.00 (0-8490-4590-8) Gordon Pr.

Controlled Substance Act see Controlled Substances!: Chemical & Legal Guide to the Federal Drug Laws

Controlled Substances! Chemical & Legal Guide to the Federal Drug Laws. rev. ed. Alexander Shulgen. Orig. Title: The Controlled Substance Act. 554p. 1992. pap. 59.95 (0-914171-50-X) Ronin Pub.

Controlled Thermonuclear Reactions. Ed. by L. A. Artsimovich et al. (Illus.). 422p. 1964. text ed. 270.00 (0-677-20020-X) Gordon & Breach.

Controlled Thermonuclear Reactions: An Introduction to Theory & Experiment. Samuel Glasstone & Ralph H. Lovberg. LC 75-11911. 540p. 1975. reprint ed. 54.50 (0-88275-326-6) Krieger.

Controlled Volume Pump Standard for Nomenclature, Definitions, Application & Operation, No. 7.1-7.5. (Hydraulic Institute Ser.: No. 7.1-7.5). 1994. 39.00 (1-880952-12-2, S116) Hydraulic Inst.

Controlled Wildlife II: Federally Controlled Species. Ed. by Carol Estes & Keith W. Sessions. 1983. pap. 40.00 (0-942924-06-1) Assn Syst Coll.

Controlled Wildlife III: State Permit Procedures. Stephen T. King & John R. Schrock. 315p. 1985. pap. 40.00 (0-942924-07-X) Assn Syst Coll.

Controlled Wildlife, Vol. I: Federal Permit Procedures. 2nd ed. Ed. by Richard Littell. (Orig.). 1993. pap. 40.00 (0-942924-16-9) Assn Syst Coll.

Controllers: A View of Our Responsibility. Jim Cole. (Illus.). (C). 1971. pap. 6.95 (0-88310-004-5) Publishers Consult.

Controllers: A View of Our Responsibility. 2nd ed. Jim Cole. (Illus.). 100p. 1989. reprint ed. pap. 4.95 (0-9601200-0-9) Growing Images.

Controller's & Treasurer's Desk Reference. Christopher R. Malburg. 1994. text ed. 69.95 (0-07-911604-3) McGraw.

***Controller's Business Adviser.** Stephen H. Collins. 1008p. 1994. 125.00 (0-7913-2070-7) Warren Gorham & Lamont.

Controller's Guide to Personnel Management, 2 vols., 1. 1992. write for info. (1-56433-138-5) Prctnrs Pub Co.

Controller's Guide to Personnel Management, 2 vols., 1. Van A. Thaxton et al. 1993. ring bd. write for info. (1-56433-375-2) Prctnrs Pub Co.

Controller's Guide to Personnel Management, 2 vols., 2. 1992. write for info. (1-56433-139-3) Prctnrs Pub Co.

Controller's Guide to Personnel Management, 2 vols., 2. Van A. Thaxton et al. 1993. ring bd. write for info. (1-56433-376-0) Prctnrs Pub Co.

Controller's Guide to Personnel Management, 2 vols., Set. 1992. ring bd. 120.00 (1-56433-137-7) Prctnrs Pub Co.

Controller's Guide to Personnel Management, 2 vols., Set. 1994. ring bd. 129.00 (1-56433-454-6) Prctnrs Pub Co.

Controller's Guide to Personnel Management, 2 vols., Set. Van A. Thaxton et al. 1993. ring bd. 120.00 (1-56433-374-4) Prctnrs Pub Co.

Controller's Guide to Personnel Management, Vol. 1. 1994. write for info. (1-56433-455-4) Prctnrs Pub Co.

Controller's Guide to Personnel Management, Vol. 2. 1994. write for info. (1-56433-456-2) Prctnrs Pub Co.

Controller's Manual of Forms. Paul Wendell. 1993. ring bd. 125.00 (0-685-69587-5, CMOF) Warren Gorham & Lamont.

Controllership: The Work of the Managerial Accountant. 4th ed. James D. Willson & James P. Colford. 1218p. 1990. text ed. 135.00 (0-471-63278-3) Wiley.

Controlling Absenteeism & Turnover. John R. Hinrichs. (Studies in Productivity: Highlights of the Literature Ser.: Vol. 17). 46p. (Orig.). 1980. pap. 55.00 (0-89361-024-0) Work in Amer.

Controlling Absenteeism & Turnover, Vol. 17. John R. Hinrichs. LC 80-21049. (Work in America Institute Studies in Productivity). (Orig.). 1982. pap. 35.00 (0-685-05444-6, Pergamon Pr) Elsevier.

Controlling Acid Rain: A New View of Responsibility. James S. Cannon. LC 87-401537. 56p. 1987. pap. 9.95 (0-918780-41-1) INFORM NY.

Controlling Air Emissions from POTWS: Guidance Manual for Evaluating Technology. 206p. 1994. pap. 45.00 (1-881369-55-2) Water Environ.

Controlling Air Movement: A Manual for Architects & Builders. T. Boutet. 336p. 1988. text ed. 50.00 (0-07-006713-9) McGraw.

Controlling Air Pollution: A Primer on Stationary Source Control Techniques. (Illus.). 52p. 6.00 (0-685-11548-8, 0021) Am Lung Assn.

Controlling Airborne Contaminants in the Workplace. M. Piney et al. 173p. (C). 1992. 225.00 (0-905927-42-7, Pub. by H&H Sci Cnslts UK) St Mut.

Controlling & Analyzing Costs in Food-Service Operations. 3rd ed. James Keiser & Frederick DeMicco. LC 92-27725. 560p. (C). 1993. write for info. (0-02-362231-8) Macmillan.

Controlling & Ending Conflict: Issues Before & after the Cold War. Ed. by Stephen J. Cimbala & Sidney R. Waldman. LC 91-27741. 296p. 1991. text ed. 59.95 (0-313-27477-0, CCQ, Greenwood Pr) Greenwood.

Controlling Anger: The Sociology of Gisu Violence. Suzette Heald. LC 89-14546. (International African Library). 320p. 1990. text ed. 75.00 (0-7190-2566-4, Pub. by Manchester Univ Pr UK) St Martin.

Controlling Asbestos in Buildings: An Economic Investigation. Donald N. Dewees. LC 86-42611. 106p. 1986. pap. 12.95 (0-915707-27-6) Resources Future.

Controlling Broadcast: Access Policy & Practice in North America & Europe. Ed. by Meryl Aldridge & Nicholas Hewitt. LC 93-37271. (Fulbright Papers: No. 13). 1994. text ed. 79.95 (0-7190-4277-1, Pub. by Manchester Univ Pr UK) St Martin.

Controlling Bureaucracies: Dilemmas in Democratic Governance. Judith E. Gruber. 150p. 1986. 40.00 (0-520-05646-9); pap. 12.00 (0-520-06461-5) U CA Pr.

Controlling Chemicals: The Politics of Regulation in Europe & the United States. Ronald Brickman et al. LC 84-29340. 336p. (C). 1985. 42.50 (0-8014-1677-9) Cornell U Pr.

Controlling Cholesterol: Preventive Medicine Program. Kenneth H. Coopers. 1989. pap. 6.50 (0-553-27775-8) Bantam.

Controlling Color: A Practical Introduction for Designers & Artists. Patricia Lambert. 1991. pap. text ed. 16.95 (0-07-036088-X) McGraw.

Controlling Color: A Practical Introduction for Designers & Artists. Patricia Lambert. (Illus.). 96p. 1991. pap. 16.95 (0-8306-3559-9, NO. 3559, Design Pr) TAB Bks.

Controlling Common Property Regulating Canada's East Coast Fishery. David R. Matthews. LC 93-93870. 277p. 1993. 55.00 (0-8020-2932-9) U of Toronto Pr.

Controlling Consulting: A Manual for Native American Governments & Organizations. Idrian N. Resnick. 75p. 1990. reprint ed. pap. 10.00 (0-9626861-1-5) First Nations Finan.

Controlling Contractors' Services on Prince Project. 98p. 1993. pap. 70.00 (0-11-330588-5, HM05885, Pub. by HMSO UK) UNIPUB.

Controlling Conventional Arms Transfers: A New Approach with Application to the Persian Gulf. Kenneth Watman. LC 93-41491. 1994. write for info. (0-8330-1488-9, MR-369-USDP) Rand Corp.

Controlling Corporate Illegality: The Regulatory Justice System. Frank & Lombness. 147p. 1988. pap. 14.95 (0-932930-78-6) Anderson Pub Co.

Controlling Corporate Legal Costs: Negotiation & ADR Techniques for Executives. Kenneth J. Thygerson. LC 93-11893. 192p. 1994. text ed. 55.00 (0-89930-876-7, Quorum Bks) Greenwood.

Controlling Corruption. Robert Klitgaard. 240p. 1988. 32.00 (0-520-05985-9) U CA Pr.

Controlling Corruption. Robert Klitgaard. (Illus.). 230p. 1991. pap. 14.00 (0-520-07408-4) U CA Pr.

***Controlling Costs & Changing Patient Care? The Role of Utilization Management.** fac. ed. Institute of Medicine (US) Staff. Ed. by Bradford H. Gray & Marilyn J. Field. LC 89-39638. 320p. 1994. pap. 91.20 (0-7837-7568-7, 2047321) Bks Demand.

Controlling Costs in Food Service: Student Manual. Educational Foundation of the National Restaurant Association Staff. 83p. (Orig.). 1991. pap. write for info. (0-915452-65-0) Educ Found.

Controlling Costs in Japanese Health Care. Ed. by Naoki Ikegami & John C. Campbell. 376p. 1994. text ed. 45.00 (0-472-10538-8) U of Mich Pr.

Controlling Credit Department Functions. Morris, Robert, Associates Staff. LC 86-5115. (Illus.). 52p. (Orig.). 1986. pap. text ed. 32.00 (0-936742-29-1) Robt Morris Assocs.

Controlling Crime: The Classical Perspective in Criminology. Bob Roshier. LC 89-8022. 153p. (C). 1989. 38.95 (0-925065-24-2); pap. text ed. 19.95 (0-925065-19-6) Lyceum IL.

Controlling Diabetes the Easy Way. Stanley Mirsky & Joan R. Hellman. 1985. pap. 12.95 (0-394-72674-X) Random.

Controlling Dietary Fibers in Food Products. Leon Prosky & Jonathan DeVries. (Illus.). 152p. 1991. text ed. 52.95 (0-442-00239-4) Chapman & Hall.

Controlling Drug Expenditure in Canada: The Ontario Experience. Paul K. Gorecki. 160p. (Orig.). 1992. pap. 24.65 (0-660-14437-9, Pub. by Canada Commun Grp CN) Accents Pubns.

Controlling East-West Trade & Technology Transfer: Power, Politics & Policies. Ed. by Gary K. Bertsch. LC 88-4101. (Duke Press Policy Studies). xiv, 506p. (C). 1988. lib. bdg. 65.50 (0-8223-0829-0); pap. text ed. 23.95 (0-8223-0843-6) Duke.

Controlling Eating Disorders with Facts, Advice, & Resources. Ed. by Raymond Lemberg. (Illus.). 240p. 1992. pap. 29.50 (0-89774-691-0) Oryx Pr.

Controlling Electrohydraulic Systems. Anderson. (Fluid Power & Control Ser.: Vol. 7). 352p. 1988. 140.00 (0-8247-7825-1) Dekker.

***Controlling Environmental Policy: The Limits of Public Law in Germany & the United States.** Susan Rose-Ackerman. 1995. write for info. (0-300-06065-3) Yale U Pr.

Controlling Florida's Development. Lance DeHaven-Smith. LC 91-13070. 130p. 1991. 25.00 (0-89341-683-5, Longwood Academic) Hollowbrook.

Controlling from Afar: The Daoguahg Emperor's Management of the Grand Canal Crisis, 1824-1826. Jane K. Leonard. (Michigan Monographs in Chinese Studies: No. 69). 1994. write for info. (0-89264-114-2); pap. write for info. (0-89264-115-0) Ctr Chinese Studies.

Controlling Health Professionals: The Future of Work & Organization in the National Health Service. Stephen Harrison & Christopher Pollitt. LC 93-2325. (State of Health Ser.). 160p. 1994. 90.00 (0-335-09644-1, Open Univ Pr); pap. 27.50 (0-335-09643-3, Open Univ Pr) Taylor & Francis.

Controlling Healthcare Costs with Medical Savings Accounts. John C. Goodman & Gerald L. Musgrave. (Illus.). 40p. (C). 1992. pap. 10.00 (0-943802-71-7, 168) Natl Ctr Pol.

Controlling High Blood Pressure. Ed. by Frans H. Leenen & R. Brian Haynes. 200p. 1989. reprint ed. 15.95 (0-914629-87-5) Prima Pub.

Controlling High Blood Pressure. Ed. by Frans H. Leenen et al. 200p. 1991. reprint ed. pap. 8.95 (1-55958-087-9) Prima Pub.

Controlling Hip & Tummy Fat Through Yogactivity. Kareen Zebroff. (Illus.). (Orig.). 1989. pap. 11.95 (0-88976-071-3) Gordon Soules Bk.

Controlling Hospital Costs: The Role of Government Regulation. Paul L. Joskow. (Health & Public Policy Ser.). 224p. 1984. reprint ed. pap. 10.95 (0-262-60012-9) MIT Pr.

Controlling Hospital Supply Inventories. Ed. by Charles E. Housley. LC 83-11738. 192p. 1983. 60.00 (0-89443-818-2) Aspen Pub.

Controlling Hotel Payroll Costs. Ad Wittemann. (Illus.). 29p. 1976. pap. 50.00 (0-938481-13-4) Camelot Consult.

***Controlling Human Heredity: 1865 to the Present.** Diane B. Paul. LC 95-12762. (Control of Nature Ser.). (Illus.). 144p. (C). 1995. text ed. 39.95 (0-391-03915-6); pap. 12.50 (0-391-03916-4) Humanities.

Controlling Hunger Response Cues: The Advance Plan. S. Mikielle Chatman. (Fat Chance Series Book Group: No. 12). 42p. 1992. pap. 3.99 (1-881146-15-4) Fat Chance.

***Controlling Immigration: A Global Perspective.** Ed. by Wayne A. Cornelius et al. 1995. 49.50 (0-8047-2497-0); pap. 17.95 (0-8047-2498-9) Stanford U Pr.

Controlling In-Plant Airborne Contaminants. Constance. (Mechanical Engineering Ser.: Vol. 21). 368p. 1983. 115.00 (0-8247-1900-X) Dekker.

Controlling Industrial Economies. Ed. by Stephen F. Frowden. LC 83-40071. 390p. 1984. text ed. 45.00 (0-312-16913-2) St Martin.

Controlling Industrial Pollution: The Economics & Politics of Clean Air. Robert W. Crandall. LC 82-45982. (Studies on the Regulation of Economic Activity). 199p. 1983. 29.95 (0-8157-1604-4); pap. 10.95 (0-8157-1603-6) Brookings.

Controlling Intelligence. Ed. by Glenn P. Hastedt. (Studies in Intelligence). 190p. 1991. 42.50 (0-7146-3394-1, Pub. by F Cass Pubs UK) Intl Spec Bk.

Controlling Interests. 2nd ed. Charles Bernstein. 88p. 1985. pap. text ed. 6.00 (0-685-12315-4) Segue NYC.

Controlling Iodine Deficiency Disorders in Developing Countries. David Phillips. (C). 1989. pap. text ed. 21.00 (0-85598-107-5, Pub. by Oxfam Pubns UK) St Mut.

Controlling Legal Addictions: Proceedings of the Twenty-Fifth Annual Symposium of the Eugenics Society, London, 1988. Ed. by David Robinson et al. LC 89-34300. 230p. 1989. text ed. 49.95 (0-312-03253-6) St Martin.

Controlling Life: Jacques Loeb & the Engineering Ideal in Biology. Philip J. Pauly. (Monographs in History & Philosophy of Biology). (Illus.). 260p. 1987. 29.95 (0-19-504244-1) OUP.

Controlling Life: Jacques Loeb & the Engineering Ideal in Biology. Philip J. Pauly. 1990. pap. 14.00 (0-520-06974-9) U CA Pr.

Controlling Marketing: Marketing Success Through Marketing Controls. Craig A. Bond. LC 88-63028. 186p. 1989. text ed. 32.00 (0-614-07355-3, 0306, Pluribus) Health Admin Pr.

Controlling Medical Professionals: The Comparative Politics of Health Governance. Ed. by Giorgio Freddi & James W. Bjorkman. (Modern Politics Ser.: Vol. 21). 250p. 1989. 45.00 (0-8039-8198-8) Sage.

Controlling Money: The Federal Reserve & Its Critics. Ralph C. Bryant. LC 82-45983. 155p. 1983. pap. 9.95 (0-8157-1135-2) Brookings.

Controlling Movement: A Therapeutic Approach to Early Intervention. Margaret J. Baker et al. 352p. 1991. 80.00 (0-8342-0192-5) Aspen Pub.

Controlling Multivariable Processes. F. G. Shinskey. LC 81-81497. (Independent Learning Module Ser.). 204p. (C). 1981. text ed. 50.00 (0-87664-529-5, 1529-5) Instru Soc.

Controlling Nonpoint-Source Water Pollution: A Citizen's Handbook. Conservation Foundation Staff & National Audubon Society Staff. LC 88-3678. (Illus.). 170p. (Orig.). 1988. pap. 7.50 (0-89164-105-X) World Wildlife Fund.

Controlling Nuclear Weapons. Robert Dahl. 1985. 39.95 (0-8156-2334-8); pap. 16.95 (0-8156-0196-4) Syracuse U Pr.

Controlling Our Reproductive Destiny: A Technological & Philosophical Perspective. Lawrence J. Kaplan & Rosemarie Tong. LC 92-38060. (Sloan New Liberal Arts - Textbook Ser.). (Illus.). 456p. 1993. 39.95 (0-262-11176-4) MIT Pr.

Controlling Parents: How to Leave Them & Love Them. B. D. Hyman & Jeremy A. Hyman. 64p. (Orig.). 1992. pap. 6.00 (1-881419-00-2) B D Hyman Minist.

Controlling Pests & Diseases. Patricia S. Michalak & Linda A. Gilkeson. LC 93-6103. (Rodale's Successful Organic Gardening Ser.). 1994. 24.95 (0-87596-611-X); 14.95 (0-87596-612-8) Rodale Pr Inc.

Controlling Prison Populations: An Assessment of Current Mechanisms, 1982. Robert Mathias & Diane Steelman. 1982. 1.50 (0-318-02050-5) Natl Coun Crime.

Controlling Psychotropic Drugs: The Nordic Experience. Kettil Bruum. LC 83-2970. 305p. 1983. text ed. 39.95 (0-312-16926-4) St Martin.

Controlling Regulatory Sprawl: Presidential Strategies from Nixon to Reagan. Howard Ball. LC 82-8541. (Contributions in Political Science Ser.: No. 105). xviii, 206p. 1984. text ed. 55.00 (0-313-23525-2, BCF/, Greenwood Pr) Greenwood.

Controlling Reproduction. J. S. Hutchinson. (Illus.). 256p. 1993. 49.95 (0-412-44310-4) Chapman & Hall.

Controlling Retailers. Ruth P. Mack. LC 77-76646. (Columbia University. Studies in the Social Sciences: No. 423). reprint ed. 34.00 (0-404-51423-5) AMS Pr.

Controlling Skills see Productive Supervisor: A Program of Practical Managerial Skills

Controlling Software Projects: Management Measurement & Estimation. Tom DeMarco. (Illus.). 296p. 1986. pap. text ed. 61.33 (0-13-171711-1, Yourdon) P-H.

Controlling Soviet Labour: Experimental Change from Brezhnev to Gorbachev. Robert Arnot. LC 87-32364. 328p. 1988. 62.95 (0-87332-470-6) M E Sharpe.

Controlling Stagefright: Presenting Yourself to Audiences from One to One Thousand. Peter Desberg & George D. Marsh. 152p. (Orig.). 1989. 19.95 (0-934986-62-2); pap. 11.95 (0-934986-61-4) New Harbinger.

***Controlling State Crime: An Introduction.** Ed. by Jeffrey I. Ross. LC 94-27125. (Current Issues in Criminal Justice Ser.: Vol. 9). 430p. 1995. 67.00 (0-8153-1546-5, SS933) Garland.

Controlling Stress & Tension: A Holistic Approach. 4th ed. Daniel A. Girdano et al. 352p. 1992. pap. text ed. 31.00 (0-13-175506-4) P-H.

***Controlling Stress in Children.** James H. Humphrey & Joy N. Humphrey. 210p. 1985. pap. 19.95 (0-398-06159-9) C C Thomas.

Controlling Stress in Children. James H. Humphrey & Joy N. Humphrey. 210p. (C). 1985. 34.95x (0-398-05050-3) C C Thomas.

Controlling Stress in the Workplace: Turning Stress into Productivity. Rex P. Gatto. LC 92-51020. 123p. 1993. pap. 12.95 (0-89384-218-4) Pfeiffer & Co.

Controlling Technology: Contemporary Issues. Ed. by William B. Thompson. 465p. (Orig.). (C). 1990. pap. text ed. 24.95x (0-87975-616-0) Prometheus Bks.

Controlling Technology: Ethics & the Responsible Engineer. 2nd ed. Stephen H. Unger. 300p. 1994. pap. text ed. 39.95 (0-471-59181-5) Wiley.

Controlling Technology: Genetic Engineering & the Law. Yvonne M. Cripps. LC 80-13754. 170p. 1980. text ed. 49.95 (0-275-90465-2, C0465, Praeger Pubs) Greenwood.

Controlling the Atom: The Beginnings of Nuclear Regulation, 1946-1962. George T. Mazuzan & J. Samuel Walker. LC 84-2485. (Illus.). 500p. (C). 1985. 55.00 (0-520-05182-3) U CA Pr.

Controlling the Atom in the Twenty-First Century. David P. O'Very. 397p. (C). 1993. text ed. 59.85 (0-8133-8816-3) Westview.

Controlling the Bomb: Nuclear Proliferation in the 1980s. Lewis A. Dunn. LC 81-16086. 223p. reprint ed. pap. 63.60 (0-7837-5307-1, 2080328) Bks Demand.

***Controlling the Bureaucracy: Institutional Constraints in Theory & Practice.** William F. West. (Bureaucracies, Public Administration & Public Policy Ser.). (Illus.). 272p. 1995. 55.00 (1-56324-513-2); pap. text ed. 25.00 (1-56324-514-0) M E Sharpe.

Controlling the Constable. Tony Jefferson & Roger Grimshaw. (C). 1988. 40.00 (0-584-11088-X, Pub. by NCCL UK) St Mut.

Controlling the Contexts of Consciousness: The I, the We, the All of Us. Barry Oshry. LC 75-9952. (Notes on Power Ser.). (Orig.). 1976. pap. 5.00 (0-910411-02-6) Power & Sys.

***Controlling the Decaying Infrastructure.** Ed. by Victor Chaker. LC 95-74995. 300p. 1995. 80.00 (1-877914-83-5) NACE Intl.

Controlling the Development & Spread of Military Technology: Lessons from the Past & Challenges for the 1990's. Ed. by Hans G. Brauch et al. 446p. (Orig.). 1992. pap. text ed. 49.50 (90-5383-103-7, Pub. by VU Univ Pr NE) Paul & Co Pubs.

Controlling the Difficult Adolescent: The REST Program (The Real Economy for Teens) David B. Stein. 116p. (Orig.). (C). 1990. lib. bdg. 39.00 (0-8191-7829-2); pap. text ed. 17.50 (0-8191-7830-6) U Pr of Amer.

Controlling the Federal Bureaucracy. Dennis D. Riley. LC 86-14469. 216p. 1987. 32.95 (0-87722-455-2) Temple U Pr.

Controlling the Federal Bureaucracy. Dennis D. Riley. 216p. 1990. pap. 14.95 (0-87722-704-7) Temple U Pr.

Controlling the Future: Managing Technology Driven Change. Stewart L. Stokes. LC 90-44473. 1991. pap. 29.95 (0-89435-293-8) Wiley.

Controlling the Future: Managing Technology-Driven Change. Stewart L. Stokes, Jr. 189p. 1993. pap. text ed. 29.95 (0-471-60164-0) Wiley.

Controlling the Game: Controlling Your Attitude in Sales. Clark T. Cameron & Sharon M. Cameron. 100p. 1993. pap. 10.00 (0-9635820-0-3) Watershed CA.

Controlling the Growth of Monetary Aggregates. Robert H. Rasche & James M. Johannes. (C). 1987. lib. bdg. 65.50 (0-89838-226-2) Kluwer Ac.

Controlling the Image - How to Choose & Use Lenses. Jerry Katz. 160p. 1993. write for info. (0-87100-249-3) Morgan.

***Controlling the International Transfer of Weaponry & Related Technology.** Ed. by Carlton David et al. 1995. 59.95 (1-85521-535-7, Pub. by Dartmth Pub UK) Ashgate Pub Co.

Controlling the "Out of Control" Costs of Education: The Critical Changes. Don Stewart. (Chance for Instructional Excellence Ser.: Bk. 4). (Illus.). 432p. (Orig.). 1989. 17.45 (0-913448-20-6); pap. 13.45 (0-913448-21-4) SLATE Servs.

Controlling the Sword: The Democratic Governance of National Security. Bruce M. Russett. (Illus.). 201p. 1990. 29.00 (0-674-16990-5) HUP.

Controlling the Uncontrollable: The Fiction of Alice Munro. Ildiko De Papp Carrington. 251p. 1989. text ed. 28.00 (0-87580-149-8) N Ill U Pr.

Controlling the Uncontrollable Elements in Court Budgets. National Center for State Courts Staff. (Paul Reardon Ser.). 6p. 1981. 0.36 (0-685-15171-9, PRS-007) Natl Ctr St Courts.

Controlling the Waves: Dean Acheson & U. S. Foreign Policy in Asia. Ronald L. McGlothlen. LC 92-38848. 352p. 1993. 27.95 (0-393-03520-4) Norton.

Controlling the World with Your PC. Paul Bergsman. 1994. pap. 29.95 (1-878707-15-9) HighText.

C

An Asterisk (*) at the beginning of an entry indicates that the title is appearing in BIP for the first time.

C

An Asterisk (*) at the beginning of an entry indicates that the title is appearing in BIP for the first time.

Controversies over the Imitation of Cicero in the Renaissance: With Translations of Letters Between Pietro Bembo & Gianfrancesco Pico "On Imitation" & a Translation of Desiderius Erasmus, "The Ciceronian" Izora Scott. x, 284p. (C). 1991. reprint ed. text ed. 18.50 (*0-9611800-9-9*); reprint ed. pap. text ed. 10.50 (*0-9611800-8-0*) Hermagoras Pr.

Controversy: Politics of Technical Decisions. 3rd ed. Ed. by Dorothy Nelkin. (Focus Editions Ser.: Vol. 8). (Illus.). 320p. 1992. 49.95 (*0-8039-4466-7*); pap. 24.95 (*0-8039-4467-5*) Sage.

Controversy: Roots of the Creation-Evolution Conflict. Donald E. Chittick. 280p. 1994. reprint ed. pap. 7.95 (*0-9640978-0-X*) Creation Compass.

Controversy about American Hopsitals: Funding, Ownership, & Performance. J. Rogers Hollingsworth & Ellen J. Hollingsworth. LC 87-19523. (AEI Studies: No. 463). (Illus.). 176p. (C). 1988. lib. bdg. 34.50 (*0-8447-3637-6*, Am Enterprise); pap. text ed. 17.25 (*0-8447-3638-4*, Am Enterprise) U Pr of Amer.

***Controversy & Coalition.** rev. ed. Myra M. Ferree & Beth B. Hess. (Twayne's Social Movements Past & Present Ser.). (Illus.). 240p. 1994. text ed. 26.95x (*0-8057-3881-9*, Twayne) Macmillan.

***Controversy & Coalition.** rev. ed. Myra M. Ferree & Beth B. Hess. (Twayne's Social Movements Past & Present Ser.). (Illus.). 240p. 1994. pap. 15.95 (*0-8057-3882-7*, Twayne) Macmillan.

Controversy & Coalition: New Feminist Movement. Myra M. Ferree & Beth B. Hess. (Social Movements Past & Present Ser.). 222p. 1985. text ed. 23.95 (*0-8057-9707-6*, Twayne); pap. 14.95 (*0-8057-9713-0*, Twayne) Macmillan.

***Controversy & Complexity: Canadian Immigration Policy During the 1980s.** Gerald E. Dirks. 200p. 1995. 39.95 (*0-7735-1238-1*) U of Toronto Pr.

Controversy & Conciliation: The Reformation & the Palatinate 1559 - 1583. Ed. by Derk Visser. LC 85-32076. (Pittsburgh Theological Monographs: No. 18). (Orig.). (C). 1986. pap. 15.00 (*0-915138-73-5*) Pickwick.

Controversy Between the Puritans & the Stage. Elbert N. Thompson. LC 76-176150. reprint ed. 41.50 (*0-404-06396-9*) AMS Pr.

***Controversy, Courts, & Community: The Rhetoric of Judge Miles Welton Lord.** Verna C. Corgan. LC 94-39472. (Contributions in Legal Studies: Vol. 79). 216p. 1995. text ed. 59.95 (*0-313-29247-7*, Greenwood Pr) Greenwood.

Controversy in American Education: An Anthology of Crucial Issues. 2nd ed. Harold Full. 448p. (C). 1972. pap. text ed. write for info. (*0-02-339960-0*) Macmillan.

Controversy in Psychotherapy. Ed. by Herbert S. Strean. LC 81-18490. 313p. 1982. lib. bdg. 20.00 (*0-8108-1498-6*) Scarecrow.

Controversy in the Twenties: Fundamentalism, Modernism, & Evolution. Ed. by Willard B. Gatewood. LC 69-11279. 469p. reprint ed. pap. 133.70 (*0-8357-3254-1*, 2039475) Bks Demand.

Controversy in Victorian Geology: The Cambrian-Silurian Dispute. James A. Secord. LC 85-43310. (Illus.). 375p. (Orig.). 1990. pap. text ed. 19.95 (*0-691-02441-3*) Princeton U Pr.

Controversy of Images from Calvin to Baronius. Giuseppe Scavizzi. LC 92-6443. (Toronto Studies in Religion: Vol. 14). 301p. 1993. 53.95 (*0-8204-1873-0*) P Lang Pubs.

Controversy of Zion. D. Reed. 1982. lib. bdg. 250.00 (*0-87700-419-6*) Revisionist Pr.

Controversy of Zion. Douglas Reed. 588p. 1987. 12.95 (*0-939482-03-7*) Noontide.

Controversy of Zion. Claude Duvernoy. LC 86-6386. 224p. 1987. reprint ed. pap. 7.95 (*0-89221-144-X*) New Leaf.

Controversy over Capitalism: Studies in the Social Philosophy of the Russian Populists. Andrzej Walicki. LC 88-23204. (C). 1989. pap. text ed. 12.95 (*0-268-00770-5*) U of Notre Dame Pr.

Controversy over German Industrialization, 1890-1902. Kenneth D. Barkin. LC 78-101359. (Illus.). 317p. reprint ed. pap. 90.40 (*0-8357-8852-0*, 2056750) Bks Demand.

Controversy over the Distribution of Abolition Literature, 1830-1860. William S. Savage. (History - United States Ser.). 141p. 1993. reprint ed. lib. bdg. 69.00 (*0-7812-4894-9*) Rprt Serv.

Contructive Analysis. E. Bishop & Douglas Bridges. (Grundlehren der Mathematischen Wissenschaften Ser.: Vol. 279). 500p. 1985. 98.00 (*0-387-15066-8*) Spr-Verlag.

Contu's Final Report & Recommendations see Copyright, Congress & Technology: The Public Record

Conundrum. Jan Morris. LC 87-8668. 192p. 1987. pap. 9.95 (*0-8050-0361-4*, Owl) H Holt & Co.

***Conundrum of Class: Public Discourse on the Social Order in America.** Martin J. Burke. LC 95-7081. 1995. lib. bdg. 42.95 (*0-226-08080-3*); pap. text ed. 16.95 (*0-226-08081-1*) U Ch Pr.

Conundrum, Vol. 1: A Cartoon Collection of Concepts, College, & Confounded Connotations. B. Jay Martin. (Illus.). 160p. (Orig.). (YA). (gr. 12 up). 1988. pap. 5.95 (*0-922073-00-7*) Thought Wave Pr.

***Conundrums: A Book of Philosophical Questions.** Charles W. Harvey. (Illus.). 198p. (Orig.). (C). 1994. pap. text ed. 9.75 (*0-8191-9776-9*) U Pr of Amer.

Conures. Tony Silva & Barbara Kotlar. (Illus.). 96p. 1980. 9.95 (*0-86622-739-3*, KW-121) TFH Pubns.

Conures. Matthew Vriends. (Complete Pet Owner's Manuals Ser.). (Illus.). 64p. 1992. pap. 5.95 (*0-8120-4880-6*) Barron.

Conures: A Complete Introduction. Al David. (Illus.). 93p. (Orig.). 1987. pap. 5.95 (*0-86622-296-0*, CO-014S) TFH Pubns.

Conus Medullaris & Cauda Equina in Man. Henry V. Corck et al. (Illus.). 85p. 1986. 66.00 (*0-387-81906-1*) Spr-Verlag.

***Convair: Into the Sunset.** William P. Yenne. Ed. by Ceila D. Robbins. (Illus.). 96p. 1995. write for info. (*0-944641-09-1*) Greenwich Pub Group.

Convair F-106 Delta Dart. William G. Holder. LC 75-15272. (Aero Ser.: Vol. 27). 104p. 1977. pap. 9.95 (*0-8168-0600-4*, 20600, TAB-Aero) TAB Bks.

Convair T-29 Flying Classroom, C-131-R4Y Samaritan, CC-109 Cosmopolitan. Steven J. Ginter & Nick Williams. (Naval Fighters Ser.: No. 14). (Illus.). 114p. (Orig.). 1987. pap. text ed. 16.95 (*0-942612-14-0*) Naval Fighters.

***Convair XFY-1 Pogo.** Skeets Coleman et al. (Naval Fighter Ser.: No. 27). (Illus.). 34p. (Orig.). 1994. pap. text ed. 6.95 (*0-942612-27-2*) Naval Fighters.

Convection: A Current Event. Alan Gould. Ed. by Lincoln Bergman & Kay Fairwell. (Great Explorations in Math & Science (GEMS) Ser.). (Illus.). 38p. (Orig.). (J). (gr. 6-9). 1988. pap. 10.00 (*0-912511-15-X*) Lawrence Science.

Convection & Chaos in Fluids. J Bhattacharjee. 256p. 1987. text ed. 58.00 (*9971-5-0224-0*) World Scientific Pub.

Convection & Inhomogeneities in Crystal Growth from the Melt. G. Muller. (Crystals - Growth, Properties & Applications Ser.). 140p. 1988. 98.00 (*0-387-18603-4*) Spr-Verlag.

Convection & Substorms: Paradigms of Magnetospheric Phenomenology. Charles F. Kennel. (International Series in Astronomy & Astrophysics: Vol. I). (Illus.). 368p. 1995. 85.00 (*0-19-508529-9*) OUP.

Convection Cuisine: Great Taste & Maximum Results from Your Convection Oven, Including 250 Newly Created Recipes. Jacqueline Mallorca & Renee Verdon. LC 88-16359. (Illus.). 320p. 1988. 22.95 (*0-688-08100-2*) Hearst Bks.

Convection Heat Transfer. Adrian Bejan. LC 84-3583. 477p. (C). 1984. text ed. 74.95 (*0-471-89612-8*) Wiley.

Convection Heat Transfer. 2nd ed. Adrian Bejan. LC 94-14045. 1994. text ed. 69.95 (*0-471-57972-6*) Wiley.

Convection in Liquids. J. K. Platten & J. C. Legros. (Illus.). 700p. 1983. 139.00 (*0-387-12637-6*) Spr-Verlag.

Convection in Porous Media. D. A. Nield & Adrian Bejan. (Illus.). 424p. 1991. 69.00 (*0-387-97651-5*) Spr-Verlag.

***Convection in Rotating Fluids.** B. M. Buobnov & G. S. Golitsyn. LC 95-3068. (Fluid Mechanics & Its Applications Ser.: Vol. 29). 232p. (C). 1995. lib. bdg. 107.00 (*0-7923-3371-3*) Kluwer Ac.

Convection Oven Cookbook. Linda Verkler & Edward Zempel. LC 83-4015. (Orig.). 1983. reprint ed. pap. 10.95 (*0-88289-377-7*) Pelican.

Convection Oven Cookery. Christie Katona & Thomas Katona. 176p. 1993. pap. 8.95 (*1-55867-070-X*, Nitty Gritty Ckbks) Bristol Pub Ent CA.

Convections. Robert Kelly. 170p. 1978. pap. 10.00 (*0-87685-312-2*) Black Sparrow.

Convective Boiling & Condensation. 3rd ed. John G. Collier & John R. Thome. LC 93-33482. (Engineering Science Ser.: No. 38). (Illus.). 624p. 1994. 135.00 (*0-19-856282-9*, Clarendon Pr) OUP.

Convective Heat & Mass Transfer. 3rd ed. William M. Kays & Michael E. Crawford. LC 92-24670. (Mechanical Engineering Ser.). 576p. 1993. text ed. write for info. (*0-07-033721-7*) McGraw.

Convective Heat & Mass Transfer in Porous Media. Ed. by Sadik Kakac et al. (C). 1991. lib. bdg. 290.00 (*0-7923-1228-7*) Kluwer Ac.

Convective Heat Transfer. 2nd ed. Louis C. Burmeister. 576p. 1993. text ed. 89.95 (*0-471-57709-X*) Wiley.

Convective Heat Transfer. 2nd ed. Sadik Kakac & Yaman Yener. LC 94-15135. (Orig.). 1994. write for info. (*0-8493-9939-4*) CRC Pr.

Convective Instabilities in Systems with Interface. I. B. Simanovskii & A. A. Nepomnyashchy. LC 92-43821. 1993. text ed. 120.00 (*2-88124-924-8*) Gordon & Breach.

Convective Motions in a Free Atmosphere. N. I. Vul'fson. 200p. 1964. text ed. 50.00 (*0-7065-0287-6*, Pub. by Keter Pub IS) Coronet Bks.

Convenanters. David Stevenson. 1989. 29.00 (*0-685-31782-X*, Pub. by Saltire Soc) St Mut.

Convencao Interamericana Sobre Extradicao. OAS, General Secretariat for Juridical Affairs. (Serie Sobre Tratados: No. 60). 16p. (POR.). 1981. pap. 2.00 (*0-8270-1331-0*) OAS.

Convencion Americana Sobre Derechos Humanos. OAS, General Secretariat, Inter-American Commission of Human Rights. (Human Rights Ser.). 248p. 1980. 9.00 (*0-8270-1222-5*) OAS.

Convencion Interamericana Sobre Arbitraje Comercial Internacional. (Treaty Ser.: No. 42). (ENG, FRE, POR & SPA.). 1975. pap. 1.00 (*0-8270-0520-2*) OAS.

Convencion Interamericana Sobre Conflictos De Leyes En Materia De Letras De Cambio, Pagares y Facturas. (Treaty Ser.: No. 40). (ENG, FRE, POR & SPA.). 1975. pap. 1.00 (*0-8270-0510-5*) OAS.

Convencion Interamericana Sobre Exhortos O Cartas Rogatorias. (Treaty Ser.: No. 43). (ENG, FRE, POR & SPA.). 1975. pap. 1.00 (*0-8270-0525-3*) OAS.

Convencion Interamericana Sobre Extradiction. OAS, General Secretariat for Juridical Affairs. (Serie Sobre Tratados: No. 60). 16p. (SPA.). (C). 1981. pap. 2.00 (*0-8270-1328-0*) OAS.

Convencion Interamericana Sobre Recepcion De Pruebas En el Extranjero. (Treaty Ser.: No. 44). (ENG, FRE, POR & SPA.). 1975. pap. 1.00 (*0-8270-0530-X*) OAS.

Convencion Interamericana Sobre Regimen Legal De Poderes Para Ser Utitizados En el Extranjero. (Treaty Ser.: No. 45). (ENG, FRE, POR & SPA.). 1975. pap. 1.00 (*0-8270-0535-0*) OAS.

Convencion Para el Fomento De las Relaciones Culturales Interamericanas. (Treaty Ser.: No. 20). (ENG, FRE, POR & SPA.). 1954. pap. 1.00 (*0-8270-0370-6*) OAS.

Convencion Sobre Asilo Diplomatico. (Treaty Ser.: No. 18). (ENG, FRE, POR & SPA.). 1954. pap. 1.00 (*0-8270-0360-9*) OAS.

Convencion Sobre Defensa Del Patrimonio Arqueologico, Historico y Artistico De las Naciones Americanas. (Treaty Ser.: No. 47). (ENG, FRE, POR & SPA.). 1977. pap. text ed. 1.00 (*0-8270-0565-2*) OAS.

Convenience & Prepared Foods. Euromonitor Staff. 160p. (C). 1987. 975.00 (*0-86338-292-4*, Pub. by Euromonitor Pubns UK) Gale.

Convenience & Take-Away Foods. 120p. 1981. 160.00 (*0-686-71863-1*, Pub. by Euromonitor Pubns UK) St Mut.

Convenience Food Facts: Help for the Healthy Meal Planner. enl. rev. ed. Arlene Monk & Marion Franz. LC 91-40471. 472p. 1991. reprint ed. pap. 10.95 (*0-937721-77-8*) Chronimed.

***Convenience Foods Market.** 210p. (Orig.). 1995. pap. 2,295.00 (*0-7605-2245-6*) Rector Pr.

***Convenience of the Minuscule: Informality & Microenterprise in Latin America.** Carlos A. Vega & Dirk Kruijt. (Latin America Ser.: No. 3). 140p. 1994. pap. 18.50 (*90-5538-006-7*, Pub. by Thesis Pubs NE) IBD Ltd.

***Convenience Store Retailing International Market Handbook.** (Illus.). 500p. (Orig.). 1994. pap. 9,950.00 (*0-7605-0941-7*) Rector Pr.

Convenience Stores in the UK. Euromonitor Staff. 80p. (C). 1988. 975.00 (*0-86338-252-5*, Pub. by Euromonitor Pubns UK) Gale.

***Convenient Arrangement.** Judith Janeway. (Romance Ser.). 1995. mass mkt. 2.99 (*0-373-19089-1*, 1-19089-1) Silhouette.

Convenient Husband. Joan Hohl. (Silhouette Desire Ser.: No. 732). 1992. pap. 2.89 (*0-373-05732-6*) Silhouette.

Convenient Marriage. Georgette Heyer. Date not set. 21.95 (*0-8488-0812-6*) Yestermorrow.

Convenient Marriage. Ellen Rawlings. 208p. (Orig.). 1993. pap. 3.99 (*1-55773-918-8*) Diamond.

Convent at Auschwitz. Wladyslaw T. Bartoszewski. 169p. 1991. 17.95 (*0-8076-1267-7*) Braziller.

Convent Poems, 1943-1961. Mary C. Rodgers. LC 92-32473. 76p. 1992. pap. 12.95 (*0-7734-0037-0*) E Mellen.

Convent School. Barbara Frischmuth. Tr. by Gerald Chapple & James B. Lawson. LC 93-2226. (Studies in Austrian Literature, Culture, & Thought. Translation Ser.). 1993. 15.95 (*0-929497-75-9*) Ariadne CA.

Convention: A Parable. Will D. Campbell. 208p. 1988. 14.95 (*0-934601-54-2*) Peachtree Pubs.

Convention: A Parable. Will D. Campbell. LC 88-61455. 414p. reprint ed. pap. 118.00 (*0-7837-6555-X*, 2046120) Bks Demand.

Convention: A Philosophical Study. David Lewis. LC 69-12727. 227p. 1987. pap. 14.50 (*0-674-17026-1*) HUP.

Convention: A Philosophical Study. David K. Lewis. LC 69-12727. (Illus.). 1969. 15.00 (*0-674-17025-3*) HUP.

Convention & Choices: A Brief Book of Style & Usage. Stephen M. Foley & Joseph W. Gordon. LC 85-80168. 179p. (C). 1986. text ed. 14.50 (*0-669-07544-2*) Heath.

Convention & Innovation in Literature. Ed. by Theo D'Haen et al. LC 89-355. (Utrecht Publications in General & Comparative Literature: No. 24). xxii, 434p. 1989. 106.00x (*90-272-2209-6*) Benjamins North Am.

Convention & Meeting Planner's Handbook: A Step-by-Step Guide to Making Your Event a Success. Michelle Voso. 192p. 1990. 35.00 (*0-669-21153-2*) Free Pr.

Convention & Revolt in Poetry. John L. Lowes. 1972. 59.95 (*0-87968-943-9*) Gordon Pr.

***Convention & the Art of Jane Austen's Heroines.** William H. Magee. 320p. (Orig.). 1995. text ed. 69.95x (*1-883255-85-6*); pap. text ed. 49.95x (*1-883255-84-8*) Intl Scholars.

Convention & the Crisis: Chicago 1968. Gerald Kurland. Ed. by D. Steve Rahmas. LC 72-89229. (Events of Our Times Ser.: No. 6). 32p. (Orig.). (gr. 7-12). 1973. lib. bdg. 4.95 (*0-87157-706-2*) SamHar Pr.

Convention Articles of Will Rogers, Ser. II, Vol. I. Will Rogers. Ed. by Joseph A. Stout, Jr. & Peter C. Rollins. LC 76-5609. (Writings of Will Rogers Ser.: Vol. 2). 174p. 1976. 10.50 (*0-914956-08-6*) Okla State Univ Pr.

Convention Centers, Stadiums, & Arenas. David C. Petersen. LC 89-50266. 168p. (Orig.). 1989. pap. text ed. 53.95 (*0-87420-679-0*, C37) Urban Land.

Convention Decisions & Voting Records. 2nd ed. Richard C. Bain & Judith H. Parris. LC 73-1082. (Brookings Institution Studies in Presidential Selection). 480p. reprint ed. pap. 136.80 (*0-317-30178-0*, 2025360) Bks Demand.

***Convention Directory U. S. A., 4 vols., Set.** 1200p. (Orig.). 1995. pap. 495.00 (*0-7605-1515-8*) Rector Pr.

Convention Essays. C. F. Walther. Tr. by August R. Seuflow. (Selected Writings of C. F. W. Walther Ser.). 1981. 15.95 (*0-570-08277-3*, 15-2735) Concordia.

***Convention Establishing the Multilateral Investment Guarantee Agency & Commentary on the Convention.** 82p. Date not set. write for info. (*0-8213-1487-4*, 11487) World Bank.

***Convention Establishing the Multilateral Investment Guarantee Agency & Commentary on the Convention.** 82p. (FRE.). Date not set. write for info. (*0-8213-1488-2*, 11488) World Bank.

***Convention Establishing the Multilateral Investment Guarantee Agency & Commentary on the Convention.** 82p. (SPA.). Date not set. write for info. (*0-8213-1489-0*, 11489) World Bank.

Convention, Fifteen Hundred to Seventeen Fifty. Lawrence Manley. LC 79-27773. 365p. 1980. 37.50 (*0-674-17015-6*) HUP.

Convention for the International Sale of Goods: A Handbook of Basic Materials. 246p. 1990. pap. 60.00 (*0-89707-588-9*, 521-0067) Amer Bar Assn.

Convention Girls. Ellen Evans. 224p. 1983. pap. 2.50 (*0-8439-2021-1*) Dorchester Pub Co.

Convention in Eighteenth- & Nineteenth-Century Music: Essays in Honor of Leonard G. Ratner. Ed. by Wye Allanbrook et al. LC 92-28766. (Festschrift Ser.: No. 10). (Illus.). 550p. 1992. lib. bdg. 48.00 (*0-945193-28-9*) Pendragon NY.

Convention Interamericaine Sur L'extradition. OAS, General Secretariat for Juridical Affairs. (Serie Sur les Traites: No. 60). 16p. (FRE.). (C). 1981. pap. 2.00 (*0-8270-1330-2*) OAS.

Convention of Delegates: The Creation of the Constitution. Denis J. Hauptly. LC 86-17260. (Illus.). 160p. (J). (gr. 3-7). 1987. text ed. 14.95 (*0-689-31148-6*, Atheneum Bks Young) S&S Childrens.

Convention of Facilitation of International Maritime Traffic (FAL) 1989 Edition. International Maritime Organization Staff. 1991. text ed. 80.00 (*0-89771-886-0*, Pub. by Intl Maritime Org UK) St Mut.

Convention of May Twenty-Ninth Eighteen Fifty-Six: That Organized the Republican Party in the State of Illinois. Ed. by Ezra M. Prince. (Transactions of the Mclean County Historical Society Ser.: Vol. III). (Illus.). 184p. 1900. 25.00 (*0-943788-03-X*) McLean County.

Convention on Civil Liability for Damage Caused During Carriage of Dangerous Goods by Road, Rail & Inland Navigation Vessels: Explanatory Report. 78p. 35.00 (*92-1-116497-4*) UN.

Convention on Climate Change: Economic Aspects of Negotiations. OECD Staff. 98p. (Orig.). 1992. pap. 23.00 (*92-64-13668-1*) OECD.

Convention on Facilitation of International Maritime Traffic (FAL) 1965. International Maritime Organization Staff. 1991. text ed. 140.00 (*0-89771-885-2*, Pub. by Intl Maritime Org UK) St Mut.

Convention on International Trade in Endangered Species of Wild Fauna & Flora 1989. (EC Annual Report Ser.). 523p. 1992. pap. 90.00 (*92-826-3931-2*, CR-73-92-990-EN-C, Pub. by Europ Com) UNIPUB.

Convention on Territorial Asylum. (Treaty Ser.: No. 19). (ENG, FRE, POR & SPA.). 1954. pap. 1.00 (*0-8270-0365-X*) OAS.

Convention on the Elimination of All Forms of Discrimination Against Women. (Illus.). 75p. (Orig.). (C). 1993. pap. text ed. 25.00 (*1-56806-440-3*) Diane Pub.

Convention on the Inter-American Institute of Agricultural Sciences & the Protocol of Amendment. (Treaty Ser.). 63p. 1966. 1.00 (*0-8270-0330-7*) OAS.

Convention on the Privileges & Immunities of the United Nations Adopted by the General Assembly of the United Nations on 13 February 1946. 2.00 (*92-1-045001-9*, MULT.75.X.1); write for info. (*92-1-045002-7*) UN.

Convention on the Regulation of Antarctic Mineral Resource Activities: An Attempt to Break New Ground. R. Wolfrum. Ed. by R. Bernhardt et al. (Beiträge Zum Auslandischen Offentlichen Rechtund Volkerecht Ser.: Vol. 102). 180p. 1991. 59.00 (*0-387-54219-1*) Spr-Verlag.

Convention on the Rights of the Child. Lawrence J. LeBlanc. LC 94-11887. (Human Rights in International Perspective Ser.: Vol. 3). xvi, 338p. 1995. text ed. 45.00 (*0-8032-2909-7*) U of Nebr Pr.

Convention on the Rights of the Child: World Campaign for Human Rights. 54p. 1991. 5.00 (*92-1-100465-9*, 91.I.51) UN.

Convention Parliament, 1689: A Biographical Study of Its Members. George L. Cherry. LC 65-24394. 218p. 1966. text ed. 29.00 (*0-8290-0163-8*) Irvington.

Convention Problem: Issues in Reform of Presidential Nominating Procedures. Judith H. Parris. LC 72-143. (Brookings Institution Studies in Presidential Selection). 208p. reprint ed. pap. 59.30 (*0-317-26344-7*, 2025399) Bks Demand.

Convention Proceedings. 1,987th ed. 137p. 1993. 5.00 (*0-318-15964-3*) Newspaper Guild.

***Convention Proceedings for the Twenty-Eighth Annual AABT Convention.** 362p. 1994. pap. 10.00 (*0-614-04146-5*) Assn Advance Behav Therapy.

Convention Sales: A Book of Readings. Ed. by Margaret Shaw. LC 89-25984. 247p. 1990. pap. text ed. 40.95 (*0-86612-056-4*) Educ Inst Am Hotel.

***Convention Sales & Services.** 4th ed. Milton T. Astroff & James R. Abbey. 580p. 1995. pap. 44.95 (*0-9620710-2-1*) Waterbury Pr.

Convention to Prevent & Punish the Acts of Terrorism Taking the Form of Crimes Against Persons & Related Extortion That Are of International Significance. (Treaty Ser.: No. 37). 18p. (ENG, FRE, POR & SPA.). 1971. pap. 1.00 (*0-8270-0480-X*) OAS.

Convention, Translation, & Understanding: Philosophical Problems in the Comparative Study of Culture. Robert Feleppa. LC 87-12176. (SUNY Series in Logic & Language). 317p. 1988. 64.50 (*0-88706-673-9*); pap. 21.95 (*0-88706-674-7*) State U NY Pr.

Conventional & FHA Mortgage Payment Table. Financial Publishing Co. Staff. 256p. 1991. pap. 8.18 (*0-87600-491-5*) Finan Pub.

Conventional Armed Forces in Europe Treaty: The Cold War Endgame. Stuart Croft. 304p. (C). 1994. text ed. 57.95 (*1-85521-504-7*, Pub. by Dartmth Pub UK) Ashgate Pub Co.

Conventional Arms Control: Perspectives on Verification. Sergey Koulik & Richard Kokoski. LC 92-37898. 230p. (C). 1995. 49.95 (*0-19-829149-3*) OUP.

An Asterisk (*) at the beginning of an entry indicates that the title is appearing in BIP for the first time.

Conventional Arms Control: The Limits & Their Verification. Ivan Oelrich. (Occasional Papers: No. 8). (Illus.). 92p. (C). 1990. lib. bdg. 38.50 (*0-8191-7833-0*); pap. text ed. 19.00 (*0-8191-7834-9*) U Pr of Amer.

Conventional Arms Control & Defense Acquisition: Catching the Caboose? Michael Moodie. (Significant Issues Ser.). (Orig.). 1990. pap. text ed. 1.00 (*0-89206-148-0*) CSI Studies.

Conventional Arms Control & East-West Security. Ed. by Stephen Larrabee. LC 89-7685. (Duke Press Policy Studies). 491p. 1989. lib. bdg. 70.50 (*0-8223-0980-7*); pap. text ed. 21.95 (*0-8223-0992-0*) Duke.

Conventional Arms Control & Europe's Future. Stanley R. Sloan. LC 89-80206. (Headline Ser.: No. 287). (Illus.). 72p. (Orig.). 1989. pap. 5.95 (*0-87124-124-2*) Foreign Policy.

Conventional Arms Transfers to the Third World, 1983-1990. Richard F. Grimmett. (Illus.). 82p. (Orig.). (C). 1993. pap. text ed. 30.00 (*1-56806-429-2*) Diane Pub.

***Conventional Bidding Explained.** Freddie North. 144p. 1995. pap. 16.95 (*0-7134-7643-5*, Pub. by Batsford UK) Trafalgar.

Conventional Cardweaving How-to Booklet. Herbi Gray. (Illus.). 12p. (Orig.). 1985. 2.50 (*0-9608406-1-3*) H Gray.

Conventional Combat Priorities: An Approach for the New Strategic Era. Dave McCurdy et al. (CSIS Panel Report). 100p. (Orig.). 1990. pap. text ed. 14.95 (*0-89206-160-X*) CSI Studies.

Conventional Defense & Total Deterrence: Assessing NATO's Strategic Options. Robert B. Killebrew. LC 85-19612. 174p. 1986. 40.00 (*0-8420-2248-1*) Scholarly Res Inc.

Conventional Defense of Europe: New Technologies & New Strategies. Ed. by Andrew J. Pierre. 200p. 1986. pap. 6.95 (*0-87609-015-3*) Coun Foreign.

Conventional Deterrence. John J. Mearsheimer. LC 83-5317. (Cornell Studies in Security Affairs). 296p. (C). 1983. 39.95 (*0-8014-1569-1*); pap. 14.95 (*0-8014-9346-3*) Cornell U Pr.

Conventional Deterrence into the 1990s. Ed. by Thomas Boyd-Carpenter. LC 88-30617. 220p. 1989. text ed. 49.95 (*0-312-02511-4*) St Martin.

Conventional Disarmament in Europe. (ENG & GER.). 1988. 14.00 (*92-9045-027-4*, EGV.88.0.6) UN.

Conventional Force Reductions: A Dynamic Assessment. Joshua M. Epstein. 150p. 1990. 34.95 (*0-8157-2462-4*); pap. 14.95 (*0-8157-2461-6*) Brookings.

Conventional Forces & Arms Limitations in Europe. 90p. 1989. 24.00 (*92-9045-036-3*, GV.89.0.6) UN.

Conventional Functions of Black English in American Literature. Richard O. Lewis. 100p. 1995. 44.95 (*1-880921-64-2*); pap. 24.95 (*1-880921-53-7*) Austin & Winfield.

Conventional Lies of Our Civilization. Max Nordau. LC 74-29511. (Modern Jewish Experience Ser.). (ENG.). 1975. reprint ed. 34.95 (*0-405-06737-2*) Ayer.

Conventional Wisdom: A Television Viewer's Guide to the 1992 National Political Conventions. Eugene Alpert. 36p. 1992. pap. 6.95 (*1-881846-00-8*) C-Span.

Conventionalism in Logic: A Study in the Linguistic Foundation of Logical Reasoning. Carlo B. Giannoni. (Janua Linguarum, Ser. Major: No. 46). 157p. 1971. text ed. 33.85 (*3-10-800056-X*) Mouton.

Conventions at a Glance. Pamela Granovetter & Matthew Granovetter. 92p. (Orig.). 1993. pap. 8.95 (*0-940257-15-7*) Granovetter Bks.

Conventions on the Law of the Sea. Hearing Before the Committee on Foreign Relations, United States Senate. U. S. Congress, Senate Committee on Foreign Relations. iii, 129p. 1985. lib. bdg. 22.50 (*0-8377-1236-X*) Rothman.

Conventions, the Australian Constitution & the Future. L. J. Cooray. xix, 235p. 1979. 24.00 (*0-9596568-1-2*) Rothman.

Conventual Buildings of Blackfriars, London, & the Playhouses Constructed Therein. Joseph Q. Adams. LC 76-113537. reprint ed. 32.50 (*0-404-00289-7*) AMS Pr.

***Converbs in Cross-Linguistic Perspective: Structure & Meaning of Adverbial Forms-- Adverbial Participles, Gerunds.** Ed. by Martin Haspelmath & Ekkehard Konig. LC 94-44536. (Empirical Approaches to Language Typology Ser.: Vol. 13). 1995. 229.25 (*3-11-014357-7*) Mouton.

Convergence. Jack Fuller. LC 90-47482. (Phoenix Fiction Ser.). 360p. 1990. pap. 12.95 (*0-226-26881-0*) U Ch Pr.

Convergence. Irene Zimmerman. LC 82-62906. (Illus.). 94p. 1983. 5.95 (*0-938232-23-1*) Winston-Derek.

Convergence: A Futuristic Thriller of Environmental Intrigue. James Miller. 1994. pap. 5.50 (*1-56171-164-0*, S P I Bks) Sure Sellers.

Convergence: Proceedings of the Second National Conference of the Library & Information Technology Association. Ed. by Michael Gorman. LC 90-804. (Library & Information Technology Ser.: No. 3). 285p. 1991. pap. 20.00 (*0-8389-3382-3*) ALA.

Convergence: The Reconciliation of Judaism & Christianity in the Life of One Woman. Judith Bruder. LC 92-26214. 1993. 20.00 (*0-385-46874-1*) Doubleday.

Convergence - International Congress on Transportation Electronics, 1992. IEEE, Vehicular Technology Staff. Ed. by Institute of Electrical & Electronics Engineers, Inc. Staff. LC 92-80986. 536p. 1992. lib. bdg. write for info. (*0-7803-0881-6*, 92CH3231-8); pap. text ed. write for info. (*0-7803-0882-4*) Inst Electrical.

***Convergence - International Congress on Transportation Electronics 1994.** Institute of Electrical & Electronics Engineers, Inc. Staff. 200p. 1994. lib. bdg. write for info. (*0-7803-2421-8*); fiche write for info. (*0-7803-2422-6*, 94CH35729) Inst Electrical.

Convergence & System Change: The Convergence Hypothesis in the Light of Transition in Central & Eastern Europe. Ed. by Bruno Dallago et al. 200p. 1992. 59.95 (*1-85521-218-8*, Pub. by Dartmth Pub UK) Ashgate Pub Co.

Convergence & Uniformity in Topology. J. W. Tukey. (Annals of Mathematics Studies). 1940. 15.00 (*0-527-02718-9*) Periodicals Srv.

Convergence Between Communications Technologies: Case Studies from North America & Europe. OECD Staff. (Information Computer Communications Policy Ser.: No. 28). 148p. (Orig.). 1992. pap. 37.00 (*92-64-13633-9*) OECD.

***Convergence, Cohesion & Intergration in the European Union.** Robert Leonardi. LC 94-31779. 1995. write for info. (*0-312-12384-1*) St Martin.

Convergence in Career Development Theories: Implications for Science & Practice. Ed. by Mark Savickas & Robert Lent. LC 93-42895. 304p. 1994. 32.95 (*0-89106-066-9*) Consulting Psychol.

Convergence in Distribution of Stochastic Processes. Lucien M. LeCam. LC 57-9424. (University of California Publications in Social Welfare: Vol. 2, No. 11). 32p. reprint ed. pap. 25.00 (*0-317-08319-8*, 2021183) Bks Demand.

Convergence of Civilizations: Beyond Marxism Liberalism & Ultra-Nationalism. Oroon K. Ghosh. (C). 1988. 38.00 (*81-85195-11-0*, Pub. by Minerva II) S Asia.

Convergence of International & Domestic Markets. Ed. by David B. Audretsch et al. (Contributions to Economic Analysis Ser.: Vol. 180). 318p. 1989. 87.25 (*0-444-87346-5*, North Holland) Elsevier.

Convergence of Iterations for Linear Equations. Olavi Nevalinna. LC 93-3187. (Lectures in Mathematics ETH Zurich). vii, 177p. 1993. Alk. paper. 29.00 (*0-8176-2865-7*); Alk. paper. pap. write for info. (*0-318-70050-6*) Birkhauser.

Convergence of Lives: Sofia Kovalevskaia - Scientist, Writer, Revolutionary. rev. ed. Ann H. Koblitz. LC 92-41715. (Lives of Women in Science Ser.). (Illus.). 305p. (C). 1993. reprint ed. text ed. 40.00 (*0-8135-1962-4*); reprint ed. pap. text ed. 15.00 (*0-8135-1963-2*) Rutgers U Pr.

***Convergence of Machine & Human Nature: A Critique of the Computer Metaphor of Mind & Artificial Intelligence.** Ed. by Alexander McClintock. 152p. 1995. 55.95 (*1-85628-997-4*, Pub. by Avebury Pub UK) Ashgate Pub Co.

Convergence of Probability Measures. Patrick Billingsley. (Probability & Mathematical Statistics Ser.). 253p. 1968. text ed. 115.00 (*0-471-07242-7*) Wiley.

Convergence of Productivity: Cross-National Studies & Historical Evidence. Ed. by William J. Baumol et al. (Illus.). 480p. 1994. pap. 26.00 (*0-19-508390-3*) OUP.

Convergence of Solutions of the Kolmogorov Equation of Travelling Waves. Maury Bramson. LC 83-6437. (Memoirs of the American Mathematical Society Ser.: No. 44/285). 196p. 1983. pap. 24.00 (*0-8218-2285-3*, MEMO 44/285) Am Math.

Convergence of Stochastic Processes. D. Pollard. (Series in Statistics). (Illus.). 280p. 1984. 49.00 (*0-387-90990-7*) Spr-Verlag.

Convergence or Divergence? Britain & the Continent. Jeremy Black. LC 93-39439. 1994. text ed. 45.00 (*0-312-12088-5*) St Martin.

***Convergence or Divergence? Comparing Recent Social Trends in Industrial Societies.** Ed. by Simon Langlois et al. (Comparative Charting of Social Change Ser.). 360p. 1995. 55.00 (*0-7735-1264-0*) U of Toronto Pr.

Convergence Problems of Orthogonal Series. G. Alexits & I. Foldes. LC 61-14566. (International Series of Monographs on Pure & Applied Mathematics: Vol. 20). 1961. 149.00 (*0-08-013811-X*, Pub. by Pergamon Repr UK) Franklin.

Convergence Problems of Orthogonal Series. G. Alexits & I. N. Sneddon. LC 61-145660. (International Series of Monographs on Pure & Applied Mathematics: Vol. 20). 1962. 152.00 (*0-08-009542-9*, Pub. by Pergamon Repr UK) Franklin.

Convergence Structures, Nineteen Eighty-Four. Ed. by J. Novak. 2545p. (C). 1985. 100.00 (*0-685-36901-3*, Pub. by Collets) St Mut.

Convergence Structures 1984. Ed. by Collet's Holdings, Ltd. Staff. 1984. 77.00 (*0-317-46602-X*, Pub. by Collets UK) Pro-Am Music.

Convergence Theory of Feasible Direction Methods. Du Dingzhu. (Applied Discrete Mathematics & Theoretical Computer Science Ser.: Vol. 1). 118p. 1991. text ed. 31.00 (*1-880132-00-1*) Sci Pr NY.

Convergences. Paz. 1991. pap. 10.95 (*0-15-622586-7*, Harvest Bks) HarBrace.

Convergences: Essays on Art & Literature. Octavio Paz. Tr. by Helen Lane. 1987. 19.95 (*0-15-122585-0*) HarBrace.

Convergences: Rhetoric & Poetic in Seventeenth-Century France, Essays for Hugh M. Davidson. Ed. by David L. Rubin & Mary B. McKinley. 240p. 1989. text ed. 56.50 (*0-8142-0468-6*) Ohio St U Pr.

Convergences: To the Source of Christian Mystery. Hans U. Von Balthasar. Tr. by E. A. Nelson. LC 83-81853. Orig. Title: Einfaltungen: Auf Wegen der Christlichen Einigung. 153p. (Orig.). 1984. pap. 9.95 (*0-89870-032-9*) Ignatius Pr.

Convergent Issues in Genetics & Demography. Julian Adams et al. (Illus.). 376p. 1990. 49.95 (*0-19-506287-6*) OUP.

Convergent Strabismus. L. Evans. 1982. lib. bdg. 154.50 (*90-6193-806-6*) Kluwer Ac.

Converging Themes in Psychotherapy: Trends in Psychodynamic Humanistic & Behavioral Practice. Ed. by Marvin R. Goldfried. 416p. 1982. 37.95 (*0-8261-3620-6*) Springer Pub.

Converging Voice-Data-Video Technologies at the Work Station. Business Communications Co., Inc. Staff. (Illus.). 119p. 1986. pap. 1,750.00 (*0-89336-466-5*, G-096) BCC.

***Conversacion En el Quijote: Subdialogo, Memoria y Asimetria.** Alberto Rodriguez. LC 94-67394. 180p. (SPA.). (C). 1995. 30.00x (*0-938972-26-X*) Spanish Lit Pubns.

Conversacion y Controversia Topicos de hoy y de Siempre. 2nd ed. Andres C. Diaz & Nino R. Iorillo. 288p. (C). 1990. pap. text ed. write for info. (*0-13-172982-9*) P-H.

***Conversaciones Creadoras.** Joan L. Brown & Carmen M. Gaite. 247p. (SPA.). (C). 1994. pap. text ed. write for info. (*0-669-17373-8*) Heath.

Conversaciones, Situaciones. Heather Leigh & Salvador Ortiz-Carboneres. 1984. pap. text ed. 8.55 (*0-582-22178-1*, 70890); audio 22.61 (*0-582-24270-3*, 70971) Longman.

Conversando: Early Intermediate Through Advanced. Juan Kattan-Ibarra. 140p. (YA). 1993. teacher ed 10.60 (*0-8442-7151-9*, Natl Textbk); pap. 19.95 (*0-8442-7150-0*, Natl Textbk); audio 39.95 (*0-8442-7153-5*, Natl Textbk) NTC Pub Grp.

Conversando en Ingles: English Conversational Grammar for Spanish Speakers. Jaime G. Bores. (ENG & SPA.). 1993. pap. 7.95 (*0-8442-7101-2*, Natl Textbk) NTC Pub Grp.

Conversant Essays: Contemporary Poets & Poetry. Ed. by James McCorkle. LC 89-32152. 597p. (C). 1990. 45.00 (*0-8143-2099-6*); pap. text ed. 23.95 (*0-8143-2100-3*) Wayne St U Pr.

Conversar Sin Parar. George Rooks et al. 144p. (C). 1982. pap. 25.95 (*0-8384-3474-6*, Newbury) Heinle & Heinle.

Conversating with the Lord! Zelphia Barkley. Ed. by Karen Mayes. 72p. (Orig.). 1994. 9.95 (*1-882368-06-1*) Quantum Christ.

Conversation: An Interdisciplinary Approach. Ed. by Peter Bull & Derek Roger. 1988. 99.00 (*0-905028-87-2*, Pub. by Multilingual Matters UK); pap. 39.95 (*0-905028-86-4*, Pub. by Multilingual Matters UK) Taylor & Francis.

Conversation about Christmas. Dylan Thomas. (Classic Short Stories Ser.). (J). 1991. lib. bdg. 13.95 (*0-88682-468-0*) Creative Ed.

Conversation Against Death. Eve Merriam. 25p. 1991. 3.95 (*0-930194-24-1*) Ctr Thanatology.

Conversation Analysis: The Sociology of Talk. Donald Allen & Rebecca Guy. (Janua Linguarum, Ser. Minor: No. 200). 284p. 1978. pap. text ed. 41.55 (*90-279-3002-3*) Mouton.

***Conversation Analysis: The Study of Talk-in-Interaction.** George Psathas. (Qualitative Research Methods: Vol. 35). 96p. 1994. 21.50 (*0-8039-5746-7*); pap. 9.50 (*0-8039-5747-5*) Sage.

Conversation Analysis of Therapeutic Discourse. Jerry E. Gale. Ed. by Roy Freedle. LC 90-14423. (Advances in Discourse Processes Ser.: Vol. 41). 176p. 1991. text ed. 39.50 (*0-89391-705-2*) Ablex Pub.

Conversation & Dialogues in Action. Zoltan Dornyei & Sarah Thurrell. LC 92-12368. 1992. 17.00 (*0-13-175035-6*) P-H.

Conversation Between James Comer & Ronald Edmonds. N.C.E.S.R.D. Staff. 96p. 1989. pap. text ed. 12.00 (*0-8403-5281-6*) Kendall-Hunt.

Conversation Book. 3rd ed. Tina K. Carver & Sandra D. Fotinos. 1994. pap. text ed. 12.25 (*0-13-053174-X*) P-H.

Conversation Book: English in Everyday Life, Bk. I. 2nd ed. Tina K. Carver & Sandra D. Fotinos. (Illus.). 224p. (C). 1985. pap. text ed. 8.50 (*0-13-172362-6*) P-H.

Conversation Book: English in Everyday Life, Bk. 2. 2nd ed. Tina K. Carver & Sandra D. Fotinos. (Illus.). 208p. (C). 1986. pap. text ed. 12.00 (*0-13-172370-7*) P-H.

Conversation Club. Diane Stanley. LC 89-18665. (Illus.). 32p. (J). (gr. k-2). 1990. reprint ed. pap. 3.95 (*0-689-71401-7*, Aladdin Paperbacks) S&S Childrens.

Conversation et Vocabulaire: Cours Soixante-Quinze. Pierre Thomas. (FRE.). 1948. pap. 3.75 (*0-910408-06-8*) Coll Store.

Conversation Failure: Case Studies in Doctor-Patient Communication. Frederic W. Platt. LC 92-15049. 1992. 16.95 (*0-943685-16-8*) Life Sci Pr.

Conversation Games: Vol. I-People Times. Illus. by Nathaniel Pinkney. 87p. (Orig.). (J). (ps-6). 1978. pap. 15.00 (*0-939632-17-9*) ILM.

Conversation Games: Vol. II-Experiences. Illus. by Nathaniel Pinkney. 87p. (Orig.). (J). (ps-6). 1978. pap. 15.00 (*0-939632-20-9*) ILM.

Conversation Games: Vol. III, Solutions. rev. ed. Illus. by Margie Frem. 134p. (J). (ps-6). 1981. pap. 17.00 (*0-939632-23-3*) ILM.

Conversation Handbook for Policeman. B. Brechbuhl. 1990. pap. 41.00 (*0-7121-5625-9*, Pub. by Northcote UK) St Mut.

Conversation in English: Points of Departure. 2nd ed. Julia M. Dobson & Frank Sedwick. (Illus.). 112p. (C). 1981. pap. 18.95 (*0-88018-076-5*) Heinle & Heinle.

Conversation in French: Points of Departure. 5th ed. Frank Sedwick & Isabelle S. Gorrell. 120p. 1989. pap. 28.95 (*0-8384-1716-7*) Heinle & Heinle.

Conversation in German: Points of Departure. 5th ed. Frank Sedwick & Nancy M. Decker. 120p. 1989. pap. 28.95 (*0-8384-1717-5*) Heinle & Heinle.

Conversation in Italian: Points of Departure. 3rd ed. Gabriel Paolozzi & Frank Sedwick. 120p. (C). 1985. pap. 26.95 (*0-8384-1276-9*) Heinle & Heinle.

Conversation in Portuguese: Points of Departure. 2nd rev. ed. Neil Miller. LC 80-83025. (Illus.). 1980. pap. text ed. 7.95 (*0-9601444-2-0*) N Miller.

Conversation in Spanish: Points of Departure. 5th ed. Frank Sedwick. 117p. 1989. pap. 28.95 (*0-8384-1715-9*) Heinle & Heinle.

Conversation Inspirations for ESL. Nancy E. Zelman. (Supplementary Materials Handbook Ser.: No. 3). (Illus.). 96p. (Orig.). 1986. pap. 11.00 (*0-86647-015-8*) Pro Lingua.

Conversation Made Easy. Elliot Russell. 1979. pap. 5.00 (*0-87980-024-0*) Wilshire.

Conversation of Journalism: Communication, Community, & News. Rob Anderson et al. LC 93-40573. 232p. 1994. text ed. 49.95 (*0-275-94448-4*, Praeger Pubs) Greenwood.

Conversation of Journalism: Communication, Community, & News. Rob Anderson et al. 1994. write for info. (*0-318-72320-4*, Praeger Pubs) Greenwood.

Conversation on Music. Anton Rubinstein. Tr. by Morgan. LC 81-12547. (Music Ser.). 146p. 1982. reprint ed. lib. bdg. 23.50 (*0-306-76121-1*) Da Capo.

Conversation on the Liberalism & the Church. Orestes A. Brownson. (Works of Orestes Augustus Brownson). 1989. reprint ed. lib. bdg. 79.00 (*0-7812-2112-9*) Rprt Serv.

Conversation Piece. Molly Keane. 273p. 1992. pap. 10.95 (*1-85381-347-8*, Pub. by Virago Pr UK) Trafalgar.

***Conversation Piece: 200 Creative & Thought-Provoking Questions.** rev. ed. Paul Lowrie & Bret Nicholaus. LC 94-65462. 64p. 1994. pap. 3.95 (*0-9634251-1-0*) Questmarc Pub.

***Conversation Pieces.** Ivy Barsky & Patrick Murphy. (Illus.). 48p. 1994. 30.00 (*0-88454-076-6*) U of Pa Contemp Art.

Conversation Pieces: A Survey of the Informal Group Portrait in Europe & America. Mario Praz. LC 76-127380. (Illus.). 285p. 1971. Individually boxed. 70.00 (*0-271-00132-1*) A Wofsy Fine Arts.

***Conversation Repair.** Frederic W. Platt. LC 95-835. 1995. 24.95 (*0-316-71082-2*) Little.

Conversation with a Cat & Others. Hilaire Belloc. LC 69-18920. (Essay Index Reprint Ser.). 1977. 19.95 (*0-8369-0035-9*) Ayer.

Conversation with a Sphinx. Maurice Valency. 1980. pap. 2.75 (*0-8222-0239-5*) Dramatists Play.

Conversation with an Angel & Other Essays. Hilaire Belloc. 1976. lib. bdg. 59.95 (*0-8490-1672-X*) Gordon Pr.

Conversation with an Angel, & Other Essays. Hilaire Belloc. LC 68-16907. (Essay Index Reprint Ser.). 1977. reprint ed. 23.95 (*0-8369-0187-8*) Ayer.

***Conversation with Anne Rice.** Riley. write for info. (*0-345-39636-7*) Ballantine.

Conversation with Christ. Peter T. Rohrbach. LC 82-50586. 171p. 1982. reprint ed. pap. 8.00 (*0-89555-180-2*) TAN Bks Pubs.

Conversation with God. Lloyd J. Ogilvie. 1993. pap. 9.99 (*1-56507-048-8*) Harvest Hse.

Conversation with Jesus. Stephen Seamands. 144p. 1994. 10.99 (*1-56476-202-5*, Victor Books) SP Pubns.

Conversational Arabic. (Orig.). (ARA & ENG.). Date not set. pap. 3.50 (*0-933511-10-8*) Kazi Pubns.

Conversational Arabic in Seven Days. (BBC Phrase Bks.). 1995. 5.95 (*0-8442-4568-2*, Passport Bks) NTC Pub Grp.

Conversational Arabic in Seven Days. (BBC Phrase Bks.). 1995. audio 12.95 (*0-8442-9145-5*, Passport Bks) NTC Pub Grp.

Conversational Brazilian-Portuguese. Cortina Staff. (Cortina Language Ser.). 192p. 1990. pap. 7.95 (*0-8050-1503-5*) H Holt & Co.

Conversational Cajun French I. Randall P. Whatley & Harry Jannise. LC 81-19943. 80p. (Orig.). 1982. pap. 10.95 (*0-88289-316-5*); audio 29.95 (*0-88289-405-6*) Pelican.

Conversational Chinese for Beginners. Morris H. Swadesh. Orig. Title: Chinese in Your Pocket II. 1948. pap. 3.95 (*0-486-21123-1*) Dover.

***Conversational Classroom: Lesson Plans for Preschool Language Learning Through Interaction.** Jennifer Y. Carroll. Ed. by Dianne Young. (Illus.). 610p. (Orig.). 1995. pap. text ed. 49.95 (*0-9645202-0-6*) Commun Counts.

Conversational Competence & Social Development. Ioanna Dimitracopoulou. (Illus.). 208p. (C). 1990. 59.95 (*0-521-37551-7*) Cambridge U Pr.

Conversational Computers. William D. Orr. LC 68-30916. 261p. reprint ed. pap. 74.40 (*0-317-08453-4*, 2011954) Bks Demand.

Conversational English. Cortina Staff. (Cortina Language Ser.). 192p. 1990. pap. 7.95 (*0-8050-1504-3*) H Holt & Co.

Conversational English: English-Azerbaijan Conversation Book. K. Gasymov. 96p. (C). 1988. 40.00 (*0-685-37241-3*, Pub. by Collets) St Mut.

Conversational English for Chinese Speakers: Learn Idiomatic English at Home or on the Go. A. Penruddocke. 1994. 25.00 (*0-517-59854-X*, Living Language) Crown Pub Group.

Conversational English for Japanese Speakers: Learn Idiomatic English at Home or on the Go. A. Penruddocke. 1994. 25.00 (*0-517-59832-9*, Living Language) Crown Pub Group.

Conversational English for Korean Speakers: Learn Idiomatic English at Home or on the Go. A. Penruddocke. 1994. 25.00 (*0-517-59853-1*, Living Language) Crown Pub Group.

Conversational English for Russian Speakers: Learn Idiomatic English at Home or on the Go. A. Penruddocke. 1994. 25.00 (*0-517-59855-8*, Living Language) Crown Pub Group.

Conversational English-Hindi Dictionary. Anil Gupta. (C). 1994. text ed. 14.00 (*81-7030-393-1*) S Asia.

***Conversational English Tibetan Dictionary.** Anil Gupta. 131p. (Orig.). (ENG & TIB.). 1995. pap. 14.95 (*0-7818-0375-6*) Hippocrene Bks.

C

An Asterisk (*) at the beginning of an entry indicates that the title is appearing in BIP for the first time. 1603

Conversational French. Cortina Staff. (Cortina Language Ser.). 384p. 1990. pap. 7.95 (*0-8050-1497-7*) H Holt & Co.

Conversational French. Simone Oudot & David Gobert. 320p. 1988. pap. 20.95 (*0-8442-1505-8*, Passport Bks) NTC Pub Grp.

Conversational French: Quick & Easy. Barbara B. Saloom. (Illus.). 135p. (Orig.). 1993. pap. text ed. 12.95 (*0-9627755-1-7*) B B Saloom.

Conversational French in Seven Days. Shirley Baldwin & Sarah Boas. (Language in Seven Days Ser.). (Illus.). 96p. 1991. audio 12.95 (*0-8442-4466-X*, Passport Bks); pap. 5.95 (*0-8442-4467-8*, Passport Bks) NTC Pub Grp.

Conversational French in Twenty Lessons. Cortina Schools Staff. 1990. pap. 6.95 (*0-8327-0011-8*) Cortina.

Conversational French Manual. 1988. pap. 5.00 (*0-517-55784-3*, Living Language) Crown Pub Group.

Conversational German. Cortina Staff. (Cortina Language Ser.). 384p. 1990. pap. 7.95 (*0-8050-1498-5*) H Holt & Co.

Conversational German in Seven Days. Shirley Baldwin & Sarah Boas. (Language in Seven Days Ser.). (Illus.). 96p. 1991. audio 12.95 (*0-8442-4483-X*, Passport Bks); pap. 5.95 (*0-8442-4484-8*, Passport Bks) NTC Pub Grp.

Conversational German in Twenty Lessons. Cortina Schools Staff. 1990. pap. 6.95 (*0-8327-0012-6*) Cortina.

Conversational German Manual. 1988. pap. 5.00 (*0-517-55781-9*, Living Language) Crown Pub Group.

Conversational Greek in Seven Days. Howard Middle & Hara G. Middle. (Language in Seven Days Ser.). (Illus.). 96p. 1991. audio 12.95 (*0-8442-4502-X*, Passport Bks); pap. 5.95 (*0-8442-4503-8*, Passport Bks) NTC Pub Grp.

Conversational Introduction to French. 2nd ed. Edward T. Heise & Rene F. Muller. (Illus.). 424p. 1987. reprint ed. pap. text ed. 29.00 (*0-8191-6430-5*) U Pr of Amer.

Conversational Italian. Cortina Staff. (Cortina Language Ser.). 352p. 1990. pap. 7.95 (*0-8050-1499-3*) H Holt & Co.

Conversational Italian in Seven Days. Shirley Baldwin & Sarah Boas. (Language in Seven Days Ser.). (Illus.). 96p. 1991. audio 12.95 (*0-8442-4497-X*, Passport Bks); pap. 5.95 (*0-8442-4498-8*, Passport Bks) NTC Pub Grp.

Conversational Italian Manual. 1988. pap. 5.00 (*0-517-55790-8*, Living Language) Crown Pub Group.

Conversational Japanese. Cortina Staff. (Cortina Language Ser.). 256p. 1990. pap. 7.95 (*0-8050-1502-7*) H Holt & Co.

Conversational Japanese in Seven Days. Etsuko Sujita & Colin Lloyd. (Language in Seven Days Ser.). (Illus.). 96p. 1991. audio 12.95 (*0-8442-4516-X*, Passport Bks); pap. 5.95 (*0-8442-4517-8*, Passport Bks) NTC Pub Grp.

Conversational Joking: Forms & Functions of Humor in Everyday Talk. Neal R. Norrick. LC 92-19471. 192p. 1993. 29.95 (*0-253-34111-6*) Ind U Pr.

Conversational Languages. Ingbert Kupka & N. Wilsing. LC 80-40120. (Wiley Series in Computing). 127p. reprint ed. pap. 36.20 (*0-685-20592-4*, 2030525) Bks Demand.

Conversational Management with Language-Impaired Children: Pragmatic Assessment & Intervention. Bonnie Brinton & Martin Fujiki. LC 89-17488. (Excellence in Practice Ser.). 240p. (C). 1989. 54.00 (*0-8342-0092-9*) Aspen Pub.

Conversational Manx. John Gell. pap. 7.50 (*0-89979-006-2*) British Am Bks.

***Conversational Medical Spanish.** Larry Purnell. 240p. (C). 1995. pap. text ed. 27.95 (*0-7872-0740-3*) Kendall-Hunt.

Conversational Modern Greek. Cortina Staff. (Cortina Language Ser.). 288p. 1990. pap. 7.95 (*0-8050-1500-0*) H Holt & Co.

Conversational Organization & Its Development. Ed. by Bruce Dorval & Roy O. Freedle. LC 89-78241. (Advances in Discourse Processes Ser.: Vol. 38). 376p. (C). 1990. text ed. 69.50 (*0-89391-582-3*); pap. text ed. 39.50 (*0-89391-663-3*) Ablex Pub.

Conversational Portuguese in Seven Days. Hilary Fleming & Izo M. Rainbow. (Language in Seven Days Ser.). (Illus.). 96p. 1991. audio 12.95 (*0-8442-4547-X*, Passport Bks); pap. 5.95 (*0-8442-4548-8*, Passport Bks) NTC Pub Grp.

Conversational Portuguese Manual (Continental) Oscar Fernandez. 1987. pap. 5.00 (*0-517-56163-8*, Living Language) Crown Pub Group.

Conversational Power. James K. Van Fleet. 1991. pap. 10.95 (*0-13-529637-4*) P-H.

***Conversational Prayer.** Craig Driscoll. 64p. Date not set. pap. 2.95 (*1-882972-46-5*) Queenship Pub.

Conversational Realities. John Shotter. (Inquiries in Social Construction Ser.). (Illus.). 224p. (C). 1993. text ed. 55.00 (*0-8039-8932-6*); pap. text ed. 19.95 (*0-8039-8933-4*) Sage.

Conversational Routine. Ed. by Florian Coulmas. (Janua Linguarum, Series Major: Vol. 2). 1980. text ed. 70.80 (*90-279-3098-8*) Mouton.

Conversational Russian. 2nd rev. ed. Helen Yakobson. LC 85-17575. (Illus.). 224p. (C). 1985. pap. 8.50 (*0-938920-59-6*) Hermitage.

Conversational Russian in Seven Days. Shirley Baldwin & Sarah Boas. (Language in Seven Days Ser.). (Illus.). 96p. 1991. audio 12.95 (*0-8442-4533-X*, Passport Bks); pap. 5.95 (*0-8442-4534-8*, Passport Bks) NTC Pub Grp.

Conversational Russian in Twenty Lessons. Cortina Institute of Languages Staff. (Cortina Language Ser.). 488p. 1990. pap. 6.95 (*0-8050-1501-9*) H Holt & Co.

Conversational Russian in Twenty Lessons. Cortina Schools Staff. 1990. pap. 6.95 (*0-8327-0015-0*) Cortina.

Conversational Sign Language II: An Intermediate-Advanced Manual. Willard J. Madsen. 220p. 1972. pap. 10.95 (*0-913580-00-7*, Clerc Bks) Gallaudet Univ Pr.

***Conversational Sociology: An Intercultural Bridge Where East Meets West.** Caycedo. (C). 1995. text ed. 39.95 (*0-391-03937-7*) Humanities.

Conversational Spanish. Cortina Staff. (Cortina Language Ser.). 384p. 1990. pap. 7.95 (*0-8050-1496-9*) H Holt & Co.

Conversational Spanish: Quick & Easy. Barbara B. Saloom. Ed. by Virginia Cogger & Jose Ricardo-Gil. (Illus.). 120p. (Orig.). (YA). 1988. pap. text ed. 12.95 (*0-9627755-0-9*) B B Saloom.

Conversational Spanish for Everyday Use. Stephen H. Richman. 304p. (C). 1994. per., pap. text ed. 36.95 (*0-8403-9510-8*) Kendall-Hunt.

***Conversational Spanish for Hospitality Managers & Supervisors: Basic Language Skills for Daily Operations.** Matt A. Casado. LC 94-37418. 1995. pap. text ed. 27.95 (*0-471-05959-5*) Wiley.

Conversational Spanish for Medical Personnel: Essential Expressions, Questions & Directions for Medical Personnel to Facilitate Conversation with Spanish-Speaking Patients & Coworkers. 2nd ed. Rochelle K. Kelz. LC 82-4917. 538p. 1982. pap. text ed. 29.95 (*0-8273-4265-9*) Delmar.

Conversational Spanish for the Medical & Health Professions. Cynthia A. Teed et al. 255p. (ENG & SPA.). (C). 1983. pap. text ed. 26.75 (*0-03-059287-9*) HB Coll Pubs.

Conversational Spanish in Seven Days. Shirley Baldwin & Sarah Boas. (Language in Seven Days Ser.). (Illus.). 96p. 1991. audio 12.95 (*0-8442-4452-X*, Passport Bks); pap. 5.95 (*0-8442-4453-8*, Passport Bks) NTC Pub Grp.

Conversational Spanish Manual. 1988. pap. 5.00 (*0-517-55787-8*, Living Language) Crown Pub Group.

Conversational Style. Deborah Tannen. Ed. by Cynthia Wallat & Judith Green. LC 83-25697. (Language & Learning for Human Service Professions Ser.: Vol. 1). 208p. 1984. text ed. 39.50 (*0-89391-188-7*); pap. text ed. 26.95 (*0-89391-200-X*) Ablex Pub.

Conversational Tagalog: A Functional-Situational Approach. Teresita V. Ramos. LC 84-8612. 358p. 1985. pap. text ed. 15.00 (*0-8248-0944-0*) UH Pr.

Conversational Thai in Seven Days. Somsong Buasai & David Smyth. 96p. 1992. pap. 5.95 (*0-8442-4551-8*, Natl Textbk); boxed 12.95 (*0-8442-4550-X*, Natl Textbk) NTC Pub Grp.

Conversational Turkish in Seven Days. 1992. audio 12.95 (*0-8442-4564-X*) NTC Pub Grp.

Conversational Turkish in Seven Days. Tayfun Caga. 1992. pap. 5.95 (*0-8442-4565-8*, Passport Bks) NTC Pub Grp.

Conversational Word of God: A Commentary on the Doctrine of St. Ignatius of Loyola Concerning Spiritual Conversation, with Four Early Jesuit Texts. Thomas H. Clancy. LC 78-51343. (Studies on Jesuit Topics Series IV: No. 8). xii, 71p. 1978. 5.00 (*0-912422-33-5*); pap. 2.50 (*0-912422-34-3*) Inst Jesuit.

***Conversational Zulu for Beginners.** 2nd ed. Du Goslin. 109p. (ENG & ZUL.). 1988. 21.95 (*0-7859-7486-5*) Fr & Eur.

Conversational Zulu for Beginners. 2nd ed. B. Du Goslin. 109p. 1988. pap. 21.00 (*0-86985-937-4*) IBD Ltd.

Conversationally Speaking: Tested New Ways to Increase Your Personal & Social Effectiveness. Alan Garner. (Orig.). 1991. reprint ed. pap. 10.95 (*0-929923-72-3*) Lowell Hse.

Conversations. 1979. pap. 2.00 (*0-89744-935-5*) Auromere.

Conversations. John Hatcher. (Illus.). 208p. (YA). (gr. 8-10). 1988. pap. 12.95 (*0-85398-275-9*) G Ronald Pub.

Conversations. Idaho Educational Public Broadcasting Foundation Staff. LC 90-83688. (Illus.). 1990. 29.95 (*1-56221-014-9*); pap. 19.95 (*1-56221-015-7*) ID Educ Public.

Conversations. William A. Miller. LC 80-54283. 96p. 1980. pap. 5.50 (*0-934104-04-2*) Woodland.

Conversations. 2nd ed. Jack Selzer. 1088p. (C). 1994. pap. write for info. (*0-02-408961-3*) Macmillan.

Conversations: Contemporary Critical Theory & the Teaching of Literature. Ed. by Charles Moran & Elizabeth Penfield. 237p. 1990. pap. 18.95 (*0-8141-0860-1*) NCTE.

***Conversations: Essays, Addresses, & Interviews 1953-1990.** George Lamming. Ed. by Richard Drayton & Andaiye. 300p. 1995. text ed. 42.50 (*0-472-09575-7*); pap. 14.95 (*0-472-06575-0*) U of Mich Pr.

Conversations: Straight Talk with America's Sister President. Johnetta B. Cole. 1993. 17.50 (*0-385-42130-3*) Doubleday.

Conversations: Straight Talk with America's Sister President. Johnetta B. Cole. LC 93-27254. 1994. 9.00 (*0-385-41160-X*, Anchor NY) Doubleday.

***Conversations: The Autobiography of Surrealism.** Andre Breton. LC 92-28131. 1995. pap. 12.95 (*1-56924-854-0*) Marlowe & Co.

Conversations about Bernstein. Intro. by William W. Burton. LC 94-9480. (Illus.). 256p. 1995. 25.00 (*0-19-507947-7*) OUP.

Conversations about God from the Journal of Willis F. Cox. Willis F. Cox. LC 85-91148. (Illus.). (Orig.). 1985. 11.95 (*0-9610758-2-1*); pap. 6.95 (*0-9610758-3-X*); pap. text ed. 6.95 (*0-9610758-1-3*) W F Cox.

Conversations & Constructions. Intro. by Barbara Clark. 64p. (J). (gr. k-12). 1978. pap. 4.95 (*0-945349-01-7*) Journeys Into Language.

Conversations at Midnight: Coming to Terms with Death & Dying. Kay Kramer & Herbert Kramer. 240p. 1994. pap. 10.00 (*0-380-72007-8*) Avon.

Conversations at Midnight: Coming to Terms with Dying & Death. Herb Kramer & Kay Kramer. LC 92-19961. 1993. 18.00 (*0-688-12084-9*) Morrow.

Conversations at Random: Survey Research as Interviewers See It. Jean M. Converse & Howard Schuman. LC 73-15840. (Illus.). 121p. 1974. pap. 8.00 (*0-87944-248-4*) Inst Soc Res.

***Conversations Before the End of Time.** Suzi Gablik. LC 95-60205. 496p. 1995. 24.95 (*0-500-01673-9*) Thames Hudson.

***Conversations Beyond the Light: With Departed Friends & Colleagues by Electronic Means.** Pat Kubis & Mark Macy. Ed. by Richard Burns. (Illus.). 192p. (Orig.). 1995. pap. 12.95 (*1-882180-47-X*) Griffin CA.

Conversations Chinoises Prises sur le Vif, 2 vols. Charles Ray. (Asian Folklore & Social Life Monographs: Nos. 47-48). 746p. (FRE.). 1973. 24.00 (*0-89986-045-1*) Oriental Bk Store.

Conversations dans le Coir-et-Cher. Paul Claudel. 182p. (FRE.). 1984. pap. 10.95 (*0-7859-1157-X*, 2070701913) Fr & Eur.

Conversations in a Clinic. Helen Forelle. 32p. 1981. 1.50 (*1-877649-01-5*) Tesseract SD.

***Conversations in Bloomsbury.** Mulk R. Anand. 175p. 1995. pap. 6.95 (*0-19-563678-3*) OUP.

Conversations in Exile: Russian Writers Abroad. Ed. by John Glad. Tr. by Richard M. Robin & Joanna Robin. LC 92-14797. (Illus.). 328p. 1993. lib. bdg. 52.00 (*0-8223-1277-8*); pap. 16.95 (*0-8223-1298-0*) Duke.

Conversations in Maine: Explaining Our Nation's Future. James Boggs et al. LC 78-55014. 299p. 1978. pap. 8.50 (*0-89608-008-0*) South End Pr.

Conversations in Modern Standard Arabic. Belkacem Baccouche & Sanaa Azmi. LC 84-40188. (Language Ser.). 432p. 1984. text ed. 47.00 (*0-300-03219-6*) Yale U Pr.

Conversations in Psychotherapy: Ways of Working with Individuals, Couples, & Families. R. V. Fitzgerald. LC 91-33335. 384p. 1992. 37.50 (*0-87668-561-0*) Aronson.

Conversations in Rome Between an Artist, a Catholic & a Critic. William E. Channing, II. (Works of William Ellery Channing II). 1990. reprint ed. lib. bdg. 79.00 (*0-7812-2269-9*) Rprt Serv.

Conversations in Spirit. John Allan et al. LC 81-66244. 112p. (Orig.). 1981. pap. 4.95 (*0-87516-452-8*) DeVorss.

Conversations in the Gallery. Wendy Parrish. (Illus.). 1977. per. 3.00 (*0-912284-92-7*) New Rivers Pr.

Conversations in the Wings: Talking about Acting. Roy Harris. LC 93-46703. (Illus.). 200p. 1994. pap. 18.95 (*0-435-08638-3*) Heinemann.

Conversations in Umbria. Aberic Dubois. 1980. 5.95 (*0-8199-0784-7*, Frncscn Herld) Franciscan Pr.

Conversations of Friends: Speculations on Affective Development. Ed. by John M. Gottman & Jeffery G. Parker. (Studies in Emotion & Social Interaction). (Illus.). 416p. 1987. 69.95 (*0-521-26321-2*) Cambridge U Pr.

Conversations of Miguel & Maria. Linda Ventriglia. (A-W Second Language Professional Library). (Illus.). (C). 1982. text ed. 26.39 (*0-201-08147-4*) Addison-Wesley.

***Conversations of Silence.** S. Harold Nickerson. LC 94-45897. 226p. (Orig.). 1995. pap. 18.95 (*0-86534-231-8*) Sunstone Pr.

Conversations of Socrates: Xenophon. Ed. & Tr. by Robin A. Waterfield. Tr. by Hugh Tredennick. (Classics Ser.). 384p. 1990. pap. 10.95 (*0-14-044517-X*, Penguin Classics) Viking Penguin.

Conversations of the Heart. Woodie W. White. LC 90-48507. 144p. 1991. 12.95 (*0-687-09637-5*) Abingdon.

Conversations on Chelation: Mineral Nutrition. H. DeWayne Ashmead. 204p. (Orig.). 1989. pap. 15.95 (*0-87983-501-X*) Keats.

Conversations on Communication Ethics. Ed. by Karen Greenberg. LC 90-49965. (Communication & Information Science Ser.). 208p. (C). 1991. text ed. 32.50 (*0-89391-656-0*) Ablex Pub.

Conversations on Communications. 1983. 1.50 (*0-939418-51-7*) Ferguson-Florissant.

Conversations on Contemporary Drama. Clayton M. Hamilton. LC 70-99700. (Essay Index Reprint Ser.). 1977. 21.95 (*0-8369-1354-X*) Ayer.

Conversations on Counselling: Between a Doctor & a Priest. 3rd ed. Marcus Lefebure & Hans Schauder. 288p. 1990. pap. 25.95 (*0-567-29164-2*, Pub. by T & T Clark UK) Bks Intl VA.

Conversations on Freemasonry. Henry W. Coil. ix, 282p. 1980. reprint ed. pap. 13.50 (*0-88053-035-9*, M084) Macoy Pub.

***Conversations on Mind, Matter, & Mathematics.** Jean-Pierre Changeux & Alain Connes. LC 94-37370. 1995. 24.95 (*0-691-08759-8*) Princeton U Pr.

Conversations on Modernism: With Reference to English, Hindi, & Urdu Fiction. Sukrita P. Kumar. (C). 1990. 16.00 (*0-685-53627-0*, Pub. by Allied II) S Asia.

***Conversations on Science, Culture & Time.** Michael Serres. Tr. by Roxanne Lapidus. LC 95-2706. (Studies in Literature & Science). 1995. 39.50 (*0-472-09548-X*); pap. 16.95 (*0-472-06548-3*) U of Mich Pr.

Conversations on Some of the Old Poets. James Russell Lowell. 1977. 18.95 (*0-8369-7226-0*, 8025) Ayer.

Conversations on the Dark Secrets of Physics. Edward Teller et al. (Illus.). 238p. 1991. 23.95 (*0-306-43772-4*, Plenum Pr) Plenum.

Conversations on the Dresden Gallery. Louis Aragon & Jean Cocteau. Tr. by Francis Scarfe. LC 81-6640. (Illus.). 288p. 1982. 58.50 (*0-8419-0730-7*) Holmes & Meier.

Conversations on the Plurality of Worlds. Bernard le Bovier de Fontenelle. Tr. by H. A. Hargreaves. LC 90-31220. 132p. 1990. 30.00 (*0-520-06361-9*); pap. 12.00 (*0-520-07171-9*) U CA Pr.

Conversations on the Written Word: Essays on Language & Literacy. Ed. by Jay L. Robinson. (Illus.). 335p. (Orig.). 1990. pap. text ed. 21.00 (*0-86709-252-1*) Boynton Cook Pubs.

Conversations on Therapy. David R. Grove & Jay Haley. (C). 1993. 22.95 (*0-393-70155-7*) Norton.

Conversations on Writing Fiction: Interviews with 13 Distinguished Teachers of Fiction Writing in America. Alexander Neubauer. LC 93-25533. (Illus.). 256p. (Orig.). 1994. pap. 12.00 (*0-06-273223-4*, Harper Ref) HarpC.

Conversations, Situations. Taylor. 1978. pap. text ed. 8.55 (*0-582-22042-4*, 70865) Longman.

Conversations to Foster Parents from Mary Reistroffer, 3 vols., Set. 18.00 (*0-685-72273-2*, 9796) Child Welfare.

Conversations to Foster Parents from Mary Reistroffer, No. 1: What You Always Wanted to Discuss about Foster Care but Didn't Have the Chance or the Time to Bring Up. LC 72-166581. 41p. 1971. pap. 7.00 (*0-87868-087-X*, 0870) Child Welfare.

Conversations to Foster Parents from Mary Reistroffer, No. 2: What's So Special about Teenagers? LC 75-75120. 40p. 1972. pap. 7.00 (*0-87868-095-0*) Child Welfare.

Conversations to Foster Parents from Mary Reistroffer, No. 3: Foster Parents & Social Workers - on the Job Together. Mary Reistroffer. LC 73-93881. 1974. pap. 7.00 (*0-87868-111-6*) Child Welfare.

Conversations with a Bible Scholar: Interviews with Frank Moore Cross. Ed. by Hershel Shanks. (Illus.). 150p. (Orig.). (C). Date not set. text ed. write for info. (*1-880317-18-4*) Biblical Arch Soc.

Conversations with a Dying Friend. John Carmody. LC 92-19560. 96p. 1992. pap. 5.95 (*0-8091-3173-0*) Paulist Pr.

Conversations with a Pocket Gopher: And Other Outspoken Neighbors. Jack Schaefer. LC 91-38797. (Illus.). 128p. 1992. reprint ed. pap. 8.95 (*0-88496-348-9*) Capra Pr.

Conversations with a Pocket Gopher & Other Outspoken Neighbors. Jack Schaefer. 128p. 1992. reprint ed. lib. bdg. 25.00x (*0-8095-4096-7*) Borgo Pr.

***Conversations with Adolf Hitler 1992-1994.** Michael L. Schuster. Ed. by Ray C. Hearne & Susan Rotondo. (Illus.). 340p. 1994. pap. 16.95 (*0-9627390-8-1*) Sufra Pubns.

Conversations with Amber. Gladys Taber. 17.95 (*0-8488-1186-0*) Amereon Ltd.

Conversations with Amiri Baraka. Ed. by Charlie Reilly. (Literary Conversations Ser.). 288p. 1994. 37.50 (*0-87805-686-6*); pap. 15.95 (*0-87805-687-4*) U Pr of Miss.

Conversations with an Alzheimer's Patient: An Interactional Sociolinguistic Study. Heidi E. Hamilton. 166p. (C). 1994. 44.95 (*0-521-42101-2*) Cambridge U Pr.

Conversations with an Unbelieving Friend. John T. Carmody. 1991. pap. 5.95 (*0-8091-3210-9*) Paulist Pr.

Conversations with Anais Nin. Ed. by Wendy DuBow. (Literary Conversations Ser.). 238p. 1994. text ed. 37.50 (*0-87805-719-6*); pap. 15.95 (*0-87805-720-X*) U Pr of Miss.

Conversations with Anatole France. Nicolas Segur. 1977. lib. bdg. 59.95 (*0-8490-1673-8*) Gordon Pr.

Conversations with Anorexics: A Compassionate & Hopeful Journey through the Therapeutic Process. Hilde Bruch. LC 94-70808. 238p. 1994. pap. 30.00 (*1-56821-261-5*) Aronson.

Conversations with Antoni Tapies. Ed. by Barbara Catoir. (Illus.). 168p. (Orig.). 1991. pap. 25.95 (*3-7913-1149-2*, Pub. by Prestel) TeNeues.

Conversations with Arrau. Joseph Horowitz. LC 84-4375. (Illus.). 336p. 1984. reprint ed. pap. 17.95 (*0-87910-013-3*) Limelight Edns.

Conversations with Arthur Miller. Ed. by Matthew C. Roudane. LC 87-17931. (Literary Conversations Ser.). 1987. 37.50 (*0-87805-322-0*); pap. 15.95 (*0-87805-323-9*) U Pr of Miss.

Conversations with Bernard Malamud. Ed. by Lawrence Lasher. LC 90-49374. (Literary Conversations Ser.). 1991. 37.50 (*0-87805-489-8*); pap. 15.95 (*0-87805-490-1*) U Pr of Miss.

Conversations with Bigfoot. (Orig.). 1995. pap. 5.00 (*0-912449-16-0*) Floating Island.

Conversations with Bugs: A Journal with Words & Drawings. Gwynn Popovac. (Illus.). 128p. 1993. 17.95 (*1-56640-681-1*) Pomegranate Calif.

Conversations with Capote. Lawrence Grobel. 256p. 1986. pap. 7.95 (*0-425-25802-5*, Plume) NAL-Dutton.

Conversations with Carl Henry: Christianity for Today. Carl F. Henry. LC 86-666. (Symposium Ser.: Vol. 18). 204p. 1986. lib. bdg. 89.95 (*0-88946-709-9*) E Mellen.

Conversations with Celestin Deliege. Pierre Boulez. (Eulenburg Music Ser.). 123p. 1985. pap. 17.50 (*0-903873-22-2*) Da Capo.

***Conversations with Chester Himes.** Ed. by Michel Fabre & Robert E. Skinner. (Literary Conversations Ser.). 320p. 1995. text ed. 39.50 (*0-87805-818-4*); pap. 15.95 (*0-87805-819-2*) U Pr of Miss.

Conversations with Chester I. Barnard. William B. Wolf. LC 72-619666. (ILR Paperback Ser.: No. 12). 68p. 1973. pap. 1.00 (*0-87546-047-X*) ILR Pr.

Conversations with Children. James A. Jones, III. LC 85-40201. (Illus.). 96p. (J). (gr. 4-8). 1985. 8.95 (*0-938232-72-X*) Winston-Derek.

Conversations with Children on the Gospel. Amos B. Alcott. (Works of Amos Bronson Alcott). 1989. reprint ed. lib. bdg. 79.00 (*0-7812-0300-7*) Rprt Serv.

Conversations with Children on the Gospels (Record of Conversations on the Gospels, Held in Mr. Alcott's School; Unfolding the Doctrine & Discipline of Human Culture), 2 vols. in 1. Ed. by A. Bronson Alcott. LC 72-4948. (Romantic Tradition in American Literature Ser.). 616p. 1976. reprint ed. 44.95 (*0-405-04621-9*) Ayer.

Conversations with Claude Levi-Strauss. Claude Levi-Strauss & Didier Eribon. Tr. by Paula Wissing. LC 90-11052. 192p. 1991. 19.95 (*0-226-47475-5*) U Ch Pr.

Conversations with Contemporary Armenian Artists. Jackie Abramiam. (Illus.). 200p. (Orig.). (C). 1990. pap. 12.50 (*0-915597-78-0*) Amana Bks.

An Asterisk (*) at the beginning of an entry indicates that the title is appearing in BIP for the first time.

C

An Asterisk (*) at the beginning of an entry indicates that the title is appearing in BIP for the first time.

Conversations 1929, 1930-1931: The Mother. 179p. 1989. pap. 5.00 (*81-7058-131-1*) Aurobindo Assn.

Converse Chart. Wanda Whitcraft. 16p. 1974. 4.50 (*0-86690-197-3*, W1516-014) Am Fed Astrologers.

Converse Kiswahili Ongea. Sharifa M. Zawawi. LC 91-70722. 1992. 24.95 (*0-86543-228-7*); pap. 9.95 (*0-86543-229-5*) Africa World.

Converse of the Pen: Acts of Intimacy in the Eighteenth Century Familiar Letter. Bruce Redford. LC 86-11237. (Illus.). 252p. 1987. lib. bdg. 28.00 (*0-226-70678-8*); pap. text ed. 11.95 (*0-226-70679-6*) U Ch Pr.

***Conversemos!** Ana C. Jarvis & Raquel Lebredo. 248p. (SPA.). (C). 1995. pap. text ed. write for info. (*0-669-24672-7*) Heath.

Conversemos: First Book for Spanish Conversation. Edin Brenes & D. H. Patterson. (Illus.). (SPA.). 1942. text ed. 14.00 (*0-89197-112-2*); pap. text ed. 6.95 (*0-89197-714-7*) Irvington.

Conversing with Cage. Richard Kostelanetz. LC 87-22853. 352p. (Orig.). 1988. pap. 16.95 (*0-87910-100-8*) Limelight Edns.

Conversing with Stones. Mark Miller. 64p. (C). 1989. 50.00 (*0-685-41002-1*, Pub. by Five Islands Pr AT) St Mut.

Conversing with Stones. Mark Miller. (C). 1990. 55.00 (*0-86418-085-3*, Pub. by Pascoe Pub AT) St Mut.

Conversing with the Planets: How Sicence & Myth Invented the Cosmos. Anthony Aveni. (Illus.). 272p. 1994. pap. 14.00 (*1-56836-021-5*) Kodansha.

Conversing with Uncertainty: Practicing Psychotherapy in a Hospital Setting. Rita W. McCleary. 160p. 1992. text ed. 26.95 (*0-88163-148-5*) Analytic Pr.

Conversion. C. H. Spurgeon. 1994. pap. 3.00 (*1-56186-421-8*) Pilgrim Pubns.

Conversion. deluxe ed. Kelly Cherry. (Treacle Story Ser.: No. 8). (Illus.). 52p. 1979. 8.00 (*0-914232-29-0*) McPherson & Co.

Conversion. E. Stanley Jones. (Abingdon Classics Ser.). 253p. 1992. reprint ed. pap. 5.95 (*0-687-08396-6*) Abingdon.

Conversion: A Program for Medical SI Unit Conversion. H. Peter Lehman & Paul G. Catrou. 1987. disk 47.00 (*0-685-54501-6*); write for info. (*0-89189-250-8*, 68-9-022-20(IBM)); write for info. (*0-89189-249-4*) Am Soc Clinical.

Conversion: Perspectives on Personal & Social Transformation. Walter E. Conn. LC 78-19079. 1978. pap. 10.95 (*0-8189-0368-6*) Alba.

Conversion: Reflections on Life & Faith. James Turro. 128p. 1993. 9.40 (*0-7829-0401-7*) Tabor Pub.

Conversion among the Intermarried: Choosing to Become Jewish. Egon Mayer & Amy Avgar. LC 87-70999. 44p. (Orig.). 1987. pap. 5.00 (*0-87495-091-0*) Am Jewish Comm.

Conversion & Community: A Catechumenal Model for Total Parish Formation. Thomas P. Ivory. 1988. pap. 7.95 (*0-8091-3019-X*) Paulist Pr.

Conversion & Economic Adjustments in an Era of Arms Reduction, 2 vols., Set, Vols. I & II. (Topical Papers Ser.: No. 5). 1991. Set. 22.00 (*92-1-142169-1*, 91.IX.6-7) UN.

Conversion & Economic Adjustments in an Era of Arms Reduction, Vol. I. (Disarmament Topical Papers: No. 5). 188p. 1991. 13.50 (*92-1-142167-5*, E.91.IX.6) UN.

Conversion & Economic Adjustments in an Era of Arms Reduction, Vol. II. (Topical Papers Ser.: No. 5). 198p. 1991. 13.50 (*92-1-142168-3*, 91.IX.7) UN.

Conversion & Experiences After Conversion. C. H. Spurgeon. 1977. pap. 2.95 (*1-56186-326-2*) Pilgrim Pubns.

Conversion & Jesuit Schooling in Zambia. Brendan P. Carmody. LC 91-27038. (Studies in Christian Mission: Vol. 4). (Illus.). xxix, 179p. 1992. 63.00 (*90-04-09428-8*) E J Brill.

Conversion & Seasoning of Wood. William Brown. LC 89-32562. (Illus.). 222p. 1989. reprint ed. pap. 16.95 (*0-941936-14-7*) Linden Pub Fresno.

Conversion & Social Equality in India: The London Missionary Society in S. Travancore in the 19th Century. Dick Kooiman. (C). 1989. 28.50 (*0-945921-04-7*, Pub. by S Asia Pubs II) S Asia.

Conversion & Text: The Cases of Augustine of Hippo, Herman-Judah, & Constantine Tsatsos. Karl F. Morrison. 208p. 1992. text ed. 35.00 (*0-8139-1359-4*); pap. 16.95 (*0-8139-1393-4*) U Pr of Va.

Conversion & the Enneagram: Transformation of the Self in Christ. Bernard Tickerhoof. 1991. pap. 11.95 (*0-87193-275-X*) Dimension Bks.

Conversion, Catechumenate, & Baptism in the Early Church. Ed. by Everett Ferguson. LC 92-40951. (Studies in Early Christianity: Vol. 11). 456p. 1993. 70.00 (*0-8153-1071-4*) Garland.

Conversion Courts. 10p. 1985. pap. 1.00 (*0-938822-64-0*) USTA.

Conversion Crisis: Essays from the Pages of Tradition. Ed. by Emanuel Feldman & Joel Wolowelsky. pap. 9.95 (*0-685-53274-7*) Ktav.

Conversion Experience: A Biblical Study of the Blood, Water & Spirit. Gary D. Erickson. LC 87-6157. (Illus.). 185p. (Orig.). 1987. pap. 5.99 (*0-932581-13-7*) Word Aflame.

Conversion Experience in America: A Sourcebook on American Religious Conversion Autobiography. James C. Holte. LC 91-32173. 256p. 1992. text ed. 65.00 (*0-313-26680-8*, HRD/, Greenwood Pr) Greenwood.

Conversion Factor Report, 1994. Innervation Technology Corporation Staff. 1995. ring bd. 95.00 (*0-07-600721-9*); disk, ring bd. 175.00 (*0-07-809978-1*) Hlthcare Mgmt Grp.

Conversion Factors. James L. Cook. (Illus.). 176p. 1991. 14.95 (*0-19-856349-3*, 12269) OUP.

Conversion Factors: SI Units & Many Others. Colin J. Pennycuick. 48p. 1988. pap. text ed. 7.95 (*0-226-65507-5*) U Ch Pr.

Conversion Factors & Tables. O. T. Zimmerman. 1961. 30.00 (*0-318-37567-2*) Indus Res Serv.

Conversion from War to Peace: Social, Economic, & Political Problems. Ed. by W. Meyers & M. V. Hayes. 132p. 1973. text ed. 76.00 (*0-677-15220-5*) Gordon & Breach.

Conversion in the New Testament. Ronald D. Witherup. (Zaachaeus Studies: New Testament). 136p. (Orig.). 1994. pap. text ed. 9.95 (*0-8146-5837-7*, M Glazier) Liturgical Pr.

Conversion-Initiation & the Baptism in the Holy Spirit. Howard M. Ervin. 108p. 1985. pap. 9.95 (*0-913573-12-4*) Hendrickson MA.

Conversion Management Handbook. Comp. by Mary J. Bitting. 109p. 1989. per., pap. 6.00 (*0-16-003299-7*, 022-003-01163-3) USGPO.

Conversion of an Oil Fired Boiler to an Atmospheric Fluidized Bed Burning Coal, EUR 14322. G. H. Lindsay. 90p. 1993. pap. 16.00 (*92-826-5487-7*, CS-NA-14322-EN-C, Pub. by Europ Com) UNIPUB.

Conversion of Armenia. Valerie G. Zahirsky. (Armenian Church Classics Ser.). (Illus.). 48p. (Orig.). 1985. pap. 5.00 (*0-934728-16-X*) D O A C.

***Conversion of Buster Drumwright: The Television & Stage Scripts.** Jesse H. Ford. LC 64-18961. 174p. 1964. 16.95 (*0-910278-99-7*) Boulevard.

Conversion of Henri the Fourth: Politics, Power & Religious Belief in Early Modern France. Michael Wolfe. (Historical Studies: Vol. 114). 265p. (C). 1993. text ed. 39.95 (*0-674-17031-8*) HUP.

Conversion of Rental Housing to Condominiums & Cooperatives: Study of Scope, Causes & Impacts. 1986. lib. bdg. 95.00 (*0-8490-3532-5*) Gordon Pr.

Conversion of the Defense Industry in the Former Soviet Union. Thierry Malleret. LC 92-11692. (Occasional Papers: Vol. 23). 1992. 12.85 (*0-913449-30-X*) Inst EW Stud.

Conversion of the Jews. Philip Roth. (Short Stories Ser.). (J). (gr. 5 up). 1992. lib. bdg. 13.95 (*0-88682-506-7*) Creative Ed.

Conversion of the Jews & Other Essays. Mark Shechner. LC 89-77795. 290p. 1990. text ed. 45.00 (*0-312-04619-7*) St Martin.

Conversion of the Slovenes & the German-Slav Ethnic Boundary in the Eastern Alps. Aloysius L. Kuhar. LC 60-23462. 231p. 1967. reprint ed. 12.00 (*0-686-28374-0*) Studia Slovenica.

Conversion of Ukraine: The Continuing Story. Appleyard et al. Ed. by Anthony A. Laszok & Joseph Stoutenberger. 56p. (Orig.). 1988. pap. write for info. (*0-318-64347-2*) Ukrain Cath Diocese Parma.

Conversion Power of the Book of Morman. Grant Von Harrison. (Missionary Success Ser.). 78p. (Orig.). 1991. pap. write for info. (*0-910613-16-8*) Millenial Pr.

Conversion Road. John J. Weigand. 80p. 1991. pap. 7.95 (*0-940169-10-X*); audio 24.95 (*0-685-56387-1*) Liturgical Pubns.

Conversion Tables: LC-Dewey; Dewey-LC. Mona L. Scott & Christine E. Alvey. 350p. 1993. lib. bdg. 60.00 (*1-56308-017-6*) Libs Unl.

Conversion Tables: LC-Dewey; Dewey-LC. Mona L. Scott & Christine E. Alvey. 350p. 1994. disk 65.00 (*1-56308-152-0*) Libs Unl.

Conversion Through Penance in the Italian Church of the Fourth & Fifth Centuries: New Approaches to the Experience of Conversion from Sin. Allan Fitzgerald. LC 88-9247. (Studies in the Bible & Early Christianity: Vol. 15). 580p. 1988. lib. bdg. 119.95 (*0-88946-615-7*) E Mellen.

Conversion to Christianity: Historical & Anthropological Perspectives on a Great Transformation. Ed. by Robert W. Hefner. 345p. (C). 1993. 45.00 (*0-520-07835-7*); pap. 15.00 (*0-520-07836-5*) U CA Pr.

Conversion to Greater Freedom? Women, Church & Social Change in North-Western Tanzania under Colonial Rule. Birgitta Larsson. (Studia Historica Upsaliensia: No. 162). (Illus.). 230p. (Orig.). 1991. pap. 46.50x (*91-554-2684-0*, Pub. by Almqv & Wiksell SW) Coronet Bks.

Conversion to Islam. Ed. by Nehemia Levtzion. LC 77-26771. 265p. 1979. 42.95 (*0-8419-0343-3*) Holmes & Meier.

Conversion to Islam: Untouchables Strategy for Protest in India. Abdulmalik Mujahid. LC 88-2445. 1989. 16.95 (*0-89012-050-1*) Anima Pubns.

Conversion to Islam in the Medieval Period: An Essay in Quantitative History. Richard W. Bulliet. LC 79-14411. (Illus.). 158p. reprint ed. pap. 48.50 (*0-7837-1676-1*, 2057208) Bks Demand.

Conversion to Judaism: A Guidebook. Lawrence J. Epstein. LC 94-25. 304p. 1994. pap. 25.00 (*1-56821-128-7*) Aronson.

Conversion to Judaism: A History & Analysis. David M. Eichhorn. 1966. 20.00 (*0-87068-019-6*) Ktav.

Conversion to Judaism: From the Biblical Period to the Present. Joseph R. Rosenbloom. LC 78-9409. 192p. reprint ed. pap. 54.80 (*0-7837-2999-5*, 2042942) Bks Demand.

Conversion to Judaism in Jewish Law. Ed. by Walter Jacob & Moshe Zemer. (Studies in Progressive Halakhah: Vol. 3). xiii, 216p. (Orig.). 1994. pap. 12.50 (*0-929699-05-X*) Rodef Shalom Pr.

***Conversion to Modernities: The Globalization of Christian Modernities.** Peter Van Der Veer. LC 95-11009. 1995. write for info. (*0-415-91273-3*, Routledge NY) Routledge.

Conversion to One-Person Operation of Rapid-Transit Trains. (National Cooperative Transit Research Program Synthesis Ser.: No. 13). 49p. 1986. 8.40 (*0-309-03863-4*) Transport Res Bd.

Conversion to Separate Electric Metering. 77p. 1982. 15.00 (*0-318-17719-6*, DG 82-312) Pub Tech Inc.

Conversions. (Road to Avonlea Ser.: No. 6). (J). (gr. 3-7). 1992. mass mkt. 3.99 (*0-553-48032-4*) Bantam.

Conversions: A Philosophical Memoir. Abigail L. Rosenthal. LC 93-44719. 240p. (C). 1994. text ed. 44.95 (*1-56639-219-5*) Temple U Pr.

Conversions: A Philosophical Memoir. Abigail L. Rosenthal. LC 93-44719. 240p. (C). 1994. pap. 19.95 (*1-56639-220-9*) Temple U Pr.

Conversions & Visions in the Writings of African-American Women. Kimberly R. Connor. LC 93-14499. 328p. (C). 1994. text ed. 34.00 (*0-87049-818-5*) U of Tenn Pr.

***Conversos, Inquisition & the Expulsion of the Jews from Spain.** Norman Roth. LC 94-23486. 448p. 1995. text ed. 50.00 (*0-299-14230-2*) U of Wis Pr.

ConverStations: The Go Anywhere Speech Book. Janet Shaw DeVaney. (Illus.). 48p. 1986. 18.95 (*0-937857-00-9*, 1551) Speech Bin.

Convert. Elizabeth Robins. 320p. 1980. pap. 11.95 (*0-912670-83-5*) Feminist Pr.

Convert: Genuine Jew? Morton K. Siegel. 24p. (Orig.). 1981. pap. text ed. 1.95 (*0-8381-2116-0*) United Synagogue.

Convert & the Counsellor. Okey Onuzo. Ed. by Femi Ogundipe. 120p. (Orig.). (C). 1990. pap. 5.00 (*978-30915-0-6*) Life Link.

Convert & the Counsellor: Following up New Christians. 2nd ed. Okey Onuzo. Ed. by Anne Ndego. 122p. 1992. pap. text ed. 6.99 (*1-880608-00-6*) Life Link.

***Convert Cardinals: Newman & Manning.** David Newsome. (Illus.). 384p. 1995. 55.00 (*0-7195-4635-4*, Pub. by John Murray UK) Trafalgar.

Convert It! 3rd ed. Michael Brown & Shari Prange. (Illus.). 128p. (Orig.). 1993. pap. 24.95 (*1-879857-94-4*) SFEAA.

Convert: or Leaves from My Experience. Orestes A. Brownson. (Works of Orestes Augustus Brownson). 1989. reprint ed. lib. bdg. 79.00 (*0-7812-2110-2*) Rprt Serv.

Convert Your Car to Alcohol. Keat B. Drane. LC 80-81750. (Illus.). 64p. (Orig.). 1980. pap. 7.95 (*0-915216-54-X*) Marathon Intl Bk.

Convert Your Oil Furnace to Wood. 2nd ed. Bill White. LC 76-58642. (Illus.). 1977. 3.50 (*0-9601794-1-0*) FireBuilders.

Converted to Christ Through the Book of Mormon. Ed. by Eugene England. LC 89-36275. 201p. 1989. 10.95 (*0-87579-268-5*) Deseret Bk.

Convertible Cooking for a Healthy Heart: How to Turn Your Favorite Recipes into Lowfat, Low Cholesterol, Delicious Dishes. Joanne D'Agostino. LC 91-73926. (Healthy Heart Ser.). (Illus.). 151p. 1992. 17.95 (*0-8038-9338-8*) Hastings.

Convertible Counterpoint. Serge I. Taneiev. 50.95 (*0-8283-1415-2*) Branden Pub Co.

Convertible Debentures & Related Securities. Michael L. Tennican. LC 74-20369. 365p. reprint ed. pap. 104.10 (*0-8357-6309-9*, 2035582) Bks Demand.

***Convertibles.** Gil Chandler. (Cruisin' Ser.). 48p. (J). (gr. 3-9). 1995. lib. bdg. 13.35 (*1-56065-256-X*) Capstone Pr.

Convertibles. Ian Kuah. (Illus.). 144p. 1993. 14.98 (*0-8317-1797-1*) Smithmark.

Converting Basements, Garages & Attics: Expanding Your Usable Space Easily, Attractively & Affordably. R. Dodge Woodson. LC 92-37688. (Illus.). 256p. 1993. 19.95 (*0-8069-8740-5*) Sterling.

Converting C to Turbo C. Len Dorfman. 1992. text ed. 29.95 (*0-07-017802-X*); pap. text ed. 39.95 (*0-07-017801-1*) McGraw.

Converting C to Turbo C-Plus Plus. Len Dorfman. 352p. 1992. 39.95 (*0-8306-3754-0*, 1566, Windcrest); pap. 29.95 (*0-8306-3725-7*, 1566, Windcrest) TAB Bks.

Converting Existing Hydro-Electric Dams & Reservoirs into Pumped Storage Facilities. Comp. by American Society of Civil Engineers Staff. 607p. 1975. pap. 21.00 (*0-87262-120-0*) Am Soc Civil Eng.

Converting, Fire Refining & Casting: Proceedings. Ed. by J. D. McCain & J. M. Floyd. LC 94-81060. 381p. 1994. 42.00 (*0-87339-263-9*) Minerals Metals.

Converting for Flexible Packaging: A Primer. Adolph Miller. LC 93-61005. 185p. 1993. pap. text ed. 49.00 (*1-56676-061-5*) Technomic.

Converting from a Manual System to an Automated System: A Guideline. 15p. 1992. pap. 27.00 (*0-933887-44-2*, A4548) Assn Recs Mgrs & Admin.

Converting Imagination: Linguistic Theory & Swift's Satiric Prose. Marilyn Francus. LC 93-16890. 260p. (C). 1994. 39.95 (*0-8093-1890-3*) S Ill U Pr.

Converting Land from Rural to Urban Uses. Alfred A. Schmid. LC 68-16165. 117p. reprint ed. pap. 33.40 (*0-317-26481-8*, 2023815) Bks Demand.

Converting Microsoft C to Microsoft C - C Plus Plus 7.0. Len Dorfman. LC 92-28869. (Illus.). 204p. 1992. pap. 34.95 (*0-8306-4320-6*, 4341, Windcrest) TAB Bks.

Converting Microsoft C to Microsoft C C. Len Dorfman. 1992. pap. text ed. 34.95 (*0-07-017829-1*) McGraw.

Converting New York State Utilities to Coal: A Study of the Costs & Environmental Impacts of Conversion. James S. Cannon. (INFORM Report Ser.). 45p. reprint ed. pap. 25.00 (*0-7837-0327-9*, 2040646) Bks Demand.

Converting Nine to Five: Bringing Spirituality to Your Daily Work. John C. Haughey. 192p. 1994. pap. 14.95 (*0-8245-1446-7*) Crossroad NY.

Converting OCL to AS-400 CL. Joe Lackie & Bill Tansi. (Fastpath Bks.). 203p. 1993. pap. text ed. 99.95 (*1-884322-04-2*) Comp Applicatns.

Converting the Baptized: A Survival Manual for Parents, Teachers, & Pastors. William O'Malley. 265p. (Orig.). 1991. pap. 9.40 (*1-55924-490-9*, 22038) Tabor Pub.

Converting the Past: Studies in Ancient Israelite & Moabite Historiography. Klaas A. Smelik. (Oudtestamentische Studien Ser.: No. 28). viii, 210p. 1992. 54.50 (*90-04-09480-6*) E J Brill.

Converting the Wasteplaces of Zion: The Maine Missionary Society (1807-1816) Michael D. Carter. LC 90-46235. 185p. 1990. text ed. 21.50 (*0-89341-633-9*, Longwood Academic) Hollowbrook.

Converting the West: A Biography of Narcissa Whitman. Julie R. Jeffrey. LC 91-12326. (Oklahoma Western Biographies Ser.: Vol. 3). (Illus.). 256p. 1991. 24.95 (*0-8061-2359-1*) U of Okla Pr.

Converting the West: A Biography of Narcissa Whitman. Julie R. Jeffrey. LC 91-12326. (Oklahoma Western Biographies Ser.: Vol. 3). (Illus.). 256p. 1994. pap. 12.95 (*0-8061-2623-X*) U of Okla Pr.

Converting Thousands. Grant Von Harrison. (Missionary Success Ser.). 44p. (Orig.). 1991. pap. write for info. (*0-910558-08-6*) Ensign Pub.

Converting Thousands: A Guide for Missionaries. Grant Von Harrison. 28p. (Orig.). (YA). (gr. 12). 1981. pap. 2.50 (*0-910558-06-X*, 8156) Pubs Bk Sales.

Converting with the Book of Morman. 21p. (Orig.). 1991. pap. write for info. (*0-318-68389-X*) Jackman Pubng.

Convert's Catechism of Catholic Doctrine. Peter Geiermann. 1977. reprint ed. pap. 3.00 (*0-89555-029-6*) TAN Bks Pubs.

Convex Analysis. R. Tyrrell Rockafellar. LC 68-56318. (Mathematical Ser.: No. 28). 1969. 69.50 (*0-691-08069-0*) Princeton U Pr.

Convex Analysis: An Introductory Text. Jan Van Tiel. LC 83-10176. 125p. 1984. text ed. 79.95 (*0-471-90263-2*) Wiley.

Convex Analysis & Mathematical Economics. Ed. by J. Kriens. (Lecture Notes in Economics & Mathematical Systems Ser.: Vol. 168). 1979. pap. 26.00 (*0-387-09247-1*) Spr-Verlag.

Convex Analysis & Minimization Algorithms: Advanced Theory & Bundle Methods, 2. Jean-Baptiste Hiriart-Urruty & Claude Lemarechal. LC 93-6137. (Grundlehren der Mathematischen Wissenschaften Ser.: Vol. 306). (Illus.). vii, 346p. 1993. 89.00 (*0-387-56852-2*) Spr-Verlag.

Convex Analysis & Minimization Algorithms: Fundamentals, 2 vols., 1. Jean-Baptiste Hiriart-Urruty & Claude Lemarechal. LC 93-6137. (Grundlehren der Mathematischen Wissenschaften Ser.: Vol. 305). (Illus.). 440p. 1993. 89.00 (*0-387-56850-6*) Spr-Verlag.

***Convex Analysis & Nonlinear Geometric Elliptic Equations.** I. Bakelman. 613p. 1994. 114.00 (*0-387-13620-7*) Spr-Verlag.

Convex Bodies: The Brunn-Minkowski Theory. Rolf Schneider. (Encyclopedia of Mathematics & Its Applications Ser.: No. 44). (Illus.). 450p. (C). 1993. 94.95 (*0-521-35220-7*) Cambridge U Pr.

Convex Bodies & Algebraic Geometry. Tadao Oda. (Ergebnisse der Mathematik und Ihrer Grenzgebiete Ser.: Vol. 15, 3 Folge). (Illus.). 280p. 1987. 89.00 (*0-387-17600-4*) Spr-Verlag.

***Convex Functions & Optimization Methods on Riemannian Manifolds.** Constantin Udriste. (Mathematics & Its Applications Ser.). 368p. (C). 1994. lib. bdg. 154.00 (*0-7923-3002-1*) Kluwer Ac.

Convex Functions, Monotone Operators & Differentiability. R. R. Phelps. (Lecture Notes in Mathematics Ser.: Vol. 1364). 115p. 1989. pap. 18.30 (*0-387-50735-3*) Spr-Verlag.

Convex Functions, Monotone Operators, & Differentiability. 2nd ed. Robert R. Phelps. LC 93-15613. (Lecture Notes in Mathematics Ser.: Vol. 1364). (Illus.). xii, 117p. 1993. pap. 27.00 (*0-387-56715-1*) Spr-Verlag.

Convex Functions, Partial Orderings & Statistical Applications. Josip E. Pecaric et al. (Mathematics in Science & Engineering Ser.). (Illus.). 467p. 1992. text ed. 69.95 (*0-12-549250-2*) Acad Pr.

Convex Geometry, 2 vol. Ed. by P. M. Gruber & J. M. Wills. LC 93-6496. (Handbook of Geometry Ser.: Vol. A-B). 1993. Vol. A, alk. paper. write for info. (*0-444-89596-5*, North Holland); Vol. B, alk. paper. write for info. (*0-444-89597-3*, North Holland) Elsevier.

Convex Geometry, 2 vol., Set. Ed. by P. M. Gruber & J. M. Wills. LC 93-6496. (Handbook of Geometry Ser.: Vol. A-B). 1993. write for info. (*0-444-89598-1*, North Holland) Elsevier.

Convex Mirror: Collected Poems. Samuel Yellen. LC 72-135016. reprint ed. pap. 28.80 (*0-317-09641-9*, 2055198) Bks Demand.

Convex Models of Uncertainty in Applied Mechanics. Yakov Ben-Haim & I. Elishakoff. (Studies in Applied Mechanics: No. 25). 222p. 1990. 95.00 (*0-444-88406-8*) Elsevier.

Convex Polytopes. Branko Grunbaum. LC 67-20423. (Pure & Applied Mathematics (Wiley) Ser.: Vol. 16). 470p. reprint ed. pap. 134.00 (*0-317-08683-9*, 2022541) Bks Demand.

Convex Sets & Their Applications. rev. ed. Steven R. Lay. LC 90-49488. 262p. (C). 1992. reprint ed. 49.95 (*0-89464-537-4*) Krieger.

Convex Structures & Economic Theory. Hukukane Nikaido. (Mathematics in Science & Engineering Ser.: Vol. 51). 1969. text ed. 136.00 (*0-12-519450-1*) Acad Pr.

Convexity. R. J. Webster. (Illus.). 400p. 1995. 69.95 (*0-19-853147-8*) OUP.

C

An Asterisk (*) at the beginning of an entry indicates that the title is appearing in BIP for the first time.

An Asterisk (*) at the beginning of an entry indicates that the title is appearing in BIP for the first time.

1607

C

Cooke Book: A Seasoning of Poets, No. XI. Ed. by Michael S. Glaser. LC 87-14143. 1987. pap. 7.00 (0-930526-10-4) SCOP Pubns.

*Cooke County, Texas. William Powell. (Illus.). 681p. 1992. 61.00 (0-88107-212-5) Curtis Media.

Cooked: Dope Poems. Bart Quinet. 32p. 1992. pap. 5.00 (1-885710-09-7) Geekspeak Unique.

Cooked Books. E. Kevin Hart. 1993. 19.95 (0-9632571-3-7); pap. 6.95 (0-9632571-1-0) Inst Am Democracy.

Cookery Americana, 15 bks, Set. Ed. by Louis Szathmary. 1973. 189.95 (0-405-05040-2) Ayer.

Cookery & Dining in Imperial Rome. Apicius. Ed. & Tr. by Joseph D. Vehling. LC 77-89410. Orig. Title: Apicius De Re Coquinaria. 301p. 1977. pap. 8.95 (0-486-23563-7) Dover.

Cookery Around India. Aroona Reejhsinghani. 184p. 1984. pap. 4.50 (0-86578-232-6) Ind-US Inc.

Cookery Book: From the Lukas Clinic for Patients with Cancer or Pre-Cancerous Conditions. Society for Cancer Research Staff. Tr. by Anna R. Meuss. 72p. (Orig.). 1988. pap. 7.95 (0-85440-716-2, Steinerbks) Anthroposophic.

Cookery for Lovers: Aphrodisiacs in the Kitchen. Bettie L. Furuta. LC 84-9329. (Illus.). 235p. (Orig.). 1984. pap. 14.95 (0-916129-00-4) Furuta.

Cookery for the Catering Industry. Douglas Sutherland & Stuart Rhodes. (Illus.). 320p. (Orig.). 1991. pap. 27.50 (0-7463-0573-7, Pub. by Northcote House UK) Trans-Atl Phila.

Cookery for the Catering Industry. S. Sutherland & R. Rhodes. (Orig.). 1990. pap. 60.00 (0-685-67967-5, Pub. by Northcote UK) St Mut.

Cooke's Peak - Pasaron Por Aqui: A Focus on United States History in Southwestern New Mexico. Donald H. Couchman. (Cultural Resources Ser.: No. 7). (Illus.). 268p. (Orig.). 1990. pap. write for info. (1-878178-08-3) Bureau of Land Mgmt NM.

Cookie. Linda C. Kneeland. (Illus.). 32p. (J). (ps-2). 1989. pap. 6.95 (0-944727-05-0) Jason & Nordic Pubs.

Cookie. Linda Kneeland. (Illus.). 32p. (J). (ps-3). 1992. reprint ed. 13.95 (0-944727-16-6) Jason & Nordic Pubs.

Cookie & Cracker Technology. 3rd ed. S. Matz. 1992. text ed. 79.95 (0-442-30892-2) Chapman & Hall.

Cookie & Cracker Technology. 3rd ed. Samuel A. Matz. (Illus.). 420p. 1992. 79.00 (0-942849-09-4) Pan Tech Intl.

Cookie Aura: Poems. 3rd ed. Bert Glick. 1977. pap. 6.99 (0-931020-07-7) Crosscut Saw.

*Cookie Book. Elizabeth W. Cohen. 1994. 12.98 (0-7858-0164-2) Bk Sales Inc.

Cookie Chemistry & Technology. Ed. by Carel Kulp. 468p. 1994. 89.00 (1-880877-08-2) Am Inst Baking.

Cookie Christmas. Faith Carlson. (Illus.). 28p. (Orig.). (J). (ps-2). 1986. pap. 5.00 (0-932591-05-1) Baggeboda Pr.

Cookie Cookbook. Lorna Rhodes. 1994. 9.98 (0-681-45460-1) Longmeadow Pr.

Cookie Cutters & Cookie Molds: Art in the Kitchen. Phyllis S. Wetherill. LC 85-61519. (Illus.). 224p. 1985. pap. 19.95 (0-88740-050-7) Schiffer.

*Cookie Exchange. Cyndi Duncan & Georgie Patrick. (Colorado Collection Ser.: Vol. 3). 160p. (Orig.). 1994. pap. 12.95 (0-9626335-4-2) C&G Pub CO.

*Cookie for the President. Anita F. Bott. LC 95-78157. (Illus.). (J). (ps-3). 1995. 14.95 (1-880851-20-2) Greene Bark Pr.

Cookie Fun. Judith H. Corwin. (Holiday Library). (Illus.). 64p. (J). (gr. 3 up). 1985. lib. bdg. 10.98 (0-671-50797-4, Julian Messner); lib. bdg. 5.95 (0-671-55019-5, Julian Messner); lib. bdg. 7.71 (0-685-47050-4, Julian Messner); pap. 3.71 (0-685-47051-2, Julian Messner) Silver Burdett Pr.

*Cookie Gets an "A" Misty Taggart. LC 94-45108. (Angel Academy Ser.: Vol. 5). (Illus.). (J). 1995. pap. 4.99 (0-8499-5084-8) Word Pub.

Cookie House. Margaret Hillert. (Illus.). (J). (ps-00). 1978. lib. bdg. 8.99 (0-8136-5012-7, TK2290); pap. 4.79 (0-8136-5512-9, TK2291) Modern Curr.

*Cookie Jar. Leisure Arts Staff. 1995. 19.95 (0-942237-50-1) Leisure AR.

Cookie Jar Cookbook. Steffif Berne. 1993. pap. 7.99 (0-517-10611-6) Random Hse Value.

Cookie Looker. 2nd ed. Anna L. Carlson. LC 80-82182. (Illus.). (J). (gr. k-4). 1980. pap. 1.95 (0-939938-01-4) Karwyn Ent.

*Cookie Market. 120p. (Orig.). 1995. pap. 2,195.00 (0-7605-2214-6) Rector Pr.

Cookie McCorkle & the Case of the Crooked Key. Sharon Cadwallader. 112p. (Orig.). (J). 1993. pap. 3.50 (0-380-76896-8, Camelot Young) Avon.

Cookie McCorkle & the Case of the Emerald Earrings. Sharon Cadwallader. 128p. (Orig.). (J). (gr. 3-4). 1991. pap. 2.95 (0-380-76098-3, Camelot Young) Avon.

Cookie McCorkle & the Case of the King's Ghost. Sharon Cadwallader. 112p. (Orig.). (J). 1991. pap. 2.99 (0-380-76350-8, Camelot) Avon.

Cookie McCorkle & the Case of the Missing Castle. Sharon Cadwallader. 128p. (J). 1991. pap. 2.99 (0-380-76348-6, Camelot) Avon.

Cookie McCorkle & the Case of the Mystery Map. Sharon Cadwallader. 128p. (Orig.). (YA). 1993. pap. 3.50 (0-380-76895-X, Camelot Young) Avon.

Cookie McCorkle & the Case of the Polka-Dot Safecracker. Sharon Cadwallader. 128p. (Orig.). (J). (gr. 3-4). 1991. pap. 2.95 (0-380-76099-1, Camelot Young) Avon.

Cookie Monster, Where Are You? Sesame Street Staff. LC 75-39342. (Sesame Street Pop-up Ser.: No. 10). (Illus.). (J). (ps-3). 1976. 8.99 (0-394-83257-4) Random Bks Yng Read.

Cookie Monster's Good Time to Eat! Richard Brown. (Golden Sturdy Shape Bks.). (Illus.). 14p. (J). (ps-00). 1989. write for info. (0-307-12259-X, Golden Bks) Western Pub.

Cookie Mueller, No. 11. Ed. by Kyoichi Tsuzuki. (Art Random Ser.). (Illus.). 48p. 1990. 32.95 (4-7636-8544-9, Pub. by Kyoto Shoin JA) Bks Nippan.

Cookie Sampler. Jan Siegrist. (Illus.). 48p. (Orig.). 1987. pap. 3.95 (0-933050-53-4) New Eng Pr VT.

Cookie, Snack, Bakery, Chemical Set. Matz. 1992. text ed. 383.80 (0-442-30902-3) Van Nos Reinhold.

Cookie Soup & Other Good-night Stories. Michaela Muntean. (Big Golden Book Ser.). (J). (ps-3). 1990. write for info. (0-307-12114-3) Western Pub.

*Cookies. Date not set. pap. 7.99 (0-517-12438-6) Random.

Cookies. E. Alston. Date not set. 12.50 (0-06-016994-X, HarpT) HarpC.

Cookies! DeCosse, Cy, Incorporated Staff. LC 93-45908. 256p. 1994. 24.95 (0-86573-924-2) Cy De Cosse.

Cookies. Friberg. 1993. text ed. 22.95 (0-442-01742-1) Van Nos Reinhold.

Cookies. William Jaspersohn. LC 91-45023. (Illus.). 48p. (J). (gr. 3-7). 1993. text ed. 14.95 (0-02-747822-X, Mac Bks Young Read) S&S Childrens.

*Cookies. Land o'Lakes Staff. LC 94-29050. (Land o'Lakes Collector Ser.). (Illus.). 128p. 1994. 14.95 (0-86573-954-4); pap. 9.95 (0-86573-955-2) Cy De Cosse.

Cookies! Ed. by Marian Levine. 64p. 1989. pap. 3.49 (0-942320-33-6) Am Cooking.

Cookies. Sunset Magazine & Book Editors. LC 84-82287. (Illus.). 96p. (Orig.). 1985. pap. 8.99 (0-376-02387-2) Sunset Menlo Pk.

Cookies. Joanne Van Roden. 36p. (Orig.). 1981. pap. 2.75 (0-940844-05-2) Wellspring.

*Cookies: Creative Cookie Baking. Sunset Books Staff. (Creative Cooking Library). 1994. 6.99 (0-376-00903-9) Sunset Menlo Pk.

*Cookies: For Youthful Appetites. Ed. by G & R Publishing Staff. (Uni-Book Ser.). 160p. (Orig.). 1994. pap. text ed. 3.00 (1-56383-008-6, 1100) G & R Pub.

Cookies: From Amish & Mennonite Kitchens. Ed. by Phyllis P. Good & Rachel T. Pellman. (Pennsylvania Dutch Cookbooks Ser.). (Illus.). 32p. (Orig.). 1982. pap. 2.95 (0-934672-05-9) Good Bks PA.

Cookies: Miniature Book of Food. Jane Donovan. 1991. 4.99 (0-517-06541-X) Random Hse Value.

Cookies & Bars...with Love. Jeannine B. Browning. 1994. pap. write for info. (0-9627729-5-X) J B Browning.

Cookies & Biscotti. Kristine Kidd. Ed. by Laurie Wertz. LC 93-28230. (Williams-Sonoma Kitchen Library). (Illus.). 108p. 1994. 17.95 (0-7835-0266-4); lib. bdg. write for info. (0-7835-0267-2) Time-Life.

*Cookies & Cakes. Rachel Master. (You Can Do It! Ser.). (Illus.). 80p. (Orig.). (J). (ps up). Date not set. pap. 12.95 (1-56530-069-6) Summit TX.

Cookies & Conversation: Tasty & Nutritious Recipes from Judy's Kitchen. Judy Wandschneider. (Illus.). 112p. (Orig.). 1988. pap. 9.95 (0-918957-03-6); spiral bd. 9.95 (0-918957-04-4) Pika Oregon.

Cookies & Crackers. (Good Cook Ser.). (Illus.). 176p. 1982. 19.93 (0-8094-2939-X); lib. bdg. 25.93 (0-8094-2938-1) Time-Life.

Cookies & Crutches. Judy Delton. (Pee Wee Scouts Ser.: No. 1). 80p. (Orig.). (J). (gr. k-6). 1988. pap. 3.25 (0-440-40010-4, YB) Dell.

Cookies & Squares with Schmecks Appeal. Edna Staebler. (Schmecks Appeal Cookbook Ser.). (Illus.). 96p. 1991. pap. 9.95 (0-7710-8277-0, Pub. by McClelland & Stewart CN) Firefly Bks Ltd.

Cookies at the Academy. 3rd ed. Cynthia Scheer. LC 92-30277. (California Culinary Academy Ser.). 128p. 1993. reprint ed. pap. 11.95 (1-56426-035-6, Calif Culinary Acad) Cole Group.

*Cookies by the Dozen: Over 75 Irresistible Recipes for Just a Dozen Cookies Each. Delores Kosteini. 176p. 1995. pap. 10.99 (0-446-67027-8) Warner Bks.

Cookies, Cakes, & Pies. Ariel Books Staff. 1993. 4.95 (0-8362-3032-9) Andrews & McMeel.

Cookies, Cookies, Cookies. Better Homes & Gardens Staff. 144p. 1992. 14.95 (0-696-01987-6); pap. 11.95 (0-696-00054-7) Meredith Bks.

Cookies for Christmas: Fifty of the Best Cookie Recipes for Holiday Gift Giving, Decorating, & Eating. Maria P. Robbins. (Illus.). 144p. (Orig.). 1993. pap. 6.95 (0-312-09775-1) St Martin.

Cookies for Kids (Cookbook) Ed. by Sharon Krall. (Illus.). 28p. (Orig.). (J). 1994. pap. 5.95 (0-944943-26-8, 23043-1) Current Inc.

Cookies from Many Lands. Josephine Perry. (Cookbook Ser.). 160p. (J). (gr. 6-12). 1972. reprint ed. pap. 4.95 (0-486-22832-0) Dover.

Cookies from the Amish & Mennonite Kitchen. Phyllis P. Good. 1991. pap. 2.95 (1-56148-035-5) Good Bks PA.

Cookies in Minutes. Mable Hoffman & Gar Hoffman. LC 92-31059. 144p. (Orig.). 1992. pap. 9.95 (1-55561-047-1) Fisher Bks.

Cookie's Week. Cindy Ward. (Illus.). 32p. (J). (ps-1). 1988. 11.95 (0-399-21498-4, Putnam) Putnam Pub Group.

Cookie's Week. Cindy Ward. (Sandcastle Ser.). (Illus.). 32p. (J). (ps). 1992. pap. 4.95 (0-399-22406-8, Putnam) Putnam Pub Group.

Cookies You Can Make: A Step-by-Step Illustrated Cookbook. Sachiko Moriyama. (Illus.). 48p. (Orig.). 1989. pap. 10.95 (0-87040-801-1) Japan Pubns USA.

Cookin' Cheap. Larry Bly & Laban Johnson. 160p. 1987. pap. 7.95 (0-87833-595-1) Taylor Pub.

*Cookin' Cousins. Ed. & Intro. by Martha F. Smith. 340p. (Orig.). 1995. pap. write for info. (1-885676-07-7) Meltdown Intl.

Cookin' Healthy with One Foot Out the Door: Quick Meals for Fast Times. Polly Pitchford & Delia Quigley. LC 93-43471. 160p. 1994. 8.95 (0-913990-86-8) Book Pub Co.

Cookin' in Fairfield County. Shirley M. Heston. 100p. 1993. Spiral bdg. spiral bd. 7.00 (0-9641411-0-8) Shirleys Ckbooks.

*Cookin' in High Cotton. (Orig.). Date not set. pap. write for info. (1-56944-075-1) Terrell Missouri.

*Cookin' in the Ozarks Branson Style. (Orig.). Date not set. pap. write for info. (1-56944-076-X) Terrell Missouri.

*Cookin' in Ventura. Gail Hobbs. (Illus.). 129p. (Orig.). 1994. pap. 9.95 (0-9642012-0-8) Gold Coast Pr.

Cookin N'Awlins Style. (Orig.). Date not set. write for info. (1-56944-014-X); pap. write for info. (1-56944-012-3) Terrell Missouri.

Cookin' on Special: Recipe Reminder System. Maureen R. Rosenthal. 97p. (Orig.). 1993. pap. text ed. 6.95 (0-9634217-1-9) MorFor Pubns.

*Cookin' Up the Blues: With TABASCO Brand Pepper Sauce. Marva Wright et al. (Illus.). (Orig.). 1993. per. 10.00 (0-9639571-0-4) McIlhenny Co.

Cookin' with Queen Ida: "Bon Temps" Creole Recipes (& Stories) from the Queen of Zydeco Music. Ida Guillory & Naomi Wise. 250p. (Orig.). 1990. pap. 14.95 (1-55958-050-X) Prima Pub.

*Cookin' with Queen Ida: "Bon Temps" Creole Recipes (& Stories) from the Queen of Zydeco Music. 2nd ed. Ida Guillory & Naomi Wise. LC 95-1517. 1995. write for info. (0-7615-0006-5) Prima Pub.

Cookin' with the Lion: A Pinch of Blue, a Dash of White. Illus. by Michael Chesworth. 304p. 1988. 19.95 (0-9620696-0-4) Penn St Alumni.

Cookin' Woman: Irish Country Recipes. Florence Irwin & John Irvin. LC 86-17594. 229p. 1992. reprint ed. pap. 12.95 (0-85640-373-3, Pub. by Blackstaff Pr IE) Dufour.

Cookin' Yankees Ain't Et. 2.95 (0-936672-35-8) Aerial Photo.

Cooking. Henry Beard & Roy McKie. LC 84-40678. (Illus.). 112p. (Orig.). 1985. pap. 6.95 (0-89480-843-5, 843) Workman Pub.

Cooking. Boy Scouts of America. LC 19-600. (Illus.). 80p. (J). (gr. 6-12). 1986. pap. 1.85 (0-8395-3257-1, 33257) BSA.

Cooking A to Z. Jane Horn. (California Culinary Academy Ser.). 1992. 39.95 (1-56426-003-8, Calif Culinary Acad); pap. 29.95 (1-56426-002-X, Calif Culinary Acad) Cole Group.

*Cooking A to Z: The Complete Culinary Reference. rev. ed. Jane Horn. 1996. write for info. (1-56426-577-3) Cole Group.

Cooking Aboard Your RV. Janet Groene. LC 92-30798. 1993. 12.95 (0-87742-339-3) Intl Marine.

Cooking Aboard Your Rv. Janet Groene. 1992. pap. text ed. 12.95 (0-07-024900-8) McGraw.

Cooking Aboard Your Yacht. (Orig.). pap. 13.95 (0-937070-09-2) Crabtree.

Cooking Adventures with Pat Hutt & the Magical Clay Pot. Patricia E. Hutt. 1985. 8.50 (0-9613884-1-2) A Thomas Pub.

Cooking Ala Heart Cookbook: Delicious Heart Healthy Recipes to Reduce Risk of Heart Disease & Stroke. 2nd ed. Linda Hachfeld & Betsy Eykyn. (Illus.). 456p. 1992. 24.95 (0-9620471-2-0); pap. 19.95 (0-9620471-3-9) Appletree MN.

Cooking Alaskan. LC 83-11865. (Illus.). 512p. 1983. pap. 16.95 (0-88240-237-4) Alaska Northwest.

Cooking & Chatting with Sadie. Jane A. Bordelon. Ed. by Paula Berumen. LC 92-97229. (Illus.). 200p. 1993. pap. 12.95 (0-9638092-0-2) J A Bordelon.

Cooking & Cruising Italian Style: Light & Healthy Cuisine. Costa Cruises, Inc. Staff. Ed. by Lucy Cooper. (Illus.). 150p. (Orig.). 1989. pap. 10.95 (0-942084-89-6) SeaSide Pub.

Cooking & Curing with Herbs in Mexico. Dolores L. Latorre. (Illus.). 1977. 20.00 (0-88426-051-8) Encino Pr.

Cooking & Eating with Children. 1974. 4.90 (0-87173-006-5) ACEI.

Cooking & Memories. Phyllis P. Good. LC 82-84537. (People's Place Book Ser.: No. 5). (Illus.). 96p. (Orig.). 1983. pap. 5.95 (0-934672-16-4) Good Bks PA.

Cooking & Traveling Inn Style: A Recipe Guide Book to the Finest Inns in Northern California. Bed & Breakfast Innkeepers of Northern California Staff. 204p. 1990. 12.95 (0-9617881-1-9) Bed & Breakfast Inn.

Cooking Apples: Recipes Inspired by the Orchards of Ampleforth Abbey. Ampleforth Abbey Staff. 1990. pap. 7.95 (0-85244-194-0, Pub. by Gracewing UK) Morehouse Pub.

Cooking at Home with the Master Chefs. Julia Child. LC 93-20241. 1993. pap. 17.95 (0-679-74829-6) Knopf.

*Cooking at Rosedown. Lynda K. Underwood. Ed. by Jacquelyn Todaro. (Illus.). 188p. 1984. 12.95 (0-614-06257-8) Rosedown Plantation.

Cooking at the Academy: Techniques & Recipes. California Culinary Academy Staff. LC 91-60965. (Illus.). 188p. (Orig.). 1991. pap. 14.95 (0-912333-09-X) KQED.

Cooking at the Cafe: Lunch & Dinner Fare. Francie J. O'Shea. (Illus.). 189p. (Orig.). 1992. pap. 14.95 (0-9634342-0-9, TXU 528 816) F OShea.

Cooking at the Natural Cafe in Santa Fe. Lynn Walters. LC 92-2255. (Illus.). 1992. pap. 14.95 (0-89594-560-6) Crossing Pr.

Cooking at the Natural Gourmet. Debra Stark. 345p. (Orig.). 1991. pap. 18.95 (0-929627-04-0) Scarecrow Enter.

Cooking Atlanta Style: Delicious Recipes from Atlanta's Best Restaurants, Hotels, & Caterers. Margaret E. Norman. LC 93-79666. (Illus.). 208p. 1993. pap. 14.95 (1-56352-096-6) Longstreet Pr Inc.

Cooking By Degrees: The Boston University Cookbook. Ed. by Laura Freid & Terence Janericco. LC 81-3862. (Illus.). 400p. 1986. reprint ed. pap. 14.95 (0-916782-85-9) Harvard Common Pr.

Cooking by the Book: Food in Literature & Culture. enl. rev. ed. Ed. by Mary A. Schofield. 228p. (C). 1989. lib. bdg. 32.95 (0-87972-443-9); pap. 16.95 (0-87972-444-7) Bowling Green Univ.

Cooking Caribe. Christopher Idone & Helen McEachrane. 1992. 25.00 (0-517-57664-3, C P Pubs) Crown Pub Group.

Cooking Chinese. Better Homes & Gardens Editors. (Better Homes & Gardens Bks.). (Illus.). 96p. 1983. 9.95 (0-696-01097-6) Meredith Bks.

Cooking Class. Marjorie W. Sharmat. (Kids on the Bus Ser.: No. 2). (J). (gr. 4-7). 1991. pap. 2.99 (0-06-106026-7, PL) HarpC.

Cooking Class: Learning about Food Preparation. Mary J. Haugen. (Life Skills Educational Board Game Ser.: No. 1). 50p. 1991. teacher ed, text ed. 49.95 (1-884074-00-6) Program Concepts.

Cooking Class Appetizers Cookbook. (Illus.). 96p. 1993. 9.98 (0-7853-0190-9, 2019602) Pubns Intl Ltd.

Cooking Class Chicken Cookbook. (Illus.). 96p. 1993. 9.98 (0-7853-0191-7, 2020102) Pubns Intl Ltd.

Cooking Class Chinese Cookbook. (Illus.). 96p. 1993. 9.98 (1-56173-986-3, 2019002) Pubns Intl Ltd.

Cooking Class Italian Cookbook. (Illus.). 96p. 1993. 9.98 (1-56173-987-1, 2018902) Pubns Intl Ltd.

Cooking Class Mexican Cookbook. (Illus.). 96p. 1993. 9.98 (1-56173-985-5, 2018802) Pubns Intl Ltd.

Cooking Class Pasta Cookbook. (Illus.). 96p. 1993. 9.98 (0-7853-0192-5, 2020902) Pubns Intl Ltd.

Cooking Class Puzzle Game. Mary J. Haugen. (Life Skills Educational Puzzle Game Ser.: No. 1). 4p. 1992. text ed. 19.95 (1-884074-10-3) Program Concepts.

Cooking Country with Shotgun Red. Carlo DiNapoli. Ed. by R. Constantine. (Illus.). 275p. (Orig.). 1993. pap. 15.95 (0-9627946-8-6) Hawk FL.

Cooking Cousins: The Karl Wolfer Family Collection of Recipes & Memories. Bonnie L. Scherer. (Illus.). 220p. 1994. pap. write for info. (0-9622421-2-8) B Scherer.

*Cooking Creole, Cajun, & Southern Chicago Style. Bernice Coleman. (Orig.). 1988. pap. 12.00 (0-9645268-0-8) B Coleman.

Cooking Cues from A to Z. Roslyn Nemet. (Orig.). 1981. pap. 1.95 (0-8439-8013-3) Dorchester Pub Co.

Cooking Down East. 12th ed. Marjorie Standish. (Illus.). 260p. 1980. 13.95 (0-930096-14-2) G Gannett.

Cooking, Eating, Thinking: Transformative Philosophies of Food. Ed. by Deane W. Curtin & Lisa M. Heldke. LC 91-23622. (Illus.). 416p. 1992. text ed. 45.00 (0-253-31599-9); pap. text ed. 19.95 (0-253-20704-5, MB-704) Ind U Pr.

Cooking Energy in India. P. P. Gusain. (Development Alternatives Ser.). 1990. text ed. 25.00 (0-7069-4939-0, Pub. by Vikas II) S Asia.

Cooking for a Big Family & Large Groups. Marilyn Meredith. (Illus.). 112p. 1990. pap. 7.95 (0-929935-05-5) Countrywomans Pr.

Cooking for a Crowd. Tana Reiff. LC 94-76146. (Working for Myself Ser.). 80p. 1994. pap. 4.50 (1-56103-908-X) Lake Pub Co.

Cooking for A Crowd: Menus, Recipes, & How-to's For Church Kitchens. Mary Ray. LC 94-33297. 128p. (Orig.). 1995. pap. 9.95 (0-687-00253-2) Abingdon.

Cooking for a Crowd Naturally: Over 200 Recipes for Large Groups & Institutions. Barbara F. Meyer. 192p. (Orig.). pap. 29.95 (0-9614339-0-6) Stamlyn Pub Co.

Cooking for a Healthier Ever. Stevens. 1990. 16.95 (0-9624784-1-5) HealthMark.

*Cooking for a Healthy Family: Inspired Vegetarian Meals. Simon Hope. (Illus.). 160p. 1995. 29.95 (1-55670-427-5) Stewart Tabori & Chang.

Cooking for a New Earth: A New Approach to Home Cooking That Promotes Wholesome Eating & Healthy Living. Carl Jerome. LC 92-8345. 352p. 1993. 25.00 (0-8050-1996-0) H Holt & Co.

Cooking for Absolute Beginners. Muriel Fitzsimmons. LC 75-35405. Orig. Title: You Can Cook If You Can Read. 380p. 1976. reprint ed. pap. 5.95 (0-486-23311-1) Dover.

Cooking for All Seasons. Jimmy Schmidt. (Illus.). 320p. 1991. text ed. 24.95 (0-02-607131-2) Macmillan.

Cooking for Camp & Trail. Hasse Bunnelle & Shirley Sarvis. LC 77-189535. (Totebook Ser.). 194p. 1972. pap. 12.00 (0-87156-066-6) Sierra.

Cooking for Consciousness: Whole Food Recipes for the Vegetarian Kitchen. Joy McClure & Kendall Layne. Ed. by Vimala McClure. LC 93-18069. (Illus.). 272p. (Orig.). 1993. reprint ed. pap. 14.00 (0-945934-12-2) New Wrld Lib.

Cooking for Diabetics: A Complete Guide to Easy Menu Planning & Enjoyable Eating for Healthy Living. Kitty Maynard et al. LC 88-32374. (Illus.). 1989. 17.95 (1-55853-000-2) Rutledge Hill Pr.

Cooking for Elderly People. Ed. by Alan Stewart. (C). 1989. 69.00 (0-86388-067-3, Pub. by Age Concern Eng UK) St Mut.

Cooking for Family & Friends. Margaret Fulton. (Illus.). 400p. 1994. 35.00 (0-207-18340-6, Pub. by Angus & Robertson AT) HarpC.

Cooking for Fifty: The Complete Reference & Cookbook. Chet Holden. LC 92-27314. 600p. 1993. text ed. 64.95 (0-471-57015-X) Wiley.

Cooking for Friends. Raymond Blanc. (Illus.). 320p. 1993. 50.00 (0-7472-0367-9, Pub. by Headline UK) Trafalgar.

Cooking for Good Health: Creative Recipes Without Added Fat, Sugar, or Salt. Gloria Rose. LC 93-617. 384p. 1993. pap. 13.95 (0-89529-577-6) Avery Pub.

---

*Cooking Healthy & Fast. large type ed. Rachel Rudel. 1994. 14.95 (0-9642510-0-0) Apple a Day. Where else but in this new cookbook can you find bison recipes as unique, scrumptious, & healthy as these? Rachel Rudel, a registered dietician in Fargo, ND, has birthed COOKING HEALTHY & FAST with hopes of improving people's health as well as the state's agricultural market. This self-produced & promoted cookbook contains 250 recipes involving bison, as well as other local commodities. Rudel relays the nutritional benefits of eating bison meat; in which North Dakota has the only bison producing facility within North America. She also promotes "Pasta Growers" brand pasta, a Carrington-based, farmer-owned cooperative. Besides containing local products, this book appeals to those with an interest in health. Rudel educates her readers on how to be "fat smart" by contrasting the difference in products that are non-fat, fat-free, & traditional foods. The elderly are cautioned against falling prey to the recent "fat scare," & are encouraged to maintain a healthy balance in the foods they consume. The one-recipe-per-page, large print, easy-to-read cookbook is designed for the time-conscious people who do not want a lot of extra fuss (or fat) in their lives. This book is "user friendly." COOKING HEALTHY & FAST retails for $14.95 & is available by mail order for $18.65 (which includes tax, shipping & handling). Send orders to Rachel Rudel, RD, LRD, P.O. Box 11336, Fargo, ND 58106-1336. *Publisher Provided Annotation.*

An Asterisk (*) at the beginning of an entry indicates that the title is appearing in BIP for the first time.

1609

C

Cooking the Caribbean Way. Cheryl Kaufman. (Easy Menu Ethnic Cookbooks Ser.). (Illus.). 48p. (J). (gr. 5 up). 1988. lib. bdg. 14.95 (0-8225-0920-2, Lerner Publctns) Lerner Group.

Cooking the Chinese Way. Ling Yu. LC 82-263. (Easy Menu Ethnic Cookbooks Ser.). (Illus.). 48p. (J). (gr. 5 up). 1982. lib. bdg. 14.95 (0-8225-0902-4, Lerner Publctns) Lerner Group.

Cooking the Chinese Way. Ling Yu. (YA). (gr. 5 up). 1993. pap. 5.95 (0-8225-9631-8, Lerner Publctns) Lerner Group.

Cooking the Country Way. Robin Page. 1993. pap. 21.00 (1-85183-061-8, Silent Bks) St Mut.

Cooking the Dutch Oven Way. 2nd expanded ed. Woody Woodruff. LC 89-7552. (Illus.). 176p. 1989. pap. 11.99 (0-934802-51-3) ICS Bks.

Cooking the English Way. Barbara Hill. LC 82-257. (Easy Menu Ethnic Cookbooks Ser.). (Illus.). 48p. (J). (gr. 5 up). 1982. lib. bdg. 14.95 (0-8225-0903-2, Lerner Publctns) Lerner Group.

Cooking the French Way. Lynne M. Waldee. LC 82-258. (Easy Menu Ethnic Cookbooks Ser.). (Illus.). 48p. (J). (gr. 5 up). 1982. lib. bdg. 14.95 (0-8225-0904-0, Lerner Publctns) Lerner Group.

Cooking the German Way. Helga Parnell. (Easy Menu Ethnic Cookbooks Ser.). (Illus.). 48p. (J). (gr. 5 up). 1988. lib. bdg. 14.95 (0-8225-0918-0, Lerner Publctns) Lerner Group.

Cooking the Greek Way. Lynne W. Villios. (Easy Menu Ethnic Cookbooks Ser.). (Illus.). 52p. (J). (gr. 5 up). 1984. lib. bdg. 14.95 (0-8225-0910-5, Lerner Publctns) Lerner Group.

Cooking the Health Way. G. Padma Vijay. 96p. (Orig.). (C). 1992. pap. text ed. 5.95x (81-207-1354-0, Pub. by Sterling Pubs II) Apt Bks.

Cooking the Hungarian Way. Magdolna Hargittai. (Easy Menu Ethnic Cookbooks Ser.). (Illus.). 48p. (J). (gr. 5 up). 1986. lib. bdg. 14.95 (0-8225-0916-4, Lerner Publctns) Lerner Group.

Cooking the Indian Way. Vijay Madavan. (Easy Menu Ethnic Cookbooks Ser.). (Illus.). 52p. (J). (gr. 5 up). 1985. lib. bdg. 14.95 (0-8225-0911-3, Lerner Publctns) Lerner Group.

Cooking the Israeli Way. Josephine Bacon. LC 85-18059. (Easy Menu Ethnic Cookbooks Ser.). (Illus.). 48p. (J). (gr. 5 up). 1986. lib. bdg. 14.95 (0-8225-0912-1, Lerner Publctns) Lerner Group.

Cooking the Italian Way. Alphonse Bisignano. LC 82-12641. (Easy Menu Ethnic Cookbooks Ser.). (Illus.). 48p. (J). (gr. 5 up). 1982. lib. bdg. 14.95 (0-8225-0906-7, Lerner Publctns) Lerner Group.

Cooking the Japanese Way. Dorothy Kent. (Illus.). 128p. (Orig.). Date not set. pap. 12.00 (0-87573-052-3) Jain Pub Co.

Cooking the Japanese Way. Reiko Weston. LC 81-12656. (Easy Menu Ethnic Cookbooks Ser.). (Illus.). 48p. (J). (gr. 5 up). 1983. lib. bdg. 14.95 (0-8225-0905-9, Lerner Publctns) Lerner Group.

Cooking the Korean Way. Okwha Chung & Judy Monroe. (Easy Menu Ethnic Cookbooks Ser.). (Illus.). 48p. (J). (gr. 5 up). 1988. lib. bdg. 14.95 (0-8225-0921-0, Lerner Publctns) Lerner Group.

Cooking the Lebanese Way. Suad Amari. (Easy Menu Ethnic Cookbooks Ser.). (Illus.). 48p. (J). (gr. 5 up). 1985. lib. bdg. 14.95 (0-8225-0913-X, Lerner Publctns) Lerner Group.

Cooking the Lite Fantastic. Eileen Dardick & Sheila Ferrendelli. 1994. 14.95 (0-9641615-0-8) Ideal Image.

Cooking the Mexican Way. Rosa Coronado. LC 82-254. (Easy Menu Ethnic Cookbooks Ser.). (Illus.). 48p. (J). (gr. 5 up). 1982. lib. bdg. 14.95 (0-8225-0907-5, Lerner Publctns) Lerner Group.

Cooking the Mexican Way. Rosa Coronado. (YA). (gr. 5 up). 1992. pap. 5.95 (0-8225-9614-8, Lerner Publctns) Lerner Group.

Cooking the Norwegian Way. Sylvia Munsen. LC 82-259. (Easy Menu Ethnic Cookbooks Ser.). (Illus.). 48p. (J). (gr. 5 up). 1982. lib. bdg. 14.95 (0-8225-0901-6, Lerner Publctns) Lerner Group.

Cooking the Nouvelle Cuisine in America. Michele Urvater & David Liedermann. LC 79-64785. (Illus.). 480p. 1982. reprint ed. pap. 12.95 (0-89480-215-1, 452) Workman Pub.

Cooking the One-Burner Way: Gourmet Cuisine for the Backcountry Chef. Melissa Gray & Buck Tilton. LC 93-50701. (Illus.). 160p. (Orig.). 1994. pap. 11.99 (0-934802-91-2) ICS Bks.

Cooking the Polish Way. Danuta Zamojska-Hutchins. LC 84-11226. (Easy Menu Ethnic Cookbooks Ser.). (Illus.). 52p. (J). (gr. 5 up). 1984. lib. bdg. 14.95 (0-8225-0909-1, Lerner Publctns) Lerner Group.

Cooking the Punjabi Way. Aroona Reejhsinghani. 137p. 1990. 6.95 (0-318-36283-X) Asia Bk Corp.

Cooking the Russian Way. Gregory Plotkin & Rita Plotkin. (Easy Menu Ethnic Cookbooks Ser.). (Illus.). 48p. (J). (gr. 5 up). 1986. lib. bdg. 14.95 (0-8225-0915-6, Lerner Publctns) Lerner Group.

Cooking the Shore Catch. R. Marilyn Schmidt. (Illus.). 133p. 1986. pap. 8.95 (0-937996-08-4) Barnegat.

***Cooking the Sourdough Way: Tips, Stores & Recipes.** Scott E. Power. LC 94-41249. (Illus.). 1995. 9.99 (1-57034-008-0) ICS Bks.

Cooking the South American Way. Helga Parnell. (Easy Menu Ethnic Cookbooks Ser.). (Illus.). 48p. (J). (gr. 5 up). 1991. lib. bdg. 14.95 (0-8225-0925-3, Lerner Publctns) Lerner Group.

Cooking the Southern Way. Gladys M. Thrift. 1991. 16.95 (0-9631645-0-3) G Thrift Pubns.

Cooking the Spanish Way. Rebecca Christian. LC 82-4709. (Easy Menu Ethnic Cookbooks Ser.). (Illus.). 48p. (J). (gr. 5 up). 1982. lib. bdg. 14.95 (0-8225-0908-3, Lerner Publctns) Lerner Group.

***Cooking the Swiss Way.** Helga Hughes. LC 94-25397. (Easy Menu Ethnic Cookbooks Ser.). (Illus.). (J). 1995. 14.95 (0-8225-0930-X, Lerner Publctns) Lerner Group.

Cooking the Thai Way. Supenn Harrison & Judy Monroe. (Easy Menu Ethnic Cookbooks Ser.). (Illus.). 48p. (J). (gr. 5 up). 1986. lib. bdg. 14.95 (0-8225-0917-2, Lerner Publctns) Lerner Group.

Cooking the Vietnamese Way. Chi Nguyen & Judy M. Monroe. (Easy Menu Ethnic Cookbooks Ser.). (Illus.). 48p. (J). (gr. 5 up). 1985. lib. bdg. 14.95 (0-8225-0914-8, Lerner Publctns) Lerner Group.

Cooking the Vietnamese Way. Chi Nguyen. (YA). (gr. 5 up). 1993. pap. 5.95 (0-8225-9647-4, Lerner Publctns) Lerner Group.

***Cooking Through the Year.** Shirley Gill. 160p. 1994. 15.98 (0-8317-5655-1) Smithmark.

Cooking to Your Heart's Content: A Low Cholesterol Cookbook for the Ordinary Kitchen. Barbara Taylor. LC 89-34523. 130p. 1990. 20.00 (1-55728-128-9) U of Ark Pr.

Cooking Today's Beef. National Live Stock & Meat Board Staff. LC 88-700115. 1988. teacher ed, vhs 10.00 (0-88700-008-8) Natl Live Stock.

Cooking under Pressure. Lorna J. Sass. LC 89-31707. 1989. 18.95 (0-688-08814-7) Morrow.

***Cooking under the Volcanoes: Communal Kitchens in the Southern Peruvian City of Arequipa.** Roelie Lenten. (CEDLA Latin America Studies (CLAS): No. 68). 232p. 1993. pap. 23.50 (90-70280-15-9, Pub. by Thesis Pubs NE) IBD Ltd.

Cooking under Wraps: The Art of Wrapping Hors D'Oeuvres, Main Courses, & Desserts. Nicole Routhier. LC 92-26605. 1993. 27.00 (0-688-10867-9) Morrow.

Cooking up a Storm. Brookwood Guild Staff. LC 93-73243. 1993. write for info. (0-87197-390-1) Favorite Recipes.

***Cooking up the Creek: Recipes from a Rural New York Valley.** Ed. by Janet W. Bowers. (Illus.). 314p. 1994. pap. 24.95 (0-9638958-0-X) Bowers Fnd.

***Cooking up Trouble.** Pence. 1995. mass mkt. 4.50 (0-06-108200-7, Harp PBks) HarpC.

Cooking up U.S. History: Recipes & Research to Share with Children. Suzanne I. Barchers & Patricia C. Marden. 175p. 1991. pap. text ed. 20.00 (0-87287-782-5) Teacher Ideas Pr.

Cooking up World History: Multicultural Recipes & Resources. Patricia C. Marden & Suzanne I. Barchers. (Illus.). 225p. 1994. pap. text ed. 22.50 (1-56308-116-4) Teacher Ideas Pr.

Cooking What Comes Naturally. rev. ed. Nikki Goldbeck. (Illus.). 192p. 1981. reprint ed. pap. 4.95 (0-9606138-0-3) Ceres Pr.

Cooking Wild. Ken Allen. (Illus.). 200p. 1985. pap. 11.95 (0-930096-53-3) G Gannett.

Cooking with a Handful of Ingredients: Delicious Meals in the Palm of Your Hand. Agnesa Reeve & Jack Reeve. LC 91-77268. 272p. (Orig.). 1992. pap. 15.95 (0-9631401-6-7) Cimarron NM.

Cooking with All Your Faculties: Menus from Around the World. University of Washington, Faculty Auxiliary Staff. Ed. by Betty Orians & Sue Christian. (Illus.). 200p. (Orig.). 1990. pap. text ed. 12.95 (0-89716-362-1) P B Pubng.

***Cooking with Angels: More Than 125 Heavenly & Healthy Recipes.** Julie Abbinante & M. J. Smith. 250p. 1995. 12.95 (1-56561-065-2) Chronimed.

Cooking with Beer: In the Spirit of Things. Barbara L. Lacy. (Illus.). 56p. 1987. pap. 5.95 (0-9617721-0-7) Golightly Pubns.

***Cooking with Booze: Your House or Mine.** E. E. Barbee. 102p. 1995. 14.95 (0-9647146-0-4) Pleasure Foods.

Cooking with Cannabis: The Art & Science. Adam Gottlieb. 72p. 1993. reprint ed. pap. 9.95 (0-914171-55-0) Ronin Pub.

Cooking with Care: A Feast of Healthy Recipes. Bob Farentinos et al. (Illus.). 96p. 1987. pap. 7.50 (0-9619582-0-0) Amer Diabetes Denver.

***Cooking with Chef Dinosaur.** J. E. Nicks. Ed. by Mary Nicks. (Illus.). 200p. 1995. pap. 11.95 (0-9642743-6-1) Jensen Pubng.

***Cooking with Children: 15 Lessons for Children, Ages 7 & Up, Who Really Want to Learn to Cook.** Marion Cunningham. LC 95-13580. (Illus.). (J). (gr. 2 up). 1995. 18.00 (0-679-42297-8) Knopf.

Cooking with Class. El Paso Country Day School Staff. (Illus.). 466p. (Orig.). 1990. pap. 15.00 (0-9626469-0-3) El Paso Ctry Day Schl.

***Cooking with Colorado's Greatest Chefs.** Lynn Booth. (Illus.). 160p. 1995. 35.00 (1-56579-127-4) Westcliffe Pubs Inc.

Cooking with Country Music Stars. Ed. by Country Music Foundation Staff. LC 89-49642. (Illus.). 1990. reprint ed. 19.95 (0-88289-793-4) Pelican.

Cooking with Craig Claiborne & Pierre Franey. Craig Claiborne & Pierre Franey. 1985. pap. 9.95 (0-449-90130-0, Columbine) Fawcett.

Cooking with Cream--the Versatile Ingredient. Phyllis M. Letellier. LC 83-90266. (Illus.). 76p. (Orig.). 1983. pap. 4.00 (0-9611138-4-7) P M Letellier.

Cooking with Curtis Grace. Curtis Grace. LC 85-62174. (Illus.). 187p. 1985. pap. 14.00 (0-913383-05-8) McClanahan Pub.

Cooking with Daniel Boulud. Daniel Boulud. 1993. 40.00 (0-679-40409-0) Random.

Cooking with David Burke. David Burke & Carmel B. Reingold. LC 93-48909. 1995. 27.50 (0-394-58343-4) Knopf.

Cooking with Fire. Helen Brody & Patricia Morris. 100p. 1993. pap. 10.00 (0-9638885-0-1) Fairfield Hist.

Cooking with Fire & Smoke. Phillip S. Schulz. 1991. pap. 10.95 (0-671-73309-5, Fireside) S&S Trade.

Cooking with Fresh Sausage. Charles Reavis. 1989. pap. 2.95 (0-88266-530-8, Garden Way Pub) Storey Comm Inc.

Cooking with Fruit. Mary Norwak. 1960. 7.95 (0-685-20569-X) Transatl Arts.

Cooking with Fruit. R. Payne & D. Payne, Sr. 1993. pap. 7.99 (0-517-11278-7) Random Hse Value.

Cooking with Fruit: The Complete Guide to Using Fruit Throughout the Meal, the Day, the Year. Rolce Payne. 1992. 22.00 (0-517-58406-9, Crown) Crown Pub Group.

***Cooking with Fruit: The Complete Guide to Using Fruit Throughout the Meal, the Day, the Year.** Rolce R. Payne & Dorrit Speyer, Jr. LC 94-41545. 1995. write for info. (0-517-12353-3) Wings Bks.

Cooking with Gluten & Seitan. Dorothy R. Bates & Colby Wingate. LC 92-44423. 128p. 1993. pap. 7.95 (0-913990-95-7) Book Pub Co.

Cooking with Grains. Susan Slack. 128p. 1993. pap. 8.95 (1-55788-079-4, HP Books) Berkley Pub.

Cooking with Hawaiian Magic. Mae Keao & Lee Keao. LC 89-81703. (Illus.). 160p. 1990. pap. 9.95 (0-935848-77-0) Bess Pr.

Cooking with Herb Scents. Western Reserve Herb Society Staff. Ed. by Donna D. Agan. (Illus.). 350p. 1991. spiral bd. 16.95 (1-880022-00-1) WRHS.

Cooking with Herbs. Nancy Glenn. Ed. by Vernon Taylor. (Illus.). 140p. 1994. spiral bd. 9.95 (1-878816-04-7) Schildge Pub.

***Cooking with Herbs.** E. Tolley & C. Mead. 1995. 24.00 (0-517-88380-5) Random.

Cooking with Herbs. Emilie Tolley & Chris Mead. (Illus.). 1989. 40.00 (0-517-57139-0, C P Pubs) Crown Pub Group.

Cooking with Herbs & Spices. Craig Claiborne. LC 82-48224. (Illus.). 400p. 1984. pap. 20.00 (0-06-090998-6, CN 998, PL) HarpC.

Cooking with Herbs & Spices. Milo Miloradovich. 320p. 1990. pap. 6.95 (0-486-26177-8) Dover.

Cooking with Herbs Dictionary. Mary Hartman. 116p. 9.95 (0-935069-30-5) White Oak Pr.

Cooking with Honey. Joanne Barrett. 1981. pap. 2.95 (0-88266-276-7, Garden Way Pub) Storey Comm Inc.

Cooking with Honey. Judy Powers. 64p. 1984. pap. 3.49 (0-942320-12-3) Am Cooking.

Cooking with Honey: The Natural Way to Health & Better Eating. Marge Davenport. Ed. by L. B. Cady. (Illus.). (Orig.). 1991. pap. 13.55 (0-938274-05-8) Paddlewheel.

Cooking with Humor: A Unique Recipe Collection. Robin C. Benzle. LC 91-90952. 160p. 1991. pap. 15.00 (0-9629398-4-6) VanTine Pub.

Cooking with Hypertalk 2.0. Dan Knaster & Scott Knaster. 352p. 1990. disk. 39.95 (0-553-34738-1) Bantam.

Cooking with HyperTalk 2.0. Dan Winkler. 1990. disk, pap. 39.95 (0-679-79017-9) Random.

Cooking with Japanese Foods: A Guide to the Traditional Natural Foods of Japan. Jan Belleme & John Belleme. (Illus.). 220p. (Orig.). 1986. pap. 12.95 (0-936184-04-3) E W-Nat Hlth Bks.

Cooking with Japanese Foods: A Guide to the Traditional Natural Foods of Japan. John Belleme & Jan Belleme. 232p. (Orig.). 1993. pap. 13.95 (0-89529-583-0) Avery Pub.

Cooking with Jenn-Air. LC 79-54943. (Orig.). 12.95 (0-87502-072-0) Benjamin Co.

Cooking with Katherine Wise. Fisher Broadcasting Staff. Ed. by Katherine Wise. 310p. (Orig.). 1984. pap. 9.95 (0-89716-133-5) P B Pubng.

Cooking with Kay McCarty. 154p. 1983. 22.50 (0-87559-205-8); spiral bd. 12.50 (0-87559-204-X) Shalom.

Cooking with Light. Ed. by Laurie Van Valkenburgh. LC 77-71228. 221p. 1981. pap. 7.00 (0-89142-032-0) Sant Bani Ash.

Cooking with Love: Lacto-Vegetarian Recipes. Ruth D. Thompson. 270p. (Orig.). 1989. pap. 9.95 (0-937067-11-3) Insti Study Aware.

Cooking with Love & Cereal. pap. 5.95 (1-55748-077-X) Barbour & Co.

Cooking with Love Italian Style. Francis Anthony. LC 93-43045. 1994. 20.00 (0-688-12754-1) Hearst Bks.

Cooking with Marijuana. Evelyn Schmevelyn. (Illus.). 1976. per. 4.95 (0-686-25124-5) Pacific Pipeline.

Cooking with Marilyn. Marilyn Harris. LC 94-15962. (Illus.). 256p. 1994. 19.95 (1-56554-075-1) Pelican.

Cooking with Master Chefs. Julia Child. Date not set. pap. write for info. (0-679-75089-4) Random.

Cooking with Mrs. Appleyard. Louise A. Kent & Elizabeth K. Gay. LC 92-30293. 1993. 19.95 (0-87983-597-4) Keats.

Cooking with Natural Foods, Vol. II. 2nd ed. Muriel Beltz. 138p. 1990. spiral bd. 14.95 (0-912145-18-8) MMI Pr.

Cooking with "Nature's Pre-Sweeten Vegetable" Velma W. Wall. (Illus.). 142p. (Orig.). 1993. 9.95 (0-9637834-0-8) VATCO Gifts.

Cooking with Oats: Oat Bran, Oatmeal, & More. Ed. by Kim Foster & Connie Parkinson. (Country Wisdom Bulletin Ser.). 32p. 1991. 2.95 (0-88266-674-6, Storey Pub) Storey Comm Inc.

Cooking with Old Bay. Ed. by Marian Levine. (Collector's Ser.: Vol. 27). 64p. (Orig.). 1989. pap. 3.49 (0-942320-34-4) Am Cooking.

***Cooking with Olive Oil.** Diane Seed. LC 94-46990. 1995. write for info. (0-688-12788-6) Morrow.

Cooking with Parchment Paper. David DiResta. (Illus.). 176p. (Orig.). 1994. pap. 8.95 (1-55867-101-3, Nitty Gritty Ckbks) Bristol Pub Ent CA.

***Cooking with Pomiane.** Edouard De Pomiane. 1994. pap. 10.00 (0-86547-481-8, North Pt Pr) FS&G.

Cooking with Potatoes. Dorothy Parker. 1990. pap. 2.95 (0-88266-601-0, Garden Way Pub) Storey Comm Inc.

Cooking with Pride. Ed. by Bryon Predika & Jon Dehart. (Illus.). 104p. (Orig.). 1989. pap. text ed. 8.25 (0-9623939-0-8) Act One.

Cooking with Pride: Celebrating Fifty Years. Odoms Tennessee Pride Staff. LC 93-70328. 1993. 12.95 (0-87197-366-9) Favorite Recipes.

***Cooking with Prozac: From Nuts to Soup.** Robin Cohn. Ed. by Richard Courtney & Maryglenn McCombs. LC 94-61991. 150p. (Orig.). 1995. pap. 12.95 (1-886371-07-5) Eggman Pub.

Cooking with Rachel. Rachel Albert. Ed. by Laurel Ruggles. LC 89-85012. (Illus.). 328p. 1989. pap. 12.95 (0-918860-49-0) G Ohsawa.

Cooking with Regis & Kathie Lee: Quick & Easy Recipes from America's Favorite TV Personality. Regis Philbin & Kathie L. Gifford. (Illus.). 272p. 1993. 19.95 (1-56282-930-0) Hyperion.

Cooking with Regis & Kathie Lee: Quick & Easy Recipes from America's Favorite TV Personality. Regis Philbin & Kathie L. Gifford. (Illus.). 272p. 1993. pap. 9.95 (1-56282-752-9) Hyperion.

Cooking with Rice: More Than Thirty Favorite Recipes. Ed. by Kim Foster & Connie Parkinson. (Country Wisdom Bulletin Ser.). 32p. 1991. 2.95 (0-88266-675-4, Storey Pub) Storey Comm Inc.

Cooking with Sea Vegetables: A Collection of Naturally Delicious Recipes Using to the Full the Bountiful Harvest of the Oceans. Peter Bradford & Montse Bradford. (Illus.). 128p. (Orig.). 1985. pap. 9.95 (0-89281-283-4) Inner Tradit.

Cooking with Seitan: A Delicious Meat Substitute Made from Whole Grains. Barbara Jacobs & Leonard Jacobs. LC 94-342. 200p. 1994. pap. 12.95 (0-89529-599-7) Avery Pub.

Cooking with Seitan: The Delicious Natural Foods from Whole Grain. Barbara Jacobs & Leonard Jacobs. LC 85-80537. 240p. (Orig.). 1987. pap. 19.00 (0-87040-637-X) Japan Pubns USA.

Cooking with Sex in Mind: Survival for the Divorced & Single Male. Maxx Walters. (Illus.). 160p. 1982. pap. 4.95 (0-930990-02-1) Seville Pub.

Cooking with Shakespeare: Chefspearean & Pan-Cultural Cuisine. Ed. by Robert D. Bernoskie. LC 91-66176. (Illus.). 1991. pap. 18.95 (0-9628283-2-7) Orig Traveling Chef.

***Cooking with Sourdough: A Tribute to the Oregon Trail Pioneers.** Alene A. Roy. (Illus.). 1995. spiral bd. 7.95 (0-9635069-2-7) Closer Walk.

Cooking with Southern Accents: A Collection of Old & New Recipes. Mary E. Marks. (Illus.). (Orig.). 1988. pap. 10.00 (0-9621561-0-8) M E Marks.

***Cooking with Spirits.** B. Carlson. (Illus.). 176p. 1995. 5.95 (1-57166-017-8) Quixote Pr IA.

Cooking with St. Clair. Fredric DeClouet. Ed. by Will Jones. LC 78-74175. 1978. pap. 10.95 (0-9602228-0-4) Dectur Corp.

Cooking with St. Francis by the Sea. St. Francis by the Sea Staff. Ed. by Suzanne Decrow. LC 91-62054. (Illus.). 178p. (Orig.). 1992. pap. 10.00 (0-9630061-0-X) St Francis Sea.

Cooking with Stone Ground Flour. 3rd ed. Arlene Kovash & Marcie Anderson. (Illus.). 48p. 1991. 2.95 (0-9605394-1-7) A & M Kovash.

Cooking with Strawberries: Delicious Ways to Eat Strawberries. Margaret Clark & Virginia Clark. LC 94-37121. (Illus.). 112p. (Orig.). 1994. pap. text ed. 10.95 (1-879415-26-7) Mtn n Air Bks.

Cooking with Sun-Dried Tomatoes. Lois Dribin et al. LC 90-13999. (Illus.). 160p. 1990. pap. 9.95 (1-55561-033-1) Fisher Bks.

Cooking with the Bad Guys: Recipes from the World's Most Notorious Kitchens. Don Abel. (Illus.). 128p. 1995. 13.95 (0-87951-564-3) Overlook Pr.

Cooking with the Chicken Breast: Delicious Main Dishes Starring the Delectable Skinless & Boneless White Meat. Stephen M. Lehrer. LC 89-91671. (Illus.). 224p. (Orig.). 1990. pap. 11.95 (0-9623104-8-4) Madeira-Hudson Pub.

Cooking with the Danes. 5th ed. Astrid Slebsager. 78p. (Orig.). (DAN.). 1991. text ed. 25.00 (87-14-28592-4, D-760) Vanous.

***Cooking with the Dead: Recipes & Stories from Fans on the Road.** Zipern. 1995. pap. 7.99 (0-312-95483-2) St Martin.

***Cooking with the Horse & Buggy People.** 255p. 1994. 7.95 (0-9642548-0-8) Carlisle Press.

Cooking with the Master Chefs. Julia Child. (Illus.). 1993. 30.00 (0-679-42993-X) Knopf.

Cooking with the Right Side of the Brain: Creative Vegetarian Cooking. Vicki R. Chelf. LC 89-17807. (Illus.). 296p. 1991. pap. 16.95 (0-89529-431-1) Avery Pub.

Cooking with the Seasons. Lesa Heebner. (Illus.). 156p. (Orig.). 1993. pap. 11.95 (1-55850-274-2) Adams Pubng.

Cooking with the Stars: Healthy, Delicious Recipes from Celebrities' Own Kitchens. Ed. by Jennifer Douglas. (Illus.). 224p. (Orig.). 1993. pap. 12.95 (0-89329-031-9) Ctr Sci Public.

Cooking with the Sun: How to Make & Use Solar Cookers. rev. ed. Beth Halacy & Dan Halacy. Orig. Title: Solar Cookery Book. (Illus.). 116p. (YA). (gr. 7 up). 1992. reprint ed. pap. 7.95 (0-9629069-2-1) Morn Sun Pr.

***Cooking with Things That Go Moo.** B. Carlson. (Illus.). 176p. 1994. 5.95 (1-57166-016-X) Quixote Pr IA.

***Cooking with Things That Go Splash.** B. Carlson. (Illus.). 176p. 1995. 5.95 (1-57166-015-1) Quixote Pr IA.

C

An Asterisk (*) at the beginning of an entry indicates that the title is appearing in BIP for the first time.

C

An Asterisk (*) at the beginning of an entry indicates that the title is appearing in BIP for the first time.

Cooling Water Discharges from Coal Fired Power Plants: Water Pollution Problems: Part of an IAWPRC International Conference on Coal Fired Power Plants & the Aquatic Environment, 16-18 August 1982, Copenhagen, Vol. 15-10. Ed. by S. H. Jenkins & P. Schjodtz Hansen. LC 83-19445. (Illus.). 276p. 1983. pap. 44.00 (*0-08-031025-7*, Pergamon Pr) Elsevier.

***Cooling Water Treatment Manual, TPC 1.** (Illus.). 1990. 41.00 (*0-915567-69-5*) NACE Intl.

Cooling with Ventilation. Subrato Chandra et al. (Illus.). 88p. 1986. pap. 4.25 (*0-16-006550-X*, S/N 061-000-00688-5) USGPO.

Coolings Flows in Clusters & Galaxies. Ed. by Andrew C. Fabian. (C). 1988. lib. bdg. 125.50 (*90-277-2707-4*) Kluwer Ac.

***Coolmore.** William L. Everett. LC 95-90243. 382p. 1995. 23.95 (*0-9646745-0-5*) E&E Pubs.

CoolPose: The Dilemmas of Black Manhood in America. Richard Majors & Janet M. Billson. 132p. 1992. text ed. 19.95 (*0-669-24523-2*) Free Pr.

Coomaraswamy. Coomaraswamy. Ed. by Roger Lipsey. Incl. Vol. 2. Selected Papers: Metaphysics. LC 76-41158. 1977. text ed. 75.00 (*0-691-09932-4*); LC 76-41158. (Bollingen Ser.: No. 89). (Illus.). 1977. write for info. (*0-318-55352-X*) Princeton U Pr.

Coomaraswamy, Vol. 3: His Life & Work. Ananda K. Coomaraswamy. Ed. by Roger Lipsey. LC 76-41158. (Bollingen Ser.: No. 89). 331p. reprint ed. pap. 94.40 (*0-7837-0234-5*, 2040542) Bks Demand.

Coomassie & Magdala: The Story of Two British Campaigns in Africa. Henry M. Stanley. LC 78-157355. (Select Bibliographies Reprint Ser.). (Illus.). 1977. reprint ed. 45.95 (*0-8369-5816-0*) Ayer.

Coombs Site, 3 pts. in 2 vols. Robert H. Lister et al. (Glen Canyon Ser.). reprint ed. Pts. I-II. 65.00 (*0-404-60720-9*); reprint ed. Pt. III. 32.50 (*0-404-60721-7*) AMS Pr.

Coombs Site, 3 pts. in 2 vols., Set. Robert H. Lister et al. (Glen Canyon Ser.). reprint ed. 97.50 (*0-404-60641-5*) AMS Pr.

Coon: The Koon-Coons Families of Eastern N.Y. W. S. Coons. (Illus.). 502p. 1991. reprint ed. lib. bdg. 88.50 (*0-8328-2126-8*); reprint ed. pap. 78.50 (*0-685-50981-8*) Higginson Bk Co.

Coon Creek. Jim McCrary. 20p. (Orig.). 1972. ring bd. 1.00 (*0-685-30031-5*) Cottonwood KS.

Coon Holler. abr. ed. J. H. Cheshire. 216p. 1994. pap. 9.95 (*1-56901-214-8*) NW Pub.

Coon Mountain Controversies: Meteor Crater & the Development of Impact Theory. William G. Hoyt. LC 87-5009. (Illus.). 442p. 1987. 50.00 (*0-8165-0968-9*) U of Ariz Pr.

Coon Tree Summer: Merry Brook Farm Story. Mary M. Landis. (J). (gr. 5 up). 1978. 9.05 (*0-686-22987-8*) Rod & Staff.

***Coonridge Digest.** Freida M. Crump. Ed. by Robert L. Crowe. 96p. (Orig.). 1994. pap. 9.95 (*0-9644681-0-7*) Consortium IL.

Coonskin Boys: Men & Mustangs of the 167th Fighter Squadron - West Virginia Air National Guard. Jack H. Smith. LC 87-90431. (Illus.). 54p. 1987. pap. 8.95 (*0-933126-86-7*) Pictorial Hist.

Coop Himmelblau: Architectural Monograph, No. 27. Academy Editions Staff. 1993. 50.00 (*1-85490-161-3*, Academy Edits); pap. 38.00 (*1-85490-162-1*, Academy Edits) St Martin.

Cooper. Linda Turner. (Silhouette Intimate Moments Ser.). 1994. mass mkt. 3.50 (*0-373-07553-7*, 5-07553-6) Silhouette.

Cooper. Hilary Masters. 1993. reprint ed. pap. text ed. 11.00 (*0-941038-08-4*) Coyne & Chenoweth.

Cooper & His Trade. Kenneth Kilby. LC 89-14518. (Illus.). 192p. 1989. reprint ed. pap. 19.95 (*0-941936-16-3*) Linden Pub Fresno.

Cooper-Clayton Method to Stop Smoking: New Hope for Heavy Smokers. Thomas M. Cooper & Richard R. Clayton. 160p. (Orig.). 1988. pap. 10.00 (*0-685-44323-X*) SBC SBC.

Cooper Henderson & the Open Road. Charles Lane. 128p. 1990. 100.00 (*0-85131-392-2*, Pub. by J A Allen & Co UK) St Mut.

Cooper in Germany. Preston A. Barba. 1973. 59.95 (*0-87968-944-7*) Gordon Pr.

Cooper-Juan Bautista Rogers Cooper. John Woolfenden & Amelie Elkinton. (Illus.). (Orig.). 1983. pap. 7.95 (*0-910286-95-7*) Boxwood.

Cooper, Lafayette & the French National Budget. James F. Beard. 1985. reprint ed. pap. 4.50 (*0-912296-74-7*, U Pr of Va) Am Antiquarian.

Cooper Street. P. D. Jordan. 147p. (Orig.). (YA). (gr. 5-12). 1989. pap. 4.25 (*0-929885-21-X*) Haypenny Pr.

Cooperacion Financiera y Empresarial Entre America Latina y el Japon. 1990. write for info. (*0-318-69856-0*) IADB.

Cooperate with Others Module, Connections: School & Work Transitions - Work Skills-Work Maturity Skills. National Center for Research in Vocational Education Staff. 1987. write for info. (*0-318-67161-1*, SP100CB13) Ctr Educ Trng Employ.

Cooperating. Mary A. McElmurry. 64p. (J). (gr. 3-8). 1985. student ed 8.95 (*0-86653-334-6*, GA 680) Good Apple.

***Cooperating Expert Systems in Mechanical Design.** John A. Brandon & Guo Q. Huang. (Research Studies Advanced Software). 1993. text ed. 89.95 (*0-471-94157-3*) Wiley.

Cooperating for Peace: The Global Agenda for the 1990s & Beyond. Gareth Evans. 160p. 1994. pap. 17.95 (*1-86373-623-9*, Pub. by Allen Unwin AT) Paul & Co Pubs.

***Cooperating Heterogeneous Systems.** David G. Schwartz. (International Series in Engineering & Computer Science, Natural Language Processing & Machine Translation). 224p. (C). 1994. lib. bdg. 92.00 (*0-7923-9535-2*) Kluwer Ac.

Cooperating Teacher: A Practical Approach for the Supervision of Student Teachers. Pamela M. Balch & Patrick E. Balch. LC 87-10585. 196p. (Orig.). (C). 1987. lib. bdg. 43.50 (*0-8191-6424-0*); pap. text ed. 21.00 (*0-8191-6425-9*) U Pr of Amer.

Cooperation. (Values Library). (YA). (gr. 7-12). 1991. lib. bdg. 14.95 (*0-8239-1232-9*) Rosen Group.

Cooperation. Janet Reihecky. LC 89-48284. (Values to Live By Ser.). (Illus.). 32p. (ENG & SPA.). (J). (ps-2). 1990. lib. bdg. 21.36 (*0-89565-565-9*) Childs World.

***Cooperation.** Janet Riehecky. LC 89-48284. (Values to Live By Ser.). (Illus.). 32p. (ENG & SPA.). (J). (ps-2). 1990. lib. bdg. 14.95 (*0-89565-947-6*) Childs World.

Cooperation, Reading Level 2. Goley. (Learn the Value Ser.: Set II). (Illus.). 32p. (J). (gr. 1-4). 1989. lib. bdg. 15.94 (*0-86592-390-6*) Rourke Corp.

Cooperation among Nations: Europe, America & Non-Tariff Barriers to Trade. Joseph M. Grieco. LC 89-46166. (Cornell Studies in Political Economy). (Illus.). 272p. 1990. pap. 14.95 (*0-8014-9699-3*) Cornell U Pr.

Cooperation among Organizations: The Potential of Computer Supported Cooperative Work. Ed. by R. J. Power. (Research Reports ESPRIT, Project 688, AMICE: Vol. 1). vii, 140p. 1993. pap. 29.00 (*0-387-56263-X*) Spr-Verlag.

Cooperation & Coercion as Methods of Social Change. Vincent D. Nicholson. (C). 1934. pap. 3.00 (*0-87574-001-4*) Pendle Hill.

Cooperation & Competition: An Experimental Study in Motivation. Julius B. Maller. LC 74-177049. (Columbia University. Teachers College. Contributions to Education Ser.: No. 384). reprint ed. 37.50 (*0-404-55384-2*) AMS Pr.

Cooperation & Competition among Primitive Peoples. enl. ed. Margaret Mead. 13.25 (*0-8446-2570-1*) Peter Smith.

Cooperation & Conflict: The Public & Private Sectors in Higher Education. John W. Gardner et al. 72p. 1985. 12.00 (*0-318-21458-X*) Assn Gov Bds.

***Cooperation & Conflict in General Evolutionary Processes.** Ed. by John L. Casti & Anders Karlqvist. 1994. text ed. 69.95 (*0-471-59487-3*) Wiley.

Cooperation & Conflict in Occupational Safety & Health: A Multination Study of the Automotive Industry. Richard E. Wokutch. LC 89-77106. 336p. 1990. text ed. 55.00 (*0-275-93530-2*, C3530, Praeger Pubs) Greenwood.

Cooperation & Conflict in South Asia. Partha S. Ghosh. 1989. 29.00 (*0-945921-07-1*) South Asia Pubns.

Cooperation & Discord in U. S. - Soviet Arms Control. Steve Weber. (Illus.). 349p. 1993. text ed. 47.50 (*0-691-07837-8*); pap. text ed. 16.95 (*0-691-02766-8*) Princeton U Pr.

Cooperation & Governance in International Trade. Beth V. Yarborough. (C). 1992. 35.00 (*0-691-04263-2*) Princeton U Pr.

Cooperation & Helping Behavior: Theories & Research. Ed. by Valerian J. Derlega & Janusz Grzelak. LC 81-19130. 1981. text ed. 60.00 (*0-12-210820-5*) Acad Pr.

***Cooperation & Productivity for Growth.** Asian Productivity Organization Staff. (Monograph Ser.: No. 14). (Illus.). 112p. 1993. pap. text ed. 7.50 (*92-833-1814-5*, 318145, Pub. by Asian Productvty Org JA) Qual Resc.

Cooperation & Prosocial Behaviour. Ed. by Robert A. Hinde & Jo Groebel. (Illus.). 415p. (C). 1991. 84.95 (*0-521-39110-5*); pap. 34.95 (*0-521-39999-8*) Cambridge U Pr.

Cooperation & the Working Class: Theoretical Contributions, 1827-1834. LC 72-2521. (British Labour Struggles Before 1850 Ser.). 1974. 20.95 (*0-405-04414-3*) Ayer.

Cooperation at Work: The Mondragon Experience. Keith Bradley & Alan Gelb. vii, 102p. (Orig.). 1983. 57.95 (*0-435-83109-7*); pap. 22.95 (*0-435-83110-0*) Ashgate Pub Co.

Cooperation Between Higher Education & Industry: Proceedings from the Seminar in Uppsala, April 24-25, 1986. Ed. by Allan Klingstrom. 145p. (Orig.). 1987. pap. text ed. 45.00x (*91-506-0604-2*, Pub. by Almqv & Wiksell SW) Coronet Bks.

Cooperation Between the Faculty of the Campus Elementary Training School & the Other Departments of Teachers Colleges & Normal Schools. Mary I. Cole. LC 76-176658. (Columbia University. Teachers College. Contributions to Education Ser.: No. 746). reprint ed. 37.50 (*0-404-55746-5*) AMS Pr.

Cooperation Between the Sexes: Writings on Women & Men, Love & Marriage, & Sexuality. abr. ed. Alfred Adler. Ed. by Heinz L. Ansbacher & Rowena R. Ansbacher. 192p. 1982. reprint ed. pap. 7.95 (*0-393-30019-6*) Norton.

Cooperation Between Theologians & the Ecclesiastical Magisterium: A Report of the Joint Committee of the Canon Law Society of America & the Catholic Theological Society of America. Ed. by Leo J. O'Donovan. 200p. (Orig.). 1982. pap. 5.00 (*0-943616-12-3*) Canon Law Soc.

Cooperation Between Types of Libraries, 1940-1968: An Annotated Bibliography. LC 71-140212. 167p. reprint ed. pap. 47.60 (*0-317-26286-6*, 2024260) Bks Demand.

***Cooperation Booklet.** (Teacher Aids Ser.). (Illus.). 48p. (J). 1995. teacher ed, pap. 4.95 (*0-614-06824-X*, WPH 0010) Totline Bks.

Cooperation Financiere Internationale. Bd. with Distortion des Echanges en Europe Occidentale. (Economies et Societes Series R: No. 7). 1962. Set pap. 19.00 (*0-8115-0787-4*) Periodicals Srv.

Cooperation in a World Without Enemies: Solving the Public Goods Problem in International Relations. Richard Rosecrance. (CISA Working Paper Ser.: No. 2). 54p. Date not set. 10.00 (*0-86682-092-2*) Ctr Intl Relations.

Cooperation in Academic Negotiations: A Guide to Mutual Gains Bargaining. Robert Birnbaum et al. 70p. 1985. pap. 7.00 (*0-88111-006-X*) Inst Mgmt & Labor.

Cooperation in Education: Based on the Proceedings of the First International Conference on Cooperation in Education, Tel-Aviv, Israel. Ed. by Shlomo Sharan et al. LC 80-20192. (Illus.). 420p. (Orig.). 1980. pap. text ed. 14.95 (*0-8425-1836-3*) BYU Scholarly.

Cooperation in Industrial Muti-Agent Systems. N. Jennings. (Series in Computer Science). 188p. 1994. text ed. 48.00 (*981-02-1652-1*) World Scientific Pub.

Cooperation in Library Service to Children. Esther R. Dyer. LC 77-28190. 160p. reprint ed. pap. 45.60 (*0-317-52026-1*, 2027491) Bks Demand.

Cooperation in New England. Edward W. Bemis. LC 73-119926. (Select Bibliographies Reprint Ser.). 1977. 18.95 (*0-8369-5369-X*) Ayer.

Cooperation in the Baltic Sea Region. Ed. by Pertti Joenniemi. LC 92-43745. 175p. 1993. 49.50 (*0-8448-1731-7*, Crane Russak) Taylor & Francis.

Cooperation in the Classroom: Students & Teachers Together. 2nd ed. James S. Cangelosi. 80p. 1990. 9.95 (*0-8106-3072-9*) NEA.

***Cooperation in the Multi-Ethnic Classroom: The Impact of Cooperative Group Work on Social Relationships in Middle Schools.** Helen Cowie et al. 144p. 1994. pap. 27.00x (*1-85346-284-5*, Pub. by D Fulton UK) Taylor & Francis.

Cooperation, Social Responsibility & Other Skills: Using the Four Conditions of Self-Esteem in Elementary & Middle Schools. Reynold Bean. LC 92-488. 1992. write for info. (*1-56071-069-1*) ETR Assocs.

Cooperation to Competition: English Perspective & Policy on Anglo-Dutch Economic Relations During the Reign of James I. Joel D. Benson. LC 89-13034. (American University Studies: History: Ser. IX, Vol. 81). 272p. 1990. text ed. 49.95 (*0-8204-1147-7*) P Lang Pubs.

Cooperation under Anarchy. Ed. by Kenneth A. Oye. LC 85-42936. 330p. 1985. 42.50 (*0-691-07695-2*); pap. 13.95 (*0-691-02240-2*) Princeton U Pr.

***Cooperation under Fire: Anglo-German Restraint During World War II.** Jeffrey W. Legro. LC 94-35482. (Studies in Security Affairs). 272p. 1995. 35.00x (*0-8014-2938-2*) Cornell U Pr.

Cooperation under the Security Dilemma. Robert Jervis. (CISA Working Paper Ser.: No. 4). 71p. (Orig.). Date not set. pap. 10.00 (*0-86682-003-5*) Ctr Intl Relations.

Cooperative Adoption: A Handbook. Mary J. Rillera & Sharon Kaplan. 158p. 1985. pap. 14.95 (*0-941770-03-6*) Triadoption Lib.

Cooperative Adoption: A Handbook. 2nd ed. Mary J. Rillera & Sharon Kaplan. 158p. 1991. pap. 14.95 (*0-685-54343-9*) Pure CA.

Cooperative Africana Microform Project: CAMP Catalog, 1985 Cumulative. 642p. 1985. 45.50 (*0-932486-32-0*) Ctr Res Lib.

Cooperative & Commune: Group Farming in the Economic Development of Agriculture. Ed. by Peter Dorner. LC 76-53651. 408p. 1977. 37.50 (*0-299-07380-7*) U of Wis Pr.

***Cooperative & Humble.** Ellen Larson. Ed. by Debbie Bible. (Value Builders Ser.). (J). 1995. 7.95 (*0-7814-5089-6*, 09563) Cook.

Cooperative Attack on Illiteracy: Transcript of Presentations Given at a Conference. Ed. by Sally M. Corngold & Monika Goodwin. (Illus.). (Orig.). 1990. lib. bdg. 18.00 (*0-943599-13-X*) OEPF.

Cooperative Bibliography: An Annotated Guide to Works in English on Cooperatives & Cooperation. Patricia M. Hill et al. LC 81-71526. 208p. (Orig.). 1982. pap. 15.00 (*0-942288-00-9*) U WI Ctr Coop.

Cooperative Breeding in Birds: Long Term Studies of Ecology & Behaviour. P. B. Stacey & W. D. Koenig. (Illus.). 500p. (C). 1990. 99.95 (*0-521-37298-4*); pap. 44.95 (*0-521-37890-7*) Cambridge U Pr.

Cooperative Cataloging: Past, Present & Future. Intro. by Barry B. Baker. LC 93-44337. (Cataloging & Classification Quarterly Ser.). (Illus.). 281p. 1994. lib. bdg. 49.95 (*1-56024-582-4*) Haworth Pr.

Cooperative Classroom: Social & Academic Activities. Jacqueline Rhoades & Margaret E. McCabe. 151p. (Orig.). 1992. pap. 19.95 (*1-879639-16-5*) Natl Educ Serv.

Cooperative Classroom Learner: A Teacher's Resource Book. Carolyn Kessler. 272p. (C). 1991. pap. text ed. write for info. (*0-13-173618-3*) P-H.

Cooperative Collective Management: The Conspectus Approach. Ed. by Georgine N. Olson & Barbara Allen. LC 94-20036. 1994. write for info. (*1-55570-200-7*) Neal-Schuman.

Cooperative Communities: Plans & Descriptions, 1825-1847. LC 72-2522. (British Labour Struggles Before 1850 Ser.). 1974. reprint ed. 28.95 (*0-405-04415-1*) Ayer.

***Cooperative Computer-Aided Authoring & Learning: A Systems Approach.** Ed. by Max Muhlhauser. 351p. (C). 1994. lib. bdg. 95.00 (*0-7923-9527-1*) Kluwer Ac.

Cooperative Consumer Credit. Morris R. Neifeld. Ed. by Stuart Bruchey & Vincent P. Carosso. LC 78-18972. (Small Business Enterprise in America Ser.). (Illus.). 1979. reprint ed. lib. bdg. 19.95 (*0-405-11475-3*) Ayer.

Cooperative-Credit Union Dictionary & Reference. Jack McLanahan & Connie McLanahan. LC 90-80911. 416p. (Orig.). 1990. 23.50 (*0-9625894-0-3*); pap. 14.50 (*0-9625894-1-1*) Coop Alumni Assn.

Cooperative Development. Julian Edge. 1994. pap. text ed. 14.95 (*0-582-06465-1*) Longman.

Cooperative Discipline Handbook. Linda Albert. (Cooperative Discipline Ser.). 1990. teacher ed 14.95 (*0-88671-362-5*, 4002) Am Guidance.

Cooperative Discipline Leaders Guide. Linda Albert. (Cooperative Discipline Ser.). 1990. teacher ed 34.95 (*0-88671-363-3*, 4001) Am Guidance.

Cooperative Edge: The Internal Politics of International Cartels. Debora L. Spar. LC 93-34801. (Cornell Studies in Political Economy). 288p. 1994. 29.95 (*0-8014-2658-8*) Cornell U Pr.

Cooperative Education. (National Teacher Examination Ser.: NT-52). 23.95 (*0-8373-8472-9*, NT-52) Nat Learn.

Cooperative Education. Jack T. Humbert & Carl A. Woloszyk. 66p. 1983. 5.75 (*0-318-22066-0*, IN253) Ctr Educ Trng Employ.

Cooperative Education: Vocational, Occupational Career. Ronald W. Stadt & Bill Gooch. LC 75-36971. 1977. write for info. (*0-672-97110-0*) Macmillan.

Cooperative Education Across the Disciplines: A Faculty Perspective. Ed. by Patricia T. Van der Vorm & Nancy Jones. 96p. (Orig.). 1985. lib. bdg. 41.50 (*0-8191-4627-7*); pap. text ed. 15.00 (*0-8191-4628-5*) U Pr of Amer.

Cooperative Education Handbook. Michael Pierson & Stephen Springer. 74p. 1990. pap. 17.95 (*0-945483-02-3*) E Bowers Pub.

Cooperative Education in a New Era: Understanding & Strengthening the Links Between College & the Workplace. Kenneth G. Ryder & James W. Wilson. LC 87-45500. (Higher Education Ser.). 363p. 1987. 46.95x (*1-55542-072-9*) Jossey-Bass.

Cooperative Education in Community Colleges: A Sourcebook for Occupational & General Education. Barry Heermann. LC 73-9072. (Jossey-Bass Higher Education Ser.). 235p. reprint ed. pap. 67.00 (*0-317-20791-1*, 2023877) Bks Demand.

Cooperative Education Student Handbook. Steven H. Eichmeier. 124p. 1989. spiral bd. 13.20 (*0-8403-5070-8*) Kendall-Hunt.

Cooperative Education Student Journal. Melinda J. Portlock. 48p. 1993. spiral bd. 12.95 (*0-8403-8790-3*) Kendall-Hunt.

Cooperative Effects in Optics: Superradiance & Phase Transitions. A. V. Andreev et al. (Malvern Physics Ser.). (Illus.). 470p. 1993. 124.50 (*0-7503-0219-4*) IOP Pub.

Cooperative Extension Service: Paradoxical Servant. P. Miller. LC 73-8308. (Landmark Ser.: No. 2). 1973. pap. text ed. 2.00 (*0-87060-060-5*, LNH 2) Syracuse U Cont Ed.

Cooperative Federalism in Employment Security: The Interstate Conference. David G. Williams. LC 74-620188. 1974. pap. 5.00 (*0-87736-323-4*) U of Mich Inst Labor.

Cooperative Grouping for Interactive Learning: Students, Teachers, & Administrators. Lawrence Lyman & Harvey C. Foyle. 96p. 1990. 11.95 (*0-8106-1842-7*) NEA.

Cooperative Healing: The Curative Properties of Human Radiations. L. E. Eeman. (Alternative Energy & Medicine Ser.). 1991. lib. bdg. 79.95 (*0-8490-4259-3*) Gordon Pr.

Cooperative Home Care Associates: A Status Report. Rick Surpin. 21p. 1987. pap. text ed. 5.00 (*0-88156-060-X*) Comm Serv Soc NY.

Cooperative Housing: Law & Practice-Forms, 4 vols. Patrick J. Rohan & Melvin A. Reskin. (Real Estate Transactions Ser.). 1967. Updates. ring bd. write for info. (*0-8205-1239-7*) Bender.

Cooperative Intelligent Robotics in Space, Vol. 1387. W. E. Stoney & R. J. De Figueiredo. 1991. 62.00 (*0-8194-0454-3*) SPIE.

Cooperative Intelligent Robotics in Space II. Ed. by W. E. Stoney. 1992. 70.00 (*0-8194-0749-6*, 1612) SPIE.

Cooperative Interfaces to Information Systems. Leonard Bolc. Ed. by Matthias Jarke. (Topics in Information Systems Ser.). (Illus.). 400p. 1986. 69.00 (*0-387-16599-1*) Spr-Verlag.

Cooperative Land Settlements in Israel & Their Relevance to African Countries. Michael Frank. 180p. 1968. lib. bdg. 36.50 (*0-685-43628-4*, Pub. by J C B Mohr GW) Coronet Bks.

Cooperative Language Arts. Murray Suid. (Illus.). 128p. (J). (gr. 2-6). 1993. 12.95 (*1-878279-51-3*) Monday Morning Bks.

Cooperative Learing in Social Studies: Making it Work in the Social Studies Classroom. Robert J. Stahl. 1992. pap. 32.00 (*0-201-81786-1*) Addison-Wesley.

Cooperative Learning. Eileen V. Hilke. LC 90-60220. (Fastback Ser.: No. 299). 40p. (Orig.). (C). 1990. pap. 1.25 (*0-87367-299-2*) Phi Delta Kappa.

Cooperative Learning. P. H. Vedder. (Selecta Reeks Ser.: Vol. 38). viii, 136p. 1985. 19.00 (*90-6472-063-0*, Pub. by Swets Pub Serv NE) Taylor & Francis.

Cooperative Learning. rev. ed. Spencer Kagan. (Illus.). 561p. 1992. pap. text ed. 29.00 (*1-879097-10-9*) Kagan Cooperative.

Cooperative Learning: A Classroom Guide. Arlene Sego. 32p. (C). 1991. pap. text ed. 4.95 (*0-940017-17-2*) Info Tec OH.

Cooperative Learning: A Guide to Research. Ed. by Samuel Totten et al. LC 90-28902. (Bibliographies in Contemporary Education Ser.: Vol. 12). 400p. 1992. 48.00 (*0-8240-7222-7*, 674) Garland.

C

An Asterisk (*) at the beginning of an entry indicates that the title is appearing in BIP for the first time.

C

An Asterisk (*) at the beginning of an entry indicates that the title is appearing in BIP for the first time.

1613

***Coordinated Science 2.** Peter Wilding et al. (Cambridge Coordinated Science Ser.). (Illus.). 344p. (C). 1995. 25.95 (*0-521-48116-3*) Cambridge U Pr.

Coordinated Service Delivery Systems for the Elderly: New Approaches for Care & Referral in New York State. Ed. by Ruth Bennett et al. LC 83-13041. (Advanced Models & Practice in Aged Care Ser.: No. 2). 198p. 1984. text ed. 39.95 (*0-86656-157-9*) Haworth Pr.

Coordinated Urban Economic Development: A Case Study Analysis. Lawrence Malone. Ed. by Juyne Linger. 269p. (Orig.). 1978. pap. 17.50 (*0-317-04920-8*) Natl Coun Econ Dev.

Coordinates: Placing Science Fiction & Fantasy. Ed. by George E. Slusser et al. LC 82-19469. (Alternatives Ser.). 264p. 1983. 19.95 (*0-8093-1105-4*) S Ill U Pr.

Coordinates in Geodesy. S. Heitz. (Illus.). xii, 255p. 1988. pap. 42.00 (*0-387-50088-X*) Spr-Verlag.

Coordinates of Anglo-American Romanticism: Wesley, Edwards, Carlyle, & Emerson. Richard E. Brantley. LC 92-22954. 219p. 1993. 29.95 (*0-8130-1169-8*) U Press Fla.

***Coordinating Auditory Information.** Jean G. DeGaetano. 75p. 1994. pap. text ed. 22.00 (*1-886143-13-7*) Grt Ideas Tching.

Coordinating Child Sexual Abuse Services in Rural Communities. Barry Trute et al. 240p. (C). 1994. 45.00 (*0-8020-2999-X*); pap. 18.95 (*0-8020-7450-2*) U of Toronto Pr.

Coordinating Community Care: Organising Multidisciplinary Teams & Care Management in Community Health & Social Services. John Vretveit. LC 92-46225. 1993. 79.00 (*0-335-19048-0*, Open Univ Pr); pap. 36.00 (*0-335-19047-2*, Open Univ Pr) Taylor & Francis.

Coordinating Cooperative Collection Development: A National Perspective. Wilson Luquire. LC 85-24847. (Resource Sharing & Information Networks Ser.: Vol. 2, Nos. 3-4). 253p. 1986. text ed. 49.95 (*0-86656-543-4*) Haworth Pr.

Coordinating Observers for Niger's 1993 Elections. National Democratic Institute for International Affairs Staff. 170p. (ENG & FRE.). 1993. pap. 10.95 (*1-880134-22-5*) Natl Demo Inst.

Coordinating Plans of Autonomous Agents. F. Von Martial. LC 92-18969. (Lecture Notes in Artificial Intelligence Ser.: Vol. 610). xii, 246p. 1992. pap. 47.00 (*0-387-55615-X*) Spr-Verlag.

Coordinating Prenatal Care. Ian T. Hill & Janine Breyel. Ed. by Karen Glass. (Strategies for Improving State Perinatal Programs Ser.). 95p. (Orig.). 1989. pap. text ed. 15.00 (*1-55877-058-5*) Natl Governor.

Coordinating Rural Transit: Stretching State Resources for Better Service. Michael J. Greene. (Publication Ser.: No. C84). 52p. reprint ed. pap. 25.00 (*0-7837-2660-0*, 2043020) Bks Demand.

***Coordinating Stabilization & Structural Reform: Proceedings of the Seminar Coordination of Structural Reform & Macroeconomic Stabilization, Washington, D. C., June 17-26, 1993.** Ed. by Richard C. Barth et al. 1994. write for info. (*0-615-00126-2*) Intl Monetary.

Coordinating the Organization of Library Services in Metropolitan Milwaukee. Ernest R. Alexander & Lynne B. Judd. (Publications in Architecture & Urban Planning: No. R83-1). (Illus.). 97p. 1983. 4.00 (*0-938744-24-0*) U of Wis Ctr Arch-Urban.

Coordinating Total Audit Coverage: Trends & Practices. Leonard E. Berry & Richard Holman. 112p. 1984. pap. text ed. 33.00 (*0-89413-110-9*, 523) Inst Inter Aud.

Coordinating User Interfaces for Consistency. Ed. by Jakob Nielsen. 144p. 1989. text ed. 43.00 (*0-12-518400-X*) Acad Pr.

***Coordination among Schools, Families & Communities: Prospects for Educational Reform.** Ed. by James G. Cibulka & William J. Kritek. LC 95-8929. (Educational Leadership Ser.). 1996. write for info. (*0-7914-2857-5*); pap. write for info. (*0-7914-2858-3*) State U NY Pr.

Coordination & Child Protection: A Review of the Literature. C. Hallett & E. Birchall. 368p. 1992. 65.00 (*0-11-494165-3*, HM41653, Pub. by HMSO UK) UNIPUB.

***Coordination & Information: Historical Perspectives on the Organization of Enterprise.** Ed. by Naomi R. Lamoreaux & Daniel M. Raff. LC 94-41674. 1995. pap. text ed. 22.50 (*0-226-46821-6*) U Ch Pr.

***Coordination & Information: Historical Perspectives on the Organization of Enterprise.** Ed. by Naomi R. Lamoreaux & Daniel M. Raff. LC 94-41674. (National Bureau of Economic Research Conference Report Ser.). 1995. lib. bdg. 68.00 (*0-226-46820-8*) U Ch Pr.

Coordination & Regulation of Movements. N. Bernstein. LC 66-25078. 1967. 88.00 (*0-08-011940-9*, Pub. by Pergamon Repr UK) Franklin.

***Coordination Chemistry.** Contrib by N. W. Alcock. LC 94-47046. (Structure & Bonding Ser.: Vol. 82). 1995. write for info. (*0-387-58761-6*) Spr-Verlag.

Coordination Chemistry, Vol. 9. Ed. by M. E. Vol'pin. (Soviet Scientific Reviews Ser.: Section B, Chemistry). 542p. 1987. text ed. 295.00 (*3-7186-0223-7*) Gordon & Breach.

Coordination Chemistry, Vols. 1-2. Ed. by Arthur E. Martell. LC 74-151255. (ACS Monograph: No. 168 & 174). Vol. 1 1971. 49.95 (*0-8412-0275-3*); Vol. 2 1978. 89.95 (*0-8412-0292-3*) Am Chemical.

***Coordination Chemistry: A Century of Progress : Developed from a Symposium Sponsored by the Division of the History of Chemistry, Chemical Education, Inc., at the 205th National Meeting of American Chemical Society, Denver, Colorado, March 28-April 2, 1993.** Ed. by George B. Kauffman. LC 94-34445. (Symposium Ser.: No. 565). (Illus.). 480p. 1994. 99.95 (*0-8412-2950-3*) Am Chemical.

***Coordination Chemistry: A Century of Progress : Developed from a Symposium Sponsored by the Division of the History of Chemistry, Chemical Education, Inc., at the 205th National Meeting of American Chemical Society, Denver, Colorado, March 28-April 2, 1993.** Ed. by George B. Kauffman. LC 94-34445. (ACS Symposium Ser.: No. 565). 1994. pap. 59.95 (*0-8412-2958-9*) Am Chemical.

Coordination Chemistry: Twentieth International Conference on Coordination Chemistry, Calcutta, India, 10-14 Dec. 1979, Proceedings, Vol. 20. D. Banerjea. LC 80-41163. 286p. 1980. 122.00 (*0-08-023942-0*, Pub. by Pergamon Repr UK) Franklin.

Coordination Chemistry Fourteen: Plenary Lecture 14th International Conference Coordination Chemistry, Toronto 6-72. IUPAC Staff & A. Lever. (IUPAC Ser.). 1973. 92.00 (*0-08-020755-3*, Pub. by Pergamon Repr UK) Franklin.

Coordination Chemistry in Non-Aqueous Solutions. Viktor Gutmann. LC 68-13490. (Illus.). 1968. 39.00 (*0-387-80867-1*) Spr-Verlag.

Coordination Chemistry of Aluminum. Ed. by Gregory H. Robinson. LC 93-12703. 1993. write for info. (*1-56081-059-9*); pap. write for info. (*1-56081-656-2*) VCH Pubs.

Coordination Chemistry of Metalloenzymes: The Role of Metals in Reaction Involving Water, Dioxygen & Related Species. Ivano Bertini et al. 1983. lib. bdg. 121.50 (*90-277-1530-0*) Kluwer Ac.

Coordination Chemistry-Twenty One: Twenty-First International Conference on Coordination Chemistry, Toulouse, France, 1980. Ed. by J. P. Laurent. (IUPAC Symposium Ser.). 200p. 1981. 88.00 (*0-08-025300-8*, Pub. by Pergamon Repr UK) Franklin.

Coordination Compounds. S. Kettle. 1994. pap. write for info. (*0-632-03051-8*) Blackwell Sci.

Coordination Compounds. Sidney F. Kettle. (Studies in Modern Chemistry). 227p. reprint ed. pap. 64.70 (*0-317-26219-X*, 2055687) Bks Demand.

Coordination Compounds: Synthesis & Medical Application. (Structure & Bonding Ser.: Vol. 67). (Illus.). 160p. 1987. 83.00 (*0-387-17881-3*) Spr-Verlag.

Coordination Compounds of Porphyrins & Phthalocyanine. B. D. Berezin. LC 80-40958. 286p. 1981. text ed. 165.00 (*0-471-27857-2*, Wiley-Interscience) Wiley.

Coordination Compounds of Porphyrins & Phthalocyanines. Boris D. Berezin. Tr. by V. G. Vopian. LC 80-40958. (Illus.). 300p. reprint ed. pap. 85.50 (*0-685-20734-X*, 2030371) Bks Demand.

Coordination of Agricultural Research: African Swine Fever, No. EUR 14209. Ed. by A. Galo. (Agricultural Ser.). 280p. 1993. pap. 45.00 (*92-826-5148-7*, CH-NA-14209-EN-C, Pub. by Europ Com) UNIPUB.

Coordination of Building Services. H. Butler. (C). 1977. 45.00 (*0-86022-043-5*, Pub. by Build Servs Info Assn UK) St Mut.

Coordination of Building Services. S. Loyd & D. Jerdin. (C). 1983. 60.00 (*0-86022-156-3*, Pub. by Build Servs Info Assn UK) St Mut.

Coordination of Building Services: Design Stage Methods. A. Michie. (C). 1982. 42.00 (*0-86022-150-4*, Pub. by Build Servs Info Assn UK) St Mut.

Coordination of Distributed Problem Solvers. Edmund H. Durfee. (C). 1988. lib. bdg. 75.00 (*0-89838-284-X*) Kluwer Ac.

Coordination of Economic & Social Activities, Vol. 2. LC 78-2882. (Carnegie Endowment for International Peace, United Nations Studies: No. 2). 109p. 1978. reprint ed. text ed. 45.00 (*0-313-20329-6*, CESA, Greenwood Pr) Greenwood.

Coordination of Education & Social Services for At-Risk Youth: A Study of Early Intervention, Substance Abuse, & Teen Pregnancy Programs. William A. Firestone & Dale H. Drews. 31p. 1990. reprint ed. pap. 7.95 (*1-56602-018-2*) Research Better.

Coordination of Foreign Language Teaching see **Language Teaching: Broader Contexts**

Coordination of Observational Projects in Astronomy. Carlos Jaschek & Christian Sterken. 1988. 59.95 (*0-521-36157-5*) Cambridge U Pr.

Coordination of State & Federal Apprenticeship Administration, Vol. II. Kenneth W. Tolo. 81p. 1980. pap. 4.95 (*0-89940-804-4*) LBJ Sch Pub Aff.

Coordination of the Laws of Distribution. Ed. by Ian Steedman. (Classics in the History of Economics Ser.). 128p. 1992. 59.95 (*1-85278-684-1*, Pub. by E Elgar Pub UK) Ashgate Pub Co.

Coordination Plan of Marin County Superior & Municipal Courts: An Assessment of Staffing Implications. Alex Aikman & Genevra K. Loveland. 66p. 1992. 4.00 (*0-685-64940-7*, WRO-138) Natl Ctr St Courts.

Coordination Without Hierarchy: Informal Structures in Multiorganizational Systems. Donald Chisholm. 1989. 42.00 (*0-520-06368-6*) U CA Pr.

Coordination Without Hierarchy: Informal Structures in Multiorganizational Systems. Donald Chisholm. (C). 1989. pap. 15.00 (*0-520-08037-8*) U CA Pr.

Coordinative Interactions. Incl. Metal Complexes of Chelating Olefin-Group V Ligands. R. J. Williams et al. 1973. (*0-318-55768-1*); Structural Radii, Electron-Cloud Radii, Ionic Radii & Solvation. E. C. Baughan. 1973. (*0-318-55769-X*); Quantitative Evaluation & Prediction of Donor-Acceptor Interactions. R. S. Drago. 1973. (*0-318-55770-3*); Redox Properties: Changes Affected by Coordination. V. Gutmann. 1973. (*0-318-55771-1*); Thermodynamics of the Stepwise Formation of Metal-Ion Complexes in Aqueous Solution. S. Ahrland. 1973. (*0-318-55772-X*); (Structure & Bonding Ser.: Vol. 15). (Illus.). 189p. 1973. Set pap. 40.00 (*0-387-06410-9*) Spr-Verlag.

Coordinator of Child Support Enforcement. Jack Rudman. (Career Examination Ser.: C-927). 1994. pap. 39.95 (*0-8373-0927-1*) Nat Learn.

Coordinator of Community Mental Health Services. Jack Rudman. (Career Examination Ser.: C-1228). 1994. pap. 39.95 (*0-8373-1228-0*) Nat Learn.

Coordinator of Drainage Designing. Jack Rudman. (Career Examination Ser.: C-3124). 1994. pap. 39.95 (*0-8373-3124-2*) Nat Learn.

Coordinator of Drug Abuse Educational Programs. Jack Rudman. (Career Examination Ser.: C-1767). 1994. pap. 39.95 (*0-8373-1767-3*) Nat Learn.

Coordinator of Educational Affairs. Jack Rudman. (Career Examination Ser.: C-2209). 1994. pap. 39.95 (*0-8373-2209-X*) Nat Learn.

Coordinator of Human Services. Jack Rudman. (Career Examination Ser.: Series 1). 1991. pap. 39.95 (*0-8373-3706-2*) Nat Learn.

Coordinator of Laboratory Services. Jack Rudman. (Career Examination Ser.: C-1227). 1994. pap. 39.95 (*0-8373-1227-2*) Nat Learn.

Coordinator of Nursing Education. Jack Rudman. (Career Examination Ser.: C-1843). 1994. pap. 39.95 (*0-8373-1843-2*) Nat Learn.

Coordinator of Surveying Services. Jack Rudman. (Career Examination Ser.: C-3022). 1994. pap. 39.95 (*0-8373-3022-X*) Nat Learn.

Coordinator of Volunteer Services. Jack Rudman. (Career Examination Ser.: C-3110). 1994. pap. 39.95 (*0-8373-3110-2*) Nat Learn.

Coordinator, Senior Citizen Planning & Research. Jack Rudman. (Career Examination Ser.: C-2939). 1994. pap. 39.95 (*0-8373-2939-6*) Nat Learn.

***Coordinator's Manual.** Thomas Zanzig. Ed. by Robert Stamschror. (Confirmed in a Faithful Community Ser.). (Illus.). 124p. (Orig.). 1995. teacher ed, spiral bd. 14.90 (*0-88489-315-4*) St Marys.

Coordinators of Children's & Young Adult Services in Public Library Systems Serving at Least 100,000 People. ALA Association for Library Service to Children Staff. 42p. 1989. pap. text ed. 10.00 (*0-8389-7297-7*) ALA.

Coors Connection: How Coors Family Philanthropy Undermines Democratic Pluralism. Russ Bellant. (Illus.). 100p. 1990. spiral bd. 7.50 (*0-915987-06-6*) Political Rsch Assocs.

Coors Connection: How Coors Family Philanthropy Undermines Democratic Pluralism. Russ Bellant. (Political Research Associates Book Ser.). 144p. 1991. 25.00 (*0-89608-417-5*); pap. 9.00 (*0-89608-416-7*) South End Pr.

Coos Texts. Leo J. Frachtenberg. LC 74-82355. (Columbia Univ. Contributions to Anthropology Ser.: Vol. 1). 1969. reprint ed. 27.50 (*0-404-50551-1*) AMS Pr.

Coot Club. Arthur Ransome. LC 88-46106. (Illus.). 352p. (J). (gr. 4-6). 1989. pap. 11.95 (*0-87923-787-2*) Godine.

Cootie Dragons. Eliza Toussant. (Illus.). 120p. (J). (gr. 4 up). 1993. pap. text ed. write for info. (*0-9630583-2-0*) E Toussant.

***Coots, Codgers & Curmudgeons: Things Were More Like They Used to Be Then Than They Are Now.** H. Sisson & D. Rowe. 176p. (Orig.). 1994. pap. 10.95 (*1-55143-012-6*) Orca Bk Pubs.

Coozan Dudley LeBlanc. Floyd M. Clay. LC 86-30628. 280p. 1987. reprint ed. pap. 13.95 (*0-88289-646-6*) Pelican.

Cop: A True Story. Michael L. Middleton. 256p. 1994. 19.95 (*0-8092-3736-9*) Contemp Bks.

***Cop: A True Story.** Mike Middleton. 288p. 1995. pap. 12.95 (*0-8092-3437-8*) Contemp Bks.

Cop-a-Form Charts & Graphs. Richard D. Dawson. (Office Copier Library Ser.). 64p. 1983. pap. text ed. 8.95 (*0-914567-04-7*) Cop-A-Form.

Cop-a-Form Columnar & Data Grid Sheets. Richard D. Dawson. (Office Copier Library Ser.). 64p. (Orig.). 1983. pap. text ed. 8.95 (*0-914567-03-9*) Cop-A-Form.

Cop-a-Form General Office Forms. Richard D. Dawson. (Office Copier Library Ser.). 64p. (Orig.). 1983. pap. 8.95 (*0-914567-01-2*) Cop-A-Form.

Cop-a-Form States & U. S. Maps. Richard D. Dawson. (Office Copier Library Ser.). 64p. (Orig.). 1983. pap. text ed. 8.95 (*0-914567-02-0*) Cop-A-Form.

***Cop & the Anthem.** O. Henry. 1972. 3.00 (*0-87129-513-X*, C33) Dramatic Pub.

***Cop & the Chorus Girl: (Opposites Attract)** Nancy Martin. (Desire Ser.). 1995. mass mkt. 3.25 (*0-373-05927-2*, 1-05927-8) Silhouette.

***Cop & the Mother-to-Be.** Charlotte Hughes. (Loveswept Ser.: No. 719). 1994. pap. 3.50 (*0-553-44390-9*, Loveswept) Bantam.

Cop Hater. Ed McBain. (Eighty-Seventh Precinct Mysteries Ser.). 160p. 1987. pap. 3.99 (*0-451-15079-1*, Sig) NAL-Dutton.

Cop Hater. deluxe ed. Ed McBain. LC 89-18327. 184p. 1990. reprint ed. Collector edition. 25.00 (*0-922890-12-9*) Armchair Detective.

Cop Hater. limited ed. Ed McBain. LC 89-18327. 184p. 1990. reprint ed. Limited edition. 75.00 (*0-922890-13-7*) Armchair Detective.

Cop Hater. Ed McBain. LC 89-18327. 184p. 1990. reprint ed. 17.95 (*0-922890-06-4*) Armchair Detective.

Cop Hunter. Vincent Murano & William Hoffer. 320p. 1991. reprint ed. mass mkt. 4.95 (*0-671-66959-1*, Pocket Star Bks) PB.

Cop Killer: The Story of a Crime. Maj Sjowall & Per Wahloo. 21.95 (*0-89190-377-1*, Am Repr) Amereon Ltd.

Cop Out. Claire McNab. (Orig.). 1991. pap. 9.95 (*0-941483-84-3*) Naiad Pr.

Cop Out. Ellery Queen. Bd. with Last Woman in His Life. 1982. Set pap. 2.50 (*0-451-11562-7*, AE1562, Sig) NAL-Dutton.

Cop Shop: Covering Crime on the Streets of Chicago. Robert Blau. (Illus.). 288p. 1993. 19.18 (*0-201-58113-2*) Addison-Wesley.

Cop Shot: The True Story of a Murder That Shocked the Nation. Mike McAlary. 288p. (Orig.). 1992. mass mkt. 4.99 (*0-515-10992-4*) Jove Pubns.

***COP Talk.** Count. 1995. mass mkt. 5.99 (*0-671-78341-6*) PB.

Cop-Talk: Monitoring Law Enforcement Communications. Laura E. Quarantiello. 80p. 1992. pap. 17.95 (*0-936653-42-6*) Tiare Pubns.

Cop Talk: True Detective Stories from the NYPD. E. W. Count. Ed. by Dana Isaacson. LC 93-48588. 400p. 1994. 22.00 (*0-671-78336-X*) PB.

Cop to Call Girl. Norma J. Almodovar. 360p. 1994. mass mkt. 5.50 (*0-380-72304-2*) Avon.

Cop to Call Girl: Why I Left the LAPD to Make an Honest Living As a Beverly Hills Prostitute. Norma J. Almodovar. LC 93-20149. (Illus.). 288p. 1993. 21.00 (*0-671-79425-6*) S&S Trade.

***Cop Without a Badge.** Charles Kipps. 368p. 1996. 23.00 (*0-7867-0246-X*) Carroll & Graf.

Cop World: Policing the Streets of San Diego. James McClure. LC 85-217205. 1984. write for info. (*0-333-30688-0*) Macmillan.

Copains. Jules Romains. (FRE.). 1982. pap. 10.95 (*0-7859-3987-3*) Fr & Eur.

Copains. Jules Romains. (Folio Ser.: No. 182). 160p. (FRE.). 1972. pap. 6.95 (*2-07-036182-9*) Schoenhof.

Copan Ceramics: A Study of Southeastern Maya Pottery. John M. Longyear. LC 77-11503. (Carnegie Institution of Washington. Publications: No. 597). reprint ed. 28.50 (*0-404-16267-3*) AMS Pr.

Copasetic: Adventures of Bojangles Robinson. Pepper Bird Staff. (Multicultural Historical Fiction Ser.). (Illus.). 48p. (Orig.). (J). (gr. 4-7). 1993. pap. 3.95 (*1-56817-000-9*) Pepper Bird.

***COPE: Client-Oriented, Provider-Efficient Services.** AVSC International Staff. Ed. by Joanne Tzanis. (Orig.). 1995. pap. text ed. write for info. (*1-885063-01-6*) AVSC Int.

Cope Community, Colorado. Cope Homemakers Club Staff. (Illus.). 295p. 1988. 42.50 (*0-88107-112-9*) Curtis Media.

Cope: Master Naturalist: Life & Letters of Edward Drinker Cope, with a Bibliography of His Writings. Henry F. Osborn. LC 77-81135. (Biologists & Their World Ser.). (Illus.). 1978. reprint ed. lib. bdg. 65.95 (*0-405-10735-8*) Ayer.

Copeau on the Theatre. Jacques Copeau. Ed. by John Rudlin & Norman Paul. (Illus.). 272p. 1991. 35.00 (*0-415-05253-X*, A4741) Routledge.

Copeland, Bostick, Patton, & Allied Families. Virginia C. Jantz. LC 81-83976. (Illus.). 430p. 1981. 25.00 (*0-9607170-0-5*) V C Jantz.

Copeland Collection, Chinese & Japanese Ceramic Figures. William R. Sargent. 70.00 (*0-87577-157-2*, Peabody Museum); pap. 35.00 (*0-87577-158-0*, Peabody Museum) Peabody Essex Mus.

Copeland Killings. Tom Miller. (Illus.). 304p. 1993. mass mkt. 4.99 (*1-55817-675-6*, Pinnacle NY) Windsor NY.

Copenhagen. (Panorama Bks.). (Illus.). (FRE.). 3.95 (*0-685-11107-5*) Fr & Eur.

Copenhagen. Karl Baedeker. (Baedeker's City Guides Ser.). (Illus.). 1986. pap. 10.95 (*0-685-17130-2*) P-H.

Copenhagen - Wonderful. P. Gronlund & J. Gronlund. 76p. 1987. pap. 18.50 (*87-87108-13-5*, D762) Vanous.

Copenhagen Chansonnier. Ed. by Knud Jeppesen & Viggo Brondal. (Illus.). 276p. (GER.). 1965. reprint ed. lib. bdg. 95.00 (*0-8450-0004-7*) Broude.

Copenhagen Connection. Elizabeth Peters. 224p. 1994. mass mkt. 5.50 (*0-446-36483-5*) Warner Bks.

Copenhagen Pocket Guide. Berlitz Staff. 1993. pap. 7.95 (*2-8315-2368-0*) Berlitz.

Copernican Plan: Restructuring the American High School. Joseph M. Carroll. (Orig.). 1989. pap. write for info. (*0-318-65833-X*) Reg Lab Educ IOT NE Isls.

Copernican Plan Evaluated: The Evolution of a Revolution. Joseph M. Carroll. 200p. Date not set. pap. 24.95 (*0-9641442-0-4*) Copernican.

Copernican Revolution. Paul Goodman. 1947. pap. 4.50 (*0-910664-37-4*) Gotham.

Copernican Revolution: Planetary Astronomy in the Development of Western Thought. Thomas S. Kuhn. LC 57-76121. (Illus.). 315p. 1957. pap. text ed. 11.95 (*0-674-17103-9*) HUP.

Copernicus & the Changing World. Wanda Stachiewicz. 64p. 1973. 2.00 (*0-940962-04-7*) Polish Inst Art & Sci.

Copernicus & the Scientific Revolution. Edward Rosen. LC 83-9380. (Anvil Ser.). 220p. (Orig.). 1984. pap. text ed. 11.50 (*0-89874-573-X*) Krieger.

Cope's Early Diagnosis of the Acute Abdomen. 18th ed. Ed. by William Silen. (Illus.). 336p. 1991. pap. 23.95 (*0-19-506735-5*) OUP.

***Cope's Early Diagnosis of the Acute Abdomen.** 19th ed. William Silen. (Illus.). 320p. 1995. 49.95 (*0-19-509758-0*) OUP.

***Cope's Early Diagnosis of the Acute Abdomen.** 19th ed. William Silen. (Illus.). 320p. 1995. pap. 24.95 (*0-19-509759-9*) OUP.

Copi: Plays, Vol. 1: Includes Eva Peron; Homosexual; Four Twins; Loretta Strong. Copi. Tr. by Lee Taylor. 1980. pap. 9.95 (*0-7145-3563-X*) Riverrun NY.

***Copiah County, Mississippi Taxpayers, 1825-1841.** T.L.C. Genealogy. LC 90-71589. 123p. (Orig.). 1990. spiral bd., pap. 12.00 (*1-886633-27-4*) TLC Genealogy.

Copie of a Letter Sent from Sea by a Gentleman. LC 72-5984. (English Experience Ser.: No. 511). 1973. reprint ed. 6.00 (*90-221-0511-3*) Walter J Johnson.

An Asterisk (*) at the beginning of an entry indicates that the title is appearing in BIP for the first time.

An Asterisk (*) at the beginning of an entry indicates that the title is appearing in BIP for the first time.

1615

C

Coping with Climate Change: Proceedings of the Second North American Conference on Preparing for Climate Change: A Cooperative Approach. Climate Institute Staff. LC 89-62291. (Illus.). 710p. (Orig.). (C). 1989. pap. 35.00 (*0-9623610-0-3*) Climate Inst.

Coping with Cliques. Lee Peck. Ed. by Ruth Rosen. LC 92-12380. (Coping Ser.). (YA). (gr. 7-12). 1992. 15.95 (*0-8239-1412-7*) Rosen Group.

Coping with Closures: An International Comparison of Mine Town Experiences. Ed. by Cecily Neil et al. LC 91-12918. (Illus.). 416p. 1991. 99.50 (*0-415-06651-4*, A6471) Routledge.

Coping with Clouters, Culture & Crisis. Joe Stanka & Jean Stanka. (Illus.). 176p. 1987. pap. 9.95 (*0-933704-57-7*) Dawn Pr.

Coping with College: A Guide for Academic Success. Alice L. Hamachek. LC 94-19866. (C). 1994. write for info. (*0-205-16579-6*) Allyn.

Coping with Communication Challenges in Alzheimer's Disease. Marie T. Rau. LC 92-41712. (Coping with Aging Ser.). (Illus.). 222p. (Orig.). (C). 1993. pap. text ed. 18.95 (*1-879105-76-4*) Singular Publishing.

***Coping with Compassion Fatigue.** Concordia Publishing Staff. (Master's Touch Ser.). 1994. pap. 3.99 (*0-570-09434-8*) Concordia.

Coping with Complexity. Hans W. Gottinger. 1983. lib. bdg. 94.00 (*90-277-1510-6*) Kluwer Ac.

Coping with Complexity in the International System. Ed. by Jack Snyder & Robert Jervis. LC 92-26066. (Pew Studies in Economics & Security). 366p. (C). 1992. text ed. 67.00 (*0-8133-8607-1*) Westview.

Coping with Compulsive Behavior. Margot Webb. LC 93-29403. (J). 1993. 15.95 (*0-8239-1604-9*) Rosen Group.

Coping with Computers in the Elementary & Middle Schools. C. Alan Reidesel & Douglas H. Clements. (Illus.). 384p. (C). 1985. pap. text ed. 35.00 (*0-13-172420-7*) P-H.

Coping with Conflict: Reproductive Choices & Community Controversy. League of Women Voters Education Fund Staff. 36p. (Orig.). 1986. pap. 2.50 (*0-89959-367-4*, 802) LWVUS.

Coping with Crime on Campus. Michael C. Smith. (ACE-Oryx Series on Higher Education). 264p. (C). 1988. 27.95 (*0-02-929440-1*, ACE-Oryx) Oryx Pr.

Coping with Crime on Campus. 2nd ed. Michael C. Smith & Richard W. Fossey. (American Council on Education-Oryx Press Series on Higher Education). 264p. 1995. boxed 34.95 (*0-89774-846-8*) Oryx Pr.

Coping with Crises. Glenys Parry. (Problems in Practice Ser.). (Illus.). 276p. 1990. pap. 18.95 (*0-415-03546-5*, A4925) Routledge.

Coping with Crises: How Governments Deal with Emergencies, Vol. II. Ed. by Shao-Chuan Leng. LC 89-16734. (Miller Center Series on Asian Political Leadership). 242p. (Orig.). (C). 1990. lib. bdg. 47.00 (*0-8191-7584-6*, Pub. by White Miller Center); pap. text ed. 24.00 (*0-8191-7585-4*, Pub. by White Miller Center) U Pr of Amer.

Coping with Crises: The Management of Disasters, Riots & Terrorism. Ed. by Uriel Rosenthal et al. (Illus.). 498p. (C). 1989. text ed. 86.95x (*0-398-05597-1*) C C Thomas.

***Coping with Crises: The Management of Disasters, Riots & Terrorism.** Ed. by Uriel Rosenthal et al. (Illus.). 198p. 1989. pap. 45.95 (*0-398-06408-3*) C C Thomas.

Coping with Crisis: Understanding & Helping People in Need. Stephen Murgatroyd & Ray Woole. 180p. 1982. pap. 29.00 (*0-335-09819-3*, Open Univ Pr) Taylor & Francis.

Coping with Crisis in Eastern Europe's Environment: Coping with Challenge. Ed. by J. Alcamo. (Illus.). 330p. (C). 1992. text ed. 85.00 (*1-85070-433-3*) Prthnon Pub.

Coping with Criticism. Jamie Buckingham. LC 78-60994. 158p. 1978. 3.95 (*0-88270-502-4*) Bridge Pub.

Coping with Crossdressing. 2nd ed. JoAnn Roberts. 80p. (Orig.). 1992. pap. 12.00 (*1-880715-10-4*) Creat Des Srvs.

***Coping with Crossdressing.** 3rd rev. ed. JoAnn Roberts. 84p. (Orig.). 1995. pap. 12.00 (*1-880715-12-0*) Creat Des Srvs.

Coping with Cultural & Racial Diversity in Urban America. Wallace E. Lambert & Donald M. Taylor. LC 89-16097. 214p. 1990. text ed. 49.95 (*0-275-93174-9*, C3174, Praeger Pubs) Greenwood.

Coping with Date Rape & Acquaintance Rape. rev. ed. Andrea Parrot. Ed. by Roger Rosen. (Coping Ser.). (YA). (gr. 7 up). 1993. lib. bdg. 15.95 (*0-8239-1649-9*) Rosen Group.

Coping with Death. rev. ed. Robert A. Raab. Ed. by Ruth Rosen. (Coping Ser.). (YA). (gr. 7-12). 1989. lib. bdg. 15.95 (*0-8239-0960-3*) Rosen Group.

Coping with Death & Dying: An Interdisciplinary Approach. Ed. by John T. Chirban. 108p. 1986. pap. text ed. 15.00 (*0-8191-4985-3*) U Pr of Amer.

Coping with Death & Grief. Marge E. Heegaard. (Coping with Modern Problems Ser.). (Illus.). 64p. (J). (gr. 4 up). 1990. lib. bdg. 17.50 (*0-8225-0043-4*, Lerner Publctns) Lerner Group.

Coping with Death & Grief. Nancy H. Sahlein & Ron Kerner. (Family Forum Library Ser.). 16p. 1992. 1.95 (*1-56688-008-4*) Bur For At-Risk.

Coping with Death in the Family. 3rd ed. Gerald Schneiderman. 168p. 1989. pap. 12.95 (*1-55021-055-6*, Pub. by NC Press CN) U of Toronto Pr.

***Coping with Decision Making.** rev. ed. Sandra L. Smith. Ed. by Ruth Rosen. (Coping Ser.). (YA). (gr. 7 up). Date not set. lib. bdg. 15.95 (*0-8239-1839-4*) Rosen Group.

Coping with Depression. rev. ed. Lawrence Clayton & Sharon Carter. Ed. by Ruth Rosen. (Coping Ser.). (YA). (gr. 7-12). 1992. 15.95 (*0-8239-1488-7*) Rosen Group.

Coping with Depression & Elation. large type ed. Patrick McKeon. (Illus.). 160p. 1991. 18.95 (*1-85089-155-9*, Pub. by ISIS UK) Transaction Pubs.

Coping with Depression Course: A Psychoeducational Intervention for Unipolar Depression. Peter M. Lewinsohn et al. 223p. 1984. 21.95 (*0-916154-11-4*) Castalia Pub.

Coping with Destitution: Poverty & Relief in Western Europe. Rosalind Mitchison. (Joanne Goodman Lectures). 96p. 1991. text ed. 30.00 (*0-8020-5912-0*); pap. text ed. 13.95 (*0-8020-6859-6*) U of Toronto Pr.

Coping with Diet Fads. June K. Kane. Ed. by Ruth Rosen. (Coping Ser.). (YA). (gr. 7-12). 1990. lib. bdg. 15.95 (*0-8239-1005-9*) Rosen Group.

Coping with Difficult Bosses. Robert Bramson. LC 92-17492. 192p. 1992. 16.95 (*1-55972-139-1*, Birch Ln Pr) Carol Pub Group.

Coping with Difficult Bosses. Robert M. Bramson. LC 93-7866. 1994. pap. 11.00 (*0-671-79790-5*) S&S Trade.

Coping with Difficult People. Robert M. Bramson. 1988. mass mkt. 5.99 (*0-440-20201-9*) Dell.

***Coping with Difficult Teachers.** Angela V. Woodhull. 200p. 1995. text ed. 19.95x (*0-87047-102-3*) Schenkman Bks Inc.

Coping with Discrimination. rev. ed. Gabrielle I. Edwards. LC 86-6727. (Coping Ser.). 120p. (gr. 7-12). 1992. lib. bdg. 15.95 (*0-8239-1426-7*) Rosen Group.

Coping with Discrimination. rev. ed. Gabrielle I. Edwards. LC 86-6727. (Coping Ser.). 120p. (YA). (gr. 7-12). 1992. teacher ed 5.95 (*0-8239-0853-4*) Rosen Group.

Coping with Disruptive Behavior in Group Care. Eva M. Russo & Ann W. Shyne. LC 79-23739. 74p. (Orig.). (C). 1980. 13.50 (*0-87868-137-X*, 1370) Child Welfare.

Coping with Divorce. rev. ed. Robert A. Raab. (J). (gr. 7-12). 1984. lib. bdg. 15.95 (*0-8239-0428-8*) Rosen Group.

Coping with Drinking & Driving. rev. ed. Janet Grosshandler. Ed. by Ruth Rosen. (Coping Ser.). (YA). (gr. 7-12). 1994. lib. bdg. 15.95 (*0-8239-1603-0*) Rosen Group.

Coping with Drought in Kenya: National & Local Strategies. Ed. by Thomas E. Downing et al. LC 89-30952. (Food in Africa Ser.). 412p. 1989. lib. bdg. 42.00 (*1-55587-151-8*) Lynne Rienner.

Coping with Droughts. L. V. Da Cunha et al. Ed. by Vujica Yevjevich. LC 83-50242. 450p. 1984. 40.00 (*0-918334-52-7*) WRP.

Coping with Drug Abuse. rev. ed. Gabrielle I. Edwards. Ed. by Roger Rosen. (Coping Ser.). (YA). (gr. 7 up). 1990. lib. bdg. 15.95 (*0-8239-1144-6*) Rosen Group.

Coping with Drug Abuse: A Lifeline for Parents. Joe Baker. LC 82-12723. (Illus.). 60p. 1982. pap. 7.95 (*0-943690-00-5*) DARE.

Coping with Drugs & Sports. Elizabeth Nelson. (Coping Ser.). (YA). (gr. 7-12). 1992. lib. bdg. 15.95 (*0-8239-1342-2*) Rosen Group.

Coping with Eating Disorders. Barbara Moe. (Coping Ser.). (YA). (gr. 7-12). 1991. lib. bdg. 15.95 (*0-8239-1343-0*) Rosen Group.

Coping with Endometriosis. Lyle J. Breitkopf & Marion G. Bakoulis. LC 87-43148. (Illus.). 256p. 1988. student ed 9.50 (*0-929655-63-X*) P-H.

Coping with Ethical Dilemmas. Martin Lakin. (Practitioner Guidebook Ser.). (C). 1991. 31.95 (*0-205-14402-0*, H4402, Longwood Div); pap. 21.95 (*0-205-14401-2*, H4401) Allyn.

Coping with Faculty Stress. Walter H. Gmelch. (Survival Skills for Scholars Ser.: Vol. 5). (Illus.). 128p. (C). 1993. text ed. 27.50 (*0-8039-4969-3*); pap. text ed. 12.95 (*0-8039-4970-7*) Sage.

Coping with Faculty Stress. Ed. by Peter Seldin. LC 85-644763. (New Directions for Teaching & Learning Ser.: No. TL 29). 1987. 16.95 (*1-55542-975-0*) Jossey-Bass.

Coping with Failure: The Therapeutic Uses of Rhetoric. David Payne. Ed. by Carroll C. Arnold. (Studies in Rhetoric-Communication). 173p. 1989. text ed. 34.95 (*0-87249-593-0*) U of SC Pr.

Coping with Family Expectations. Margaret Hill. Ed. by Ruth Rosen. (Coping Ser.). (YA). (gr. 7-12). 1990. lib. bdg. 15.95 (*0-8239-1159-4*) Rosen Group.

Coping with Family Stress. Kimberly W. Gooden. Ed. by Ruth Rosen. (Coping Ser.). (YA). (gr. 7-12). 1989. lib. bdg. 15.95 (*0-8239-0980-8*) Rosen Group.

Coping with Family Violence. rev. ed. Morton L. Kurland. Ed. by R. Rosen. (Coping Ser.). 141p. (YA). (gr. 7-12). 1990. lib. bdg. 15.95 (*0-8239-1050-4*) Rosen Group.

Coping with Family Violence: Research & Policy Perspectives. Ed. by Gerald T. Hotaling et al. 336p. (C). 1988. text ed. 49.95 (*0-8039-2722-3*); pap. text ed. 22.95 (*0-8039-2723-1*) Sage.

Coping with Floods. Ed. by Giuseppe Rossi et al. LC 94-2615. (NATO Advanced Study Institutes Series E, Applied Sciences: Vol. 257). 1994. lib. bdg. 282.00 (*0-7923-2706-3*) Kluwer Ac.

Coping with Foreign Dependence: The Simple Analytics of Stockpiling versus Protection. Martin C. McQuire. 21p. 1990. pap. text ed. 12.50 (*981-3035-53-6*, Pub. by Inst SE Asian Studies SI) Ashgate Pub Co.

Coping with Germany. 2nd ed. John A. Abecasis-Phillips. (Illus.). 1992. pap. 13.95 (*0-631-18235-7*) Blackwell Pubs.

***Coping with Global Unemployment: Putting People Back to Work.** Ed. by John Eatwell. (Illus.). 253p. 1995. 55.00 (*1-56324-581-7*) M E Sharpe.

***Coping with Global Unemployment: Putting People Back to Work.** Ed. by John Eatwell. (Illus.). 253p. 1995. pap. 21.95 (*1-56324-582-5*) M E Sharpe.

Coping with Gorbachev's Soviet Union. Stephen R. Sestanovich et al. (Significant Issues Ser.). 1988. 1.00 (*0-318-35436-5*) CSI Studies.

Coping with Gravity. Maxine Clair. LC 87-37162. 1988. pap. 7.00 (*0-931846-32-3*) Wash Writers Pub.

Coping with Hazardous Waste: Local Officials Guide to the Small Quantity Generator Regulations. 71p. 1987. pap. 10.00 (*0-933729-20-0*) Natl League Cities.

Coping with Hazardous Waste: Local Officials Guide to the Underground Tank Regulations. 58p. 1987. pap. 10.00 (*0-933729-21-9*) Natl League Cities.

Coping with Health Risks & Risky Behavior. Alan R. Bleich. Ed. by Roger Rosen. (Coping Ser.). (YA). (gr. 7-12). 1990. lib. bdg. 15.95 (*0-8239-1072-5*) Rosen Group.

Coping with Hearing Loss: A Guide for Adults & Their Families. rev. ed. Susan V. Rezen & Carl Hausman. LC 92-36728. 1993. 17.95 (*0-942637-83-6*) Barricade Bks.

Coping with Hearing Loss & Hearing Aids. Debra A. Shimon. (Coping with Aging Ser.). (Illus.). 224p. (Orig.). (C). 1991. pap. text ed. 18.95 (*1-879105-45-4*, 0229) Singular Publishing.

Coping with High Blood Pressure. Sandy Sorrentino & Carl Hausman. LC 86-6239. (Illus.). 1986. 16.95 (*0-934878-76-5*, Dembner NY) Barricade Bks.

Coping with High Blood Pressure. Sandy Sorrentino & Carl Hausman. LC 86-6239. 1990. pap. 9.95 (*0-942637-25-9*, Dembner NY) Barricade Bks.

***Coping with Illness.** Helen Garvy. (Illus.). 240p. (Orig.). 1995. pap. 12.00 (*0-918828-18-X*) Shire Pr.

Coping with Impaired Mobility. Jane Mahoney & Reenie Euhardy. LC 93-40443. (Coping with Aging Ser.). 1994. 18.95 (*1-879105-65-9*) Singular Publishing.

Coping with Incest. rev. ed. Deborah Miller. (J). (gr. 4-7). 1995. 15.95 (*0-8239-1949-8*) Rosen Group.

Coping with Increasing Complexity: Implications of General Semantics & General Systems. Ed. by Donald E. Washburn & Dennis R. Smith. 408p. 1974. text ed. 154.00 (*0-677-14940-9*) Gordon & Breach.

Coping with India. Robert Wood. (Coping with...Ser.). (Illus.). 192p. 1990. pap. 13.95 (*0-631-16477-4*) Blackwell Pubs.

Coping with Infant or Fetal Loss: The Couple's Healing Process. Kathleen R. Gilbert & Laura S. Smart. LC 92-16166. (Psychosocial Stress Ser.: Vol. 22). 224p. 1992. 30.95 (*0-87630-679-2*); pap. 17.95 (*0-87630-694-6*) Brunner-Mazel.

Coping with Information Illiteracy: Bibliographic Instruction for the Information Age. Ed. by Glenn E. Mensching, Jr. & Teresa B. Mensching. (Library Orientation Ser.: No. 20). 1990. pap. 35.00 (*0-87650-267-2*) Pierian.

Coping with Interracial Dating. Renea D. Nash. LC 93-6895. (YA). 1994. 15.95 (*0-8239-1606-5*) Rosen Group.

Coping with Japan. John Randle & Mariko Watanabe. 184p. 1987. pap. 13.95 (*0-631-15443-4*) Blackwell Pubs.

Coping with Jealousy. Beth Wilkinson. Ed. by Ruth Rosen. (Coping Ser.). (YA). (gr. 7-12). 1992. 15.95 (*0-8239-1516-6*) Rosen Group.

Coping with Job Loss. Loyd D. White. Ed. by Dennis W. Wootan. (Minority Outplacement Workshop Ser.). (Illus.). 70p. (Orig.). (C). 1991. pap. text ed. 19.95 (*1-880409-03-8*) Pacific Servs.

Coping with Job Loss: How Individuals, Corporations, Unions & Communities Respond to a Layoff. Carrie R. Leana. 1992. text ed. 24.95 (*0-669-16569-7*) Free Pr.

Coping with Joyce: Essays from the Copenhagen Symposium. Ed. by Morris Beja & Shari Benstock. 296p. 1989. text ed. 42.50 (*0-8142-0467-8*) Ohio St U Pr.

Coping with Kidney Failure: A Guide to Living with Kidney Failure for You & Your Family. Robert H. Phillips. LC 87-17477. 320p. 1987. pap. 12.95 (*0-89529-370-6*) Avery Pub.

Coping with Learning Difficulties. Kathleen Clark. (C). 1989. 30.00 (*1-85098-118-3*, Pub. by Jordanhill College UK) St Mut.

Coping with Life. Ed. by Hugh Douglas. (C). 1990. pap. 45.00 (*0-85305-282-4*, Pub. by J Arthur Ltd UK) St Mut.

Coping with Life after High School. Michael Dumond. Ed. by Roger Rosen. (Coping Ser.). (YA). (gr. 7 up). 1988. lib. bdg. 15.95 (*0-8239-0781-3*) Rosen Group.

Coping with Life after Your Mate Dies. Donald C. Cushenberry & Rita C. Cushenberry. 96p. (Orig.). 1991. pap. 6.99 (*0-8010-2557-5*) Baker Bk.

Coping with Life Challenges. Chris L. Kleinke. 272p. (C). 1991. pap. 22.95 (*0-534-14424-1*) Brooks-Cole.

Coping with Life Crises: An Integrated Approach. Ed. by Rudolf H. Moos. LC 85-28149. (Stress & Coping Ser.). 444p. 1986. 60.00 (*0-306-42133-X*, Plenum Pr); pap. 32.50 (*0-306-42144-5*, Plenum Pr) Plenum.

Coping with Life the Principle Way: A Plain-English Common-Sense Approach to Solving the Problems of Everyday Living. rev. ed. Merritt W. Borden. (Illus.). 119p. (YA). (gr. 7-12). 1993. spiral bd. 12.95 (*0-929393-11-2*) Diogenes Pub Co.

***Coping with Limb Loss: A Practical Guide to Successfully Living with Amputation.** Ellen Winchell. LC 95-5445. 1995. pap. 14.95 (*0-89529-646-2*) Avery Pub.

Coping with Living: How to Handle Your Emotional Problems. B. Katz & M. L. Kurland. LC 75-14947. 256p. reprint ed. 73.00 (*0-8357-9519-5*, 2012417) Bks Demand.

***Coping with Loss: A Guide for Caregivers.** Shirley A. Locke. LC 94-7441. 238p. 1994. pap. 29.95 (*0-398-06244-7*) C C Thomas.

Coping with Loss: A Guide for Caregivers. Shirley A. Locke. LC 94-7441. 238p. (C). 1994. text ed. 48.95 (*0-398-05912-8*) C C Thomas.

Coping with Loss: Psychotherapeutic Use of Leave-Taking Rituals. Ed. by Onno Van Der Hart. 300p. (C). 1988. text ed. 29.95 (*0-8290-1596-5*); audio 14.00 (*0-8290-2304-6*) Irvington.

Coping with Loss of Independence. Michael J. Siebers et al. LC 92-42197. (Coping with Aging Ser.). (Illus.). 238p. (Orig.). (C). 1993. pap. text ed. 18.95 (*1-879105-60-8*) Singular Publishing.

Coping with Low Vision. Marshall E. Flax et al. LC 92-31826. (Coping with Aging Ser.). (Illus.). 213p. (Orig.). (C). 1993. pap. text ed. 18.95 (*1-879105-71-3*) Singular Publishing.

Coping with Lupus: A Guide to Living with Lupus for You & Your Family. 2nd ed. Robert H. Phillips. LC 90-1270. 288p. 1991. pap. 12.95 (*0-89529-475-3*) Avery Pub.

Coping with Lyme Disease: A Practical Guide to Dealing with Diagnosis & Treatment. Denise Lang & Derrick M. DeSilva, Jr. LC 93-16442. 288p. (Orig.). 1993. pap. 12.95 (*0-8050-2650-9*, Owl) H Holt & Co.

Coping with Mandates: What Are the Alternatives? Ed. by Michael Fix & Daphne A. Kenyon. LC 89-28319. (Illus.). 126p. (Orig.). (C). 1990. lib. bdg. 28.00 (*0-87766-434-X*); pap. text ed. 15.50 (*0-87766-435-8*) Urban Inst.

Coping with Marital Conflict: An Adlerian Approach to Succeeding in Marriage. Charles H. Huber & Leroy G. Baruth. 160p. (C). 1981. pap. text ed. 6.00 (*0-87563-201-7*) Stipes.

Coping with Marital Transitions: A Family Systems Perspective. E. Mavis Hetherington et al. (Illus.). 300p. 1992. pap. text ed. 14.50 (*0-226-33168-7*) U Ch Pr.

Coping with Medical Emergencies. rev. ed. Sharon Carter et al. (Coping Ser.). 121p. (YA). (gr. 7-12). 1988. lib. bdg. 15.95 (*0-8239-0782-1*) Rosen Group.

Coping with Medications. Maren E. Meyer. LC 92-25613. (Coping with Aging Ser.). (Illus.). (Orig.). (C). 1993. pap. text ed. 18.95 (*1-879105-67-5*) Singular Publishing.

Coping with Miscarriage: A Simple, Reassuring Guide to Emotional & Physical Healing. Mimi Luebbermann. 1994. pap. 9.95 (*1-55958-503-X*) Prima Pub.

Coping with Mitral Valve Prolapse: A Guide to Living with MVP for You & Your Family. Robert H. Phillips. LC 91-46165. 286p. 1992. pap. 9.95 (*0-89529-514-8*) Avery Pub.

Coping with Money. Mary P. Lee. Ed. by Ruth Rosen. (Coping Ser.). (YA). (gr. 7 up). 1988. lib. bdg. 15.95 (*0-8239-0783-X*) Rosen Group.

Coping with Moving. Dorothy Greenwald. Ed. by Ruth Rosen. (Coping Ser.). 128p. (YA). (gr. 7 up). 1987. lib. bdg. 15.95 (*0-8239-0683-3*) Rosen Group.

Coping with Natural Disasters. Caroline Arnold. (J). (gr. 5 up). 1988. 13.95 (*0-8027-6716-8*); lib. bdg. 14.85 (*0-8027-6717-6*) Walker & Co.

Coping with Negative Life Events: Clinical & Social Psychological Perspectives. Ed. by C. R. Snyder & Carol E. Ford. LC 87-2483. (Stress & Coping Ser.). (Illus.). 436p. 1987. 59.50 (*0-306-42432-0*, Plenum Pr) Plenum.

Coping with Noncompliance in the Classroom: A Positive Approach for Teachers. Hill M. Walker & Janet E. Walker. LC 90-27492. 70p. (Orig.). 1991. pap. text ed. 9.00 (*0-89079-457-X*, 1947) PRO-ED.

Coping with Numbers. David Targett. 250p. 1984. pap. 16.95 (*0-631-14123-5*) Blackwell Pubs.

Coping with Osteoarthritis: A Guide to Living with Arthritis for You & Your Family. Robert H. Phillips. LC 89-175. 224p. (Orig.). 1989. pap. 9.95 (*0-89529-393-5*) Avery Pub.

Coping with Parent Burnout. Anthony Coletta. 40p. (Orig.). 1992. pap. text ed. 6.00 (*0-935493-86-7*) Programs Educ.

Coping with Parents Who Are Activists. Margot Webb. Ed. by Ruth Rosen. (Coping Ser.). (YA). (gr. 7-12). 1992. 15.95 (*0-8239-1416-X*) Rosen Group.

Coping With Pediatric Illness. Ed. by Charles E. Hollingworth. LC 82-10743. 266p. 1983. text ed. 35.00 (*0-88331-126-7*) Luce.

Coping with Peer Pressure. Leslie S. Kaplan. (Coping Ser.). 140p. 1989. teacher ed 5.95 (*0-8239-0852-6*) Rosen Group.

Coping with Peer Pressure. rev. ed. Leslie S. Kaplan. (Coping Ser.). 140p. (J). 1993. lib. bdg. 15.95 (*0-8239-1650-2*) Rosen Group.

Coping with Physical Illness, Vol. 2: New Perspectives. Ed. by Rudolf H. Moos. (Illus.). 452p. 1984. 49.50 (*0-306-41681-6*, Plenum Med Bk) Plenum.

Coping with Physical Illness, Vol. 2: New Perspectives. Ed. by Rudolf H. Moos. (Illus.). 452p. 1989. pap. 29.50 (*0-306-43350-8*, Plenum Med Bk) Plenum.

Coping with Police Stress. 52p. (Orig.). (C). 1993. pap. text ed. 20.00 (*1-56806-833-6*) Diane Pub.

***Coping with Postnatal Depression.** Bryanne Barnett. 129p. (Orig.). 1995. pap. 14.95 (*0-85091-471-X*, Pub. by Lothian Pub AT) Seven Hills Bk.

Coping with Poverty: Pentecostals & Christian Base Communities in Brazil. Cecilia L. Mariz. LC 93-12511. 224p. (C). 1993. 39.95 (*1-56639-112-1*); pap. 16.95 (*1-56639-113-X*) Temple U Pr.

Coping with Prostate Cancer: A Guide to Living with Prostate Cancer for You & Your Family. Robert H. Phillips. LC 93-43373. 294p. 1994. pap. 11.95 (*0-89529-564-4*) Avery Pub.

Coping with Psychiatric & Psychological Testimony, 3 vols. 4th ed. Jay Ziskin & David Faust. LC 87-83111. 560p. 1988. Vol. I, 560p. write for info. (*0-9603630-7-6*); Vol. 2, 584p. write for info. (*0-9603630-8-4*); Vol. 3, 904p. write for info. (*0-9603630-9-2*) Law & Psych.

Coping with Psychiatric & Psychological Testimony, 3 vols., Set. 4th ed. Jay Ziskin & David Faust. LC 87-83111. 1988. 240.00 (*0-9603630-6-8*) Law & Psych.

Coping with Radiation Therapy: A Ray of Hope. Daniel Cukier & Virginia E. McCullough. 240p. 1994. pap. 14.95 (*1-56565-147-2*) Lowell Hse.

Coping with Reality: Handling Money, In-Laws, Babies & Other Details of Daily Life. Jeanne W. Lindsay. (Teenage Couples Ser.). (Illus.). (Orig.). (YA). (gr. 7 up). 1995. student ed 2.50 (*0-930934-88-1*) Morning Glory.

An Asterisk (*) at the beginning of an entry indicates that the title is appearing in BIP for the first time.

Coping with Reality: Handling Money, In-Laws, Babies & Other Details of Daily Life. Jeanne W. Lindsay. (Teenage Couples Ser.). (Illus.). 192p. (Orig.). (YA). (gr. 7 up). 1995. 15.95 (*0-930934-87-3*); pap. 9.95 (*0-930934-86-5*) Morning Glory.

Coping with Rheumatoid Arthritis: A Guide to Living with Arthritis for You & Your Family. Robert H. Phillips. LC 88-3450. 272p. 1988. pap. 9.95 (*0-89529-371-4*) Avery Pub.

Coping with Romantic Breakup. Allen J. Ottens. (Coping Ser.). 147p. (YA). (gr. 7-12). 1987. lib. bdg. 15.95 (*0-8239-0649-3*) Rosen Group.

Coping with Safer Sex. Ellen V. Mahoney. Ed. by Ruth Rosen. (Coping Ser.). (YA). (gr. 7-12). 1989. lib. bdg. 15.95 (*0-8239-0999-9*) Rosen Group.

Coping with Satanism. Allen Ottens & Rick Myer. Ed. by Ruth Rosen. (Coping Ser.). (YA). (gr. 7-12). 1994. 15.95 (*0-8239-1423-2*) Rosen Group.

Coping with Schizophrenia. Mona Wasow. LC 81-86713. 1982. pap. 9.95 (*0-8314-0062-5*) Sci & Behavior.

***Coping with Schizophrenia: A Guide for Families.** Kim T. Mueser & Susan Gingerich. LC 94-67043. (Illus.). 355p. 1994. text ed. 24.95 (*1-879237-79-2*); pap. 13.95 (*1-879237-78-4*) New Harbinger.

Coping with School Age Fatherhood. rev. ed. Michael Pennetti. LC 86-20288. (Coping Ser.). 148p. (gr. 7-12). 1988. lib. bdg. 15.95 (*0-8239-0824-0*) Rosen Group.

Coping with School-Age Motherhood. rev. ed. Nancy Minor & Patricia Bradley. (J). (gr. 7-12). 1988. lib. bdg. 15.95 (*0-8239-0923-9*) Rosen Group.

Coping with Science. Gernot Bohme. 122p. (C). 1992. text ed. 42.50 (*0-8133-1237-X*) Westview.

Coping with Seasonality & Drought. Martha A. Chen. 258p. (C). 1991. text ed. 29.95 (*0-8039-9689-6*) Sage.

Coping with Severe Mental Illness: Families Speak Out. Martha B. Mermier. LC 93-20490. (Studies in Health & Human Services: Vol. 23). 212p. 1993. text ed. 89.95 (*0-7734-9285-2*) E Mellen.

Coping with Sexism in the Military. Mary Stremlow. 1990. 14.95 (*0-8239-1025-3*) Rosen Group.

Coping with Sexual Abuse. rev. ed. Judith Cooney. Ed. by R. Rosen. (Coping Ser.). 118p. (YA). (gr. 7-12). 1991. teacher ed 5.95 (*0-8239-0846-1*); lib. bdg. 15.95 (*0-8239-1336-8*) Rosen Group.

Coping with Sexual Harassment. rev. ed. Beryl Black. Ed. by Ruth Rosen. (Coping Ser.). 149p. (YA). (gr. 7 up). 1992. lib. bdg. 15.95 (*0-8239-1174-8*); pap. 8.95 (*0-8239-0764-3*) Rosen Group.

Coping with Sibling Rivalry. Shari Cohen. Ed. by Ruth Rosen. (Coping Ser.). (YA). (gr. 7-12). 1989. lib. bdg. 15.95 (*0-8239-0977-8*) Rosen Group.

***Coping with Sleep Disorders.** Carolyn Simpson. LC 95-6509. (Coping Ser.). (J). 1995. write for info. (*0-8239-2068-2*) Rosen Group.

Coping with Social Change: Programs That Work: Proceedings of a Conference. Ed. by Irene Hoskins. (ENG & SPA.). 1990. pap. (*0-910473-20-X*) Intl Fed Ageing.

Coping with Sorrow on the Loss of Your Pet. 2nd rev. ed. Moira Anderson. LC 87-29128. 184p. (Orig.). 1994. pap. 10.95 (*0-9619232-2-9*) Peregrine Pr.

Coping with Spain. Garry Marvin. (Coping with... Ser.). (Illus.). 192p. 1990. pap. 13.95 (*0-631-16832-X*) Blackwell Pubs.

Coping with Special-Needs Classmates. Sherri N. McCarthy-Tucker. LC 92-40662. 1993. 15.95 (*0-8239-1598-0*) Rosen Group.

Coping with Speech Anxiety. Joe Ayres & Tim Hopf. LC 92-30164. (Communication & Information Science Ser.). 144p. 1993. text ed. 39.50 (*0-89391-882-2*); pap. text ed. 19.95 (*0-89391-986-1*) Ablex Pub.

Coping with Sports Injuries. Lawrence Clayton. (YA). 1992. 15.95 (*0-8239-1453-4*) Rosen Group.

Coping with Stage Fright. Gerald L. Ratliff. (Illus.). 119p. (gr. 7-12). 1985. 15.95 (*0-8239-0638-8*) Rosen Group.

Coping with Stigma. Rhoda McFarland. Ed. by Ruth Rosen. (Coping Ser.). (YA). (gr. 7-12). 1989. lib. bdg. 15.95 (*0-8239-0998-0*) Rosen Group.

***Coping with Street Gangs.** Margot Webb. Ed. by Roger Rosen. (Coping Ser.). 64p. (YA). (gr. 7-12). 1995. lib. bdg. 15.95 (*0-8239-2145-X*) Rosen Group.

Coping with Stress: A Guide to Living. James W. Mills. LC 82-16044. 151p. 1982. pap. text ed. 16.95 (*0-471-87678-X*) Wiley.

Coping with Stress: A Workbook. 44p. 7.95 (*0-317-05943-2*) WFS.

***Coping with Stress & Anxiety: An Interactional Perspective.** Norman Endler & James Parker. (International Series in Experimental Social Psychology: Vol. 32). 250p. 1995. text ed. 72.01 (*0-08-041938-0*, Pergamon Pr) Elsevier.

Coping with Stress & Distress. Desmond Ford. 84p. (Orig.). 1984. pap. text ed. 5.00 (*1-883619-07-6*) D Ford Pubns.

Coping with Stress at Work. Ed. by Judi Marshall & Cary L. Cooper. 256p. 1981. text ed. 59.95 (*0-566-02338-5*) Ashgate Pub Co.

Coping with Stress in Childhood. J. Frederick Garman & Charlotte G. Garman. 20p. 1990. 2.95 (*1-56456-035-X*, 239) W Gladden Found.

Coping with Stress in College. Mark Rowh. 172p. 1989. pap. 9.95 (*0-87447-334-9*) College Bd.

Coping with Stress in Teaching. Joy N. Humphrey & James H. Humphrey. LC 86-47685. (Stress in Modern Society Ser.: No. 3). 1986. 32.50 (*0-404-63253-X*) AMS Pr.

Coping with Stress in the Health Professions: A Practical Guide. Philip Burnard. (Therapy in Practice Ser.: No. 21). pap. 22.50 (*0-412-38910-X*) Chapman & Hall.

Coping with Study Strategies. rev. ed. Gary Bergreen. (Coping Ser.). (YA). (gr. 7-12). 1990. 15.95 (*0-8239-1140-3*) Rosen Group.

Coping with Substance Abuse. rev. ed. Rhoda McFarland. Ed. by Ruth Rosen. (Coping Ser.). 144p. (YA). (gr. 7 up). 1990. lib. bdg. 15.95 (*0-8239-1135-7*) Rosen Group.

Coping with Suicide. rev. ed. Judie Smith. LC 86-10076. (Coping Ser.). 128p. (YA). (gr. 7-12). 1990. lib. bdg. 15.95 (*0-8239-1052-0*) Rosen Group.

Coping with Suicide: A Pastoral Aid. Gerard Green. 112p. (Orig.). 1992. pap. 7.95 (*1-85607-046-8*, Pub. by Columba Pr IE) Twenty-Third.

Coping with Surgery: A Guide to Self Help. Gary Boyd. 56p. (Orig.). 1990. pap. 6.95 (*0-910467-09-9*) Heritage Assocs.

Coping with Sustained Low Fertility in France & the Netherlands. N. Van Nimwegen et al. 252p. 1993. pap. 60.00 (*90-265-1343-7*, Pub. by Swets Pub Serv NE) Taylor & Francis.

Coping with Tax Reform. Carol A. Myers & Ronald G. Weiner. LC 87-406325. 51p. reprint ed. pap. 25.00 (*0-7837-6626-2*, 2046208) Bks Demand.

Coping with Technological Dualism in the Farm Equipment Sector of the Sudan. vii, 97p. (Orig.). 1987. pap. 16.00 (*92-2-105481-0*) Intl Labour Office.

Coping with Teen Gambling. Jane Haubrich-Casperson & Doug Van Nispen. LC 92-41549. (YA). 1993. 15.95 (*0-8239-1512-3*) Rosen Group.

Coping with Teen Parenting. rev. ed. Kay Beyer. Ed. by Ruth Rosen. (Coping Ser.). (YA). (gr. 7-12). 1992. lib. bdg. 15.95 (*0-8239-1525-5*) Rosen Group.

Coping with Teenage Motherhood. Carolyn Simpson. Ed. by Ruth Rosen. LC 92-8168. (Coping Ser.). (YA). (gr. 7-12). 1992. 15.95 (*0-8239-1458-5*) Rosen Group.

Coping with Teenagers. Judith Wolfe. 231p. 22.00 (*0-932966-30-6*) Permanent Pr.

Coping with Texas & Other Staggering Feets: The Autobiography of an Ancient Statue. Fray A. Chavez. LC 91-33930. (Illus.). 96p. (Orig.). 1992. pap. 6.95 (*0-86534-169-9*) Sunstone Pr.

Coping with the Biomedical Literature: A Primer for the Scientist & the Clinician. Ed. by Kenneth S. Warren. LC 81-5149. 246p. 1981. text ed. 69.50 (*0-275-91355-4*, C1355, Praeger Pubs) Greenwood.

Coping with the Crises in Your Life. Edgar Jackson. LC 73-369. 232p. 1986. 25.00 (*0-87668-413-4*) Aronson.

Coping with the Cults: Practical Insights for Concerned Christians. Lorri MacGregor. 160p. (Orig.). 1992. pap. 6.99 (*0-89081-940-8*) Harvest Hse.

Coping with the Disruptive College Student: A Practical Model. Gerald Amada. LC 93-34165. 124p. 1994. pap. 16.95 (*0-912557-16-8*) Coll Admin Pubns.

Coping with the Economic Crisis: Alternative Responses to Economic Recession in Advanced Industrial Societies. Ed. by Hans Keman et al. (Modern Politics Ser.: Vol. 17). 240p. (C). 1988. text ed. 45.00 (*0-8039-8118-X*); pap. text ed. 17.95 (*0-8039-8119-8*) Sage.

Coping with the Final Tragedy: Dying & Grieving in Cross Cultural Perspective. Ed. by David Counts & Dorothy Counts. (Perspectives on Death & Dying Ser.). 366p. 1991. text ed. 35.95 (*0-89503-082-9*); pap. text ed. 25.95 (*0-89503-081-0*) Baywood Pub.

Coping with the Gluten-Free Diet. Marion N. Wood. (Illus.). 164p. 1982. spiral bd., pap. 33.95 (*0-398-04718-9*) C C Thomas.

Coping with the Latin American Debt. Ed. by Robert Wesson. LC 87-2745. 218p. 1988. text ed. 55.00 (*0-275-92996-5*, C2996, Praeger Pubs) Greenwood.

Coping with the Loss of a Pet: A Gentle Guide for All Who Love a Pet. rev. ed. Christina M. Lemieux. (Illus.). 60p. (Orig.). 1989. 14.95 (*0-9622158-0-5*); pap. 9.95 (*0-9622158-1-3*) W R Clark Co.
This gentle & caring guide was written to assist & comfort those who have experienced the loss of a cherished pet. COPING WITH THE LOSS OF A PET is a "how to" book & contains specific strategies to assist the bereaved pet owner & those supportive friends who are attempting to comfort one who has lost a pet. The death of a beloved pet can be a devastating emotional experience & is an experience faced by all who love & cherish a pet. Unlike other areas where loss & death occur, the grief & pain felt at the loss of a beloved pet is little understood & only slight guidance or comfort has been available. Authored by thanatologist & cultural anthropologist Christina M. Lemieux, COPING WITH THE LOSS OF A PET helps us understand the dimensions & effects of bereavement with regard to ourselves & those whom we care about. By drawing on her own background of compassion, experience, & practical wisdom, Dr. Lemieux is able to combine encouragement with insight as she provides help & counsel while accompanying us through the experience of aloneness, grieving, & ultimately the process of healing. Dr. Lemieux has devoted much of her professional career to the subject of death & dying. She is an Associate Professor of Anthropology at Kutztown University of Pennsylvania & maintains an extensive involvement in fieldwork, classroom instruction, educational programs for health care professionals, & involvement in hospice training programs. ***Publisher Provided Annotation.***

Coping with the Male Ego in the Workplace. Sandra Grymes & Mary Stanton. 192p. 1993. 15.95 (*0-681-41454-5*) Longmeadow Pr.

Coping with the Miracle: Japan's Unions Explore New International Relations. Hugh Williamson. LC 94-18236. (International Labour Ser.). (C). 1994. pap. text ed. 19.95 (*0-7453-0937-2*) Westview.

Coping with the Miracle: Japan's Unions Explore New International Relations. Hugh Williamson. LC 94-18236. (International Labour Ser.). (C). 1995. text ed. 67.95 (*0-7453-0938-0*) Westview.

Coping with the Multi-Handicapped Hearing Impaired: A Practical Approach. Ed. by Hugh T. Prickett & Earlene Duncan. 90p. (C). 1988. text ed. 28.95x (*0-398-05412-6*) C C Thomas.

***Coping with the Multi-Handicapped Hearing Impaired: A Practical Approach.** Ed. by Hugh T. Prickett & Earlene Duncan. 90p. 1988. pap. 15.95 (*0-398-06333-8*) C C Thomas.

Coping with the Oil Crisis: French & German Experiences. Horst Mendershausen. LC 75-35485. 127p. reprint ed. pap. 36.20 (*0-7837-3048-9*, 2023807) Bks Demand.

Coping with the Past: Germany & Austria after 1945. Ed. by Kathy Harms et al. LC 90-13031. 280p. 1991. 17.50 (*0-299-97072-8*) U of Wis Pr.

Coping with the Purple Menace: A Barney Apathy Therapy Kit. Kevin R. Haff. (Illus.). 64p. (Orig.). 1993. pap. 6.99 (*0-9639362-0-4*) Schone Bks.

Coping with the Stressed-out People in Your Life. Ronald G. Nathan & Marian R. Stuart. 288p. (Orig.). 1994. pap. 10.00 (*0-345-38186-6*) Ballantine.

Coping with Threatened Identities. Glynis M. Breakwell. 280p. 1987. 33.00 (*0-416-37120-5*, 9852) Routledge Chapman & Hall.

***Coping with Tourists: European Reactions to Mass Tourism.** Jeremy Boisservain. (New Directions in Anthropology Ser.: Vol. 1). (Illus.). 240p. 1995. 39.95 (*1-57181-878-2*); pap. 19.95 (*1-57181-900-2*) Berghahn Bks.

***Coping with Trauma: A Guide to Self-Understanding.** Jon G. Allen. 384p. 1995. boxed 23.95 (*0-88048-720-8*, 8720) Am Psychiatric.

Coping with Trauma: Theory, Prevention & Treatment. Rolf J. Kleber et al. 328p. 1992. 59.90 (*90-265-1227-9*, Pub. by Swets Pub Serv NE) Taylor & Francis.

Coping with Traumas of Family Life. (Dialog Ser.). 120p. 1989. student ed, pap. 4.95 (*0-8341-1263-9*); teacher ed, pap. 3.95 (*0-8341-1262-0*) Beacon Hill.

Coping with Trouble: How Science Reacts to Political Disturbances of Research Conditions. Ed. by Uwe Schimank & Andreas Stucke. LC 94-31141. 400p. 1994. text ed. 59.95 (*0-312-12240-3*) St Martin.

Coping with Two Cultures: British Asian & Indo-Canadian Adolescents. Ed. by P. A. Singh Ghuman. (Multilingual Matters Ser.: No. 99). 160p. 1993. 69.00 (*1-85359-202-1*, Pub. by Multilingual Matters UK); pap. 24.95 (*1-85359-201-3*, Pub. by Multilingual Matters UK) Taylor & Francis.

Coping with U. S. Export Controls, 2 vols, Set. (Commercial Law & Practice Ser.). 1145p. 1992. pap. text ed. 80.00 (*0-685-56867-9*, A4-4366) PLI.

Coping with Uncertainty: Behavioral & Developmental Perspectives. Ed. by David S. Palermo. (Penn State Series on Child & Adolescent Development). 224p. 1989. 45.00 (*0-8058-0157-X*) L Erlbaum Assocs.

Coping with Uncertainty: Insights from the New Sciences of Chaos, Self-Organization. Uria Merry. LC 94-16996. 224p. 1995. text ed. 59.95 (*0-275-94910-9*, Praeger Pubs) Greenwood.

***Coping with Uncertainty: Insights from the New Sciences of Chaos, Self-Organization & Complexity.** Uri Merry. LC 94-16996. 209p. 1995. pap. text ed. 18.95 (*0-275-95152-9*) Greenwood.

Coping with Uncertainty: Policy & Politics in the National Health Service. David J. Hunter. LC 80-41270. (Social Policy Research Monograph Ser.: No. 2). 312p. reprint ed. pap. 89.00 (*0-8357-8853-9*, 2033340) Bks Demand.

Coping with Unemployment. 1992. lib. bdg. 250.00 (*0-8490-5615-2*) Gordon Pr.

Coping with Unemployment. Brian Jud. Ed. by Charles Lipka. (Illus.). 292p. (Orig.). (C). 1993. pap. 14.95 (*1-880218-03-8*) Mktg Dir Inc.

Coping with Unhappy Children. Ed. by Ved Varma. LC 92-38453. (Education Ser.). 192p. 1993. text ed. 70.00 (*0-304-32414-0*); pap. text ed. 24.95 (*0-304-32436-1*) Cassell.

Coping with Venereal Disease. rev. ed. Gabrielle Edwards. (Coping Ser.). (Illus.). (gr. 7-12). 1988. lib. bdg. 15.95 (*0-8239-0926-3*) Rosen Group.

Coping with Verbal Abuse. Janet Grosshandler. Ed. by Ruth Rosen. (Coping Ser.). (YA). (gr. 7-12). 1989. lib. bdg. 15.95 (*0-8239-0979-4*) Rosen Group.

***Coping with Violence: A Guide for Human Service Workers.** Vaughan Bowie. (Illus.). 1995. pap. 25.00 (*1-871177-46-4*, Pub. by Whiting & Birch UK) Paul & Co Pubs.

***Coping with War-Induced Stress: The Gulf War & the Israeli Response.** Zahava Solomon. LC 94-43373. (Stress & Coping Ser.). 250p. 1995. 39.50 (*0-306-44788-6*, Plenum Pr) Plenum.

Coping with Weapons & Violence in School & on Your Streets. Maryann Miller. Ed. by Ruth Rosen. (Coping Ser.). (YA). (gr. 7-12). 1993. 15.95 (*0-8239-1435-6*) Rosen Group.

Coping with Weight Problems. Paul J. Gelinas. (Coping Ser.). 131p. (YA). (gr. 7-12). 1983. lib. bdg. 15.95 (*0-8239-0598-5*) Rosen Group.

***Coping with Workplace Change.** J. Shep Jeffries. Ed. by Philip Gerould. (Fifty-Minute Ser.). (Illus.). 100p. (Orig.). 1995. pap. 9.95 (*1-56052-308-5*) Crisp Pubns.

***Coping with Your Adolescent.** Larry Waldman. 104p. (Orig.). 1994. pap. 10.95 (*1-57174-002-3*) Hampton Roads Pub Co.

Coping with Your Anger: A Christian Guide. Andrew D. Lester. LC 82-24730. 114p. 1983. pap. 8.99 (*0-664-24471-8*, Westminster) Westminster John Knox.

Coping with Your Grown Children. Edwin L. Klingelhofer. LC 88-13734. 304p. 1989. 18.95 (*0-89603-159-4*) Humana.

Coping with Your Headaches. Seymour Diamond. 1988. pap. 9.95 (*0-8236-1083-7*) Intl Univs Pr.

Coping Within the Alcoholic Family. Joseph Perez. LC 86-70658. xiii, 178p. 1986. pap. text ed. 9.45 (*0-915202-63-8*) Accel Devel.

Copito: The Christmas Chihuahua. Jean Nelson-Erichsen. LC 82-72080. (Copito Stories). (Illus.). 80p. (J). (gr. k-5). 1982. pap. 3.50 (*0-943864-07-0*) Davenport.

Copland: Since 1943. Aaron Copland & Vivian Perlis. (Illus.). 480p. 1990. pap. 14.95 (*0-312-05066-6*) St Martin.

***Copland: Since 1943.** Aaron Copland & Vivian Perlis. 1049p. 1994. text ed. 83.92 (*1-56956-497-3*, BR9226) W A T Braille.

***Copland: 1900 through 1942.** Aaron Copland & Vivian Perlis. 917p. 1994. text ed. 73.36 (*1-56956-496-5*, BR9225) W A T Braille.

Copland: 1900-1942. Aaron Copland & Vivian Perlis. (Illus.). 408p. 1987. pap. 12.95 (*0-312-01149-0*) St Martin.

Coplas de los Siete Pecados Mortales: Second & Third Continuations. Juan De Mena. Ed. by Gladys Rivera. 25.50 (*0-916379-16-7*) Scripta.

Coplas de Mingo Revulgo. Vivana Brodey. (Spanish Ser.: No. 30). 308p. 1986. 25.00 (*0-942260-74-0*) Hispanic Seminary.

Copp for Hire. Don Pendleton. LC 87-81420. 272p. 1987. 16.95 (*1-55611-064-2*) D I Fine.

Copp in Deep. Don Pendleton. 252p. 1989. 17.95 (*1-55611-141-X*) D I Fine.

Copp in Deep. Don Pendleton. 1991. mass mkt. 4.50 (*0-06-100248-8*, Harp PBks) HarpC.

Copp in Shock. Don Pendleton. LC 91-58661. 256p. 1992. 19.95 (*1-55611-287-4*) D I Fine.

Copp in Shock. Don Pendleton. 1993. mass mkt. 4.99 (*0-06-100459-6*, Harp PBks) HarpC.

Copp in the Dark. Don Pendleton. (Joe Copp Ser.: No. 4). 1990. 18.95 (*1-55611-210-6*) D I Fine.

Copp in the Dark. Don Pendleton. 1992. mass mkt. 4.99 (*0-06-100347-6*, Harp PBks) HarpC.

Copp on Fire. Don Pendleton. LC 87-46278. 1988. 16.95 (*1-55611-088-X*) D I Fine.

Copp on Fire. Don Pendleton. 1990. mass mkt. 4.50 (*0-06-100036-1*, Harp PBks) HarpC.

Copp on Ice. Don Pendleton. 1991. 18.95 (*1-55611-235-1*) D I Fine.

Copp on Ice. Don Pendleton. 1992. mass mkt. 4.99 (*0-06-100458-8*, Harp PBks) HarpC.

Coppelia see Little Box of Ballet Stories

Copper. (Metals & Minerals Ser.). 1993. lib. bdg. 259.95 (*0-8490-9001-6*) Gordon Pr.

Copper. M. Lambert. (Spotlight on Resources Ser.). (Illus.). 48p. (J). (gr. 5 up). 1985. lib. bdg. 17.27 (*0-86592-270-5*); lib. bdg. 12.95 (*0-685-58324-4*) Rourke Corp.

Copper Alloys to Distillations see Encyclopedia of Chemical Technology

Copper & Bronze Ages in South America. Erland Nordenskiold. LC 75-46057. (Comparative Ethnographical Studies: Vol. 4). reprint ed. 35.50 (*0-404-15144-2*) AMS Pr.

Copper & Coordination Chemistry: Biochemical & Inorganic Perspectives. Ed. by Kenneth D. Karlin & Jon Zubieta. (Illus.). 512p. (C). 1983. lib. bdg. 120.00 (*0-940030-03-9*) Adenine Pr.

Copper & Copper Alloys Including Electrical Conductors (179 Standards) see ASTM Annual Book of Standards, 1986

Copper & Copper Mining. R. L. Atkinson. 1989. pap. 25.00 (*0-85263-895-7*, Pub. by Shire UK) St Mut.

Copper & Lymphomas. M. Hrgovcic & C. Shullenberger. LC 83-14335. 1984. 141.00 (*0-8493-6331-4*, CRC Reprint) Franklin.

Copper & Nickel Converters: Proceedings of a Symposium on Converter Operating Practices Sponsored by the TMS-AIME Pyrometallurgy Committee at the 108th AIME Annual Meeting in New Orleans, LA, February 19-21, 1979. Metallurgical Society of AIME Staff. Ed. by Robert E. Johnson. LC 79-87441. (Illus.). 411p. reprint ed. pap. 117.20 (*0-8357-3202-9*, 2052362) Bks Demand.

Copper & Tin: The Distribution of Mineral Resources & the Nature of the Metals Trade in the Bronze Age, Including Supplement. James D. Muhly. (Connecticut Academy of Arts & Sciences Ser., Trans.: Vol. 43). 380p. 1973. pap. 69.50 (*0-685-22879-7*) Elliots Bks.

***Copper & Uranium in Pennsylvanian & Permian Sedimentary Rocks, Northern Sangre de Cristo Range, Colorado.** David A. Lindsey & Ralph E. Clark. LC 94-41507. (Bulletin Ser.: No. 2116). 1995. write for info. (*0-615-00389-3*) US Geol Survey.

C

An Asterisk (*) at the beginning of an entry indicates that the title is appearing in BIP for the first time.

Copper & Zinc in Inflammation. Ed. by R. Milanino et al. (Inflammation & Drug Therapy Ser.). 160p. (C). 1989. lib. bdg. 70.50 (*0-7462-0079-X*) Kluwer Ac.

Copper Angel of Piper's Mill & How She Saved Her Town. Linda Cunningham. LC 89-83406. (Illus.). 48p. (J). (gr. 3-5). 1989. 12.95 (*0-89272-274-6*) Down East.

Copper Art Jewelry: A Different Luster. Mathew L. Burkholz & Linda L. Kaplan. LC 92-60623. (Illus.). 176p. 1992. text ed. 49.95 (*0-88740-419-7*) Schiffer.

Copper Artifacts in Late Eastern Woodlands Prehistory. Claire G. Goodman. Ed. by Anne-Marie Cantwell. 104p. (C). 1984. 11.00 (*0-942118-16-2*, E78.E2G66) Ctr Amer Arche.

Copper Base Powder Metallurgy. Metal Powder Industries Federation Staff. Ed. by Pierre W. Taubenblat. LC 80-81464. (New Perspectives in Powder Metallurgy: Fundamentals, Methods, & Applications Ser.: No. 7). (Illus.). 227p. reprint ed. pap. 64.70 (*0-7837-5161-3*, 2044890) Bks Demand.

Copper Beech. Maeve Binchy. LC 92-18601. 1992. 22.50 (*0-385-30775-6*) Delacorte.

Copper Beech. Maeve Binchy. 1993. mass mkt. 5.99 (*0-440-21329-0*) Dell.

Copper Beech. large type ed. Maeve Binchy. LC 92-18601. 1992. pap. 28.00 (*0-385-30853-1*, Delacorte LT) BDD LT Grp.

Copper Beech. large type ed. Maeve Binchy. LC 93-36334. 1994. pap. 17.95 (*0-8161-5810-X*, Large Print Bks) Hall.

Copper Bioavailabity & Metabolism. C Kies. (Advances in Experimental Medicine & Biology Ser.: Vol. 258). (Illus.). 314p. 1989. 85.00 (*0-306-43373-7*, Plenum Pr) Plenum.

Copper Bronze Age in India. D. P. Agarwal. (Illus.). 286p. 1971. text ed. 27.00 (*0-685-13646-9*) Coronet Bks.

Copper Camp. Writers' Program, Montana Staff. LC 73-3632. (Illus.). reprint ed. write for info. (*0-404-57933-7*) AMS Pr.

Copper Canyon Conspiracy. Carolyn Keene. Ed. by Anne Greenberg. (HB - ND Supermystery Ser.). 224p. (Orig.). (J). 1994. mass mkt. 3.99 (*0-671-88514-6*, Archway) PB.

Copper Coinage of Tsar Peter I, Seventeen Hundred to Seventeen Twenty-Five: In Russian, with Preface in English. A. A. Ilyin. Ed. by Russian Numismatic Society Staff. (Illus.). 62p. 1984. pap. 13.00 (*0-912710-60-8*) Russian Numis.

C

Copper Coins of Europe till 1892. Frank C. Higgins. 1970. 4.00 (*0-685-51545-1*) S J Durst.

Copper Coins of India. W. H. Valentine. 1978. 25.00 (*0-685-51122-7*) S J Durst.

Copper Coins of Massachusetts. Hillyer Ryder. (Illus.). 1981. reprint ed. pap. 6.00 (*0-915262-66-5*) S J Durst.

Copper Contacts: A True Account of Extraterrestrial Events. John I. Norkin. 1994. 15.95 (*0-533-10845-4*) Vantage.

Copper-Containing Composites. Rutgers University Staff. 74p. 1970. 11.10 (*0-317-34502-8*, 65) Intl Copper.

Copper Country. John S. Penrod. (Orig.). 1990. pap. 4.49 (*0-942618-23-8*) Penrod-Hiawatha.

Copper Country Adventure. Ethel C. Brill. LC 87-31485. 213p. (J). (gr. 4 up). 1988. 8.50 (*0-933249-05-5*) Mid-Peninsula Lib.

Copper Country Journal: The Diary of Schoolmaster Henry Hobart, 1863-1864. Henry Hobart. Ed. by Philip P. Mason. LC 91-11188. (Great Lakes Bks.). 351p. (C). 1991. text ed. 34.95 (*0-8143-2341-3*, Great Lks Bks); pap. text ed. 16.95 (*0-8143-2342-1*, Great Lks Bks) Wayne St U Pr.

Copper Country Logger's Tale. rev. ed. (Copper Country Local History Ser.: Vol. 2). (Illus.). 28p. 1976. 1.00 (*0-942363-01-9*) C J Monette.

Copper Crown. Patricia Kennealy. (Tale of Aeron Ser.: Bk. 1). 432p. 1986. pap. 5.50 (*0-451-45050-7*, ROC) NAL-Dutton.

Copper Crown. Lane Von Herzen. LC 92-53572. (Contemporary Fiction Ser.). 240p. 1992. pap. 10.00 (*0-452-26916-4*, Plume) NAL-Dutton.

Copper Crown. large type ed. Lane Von Herzen. 395p. 1992. reprint ed. lib. bdg. 17.95 (*1-56054-370-1*) Thorndike Pr.

***Copper Crucible: How the Arizona Miners' Strike of 1983 Recast Labor-Management Relations in America.** Jonathan D. Rosenblum. LC 94-27852. 264p. 1994. 38.00 (*0-87546-331-2*) ILR Pr.

***Copper Crucible: How the Arizona Miners' Strike of 1983 Recast Labor-Management Relations in America.** Jonathan D. Rosenblum. LC 94-27852. 264p. 1994. pap. 16.95 (*0-87546-332-0*) ILR Pr.

Copper Deficiency & Toxicity: Acquired & Inherited, in Plants, Animals, & Man. Charles A. Owen, Jr. LC 81-11061. (Copper in Biology & Medicine Ser.). 189p. 1982. 28.00 (*0-8155-0868-9*) Noyes.

Copper Enameling. Jo Robert & Jean O'Hara. 1956. 2.95 (*0-934706-00-X*) Prof Pubns Ohio.

Copper Falls - Just a Memory. (Copper Country Local History Ser.: Vol. 13). (Illus.). 96p. 1978. 2.50 (*0-942363-12-4*) C J Monette.

Copper in Animal Wastes & Sewage Sludge. Ed. by P. L. L'Hermite & J. Handtschutter. xiv, 378p. 1981. lib. bdg. 74.50 (*90-277-1293-X*) Kluwer Ac.

Copper in Feedwater to Supercritical Steam Generating Units. Cyrus William Rice & Co. 55p. 1965. 8.25 (*0-317-34503-6*, 69) Intl Copper.

Copper in Iron & Steel. Ed. by Iain LeMay & McDonald Schetky. LC 82-17615. 446p. 1982. 59.50 (*0-471-05913-7*) Wiley.

Copper in Soils & Plants. J. F. Loneragan. 1981. text ed. 103.00 (*0-12-455520-9*) Acad Pr.

Copper in the Environment, 2 pts. Jerome O. Nriagu. Incl. Pt. 1. Ecological Cycling. 536p. 1980. reprint ed. 94.00 (*0-471-04778-3*); (Environmental Science & Technology Texts & Monographs Ser.). 1980. write for info. (*0-318-56422-X*, Wiley-Interscience) Krieger.

Copper in the World Economy. Dorothea Mezger. LC 79-3883. 282p. 1980. 16.00 (*0-85345-544-9*); pap. 8.00 (*0-85345-545-7*) Monthly Rev.

Copper Indium Diselenide for Photovoltaic Applications. Ed. by T. J. Coutts et al. (Materials Science Monographs: No. 37). 640p. 1986. 164.00 (*0-444-42673-6*) Elsevier.

Copper Industry in Zambia: Foreign Mining Companies in a Developing Country. Simon Cunningham. LC 81-11869. 366p. 1981. text ed. 75.00 (*0-275-90602-7*, C0602, Praeger Pubs) Greenwood.

***Copper Jack: My Life on the Force.** Jack Webster & Rosemary Aubert. (Illus.). 220p. Date not set. pap. 19.99 (*0-614-06792-8*) Dun.

Copper King's Daughter: From Cape Cod to Crooked River. Dorothy L. McCall. LC 74-188836. (Illus.). 200p. 1972. pap. 9.95 (*0-8323-0203-1*) Binford Mort.

Copper Lantern. Karlis Freivals. Ed. by Bradley R. Strahan. (Black Buzzard Illustrated Poetry Chapbook Ser.). (Illus.). 28p. 1982. reprint ed. pap. 3.50 (*0-938872-01-X*) Black Buzzard.

Copper Mandarina: A Memoir. Gerald Murphy. 144p. 1984. 34.00 (*0-7212-0674-3*, Pub. by Regency Press) St Mut.

Copper Metallurgy. Ed. by Reinhart P. Ehrlich. LC 70-633878. 379p. reprint ed. pap. 108.10 (*0-317-10290-7*, 2012652) Bks Demand.

Copper Mining & Management. Thomas R. Navin. LC 78-2669. 450p. reprint ed. pap. 128.30 (*0-317-28914-4*, 2020438) Bks Demand.

Copper, Molybdenum, & Vanadium in Biological Systems: Structure & Bonding, Vol. 53. M. J. Clarke et al. (Illus.). 166p. 1983. 63.00 (*0-387-12042-4*) Spr-Verlag.

Copper Moons. Susan Y. Ackerman. LC 89-37901. 264p. (Orig.). 1990. pap. 9.95 (*0-8361-3510-5*) Herald Pr.

Copper Mountain Mandala: Mystic Land of Odiyan. (Illus.). 500p. Date not set. write for info. (*0-913546-93-3*) Dharma Pub.

Copper Oxide Superconductors. Charle P. Poole et al. LC 88-18569. 289p. 1988. text ed. 79.95 (*0-471-62342-3*) Wiley.

Copper Peacock. large type ed. Ruth Rendell. 1993. pap. 16.95 (*0-7927-1262-5*, Paragon Lrg Print) Chivers N Amer.

Copper Peacock & Other Stories. Ruth Rendell. 1991. 17.95 (*0-89296-465-0*) Mysterious Pr.

Copper Peacock & Other Stories. Ruth Rendell. 192p. 1992. mass mkt. 4.99 (*0-446-40055-6*, Mysterious Paperbk) Warner Bks.

Copper Peacock & Other Stories. large type ed. Ruth Rendell. 1992. 18.95 (*0-7927-1263-3*, Eagle Lrg Print) Chivers N Amer.

Copper Pieces. Fay P. LeCompte. LC 86-72349. 100p. 1987. 10.00 (*0-934943-08-7*) Thirteen Colonies Pr.

Copper Proteins. Ed. by Thomas G. Spiro. LC 81-7465. 376p. 1981. 78.50 (*0-471-04400-8*) Wiley.

Copper Proteins & Copper Enzymes, Vol. I. Ed. by Rene Lontie. 256p. 1984. 168.00 (*0-8493-6470-1*, QP552) CRC Pr.

Copper Proteins & Copper Enzymes, Vol. II. Ed. by Rene Lontie. 304p. 1984. 191.00 (*0-8493-6471-X*, QP552) CRC Pr.

Copper Proteins & Copper Enzymes, Vol. III. Ed. by Rene Lontie. 272p. 1984. 168.00 (*0-8493-6472-8*, QP552, CRC Reprint) Franklin.

Copper Range Railroad. (Copper Country Local History Ser.: Vol. 37). (Illus.). 120p. 1989. 3.00 (*0-942363-36-1*) C J Monette.

Copper Sands & The N. P. M. W. A. R. A. Dean Nichols. LC 93-71480. (Illus.). 1994. pap. 14.95 (*0-8323-0503-0*) Binford Mort.

***Copper Silhouette.** Candace R. Curran. 12p. (Orig.). 1995. pap. text ed. 3.50 (*1-884540-11-2*) Haleys.

Copper, Silver, Brass & Glass. Susan Jenkins. 100p. 1989. pap. 6.50 (*1-56770-211-2*) S Scheewe Pubns.

Copper, Silver, Gold & Zinc, Cadmium, Mercury Oxides & Hydroxides. Ed. by T. P. Dirkse. (Solubility Data Ser.: Vol. 23). 380p. 1986. 155.00 (*0-08-032497-5*, E125, E120, Pub. by PPL UK) Elsevier.

Copper Smelting, an Update: Proceedings of a Symposium Held at the 111th AIME Annual Meeting, Dallas, Texas, February 14-18, 1982. Metallurgical Society of AIME Staff. Ed. by David B. George & John C. Taylor. LC 81-86302. (Conference Proceedings Ser.). 353p. reprint ed. pap. 100.70 (*0-8357-2500-6*, 2052380) Bks Demand.

Copper, the Next Fifteen Years: A United Nations Study. Wolfgang Gluschke et al. 1978. lib. bdg. 51.50 (*90-277-0898-3*); pap. text ed. 26.50 (*90-277-0899-1*) Kluwer Ac.

Copper Times. Jack Fleming. LC 87-90762. (Illus.). 260p. 1987. 20.00 (*0-9617753-1-9*); pap. 12.95 (*0-9617753-0-0*) J Fleming Prodns.

Copper-Tints: A Book of Cordova Sketches. Katherine Wilson. (Shorey Historical Ser.). (Illus.). 44p. 1976. reprint ed. pap. 3.95 (*0-8466-0132-X*, S-132) Shorey.

Copper-Toed Boots. Marguerite De Angeli. LC 88-34417. (Great Lakes Bks.). (Illus.). 96p. (J). (gr. 4 up). 1989. reprint ed. 14.95 (*0-8143-1922-X*) Wayne St U Pr.

Copper Trail. Alaska Geographic Staff. Ed. by Penny Rennick. (Alaska Geographic Ser.: Vol. 16, No. 4). (Illus.). 96p. (Orig.). 1989. pap. 17.95 (*0-88240-191-2*) Alaska Geog Soc.

Copper Trails & Iron Rails. 4th ed. Larry Massie. LC 89-83953. (Illus.). 1990. pap. 11.95 (*0-932212-60-3*) Avery Color.

Copper Wire & Electrical Conductors: The Shaping of a Technology. B. C. Blake-Colman. LC 91-40910. 284p. 1992. text ed. 70.00 (*3-7186-5200-5*) Gordon & Breach.

Copperfield Checklist of Mystery Authors. 2nd ed. Karen T. McCallum & Pamela Granovetter. (Copperfield Collection Ser.: Vol. 2). 160p. (Orig.). 1992. reprint ed. pap. 6.95 (*0-9617037-1-7*) Copperfld NY.

***Copperhead.** Bernard Cornwell. LC 94-749. 1994. pap. 5.99 (*0-06-109196-0*, Harp PBks) HarpC.

Copperhead. large type ed. Bernard Cornwell. LC 94-749. (Starbuck Chronicles Ser.: Vol. 2). 1994. lib. bdg. 21.95 (*0-7862-0186-X*) Thorndike Pr.

Copperhead. Harold Frederic. 1972. reprint ed. 9.00 (*0-8422-8050-2*) Irvington.

Copperhead. Harold Frederic. (Collected Works of Harold Frederic). 1988. reprint ed. lib. bdg. 59.00 (*0-7812-1189-1*) Rprt Serv.

Copperhead: A Novel of the Civil War. Bernard Cornwell. LC 93-29421. (Starbuck Chronicles Ser.: Vol. 2). (Illus.). 352p. 1994. 15.95 (*0-06-017766-7*, HarpT) HarpC.

Copperhead see Collected Works of Harold Frederic

***Copperhead Cane.** Jim W. Miller. Ed. by Mary O'Dell. Tr. by Thomas Dorsett. (Library Poetry Ser.). 80p. (GER.). 1995. 17.50 (*0-9623666-5-X*); pap. 11.95 (*0-9623666-6-8*) Green Rvr Writers.

***Copperhead Cane.** deluxe ed. Jim W. Miller. Ed. by Mary O'Dell. Tr. by Thomas Dorsett. (Library Poetry Ser.). 80p. (GER.). 1995. boxed 50.00 (*0-614-01860-9*) Green Rvr Writers.

Copperhead Summer. Garry Barker. LC 85-50639. 233p. 1985. pap. 7.95 (*0-935680-15-2*) Kentucke Imprints.

Copperheads, Reading Level 2. Barger & Johnson. (Snake Discovery Library: Set I). (Illus.). 24p. (J). (gr. k-5). 1986. lib. bdg. 11.94 (*0-86592-957-2*) Rourke Corp.

Copperheads in the Middle West. Frank L. Klement. (Illus.). 15.75 (*0-8446-0167-5*) Peter Smith.

Copperplate Calligraphy. Dick Jackson. 1979. pap. 9.95 (*0-02-011710-8*, Collier S&S) S&S Trade.

Copperplate Calligraphy Kit, Set. (J). (gr. 7 up). 1988. Boxed set. 17.95 (*0-939564-11-4*) Pen Notes.

Copperplate Manual: An Introduction to Writing with the Pointed Pen. Gerald Krimm. LC 78-20703. (Illus.). 1979. pap. 6.95 (*0-8008-1865-2*) Taplinger.

Copperplate Workbook: Step by Step for Calligraphers. Karol Zaleski. Ed. by Daniel Zaleski & Judy Murphy. (Illus.). 61p. (Orig.). 1993. pap. 12.95 (*1-884107-01-X*) Lovely Nails.

Coppers of the Northwest Coast Indians: Their Origin, Development, & Possible Antecedents. Carol F. Jopling. LC 87-72871. (Transactions Ser.: Vol. 79, Pt. 1). (Illus.). (C). 1989. pap. 25.00 (*0-87169-791-2*, T791-JOC) Am Philos.

Coppery-Tailed Trogan "Arizona Bird of Paradise" see Trogons of the Arizona Borderlands

Coppola: A Biography. Peter Cowie. LC 94-16270. (Illus.). 352p. 1994. reprint ed. pap. 14.95 (*0-306-80598-7*) Da Capo.

Coppola & Eiko on Dracula. Francis F. Coppola & Eiko Ishioka. 1993. pap. 25.00 (*0-00-638243-6*) Collins SF.

Coprehensive Foundation in Accountancy. M Nazim. 1985. 90.00 (*0-946796-04-1*) St Mut.

Cops: The Men & Women Behind the Badge. Stuart Gellman. LC 90-84549. 288p. (Orig.). 1992. text ed. 12.95 (*0-9627628-4-9*) Horizon Pr AZ.

Cops Across Borders: The Internationalization of U. S. Criminal Law Enforcement. Ethan A. Nadelmann. LC 93-1305. 480p. 1993. 55.00 (*0-271-01094-0*); pap. 16.95 (*0-271-01095-9*) Pa St U Pr.

Cops & Computers: Microcomputer Use in Criminal Justice Agencies. (Illus.). 81p. (Orig.). (C). 1992. pap. text ed. 45.00 (*0-941375-44-7*) Diane Pub.

Cops & Constables: American & British Fictional Policemen. Earl Bargainnier & George N. Dove. LC 86-71642. 204p. 1986. 24.95 (*0-87972-333-5*); pap. 12.95 (*0-87972-334-3*) Bowling Green Univ.

Cops & Neighbors: An Evaluation of the Whittier Community-Based Policing Project. Sharon Ramirez & David Scheie. 70p. (Orig.). (C). 1994. pap. text ed. 40.00 (*0-7881-0753-4*) Diane Pub.

Cops & Robbers. Donald E. Westlake. 256p. 1993. mass mkt. 5.50 (*0-446-40133-1*, Mysterious Paperbk) Warner Bks.

Cops Are Robbers: A Convicted Cop's True Story of Police Corruption. Gerald W. Clemente & Kevin Stevens. 208p. 1989. pap. 3.95 (*0-380-70626-1*) Avon.

Cop's Cop. Edward Connolly & Christopher S. Harding. 288p. 1987. pap. 3.95 (*0-380-70169-3*) Avon.

Cops, Crooks, & Politicians. Neil W. Moloney. 340p. pap. write for info. (*0-318-72640-8*) Peanut Butter.

***Cops, Crooks & Politicians.** Neil W. Moloney. Date not set. pap. 17.95 (*0-89716-467-9*) Peanut Butter.

***Cops, Crooks & Politicians: A Bank Heist Exposed a Major Political Scandal.** Neil W. Moloney. (Illus.). 340p. 1994. pap. text ed. 17.95 (*0-89716-510-1*) P B Pubng.

***Cops, Killers & Staying Alive: The Murder of Police Officers in America.** Samuel G. Chapman. 174p. 1986. pap. 19.95 (*0-398-06052-5*) C C Thomas.

Cops, Killers & Staying Alive: The Murder of Police Officers in America. Samuel G. Chapman. 174p. (C). 1986. 36.95x (*0-398-05222-0*) C C Thomas.

Cops Said What? Everett Evansky. 74p. 1990. pap. 6.95 (*0-9621570-0-7*) North Lights.

Copse 125. Ernst Junger. Tr. by B. Creighton. 262p. 1988. reprint ed. lib. bdg. 39.50 (*0-86527-379-0*) Fertig.

Coptic Apocrypha in the Dialect of Upper Egypt. Ed. by Ernest A. Budge. LC 77-3589. (Coptic Texts Ser.: Vol. 3). (Illus.). reprint ed. 76.50 (*0-404-11553-5*) AMS Pr.

Coptic Biblical Texts in the Dialect of Upper Egypt. Ed. by Ernest A. Budge. LC 77-3590. (Coptic Texts Ser.: Vol. 2). (Illus.). 1977. reprint ed. 72.50 (*0-404-11552-7*) AMS Pr.

Coptic Dictionary. Ed. by Walter E. Crum. 1962. reprint ed. 175.00 (*0-19-864404-3*) OUP.

Coptic Egypt. Jill Kamil. 1987. pap. 15.00 (*0-685-43965-8*, Pub. by Am Univ Cairo Pr UA) Col U Pr.

Coptic Egypt: A History & Guide. Jill Kamil. 1987. pap. 15.00 (*977-424-104-5*, Pub. by Am Univ Cairo Pr UA) Col U Pr.

Coptic Encyclopedia, 8 vols., Set. Aziz S. Aitya. (Illus.). 2944p. 1991. text ed. 950.00 (*0-02-897025-X*) Macmillan.

Coptic Etymological Dictionary. Jaroslav Cerny. LC 69-10192. 350p. 1976. 210.00 (*0-521-07228-X*) Cambridge U Pr.

Coptic Future Tenses: Syntactical Studies in Sahidic. M. R. Wilson. (Janua Linguarum, Ser. Practica: No. 64). (Orig.). 1970. text ed. 60.00 (*3-11-000269-8*) Mouton.

Coptic Grammar. Henry Tattam. 15.00 (*0-89979-007-0*) British Am Bks.

Coptic Homilies in the Dialect of Upper Egypt. Ed. by Ernest A. Budge. LC 77-3585. (Coptic Texts Ser.: Vol. 1). (Illus.). reprint ed. 76.50 (*0-404-11551-9*) AMS Pr.

Coptic Hymns-Fragments from the Wadi n Narrun, Pt. 1, Translation. De Lacy O'Leary. pap. 3.95 (*0-89979-008-9*) British Am Bks.

Coptic Language Analysis of St. Basil Coptic Liturgy. Monir Barsoum Raphael. 160p. 1994. pap. 20.00 (*0-9644158-0-1*) M B Raphael. St. Basil Coptic Liturgy for the Catechumen, 70 p. (Orig.). Jan. 1995, pap. $8.00. (0-9644158-1-X) (Prices do not include shipping & handling). Other books hopefully will follow. Every word gets a consecutive number, which will keep in all these books & every new word is translated in English & Arabic, analyzed, explained & examples from the Bible are given whenever seen adequate. Aims in these books are to feel the meaning of every word, to teach the Coptic Language by the most common passages we have, & to collect a Dictionary - not dry - of the Coptic Language, & Greek words in it. Greek words (New Testament & Patrological) are dealt with precisely, briefly & carefully arranged grammatically in the Analysis & in their own Appendix #4 in the first book. Other Appendices are for Coptic (1) conjunctive pronouns, (2) numbering, (3) comprehensive analogy & a table of all Coptic Tenses. A brief Introduction is for Pronunciation, Conventional Notes & About Greek Words. The Analysis itself is literally - as possible - translated into English & Arabic. Alphabeticals are for Coptic Words, Verbs, Inflections & Greek Words. Call: (312) 728-2867 or write COPTS IN, 850 W. Eastwood #1509, Chicago, IL 60640.** ***Publisher Provided Annotation.

Coptic Life of Anthony. Tr. & Intro. by Tim Vivian. LC 93-45980. 1994. 64.95 (*1-883255-29-5*); pap. 44.95 (*1-883255-28-7*) Intl Scholars.

Coptic Martyrdoms, Etc. in the Dialect of Upper Egypt. Ed. by Ernest A. Budge. LC 77-3588. (Coptic Texts Ser.: Vol. 4). (Illus.). reprint ed. 76.50 (*0-404-11554-3*) AMS Pr.

Coptic Morning Service for the Lord's Day. Coptic Church Staff. Tr. by John P. Crichton-Stuart. LC 72-39871. reprint ed. 47.50 (*0-404-01247-7*) AMS Pr.

Coptic Perspective on Late Antiquity. Leslie S. MacCoull. LC 92-41249. (Collected Studies: Vol. CS398). 256p. 1993. 82.50 (*0-86078-364-2*, Pub. by Variorum UK) Ashgate Pub Co.

Coptic Share Pattern & Its Ancient Egyptian Ancestors: A Reassessment of the Aorist Pattern in the Egyptian Language. Green. 1987. pap. 29.95 (*0-85668-380-9*, Pub. by Aris & Phillips UK) David Brown.

***Coptic Synaxarium: Baounah, Abib, Misra, Vol. IV.** 1995. pap. text ed. 7.00 (*1-881577-05-8*) St George Coptic OC.

Coptic Synaxarium: Baramhat, Baramouda, Bashans, Vol. III. 165p. 1992. pap. text ed. 6.00 (*1-881577-03-1*) St George Coptic OC.

Coptic Synaxarium: Kiahk, Tubah, Amshir, Vol. 2. 1989. 4.75 (*1-881577-02-3*) St George Coptic OC.

Coptic Textile Designs. M. Gerspach. 1975. pap. 3.95 (*0-486-22849-5*) Dover.

Coptic Textiles in The Brooklyn Museum. Deborah Thompson. LC 73-114336. (Wilbour Monographs: No. 2). (Illus.). 1971. 15.00 (*0-913696-11-0*) Bklyn Mus.

Coptic Texts Edited with Introductions & English Translations, 5 vols., Set. Ernest A. Budge. reprint ed. 452.00 (*0-404-11550-0*) AMS Pr.

Copulantes. Rafael Catala. LC 83-62039. (Serie de Poesia Guampara: No. 2). 80p. (Orig.). (SPA.). 1984. pap. text ed. 5.95 (*0-910235-03-1*) Prisma Bks.

An Asterisk (*) at the beginning of an entry indicates that the title is appearing in BIP for the first time.

Copy & Create: Clip Art for Primary, Young Women, & Relief Society. Annette Ward. 1994. pap. 3.95 (*0-88494-924-9*) Bookcraft Inc.

Copy-Book of Letters Outward Etc. Begins 29 May, 1680, Ends 5 July, 1687. Ed. by E. E. Rich. (Hudson's Bay Record Society Publications Ser.: Vol. 11). 1972. reprint ed. pap. 58.00 (*0-8115-3185-6*) Periodicals Srv.

***Copy Cat.** Dawn Goodrich. 1994. 7.95 (*0-614-03067-6*) Vantage.

Copy-Cat, & Other Stories. Mary E. Wilkins Freeman. LC 71-122707. (Short Story Index Reprint Ser.). 1977. 21.95 (*0-8369-3540-3*) Ayer.

***Copy Cat Crimes.** Karen A. Wilson. 256p. (Orig.). 1995. pap. text ed. 4.99 (*0-425-14932-3*) Berkley Pub.

Copy Cat Mystery. Carol Adorjan. 128p. (J). 1990. pap. 2.95 (*0-380-75743-5*, Camelot) Avon.

Copy Chasers on Creating Business-to-Business Ads. Edmund O. Lawler. LC 93-4045. 220p. 1994. 39.95 (*0-8442-3470-2*, NTC Busn Bks) NTC Pub Grp.

Copy Editing: Making Good Writing Better. Boyd Miller. 64p. 1992. pap. text ed. 5.95 (*0-9615971-1-9*) Wordpix Serv.

Copy-Editing: The Cambridge Handbook for Authors, Editors & Indexers. 3rd ed. Judith Butcher. (Illus.). 384p. (C). 1992. 50.00 (*0-521-40074-0*) Cambridge U Pr.

Copy Machine Dealers, 1995. American Business Directories Staff. 1995. spiral bd., pap. 810.00 (*1-56105-610-3*) Am Busn Direct.

Copy of Letters Sent to Great Britain. Thomas Hutchinson. (Notable American Authors Ser.). 1992. reprint ed. lib. bdg. 75.00 (*0-7812-3299-6*) Rprt Serv.

Copy of the Letters Wherein Kyng Henry the Eyght Made Answere into a Certayn Letter of Martyn Luther. Henry VIII. LC 72-204. (English Experience Ser.: No. 322). 100p. 1971. reprint ed. 45.00 (*90-221-0322-6*) Walter J Johnson.

Copy of the Old Records of the Town of Duxbury, Mass., from 1642 to 1770. George Etheridge. (Illus.). 350p. (Orig.). reprint ed. pap. 22.50 (*1-55613-632-3*) Heritage Bk.

Copy Preparation & Design. Incl. What Every Editor Should Know about Layout & Typography. 5.95 (*0-318-02559-0*); Eighteen Ready-to-Use Grids. 20.00 (*0-318-02560-4*); write for info. (*0-318-58035-7*) Print Indus Am.

Copy Service Business Possibilities. Lamp Light Press Staff. 112p. (C). 1993. 32.95 (*0-917593-14-6*, Lamp Light Pr) Prosperity & Profits.

Copy Stimulators. Edmund J. Gross. (Illus.). 128p. 1975. pap. 8.50 (*0-912256-07-9*) Halls of Ivy.

***Copy the Cat.** Carol Cummings. (Learn with Me Ser.). (Illus.). 24p. (J). 1994. pap. 4.99 (*1-881660-01-X*) Teaching WA.

Copy Workshop Workbook. Bruce Bendinger. (Illus.). 350p. (Orig.). (C). 1988. pap. 30.00 (*0-9621415-0-X*) Copy Wrkshp.

Copy Workshop Workbook. 2nd ed. Bruce Bendinger. 396p. (Orig.). (C). 1993. pap. 33.00 (*0-9621415-4-2*) Copy Wrkshp.

Copy-Write: Basic Training Through Controlled Composition. Donna Gorrell. (C). 1987. pap. text ed. 15.25 (*0-673-39264-3*) HarpCollege.

Copy-Write: Basic Writing Through Controlled Composition. Donna Gorrell. (Orig.). (C). 1982. teacher ed write for info. (*0-318-54086-X*); pap. 12.95 (*0-316-32133-8*) Little.

Copybook for Japanese Ink Painting. Ed. by Reiko Chiba. LC 64-14192. (Illus.). 71p. 1964. bds. 14.95 (*0-8048-0124-X*) C E Tuttle.

Copycat. Ruth Brown. LC 94-20451. (Illus.). 32p. (J). (ps-1). 1994. 14.99 (*0-525-45326-1*, DCB) Dutton Child Bks.

Copycat. ALison A. McMaster. (Linford Romance Library). 256p. 1992. pap. 14.95 (*0-7089-7210-1*, Trailtree Bookshop) Ulverscroft.

***Copycat Cookbook (of Secret Recipes)** Gloria Pitzer. (Illus.). 120p. 1995. pap. write for info. (*1-886138-04-4*) G Pitzers.

Copycat Dog. Michael J. Pellowski. LC 85-14128. (Illus.). 48p. (Orig.). (J). (gr. 1-3). 1986. lib. bdg. 10.59 (*0-8167-0652-2*); pap. text ed. 3.50 (*0-8167-0653-0*) Troll Assocs.

Copycat Sam: Developing Ties with a Special Child. Alfred Stefanik. LC 81-20212. (Illus.). 32p. (J). (gr. k-5). 1982. 16.95 (*0-89885-058-4*) Human Sci Pr.

Copycats. Nicola Bayley. LC 91-58722. (Illus.). 96p. (J). (ps up). 1992. 14.95 (*1-56402-114-9*) Candlewick Pr.

Copyediting: A Practical Guide. 2nd ed. Karen Judd. LC 90-45746. 317p. 1991. 22.95 (*0-931961-94-7*); pap. 15.95 (*1-56052-143-0*) Crisp Pubns.

Copyfitting with a Small Calculator. Leslie Rasberry. LC 77-83812. 83p. 1977. 11.50 (*0-910158-26-6*) Art Dir.

Copyhold, Equity, & the Common Law. Charles M. Gray. LC 63-11420. (Historical Monographs: No. 53). 264p. 1963. 20.00 (*0-674-17150-0*) HUP.

Copying Other Nations' Policies: Two American Case Studies. Jerold Waltman. LC 80-12083. 126p. 1981. text ed. 18.95 (*0-87073-832-1*) Schenkman Bks Inc.

Copykat. Karen Kijewski. 1993. mass mkt. 4.99 (*0-553-29883-6*) Bantam.

Copyright, Vol. 1. Goldstein. 1988. 150.00 (*0-316-31963-5*) Little.

Copyright, Vol. 2. Goldstein. 1989. 150.00 (*0-316-31964-3*) Little.

Copyright, Vol. 3. Goldstein. 1989. 150.00 (*0-316-31965-1*) Little.

Copyright: Adaptable to Courses Utilizing Nimmer, M, M & N's Casebook on Copyright & Other Aspects of Law Pertaining to Literary, Musical & Artistic Works. Casenotes Publishing Co., Inc. Staff. Ed. by Norman S. Goldenberg et al. (Legal Briefs Ser.). 1991. pap. write for info. (*0-87457-045-X*, 1501) Casenotes Pub.

Copyright: Its Law & Its Literature, Being a Summary of the Principles & Law of Copyright, with Especial Reference to Books. R. R. Bowker. 60p. 1986. reprint ed. lib. bdg. 25.00 (*0-8377-1942-9*) Rothman.

Copyright: The Complete Guide for Music Educators. Jay Althouse. 76p. (Orig.). 1984. pap. 6.95 (*0-939139-01-4*) Music In Action.

Copyright a Praction. Harry G. Henn. 895p. 1988. 15.00 (*0-685-69402-X*) PLI.

Copyright Act & Regulations, 1992: An Office Consolidation. 1992. pap. 20.00 (*0-409-91058-9*) Butterworth Legal Pubs.

Copyright: Adaptable to Courses Utilizing Goldstein's Casebook on Copyright, Patent & Trademark Casenotes Legal Briefs. Casenotes Publishing Co., Inc. Staff. Ed. by Norman S. Goldenberg et al. (Legal Briefs Ser.). (Orig.). (C). 1992. pap. text ed. write for info. (*0-87457-173-1*, 1502) Casenotes Pub.

Copyright & Designs Law: A Question of Balance. Peter Groves. (C). 1991. lib. bdg. 180.00 (*1-85333-364-6*, Pub. by Graham & Trotman UK) Kluwer Ac.

Copyright & Educational Media: A Guide to Fair Use & Permissions Procedures. Association for Educational Communications & Technology & Association of Media Producers. 1977. pap. 4.95 (*0-89240-004-8*) Assn Ed Comm Tech.

Copyright & Information Limits to the Protection of Literary & Pseudo-Literary. European Commission Staff. 246p. 1992. pap. 40.00 (*92-826-3666-6*, CM-75-92-049-EN-C, Pub. by Europ Com) UNIPUB.

Copyright & Photocopying: Papers on Problems & Solutions, Design for a Clearinghouse, & a Bibliography. Laurence B. Heilprin. LC 77-620028. (Student Contribution Ser.: No. 10). 1977. pap. 6.00 (*0-911808-14-0*) U of Md Lib Serv.

***Copyright & Preservation: A Serious Problem in Need of a Thoughtful Solution.** Robert Oakley. 58p. 1990. pap. 15.00 (*1-887334-04-1*) Comm Preserv & Access.

Copyright & Public Performance of Music. Stanley Rothenberg. xii, 188p. 1987. reprint ed. lib. bdg. 32.50 (*0-8377-2535-6*) Rothman.

***Copyright & the GATT - an Interpretation & Legislative History of the Uruguay Round Agreements Act: 1995 Supplement to Copyright Law & Practice.** William F. Patry. LC 95-10477. 1995. pap. write for info. (*0-87179-886-7*) BNA.

Copyright Book: A Practical Guide. 4th ed. William S. Strong. (Illus.). 264p. 1992. 23.50 (*0-262-19330-2*) MIT Pr.

Copyright Book: Supplemental Copy. 4th ed. William S. Strong. (Illus.). 200p. 1993. pap. 30.00x (*0-262-69170-1*) MIT Pr.

Copyright, Cases & Materials. Sheldon W. Halpern et al. (American Casebook Ser.). 649p. 1992. text ed. 44.00 (*0-314-00328-2*) West Pub.

Copyright, Competition & Industrial Design. Hector L. MacQueen. (David Hume Papers: No. 14). 117p. 1990. pap. text ed. 14.00 (*0-08-037965-6*, Pub. by Aberdeen U Pr) Macmillan.

Copyright, Congress & Technology: The Public Record, 5 vols. Incl. Vol. I. Formative Years, 1958-1966. Ed. & Contrib by Nicholas L. Henry. LC 78-2347. 1979. 49.50 (*0-912700-29-7*); Vol. II. Political Years, 1967-1973. Ed. & Contrib by Nicholas L. Henry. LC 78-2347. 1979. 49.50x (*0-912700-30-0*); Vol. III. Future of Copyright, 1973-1977. Ed. & Contrib by Nicholas L. Henry. LC 78-2347. 1980. 49.50 (*0-912700-31-9*); Vol. IV. Contu: The Future of Information Technology. Ed. & Contrib by Nicholas L. Henry. LC 78-2347. 1980. 49.50 (*0-912700-32-7*); Vol. V. Contu's Final Report & Recommendations. Ed. by Nicholas L. Henry. LC 78-2347. 1980. 49.50 (*0-912700-74-2*); LC 78-2347. Set. 85.00 (*0-912700-13-0*) Oryx Pr.

Copyright, Defamation & Privacy in Soviet Civil Law, No. 22. Serge L. Levitsky. (Law in Eastern Europe Ser.). 517p. 1979. lib. bdg. 91.50 (*90-286-0139-2*) Kluwer Ac.

Copyright, Designs & Patents Act, 1988. Gerald Dworkin & Richard Taylor. 464p. 1989. pap. 46.00 (*1-85431-023-2*, Pub. by Blackstone Pr UK) W W Gaunt.

Copyright Directory, 1990-91. 125p. 1990. 79.95 (*0-914143-22-0*, Copy Info Svc) Assn Ed Comm Tech.

Copyright, Fair Use, & the Challenge for Universities: Promoting the Progress of Higher Education. Kenneth D. Crews. LC 93-3839. (Illus.). 256p. 1993. 22.50 (*0-226-12055-4*) U Ch Pr.

Copyright for School Libraries: A Practical Guide. Carol M. Simpson. LC 93-50802. (Professional Growth Ser.). 85p. 1994. pap. text ed. 16.95 (*0-938865-31-5*) Linworth Pub.

***Copyright for the Nineties.** Robert A. Gorman & Jane C. Ginsburg. 983p. 1994. 50.00 (*1-55834-110-2*) Michie Butterworth.

Copyright for the Nineties. 3rd ed. Alan Latman et al. (Contemporary Legal Education Ser.). 881p. 1989. 47.00 (*0-87473-444-4*) Michie Butterworth.

Copyright for the Nineties. 3rd suppl. ed. Alan Latman et al. (Contemporary Legal Education Ser.). 881p. 1989. 6.00 (*0-87473-773-7*) Michie Butterworth.

Copyright Game, Etc. A Strategic Guide for the Computer Software User. Albert Silverman. 331p. (Orig.). 1991. pap. 23.94 (*0-9627435-1-8*) Intellogic Pr.

Copyright Handbook. James S. Heller & Sarah K. Wiant. LC 84-17764. (AALL Publications Ser.: No. 23). vii, 68p. 1984. 15.00 (*0-317-01170-7*) Am Assn Law Libs.

Copyright Handbook. James S Heller & Sarah K. Wiant. (American Association of Law Libraries Publications Ser.: No. 23). vil, 68p. 1984. 20.00 (*0-8377-0121-X*) Rothman.

Copyright Handbook. 2nd ed. Stephen Fishman. LC 94-975. 320p. 1994. pap. 24.95 (*0-87337-241-7*) Nolo Pr.

Copyright Handbook. 2nd ed. Donald Johnston. LC 77-27449. 381p. 1982. 39.95 (*0-8352-1488-5*) Bowker.

Copyright in Historical Perspective. Lyman R. Patterson. LC 68-22415. 1968. 19.95 (*0-8265-1120-1*) Vanderbilt U Pr.

***Copyright Industries in the U. S. Economy: 1977 - 1993.** Stephen E. Siwek & Harold Furchtgott-Roth. 37p. 1995. pap. write for info. (*0-9634708-8-4*) Intl Intell Prop.

Copyright, Information Technology, Public Policy, 2 pts. Nicholas Henry. LC 74-83417. (Books in Library & Information Science: No. 17). 152p. reprint ed. Pt. 1, 152p. pap. 41.10 (*0-7837-0840-8*, 2041154); reprint ed. Pt. 2, 176p. pap. 50.20 (*0-7837-0841-6*) Bks Demand.

Copyright Law. 2nd ed. Joyce. 1991. write for info. (*0-8205-0115-8*, 210) Bender.

Copyright Law. 3rd ed. Craig Joyce et al. LC 94-102. (Cases & Materials Ser.). 1994. write for info. (*0-256-16446-0*) Bender.

Copyright Law: A Guide for Public Schools. 128p. 1986. 10.00 (*0-88364-112-7*) Natl Sch Boards.

Copyright Law: A Practitioner's Guide & 1992 Supplement. Harry G. Henn. LC 87-63438. 895p. 1988. 110.00 (*0-685-69403-8*) PLI.

Copyright Law: What You Don't Know Can Cost You! Woody Young. Ed. by Kathy Dongarra. (Illus.). 112p. 1988. text ed. 24.95 (*0-939513-70-6*); pap. text ed. 14.95 (*0-939513-71-4*) Joy Pub SJC.

Copyright Law & Practice. 6th ed. William F. Patry. LC 88-17494. 687p. 1986. text ed. 75.00 (*0-87179-506-X*, 0506) BNA.

Copyright Law & Practice, 3 vols., 1. William F. Patry. LC 94-12208. 1994. write for info. (*0-87179-854-9*) BNA.

Copyright Law & Practice, 3 vols., 2. William F. Patry. LC 94-12208. 1994. write for info. (*0-87179-855-7*) BNA.

Copyright Law & Practice, 3 vols., 3. William F. Patry. LC 94-12208. 1994. 225.00 (*0-87179-856-5*) BNA.

Copyright Law & Practice, 3 vols., Set, Vols. I, II, & III. 7th ed. William F. Patry. LC 94-12208. 2238p. 1994. text ed. 225.00 (*0-87179-685-6*, S685) BNA.

Copyright Law & the Health Sciences Librarian. rev. ed. 1989. pap. 15.00 (*0-912176-28-8*) Med Lib Assn.

Copyright Law for Unpublished Manuscripts & Archival Collections. Robert E. Cogswell. Ed. by Roy M. Mersky. (Law Library Information Reports: Vol. 14). 150p. 1992. pap. text ed. 100.00 (*0-87802-091-8*) Glanville.

Copyright Law in Business & Practice. John W. Hazard. 600p. 1989. 96.00 (*0-13-172446-0*) P-H.

Copyright Law in Business & Practice. John W. Hazard, Jr. 1989. text ed. 110.00 (*0-685-69656-1*, CLIB) Warren Gorham & Lamont.

***Copyright Law in Malaysia: An Outline.** Khaw Lake Tee. xxiv, 241p. 1994. write for info. (*0-409-99684-X*, SI) Butterworth Legal Pubs.

Copyright Law in the United Kingdom & the European Community. Peter B. Stone. LC 89-77147. (European Community Law Ser.). 240p. (C). 1990. text ed. 85.00 (*0-485-70004-2*, Pub. by Athlone Pr UK) Humanities.

Copyright Law of the United States of America. rev. ed. 142p. (C). 1994. pap. text ed. 30.00 (*0-7881-0593-0*) Diane Pub.

Copyright Law Symposium, Vol. 30. ASCAP Staff. 1983. text ed. 40.00 (*0-231-05582-X*) Col U Pr.

Copyright Law Symposium, Vol. 37. ASCAP Staff. 1990. text ed. 31.50 (*0-231-07310-0*) Col U Pr.

Copyright Law Symposium: Proceedings. American Society of Composers, Authors & Publishers Staff. Incl. No. 6. LC 40-8341. 1955. text ed. 42.00 (*0-231-02091-0*); LC 40-8341. 1958. 38.00 (*0-231-02318-9*); No. 10. LC 40-8341. 1959. text ed. 40.00 (*0-231-02351-0*); No. 17. LC 40-8341. 1969. text ed. 40.00 (*0-231-03235-8*); LC 40-8341. write for info. (*0-318-51405-2*) Col U Pr.

Copyright Laws & Treaties of the World: 25th Supplement, 1987-88. UNESCO Staff & BNA Staff. 925p. 1990. 245.00 (*0-87179-644-9*, 0644) BNA.

***Copyright Laws & Treaties of the World: 27th Supplement.** UNESCO Staff. 1995. text ed. write for info. (*0-614-04036-1*) BNA.

***Copyright Laws & Treaties of the World, Sup. 26 (1989-1990)** UNESCO Staff. 475p. 1992. ring bd. 325.00 (*0-87179-739-9*) BNA.

Copyright Laws & Treaties of the World with New Twenty-Sixth Supplement. UNESCO Staff & WIPO Staff. 1992. 695.00 (*0-87179-689-9*, 0689) BNA.

Copyright, Patent, Trademark, & Related State Doctrines: Cases & Materials on the Law of Intellectual Property. Paul Goldstein. LC 92-37619. (University Casebook Ser.). 1992. text ed. 43.95 (*1-56662-048-1*) Foundation Pr.

Copyright, Patent, Trademark & Related State Doctrines: Cases & Materials on the Law of Intellectual Property. 2nd ed. Paul Goldstein. (University Casebook Ser.). 33p. reprint ed. pap. text ed. 4.00 (*0-88277-482-4*) Foundation Pr.

Copyright, Patent, Trademark & Related State Doctrines: Cases & Materials on the Law of Intellectual Property. 3rd ed. Paul Goldstein. (University Casebook Ser.). 982p. 1991. reprint ed. text ed. 40.50 (*0-88277-792-0*) Foundation Pr.

Copyright, Patent, Trademark & Related State Doctrines: Teacher's Guide to Accompany Cases & Materials on the Law of Intellectual Property. 2nd ed. Paul Goldstein. (University Casebook Ser.). 183p. 1982. pap. text ed. write for info. (*0-88277-105-1*) Foundation Pr.

Copyright Piracy in Latin America: Trade Losses Due to Piracy & the Adequacy of Copyright Protection in 16 Central & South American Countries. International Intellectual Property Alliance Staff. 177p. 1992. 15.00 (*0-9634708-9-2*) Intl Intell Prop.

Copyright Policy Development: A Resource Book for Educators. Charles W. Vlcek. (Copyright Information Bulletin Ser.: No. 2). 164p. 1987. 19.45 (*0-914143-08-5*, Copy Info Svc) Assn Ed Comm Tech.

Copyright Practice & Procedure. S. Durst. LC 83-71260. 1984. lib. bdg. 15.00 (*0-942666-22-4*); pap. 10.00 (*0-685-10798-1*) S J Durst.

Copyright Primer for Educational & Industrial Media Producers. Esther R. Sinofsky. LC 87-15423. (Copyright Information Bulletin Ser.: No. 4). 1988. 29.95 (*0-914143-12-3*, Copy Info Svc) Assn Ed Comm Tech.

Copyright Primer for Librarians & Educators. 2nd ed. Janis Bruwelheide. 100p. 1995. pap. text ed. 22.00 (*0-8389-0642-7*) ALA.

Copyright Principles, Law & Practice, 3 vols. Paul Goldstein. 2300p. 1989. 375.00 (*0-316-31967-8*) Little.

Copyright Protection of Computer Programs. Beth Gaze. 220p. 1989. 58.00 (*1-86287-014-4*, Pub. by Federation Pr AU) W W Gaunt.

Copyright Reference Guide: For Genealogists. 3rd ed. Daniel J. Hay. 26p. (C). 1993. reprint ed. pap. 3.45 (*1-879079-04-6*) Advnced Rescs.

Copyright Registration Practice. James E. Hawes. LC 90-334. 1990. ring bd. 140.00 (*0-87632-735-8*) Clark Boardman Callaghan.

Copyright Society of the U. S. A. Bulletin: Cumulative Index, Vols. 1-20, 1953-1973. Ed. by Meira G. Pimsleur. LC 74-25274. x, 229p. 1975. text ed. 32.50 (*0-8377-0421-9*) Rothman.

Copyright Thought in Continental Europe: A Selected Bibliography. Francis J. Kase. x, 85p. 1967. pap. text ed. 8.50 (*0-8377-0725-0*) Rothman.

Copyright Through Cases. G. McFarlane. 352p. 1986. pap. 30.00 (*0-08-039208-3*, Pergamon Pr) Elsevier.

Copyright Tyranny. Francis Neilson. 1979. lib. bdg. 39.95 (*0-685-96615-1*) Revisionist Pr.

Copyright, Unfair Competition, & Other Topics Bearing on the Protection of Literary, Musical, & Artistic Works, Fifth Edition, Cases On. 5th ed. Ralph S. Brown & Robert C. Denicola. (University Casebook Ser.). 754p. 1989. text ed. 40.50 (*0-88277-744-0*) Foundation Pr.

Copyright, Unfair Competition, & Other Topics Bearing on the Protection of Literary, Musical, & Artistic Works, 1993: Statutory & Case Supplement to Cases On. 5th ed. Ralph S. Brown & Robert C. Denicola. (University Casebook Ser.). 364p. 1993. pap. text ed. 14.95 (*1-56662-072-4*) Foundation Pr.

***Copyright Your Software.** Stephen Fishman. (Illus.). 256p. 1994. pap. 39.95 (*0-87337-260-3*) Nolo Pr.

Copyright's Highway: From Gutenberg to the Celestial Jukebox. Paul Goldstein. LC 94-10831. 1995. 21.00 (*0-8090-5381-0*) Hill & Wang.

Copyrights in the World Marketplace: Successful Approaches to International Media Rights. Richard Wincor. 214p. 1990. 85.00 (*0-13-173956-5*) Aspen Law.

Copyrights, Patents & Trademarks. 2nd ed. Hoyt L. Barber. 1995. text ed. 32.95 (*0-07-005103-8*) McGraw.

Copyrights, Patents & Trademarks: Protect Your Rights Worldwide. Hoyt L. Barber. 256p. 1989. pap. 16.95 (*0-8306-0233-X*, Liberty Hse) TAB Bks.

Copyrights, Patents & Trademarks: Protect Your Rights Worldwide. 2nd ed. Hoyt L. Barber. 1995. pap. text ed. 16.95 (*0-07-005104-6*) McGraw.

Copywriter's Handbook. Robert Bly. LC 89-38563. 368p. 1990. pap. 13.95 (*0-8050-1194-3*, Owl) H Holt & Co.

Copywriting Assignments from America's Best Advertising Copywriters. Haberstroh & Wright. 163p. (C). 1989. pap. text ed. write for info. (*0-13-172693-5*) P-H.

Copywriting for the Electronic Media: A Practical Guide. 2nd ed. Milan D. Meeske & R. C. Norris. 377p. (C). 1992. pap. 34.95 (*0-534-15624-X*) Intl Thomson.

Copywriting Secrets & Tactics. Herschell G. Lewis. (Illus.). 420p. 1992. ring bd. 91.50 (*0-85013-193-6*) Dartnell Corp.

Coq de Bruyere. Michel Tournier. (Folio Ser.: No. 1229). 340p. (FRE.). 1987. pap. 9.95 (*2-07-037229-4*) Schoenhof.

Coq de Bruyere. Michel Tournier. (FRE.). 1980. pap. 11.95 (*0-8288-3794-5*, M14977) Fr & Eur.

Coquecigrues see Oeuvres

Coquecigres see Oeuvres

Coqui. Ester Feliciano-Mendoza. LC 82-4884. (Ninos y Letras Ser.). (Illus.). 68p. (gr. 4-7). 1982. reprint ed. pap. 5.00 (*0-8477-3505-2*) U of PR Pr.

Coquille Indians: Yesterday, Today & Tomorrow. Roberta L. Hall. (Western Americana Bks.). (Illus.). 214p. (Orig.). 1984. pap. 9.95 (*0-913626-21-X*) S S S Pub Co.

Cor-Ago, a Lake Linden Medicine Company. rev. ed. (Copper Country Local History Ser.: Vol. 1). (Illus.). 25p. 1974. 1.00 (*0-942363-00-0*) C J Monette.

Cor Pulmonale in Chronic Bronchitis & Emphysema. Ed. by Marvin L. Murphy & Roger C. Bone. LC 84-80453. (Illus.). 296p. 1984. 37.50 (*0-87993-226-0*) Futura Pub.

Cora: People of the Sierra Madre. Sarah Lane et al. 51p. (J). (gr. 6-12). 1989. pap. 9.95 (*0-941379-06-X*, 5114) World Eagle.

Cora Fry. Rosellen Brown. 100p. 1989. reprint ed. 19.95 (*0-87775-210-9*); reprint ed. pap. 9.95 (*0-87775-211-7*) Unicorn Pr.

Cora Fry's Pillow Book. Rosellen Brown. LC 94-14729. 1994. 15.00 (*0-374-14402-8*) FS&G.

***Cora Fry's Pillow Book.** Rosellen Brown. 179p. Date not set. 9.00 (*0-374-52443-2*) FS&G.

An Asterisk (*) at the beginning of an entry indicates that the title is appearing in BIP for the first time.

1619

Cora Gage Sayre: Memories of Smith Valley. Ed. by Mary E. Glass. (Illus.). 1977. lib. bdg. 23.00 (*1-56475-169-4*); fiche write for info. (*1-56475-170-8*) U NV Oral Hist.

Cora Sandel: Seeker of Truth. Ruth Essex. LC 94-9796. (Writing about Women Ser.: Vol. 10). 264p. (C). 1995. text ed. 49.95 (*0-8204-2229-0*) P Lang Pubs.

Cora Sandel: Selected Short Stories. Cora Sandel. Tr. & Intro. by Barbara Wilson. LC 85-22295. (Women in Translation Ser.). 256p. (Orig.). 1985. 16.95 (*0-931188-31-8*); pap. 8.95 (*0-931188-30-X*) Seal Pr Feminist.

Coracle: Coracle Press Gallery, 1975-1987. Simon Cutts et al. (Illus.). 132p. (Orig.). 1989. pap. 12.95 (*0-685-38946-4*) Yale Ctr Brit Art.

Coracle & Other Poems. Martin C. Rosner. LC 75-146469. 1971. 3.95 (*0-87212-001-5*) Libra.

Coracle-Rebuilding the Common Life. Wild Goose Publications Staff. (C). 1990. 20.00 (*0-947988-25-4*, Pub. by Wild Goose Pubns UK) St Mut.

Coraje y Sumision: Courage & Submission. Stanley Collins. (SPA.). 3.95 (*84-7228-421-2*, 220191, Pub. by Edit Clie SP) TSELF.

Coral & Brass. Holland M. Smith. (Elite Unit Ser.: No. 21). (Illus.). 289p. 1989. reprint ed. 27.50 (*0-89839-136-9*) Battery Pr.

Coral & Brass. Holland M. Smith & Percy Finch. LC 79-17252. reprint ed. 19.95 (*0-89201-051-7*) Zenger Pub.

Coral Boatmen. Elizabeth De Vegh. Ed. by Julie Reynolds & Sandy Darlington. LC 81-70080. (Illus.). 176p. (Orig.). 1982. pap. 3.95 (*0-9604152-3-8*) Arrowhead Pr.

Coral Buildings of Suakin. Jean-Pierre Greenlaw. LC 94-7372. 1994. write for info. (*0-7103-0489-7*, Pub. by Kegan Paul Intl UK) Routledge Chapman & Hall.

***Coral Comes High.** George P. Hunt. (Elite Unit Ser.: No. 32). (Illus.). 169p. 1995. reprint ed. 22.00 (*0-89839-214-4*) Battery Pr.

Coral Gables Conference on Fundamental Interactions at High Energy, Vol. 2. A. Perlmutter et al. 380p. (C). 1970. text ed. 255.00 (*0-677-14380-X*) Gordon & Breach.

Coral Gables in Postcards: Scenes from Florida's Yesterday. Samuel D. LaRoue, Jr. & Ellen J. Uguccioni. LC 88-71025. (Illus.). 56p. (Orig.). 1988. pap. 12.95 (*0-9620565-0-2*) Dade Heritage Trust.

Coral Island. R. M. Ballantyne. (World's Classics Ser.). 384p. 1990. pap. 7.95 (*0-19-282644-1*) OUP.

Coral Kingdom. Douglas Niles. (Druidhome Trilogy Ser.: Bk. 2). 320p. (Orig.). 1992. pap. 4.95 (*1-56076-332-9*) TSR Inc.

Coral Kingdoms. Carl Roessler. (Illus.). 244p. 1990. 39.95 (*0-8109-0774-7*); pap. 19.98 (*0-8109-8095-9*) Abrams.

Coral Kiss. Jayne A. Krentz. 384p. (Orig.). 1992. mass mkt. 5.99 (*0-446-36349-9*) Warner Bks.

Coral Kiss. Jayne A. Krentz. 384p. (Orig.). 1992. reprint ed. 20.00 (*0-7278-4299-4*) Severn Hse.

Coral Peregrino: Del Caribe Mexicano a Biosfera-2. Fernando Ortiz & Tatiana Ortiz. 88p. (SPA.). 1994. 8.95 (*1-882428-15-3*) Biosphere Pr.

Coral Reef. Norman S. Barrett. LC 90-42931. (Picture Library). (Illus.). 32p. (J). (gr. k-4). 1991. lib. bdg. 12.53 (*0-531-14110-1*) Watts.

Coral Reef. Michael George. (Images Ser.). (J). (gr. 5 up). 1992. lib. bdg. 18.95 (*0-88682-430-3*) Creative Ed.

Coral Reef. Michael George. 40p. (J). (gr. 4-7). 1993. 15.95 (*1-56846-059-7*) Creative Ed.

Coral Reef. Jerry Greenberg. 64p. 6.95x (*0-913008-06-0*) Seahawk Pr.

Coral Reef. Bob Reese. LC 82-23610. (Critterland Ocean Adventures Ser.). (Illus.). 24p. (J). (ps-2). 1983. pap. 2.95 (*0-516-42312-6*) Childrens.

Coral Reef. Barbara Taylor. LC 91-58198. (Look Closer Ser.). (Illus.). 32p. (J). (gr. 1-4). 1992. 9.95 (*1-879431-92-0*) Dorling Kindersley.

***Coral Reef: A City That Never Sleeps.** Illus. by Jeffrey L. Rotman. LC 95-6635. (J). 1996. 15.99 (*0-525-65193-4*, Cobblehill Bks) Dutton Child Bks.

Coral Reef at Night. Joseph Levine. LC 93-12277. (Illus.). 1993. 39.95 (*0-8109-3190-7*) Abrams.

Coral Reef Coloring Book. Illus. by Idaz Greenberg. 32p. 1988. 4.00 (*0-913008-21-4*) Seahawk Pr.

Coral Reef Coloring Book. Katherine Orr. (NaturEncyclopedia Library). (Illus.). 48p. (J). (gr. 2 up). 1988. pap. 5.95 (*0-88045-090-8*) Stemmer Hse.

Coral Reef Ecology. Yu. I. Sorokin. 475p. 1994. 198.00 (*0-387-56427-6*) Spr-Verlag.

Coral Reef Ecosystems. Gerald J. Bakus et al. (Illus.). 260p. (C). 1994. text ed. 45.00 (*90-6191-953-3*, Pub. by A A Balkema NE) Ashgate Pub Co.

Coral Reef Geomorphology. Andre Guilcher. LC 87-25422. (Coastal Morphology & Research Ser.). 228p. 1988. text ed. 125.00 (*0-471-91755-9*) Wiley.

Coral Reef Handbook. Ed. by Patricia Mather. 80p. (C). 1992. text ed. 100.00 (*0-949324-47-7*, Pub. by Surrey Beatty & Sons AT) St Mut.

***Coral Reef Hideaway: The Story of a Clown Anemonefish.** Doe Boyle. (Smithsonian Oceanic Collection). (Illus.). 32p. (J). (ps-3). 1995. 15.95 (*1-56899-182-7*); 4.95 (*1-56899-183-5*); 26.95 (*1-56899-184-3*); 9.95 (*1-56899-185-1*); audio 19.95 (*1-56899-186-X*) Soundprints.

Coral Reef Problem. William M. Davis. reprint ed. 37.50 (*0-404-01998-6*) AMS Pr.

Coral Reef Problem. William M. Davis. LC 75-45469. 612p. 1977. reprint ed. 48.50 (*0-88275-383-5*) Krieger.

Coral Reefs. Jason Cooper. LC 92-16077. (Discovery Library of the Sea). (J). 1992. 12.67 (*0-86593-229-8*); lib. bdg. 9.50 (*0-685-59719-9*) Rourke Corp.

Coral Reefs. Alberto De Larramendi Ruis. LC 93-3438. (World Heritage Ser.). (Illus.). 36p. (J). (gr. 3 up). 1993. lib. bdg. 15.00 (*0-516-08384-8*); pap. 6.95 (*0-516-48384-6*) Childrens.

Coral Reefs. Ed. by Z. Dubinsky. (Ecosystems of the World Ser.: No. 25). 562p. 1991. 220.00 (*0-444-87392-9*) Elsevier.

***Coral Reefs.** Dwight Holing et al. Ed. by Vicki Leon. LC 94-30868. (Close up: A Focus on Nature Ser.). (Illus.). 40p. (YA). (gr. 5 up). 1994. lib. bdg. 14.95 (*0-382-24857-0*); pap. 7.95 (*0-382-24858-9*) Silver Burdett Pr.

Coral Reefs. Les Holliday. (Illus.). 207p. 31.95 (*3-89356-034-3*, 16098) Tetra Pr.

Coral Reefs. Sylvia A. Johnson. LC 84-816. (Lerner Natural Science Bks.). (Illus.). 48p. (J). (gr. 4 up). 1984. lib. bdg. 19.95 (*0-8225-1451-6*, Lerner Publctns); pap. 5.95 (*0-8225-9545-1*, Lerner Publctns) Lerner Group.

Coral Reefs. Lawrence Pringle. LC 94-5875. (J). (gr. 3 up). 1995. write for info. (*0-671-79166-4*, S&S Bks Young Read) S&S Childrens.

Coral Reefs. Jenny Wood. (Wonderworks of Nature Ser.). (Illus.). 32p. (J). (gr. 3-4). 1991. lib. bdg. 17.27 (*0-8368-0630-1*) Gareth Stevens Inc.

***Coral Reefs: Exploring the World Below.** Joseph Wallace. LC 94-26775. 1995. pap. write for info. (*1-56799-155-6*, Friedman-Fairfax) M Friedman Pub Grp Inc.

***Coral Reefs: Nature's Richest Realm.** Roger Steene. 1994. 39.99 (*0-517-10272-2*) Random Hse Value.

Coral Reefs: Valuable Resources of Southeast Asia. Alan T. White. (Education Ser.: No. 1). 36p. 1987. pap. 5.00 (*971-10-2233-8*, Pub. by ICLARM PH) Intl Spec Bk.

Coral Reefs in Danger. Christopher Lampton. LC 91-41441. (Illus.). 64p. (J). (gr. 4-8). 1992. lib. bdg. 15.90 (*1-56294-091-0*) Millbrook Pr.

Coral Reefs of Florida. Gilbert L. Voss. LC 88-9946. (Illus.). 96p. 1988. 14.95 (*0-910923-56-6*); pap. 10.95 (*0-910923-57-4*) Pineapple Pr.

Coral Reefs of the World. Ed. by Sue Wells et al. (International Union for the Conservation of Nature & Natural Resources: A Belhaven Press Book Ser.). (Illus.). 500p. 1988. Vol. 1: Atlantic & Eastern Pacific. 45.00 (*2-88032-943-4*, Pub. by IUCN SZ); Vol. 2: Indian Ocean, Red Sea, & Gulf. 45.00 (*2-88032-944-2*, Pub. by IUCN SZ); Vol. 3: Central & Western Pacific. 45.00 (*2-88032-945-0*, Pub. by IUCN SZ) Island Pr.

Coral Reefs of the World, 3 vols., Set. Ed. by Sue Wells et al. (International Union for the Conservation of Nature & Natural Resources: A Belhaven Press Book Ser.). (Illus.). 500p. 1988. 100.00 (*2-88032-958-2*, Pub. by IUCN SZ) Island Pr.

***Coral Sea.** Patti Smith. (Illus.). 72p. 1995. 18.00 (*0-393-03908-0*) Norton.

Coral Snakes. Bargar & Johnson. (Snake Discovery Library: Set II). (Illus.). 24p. (J). (gr. 1-4). 1987. lib. bdg. 11.94 (*0-86592-246-2*) Rourke Corp.

Coral Snakes: Biology, Identification, Venoms. Janis A. Roze. LC 93-1912. 1995. write for info. (*0-89464-847-0*) Krieger.

Coralline Algae: A First Synthesis. Ed. by H. William Johansen. 256p. 1981. 119.00 (*0-8493-5261-4*, QK569, CRC Reprint) Franklin.

Coralroot. Cynthia Chinelly. 24p. 1987. pap. 5.95 (*0-942979-01-X*) Livingston U Pr.

Corals: The Sea's Great Builders. Cousteau Society Staff. LC 91-34458. (Illus.). 32p. (J). (gr. 1-5). 1992. pap. 12.00 (*0-671-77068-3*, S&S Bks Young Read) S&S Childrens.

Corals & Coral Islands. James D. Dana. (Notable American Authors Ser.). 1992. reprint ed. lib. bdg. 75.00 (*0-7812-2607-4*) Rprt Serv.

Corals & Coral Reefs of the Galapagos Islands. Peter W. Glynn & Gerard M. Wellington. LC 82-25161. (Illus.). (C). 1984. 60.00 (*0-520-04713-3*) U CA Pr.

***Corals in Space & Time: Biogeography & Evolution of the Scleractinia.** J. E. Veron. LC 94-33540. 1995. write for info. (*0-8014-3141-7*) Cornell U Pr.

***Corals in Space & Time: Biogeography & Evolution of the Scleractinia.** J. E. Veron. (Comstock Book Ser.). (Illus.). 336p. 1995. pap. 35.00x (*0-8014-8263-1*) Cornell U Pr.

Corals of Australia & the Indo-Pacific. John E. Veron. LC 92-24064. (Illus.). 656p. 1993. reprint ed. text ed. 90.00 (*0-8248-1504-1*) UH Pr.

Corals of Australia & the Indo-Pacific: Best Australian Natural History Book, Whitley Medal 1988. J. E. N. Veron. 1993. 90.00 (*0-8245-1504-8*, Kolowalu Bk) UH Pr.

Corals of Hong Kong. P. J. Scott. (Illus.). 120p. (Orig.). 1984. pap. 36.50 (*962-209-033-8*, Pub. by Hong Kong Univ Pr HK) Coronet Bks.

Coral's Reef. Dee Scarr. 1985. pap. 2.50 (*0-380-89951-5*, Camelot) Avon.

Coram's Children: The London Foundling Hospital in the Eighteenth Century. Ruth K. McClure. LC 80-21375. (Illus.). 322p. (C). 1981. text ed. 42.00 (*0-300-02465-7*) Yale U Pr.

Coran. Tr. by Julio Cortes. LC 85-52262. 672p. (SPA.). 1986. 24.00 (*0-940368-71-4*, 127); Spanish only. 12.00 (*0-685-73758-6*); pap. 14.00 (*0-940368-70-6*, 127A) Tahrike Tarsile Quran.

Cora's Country Cookbook. Cora. 1985. 11.95 (*0-02-528150-X*) Macmillan.

Corasius & the Renaissance Systematization of Roman Law. A. London Fell. LC 81-22332. (Origins of Legislative Sovereignty & the Legislative State Ser.: Vol. 1). 368p. 1991. text ed. 45.00 (*0-275-93971-5*, C3971, Praeger Pubs) Greenwood.

Corazon. 6th ed. J. Willis Hurst. 1988. text ed. 120.00 (*0-07-104000-5*) McGraw.

Corazon Aquino. Howard Chua-Eoan. (World Leaders - Past & Present Ser.). (Illus.). 112p. (J). (gr. 5 up). 1988. 17.95 (*1-55546-825-X*) Chelsea Hse.

Corazon Aquino. Jill Wheeler. LC 91-73025. (Leading Ladies Ser.). 202p. (J). 1991. lib. bdg. 12.94 (*1-56239-082-1*) Abdo & Dghtrs.

Corazon Aquino: Journey to Power. Laurie Nadel. LC 86-33266. 93p. (J). (gr. 6 up). 1987. lib. bdg. 13.98 (*0-671-63950-1*, Julian Messner) Silver Burdett Pr.

Corazon Aquino: Leader of the Philippines. James Haskins. LC 87-24440. (Contemporary Women Ser.). (Illus.). 128p. (J). (gr. 6 up). 1988. lib. bdg. 17.95 (*0-89490-152-4*) Enslow Pubs.

Corazon Aquino: The Miracle of a President. Cecilia K. Gullas. LC 87-61979. (Orig.). 1987. pap. 7.95 (*0-943949-00-9*) Cultural Hse.

***Corazon Aquino & the Brushfire Revolution.** Robert H. Reid & Eileen Guerrero. (Illus.). 248p. (C). 1995. 29.95 (*0-8071-1980-6*) La State U Pr.

Corazon con Que Vivo: Nuevos Poemas y Relatos "Desde Mi Silla de Ruedas" Armando F. Valladares. LC 79-56383. (Coleccion Espejo de Paciencia Ser.). (Illus.). 144p. (Orig.). (SPA.). 1980. pap. 9.95 (*0-89729-245-6*) Ediciones.

Corazon de Dios. G. Campbell Morgan. (SPA.). 1980. pap. 3.75 (*0-8254-1494-6*) Kregel.

Corazon de Espana. Augusto Centano. (Illus.). (C). 1957. text ed. 30.75 (*0-03-015080-9*) HB Coll Pubs.

***Corazon de Oro.** Harold Klemp. Orig. Title: The Golden Heart. 312p. (SPA.). (J). 1994. pap. 14.00 (*1-57043-098-5*) ECKANKAR.

Corazon de Piedra Verde, I. Salvador de Madariaga. (Nueva Austral Ser.: Vol. 55). (SPA.). 1991. pap. text ed. 34.95x (*84-239-1855-6*) Elliots Bks.

Corazon de Piedra Verde, II. Salvador de Madariaga. (Nueva Austral Ser.: Vol. 56). (SPA.). 1991. pap. text ed. 29.95x (*84-239-1864-5*) Elliots Bks.

Corazon del Barrio. Jorge Argueta. 28p. (Orig.). 1994. pap. 4.00 (*0-916397-29-7*) Manic D Pr.

Corazon Oyente y Entendido: Hearing Heart. Hanna Hurnard. (SPA.). 3.95 (*84-7228-574-X*, 220194, Pub. by Edit Clie SP) TSELF.

Corazon Paternal de Dios. Floyd McClung, Jr. Tr. by Francisco B. Guerra. 96p. 1988. reprint ed. pap. 3.50 (*0-88113-027-3*) Edit Betania.

Corazon y Pensamientos. Luis A. Algarra. 630p. (Orig.). 1989. pap. 15.00 (*0-685-28126-4*) L A A Algarra.

***CORBA: A Guide to Common Object Request Broker Architecture.** Ron Ben-natan. 1995. pap. text ed. 45.00 (*0-07-005427-4*) McGraw.

Corbaccio: Giovanni Boccaccio: Or, The Labyrinth of Love. 2nd ed. Ed. & Tr. by Anthony K. Cassell. LC 92-42698. 120p. 1993. 8.00 (*0-86698-154-3*) MRTS.

Corbiere, Mallarme, Valery: Preservations & Commentary. Robert L. Mitchell. (Stanford French & Italian Studies: Vol. 23). viii, 149p. 1981. pap. 46.50 (*0-915838-16-8*) Anma Libri.

Corbillard De Jules. Alphonse Boudard. (FRE.). 1981. pap. 10.95 (*0-7859-1935-X*, 2070372820) Fr & Eur.

Corbin on Contracts. write for info. (*0-318-57510-8*) West Pub.

Corbin on Contracts: (SS1-108), Vol. 1. rev. ed. Joseph M. Perillo. 700p. 1993. text ed. write for info. (*0-314-01881-6*) West Pub.

***Corbin's Fancy.** Miller. 1995. mass mkt. 5.99 (*0-671-53421-1*) PB.

Corbin's Fancy. Linda L. Miller. Ed. by Linda Marrow. 320p. 1991. mass mkt. 5.99 (*0-671-73767-8*) PB.

Corbin's Rubi-Yacht. Benjamin W. Farley. 1992. 14.95 (*0-87844-111-5*); pap. 9.95 (*0-87844-114-X*) Sandlapper Pub Co.

Corbould Genealogy, in England. G. C. Poulter. 165p. 1994. reprint ed. lib. bdg. 35.00 (*0-8328-4143-9*); reprint ed. pap. 25.00 (*0-8328-4144-7*) Higginson Bk Co.

Corbusier: A Marriage of Contours. Ed. by Richard Ingersoll. (Illus.). 38p. (Orig.). 1991. pap. 10.95 (*1-878271-22-9*) Princeton Arch.

Corbusier: An Analysis of Form. 2nd ed. Geoffrey Baker. (Illus.). 336p. 1989. pap. 49.95 (*0-7476-0028-7*) Chapman & Hall.

Corbusier: An Annotated Bibliography. Darlene Brady. LC 82-49267. (Reference Library of the Humanities). 320p. 1985. lib. bdg. 71.00 (*0-8240-9134-5*) Garland.

Corbusier: Early Works at La Chaux-de-Fonds. Geoffrey H. Baker & Jacques Gubler. (Academy Architecture Bks.). (Illus.). 128p. 1987. 45.00 (*0-312-47582-9*); pap. 30.00 (*0-312-47583-7*) St Martin.

Corbusier: Ideas & Forms. William J. Curtis. LC 86-6499. (Illus.). 224p. 1992. pap. 35.00 (*0-8478-1556-0*) Rizzoli Intl.

***Corbusier: Ideas & Forms.** rev. ed. William J. Curtis. (Illus.). 240p. (C). 1995. pap. 29.95 (*0-7148-2790-8*, Pub. by Phaidon Press UK) Chronicle Bks.

***Corbusier: Les Voyages D'Allemagne, Carnets, 5 vols., Set.** Le Corbusier. Ed. by Giuliano Gresleri. Tr. by Mila Dau. (Illus.). 1995. boxed 250.00 (*1-885254-15-6*) Monacelli Pr.

Corbusier: The City of Refuge, Paris 1929-33. Brian B. Taylor. (Illus.). 176p. 1988. 32.50 (*0-226-79134-3*) U Ch Pr.

Corbusier: To Live with the Light. 1987. 72.95 (*0-85139-804-9*) Buttrwrth-Heinemann.

Corbusier & the Tragic View of Architecture. Charles Jencks. LC 73-84322. (Illus.). 191p. 1974. 25.00 (*0-674-51860-8*); pap. text ed. 14.95 (*0-674-51861-6*) HUP.

Corbusier at Work: The Genesis of the Carpenter Center for the Visual Arts. Eduard F. Sekler & William Curtis. LC 77-7315. (Illus.). 490p. 1978. 49.00 (*0-674-52059-9*) HUP.

Corbusier Sketchbooks. Ed. by Fondation Le Corbusier Staff & Architectural History Foundation Staff. (Illus.). 520p. (ENG & FRE.). 1982. 200.00x (*0-262-03078-0*); Vol. 1, 1914-1948. 200.00 (*0-262-12090-9*); Vol. 3, 1954-1957, 1982. 200.00 (*0-262-12092-5*); Vol. 4, 1957-1964. 200.00 (*0-262-12093-3*) MIT Pr.

***Corbusier: The Creative Search: The Formative Years of Charles-Edouard Jeanneret.** Baker. 1995. (*0-419-17730-2*) Routledge Chapman & Hall.

Corcoran: A Tribute to William Wilson Corcoran, the Founder of the Corcoran Gallery. (Illus.). 1976. 3.00 (*0-686-20538-3*) Corcoran.

Cord: Twenty-Five Year Index 1950-1975. 1977. 4.00 (*0-686-19080-7*) Franciscan Inst.

CORD Applied Mathematics - Metric Version, Unit A: "Getting to Know Your Calculator" Center for Occupational Research & Development Staff. (Illus.). 1994. teacher ed write for info. (*1-55502-522-6*); pap. text ed. write for info. (*1-55502-521-8*) CORD Commns.

CORD Applied Mathematics - Metric Version, Unit B: "Naming Numbers in Different Ways" Center for Occupational Research & Development Staff. (Illus.). 1994. teacher ed write for info. (*1-55502-524-2*); pap. text ed. write for info. (*1-55502-523-4*) CORD Commns.

CORD Applied Mathematics - Metric Version, Unit C: "Finding Answers with Your Calculator" Center for Occupational Research & Development Staff. (Illus.). 1994. teacher ed write for info. (*1-55502-526-9*); pap. text ed. write for info. (*1-55502-525-0*) CORD Commns.

CORD Applied Mathematics - Metric Version, Unit 1: "Learning Problem-solving Techniques" Center for Occupational Research & Development Staff. (Illus.). 1994. teacher ed write for info. (*1-55502-528-5*); pap. text ed. write for info. (*1-55502-527-7*) CORD Commns.

CORD Applied Mathematics - Metric Version, Unit 10: "Working with Scale Drawings" Center for Occupational Research & Development Staff. (Illus.). 1994. teacher ed write for info. (*1-55502-546-3*); pap. text ed. write for info. (*1-55502-545-5*) CORD Commns.

CORD Applied Mathematics - Metric Version, Unit 11: "Using Signed Numbers & Vectors" Center for Occupational Research & Development Staff. (Illus.). 1994. teacher ed write for info. (*1-55502-548-X*); pap. text ed. write for info. (*1-55502-547-1*) CORD Commns.

CORD Applied Mathematics - Metric Version, Unit 12: "Using Scientific Notation" Center for Occupational Research & Development Staff. (Illus.). 1994. teacher ed write for info. (*1-55502-550-1*); pap. text ed. write for info. (*1-55502-549-8*) CORD Commns.

CORD Applied Mathematics - Metric Version, Unit 13: "Precision, Accuracy, & Tolerance" Center for Occupational Research & Development Staff. (Illus.). 1994. teacher ed write for info. (*1-55502-552-8*); pap. text ed. write for info. (*1-55502-551-X*) CORD Commns.

CORD Applied Mathematics - Metric Version, Unit 14: "Solving Problems with Powers & Roots" Center for Occupational Research & Development Staff. (Illus.). 1994. teacher ed write for info. (*1-55502-554-4*); pap. text ed. write for info. (*1-55502-553-6*) CORD Commns.

CORD Applied Mathematics - Metric Version, Unit 15: "Using Formulas to Solve Problems" Center for Occupational Research & Development Staff. (Illus.). 1994. teacher ed write for info. (*1-55502-556-0*); pap. text ed. write for info. (*1-55502-555-2*) CORD Commns.

CORD Applied Mathematics - Metric Version, Unit 2: "Estimating Answers" Center for Occupational Research & Development Staff. (Illus.). 1994. teacher ed write for info. (*1-55502-530-7*); pap. text ed. write for info. (*1-55502-529-3*) CORD Commns.

CORD Applied Mathematics - Metric Version, Unit 3: "Measuring in English & Metric Units" Center for Occupational Research & Development Staff. (Illus.). 1994. teacher ed write for info. (*1-55502-532-3*); pap. text ed. write for info. (*1-55502-531-5*) CORD Commns.

CORD Applied Mathematics - Metric Version, Unit 4: "Using Graphs, Charts, & Tables" Center for Occupational Research & Development Staff. (Illus.). 1994. teacher ed write for info. (*1-55502-534-X*); pap. text ed. write for info. (*1-55502-533-1*) CORD Commns.

CORD Applied Mathematics - Metric Version, Unit 5: "Dealing with Data" Center for Occupational Research & Development Staff. (Illus.). 1994. teacher ed write for info. (*1-55502-536-6*); pap. text ed. write for info. (*1-55502-535-8*) CORD Commns.

CORD Applied Mathematics - Metric Version, Unit 6: "Working with Lines & Angles" Center for Occupational Research & Development Staff. (Illus.). 1994. teacher ed write for info. (*1-55502-538-2*); pap. text ed. write for info. (*1-55502-537-4*) CORD Commns.

CORD Applied Mathematics - Metric Version, Unit 7: "Working with Shapes in Two Dimensions" Center for Occupational Research & Development Staff. (Illus.). 1994. teacher ed write for info. (*1-55502-540-4*); pap. text ed. write for info. (*1-55502-539-0*) CORD Commns.

CORD Applied Mathematics - Metric Version, Unit 8: "Working with Shapes in Three Dimensions" Center for Occupational Research & Development Staff. (Illus.). 1994. teacher ed write for info. (*1-55502-542-0*); pap. text ed. write for info. (*1-55502-541-2*) CORD Commns.

CORD Applied Mathematics - Metric Version, Unit 9: "Using Ratios & Proportions" Center for Occupational Research & Development Staff. (Illus.). 1994. teacher ed write for info. (*1-55502-544-7*); pap. text ed. write for info. (*1-55502-543-9*) CORD Commns.

Cord Model 810 & 812 Owner's Companion. Ed. by Dan R. Post. 224p. 1975. 18.95 (*0-911160-54-X*) Post Group.

Cord of Three Strands. Audrey L. Thomas. LC 90-72026. (Illus.). 192p. (Orig.). 1990. pap. 10.95 (*0-9628656-0-5*) Wildberry Pr.

1620

An Asterisk (*) at the beginning of an entry indicates that the title is appearing in BIP for the first time.

Cord-Without Tribute to Tradition: The Front Drive Legend. Dan R. Post. LC 72-96734. (Illus.). 224p. 1974. 21.95 (*0-911160-50-7*) Post Group.

***Cordage: Industry & Trade Summary.** C. Lee Cooke. (Illus.). 51p. (Orig.). (C). 1995. pap. text ed. 25.00x (*0-7881-1565-0*) Diane Pub.

Cordage & Cables: Their Uses at Sea. P. J. Stofrod. (C). 1987. 50.00 (*0-85174-531-8*, Pub. by Brwn Son Ferg) St Mut.

Cordage & Cables: Their Uses at Sea. P. J. Stopford. 109p. 1968. reprint ed. pap. 14.50 (*0-85174-163-0*) Sheridan.

Corday. Michael Mott. 90p. 1987. lib. bdg. 13.95 (*0-933833-15-6*) Beacham Pub.

***Corday.** rev. ed. Michael Mott. (International-Visions Ser.). (Illus.). 84p. 1995. pap. 7.95 (*0-938872-21-4*) Black Buzzard.

Corde et les Souris: Avec Les Hotes de Passage, Les Chenes Qu'On Abat (Version Difinitive), La Tete d'Obsidienne (Version Definitive), Lazare. Andre Malraux. 1976. 4.95 (*0-686-56322-0*) Fr & Eur.

Cordelia. Robert Johnston. LC 91-90446. 160p. (Orig.). 1991. pap. 7.95 (*0-9625321-4-2*) Sand Castle Bks.

Cordelia? Garson Kanin. 1983. pap. 3.25 (*0-8217-1266-7*) Zebra.

Cordelia. Francoise Mallet-Joris. 300p. (FRE.). 1956. 8.95 (*0-8288-9837-5*, F110730) Fr & Eur.

Cordia Alliodora 1922-1988. A. Greaves & P. S. McCarter. 28p. (Orig.). 1988. pap. text ed. 28.00 (*0-85198-624-2*) CAB Intl.

Cordial Concurrence: Orchestrating National Party Conventions in the Telepolitical Age. Larry D. Smith & Dan Nimmo. LC 91-3549. (Praeger Series in Political Communication). 264p. 1991. text ed. 65.00 (*0-275-93863-8*, C3863, Praeger Pubs); pap. text ed. 17.95 (*0-275-93864-6*, Praeger Pubs) Greenwood.

Cordillera Tales. Maria L. Aguilar-Carino. (Illus.). vii, 122p. 1990. pap. 8.50 (*971-10-0379-1*, Pub. by New Day Pub PH) Cellar.

Cordilleran Metamorphic Core Complexes. Ed. by Max D. Crittenden, Jr. et al. LC 80-67489. (Geological Society of America, Memoir Ser.: No. 153). (Illus.). 496p. reprint ed. pap. 141.40 (*0-7837-5360-8*, 2045123) Bks Demand.

Cordilleran Orogen: Conterminous U. S. Ed. by B. C. Burchfiel et al. (DNAG, Geology of North America Ser.: Vol. G3). (Illus.). 1992. 105.00 (*0-8137-5217-5*) Geol Soc.

Cordilleran Section Field Guide. Ed. by M. L. Hill. (DNAG Centennial Field Guides Ser.: No. 1). (Illus.). 532p. 1987. 43.50 (*0-8137-5401-1*) Geol Soc.

Cordless Telecommunications in Europe: The Evolution of Personal Communications. Ed. by W. H. Tuttlebee. (Illus.). xviii, 82p. 1991. 98.00 (*0-387-19633-1*) Spr-Verlag.

Cordoba. Tom Burns. (Everything under the Sun Ser.). (Illus.). 176p. 1988. pap. 6.95 (*0-8442-9209-5*, Passport Bks) NTC Pub Grp.

Cordon & Search: With the 6th Airborne Division in Palestine. 18th ed. R. Dare Wilson. (Airborne Ser.). 275p. 1984. reprint ed. 24.95 (*0-89839-083-4*) Battery Pr.

Cordon Bleu at Home. Intro. by Andre Cointreau. (Illus.). 592p. 1991. 40.00 (*0-688-09750-2*) Hearst Bks.

Cordon Bleu Classic French Cookbook. LC 94-7360. (Illus.). 160p. 1994. 24.95 (*1-56458-643-X*) Dorling Kindersley.

***Cordon of Steel: The U. S. Navy & the Cuban Missile Crisis.** (Military History Ser.). 1995. lib. bdg. 250.75 (*0-8490-7425-8*) Gordon Pr.

Cordon of Steel: The U. S. Navy & the Cuban Missile Crisis. Curtis A. Utz. LC 93-35708. (U. S. Navy in the Modern World Ser.: No. 1). 48p. 1993. 5.50 (*0-945274-23-8*) Naval Hist Ctr.

CordonBluegrass. Junior League of Louisville. (Illus.). 1987. bds. 16.95 (*0-9613330-0-6*) Jr League KY.

Cordova: The First Seventy-Five Years. Rose C. Arvidson. LC 84-80040. (Illus.). 98p. 1984. pap. 11.95 (*0-9607358-3-6*) Fathom Pub.

Cordova to Kennecott, Alaska. National Parks Service - Cordova Historical Society Staff. Ed. by Robert Spude et al. (Illus.). 52p. (C). 1988. pap. 8.95 (*0-9623320-0-3*) Cordova Historical.

Cordova's Historic Buildings. Nancy Ross. LC 83-81337. (Illus.). 20p. 1983. pap. 3.50 (*0-9607358-1-X*) Fathom Pub.

Cords of Vanity. large type ed. Miles Tripp. 1991. 21.95 (*0-7089-2471-9*) Ulverscroft.

Corduroy. (Story Tapes Ser.). (Illus.). (J). (ps-3). 1988. pap. 6.95 (*0-14-095063-X*, Puffin) Puffin Bks.

Corduroy. Don Freeman. (Illus.). (J). (gr. k-3). 1982. audio 19.95 (*0-941078-08-6*); 27.95 (*0-941078-07-8*); audio, pap. 12.95 (*0-941078-06-X*) Live Oak Media.

Corduroy. Don Freeman. (Picture Puffins Ser.). (Illus.). (J). (gr. k-1). 1976. pap. 3.99 (*0-14-050173-8*, Puffin) Puffin Bks.

Corduroy. Don Freeman. (Picture Puffins Ser.). (Illus.). (J). (gr. k-1). 1993. audio 6.99 (*0-14-095114-8*, Puffin) Puffin Bks.

Corduroy. Don Freeman. LC 68-16068. (Illus.). 32p. (J). 1968. 13.99 (*0-670-24133-4*) Viking Child Bks.

Corduroy: (Edicion Espanola) Don Freeman. (Illus.). (SPA.). (J). (ps-3). 1990. reprint ed. audio, pap. 12.95 (*0-87499-213-3*) Live Oak Media.

Corduroy: (Edicion Espanola) Bernard Most & Don Freeman. (Illus.). (SPA.). (J). (gr. 4-6). 1993. reprint ed. audio 22.95 (*0-87499-192-7*) Live Oak Media.

Corduroy: (Edicion Espanola), 4 bks., Set. Bernard Most & Don Freeman. (Illus.). (SPA.). (J). (gr. 4-6). 1993. reprint ed. audio, pap. 33.95 (*0-87499-193-5*) Live Oak Media.

Corduroy: A Study Guide. Garrett Christopher. Ed. by Joyce Friedland & Rikki Kessler. (Little Novel-Ties Ser.). (J). (gr. k-3). 1991. pap. text ed. 14.95 (*0-88122-588-6*) Lrn Links.

Corduroy: Edicion Espanola. Don Freeman. (Illus.). 32p. (J). (ps-3). 1990. pap. 4.99 (*0-14-054252-3*, Puffin) Puffin Bks.

Corduroy, Edicion Espanola. Don Freeman. (Illus.). 32p. (SPA.). (J). (ps-3). 1988. 11.95 (*0-670-82265-5*) Viking Child Bks.

Corduroy Goes to the Doctor. Lisa McCue. (Illus.). (J). (ps). 1987. pap. 3.99 (*0-670-81495-4*) Viking Child Bks.

Corduroy on the Go. Lisa McCue. (Illus.). (J). (ps). 1987. pap. 3.50 (*0-670-81497-0*) Viking Child Bks.

Corduroy Road. Patricia E. Clyne. (Illus.). (J). (gr. 5-9). 1984. 15.25 (*0-8446-6163-5*) Peter Smith.

Corduroy's Busy Street. Lisa McCue. (Illus.). (J). (ps). 1987. pap. 3.99 (*0-670-81496-2*) Viking Child Bks.

Corduroy's Busy Street & Corduroy Goes to the Doctor, 2 bks. Don Freeman. (Illus.). (J). (ps-00). 1989. reprint ed. audio, bds. 12.95 (*0-87499-133-1*) Live Oak Media.

Corduroy's Christmas. Illus. by Lisa McCue. 16p. (J). (ps-1). 1992. 10.99 (*0-670-84477-2*) Viking Child Bks.

Corduroy's Day. Lydia Freeman. LC 84-40477. (Illus.). 14p. (J). (ps). 1985. pap. 3.99 (*0-670-80521-1*) Viking Child Bks.

Corduroy's Day. Intro. by Lisa McCue. (J). (ps-k). 1987. Incl. cass. audio 12.95 (*0-87499-041-6*) Live Oak Media.

***Corduroy's Halloween: A Lift-the-Flap Book.** Illus. by Lisa McCue. 16p. (J). 1995. 10.99 (*0-670-86193-6*) Viking Child Bks.

Corduroy's Party. Lydia Freeman. LC 84-40476. (Illus.). 14p. (J). (ps). 1985. pap. 3.99 (*0-670-80520-3*) Viking Child Bks.

Corduroy's Toys. Lydia Freeman. LC 84-40478. (Illus.). 24p. (J). 1985. pap. 3.50 (*0-670-80522-X*) Viking Child Bks.

Cordwainer Smith Checklist. Mike Bennett. (Booklet Ser.: No. 37). 28p. 1991. pap. text ed. 3.00 (*0-936055-49-9*) C Drumm Bks.

***Cordwood Masonry Houses.** Roy. 1980. pap. text ed. (*0-8069-8944-0*) Sterling.

Core. Paul Preuss. 400p. 1994. mass mkt. 5.99 (*0-380-71182-6*, AvoNova) Avon.

Core: A Novel. Paul Preuss. LC 93-12167. 1993. 23.00 (*0-688-09662-X*) Morrow.

CORE: A Study in the Civil Rights Movement, 1942-1968. August Meier & Elliott Rudwick. LC 72-92294. 580p. 1975. reprint ed. pap. 15.95 (*0-252-00567-8*) U of Ill Pr.

Core, a Symposium on Contemporary Visual Poetry. Ed. by Crag Hill. (Illus.). 160p. (Orig.). 1993. pap. text ed. 12.00 (*0-945112-16-5*) Generator Pr.

Core & Log Analyses of Depositional Systems & Reservoir Properties of Gulf Coast Natural Gas Reservoirs: An Integrated Approach to Infield Reserve Growth in Frio, Vicksburg, & Wilcox Sandstones. Ed. by R. A. Levey. (Illus.). 56p. 1992. pap. 3.50 (*0-317-05170-9*, GC92-1) Bur Econ Geology.

Core & Splice Waste. (Waste Reduction & Control in a Corrugated Boxplant Ser.). 1989. student ed, vhs 149.00 (*0-685-45517-3*, 1207CORE) TAPPI.

Core & the Canon: A National Debate. Ed. by L. Robert Stevens et al. LC 92-33431. 540p. (Orig.). 1993. pap. 19.95 (*0-929398-49-1*) UNTX Pr.

Core & the Elephants. Lissa. LC 94-9153. (J). (gr. 3 up). 1995. 14.99 (*0-670-84335-0*, Viking) Viking Penguin.

Core Bibliography on Technology & Social Change in Foreign Cultures. Marsha Armstrong. (Reports on Technology & Social Change Ser.). 133p. 1973. 10.00 (*0-945271-22-0*) ISU-TSCP.

Core Cases in Torts. Jane Swanton et al. 550p. 1992. pap. 59.00 (*1-86287-076-4*, Pub. by Federation Pr AU) W W Gaunt.

Core Collection in Preservation. 2nd ed. Lisa L. Fox. LC 92-30517. 1992. 5.00 (*0-8389-7633-6*) ALA.

Core Competency Objectives in Behavioral Science Education. Comp. by STFM Task Force on Behavioral Science Education. 58p. 1986. 5.00 (*0-942295-02-1*) Soc Tchrs Fam Med.

***Core Concepts: Marketing.** Roy T. Shaw. Ed. by Richard J. Semenik. 1995. text ed. 24.95 (*0-538-83659-8*) S-W Pub.

Core Concepts in Health. 7th ed. Ed. by Walton T. Roth. 1994. 15.95 (*1-55934-342-7*); pap. 39.95 (*1-55934-210-2*) Mayfield Pub.

Core Concepts in Health: Brief Edition. 7th ed. Paul M. Insel & Walton T. Roth. LC 93-28086. (Illus.). 432p. (C). 1994. pap. text ed. 28.95 (*1-55934-316-8*) Mayfield Pub.

***Core Concepts of Business Law.** William Eldridge. 1995. text ed. 25.95 (*0-538-83869-8*) S-W Pub.

Core Conversation Course: Beginning Text. 2nd ed. Steven J. Molinsky & Bill Bliss. 208p. (C). 1989. pap. text ed. 15.95 (*0-13-811860-4*) P-H.

Core Curriculum. Deakin University Press Staff. 69p. (C). 1985. 38.00 (*0-7300-0313-2*, Pub. by Deakin Univ AT) St Mut.

Core Curriculum: Making Mathematics Count for Everyone. Steven P. Meiring et al. Ed. by Christian R. Hirsch. LC 92-6996. (Curriculum & Evaluation Standards for School Mathematics Addenda Ser.). (Illus.). 150p. (Orig.). 1992. pap. 17.00 (*0-87353-328-3*) NCTM.

Core Curriculum: Making the Connections. (Illus.). 75p. (Orig.). (C). 1994. pap. text ed. 40.00 (*0-7881-0319-9*) Diane Pub.

Core Curriculum for Critical Care Nursing. 4th ed. AACN Staff. (Illus.). 992p. 1991. text ed. 44.00 (*0-7216-3074-X*) Saunders.

***Core Curriculum for Diabetes Education.** 2nd ed. Ed. by V. Pergallo-Dittko et al. (Illus.). 732p. (C). 1994. pap. text ed. 85.00 (*1-881876-01-2*) Am Assn Diabetes Ed.

***Core Curriculum for Home Health Care Nursing, 1995.** Kathy J. Morgan & Sandra L. McClain. 1995. 79.00 (*0-8342-0725-7*) Aspen Pub.

Core Curriculum for Intravenous Nursing. Crudi & Patricia Larkin. 368p. 1984. text ed. 26.00 (*0-397-54516-9*, Lippincott Nursing) Lippincott.

Core Curriculum for Maternal-Newborn Nursing. Organization for Obstetric, Gynecologic & Neonatal Nurses Staff. Ed. by Susan Mattson & Judy E. Smith. (Illus.). 816p. 1992. pap. text ed. 54.50 (*0-7216-3122-3*) Saunders.

Core Curriculum for Neonatal Intensive Care Nursing. Organization for Obstetric, Gynecologic & Neonatal Nurses Staff. Ed. by Patricia O. Beachy & Jane Deacon. (Illus.). 746p. 1992. pap. text ed. 55.50 (*0-7216-3121-5*) Saunders.

Core Curriculum for Neuroscience Nursing. 3rd rev. ed. Ed. by Margarethe Cammermeyer & Claudia Appeldorn. (Illus.). 326p. 1990. 49.95 (*0-9625729-1-8*) Am Assoc Neuroscience.

Core Curriculum for Oncology Nursing. 2nd ed. Ed. by Jane C. Clark & Rose McGee. LC 92-11722. 1992. pap. text ed. 44.00 (*0-7216-3486-9*) Saunders.

Core Curriculum for Perioperative Nursing. Billie Fernsebner. 168p. (Orig.). 1992. pap. 52.00 (*0-945970-02-1*) O R Manager.

Core Curriculum for Post Anesthesia Nursing Practice. 3rd ed. Ed. by Kim Litwack. LC 94-13579. (Illus.). 544p. 1994. pap. text ed. 42.50 (*0-7216-5051-1*) Saunders.

Core Curriculum for Surgical First Assisting. Ed. by Association of Surgical Technologists Staff. 131p. (Orig.). (C). 1993. pap. text ed. 65.00 (*0-926805-03-7*) Assn Surgical.

Core Curriculum for Surgical Technology. 3rd ed. 168p. (C). 1990. text ed. 44.95 (*0-926805-01-0*) Assn Surgical.

***Core Curriculum for the RN First Assistant.** rev. ed. AORN Staff. Ed. by Ruth Vaiden et al. (Illus.). 220p. 1994. pap. text ed. 35.00 (*0-939583-86-0*) Assn Oper Rm Nurses.

Core Curriculum for the RN First Assistant. rev. ed. Ed. by Ruth E. Vaiden et al. (Illus.). 299p. 1994. pap. text ed. 43.75 (*0-939583-66-6*) Assn Oper Rm Nurses.

Core Curriculum in Architectural Education. Michael A. Bunch. LC 93-8671. 1993. 89.95 (*0-7734-2211-0*, Mellen Univ Pr) E Mellen.

Core Curriculum in Professional Psychology. Ed. by Roger L. Peterson et al. 187p. 1992. pap. text ed. 30.00 (*1-55798-143-4*) Am Psychol.

Core Curriculum of Addictions Nursing. Intro. by Lynette Jack. 188p. (Orig.). 1990. pap. text ed. 60.00 (*0-317-05723-5*) Ntl Nurses Soc.

Core Diet for Kids. 2nd ed. Stephen Gislason. 250p. 1989. pap. 15.95 (*0-9694145-0-1*) Gordon Soules Bk.

Core Energetics: Developing the Capacity to Love & Heal. John C. Pierrakos. (Illus.). 304p. 1990. write for info. (*0-940795-00-0*); pap. 18.95 (*0-940795-08-6*) LifeRhythm.

Core Geography: Leisure. M. Martin & W. Whittle. (C). 1982. 50.00 (*0-09-144451-9*, Pub. by S Thornes Pubs UK) St Mut.

Core Geography: Physical. M. Martin & W. Whittle. (C). 1987. 55.00 (*0-09-164201-9*, Pub. by S Thornes Pubs UK) St Mut.

Core Geography: The Developing World. M. Martin & W. Whittle. (C). 1985. 55.00 (*0-09-156621-5*, Pub. by S Thornes Pubs UK) St Mut.

Core Geography: United Kingdom. M. Martin & W. Whittle. (C). 1986. 60.00 (*0-09-160691-8*, Pub. by S Thornes Pubs UK) St Mut.

Core Geography Cities. M. Martin & W. Whittle. (C). 1983. 50.00 (*0-09-147521-X*, Pub. by S Thornes Pubs UK) St Mut.

Core Geography Work. M. Martin & W. Whittle. (C). 1983. 50.00 (*0-09-144461-6*, Pub. by S Thornes Pubs UK) St Mut.

Core Gospel. Bill R. Love. LC 91-76128. 319p. 1992. pap. 14.95 (*0-89112-151-X*) Abilene Christ U.

Core Hole Book. 35.00 (*0-318-40071-5*) Munger Oil.

Core Images of the Self: A Symbolic Approach to Healing & Wholeness. Jean D. Clift. 160p. 1992. 17.95 (*0-8245-1218-9*) Crossroad NY.

Core Inflation. Otto Eckstein. (Illus.). 128p. (C). 1981. pap. text ed. write for info. (*0-13-172635-8*) P-H.

Core Language Engine. Ed. by Hiyan Alshawi. (Bradford Books-MITP-ACL Series Natural Language Processing). (Illus.). 280p. 1992. 39.95 (*0-262-01126-3*) MIT Pr.

Core-Level Spectroscopy in Condensed Systems. Ed. by J. Kanamori & A. Kotani. (Solid-State Sciences Ser.: Vol. 81). (Illus.). 320p. 1988. 69.00 (*0-387-19112-7*) Spr-Verlag.

Core Library for Literacy - Conversational English Programs: A Bibliography. Ed. by V. K. Lawson & Barbara J. MacDonald. 34p. 1984. pap. text ed. 5.00 (*0-930713-35-4*) Lit Vol Am.

Core List of Academic Planning Periodicals & Their Indexes. Deborah Thompson-Wise. LC 92-29512. (CPL Bibliographies Ser.: No. 285). 1992. write for info. (*0-86602-285-6*) Coun Plan Librarians.

Core List of Books & Journals in Education. Nancy P. O'Brien & Emily S. Fabiano. 136p. 1991. 39.95 (*0-89774-559-0*) Oryx Pr.

Core List of Books & Journals in Science & Technology. Ed. by Russell H. Powell & James R. Powell, Jr. LC 87-10970. 144p. 1987. 38.50 (*0-89774-275-3*) Oryx Pr.

Core List of Books & Journals in Science & Technology. 2nd ed. James R. Powell, Jr. & Russell H. Powell. 176p. Date not set. 45.00 (*0-89774-730-5*) Oryx Pr.

Core of Christian Faith: D. F. Strauss & His Catholic Critics. William Madges. (American University Studies: Theology & Religion: Ser. VII, Vol. 38). 224p. (C). 1988. text ed. 33.00 (*0-8204-0521-3*) P Lang Pubs.

Core of Creation: An Investigation into the Fundamentals of Reality & the Foundation of Existence. Albert G. Choate. LC 82-80727. (Illus.). 128p. 1982. pap. 7.50 (*0-943108-00-4*) Syzygy.

Core of the Cosmos. Alnita H. Dyall. (Pilate Said to Him: "What Is Truth?" Ser.). (Illus.). 144p. (Orig.). 1991. pap. 6.95 (*1-879539-03-9*) Word Serv CA.

Core of the Curriculum for Accounting Majors, Vol. 3. Ed. by Richard E. Flaherty. (Studies in Accounting Education). 234p. 1979. 12.00 (*0-86539-031-2*) Am Accounting.

Core Otolaryngology. Koufman. (Illus.). 370p. 1989. text ed. 19.95 (*0-397-51026-8*) Lippincott.

Core Package. Richard C. Mentzer. Ed. by Danny G. Longdom. LC 79-23416. (Instructional Design Library). 124p. 1980. 23.95 (*0-87778-141-9*) Educ Tech Pubns.

Core Poetry Collection Index, 3 vols., Set. Roth Publishing Editorial Board. (Corefiche Ser.). 1127p. (Orig.). (YA). (gr. 9). 1993. pap. text ed. 75.00 (*0-89609-325-5*) Roth Pub Inc.

Core Program Diet Revision Cooking & Meal Planning. Stephen Gislason. 173p. (Orig.). 1991. pap. 14.95 (*0-9694145-1-X*) Gordon Soules Bk.

Core Questions in Philosophy: A Text with Readings. Elliott Sober. 592p. (C). 1990. text ed. write for info. (*0-02-413151-2*) Macmillan.

Core Questions in Philosophy: A Text with Readings. 2nd ed. Elliott Sober. 592p. (C). 1995. text ed. write for info. (*0-02-413161-X*) Macmillan.

***Core Readings in Psychiatry: An Annotated Guide to the Literature.** Ed. by Michael J. Sacks et al. 896p. 1995. boxed 85.00 (*0-88048-559-0*, 8559) Am Psychiatric.

Core Review for Critical Care Nursing. 2nd ed. AACN Staff. 192p. 1991. pap. text ed. 25.50 (*0-7216-3228-9*) Saunders.

Core Review in Emergency Nursing: A CEN Study Guide & Practice Examination. 2nd ed. Nancy Townsend & Pam Pourciau. 207p. (C). 1989. pap. text ed. 19.95 (*0-9622174-4-1*) Nursing Knowledge.

Core Rules, Incl. Bughunters supplement. TSR Staff. (Amazing Engine Ser.). (Illus.). 1993. Incl. Bughunters Supplement. pap. 24.95 (*1-56076-689-1*) TSR Inc.

Core Spanish. Collier & Davis. 112p. 1987. spiral bd. 22.95 (*0-8403-4270-5*) Kendall-Hunt.

Core Technology for Long-Term Care: Team Delivery. William E. Aaronson & Ruby Neuhaus. (Learning the Continuum: AUPHA Modules for Management Education Ser.). (Illus.). 84p. (Orig.). (C). 1989. pap. text ed. 45.00 (*0-910591-19-9*) AUPHA Pr.

Core Text of Neuroanatomy. 4th ed. Malcolm B. Carpenter. (Illus.). 496p. 1991. pap. 38.00 (*0-683-01457-9*) Williams & Wilkins.

***Core Text of Substance Abuse.** Ed. by Lawrence Friedman et al. LC 95-10767. 1995. write for info. (*0-683-04292-0*) Williams & Wilkins.

Core Textbook for Respiratory Care Practice. 2nd rev. ed. Ed. by Thomas A. Barnes. LC 93-32911. 916p. 1993. 51.95 (*0-8016-6550-7*) Mosby Yr Bk.

Core Textbook of Pediatrics. 3rd ed. Robert Kaye et al. LC 65-10887. (Illus.). 544p. 1988. text ed. 36.00 (*0-397-50923-5*, Lippincott Medical) Lippincott.

Core Topics in Biochemistry. Jochanan Stenesh. LC 92-72175. (Illus.). 599p. (Orig.). (C). 1992. pap. text ed. 33.95 (*0-9633552-0-1*) Cogno Pr.

Core Transformation: Reaching the Wellspring Within. Connirae Andreas & Tamara Andreas. LC 93-41068. 1994. 21.50 (*0-911226-32-X*) Real People.

Core Writing 6000. Patrick Sebranek et al. (Illus.). 50p. 1993. student ed 4.95 (*0-939045-85-0*) Write Source.

Core Writing 7000. Patrick Sebranek et al. (Illus.). 49p. 1993. student ed 4.95 (*0-939045-86-9*) Write Source.

Core Writing 8000. Patrick Sebranek et al. (Illus.). 58p. 1993. student ed 4.95 (*0-939045-87-7*) Write Source.

Corea: The Hermit Nation. William E. Griffis. (Notable American Authors Ser.). 1992. reprint ed. lib. bdg. 75.00 (*0-7812-2959-6*) Rprt Serv.

Corea, the Hermit Nation. 9th enl. rev. ed. William E. Griffis. LC 74-158615. reprint ed. 65.00 (*0-404-02916-7*) AMS Pr.

Corectec's Comprehensive Set of Review Questions for Radiography. 2nd ed. Gerald R. Cummings & Elizabeth Meixner. 300p. (C). 1991. pap. text ed. 18.50 (*1-880890-00-3*) Corectec.

Corectec's Comprehensive Set of Review Questions for Radiography. 3rd ed. Gerald R. Cummings & Elizabeth Meixner. (Illus.). 284p. (C). 1993. pap. text ed. 22.00 (*1-880890-03-8*) Corectec.

Corel Artshow Three: Graphics from Coreldraw. (Illus.). 210p. (Orig.). 1993. pap. 29.99 (*1-56496-046-3*) Rockport Pubs.

Corel Draw: A User's Guide. Alan Balfe. 400p. 1991. pap. text ed. write for info. (*0-13-176314-8*) P-H.

Corel Draw: Step-by-Step. John Campbell & Marion Pye. (Illus.). 289p. 1992. pap. 37.95 (*0-7506-0503-0*) Buttrwrth-Heinemann.

Corel Draw! Four Unleashed. Foster Coburn et al. 1044p. 1993. cd-rom, disk 39.95 (*0-672-30371-X*) Sams.

Corel Draw It! Steve Rimmer. 552p. 1993. pap. (*0-201-62637-3*) Addison-Wesley.

Corel DRAW! Unleashed, New Edition: Five Tools Unleashed with CD-ROM. Coburn et al. (Illus.). 1200p. (Orig.). 1994. pap. 49.95 (*0-672-30517-8*) Sams.

***Corel Draw 5: Visual Quickstart Guide.** Glen Waller & Webster & Associates. 352p. 1994. pap. 16.95 (*1-56609-167-5*) Peachpit Pr.

Corel Photo-Paint 5 Unleashed: Five Tools Unleashed with CD-ROM. David Huss. (Illus.). 800p. (Orig.). 1995. pap. text ed. 45.00 (*0-672-30516-X*) Sams.

***Corel Ventura 5: Visual Quickstart Guide.** Jan Tolman. 320p. 1995. pap. 18.95 (*1-56609-145-4*) Peachpit Pr.

C

An Asterisk (*) at the beginning of an entry indicates that the title is appearing in BIP for the first time. 1621

***Corel Ventura 5 Quick & Easy.** Robbin Merrin. LC 94-69702. 200p. 1995. 16.99 (*0-7821-1666-3*) Sybex.

CorelDRAW by Example: Including Comprehensive Chapters on CorelDRAW, CorelCHART, CorelPHOTO-PAINT, & CorelSHOW. Webster & Associates Staff. (By Example Ser.). (Illus.). 625p. (Orig.). 1993. pap. 34.95 (*0-947302-88-3*) Prima Pub.

***CorelDraw F-X.** Gary Priester. 300p. 1995. cd-rom 39.95 (*1-56604-274-7*) Ventana Pr.

CorelDRAW! for Beginners. Gary Bouton. (Illus.). 600p. (Orig.). 1994. pap. 24.95 (*1-56205-327-2*) New Riders Pub.

CorelDraw! for Dummies. Deke McClelland. 424p. 1993. pap. 19.95 (*1-56884-042-X*) IDG Bks.

CorelDRAW! for Non-Nerds. Gary D. Bouton. LC 93-22383. 1993. pap. 18.95 (*1-56205-174-1*) New Riders Pub.

CorelDRAW! for the Macintosh by Example. Paul Webster & Webster & Associates Staff. 500p. (Orig.). 1993. pap. 24.95 (*1-86398-002-4*) Prima Pub.

Coreldraw for the Macintosh Revealed. William Harrel. 1994. pap. 24.95 (*1-55958-510-2*) Prima Pub.

CorelDRAW! for Windows at a Glance: The Fastest & Easiest Way to Learn CorelDRAW! 4.0 for Windows. Nesbit Group Staff & Diane E. Brown. LC 93-49610. 128p. (Orig.). 1994. pap. 15.95 (*1-55622-409-5*) Wordware Pub.

CorelDRAW! Now! New Riders Publishing Staff. 310p. 1993. 21.95 (*1-56205-131-8*) New Riders Pub.

***Coreldraw! Revealed Vol. 1.** William D. Harrel. 1994. pap. 24.95 (*1-55958-599-4*) Prima Pub.

Coreldraw Special Effects. Dan Gray. 350p. 1993. pap. 39.95 (*1-56205-123-7*) New Riders Pub.

CorelDRAW! Three Made Easy. Emil Ihrig. 1992. pap. text ed. 29.95 (*0-07-881838-9*) Osborne-McGraw.

Coreldraw to the Macs. Emil Ihrig. 1993. pap. 29.95 (*0-07-881867-2*) McGraw.

CorelDRAW! VisiRef. Que Development Group Staff. (Illus.). 168p. (Orig.). 1994. pap. 12.99 (*1-56529-861-6*) Que.

CorelDRAW! 2.0 Made Easy. 2nd ed. Emil Ihrig & Sybil Ihrig. 500p. 1991. pap. text ed. 24.95 (*0-07-881726-9*) Osborne-McGraw.

CorelDraw 3 Acceso Facil. Len Gilbert. 312p. 1993. pap. text ed. 16.95 (*968-6346-84-8*, Pub. by Ventura Ediciones MX) Computer & Tech.

CorelDRAW 3 Walkabout (Training Software) Training Software & Manual. Webster & Associates Staff. 96p. 1993. disk, pap. 35.00 (*1-56609-075-X*) Peachpit Pr.

CorelDRAW! 3.0: A User's Guide. Alan Balfe. LC 92-18189. 1992. pap. 45.00 (*0-13-014581-5*) P-H.

CorelDRAW 3.0: Advanced Guide. Alan Balfe. LC 93-210. 484p. 1993. pap. 29.95 (*0-13-074964-8*) P-H.

CorelDraw 4: A User's Guide. Alan Balfe. 1993. pap. 27.95 (*0-13-207770-1*) P-H.

CorelDRAW 4: Visual QuickStart Guide. Webster & Associates Staff. (Illus.). 360p. (Orig.). 1993. pap. 15.00 (*1-56609-086-5*) Peachpit Pr.

CorelDraw 4 Instance Reference. Gordon Padwick. LC 93-85060. 471p. 1993. pap. 12.99 (*0-7821-1307-9*) Sybex.

CorelDraw! 4 Revealed. William D. Harrel. LC 93-17267. 1993. pap. 24.95 (*1-55958-391-6*) Prima Pub.

CorelDRAW! 5: The Professional Reference. 1300p. 1994. 50.00 (*1-56205-297-7*) New Riders Pub.

CorelDraw! 5 for Dummies. Deke McClelland. 1994. pap. 19.95 (*1-56884-157-4*) IDG Bks.

***CorelDRAW! 5 for Windows at a Glance.** Diane E. Brown. (At a Glance Ser.). 128p. (Orig.). 1995. pap. 15.95 (*1-55622-451-6*) Wordware Pub.

CorelDRAW 5 Quick & Easy. Robin Merrin. LC 94-67201. 167p. 1994. pap. 19.99 (*0-7821-1461-X*) Sybex.

***Coreldraw 5.0.** (Prisma Computer Courses Ser.). (Illus.). 200p. (Orig.). 1995. pap. 12.95 (*1-85365-396-9*, Pub. by Spectrum UK) Seven Hills Bk.

Corelli: His Life & His Music. Marc Pincherle. LC 79-9155. (Music Reprint Ser.). 1979. reprint ed. lib. bdg. 32.50 (*0-306-79576-0*) Da Capo.

Corelli & His Contemporaries: Sonatas for Violin. Ed. by Jane Adas. LC 91-751665. (Eighteenth-Century Continuo Sonata). 288p. 1991. 80.00 (*0-8153-0174-X*) Garland.

Corelli's Mandolin: A Novel. Louis De Bernieres. LC 94-4783. 1994. 24.00 (*0-679-43644-8*) Pantheon.

Coremaking, Dry-Sand & Loan Molding. 1983. reprint ed. pap. 6.50 (*0-917914-11-2*) Lindsay Pubns.

Corentyne Thunder. Edgar Mittleholzer. (Caribbean Writers Ser.). 229p. 1970. pap. 8.95 (*0-435-98593-0*) Heinemann.

Coreone. Francis M. Crawford. (Works of Francis Marion Crawford Ser.). 1990. reprint ed. lib. bdg. 79.00 (*0-7812-2549-3*) Rprt Serv.

Corepresentation of Grammatical Structure. Michael B. Kac. LC 77-75632. (Illus.). 169p. reprint ed. pap. 48.20 (*0-318-39679-3*, 2033262) Bks Demand.

Cores & Spools for Recording Equipment - Dimensions: ANSI AIIM MS29-1992. Association for Information & Image Management Staff. 1992. pap. 30.00 (*0-685-65906-2*, MS29) Assn Inform & Image Mgmt.

Coretta Scott King. Diane Patrick. LC 91-17032. (Impact Biographies Ser.). (Illus.). 144p. (YA). (gr. 9-12). 1991. lib. bdg. 15.47 (*0-531-13005-3*) Watts.

Coretta Scott King. Jill C. Wheeler. LC 92-16677. (Leading Ladies Ser.). (J). 1992. lib. bdg. 12.94 (*1-56239-116-X*) Abdo & Dghtrs.

***Coretta Scott King: Civil Rights Leader.** (Junior Black Americans of Achievement Ser.). (Illus.). 80p. (J). (gr. 3-6). Date not set. lib. bdg. 14.95 (*0-7910-2384-2*) Chelsea Hse.

***Coretta Scott King: Civil Rights Leader.** Ed. by Nathan I. Huggins. (Black Americans of Achievement Ser.). (Illus.). 144p. (YA). (gr. 5 up). 1995. 18.95 (*0-7910-1874-1*) Chelsea Hse.

Coretta Scott King: Keeper of the Dream. Sondra Henry & Emily Taitz. LC 91-31082. (Contemporary Women Ser.). (Illus.). 128p. (J). (gr. 6 up). 1992. lib. bdg. 17.95 (*0-89490-334-9*) Enslow Pubs.

Coretta Scott King Awards Book: From Vision to Reality. American Library Association's Social Responsibility Roundtable Staff. Ed. by Henrietta Smith. (Illus.). 130p. (Orig.). 1994. pap. text ed. 25.00 (*0-8389-3441-2*) ALA.

Coretta, the Story of Mrs. Martin Luther King Jr. Octavia Vivian. LC 72-119765. 123p. reprint ed. pap. 35.10 (*0-685-15989-2*, 2026921) Bks Demand.

Corey Ford Sporting Treasury. Corey Ford. Ed. by Chuck Petrie. LC 87-2202. (Illus.). 351p. 1987. 25.00 (*0-932558-37-2*) Willow Creek Pr.

Corey Ford Sporting Treasury: Minutes of the "Lower Forty" & Other Treasured Stories. Corey Ford. 351p. 1994. 25.00 (*1-57223-002-9*) Outlook Pubng.

Corey Guide to Postal Exams. 3rd ed. Richard J. Corey. 256p. 1988. student ed, pap. 12.95 (*0-13-172651-X*) P-H.

Corey's Fire. Lee Wardlaw. 160p. (J). (gr. 5). 1990. pap. 2.95 (*0-380-75791-5*, Flare) Avon.

CORFA: Constitutional Rebirth for America. Sam C. Polk. LC 88-71961. (Illus.). 240p. (Orig.). (C). 1989. pap. 10.95 (*0-9621836-0-1*) Corfa Bks.

Corfu. Nigel Coleman & Conrad Mewton. (Illus.). 144p. 1991. 12.95 (*0-900075-07-4*, Pub. by Windrush Pr UK) Interlink Pub.

Corfu: The Garden Isle. Frank Giles. 1994. 67.50 (*1-55859-845-6*) Abbeville Pr.

Corfu Pocket Guide. Berlitz Editors. (Pocket Guides Ser.). 1989. pap. 7.95 (*2-8315-2270-6*) Berlitz.

Corgi Toys. rev. ed. Edward Force. LC 83-51211. (Illus.). 208p. 1991. pap. 16.95 (*0-88740-364-6*) Schiffer.

Corgi Toys the Ones with Windows. Ed Force & James Wieland. write for info. (*0-87938-123-X*) J Wieland.

Cori Spezzati, 2 vols. Anthony F. Carver. (Illus.). 160p. 1989. Vol. 2: An Anthology of Sacred Polychoral Music, 160p. 69.95 (*0-521-30399-0*) Cambridge U Pr.

Coriander. Barbara Victor. 1994. mass mkt. 5.99 (*0-345-38454-7*) Ballantine.

Coriander. Barbara Victor. LC 92-54470. 1993. 22.00 (*1-55611-353-6*) D I Fine.

Corinair Working Group on Emission Factors for Calculating Emissions, 1990, 2 vols., Vols. 1-2. 1993. Set, Vol. 1: Methodology & Emission Factors, 122p.; Vol. 2: CPORET Computer Program, 187p. pap. 35.00 (*92-826-5770-1*, CR-18-93-000-EN-C) UNIPUB.

Corine Soil Erosion Risk & Important Land Resources (with Two Maps on Soil Erosion & Land Resources), EUR 13233. European Communities Staff. (Illus.). 97p. 1992. pap. 14.00 (*92-826-2545-1*, CD-NA-13233-EN, Pub. by Europ Com) UNIPUB.

Coring & Core Analysis. Tamara Kull. LC 83-61932. (Illus.). 80p. (Orig.). 1984. pap. text ed. 15.00 (*0-88698-041-0*, 3.30910) PETEX.

Coring & Core Analysis Handbook. Gene Anderson. LC 74-33713. 200p. 1975. 15.00 (*0-87814-058-1*, P4029) PennWell Bks.

Coring Operations: Procedures for Sampling & Analysis of Bottomhole & Sidewall Cores. EXLOG Staff. Ed. by Alun Whittaker. LC 85-2289. (EXLOG Series of Petroleum Geology & Engineering Handbks.). (Illus.). 174p. 1985. text ed. 30.00 (*0-88746-053-4*) Intl Human Res.

Corinna 175th Anniversary 1816-1991. Ed. by Everett E. Simpson. (Illus.). 112p. 1992. per. 10.00 (*0-9633754-0-7*) Town of Corinna.

***Corinna's Cause.** large type ed. Joanna Makepeace. (Historical Romance Ser.). 1994. 18.95 (*0-263-14008-3*, Pub. by Mills & Boon Ltd UK) Chivers N Amer.

Corinne: Or, Italy. Anne L. Stael-Holstein. Tr. by Isabel Hill. LC 77-162890. (Bentley's Standard Novels Ser.: No. 24). reprint ed. 17.00 (*0-404-54424-X*) AMS Pr.

Corinne ou l'Italie. Madame De Stael. (Folio Ser.: No. 1632). 632p. (FRE.). 1985. pap. 16.95 (*2-07-037632-X*) Schoenhof.

Corinne T. Netzer Carboyhydrate Gram Counter. Corinne T. Netzer. 1994. mass mkt. 4.99 (*0-440-21665-6*) Dell.

Corinne T. Netzer Dieter's Diary. Corinne T. Netzer. 1992. mass mkt. 6.95 (*0-440-50410-4*) Dell.

Corinne T. Netzer Encyclopedia of Food Values. Corinne T. Netzer. 1992. pap. 25.00 (*0-440-50367-1*) Dell.

Corinne T. Netzer Fat Gram Counter. Corinne T. Netzer. 1992. mass mkt. 4.99 (*0-440-20740-1*) Dell.

***Corinne T. Netzer Low-Fat Diary.** Corinne T. Netzer. 1995. pap. 6.95 (*0-440-50695-6*) Dell.

***Corinne T. Netzer 1995 Calorie Counter.** Corinne T. Netzer. 1995. pap. 4.99 (*0-440-21760-1*) Dell.

Corinne T. Netzer's, 3 vols. Corinne T. Netzer. 1990. boxed 12.85 (*0-440-36012-9*) Dell.

Corinne, the Gentile Capital of Utah. Brigham D. Madsen. LC 80-50202. (Illus.). xii, 331p. 1980. 17.50 (*0-913738-30-1*) Utah St Hist Soc.

Corinne True: Faithful Handmaid of 'Abdu'l Baha. Nathan Rutstein. (Illus.). 272p. 1987. 19.95 (*0-85398-263-5*); pap. 12.95 (*0-85398-264-3*) G Ronald Pub.

Corinth. Joanne Lowery. LC 90-70445. 59p. (Orig.). 1991. pap. 7.00 (*1-56002-102-0*) Aegina Pr.

Corinth: The Red-Figure Pottery. Sharon Herbert. LC 77-3070. (Corinth Ser.: Vol. 7, Pt. 4). x, 88p. 1977. 35.00 (*0-87661-074-2*) Am Sch Athens.

Corinth-Mycenae-Nauplion-Tiryns-Epidauros. Old Vicarage Publications Staff. 50p. (C). 1982. pap. text ed. 33.00 (*0-9508635-7-2*, Pub. by Old Vicarage UK) St Mut.

Corinthiaca: Studies in Honor of Darrell A. Amyx. Ed. by Mario A. Del Chiaro & William R. Biers. LC 86-4375. (Illus.). 200p. 1987. text ed. 32.50 (*0-8262-0617-4*) U of Mo Pr.

Corinthian. Georgette Heyer. 334p. 1981. reprint ed. lib. bdg. 27.95x (*0-89966-297-8*) Buccaneer Bks.

***Corinthian Body.** Dale B. Martin. LC 94-44947. 1995. write for info. (*0-300-06205-2*) Yale U Pr.

Corinthian Catastrophe. George E. Gardiner. LC 74-75106. 64p. 1975. pap. 4.99 (*0-8254-2708-8*) Kregel.

Corinthian Catastrophe: How to Ruin a Church Quickly. Dino Pedrone. 63p. (Orig.). 1987. pap. 1.00 (*0-929961-16-1*) Open Door Ch.

Corinthian Catastrophe see Catastrofe de Corinto

Corinthian Correspondence. Russell P. Spittler. LC 75-43157. (Radiant Life Ser.). 128p. 1976. teacher ed 4.50 (*0-88243-166-8*, 32-0166); pap. 2.95 (*0-88243-892-1*, 02-0892) Gospel Pub.

Corinthian Hellenistic Pottery. G. Roger Edwards. LC 74-10623. (Corinth Ser.: Vol. 7, Pt. 3). (Illus.). xviii, 254p. 1975. 45.00 (*0-87661-073-4*) Am Sch Athens.

Corinthian Letters of Paul. G. Campbell Morgan. 288p. 1946. 16.99 (*0-8007-0051-1*) Revell.

Corinthian Vase-Painting of the Archaic Period, 3 Vol., Set. D. A. Amyx. (California Studies in the History of Art: No. XXV). 1989. Vol. I: Catalogue; Vol. II: Commentary; Vol. III: Indexes, Concordances & Plates. 300.00 (*0-520-03166-0*) U CA Pr.

Corinthian Women Prophets. Antoinette C. Wire. LC 90-35519. 328p. 1990. 30.00 (*0-8006-2434-3*, 1-2434) Augsburg Fortress.

Corinthians. William Barclay. 288p. 1993. pap. 25.00 (*0-7152-0278-2*) St Mut.

Corinthians. F. Fallon. 1989. pap. 25.00 (*0-86217-025-7*, Pub. by Veritas IE) St Mut.

Corinthians. Murphy-O'Connor. 1989. pap. 21.00 (*0-86217-014-1*, Pub. by Veritas IE) St Mut.

Corinthians: A Commentary on the New Testament in Modern English. (J. B. Phillips New Testament Commentaries Ser.). 102p. 1973. reprint ed. write for info. (*0-685-29328-9*) Macmillan.

Corinthians I. William F. Orr. LC 75-42441. (Anchor Bible Ser.: Vol. 32). 1976. pap. 34.00 (*0-385-02853-9*) Doubleday.

Corinthians I: The Challenge of Life Together. Paul Stevens & Dan Williams. (LifeGuide Bible Studies). 64p. (Orig.). 1988. pap. 4.99 (*0-8308-1009-9*, 1009) InterVarsity.

Corinthians I see Commentaries on the New Testament

***Corinthians II.** Linda L. Belleville. Ed. by Grant R. Osborne et al. (IVP New Testament Commentary Ser.). 272p. 1995. text ed. 16.99 (*0-8308-1808-1*, 1808, Pub. by IVP UK) InterVarsity.

Corinthians II. Paul Stevens. (LifeGuide Bible Studies). 64p. 1990. pap. 4.99 (*0-8308-1010-2*, 1010) InterVarsity.

Corinthians II: Critical & Exegetical Commentary. Alfred Plummer. Ed. by Samuel R. Driver & Charles A. Briggs. (International Critical Commentary Ser.). 462p. 1915. 36.95 (*0-567-05028-9*, Pub. by T & T Clark UK) Bks Intl VA.

Corinthians II - Galatians see Commentaries on the New Testament

Corinthians One. H. A. Ironside. 1938. 18.99 (*0-87213-354-0*) Loizeaux.

Corinthians One: Critical & Exegetical Commentary. Archibald Robertson & Alfred Plummer. Ed. by Samuel R. Driver & Charles A. Briggs. (International Critical Commentary Ser.). 496p. 1914. 36.95 (*0-567-05027-0*, Pub. by T & T Clark UK) Bks Intl VA.

Corinthians Two. H. A. Ironside. 1939. 14.99 (*0-87213-355-9*) Loizeaux.

Corinthians 1 & 2. Charles Hodge. (Geneva Commentaries Ser.). 1978. 26.95 (*0-85151-185-6*) Banner of Truth.

Coriolano. William Shakespeare. Ed. & Tr. by Angel-Luis Pujante. (Nueva Austral Ser.: Vol. 163). (SPA.). 1991. pap. text ed. 24.95x (*84-239-1963-3*) Elliots Bks.

Coriolanus. Bruce King. LC 88-38994. (Critics Debate Ser.). (C). 1989. text ed. 35.00 (*0-391-03643-2*) Humanities.

Coriolanus. Adrian Poole. LC 88-18051. 192p. 1988. text ed. 22.95 (*0-8057-8709-7*, Twayne); pap. 13.95 (*0-8057-8713-5*, Twayne) Macmillan.

Coriolanus. Shakespeare. (BBC Television Plays Ser.). 1984. pap. 5.95 (*0-563-20188-6*, Pub. by BBC UK) Parkwest Pubns.

Coriolanus. William Shakespeare. (Airmont Shakespeare Ser.). (YA). (gr. 10 up). 1968. pap. 0.60 (*0-8049-1021-9*, S-21) Airmont.

Coriolanus. William Shakespeare. Ed. by Brian Parker. (Oxford Shakespeare Ser.). (Illus.). 400p. 1994. 65.00 (*0-19-812923-8*) OUP.

Coriolanus. William Shakespeare. Ed. by Philip Brockbank. LC 76-9167. (Arden Shakespeare Ser.). 300p. 1976. 55.00 (*0-415-02682-2*, NO.2448); pap. 8.95 (*0-416-17880-4*, NO.2449) Routledge.

Coriolanus. William Shakespeare. 1988. pap. 3.95 (*0-671-49966-1*) S&S Trade.

Coriolanus. William Shakespeare. Ed. by G. R. Hibbard. (New Penguin Shakespeare Ser.). 1981. mass mkt. 5.50 (*0-14-070703-4*, Penguin Classics) Viking Penguin.

Coriolanus. rev. ed. William Shakespeare. Ed. by Reuben A. Brower. 1966. pap. 4.95 (*0-451-52296-6*, Sig Classics) NAL-Dutton.

Coriolanus. rev. ed. William Shakespeare. Ed. by Harry T. Levin. (Pelican Shakespeare Ser.). 1956. pap. 4.95 (*0-14-071402-2*, Pelican Bks) Viking Penguin.

Coriolanus. William Shakespeare. Ed. by Brian Parker. (Shakespeare Ser.). (Illus.). 384p. 1994. reprint ed. pap. 6.95 (*0-19-281452-4*) OUP.

***Coriolanus: Critical Essays.** Ed. by David Wheeler. LC 94-30211. (Shakespeare Criticism Ser.: Vol. 11). 472p. 1995. 70.00 (*0-8153-1057-9*, H1646) Garland.

***Coriolanus: Granville Barker's Prefaces to Shakespeare.** Granville Barker. 240p. 1995. pap. 6.95 (*0-435-08646-4*) Heinemann.

Coriolanus at the National: The Interpretation of the Time. Kristina Bedford. LC 90-55697. (Illus.). 352p. 1992. 55.00 (*0-945636-18-0*) Susquehanna U Pr.

Coriolis Effect. Chuck Wachtel. 120p. 1985. pap. 7.00 (*0-914610-40-6*) Hanging Loose.

Coritani. rev. ed. Malcolm Todd. (Peoples of Roman Britain Ser.). 176p. 1991. 30.00 (*0-86299-878-6*) A Sutton Pub.

Corithian. Georgette Heyer. 1976. 20.95 (*0-8488-1052-X*) Amereon Ltd.

Corixidae of the Western Hemisphere (Hemiptera) H. B. Hungerford & Reece I. Sailer. LC 75-43673. (Illus.). 827p. 1977. reprint ed. 25.00 (*0-911836-07-1*) Entomological Repr.

Cork: Anything Book. 1993. 3.99 (*0-517-09388-X*) Random Hse Value.

Cork & the Cork Tree. G. Cooke & R. Rollins. LC 61-9780. (International Series of Monographs on Pure & Applied Mathematics: Vol. 4). 1961. 56.00 (*0-08-009370-1*, Pub. by Pergamon Repr UK) Franklin.

Cork & Wood Crafts. Arden Newsome. LC 72-112370. (Illus.). 64p. (J). (gr. k-3). 1971. lib. bdg. 12.95 (*0-87460-229-7*) Lion Bks.

Cork Dramatic Society: Lost Plays of the Irish Renaissance, Vol. III. R. Burnham & R. Hogan. 1985. pap. 3.95 (*0-912262-82-6*) Proscenium.

Cork Millner's Recipe of the Winemakers. Cork Millner. 64p. 1986. pap. 6.50 (*0-87461-064-8*) McNally & Loftin.

Cork of the Colonies: The First American Detective. S. S. Rafferty. LC 84-80232. 314p. 1984. pap. 4.95 (*0-930330-11-0*) Intl Polygonics.

Cork on a String. David Casper. LC 91-65708. 270p. 1992. 12.95 (*1-55523-444-5*) Winston-Derek.

Corker. Anya Bateman. pap. 3.95 (*0-88494-750-5*) Bookcraft Inc.

Corker's Freedom. John Berger. 288p. 1981. 5.95 (*0-906495-08-3*); pap. 5.95 (*0-904613-40-2*) Writers & Readers.

***Corkers Freedom.** John Berger. 1995. pap. 11.00 (*0-679-75513-6*, Vin) Random.

Corker's Freedom: A Novel. John Berger. LC 93-17128. 1993. 21.00 (*0-679-42722-8*) Pantheon.

Corkscrews: An Introduction to Their Appreciation. Manfred Heckmann. Ed. by Maurice Sullivan. (Illus.). 124p. 1981. 12.95 (*0-686-69566-6*) Wine Appreciation.

Corkscrews & Bottle Openers. Evan Perry. (Album Ser.). (Illus.). 32p. 1980. pap. text ed. 5.25 (*0-85263-534-6*, Pub. by Shire Pubns UK) Lubrecht & Cramer.

Corkscrews for Collectors. Bernard M. Watney & Homer D. Babbidge. (Illus.). 176p. 1993. 39.95 (*0-85667-431-1*, Pub. by P Wilson Pubs) Sothebys Pubns.

***Corkscrews of the Eighteenth Century: Artistry in Iron & Steel.** Bertrand B. Giulian. (Illus.). 236p. 1994. 60.00 (*0-9639201-1-1*) WhiteSpace Pubng.

Corky: Kel, Pt. 2. Mark Dunster. (Rin Ser.: Pt. 29). 82p. (Orig.). 1981. pap. 5.00 (*0-89642-072-8*) Linden Pubs.

Corm. Frank Cebulski. 1974. 5.00 (*0-685-48373-8*); pap. 2.50 (*0-685-48374-6*) Oyez.

***Cormac Mac Art.** Robert E. Howard. 224p. 1995. mass mkt. 5.99 (*0-671-87651-1*) Baen Bks.

Cormack Came Back. large type ed. Marshall Grover. (Linford Western Library). 240p. 1987. pap. 11.95 (*0-7089-6398-6*, Linford) Ulverscroft.

***Cormany Diaries: A Northern Family in the Civil War.** Ed. by James C. Mohr & Richard E. Winslow, 3rd. LC 81-16345. 623p. 1982. pap. 177.60 (*0-7837-8550-X*, 2049365) Bks Demand.

Cormorant-Fisherman Conflict in Tillamook County, Oregon. Range D. Bayer. LC 89-80373. (Studies in Oregon Ornithology: No. 6). (Illus.). 99p. 1989. pap. 9.50 (*0-939819-05-8*) Gahmken Pr.

Cormorant's Brood. Inglis Fletcher. (Albemarle Ser.). 324p. 1976. reprint ed. lib. bdg. 23.95 (*0-89244-002-3*) Queens Hse-Focus Serv.

Cormorants, Darters, & Pelicans of the World. Paul A. Johnsgard. LC 92-31997. (Illus.). 448p. 1993. 49.00 (*1-56098-216-0*) Smithsonian.

Cormyr. TSR, Inc. Staff. Date not set. 9.95 (*1-56076-818-5*) TSR Inc.

***Corn: A Country Garden Cookbook.** David Tanis. LC 94-39172. (Illus.). 1995. 14.95 (*0-00-255450-X*) Collins SF.

Corn: Chemistry & Technology. Ed. by S. A. Watson & P. E. Ramstad. LC 87-70831. (Monograph Ser.). (Illus.). 605p. 1987. 145.00 (*0-913250-48-1*) Am Assn Cereal Chem.

***Corn: Country Garden Book Club Edition.** David Tonis. Date not set. 14.95 (*0-00-225101-9*, HarpT) HarpC.

Corn: Improvement, Seed Production & Uses. Robert W. Jugenheimer. LC 83-17491. 832p. 1985. reprint ed. 83.50 (*0-89874-662-0*) Krieger.

Corn: Its Origin, Evolution, & Development. Paul C. Mangelsdorf. LC 72-95454. 288p. 1974. 30.00 (*0-674-17175-6*) HUP.

Corn: The American Grain. Richard V. Humphrey. (Antique Eating Ser.). 74p. (Orig.). 1985. pap. 4.95 (*0-9610602-2-0*) Teaparty Bks.

Corn: What It Is, What It Does. Cynthia Kellogg. LC 88-18784. (Illus.). 48p. (J). 1989. 11.95 (*0-688-08024-3*); lib. bdg. 11.88 (*0-688-08026-X*) Greenwillow.

Corn - On & Off the Cob. Allan Fowler. LC 94-10471. (Rookie Read-about Science Ser.). (Illus.). 32p. (J). (ps-2). 1994. lib. bdg. 11.93 (*0-516-06027-9*); pap. 3.95 (*0-516-46027-7*) Childrens.

Corn & Corn Improvement. 3rd ed. Ed. by George F. Sprague & J. W. Dudley. 986p. 1988. 66.00 (*0-89118-099-0*) Am Soc Agron.

Corn & Culture in the Prehistoric New World. Ed. by Sissel Johannessen & Christine A. Hastorf. 623p. (C). 1994. pap. text ed. 61.00 (*0-8133-8375-7*) Westview.

An Asterisk (*) at the beginning of an entry indicates that the title is appearing in BIP for the first time.

Corn & Its Early Fathers. rev. ed. William L. Brown & Henry A. Wallace. (Henry A. Wallace Series on Agricultural History & Rural Studies). (Illus.). 158p. 1988. reprint ed. text ed. 23.95 (0-8138-0012-9) Iowa St U Pr.

***Corn & Ivy: Spiritual Reading in Ruth & Jonah.** Denise L. Carmody & John T. Carmody. 176p. (Orig.). (C). 1995. pap. write for info. (1-56338-134-6) TPI PA.

Corn & Sage. Allen Bennett. 160p. 1991. pap. 10.98 (1-880899-00-0) Melville & Co.

Corn Belt Harvest. Raymond Bial. (Illus.). 48p. (J). (gr. 3-6). 1991. 14.95 (0-395-56234-1, Sandpiper) HM.

Corn Belt Route: A History of the Chicago Great Western Railroad Company. H. Roger Grant. LC 83-17461. (Illus.). 231p. 1984. 30.00 (0-87580-095-5) N Ill U Pr.

Corn Bread & Beans for Breakfast: Alabama Boyhood in the Thirties & Forties. James M. Hanna. 170p. 1994. 8.95 (0-9640458-0-X) Cherokee DE.

Corn Cookery. Sheila Buff. 160p. 1993. pap. 13.95 (1-55821-245-0) Lyons & Burford.

Corn, Cucurbits & Cotton from Glen Canyon. Hugh C. Cutler. (Glen Canyon Ser.: No. 30). reprint ed. 26.00 (0-404-60680-6) AMS Pr.

***Corn Dance.** Jeri Theriault. Ed. by R. Zarucchi. (Poetry Chapbook Ser.). (Illus.). 36p. (Orig.). 1994. pap. 6.95 (1-879205-53-X) Nightshade Pr.

Corn Economy of Indonesia. Ed. by C. Peter Timmer. LC 86-23939. (Illus.). 304p. 1987. 32.50 (0-8014-1961-1) Cornell U Pr.

***Corn Fed Giants: Step by Step Guide to Locating & Harvesting Whitetails in Farmland.** Bernie Barringer & Tom Miranda. (Illus.). 192p. (Orig.). 1993. pap. 14.95 (1-885149-01-8) Moving Mtn.

Corn Grows Ripe. Dorothy Rhoads. (J). 1994. 17.75 (0-8446-6756-0) Peter Smith.

Corn Grows Ripe. Dorothy Rhoads. LC 92-24888. (J). (gr. 8-12). 1993. 4.99 (0-14-036313-0, Puffin) Puffin Bks.

Corn into Alcohol: Its Chemistry. 1991. lib. bdg. 69.00 (0-8490-4561-4) Gordon Pr.

Corn Is Green. Emlyn Williams. 1945. pap. 4.75 (0-8222-0240-9) Dramatists Play.

Corn Is Maize: The Gift of the Indians. Aliki. LC 75-6928. (Let's-Read-&-Find-Out Science Bk.). (Illus.). 40p. (J). (gr. k-3). 1976. lib. bdg. 14.89 (0-690-00975-5, Crowell Jr Bks) HarpC Child Bks.

Corn Is Maize: The Gift of the Indians. Aliki. LC 75-6928. (Let's-Read-&-Find-Out Science Bk.). (Illus.). 40p. (J). (gr. k-3). 1986. pap. 4.95 (0-06-445026-0, Trophy) HarpC Child Bks.

Corn Is Our Blood: Culture & Ethnic Identity in a Contemporary Aztec Indian Village. Alan R. Sandstrom. LC 91-50307. (Civilization of the American Indian Ser.: Vol. 206). (Illus.). 448p. (C). 1992. 39.95 (0-8061-2399-0); pap. 21.95 (0-8061-2403-2) U of Okla Pr.

Corn King & Spring Queen. Naomi Mitchison. 720p. 1990. 24.95 (0-87951-377-2) Overlook Pr.

Corn King & Spring Queen. Naomi Mitchell. 1988. reprint ed. lib. bdg. 89.00 (0-7812-0167-5) Rprt Serv.

Corn King & the Spring Queen. Naomi Mitchison. LC 93-17897. (Hera Ser.). 721p. 1994. pap. 17.00 (0-939149-99-0) Soho Press.

Corn King & the Spring Queen. Naomi Mitchinson. LC 73-145186. 1971. reprint ed. 69.00 (0-403-01111-6) Scholarly.

***Corn Pone: Half-Baked, Half-Fried Staple Corn Bread Patties.** Jimmie McWilliams. (Illus.). 216p. (Orig.). 1992. pap. 19.95 (0-9633194-1-8) D R Virtue Pr.

Corn Recipes from the Indians. Frances Gwaltney. (Illus.). 32p. 1991. pap. 3.50 (0-935741-15-1) Cherokee Pubns.

***Corn Silage Production, Management, & Feeding.** Ed. by Greg Roth et al. LC 95-1562. 1995. write for info. (0-89118-124-5) Am Soc Agron.

Corn Uses: Uses for Corn. rev. ed. Recycling Consortium Staff. 1992. pap. text ed. 14.95 (0-317-04792-2, Recycling Consort) Prosperity & Profits.

Corn Woman: Stories & Legends to the Hispanic South. Angel Vigil. (World Folklore Ser.). (Illus.). 175p. 1994. lib. bdg. 28.00 (1-56308-194-6) Libs Unl.

Cornaceae & Allies in the Marquesas & Neighboring Islands. F. B. Brown. (BMB Ser.). 1972. reprint ed. pap. 15.00 (0-527-02158-X) Periodicals Srv.

Cornballs: Cereal Box Joke Book. Aristides Ruiz. LC 92-60581. 400p. (J). (gr. 4-7). 1993. pap. 2.99 (0-679-83455-9) Random Bks Yng Read.

Cornbread & Caviar. Bob Jones. (Illus.). 236p. 1985. 14.95 (0-89084-305-8); pap. 9.95 (0-89084-306-6) Bob Jones Univ Pr.

***Cornbread & Maggots, Cloak & Dagger, Union Prisoners & Spies in Civil War Richmond.** David D. Ryan. 1994. 24.95 (0-87517-083-8) Dietz.

Cornbread Chronicles. Ludlow Porch. LC 83-61914. 208p. 1983. 12.95 (0-931948-48-7) Peachtree Pubs.

Cornbread Whistle: Oral History of a Texas Timber Company Town. Megan Biesele. Ed. by Bob Bowman. (Illus.). 200p. 1987. 15.00 (0-9617904-0-7) Diboll Hist Soc.

Concribs of Buzet: Modernizing Agriculture in the French Southwest. Peter H. Amann. (Illus.). 282p. (C). 1990. text ed. 45.00 (0-691-05563-7) Princeton U Pr.

Cornea. Ed. by Herbert E. Kaufman et al. (Illus.). 952p. 1988. text ed. 220.00 (0-443-08374-6) Churchill.

Cornea. 2nd ed. Ed. by Gilbert Smolin & Richard A. Thoft. 600p. 1987. text ed. 85.00 (0-685-17573-1, Little Med Div) Little.

Cornea: Scientific Foundations & Clinical Practice. 3rd ed. Ed. by Gilbert Smolin & Richard A. Thoft. LC 93-4460. 1994. 235.00 (0-316-80270-0) Little.

Cornea: Transactions of the World Congress on the Cornea III. Ed. by H. Dwight Cavanagh. (Illus.). 672p. 1988. text ed. 142.50 (0-88167-373-0) Raven.

***Cornea Color Atlas.** Jay H. Krachmer & David A. Palay. LC 95-6803. 1995. write for info. (0-615-00666-3) Mosby Yr Bk.

Cornea in Measles. N. W. Dekkers. (Monographs in Ophthalmology: No. 3). 121p. 1981. lib. bdg. 51.50 (90-6193-803-1) Kluwer Ac.

Cornea in Normal Condition & in Groenouw's Macular Dystrophy. J. Francois & V. Victoria-Troncoso. (Illus.). x, 198p. 1980. lib. bdg. 94.00 (90-6193-161-4) Kluwer Ac.

Cornea, Refractive Surgery, & Contact Lens. (Transactions of the New Orleans Academy of Ophthalmology Ser.). (Illus.). 336p. 1987. text ed. 113.50 (0-88167-307-2) Raven.

Corneal Alterations with Contact Lens Wear. A. J. Rouwen. (Illus.). 168p. 1992. lib. bdg. 43.00 (90-6299-080-0, Pub. by Kugler NE) Kugler Pubns.

Corneal & External Disorders: Refractive Surgery. Gerhard K. Lang & Gottfried O. Naumann. (Current Opinion in Ophthalmology Ser.). (Illus.). 115p. (Orig.). 1993. pap. text ed. 59.95 (1-870485-70-X) Current Science.

***Corneal & External Disorders & Refractive Disorders.** Gerhard K. Lang & Gotfried. Ed. by O. H. Naumann. (Current Opinion in Ophthalmology Ser.). (Illus.). (Orig.). 1994. pap. text ed. 59.95 (1-85922-627-2) Current Science.

Corneal & External Eye Disease. Foster. 1991. 39.95 (0-8151-3270-0, Yr Bk Med Pubs) Mosby Yr Bk.

Corneal & Refractive Surgery. Sherwin A. Kaufman et al. (Illus.). 337p. 1991. text ed. 99.50 (0-397-51073-X) Lippincott.

Corneal Angiogenesis: A Comprehensive Critical Review. G. K. Klintworth. (Illus.). 144p. 1990. 72.00 (0-387-97440-7) Spr-Verlag.

Corneal Astigmatism: Etiology, Prevention & Management. Troutman. (Illus.). 506p. 1992. 110.00 (0-8016-5531-5) Mosby Yr Bk.

Corneal Disorders: Clinical Diagnosis & Management. Howard M. Leibowitz. (Illus.). 550p. 1984. text ed. 185.00 (0-7216-5727-3) Saunders.

Corneal Graft Failure. Ciba Foundation Staff. LC 73-82445. (Ciba Foundation Symposium: New Ser.: No. 15). 371p. reprint ed. pap. 105.80 (0-317-28298-0, 2022146) Bks Demand.

Corneal Grafting: Principles & Practice. 2nd ed. Thomas A. Casey et al. (Illus.). 352p. 1984. text ed. 155.00 (0-7216-2448-0) Saunders.

***Corneal Laser Surgery.** Ed. by James J. Salz et al. LC 94-26527. 1994. write for info. (0-8151-7510-8) Mosby Yr Bk.

Corneal Sensitivity: Measurement & Clinical Importance. J. Draeger. (Illus.). 160p. 1984. 56.00 (0-387-81794-8) Spr-Verlag.

Corneal Surgery: Theory, Technique, & Tissue. 2nd ed. Ed. by Frederick S. Brightbill. LC 92-23630. 763p. 1992. 189.00 (0-8016-6487-X) Mosby Yr Bk.

Corneal Topography: Measuring & Modifying the Cornea. Ed. by D. J. Schanzlin & J. B. Robin. (Illus.). 288p. 1991. 108.00 (0-387-97539-X) Spr-Verlag.

***Corneal Topography: State of the Art.** Donald R. Sanders. 1995. 135.00 (1-55642-268-7) SLACK Inc.

Corneal Transplantation in Complicated Leucomas. N. Puchkovskaya. (Illus.). 303p. 1969. 26.95 (0-8464-1083-4) Beekman Pubs.

Corneille. Gustave Lanson. LC 75-41170. reprint ed. 36.00 (0-404-14797-6) AMS Pr.

Corneille: Le Cid. P. Nurse. (Bristol French Texts Ser.). (FRE.). 1992. 14.95 (0-685-49971-5, Pub. by Brstl Class Pr UK) Focus Info Gr.

Corneille: Polyeucte. Pierre Corneille. Ed. by R. A. Sayce. (Bristol French Texts Ser.). 112p. (FRE.). 1992. reprint ed. 11.95 (0-631-00480-7, Pub. by Brstl Class Pr UK) Focus Info Gr.

Corneille & the Spanish Drama. J. B. Segall. 1976. lib. bdg. 59.95 (0-8490-1674-6) Gordon Pr.

Corneille, Classicism & the Ruses of Symmetry. Mitchell Greenberg. (Cambridge Studies in French: No. 17). 208p. 1986. 64.95 (0-521-32554-4) Cambridge U Pr.

Corneille et la Vie Litteraire de Son Temps see Heroisme Cornelien: Genese et Signification

Corneille, Tasso & Modern Poetics. A. Donald Sellstrom. LC 86-2539. 165p. 1986. 36.50 (0-8142-0410-4) Ohio St U Pr.

Corneille's Tragedies: The Role of the Unexpected. R. C. Knight. 144p. (C). 1991. text ed. 59.00 (0-389-20960-0) B&N Imports.

Cornelian Theater: The Metadramatic Dimension. Mary J. Muratore. LC 90-70978. 117p. 1990. lib. bdg. 23.95 (0-917786-84-X) Summa Pubns.

Cornelii Taciti Annalium Libri I-IV. Cornelius Tacitus. LC 75-41270. 1976. reprint ed. 18.00 (0-404-14615-5) AMS Pr.

***Cornelis Cort: "Accomplished Plate-Cutter from Hoorn in Holland"** Manfred Sellink. (Illus.). 232p. 1995. pap. 35.00 (90-6918-121-5) U of Wash Pr.

Cornelis Saftleven: 1607-1682 Leben und Werke. Wolfgang Schulz. (Beitraege zur Kunstgeschichte Ser.: No. 14). (Illus.). (C). 1978. 192.35 (3-11-007474-5) De Gruyter.

Cornelius. Leo Lionni. LC 82-6442. (Dragonfly Bks.). (Illus.). (J). (ps-2). 1994. pap. 4.99 (0-679-86040-1) Knopf Bks Yng Read.

***Cornelius & the Dog Star.** Diana Spyropulos. LC 94-32335. (Illus.). 48p. (J). (gr. k-5). 1995. 15.95 (0-935699-08-2) Illum Arts.

Cornelius Chronicles, Vol. I. Michael Moorcock. 992p. 1977. mass mkt. 4.95 (0-380-00878-5) Avon.

Cornelius Chronicles, Vol. II. Michael Moorcock. 352p. 1986. pap. 3.50 (0-380-75003-1) Avon.

Cornelius Chronicles, Vol. III. Michael Moorcock. 352p. 1987. pap. 3.50 (0-380-70255-X) Avon.

Cornelius Harnett: An Essay in North Carolina History. Robert D. Connor. LC 76-148876. (Select Bibliographies Reprint Ser.). 1977. reprint ed. 20.95 (0-8369-5647-8) Ayer.

Cornelius: History of the Cornelius Family in America: Historical, Genealogical & Biographical. C. S. Cornelius & S. F. Cornelius. (Illus.). 292p. 1991. reprint ed. 56.00 (0-8328-1855-0); reprint ed. pap. 46.00 (0-8328-1856-9) Higginson Bk Co.

Cornelius in Charge. Mary Flynn. (Illus.). (Orig.). (J). (gr. 1-6). 1990. 10.95 (0-947962-53-0, Pub. by Anvil Bks Ltd IE); pap. 7.95 (0-947962-54-9, Pub. by Anvil Bks Ltd IE) Irish Bks Media.

Cornelius Jansen Family History, 1822-1973. Betty A. Miller & Oscar R. Miller. (Illus.). 73p. 1974. pap. 4.50 (0-685-64818-4) O R Miller.

Cornelius Matthews. Allen F. Stein. Ed. by Sylvia E. Bowman. LC 72-11012. (Twayne's United States Authors Ser.). 171p. (C). 1974. lib. bdg. 17.95 (0-8290-1720-8) Irvington.

Cornelius Nepos. Cornelius Nepos. Tr. by J. C. Rolfe. (Loeb Classical Library: No. 467). 366p. 1929. text ed. 18.95 (0-674-99514-7) HUP.

Cornelius Nepos: A Selection, Including the Lives of Cato & Atticus. Ed. by N. M. Horsfall. (Clarendon Ancient History Ser.). 160p. 1990. 45.00 (0-19-814903-4) OUP.

Cornelius Nepos: Lives of Famous Men. Ed. by Gareth Schmeling. 144p. 1971. pap. 5.00 (0-87291-023-7) Coronado Pr.

Cornelius Nepos: Three Lives, Alcibiades-Dion-Atticus. R. Roebuck. (Illus.). 138p. (ENG & LAT.). 1987. reprint ed. pap. 11.00 (0-86516-207-7) Bolchazy-Carducci.

Cornelius Nepos & Ancient Political Biography. Joseph Geiger. 128p. (Orig.). 1985. pap. text ed. 34.50 (3-515-04414-0) Coronet Bks.

Cornelius Van Til: The Man & the Myth. John W. Robbins. 42p. (Orig.). 1986. pap. 2.45 (0-940931-15-X) Trinity Found.

Cornell & Ithaca in Postcards. Harvey N. Roehl. LC 86-18937. (Illus.). 112p. (Orig.). 1986. pap. 11.95 (0-911572-59-7) Vestal.

Cornell Book of Cats. Ed. by Siegal Mordecai. LC 89-40195. 1989. 30.00 (0-394-56787-0) Random.

Cornell Book of Cats: A Comprehensive Medical Reference for Every Cat & Kitten. Cornell Feline Health Center Staff. Ed. by Mordecai Siegal. (Illus.). 1989. write for info. (0-394-56786-2, Villard Bks) Random.

Cornell Bread Book: Fifty-Four Recipes for Nutritious Loaves, Rolls & Coffee Cakes. rev. ed. Clive M. McCay & Jeannette B. McCay. (Illus.). 52p. 1980. reprint ed. pap. 2.95 (0-486-23995-0) Dover.

Cornell Collects: A Celebration of American Art from the Collections of Alumni & Friends. Frank H. Rhodes et al. LC 90-82601. (Illus.). 196p. (Orig.). (C). 1990. pap. 31.95 (0-8122-1507-9) U of Pa Pr.

***Cornell Cooks: Recipes & Rememberances of Cornell University.** Cornell Club of Central New York Staff. (Illus.). 1995. 14.95 (0-9644413-0-6) Cornell Alum Assoc.

Cornell Geology Through the Years. William R. Brice. 240p. 1989. write for info. (0-918531-03-9) Cornell Coll Eng.

Cornell International Law Journal: 1968-1992, 26 vols. mic. film write for info. (0-318-57428-4) Rothman.

Cornell International Law Journal: 1968-1992, 26 vols., Set. 920.00 (0-8377-9045-X) Rothman.

Cornell Law Review: 1915-1992, 78 vols. fiche, mic. film write for info. (0-318-57429-2) Rothman.

Cornell Law Review: 1915-1992, 78 vols., Set. 3,840.00 (0-8377-9046-8) Rothman.

Cornell Manual for Lifeboatmen, Able Seamen, & Qualified Members of Engine Department. William B. Hayler et al. LC 83-46036. (Illus.). 166p. 1984. pap. text ed. 7.50 (0-87033-313-5) Cornell Maritime.

Cornell Woolrich-Morkrets Poet. Francis M. Nevins, Jr. LC 86-2266. 46p. 1986. reprint ed. lib. bdg. 27.00x (0-89370-538-1) Borgo Pr.

Corneo-Plastic Surgery. Ed. by P. V. Rycroft. LC 68-58885. 1969. 264.00 (0-08-013013-5, Pub. by Pergamon Repr UK) Franklin.

Corner. Ed. by Theo Lancaster. 128p. (C). 1988. pap. 35.00 (0-7212-0769-3, Pub. by Regency Press) St Mut.

***Corner Boys.** Stanley Sunabe. (Illus.). 102p. (Orig.). Date not set. pap. 9.95 (0-9645874-0-8) Bons Pub.

Corner Boys: A Study of Clique Behavior. William F. Whyte. (Reprint Series in Social Sciences). (C). 1993. reprint ed. pap. text ed. 1.90 (0-8290-3095-6, S-311) Irvington.

Corner Grocery Store. Catherine Otten. (Illus.). 148p. (Orig.). 1980. pap. 4.95 (0-937816-02-7) Tech Data.

***Corner Is No Place for Hiding.** Jonetta R. Barras. Ed. by Cindy Comitz & Grace Cavalieri. 67p. (Orig.). 1995. pap. write for info. (0-938572-13-X) Bunny Crocodile.

Corner Men: Great Boxing Trainers. Ronald K. Fried. LC 90-49705. (Illus.). 414p. 1991. 21.95 (0-941423-48-4) FWEW.

Corner of Paradise. Peter Davies. (Illus.). 136p. 1992. 29.95 (0-233-98765-7, Pub. by A Deutsch UK) Trafalgar.

Corner of Paradise. 2nd large type ed. Peter Davies. 153p. 1993. 19.95 (1-85695-130-8, Pub. by ISIS UK) Transaction Pubs.

Corner of the Tapestry: A History of the Jewish Experience in Arkansas, 1820s - 1990s. Carolyn G. LeMaster. LC 93-48940. 622p. 1994. 60.00 (1-55728-304-4) U of Ark Pr.

Corner of Time. John Kirkhoff. 116p. 1992. 15.95 (1-878208-20-9) Guild Pr IN.

Corner on Main Street. Al Tingley. 260p. 1984. 14.95 (0-9613811-0-8) Creative Concepts.

Corner People. Harri P. Jones. 97p. (C). 1991. pap. 22.00x (0-86383-642-9, Pub. by Gomer Pr UK) St Mut.

Corner Restoration Circulars, 1883-1974. 1977. 25.00 (0-686-23344-1, 507) CARBEN Survey.

Corner Stone. Walter Hinz. 192p. Date not set. 9.95 (0-8464-4197-7) Beekman Pubs.

Cornered Animals. Randall Borchers. (Orig.). 1988. pap. 9.95 (1-55774-031-3) Modan-Adama Bks.

Cornerless People. John H. Williams. 64p. 1990. pap. 15.95 (1-85224-101-2, Pub. by Bloodaxe Bks UK) Dufour.

Corners. Grace Nettles & Bea Nettles. (Illus.). 104p. 1989. pap. 14.95 (0-930810-03-1) Inky Pr.

Corners in the Cabin. Paulette Peters. LC 92-8659. 1992. 12.95 (1-56477-011-7) That Patchwork.

Corners of Black History. Reginald Larrie. (Illus.). 70p. 1986. reprint ed. 9.95 (0-9615662-0-5); reprint ed. teacher ed write for info. (0-9615662-1-3) Olympian King Co.

Corners of My Mind. Chriscilla A. Lasseter. 1993. 8.95 (0-533-10399-1) Vantage.

***Corners of New York.** Frank H. Wallis. LC 94-69813. (Illus.). 98p. (Orig.). 1995. pap. 25.95 (0-9638332-4-3) Source Pub CT.

Corners of Texas. Ed. by Francis E. Abernethy. LC 93-7447. (Publications of the Texas Folklore Society: No. 52). (Illus.). 320p. 1993. 29.95 (0-929398-57-2) UNTX Pr.

Corners of the Heart. Leslie Grey. Ed. by Lee Boojamra & Alice Frier. LC 92-62810. 208p. (Orig.). 1993. pap. 9.95 (0-9628938-3-8) Rising NY.

Cornerstone. 1981. 8.95 (0-685-68408-3, MB-501); audio 12.98 (0-685-68409-1, TA-9033C) Lillenas.

***Cornerstone.** Darla Jasmine. 200p. Date not set. pap. 8.95 (0-7610-0317-7) NW Pub.

Cornerstone. Mille Kirn. (Account Ability Ser.). 150p. 1992. student ed 18.00 (0-9632915-0-5) Ellim & Ange.

Cornerstone. Kevin Nichols. (C). 1988. 39.00 (0-85439-157-6, Pub. by St Paul Pubns UK) St Mut.

Cornerstone: A Story About 'Abdu'l-Baha in America. Anthony A. Lee. (Stories About 'Abdu'l-Baha Ser.). (Illus.). 24p. (Orig.). (J). (gr. k-5). 1979. pap. 3.00 (0-933770-01-4) Kalimat.

Cornerstone: Foundations for Writing. Harriet Spiegel. 280p. (C). 1986. pap. text ed. 18.50 (0-669-04522-5); Instr.'s guide. teacher ed 2.00 (0-669-04524-1) Heath.

***Cornerstone - Sparks Fly Upward, Bk. 1.** Terri Blackstock. 272p. 1995. pap. 11.99 (0-310-20015-6) Zondervan.

Cornerstone Book: Twenty Blueprints for Applications. Laura Buddine. write for info. (0-318-60211-3) Addison-Wesley.

Cornerstone Cookery. St. Vincent Infirmary Employee Council Staff. 293p. 1984. 10.95 (0-9613342-0-7) St Vincent Infir.

Cornerstone for Nursing Education: A History of the Division of Nursing Education at Teachers College, Columbia University, 1899-1947. Teresa E. Christy. LC 79-96868. 137p. reprint ed. pap. 39.10 (0-685-10689-6, 2052126) Bks Demand.

Cornerstone of Living. I. Parker Maxey. 1991. pap. 8.99 (0-88019-276-3) Schmul Pub Co.

Cornerstone on College Hill: An Illustrated History of the University of Alaska, Fairbanks. Terrence Cole. LC 93-40545. (Illus.). xii, 394p. 1994. 35.00 (0-912006-57-9) U of Alaska Pr.

Cornerstone Reggae Music Book of Light: Matshafa Berhan. Ricardo A. Scott. (Illus.). 110p. (Orig.). (YA). Date not set. write for info. (1-883427-18-5) Crnerstone GA.

***Cornerstones.** Mel Donaldson. 800p. (C). 1995. pap. text ed. 36.58 (0-312-09530-9) St Martin.

Cornerstones: A Journal with Inspiration from the Twelve Step Spoken Tradition. 96p. (Orig.). 1992. pap. 6.95 (0-89486-616-8, 8300) Hazelden.

Cornerstones: An Anthology. Jeanne H. Heritage et al. Ed. by Rosemary J. Schmidt. (Illus.). 100p. (Orig.). 1991. pap. text ed. 10.95 (0-9628611-6-2) Blue Denim.

Cornerstones: Twenty-Six Masterpieces of Western Architecture. Ralph Lieberman. 1989. 25.95 (0-525-24461-1, Dutton); pap. 15.95 (0-525-48259-8, Dutton) NAL-Dutton.

Cornerstones for a New Century. Ernest Boyer. 48p. 1992. 7.95 (0-8106-1846-X) NEA.

***Cornerstones of American Democracy.** LC 94-32614. 1994. write for info. (1-880875-06-3) National Archives & Recs.

Cornerstones of Astrology. Schwickert & Weiss. 342p. 1972. 16.50 (0-86690-159-0, S1458-014) Am Fed Astrologers.

***Cornerstones of Georgia History: Documents That Formed the State.** Scott. 1995. pap. text ed. (0-8203-1743-8) U of Ga Pr.

***Cornerstones of Georgia History: Documents that Formed the State.** Ed. by Thomas A. Scott. LC 94-21880. 244p. 1995. 30.00 (0-8203-1706-3) U of Ga Pr.

Cornerstones of Leadership for Health Services Executives. Austin Ross. LC 91-35345. 220p. 1992. text ed. 42.00 (0-910701-58-X, 0818) Health Admin Pr.

***Cornerstones of Peace: Jewish Identity Politics & Democratic Theory.** Marla Brettschneider. LC 95-16068. 250p. (C). 1996. text ed. 48.00 (0-8135-2215-3); pap. text ed. 16.95 (0-8135-2216-1) Rutgers U Pr.

Cornerstones of Reference Work. 1974. pap. 8.95 (0-913308-05-6) Fordham Pub.

Cornerstones of Undecidability. Grzegorz Rozenberg & Arto Salomaa. LC 93-46737. 250p. 1994. pap. text ed. 39.00 (0-13-297425-8) P-H.

Cornet a Des. M. Jacob. (FRE.). 1967. pap. 10.95 (0-8288-3860-7, F106150) Fr & Eur.

Cornewall: The House of Cornewall Family in England. C. Reade. (Illus.). 316p. 1993. reprint ed. lib. bdg. 57.50 (0-8328-3659-1); reprint ed. pap. 47.50 (0-8328-3660-5) Higginson Bk Co.

C

An Asterisk (*) at the beginning of an entry indicates that the title is appearing in BIP for the first time.

Cornfields. Dave Etter. LC 80-52084. 80p. 1980. pap. 3.95 (*0-933180-18-7*) Spoon Riv Poetry.

***Cornfields of Coaley Creek: Tales from Southwest Virginia.** Denvil Mullins. 224p. (Orig.). 1994. pap. 9.95 (*1-57072-011-8*) Overmountain Pr.

Cornflake Crusade. Gerald Carson. LC 75-39240. (Getting & Spending: the Consumer's Dilemma Ser.). (Illus.). 1976. reprint ed. 28.95 (*0-405-08013-1*) Ayer.

***Cornhill to Grand Cairo.** William M. Thackeray. (Illus.). 160p. (Orig.). 1994. pap. 29.95 (*1-873054-01-7*) Seven Hills Bk.

Cornhusk Bags of the Plateau Indians. Cheney Cowles Memorial Museum of the Eastern Washington State Historical Society Staff. LC 76-9025. 1976. fiche, lib. bdg. 30.00 (*0-226-68987-5*) U Ch Pr.

Corning Flood: Museum Under Water. Ed. by John H. Martin. LC 77-73627. (Illus.). 72p. 1977. pap. 6.00 (*0-87290-063-0*) Corning.

Cornish Captain's Tale. Laurence O'Toole. (C). 1989. 50.00 (*1-85022-011-5*, Pub. by Dyllansow Truran UK) St Mut.

Cornish Carols from Australia. Philip Payton. (C). 1989. 45.00 (*0-907566-92-8*, Pub. by Dyllansow Truran UK) St Mut.

Cornish Cookery: Recipes of Today & Yesteryear. Ed. by Vida Heard. (C). 1989. 45.00 (*0-907566-91-X*, Pub. by Dyllansow Truran UK) St Mut.

Cornish-English Dictionary. (COR & ENG.). 35.00 (*0-89979-009-7*) British Am Bks.

Cornish-English Dictionary. 1974. 42.50 (*0-87557-011-9*, 001-9) Saphrograph.

Cornish Farmer in Australia. Philip Payton. (C). 1989. 90.00 (*1-85022-029-8*, Pub. by Dyllansow Truran UK) St Mut.

Cornish Ghosts & Legends. (Ghost Ser.). (Illus.). 144p. 1993. pap. 7.95 (*1-85306-960-4*) Seven Hills Bk.

Cornish Gurnseys & Knit-Frocks. Mary Wright. 1977. 9.00 (*0-906720-05-2*) Dos Tejedoras.

Cornish Hearth. large type ed. Isobel Chace. (Linford Romance Library). 333p. 1984. pap. 11.95 (*0-7089-6024-3*, Trailtree Bookshop) Ulverscroft.

Cornish Heraldry & Symbolism. Ed. by Dennis E. Ivall. (C). 1989. 200.00 (*1-85022-043-3*, Pub. by Dyllansow Truran UK) St Mut.

Cornish Hotchpotch. Kathleen Hawke. (C). 1989. 35.00 (*1-85022-048-4*, Pub. by Dyllansow Truran UK) St Mut.

Cornish in America: Linden, Wis. Jim Jewell. (Illus.). 130p. 1990. pap. 8.50 (*1-878053-00-0*) Cornish Miner.

Cornish Language. P. Berresford Ellis. (C). 1990. pap. 24.95 (*0-85025-310-1*, Pub. by Tor Mark Pr UK) St Mut.

Cornish Legends. Robert Hunt. (C). 1990. pap. text ed. 24.95 (*0-85025-313-6*, Pub. by Tor Mark Pr UK) St Mut.

Cornish Literature. Brian Murdoch. 192p. (C). 1993. text ed. 45.00 (*0-85991-364-3*) Boydell & Brewer.

Cornish Mine Disasters. Cyril Noall. (C). 1989. 100.00 (*1-85022-032-8*, Pub. by Dyllansow Truran UK) St Mut.

Cornish Miner in Australia: Cousin Jack Down Under. Philip Payton. (C). 1989. 90.00 (*0-907566-51-0*, Pub. by Dyllansow Truran UK); 50.00 (*0-907566-52-9*, Pub. by Dyllansow Truran UK) St Mut.

Cornish Miners. John Vivian. (C). 1990. pap. text ed. 24.95 (*0-85025-318-7*, Pub. by Tor Mark Pr UK) St Mut.

***Cornish Mines (Metalliferous & Associated Minerals 1845-1913)** R. Burt et al. 562p. 1990. 75.00x (*0-85989-287-5*, Pub. by Northern Mine Res UK) St Mut.

Cornish Mining Families of Grass Valley, California. Shirley Ewart. LC 87-45792. (Immigrant Communities & Ethnic Minorities in the U. S. & Canada Ser.: No. 27). 1988. 39.50 (*0-404-19437-0*) AMS Pr.

Cornish Mistress. Sheila Reddicliffe. 148p. (C). 1992. pap. 29.95 (*1-871330-04-1*, Pub. by Lightbody Pubns UK) St Mut.

Cornish Names for Cornish Homes. Crysten Fudge. (C). 1989. text ed. 35.00 (*0-9506431-0-6*, Pub. by Dyllansow Truran UK) St Mut.

Cornish Ordinalia: A Medieval Dramatic Trilogy. Markham Harris. LC 69-19368. 306p. reprint ed. pap. 87.30 (*0-685-17853-6*, 2029513) Bks Demand.

Cornish Ordinalia: Religion & Dramaturgy. Robert Longsworth. LC 67-22869. 185p. reprint ed. pap. 52.80 (*0-7837-5935-5*, 2045734) Bks Demand.

Cornish Phrase Book: Lyver Lavarow Kernewek. Christopher Bice. pap. 7.50 (*0-89979-012-7*) British Am Bks.

Cornish Primitive: Alfred Wallis. Edmund Mullins. (Illus.). 64p. 1994. 24.95 (*1-85793-274-9*, Pub. by Pavilion UK) Trafalgar.

Cornish Quiz. R. Best. (C). 1989. 30.00 (*0-9506431-4-9*, Pub. by Dyllansow Truran UK) St Mut.

Cornish Rapture. large type ed. Sally Douglas. (Dales Romance Ser.). 223p. 1993. pap. 16.95 (*1-85389-405-2*, Medcom-Trainex) Ulverscroft.

Cornish Recipes. Tony Fairclough. (C). 1989. pap. text ed. 35.00 (*0-85025-320-9*, Pub. by Tor Mark Pr UK) St Mut.

Cornish Sayings Supersitutations & Remedies. Ed. by Kathleen Hawke. (C). 1989. 22.00 (*0-907566-04-9*, Pub. by Dyllansow Truran UK) St Mut.

Cornish Simplified, Pt. 2. A. S. Smith. Ed. by Talek. (C). 1989. pap. 30.00 (*0-907566-69-3*, Pub. by Dyllansow Truran UK) St Mut.

Cornish Smugglers. John Vivian. (C). 1990. pap. 24.95 (*0-85025-301-2*, Pub. by Tor Mark Pr UK) St Mut.

Cornish Trilogy: The Rebel Angels; What's Bred in the Bone; The Lyre of Orpheus. Robertson Davies. LC 91-50242. 1200p. 1992. pap. 17.95 (*0-14-015850-2*, Penguin Bks) Viking Penguin.

Cornish Voices. Ed. by Dyllansow Truran Staff. (C). 1989. 50.00 (*0-907566-21-9*, Pub. by Dyllansow Truran UK) St Mut.

Cornish Wreckers. John Vivian. (C). 1989. pap. text ed. 30.00 (*0-85025-311-X*, Pub. by Tor Mark Pr UK) St Mut.

***Corno Emplumado-The Plumed Horn: A Voice of the Sixties.** Alan R. Davison. 130p. (C). 1994. pap. text ed. 14.95 (*0-9643576-0-7*) Textos toledanes.

Cornovii. rev. ed. Graham Webster. (Peoples of Roman Britain Ser.). 192p. 1991. 30.00 (*0-86299-877-8*) A Sutton Pub.

Cornrows. Camille Yarbrough. (Illus.). (Orig.). (J). (gr. 2-6). 1992. pap. 6.95 (*0-698-20709-2*, Sandcastle Bks) Putnam Pub Group.

Cornshucks, Spanish Moss & Feathers: More Tales of the Cajun Wetlands. Verne Pitre. (Illus.). 96p. (Orig.). (J). (gr. 5-7). 1993. pap. 7.95 (*0-9621724-9-9*) Blue Heron LA.

Cornstalk Militia of Kentucky (1792-1811) Garrett G. Clift. 248p. 1982. reprint ed. 30.00 (*0-89308-318-6*) Southern Hist Pr.

Cornstarch & Cornmeal Uses: A How to Find or Locate Workbook. rev. ed. Center for Self-Sufficiency, Research Division Staff. 53p. 1992. pap. 16.95 (*0-685-57330-3*) Ctr Self Suff.

Cornucopia: A Source Book of Edible Plants. Stephen Facciola. LC 90-92097. 677p. (Orig.). (C). 1990. pap. 35.00 (*0-9628087-0-9*) Kampong Pubns.

***Cornucopia for Windows.** 1994. 70.00 (*0-9628087-1-7*) Kampong Pubns.

Cornucopia of Design & Illustration for Decoupage & Other Arts & Crafts. Ed. by Eleanor H. Rawlings. (Illus.). 160p. (Orig.). 1984. pap. 8.95 (*0-486-24486-5*) Dover.

Cornucopian Mind & the Baroque Unity of the Arts. Giancarlo Maiorino. LC 89-3894. (Illus.). 224p. 1990. lib. bdg. 32.50 (*0-271-00679-X*) Pa St U Pr.

Cornucopian Text: Problems of Writing in the French Renaissance. Terence Cave. 1985. pap. 24.95 (*0-19-815835-1*) OUP.

Cornutor of Seventy-Five, Being a Genuine Narrative of the Life, Adventures, & Amours, of Don Ricardo Honeywater: And Don Ricardo Honeywater Vindicated, in a Letter to Doctor Salguod, Pysician in Ordinary. William Douglas & Tobias Smollett. LC 92-22023. (Augustan Reprints Ser.: Nos. 244-245 (1987)). reprint ed. 18.50 (*0-404-70244-9*, R489) AMS Pr.

***Cornwall.** (Journey Through...Ser.). (Illus.). 64p. (Orig.). 1994. pap. 8.95 (*0-7117-0508-9*) Seven Hills Bk.

Cornwall. Automobile Association Staff. (AA - Ordnance Survey Leisure Guide Ser.). (Illus.). 128p. (Orig.). 1992. pap. 14.95 (*0-7495-0371-8*) Hunter NJ.

Cornwall: Its Mines & Miners. J. R. Leifchild. 304p. 1968. reprint ed. 35.00 (*0-7146-1402-5*, Pub. by F Cass Pubs UK) Intl Spec Bk.

Cornwall: The People & Culture of an Industrial Camelot, 1890-1980. Carl Oblinger. (Illus.). 123p. 1984. pap. text ed. 6.95 (*0-89271-028-4*) Pa Hist & Mus.

***Cornwall Coast Path Guide: Lands End to Lizard Point.** Richard Hayward. (British Footpath Guides Ser.: No.1). (Illus.). 100p. (Orig.). 1995. pap. 6.95 (*1-880848-08-2*) Brit Footpaths.

***Cornwall in the Age of Steam.** A. Guthrie. (Illus.). 211p. (Orig.). 1995. pap. 19.95 (*1-873951-16-7*, Pub. by Tabb Hse Pubs UK) Seven Hills Bk.

***Cornwall Mineral Industry: Past Performance & Future Prospects; A Personal View 1937-1951.** R. Burt et al. 119p. 1989. 75.00x (*0-85989-334-0*, Pub. by Northern Mine Res UK) St Mut.

***Cornwall, New York: Images from the Past, 1788-1920.** rev. ed. Janet Dempsey et al. LC 94-35515. (Illus.). 142p. 1994. 25.00 (*0-912526-73-4*) Lib Res.

Cornwall since the War. Ed. by Philip Payton. (C). 1993. 39.00 (*1-85022-073-5*, Pub. by Dyllansow Truran UK) St Mut.

Cornwall Walks. (Ordnance Survey Pathfinder Guides Ser.). 80p. 1993. pap. 12.95 (*0-7117-0457-0*) Seven Hills Bk.

Cornwallis: The Imperial Years. Franklin B. Wickwire & Mary B. Wickwire. LC 79-9943. xi, 340p. 1980. 34.95 (*0-8078-1387-7*) U of NC Pr.

Coroebus Triumphs: The Alliance of Sport & the Arts. Ed. by Susan J. Bandy. (Illus.). 303p. 1989. pap. 18.75 (*0-916304-76-0*) SDSU Press.

Corollaries on Place & Time. Simplicius. Tr. by J. O. Urmson. LC 91-21147. (Ancient Commentators on Aristotle Ser.). 160p. 1992. 47.95 (*0-8014-2713-4*) Cornell U Pr.

Coromandel. large type ed. Pat Barr. 1990. 21.95 (*0-7089-2273-2*) Ulverscroft.

Coromandel Sea Change. Rumer Godden. 1993. pap. 9.00 (*0-688-12572-7*, Quill) Morrow.

Coromandel Sea Change. large type ed. Rumer Godden. LC 91-44757. 388p. 1992. reprint ed. lib. bdg. 17.95 (*1-56054-346-9*) Thorndike Pr.

Coromandel Sea Change: A Novel. Rumer Godden. 224p. 1991. 18.00 (*0-688-10397-9*) Morrow.

Corona. Greg Bear. LC 85-8031. 192p. 1985. 20.00 (*0-89366-246-1*) Ultramarine Pub.

Corona. Greg Bear. (Star Trek Ser.: No. 15). 1991. reprint ed. mass mkt. 5.50 (*0-671-74353-8*) PB.

Corona: Bullfighter & Artist. Corinne H. Milton. LC 87-33677. (Illus.). 64p. (Orig.). 1988. pap. 16.95 (*0-86534-119-2*) Sunstone Pr.

Corona: Studies in Celebration of the Eightieth Birthday of Samuel Singer. Ed. by A. Schirokauer & W. Paulsen. LC 68-14901. (Essay Index Reprint Ser.). 1977. 23.95 (*0-8369-0338-2*) Ayer.

Corona Blue. J. F. Trainor. 1994. 16.95 (*0-8217-4739-8*) Zebra.

Corona Class Lessons. Jesus & Kuthumi. Ed. by Mark L. Prophet & Elizabeth C. Prophet. LC 83-51445. 504p. (Orig.). 1983. pap. 12.95 (*0-916766-65-9*) Summit Univ.

Corona de Fuego: Primer Esquema para una Tragedia Antihistorica Americana. Rodolfo Usigli. Ed. by Rex E. Ballinger. LC 72-167893. (SPA.). 1972. reprint ed. pap. text ed. 9.95 (*0-672-63025-7*) Irvington.

Corona Tragica de Lope de Vega. Michael G. Paulson & Tamara Alvarez-Detrell. LC 81-51027. (Illus.). 275p. (SPA.). 1982. 17.00 (*0-938972-01-4*) Spanish Lit Pubns.

Coronado: A Dreamer in Golden Armor. William J. Jacobs. (First Bks.). (Illus.). 64p. (J). (gr. 4-6). 1994. pap. 5.95 (*0-531-15722-9*) Watts.

Coronado: Dreamer in Golden Armor. William J. Jacobs. LC 93-31174. (First Bks.). (Illus.). 64p. (J). (gr. 5-8). 1994. lib. bdg. 13.93 (*0-531-20140-6*) Watts.

Coronado & the Myth of Quivira. Ed. by Dianna Everett. (Illus.). 88p. (Orig.). 1986. pap. 6.98 (*0-913463-01-9*) Panhandle.

Coronado: Knight of Pueblos & Plains: Published in Observation of the 450th Anniversary of the Coronado Expedition & the 500th Anniversary of Spain's Discovery of the New World. Herbert E. Bolton. LC 89-78224. (Illus.). 525p. 1981. reprint ed. pap. 18.95 (*0-8263-0007-3*) U of NM Pr.

Coronado Project Archaeological Investigations: The Coronado Generating Station Plant Site & Access Road. James E. Bradford. 139p. 1980. pap. 7.50 (*0-685-14701-0*, RS-17) Mus Northern Ariz.

Coronado's Children. J. Frank Dobie. 1993. reprint ed. lib. bdg. 75.00 (*0-7812-5927-4*) Rprt Serv.

Coronado's Children: Tales of Lost Mines & Buried Treasures of the Southwest. J. Frank Dobie. (Barker Texas History Center Ser.: No. 3). (Illus.). 351p. 1978. reprint ed. 22.95 (*0-292-71050-X*); reprint ed. pap. 10.95 (*0-292-71052-6*) U of Tex Pr.

Coronado's Children: Tales of Lost Mines & Buried Treasures of the Southwest. James F. Dobie. (BCL1 - United States Local History Ser.). 367p. 1991. reprint ed. text ed. 89.00 (*0-7812-6332-8*) Rprt Serv.

Coronado's Friars: The Franciscans in the Coronado Expedition. Angelico Chavez. (Monograph Ser.). (Illus.). 1968. 20.00 (*0-88382-058-7*) AAFH.

Coronado's Golden Quest. Barbara Weisberg. LC 92-18078. (Stories of America Ser.). (Illus.). 79p. (J). (gr. 2-5). 1992. lib. bdg. 22.13 (*0-8114-7232-9*); pap. 4.95 (*0-8114-8072-0*) Raintree Steck-V.

Coronado's Land: Essays on Daily Life in Colonial New Mexico. Marc Simmons. LC 91-21689. (Illus.). 195p. 1991. 22.50 (*0-8263-1313-2*) U of NM Pr.

Coronado's Quest: Discovery of the American Southwest. A. Grove Day. 322p. 1987. reprint ed. pap. 5.95 (*0-935180-37-0*) Mutual Pub HI.

Coronado's Quest: The Discovery of the Southwestern States. Arthur G. Day. LC 81-13443. xvi, 419p. 1982. reprint ed. text ed. 65.00 (*0-313-23207-5*, DACO, Greenwood Pr) Greenwood.

Coronal Disturbances: Proceedings of the I.A.U. Symposium, No. 57, Surfer's Paradise , Queensland, Australia, Sept. 7-11, 1973. International Astronomical Union Staff. Ed. by G. Newkirk. LC 74-80521. (Symposia of the International Astronomical Union Ser.: No. 57). 1974. lib. bdg. 149.50 (*90-277-0491-0*); pap. text ed. 99.00 (*90-277-0492-9*) Kluwer Ac.

Coronal Holes & High Speed Wind Streams: A Monograph from Skylab Solar Workshop I. Skylab Solar Workshop Staff. Ed. by Jack B. Zirker. LC 77-84528. (Illus.). 454p. reprint ed. pap. 129.40 (*0-8357-5517-7*, 2035133) Bks Demand.

***Coronal Magnetic Energy Releases: Proceedings of the CESRA Workshop Held in Caputh - Potsdam, Germany 16-20 May 1994.** Ed. by Arnold O. Benz & Albrecht Kruger. LC 95-12156. (Lecture Notes in Physics Ser.: Vol. 444). 1995. write for info. (*3-540-59109-5*) Spr-Verlag.

Coronal Polish see D.A.E Project: Instructional Materials for Dental Health Professions

Coronal Polishing for the Registered Dental Assistant. Catherine M. Germano & Mona L. Spicer. (Course Syllabus Ser.). (Illus.). 78p. (Orig.). (C). 1987. pap. text ed. 16.95 (*0-942801-01-6*) Apogee Pr.

Coronal Section Atlas, Human Larynx. Gabriel F. Tucker, Jr. (Illus.). 70p. 1990. per., pap. 2.25 (*0-16-001841-2*, S/N 008-023-000) USGPO.

Coronaries, Cholesterol & Chlorine. Joseph M. Price. 100p. 1984. pap. 3.95 (*0-515-09461-7*) Jove Pubns.

Coronary & Cerebral Vascular Disease: A Practical Guide. Ed. by Loren A. Rolak & Roxann Rokey. (Illus.). 400p. 1990. 52.00 (*0-87993-353-4*) Futura Pub.

Coronary & Peripheral Angiography & Angioplasty. Leachman. (Illus.). 200p. 1989. text ed. 37.50 (*0-397-58311-7*) Lippincott.

Coronary Angiography. Curtis E. Green. (Illus.). 350p. 1994. 125.00 (*0-397-51301-1*) Lippincott.

Coronary Angiography: Ratings of Appropriateness & Necessity by a Canadian Panel. Lucian L. Leape et al. LC 93-34519. 1993. write for info. (*0-8330-1453-6*, MR-129-CWF) Rand Corp.

Coronary Angiography for the Interventionalist. George W. Vetrovec & Evelyne Goudreau. 1993. 100.00 (*0-412-04461-7*) Chapman & Hall.

Coronary Angiography for the Interventionalist. George W. Vetrovec & Evelyne Goudreau. LC 92-48409. 1993. write for info. (*0-444-01667-8*) Elsevier.

Coronary Angioplasty. Susan D. Allen. Ed. by Colleen A. Holloran. (Illus.). 32p. 1992. pap. text ed. 2.85 (*0-916999-12-2*) HERC Inc.

Coronary Angioplasty. Ed. by Sheldon Goldberg. LC 70-6558. (Cardiovascular Clinics Ser.: Vol. 19, No. 2). (Illus.). 285p. (C). 1988. text ed. 66.00 (*0-8036-4162-1*) Davis Co.

Coronary Angioplasty. Meier. 1987. text ed. 76.95 (*0-8089-1892-3*, Grune) Saunders.

Coronary Angioplasty. 2nd ed. Ed. by David A. Clark. 1991. text ed. 94.95 (*0-471-56074-X*) Wiley.

Coronary Angioplasty: A Controlled Model for Ischemia. Ed. by Patrick W. Serruys & Greert T. Meester. (Developments in Cardiovascular Medicine Ser.). 1986. lib. bdg. 128.00 (*0-89838-819-8*) Kluwer Ac.

Coronary Angioplasty: Book & Video Tutorial. 2nd ed. David A. Clark. 316p. 1991. 495.00 (*0-471-56109-6*, Wiley-Liss) Wiley.

Coronary Arteriography. Herbert L. Abrams. 1982. 102.00 (*0-316-00469-3*) Little.

Coronary Artery. Ed. by Stanley Kalsner. (Illus.). (C). 1982. text ed. 95.00 (*0-19-520398-4*) OUP.

Coronary Artery Bypass Graft Surgery & Percutaneous Transluminal Coronary Angioplasty: Ratings of Appropriateness & Necessity by a Canadian Panel. David Naylor et al. LC 93-33095. 1993. write for info. (*0-8330-1452-8*, MR-128-CWF) Rand Corp.

Coronary Artery Bypass Surgery. Lawrie & Morris. 1991. 45.00 (*0-8151-5334-1*, Yr Bk Med Pubs) Mosby Yr Bk.

Coronary Artery Bypass Surgery. Lawrence H. Patzelt & Nancy L. Berends. Ed. by Oliver D. Grin & Dorothy Bouwman. (Patient Education Ser.). (Illus.). 34p. (Orig.). 1991. pap. text ed. 3.00 (*0-929689-41-0*) Ludann Co.

Coronary Artery Disease in Infants & Children. Henry N. Neufeld & Adam Schneeweiss. LC 83-766. (Illus.). 189p. reprint ed. pap. 53.90 (*0-7837-1491-2*, 2057187) Bks Demand.

Coronary Artery Graft Disease: Mechanism & Prevention. Ed. by T. Luscher et al. LC 94-16135. 1994. 99.00 (*0-387-57438-7*) Spr-Verlag.

Coronary Artery Spasm: Pathophysiology, Diagnosis & Treatment. Ed. by C. Richard Conti. LC 86-4592. (Basic & Clinical Cardiology Ser.: No. 6). 363p. reprint ed. pap. 103.50 (*0-7837-3352-6*, 2043310) Bks Demand.

Coronary Artery Stenosis. Ed. by L. K. Gould. 272p. 1990. 104.00 (*0-444-01544-2*) Elsevier.

Coronary Artery Stenting. Gary S. Roubin. 400p. 1994. write for info. (*0-86542-283-4*) Blackwell Sci.

Coronary Artery Surgery: A Critical Review. Thomas A. Preston. LC 76-51977. 278p. reprint ed. pap. 79.30 (*0-7837-7117-7*, 2046946) Bks Demand.

Coronary Artery Surgery: Application of New Technologies. Ed. by Arthur J. Roberts. LC 82-23905. (Illus.). 495p. reprint ed. pap. 141.10 (*0-8357-7630-1*, 2056953) Bks Demand.

Coronary Artery Surgery: Imaging & Echocardiography. Magdi Yacoub. Ed. by Robert A. Vogel. (Current Opinion in Cardiology, 1993 Ser.). (Illus.). 1076p. (Orig.). 1993. pap. text ed. 39.95 (*1-870485-98-X*) Current Science.

***Coronary Artery Surgery: Imaging & Echocardiography.** Magdi Yacoub. Ed. by Robert A. Vogel. (Current Opinion in Cardiology Ser.). (Illus.). 746p. (Orig.). 1994. pap. text ed. 39.95 (*1-85922-605-1*) Current Science.

Coronary Balloon Angioplasty. Ed. by Ronald E. Vlietstra & David R. Holmes, Jr. LC 93-33051. (Series in Interventional Cardiology). 1993. 75.00 (*0-86542-295-8*) Blackwell Sci.

Coronary Blood Flow: Mechanics, Distribution, & Control. Joe A. Spaan. (Developments in Cardiovascular Medicine Ser.). 416p. 1991. lib. bdg. 174.00 (*0-7923-1210-4*) Kluwer Ac.

Coronary Bypass Surgery. Shahbudin H. Rahimtoola. LC 77-8284. (Cardiovascular Clinics Ser.: Vol. 8, No. 2). 287p. 1977. text ed. 35.00 (*0-8036-7270-5*) Davis Co.

Coronary Bypass Surgery: The Late Results. Ed. by Karl E. Hammermeister. LC 82-13302. 464p. 1983. text ed. 79.50 (*0-275-91392-9*, C1392, Praeger Pubs) Greenwood.

***Coronary Bypass Surgery in the Elderly: Ethical, Economical, & Quality of Life Aspects.** Ed. by Paul J. Walter. LC 94-37708. (Developments in Cardiovascular Medicine Ser.). 280p. (C). 1995. lib. bdg. 127.00 (*0-7923-3188-5*) Kluwer Ac.

Coronary Care. William E. Boden & Robert J. Capone. (Blue Book Ser.). (Illus.). 224p. 1984. pap. text ed. 31.50 (*0-7216-1072-2*) Saunders.

Coronary Care Manual: A Practical Guide to the Management of Acute Cardiac Problems & Their Subsequent Follow-Up. James Nolan & David P. Lipkin. LC 92-49665. (Pocket Medical Reference Ser.). (Illus.). 134p. 1993. 25.95 (*0-19-262315-X*) OUP.

Coronary Care Manual: A Practical Guide to the Management of Acute Cardiac Problems & Their Subsequent Follow-Up. James Nolan & David P. Lipkin. LC 92-49665. (Pocket Medical Reference Ser.). (Illus.). 134p. 1993. pap. 24.95 (*0-19-262314-1*) OUP.

Coronary Care Medicine. Elliott M. Antman & John D. Rutherford. 1986. lib. bdg. 108.00 (*0-89838-788-4*) Kluwer Ac.

Coronary Care Nursing. 2nd ed. Paul L. Huang et al. 480p. 1989. pap. text ed. 37.50 (*0-7216-2627-0*) Saunders.

Coronary Care Unit Manual. Hodges. 1991. write for info. (*0-8151-4492-X*, Yr Bk Med Pubs) Mosby Yr Bk.

Coronary Care Units. Ed. by Attilio Maseri. 292p. 1981. lib. bdg. 89.00 (*90-247-2456-2*) Kluwer Ac.

Coronary Circulation: From Basic Mechanisms to Clinical Implications. Ed. by Joe A. Spaan et al. (Developments in Cardiovascular Medicine Ser.). (C). 1987. lib. bdg. 103.00 (*0-89838-978-X*) Kluwer Ac.

Coronary Circulation in Physiological & Pathophysiological States. Ed. by M. Nakamura & Paul M. Vanhoutte. (Illus.). xiii, 178p. 1991. 69.00 (*0-387-70053-6*) Spr-Verlag.

Coronary Collaterals: Clinical & Experimental Observations. Michael V. Cohen. (Illus.). 468p. 1985. 69.50 (*0-87993-168-X*) Futura Pub.

An Asterisk (*) at the beginning of an entry indicates that the title is appearing in BIP for the first time.

An Asterisk (*) at the beginning of an entry indicates that the title is appearing in BIP for the first time.

1625

C

Corporate Board: Confronting the Paradoxes. Ada Demb & Franz-Freidrich Neubauer. (Illus.). 232p. 1992. 35.00 (*0-19-507039-9*) OUP.

Corporate Board of Directors in Girl Scouting. rev. ed. 47p. 1984. reprint ed. pap. 6.50 (*0-88441-453-1*, 26-189) Girl Scouts USA.

Corporate Bodies. Simon Brett. (Mystery Ser.). 1993. mass mkt. 3.99 (*0-373-26130-6*, 1-26130-4) Harlequin Bks.

Corporate Bodies. large type ed. Simon Brett. LC 92-23382. 1993. pap. 20.95 (*0-7927-1417-2*, Curley Lrg Print) Chivers N Amer.

Corporate Bodies: A Charles Paris Mystery. Simon Brett. 256p. 1992. text ed. 19.00 (*0-684-19397-3*, Scribners) S&S Trade.

Corporate Body. R. Thomas Dickman. LC 82-90980. 1983. 9.95 (*0-87212-168-2*) Libra.

Corporate Bond Financing. 2nd ed. Tom Arthur. (Corporate Practice Ser.: No. 13). 1988. 92.00 (*0-87179-982-0*) BNA.

Corporate Bond Quality & Investor Experience. W. Braddock Hickman. (Financial Research Program V: Studies in Corporate Bond Financing: No. 2). 566p. 1958. reprint ed. 147.20 (*0-87014-146-5*) Natl Bur Econ Res.

Corporate Bond Rating Drift: An Examination of Rating Agency Credit Quality Changes over Time. Edward I. Altman & Duen L. Kao. (Orig.). 1991. pap. text ed. 20.00 (*0-943205-12-3*) ICFARF.

Corporate Bonds: Quality & Investment Performance. W. Braddock Hickman. (Occasional Papers: No. 59). 43p. 1957. reprint ed. 20.00 (*0-87014-373-5*); reprint ed. mic. film 20.00 (*0-685-61314-3*) Natl Bur Econ Res.

Corporate Book Reserving for Postretirement Healthcare Benefits. Ed. by Dwight K. Bartlett. (Pension Research Council Publications). 128p. (C). 1991. text ed. 29.95 (*0-256-09142-0*) U of Pa Pr.

Corporate Buy-Sell Handbook: An Essential Guide to Business Succession Planning. Stephan Leimberg et al. 333p. (Orig.). 1992. pap. 32.95 (*0-7931-0405-X*, 2402-34) Dearborn Finan.

Corporate Cabling Guide. Mark W. McElroy. LC 92-32245. (Telecommunications Ser.). 110p. (C). 1992. text ed. 60.00 (*0-89006-663-9*) Artech Hse.

Corporate Capital: Control, Ownership, Savings & Crisis. Christos N. Pitelis. 136p. 1987. 49.95 (*0-521-32848-9*) Cambridge U Pr.

Corporate Cash Balances, 1914-43: Manufacturing & Trade. Friedrich A. Lutz. (Financial Research Program III: Studies in Business Financing: No. 8). 148p. 1945. reprint ed. 38.50 (*0-87014-136-8*); reprint ed. mic. film 20.00 (*0-685-61257-0*) Natl Bur Econ Res.

***Corporate Cash Handbook.** Richard Bort. LC 93-60954. 1994. 135.00 (*0-7913-1751-X*) Warren Gorham & Lamont.

Corporate Cash Management. Phillipa L. Back. 192p. 1988. 42.50 (*0-89397-294-0*) Nichols Pub.

Corporate Cash Management: Including Electronic Funds Transfer. Alfred Hunt. LC 78-16648. 240p. reprint ed. pap. 68.40 (*0-317-26017-0*, 2023889) Bks Demand.

Corporate Cash Management Handbook. Richard Bort. 560p. 1989. Supplemented annually. 130.00 (*0-7913-0239-3*) Warren Gorham & Lamont.

Corporate Cash Management Handbook, No. 1. suppl. ed. Richard Bort. 560p. 1991. 49.75 (*0-7913-1015-9*) Warren Gorham & Lamont.

Corporate Casino: How Managers Win & Lose at the Biggest Game in Town. Dean B. Peskin. LC 78-12779. 251p. reprint ed. pap. 71.60 (*0-317-19937-4*, 2023570) Bks Demand.

Corporate Class Ethics & Apartheid. Omenana Staff. 120p. (Orig.). 1982. pap. 3.95 (*0-943324-04-1*) Omenana.

Corporate Classrooms: The Learning Business. Nell P. Eurich. LC 85-3845. 163p. 1985. pap. text ed. 8.00 (*0-931050-25-1*) Carnegie Fnd Advan Teach.

Corporate Clients & Their Lawyers: A Colloquy. Ed. by Joel Henning & Joan Hamby. 1986. pap. text ed. 25.00 (*0-914239-08-2*) LawLetters.

Corporate Closet. James D. Woods. 1994. pap. 12.95 (*0-02-935604-0*) Free Pr.

Corporate Closet: The Professional Lives of Gay Men in America. James D. Woods & Jay H. Lucas. 288p. 1993. text ed. 24.95 (*0-02-935603-2*) Free Pr.

Corporate Coach. James B. Miller & Paul B. Brown. LC 93-9669. (Illus.). 256p. 1993. 21.95 (*0-312-09262-8*) St Martin.

Corporate Coach: How to Build a Team of Loyal Customers & Happy Employees. James B. Miller & Paul B. Brown. 256p. 1994. reprint ed. pap. 12.00 (*0-88730-685-3*) Harper Busn.

Corporate Codes of Conduct. Stephen Landekich. Ed. by Claire Barth. (Bold Step Ser.). 130p. (Orig.). 1989. pap. 24.95 (*0-86641-175-5*, 89237) Inst Mgmt Account.

Corporate Communication. Paul A. Argenti. LC 93-1310. 224p. (C). 1993. text ed. 29.95 (*0-256-05705-2*) Irwin.

Corporate Communication: Theory & Practice. Ed. by Michael B. Goodman. LC 93-39171. (Series, Human Communication Processes). 408p. (C). 1994. 64.50x (*0-7914-2055-8*); pap. 21.95x (*0-7914-2056-6*) State U NY Pr.

Corporate Communications: A Comparison of Japanese & American Practices. William V. Ruch. LC 84-1973. (Illus.). xiv, 298p. 1984. text ed. 59.95 (*0-89930-028-6*, RCC/, Quorum Bks) Greenwood.

Corporate Communications Handbook. Wesley S. Walton & Charles P. Brissman. 1990. pap. 125.00 (*0-87632-697-1*) Clark Boardman Callaghan.

Corporate Communications Management: The Renaissance Communicator in Information Age Organizations. Diane Gayeski. LC 93-6592. (Illus.). 208p. 1993. 37.50 (*0-240-80139-3*, Focal) Buttrwrth-Heinemann.

Corporate Communicator's Quick Reference. Peter Lichtgarn. LC 92-42083. 192p. 1993. text ed. 20.00 (*1-55623-892-4*) Irwin Prof Pubng.

***Corporate Compliance with the Plant Closing Law: Legal Overview & Selected Legislative History.** 780p. 1989. 65.00 (*0-916559-18-1*, 2014-MO-4035) EPF.

Corporate Computer Insurance. Yvo Henniker-Heaton. 80p. (C). 1990. 420.00 (*1-85271-167-1*, Pub. by IBC Tech Srvs UK) St Mut.

Corporate Conflicts: Proxy Fights in the 1980s. Ronald E. Schrager. 203p. (Orig.). 1986. pap. 50.00 (*0-931035-06-6*) IRRC Inc DC.

Corporate Contributions Handbook: Devoting Private Means to Public Needs. Ed. by James P. Shannon. LC 90-28637. (Nonprofit Sector-Public Administration Ser.). 440p. 1991. 42.95 (*1-55542-320-5*) Jossey-Bass.

Corporate Contributions, 1991, Report No. 1014. Anne Klepper. (Illus.). 62p. (Orig.). 1992. pap. text ed. 100.00 (*0-8237-0462-9*) Conference Bd.

***Corporate Contributions, 1993.** Audris D. Tillman. (Report Ser.: No. 1098-94-RR). (Illus.). 60p. (Orig.). 1994. pap. text ed. 100.00 (*0-8237-0545-5*) Conference Bd.

***Corporate Control & Accountability: Changing Structures & Dynamics of Regulation.** Ed. by Joseph McCahery et al. (Illus.). 272p. 1995. pap. 32.00 (*0-19-825990-5*) OUP.

Corporate Control & Accountability: Changing Structures & the Dynamics of Regulation. Ed. by Joseph McCahery et al. LC 92-19420. 1994. 45.00 (*0-19-825827-5*, Clarendon Pr) OUP.

Corporate Control & Capital Structure: Essays on Property Rights & Financial Contracts. Erik Berglof. 193p. (Orig.). 1991. pap. 115.00x (*91-971005-6-0*, Pub. by Almqv & Wiksell SW) Coronet Bks.

Corporate Controller's Handbook of Financial Management. Joel G. Siegel. 1991. 89.95 (*0-13-174459-3*, Busn) P-H.

Corporate Controller's Manual. 2nd ed. Paul J. Wendell. Supplemented annually. boxed 142.00 (*0-685-51108-1*, CCM) Warren Gorham & Lamont.

Corporate Controller's Manual, No. 1. 2nd suppl. ed. Paul J. Wendell. 1991. 71.75 (*0-7913-0744-1*) Warren Gorham & Lamont.

Corporate, Corporation. abr. ed. Intro. by Luanna C. Blagrove. (Illus.). 250p. 1988. 24.95 (*0-939776-21-9*) Blagrove Pubns.

Corporate Counsel: A Role Study. John D. Donnell. LC 78-633785. (Business Study Ser.: No. 40). 1971. 15.00 (*0-685-03851-3*, IBS40) Ind U Busn Res.

Corporate Counsel Environmental Law Guide. Theodore L. Garrett. LC 93-1400. 555p. 1993. 115.00 (*0-87179-772-0*) BNA.

***Corporate Counseling: Transfer of Wealth.** Peter W. Schmidt & David J. McCabe. LC 93-83652. 166p. 1993. pap. text ed. 25.00 (*0-942954-57-2*) NYS Bar.

Corporate Counseling Monography Series: New York Securities Law: Practice & Policy. Catherine J. Douglass & Ellen Lieberman. Ed. by Raymond W. Merritt & Clifford M. Ennico. 125p. 1990. pap. 25.00 (*0-942954-27-0*) NYS Bar.

Corporate Counseling, Vols. One & Two, 2 vols. Ed. by Raymond W. Merritt & Clifford R. Ennico. 1400p. 1988. 110.00 (*0-942954-20-3*) NYS Bar.

Corporate Counsellor's Deskbook. 4th ed. Ed. by Dennis J. Block & Michael A. Epstein. 954p. 1992. ring bd. 116.00 (*0-13-225079-9*) Aspen Law.

Corporate Counsel's Annual, 1966-1985, Set. 1,450.00 (*0-8377-9047-6*) Rothman.

Corporate Counsel's Construction Contracts Deskbook, No. 88. Ed. by William A. Hancock. 600p. 1991. ring bd. 115.00 (*0-929576-66-7*) Busn Laws Inc.

Corporate Counsel's Consulting Agreements Deskbook, No. 85. 600p. 1991. 139.00 (*0-929576-63-2*) Busn Laws Inc.

***Corporate Counsel's Consulting Agreements Deskbook, No. 85.** 1991. disk write for info. (*0-614-07056-2*) Busn Laws Inc.

Corporate Counsel's Guide to Acquisitions & Divestitures, 3 vols., Set. 1400p. 1990. 270.00 (*0-929576-49-7*) Busn Laws Inc.

Corporate Counsel's Guide to Alternative Dispute Resolution Techniques, No. 64. 800p. 1989. 115.00 (*0-929576-01-2*) Busn Laws Inc.

Corporate Counsel's Guide to Attorney-Client, Work Product & Self-Evaluative Privileges, No. 91. 200p. 1991. ring bd. 95.00 (*0-929576-68-3*) Busn Laws Inc.

Corporate Counsel's Guide to Bankruptcy Law, No. 102. 600p. 1992. ring bd. 115.00 (*0-929576-79-9*) Busn Laws Inc.

Corporate Counsel's Guide to Business Ethics Policies, No. 84. 600p. 1991. ring bd. 115.00 (*0-929576-60-8*) Busn Laws Inc.

Corporate Counsel's Guide to Business-Related Visas, No. A99. 300p. 1991. ring bd. 95.00 (*0-929576-77-2*) Busn Laws Inc.

Corporate Counsel's Guide to Dealing with Financially Troubled Companies, No. 51. 500p. 1987. ring bd. 95.00 (*0-929576-24-1*) Busn Laws Inc.

Corporate Counsel's Guide to Director & Officer Liability Insurance, No. 100. 400p. 1992. ring bd. 95.00 (*0-929576-76-4*) Busn Laws Inc.

Corporate Counsel's Guide to Distribution Counseling, No. 74. 1990. ring bd. 115.00 (*0-929576-53-5*) Busn Laws Inc.

Corporate Counsel's Guide to Employee Relations Law, 4 vols., Set. 1991. ring bd. 350.00 (*0-929576-59-4*) Busn Laws Inc.

Corporate Counsel's Guide to Employment Contracts, No. 73. 1990. ring bd. 115.00 (*0-929576-52-7*) Busn Laws Inc.

Corporate Counsel's Guide to Environmental Compliance & Audits, No. 105. 550p. 1992. ring bd. 115.00 (*0-929576-83-7*) Busn Laws Inc.

Corporate Counsel's Guide to Environmental Law, 4 vols., Set. 1200p. 1989. ring bd. 320.00 (*0-929576-48-9*) Busn Laws Inc.

Corporate Counsel's Guide to European Economic Community Law, No. A89. 600p. 1991. ring bd. 115.00 (*0-929576-62-4*) Busn Laws Inc.

Corporate Counsel's Guide to Gender-Based Discrimination, No. 95. 600p. 1992. ring bd. 115.00 (*0-929576-74-8*) Busn Laws Inc.

Corporate Counsel's Guide to Government Contracting, No. 80. 900p. 1991. ring bd. 115.00 (*0-929576-58-6*) Busn Laws Inc.

Corporate Counsel's Guide to Handling Government Investigations, No. 53. 500p. 1987. ring bd. 95.00 (*0-929576-20-9*) Busn Laws Inc.

Corporate Counsel's Guide to Importing under the U. S. Customs Law, No. 101. 550p. 1992. ring bd. 115.00 (*0-929576-78-0*) Busn Laws Inc.

Corporate Counsel's Guide to International Antitrust Laws, No. 83. 800p. 1991. ring bd. 125.00 (*0-929576-61-6*) Busn Laws Inc.

Corporate Counsel's Guide to Labor Law, No. 97. 500p. 1992. ring bd. 115.00 (*0-929576-75-6*) Busn Laws Inc.

Corporate Counsel's Guide to Legal Audits & Investigations, No. 93. 600p. 1992. ring bd. 125.00 (*0-929576-72-1*) Busn Laws Inc.

Corporate Counsel's Guide to Litigation Management, No. 71. 500p. 1990. ring bd. 115.00 (*0-929576-51-9*) Busn Laws Inc.

Corporate Counsel's Guide to Merger Analysis under the Antitrust Laws, No. 104. 500p. 1992. ring bd. 115.00 (*0-929576-80-2*) Busn Laws Inc.

Corporate Counsel's Guide to Protecting Trade Secrets, No. 50. 500p. 1987. ring bd. 95.00 (*0-929576-36-5*) Busn Laws Inc.

Corporate Counsel's Guide to Reductions in Force, No. 106. 550p. 1992. ring bd. 115.00 (*0-929576-84-5*) Busn Laws Inc.

Corporate Counsel's Guide to Securities Regulation, No. 96. 600p. 1992. ring bd. 115.00 (*0-929576-73-X*) Busn Laws Inc.

Corporate Counsel's Guide to the Immigration Reform & Control Act, No. 98. 300p. 1992. ring bd. 95.00 (*0-929576-70-5*) Busn Laws Inc.

Corporate Counsel's Guide to the Occupational Safety & Health Law, No. 94. W. Kenworthy. 550p. 1992. ring bd. 115.00 (*0-929576-71-3*) Busn Laws Inc.

Corporate Counsel's Guide to the Robinson-Patman Act, No. 87. Ed. by William A. Hancock. 600p. 1991. ring bd. 115.00 (*0-929576-67-5*) Busn Laws Inc.

Corporate Counsel's Guide to Unfair Competition, No. 48. 800p. 1986. ring bd. 115.00 (*0-929576-16-0*) Busn Laws Inc.

Corporate Counsel's Managerial Guide, No. 57. 500p. 1988. ring bd. 105.00 (*0-929576-04-7*) Busn Laws Inc.

Corporate Cowgirl. Stella Bagwell. (Silhouette Romance Ser.). 1994. pap. 2.75 (*0-373-08991-0*, 5-08991-7) Silhouette.

Corporate Creativity: Robust Companies & the Entrepreneurial Spirit. Ed. by W. Raymond Smilor. LC 83-24525. 174p. 1984. text ed. 49.95 (*0-275-91271-X*, C1271, Praeger Pubs) Greenwood.

Corporate Crime. Marshall B. Clinard & Peter C. Yeager. LC 80-2156. 1983. pap. 16.95 (*0-02-905880-5*) Free Pr.

***Corporate Crime: Contemporary Debates.** Ed. by Frank Pearce & Laureen Snider. 416p. 1995. 60.00 (*0-8020-0667-1*) U of Toronto Pr.

***Corporate Crime: Contemporary Debates.** Ed. by Frank Pearce & Laureen Snider. 416p. 1995. pap. 19.95 (*0-8020-7621-1*) U of Toronto Pr.

***Corporate Crime & Sentencing.** Richard S. Gruner. 1050p. 1994. 105.00 (*1-55834-162-5*) Michie Butterworth.

Corporate Crime & Violence: Big Business Power & the Abuse of the Public Trust. Russell Mokhiber. LC 87-4730. 384p. 1989. pap. 16.00 (*0-87156-608-7*) Sierra.

Corporate Crime under Attack: The Ford Pinto Case & Beyond. Frank Cullen et al. 1987. 22.95 (*0-87084-177-7*) Anderson Pub Co.

Corporate Criminal Liability, 3 vols. Kathy Brickey. LC 84-9465. 1990. 350.00 (*0-685-09046-9*) Clark Boardman Callaghan.

Corporate Criminal Liability, 3 vols. annuals suppl. ed. Kathy Brickey. 1990. write for info. (*0-318-58076-4*) Clark Boardman Callaghan.

Corporate Criminal Liability: Representing Corporations, CEOs, Corporate Officers & the Impact of the Sentencing Guidelines. (Litigation & Administrative Practice Ser.). 464p. 1991. pap. text ed. 70.00 (*0-685-56928-4*) PLI.

Corporate Crisis Management. Stephen J. Andriole. LC 84-19068. (Illus.). 250p. 1984. text ed. 32.95 (*0-89433-216-3*) Petrocelli.

Corporate Crisis Management. TAB Books Staff. 1984. text ed. 32.95 (*0-07-158572-9*) McGraw.

Corporate Crocodiles & Other Tales. Graham Nicoll. 1993. pap. 11.95 (*1-875680-05-5*, Pub. by Busn & Prof Pubng AT) Pubs Dist MI.

Corporate Culture & Change: Highlights of a Conference. Ed. by Melissa A. Berman. (Report Ser.: No. 888). v, 65p. (Orig.). 1986. pap. text ed. 60.00 (*0-8237-0330-4*) Conference Bd.

Corporate Culture & Organizational Effectiveness. Daniel R. Denison. 267p. 1990. text ed. 60.00 (*0-471-80021-X*) Wiley.

Corporate Culture & Organizational Symbolism: An Overview. Mats Alvesson & Per O. Breg. (Studies in Organization: No. 34). xii, 258p. (C). 1992. lib. bdg. 57.95 (*3-11-012154-9*); pap. text ed. 24.95 (*3-11-013607-4*) De Gruyter.

Corporate Culture & Performance. John P. Kotter. 1992. text ed. 27.95 (*0-02-918467-3*) Free Pr.

Corporate Culture Sourcebook. Ed. by Richard Bellingham et al. (Illus.). 264p. (Orig.). 1989. pap. 39.95 (*0-87425-117-6*) Human Res Dev Pr.

Corporate Cultures: The Rites & Rituals of Corporate Life. Terrence E. Deal & Allan A. Kennedy. 1982. pap. 13.46 (*0-201-10287-0*) Addison-Wesley.

Corporate Dandelions: How the Weed of Bureaucracy Is Choking American Companies - & What You Can Do to Uproot It. Craig J. Cantoni. LC 93-7663. 176p. 1993. 19.95 (*0-8144-5119-5*) AMACOM.

***Corporate Debt Securitization: Regulation & Documentation.** Hairani Saban. xxviii, 427p. 1994. text ed. write for info. (*0-409-99678-5*) Butterworth Legal Pubs.

Corporate Decision Making in the World Economy. Michael G. Rukstad. 640p. (C). 1992. pap. text ed. 41.25 (*0-03-076526-9*) Dryden Pr.

Corporate Decline in Advanced Capitalism. Mark J. Gobeyn. LC 93-7706. (Contributions in Political Science Ser.: No. 332). 184p. 1993. text ed. 49.95 (*0-313-28883-6*, GM8883, Greenwood Pr) Greenwood.

***Corporate Diagnosis: Meeting International Standards for Excellence.** Thomas L. Jackson. (Illus.). 100p. 1995. text ed. 15.95 (*1-56327-086-2*) Prod Press.

Corporate Director: A Guide to Law, Economics, & Strategy in the Boardroom. Leo Herzel. 1994. text ed. 49.95 (*0-07-028438-5*) McGraw.

***Corporate Director's & Officer's: Liability, Insurance & Risk Management.** Paul Cottrell & Joseph P. Monteleone. 1994. pap. text ed. 59.95 (*0-471-11245-3*) Wiley.

Corporate Director's & Officers Liability, Insurance & Risk Management. Paul Cottrell & Joseph P. Monteleone. 1989. pap. 75.00 (*1-55840-129-6*) Exec Ent Pubns.

Corporate Director's Financial Handbook. John P. Fertakis. LC 88-11318. 201p. 1988. text ed. 55.00 (*0-89930-289-0*, FCD/, Quorum Bks) Greenwood.

Corporate Directorship Practices: Role, Selection & Legal Status of the Board. Jeremy Bacon & James K. Brown. (Report Ser.: No. 646). 161p. (Orig.). 1975. pap. text ed. 40.00 (*0-8237-0065-8*) Conference Bd.

Corporate Directory of U. S. Public Companies, 1993. R. Walsh. 3200p. 1993. 360.00 (*1-879346-10-9*, 101853); cd-rom 595.00 (*1-879346-13-3*) Walkers Western.

***Corporate Directory of U. S. Public Companies, 1994.** E. Nash. 1994. cd-rom 595.00 (*1-879346-16-8*) Walkers Western.

Corporate Directory of U. S. Public Companies, 1994. E. Walsh. 1994. 360.00 (*1-879346-15-X*) Walkers Western.

***Corporate Directory of U. S. Public Companies, 1995.** 1994. cd-rom 595.00x (*1-879346-25-7*) Walkers Western.

Corporate Directory of U. S. Public Companies, 1995. 7th ed. Ed. by Walker's Western Research Staff & E. Walsh. 2500p. 1995. 360.00x (*1-879346-22-2*) Walkers Western.

Corporate Disclosure of Environmental Risks: U. S. & European Law. Michael S. Baram & Daniel G. Partan. 320p. 1990. boxed 105.00 (*0-88063-258-5*) Michie Butterworth.

Corporate Divestment. Gordon Bing. LC 77-86528. 180p. reprint ed. pap. 51.30 (*0-685-23766-4*, 2032843) Bks Demand.

Corporate Dividend Policy. John A. Brittain. LC 66-15642. (Studies of Government Finance). 272p. reprint ed. pap. 77.60 (*0-685-15988-4*, 2026400) Bks Demand.

Corporate Dividends: Legal & Accounting Problems Pertaining to Corporate Distributions. Donald Kehl. LC 75-18473. (History of Accounting Ser.). (Illus.). 1978. reprint ed. 26.95 (*0-405-07555-3*) Ayer.

Corporate Dividends & Stock Repurchases. Barbara Black. 1990. ring bd. 130.00 (*0-685-44912-2*) Clark Boardman Callaghan.

Corporate Downsizing: An Employee's Diary. Arthur G. Sharp. LC 89-84389. 307p. (Orig.). 1989. pap. text ed. 12.95 (*0-945510-01-2*) Intl Info Assocs.

Corporate Dream: Making It Big in Business. Hank Johnson. 288p. 1990. 19.95 (*0-8184-0517-1*) Carol Pub Group.

Corporate Dream: Making It Big in Business. Hank Johnson. 1990. 19.95 (*0-685-45109-7*, L Stuart) Carol Pub Group.

Corporate Dynamic Worship. Callahan. Date not set. 16.00 (*0-685-69292-2*, HarpT) HarpC.

Corporate Dynamism: How World Class Companies Became World Class. Cuno Pumpin. 230p. 1991. text ed. 59.95 (*0-566-07277-7*, Pub. by Gower UK) Ashgate Pub Co.

Corporate Economy: Growth, Competition, & Innovative Potential. Ed. by Robin Marris & Adrian Wood. (Studies in Technology & Society). 479p. 1971. 46.50 (*0-674-17252-3*) HUP.

Corporate Encounters: Law & Ethics in the Business Environment. Clarence Walton. 480p. (C). 1992. text ed. 43.25 (*0-03-074822-4*) Dryden Pr.

Corporate Energy Management Manual. pap. 14.00 (*0-915586-21-5*) Fairmont Pr.

Corporate Environment. David Farnham. 250p. (C). 1990. 75.00 (*0-85292-439-9*, Pub. by IPM Hse UK) St Mut.

Corporate Environmental Management II. (Mineral Law Ser.). 1994. student ed. 75.00 (*0-929047-45-1*) Rocky Mtn Mineral Law Found.

Corporate Environmental Policy & Government Regulation. Ed. by L. R. Jones & John H. Baldwin. LC 94-14651. (Monographs in Organizational Behavior & Industrial Relations: Vol. 17). 1994. write for info. (*1-55938-759-9*) Jai Pr.

***Corporate Environmental Profiles Directory - 1994, 3 vols., Set.** Environmental Information Service Staff. (Illus.). 2000p. Date not set. ring bd. write for info. (*1-879775-19-0*) IRRC Inc DC.

An Asterisk (*) at the beginning of an entry indicates that the title is appearing in BIP for the first time.

Corporate Environmental Profiles Directory, 1992. Environmental Information Staff. Ed. by Scott Fenn. 1100p. 1992. ring bd. 3,000.00 (*0-931035-97-X*) IRRC Inc DC.

Corporate Environmental Profiles Directory 1993, 3 vols., Set. Environmental Information Service Staff. (Illus.). 1600p. ring bd. write for info. (*1-879775-12-3*) IRRC Inc DC.

Corporate Environmental Responsibilities. Osler et al. 256p. Date not set. 130.00 (*0-409-89718-3*) Butterworth Legal Pubs.

Corporate Environmental Responsibility. John Salter. 1992. 130.00 (*0-406-00138-3*, U.K.) Butterworth Legal Pubs.

*__Corporate Environmental Strategy: The Avalanche of Change since Bhopal.__ Bruce W. Piasecki. LC 94-38131. 1995. text ed. 24.95 (*0-471-10627-5*) Wiley.

Corporate Environmentalism in a Global Economy: Societal Values in International Technology Transfer. Halina S. Brown et al. LC 92-19851. 264p. 1993. text ed. 52.95 (*0-89930-802-3*, Q802, Quorum Bks) Greenwood.

Corporate Eponymy: A Biographical Dictionary of the Persons Behind the Names of Major American, British, European & Asian Businesses. Adrian Room. LC 92-53502. 302p. 1992. lib. bdg. 38.50x (*0-89950-679-8*) McFarland & Co.

Corporate Espionage: How to Stop Thieves, Saboteurs & Spies from Bankrupting Your Business. Mark Nestmann & Paul Nelson. (Orig.). 1991. pap. write for info. (*0-9627953-0-5*) LPP.

Corporate Ethics. Ronald E. Berenbeim. (Report Ser.: No. 900). (Illus.). viii, 31p. (Orig.). 1987. pap. text ed. 60.00 (*0-8237-0343-6*) Conference Bd.

Corporate Ethics: Developing New Standards of Accountability. Ed. by Theresa Brothers. (Report Ser.: No. 980). 55p. (Orig.). 1991. pap. text ed. 100.00 (*0-8237-0428-9*) Conference Bd.

Corporate Ethics in Healthcare: Models & Processes. 66p. 1991. pap. 7.00 (*0-87125-209-0*, 210) Cath Health.

Corporate Excellence Through Grid Organization Development. Robert R. Blake & Jane S. Mouton. LC 68-21510. 394p. reprint ed. pap. 112.30 (*0-8357-2575-8*, 2040266) Bks Demand.

*__Corporate Experiential Learning.__ Christopher Roland et al. 256p. 1994. boxed, per. 50.00 (*0-7872-0308-4*) Kendall-Hunt.

Corporate Facility Planning. Ed. by H. McKinley Conway & Linda L. Liston. 450p. 1981. 14.95 (*0-910436-21-5*) Conway Data.

Corporate Finance. Sabine. 1987. 104.00 (*0-409-99541-X*) Butterworth Legal Pubs.

Corporate Finance. 2nd ed. Martin Sabine. 1993. 110.00 (*0-406-00107-3*, U.K.) Butterworth Legal Pubs.

Corporate Finance. 3rd ed. Stephen A. Ross et al. LC 92-25582. (Finance Taking the Lead Ser.). 992p. (C). 1992. text ed. 69.95 (*0-256-09487-X*) Irwin.

*__Corporate Finance: Cases & Materials, 1994 Supplement.__ 4th ed. Victor Brudney & William W. Bratton. (University Casebook Ser.). 118p. 1994. pap. text ed. 8.50 (*1-56662-200-X*) Foundation Pr.

Corporate Finance: Concepts & Policies. Fred R. Kaen. (Illus.). 1500p. (C). 1994. text ed. 49.95 (*1-55786-512-4*) Blackwell Pubs.

*__Corporate Finance: Legal Practice Course Guides.__ Richard King. 211p. 1995. pap. 34.00 (*1-85431-393-2*, Pub. by Blackstone Pr UK) W W Gaunt.

Corporate Finance: Theory, Method & Applications. Cheng F. Lee & Joseph E. Finnerty. 765p. (C). 1989. text ed. 50.00 (*0-15-514085-X*) Dryden Pr.

Corporate Finance & Fiscal Policy in Ireland. J. Stewart. 177p. 1982. text ed. 59.95 (*0-566-05441-8*, Pub. by Avebury Pub UK) Ashgate Pub Co.

Corporate Finance & Governance: Cases, Materials, & Problems for an Advanced Course in Corporations. Lawrence E. Mitchell & Lewis D. Solomon. LC 91-76746. 1140p. 1992. 75.00 (*0-89089-469-8*) Carolina Acad Pr.

Corporate Finance & the Capital Markets. Harvard Business Review Staff. (Financial Manager Ser.). 122p. 1991. pap. 19.95 (*0-87584-293-3*) Harvard Busn.

Corporate Finance & the Capital Markets. Harvard Business School Press Staff. 1991. pap. text ed. 19.95 (*0-07-103353-X*) McGraw.

Corporate Finance & the Securities Laws. Charles J. Johnson, Jr. 848p. 1990. 116.00 (*0-13-173857-7*) Aspen Law.

Corporate Finance, Cases & Materials On. 2nd ed. Robert W. Hamilton. (American Casebook Ser.). 1221p. 1989. text ed. 51.00 (*0-314-55036-4*) West Pub.

Corporate Finance, Cases & Materials On. 4th ed. Victor Brudney et al. (University Casebook Ser.). 1200p. (C). 1993. text ed. 47.95 (*1-56662-059-7*) Foundation Pr.

*__Corporate Finance in the Euromarkets & the Economics of Intermediation.__ fac. ed. E. P. Davis & C. P. Mayer. (Bank of England, Discussion Papers, Technical Ser.: No. 45). 44p. 1994. pap. 25.00 (*0-7837-7648-9*, 2047401) Bks Demand.

*__Corporate Finance, International.__ 3rd ed. Stephan A. Ross et al. (C). 1992. text ed. 35.50 (*0-256-10827-7*) Irwin.

Corporate Finance Reader. Ed. by Robert W. Kolb. LC 91-90007. 216p. (C). 1991. pap. text ed. 16.00 (*1-878975-04-8*) Kolb Pub.

Corporate Finance Reporting: Text & Cases. 2nd ed. Richard Brownlee, II et al. LC 93-8384. 896p. (C). 1993. text ed. 69.95 (*0-256-12405-1*) Irwin.

Corporate Finance Sourcebook, 1994. National Register Publishing Staff. LC 86-642719. 1878p. 1994. pap. 450.00 (*0-87217-943-5*) Natl Register.

*__Corporate Finance Sourcebook 1995: The Guide to Major Capital Investment Sources & Related Financial Services.__ Ed. by National Register Press Editing Staff. LC 86-642719. 2200p. (Orig.). 1995. pap. 479.00 (*0-87217-944-3*) Natl Register.

Corporate Finance, 1993-94. Richard King. (Legal Practice Course Guides Ser.). 189p. 1994. pap. 34.00 (*1-85431-347-9*, Pub. by Blackstone Pr UK) W W Gaunt.

Corporate Financial Accounting. 4th ed. Warren et al. (C). 1994. text ed. 48.95 (*0-538-83719-5*) S-W Pub.

Corporate Financial Analysis. 3rd ed. Diana R. Harrington & Brent D. Wilson. 256p. 1989. text ed. 44.95 (*1-55623-195-4*) Irwin Prof Pubng.

Corporate Financial Analysis. 4th ed. Diana R. Harrington & Brent D. Wilson. LC 92-25583. (Finance Taking the Lead Ser.). 352p. (C). 1993. pap. text ed. 39.95 (*0-256-08302-9*) Irwin.

Corporate Financial Analysis: Decisions in a Global Environment. 4th ed. Diana R. Harrington & Brent D. Wilson. LC 92-45763. 335p. 1993. text ed. 45.00 (*1-55623-900-9*) Irwin Prof Pubng.

Corporate Financial Decisions. James C. Mao. LC 75-18149. (Illus.). 600p. (C). 1976. text ed. 19.95 (*0-915944-00-6*) Pavan Pubs.

Corporate Financial Distress & Bankruptcy: A Complete Guide to Predicting & Avoiding Distress & Profiting from Bankruptcy. 2nd ed. Edward I. Altman. LC 92-26897. 384p. 1993. text ed. 79.95 (*0-471-55253-4*) Wiley.

*__Corporate Financial Patterns in Industrializing Economies: A Comparative International Study.__ Ajit Singh. LC 95-12256. (Technical Paper - International Finance Corporation Ser.: No. 2). 1995. write for info. (*0-8213-3231-7*) World Bank.

Corporate Financial Planning & Management in a Deficit Economy. Louis E. Nevaer & Steven A. Deck. LC 86-25582. 190p. 1987. text ed. 59.95 (*0-89930-202-5*, NCF/, Quorum Bks) Greenwood.

Corporate Financial Policies: A Review & Analysis of Existing Literature. Jerry L. Arnold & Michael A. Diamond. 120p. (Orig.). 1989. pap. 6.00 (*0-910586-75-6*, 083-89) Finan Exec.

Corporate Financial Policy & Taxation. Mariateresa Fiocca. 142p. 1990. text ed. 51.95 (*1-85521-088-6*, Pub. by Dartmth Pub UK) Ashgate Pub Co.

Corporate Financial Reporting: Public or Private Control? Robert Chatov. LC 74-15368. 1975. 24.95 (*0-02-905410-9*) Free Pr.

Corporate Financial Reporting: Text & Cases. E. Richard Brownlee et al. 928p. (C). 1989. text ed. 65.95 (*0-256-07194-2*) Irwin.

Corporate Financial Reporting & Analysis: Text & Cases. 3rd ed. David F. Hawkins. 1072p. (C). 1986. text ed. 69.95 (*0-256-02587-8*) Irwin.

Corporate Financial Risk Management: Practical Techniques of Financial Engineering. Diane B. Wunnicke et al. (Finance Editions Ser.: No. 1935). 368p. 1992. text ed. 65.00 (*0-471-52914-1*) Wiley.

Corporate Financial Services in Wales 1988-89. Ed. by J. Carr & G. Bricault. (C). 1989. lib. bdg. 74.50 (*1-85333-094-9*, Pub. by Graham & Trotman UK) Kluwer Ac.

Corporate Financial Services in Wales, 1990. Ed. by G. Bricault. (C). 1990. lib. bdg. 66.00 (*1-85333-311-5*, Pub. by Graham & Trotman UK) Kluwer Ac.

Corporate Financial Strategy. Ward. 1993. 39.95 (*0-7506-0657-6*) Buttrwrth-Heinemann.

Corporate Financial Structures in Developing Countries. Ajit Singh & Javed Hamid. (IFC Technical Paper Ser.: No. 1). 161p. 1992. 10.95 (*0-8213-1874-8*, 11874) World Bank.

Corporate Firm in a Changing World Economy. Ed. by Marc De Smidt & Egbert Wever. 228p. 1990. 74.50 (*0-415-03497-3*, A4647) Routledge.

Corporate First Amendment Rights & the SEC. Nicholas Wolfson. LC 90-8412. 184p. 1990. text ed. 55.00 (*0-89930-450-8*, WCZ, Quorum Bks) Greenwood.

Corporate Five Hundred: Directory of Corporate Philanthropy. 10th ed. Public Management Staff. Ed. by Debbie Zuver & Tracy Fetters. 1350p. 1991. pap. 355.00 (*0-916664-55-4*) Datarex Corp.

Corporate Five Hundred: Directory of Corporate Philanthropy. 12th ed. Public Management Staff. Ed. by D. L. Conrad. 1400p. pap. 375.00 (*0-916664-57-0*) Datarex Corp.

Corporate Five Hundred: The Directory of Corporate Philanthropy. 9th ed. 1125p. 1995. text ed. write for info. (*0-8103-9863-X*, Pub Mgmt Inst) Gale.

*__Corporate 500: The Directory of Corporated Pilanthropy.__ 1400p. 1995. 375.00 (*0-615-00669-8*) Datarex Corp.

Corporate Five Hundred 1993: Directory of Corporate Philanthropy. 11th ed. Public Management Staff. Ed. by Julie Berriault. 1350p. 1992. pap. 365.00 (*0-916664-56-2*, 071056) Datarex Corp.

*__Corporate Formation: A Primer for Legal Assistants.__ Dris. 1995. text ed. 98.00 (*0-471-08646-0*) Wiley.

*__Corporate Forms Kit.__ Ted Nicholas. 1995. pap. 19.95 (*0-936894-91-1*) Upstart Pub.

Corporate Foundation Profiles. 8th ed. Foundation Center Staff. 1994. pap. 145.00 (*0-87954-505-4*) Foundation Ctr.

Corporate Fraud. Michael J. Comer. LC 85-11686. 1985. text ed. 31.95 (*0-07-084791-6*) McGraw.

Corporate Fraud: The Basics of Prevention & Detection. Jack Bologna. 232p. 1984. text ed. 32.95 (*0-409-95129-3*) Buttrwrth-Heinemann.

*__Corporate Funders Operating in Missouri.__ Grants Link. 1994. pap. 50.00 (*0-9631907-1-7*) Grants Link.

Corporate Game: A Computer Adventure for Developing Business Decision-Making Skills. David Rye. 1994. disk, pap. text ed. 34.95 (*0-07-911763-5*) McGraw.

*__Corporate Geography: Business Location Principles & Cases.__ Risto Laulajainen & Howard A. Stafford. LC 94-42236. 1995. lib. bdg. 205.00 (*0-7923-3326-8*) Kluwer Ac.

Corporate Giants & the Power Structure. Morton S. Baratz. (Reprint Series in Social Sciences). (C). 1993. reprint ed. pap. text ed. 1.00 (*0-8290-3141-3*, PS-13) Irvington.

Corporate Giving Directory 1995. Bohdan R. Romaniuk. 1994. 365.00 (*1-56995-002-4*) Taft Group.

Corporate Giving Directory 1996. Bohdan R. Romaniuk. 1995. 375.00 (*1-56995-003-2*) Taft Group.

Corporate Giving Directory 1997. Bohdan R. Romaniuk. Date not set. 350.00 (*1-56995-004-0*) Taft Group.

Corporate Giving in the Reagan Years. Kenneth A. Bertsch. 97p. (Orig.). 1985. pap. 20.00 (*0-931035-04-X*) IRRC Inc DC.

Corporate Giving Yellow Page 1995, Vol. 1. Bohdan R. Romaniuk. 1994. 88.00 (*1-56995-005-9*) Taft Group.

Corporate Giving Yellow Pages 1996. Bohdan R. Romaniuk. 1995. 90.00 (*1-56995-006-7*) Taft Group.

Corporate Giving Yellow Pages 1997. Bohdan R. Romaniuk. Date not set. 82.00 (*1-56995-007-5*) Taft Group.

Corporate Globalization Through Mergers & Acquisitions. Ed. by Leonard Waverman. 252p. (Orig.). 1992. pap. text ed. 26.95 (*1-895176-12-3*, Pub. by Univ Calgary CN) Paul & Co Pubs.

*__Corporate Governance.__ 200p. 1995. pap. write for info. (*0-615-00307-9*) West Pub.

*__Corporate Governance.__ Douglas M. Branson. 900p. 1993. 125.00 (*1-55834-072-6*) Michie Butterworth.

*__Corporate Governance.__ Robert Monks & Nell Minow. (Illus.). 400p. 1994. pap. 34.95 (*1-55786-490-X*) Blackwell Pubs.

Corporate Governance: A Review of the Literature. Philip L. Cochran & Steven L. Wartick. LC 88-81702. (Illus.). 72p. (Orig.). 1988. pap. 6.00 (*0-910586-69-1*, 075-88) Finan Exec.

Corporate Governance: An Action Plan for Profitability & Business Success. Nigel Kendall & Tom Sheridan. (Financial Times Management Ser.). 240p. 1992. 111.00x (*0-273-03870-2*, Pub. by Pitman Pubng UK) St Mut.

Corporate Governance: Practices, Procedures & Powers in British Companies & Their Boards of Directors. R. Ian Tricker. LC 84-4071. 319p. 1984. 79.95 (*0-566-00749-5*) Ashgate Pub Co.

Corporate Governance & Directors' Liabilities: Legal, Economic, & Sociological Analyses on Corporate Social Responsibility. Ed. by Klaus J. Hopt & Gunther Teubner. LC 84-23212. (European University Institute, Series A (Law): No. 1). xii, 462p. 1985. 150.00 (*3-11-010027-4*) De Gruyter.

Corporate Governance & Shareholder Rights: Voting by Institutional Investors & 1986 Annual Meeting Results. Karen Mathiasen. LC 86-230362. (Corporate Governance Service). 96p. 1986. pap. 50.00 (*0-931035-57-0*) IRRC Inc DC.

*__Corporate Governance in the Age of Relationship Investing.__ John Kensinger & John Martin. 100p. (Orig.). 1995. pap. text ed. 15.00 (*1-885065-05-1*) Finan Exec.

*__Corporate Governance in Transitional Economies: Insider Control & the Role of Banks.__ Hyung-Ki Kim & Mashiko Aoki. LC 94-42709. (EDI Development Studies). 492p. 1995. 29.95 (*0-8213-2990-1*, 12990) World Bank.

Corporate Grammar, Incl. cass. Margaret M. Bynum. 72p. 1983. Includes audiocassettes. audio, pap. text ed. 39.95 (*0-913286-75-3*) Learn Inc.

Corporate Grantmaking: Giving to Racial - Ethnic Populations. Steven L. Paprocki & Robert O. Bothwell. LC 94-20702. (Illus.). 643p. (C). reprint ed. pap. text ed. 55.00 (*0-8191-9573-1*) U Pr of Amer.

*__Corporate Graphics Vol. 1.__ Mike Quon & Graphic Design U. S. A. Editors. (Illus.). 240p. 1995. 42.50 (*0-86636-232-0*) PBC Intl Inc.

Corporate Groups: Procedural Law. Phillip I. Blumberg. 1983. 145.00 (*0-316-10025-0*) Little.

Corporate Growth & Common Stock Risk. David R. Fewings. Ed. by Edward I. Altman & Ingo Walter. LC 76-52014. (Contemporary Studies in Economic & Financial Analysis: Vol. 12). (Orig.). 1979. lib. bdg. 73.25 (*0-89232-053-2*) Jai Pr.

Corporate Growth Strategies. Ed. by Isay Stemp. LC 75-103426. 445p. reprint ed. pap. 126.90 (*0-317-29940-9*, 2051694) Bks Demand.

*__Corporate Growth Strategies: How to Find-Exploit New Technology & Products.__ 3rd ed. 375p. 1995. spiral bd., vinyl bd. 1,270.00 (*1-56217-011-2*) Tech Insights.

Corporate Guide: A Manual for Filing Corporate Documents in Pennsylvania. Pennsylvania State Department Staff. 31p. 1985. write for info. (*0-318-58006-3*) Penna Secy.

Corporate Guide to Parental Leaves. rev. ed. 77p. 1992. 85.00 (*0-89584-152-5*) Catalyst.

*__Corporate Guide to Payments System Risk: Assessing & Controlling Payments Risk.__ Jack M. Meckler & Treasury Management Association Staff. (Illus.). 186p. 1995. 60.00 (*1-55738-885-7*) Probus Pub Co.

Corporate Guide to the Malcolm Baldrige National Quality Award: Proven Strategies for Building Quality into Your Organization. 2nd ed. Marion M. Steeples. LC 92-26216. (Malcolm Baldridge National Quality Award Ser.). 384p. 1992. text ed. 35.00 (*1-55623-957-2*) Irwin Prof Pubng.

Corporate Healing: Solutions to the Impact of the Addictive Personality in the Workplace. Mary Riley. 1990. pap. 8.95 (*1-55874-058-9*) Health Comm.

Corporate Health Care Revolution: Strategies for Preventive Medicine at Work. David Ashton. 400p. 1989. text ed. 89.95 (*0-8464-1367-1*) Beekman Pubs.

Corporate Healthcare Revolution: Strategies for Preventive Medicine at Work. David Ashton. 372p. (C). 1989. 225.00 (*1-85091-694-2*, Pub. by IPM Hse UK) St Mut.

Corporate Hegemony: Contributions in Economics & Economic History, No. 97. William M. Dugger. LC 89-2188. 224p. 1989. text ed. 49.95 (*0-313-26711-1*, DCT/, Greenwood Pr) Greenwood.

Corporate History & the Chemical Industries: A Resource Guide Published on the Occasion of a CHOC Conference on Corporate History. Ed. by Jeffrey L. Sturchio. (BCHOC Publication Ser.: No. 4). (Illus.). 53p. (Orig.). 1985. pap. 10.00 (*0-941901-02-5*, HD9650.5 S78 1985) Chem Heritage Fnd.

Corporate Human Resources Development: A Management Tool. Leonard Nadler. 217p. 16.95 (*0-318-13267-2*, NACB); 13.50 (*0-318-13268-0*) Am Soc Train & Devel.

Corporate Ideal in the Liberal State: 1900-1918. James Weinstein. LC 80-22211. xvii, 263p. 1981. reprint ed. text ed. 45.00 (*0-313-22709-8*, WECI, Greenwood Pr) Greenwood.

Corporate Identity: Making Business Strategy Visible Through Design. Wally Olins. 224p. (C). 1992. pap. 24.95 (*0-87584-368-9*) Harvard Busn.

Corporate Identity: Making Business Strategy Visible Through Design. Wally Olins. 1990. text ed. 50.00 (*0-07-103301-7*); pap. text ed. 39.95 (*0-07-103300-9*) McGraw.

Corporate Identity: Making Business Strategy Visible Through Design. Wally Olins. 1992. pap. text ed. 24.95 (*0-07-103378-5*) McGraw.

Corporate Identity: Making Business Strategy Visible Through Design. Wally Olins. 224p. 1992. reprint ed. 50.00 (*0-87584-250-X*) Harvard Busn.

Corporate Identity Manuals. Ed. by David E. Carter. LC 75-44679. (Illus.). 460p. 1978. reprint ed. 41.50 (*0-910158-33-9*) Art Dir.

Corporate Image: A Practical Guide to the Implementation of a Corporate Identity Program. Nicholas Ind. 230p. 1990. pap. 44.95 (*0-685-74200-8*) Beekman Pubs.

Corporate Image: A Practical Guide to the Implementation of a Corporate Identity Program. rev. ed. Nicholas Ind. 206p. 1992. pap. 44.95x (*0-8464-1349-3*) Beekman Pubs.

Corporate Image: Communicating Visions & Values. Ed. by Allyson LaBorde. (Report Ser.: No. 1038). 57p. (Orig.). 1993. pap. text ed. 100.00 (*0-8237-0510-2*) Conference Bd.

*__Corporate Image: For Professional Communicators.__ Amanda Barrett. (Illus.). 96p. 1995. 34.95 (*0-7134-7476-9*, Pub. by Batsford UK) Trafalgar.

Corporate Image: Strategies for Effective Identity Programmes. rev. ed. Nicholas Ind. pap. text ed. write for info. (*0-7494-0768-9*, Pub. by Kogan Page Educ UK) Taylor & Francis.

Corporate Images: Photography & the Dupont Company, 1865-1972. Dan Muir & Jon Williams. 72p. 1984. pap. 5.00 (*0-914650-24-6*) Hagley Museum.

Corporate Imagination. James F. Bandrowski. 1990. text ed. 29.95 (*0-02-901501-4*) Free Pr.

Corporate Imperialism: Conflict & Expropriation. Transnational Corporations & Economic Nationalism in the Third World. Norman Girvan. LC 78-11411. 241p. 1978. pap. 5.95 (*0-85345-472-8*) Monthly Rev.

Corporate Income Retention, 1915-43. Sergei P. Dobrovolsky. (Financial Research Program III: Studies in Business Financing: No. 10). 142p. 1951. reprint ed. 37.00 (*0-87014-138-4*); reprint ed. mic. film 20.00 (*0-685-61284-8*) Natl Bur Econ Res.

Corporate Income Taxation & Foreign Direct Investment in Central & Eastern Europe. Jack M. Mintz & Thomas Tsiopoulos. LC 92-37602. (FIAS Occasional Paper Ser.: No. 4). 28p. 1992. 6.95 (*0-8213-2301-6*, 12301) World Bank.

Corporate Information Committee Report, 1985-1986. Ed. by Financial Analysts Federation Staff. 79p. 1990. pap. text ed. 30.00 (*0-938367-04-8*) Assn I M&R.

Corporate Information Committee Report, 1986-1987. Ed. by Financial Analysts Federation Staff. LC 02-249. 105p. 1990. pap. text ed. 30.00 (*0-938367-05-6*) Assn I M&R.

Corporate Information Committee Report, 1987-1988. Ed. by Financial Analysts Federation Staff. 108p. 1990. pap. text ed. 30.00 (*0-938367-07-2*) Assn I M&R.

Corporate Information Committee Report, 1988-1989. Ed. by Financial Analysts Federation Staff. 127p. 1990. pap. text ed. 30.00 (*0-938367-08-0*) Assn I M&R.

Corporate Information Committee Report, 1989-90. Ed. by Association for Investment Management & Research Staff. 128p. 1990. pap. text ed. 30.00 (*0-938367-10-2*) Assn I M&R.

Corporate Information Committee Report, 1990-91. Ed. by Association for Investment Management & Research Staff. 121p. 1991. pap. text ed. 30.00 (*0-938367-11-0*) Assn I M&R.

Corporate Information Committee Report, 1991-92. Ed. by Association for Investment Management & Research Staff. 122p. 1992. pap. text ed. 30.00 (*0-938367-12-9*) Assn I M&R.

*__Corporate Information Committee Report, 1992-93.__ 1994. write for info. (*1-879087-33-2*) Assn I M&R.

Corporate Information Systems Management: Issues Facing Senior Executives. 3rd ed. James I. Cash, Jr. et al. (Illus.). 320p. (C). 1992. pap. text ed. 38.95 (*0-256-09008-4*, 14-1601-03) Irwin.

Corporate Information Systems Management: Text & Cases. 3rd ed. James I. Cash et al. 704p. (C). 1992. text ed. 71.50 (*0-256-08705-9*) Irwin.

C

An Asterisk (*) at the beginning of an entry indicates that the title is appearing in BIP for the first time. 1627

Corporate Information Systems Management: The Issues Facing Senior Executives. 3rd ed. James I. Cash, Jr. et al. Ed. by Susan Glinert. 450p. 1992. text ed. 45.00 (*1-55623-615-8*) Irwin Prof Pubng.

Corporate Innovation: Marketing & Strategy. Gordon R. Foxall. LC 83-40096. 240p. 1984. text ed. 29.95 (*0-312-16995-7*) St Martin.

Corporate Insolvency - Law & Practice. Edward Bailey et al. 726p. 1992. U.K. text ed. 170.00 (*0-406-14501-6*) Butterworth Legal Pubs.

Corporate Insolvency & Rescue: The International Dimension. Ed. by Dennis Campbell & Anthony E. Collins. LC 92-45136. 1993. 94.00 (*90-6544-685-0*) Kluwer Law Tax Pubs.

Corporate Insolvency in Practice: An Analytical Approach. Clare Campbell & Brian Underdown. 208p. (C). 1991. pap. text ed. 36.00 (*1-85396-085-3*, Pub. by P Chapman Pub UK) Taylor & Francis.

Corporate Intelligence & Espionage: A Blueprint for Executive Decision Making. Richard Eells & Peter Nehemkis. LC 84-43214. 288p. 1984. 35.00 (*0-02-909240-X*) Free Pr.

Corporate Intensive Care: Why Businesses Fail & How to Make Them Succeed. Larry Goddard. Ed. by Bryan Aubrey & Laura S. Bell. LC 92-62451. 316p. (C). 1993. 49.95 (*0-9634940-0-7*); pap. 19.95 (*0-9634940-1-5*) York Pub.

Corporate Interaction with Five Urban Education Systems in Connecticut. Jane M. Metzler. (Urban Education Reports Ser.: No. 4). 21p. 1983. 2.50 (*0-685-09451-0*) I N Thut World Educ Ctr.

Corporate Internal Affairs: A Corporate & Securities Law Perspective. Marc I. Steinberg. LC 82-16619. xiii, 294p. 1983. text ed. 49.95 (*0-89930-039-1*, SCS/, Quorum Bks) Greenwood.

Corporate Internal Investigations. Dan K. Webb et al. 1993. ring bd. 85.00 (*0-317-05394-9*, 00620) NY Law Pub.

Corporate Investment Manual: Short & Intermediate Term Securities. Alan G. Seidner. 528p. 1989. 145.00 (*0-88712-843-2*) Warren Gorham & Lamont.

Corporate Investment Manual: Short & Intermediate Term Securities, No. 1. suppl. ed. Alan G. Seidner. 528p. 1991. 49.75 (*0-685-32267-X*) Warren Gorham & Lamont.

Corporate Law. Robert Clark. 900p. 1986. 37.00 (*0-316-14494-0*) Little.

***Corporate Law.** 2nd ed. H. S. Cillers. 816p. 1992. boxed 132.00 (*0-409-01968-2*, SA) Butterworth Legal Pubs.

***Corporate Law.** 2nd ed. H. S. Cillers. 816p. 1992. pap. 92.00 (*0-409-01969-0*, SA) Butterworth Legal Pubs.

Corporate Law: The European Dimension. Butterworths European Information Services Staff. 600p. 1991. pap. 140.00 (*0-406-00296-7*, U.K.) Butterworth Legal Pubs.

Corporate Law & Economic Analysis. Ed. by Lucian A. Bebchuk. (Illus.). (C). 1990. 49.95 (*0-521-36054-4*) Cambridge U Pr.

Corporate Law & Practice Series, 1992-1993, 31 vols., Set. 1993. pap. 1,025.00 (*0-685-69405-4*) PLI.

Corporate Law Department Series, 2 vols. Incl. Recruiting, Training, & Compensating Attorney Staff. 1986. (*0-318-62382-X*); Getting the Most from Your Support Staff. 1986. (*0-318-62383-8*); 1986. Set. Set pap. 24.95 (*0-685-19012-9*) Amer Bar Assn.

***Corporate Law for the Healthcare Provider: Organization, Operation, Merger & Bankruptcy.** Ed. by Ann Huckstep et al. 239p. 1993. 55.00 (*0-918945-15-1*) Natl Health Lawyers.

Corporate Law in Canada: The Governing Principles. 2nd ed. Bruce L. Welling. 820p. 1991. 125.00 (*0-409-89639-X*) Butterworth Legal Pubs.

Corporate Law of Banks: Regulation of Corporate & Securities Activities of Depository Institutions, 2 vols., Set. Michael P. Malloy. 1800p. 1987. 160.00 (*0-316-54462-0*) Little.

Corporate Lawbreaking & Interactive Compliance: Resolving the Regulation-Deregulation Dichotomy. Ed. by Jay A. Sigler & Joseph E. Murphy. LC 90-26209. 224p. 1991. text ed. 55.00 (*0-89930-490-7*, SGB/, Quorum Bks) Greenwood.

Corporate Laws: Covering Companies Act, Capital Issues Act, Securities Contracts, Regulation Act, FERA, MRTP Act & IDRA. Ed. by T. Taxmann. (C). 1990. 35.00 (*0-89771-213-7*) St Mut.

Corporate Lease Analysis: A Guide to Concepts & Evaluation. Bennie H. Nunnally, Jr. et al. LC 90-45147. 256p. 1991. text ed. 59.95 (*0-89930-513-X*, NCC, Quorum Bks) Greenwood.

Corporate Legends & Lore: The Power of Storytelling as a Management Tool. Peg C. Neuhauser. LC 93-14759. 240p. 1993. text ed. 22.95 (*0-07-046326-3*) McGraw.

Corporate-Level Strategy: Creating Value in the Multibusiness Company. Michael Goold. LC 94-6805. 1994. text ed. 34.95 (*0-471-04716-3*) Wiley.

Corporate Liberalism: The Origins of Modern American Political Theory, 1890-1920. R. J. Lustig. LC 81-16376. 350p. (C). 1982. pap. 15.00 (*0-520-05894-1*) U CA Pr.

Corporate Library Excellence. James Matarazzo. 137p. 1990. 31.25 (*0-87111-367-8*) SLA.

Corporate Lifecycles. Ichak Adizes. 1990. pap. 11.95 (*0-13-174426-7*) P-H.

Corporate Lifecycles: How & Why Corporations Grow & Die & What to Do about It. Ichak Adizes. (Illus.). 336p. 1988. 22.95 (*0-13-174400-3*, Busn) P-H.

Corporate Liquidations for the Lawyer & Accountant. 5th ed. Howard A. Rumpf. LC 82-5298. 256p. 1982. text ed. 39.50 (*0-13-174383-X*, Busn) P-H.

Corporate Liquidity: A Guide to Managing Working Capital. Kenneth L. Parkinson & Jarl G. Kallberg. LC 93-21755. 500p. 1993. text ed. 55.00 (*1-55623-864-9*) Irwin Prof Pubng.

Corporate Liquidity: Management & Measurement. Jarl G. Kallberg & Kenneth L. Parkinson. LC 92-31866. 576p. (C). 1992. text ed. 65.95 (*0-256-11844-2*) Irwin.

Corporate Litigator. 952p. 1989. 150.00 (*0-89707-427-0*, 531-0063-01) Amer Bar Assn.

Corporate Lobbying: Federal & State Regulation. Frederic J. Krebs. (Corporate Practice Ser.: No. 25). 1981. 92.00 (*1-55871-202-X*) BNA.

Corporate Madness. Mark Lineback. (Illus.). 104p. (Orig.). 1994. pap. 9.95 (*0-9641121-0-8*) Madness.

Corporate Madness: How to Change the System When the System Refuses to Change. William D. Stinnett & Russell G. Hanson. Ed. by Mary Westheimer. LC 90-60205. (Illus.). 208p. 1990. pap. 17.95 (*0-9625630-0-5*) Leadership AZ.

Corporate Magazines of the United States: Historical Guides to the World's Periodicals & Newspapers. Ed. by Sam G. Riley. LC 91-33481. 296p. 1992. text ed. 79.50 (*0-313-27569-6*, RCG, Greenwood Pr) Greenwood.

***Corporate Management in Developing Countries: The Challenge of International Competitiveness.** Alvin G. Wint. LC 95-7519. 232p. 1995. text ed. 59.95 (*0-89930-929-1*, Quorum Bks) Greenwood.

Corporate Manager's Guide to Speechwriting. Burton Kaplan. 250p. 1988. text ed. 29.95 (*0-02-916951-8*) Free Pr.

Corporate Marketing Planning. John M. Brion. LC 67-19446. (Wiley Marketing Ser.). 591p. reprint ed. 168.50 (*0-8357-9867-4*, 2017001) Bks Demand.

Corporate Meeting Planners, 1994. Ed. by Edgar Adcock et al. 1148p. (Orig.). 1994. pap. 297.00 (*0-87228-052-7*) Salesmans.

Corporate Memory: A Profitable & Practical Approach to Information Management & Retention Systems. Barbara N. Weaver & Wiley L. Bishop. LC 80-20187. 282p. 1981. reprint ed. text ed. 29.50 (*0-89874-245-5*) Krieger.

***Corporate Misconduct: The Legal, Societal, & Management Issues.** Margarate P. Spencer & Ronald R. Sims. LC 94-32083. 232p. 1995. text ed. 59.95 (*0-89930-879-1*, Quorum Bks) Greenwood.

***Corporate Misconduct: The Legal, Societal, & Management Issues.** Ed. by Margaret P. Spencer & Ronald R. Sims. LC 94-32083. 272p. 1995. text ed. 65.00 (*0-89930-840-6*, Quorum Bks) Greenwood.

Corporate Mobility & Paths to the Top: Studies for Human Resource & Management Development Specialists. J. Benjamin Forbes & James E. Piercy. LC 90-42967. 224p. 1991. text ed. 55.00 (*0-89930-524-5*, FPT/, Quorum Bks) Greenwood.

Corporate Mule. Robert Gerard. Ed. by Sara Benjamin. 147p. (Orig.). 1995. pap. 10.95 (*1-880666-04-9*) Oughten Hse.

Corporate Museums, Galleries, & Visitor Centers: A Directory. Victor J. Danilov. LC 91-11324. 224p. 1991. text ed. 55.00 (*0-313-27658-7*, DCI/, Greenwood Pr) Greenwood.

Corporate Negaholic: How to Deal Successfully with Negative Colleagues, Managers & Corporation. Cherie Carter-Scott. 1991. 19.50 (*0-394-58622-0*, Villard Bks) Random.

Corporate Networking: Building Channels of Communication. Robert K. Mueller. 176p. 1986. text ed. 32.95 (*0-02-922150-1*) Free Pr.

Corporate Networks: The Strategic Use of Telecommunications. Thomas S. Valovic. LC 92-19581. (Telecommunications Ser.). 150p. 1992. text ed. 59.00 (*0-89006-484-9*) Artech Hse.

Corporate Networks & Corporate Control: The Case of the Delaware Valley. Ralph M. Faris. LC 90-20596. (Contributions in Economics & Economic History Ser.: No. 119). 208p. 1991. text ed. 49.95 (*0-313-27553-X*, FCK/, Greenwood Pr) Greenwood.

Corporate Networks in the Information Economy. Ed. by Howard Williams & John Taylor. (Illus.). 256p. 1993. text ed. 59.00 (*1-85293-142-6*, Pub. by Pinter Pubs UK) St Martin.

***Corporate Networks, International Telecommunications & Interdependence: Perspectives from Geography & Information Systems.** H. Bakis. 1994. text ed. 59.95 (*0-471-94802-0*) Wiley.

Corporate Nonunion Complaint Procedures & Systems: A Strategic Human Resources Management Analysis. Douglas M. McCabe. LC 88-11758. 220p. 1988. text ed. 55.00 (*0-275-93059-9*, C3059, Praeger Pubs) Greenwood.

Corporate Oligarch. David Finn. LC 83-10449. 320p. (C). 1983. reprint ed. pap. text ed. 24.00 (*0-8191-3346-9*) U Pr of Amer.

Corporate Operational Analysis: A Procedure for Evaluating Key Factors in Internal Operations, Acquisitions, & Takeovers. Jerry W. Anderson, Jr. & John B. Camealy. LC 90-47592. 362p. 1991. text ed. 75.00 (*0-89930-535-0*, ACB/, Quorum Bks) Greenwood.

Corporate PACs & Federal Campaign Financing Laws: Use or Abuse of Power? Ann B. Matasar. LC 85-12280. (Illus.). 171p. 1986. text ed. 55.00 (*0-89930-086-3*, MTP/, Quorum Bks) Greenwood.

***Corporate Partnering: Structuring & Negotiating Domestic & International Strategic Alliances.** 2nd ed. Thomas F. Villeneuve et al. LC 94-35075. 1994. ring bd. 140.00 (*0-13-349580-9*) Aspen Law.

***Corporate, Partnership, Estate, & Gift Taxation.** 8th ed. James W. Pratt & William N. Kulsrud. 1088p. (C). 1994. text ed. 67.95 (*0-256-12739-5*) Irwin Prof Pubng.

Corporate, Partnership, Estate & Gift Taxation, 1992. Ed. by James W. Pratt et al. (C). 1991. text ed. 61.95 (*0-256-10043-8*) Irwin.

Corporate, Partnership, Estate & Gift Taxation, 1993. James W. Pratt & William Kulsrud. 1120p. 1992. text ed. 61.95 (*0-256-10842-0*) Irwin.

***Corporate Partnership Estate & Gift Taxation, 1994.** 7th ed. James Pratt & William Kulsrud. (C). 1993. text ed. 62.95 (*0-256-10940-0*) Irwin.

***Corporate Partnership Estate & Gift Taxation 1994.** 7th ed. Steven Thompson. (C). 1993. student ed. text ed. 21.50 (*0-256-12148-6*) Irwin.

Corporate Personality in Ancient Israel. rev. ed. Henry W. Robinson. LC 79-8887. 64p. reprint ed. pap. 25.00 (*0-317-55504-9*, 2029603) Bks Demand.

Corporate Philanthropy. Kenneth A. Bertsch. 84p. 1982. 15.00 (*0-931035-58-9*) IRRC Inc DC.

Corporate Philanthropy in New England: Maine 1987-88. Ed. by Michael Burns. 120p. 1987. pap. text ed. 8.00 (*1-882445-01-5*) D A T A.

Corporate Philanthropy in New England: New Hampshire 1987-88. Ed. by Michael Burns. 171p. 1987. pap. text ed. 8.00 (*1-882445-03-1*) D A T A.

Corporate Philanthropy in New England: Vermont 1987-88. Ed. by Michael Burns. 100p. 1987. pap. text ed. 8.00 (*1-882445-02-3*) D A T A.

Corporate Philanthropy in Rhode Island. Ed. by Michael Burns. 100p. 1989. pap. text ed. 19.95 (*1-882445-07-4*) D A T A.

Corporate Philosophies & Mission Statements: A Survey & Guide for Corporate Communicators & Management. Thomas A. Falsey. LC 88-18257. 169p. 1989. text ed. 55.00 (*0-89930-313-7*, FYC/, Quorum Bks) Greenwood.

Corporate Planner's Yearbook, 1978-79. Ed. by David E. Hussey. 1978. text ed. 110.00 (*0-08-022255-2*, Pub. by Pergamon Repr UK) Franklin.

Corporate Planning: A Systems View. Lloyd R. Amey. LC 86-8110. 287p. 1986. text ed. 65.00 (*0-275-92077-1*, C2077, Praeger Pubs) Greenwood.

Corporate Planning: Techniques & Applications. Ed. by Robert J. Allio & Malcom W. Pennington. LC 78-25803. 446p. reprint ed. pap. 127.20 (*0-317-27068-0*, 2023537) Bks Demand.

Corporate Planning: The Human Factor. David E. Hussey & M. J. Langham. LC 78-40532. (Pergamon International Library Science Technology Engineering & Social Studies). 1979. text ed. 132.00 (*0-08-022464-4*, Pub. by Pergamon Repr UK) Franklin.

Corporate Planning: Theory & Practice. 2nd ed. David E. Hussey. (Illus.). 468p. 1982. text ed. 61.00 (*0-08-024073-9*, Pergamon Pr) Elsevier.

Corporate Planning & LAN: Information Systems As Forums. Ru M. Sabre & J. Edward Ketz. (Illus.). 213p. 1992. text ed. 49.95 (*0-12-613730-7*) Acad Pr.

Corporate Planning & Modeling with Simplan. 2nd ed. Simplan Systems, Inc. Staff. 598p. 1982. pap. text ed. write for info. (*0-201-07830-9*) Addison-Wesley.

Corporate Planning & Policy. Sampat Mukhopadhyay. (C). 1989. 45.00 (*0-89771-438-5*, Current Dist) St Mut.

Corporate Planning & Policy Planning in the Pacific. Gavin Boyd. LC 92-27122. 248p. 1993. text ed. 45.00 (*0-312-06767-4*) St Martin.

Corporate Planning & Procurement. David Farmer & Bernard Taylor. 271p. (C). 1975. 145.00 (*0-685-39880-3*, Inst Pur & Supply) St Mut.

Corporate Planning & Procurement. David Farmer & Bernard Taylor. 271p. (C). 1988. 74.00 (*0-685-29234-7*, Inst Pur & Supply) St Mut.

Corporate Planning & Strategies in Forest Industries. Pentti Sierila. LC 87-50439. 146p. 1987. pap. 72.00 (*0-89852-441-5*, 0101R141) TAPPI.

Corporate Planning & Strategies in Forest Industries. Pentti Sierila. LC 87-50439. 146p. reprint ed. pap. 41.70 (*0-318-34987-6*, 2030833) Bks Demand.

Corporate Planning, Human Behavior, & Computer Simulation: Forecasting Business Cycles. Roy L. Nersesian. LC 89-37650. 249p. 1990. text ed. 59.95 (*0-89930-458-3*, NCB/, Greenwood Pr) Greenwood.

Corporate Planning in Girl Scouting. 216p. 1994. pap. 31.00 (*0-88441-478-7*, 26-162) Girl Scouts USA.

Corporate Planning Models. Thomas H. Naylor. LC 77-93329. 1979. text ed. write for info. (*0-201-05226-1*) Addison-Wesley.

Corporate Policy & the Investment Community. Martin Zausner. LC 68-13476. 242p. reprint ed. 69.00 (*0-8357-9520-9*, 2012485) Bks Demand.

Corporate Policy, Values & Social Responsibility. Anthony F. Buono & Lawrence T. Nichols. LC 85-6422. 240p. 1985. text ed. 65.00 (*0-275-90068-1*, C0068, Praeger Pubs) Greenwood.

Corporate Politeia: A Conceptual Approach to Business, Government & Society. James M. Buxbaum. LC 81-40313. (Illus.). 96p. (Orig.). 1981. pap. text ed. 16.00 (*0-8191-1764-1*) U Pr of Amer.

Corporate Political Activities, 1992: Complying with Campaign Finance & Ethics Laws. (Corporate Law & Practice Ser.). 423p. 1992. pap. text ed. 70.00 (*0-685-56898-9*, B4-6996) PLI.

Corporate Political Activity. Ed. by Barry M. Mitnick. (Focus Editions Ser.: Vol. 163). (Illus.). 312p. 1993. 49.95 (*0-8039-4348-2*); pap. 24.95 (*0-8039-4349-0*) Sage.

Corporate Power: A Personal Program for Success in the Business World. Donald V. Seibert & William Proctor. 7.75 (*0-317-03178-3*, Fireside) S&S Trade.

***Corporate Power & Responsibility: Issues in the Theory of Company Law.** J. E. Parkinson. 496p. 1995. pap. 32.00 (*0-19-825989-1*) OUP.

Corporate Power & Social Change: The Politics of the Life Insurance Industry. Karen Orren. LC 73-8118. (Illus.). 224p. reprint ed. pap. 63.90 (*0-317-41753-3*, 2025862) Bks Demand.

Corporate Power & Social Responsibility: Issues in the Theory of Company Law. John E. Parkinson. (Clarendon Press Ser.). 540p. 1994. 75.00 (*0-19-825288-9*) OUP.

Corporate Power & Urban Crisis in Detroit. Lynda Ann Ewen. LC 77-71981. 1978. 52.50x (*0-691-09373-3*) Princeton U Pr.

***Corporate Power & Urban Crisis in Detroit.** Lynda A. Ewen. LC 77-71981. reprint ed. pap. 94.70 (*0-7837-9334-0*, 2060075) Bks Demand.

Corporate Practice Commentator, 1966-1990, 25 vols. Ed. by F. O'Neal. (*0-318-61075-2*); 135.00 (*0-685-14553-0*) Clark Boardman Callaghan.

Corporate Practice Commentator, 1966-1990, 25 vols., Set. Ed. by F. O'Neal. LC 68-3938. 515.00 (*0-685-14552-2*) Clark Boardman Callaghan.

***Corporate Practice Handbook.** New York State Bar Association Staff. Ed. by Raymond W. Merritt & Clifford R. Ennico. LC 92-61676. 995p. (Orig.). 1992. text ed. 95.00 (*0-942954-55-6*) NYS Bar.

Corporate Practice Series. BNA's Legal Services Staff. 1978. ring bd. 1,389.00 (*1-55871-247-X*) BNA.

Corporate Prenatal Programs: Healthier Babies, Healthier Bottom Line. Marcy Swerdlin. (BNA Special Report Series on Work & Family: No. 37). 32p. 1991. 35.00 (*1-55871-207-0*, BSP205) BNA.

Corporate Productivity Atlas. 2nd ed. C. N. Athanasopoulos. LC 82-150492. 220p. (C). 1983. pap. 30.00 (*0-916987-00-0*) Delphi Res.

Corporate Productivity in Action: How Top American Firms Manage the Competitive Challenge. Doris Martin. LC 85-90460. (Management Ser.). (Illus.). 92p. (Orig.). 1987. pap. 12.95 (*0-9615541-1-8*) Martin Mgmt.

***Corporate Profile Graphics.** (Illus.). 224p. 1995. 64.95 (*4-938586-73-8*, Pub. by PIE Bks JA) Bks Nippan.

Corporate Profitability & Logistics: Innovative Guidelines for Executives. Comp. by National Association of Accountants. 1987. 60.00 (*0-318-33301-5*) Coun Logistics Mgt.

Corporate Profits As Shown by Audit Reports. W. A. Paton. (General Ser.: No. 28). 165p. 1935. reprint ed. 42.90 (*0-87014-027-2*); reprint ed. mic. film 21.50 (*0-685-61167-1*) Natl Bur Econ Res.

Corporate Promotion & Reorganizations. Arthur S. Dewing. LC 14-6465. (Business Enterprises Reprint Ser.). ix, 615p. 1986. reprint ed. lib. bdg. 49.50 (*0-89941-444-3*, 303830) W S Hein.

Corporate Protocol: A Brief Case for Business Etiquette. Valerie Sokolosky. 208p. (Orig.). 1986. pap. 6.95 (*1-56292-417-6*) Honor Bks OK.

Corporate Public Relations: A New Historical Perspective. Marvin N. Olasky. 192p. 1987. pap. 36.00 (*0-8058-0052-2*) L Erlbaum Assocs.

Corporate Punishment. Stewart W. White. (Illus.). 432p. (Orig.). (C). 1985. pap. 14.95 (*0-9614794-1-8*) SW White.

Corporate Quality Universities: Lessons Learned from Programs That Produce Results. Jeanne C. Meister. 276p. 1993. text ed. 40.00 (*1-55623-790-1*) Irwin Prof Pubng.

Corporate Real Estate Handbook: Strategies for Improving Bottom-Line Performance. Ed. by Robert A. Silverman et al. (Illus.). 224p. 1987. text ed. 33.50 (*0-07-045900-2*) McGraw.

***Corporate Realities: The Dynamics of Large & Small Organizations.** Robert Goffee & Richard Scase. LC 94-38295. (Organizational Behavior & Management Ser.). 208p. 1995. 59.95x (*0-415-05351-X*, B0192); pap. 18.95 (*0-415-05352-8*, B0196) Routledge.

Corporate Realities & Environmental Truths: Strategies for Leading Your Business in the Environmental ERA. Steven J. Bennett et al. LC 93-3481. 1993. text ed. 24.95 (*0-471-53073-5*) Wiley.

Corporate Reconstruction of American Capitalism, 1890-1916: The Market, the Law & Politics. Martin J. Sklar. 496p. 1988. 74.95 (*0-521-30921-2*); pap. 19.95 (*0-521-31382-1*) Cambridge U Pr.

Corporate Record Book. David Waldman. 1990. ring bd. 35.95 (*1-879191-37-7*) Forms Man.

Corporate Renaissance: Business As an Adventure in Human Development. Rolf Osterberg. 196p. 1993. 18.95 (*1-882591-12-7*) Nataraj Pub.

Corporate Renaissance: The Art of Reengineering. Kelvin F. Cross et al. (Illus.). 1994. 336p. (Orig.). 1994. pap. 19.95 (*1-55786-471-3*) Blackwell Pubs.

Corporate Reports. B. Bond & W. Walton. (C). 1986. 120.00 (*0-09-164231-0*, Pub. by S Thornes Pubs UK) St Mut.

Corporate Rescues & Insolvencies. 2nd ed. James R. Lingard. 1989. 84.00 (*0-406-10601-0*, U.K.) Butterworth Legal Pubs.

Corporate Resource Allocation: Integrating Finance & Strategy. Cyril Tomkins. (C). 1991. pap. write for info. (*0-631-17822-8*) Blackwell Pubs.

Corporate Responses to Environmental Challenges: Initiatives by Multinational Management. Ann Rappaport & Margaret F. Flaherty. LC 91-44706. 216p. 1992. text ed. 49.95 (*0-89930-715-9*, RMJ/, Quorum Bks) Greenwood.

Corporate Responses to Import Competition in the U. S. Apparel Industry. Michael J. Jedel et al. LC 78-17149. (Research Monograph: No. 74). 221p. (C). 1978. spiral bd. 19.95 (*0-88406-111-6*) GA St U Busn Pr.

Corporate Responsibility. Tom Cannon. (Financial Times Management Ser.). 256p. 1992. 96.00x (*0-273-03727-7*, Pub. by Pitman Pubng UK) St Mut.

Corporate Responsibility: Issues in Business Ethics, Governance & Responsibilities. Tom Cannon. 384p. (Orig.). 1994. pap. 53.50 (*0-273-60270-5*, Pub. by Pitman Pub Ltd UK) Trans-Atl Phila.

***Corporate Responsibility & Financial Performance: The Paradox of Social Cost.** Moses L. Pava & Joshua Krausz. LC 94-45284. 192p. 1995. text ed. 55.00 (*0-89930-921-6*, Quorum Bks) Greenwood.

C

An Asterisk (*) at the beginning of an entry indicates that the title is appearing in BIP for the first time.

An Asterisk (*) at the beginning of an entry indicates that the title is appearing in BIP for the first time.

1629

C

Corporation Law Review: 1978-1986, 9 vols., Set. 430.00 (0-8377-9048-4) Rothman.

***Corporation Laws of Ohio.** Ed. by Ronald C. Allan & Adam M. Ekonomon. 996p. 1994. pap. text ed. 65.00 (0-8322-0489-7) Banks-Baldwin.

Corporation of the 1990s: Information Technology & Organizational Transformation. Ed. by Michael S. Morton. (Illus.). 352p. 1991. 27.50 (0-19-506358-9) OUP.

Corporation, Partnership & Fiduciary Federal Income Tax Specimen Returns. Prentice-Hall Editorial Staff. 72p. 1989. pap. text ed. 8.00 (0-13-308651-8, Busn) P-H.

***Corporation Report 2020.** William Moss. (Cyberpunk Ser.). (Illus.). 88p. (Orig.). 1991. pap. 10.00 (0-614-02724-1, CP3111) R Talsorian.

***Corporation Report 2020, Vol. 3.** William Moss. (Cyberpunk Ser.). (Illus.). 88p. (Orig.). 1992. pap. 10.00 (0-937279-24-2, CP3161) R Talsorian.

***Corporation Report 2020 Vol. 2.** William Moss. (Cyberpunk Ser.). (Illus.). 80p. (Orig.). 1992. pap. 10.00 (0-937279-20-X, CP3151) R Talsorian.

Corporation Take-over. Ed. by Andrew Hacker. LC 77-117799. (Essay Index Reprint Ser.). 1977. 20.95 (0-8369-1945-9) Ayer.

Corporation Tax Manual. K. S. Carmichael. Date not set. pap. write for info. (0-406-50261-7) Butterworth Legal Pubs.

Corporation Tax Set. Daniel Q. Posin. 1990. 155.00 (0-316-71405-4) Little.

Corporation under Russian Law, 1800-1917: A Study in Tsarist Economic Policy. Thomas C. Owen. 240p. (C). 1991. 59.95 (0-521-39126-1) Cambridge U Pr.

Corporations. (Essential Principles Ser.). 1982. 12.95 (0-940366-30-4) Sum & Substance.

Corporations. Steven Emanuel. 593p. 1992. pap. text ed. 17.95 (1-56542-025-X) E Law Outlines.

Corporations. 2nd ed. Lattin. 1971. text ed. 27.00 (0-88277-411-5) Foundation Pr.

Corporations. 3rd ed. Robert W. Hamilton. (Black Letter Ser.). 723p. 1992. pap. text ed. 22.50 (0-314-00741-5) West Pub.

Corporations. 3rd ed. Harry G. Henn. (Hornbook Ser.). 1371p. 1991. student ed, text ed. 39.00 (0-314-69870-1) West Pub.

C

Corporations. 5th ed. (Sum & Substance Ser.). 1988. 17.95 (0-685-47933-1) Sum & Substance.

Corporations: A Study of the Origin & Development of Great Business Combinations & of Their Relation to the Authority of the State, 2 vols., Set. John P. Davis. (Business Enterprises Reprint Ser.). 628p. 1986. reprint ed. lib. bdg. 105.00 (0-89941-443-5, 303820) W S Hein.

Corporations: Adaptable to Courses Utilizing Cary & Eisenberg's Casebook on Corporations. Casenotes Publishing Co., Inc. Staff. Ed. by Norman S. Goldenberg et al. (Legal Briefs Ser.). 1988. pap. write for info. (0-87457-046-8, 1050) Casenotes Pub.

Corporations: Adaptable to Courses Utilizing Choper, Morris & Coffee's Casebook on Corporations. Casenotes Publishing Co., Inc. Staff. Ed. by Norman S. Goldenberg et al. (Legal Briefs Ser.). 1989. pap. write for info. (0-87457-047-6, 1054) Casenotes Pub.

Corporations: Adaptable to Courses Utilizing Hamilton's Casebook on Corporations-Including Partnerships & Limited Partnerships. Casenotes Publishing Co., Inc. Staff. Ed. by Norman S. Goldenberg et al. (Legal Briefs Ser.). 1994. pap. write for info. (0-87457-048-4, 1053) Casenotes Pub.

Corporations: Adaptable to Courses Utilizing Materials by Frey. Alexander H. Frey. LC 87-114670. (Legalines Ser.). 11.50 (0-685-18525-7) HarBrace.

Corporations: Adaptable to Courses Utilizing O'Kelley & Thompson's Casebook on Corporations & Other Business Associations. Casenote Publishing Co., Inc. Staff et al. (Legal Briefs Ser.). (Orig.). 1994. pap. text ed. write for info. (0-87457-203-7, 1057) Casenotes Pub.

Corporations: Adaptable to Courses Utilizing Solomon, Schwartz, Bauman & Weiss' Casebook on Corporations. Casenotes Publishing Co., Inc. Staff. Ed. by Norman S. Goldenberg et al. (Legal Briefs Ser.). 1994. pap. write for info. (0-87457-158-8, 1056) Casenotes Pub.

Corporations: Adaptable to Courses Utilizing Vagt's Casebook on Basic Corporation Law. Casenotes Publishing Co., Inc. Staff. Ed. by Norman S. Goldenberg et al. (Legal Briefs Ser.). 1988. pap. write for info. (0-87457-051-4, 1052) Casenotes Pub.

***Corporations: Cases & Materials.** 7th unabridged ed. Melvin A. Eisenberg. (Illus.). 1995. text ed. write for info. (1-56662-257-3) Foundation Pr.

Corporations: Cases & Materials On. 6th abr. ed. William L. Cary & Melvin A. Eisenberg. (University Casebook Ser.). 1016p. 1991. reprint ed. text ed. 39.50 (0-88277-662-2) Foundation Pr.

Corporations: Cases & Materials, 1994 Supplement. 6th ed. Melvin A. Eisenberg. (University Casebook Ser.). 343p. 1994. pap. text ed. 11.95 (1-56662-175-5) Foundation Pr.

***Corporations: Complete Tax Practice & Planning Guide.** Robert W. Wood. 700p. 1994. ring bd. 125.00 (1-886035-03-2) Pro Tax & Business.

Corporations: Jennings & Buxbaum's Casebook on Corporations. Casenotes Publishing Co., Inc. Staff. Ed. by Norman s. Goldenberg et al. (Legal Briefs Ser.). 1980. pap. write for info. (0-87457-050-6, 1055) Casenotes Pub.

Corporations: Tax Choices for Business Planning-Explanation, Law & Regulations, Legislative History, Cases & Rulings, Indexes. Prentice-Hall Editorial Staff. (Illus.). ring bd. write for info. (0-318-57847-6) P-H.

Corporations: Unabridged, Cases & Materials. 6th ed. Melvin A. Eisenberg. (University Casebook Ser.). 1619p. 1991. reprint ed. text ed. 45.50 (0-88277-649-5) Foundation Pr.

Corporations - Including Partnerships & Limited Partnerships: Statutory Supplement to Cases & Materials on. 4th ed. Robert W. Hamilton. (American Casebook Ser.). 70p. 1993. pap. text ed. 14.00 (0-314-74328-6) West Pub.

Corporations - Including Partnerships & Limited Partnerships, Statutory Supplement to Cases & Materials on. Robert W. Hamilton. (American Casebook Ser.). 175p. 1994. pap. text ed. 12.00 (0-314-03911-2) West Pub.

Corporations - Law & Policy, Materials & Problems. 2nd ed. Lewis D. Solomon et al. (American Casebook Ser.). 269p. (C). 1992. pap. text ed. 14.00 (0-314-01095-5) West Pub.

Corporations & Alternative Business Vehicles. Lewis D. Solomon et al. Ed. by Robert J. Switzer. (Law Outlines Ser.). 320p. (Orig.). 1993. pap. text ed. 17.95 (0-87457-181-2, 5050) Casenotes Pub.

***Corporations & Associations Law: Principles & Issues.** 2nd ed. J. Gooley. 292p. 1992. pap. 40.00 (0-409-31007-7, Austral) Butterworth Legal Pubs.

***Corporations & Business Associations: Statutes, Rules, Materials & Forms, 1994.** Melvin A. Eisenberg. (Illus.). 1004p. 1994. pap. text ed. 19.95 (1-56662-174-7) Foundation Pr.

Corporations & Business Associations - Statutes, Rules, & Forms, 1993. Melvin A. Eisenberg. 825p. 1993. pap. text ed. 19.95 (1-56662-088-0) Foundation Pr.

Corporations & Child Care: Profit-Making Day Care, Workplace Day Care & a Look at the Alternatives. Georgia Sassen & Cookie Avrin. LC 76-17319. (Illus.). 1974. pap. 3.50 (0-685-85529-5) Womens Research Act.

Corporations & Criminal Responsibility. Celia Wells. (Monographs on Criminal Law & Justice). 192p. 1995. reprint ed. pap. 24.00 (0-19-825947-6) OUP.

Corporations & Other Business Entities. (Texas Legal Assistant Education Ser.). 1991. write for info. (0-8205-0636-2) Bender.

Corporations & Other Business Entities. 2nd ed. Diane M. Baldwin & Frances B. Whiteside. LC 93-11321. (Texas Legal Assistant Education Ser.). 1993. reprint ed. write for info. (0-8205-0637-0) Bender.

Corporations & Partnerships. Ed. by K. Geens. (International Encyclopedia of Laws Ser.). 1991. 157.00 (0-685-58991-9) Kluwer Law Tax Pubs.

Corporations & Partnerships. Ed. by Koen Geens. (International Encyclopedia of Laws Ser.). 1992. ring bd. 156.00 (90-6544-946-9) Kluwer Law Tax Pubs.

Corporations & Political Accountability. Mark V. Nadel. 265p. (C). 1976. pap. text ed. 13.00 (0-669-93013-X) Heath.

Corporations & Society: Power & Responsibility. Arthur S. Miller. Ed. by Warren J. Samuels. LC 86-19451. (Contributions in American Studies: No. 88). 343p. 1987. text ed. 69.50 (0-313-25072-3, SCI/, Greenwood Pr) Greenwood.

Corporations & the Cold War. Ed. by David Horowitz. LC 78-81793. 256p. 1970. pap. 4.50 (0-85345-160-5) Monthly Rev.

Corporations & the Common Good. Ed. by Robert B. Dickie & Leroy S. Rouner. LC 85-40597. 160p. 1986. text ed. 19.95 (0-268-00754-3); pap. text ed. 8.95 (0-268-00761-6) U of Notre Dame Pr.

Corporations As Criminals. Ed. by Ellen Hochstedler. LC 83-19093. (Perspectives in Criminal Justice Ser.: No. 6). 168p. reprint ed. pap. 47.90 (0-8357-8418-5, 2034683) Bks Demand.

Corporations, Businesses & Families. Ed. by Roma S. Hanks & Marvin B. Sussman. (Marriage & Family Review Ser.). 251p. 1990. text ed. 39.95 (0-86656-863-8) Haworth Pr.

Corporations, Cases & Materials: Teachers Manual. 2nd ed. Harry G. Henn. (American Casebook Ser.). 397p. 1986. pap. text ed. write for info. (0-314-32188-8) West Pub.

Corporations Collect One. Ann Williams. 58p. 1991. 4.50 (0-9613046-6-9) Morris Mus.

Corporations, Crime & Accountability. Brent Fisse & John Braithwaite. (Theories of Institutional Design Ser.). 288p. (C). 1994. 59.95 (0-521-44130-7); pap. 17.95 (0-521-45923-0) Cambridge U Pr.

Corporations in & under International Law. Ignaz Seidl-Hohenveldern. 158p. (C). 1987. 114.00 (0-949009-09-1, Pub. by Grotius Pubns UK) St Mut.

Corporations in Conflict ... the Tender Offer. Douglas V. Austin & Jay A. Fishman. LC 75-94688. 1970. 21.50 (0-912164-08-5) Masterco Pr.

Corporations in Crisis: Behavioral Observations for Bankruptcy Policy. Philip B. Nelson. LC 81-1415. 222p. 1981. text ed. 49.95 (0-275-90687-6, C0687, Praeger Pubs) Greenwood.

Corporations in Perspective. Alfred F. Conard. (University Textbook Ser.). 456p. 1991. reprint ed. text ed. 28.00 (0-88277-405-0) Foundation Pr.

Corporations in the Moral Community. Peter A. French et al. 176p. (C). 1992. pap. text ed. 22.00 (0-03-030782-1) HB Coll Pubs.

Corporations, Including Partnerships & Limited Partnerships: Cases & Materials. 4th ed. Robert W. Hamilton. (American Casebook Ser.). 1248p. 1991. reprint ed. text ed. 50.50 (0-314-74327-8) West Pub.

Corporations, Including Partnerships & Limited Partnerships: Teacher's Manual to Accompany Cases & Materials On. 4th ed. Robert Hamilton. (American Casebook Ser.). 297p. 1990. pap. text ed. write for info. (0-314-79519-7) West Pub.

Corporations, Including Partnerships & Limited Partnerships, Cases & Materials on. 5th ed. Robert W. Hamilton. (American Casebook Ser.). 1289p. 1994. text ed. 52.00 (0-314-03909-0) West Pub.

Corporations Law & Policy, Materials & Problems. 2nd ed. Lewis D. Solomon et al. (American Casebook Ser.). 1391p. (C). 1990. reprint ed. text ed. 47.00 (0-314-36116-2) West Pub.

Corporations, Law & Policy, Materials & Problems. 3rd ed. Lewis D. Solomon et al. (American Casebook Ser.). 1306p. 1994. text ed. 53.00 (0-314-03717-9) West Pub.

Corporations Law & Policy, Materials & Problems. Lewis D. Solomon et al. (American Casebook Ser.). 1391p. (C). 1990. reprint ed. pap. text ed. write for info. (0-314-46966-4) West Pub.

***Corporations Law & Policy, Materials & Problems: Teacher's Manual to Accompany.** 3rd ed. Lewis D. Solomon et al. (American Casebook Ser.). 215p. 1994. pap. text ed. write for info. (0-314-04421-3) West Pub.

***Corporations Law in Australia.** Roman Tomasic & Stephen Bottomley. 1056p. 1995. 129.00 (1-86287-152-3, Pub. by Federation Pr AU); pap. 79.00 (1-86287-151-5, Pub. by Federation Pr AU) W W Gaunt.

***Corporations Law Workbook.** 2nd ed. Lorraine Griffiths. 346p. 1994. pap. 29.00 (0-455-21241-4, Pub. by Law Bk Co) W W Gaunt.

Corporations Legislation Index. Kathryn Fitzhenry. 100p. 1989. pap. 30.00 (1-86287-022-5, Pub. by Federation Pr AU) W W Gaunt.

***Corporations, Teacher's Manual to Accompany Cases & Materials On.** 5th ed. Robert W. Hamilton. (American Casebook Ser.). 342p. 1994. pap. text ed. write for info. (0-314-03910-4) West Pub.

Corporations, 1993 Supplement to Cases & Materials On. 6th ed. Melvin A. Eisenberg. (University Casebook Ser.). 250p. 1993. pap. text ed. 10.95 (1-56662-093-7) Foundation Pr.

Corporatism & Accountability: Organized Interests in British Public Life. Ronald Dore. Ed. by Colin Crouch. (Illus.). 312p. 1990. 65.00 (0-19-827590-0) OUP.

Corporatism & Change: Austria, Switzerland, & the Politics of Industry. Peter J. Katzenstein. LC 84-7676. (Cornell Studies in Political Economy). 334p. 1984. 47.50 (0-8014-1716-3); pap. 16.95 (0-8014-9467-2) Cornell U Pr.

Corporatism & Development: The Portuguese Experience. Howard J. Wiarda. LC 76-8761. 464p. 1977. 37.50 (0-87023-221-5) U of Mass Pr.

Corporatism & Economic Performance: A Comparative Analysis of Market Economics. Andrew Henley & Euclid Tsakalotos. (New Directions in Modern Economics Ser.). 224p. 1994. 59.95 (1-85278-539-X, Pub. by E Elgar Pub UK) Ashgate Pub Co.

Corporatism & Protest: Organizational Politics in the Norwegian Trade Unions. Don S. Schwerin. LC 82-114439. (Illus.). 79p. 1981. pap. text ed. 3.95 (0-933522-10-X) Kent Popular.

Corporatism & the Rule of Law: A Study of the National Recovery Administration. Donald R. Brand. LC 88-7167. 352p. 1988. 47.50 (0-8014-2169-1); pap. 16.95 (0-8014-9495-8) Cornell U Pr.

Corporatism & the Stability of Capitalist Democracies. Marco Wilke. Ed. by Peter Flaschel & Michael Kruger. (Dynamische Wirtschaftstheorie Ser.: Vol. 10). (Illus.). 225p. 1991. pap. 49.80 (3-631-43709-9) P Lang Pubs.

Corporatism & the Welfare State. Ed. by M. L. Harrison. 157p. 1984. text ed. 55.95 (0-566-00657-X) Ashgate Pub Co.

Corporatism in Perspective: An Introductory Guide to Corporatist Theory. Peter J. Williamson. (Studies in Neo-Corporatism). 272p. (C). 1989. text ed. 49.95 (0-8039-8222-4); pap. text ed. 17.95 (0-8039-8223-2) Sage.

Corporative Identity Design. V. Napoles. 1988. pap. 24.95 (0-442-26844-0) Van Nos Reinhold.

Corporatization & Privatization: Lessons from New Zealand. Ian Duncan & Alan Bollard. (Illus.). 208p. (C). 1993. pap. 28.00 (0-19-558267-5, 14486) OUP.

Corporeal Self. Sharon Cameron. 1991. text ed. 35.00 (0-231-07568-5); pap. text ed. 13.50 (0-231-07569-3) Col U Pr.

***Corporealities: Body, Knowledge, Culture, Power.** Ed. by Susan L. Foster. LC 94-41406. (Illus.). 272p. 1995. 59.95x (0-415-12138-8, C0284); pap. 16.95 (0-415-12139-6, C0283) Routledge.

***Corps: Three Complete Novels.** W. E. B. Griffin. LC 94-33371. 1995. write for info. (0-615-00142-4, Putnam) Putnam Pub Group.

Corps Book, No. 4: Battleground. W. E. B. Griffin. 1991. mass mkt. 5.95 (0-515-10640-2) Jove Pubns.

Corps Book One: Semper Fi. W. E. B. Griffin. 352p. 1986. mass mkt. 5.99 (0-515-08749-1) Jove Pubns.

Corps Book Three: Counterattack. W. E. B. Griffin. 1990. mass mkt. 6.50 (0-515-10417-5) Jove Pubns.

Corps Book Two: Call to Arms. W. E. B. Griffin. 1987. mass mkt. 5.99 (0-515-09349-1) Jove Pubns.

Corps De Jeune Fille. Elisabeth Barille. 182p. (FRE.). 1988. pap. 10.95 (0-7859-2091-9, 2070380394) Fr & Eur.

Corps de Mon Enemi. Felicien Marceau. (FRE.). 1978. pap. 10.95 (0-7859-4096-0) Fr & Eur.

Corps Diplomatique Accredite Aupres des Communautes Europeennes, April 1990. 196p. (FRE.). 1990. pap. 8.00 (92-826-0896-4, CB-57-89-071-FR-C) UNIPUB.

Corps et Biens. Robert Desnos. (FRE.). 1968. pap. 11.95 (0-7859-2761-1) Fr & Eur.

Corps et Biens. Robert Desnos. (Poesie Ser.). 192p. (FRE.). 1968. 9.95 (2-07-030085-4) Schoenhof.

Corps Humain - The Human Body. (Gallimard - Encyclopedie Vis. Bilingue Ser.). 63p. (ENG & FRE.). (J). 1991. 24.95 (2-07-057511-X) Schoenhof.

Corps Infirme, Corps Infame: La Femme Dans le Roman Balzacien. Brenda Mehta. LC 92-81520. 128p. (FRE.). 1992. lib. bdg. 29.95 (0-917786-86-6) Summa Pubns.

Corps Memorable. Paul Eluard. (FRE.). 43.95 (0-7859-0044-6, F99930) Fr & Eur.

Corps Perdu see Cadastre

***Corps Roots the Loudest: A History of VMI Athletics.** fac. ed. Thomas W. Davis. LC 85-13446. 351p. 1986. reprint ed. pap. 100.10 (0-7837-8292-6, 2049074) Bks Demand.

Corps Universel Diplomatique: Supplement, 5 Vols, Set. Ed. by Jean Dumont et al. LC 72-953. reprint ed. lib. bdg. write for info. (0-404-01820-3) AMS Pr.

Corps Universel Diplomatique du Droit des Gens, 8 Vols, Set. Ed. by Jean Dumont et al. LC 72-164796. reprint ed. lib. bdg. write for info. (0-404-01810-6) AMS Pr.

Corps V: Line of Fire. W. E. B. Griffin. 480p. (Orig.). 1993. mass mkt. 5.99 (0-515-11013-2) Jove Pubns.

Corpse. large type ed. Philip MacCutchan. 317p. 1992. 21.95 (0-7505-0309-2) Ulverscroft.

Corpse at Camp Two. large type ed. Glyn Carr. 426p. 1973. 15.95 (0-85456-216-8) Ulverscroft.

Corpse at the Opera House. Stephen Knight. (Crimes for a Summer Christmas Ser.: No. 3). 240p. (Orig.). 1993. pap. 14.95 (1-86373-321-3, Pub. by Allen & Unwin Aust Pty AT) IPG Chicago.

Corpse Diplomatique. Delano Ames. (Black Dagger Crime Ser.). 216p. 1989. reprint ed. 16.50 (0-86220-743-6, Black Dagger) Chivers N Amer.

Corpse Dream of N. Petkov. Thomas McGonigle. LC 86-72661. 134p. 1987. 20.00 (0-916583-19-8) Dalkey Arch.

Corpse for a Candidate. large type ed. Michael Geller. 1990. pap. 10.95 (0-7927-0124-0, C0202, Atlantic Lrg Print) Chivers N Amer.

Corpse Had a Familiar Face. Edna Buchanan. 1991. mass mkt. 5.99 (0-425-12994-2) Berkley Pub.

Corpse Had a Familiar Face: Covering Miami, America's Hottest Beat. Edna Buchanan. LC 86-26185. 288p. 1987. 17.95 (0-394-55794-8) Random.

Corpse in Ozzak's Pond. Charlotte MacLeod. 224p. 1988. mass mkt. 4.99 (0-445-40683-6, Mysterious Paperbk) Warner Bks.

Corpse in the Kitchen. Sarah J. Mason. 224p. (Orig.). 1993. pap. 4.50 (0-425-14006-7) Berkley Pub.

Corpse Moved Upstairs. large type ed. Frank Gruber. (Linford Mystery Library). 352p. 1992. pap. 14.95 (0-7089-7236-5, Trailtree Bookshop) Ulverscroft.

***Corpse Mows at Midnight.** Warren M. Evans. 269p. (Orig.). 1995. pap. 6.99 (1-880664-09-7) E M Pr.

Corpse of One's Own (Una Ombra Fosca, com un Vuvol de Tempesta) Isabel-Clara Simo. Tr. by Patricia Hart. LC 92-36500. (Catalan Studies: Vol. 7). 167p. (Orig.). (C). 1993. pap. text ed. 39.95 (0-8204-2048-4) P Lang Pubs.

Corpse on the Cruise. large type ed. Freda Bream. 1990. pap. 12.95 (0-7089-6896-1, Trailtree Bookshop) Ulverscroft.

***Corpse on the Dike.** Janwillem Van de Wetering. 215p. 1995. pap. 10.00 (1-56947-049-9) Soho Press.

Corpse Road. large type ed. Gwen Moffat. (Mystery Ser.). 400p. 1993. 21.95 (0-7089-2990-7) Ulverscroft.

Corpse Steps Out. Craig Rice. LC 89-85720. 186p. 1989. reprint ed. pap. 7.95 (1-55882-022-1, Lib Crime Classics) Intl Polygonics.

Corpsman Up. Paul M. Baviello. Ed. by James B. Van Treese. 216p. 1994. pap. 8.95 (1-56901-121-4) NW Pub.

***CorpTech Directory of Technology Companies: 1995 Edition, 4 vols., Set.** Ed. by Steven W. Parker. 1995. 575.00 (1-57114-008-5) CorpTech.

Corpus: An Anthology of Poets in Search of God. Alfrredo N. Salanga. 125p. (Orig.). (C). 1990. pap. 8.00 (971-10-0400-3, Pub. by New Day Pub PH) Cellar.

Corpus Christi: An Encyclopedia of the Eucharist. Michael O'Carroll. LC 88-45354. (Illus.). 232p. 1988. 42.00 (0-8146-5687-0) Liturgical Pr.

Corpus Christi: The Eucharist in Late Medieval Culture. Miri Rubin. (Illus.). 435p. (C). 1992. pap. 24.95 (0-521-43805-5) Cambridge U Pr.

Corpus Christi, Texas: A Picture Postcard History. Anita Eisenhauer & Gigi Starnes. 80p. 1987. 20.00 (0-318-23803-9) Anitas Antiques.

Corpus Cultus Cybelae Attidisque (CCCA), V: Aegyptus, Africa, Hispania, Gallia et Britannia. M. J. Vermaseren. (Etudes Preliminaires aux Religions Orientales dans l'Empire Romain Ser.: Vol. 50/5). (Illus.). xxiv, 224p. 1986. 68.75 (90-04-07679-4) E J Brill.

Corpus Cultus Iovis Dolicheni (CCID) Monika Horig & Elmar Schwertheim. (Etudes Preliminaires aux Religions Orientales dans l'Empire Romain Ser.: No. 106). (Illus.). xxiv, 422p. 1987. 125.75 (90-04-07665-4) E J Brill.

Corpus Delicious: The Fordham Law School Cookbook. Ed. by Janet Tracy. LC 93-70289. 150p. 1993. pap. 12.95 (0-8232-1498-2) Fordham.

Corpus Delicti. Diane Wagner. 1987. mass mkt. 4.95 (0-312-92363-5) St Martin.

Corpus der Griechisch Christlichen Inschriften von Hellas. N. A. Bees. 1978. 30.00 (0-89005-238-7) Ares.

Corpus der Hieroglyphischen Inschriften aus dem Grab des Tutanchamun: Tutankhamuns Tomb. Beinlich. 110.00 (0-900416-53-X, Pub. by Aris & Phillips UK) David Brown.

Corpus Dionysiacum, Band 1: Pseudo-Dionysius Areopagita, de Divinis Nominibus. Ed. by Beate R. Suchia. (Patristische Texte und Studien Ser.: Band 33). xxix, 237p. 1990. lib. bdg. 136.95x (3-11-012042-9) De Gruyter.

An Asterisk (*) at the beginning of an entry indicates that the title is appearing in BIP for the first time.

Corpus Dionysiacum Vol. II: Pseudo-Dionysius Areopagita, De Coelesti Hierarchia, De Ecclesiastica Heirarchia, De Mystica Theologia, Epistulae. Ed. by Gunther Heil & Adolf M. Ritter. (Patristische Texte und Studien Ser.: Vol. 36). xvi, 300p. (GER.). (C). 1991. lib. bdg. 152.35 (*3-11-012041-0*) De Gruyter.

Corpus in the Library & Other Stories. Alf MacLochlainn. (Illus.). 170p. 1996. 19.95 (*1-56478-068-6*) Dalkey Arch.

Corpus Inscriptionum Graecarum, 5 vols. in 4, Set. Ed. by A. Boeckh et al. (Subsidia Epigraphica Ser.). lxxii, 4090p. (GER.). 1977. reprint ed. write for info. (*3-487-06286-0*, Pub. by Georg Olms GW) Lubrecht & Cramer.

***Corpus Inscriptionum Latinarum Vol. II, Part 14, Fascicle I: Consilio et Auctoritate Academiae Scientiarum.** Ed. by Geza Alfoeldy et al. 197p. (C). 1994. pap. text ed. 398.50 (*3-11-014304-6*) De Gruyter.

Corpus Iuris Civilis, Vol. I: Institutiones. Ed. by Paul Kruger & Theodor Mommsen. xxiv, 56p. (GER.). 1988. write for info. (*3-296-12101-3*, Pub. by Georg Olms GW) Lubrecht & Cramer.

Corpus Iuris Civilis, Vol. II: Codex Iustinianus. Ed. by Paul Kruger. xxx, 513p. (GER.). 1989. write for info. (*3-296-12102-1*, Pub. by Georg Olms GW) Lubrecht & Cramer.

Corpus Iuris Civilis, Vol. III: Novellae. Ed. by Rudolf Schoell & Wilhelm Kroll. xxiv, 813p. (GER.). 1988. write for info. (*3-296-12103-X*, Pub. by Georg Olms GW) Lubrecht & Cramer.

Corpus Juris Civilis. The Civil Law: Including the Twelve Tables, the Institutes of Gaius, the Rules of Ulpian, the Opinions of Paulus, the Enactments of Justinian, & the Constitutions of Leo, 17 vols. in 7, Set. Ed. by Samuel P. Scott. LC 72-8392. reprint ed. 845.00 (*0-404-11026-6*) AMS Pr.

Corpus Juris Humorous: A Compilation of Humorous, Extraordinary, Outrageous, Unusual, Colorful, Infamous, Clever & Witty Reported Judicial Opinions & Related Materials Dating from 1256 A.D. to the Present. 724p. 1991. 28.95 (*0-9631488-0-X*) Mac-Mat.

***Corpus Juris Humorous: In Brief: A Compilation of Outrageous, Unusual, Infamous & Witty Judicial Opinions from 1256 A.D. to the Present.** John B. McClay & Wendy L. Matthews. 288p. 1994. 9.95 (*0-9631488-1-8*) Mac-Mat.

Corpus Juris Secundum: Criminal Law, 7 vols. write for info. (*0-318-57505-1*) West Pub.

Corpus Nummorum Romanorum: Roman Republican Coins, 9 vols., Set. Alberto Banti. reprint ed. 400.00 (*0-686-35946-1*) Numismatic Fine Arts.

Corpus Nummorum Romanorum (Roman Imperial Coins), 18 vols., Set. Alberto Banti & L. Simonetti. 1979. 800.00 (*0-686-37929-2*) Numismatic Fine Arts.

Corpus Nummorum Siculorum: The Bronze Coinage, Vol. I. Romolo Calciati. 1983. 180.00 (*0-318-19581-X*) Numismatic Fine Arts.

Corpus Nummorum Siculorum: The Bronze Coinage Syrakosai-Symmachia, Vol. II. Romolo Calciati. 1986. 180.00 (*0-318-19607-7*) Numismatic Fine Arts.

Corpus Nummorum Siculorum Vol. III: The Bronze Coinage, 3 vols., Set. Romola Calciati. (Illus.). 400p. 1988. lib. bdg. 180.00 (*0-317-01701-2*, Pub. by R Calciati IT) Numismatic Fine Arts.

Corpus of Ammonite Inscriptions. Walter E. Aufrecht. LC 88-1535. (Ancient Near Eastern Texts & Studies: Vol. 4). (Illus.). 516p. 1989. lib. bdg. 119.95 (*0-88946-089-2*) E Mellen.

Corpus of Anglo-Saxon Stone Sculpture Vol. III: York & Eastern Yorkshire. James T. Lang. (British Academy Ser.). (Illus.). 456p. 1991. 195.00 (*0-19-726079-9*) OUP.

***Corpus of Anglo-Saxon Stone Sculpture Vol. IV: South-East England.** Ed. by Dominic Tweddle et al. (Corpus of Anglo-Saxon Stone Sculpture British Academy Ser.). (Illus.). 550p. 1995. 150.00 (*0-19-726129-9*) OUP.

Corpus of Celtic Finds in Hungary, Vol. 1. T. Kovacs. (Illus.). 248p. (C). 1987. 400.00 (*0-569-09045-8*, Pub. by Collets UK) Pro-Am Music.

Corpus of Clandestine Literature in France, 1769-1789. Robert Darnton. 1995. 32.50 (*0-393-03745-2*) Norton.

Corpus of Early Christian Inscribed Stones. Elisabeth Okasha. LC 93-9951. (Studies in the Early History of Britain). 256p. 1993. 95.00 (*0-7185-1475-0*, Pub. by Leicester Univ Pr) St Martin.

Corpus of Inscribed Egyptian Funerary Cones, Vol. 1. Davies. (Plates Ser.). 1957. 49.95 (*0-900416-12-2*, Pub. by Aris & Phillips UK) David Brown.

Corpus of Mycenaean Inscriptions from Knossos. John Chadwick et al. (Illus.). 288p. (C). 1994. 250.00 (*0-521-32024-0*) Cambridge U Pr.

Corpus of Mycenaean Inscriptions from Knossos, 1-1063, Vol. I. John Chadwick et al. (Illus.). 520p. 1987. 240.00 (*0-521-32022-4*) Cambridge U Pr.

Corpus of Mycenaean Inscriptions from Knossos, 1064-4495, Vol. II. John Chadwick et al. (Illus.). 264p. (C). 1992. 185.00 (*0-521-32023-2*) Cambridge U Pr.

Corpus of Rembrandt Paintings, Vol. 1. J. Bruyn. 1982. lib. bdg. 643.50 (*90-247-2614-X*) Kluwer Ac.

Corpus of Rembrandt Paintings, Vol. III: 1635-1642. Rembrandt Research Project Staff. (C). 1990. lib. bdg. 625.00 (*90-247-3781-8*) Kluwer Ac.

Corpus of the Aramaic Incantation Bowls. Charles D. Isbell. LC 75-15949. (Society of Biblical Literature. Dissertation Ser.: No. 17). 214p. reprint ed. pap. 61.00 (*0-317-10143-9*, 2017519) Bks Demand.

Corpus Papyrorum Aegypti, 3 vols. in 1. Eugene Revillout & Eisenlohr. xii, 67p. 1978. reprint ed. write for info. (*3-487-06440-5*, Pub. by Georg Olms GW) Lubrecht & Cramer.

Corpus Paroemiograhorum Graecorum, 2 vols., Set. Ed. by E. L. Von Leutsch & F. W. Schneidewin. 1468p. 1958. reprint ed. write for info. (*0-318-70961-9*, Pub. by Georg Olms GW) Lubrecht & Cramer.

Corpus Paroemiographorum Graecorum. Ed. by E. Leutsch & F. G. Schneidewin. Bd. 21-22. pap. write for info. (*0-318-70795-0*, Pub. by Georg Olms GW) Lubrecht & Cramer.

Corpus Paroemiographorum Graecorum. Ed. by E. L. Von Leutsch & F. W. Schneidewin. Bd. 21-22. 1468p. 1958. reprint ed. pap. write for info. (*0-318-70962-7*, Pub. by Georg Olms GW) Lubrecht & Cramer.

Corpus Paroemiographorum Graecorum, 2 vols., Set. E. L. Leutsch & F. Schneidewin. 1468p. (GER.). 1958. reprint ed. pap. write for info. (*0-318-70499-4*, Pub. by Georg Olms GW) Lubrecht & Cramer.

Corpus Paroemiographorum Graecorum Supplementum. Ed. by E. L. Von Leutsch & F. W. Schneidewin. xxiv, 904p. 1991. reprint ed. write for info. (*3-487-00086-5*, Pub. by Georg Olms GW) Lubrecht & Cramer.

Corpus Signorum Imperii Romani: Great Britain: Roman Sculpture from Eastern England. Jane Huskinson. (British Academy, Corpus Signorum Imperii Romani Ser.: Vol. I, Fascicule 8). (Illus.). 62p. 1994. 80.00 (*0-19-726140-X*) OUP.

Corpus Signorum Imperii Romani: Great Britain, Vol. I Fascicule 7: Roman Sculpture from the Cotswold Region with Devon & Cornwall. Martin Henig. (British Academy Ser.). (Illus.). 180p. 1994. 125.00 (*0-19-726135-3*) OUP.

Corpus Signorum Imperii Romani: Great Britian, Vol. I, Fascicule 4, Scotland. Lawrence Keppie & Beverly Arnold. (Illus.). 1984. 79.00 (*0-19-726026-8*) OUP.

Corpus Signorum Imperii Romani, Vol. I: Fascicule 5: Wales. R. J. Brewer. (Corpus Signorum Imperii Romani Ser.). (Illus.). 116p. 1986. 69.00 (*0-19-726045-4*) OUP.

Corpus Signorum Imperii Romanii - Hadrian's Wall West of the North Tyne, & Carlisle, Vol. I, Fascicule 6. J. C. Coulston & E. J. Phillips. (Corpus Signorum Imperii Romani Ser.). (Illus.). 240p. 1988. 198.00 (*0-19-726058-6*) OUP.

Corpus Speculorum Etruscorum: Great Britain 2 Cambridge. Richard Nicholls. Ed. by Judith Swaddling & Tom Rasmussen. LC 92-35756. (Illus.). 144p. (C). 1994. 95.00 (*0-521-43380-0*) Cambridge U Pr.

Corpus Speculorum Etruscorum: U. S. A. 1 - Midwestern Collections. Richard D. De Puma. LC 86-31135. 242p. 1987. text ed. 47.95 (*0-8138-0363-2*) Iowa St U Pr.

Corpus Speculorum Etruscorum, U. S. A. 2: Boston & Cambridge. Richard DePuma. LC 86-31135. (U. S. A. Ser.). (Illus.). 208p. 1993. text ed. 69.95 (*0-8138-0354-3*) Iowa St U Pr.

Corpus Vasorum Antiquorum, Fasc. 1. Stephen B. Luce. (Illus.). 1933. 5.00 (*0-911517-16-2*) Mus of Art RI.

Corpus Vasorum Antiquorum: Great Britain, Fascicule 16, National Museums of Scotland, Edinburgh. Elizabeth Moignard. (British Academy Ser.). (Illus.). 128p. 1990. 115.00 (*0-19-726077-2*) OUP.

Corpus Vasorum Antiquorum: Great Britain Fascicule 12. Percy N. Ure & Annie D. Ure. Bd. with University of Reading, Fascicule 1 61p. 1979. 42.00 (*0-686-27266-8*) St Mut.

Corpus Vasorum Antiquorum: Joslyn Art Museum Fascisule 1, (U. S. A. Fascicule 21) Ann Steiner. LC 85-60881. (Corpus Vasorum Antiquorum Ser.). (Illus.). xii, 51p. 1986. write for info. (*0-936364-14-9*) Joslyn Art.

Corpus Vasorum Antiquorum: The Netherlands, Leiden, Rijksmuseum van Oudheden. Ed. by M. J. Jongkees-Vos. (CVA Ser.: Nos. 7 & 4). (Illus.). 99p. 1991. 183.00 (*90-04-09412-1*) E J Brill.

Corpus Vasorum Antiquorum: The South Italian Pottery, Pt. I. J. R. Green. (University Museum Fascicule I Ser.: USA Fascicule 22). (Illus.). xiv, 72p. 1986. text ed. 76.00 (*0-934718-83-0*) U PA Mus Pubns.

***Corpus Vasorum Antiquorum: United States of America.** Richard De Puma. (J. Paul Getty Museum Ser.: Fascicule 6). (Illus.). 90p. 1995. 85.00 (*0-89236-293-6*, J P Getty Museum) J P Getty Trust.

Corpus Vasorum Antiquorum, U. S. A. Fasc. 15 Cleveland Museum of Art, Fasc. 1. Cedric G. Boulter. LC 70-148348. (Corpus Vasorum Antiquorum Ser.: Fascicule 1, U. S. A.). (Illus.). 1971. 62.50x (*0-691-03540-7*) Princeton U Pr.

Corpus Vasorum Antiquorum, United States of America, Fascicule 1: The J. Paul Getty Museum, Fascule 1. Andrew J. Clark. LC 88-12781. (Illus.). 88p. 1988. 85.00 (*0-89236-134-4*) J P Getty Trust.

Corpus Vasorum Antiquorum, United States of America, Fascicule 2. Andrew Clark. (Illus.). 100p. 1990. 85.00 (*0-89236-170-0*) J P Getty Trust.

Corpus Vasorum Antiquorum, United States of America, Fascicule 3. Marit-Jentoft Nilsen & A. D. Trendall. (Illus.). 50p. 1990. 85.00 (*0-89236-172-7*) J P Getty Trust.

Corpus Vasorum Antiquorum, United States of America, Fascicule 4, No. 4. Marit Jentoft-Nilsen & A. D. Trendall. (Illus.). 50p. 1991. 85.00 (*0-89236-190-5*) J P Getty Trust.

Corpus Vasorum Antiquorum, United States of America, Fascicule 5. Marit Jentoft-Nilsen & A. D. Trendall. (Illus.). 60p. 1994. 85.00 (*0-89236-278-2*) J P Getty Trust.

Corpus Vitrearum: Studies on Medieval Stained Glass. Madeline E. Caviness & Timothy Husband. (Occasional Papers: No. 1). (Illus.). 160p. 1985. 19.95 (*0-87099-391-7*) Metro Mus Art.

Corpus Vitrearum Medii Aevi: Great Britain. Summary Catalogue 1: A Catalogue of Netherlandish & North European Roundels in Britain. William E. Cole. (British Academy Ser.). (Illus.). 320p. 1993. 115.00 (*0-19-726116-7*) OUP.

Corpus Vitrearum Medii Aevi. Great Britain, Vol. III: The Medieval Stained Glass of York Minster: Fascicule I, the Glazing of the West wall. T. W. French & D. E. O'Connor. (Illus.). 160p. 1987. fiche 62.00 (*0-19-726053-5*) OUP.

Corpus Vitrearum Occasional Papers I: Studies on Medieval Stained Glass. Madeline E. Caviness. 1994. 19.95 (*0-8109-6454-6*) Abrams.

Corpuscles: Adventurers in Inner Space. John Benziger. LC 88-92390. (Illus.). 64p. (J). (gr. k-6). 1989. 11.95 (*0-9620961-0-5*) Corpuscles Intergalactica.

Corpuscles & Radiation in Matter I. T. Aberg et al. (Encyclopedia of Physics Ser.: Vol. 31). (Illus.). 670p. 1982. 257.00 (*0-387-11313-4*) Spr-Verlag.

Corpuscles Meet the Virus Invaders. John Benziger. LC 90-80327. (Illus.). 30p. (J). (gr. 3-6). 1990. 14.95 (*0-9620961-1-3*) Corpuscles Intergalactica.

Corrado Lovi. Kyoichi Tsuzuki. (Art Random Ser.: No. 56). (Illus.). 48p. 1991. 32.95 (*4-7636-8562-7*, Pub. by Kyoto Shoin JA) Bks Nippan.

Corrales De Comedias De Madrid: 1632-1745. Repraciones Y Obras Nuevas: Estudio Y Documentos. N. D. Shergold. (Series C: Fuentes Para La Historia Del Teatro En Espana: No. 10). (Illus.). 335p. (C). 1990. 63.00 (*0-7293-0306-3*, Pub. by Tamesis Bks Ltd UK) Boydell & Brewer.

Corre Contus Suenos. Maureen A. Burns. (Illus.). 60p. 1987. pap. 8.00 (*0-9613084-1-9*) Empey Ent.

Corre, Perro, Corre! P. D. Eastman. Tr. by Teresa Mlawer. (Illus.). 64p. (J). (gr. 1-2). 1992. 8.95 (*1-880507-02-1*) Lectorum Pubns.

Correa: Extracts see Portuguese Expedition to Abyssinia in 1541-1543

Correct Dress for Riding. Pony Club Staff. (C). 1990. pap. 21.00 (*0-900226-30-7*, Pub. by J A Allen & Co UK) St Mut.

Correct Food Combining for Easy Digestion: How to Get Rid of Indigestion, Gas, Bloating, Belching & Bad Breath. 1992. lib. bdg. 88.95 (*0-8490-8806-2*) Gordon Pr.

Correct Hardware Design & Verification Methods: IFIP WG10.2 Advanced Research Working Conference CHARME '93, Arles, France, May 24-26, 1993. Ed. by G. J. Milne & L. Pierre. (Lecture Notes in Computer Science Ser.: Vol. 683). viii, 269p. 1993. pap. 44.00 (*0-387-56778-X*) Spr-Verlag.

Correct Me If I'm Wrong: A Practical Approach to Improving Written English. Rosemary Moor. 96p. (Orig.). 1988. pap. 11.95 (*0-85950-713-0*, Pub. by Stanley Thornes UK) Trans-Atl Phila.

Correct Mispronunciations of Some South Carolina Names. Claude Neuffer & Irene Neuffer. LC 83-5947. 191p. 1983. 15.95 (*0-87249-424-1*); pap. 9.95 (*0-87249-556-6*) U of SC Pr.

***Correct Sadist.** 3rd ed. Terence Sellers. 192p. 1995. mass mkt., pap. 6.95 (*1-56201-077-8*) Blue Moon Bks.

Correct Sadist: The Memoirs of Angel Stern. Terence Sellers. LC 84-180950. (Illus.). 164p. (Orig.). 1983. 20.00 (*0-930635-41-8*); pap. 13.00 (*0-930635-40-X*) Vitriol Pubns.

Correct Spelling Made Easy. rev. ed. Norman Lewis. 1987. mass mkt. 4.99 (*0-440-31501-8*, LE) Dell.

Correct the Ten Most Common Golf Problems in Ten Days. Walter Ostroske & John Devaney. (Illus.). 128p. 1991. pap. 8.95 (*0-399-51656-5*, Perigree Bks) Berkley Pub.

Correct Use of VHF Channels. ICS Staff. (C). 1989. 45.00 (*0-685-31786-2*, Pub. by Witherby & Co UK) St Mut.

Correct Writing. 3rd ed. Eugenia W. Butler et al. 384p. 1983. 2.00 (*0-669-05438-0*); pap. text ed. 18.00 (*0-669-05437-2*) Heath.

Correct Writing. 4th ed. Eugenia W. Butler et al. LC 86-81265. 405p. (C). 1987. pap. text ed. 18.00 (*0-669-11770-6*); Answer key. 2.00 (*0-669-11771-4*) Heath.

Correct Writing. 5th ed. Eugenia W. Butler et al. 494p. (C). 1991. pap. text ed. write for info. (*0-669-20474-9*); Instr.'s guide. teacher ed write for info. (*0-669-24714-6*) Heath.

***Correct Writing.** 6th ed. Eugenia Butler et al. 484p. (C). 1995. pap. text ed. write for info. (*0-669-34073-1*) Heath.

Correctable Renal Hypertension. Chester C. Winter. LC 64-14483. (Illus.). 190p. reprint ed. pap. 54.20 (*0-317-07832-1*, 2014590) Bks Demand.

Corrected Impressions: Essays on Victorian Writers. George E. Saintsbury. LC 74-39073. (Essay Index Reprint Ser.). 1977. reprint ed. 18.95 (*0-8369-2716-8*) Ayer.

Corrected Opinion of Harold R. Medina, United States Circuit Judge in United States of America, Plaintiff, v. Henry S. Morgan, Harold Stanley et al... Harold R. Medina. LC 75-2647. (Wall Street & the Security Market Ser.). 1975. reprint ed. 35.95 (*0-405-06972-3*) Ayer.

Correcting the Code: Inventing the Genetic Cure for the Human Body. Larry Thompson. 1994. 23.00 (*0-671-77082-9*) S&S Trade.

Correction. Thomas Bernhard. Tr. by Sophie Wilkins. LC 89-27656. (Phoenix Fiction Ser.). viii, 272p. 1990. pap. 14.95 (*0-226-04393-2*) U Ch Pr.

Correction & Nomenclatural Changes to the Forest Flora of the Bombay Presidency & Sind, 2 vols., Set. Ed. by M. B. Raizada. (C). 1976. text ed. 65.00 (*0-89771-645-0*, Pub. by Intl Bk Distr II) St Mut.

Correction Captain. Jack Rudman. (Career Examination Ser.: C-165). 1994. pap. 29.95 (*0-8373-0165-3*) Nat Learn.

Correction Counselor. Jack Rudman. (Career Examination Ser.: C-2593). 1994. pap. 29.95 (*0-8373-2593-5*) Nat Learn.

Correction Counselor Trainee. Jack Rudman. (Career Examination Ser.: C-2999). 1994. pap. 27.95 (*0-8373-2999-X*) Nat Learn.

Correction Hospital Officer (Men) Jack Rudman. (Career Examination Ser.: C-956a). 1994. pap. 27.95 (*0-8373-0956-5*) Nat Learn.

Correction Hospital Officer (Women) Jack Rudman. (Career Examination Ser.: C-956b). 1994. pap. 27.95 (*0-685-03521-2*) Nat Learn.

Correction Law Plus Text, Statute & Appendix, N.Y.S. 320p. 1994. ring bd. 10.95 (*0-930137-45-0*) Looseleaf Law.

Correction Lieutenant. Jack Rudman. (Career Examination Ser.: C-166). 1994. pap. 29.95 (*0-8373-0166-1*) Nat Learn.

Correction Matron. Jack Rudman. (Career Examination Ser.: C-1219). 1994. pap. 23.95 (*0-8373-1219-1*) Nat Learn.

Correction Officer. Jack Rudman. (Career Examination Ser.: C-3019). 1994. pap. 23.95 (*0-8373-3019-X*) Nat Learn.

Correction Officer. 9th ed. E. P. Steinberg. 288p. 1992. pap. 15.00 (*0-13-178419-6*, Arco Test) P-H Gen Ref & Trav.

Correction Officer. 10th ed. Eve P. Steinberg. LC 94-9419. 1994. 15.00 (*0-671-89230-4*) P-H.

Correction Officer I. Jack Rudman. (Career Examination Ser.: C-837). 1994. pap. 23.95 (*0-8373-0837-2*) Nat Learn.

Correction Officer II. Jack Rudman. (Career Examination Ser.: C-838). 1994. pap. 27.95 (*0-8373-0838-0*) Nat Learn.

Correction Officer III. Jack Rudman. (Career Examination Ser.: C-839). 1994. pap. 27.95 (*0-8373-0839-9*) Nat Learn.

Correction Officer IV. Jack Rudman. (Career Examination Ser.: C-840). 1994. pap. 29.95 (*0-8373-0840-2*) Nat Learn.

Correction Officer (Men) Jack Rudman. (Career Examination Ser.: C-167). 1994. pap. 23.95 (*0-8373-0167-X*) Nat Learn.

Correction Officer Trainee. Jack Rudman. (Career Examination Ser.: C-957). 1994. pap. 19.95 (*0-8373-0957-3*) Nat Learn.

Correction Officer (Women) Jack Rudman. (Career Examination Ser.: C-168). 1994. pap. 23.95 (*0-8373-0168-8*) Nat Learn.

***Correction Promotion Course.** Jack Rudman. (General Aptitude & Abilities Ser.: CS-25). 1994. pap. 29.95 (*0-8373-6725-5*) Nat Learn.

Correction Sergeant. Jack Rudman. (Career Examination Ser.: C-169). 1994. pap. 27.95 (*0-8373-0169-6*) Nat Learn.

Correction Youth Camp Officer (Men) Jack Rudman. (Career Examination Ser.: C-958a). 1994. pap. 23.95 (*0-8373-0958-1*) Nat Learn.

Correction Youth Camp Officer (Women) Jack Rudman. (Career Examination Ser.: C-958b). 1994. pap. 23.95 (*0-685-03522-0*) Nat Learn.

Correctional Administration: Theory & Practice. Clemens Bartollas & Stuart J. Miller. (Illus.). 1978. text ed. 43.95 (*0-07-003950-X*) McGraw.

***Correctional Administration Vocabulary.** Estelle Beauregard. (Terminology Bulletin Ser.: No. 224). 325p. (Orig.). 1994. pap. 38.95x (*0-660-59111-1*, Pub. by Canada Commun Grp CN) Accents Pubns.

***Correctional Alternatives Program Representative.** (Career Examination Ser.: Series 1). Date not set. pap. 34.95 (*0-8373-3622-8*) Nat Learn.

Correctional & Juvenile Justice Training Directory of North America. 50p. (Orig.). (C). 1993. pap. text ed. 30.00 (*1-56806-868-9*) Diane Pub.

Correctional Assessment, Casework, & Counseling. 2nd ed. Anthony Walsh. (Illus.). 332p. (Orig.). 1992. pap. 25.00 (*0-929310-75-6*, 450) Am Correctional.

Correctional Counseling. 2nd ed. David Lester et al. LC 91-72940. 271p. (C). 1992. pap. 21.95 (*0-87084-372-9*) Anderson Pub Co.

Correctional Counseling & Treatment. 3rd rev. ed. Peter Kratcoski. (Illus.). 591p. (Orig.). (C). 1994. pap. text ed. 24.95 (*0-88133-772-2*) Waveland Pr.

Correctional Education: Perspective on Programs for Adult Offenders. Osa D. Coffey et al. Ed. by Bruce I. Wolford. (Eric Information Analysis Ser.). 53p. 1986. 7.00 (*0-318-22356-2*, IN 310) Ctr Educ Trng Employ.

Correctional Education: Theory & Practice. D. R. Werner. 250p. 1990. pap. 18.95 (*0-8134-2882-3*) Interstate.

Correctional Facility Law Libraries: An A to Z Resource Guide. rev. ed. American Correctional Association Staff. 146p. 1991. pap. 14.75 (*0-929310-55-1*, 203) Am Correctional.

Correctional Facility Planning & Design. 2nd ed. J. Faberstein. 64.95 (*0-685-19095-1*) Van Nos Reinhold.

Correctional Food Service Correspondence Course, 2 Vols., Set. Ed. by Rosalie Rosetti & Diane Geiman. (Illus.). (Orig.). 1985. pap. 54.00 (*0-942974-67-0*, 166) Am Correctional.

Correctional Industries Handbook for Line Supervisors. 184p. 1990. ring bd. 40.45 (*0-929310-34-9*, 421) Am Correctional.

Correctional Industries Handbook for Line Supervisors Test Packet. 1990. 21.00 (*0-929310-48-9*, 421T) Am Correctional.

Correctional Law for the Correctional Officer. rev. ed. William C. Collins. 144p. 1993. pap. text ed. 15.00 (*0-929310-98-5*, 523) Am Correctional.

Correctional Management. (Correctional Issues Ser.). 88p. 1990. pap. 13.65 (*0-929310-38-1*, 430) Am Correctional.

Correctional Management. James Houston. 1994. text ed. 36.95 (*0-8304-1309-X*) Nelson-Hall.

Correctional Management: Change & Control in Correctional Organizations. David E. Duffee. (Criminal Justice Ser.). (Illus.). 1980. text ed. 25.95 (*0-685-03805-X*) P-H.

Correctional Management: Change & Control in Correctional Organizations. David Duffee. 407p. (C). 1986. reprint ed. pap. text ed. 19.95 (*0-88133-246-1*) Waveland Pr.

Correctional Mid-Management Skills Correspondence Course, 2 vols., Set. American Correctional Association Staff. Ed. by Rosalie Rosetti & Diane Geiman. (Correspondence Courses Ser.). (Orig.). 1988. pap. 68.00 (*0-942974-94-8*, 168) Am Correctional.

Correctional Officer Correspondence Course. rev. ed. American Correctional Association Staff. 146p. (Orig.). 1989. Bk. I, 146p. write for info. (*0-318-66690-1*); Bk. II, 110p. write for info. (*0-318-66691-X*); Bk. III, 182p. write for info. (*0-318-66692-8*); Bk. IV, 166p. write for info. (*0-318-66693-6*) Am Correctional.

Correctional Officer Correspondence Course. rev. ed. American Correctional Association Staff. 124p. (Orig.). 1989. pap. 68.00 (*0-929310-19-5*, 165) Am Correctional.

Correctional Officer Correspondence Course, Set, Bks. I-IV. rev. ed. Ed. by American Correctional Association, Capitol Communication Systems, Inc. Staff. (Orig.). 1989. pap. 68.00 (*0-929310-18-7*, 165) Am Correctional.

Correctional Officer Correspondence Course: Final Tests. rev. ed. American Correctional Association Staff. 44p. (Orig.). 1989. Final Tests, 44p. write for info. (*0-318-66694-4*) Am Correctional.

***Correctional Officer Correspondence Course - Final Test.** rev. ed. Ed. by American Correctional Association, Capitol Communication Systems, Inc. Staff. 24p. 1992. pap. 35.00 (*1-56991-028-6*) Torah Aura.

Correctional Officer II: Correspondence Course, Bk. III: Trends in Corrections. ACA Staff. 96p. 1990. write for info. (*0-318-68216-8*) Am Correctional.

Correctional Officer II: Correspondence Course, 3 bks., Bks. I, II & III. ACA Staff. 348p. 1990. Bk. I: Personal & Professional Growth in Corrections, 108p. write for info. (*0-318-68214-1*); Bk. II: Advanced Topics in Corrections, 144p. write for info. (*0-318-68215-X*) Am Correctional.

Correctional Officer II: Correspondence Course, Final Test. ACA Staff. 20p. 1990. write for info. (*0-318-68217-6*) Am Correctional.

Correctional Officer II: Correspondence Course, 3 bks., Set. 1990. pap. 68.00 (*0-929310-39-X*, 172) Am Correctional.

***Correctional Officer II Correspondence Course - Final Test.** rev. ed. Ed. by Diane Geiman & Denise Flannery. 11p. 1993. pap. 35.00 (*1-56991-029-4*) Torah Aura.

Correctional Officer Resource Guide. rev. ed. Ed. by Richard L. Phillips & Ann Dargis. (Illus.). 140p. 1989. pap. 20.95 (*0-929310-21-7*, 130) Am Correctional.

Correctional Policy Inventory. National Council on Crime & Delinquency Staff & Vincent O'Leary. 1970. ring bd. 4.10 (*0-318-02051-3*) Natl Coun Crime.

***Correctional Populations in the United States, 1992.** 8th ed. (Illus.). 350p. (YA). (gr. 12 up). 1994. pap. text ed. 50.00 (*0-7881-0845-X*) Diane Pub.

Correctional Psychiatry. Ed. by Richard Rosner & R. B. Harmon. LC 88-657025. (Critical Issues in American Psychiatry & the Law Ser.: Vol. 6). (Illus.). 320p. 1989. 65.00 (*0-306-43070-3*, Plenum Pr) Plenum.

Correctional Rehabilitation & Management: A Psychological Approach. Teodoro Ayllon & Michael A. Milan. LC 78-21703. (Wiley Series in Behavior). 293p. reprint ed. pap. 84.40 (*0-7837-3424-7*, 2057745) Bks Demand.

Correctional Supervision Correspondence Course, Bks. I-III. rev. ed. 1993. Set, Bk. 1: Supervision in the 90s, 200p; Bk. 2: Working with Staff, 180p; Bk. 3: Legal Issues, 190p. 65.00 (*0-929310-95-0*, 162) Am Correctional.

Correctional Supervision II Correspondence Course, 3 bks., Set. Alvin W. Cohn. Ed. by Diane Geiman & Denise Flannery. (Orig.). 1990. 60.00 (*0-929310-24-1*, 171) Am Correctional.

***Correctional Supervision II Correspondence Course - Final Test.** rev. ed. Alvin Cohn & D. Crim. Ed. by Diane Geiman & Denise Flannery. 12p. 1994. pap. 38.00 (*1-56991-030-8*) Torah Aura.

Correctional Supervisory Management: Principles of Organization, Policy & Law. William G. Archambeault & Betty J. Archambeault. (Criminal Justice Ser.). (Illus.). 448p. 1981. text ed. 73.00 (*0-13-178269-X*) P-H.

Correctional System: An Introduction. Sue T. Reid. 592p. (C). 1981. text ed. 46.75 (*0-03-042331-7*) HB Coll Pubs.

Correctional Theory & Practice. Ed. by Clayton A. Hartjen & Edward E. Rhine. (Law, Crime, & Justice Ser.). 350p. (C). 1992. pap. text ed. 20.95 (*0-8304-1248-4*) Nelson-Hall.

Correctional Treatment Specialist. Jack Rudman. (Career Examination Ser.: C-959). 1994. pap. 34.95 (*0-8373-0959-X*) Nat Learn.

Corrections. Ed. by Eleanor C. Goldstein. (Resources Ser.). 1995. 38.00 (*0-89777-181-8*) Sirs Inc.

Corrections: An Introduction. Stan Stojkovic & Rick Lovell. LC 91-70609. 667p. (C). 1992. text ed. 39.95 (*0-87084-814-3*) Anderson Pub Co.

Corrections: An Issues Approach. 3rd ed. Lawrence F. Travis, III et al. LC 91-70610. 323p. (C). 1991. pap. text ed. 24.95 (*0-87084-847-X*) Anderson Pub Co.

Corrections: Practice & Policy. David E. Duffee. (Illus.). 550p. (C). 1989. pap. text ed. 32.50 (*0-394-34714-5*) Random.

Corrections: Treatment & Philosophy. Louis P. Carney. (Criminal Justice Ser.). (Illus.). 1980. text ed. 25.95 (*0-685-03806-8*) P-H.

Corrections & Additions to Arsenault's Histoire et Genealogie des Acadiens. Janet B. Jehn. LC 73-153975. 138p. (Orig.). 1988. pap. 21.95 (*0-939444-09-7*) Acadian Genealogy.

Corrections & Additions to the Dictionary of National Biography Cumulated from the Bulletin of the Institute of Historical Research Covering the Years 1923-1963. University of London, Institute of Historical Research Staff. 1970. lib. bdg. 85.00 (*0-8161-0723-8*, Hall Library) G K Hall.

Corrections & Prisoners' Rights, Cases & Materials on the Law of Sentencing. 4th ed. Sheldon Krantz & Lynn S. Branham. (American Casebook Ser.). 619p. 1990. text ed. 43.00 (*0-314-78585-X*) West Pub.

Corrections & Prisoner's Rights in a Nutshell. 3rd ed. Sheldon Krantz. (Nutshell Ser.). 407p. 1991. reprint ed. pap. text ed. 18.50 (*0-314-46561-8*) West Pub.

***Corrections & Prisoners' Rights in a Nutshell.** 4th ed. Lynn S. Branham. (Nutshell Ser.). 338p. (C). 1995. pap. text ed. 17.00 (*0-314-04514-7*) West Pub.

Corrections at the Crossroads: Designing Policy. Ed. by Sherwood E. Zimmerman & Harold D. Miller. LC 80-28847. (Perspectives in Criminal Justice Ser.: No. 1). 176p. reprint ed. pap. 50.20 (*0-8357-8409-6*, 2034680) Bks Demand.

Corrections Directories Series, Set. American Correctional Association Staff. Ed. by Glenda J. Beal. 1800p. (Orig.). Date not set. pap. 200.00 (*0-929310-96-9*) Am Correctional. Four directories with the most up-to-date information available on the corrections field. Names, titles, addresses, phone & fax numbers of key personnel in an easy-to-use format. Includes statistical summaries on number & types of facilities, budgets, capital expenditures & projects, population characteristics & movement, per capita costs, caseloads, programs & services, & staffing & personnel information. 1. 1995 DIRECTORY OF JUVENILE & ADULT CORRECTIONAL DEPARTMENTS, INSTITUTIONS, AGENCIES, & PAROLING AUTHORITIES covers more than 4,000 U.S. & Canadian provincial, state & federal systems. (1-56991-000-6, 625 pages, $75.00). 2. 1993-1995 NATIONAL JAIL & ADULT DETENTION DIRECTORY lists facilities by state & includes information on construction & use of jail & detention center space. Also lists jail inspection officials. (0-929310-58-6, 500 pages, $60.00). 3. 1992-1994 PROBATION & PAROLE DIRECTORY includes more than 1,600 probation & parole commissions, boards & local offices plus more than 1,700 state, district & satellite offices. (0-929310-80-2, 452 pages, $60.00). 4. NATIONAL JUVENILE DETENTION DIRECTORY lists more than 850 facilities by state & includes an alphabetical index of all facilities. (0-929310-69-1, 306 pages, $40.00). ***Publisher Provided Annotation.***

Corrections in America. Harry E. Allen & Clifford E. Simonsen. (Illus.). 768p. (C). 1994. teacher ed write for info. (*0-318-72450-2*) Macmillan.

Corrections in America. 7th ed. Harry E. Allen & Clifford E. Simonsen. (Illus.). 768p. (C). 1995. text ed. write for info. (*0-02-301741-4*) Macmillan.

Corrections in America: An Introduction. 6th ed. Harry E. Allen & Clifford E. Simonsen. (Illus.). 752p. (C). 1992. text ed. write for info. (*0-02-301725-2*) Macmillan.

Corrections in the Community. 2nd ed. George G. Killinger & Paul F. Cromwell, Jr. (Criminal Justice Ser.). 357p. 1978. pap. text ed. 45.50 (*0-8299-0155-8*) West Pub.

Corrections in the United States: A Contemporary Perspective. Dean J. Champion. 560p. 1989. text ed. 62.00 (*0-13-176249-4*) P-H.

Corrections Profession. Harold E. Williamson. (Illus.). 200p. (C). 1990. 39.95 (*0-8039-3848-9*); pap. 18.50 (*0-8039-3849-7*) Sage.

Corrections: State of the Art: Critical Issues, Developments & Concerns. Ed. by Alvin W. Cohn. 94p. (Orig.). (C). 1993. pap. text ed. 40.00 (*1-56806-351-2*) Diane Pub.

Corrections to "Brewington" Notes & Revisions to...Kendall Whaling Museum Paintings. Stuart M. Frank. (Museum Monograph Ser.). 8p. 1988. pap. text ed. 3.00 (*0-937854-27-1*) Kendall Whaling.

Corrections, Vol. 4: (Incl. 1988-1992 Supplements) Ed. by Eleanor C. Goldstein. (Social Issues Resources Ser.). 1993. 95.00 (*0-89777-135-4*) Sirs Inc.

Corrective Action Response Guide for Leaking Underground Storage Tanks. Albert D. Young. 150p. 1990. pap. text ed. 55.00 (*0-86587-209-0*) Gov Insts.

Corrective & Protective Eyewear Markets: New Technologies Alter Marketing Strategies. Market Intelligence Staff. 297p. 1993. 1,695.00 (*1-56753-481-3*) Frost & Sullivan.

Corrective & Reconstructive Rhinoplasty. H. J. Denecke & R. Meyer. Tr. by L. Oxtoby. (Plastic Surgery of Head & Neck Ser.: Vol. 1). (Illus.). 1967. 354.00 (*0-387-03757-8*) Spr-Verlag.

Corrective & Remedial Instruction in Reading. Jack Rudman. (College Proficiency Examination Ser.: CPEP-31). 1994. pap. 23.95 (*0-8373-5431-5*) Nat Learn.

Corrective & Remedial Instruction in Reading. Jack Rudman. (ACT Proficiency Examination Program Ser.: PEP-32). 1994. pap. 23.95 (*0-8373-5532-X*) Nat Learn.

Corrective Haircoloring: A Hands-on Approach. Tom Sollock. LC 92-12759. 1992. text ed. 16.95 (*1-56253-083-6*) Milady Pub.

***Corrective Love: The Power of Communion Discipline.** Thomas C. Oden. LC 95-4150. (Scholarship Today Ser.). 1995. write for info. (*0-570-04803-6*) Concordia.

Corrective Osteotomies of the Lower Extremity after Trauma. Ed. by G. Hierholzer & K. H. Muller. Tr. by Terry C. Telger. (Illus.). 432p. 1985. 133.00 (*0-387-15879-0*) Spr-Verlag.

Corrective Reading. 6th ed. Zelda R. Maggart & Miles V. Zintz. 568p. (C). 1990. pap. write for info. (*0-697-10426-5*) Brown & Benchmark.

***Corrective Reading Techniques for Classroom Teachers.** 3rd ed. Joan P. Gipe. LC 94-31403. 1995. per. 36.00 (*0-89787-537-0*) Gorsuch Scarisbrick.

Corrective Services in New South Wales. Ed. by Bill Cullen et al. xxii, 347p. 1988. pap. 43.00 (*0-455-20781-X*, Pub. by Law Bk Co) W W Gaunt.

Corrective Therapist. Jack Rudman. (Career Examination Ser.: C-960). 1994. pap. 29.95 (*0-8373-0960-3*) Nat Learn.

Corrective Thinking. Lucille Cedercrans. 270p. 1992. student ed 174.95 (*1-883493-04-8*) Wisdom Impress.

Corrective Thinking. Lucille Cedercrans. 600p. 1993. text ed. 49.95 (*1-883493-05-6*); pap. text ed. 16.95 (*1-883493-06-4*); 3.5 hd 24.95 (*1-883493-07-2*) Wisdom Impress.

Corrective Vision: Explorations in Moral Theology. Richard A. McCormick. LC 93-21332. 256p. (Orig.). 1994. pap. 15.95 (*1-55612-601-8*) Sheed & Ward MO.

***Correctness & Effectiveness of English Expression (G. E. D.)** Jack Rudman. (General Aptitude & Abilities Ser.: CS-35). 1994. pap. 17.95 (*0-8373-6735-2*) Nat Learn.

Correctness Problem in Computer Science. Robert S. Boyer & J. Strother Moore. LC 81-67887. (International Lecture Series in Computer Mathematics). 1982. text ed. 92.00 (*0-12-122920-3*) Acad Pr.

Corrector of Destinies: Vol. 3 of Randolph Mason Stories. Melville D. Post. LC 72-150559. (Short Story Index Reprint Ser.). 1977. reprint ed. 20.95 (*0-8369-3856-9*) Ayer.

Correggio. Lucia F. Schianchi. Tr. by Christopher Evans. (Library of Great Masters). (Illus.). 80p. (Orig.). 1994. pap. 12.99 (*1-878351-46-X*) Riverside NY.

Corregidor Tape. Charles Ryan. 416p. (Orig.). 1992. pap. 5.99 (*0-451-40345-2*, Onyx) NAL-Dutton.

Corregidora. Gayl Jones. LC 86-47512. (Black Women Writers Ser.). 185p. 1986. reprint ed. pap. 12.00 (*0-8070-6315-0*, BP727) Beacon Pr.

Correlated Electron Systems: Proceedings of the 9th Jerusalem Winter Schedule for Theoretical Physics, Jerusalem, Israel, Dec. 30, '91-Jan. 8, 1992. V. J. Emery. LC 93-23180. 200p. 1993. text ed. 81.00 (*981-02-1232-1*); pap. text ed. 48.00 (*981-02-1269-0*) World Scientific Pub.

Correlated Interplanetary & Magnetospheric Observations: Proceedings of the ESLAB Symposium, 7th, Saulgau, Germany, May 22-25, 1973. ESLAB-ESRIN Symposium Staff. Ed. by D. E. Page. LC 73-91433. (Astrophysics & Space Science Library: No. 42). 676p. 1974. lib. bdg. 210.00 (*90-277-0429-5*) Kluwer Ac.

Correlates of War I: Research Origins & Rationale. Ed. by David J. Singer. LC 77-18431. 1979. text ed. 35.00 (*0-02-928960-2*) Free Pr.

***Correlating Museum & Exhibition Attendance with Book & Catalog Sales.** Laing Research Services Staff. 105p. 1991. 95.00 (*0-938106-07-4*) Laing Res Servs.

Correlating Sensory Objective Measurements - STP 594. 133p. 1976. pap. 13.00 (*0-8031-0312-3*, 04-594000-36) ASTM.

Correlation Analysis of Chemical Data. Otto Exner. LC 83-60259. (Illus.). 276p. 1988. 75.00 (*0-306-41559-3*, Plenum Pr) Plenum.

Correlation Analysis of Simulated Voltage Responses in Printed Circuit Board Transmission Lines. Don Atkins. LC 92-2341. (Six Sigma Research Institute Ser.). 1992. pap. write for info. (*0-201-63421-X*) Addison-Wesley.

Correlation & Conservation of Forces. Edward L. Youmans. Ed. by I. Bernard Cohen. LC 80-2152. (Development of Science Ser.). (Illus.). 1981. lib. bdg. 44.95 (*0-405-13961-6*) Ayer.

Correlation & Regression Analysis: A Historian's Guide. Thomas J. Archdeacon. LC 92-56927. (Illus.). 374p. (Orig.). (C). 1994. 50.00 (*0-299-13650-7*); pap. text ed. 22.50 (*0-299-13654-X*) U of Wis Pr.

Correlation & Regression in Industrial & Organizational Psychology & Management. Philip Bobko. LC 94-4096. 1994. text ed. write for info. (*0-07-006223-4*) McGraw.

Correlation Between Memory & Perception see Study & Analysis of the Conditional Reflex

Correlation Effects in Low-Dimensional Electron Systems: Proceedings of the 16th Taniguchi Symposium, Kashkojima, Japan, October 25-29, 1993. Ed. by A. Okiji & N. Kawakami. LC 94-8947. (Springer Series in Solid-State Sciences: Vol. 118). 1994. 79.00 (*0-387-57878-1*) Spr-Verlag.

Correlation Equations for Statistical Computations. Aristarkh K. Mitropol'skii. LC 65-25246. 111p. reprint ed. pap. 31.70 (*0-317-30339-2*, 2024712) Bks Demand.

Correlation in Hydrocarbon Exploration. Ed. by John Collinson. (C). 1990. lib. bdg. 219.50 (*1-85333-284-4*, Pub. by Graham & Trotman UK) Kluwer Ac.

Correlation of Behavioral Traits with Specific Property Management Tasks. (Illus.). 101p. 1986. pap. 27.00 (*0-944298-27-3*, 930) Inst Real Estate.

Correlation of Bridge Load Capacity Estimates with Test Data. (National Cooperative Highway Research Program Report Ser.: No. 306). 75p. 1988. 11.20 (*0-309-04603-3*) Transport Res Bd.

Correlation of Destructive Testing of Steel Castings with Stress Analysis & Mechanical Properties: A Summary Report. 1962. 20.00 (*0-686-44994-0*) Steel Founders.

Correlation of Forces: An Analysis of Marxist-Leninist Concepts. Julian Lider. LC 85-27841. 320p. 1986. text ed. 45.00 (*0-312-17004-1*) St Martin.

Correlation of Forces: Four Decades of Soviet Military Development. James H. Hansen. LC 86-30682. 255p. 1987. text ed. 55.00 (*0-275-92657-5*, C2657, Praeger Pubs) Greenwood.

Correlation of Mental & Physical Tests see On Inhibition

Correlation of Subjective-Objective Methods in the Study of Odors & Taste - STP 440. 112p. 1968. pap. 13.00 (*0-8031-0017-5*, 04-440000-36) ASTM.

***Correlation of the Bible & Science.** Edward F. Blick. 50p. (Orig.). 1994. pap. 2.50 (*1-879366-70-3*) Hearthstone OK.

Correlation of the Silurian Rocks of Australia, New Zealand, & New Guinea. John A. Talent et al. LC 74-75784. (Geological Society of America, Special Paper Ser.: No. 150). 138p. reprint ed. pap. 39.40 (*0-317-51969-7*, 2027371) Bks Demand.

Correlation of the Silurian Rocks of China. Mu En-zhi et al. Ed. by A. J. Boucot & W. B. Berry. (Special Paper Ser.: No. 202). (Illus.). 88p. 1985. pap. 2.00 (*0-8137-2202-0*) Geol Soc.

Correlation of the Silurian Rocks of the British Isles. Alfred M. Ziegler et al. LC 74-83052. (Geological Society of America, Special Paper Ser.: No. 154). 166p. reprint ed. pap. 47.40 (*0-685-16457-8*, 2027369) Bks Demand.

Correlation of the West Canyon, Lake Point & Bannock Peak Limestones, Upper Mississippian to Middle Pennsylvanian: Basal Formations of the Oquirrh Group, Northern Utah & Southeastern Idaho. L. E. Davis et al. LC 94-4948. Date not set. write for info. (*0-318-72646-7*) USGPO.

Correlation Theory of Stationary & Related Random Functions II. A. M. Yaglom. (Series in Statistics). (Illus.). 250p. 1987. 64.00 (*0-387-96331-6*) Spr-Verlag.

Correlation Theory of Stationary & Related Random Functions One. A. M. Yaglom. (Series in Statistics). (Illus.). 512p. 1987. 64.00 (*0-387-96268-9*) Spr-Verlag.

Correlations & Connectivity: Geometric Aspects of Physics, Chemistry & Biology. Ed. by H. Eugene Stanley & Nicole Ostrowsky. (C). 1990. lib. bdg. 133.00 (*0-7923-1010-1*); pap. text ed. 58.00 (*0-7923-1011-X*) Kluwer Ac.

Correlations & Entropy in Classical Statistical Mechanics. J. Yvon. 1969. 86.00 (*0-08-012755-X*, Pub. by Pergamon Repr UK) Franklin.

Correlations & Multiparticle Production. Ed. by M. Plumar et al. 480p. (C). 1991. text ed. 147.00 (*981-02-0331-4*) World Scientific Pub.

Correlations & Polarization in Electronic & Atomic Collisions & (E, 2E) Reactions: Satellite Meeting of the XVII ICPEAC. P. J. Teubner & E. Weigold. (Institute of Physics Conference Ser.: No. 122). (Illus.). 360p. 1992. 106.00 (*0-85498-412-7*) IOP Pub.

Correlations Between Ash Compositions from Coal Combustion & Tendencies Toward Slagging, Fouling & Incomplete Combustion. 1984. write for info. (*0-318-57809-3*) Elsevier.

***Correlations Between In Vitro & In Vivo Investigations in Inhalation Toxicology.** Ed. by U. Mohr et al. (Illus.). Date not set. write for info. (*0-944398-47-2*) ILSI.

Correlations in Rosenzweig & Levinas. Robert Gibbs. 312p. 1992. text ed. 39.50 (*0-691-07415-1*) Princeton U Pr.

***Correlations in Rosenzweig & Levinas.** Robert Gibbs. 1994. pap. 16.95 (*0-691-02964-4*) Princeton U Pr.

Correlations of Cosmic & Human Constitutions. G. De Purucker & W. Emmett Small. (Esoteric Teachings Ser.: Vol. IX). 136p. 1987. pap. 7.00 (*0-913004-60-X*) Point Loma Pub.

Correlations, Transformations, & Interactions in Organic Crystal Chemistry. Ed. by D. W. Jones & A. Katrusiak. (IUCr Crystallographic Symposia: Vol. 7). (Illus.). 328p. 1994. bds. 75.00 (*0-19-855826-0*) OUP.

Correlative Atlas of Adult Cardiac Disorders: Noninvasive Diagnostic Techniques. Michael V. Cohen. LC 80-66333. (Illus.). 432p. 1980. 48.50 (*0-87993-149-3*) Futura Pub.

Correlative Brain: Theory & Experiment in Neural Interaction. J. J. Eggermont. (Studies of Brain Function: Vol. 16). (Illus.). xii, 309p. 1990. 173.00 (*0-387-52326-X*) Spr-Verlag.

Correlative Microscopy in Biology: Instruments & Methods. Ed. by M. A. Hayat. 437p. 1987. text ed. 99.00 (*0-12-333922-7*) Acad Pr.

***Correlative Neuroanatomy.** 2nd ed. Waxman. (C). 1994. pap. text ed. 29.95 (*0-8385-1091-4*) Appleton & Lange.

Correlative Neuroanatomy of Computed Tomography & Magnetic Resonance Imaging. J. De Groot. LC 83-22175. 260p. reprint ed. pap. 74.10 (*0-7837-2698-8*, 2043077) Bks Demand.

Correlative Observations in Dementia. John S. Woodward. (Illus.). 110p. (Orig.). 1985. pap. text ed. 14.00 (*0-9615638-0-X*) CA Med Pubns.

Correlative Urinalysis: The Body Knows Best. M. T. Morter, Jr. LC 87-51116. 150p. 1988. 32.00 (*0-944994-00-8*) BEST Research.

An Asterisk (*) at the beginning of an entry indicates that the title is appearing in BIP for the first time.

Correlative Urinalysis: The Body Knows Best. M. T. Morter, Jr. LC 87-51116. 200p. 1988. pap. 32.00 (0-944994-02-4) BEST Research.

Correspondance, 3 vols. Pierre De Beaumarchais. Ed. by Brian N. Morton. 250p. (FRE.). 1969. Vol. 3, 1777. write for info. (0-318-51967-4) Fr & Eur.

Correspondance, 3 vols. Pierre-Augustin C. De Beaumarchais. Ed. by Brian N. Morton. 250p. (FRE.). 1969. pap. 24.95 (0-7859-5280-2); Vol. 1, 1745-1772. pap. 24.95 (0-685-73257-6); Vol. 2, 1773-1776. pap. 24.95 (0-685-73258-4) Fr & Eur.

Correspondance, 2 vols. Jean Du Bellay. 549p. 1969. Vol. 1, 1529-1535. 25.95 (0-7859-0064-0, M1364); Vol. 2, 1535-Dec. 1536.139.95. 39.95 (0-686-56035-3) Fr & Eur.

Correspondance, 3 tomes. Stephane Mallarme. Ed. by Mondor. Incl. Tome I. 1862-1871. 15.95 (0-7859-0022-5, F67220); Tome II. 1871-1885. 15.95 (0-7859-0023-3, F67221); Tome III. 1886-1889. 19.95 (0-7859-0024-1, F67222); (FRE.). write for info. (0-318-51969-0) Fr & Eur.

Correspondance, 17 tomes. Prosper Merimee. Ed. by Parturier. Incl. 1832-1835(FRE.). 1972. pap. 50.00 (0-7859-1522-2, 2708926012); 1836-1840(FRE.). 658p. 1964. pap. 50.00 (0-7859-1523-0, 2708926020); 1844-1846(FRE.). 584p. 1943. pap. 45.00 (0-7859-1524-9, 2708926047); 1847-1849(FRE.). 567p. 1945. pap. 45.00 (0-7859-1525-7, 2708926055); 1850-1852(FRE.). 492p. 1946. pap. 40.00 (0-7859-1526-5, 2708926063); 1853-1855(FRE.). 560p. 1947. pap. 45.00 (0-7859-1527-3, 2708926071); 1856-1858(FRE.). 1964. pap. 50.00 (0-7859-1611-3, 270892608X); 1859-1860(FRE.). 574p. 1955. pap. 45.00 (0-7859-1528-1, 2708926098); 1860-1861(FRE.). 450p. 1961. pap. 35.00 (0-7859-1529-X, 2708926101); 1862-1863(FRE.). 596p. 1962. pap. 45.00 (0-7859-1612-1); 1864-1865(FRE.). 640p. 1964. pap. 52.00 (0-7859-1530-3, 2708926128); 1866-1867(FRE.). 650p. 1958. pap. 55.00 (0-7859-1531-1, 2708926136); 1868-1869(FRE.). 712p. 1960. pap. 60.00 (0-7859-1532-X, 2708926144); 1870(FRE.). 256p. 1960. pap. 25.00 (0-7859-1533-8, 2708926152); Supplement(FRE.). 468p. 1961. pap. 35.00 (0-7859-1534-6, 2708926160); Tome XVII. Supplement, Additions et Corrections, Index et Tables. (FRE.). 538p. 1962. pap. 50.00 (0-685-35900-X, 2708926179); (FRE.). 1964. Set pap. write for info. (0-318-51970-4) Fr & Eur.

Correspondance, 12 vols. Voltaire. Ed. by Besterman. Incl. 1739-174865.95 (2-07-010929-1); Vol. III. 1749-1753. 61.95 (2-07-010807-4); Vol. IV. 1754-1757. 65.05 (2-07-010819-8); 1704-173865.95 (2-07-010928-3); (Pleiade Ser.). 385.00 (0-685-01694-3) Schoenhof.

Correspondance, 3 vols. Marie De Sevigne. Incl. 1646-167573.95 (2-07-010524-5); 1675-1680 deluxe ed. 75.95 (2-07-010525-3); 1680-169678.95 (2-07-010935-6); (Pleiade Ser.). (FRE.). write for info. (0-318-51968-2) Schoenhof.

Correspondance, 3 vols. deluxe ed. Gustave Flaubert. (Pleiade Ser.). 1220p. (FRE.). Vol. 1, 1830-1851. 69.95 (2-07-010667-5); Vol. 2, 1851-1858. 72.95 (2-07-010668-3) Schoenhof.

Correspondance, Vol. 1. Balzac. 851p. 1960. 49.95 (0-8288-7466-2) Fr & Eur.

Correspondance, Vol. 3. Balzac. 927p. 1964. 49.95 (0-8288-7467-0) Fr & Eur.

Correspondance, 3 vols., Vol. 3. deluxe ed. Gustave Flaubert. (Pleiade Ser.). 1220p. (FRE.). 105.95 (2-07-010669-1) Schoenhof.

Correspondance, Vol. 4. Balzac. 930p. 1966. 49.95 (0-8288-7468-9) Fr & Eur.

Correspondance, Vol. 5. Balzac. 1009p. 1969. 49.95 (0-8288-7469-7) Fr & Eur.

Correspondance: Annees 1521-1522, Vol. 1. Marguerite d'Angouleme. Ed. by Guillaume Briconnet et al. 238p. (FRE.). 1975. pap. 49.95 (0-7859-5530-5) Fr & Eur.

Correspondance: Janvier 1832-Fevrier 1860, Vol. 1. deluxe ed. Charles Baudelaire. (Pleiade Ser.). (FRE.). 1973. 63.95 (2-07-010782-5) Schoenhof.

Correspondance: Mars 1860-Mars 1866, Vol. 2. deluxe ed. Charles Baudelaire. (Pleiade Ser.). (FRE.). 1973. 63.95 (2-07-010783-3) Schoenhof.

***Correspondance Vol. IV: 1527-1529, Publie Par C. Krieger et J. Rott.** Martin Bucer. (Studies in Medieval & Reformation Thought: No.56). 480p. 1995. 139.50 (90-04-10369-4) E J Brill.

Correspondance, Andre Gide-Francois Mauriac, 1912-1950. Andre Gide & Francois Mauriac. 280p. (FRE.). 1971. 55.00 (0-8288-9782-4, F103041) Fr & Eur.

Correspondance avec Andre Gide: 1899-1926. Paul Claudel. 400p. (FRE.). 1949. pap. 10.95 (0-7859-1128-6, 2070215326) Fr & Eur.

Correspondance avec Andre Rouveyre (1909-1951) Andre Gide. 288p. (FRE.). 1967. pap. 36.95 (0-7859-5301-9) Fr & Eur.

Correspondance avec Andre Suares: 1904-1938. Paul Claudel. 272p. (FRE.). 1951. pap. 10.95 (0-7859-1129-4, 2070215334) Fr & Eur.

Correspondance avec Arnauld et Morus. 190p. (FRE & LAT.). 1953. pap. 32.95 (0-7859-5494-5, 271160179X) Fr & Eur.

***Correspondance avec Arnold Bennett, Vingt Ans d'Amitie Litteraire (1911-1931)** Andre Gide. (Textes Litteraires Francais Ser.). 224p. 1964. pap. 24.95 (0-7859-5261-6) Fr & Eur.

Correspondance avec Elisabeth, et Autres Lettres. Rene Descartes. Ed. by Beysade. (FRE.). 1989. pap. 12.95 (0-7859-3400-6) Fr & Eur.

Correspondance avec Francis Jammes et Gabriel Frizeau: 1897-1938. Paul Claudel. 468p. (FRE.). 1952. pap. 10.95 (0-7859-1130-8, 2070215342) Fr & Eur.

Correspondance avec Francis Jammes (1893-1938) Andre Gide. (FRE.). 6.95 (0-8288-9776-X, F10253) Fr & Eur.

Correspondance avec Francois Mauriac (1912-1951) Andre Gide. 15.75 (0-685-34137-2) Fr & Eur.

Correspondance avec G. Fourment 1887-1933. Paul Valery. 272p. (FRE.). 1957. pap. 11.95 (0-7859-1284-3, 2070224880) Fr & Eur.

Correspondance Avec Gaston Gallimard. Marcel Proust. (Gallimard Ser.). (FRE.). pap. 49.95 (2-07-071629-5) Schoenhof.

Correspondance avec les Tronchin: Edition Critique. Francois-Marie de Voltaire. Ed. by Andre Delattre. 720p. (FRE.). 1950. pap. 85.00 (0-7859-5510-0) Fr & Eur.

Correspondance avec Paul Valery (1890-1942) Andre Gide. 560p. (FRE.). 1942. pap. 39.95 (0-7859-4590-3) Fr & Eur.

Correspondance avec Roger Martin du Gard (1913-1951), 2 tomes, Set. Andre Gide. 744p. (FRE.). 1968. pap. 36.95 (0-7859-4589-X) Fr & Eur.

Correspondance avec Roger Martin du Gard (1913-1951), Vol. 1: 1913-1934. 192p. 1944. 11.95 (0-7859-4592-X) Fr & Eur.

Correspondance avec Sa Mere. Marcel Proust. (FRE.). 1992. pap. 16.95 (0-7859-3205-4, 2264017929) Fr & Eur.

Correspondance (Avril 1622-Fevrier 1638) see Oeuvres

Correspondance Choisie. Francois-Marie de Voltaire. (FRE.). 1990. pap. 32.95 (0-7859-3157-0, 2253054437) Fr & Eur.

Correspondance Commerciale en Espagnol. E. Jimenez & Martin Juarrero. 254p. (FRE & SPA.). 1988. pap. 39.95 (0-8288-0994-1, F 14580) Fr & Eur.

Correspondance Complete de Diderot, 16 vols. Denis Diderot. Incl. Vol. 1. 1713-1757. 1970. pap. 24.95 (0-8288-9582-1); Vol. 3. 1759-1761. 1970. pap. 24.95 (0-8288-9584-8); Vol. 5. 1765-1766. 1958. pap. 24.95 (0-8288-9586-4, 2707304409); Vol. 6. 1766. 1970. pap. 24.95 (0-8288-9587-2); Vol. 7. 1767. 1970. pap. 24.95 (0-8288-9588-0); Vol. 8. 1768. 1970. pap. 24.95 (0-8288-9589-9); Vol. 9. 1769. 1970. pap. 24.95 (0-8288-9590-2); Vol. 10. 1770-1771. 1970. pap. 24.95 (0-8288-9591-0); Vol. 11. 1771. 1970. pap. 24.95 (0-8288-9592-9); Vol. 12. 1771-1772. 1970. pap. 24.95 (0-8288-9593-7); Vol. 13. 1773-1774. 1970. pap. 24.95 (0-8288-9594-5); Vol. 15. 1776-1784. 1970. pap. 24.95 (0-8288-9596-1); Vol. 16. Complement, Corrections, Listes et Index General. 1970. pap. 24.95 (0-8288-9597-X); (FRE.). 1970. Set pap. write for info. (0-318-51971-2) Fr & Eur.

Correspondance Complete de Diderot, Vol. 14: 1774-1776. Denis Diderot. 276p. (FRE.). 1968. pap. 24.95 (0-7859-5255-1, 2707304492) Fr & Eur.

Correspondance Complete de Diderot, Vol. 2: 1757-1759. 348p. (FRE.). 1956. pap. 24.95 (0-7859-5252-7, 2707304379) Fr & Eur.

Correspondance Complete de Diderot, Vol. 4: 1762-1764. Denis Diderot. (FRE.). 1958. pap. 24.95 (0-7859-5253-5, 2707304395) Fr & Eur.

Correspondance Complete de Diderot, Vol. 5: 1765-1766. Denis Diderot. 272p. (FRE.). 1958. pap. 24.95 (0-7859-5254-3, 2707304409) Fr & Eur.

Correspondance de Martin Bucer Tome II (1524-1526) Ed. by Jean Rott. (Studies in Medieval & Reformation Thought: No. 43). (Illus.). (FRE & LAT.). (C). 1989. text ed. 74.50 (90-04-08636-6) E J Brill.

Correspondance de Napoleon Ier; Publiee par Ordre de l'empereur Napoleon III, 32 vols., 26. Napoleon I. Incl. Set. 3,060.00 (0-404-07400-6); 40.00 (0-685-73117-0); 1. 95.65 (0-404-07401-4); 2. 95.65 (0-404-07402-2); 3. 95.65 (0-404-07403-0); 4. 95.65 (0-404-07404-9); 5. 95.65 (0-404-07405-7); 6. 95.65 (0-404-07406-5); 7. 95.65 (0-404-07407-3); 8. 95.65 (0-404-07408-1); 9. 95.65 (0-404-07409-X); 10. 95.65 (0-404-07410-3); 11. 95.65 (0-404-07411-1); 12. 95.65 (0-404-07412-X); 13. 95.65 (0-404-07413-8); 14. 95.65 (0-404-07414-6); 15. 95.65 (0-404-07415-4); 16. 95.65 (0-404-07416-2); 17. 95.65 (0-404-07417-0); 18. 95.65 (0-404-07418-9); 19. 95.65 (0-404-07419-7); 20. 95.65 (0-404-07420-0); 21. 95.65 (0-404-07421-9); 22. 95.65 (0-404-07422-7); 23. 95.65 (0-404-07423-5); 24. 95.65 (0-404-07424-3); 25. 95.65 (0-404-07425-1); reprint ed. 95.65 (0-404-07426-X) AMS Pr.

Correspondance de Napoleon Ier; Publiee par Ordre de l'empereur Napoleon III, 32 vols., 27. Napoleon I. Incl. Set. 3,060.00 (0-404-07400-6); 40.00 (0-685-73117-0); 1. 95.65 (0-404-07401-4); 2. 95.65 (0-404-07402-2); 3. 95.65 (0-404-07403-0); 4. 95.65 (0-404-07404-9); 5. 95.65 (0-404-07405-7); 6. 95.65 (0-404-07406-5); 7. 95.65 (0-404-07407-3); 8. 95.65 (0-404-07408-1); 9. 95.65 (0-404-07409-X); 10. 95.65 (0-404-07410-3); 11. 95.65 (0-404-07411-1); 12. 95.65 (0-404-07412-X); 13. 95.65 (0-404-07413-8); 14. 95.65 (0-404-07414-6); 15. 95.65 (0-404-07415-4); 16. 95.65 (0-404-07416-2); 17. 95.65 (0-404-07417-0); 18. 95.65 (0-404-07418-9); 19. 95.65 (0-404-07419-7); 20. 95.65 (0-404-07420-0); 21. 95.65 (0-404-07421-9); 22. 95.65 (0-404-07422-7); 23. 95.65 (0-404-07423-5); 24. 95.65 (0-404-07424-3); 25. 95.65 (0-404-07425-1); reprint ed. 95.65 (0-404-07427-8) AMS Pr.

Correspondance de Napoleon Ier; Publiee par Ordre de l'empereur Napoleon III, 32 vols., 28. Napoleon I. Incl. Set. 3,060.00 (0-404-07400-6); 40.00 (0-685-73117-0); 1. 95.65 (0-404-07401-4); 2. 95.65 (0-404-07402-2); 3. 95.65 (0-404-07403-0); 4. 95.65 (0-404-07404-9); 5. 95.65 (0-404-07405-7); 6. 95.65 (0-404-07406-5); 7. 95.65 (0-404-07407-3); 8. 95.65 (0-404-07408-1); 9. 95.65 (0-404-07409-X); 10. 95.65 (0-404-07410-3); 11. 95.65 (0-404-07411-1); 12. 95.65 (0-404-07412-X); 13. 95.65 (0-404-07413-8); 14. 95.65 (0-404-07414-6); 15. 95.65 (0-404-07415-4); 16. 95.65 (0-404-07416-2); 17. 95.65 (0-404-07417-0); 18. 95.65 (0-404-07418-9); 19. 95.65 (0-404-07419-7); 20. 95.65 (0-404-07420-0); 21. 95.65 (0-404-07421-9); 22. 95.65 (0-404-07422-7); 23. 95.65 (0-404-07423-5); 24. 95.65 (0-404-07424-3); 25. 95.65 (0-404-07425-1); reprint ed. 95.65 (0-404-07428-6) AMS Pr.

Correspondance de Napoleon Ier; Publiee par Ordre de l'empereur Napoleon III, 32 vols., 29. Napoleon I. Incl. Set. 3,060.00 (0-404-07400-6); 40.00 (0-685-73117-0); 1. 95.65 (0-404-07401-4); 2. 95.65 (0-404-07402-2); 3. 95.65 (0-404-07403-0); 4. 95.65 (0-404-07404-9); 5. 95.65 (0-404-07405-7); 6. 95.65 (0-404-07406-5); 7. 95.65 (0-404-07407-3); 8. 95.65 (0-404-07408-1); 9. 95.65 (0-404-07409-X); 10. 95.65 (0-404-07410-3); 11. 95.65 (0-404-07411-1); 12. 95.65 (0-404-07412-X); 13. 95.65 (0-404-07413-8); 14. 95.65 (0-404-07414-6); 15. 95.65 (0-404-07415-4); 16. 95.65 (0-404-07416-2); 17. 95.65 (0-404-07417-0); 18. 95.65 (0-404-07418-9); 19. 95.65 (0-404-07419-7); 20. 95.65 (0-404-07420-0); 21. 95.65 (0-404-07421-9); 22. 95.65 (0-404-07422-7); 23. 95.65 (0-404-07423-5); 24. 95.65 (0-404-07424-3); 25. 95.65 (0-404-07425-1); reprint ed. 95.65 (0-404-07429-4) AMS Pr.

Correspondance de Napoleon Ier; Publiee par Ordre de l'empereur Napoleon III, 32 vols., 30. Napoleon I. Incl. Set. 3,060.00 (0-404-07400-6); 40.00 (0-685-73117-0); 1. 95.65 (0-404-07401-4); 2. 95.65 (0-404-07402-2); 3. 95.65 (0-404-07403-0); 4. 95.65 (0-404-07404-9); 5. 95.65 (0-404-07405-7); 6. 95.65 (0-404-07406-5); 7. 95.65 (0-404-07407-3); 8. 95.65 (0-404-07408-1); 9. 95.65 (0-404-07409-X); 10. 95.65 (0-404-07410-3); 11. 95.65 (0-404-07411-1); 12. 95.65 (0-404-07412-X); 13. 95.65 (0-404-07413-8); 14. 95.65 (0-404-07414-6); 15. 95.65 (0-404-07415-4); 16. 95.65 (0-404-07416-2); 17. 95.65 (0-404-07417-0); 18. 95.65 (0-404-07418-9); 19. 95.65 (0-404-07419-7); 20. 95.65 (0-404-07420-0); 21. 95.65 (0-404-07421-9); 22. 95.65 (0-404-07422-7); 23. 95.65 (0-404-07423-5); 24. 95.65 (0-404-07424-3); 25. 95.65 (0-404-07425-1); reprint ed. 95.65 (0-404-07430-8) AMS Pr.

Correspondance de Napoleon Ier; Publiee par Ordre de l'empereur Napoleon III, 32 vols., 31. Napoleon I. Incl. Set. 3,060.00 (0-404-07400-6); 40.00 (0-685-73117-0); 1. 95.65 (0-404-07401-4); 2. 95.65 (0-404-07402-2); 3. 95.65 (0-404-07403-0); 4. 95.65 (0-404-07404-9); 5. 95.65 (0-404-07405-7); 6. 95.65 (0-404-07406-5); 7. 95.65 (0-404-07407-3); 8. 95.65 (0-404-07408-1); 9. 95.65 (0-404-07409-X); 10. 95.65 (0-404-07410-3); 11. 95.65 (0-404-07411-1); 12. 95.65 (0-404-07412-X); 13. 95.65 (0-404-07413-8); 14. 95.65 (0-404-07414-6); 15. 95.65 (0-404-07415-4); 16. 95.65 (0-404-07416-2); 17. 95.65 (0-404-07417-0); 18. 95.65 (0-404-07418-9); 19. 95.65 (0-404-07419-7); 20. 95.65 (0-404-07420-0); 21. 95.65 (0-404-07421-9); 22. 95.65 (0-404-07422-7); 23. 95.65 (0-404-07423-5); 24. 95.65 (0-404-07424-3); 25. 95.65 (0-404-07425-1); reprint ed. 95.65 (0-404-07431-6) AMS Pr.

Correspondance de Napoleon Ier; Publiee par Ordre de l'empereur Napoleon III, 32 vols., 32. Napoleon I. Incl. Set. 3,060.00 (0-404-07400-6); 40.00 (0-685-73117-0); 1. 95.65 (0-404-07401-4); 2. 95.65 (0-404-07402-2); 3. 95.65 (0-404-07403-0); 4. 95.65 (0-404-07404-9); 5. 95.65 (0-404-07405-7); 6. 95.65 (0-404-07406-5); 7. 95.65 (0-404-07407-3); 8. 95.65 (0-404-07408-1); 9. 95.65 (0-404-07409-X); 10. 95.65 (0-404-07410-3); 11. 95.65 (0-404-07411-1); 12. 95.65 (0-404-07412-X); 13. 95.65 (0-404-07413-8); 14. 95.65 (0-404-07414-6); 15. 95.65 (0-404-07415-4); 16. 95.65 (0-404-07416-2); 17. 95.65 (0-404-07417-0); 18. 95.65 (0-404-07418-9); 19. 95.65 (0-404-07419-7); 20. 95.65 (0-404-07420-0); 21. 95.65 (0-404-07421-9); 22. 95.65 (0-404-07422-7); 23. 95.65 (0-404-07423-5); 24. 95.65 (0-404-07424-3); 25. 95.65 (0-404-07425-1); reprint ed. 95.65 (0-404-07432-4) AMS Pr.

Correspondance de Napoleon Ier, Supplement: Lettres Curieuses Omises par le Comite de Publication, Rectifications. Napoleon First. LC 77-173013. 1975. reprint ed. 96.00 (0-404-07148-1) AMS Pr.

Correspondance D'Erasme, 12 vols., Set. Desiderius Erasmus. Ed. by Alois Gerlo et al. 7427p. (FRE.). 1982. text ed. 995.00 (0-317-55851-X, Pub. by B De Graaf NE) Coronet Bks.

Correspondance Diplomatique de Bertrand de Salignac de la Mothe-Fenelon, 7 vol. set. Bertrand D. Fenelon. LC 73-168014. (Bannatyne Club, Edinburgh. Publications: No. 67). reprint ed. 345.00 (0-404-52780-9) AMS Pr.

Correspondance Generale, 9 tomes. George Sand, pseud. Ed. by Georges Lubin. Incl. 1812-1831pap. 24.50 (0-685-34977-2); Juin 1832-Juin 1835pap. 24.50 (0-685-34978-0); Juillet 1835-Avril 1837pap. 24.50 (0-685-34979-9); Mai 1837-Mars 1840pap. 24.50 (0-685-34980-2); Avril 1840-Decembre 1842pap. 24.50 (0-685-34981-0); 1843-Juin 1845pap. 25.95 (0-685-34982-9); Juillet 1845-Juillet 1847pap. 22.95 (0-685-34983-7); Juillet 1847-Decembre 1848pap. 22.95 (0-685-34984-5); 1849-1850pap. 29.95 (0-685-34985-3); (Class. Garnier Ser.). Set pap. write for info. (0-318-51973-9); Incl. pap. 24.50 (0-685-34977-2); pap. 24.50 (0-685-34978-0); pap. 24.50 (0-685-34979-9); pap. 24.50 (0-685-34980-2); pap. 24.50 (0-685-34981-0); pap. 25.95 (0-685-34982-9); pap. 22.95 (0-685-34983-7); pap. 22.95 (0-685-34984-5); pap. 29.95 (0-685-34985-3); write for info. (0-318-51974-7) Fr & Eur.

Correspondance Generale, 3 tomes. Madame De Stael. Ed. by Jasinski. Incl. Tome I, Pt. 1. Lettres de Jeunesse de 1777 a Aout 1788. 20.95 (0-8288-9660-7, F73290); Tome I, Pt. 2. 1788-1791. 20.95 (0-8288-9661-5, F73291); Tome II, Pt. 1. Lettres Inedites a Louis de Norbonne. 26.95 (0-8288-9662-3, F73292); Tome II, Pt. 2. Lettres Diverses de 1792 a Mai 1794. 31.95 (0-8288-9663-1, F73293); Tome III, Pt. 1. Lettres de Mezery et de Coppet (16 Mai 1794-16 Mai 1795) 27.95 (0-8288-9664-X, F73294); Tome III, Pt. 2. Lettres d'une Nouvelle Republicaine. 39.95 (0-8288-9665-8, F73295); write for info. (0-318-51972-0) Fr & Eur.

Correspondance Generale, 2 vols. Auguste de Villiers De L'Isle Adam. 620p. (FRE.). 1962. pap. 59.95 (0-7859-5502-X) Fr & Eur.

Correspondance Generale: 1789-1807, Vol. 1. Rene de Chateaubriand et al. 682p. (FRE.). 1977. 89.95 (0-7859-1141-3, 2070291154) Fr & Eur.

Correspondance generale d'Helvetius, Vol. I: 1737-1756 - Lettres 1-249. David Smith et al. (Romance Ser.). 361p. 1981. 60.00 (0-8020-5517-6) U of Toronto Pr.

Correspondance (Janvier 1640-Juin 1643) see Oeuvres

Correspondance (Juillet 1643-Avril 1647) see Oeuvres

Correspondance (Mai 1647 - Fevrier 1650) see Oeuvres

Correspondance (Mars 1638 - Decembre 1639) see Oeuvres

Correspondance, Vol. 1: 1904-1939. 570p. (FRE.). 1971. pap. 16.95 (0-7859-4885-6) Fr & Eur.

Correspondance, Vol. 2: 1773-1776. Pierre de Beaumarchais. 282p. (FRE.). 1970. pap. 24.95 (0-7859-6522-X) Fr & Eur.

Correspondance, Vol. 3: 1777. Pierre de Beaumarchais. 256p. (FRE.). 1972. pap. 24.95 (0-7859-6523-8) Fr & Eur.

Correspondance, Vol. 4: 1778. Pierre de Beaumarchais. 334p. (FRE.). 1978. pap. 36.95 (0-7859-6524-6) Fr & Eur.

Correspondance 1812-1831, Vol. 1. George Sand. 1093p. 1964. 19.95 (0-8288-7482-4) Fr & Eur.

Correspondance 1827-1857. Alfred De Musset. 293p. (FRE.). 1977. 89.95 (0-7859-5489-9) Fr & Eur.

Correspondance 1827-1857. Alfred De Musset. 300p. reprint ed. 25.00 (0-686-55545-7) Fr & Eur.

Correspondance, 1851-1852, Vol. 10. George Sand. Ed. by Georges Lubin. (Illus.). 992p. (FRE.). 1974. pap. 75.00 (0-7859-5394-9) Fr & Eur.

Correspondance 1888-1891. Arthur Rimbaud. 228p. (FRE.). 1965. pap. 18.95 (0-7859-1303-3, 2070254364) Fr & Eur.

Correspondance 1891-1938. Andre Gide et al. 351p. (FRE.). 1975. pap. 59.95 (0-7859-5528-3) Fr & Eur.

Correspondance 1897-1944, 2 vols., Vol. 1. Andre Gide et al. 1064p. (FRE.). 1976. 75.00 (0-7859-1143-X, 2070293947) Fr & Eur.

Correspondance 1914-1922. Marcel Proust & Jacques Riviere. Ed. by Phillip Kolb. 353p. (FRE.). 1976. pap. 18.95 (0-7859-1594-X, 207029420X) Fr & Eur.

Correspondance 1916-1942. Francois Mauriac & Jacques-Emile Blanche. Ed. by Georges-Paul Collet. 256p. (FRE.). 1976. 13.95 (0-7859-0108-6, M3746) Fr & Eur.

Correspondance, 1936-1959. Jules Supervielle et al. 196p. 1969. 9.95 (0-686-55091-9) Fr & Eur.

Correspondances a l'exception Ides Lettres de Mme. Hanska, 5 vols. Honore De Balzac. Ed. by Pierrot. Tome 1, (1809-Mai 1832. write for info. (0-8288-9326-8); Tome 2, (juin 1832-1835. write for info. (0-8288-9327-6); Tome 3, (1836-1837). write for info. (0-8288-9328-4); Tome 4,(1840-Avril 1845). write for info. (0-8288-9329-2); Tome 5, (mai 1845-1850). write for info. (0-8288-9330-6) Fr & Eur.

Correspondances a l'exception Ides Lettres de Mme. Hanska, 5 vols., Set. Honore De Balzac. Ed. by Pierrot. pap. 65.00 (0-685-57707-4) Fr & Eur.

Correspondances de Howe sur un Corps P-adique. C. Moeglin et al. (Lecture Notes in Mathematics Ser.: Vol. 1291). vii, 163p. 1987. pap. 35.30 (0-387-18699-9) Spr-Verlag.

Correspondant & the Founding of the French Third Republic. Caroline A. Gimpl. LC 74-5773. 239p. 1974. reprint ed. text ed. 52.50 (0-8371-7517-8, GITR, Greenwood Pr) Greenwood.

Correspondence. Jerry Belch. Ed. by Valerie Harris. (Simulating the Medical Office). 92p. 1993. Correspondence, 92p. 7.98 (0-89262-314-4) Career Pub.

Correspondence. Frederic. Ed. by G. E. Fortenberry et al. LC 76-3562. (Harold Frederic Edition Ser.: Vol. 1). (Illus.). xxvi, 615p. 1977. 40.00 (0-912646-15-2) U of Nebr Pr.

Correspondence. Herman Melville. Ed. by Lynn Horth. (Northwestern-Newberry Edition of the Writings of Herman Melville: Vol. 14). (Illus.). 924p. (Orig.). 1993. 89.95 (0-8101-0981-6); pap. 29.95 (0-8101-0995-6) Northwestern U Pr.

An Asterisk (*) at the beginning of an entry indicates that the title is appearing in BIP for the first time.

Correspondence, 4 vols. Isaac Newton. Ed. by H. W. Turnbull & J. F. Scott. 1967. 74.50 (*0-685-42030-2*) Cambridge U Pr.

Correspondence. Evelin Sullivan. LC 93-18194. 336p. 1993. 20.00 (*0-88064-143-6*) Fromm Intl Pub.

Correspondence. Sue Thomas. LC 92-24591. 1993. 19.95 (*0-87951-480-9*) Overlook Pr.

Correspondence. Sue Thomas. 160p. 1994. pap. 10.95 (*0-87951-529-5*) Overlook Pr.

Correspondence, 5 vols. Walt Whitman. Ed. by Edwin H. Miller. Incl. Vol. 4. 1886-1889. LC 60-15980. 458p. 1969. 125.00 (*0-8147-0438-7*); Vol. 5. 1890-1892. 365p. 1969. 125.00 (*0-8147-0439-5*); LC 60-15980. (Illus.). 50.00 (*0-685-03615-4*) NYU Pr.

Correspondence, 2 vols. in 1. Richard Bentley. Ed. by C. Wordsworth. (Anglistica & Americana Ser.: No. 93). xxxii, 838p. 1977. reprint ed. 128.70 (*3-487-06320-4*, Pub. by Georg Olms GW) Lubrecht & Cramer.

Correspondence. John C. Calhoun. (Works of John Calswell Calhoun Ser.). 1990. reprint ed. lib. bdg. 79.00 (*0-7812-2241-9*) Rprt Serv.

Correspondence, 2 vols., 1. Fronto. (Loeb Classical Library: No. 112-113). 378p. 1920. 18.95 (*0-674-99124-9*) HUP.

Correspondence, 8 Vols., 1. Voltaire. Ed. by Theodore Besterman. 1978. lib. bdg. 125.00 (*0-7859-3838-9*) Fr & Eur.

Correspondence, 2 vols., 2. Fronto. (Loeb Classical Library: No. 112-113). 15.50 (*0-674-99125-7*) HUP.

Correspondence, 8 Vols., 2. Voltaire. Ed. by Theodore Besterman. 1978. lib. bdg. 125.00 (*0-7859-3839-7*) Fr & Eur.

Correspondence, 4 vols., 4. Isaac Newton. Ed. by H. W. Turnbull & J. F. Scott. 1967. 79.95 (*0-521-05815-5*) Cambridge U Pr.

Correspondence, 2 vols, Set. Robert Kerr. LC 78-171062. (Bannatyne Club, Edinburgh. Publications). reprint ed. 62.00 (*0-404-52896-1*) AMS Pr.

Correspondence, Vol. 5, 1758-1760. Voltaire. Ed. by Theodore Besterman. 1978. lib. bdg. 125.00 (*0-7859-3847-8*) Fr & Eur.

Correspondence, Vol. 6, 1760-1762. Voltaire. Ed. by Theodore Besterman. 1978. lib. bdg. 125.00 (*0-7859-3850-8*) Fr & Eur.

Correspondence, Vol. 7, 1763-1765. Voltaire. Ed. by Theodore Besterman. 1978. lib. bdg. 125.00 (*0-7859-3853-2*) Fr & Eur.

Correspondence, 8 Vols., Vol. 8, 1765-1767. Voltaire. Ed. by Theodore Besterman. 1978. lib. bdg. 125.00 (*0-7859-3856-7*) Fr & Eur.

***Correspondence: Italian Poetry.** Gianni Diecidue. 54p. 1988. pap. 7.50 (*0-89304-666-3*) Cross-Cultrl NY.

Correspondence: The Berlin & Jena Years (1764-1802), Schlegel Translations, Vol. 3. Dorothea M. Schlegel. Tr. by Edwina Lawler & Ruth Richardson. 1987. write for info. (*0-88946-366-2*) E Mellen.

Correspondence: With an Account of His Life & Work. John Owen. Ed. by Peter Toon. 215p. 1970. 14.00 (*0-227-67746-3*) Attic Pr.

Correspondence: 1821-1836, Vol. 1. Charles Darwin. Ed. by Frederick Burkhardt & Sydney Smith. 672p. 1985. 59.95 (*0-521-25587-2*) Cambridge U Pr.

Correspondence: 1837-1843, Vol. 2. Charles Darwin. Ed. by Frederick Burkhardt & Sydney Smith. 1987. 59.95 (*0-521-25588-0*) Cambridge U Pr.

Correspondence: 1843-1846, Vol. 3. Charles Darwin. Ed. by Frederick Burkhardt & Sydney Smith. 550p. 1988. 59.95 (*0-521-25589-9*) Cambridge U Pr.

Correspondence: 1847-1850, Vol. 4. Charles Darwin. Ed. by Frederick Burkhardt & Sydney Smith. (Illus.). 500p. 1989. 59.95 (*0-521-25590-2*) Cambridge U Pr.

Correspondence: 1851-1855, Vol. 5. Charles Darwin. Ed. by Frederick Burkhardt & Sydney Smith. (Illus.). (C). 1990. 59.95 (*0-521-25591-0*) Cambridge U Pr.

Correspondence: 1856-1857, Vol. 6. Charles Darwin. Ed. by Frederick Burkhardt & Sydney Smith. 1990. 59.95 (*0-521-25586-4*) Cambridge U Pr.

Correspondence: 1858-1859, Vol. 7. Charles Darwin. Ed. by Frederick Burkhardt & Sydney Smith. (Illus.). 700p. (C). 1992. 59.95 (*0-521-38564-4*) Cambridge U Pr.

Correspondence: 1861, Vol. 9. Charles Darwin. Ed. by Frederick Burkhardt et al. (Illus.). 700p. (C). 1994. 59.95 (*0-521-45156-6*) Cambridge U Pr.

Correspondence: 1862, Vol. 8. Charles Darwin. Ed. by Frederick Burkhardt et al. (Illus.). 800p. (C). 1993. 59.95 (*0-521-44241-9*) Cambridge U Pr.

Correspondence Across a Room. V. I. Ivanov & M. O. Gershenzon. Tr. by Lisa Sergio. LC 84-60879. 96p. 1984. pap. 7.25 (*0-910395-11-X*) Marlboro Pr.

Correspondence Analysis Handbook. Ed. by Benzecri & Gopalan. (Statistics Ser.: Vol. 125). 688p. 1992. 150.00 (*0-8247-8437-5*) Dekker.

Correspondence Analysis in Practice. Michael Greenacre. (Illus.). 195p. 1993. pap. text ed. 39.95 (*0-12-299052-8*) Acad Pr.

Correspondence Analysis in the Social Sciences. Michael Greenacre & Jorg Blasius. 392p. 1994. text ed. 67.50 (*0-12-104570-6*) Acad Pr.

Correspondence & Conversations of Alexis de Tocqueville with Nassau W. Senior from 1834 to 1859, 2 vols. in 1. 2nd ed. Alexis De Tocqueville. Ed. by M. C. Simpson. LC 68-30544. 1968. reprint ed. 57.50 (*0-678-00444-7*) Kelley.

Correspondence & Disquotation: An Essay on the Nature of Truth. Marian A. David. 224p. 1994. 35.00 (*0-19-507924-8*) OUP.

Correspondence & Documents, 1901-1925. Rudolf Steiner & Marie Steiner Von Sivers. Ed. by Joan M. Thompson. Tr. by Christian Von Arnim & Ingrid Von Arnim. 342p. (Orig.). 1988. 35.00 (*0-88010-208-X*); pap. 25.00 (*0-88010-207-1*) Anthroposophic.

Correspondence & Journals of Captain Nathaniel J. Wyeth, 1831-6. Ed. by Frank G. Young. LC 72-9474. (Far Western Frontier Ser.). (Illus.). 288p. 1973. reprint ed. 25.95 (*0-405-05001-1*) Ayer.

Correspondence & Journals of Samuel Blachley Webb, 3 Vols, 1. Samuel B. Webb. Ed. by Worthington Ford. LC 78-79947. (Eyewitness Accounts of the American Revolution Ser., No. 1). 1969. reprint ed. 31.95 (*0-405-01154-7*) Ayer.

Correspondence & Journals of Samuel Blachley Webb, 3 Vols, 2. Samuel B. Webb. Ed. by Worthington Ford. LC 78-79947. (Eyewitness Accounts of the American Revolution Ser., No. 1). 1969. reprint ed. 31.95 (*0-405-01155-5*) Ayer.

Correspondence & Journals of Samuel Blachley Webb, 3 Vols, 3. Samuel B. Webb. Ed. by Worthington Ford. LC 78-79947. (Eyewitness Accounts of the American Revolution Ser., No. 1). 1969. reprint ed. 31.95 (*0-405-01156-3*) Ayer.

Correspondence & Journals of Samuel Blachley Webb, 3 Vols, Set. Samuel B. Webb. Ed. by Worthington Ford. LC 78-79947. (Eyewitness Accounts of the American Revolution Ser., No. 1). 1969. reprint ed. 93.95 (*0-405-01153-9*) Ayer.

Correspondence & Minutes of the SPCK Relating to Wales. Ed. by Mary Clement. xi, 369p. 1952. 28.50 (*0-7083-0109-6*, Pub. by U of Wales UK) Bks Intl VA.

Correspondence & Miscellaneous Papers of Benjamin Henry Latrobe. Benjamin H. Latrobe. Ed. by John C. Van Horne & Lee W. Formwalt. LC 83-27423. (Series No. IV: Vol. I). (Illus.). 640p. 1985. text ed. 80.00 (*0-300-02901-2*) Yale U Pr.

Correspondence & Miscellaneous Papers of Benjamin Henry Latrobe, Vol. 3. Benjamin H. Latrobe. LC 83-27423. 1024p. (C). 1988. text ed. 140.00 (*0-300-03521-7*) Yale U Pr.

Correspondence & Miscellaneous Papers of Benjamin Henry Latrobe: 1805-1810, Ser. IV, Vol. II. Benjamin H. Latrobe. Ed. by John C. Van Horne et al. LC 83-27423. (Papers of Benjamin Henry Latrobe). 1018p. 1987. text ed. 95.00 (*0-300-03229-3*) Yale U Pr.

Correspondence & Papers of Edmond Halley. Edmond Halley. LC 74-26268. (History, Philosophy & Sociology of Science Ser.). 1975. reprint ed. 33.95 (*0-405-06596-5*) Ayer.

Correspondence & Public Papers, 4 vols. in 1, Set. John Jay. (American Biography Ser.). 1991. reprint ed. lib. bdg. 99.00 (*0-7812-8215-2*) Rprt Serv.

Correspondence & Public Papers of John Jay, 1763-1781. Ed. by Henry P. Johnston. LC 69-16639. (American Public Figures Ser.). 1971. reprint ed. lib. bdg. 72.50 (*0-306-71124-9*) Da Capo.

Correspondence Art: Source Book for the Network of International Postal Art Activity. Ed. by Mary Stofflet & Michael Crane. LC 81-68049. (Contemporary Documents Ser.: Vol. 2). (Illus.). 544p. (Orig.). (C). 1984. pap. 15.95 (*0-931818-02-8*) Contemporary Arts.

Correspondence avec Roger Martin du Gard, 1935-1951, Vol. 2. Andre Gide. (FRE.). 1968. pap. 36.95 (*0-7859-3968-7*) Fr & Eur.

Correspondence Betweeen Leon Green & Charles McCormick, 1927-1962. Ed. by David W. Robertson & Robin Meyer. x, 222p. 1988. 27.50 (*0-8377-1046-4*) Rothman.

Correspondence Between A. A. Markov & A. A. Chuprov on the Theory of Probability & Mathematical Statistics. Ed. by O. Ondar. 192p. 1981. pap. 79.00 (*0-387-90585-5*) Spr-Verlag.

Correspondence Between Albrecht von Haller & Charles Bonnet. Ed. by O. Sonntag. (Studia Halleriana Ser.: Vol. 1). 1338p. 1983. 165.00 (*3-456-81138-1*) Hogrefe & Huber Pubs.

Correspondence Between Albrecht von Haller & Horace-Benedict de Saussure. Ed. by O. Sonntag. (Studia Halleriana Ser.: Vol. 3). 520p. (ENG & FRE.). 1990. 52.00 (*3-456-81935-8*) Hogrefe & Huber Pubs.

Correspondence Between Goethe & Carlyle. C. Norton. 1972. 59.95 (*0-87968-945-5*) Gordon Pr.

Correspondence Between Goethe & Schiller Vol. 60. Johann W. Von Goethe. Tr. by Liselotte Dieckmann. LC 93-42014. (Studies in Modern German Literature: Vol. 60). 320p. (C). 1994. text ed. 48.95 (*0-8204-2314-9*) P Lang Pubs.

Correspondence Between Henry Stephens Randall & Hugh Blair Grigsby 1856-1861. F. J. Klingberg & F. W. Klingberg. LC 73-37530. (American Scene Ser.). 196p. 1972. reprint ed. lib. bdg. 29.50 (*0-306-70429-3*) Da Capo.

Correspondence Between Jerome & Augustine of Hippo (394-419) Tr. by Carolinne White. LC 90-23420. (Studies in the Bible & Early Christianity: Vol. 23). 264p. 1991. lib. bdg. 89.95 (*0-88946-599-1*) E Mellen.

Correspondence Between John Adams & Mercy Warren. John Adams. (American Biography Ser.). 436p. 1991. reprint ed. lib. bdg. 89.00 (*0-7812-8007-9*) Rprt Serv.

Correspondence Between John Adams & Mercy Warren Relating to Her History of the American Revolution, July-August, 1807. Ed. by Charles F. Adams, Jr. LC 72-2586. (American Women Ser.: Images & Realities). 202p. 1976. reprint ed. 21.95 (*0-405-04487-9*) Ayer.

Correspondence Between Ralph Waldo Emerson & Hermaan Grimm. Ralph Waldo Emerson. (American Biography Ser.). 90p. 1991. reprint ed. lib. bdg. 59.00 (*0-7812-8123-7*) Rprt Serv.

Correspondence Between Sir George Gabriel Stokes & Sir William Thomson, Baron Kelvin of Largs, Vols. 1-2. Ed. by David B. Wilson. (Illus.). 900p. (C). 1990. 220.00 (*0-521-32831-4*) Cambridge U Pr.

Correspondence Between the Honorable F. H. Elmore & James G. Birney. Ed. by James G. Birney. LC 75-82173. (Anti-Slavery Crusade in America Ser.). 1970. reprint ed. 17.95 (*0-405-00612-8*) Ayer.

Correspondence Between the Stonehaulers. Jack Agueros. 1991. 15.00 (*0-914610-94-5*); pap. 9.00 (*0-914610-93-7*) Hanging Loose.

Correspondence Between Thomas Jefferson & Pierre Samuel Du Pont de Nemours, 1798-1817. Thomas Jefferson. Ed. by Dumas Malone. Tr. by Linwood Lehmann. LC 78-75282. (American Scene Ser.). 1970. reprint ed. lib. bdg. 42.50 (*0-306-71301-2*) Da Capo.

Correspondence Between Thomas Jefferson & Pierre Samuel du Pont de Nemours, 1798-1817. Thomas Jefferson. (American Biography Ser.). 210p. 1991. reprint ed. lib. bdg. 69.00 (*0-7812-8218-7*) Rprt Serv.

Correspondence Between William Penn & James Logan, 2 vols., Set. James Logan. 1993. reprint ed. lib. bdg. 150.00 (*0-7812-5484-1*) Rprt Serv.

Correspondence Between William Penn & James Logan & Others, 2 Vols, Set. William Penn. Ed. by Deborah Logan & Edward Armstrong. LC 72-173943. reprint ed. 115.00 (*0-404-04985-0*) AMS Pr.

Correspondence Commerciale Anglaise. Dominique Daugeras & Patricia Janiaud-Powell. 157p. (ENG & FRE.). 1992. 24.95 (*0-7859-0968-0*, 2091760730) Fr & Eur.

Correspondence Concerning Claims Against Great Britain, 7 vols., Set. U. S. Department of State Staff. LC 06-9813. 1976. 350.00 (*0-527-91930-6*) Periodicals Srv.

Correspondence, Conferences, Documents, Vol. 1. Vincent De Paul. Ed. by Jacqueline Kilar. Tr. by Helen M. Law et al. LC 83-63559. 675p. 1985. 33.00 (*0-911782-50-8*) New City.

Correspondence, Conferences, Documents, Vol. II. Vincent De Paul. Ed. by Marie Poole. Tr. by Helen M. Law et al. 725p. 1990. 33.00 (*0-911782-79-6*) New City.

Correspondence, Conferences, Documents, Vol. 3. Vincent De Paul. Ed. by Marie Poole. 620p. 1992. 33.00 (*1-56548-022-8*) New City.

***Correspondence, Conferences Documents Vol. 4.** Vincent De Paul. Ed. & Tr. by Marie Poole. 620p. 1994. lib. bdg. 33.00 (*1-56548-063-5*) New City.

Correspondence Course. Ed. by Joseph L. Cavinato, Jr. Orig. Title: Transportation-Distribution Costs and Cost Analysis. 114p. 1982. pap. 225.00 (*0-318-16888-X*); pap. 175.00 (*0-318-16889-8*) Am Soc Transport.

Correspondence Course in Zone Therapy, Reflex Technique & Hook Work. Joe S. Riley. 13p. 1959. reprint ed. spiral bd. 9.35 (*0-7873-1179-0*) Mokelumne.

Correspondence Education in Central Africa: An Alternative Route to Higher Education in Developing Countries. M. A. Wakatama. LC 83-1327. (Illus.). 556p. (Orig.). (C). 1983. pap. text ed. 41.00 (*0-8191-3097-4*) U Pr of Amer.

Correspondence Education Moves to the Year 2000: National Invitational Forum on Correspondence Education. Ed. by Thrane Lucille Campbell. 187p. 1984. 16.50 (*0-318-17783-8*, SN47) Ctr Educ Trng Employ.

Correspondence generale d'Helvetius, Vol. II: 1757-1760 - Lettres 250-464. David Smith et al. (Romance Ser.). 433p. 1984. 75.00 (*0-8020-5641-5*) U of Toronto Pr.

Correspondence generale d'Helvetius, Vol. III: Lettres 465-719 (1761-74) Ed. by David W. Smith et al. (Romance Ser.: No. 63). 592p. 1991. 120.00 (*0-8020-2778-4*) U of Toronto Pr.

Correspondence Ine, Vol. XI. Ed. by Robert Amadou. 330p. write for info. (*0-318-71422-1*, Pub. by Georg Olms GW) Lubrecht & Cramer.

Correspondence, Invariance, & Heuristics: Essays in Honour of Heinz Post. Ed. by Steven French & Harmke Kamminga. LC 92-40985. (Boston Studies in the Philosophy of Science: Vol. 148). 388p. (C). 1993. lib. bdg. 137.00 (*0-7923-2085-9*) Kluwer Ac.

Correspondence of Abel Boyer, Huguenot Refugee. Rex A. Barrell. LC 92-3521. 240p. 1992. lib. bdg. 89.95 (*0-7734-9488-X*) E Mellen.

Correspondence of Adam Smith. 2nd ed. Adam Smith. Ed. by Ernest C. Mossner & Ian S. Moss. 496p. 1987. 98.00 (*0-19-828570-1*) OUP.

Correspondence of Adam Smith: Glasgow Edition. Adam Smith. LC 83-25559. 495p. 1987. 7.50 (*0-913966-99-1*) Liberty Fund.

Correspondence of Boris Pasternak & Olga Friedenberg, 1910-1954. Tr. by Margaret Wettlin. LC 81-48017. (Helen & Kurt Wolff Bk.). (Illus.). 416p. 1983. pap. 9.95 (*0-15-622597-2*, Harvest Bks) HarBrace.

Correspondence of Captain Nathan & Lois Peters, April 25, 1775-Febuary 5, 1777. Ed. by William H. Guthman. (Illus.). 1980. 6.50 (*0-940748-58-4*) Conn Hist Soc.

Correspondence of Edmund Burke, 8 vols. Incl. Ed. by R. B. McDowell. LC 58-5615. 1970. lib. bdg. 32.00 (*0-226-11560-7*); Ed. by R. B. McDowell & John A. Woods. LC 58-5615. 1971. lib. bdg. 32.00 (*0-226-11561-5*); Index. Edmund E. Burke. Ed. by Barbara Lowe. LC 58-5615. 1978. lib. bdg. 40.00x (*0-226-11562-3*); LC 58-5615. write for info. (*0-318-56026-7*) U Ch Pr.

Correspondence of Emerson & Carlyle. Ralph Waldo Emerson & Thomas Carlyle. Ed. by Joseph Slater. LC 63-17539. 632p. reprint ed. pap. 180.00 (*0-8357-9063-0*, 2017253) Bks Demand.

Correspondence of Erasmus: Collected Works of Erasmus Letters 1356 to 1534 (1523-1524) Desiderius Erasmus. (Collected Works of Erasmus: No. 10). 560p. 1992. 100.00 (*0-8020-5976-7*) U of Toronto Pr.

Correspondence of Erasmus: Letters 1252-1355 (1522-1523) Desiderius Erasmus. Tr. by R. A. Mynors. (Collected Works of Erasmus: No. 9). 496p. 1989. 90.00 (*0-8020-2604-4*) U of Toronto Pr.

Correspondence of Erasmus, Letters, 1501-1514, Vol. 2. Desiderius Erasmus. Ed. by Beatrice Corrigan. LC 72-47422. (Collected Works of Erasmus: Vol. 2). (Illus.). 1975. 85.00 (*0-8020-1983-8*) U of Toronto Pr.

Correspondence of Erasmus: Letters 1535 to 1657 (1525) Tr. by Alexander Dalzell. (Collected Works of Erasmus: No. 11). 544p. 1993. 110.00 (*0-8020-0536-5*) U of Toronto Pr.

Correspondence of Erasmus: Letters 993 to 1121 (1519-1520) Desiderius Erasmus. Tr. by R. A. Mynors. (Collected Works of Erasmus: No. 7). 500p. 1988. 85.00 (*0-8020-5607-5*) U of Toronto Pr.

Correspondence of Erasmus, Vol. 1: Letters 1 to 141, 1484-1500. annot. ed. Desiderius Erasmus. Tr. by R. A. Mynors & D. F. Thomson. LC 72-97422. (Collected Works of Erasmus: No. 1). (Illus.). 396p. reprint ed. pap. 112.90 (*0-8357-4724-7*, 2037639) Bks Demand.

Correspondence of Erasmus, Vol. 3: Letters 298-445 (1514-1516) Mynors. Desiderius Erasmus. Tr. by R. A. Mynors & D. F. Thomson. LC 72-97422. (Collected Works of Erasmus: Vol. 3). (Illus.). 1976. 85.00 (*0-8020-2202-2*) U of Toronto Pr.

Correspondence of Erasmus, Vol. 4: Letters 446-593. Desiderius Erasmus. Tr. by R. A. Mynors & D. F. Thomson. LC 72-97422. (Collected Works of Erasmus: Vol. 4). 1977. 85.00 (*0-8020-5366-1*) U of Toronto Pr.

Correspondence of Erasmus, Vol. 5: Letters 594-841 (July 1517 - April 1518) Desiderius Erasmus. Tr. by R. A. Mynors & D. F. Thomson. LC 78-6904. (Collected Works of Erasmus: Vol. 5). 1979. 85.00 (*0-8020-5429-3*) U of Toronto Pr.

Correspondence of Erasmus, Vol. 6: Letters 842-992 (May 1518 - June 1519) Desiderius Erasmus. Tr. by R. A. Mynors & D. F. Thomson. (Collected Works of Erasmus: Vol. 6). 1981. 85.00 (*0-8020-5500-1*) U of Toronto Pr.

Correspondence of Erasmus, Vol. 8: Letters 1122-1251 (1520-1521) Ed. by Peter G. Bietenholz. Tr. by R. A. Mynors. 1988. 85.00 (*0-8020-2607-9*) U of Toronto Pr.

Correspondence of Flannery O'Connor & the Brainard Cheneys. Ed. by C. Ralph Stephens. LC 85-26512. 220p. 1986. 32.00 (*0-87805-292-5*) U Pr of Miss.

Correspondence of Ford Madox Ford & Stella Bowen. Ed. by Sondra J. Stang & Karen Cochran. (Illus.). 496p. (C). 1993. 65.00 (*0-253-35494-3*) Ind U Pr.

Correspondence of G. E. Morrison, 2 Vols., Set. G. E. Morrison. Ed. by Lo Hui-Min. LC 74-31805. 825p. 1978. 265.00 (*0-521-08779-1*) Cambridge U Pr.

Correspondence of George Baillie of Jerviswood. George Baillie. Ed. by Earl Of Minto. LC 76-161744. (Bannatyne Club, Edinburgh. Publications: No. 72). reprint ed. 40.00 (*0-404-52792-2*) AMS Pr.

Correspondence of Gov. Samuel Ward, May 1775-March 1776. Ed. by Bernhardt Knollenberg. Bd. with Genealogy of the Ward Family. (Illus.). 8.00 (*0-685-67898-9*) RI Hist Soc.

***Correspondence of Heinrich Melchior Muhlenberg Vol. 2: 1748-1752.** Heinrich M. Muhlenberg. Tr. by Helmut T. Lehmann & John W. Kleiner. 400p. Date not set. write for info. (*0-89725-227-6*, 494) Picton Pr.

Correspondence of Heinrich Melchior Muhlenberg, Vol. 1: 1740-1748. Tr. by Helmut Lehmann & John Kleiner. LC 93-86108. 750p. 1993. 59.50 (*0-89725-096-6*) Picton Pr.

Correspondence of Henrik Ibsen. Henrik Ibsen. Ed. by Mary Morrison. LC 75-124394. (Studies in European Literature: No. 56). 1970. reprint ed. lib. bdg. 75.00 (*0-8383-1098-2*) M S G Haskell Hse.

Correspondence of Henry & Sarah Fielding. Henry Fielding & Sarah Fielding. Ed. by Martin C. Battestin & Clive T. Probyn. LC 92-27584. (Illus.). 280p. 1993. 58.00 (*0-19-811273-4*, Clarendon Pr) OUP.

Correspondence of Henry David Thoreau. Henry David Thoreau. Ed. by Carl Bode & Walter Harding. LC 73-16954. 665p. 1974. reprint ed. text ed. 47.50 (*0-8371-7247-0*, THCO, Greenwood Pr) Greenwood.

Correspondence of Henry James & Henry Adams, 1877-1914. Ed. by George Monteiro. LC 91-5175. (Illus.). 128p. (C). 1992. text ed. 22.50 (*0-8071-1729-3*) La State U Pr.

Correspondence of Henry James & the House of Macmillan, 1877-1914: "All the Links in the Chain" Ed. by Rayburn S. Moore. LC 92-28962. xxvi, 275p. 1993. text ed. 40.00x (*0-8071-1834-6*) La State U Pr.

Correspondence of Henry Oldenburg, Vol. XIII. Tr. by A. R. Hall & M. B. Hall. (Illus.). 450p. 1986. 145.00 (*0-8002-3082-5*) Taylor & Francis.

Correspondence of Henry Oldenburg, 9 vols. Tr. by Rupert A. Hall & Marie B. Hall. Incl. Vol 1. 1641-1662. 1965. 0.35 (*0-299-03760-6*); Vol 2. 1663-1665. 1966. 0.35 (*0-299-03770-3*); Vol. 3. 1666-1667. 1966. 35.00 (*0-299-03780-0*); Vol. 4. 1667-1668. 1968. 0.35 (*0-299-04650-8*); Vol. 5. 1668-1669. 1968. 35.00 (*0-299-04890-X*); Vol. 6. 1669-1670. 1969. 35.00 (*0-299-05280-X*); Vol. 7. 1670-1671. 1970. 35.00 (*0-299-05630-9*); Vol. 8. 1671-1672. 1971. 35.00 (*0-299-05950-2*); Vol. 9. 1672-1673. 1973. 35.00 (*0-299-06390-9*); (Illus.). (C). write for info. (*0-318-56168-9*) U of Wis Pr.

Correspondence of Henry Oldenburg, Vol. XII. Comp. by A. R. Hall & M. B. Hall. 450p. 1986. 145.00 (*0-85066-236-2*) Taylor & Francis.

Correspondence of Isaac Newton, Vol. 3, 1688-1694. Isaac Newton. Ed. by H. W. Turnbull. LC 59-65134. 465p. reprint ed. pap. 132.60 (*0-317-26385-4*, 2024527) Bks Demand.

Correspondence of James Fenimore Cooper, 2 vols, Set. James Fenimore Cooper. LC 70-164597. (Select Bibliographies Reprint Ser.). 1977. reprint ed. 58.95 (*0-8369-5881-0*) Ayer.

C

An Asterisk (*) at the beginning of an entry indicates that the title is appearing in BIP for the first time.

C

An Asterisk (*) at the beginning of an entry indicates that the title is appearing in BIP for the first time.

1635

Correspondence with Madame du Deffand & Wiart, 6. Horace Walpole. Ed. by W. S. Lewis & Warren H. Smith. (Horace Walpole's Correspondence Ser.: Vols. 3, 6 & 7). (Illus.). 1939. 75.00x (*0-300-00691-8*) Yale U Pr.

Correspondence with Madame du Deffand & Wiart, 7. Horace Walpole. Ed. by W. S. Lewis & Warren H. Smith. (Horace Walpole's Correspondence Ser.: Vols. 3, 6 & 7). (Illus.). 1939. 75.00 (*0-300-00692-6*) Yale U Pr.

Correspondence with Mary & Agnes Berry & Barbara Cecilia Seton 1st. Horace Walpole. Ed. by W. S. Lewis et al. (Horace Walpole's Correspondence Ser.: Vol. 11). (Illus.). 1944. 70.00 (*0-300-00696-9*) Yale U Pr.

Correspondence with Seymour Conway, Lady Ailesbury, Lord & Lady Hertford, Lord Beauchamp, & Henrietta Seymour Conway. Horace Walpole. (Horace Walpole's Correspondence Ser.: Vol. 38). 1974. 75.00 (*0-300-01764-2*) Yale U Pr.

Correspondence with Sir David Dalrymple, Conyers Middleton, Daniel Lysons, William Robertson, William Roscoe, William Beloe, the Earle of Buchan, Samuel Lysons, Robert Henry, James Edwards-Robert Nares. Horace Walpole. Ed. by Wilmarth S. Lewis & Charles H. Bennett. (Horace Walpole's Correspondence Ser.: Vol. 15). (Illus.). 1951. 70.00 (*0-300-00699-3*) Yale U Pr.

Correspondence with Sir Horace Mann, 1. Horace Walpole. (Horace Walpole's Correspondence Ser.: Vol. 17). 1954. 75.00 (*0-300-00701-9*) Yale U Pr.

Correspondence with Sir Horace Mann, 10-11, Set. Horace Walpole. (Horace Walpole's Correspondence Ser.: Vols. 26-27). 1971. 150.00 (*0-300-01520-8*) Yale U Pr.

Correspondence with Sir Horace Mann, 2. Horace Walpole. (Horace Walpole's Correspondence Ser.: Vol. 18). 1954. 75.00 (*0-300-00702-7*) Yale U Pr.

Correspondence with Sir Horace Mann, 3. Horace Walpole. (Horace Walpole's Correspondence Ser.: Vol. 19). 1954. 75.00 (*0-300-00703-5*) Yale U Pr.

Correspondence with Sir Horace Mann, 4. Horace Walpole. (Horace Walpole's Correspondence Ser.: Vol. 20). 1960. 75.00 (*0-300-00704-3*) Yale U Pr.

Correspondence with Sir Horace Mann, 5. Horace Walpole. (Horace Walpole's Correspondence Ser.: Vol. 21). 1960. 75.00 (*0-300-00705-1*) Yale U Pr.

Correspondence with Sir Horace Mann, 6. Horace Walpole. (Horace Walpole's Correspondence Ser.: Vol. 22). 1960. 75.00 (*0-300-00707-8*) Yale U Pr.

Correspondence with Sir Horace Mann, 8. Horace Walpole. (Horace Walpole's Correspondence Ser.: Vol. 24). 1967. 75.00 (*0-300-00709-4*) Yale U Pr.

Correspondence with Sir Horace Mann, 9. Horace Walpole. (Horace Walpole's Correspondence Ser.: Vol. 25). 1971. 75.00 (*0-300-01298-5*) Yale U Pr.

Correspondence with the Countess of Upper Ossory, 33. Horace Walpole. Ed. by Wilmarth S. Lewis et al. (Horace Walpole's Correspondence Ser.: Vols. 32-34). (Illus.). 1965. 75.00x (*0-300-00715-9*) Yale U Pr.

Correspondence with the Rev. William Cole 1st & 2nd, Vol. 1. Horace Walpole. Ed. by W. S. Lewis & A. Dayle Wallace. (Horace Walpole's Correspondence Ser.: Vols. 1 & 2). (Illus.). 1937. 70.00 (*0-300-00684-5*) Yale U Pr.

Correspondence with the Rev. William Cole 1st & 2nd, Vol. 2. Horace Walpole. Ed. by W. S. Lewis & A. Dayle Wallace. (Horace Walpole's Correspondence Ser.: Vols. 1 & 2). (Illus.). 1937. 75.00 (*0-300-00685-3*) Yale U Pr.

Correspondence with the Walpole Family. Horace Walpole. (Horace Walpole's Correspondence Ser.: Vol. 36). 1973. 75.00 (*0-300-01667-0*) Yale U Pr.

Correspondence with Thomas Chatterton, Michael Lort, John Pinkerton, John Fenn & Mrs. Fenn, William Bewley, Nathaniel Hillier, & Henry Zouch. Horace Walpole. Ed. by W. S. Lewis & Ralph M. Williams. (Horace Walpole's Correspondence Ser.: Vol. 16). (Illus.). 1951. 75.00 (*0-300-00700-0*) Yale U Pr.

Correspondence with Thomas Gray, Richard West, & Thomas Ashton, Set. Horace Walpole. Ed. by W. S. Lewis et al. (Horace Walpole's Correspondence Ser.: Vols. 13 & 14). (Illus.). 1948. 140.00 (*0-300-00698-5*) Yale U Pr.

Correspondence, 1646-1675, Vol. 1. Madame De Sevigne. Ed. by Raphael Duchenen. 1973. lib. bdg. 115.00 (*0-7859-3792-7*) Fr & Eur.

Correspondence, 1675-1680, Vol. 2. Madame De Sevigne. Ed. by Roger Duchene. 1987. lib. bdg. 120.00 (*0-7859-3793-5*) Fr & Eur.

Correspondence, 1709-1713, Vol. 5. Isaac Newton. Ed. by A. R. Hall & Laura Tilling. 1975. 120.00 (*0-521-08721-X*) Cambridge U Pr.

Correspondence, 1713-1718, 6. Isaac Newton. Ed. by A. R. Hall & Laura Tilling. (Illus.). 500p. 1976. 120.00 (*0-521-08722-8*) Cambridge U Pr.

Correspondence, 1713-1718, 7. Isaac Newton. Ed. by A. R. Hall & Laura Tilling. (Illus.). 500p. 1976. 120.00 (*0-318-51278-5*) Cambridge U Pr.

Correspondence, 1733-1764. Robert Dodsley. Ed. by James E. Tierney. (Cambridge Studies in Publishing & Printing History). (Illus.). 620p. (C). 1989. 110.00 (*0-521-25925-8*) Cambridge U Pr.

Correspondence, 1749-1753, Vol. 3. Francois-Marie de Voltaire. Ed. by Theodore Besterman. (FRE.). 1975. lib. bdg. 120.00 (*0-7859-3828-1*) Fr & Eur.

Correspondence, 1767-1769, Vol. 9. Francois-Marie de Voltaire. Ed. by Theodore Besterman. (FRE.). 1986. lib. bdg. 135.00 (*0-7859-3867-2*) Fr & Eur.

Correspondence, 1769-1772, Vol. 10. Francois-Marie de Voltaire. Ed. by Theodore Besterman. (FRE.). 1985. lib. bdg. 140.00 (*0-7859-3870-2*) Fr & Eur.

Correspondence, 1772-1774, Vol. 11. Francois-Marie de Voltaire. Ed. by Theodore Besterman. (FRE.). 1987. lib. bdg. 140.00 (*0-7859-3874-5*) Fr & Eur.

Correspondence, 1821-1834, Vol. 2. Stendhal, pseud. Ed. by Henri Martineau. 1967. lib. bdg. 100.00 (*0-7859-3797-8*) Fr & Eur.

Correspondence, 1830-1851, Vol. 1. Gustave Flaubert. Ed. by Jean Bruneau. (FRE.). 1973. lib. bdg. 115.00 (*0-7859-3812-5*) Fr & Eur.

Correspondence, 1835-1842, Vol. 3. Stendhal. Ed. by Henri Martineau. 1969. lib. bdg. 100.00 (*0-7859-3798-6*) Fr & Eur.

Correspondence, 1859-1868, Vol. 3. Gustave Flaubert. Ed. by Jean Bruneau. (FRE.). 1991. lib. bdg. 195.00 (*0-7859-3816-8*) Fr & Eur.

Correspondence, 1890-1891, Vol. 4. Stephane Mallarme. (FRE.). 1973. pap. 65.00 (*0-7859-3969-5*) Fr & Eur.

Correspondence, 1893-1894, Vol. 6. Stephane Mallarme. (FRE.). 1981. pap. 55.00 (*0-7859-3959-8*) Fr & Eur.

Correspondence, 1894-1895, Vol. 7. Stephane Mallarme. (FRE.). 1982. pap. 75.00 (*0-7859-3965-2*) Fr & Eur.

Correspondence, 1896, Vol. 8. Stephane Mallarme. (FRE.). 1983. pap. 65.00 (*0-685-68103-3*) Fr & Eur.

Correspondence, 1897, Vol. 9. Stephane Mallarme. (FRE.). 1983. pap. 75.00 (*0-7859-3966-0*) Fr & Eur.

Correspondence, 1926-1969. Hannah Arendt. 1992. 49.95 (*0-15-107887-4*) HarBrace.

Correspondence, 1945-1984. Francois Truffaut. Ed. by Gilles Jacob & Claude De Givray. Tr. by Gilbert Adair. 1990. 50.00 (*0-374-13001-9*) FS&G.

Correspondencia Comercial Moderna. 4th ed. Marjorie Hunsinger. 232p. 1982. text ed. 19.75 (*0-07-031282-6*) McGraw.

Correspondent Breeze: Essays on English Romanticism. Meyer H. Abrams. LC 83-19359. 296p. 1984. reprint ed. 22.50 (*0-393-01837-7*) Norton.

***Correspondent Colorings: Melville in the Marketplace.** Sheila Post-Lauria. (Illus.). 272p. (C). 1996. text ed. 50.00 (*1-55849-002-7*); pap. 17.95 (*1-55849-003-5*) U of Mass Pr.

Correspondent in Spain. H. Knoblaufgh. 1973. 59.95 (*0-87968-946-3*) Gordon Pr.

Corresponding Dates of Hebrew & Civil Calendar for 216 Years & Family Record. 32.50 (*0-87559-198-1*) Shalom.

Corrida. Michel Deon. (FRE.). 1982. pap. 10.95 (*0-7859-1948-1*, 2070373509) Fr & Eur.

Corrida at San Feliu. Paul Scott. 224p. 1986. 3.95 (*0-88184-274-5*) Carroll & Graf.

Corrida du 1er Mai. Jean Cocteau. 214p. (FRE.). 1957. 17.95 (*0-8288-9120-6*) Fr & Eur.

Corridor: Poems. Jonathan Aaron. LC 91-50807. (Wesleyan Poetry Ser.). 59p. (C). 1992. 22.50 (*0-8195-2200-7*, Wesleyan Univ Pr); pap. 10.95 (*0-8195-1203-6*, Wesleyan Univ Pr) U Pr of New Eng.

Corridor of Storms, Bk. 2. William Sarabande. (First Americans Ser.). 416p. (Orig.). 1988. pap. 5.99 (*0-553-27159-8*) Bantam.

***Corridor Seven Official Guide.** 1994. cd-rom, pap. 19.99 (*1-56686-219-1*) Brady Compu Bks.

Corridors of Deceit: The World of John le Carre. Peter Wolfe. LC 87-70354. 282p. 1987. 32.95 (*0-87972-381-5*); pap. text ed. 16.95 (*0-87972-382-3*) Bowling Green Univ.

Corridors of Guilt. John B. Hilton. 208p. 1993. pap. 3.99 (*1-55773-943-9*) Diamond.

Corridors of Healing. large type ed. Elizabeth Harrison. 390p. 1982. 15.95 (*0-7089-0790-3*) Ulverscroft.

Corridors of Time: New Haven & London, 1927-1956, 10 vols., Set. Harold J. Peake & Herbert J. Fleure. Incl. Vol. 1. Apes & Men. (*0-404-18251-8*); Vol. 2. Hunters & Artists. (*0-404-18252-6*); Vol. 3. Peasants & Potters. (*0-404-18253-4*); Vol. 4. Priests & Kings. (*0-404-18254-2*); Vol. 5. Steppe & the Sown. (*0-404-18255-0*); Vol. 6. Way of the Sea. (*0-404-18256-9*); Vol. 7. Merchant Venturers in Bronze. (*0-404-18257-7*); Vol. 8. Horse & the Sword. (*0-404-18258-5*); Vol. 9. Law & the Prophets. (*0-404-18259-3*); Vol. 10. Times & Places. (*0-404-18260-7*); write for info. (*0-404-18250-X*) AMS Pr.

Corridors Through Time. J. Selby Mines & Energy Staff. (C). 1989. pap. text ed. 30.00 (*0-89771-035-5*, Pub. by Bob Mossel AT) St Mut.

Corridors to Communication. Ranu Vanikar. 160p. 1984. pap. text ed. 5.95 (*0-86131-476-X*, Pub. by Orient Longman Ltd II) Apt Bks.

Corrie Ten Boom. Kjersti H. Baez. (Young Reader's Christian Library). (Illus.). 224p. (J). (gr. 3 up). 1989. per., pap. 2.50 (*1-55748-102-4*) Barbour & Co.

Corrie Ten Boom. Sue Shaw. (Illus.). 30p. (SPA.). 1994. pap. 6.99 (*0-8254-1661-2*) Kregel.

Corrie Ten Boom. Kathleen White. (Women of Faith Ser.). 112p. (Orig.). 1991. 4.99 (*1-55661-194-3*) Bethany Hse.

Corrientes Actuales en la Dialectologia del Caribe Hispanico: Actas de un Simposio. Ed. by Humberto Lopez-Morales. LC 77-12823. 247p. 1978. pap. 6.00 (*0-8477-3186-3*) U of PR Pr.

Corrientes Neo-Teologicas: Neo-Theological Trends. Guido Feliz. (SPA.). 5.95 (*84-7228-351-8*, 220190, Pub. by Edit Clie SP) TSELF.

Corrie's Secret Pal. Jane O'Connor. LC 92-35602. (Here Come the Brownies, Brownie Girl Scout Bks.). (Illus.). 64p. (J). (gr. 1-4). 1993. 7.99 (*0-448-40161-4*, G&D); pap. 3.95 (*0-448-40160-6*, G&D) Putnam Pub Group.

Corrigan. large type ed. Cameron Judd. 230p. 1992. reprint ed. lib. bdg. 16.95 (*1-56054-413-9*) Thorndike Pr.

Corrigan's Island. large type ed. Marian Hipwell. 1991. 21.95 (*0-7089-2349-6*) Ulverscroft.

Corrigan's Range. large type ed. Jed Norton. (Linford Western Library). 240p. 1988. pap. 11.95 (*0-7089-6607-1*, Linford) Ulverscroft.

Corrigan's Revenge. large type ed. J. D. Kincaid. (Linford Western Library). 1991. pap. 13.95 (*0-7089-7123-7*) Ulverscroft.

Corrine, Italy. Germaine De Stael. Ed. by Avriel Goldberger. 434p. (FRE.). 1987. text ed. 50.00 (*0-8135-1207-7*); pap. text ed. 17.00 (*0-8135-1208-5*) Rutgers U Pr.

Corroboration of Evidence in Criminal Trials. (Law Commission Working Paper Ser.: No. 115). 137p. 1990. pap. 12.00 (*0-11-730197-3*, HM7913) UNIPUB.

Corroboree. Kenneth Gangemi. LC 76-27241. 96p. 1977. pap. 2.95 (*0-915066-22-X*) Assembling Pr.

Corrosion. (Illus.). 250p. 1981. ring bd. 95.00 (*0-87683-343-1*); trans. 95.00 (*0-87683-345-8*); 495.00 (*0-87683-344-X*); 195.00 (*0-87683-346-6*); 795.00 (*0-87683-342-3*) GP Pub.

Corrosion, 2 vols. 3rd rev. ed. L. L. Shreir et al. LC 93-13859. 2700p. 1994. 275.00 (*0-7506-1077-8*) Buttrwrth-Heinemann.

Corrosion. American Society for Metals Staff. Ed. by Seymour K. Coburn. LC 83-7371. (Source Book Ser.). (Illus.). 452p. reprint ed. pap. 128.90 (*0-7837-1860-8*, 2042061) Bks Demand.

Corrosion - Erosion of Coal Conversion System Materials. LC 79-88421. (Illus.). 945p. 1979. 10.00 (*0-915567-68-7*) NACE Intl.

Corrosion & Chemical Resistant Masonry Materials Handbook. Ed. by Walter L. Sheppard, Jr. LC 85-25929. (Illus.). 722p. 1986. 89.00 (*0-8155-1053-5*) Noyes.

Corrosion & Corrosion Control: An Introduction to Corrosion Science & Engineering. 3rd ed. Herbert H. Uhlig & R. Winston Revie. (Illus.). 409p. (C). 1985. 72.00 (*0-471-07818-2*) NACE Intl.

Corrosion & Corrosion Control for Offshore & Marine Constructions: Proceedings of the International Conference on Corrosion & Corrosion Control for the Offshore & Marine Constructions, Xiamen, PRC, 6-9 September 1988. Ed. by Chinese Society of Corrosion & Protection Staff. (International Academic Publishers Ser.). (Illus.). 1000p. 1989. 150.00 (*0-08-036626-0*, Pergamon Pr) Elsevier.

Corrosion & Corrosion Control in Drinking Water Systems. Ed. by E. A. Vik & T. Hedberg. (Illus.). 72p. 1991. 10.00 (*1-877914-26-6*) NACE Intl.

***Corrosion & Corrosion Control of Aluminum & Steel in Lightweight Automotive Applications: CORROSION-95 Symposium, Castricum, the Netherlands.** Ed. by Theresa C. Simpson & James P. Moran. LC 95-62139. 1995. pap. 65.00 (*1-877914-88-6*) NACE Intl.

***Corrosion & Corrosion Protection: Proceedings of an International Symposium Honoring Professor H. H. Uhlig on His Seventy-Fifth Birthday.** Electrochemical Society Staff. Ed. by Robert P. Frankenthal & Florian Mansfeld. LC 81-68456. (Electrochemical Society. Proceedings Ser.: Vol. 81-8). (Illus.). 304p. 1981. pap. 86.70 (*0-7837-9003-1*, 2059268) Bks Demand.

Corrosion & Corrosion Protection Handbook. 2nd enl. rev. ed. Schweitzer. (Corrosion Technology Ser.: Vol. 1). 680p. 1989. 175.00 (*0-8247-7998-3*) Dekker.

***Corrosion & Corrosivity Sensors.** Ed. by V. S. Agarwala & G. K. Brown. (Illus.). 295p. 1994. 85.00 (*1-877914-73-8*) NACE Intl.

Corrosion & Degradation of Implant Materials - STP 684. Ed. by B. C. Syrett & A. Acharya. 369p. 1979. 37.75 (*0-8031-0313-1*, 04-684000-27) ASTM.

Corrosion & Degradation of Implant Materials: Second Symposium - STP 859. Ed. by Anna C. Fraker & Charles D. Griffin. LC 84-70337. (Illus.). 470p. 1985. text ed. 62.00 (*0-8031-0427-8*, 04-859000-27) ASTM.

Corrosion & Deposits from Combustion Gases: Abstracts & Index. Ed. by Jerrold E. Radway. LC 66-52838. 575p. 1985. 136.00 (*0-89116-301-8*) Hemisp Pub.

Corrosion & Incrustation of Water Wells: Anthology. 114p. 1983. 6.25 (*1-56034-004-5*, K064) Natl Water Well.

Corrosion & Its Control: An Introduction to the Subject. LC 82-62108. (Illus.). 202p. 1982. 45.00 (*0-915567-94-6*) NACE Intl.

***Corrosion & Its Control: An Introduction to the Subject.** H. Van Droffelaar & J. T. Atkinson. LC 95-87424. 332p. 1995. 91.00 (*1-877914-71-1*) NACE Intl.

Corrosion & Mechanical Stress at High Temperatures. Ed. by V. Guttman & M. Merz. (Illus.). 477p. 1981. 117.00 (*0-85334-956-8*, Pub. by Elsevier Applied Sci UK) Elsevier.

Corrosion & Particle Erosion at High Temperatures. Ed. by V. Srinivasan & K. Vedula. LC 89-60379. (Illus.). 650p. 1989. 20.00 (*0-87339-093-8*, 360) Minerals Metals.

Corrosion & Particle Erosion at High Temperatures: Proceedings of a Symposium Sponsored by the TMS-ASM Joint Corrosion & Environmental Effects Committee, Held at the 118th Annual Meeting of the Minerals, Metals & Materials Society in Las Vegas, Nevada, February 27-March 3, 1989. Minerals, Metals & Materials Society Staff. Ed. by V. Srinivasan & K. Vedula. LC 89-60379. (Illus.). 651p. reprint ed. pap. 180.00 (*0-7837-6061-2*, 2052507) Bks Demand.

Corrosion & Protection of Metals. G. Bakhvalov & A. Turkovskaya. LC 63-10103. 1965. 143.00 (*0-08-009995-5*, Pub. by Pergamon Repr UK) Franklin.

Corrosion & Related Aspects of Materials for Potable Water Supplies. Ed. by P. McIntyre & A. D. Mercer. (Illus.). 285p. 1994. 160.00 (*0-901716-47-2*, Pub. by Inst Materials UK) Ashgate Pub Co.

Corrosion & Water Technology for Petroleum Producers. Lloyd W. Jones. LC 88-60130. 202p. 1988. 50.00 (*0-930972-09-0*, P7149) Oil & Gas.

Corrosion & Wear. Joseph E. Shigley & Charles R. Mischke. (Mechanical Designer's Workbook Ser.). 256p. 1989. pap. text ed. 31.95 (*0-07-056923-1*) McGraw.

***Corrosion Asia, 94: Proceedings, 2 vols., Set.** 91p. 1994. 79.00 (*0-614-07124-0*) NACE Intl.

Corrosion Atlas. Ed. by E. D. During. (Illus.). 300p. 1988. 333.50 (*0-444-42804-6*) Elsevier.

***Corrosion Atlas, 2 vols., Set.** Ed. by E. D. During. (Illus.). 480p. 1991. ring bd. 575.00 (*0-444-89094-7*) NACE Intl.

Corrosion Basics - An Introduction. LC 84-61042. (Illus.). 364p. 1984. 66.00 (*0-915567-02-4*) NACE Intl.

Corrosion Chemistry. Ed. by George R. Brubaker & P. Beverley Phipps. LC 78-25554. (ACS Symposium Ser.: No. 89). 1979. 32.95 (*0-8412-0471-3*) Am Chemical.

Corrosion, Concrete, & Chlorides-Steel Corrosion in Concrete: Causes & Restraints. 175p. 1987. pap. 68.75 (*0-318-35480-2*, SP102) ACI.

Corrosion Control. S. Bradford. 1992. text ed. 59.95 (*0-442-01088-5*) Chapman & Hall.

Corrosion Control. Ed. by Charles Kirkley. (Oil & Gas Production Ser.). (Illus.). 76p. (Orig.). (C). 1982. pap. text ed. 15.00 (*0-88698-110-7*, 3.30110) PETEX.

Corrosion Control & System Protection. American Gas Association Operating Section Corrosion Control & System Protection Committee. Ed. by Robert L. Parker. (Gas Engineering & Operating Services Ser.). 276p. 1986. 30.00 (*0-87257-001-0*) Am Gas Assn.

Corrosion Control by Organic Coatings. Ed. by H. Leidheiser, Jr. LC 81-84733. (Illus.). 300p. 1981. 53.00 (*0-915567-93-8*) NACE Intl.

Corrosion Control for Operators. 128p. 1986. pap. 26.50 (*0-89867-350-X*, 20232) Am Water Wks Assn.

Corrosion Control in Petrolem Production (TPC-5) LC 79-88179. (Illus.). 100p. 1979. 44.00 (*0-915567-92-X*) NACE Intl.

***Corrosion Control in the Chemical Process Industries, Pub. No. 45.** C. P. Dillon. (Illus.). 420p. 1994. 93.00 (*1-877914-58-4*) NACE Intl.

Corrosion Control of Metals by Organic Coatings. Van Ooij. 1995. write for info. (*0-8493-8958-5*) CRC Pr.

Corrosion Damaged Concrete: Assessment & Control. Peter Pullar-Strecker. (Illus.). 99p. 1987. text ed. 36.95 (*0-408-02556-5*) Buttrwrth-Heinemann.

Corrosion Data from Polarization Measurements. Rudolf Stefec. 385p. 1991. text ed. write for info. (*0-13-173725-2*) P-H.

Corrosion Data Survey - Nonmetals Section. 5th ed. Ed. by N. E. Hamner. LC 74-30949. (Illus.). 494p. 1975. 111.00 (*0-915567-91-1*) NACE Intl.

Corrosion Effect of Stray Currents & the Technique for Evaluating Corrosion of REBARS in Concrete-STP 906. Ed. by Victor Chaker. LC 85-30618. (Illus.). 145p. 1986. text ed. 29.00 (*0-8031-0468-5*, 04-906000-27) ASTM.

Corrosion Engineering. 3rd ed. Mars G. Fontana. (Illus.). 544p. 1986. 74.00 (*0-07-021463-8*) NACE Intl.

Corrosion-Erosion Behavior of Materials: Proceedings of a Symposium - Sponsored by the TMS-AIME Corrosion Resistant Metals Committee & the Oxidation Activity Committee of American Society for Metals at the Fall Meeting of the Metallurgical Society of AIME, St. Louis, Missouri, October 17-18, 1978. Metallurgical Society of AIME Staff. Ed. by K. Natesan. LC 80-81518. (Illus.). 320p. reprint ed. pap. 91.20 (*0-8357-7563-1*, 2052327) Bks Demand.

Corrosion Fatigue: Mechanics, Metallurgy, Electrochemistry, & Engineering - STP 801. Ed. by T. W. Crooker & Brian N. Leis. LC 82-83519. 522p. 1983. text ed. 62.00 (*0-8031-0245-3*, 04-801000-30) ASTM.

Corrosion Fatigue (NACE Reference Book 2) Ed. by O. F. Devereux et al. (Illus.). 762p. 1972. 92.00 (*0-915567-58-X*) NACE Intl.

Corrosion Fatigue Technology - STP 642. 1978. 32.00 (*0-8031-0314-X*, 04-642000-27) ASTM.

Corrosion for Students of Science & Engineering. Kenneth R. Trethewey & John Chamberlain. LC 86-34417. 382p. 1988. pap. text ed. 59.95 (*0-470-20794-9*) Halsted Pr.

Corrosion Forms & Control for Infrastructure. Ed. by Victor Chaker. LC 92-35015. (Special Technical Publication Ser.: Vol. 1137). (Illus.). 430p. 1992. text ed. 55.00 (*0-8031-1432-X*, 04-011370-27) ASTM.

Corrosion Guide. 2nd rev. ed. Erich Rabald. 900p. 1968. 233.50 (*0-444-40465-1*) Elsevier.

Corrosion Handbook. Herbert H. Uhlig. (Electrochemical Society Ser.). 1188p. 1948. text ed. 180.00 (*0-471-89562-8*) Wiley.

Corrosion in Flue Gas Desulfurization Systems. Ed. by G. H. Koch & N. G. Thompson. LC 84-61873. 479p. 1984. 54.00 (*0-915567-05-9*) NACE Intl.

Corrosion in Natural Environments - STP 558. 352p. 1974. 29.75 (*0-8031-0315-8*, 04-558000-27) ASTM.

Corrosion in Natural Waters. Ed. by Calvin H. Baloun. LC 90-665. (Special Technical Publication (STP) Ser.: No. 1086). (Illus.). 160p. 1990. text ed. 45.00 (*0-8031-1383-8*, 04-01860-27) ASTM.

Corrosion in Seawater Systems. Alan D. Mercer. 176p. 1991. text ed. write for info. (*0-13-388703-0*) P-H.

Corrosion in Sulfuric Acid. LC 85-61573. (Illus.). 106p. 1985. 40.00 (*0-915567-11-3*) NACE Intl.

Corrosion in the Petrochemical Industry. Ed. by Linda Garverick. LC 94-10847. (Illus.). 400p. 1994. 128.00 (*0-87170-505-2*, 6393U) ASM.

Corrosion-Industrial Problems, Treatment & Control Techniques: Proceedings of the 1st Arabian Conference on Corrosion, Kuwait, 1984. Ed. by V. Ashworth. (Kuwait Foundation for the Advancement of Science Ser.: Vol. 2). (Illus.). 450p. 1987. 265.00 (*0-08-032576-9*) Macmillan.

Corrosion Inhibition - Theory & Practice. (NACE Reference Bks.: No. 7). (Illus.). 208p. 1988. 107.00 (*0-915567-67-9*) NACE Intl.

Corrosion Inhibitors. 179p. 1993. 2,650.00 (*0-89336-961-6*, C) BCC.

Corrosion Inhibitors. LC 73-85564. 260p. 1973. 57.00 (*0-915567-89-X*) NACE Intl.

C

An Asterisk (*) at the beginning of an entry indicates that the title is appearing in BIP for the first time.

An Asterisk (*) at the beginning of an entry indicates that the title is appearing in BIP for the first time.

1637

C

Corruptrice. Guy Des Cars. 384p. (FRE.). 1985. pap. 10.95 (0-7859-4791-4) Fr & Eur.

Corry: History of the Corry Family of Castlecoole. Earl of Belmore. (Illus.). xiii, 296p. 1993. reprint ed. lib. bdg. 56.50 (0-8328-3661-3); reprint ed. pap. 46.50 (0-8328-3662-1) Higginson Bk Co.

Corsair: The F-4U in World War II. Barrett Tillman. LC 79-87685. 235p. 1979. 26.95 (0-87021-131-5) Naval Inst Pr.

***Corsair Aces of World War II.** (Aircraft of the Aces Ser.: Vol. 8). (Illus.). 96p. 1995. pap. 14.95 (1-85532-583-7, Pub. by Osprey Pubng Ltd UK) Motorbooks Intl.

Corsair Affair. Soren Kierkegaard. Tr. by H. V. Hong & E. Hong. (Kierkegaard's Writings: Vol. XIII). 1981. 47.50 (0-691-07246-9) Princeton U Pr.

Corsair Affair. Ed. by Robert L. Perkins. LC 84-161455. (International Kierkegaard Commentary Ser.: No. 13). xxv, 193p. (C). 1990. 24.95 (0-86554-363-1, MUP-H301) Mercer Univ Pr.

***Corsair Years.** Turner Publishing Company Staff. LC 95-60329. 104p. 1995. 48.00 (1-56311-181-0) Turner Pub KY.

Corsairs & Navies, 1660-1760. J. S. Bromley. 517p. 1988. text ed. 70.00 (0-907628-77-X) Hambledon Press.

Corsaro. Giovanni Pacini. Ed. by Philip Gossett. (Italian Opera 1810-1840 Ser.: Vol. 34). 330p. 1985. 108.00 (0-8240-6583-2) Garland.

Corse Green Guide. (FRE.). Date not set. pap. 18.00 (2-06-700319-4, 319) Michelin.

***Corse Green Guide French Edition.** Michelin Staff. (FRE.). Date not set. pap. 17.95 (0-7859-7226-9) Fr & Eur.

Corse Sans Peine: Corsican for French Speakers. Assimil Staff. (FRE.). 1990. 28.95 (0-8288-4463-1, M10750); audio 125.00 (0-8288-9038-2, M4591) Fr & Eur.

Corset. Lewis Warsh. 28p. (Orig.). 1986. pap. 3.95 (0-932597-04-1) In Camera.

Corsets: A Visual History. R. L. Shep. LC 93-21419. (Illus.). 272p. (Orig.). 1993. pap. 26.95 (0-914046-20-9) R L Shep.

Corsets & Crinolines. Norah Waugh. LC 69-11134. (Illus.). 1954. pap. 18.95 (0-87830-526-2, Theatre Arts Bks) Routledge Chapman & Hall.

Corsham Boyhood: The Diary of Herbert Spackman, 1877-1891. Herbert Spackman. Ed. by Faith Sharp & Heather Tanner. 270p. (C). 1987. 41.00 (0-902633-71-6, Pub. by Picton UK) St Mut.

Corsica. (Insight Guides, Windows on the World Ser.). (Illus.). 350p. 1993. pap. 21.95 (0-395-65777-6) HM.

Corsica. (Visitor's Guides Ser.). (Illus.). 192p. 1993. pap. 13.95 (1-55650-587-6) Hunter NJ.

Corsican. William Heffernan. 448p. 1987. pap. 5.99 (0-451-16840-2, Sig) NAL-Dutton.

Corsican Brothers. Alexandre Dumas. 1976. 18.95 (0-8488-1291-3) Amereon Ltd.

Corsican Brothers. Alexandre Dumas. 68p. 1983. reprint ed. lib. bdg. 12.95 (0-89966-317-6) Buccaneer Bks.

Corsican Gambit. Sandra Marton. (Presents Ser.). 1994. mass mkt. 2.99 (0-373-11637-3, 1-11637-5) Harlequin Bks.

Corsican Gambit. large type ed. Sandra Marton. 1992. lib. bdg. 18.95 (0-263-13030-4, Pub. by Mills & Boon UK) Thorndike Pr.

Corsican Honor. William Heffernan. 480p. 1993. pap. 5.99 (0-451-17628-6, Sig) NAL-Dutton.

Corsican Woman. Madge Swindells. LC 87-40411. 384p. 1989. 18.45 (0-446-51371-7) Warner Bks.

Corson of the J. C. Clarence Mulford. (Hopalong Cassidy Ser.). 340p. 1974. reprint ed. lib. bdg. 22.95 (0-685-00358-2, Aeonian Pr) Amereon Ltd.

CoRT Thinking Program: CoRT 1 - Breadth. Edward De Bono. 80p. 1987. teacher ed. 12.50 (0-685-17432-8, Pergamon Pr) Elsevier.

Corte de los Milagros. Ramon Del Valle-Inclan. Ed. by Jose M. Garcia de la Torre. (Nueva Austral Ser.: Vol. 108). (SPA.). 1991. pap. text ed. 24.95x (84-239-1908-0) Elliots Bks.

***Cortege.** Carl Phillips. 96p. 1995. pap. 12.95 (1-55597-230-6) Graywolf.

***Cortege: A Poem.** Carl Phillips. Ed. by Gloria V. Hickok. 10p. (Orig.). 1994. pap. 3.00 (1-884235-00-X) Helicon Nine Eds.

***Cortes.** Steve Lilley. LC 95-1279. (Importance of Ser.). (J). 1995. 16.95 (1-56006-066-2) Lucent Bks.

Cortes: Conquerer of Mexico. William J. Jacobs. LC 93-31177. (Illus.). 64p. (J). (gr. 5-8). 1994. lib. bdg. 13.93 (0-531-20138-4) Watts.

Cortes: Conqueror of Mexico. William J. Jacobs. (First Bks.). (Illus.). 64p. (J). (gr. 4-6). 1994. pap. 5.95 (0-531-15723-7) Watts.

Cortes: The Great Adventurer & the Fate of Aztec Mexico. Richard L. Marks. LC 92-37170. 1993. 27.50 (0-679-40609-3) Knopf.

Cortes: The Life of the Conqueror of Mexico by His Secretary, Francisco Lopez de Gomara. Francisco Lopez de Gomara. Ed. & Tr. by Lesley B. Simpson. LC 64-13474. 1964. pap. 14.00 (0-520-00493-0) U CA Pr.

Cortes & the Downfall of the Aztec Empire. Jon M. White. (Illus.). 351p. 1989. pap. 10.95 (0-88184-461-6) Carroll & Graf.

Cortes & the Fall of the Aztec Empire. Caesar C. Cantu. (Illus.). 1966. 12.95 (0-685-16803-4, 0-910978-1-3) Modern World.

***Cortex Cerebri: Performance, Structural & Functional Organisation of the Cortex.** O. Creutzfeldt. Tr. by Mary Creutzfeldt. (Illus.). 672p. 1995. 98.00 (0-19-852324-6) OUP.

Cortex of the Rat. K. Zilles. (Illus.). 145p. 1985. 79.00 (0-387-15570-8) Spr-Verlag.

Cortez Peters Championship Formatting. Cortez W. Peters, Jr. LC 92-21574. 1992. write for info. (0-02-802300-5) Glencoe.

Cortez Peters Championship Keyboarding. Cortez W. Peters, Jr. (Illus.). 192p. 1988. text ed. 19.96 (0-07-049635-8) McGraw.

Cortez Peters Championship Typing Drills. Cortez W. Peters, Jr. 1979. text ed. 14.96 (0-07-049590-4) McGraw.

Cortez Peters Championship Typing Drills. 2nd ed. Cortez W. Peters, Jr. 112p. 1987. pap. text ed. 13.84 (0-07-049637-4) McGraw.

Cortical Circuits: Synaptic Organization & Cerebral Cortex - Structure, Function & Theory. Edward L. White. 264p. 1989. 52.50 (0-8176-3402-9) Birkhauser.

***Cortical Integration: Basic, Archicortical, & Cortical Association Levels of Neural Integration.** Ed. by Fernando Reinoso-Suarez & Cosimo Ajmone-Marsan. LC 84-17798. (International Brain Research Organization Monograph Ser.: No. 11). (Illus.). Date not set. reprint ed. pap. 129.40 (0-7837-9555-6, 2060304) Bks Demand.

Cortical Memory Functions. C. M. Fair. (Illus.). x, 210p. 1992. 64.50 (0-8176-3615-3) Spr-Verlag.

Cortical Monkey & Healing. Majid Ali. 352p. 1995. pap. 14.99 (1-879131-00-5) Inst of Prev Med.

***Cortical Neuron.** Ed. by Michael J. Gutnick & Istvan Mody. (Illus.). 448p. 1995. text ed. 65.00 (0-19-508330-X) OUP.

Cortical Sensory Organization: Multiple Auditory Areas, Vol. 3. Ed. by Clinton N. Woolsey. LC 81-81433. (Illus.). 280p. 1982. 69.50 (0-89603-032-6) Humana.

Cortical Sensory Organization: Multiple Somatic Areas, Vol. 1. Ed. by Clinton N. Woolsey. LC 81-81433. (Illus.). 264p. 1981. 69.50 (0-89603-030-X) Humana.

Cortical Sensory Organization: Multiple Visual Areas, Vol. 2. Ed. by Clinton N. Woolsey. LC 81-81433. (Illus.). 240p. 1981. 69.50 (0-89603-031-8) Humana.

Corticiaceae of North Europe, 8 vols., Set. J. Eriksson & Leif Ryvarden. (Illus.). 1631p. 1987. pap. text ed. 165.00 (0-685-47183-7, Pub. by Fungi-Flora NO) Lubrecht & Cramer.

Cortico-Hippocampal Interplay & the Representation of Contexts in the Brain. R. Miller. (Studies of Brain Function: Vol. 17). (Illus.). 288p. 1991. 70.00 (0-387-53109-2) Spr-Verlag.

Corticonics: Neural Circuits of the Cerebral Cortex. M. Abeles. (Illus.). 377p. (C). 1991. 59.95 (0-521-37476-6); pap. 27.95 (0-521-37617-3) Cambridge U Pr.

Corticospinal Function & Voluntary Movement. Robert Porter & Roger Lemon. (Monographs of the Physiological Society: No. 45). (Illus.). 440p. 1993. 90.00 (0-19-857745-1) OUP.

Corticothalamic Projections & Sensorimotor Activities. T. Frigrjesi. 1972. 36.50 (0-7204-7029-3) Elsevier.

Corticotropin: Its Pharmacologic Effects in Man & Practical Therapeutic Utilization. Gordon B. Myers & William Q. Wolfson. LC 55-7773. (Illus.). 83p. reprint ed. pap. 25.00 (0-7837-3823-4, 2043643) Bks Demand.

Corticotropin-Releasing Factor. CIBA Foundation Staff. LC 92-36532. (CIBA Foundation Symposia Ser.: No. 172). 357p. 1993. text ed. 72.00 (0-471-93448-8) Wiley.

Corticotropin-Releasing Factor: Basic & Clinical Studies of Neuropeptides. Ed. by Errol B. De Souza & Charles B. Nemeroff. 368p. 1989. 236.00 (0-8493-4550-2, QP572) CRC Pr.

Corticotropin-Releasing Factor & Cytokines: Role in the Stress Response. Ed. by Yvette Tache & Catherine Rivier. LC 93-35701. (Annals Ser.: Vol. 697). 1993. write for info. (0-89766-815-4); pap. write for info. (0-89766-816-2) NY Acad Sci.

Corticovisceral Theory Pathogenesis of Peptic Ulcer. K. M. Bykov & I. T. Kurtsin. LC 65-8089. (International Series of Monographs on Cerebrovisceral & Behavior Physical & Conditioned Reflexes: No. 2). 1966. 141.00 (0-08-011489-X, Pub. by Pergamon Repr UK) Franklin.

Cortina - Holt Traveler's French Dictionary: English-French - French-English. Teresa Nutting & Michel Marcy. LC 93-3672. 1993. pap. 6.95 (0-8327-0722-8) Cortina.

Cortina - Holt Traveler's German Dictionary: English-German - German-English. Josefa Zotter. Ed. by Dilaver Berberi & Edel A. Winje. LC 93-3679. 1993. write for info. (0-8327-0723-6) Cortina.

Cortina - Holt Traveler's Spanish Dictionary: English-Spanish - Spanish-English. Luis M. Laita & Carmen Gil de Montes. Ed. by Dilaver Berberi & Edel A. Winje. LC 93-3673. 1993. pap. 6.95 (0-8327-0721-X) Cortina.

***Cortina De Bagazo.** Zilia L. Laje. LC 95-94272. 576p. (Orig.). (SPA.). 1995. pap. 19.00 (0-9646224-0-8) Z L Laje.

Cortina Handy Spanish-English - English-Spanish Dictionary. Cortina Institute of Languages Staff. (Cortina Language Ser.). 574p. (ENG & SPA.). 1990. pap. 7.95 (0-8050-1505-1, Owl) H Holt & Co.

***Cortinariaceae p.p., Galerina, Gymnopilus, Leucocortinarius, Phaeogalera, Phaeolepiota, Phaeomarasmius, Pleuroflammula, Rozites & Stagnicola, Gymnopilus by P. D. Orton.** Roy Watling & Norma M. Gregory. (British Fungus Flora, Agarics & Boleti Ser.: 7). (Illus.). 131p. 1993. pap. 26.95x (1-872291-09-0) Lubrecht & Cramer.

Cortinarius Fr. und Nahe Verwandte Gottungen in Suedamerika. M. Moser & E. Horak. 1975. 162.50 (3-7682-5452-6) Lubrecht & Cramer.

Cortinas de Humo. Jack T. Chick. (Illus.). (Orig.). (SPA.). 1984. pap. 3.95 (0-937958-20-4) Chick Pubns.

***Cortland-Ithaca Dine-a-Mate.** 224p. 1994. pap. 20.00 (1-57393-004-0) Dine-A-Mate.

Corvair, 1960-1969. Wayne Machan & Bill Bruggen. LC 89-63378. (Authenticity Ser.). (Illus.). 128p. (Orig.). (YA). 1991. pap. 19.95 (0-929758-07-2) Beeman Jorgensen.

Corval Formula. V. G. Marketing. (Illus.). 56p. 1994. 14.95 (0-9641184-0-8) V G Mktg.

Corvette. Consumer Guide Auto Editors. (Illus.). 96p. 1993. 12.98 (1-56173-273-7, 1011400) Pubns Intl Ltd.

Corvette. Jay Schleifer. LC 91-18096. (Cool Classics Ser.). (Illus.). 48p. (J). (gr. 5). 1992. text ed. 13.95 (0-89686-697-1, Crstwood Hse) Silver Burdett Pr.

Corvette: A Piece of the Action. 2nd ed. Automobile Quarterly Staff. LC 84-61085. (Illus.). 240p. 1985. 39.95 (0-915038-44-7, 3-AQ-1086) Auto Quarterly.

Corvette: America's Sports Car. Consumer Guide Staff. 1990. 19.99 (0-517-02036-X) Random Hse Value.

Corvette: America's Star-Spangled Sports Car, Complete History. 3rd ed. Karl Ludvigsen. LC 72-85847. (Illus.). 324p. 1978. 49.95 (0-915038-06-4, 3-AQ-0006) Auto Quarterly.

Corvette: An American Legend. Roy D. Query. LC 86-70357. (Bloomington Gold Corvettes Ser.: Vol. I). (Illus.). 184p. 1986. 49.95 (0-915038-51-X, 3-AQ-0046) Auto Quarterly.

Corvette: Cream of the Crop. Photos & Text by Henry Rasmussen. (Top Ten Ser.). (Illus.). 132p. 1992. 29.95 (1-879301-01-6) Top Ten Pub.

Corvette: The American Sports Car. Shirley Haines & Harry Haines. LC 93-18066. (J). 1993. 17.26 (0-86593-253-0); 12.95 (0-685-66578-X) Rourke Corp.

Corvette: The Legend Lives On. Roy D. Query. LC 86-70357. (Bloomington Gold Corvettes Ser.: Vol. II). (Illus.). 192p. 1987. 49.95 (0-915038-52-8, 3-AQ-0048) Auto Quarterly.

Corvette! Thirty Years of Great Advertising, the Collection of William & Sharon Landis. Automobile Quarterly Staff, Jr. LC 82-73577. (Illus.). 176p. 1983. 19.95 (0-915038-38-2, 3-AQ-0031) Auto Quarterly.

Corvette: 1984-86. Chilton Automotives Editorial Staff. LC 85-47982. 232p. (Orig.). 1986. pap. 16.95 (0-8019-7682-0) Chilton.

***Corvette - America's Supercar.** Lamm. 1995. (0-7858-0341-6) Bk Sales Inc.

Corvette Black Book, 1953-1993. Michael Antonick. (Illus.). 128p. 1992. pap. 11.95 (0-933534-35-3) M Bruce Assocs.

Corvette Black Book, 1953-1994. Michael Antonick. (Illus.). 128p. 1993. pap. 11.95 (0-933534-36-1) M Bruce Assocs.

***Corvette Black Book 1953-1995.** Michael Antonick. (Illus.). 128p. 1994. pap. 11.95 (0-933534-37-X) M Bruce Assocs.

***Corvette Black Book 1953-1996.** Michael Bruce. (Illus.). 128p. 1995. pap. 11.95 (0-933534-38-8) Bruce Michael Assoc.

Corvette Cartoon Book. Wally Davis. (Illus.). 96p. (Orig.). 1991. pap. 5.95 (0-938417-02-9) Copouts Ink.

Corvette Chassis Restoration Guide, 1953 Through 1972, Vol. 1. Joseph A. Tripoli, Jr. 125p. (Orig.). (C). 1989. pap. 25.00 (0-9624817-0-X) J A Tripoli.

Corvette Chronicle. Consumer Guide Auto Editors & James Flammang. (Illus.). 192p. 1993. 19.98 (0-7853-0068-6, 1013800) Pubns Intl Ltd.

***Corvette Coloring Book: Official Coloring Book of the National Corvette Museum.** R. Bataglini, Sr. (Illus.). 24p. (Orig.). (J). 1995. pap. text ed. 5.00 (0-9647030-0-9) Tin Type.

Corvette Essentials: A Collector's Guide, 1956-1967. Chuck Brigermann. 1993. pap. 19.95 (0-89709-207-4) Liberty Pub.

Corvette Grand Sport: Photographic Race Log of the Magnificent Chevrolet Corvette Factory Specials, 1962-67. Dave Friedman & Lowell C. Paddock. (Illus.). 160p. 1989. 29.95 (0-87938-382-8) Motorbooks Intl.

Corvette Racers. Gregory Van Dare. (Illus.). 192p. 1992. pap. 19.95 (0-87938-574-X) Haynes Pubns.

Corvette Restoration & Technical Guide, 2 vols. 2nd ed. Noland Adams. (Illus.). 1987. write for info. (0-318-60843-X); Vol. 2, 1963-1967, 456p. 69.95 (0-915038-42-0, 3AQ0044) Auto Quarterly.

Corvette Restoration & Technical Guide, Vol. 1, 1953-1962. 2nd ed. Noland Adams. LC 80-65894. (Illus.). 432p. 1987. 69.95 (0-915038-57-9, 3AQ0051) Auto Quarterly.

Corvette Seatbelts: 1956-1976. Barbara Spear. 127p. 1989. pap. 15.95 (0-9630588-0-0) B Spear.

Corvette Specifications Guide, 1953-1972. John Amgwert. (Illus.). 168p. (Orig.). 1989. pap. 19.95 (0-685-29080-8) Natl Corvette.

Corvette Sports Car of America, C505. Michael Antonick. 1980. 37.95 (0-933534-11-6) M Bruce Assocs.

Corvette Sting Ray 1963-1967. Mike Mueller. (Illus.). 128p. 1994. pap. 19.95 (0-87938-788-2) Motorbooks Intl.

Corvette Stingray, 1963-1967 G-P. R. M. Clarke. (Gold Portfolio Ser.). (Illus.). 180p. 1990. pap. 24.95 (1-85520-024-4, Pub. by Brooklands Bks UK) Motorbooks Intl.

Corvina History of Hungary. P. Hanak. 243p. (C). 1991. 83.00 (0-685-60803-4, Pub. by Collets) St Mut.

Corvinus Press: A History & Bibliography. A. J. Flavell & Paul Nash. LC 93-33291. 301p. 1994. 79.95 (0-85967-952-7, Pub. by Scolar Pr UK) Ashgate Pub Co.

***Corvus.** Anselm Hollo. 96p. (Orig.). 1995. pap. 11.95 (1-56689-039-X) Coffee Hse.

Corwin Genealogy (Curwin, Curwen, Corwine) in the United States. E. T. Corwin. (Illus.). 318p. 1989. reprint ed. lib. bdg. 57.50 (0-8328-0428-2); reprint ed. pap. 47.50 (0-8328-0429-0) Higginson Bk Co.

Corwin on the Constitution, Vol. One: The Foundations of American Constitution & Political Thought, the Powers of Congress, & the President's Power of Removal. Edward S. Corwin. Ed. by Richard Loss. 392p. 1981. 47.50 (0-8014-1381-8) Cornell U Pr.

Corwin on the Constitution, Vol. Three: On Liberty against Government. Edward S. Corwin. Ed. by Richard Loss. LC 80-69823. 272p. 1988. 47.50 (0-8014-2176-4) Cornell U Pr.

Corwin on the Constitution, Vol. Two: The Judiciary. Edward S. Corwin. Ed. by Richard Loss. LC 80-69823. 400p. (C). 1987. 47.50 (0-8014-1996-4) Cornell U Pr.

Corwin's Constitution: Essays & Insights of Edward S. Corwin. Edward S. Corwin & Kenneth D. Crews. LC 86-7590. (Contributions in Legal Studies: No. 34). 285p. 1986. text ed. 55.00 (0-313-24903-2, CCU, Greenwood Pr) Greenwood.

Cory. Mark Dunster. (Rin Ser.: Pt. 51). 55p. (Orig.). 1984. pap. 4.00 (0-89642-117-1) Linden Pubs.

Cory - Profile of a President. Isabelo T. Crisostomo. 340p. 1987. reprint ed. 22.95 (0-8283-1913-8) Branden Pub Co.

Cory & the Horned Toad. Blaine Yorgason & Brenton Yorgason. (Gospel Power Ser.). 33p. (Orig.). 1990. pap. 3.50 (0-929985-20-6) Jackman Pubng.

Cory Aquino & the People of the Philippines. Claude Buss. (Portable Stanford Book Ser.). (Illus.). 189p. 1987. 16.95 (0-916318-25-7); pap. 10.95 (0-916318-24-9) Stanford Alumni Assn.

Cory Coleman, Grade 2. Larry D. Brimner. LC 89-24694. (Illus.). 80p. (J). (gr. 2-4). 1991. pap. 4.95 (0-8050-1844-1, Bks Young Read) H Holt & Co.

Cory Everson's Fat-Free & Fit: A Complete Program for Fitness, Exercise, & Healthy Living. Cory Everson & Carole Jacobs. LC 93-36944. (Illus.). 240p. (Orig.). 1994. pap. 15.00 (0-399-51858-4, Perigree Bks) Berkley Pub.

Cory Everson's Workout. Corinna Everson & Jeff Everson. (Illus.). 192p. (Orig.). 1991. pap. 15.95 (0-399-51684-0, Perigree Bks) Berkley Pub.

Cory, Pts. 1 & 2: Lineal Ancestors of Rhoda Axtell Cory. C. H. Cory, Jr. (Illus.). 300p. 1991. reprint ed. lib. bdg. 54.00 (0-8328-2132-2); reprint ed. pap. 44.00 (0-8328-2133-0) Higginson Bk Co.

Cory, Pts. 1 & 2: Lineal Ancestors of Susan Kitchell Mulford. C. H. Cory, Jr. 295p. 1991. reprint ed. lib. bdg. 53.50 (0-8328-2128-4); reprint ed. pap. 43.50 (0-8328-2129-2) Higginson Bk Co.

Cory, Pts. 1 & 2: Lineal Ancestors of Susan Mulford Cory. C. H. Cory, Jr. 437p. 1991. reprint ed. lib. bdg. 74.00 (0-8328-2130-6); reprint ed. pap. 64.00 (0-8328-2131-4) Higginson Bk Co.

Cory the Cormorant. Jane Weinberger. LC 91-68128. (Illus.). 40p. (J). (ps-3). 1992. pap. 8.95 (0-932433-92-8) Windswept Hse.

Cory the Crocodile. Illus. by Bob Storms. (World of Animals Ser.). 24p. (Orig.). (J). (gr. k-4). 1993. pap. 4.95 (0-89346-530-5) Heian Intl.

Corydon. Andre Gide. 148p. (FRE.). 1991. pap. 10.95 (0-7859-2604-6, 2070383350) Fr & Eur.

Corydon. Andre Gide. (Folio Ser.: No. 2235). pap. 24.95 (2-07-038335-0) Schoenhof.

Corydon - The Forgotten Battle of the Civil War. W. Fred Conway, Sr. (Illus.). 128p. (Orig.). 1991. pap. 9.95 (0-925165-03-4) Fire Buff Hse.

Coryneform Bacteria. Ed. by I. J. Bousfield & A. G. Callely. (Society for General Microbiology Special Publications). 1979. text ed. 99.00 (0-12-119650-X) Acad Pr.

***Cory's Big Step.** Carol A. Hanshaw. (Play Along Ser.). 16p. (J). (ps-2). 1995. write for info. (1-57234-059-2) YES Ent.

Cory's Counting Game. (Surprise Bks.). (Illus.). 24p. (J). (ps). 1979. 6.95 (0-8431-0629-8) Price Stern.

Corythosaurus. William Lindsay. LC 92-54309. (American Museum of Natural History Ser.). (Illus.). 32p. (J). (gr. 3 up). 1993. 12.95 (1-56458-225-6) Dorling Kindersley.

Corythosaurus. F. Swann. (Dinosaur Library). (Illus.). 24p. (J). (gr. 3 up). 1989. lib. bdg. 14.60 (0-86592-521-6); lib. bdg. 10.95 (0-685-58283-3) Rourke Corp.

Cosa: The Lamps. Cleo R. Fitch & Norma W. Goldman. LC 93-48547. (Memoirs of the American Academy in Rome Ser.: No. 39). (Illus.). 500p. 1994. text ed. 64.00 (0-472-10518-3) U of Mich Pr.

Cosa: The Making of a Roman Town. Frank E. Brown. (Illus.). 150p. 1980. 37.50 (0-472-04100-2) U of Mich Pr.

Cosa III: The Buildings of the Forum: Colony, Municipium, & Village. Frank E. Brown et al. LC 92-20337. (Memoirs of the American Academy in Rome Ser.: Vol. XXXVII). (Illus.). 256p. 1993. 65.00 (0-271-00825-3) Pa St U Pr.

Cosas Cambian. Phyllis M. Bourne. (Que Maravilla! Ser.). (Illus.). 24p. (Orig.). (SPA.). (J). (gr. 1-3). 1992. pap. text ed. 29.95 (1-56334-028-3); pap. text ed. 6.00 (1-56334-042-9) Hampton-Brown.

Cosas Cambian: Level 2. Phyllis M. Bourne. (Que Maravilla! Ser.). 24p. (Orig.). (SPA.). 1992. pap. 6.00 (1-56334-219-7) Hampton-Brown.

Cosas de Cada Dia - Everyday Things. Ed. by Maria Puncel. Tr. by Javier F. Aixela. (Diccionarios Visuales Altea Ser. - Visual Dictionary Ser.). (Illus.). 64p. (SPA.). (YA). (gr. 5-12). 1992. write for info. (84-372-4527-3) Santillana.

Cosas De Katy. (Spanish Children's Classics Ser.: No. 800-6). (SPA.). (J). 1990. boxed 3.50 (0-7214-1401-X) Ladybird Bks.

Cosas Grandes y Chicas. (SPA.). (J). (ps-3). 1993. pap. 2.25 (0-307-50073-X, Golden Pr) Western Pub.

Cosas que Conejito Ve. (SPA.). (J). (ps-3). 1993. pap. 5.95 (0-307-91591-3, Golden Pr) Western Pub.

Cosas Que Hacer para Navidad. Meg Braga. (Editorial Mundo Hispano Ser.). (YA). (gr. 4-6). 1989. reprint ed. 2.75 (0-311-26607-X) Casa Bautista.

Cosas y Casos de los Albores del Siglo XVII Espanol. Federico Sanchez & Escribano Sanchez. 157p. (SPA.). 2.25 (0-318-14251-1) Hispanic Inst.

An Asterisk (*) at the beginning of an entry indicates that the title is appearing in BIP for the first time.

An Asterisk (*) at the beginning of an entry indicates that the title is appearing in BIP for the first time.

C

Cosmic Messenger. Graham Radcliffe. 160p. (C). 1990. 90.00 (*0-86439-140-4*, Pub. by Boolarong Pubns AT) St Mut.

Cosmic Microwave Background: Twenty-Five Years Later. Ed. by N. Mandolesi & N. Vittorio. (C). 1990. lib. bdg. 115.50 (*0-7923-0849-2*) Kluwer Ac.

Cosmic Mind-Boggling Book. Neil McAleer. 320p. (Orig.). 1989. pap. 11.95 (*0-446-39046-1*) Warner Bks.

Cosmic Mission Fulfilled. 3rd ed. Ralph M. Lewis. LC 66-25243. 364p. 1978. 18.95 (*0-912057-22-X*, 501790) AMORC.

Cosmic Mission Fulfilled: The Life of Dr. H. Spencer Lewis - a 20th Century Mystic. Ralph M. Lewis. LC 66-25243. (Illus.). 364p. Date not set. pap. 16.95 (*0-912057-90-4*, 501790) AMORC.

Cosmic Moral Law. 3rd ed. Omraam M. Aivanhov. (Complete Works: Vol. 12). 284p. 1984. pap. 14.95 (*2-85566-445-4*) Prosveta USA.

Cosmic Mountain in Canaan & the Old Testament. Richard J. Clifford. LC 71-188968. (Harvard Semitic Monographs: No. 4). (Illus.). 221p. reprint ed. pap. 67.00 (*0-7837-1685-0*, 2057215) Bks Demand.

Cosmic Music: Keys for the Musical Interpretation of Reality. Ed. by Joscelyn Godwin. 260p. (Orig.). 1989. pap. 16.95 (*0-89281-070-X*) Inner Tradit.

Cosmic Mutons & Neutrinos. T. J. De Graaf. write for info. (*0-318-55151-9*, Pergamon Pr) Elsevier.

Cosmic Mysteries. rev. ed. (Voyage Through the Universe Ser.). 1992. write for info. (*0-8094-9062-5*); lib. bdg. write for info. (*0-8094-9063-3*) Time-Life.

Cosmic Octave: Origin of Harmony. Cousto. Tr. by Chris Baker & Judith Harrison. (Illus.). 200p. 1988. pap. 12.95 (*0-940795-04-3*) LifeRhythm.

Cosmic Odyssey. Jean Heidmann. Tr. by Simon Mitton. (Illus.). 220p. 1989. 21.95 (*0-521-34377-1*) Cambridge U Pr.

Cosmic Omelet. John C. Anderson. LC 79-89328. 1980. 5.95 (*0-87212-102-X*) Libra.

Cosmic Onion: Quarks & the Nature of the Universe. Frank Close. LC 86-3646. (Illus.). 192p. reprint ed. text ed. 34.00 (*0-88318-491-5*) Am Inst Physics.

Cosmic Optimism: A Study of the Interpretation of Evolution. Frederick Conner. (BCL1-PS American Literature Ser.). 458p. 1993. reprint ed. lib. bdg. 99.00 (*0-7812-6584-3*) Rprt Serv.

***Cosmic Patent.** Proctor Jones. LC 94-78062. 250p. (Orig.). 1995. pap. write for info. (*0-9608860-8-7*) Proctor Jones.

Cosmic Patriot Files, 2 vols., Set. Ed. by Commander X. 1993. 29.95 (*0-938294-06-7*) Glob Comm-Inner Lght.

Cosmic Patterns. John H. Nelson. 80p. 1974. 6.00 (*0-86690-133-7*, N1355-014) Am Fed Astrologers.

Cosmic Patterns, Vol. 1: An Explanation of the Underlying Intuitive Structure of the World in Its Mythical, Natural, Historical, & Cultural Manifestations. Robert Navon. 303p. (Orig.). 1993. pap. 25.00 (*0-933601-22-0*) Selene Bks.

Cosmic Perspective. Brian Stableford. Bd. with Custer's Last Stand. (Drumm Booklet Ser.: No. 21). 44p. (Orig.). 1985. Set pap. 2.00 (*0-936055-21-9*) C Drumm Bks.

Cosmic Perspective. deluxe limited ed. Brian Stableford. Bd. with Custer's Last Stand. (Drumm Booklet Ser.: No. 21). 44p. (Orig.). 1985. 5.00 (*0-936055-22-7*) C Drumm Bks.

Cosmic Perspectives. Ed. by S. K. Biswas et al. (Illus.). 300p. (C). 1989. 59.95 (*0-521-34354-2*) Cambridge U Pr.

Cosmic Pinball. Susan Kern & Phil Kern. (Illus.). 125p. 1991. pap. 69.95 (*1-56516-010-X*) Houston IN.

Cosmic Plasma. Hannes Alfven. 1981. lib. bdg. 70.00 (*90-277-1151-8*) Kluwer Ac.

Cosmic Power Within You. Joseph Murphy. 203p. 1988. pap. 7.95 (*0-13-179128-1*) P-H.

Cosmic Power Within You. Joseph Murphy. 1986. 5.95 (*0-13-179176-1*, Reward) P-H.

Cosmic Pulse of Life: The Revolutionary Biological Power Behind UFOs. rev. ed. Trevor J. Constable. LC 90-60345. (Illus.). 504p. 1990. pap. 24.95 (*0-945685-07-6*) Borderland Sciences.

Cosmic Pulse of Life, Vol. 1: The Revolutionary Biological Power Behind UFOs. Trevor J. Constable. (Illus.). 450p. 1989. 24.95 (*0-9622677-0-8*) Merlin.

Cosmic Questions: Galactic Halos, Cold Dark Matter, & the End of Time. Richard Morris. LC 93-13373. 208p. 1993. text ed. 24.95 (*0-471-59521-7*) Wiley.

Cosmic Radiation in Contemporary Astrophysics. Ed. by Maurice M. Shapiro. 1985. lib. bdg. 101.50 (*90-277-2144-0*) Kluwer Ac.

Cosmic Ray - Invited & Rapporteur Papers: Proceedings of the XXIII International Conference. R. B. Hicks et al. 532p. 1994. text ed. 121.00 (*981-02-1519-3*) World Scientific Pub.

Cosmic Rays. Ed. by L. I. Dorman. 675p. 1974. 110.25 (*0-444-10480-1*, North Holland) Elsevier.

Cosmic Rays. Michael W. Friedlander. LC 88-24371. (Illus.). 176p. 1989. 34.00 (*0-674-17458-5*) HUP.

Cosmic Rays. Michael W. Friedlander. (Illus.). 176p. 1990. pap. 14.95 (*0-674-17459-3*) HUP.

Cosmic Rays. A. M. Hillas. 306p. (C). 1972. 131.00 (*0-08-016724-1*, Pub. by Pergamon Repr UK) Franklin.

Cosmic Rays. J. G. Wilson & G. E. Perry. LC 75-38743. (Wykeham Science Ser.: No. 40). 150p. (C). 1976. 18.00 (*0-8448-1167-X*, Crane Russak) Taylor & Francis.

Cosmic Rays & Particle Physics. Thomas K. Gaisser. 320p. (C). 1991. 79.95 (*0-521-32667-2*); pap. 34.95 (*0-521-33931-6*) Cambridge U Pr.

Cosmic Rays & Particle Physics - Nineteen Seventy-Eight: Bartol Conference. Ed. by T. K. Gaisser. LC 79-50489. (AIP Conference Proceedings Ser.: No. 49). (Illus.). 1979. lib. bdg. 23.50 (*0-88318-148-7*) Am Inst Physics.

Cosmic Rays & Problems of Space Physics. Ed. by Y. G. Shafer. 320p. 1967. text ed. 82.00 (*0-7065-0458-5*, Pub. by Keter Pub IS) Coronet Bks.

Cosmic Rays in Interplanetary Magnetic Fields. I. N. Toptygin. 1985. lib. bdg. 149.50 (*90-277-1863-6*) Kluwer Ac.

Cosmic Rays in the Heliosphere. Ed. by A. J. Somogyi. (Advances in Space Research Ser.: Vol. 1, No. 3). (Illus.). 177p. 1981. pap. 25.00 (*0-08-027159-6*, Pergamon Pr) Elsevier.

Cosmic Rays, Supernovae & the Interstellar Medium. Ed. by Maurice M. Shapiro et al. (C). 1991. lib. bdg. 112.50 (*0-7923-1278-3*) Kluwer Ac.

Cosmic Rays, the Sun, & Geomagnetism: The Works of Scott E. Forbush. Ed. by James A. Van Allan. LC 93-26144. 472p. 1993. 48.50 (*0-87590-833-0*) Am Geophysical.

Cosmic Reader of the Southwest for Young People. Ruben D. Salaz. (Illus.). (J). (gr. 4 up). 1976. pap. 6.95 (*0-932492-00-2*) Cosmic Hse NM.

Cosmic Retribution: The Infernal Art of Joe Coleman. Joe Coleman. 1991. pap. 19.95 (*0-922915-06-7*) Feral Hse.

Cosmic Revelation: The Hindu Way to God. Bede Griffiths. 128p. 1983. pap. 9.95 (*0-87243-119-3*) Templegate.

Cosmic Scents One. Ralph E. Vaughn. LC 77-79575. 1979. 8.95 (*0-87212-096-1*) Libra.

Cosmic Science of the Ancient Masters. 2nd ed. Hilton Hotema. 97p. 1969. reprint ed. spiral bd. 9.35 (*0-7873-1281-9*) Mokelumne.

Cosmic Shakti Kundalini: The Universal Mother. Satguru S. Keshavadas. LC 76-11347. (Illus.). 112p. (Orig.). 1976. pap. 8.00 (*0-942508-04-1*) Vishwa.

***Cosmic Shocks.** Torkom Saraydarian. LC 89-192439. (Illus.). 192p. (Orig.). 1989. pap. 18.00 (*0-929874-09-9*) TSG Pub Found.

Cosmic Software Catalog, 1993: A Comprehensive Directory of All Available NASA Computer Programs. 220p. (Orig.). (C). 1994. pap. text ed. 60.00 (*0-7881-0482-9*) Diane Pub.

Cosmic Strings: The Current Status. Ed. by Lawrence M. Krauss & F. S. Accetta. 256p. (C). 1989. pap. 40.00 (*9971-5-0736-6*) World Scientific Pub.

Cosmic Strings & Other Topological Defects. Alexander Vilenkin & E. Paul Shellard. (Cambridge Monographs on Mathematical Physics). (Illus.). 518p. (C). 1995. 100.00 (*0-521-39153-9*) Cambridge U Pr.

Cosmic Symbolism. Sepharial. 294p. 1981. pap. 26.00 (*0-89540-071-5*, SB-071) Sun Pub.

Cosmic Tarot. Norbert Losche. 36p. 1988. 16.00 (*0-88079-395-3*) US Games Syst.

Cosmic-The La Raza Sketchbook. Ruben D. Salaz. 1975. pap. 6.95 (*0-932482-00-7*) Blue Feather.

Cosmic-The Raza Sketchbook. Ruben D. Salaz. 1975. pap. 6.95 (*0-317-62203-X*) Cosmic Hse NM.

Cosmic Time Travel: A Scientific Odyssey. Barry Parker. (Illus.). 320p. 1991. 24.50 (*0-306-43966-2*, Plenum Pr) Plenum.

Cosmic Top Secret. William Hamilton, III. 150p. 1992. 8.95 (*0-938294-75-X*) Glob Comm-Inner Lght.

Cosmic Top Secret. William F. Hamilton, III. 8.95 (*0-685-64741-2*) Glob Comm-Inner Lght.

Cosmic Tour Ba Gua. Hua-Ching Ni. (Master's Series of Taoist Internal Arts). 1994. pap. write for info. (*0-937064-43-2*) SevenStar Comm.

***Cosmic Trigger III.** Robert A. Wilson. (Illus.). 256p. (Orig.). 1995. pap. 14.95 (*1-56184-112-9*) New Falcon Pubns.

Cosmic Trigger, Vol. I: Final Secret of the Illuminati. rev. ed. Robert A. Wilson. LC 77-89429. (Illus.). 280p. (C). 1991. reprint ed. pap. 12.95 (*1-56184-003-3*) New Falcon Pubns.

Cosmic Trigger, Vol. II: Down to Earth. Robert A. Wilson. LC 91-68040. 300p. (Orig.). 1991. pap. 12.95 (*1-56184-011-4*) New Falcon Pubns.

Cosmic Understanding. Carl Unger. 1982. reprint ed. pap. 2.50 (*0-916786-62-5*) R Steiner Col Pubns.

Cosmic Understanding: Philosophy & Science of the Universe. Milton K. Munitz. 296p. (Orig.). 1990. text ed. 45.00 (*0-691-07312-0*) Princeton U Pr.

Cosmic Unfoldment: The Individualizing Process As Mirrored in the Life of Jesus. Diane K. Pike. LC 76-45344. 99p. 1976. pap. 4.95 (*0-916192-08-3*) L P Pubns.

Cosmic Verses: PTL? Heaven? Hell? Superlove. LC 89-91094. 200p. (Orig.). 1991. spiral bd. 17.00 (*0-9602334-2-3*) Superlove.

Cosmic Voice, 1. Ed. by George King. LC 86-215795. 91p. 1957. pap. 10.00 (*0-937249-00-9*) Aetherius Soc.

Cosmic Voice, 2. Ed. by George King. LC 86-215795. 91p. 1957. write for info. (*0-937249-01-7*) Aetherius Soc.

Cosmic Voyage: Through Time & Space, 1992 Edition. William K. Hartmann. 500p. (C). 1992. pap. 42.95 (*0-534-17376-4*) Intl Thomson.

Cosmic Web: Scientific Field Models & Literary Strategies in the Twentieth Century. N. Katherine Hayles. LC 84-45141. 232p. 1984. 34.95 (*0-8014-1742-2*); pap. 13.95 (*0-8014-9290-4*) Cornell U Pr.

Cosmic Winter. Victor Clube & Bill Napier. (Illus.). 288p. 1990. 34.95 (*0-631-16953-9*) Blackwell Pubs.

Cosmic Wisdom Beyond Astrology: Towards a New Gnosis of the Stars. Adrian G. Gilbert. (Illus.). 208p. 1995. pap. 9.95 (*1-873616-00-7*, Pub. by Solos UK) Atrium Pubs.

Cosmic Wisdom of Joe Bob Briggs. Joe B. Briggs. 1991. 17.95 (*0-394-58890-8*) Random.

Cosmic Womb: An Interpretation of Man's Relationship to the Infinite. Arthur W. Osborn. LC 69-17714. (Orig.). 1969. pap. 4.95 (*0-8356-0001-7*, Quest) Theos Pub Hse.

Cosmic Wormholes: The Search for Interstellar Shortcuts. Paul Halpern. LC 93-17393. 1993. write for info. (*0-525-27029-9*, Plume); pap. 11.00 (*0-452-27029-4*, Plume) NAL-Dutton.

***Cosmic X-Ray Astronomy.** fac. ed. David J. Adams. LC 80-491685. (Monographs on Astronomical Subjects: No. 6). (Illus.). 160p. 1980. reprint ed. pap. 45.60 (*0-7837-8001-X*, 2047757) Bks Demand.

Cosmic Zygote: Cosmology in the Amazon Basin. Peter G. Roe. (Illus.). 451p. 1982. 50.00 (*0-8135-0896-7*) Rutgers U Pr.

Cosmical Gas Dynamics: Proceedings of the Manchester Conference, April, 1985. Ed. by F. D. Kahn. 338p. 1986. lib. bdg. 102.00 (*90-6764-053-0*, Pub. by VSP NE) Coronet Bks.

Cosmical Magnetism: Proceedings of the NATO Advanced Research Workshop, Cambridge, England, July 5-9, 1993. Ed. by D. Lynden-Bell. LC 94-668. (NATO Advanced Study Institutes Series C, Mathematical & Physical Sciences: Vol. 422). 228p. (C). 1994. lib. bdg. 89.00 (*0-7923-2730-6*) Kluwer Ac.

Cosmically Yours. deluxe limited ed. Susan Mary Gardner. 64p. 1990. Collector's Ed., Signed & Numbered. 34.95 (*0-9625307-0-0*) Inner Garden Pathways.

Cosmicomics. Italo Calvino. Tr. by William Weaver. LC 76-14795. 153p. 1976. pap. 6.95 (*0-15-622600-6*, Harvest Bks) HarBrace.

Cosmo-Biological Birth Control. Shalila Sharamon & Bodo Baginski. 240p. (Orig.). 1989. pap. 14.95 (*0-941524-82-5*) Lotus Light.

Cosmo-Creative Society: Logistical Networks in a Dynamic Economy. David F. Batten et al. Ed. by K. Kobayashi & K. Yoshikawa. LC 93-34383. (Advances in Spatial & Network Economics Ser.). (Illus.). viii, 296p. 1993. 99.00 (*0-387-57158-2*) Spr-Verlag.

Cosmo Dictionary of English Nepali. H. C. Duncan & G. P. Pradhan. 399p. (C). 1991. 60.00 (*0-89771-071-1*, Pub. by Ratna Pustak Bhandar) St Mut.

***Cosmo Gets an Ear.** Gary Clemente. LC 94-75586. (Illus.). 54p. (J). (gr. 1-6). 1994. 9.95 (*0-916708-24-1*) Modern Signs.

Cosmo 101: The Four-Dimensional Universe. Michael R. Feltz. LC 92-97463. (Illus.). 176p. (Orig.). 1993. pap. 9.95 (*0-9635950-0-8*) Cosmos Pub.

Cosmobiology: A Modern Approach in Astrology. Doris Greaves. 136p. 1980. 10.00 (*0-86690-110-8*, G1152-014) Am Fed Astrologers.

Cosmochemical Evolution & the Origins of Life: Proceedings of the International Conference on the Origin of Life with Invited Papers & Contributed Papers, 4th, 1973, 2 vols, 2. International Conference on the Origin of Life Staff et al. Ed. by J. Oro et al. LC 74-77967. vii, 755p. 1974. lib. bdg. 80.50 (*90-277-0518-6*) Kluwer Ac.

Cosmochemistry: Proceedings of the Symposium, Cambridge, MA, Aug. 1972. Cosmochemistry Symposium Staff. Ed. by A. G. Cameron. LC 73-88588. (Astrophysics & Space Science Library: No. 40). 180p. 1973. lib. bdg. 62.00 (*90-277-0394-9*) Kluwer Ac.

Cosmochemistry & the Origin of Life. Ed. by Cyril Ponnamperuma. 1983. lib. bdg. 136.50 (*90-277-1544-0*) Kluwer Ac.

Cosmogenesis: The Growth of Order in the Universe. David Layzer. (Illus.). 336p. 1990. 27.95 (*0-19-505528-4*) OUP.

Cosmogenesis: The Growth of Order in the Universe. David Layzer. (Illus.). 336p. 1991. reprint ed. pap. 13.95 (*0-19-506908-0*) OUP.

Cosmogonical Processes: Proceedings of the Symposium Held in Boulder, Colorado, March 1985. Ed. by W. D. Arnett et al. 310p. 1986. lib. bdg. 114.00 (*90-6764-054-9*, Pub. by VSP NE) Coronet Bks.

Cosmogony & Ethical Order: New Studies in Comparative Ethics. Ed. by Robin W. Lovin & Frank E. Reynolds. LC 85-1159. viii, 448p. 1985. lib. bdg. 55.00 (*0-226-49416-0*) U Ch Pr.

Cosmogony & Evolution. 2nd ed. Richard Ingalese & Isabella Ingalese. 276p. 1972. reprint ed. spiral bd. 9.35 (*0-7873-0463-8*) Mokelumne.

***Cosmographers and Pilots of the Spanish Maritime Empire.** Ursula Lamb. (Jvariorum Collected Studies Ser.: Vol. 499). 280p. 1995. 82.50 (*0-86078-473-8*, Pub. by Variorum UK) Ashgate Pub Co.

Cosmographia of Bernardus Silvestris. Winthrop Wetherbee. 180p. 1990. text ed. 58.00 (*0-231-03673-6*); pap. text ed. 12.50 (*0-231-09625-9*) Col U Pr.

Cosmographiae Introductio of Martin Waldseemuller in Facsimile. Martin Waldseemuller. LC 77-102258. (Select Bibliographies Reprint Ser.). 1977. 31.95 (*0-8369-5143-3*) Ayer.

Cosmographical Glass: Renaissance Diagrams of the Universe. S. K. Heninger. LC 76-62637. (Illus.). 227p. reprint ed. pap. 64.70 (*0-8357-2932-X*, 2039171) Bks Demand.

Cosmography: A Blueprint for the Science & Culture of the Future. R. Buckminster Fuller. 320p. 1992. text ed. 24.95 (*0-02-541850-5*) Macmillan.

Cosmologia: El Humanismo Cristiano. Jose D. Oropesa. LC 90-82885. (Coleccion Polymita Ser.). 140p. (Orig.). 1990. pap. 9.95 (*0-89729-573-0*) Ediciones.

***Cosmological Aspects of X-Ray Clusters of Galaxies: Proceedings of the NATO Advanced Study Institute, Velen, Germany June 6 - June 18, 1993.** Ed. by Waltraut C. Seitter. (NATO ASI, Series C, Mathematical & Physical Sciences Ser.). 516p. (C). 1994. lib. bdg. 225.00 (*0-7923-3058-7*) Kluwer Ac.

Cosmological Constants: Papers In Modern Cosmology. Jeremy Bernstein & Gerald Feinberg. LC 86-2220. 352p. 1989. text ed. 53.00 (*0-231-06376-8*); pap. text ed. 26.50 (*0-231-06377-6*) Col U Pr.

Cosmological Dark Matter: Proceedings of the International School. J. W. Valle & A. Perez. 344p. 1994. text ed. 112.00 (*981-02-1879-6*) World Scientific Pub.

Cosmological Eye. Henry Miller. LC 75-88729. 1969. reprint ed. pap. 12.95 (*0-8112-0110-4*, NDP109) New Directions.

Cosmological Milkshake: A Semi-Serious Look at the Size of Things. Robert Ehrlich. LC 93-28135. (Illus.). 250p. (J). 1994. 24.95 (*0-8135-2045-2*) Rutgers U Pr.

Cosmological Milkshake: A Semi-Serious Look at the Size of Things. Robert Ehrlich. LC 93-28135. (Illus.). 259p. (C). 1995. pap. 14.95 (*0-8135-2046-0*) Rutgers U Pr.

Cosmologies in the Making: A Generative Approach to Cultural Variation in Inner New Guinea. Fredrik Barth. (Cambridge Studies in Social & Cultural Anthropology: No. 64). (Illus.). 128p. 1987. 49.95 (*0-521-34279-1*) Cambridge U Pr.

Cosmologies in the Making: A Generative Approach to Cultural Variation in Inner New Guinea. Fredrik Barth. (Cambridge Studies in Social & Cultural Anthropology: No. 64). (Illus.). 112p. (C). 1990. pap. 13.95 (*0-521-38735-3*) Cambridge U Pr.

Cosmologies of Consciousness. E. C. Barksdale. 148p. 1980. text ed. 18.95 (*0-87073-969-7*); pap. text ed. 11.95 (*0-87073-970-0*) Schenkman Bks Inc.

Cosmologists Second: The Riddle of Time in Theories of the Universe. Konrad Rudnicki. Tr. by Michael Lipson. 128p. (Orig.). 1991. pap. 12.95 (*0-940262-41-X*) Lindisfarne Pr.

Cosmology. G. Contopoulos & D. Kotsakis. (Illus.). 250p. 1987. pap. 44.00 (*0-387-16922-9*) Spr-Verlag.

Cosmology. William Kaufman. (C). 1995. text ed. write for info. (*0-7167-2486-3*) W H Freeman.

***Cosmology: A First Course.** Marc Lachieze-Rey. (Illus.). 140p. (C). 1995. write for info. (*0-521-47441-8*); pap. write for info. (*0-521-47966-5*) Cambridge U Pr.

Cosmology: Historical, Literary, Philosophical, Religious, & Scientific Perspectives. Ed. by Norriss S. Hetherington. LC 92-46276. (Illus.). 648p. 1993. 85.00 (*0-8153-1085-4*, H1634); pap. 18.95 (*0-8153-0934-1*) Garland.

***Cosmology: Science & the Meanings of the Universe.** John McLeish. (Illus.). 212p. 1995. 39.95 (*0-7475-1145-4*, Pub. by Bloomsbury Pub Ltd UK) Trafalgar.

***Cosmology: The Origin & Evolution of Cosmic Structure.** Peter Coles & Francesco Lucchin. LC 94-46441. 1995. text ed. 54.95 (*0-471-95473-X*) Wiley.

Cosmology: The Science of the Universe. Edward R. Harrison. LC 80-18703. (Illus.). 480p. 1981. 49.95 (*0-521-22981-2*) Cambridge U Pr.

Cosmology & Astrophysics: Essays in Honor of Thomas Gold on His 60th Birthday. Ed. by Yervant Terzian & Elizabeth Bilson. (Illus.). 168p. 1982. 39.95 (*0-8014-1497-0*) Cornell U Pr.

Cosmology & Elementary Particles: Proceedings of the 2nd Winter School of Physics. Ed. by D. R. Altschuler et al. 400p. (C). 1992. text ed. 114.00 (*981-02-0808-1*) World Scientific Pub.

***Cosmology & Geophysics.** fac. ed. Paul S. Wesson. LC 78-10133. (Monographs on Astronomical Subjects: No. 3). 248p. 1978. reprint ed. pap. 70.70 (*0-7837-8018-4*, 2047774) Bks Demand.

Cosmology & Gravitation: Proceedings of the 6th Brazilian Sch. M. Novello et al. 1993. text ed. 103.00 (*981-02-0123-0*) World Scientific Pub.

Cosmology & Large-Scale Structure in the Universe. Ed. by R. De Carvalho. (ASP Conference Series Publications: Vol. 24). 225p. 1992. 40.00 (*0-937707-43-0*) Astron Soc Pacific.

Cosmology & Particle Physics. Ed. by L. Fang & A. Zee. (CCAST Ser.). xii, 446p. 1988. pap. text ed. 35.00 (*2-88124-691-5*) Gordon & Breach.

Cosmology & Particle Physics. Ed. by David Lindley et al. 1991. 18.00 (*0-917853-42-3*, RB-57) Am Assn Physics.

Cosmology & Particle Physics: Proceedings of the NATO Advanced Study Institute on Cosmology & Particle Physics (13th Course on the International School of Cosmology & Gravitatio of the Ettore Majorana Centre for Scientific Culture), Erice, Italy, May 3-14, 1993. Ed. by Venzo De Sabbata. LC 94-8301. (NATO Advanced Study Institutes Series C, Mathematical & Physical Sciences). 352p. (C). 1994. lib. bdg. 137.00 (*0-7923-2768-3*) Kluwer Ac.

Cosmology & Particle Physics: Proceedings of the Workshop, Berkeley, July 28-August 15, 1987. Ed. by I. Hinchliffe. 216p. 1987. pap. 45.00 (*9971-5-0215-1*) World Scientific Pub.

Cosmology & Religion. Kipley A. Farr. 320p. 1994. pap. 9.95 (*1-56901-301-2*) NW Pub.

Cosmology, Fusion & Other Matters: George Gamow Memorial Volume. Ed. by Frederick Reines. LC 77-159018. (Illus.). 334p. reprint ed. pap. 95.20 (*0-8357-5503-7*, 2035118) Bks Demand.

***Cosmology in Antiquity.** M. R. Wright. LC 94-45131. (Sciences of Antiquity Ser.). 1995. write for info. (*0-415-08372-9*); pap. write for info. (*0-415-12183-3*) Routledge.

Cosmology in (2 Plus 1)-Dimensions, Cyclic Models, & Deformations of M2,1. Victor Guillemin. 228p. 1989. text ed. 59.50 (*0-691-08513-7*); pap. text ed. 19.95 (*0-691-08514-5*) Princeton U Pr.

***Cosmology of Freedom.** Robert C. Neville. 385p. (C). 1994. text ed. 59.50x (*0-7914-2757-9*); pap. text ed. 19.95x (*0-7914-2758-7*) State U NY Pr.

***Cosmology of John Ross.** Patrick B. O'Neil. LC 94-61226. 136p. (Orig.). 1995. 10.00 (*1-884570-14-3*) Research Triangle.

Cosmology of the Early Universe. Fang Lizhi & Remo Ruffini. (Advanced Series in Astrophysics & Cosmology: Vol. 1). 316p. (C). 1984. 54.00 (*9971-950-92-8*); pap. 30.00 (*9971-950-93-6*) World Scientific Pub.

Cosmology, Ontology, & Human Efficacy: Essays in Chinese Thought. Ed. by Richard J. Smith & D. W. Kwok. LC 92-31229. 258p. (C). 1993. text ed. 38.00 (*0-8248-1443-6*) UH Pr.

An Asterisk (*) at the beginning of an entry indicates that the title is appearing in BIP for the first time.

Cosmology, Physics & Philosophy. 2nd ed. Or Gal. 1987. 69.00 (*0-387-96526-2*) Spr-Verlag.

Cosmology, Religion, & Philosophy. Rudolf Steiner. 88p. 1994. pap. 7.00 (*0-89540-245-9*, SB-245) Sun Pub.

Cosmonautics: a Colorful History: History of Soviet-Russian Space Programs. Ed. by Wayne R. Matson. 212p. 1994. 49.95 (*1-885609-01-9*) Cosmos Books.

***Cosmonauts Autographs Identification Guide.** (Illus.). 80p. 1994. pap. 14.95x (*0-9643667-0-3*) Sanabria.

Cosmopolis. Stephen E. Toulmin. 1990. text ed. 27.95 (*0-02-932631-1*) Free Pr.

Cosmopolis: The Hidden Agenda of Modernity. Stephen E. Toulmin. LC 92-18478. xii, 228p. 1992. pap. 13.95 (*0-226-80838-6*) U Ch Pr.

Cosmopolis: Urban Stories by Women. Ed. & Tr. by Ines Rieder. 200p. (Orig.). 1990. 24.95 (*0-939416-36-0*); pap. 9.95 (*0-939416-37-9*) Cleis Pr.

Cosmopolis: Urban Stories by Women. Ed. by Ines Rieder. 192p. (C). 1990. pap. 15.99 (*1-85594-013-2*, Pub. by Attic IE) InBook.

Cosmopolis: Yesterday's Cities of the Future. Howard Mansfield. LC 89-25159. 172p. (C). 1990. 10.00 (*0-88285-131-4*) Ctr Urban Pol Res.

***Cosmopolitan Democracy: An Agenda for a New World Order.** Ed. by Daniele Archibugi & David Held. LC 94-44706. 1995. write for info. (*0-7456-1380-2*, Pub. by Polity Pr UK); pap. write for info. (*0-7456-1381-0*, Pub. by Polity Pr UK) Blackwell Pubs.

Cosmopolitan Greetings. Allen Ginsberg. 128p. 1994. 20.00 (*0-06-016770-X*, HarpT) HarpC.

***Cosmopolitan Greetings.** Allen Ginsberg. 1995. pap. 12.00 (*0-06-092623-6*, PL) HarpC.

Cosmopolitan World Atlas. rev. ed. LC 94-15785. 1994. 70.00 (*0-528-83674-9*) Rand McNally.

Cosmopolitan World of Henry James: An Intertextual Study. Adeline R. Tintner. LC 91-2026. 352p. 1991. text ed. 39.95 (*0-8071-1663-7*); pap. text ed. 16.95 (*0-8071-1692-0*) La State U Pr.

Cosmopolitans & Parochials: Modern Orthodox Jews in America. Samuel C. Heilman & Steven M. Cohen. 216p. 1989. lib. bdg. 32.00 (*0-226-32495-8*); pap. text ed. 13.95 (*0-226-32496-6*) U Ch Pr.

Cosmopolitan's Guide to Marvelous Men. 1977. reprint ed. pap. 3.00 (*0-87980-336-3*) Wilshire.

Cosmopolitan's Hang-up Handbook. 1977. reprint ed. pap. 4.00 (*0-87980-338-X*) Wilshire.

Cosmopolitan's Love Book: A Guide to Ecstasy in Bed. Helen Gurley Brown. 1978. pap. 7.00 (*0-87980-355-X*) Wilshire.

Cosmopolitan's New Etiquette Guide. 1977. reprint ed. pap. 4.00 (*0-87980-337-1*) Wilshire.

Cosmos. (Voyage Through the Universe Ser.). (Illus.). 144p. 1989. 17.27 (*0-8094-6862-X*); lib. bdg. 24.60 (*0-8094-6863-8*) Time-Life.

Cosmos. Louis Bouyer. Tr. by Pierre De Fontnouvelle. LC 88-18592. (Orig.). 1988. pap. 17.95 (*0-932506-66-6*) St Bedes Pubns.

Cosmos. Witold Gombrowicz. 224p. (FRE.). 1989. pap. 10.95 (*0-7859-2312-8*, 2070364003) Fr & Eur.

Cosmos. Carl Sagan. 400p. 1985. mass mkt. 5.99 (*0-345-33135-4*) Ballantine.

Cosmos. Carl Sagan & Gentry Lee. (C). 1980. 8.76 (*0-07-554277-3*); pap. text ed. 3.00 (*0-685-04225-1*); 8.95 (*0-685-04226-X*) McGraw.

Cosmos. Carl Sagan. 1993. 35.50 (*0-8446-6698-X*) Peter Smith.

Cosmos. Carl Sagan. 1983. pap. 30.00 (*0-394-71596-9*) Random.

***Cosmos.** Carl Sagan. LC 94-36838. 1995. 19.99 (*0-517-12355-X*) Wings Bks.

Cosmos. Richard J. Pendergast. LC 72-82897. 223p. reprint ed. pap. 63.60 (*0-7837-0462-3*, 2040785) Bks Demand.

Cosmos: A Book of Poetry. Yushu Pu. (Illus.). 24p. (Orig.). 1989. pap. 2.95 (*0-9612480-0-9*) Mount Pr DE.

Cosmos: International Affairs in the Modern Age. Carl Sagan. 1980. 34.95 (*0-394-50294-9*) Random.

Cosmos & Anthropos: A Philosophical Interpretation of the Anthropic Cosmological Principle. Errol E. Harris. LC 90-37036. 208p. (C). 1991. text ed. 45.00 (*0-391-03694-7*) Humanities.

Cosmos & Epic Representation: Dante, Spenser, Milton & the Transformation of Renaissance Heroic Poetry. John G. Demaray. LC 90-21022. (Duquesne Studies: Language & Literature Ser.: Vol. 11). (Illus.). 284p. 1991. text ed. 48.00 (*0-8207-0231-5*) Duquesne.

Cosmos & Pornografia. Witold Gombrowicz. LC 85-81780. 608p. (POL.). 1986. pap. 10.00 (*0-8021-5159-0*) Grove-Atltic.

Cosmos & Theos: Ethical & Theological Implications of the Anthropic Cosmological Principle. Errol E. Harris. LC 91-33157. 232p. (C). 1992. text ed. 45.00 (*0-391-03744-7*) Humanities.

Cosmos & Transcendence: Breaking Through the Barriers of Scientistic Belief. Wolfgang Smith. 168p. (Orig.). 1984. pap. 10.95 (*0-89385-028-4*) Sugden.

Cosmos, Bios, Theos: Scientists Reflect on Science, Religion, & the Origins of the Universe, Life, & Homo Sapiens. Ed. by Henry Margenau & Roy A. Varghese. LC 92-7685. 299p. (C). 1992. pap. 17.95 (*0-8126-9186-5*) Open Court.

Cosmos, Chaos, & the World to Come: The Ancient Roots of Apocalyptic Faith. Norman Cohn. 320p. 1993. 30.00 (*0-300-05598-6*) Yale U Pr.

Cosmos Crumbling: American Reform & Religious Imagination. Robert H. Abzug. 1994. 30.00 (*0-19-503752-9*) OUP.

Cosmos Crumbling: American Reform & the Religious Imagination. Robert H. Abzug. 320p. (C). 1994. reprint ed. pap. text ed. 14.95 (*0-19-504568-8*) OUP.

Cosmos de Fernando Arrabal: Lo Cosmicocidico en El Arquitecto y el Emperador de Asiria. Rino Cassanelli. LC 90-34853. (American University Studies: Romance Languages & Literature: Ser. II, Vol. 143). 149p. (SPA.). (C). 1991. text ed. 32.95 (*0-8204-1302-X*) P Lang Pubs.

Cosmos de Lydia Cabrera: Dioses, Animales y Hombres. Mariela Gutierrez. LC 89-83955. (Coleccion Ebano y Canela Ser.). 137p. (Orig.). (SPA.). 1991. pap. 19.00 (*0-89729-535-8*) Ediciones.

Cosmos, Earth & Man: A Short History of the Universe. Preston Cloud. LC 78-2666. (Illus.). 1980. pap. 18.00x (*0-300-02594-7*) Yale U Pr.

***Cosmos from Space.** fac. ed. David H. Clark. LC 87-34410. 178p. 1987. reprint ed. pap. 50.80 (*0-7837-8002-8*, 2047758) Bks Demand.

Cosmos, God & Philosophy. Ralph J. Moore & Brooke N. Moore. (American University Studies: Philosophy: Ser. V, Vol. 49). 312p. (C). 1989. text ed. 41.50 (*0-8204-0610-4*) P Lang Pubs.

Cosmos in Man. Torkom Saraydarian. LC 73-77838. 1973. 15.00 (*0-911794-31-X*); pap. 12.00 (*0-911794-32-8*) Aqua Educ.

Cosmos in Transition: Studies in the History of Cosmology. S. J. Jaki. (History of Astronomy Ser.: Vol. 5). 256p. 1990. pap. 24.00 (*0-88126-222-6*) Pachart Pub Hse.

Cosmo's Law: The Timebook, Bk. 1. T. Byron G. 128p. 1993. pap. 5.98 (*1-879352-03-6*) Mini-Novel Pub.

Cosmos, Man & Society. Edmond B. Szekely. 152p. 1973. pap. 6.80 (*0-89564-070-8*) IBS Intl.

Cosmos of My Own: Faulkner & Yoknapatawpha. Ed. by Doreen Fowler & Ann Abadie. LC 81-7430. (Faulkner & Yoknapatawpha Ser.). 284p. 1981. 30.00 (*0-87805-142-2*); pap. 15.95 (*0-87805-143-0*) U Pr of Miss.

Cosmotheandric Experience: Emerging Religious Consciousness. Raimon Panikkar. LC 92-46195. 150p. 1993. 24.95 (*0-88344-862-9*) Orbis Bks.

Cosmotherapy of the Essenes. Edmond B. Szekely. (Illus.). 64p. 1975. pap. 3.50 (*0-89564-012-0*) IBS Intl.

Cosmovision Poetica De Jose Lezama Lima En "Paraiso" y "Oppiano Licario" Alina Camacho-Gingerich. LC 88-82892. (Coleccion Polymita Ser.). 169p. (Orig.). (SPA.). 1991. pap. 19.95 (*0-89729-511-0*) Ediciones.

***Coson Carriage Collection at Beechdale.** Thomas Ryder. Ed. by Rodger Morrow. (Illus.). 175p. (Orig.). Date not set. boxed, pap. 25.00 (*1-880499-03-7*) S Green PA.

Cospaia. Giuseppe Risso. Tr. by Claudette Asselin. LC 78-70626. (Illus.). 1979. pap. 7.95 (*0-915570-14-9*) Oolp Pr.

Cospar International Reference Atmosphere: 1986: Middle Atmosphere Models, Pt. II. Ed. by D. Rees et al. (Advances in Space Research Ser.: No. 10). (Illus.). 528p. 1991. pap. 105.00 (*0-08-040789-7*, Pergamon Pr) Elsevier.

COSPAR Space Research XIV: Proceedings of the Fourteenth Plenary Meeting of COSPAR, Washington, U. S. A. & Selected Symposia. Ed. by S. A. Bowhill et al. (Space Research Ser.). (Illus.). 1815p. 1977. 140.00 (*0-08-021786-9*, Pergamon Pr) Elsevier.

Cossack! Warrior Riders of the Steppes. M. A. Groushko. (Illus.). 144p. 1992. 24.95 (*0-8069-8703-0*) Sterling.

Cossack Administration of the Hetmanate, 2 vols. George Gajecky. LC 77-73708. (Sources & Documents Ser.). (Illus.). 1978. pap. 5.00 (*0-916458-02-4*) Harvard Ukrainian.

Cossack Hero in Russian Literature: A Study in Cultural Mythology. Judith D. Kornblatt. LC 92-50254. (Illus.). 244p. (Orig.). (C). 1992. lib. bdg. 47.50 (*0-299-13520-9*); pap. 22.50 (*0-299-13524-1*) U of Wis Pr.

Cossacks. Leo Tolstoy. (Orig.). 1994. 15.00 (*0-679-43131-4*) Knopf.

Cossacks. Leo Tolstoy. Tr. by Rosemary Edmonds. (Classics Ser.). (Orig.). 1961. pap. 2.95 (*0-14-044109-3*, Penguin Bks) Viking Penguin.

Cossacks: Their History & Country. William P. Cresson. LC 77-87541. reprint ed. 29.50 (*0-404-16608-3*) AMS Pr.

Cossacks in the German Army, 1941-1945. Samuel J. Newland. 1991. 39.50 (*0-7146-3351-8*, Pub. by F Cass Pubs UK) Intl Spec Bk.

Cossacks of the Brotherhood: The Zaporog Kosh of the Dniepr River. George P. March. LC 89-27980. (American University Studies: History: Ser. IX, Vol. 86). 264p. 1990. text ed. 51.00 (*0-8204-1191-4*) P Lang Pubs.

Cossacks of the Ukraine. Henryk Krasinski. LC 77-87543. (BCL Ser.). 320p. 1985. reprint ed. 62.50 (*0-404-16609-1*) AMS Pr.

Cossacks, Sevastopol, the Invaders & Other Stories. Leo Tolstoy. (Short Story Index Reprint Ser.). 1977. 35.95 (*0-8369-3416-4*) Ayer.

Cost. David C. Phillips. (Collected Works of David G. Phillips). 1988. reprint ed. lib. bdg. 79.00 (*0-7812-1326-6*) Rprt Serv.

Cost. David G. Phillips. (American Author Ser.). reprint ed. lib. bdg. 69.00 (*0-685-47615-4*) Scholarly.

Cost - Price Analysis: Tools to Improve Profit Margins. LeRoy H. Graw. LC 93-12856. 210p. 1993. text ed. 49.95 (*0-442-01717-0*) Van Nos Reinhold.

Cost Accounting. American Foundrymen Society. 81p. 60.00 (*0-317-32611-2*, GM7001) Am Foundrymen.

***Cost Accounting.** Lane Anderson & Donald Clancy. (C). 1990. student ed, text ed. 23.95 (*0-256-08685-0*) Irwin.

Cost Accounting. Lane K. Anderson & Donald K. Clancy. 1026p. (C). 1990. text ed. 64.95 (*0-256-08683-4*, 01-3242-01) Irwin.

Cost Accounting. B. Batty. 1990. pap. 21.00 (*0-7463-0481-1*, Pub. by Northcote UK) St Mut.

Cost Accounting. James A. Cashin & Ralph S. Polimeni. 1981. Study Guide. student ed, pap. text ed. write for info. (*0-07-010257-0*) McGraw.

Cost Accounting. Michael Chatfield & Denis P. Nielson. 1172p. (C). 1983. student ed write for info. (*0-318-56981-7*); write for info. (*0-15-514142-2*) HB Coll Pubs.

***Cost Accounting.** Robert L. Dansby & Michael D. Lawrence. LC 94-43266. 1995. text ed. 47.95 (*0-538-83121-9*) S-W Pub.

Cost Accounting. Mark Frigo. LC 86-285. (College Outline Ser.). 259p. (C). 1986. pap. text ed. 12.50 (*0-15-601566-8*) HB Coll Pubs.

Cost Accounting. M. W. Glautier & B. Underdown. 352p. (Orig.). 1988. pap. text ed. 32.50 (*0-273-02500-7*, Pub. by Pitman Pub Ltd UK); Solution Manual, 160p. 32.50 (*0-273-02920-7*, Pub. by Pitman Pub Ltd UK) Trans-Atl Phila.

Cost Accounting. Lester E. Heitger. 896p. 1985. text ed. 47.95 (*0-07-027991-8*); student ed 17.95 (*0-07-027992-6*) McGraw.

Cost Accounting. 3rd ed. Incl. 536p. 1991. 46.00 (*0-471-51396-2*); 848p. 42.50 (*0-471-51394-6*); 4p. 2.00 (*0-471-54543-0*); 1991. Net. 66.95 (*0-471-62331-8*); 20.00 (*0-471-54506-6*); 20.00 (*0-471-54505-8*); 20.00 (*0-471-54501-5*); 10.00 (*0-471-54791-3*); 10.00 (*0-471-54790-5*); 440p. 28.00 (*0-471-51395-4*); No. 3I. teacher ed, disk 20.00 (*0-471-54820-0*); No. 5I. teacher ed, disk 20.00 (*0-471-54837-5*); 384p. trans. 257.00 (*0-471-51397-0*); 1991. Net. Set text ed. write for info. (*0-471-52425-5*); Incl. 46.00 (*0-471-51396-2*); 42.50 (*0-471-51394-6*); 2.00 (*0-471-54543-0*); Net. 66.95 (*0-471-62331-8*); 20.00 (*0-471-54506-6*); 20.00 (*0-471-54505-8*); 20.00 (*0-471-54501-5*); 10.00 (*0-471-54791-3*); 10.00 (*0-471-54790-5*); 28.00 (*0-471-51395-4*); No. 3I. teacher ed, disk 20.00 (*0-471-54820-0*); No. 5I. teacher ed, disk 20.00 (*0-471-54837-5*); trans. 257.00 (*0-471-51397-0*); Net. Set text ed., 5.25 hd 66.96 (*0-471-54729-8*); Incl. 46.00 (*0-471-51396-2*); 42.50 (*0-471-51394-6*); 2.00 (*0-471-54543-0*); Net. 66.95 (*0-471-62331-8*); 20.00 (*0-471-54506-6*); 20.00 (*0-471-54505-8*); 20.00 (*0-471-54501-5*); 10.00 (*0-471-54791-3*); 10.00 (*0-471-54790-5*); 28.00 (*0-471-51395-4*); No. 3I. teacher ed, disk 20.00 (*0-471-54820-0*); No. 5I. teacher ed, disk 20.00 (*0-471-54837-5*); trans. 257.00 (*0-471-51397-0*); Net. Set text ed., 3.5 hd 66.96 (*0-471-54730-1*); Incl. 46.00 (*0-471-51396-2*); 42.50 (*0-471-51394-6*); 2.00 (*0-471-54543-0*); Net. 66.95 (*0-471-62331-8*); 20.00 (*0-471-54506-6*); 20.00 (*0-471-54505-8*); 20.00 (*0-471-54501-5*); 10.00 (*0-471-54791-3*); 10.00 (*0-471-54790-5*); 28.00 (*0-471-51395-4*); No. 3I. teacher ed, disk 20.00 (*0-471-54820-0*); No. 5I. teacher ed, disk 20.00 (*0-471-54837-5*); trans. 257.00 (*0-471-51397-0*); Case Set. Net. Set text ed. write for info. (*0-471-54924-X*) Wiley.

***Cost Accounting.** 3rd ed. Edward Deakin & Michael Maher. (C). 1991. student ed, text ed. 23.95 (*0-256-06917-4*) Irwin.

Cost Accounting. 3rd ed. Edward B. Deakin & Michael W. Maher. 1059p. (C). 1991. text ed. 65.95 (*0-256-06919-0*, 01-1551-03) Irwin.

Cost Accounting. 3rd ed. W. M. Harper. 480p. 1993. pap. 37.50 (*0-7121-1043-7*, Pub. by Pitman Pub Ltd UK) Trans-Atl Phila.

Cost Accounting. 3rd ed. Mark L. Inman. (CIMA Ser., Stage 2). 1993. pap. 31.50 (*0-7506-0991-5*) Buttrwrth-Heinemann.

***Cost Accounting.** 4th ed. Michael Maher & Edward Deakin. 1016p. (C). 1993. text ed. 69.95 (*0-256-11657-1*) Irwin.

Cost Accounting: A Managerial Approach. J. Owen Cherrington et al. 1036p. (C). 1988. text ed. 69.75 (*0-314-64832-1*) West Pub.

Cost Accounting: A Managerial Emphasis. 8th ed. Charles T. Horngren et al. LC 93-31195. 1993. text ed. 75.00 (*0-13-181066-9*) P-H.

Cost Accounting: Accumulation, Analysis, & Use. 3rd ed. Maurice L. Hirsch, Jr. & Joseph G. Louderback, III. 950p. (C). 1992. text ed. 65.95 (*0-538-82174-4*, AE64CA) S-W Pub.

Cost Accounting: Concepts & Applications for Managerial Decision Making. 3rd ed. Ralph S. Polimeni et al. 1991. pap. text ed. write for info. (*0-07-837443-X*) McGraw.

Cost Accounting: Concepts & Applications for Managerial Decision Making. 3rd ed. Ralph S. Polimeni et al. 1991. Practice sets: Job Order Costing & Process Costing. pap. text ed. write for info. (*0-07-010559-6*) McGraw.

Cost Accounting: Concepts & Applications for Managerial Decision Making. 3rd ed. Ralph S. Polimeni et al. 1991. text ed. write for info. (*0-07-010553-7*); Study guide. student ed, pap. text ed. write for info. (*0-07-010554-5*) McGraw.

Cost Accounting: Concepts & Applications for Managerial Decision Making. 3rd ed. Ralph S. Polimeni et al. 1991. pap. text ed. write for info. (*0-07-834990-7*) McGraw.

Cost Accounting: Concepts & Applications for Managerial Decision Making. 3rd ed. Ralph S. Polimeni et al. 1991. Microtest III Macintosh. pap. text ed. write for info. (*0-07-836431-0*) McGraw.

Cost Accounting: Concepts & Techniques for Management. Larry N. Killough & Wayne E. Leininger. LC 86-26677. (Illus.). 870p. (C). 1987. teacher ed, pap. text ed. write for info. (*0-314-35102-7*); student ed, pap. text ed. 20.50 (*0-314-35103-5*) West Pub.

Cost Accounting: Concepts & Techniques for Management. 2nd ed. Larry N. Killough & Wayne E. Leininger. LC 86-26677. (Illus.). 870p. (C). 1987. text ed. 68.50 (*0-314-25865-5*) West Pub.

Cost Accounting: Planning & Control. Milton F. Usry et al. 960p. (C). 1990. text ed. write for info. (*0-538-80925-6*, AE88JA) S-W Pub.

Cost Accounting: Planning & Control. 9th ed. Milton F. Usry et al. 960p. (C). 1988. text ed. write for info. (*0-538-01881-X*, A88) S-W Pub.

Cost Accounting: Planning & Control. 11th ed. Milton F. Usry et al. LC 93-11101. (C). 1994. text ed. 62.95 (*0-538-82807-2*, AE88KA) S-W Pub.

Cost Accounting: Principles & Applications. Horace R. Brock et al. 1989. Study Guide. student ed, pap. text ed. write for info. (*0-07-008287-1*) McGraw.

Cost Accounting: Principles & Applications. 4th ed. Horace R. Brock & Charles E. Palmer. (Illus.). 512p. (C). 1984. text ed. 25.95 (*0-07-008045-3*); student ed 14.30 (*0-07-008046-1*) McGraw.

Cost Accounting: Principles & Applications. 5th ed. Horace R. Brock et al. 592p. (C). 1988. text ed. 28.55 (*0-07-008152-2*) McGraw.

Cost Accounting: Principles & Applications. 5th ed. Horace R. Brock et al. 1989. text ed. write for info. (*0-07-008286-3*) McGraw.

Cost Accounting: Processing, Evaluating, & Using Cost Data. 3rd ed. Wayne J. Morse & Harold P. Roth. LC 85-6153. 1040p. (C). 1986. teacher ed write for info. (*0-201-13997-9*); text ed. 51.95 (*0-201-13995-2*); Study guide. student ed 24.75 (*0-201-13996-0*); write for info. (*0-201-13979-0*); write for info. (*0-201-13998-7*); Check list key figure. 27.95 (*0-201-13745-3*) Addison-Wesley.

Cost Accounting: Theory & Practice. Jerome L. Nicholson. Ed. by Richard P. Brief. LC 77-87283. (Development of Contemporary Accounting Thought Ser.). 1978. reprint ed. lib. bdg. 31.95 (*0-405-10911-3*) Ayer.

Cost Accounting: Traditions & Innovations. Jesse T. Barfield et al. Ed. by Leyh. 965p. (C). 1991. text ed. 64.25 (*0-314-77474-2*) West Pub.

Cost Accounting: Traditions & Innovations. 2nd ed. Jesse T. Barfield et al. Ed. by Leyh. LC 93-41871. 1131p. (C). 1993. text ed. 72.25 (*0-314-02904-4*) West Pub.

Cost Accounting: With Managerial Applications. 5th ed. Stephen A. Moscove et al. LC 84-80701. 928p. (C). 1985. 6.36 (*0-685-09608-4*) HM.

Cost Accounting - Principles, Practice & Problems. S. P. Arora & T. S. Soni. 873p. 1990. pap. 48.00 (*81-209-0007-3*, Pub. by Pitambar Pub II) St Mut.

***Cost Accounting & Analysis.** (ACT Proficiency Examination Program (PEP) Ser.). Date not set. 39.95 (*0-8373-5562-1*) Nat Learn.

Cost Accounting & Burden Application. Clinton H. Scovell. Ed. by Richard P. Brief. LC 80-1578. (Dimensions of Accounting Theory & Practice Ser.). 1980. reprint ed. lib. bdg. 36.95 (*0-405-13544-0*) Ayer.

Cost Accounting Check Figures: Concepts & Managerial Applications. 2nd ed. Thomas R. Dyckman. (C). 1994. text ed. 64.95 (*0-538-82533-2*, AE66BA) S-W Pub.

Cost Accounting for Financial Institutions. 149p. 200.00 (*0-318-16999-1*); 150.00 (*0-318-17000-0*) Finan Mgrs Soc.

***Cost Accounting for Financial Institutions: The Complete Desktop Reference Guide.** rev. ed. Leonard P. Cole. 1994. 60.00 (*1-55738-739-7*) Probus Pub Co.

Cost Accounting for Health Care Organizations: Concepts & Applications. Steven A. Finkler. LC 93-7175. 800p. 1993. 130.00 (*0-8342-0378-2*, 20378) Aspen Pub.

Cost Accounting for Law Firms. American Bar Association Staff. LC 83-73344. 59p. 1984. pap. 29.95 (*0-89707-127-1*, 511-0088) Amer Bar Assn.

Cost Accounting for Managerial Planning, Decision Making & Control. 4th ed. Woody M. Liao & James L. Boockholdt. LC 91-73135. 744p. 1992. 53.95 (*0-87393-136-X*); student ed 17.95 (*0-87393-137-8*) Dame Pubns.

Cost Accounting in the Clinical Laboratory: Proposed Guideline. 1990. 40.00 (*1-56238-098-2*, GP11-P) Natl Comm Clin Lab Stds.

***Cost Accounting in the Service Industry: A Critical Assessment.** Otto B. Martinson. Ed. by Claire Barth. 125p. 1994. pap. 25.00 (*0-86641-228-X*, 94291) Inst Mgmt Account.

***Cost Accounting, International.** 3rd ed. Edward Deaking & Michael Maher. (C). 1991. student ed, text ed. 30.95 (*0-256-11407-2*) Irwin.

***Cost Accounting, International: Using a Cost Management Approach.** 5th ed. L. Gayle Rayburn. 1024p. (C). 1992. text ed. 36.50 (*0-256-10809-9*) Irwin.

Cost Accounting Methods for Iron Foundries. 186p. 1987. pap. 15.00 (*0-317-59806-6*, OS8200) Am Foundrymen.

***Cost Accounting Standards.** Margaret M. Worthington. 104p. (Orig.). 1994. pap. 37.45 (*0-940343-66-5*) Natl Contract Mgmt.

Cost Accounting with Managerial Applications. 6th ed. Stephen A. Moscove & Arnold Wright. LC 88-81349. 1989. text ed. 49.16 (*0-318-36900-1*) HM.

Cost Allocation: Methods, Principles, Applications. Ed. by H. P. Young. 206p. 1986. 77.00 (*0-444-87863-7*, North Holland) Elsevier.

Cost Allocation & Rate Design for Water Utilities. 210p. 1991. pap. 36.00 (*0-89867-568-5*, 90590) Am Water Wks Assn.

Cost Allocation for Electric Utilities Conservation & Load Management Programs. 146p. 1993. 7.50 (*0-317-05191-1*) NARUC.

Cost Analysis Module 8: Facilitator's Guide. Mary Millar. (Primary Health Care Management Advancement Programme (PHC MAP) Modules Ser.). 53p. 1993. pap. text ed. write for info. (*1-882839-14-5*) Aga Khan Fnd.

Cost Analysis Module 8: User's Guide. Jack Reynolds. (Primary Health Care Management Advancement Programme (PHC MAP) Modules Ser.). 97p. 1993. pap. text ed. write for info. (*1-882839-06-4*) Aga Khan Fnd.

Cost Analysis & Estimating: Shifting U. S. Priorities. Ed. by R. Kankey & J. Robbins. (Illus.). v, 154p. 1991. 28.00 (*0-387-97659-0*) Spr-Verlag.

An Asterisk (*) at the beginning of an entry indicates that the title is appearing in BIP for the first time.

1641

Cost Analysis & Estimating: Tools & Techniques. Ed. by W. R. Greer, Jr. & D. Nussbaum. (Illus.). x, 306p. 1990. 37.00 (*0-387-97325-7*) Spr-Verlag.

Cost Analysis, Cost Recovery, Marketing & Fee-Based Services: A Guide for the Health Sciences Librarian. Ed. by M. Sandra Wood. LC 85-888. (Medical Reference Services Quarterly Ser.: Supplement Vol. 1). 268p. 1985. text ed. 49.95 (*0-86656-353-9*) Haworth Pr.

Cost Analysis for Capital Investment Decisions. Lang. (Cost Engineering Ser.: Vol. 14). 400p. 1989. 175.00 (*0-8247-7894-4*) Dekker.

Cost Analysis in Education: A Tool for Policy & Planning. Philip H. Coombs & Jacques Hallak. LC 87-26105. (EDI Series in Economic Development). 116p. 1988. text ed. 14.50 (*0-8018-3648-4*) Johns Hopkins.

Cost Analysis of Library Functions: A Total Systems Approach. Betty J. Mitchell et al. Ed. by Robert D. Stuwart. LC 77-2110. (Foundations in Library & Information Science: Vol. 6). 192p. 1978. lib. bdg. 73.25 (*0-89232-072-9*) Jai Pr.

Cost & Benefit of Fluoride in the Prevention of Dental Caries. G. N. Davies. (Offset Publication Ser.: No. 9). 1974. pap. 8.00 (*92-4-170009-2*) World Health.

Cost & Benefits of Community Care: A Case Study of People with Learning Difficulties. Alan Haycox. (Studies of Care in the Community). 128p. 1995. 55.95 (*1-85628-433-6*, Pub. by Avebury Pub UK) Ashgate Pub Co.

Cost & Choice: An Inquiry in Economic Theory. James M. Buchanan. LC 78-70150. (Midway Reprint Ser.). 1979. pap. text ed. 12.95 (*0-226-07818-3*) U Ch Pr.

***Cost & Competition in American Medicine: Theory, Policy, & Institutions.** Les Seplaki. LC 94-22105. 1994. write for info. (*0-8191-9639-8*); pap. 37.50 (*0-8191-9640-1*) U Pr of Amer.

Cost & Economics. 1987. 14.95 (*0-685-31035-3*, 108705) Hazardous Mat Control.

Cost & Financial Accounting in Forestry. K. Openshaw. 1980. reprint ed. text ed. 94.00 (*0-08-021456-8*, CRC Reprint) Franklin.

Cost & Management Accountancy (M&T) R. Roychowdhury & B. Bhattacharyya. (C). 1989. 80.00 (*0-89771-436-9*, Current Dist) St Mut.

***Cost & Management Accounting.** W. M. Harper. 544p. (Orig.). 1995. pap. 39.50 (*0-7121-1053-4*) Trans-Atl Phila.

Cost & Management Accounting. Ed. by R. Hussey. 217p. (C). 1989. 90.00 (*0-685-39824-2*, Inst Pur & Supply) St Mut.

Cost & Management Accounting: A Modern Approach. John G. Burch. Ed. by Horan. LC 93-27986. 1100p. (C). 1993. text ed. 72.25 (*0-314-02773-4*) West Pub.

Cost & Management Accounting Made Simple. Joseph Baggott. 395p. (C). 1988. 45.00 (*0-685-29262-2*, Inst Pur & Supply) St Mut.

Cost & Management Accounting Made Simple. Joseph Baggott. 395p. (C). 1989. 70.00 (*0-685-39825-0*, Inst Pur & Supply) St Mut.

Cost & Quality of Fuels for Electric Utility Plants. (Illus.). 168p. (Orig.). (C). 1994. pap. text ed. 45.00 (*0-7881-0285-0*) Diane Pub.

Cost & Quality of Fuels for Electric Utility Plants. (Orig.). 1994. lib. bdg. 250.00 (*0-8490-5742-6*) Gordon Pr.

***Cost & Quality of Fuels for Electric Utility Plants 1993.** (Illus.). 188p. (Orig.). (C). 1994. pap. text ed. 50.00x (*0-7881-1278-3*) Diane Pub.

Cost & Revenue Constrained Production. Rolf Fare & Shawna Grosskopf. LC 93-32408. (Bilkent University Lecture Ser.: Vol. 4). 184p. 1993. 42.95 (*0-387-94175-4*) Spr-Verlag.

Cost & Revenue of the Superior & Justice of the Peace Courts in Arizona. National Center for State Courts Staff. 105p. 1981. 6.30 (*0-685-15172-7*, WRO-031) Natl Ctr St Courts.

Cost & Safety Effectiveness of Highway Design Elements. (National Cooperative Highway Research Program Report Ser.: No. 197). 237p. 1978. 10.60 (*0-309-02858-2*) Transport Res Bd.

Cost & Schedule Control Techniques Handbook. Thomas C. Charland. (Illus.). 104p. (C). 1995. spiral bd. 79.95 (*0-9610754-0-6*) Manage Co In.

Cost & Statistical Analyst. Jack Rudman. (Career Examination Ser.: C-3561). 1994. 39.95 (*0-8373-3561-2*) Nat Learn.

Cost & Value of Your Retirement Fund. Mark Smith. LC 83-63498. 68p. (Orig.). 1984. pap. 8.95 (*0-9604302-1-0*) Perfas.

Cost Behavior & Price Policy. Conference on Price Research & Committee on Price Determination. 1975. 26.95 (*0-405-19043-3*, 7) Ayer.

Cost Behavior & Price Policy. Committee on Price Determination. (Conference on Price Research Ser.: No. 4). 382p. 1943. reprint ed. 99.40 (*0-87014-190-2*) Natl Bur Econ Res.

Cost Benefit Analysis. Ed. by Richard Layard & Stephen Glaister. LC 93-37740. (Illus.). 500p. (C). 1994. pap. 22.95 (*0-521-46674-1*) Cambridge U Pr.

Cost Benefit Analysis. 2nd ed. Ed. by Richard Layard & Stephen Glaister. LC 93-37740. (Illus.). 500p. (C). 1994. 59.95 (*0-521-46128-6*) Cambridge U Pr.

Cost Benefit Analysis. 4th ed. E. J. Mishan. 384p. 1988. pap. text ed. 24.95 (*0-04-445092-3*) Routledge Chapman & Hall.

Cost-Benefit Analysis: Issues & Methodologies. Anandarup Ray. LC 83-49367. 176p. 1984. pap. text ed. 11.95 (*0-8018-3069-9*) Johns Hopkins.

***Cost Benefit Analysis: Issues & Methodologies.** Anandarup Ray. 208p. 1984. 11.95 (*0-614-02764-0*, 43069) World Bank.

Cost-Benefit Analysis: Issues & Methodologies. Anandarup Ray. LC 83-49367. 166p. reprint ed. pap. 47.40 (*0-685-15553-6*, 2026707) Bks Demand.

Cost Benefit Analysis & Economic Theory. Jacques Lesourne. LC 74-84213. (Studies in Mathematical & Managerial Economics: Vol. 19). 521p. 1976. pap. 92.50 (*0-7204-3097-6*, North Holland) Elsevier.

***Cost Benefit Analysis & Sales Automation: A Guide to Financial Justification.** Paul H. Selden. Ed. by Charles Barr. (Illus.). 200p. 1995. 79.00 (*1-887407-00-6*) P H Selden.

Cost-Benefit Analysis & the Environment. Nick Hanley & Clive L. Spash. 304p. 1993. 59.95 (*1-85278-455-5*, Pub. by E Elgar Pub UK) Ashgate Pub Co.

Cost-Benefit Analysis & the Environment. Nick Hanley & Clive L. Spash. 288p. 1994. pap. 22.95 (*1-85278-947-6*, Pub. by E Elgar Pub UK) Ashgate Pub Co.

Cost-Benefit Analysis for Executive Decision Making: The Danger of Plain Common Sense. Alfred R. Oxenfeldt. LC 79-14617. 442p. reprint ed. pap. 126.00 (*0-317-28147-X*, 2055748) Bks Demand.

Cost Benefit Analysis for Irrigation & Drought Proofing. K. Puttaswamaiah. (C). 1988. 27.50 (*81-204-0369-X*, Pub. by Oxford IBH II) S Asia.

Cost-Benefit Analysis in Urban & Regional Planning. John A. Schofield. 272p. 1990. text ed. 55.00 (*0-04-338145-6*); pap. text ed. 27.95 (*0-04-445683-2*) Routledge Chapman & Hall.

Cost-Benefit Analysis of Environmental Change. Per-Olov Johansson. LC 92-38887. (Illus.). 256p. (C). 1993. 49.95 (*0-521-44318-0*); pap. 17.95 (*0-521-44792-5*) Cambridge U Pr.

***Cost-Benefit Analysis of the Onchoceriasis Program (OCP)** Aehyung Kim & Bruce Benton. LC 95-13778. (Technical Paper Ser.). 1995. write for info. (*0-8213-3235-X*) World Bank.

Cost-Benefit & Cost-Effectiveness Analyses: Their Application in Evaluating Investment Decisions in Urban Public Services & Facilities. David A. Good. (Discussion Paper Ser.: No. 47). 1971. pap. 10.00 (*1-55869-018-2*) Regional Sci Res Inst.

Cost-Benefit & Cost-Effectiveness Analysis in Health Care: Principles, Practice, & Potential. Kenneth E. Warner & Bryan R. Luce. LC 81-30165. (Illus.). 338p. 1982. text ed. 37.00 (*0-914904-81-7*, 0847) Health Admin Pr.

Cost-Benefit & Predictive Value of Radioimmunoassay. Ed. by Alberto Albertini et al. (Giovanni Lorenzini Foundation Symposia Ser.: Vol. 18). 270p. 1984. 95.50 (*0-444-80618-0*) Elsevier.

Cost-Benefit Methodology for Evaluation of State Judicial Information Systems. National Center for State Courts Staff. 200p. 1979. 12.00 (*0-89656-033-3*, F-002) Natl Ctr St Courts.

Cost, Choice & Political Economy. Jack Wiseman. 1989. text ed. 74.95 (*1-85278-165-3*, Pub. by E Elgar Pub UK) Ashgate Pub Co.

Cost Comparison of Selected U. S. & Indonesian Coal Mines. Ed. by Erik Sherer. 1994. write for info. (*0-318-72790-0*) US Interior.

Cost Comparison of Selected U. S. & Polish Coal Mines. U. S. Department of Commerce, International Trade Administration Staff & U. S. Department of the Interior, Bureau of Mines Staff. 1993. write for info. (*0-318-72128-7*) US Interior.

Cost-Conscious Home-Buyer's Guide. Jane White. 1991. pap. text ed. 12.95 (*0-471-52656-8*) Wiley.

Cost Containment: The Ultimate Advantage. Peter R. Richardson. (Illus.). 304p. 1988. text ed. 35.00 (*0-02-926432-4*) Free Pr.

Cost Containment & New Priorities in Health Care: A Study of the European Community. Brian Abel-Smith. 160p. 1992. 55.95 (*1-85628-319-4*, Pub. by Avebury Pub UK) Ashgate Pub Co.

Cost Containment for Higher Education: Strategies for Public Policy & Institutional Administration. William B. Simpson. LC 91-15317. 272p. 1991. text ed. 55.00 (*0-275-94066-7*, C4066, Praeger Pubs) Greenwood.

Cost Containment in the Clinical Laboratory. Evans et al. Ed. by Edith Helman. (Illus.). 250p. 1995. pap. text ed. 54.95 (*0-910224-16-1*) Berkeley Sci.

Cost Containment Learning Module, No. 1. Jake Elwood. (Orig.). 1985. pap. text ed. 47.50 (*0-931369-03-7*) Southern IL Univ Sch.

Cost Containment Learning Module, No. 2. Ruth Fane. (Orig.). 1985. pap. text ed. 47.50 (*0-931369-04-5*) Southern IL Univ Sch.

Cost Containment Learning Module, No. 3. Jan Garber. (Orig.). 1985. pap. text ed. 47.50 (*0-931369-05-3*) Southern IL Univ Sch.

Cost Containment Learning Module, No. 5. Ivan Johnson. (Orig.). 1985. pap. text ed. 47.50 (*0-931369-07-X*) Southern IL Univ Sch.

Cost Containment Learning Module, No. 6. Marie Johnson. (Orig.). 1985. pap. text ed. 47.50 (*0-931369-08-8*) Southern IL Univ Sch.

Cost Containment Learning Module, No. 7. Paula Malcolm. (Orig.). 1985. pap. text ed. 47.50 (*0-931369-09-6*) Southern IL Univ Sch.

Cost Containment Learning Module, No. 8. Ed Martin. (Orig.). 1985. pap. text ed. 47.50 (*0-931369-10-X*) Southern IL Univ Sch.

Cost Containment Learning Module, No. 9. Susan Scott. (Orig.). 1985. pap. text ed. 47.50 (*0-931369-11-8*) Southern IL Univ Sch.

Cost Containment Learning Module, No. 10. Dorothy Simpson. (Orig.). 1985. pap. text ed. 47.50 (*0-931369-12-6*) Southern IL Univ Sch.

Cost Containment Learning Module, No. 11. Ed Smith. (Orig.). 1985. pap. text ed. 47.50 (*0-931369-13-4*) Southern IL Univ Sch.

Cost Containment Learning Module, No. 12. David Sprague. (Orig.). 1985. pap. text ed. 47.50 (*0-931369-14-2*) Southern IL Univ Sch.

Cost Containment Learning Module, No. 13. Harold B. Stahl. (Orig.). 1985. pap. text ed. 47.50 (*0-931369-15-0*) Southern IL Univ Sch.

Cost Containment Learning Module, No. 14. Marianne Stiehl. (Orig.). 1985. pap. text ed. 47.50 (*0-931369-16-9*) Southern IL Univ Sch.

Cost Containment Learning Modules Series, 14 modules, Set. (Orig.). 1985. pap. text ed. 570.00 (*0-931369-02-9*) Southern IL Univ Sch.

***Cost Control for Builders, Remodelers, & Developers.** Jerry Householder & Timothy J. Wait. Ed. by Dorris Tennyson. LC 93-39104. (Illus.). 112p. (Orig.). 1994. 25.00 (*0-86718-405-1*) Home Builder.

Cost Control for Foodservice Managers Skillbook. Educational Foundation of the National Restaurant Association Staff. (Management Skills Program Ser.). 54p. (Orig.). 1992. pap. text ed. 10.95 (*0-915452-93-6*) Educ Found.

Cost Control for the Hospitality Industry. 2nd ed. Michael M. Coltman. 1989. text ed. 44.95 (*0-442-20591-0*) Van Nos Reinhold.

Cost Control Handbook. 2nd ed. R. M. Wilson. 624p. 1983. text ed. 79.95 (*0-566-02250-8*) Ashgate Pub Co.

Cost Control in Business. 5.95 (*0-686-02551-2*); pap. 1.95 (*0-686-02552-0*) Dun.

Cost Control Using Lotus 1-2-3. Rainey Rissman. (Illus.). 112p. 1992. disk, pap. 15.95 (*1-55622-218-1*) Wordware Pub.

Cost Cuts Manual: Nailing Down Savings for Least-Cost Housing. Robert M. Santucci & Peter Werwath. Ed. by Jim Thomas & Cecilia Cassidy. (Illus.). 336p. (Orig.). 1988. 55.00 (*0-317-89774-8*); pap. 45.00 (*0-942901-00-2*) Enterprise Foundation.

Cost Cuts Manual: Nailing Down Savings for Least-Cost Housing. Robert M. Santucci et al. (Illus.). 336p. (Orig.). 1988. lib. bdg. 55.00 (*0-942850-14-9*) Intermediate Tech.

***Cost Drivers in Missouri.** John A. Gardner. 1994. 40.00 (*0-935149-49-X*) Workers Comp Res Inst.

Cost Drivers in New Jersey. John A. Gardner et al. 1994. 40.00 (*0-935149-47-3*, WC-94-4) Workers Comp Res Inst.

Cost Drivers in Six States. Richard A. Victor et al. LC 92-33152. 1992. 75.00 (*0-935149-39-2*, WC92-9) Workers Comp Res Inst.

Cost Effective Control of Urban Smog. Richard F. Kosobud et al. Ed. by William A. Testa. (Orig.). 1993. write for info. (*0-9614358-4-4*) FRB Chicago.

Cost-Effective Control Systems for Colleges & Universities: A New Paradigm. Jennifer D. Dougherty & Loren L. Hubbell. LC 92-34574. 1992. 44.00 (*0-915164-73-6*) NACUBO.

Cost Effective Decision Making. Robert H. Pearson. 1973. 6.95 (*0-912164-12-3*) Masterco Pr.

***Cost-Effective Design & Delivery.** Jerome M. Rosow et al. Ed. by Jill Casner-Lotto. (Training for New Technology Ser.: Part III). 118p. 1986. 95.00 (*0-89361-056-9*) Work in Amer.

Cost Effective Design-Build Construction. Anthony J. Branca. (Illus.). 420p. 1987. 54.95 (*0-87629-088-8*, 67242) R S Means.

Cost Effective Electronic Recording System. National Center for State Courts Staff. (Paul Reardon Ser.). 9p. 1983. 0.54 (*0-685-16323-7*, PRS-042) Natl Ctr St Courts.

Cost-Effective Financial Management of CE Departments. Ed. by Allan F. Pacela. (Journal of Clinical Engineering Reprint Ser.: No. 4). 32p. (Orig.). 1991. pap. 20.00 (*0-685-62309-2*) Quest Pub.

Cost-Effective Home Building: A Design & Construction Handbook. Jerry Householder & Timothy J. Wait. Orig. Title: Reducing Home Building Costs with Optimum Value Engineered Design & Construction. (Illus.). 144p. (Orig.). 1994. 20.00 (*0-86718-391-8*) Home Builder.

Cost-Effective Home Upgrades. James Carey & Morris Carey. Ed. by Barbara Feller-Roth. LC 91-73777. (Illus.). 112p. (Orig.). 1992. pap. text ed. 9.95 (*0-89721-240-1*) Ortho Info.

Cost-Effective Information Systems. Burton J. Cohen. LC 78-152375. 71p. reprint ed. pap. 25.00 (*0-317-10661-9*, 2050389) Bks Demand.

Cost Effective Maintenance. Ed. by W. T. File. 143p. 1991. text ed. 74.95 (*0-7506-1006-9*) Buttrwrth-Heinemann.

Cost Effective Management of Reclaimed Derelict Sites. 96p. 1990. pap. 47.00 (*0-11-752258-9*, HM2589) UNIPUB.

Cost-Effective Marketing Research: A Guide for Marketing Managers. Eric J. Soares. LC 88-18526. 177p. 1988. text ed. 45.00 (*0-89930-278-5*, SCU/, Quorum Bks) Greenwood.

Cost Effective Nursing Practice: Guidelines for Nurse Managers. Blaney & Hobson. LC 65-5559. (Nursing Management Ser.). (Illus.). 349p. 1988. text ed. 44.50 (*0-397-54649-1*, Lippincott Nursing) Lippincott.

Cost-Effective Organization: How to Create It, How to Maintain It. James K. Hickel. LC 93-77879. 210p. 1994. text ed. 19.95 (*0-944435-22-X*) Glenbridge Pub.

Cost Effective Pension Planning. Robert L. Clark. (Studies in Productivity: Highlights of the Literature Ser.: Vol. 20). 1982. pap. 55.00 (*0-89361-030-5*) Work in Amer.

Cost Effective Personnel Decisions. James Cannon. 250p. (C). 1979. 75.00 (*0-85292-253-1*) St Mut.

Cost Effective Problem Solving Through Creativity: 39th Annual Technical Meeting, Las Vegas, Nevada, May 2-7th 1993, 2 vols., Set. Institute of Environmental Sciences Staff. 1155p. 1993. pap. text ed. 175.00 (*1-877862-18-5*) Inst Environ Sci.

Cost Effective Quality Control: Managing the Quality & Productivity of Analytical Processes. Ed. by James O. Westgard & Patricia L. Barry. (Illus.). 229p. 1986. 40.00 (*0-915274-35-3*) Am Assn Clinical Chem.

Cost Effective Recipes for Ten to One-Hundred. Carolyn Breeding & Donna Foster. 368p. 1989. text ed. 49.95 (*0-442-22119-3*) Van Nos Reinhold.

Cost Effective Regulation by EPA & Small Business Impacts: Includes Addendum & Individual Case Studies. 430p. (Orig.). (C). 1993. pap. text ed. 95.00 (*1-56806-510-8*) Diane Pub.

***Cost-Effective Risk Assessment for Process Design.** Ed. by Robert L. Deshotels & Robert D. Zimmerman. LC 94-43007. 1995. text ed. 55.00 (*0-07-006463-6*) McGraw.

Cost Effective Strategies for Managing the Human Resources Function. Ronald Bouchard et al. 79p. 1992. 15.00 (*1-878240-12-9*) Coll & U Personnel.

Cost-Effective Surgical Management: Serving Two Masters. Ben E. Eiseman. (Illus.). 304p. 1987. text ed. 66.50 (*0-7216-2102-3*) Saunders.

Cost-Effective Technical Services: How to Track, Manage, & Justify Internal Operations. Ed. by Gary M. Pitkin. 325p. (Orig.). 1989. pap. text ed. 39.50 (*1-55570-041-1*) Neal-Schuman.

Cost-Effective Telecommunications. Richard A. Kuehn. 160p. reprint ed. pap. 45.60 (*0-317-10065-3*, 2051841) Bks Demand.

Cost Effective Use of Computer Aided Technologies & Integration Methods in Small & Medium Sized Companies: IFAC Workshop, Vienna, Austria, September 1992. Ed. by C. Kopacek. LC 93-5238. 1993. pap. 85.00 (*0-08-042061-3*, Pergamon Pr) Elsevier.

Cost-Effective Use of Once-Daily Ceftriaxone in the Treatment of Moderate to Severe Infections, Vol. 37, Supplement 3, 1991: Journal: Chemotherapy. Ed. by V. T. Andriole. (Illus.). iv, 28p. 1991. pap. 9.75 (*3-8055-5450-8*) S Karger.

Cost-Effectiveness: A Primer. Henry M. Levin. (New Perspectives in Evaluation Ser.: Vol. 4). 168p. 1983. 39.95 (*0-8039-2152-7*); pap. 17.95 (*0-8039-2153-5*) Sage.

Cost Effectiveness: Economic Evaluation of Engineered Systems. J. M. English. LC 68-28500. 315p. reprint ed. 89.80 (*0-8357-9868-2*, 2013052) Bks Demand.

Cost Effectiveness in the Environmental Sciences: 1974 Proceedings. 539p. 1974. 26.00 (*0-915414-14-7*) Inst Environ Sci.

Cost-Effectiveness in the Nonprofit Sector: Methods & Examples from Leading Organizations. Ed. by Gerald L. Schmaedick. LC 92-1746. 208p. 1993. text ed. 47.95 (*0-89930-627-6*, RES, Quorum Bks) Greenwood.

***Cost-Effectiveness of GEF Projects.** Dennis Anderson & Robert H. Williams. (Global Environment Facility Working Paper Ser.: No. 6). 44p. 1994. 6.95 (*1-884122-05-1*, 72051) World Bank.

Cost Effectiveness of Occupational Employee Assistance Programs: Test of an Evaluation Method. Andrea E. Foote et al. 110p. 1978. 7.00 (*0-87736-328-5*) U of Mich Inst Labor.

Cost-Effectiveness of Rehabilitation: A Guide to Research Relevant to Occupational Therapy. Ed. by Patricia C. Ostrow et al. 284p. 1987. pap. 32.50 (*0-910317-43-7*) Am Occup Therapy.

Cost Effectiveness of Science Journals: Supplement to the Report of the Advisory Panel for Scientific Publications. rev. ed. 100p. 1992. pap. text ed. 35.00 (*0-9633325-0-3*) Fnd Intl Sci.

Cost-Effectiveness of Transportation Services for Handicapped Persons - Research Report. (National Cooperative Highway Research Program Report Ser.: No. 261). 130p. 1983. 9.60 (*0-309-03602-X*) Transport Res Bd.

Cost-Effectiveness Study of Clinical Methods of Birth Control: With Special Reference to Puerto Rico. William J. Kelly. LC 72-79559. (Special Studies in International Economics & Development). 1972. 29.50 (*0-275-28637-1*) Irvington.

Cost-Efficient Network Management. Larry Ball. 320p. 1992. text ed. 35.00 (*0-07-003484-2*) McGraw.

Cost Engineering for Effective Project Control. Sol A. Ward. (Construction Business & Management Library: No. 1982). 240p. 1991. text ed. 69.95 (*0-471-52851-X*) Wiley.

Cost Engineering in Printed Circuit Board Manufacturing. Hedden. (Cost Engineering Ser.: Vol. 11). 240p. 1987. 99.75 (*0-8247-7574-0*) Dekker.

Cost Engineering Management Techniques. Black. (Cost Engineering Ser.: Vol. 4). 272p. 1984. 99.75 (*0-8247-7088-9*) Dekker.

Cost Engineers' Notebook, 2 vols., Set, Vols. 1-2. 1991. Set. ring bd. 175.00 (*0-317-04231-9*) AACE Intl.

***Cost Estimates for Expanded Substance Abuse Benefits for Medicaid-Eligible Pregnant Women.** (Illus.). 210p. (Orig.). (C). 1994. pap. text ed. 75.00x (*0-7881-1272-4*) Diane Pub.

Cost Estimating. 2nd ed. Rodney D. Stewart. 1991. text ed. 69.95 (*0-471-85707-6*) Wiley.

Cost Estimating for Government Contracts: Course Manual. write for info. (*0-318-61723-4*) Fed Pubns Inc.

Cost Estimating for Metal Stampers & Fabricators. J. E. Nicks. Ed. by Amy Boeselager. (Illus.). 160p. (Orig.). (C). 1993. pap. 29.95 (*1-881113-04-3*) Croydon Grp.

Cost Estimating Man-Hour Manual for Pipelines & Marine Structures. John Page. LC 76-40868. 336p. 1977. 49.00 (*0-87201-157-7*) Gulf Pub.

Cost Estimation for Software Development. Bernard Londeix. 209p. (C). 1987. text ed. 29.25 (*0-201-17451-0*) Addison-Wesley.

Cost Estimator's Reference Manual. Rodney D. Stewart & Richard M. Wyskida. LC 86-15884. 620p. 1987. text ed. 110.00 (*0-471-83082-8*) Wiley.

An Asterisk (*) at the beginning of an entry indicates that the title is appearing in BIP for the first time.

*Cost Estimator's Reference Manual. 2nd ed. Ed. by Rodney D. Stewart et al. LC 94-23415. (New Dimensions in Engineering Ser.). 1995. text ed. 89.95 (0-471-30510-3) Wiley.

Cost Factors in the Army, Vol. 2: Factors, Methods, & Models. Adele R. Palmer & Eric V. Larson. LC 92-15576. 1992. write for info. (0-8330-1241-X, R-4078/2-PA&E) Rand Corp.

Cost Finding for Public Libraries: A Manager's Handbook. Philip Rosenberg. LC 85-20091. 112p. 1986. pap. 5.00 (0-8389-0442-4) ALA.

*Cost Finding for Records Management Activities: A Guide to Unit Costing for the Records Manager, Vol. II. Jose-Marie Griffiths & Donald W. King. Ed. by Elizabeth Atwood-Gailey & Paul Gailey. 107p. 1995. disk, spiral bd. 151.00 (0-933887-51-5, A4592) Assn Recs Mgrs & Admin.

Cost Forum Transnational Cooperation in Science & Technology with New European, EUR 14188. A. Klose & I. Dusak. 203p. 1992. pap. 25.00 (92-826-4376-X, CG-NA-14188-EN-C, Pub. by Europ Com) UNIPUB.

Cost Guide for Automatic Finishing Processes. Ed. by Lawrence J. Rhoades. LC 80-52614. 219p. reprint ed. pap. 62.50 (0-317-41902-1, 2026159) Bks Demand.

Cost Indicators for Selected Records Management Activities: A Guide to Unit Costing for the Records Manager, Vol. I. Jose-Marie Griffiths & Donald W. King. Ed. by Elizabeth Atwood-Gailey. 74p. 1993. disk, spiral bd. 151.00 (0-933887-47-7, A4591) Assn Recs Mgrs & Admin.

Cost-Justifying Usability. Ed. by Randolph G. Bias & Deborah J. Mayhew. (Illus.). 334p. 1994. text ed. 49.95 (0-12-095810-4) Acad Pr.

*Cost Management: Accounting & Control. Don R. Hansen & Maryanne M. Mowen. LC 94-23365. 1000p. 1995. text ed. 62.95 (0-538-83227-4) S-W Pub.

Cost Management for Long-Term Care Facilities. Mike Jacobs. 208p. (C). 1986. 49.95 (0-929442-01-6) Publicare Pr.

Cost Management for Today's Advanced Manufacturing: The Cam-I Conceptual Design. Callie Berliner & James A. Brimson. 1988. text ed. 35.00 (0-07-103210-X) McGraw.

Cost Management for Tomorrow: Seeking the Competitive Edge. Robert A. Howell et al. (Innovative Management Ser.). 525p. (Orig.). 1992. 30.00 (0-910586-85-3) Finan Exec.

Cost Management in Engineering Construction Projects: Guidance Notes. RICS Staff. (C). 1992. pap. text ed. 90.00 (0-85406-524-5, Pub. by R-I-C-S Bks UK) St Mut.

Cost Management in the New Manufacturing Age: Innovations in the Japanese Automotive Industry. Yasuhiro Monden. Tr. by Stephen Vitek. (Illus.). 198p. 1992. 45.00 (0-915299-90-9) Prod Press.

Cost Management Strategies for Smaller Hospitals. Malcolm R. Hastings. LC 91-1908. 124p. 1993. 45.00 (1-55648-105-5, 184131) AHPI.

Cost-Managerial Accounting: Comptech Manufacturer Standard Costs & Budgeting. V. A. Pacsy & J. V. Bennett. 64p. 1986. 10.05 (0-07-004704-9) McGraw.

Cost-Managerial Accounting: Robotor Inc. Job Order System & Cost Control. V. A. Pacsy & J. V. Bennet. 96p. 1986. 10.05 (0-07-004702-2) McGraw.

Cost Manual for Piping & Mechanical Construction. Herbert Herkimer. 1958. 37.50 (0-8206-0029-6) Chem Pub.

Cost, Markup & Profit Tables for Bars. 1988. 3.95 (0-318-33254-X, 101) Am Bartenders.

Cost of Accessible Housing: An Analysis of the Estimated Cost of Compliance with the Fair Housing Accessibility Guidelines & ANSI A 117.1. (Illus.). 230p. (Orig.). (C). 1993. pap. text ed. 65.00 (0-7881-0065-3) Diane Pub.

Cost of American Almshouses. Estelle M. Stewart. LC 75-17245. (Social Problems & Social Policy Ser.). (Illus.). 1976. reprint ed. 13.95 (0-405-07516-2) Ayer.

Cost of Being Human. Corona Bamberg. 1984. 11.95 (0-87193-128-1) Dimension Bks.

Cost of Capital: Estimating the Rate of Return for Public Utilities. Lawrence A. Kolbe et al. 256p. 1984. 33.00x (0-262-11094-6) MIT Pr.

*Cost of Capital: Theory & Estimation. Cleveland S. Patterson. LC 94-32081. 344p. 1995. text ed. 75.00 (0-89930-862-7, Quorum Bks) Greenwood.

Cost of Capital in Receivables Management. 33p. 1978. 40.00 (0-939050-11-0) Credit Res NYS.

Cost of Capital to a Public Utility. Myron J. Gordon. LC 73-620076. (MSU Public Utilities Papers). 243p. reprint ed. pap. 69.30 (0-317-55816-1, 2029403) Bks Demand.

Cost of Children in Urban U. S., Vol. 11. Thomas J. Espenshade. LC 76-4798. (Population Monograph Ser.: No. 14). 94p. 1976. reprint ed. text ed. 45.00 (0-8371-8835-0, ESCC, Greenwood Pr) Greenwood.

Cost of Courage: The Journey of an American Congressman. Carl Elliot. 1992. 22.00 (0-385-42091-9) Doubleday.

*Cost of Credit: Regulation & Legal Challenges. Kathleen E. Keest. LC 94-69831. (Consumer Credit & Sales Legal Practice Ser.). 528p. 1995. pap. 70.00 (1-881793-29-X) Nat Consumer Law.

Cost of Culture: Patterns & Prospects of Private Arts Patronage. Ed. by Margaret J. Wyszomirski & Pat Clubb. LC 88-27289. (ACA Arts Research Seminar Series Paper). 102p. 1989. pap. 9.95 (0-915400-76-6, ACA Bks) Am Council Arts.

Cost of Democracy. Alexander Heard. LC 60-10532. 519p. reprint ed. pap. 148.00 (0-8357-4401-9, 2037221) Bks Demand.

Cost of Dictatorship: The Somali Experience. Jama M. Ghalib. 240p. 1993. pap. text ed. 18.95 (0-936508-32-9) Barber Pr.

Cost of Dictatorship: The Somali Experience. Jama M. Ghalib. 240p. 1994. lib. bdg. 14.95 (0-936508-30-2) Barber Pr.

Cost of Discipleship. 36p. 1986. pap. 2.00 (0-934803-56-0) J Van Impe.

Cost of Discipleship. Dietrich Bonhoeffer. 352p. 1963. pap. 6.95 (0-02-083850-6, Collier S&S) S&S Trade.

Cost of Discipleship. Dietrich Bonhoeffer. 1983. 19.75 (0-8446-5960-6) Peter Smith.

Cost of Doing Business: Legal & Regulatory Issues in the U. S. & Abroad. Peter Chinloy. LC 89-3650. 194p. 1989. text ed. 55.00 (0-275-93332-6, C3332, Praeger Pubs) Greenwood.

Cost of Education: An Investment in America's Future. Glen E. Robinson & Nancy J. Protheroe. 102p. 1987. 26.00 (0-318-37608-3) Ed Research.

Cost of Empire: Neapolitan Finance During the Period of Spanish Rule. Antonio Calabria. (Studies in Early Modern History). 208p. (C). 1991. 49.95 (0-521-39176-8) Cambridge U Pr.

Cost of Energy & a Clean Environment. Ed. by Russell Thompson et al. LC 77-71491. (Illus.). 564p. reprint ed. pap. 160.80 (0-685-20482-0, 2029916) Bks Demand.

Cost of Environmental Protection: Regulating Housing Development in the Coastal Zone. Dan K. Richardson. 219p. 1976. pap. text ed. 17.95 (0-87855-614-1) Transaction Pubs.

Cost of Freedom: A New Look at Capitalism. Henry C. Wallich. LC 78-27775. 178p. 1979. reprint ed. text ed. 49.75 (0-313-20935-9, WACF, Greenwood Pr) Greenwood.

Cost of Future Freedom: Energy Economics. Samuel M. Dix. 1982. 30.00 (0-918998-05-0) Energy Educ.

Cost of Government & the Support of Education: An Intensive Study of New York State with Results Applicable Over the Entire Country. Harold F. Clark. LC 79-17668. (Columbia University. Teachers College. Contributions to Education Ser.: No. 145). reprint ed. 37.50 (0-404-55145-9) AMS Pr.

Cost of High-Level Waste Disposal in Geological Repositories: An Analysis of Factors Affecting Cost Estimates. OECD Staff. 136p. (Orig.). 1993. pap. 36.00 (92-64-13914-1) OECD.

Cost of Honor. Emma Lange. 224p. 1988. pap. 3.99 (0-451-15188-7, Sig) NAL-Dutton.

Cost of Human Neglect: America's Welfare Failure. Harrell R. Rodgers, Jr. LC 82-10390. 236p. 1982. pap. text ed. 22.95 (0-87332-238-X) M E Sharpe.

Cost of Inefficiency in Fluid Machinery: Presented at the Winter Annual Meeting of the ASME, New York, NY, November 17-21, 1974 (Sponsored by the Fluid Machinery Committee of the Fluids Engineering Division, ASME) Ed. by David Japikse. LC 75-153. 82p. reprint ed. pap. 25.00 (0-317-10979-0, 2016811) Bks Demand.

Cost of Libel: Economic & Policy Implications. Ed. by Eli M. Noam & Everette Dennis. (Columbia Studies in Business, Government & Society). 320p. 1989. text ed. 40.00 (0-231-06692-9) Col U Pr.

Cost of Living. Robert Chesshyre. 1991. pap. 24.95 (0-89381-439-3) Aperture.

*Cost of Living. Kenneth Sherman. 48p. 1995. lib. bdg. 23.00 (0-8095-4535-7) Borgo Pr.

Cost of Living Index Numbers: Practice, Precision, & Theory. Kali S. Banerjee. LC 75-985. (Statistics, Textbooks & Monographs: No. 11). 197p. reprint ed. pap. 56.20 (0-7837-0734-7, 2041058) Bks Demand.

Cost of Living of Teachers in the State of New York. David P. Harry. LC 70-176844. (Columbia University. Teachers College. Contributions to Education Ser.: No. 320). reprint ed. 37.50 (0-404-55320-6) AMS Pr.

Cost of Love. Alexis Rogers. 160p. (Orig.). 1990. pap. 8.95 (0-938743-10-4) Lavender CT.

Cost of Loving. large type ed. Juliet Gray. (Linford Romance Library). 1991. pap. 13.95 (0-7089-7044-3) Ulverscroft.

Cost of Mississippi: Its Past & Progress. Jerry Kinser. Ed. by Doug Woolfolk. 1981. 10.00 (0-86518-018-0) Moran Pub Corp.

Cost of Nursing Education: A Manual for Analysis of Expenditures. Ed. by Lucille Knopf. Incl. Pt. I. Method, Directions, & Examples: Baccalaureate Program. 66p. 1982. 35.00 (0-88737-081-0, 19-1909); Pt. I. Methods, Directions, & Examples: Associate Degree Program. 74p. 1982. 35.00 (0-88737-082-9, 19-1910); Pt. I. Method, Directions, & Examples: Diploma Program. 59p. 1982. 35.00 (0-88737-083-7, 19-1911); Pt. II. Data-Gathering Instruments. 49p. 1982. 15.00 (0-88737-084-5, 19-1912); 1982. write for info. (0-318-57625-2) Natl League Nurse.

Cost of Our National Government: A Study in Political Pathology. Henry J. Ford. LC 73-19145. (Politics & People Ser.). 164p. 1974. reprint ed. 16.95 (0-405-05869-1) Ayer.

Cost of Personal Borrowing in the United States. Ed. by Financial Publishing Company Staff & Charles H. Gushee. (Illus.). 525p. 1985. per. 75.00 (0-87600-830-9, 830) Finan Pub.

Cost of Providing Consumer Credit: A Study of Four Major Types of Financial Institutions. Paul F. Smith. (Occasional Papers: No. 83). 32p. 1962. reprint ed. 20.00 (0-87014-397-2) Natl Bur Econ Res.

Cost of Quality Guideline. Tien Hou. Ed. by Valerie Rothlein. (AT&T Quality Library). (Illus.). 46p. (Orig.). 1990. pap. 19.95 (0-932764-25-8, 500-746) AT&T Customer Info.

Cost of Raising Children in Canada. Douthitt & Fedyk. 224p. 1990. pap. 54.00 (0-409-88957-1) Butterworth Legal Pubs.

Cost of Recreation & Leisure Activities. Kathleen O'Brien. 1988. pap. text ed. 25.00 (0-89478-056-5) U CO Busn Res Div.

Cost of Regulated Loans: An Analysis of Chapter 3 of the Texas Credit Code. Contrib by John Gronovski. (Policy Research Project Report Ser.: No. 45). 64p. 1981. 2.95 (0-89940-647-5) LBJ Sch Pub Aff.

Cost of Regulated Pricing: A Critical Analysis of Auto Insurance Premium Rate - Setting in Massachusetts. Simon Rottenberg. LC 89-22939. (Pioneer Paper Ser.: No. 2). 50p. (Orig.). 1989. pap. 10.00 (0-929930-02-9) Pioneer Inst.

*Cost of Revival. Rob Lindsted. 40p. (Orig.). 1994. pap. 2.50 (1-879366-46-0) Hearthstone OK.

*Cost of Select Recreation & Leisure Activities 1993. David A. Olson. 78p. 1994. pap. text ed. 25.00 (0-614-06283-7) U CO Busn Res Div.

Cost of Social Security: Thirteenth International Inquiry, 1984-1986, Comparative Tables. 13th ed. International Labour Office Staff. (Illus.). iv, 212p. (ENG, FRE & SPA.). 1992. pap. 56.00 (92-2-006430-8) Intl Labour Office.

Cost of Something for Nothing. John P. Altgeld. 1974. 59.95 (0-87968-948-X) Gordon Pr.

Cost of Something for Nothing. John P. Altgeld. (Illus.). 135p. reprint ed. 12.95 (0-88286-152-2) C H Kerr.

Cost of Strangeness: Essays on the English Poets in Wales. Ed. by Anthony Conran. 330p. (C). 1982. pap. text ed. 20.00x (0-85088-865-4, Pub. by Gomer Pr UK) St Mut.

Cost of Talent: How Executives & Professionals Are Compensated & How It Affects America. Derek C. Bok. 320p. 1993. text ed. 22.95 (0-02-903755-7) Free Pr.

Cost of the War to Russia. S. Kohn & Alexander F. Meyendorff. 40.00 (0-86527-034-1) Fertig.

Cost of Thinking: Information Economics of Ten Pacific Countries. Ed. by Meheroo Jussawalla et al. LC 87-22937. (Communication & Information Science Ser.). 272p. 1988. text ed. 55.00 (0-89391-419-3) Ablex Pub.

Cost of War, Vol. 1. Craig Reed. Ed. by Janet Strunk. 240p. (Orig.). (C). 1989. pap. text ed. write for info. (0-318-65794-5) Hurricane Ridge.

Cost, Prices, & Profits: Their Cyclical Relations. Thor Hultgren & Maude R. Pech. (Business Cycles Ser.: No. 14). 255p. 1965. 66.30 (0-87014-098-1) Natl Bur Econ Res.

Cost, Prices, & Profits, Their Cyclical Relations. Thor Hultgren. LC 65-11218. (National Bureau of Economic Research, Studies in Business Cycles: No. 14). (Illus.). 255p. reprint ed. pap. 72.70 (0-8357-7568-2, 2056889) Bks Demand.

Cost, Quality, & Access in Health Care: New Roles for Health Planning in a Competitive Environment. Ed. by Frank A. Sloan et al. LC 87-46349. (Health-Management Ser.). 317p. 1988. 39.95 (1-55542-094-X) Jossey-Bass.

Cost Records for Construction Estimating. W. P. Jackson. LC 84-14271. 208p. (Orig.). 1984. pap. 15.75 (0-910460-41-8) Craftsman.

*Cost Recovery in Public Health Services in Sub-Saharan Africa. Brian Nolan & Vincent Turbat. LC 95-14406. (EDI Technical Materials Ser.). 1995. write for info. (0-8213-3240-6) World Bank.

Cost Recovery in the Health Care Sector: Selected Country Studies in West Africa. Ronald J. Vogel. (Technical Paper Ser.: No. 82). 206p. 1988. 12.95 (0-8213-1051-8, BK1051) World Bank.

Cost Reduction in Offshore Engineering: Proceedings of a Conference Organized by the Offshore Engineering Society of the Institution of Civil Engineers. 136p. 1988. 54.00 (0-7277-1349-3, Pub. by T Telford UK) Am Soc Civil Eng.

Cost Reduction Offshore: The Way Ahead: Papers Presented at a Conference Organised by the Exploration & Production Group on November 16, 1989. Institute of Petroleum, London Staff. Ed. by A. E. Lodge. LC 91-17900. (Illus.). 214p. reprint ed. pap. 61.00 (0-7837-6838-9, 2046667) Bks Demand.

*Cost Reduction System: Target Costing & Kaizen Costing. Yasuhiro Monden. (Illus.). 400p. (JPN.). 1995. text ed. 50.00 (1-56327-068-4) Prod Press.

Cost Reimbursement Contracting. 2nd ed. John Cibinic, Jr. & Ralph C. Nash, Jr. 1450p. 1993. 90.00 (0-935165-20-7); pap. 65.00 (0-935165-28-2) GWU Gov Contracts.

Cost-Saving Ideas for Local Governments. 100p. 1993. student ed 29.95 (1-882403-12-6) Innovation Grps.

Cost Schedule Control System: Principle & Practices. Charles M. Slemaker. (Illus.). 450p. 1984. text ed. 39.95 (0-89433-227-9) Petrocelli.

Cost Shifting in Health Care: Separating Evidence from Rhetoric. Michael A. Morrisey. LC 94-14605. Date not set. pap. write for info. (0-8447-3861-1) Am Enterprise.

Cost Shifting in Health Care: Separating Evidence from Rhetoric. Michael A. Morrisey. LC 94-14605. 1994. 19.95 (0-8447-3860-3, AEI Pr) Am Enterprise.

Cost Study for Sheetfed Presses. (Illus.). 779p. 1989. 100.00 (0-318-14963-X, B103) NAPL.

Cost Study in Lithographic Preparatory Operations. 524p. 1991. 100.00 (0-318-21975-1, B102) NAPL.

Cost Study of Resident Camps. 66p. 1985. 15.00 (0-87603-081-9) Am Camping.

Cost Study on Bindery, Finishing & Mailing Operations. 1993. 100.00 (0-318-21976-X, B105) NAPL.

Cost Study on Phototypesetting & Automated Composition. 147p. 1989. 100.00 (0-318-21979-4, B101) NAPL.

Cost Study on Web Presses. (Illus.). 389p. 1990. 100.00 (0-317-01440-4, B104) NAPL.

Cost Study on Web Presses. (Illus.). 389p. 1990. pap. 125.00 (0-318-14965-6, B104) NAPL.

Cost Three Hundred Seven Rational Use of Energy in Interregional Transport, EUR 14909. J. L. Alfaro et al. 278p. 1993. pap. 45.00 (92-826-5489-3, CG-NA-14909-EN-C, Pub. by Europ Com) UNIPUB.

Cost Versus Benefit in Cancer Care. Ed. by Basil A. Stoll. LC 88-9074. (Johns Hopkins Series in Contemporary Medicine & Public Health). 128p. 1989. text ed. 40.00 (0-8018-3774-X) Johns Hopkins.

Cost Watch at Average Litho. 2nd rev. ed. 37p. 1987. 45.00 (0-318-21978-6, XP110) NAPL.

Cost 202 Bis Wideband Digital Telecommunications Networks. Ed. by W. Maggi. 429p. 1991. pap. 50.00 (92-826-1997-4, CD-NA-13195-EN-C) UNIPUB.

Cost 206 Coding & Transmission of High-Definition T.V. Signals. Ed. by L. Stenger. (EUR Ser.: No. 14654). 172p. 1993. 25.00 (92-826-4877-X, CD-NA-14654-EN-C, Pub. by Europ Com) UNIPUB.

Cost 210 Influence of the Atmosphere on Interference Between Radio Communication, EUR 13407. Ed. by E. Ballabio. 664p. 1991. 70.00 (92-826-2400-5, CD-NA-13407-EN-C) UNIPUB.

Cost 212: Human Factors in Information Services, EUR 13189. Ed. by A. Orlando. 125p. 1991. pap. 16.00 (92-826-2020-4, CD-NA-13189-EN-C) UNIPUB.

Cost 212 Human Factors in Information Services, EUR 14277. Ed. by A. Orlando. 175p. 1992. 25.00 (92-826-4132-5, CG-NA-14277-EN-C, Pub. by Europ Com) UNIPUB.

Cost 305 European Passenger Transport Demand Today & Tomorrow Data Requirements, Transport Research. F. Fabre & A. Klose. 196p. 1993. pap. 30.00 (92-826-4416-2, CG-NA-14381-EN-C, Pub. by Europ Com) UNIPUB.

*Costa. Bill Costa. 1995. 12.00 (0-312-11809-0, Stonewall Inn) St Martin.

Costa Blanca Pocket Guide. Berlitz Editors. (Pocket Guides Ser.). (Illus.). 1989. pap. 7.95 (2-8315-2271-4) Berlitz.

Costa Brava. (Baedeker's Travel Guide Ser.). 1988. pap. 12.95 (0-13-055880-X, P-H Travel) P-H Gen Ref & Trav.

Costa Brava Travel Guide. Berlitz Editors. (Pocket Guides Ser.). 1989. pap. 6.95 (2-8315-0065-6) Berlitz.

Costa del Sol. (Panorama Books Collection). (FRE.). 3.95 (0-685-36096-2) Fr & Eur.

Costa del Sol Pocket Guide. Berlitz Editors. (Pocket Guides Ser.). (Illus.). 1989. pap. 7.95 (2-8315-2573-X) Berlitz.

Costa-Gavras: The Political Fiction Film. John J. Michalczyk. (Illus.). 296p. 1984. 48.50 (0-87982-029-2) Art Alliance.

Costa Rica. John A. Booth. 175p. 1929. text ed. 29.95 (0-8133-7631-9) Westview.

Costa Rica. S. May. 1976. lib. bdg. 59.95 (0-8490-1677-0) Gordon Pr.

Costa Rica. Charles L. Stansifer. (World Bibliographical Ser.). 1991. lib. bdg. 83.50 (1-85109-027-4) ABC-CLIO.

Costa Rica. 3rd ed. Paul Glassman. (Illus.). 288p. 1989. pap. 13.95 (0-930016-12-2) Passport Pr.

Costa Rica: A Country Study. 2nd ed. Ed. by Harold D. Nelson. LC 84-16888. (Area Handbook Ser.: DA Pam 550-90). 367p. 1984. 14.00 (0-16-001610-X, S/N 008-020-01009-0) USGPO.

Costa Rica: A Natural Destination. 2nd ed. Ree S. Sheck. 288p. (Orig.). 1992. pap. 16.95 (1-56261-014-7) John Muir.

Costa Rica: A Natural Destination. 3rd ed. Ree S. Sheck. 320p. (Orig.). 1994. pap. 16.95 (1-56261-144-5) John Muir.

Costa Rica: A Travel Survival Kit. 2nd ed. Rob Rachowiecki. (Illus.). 420p. (Orig.). 1994. pap. 14.95 (0-86442-205-9) Lonely Planet.

Costa Rica: A Traveler's Literary Companion. Intro. by Barbara Ras. (Traveler's Literary Companions Ser.). 256p. (Orig.). 1994. pap. 12.95 (1-883513-00-6) Whereabouts.

*Costa Rica: Commercial Law. 300p. (Orig.). 1994. pap. 295.00 (0-7605-1240-X) Rector Pr.

Costa Rica: Foreign Financing Reporter. Ed. by Lewis B. Sckolnick. (Illus.). 60p. (Orig.). 1994. pap. 225.00 (1-57205-238-4) Rector Pr.

Costa Rica: Gem of American Republics. Richard Villafranca. 1976. lib. bdg. 59.95 (0-8490-1679-7) Gordon Pr.

Costa Rica: The Last Country the Gods Made. Adrian Colesberry et al. LC 93-71977. 152p. (Orig.). 1993. 35.00 (1-56044-251-4) Falcon Pr MT.

Costa Rica: Trade, Licensing & Investing Rules & Regulations. Ed. by Lewis B. Sckolnick. (Illus.). 80p. (Orig.). (C). 1994. pap. 225.00 (1-57205-060-8) Rector Pr.

Costa Rica see American Nations Past & Present

Costa Rica see Statements of the Laws of the OAS Member States in Matters Affecting Business

Costa Rica & Civilization in the Caribbean. Chester L. Jones. 1976. lib. bdg. 59.95 (0-8490-1678-9) Gordon Pr.

Costa Rica Before Coffee: Society & Economy on the Eve of the Export Boom. Lowell Gudmundson. LC 86-2789. (Illus.). xvi, 204p. 1986. text ed. 32.50 (0-8071-1274-7) La State U Pr.

Costa Rica, Belize, Guatemala, 1995: The Complete Guide with the Rainforests, Maya Ruins & Beaches. 2nd ed. Fodor's Travel Staff. (Illus.). 1994. pap. 15.00 (0-679-02709-2) Fodors Travel.

Costa Rica Business Forecaster. Ed. by Lewis B. Sckolnick. 70p. (Orig.). (C). 1994. pap. 675.00 (1-57205-370-4) Rector Pr.

*Costa Rica Business Intelligence Handbook. (Illus.). 70p. (Orig.). 1994. pap. 295.00 (0-7605-1075-X) Rector Pr.

*Costa Rica Business Risk Outlook. 70p. (Orig.). 1994. pap. 495.00 (0-7605-1382-1) Rector Pr.

*Costa Rica Commercial Tax. 150p. (C). 1994. pap. 295.00 (0-7605-0102-5) Rector Pr.

C

An Asterisk (*) at the beginning of an entry indicates that the title is appearing in BIP for the first time. 1643

Costa Rica Guide. 5th rev. ed. Paul Glassman. (Passport Ser.). 448p. 1993. pap. 13.95 (*1-883323-03-7*) Open Rd Pub.

Costa Rica Guide: New Authorized Edition (Description & Travel) Paul Glassman. (Illus.). 416p. 1994. lib. bdg. 13.95 (*0-930016-18-1*) Passport Pr.

Costa Rica Guide (Description & Travel) 4th ed. Paul Glassman. LC 90-91856. (Illus.). 352p. 1991. pap. 13.95 (*0-930016-16-5*) Passport Pr.

Costa Rica Handbook. Christopher P. Baker. LC 93-13797. (Moon Handbooks Ser.). 574p. 1994. 17.95 (*1-56691-008-0*) Moon Pubns CA.

***Costa Rica Handbook.** 2nd ed. Christopher P. Baker. (Moon Travel Handbooks Ser.). (Illus.). 574p. 1995. pap. 18.95 (*1-56691-035-8*) Moon Pubns CA.

Costa Rica in Pictures. Lerner Publications, Department of Geography Staff. (Visual Geography Ser.). (Illus.). 64p. (YA). (gr. 5 up). 1987. lib. bdg. 18.95 (*0-8225-1805-8*, Lerner Publctns) Lerner Group.

Costa Rica Is My Home. Photos by Rose Welch. LC 92-17727. (My Home Country Ser.). (Illus.). (J). 1992. lib. bdg. 18.60 (*0-8368-0847-9*) Gareth Stevens Inc.

Costa Rica, Panama: Business Risk Overview. Ed. by Lewis B. Sckolnick. 125p. (Orig.). (C). 1994. pap. text ed. 495.00 (*1-57205-573-1*) Rector Pr.

***Costa Rica Postal Catalogue.** Hector R. Mena. 216p. 1994. 12.00 (*0-9645247-2-4*) SCRC.

Costa Rica Reader. Ed. by Mark Edelman & Joanne Kenan. 416p. 1989. pap. 16.95 (*0-8021-3124-7*) Grove-Atltic.

***Costa Rica Tax.** 150p. (C). 1994. pap. 295.00 (*0-7605-0101-7*) Rector Pr.

Costa Rica Traveler. Ellen Searby. 1990. 11.95 (*0-317-99658-4*) Windham Bay.

***Costa Rica Traveler.** rev. ed. Ellen Searby. (Illus.). 400p. 1995. 17.95 (*0-942297-10-5*) Windham Bay.

Costa Rica Traveler: Getting Around in Costa Rica. 2nd ed. Ellen Searby. LC 87-51454. (Illus.). 256p. 1988. pap. 11.95 (*0-9605526-9-3*) Windham Bay.

Costa Rica Traveler: Getting Around in Costa Rica. 3rd ed. Ellen Searby. (Illus.). 304p. 1991. pap. 14.95 (*0-942297-04-0*) Windham Bay.

Costa Rica Travellers Guide. Berlitz Editors. (Travellers Guides Ser.). (Illus.). 256p. 1993. pap. 11.95 (*2-8315-1702-8*) Berlitz.

Costa Rican Laboratory: A Twentieth-Century Fund Paper. Sol W. Sanders. (International Debt Ser.). 74p. (Orig.). (C). 1986. pap. text ed. 7.00 (*0-87078-170-7*) TCFP-PPP.

Costa Rican Life. John B. Biesanz & Mavis Biesanz. LC 78-12865. (Illus.). 272p. 1979. text ed. 35.00 (*0-313-21125-6*, BICR, Greenwood Pr) Greenwood.

Costa Rican Natural History. Ed. by Daniel H. Janzen. LC 82-17625. (Illus.). 832p. 1983. pap. text ed. 35.00 (*0-226-39334-8*) U Ch Pr.

Costa Rican Women's Movement: A Reader. Ed. & Tr. by Ilse A. Leitinger. (Pitt Latin American Ser.). (Illus.). 384p. (C). 1995. 49.95 (*0-8229-3862-6*); pap. 19.95 (*0-8229-5543-1*) U of Pittsburgh Pr.

Costa Ricans. Richard Biesanz et al. (Illus.). 250p. (C). 1988. reprint ed. pap. text ed. 9.95 (*0-88133-340-9*) Waveland Pr.

Costa Rica's National Parks & Preserves: A Visitor's Guide. Joseph Franke. (Illus.). 224p. (Orig.). 1993. pap. 16.95 (*0-89886-321-X*) Mountaineers.

Costal Resources Management Guidelines. Samuel C. Snedaker & Charles D. Getter. (Renewable Resources Information Series: Coastal Management Publication: No. 2). 220p. 1985. pap. write for info. (*0-931531-01-2*) Res Plan Inst.

Costanso Narrative of the Portola Expedition: First Chronicle of the Spanish Conquest of Alta California. Miguel Costanso. Tr. by Ray Brandes. LC 79-112869. 112p. 1983. reprint ed. lib. bdg. 33.00x (*0-89370-753-8*) Borgo Pr.

Costimator Standards Handbook: Practical Labor & Machine Time Standards. Thomas Charkiewicz. (Orig.). 1985. pap. 49.95 (*0-9614980-0-5*) Manu Technologies.

Costimulatory Pathway for T Cell Responses. Yang Liu. LC 93-45549. (Molecular Biology Intelligence Unit Ser.). 128p. 1993. 89.95 (*1-57059-052-4*) R G Landes.

Costing: An Introduction. 2nd ed. Colin Drury. 416p. 1990. pap. 30.00 (*0-412-35800-X*, A4881) Chapman & Hall.

Costing Community Care: Theory & Practice. Ann Netten & Jeni Beecham. LC 93-16351. 180p. 1993. 58.95 (*1-85742-098-5*, Pub. by Ashgate UK); pap. 27.95 (*1-85742-102-7*, Pub. by Ashgate UK) Ashgate Pub Co.

Costing Data for Fire Protection in Complex Industrial Occupancies. David S. Mowrer. 1982. 4.65 (*0-686-37671-4*, TR 82-7) Society Fire Protect.

Costing for Negotiated Government Contracts. rev. ed. Stanley Fishner. 182p. (C). 1986. pap. 29.95 (*0-9606848-1-6*) Fishner Bks.

Costing Heritage: Studies in Honor of S. Paul Garner. Ed. by O. Finley Graves. LC 91-11291. (Monograph Series of the Academy of Accounting Historians). 1991. pap. 20.00 (*1-879750-04-X*) Acad Acct Hist.

Costing Human Resources. 3rd ed. Wayne F. Cascio. 300p. (C). 1991. pap. 22.95 (*0-534-91938-3*) Intl Thomson.

Costing in the Furniture Industry. V. Parker & W. Kape. LC 65-14786. (Pergamon Series of Monographs on Furniture & Timber: Vol. 2). 1965. 71.00 (*0-08-013776-8*, Pub. by Pergamon Repr UK) Franklin.

Costing Labor Contracts & Judging Their Financial Impact. Stephen J. Holoviak. LC 84-15880. 208p. 1984. text ed. 55.00 (*0-275-91193-4*, C1193, Praeger Pubs) Greenwood.

Costing Matters for Managers. E. G. Wood. 1977. reprint ed. 29.00 (*0-8464-0294-7*) Beekman Pubs.

Costing out Nursing: Pricing Our Product. Ed. by Franklin Shaffer. 272p. 1985. 18.95 (*0-88737-167-1*, 20-1982) Natl League Nurse.

Costing Sectoral Outputs in a General Hospital: A General Economic Systems Approach. Robert E. Kuenne. (Discussion Paper Ser.: No. 27). 1969. pap. 10.00 (*1-55869-019-0*) Regional Sci Res Inst.

Costing System for Public Libraries. (Library Information Ser.: No. 17). 33p. (Orig.). 1987. pap. text ed. 10.00 (*0-11-430018-6*, HM44, Pub. by HMSO UK) UNIPUB.

Costing the Earth. Ed. by Ronald Banks. 196p. (Orig.). 1989. pap. 10.00 (*0-85683-111-5*, Pub. by Shephrd-Walwyn UK) Schalkenbach.

Costing the Earth: The Challenge for Governments, the Opportunities for Business. Frances Cairncross. LC 91-33750. 368p. 1992. 24.95 (*0-87584-315-8*) Harvard Busn.

Costing the Earth: The Challenge for Governments, the Opportunities for Business. Frances Cairncross. 368p. 1993. pap. 14.95 (*0-87584-410-3*) Harvard Busn.

Costing the Earth: The Challenge for Governments, the Opportunities for Business. Frances Cairncross. 1992. text ed. 24.95 (*0-07-103367-X*) McGraw.

Costing the Earth: The Challenge for Governments, the Opportunities for Business. rev. ed. Frances Cairncross. 1993. pap. text ed. 14.95 (*0-07-103396-3*) McGraw.

Costly Anointing. Lori Wilke. 182p. (Orig.). 1992. pap. 8.99 (*1-56043-051-6*) Destiny Image.

Costly Grace: An Illustrated Introduction to Dietrich Bonhoeffer in His Own Words. Eberhard Bethge. LC 78-19492. (Illus.). 1979. pap. 4.95i (*0-06-060773-4*, RD294) Harper SF.

Costly Monuments: Representations of the Self in George Herbert's Poetry. Barbara L. Harman. 240p. 1982. 29.00 (*0-674-17465-8*) HUP.

Costly Obedience: Sermons by Women of Steadfast Spirit. Ed. by Elizabeth S. Bellinger. LC 93-45873. 1994. pap. 13.00 (*0-8170-1205-2*) Judson.

Costly Policies: State Regulation & Antitrust Exemption in Insurance Markets. Jonathan R. Macey & Geoffrey P. Miller. 123p. 1993. 24.75 (*0-8447-3831-X*); pap. 9.75 (*0-8447-3830-1*) Am Enterprise.

***Costly Reflections in a Midas Mirror.** Iris W. Collett & Dana Forgione. LC 94-77805. 182p. (Orig.). (C). 1994. pap. text ed. 9.95 (*0-913878-54-5*) T Horton & Dghts.

Costly Returns: Burdens of the U. S. Tax System. James L. Payne. LC 92-19854. 272p. 1993. 34.95 (*1-55815-202-4*); pap. 14.95 (*1-55815-215-6*) ICS Pr.

Costly Tradeoffs: Reconciling Trade & the Environment. Hilary F. French. 70p. (Orig.). 1993. pap. 5.00 (*1-878071-14-9*) Worldwatch Inst.

Costs & Benefits in Health Care & Prevention: An International Approach to Priorities in Medicine. Ed. by U. Laaser et al. (Illus.). 180p. 1990. pap. 31.00 (*0-387-52708-7*) Spr-Verlag.

Costs & Benefits of Deferred Giving. Norman S. Fink & Howard C. Metzler. LC 81-21565. 224p. 1982. text ed. 39.50 (*0-231-05478-5*) Col U Pr.

Costs & Benefits of Foreign Investment from a State Perspective. Cedric L. Suzman et al. 205p. (Orig.). 1982. pap. 5.00 (*0-686-46057-X*) Southern Ctr Intl Stud.

Costs & Benefits of Openness: Sunshine Laws & Higher Education. Association of Governing Boards of Universities & Colleges Staff & Harlan Cleveland. LC 85-239957. (AGB Special Report Ser.). ix, 58p. 12.00 (*0-685-13374-5*) Assn Gov Bds.

Costs & Benefits of U. S. Agricultural Policies with Imperfect Competition in Food Manufacturing. Leo Maier. LC 92-36023. (Government & the Economy Ser.). 328p. 1993. 70.00 (*0-8153-1233-4*) Garland.

Costs & Compensation Paid in Tort Litigation. James S. Kakalik & Nicholas M. Pace. LC 86-31436. 1986. 15.00 (*0-8330-0781-5*, R-3391-ICJ) Rand Corp.

Costs & Effectiveness of Cervical Cancer Screening in Elderly Women. Charlotte Muller et al. (Illus.). 93p. 1990. pap. 4.25 (*0-16-019038-X*, S/N 052-003-01176-0) USGPO.

Costs & Effectiveness of Colorectal Cancer Screening in the Elderly. Judith L. Wagner. (Illus.). 62p. 1990. pap. 3.00 (*0-16-025928-2*, S/N 052-003-01213-8) USGPO.

***Costs & Indices for Domestic Oil & Gas Field Equipment & Production Operations.** (Illus.). 124p. (Orig.). (C). 1994. pap. text ed. 50.00x (*0-7881-1279-1*) Diane Pub.

Costs & Productivity in Automobile Production: The Challenge of Japanese Efficiency. Melvyn A. Fuss & Leonard Waverman. (Illus.). 240p. (C). 1992. 49.95 (*0-521-34141-8*) Cambridge U Pr.

Costs & Returns for Agricultural Commodities: Advances in Concepts & Measurement. Ed. by Mary Ahearn & Utpal Vasavada. 395p. (C). 1992. pap. text ed. 52.00 (*0-8133-0369-9*) Westview.

Costs & Returns on Farm Mortgage Lending by Life Insurance Companies, 1945-1947. Raymond J. Saulnier. (Occasional Papers: No. 30). 67p. 1949. reprint ed. 20.00 (*0-87014-345-X*) Natl Bur Econ Res.

Costs & Taxations in Family Law. G. Pesce. xxi, 201p. 1988. 45.50 (*0-455-20796-8*, Pub. by Law Bk Co) W W Gaunt.

Costs, Benefits, & Productivity in Training Systems. Greg P. Kearsley. LC 82-22846. (Illus.). 160p. 1982. text ed. write for info. (*0-201-10332-X*) Addison-Wesley.

Costs for Hazardous Waste Incineration: Capital, Operation & Maintenance, Retrofit. R. J. McCormick et al. LC 85-16839. (Pollution Technology Review Ser.: No. 123). (Illus.). 274p. 1986. 39.00 (*0-8155-1047-0*) Noyes.

Costs of Accidents: Legal & Economic Analysis. Guido Calabresi. 1970. pap. text ed. 17.00x (*0-300-01115-6*) Yale U Pr.

Costs of Alternative Development Patterns: A Review of the Literature. James E. Frank. LC 89-51660. 1990. 18.95 (*0-87420-695-2*) Urban Land.

Costs of Asbestos Litigation. James S. Kakalik et al. LC 83-16032. 1983. 4.00 (*0-8330-0521-9*, R-3042-ICJ) Rand Corp.

Costs of Compulsory Attendance Service in the State of New York & Some Factors Affecting the Cost. Whittier L. Hanson. LC 78-176838. (Columbia University. Teachers College. Contributions to Education Ser.: No. 158). reprint ed. 37.50 (*0-404-55158-0*) AMS Pr.

Costs of Controls on Farmers' Use of Nitrogen: A Study Applied to Gotland. Ing-Marie Andreasson. 176p. (Orig.). 1988. pap. 85.00x (*91-7258-272-3*, Pub. by Almqv & Wiksell SW) Coronet Bks.

Costs of Crime. Ed. by Charles M. Gray. LC 79-18871. (Sage Criminal Justice System Annuals Ser.: No. 12). (Illus.). 280p. reprint ed. pap. 79.80 (*0-8357-8464-9*, 2034732) Bks Demand.

Costs of Cutting Carbon Emissions: Results from Global Models. OECD Staff. 160p. (Orig.). 1993. pap. 19.00 (*92-64-03875-2*) OECD.

Costs of Default: A Twentieth Century Fund Paper. Anatole Kaletsky. (International Debt Ser.). 116p. (Orig.). (C). 1985. pap. text ed. 8.95 (*0-87078-159-6*) TCFP-PPP.

Costs of Economic Growth. 2nd rev. ed. E. J. Mishan. LC 93-19231. 320p. 1993. text ed. 57.95 (*0-275-94703-3*, Praeger Pubs) Greenwood.

Costs of Educational Media: Guidelines for Planning & Evaluation. Dean Jamison et al. LC 77-17782. (People & Communication Ser.: No. 3). (Illus.). 255p. reprint ed. pap. 72.70 (*0-8357-8434-7*, 2034697) Bks Demand.

Costs of Evaluation. Ed. by Marvin C. Alkin & Lewis C. Solmon. LC 83-2857. (Sage Focus Editions Ser.: No. 60). 199p. reprint ed. pap. 56.80 (*0-7837-1119-0*, 2041649) Bks Demand.

***Costs of Excess Medical Claims for Automobile Personal Injuries.** Stephen Carroll et al. (Illus.). 28p. Date not set. pap. text ed. 6.00 (*0-8330-1649-0*, DB-139-ICJ) Rand Corp.

***Costs of Facility Development: A Comparative Analysis of Public & Private Sector Facility Development Processes & Costs.** Jeffery A. Lackney et al. (Illus.). vi, 175p. (C). 1995. 20.00 (*0-938744-90-9*, R94-9) U of Wis Ctr Arch-Urban.

Costs of Federalism: Essays in Honor of James W. Fesler. Robert T. Golembiewski & Aaron Wildavsky. 320p. 1984. 34.95x (*0-88738-000-X*) Transaction Pubs.

Costs of Further Education: British Analysis. C. Smith & R. Robinson. LC 76-124058. (Commonwealth & International Library). 1970. 93.00 (*0-08-016163-4*, Pub. by Pergamon Repr UK) Franklin.

Costs of Higher Education: How Much Do Colleges & Universities Spend Per Student & How Much Should They Spend? Howard R. Bowen. LC 80-8321. (Carnegie Council Ser.). 313p. reprint ed. pap. 89.30 (*0-7837-0163-2*, 2040460) Bks Demand.

Costs of Illness & Benefits of Drug Treatment. Ed. by U. Abshagen & F. E. Munnich. (Clinical Pharmacology Ser.: Vol. 4). (Illus.). 112p. 1990. text ed. 42.00 (*3-88603-364-3*, Pub. by W Zuckschwerdt GW) Scholium Intl.

Costs of Living: How Market Freedom Erodes the Best Things in Life. Barry Schwartz. LC 93-37328. 1994. 25.00 (*0-393-03646-4*) Norton.

Costs of Medical Care: A Summary of Investigations on the Economic Aspects of the Prevention & Care of Illness, No. 27. Isidore S. Falk et al. LC 71-180568. (Medicine & Society in America Ser.). 652p. 1972. reprint ed. 37.95 (*0-405-03950-6*) Ayer.

Costs of Not Knowing...EDRA Proceedings, 1986. Ed. by Jean Wineman et al. 1986. 35.00 (*0-939922-09-6*) EDRA.

Costs of Poor Health Habits. Willard G. Manning et al. 223p. (C). 1991. 34.50 (*0-674-17485-2*) HUP.

Costs of Privacy: Reputation & Surveillance in America. Steven L. Nock. LC 92-35480. 158p. 1993. lib. bdg. 39.95 (*0-202-30454-X*); pap. 18.95 (*0-202-30455-8*) Aldine de Gruyter.

Costs of Regime Survival: Racial Mobilization, Elite Domination & Control of the State in Guyana & Trinidad. Percy C. Hintzen. (American Sociological Assn. Rose Monograph Ser.). (Illus.). (C). 1989. 59.95 (*0-521-36378-0*) Cambridge U Pr.

Costs of Restricting Imports: The Automobile Industry. OECD Staff. 174p. (Orig.). 1988. pap. 18.00 (*92-64-13037-3*) OECD.

Costs of the Civil Justice System: Court Expenditures for Various Types of Civil Cases. James S. Kakalik & Randy L. Ross. LC 83-16007. 125p. 1983. 10.00 (*0-8330-0517-0*, R-2985-ICJ) Rand Corp.

Costs of the World War to the American People. John M. Clark. LC 68-55507. (Reprints of Economic Classics Ser.). xii, 316p. 1970. reprint ed. 37.50 (*0-678-00662-8*) Kelley.

Costs of Welfare. Nicholas Deakin & Robert Page. 264p. 1993. 59.95 (*1-85628-513-8*, Pub. by Avebury Pub UK) Ashgate Pub Co.

Costs of Worker Dislocations. Louis Jacobson et al. LC 93-23613. 158p. 1993. text ed. 23.00 (*0-88099-144-5*); pap. text ed. 13.00 (*0-88099-143-7*) W E Upjohn.

Costs to Americans of Lack of Family Leave. Roberta M. Spalter-Roth. 10p. 1989. pap. 5.00 (*0-685-29937-6*) Inst Womens Policy Rsch.

Costs to Women & Their Families of Childbirth & the Lack of Parental Leave. Roberta M. Spalter-Roth & Heidi Hartmann. 27p. 1989. pap. 8.00 (*0-685-29935-X*) Inst Womens Policy Rsch.

Costside Memories: Motoring South of San Francisco, 1850-1950. June Morrall. Ed. by Luana Mannett. (Illus.). 176p. (Orig.). 1994. write for info. (*0-9602088-2-8*) Moonbeam CA.

***Costumbre en Santa Eulalia.** Oliver La Farge. Tr. by Fernando Penalosa. (Illus.). 242p. (Orig.). (SPA.). 1994. pap. 11.95 (*1-886502-06-4*, Ediciones Yax Te) Yax Te Press.

Costumbre Nacionales 1809-1883. Ramon T. Mendez. (Illus.). (SPA.). 1978. lib. bdg. 35.00 (*0-8288-3941-7*) Fr & Eur.

Costume. (Ultimate Sticker Ser.). (Illus.). 16p. (J). (gr. 3 up). 1993. 6.95 (*1-56458-400-3*) Dorling Kindersley.

Costume. L. Rowland-Warne. LC 91-53135. (Eyewitness Bks.). (Illus.). 64p. (J). (gr. 5 up). 1992. 16.00 (*0-679-81680-1*); lib. bdg. 16.99 (*0-679-91680-6*) Knopf Bks Yng Read.

Costume: An Illustrated Survey from Ancient Times to the Twentieth Century. Margot Lister. LC 67-29412. (Illus.). 1968. 30.00 (*0-8238-0096-2*) Plays.

Costume: The Performing Partner. Jac Lewis & Miriam S. Lewis. Ed. by Arthur L. Zapel. LC 90-53279. (Illus.). 192p. (Orig.). 1990. pap. text ed. 11.95 (*0-916260-71-2*, B162) Meriwether Pub.

***Costume & Clothes.** Penelope Paul. LC 94-44417. (Legacies Ser.). (Illus.). 48p. (J). (gr. 4-6). 1995. 15.95 (*1-56847-274-9*) Thomson Lrning.

Costume & Culture: Vanishing Textiles of Some of the Tai Groups in Laos P. D. R. Patricia C. Naenna. (Illus.). 48p. 1992. pap. text ed. 20.00 (*0-8248-1454-1*) UH Pr.

Costume & Fashion. James Laver. LC 84-51360. (World of Art Ser.). (Illus.). 288p. 1985. pap. 12.95 (*0-500-20190-0*) Thames Hudson.

***Costume & Fashion: A Concise History.** rev. ed. James Laver. LC 94-61062. (World of Art Ser.). (Illus.). 296p. 1995. pap. 14.95 (*0-500-20266-4*) Thames Hudson.

Costume & Makeup, Vol. 4. Michael Holt. Ed. by David Mayer. (Theatre Manuals Ser.). 1991. pap. 8.95 (*0-02-871345-1*) Schirmer Bks.

Costume Construction. Katherine S. Holkeboer. 300p. 1988. pap. text ed. 41.00 (*0-13-181207-6*) P-H.

Costume Crafts. Chris Deshpande & Iain Macleod-Brudenell. (Worldwide Crafts). (Illus.). 32p. 1994. lib. bdg. 18.60 (*0-8368-1152-6*) Gareth Stevens Inc.

Costume Design. Barbara B. Anderson & Cletus Anderson. 416p. (C). 1984. text ed. 41.25 (*0-03-060383-8*) HB Coll Pubs.

Costume Design: From Conception to Curtain. Rebecca Cunningham. (Illus.). 288p. 1986. 29.95 (*0-671-61266-2*) P-H.

Costume Design: Techniques of Modern Masters. Lynn Pecktal. LC 92-41428. (Illus.). 256p. 1993. 49.95 (*0-8230-8311-X*, Back Stage Bks) Watsn-Guptill.

Costume Design in the Movies: An Illustrated Guide to the Work of 158 Great Designers. Elizabeth Leese. 1990. pap. 13.95 (*0-486-26548-X*) Dover.

Costume Design on Broadway: Designers & Their Credits, 1915-1985. Bobbi Owen. LC 87-7515. (Bibliographies & Indexes in the Performing Arts Ser.: No. 5). (Illus.). 269p. 1987. text ed. 79.50 (*0-313-25524-5*, OCD/, Greenwood Pr) Greenwood.

Costume Designer's Handbook: A Complete Guide for Amateur & Professional Costume Designers. 2nd ed. Rosemary Ingham & Liz Covey. LC 92-15238. (Illus.). 286p. 1992. pap. 24.95 (*0-435-08607-3*) Heinemann.

Costume History & Style. Douglas A. Russell. (Illus.). 576p. 1982. text ed. write for info. (*0-13-181214-9*) P-H.

Costume in Aristophanic Comedy. rev. ed. Laura M. Stone. Ed. by W. R. Connor. LC 80-2669. (Monographs in Classical Studies). (Illus.). 1981. lib. bdg. 39.95 (*0-405-14052-5*) Ayer.

Costume in Context: Medieval Times. Jennifer Ruby. (Costume in Context Ser.). (Illus.). 64p. (YA). (gr. 7-11). 1990. 24.95 (*0-7134-6075-X*, Pub. by Batsford UK) Trafalgar.

Costume in Context: The 1940s & 1950s. Jennifer Ruby. (Costume in Context Ser.). (Illus.). 64p. (YA). (gr. 7-11). 1990. 24.95 (*0-7134-6016-4*, Pub. by Batsford UK) Trafalgar.

Costume in Context: The 1980s. Jennifer Ruby. (Illus.). 72p. (YA). (gr. 7-11). 1991. 24.95 (*0-7134-6539-5*, Pub. by Batsford UK) Trafalgar.

Costume in Detail. 1,983th ed. Nancy Bradfield. (Illus.). 391p. 1983. 47.50 (*0-8238-0260-4*) Plays.

Costume in England, 2 vols. Frederick W. Fairholt. 1995. reprint ed. 48.00 (*1-55888-945-0*) Omnigraphics Inc.

Costume in France. Ary Renan. (Illus.). 274p. 1984. reprint ed. pap. 25.00 (*0-87556-689-8*) Saifer.

Costume in Greek Classic Drama. Iris Brooke. LC 73-3010. (Illus.). 112p. 1973. reprint ed. text ed. 35.00 (*0-8371-6828-7*, BRGC, Greenwood Pr) Greenwood.

Costume in Roman Comedy. Catharine Saunders. LC 09-19854. reprint ed. 31.50 (*0-404-05563-X*) AMS Pr.

Costume Jewelers: The Golden Age of Design. Joanne D. Ball. LC 90-60601. (Illus.). 208p. 1990. 39.95 (*0-88740-255-0*) Schiffer.

Costume Jewelry: Identification & Price Guide. 2nd ed. Harrice S. Miller. 344p. (Orig.). 1994. pap. 15.00 (*0-380-77078-4*, Confident Collect) Avon.

Costume Jewelry: The Fun of Collecting. Nancy Schiffer. LC 87-63483. (Illus.). 200p. 1988. pap. 24.95 (*0-88740-125-2*) Schiffer.

Costume of Ancient Egypt. Philip J. Watson. (Costume Reference Ser.). (Illus.). 80p. 1987. lib. bdg. 14.95 (*1-55546-771-7*) Chelsea Hse.

Costume of Ancient Rome. David J. Symons. (Costume Reference Ser.). (Illus.). 64p. 1987. 14.95 (*1-55546-768-7*) Chelsea Hse.

Costume of Colonial Times. Alice M. Earle. 1995. reprint ed. 48.00 (*1-55888-946-9*) Omnigraphics Inc.

Costume of Old Testament Peoples. Philip J. Watson. (Costume Reference Ser.). (Illus.). 80p. 1987. lib. bdg. 14.95 (*1-55546-770-9*) Chelsea Hse.

Costume of the Classical World. Marion Sichel. 1986. lib. bdg. 14.95 (*1-55546-761-X*) Chelsea Hse.

An Asterisk (*) at the beginning of an entry indicates that the title is appearing in BIP for the first time.

C

An Asterisk (*) at the beginning of an entry indicates that the title is appearing in BIP for the first time.

1645

Cotton Club. rev. ed. James Haskins. (Illus.). 213p. 1994. pap. 14.95 (0-7818-0248-2) Hippocrene Bks.

***Cotton, Colonialism & Social History in Sub-Saharan Africa.** Ed. by Allen Isaacman & Richard Roberts. LC 94-45083. (Social History of Africa Ser.). 1995. 55.00 (0-435-08966-8) Heinemann.

***Cotton, Colonialism & Social History in Sub-Saharan Africa.** Ed. by Allen Isaacman & Richard Roberts. LC 94-45083. (Social History of Africa Ser.). 1995. pap. 24.95 (0-435-08968-4) Heinemann.

Cotton Comes to Harlem. Chester Himes. (Crime Ser.). 159p. 1988. pap. 9.00 (0-394-75999-0, Vin) Random.

***Cotton Comes to Harlem.** Chester B. Himes. 1994. lib. bdg. 24.95x (1-56849-422-X) Buccaneer Bks.

Cotton Control Board. Herbert D. Henderson. (Economic & Social History of the World War Ser.). 1922. 89.50 (0-686-83513-1) Elliots Bks.

Cotton Country Collection. 14th ed. Junior League of Monroe, Louisiana, Inc. Staff. (Illus.). 491p. 1972. 16.95 (0-9602364-0-6) Jun League Mon.

Cotton Country Cooking. Junior League of Morgan County, Inc. Staff. (Illus.). 407p. 1992. reprint ed. 14.95 (0-9614406-0-0) Decatur Jr Serv.

Cotton Crisis. Robert E. Snyder. LC 83-14747. (Fred W. Morrison Series in Southern Studies). 192p. reprint ed. pap. 54.80 (0-7837-2449-7, 2042598) Bks Demand.

Cotton Diseases. Ed. by R. J. Hillocks. (Illus.). 415p. 1992. 114.00 (0-85198-749-4) CAB Intl.

Cotton Dust: Controlling an Occupational Health Hazard. Ed. by Joseph G. Montalvo, Jr. LC 82-6857. (ACS Symposium Ser.: No. 189). 1982. 49.95 (0-8412-0716-X) Am Chemical.

Cotton Dust & Byssinosis. Shirley Institute Staff. (C). 1984. 150.00 (0-685-36022-9, Pub. by British Textile Tech UK) St Mut.

Cotton Dust, Sampling, Monitoring, & Control: Proceedings of the Symposium: Presented at Textile Engineering Industries Conference & Exhibit, October 7-8, 1980, Atlanta, GA. Symposium on Cotton Dust: Sampling, Monitoring, & Control Staff. Ed. by K. Q. Robert & S. K. Batra. LC 80-68345. 71p. reprint ed. pap. 25.00 (0-8357-8700-1, 2033651) Bks Demand.

Cotton-Eye Joe. (Ballroom Dance Ser.). 1985. lib. bdg. 64.00 (0-87700-730-6) Revisionist Pr.

Cotton-Eyed Joe. (Ballroom Dance Ser.). 1986. lib. bdg. 79.95 (0-8490-3337-3) Gordon Pr.

***Cotton Fiber Characteristics.** (Illus.). 250p. (Orig.). 1994. per. 195.00 (0-7605-0691-4) Rector Pr.

Cotton Fibre Impurities: Neps, Motes & Seed Coat Fragments, No. 1. L. Verschraege. (International Cotton Advisory Committee Review Articles on Cotton Production Research Ser.). 55p. (Orig.). 1989. pap. text ed. 30.50 (0-85198-633-1) CAB Intl.

Cotton Fields & Skyscrapers: Southern City & Region. David R. Goldfield. LC 89-8204. 256p. 1989. reprint ed. pap. text ed. 14.95x (0-8018-3946-7) Johns Hopkins.

Cotton Fields No More: Southern Agriculture, 1865-1980. Gilbert C. Fite. LC 84-7439. 295p. reprint ed. pap. 84.10 (0-7837-5803-0, 2045469) Bks Demand.

Cotton Genesis: British Library, Codex Cotton Otho B VI, the Illustrations in the Manuscripts of the Septuagint, Vol. I. Kurt Weitzmann & Herbert L. Kessler. LC 85-550. (Illus.). 430p. 1985. text ed. 190.00x (0-691-04031-1) Princeton U Pr.

Cotton Ginning. Indra Doraiswamy & A. Pavendham. 1993. 130.00 (1-870812-48-4, Pub. by Textile Institue UK) St Mut.

Cotton in a Competitive World. P. W. Harrison. 311p. 1979. 90.00 (0-686-63757-7) St Mut.

Cotton in a Competitive World. P. W. Harrison. 311p. (C). 1979. pap. text ed. 90.00 (0-900739-30-4, Pub. by Textile Institue UK) St Mut.

***Cotton in My Ears.** Frances Warfield. (American Autobiography Ser.). 152p. 1995. reprint ed. lib. bdg. 69.00 (0-7812-8657-3) Rprt Serv.

Cotton in Your T-Shirt. Aline Riquier. (Young Discovery Library). (Illus.). 40p. (J). (gr. k-5). 1993. lib. bdg. 9.95 (1-56674-058-4, HTS Bks) Forest Hse.

Cotton in Your T-Shirt. Aline Riquier. Tr. by Vicki Bogard. LC 91-45786. (Illus.). 38p. (J). (gr. k-5). 1992. 5.95 (0-944589-40-5) Young Discovery Lib.

Cotton Industry. Chris Aspin. 1989. pap. 25.00 (0-85263-545-1, Pub. by Shire UK) St Mut.

Cotton Is King: Or, the Culture of Cotton, & Its Relation to Agriculture, Manufactures & Commerce. 2nd enl. rev. ed. David Christy. LC 70-136634. (Reprints of Economic Classics Ser.). xxiii, 298p. 1974. reprint ed. 39.50 (0-678-00807-8) Kelley.

***Cotton Is the Mother of Poverty: Peasants, Work, & Rural Struggle in Colonial Mozambique, 1938-1961.** Allen Isaacman. LC 95-14471. (Social History of Africa Ser.). 1995. 55.00 (0-435-08976-5); pap. 24.95 (0-435-08978-1) Heinemann.

Cotton Kingdom. Frederick L. Olmsted. Ed. by Lawrence Powell et al. (Modern Library College Editions). 708p. (C). 1983. pap. text ed. write for info. (0-07-554413-X) McGraw.

Cotton Kingdom: A Chronicle of the Old South. William E. Dodd. (BCL1 - United States Local History Ser.). 161p. 1991. reprint ed. lib. bdg. 69.00 (0-7812-6287-9) Rprt Serv.

Cotton Knitting. Sally Harding. 120p. 1987. 20.95 (0-8120-5816-X) Barron.

Cotton Manufacturing Industry of the United States. Melvin T. Copeland. LC 66-23981. (Reprints of Economic Classics Ser.). 1966. reprint ed. lib. bdg. 45.00 (0-678-00196-0) Kelley.

Cotton Mather. Otho T. Beall & Richard H. Shryock. 1979. 23.95 (0-405-10580-0) Ayer.

Cotton Mather. Barrett Wendell. LC 80-23335. (American Men & Women of Letters Ser.). Orig. Title: Cotton Mather: the Puritan Priest. 328p. 1981. reprint ed. pap. 5.95 (0-87754-166-3) Chelsea Hse.

Cotton Mather: The Young Life of the Lord's Remembrancer, 1663-1703. David Levin. LC 78-2355. (Illus.). 382p. 1978. 37.50 (0-674-17507-7) HUP.

Cotton Mather & American Science & Medicine: With Studies & Documents Concerning the Introduction of Inoculation or Variolation, 2 vols. Ed. by I. Bernard Cohen. LC 79-7974. (Three Centuries of Science in America Ser.). (Illus.). 1980. lib. bdg. 82.95 (0-405-12556-9) Ayer.

Cotton Mather & American Science & Medicine: With Studies & Documents Concerning the Introduction of Inoculation or Variolation, Vol. 1. I. Bernard Cohen. 1980. 41.95 (0-405-12520-8) Ayer.

Cotton Mather & American Science & Medicine: With Studies & Documents Concerning the Introduction of Inoculation or Variolation, Vol. 2. I. Bernard Cohen. 1980. 41.95 (0-405-12521-6) Ayer.

Cotton Mather, Keeper of the Puritan Conscience. Ralph P. Boas & Louise Boas. (BCL1 - United States Local History Ser.). 271p. 1991. reprint ed. lib. bdg. 79.00 (0-7812-6265-8) Rprt Serv.

Cotton Mather on Witchcraft. Cotton Mather. (Dorset Classic Reprints Ser.). (Illus.). 180p. 1991. 19.95 (0-88029-672-0) Dorset Pr.

Cotton Mather: the Puritan Priest see Cotton Mather

Cotton Mather's Verse in English. Ed. by Denise D. Knight. LC 88-40313. 176p. 1989. 32.50 (0-87413-349-1) U Delaware Pr.

Cotton Mill Movement in Antebellum Alabama. Randall M. Miller. LC 77-14771. (Dissertations in American Economic History Ser.). 1978. 30.95 (0-405-11049-9) Ayer.

Cotton Patch Cooking. Esther Nelson. (Black Folktales & Recipes Ser.: No. 1). (Illus.). 80p. 1981. pap. 3.00 (0-686-32790-X) Folks Pubns.

Cotton Patch Gospel: Musical. Tom Key & Russell Treyz. 1983. 5.45 (0-87129-244-0, C05) Dramatic Pub.

Cotton Patch Parables of Liberation. Clarence Jordon & Bill L. Doulos. 176p. 1976. pap. 4.95 (0-8361-1334-9) Herald Pr.

Cotton-Patch Schoolhouse. Susie P. Tompkins. LC 91-23331. 224p. (Orig.). (J). 1992. pap. 19.95 (0-8173-0563-7) U of Ala Pr.

***Cotton-Pickers.** B. Traven. LC 94-43051. 1995. write for info. (1-56663-075-4) I R Dee.

Cotton Planter's Manual. J. A. Turner. LC 74-90138. 320p. 1970. reprint ed. text ed. 52.50 (0-8371-1996-0, TUC&, Negro U Pr) Greenwood.

***Cotton Plenary Meeting Report.** (Illus.). 250p. (Orig.). 1994. pap. 275.00 (0-7605-0690-6) Rector Pr.

***Cotton Plenary Report No. 53.** (Illus.). 250p. (Orig.). 1994. pap. 295.00 (0-7605-0692-2) Rector Pr.

***Cotton Production.** Ed. by Tom Kerby et al. (Illus.). 300p. 1995. pap. write for info. (1-879906-09-0, 3352) ANR Pubns CA.

Cotton Production Prospects for the Decade to 2002: A Global Review. Hamdy M. Eisa et al. (Technical Paper Ser.: No. 231). 130p. 1994. 8.95 (0-8215-2715-0, 12715) World Bank.

Cotton Production Prospects for the Decade to 2002: A Global Review. Hamdy M. Eisa et al. LC 93-43822. (Technical Paper Ser.: No. 231). 130p. 1994. write for info. (0-8213-2715-1) World Bank.

Cotton Sailboats (Poems) Edith Witmer. 78p. 1988. pap. 4.05 (0-318-41777-4) Rod & Staff.

***Cotton Statistics International.** 60p. (Orig.). 1994. pap. 245.00 (0-614-03355-1) Rector Pr.

***Cotton Supply 1994-1995.** (Illus.). 240p. (Orig.). 1994. pap. 295.00 (0-7605-0687-6) Rector Pr.

Cotton-Textile Diplomacy: Japan, Great Britain & the United States, 1930-1936. Osamu Ishii. Ed. by Stuart Bruchey. LC 80-2813. (Dissertations in European Economic History Ser.). 1981. lib. bdg. 54.95 (0-405-13996-9) Ayer.

***Cotton, the Nosey Horse.** large type ed. William O. Beazley. (Illus.). 48p. (J). (gr. k-5). 1993. reprint ed. spiral bd., pap. 7.95 (1-884758-01-0) W O Beazley.

Cotton Trade & Industrial Lancashire 1600-1780. Alfred P. Wadsworth & Julia Mann. LC 68-6121. (Illus.). 1968. reprint ed. 49.50 (0-678-06768-6) Kelley.

***Cotton Trade International.** 96p. (Orig.). 1994. pap. 295.00 (0-614-03356-X) Rector Pr.

Cotton Trade of Great Britain: Its Rise, Progress & Present Extent. J. A. Mann. (Illus.). 134p. 1968. reprint ed. 29.50 (0-7146-1405-X, Pub. by F Cass Pubs UK) Intl Spec Bk.

Cotton Versus Conscience. Kinley J. Brauer. 1967. 15.00 (0-87018-071-1) Ross.

Cotton Woods. Ray Gotto. Ed. by Dave Schreiner & Max A. Collins. LC 91-19437. (Illus.). 160p. (Orig.). 1991. pap. 14.95 (0-87816-145-7) Kitchen Sink.

Cotton Woods. deluxe limited ed. Ray Gotto. Ed. by Dave Schreiner & Max A. Collins. LC 91-19437. (Illus.). 160p. (Orig.). 1991. 25.00 (0-87816-151-1) Kitchen Sink.

***Cotton World Situation.** (Illus.). 250p. (Orig.). 1994. pap. 225.00 (0-7605-0688-4) Rector Pr.

Cottonmouth. Julian L. Rayford. (Library of Alabama Classics). 424p. 1991. pap. 19.95 (0-8173-0529-7) U of Ala Pr.

Cottonmouths, Reading Level 2. Barger & Johnson. (Snake Discovery Library: Set I). (Illus.). 24p. (J). (gr. k-5). 1986. lib. bdg. 11.94 (0-86592-958-0) Rourke Corp.

Cotton's Journey from Seed. Janette Yribarren & Rick Yribarren. Ed. & Illus. by Alaca Company Staff. 37p. (Orig.). (C). 1993. teacher ed 20.00 (0-9641484-1-2, 37-CFR-202.20(D)) Alaca.

Cotton's Journey from Seed to You, Vol. II. Janette Yribarren & Rick Yribarren. Ed. & Illus. by Alaca Company Staff. 37p. (C). 1995. teacher ed 25.00 (0-9641484-2-0) Alaca.

Cotton's Journey from Seed to You Educational Kit. janetteff Yribarren & Rick Yribarren. Ed. by Alaca Company Staff. (Illus.). 45p. 1993. 65.00 (0-9641484-0-4) Alaca.

Cotton's Journey from Seed to You Presented by Clever Cotton. Ed. by Alaca Company Staff. (Illus.). 8p. 1993. student ed 1.25 (0-9641484-3-9) Alaca.

Cotton's Journey from Seed to You Presented by Clever Cotton, No. II. Ed. by Alaca Company Staff. (Illus.). 8p. 1994. student ed 1.25 (0-9641484-4-7) Alaca.

Cotton's Journey from Seed to You Presented by Clever Cotton, No. III. Ed. by Alaca Company Staff. (Illus.). 8p. 1995. student ed 1.50 (0-9641484-5-5) Alaca.

Cottons of Catahoula & Related Families. William D. Cotton. Ed. by Carole Cotton-Winn & Carolyn P. Gorman. (Illus.). 300p. 1987. text ed. 35.00 (0-9618464-0-2) Wm Davis Cotton.

***Cottontail at Clover Crescent.** C. Drew Lamm. LC 94-28697. (Smithsonian's Backyard Ser.). (Illus.). 32p. (J). (ps-2). 1995. 15.95 (1-56899-108-8); 4.95 (1-56899-109-6) Soundprints.

***Cottontail at Clover Crescent.** C. Drew Lamm. LC 94-28697. (Smithsonian's Backyard Ser.). (Illus.). 32p. (J). (ps-2). 1995. audio 19.95 (1-56899-112-6); audio write for info. (1-56899-113-4) Soundprints.

***Cottontail at Clover Crescent, Incl. 12" plush toy.** C. Drew Lamm. LC 94-28697. (Smithsonian's Backyard Ser.). (Illus.). 32p. (J). (ps-2). 1995. 29.95 (1-56899-110-X) Soundprints.

***Cottontail at Clover Crescent, Mini-sized bk., incl. 6" plush toy.** C. Drew Lamm. LC 94-28697. (Smithsonian's Backyard Ser.). (Illus.). 32p. (J). (ps-2). 1995. 12.95 (1-56899-111-8) Soundprints.

Cottontail Caper: The Pet Lovers Club. Stephen Roos. (J). (gr. 4-7). 1994. pap. 3.50 (0-440-40925-X) Dell.

Cottonwood Collection: A History of Sinclair Island. Mary M. Leach. (Illus.). 160p. (Orig.). 1988. pap. write for info. (0-318-63124-5) M M Leach.

Cottonwood County. William Kloefkorn & Ted Kooser. 1980. pap. 5.95 (0-931534-08-9) Windflower Pr.

Cottonwood Gulch. Clarence E. Mulford. 1976. 23.95 (0-88411-204-7) Amereon Ltd.

Cottonwood Gulch. large type ed. Clarence Mulford. (Hopalong Cassidy Ser.). 348p. 1974. reprint ed. lib. bdg. 23.95 (0-88411-233-0, Aeonian Pr) Amereon Ltd.

Cottonwood Pass: A Celebration of Flowers in Fabric. Barbara Barr. Ed. & Illus. by Sharon Holmes. 36p. 1993. pap. 8.95 (1-880972-07-7, DreamSpinners) Pssblts Denver.

Cottonwood Roots. Kem Luther. LC 92-44167. (Illus.). xii, 152p. 1993. 20.00 (0-8032-2906-2) U of Nebr Pr.

***Cottonwood Stage.** Ross Paden. (Black Horse Westerns Ser.). 159p. 1995. 14.95 (0-7090-5227-8) Parkwest Pubns.

***Cottonwood Station.** Michael Zimmer. 1994. pap. 3.99 (0-06-100794-3, Harp PBks) HarpC.

Cottonwood Station. Michael Zimmer. 182p. 1993. 19.95 (0-8027-1273-8) Walker & Co.

Cottonwood Station. large type ed. Michael Zimmer. LC 93-42268. 1994. write for info. (0-8161-5920-3) G K Hall.

Cottonwood Summer. Jean Z. Liebenthal. pap. 6.95 (0-88494-825-0) Bookcraft Inc.

Cottonwoods: Photographs by Robert Adams. Ed. by Constance Sullivan. (Photographs at Work Ser.). (Illus.). 60p. (Orig.). 1994. pap. 15.95 (1-56098-506-2) Smithsonian.

Cottrell: Samaritan of Science. Frank Cameron. 416p. 1993. reprint ed. pap. 19.95 (0-9633504-2-0) Res Corp.

Cotylosauria. O. Kuhn. (Encyclopedia of Paleoherpetology Ser.: Pt. 6). (Illus.). 89p. 1969. text ed. 50.70 (3-437-30029-6) Lubrecht & Cramer.

Coubertin's Olympics: How the Games Began. Davida Kristy. LC 94-12889. (Sports Legacy Ser.). (Illus.). 128p. (YA). (gr. 5 up). 1995. lib. bdg. 22.95 (0-8225-3327-8, Lerner Publctns) Lerner Group.

Couch. Lynne Kaufman. 1986. pap. 4.75 (0-8222-0241-7) Dramatists Play.

Couch: Its Use & Meaning in Psychotherapy. Harold Stern. LC 77-15610. 215p. 1978. 32.95 (0-87705-303-0) Human Sci Pr.

Couch Book: Finding & Buying the Couch of Your Dreams. Fayal Greene. LC 92-36409. 1993. 20.00 (0-688-11363-X) Hearst Bks.

Couch on Insurance, 33 vols., Set. 2nd ed. Ronald Anderson. LC 59-1915. 1984. 2,900.00 (0-685-59868-3) Clark Boardman Callaghan.

Couch Potato Guide to Life. Jack Mingo. 1988. pap. 3.50 (0-380-75596-3) Avon.

Couch Potato Kids. Lee Canter. (Illus.). 48p. (Orig.). 1993. pap. 5.95 (0-939007-76-2) Lee Canter & Assocs.

Couche dans le Pain. Chester Himes. 256p. (FRE.). 1987. pap. 10.95 (0-7859-2534-1, 2070378144) Fr & Eur.

***Couches from the Underworld: Cartoons & Stories from Moe's Notebook.** Erik Moe. 128p. 1994. pap. 9.95 (0-9644905-0-1) E Moe.

Couching Resistance: Women, Film, & Psychoanalytic Psychiatry. Janet Walker. LC 92-23509. (Illus.). 238p. (C). 1993. text ed. 44.95 (0-8166-2232-9); pap. text ed. 16.95 (0-8166-2233-7) U of Minn Pr.

Couette-Taylor Problem. Pascal Chossat & Gerard Iooss. LC 93-21048. (Applied Mathematical Sciences Ser.: Vol. 102). 1994. 44.50 (0-387-94154-1) Spr-Verlag.

Couey Genealogy: Some Descendants of Joseph Couey (1764-1844) Stanley D. Couey. 244p. (Orig.). 1988. pap. write for info. (0-318-63231-4) S Couey.

Cougar: Ghost of the Rockies. Karen McCall. LC 92-3691. (Illus.). 160p. 1993. reprint ed. pap. 20.00 (0-87156-463-7) Sierra.

Cougar: The American Lion. Kevin Hansen. LC 92-15344. (Western Horizons Book Ser.). (Illus.). 144p. (Orig.). 1992. pap. 19.95 (0-87358-544-5) Northland AZ.

Cougar & Her Babies. Curt Jansen et al. Vol. 1. (Orig.). (J). (gr. k-4). write for info. (0-318-61886-9) Adventure Prods.

Cougar Canyon. Peter Field. 176p. 1989. pap. 2.75 (0-380-70710-1) Avon.

Cougar Canyon. large type ed. Peter Field. 286p. 1980. 15.95 (0-7089-0503-X) Ulverscroft.

Cougar City. large type ed. Ron Pritchett. (Linford Western Library). 256p. 1992. pap. 14.95 (0-7089-7150-4, Traitree Bookshop) Ulverscroft.

Cougar Dawn. Jon Sharpe. (Trailsman Ser.: No. 134). 176p. (Orig.). 1993. pap. 3.50 (0-451-17503-4, Sig) NAL-Dutton.

***Cougar Kittens.** Victoria Miles. (Illus.). 24p. (Orig.). (J). (gr. 1-4). 1995. pap. 5.95 (1-55143-026-6) Orca Bk Pubs.

Cougar Moon, 4 bks., Bk. 1. Tom Gilmore. 192p. (Orig.). (C). 1991. pap. 3.50 (1-879352-09-5) Mini-Novel Pub.

Cougar of Canyon Caballo. Paul E. Lehman. Bd. with Devil's Doorstep. Paul E. Lehman. (Double Western Ser.). 1979. reprint ed. Set pap. 2.25 (0-8439-0688-X) Dorchester Pub Co.

Cougar-Tamer & Other Stories of Adventure. Franklin W. Calkins. LC 79-153541. (Short Story Index Reprint Ser.). 1977. reprint ed. 17.95 (0-8369-3795-3) Ayer.

Cougars. L. Stone. (Big Cat Discovery Library). (Illus.). 24p. (J). (gr. k-5). 1989. lib. bdg. 11.94 (0-86592-505-4) Rourke Corp.

Cough. Pier C. Braga & Luigi Allegra. 254p. 1989. 60.00 (0-88167-538-5) Raven.

Cough & Other Respiratory Reflexes. J. Korpas & Z. Tomori. (Progress in Respiration Research Ser.: Vol. 12). (Illus.). 1979. 131.25 (3-8055-3007-2) S Karger.

Coughlin-Fahey Connection: Father Denis Fahey, C. S. Sp., & Religious Anti-Semiticism in the United States, 1938-1954. Mary C. Athans. LC 91-3821. (American University Studies: Theology & Religion: Ser. VII, Vol. 102). 250p. 1992. 43.95 (0-8204-1534-0) P Lang Pubs.

***Coughs & Wheezes.** Speight. 1995. pap. 7.95 (0-85207-252-X) Atrium Pubs.

Coughs & Wheezes: Their Treatment by Homoeopathy. Phyllis Speight. 80p. (Orig.). Date not set. pap. 11.95 (0-8464-4194-2) Beekman Pubs.

Could Be Worse! James Stevenson. LC 76-28534. (Illus.). 32p. (J). (gr. k-3). 1977. 13.95 (0-688-80075-0); lib. bdg. 13.88 (0-688-84075-2) Greenwillow.

Could Be Worse! James Stevenson. LC 76-28534. (Illus.). 32p. (J). (gr. k up). 1987. reprint ed. pap. 3.95 (0-688-07035-3, Mulberry) Morrow.

Could I Be a Pastor. Marilee Schmidt. 1985. 2.95 (0-8100-0199-3, 16N0781) Northwest Pub.

Could I Be a Teacher. Marilee Schimidt. 1985. 2.95 (0-8100-0200-0, 16N0782) Northwest Pub.

Could I Have Your Recipe? Janice Porter. (Illus.). 115p. (Orig.). 1981. pap. 5.95 (0-9607670-0-2) J Porter Bks.

Could It Be - Bank Street. Joanne Oppenheim. (J). (ps-3). 1990. mass mkt. 3.99 (0-553-34924-4, Little Rooster) Bantam.

Could It Be Old Hiari. Marjorie Vandervelde. (Indian Culture Ser.). (J). (gr. 5-9). 1975. 4.95 (0-89992-040-3) Coun India Ed.

***Could It Be Stress? Reflections on Psychosomatic Illness.** Cameron Macdonald. 192p. (C). 1992. pap. 32.00x (1-874640-10-6, Pub. by Argyll Pubng UK) St Mut.

Could It Be You? Mary A. Wilson. (American Romance Ser.). 1994. mass mkt. 3.50 (0-373-16523-4, 1-16523-2) Harlequin Bks.

Could the British Have Won the War of Independence? Piers Mackesy. Ed. by George A. Billias. LC 76-41409. (Bland-Lee Lectures in History Ser.). 1976. pap. 1.00 (0-914206-08-7) Clark U Pr.

Could the Military Govern the Philippines? Viberto Selochan. (Illus.). 63p. (Orig.). 1990. pap. 6.50 (971-10-0399-6, Pub. by New Day Pub PH) Cellar.

Could This Be Love? Melissa Brennan. (Pizza Paradise Ser.: No. 3). (YA). 1991. mass mkt. 3.50 (0-06-106067-4, Harp PBks) HarpC.

Could UFOs Be Real? Larry Koss. (Illus.). 48p. (J). (gr. 3-6). 1991. 11.95 (1-56065-093-1) Capstone Pr.

Could You Ever Build a Time Machine? David Darling. (Could You Ever Ser.). (Illus.). 60p. (J). (gr. 5 up). 1991. text ed. 14.95 (0-87518-456-1, Dillon Silver Burdett) Silver Burdett Pr.

Could You Ever Dig a Hole to China? David Darling. (Could You Ever Ser.). (Illus.). 60p. (J). (gr. 5 up). 1991. text ed. 14.95 (0-87518-449-9, Dillon Silver Burdett) Silver Burdett Pr.

Could You Ever Fly to the Stars? David Darling. (Could You Ever Ser.). (Illus.). 60p. (J). (gr. 5 up). 1991. text ed. 14.95 (0-87518-446-4, Dillon Silver Burdett) Silver Burdett Pr.

Could You Ever Live Forever? David Darling. (Could You Ever Ser.). (Illus.). 60p. (J). (gr. 5 up). 1991. text ed. 14.95 (0-87518-457-X, Dillon Silver Burdett) Silver Burdett Pr.

Could You Ever Meet an Alien? David Darling. (Could You Ever Ser.). (Illus.). 60p. (J). (gr. 5 up). 1991. text ed. 14.95 (0-87518-447-2, Dillon Silver Burdett) Silver Burdett Pr.

Could You Ever Speak Chimpanzee? David Darling. (Could You Ever Ser.). (Illus.). 60p. (J). (gr. 5 up). 1991. text ed. 14.95 (0-87518-448-0, Dillon Silver Burdett) Silver Burdett Pr.

An Asterisk (*) at the beginning of an entry indicates that the title is appearing in BIP for the first time.

Could You Hurry up the Dawn, Lord? Poems, Prayers, & Lively Conversations with a Loving God. Joy M. Davis. LC 93-27134. 112p. (Orig.). 1994. pap. 6.99 (*0-8007-5507-3*) Revell.

***Could You Love Me Like My Dog?** Beth Fowler. 160p. 1994. pap. 7.95 (*0-9642776-0-3*) In the Weeds.

Could You Stop Josephine? Stephane Poulin. LC 88-50260. (Josephine Ser.). (Illus.). 24p. (J). (ps-3). 1988. 12.95 (*0-88776-216-6*); pap. 6.95 (*0-88776-227-1*) Tundra Bks.

Could Your Kid Die "Laughing"? AIDS & Today's Adolescent. Carole Marsh. (Smart Sex Stuff Ser.). (Orig.). 1994. 24.95 (*1-55609-262-8*); pap. 14.95 (*1-55609-225-3*) Gallopade Pub Group.

Couldn't I Start Over? Jean Thesman. 176p. (Orig.). (YA). (gr. 7 up). 1989. pap. 2.95 (*0-380-75717-6*, Flare) Avon.

Couleur. Illus. by P. M. Valat & S. Perols. (Gallimard - Mes Premieres Decouvertes Ser.: No. 8). (FRE.). (J). (ps-1). 1989. 13.95 (*2-07-035706-6*) Schoenhof.

Coulomb & the Evolution of Physics & Engineering in Eighteenth Century France. C. Stewart Gillmor. LC 79-155006. (Illus.). 1971. 52.50x (*0-691-08095-X*) Princeton U Pr.

***Coulomb & the Evolution of Physics & Engineering in Eighteenth-Century France.** C. Stewart Gillmor. LC 79-155006. reprint ed. pap. 98.10 (*0-7837-9343-X*, 2060084) Bks Demand.

Coulomb Excitation of Vibrational Muclei. Lars E. Svensson. (Uppsala Dissertations from the Faculty of Science Ser.: No. 27). (Illus.). 169p. (Orig.). 1989. 41.50x (*91-554-2429-5*, Pub. by Almqv & Wiksell SW) Coronet Bks.

***Coulomb Interactions in Nuclear & Atomic Few-Body Collisions.** Ed. by F. S. Levin & D. A. Micha. (Finite Systems & Multiparticle Dynamics Ser.). (Illus.). 335p. (C). 1995. write for info. (*0-306-45149-2*, Plenum Pr) Plenum.

Coulomb Liquids: Monograph. Norman H. March & Mario P. Tosi. 1984. text ed. 129.00 (*0-12-470520-0*) Acad Pr.

Coulombic Interactions in Macromolecular Systems. Ed. by Adi Eisenberg & Fred E. Bailey. LC 86-3641. (ACS Symposium Ser.: No. 302). (Illus.). vii, 282p. 1986. 65.95 (*0-8412-0960-X*) Am Chemical.

Coulometric Analysis. E. Pungor. 302p. 1979. 175.00 (*0-569-08551-9*, Pub. by Collets) St Mut.

***Coulometric Analysis: Conference Held at Matrafured, Hungary 17-19 October, 1978.** E. Pungor & I. Buzas. 301p. (C). 1979. 81.00x (*963-05-2021-4*, Pub. by Akad Kiado HU) St Mut.

Coulometry in Analytical Chemistry. G. W. Milner & G. Phillips. 1968. 95.00 (*0-08-012439-9*, Pub. by Pergamon Repr UK) Franklin.

***Coulor Compass.** Skerry. 1995. pap. 24.95 (*0-646-15176-2*) Atrium Pubs.

Coulson & Richardson's Chemical Engineering, Vol. 3. 3rd ed. Richardson & Peacock. (Chemical Engineering Technical Ser.: No. 3). 1994. text ed. 135.00 (*0-08-041002-2*, Pergamon Pr); pap. text ed. 46.00 (*0-08-041003-0*, Pergamon Pr) Elsevier.

Coulson & Richardson's Chemical Engineering: Chemical Engineering Design, Vol. 6. 2nd ed. R. K. Sinnott. 1000p. 1993. text ed. 133.00 (*0-08-041865-1*, Pergamon Pr); pap. text ed. 48.00 (*0-08-041866-X*) Elsevier.

***Coulson & Richardsons Chemical Engineering V-4, Vol. 4.** 2nd ed. Backhurst & Harker. (Chemical Engineering Technical Ser.). 1994. pap. text ed. 28.00 (*0-08-042083-4*, Pergamon Pr) Elsevier.

***Coulson & Richardsons Chemical Engineering V-4, Vol. 4.** 2nd ed. Backhurst & Harker. (Chemical Engineering Technical Ser.). 1994. text ed. 76.00 (*0-08-042082-6*, Pergamon Pr) Elsevier.

Coulson's Valence. 3rd ed. Charles A. Coulson. Ed. by Roy McWeeny. (Illus.). 1980. pap. 35.00 (*0-19-855145-2*) OUP.

Councel from the Ancients: A Study of Badaga Proverbs, Prayers, Omens & Curses. Ed. by Paul Hockings. (Trends in Linguistics Ser.: No. 4). 810p. (C). 1988. text ed. 161.55 (*0-89925-410-1*) Mouton.

Council & Commune: The Conciliar Movement & the Council of Basle. Antony Black. 264p. 1990. 60.00 (*0-86012-077-5*, Pub. by Srch Pr UK) St Mut.

Council & Commune: The Conciliar Movement & the Fifteenth-Century Heritage. Antony Black. LC 79-89220. x, 253p. 1979. 25.95 (*0-915762-08-0*) Patmos Pr.

Council & Hierarchy: The Political Thought of William Durant the Younger. Constantin Fasolt. (Cambridge Studies in Medieval Life & Thought: No. 16). 416p. (C). 1991. 69.95 (*0-521-39285-3*) Cambridge U Pr.

Council Fires on the Upper Ohio. Randolph C. Downes. LC 40-34394. (Illus.). 384p. (C). 1969. reprint ed. pap. 14.95 (*0-8229-5201-7*) U of Pittsburgh Pr.

Council for Mutual & Economic Assistance: Foreign Trade among Soviet Union & other Eastern European Countries, Transfer of Technology in the Socialist State, 3 vols., Set. 1979. reprint ed. lib. bdg. 195.00 (*0-930342-90-9*, 300180) W S Hein.

Council for Mutual Economic Assistance: The Thorny Path from Political to Economic Integration. Adam Zwass. LC 89-4198. 288p. 1989. 67.95 (*0-87332-496-X*) M E Sharpe.

Council House. Ed. by Lee Nordness. LC 80-82639. (Illus.). 230p. (C). 1980. 39.00 (*0-937486-01-9*) Perimeter Pr.

Council Meetings in South Australia. Matthew Goode & David Williams. 257p. 1992. pap. 53.00 (*0-685-62414-5*, Pub. by Federation Pr AU); pap. 52.50 (*0-86287-054-2*, Pub. by Federation Pr AU) W W Gaunt.

Council Minutes, 1655-1656. Ed. & Tr. by Charles T. Gehring. (New Netherland Project Ser.). 384p. (C). 1994. text ed. 75.00 (*0-8156-2646-0*) Syracuse U Pr.

Council of Chalcedon & the Armenian Church: With Maps. Karekin Sarkissian. LC 82-45823. (Orthodoxies & Heresies in the Early Church Ser.). (Illus.). reprint ed. 32.00 (*0-404-62393-X*) AMS Pr.

Council of Florence. Joseph Gill. LC 78-63345. (Crusades & Military Orders Ser.: Second Series). (Illus.). 480p. reprint ed. 71.50 (*0-404-17016-1*) AMS Pr.

Council of Logistics Management Conference Proceedings, 2 vols., Set. 1987. 25.00 (*0-318-33433-X*) Coun Logistics Mgt.

Council of Logistics Management Supplement to Bibliography on Logistics & Physical Distribution Management. Bernard J. LaLonde. 1988. 15.00 (*0-318-33304-X*) Coun Logistics Mgt.

Council of Revision in the State of New York. Alfred B. Street. reprint ed. 35.00 (*0-89201-055-X*) Zenger Pub.

Council of Ten. Jon Land. 352p. (Orig.). 1987. mass mkt. 5.99 (*0-449-13117-3*, GM) Fawcett.

Council of the European Community. 70p. 1992. pap. 7.00 (*92-72-40969-1*, BX-73-92-877-EN-C, Pub. by Europ Com) UNIPUB.

Council of the Rainmakers: Address Book. David Dawangyumptewa. (Illus.). 110p. 1993. 12.95 (*0-87358-568-2*) Northland AZ.

Council of the Sanhedrims: They Divided My Garments among Them. Ricardo Scott. (Reggae Book of Light Ser.). (Illus.). 70p. (Orig.). Date not set. pap. write for info. (*1-883427-26-6*) Crnerstone GA.

***Council of Wyrms.** Bill Slavicsek. 1994. 25.00 (*1-56076-857-6*) TSR Inc.

Council on Environmental Quality, Annual Report, 1986. (Illus.). 432p. 1988. pap. 14.00 (*0-16-004348-4*, S/N 041-011-00081-5) USGPO.

Council on Foreign Relations & American Foreign Policy in the Early Cold War. Michael Wala. LC 94-29652. 256p. (C). 1994. text ed. 49.95 (*1-57181-003-X*) Berghahn Bks.

Council on Tribunals Report: Model Rules of Procedure for Tribunals. HMSO Staff. (Command Paper Ser.: No. 1434). 164p. 1991. pap. 35.00 (*0-10-114342-7*, HM2437) UNIPUB.

Council to Save the Planet. Conrad Lawrence. Tr. by Ingram. 364p. (Orig.). 1994. pap. 9.95 (*1-56901-189-3*) NW Pub.

Councillor. John Propher. (C). 1987. pap. 50.00 (*0-7219-0851-9*, Scientific) St Mut.

Councilman & Other Stories. Sky H. Tyler. 1993. 17.95 (*0-533-10449-1*) Vantage.

Councilman Speaks. Arthur W. Bromage. 1951. 3.00 (*0-911586-04-0*) Wahr.

Councilmen at Work. Arthur W. Bromage. 1954. 3.00 (*0-911586-05-9*) Wahr.

Councils, Committees, & Boards. 6th ed. Ed. by I. G. Anderson. 440p. 1985. 130.00 (*0-900246-43-X*) Gale.

Councils, Committees & Boards. 7th ed. Anderson. 1995. 130.00 (*0-900246-52-9*) Gale.

Councils in Action. Ed. by Audrey I. Richards & Adam Kuper. LC 76-160101. (Cambridge Papers in Social Anthropology: No. 6). 222p. reprint ed. pap. 63.30 (*0-317-27985-8*, 2025594) Bks Demand.

Counsel & Strategy in Middle English Romance. Geraldine Barnes. LC 92-43903. 192p. (C). 1993. text ed. 65.00 (*0-85991-362-7*) Boydell & Brewer.

Counsel for Catholic Parents. Ed. by Brett Brannen. 1992. 1.00 (*1-56036-017-8*) AMI Pr.

Counsel for Pastor's Wives. Diane M. Langberg. 128p. (Orig.). 1988. pap. 9.99 (*0-310-37621-1*, 12086P) Zondervan.

Counsel Individuals & Groups Module, Competency-Based Career Guidance (CBCG) - Category C: Implementing. National Center for Research in Vocational Education Staff. 1985. 7.95 (*0-317-03869-9*, CG100C01) Ctr Educ Trng Employ.

Counsel to the President. Clark A. Clifford. 1990. 25.00 (*0-395-56997-4*) HM.

Counsel to the President. Clark M. Clifford. 1991. 25.00 (*0-394-56995-4*) Random.

Counsel to the President: A Memoir. Clark Clifford. 1992. pap. 15.00 (*0-385-42398-5*, Anchor NY) Doubleday.

Counseled by God. Mark Virkler. 140p. (Orig.). 1989. pap. 8.99 (*1-56043-003-6*) Destiny Image.

Counselfile. Sabina Dunton & Kathy A. Miller. Ed. by Richard A. McNeely. LC 82-50626. (Illus.). 150p. (Orig.). (C). 1982. 27.50 (*0-943562-50-3*) Well Aware.

***Counseling: A Comprehensive Profession.** 3rd ed. Samuel T. Gladding. LC 95-7665. 1995. write for info. (*0-02-344145-3*, Merrill Pub Co) Macmillan.

Counseling: An Introduction, 2 Vols. 2nd ed. John J. Pietrofesa et al. LC 83-82703. 544p. (C). 1983. text ed. 58.76 (*0-395-35147-2*) HM.

Counseling: Group Theory & System. 2nd ed. Daniel W. Fullmer. LC 78-9058. 1978. 32.50 (*0-910328-12-9*); pap. 22.50 (*0-910328-13-7*) Sulzburger & Graham Pub.

Counseling: Offering a Needed Touch in Times of Trouble, a Guide for Personal Care-Giving. Walter Major & David Hoagland. Ed. by Cindy G. Spear & Tamara Johnson. 144p. (Orig.). 1993. pap. 8.95 (*0-941005-91-7*) Chrch Grwth VA.

***Counseling: The Spiritual Dimension.** Mary T. Burke & Judith Miranti. 1995. write for info. (*1-55620-145-1*) Am Coun Assn.

Counseling: Theory & Practice. 4th ed. Rickey L. George & Therese S. Cristiani. LC 94-11091. 1994. text ed. write for info. (*0-205-15252-X*) Allyn.

Counseling: Theory & Process. 5th ed. James H. Hansen et al. LC 92-42153. 403p. 1993. text ed. 47.00 (*0-205-14819-0*) Allyn.

Counseling--Guidance, Intervention, Skills, Management & Sex Infections. Peter P. Richey. 150p. 1994. 44.50 (*0-7883-0146-2*); pap. 39.50 (*0-7883-0147-0*) ABBE Pubs Assn.

Counseling Across Cultures. 3rd ed. Ed. by Paul B. Pedersen et al. LC 88-39249. (Illus.). 384p. (Orig.). (C). 1989. pap. text ed. 15.95 (*0-8248-1231-X*) UH Pr.

***Counseling Adults in Transition: A Compassionate Approach.** Ed. by Nancy K. Schlossberg et al. (Illus.). 304p. 1995. write for info. (*0-8261-4231-1*) Springer Pub.

Counseling Adults in Transition: Linking Practice with Theory. Nancy K. Schlossberg. 224p. 1984. 25.95 (*0-8261-4230-3*) Springer Pub.

Counseling American Minorities: A Cross-Cultural Perspective. 4th ed. Donald R. Atkinson et al. 400p. (C). 1993. pap. text ed. write for info. (*0-697-10444-3*) Brown & Benchmark.

Counseling & Accountability: Methods & Critique. H. D. Burck et al. 224p. (C). 1973. 124.00 (*0-08-017029-3*, Pub. by Pergamon Repr UK) Franklin.

Counseling & Basic Needs see Lay Counseling Series

***Counseling & Community: Using Church Relationships to Reinforce Counseling.** Wilson. 1995. (*0-8499-1051-X*) Word Inc.

Counseling & Confession. Walter J. Koehler. 1982. pap. 7.95 (*0-570-03849-9*, 12-2804) Concordia.

Counseling & Demonization: The Missing Link. Grayson H. Ensign & Edward Howe. 350p. 1989. pap. text ed. 9.95 (*0-9613185-1-1*) Recovery Pubns.

Counseling & Development in a Multicultural Society. 2nd ed. John A. Axelson. LC 92-26095. 1993. text ed. 44.95 (*0-534-19902-X*) Brooks-Cole.

Counseling & Guidance in the Schools: Three Exemplary Guidance Approaches. Garry Walz. 72p. 1992. 9.95 (*0-8106-1541-X*) NEA.

Counseling & Life-Style Development. R. Murray Thomas. 320p. (C). 1989. text ed. 46.00 (*0-8039-3613-3*); pap. text ed. 22.50 (*0-8039-3614-1*) Sage.

***Counseling & Psychology for Health Professionals.** Bayne. 1992. pap. 41.50 (*1-56593-117-3*, 0420) Singular Publishing.

Counseling & Psychotherapy: A Behavioral Approach. Ewing L. Phillips. LC 77-1771. (Wiley Series on Personality Processes). 303p. reprint ed. pap. 86.40 (*0-317-08440-2*, 2019850) Bks Demand.

Counseling & Psychotherapy: A Multicultural Perspective. 3rd ed. Allen E. Ivey et al. LC 92-20262. 1992. text ed. 55.00 (*0-205-14226-5*) Allyn.

Counseling & Psychotherapy: A Transpersonal Approach. Ed. by Barry Weinhold & Gay Hendricks. LC 91-77046. 233p. 1993. pap. 19.95 (*0-89108-224-7*, 9205) Love Pub Co.

Counseling & Psychotherapy: Classics on Theories & Issues, 2 vols. Ed. by Ben N. Ard, Jr. LC 93-390. 274p. 1993. Vol. I: Theories. pap. text ed. 39.95 (*0-7734-9932-6*); Vol. II: Issues. pap. text ed. 39.95 (*0-7734-9934-2*) E Mellen.

Counseling & Psychotherapy: Integrating Skills, Theory, & Practice. 2nd ed. Allen E. Ivey et al. (Illus.). 512p. 1987. text ed. 44.00 (*0-13-183138-0*) P-H.

Counseling & Psychotherapy: Theoretical Analysis & Skills Applications. Leroy G. Baruth & Charles Huber. 480p. (C). 1985. write for info. (*0-675-20299-X*, Merrill Pub Co) Macmillan.

Counseling & Psychotherapy: Theories & Interventions. David Capuzzi & Douglas R. Gross. (Illus.). 544p. (C). 1994. teacher ed write for info. (*0-318-72454-5*); text ed. write for info. (*0-02-319211-9*) Macmillan.

***Counseling & Psychotherapy of Religious Clients: A Developmental Approach.** Vicky Genia. LC 94-37888. 129p. 1995. text ed. 49.95 (*0-275-95107-3*, Praeger Pubs) Greenwood.

Counseling & Psychotherapy of Work Dysfunctions. Rodney L. Lowman. (Illus.). 348p. 1993. text ed. 39.95 (*1-55798-204-X*); pap. text ed. 24.95 (*1-55798-205-8*) Am Psychol.

Counseling & Psychotherapy with Children & Adolescents: Theory & Practice for School & Clinic Settings. 2nd ed. Douglas T. Brown & H. Thompson Prout. LC 89-62094. (Illus.). 434p. (C). 1989. text ed. 49.50 (*0-88422-104-0*) Clinical Psych.

Counseling & Psychotherapy with College Students: A Guide to Treatment. Ed. by Joseph E. Talley & W. J. Rockwell. LC 85-16957. 208p. 1985. text ed. 49.95 (*0-275-90033-9*, C0033, Praeger Pubs) Greenwood.

Counseling & Psychotherapy with Persons with Mental Retardation & Borderline Intelligence. Ed. by Douglas C. Strohmer & H. Thompson Prout. LC 93-12016. 312p. 1994. lib. bdg. 34.95 (*0-88422-121-0*) Clinical Psych.

Counseling & Social Support: Perspectives & Practice. Richard E. Pearson. (Illus.). 240p. (C). 1990. 46.00 (*0-8039-3210-3*); pap. 21.95 (*0-8039-3211-1*) Sage.

***Counseling & Social Work.** Judith Brearley. LC 94-22205. (Counselling in Context Ser.). 1994. write for info. (*0-335-19002-2*) Open Univ Pr.

Counseling & Spiritual Issues: An Annotated Bibliography. Ed. by Milton G. Spann, Jr. & N. Beverly Nickles. 170p. 1992. 14.00 (*1-55620-115-X*, 72292) Am Coun Assn.

Counseling & the Human Predicament: A Study of Sin, Guilt, & Forgiveness. Ed. by LeRoy Aden & David G. Benner. LC 89-38661. (Psychology & Christianity Ser.). 192p. (Orig.). 1989. pap. 12.99 (*0-8010-0218-4*) Baker Bk.

Counseling & Therapy for Children. Jim Gumaer. 384p. (C). 1984. text ed. 29.95 (*0-02-913350-5*) Free Pr.

Counseling & Therapy Skills. David G. Martin. 289p. (C). 1989. reprint ed. pap. text ed. 16.95x (*0-88133-409-X*) Waveland Pr.

Counseling & Values: A Philosophical Examination. 2nd ed. James A. Peterson. LC 89-38243. 1989. pap. 21.85 (*0-910328-43-9*) Sulzburger & Graham Pub.

Counseling As an Art: The Creative Arts in Counseling. Samuel T. Gladding. 1992. 25.95 (*1-55620-091-9*) Am Coun Assn.

Counseling California Corporations. Ed. by Margaret Shulenberger & Edward Giacomini. LC 90-80013. 765p. 1990. text ed. 115.00 (*0-88124-264-0*, BU-39230) Cont Ed Bar-CA.

Counseling Chemically Dependent People with HIV Illness. Ed. by Michael Shernoff. LC 91-35376. (Journal of Chemical Dependency Treatment). 174p. 1992. pap. text ed. 14.95 (*1-56023-016-9*) Harrington Pk.

Counseling Chemically Dependent People with HIV Illness. Ed. by Michael Shernoff. LC 91-35375. (Journal of Chemical Dependency Treatment). 174p. 1992. lib. bdg. 39.95 (*1-56024-259-0*) Haworth Pr.

Counseling Children. 3rd ed. Charles L. Thompson & Linda B. Rudolph. LC 91-24926. 480p. (C). 1992. text ed. 50.95 (*0-534-17196-6*) Brooks-Cole.

Counseling Children & Adolescents. Ann Vernon. LC 92-74808. 323p. 1993. text ed. 37.95 (*0-89108-228-X*, 9304) Love Pub Co.

Counseling Clients in the Entertainment Industry. 1990. 17.50 (*0-685-69408-9*) PLI.

Counseling Clients in the Entertainment Industry, 1989. (Patents, Copyrights, Trademarks, & Literary Property Ser.). 268p. 1989. 17.50 (*0-685-69406-2*) PLI.

Counseling Clients in the Entertainment Industry, 1990. LC 73-157034. 903p. 1990. 17.50 (*0-685-69407-0*) PLI.

Counseling Clients in the Entertainment Industry 1992, 2 vols., Set. (Patents, Copyrights, Trademarks, & Literary Property Ser.). 1253p. 1992. pap. text ed. 80.00 (*0-685-56910-1*, G4-3879) PLI.

Counseling Clients in the Entertainment Industry 1993, 2 vols., Set. (Patents, Copyrights, Trademarks, & Literary Property Ser.: Vols. 359-360). 1659p. 1993. 80.00 (*0-685-65519-9*, G4-3896) PLI.

Counseling College Student-Athletes: Issues & Interventions. Ed. by Edward F. Etzel, Jr. et al. LC 91-73215. 272p. (C). 1991. text ed. 36.00 (*0-9627926-1-6*) Fit Info Tech.

Counseling College Students: A Practical Guide for Teachers, Parents, & Counselors. James Archer, Jr. 192p. 1991. 17.95 (*0-8245-1300-2*) Crossroad NY.

Counseling Couples. Donald Bubenzer & John West. (Counselling in Action Ser.). 160p. (C). 1993. text ed. 44.00 (*0-8039-8420-0*); pap. text ed. 19.95 (*0-8039-8421-9*) Sage.

Counseling Criminal Justice Offenders. Ruth E. Masters. 264p. (C). 1994. text ed. 46.00 (*0-8039-5532-4*); pap. text ed. 19.95 (*0-8039-5533-2*) Sage.

Counseling Diverse Client Groups: An International Perspective on Human Social Functioning. Margaret Rodway. LC 89-9297. (Studies in Health & Human Services). 376p. 1989. lib. bdg. 99.95 (*0-88946-139-2*) E Mellen.

***Counseling Effectively in Groups.** John Vriend & Wayne W. Dyer. LC 73-7937. 384p. 1973. 37.95 (*0-87778-062-5*) Educ Tech Pubns.

Counseling Elders & Their Families: Practical Techniques for Applied Gerontology. John J. Herr & John H. Weakland. LC 78-26365. (Adulthood & Aging Ser.: Vol. 2). 320p. 1979. 32.95 (*0-8261-2510-7*) Springer Pub.

Counseling Exceptional Students. Ed. by Anthony F. Rotatori et al. 334p. (C). 1986. 45.95 (*0-89885-274-9*); pap. 21.95 (*0-89885-275-7*) Human Sci Pr.

Counseling Experience. Jay T. Willis. 42p. (Orig.). 1987. pap. text ed. 5.95 (*0-9618486-0-X*) J T Willis.

Counseling Experience: A Theoretical & Practical Approach. Michael E. Cavanagh. 383p. (C). 1990. reprint ed. pap. text ed. 21.95 (*0-88133-531-2*) Waveland Pr.

Counseling Families: An Introduction to Marriage & Family Therapy. David L. Fenell & Barry K. Weinhold. LC 88-80211. 339p. 1989. pap. text ed. 24.95 (*0-89108-203-4*) Love Pub Co.

***Counseling Families with Chronic Illness.** Susan McDaniel. 1995. 17.95 (*1-55620-144-3*) Am Coun Assn.

Counseling for Career Development: Theories, Resources, & Practice. Carl McDaniels & Norman C. Gysbers. LC 91-25851. (Management Ser.). 485p. 1992. 36.95 (*1-55542-399-X*) Jossey-Bass.

***Counseling for College.** rev. ed. Eileen Matthay. Ed. by Erika Pendleton. 432p. 1995. pap. 29.95 (*1-56079-534-4*) Petersons Guides.

Counseling for Diversity: A Guide for School Counselors & Related Professionals. Ed. by Courtland C. Lee. 1994. 32.95 (*0-205-15321-6*, Longwood Div) Allyn.

Counseling for Empowerment. Ellen H. McWhirter. LC 94-3945. 270p. 1994. 33.95 (*1-55620-135-4*) Am Coun Assn.

Counseling for Family Problems. Eddy Street. (Counselling in Action Ser.). 192p. 1994. 44.00 (*0-8039-8854-0*); pap. 19.95 (*0-8039-8855-9*) Sage.

Counseling for Racial Understanding. Comp. by Brenda K. Bryant. LC 93-36424. 100p. 1994. pap. text ed. 17.95 (*1-55620-126-5*) Am Coun Assn.

Counseling for Relapse Prevention. Terence T. Gorski & Merlene Miller. 1982. pap. 10.75 (*0-8309-0367-4*) Herald Hse.

Counseling for Results: Principles & Practices of Helping. Edward Scissons. LC 92-13414. 272p. (C). 1993. text ed. 39.95 (*0-534-19476-1*) Brooks-Cole.

***Counseling for Spiritually Empowered Wholeness: A Hope-Centered Approach.** Howard Clinebell. LC 94-30384. 1994. pap. 14.95 (*1-56024-903-X*) Haworth Pr.

Counseling for Spiritually Empowered Wholeness: A Hope-Centered Approach. Howard Clinebell. LC 94-30384. 185p. (C). 1994. lib. bdg. 29.95 (*1-56024-902-1*) Haworth Pr.

Counseling for the Gifted see Reaching for the Stars: A Minicourse for Education of Gifted Students

Counseling Futures. Ed. by Garry R. Walz. 80p. 1990. pap. 8.95 (*1-56109-005-0*) ERIC Clearinghouse.

C

An Asterisk (*) at the beginning of an entry indicates that the title is appearing in BIP for the first time.

1647

Counseling Gay Men & Lesbians: Journey to the End of the Rainbow. Ed. by Sari H. Dworkin & Fernando J. Gutierrez. 1992. 28.95 (*1-55620-089-7*) Am Coun Assn.

Counseling Gems: Thoughts for the Practitioner. J. Carnevale. LC 89-6588. vii, 176p. (Orig.). (C). 1989. pap. text ed. 17.95 (*0-915202-88-3*) Accel Devel.

Counseling Gifted & Talented Children: A Guide for Teachers, Counselors, & Parents. Ed. by Roberta M. Milgram & Mark Runco. (Creativity Research Ser.). 288p. 1991. text ed. 47.50 (*0-89391-724-9*); pap. text ed. 24.95 (*0-89391-773-7*) Ablex Pub.

***Counseling Gifted, Creative & Talented Youth Through the Arts.** Adele Kenny. 1989. pap. text ed. 9.97 (*0-937659-35-5*) GCT.

Counseling Helpsheets. Tom Klaus. 1994. 14.99 (*1-55945-007-X*) Group Pub.

Counseling in a Dynamic Society: Opportunities & Challenges. Edwin L. Herr. 1989. 31.95 (*1-55620-062-5*) Am Coun Assn.

Counseling in Abortion Services: Physician-Nurse-Social Worker. Columbia University , School of Social Work Staff. 1974. 3.00 (*0-686-09562-6*) Univ Bk Serv.

***Counseling in Child Disability: Skills for Working with Parents.** G. Hornby. 212p. 1994. 44.95 (*1-56593-308-7*, 0632) Singular Publishing.

Counseling in Correctional Environments. Lawrence A. Bennett. LC 77-21269. (New Vistas in Counseling Ser.: Vol. VI). 94p. 1978. 24.95 (*0-87705-319-7*) Human Sci Pr.

Counseling in Schools: Essential Services & Comprehensive Programs. John J. Schmidt. LC 92-14011. 1992. text ed. 54.00 (*0-205-14350-4*) Allyn.

***Counseling in Schools: Essential Services & Comprehensive Programs.** 2nd ed. John J. Schmidt. LC 94-46178. 1995. text ed. write for info. (*0-205-16553-2*) Allyn.

Counseling in the Asia-Pacific Region. Ed. by Abdul H. Othman & Amir Awang. LC 92-45074. (Contributions in Psychology Ser.: No. 20). 168p. 1993. text ed. 55.00 (*0-313-28799-6*, GM8799, Greenwood Pr) Greenwood.

Counseling in the Elementary School: A Comprehensive Approach. Robert L. Gibson et al. LC 92-29659. 1993. text ed. write for info. (*0-205-14706-2*) Allyn.

***Counseling Individual Handbook.** 2nd ed. Dryden. 1993. 65.00 (*1-56593-524-1*, 0314) Singular Publishing.

Counseling Individuals: The Rational-Emotive Approach. Wendy Dryden. 240p. 1987. 49.00 (*0-85066-666-X*); pap. 27.00 (*0-85066-665-1*) Singular Publishing.

Counseling Interactions with Traumatically Brain Injured Clients. Keith D. Cicerone. Ed. by Robert Fraser & David Clemmons. LC 91-73658. (Traumatic Brain Injury Rehabilitation Training Ser.). 43p. (Orig.). 1991. spiral bd., pap. 14.95 (*1-878205-20-X*) GR Press.

Counseling Issues in Catholic Schools: Moral, Ethical & Legal Dimensions. Mary A. Shaughnessy et al. 80p. (Orig.). 1993. pap. 9.95 (*0-9636790-0-7*) Catholic Schl.

Counseling Juvenile Offenders in Institutional Settings. Ed. by Sol Chaneles. (Journal of Offender Counseling, Services & Rehabilitation: Vol. 6, No. 3). 85p. 1983. pap. text ed. 14.95 (*0-86656-170-6*) Haworth Pr.

Counseling Kids. Donald L. Peters. LC 91-70334. 348p. (Orig.). 1991. pap. text ed. 27.95 (*1-55959-030-0*) Accel Devel.

Counseling Layman see Lay Counseling Series

Counseling Lesbian Women & Gay Men: A Life-Issues Approach. A. Elfin Moses & Robert O. Hawkins, Jr. 263p. (C). 1982. pap. write for info. (*0-675-20599-9*, Merrill Pub Co) Macmillan.

Counseling Manual in Astrology. M. Jones. LC 79-92997. 206p. 1982. 15.00 (*0-685-08836-7*, J2425-014) Am Fed Astrologers.

Counseling Manual in Astrology: A Long-Tested Method for Accuracy. Marc E. Jones. (Illus.). 197p. 1982. 15.00 (*0-87878-017-3*) Sabian Pub.

Counseling Men. Philip L. Culbertson. LC 94-2825. 1994. 9.00 (*0-8006-2786-5*, Fortress Pr) Augsburg Fortress.

Counseling Midlife Career Changers. Loretta J. Bradley. LC 89-25914. (Illus.). 70p. (Orig.). 1990. pap. 6.50 (*0-912048-70-0*) Garrett Pk.

Counseling Model for Minority & Ethnic Students. Pasquale F. Amendolia. 25p. (Orig.). 1988. pap. write for info. (*0-318-63708-1*) Amer Italian Descent.

***Counseling Older Persons: A Professional Handbook.** George Thorman. LC 95-2561. (Illus.). 110p. (C). 1995. text ed. 34.95x (*0-398-05993-4*); pap. text ed. 19.95x (*0-398-05994-2*) C C Thomas.

***Counseling Older Persons: An Annotated Bibliography.** Ed. by Valerie L. Schwiebert & Jane E. Myers. LC 94-44351. (Bibliographies & Indexes in Gerontology Ser.: No. 26). 136p. 1995. text ed. 49.95 (*0-313-29277-9*, Greenwood Pr) Greenwood.

Counseling Older Persons: Careers, Retirement, Dying. Daniel Sinick. LC 77-21963. (New Vistas in Counseling Ser.: Vol. IV). 112p. 1978. 24.95 (*0-87705-312-X*) Human Sci Pr.

Counseling on Early Sexual Memories. Joan Karp. 1992. pap. 3.00 (*0-913937-54-1*) Rational Isl.

***Counseling on Early Sexual Memories.** Joan Karp. (ITA.). 1994. pap. 3.00 (*1-885357-00-1*) Rational Isl.

Counseling Our Own: Lesbian-Gay Subculture Meets the Mental Health System. Charna Klein. (Illus.). 240p. (Orig.). (C). 1986. pap. 9.99 (*0-9617216-0-X*) Consult Serv NW.

Counseling Our Own: The Lesbian-Gay Subculture Meets the Mental Health System. 2nd ed. Charna Klein. 263p. 1991. pap. 12.95 (*0-9617216-1-8*) Consult Serv NW.

Counseling Parents of Exceptional Children. Ed. by Jack C. Stewart. LC 74-10596. 136p. 1974. pap. text ed. 12.95 (*0-8422-0422-9*) Irvington.

Counseling Parents of Exceptional Children. 2nd ed. Jack Stewart. 224p. (C). 1986. pap. write for info. (*0-675-20510-7*, Merrill Pub Co) Macmillan.

Counseling Parents of Hearing-Impaired Children. David Luterman. 1979. text ed. 15.00 (*0-316-53750-0*, Little Med Div) Little.

Counseling Patients on Their Medications: One of the Principle Responsibilities of the Pharmacist. Arnold W. Karig & Edward A. Hartshorn. (Illus.). xvi, 580p. 1991. pap. 59.00 (*0-914768-48-4*, BK. #4) Drug Intell Pubns.

Counseling People with Communication Problems. Peggy Dalton. (Counselling in Action Ser.). 192p. 1994. 44.00 (*0-8039-8894-X*); pap. 19.95 (*0-8039-8895-8*) Sage.

Counseling Persons with Cancer. John V. Conti. 136p. 1989. 31.95 (*0-398-05590-4*) C C Thomas.

***Counseling Persons with Cancer.** John V. Conti. 136p. 1989. pap. 16.95 (*0-398-06072-X*) C C Thomas.

Counseling Persons with Physical Disabilities: Theoretical & Clinical Perspectives. Laura E. Marshak & Milton Seligman. LC 92-35809. (Orig.). (C). 1993. pap. text ed. 27.00 (*0-89079-580-0*, 6594) PRO-ED.

Counseling Powers & Passions: More Counseling Techniques that Work. John Vriend. 327p. 18.95 (*0-911547-96-7*) Am Coun Assn.

Counseling Principles for Christian Leaders. James A. Jones. 1982. 7.50 (*0-89137-534-1*) Quality Pubns.

Counseling Process. 4th ed. Lewis E. Patterson & Elizabeth R. Welfel. LC 93-37295. 1994. pap. 29.95 (*0-534-23268-X*) Brooks-Cole.

Counseling Process: A Cognitive-Behavioral Approach. John M. Lembo. LC 76-4232. 1976. 10.95 (*0-87212-060-0*) Libra.

Counseling Programs: A Guide to Evaluation. L. DiAnne Borders & Sandra M. Drury. (Essential Tools for Educators Ser.). 104p. 1992. pap. 16.95 (*0-8039-6036-0*) Corwin Pr.

Counseling Psychology. Charles J. Gelso & Bruce R. Fretz. (William James Centennial Ser.). (Illus.). 480p. (C). 1992. text ed. 42.75 (*0-03-027858-9*) HB Coll Pubs.

Counseling Psychology: Strategies & Services. Robert H. Woody et al. LC 88-31705. 306p. (C). 1989. text ed. 42.95 (*0-534-10002-3*) Brooks-Cole.

***Counseling Research & Program Evaluation.** 5th ed. Robert G. Hadley & Lynda K. Mitchell. LC 94-36135. 544p. 1995. text ed. 49.95 (*0-534-25650-3*) Brooks-Cole.

Counseling Same-Sex Couples. Douglas Carl. 160p. (C). 1990. 19.95 (*0-393-70107-7*) Norton.

***Counseling Single Adults: A Handbook of Principles & Advice.** Douglas L. Fagerstrom. 368p. 1995. text ed. 22.99 (*0-8010-9008-3*) Baker Bk.

Counseling Single Parents. Joan D. Atwood & Frank Genovese. LC 93-21659. 238p. (C). 1993. pap. 26.95 (*1-55620-125-7*, 72516) Am Coun Assn.

Counseling Single Parents: Meeting the Challenges of Single Parent Families. David R. Miller. LC 93-46347. 1994. 15.99 (*0-8499-1062-5*) Word Inc.

***Counseling Skills for Health Professionals.** P. Burnard. 272p. 1994. 42.50 (*1-56593-312-5*, 0635) Singular Publishing.

Counseling Skills for Health Professionals. Philip Burnard. (Therapy in Practice Ser.). 250p. 1989. pap. 15.95 (*0-412-32000-2*) Chapman & Hall.

Counseling Skills in Family Planning. Deborah E. Bender & Cydne Bean. 1982. pap. 14.00 (*0-686-47616-6*); pap. 4.00 (*0-685-55671-9*) Carolina Pop Ctr.

Counseling Sourcebook: A Practical Reference on Contemporary Issues. Ed. by Judah L. Ronch et al. 536p. (Orig.). 1994. pap. 21.95 (*0-8245-1241-3*) Crossroad NY.

Counseling Specialist. (Career Examination Ser.: C-3440). 1994. pap. 29.95 (*0-8373-3440-3*) Nat Learn.

Counseling Strategies & Intervention Techniques for the Human Services. 4th ed. Richard D. Parsons & Robert J. Wicks. LC 93-1560. 1993. pap. text ed. 30.00 (*0-205-14791-7*) Allyn.

Counseling Strategies & Interventions. 4th ed. Harold L. Hackney & Sherry Cormier. LC 92-33891. 1993. pap. text ed. write for info. (*0-205-14800-X*) Allyn.

Counseling Students: Lessons from Northfield, Echoes from Fountain Valley. Preston K. Munter. LC 87-35130. 220p. 1988. text ed. 45.00 (*0-86569-172-X*, Auburn Hse) Greenwood.

Counseling Stutterers. Jane F. Gruss. (Publications on Stuttering: No. 18). 80p. 1982. pap. 2.00 (*0-933388-18-7*) Stuttering Fnd Am.

Counseling Survivors of Childhood Sexual Abuse. Claire B. Draucker. (Counselling in Practice Ser.). (Illus.). 160p. (C). 1992. 44.00 (*0-8039-8570-3*); pap. 19.95 (*0-8039-8571-1*) Sage.

Counseling Techn-Astro. rev. ed. Stephanie Ennis. 1990. pap. 12.95 (*0-685-47196-9*, 2584-014) Am Fed Astrologers.

Counseling Techniques: An Outline & Overview. Frederick D. Harper & Gail C. Bruce. 225p. (C). 1989. pap. text ed. write for info. (*0-935392-04-1*) Douglass Pubs.

Counseling Techniques in Astrology. rev. ed. Stephanie Ennis. LC 81-71393. 98p. 1982. 12.95 (*0-86690-026-8*, E2584-014) Am Fed Astrologers.

Counseling Techniques that Work. Wayne Dyer & John Vriend. 270p. 1975. 15.95 (*0-686-34289-5*) Am Coun Assn.

Counseling Techniques that Work. Wayne Dyer & John Vriend. 288p. 1988. 15.95 (*0-911547-26-6*, 72044) Am Coun Assn.

Counseling Teenagers. G. Keith Olson. 528p. 1984. pap. 21.99 (*0-931529-67-0*) Group Pub.

Counseling the Able Disabled: Rehabilitation Consulting in Disability Compensation Systems. Lawrence J. Deneen & Thorvald A. Hessellund. 344p. (Orig.). 1986. 34.95 (*0-9614877-1-2*) Rehab Pubns.

Counseling the Adolescent: Individual, Family, & School Interventions. 2nd ed. Ed. by Jon Carlson & Judith Lewis. LC 92-72337. 316p. 1993. pap. text ed. 29.95 (*0-89108-226-3*, 9302) Love Pub Co.

Counseling the Adolescent Substance Abuser in the School Setting: School Based Intervention & Prevention. Marlene M. Gonet. (Sourcebooks for the Human Services Ser.: Vol. 29). 232p. (C). 1994. text ed. 49.95 (*0-8039-4865-4*); pap. text ed. 24.00 (*0-8039-4866-2*) Sage.

Counseling the Alcoholic Group. Joseph F. Perez. 145p. 1986. text ed. 22.95 (*0-89876-131-X*) Gardner Pr.

Counseling the Alcoholic Woman. Joseph Perez. 225p. (C). 1993. pap. text ed. 22.95 (*1-55959-055-6*) Accel Devel.

Counseling the Bereaved. Dersheimer. (Practitioner Guidebook Ser.). (C). 1990. 29.95 (*0-205-14311-3*, H4311, Longwood Div) Allyn.

Counseling the Chemically Dependent. Rickey L. George & Therese S. Cristiani. 320p. (C). 1990. Casebound. text ed. 36.00 (*0-13-181330-7*) P-H.

Counseling the Childless Couple. William T. Bassett. LC 63-14722. (Successful Pastoral Counseling Ser.). 139p. reprint ed. pap. 39.70 (*0-685-16015-7*, 2026938) Bks Demand.

Counseling the Communicatively Disordered & Their Families. 2nd ed. David Luterman. LC 90-45168. 187p. (C). 1991. pap. text ed. 25.00 (*0-89079-414-6*, 1585) PRO-ED.

Counseling the Culturally Different: Theory & Practice. 2nd ed. Donald W. Sue. 1990. text ed. 37.50 (*0-471-84269-9*) Wiley.

Counseling the Defiant Child: A Basic Guide to Helping Troubled & Aggressive Youth. John B. Mordock. LC 93-47043. (Formerly Counseling Children Ser.). 240p. 1994. reprint ed. pap. 12.95 (*0-8245-1407-6*) Crossroad NY.

Counseling the Dying. Margaretta K. Bowers et al. LC 74-33146. 192p. 1994. pap. 25.00 (*1-56821-286-0*) Aronson.

Counseling the Elderly Client in Minnesota. Center for Public Representation Staff. Ed. by Lynn K. Klobucher. 1992. 150.00 (*0-317-05374-4*) Lawyers Cooperative.

Counseling the Elderly Client in Virginia, 2 vols., Set. Center for Public Representation Staff. Ed. by Laura Wagner & Robert Wagner. 1992. ring bd. 150.00 (*0-317-05371-X*) Lawyers Cooperative.

Counseling the Gifted: Developing the Whole Child. Cal Ross. 1990. pap. 6.00 (*0-89824-710-1*) Trillium Pr.

Counseling the Gifted & Talented. Ed. by Linda K. Silverman. LC 92-74350. 372p. 1993. text ed. 39.95 (*0-89108-227-1*, 9303) Love Pub Co.

Counseling the Homosexual. Bill Flatt et al. 1982. 12.00 (*0-934916-49-7*) Natl Christian Pr.

Counseling the Homosexual. Mike Saia. LC 87-35524. 240p. (Orig.). (C). 1988. pap. 9.99 (*0-87123-989-2*) Bethany Hse.

Counseling the Involuntary & Resistant Client. George A. Harris & David Watkins. 112p. 1987. pap. 23.25 (*0-942974-87-5*, 350) Am Correctional.

Counseling the Nursing Mother. 2nd ed. Childbirth Education Association of Greater Philadelphia, Inc. Staff. (Avery's Childbirth Reference Ser.). 538p. 1990. ring bd. 36.95 (*0-89529-448-6*) Avery Pub.

Counseling the Nursing Mother: Supplement to 1st Edition. Childbirth Education Association of Greater Philadelphia, Inc. Staff. (Avery's Childbirth Reference Ser.). 128p. 1989. ring bd. 8.95 (*0-89529-401-X*) Avery Pub.

Counseling the Older Adult: A Training Manual for Paraprofessionals & Beginning Counselors. 2nd ed. Patricia A. McDonald & Margaret Haney. 224p. (Orig.). 1988. pap. 27.95 (*0-669-16970-6*) Free Pr.

***Counseling the Older Patient.** E. O'Leary. 160p. 1995. 41.50 (*1-56593-281-1*, 0605) Singular Publishing.

Counseling the Sexual Addict. Patrick Carnes. 1994. pap. 3.95 (*0-89638-137-4*) Hazelden.

Counseling Theories & Techniques: Summarized & Critiqued. Lester N. Downing. LC 74-23725. 264p. 1975. 28.95 (*0-88229-203-X*); pap. 19.95 (*0-88229-502-0*) Nelson-Hall.

Counseling Through Group Process. Joseph Anderson. 288p. (C). 1984. 27.95 (*0-8261-4620-1*) Springer Pub.

Counseling Today's Families. Herbert Goldenberg & Irene Goldenberg. 290p. (C). 1989. pap. 26.95 (*0-534-11934-4*) Brooks-Cole.

Counseling Today's Families. 2nd ed. Herbert Goldenberg & Irene Goldenberg. LC 93-29235. 1994. pap. 27.95 (*0-534-20526-7*) Brooks-Cole.

***Counseling Toward Solutions: A Practical Solution-Focused Program for Working with Students.** Linda Metcalf. 1994. spiral bd. 29.95 (*0-87628-267-2*) Ctr Appl Res.

Counseling Victims of Violence. Sandra L. Brown. 243p. 1991. 28.95 (*1-55620-083-8*) Am Coun Assn.

Counseling with Gay Men & Women: A Guide for Facilitating Positive Life-Styles. Natalie J. Woodman & Harry R. Lenna. LC 80-8002. (Jossey-Bass Social & Behavioral Science Ser.). 160p. reprint ed. pap. 45.60 (*0-7837-0190-X*, 2040486) Bks Demand.

Counseling with Senior Citizens. J. Paul Brown. LC 64-15217. (Successful Pastoral Counseling Ser.). 144p. reprint ed. pap. 41.10 (*0-685-15384-3*, 2027174) Bks Demand.

Counseling Women: A Guide for Therapists. Helen V. Collier. (Illus.). 352p. 1982. text ed. 32.95 (*0-02-905840-6*) Free Pr.

Counseling Women over the Life Span. Judith A. Lewis et al. LC 91-77048. 307p. 1992. pap. 29.95 (*0-89108-222-0*, 9203) Love Pub Co.

Counselling: A Guide to Practice in Nursing. Philip Bornard. 214p. 1992. pap. 29.95 (*0-7506-0643-6*) Buttrwrth-Heinemann.

Counselling: A Practical Guide for Employers. Mike Megranahan. 304p. (C). 1989. 94.00 (*0-85292-397-X*, Pub. by IPM Hse UK) St Mut.

***Counselling: Approaches & Issues in Education.** Helen Cowie & Andrea Pecherek. 176p. 1994. pap. 27.00x (*1-85346-293-4*, Pub. by D Fulton UK) Taylor & Francis.

Counselling: Interdisciplinary Perspectives. Ed. by Brian Thorne & Wendy Dryden. LC 93-18531. 1993. pap. 36.00 (*0-335-15678-9*, Open Univ Pr) Taylor & Francis.

***Counselling - The Deaf Challenge.** Mairian Corker. 250p. 1995. pap. 24.95x (*1-85302-321-3*, Pub. by J Kingsley Pubs UK) Taylor & Francis.

Counselling Adult Survivors of Child Sexual Abuse. Christiane Sanderson. 240p. 1990. 57.00 (*1-85302-045-1*); pap. 32.00 (*1-85302-138-5*) Taylor & Francis.

***Counselling Adult Survivors of Child Sexual Abuse.** 2nd ed. Christiane Sanderson. 288p. 1994. pap. 29.50x (*1-85302-252-7*, Pub. by J Kingsley Pubs UK) Taylor & Francis.

Counselling & Communication in Health Care. Ed. by Hilton Davis & Lesley Fallowfield. 358p. 1991. text ed. 108.00 (*0-471-92818-6*) Wiley.

Counselling & Long Term Unemployment: Report on Phase 1 of the Eurocounsel Action Research Programme. European Communities Staff. 68p. 1992. pap. 11.00 (*92-826-4981-4*, SY-76-92-883-EN-C, Pub. by Europ Com) UNIPUB.

Counselling & School Social Work: An Experimental Study. Gordon Rose & Tony F. Marshall. LC 74-2449. 355p. reprint ed. pap. 101.20 (*0-317-09856-X*, 2016524) Bks Demand.

Counselling & Spiritual Development & Other Essays from the "Golden Blade" Adam Bittleston. 270p. 1990. 29.50 (*0-86315-074-8*, 1316, Pub. by Floris Books UK) Anthroposophic.

Counselling & Therapy with Refugees: Psychological Problems of Victims of War, Torture & Repression. Guus Van der Veer. (Series in Psychotherapy & Counselling). 275p. 1992. text ed. 56.95 (*0-471-93414-3*) Wiley.

***Counselling & Therapy with Refugees: Psychological Problems of Victims of War, Torture & Repression.** Guus Van der Veer. (Series in Psychotherapy & Counselling). 1995. pap. text ed. 35.00 (*0-471-95175-7*) Wiley.

Counselling As a Christian Challenge. Andrew Monaghan. 183p. pap. 19.95 (*0-7171-1831-2*, CC-01831) Chr Classics.

Counselling Drug Users about HIV & AIDS. Geraldine Mulleady. (Illus.). 192p. 1992. pap. 36.95 (*0-632-02939-0*) Blackwell Sci.

Counselling for Alcohol Problems. Richard Velleman. (Counselling in Practice Ser.). (Illus.). 160p. (C). 1992. 44.00 (*0-8039-8468-5*); pap. 19.95 (*0-8039-8469-3*) Sage.

Counselling for Anxiety Problems. Richard Hallam. (Counselling in Practice Ser.). (Illus.). 160p. (C). 1992. 44.00 (*0-8039-8460-X*); pap. 19.95 (*0-8039-8461-8*) Sage.

***Counselling for Change: Coaching & Motivating Your Team.** Nicola Phillips. (Institute of Management Ser.). 250p. 1995. pap. 43.50 (*0-273-61176-3*, Pub. by Pitman Pub Ltd UK) Trans-Atl Phila.

Counselling for Depression. Paul Gilbert. (Counselling in Practice Ser.). (Illus.). 160p. (C). 1992. 44.00 (*0-8039-8497-9*); pap. 19.95 (*0-8039-8498-7*) Sage.

***Counselling for Fertility Problems.** Jane Read. (Counselling in Practice Ser.). 240p. 1995. text ed. 44.00 (*0-8039-8949-0*); pap. text ed. 19.95 (*0-8039-8950-4*) Sage.

Counselling for Heart Disease. Paul Bennett. 144p. (Orig.). (C). 1993. pap. text ed. 25.00 (*1-85433-096-9*, Pub. by Brit Psychol Soc UK) P H Brookes.

***Counselling for Managers.** John M. Hughes. 77p. (C). 1991. pap. 21.00x (*0-85171-094-8*, Pub. by IPM Hse UK) St Mut.

Counselling for Post-Traumatic Stress Disorder. Michael J. Scott & Stephen G. Stradling. (Counselling in Practice Ser.). (Illus.). 192p. (C). 1992. 44.00 (*0-8039-8408-1*); pap. 19.95 (*0-8039-8409-X*) Sage.

***Counselling for Sexual Abuse: A Therapist's Guide to Working with Adults, Children & Families.** Kathy MacDonald et al. 320p. 1995. 39.95 (*0-19-558315-9*) OUP.

***Counselling for Stress Problems.** Stephen Palmer & Windy Dryden. (Counselling in Practice Ser.). 240p. 1995. text ed. 44.00 (*0-8039-8862-1*); pap. text ed. 19.95 (*0-8039-8863-X*) Sage.

Counselling for Women. Janet Perry. LC 93-15402. (Counselling in Context Ser.). 128p. 1993. pap. 23.00 (*0-335-19034-0*, Open Univ Pr) Taylor & Francis.

***Counselling for Young People.** Judith Mabey & Bernice Sorensen. LC 94-41293. 160p. 1995. pap. 19.95 (*0-335-19298-X*, Open Univ Pr) Taylor & Francis.

***Counselling Heroin & Other Drug Users.** Paul Lockley. 315p. 1995. 50.00 (*1-85343-312-8*); pap. 24.95 (*1-85343-304-7*) NYU Pr.

Counselling in General Practice. Ed. by Roslyn Corney & Rachel Jenkins. 144p. 1995. pap. 17.95x (*0-415-05956-9*, A7790) Routledge.

Counselling in HIV Infection & AIDS. 2nd ed. J. Green & A. McCreaner. 320p. 1994. pap. write for info. (*0-632-03605-2*) Blackwell Sci.

Counselling in Independent Practice. Gabrielle Syme. LC 93-29252. (Counselling in Context Ser.). 128p. 1994. pap. 23.00 (*0-335-19049-9*, Open Univ Pr) Taylor & Francis.

Counselling in Infertility. S. Jennings. 1994. pap. write for info. (*0-632-03866-7*) Blackwell Sci.

An Asterisk (*) at the beginning of an entry indicates that the title is appearing in BIP for the first time.

C

An Asterisk (*) at the beginning of an entry indicates that the title is appearing in BIP for the first time.

1649

Count Your Dead, They Are Alive. Wyndham Lewis. LC 72-82185. 1972. reprint ed. lib. bdg. 250.00 (0-87968-007-5) Gordon Pr.

Count Your Money with the Polk Street School. Patricia R. Giff. (J). (ps-3). 1994. mass mkt. 3.99 (0-440-40929-2) Dell.

Count Your Way Through Africa. Jim Haskins. (Count Your Way Bks.). (Illus.). 24p. (J). (gr. 1-4). 1989. 17.50 (0-87614-347-8, Carolrhoda); pap. 5.95 (0-87614-514-4, Carolrhoda) Lerner Group.

Count Your Way Through Canada. Jim Haskins. (Count Your Way Bks.). (Illus.). 24p. (J). (gr. 1-4). 1989. 17.50 (0-87614-350-8, Carolrhoda); pap. 5.95 (0-87614-515-2, Carolrhoda) Lerner Group.

Count Your Way Through China. Jim Haskins. (Count Your Way Bks.). (Illus.). 24p. (J). (gr. 1-4). 1987. lib. bdg. 17.50 (0-87614-302-8, Carolrhoda) Lerner Group.

Count Your Way Through China. Jim Haskins. (Count Your Way Picture Bks.). (Illus.). 24p. (J). (gr. 1-4). 1988. pap. 5.95 (0-87614-486-5, Lerner Publctns) Lerner Group.

Count Your Way Through Germany. Jim Haskins. (Count Your Way Bks.). (Illus.). 24p. (J). (gr. 1-4). 1990. lib. bdg. 17.50 (0-87614-407-5, Carolrhoda) Lerner Group.

Count Your Way Through Germany. Jim Haskins. LC 89-22232. (J). (gr. 1-4). 1991. pap. 5.95 (0-87614-532-2, Carolrhoda) Lerner Group.

Count Your Way Through India. Jim Haskins. (Count Your Way Bks.). (Illus.). 24p. (J). (gr. 1-4). 1990. lib. bdg. 17.50 (0-87614-414-8, Carolrhoda) Lerner Group.

Count Your Way Through India. Jim Haskins. (J). (gr. 1-4). 1992. pap. 5.95 (0-87614-577-2, Carolrhoda) Lerner Group.

Count Your Way Through Israel. Jim Haskins. (Count Your Way Bks.). (Illus.). 24p. (J). (gr. 1-4). 1990. lib. bdg. 17.50 (0-87614-415-6, Carolrhoda) Lerner Group.

Count Your Way Through Israel. Jim Haskins. (J). (ps-3). 1992. pap. 5.95 (0-87614-558-6, Carolrhoda) Lerner Group.

Count Your Way Through Italy. Jim Haskins. (Count Your Way Bks.). (Illus.). 24p. (J). (gr. 1-4). 1990. lib. bdg. 17.50 (0-87614-406-7, Carolrhoda) Lerner Group.

Count Your Way Through Italy. Jim Haskins. LC 89-37455. (J). (ps-3). 1991. pap. 5.95 (0-87614-533-0, Carolrhoda) Lerner Group.

Count Your Way Through Japan. Jim Haskins. (Count Your Way Bks.). (Illus.). 24p. (J). (gr. 1-4). 1987. lib. bdg. 17.50 (0-87614-301-X, Carolrhoda); pap. 5.95 (0-87614-485-7, Carolrhoda) Lerner Group.

Count Your Way Through Korea. Jim Haskins. (Count Your Way Bks.). (Illus.). 24p. (J). (gr. 1-4). 1989. 17.50 (0-87614-348-6, Carolrhoda); pap. 5.95 (0-87614-516-0, Carolrhoda) Lerner Group.

Count Your Way Through Mexico. Jim Haskins. (Count Your Way Bks.). (Illus.). 24p. (J). (gr. 1-4). 1989. 17.50 (0-87614-349-4, Carolrhoda); pap. 5.95 (0-87614-517-9, Carolrhoda) Lerner Group.

Count Your Way Through Russia. Jim Haskins. (Count Your Way Bks.). (Illus.). 24p. (J). (gr. 1-4). 1987. lib. bdg. 17.50 (0-87614-303-6, Carolrhoda); pap. 5.95 (0-87614-488-1, Carolrhoda) Lerner Group.

Count Your Way Through the Arab World. Jim Haskins. (Count Your Way Bks.). (Illus.). 24p. (J). (gr. 1-4). 1987. lib. bdg. 17.50 (0-87614-304-4, Carolrhoda); pap. 5.95 (0-685-13264-1, Carolrhoda) Lerner Group.

Count Your Way Through the Arab World. Jim Haskins. (Count Your Way Picture Bks.). (Illus.). 24p. (J). (gr. 1-4). 1988. pap. 5.95 (0-87614-487-3, Lerner Publctns) Lerner Group.

Count Zeppelin - A System Builder: The Zeppelin Company & Its Subsidiaries. John Provan. (Illus.). 128p. (Orig.). 1988. pap. 11.75 (0-945794-07-X) Luftschiff-Zeppelin.

Count Zero. William Gibson. 256p. 1987. mass mkt. 5.99 (0-441-11773-2) Ace Bks.

Count Zinzendorf: The Story of His Life & Leadership in the Renewed Moravian Church. John R. Weinlick. LC 56-5375. (Illus.). 240p. 1989. reprint ed. pap. 8.00 (0-685-29863-9) Moravian Ch in Amer.

Countdown. Jerry Ahern. (Survivalist Ser.: No. 26). 352p. 1993. pap. 3.50 (0-8217-4229-9) Zebra.

Countdown. Keith Douglass. (Carrier Ser.: No. 6). 336p. (Orig.). 1994. mass mkt. 4.99 (0-515-11309-3) Jove Pubns.

Countdown. William Doxey. 352p. (Orig.). 1986. pap. 3.50 (0-8439-2321-0) Dorchester Pub Co.

Countdown. David Hagberg. 1991. mass mkt. 4.95 (0-8125-0964-1) Tor Bks.

Countdown. Lindsay McKenna. 1994. mass mkt. 3.50 (0-373-09890-1, 5-09890-0) Harlequin Bks.

Countdown. Dorothy Montgomery. (Illus.). (J). (gr. k-6). 1966. 4.50 (3-901170-10-3) CEF Press.

Countdown. Joe M. Parkhill & Theodore Perry. (Orig.). 1983. spiral bd. 4.95 (0-936744-09-X) Country Bazaar.

Countdown! Rice. 1990. pap. 18.95 (0-8384-3379-0) Heinle & Heinle.

Countdown! Thirty-Five Missions over Germany. Fred Koger. 224p. 1990. 18.95 (0-945575-17-3) Algonquin Bks.

Countdown see Cuenta Regresiva

Countdown at Eighty: An American Perspective. Henry Chapin. LC 77-4360. (Illus.). 1977. pap. 8.95 (0-87233-041-9) Bauhan.

***Countdown at Sheperd Square.** Dalton Stephenson. 112p. (Orig.). 1994. pap. write for info. (1-56167-178-9) Am Literary Pr.

***Countdown Cooking: Recipes Low in Cholesterol, Calories, Sodium, Sugar & Fat.** Rae Udy. 200p. 1994. pap. 14.95 (0-9642434-0-7) Weese Ent.

Countdown to Better Bridge. H. W. Kelsey. 190p. 1991. pap. 9.95 (0-910791-22-8) Devyn Pr.

Countdown to Black Genocide. Saggittarus. LC 73-78108. 128p. reprint ed. 5.95 (0-912444-14-2) DARE Bks.

Countdown to Cassino: The Battle of Mignano Gap, 1943. Alex Bowlby. (Illus.). 256p. 1994. 42.50 (0-85052-410-5, Pub. by L Cooper Bks UK) Trans-Atl Phila.

***Countdown to Cassino: The Battle of Mignano Gap, 1943.** Alex Bowlby. (Illus.). 276p. 1995. 24.95 (1-885119-16-X) Sarpedon.

Countdown to Christmas. Illus. by Joe Boddy. (Counting Book Ser.). 48p. (J). (ps). 1992. 6.95 (0-88101-230-0) Unicorn Pub.

Countdown to Christmas. Bill Peet. LC 72-78394. (Illus.). 48p. (J). (gr. k-8). 1972. lib. bdg. 12.00 (0-516-08716-9, Golden Gate) Childrens.

***Countdown to Christmas: Advent Thoughts, Prayers & Activities.** Susan H. O'Keefe. LC 95-16257. (Illus.). 80p. (Orig.). (J). (gr. 4-8). 1995. pap. 4.95 (0-8091-6628-3) Paulist Pr.

Countdown to Christmas: On Its Way. Better Homes & Gardens Staff. 1994. 19.95 (0-696-00047-4) Meredith Bks.

Countdown to Christmas: Round the Corner. Better Homes & Gardens Staff. 1994. 19.95 (0-696-00048-2) Meredith Bks.

Countdown to Christmas: Tis the Season. Better Homes & Gardens Staff. 1994. 19.95 (0-696-00049-0) Meredith Bks.

Countdown to College. Zola D. Schneider & Phyllis B. Kalb. 140p. 1989. pap. 9.95 (0-87447-335-7) College Bd.

***Countdown to Dinosaur Doom!** Graham Coleman. LC 95-3826. (Illus.). (J). 1995. write for info. (0-8120-9415-8) Barron.

Countdown to Eternity: Prologue to Destiny. Woody Young & Chuck Missler. 208p. 1992. 19.95 (0-939513-53-6) Joy Pub SJC.

***Countdown to Flight.** Steve Englehart. LC 95-6193. (J). 1995. write for info. (0-380-77918-8, Camelot Young) Avon.

Countdown to Halloween. Dan Witkowski. (Illus.). (J). (ps up). 1994. 7.99 (0-679-86948-4) Random Bks Yng Read.

***Countdown to His Coming.** Bob Yandian. 1995. pap. 9.99 (0-88419-390-X) Strang Comms Co.

Countdown to Manassas. Ken Drew. (Illus.). 56p. (Orig.). 1989. pap. 2.35 (0-9622714-1-1) K Drew.

Countdown to Nineteen Ninety-Seven: Report of a Mission to Hong-Kong. International Commission of Jurists Staff & William Goodhart. 132p. reprint ed. pap. 37.70 (0-7837-6982-2, 2046794) Bks Demand.

Countdown to Perfection: Take a Giant Step Forward - in This Lifetime! rev. ed. Richard S. Clarke. (Illus.). 256p. 1992. pap. 9.99 (0-934363-10-2) Lance Pubns.

Countdown to Rapture. Salem Kirban. (Illus.). 1977. pap. 5.95 (0-912582-26-X) Kirban.

Countdown to Rebellion: British Policy in Cyprus, 1939-1955. George H. Kelling. LC 89-26002. (Contributions in Comparative Colonial Studies: No. 27). 200p. 1990. text ed. 49.95 (0-313-26848-7, KBP/, Greenwood Pr) Greenwood.

Countdown to Retirement for Educators. Wilson Riles & Jessie Heizman. 240p. 1985. pap. 9.95 (0-944223-00-1, BoothMark Bks) Moonlght Pr.

Countdown to Space Fleet Landing. Ruth E. Norman. (Tesla Speaks Ser.: Vol. VII). (Illus.). 1974. pap. 7.95 (0-932642-28-4) Unarius Acad Sci.

***Countdown to Space Ser., 6 vols.** Michael D. Cole. Incl. Apollo 11: First Moon Landing. LC 94-30001. (Illus.). 48p. (J). (gr. 4-10). 1995. lib. bdg. 15.95 (0-89490-539-2); Friendship 7: First American in Orbit. LC 94-29433. (Illus.). 48p. (J). (gr. 4-10). 1995. lib. bdg. 15.95 (0-89490-540-6); Columbia: First Flight of the Space Shuttle. LC 94-41181. (Illus.). 48p. (J). (gr. 4-10). 1995. lib. bdg. 15.95 (0-89490-543-0); Apollo 13: Space Emergency. LC 94-41179. (Illus.). 48p. (J). (gr. 4-10). 1995. lib. bdg. 15.95 (0-89490-542-2); Vostok 1: First Human in Space. LC 94-41180. (Illus.). 48p. (J). (gr. 4-10). 1995. lib. bdg. 15.95 (0-89490-541-4); Challenger: America's Space Tragedy. LC 94-41177. (Illus.). 48p. (J). (gr. 4-10). 1995. lib. bdg. 15.95 (0-89490-544-9); 95.70 (0-89490-562-7) Enslow Pubs.

Countdown to the First Day of School. Leo M. Schell & Paul Burden. LC 92-24110. (Checklist Ser.). 56p. 1992. 4.95 (0-8106-2150-9, NEA Prof Lib) NEA.

Countdown to the Millennium: Demystifying the Drama of These Last Days. Mona Johnian. 242p. (Orig.). 1994. pap. 7.95 (0-88270-719-1) Bridge Pub.

Countdown to the Moon. Steve Englehart. LC 94-5135. (Avon Camelot Book Ser.). (Illus.). 96p. (Orig.). (J). 1994. pap. 3.99 (0-380-77538-7, Camelot) Avon.

Countdown to the Moon. Susan D. Gold. LC 91-30360. (Adventures in Space Ser.). (Illus.). 48p. (J). (gr. 5-6). 1992. text ed. 12.95 (0-89686-689-0, Crstwood Hse) Silver Burdett Pr.

***Countdown to the Second Coming.** Dave Hunt. (Orig.). 1991. pap. 2.50 (0-614-05560-1) Harvest Hse.

Countdown to the Third Millennium: Your Unique, Personal Calendar-Journal from Now Through 2000. Peter Tracy et al. 218p. (Orig.). 1993. pap. text ed. 14.95 (0-9636404-0-2) Millennium IL.

Countdown to Violence: The Charlestown Convent Riot of 1834. Wilfred J. Bisson. (Nineteenth Century American Political & Social History Ser.). 154p. 1989. reprint ed. 54.00 (0-8240-4064-3) Garland.

Countdown to 1900: World Evangelization at the End of the Nineteenth Century. Todd M. Johnson. (AD 2000 Ser.). 73p. (Orig.). 1988. pap. text ed. 5.95 (0-936625-69-4, New Hope AL) Womans Mission Union.

Counted Cross Stitch. Angela Wainwright. (Letts Creative Needlecrafts Ser.). (Illus.). 92p. 1992. 16.95 (1-85238-105-1, Pub. by New Holland Pubs UK) Sterling.

Counted-Thread Embroidery. Helen Fairfield. (Illus.). 160p. 1987. pap. 10.95 (0-312-00965-8) St Martin.

***Countee Cullen: Poet.** Ed. by Nathan I. Huggins. (Black Americans of Achievement Ser.). (Illus.). 144p. (YA). (gr. 5 up). 1995. 18.95 (0-7910-1869-5) Chelsea Hse.

Counter-Arts Conspiracy: Art & Industry in the Age of Blake. Morris Eaves. LC 92-52749. (Illus.). 320p. (C). 1992. 37.95 (0-8014-2489-5) Cornell U Pr.

***Counter Attack.** David Galerstein. 300p. 1996. pap. 9.95 (0-7610-0459-9) NW Pub.

Counter Attack: Beating Football's Attack Defenses. Michael D. Koehler. LC 86-773. 199p. 1986. text ed. 21.95 (0-13-183575-0, Parker Publishing Co) P-H.

Counter-Attack: Isshinryu Self Defense for Men & Women. Harold Long & Allen Wheeler. Ed. by Steve Condry. (Illus.). 96p. 1983. pap. 5.95 (0-89826-010-8) Natl Paperback.

Counter-Clockwise. John M. Lee. LC 73-18591. reprint ed. 29.50 (0-404-11402-4) AMS Pr.

Counter Colon-Ialismo. Patricio Chavez et al. 96p. 1991. 15.00 (0-9631354-0-6) C C De La Raza.

Counter Cultures: Saleswomen, Managers, & Customers in American Department Stores, 1890-1940. Susan P. Benson. LC 85-21012. (Working Class in American History Ser.). (Illus.). 344p. 1986. 27.50 (0-252-01252-6) U of Ill Pr.

Counter Cultures: Saleswomen, Managers, & Customers in American Department Stores, 1890-1940. Susan P. Benson. LC 85-21012. (Working Class in American History Ser.). (Illus.). 344p. 1988. pap. 12.95 (0-252-06013-X) U of Ill Pr.

Counter Current Extraction. S. Hartland. LC 69-17867. (C). 1970. 120.00 (0-08-012976-5, Pub. by Pergamon Repr UK) Franklin.

Counter-Currents. Agnes Repplier. LC 73-121504. (Essay Index Reprint Ser.). 1977. 23.95 (0-8369-2026-0) Ayer.

Counter-Dependency: The Flight from Intimacy. Barry K. Weinhold & Janae B. Weinhold. 251p. (Orig.). 1992. pap. 12.95 (1-882056-00-0) CICRCL Pr.

Counter-Examples in Differential Equations & Related Topics. J. M. Rassias. 192p. 1991. text ed. 48.00 (981-02-0460-4); pap. text ed. 25.00 (981-02-0461-2) World Scientific Pub.

Counter Force. Dan Streib. 192p. (Orig.). 1983. pap. 2.50 (0-449-12387-1, GM) Fawcett.

Counter-Guerilla Operations. 1991. lib. bdg. 79.95 (0-8490-4073-6) Gordon Pr.

Counter-Insurgency: Armies & Guerilla Warfare. 1991. lib. bdg. 88.95 (0-8490-4981-4) Gordon Pr.

Counter-Insurgency in Kenya: A Study of Military Operations Against Mau Mau, 1952-1960. Anthony Clayton. 64p. 1984. pap. text ed. 5.00 (0-89745-061-2) Sunflower U Pr.

Counter-Measures. W. Michael Gear. (Forbidden Borders Ser.: No. 3). 648p. (Orig.). 1993. mass mkt. 5.99 (0-88677-564-7) DAW Bks.

Counter Meditation. Kit Robinson. 42p. 1991. pap. 7.00 (84-87467-09-1) SPD-Small Pr Dist.

Counter-Modernism in Current Critical Theory. Geoffrey Thurley. LC 83-23107. 266p. 1983. text ed. 29.95 (0-312-17020-3) St Martin.

Counter Play. Anne Snyder. 176p. (Orig.). 1981. pap. 2.25 (0-451-11898-7, AE1898, Sig) NAL-Dutton.

Counter-Poyson..., to the Objections & Reproaches, Wherewith the Answerer to the Abstract, Would Disgrace the Holy Discipline of Christ. Dudley Fenner. LC 74-28854. (English Experience Ser.: No. 735). 1975. reprint ed. 20.00 (90-221-0735-3) Walter J Johnson.

Counter-Reformation. Nicholas S. Davidson. 96p. 1987. pap. text ed. 12.95 (0-631-14888-4) Blackwell Pubs.

Counter-Reformation. A. G. Dickens. (Library of World Civilization). (Illus.). (C). 1979. pap. text ed. 9.95 (0-393-95086-7) Norton.

***Counter Reformation: Religion & Society in Early Modern Europe.** Martin D. Jones. (Cambridge Topics in History Ser.). (Illus.). 128p. (C). 1995. pap. 14.95 (0-521-43993-0) Cambridge U Pr.

Counter-Reformation & Price Revolution, 1559-1610 see New Cambridge Modern History

Counter-Reformation in the Villages: Religion & Reform in the Bishopric of Speyer, 1560-1720. Marc R. Forster. LC 91-55564. (Illus.). 288p. 1992. 39.95 (0-8014-2566-2) Cornell U Pr.

Counter-Reformation Prince: Anti-Machiavellianism or Catholic Statecraft in Early Modern Europe. Robert Bireley. LC 90-31805. (Illus.). xiv, 310p. (C). 1990. 45.00 (0-8078-1925-5) U of NC Pr.

Counter-Reformation, 1550-1600. Beresford J. Kidd. LC 79-8713. 270p. 1980. reprint ed. text ed. 59.75 (0-313-22193-6, KICR, Greenwood Pr) Greenwood.

Counter-Revolution: Doctrine & Action, 1789-1804. Jacques L. Godechot. LC 70-159820. 415p. reprint ed. pap. 118.30 (0-8357-3420-X, 2039677) Bks Demand.

***Counter-revolution: The Second Civil War & Its Origins, 1646-48.** Robert Ashton. LC 94-19546. 1995. 45.00 (0-300-06114-5) Yale U Pr.

Counter-Revolution in France, 1787-1830. James Roberts. LC 89-70226. 134p. 1990. text ed. 45.00 (0-312-04568-9) St Martin.

Counter-Revolution in Hungary, Nineteen Fifty-Six: Words & Weapons. Janos Berecz. 224p. (C). 1986. 115.00x (0-569-08926-3, Pub. by Collets UK) Pro-Am Music.

Counter Revolution in Hungary 1956. Janos Berecz. (Words & Weapons Ser.). 1986. 60.00 (0-685-18360-2, Pub. by Collets UK) Pro-Am Music.

Counter-Revolution of Science. Friedrich A. Hayek. LC 79-21045. 416p. 1980. reprint ed. pap. 4.00 (0-913966-67-3) Liberty Fund.

Counter Sniper Guide. 1986. lib. bdg. 79.95 (0-8490-3494-9) Gordon Pr.

Counter Sniper Guide. U. S. Army Staff. (Illus.). 36p. 1977. reprint ed. pap. 8.00 (0-87364-069-1) Paladin Pr.

Counter-Statement. Kenneth Burke. LC 68-20356. 1968. pap. 11.00 (0-520-00196-6) U CA Pr.

Counter-Terra. Frederick Turner. 1977. 5.00 (0-87922-053-8) Christophers Bks.

Counter-Terrorism Handbook: Tactics, Procedures, & Techniques. F. Bolz et al. (Practical Aspects of Criminal & Forensic Investigations Ser.). 248p. 1992. 45.00 (0-444-01524-8, HV6431) CRC Pr.

Counter-Terrorist. Sam Hall. LC 87-81425. 336p. 1987. 18.95 (1-55611-049-9) D I Fine.

Counterattack: Taking Back Ground Lost to Sin. Jay Carty. Ed. by Liz Heaney. LC 88-5210. 208p. 1988. pap. 8.99 (0-88070-233-8, Multnomah Bks) Questar Pubs.

Counterattack: The West's Battle Against the Terrorists. Christopher Dobson & Ronald Payne. LC 82-1589. 220p. reprint ed. pap. 62.70 (0-8357-4238-5, 2037025) Bks Demand.

Counterattack on the Naktong 1950. William G. Robertson. LC 86-2637. (Leavenworth Papers: No. 13). (Illus.). 149p. (Orig.). 1985. pap. 7.00 (0-16-001643-6, S/N 008-020-01079-1) USGPO.

Counterbomb: Protecting Yourself Against Car, Mail, & Area-Emplaced Bombs. Lawrence W. Myers. (Illus.). 96p. 1991. pap. 14.00 (0-87364-608-8) Paladin Pr.

Counterclockwise: Perspectives on Communication from Dallas Smythe. Dallas Smythe. Ed. by Thomas Guback. LC 93-24880. (Critical Studies in Communication & in the Cultural Industries). 1993. text ed. 63.00 (0-8133-1561-1) Westview.

Counterclockwise: Perspectives on Communication from Dallas Smythe. Dallas Smythe. Ed. by Thomas Guback. LC 93-24880. (Critical Studies in Communication & in the Cultural Industries). (C). 1993. pap. text ed. 21.50 (0-8133-1907-2) Westview.

Counterclockwise: Reflections of a Maverick. Michael Drury. 1987. 12.95 (0-8027-0942-7) Walker & Co.

Countercultural Communes: A Sociological Perspective. Gilbert Zicklin. LC 82-21086. (Contributions in Sociology Ser.: No. 44). xv, 198p. 1983. text ed. 49.95 (0-313-20709-7, ZIC/, Greenwood Pr) Greenwood.

***Countercultural South.** Jack T. Kirby. (Mercer University Lamar Memorial Lectures: Vol. 38). 1995. write for info. (0-8203-1723-3) U of Ga Pr.

Counterculture. George Bailin. Ed. by Eric Friedman et al. (C). 1982. pap. 7.50 (0-942856-00-7) Seaport Poets & Writers.

***Countercultures: A Sociological Analysis.** William W. Zellner. 224p. 1994. pap. text ed. 12.50 (0-312-08084-0) St Martin.

Countercultures: The Promise & the Peril of a World Turned Upside Down. J. Milton Yinger. LC 81-17276. 371p. (C). 1984. pap. 16.95 (0-02-934010-1) Free Pr.

Countercurrent Chromatography: Apparatus, Theory & Applications. Walter D. Conway. LC 89-14697. 475p. 1990. text ed. 80.00 (0-89573-331-5) VCH Pubs.

Countercurrent Chromatography: Theory & Practice. Mandava & Ito. (Chromatographic Science Ser.: Vol. 44). 752p. 1988. 199.00 (0-8247-7815-4) Dekker.

Countercurrents: On the Primacy of Texts in Literary Criticism. Raymond A. Prier. LC 91-13268. (SUNY Series, The Margins of Literature). 302p. 1992. 59.50 (0-7914-0941-4); pap. 19.95 (0-7914-0942-2) State U NY Pr.

Counterexamples in Probability. Jordan M. Stoyanov. LC 87-1330. (Probability & Mathematical Statistics Ser.). 313p. 1988. text ed. 250.00 (0-471-91649-8) Wiley.

Counterexamples in Probability & Real Analysis. Gary L. Wise & Eric B. Hall. 256p. 1993. 39.95 (0-19-507068-2) OUP.

Counterexamples in Probability & Statistics. Joseph P. Romano & Andrew F. Siegel. LC 85-19024. (Statistics Ser.). 303p. (C). 1986. boxed 46.50 (0-534-05568-0) Chapman & Hall.

***Counterexamples in Topology.** Lynn A. Steen & J. Arthur Seebach, Jr. LC 95-12763. 1995. pap. write for info. (0-486-68735-X) Dover.

Counterfactuals. David Lewis. LC 72-78430. 1973. 10.00 (0-674-17540-9) HUP.

Counterfactuals. David Lewis. LC 72-78430. 160p. 1987. pap. 12.95 (0-674-17541-7) HUP.

Counterfeit Blessings: The Anti-Christ by Any Name: Khazars. Gyeorgos C. Hatonn. Tr. by Dharma. 257p. (Orig.). (C). 1991. pap. 10.00 (0-922356-36-X) Amer West Pubs.

Counterfeit Bride. Vivian Connolly. (Coventry Romance Ser.: No. 68). 224p. 1980. pap. 1.75 (0-449-50099-3, Coventry) Fawcett.

Counterfeit Caress. Elizabeth Leigh. 1991. mass mkt. 4.25 (0-8217-3585-3) Zebra.

Counterfeit Christ of the New Age Movement. Ron Rhodes. LC 90-43495. 256p. (Orig.). 1990. pap. 11.99 (0-8010-7757-5) Baker Bk.

Counterfeit Christmas. Carolyn Keene. Ed. by Ruth Ashby. (NDF Ser.: No. 102). 160p. (Orig.). (J). 1994. mass mkt. 3.99 (0-671-88193-0, Archway) PB.

Counterfeit Coachman. Elisabeth Fairchild. 224p. (Orig.). 1994. pap. 3.99 (0-451-18155-7) NAL-Dutton.

Counterfeit Cowgirl: Back to the Ranch. Heather Allison. (Romance Ser.). 1994. mass mkt. 2.99 (0-373-03309-5, 1-03309-1) Harlequin Bks.

Counterfeit Currency: How to Really Make Money. M. Thomas Collins. LC 90-62407. (Illus.). 144p. (Orig.). 1990. pap. 15.00 (1-55950-042-5, 40069) Loompanics.

Counterfeit Detection, Vol. 1. 1983. reprint ed. 7.50 (0-317-12575-3) American Numismatic.

Counterfeit Detection, Vol. II. 1988. reprint ed. 9.95 (0-318-41034-6) American Numismatic.

An Asterisk (*) at the beginning of an entry indicates that the title is appearing in BIP for the first time.

C

An Asterisk (*) at the beginning of an entry indicates that the title is appearing in BIP for the first time.

1651

Countesse of Lincolnes Nurserie. Elizabeth Clinton. LC 74-28838. (English Experience Ser.: No. 720). 1975. reprint ed. 25.00 (*90-221-0720-5*) Walter J Johnson.

Countesse of Pembroke's Arcadia, 2 vols., Set. Philip Sidney. LC 82-10288. 1983. 80.00 (*0-8201-1382-4*) Schol Facsimiles.

Counties & Regions of the U. K. 3rd ed. David Mort & Marcus Woolley. 250p. 1994. 76.95 (*0-566-02972-3*, Pub. by Avebury Pub UK) Ashgate Pub Co.

Counties & Regions of the UK. University of Warwick Business Information Service Staff. 176p. 1988. text ed. 54.95 (*0-566-02755-0*, Pub. by Gower UK) Ashgate Pub Co.

***Counties in Court: Jail Overcrowding & Court-Ordered Reform.** Wayne N. Welsh. LC 94-47139. 288p. (C). 1995. lib. bdg. 49.95 (*1-56639-340-X*); pap. text ed. 22.95 (*1-56639-341-8*) Temple U Pr.

***Counties of Britain: A Tudor Atlas.** John Speed. (Illus.). 228p. 1995. pap. 24.95 (*1-85793-612-4*, Pub. by Pavilion UK) Trafalgar.

Counties of Clay & Owen, Indiana. Charles Blanchard. (Illus.). 966p. 1992. reprint ed. lib. bdg. 95.00 (*0-8328-2535-2*) Higginson Bk Co.

Counties of Cumberland, Jasper & Richland, Illinois. (Illus.). 839p. 1993. reprint ed. lib. bdg. 84.00 (*0-8328-3512-9*) Higginson Bk Co.

Counties of La Grange & Noble, Indiana. (Illus.). 502p. 1993. reprint ed. lib. bdg. 52.50 (*0-8328-3450-5*) Higginson Bk Co.

Counties of Morgan, Monroe, & Brown, Indiana. Ed. by Charles Blanchard. (Illus.). 800p. 1992. reprint ed. lib. bdg. 79.50 (*0-8328-2550-6*) Higginson Bk Co.

Counties of Tennessee. Austin P. Foster. (Illus.). 124p. 1992. reprint ed. pap. 14.00 (*0-685-62592-3*, 9086) Clearfield Co.

Counties of Warren, Benton, Jasper & Newton, Indiana. (Illus.). 810p. 1992. reprint ed. lib. bdg. 81.00 (*0-8328-2562-X*) Higginson Bk Co.

Counties of White & Pulaski, Indiana. (Illus.). 772p. 1992. reprint ed. lib. bdg. 78.00 (*0-8328-2574-3*) Higginson Bk Co.

Counties of Whitley & Noble, 2 pts. Ed. by Weston A. Goodspeed & Charles Blanchard. (Illus.). 428p. 1992. reprint ed. Pt. I, 428p. lib. bdg. 49.00 (*0-8328-2571-9*); reprint ed. Pt. II, 502p. lib. bdg. 49.00 (*0-8328-2572-7*) Higginson Bk Co.

Counting. (Sticker Activity Ser.). (Illus.). 16p. (J). (gr. 3 up). 1993. 6.95 (*1-56458-395-3*) Dorling Kindersley.

Counting. (Ready to Learn Ser.: No. S813-3). (J). 1989. pap. 1.95 (*0-7214-5180-2*) Ladybird Bks.

Counting. (Look & Learn Ser.). (Illus.). 24p. (J). 1993. 7.98 (*1-56173-908-1*) Pubns Intl Ltd.

***Counting.** (Tab Board Bks.). (J). Date not set. bds. 4.95 (*0-7894-0232-7*, 5-70644) Dorling Kindersley.

Counting. Liz Jonson & Emery Silliman. Ed. by Judith E. Nayer. (Learn Today for Tomorrow Ser.). (Illus.). 32p. (J). (gr. k-1). 1991. student ed 1.95 (*1-878624-54-7*) McClanahan Bk.

Counting. Photos by Stephen Oliver. LC 90-8577. (My First Look At Ser.). (Illus.). 24p. (J). (ps-00). 1991. 7.00 (*0-679-81163-X*) Random Bks Yng Read.

Counting. Istar Schwager. (Look & Learn Ser.). (Illus.). 24p. (J). (ps-3). 1993. lib. bdg. 12.95 (*1-56674-067-3*, HTS Bks) Forest Hse.

***Counting: A Book about Counting.** Anne M. Miranda. Ed. by Jean Crawford. (Snugglebug Bks.). (Illus.). 24p. (J). (ps). 1994. lib. bdg. write for info. (*0-7835-4502-9*) Time-Life.

Counting: A Turn-the-Wheel Book. Mavis Smith. (Wheelies Ser.). (Illus.). 12p. (J). 1994. 4.50 (*0-307-17376-3*, Artsts Writrs) Western Pub.

***Counting: The Story of the Lost Coin.** Mack Thomas. (J). 1995. 4.99 (*0-88070-758-5*, Gold & Honey) Questar Pubs.

Counting & Coloring Dinosaurs: An Educational Coloring Book. Spizzirri Publishing Co. Staff. Ed. by Linda Spizzirri. (Illus.). 32p. (J). (gr. 1-8). 1982. pap. 1.75 (*0-86545-044-7*) Spizzirri.

Counting Back: Voices of the Lakota & Pioneer Settlers. Sylvia G. Wheeler. LC 91-37984. 120p. 1992. 12.95 (*0-933532-85-7*) BkMk.

Counting Bears. Lucinda McQueen. (Wee Pudgy Board Bks.). (Illus.). 24p. (J). (gr. 1-3). 1990. bds. 2.50 (*0-448-02263-X*, G&D) Putnam Pub Group.

Counting Books Are More Than Numbers: An Annotated Action Bibliography. Patricia L. Roberts. x, 264p. (C). 1989. lib. bdg. 36.00 (*0-208-02216-3*, Lib Prof Pubns) Shoe String.

***Counting by Kangaroos.** Joy N. Hulme. LC 95-13880. (Illus.). (J). 1995. text ed. write for info. (*0-7167-6602-7*, Sci Am Yng Rdrs) W H Freeman.

Counting by Tens & Fives. Renee Z. Novit. (Kidz & Katz Educational Learning Book Ser.). (Illus.). 16p. (J). (ps-00). Date not set. pap. 7.95 (*1-883371-02-3*) Kidz & Katz.

Counting Caterpillars. Barbara Gregorich. Ed. by Joan Hoffman. (Fast Forward Enrichment Ser.). 32p. (Orig.). (J). (ps-1). 1986. student ed 1.99 (*0-88743-126-7*) Sch Zone Pub Co.

***Counting Cats.** Michi Fujimoto. LC 94-68592. (Beethoven Ser.: No. 1). (Illus.). 24p. (J). (ps up). 1995. pap. 2.95 (*0-8431-3839-4*) Price Stern.

Counting Coup & Cutting Horses: Intertribal Warfare on the Northern Plains, 1738-1889. Anthony McGinnis. LC 90-45306. (Illus.). 250p. 1990. pap. 14.95 (*0-917895-29-0*) Cordillera CO.

***Counting Cows.** Woody Jackson. LC 94-22927. (J). (gr. 1-8). 1994. write for info. (*0-15-220165-3*) HarBrace.

***Counting Cows.** Dyan Sheldon. (Illus.). 32p. (J). (ps-1). 1994. 19.95 (*0-09-176467-X*, Pub. by Batsford UK) Trafalgar.

Counting Cranes. Mary B. Owens. (J). (ps-3). 1993. 14.95 (*0-316-67719-1*) Little.

Counting Down the Days in the Mechlenburg County Jail. Ron Watson. 1994. pap. 5.95 (*0-685-72047-0*) Pudding Hse Pubns.

Counting for Something: Effective User Feedback in Mental Health Services. Ed. by Rob Leiper & Vida Field. 160p. 1993. 54.95 (*1-85628-477-8*, Pub. by Avebury Pub UK) Ashgate Pub Co.

Counting for Something: Statistical Principles & Personalities. W. S. Peters. (Texts in Statistics Ser.). (Illus.). 305p. 1986. 39.00 (*0-387-96364-2*) Spr-Verlag.

Counting Friends. Rebecca Gryspeerdt. (Illus.). 24p. (J). (ps-1). 1993. 13.95 (*1-85681-092-5*, Pub. by J MacRae UK) Trafalgar.

Counting Gypsies. Hazel Green. 156p. 1991. pap. 25.00 (*0-11-752444-1*, HM8852) UNIPUB.

Counting Hawaiian Petroglyphs. Cassandra Land-Nellist. (Hawaiian Treasures Ser.). (Illus.). 10p. (J). (ps). 1993. 3.95 (*0-916630-74-9*) Pr Pacifica.

Counting House: Thomas Thompson of Hull & His Family, 1751-1828. Ed. by A. R. Robinson. (C). 45.00 (*1-85072-102-5*, Pub. by W Sessions UK) St Mut.

Counting-House Days in South Street: New York's Early Brick Seaport Buildings. Ellen F. Rosebrock. (Illus.). (Orig.). 1975. pap. 2.50 (*0-913344-18-4*) South St Sea Mus.

Counting Jennie. Helena C. Pittman. (J). (ps-3). 19.95 (*0-87614-745-7*, Carolrhoda) Lerner Group.

Counting Kangaroos, A Book about Numbers. Marcia Leonard. LC 89-4960. (Illus.). 24p. (J). (gr. k-2). 1990. lib. bdg. 9.59 (*0-8167-1722-2*); pap. text ed. 2.50 (*0-8167-1723-0*) Troll Assocs.

Counting Kids. Annie Kubler. LC 90-1978. (Bead Frame Ser.). (J). 1989. 11.95 (*0-85953-241-0*) Childs Play.

***Counting Lift the Flap Book.** 1995. 9.99 (*0-88705-642-3*) Joshua Morris.

Counting Molecules-Approaching the Limit of Chemical Analysis. 1982. 9.50 (*0-910362-20-3*) Chem Educ.

Counting Money. Fred Justus. (Math Ser.). 24p. (gr. 2-4). 1979. student ed 5.00 (*0-8209-0113-X*, A-23) ESP.

Counting Money. John McNutt. 1992. 149.00 (*1-56304-032-8*) J Stanfield.

Counting Myself Lucky: Selected Poems, 1963-1992. Edward Field. LC 92-32538. 307p. (Orig.). (C). 1992. 25.00 (*0-87685-891-4*); pap. 12.50 (*0-87685-890-6*) Black Sparrow.

Counting Myself Lucky: Selected Poems, 1963-1992, signed ed. deluxe ed. Edward Field. LC 92-32538. 307p. (Orig.). (C). 1992. 30.00 (*0-87685-892-2*) Black Sparrow.

Counting of Grains. Joan LaBombard. Ed. by Kathleen Iddings. LC 90-60172. (American Book Ser.). 99p. (Orig.). 1983. per., pap. text ed. 10.00 (*0-931289-03-3*) San Diego Poet Pr.

Counting on a Small Planet: Activities for Environmental Mathematics. Ann Baker & Johnny Baker. LC 91-30571. 96p. 1992. pap. text ed. 15.00 (*0-435-08327-9*, 08327) Heinemann.

***Counting on Calico.** Phyllis L. Tildes. Ed. by Elena D. Wright. (Illus.). 32p. (J). (gr. k-4). 1995. 14.95 (*0-88106-863-2*); lib. bdg. 15.88 (*0-88106-864-0*); pap. 6.95 (*0-88106-862-4*) Charlesbridge Pub.

Counting on Computer Equity: A Quick & Easy Guide for Finding Out If Your School Has a Computer Gender Gap. Jo Sanders & Mary McGinnis. (Computer Equity Ser.). 16p. 1991. pap. 4.95 (*0-8108-2369-1*) Scarecrow.

Counting on Frank. Rod Clement. LC 90-27558. (Illus.). 32p. (J). (gr. 1-3). 1991. lib. bdg. 18.60 (*0-8368-0358-2*) Gareth Stevens Inc.

***Counting on Frank: Macintosh.** (J). 1995. cd-rom 85.20 (*0-8368-1333-2*) Gareth Stevens Inc.

***Counting on Frank: Windows.** LC 90-27558. (J). 1995. cd-rom 85.20 (*0-8368-1351-0*) Gareth Stevens Inc.

Counting on Kindness: An Exploration of Dependency. Wendy Lustbader. 160p. 1991. text ed. 18.95 (*0-02-919515-2*) Free Pr.

Counting on Literature. Kathy E. Danielson. (Illus.). 32p. 1990. pap. 5.95 (*0-913839-82-5*) Bk Lures.

Counting on Math. Kathy Faggella et al. (Illus.). 108p. 1988. pap. 10.95 (*0-9615005-9-X*) First Teacher.

Counting on People: Elementary Population & Environmental Activities. Pamela Wasserman & Anne Scullard. (Reporter Ser.). (Illus.). 148p. (Orig.). 1994. teacher ed, spiral bd. 19.95 (*0-945219-04-0*) Zero Pop Growth.

Counting One to Ten. Barbara Gregorich. Ed. by Joan Hoffman. (Get Ready! Bks.). (Illus.). 32p. (J). (ps). 1983. student ed 1.99 (*0-938256-56-4*) Sch Zone Pub Co.

Counting One to Twenty. Renee Z. Novit. (Kidz & Katz Educational Learning Book Ser.). (Illus.). 16p. (J). (ps-00). Date not set. pap. 7.95 (*1-883371-01-5*) Kidz & Katz.

Counting One, Two, Three. (Picture-Word Boards Bks.). (Illus.). (J). (ps). 1985. bds. 2.98 (*0-517-47338-0*) Random Hse Value.

Counting One-Two-Three. (Illus.). 32p. (J). (gr. k-2). 1991. pap. 4.95 (*0-87449-834-1*) Modern Pub NYC.

***Counting Our Way to Maine.** Maggie Smith. LC 94-24874. (Illus.). 32p. (J). (ps-1). 1995. 14.95 (*0-531-06884-6*); lib. bdg. 14.99 (*0-531-08734-4*) Orchard Bks Watts.

Counting-Out Rhymes: A Dictionary. Ed. by Roger D. Abrahams & Lois Rankin. LC 79-22260. (American Folklore Society Bibliographical & Special Ser.: Vol. 33). 263p. 1980. text ed. 22.95 (*0-292-71057-7*) U of Tex Pr.

Counting-Out Rhymes: A Dictionary. Ed. by Roger D. Abrahams & Lois Rankin. LC 79-22260. (Publications of the American Folklore Society, Bibliographical & Special Ser.: No. 33). 263p. reprint ed. pap. 75.00 (*0-7837-0090-3*, 2040365) Bks Demand.

Counting-Out Rhymes Coloring Book. Victoria Fremont. (Illus.). (J). (gr. k-3). 1992. pap. 1.00 (*0-486-27221-4*) Dover.

Counting-Out Rhymes of Children. Henry C. Bolton. 1972. 59.95 (*0-87968-950-1*) Gordon Pr.

***Counting People in the Information Age: Final Report.** National Research Council, Panel to Evaluate the Survey of Income & Program Participation, Committee on National Statistics Commission on Behavioral &. Ed. by Duane L. Steffey & Norman M. Bradburn. 240p. (Orig.). (C). 1994. pap. text ed. 29.00 (*0-309-05178-9*) Natl Acad Pr.

Counting Processes & Survival Analysis. Thomas R. Fleming & David P. Harrington. (Series in Probability & Mathematics). 429p. 1991. text ed. 79.95 (*0-471-52218-X*) Wiley.

Counting Rhymes. (Tiny Tots Rhymes Ser.). (J). (ps). 1982. 2.95 (*0-86112-085-X*) Borden.

Counting Rhymes. Sel. by Shona McKellar. LC 93-12383. (Illus.). 32p. (J). (ps-3). 1993. 12.95 (*1-56458-309-0*) Dorling Kindersley.

Counting Sheep. Barbara McGee. (Illus.). 24p. (J). (gr. k-3). 1991. 12.95 (*1-55037-157-6*, Pub. by Annick CN); pap. 4.95 (*1-55037-160-6*, Pub. by Annick CN) Firefly Bks Ltd.

***Counting Sheep.** Suzy-Jane Tanner. (Illus.). 10p. (J). (ps). 1994. 11.97 (*1-881445-26-7*) Sandvik Pub.

Counting Sheep: From Open Range to Agribusiness on the Columbia Plateau. Alexander C. McGregor. LC 82-15903. (Illus.). 516p. 1989. pap. 14.95 (*0-295-96814-1*) U of Wash Pr.

Counting Sheep: Twenty Ways of Seeing Desert Bighorn. Ed. by Gary P. Nabhan. LC 93-12477. (Southwest Center Ser.). 260p. (Orig.). 1993. lib. bdg. 29.95 (*0-8165-1385-6*); pap. 16.95 (*0-8165-1398-8*) U of Ariz Pr.

Counting-Spanish Contando Del 1 Al 10: Counting 1 to 10. Barbara Gregorich. Ed. by Joan Hoffman. Tr. by Shepherd-Bartman. (Get-Ready Spanish Ser.). (Illus.). 32p. (Orig.). (SPA.). (J). 1987. student ed 1.99 (*0-938256-79-3*) Sch Zone Pub Co.

Counting Statistics. (Advanced Health Physics Training Ser.). (Illus.). 110p. 1981. ring bd. 69.50 (*0-87683-183-8*) GP Pub.

***Counting Survivors.** Walter McDonald. LC 94-43044. 1995. write for info. (*0-8229-3874-X*); pap. write for info. (*0-8229-5555-5*) U of Pittsburgh Pr.

Counting the Black Angels: Poems. Len Roberts. LC 93-30476. 96p. 1994. pap. 12.95 (*0-252-06381-3*) U of Ill Pr.

Counting the Camels: The Economics of Transportation in Pre-Industrial Nigeria. G. O. Ogunremi. LC 79-88989. (Illus.). 1982. 21.50 (*0-88357-092-0*) NOK Pubs.

***Counting the Change.** Joseph Powell. (QRL Poetry Book Ser.: Vol. XXVI). 20.00 (*0-614-06417-1*) Quarterly Rev.

Counting the Cost. David Drake. (Hammer's Slammers Ser.). 288p. 1987. mass mkt. 4.95 (*0-671-65355-5*) Baen Bks.

Counting the Cost: The Economics of Christian Stewardship. Robin K. Klay. LC 86-16212. (Illus.). 195p. (Orig.). reprint ed. pap. 55.60 (*0-8357-4363-2*, 2037192) Bks Demand.

Counting the Cost: The Life of Alexander Mack. William G. Willoughby. 1979. 10.95 (*0-87178-161-1*); pap. 6.95 (*0-87178-159-X*) Brethren.

Counting the Cost of Global Warming. John Broome. 150p. 1993. 50.00 (*1-874267-01-4*, Pub. by White Horse Pr UK); pap. 19.95 (*1-874267-00-6*, Pub. by White Horse Pr UK) Paul & Co Pubs.

Counting the Days: Twenty-Five Ways. Phyllis Vos Wezeman & Jude D. Fournier. 51p. (Orig.). (J). 1989. pap. 9.95 (*0-940754-77-0*) Ed Ministries.

Counting the Dead: The Epidemiology of Skeletal Populations. Tony Waldron. LC 94-8477. 1994. pap. text ed. 19.95 (*0-471-95138-2*) Wiley.

Counting the Hours: City Poems. Tom Wayman. 160p. (Orig.). (C). 1983. pap. text ed. 9.95 (*0-7710-8873-6*) Left Bank.

Counting the Internet: Monitoring Pornographic Transmissions on the Internet in the Coming Decade. Linda Bellow. Ed. by Mike Heinz. (Illus.). 84p. (Orig.). 1993. pap. 8.95 (*0-9625476-3-8*) Carnegie.

***Counting the Sums.** Rita S. Quillen. 64p. (Orig.). 1995. pap. 11.00 (*1-885912-04-8*) Sows Ear Pr.

Counting the Ways, & Listening: Two Plays. Edward Albee. 1977. pap. 4.75 (*0-8222-0242-5*) Dramatists Play.

Counting the Ways & Listening see **Plays**

Counting to Zero: Poems on Repeated Miscarriage. Marion D. Cohen. LC 88-72229. 102p. 1989. pap. 8.95 (*0-930194-18-7*) Ctr Thanatology.

Counting up to Ten. J. Tyler & G. Round. (First Learning Ser.). (Illus.). 24p. (J). (ps up). 1987. pap. 3.50 (*0-7460-0217-3*) EDC.

Counting Wildflowers. Bruce McMillan. LC 85-16607. (Illus.). 32p. (J). (ps-1). 1986. 16.00 (*0-688-02859-4*); lib. bdg. 15.93 (*0-688-02860-8*) Lothrop.

Counting Wildflowers. Bruce McMillan. Ed. by Amy Cohn. LC 85-16607. (Illus.). 32p. (J). (ps up). 1995. reprint ed. pap. 4.95 (*0-688-14027-0*, Mulberry) Morrow.

Counting with Buster Bear. Kaitlin M. Smith. (Illus.). 15p. (J). (gr. k-3). 1992. pap. 12.95 (*1-895583-15-2*) MAYA Pubs.

***Counting Zoo.** (J). Date not set. 16.98 (*0-7853-0744-3*) Pubns Intl Ltd.

Counting Zoo: A Pop-up Number Book. Lynette Ruschak. LC 91-42462. (Illus.). 24p. (J). (ps-2). 1992. pap. 13.95 (*0-689-71619-2*, Aladdin Paperbacks) S&S Childrens.

Countless Silken Ties: Collections of Poems by Writers in Maryland, Virginia & the District of Columbia. Comp. & Pref. by Joseph D. Adams. (Poet's Domain Ser.: Vol. 3). xii, 76p. 1991. pap. 5.95 (*1-880016-04-4*) Road Pubs.

Countrey Justice, Containing the Practise of the Justices of the Peace out of Their Sessions. Michael Dalton. LC 70-37969. (American Law Ser.: The Formative Years). 406p. 1972. reprint ed. 30.95 (*0-405-03996-4*) Ayer.

Countrey Justice, Containing the Practise of the Justices of the Peace Out of Their Sessions. Michael Dalton. LC 74-28844. (English Experience Ser.: No. 725). 1975. reprint ed. 42.00 (*90-221-0725-6*) Walter J Johnson.

***Countries & Concepts: An Introduction to Comparative Politics.** 5th ed. Michael G. Roskin. LC 94-32876. 464p. 1994. text ed. 32.00 (*0-13-176025-4*) P-H.

Countries & Tribes of the Persian Gulf. Samuel B. Miles. 634p. 1994. 100.00 (*1-873938-56-X*, Pub. by Garnet Pubng Ltd UK) Paul & Co Pubs.

Countries Facts. (Facts & Lists Ser.). (Illus.). 48p. (J). (gr. 3-7). 1986. lib. bdg. 12.96 (*0-88110-227-X*); pap. 5.95 (*0-86020-977-6*) EDC.

Countries of Community Europe: A Geographical Survey of Contemporary Issues. Geoffrey Parker. LC 78-23239. 1979. text ed. 29.95 (*0-312-17037-8*) St Martin.

Countries of South Asia: Boundaries, Extensions, & Interrelations. Ed. by Peter Gaeffke & David A. Utz. (Proceedings of the South Asia Seminar Ser.: No. 3). (Illus.). 167p. (Orig.). 1988. pap. 10.00 (*0-936115-02-5*) U Penn South Asia.

Countries of the Mind: Essays in Literary Criticism, 1st Series. John M. Murry. LC 68-22111. (Essay Index Reprint Ser.). 1980. 18.95 (*0-8369-0729-9*) Ayer.

Countries of the Mind: Essays in Literary Criticism, 2nd Series. John M. Murry. LC 68-22112. (Essay Index Reprint Ser.). 1977. 18.95 (*0-8369-0730-2*) Ayer.

Countries of the Mind: Literary Explorations. Monroe K. Spears. LC 92-19188. 312p. 1992. text ed. 37.50 (*0-8262-0856-8*) U of Mo Pr.

Countries of the Mind: The Fiction of J. M. Coetzee. Dick Penner. LC 88-34731. (Contributions to the Study of World Literature Ser.: No. 32). 167p. 1989. text ed. 45.00 (*0-313-26684-0*, PCD/, Greenwood Pr) Greenwood.

Countries of the Mind: The Meaning of Place to Writers. Gillian Tindall. 263p. 1991. text ed. 27.50 (*1-55553-116-4*) NE U Pr.

***Countries of the World.** LC 94-37199. (J). 1995. 35.00 (*1-85697-561-4*, Kingfisher LKC) LKC.

Countries of the World: A Visual Factfinder. Brian Williams. LC 92-40367. (Visual Factfinders Ser.). (Illus.). 96p. (J). (gr. 5 up). 1993. 15.95 (*1-85697-844-3*, Kingfisher LKC); pap. 9.95 (*1-85697-816-8*, Kingfisher LKC) LKC.

***Countries of the World Yearbook, 1995.** suppl. ed. Ed. by Brian Rajewski. 450p. 1995. 85.00 (*0-8103-6843-9*) Gale.

Countries with No Names. Mary Sternbach. 32p. (Orig.). 1982. pap. 4.00 (*0-941062-08-2*) Begos & Rosenberg.

Country, Vol. 1. (Ultimate Ser.). 264p. 1982. pap. 17.95 (*0-88188-160-0*, 00361401) H Leonard.

Country, Vol. 2. (Ultimate Ser.). 304p. 1983. pap. 17.95 (*0-88188-274-7*, 00361403) H Leonard.

Country! Cowboys, Rodeo, Women Like Never Before. Tom Raley. (Illus.). 170p. (Orig.). 1993. pap. 9.95 (*0-935752-03-X*) Latigo Pr.

Country: The Music & the Musicians. Country Music Foundation Staff. (Illus.). 592p. 1988. 85.00 (*0-89659-868-3*) Abbeville Pr.

Country: The Music & the Musicians. exp. rev. ed. Country Music Foundation Staff. 1994. 45.00 (*1-55859-879-0*) Abbeville Pr.

***Country: The Music of America.** Ariel Bks. Staff. (Illus.). 80p. 1995. 4.95 (*0-8362-3113-9*) Andrews & McMeel.

Country Adventures in Maryland, Virginia & West Virginia. Elizabeth C. Mooney. 164p. (Orig.). 1984. pap. 5.95 (*0-915168-01-4*) Wash Bk Trad.

***Country Afghans.** Vanessa Ann Collection Staff. 1994. pap. 14.95 (*0-8487-1418-0*) Oxmoor Hse.

Country Airport. Peter Schmitt. LC 89-32124. 51p. (Orig.). 1989. pap. 6.95 (*0-914278-52-5*) Copper Beech.

Country Almanac. Lucille Noltensmeier. (Illus.). 160p. 1982. 10.50 (*0-943782-00-7*, Pantagraph Bks); pap. 5.00 (*0-943782-01-5*, Pantagraph Bks) Evergreen Comm.

***Country America: A Pictorial History.** Mary Shafer. 160p. 1995. 29.50 (*1-57223-021-5*) Outlook Pubng.

Country & Blues Harmonica for the Musically Hopeless. Jon Gindick. (Illus.). 128p. 1984. pap. 13.95 (*0-932592-08-2*) Klutz Pr.

Country & Calling. William K. Hancock. LC 78-6026. 246p. 1978. reprint ed. text ed. 59.75 (*0-313-20447-0*, HACAC, Greenwood Pr) Greenwood.

***Country & Folk Antiques.** Don Raycraft & Carol Raycraft. (Illus.). 176p. (Orig.). 1995. pap. 29.95 (*0-88740-828-1*) Schiffer.

Country & Suburban Homes of the Prairie School Period: 408 Examples, Photographs & Floor Plans. H. V. Von Holst. (Architecture Ser.). (Illus.). 128p. 1983. reprint ed. pap. 7.95 (*0-486-24373-7*) Dover.

Country & the City. Raymond Williams. LC 72-98128. 1975. reprint ed. pap. 11.95 (*0-19-519810-7*) OUP.

Country & Western Dancing. Larre Bryant. (Illus.). 30p. (Orig.). pap. text ed. 3.00 (*0-685-54791-4*) Bryant Assocs.

Country & Western Music. Charles T. Brown. (Illus.). 250p. (C). 1985. text ed. 22.95 (*0-685-10423-0*); pap. 12.95 (*0-685-10424-9*) P-H.

Country Animals. Lucy Cousins. LC 90-35894. (Illus.). (J). (ps). 1991. bds. 3.95 (*0-688-10070-8*, Tambourine Bks) Morrow.

Country Antiques: A Child's Guide. Brad R. Smith. (Illus.). 64p. (Orig.). (J). (gr. 1-3). 1987. pap. 11.95 (*0-9618645-0-8*) Sanford Hse Pr.

Country Artist: A Story about Beatrix Potter. David R. Collins. (Illus.). 56p. (J). (gr. 3-6). 1989. 15.95 (*0-87614-344-3*, Carolrhoda); pap. 5.95 (*0-87614-509-8*, Carolrhoda) Lerner Group.

An Asterisk (*) at the beginning of an entry indicates that the title is appearing in BIP for the first time.

Country at My Shoulder. Moniza Alvi. 64p. (C). 1993. pap. 11.95 (*0-19-283125-9*, 1078) OUP.

*__Country Auctioneer: Anecdotes, Admonitions, & Advice.__ Thomas M. Martin. Ed. by Amy G. Moore. (Illus.). 96p. (Orig.). 1994. pap. 12.95 (*1-883912-00-8*) Hamiltons.

Country Bairns: Growing up in Rural Scotland in the Early 1900s. Lynn Jamieson & Claire Toynbee. (Edinburgh Education & Society Ser.). 176p. 1992. text ed. 35.00 (*0-7486-0373-5*, Pub. by Edinburgh U Pr UK) Col U Pr.

Country Baker, 4 vols., Vol. 1. 1993. Boxed. boxed 35.00 (*0-688-10621-8*) Morrow.

Country Baking. (Illus.). 64p. 1988. pap. 3.95 (*0-8249-3078-9*) Ideals.

Country Baking. (American Country Ser.). (Illus.). 176p. 1990. lib. bdg. 25.93 (*0-8094-6788-7*) Time-Life.

*__Country Baking: Simple Home Baking with Wholesome Grains & the Pick of the Harvest.__ Ken Haedrich. 1994. pap. 14.95 (*0-553-37414-1*) Bantam.

Country Beans. Rita Bingham. (Natural Meals in Minutes Ser.: Bk. 4). 192p. (Orig.). 1992. 12.95 (*1-882314-07-7*) Nat Meals Minutes.

*__Country Before Party: Coalition & the Idea of "National Government" in Modern Britain, 1885-1987.__ G. R. Searle. LC 94-22618. (Studies in Modern History). 352p. (C). 1996. text ed. 53.95 (*0-582-20952-8*, 77012, Pub. by Longman UK); pap. text ed. 23.95 (*0-582-20951-X*, 77011, Pub. by Longman UK) Longman.

Country Between: The Upper Ohio Valley & Its Peoples, 1724-1774. Michael N. McConnell. LC 91-42867. (Illus.). xiv, 357p. 1992. 40.00 (*0-8032-3142-3*) U of Nebr Pr.

Country Between Us. Carolyn Forche. 1982. pap. 10.00 (*0-06-090926-9*, PL) HarpC.

*__Country Beyond.__ Sherwood. 1995. pap. 17.95 (*0-85207-254-6*) Atrium Pubs.

Country Beyond. Jane Sherwood. 256p. (Orig.). Date not set. pap. 26.95 (*0-8464-4193-4*) Beekman Pubs.

Country Blues. large type ed. Marjorie Everitt. 297p. 1992. reprint ed. lib. bdg. 13.95 (*1-56054-479-1*) Thorndike Pr.

Country Blues. Samuel B. Charters. LC 75-14114. (Roots of Jazz Ser.). (Illus.). 288p. 1975. reprint ed. lib. bdg. 29.50 (*0-306-70678-4*); reprint ed. pap. 13.95 (*0-306-80014-4*) Da Capo.

Country Blues Guitar. Tommy Flint. 1993. 6.95 (*0-87166-779-7*, 93346); 9.98 (*1-56222-437-9*, 93346) Mel Bay.

Country Blues Guitar. Intro. by Happy Traum. (Illus.). 120p. 1968. pap. 14.95 (*0-8256-0129-0*, OK61929, Oak) Music Sales.

Country Blues Guitar for the Musically Hopeless. Carol McComb. (Illus.). 96p. (Orig.). 1986. audio, pap. 12.95i (*0-932592-12-0*) Klutz Pr.

Country Blues Songbook. Stefan Grossman et al. (Illus.). 208p. 1973. pap. 17.95 (*0-8256-0137-1*, OK62588, Oak) Music Sales.

Country Book Herbs & Spices. Joanna Sheen. 144p. 1994. 12.98 (*0-8317-1159-0*) Smithmark.

Country Bound! Trade Your Business Suit Blues for Blue Jean Dreams. Marilyn Ross & Tom Ross. 1993. audio 59.95 (*0-918880-32-7*) Comm Creat.

Country Bound! Trade Your Business Suit Blues for Blue Jean Dreams. Marilyn Ross & Tom Ross. 430p. 1992. pap. 19.95 (*0-918880-30-0*) Comm Creat.

*__Country Boy.__ Dale E. Coons. 37p. (J). (gr. 2-8). 1993. pap. text ed. 8.95 (*1-882241-75-4*) Alleycat.

Country Boy. Max Westbrook. (Orig.). 1979. pap. 3.50 (*0-914476-87-4*) Thorp Springs.

Country Boys, City Boys. J. Medley. 448p. (Orig.). 1994. pap. 12.95 (*1-877978-51-5*) Woldt.

Country Breakfasts. Ken Haedrich. LC 94-17330. 1994. pap. 14.95 (*0-553-37246-7*) Bantam.

Country Bride Quilt. Craig N. Heisey & Rachel T. Pellman. LC 88-82139. (Illus.). 96p. 1988. pap. 12.95 (*0-934672-72-5*) Good Bks PA.

Country Bride Quilt Collection. Cheryl A. Benner & Rachel T. Pellman. LC 91-70666. (Country Quilt Ser.). (Illus.). 102p. (Orig.). 1991. pap. 12.95 (*1-56148-015-0*) Good Bks PA.

Country Builder's Assistant. Asher Benjamin. 64p. 1989. pap. 7.95 (*1-55709-104-8*) Applewood.

Country Builder's Assistant: 1797 see Works of Asher Benjamin: Boston, 1806-1843

*__Country Bumpkin Gang: A Those Were the Days Book.__ Wendell Trogdon. (Illus.). 176p. 1995. pap. 10.00 (*0-9642371-1-3*) Backroads Pr.

Country Bunny & the Little Gold Shoes. Du Bose Heyward. (Illus.). 48p. (J). (gr. k-3). 1974. 14.95 (*0-395-15990-3*, Sandpiper); pap. 4.95 (*0-395-18557-2*, Sandpiper) HM.

Country Bunny & the Little Gold Shoes. DuBose Heyward. (Illus.). (J). (ps-3). 1989. audio, pap. 7.95 (*0-395-52140-8*) HM.

Country Bunny Quilt. Jean Wells. Ed. by Barbara K. Kuhn & Joyce E. Lytle. (Patchwork Quilts Made Easy Ser.: No. II). (Illus.). 24p. 1994. pap. 8.95 (*0-914881-72-8*, CT175) C & T Pub.

*__Country Business Patterns.__ 1995. lib. bdg. 250.00 (*0-8490-5863-5*) Gordon Pr.

Country By-Ways. Sarah O. Jewett. LC 76-94735. (Short Story Index Reprint Ser.). 1977. 18.95 (*0-8369-3115-7*) Ayer.

Country By-Ways. Sarah O. Jewett. (Collected Works of Sarah O. Jewett). 1988. reprint ed. lib. bdg. 79.00 (*0-7812-1304-5*) Rprt Serv.

Country By-Ways see Collected Works of Sarah Orne Jewett

Country Cakes. Bevelyn W. Blair. LC 84-72948. (Illus.). 240p. 1984. 13.95 (*0-9613709-0-4*) Blair Columbus.

Country Cakes. Lisa Yockelson. 1989. 10.00 (*0-06-016092-6*, HarpT) HarpC.

***Country Calendar. Wilbur Willey. 93p. (Orig.). 1995. pap. 11.95 (*0-9645740-2-0*) Wldwood W.**
Selected from the author's columns, "Where There's a Will...", these essays deal with rural life, not only today, but in his nearly 70 years living on the family farm in Northern New Hampshire. They reflect both the joys & the frustrations of a way of life struggling to maintain the values of an earlier time. He touches on flowers & gardens, problems with animals & delight with birds, & the changes in farming methods. With wit & understanding he comments on the seasons from the untouched year, through sugaring time & haying, to the harvest & the onslaught of winter. The topics range widely from valentines & parades to tulips & weeds, from cutting ice & sounds in the winter night, to a walk in the woods & cross country skiing, from marauding raccoons to beetle infestations, from potato digging to where to find the thrill of fall foliage. For information or ordering, write Wildwood West, RR2, Foster Hill Road, Littleton, NH 03561, Tel. (603) 444-2076. ***Publisher Provided Annotation.***

Country Calendar. 2nd large type ed. Flora Thompson. 192p. 1993. 19.95 (*1-85695-115-4*, Pub. by ISIS UK) Transaction Pubs.

***Country Capers from Cockriel Farm. Frankie M. Bush. (Illus.). 58p. (Orig.). (J). (gr. k-4). 1995. pap. 5.95 (*0-933865-23-6*) Doris Pubns.**
Storyteller Frankie M. Bush is known throughout Leitchfield in southwestern Kentucky as "Aunt Frankie". In her first published work, COUNTRY CAPERS FROM COCKRIEL FARM, she introduces four charming read-aloud short stories for children ages four through nine. In this collection you will enjoy JUG-O-RUM, the story of the unstoppable mission of young Stephen Blake. RANDY, THE LITTLE CITY HOUSE MOUSE, acquires a valuable lesson in self-esteem, & Little Roy in DOGGIE DOG sets up for a wonderful surprise. A HOME FOR JOHN HENRY contains the simple, kind deed of Ryan Christopher & his animal friends. Aunt Frankie's tales have fascinated children of all ages, the young & not so young, for many years. You will be delighted at these simple, wonderful examples of the oral tradition. The author & her husband Charles have one son, now grown. To order: Doris Publications, P.O. Box 11725, Louisville, KY 40251. $5.95 plus $2.00 shipping & handling per copy. ***Publisher Provided Annotation.***

Country Careers: Successful Ways to Live & Work in the Country. Jerry Germer. 288p. 1993. text ed. 40.00 (*0-471-57583-6*) Wiley.

Country Careers: Successful Ways to Live & Work in the Country. Jerry Germer. 288p. 1993. pap. text ed. 14.95 (*0-471-57582-8*) Wiley.

Country Carving: Hound Dogs, Raccoon, Coon Hunter. Tom Wolfe. LC 87-61435. (Illus.). 136p. 1987. pap. 15.95 (*0-88740-105-8*) Schiffer.

Country Carving (Pig Pickin'). Tom Wolfe. LC 88-61478. (Illus.). 136p. 1988. pap. 15.95 (*0-88740-130-9*) Schiffer.

Country Casseroles. Ed. by Sandy Trzesniewski. LC 93-84019. 52p. 1993. 4.98 (*0-89821-110-7*) Reiman Pubns.

Country Catalog of Memories: A Childhood on a German-American Farm in the Late 1920s & Early 1930s. rev. ed. Helen E. Ouimette. (Illus.). 204p. (Orig.). 1987. pap. 14.95 (*0-9617116-1-2*) H Ouimette.

Country Cellar. Ruth Blackett & Bonnie Millhollin. Ed. by Kathey Shreves. (Illus.). 114p. (C). 1981. spiral bd. 5.95 (*0-940158-01-9*) Zucchini Patch.

Country Changes. Lee Rudolph. LC 78-60470. 72p. 1978. pap. 9.95 (*0-914086-23-5*) Alicejamesbooks.

Country Chartbusters - Five of the Best. Ed. by Milton Okun. pap. 6.95 (*0-89524-641-4*) Cherry Lane.

Country Child. 2nd large type ed. Alison Uttley. 261p. 1993. 22.95 (*1-85695-316-5*, Pub. by ISIS UK) Transaction Pubs.

Country Child: An Illustrated Reminiscence. Ed. by Piers Dudgeon. (Illus.). 192p. 1993. 29.95 (*0-7472-0677-5*, Pub. by Headline UK) Trafalgar.

Country Childhoods. Ed. by Geoffrey Dutton. (Orig.). 1992. pap. 14.95 (*0-7022-2434-0*, Pub. by Univ Queensland Pr AT) Intl Spec Bk.

Country Christmas. (American Country Ser.). (Illus.). 176p. 1989. lib. bdg. 25.93 (*0-8094-6780-1*) Time-Life.

Country Christmas. Emily Bradshaw et al. 352p. 1993. pap. 4.99 (*0-451-17725-8*, Sig) NAL-Dutton.

Country Christmas. Ed. by Ideals Staff. (Illus.). 1993. 22.95 (*0-8249-4050-4*) Ideals.

Country Christmas. Nancy Marie. (Jimmy & Sweet Sue's Bks.). (Illus.). 36p. (J). (gr. k-5). 1979. 5.95 (*0-941595-00-5*) Heldreth Pub.

*__Country Christmas: As Remembered by a Former Kid.__ Bob Artley. LC 94-13179. (Illus.). 40p. 1994. 12.95 (*0-8138-2778-7*) Iowa St U Pr.

Country Christmas Carol. Ken Nelson & Jack Dyville. (Illus.). 36p. (Orig.). 1985. pap. 3.50 (*0-88680-235-0*); 12.50 (*0-88680-247-4*) I E Clark.

Country Christmas Cross-Stitch. Lisbeth Perrone. (Illus.). 192p. 1986. write for info. (*0-02-595920-4*) Macmillan.

Country Chronicle. Gladys Taber. reprint ed. lib. bdg. 20.95 (*0-89190-596-0*, Rivercity Pr) Amereon Ltd.

*__Country Chuckles, Cracks & Kneeslappers.__ 1995. 11.95 (*0-614-04393-X*) Lessiter Pubns.

Country Classics. Ed. by Bill Thompson. LC 85-63462. 60p. (Orig.). 1985. 3.98 (*0-916809-04-8*) Scott Pubns MI.

*__Country Classics.__ Patsy Tompkins & Ginger Mitchell. 1995. 12.95 (*0-9646160-0-9*) Country Classics.

Country Classics: Authentic Projects You Can Build in One Weekend. John A. Nelson. Ed. by Sally Atwater. LC 88-20027. (Illus.). 224p. (Orig.). 1989. pap. 16.95 (*0-8117-2277-5*) Stackpole.

Country Classics: Twenty-Five Early American Projects. Gloria Saberin. (Illus.). 160p. 1991. 19.95 (*0-8306-7587-6*, 3587) TAB Bks.

Country Cloth to Coverlets: Textile Traditions in Nineteenth Century Central Pennsylvania. Sandra R. Walker. LC 81-39246. (Illus.). 64p. (Orig.). 1981. pap. 12.50 (*0-271-00290-5*) Pa St U Pr.

Country Club. Nancy Bruff. 400p. 1986. reprint ed. pap. 3.95 (*0-8439-2320-2*) Dorchester Pub Co.

Country Club: Why Switching from the Big City to the Boondocks Could Be Your Smartest Move Ever. Dale Wildman. LC 92-61455. 138p. (Orig.). 1992. pap. 8.95 (*0-9624945-5-0*) Silvercat Pubns.

Country Club People. Margaret C. Banning. 1976. lib. bdg. 14.85 (*0-89968-006-2*, Lghtyr Pr) Buccaneer Bks.

Country Collections. (American Country Ser.). (Illus.). 176p. 1989. 19.93 (*0-8094-6783-6*); lib. bdg. 25.93 (*0-8094-6784-4*) Time-Life.

Country Commitment to Development Projects. Richard Heaver & Arturo Israel. (Discussion Paper Ser.: No. 4). 38p. 1986. 6.95 (*0-8213-0860-2*, 20004) World Bank.

Country Competitiveness: Technology & the Organizing of Work. Ed. by Bruce Kogut. LC 92-22897. 250p. 1993. 42.00 (*0-19-507277-4*) OUP.

Country, Conscience & Caviar: A Diplomat's Journey in the Company of History. Alfred L. Jenkins. (Illus.). 360p. 1994. write for info. (*0-9622269-4-7*) BookPartners.

Country Consultant. Brian R. Smith. 310p. 1982. 8.95 (*0-916654-23-0*) Kennedy Pubns.

*__Country Cookies.__ Ed. by Nancy Mack. 48p. Date not set. 4.98 (*0-89821-114-X*) Reiman Pubns.

Country Cookies: An Old-Fashioned Collection. Lisa Yockelson. LC 89-46131. (Illus.). 144p. 1990. 12.50 (*0-06-016258-9*, HarpT) HarpC.

Country Cooking. (Americana Book Ser.). (Illus.). 1975. 3.50 (*0-911410-38-4*) Applied Arts.

Country Cooking. (American Country Ser.). (Illus.). 176p. 1989. lib. bdg. 25.93 (*0-8094-6776-3*) Time-Life.

Country Cooking. Helen Hale. LC 85-70622. (Orig.). 1985. pap. 5.95 (*0-910042-48-9*) Allegheny.

Country Cooking. large type ed. Miss Read. 296p. 1993. 21.95 (*0-7505-0217-7*) Ulverscroft.

Country Cooking from Farthinghoe. Nicola Cox. (Illus.). 156p. 1984. 29.95 (*0-575-03504-8*, Pub. by V Gollancz UK) Trafalgar.

Country Cooking with A-Peel: A Treasury of Apple Cookery - Over 300 Ways to Use Fresh & Dried Apples. Margaret Gubin. 234p. 1988. spiral bd. 14.95 (*0-9621883-0-1*) Country Cupboard.

Country Cooking...California Style. California Farm Bureau Federation Staff. 320p. 1981. pap. 10.25 (*0-686-31491-3*) Cal Farm Bureau.

*__Country Cooks.__ 1994. pap. 6.50 (*0-00-225031-4*, Harp PBks) HarpC.

Country Cook's Companion. Jocasta Innes. LC 93-29787. (Country Companion Ser.). 64p. 1994. 12.95 (*0-00-255363-5*) Collins SF.

Country Cop. Terrence C. Parker. 138p. (Orig.). 1989. pap. 8.95 (*0-685-30391-8*) Tihtiyas Pub.

Country Cotillion. Sandra Heath. (Regency Romance Ser.). 224p. 1992. 3.99 (*0-451-17124-1*, Sig) NAL-Dutton.

Country Cousins. Michael Brownstein. (New American Fiction Ser.: No. 9). 349p. 1986. pap. 11.95 (*0-940650-74-6*) Sun & Moon CA.

Country Crafts. (American Country Ser.). (Illus.). 176p. 1989. lib. bdg. 25.93 (*0-8094-6771-2*) Time-Life.

Country Crafts: From Storey's Country Wisdom Collection. Storey Publishing Editors Staff. Ed. by Kim Foster & Gwen Steege. LC 90-50025. 160p. (Orig.). 1990. pap. text ed. 10.95 (*0-88266-628-2*) Storey Comm Inc.

Country Crafts Decoupage. Kaye Healey. 1993. 5.99 (*0-517-08798-7*) Random Hse Value.

Country Crafts for Kids. Ed. by Neva Hickerson. LC 93-6383. 1994. write for info. (*0-8307-1610-6*) Regal.

Country Creations: Club Edition. Yaklick Seitz. 1991. 27.95 (*0-8306-2562-3*) TAB Bks.

Country Creations: Woodworking Projects to Make & Sell. James E. Seitz & Linda S. Yaklich. (Illus.). 128p. 1991. pap. 9.95 (*0-8306-2144-X*) TAB Bks.

Country Cross-Stitch. Sharon Perna. (Illus.). 144p. 1992. pap. 12.95 (*0-8069-5769-7*) Sterling.

*__Country Crossing.__ Aylesworth. (J). 1995. pap. 4.95 (*0-689-71895-0*, Aladdin Paperbacks) S&S Childrens.

Country Crossing. Jim Aylesworth. LC 89-78184. (Illus.). 32p. (J). (ps-2). 1991. text ed. 13.95 (*0-689-31580-5*, Atheneum Bks Young) S&S Childrens.

Country Cuisine from Maxine: Country Cuisine Cookbooks. 2nd ed. Maxine Henderson. (Illus.). 237p. 1989. reprint ed. 9.50 (*0-9625024-0-5*) Ctry Cuisine Cookbks.

Country Cut-Outs Pattern Book. John Drogemuller & Barbara Drogemuller. (Illus.). 64p. (Orig.). 1993. pap. 10.95 (*0-86417-517-5*, Pub. by Kangaroo Pr AT) Seven Hills Bk.

*__Country Dance.__ Henry Brewis. (Illus.). 208p. 1992. pap. 12.95 (*0-85236-244-7*, Pub. by Farming Pr UK) Diamond Farm Bk.

Country Dance Book: Parts 1 & 2. Cecil J. Sharp. (Illus.). 1978. reprint ed. 13.00 (*0-85409-928-X*) Charles River Bks.

Country Dance Book: Parts 3 & 4. Cecil J. Sharp & George Butterworth. (Illus.). 1978. reprint ed. 13.00 (*0-7158-1062-6*) Charles River Bks.

Country Dance Books: Parts 5 & 6. Cecil J. Sharp & Maud Karpeles. (Illus.). 1976. reprint ed. 13.00 (*0-7158-1143-6*) Charles River Bks.

Country Dances of Colonial America. John F. Millar. LC 90-49922. (Illus.). 160p. (Orig.). 1990. pap. 20.00 (*0-934943-28-1*) Thirteen Colonies Pr.

Country Dances of Today: Book 2. May Gadd. 1951. pap. 2.00 (*0-917024-01-X*) Country Dance & Song.

*__Country Days.__ Alice Taylor. 1995. 16.95 (*0-312-11763-9*) St Martin.

Country Days & Southern Ways. Dwight Holt. (Illus.). 202p. (Orig.). 1991. pap. 8.95 (*0-943487-28-5*) Sevgo Pr.

Country Days in New York City. Divya Symmers. LC 93-29547. (Country Roads Ser.). (Illus.). 120p. (Orig.). 1993. pap. 9.95 (*1-56626-030-2*) Country Rds.

Country Decorating. (American Country Ser.). (Illus.). 176p. 1988. lib. bdg. 25.93 (*0-8094-6759-3*) Time-Life.

Country Decorating with Fabric: More Than Eighty Projects to Add Country Style, Charm & Color to Every Room in Your Home. Chris Rankin. (Illus.). 160p. 1992. 24.95 (*0-8069-8380-9*) Sterling.

Country Decorating with Fabric: More Than 80 Projects to Add Country Style, Charm & Color to Every Room in Your Home. Chris Rankin. (Illus.). 160p. 1993. pap. 14.95 (*0-8069-8381-7*) Sterling.

C

*__Country Decorative Painting Companion.__ Judith Miller & Martin Miller. LC 94-24446. 1995. 12.95 (*0-00-255490-9*) Collins SF.

*__Country Decorator.__ Francine Lawrence. 1994. 19.99 (*0-517-08795-2*) Random Hse Value.

Country Desserts. Friberg. 1993. text ed. 22.95 (*0-442-01741-3*) Van Nos Reinhold.

Country Diary. Matt Mundell. 208p. (C). 1989. 45.00 (*0-903065-33-9*, Pub. by G Wright Pub Ltd) St Mut.

*__Country Diary.__ Ed. by Jeanette Page. (Illus.). 160p. 1995. 19.95 (*1-85702-254-8*, Pub. by Fourth Estate UK) Trafalgar.

Country Diary: The Year in Kerry. Patrick O'Sullivan. (Illus.). 160p. (Orig.). 1993. pap. 13.95 (*0-947962-76-X*, Pub. by Anvil Bks Ltd IE) Irish Bks Media.

Country Diary Book of Creating a Butterfly Garden. E. J. Warren. 1988. 19.95 (*0-8050-0814-4*) H Holt & Co.

Country Diary Book of Flowers: Drying, Pressing, & Pot Pourri. Carol Petelin. (Illus.). 160p. 1991. 24.95 (*0-8050-1770-4*) H Holt & Co.

*__Country Diary Herbal.__ Sarah Hollis. LC 90-55157. 1995. 12.99 (*0-517-12292-8*) Random Hse Value.

Country Diary of an Edwardian Lady. Edith Holden. LC 77-71198. (Illus.). 192p. 1977. 24.95 (*0-8050-1232-X*) H Holt & Co.

Country Divorce. Ann T. Jones. 310p. 1992. 20.00 (*1-883285-11-9*) Delphinium.

Country Dobro Guitar Styles. Ken Eidson & Tom Swatzell. 1993. 7.95 (*0-87166-788-6*, 93350) Mel Bay.

Country Doctor. John G. Hipps. LC 89-50844. 112p. (Orig.). (C). 1989. pap. text ed. 8.95 (*0-685-27235-4*) Country Dr Enter.

Country Doctor. Sarah O. Jewett. 1986. mass mkt. 9.95 (*0-452-00805-0*, Mer) NAL-Dutton.

Country Doctor. large type ed. Paula Lindsay. (Linford adj Romance Library). 1988. pap. text ed. 10.95 (*0-7089-6540-7*, Linford) Ulverscroft.

Country Doctor. Sarah O. Jewett. LC 84-60955. (Illus.). 371p. 1984. reprint ed. 25.00 (*0-89725-048-6*) Picton Pr.

Country Doctor. Sarah O. Jewett. (Collected Works of Sarah O. Jewett). 1988. reprint ed. lib. bdg. 79.00 (*0-7812-1306-1*) Rprt Serv.

Country Doctor see Collected Works of Sarah Orne Jewett

Country Dogs & City Cousins: The Care & Loving of All Puppies. Marion Damroth. LC 80-81371. (Illus.). 125p. write for info. (*0-937118-01-X*) Home Frosted.

Country Dollmaking. Nancy Wolfe & Tom Wolfe. LC 88-61479. (Illus.). 136p. 1988. pap. 14.95 (*0-88740-129-5*) Schiffer.

Country Dolls. Ed. by Better Homes & Gardens Staff. (Illus.). 80p. 1991. pap. 9.95 (*0-696-01916-7*) Meredith Bks.

Country Dreams: Your Guide to Saving Time & Money, While Still Getting What You Want & Need in Country Property. Alan R. Schabilion. (Illus.). 150p. (Orig.). 1991. pap. 10.00 (*0-9628610-0-6*) Misty Mt Pr.

*__Country Dried Flower Companion.__ Stephen Woodhams. LC 94-42867. 1995. 12.95 (*0-00-255492-5*) HarpC West.

Country Editor. Henry B. Hough. LC 40-27604. 1974. reprint ed. pap. 9.95 (*0-85699-091-4*) Chatham Pr.

Country Elegance: Projects for Woodworkers. Edward A. Baldwin. (Illus.). 256p. 1991. 26.95 (*0-8306-0579-7*, 3768); pap. 14.95 (*0-8306-0527-4*) TAB Bks.

An Asterisk (*) at the beginning of an entry indicates that the title is appearing in BIP for the first time.

1653

***Country Entertaining.** Pat Ross. LC 95-15983. (Illus.). 1995. 24.99 (*0-517-14695-9*, Pub. by Wings Bks) Random.

Country Estate Development: The Report of a Seminar Organized by the Royal Town Planning Institute. Martin J. Elson. (C). 1980. 29.00 (*0-685-30296-2*, Pub. by Oxford Polytechnic UK) St Mut.

Country Estates Around Moscow from the History of Russian Estate Culture of the 17th, 18th, & 19th Centuries. M. Anikst & V. Turchin. 398p. 1979. 150.00 (*0-317-14227-5*, Pub. by Collets UK) St Mut.

Country Experiences with Water Resources Management: Economic, Institutional, Technological, & Environmental Issues. Ed. by Guy Le Moigne et al. LC 92-18831. (Technical Paper Ser.: No. 175). 223p. 1992. 11.95 (*0-8213-2159-5*, 12159) World Bank.

Country Fact Files, 6 vols., Set. (J). (gr. 4-7). 1994. 95.76 (*0-8114-1872-3*) Raintree Steck-V.

Country Fair. Gail Gibbons. LC 93-30289. (J). 1994. 14.95 (*0-316-30951-6*) Little.

Country Fair. Mark Publishing Staff. 1991. pap. 8.95 (*0-937769-19-3*) Mark Inc CA.

***Country Fair Cookbook.** Alison M. Boteler. LC 94-42420. 1995. write for info. (*0-8120-6522-0*) Barron.

***Country Fair Craft Book.** Alison Boteler. LC 94-40846. 1995. write for info. (*0-8120-9173-6*) Barron.

Country Fair, Food & Crafts. Smithmark Publishers Staff. 1994. 9.98 (*0-8317-1228-7*) Smithmark.

Country Far Away. Nigel Gray. LC 88-22360. (Illus.). 32p. (J). (ps-1). 1989. 14.95 (*0-531-05792-5*); lib. bdg. 14.99 (*0-531-08392-6*) Orchard Bks Watts.

Country Far Away. Nigel Gray. LC 88-22360. (Illus.). 32p. (J). (ps-1). 1991. pap. 5.95 (*0-531-07024-7*) Orchard Bks Watts.

Country Fare for City Folks. Cathy Sillman. 256p. 1993. pap. 14.95 (*0-9635565-0-9*) Fuzzy Tekky.

***Country Favorites.** Ed. by Carol Cuellar. (Warner Bros. Presents Ser.). 304p. (Orig.). (YA). 1995. pap. text ed. 18.95 (*0-89724-521-0*) Warner Brothers.

Country Features by Natalie. Natalie Howard. 9.95 (*0-932298-38-9*) Tri-State Pr Corp.

Country Fiddle. Marilyn Bos. 68p. 1988. pap. text ed. 7.95 (*0-931759-21-8*) Centerstream Pub.

Country Finishes: Simple Paint Treatments for Found & Unfinished Furniture. Richard Kollath. LC 92-45280. (Illus.). 144p. 1993. 24.95 (*0-8212-1994-4*) Bulfinch Pr.

Country Flag Wallhanging & Placemats. Eleanor Burns. (Illus.). 18p. 1991. 5.95 (*0-922705-25-9*) Quilt Day.

Country Flat Carving with Tom Wolfe. Tom Wolfe & Douglas Congdon-Martin. LC 90-61505. 64p. (Orig.). 1990. pap. 9.95 (*0-88740-278-X*) Schiffer.

Country Flavor. Haydn S. Pearson. 1977. 18.95 (*0-8369-7324-0*, 8117) Ayer.

***Country Flavor.** Hayden Pearson. (American Autobiography Ser.). 112p. 1995. reprint ed. lib. bdg. 69.00 (*0-7812-8611-5*) Rprt Serv.

***Country Floors Decorating with Tiles.** Roslyn Siegel. LC 94-22875. (Illus.). 1995. write for info. (*1-56799-150-5*, Friedman-Fairfax) M Friedman Pub Grp Inc.

Country Flower Companion. Tricia Guild. LC 93-20762. (Country Companion Ser.). 1994. 12.95 (*0-00-255365-1*) Collins SF.

Country Flower Drying. Beverly Olson & Judy Lazzara. LC 87-26705. (Illus.). 132p. 1988. pap. 9.95 (*0-8069-6746-3*) Sterling.

***Country Flower Style: Creating the Natural Look.** Jane Newdick. (Illus.). 120p. 1995. 24.95 (*0-7892-0013-9*) Abbeville Pr.

Country Flowers. Jane Sharp. (Illus.). 106p. 1992. 14.95 (*1-85238-317-8*, Pub. by New Holland Pubs UK) Sterling.

Country Folk: Butte Falls, Derby, Dudley. Barbara M. Hegne. (Illus.). 119p. 1989. spiral bd., pap. 11.00 (*0-9623847-2-0*) B Hegne.

***Country Folk Medicine.** Janos. 1995. 6.98 (*0-88365-903-4*) Galahad Bks.

Country Fresh Gifts: Recipes & Projects from Your Garden & Country Kitchen. Storey Publishing Editors. Ed. by Gwen Steege. LC 90-50606. (Illus.). 160p. 1991. pap. 12.95 (*0-88266-660-6*) Storey Comm Inc.

Country Furnishings: Projects for Woodworkers. Edward A. Baldwin. 1991. text ed. 26.95 (*0-07-157731-9*) McGraw.

Country Furniture. (American Country Ser.). (Illus.). 176p. 1989. lib. bdg. 25.93 (*0-8094-6767-4*) Time-Life.

Country Furniture. Aldren A. Watson. 1976. mass mkt. 4.95 (*0-452-25130-3*, Z5130, Plume) NAL-Dutton.

Country Furniture. Aldren A. Watson. LC 93-32912. (Illus.). 288p. 1994. reprint ed. pap. 18.95 (*1-55821-286-8*) Lyons & Burford.

Country Furniture: A Walker-Homestead Price Guide. Ellen M. Plante & Ted Plante. LC 92-32289. (Illus.). 160p. 1993. pap. 14.95 (*0-87069-640-8*, Wallace-Hmestead) Chilton.

Country Furniture & Accessories from Quebec. Warren I. Johansson. LC 90-61512. (Illus.). 160p. (Orig.). 1990. pap. 24.95 (*0-88740-276-3*) Schiffer.

Country Gals. Mark Bego. 352p. 1994. pap. 4.50 (*0-7860-0014-7*, Pinnacle NY) Windsor NY.

Country Garden. (American Country Ser.). (Illus.). 176p. 1990. 19.93 (*0-8094-6791-7*); lib. bdg. 25.93 (*0-8094-6792-5*) Time-Life.

Country Garden. John Brookes. (Illus.). 208p. 1987. 35.00 (*0-517-56704-0*, Crown) Crown Pub Group.

Country Garden. Trisha Dixon. (Illus.). 150p. 1993. 35.00 (*0-207-17481-4*, Pub. by HarpC UK) HarpC.

Country Garden for Your Backyard: Projects, Plans, & Plantings for a Country Look. Marny Smith & Nancy DuBrule. (Illus.). 256p. 1992. 26.95 (*0-87596-135-5*, 01-794-0) Rodale Pr Inc.

Country Gardens: Country Living. Nina Williams & Rebecca Sawyer. LC 92-17207. 1993. 25.00 (*0-688-10619-6*) Hearst Bks.

Country Gentleman. Fiona Hill. 304p. 1989. pap. 3.50 (*0-449-21758-2*, Crest) Fawcett.

Country Gentleman: Biography Chet Atkins. Red O'Donnell. 1976. 19.95 (*0-8488-1115-1*) Amereon Ltd.

Country Gifts: Handmade & Homebaked. Eileen Westfall. 1994. 24.95 (*0-696-04666-0*) Meredith Bks.

Country Girl. Clifford Odets. 1953. pap. 4.75 (*0-8222-0243-3*) Dramatists Play.

Country Girls Trilogy. Edna O'Brien. 1987. pap. 14.00 (*0-452-26394-8*, Plume) NAL-Dutton.

Country Girls Trilogy: And Epilogue. Edna O'Brien. LC 86-28557. 544p. 1987. pap. 9.95 (*0-452-26182-1*, Plume) NAL-Dutton.

Country Girls Trilogy: Second Epilogue. Edna O'Brien. 1989. pap. 8.95 (*0-452-25926-6*) NAL-Dutton.

Country Girls Trilogy & Epilogue. Edna O'Brien. 1986. 18.95 (*0-374-13027-2*) FS&G.

Country Ground Beef. Ed. by Linda Piepenbrink. LC 93-83939. 100p. 1993. 9.98 (*0-89821-104-2*) Reiman Pubns.

Country Guitar. Alan Warner. (Illus.). 1993. pap. 15.95 (*0-7119-3166-6*) Music Sales.

Country-Harbor-Quiet-Act-Around. Larry Eigner. 1988. 20.00 (*0-935074-16-3*); 10.00 (*0-935074-15-5*); pap. 7.50 (*0-935074-14-7*) This Pr.

Country Hardball: The Autobiography of Enos "Country" Slaughter. Enos Slaughter & Kevin Reid. (Illus.). 208p. 1991. 18.95 (*0-936389-23-0*) Tudor Pubs.

Country Harvest. Jean Rood. (Illus.). (Orig.). 1984. pap. 6.50 (*0-941284-23-9*) J Shaw Studio.

Country Heartbeat. Louise M. Gabler. (Illus.). 200p. 1990. write for info. (*0-939116-22-7*) Frontier OR.

Country Hoard. large type ed. Alison Uttley. (Isis Reminiscence Ser.). (Illus.). 170p. 1992. 18.95 (*1-85695-305-X*, Pub. by ISIS UK) Transaction Pubs.

Country Home. (American Country Ser.). (Illus.). 176p. 1988. lib. bdg. 25.93 (*0-8094-6751-8*) Time-Life.

Country Home: An Old Fashioned Christmas. Country Home Staff. 192p. 1992. 24.95 (*0-696-01965-5*) Meredith Bks.

Country Home Book of Herbs. (Illus.). 192p. 1994. 24.95 (*0-696-00083-0*) Meredith Bks.

Country Home Decorating Book. Miranda Innes. 1993. 19.99 (*0-517-08793-6*) Random Hse Value.

***Country Home Plans.** (Illus.). 256p. 1995. pap. text ed. 6.95 (*0-938708-62-7*) L F Garlinghouse Co.

Country Home Stay for Supper. 1993. 19.95 (*0-696-01994-9*) Meredith Bks.

Country Homes & Seaside Cottages of the Victorian Era. William T. Comstock. (Illus.). 64p. 1989. pap. 4.95 (*0-486-25972-2*) Dover.

Country House: How It Worked. John Vince. (Illus.). 144p. 1991. pap. 22.95 (*0-7195-4769-5*, Pub. by John Murray UK) Trafalgar.

Country House at War. John M. Robinson. (Illus.). 184p. 1990. 29.95 (*0-370-31306-2*, Pub. by Jonathan Cape UK) Trafalgar.

Country-House Burglar: A Perennial British Mystery. Michael Gilbert. LC 88-45116. 320p. 1988. reprint ed. pap. 4.95 (*0-318-35204-4*, P 937, PL) HarpC.

Country House Described: An Index to the Country Houses of Great Britain & Ireland. Ed. by Michael Holmes. (Illus.). 328p. 1986. 40.00 (*0-906795-39-7*) Oak Knoll.

Country House Establishment: Family & Servants, 1815-1914. Jessica Gerard. (Family, Sexuality & Social Relations in Past Times Ser.). (Illus.). 352p. 1994. 49.95 (*0-631-15566-X*) Blackwell Pubs.

***Country House Garden: A Grand Tour.** Gervase Jackson-Stops. (Illus.). 216p. 1995. pap. 24.95 (*1-85793-619-1*, Pub. by Pavilion UK) Trafalgar.

Country House in English Renaissance Poetry. William A. McClung. 1977. 45.00 (*0-520-03137-7*) U CA Pr.

Country House Poem: A Cabinet of Seventeenth-Century Estate Poems & Related Items. Alastair Fowler. (Illus.). 448p. 1994. 75.00 (*0-7486-0440-5*, Pub. by Edinburgh U Pr UK) Col U Pr.

Country House Tour. Time Life Staff. (American Country Ser.). 1990. lib. bdg. 25.93 (*0-8094-6838-7*) Time-Life.

Country Houses: A Portfolio of Floor Plans, Exteriors & Furnishing Ideas for 80 Beautiful Country Houses. A. B. Thorne. (Illus.). 208p. 1988. pap. 10.95 (*0-918894-65-4*) Home Planners.

Country Houses from the Air. Adrian Tinniswood. (Illus.). 160p. 1994. 39.95 (*0-297-83263-8*) Trafalgar.

Country Hunks. Mark Bego. 96p. 1994. pap. 7.95 (*0-8092-3641-9*) Contemp Bks.

Country I Come From: Stories. Maura Stanton. LC 88-42977. 112p. (Orig.). 1988. pap. 9.95 (*0-915943-33-6*) Milkweed Ed.

Country Ideals Magazine, 1993. (Illus.). 80p. 1993. pap. 4.95 (*0-8249-1109-1*) Ideals.

***Country Images.** Lowell Long. 37p. 1995. per., pap. 4.95 (*0-614-04034-5*) Sage Pr OK.

Country Index, Vol. I: Interpretations for Use in the Evaluation of Foreign Educational Credentials. rev. ed. Ed. by Inez H. Sepmeyer. LC 86-90408. 327p. 1986. pap. 70.00 (*0-9615028-0-0*) F Severy Pub.

Country Information. Ed. by Linda Piepenbrink. LC 92-63184. 148p. 1993. 8.98 (*0-89821-103-4*) Reiman Pubns.

Country Inn Breakfast: Favorite Recipes from America's Bed & Breakfast Inns. Gail Greco. 6.95 (*0-942320-40-9*) Am Cooking.

Country Inn Cookbook. Anita Stewart. (Illus.). 208p. 1987. 14.95 (*0-7737-5099-1*, Pub. by Stoddart Pubng CN) Genl Dist Srvs.

Country Inn Cookbook. Anita Stewart. (Illus.). 208p. 1990. 18.95 (*0-7737-5339-7*, Pub. by Stoddart Pubng CN) Genl Dist Srvs.

***Country Inn Cooking with Gail Greco.** Gail Greco. (Illus.). 320p. (Orig.). 1995. pap. 17.95 (*1-55853-361-3*) Rutledge Hill Pr.

Country Innkeepers' Cookbook. Ed. by Wilf Copping & Lois Copping. LC 92-74911. 224p. 1992. pap. 12.95 (*1-56626-015-9*) Country Rds.

Country Inns: America Revisited. N. W. Adler & K. L. Mielke. (Illus.). 515p. 1987. pap. 12.95 (*0-944790-00-3*) LouMax Enterp.

***Country Inns & Backroads Cookbook.** Linda G. Conway. LC 95-12024. (Illus.). 270p. 1995. 29.95 (*0-936399-69-4*) Berkshire Hse.

Country Inns of Maryland, Virginia & West Virginia. 4th ed. Lewis Perdue. (Illus.). 210p. 1988. pap. 7.95 (*0-915168-06-5*) Wash Bk Trad.

Country Inspiration: Twenty-One Songs with a Message. (Piano-Vocal-Guitar Ser.). 104p. (Orig.). 1993. pap. 9.95 (*0-7935-2156-4*, 00311616) H Leonard.

Country Is My Music! Lazarus. (J). Date not set. 15.00 (*0-671-86773-3*, S&S Bks Young Read) S&S Childrens.

***Country Jake: American Autobiography.** Charles Driscoll. 256p. 1995. lib. bdg. 79.00 (*0-7812-8503-8*) Rprt Serv.

Country Jam Trax. Ralph Agresta. (JamTrax Ser.). (Illus.). 1992. pap. 11.95 (*0-8256-1324-8*, AM87432) Music Sales.

Country Journal. David Grayson. (Illus.). 1989. pap. 9.95 (*1-55838-113-9*) R H Pub.

Country Journal Book of Vegetable Gardening. Nancy Bubel. (Illus.). 256p. (Orig.). 1983. pap. 9.95 (*0-918678-03-X*) Natl Hist Soc.

Country Kids' Encounter with Buttsy. Donald D. McGuire. (J). 1992. 7.95 (*0-533-10346-0*) Vantage.

Country Killing. Max F. Harris. 1980. pap. 1.95 (*0-8439-0836-X*) Dorchester Pub Co.

Country Kiss. Sharon Harlow. (Homespun Ser.). 336p. (Orig.). 1993. mass mkt. 4.99 (*1-55773-852-1*) Diamond.

Country Kitchen. (American Country Ser.). (Illus.). 176p. 1988. lib. bdg. 25.93 (*0-8094-6755-0*) Time-Life.

Country Kitchen. Della T. Lutes. (American Biography Ser.). 264p. 1991. reprint ed. lib. bdg. 69.00 (*0-7812-8254-3*) Rprt Serv.

Country Kitchen. Della T. Lutes. LC 92-26831. (Great Lakes Bks.). 269p. (C). 1992. reprint ed. pap. text ed. 14.95 (*0-8143-2438-X*, Great Lks Bks) Wayne St U Pr.

Country Kitchen Cutouts. Lee Lindeman & Pat Harste. LC 93-43891. (Illus.). 136p. 1994. pap. 12.95 (*0-8069-0370-8*) Sterling.

Country Kitchen Stoneware Cookbook. Ed. by Kay E. Powell. (Illus.). 100p. (Orig.). 1983. pap. 6.00 (*0-930528-05-0*) Sassafras Pr.

Country Kitchens. Jocasta Innes. LC 91-6438. (Illus.). 180p. 1991. 40.00 (*0-8478-1379-7*) Rizzoli Intl.

Country Kitchens: Decorating, Cooking & Entertaining. Barbara Randolf. (American Country Living Ser.). 1992. 14.99 (*0-517-06115-5*) Random Hse Value.

Country Ladies. Ed. by Milton Okun. (Illus.). 128p. (Orig.). 1995. pap. 12.95 (*0-89524-819-0*, HL02502129) Cherry Lane.

Country Land & Its Uses. Howard Orem & Suzen Snyder. LC 74-22154. (Illus.). 310p. 1975. 16.95 (*0-87961-031-X*); pap. 8.95 (*0-87961-030-1*) Naturegraph.

Country Landscapes. Jacques-Pierre Amette. Tr. by Stuart Seide. (Publications Ser.: No. 20). 45p. (Orig.). 1987. pap. text ed. 8.95 (*0-913745-23-5*) Ubu Repertory.

Country Lawyer. Fred Whitaker. (Illus.). 250p. Date not set. 19.95 (*1-878096-28-1*) Best E TX Pubs.

Country Lawyer. Francis L. Windolph. LC 77-107743. (Essay Index Reprint Ser.). 1977. 19.95 (*0-8369-1638-7*) Ayer.

Country Lawyer & Other Stories for the Screen. William Faulkner. Ed. by Louis D. Brodsky & Robert W. Hamblin. LC 86-21201. 96p. 1987. 17.95 (*0-87805-308-5*) U Pr of Miss.

Country Lawyers: The Impact of Context on Professional Practice. Donald L. Landon. LC 89-16220. 192p. 1990. text ed. 49.95 (*0-275-93042-4*, C3042, Praeger Pubs) Greenwood.

Country Lead Guitar. Larry McCabe. 1993. 8.95 (*0-87166-935-8*, 94079); audio 9.98 (*1-56222-623-1*, 94079) Mel Bay.

***Country Life.** William S. Morse. LC 94-43017. (Illus.). 136p. (Orig.). 1995. pap. 9.95 (*0-9642213-1-4*) Moose Cntry.

***Country Life.** Roy Strong. (Illus.). 160p. 1995. 29.95 (*1-85793-443-1*, Pub. by Pavilion UK) Trafalgar.

Country Life: Counted Cross-Stitch. Polly Carboni & Jean D. Crowther. (Illus.). 8p. (Orig.). 1987. pap. 5.98 (*0-88290-294-6*) Horizon Utah.

Country Life Collector's Pocket Book. G. Bernard Hughes. 1976. 16.95 (*0-600-43055-3*) Transatl Arts.

Country Life Diary. Josh Pons. (Illus.). 516p. (Orig.). 1992. pap. 19.95 (*0-939049-49-X*) Blood-Horse.

Country Life in America. (Illus.). 160p. 1992. 22.95 (*0-8249-4044-X*) Ideals.

Country Life in Classical Times. Ed. by K. D. White. LC 77-74923. (Illus.). 224p. 1977. 32.95 (*0-8014-1114-9*) Cornell U Pr.

Country Life in Georgia in the Days of My Youth. Rebeca L. Felton. Ed. by Annette K. Baxter. LC 79-8792. (Signal Lives Ser.). 1980. reprint ed. lib. bdg. 34.95 (*0-405-12839-8*) Ayer.

Country Life in Scotland. Alexander Fenton. 232p. (C). 1989. pap. 35.00 (*0-85976-188-6*, Pub. by J Donald) St Mut.

Country Life Natural Foods: Something Better Nutrition Seminar Cookbook. LC 84-62260. (Illus.). 108p. (Orig.). 9.95 (*0-912145-05-6*) MMI Pr.

Country Life Picture Book of Ireland. Elgy Gillespie. (Illus.). 1982. 19.95 (*0-393-01627-7*) Norton.

Country Life "Something Better" Cookbook. 6th ed. Country Life Restaurant Staff. LC 93-61526. 112p. ring bd. 12.95 (*0-945383-67-3*) Teach Servs.

Country Life Vegetarian Cookbook: Delicious Recipes from the Kitchens of the Country Life Vegetarian Restaurants. Ed. by Diana Fleming. 192p. (Orig.). 1990. pap. 9.95 (*1-878726-00-5*) Fam Hlth Pubns.

Country Lily Quilt. Cheryl A. Benner & Rachel T. Pellman. LC 90-3078. (Illus.). 104p. 1990. pap. 12.95 (*0-934672-88-1*) Good Bks PA.

***Country Living: Notes from a Country Cupboard.** 1994. pap. 14.95 (*0-688-13408-4*) Hearst Bks.

Country Living & Country Thinking. Mary A. Dodge. (Notable American Authors Ser.). 1992. reprint ed. lib. bdg. 75.00 (*0-7812-2656-2*) Rprt Serv.

Country Living at Its Best. Rea W. Yarnall. Ed. by Gary Yarnall. (Illus.). 176p. 1990. 14.95 (*0-9621821-2-5*) Lil Jewel Enterp.

Country Living Book of Country Kitchens. Bo Niles. LC 85-60098. (Illus.). 1985. 29.95 (*0-688-04267-8*) Hearst Bks.

Country Living, Country Baker: Breads & Muffins. Text by Lucy Wing. LC 92-33224. 1993. 10.00 (*0-688-12544-1*) Hearst Bks.

Country Living, Country Baker: Cakes & Cupcakes. Text by Lucy Wing. LC 92-33221. 1993. 10.00 (*0-688-12541-7*) Hearst Bks.

Country Living, Country Baker: Cookies & Crackers. Text by Lucy Wing. LC 92-33223. 1993. 10.00 (*0-688-12542-5*) Hearst Bks.

Country Living, Country Baker: Pies & Tarts. Text by Lucy Wing. LC 92-33222. 1993. 10.00 (*0-688-12543-3*) Hearst Bks.

Country Living Country Bears. Bo Niles. (Illus.). 96p. 1991. 13.95 (*0-688-10016-3*, Hearst Marine Bks) Morrow.

Country Living Country Cats. Country Living Staff. 1992. 14.00 (*0-688-11182-3*) Morrow.

Country Living Country Christmas. Country Living Magazine Editors. LC 90-80313. (Illus.). 176p. 1990. 21.95 (*0-688-09738-3*) Hearst Bks.

Country Living Country Decorating: Achieving the Country Look, Room by Room. Bo Niles. Ed. by Ann Bramson. LC 88-4112. (Illus.). 256p. 1988. 29.95 (*0-688-08073-1*) Hearst Bks.

Country Living Country Mornings Cookbook. Country Living Magazine Editors & Lucy Wing. LC 90-82433. 1989. 23.95 (*0-688-06639-9*) Hearst Bks.

Country Living Country Stencils. Candie Frankel. 1994. pap. 20.00 (*0-688-13126-3*) Hearst Bks.

Country Living, Living with Folk Art. Country Living Magazine Editors. LC 94-6366. 1994. 25.00 (*0-688-11666-3*) Hearst Bks.

***Country Living New Country Kitchens.** Rebecca Sayer-Faye. LC 95-10885. (Illus.). 1995. write for info. (*0-688-12586-7*) Hearst Bks.

Country Living's Country Look & How to Get It. Country Living Editors. (Illus.). 192p. 1991. 25.00 (*0-688-09358-2*) Hearst Bks.

Country Living's Country Quilts. Mary S. Sears. (Illus.). 208p. 1992. 25.00 (*0-688-10620-X*) Hearst Bks.

Country Love Quilt. Cheryl A. Benner & Rachel T. Pellman. LC 89-23374. 192p. 1989. pap. 12.95 (*0-934672-65-2*) Good Bks PA.

Country Lovin' Pat McClure. (Illus.). 40p. 1985. pap. 7.50 (*0-941284-29-8*) J Shaw Studio.

Country Made by War: A Story of America's Rise to Power. Geoffrey Perret. 1989. 22.50 (*0-394-55398-5*) Random.

Country Made by War: From the Revolution to Vietnam - The Story of America's Rise to Power. Geoffrey Perret. LC 89-40548. 640p. 1990. pap. 14.95 (*0-679-72698-5*, Vin) Random.

Country Mailboxes: Patterns & Techniques. Patrick Spielman & Paul Meisel. LC 92-41648. (Illus.). 160p. 1993. pap. 12.95 (*0-8069-8673-5*) Sterling.

Country Manors of Portugal. Marcus Binney. (Illus.). 229p. 1993. 55.00 (*0-935748-74-1*) M T Train.

Country Matters. Jo Northrop. (Illus.). 208p. 1994. 21.95 (*1-55591-150-1*) Fulcrum Pub.

Country Medallion Sampler. Carol Doak. LC 93-32533. 1993. 7.95 (*1-56477-046-X*) That Patchwork.

Country Men. John C. Moore. LC 69-17585. (Essay Index Reprint Ser.). 1977. 20.95 (*0-8369-0088-X*) Ayer.

Country Mother Cookbook. Jane Hopping. 1993. pap. 7.99 (*0-517-11230-2*) Random Hse Value.

Country Mothers Cookbook: A Celebration of Motherhood & Old-Fashioned Cooking. Jane W. Hopping. 1991. 20.00 (*0-679-40274-8*, Villard Bks) Random.

Country Mothers Cookbook: A Celebration of Motherhood & Old-Fashioned Cooking by Jane Watson. Jane W. Hopping. 1991. 19.50 (*0-394-58874-6*, Villard Bks) Random.

***Country Mouse.** large type ed. Petra Nash. (Historical Romance Ser.). 1994. 18.95 (*0-263-14009-1*, Pub. by Mills & Boon Ltd UK) Chivers N Amer.

Country Mouse: A Cookbook for Cheese Lovers. Sally Walton & Faye Wilkinson. (Cookbook Ser.: No. 6). (Illus.). 80p. 1981. pap. 5.95 (*0-937552-10-0*) Quail Ridge.

Country Mouse & City Mouse. Patricia McKissack & Fredrick McKissack. LC 85-12759. (Start-Off Stories Ser.). (Illus.). (J). (ps-2). 1985. lib. bdg. 10.35 (*0-516-02362-4*); pap. 3.95 (*0-516-42362-2*) Childrens.

***Country Mouse & the City Mouse.** Ret. by Jean Warren. (Cut & Tell Cutouts Ser.). (Illus.). 8p. (J). Date not set. 8.85 (*0-614-07350-2*) Totline Bks.

Country Mouse & the City Mouse: "Christmas Is Where the Heart Is" Maxine P. Fisher. LC 93-26488. (Illus.). 48p. (J). (ps-2). 1994. 13.00 (*0-679-84684-0*) Random Bks Yng Read.

An Asterisk (*) at the beginning of an entry indicates that the title is appearing in BIP for the first time.

An Asterisk (*) at the beginning of an entry indicates that the title is appearing in BIP for the first time.

1655

C

Country Roads of New Jersey. Judi Dash & Jill Schensul. LC 93-70215. (Country Roads Ser.). (Illus.). 140p. (Orig.). 1994. pap. 9.95 (*1-56626-019-1*) Country Rds.

Country Roads of New York. Deborah Williams. LC 93-70217. (Country Roads Ser.). (Illus.). 140p. (Orig.). 1993. pap. 9.95 (*1-56626-018-3*) Country Rds.

Country Roads of North Carolina. Glen Morris. LC 94-14329. (Illus.). 144p. (Orig.). 1994. pap. 9.95 (*1-56626-067-1*) Country Rds.

Country Roads of Ohio. Janet Groene. LC 93-70214. (Country Roads Ser.). (Illus.). 140p. (Orig.). 1993. pap. 9.95 (*1-56626-020-5*) Country Rds.

Country Roads of Ontario. Iris S. Jones. LC 93-47477. (Country Roads Ser.). (Illus.). 140p. (Orig.). 1994. pap. 9.95 (*1-56626-066-3*) Country Rds.

Country Roads of Oregon. Archie Satterfield. LC 93-70218. (Country Roads Ser.). (Illus.). 140p. (Orig.). 1993. pap. 9.95 (*1-56626-017-5*) Country Rds.

Country Roads of Pennsylvania. Sally Moore. LC 93-11611. (Country Roads Ser.). (Illus.). 140p. (Orig.). 1993. pap. 9.95 (*1-56626-032-9*) Country Rds.

***Country Roads of Southern California.** Arlene Inge. (Country Roads Ser.). (Illus.). 180p. (Orig.). 1995. pap. 9.95 (*1-56626-076-0*) Country Rds.

Country Roads of Tennessee. Fronda Throckmorton. LC 93-44334. (Country Roads Ser.). (Illus.). 148p. (Orig.). 1994. pap. 9.95 (*1-56626-041-8*) Country Rds.

Country Roads of Texas. Eleanor Morris. LC 94-4403. (Country Roads Ser.). 140p. 1994. pap. 9.95 (*1-56626-100-7*) Country Rds.

Country Roads of the Maritimes. Ed. by Diana Haynes. LC 93-44946. (Country Roads Ser.). (Illus.). 160p. (Orig.). 1995. pap. 12.95 (*1-56626-085-X*) Country Rds.

Country Roads of Vermont. Molly Walsh & Joe Cutts. LC 93-70216. (Country Roads Ser.). (Illus.). 140p. 1993. pap. 9.95 (*1-56626-021-3*) Country Rds.

Country Roads of Virginia. W. Lynn Seldan. LC 93-32313. (Country Roads Ser.). (Illus.). 148p. (Orig.). 1994. pap. 9.95 (*1-56626-038-8*) Country Rds.

Country Roads of Washington. Archie Satterfield. (Illus.). 168p. (Orig.). 1989. pap. 12.95 (*0-942381-02-5*) Sammamish Pr.

Country Roads of Washington. Ardie Satterfield. LC 93-24842. (Country Roads Ser.). (Illus.). 140p. (Orig.). 1993. pap. 9.95 (*1-56626-034-5*) Country Rds.

Country Roads Revisited: The Cultural Imprint of Madison County. Ed. by Barbara J. Giambastiani. (Illus.). 148p. (Orig.). 1984. pap. 12.95 (*0-317-04086-3*) Mad Ct Hist.

***Country Rouges: Short Story Anthology.** Ed. by Bill Lee. (Rogues Ser.: No. 4). 211p. 1995. pap. 12.95 (*1-879194-19-8*) GLB Pubs.

Country Rugs. Pat Hornafius. 1992. 25.75 (*0-8446-6639-4*) Peter Smith.

Country Rugs: How to Design & Hook Traditional Wool Rugs & Hangings. Pat Hornafius. LC 91-17240. (Illus.). 216p. 1992. pap. 19.95 (*0-8117-3042-5*) Stackpole.

Country Rustic Home Plans. National Plan Service, Inc. (Illus.). 32p. (Orig.). reprint ed. pap. 3.95 (*0-934039-03-8*, A48) Natl Plan Serv.

Country Sayings. Fred Archer. (Illus.). 192p. 1991. 26.00 (*0-86299-837-9*) A Sutton Pub.

Country School: Marion No. 7. Bob Artley. LC 89-15516. (Illus.). 104p. (Orig.). 1989. pap. 10.95 (*0-8138-1077-9*) Iowa St U Pr.

Country School Memories. Bonnie H. Falk. LC 86-91104. (Illus.). 94p. 1986. pap. 7.95 (*0-9614108-1-7*) BHF Memories.

Country Schoolteacher: A Kansas Legacy. Vera E. Rodecap. 141p. (Orig.). 1993. pap. text ed. 12.00 (*0-9639944-0-9*) V E Rodecap.

Country Seasons. Katharine H. Annin. 256p. (Orig.). 1989. pap. 9.95 (*0-9611118-3-6*) Cardamom.

Country Seasons Cookbook. Gladys Manyan. LC 74-80292. (Illus.). 184p. 1985. reprint ed. pap. 8.95 (*0-941216-25-X*) Cay-Bel.

***Country Sermons.** J. R. Ivie. Ed. by Joan Ivie. (Illus.). 120p. 1994. 19.95 (*1-882935-07-1*) Rolla Fine Arts.

Country Showstoppers. Ed. by Carol Cuellar. 312p. (Orig.). (YA). 1992. pap. text ed. 18.95 (*0-89898-595-1*) CPP Belwin.

Country Showstoppers, Vol. 2. Ed. by Carol Cuellar. 292p. (Orig.). (YA). 1993. pap. text ed. 18.95 (*0-89898-596-X*) CPP Belwin.

Country So Full of Game: The Story of Wildlife in Iowa. James J. Dinsmore. LC 93-34775. (Bur Oak Original Ser.). (Illus.). 261p. 1994. 32.95 (*0-87745-453-1*); pap. 14.95 (*0-87745-454-X*) U of Iowa Pr.

Country So Interesting: The Hudson's Bay Company & Two Centuries of Mapping, 1670-1870. Richard I. Ruggles. (Rupert's Land Record Society Ser.). (Illus.). 304p. (C). 1991. text ed. 55.00 (*0-7735-0678-0*, Pub. by McGill CN) U of Toronto Pr.

***Country Songbird.** Anne Silkman. Ed. by Doghouse Press Inc. Staff. (Togetherness Ser.). (Illus.). 200p. (YA). Date not set. pap. write for info. (*1-885531-34-6*) Doghouse Pubng.

Country Songbird Quilt. Cheryl A. Benner & Rachel T. Pellman. LC 90-71120. (Illus.). 104p. 1990. pap. 12.95 (*1-56148-006-1*) Good Bks PA.

Country Spunky Gets Lost. Sheila B. Jones. LC 92-56938. (Illus.). 40p. (J). (gr. k-3). 1993. 6.95 (*1-55523-582-4*) Winston-Derek.

Country Squire in the White House. John Thomas Flynn. LC 77-167846. (FDR & the Era of the New Deal Ser.). 122p. 1972. reprint ed. lib. bdg. 22.50 (*0-306-70324-6*) Da Capo.

***Country Stars Shine: Insights to Your Favorite Country Artists...Their Lives, Loves & Reflections.** Lisa M. Chapman. Ed. by Richard Courtney & Maryglenn McCombs. (Illus.). 128p. (Orig.). 1995. pap. 5.95 (*1-886371-03-2*) Eggman Pub.

Country Stencils. Tim Frew. (American Country Living Ser.). 1991. 14.99 (*0-517-02016-5*) Random Hse Value.

Country Stoneware & Pottery. Don Raycraft & Carol Raycraft. (Illus.). 160p. 1989. pap. 9.95 (*0-89145-289-3*) Collector Bks.

Country Store Antiques: From Cradles to Caskets. Ed. by Douglas Congdon-Martin. LC 91-65652. (Illus.). 160p. 1991. pap. 29.95 (*0-88740-331-X*) Schiffer.

Country Store Collectibles. Douglas Congdon-Martin & Bob Biondi. LC 90-61510. (Illus.). 160p. (Orig.). 1990. pap. 24.95 (*0-88740-274-7*) Schiffer.

Country Stores. Jim Harrison. LC 92-84008. (Illus.). 128p. 1993. 20.00 (*1-56352-067-2*) Longstreet Pr Inc.

Country Stores of East Texas: Everything You Need from the Cradle to the Grave. Ed. by Larry Thompson & Jean Pamplin. (Illus.). 160p. (Orig.). 1990. pap. 9.95 (*0-9627304-1-6*) Thompson & Sons.

Country Stories. Mary R. Mitford. LC 70-110208. (Short Story Index Reprint Ser.). 1977. 20.95 (*0-8369-3359-1*) Ayer.

Country Studies on the Financing of Vocational Training. Cedefop. 120p. 1992. pap. 10.00 (*92-826-3637-2*, HX-60-91-539-EN-C, Pub. by Europ Com) UNIPUB.

Country Style. (American Country Ser.). (Illus.). 176p. 1990. 19.93 (*0-8094-6834-4*) Time-Life.

Country Style Appliques. Mary Mulari. (Illus.). 42p. (Orig.). 1987. pap. 7.95 (*0-9613569-5-2*) Mary Prodns.

Country Style Decorating Ideas. rev. ed. (Illus.). 64p. 1986. pap. 2.95 (*0-685-08974-6*) Simplicity.

Country Style Flowers. Date not set. 17.99 (*0-517-10334-6*) Random Hse Value.

Country Style Sewing for the Home. Chilton Book Staff. 128p. 1992. pap. 14.95 (*0-8019-8361-4*) Chilton.

Country Sunshine. Teresa Warfield. (Homespun Ser.). 336p. (Orig.). 1994. pap. text ed. 4.99 (*0-7865-0042-5*) Diamond.

***Country Sunshine.** Teresa Warfield. 336p. (Orig.). 1994. pap. 4.99 (*0-614-01377-1*) Diamond.

***Country Sunshine: The Dottie West Story.** Frances Meeker & Judy Berryhill. Ed. by Richard Courtney & Maryglenn McCombs. LC 94-62009. 128p. (Orig.). 1995. pap. text ed. 12.95 (*1-886371-08-3*) Eggman Pub.

Country Suppers: From Uphill Farm. Carol Lowe-Clay. (Illus.). 160p. 1993. pap. 10.95 (*0-913589-74-8*) Williamson Pub Co.

Country Talk. Diane Suchetka. LC 93-70210. 140p. 1993. 12.95 (*1-56626-029-9*) Country Rds.

Country Talk. Dick Syatt. 1980. 8.95 (*0-8065-0684-9*, Citadel Pr) Carol Pub Group.

Country Tea Rose Quilt. Des. by Cheryl A. Benner. (Illus.). 81p. (Orig.). 1993. pap. 12.95 (*1-56148-097-5*) Good Bks PA.

Country Teacher. Katai Tayama. Tr. by Kenneth Henshall. LC 83-24322. 231p. 1984. text ed. 16.95 (*0-8248-0869-X*) UH Pr.

***Country Textiles of Japan: The Art of Tsutsugaki.** Reiko M. Brandon. (Illus.). 152p. 1995. pap. 12.50 (*0-937426-22-9*, 777) Honolu Arts.

***Country Things.** Bob Artley. LC 94-21239. (Illus.). 136p. 1994. pap. 10.95 (*0-8138-2650-0*) Iowa St U Pr.

Country Threads. Connie Tesene & Mary Tendall. Ed. by Barbara Weiland. LC 91-47908. (Quilt Shop Ser.). (Illus.). 80p. 1992. pap. 19.95 (*1-56477-007-9*) That Patchwork.

***Country 'til I Die: John Anderson.** Ed. by Jeannette DeLisa. 44p. (Orig.). (YA). 1995. pap. text ed. 16.95 (*0-89724-537-7*) Warner Brothers.

Country to City: The Urbanization of a Japanese Hamlet. Edward Norbeck. LC 77-14737. 381p. reprint ed. pap. 108.60 (*0-8357-3272-X*, 2039493) Bks Demand.

Country to Play With: Level of Industry Negotiations in Berlin in 1945-46. Alec Cairncross. LC 87-63151. 72p. (Orig.). 1987. pap. 13.95 (*0-86140-274-X*, Pub. by Colin Smythe Ltd UK) Dufour.

Country Town: A Study of Rural Evolution. Wilbert L. Anderson. LC 73-11914. (Metropolitan America Ser.). 318p. 1979. reprint ed. 21.95 (*0-405-05382-7*) Ayer.

Country Town Nexus. Ed. by K. L. Sharma & Dipankar Gupta. (C). 1991. text ed. 26.00 (*81-7033-099-8*, Pub. by Rawat II) S Asia.

Country Town Sayings. E. W. Howe. (Collected Works of E. W. Howe). 1988. reprint ed. lib. bdg. 59.00 (*0-7812-1293-6*) Rprt Serv.

Country Town Sayings see Collected Works of E. W. Howe

Country Towns of Arkansas. Archie Satterfield. LC 94-37414. (Country Towns Ser.). (Illus.). 180p. (Orig.). 1995. pap. 9.95 (*1-56626-105-8*) Country Rds.

***Country Towns of Florida.** Anne Johnson. LC 93-48132. (Country Towns Ser.). (Illus.). 180p. (Orig.). 1995. pap. 9.95 (*1-56626-077-9*) Country Rds.

Country Towns of Georgia. William Schemmel. LC 93-48132. (Country Towns Ser.). (Illus.). 148p. (Orig.). 1994. pap. 9.95 (*1-56626-058-2*) Country Rds.

Country Towns of Michigan. Doris Scharfenberg. LC 93-49834. (Country Towns Ser.). (Illus.). (Orig.). 1994. pap. 9.95 (*1-56626-048-5*) Country Rds.

Country Towns of New York. Bill Kauffman. LC 93-42263. (Country Towns Ser.). (Illus.). 148p. (Orig.). 1994. pap. 9.95 (*1-56626-061-2*) Country Rds.

Country Towns of Northern California. Eleanor Morris. LC 94-11543. (Country Towns Ser.). (Illus.). (Orig.). 1995. pap. 9.95 (*1-56626-101-5*) Country Rds.

Country Towns of Pennsylvania. Marcus Schneck. LC 94-26344. (Country Towns Ser.). 140p. 1994. pap. 9.95 (*1-56626-102-3*) Country Rds.

***Country Towns of Texas.** Eleanor Morris. (Illus.). (Orig.). 1995. pap. 9.95 (*0-614-00764-X*) Country Rds.

***Country Toys & Children's Furniture: XX Antique Designs with Complete Plans & Instructions.** Ken Folk. (Illus.). 160p. 1996. pap. 19.95 (*0-8117-2428-X*) Stackpole.

Country Traditions. (American Country Ser.). (Illus.). 176p. 1991. lib. bdg. 25.93 (*0-8094-7059-4*) Time-Life.

Country Traveler. Time Life Staff. (American Country Ser.). 1990. lib. bdg. 25.93 (*0-8094-6796-8*) Time-Life.

***Country Treasury.** Ed. by Allen D. Bragdon. (Allen D. Bragdon Brownstone Library Bk.). (Illus.). 168p. 1995. 24.95 (*0-8317-1434-4*) A D Bragdon.

Country Twelvemonth. Fred Archer. LC 92-35772. 1992. 30.00 (*0-7509-0268-X*) A Sutton Pub.

Country, U. S. A. Richard Brooks. 1990. 39.95 (*0-9624617-0-9*) Silver Image.

Country-U. S. A. Twenty-Four Hours in Rural America. Pref. by Richard E. Brooks. (Illus.). 192p. 1989. 40.00 (*0-685-29335-1*) Silver Image.

Country Undertaker's Wife. Cora Dodd. LC 93-83445. (Illus.). 112p. 1993. 15.00 (*0-9631855-5-1*) Still Waters Pr.

Country Vet. Danniel S. Dennis. Tr. by Ingram. 372p. 1994. pap. 9.95 (*1-56901-234-2*) NW Pub.

Country Voices, the Oral History of a Japanese American Family Farm Community. David M. Masumoto. LC 87-3126. (Illus.). 256p. (Orig.). 1987. pap. 14.95 (*0-9614541-0-5*) Inaka-Countryside Pubns.

Country Waif. George Sand. 17.95 (*0-8488-0623-9*) Amereon Ltd.

Country Waif (Francois le Champi) George Sand. Tr. by Eirene Collis. LC 76-14125. (Bison Book Ser.). 209p. reprint ed. pap. 59.60 (*0-7837-1901-9*, 2042105) Bks Demand.

***Country Walks & Bikeways in the Philadelphia Region.** Alan Fisher. (Country Walks Ser.). (Illus.). 239p. 1994. pap. 11.95 (*0-614-04934-2*) Rambler Bks.

Country Walks in Connecticut: A Guide to the Nature Conservancy Preserves. 2nd ed. Susan D. Cooley. LC 88-36701. (Country Walks Ser.). (Illus.). 240p. 1989. pap. 8.95 (*0-910146-78-0*) AMC Books.

***Country Walks Near Baltimore.** 3rd ed. Alan Fisher. (Country Walks Ser.). (Illus.). 287p. 1993. pap. 8.95 (*0-9614963-4-7*) Rambler Bks.

Country Walks Near Boston. 2nd ed. Alan Fisher. (Country Walks Ser.). (Illus.). 176p. 1986. pap. 8.95 (*0-910146-58-6*) AMC Books.

Country Walks Near Chicago. Alan Fisher. (Illus.). 207p. 1987. pap. 9.95 (*0-9614963-1-2*) Rambler Bks.

Country Walks Near Montreal. William G. Scheller. (Country Walks Ser.). (Illus.). 160p. 1982. pap. 8.95 (*0-910146-40-3*) AMC Books.

Country Walks Near New York. 2nd ed. William G. Scheller. (Country Walks Ser.). (Illus.). 208p. (Orig.). 1986. pap. 8.95 (*0-910146-59-4*) AMC Books.

Country Ways. Reader's Digest Editors. LC 87-23308. (Illus.). 304p. 1988. 25.95 (*0-89577-290-6*, Random) RD Assn.

Country Ways in Hampshire & Dorset. Anthony Howard. 80p. 1987. 30.00 (*0-905392-66-3*) St Mut.

Country Ways in Kent. Anthony Howard. 80p. 1987. 30.00 (*0-905392-67-1*) St Mut.

Country Ways in Sussex & Surrey. Anthony Howard. 80p. 1987. 30.00 (*0-905392-68-X*) St Mut.

Country Wedding. Berry Fleming. 128p. 1983. 8.95 (*0-932298-29-X*) Tri-State Pr Corp.

Country Wedding. Berry Fleming. LC 88-92615. 128p. 1989. reprint ed. 22.00 (*0-933256-74-4*) Second Chance.

***Country Wedding Favorites.** Ed. by Carol Cuellar & Manny Quinones. 96p. (Orig.). (YA). 1994. pap. text ed. 12.95 (*0-89898-876-4*) CPP Belwin.

***Country Wedding Favorites.** rev. ed. Ed. by Carol Cuellar & Manny Quinones. 96p. (Orig.). (YA). 1995. pap. text ed. 12.95 (*0-89724-467-2*) Warner Brothers.

Country Western Dancing. Marilyn Argus & Diane Glynn. Ed. by Suzanne Rafer. (Illus.). 128p. (Orig.). 1994. pap. 8.95 (*1-56305-548-1*) Workman Pub.

Country-Western Dancing. Barry Nelson. (Illus.). 72p. (Orig.). 1993. pap. 6.95 (*0-911007-29-6*) Prairie Hse.

Country-Western Guide to Life: From Down-Home Talkin' to Steppin' Tall in Your Boots. Mickey Flodin & Carol Flodin. 128p. (Orig.). 1993. pap. 7.95 (*0-8092-3776-8*) Contemp Bks.

***Country Western Line Dancing: Run to the Floor For.** Hilton Osborne. (Illus.). 192p. (Orig.). 1994. pap. 19.95 (*1-882180-37-2*) Griffin CA.

Country Wife. 2nd ed. William Wycherley. Ed. by James Ogden. (New Mermaid Ser.). 152p. (C). 1991. pap. text ed. 6.95 (*0-393-90063-0*) Norton.

Country Wife see Restoration Plays

Country Wife see Six Restoration Plays

Country Winemaker & Brewer. Ed. by Richard Humphrey. 160p. 1990. pap. write for info. (*0-9610602-7-1*) Teaparty Bks.

Country Winemaking. Barbara B. Johanns. (Illus.). 112p. 1990. pap. 7.95 (*0-929935-01-2*) Countrywomans Pr.

Country Wines: Making & Using Wines from Herbs, Fruits, Flowers & More. Pattie Vargas & Rich Gulling. Ed. by Jill Mason. LC 91-746. (Illus.). 176p. 1992. pap. 12.95 (*0-88266-749-1*) Storey Comm Inc.

Country Wines to Make, Drink & Cook With. Mollie Harris & Helen Peacocke. (Illus.). 160p. 1991. 26.00 (*0-86299-992-8*) A Sutton Pub.

Country Wisdom: Counted Cross-Stitch. Polly Carboni & Jean D. Crowther. (Illus.). 8p. (Orig.). 1987. pap. 5.98 (*0-88290-295-4*) Horizon Utah.

Country Wisdom Best Fences. 1984. pap. 2.95 (*0-88266-335-6*) Storey Comm Inc.

***Country Wisdom Journal.** Storey Publishing Editors Staff. 128p. 1995. 16.95 (*0-88266-882-X*, Storey Pub) Storey Comm Inc.

Country Wit. rev. ed. Reinhart B. Fischer. 10p. 1991. pap. 6.95 (*1-880718-00-6*) Genius New.

Country Woman's Christmas. Louisa V. Kyle. 72p. (Orig.). 1993. pap. 9.95 (*0-927044-03-X*) Four OClock Farms.

Country Woman's Scrapbook. Louisa V. Kyle. Ed. by Joseph Dunn. (Illus.). 112p. 1980. 12.95 (*0-927044-01-3*) Four OClock Farms.

Country Wood Projects. Lavon B. Smith. LC 93-17329. (Illus.). 164p. 1993. pap. 12.95 (*0-8069-0318-X*) Sterling.

Country Woodcraft Patterns. Doris Pugh & Charles W. Pugh. LC 90-39880. (Illus.). 168p. (Orig.). (YA). (gr. 10-12). 1990. pap. 12.95 (*0-8069-7360-9*) Sterling.

***Country Woodworking: How to Make Rustic Furniture, Utensils & Decorations.** Jack Hill. LC 94-44479. 1995. 22.95 (*0-8118-1086-0*) Chronicle Bks.

Country Worth Saving. Guy V. Jagt. LC 85-149644. 128p. 1984. 10.95 (*0-915463-04-0*) Green Hill.

Country Wreath Kit Book. Richard Kollath & Tim Frew. 48p. 1990. 39.98 (*0-9627134-0-6*, Friedman-Fairfax) M Friedman Pub Grp Inc.

Country Wreaths from Caprilands. Adelma G. Simmons. (Illus.). 176p. 1989. 17.95 (*0-318-42365-0*) Wieser & Wieser.

Country Year: Living the Questions. Sue Hubbell. LC 85-10784. (Illus.). 240p. 1986. 17.95 (*0-394-55146-X*) Random.

Countryblast: Your Countryside Needs You Now. Clive Aslet. (Illus.). 128p. 1992. 22.95 (*0-7195-4945-0*, Pub. by John Murray UK) Trafalgar.

Countryman Family. Ardell Countryman & Grace Countryman. (Illus.). 414p. 1987. 55.00 (*0-88107-081-5*) Curtis Media.

Countryman's Tale. Syd Tyrrell. (National Trust Classic Ser.). (Illus.). 286p. 1992. pap. 15.95 (*0-7126-4673-6*, Pub. by Century UK) Trafalgar.

Countryman's Year. write for info. (*0-318-58220-1*) P-H.

Countryman's Year. large type ed. Thurlow Craig. 1991. 21.95 (*0-7089-2364-X*) Ulverscroft.

***Countryman's Year.** Hayden Pearson. (American Autobiography Ser.). 192p. 1995. reprint ed. lib. bdg. 69.00 (*0-7812-8612-3*) Rprt Serv.

Countrymen of Bones. Robert O. Butler. LC 93-37099. 1994. 25.00 (*0-8050-3202-9*); pap. 11.00 (*0-8050-3142-1*) H Holt & Co.

***Country's Angels' Christmas.** Tomie DePaola. LC 94-37433. 1995. write for info. (*0-399-22817-9*, Putnam) Putnam Pub Group.

Country's Edge, Vol. 1. Shirley Koenig. 100p. 1987. pap. 7.50 (*1-56770-179-5*) S Scheewe Pubns.

Country's Edge, Vol. 2. Shirley Koenig. 100p. 1989. pap. 6.50 (*1-56770-212-0*) S Scheewe Pubns.

Countryscapes. Donna Bell. 100p. 1992. pap. 7.50 (*1-56770-249-X*) S Scheewe Pubns.

Countryside. Maria Rius & J. M. Parramon. (Let's Discover Ser.). (J). (ps). 1986. 6.95 (*0-8120-5749-X*); pap. 6.95 (*0-8120-3701-4*) Barron.

Countryside, Garden & Table: A New England Seasonal Diary. Martha A. Rubin. LC 92-54761. (Illus.). 260p. 1993. 19.95 (*1-55591-137-4*) Fulcrum Pub.

Countryside Ideal: Anglo-American Images of Landscape. Michael Bunce. LC 93-33662. (Illus.). 256p. 1994. 65.00x (*0-415-10434-3*, B7043); pap. 18.95 (*0-415-10435-1*, B7047) Routledge.

***Countryside, Illustrated Treasuries.** Lovric. (Illus.). 1995. 6.98 (*1-56138-524-7*) Courage Bks.

Countryside in the Age of Capitalist Transformation: Essays in the Social History of Rural America. Ed. by Steven Hahn & Jonathan Prude. LC 85-2847. xii, 355p. 1985. 45.00 (*0-8078-1666-3*); pap. 14.95 (*0-8078-4139-0*) U of NC Pr.

Countryside in Trust: Land Management by Conservation, Recreation & Amenity Organization. Janet Dwyer & Ian Hodge. 224p. 1994. text ed. 49.95 (*0-470-21997-1*) Halsted Pr.

***Countryside in Trust: Land Management by Conservation, Recreation & Organization.** Janet Dwyer & Ian Hodge. Date not set. text ed. 49.95 (*0-471-94871-3*) Wiley.

Countryside Law. B. L. Jones & J. F. Garner. 1987. pap. 100.00 (*0-7219-1060-2*, Scientific) St Mut.

Countryside, Mirror of Ourselves. 2nd ed. Joseph Amato. (Illus.). 60p. 1983. pap. 3.50 (*0-685-08703-4*) Crossings Pr.

Countryside, Mirror of Ourselves: Essays about Calling Farmers Names, Peasants Living in the City, & Other Rural Gleanings. Joseph Amato. (Illus.). vi, 49p. 1992. reprint ed. 6.95 (*0-9614119-5-3*) Crossings Pr.

Countryside of Medieval England. Grenville Astill & Annie Grant. (Illus.). 300p. 1988. text ed. 21.95 (*0-631-18442-2*) Blackwell Pubs.

Countryside of Nijar. Juan Goytisolo. Tr. by Luigi Luccarelli. Bd. with Chanca. LC 86-7929. 160p. 1987. 16.00 (*0-934184-19-4*); Bd. with Set pap. 9.00 (*0-934184-20-8*) Alembic Pr.

Countryside Planning Policies for the Nineteen Nineties. Andrew W. Gilg. 300p. 1991. 76.00 (*0-85198-744-3*) CAB Intl.

Countryside Reflections. Susan Scheewe. 48p. 1986. pap. 6.50 (*1-56770-161-2*) S Scheewe Pubns.

***Countrysides at Risk: The Political Geography of Sustainable Agriculture.** Robert L. Paarlberg. LC 94-43973. (Policy Essay Ser.: Vol. 16). 1994. pap. 9.95 (*1-56517-021-0*) Overseas Dev Council.

Countrysport Wingshooter's Journal: A Bird Hunter's Personal Diary. 72p. 1992. 34.50 (*0-924357-30-4*, 1033) Countrysport Pr.

Countrywoman-Surgeon. Lynn Strongin. LC 79-12821. 70p. 1979. 6.95 (*0-934332-17-7*) LEpervier Pr.

***Countrywoman's Calendar.** Bessie Skea. 60p. 1988. pap. 4.95 (*0-9606262-2-0*) Yesnaby Inc.

Countrywoman's Year. Rosemary Verey. 1991. 19.95 (*0-316-89977-1*) Little.

County Agent. Arnold Barber. (UED 85 Ser.). (Illus.). 1989. pap. 9.95 (*0-933842-11-2*) Extension Div.

County Agents Directory. 62th ed. Ed. by M. J. Mast. 1977. 6.50 (*0-686-20517-0*) C L Mast.

C

An Asterisk (*) at the beginning of an entry indicates that the title is appearing in BIP for the first time.

An Asterisk (*) at the beginning of an entry indicates that the title is appearing in BIP for the first time.

1657

Coupleship: How to Build a Relationship. Sharon Wegscheider-Cruse. (Illus.). (Orig.). 1988. pap. 8.95 (*0-932194-64-8*) Health Comm.

Couples's Guide to Fertility. R. Huneger. 1986. 5.00 (*0-685-59737-7*, J602) Human Life Intl.

Couplets from Kabir. G. N. Das. (C). 1991. 17.50 (*81-208-0935-1*, Pub. by Motilal Banarsidass II) S Asia.

***Coupling.** I. M. Alethia. 300p. (Orig.). 1995. pap. 18.95 (*0-9646354-0-2*) Epiphany CA.

Coupling ... What Makes Permanance: A Feminine Perspective. Ed. by Barbara J. Brothers. LC 91-123880. (Journal of Couples Therapy). (Illus.). 109p. 1992. text ed. 24.95 (*1-56024-186-1*) Haworth Pr.

Coupling Alignment (Reference Card) Tel-A-Train, Inc. Staff. 1979. student ed 0.15 (*1-56355-232-9*) Tel-A-Train.

Coupling Convention: Tradition & the Black Female Talent. Ann DuCille. LC 93-19916. 1993. pap. 16.95 (*0-19-508509-4*) OUP.

Coupling of External Electromagnetic Fields to Transmission Lines. Albert A. Smith, Jr. LC 76-49504. (Illus.). 133p. 1977. 49.00 (*0-471-01995-X*) D White Consult.

Coupling Processes in the Lower & Middle Atmosphere: Proceedings of the NATO Advanced Research Workshop, Loen, Norway May 25-30, 1992. Ed. by Eivind V. Thrane et al. LC 92-43798. (NATO Advanced Science Institutes Series C: Mathematical & Physical Sciences: No. 387). 420p. (C). 1993. lib. bdg. 169.00 (*0-7923-2127-8*) Kluwer Ac.

Coupling Symbolic & Numerical Computing in Expert System, II: Papers from the Workshop, Bellevue, Washington 20-22 July, 1987. Ed. by Janusz S. Kowalik & C. T. Kitzmiller. 282p. 1988. 72.00 (*0-444-70401-9*, North Holland) Elsevier.

Coupling Symbolic & Numerical Computing in Expert Systems: Papers from the Workshop, Bellevue, WA, 27-29 August 1985. Ed. by Janusz S. Kowalik. 336p. 1986. 72.00 (*0-444-87988-9*) Elsevier.

***Couplings.** Peter Schneider. Tr. by Philip Boehm. 356p. Date not set. 24.00 (*0-374-13053-1*) FS&G.

Couplings: A Book of Stories. Richard Hall. LC 80-26609. 202p. 1981. pap. 7.95 (*0-912516-58-5*) Grey Fox.

Couplings & Joints: Design, Selection & Application. Mancuso. (Mechanical Engineering Ser.: Vol. 45). 488p. 1986. 140.00 (*0-8247-7400-0*) Dekker.

Coupon & Refund Guide. Jana Mahon. (Illus.). 52p. (Orig.). 1989. pap. 4.00 (*0-685-25744-4*) J L Mahon.

Coupon Bonds & Other Stories. John T. Trowbridge. 1972. reprint ed. 19.00 (*0-8422-8119-3*) Irvington.

Coupon Clippers. Mark Doeffinger. 98p. (Orig.). 1985. pap. 4.95 (*0-9615463-0-1*) Ross St.

Coupon Interest Calendar. Financial Publishing Co. Staff. 760p. 1994. pap. 50.00 (*0-87600-360-9*) Finan Pub.

Coupon Networking: A Workbook. Training Manuals, Research Division Staff. 1985. 19.95 (*0-318-04430-7*, Training Manuals) Prosperity & Profits.

Coupon Search - How to Obtain Coupons, Forms, Etc. A Workbook. rev. ed. 70p. 1993. 19.95 (*0-913597-96-1*) Prosperity & Profits.

Couponing for Wealth: The Only Couponing & Money Guide that Shows You How to Quickly Organize & Turn Cents-off Coupons into Thousands of Extra Dollars. Steven W. Caudill & L. Susan Caudill. LC 90-61928. 140p. 1990. pap. 9.95 (*0-9627101-0-5*) Money Watchers Pub.

Coups & Army Rule in Africa: Motivation & Constraints. 2nd ed. Samuel Decalo. 368p. (C). 1990. text ed. 42.00 (*0-300-04043-1*); pap. 19.00 (*0-300-04045-8*) Yale U Pr.

Coups & Cocaine: Journeys in South America. Anthony Daniels. LC 86-18054. (Illus.). 240p. 1987. reprint ed. 17.95 (*0-87951-263-6*); reprint ed. pap. 9.95 (*0-87951-311-X*) Overlook Pr.

***Coups de Marteau: Hammer Blows.** Afrikadzata Deku (Afrikan Culture Institute) Staff. LC 91-72690. (Afrikan Poetry in French Ser.). 90p. 1995. write for info. (*1-56454-028-6*) Cont Afrikan.

Coups de Soleil: Textes. Henry de Montherlant. 344p. (FRE.). 1976. pap. 19.95 (*0-7859-1346-7*, 2070293637) Fr & Eur.

Cour et l'Opera sous Louis XVI: Marie-Antoinette et Sacchini; Salieri; Favart et Gluck. Adolphe Jullien. LC 76-43947. (Music & Theatre in France in the 17th & 18th Centuries Ser.). reprint ed. 55.00 (*0-404-60166-9*) AMS Pr.

Courage. J. M. Barrie. 12.95 (*0-89190-519-7*, Am Repr) Amereon Ltd.

Courage. Elaine Goley. (Learn the Value Ser.). (Illus.). 32p. (J). (gr. 1-4). 1987. lib. bdg. 15.94 (*0-86592-377-9*); lib. bdg. 11.95 (*0-685-67576-9*) Rourke Corp.

Courage. Ellen Kahaner. (Illus.). 64p. (YA). (gr. 7-12). 1990. lib. bdg. 14.95 (*0-8239-1112-8*) Rosen Group.

Courage! Nachman of Breslov & Nathan of Breslov. 119p. (Orig.). 1983. pap. 3.00 (*0-930213-23-8*) Breslov Res Inst.

Courage. rev. ed. Edwin L. Cole. 170p. 1991. pap. 4.95 (*0-89274-873-7*, HH-873) Harrison Hse.

Courage. rev. ed. Jane B. Moncure. LC 80-39515. (Values to Live By Ser.). (Illus.). 32p. (ENG & SPA.). (J). (ps-2). 1981. lib. bdg. 21.36 (*0-89565-202-1*) Childs World.

***Courage.** rev. ed. Jane B. Moncure. LC 80-39515. (Values to Live By Ser.). (Illus.). 32p. (ENG & SPA.). (J). (ps-2). 1981. pap. text ed. 21.36 (*0-89565-935-2*) Childs World.

Courage: How to Make Things Happen. Clifford Self. 160p. (Orig.). 1991. pap. 7.95 (*0-917595-37-8*) Kingdom Pubs.

Courage: The Story of Courage Center. Mavis A. Voigt. LC 89-60274. (Illus.). xii, 112p. 1989. 14.95 (*0-9622455-0-X*) Courage Ctr.

Courage a Grace - A Biography of Dame Mary Gilmore. W. H. Wilde. 1988. 45.95 (*0-522-84368-9*) Intl Spec Bk.

***Courage & Air Warfare.** M. E. Wells. 256p. 1995. pap. 22.50 (*0-7146-4148-0*, Pub. by F Cass Pubs UK) Intl Spec Bk.

***Courage & Air Warfare: The Allied Aircrew Experience in the Second World War.** M. E. Wells. LC 95-3290. (Studies in Air Power). 256p. 1995. 40.00 (*0-7146-4618-0*, Pub. by F Cass Pubs UK) Intl Spec Bk.

Courage & Conscience: Black & White Abolitionists in Boston. Ed. by Donald M. Jacobs. LC 92-31395. (Illus.). 1993. 39.95 (*0-253-33198-6*); pap. 19.95 (*0-253-20793-2*) Ind U Pr.

Courage & Love. Gisela Konopka. (Orig.). (YA). (gr. 7 up). 1988. pap. 10.95 (*0-9621328-0-2*) G Konopka.

Courage & Tools: The Florence Howe Award for Feminist Scholarship, 1974-1989. Ed. by Joanne Glasgow. LC 90-44932. xxx, 275p. 1990. text ed. 37.50 (*0-87352-344-X*, B821C); pap. text ed. 17.50 (*0-87352-345-8*, B821P) Modern Lang.

Courage at Indian Deep. Jane R. Thomas. (J). (gr. 4-7). 1990. pap. 5.95 (*0-395-55699-6*, Clarion Bks) HM.

Courage by Darkness. Jeri Massi. (Light Line Ser.). 157p. (Orig.). (J). 1987. pap. 5.95 (*0-89084-412-7*) Bob Jones Univ Pr.

Courage Covenant see **And Should She Die**

Courage, etc. see **Works of J. M. Barrie**

Courage for Today Hope for Tomorrow. Esther Onstad. LC 75-2829. 144p. 1993. pap. 10.99 (*0-8066-2651-8*, 9-2651) Augsburg Fortress.

Courage for Truth. Thomas Merton. 1994. pap. 15.95 (*0-15-600004-0*) HarBrace.

Courage for Truth: Letters to Writers. Thomas Merton. Ed. by Christine M. Bochen. LC 92-37078. 1993. 25.00 (*0-374-13055-8*) FS&G.

Courage High. Sally Holloway. 280p. 1992. pap. 35.00 (*0-11-701689-6*, HM16896, Pub. by HMSO UK) UNIPUB.

Courage in Adversity. Michael Forsyth-Grant. 229p. (C). 1989. text ed. 60.00 (*0-946270-81-3*, Pub. by Pentland Pr UK) St Mut.

Courage in Mission: Presidential Leadership in the Church-Related College. Ed. by Duane H. Dagley. 165p. 1988. 32.00 (*0-89964-256-X*) Coun Adv & Supp Ed.

Courage in Politics & Other Essays, 1885-1896. Coventry K. Patmore. LC 68-26464. (Essay Index Reprint Ser.). 1977. reprint ed. 19.95 (*0-8369-0774-4*) Ayer.

Courage in the Ashes. William W. Johnstone. 1991. mass mkt. 3.99 (*0-8217-3574-8*) Zebra.

Courage in the Skies: Great Air Battles from the Somme to Desert Storm. J. E. Johnson & P. B. Lucas. (Illus.). 208p. 1993. 39.95 (*0-09-174676-0*, Pub. by S Paul UK) Trafalgar.

Courage Is a Three-Letter Word. Walter Anderson. LC 85-25711. 320p. 1986. 17.95 (*0-394-54656-3*) Random.

***Courage, Mere Afrique: Worry Not, Mother Afrika.** Afrikadzata Deku (Afrikan Culture Institute) Staff. LC 91-72689. (Afrikan Poetry in French Ser.). 80p. 1995. write for info. (*1-56454-027-8*) Cont Afrikan.

Courage, My Love: Women Who Dare. Lynn Leslie. (Superromance Ser.). 1993. mass mkt. 3.50 (*0-373-70566-2*, 1-70566-4) Harlequin Bks.

Courage of a Critic: Edgar Poe As Editor. Robert D. Jacobs. 1971. pap. 2.00 (*0-910556-04-0*) Enoch Pratt.

Courage of a Southern Unionist: A Biography of Isaac Murphy, Governor of Arkansas, 1864-1868. John I. Smith. LC 79-64703. 152p. 1979. 6.95 (*0-914546-24-4*) Rose Pub.

Courage of Captain Plum. James O. Curwood. LC 71-144593. (BCL Ser. I). (Illus.). reprint ed. 18.00 (*0-404-01895-5*) AMS Pr.

Courage of Conviction. Ed. by Phillip L. Berman. 1986. pap. 9.95 (*0-345-33296-2*, Ballantine Trade) Ballantine.

Courage of Girls. Jean McGarry. LC 91-23149. (Fiction Ser.). 250p. 1992. 22.95 (*0-8135-1771-0*) Rutgers U Pr.

Courage of Helen Keller. Francene Sabin. LC 81-23109. (Illus.). 48p. (J). (gr. 4-6). 1982. lib. bdg. 10.79 (*0-89375-754-3*); pap. text ed. 3.50 (*0-89375-755-1*) Troll Assocs.

Courage of Judgment: Essays in Criticism, Culture & Society. George A. Panichas & Austin Warren. LC 81-4050. 318p. 1982. text ed. 36.00x (*0-87049-325-6*) U of Tenn Pr.

Courage of Magic Johnson. Peter Pascarelli. 1992. mass mkt. 3.99 (*0-553-29915-8*) Bantam.

***Courage of Sarah Noble.** Garrett Christopher. Ed. by J. Friedland & R. Kessler. (Novel-Ties Ser.). (J). (gr. 2-4). 1992. student ed, pap. text ed. 15.95 (*0-88122-722-6*) Lrn Links.

Courage of Sarah Noble. 2nd ed. Alice Dalgliesh. LC 91-15531. (Illus.). 64p. (J). (gr. 1-5). 1991. reprint ed. pap. 4.95 (*0-689-71540-4*, Aladdin Paperbacks) S&S Childrens.

Courage of Sarah Noble. Alice Dalgliesh. LC 54-5922. (Illus.). 64p. (J). (gr. 1-5). 1987. reprint ed. text ed. 13.95 (*0-684-18830-9*, C Scribner Sons Young) S&S Childrens.

Courage of the Early Morning. W. A. Bishop. 211p. 1991. pap. 5.95 (*0-7710-1522-4*, Pub. by McClelland & Stewart CN) Firefly Bks Ltd.

Courage of the Mountain Man. William W. Johnstone. 1992. pap. 3.50 (*0-8217-3720-1*) Zebra.

***Courage of the Mountain Man.** William W. Johnstone. 224p. 1995. pap. 4.50 (*0-8217-5058-5*) Zebra.

Courage of the Rainbow: Selected Poems. Bronislava Volkova et al. Tr. by Willis Barnstone & Gregory Oir. LC 92-34198. 120p. (Orig.). 1993. pap. 12.95 (*1-878818-20-1*) Sheep Meadow.

Courage of Their Convictions: Sixteen Americans Who Fought Their Way to the Supreme Court. Peter Irons. (Illus.). 380p. 1988. text ed. 27.95 (*0-02-915670-X*) Free Pr.

Courage of Their Convictions: Sixteen Americans Who Fought Their Way to the Supreme Court. Peter Irons. 432p. 1990. pap. 12.95 (*0-14-012810-7*, Penguin Bks) Viking Penguin.

Courage of Turtles. Edward Hoagland. 256p. 1993. pap. 14.95 (*1-55821-215-9*) Lyons & Burford.

Courage on Mirror Mountain. W. Fraser. LC 89-31978. (White Horse Ser.). 128p. (J). (gr. 3-7). 1989. pap. 4.99 (*1-55513-039-9*, Chariot Bks) Chariot Family.

Courage Seed. Jean Richardson. LC 93-20182. (Illus.). 76p. (J). (gr. 3-6). 1993. 14.95 (*0-89015-902-5*) Sunbelt Media.

Courage to Achieve: Why America's Brightest Women Struggle to Fulfill Their Promise. Betty A. Walker & Marilyn Mehr. LC 92-20951. 1992. 20.00 (*0-671-73642-6*) S&S Trade.

Courage to Be. Paul Tillich. (Terry Lecture Ser.). (C). 1959. pap. 11.00 (*0-300-00241-6*, Y11) Yale U Pr.

Courage to Be Chaste. Benedict J. Groeschel. 128p. (Orig.). 1985. pap. 5.95 (*0-8091-2705-9*) Paulist Pr.

Courage to Be Gifted. Landau. pap. 10.00 (*0-89824-527-3*) Trillium Pr.

Courage to Be Rich. Ed. by Dianne Higginson & Diane Reverand. 1983. 14.95 (*0-317-61523-8*) M O Haroldsen.

Courage to Be Yourself: A Woman's Guide to Growing Beyond Emotional Dependence. rev. ed. Sue P. Thoele. 220p. 1991. reprint ed. lib. bdg. 29.00x (*0-8095-5850-5*) Borgo Pr.

Courage to Be Yourself: A Woman's Guide to Growing Beyond Emotional Dependence. rev. ed. Sue P. Thoele. 240p. 1991. reprint ed. pap. 10.95 (*0-943233-25-9*) Conari Press.

Courage to Care. Judy Ransom. 192p. 1994. pap. 9.95 (*0-8358-0701-0*) Upper Room Bks.

Courage to Care: Helping the Aging, Grieving, & Dying. Jeffrey A. Watson. LC 91-47537. 208p. (Orig.). 1992. pap. 10.99 (*0-8010-9715-0*) Baker Bk.

Courage to Care: Rescuers of Jews During the Holocaust. Carol Rittner & Sondra Myers. 176p. 1989. 35.00x (*0-8147-7397-4*); pap. 19.50 (*0-8147-7406-7*) NYU Pr.

Courage to Care: Responding to the Crisis of Children with Aids. Gary Anderson. 1990. pap. 15.95 (*0-87868-401-8*) Child Welfare.

Courage to Care, Strength to Serve: Reflections on Community Service. Geoffrey Comber et al. 161p. (Orig.). 1989. pap. 11.00 (*1-878461-19-2*) CZM Pr.

Courage to Change. Dennis Wholey. 320p. 1988. mass mkt. 5.99 (*0-446-35758-8*) Warner Bks.

Courage to Change: A Paradigm for Success. Shirley Summer. 160p. (Orig.). 1993. pap. 12.95 (*0-9635039-3-6*) SummerTime.

Courage to Change: An Introduction to the Life & Thought of Reinhold Niebuhr. June Bingham. LC 92-484. 1992. pap. 24.50 (*0-8191-8731-3*) U Pr of Amer.

Courage to Change: One Day at a Time in Al-Anon II. Al-Anon Family Group Headquarters, Inc. Staff. LC 92-71379. 384p. 1992. 9.00 (*0-910034-79-6*) Al-Anon.

Courage to Change: One Day at a Time in Al-Anon II. large type ed. LC 92-71379. 384p. 1992. 11.00 (*0-910034-84-2*) Al-Anon.

Courage to Change: The Christian Roots of the 12-Step Movement, Samuel M. Shoemaker. Dick B. LC 93-5984. 223p. (Orig.). 1994. pap. text ed. 9.99 (*0-8007-5499-9*) Revell.

***Courage to Change for Tomorrow.** Robert E. Staub. 300p. Date not set. 17.95 (*0-7610-0264-2*) NW Pub.

Courage to Conquer: Studies in Daniel. Doris W. Greig. Ed. by Mary Beckwith. LC 88-4398. (Joy of Living Bible Study Ser.). 180p. (Orig.). 1988. pap. 5.99 (*0-8307-1285-2*, 5419489) Regal.

***Courage to Create.** Rollo May. 1995. 20.50 (*0-8446-6854-0*) Peter Smith.

Courage to Create. Rollo May. LC 93-43718. 144p. 1994. pap. 9.95 (*0-393-31106-6*) Norton.

Courage to Doubt. Robert Davidson. LC 89-5023. 1989. pap. 14.95 (*0-334-01957-5*) TPI PA.

Courage to Fail: Art Mortell's Secrets for Business Success. Art Mortell. 1993. text ed. 18.95 (*0-07-043392-5*) McGraw.

Courage to Go On: Life after Addiction. Cynthia R. McClure. 192p. (Orig.). 1990. pap. 8.99 (*0-8010-6263-2*) Baker Bk.

Courage to Grieve: Creative Living, Recovery, & Growth Through Grief. Judy Tatelbaum. LC 84-47621. 160p. 1984. pap. 12.00 (*0-06-091185-9*, CN1185, PL) HarpC.

Courage to Heal: A Guide for Women Survivors of Child Sexual Abuse. Ellen Bass & Laura Davis. LC 91-58463. 544p. 1989. audio 18.00 (*0-89845-833-1*, PL) HarpC.

Courage to Heal: A Guide for Women Survivors of Child Sexual Abuse. 3rd rev. ed. Ellen Bass & Laura Davis. LC 93-48353. 592p. 1994. pap. 22.50 (*0-06-095066-8*, PL) HarpC.

Courage to Heal Workbook: For Men & Women Survivors of Child Sexual Abuse. Laura Davis. LC 89-45646. 352p. (Orig.). 1990. pap. 20.00 (*0-06-096437-5*, PL) HarpC.

***Courage to Inquire: Ideals & Realities in Higher Education.** Thomas Ehrlich & Juliet Frey. LC 95-3436. 1995. write for info. (*0-253-32913-2*) Ind U Pr.

Courage to Lead. Charles E. Farrell. (Illus.). 160p. (Orig.). 1994. 14.95 (*0-9642047-0-3*); pap. 9.95 (*0-9642047-1-1*) Falcon Bks.

Courage to Love...When Your Marriage Hurts. Gerald Foley. LC 92-71816. 160p. (Orig.). 1992. pap. 6.95 (*0-87793-488-6*) Ave Maria.

Courage to Pray. 3rd ed. Anthony Bloom & George LeFebvre. Tr. by Dinah Livingstone. 123p. (Orig.). 1984. reprint ed. pap. text ed. 8.95 (*0-88141-031-4*) St Vladimirs.

Courage to Question. Ed. by Caryn M. Musil. 224p. 1992. 15.00 (*0-911696-55-5*) Assn Am Coll.

***Courage to Raise Good Men.** Olga Silverstein & Beth Rashbaum. 288p. 1995. 11.95 (*0-14-017567-9*, Penguin Bks) Viking Penguin.

Courage to Raise Good Men: A Manifesto for Change. Olga Silverstein & Beth Rashbaum. LC 93-30253. 288p. 1994. 21.95 (*0-670-84836-0*, Viking) Viking Penguin.

***Courage to Remember: The Holocaust 1933-1945.** Simon Wiesenthal Center Staff. 50p. (Orig.). (RUS.). 1989. pap. text ed. write for info. (*0-943058-09-0*) S Wiesenthal Ctr.

Courage to Write. Ralph Keyes. 1995. 17.95 (*0-8050-3188-X*) H Holt & Co.

Courage under Fire: Testing Epictetus's Doctrines in a Laboratory of Human Behavior. James B. Stockdale. LC 93-42455. (Hoover Essays Ser.: No. 6). 1993. write for info. (*0-8179-3692-0*) Hoover Inst Pr.

Courage under Siege: Starvation, Disease, & Death in the Warsaw Ghetto. Charles G. Roland. (Studies in Jewish History). (Illus.). 352p. 1992. 30.00 (*0-19-506285-X*) OUP.

***Courageous & Holy.** Ellen Larson. Ed. by Debbie Bible. (Value Builders Ser.). (J). 1995. 7.95 (*0-7814-5096-9*, 10173) Cook.

Courageous Breed. large type ed. Peter Taylor. (Linford Western Library). 288p. 1992. pap. 14.95 (*0-7089-7260-8*, Trailtree Bookshop) Ulverscroft.

Courageous Captain. (Jataka Tales Ser.). (Illus.). 32p. (Orig.). (J). (gr. 1-5). 1989. 15.95 (*0-89800-194-3*); pap. 7.95 (*0-89800-195-1*) Dharma Pub.

***Courageous Crimefighters.** Robert Italia. LC 94-22098. (Profiles Ser.). (Illus.). 160p. (YA). 1995. 14.95 (*1-881508-21-8*) Oliver Pr MN.

***Courageous Follower: Standing up to & for Our Leaders.** Ira Chaleff. 208p. 1995. 24.95 (*1-881052-66-4*) Berrett-Koehler.

***Courageous Hearts: The Women of July 1944.** Dorothee Von Meding. Tr. & Anno. by Michael Balfour. (Illus.). 288p. 1995. 39.95 (*1-57181-853-7*); pap. 19.95 (*1-57181-879-0*) Berghahn Bks.

Courageous Incarnation: In Intimacy, Work, Childhood, & Aging. Fredrica H. Thompsett. LC 92-45781. 158p. 1993. 11.95 (*1-56101-075-8*) Cowley Pubns.

Courageous Overcomers: Old Testament Women. Sara Buswell. 1993. pap. 4.99 (*0-8010-1047-0*) Baker Bk.

Courageous Pacers: The Complete Guide to Running, Walking & Fitness for Kids (Ages 8-108), Incl. logbook & journal. Tim Erson. (Illus.). 224p. (Orig.). (J). (gr. 2 up). 1993. otabind 18.95 (*0-9636547-0-5*) PRO-ACTIV Pubns.

Courageous Pacers Classroom Fitness Program. Tim Erson. (Illus.). 1994. teacher ed 14.95 (*0-9636547-1-3*) PRO-ACTIV Pubns.

***Courageous Spirits: Aboriginal Heroes of Our Children.** Ed. by Mokakit Indian Education Research Association Staff. 180p. (Orig.). 1993. student ed, pap. 8.95 (*0-919441-50-5*, Pub. by Theytus Bks Ltd CN) Orca Bk Pubs.

***Courageous Spirits: Aboriginal Heroes of Our Children.** Mokakit Indian Education Research Association Staff. 76p. (Orig.). 1993. teacher ed, pap. 5.95 (*0-919441-51-3*, Pub. by Theytus Bks Ltd CN) Orca Bk Pubs.

***Courageous Teaching: Creating a Caring Environment for Learning.** Jim Andersen. (Illus.). 128p. 1995. pap. 24.95 (*0-8039-6239-8*) Corwin Pr.

Courageous Turke, or Amvrath the Third see **Raging Turke, or Baiazet the Second**

Courageous Universality: The Work of Schmuel Hugo Bergman. William Kluback. LC 92-1757. (Brown Judaic Studies: No. 245). 170p. 1992. 59.95 (*1-55540-693-9*, 140245) Scholars Pr GA.

***Courageous Walk Through Life: The Story of Aunt Fannie.** Jeannine W. Hamburg. LC 95-94355. (Illus.). 211p. (Orig.). 1995. 19.95 (*0-9623501-2-5*) Myrte Pr.

***Courageous Walk Through Life: The Story of Aunt Fannie.** Jeannine W. Hamburg. Ed. by Gloria Delamar. LC 95-94355. (Illus.). 211p. (Orig.). 1995. pap. 12.95 (*0-9623501-1-7*) Myrte Pr.

Courant: In Goettingen & New York. C. Reid. LC 76-17062. (Illus.). 1976. 49.00 (*0-387-90194-9*) Spr-Verlag.

Courant Ascendant. Harvey Jackins. 1981. pap. 10.00 (*0-911214-78-X*) Rational Isl.

Courant Computer Science Symposia, Vols. 7-9. Ed. by Randall Rustin. Incl. Vol. 7. Computational Complexity. 30.00 (*0-686-46259-9*); Vol. 8. Natural Language Processing. 36.00 (*0-686-46260-2*); Vol. 9. Combinatorial Algorithms. 40.00 (*0-686-46261-0*); 91.00 (*0-686-46258-0*) Algorithmics.

Courant Computer Science, Symposium 7: Computational Complexity. Ed. by Randall Rustin. (Illus.). 268p. 1973. 40.00 (*0-917448-01-4*) Algorithmics.

Courant Computer Science, Symposium 8: Natural Language Processing. Ed. by Randall Rustin. (Illus.). 350p. 1973. 40.00 (*0-917448-02-2*) Algorithmics.

Courant Computer Science Symposium 9: Combinatorial Algorithms. Ed. by Randall Rustin. (Illus.). 126p. 1973. 40.00 (*0-917448-03-0*) Algorithmics.

Courante of Newes from the East India. LC 74-28848. (English Experience Ser.: No. 729). 1975. reprint ed. 3.50 (*90-221-0729-9*) Walter J Johnson.

Courbet. Sarah Faunce. LC 92-21998. (Masters of Art Ser.). 1993. 22.95 (*0-8109-3182-6*) Abrams.

Courbet: The Complete Paintings, 2 vols., Set. Robert Fernier. (Illus.). (FRE.). 1988. 1,200.00 (*1-55660-016-X*) A Wofsy Fine Arts.

Courbet: To Venture Independence. Klaus Herding. Tr. by John W. Gabriel. (Illus.). 272p. (C). 1991. text ed. 55.00x (*0-300-03744-9*) Yale U Pr.

Courbet's Realism. Michael Fried. LC 89-35432. (Illus.). 350p. 1992. pap. text ed. 24.95 (*0-226-26215-4*) U Ch Pr.

An Asterisk (*) at the beginning of an entry indicates that the title is appearing in BIP for the first time.

An Asterisk (*) at the beginning of an entry indicates that the title is appearing in BIP for the first time.

Course in Miracles. 2nd ed. 1296p. 1992. pap. 25.00 (*0-9606388-8-1*) Found Inner Peace.

***Course in Miracles.** 2nd ed. 1992. 40.00 (*0-9606388-7-3*) Found Inner Peace.

Course in Miracles. 2nd rev. ed. 1296p. 1992. 30.00 (*0-9606388-9-X*) Found Inner Peace.

Course in Miracles, 3 vols., Set. LC 76-20363. 1975. teacher ed 40.00 (*0-9606388-0-6*) Found Inner Peace.

Course in Miracles: A Gift for all Mankind. 2nd ed. Tara Singh. 1992. pap. 9.95 (*1-55531-262-4*) Life Action Pr.

Course in Miracles & Christianity: A Dialogue - Kenneth Wapnick, Ph.D., W. Norris Clarke, S.J., Ph.D. Kenneth Wapnick & W. Norris Clarke. LC 94-10394. 113p. (Orig.). 1995. pap. 5.00 (*0-933291-18-3*) Foun Miracles.

Course in Miracles in Five Minutes. Jerry Sears. (Orig.). 1994. pap. 12.95 (*0-9639741-0-6*) Assocs Press.

Course in Modern Algebra. Peter J. Hilton & Yel-Chiang Wu. 1989. pap. text ed. 49.95 (*0-471-50405-X*) Wiley.

Course in Modern Bulgarian, Pt. 1. Milka Hubenova et al. (Illus.). viii, 303p. (C). 1983. reprint ed. pap. text ed. 17.95 (*0-89357-104-0*) Slavica.

Course in Modern Bulgarian, Pt. 2. Milka Hubenova & Ana Dzhumadanova. (Illus.). ix, 303p. 1983. reprint ed. pap. text ed. 17.95 (*0-89357-105-9*) Slavica.

Course in Modern Business Statistics. 2nd ed. Terry Sincich. Orig. Title: Contemporary Business Statistics. 832p. (C). 1994. write for info. (*0-02-410481-7*) Dellen Pub.

Course in Modern Business Statistics, Minitap Computer Supplement. 2nd ed. Ruth K. Meyer & David D. Krueger. (C). 1994. pap. write for info. (*0-02-380837-3*) Dellen Pub.

Course in Modern Business Statistics, Student's Solutions Manual. 2nd ed. Mark Dummeldinger. Orig. Title: Contemporary Business Statistics, Student's Solutions Manual. 144p. (C). 1994. pap. write for info. (*0-02-330741-2*) Dellen Pub.

Course in Modern Geometries. J. N. Cederberg. Ed. by J. H. Ewing et al. (Undergraduate Texts in Mathematics Ser.). (Illus.). xii, 232p. 1991. reprint ed. text ed. 42.00 (*0-387-96922-5*) Spr-Verlag.

Course in Modern Icelandic. J. Fridjonsson. 333p. 1978. pap. text ed. 62.00 (*0-88431-653-X*) IBD Ltd.

Course in Modern Western Armenian: Dictionary & Linguistic Notes. Thomas J. Samuelian. LC 88-38110. 288p. 1989. 19.50 (*0-9617933-2-5*) Armenian Natl Educ.

Course in Modern Western Armenian: Exercises & Commentary. Thomas J. Samuelian. LC 88-33309. 864p. 1989. 40.00 (*0-9617933-1-7*) Armenian Natl Educ.

Course in Nepali. David Matthews. 1984. pap. 42.50 (*0-8364-1061-0*, Pub. by Sch Orient & African Stud UK) S Asia.

***Course in Number Theory.** 2nd ed. H. E. Rose. 416p. (C). 1995. text ed. 46.95 (*0-19-853479-5*) OUP.

Course in Number Theory & Cryptography. Neal Koblitz. (Graduate Texts in Mathematics Ser.: Vol. 114). (Illus.). 210p. 1993. 39.00 (*0-387-96576-9*, 788) Spr-Verlag.

***Course in Number Theory & Cryptography No. 114.** N. I. Koblitz. 248p. 1994. 39.95 (*0-387-94293-9*) Spr-Verlag.

Course in Ocean Engineering. Sverre Gran. LC 92-18205. (Developments in Marine Technology Ser.: Vol. 8). 1992. write for info. (*0-444-88143-3*) Elsevier.

Course in Phonetics. 2nd ed. Peter Ladefoged. 300p. (Orig.). (C). 1982. pap. text ed. 24.00 (*0-15-515178-9*) HB Coll Pubs.

Course in Phonetics. 3rd ed. Peter Ladefoged. LC 91-78390. (Illus.). 300p. (Orig.). (C). 1993. pap. text ed. 26.75 (*0-15-500173-6*) HB Coll Pubs.

Course in Probability Theory. 2nd ed. Kai L. Chung. (Probability & Mathematical Statistics Ser.). 1974. text ed. 59.50 (*0-12-174650-X*) Acad Pr.

Course in Ring Theory. Donald Passman. (C). 1991. text ed. 60.00 (*0-534-13776-8*) Van Nos Reinhold.

Course in Romance Linguistics, Vol. 1: A Synchronic View. Frederick B. Agard. LC 83-20817. 254p. (Orig.). (C). 1984. pap. 22.95 (*0-87840-088-5*) Georgetown U Pr.

Course in Romance Linguistics, Vol. 2: A Diachronic View. Frederick B. Agard. LC 93-20817. 256p. 1984. text ed. 22.95 (*0-87840-089-3*) Georgetown U Pr.

Course in Russian History: The 17th Century. V. O. Kliuchevsky. Tr. by Natalie Duddington. 448p. (C). 1994. text ed. 49.95 (*1-56324-316-4*); pap. text ed. 19.95 (*1-56324-317-2*) M E Sharpe.

Course in Scientific German. Hans Meinel. 248p. 1972. 32.75 (*3-19-001103-6*) Adlers Foreign Bks.

Course in Simulation. Sheldon M. Ross. 326p. (C). 1990. write for info. (*0-02-403891-1*) Macmillan.

Course in Spoken Arabic. Shafti Shaikh. (Orig.). (C). 1980. pap. text ed. 8.95 (*0-19-561067-9*) OUP.

Course in Spoken Tamazight: Berber Dialects of the Middle Atlas. Ernest T. Abdel-Massih. LC 79-32218. (C). 1970. pap. text ed. 16.00 (*0-932098-04-5*) UM Ctr MENAS.

Course in Statistical Mechanics. Harold L. Friedman. (Illus.). 272p. (C). 1985. text ed. 89.00 (*0-13-184565-9*) P-H.

Course in the Art of Measurement with Compass & Ruler. Albrecht Durer. (Printed Sources of Western Art Ser.). (Illus.). 180p. (GER.). 1981. reprint ed. boxed 65.00 (*0-915346-52-4*) A Wofsy Fine Arts.

Course in the Theory of Groups. D. J. Robinson. (Graduate Texts in Mathematics Ser.: Vol. 80). 480p. 1982. 59.00 (*0-387-90600-2*) Spr-Verlag.

Course in the Theory of Groups. 2nd ed. D. J. Robinson. (Graduate Texts in Mathematics Ser.: Vol. 80). (Illus.). 500p. 1993. pap. text ed. write for info. (*3-540-94092-8*) Spr-Verlag.

***Course in the Theory of Groups.** 2nd ed. Derek J. Robinson. LC 95-4025. (Graduate Texts in Mathematics: Vol. 80). 1995. write for info. (*0-387-94461-3*) Spr-Verlag.

Course in the Theory of Groups. D. J. Robinson. Ed. by J. H. Ewing et al. (Graduate Texts in Mathematics Ser.: Vol. 80). (Illus.). 502p. 1994. reprint ed. pap. 42.50 (*0-387-94092-8*) Spr-Verlag.

Course in Theoretical Statistics. N. A. Rahman. 542p. 1968. text ed. 26.95 (*0-85264-068-4*) Lubrecht & Cramer.

Course in Thermodynamics, Vol. 1. rev. ed. Joseph Kestin. 725p. 1979. pap. 63.00 (*0-89116-640-8*) Hemisp Pub.

Course in Thermodynamics, Vol. 2. Joseph Kestin. 617p. 1979. 63.00 (*0-89116-641-6*) Hemisp Pub.

Course in Triangulations for Solving Equations with Deformations. B. C. Eaves. (Lecture Notes in Economics & Mathematical Systems Ser.: Vol. 234). 302p. 1984. pap. 41.00 (*0-387-13876-5*) Spr-Verlag.

Course in Tswana. Desmond T. Cole & Dingaan M. Mokaila. LC 70-278557. 146p. reprint ed. pap. 41.70 (*0-7837-6311-5*, 2046026) Bks Demand.

Course in Universal Algebra. S. Burris & H. P Sankappanavar. (Graduate Texts in Mathematics Ser.: Vol. 78). (Illus.). 320p. 1981. 49.00 (*0-387-90578-2*) Spr-Verlag.

Course Leader's Cookbook: With Recipes for Successful Learning Experiences. Richard D. Colvin & Naomi C. Steinberg. 89p. 1985. spiral bd. 19.95 (*0-88390-303-2*) Pfeiffer & Co.

Course Materials on Buying, Selling, & Merging Businesses. John H. McCord et al. 351p. 1975. Supplement 1978. 3.00 (*0-317-30795-9*, B145) Am Law Inst.

Course Materials on Buying, Selling, & Merging Businesses, Incl. 1978 suppl. John H. McCord et al. 351p. 1975. Incl. 1978 supplement. 51.00 (*0-317-30793-2*, B145/B146) Am Law Inst.

Course Materials on Lifetime & Testamentary Estate Planning. 4th ed. Edward M. David & Maurice D. Lee, III. 174p. 1982. pap. 37.00 (*0-8318-0409-2*, B409) Am Law Inst.

Course Materials on the Law of European Economic Community. George A. Bermann et al. (American Casebook Ser.). 1200p. (C). 1993. text ed. 55.00 (*0-314-01170-6*) West Pub.

Course Mathematical Analysis, Pt. II. A. Bermant & D. Brown. LC 62-9695. (On Pure & Applied Mathematics Ser.). 1963. 162.00 (*0-08-009817-7*, Pub. by Pergamon Repr UK) Franklin.

Course Models for the History - Social Science Framework, Grade Six - World History & Geography: Ancient Civilizations. California Department of Education Staff. (Illus.). 128p. 1993. pap. 9.50 (*0-8011-1034-3*) Calif Education.

Course Models for the History-Social Science Framework, Grade Five - United States History & Geography: Making a New Nation. California Department of Education Staff. (Illus.). 126p. 1991. pap. 9.50 (*0-8011-0978-7*) Calif Education.

Course Models for the History-Social Science Framework, Grade Seven - World History & Geography: Medieval & Early Modern Times. California Department of Education Staff. (Illus.). 386p. 1994. pap. 12.75 (*0-8011-1132-3*) Calif Education.

Course Notes for Financial Accounting: Spring 1994 Version. Alvin Arens. 256p. (C). 1994. spiral bd. 7.49 (*0-8403-9303-2*) Kendall-Hunt.

Course Notes for Financial Accounting Fall 1993. Alvin A. Arens. 256p. (C). 1993. pap. text ed., spiral bd. 7.49 (*0-8403-9014-9*) Kendall-Hunt.

Course of Advanced Lessons in Clairvoyance & Occult Powers. Swami Panchadasi. 319p. 1976. reprint ed. spiral bd. 11.00 (*0-7873-0653-3*) Mokelumne.

Course of American Democratic Thought. 3rd ed. Ralph H. Gabriel & Robert H. Walker. LC 85-27161. (Contributions in American Studies: No. 87). (Illus.). 587p. 1986. text ed. 75.00 (*0-313-24999-7*, GCD, Greenwood Pr) Greenwood.

Course of American Diplomacy: From the Revolution to the Present. 2nd ed. Howard Jones. 475p. (C). 1988. Vol. 2: From 1897, 475p. pap. 26.95 (*0-534-10606-4*) Intl Thomson.

Course of British History: Tudors & Stuarts. John Ray & James Hagerty. (Illus.). 96p. 1987. pap. 13.95 (*0-09-170781-1*, Pub. by S Thornes UK) Dufour.

Course of British History, Bk. 1: The Romans to the Middle Age. Ray Hagerty. (C). 1987. pap. 13.95 (*0-09-167961-3*, Pub. by S Thornes UK) Dufour.

Course of British History, Bk. 2: Tudors & Stuarts. Stanley Thornes. (C). 1987. 40.00 (*0-685-47490-9*, Pub. by S Thornes Pubs UK) St Mut.

Course of British History, Bk. 3: 1714 to the Present Day. Ed. by J. Ray & J. Hagerty. (C). 1987. 40.00 (*0-09-172701-4*, Pub. by S Thornes Pubs UK) St Mut.

Course of Empire. American Friends Service Committee Staff. 1992. pap. 2.00 (*0-910082-22-7*) Am Fr Serv Comm.

Course of Empire. Bernard A. De Voto. (American Heritage Library). 640p. 1989. pap. 11.95 (*0-395-51014-7*) HM.

Course of Empire. Bernard Devoto. 21.75 (*0-8446-6784-6*) Peter Smith.

Course of Empire, Voyage of Life, & Other Pictures of Thomas Cole. Louis Noble. 415p. 1993. reprint ed. lib. bdg. 99.00 (*0-7812-5281-4*) Rprt Serv.

Course of English Classicism. Sherard Vines. (BCL1-PR English Literature Ser.). 160p. 1992. reprint ed. lib. bdg. 69.00 (*0-7812-7029-4*) Rprt Serv.

Course of English Classicism: From the Tudor to the Victorian Age. Sherard Vines. LC 70-91351. 160p. (C). 1969. reprint ed. 50.00 (*0-87753-041-6*) Phaeton.

Course of English Surrealist Poetry since the 1930's. Rob Jackaman. LC 89-9361. (Studies in British Literature: Vol. 5). 336p. 1989. lib. bdg. 99.95 (*0-88946-932-6*) E Mellen.

Course of Exclusion, 1882-1924: San Francisco Newspaper Coverage of the Chinese & Japanese in the United States. Jules Becker. LC 91-25795. 344p. 1991. lib. bdg. 99.95 (*0-7734-9874-5*) E Mellen.

Course of French History. Pierre Goubert. (Illus.). 336p. 1991. pap. 16.95 (*0-415-06671-9*, A6357) Routledge.

Course of German Nationalism: From Frederick the Great to Bismarck, 1763-1867. Hagen Schulze. Tr. by Sarah Hanbury-Tenison. 224p. (C). 1991. 49.95 (*0-521-37379-4*); pap. 14.95 (*0-521-37759-5*) Cambridge U Pr.

Course of Group Theory. John S. Rose. LC 76-22984. 320p. reprint ed. pap. 91.20 (*0-318-34665-6*, 2031721) Bks Demand.

Course of H Control Theory. B. A. Francis. (Lecture Notes in Control & Information Sciences Ser.: Vol. 88). xi, 156p. 1991. pap. 29.00 (*0-387-17069-3*) Spr-Verlag.

Course of Higher Math, Vol. 5. V. Smirnov & D. Brown. LC 63-10134. (Adiwes International Series in Math: Vol. 62). 1964. 262.00 (*0-08-013719-9*, Pub. by Pergamon Repr UK) Franklin.

Course of Higher Math, Vol. 3, Pt. 1: Linear Algebra. V. Smirnov & D. Brown. LC 63-10134. (Adiwes International Series in Math: Vol. 59). 1964. 142.00 (*0-08-010208-5*, Pub. by Pergamon Repr UK) Franklin.

Course of Higher Mathematics, Vol. 1. V. Smirnov & D. Brown. LC 63-10134. (International Series of Monographs on Pure & Applied Mathematics: Vol. 57). 1964. 224.00 (*0-08-010206-9*, Pub. by Pergamon Repr UK) Franklin.

Course of Higher Mathematics, Vol. 2. V. Smirnov & D. Brown. LC 63-10340. (International Series of Monographs on Pure & Applied Mathematics: Vol. 58). 1964. 272.00 (*0-08-010207-7*, Pub. by Pergamon Repr UK) Franklin.

Course of Higher Mathematics: Integral Equations & Partial Differential Equations. V. Smirnov & D. Brown. LC 63-10134. (International Series of Monographs on Pure & Applied Mathematics: Vol. 61). 333.00 (*0-08-013718-0*, Pub. by Pergamon Repr UK) Franklin.

Course of Higher Mathematics Series, 6 vols., Set. V. Smirnov & D. Brown. 1964. 1,523.00 (*0-08-010212-3*, Pub. by Pergamon Repr UK) Franklin.

Course of Human Development: Selected Papers from the Longitudinal Studies, Institute of Human Development, the University of California, Berkeley. Ed. by Mary C. Jones et al. LC 70-133268. (Illus.). 504p. reprint ed. pap. 143.70 (*0-317-10431-4*, 2012549) Bks Demand.

Course of Ideas. 2nd ed. Jeanne Gunner & Frankel. (C). 1990. pap. text ed. 27.00 (*0-06-042550-4*) HarpCollege.

Course of Industrial Decline: The Boott Cotton Mills of Lowell, Massachusetts, 1835-1955. Laurence F. Gross. LC 92-25128. (Studies in the History of Technology). (Illus.). 304p. (C). 1993. text ed. 42.00 (*0-8018-4453-3*) Johns Hopkins.

Course of Initiatory & Progressive Lessons for the Use of the Deaf & Dumb. J. Weir. 1972. 69.95 (*0-87968-951-X*) Gordon Pr.

Course of Instruction for the Deaf & Dumb. Harvey P. Peet. 1971. 69.95 (*0-87968-952-8*) Gordon Pr.

Course of Instruction in the Development of Power Through Clairvoyance. Lloyd K. Jones. 42p. 1968. reprint ed. spiral bd. 4.40 (*0-7873-0480-8*) Mokelumne.

Course of Instruction in the Development of Power Through Clairvoyance Including Personal Magnetism, Self Control, Will-Power, Auto-Suggestion, Mind Reading & Concentration. L. K. Jones. 1991. lib. bdg. 250.00 (*0-87700-984-8*) Revisionist Pr.

Course of Instructions in the Biochemic Pathology of Disease. George W. Carey. 31p. 1959. reprint ed. spiral bd. 7.70 (*0-7873-0145-0*) Mokelumne.

Course of Irish History. Ed. by T. W. Moody & F. X. Martin. (Illus.). 479p. 1989. pap. 25.95 (*0-85342-710-0*, Pub. by Mercier Pr IE) Dufour.

***Course of Irish History.** rev. ed. Ed. by T. W. Moody & F. X. Martin. (Illus.). 504p. (C). 1995. pap. 16.95 (*1-57098-015-2*) R Rinehart.

Course of Later Life: Research & Reflections. Ed. by Vern Bengtson & K. Warner Schaie. 192p. 1989. 28.95 (*0-8261-6220-7*) Springer Pub.

Course of Lectures on Dramatic Art & Literature. Augustus W. Von Schlegel. Tr. by John Black. LC 11-18702. reprint ed. 47.50 (*0-404-05605-9*) AMS Pr.

Course of Lectures on Elocution. Thomas Sheridan. LC 67-23853. 1972. reprint ed. 23.95 (*0-405-08964-3*) Ayer.

Course of Lectures on Elocution. Thomas Sheridan. (American Linguistics, 1700-1900 Ser.). 1991. reprint ed. 50.00 (*0-8201-1453-7*) Schol Facsimiles.

Course of Lectures on Elocution: Together with Two Dissertations on Language; & Some Other Tracts Relative to Those Subjects. Thomas Sheridan. (Anglistica & Americana Ser.: No. 38). xviii, 262p. 1970. reprint ed. 44.20 (*0-685-66515-1*, 05102434, Pub. by Georg Olms GW) Lubrecht & Cramer.

Course of Lectures on the English Law Delivered at the University of Oxford 1767-1773, 2 Vols. Robert Chambers & Samuel Johnson. Ed. by Thomas M. Curley. 700p. 1987. write for info. (*0-318-61115-5*) U of Wis Pr.

Course of Lectures on the English Law Delivered at the University of Oxford 1767-1773, 2 Vols., 1. Robert Chambers & Samuel Johnson. Ed. by Thomas M. Curley. LC 84-40493. 700p. 1987. text ed. 40.00 (*0-299-10011-1*) U of Wis Pr.

Course of Lectures on the English Law Delivered at the University of Oxford 1767-1773, 2 Vols., 2. Robert Chambers & Samuel Johnson. Ed. by Thomas M. Curley. LC 84-40493. 700p. 1987. text ed. 40.00 (*0-299-10012-X*) U of Wis Pr.

Course of Lectures on the Jews: By Ministers of the Established Church in Glasgow. Ed. by Gerald Grob. LC 76-46095. (Anti-Movements in America Ser.). 1977. lib. bdg. 41.95 (*0-405-09968-1*) Ayer.

Course of Legal Study, Addressed to Students & the Profession Generally, 2 vols. in 1. David Hoffman. LC 72-37980. (American Law Ser.: The Formative Years). 888p. 1972. reprint ed. 56.95 (*0-405-04023-7*) Ayer.

Course of Lessons for the Deaf & Dumb, 3 vols., Set. Joseph Watson. 1972. 300.00 (*0-87968-953-6*) Gordon Pr.

Course of Life, Vol. V: Early Adulthood. Ed. by George H. Pollock & Stanley I. Greenspan. 430p. 1993. text ed. 55.00 (*0-8236-1127-2*) Intl Univs Pr.

Course of Life, Vol. VI: Late Adulthood. Ed. by George H. Pollock & Stanley I. Greenspan. 550p. 1993. text ed. 65.00 (*0-8236-1128-0*) Intl Univs Pr.

Course of Life, Vol. 1: Infancy. enl. rev. ed. Ed. by Stanley I. Greenspan & George H. Pollock. LC 88-28465. 706p. 1989. 55.00x (*0-8236-1123-X*) Intl Univs Pr.

Course of Life, Vol. 2: Early Childhood. enl. rev. ed. Ed. by Stanley I. Greenspan & George H. Pollock. (Course of Life Ser.: Vol. II). 475p. 1990. 55.00 (*0-8236-1124-8*, BN 01124) Intl Univs Pr.

Course of Life, Vol. 3: Middle & Late Childhood. enl. rev. ed. Ed. by Stanley I. Greenspan & George H. Pollock. (Course of Life Ser.: Vol. III). 572p. 1991. 70.00 (*0-8236-1125-6*, BN 01125) Intl Univs Pr.

Course of Life, Vol. 4: Adolescence. enl. rev. ed. Ed. by Stanley I. Greenspan & George H. Pollock. LC 88-28465. 530p. 1991. 65.00 (*0-8236-1126-4*) Intl Univs Pr.

Course of Mathematical Analysis. A. I. Khinchin. 680p. 1960. text ed. 290.00 (*0-677-20130-3*) Gordon & Breach.

Course of Mathematical Analysis, 2 Vols. S. M. Nikolsky. 460p. 1985. 110.00 (*0-317-46603-8*, Pub. by Collets UK) Pro-Am Music.

Course of Mathematical Analysis, Pt. 1. A. Bermant & D. Brown. LC 62-9695. (International Series of Monographs on Pure & Applied Mathematics: Vol. 44). 1963. 210.00 (*0-08-010013-9*, Pub. by Pergamon Repr UK) Franklin.

Course of Mathematical Analysis, Pt. 1. A. Bermant & I. N. Sneddon. LC 62-9695. (International Series of Monographs on Pure & Applied Mathematics: No. 44). 1963. 210.00 (*0-08-013471-8*, Pub. by Pergamon Repr UK) Franklin.

Course of Mathematical Logic: Model Theory, Vol. 2. R. Fraisse. Tr. by David Louvish. LC 72-95893. (Synthese Library: No. 69). Orig. Title: Cours De Logique Mathematique. 212p. 1974. pap. text ed. 37.50 (*90-277-0510-0*) Kluwer Ac.

Course of Mathematics for Engineers & Scientists. B. H. Chirgwin & C. A. Plumpton. LC 62-9696. (Course of Mathematics for Engineers & Scientists Ser.: Vol. 5). 1964. 92.00 (*0-08-025060-2*, Pub. by Pergamon Repr UK) Franklin.

Course of Mathematics for Engineers & Scientists. 2nd ed. B. H. Chirgwin & C. A. Plumpton. 1982. Vol. 1, 1970. 232.00 (*0-08-006388-8*, Pub. by Pergamon Repr UK); Vol. 2, 1972. text ed. 226.00 (*0-08-015970-2*, Pub. by Pergamon Repr UK) Franklin.

Course of Mathematics for Engineers & Scientists, Vol. 5. B. H. Chirgwin & C. A. Plumpton. LC 92-9696. 1962. 93.00 (*0-08-009378-7*, Pub. by Pergamon Repr UK) Franklin.

Course of Mathematics for Engineers & Scientists, Vol. 3: Theoretical Mechanics. rev. ed. B. H. Chirgwin & C. A. Plumpton. LC 60-13894. 1963. 154.00 (*0-08-009376-0*, Pub. by Pergamon Repr UK) Franklin.

Course of Mathematics for Engineers & Scientists, Vol. 6. B. H. Chirgwin. 506p. 1980. text ed. 216.00 (*0-08-009379-5*) Franklin.

Course of Mexican History. 5th ed. Michael C. Meyer & William L. Sherman. (Illus.). 768p. (C). 1995. 49.95 (*0-19-508979-0*); pap. text ed. 24.95 (*0-19-508980-4*) OUP.

Course of Modern Analysis. 4th ed. Edmund T. Whittaker & George N. Watson. (C). 1927. pap. 49.95 (*0-521-09189-6*) Cambridge U Pr.

Course of Modern Analysis. Edmund T. Whittaker. LC 75-41296. reprint ed. 89.50 (*0-404-14736-4*) AMS Pr.

Course of Modern Jewish History. Howard M. Sachar. LC 89-40528. 912p. 1990. pap. 21.00 (*0-679-72746-9*, Vin) Random.

Course of Pure Mathematics. 10th ed. G. H. Hardy. (Cambridge Mathematical Library). (C). 1993. 99.95 (*0-521-05203-3*); pap. 24.95 (*0-521-09227-2*) Cambridge U Pr.

Course of Pure Mathematics. 10th ed. Godfrey H. Hardy. (Cambridge Mathematical Library). (Illus.). 522p. (C). 1993. text ed. 22.95 (*0-521-09275-2*) Cambridge U Pr.

Course of Russian History. 5th ed. Melvin Wren & Taylor Stults. (Illus.). 617p. (C). 1993. pap. text ed. 22.95 (*0-88133-750-1*) Waveland Pr.

Course of Study for Television Commercials. Ruth Tolman. 118p. 1973. 100.00 (*0-318-16873-1*) World Modeling.

Course of Study Outlines for Bible Class Leaders. C. H. Dodd. 1973. 59.95 (*0-87968-954-4*) Gordon Pr.

Course of the Melting Pot Idea to 1910. Richard C. Harper. Ed. by Francesco Cordasco. LC 80-862. (American Ethnic Groups Ser.). 1981. lib. bdg. 47.95 (*0-405-13425-8*) Ayer.

Course of the Seeker. Omar A. Shah. Ed. by Richard Weaver & Ron Baron. 150p. (C). 1988. pap. 11.95 (*0-942139-07-0*) Tale Weaver.

An Asterisk (*) at the beginning of an entry indicates that the title is appearing in BIP for the first time.

Course of Theoretical Physics, 10 vols. Incl. Vol. 1. Course of Theoretical Physics: Mechanics. 3rd ed. L. D. Landau et al. 1976. text ed. 50.00 (*0-08-021022-8*); Vol. 1. Course of Theoretical Physics: Mechanics. 3rd ed. L. D. Landau et al. 1982. pap. text ed. 27.00 (*0-08-029141-4*); Vol. 3. Quantum Mechanics - Non-Relativistic Theory. 3rd ed. Landau et al. 1981. pap. text ed. 37.00 (*0-08-029140-6*, Pergamon Pr); Vol. 6. Fluid Mechanics. L. D. Landau et al. 1959. (*0-318-55153-5*); Vol. 7. Elasticity Theory. 2nd ed. L. D. Landau et al. 1970. (*0-318-55154-3*); Vol. 8. Electrodynamics of Continuous Media. L. D. Landau et al. 1960. (*0-318-55155-1*); Vol. 9. 3rd ed. L. D. Landau et al. 1980. text ed. 130.00 (*0-08-023073-3*); Vol. 9. L. D. Landau et al. 1980. pap. text ed. 40.00 (*0-08-023072-5*); Set text ed. write for info. (*0-318-55152-7*, Pergamon Pr) Elsevier.

Course of Theoretical Physics: Fluid Mechanics. 2nd ed. L. D. Landau & E. M. Lifshitz. LC 86-30498. (Course of Theoretical Physics Ser.: No. 6). (Illus.). 551p. 1987. text ed. 130.00 (*0-08-033933-6*, Pergamon Pr); pap. text ed. 48.00 (*0-08-033932-8*, Pergamon Pr) Elsevier.

Course of Theoretical Physics: The Classical Theory of Fields, Vol. 2. L. D. Landau. LC 75-4737. (Course of Theoretical Physics Ser.). (Illus.). 1980. pap. text ed. 36.00 (*0-08-025072-6*, Pergamon Pr) Elsevier.

Course of Time. Mark Insingel. Tr. by Adrienne Dixon. LC 76-56575. Orig. Title: Een Tijdsverloop. 1977. 4.95 (*0-87376-029-8*) Red Dust.

Course on Aesthetics. Renato Barilli. Tr. by Karen Pinkus. LC 93-21779. 186p. (C). 1993. text ed. 44.95 (*0-8166-2118-7*); pap. text ed. 16.95 (*0-8166-2119-5*) U of Minn Pr.

Course on Damage Mechanics. Jean P. Lemaitre. (Illus.). 250p. 1992. 89.00 (*0-387-53609-4*) Spr-Verlag.

Course on Group Theory. unabridged ed. John S. Rose. LC 94-20435. 310p. 1994. reprint ed. pap. text ed. 8.95 (*0-486-68194-7*) Dover.

Course on Instabilities & Confinement in Toroidal Plasmas. International School of Plasma Physics, Varenna (Como), Italy, 1971. 1975. pap. 193.00 (*0-08-020452-X*, Pub. by Pergamon Repr UK) Franklin.

Course on Integral Equations. A. C. Pipkin. (Texts in Applied Mathematics Ser.: Vol. 9). (Illus.). xiii, 268p. 1991. 39.00 (*0-387-97557-8*) Spr-Verlag.

Course on Many-Body Theory Applied to Solid-State Physics. C. P. Enz. LC 92-30895. (Lecture Notes in Physics Ser.: Vol. 11). 440p. 1992. text ed. 90.00 (*9971-5-0336-0*); pap. text ed. 44.00 (*9971-5-0337-9*) World Scientific Pub.

Course on Nonlinear Waves. Samuel S. Shen. LC 93-19296. (Nonlinear Topics in the Mathematical Sciences Ser.). 344p. (C). 1993. lib. bdg. 129.00 (*0-7923-2292-4*) Kluwer Ac.

***Course on PC-Based Seismic Networks.** Ed. by W. H. Lee & D. A. Dodge. (Illus.). 535p. (Orig.). (C). 1994. pap. text ed. 145.00x (*0-7881-1247-3*) Diane Pub.

Course on Plasma Diagnostics & Data Acquisition Systems. Ed. by H. Eubank & E. Sindoni. (Commission of the European Communities Ser.). (Illus.). 1975. pap. 193.00 (*0-08-024462-9*, Pub. by Pergamon Repr UK) Franklin.

Course on Point Processes. R. D. Reiss et al. Ed. by Stephen E. Fienberg et al. LC 92-29587. (Series in Statistics). (Illus.). 264p. 1992. 54.95 (*0-387-97924-7*) Spr-Verlag.

Course on Power Electronics. Vedam Subrahmanyam. LC 93-36010. 1995. text ed. 49.95 (*0-470-23341-9*) Halsted Pr.

Course on Stationary & Quasi-Stationary Toroidal Reactors. International School of Fusion Reactor Technology, Erice (Trapani), Italy, Sept. 4-15, 1972. 1975. pap. 206.00 (*0-08-020455-4*, Pub. by Pergamon Repr UK) Franklin.

Course on the Application of Group Theory to Quantum Mechanics. Irene V. Schensted. 300p. 1975. 12.00 (*0-911014-24-1*); pap. 6.00 (*0-911014-25-X*) Neo Pr.

Course on Theoretical Physics: Statistical Physics, Vol. 5, Pt. 1. 3rd ed. L. D. Landau & E. M. Lifshitz. (Illus.). 1980. text ed. 160.00 (*0-08-023039-3*, Pergamon Pr); pap. text ed. 40.00 (*0-08-023038-5*, Pergamon Pr) Elsevier.

Course on Words. rev. ed. Waldo Sweet & Glenn Knudsvig. 356p. 1989. reprint ed. pap. text ed. 17.95 (*0-472-08101-2*) U of Mich Pr.

Course on Writing. Columbia Pacific University Faculty Staff & Richard L. Crews. 29p. (C). 1989. student ed write for info. (*0-945864-17-5*); pap. text ed. write for info. (*0-945864-16-7*) Columbia Pacific U Pr.

Course Outlines on Women & Politics. Ed. by Janice Newton. 293p. (C). 1993. pap. 25.00 (*0-88920-236-2*, Pub. by Wilfrid Laurier CN) Humanities.

Course Pak for English 203: Advanced Communication Skills. Maurice M. Henderson. 48p. (C). 1994. 6.25 (*0-8403-8047-X*) Kendall-Hunt.

Course Pak for English 303: Technical & Professional Writing. Maurice M. Henderson. 48p. (C). 1992. 5.25 (*0-8403-8054-2*) Kendall-Hunt.

***Course Set for Manito-Wish: The History.** Jon Helminiak. 102p. (Orig.). 1994. pap. text ed. write for info. (*0-9641794-0-7*) Hare Strigenz.

Course 095 to Eternity. 2nd ed. Elwyn E. Overshiner. LC 80-82005. (Illus.). 256p. 1989. 10.95 (*0-936940-07-7*) Helm Pub.

Courses for Change in Writing: A Selection from the NEH Iowa Institute. Ed. by Carl H. Klaus & Nancy Jones. 296p. (Orig.). 1984. pap. text ed. 14.50 (*0-86709-121-5*) Boynton Cook Pubs.

Courses for Horses. Keith Noud. 159p. (C). 1990. pap. 60.00 (*0-7316-7935-0*, Pub. by Boolarong Pubns AT) St Mut.

Courses for Horses: A Complete Guide to Construction Show Jumping Courses. Christopher Coldrey. 128p. 1990. 60.00 (*0-85131-541-0*, Pub. by J A Allen & Co UK) St Mut.

Courses of Study: Clues to the Independent Study of Important Subjects. Ed. by J. M. Robertson. 1977. lib. bdg. 59.95 (*0-8490-1680-0*) Gordon Pr.

Courses of Study for SLC Exam, 1951: Outlines of Content. Controller of Exams Staff. 64p. 1951. 6.00 (*0-318-04182-0*) Am-Nepal Ed.

Courses of Study for SLC Exam, 1965: Expanded Outlines; Recommended Texts Included. Min Education Staff. 106p. 1965. 10.00 (*0-318-04183-9*) Am-Nepal Ed.

Courses on Population & Development: Aspects of Technical Co-Operation. 54p. 7.00 (*92-1-104231-3*) UN.

Courseware Evaluation: Form & Guide for Vocational & Technical Education. Shirley A. Chase et al. 24p. 1984. 2.50 (*0-318-22068-7*, SN44) Ctr Educ Trng Employ.

Courseware in the Classroom: Selecting, Organizing, & Using Educational Software. Ann Lathrop & Bobby Goodson. 1983. text ed. 12.95 (*0-201-20007-4*) Addison-Wesley.

Coursework Explained: Child Development. Stanley Thornes. (C). 1990. 40.00 (*0-7487-0177-X*, Pub. by S Thornes Pubs UK) St Mut.

Court. Elizabeth Walker. 1990. 19.95 (*0-446-51596-5*) Warner Bks.

Court. Elizabeth Walker. 1991. mass mkt. 5.99 (*0-446-36157-7*) Warner Bks.

Court Administration: Issues & Responses. Charles R. Swanson & Susette M. Talarico. LC 86-30760. 113p. 1987. pap. 14.95 (*0-89854-119-0*, KF8732.A75C68) U of GA Inst Govt.

Court Administration in New Mexico. National Center for State Courts Staff. 115p. 1975. pap. write for info. (*0-318-61207-0*, MAB-029) Natl Ctr St Courts.

***Court & Bakufu in Japan: Essays in Kamakura History.** Ed. by Jeffrey P. Mass. 342p. (C). 1995. 49.50x (*0-8047-2532-2*); pap. 16.95 (*0-8047-2473-3*) Stanford U Pr.

Court & Country Politics in the Plays of Beaumont & Fletcher. Philip J. Finkelpearl. 250p. (Orig.). 1990. pap. text ed. 39.50 (*0-691-06825-9*) Princeton U Pr.

Court & Culture: Dutch Literature, 1350-1450. Frits P. Van Oostrom. Tr. by Arnold J. Pomerans. (C). 1992. 45.00 (*0-520-06777-0*) U CA Pr.

Court & Culture in Renaissance Scotland: Sir David Lindsay of the Mount. Carol Edington. LC 94-14813. (Massachusetts Studies in Early Modern Culture). 288p. (C). 1995. lib. bdg. 40.00 (*0-87023-934-1*) U of Mass Pr.

Court & Family in Sung China, 960-1279: Bureaucratic Success & Kinship Fortunes for the Shih of Ming-Chou. Richard L. Davis. LC 85-20656. xvi, 354p. 1986. text ed. 42.95 (*0-8223-0512-7*) Duke.

Court & Free-Lance Reporter Profession: Improved Management Strategies. David J. Saari. LC 87-13093. 192p. 1988. text ed. 49.95 (*0-89930-234-3*, SRN/, Quorum Bks) Greenwood.

Court & Garden: From the French Hotel to the City of Modern Architecture. Michael Dennis. (Graham Foundation Architecture Ser.). 412p. (Orig.). 1986. pap. 30.00 (*0-262-54051-7*) MIT Pr.

Court & Samurai in an Age of Transition: Medieval Paintings & Blades from the Gotoh Museum, Tokyo. Miyeko Murase et al. LC 89-63130. (Illus.). 128p. 1990. 36.00 (*0-913304-28-X*) Japan Soc.

Court & Samurai in an Age of Transition: Medieval Paintings & Blades from the Gotoh Museum, Tokyo. Miyeko Murase et al. LC 89-63130. (Illus.). 127p. 1995. pap. 25.00 (*0-913304-29-8*, 298) Japan Soc.

Court & the Constitution. Archibald Cox. (C). 1989. 80.00 (*0-685-27943-X*) St Mut.

Court & the Constitution. Archibald S. Cox. 432p. 1988. pap. 13.95 (*0-395-48071-X*) HM.

Court & the Kingdom. Rosemary Upton. 288p. (Orig.). 1993. pap. 8.99 (*0-87788-159-6*) Shaw Pubs.

Court & Times of James the First, 2 Vols, Set. Thomas Birch. LC 74-113558. reprint ed. 115.00 (*0-404-00906-9*) AMS Pr.

Court Appointed Special Advocate (CASA) Manual. National CASA Association Staff & National Council of Juvenile & Family Court Judges. 239p. 1984. 20.00 (*0-318-21317-6*) Natl Juv & Family Ct Judges.

Court Artist: On the Ancestry of the Modern Artist. Martin Warnke. Tr. by David McLintock. LC 92-29567. (Ideas in Context Ser.). 288p. (C). 1993. 59.95 (*0-521-36375-6*) Cambridge U Pr.

Court Assistant. Jack Rudman. (Career Examination Ser.: C-1226). 1994. pap. 19.95 (*0-8373-1226-4*) Nat Learn.

Court Assistant I. Jack Rudman. (Career Examination Ser.: C-961). 1994. pap. 23.95 (*0-8373-0961-1*) Nat Learn.

Court Assistant II. Jack Rudman. (Career Examination Ser.: C-962). 1994. pap. 27.95 (*0-8373-0962-X*) Nat Learn.

Court Attendant. Jack Rudman. (Career Examination Ser.: C-170). 1994. pap. 23.95 (*0-8373-0170-X*) Nat Learn.

Court Automation Report: Ninth Judicial Circuit of Florida. National Center for State Courts Staff. 20p. 1984. write for info. (*0-318-61281-X*, NCSC-044) Natl Ctr St Courts.

Court Awarded Attorney Fees, 3 vols. Mary F. Derfner & Arthur D. Wolf. 1983. Updates. ring bd. write for info. (*0-8205-1168-4*) Bender.

Court Awarded Attorney Fees: Report of the Third Crcuit Task Force. 54p. 1985. pap. 5.00 (*0-685-29760-8*, 40, 750) NCLS Inc.

Court Case Management Information Systems Manual. Mary Louise Clifford & Lynn A. Jensen. LC 83-17382. (Illus.). 342p. 1983. pap. 15.00 (*0-89656-071-6*, R-082) Natl Ctr St Courts.

***Court Cases of Consequence.** John Miller. 84p. (Orig.). 1978. pap. text ed. 15.00 (*1-886536-00-7*) Elevator Wrld.

Court Circles of the Republic, or the Beauties & Celebrities of the Nation. Elizabeth F. Ellet. LC 75-1841. (Leisure Class in America Ser.). (Illus.). 1975. reprint ed. 42.95 (*0-405-06910-3*) Ayer.

Court Clerk. Jack Rudman. (Career Examination Ser.: C-171). 1994. pap. 27.95 (*0-8373-0171-8*) Nat Learn.

Court Clerk I. Jack Rudman. (Career Examination Ser.: C-963). 1994. pap. 27.95 (*0-8373-0963-8*) Nat Learn.

Court Clerk II. Jack Rudman. (Career Examination Ser.: C-964). 1994. pap. 29.95 (*0-8373-0964-6*) Nat Learn.

***Court, Cloister & City: The Art & Culture of Central Europe, 1450-1800.** Thomas D. Kaufmann. LC 95-10237. (Illus.). 584p. 1995. 45.00 (*0-226-42729-3*); pap. 24.95 (*0-226-42730-7*) U Ch Pr.

***Court Companion 1995.** rev. ed. Stephen Adams & Nancy Sevitch. 184p. 1995. 75.00 (*0-932663-77-X*) CA Fam Law.

Court Congestion, Some Remedial Approaches: Conciliation, Pretrial Training, Use of Auxiliaries & Electronic Devices. World Association of Judges Staff & International Legal Center Staff. iii, 203p. 1971. pap. 9.50 (*0-8377-0420-0*) Rothman.

Court Consultation Specialist. Jack Rudman. (Career Examination Ser.: Series 1). 1991. pap. 34.95 (*0-8373-3707-0*) Nat Learn.

Court Coordination of Family Cases. H. Ted Rubin & Victor E. Flango. 83p. 1992. pap. text ed. 6.95 (*0-89656-120-8*, R-144) Natl Ctr St Courts.

Court, Country & Culture: Essays on Early Modern British History in Honor of Perex Zagorin. Ed. by Bonnelyn Y. Kunze & Dwight Brautigam. 352p. 1992. text ed. 79.00 (*1-878822-05-5*) Univ Rochester Pr.

Court Culture & the Origins of a Royalist Tradition in Early Stuart England. R. Malcolm Smuts. LC 86-27243. (Illus.). 320p. 1987. text ed. 46.95x (*0-8122-8039-3*) U of Pa Pr.

Court Decisions: Coverage Interpretations That Help You Understand & Sell Insurance. 1991. 27.50 (*1-56461-004-7*, 30035) Rough Notes.

Court Divided: The Fifth Circuit Court of Appeals & the Politics of Judicial Reform. Deborah J. Barrow & Thomas G. Walker. 288p. (C). 1990. reprint ed. 16.00x (*0-300-04896-3*) Yale U Pr.

Court Facilities in Barnstable, Dukes, Nantucket, & Plymouth Counties, Massachusetts. National Center for State Courts Staff. 530p. 1975. 31.80 (*0-685-15350-9*, MAB-030) Natl Ctr St Courts.

Court Facilities in Berkshire, Franklin, Hampden, & Hampshire Counties, Massachusetts. National Center for State Courts Staff. 510p. 1975. 30.60 (*0-685-15354-1*, MAB-031) Natl Ctr St Courts.

Court Facilities in Bristol County (Massachusetts) Final Report. National Center for State Courts Staff. (On Loan Through NCSC Library). 212p. 1975. 12.72 (*0-685-15356-8*, MAB-032) Natl Ctr St Courts.

Court Facilities in Essex County (Massachusetts) National Center for State Courts Staff. 375p. 1975. 22.50 (*0-685-15359-2*, MAB-033) Natl Ctr St Courts.

Court Facilities in Middlesex County (Massachusetts) National Center for State Courts Staff. 524p. 1975. write for info. (*0-318-61245-3*, NERO-011) Natl Ctr St Courts.

Court Facilities in Norfolk County (Massachusetts) National Center for State Courts Staff. 219p. 1975. 13.14 (*0-685-15365-7*, NERO-022) Natl Ctr St Courts.

Court Facilities in Suffolk County (Massachusetts) National Center for State Courts Staff. 214p. 1975. 12.84 (*0-685-15368-1*, MAB-034) Natl Ctr St Courts.

Court Facilities in Worcester County (Massachusetts) National Center for State Courts Staff. 469p. 1975. 28.14 (*0-685-15372-X*, MAB-035) Natl Ctr St Courts.

Court Facilities Needs of the Hudson County (NJ) Superior Court: Final Report. 174p. 1988. 11.00 (*0-685-19937-1*, NERO-215) Natl Ctr St Courts.

Court Facility Evaluation, Greene County Courthouse, Springfield, Missouri: A Technical Assistance Report. Don Hardenbergh & James R. James. 101p. 1989. 6.00 (*0-685-33612-3*, SERO, T/A-508) Natl Ctr St Courts.

Court for Owls. Richard Adicks. LC 89-3466. 270p. 1989. 17.95 (*0-910923-65-5*) Pineapple Pr.

Court Fox. Jacques Melek. 500p. 1983. pap. 24.95 (*0-942330-49-8*, Sunrise Pubns) J Melek.

Court Guide. Ed. by Andrew Goodman. 152p. (C). 1990. 70.00 (*1-85431-065-8*, Pub. by Blackstone Pr UK) St Mut.

Court Guide, 1992. A. Goodman. (C). 1992. 60.00 (*0-685-52534-1*, Pub. by Blackstone Pr UK) W W Gaunt.

Court Guide, 1993. Andrew Goodman. 188p. (C). 1993. text ed. 24.00 (*1-85431-235-9*, Pub. by Blackstone Pr UK) W W Gaunt.

Court Hearing Reporter. Jack Rudman. (Career Examination Ser.: C-172). 1994. pap. 23.95 (*0-8373-0172-6*) Nat Learn.

Court Historians Versus Revisionism. Harry E. Barnes. 1971. 250.00 (*0-87700-193-6*) Revisionist Pr.

Court House Square, A Social History. (Illus.). 134p. 1984. 7.00 (*0-317-00951-6*) M B Hinman.

Court, Household & Itinerary of King Henry II. Robert W. Eyton. xii, 344p. 1974. reprint ed. 63.70 (*3-487-05513-9*, Pub. by Georg Olms GW) Lubrecht & Cramer.

Court Houses of Plymouth. Rose T. Briggs. (Pilgrim Society Notes Ser.: No. 17). 1966. 2.00 (*0-940628-11-2*) Pilgrim Soc.

Court Improvement Programs: A Guidebook for Planners. National Center for State Courts Staff. 308p. 1972. pap. write for info. (*0-318-61214-3*, R-002) Natl Ctr St Courts.

Court Jesters. Avigdor Dagan. Tr. by Barbara Harshav. 184p. 1990. 16.95 (*0-8276-0324-X*) JPS Phila.

Court Jew: A Contribution to the History of Absolutism in Europe. Selma Stern. 316p. 1985. 39.95x (*0-88738-019-0*) Transaction Pubs.

Court, Kirk, & Community: Scotland, 1470-1625. Jenny Wormald. 224p. 1991. pap. text ed. 20.00 (*0-7486-0276-3*, Pub. by Edinburgh U Pr UK) Col U Pr.

Court, Kirk & Community: Scotland, 1470-1625. Jenny Wormald. (New History of Scotland Ser.: No. 4). 224p. reprint ed. pap. 63.90 (*0-685-15912-4*, 2026391) Bks Demand.

Court Law Stenographer. Jack Rudman. (Career Examination Ser.: C-173). 1994. pap. 23.95 (*0-8373-0173-4*) Nat Learn.

Court Life under the Plantagenets: Reign of Henry the Second. Hubert Hall. LC 70-109627. (Select Bibliographies Reprint Ser.). 1977. 24.95 (*0-8369-5236-7*) Ayer.

Court Martial. Marszalek. 326p. 1994. pap. 12.00 (*0-02-034515-1*, Collier S&S) S&S Trade.

Court-Martial: A Black Man in America. John F. Marszalek. LC 73-38282. 336p. reprint ed. pap. 95.80 (*0-317-29835-6*, 2051954) Bks Demand.

Court Martial of Capt. John Moutray. Great Britain Navy Court, 1781 Staff et al. 19.95 (*0-405-01163-6*, 13252) Ayer.

Court Martial of General George Armstrong Custer. Lawrence A. Frost. (Illus.). 280p. 1979. pap. 15.95 (*0-8061-1608-0*) U of Okla Pr.

Court Martial of Lieutenant Henry Flipper. Charles M. Robinson, III. LC 93-60328. (Southwestern Studies: No. 100). (Illus.). 120p. (Orig.). 1994. pap. 12.50 (*0-87404-196-1*) Tex Western.

***Court-Martial of Mother Jones.** Ed. by Edward M. Steel. (Illus.). 416p. (Orig.). 1995. text ed. 49.95 (*0-8131-1941-3*); pap. 18.95 (*0-8131-0857-8*) U Pr of Ky.

Court-Martial of Robert E. Lee. Douglas Savage. 448p. 1993. 24.95 (*0-938289-26-8*, 7342) Combined Bks.

Court Martial of Robert E. Lee. Douglas Savage. 480p. 1995. pap. 13.99 (*0-446-67056-1*) Warner Bks.

Court-Martial Procedure, 2 vols., Set. suppl. ed. Francis A. Gilligan & Fredric I. Lederer. (Orig.). 1993. 160.00 (*0-87473-749-4*) Michie Butterworth.

***Court Masques.** Ed. by David Lindley. (World's Classics Ser.). (Illus.). 400p. 1995. 56.00 (*0-19-812164-4*); pap. 13.95 (*0-19-282569-0*) OUP.

Court of a Saint: St. Louis of France. W. F. Knox. 1976. lib. bdg. 59.95 (*0-8490-1681-9*) Gordon Pr.

Court of a Thousand Suns. Allan Cole & Chris Bunch. 288p. (Orig.). 1985. mass mkt. 4.99 (*0-345-31681-9*, Del Rey) Ballantine.

Court of Appeals at Austin: 1892-1992. Deborah D. Powers. LC 92-28116. (Illus.). 86p. 1992. 24.95 (*0-938349-92-9*) State House Pr.

Court of Appeals for the Federal Circuit: Review of Patent & Trademark Cases, 2 vols., Set. Donald R. Dunner & Charles L. Gholz. (Patent Law & Practice Ser.). 1973. ring bd. write for info. (*0-8205-1261-3*) Bender.

Court of Blue Shadows: A Novel. Maynard Allington. LC 94-20236. 288p. 1995. 23.00 (*0-02-881104-6*) Brasseys Inc.

Court of Boyville. William A. White. LC 77-116968. (Short Story Index Reprint Ser.). 1977. 24.95 (*0-8369-3472-5*) Ayer.

Court of Burgundy. Otto Cartellieri. LC 70-132437. (World History Ser.: No. 48). 1970. reprint ed. lib. bdg. 75.00 (*0-8383-1197-0*) M S G Haskell Hse.

Court of First Instance of the European Communities. Timothy Millett. 1991. 76.00 (*0-406-20222-2*, U.K.) Butterworth Legal Pubs.

Court of France, 1789-1830. Philip Mansel. (Illus.). 236p. (C). 1991. pap. 22.95 (*0-521-42398-8*) Cambridge U Pr.

***Court of Honor.** Paula B. Gorgas. Ed. by Jane Weinberger. 140p. (YA). 1995. pap. 9.95 (*1-883650-15-1*) Windswept Hse.

Court of Honor. William P. Wood. Ed. by Claire Zion. 384p. 1992. reprint ed. mass mkt. 5.99 (*0-671-73177-7*) PB.

Court of Last Resort. Elmer Rice. (Lost Play Ser.). 1985. pap. 3.95 (*0-912262-87-7*) Proscenium.

Court of Last Resort: Mental Illness & the Law. Carol A. Warren. LC 82-1839. (Illus.). (C). 1984. pap. text ed. 8.95 (*0-226-87389-7*) U Ch Pr.

Court of Memory. James McConkey. 1993. pap. 13.95 (*0-87923-983-2*) Godine.

Court of Sapience. Ed. by E. Ruth Harvey. (Medieval Texts & Translations Ser.: No. 2). 272p. 1984. 40.00 (*0-8020-5628-8*) U of Toronto Pr.

Court of the Damned. J. Gladston Emery. Ed. by Ralph Marsh. (Illus.). 232p. 1992. 20.00 (*0-9632699-0-9*) Yellow Dog Pr.

Court of the Lion. Eleanor Cooney & Daniel Altieri. 1024p. 1990. mass mkt. 6.50 (*0-380-70985-6*) Avon.

Court of the Lost Woods. Joseph D. Ossorio et al. (Under Twenty Writing Society Ser.). (Illus.). 48p. (J). (gr. 3-5). 1994. pap. 6.95 (*1-56721-052-X*) Twnty-Fifth Cent Pr.

Court of the Palms: A Functional Interpretation of the Mari Palace. Yasin M. Al-Khalesi. LC 77-94987. (Bibliotheca Mesopotamica Ser.: Vol. 8). (Illus.). viii, 90p. 1978. 31.25 (*0-89003-029-4*) Undena Pubns.

Court of the Stone Children. Eleanor Cameron. (J). 1994. 17.75 (*0-8446-6757-9*) Peter Smith.

Court of the Stone Children. Eleanor Cameron. 192p. (J). (gr. 4 up). 1990. pap. 4.99 (*0-14-034289-3*, Puffin) Puffin Bks.

***Court of the Winged Serpent.** Russell Hoban & Patrick Benson. (Illus.). 32p. (J). 1995. 19.95 (*0-224-03614-9*, Pub. by Jonathan Cape UK) Trafalgar.

C

Court of Three Sisters. M. Willman. 1994. mass mkt. 5.50 (*0-06-108053-5*, Harp PBks) HarpC.

Court of Two Sisters Cookbook. Joseph Fein, III et al. LC 91-17110. (Illus.). 112p. 1991. 14.95 (*0-88289-866-3*) Pelican.

Court of Venus. 1987. pap. 3.95 (*0-88184-300-8*) Carroll & Graf.

Court Office Assistant. Jack Rudman. (Career Examination Ser.: C-965). 1994. pap. 23.95 (*0-8373-0965-4*) Nat Learn.

Court Officer. Jack Rudman. (Career Examination Ser.: C-966). 1994. pap. 19.95 (*0-8373-0966-2*) Nat Learn.

***Court Officer: Senior Court Officer, Court Clerk.** 8th ed. E. P. Steinberg. 1995. pap. 14.95 (*0-02-860012-6*) Macmillan.

***Court Officer: Senior Court Officer, Court Clerk.** 8th ed. Eve P. Steinberg. LC 94-36241. 1994. write for info. (*0-671-84801-1*, Arco Test) P-H Gen Ref & Trav.

Court Officer Sergeant. Jack Rudman. (Career Examination Ser.: No. C-3508). 1994. 27.95 (*0-8373-3508-6*) Nat Learn.

***Court on God: When Your Life Doesn't Add.** James P. Keener. LC 94-43714. 224p. (Orig.). 1995. pap. 10.99 (*0-929239-94-6*) Discovery Hse Pubs.

Court-Ordered Arbitration in North Carolina: An Evaluation of Its Effects. Stevens H. Clarke et al. 82p. (Orig.). (C). 1989. pap. text ed. 11.00 (*1-56011-158-5*) Institute Government.

Court-Ordered Insanity: Interpretive Practice & Involuntary Commitment. James A. Holstein. LC 92-35481. (Social Problems & Social Issues Ser.). 245p. 1993. lib. bdg. 44.95 (*0-202-30448-5*); pap. 22.95 (*0-202-30449-3*) Aldine de Gruyter.

Court Orders, Vol. 1: Guidance & Regulations Children Act, 1989. HMSO Staff. 80p. 1991. pap. 25.00 (*0-11-321371-9*, HM2794) UNIPUB.

Court Over Constitution: A Study of Judicial As an Instrument of Popular Government. Edward S. Corwin. 11.75 (*0-8446-1129-8*) Peter Smith.

Court Paintings of India. Pratapaditya Pal. (Illus.). 344p. 1983. 140.00 (*0-9611400-0-3*) N Kumar.

Court Patronage & Corruption in Early Stuart England. Linda L. Peck. 320p. 1993. pap. 17.95 (*0-415-09368-6*, B0617) Routledge.

Court Patronage & Corruption in Early Stuart England. Linda L. Peck. 320p. 1990. text ed. 55.00 (*0-04-942195-6*) Routledge Chapman & Hall.

Court Poetry & Literary Miscellanea. Ed. by Alasdair Livingstone. (State Archives of Assyria Ser.: Vol. 3). (Illus.). xxxvii, 183p. 1989. text ed. 49.50 (*951-570-044-2*, Pub. by Helsinki Univ Pr FI); pap. 36.00 (*951-570-043-4*, Pub. by Helsinki Univ Pr FI) Eisenbrauns.

Court Records Supervisor. Jack Rudman. (Career Examination Ser.: C-3160). 1994. pap. 29.95 (*0-8373-3160-9*) Nat Learn.

***Court Reform & Judicial Leadership: Judge George Nicola & the New Jersey Justice System.** Paul B. Wice. LC 94-33260. 224p. 1995. text ed. 57.95 (*0-275-95038-7*, Praeger Pubs) Greenwood.

Court Reform in Seven States. National Center for State Courts Staff. 171p. 1980. pap. write for info. (*0-89656-046-5*, R-054) Natl Ctr St Courts.

Court-Related Data Processing in Montgomery County, Pennsylvania: A Technical Assistance Assessment Report. National Center for State Courts Staff. 24p. 1983. 2.00 (*0-685-16650-3*, NERO, T/A-523) Natl Ctr St Courts.

Court Reporter. Jack Rudman. (Career Examination Ser.: C-174). 1994. pap. 23.95 (*0-8373-0174-2*) Nat Learn.

Court Reporter I. Jack Rudman. (Career Examination Ser.: C-967). 1994. pap. 23.95 (*0-8373-0967-0*) Nat Learn.

Court Reporter II. Jack Rudman. (Career Examination Ser.: C-968). 1994. pap. 27.95 (*0-8373-0968-9*) Nat Learn.

***Court Reporters & Stress: How to Find the Time to Live.** Barbara Barnett. 162p. 1993. pap. text ed. 24.95 (*1-881859-04-5*) Natl Ct Report.

Court Reporter's Language Arts Workbook. Marcella J. Kocar. 224p. (C). 1992. pap. text ed. write for info. (*0-13-184391-5*) P-H.

Court Reporters Manual, State of Tennessee. National Center for State Courts Staff. 123p. 1975. 7.38 (*0-685-16328-8*, MAB-036) Natl Ctr St Courts.

Court Reporting: Grammar & Punctuation. Diane Castilaw-Palliser. (C). 1987. text ed. 24.95 (*0-538-11610-2*, K61) S-W Pub.

Court Reporting: Lessons from Alaska & Australia. National Center for State Courts Staff. 114p. 1974. write for info. (*0-318-61258-5*, R-010) Natl Ctr St Courts.

Court Reporting in a Fast-Paced World: A Procedures Manual & Form Book for Freelance Reporters, Version 2. Karen L. Schoeve. 258p. (C). 1992. spiral bd. 29.95 (*0-9635731-0-1*) Fast Pace Report.

Court Reporting Services in Maryland. National Center for State Courts Staff. 148p. 1976. 8.88 (*0-685-16338-5*, MARO-007) Natl Ctr St Courts.

Court Reporting Services in New Jersey. National Center for State Courts Staff. 242p. 1978. 14.52 (*0-685-16346-6*, NERO-017) Natl Ctr St Courts.

Court Reporting Services in New Jersey. David Steelman & Sam Conti. 242p. 1978. 14.52 (*0-685-55347-7*, NERO017) Natl Ctr St Courts.

Court Reporting Services in South Dakota: Findings & Recommendations. National Center for State Courts Staff. 133p. 1977. 7.98 (*0-685-16350-4*, MAB-037) Natl Ctr St Courts.

Court Reporting Services in the Lackawanna County (PA) Court of Common Pleas: Technical Assistance Report. National Center for State Courts Staff. 90p. 1982. 5.40 (*0-685-16356-3*, NERO, T/A-512) Natl Ctr St Courts.

Court Revels: 1485-1559. W. R. Streitberger. (Studies in Early English Drama: No. 3). 488p. (C). 1994. 75.00 (*0-8020-0590-X*) U of Toronto Pr.

Court Rules of Michigan Annotated, 7 vols. 3000p. 1991. Suppls. only. write for info. (*0-318-68093-9*) U MI Law CLE.

Court Rules of Michigan Annotated, 7 vols., Set. LC 91-75608. 3000p. 1991. ring bd. 185.00 (*0-685-38201-X*, 85-001) U MI Law CLE.

***Court Security Supervisor.** (Career Examination Ser.: Series 1). Date not set. pap. 29.95 (*0-8373-3632-5*) Nat Learn.

Court Selection: Student Litigation in State & Federal Courts. National Center for State Courts Staff. 220p. 1982. 13.20 (*0-685-16952-9*, NCSC-014) Natl Ctr St Courts.

Court Services Package. National Center for State Courts Staff. 67p. 1973. pap. write for info. (*0-318-61220-8*, MAB-038) Natl Ctr St Courts.

Court Space Needs for Cape May County, New Jersey. National Center for State Courts Staff. 168p. 1981. 10.08 (*0-685-15381-9*, NERO-086) Natl Ctr St Courts.

Court Staffing Guidelines: A Survey with Recommendations. National Center for State Courts Staff. 59p. 1980. 3.54 (*0-685-15228-6*, NERO-049) Natl Ctr St Courts.

Court System. 2nd ed. Meridith B. Cox. (Introduction to the Law, Legal System & Legal Liability Ser.: Vol. II). (Illus.). (C). 1988. pap. text ed. 35.00 (*0-912665-19-X*) Cox Pubns.

Court Technology Reports, Transferable Systems, 1988. 98p. 1989. 6.00 (*0-89656-104-6*, R-122) Natl Ctr St Courts.

***Court Testimony in Mental Health: A Guide for Mental Health Professionals & Attorneys.** Gerald H. Vandenberg. LC 92-31403. 162p. 1993. pap. 19.95 (*0-398-06471-7*) C C Thomas.

Court Testimony in Mental Health: A Guide for Mental Health Professionals & Attorneys. Gerald H. Vandenberg. LC 92-31403. 162p. (C). 1993. text ed. 34.95x (*0-398-05825-3*) C C Thomas.

Court Theatre, 1904-1907: A Commentary & Criticism. Desmond MacCarthy. Ed. by Stanley Weintraub. LC 66-27969. (Books of the Theatre: No. 6). 182p. 1966. 10.95 (*0-87024-068-4*) U of Miami Pr.

Court Theatres of Drottningholm & Gripsholm. Agne Beijer. LC 77-180032. (Illus.). 1972. reprint ed. 38.95 (*0-405-08260-6*) Ayer.

Court Traite de l'Existence et de l'Existant. Jacques Maritain. 238p. (FRE.). 1964. 11.95 (*0-8288-9846-4*, F111680) Fr & Eur.

***Court TV's Cradle-to-Grave Legal Survival Guide: A Complete Resource for Any Question You Might Have about the Law.** Ed. by Court TV Staff & American Lawyer Staff. 1995. 40.00 (*0-316-03699-4*); pap. 19.95 (*0-316-03663-3*) Little.

Court vs. Congress: Prayer, Busing, & Abortion. Edward Keynes & Randall K. Miller. LC 89-33442. 401p. (C). 1989. pap. text ed. 19.95 (*0-8223-0968-8*) Duke.

Courtauld Institute Galleries. Dennis Farr. (Illus.). 128p. 1990. 29.95 (*1-870248-39-2*) Scala Books.

Courtaulds Vocabulary of Textile Terms. P. W. Harrison. 311p. (C). 1972. pap. text ed. 100.00 (*0-685-46408-3*, Pub. by Textile Institue UK) St Mut.

Courte Lettre pour Un Long Adieu. Peter Handke. 177p. (FRE.). 1986. pap. 10.95 (*0-7859-2512-0*, 2070377164) Fr & Eur.

Courtesan. Diane Haeger. Ed. by Linda Marrow. 576p. (Orig.). 1993. mass mkt. 5.99 (*0-671-74065-2*, Pocket Star Bks) PB.

Courtesan of Lucknow. Mirza Ruswa. Tr. by Khushwant Singh & M. A. Husaini. 240p. 1970. pap. 4.00 (*0-88253-076-3*) Ind-US Inc.

Courtesan of Seizure. Phillip Foss. (Light & Dust Bks.). 64p. (Orig.). 1993. pap. 8.00 (*0-685-69806-8*) Membrane Pr.

Courtesan's Jewel Box, Chinese Stories of the Xth-XVIIth Centuries. Tr. by Xian-yi Yang et al. (Illus.). 520p. (C). 1981. 19.95 (*0-917056-65-5*, Pub. by Foreign Lang Pr CH) Cheng & Tsui.

Courtesy. Alan Shapiro. LC 82-24837. (Phoenix Poets Ser.). 72p. 1984. 12.95 (*0-226-75026-4*); pap. 5.95 (*0-226-75027-2*) U Ch Pr.

Courtesy Book. Nancy Dunlea. LC 93-80030. (Illus.). 128p. (J). (gr. 4-8). reprint ed. pap. 7.95 (*1-882420-07-1*) Hearth KS.

Courtesy, Service, Protection: The Iowa State Patrol. Scott M. Fisher. 240p. 1993. per. 25.00 (*0-8403-8956-6*) Kendall-Hunt.

Courtesy Workbook. Melinda Schmidt. (Illus.). 52p. (Orig.). (J). (gr. 1-6). 1994. pap. 4.95 (*1-882420-18-7*) Hearth KS.

Courtezan Olympia: An Intimate Survey of Artists & Their Mistress Models. C. J. Bulliet. 1971. 59.95 (*0-87968-955-2*) Gordon Pr.

Courthouse: A Planning & Design Guide for Court Facilities. Don Hardenbergh. (Illus.). 154p. (Orig.). 1992. pap. text ed. 54.95 (*0-89656-112-7*, R131) Natl Ctr St Courts.

Courthouse at Edenton: A History of the Chowan County Courthouse of 1767. Marc D. Brodsky. LC 89-60832. (Illus.). 142p. (Orig.). 1989. 22.00 (*0-9622742-0-8*); pap. 16.00 (*0-9622742-1-6*) Chowan County.

Courthouse Cavalcade, 1786-1986: A Political History of the Courts of Chester County. Wayne C. Woodward. (Illus.). 240p. 1988. 29.95 (*0-929706-00-5*) Chester Co Hist Soc.

Courthouse Design: The First International Conference. Simpson Lawson et al. LC 93-28652. (Illus.). 100p. 1993. pap. 20.00 (*1-55835-118-3*) AIA Press.

Courthouse over White House: Chicago & the Presidential Election of 1960. Edmund F. Kallina, Jr. LC 87-13100. 309p. 1988. 32.95 (*0-8130-0864-6*) U Press Fla.

Courthouse Security Screening. Charles Garrett. LC 92-61123. (Illus.). 120p. 1993. pap. 5.95 (*0-915920-80-8*) Ram Pub.

Courthouse Steps Quilt. Judy Knoechel. (Illus.). 64p. 1995. 12.95 (*0-922705-46-1*) Quilt Day.

Courthouses of Shawnee County. 98p. 1965. write for info. (*0-318-57062-9*) Shawnee County Hist.

Courthouses of Texas: A Guide. Mavis P. Kelsey, Sr. & Donald H. Dyal. LC 93-7022. (Illus.). 342p. (C). 1993. 29.50 (*0-89096-546-3*); pap. 15.95 (*0-89096-547-1*) Tex A&M Univ Pr.

Courthouses of Texas: A Guide. limited ed. Mavis P. Kelsey, Sr. & Donald H. Dyal. LC 93-7022. (Illus.). 342p. (C). 1993. write for info. (*0-89096-558-7*) Tex A&M Univ Pr.

Courthouses of the Commonwealth. Ed. by Robert Brink. LC 84-8752. (Illus.). 136p. 1984. lib. bdg. 35.00 (*0-87023-438-2*) U of Mass Pr.

Courtier & Commoner in Ancient China: Selections from the History of Former Han by Pan Ku. Tr. by Burton Watson. LC 73-18003. 272p. 1977. pap. text ed. 17.00 (*0-231-08354-8*) Col U Pr.

Courtier & the King: Ruy Gomez de Silva, Philip II, & the Court of Spain. James M. Boyden. LC 93-41011. 1995. 35.00 (*0-520-08622-8*) U CA Pr.

Courtiers of American Business. W. T. Brahmstedt. 192p. 1987. pap. 12.95 (*0-88280-118-X*) ETC Pubns.

Courting Danger. Alice Marble. 1992. mass mkt. 5.99 (*0-312-92813-0*) St Martin.

Courting Danger: Injury & Law in New York City, 1870-1910. Randolph E. Bergstrom. LC 92-52744. 232p. (C). 1992. 33.95 (*0-8014-2607-3*) Cornell U Pr.

Courting Disaster. Carolyn Keene. Ed. by Anne Greenberg. (Nancy Drew & Hardy Boys Supermystery Ser.). 224p. (Orig.). (J). 1993. mass mkt. 3.99 (*0-671-78168-5*, Archway) PB.

Courting Disaster: Astrology at the English Court & University in the Later Middle Ages. Hilary M. Carey. LC 91-17383. 296p. 1992. text ed. 55.00 (*0-312-06723-2*) St Martin.

***Courting Disaster: What Runaway Litigation Is Costing You & What Can Be Done to Stop the Fallout.** Joseph W. Kniskern. LC 94-46121. 1995. 14.99 (*0-8054-6162-0*) Broadman.

Courting Julia. Mary Balogh. 224p. 1993. pap. 3.99 (*0-451-17739-8*, Sig) NAL-Dutton.

Courting Miss Hattie. Pamela Morsi. 1991. mass mkt. 5.50 (*0-553-29000-2*) Bantam.

Courting of Dinah Shadd, & Other Stories. Rudyard Kipling. LC 78-144158. (Short Story Index Reprint Ser.). 1977. reprint ed. 15.95 (*0-8369-3773-2*) Ayer.

Courting of Marcus Dupree. Willie Morris. LC 92-27510. 464p. 1992. reprint ed. 37.50 (*0-87805-610-6*); reprint ed. pap. 17.95 (*0-87805-585-1*) U Pr of Miss.

Courting of Philippa. Anthea Malcolm. 1989. pap. 3.95 (*0-8217-2714-1*) Zebra.

***Courting Pleasure.** Tee A. Corinne. 1994. pap. 9.95 (*0-934411-53-0*, Banned Bks) Edward-William Austin.

Courting Season. Jo Anne Cassity. (Homespun Ser.). 304p. (Orig.). 1994. pap. 4.99 (*0-7865-0023-9*) Diamond.

***Courting Valerie.** Linda Markowiak. (Superromance Ser.). 1995. 3.50 (*0-373-70629-4*, 1-70629-0) Harlequin Bks.

Courtly Culture: Literature & Society in the High Middle Ages. Joachim Bumke. Tr. by Thomas J. Dunlap. LC 90-39790. (Illus.). 765p. 1991. 55.00 (*0-520-06634-0*) U CA Pr.

***Courtly Dance of the Renaissance: A New Translation & Edition of the Nobilta di Dame (1600)** Fabritio Caroso. (Illus.). 432p. 1995. pap. text ed. 12.95 (*0-486-28619-3*) Dover.

Courtly Literature: Culture & Context. Selected Papers from the 5th Triennial Congress of the International Courtly Literature Society, Dalfsen, The Netherlands, 9-16 August, 1986. Ed. by Keith Busby & Erik Kooper. LC 90-1072. (Utrecht Publications in General & Comparative Literature: Vol. 25). xvi, 621p. 1990. 148.00x (*90-272-2211-8*) Benjamins North Am.

Courtly Love in Chaucer & Gower. William G. Dodd. 1972. 59.95 (*0-87968-956-0*) Gordon Pr.

Courtly Love in the Shopping Mall: Humanities Programming for Young Adults. Evelyn Shaevel & Peggy O'Donnel. Ed. by Susan Goldberg & Rolly Kent. LC 90-44211. (C). 1991. pap. text ed. 15.00 (*0-8389-3387-4*, 3387-4) ALA.

Courtly Masquing Ayres, to 5 & 6 Parts, for Violins, Consorts, & Cornets. John Adson. LC 77-6842. (English Experience Ser.: No. 838). 1977. reprint ed. lib. bdg. 25.00 (*90-221-0838-4*) Walter J Johnson.

Courtly Romance: A Collection of Essays. Ed. by Guy R. Mermier. LC 84-60235. (Medieval & Renaissance Monograph Ser.: Vol. 6). 320p. reprint ed. pap. 91.20 (*0-318-34986-8*, 2030826) Bks Demand.

***Courtly Tradition in Japanese Art & Literature; Selected from the Hofer & Hyde Collections.** Ed. by John Rosenfield et al. LC 73-85473. (Illus.). 316p. 1973. 12.00 (*0-614-02674-1*) Japan Soc.

Courtney. John Burningham. LC 93-43508. (Illus.). 32p. (J). (ps-2). 1994. 16.00 (*0-517-59883-5*); lib. bdg. 16.99 (*0-517-59884-1*) Crown Bks Yng Read.

Courtney: Master Oarsman - Champion Coach. Margaret K. Look. (Illus.). 168p. 1989. pap. 9.95 (*1-55787-044-6*, NY55032) Hrt of the Lakes.

***Courtney C. Brown: In Memory.** Ed. by James W. Kuhn & Chauncey G. Olinser, Jr. 288p. 1995. 20.00 (*0-9644274-0-0*) Columbia U CBS.

Courtney Price Answers the Most Asked Questions from Entrepreneurs. Courtney Price. 1994. pap. text ed. 15.95 (*0-07-050831-3*) McGraw.

Courtneys. Wilbur Smith. 944p. 1988. 29.95 (*0-316-80182-8*) Little.

Courtneys. braille ed. Wilbur Smith. 2767p. 1992. vinyl bd. 221.36 (*1-56956-047-1*, BR8207) W A T Braille.

Courtney's Wench. large type ed. Jeanne Montague. 390p. 1994. pap. 16.95 (*1-85389-485-0*, Medcom-Trainex) Ulverscroft.

Courtoisie au Moyen Age: (d'apres les textes du XII et du XIII siecle) Henri Dupin. LC 78-63496. 176p. reprint ed. 26.00 (*0-404-17144-3*) AMS Pr.

Courtoisie in Anglo Norman Literature. C. B. West. LC 68-911. (Studies in Comparative Literature: No. 35). 1969. reprint ed. lib. bdg. 75.00 (*0-8383-0686-1*) M S G Haskell Hse.

Courtroom. Quentin Reynolds. LC 77-119943. (Select Bibliographies Reprint Ser.). 1977. 30.95 (*0-8369-5386-X*) Ayer.

Courtroom Communication Strategies with 1988 Cumulative Supplement. suppl. ed. Lawrence J. Smith & Loretta A. Malandro. 880p. 1988. 80.00 (*0-930273-07-9*); 45.00 (*0-930273-91-5*) Michie Butterworth.

***Courtroom Conflicts.** David W. Felder. 102p. 1995. 19.95 (*0-910959-19-6*, B&G 19H); teacher ed 39.95 (*0-910959-39-0*, B&G 19T) Felder Bks.

***Courtroom Criminal Evidence.** suppl. ed. Edward J. Imwinkelried et al. 1302p. 1994. 105.00 (*1-55834-127-7*) Michie Butterworth.

Courtroom Criminal Evidence with 1991 Cumulative Supplement. Edward J. Imwinkelried et al. 1040p. 1987. 95.00 (*0-87473-289-1*) Michie Butterworth.

Courtroom ESL. Nancy S. Green. (Illus.). 80p. (Orig.). 1986. 34.50 (*0-88272-275-1*); pap. text ed. 5.45 (*0-88272-276-X*) Santillana.

Courtroom Needs Assessment & Court Space Review in Rockingham County, New Hampshire. National Center for State Courts Staff. 29p. 1981. 1.74 (*0-685-15375-4*, NERO-090) Natl Ctr St Courts.

Courtroom Procedures for Court Reporters: Syllabus. Robert E. Bennett. 1977. pap. text ed. 6.50 (*0-89420-031-3*, 456010); audio 42.30 (*0-89420-137-9*, 456000) Natl Book.

Courtroom Psychology for Trial Lawyers. Thomas Sannito & Peter J. McGovern. LC 85-12006. (Trial Pract Library). 344p. 1985. text ed. 138.00 (*0-471-82649-9*); Cummulative supplement, 128p., 1992. pap. 55.00 (*0-471-57036-2*) Wiley.

Courtroom Rapport: How to Be Effective & at Ease in Court. Gusty Winds Staff. LC 93-86054. 65p. 1993. pap. 19.95 (*0-9638681-0-1*) Legal Ease.

Courtroom Security: Closed Circuit Television & Microphone Including Supporting Materials. National Center for State Courts Staff. 113p. 1975. 6.78 (*0-685-15436-X*, MAB-040) Natl Ctr St Courts.

Courtroom Survival: The Officer's Guide to Better Testimony. 2nd ed. Devallis Rutledge. LC 87-70528. (Illus.). 189p. 1989. reprint ed. pap. text ed. 14.95 (*0-942728-15-7*) Copperhouse.

***Courtroom Testimony Concepts.** Michael F. Mangiaracina. Ed. by Kathleen M. Garrison. 98p. 1994. pap. text ed. 14.95 (*0-9644837-0-X*) Garrison Desktop.

Courtroom Testimony for Skill Development. (Orig.). (C). 1990. pap. 16.95 (*0-937112-11-9*); pap. text ed. 13.95 (*0-685-31738-2*) Stenograph Corp.

Courtroom Toxicology, 7 vols., Set. Marshall Houts & Randall C. Baselt. 1981. ring bd. write for info. (*0-8205-1717-8*) Bender.

Courtroom's Finest Hour in American Cinema. Thomas J. Harris. LC 86-26073. (Illus.). 191p. 1987. 20.00 (*0-8108-1956-2*) Scarecrow.

Courtrooms of the Mind: Stories & Advice on Judging Others Favorably. 2nd ed. Hanoch Teller. 288p. (YA). (gr. 12). 1988. reprint ed. 11.95 (*0-9614772-4-5*) NYC Pub Co.

Courts: A Comparative & Political Analysis. Martin Shapiro. LC 80-18263. ix, 245p. 1986. pap. text ed. 13.95 (*0-226-75043-4*) U Ch Pr.

Courts: Fulcrum of the Justice System. 2nd ed. H. Ted Rubin. 256p. (C). 1984. pap. text ed. write for info. (*0-394-33573-2*) Random.

Courts: Separation of Powers. LC 83-61923. (Annual Chief Earl Warren Conference on Advocacy in the U.S. Ser.). 141p. 1983. pap. 25.00 (*0-933067-05-4*) Roscoe Pound Found.

Courts: The Pendulum of Federalism. LC 79-92328. (Annual Chief Justice Earl Warren Conference on Advocacy in the U.S. Ser.). 166p. 1979. pap. 25.00 (*0-933067-01-1*) Roscoe Pound Found.

Courts: The Pendulum of Federalism: Final Report of the 1979 Chief Justice Earl Warren Conference on Advocacy in the United States. Roscoe Pound-American Trial Lawyers Foundation Staff. 166p. 1979. pap. 25.00 (*0-317-57758-1*) Roscoe Pound Found.

Courts Acts (Annotated) Hilary Delany. 320p. 1993. text ed. 75.00 (*1-85800-006-8*, Pub. by Round Hall) Intl Spec Bk.

Courts & Administration of Justice under Chhatrapati Shivaji. T. T. Mahajan. (C). 1992. 18.00 (*81-7169-198-6*, Commonwealth) S Asia.

Courts & American Education Law. Tyll Van Geel. LC 86-25293. (Frontiers of Education Ser.). 502p. 1987. 38.95x (*0-87975-384-6*) Prometheus Bks.

Courts & Cabinets. George P. Gooch. LC 72-3304. (Essay Index Reprint Ser.). 1977. reprint ed. 27.95 (*0-8369-2901-2*) Ayer.

Courts & Criminals. Arthur C. Train. LC 74-3857. (Criminal Justice in America Ser.). 1974. reprint ed. 25.95 (*0-405-06173-0*) Ayer.

Courts & Education: Seventy-Seventh Yearbook, Part I, of the National Society for the Study of Education. Ed. by Clifford P. Hooker. LC 77-15768. 1978. lib. bdg. 12.00 (*0-226-60124-2*) U Ch Pr.

An Asterisk (*) at the beginning of an entry indicates that the title is appearing in BIP for the first time.

An Asterisk (*) at the beginning of an entry indicates that the title is appearing in BIP for the first time.

1663

C

Covenant Affirmations: This We Believe. Donald C. Frisk. 196p. (Orig.). 1981. pap. 9.95 (*0-910452-48-2*) Covenant.

Covenant & Causality in Medieval Thought: Studies in Philosophy, Theology & Economic Practice. William J. Courtenay. (Collected Studies: No. CS206). 350p. (C). 1984. reprint ed. text ed. 95.95 (*0-86078-154-2*, Pub. by Variorum UK) Ashgate Pub Co.

Covenant & Consensus. Cora E. Cypser. 202p. (C). 1990. pap. 11.95 (*0-9625774-9-9*) Kim Pathways.

Covenant & Creation: An Old Testament Covenantal Theology. William J. Dumbrell. LC 93-16690. 1993. reprint ed. pap. 11.99 (*0-8010-3022-6*) Baker Bk.

Covenant & Polity in Biblical Israel: Biblical Foundations & Jewish Expressions. Daniel J. Elazar. LC 93-37985. (Covenant Tradition in Politics Ser.: Vol. 1). 536p. (C). 1994. 49.95 (*1-56000-151-8*) Transaction Pubs.

Covenant & Sacrifice in the Letter to the Hebrews. John Dunnill. (Society for New Testament Studies Monographs: No. 75). 292p. (C). 1993. 64.95 (*0-521-43158-1*) Cambridge U Pr.

***Covenant & Theophany in the Bible & Ancient Near East.** Jeffrey J. Niehaus. 360p. 1995. pap. 18.99 (*0-310-49471-0*) Zondervan.

Covenant Book of Worship. 1981. 10.95 (*0-685-45351-0*) Covenant.

Covenant, Charter & Party: Traditions of Revolt & Protest in Modern Scottish History. Ed. by Terry Brotherstone. 1989. pap. text ed. 19.95 (*0-08-037736-X*, Pergamon Pr) Elsevier.

Covenant Coat. Robert H. Moss. LC 85-81312. 174p. 1985. pap. 11.98 (*0-88290-311-X*, 1959) Horizon Utah.

Covenant Community & Church: A Statement on Catholic Covenant Community & a Selection of Documents. Ed. by Stephen B. Clark. 84p. 1992. pap. 6.99 (*0-89283-806-X*) Servant.

Covenant Community in Modern Judaism. S. Daniel Breslauer. LC 88-24631. (Contributions to the Study of Religion Ser.: No. 21). 138p. 1989. text ed. 45.00 (*0-313-26605-0*, BRQ, Greenwood Pr) Greenwood.

Covenant Discipleship: Christian Formation Through Mutual Accountability. David L. Watson. LC 90-82418. 192p. 1991. pap. 9.95 (*0-88177-091-4*, DR091) Discipleship Res.

Covenant Enforced: Sermons on Deuteronomy 27 & 28. John Calvin. Ed. by James B. Jordan. LC 90-32836. 364p. 1990. 14.95 (*0-930464-33-8*) Inst Christian.

***Covenant Experience: Eleven Steps to a Better Marriage.** Bob Tomonto et al. 128p. (Orig.). 1995. pap. 10.95 (*0-89390-326-4*) Resource Pubns.

***Covenant Experience: Facilitator's Guide.** Bob Tomonto et al. 144p. (Orig.). 1995. teacher ed, pap. 21.95 (*0-89390-328-0*) Resource Pubns.

Covenant for a New Creation: Ethics, Religion, & Public Policy. Ed. by Carol S. Robb & Carl J. Casebolt. LC 90-27013. 1991. pap. 17.95 (*0-88344-740-1*) Orbis Bks.

***Covenant for All Seasons: The Marriage Journey.** Calvin Miller. LC 95-7593. 192p. 1995. 14.99 (*0-87788-386-6*) Shaw Pubs.

Covenant for Young People. Enoch N. Tanyi. (Illus.). 40p. (Orig.). (J). (gr. k-4). 1991. pap. 7.95 (*0-85398-337-2*) G Ronald Pub.

***Covenant, God's Guarantee for Victorious Living.** R. S. Bud Miller. 1995. pap. 5.00 (*1-57149-020-5*) Christ Unltd.

Covenant Hymnal. 1973. 8.95 (*0-685-45349-9*) Covenant.

***Covenant in Judaism & Paul: A Study of Ritual Boundaries As Identity Markers.** Ellen J. Christiansen. (Arbeiten zur Geschichte des Antiken Judentums und des Urchristentums Ser.: No. 27). 300p. 1995. 84.00 (*90-04-10333-3*) E J Brill.

Covenant in the Ninteenth Century: The Decline of an American Political Tradition. Ed. by Daniel J. Elazar. 244p. (C). 1994. lib. bdg. 49.50 (*0-8476-7924-1*); pap. text ed. 21.95 (*0-8476-7925-X*) Rowman.

Covenant in the Old Testament. Michael D. Guinan. (Biblical Booklets Ser.). 68p. 1975. pap. 0.75 (*0-8199-0520-8*, Frncscn Herld) Franciscan Pr.

Covenant Love: Its Nature, Commitment & Patterns. Blair Adams & Joel Stein. LC 89-51247. 225p. (Orig.). 1989. pap. 9.95 (*0-916387-18-6*) Truth Forum.

Covenant Never Revoked: Biblical Reflections on Christian-Jewish Dialogue. Norbert Lohfink. 1991. pap. 7.95 (*0-8091-3228-1*) Paulist Pr.

Covenant of Baha'u'llah. Adib Taherzadeh. (Illus.). 500p. 1992. pap. 21.95 (*0-85398-344-5*) G Ronald Pub.

***Covenant of Blood: Circumcision & Gender in Rabbinic Judaism.** Lawrence A. Hoffman. LC 95-16067. (Chicago Studies in the History of Judaism). 1996. write for info. (*0-226-34783-4*); pap. write for info. (*0-226-34784-2*) U Ch Pr.

***Covenant of Brotherhood: Building Lasting Relationships.** Richard Wright. (Illus.). 60p. Date not set. pap. 4.50 (*0-9632748-9-9*) Majesty Pubns.

Covenant of Grace. C. H. Spurgeon. 1988. pap. 4.95 (*1-56186-218-5*) Pilgrim Pubns.

Covenant of Grace: A Biblico-Theological Study. John Murray. LC 87-29117. 32p. 1987. reprint ed. pap. 2.50 (*0-87552-363-3*) Presby & Reformed.

Covenant of Grace in Puritan Thought. John Von Rohr. LC 86-13935. (American Academy of Religion, Studies in Religion). 240p. 1987. pap. 15.95 (*1-55540-038-8*) Scholars Pr GA.

Covenant of Justice. David Gerrold. 1994. mass mkt. 5.99 (*0-553-56188-X*, Spectra) Bantam.

Covenant of Love. Janina Babris. (Illus.). 228p. (Orig.). pap. 7.95 (*0-913382-19-1*, 101-25) Prow Bks-Franciscan.

Covenant of Love. Gilbert Morris. LC 92-5584. (Appomattox Saga Ser.: Vol. 1). 352p. 1992. pap. 10.99 (*0-8423-5497-2*) Tyndale.

Covenant of Love: Pope John Paul II on Sexuality, Marriage, & Family in the Modern World. rev. ed. Richard M. Hogan & John M. LeVoir. LC 91-76516. 276p. 1992. pap. 14.95 (*0-89870-399-9*) Ignatius Pr.

Covenant of Peace. Maurice Friedman. LC 60-9785. (C). 1960. pap. 3.00 (*0-87574-110-X*) Pendle Hill.

Covenant of the Church. Buford Johnson. 72p. 1988. pap. 4.50 (*0-934942-70-6*) White Wing Pub.

Covenant of the Flame. David Morrell. 1991. 19.95 (*0-446-51563-9*) Warner Bks.

Covenant of the Flame. David Morrell. 480p. 1992. mass mkt. 6.50 (*0-446-36292-1*) Warner Bks.

Covenant of the Forge. Dan Parkinson. (Dwarven Nations Trilogy Ser.). 320p. (Orig.). 1993. 4.95 (*1-56076-558-5*) TSR Inc.

Covenant of the Heart: Meditations of a Christian Hermeticist on the Mysteries of Tradition. Valentin Tomberg. 272p. 1994. reprint ed. pap. text ed. 19.95 (*0-8264-0764-1*) Continuum.

Covenant of the Poppies. Colin D. Peel. LC 93-1111. 224p. 1993. 17.95 (*0-312-09264-4*, Pub. by Thomas Dunne Bks) St Martin.

Covenant of 1996: Countdown the Last Seven Years. Robert J. Messina. (Illus.). (Orig.). 1993. pap. text ed. 8.00 (*0-685-65628-4*) Hse of Asher.

Covenant Over Middle Eastern Waters. Joyce R. Starr. LC 94-45433. (J). 1995. 25.00 (*0-8050-3019-0*) H Holt & Co.

Covenant Over Middle Eastern Waters. Joyce R. Starr. 1995. pap. write for info. (*0-8050-3056-5*) H Holt & Co.

Covenant People. W. J. Cameron. 3.00 (*0-685-08801-4*) Destiny.

Covenant People. Shirley J. Heckman & June A. Gibble. LC 93-19028. (Covenant Bible Study Ser.). (Illus.). 1993. 4.95 (*0-87178-169-7*) Brethren.

Covenant, Polity, & Constitutionalism. Daniel J. Elazar & John Kincaid. LC 83-23295. 1983. pap. text ed. 20.00 (*0-8191-3709-X*) U Pr of Amer.

Covenant Relationships: A More Excellent Way. Keith Intrater. 286p. (Orig.). 1992. pap. 14.99 (*0-914903-71-3*) Destiny Image.

Covenant Roots: Sources & Affirmations. Ed. by Glenn P. Anderson. Tr. by Fred O. Jansson et al. 238p. (Orig.). 1980. pap. 7.95 (*0-910452-46-6*) Covenant.

Covenant Sealed: The Development of Puritan Sacramental Theology in Old & New England, 1570-1720. E. Brooks Holifield. LC 73-92695. 260p. reprint ed. pap. 74.10 (*0-8357-8083-X*, 2033756) Bks Demand.

Covenant Sequence in Leviticus & Deuteronomy. James B. Jordan. 76p. 1989. pap. 5.95 (*0-930464-22-2*) Inst Christian.

***Covenant with Death: The Constitution, Law, & Equality in the Civil War Era.** Phillip S. Paludan. LC 74-34324. 325p. 1975. reprint ed. pap. 92.70 (*0-7837-8083-4*, 2047836) Bks Demand.

Covenant with Earth: A Selection from the Poetry of Lew Sarett, Including Six Poems Not Previously Published. Lew R. Sarett. LC 56-12859. 205p. reprint ed. pap. 58.50 (*0-8357-6919-4*, 2037978) Bks Demand.

Covenant with God's People. Henry R. Rust. 1990. 5.95 (*0-940754-90-8*, 3554) Ed Ministries.

Covenant with Honor. Joseph H. Hughes, Jr. LC 65-26682. 1982. 17.00 (*0-317-00001-2*); pap. 11.00 (*0-317-00002-0*) Aaron-Jenkins.

Covenant with Power: America & World Order from Wilson to Reagan. Lloyd C. Gardner. (Illus.). 268p. 1986. pap. text ed. 14.95 (*0-19-504009-0*) OUP.

Covenant with the Vampire: The Diaries of the Family Dracul. Jeanne Kalogridis. LC 94-6049. 1994. 19.95 (*0-385-31313-6*) Delacorte.

Covenantal Theology, Vol. I: The Eucharistic Order of History. Donald J. Keefe. 572p. (C). 1991. lib. bdg. 69.50 (*0-8191-8086-6*) U Pr of Amer.

Covenantal Theology, Vol. II: The Eucharistic Order of History. Donald J. Keefe. 546p. (C). 1991. lib. bdg. 69.00 (*0-8191-8087-4*) U Pr of Amer.

Covenanted People: The Religious Tradition & the Origins of American Constitutionalism. Donald S. Lutz & Jack D. Warren. (Illus.). 104p. 1987. pap. 30.00 (*0-916617-27-0*) J C Brown.

Covenanters Monuments of Scotland. Robert W. Crone. 96p. 1984. 40.00 (*0-7212-0694-8*, Pub. by Regency Press) St Mut.

Covenants. Kevin J. Conner & Ken P. Malmin. 120p. 1976. pap. 9.95 (*0-914936-77-8*) Bible Temple.

Covenants & Blessings. Murray. 176p. pap. 4.99 (*0-88368-136-6*) Whitaker Hse.

Covenants & Zoning for Research-Business Parks. Douglas R. Porter et al. 88p. 1986. pap. 43.95 (*0-87420-648-0*) Urban Land.

Covenants Not to Compete, 2 vols. Kurt H. Decker. (Employment Law Library). 432p. 1993. Vol. 1, 432p. text ed. 105.00 (*0-471-59294-3*) Wiley.

Covenants Not to Compete, 2 vols. 2nd ed. Kurt H. Decker. (Employment Law Library). 288p. 1993. Vol. 2, 288p. text ed. 105.00 (*0-471-59299-4*) Wiley.

Covenants Not to Compete, 2 vols., Vol. 2. 2nd ed. Kurt H. Decker. (Employment Law Library). 880p. 1993. Set. text ed. 232.00 (*0-471-58257-3*) Wiley.

Covenants Not to Compete: A State-by-State Survey. ABA Staff. LC 91-29351. 688p. 1991. pap. text ed. 85.00 (*0-87179-676-7*, 0676) BNA.

***Covenants Not to Compete: A State-by-State Survey Cumulative Supplement 3.** ABA Staff. 1995. pap. text ed. 75.00 (*0-87179-876-X*) BNA.

***Covenants Not to Compete: A State-by-State Survey, with Culmuative Supplement 3.** 1995. pap. text ed. 125.00 (*0-614-04037-X*) BNA.

Covenants Not to Compete, a State-by-State Survey - Cumulative Supplement 2 (1990-1992) A State-by-State Survey. suppl. ed. ABA Staff. LC 91-29361. 356p. 1994. pap. text ed. 55.00 (*0-87179-808-5*) BNA.

Covenants of God. Lester Sumrall. 66p. (C). 1982. pap. text ed. 10.00 (*0-937580-67-8*) LeSEA Pub Co.

Covenants on Campus: Covenant Discipleship Groups for College & University Students. Kim A. Hauenstein-Mallet & Kenda C. Dean. LC 90-62152. 112p. 1991. pap. 6.95 (*0-88177-099-X*, DR099) Discipleship Res.

***Covenants with Earth & Rain: Exchange, Sacrifice & Revelation in Mixtec Sociality.** John Monaghan. LC 95-2527. (Civilization of the American Indian Ser.: Vol. 219). 1995. write for info. (*0-8061-2762-7*) U of Okla Pr.

Covent Garden Fish Book. Phil Diamond & Jackie Hunt. (Illus.). 320p. 1993. pap. 22.95 (*1-85626-063-1*) Trafalgar.

Covent-Garden Journal, 2 vols., Set. Henry Fielding. (BCL1-PR English Literature Ser.). 1992. reprint ed. lib. bdg. 150.00 (*0-7812-7351-X*) Rprt Serv.

Covent-Garden Journal & A Plan of the Universal Register-Office. Henry Fielding. Ed. by Bertrand A. Goldgar. LC 87-27940. (Works of Henry Fielding Ser.). (Illus.). 561p. 1988. text ed. 75.00 (*0-8195-5167-8*, Wesleyan Univ Pr) U Pr of New Eng.

Covent Garden Theatre. Charles Macklin. LC 93-20862. (Augustan Reprints Ser.: No. 116 (1965)). 1993. reprint ed. 12.00 (*0-404-70116-7*) AMS Pr.

Coventesse of Pembrokes Arcadia. Philip Sidney. LC 78-85106. (Kent English Reprints, the Renaissance Ser.). 788p. reprint ed. pap. 180.00 (*0-7837-1346-0*, 2041494) Bks Demand.

Coventry: History & Guide. David McGrory. (History & Guide Ser.). (Illus.). 128p. 1992. pap. 16.00 (*0-7509-0194-2*) A Sutton Pub.

Coventry at War in Photographs. (C). 1987. 50.00 (*0-317-89846-9*, Pub. by Birmingham Midland Soc UK) St Mut.

Coventry Leet Book: Parts I & II, Set. Coventry, Eng. Staff. (EETS, OS Ser.: Nos. 134-35). 1972. reprint ed. 70.00 (*0-527-00132-5*) Periodicals Srv.

Coventry Leet Book: Parts III & IV, Set. Coventry, Eng. Staff. (EETS, OS Ser.: Nos. 138 & 146). 1972. reprint ed. 53.00 (*0-527-00133-3*) Periodicals Srv.

Coventry Patmore. Edmund W. Gosse. LC 71-131720. 1971. 10.00 (*0-403-00607-4*) Scholarly.

Coventry Patmore. Edmund W. Gosse. (BCL1-PR English Literature Ser.). 213p. 1992. reprint ed. lib. bdg. 79.00 (*0-7812-7615-2*) Rprt Serv.

***Coventry Pool & Garden Houses.** Coventry Pool & Garden Houses, Inc., Staff. 1995. pap. 19.95 (*0-9645844-0-9*) Coventry Pool & Grdn.

Cover Crops for Clean Water. Pref. by W. L. Hargroye. (Illus.). 197p. (C). 1991. pap. text ed. 18.00 (*0-935734-25-2*) Soil & Water Conserv.

Cover for a Traitor. large type ed. Palma Harcourt. (Charnwood Ser.). 400p. 1992. 23.95 (*0-7089-8607-2*, Trail West Pubs) Ulverscroft.

***Cover Girls & Supermodels: 1945-1965.** Jean-Noel Liaut. Tr. by Robin Buss. (Illus.). 322p. 1995. 35.00 (*0-7145-2998-2*) M Boyars Pubs.

Cover Her Face. P. D. James. 256p. 1989. mass mkt. 4.99 (*0-446-31221-5*) Warner Bks.

Cover Letters, Cover Letters, Cover Letters. Richard Fein. 192p. (Orig.). 1994. pap. 8.95 (*1-56414-093-8*) Career Pr Inc.

***Cover Letters That Knock 'em Dead.** 2nd ed. Martin J. Yate. LC 94-24021. 1995. pap. 9.95 (*1-55850-435-4*) Adams Pubng.

Cover Letters That Will Get You the Job You Want. Stanley Wynett. 192p. (Orig.). 1993. pap. 12.99 (*1-55870-275-X*) Betterway Bks.

Cover Letters They Can't Forget. Eric R. Martin & Karyn E. Langhorne. LC 92-38541. (Opportunities in...Ser.). 160p. 1993. pap. 8.95 (*0-8442-4139-3*, VGM Career Bks) NTC Pub Grp.

Cover Me. Lon Otto. LC 88-11817. 142p. (Orig.). 1988. pap. 9.95 (*0-918273-40-4*) Coffee Hse.

Cover Stories: Narrative & Ideology in the British Spy Thriller. Michael Denning. LC 86-21968. 168p. 1987. pap. 11.95 (*0-7100-9642-9*, RKP) Routledge.

Cover Story. Robert Cullen. LC 93-40751. 312p. 1994. text ed. 20.00 (*0-689-12198-9*, Atheneum S&S) S&S Trade.

***Cover Story.** Robert Cullen. 1995. pap. write for info. (*0-8041-1344-0*) Ivy Books.

***Cover Story.** Colin Forbes. 383p. (Orig.). 1986. pap. 12.95 (*0-330-29456-3*, Pub. by Pan Books UK) Trans-Atl Phila.

Cover Story Index, 1960-1991. Ed. by Robert Skapura. 480p. 1992. 32.00 (*0-917846-08-7*, 95503) Highsmith Pr.

***Cover to Cover: Creative Techniques for Making Beautiful Books, Journals & Albums.** Shereen La Plantz. Ed. by Leslie Dierks. LC 94-24439. (Illus.). 144p. 1995. 24.95 (*0-937274-81-X*, Lark Bks) Sterling.

Cover-Up. Anthony Oliver. 1988. mass mkt. 4.99 (*0-449-21466-4*, Crest) Fawcett.

Cover-up: The Governmental Conspiracy to Conceal the Facts about the Public Execution of John Kennedy. 2nd ed. J. Gary Shawwith & Larry R. Harris. (Collector's Editions Ser.). 210p. 1992. reprint ed. pap. 35.00 (*0-918487-63-3*) Thomas Pubns TX.

Cover-Up: The Jeremy Thorpe Affair. limited ed. Peter Bessell. LC 80-52089. (Illus.). 574p. 1981. pap. 12.95 (*0-937812-01-3*) Simons Bks.

Cover-Up: What You Are Not Supposed to Know About Nuclear Power. Karl Grossman. LC 80-81394. 312p. 1980. 22.00 (*0-932966-10-1*); pap. 16.00 (*0-932966-19-5*) Permanent Pr.

Cover-Up at Mojave Green. Jo-Bradley Jackson. 1980. pap. 2.25 (*0-8439-0816-5*) Dorchester Pub Co.

Cover-up Story. large type ed. Marian Babson. (Nightingale Ser.). 264p. 1991. pap. 14.95 (*0-8161-4926-7*, Nightingale) Hall.

***Cover Your Assets.** Jay Mitton. 1995. pap. 14.00 (*0-517-88518-2*, Crown) Crown Pub Group.

Cover Your Own Boat or Start Your Own Marine Canvas Business. Oliver Parker. (Illus.). 1982. pap. 24.95 (*0-937155-00-4*) O Parker Pub.

Coverage Catalog: Coverage for Mental & Nervous Disorders: a Compendium of Public & Private Sector Health Insurance Plans. 3rd ed. Comp. by Patricia Scheidemandel. LC 93-7144. 1993. 27.50 (*0-89042-209-5*) Am Psychiatric.

Coverages Applicable. Roy McCormick. 144p. 1992. 39.00 (*0-942326-28-8*, 30040) Rough Notes.

***Coverama - The Collector's Guide to Antique Hawaiian Milk Covers.** DeSoto Brown & Burl Burlingame. 1994. pap. 4.80 (*0-9629227-4-9*) Pacific Mono.

Coverdale on Management. 2nd ed. Max Taylor. 300p. 1992. pap. 42.95 (*0-7506-0150-7*) Buttrwrth-Heinemann.

Covered Animal Dishes. Everett Grist. (Illus.). 120p. 1991. pap. 14.95 (*0-89145-364-4*, 1843) Collector Bks.

Covered Bridge. Herbert W. Congdon. (Illus.). 1970. reprint ed. pap. 7.95 (*0-911570-05-5*) Vermont Bks.

Covered Bridges: Focus on Kentucky. Vernon White. LC 85-81964. (Illus.). 137p. 1985. 10.95 (*0-935680-20-9*); pap. 6.95 (*0-685-24881-X*) Kentucke Imprints.

***Covered Bridges Cookbook.** Bruce Carlson. (Illus.). 224p. 1995. 11.95 (*1-57166-029-1*) Quixote Pr IA.

Covered Bridges in Illinois, Iowa, & Wisconsin. rev. ed. Leslie C. Swanson. (Illus.). (Orig.). 1986. pap. 4.00 (*0-911466-14-2*) Swanson.

Covered Bridges of California. S. Griswold Morley. 1992. reprint ed. lib. bdg. 75.00 (*0-7812-5066-8*) Rprt Serv.

Covered Bridges of Connecticut: A Guide. Andrew R. Howard. LC 83-51726. (Covered Bridge Ser.). (Illus.). 44p. (Orig.). 1985. pap. 3.95 (*0-940310-02-3*) Village Pr.

***Covered Bridges of Massachusetts: A Guide.** Andrew R. Howard. (Covered Bridge Ser.). (Illus.). 80p. (Orig.). 1995. pap. 6.95 (*0-940310-03-1*) Village Pr.

Covered Bridges of Oregon. Suzanne F. Welt. (Illus.). 48p. 1982. 22.00 (*0-88014-044-5*) Mosaic Pr OH.

Covered Bridges of Parke County. Brenda Krekeler. 56p. 1991. pap. 6.95 (*1-879729-00-8*) Comp Soft Pubns.

Covered Bridges of Pennsylvania: A Guide. Susan M. Zacher. LC 82-623265. (Illus.). 140p. 1982. pap. 9.95 (*0-89271-019-5*) Pa Hist & Mus.

Covered Bridges of Pennsylvania Dutchland. (Pennsylvania Dutch Bks.). (Illus.). 1960. 3.00 (*0-911410-03-1*) Applied Arts.

***Covered Bridges of the Midwest: 1996 Calendar.** (Illus.). 26p. 1995. 12.95 (*1-886154-08-2*) Phoenix IL.

Covered Bridges of West Virginia. Stan Cohen. 1992. pap. 14.95 (*0-929521-55-2*) Pictorial Hist.

Covered, Not Concealed. C. Hershel Gammill. 182p. (Orig.). 1991. pap. 8.99 (*1-56043-037-0*) Destiny Image.

Covered Wagon. Emerson Hough. 24.95 (*0-89190-617-7*, Am Repr) Amereon Ltd.

Covered Wagon. Emerson Hough. (BCL1-PS American Literature Ser.). 378p. 1992. reprint ed. lib. bdg. 89.00 (*0-7812-6743-9*) Rprt Serv.

Covered Wagon & Other Adventures. Lynn H. Scott. LC 87-5857. (Illus.). x, 135p. (J). (gr. 4-7). 1987. 15.00 (*0-8032-4179-8*); pap. 7.95 (*0-8032-9222-8*) U of Nebr Pr.

Covered Wagon Days: A Journey Across the Plains in the Sixties, & Pioneer Days in the Northwest; from the Private Journals of Albert Jerome Dickson. Albert J. Dickson. (American Biography Ser.). 287p. 1991. reprint ed. lib. bdg. 69.00 (*0-7812-8108-3*) Rprt Serv.

Covered Wagon Days: From the Private Journals of Albert Jerome Dickson. Arthur Jerome Dickson. Ed. by Arthur J. Dickson. LC 89-4934. 285p. 1989. pap. 9.95 (*0-8032-6582-4*) U of Nebr Pr.

Covered Wagon Geologist. Charles N. Gould. (Illus.). 312p. reprint ed. 89.00 (*0-8357-9723-6*, 2010150) Bks Demand.

***Covered Wagon Remedy Chest.** Date not set. write for info. (*0-937844-01-2*) Caverne Pub.

***Covered Wagon Women: Diaries & Letters from the Western Trails, 1840-1849.** Ed. by Kenneth Holmes. (Latin American Women Writers Ser.). (Illus.). 288p. 1995. pap. 12.00 (*0-8032-7277-4*, Bison Books) U of Nebr Pr.

Covered Wagon Women, Vol. I, 1840-1849: Diaries & Letters from the Western Trails, 1840-1849. Ed. by Kenneth L. Holmes. LC 82-72586. (Covered Wagon Women Ser.). (Illus.). 275p. 1983. 35.00 (*0-87062-146-7*) A H Clark.

Covered Wagon Women, Vol. II: Diaries & Letters from the Western Trails, 1840-1849. Ed. by Kenneth L. Holmes. LC 82-72586. (Covered Wagon Women Ser.). (Illus.). 275p. 1983. 35.00 (*0-87062-151-3*) A H Clark.

Covered Wagon Women, Vol. III, 1851: Diaries & Letters from the Western Trails, 1840-1849. Kenneth L. Holmes. LC 82-72586. (Covered Wagon Women Ser.). (Illus.). 287p. 1984. 35.00 (*0-87062-153-X*) A H Clark.

Covered Wagon Women, Vol. IV, 1852: Diaries & Letters from the Western Trails, 1840-90. Ed. by Kenneth L. Holmes. LC 82-72586. (Illus.). 295p. 1991. The California Trail. 35.00 (*0-87062-158-0*) A H Clark.

Covered Wagon Women, Vol. 10: Diaries & Letters from the Western Trails, 1840-1890. Ed. by Kenneth L. Holmes. LC 82-72586. 272p. 1991. 35.00 (*0-87062-211-0*) A H Clark.

Covered Wagon Women, Vol. 11: Bibliography to the Series, Index to the Series, Folding Map of Routes. Ed. by Kenneth L. Holmes. 1994. 40.00 (*0-87062-223-4*) A H Clark.

An Asterisk (*) at the beginning of an entry indicates that the title is appearing in BIP for the first time.

An Asterisk (*) at the beginning of an entry indicates that the title is appearing in BIP for the first time.

1665

An Asterisk (*) at the beginning of an entry indicates that the title is appearing in BIP for the first time.

An Asterisk (*) at the beginning of an entry indicates that the title is appearing in BIP for the first time.

C

Coyote Wisdom. Ed. by J. Frank Dobie et al. LC 40-499. (Texas Folklore Society Publications: No. 14). (Illus.). 304p. 1965. reprint ed. 16.95 (*0-87074-046-6*) UNTX Pr.

Coyotes. Sandra Lee. (Nature Books Ser.). (J). (gr. 2-6). 1992. lib. bdg. 22.79 (*0-89565-843-7*) Childs World.

Coyotes. Emilie U. Lepthien. LC 92-35050. (New True Book Ser.). (Illus.). 48p. (J). (gr. k-4). 1993. lib. bdg. 12.90 (*0-516-01331-9*); pap. 4.95 (*0-516-41331-7*) Childrens.

Coyotes: A Journey Through the Secret World of America's Illegal Aliens. Ted Conover. LC 87-40066. (Vintage Departures Ser.). 256p. 1987. pap. 11.00 (*0-394-75518-9*, Vin) Random.

Coyotes: Biology, Behavior & Management. Ed. by Marc Bekoff. 1978. text ed. 99.00 (*0-12-086050-3*) Acad Pr.

Coyotes: Predators & Survivors. Charles L. Cadieux & Edward L. Kozicky. LC 82-62895. (Illus.). 240p. 1983. 21.95 (*0-913276-42-1*) Stone Wall Pr.

Coyotes & My Mom. Bethany Reid. 48p. (Orig.). 1989. pap. 4.00 (*0-944920-03-9*) Bellowing Ark Pr.

Coyotes & Town Dogs: Earth First! & the Environmental Movement. Susan Zakin. LC 92-50748. 448p. 1993. 23.50 (*0-670-83618-4*, Viking) Viking Penguin.

***Coyotes & Town Dogs: Earth First! & the Environmental Movement.** Susan Zakin. 496p. 1995. 14.95 (*0-14-014487-0*, Penguin Bks) Viking Penguin.

Coyote's Big Penis & Other Stories. Guy Mount. 80p. 1989. pap. 5.95 (*0-9604462-5-7*) Sweetlight.

Coyote's Canyon. Terry T. Williams. (Illus.). 96p. (Orig.). 1989. pap. 17.95 (*0-87905-245-7*) Gibbs Smith Pub.

***Coyote's Cool Juice Drinks Book.** Mark Miller. 1995. pap. 16.95 (*0-89815-654-8*) Ten Speed Pr.

***Coyote's Council Fire: Contemporary Shamans on Race, Gender & Community.** Loren Cruden. 192p. 1995. pap. 14.95 (*0-89281-566-3*, Destiny Bks) Inner Tradit.

***Coyotes in the Crosswalk: True Tales of Animal Life in the Wilds-- of the City!** Diane Swanson. LC 94-36665. (J). 1995. write for info. (*0-89658-272-8*) Voyageur Pr.

Coyote's Journal. Steven Nemirow et al. LC 82-70807. (Illus.). 176p. (Orig.). 1982. pap. 8.95 (*0-914728-38-5*) Wingbow Pr.

Coyote's Journal, No. 12. Ed. by James Koller. 1988. pap. 10.00 (*0-940556-04-9*) Coyote.

***Coyotes of WillBrook.** large type ed. Lee Floren. (Linford Western Large Pr. Ser.). 1994. pap. 14.95 (*0-7089-7640-9*) Ulverscroft.

Coyote's Pantry. Mark Miller & Mark Kiffen. 128p. 1993. 25.95 (*0-89815-494-4*) Ten Speed Pr.

Coyote's Pow-Wow. Hap Gilliland. (Indian Culture Ser.). (J). (gr. 1-6). 1972. 4.95 (*0-89992-022-5*) Coun India Ed.

Cozumel: Late Maya Settlement Patterns (Monograph) David A. Freidel. Ed. by Jeremy A. Sabloff. LC 83-12222. (Studies in Archaeology Ser.). 1984. text ed. 65.00 (*0-12-266980-0*) Acad Pr.

C

Cozy Book. Mary A. Hoberman. LC 93-10826. (Illus.). (J). 1995. write for info. (*0-15-276620-0*, Browndeer Pr) HarBrace.

Cozy Book of Herbal Teas: Recipes, Remedies & Folk Wisdom. Mindy Toomay. LC 94-21793. 1994. write for info. (*1-55958-568-4*) Prima Pub.

Cozy in the Woods. K. K. Ross. LC 88-63931. (Chunky Tales Ser.). (Illus.). 28p. (J). (ps). 1990. 2.95 (*0-394-85400-4*) Random Bks Yng Read.

Cozy Place. Hope Slaughter. LC 90-49715. (Illus.). 32p. (J). (ps-2). 1990. 15.95 (*0-931093-13-9*) Red Hen Pr.

***CO2 Controlled Ventilation Systems.** J. N. Potter. 1994. 125.00 (*0-86033-376-0*, Pub. by Build Servs Info Assn UK) St Mut.

CO2 Corrosion in Oil & Gas Production: Selected Papers, Abstracts, & References. Ed. by L. E. Newton, Jr. & R. H. Hausler. LC 82-60734. 687p. 1984. 137.00 (*0-915567-01-6*) NACE Intl.

CO2 Corrosion in Oil & Gas Production: Selected Papers, Abstracts, & References. 6th ed. Ed. by L. E. Newton & R. H. Hausler. LC 82-60734. 687p. 1984. 75.00 (*0-915567-06-7*) NACE Intl.

CO2 Laser. W. J. Witteman. (Optical Sciences Ser.: Vol. 53). (Illus.). 320p. 1987. 69.00 (*0-387-17657-8*) Spr-Verlag.

CO2 Lasers & Applications: 1989 Los Angeles Symposium - OE-LASE '89 (January 1989) Ed. by J. D. Evans & E. V. Locke. (Proceedings Ser.: Vol. 1042). 1989. 42.00 (*0-8194-0077-7*) SPIE.

CO2 Lasers & Applications II. Ed. by H. Opower. 1990. 70.00 (*0-8194-0323-7*, VOL. 1276) SPIE.

CO2, Temperature, Ventilation, Humidity & Odor Control: High-Tech Horticulture. D. Gold & Bud Green. Ed. by Ed Rosenthal. (Maximizer - Problem Solver Ser.). (Illus.). 100p. (C). 1989. spiral bd. 9.95 (*0-685-30058-7*, Open Mind Pub) Creston Hse.

CP-M. Heath Company Staff. (Illus.). 470p. 1981. 99.95 (*0-87119-087-7*, EC-1120) Heathkit-Zenith Ed.

CP-M 3.0 Handbook for the C128. Jurgen Huckstadt. Ed. by Susan Dorn. Tr. by Ludwig J. Prazak. 250p. (Orig.). 1987. pap. 19.95 (*0-941689-00-X*) Prog Peripherals.

***CP "Teach" Expert Coding Made Easy: 1995 Version.** rev. ed. Patrice Morin-Spatz. (Illus.). 357p. (C). 1994. pap. text ed. 44.95 (*0-923369-27-9*) MedBooks.

***CP "Teach" Instructor's Manual.** Patrice Morin-Spatz. (Illus.). 447p. (C). 1995. ring bd. 199.95 (*0-614-06571-2*) MedBooks.

***CP "Teach" Student Workbook.** rev. ed. Patrice Morin-Spatz. (Illus.). 96p. (C). 1995. pap. text ed. 19.95 (*0-923369-28-7*) MedBooks.

CP "Teach" Workbook with Answers. Patrice T. Morin. (Illus.). 96p. 1995. pap. 29.95 (*0-923369-30-9*) MedBooks.

CP Violation. Ed. by L. Wolfenstein. (Current Physics Sources & Comments Ser.: Vol. 5). 336p. 1990. 92.50 (*0-444-88081-X*, North Holland); pap. 43.75 (*0-444-88114-X*, North Holland) Elsevier.

CP Violation: The BNL Summer Study. S. Dawson & A. Soni. 392p. 1991. text ed. 101.00 (*981-02-0480-9*) World Scientific Pub.

CP Violations. Ed. by C. Jarlskog. 736p. (C). 1989. text ed. 106.00 (*9971-5-0560-6*); pap. text ed. 61.00 (*9971-5-0561-4*) World Scientific Pub.

***CPA Accounting & Reporting: Taxation, Managerial, Governmental & Not-for-Profit.** Nathan Bisk. 1994. pap. 29.95 (*0-88128-765-2*) Totaltape.

***CPA Auditing.** Nathan Bisk. 1994. pap. 29.95 (*0-88128-766-0*) Totaltape.

***CPA Business Law & Professional Responsibilites.** Nathan Bisk. 1994. pap. 29.95 (*0-88128-767-9*) Totaltape.

***CPA Collection & Billing Guide.** 240p. (Orig.). 1994. pap. 295.00 (*0-7605-1112-8*) Rector Pr.

CPA Comprehensive Exam Review, Vol. 1: Topic Summaries & Exam Preparation Guides. Nathan M. Bisk. 1994. pap. 41.95 (*0-88128-632-X*) Totaltape.

CPA Comprehensive Exam Review, Vol. 2: Questions, Problems & Essays with Solutions. Nathan M. Bisk. 1994. pap. 41.95 (*0-88128-633-8*) Totaltape.

CPA Comprehensive Examination Review: Questions, Problems & Essays with Solutions, Vol. 2. Nathan Bisk. 1994. pap. 41.95 (*0-88128-704-0*) Totaltape.

CPA Comprehensive Examination Review: Topic Summaries & Exam Preparation Guides, Vol. 1. Nathan Bisk. 1994. pap. 41.95 (*0-88128-703-2*) Totaltape.

***CPA Correspondence Guide.** 240p. (Orig.). 1994. pap. 295.00 (*0-7605-1113-6*) Rector Pr.

CPA Exam Review: Problems & Solutions, Vol. 2. 20th ed. Patrick R. Delany. 1264p. 1993. pap. text ed. 42.00 (*0-471-59439-3*) Wiley.

***CPA Exam Review Audio: Accounting & Reporting, Vol. 3.** Patrick R. Delaney. 1994. pap. text ed. 99.00 (*0-471-00802-8*) Wiley.

***CPA Exam Review Audio: Accounting & Reporting, Vol. 4.** Patrick R. Delaney. 1994. pap. text ed. 99.00 (*0-471-00805-2*) Wiley.

***CPA Exam Review Audio: Auditing, 1.** Patrick R. Delaney. (Business Law & Professional Responsibilities Ser.: Vol. 1). 1994. pap. text ed. 99.00 (*0-471-00803-6*) Wiley.

***CPA Exam Review Audio: Auditing, Vol. 2.** Patrick R. Delaney. (Business Law & Professional Responsibilities Ser.: Vol. 2). 1994. pap. text ed. 99.00 (*0-471-00804-4*) Wiley.

CPA Examination Questions & Answers: Indexed to Content Specification Outlines, 1989-1993, 4 Vols. 65.00 (*0-317-37096-0*) Am Inst CPA.

CPA Examination Review, 2 vols., Vol. 2. 21th ed. Patrick Delaney. Incl. Vol. 1. 21th ed. 1994. pap. text ed. 42.00 (*0-471-02682-4*); Vol. 2. 21th ed. 1994. pap. text ed. 42.00 (*0-471-02683-2*); 1994. Set pap. text ed. 84.00 (*0-471-02679-4*) Wiley.

***CPA Examination Review, Vol. 8, Micro-Pass MacIntosh.** Patrick R. Delaney. 1993. text ed. 199.00 (*0-471-59828-3*) Wiley.

CPA Examination Review: Auditing, 1993. Patrick R. Delaney. 1992. pap. text ed. 30.00 (*0-471-57858-4*) Wiley.

CPA Examination Review: Business Law. Edwin W. Tucker. (Orig.). 1985. 14.95 (*0-685-43074-X*) S&S Trade.

CPA Examination Review: Business Law, 1993, Vol. 2. 19th ed. Patrick R. Delaney. 670p. 1992. pap. text ed. 30.00 (*0-471-57861-4*) Wiley.

CPA Examination Review: Outline & Study Guide, Vol. 1. 20th ed. Patrick R. Delany. 1392p. 1993. pap. text ed. 42.00 (*0-471-59441-5*) Wiley.

CPA Examination Review: Theory & Practice, 1993. Patrick R. Delaney. 1596p. 1992. pap. text ed. 42.00 (*0-471-57863-0*) Wiley.

***CPA Examination Review Vol. 1: Auditing & Business Law, Micro-Pass DOS.** Patrick R. Delaney. 1993. text ed. 110.00 (*0-471-31155-3*) Wiley.

***CPA Examination Review Vol. 2: Theory & Practice, Micropass-DOS.** Patrick R. Delaney. 1993. text ed. 110.00 (*0-471-31153-7*) Wiley.

CPA Examination Review Handbook: Course Management. Irvin N. Gleim & Patrick R. Delaney. 1985. pap. text ed. 10.00 (*0-471-81651-5*) Wiley.

CPA Examination Review, Vol. 1: Outlines & Study Guides. 20th ed. Patrick R. Delaney. 1993. pap. 84.00 (*0-471-59442-3*) Wiley.

***CPA Financial Accounting & Reporting: Business Enterprises.** Nathan Bisk. 1994. pap. 32.95 (*0-88128-764-4*) Totaltape.

***CPA Firm Administration Handbook.** Marc L. Rosenberg & Paul R. Nadolny. 1995. text ed. 95.00 (*0-471-58548-3*) Wiley.

CPA Firm Mergers That Work. August J. Aquila et al. LC 93-43015. 120p. 1994. text ed. 50.00 (*0-7863-0126-0*) Irwin Prof Pubng.

CPA Firm Technology Planning Guide. L. Gary Boomer et al. LC 92-31723. 1992. 10.00 (*0-87051-125-4*) Am Inst CPA.

***CPA Guide to Personal Computers & Electronic Files.** 3rd ed. Joseph Gomolski et al. 118p. (C). 1994. pap. text ed. 49.00 (*1-878025-65-1*) Western Schls.

***CPA Management Guide.** 240p. (Orig.). 1994. pap. 295.00 (*0-7605-1114-4*) Rector Pr.

***CPA Partner's Notebook.** Ed. by Mark Carr. 62p. 1994. pap. text ed. 24.50 (*0-9616858-7-5*) Strafford Pubns.

CPA Professional Responsibilities: An Introduction. Harry T. Magill & Gary J. Previtts. 214p. (C). 1991. text ed. 23.95 (*0-538-80121-2*, AT64AA) S-W Pub.

***CPA Review: A Sstem for Success.** Irvin N. Gleim. LC 95-76486. 300p. 1995. pap. 15.00 (*0-917537-82-3*) Gleim Pubns.

***CPA Review: Auditing.** Irvin N. Gleim & William A. Hillison. LC 95-76487. 632p. (Orig.). 1995. pap. 22.50 (*0-917537-77-7*) Gleim Pubns.

***CPA Review: Business Law.** Irvin N. Gleim & Jordan B. Ray. LC 95-76488. 668p. (Orig.). 1995. pap. 22.50 (*0-917537-76-9*) Gleim Pubns.

***CPA Review: Financial.** Irvin N. Gleim. LC 95-76489. 826p. (Orig.). 1995. pap. 22.50 (*0-917537-79-3*) Gleim Pubns.

***CPA Review: TAX-MAN-GOV.** Irvin N. Gleim. 722p. 1995. pap. 22.50 (*0-917537-78-5*) Gleim Pubns.

CPA Review Manual. 5th ed. Herbert E. Miller & George C. Mead. (Illus.). 1979. 38.50 (*0-685-03807-6*); text ed. 28.95 (*0-685-03808-4*) P-H.

CPA Review of Auditing, 1983-1984, Vol. 2. Albert K. Francisco & Kenneth A. Smith. LC 83-15710. 384p. (Orig.). (C). 1984. pap. text ed. write for info. (*0-201-07812-0*) Addison-Wesley.

CPA Review of Business Law: 1983-1984, Vol. 3. Albert K. Francisco & Kenneth A. Smith. LC 83-1573. (C). 1984. write for info. (*0-201-07813-9*) Addison-Wesley.

***CPA Tax Guide.** 240p. (Orig.). 1994. pap. 295.00 (*0-7605-1115-2*) Rector Pr.

CPA's Guide to a Successful Financial Planning Practice: Selling Financial Investments & Marketing Advisory Services. Jim H. Ainsworth. LC 94-17917. 1995. text ed. 49.95 (*0-471-07687-2*) Wiley.

***CPA's Guide to Personal Computers & Electronic Filing.** 2nd ed. Joseph Gomolski & Barbara Cole-Gomolski. 100p. (C). 1993. pap. text ed. 49.00 (*1-878025-52-X*) Western Schls.

CPAs Who Sell: How to Bring in New Business. C. Goldsmith. 192p. 1985. text ed. 45.00 (*0-07-023671-2*) McGraw.

***CPC International: A Report on the Company's Environmental Policies & Practices.** (Illus.). 28p. (C). 1994. reprint ed. pap. text ed. 200.00x (*0-7881-0938-3*, Coun on Econ) Diane Pub.

CPC Minority Recruitment Sourcebook. College Placement Council, Inc. Staff. 1990. 89.95 (*0-913936-24-3*) Coll Placement.

CPCM Candidate's Workbook: Area of Concentration: Commercial Purchasing. rev. ed. Ed. by David L. Balint. 60p. 1993. pap. 15.00 (*0-940343-51-7*) Natl Contract Mgmt.

CPCM Candidate's Workbook: Area of Concentration: Contracting. rev. ed. Ed. by David L. Balint. 176p. 1993. pap. 22.50 (*0-940343-52-5*) Natl Contract Mgmt.

CPCM Candidate's Workbook: Area of Concentration: Finance, Economics, & Accounting. rev. ed. Ed. by David L. Balint. 146p. 1993. pap. 22.50 (*0-940343-53-3*) Natl Contract Mgmt.

CPCM Candidate's Workbook: Area of Concentration: Legal. rev. ed. Ed. by David L. Balint. 126p. 1993. pap. 22.50 (*0-940343-54-1*) Natl Contract Mgmt.

CPCM Candidate's Workbook: Area of Concentration: Logistics. rev. ed. Ed. by David L. Balint. 98p. 1993. pap. 22.50 (*0-940343-55-X*) Natl Contract Mgmt.

CPCM Candidate's Workbook: Area of Concentration: Production. rev. ed. Ed. by David L. Balint. 126p. 1993. pap. 22.50 (*0-940343-57-6*) Natl Contract Mgmt.

CPCM Candidate's Workbook: Area of Concentration: State & Local Government. rev. ed. Ed. by David L. Balint. 60p. 1993. pap. 15.00 (*0-940343-56-8*) Natl Contract Mgmt.

CPCM Candidate's Workbook: General Examination. rev. ed. Ed. by David L. Balint. 170p. 1993. pap. 22.50 (*0-940343-50-9*) Natl Contract Mgmt.

CPCS Training Manual. Martin R. Rosenthal. LC 89-64082. 200p. 1989. pap. 50.00 (*0-944490-19-0*) Mass CLE.

***CPI-C.** X-Open Staff. (Illus.). 174p. (C). 1994. pap. text ed. 50.00 (*0-13-353533-9*) P-H.

CPI-C Programming in C: An Application Developer's Guide to APPC. John Q. Walker. 1994. disk, pap. text ed. 49.95 (*0-07-911733-3*) McGraw.

***CPI's Instruction Book for Writers: A Step-by-Step Guide to Publishing, Marketing & Promoting Your Book.** A. M. Gates. 124p. 1995. pap. 17.95 (*1-882185-27-7*) Crnrstone Pub.

Cplus Cplusplus: Programming with Objects in C & Cplusplus. Allen I. Holub. 1992. pap. text ed. 29.95 (*0-07-029662-6*) McGraw.

CPlusPlus Programming with Macapp. David A. Wilson. 1990. pap. 24.95 (*0-201-57020-3*); pap. 34.95 (*0-201-57021-1*) Addison-Wesley.

CPLY: Reflection on a Past Life. William N. Copley. 1979. pap. 8.00 (*0-914412-15-9*) Inst for the Arts.

CPM in Construction Management. 4th ed. James J. O'Brien. LC 92-24367. 1993. text ed. 71.00 (*0-07-047921-6*) McGraw.

CPR: 1992 Guidelines. 2nd ed. National Safety Council Staff. (Emergency Care Ser.). 120p. (C). 1993. teacher ed, pap. text ed. 15.00 (*0-86720-811-2*) Jones & Bartlett.

CPR - Cardiopulmonary Resuscitation: Evaluating Performance & Potential. Ed. by Mickey Eisenberg & Lawrence Bergner. (Emergency Health Services Quarterly Ser.: Vol. 1, No. 3). 70p. 1982. pap. text ed. 19.95 (*0-917724-58-5*) Haworth Pr.

CPR Bluebook. Mary J. Newman. 148p. 1984. 11.95 (*0-317-47412-X*) Jems Comm.

CPR for Infants & Children: A Guide to Cardiopulmonary Resuscitation. Gerald M. Dworkin. (Illus.). 79p. 1989. pap. 9.95 (*0-87868-272-4*) Child Welfare.

CPR for the Professional Rescuer. American Red Cross Staff. LC 92-41664. (Illus.). 1993. write for info. (*0-8016-0706-X*) Mosby Yr Bk.

CPR Manual. National Safety Council Staff & Thygerson. (First Aid Ser.). (C). 1992. pap. text ed. 12.50 (*0-86720-192-4*); vhs 195.00 (*0-86720-159-2*); 10.00 (*0-86720-233-5*) Jones & Bartlett.

CPR Manual: 1992 Guidelines. National Safety Council Staff. LC 92-40649. 128p. 1992. pap. text ed. 12.50 (*0-86720-784-1*); vhs 225.00 (*0-86720-794-9*) Jones & Bartlett.

CPR Review Manual. National Safety Council Staff. LC 93-46698. (Emergency Care Ser.). (C). 1994. pap. text ed. 3.00 (*0-86720-849-X*) Jones & Bartlett.

***CPS Examination Review Finance & Business Law.** 3rd ed. Schroeder & Webber. (Illus.). 560p. 1994. pap. text ed. 56.00 (*0-13-312133-X*) P-H.

***CPS Examination Review Management.** 3rd ed. Schroeder & Kardoff. (Illus.). 560p. 1994. pap. text ed. 56.00 (*0-13-315441-6*) P-H.

CPS Module VI: Office Technology. 2nd ed. Betty L. Schroeder & Diane Routhier-Graf. 251p. 1986. pap. text ed. 19.95 (*0-471-84712-7*) P-H.

CPS Review for Accounting: Module 4. Betty L. Schroeder & Sally A. Webber. 260p. (C). 1984. pap. text ed. 22.95 (*0-471-86152-9*) P-H.

CPS Review for Behavioral Science in Business, Module I. 3rd ed. Betty L. Schroeder. 300p. 1993. pap. 21.00 (*0-13-188491-3*) P-H.

CPS Review for Business Law: Module 2. Betty L. Schroeder et al. 222p. (C). 1984. pap. text ed. 22.95 (*0-471-86154-5*) P-H.

CPS Review for Economics & Management: Module 3. Betty L. Schroeder et al. 275p. (C). 1984. pap. text ed. 22.95 (*0-471-86158-8*) P-H.

CPS Review for Office Administration & Communication: Module 5. Betty L. Schroeder & Diane R. Graf. 298p. (C). 1984. pap. text ed. 22.95 (*0-471-86153-7*) P-H.

CPS Review for Office Technology, Module VI. 3rd ed. Betty L. Schroeder. 300p. 1992. pap. 21.00 (*0-13-188590-1*) P-H.

CP's Selfcontrol Clinic. Chandrakant P. Desai. LC 93-72032. (Illus.). 96p. (Orig.). 1993. pap. 7.95 (*0-9634271-1-3*) Enlightening.

CPS Story: An Illustrated History of Civilian Public Service. Albert N. Keim. LC 90-71118. (Illus.). 128p. (Orig.). 1990. pap. 11.95 (*1-56148-002-9*) Good Bks PA.

CPT - HCPCS Basic Coding Handbook. Toula Nicholas. 85p. 1993. 35.00 (*0-317-05425-2*) Am Hlth Info.

CPT & HCPCS Coding Made Easy! 2nd ed. James B. Davis. 212p. 1992. text ed. 24.95 (*1-878487-43-4*) Practice Mgmt Info.

***CPT & HCPCS Coding Made Easy.** 3rd ed. James B. Davis. Ed. by Kathryn M. Swanson. 200p. 1995. student ed 24.95 (*1-57066-026-3*) Practice Mgmt Info.

CPT Clinic: Basic Procedural Coding Seminar Manual. Ed. by Gay M. Boughton-Barnes. 200p. 1992. 149.00 (*1-56329-044-8*, CPCL) St Anthony Pub.

CPT Code Book, 1992: As Presented by St. Anthony. American Medical Association Staff. Ed. by Kathy Brouch. 750p. 59.00 (*1-56329-061-8*) St Anthony Pub.

CPT Code Book 1993: As Presented by St. Anthony's. American Medical Association Staff. Ed. by Elizabeth Jordan. 750p. 1992. 59.00 (*1-56329-102-9*, CBK) St Anthony Pub.

CPT Coder's Choice 1994. deluxe rev. ed. Ed. by Gregg Rogers & Kathryn Swanson. 850p. 1993. 49.95 (*1-878487-97-3*) Practice Mgmt Info.

CPT Coder's Choice 1994. rev. ed. Ed. by Gregg Rogers & Kathryn Swanson. 850p. 1993. 42.95 (*1-878487-93-0*); spiral bd., pap. 39.95 (*1-878487-95-7*); Timesaver ver. ring bd. 49.95 (*1-878487-96-5*) Practice Mgmt Info.

CPT Coding Made Easy. Gabrielle M. Kotoski. 561p. 1991. ring bd. 200.00 (*0-8342-0284-0*, 561) Aspen Pub.

CPT-Dermatology, Plastic & Reconstructive Surgery. American Medical Association Staff. (Orig.). 1991. pap. 34.00 (*0-89970-425-5*, OP054791) AMA.

CPT-General Surgery. American Medical Association Staff. (Orig.). 1991. pap. 34.00 (*0-89970-426-3*, OP054891) AMA.

CPT-Gynecology, Obstetrics & Urology. American Medical Association Staff. (Orig.). 1991. pap. 34.00 (*0-89970-398-4*, OP054591) AMA.

CPT Handbook for Psychiatrists. Chester W. Schmidt, Jr. LC 93-3252. 110p. 1993. spiral bd. 19.50 (*0-88048-650-3*) Am Psychiatric.

CPT-Head & Neck Surgery, Otorhinolaryngology & Ophthalmology. American Medical Association Staff. (Orig.). 1991. pap. 34.00 (*0-89970-427-1*, OP054991) AMA.

CPT-Hospital Outpatient Services. American Medical Association Staff. 500p. (Orig.). 1991. pap. 34.00 (*0-89970-429-8*, OP055091) AMA.

CPT-Medical Specialties. American Medical Association Staff. (Orig.). 1991. pap. 34.00 (*0-89970-395-X*, OP054291) AMA.

CPT-Neurological & Orthopaedic Surgery. American Medical Association Staff. (Orig.). 1991. pap. 34.00 (*0-89970-399-2*, OP054691) AMA.

CPT-Pathology & Laboratory. American Medical Association Staff. (Orig.). 1991. pap. 34.00 (*0-89970-397-6*, OP054491) AMA.

CPT-Physicians Current Procedural Terminology, 1991. 1991. 34.00 (*0-89970-394-1*, 054191) AMA.

CPT, Radiology. American Medical Association Staff. (Orig.). 1991. pap. 34.00 (*0-89970-396-8*, OP054391) AMA.

***CPT 1995.** Rittenhouse. 1994. pap. text ed. 41.95 (*0-89970-651-7*) AMA.

***CPT 1995: Physician's Current Procedural Terminology.** American Medical Association Staff. Date not set. disk 129.95 (*1-56337-128-6*) Medicode Pubns.

An Asterisk (*) at the beginning of an entry indicates that the title is appearing in BIP for the first time.

***CPT 1995: Physician's Current Procedural Terminology.** American Medical Association Staff. 1994. 51.95 (*1-56337-121-9*); spiral bd. 44.95 (*1-56337-148-0*) Medicode Pubns.

CPT 1995 Coder's Choice. Ed. by Gregg Rogers & Kathryn Swanson. 850p. 1994. spiral bd., pap. 44.95 (*1-57066-016-6*) Practice Mgmt Info.

CPT 1995 Deluxe. Ed. by Gregg Rogers & Kathryn Swanson. 850p. 1994. 49.95 (*1-57066-019-0*) Practice Mgmt Info.

CPT 1995 Plain? Ed. by Gregg Rogers & Kathryn Swanson. 850p. 1994. spiral bd., pap. 41.95 (*1-57066-017-4*) Practice Mgmt Info.

CPT 1995 Timesaver. Ed. by Gregg Rogers & Kathryn Swanson. 850p. 1994. ring bd. 49.95 (*1-57066-018-2*) Practice Mgmt Info.

CP"Teach" Instructor's Manual. Patrice T. Morin. (Illus.). 350p. 1993. reprint ed. teacher ed 149.95 (*0-685-65111-8*) MedBooks.

CQ Almanac 1982. Congressional Quarterly Staff. (Almanac Ser.). 1040p. 1983. 215.00 (*0-87187-251-X*) Congr Quarterly.

CQ Almanac 1983. Congressional Quarterly Staff. (Almanac Ser.). 1000p. 1984. 215.00 (*0-87187-314-1*) Congr Quarterly.

CQ Almanac 1984. Congressional Quarterly Staff. (Almanac Ser.). 1000p. 1985. 215.00 (*0-87187-346-X*) Congr Quarterly.

CQ Almanac 1985. Congressional Quarterly Staff. (Almanac Ser.). 1099p. 1986. 215.00 (*0-87187-388-5*) Congr Quarterly.

CQ Almanac 1986. Congressional Quarterly Staff. (Almanac Ser.). 1200p. 1987. 215.00 (*0-87187-418-0*) Congr Quarterly.

CQ Almanac 1987. Congressional Quarterly Staff. (Almanac Ser.). 1017p. 1988. 215.00 (*0-87187-463-6*) Congr Quarterly.

CQ Almanac 1988. Congressional Quarterly Staff. (Almanac Ser.). 1000p. 1989. 215.00 (*0-87187-507-1*) Congr Quarterly.

CQ Almanac 1989. Congressional Quarterly Staff. (Almanac Ser.). 1288p. 1990. 215.00 (*0-87187-549-7*) Congr Quarterly.

CQ Almanac 1990. Congressional Quarterly Staff. (Almanac Ser.). 1200p. 1991. 215.00 (*0-87187-655-8*) Congr Quarterly.

CQ Almanac 1991. Congressional Quarterly Staff. (Almanac Ser.). 1200p. 1992. 215.00 (*0-685-57411-3*) Congr Quarterly.

CQ Almanac 1992. Congressional Quarterly Staff. (Almanac Ser.). 693p. 1993. 215.00 (*0-87187-931-X*) Congr Quarterly.

CQ Almanac 1993. 1204p. 1994. 215.00 (*1-56802-020-1*) Congr Quarterly.

CQ American Congressional Dictionary. W. Kravitz. LC 91-28262. 305p. 1993. pap. text ed. 25.95 (*0-87187-864-X*) Congr Quarterly.

CQ American Congressional Dictionary. W. Kravitz. LC 91-28262. 305p. 1993. 35.95 (*0-87187-861-5*) Congr Quarterly.

CQ Ghost Ship. Tompkins. 1985. pap. 5.00 (*0-87259-501-3*) Am Radio.

CQ Research. 1180p. 1994. ring bd. 137.00 (*1-56802-019-8*) Congr Quarterly.

CQ Researcher Bound Volume 1991. Orig. Title: Editorial Research Reports. 1992. 132.00 (*0-87187-695-7*) Congr Quarterly.

***CQ Researcher 1994.** Congressional Quarterly Staff. 1200p. 1995. 140.00 (*1-56802-025-2*) Congr Quarterly.

CQB (Close Quarter Battle) (Illus.). 240p. 1991. 22.00 (*0-939235-03-X*) Spec Trning Unit.

CQE Exam Study Guide. Thomas Pyzdek. 1991. 39.95 (*0-930011-01-5*) Quality Am.

***CQI System for Healthcare: How the Williamsport Hospital Brings Quality to Life.** Timothy Mannello. LC 94-46508. 1995. write for info. (*0-527-76290-3*) Qual Resc.

CQ's Guide to Congressional Redistricting, 1990, 1, Pt. 1. 178p. 1993. pap. text ed. 23.95 (*0-87187-733-3*) Congr Quarterly.

CQ's Guide to Congressional Redistricting, 1990 Part 2, 2, Pt. 2. LC 92-19904. 428p. 1993. pap. text ed. 23.95 (*0-87187-734-1*) Congr Quarterly.

CQ's Pocket Guide to the Language of Congress. LC 94-726. 127p. 1994. pap. text ed. 15.95 (*0-87187-995-6*) Congr Quarterly.

CQ's State Fact Finder: Rankings Across America. Victoria Van Son. 300p. 1993. 74.95 (*0-87187-916-6*); pap. 39.95 (*0-87187-915-8*) Congr Quarterly.

C.R. Billiards Pool Series, 7 vols. Chris Raftis. (C.R. Billiards Pool Ser.). 1992. 70.00 (*1-880135-05-1*) C R Billiards.

C.R. Mackintosh: The Poetics of Workmanship. David Brett. (Illus.). 152p. (C). 1993. pap. 18.95 (*0-674-54066-2*) HUP.

CR Manifolds & the Tangential Cauchy Riemann Complex. Albert Boggess. (Illus.). 330p. 1991. 55.00 (*0-8493-7152-X*, QA) CRC Pr.

CR Submanifolds of Kaehlerian & Sasakian Manifolds. Kentaro Yano & Masahiro Kon. (Progress in Mathematics Ser.: Vol. 30). 205p. 1982. 38.50 (*0-8176-3119-4*) Birkhauser.

CRA Compliance: A Practical Perspective. William R. Hamblin. 134p. 1991. 65.00 (*1-882097-41-6*, 12583) Sav & Comm Bank.

Crab: Finding It, Catching It & Cooking It. Tom Bailey. (Illus.). 1984. 5.95 (*0-318-19502-X*); lib. bdg. 6.95 (*0-318-19501-1*) Comtech Pubns.

***Crab Antics: A Caribbean Case Study of the Conflict Between Reputation & Respectability.** rev. ed. Peter J. Wilson. 262p. (C). 1995. pap. text ed. 9.95x (*0-88133-849-4*) Waveland Pr.

Crab Antics: The Social Anthropology of English-Speaking Negro Societies of the Caribbean. Peter J. Wilson. LC 72-91319. (Yale University, Caribbean Ser.: 14). 276p. reprint ed. pap. 78.70 (*0-317-29704-X*, 2022054) Bks Demand.

Crab Apple. Bob Reese. Ed. by Dan Wasserman. (Ten Word Book Ser.). (Illus.). (J). (gr. k-1). 1979. 7.95 (*0-89868-072-7*); pap. 2.95 (*0-89868-083-2*) ARO Pub.

Crab Apple Bathroom. Jocasta Innes & Stewart Walton. (Paintability Ser.). (Illus.). 8p. 1991. 9.99 (*0-517-05301-2*) Random Hse Value.

Crab-Bags & Other Bean-Beings. Margaret Park. (Illus.). (J). (gr. 5 up). 1979. pap. 2.95 (*0-915556-05-7*) Great Ocean.

Crab Book. Cy Liberman & Pat Liberman. (Illus.). 160p. 1986. pap. 4.95 (*0-912608-22-6*) Mid Atlantic.

Crab Cookbook. Whitey Schmidt. LC 89-81335. 224p. 1990. pap. 12.95 (*0-9613008-8-4*) Hartnett Marian Pr.

Crab Cookery Coast to Coast: Jimmys, Jonahs, Busters & Blues. Glenn Day. (Illus.). 224p. (Orig.). 1992. pap. 12.95 (*0-89594-529-0*) Crossing Pr.

***Crab Lover's Book: Recipes & More.** Mary E. Orso. 256p. 1995. 40.00 (*0-87805-801-X*); pap. 14.95 (*0-87805-796-X*) U Pr of Miss.

Crab on the Seashore. Jennifer Coldrey. LC 85-30293. (Animal Habitats Ser.). (Illus.). 32p. (J). (gr. 4-6). 1987. lib. bdg. 17.27 (*1-55532-060-0*) Gareth Stevens Inc.

Crab Orchard Site, Tazewell County, Virginia, No. 8. Howard A. Maccord, Sr. & William T. Buchanan, Jr. 156p. 1980. pap. 9.00 (*1-884626-02-5*) Archeolog Soc.

Crab with Golden Claws. Herge. 1986. 7.95 (*0-416-60500-1*) Routledge Chapman & Hall.

Crab with the Golden Claws. Herge. (Illus.). 62p. (J). (gr. 3-8). 19.95 (*0-8288-5023-2*) Fr & Eur.

Crab with the Golden Claws. Herge. LC 73-21249. (Adventures of Tintin Ser.). (Illus.). 64p. (J). (gr. k up). 1974. reprint ed. mass mkt. 7.95 (*0-316-35833-9*, Joy St Bks) Little.

Crabbe: The Critical Heritage. Arthur Pollard. (Critical Heritage Ser.). 510p. 1975. 69.50 (*0-7100-7258-9*, RKP) Routledge.

Crabby & Nabby: A Tale of Two Blue Crabs. Suzanne Tate. LC 88-61096. (Suzanne Tate's Nature Ser.: No. 1). (Illus.). 28p. (Orig.). (J). (gr. k-4). 1988. pap. 3.95 (*0-9616344-3-X*) Nags Head Art.

Crabby Gabby. Stephen Cosgrove. LC 85-14351. (Serendipity Bks.). (Illus.). 32p. (Orig.). (J). (gr. 1-4). 1985. pap. 2.95 (*0-8431-1441-X*) Price Stern.

***Crabby Road: More Thoughts on Life from Maxine: Shoebox Greetings Book.** Shoebox Greetings Staff. 1994. pap. 6.95 (*0-8362-1774-8*) Andrews & McMeel.

Crabby's Water Wish: A Tale of Saving Sea Life. Suzanne Tate. LC 91-60262. (Suzanne Tate's Nature Ser.: No. 9). (Illus.). 28p. (Orig.). (J). (gr. k-4). 1991. pap. 3.95 (*1-878405-04-7*) Nags Head Art.

Crabe aux Pinces d'or. Herge. (Illus.). (FRE.). (J). (gr. 7-9). ring bd. 19.95 (*0-8288-5025-9*) Fr & Eur.

Crabe aux Pinces D'Or. Herge. (Illus.). 64p. (FRE.). (J). 1992. reprint ed. 19.95 (*0-7859-4561-X*) Fr & Eur.

Crabgrass Frontier: The Suburbanization of America. Kenneth T. Jackson. (Illus.). 396p. 1985. 30.00 (*0-19-503610-7*) OUP.

Crabgrass Frontier: The Suburbanization of America. Kenneth T. Jackson. 1987. pap. 13.95 (*0-19-504983-7*) OUP.

Crabgrass Muffins & Pine Needle Tea: How to Identify, Enjoy, & Cook the Cornucopia of Wild Foods Growing Among us. Linda Runyon. LC 93-25247. 1994. 20.00 (*0-517-88033-4*, Harmony) Crown Pub Group.

Crabs. Christine Butterworth & Donna Bailey. LC 90-36168. (Animal World Ser.). (Illus.). 32p. (J). (gr. 1-4). 1990. lib. bdg. 19.97 (*0-8114-2640-8*) Raintree Steck-V.

***Crabs.** Elwyn Ellis. LC 94-48869. 64p. 1995. pap. 12.95 (*0-7734-2717-1*, Mellen Poetry Pr) E Mellen.

Crabs. Sylvia A. Johnson. LC 82-10056. (Lerner Natural Science Bks.). (Illus.). 48p. (J). (gr. 4 up). 1982. lib. bdg. 19.95 (*0-8225-1471-0*, Lerner Publctns) Lerner Group.

Crabs. Adapt. by Kathleen Pohl. (Nature Close-Ups Ser.). (Illus.). 32p. (J). (gr. 3-7). 1986. lib. bdg. 10.95 (*0-8172-2716-4*) Raintree Steck-V.

Crabs of Cape Cod. Stephan Berrick. (Natural History Ser.: No. 3). (Illus.). 80p. 1986. pap. 6.95 (*0-916275-01-9*) Cape Cod Mus Nat His.

Crabtree & Evelyn Cookbook: A Book of Light Meals & Small Feasts. Photos by Christopher Baker. LC 89-30646. (Illus.). 256p. 1989. 29.95 (*0-941434-99-0*) Stewart Tabori & Chang.

Crack. rev. ed. (Drug Abuse Prevention Library). (Illus.). 64p. (YA). (gr. 7-12). 1994. lib. bdg. 15.95 (*0-8239-1753-3*) Rosen Group.

Crack: Cocaine Squared. rev. ed. 1993. pap. 0.25 (*0-89230-214-3*) Do It Now.

Crack: The Broken Promise. David F. Allen & James F. Jekel. 112p. 1991. text ed. 29.95 (*0-312-05744-X*) St Martin.

Crack: The New Drug Epidemic. Gilda Berger. (Impact Bks.). (Illus.). 128p. (YA). (gr. 7-12). 1994. lib. bdg. 14.56 (*0-531-11188-1*) Watts.

Crack: The Rock of Death. Jane Scherer. 32p. (Orig.). 1988. pap. 3.95 (*0-945485-00-X*) Comm Intervention.

Crack: Treating Cocaine Addiction. George Medzerian. 140p. 1991. pap. 12.95 (*0-8306-3622-6*, 3622, TAB-Human Servs Inst) TAB Bks.

Crack-Affected Children: A Teacher's Guide. Mary B. Waller. (New Survival Skills for Teachers Ser.). 104p. 1993. pap. 9.95 (*0-8039-6051-4*) Corwin Pr.

Crack & Cocaine. Mary C. Turck. LC 89-25409. (Facts About Ser.). (Illus.). 48p. (J). (gr. 5-6). 1990. text ed. 12.95 (*0-89686-491-X*, Crstwood Hse) Silver Burdett Pr.

Crack & Ice: Treating Smokable Stimulant Abuse. Donald R. Wesson et al. 96p. (Orig.). 1992. pap. 11.95 (*0-89486-822-5*, 5094A) Hazelden.

Crack & Other Addictions: Old Realities & New Challenges. Contrib by Ira Chasnoff et al. 255p. 1991. pap. 14.95 (*0-87868-409-3*) Child Welfare.

Crack & the Evolution of Anti-Drug Policy. Steven R. Belenko. LC 93-9312. (Contributions in Criminology & Penology Ser.: No. 42). 216p. 1993. text ed. 55.00 (*0-313-28030-4*, BKE, Greenwood Pr) Greenwood.

Crack Arrest Methodology & Applications - STP 711. Ed. by G. T. Hahn & M. F. Kanninen. 452p. 1980. 44.75 (*0-8031-0317-4*, 04-711000-30) ASTM.

***Crack Babies.** Jane Scherer. 81p. (YA). (gr. 7-12). 1991. pap. write for info. (*1-57515-014-X*) PPI Pubng.

Crack Babies: A National Epidemic. (Illus.). 37p. (Orig.). 1991. pap. 20.00 (*0-941375-37-4*) Diane Pub.

Crack Busters Workbook: How to Recognize & Resist the Pressure to Use Crack. Joseph A. Wallace. 128p. (Orig.). 1988. pap. 11.95 (*0-929105-00-1*) North Amer Pubns.

***Crack Climbing.** Craig Luebben. (How to Rock Climb Ser.). (Illus.). 48p. 1995. pap. 5.95 (*0-934641-69-2*) Chockstone Pr.

Crack Cocaine: A Challenge for Prevention. Ed. by Robert L. DuPont. (Illus.). 71p. (Orig.). (C). 1994. pap. text ed. 40.00 (*0-7881-0579-5*) Diane Pub.

Crack Cocaine: A Practical Treatment Approach for the Chemically Dependent. Barbara C. Wallace. LC 90-2683. 304p. 1991. 41.95 (*0-87630-604-0*) Brunner-Mazel.

Crack Cocaine Epidemic: Consequences & Treatment. (Illus.). 44p. (Orig.). (C). 1993. pap. text ed. 20.00 (*1-56806-801-8*) Diane Pub.

Crack, Cocaine, Methamphetamine & Ice: What Every One of Us Must Know about These Public Enemies. Leslie E. Moser. 336p. 1990. 19.95 (*1-878938-00-2*) Mlti-Media Prodns.

Crack Down. Val McDermid. 1994. text ed. 20.00 (*0-684-19756-1*, Scribners) S&S Trade.

Crack Dynamics in Metallic Materials. J. R. Klepaczko. (CISM Ser.: Vol. 310). (Illus.). vii, 497p. 1990. pap. 86.00 (*0-387-82226-7*) Spr-Verlag.

Crack Growth Analysis in Anistropic Materials. A. Portela et al. 1995. disk, ring bd. 440.00 (*1-56252-270-1*) Computational Mech MA.

Crack Growth Analysis in Stiffened Sheets. A. Portela et al. 1994. disk, ring bd. 440.00 (*1-56252-271-X*) Computational Mech MA.

Crack Growth Analysis Using Boundary Elements. A. Portela & M. H. Aliabadi. LC 92-75034. 124p. 1993. disk, ring bd. 995.00 (*1-56252-115-2*) Computational Mech MA.

Crack Growth Analysis Using Boundary Elements 3 Module Set. A. Portela et al. 1995. disk, ring bd. 1,030.00 (*1-56252-272-8*) Computational Mech MA.

Crack in the Cosmic Egg: Challenging Constructs of Mind & Reality. Joseph C. Pearce. 224p. 1988. pap. 11.00 (*0-517-56661-3*, Harmony) Crown Pub Group.

Crack in the Heart. Doris Orgel. (YA). (gr. 7 up). 1989. pap. 2.95 (*0-449-70204-9*, Juniper) Fawcett.

Crack in the Ice. Joe Sheerin. 62p. 1985. pap. 10.95 (*0-318-40004-9*, Pub. by Colin Smythe Ltd UK) Dufour.

Crack in the Teacup. Michael Gilbert. 256p. 1993. pap. 3.95 (*0-88184-988-X*) Carroll & Graf.

Crack in the Teacup. large type ed. Michael Gilbert. (Keating's Choice Ser.). 344p. 1992. 12.97 (*1-85089-509-0*, Pub. by ISIS UK) Transaction Pubs.

Crack in the Wall. Mary E. Haggerty. LC 92-59952. (Illus.). 32p. (J). (gr. k-5). 1993. 14.95 (*1-880000-03-2*) Lee & Low Bks.

Crack in the Wall: Growing up under Hitler. Horst Kruger. Tr. by Ruth Hein. LC 85-25210. 242p. (C). 1985. reprint ed. pap. 9.95 (*0-88064-052-9*) Fromm Intl Pub.

***Crack in the Wall: The Unspeakable Solution.** Jim Guido. LC 95-76672. 223p. (Orig.). 1995. pap. 12.99 (*0-9646409-4-5*) Global Heart Bks.

Crack of Dawn Walkers. Amy Hest. LC 83-19597. (Illus.). 32p. (J). (ps-2). 1984. text ed. 13.95 (*0-02-743710-8*, Mac Bks Young Read) S&S Childrens.

Crack-of-Dawn Walkers. Amy Hest. (Illus.). 32p. (Orig.). (J). (ps-3). 1988. pap. 3.99 (*0-14-050829-5*, Puffin) Puffin Bks.

***Crack of Doom: The Extraordinary True Story Behind Crack-Cocaine.** Jon Silverman. (Illus.). 307p. 1995. pap. 9.95 (*0-7472-4255-0*, Pub. by Headline UK) Trafalgar.

Crack Pipe As Pimp: An Ethnographic Investigation of Sex-for-Crack Exchanges. Ed. by Mitchell S. Ratner. LC 92-29042. 1992. text ed. 35.00 (*0-02-925725-5*) Free Pr.

Crack Problems in the Classical Theory of Elasticity. Ian Sneddon & M. Lowengrub. LC 75-84971. (Siam Series in Applied Mathematics). 231p. reprint ed. pap. 65.90 (*0-317-08602-2*, 2006312) Bks Demand.

Crack-Up. F. Scott Fitzgerald. Ed. by Edmund Wilson. LC 93-1100. 1993. pap. 10.95 (*0-8112-1247-5*, NDP757) New Directions.

Crack-Ups: A Very Silly Joke Book. Mik Brown. LC 93-28644. (Illus.). 64p. (Orig.). (J). (gr. 1-4). 1994. pap. 2.95 (*1-85697-930-X*, Kingfisher LKC) LKC.

Crack Wars: Literature Addiction Mania. Avital Ronell. LC 91-18917. (Texts & Contexts Ser.). xii, 175p. 1992. 25.00 (*0-8032-3903-3*); pap. 9.95 (*0-8032-8944-8*) U of Nebr Pr.

Crackdown. Bernard Cornwell. 1991. mass mkt. 5.95 (*0-06-109924-4*, Harp PBks) HarpC.

Crackdown. large type ed. Bernard Cornwell. 448p. 1992. 23.95 (*0-7089-8606-4*, Trail West Pubs) Ulverscroft.

Crackdown in Inner Mongolia. Ed. by Human Rights Watch Staff. 36p. (Orig.). 1991. pap. 5.00 (*1-56432-035-9*) Hum Rts Watch.

Crackdown in Kashmir: Torture of Detainees & Assaults on the Medical Community. Physicians for Human Rights Staff & Asia Watch Staff. (Illus.). 38p. 1993. Glossy cover version with photo. pap. text ed. 7.00 (*1-879707-14-4*); Press copy. pap. text ed. 7.00 (*1-879707-13-6*) Phy Human Rights.

Crackdown on Cancer with Good Nutrition. 2nd rev. ed. Ruth Y. Long. 172p. 1991. reprint ed. pap. 10.00 (*0-916243-15-X*) Nutrit Educ.

Cracked Coverage: Television News, the Anti-Cocaine Crusade, & the Reagan Legacy. Jimmie L. Reeves & Richard Campbell. 360p. 1994. lib. bdg. 59.95 (*0-8223-1449-5*); pap. text ed. 19.95 (*0-8223-1491-6*) Duke.

Cracked Crystal: Jazz Poetry in Three Sets. Margareta Waterman. (Illus.). 64p. (Orig.). 1991. pap. 6.50 (*1-878888-06-4*) Nine Muses.

Cracked Lens at Sundown. Gerald Toy. Ed. by Shelia Lenahan. (Illus.). 22p. (C). 1982. pap. 3.00 (*0-911017-00-3*) Seacliffe.

Cracked Looking-Glass: James Joyce & the Nightmare of History. Albert Wachtel. LC 91-50004. 176p. 1992. 36.50 (*0-945636-27-X*) Susquehanna U Pr.

Cracked Mirror: A Novel. Edilberto K. Tiempo. 219p. (Orig.). 1984. pap. 11.50 (*971-10-0145-4*, Pub. by New Day Pub PH) Cellar.

Cracked Wheat & Other Stories. Ed. by Hugh Cook. LC 84-18878. 127p. (Orig.). (YA). (gr. 7 up). 1984. 12.95 (*0-931940-09-5*); pap. 6.95 (*0-931940-08-7*) Middleburg Pr.

***Cracked Wheat & Other Stories.** Hugh Cook. 122p. 1995. lib. bdg. 27.00 (*0-8095-4872-0*) Borgo Pr.

Cracked Wheat for Christmas. Ted C. Hindmarsh. 73p. 1985. pap. 4.98 (*0-88290-265-2*, 1964) Horizon Utah.

Cracker Barrel Old Country Store: Old Timey Recipes & Proverbs to Live By. 1983. write for info. (*0-9606192-1-6*) Hach.

Cracker-Barrel Wit & Wisdom. Emil Ksenich. 1993. 7.95 (*0-533-10322-3*) Vantage.

Cracker Cookin' & Other Favorites. Bj Altschul. 1989. pap. 12.95 (*0-942084-07-1*) SeaSide Pub.

Cracker Cookin' & Other Favorites. Ed. by Shepard et al. LC 83-82687. (Famous Florida Ser.). (Illus.). 320p. (Orig.). 1985. reprint ed. pap. 14.95 (*0-932855-28-8*) Winner Enter.

Cracker Crumb Rescue. Carolyn J. Schott & Phillipa A. Smith. 40p. (J). (gr. 3-6). 1992. lib. bdg. 16.95 (*0-9632461-0-0*) Harbour Duck.

Cracker Culture: Celtic Ways in the Old South. Grady McWhiney. LC 86-16052. (Illus.). 336p. 1989. pap. 19.50 (*0-8173-0458-4*) U of Ala Pr.

Cracker Florida. Ray Washington. 160p. 1982. pap. 7.95 (*0-916224-80-5*) Banyan Bks.

***Cracker Jack Collectibles.** Ravi Pina. (Illus.). 112p. (Orig.). 1995. pap. 19.95 (*0-88740-847-8*) Schiffer.

Cracker Jack Prizes. Alex Jaramillo. (Illus.). 96p. 1989. 21.95 (*1-55859-000-5*) Abbeville Pr.

Cracker Jackson. Betsy C. Byars. (Novels Ser.). 160p. (J). (gr. 5-9). 1986. pap. 3.99 (*0-14-031881-X*, Puffin) Puffin Bks.

Cracker Jackson. Betsy C. Byars. LC 84-24684. 168p. (J). (gr. 5-7). 1985. pap. 12.95 (*0-670-80546-7*) Viking Child Bks.

Cracker Market. Ed. by Peter Allen. 100p. 1989. pap. 795.00 (*0-318-41828-2*) FIND-SVP.

***Cracker Still Lives Here: A Story of Living, Loving & Healing. Connie Cummings. Ed. by Dan Arden. (Illus.). 128p. (Orig.). 1995. pap. 7.95 (*0-9641683-0-8*) Rivers Edge.**
A book written to enlighten & support those grieving in silence over the loss of a pet. A truly inspiring story of a young woman's quest for understanding & healing after the death of a dear friend. Society has been slow to accept & support the loving relationship that people, both young & old, have with their companion animals. It is a relationship of unconditional love that one may not have experienced in human relationships. The book covers emotions of grief involving the loss of a pet: denial, anger, depression, bargaining & resolution. It also deals with situations involving euthanasia, unexpected loss, telling a child, dealing with other pets, & other important issues. This book not only condones but encourages the expression of emotion in order to heal the pain that is often kept within the heart. A journal section is included to record special feelings & remembrances allowing you to personalize each book. Order from River's Edge Publishing, P.O. Box 7343, Fort Myers, FL 33911; 813-332-2941. ***Publisher Provided Annotation.***

Crackerbox Philosophers in American Humor & Satire. Jeannette R. Tandy. (BCL1-PS American Literature Ser.). 181p. 1992. reprint ed. lib. bdg. 69.00 (*0-7812-6644-0*) Rprt Serv.

C

An Asterisk (*) at the beginning of an entry indicates that the title is appearing in BIP for the first time.

Crackerjack. large type ed. B. J. Rockliff. (General Fiction Ser.). 432p. 1992. 21.95 (0-7089-2701-7) Ulverscroft.

Crackers. Roy Blount, Jr. 1982. pap. 3.95 (0-345-29805-5) Ballantine.

Crackers & Crumbs: Chants for Whole Language. Sonja Dunn. LC 89-78077. 96p. 1990. pap. text ed. 14.00 (0-435-08528-X, 08528) Heinemann.

Crackers & Peaches: Travels in Georgia. Jane Schnell. LC 93-8249. 1993. 11.00 (0-9626112-1-2) Milner Pr.

***Crackers for a Lycanthrope.** Robert M. Hoff. Ed. by Jamie Curtis. LC 95-94295. 312p. (Orig.). 1995. pap. 15.00 (0-9645835-0-X) Lycanthrocorp.

Crackhouse: Notes from the End of the Line. Terence T. Williams. (Illus.). 192p. 1992. 17.26 (0-201-56759-8) Addison-Wesley.

Crackhouse: Notes from the End of the Line. Terence T. Williams. 172p. 1993. pap. 10.00 (0-14-023047-5, Penguin Bks) Viking Penguin.

Cracking. Gary A. Young. LC 88-50591. 89p. (Orig.). 1989. pap. 5.95 (0-916383-64-4, Univ Edtns) Aegina Pr.

Cracking & Damage - Strain Localization & Size Effects: Proceedings of the France - U. S. Workshop Held at the Laboratoire de Mechanique et Technolgie, ENS de Cachan, France, 6-9 September 1988. Ed. by J. Mazars. 552p. 1989. 108.00 (1-85166-347-9) Elsevier.

Cracking Catalyst Activity in the Presence of Hydrogen Sulfide. H. A. Dirksen et al. (Research Bulletin Ser.: No. 4). iv, 27p. 1953. 3.50 (0-317-56779-9) Inst Gas Tech.

Cracking, Deflection, & Ultimate Load on Concrete Slab Systems: Proceedings of the International Symposium, Denver, 1971. International Symposium on the Cracking, Defection, & Ultimate Load on Slab Systems Staff. LC 70-176469. (American Concrete Institute Publication Ser.: No. SP-30). 389p. reprint ed. pap. 110.90 (0-685-09007-8, 2002902) Bks Demand.

Cracking Down: Oil Refining & Pollution Control. Gregg Kerlin & Daniel Rabovsky. LC 75-10534. 478p. 1975. 3.95 (0-318-40142-8) CEP.

Cracking Eastern Europe: Everything Marketers Must Know to Sell into the World's Newest Emerging Markets - Filled with Facts, Figures, Demographics & More. Allyn Enderlyn & Oliver C. Dziggel. 425p. 1992. 42.50 (1-55738-255-7) Probus Pub Co.

Cracking Eggs. Katherine Soniat. 96p. 1990. 16.95 (0-8130-0973-1); pap. 10.95 (0-8130-0992-8) U Press Fla.

***Cracking India.** braille ed. Bapsi Sidhwa. 519p. 1994. text ed. 41.52 (1-56956-449-3, BR9318) W A T Braille.

Cracking India: A Novel. Bapsi Sidhwa. LC 91-12967. (Illus.). 293p. 1991. reprint ed. 18.95 (0-915943-51-4); reprint ed. pap. 13.00 (0-915943-56-5) Milkweed Ed.

Cracking Jokes. Alan Dundes. 184p. 1987. 15.95 (0-89815-206-2); pap. 9.95 (0-89815-188-0) Ten Speed Pr.

Cracking Latin America: A Country-by-Country Guide to Doing Business in the World's Newest Emerging Markets. Allyn Enderlyn & Oliver C. Dziggel. 350p. 1993. 45.00 (1-55738-432-0) Probus Pub Co.

Cracking New Accounts: Quick Tips & Inside Techniques to Help You Gain Market Share & Close the Sale in Half the Time. Terry L. Booton. 235p. 1991. 25.00 (0-9633282-0-4) Advan Mktg Instruct.

***Cracking New Accounts: Tips & Techniques for Opening & Closing the Sale in Half the Time.** Terry L. Booton. 1994. 24.95 (1-55738-817-2) Probus Pub Co.

Cracking of Spines. large type ed. Roy H. Lewis. (Linford Mystery Library). 352p. 1987. pap. 11.95 (0-7089-6459-1, Linford) Ulverscroft.

***Cracking Old Testament Codes: A Guide to Interpreting Old Testament Literary Forms.** Ed. by D. Brent Sandy, Jr. & Ronald L. Giese. LC 94-39677. 1995. 14.99 (0-8054-1093-7) Broadman.

***Cracking Open a Coffin.** Gwendoline Butler. (WWL Mystery Ser.). 1995. mass mkt. 3.99 (0-373-26171-3, 1-29171-8) Harlequin Bks.

Cracking Open a Coffin. Gwendoline Butler. 240p. 1993. 18.95 (0-312-09777-8, Pub. by Thomas Dunne Bks) St Martin.

Cracking Open a Coffin. large type ed. Gwendoline Butler. 390p. 1994. lib. bdg. 17.95 (0-7862-0118-5) Thorndike Pr.

***Cracking the ACT with Sample Tests on Computer Disk, 1995-96 Edition: Mac Version.** Geoff Martz. (Princeton Review Ser.). 1995. student ed, disk 29.95 (0-679-76024-5) Random.

Cracking the Code. David Bergman. LC 85-15227. 49p. 1985. 18.95 (0-8142-0394-9); pap. 12.50 (0-8142-0405-8) Ohio St U Pr.

Cracking the Corporate Closet: The Two Hundred Best (& Worst) Companies to Work for, Buy from, & Invest in If You're Gay or Lesbian - & Even If You're Not. Daniel B. Baker & Sean O. Strub. 320p. 1995. 23.00 (0-88730-691-8) Harper Busn.

Cracking the European Markets. Timothy Harper. 288p. 1992. text ed. 24.95 (0-471-54769-7) Wiley.

Cracking the Glass Ceiling: Strategies for Success. Catalyst Staff. 1994. 40.00 (0-89584-185-1) Catalyst.

***Cracking the GMAT 1996.** Geoff Martz et al. (Princeton Review Ser.). 1995. pap. 17.00 (0-679-76135-7, Villard Bks) Random.

***Cracking the GMAT 1996: With Sample Tests on Computer Disk (WIN)** Geoff Martz et al. (Princeton Review Ser.). 1995. disk, pap. 29.95 (0-679-76137-3, Villard Bks) Random.

***Cracking the GMAT '96: With Sample Tests on Computer Disk (MAC)** Geoff Martz et al. (Princeton Review Ser.). 1995. disk, pap. 29.95 (0-679-76138-1, Villard Bks) Random.

Cracking the Gnostic Code: The Powers in Gnosticism. Walter Wink. LC 93-10143. (Society of Biblical Literature Monographs: No. 46). 69p. 1993. 29.95 (1-55540-859-1, 060046); pap. 19.95 (1-55540-860-5, 060046) Scholars Pr GA.

***Cracking the GRE Psychology Test '96.** Laurice Pearson. (Princeton Review Ser.). 1995. pap. 16.00 (0-679-76144-6, Villard Bks) Random.

Cracking the GRE (Psychology) 1995 Edition. 1994. pap. 16.00 (0-679-75364-8, Villard Bks) Random.

***Cracking the GRE 1996.** Adam Robinson & John Katzman. 1995. pap. 17.00 (0-679-76136-5, Villard Bks) Random.

***Cracking the GRE '96: With Sample Tests on Computer Disk (MAC)** Adam Robinson & John Katzman. (Princeton Review Ser.). 1995. disk, pap. 29.95 (0-679-76141-1, Villard Bks) Random.

***Cracking the GRE '96: With Sample Tests on Computer Disk (WIN)** Adam Robinson & John Katzman. (Princeton Review Ser.). 1995. disk, pap. 29.95 (0-679-76140-3, Villard Bks) Random.

Cracking the Ike Age: Aspects of Fifties America. Ed. by Dale Carter. (Dolphin Ser.: No. 23). (Illus.). 271p. (Orig.). (C). 1992. pap. 37.50 (87-7288-373-1, Pub. by Aarhus Univ Pr DK) Coronet Bks.

Cracking the Japanese Market: Strategies for Success in the New Global Economy. James C. Morgan & J. Jeffrey Morgan. 288p. 1991. 32.95 (0-02-921691-5) Free Pr.

Cracking the Language Code: French. Stanley Rundle. 1983. pap. 19.95 (0-87243-110-X) Templegate.

Cracking the Language Code: German. Stanley Rundle. 1982. pap. 19.95 (0-87243-107-X) Templegate.

Cracking the Language Code: Spanish. Stanley Rundle. 1974. pap. 19.95 (0-87243-109-6) Templegate.

***Cracking the LSAT '96.** Adam Robinson & Princeton Review Staff. (Princeton Review Ser.). 1995. pap. 17.00 (0-679-76139-X, Villard Bks) Random.

***Cracking the LSAT '96: With Sample Tests on Computer Disk (MAC)** Adam Robinson & Princeton Review Staff. (Princeton Review Ser.). 1995. disk, pap. 29.95 (0-679-76143-8, Villard Bks) Random.

***Cracking the LSAT '96: With Sample Tests on Computer Disk (WIN)** Adam Robinson & Princeton Review Staff. (Princeton Review Ser.). 1995. disk, pap. 29.95 (0-679-76142-X, Villard Bks) Random.

Cracking the Market Code Without Twenty-Twenty Hindsight. Robert H. Knapp. Ed. by Robin Reagan. (Illus.). 200p. 1985. 16.95 (0-935623-01-9) Hazard Mgmt.

***Cracking the MCAT '96.** Princeton Review Staff & Theodore Silver. (Princeton Review Ser.). 1995. pap. 20.00 (0-679-76272-8, Villard Bks) Random.

***Cracking the MCAT '96: With Sample Tests on Computer Disk (MAC)** Princeton Review Staff & Theodore Silver. (Princeton Review Ser.). 1995. disk, pap. 34.95 (0-679-76073-3, Villard Bks) Random.

***Cracking the MCAT '96: With Sample Tests on Computer Disk (WIN)** Princeton Review Staff & Theodore Silver. (Princeton Review Ser.). 1995. disk, pap. 29.95 (0-679-76072-5, Villard Bks) Random.

Cracking the Monolith: The Struggle for the Soul of America - A Peace & Justice Manifesto. William W. Rankin. 160p. (Orig.). 1994. pap. 10.95 (0-8245-1439-4) Crossroad NY.

Cracking the Monolith: U. S. Policy Against the Sino-Soviet Alliance, 1949-1955. David A. Mayers. LC 86-40. (Political Traditions in Foreign Policy Ser.). xiii, 176p. 1986. text ed. 27.50 (0-8071-1287-9) La State U Pr.

Cracking the Over-Fifty Job Market. J. Robert Connor. 240p. (Orig.). 1992. pap. 12.00 (0-452-26835-4, Plume) NAL-Dutton.

Cracking the Pacific Rim: Everything Marketers Must Know to Sell into the World's Fastest Growing Markets - Filled with Facts, Figures, Demographics & More. Allyn Enderlyn & Oliver C. Dziggel. 425p. 1992. 42.50 (1-55738-254-9) Probus Pub Co.

Cracking the Pavement. David J. Nelson, Jr. (Minority Poet Ser.). (Illus.). 57p. 1989. pap. 4.00 (1-880046-01-6) Baculite Pub.

***Cracking the SAT & PSAT '96.** Adam Robinson & John Katzman. (Princeton Review Ser.). 1995. pap. 17.00 (0-679-76132-2, Villard Bks) Random.

***Cracking the SAT & PSAT '96: With Sample Tests on Computer Disk (MAC)** Adam Robinson & John Katzman. (Princeton Review Ser.). 1995. disk, mac ld 29.95 (0-679-76134-9, Villard Bks) Random.

***Cracking the SAT & PSAT '96: With Sample Tests on Computer Disk (WIN)** Adam Robinson & John Katzman. (Princeton Review Ser.). 1995. disk, pap. 29.95 (0-679-76133-0, Villard Bks) Random.

***Cracking the SAT II: Biology Subject Test 1996 Edition.** Theodore Silver. (Princeton Review Ser.). 1995. student ed, pap. 17.00 (0-679-75913-1) Random.

***Cracking the SAT II: Chemistry Subject Test, 1996 Edition.** Theodore Silver. (Princeton Review Ser.). 1995. student ed, pap. 17.00 (0-679-75914-X) Random.

***Cracking the SAT II: English Subject Tests 1996.** Liz Buffa. (Princeton Review Ser.). 1995. student ed, pap. 17.00 (0-679-75915-8) Random.

***Cracking the SAT II: French Subject Test, 1996 Edition.** Isabel Parlett. (Princeton Review Ser.). 1995. student ed, pap. 17.00 (0-679-75916-6) Random.

***Cracking the SAT II: History Subject Test, 1996 Edition.** Grace R. Freedman. (Princeton Review Ser.). 1995. student ed, pap. 17.00 (0-679-75917-4) Random.

***Cracking the SAT II: Math Subject Tests, 1996 Edition.** Ethan Mintz. (Princeton Review Ser.). 1995. student ed, pap. 17.00 (0-679-75918-2) Random.

***Cracking the SAT II: Physics Subject Tests, 1996 Edition.** Theodore Silver. (Princeton Review Ser.). 1995. student ed, pap. 17.00 (0-679-75919-0) Random.

***Cracking the SAT II: Spanish Subject Test, 1996 Edition.** George R. Pace. (Princeton Review Ser.). 1995. student ed, pap. 17.00 (0-679-75920-4) Random.

***Cracking the Show.** Thomas Bosswell. 1995. pap. 14.95 (0-385-47713-9) Doubleday.

Cracking the Show. Thomas Bowsell. 1994. 23.00 (0-385-47286-2) Doubleday.

Cracking the TASP. Leslie Cohen & Antoinette Falco. Ed. by Yolanda L. Salazar & Emily A. Cullen. (Illus.). 198p. 1992. per. 11.95 (1-877709-21-2) ADAPT Pub Co.

Cracking the TOEFL. Liz Buffa. 1994. pap. 20.00 (0-679-74624-2, Villard Bks) Random.

Cracking the Wall: Women in Higher Education Administration. 196p. 1993. 30.00 (1-878240-21-8) Coll & U Personnel.

***Cracking Up: The Work of Unconscious Experience.** Christopher Bollas. 272p. 1995. 20.00 (0-8090-8533-X) Hill & Wang.

Crackle Creek. Mary E. Monsell. LC 89-15105. (Illus.). 64p. (J). (gr. 2-4). 1990. text ed. 12.95 (0-689-31564-3, Atheneum Bks Young) S&S Childrens.

Crackle Weave. Mary Snyder. 1990. pap. 9.50 (1-56659-007-8) Robin & Russ.

Crackle with Life. Brian Jones. LC 91-73614. (Illus.). 128p. 1991. pap. 9.95 (0-9629711-0-3) Happy Miner.

***Crackle with Life: Short Stories.** Brian Jones. (Illus.). 112p. (Orig.). 1994. pap. 7.95 (0-931892-95-3) B Dolphin Pub.

Cracklin Bread & Asfidity: Folk Recipes & Remedies. Jack Solomon & Olivia P. Solomon. LC 77-13065. 232p. 1979. pap. 16.95 (0-8173-0724-9) U of Ala Pr.

Crackling Mountain & Other Stories. Osamu Dazai. Tr. by James O'Brien. LC 89-50024. 256p. 1989. 16.95 (0-8048-1565-8) C E Tuttle.

Crackling of Thorns. John Hollander. LC 73-11023. (Yale Series of Younger Poets: No. 54). reprint ed. 18.00 (0-404-53854-1) AMS Pr.

Crackpot. John Waters. LC 87-40083. 160p. 1987. pap. 10.00 (0-394-75534-0, Vin) Random.

Crackpot. Adele Wiseman. 300p. 1993. pap. 11.95 (0-8032-9753-X, Bison Books) U of Nebr Pr.

Cracks & Fracture: 9th Conference - STP 601. Ed. by J. L. Swedlow & M. L. Williams. 1976. 51.75 (0-8031-0318-2, 04-601000-30) ASTM.

Cracks in an Earthen Vessel: An Examination of the Catalogues of Hardships in the Corinthian Correspondence. John T. Fitzgerald. LC 86-26164. (Society of Biblical Literature Ser.). 284p. 1988. 18.95 (1-55540-087-6, 06 01 99); pap. 12.95 (1-55540-088-4, 06 01 99) Scholars Pr GA.

Cracks in Concrete. 44p. 1973. pap. 11.00 (0-924659-00-9, 1310) Aberdeen Group.

Cracks in the Constitution. Ferdinand Lundberg. 1980. 15.00 (0-8184-0279-2) Carol Pub Group.

Cracks in the Empire: State Politics in the Vietnam War. Paul Joseph. (Morningside Bk.). 384p. 1987. reprint ed. pap. text ed. 16.00 (0-231-06635-X) Col U Pr.

Cracks in the Monolith: Party Power in the Brezhnev Era. Ed. by James R. Millar. LC 92-9300. (Contemporary Soviet - Post Soviet Politics Ser.). 256p. 1992. 62.95 (0-87332-885-X) M E Sharpe.

Cracks in the Parchment Curtain & Other Essays in Philippine History. William H. Scott. (Orig.). (C). 1982. pap. 15.00 (971-10-0073-3, Pub. by New Day Pub PH) Cellar.

Cracks in the Sidewalk: Children's Daily Adventures. Crystal Bowman. Ed. by Alan G. Hartman. (Illus.). 128p. (Orig.). (J). (gr. k-8). 1993. 12.00 (0-9636050-1-1); pap. 6.00 (0-9636050-0-3) Cygnet Pub.

***Cracks of Grace.** Edward Sanders. (Light & Dust Bks.). 62p. (Orig.). 1994. pap. 5.00 (0-87924-066-0) Membrane Pr.

Cracow Pontifical. Ed. by Z. Obertynski. (Henry Bradshaw Society Publication Ser.: No. C (100)). 1970. 30.00 (0-907077-17-X) Boydell & Brewer.

Cradle. Arthur C. Clarke & Gentry Lee. LC 87-40404. 1989. mass mkt. 5.99 (0-446-35061-8) Warner Bks.

***Cradle & All.** Nancy B. Jacobs. 1994. pap. 4.99 (0-06-100750-1, Harp PBks) HarpC.

Cradle & All. Rebecca York. (Intrigue Ser.). 1993. mass mkt. 2.99 (0-373-22233-5, 1-22233-0) Harlequin Bks.

Cradle & All: A Cultural & Psychoanalytic Study of Nursery Rhymes. Lucy Rollin. LC 91-38995. (Studies in Popular Culture Ser.). 176p. 1992. 28.50 (0-87805-556-8) U Pr of Miss.

Cradle & All: Everything for Welcoming the New Baby. Pamela Scurry. (Illus.). 1992. pap. 20.00 (0-517-57560-4, C P Pubs) Crown Pub Group.

Cradle & All: Women Writers on Pregnancy & Birth. Ed. by Laura Chester. 276p. 1989. pap. 12.95 (0-571-12989-7) Faber & Faber.

Cradle Book of Verse: An Anthology of Baby Poetry. Comp. by Louise Hovde. LC 72-2997. (Granger Index Reprint Ser.). 1977. reprint ed. 17.95 (0-8369-8244-4) Ayer.

Cradle of Dreams. Janice Kaiser. (Superromance Ser.). 1993. mass mkt. 3.39 (0-373-70541-7, 1-70541-7) Harlequin Bks.

Cradle of Fear. Meg Griffin. 352p. 1994. mass mkt. 4.50 (0-8217-4497-6) Zebra.

Cradle of Invasion: A History of the U. S. Naval Amphibious Training Base, Solomons, Maryland, 1942-1945. Merle T. Cole. LC 85-179786. (Illus.). 37p. (Orig.). 1984. reprint ed. pap. 3.95 (0-941647-03-X) Calvert MM Pr.

Cradle of Mankind. Mohamed Amin. (Illus.). 1983. 50.00 (0-87951-179-6) Overlook Pr.

Cradle of Rebellion. Lucien De La Hodde. Tr. by J. Bradburn. (History of Political Violence Ser.). 1985. reprint ed. lib. bdg. 60.00 (0-527-41195-7) Periodicals Srv.

Cradle of Steel Unionism: Monogahela, PA. George Powers. 163p. 1972. lib. bdg. 25.95 (0-88286-098-4) C H Kerr.

***Cradle of Texas Presbyterianism: Memorial Presbyterian Church, San Augustine, Texas.** William E. Lytch. (Illus.). 224p. 1993. 19.95 (1-881576-19-1) Providence Hse.

Cradle of the Middle Class: The Family in Oneida County, New York, 1790-1865. Mary P. Ryan. LC 80-18460. (Interdisciplinary Perspectives on Modern History Ser.). (Illus.). 336p. 1983. pap. 16.95 (0-521-27403-6) Cambridge U Pr.

Cradle of Valor: The Intimate Letters of a Plebe at West Point During the Great Depression. Dale O. Smith. (Illus.). 288p. 1988. 16.95 (0-912697-80-6) Algonquin Bks.

***Cradle of Violence: Essays on Psychiatry, Psychoanalysis & Literature.** Stephen Wilson. LC 95-14278. (Forensic Focus Ser.: No. 2). 1995. pap. write for info. (1-85302-306-X, Pub. by J Kingsley Pubs UK) Taylor & Francis.

Cradle Song. Rita A. Scotti. 224p. 1989. 16.95 (1-55611-116-9) D I Fine.

Cradle Tales of Hinduism. Nivedita. (Illus.). 329p. (J). (gr. 3-12). 1972. pap. 5.95 (0-87481-170-8, Pub. by Advaita Ashrama II); pap. 5.95 (0-87481-131-7, Pub. by Advaita Ashrama II) Vedanta Pr.

Cradle, the Cross & the Crown. George Bass. Ed. by Michael L. Sherer. (Orig.). 1986. pap. 7.60 (0-89536-817-X, 6866) CSS OH.

Cradle to College. Brannon Howse. LC 93-86325. 224p. (Orig.). 1993. pap. 9.95 (0-89221-243-8) New Leaf.

Cradle to Grave. Susan Claudia. 1983. pap. 2.95 (0-449-12551-3) Fawcett.

Cradle to Grave: Life, Work, & Death at the Lake Superior Copper Mines. Larry Lankton. (Illus.). 352p. 1993. reprint ed. pap. 16.95 (0-19-508357-1) OUP.

Cradle to Grave: Poverty in America. Jonathan Freedman. Ed. by Lee Goerner. (Illus.). 352p. 1993. text ed. 20.00 (0-689-12126-1, Atheneum S&S) S&S Trade.

Cradle Will Fall. Mary Higgins Clark. Ed. by Julie Rubenstein. 432p. 1991. pap. 6.99 (0-671-74119-5) PB.

Cradle Will Fall. Mary Higgins Clark. 1993. reprint ed. lib. bdg. 25.95 (0-89968-448-3, Lghtyr Pr) Buccaneer Bks.

Cradle Will Fall: One Woman's Story of Her Descent into Madness Following the Birth of Her Baby - & Her Remarkable, Inspiring Recovery. Michele G. Remington & Carl Burak. LC 94-71107. 240p. 1994. 21.95 (1-55611-408-7) D I Fine.

***Cradle Will Rock: An Original Screenplay.** Orson Welles. Ed. & Intro. by James Pepper. 150p. 1994. 35.00 (0-944166-06-7) Santa Teresa Pr.

Cradled & the Called. Roger E. Sargeant & Audrey R. Langer. 280p. (Orig.). 1989. pap. 6.95 (0-929827-02-3) New Saga Pubs.

Cradled in Human Hands: A Textbook on Environmental Responsibility. Eileen P. Flynn. LC 90-63483. 160p. (Orig.). (C). 1991. pap. 10.95 (1-55612-413-9, LL1413) Sheed & Ward MO.

Cradles in the Trees: The Story of Bird Nests. Patricia B. Demuth. LC 93-9114. (Illus.). 32p. (J). (ps-3). 1994. text ed. 14.95 (0-02-728466-2, Mac Bks Young Read) S&S Childrens.

Cradles, Nests & Other Backward Glances. Pearl B. Segall. Ed. by Denise Martinson. 40p. (Orig.). 1992. pap. text ed. 6.00 (1-879533-12-X) Poetic Page.

Cradlesong. Jessica Palmer. Ed. by Rebecca Todd. 320p. (Orig.). 1993. mass mkt. 4.99 (0-671-73421-0) PB.

Cradlesong. Mark Taksa. 1994. pap. 6.95 (0-685-70584-6) Pudding Hse Pubns.

Cradoc's Quest. Cherith Baldry. Ed. by Sue Reck. (Saga of the Six Worlds Ser.). 160p. (YA). (gr. 8-12). Date not set. pap. 4.99 (0-7814-0093-7, Chariot Bks) Chariot Family.

***Craft an Elegant Wedding.** Naomi Baker & Tammy Young. 144p. 1995. pap. 17.95 (0-8019-8575-7) Chilton.

Craft & Architecture. (Modulus: the Architectural Review of the University of Virginia Ser.: No. 22). (Illus.). 132p. (Orig.). 1993. pap. 24.95 (1-878271-94-6) Princeton Arch.

Craft & Art of Clay. Susan Peterson. 368p. 1992. pap. text ed. 45.33 (0-13-188475-1) P-H.

Craft & Art of Clay. Susan Peterson. 1993. 40.00 (0-13-189598-2) P-H.

***Craft & Business of Songwriting.** John Braheny. 322p. (Orig.). 1995. pap. 21.99 (0-89879-653-9) Writers Digest.

Craft & Community: Traditional Arts in Contemporary Society. Ed. by Shalom D. Staub. LC 88-72287. (Illus.). 140p. (C). 1988. reprint ed. pap. 13.95 (0-937437-05-0) U of Pa Pr.

Craft & Consciousness: Occupational Technique & the Development of World Images. 2nd ed. Joseph Bensman & Robert Lilienfeld. (Communication & Social Order Ser.). 419p. 1991. lib. bdg. 55.95 (0-202-30384-5); pap. text ed. 30.95 (0-202-30385-3) Aldine de Gruyter.

Craft & Creation of Wood Sculpture. Cecil C. Carstenson. (Illus.). 192p. 1981. reprint ed. pap. 6.95 (0-486-24094-0) Dover.

Craft & Design in Metal. Stanley Thornes. (C). 1986. 80.00 (0-09-160711-6, Pub. by S Thornes Pubs UK) St Mut.

Craft & Design in Wood, GCSE Edition. D. M. Willacy. (C). 1987. 65.00 (0-09-172711-1, Pub. by S Thornes Pubs UK) St Mut.

Craft & Hobby Airbrush Book. Peter Owen. (Illus.). 96p. 1995. pap. 17.95 (1-55821-333-3) Lyons & Burford.

C

An Asterisk (*) at the beginning of an entry indicates that the title is appearing in BIP for the first time.

An Asterisk (*) at the beginning of an entry indicates that the title is appearing in BIP for the first time.

1671

Crafts: Contemporary Design & Technique. Alice Sprintzen. LC 86-70902. (Illus.). 192p. 1987. 25.95 (*0-87192-180-4*) Davis Mass.

Crafts All Together. Karen Campbell. 1993. spiral bd., pap. 7.50 (*1-879127-26-1*) Lighten Up Enter.

Crafts & Craftsmen of New Jersey. Walter H. Van Hoesen. LC 72-421. (Illus.). 251p. 1973. 27.50 (*0-8386-1080-3*) Fairleigh Dickinson.

Crafts & Hobbies. Reader's Digest Editors. LC 79-63118. (Illus.). 456p. 1981. 24.95 (*0-89577-063-6*) RD Assn.

Crafts & More for Children's Ministry. Karyn Henley. LC 93-10755. 1993. 14.99 (*1-55945-191-2*) Group Pub.

Crafts & More Rhyming Instructions & Patterns. Patterns by Alfreda Staff. 1992. pap. text ed. 21.95 (*0-318-04425-0*, Patterns Alfreda) Prosperity & Profits.

Crafts & Traditions of the Canary Islands. Mike Eddy. 1989. pap. 25.00 (*0-7478-0011-1*, Pub. by Shire UK) St Mut.

Crafts Business Encyclopedia. rev. ed. Michael Scott. Ed. by Leonard D. DuBoff. LC 93-12997. 1993. pap. 14.95 (*0-15-622726-6*, Harvest Bks) HarBrace.

Crafts Family: A Genealogical & Biographical History of the Descendants of Griffin & Alice Craft of Roxbury, Mass., 1630-1890. James M. Crafts & W. F. Crafts. (Illus.). 807p. 1989. reprint ed. lib. bdg. 109.00 (*0-8328-0434-7*); reprint ed. pap. 99.00 (*0-8328-0435-5*) Higginson Bk Co.

Crafts for a Long, Boring, What-Do-I-Do-Now Afternoon. Jeanette Pelton & Fawn Pelton. Ed. by Dan Pelton. (Illus.). 50p. (Orig.). (J). (gr. 4-7). 1993. pap. 4.00 (*1-879564-04-1*) Long Acre Pub.

Crafts for Celebration. Ed. by Caroline Bingham & Karen Foster. (Millbrook Arts Library). (Illus.). 48p. (J). (gr. 2-6). 1993. lib. bdg. 14.40 (*1-56294-099-6*) Millbrook Pr.

*__Crafts for Christmas.__ Kathy Ross. LC 94-48304. (Holiday Crafts for Kids Ser.). (Illus.). 48p. (J). (gr. k-3). 1995. lib. bdg. 15.40 (*1-56294-536-X*) Millbrook Pr.

*__Crafts for Christmas.__ Kathy Ross. LC 94-48304. (Holiday Crafts for Kids Ser.). (Illus.). 48p. (J). (gr. k-3). 1995. pap. 5.95 (*1-56294-681-1*) Millbrook Pr.

Crafts for Decoration. Ed. by Caroline Bingham & Karen Foster. (Millbrook Arts Library). (Illus.). 48p. (J). (gr. 2-6). 1993. lib. bdg. 14.40 (*1-56294-098-8*) Millbrook Pr.

*__Crafts for Easter.__ Kathy Ross. LC 95-13510. (Holiday Crafts for Kids Ser.). (Illus.). (J). 1995. lib. bdg. write for info. (*1-56294-918-7*) Millbrook Pr.

Crafts for Everyday Life. Ed. by Caroline Bingham & Karen Foster. (Millbrook Arts Library). (Illus.). 48p. (J). (gr. 2-6). 1993. lib. bdg. 14.40 (*1-56294-097-X*) Millbrook Pr.

Crafts for Fun. Virginia Rich. (Illus.). 96p. 1986. pap. 6.00 (*0-8170-1090-4*) Judson.

*__Crafts for Girls.__ Sally Seamans. LC 95-6743. (American Girl Ser.). (Illus.). (J). 1995. write for info. (*1-56247-229-1*) Pleasant Co.

Crafts for Halloween. Kathy Ross. LC 93-37249. (Holiday Crafts for Kids Ser.). (Illus.). 48p. (J). (gr. k-3). 1994. lib. bdg. 15.40 (*1-56294-411-8*); pap. 6.95 (*1-56294-741-9*) Millbrook Pr.

Crafts for Kids: A Month-by-Month Idea Book. Barbara L. Dondiego. LC 84-16439. (Illus.). 304p. (Orig.). 1984. 17.95 (*0-8306-0784-6*); pap. 11.95 (*0-8306-1784-1*, 1784) TAB Bks.

Crafts for Kids: A Month-by-Month Idea Book. 2nd ed. Barbara L. Dondiego. (Illus.). 224p. (Orig.). 1990. pap. 22.95 (*0-8306-7573-6*, 3573); pap. 14.95 (*0-8306-3573-4*) TAB Bks.

Crafts for Kids: A Month by Month Idea Book. 2nd ed. Barbara L. Dondiego. 1990. 22.95 (*0-07-155880-2*); pap. text ed. 15.95 (*0-07-155890-X*) McGraw.

Crafts for Kids: Cross Stitch Farmyard. Jane Greenoff. (Illus.). 32p. (J). 1994. 9.95 (*0-7153-0248-5*, Pub. by D & C Pub UK) Sterling.

Crafts for Kids: Dinosaurs Monsters. Jane Greenoff. (Illus.). 32p. (J). 1994. 9.95 (*0-7153-0249-3*, Pub. by D & C Pub UK) Sterling.

Crafts for Kids: Eighty Totally Excellent Projects. Vanessa-Ann Collection Staff. 1993. 22.95 (*0-696-02387-3*); pap. 14.95 (*0-696-02498-5*) Meredith Bks.

Crafts for Kids: Cross Stitch on the Move: 10 Easy Projects. Jane Greenoff. (Illus.). 32p. (J). 1994. 9.95 (*0-7153-0070-9*, Pub. by D & C Pub UK) Sterling.

Crafts for Kids: Our World in Cross Stitch: 12 Easy Projects. Jane Greenoff. (Illus.). 32p. (J). 1994. 9.95 (*0-7153-0068-7*, Pub. by D & C Pub UK) Sterling.

Crafts for Kwanzaa. Kathy Ross. LC 93-36690. (Holiday Crafts for Kids Ser.). (Illus.). 48p. (J). (gr. k-3). 1994. 15.40 (*1-56294-412-6*); pap. 6.95 (*1-56294-740-0*) Millbrook Pr.

Crafts for Play. Ed. by Caroline Bingham & Karen Foster. (Millbrook Arts Library). (Illus.). 48p. (J). (gr. 2-6). 1993. lib. bdg. 14.40 (*1-56294-096-1*) Millbrook Pr.

Crafts for Religious Education. Barbara Albin & Julia Holek. 174p. (Orig.). 1987. pap. 10.95 (*1-55588-144-0*) TEL Pubs.

*__Crafts for Thanksgiving.__ Kathy Ross. LC 94-48301. (Holiday Crafts for Kids Ser.). (Illus.). 48p. (J). (gr. k-3). 1995. 15.40 (*1-56294-535-1*) Millbrook Pr.

*__Crafts for Thanksgiving.__ Kathy Ross. LC 94-48301. (Holiday Crafts for Kids Ser.). (Illus.). 48p. (J). (gr. k-3). 1995. pap. 5.95 (*1-56294-682-X*) Millbrook Pr.

Crafts for the Very Disabled & Handicapped: For All Ages. Jane G. Kay. (Illus.). 224p. 1977. spiral bd. pap. 38.95x (*0-398-03661-6*) C C Thomas.

Crafts for Valentine's Day. Kathy Ross. LC 94-9834. (Holiday Crafts for Kids Ser.). (Illus.). 48p. (J). (gr. k-3). 1995. lib. bdg. 15.40 (*1-56294-489-4*) Millbrook Pr.

*__Crafts for Valentine's Day.__ Kathy Ross. LC 94-9834. (Holiday Crafts for Kids Ser.). (Illus.). 48p. (J). (gr. k-3). 1995. pap. 5.95 (*1-56294-887-3*) Millbrook Pr.

Crafts from Recyclables: Great Ideas from Throwaways. Ed. by Colleen Van Blaricom. LC 91-72872. (Illus.). 48p. (J). (gr. 1-5). 1992. pap. 4.95 (*1-56397-015-5*) Boyds Mills Pr.

*__Crafts from World Cultures.__ Jan Weith & Anne Weber. (Illus.). 96p. 1994. teacher ed, pap. text ed. 9.95 (*1-878279-75-0*, MM 1996) Evan-Moor Corp.

*__Crafts from Your Microwave.__ Alison Jenkins. 1994. pap. 12.99 (*0-517-10307-9*) Random Hse Value.

Crafts in Action Series, 6 vols., Set. (Illus.). (J). (gr. 4-8). 1991. lib. bdg. 89.70 (*1-85435-404-3*) Marshall Cavendish.

Crafts in the World Market: The Impact of Global Exchange on Middle American Artisans. Ed. by June C. Nash. LC 91-21308. (SUNY Series in the Anthropology of Work). 264p. (C). 1993. 59.50 (*0-7914-1061-7*); pap. 19.95 (*0-7914-1062-5*) State U NY Pr.

Crafts in Therapy & Rehabilitation. Margaret Drake. LC 89-42919. (Illus.). 162p. (C). 1992. pap. text ed. 23.00 (*1-55642-118-4*) SLACK Inc.

Crafts Index for Young People. Mary A. Pilger. LC 92-12996. (Data Bks.). 288p. 1992. lib. bdg. 32.50 (*1-56308-002-8*) Libs Unl.

Crafts Kids Can Eat, Play with, or Wear. Eileen Morris. (J). (gr. k-3). 1991. pap. 11.99 (*0-86653-979-4*) Fearon Teach Aids.

Crafts of Egypt. Denise Ammoun. (Illus.). 125p. 1991. pap. 16.00 (*977-424-233-5*) Col U Pr.

Crafts of Gardens. Ji Cheng. LC 88-5607. (C). 1989. 40.00 (*0-300-04182-9*) Yale U Pr.

Crafts of Himachal Pradesh. Subhashini Aryan. LC 89-80993. (Living Traditions of India Ser.). (Illus.). 168p. 1994. 65.00 (*0-944142-46-X*) Mapin International Inc.

Crafts of Kashmir, Jammu & Ladakh. Ed. by Jaya Jaitly. (Illus.). 228p. 1990. 29.98 (*1-55859-116-8*) Abbeville Pr.

Crafts of the North American Indians: A Craftman's Manual. Richard C. Schneider. LC 73-13008. (Illus.). 325p. 1981. reprint ed. pap. 19.95 (*0-936984-00-7*) Schneider Pubs.

Crafts of West Bengal. Prabhas Sen. LC 89-80998. (Living Traditions of India Ser.). (Illus.). 180p. 1992. 65.00 (*0-944142-45-1*) Mapin International Inc.

Crafts Supply Sourcebook: A Comprehensive Shop-by-Mail Guide. 3rd ed. Ed. by Margaret Boyd. (Illus.). 288p. 1994. pap. 16.99 (*1-55870-355-1*) Betterway Bks.

Crafts Together: Projects for the Whole Family. Alan Bridgewater & Gill Bridgewater. 1994. pap. text ed. 14.95 (*0-07-007778-9*) McGraw.

Craftsman Bungalows - Fifty-Nine Homes from the Craftsman. Gustav Stickley. 21.00 (*0-8446-6390-5*) Peter Smith.

Craftsman Homes: Architecture & Furnishings of the American Arts & Crafts Movement. Gustav Stickley. LC 78-73519. (Illus.). 1979. reprint ed. pap. 8.95 (*0-486-23791-5*) Dover.

*__Craftsman Illustrated Dictionary of Construction Terms.__ James T. Frane. (Illus.). 416p. (Orig.). 1994. pap. 36.00 (*1-57218-008-0*) Craftsman.

Craftsman of the Cumberlands: Tradition & Creativity. Michael O. Jones. LC 89-5542. (Illus.). 304p. 1990. 32.00 (*0-8131-1672-4*); pap. 16.00 (*0-8131-0183-2*) U Pr of Ky.

Craftsman Woodturner. rev. ed. Peter Child. (Illus.). 248p. (Orig.). 1992. pap. 14.95 (*0-8069-8782-0*) Sterling.

Craftsman's Cookbook. Ed. by Lois Moran. LC 72-91347. (Illus.). 192p. 1972. 12.00 (*0-88321-000-2*) Am Craft.

Craftsman's Handbook. Cennino A. Cennini. 1933. pap. 4.50 (*0-486-20054-X*) Dover.

Craftsman's Handbook: Henry Lapp. Illus. by Henry Lapp. LC 91-70663. 100p. 1991. pap. 15.95 (*1-56148-014-2*) Good Bks PA.

Craftsmanship & Function: A Study of Metal Vessels Found in Viking Age Tombs on the Island of Gotland, Sweden. Gustaf Trotzig. (Museum of National Antiquities, Monography Ser.: No. 1). (Illus.). 278p. (Orig.). 1991. pap. 123.50x (*91-7192-817-0*, Pub. by Almqv & Wiksell SW) Coronet Bks.

Craftsmanship & the Michigan Union Carpenter. Philip Korth. LC 91-73353. (Illus.). 112p. (C). 1991. lib. bdg. 18.00 (*0-87972-533-8*); pap. text ed. 9.00 (*0-87972-534-6*) Bowling Green Univ.

Craftsmanship in Context: The Development of Ben Jonson's Poetry. Judith K. Gardiner. (Studies in English Literature: No. 110). 208p. 1975. pap. text ed. 29.35 (*90-279-3191-7*) Mouton.

Craftsmen & Interior Decoration in England 1660 - 1820. Geoffrey Beard. LC 81-2648. (Illus.). 320p. 1981. 125.00 (*0-8419-0703-X*) Holmes & Meier.

Craftsmen & Merchants: Essays in South Indian Urbanism. Narayani Gupta. (C). 1993. pap. 7.50 (*0-8364-2861-7*, Pub. by Manohar II) S Asia.

Craftsmen of Colonial America. Sharon Smith. (Social Studies Ser.). 24p. (gr. 5-8). 1977. student ed 5.00 (*0-8209-0258-6*, SS-25) ESP.

Craftsmen of Dionysus: An Approach to Acting. Jerome Rockwood. LC 92-25206. (Acting Ser.). 1992. pap. 18.95 (*1-55783-155-6*) Applause Theatre Bk Pubs.

Craftsmen of Franklin County Pennsylvania, 1784-1884. William S. Bowers. 232p. 1985. 35.00 (*0-318-04635-0*) Irwinton.

Craftsperson Speaks: Artists in Varied Media Discuss Their Crafts. Ed. by Joan Jeffri. LC 91-34696. (Contributions to the Study of Art & Architecture Ser.: No. 1). 248p. 1992. text ed. 49.95 (*0-313-27993-4*, JCP/, Greenwood Pr) Greenwood.

Craftstrip Braiding Projects. 32p. 1959. pap. 1.30 (*0-8395-3169-9*, 33169) BSA.

Craftswomen in Kerdassa, Egypt: Household Production & Reproduction. (Women, Work & Development Ser.: No. 7). iv, 91p. (Orig.). 1991. pap. 14.00 (*92-2-103625-1*) Intl Labour Office.

Craftways: On the Organization of Scholarly Work. Aaron Wildavsky. 168p. 1989. 32.95 (*0-88738-269-X*) Transaction Pubs.

Craftways: On the Organization of Scholarly Work. 2nd enl. ed. Aaron Wildavsky. 172p. (C). 1993. pap. text ed. 18.95 (*1-56000-696-X*) Transaction Pubs.

Craftways Keepsake Calendar, 1995. (Illus.). 44p. 1994. 9.95 (*0-696-20005-8*) Meredith Bks.

*__Crafty Cat Workbasket.__ Julie Hasler. (Illus.). 128p. 1995. pap. 14.95 (*0-7153-0291-4*, Pub. by D & C Pub UK) Sterling.

Crafty Chameleon. Mwenye Hadithi. (Illus.). 32p. (J). (ps-3). 1987. 15.95 (*0-316-33723-4*) Little.

*__Crafty Chameleon.__ Mwenye Hadithi. (Illus.). (J). (ps-3). 1995. pap. 4.95 (*0-316-33771-4*) Little.

Crafty Ideas for Parties. Myrna Daitz. Ed. by Margaret Montgomery. (Crafty Ideas Ser.). (Illus.). 48p. 1993. pap. 4.99 (*1-85015-391-4*) Exley Giftbooks.

Crafty Ideas for Presents. Myrna Daitz. Ed. by Margaret Montgomery. (Crafty Ideas Ser.). (Illus.). 48p. Date not set. pap. 4.99 (*1-85015-390-6*) Exley Giftbooks.

Crafty Ideas from Junk. Myrna Daitz. Ed. by Margaret Montgomery. (Crafty Ideas Ser.). (Illus.). 48p. 1993. pap. 4.99 (*1-85015-393-0*) Exley Giftbooks.

Crafty Ideas from Nature. Myrna Daitz & Shirley Williams. Ed. by Margaret Montgomery. (Crafty Ideas Ser.). (Illus.). 48p. 1993. pap. 4.99 (*1-85015-389-2*) Exley Giftbooks.

Crafty Ideas from Science. Myrna Daitz. Ed. by Margaret Montgomery. (Crafty Ideas Ser.). (Illus.). 48p. 1993. pap. 4.99 (*1-85015-392-2*) Exley Giftbooks.

Crafty Ideas in the Kitchen. Myrna Daitz. Ed. by Margaret Montgomery. (Crafty Ideas Ser.). (Illus.). 48p. Date not set. pap. 4.99 (*1-85015-394-9*) Exley Giftbooks.

Crafty Ideas with Placemats. Pam Aulson. (Illus.). 24p. (J). (gr. 6 up). 1979. pap. 3.00 (*0-9601896-3-7*) Patch As Patch.

Crafty Recycling: Wallpaper Craft from Throw-Aways. Jean Lennander. LC 93-86374. (Illus.). 192p. (Orig.). 1994. pap. 12.95 (*0-9639009-1-9*) Tassel Pr.

*__Crag Guide to England & Wales.__ 2nd ed. David Jones. (Illus.). 224p. 1995. pap. 24.95 (*1-85223-884-4*, Pub. by Crowood Pr UK) Trafalgar.

Cragside, Northumberland. Andrew Saint. (Illus.). 96p. 1992. pap. 10.95 (*0-7078-0148-6*, Pub. by Natl Trust UK) Trafalgar.

Craig Claiborne's Gourmet Diet. Craig Claiborne. 1985. mass mkt. 5.99 (*0-345-33635-6*) Ballantine.

Craig Claiborne's Gourmet Diet. Craig Claiborne. 1992. 7.99 (*0-517-08133-4*) Random Hse Value.

Craig Claiborne's Gourmet Diet. Craig Claiborne & Pierre Franey. 288p. 1980. 18.95 (*0-8129-0914-3*, Times Bks) Random.

Craig Claiborne's Kitchen Primer. Craig Claiborne. LC 68-23951. (Illus.). 1972. 12.95 (*0-394-42071-3*); pap. 8.00 (*0-394-71854-2*) Knopf.

Craig Claiborne's Kitchen Primer: A Basic Cookbook. Illus. by Tom Funk. LC 93-3828. 1993. reprint ed. 7.99 (*0-517-09362-6*, Pub. by Wings Bks) Random Hse Value.

Craig Claiborne's New New York Times Cookbook. Craig Claiborne & Pierre Franey. LC 79-51428. (Illus.). 1979. 29.95 (*0-8129-0835-X*, Times Bks) Random.

Craig Claiborne's Southern Cooking. Craig Claiborne. 1992. 12.99 (*0-517-07757-4*) Random Hse Value.

Craig Claiborne's Southern Cooking. Craig Claiborne. LC 86-14509. 384p. 1987. 23.00 (*0-8129-1599-2*, Times Bks) Random.

*__Craig Claiborne's The New New York Times Cookbook.__ Craig Claiborne & Pierre Franey. LC 94-34265. 1995. 15.99 (*0-517-12235-9*) Random Hse Value.

Craig Claiborne's The New York Times Food Encyclopedia. Comp. by Joan Whitman. LC 94-10846. 1994. write for info. (*0-517-11906-4*) Random Hse Value.

Craig Kauffman. Robert McDonald. 1989. pap. 15.00 (*0-932499-35-X*) Lapis Pr.

Craig Kauffman: A Comprehensive Survey 1957-1980. Robert McDonald. LC 80-70807. (Illus.). 95p. 1980. pap. 12.00 (*0-934418-09-8*) Mus Contemp Art.

Craig Kauffman: A Comprehensive Survey, 1957-1980. Text by Robert McDonald. LC 80-70807. (Illus.). 96p. (Orig.). 1981. pap. 15.00 (*0-911291-06-7*) Fellows Cont Art.

*__Craig Lucas: Collected Works.__ Craig Lucas. 1995. pap. 14.95 (*1-880399-17-2*) Smith & Kraus.

Craig on Theatre. Ed. by J. Michael Walton. (Illus.). 192p. 1988. pap. 19.95 (*0-413-47220-5*, A0556) Heinemann.

Craig Rubadoux: Works on Paper, 1962-1984. Mark Ormond. LC 85-80749. (Illus.). 48p. (Orig.). 1985. pap. 10.00 (*0-916758-20-6*) Ringling Mus Art.

*__Craig Scoffone 1996 Calendar.__ 1995. 14.95 (*1-886788-02-2*) Soho Gall.

Craigdarroch Girl. large type ed. Janis Coles. (Ulverscroft Ser.). 336p. 1994. 20.95 (*0-7089-3017-4*) Ulverscroft.

Craighead Family: A Genealogical Memoir of the Descendants of Rev. Thomas & Margaret Craighead, 1658-1876. James G. Craighead. LC 85-73794. 173p. 1986. reprint ed. 90.00 (*0-916497-71-2*); reprint ed. fiche 6.00 (*0-916497-70-4*) Burnett Micro.

Craighead's Country Reports: 1993 Edition. 95.00 (*0-945994-00-1*) Craighead Pubns.

*__Craighead's International Business Travel & Relocation.__ 7th ed. 1993. 460.00 (*0-8103-9633-5*) Craighead Pubns.

Craighead's International Business, Travel & Relocation Guide to Seventy-One Countries. 6th ed. 1625p. 1991. 425.00 (*0-8103-8455-8*, 071255) Craighead Pubns.

Craighead's International Business Travel & Relocation Guide to 81 Countries, 1994-95, 2 vols., Set. 7th ed. Craighead Publications, Inc., Staff. (International Business Travel-Relocation Ser.). 2676p. 1995. 460.00 (*0-8103-9759-5*, M89356-071256) Gale.

Craighead's Mobile. Erwin Craighead. Ed. by Caldwell Delaney. (Illus.). 221p. 1968. 15.00 (*0-940882-10-8*) HB Pubns.

Craigie College of Education. Brian Daniels & Anne McIntyre. (C). 1989. 40.00 (*1-85098-149-3*, Pub. by Jordanhill College UK) St Mut.

Craigmont Story. Murphy Shewchuck. (Illus.). 80p. (Orig.). pap. 6.95 (*0-88839-980-4*) Hancock House.

Craignish Tales & Others. Ed. by Archibald Campbell. LC 78-144454. (Waifs & Strays of Celtic Tradition: Argyllshire Ser.: No. 1). reprint ed. 29.50 (*0-404-53531-3*) AMS Pr.

Craig's Care of the Newly Born Infant. 8th ed. T. L. Turner et al. (Illus.). 600p. 1988. pap. text ed. 42.00 (*0-443-03342-0*) Churchill.

Crain Adventure: The Making & Building of a Family Publishing Company. Robert Goldsborough. 1992. 29.95 (*0-8442-3485-0*, NTC Busn Bks) NTC Pub Grp.

Crainquebille. Anatole France. Tr. by Winifred Stephens. LC 74-122705. (Short Story Index Reprint Ser.). 1977. 18.95 (*0-8369-3538-1*) Ayer.

Crainquebille, et Plusieurs Autres Recits Profitables. Anatole France. (FRE.). 1992. pap. 10.95 (*0-7859-3246-1*, 2266045547) Fr & Eur.

Crain's Muscle World: Workout Training Log. Rickey D. Crain. (Illus.). 125p. 1995. pap. 10.95 (*0-929994-00-0*) Crains Muscle.

Craken's Field Guide: S. Wars. 1991. 13.00 (*0-87431-118-7*, 40046) West End Games.

Cramps: The Wild Wild World Of. Ian Johnston. (Illus.). 128p. 1990. pap. 19.95 (*0-7119-2350-7*, OP46036) Omnibus NY.

Crampton Hodnet. Barbara Pym. 224p. 1986. pap. 8.95 (*0-452-25816-2*, Plume) NAL-Dutton.

Cranberries. William Jaspersohn. LC 90-41989. (Illus.). 32p. (J). (gr. 2-6). 1991. 14.95 (*0-395-52098-3*) HM.

Cranberries: Fruit of the Bogs. Diane Burns. LC 93-29620. (J). (ps-5). 1994. 19.95 (*0-87614-822-4*, Carolrhoda) Lerner Group.

Cranberries from A to Z: An Educational Picture Book. Ann Kurz. LC 89-61059. (Illus.). 32p. (J). (gr. k-8). 1989. lib. bdg. 14.95 (*0-9622784-0-8*) Cranberry Origs.

Cranberry Autumn. Wende Devlin & Harry Devlin. LC 92-23237. (Illus.). 40p. (J). (gr. k-3). 1993. text ed. 13.95 (*0-02-729936-8*, Four Winds Pr) S&S Childrens.

Cranberry Birthday. Wende Devlin & Harry Devlin. LC 88-294. (Cranberryport Ser.). (Illus.). 40p. (J). (gr. k-3). 1988. text ed. 13.95 (*0-02-729210-X*, Four Winds Pr) S&S Childrens.

Cranberry Birthday. Wende Devlin & Harry Devlin. LC 92-23541. (Illus.). 40p. (J). (ps-3). 1993. reprint ed. pap. 4.95 (*0-689-71697-4*, Aladdin Paperbacks) S&S Childrens.

Cranberry Christmas. Wende Devlin & Harry Devlin. LC 80-16971. (Illus.). 40p. (J). (ps-3). 1984. reprint ed. text ed. 13.95 (*0-02-729900-7*, Four Winds Pr) S&S Childrens.

Cranberry Christmas. Wende Devlin & Harry Devlin. LC 91-1988. (Illus.). 40p. (J). (gr. k-3). 1991. reprint ed. pap. 3.95 (*0-689-71510-2*, Aladdin Paperbacks) S&S Childrens.

Cranberry Connection. Beatrice R. Buszek. 1991. pap. 12.95 (*0-920852-30-0*, Pub. by Nimbus Publishing Ltd CN) Chelsea Green Pub.

Cranberry Cookery, II. 2nd ed. R. Marilyn Schmidt. 86p. 1991. pap. 7.95 (*0-937996-17-3*) Pine Barrens Pr.

Cranberry Easter. Wende Devlin & Harry Devlin. LC 88-21370. (Cranberryport Ser.). (Illus.). 40p. (J). (gr. k-3). 1990. text ed. 13.95 (*0-02-729935-X*, Four Winds Pr) S&S Childrens.

Cranberry Easter. Wende Devlin & Harry Devlin. LC 92-23537. (Illus.). 40p. (J). (ps-3). 1993. reprint ed. pap. 4.95 (*0-689-71698-2*, Aladdin Paperbacks) S&S Childrens.

*__Cranberry First Day of School.__ Wende Devlin & Harry Devlin. LC 94-39805. (Tales from Cranberryport Ser.). (J). 1995. write for info. (*0-689-80122-X*, Aladdin Paperbacks) S&S Childrens.

Cranberry Halloween. Wende Devlin & Harry Devlin. LC 81-22134. (Illus.). 40p. (J). (gr. k-3). 1984. text ed. 13.95 (*0-02-729910-4*, Four Winds Pr) S&S Childrens.

Cranberry Halloween. Wende Devlin & Harry Devlin. LC 89-18666. (Cranberryport Ser.). (Illus.). 40p. (J). (gr. k-3). 1990. reprint ed. pap. 3.95 (*0-689-71428-9*, Aladdin Paperbacks) S&S Childrens.

Cranberry Harvest: A History of Cranberry Growing in Massachusetts. Ed. by Joseph D. Thomas. (Illus.). 224p. 1990. text ed. 37.95 (*0-932027-10-5*); pap. text ed. 17.95 (*0-932027-11-3*) Spinner Pubns.

*__Cranberry Lost at the Fair.__ Wende Devlin & Harry Devlin. LC 94-39806. (Tales from Cranberryport Ser.). 1995. write for info. (*0-689-80123-8*, Aladdin Paperbacks) S&S Childrens.

Cranberry Moving Day. Harry Devlin & Wende Devlin. LC 93-36279. (Tales from Cranberryport Ser.). (Illus.). 24p. (J). (ps-1). 1994. pap. 2.95 (*0-689-71777-6*, Aladdin Paperbacks) S&S Childrens.

Cranberry Mystery. Wende Devlin & Harry Devlin. LC 85-16015. (Illus.). 40p. (J). (ps-3). 1984. reprint ed. text ed. 13.95 (*0-02-729920-1*, Four Winds Pr) S&S Childrens.

Cranberry Ridge Tales. Sharon Varney. 72p. (Orig.). (J). (gr. 7 up). 1986. pap. 7.95 (*0-685-17323-2*) S Varney.

Cranberry Smoke. Michael Hood. LC 89-91137. (Orig.). 1989. pap. 20.00 (*0-9622300-0-6*) Snocks Pr.

An Asterisk (*) at the beginning of an entry indicates that the title is appearing in BIP for the first time.

Cranberry Summer. Wende Devlin & Harry Devlin. LC 90-24560. (Cranberryport Ser.). (Illus.). 40p. (J). (gr. k-3). 1992. text ed. 13.95 (0-02-729181-2, Four Winds Pr) S&S Childrens.

Cranberry Tales. Frank L. Jones. LC 88-83610. 104p. 1988. pap. 9.95 (0-937226-05-X) Laugh Cat.

Cranberry Tea Room Cookbook. Richard Martinez. Ed. by Gloria Chavez. LC 92-35047. 144p. 1992. lib. bdg. 27.00x (0-8095-2950-5); pap. 17.00x (0-8095-3950-0) Borgo Pr.

Cranberry Thanksgiving. Wende Devlin & Harry Devlin. LC 80-17070. (Illus.). 48p. (J). (ps-3). 1984. reprint ed. text ed. 13.95 (0-02-729930-9, Four Winds Pr) S&S Childrens.

Cranberry Thanksgiving. Wende Devlin & Harry Devlin. LC 89-18642. (Cranberryport Ser.). (Illus.). 40p. (J). (gr. k-3). 1990. reprint ed. pap. 4.95 (0-689-71429-7, Aladdin Paperbacks) S&S Childrens.

Cranberry Trip to the Dentist. Wende Devlin & Harry Delvin. LC 93-36280. (Tales from Cranberryport Ser.). (J). (ps-1). 1994. pap. 2.95 (0-689-71779-2, Mac Bks Young Read) S&S Childrens.

Cranberry Valentine. Wende Devlin & Harry Devlin. LC 85-24047. (Illus.). 40p. (J). (gr. k-3). 1986. text ed. 14.95 (0-02-729200-2, Four Winds Pr) S&S Childrens.

Cranberry Valentine. Wende Devlin & Harry Devlin. LC 91-6915. (Illus.). 40p. (J). (gr. k-3). 1992. reprint ed. pap. 3.95 (0-689-71509-9, Aladdin Paperbacks) S&S Childrens.

Cranbrook Design: The New Discourse. Hugh Aldersey-Williams & Daralice Bales. LC 90-34704. (Illus.). 208p. 1990. 50.00 (0-8478-1252-9); pap. 35.00 (0-8478-1253-7) Rizzoli Intl.

Cranbrook Reflections: A Culinary Collection. Ed. by Geri Rinschler. (Illus.). 208p. 1991. 19.95 (0-9628714-0-0) Cranbrook Hse.

Cranbrook U. S. A. Painting & Sculpture. 51p. 1982. pap. text ed. 8.00 (1-880337-07-X) Cranbrook Acad.

Crandall: Elder John Crandall of Rhode Island & His Descendants. J. C. Crandall. 797p. 1991. reprint ed. lib. bdg. 119.00 (0-8328-1806-2); reprint ed. pap. 129.00 (0-8328-1807-0) Higginson Bk Co.

Crane. Gabriel Horn. LC 88-12031. (Wildlife Habits & Habitats Ser.). (Illus.). 48p. (J). (gr. 5). 1988. text ed. 12.95 (0-89686-393-X, Crstwood Hse) Silver Burdett Pr.

Crane Girl. Veronika M. Charles. LC 92-50843. (Illus.). 32p. (J). (ps-1). 1993. 14.95 (0-531-05485-3) Orchard Bks Watts.

Crane Hazards & Their Prevention. David V. MacCollum. LC 93-39816. (Illus.). 172p. (Orig.). 1993. pap. 34.95 (0-939874-95-4, 4348) ASSE.

Crane Log: A Documentary Life of Stephen Crane. Stanley Wertheim & Paul Sorrentino. LC 93-8872. (Reference Ser.). 554p. 1993. text ed. 75.00 (0-8161-7292-7, Hall Reference) Macmillan.

Crane Morning. Deborah R. Huso. (Illus.). 38p. 1993. pap. text ed. 6.95 (1-56315-025-5) Sterling Hse.

Crane Music: A Natural History of American Cranes. Paul A. Johnsgard. LC 90-20683. (Illus.). 160p. (C). 1991. 19.95 (1-56098-051-6) Smithsonian.

Crane Operation & Preventive Maintenance. F. David McCleskey, Jr. (Illus.). 104p. 1983. pap. text ed. 20.00 (0-934114-43-9, BK-101) Marine Educ.

Crane Operator (Any Motive Power Except Steam) (AMPES) Jack Rudman. (Career Examination Ser.: C-1749). 1994. pap. 27.95 (0-8373-1749-5) Nat Learn.

Crane Reading System, Practice Bks, A-J. Barbara J. Crane. Incl. Practice Book A. 1977. pap. text ed. 4.75 (0-89075-052-1); Practice Book B. 1977. pap. text ed. 4.75 (0-89075-054-8); Practice Book C. 1977. pap. text ed. 4.75 (0-89075-055-6); Practice Book D. 1977. pap. text ed. 4.75 (0-89075-056-4); Practice Book E. 1977. pap. text ed. 4.75 (0-89075-057-2); Practice Book F. 1977. pap. 4.95 (0-89075-058-0); Practice Book G. 1977. pap. 4.95 (0-89075-059-9); Practice Book H. 1977. pap. 4.95 (0-89075-060-2); Practice Book I. 1977. pap. 4.95 (0-89075-061-0); Practice Book J. 1977. pap. 4.95 (0-89075-062-9); (Illus.). (gr. k-2). 1977. Set pap. text ed. write for info. (0-318-51460-5) Bilingual Ed Serv.

Crane Reading System in Spanish. Incl. Level F. Libro De Lectura. 7.55 (0-89075-185-4); Level F. Libro De Ejercicios. 5.95 (0-89075-175-7); Level G. Libro De Ejercicios. 5.95 (0-89075-176-5); Level H. Libro De Ejercicios. 5.95 (0-89075-177-3); Level I. Libro De Lectura. 8.72 (0-89075-188-9); Level I. Libro De Ejercicios. 5.95 (0-89075-178-1); Level J. Libro De Lectura. 9.98 (0-89075-189-7); Level J. Libro De Ejercicios. 5.95 (0-89075-180-3); Level K. Libro De Lectura. 9.98 (0-89075-190-0); Level K. Libro De Ejercicios. 5.95 (0-89075-181-1); 1978p. Levels F-K Guidebook. 27.50 (0-89075-202-8) Bilingual Ed Serv.

Crane Research Around the World. Ed. by J. C. Lewis & H. Masatomi. (Illus.). 259p. 1981. pap. 17.00 (0-318-14550-2) Intl Crane.

Crane-Style Chi Gong & Its Therapeutic Effects. Daoshing Ni. (Illus.). 68p. (Orig.). 1984. pap. 10.95 (0-937064-10-6) SevenStar Comm.

Crane Wife. Sumiko Yagawa. Orig. Title: Tsuru-Nyobo. (J). (ps-3). 1992. 18.25 (0-8446-6589-4) Peter Smith.

Crane Wife. Sumiko Yagawa. Tr. by Katherine Paterson. LC 80-29278. Orig. Title: Tsuru-Nyobo. (Illus.). 32p. (J). (gr. k up). 1987. 4.95 (0-688-07048-5, Mulberry) Morrow.

***Cranes.** Patricia Armentrout & David Armentrout. LC 95-3979. (Heavy Equipment Ser.). (J). 1995. write for info. (1-55916-133-7) Rourke Bk Co.

Cranes & Derricks. 2nd ed. H. I. Shapiro et al. 1991. text ed. 55.00 (0-07-056422-1) McGraw.

Cranes, Dump Trucks, Bulldozers & Other Building Machines. Terry Jennings. LC 92-23370. (How Things Work Ser.). (J). 1993. 10.95 (1-85697-866-4, Kingfisher LKC); pap. 5.95 (1-85697-865-6, Kingfisher LKC) LKC.

Crane's Gift: A Japanese Folktale. Illus. by Megumi Biddle. LC 94-7573. 32p. 1994. 16.00 (1-56957-932-6) Barefoot Bks.

Crane's Rebound. Alison Jackson. LC 90-20648. (Illus.). 128p. (J). (gr. 3-7). 1991. 12.95 (0-525-44722-9, DCB) Dutton Child Bks.

Crane's Wedding Blue Book. Ed. by Steven L. Feinberg. 144p. (Orig.). 1993. pap. 12.00 (0-671-79641-0, Fireside) S&S Trade.

Cranford. Elizabeth C. Gaskell. Ed. by Elizabeth Watson. (World's Classics Paperback Ser.). 1982. pap. 4.95 (0-19-281531-8) OUP.

Cranford. braille ed. Elizabeth Gaskell. 463p. 1993. vinyl bd. 37.04 (1-56956-436-1, BR9152) W A T Braille.

***Cranford & Mr. Harrison's Confessions.** Elizabeth Gaskell. Ed. by Graham Handley. 384p. (Orig.). 1995. pap. 5.95 (0-460-87553-1, Everyman's Classic Lib) C E Tuttle.

Cranford, & Other Tales. Elizabeth C. Gaskell. LC 74-150475. (Short Story Index Reprint Ser.). 1977. reprint ed. 26.95 (0-8369-3815-1) Ayer.

Cranford-Cousin Phillis. Elizabeth C. Gaskell. Ed. by Peter Keating. (English Library). 1977. mass mkt. 6.95 (0-14-043104-7, Penguin Classics) Viking Penguin.

***Cranford's Light Division.** Ian Fletcher. (Illus.). 248p. 1994. 27.50 (1-885119-06-2) Sarpedon.

Cranial & Facial Adjusting Step-by-Step: Twenty-Two Lessons, 2 vols. Calvin Cottam. (Illus.). 439p. 1985. 116.00 (0-685-12287-5); 126.00 (0-917628-11-X); write for info. (0-917628-07-1) Coraco.

Cranial & Facial Adjusting Technique. abr. ed. 170p. 1988. spiral bd. 49.00 (0-318-37557-5) Coraco.

Cranial & Postcranial Skeletal Remains from Easter Island. Rupert I. Murrill. LC 67-10609. (Illus.). 113p. reprint ed. pap. 32.30 (0-8357-8854-7, 2033274) Bks Demand.

Cranial & Spinal Magnetic Resonance Imaging: An Atlas & Guide. Ed. by David L. Daniels et al. 332p. 1987. text ed. 157.50 (0-88167-185-1) Raven.

Cranial Computed Tomography in Infants & Children. Eric N. Faerber. (Clinics in Developmental Medicine Ser.: No. 93). (Illus.). 237p. (C). 1991. 54.95 (0-521-41213-7, Pub. by Mc Keith Pr UK) Cambridge U Pr.

***Cranial Guitar.** Bob Kaufman. 192p. (Orig.). 1996. pap. 12.95 (1-56689-038-1) Coffee Hse.

Cranial Haemorrhage in the Full-Term Newborn Infant. Ed. by Paul Govaert. (Clinics in Developmental Medicine Ser.: No. 129). (Illus.). 300p. (C). 1994. 64.95 (0-521-45149-3) Cambridge U Pr.

Cranial Magnetic Resonance Imaging. Allen D. Elster. LC 87-22428. (Illus.). 435p. reprint ed. pap. 124.00 (0-7837-6233-X, 2045947) Bks Demand.

Cranial Manipulation Roots References. 113p. 1984. 18.00 (0-685-01217-4) Coraco.

Cranial MRI: A Teaching File Approach. John H. Bisese. (Illus.). 382p. 1991. 95.00 (0-07-005405-3) Hlth Prof Div.

Cranial MRI & CT. 3rd ed. S. Howard Lee et al. (Illus.). 880p. 1992. text ed. 169.00 (0-07-037508-9) Hlth Prof Div.

***Cranial Nerves: Anatomy, Imaging, Vascularisation.** 2nd enl. rev. ed. Andre LeBlanc. Tr. by David Le Vay. LC 95-8410. Orig. Title: Anatomy & Imaging of the Cranial Nerves. (Illus.). 1995. write for info. (0-387-58702-0) Spr-Verlag.

Cranial Nerves: Gross Anatomy & Clinical Comments. Wilson-Pauwels et al. (Illus.). 178p. (C). 1988. 32.95 (1-55664-010-2) Mosby Yr Bk.

Cranial Nerves of the Coelacanth, Latimeria Chalumnae - Osteichtyes: Sarcoterygii: Actinistia - Comparisons with Other Cranista: Actinistia - Comparisons with Other Craniata. R. G. Northcutt & W. E. Bemis. (Journal: Reprint of Brain, Behavior & Evolution: Vol. 42, Suppl. 1, 1993). (Illus.). x, 76p. 1993. 74.50 (3-8055-5802-3) S Karger.

Cranial Neuroimaging & Clinical Neuroanatomy: Computed Tomography & Magnetic Resonance Imaging. 2nd rev. ed. Hans-Joachim Kretschmann & Wolfgang Weinrich. LC 92-49240. (Illus.). 1993. 229.00 (0-86577-392-0) Thieme Med Pubs.

Cranial Ultrasonography of Infants. Diane S. Babcock & Bokyung K. Han. LC 81-10340. 263p. reprint ed. pap. 75.00 (0-317-42400-9, 2056073) Bks Demand.

Cranicocerebral Trauma. Ed. by H. Krayenbuehl et al. (Progress in Neurological Surgery Ser.: Vol. 10). (Illus.). xiv, 402p. 1981. 238.50 (3-8055-0134-X) S Karger.

Craniofacial Anomalies. Ross. 1991. 79.50 (1-55664-082-X) Mosby Yr Bk.

Craniofacial Anomalies: An Interdisciplinary Approach. Brodsky et al. 272p. 1991. 61.00 (1-55664-357-8) Mosby Yr Bk.

***Craniofacial Anomalies: Growth & Development from a Surgical Perspective.** Ed. by James Goodrich & Craig D. Hall. (Illus.). 320p. 1994. 149.00 (0-86577-522-2) Thieme Med Pubs.

Craniofacial Biology. Ed. by D. S. Carlson. (Craniofacial Growth Ser.: Vol. 10). (Illus.). 269p. 1981. 43.00 (0-929921-07-0) UM CHGD.

Craniofacial Deformities. D. J. David et al. (Illus.). x, 147p. 1989. 160.00 (0-387-96969-1, 2655) Spr-Verlag.

Craniofacial Embryology. 4th ed. Geoffrey H. Sperber. (Dental Practitioners' Handbook Ser.: No. 15). (Illus.). 256p. 1989. pap. 47.50 (0-7236-1715-5, Pub. by John Wright UK) Buttrwrth-Heinemann.

Craniofacial Growth During Adolescence. Ed. by D. S. Carlson & K. A. Ribbens. (Craniofacial Growth Ser.: Vol. 20). (Illus.). 226p. 1987. 45.00 (0-929921-16-X) UM CHGD.

Craniofacial Growth in Man. R. E. Moyers & W. M. Krogman. 1971. 157.00 (0-08-016331-9, Pub. by Pergamon Repr UK) Franklin.

Craniofacial Growth Series. write for info. (0-929921-00-3) UM CHGD.

Craniofacial Growth Theory & Orthodontic Treatment. Enlow et al. Ed. by David S. Carlson. (Craniofacial Growth Ser.: Vol. 23). (Illus.). 235p. 1990. 49.00 (0-929921-19-4) UM CHGD.

Craniofacial Identification. M. Yasar Iscan & Richard P. Helmer. 238p. 1993. text ed. 69.95 (0-471-56078-2) Wiley.

Craniofacial Malformations. Ed. by M. Stricker et al. (Illus.). 656p. 1990. text ed. 249.95 (0-443-03924-0) Churchill.

Craniofacial Morphogenesis & Dysmorphogenesis. Ed. by K. L. Vig & A. R. Burdi. (Craniofacial Growth Ser.: Vol. 21). (Illus.). 221p. 1988. 39.00 (0-929921-17-8) UM CHGD.

Craniofacial Morphology of Pan Paniscus. D. L. Cramer. Ed. by F. S. Szalay. (Contributions to Primatology Ser.: Vol. 10). (Illus.). 1977. 38.50 (3-8055-2391-2) S Karger.

Craniofacial Morphology of the Sulawesi Macaques: Multivariate Analysis As a Tool in Systematics. Gene H. Albrecht. (Contributions to Primatology Ser.: Vol. 13). (Illus.). 1977. 59.25 (3-8055-2694-6) S Karger.

Craniofacial Radiological Diagnosis & Management, Vol. 1. 1988. 195.00 (0-938705-01-6) Radio Mgmt Comns Ltd.

Craniofacial Radiological Diagnosis & Management, Vol. 2. Zhao-ju Zou. Ed. by R. F. Sloan et al. (Illus.). 60p. (CHI.). (C). 1989. text ed. 30.00 (0-685-26560-9) Intl Scientific.

Craniofacial Surgery. Ernesto P. Caronni. 620p. 1985. 89.50 (0-316-12877-5) Little.

Craniofacial Surgery. Ed. by D. Marchac. (Illus.). 540p. 1987. 266.00 (0-387-16924-5) Spr-Verlag.

Craniographic Positioning with Comparison Studies. Don Q Paris. LC 82-14074. (Illus.). 162p. 1983. 25.00 (0-8036-6768-X) Davis Co.

Craniology of the North Pacific Coast. Bruno Oetteking. LC 73-3533. (Jessup North Pacific Expedition. Publications: No. 11). reprint ed. 82.50 (0-404-58111-0) AMS Pr.

Craniomandibular Disorders: Guidelines for Evaluation, Diagnosis, & Management. American Academy of Craniomandibular Disorders Staff. Ed. by Charles McNeill. 54p. 1990. pap. text ed. 18.00 (0-86715-227-3) Quint Pub Co.

Craniomandibular Disorders & Orofacial Pain: Diagnosis & Management. Iven Klineberg. (Illus.). 1992. 80.00 (0-7236-0989-6) Buttrwrth-Heinemann.

Craniomandibular Muscles: Their Role in Function & Form. Arthur Miller. (Illus.). 256p. 1991. 121.00 (0-8493-4873-0, QP325) CRC Pr.

Craniomaxillofacial Fractures: Principles of Internal Fixation Using the AO-ASIF Techniques. Alex M. Greenberg. LC 92-2423. 340p. 1993. 125.00 (0-387-97902-6) Spr-Verlag.

Craniometric Relationships among Plains Indians: Cultural-Historical & Evolutionary Implications, No. 34. Patrick J. Key. 204p. 1983. pap. 21.00x (0-87049-455-4) U of Tenn Pr.

Craniometry & Biological Distance. Judith B. Droessler. LC 81-11009. (Research Ser.: No. 1). (Illus.). 270p. 1981. 15.00 (0-942118-11-1, E78.13D76); pap. 10.00 (0-942118-12-X) Ctr Amer Arche.

Craniometry of New Guinea see Skeletal Material from San Jose Ruin, British Honduras

Craniometry of Southern New England Indians. Marian V. Knight. (Connecticut Academy of Arts & Sciences Ser., Trans.: Vol. 4). 1915. pap. 150.00 (0-685-22869-X) Elliots Bks.

Craniometry of the Orchid Site Ossuary, Fort Erie, Ontario. H. James Birx. (Monographs in Anthropology). (Illus.). 60p. (C). 1991. pap. 11.95 (0-9615462-5-5) Persimmon NY.

Craniopathy: (Cranial Adjusting) 93 Technics in 10 Folios. 1975. write for info. (0-917628-01-2) Coraco.

Craniopathy Story: Facsimile of Classic 1936 Edition. (Illus.). 1988. 3.00 (0-917628-09-8) Coraco.

***Craniopharyngioma: The Answer.** Ed. by F. J. Epstein & M. H. Handler. (Journal: Pediatric Neurosurgery Ser.: Vol. 21, Supplement 1, 1994). (Illus.). iv, 132p. 1994. pap. 54.50 (3-8055-6048-6) S Karger.

Cranioplasty. D. Stula. (Illus.). 130p. 1985. 60.00 (0-387-81808-1) Spr-Verlag.

Craniosacral Therapy. John Upledger & Jon Vredevoogd. LC 82-82505. (Illus.). 381p. 1983. 49.50 (0-939616-01-7) Eastland.

Craniosacral Therapy II: Beyond the Dura. John E. Upledger. LC 82-82505. (Illus.). 260p. (C). 1987. text ed. 45.00 (0-939616-05-X) Eastland.

Craniospinal Magnetic Resonance Imaging. Pomeranz. 624p. 1989. text ed. 179.00 (0-7216-2428-6) Saunders.

Craniospinal Trauma. Lawrence Pitts & Franklin Wagner. Ed. by Blaisdell & Trunkey. (Trauma Management Ser.: Vol. 5). (Illus.). 280p. 1989. text ed. 89.00 (0-86577-322-X) Thieme Med Pubs.

Craniosynostosis. Ed. by Guido Galli. 280p. 1984. 186.00 (0-8493-5206-1, RJ482, CRC Reprint) Franklin.

Craniovertebral Junction & Its Abnormalities. John C. VanGilder et al. (Illus.). 336p. 1987. 65.00 (0-87993-250-3) Futura Pub.

Crank 'Emup! Brilliant Sales Contests & Bright Ideas to Turn on Your Team & Turn up Results. Bruce Fuller. (Business Ser.). 176p. (Orig.). 1995. pap. 10.95 (0-88908-799-7) Self-Counsel Pr.

Crank It Up!, Incl. disk. Keith Aleshire. LC 93-8194. 1993. disk, pap. 16.95 (1-56205-173-3) New Riders Pub.

Crank Letters. Kirby Congdon. LC 85-61564. 84p. (Orig.). 1986. pap. 10.00 (0-912292-79-2) The Smith.

Crankbaits: A Guide to Trolling & Casting Depths of 200 Popular Lures. Mike McCelland. (Illus.). 84p. 1990. spiral bd. write for info. (0-318-66847-5) Fishing Enterprises.

Cranking Out Adventure; A Bike Leader's Guide to Trial & Error Touring. Karl E. Rohnke. 46p. 1977. pap. 4.50 (0-934387-04-4) Project Advent.

Cranks & Shadows. K. C. Constantine. 320p. 1995. 19.95 (0-89296-543-6) Mysterious Pr.

***Cranks & Shadows.** K. C. Constantine. 320p. 1996. mass mkt. 5.99 (0-446-40353-9, Mysterious Paperbk) Warner Bks.

Cranks, Quarks, & the Cosmos. Jeremy Bernstein. 240p. 1994. reprint ed. pap. 12.00 (0-465-01449-6) Basic.

Crankshaft. Tom Batiuk & Chuck Ayers. 128p. 1992. pap. 8.95 (0-8362-1889-2) Andrews & McMeel.

Cranky Blue Crab: A Tale in Verse. Dawn L. Watkins. Ed. by Anne Smith. (Pennant Ser.). (Illus.). 32p. (Orig.). (J). (gr. k-1). 1990. pap. 4.95 (0-89084-506-9) Bob Jones Univ Pr.

Cranmer. Hilaire Belloc. LC 72-4495. (English Biography Ser.: No. 31). 1972. reprint ed. lib. bdg. 75.00 (0-8383-1610-7) M S G Haskell Hse.

Crannied Wall: Women, Religion, & the Arts in Early Modern Europe. Ed. by Craig A. Monson. (Studies in Medieval & Early Modern Civilization). (Illus.). 300p. (C). 1992. text ed. 42.50 (0-472-10271-0) U of Mich Pr.

Crannogs of Scotland: Lake Dwellings in a Landscape. Ian Morrison. 80p. (Orig.). 1983. pap. 16.50 (0-85224-472-X, Pub. by Edinburgh U Pr UK) Col U Pr.

Crapo Certain Comeovers, 2 vols. H. H. Crapo. 1044p. 1989. reprint ed. lib. bdg. 147.00 (0-8328-0440-1); reprint ed. pap. 139.00 (0-8328-0441-X) Higginson Bk Co.

Crappie! Jim Robbins. 1991. 21.95 (1-879034-02-6) MS River Pub.

Crappie: A Fish for All Seasons. rev. ed. Dan D. Gapen, Sr. (Illus.). 120p. 1986. reprint ed. pap. text ed. 7.95 (0-932985-02-5) Whitewater Pubns.

Crappie Tactics. Larry Larsen. LC 93-79800. (Freshwater Library). (Illus.). 160p. (Orig.). 1993. pap. text ed. 9.95 (0-936513-40-3) Larsens Outdoor.

Crappie Wisdom: An In-Fisherman Handbook of Strategies. Al Lindners et al. (Illus.). 258p. (Orig.). 1985. pap. 11.95 (0-9605254-4-0) In-Fisherman.

Craps. Tony Korfman. (Playing to Win Ser.). 56p. (Orig.). 1985. pap. text ed. 2.50 (0-934047-01-4) Gaming Bks Intl.

Craps: Pressing Your Luck. Robert Spira. 32p. (Orig.). 1982. pap. 2.95 (0-911455-01-9) Quartz Pr.

***Craps: Take the Money & Run.** Henry J. Tamburin. LC 95-67044. 144p. 1995. pap. 11.95 (0-912177-10-1) Res Serv Unltd.

Craps by the Numbers. Alfred Di Mauro. (By the Numbers Ser.). (Illus.). 112p. (Orig.). 1994. pap. 9.95 (0-9631961-3-8) Sibylline Bks.

Craps Made Simple. rev. ed. Thomas B. Gallagher. (Illus.). 26p. 1992. pap. 6.95 (0-938706-05-5) Thomas Co.

***Craps System Tester.** Erick St. Germain. Ed. by Stan Johnson. 295p. (Orig.). 1994. 24.95 (0-9640595-7-6) Zumma Pubng.

Craps: There Are No Secrets to This Game! How Craps Is Played. Joubert W. Olson. 156p. 1994. pap. 19.95 (1-883067-24-3) South Shore.

***Crapshoot.** Jules Witcover. 1994. pap. 4.99 (0-517-09861-X) Random.

Crash! Dick Allen. 1989. write for info. (0-318-64980-2) HM.

Crash. J. G. Ballard. 1994. pap. 12.00 (0-374-52412-2, Noonday) FS&G.

Crash. Sarah A. Harris. 1992. pap. 8.95 (1-55673-421-2, 7901) CSS OH.

Crash. Lukyan Kary. (Ukrainian Ser.). 564p. 1985. 15.25 (0-914834-35-5) Smoloskyp.

Crash. Lisetor. 1985. pap. 2.50 (0-87879-297-X) Acad Therapy.

CRASH: Computer Assisted Hardcopy. Photos by Ralph Knasinski. (Illus.). 84p. (Orig.). (C). 1989. pap. 12.50 (1-880763-04-4) Mus Beloit Coll.

Crash & Its Aftermath: A History of Securities Markets in the United States, 1929-1933. Barrie A. Wigmore. LC 84-8961. (Contributions in Economics & Economic History Ser.: No. 58). (Illus.). xx, 731p. 1985. text ed. 55.00 (0-313-24574-6, WCF/) Greenwood.

***Crash at Corona: The Definitive Study of the Roswell Incident.** Stanton Friedman. 1994. pap. 10.00 (1-56924-863-X) Marlowe & Co.

Crash Avoidance. 1983. 19.00 (0-89883-315-9, SP544) Soc Auto Engineers.

Crash! Bang! Boom! Peter Spier. (J). (ps-1). 1990. 5.95 (0-385-26569-7) Doubleday.

Crash Cases: A Hands-On Guide to Vehicle Collision Litigation. LC 89-45148. 343p. 1989. pap. 42.95 (0-89707-432-7, 519-0087-01) Amer Bar Assn.

Crash Club. limited ed. Henry G. Felsen. 208p. (YA). (gr. 9-12). 1990. boxed, pap. 25.00 (0-917473-06-X) G P Pub MI.

Crash Course. Nicole Davidson. 224p. 1990. mass mkt. 3.99 (0-380-75964-0, Flare) Avon.

Crash Course for Study Skills: Setting Goals, Managing Time, Listening, Taking Notes, Studying, Taking Tests, Learning Attitude, Learning Style. Marty Soper. (gr. 7 up). 1993. student ed, spiral bd. 27.95 (1-55999-256-5) LinguiSystems.

***Crash Course in Access Basic.** Wyatt. 1994. pap. 19.99 (1-56529-927-2) Que.

Crash Course in Borland C Plus Plus 4.0. Que Development Staff. 1994. pap. 19.99 (1-56529-773-3) Que.

Crash Course in C. Paul J. Perry. (Illus.). 250p. (Orig.). 1993. pap. 16.95 (1-56529-149-2) Que.

An Asterisk (*) at the beginning of an entry indicates that the title is appearing in BIP for the first time.

1673

***Crash Course in C.** 2nd ed. Que Development Group Staff & Ed Toupin. (Illus.). 1994. pap. 19.99 (*1-56529-940-X*) Que.

Crash Course in CC: Mail for DOS. Que Development Group Staff. (Illus.). 288p. (Orig.). 1993. pap. 12.95 (*1-56529-527-7*) Que.

Crash Course in CC: Mail for Windows. Que Development Group Staff. (Illus.). 288p. (Orig.). 1993. pap. 12.95 (*1-56529-528-5*) Que.

Crash Course in Composition. 4th ed. Elizabeth McMahan. 256p. 1989. pap. text ed. write for info. (*0-07-045478-7*); With Readings. pap. text ed. write for info. (*0-07-045479-5*) McGraw.

***Crash Course in dBase for Windows Programming.** Chris Green. (Illus.). (Orig.). 1994. pap. 19.99 (*1-56529-938-8*) Que.

Crash Course in DOS. Que Development Group Staff. (Illus.). 256p. (Orig.). 1993. pap. 12.95 (*1-56529-529-3*) Que.

Crash Course in Microsoft Mail for Windows. Que Development Group Staff. (Illus.). 288p. (Orig.). 1993. pap. 12.95 (*1-56529-526-9*) Que.

Crash Course in Netware 4.0. Keith Brown. (Illus.). 400p. (Orig.). 1993. pap. 24.95 (*1-56529-285-5*) Que.

***Crash Course in Q Basic.** 2nd ed. Que Development Group Staff & Ed Toupin. (Illus.). 1994. pap. 19.99 (*1-56529-939-6*) Que.

Crash Course in QBasic. Greg Perry. (Illus.). 250p. (Orig.). 1993. pap. 16.95 (*1-56529-165-4*) Que.

Crash Course in Turbo C Plus Plus. Que Development Group Staff. (Illus.). 250p. (Orig.). 1993. pap. 16.95 (*1-56529-168-9*) Que.

Crash Course in Visual BASIC. Que Development Staff. 1994. pap. 19.99 (*1-56529-765-2*) Que.

Crash Course in Windows. Debbie Walkowski. (Illus.). 256p. (Orig.). 1993. pap. 12.95 (*1-56529-530-7*) Que.

Crash Course Manual. 96p. 15.00 (*0-87431-153-5*, 12020) West End Games.

Crash Course on the New Age Movement: Describing & Evaluating a Growing Social Force. Elliott Miller. 1989. 14.99 (*0-8010-6251-9*); pap. 10.99 (*0-8010-6248-9*) Baker Bk.

Crash Diet. Jill McCorkle. 1993. mass mkt. 4.99 (*0-449-22222-5*, Crest) Fawcett.

Crash Diet: Stories by Jill McCorkle. Jill McCorkle. Ed. by Shannon Ravenel. 256p. 1992. 16.95 (*0-945575-75-0*) Algonquin Bks.

Crash, Fire & Rescue Handbook. Charles Bellomo & John F. Lynch. LC 92-46755. (Training Manual Ser.). 94p. (Orig.). 1982. pap. text ed. 10.95 (*0-89100-250-2*, EA-250-2) IAP.

Crash in the Jungle. A. Alderson. (Spirals Ser.). (C). 1989. 25.00 (*0-09-136441-8*, Pub. by S Thornes Pubs UK) St Mut.

Crash Injuries: How & Why They Happen: A Primer For Anyone Who Cares About People in Cars. 1993. write for info. (*0-9637057-0-9*) Hyde Assocs.

Crash Landing. Francine Pascal. (Sweet Valley High Ser.: No. 20). 1985. 3.25 (*0-553-27454-6*) Bantam.

Crash-Landing. Peter Spielberg. LC 84-8126. 224p. 1985. pap. 7.95 (*0-914590-91-X*) Fiction Coll.

Crash Landing: Surviving a Business Crisis. Richard O. Jacobs. LC 90-84800. 316p. 1991. 24.95 (*0-944435-12-2*) Glenbridge Pub.

***Crash of Rhinoceroses: A Dictionary of Collective Nouns.** Rex Collings. (Illus.). 191p. 1995. pap. 11.95 (*1-55921-141-5*) Moyer Bell.

Crash of Rhinoceroses: A Dictionary of Collective Nouns. Rex Collings. LC 93-1053. (Illus.). 191p. 1995. reprint ed. 18.95 (*1-55921-096-6*) Moyer Bell.

Crash of Suburbia: The Coming Boom of Small Towns. rev. ed. Jack Lessinger. (Illus.). 1990. write for info. (*0-318-66598-0*) Socioeconomics.

Crash of 1929. Ronald Migneco & Timothy L. Biel. LC 89-33556. (World Disasters Ser.). (Illus.). 64p. (J). (gr. 5-8). 1989. lib. bdg. 14.95 (*1-56006-007-7*) Lucent Bks.

Crash of 1987. Gordon Hall. 247p. 1988. reprint ed. 25.00 (*0-9619878-2-0*); reprint ed. pap. write for info. (*0-9619878-0-4*) Johnson Cnty Pubs.

Crash of '79. large type ed. Paul E. Erdman. 481p. 1981. 23.95 (*0-7089-8017-1*, Trail West Pubs) Ulverscroft.

Crash Put Simply: October, 1987. Ruben J. Dunn & John Morris. LC 88-17992. 186p. 1988. text ed. 49.95 (*0-275-93133-1*, Praeger Pubs) Greenwood.

CrashCourse. Wilhelmina Baird. 288p. (Orig.). 1993. mass mkt. 4.99 (*0-441-12163-2*) Ace Bks.

***CrashCourse In Accounting Fundamentals.** HighText Multimedia Development Group. 1995. cd-rom, pap. 39.95 (*1-878707-25-6*) HighText.

***CrashCourse In Differential Calculus.** Jack W. Lewis & HighText Multimedia Development Group. 1995. cd-rom, pap. 39.95 (*1-878707-24-8*) HighText.

***CrashCourse In Integral Calculus.** Jack W. Lewis. 1995. cd-rom, pap. 39.95 (*1-878707-28-0*) HighText.

***CrashCourse In Introductory Algebra.** HighText Multimedia Development Group. 1995. cd-rom, pap. 39.95 (*1-878707-27-2*) HighText.

Crashcourse in Statistics: An Innovative Book Multimedia Approach to Collecting, Organizing. Joseph J. Carr. 1994. pap. 29.95 (*1-878707-18-3*) HighText.

Crashes & Panics: Lessons from History. Eugene N. White. 260p. 1991. pap. 17.00 (*1-55623-688-3*) Irwin Prof Pubng.

Crashing. William T. Pancoast. 187p. 1983. 7.95 (*0-9610562-0-7*) Blazing Flowers.

Crashing & Splashing. Alison Lester. (Illus.). 16p. (J). (ps-00). 1989. pap. 3.50 (*0-670-81989-1*) Viking Child Bks.

Crashing into the Wall of Vanity: Cosmetic Surgery Is It for You? Katherine Michaels. 160p. 1992. pap. 6.95 (*0-9634948-0-5*, TX3346596) Equinox Prods.

Crashlander. Larry Niven. 1994. mass mkt. 4.99 (*0-345-38168-8*, Del Rey) Ballantine.

Crashproof Your BBC: Software Tips for BBC & Electron Programs. Mike McNamara. LC 84-17343. 67p. reprint ed. pap. 25.00 (*0-685-44426-0*, 2032662) Bks Demand.

Crashworthiness. Ed. by ATLA Press Staff. 242p. 1989. pap. 32.00 (*0-941916-49-9*) ATLA Pr.

Crashworthiness & Occupant Protection in Transportation Systems. Ed. by J. D. Reid & K. H. Yang. LC 89-46297. 319p. 1993. pap. 70.00 (*0-7918-1022-4*) ASME.

Crassulacean Acid Metabolism. Ed. by Irwin P. Ting & Martin Gibbs. 332p. (C). 1982. pap. 14.00 (*0-943088-00-3*) Am Soc of Plan.

Crassulacean Acid Metabolism: Analysis of an Ecological Adaptation. M. Kluge & Irwin P. Ting. LC 78-12658. (Ecological Studies: Vol. 30). (Illus.). 1978. 65.00 (*0-387-08979-9*) Spr-Verlag.

***Crassulacean Acid Metabolism: Biochemistry, Ecophysiology & Evolution.** International Workshop on Crassulacean Acid Metabolism Staff. Ed. by Klaus Winter. LC 95-7373. (Ecological Studies: Vol. 114). 1995. write for info. (*3-540-58104-9*) Spr-Verlag.

Crassy the Crude Beastie: A Beastie Book about Good Manners. Ron Berry et al. (Good Behavior Builders Ser.). (Illus.). 48p. (J). (ps-1). 1993. write for info. (*1-883761-03-4*) Fmly Life Prods.

Crater. James Fennimore Cooper. Ed. by Doug Robillard. (Masterworks of Literature Ser.). 1995. pap. 12.95 (*0-685-71555-8*) NCUP.

Crater. James Fenimore Cooper. (Works of James Fenimore Cooper Ser.). 1990. reprint ed. lib. bdg. 79.00 (*0-7812-2396-2*) Rprt Serv.

Crater: Or, Vulcan's Peak; a Tale of the Pacific. James Fenimore Cooper. LC 76-42723. reprint ed. 37.50 (*0-404-60058-1*) AMS Pr.

Crater Lake. Terry V. Marshall. LC 23-939860. (Illus.). 70p. 1977. 16.95 (*0-939860-02-3*); pap. 6.95 (*0-939860-01-5*) Tremaine Graph & Pub.

Crater Lake. Ronald G. Warfield et al. LC 82-82579. (Illus.). (Orig.). 1982. pap. 6.95 (*0-916122-79-4*) KC Pubns.

Crater Lake: An Ecosystem Study. Ed. by Gary L. Larson et al. LC 89-63688. (Illus.). 221p. 1991. 27.95 (*0-934394-07-5*) AAASPD.

Crater Lake National Park & Vicinity. Jeffrey P. Schaffer. LC 82-62810. (Illus.). 160p. (Orig.). 1983. pap. 14.95 (*0-89997-020-6*) Wilderness Pr.

***Crater Lake National Park, OR.** Ed. by Trails Illustrated Staff. 1994. 8.99 (*1-56695-015-5*) Trails Illustrated.

Craters, Canyons & Caverns. Jon Erickson. LC 92-15626. (Changing Earth Ser.). (Illus.). 192p. 1992. lib. bdg. 24.95 (*0-8160-2590-8*) Facts on File.

Craters, Cosmos, & Chronicles: A New Theory of Earth. Herbert R. Shaw. LC 93-31725. 702p. 1995. 79.50 (*0-8047-2131-9*) Stanford U Pr.

Craters of the Moon National Monument, Idaho. National Park Service Staff. LC 89-13670. (Handbook Ser.: No. 139). (Illus.). 64p. 1991. pap. 2.75 (*0-912627-44-1*, 024-005-01077-7) Natl Park Serv.

Crating As a Business. Wendy Rosen. 160p. 1994. pap. 19.95 (*0-8019-8632-X*) Chilton.

Cratis Williams Symposium Proceedings. Ed. by Barry M. Buxton. 1989. pap. 5.95 (*0-913239-61-5*) Appalach Consortium.

Cratylus: Plato's Critique of Naming. Timothy M. Baxter. LC 92-25897. (Philosophia Antiqua Ser.: Vol. 58). 203p. 1992. 57.25 (*90-04-09597-7*) E J Brill.

Cratylus, Parmenides, Greater Hippias, Lesser Hippias, Vol. IV. Plato. (Loeb Classical Library: No. 167). 488p. 1926. text ed. 18.95 (*0-674-99185-0*) HUP.

Craufurd's Light Division. Spellmount Ltd. Publishers Staff. (C). 1986. 125.00 (*0-685-60255-9*, Pub. by Spellmount UK) St Mut.

Craufurd's Light Division: The Life of Robert Craufurd & His Command of the Light Division. Ian Fletcher. 248p. (C). 1991. 125.00 (*0-946771-01-4*, Pub. by Spellmount UK) St Mut.

***Craven County, North Carolina Marriage Bonds & Certificates, 1780-1867.** Francis T. Ingmire. 258p. 1994. lib. bdg. 54.00 (*0-8095-8025-X*); pap. 27.50 (*0-8095-8550-2*) Borgo Pr.

Cravens & Woodruff Marketing: Applied Marketing Problems Workbook. Peter F. Kaminski & David R. Rink. (C). 1986. pap. write for info. (*0-201-10872-0*) Addison-Wesley.

Craving for Ecstasy: The Consciousness & Chemistry of Escape. Harvey B. Milkman & Stanley Sunderwirth. 1987. text ed. 29.95 (*0-669-12337-4*); pap. 13.95 (*0-669-15281-1*) Free Pr.

Craving for Swan. Andrei Codrescu. LC 86-21878. 314p. 1986. pap. 17.50 (*0-8142-0452-X*) Ohio St U Pr.

Cravings of Desire. Wood Kahler. 285p. 1960. 5.95 (*0-87140-911-9*) Liveright.

***Crawdads, Doodlebugs & Creasy Greens: Songs, Stories & Lore Celebrating the Natural World.** Doug Elliott. 1995. pap. 4.95 (*0-614-04584-3*) Native Ground.

Crawfish Book. Glen Pitre. (Illus.). 160p. 1993. pap. 13.95 (*0-87805-599-1*) U Pr of Miss.

***Crawfish Cookbook.** Dalmation D. Dupre. Ed. by Sylvia J. Barbre. (Illus.). 32p. 1982. pap. 2.95 (*0-9604580-0-X*) Creole Foods.

Crawfish-Man Rescues Ron Guidry. deluxe ed. Timothy Edler. (Tim Edler's Tales from the Atchafalaya Ser.). (Illus.). (J). (gr. k-8). 1980. 6.00 (*0-931108-05-5*) Little Cajun Bks.

Crawfish-Man Rescues the Ol' Beachcomber. deluxe ed. Timothy Edler. (Tim Edler's Tales from the Atchafalaya Ser.). (Illus.). 32p. (J). (gr. k-8). 1985. 10.00 (*0-931108-13-6*) Little Cajun Bks.

Crawfish-Man's Fifty Ways to Keep Your Kids from Using Drugs. Timothy J. Edler. (Tim Edler's Tales from the Atchafalaya Ser.). (Illus.). 52p. (J). (gr. k-8). 1982. pap. 6.00 (*0-931108-08-X*) Little Cajun Bks.

Crawfish-Man's Night Befo' Christmas. Timothy J. Edler. (Illus.). 40p. (J). (gr. k-8). 1984. pap. 10.00 (*0-931108-12-8*) Little Cajun Bks.

Crawford Bequest: Chinese Objects in the Collection of the Museum of Art, Rhode Island School of Design. Maggie Bickford et al. (Illus.). 120p. (Orig.). 1993. pap. 16.00 (*0-933519-24-9*) D W Bell Gallery.

Crawford Co. & Cuba, Mo. Breuer. 10.00 (*0-911208-23-2*) Ramfre.

Crawford Collection of Early Charters & Documents Now in the Bodleian Library. Ed. by Arthur S. Napier. (Anecdota Oxoniensia Ser.: No. 7). 1988. reprint ed. 59.50 (*0-404-63957-7*) AMS Pr.

Crawford County, Ohio, Probate Records. Jane Fisher. 210p. 1988. pap. text ed. 16.50 (*0-933227-92-2*) Closson Pr.

Crawford's Directory of City Connections 1991. 1991. lib. bdg. 150.00 (*1-55862-107-5*) St James Pr.

Crawford's Proof in Criminal Cases. 4th ed. Reg Bartley. xxii, 279p. 1982. 49.00 (*0-455-20537-X*, Pub. by Law Bk Co) W W Gaunt.

***Crawfordsville: A Pictorial History.** Pat Cline. (Indiana Pictorial History Ser.). (Illus.). 1988. write for info. (*0-943963-23-0*) G Bradley.

Crawley: New Town. Jacob Fried. 350p. (Orig.). 1983. pap. 10.95 (*0-913244-60-0*) Hapi Pr.

Crawley Affair. A. H. Haley. 1990. 49.00 (*0-9511427-3-9*, Pub. by Bullfinch Pubns UK) St Mut.

Crawling Arnold. Jules Feiffer. 1963. pap. 2.75 (*0-8222-0247-6*) Dramatists Play.

Crawlspace. Linda K. Kissler. LC 91-80608. 72p. 1993. pap. 6.95 (*0-943512-19-0*) Linwood Pub.

Crawlspace: New & Selected Poems. Monty Reid. 122p. (Orig.). 1993. pap. 14.95 (*0-88784-539-8*, Pub. by Hse of Anansi Pr CN) Genl Dist Srvs.

***Crawlspace Conspiracy.** Thomas Keech. 330p. 1995. 22.00 (*1-880909-34-0*) Baskerville.

Crawshaw Paints on Holiday. Alwyn Crawshaw. (Illus.). 128p. 1993. 19.95 (*0-89134-538-8*, 30549) North Light Bks.

Cray X-MP - Model 24. K. A. Robbins & S. Robbins. (Lecture Notes in Computer Science Ser.: Vol. 374). iv, 165p. 1989. pap. 22.00 (*0-387-97089-4*, 3132) Spr-Verlag.

Craycrofts of Maryland & Kentucky Kin. Mary L. Donnelly. LC 82-90280. (Illus.). 336p. 1982. 15.00 (*0-939142-06-6*) M L Donnelly.

Crayfish. Adapt. by Kathleen Pohl. (Nature Close-Ups Ser.). (Illus.). 32p. (J). (gr. 3-7). 1986. pap. text ed. 10.95 (*0-8172-2718-0*) Raintree Steck-V.

Crayfish: An Introduction to the Study of Zoology. T. H. Huxley. 1974. pap. 12.00 (*0-262-58034-9*) MIT Pr.

Crayfish International Cookbook. Johnnye Akin. Ed. by Doug Woolfolk. (Illus.). 210p. (Orig.). 1981. spiral bd. 9.95 (*0-86518-023-7*) Moran Pub Corp.

Crayfishes & Shrimp of Wisconsin (Cambaridae, Palaemonidae) H. H. Hobbs, III & Joan P. Jass. (Special Publications in Biology & Geology: No. 5). (Illus.). 166p. 1988. pap. text ed. 14.95 (*0-89326-152-1*) Milwaukee Pub Mus.

***Crayfishes (Decapoda: Cambaridae) of West Virginia.** Raymond F. Jezerinac et al. (Bulletin New Ser.: Vol. 10, No. 1). (Illus.). 200p. 1995. 25.00 (*0-86727-113-2*) Ohio Bio Survey.

Crayfishes of Ohio. Clarence L. Turner. (Bulletin Ser.: No. 13). 1926. 2.00 (*0-86727-012-8*) Ohio Bio Survey.

***Crayola Counting Book.** Rozanne Williams. (Emergent Reader Bks.). 16p. 1995. 2.49 (*1-57471-005-2*) Creat Teach Pr.

Crayon: A Journey Devoted to the Graphic Arts, & the Literature Related to Them, 8 vols. in 1, Set. Ed. by William J. Stillman & John Durand. reprint ed. 685.00 (*0-404-19511-3*) AMS Pr.

Crayon Creations. Marina Wood. (Illus.). 40p. (Orig.). (J). (gr. 4-8). 1984. pap. 6.00 (*0-932946-12-7*) Burdett CA.

Crayon Design Workbook. Marina Anderson. (Illus.). 40p. (Orig.). 1985. pap. 6.00 (*0-932946-23-2*) Burdett CA.

Crayons & Markers: Artistic Creations, One of a Kind & Made By You. Imogene Forte. LC 86-82934. (Tabletop Learning Ser.). (Illus.). 80p. (J). (gr. k-6). 1987. pap. text ed. 3.95 (*0-86530-162-X*, IP 943) Incentive Pubns.

Crayons Crafts & Concepts. Kathy Faggella. Ed. by Lisa L. Durkin. (Illus.). 106p. 1985. pap. 10.95 (*0-9615005-0-6*) First Teacher.

***Crayons on the Wall.** James B. Likeness. 128p. 1995. ring bd. 15.00 (*0-9629765-5-5*) Frederick Pubs.

Crayonstone: The Life & Work of Bolton Brown. Clinton Adams. LC 92-30157. (Illus.). 302p. 1993. 75.00 (*0-8263-1388-4*) U of NM Pr.

Crazeology: The Autobiography of a Chicago Jazzman As Told to Robert Wolf. Bud Freeman. LC 89-4704. (Music in American Life Ser.). (Illus.). 124p. 1989. 15.95 (*0-252-01634-3*) U of Ill Pr.

***Craziest Horse.** Alison Hart. 132p. (J). 1995. pap. 3.50 (*0-679-87140-3*) Random.

Craziest Riddle Book in the World. Lori M. Fox. LC 91-13209. (Illus.). 96p. (J). (gr. 3-9). 1992. 13.95 (*0-8069-8406-6*) Sterling.

Crazing in Polymers, Vol. 2. (Advances in Polymer Science Ser.: Vol. 91-92). (Illus.). 416p. 1990. 193.00 (*0-387-51306-X*, 3161) Spr-Verlag.

Crazy. Carolyn Weathers. LC 89-81045. 110p. (Orig.). 1989. pap. 8.95 (*0-9616572-3-5*) Clothespin Fever Pr.

Crazy about Gardening: Humorous Reflections on the Sweet Seduction of a Garden. Des Kennedy. LC 93-41616. 282p. (Orig.). 1994. 14.95 (*0-88240-447-4*); pap. 14.95 (*0-88240-451-2*) Alaska Northwest.

Crazy about the Cats: From Rupp to Pitino. Jamie H. Vaught. LC 91-66564. (Illus.). 256p. (Orig.). 1991. pap. 15.95 (*0-913383-21-X*) McClanahan Pub.

Crazy Alice. Lois M. Harrod. LC 90-84847. 91p. 1991. 10.00 (*1-879462-00-1*) Belle Mead Pr.

Crazy All the Time: Life, Lessons, & Insanity on the Psych Ward of Bellevue Hospital. Frederick L. Covan & Carol Kahn. 1994. 23.00 (*0-671-79159-1*) S&S Trade.

***Crazy All the Time: On the Psyche Ward of Bellevue Hospital.** Frederick L. Covan & Carol Kahn. 1995. mass mkt. 4.99 (*0-449-22366-3*) Fawcett.

Crazy Alphabet. Lynn Cox. LC 91-3734. (Illus.). 32p. (J). (ps-1). 1992. 14.95 (*0-531-05966-9*); lib. bdg. 14.99 (*0-531-08566-X*) Orchard Bks Watts.

Crazy Al's Cook Book & Party Book. Albert Ormondroyd, III. LC 83-51789. (Illus.). 136p. 1984. pap. 8.95 (*0-915949-10-5*) Whitinsville Bk.

Crazy Ape: Sanity, Madness, Your Brain & You. David MacSweeney. 244p. 1982. 25.00 (*0-7206-0565-2*, Pub. by P Owen Ltd UK) Dufour.

Crazy As We Are. Mevlana C. Rumi. Tr. by Nevit O. Ergin. 80p. (Orig.). (C). 1992. per., pap. 9.95 (*0-934252-30-0*) Hohm Pr.

Crazy Aunt & Other Stories. James T. McCartin. LC 87-26256. 1988. pap. 7.95 (*0-9617589-2-9*) Lincoln Springs Pr.

***Crazy Baseball Game.** Illus. by James Henry. (Crazy Games Ser.). (J). (gr. 1 up). 1995. boxed 2.95 (*0-8431-3818-1*) Price Stern.

Crazy Basketball Game. (Crazy Game Ser.). (Illus.). (J). 1994. 2.95 (*0-8431-3661-8*) Price Stern.

Crazy Bear Game. (Crazy Game Ser.). (Illus.). (J). 1994. 2.95 (*0-8431-1409-6*) Price Stern.

Crazy Bombay. Gangadhar Gadgil. (C). 1991. 9.50 (*81-7154-719-2*, Pub. by Popular Prakashan II) S Asia.

Crazy Bosses. Stanley Bing. Ed. by Julie Rubenstein. LC 93-10527. 272p. 1993. reprint ed. pap. 10.00 (*0-671-79692-5*) PB.

Crazy Bosses: Spotting Them, Serving Them, Surviving Them. Stanley Bing. (Illus.). 304p. 1992. 20.00 (*0-688-07073-6*) Morrow.

Crazy Butterflies Game. (Crazy Game Ser.). (Illus.). (J). 1994. 2.95 (*0-8431-3630-8*) Price Stern.

Crazy Card Game. (Crazy Game Ser.). (Illus.). (J). 1989. 2.95 (*0-8431-2762-7*) Price Stern.

Crazy Cat. Ron Reese. Ed. by Alton Jordan. (I Can Read Ser.). (Illus.). (J). (gr. k-3). 1984. 6.95 (*0-89868-002-6*, Read Res); pap. 3.50 (*0-89868-035-2*, Read Res) ARO Pub.

Crazy Cat's Bad Day. Ron Reese. Ed. by Alton Jordan. (Buppet Bks.). (Illus.). (J). (gr. 1-4). 1980. 9.25 (*0-89868-090-5*, Read Res); pap. 3.50 (*0-89868-101-4*, Read Res) ARO Pub.

***Crazy Christmas Angel Mystery.** Beverly Lewis. (Cul-De-Sac Kids Ser.). 80p. 1995. mass mkt. 2.99 (*1-55661-627-9*) Bethany Hse.

Crazy Christmas Characters. Illus. by Bill Ross. (Orig.). (J). (ps-2). 1991. pap. 3.50 (*0-8249-8522-2*, Ideals Child) Hambleton-Hill.

Crazy Christmas Game. Illus. by Andrea Tachiera. (Crazy Games Ser.). (J). (gr. 1 up). 1994. boxed 2.95 (*0-8431-3507-7*) Price Stern.

Crazy Classroom Dictionary. 64p. (Orig.). (YA). 1994. pap. 2.99 (*0-8125-9432-0*) Tor Bks.

Crazy Classroom Jokes & Riddles. Neil Yamamoto. 1990. pap. 1.95 (*0-8125-9377-4*) Tor Bks.

Crazy Clothes. Niki Yektai. LC 93-19738. (Illus.). 32p. (J). (ps-2). 1994. reprint ed. pap. 4.95 (*0-689-71781-4*, Aladdin Paperbacks) S&S Childrens.

Crazy Clothes Book Mobile. Illus. by Miriam Schapiro. (Book Mobiles Ser.). 28p. 1993. 7.95 (*1-56640-589-0*) Pomegranate Calif.

Crazy Clowns. (Illus.). 12p. (Orig.). (J). (ps-2). 1994. pap. 3.50 (*1-57102-013-6*, Ideals Child) Hambleton-Hill.

Crazy Comet Classroom Gamebook. Carole Marsh. (Carole Marsh Bks.). (Illus.). (Orig.). (J). (gr. 3-12). 1994. pap. 19.95 (*0-935326-87-1*) Gallopade Pub Group.

Crazy Comet Silly Trivia Book. Carole Marsh. (Gallopade Galaxy Ser.). (Illus.). 60p. (Orig.). (J). (gr. 2-12). 1994. pap. 14.95 (*0-935326-64-2*) Gallopade Pub Group.

Crazy Compositions. Ron Padgett. (Orig.). 1974. 2.50 (*0-929844-01-7*) Big Sky Bolinas.

Crazy Cooks & Gold Miners. Joyce Yardley. 352p. 1993. pap. 22.95 (*0-88839-294-X*) Hancock House.

Crazy Cool Cat Combo Game. (Crazy Game Ser.). (Illus.). (J). 1989. 2.95 (*0-8431-2763-5*) Price Stern.

Crazy Cow Game. (Crazy Game Ser.). (Illus.). (J). 1989. 2.95 (*0-8431-2477-6*) Price Stern.

Crazy Cowboy Game. (Crazy Game Ser.). (Illus.). (J). 1993. 2.95 (*0-8431-3647-2*) Price Stern.

Crazy Creatures. (Surprise Bks.). (Illus.). 24p. (J). (ps). 1986. 5.95 (*0-8431-1822-9*) Price Stern.

Crazy Creatures. H. Williams. (Illus.). 32p. (J). (gr. 1-4). 1989. pap. 2.95 (*0-88625-222-9*) Durkin Hayes Pub.

***Crazy Creepy Crawlies Game.** Illus. by Cherie Sinnen. (Crazy Games Ser.). (J). (gr. 1 up). 1995. boxed 2.95 (*0-8431-3817-3*) Price Stern.

Crazy Crock: A Novel. Henry Miller. 1992. pap. 9.95 (*0-8021-3293-6*) Grove-Atltic.

Crazy Crosswords. Helene Hovanec. 48p. (J). (gr. 2 up). 1993. bds. 2.95 (*0-8431-3492-5*) Price Stern.

Crazy Dinosaur Game. (Crazy Games Ser.). (Illus.). (YA). (gr. 6 up). 1988. boxed 2.95 (*0-8431-2271-4*) Price Stern.

Crazy Dinosaurs Magnet Game. (Crazy Magnet Game Ser.). (Illus.). (J). 1994. 4.95 (*0-8431-3725-8*) Price Stern.

Crazy Dog Guide to a Happier World. Brian B. Walker. 1993. pap. 9.00 (*0-671-86573-0*, Fireside) S&S Trade.

An Asterisk (*) at the beginning of an entry indicates that the title is appearing in BIP for the first time.

Cream Cake. Chris Barton & Dee Shulman. (Illus.). 32p. (J). (ps-2). 1993. 16.95 (*0-370-31766-1*, Pub. by Bodley Head UK) Trafalgar.

Cream of Creature from the School Cafeteria. Mike Thaler. 1985. pap. 2.99 (*0-380-89862-4*, Camelot) Avon.

Cream of the Crop, Bk 1. 32p. (gr. 3-12). 1980. pap. text ed. 5.95 (*0-87487-659-1*) Summy-Birchard.

Cream of the Crop, Book 2. 32p. (gr. 4-12). 1980. pap. text ed. 5.95 (*0-87487-658-3*) Summy-Birchard.

Cream of the Crop: The Impact of Elite Education in the Decade after College. Herant Katchadourian & John Boli. LC 94-12174. 1994. 27.00 (*0-465-04343-7*) Basic.

Cream of the Jest. James B. Cabell. Ed. by Joseph M. Flora. (Masterworks of Literature Ser.). 1973. pap. 11.95x (*0-8084-0396-6*) NCUP.

Cream of the Troubadour Coffee House. Ed. by David S. Ryan. (Illus.). 112p. (Orig.). 1990. pap. 17.95 (*0-905116-19-4*, Pub. by Kozmik Pr Centre UK) Seven Hills Bk.

***Cream Peas on Toast: Comfort Food for Norwegian Lutheran Farm Kids (& Others)** Janet L. Martin & Suzann J. Nelson. (Illus.). 1994. 9.95 (*0-9613437-9-6*) Redbird Prods.

Cream School from Sixteen Forty-Five. Edward Peel. (C). 1988. 40.00 (*0-904110-02-8*, Pub. by Thornhill Pr UK) St Mut.

Cream Separator Guide. Paul W. Dettloff. (Illus.). 480p. 1993. 54.95 (*0-9632897-1-3*) Million Mile.

Cream Tortes & Other Works. Natalie McKelvy. Ed. by Charles McKelvy. LC 90-82208. 394p. (Orig.). 1992. pap. 9.95 (*0-944771-07-6*) Dunery Pr.

Creamed, Pureed, & Smashed. Marda Stoliar. Ed. by Karen Michalsen. 176p. 1991. text ed. 19.95 (*0-9628822-0-8*) Spec Cookbook.

Creatavision: Instructor-Counselor Resource Book. Astrid Berg. 64p. 10.00 (*0-9627862-6-8*) Sefa Bks.

Create. 1989. 9.95 (*0-942821-26-2*) MENU Pub.

Create! 2nd ed. Rita Foley. (Catechist Training Ser.). 1982. 4.50 (*0-8215-1230-7*) Sadlier.

Create: A Procedure Manual for Cataloging Photographs. 3rd rev. ed. Marcia Tiede. 118p. 1991. pap. 15.00 (*0-938262-20-3*) Ctr Creat Photog.

***Create a Baby's Heirloom in Battenberg Lace.** 2nd ed. Eunice S. Jurado. (Illus.). (C). 1990. 10.95 (*0-944488-03-X*) E S Jurado.

Create a Celebration. Ellen Pals. (Illus.). 368p. (J). (gr. 4-12). Date not set. pap. 22.95 (*0-9627721-0-0*) Aladdin CO.

Create a Computer Bulletin Board System. L. Myers. 1991. 30.50 (*0-8306-6225-1*) TAB Bks.

Create a Cube. Margaret A. Smart & Mary Laycock. (Illus.). 64p. (Orig.). (J). (gr. 4-12). 1985. pap. text ed. 7.95 (*0-918932-84-X*) Activity Resources.

***Create a Culture.** Carol Nordgaarden. 88p. (YA). (gr. 4-8). 1995. 9.95 (*0-88160-240-X*, LW335) Learning Wks.

***Create a Curriculum.** Jean G. DeGaetano. 139p. 1993. pap. text ed. 22.00 (*1-886143-14-5*) Grt Ideas Tching.

Create a Drama Ministry. Paul M. Miller & Dan Dunlop. 1984. 9.95 (*0-685-69281-7*, MP-625) Lillenas.

Create a Math Environment: Arithmetic Made Touchable. Vivian W. Owens. (Illus.). 192p. (Orig.). 1992. pap. 13.95 (*0-9623839-1-0*) Eschar Pubns.

Create-A-Prehistoric Kid. 1987. 3.00 (*0-88047-137-9*, 8709) DOK Pubs.

***Create-a-Story Book.** Lerner Group Staff. 1995. pap. text ed. (*0-8225-9998-8*) Lerner Group.

***Create-A-Timeline.** (J). (gr. k-12). 1994. student ed, bds. 19.95 (*1-56290-105-2*, CP-4000) Crystal.

Create a Type - Handbook Office Communication. M. Toabs. (C). 1990. 80.00 (*0-7487-0234-2*, Pub. by S Thornes Pubs UK) St Mut.

Create an Heirloom. Louise Van Dyke. (Illus.). 52p. 1983. write for info. (*0-9612778-0-7*) L & L Pubns.

***Create an Oasis with Greywater: Your Complete Guide to Managing Greywater in the Landscape.** 2nd expanded rev. ed. Art Ludwig. 49p. 1994. pap. 7.00 (*0-9643433-0-4*) Oasis Biocomp.

Create & Celebrate Your Church's Uniqueness. Harold Westing. LC 93-13813. 256p. 1993. pap. 12.99 (*0-8254-3977-9*) Kregel.

Create & Manage Your Own Mutual Fund: Buy Stocks Directly from America's Blue Chip Companies. Vita Nelson & Donald J. Korn. 220p. 1994. 15.95 (*0-8119-0773-2*) LIFETIME.

Create & Use an Individual Career Development Plan Module, Competency-Based Career Guidance (CBCG) - Category C: Implementing. National Center for Research in Vocational Education Staff. 1985. 6.95 (*0-317-03870-2*, CG100C12) Ctr Educ Trng Employ.

Create & Use Bulletin Boards That Teach. Colleen Britton. 1990. 12.95 (*0-940754-96-7*, 5410) Ed Ministries.

Create & Write. Cyndi Lauritzen. (Learning Works Creative Writing Ser.). 48p. (J). (gr. 4-6). 1982. 5.95 (*0-88160-052-0*, LW 238) Learning Wks.

Create Community with Christ. Robert Doolittle. Ed. by Robert P. Stamschror. (Youth Group Strategies Ser.). (Illus.). 167p. (Orig.). 1991. pap. 16.95 (*0-88489-247-6*) St Marys.

***Create Empowering Affirmations & Spiritual Petitions.** Kathleen L. Mendel. 40p. (Orig.). 1995. student ed 10.15 (*0-614-06622-0*); student ed, pap. 10.15 (*1-878142-42-9*) Telstar TX.

Create Excellent Video. Peter Utz. 512p. 1990. pap. 22.95 (*0-13-547142-7*) P-H.

Create in Me: Young Adult Bible Study. Arthur G. Simmons & Beborah T. Simmons. 1985. 6.00 (*0-89536-765-3*, 5872) CSS OH.

Create in Me a Youth Ministry. Ridge Burns & Pam Campbell. 204p. 1986. pap. 16.99 (*0-89693-636-8*, Victor Books) SP Pubns.

Create in Me a Youth Ministry. rev. ed. Ridge Burns & Pam Campbell. 204p. 1994. pap. 8.99 (*1-56476-322-6*, Victor Books) SP Pubns.

Create It! Kit: The Complete Desktop Publishing Software Kit for Kids. Kim Baker & Sunny Baker. 1993. pap. 25.00 (*0-679-74870-9*) Random.

Create or Abdicate: City's Human Resource Choice for the 1990's. Ed. by A. Rajan & J. Fryatt. (C). 1988. 250.00 (*0-685-32837-6*, Pub. by Witherby & Co UK) St Mut.

Create or Abdicate: The City's Human Resource Choice for the 90's. Ed. by Amin Rajan & Julie Fryatt. 240p. 1988. 250.00 (*0-948691-66-2*, Pub. by Witherby & Co UK) St Mut.

Create Public Opinion, Seize Power. 1979. 0.50 (*0-89851-032-5*) RCP Pubns.

***Create Stereograms: Discover the World of 3D Illusion.** Dan Richardson. 224p. 1994. disk, pap. 26.95 (*1-878739-75-1*) Waite Group Pr.

***Create Stereograms on Your PC.** Dan Richardson. 200p. 1994. boxed, pap. 26.95 (*1-878739-98-0*) Waite Group Pr.

Create the Best Sales & Promotion Pieces. Herman R. Holtz. LC 88-14253. (Orig.). 1988. text ed. 42.50 (*0-471-63224-4*); pap. text ed. 12.95 (*0-471-63227-9*) Wiley.

Create the Love of Your Life. Susan Scott. 208p. 1993. 16.95 (*0-8217-4180-2*) Zebra.

Create the Perfect Sales Piece: How To Produce Brochures, Catalogs, Fliers & Pamphlets. Robert W. Bly. LC 85-12457. 243p. 1985. pap. text ed. 17.95 (*0-471-82525-5*) Wiley.

Create Wealth with Quicken. Christopher Vogt. 270p. (Orig.). 1993. pap. 19.95 (*1-55958-394-0*) Prima Pub.

***Create Wealth with Quicken.** 2nd ed. Christopher E. Vogt. 1994. pap. 19.95 (*1-55958-667-2*) Prima Pub.

***Create Work You Love.** Nancy J. Hanson. LC 94-92464. 141p. (Orig.). Date not set. pap. 10.00 (*0-9644736-0-7*) Career Disc.

Create Your College Success: Activities & Exercises for Students. Robert A. Friday. 219p. (C). 1988. pap. 12.95 (*0-534-09318-3*) Intl Thomson.

Create Your Employee Handbook. (You Can Bks.). (Orig.). 1984. pap. 26.95 (*0-87280-104-7*, 3314, Asher-Gallant) Caddylak Systs.

Create Your Own Beach Sticker Picture: With Reusable Peel-&-Apply Stickers. Robbie Stillerman. (Illus.). (J). (gr. k-3). 1993. pap. 2.95 (*0-486-27450-0*) Dover.

Create Your Own Class Newspaper! A Complete Guide for Planning, Writing, & Publishing a Newspaper. Diane Crosby. Ed. by Leslie Britt. (Illus.). 64p. (Orig.). 1994. pap. text ed. 7.95 (*0-86530-289-8*) Incentive Pubns.

Create Your Own Desktop Publishing System. Harley Bjelland. 1994. pap. text ed. 24.95 (*0-07-005923-3*, Windcrest) TAB Bks.

Create Your Own Dinosaur Stickers. Christopher Santoro. (Illus.). (J). (gr. k-3). 1993. pap. 2.95 (*0-486-27773-9*) Dover.

Create Your Own Farm Stickers. Barbara Steadman. (Illus.). (J). (gr. k-3). 1993. pap. 2.95 (*0-486-27775-5*) Dover.

Create Your Own Future. Lyle E. Schaller. LC 90-19334. 160p. 1991. pap. 11.95 (*0-687-09847-5*) Abingdon.

Create Your Own Goldilocks & the Three Bears Sticker Picture: With 30 Reusable Stickers. Kristie Bollinger. (Illus.). (J). (gr. k-3). 1994. pap. 2.95 (*0-486-27946-4*) Dover.

***Create Your Own Graphics Workstation.** Horace W. LaBadie. LC 94-31175. 1995. pap. text ed. 24.95 (*0-07-035955-5*, Windcrest) TAB Bks.

Create Your Own Greeting Cards & Gift Wrap with Priscilla Hauser. Priscilla W. Hauser. 128p. 1994. 24.99 (*0-89134-519-1*) North Light Bks.

***Create Your Own Japanese Gardens.** Japanese Garden Research Association Staff. (Illus.). 144p. 1995. pap. 59.95 (*4-7661-0814-0*, Pub. by Graphic Sha JA) Bks Nippan.

Create Your Own Joy: A Guide for Transforming Your Life. Elizabeth J. Rogers. LC 94-2565. 240p. 1994. pap. 10.00 (*1-56718-354-9*) Llewellyn Pubns.

Create Your Own Jungle Sticker Picture: With Reusable Peel-&-Apply Stickers. Robbie Stillerman. (Illus.). (J). (gr. k-3). 1993. pap. 2.95 (*0-486-27505-1*) Dover.

Create Your Own Life. Tom Johnson. LC 89-51260. 276p. (Orig.). 1989. pap. 10.50 (*0-941992-16-0*) Los Arboles Pub.

Create Your Own Life's Story: The Simple Way to Record Your Personal History. Glen Walker. (Mature Reader Ser.). 96p. (Orig.). 1993. pap. 8.95 (*1-55867-087-4*) Bristol Pub Ent CA.

Create Your Own Mad Scientist's Laboratory Sticker Picture: With 32 Reusable Stickers. Frank Daniel. (Illus.). (J). (gr. k-3). 1994. pap. 2.95 (*0-486-27919-7*) Dover.

***Create Your Own Magazine.** Barbara Taylor. (Illus.). 48p. (Orig.). 1995. pap. 6.95 (*0-8069-0426-7*) Sterling.

Create Your Own Multimedia System. John A. McCormick. 1994. disk, pap. 32.95 (*0-07-046034-5*) McGraw.

Create Your Own Newsletter Handbook. Dave Bause et al. LC 83-91092. (Illus.). 80p. 1983. 24.95 (*0-9612032-0-X*) Copy Fast.

Create Your Own Noah's Ark Sticker Picture: With 52 Reusable Stickers. Jill Dubin. (Illus.). (J). (gr. k-3). 1994. pap. 2.95 (*0-486-27921-9*) Dover.

Create Your Own Pictures Coloring Book. Anna Pomaska. (Illus.). (J). 1984. pap. 2.50 (*0-486-24614-0*) Dover.

Create Your Own Virtual Reality System. Joseph R. Levy. 1994. text ed. 44.95 (*0-07-037651-4*); disk, pap. 32.95 (*0-07-037652-2*) McGraw.

Create Your Own Zoo Sticker Picture: With 32 Reusable Stickers. Barbara Steadman. (Illus.). (J). (gr. k-3). 1994. pap. 2.95 (*0-486-27953-7*) Dover.

Create Yourself - An "Experience" Waiting Just for You. Dolores Seymour. LC 92-27369. 1992. pap. 9.95 (*0-8119-8119-3*) LIFETIME.

Created. TSR Staff. (Advanced Dungeons & Dragons, Second Edition; Al-Qadim Ser.). (Illus.). 1993. pap. 6.95 (*1-56076-610-7*) TSR Inc.

Created & Natural Wetlands for Controlling Nonpoint Source Pollution. U. S. Environmental Protection Agency, Office of Wetlands, Oceans, & Watersheds Staff. 1992. 49.95 (*0-87371-943-3*, TD223) Smoley.

Created By. Richard C. Matheson. 1994. mass mkt. 5.99 (*0-553-56610-5*) Bantam.

Created by Design. Quander Wilson. 96p. (Orig.). 1994. pap. 7.99 (*1-56043-123-7*) Destiny Image.

Created Creator: Images of God Created by Human Thought, a Primer for Those Who Wonder about the Existence of God. Carl M. Schmitthausler. LC 94-72097. 275p. (Orig.). 1994. pap. 14.95 (*0-9623817-2-1*) AOP Lincoln.

Created Equal: The Lives & Ideas of Black American Innovators. James M. Brodie. LC 92-40979. 1993. 20.00 (*0-688-11536-5*) Morrow.

***Created Equal: The Lives & Ideas of Black American Innovators.** Michael Brodie. 1994. pap. 12.00 (*0-688-13790-3*, Quill) Morrow.

Created Equal: Why Gay Rights Matter to America. Michael Nava & Robert Dawidoff. 144p. 1994. 17.95 (*0-312-10443-X*, Stonewall Inn) St Martin.

***Created Equal: Why Gay Rights Matter to America.** Michael Nava. 1995. pap. 8.95 (*0-312-11764-7*, Stonewall Inn) St Martin.

Created Female. Cindy Bunch & Brian Wallace. (Created Male & Female Bible Studies). 64p. (Orig.). 1993. pap. 4.99 (*0-8308-1132-X*, 1132) InterVarsity.

Created for Commitment. A. Wetherell Johnson. 1989. 9.99 (*0-8423-0443-6*); write for info. (*0-685-32312-9*) Tyndale.

***Created for Community.** Stanley Grenz. 312p. 1996. pap. 15.99 (*1-56476-550-4*, 6-3550) SP Pubns.

Created for Relationships. Cindy Bunch. (Created Male & Female Bible Studies). 64p. (Orig.). 1993. pap. 4.99 (*0-8308-1136-2*, 1136) InterVarsity.

Created from Animals: The Moral Implications of Darwinism. James Rachels. 256p. 1990. 22.95 (*0-19-217775-3*) OUP.

***Created Images.** Marceal Clark. 150p. (Orig.). 1995. pap. text ed. 6.99 (*1-56722-137-8*) Word Aflame.

Created in God's Image. Anthony A. Hoekema. 272p. 1986. pap. 14.99 (*0-8028-0850-6*) Eerdmans.

Created in God's Image: Meditating on Our Body. Carl Koch & Joyce Heil. (Illus.). 120p. (Orig.). 1991. pap. 6.95 (*0-88489-251-4*) St Marys.

Created in Her Image: Models of the Feminine Divine. Bernice Marie-Daly & Eleanor Rae. 160p. 1990. 18.95 (*0-8245-1013-5*) Crossroad NY.

Created Legend. Feodor K. Sologub. Tr. by John Cournos. LC 76-23899. (Classics of Russian Literature Ser.). 1977. reprint ed. pap. 10.00 (*0-88355-518-2*) Hyperion Conn.

Created Male. Brian Wallace & Cindy Bunch. (Created Male & Female Bible Studies). 64p. (Orig.). 1993. pap. 4.99 (*0-8308-1131-1*, 1131) InterVarsity.

Created Male & Female Bible Studies Series, 8 vols., Set. (Orig.). 1993. pap. 39.92 (*0-8308-1130-3*, 1130) InterVarsity.

***Created Space: An Exhibition by the New England Chapter of the Guild of Book Workers.** Guild of Book Workers, New England Chapter Staff. (Illus.). 44p. (Orig.). 1995. pap. 10.00 (*1-887336-00-1*) Guild Bk Workers.

Created, the Destroyer. Warren Murphy. (Destroyer Ser.: No. 1). 1988. pap. 3.50 (*1-55817-036-7*, Pinnacle NY) Windsor NY.

Created to Worship: Hearts of Love, Hearts of Sacrifice. LC 91-70396. 1991. pap. 8.99 (*0-89636-300-7*, LifeJourney) Chariot Family.

Createurs De l'Opera Francais. Lionel D. La Laurencie. LC 80-2287. reprint ed. 26.00 (*0-404-18854-0*) AMS Pr.

Createurs de l'Opera-Comique Francais. Georges Cucuel. LC 80-2271. reprint ed. 29.50 (*0-404-18834-6*) AMS Pr.

***Creating.** Fritz. 300p. 1995. pap. write for info. (*0-7506-2107-9*, Focal) Buttrwrth-Heinemann.

Creating. Robert Fritz. 320p. 1993. pap. 12.00 (*0-449-90801-1*, Columbine) Fawcett.

Creating a Beautiful Home: From Starting Fresh to Freshening Up - Inspiring Ideas to Help You Turn Your House into a Warm & Welcoming Home. Alexandra Stoddard. (Illus.). 240p. 1992. 25.00 (*0-688-10934-9*) Morrow.

Creating a Beautiful Home: From Starting Fresh to Freshening up, Inspiring Ideas to Help You Turn Your House into a Warm & Welcoming Home. Alexandra Stoddard. 240p. 1993. pap. 12.50 (*0-380-71624-0*) Avon.

Creating a Break: A Homecare Relief Scheme for Elderly People & Their Supporters. Patricia Thornton. 208p. (C). 1989. 39.00 (*0-86242-069-5*, Pub. by Age Concern Eng UK) St Mut.

Creating a Business-Based IT Strategy. Ed. by A. Brown. LC 92-26878. (UNICOM Applied Information Technology Ser.: Vol. 14). 1992. write for info. (*0-442-31643-7*) Routledge Chapman & Hall.

Creating a Butterfly Garden: A Guide to Attracting & Identifying Butterfly Visitors. Marcus Schneck. LC 93-39582. 1994. pap. 8.95 (*0-671-89246-0*, Fireside) S&S Trade.

Creating a Caring Classroom. Pat Huggins. (ASSIST Program: Affective - Social Skills: Instructional Strategies & Techniques Ser.). (Illus.). 582p. 1991. 34.95 (*0-944584-36-5*) Sopris.

Creating a Character: A Physical Approach to Acting. Moni Yakim & Muriel Broadman. (Acting Ser.). 256p. 1993. pap. 18.95 (*1-55783-161-0*) Applause Theatre Bk Pubs.

***Creating a Child-Centered Day Care Environment for Two-Year-Olds.** Margaret A. King et al. LC 93-10146. 144p. 1993. pap. 19.95 (*0-398-06203-X*) C C Thomas.

Creating a Child-Centered Day Care Environment for Two-Year-Olds. Margaret A. King et al. LC 93-10146. 144p. (C). 1993. text ed. 34.95x (*0-398-05866-0*) C C Thomas.

Creating a Christian Lifestyle. Carl Koch. 366p. 1988. pap. text ed. 12.00x (*0-88489-184-4*); teacher ed, spiral bd. 18.95 (*0-88489-185-2*) St Marys.

Creating a Climate of Confidence. O. Bykov. 80p. (C). 1986. 60.00 (*0-685-31587-8*, Pub. by Collets UK) Pro-Am Music.

Creating a Committed Workforce. Peter Martin & John Nicholls. 224p. (C). 1987. 70.00 (*0-85292-379-1*) St Mut.

Creating a Common Profile for Mental Health. Ed. by S. Griffiths et al. 240p. 1992. pap. 45.00 (*0-11-321514-2*, HM15142, Pub. by HMSO UK) UNIPUB.

Creating a Community Association: The Developer's Role in Condominium & Homeowner Associations. 2nd rev. ed. C. James Dowden. LC 86-50785. (Illus.). 86p. reprint ed. pap. 25.00 (*0-8357-3188-X*, 2039458) Bks Demand.

Creating a Computer-Supported Writing Facility: A Blueprint for Action. Cynthia L. Selfe. Ed. by Gail E. Hawisher. (Advances in Computers & Composition Studies). (Orig.). 1989. pap. 19.95 (*0-9623392-0-2*) C&C MI.

Creating a Culturally Enriched Curriculum for Grades K-6. Cathy C. Block & Jo A. Zinke. 1994. 29.95 (*0-205-14691-0*, Longwood Div) Allyn.

***Creating a Culture of Service: Effective Service Learning: Facilitators Program Manual, Facilitators Guide, Student Manuals for Books I-VI.** Irving H. Buchen & Carl I. Fertman. 32p. 1994. teacher ed write for info. (*1-884063-29-2*) Mar Co Prods.

***Creating a Culture of Service: Effective Service Learning: Facilitators Program Manual, Facilitators Guide, Student Manuals for Books I-VI, Bklt. I.** Irving H. Buchen & Carl I. Fertman. 16p. 1994. student ed write for info. (*1-884063-38-1*) Mar Co Prods.

***Creating a Culture of Service: Effective Service Learning: Facilitators Program Manual, Facilitators Guide, Student Manuals for Books I-VI, Bklt. II.** Irving H. Buchen & Carl I. Fertman. 16p. 1994. student ed write for info. (*1-884063-39-X*) Mar Co Prods.

***Creating a Culture of Service: Effective Service Learning: Facilitators Program Manual, Facilitators Guide, Student Manuals for Books I-VI, Bklt. III.** Irving H. Buchen & Carl I. Fertman. 16p. 1994. student ed write for info. (*1-884063-40-3*) Mar Co Prods.

***Creating a Culture of Service: Effective Service Learning: Facilitators Program Manual, Facilitators Guide, Student Manuals for Books I-VI, Bklt. IV.** Irving H. Buchen & Carl I. Fertman. 16p. 1994. student ed write for info. (*1-884063-41-1*) Mar Co Prods.

***Creating a Culture of Service: Effective Service Learning: Facilitators Program Manual, Facilitators Guide, Student Manuals for Books I-VI, Bklt. V.** Irving H. Buchen & Carl I. Fertman. 16p. 1994. student ed write for info. (*1-884063-42-X*) Mar Co Prods.

***Creating a Culture of Service: Effective Service Learning: Facilitators Program Manual, Facilitators Guide, Student Manuals for Books I-VI, Bklt. VI.** Irving H. Buchen & Carl I. Fertman. 16p. 1994. student ed write for info. (*1-884063-43-8*) Mar Co Prods.

***Creating a Culture of Service: Effective Service Learning: Facilitators Program Manual, Facilitators Guide, Student Manuals for Books I-VI, Facilitator Guide I.** Irving H. Buchen & Carl I. Fertman. 16p. 1994. write for info. (*1-884063-30-6*) Mar Co Prods.

***Creating a Culture of Service: Effective Service Learning: Facilitators Program Manual, Facilitators Guide, Student Manuals for Books I-VI, Facilitator Guide II.** Irving H. Buchen & Carl I. Fertman. 16p. 1994. write for info. (*1-884063-31-4*) Mar Co Prods.

***Creating a Culture of Service: Effective Service Learning: Facilitators Program Manual, Facilitators Guide, Student Manuals for Books I-VI, Facilitator Guide III.** Irving H. Buchen & Carl I. Fertman. 16p. 1994. write for info. (*1-884063-32-2*) Mar Co Prods.

***Creating a Culture of Service: Effective Service Learning: Facilitators Program Manual, Facilitators Guide, Student Manuals for Books I-VI, Facilitator Guide IV.** Irving H. Buchen & Carl I. Fertman. 16p. 1994. write for info. (*1-884063-33-0*) Mar Co Prods.

***Creating a Culture of Service: Effective Service Learning: Facilitators Program Manual, Facilitators Guide, Student Manuals for Books I-VI, Facilitator Guide V.** Irving H. Buchen & Carl I. Fertman. 16p. 1994. write for info. (*1-884063-34-9*) Mar Co Prods.

***Creating a Culture of Service: Effective Service Learning: Facilitators Program Manual, Facilitators Guide, Student Manuals for Books I-VI, Facilitator Guide VI.** Irving H. Buchen & Carl I. Fertman. 16p. 1994. write for info. (*1-884063-35-7*) Mar Co Prods.

***Creating a Culture of Service: Effective Service Learning: Facilitators Program Manual, Facilitators Guide, Student Manuals for Books I-VI, Set.** Irving H. Buchen & Carl I. Fertman. 1994. 179.95 (*1-884063-26-8*) Mar Co Prods.

***Creating a Curriculum That Works.** Lorraine A. Ozar. (Illus.). 172p. (Orig.). 1994. pap. 16.60 (*1-55833-143-3*) Natl Cath Educ.

Creating a Customer-Centered Culture: Leadership in Quality, Innovation, & Speed. Robin L. Lawton. LC 93-15572. 180p. 1993. 21.95 (*0-87389-151-1*) ASQC Qual Pr.

An Asterisk (*) at the beginning of an entry indicates that the title is appearing in BIP for the first time.

An Asterisk (*) at the beginning of an entry indicates that the title is appearing in BIP for the first time.

Creating Communities of Good News: A Handbook for Small-Group Facilitators. Mary L. Mauren. LC 92-64035. 80p. (Orig.). 1992. pap. 8.95 (*1-55612-473-2*, LL1473) Sheed & Ward MO.

Creating Communities of the Kingdom: New Testament Models of Church Planting. David W. Shenk & Ervin R. Stutzman. LC 88-11235. 229p. (Orig.). 1988. pap. 10.95 (*0-8361-3470-2*) Herald Pr.

Creating Community Anywhere: Finding Support in a Fragmented World. Carolyn R. Shaffer & Kristin Anundsen. LC 93-14895. (Illus.). 352p. 1993. pap. 15.95 (*0-87477-746-1*, J P T-Putnam) Putnam Pub Group.

Creating Community in the City: Cooperatives & Community Gardens in Washington, D. C. Ruth H. Landman. LC 92-42899. (Contemporary Urban Studies). 168p. 1993. text ed. 45.00 (*0-89789-316-6*, H316, Bergin & Garvey) Greenwood.

Creating Community on College Campuses. Irving J. Spitzberg, Jr. & Virginia V. Thorndike. LC 91-17847. (SUNY Series, Frontiers in Education). 233p. 1992. 59.50 (*0-7914-1005-6*); pap. 19.95 (*0-7914-1006-4*) State U NY Pr.

Creating Compassion: Activities for Understanding HIV-AIDS. Phyllis Vos Wezeman. LC 94-27133. (Illus.). 176p. (Orig.). (J). (gr. k up). 1994. pap. 13.95 (*0-8298-0996-1*) Pilgrim OH.

Creating Competent Communication. Donald D. Yoder et al. 496p. (C). 1993. pap. text ed. write for info. (*0-697-13238-2*) Brown & Benchmark.

Creating Compositions. 6th ed. Harvey A. Wiener. 480p. (C). 1992. teacher ed write for info. (*0-318-68322-9*); pap. text ed. write for info. (*0-07-070178-4*) McGraw.

***Creating Computer Art Using Dabbler.** Dawn Erdos & Dennis Orlando. (Illus.). 256p. (Orig.). 1995. pap. 32.95 (*1-886801-03-7*) Chrles River Media.

Creating Computer Programs for Learning: A Guide for Trainers, Parents & Teachers. Gary Orwig. 1983. pap. 16.95 (*0-8359-1168-3*, Reston) P-H.

***Creating Confidence: The Secrets of Self-Esteem.** Rex Johnson & David Swindley. LC 94-33814. 1995. pap. text ed. 10.95 (*1-85230-577-0*) Element MA.

***Creating Connections: Learning to Appreciate Diversity.** Dorothy Michener. Ed. by Leslie Britt. (Illus.). 96p. (Orig.). (J). (gr. 3-6). 1995. pap. text ed. 9.95 (*0-86530-310-X*, 1P310-0) Incentive Pubns.

Creating Consent of the Governed: A Member of Congress & the Local Media. Stephanie G. Larson. LC 91-40750. 232p. (C). 1992. 27.50 (*0-8093-1787-7*) S Ill U Pr.

Creating Contact, Choosing Relationship: The Dynamics of Unstructured Group Therapy. Richard C. Page & Daniel N. Berkow. LC 93-48625. (Social & Behavioral Science Ser.). 360p. 1994. 34.95 (*1-55542-654-9*) Jossey-Bass.

Creating Contemporary Worship. Terry Dittmer. 80p. (Orig.). 1985. pap. 7.95 (*0-570-03954-1*, 12-2889) Concordia.

Creating Contexts: A Practical Approach to Writing. Domenick Caruso & Stephen Weidenborner. LC 76-55159. (Illus.). (C). 1977. pap. text ed. 22.95 (*0-393-09101-5*); teacher ed, pap. text ed. write for info. (*0-393-09107-4*) Norton.

Creating Contexts for Second Language Acquisition: Theory & Methods. Arnulfo G. Ramirez. LC 94-6628. 395p. (C). 1995. pap. text ed. 32.95 (*0-8013-0480-6*, 78313) Longman.

***Creating Cool Web Pages with HTML.** Dave Taylor. 1995. pap. 19.99 (*1-56884-454-9*) IDG Bks.

Creating Corporate Audio-Visual Presentations: How to Commission & Manage Client-Centered Projects. Richard Worth. LC 90-47588. 208p. 1991. text ed. 49.95 (*0-89930-497-4*, WAA/, Quorum Bks) Greenwood.

Creating Corporate Culture: From Discord to Harmony. Charles T. Hampden-Turner. (Illus.). 256p. 1992. 27.95 (*0-201-60801-4*) Addison-Wesley.

Creating Corporate Venturing: New Businesses Within the Firm. Zenas Block & Ian C. MacMillan. LC 92-28830. 272p. 1993. 35.00 (*0-87584-321-2*) Harvard Busn.

***Creating Cosmos.** rev. ed. Barbara Dewey. 110p. 1994. pap. 12.95 (*0-933123-05-1*) Bartholomew Bks.

Creating Cottage Gardens. Mary Davis. (Illus.). 185p. 1993. 30.00 (*0-207-17779-1*, Pub. by Angus & Robertson AT) HarpC.

Creating Courseware: A Beginner's Guide. Ruth K. Landa. 380p. (C). 1984. pap. text ed. 26.50 (*0-06-043837-1*) HarpCollege.

***Creating Cross-Platform Multi-Media.** Terry R. Schussler. Date not set. 34.00 (*0-679-76192-6*) Random.

Creating Curriculum: Teachers & Students As a Community of Learners. Kathy G. Short & Carolyn Burke. LC 91-15145. 72p. 1991. pap. text ed. 14.50 (*0-435-08590-5*, 08590) Heinemann.

Creating Customer Loyalty. Manchester Open Learning Staff. 216p. (Orig.). 1993. pap. text ed. 22.95 (*0-7494-1139-2*, Pub. by Kogan Page UK) Nichols Pub.

Creating Customer Satisfaction. Ed. by Earl L. Bailey. (Report Ser.: No. 944). (Illus.). vii, 64p. (Orig.). 1990. pap. text ed. 80.00 (*0-8237-0390-8*) Conference Bd.

Creating Customer Value: The Path to Sustainable Competitive Advantage. Earl Naumann. LC 94-159. 1995. text ed. 24.95 (*0-538-83847-7*) S-W Pub.

Creating Customers. Common Sense Editors & David Bangs, Jr. 176p. 1992. pap. 19.95 (*0-936894-27-X*) Upstart Pub.

***Creating Customers for Life.** Eberhard E. Scheuing. LC 95-12449. (Management Master Ser.: Vol. 14). (Illus.). 50p. 1995. 15.95 (*1-56327-093-5*) Prod Press.

Creating Demand: Powerful Tips & Tactics for Marketing Your Product or Service. Richard Ott. 250p. 1991. 30.00 (*1-55623-560-7*) Irwin Prof Pubng.

Creating Desktop Presentations That Work. Karen L. McGraw. 288p. 1991. pap. text ed. write for info. (*0-13-189390-4*) P-H.

Creating Distinctiveness: Lessons from Uncommon Colleges & Universities. Barbara K. Townsend et al. Ed. by Jonathan D. Fife. LC 93-83928. (ASHE-ERIC Higher Education Report Ser.: No. 92-6). 94p. (Orig.). 1993. pap. text ed. 17.00 (*1-878380-19-2*) GWU Schl E&HD.

Creating Drug-Free School & Communities. Fox & Forbing. (C). 1991. text ed. 37.50 (*0-673-38238-9*) HarpCollege.

Creating Dynamic Stories with Logo Writer. Ihor Charischak. Ed. by Barbara Lipkin. (Illus.). 90p. (C). 1988. pap. text ed. 19.95 (*0-685-24432-6*) Dynamic Classroom.

Creating Early American Dolls. Kay Cloud. 32p. 1990. pap. 5.95 (*0-87588-354-0*) Hobby Hse.

Creating Eden. Marilyn Barrett. Date not set. pap. 10.00 (*0-06-250091-0*, HarpT) HarpC.

Creating Eden: The Garden As a Healing Space. Marilyn Barrett. LC 91-55317. (Illus.). 160p. 1992. 18.00 (*0-06-250076-7*) Harper SF.

Creating Effective Advertising: Using Semiotics. Mihai Nadin & Richard D. Zakia. LC 94-4481. 268p. 1994. 39.95 (*0-913069-46-9*) Consultant Pr.

Creating Effective Boards for Private Enterprises: Meeting the Challenges of Continuity & Competition. John L. Ward. LC 91-8358. (Management Ser.). 281p. 1991. 27.95 (*1-55542-352-3*) Jossey-Bass.

Creating Effective Documentation for Computer Programs. G. Prentice Hastings & Kathryn J. King. LC 85-19358. 214p. 1986. text ed. 29.95 (*0-13-189192-8*, Busn) P-H.

Creating Effective Enrollment Management Systems. Don Hossler. 154p. (Orig.). 1986. pap. 12.95 (*0-87447-272-5*) College Bd.

Creating Effective Schools: An In-Service Program for Enhancing School Learning Climate & Achievement. Wilbur Brookover et al. LC 81-84659. 290p. 1982. pap. 19.95 (*0-918452-34-1*) Learning Pubns.

Creating Effective Software: Computer Program Design Using the Jackson Methodology. David King. (Illus.). 224p. (C). 1987. text ed. 54.00 (*0-13-189242-8*) P-H.

Creating Effective TV Commercials. Huntley Baldwin. 255p. 1987. 29.95 (*0-8442-3063-4*, NTC Busn Bks) NTC Pub Grp.

Creating Encaustics. Shirley L. Charnell. LC 87-70834. (Illus.). 76p. (Orig.). (C). 1987. pap. 16.00 (*0-9618514-0-6*) Artistree Studio.

Creating Environments for Effective Adult Learning. Ed. by Roger Hiemstra. LC 85-644750. (New Directions for Adult & Continuing Education Ser.: No. ACE 50). 1991. 16.95 (*1-55542-784-7*) Jossey-Bass.

Creating Ethnicity: The Process of Ethnogenesis. Eugeen E. Roosens. (Frontiers of Anthropology Ser.). 200p. (C). 1989. text ed. 49.95 (*0-8039-3422-X*); pap. text ed. 24.00 (*0-8039-3423-8*) Sage.

Creating Excellence. Craig R. Hickman & Michael A. Silva. LC 84-20612. 304p. 1986. pap. 11.95 (*0-452-26455-3*, Plume); pap. 9.95 (*0-452-25810-3*, Plume) NAL-Dutton.

Creating Excellence in Our Schools...by Taking More Lessons from America's Best Run Companies. James Lewis, Jr. LC 85-51533. 250p. 1986. 24.95 (*0-915253-04-6*) Wilkerson Pub Co.

Creating Excellence in the Boardroom: A Guide to Shaping Directorial Competence & Board Effectiveness. Colin Coulson-Thomas. LC 93-892. (Henley Management Ser.). 1993. write for info. (*0-07-707796-2*) McGraw.

Creating Exceptional Classrooms: Technology Options for All. Mary C. Male. LC 93-16215. 1993. pap. text ed. write for info. (*0-205-14695-3*) Allyn.

Creating Expert Systems for Business & Industry. Paul Harmon & Brian Sawyer. 329p. 1990. text ed. 42.95 (*0-471-61495-5*); pap. text ed. 32.95 (*0-471-61496-3*) Wiley.

Creating Fashion Accessories. Singer Staff. LC 92-32804. (Singer Sewing Reference Library). 128p. 1993. 16.95 (*0-86573-284-1*); pap. 14.95 (*0-86573-285-X*) Cy De Cosse.

Creating Faulkner's Reputation: The Politics of Modern Literary Criticisim. Lawrence H. Schwartz. LC 87-27203. 256p. 1988. 32.50 (*0-87049-565-8*); pap. 16.95 (*0-87049-645-X*) U of Tenn Pr.

Creating Five String Bass Styles with Drum Accompaniment. Brian Emmel. (Illus.). 40p. (Orig.). 1993. cd-rom, pap. text ed. 17.95 (*0-931759-75-7*) Centerstream Pub.

Creating Four-Part Harmony. Lois Bock & Fred Bock. LC 89-81184. 208p. (Orig.). 1989. pap. 9.95 (*0-916642-40-2*) Hope Pub.

Creating FoxPro Applications. George Goley. (Illus.). (Orig.). 1993. pap. 40.00 (*1-56529-093-3*) Que.

***Creating French Culture: Treasures of the Bibliotheque Nationale de France.** Ed. by Marie-Helene Tesniere & Prosser Gifford. LC 95-6886. 1995. write for info. (*0-300-06283-4*) Yale U Pr.

Creating Freshwater Wetlands. Donald A. Hammer. 256p. 1991. 59.95 (*0-87371-445-8*, TD) Lewis Pubs.

Creating Fur Teddy Bears: Mink & Fake Fur. Hazel Ulseth & Helen Shannon. 32p. 1987. spiral bd. 4.95 (*0-87588-313-3*, 3595) Hobby Hse.

Creating Georgia: Minutes of the Bray Associates, 1730-1732, & Supplementary Documents. Ed. by Rodney M. Baine. LC 94-4169. 168p. 1995. 50.00 (*0-8203-1666-0*) U of Ga Pr.

Creating Global Value: Achieving Sustainable Results from the Centre. Phillippe De Backer. (Financial Times Management Ser.). 256p. 1994. 75.00x (*0-273-60849-5*, Pub. by Pitman Pubng UK) St Mut.

***Creating Global Value: Achieving Sustainable Results from the Centre.** Phillippe De Backer. 256p. 1994. 75.00 (*0-614-04104-X*, Pub. by Pitman Pubng UK) St Mut.

***Creating Good Landscape Design: A Guide for Non-Professionals.** Glen Hunt & Eugene Smith. Ed. by Elizabeth Lake. LC 95-67927. (Illus.). 224p. (Orig.). 1995. pap. 17.95 (*0-89716-561-6*) P B Pubng.

Creating Gourmet Gifts. Barbara Beckett. (Illus.). 176p. 1993. 24.95 (*1-86373-246-2*, Pub. by Allen & Unwin Aust Pty AT) IPG Chicago.

Creating Graphical Programs in Visual C. Brian Marshall. 1995. pap. text ed. 42.95 (*0-13-305145-5*) P-H.

***Creating Great Designs on a Limited Budget.** Lee Chartier & Scott Mason. (Illus.). 128p. 1995. 28.99 (*0-89134-607-4*) North Light Bks.

Creating Growth from Change: How You React, Develop & Grow. Rupert Eales-White. LC 94-18935. 1994. pap. text ed. 24.95 (*0-07-707933-7*) McGraw.

Creating Gymnastic Pyramids & Balances. Joseph M. Fodero & Ernest E. Furblur. LC 87-33883. (Illus.). 120p. 1989. 19.00 (*0-88011-308-1*, PFOD0308) Human Kinetics.

***Creating Harmony in Your Center.** Janet Hauter. 16p. 1994. pap. text ed. 25.00 (*1-57323-004-9*) Woodhaven Pbg.

Creating Health: How to Wake up the Body's Intelligence. Deepak Chopra. 234p. 1991. pap. 11.95 (*0-395-57421-8*) HM.

Creating Healthy Organizations. Ed. by Cary L. Cooper & Steve Williams. LC 94-2441. (Work, Well-Being & Stress Ser.). 1994. text ed. 42.95 (*0-471-94345-2*) Wiley.

Creating Heaven on Earth: The Mechanics of the impossible. Robert Oates. (Illus.). 191p. 1990. pap. 12.50 (*0-685-35778-3*) Heaven On Earth.

***Creating Heaven Through Your Plate.** Shelley Summers. (Illus.). 250p. (Orig.). Date not set. pap. 19.95 (*0-9629923-5-6*) Warm Snow.

***Creating Help for Windows Applications.** Rose M. Alciere. (Popular Applications Ser.). 144p. 1995. pap. 15.95 (*1-55622-448-6*) Wordware Pub.

***Creating High-Impact Training: A Practical Guide to Successful Training Outcomes.** Richard Y. Chang. (High Impact Training Ser.). (Illus.). 120p. 1994. pap. 12.95 (*1-883553-41-5*) R Chang Assocs.

***Creating High Performance Organizations: Survey of Practices & Results of Employee Envolvement & TQM in Fortune 1000 Companies.** Edward E. Lawler, 3rd et al. (Management Ser.). 1995. pap. 65.00 (*0-7879-0171-7*) Jossey-Bass.

Creating Holiday Greeting Cards. Peggy A. Gwinn & Randy L. Womack. 48p. (gr. k-3). 1991. student ed 5.95 (*1-56500-015-3*) Gldn Educ.

Creating Inclusive Classrooms: Education for All Children. 208p. 1994. pap. text ed. 24.95 (*0-9627389-8-0*) Soc Dev Educ.

***Creating Inclusive School Communities (CISC), Set.** York et al. (Staff Development Series for General & Special Educators). 1995. spiral bd. 300.00 (*0-614-06527-5*, CISC) P H Brookes.

Creating Individual Supports for People with Developmental Disabilities: A Mandate for Changes at Many Levels. Ed. by Valerie Bradley & Bruce Blaney. 560p. 1994. pap. 35.00 (*1-55766-136-7*) P H Brookes.

Creating Innovative Classroom Materials for Teaching Young Children. Marianne Debelak et al. 362p. (C). 1981. pap. text ed. 32.00 (*0-15-515786-8*) HB Coll Pubs.

Creating Instructional Materials. 3rd ed. Robert V. Bullough, Sr. 352p. (C). 1988. pap. write for info. (*0-675-20868-8*, Merrill Pub Co) Macmillan.

***Creating Interactive CD-ROM for Windows & MacIntosh.** Scott Fisher. (Illus.). 320p. 1995. pap. text ed. 39.95 (*0-12-257565-2*) Acad Pr.

Creating Interactive Environments in the Secondary School. Lois T. Stover et al. LC 93-19041. (Interactive Resources Ser.). 104p. 1993. 16.95 (*0-8106-3351-5*) NEA.

Creating Interagency Projects: School & Community Agencies. Joseph Ringers, Jr. 56p. (Orig.). 1977. pap. 3.95 (*0-930388-01-1*) Comm Collaborators.

Creating Investor Demand for Company Stock: A Guide for Financial Managers. Richard M. Altman. LC 86-25566. 416p. 1988. text ed. 75.00 (*0-89930-173-8*, ACI/, Quorum Bks) Greenwood.

Creating Japanese Gardens. Philip Cave. (Illus.). 176p. 1993. 34.95 (*0-8048-1838-X*) C E Tuttle.

Creating Japanese Gardens. Alvin Horton. Ed. by Ortho Books Staff & Cedric Crocker. LC 87-72814. (Illus.). 112p. (Orig.). 1989. pap. 9.95 (*0-89721-148-0*) Ortho Info.

Creating Jobs: Public Employment Programs & Wage Subsidies. Ed. by John L. Palmer. LC 78-12241. (Studies in Social Economics). 379p. 1978. pap. 14.95 (*0-8157-6891-5*) Brookings.

Creating Jobs by Creating New Businesses: The Role of Business Incubators. Mary McClean. 72p. (Orig.). 1985. pap. 20.00 (*0-317-04904-6*) Natl Coun Econ Dev.

Creating Jobs, Creating Workers: Economic Development & Employment in Metropolitan Chicago. Intro. by Lawrence B. Joseph & Laurence E. Lynn, Jr. (Chicago Assembly Ser.). 300p. (C). 1990. pap. text ed. 15.00 (*0-9626755-0-4*) UC Ctr UR&PS.

Creating Labor-Management Partnerships. Christopher B. Meek & Werner P. Woodworth. (Illus.). 208p. (C). 1995. pap. text ed. 26.95 (*0-201-58823-4*) Addison-Wesley.

***Creating Leaders for Tomorrow.** Karl Albrecht. (Management Master Ser.). (Illus.). 50p. 1995. 15.95 (*1-56327-101-X*) Prod Press.

Creating Learning Places for Teachers, Too. Larry E. Frase & Sharon C. Conley. (Total Quality Education for the World's Best Schools Ser.: Vol. 3). 120p. 1994. pap. 16.00 (*0-8039-6121-9*) Corwin Pr.

Creating Life: The Aesthetic Utopia of Russian Modernism. Ed. by Irina Paperno & Joan D. Grossman. LC 93-27948. 1994. write for info. (*0-8047-2288-9*) Stanford U Pr.

Creating Line Design, Bk. 3. Randy L. Womack. (Books 1, 2, 3 & 4 Ser.). (Illus.). 48p. (gr. k-1). 1985. student ed 6.95 (*1-56500-002-1*) Gldn Educ.

Creating Line Designs, Bk. 1. Randy L. Womack. (Books 1, 2, 3 & 4 Ser.). (Illus.). 48p. (gr. 2-4). 1985. student ed 6.95 (*1-56500-000-5*) Gldn Educ.

Creating Line Designs, Bk. 2. Randy L. Womack. (Books 1, 2, 3 & 4 Ser.). (Illus.). 48p. (gr. 4-6). 1985. student ed 6.95 (*1-56500-001-3*) Gldn Educ.

Creating Line Designs, Bk. 4. Randy L. Womack. (Books 1, 2, 3 & 4 Ser.). (Illus.). 48p. (gr. 5-7). 1985. student ed 6.95 (*1-56500-003-X*) Gldn Educ.

***Creating Logos & Letterheads.** Jennifer Place. LC 95-1851. (Graphic Design Basics Ser.). 1995. write for info. (*0-89134-571-X*) North Light Bks.

Creating Lotus Notes Applications. Lisa Pyle. 1994. pap. 29.95 (*1-56529-556-0*) Que.

Creating Love: The Next Great Stage of Growth. John Bradshaw. 1994. pap. 12.95 (*0-553-37305-6*) Bantam.

Creating Love: The Next Great Stage of Growth. large type ed. John Bradshaw. LC 92-47393. 1993. 22.95 (*0-8161-5728-6*); pap. write for info. (*0-8161-5729-4*) G K Hall.

Creating, Managing, & Evaluating Multidisciplinary Teams. Paul Ching et al. (Continuing Education Course Note Ser.: No. 35). (Illus.). 95p. (Orig.). 1993. pap. 20.00 (*0-89181-184-2*) AAPG.

Creating Mandalas for Insight, Healing, & Self-Expression. Susanne F. Fincher. LC 91-52872. (Illus.). 200p. (Orig.). 1991. pap. 16.00 (*0-87773-646-4*) Shambhala Pubns.

***Creating Meaningful Funeral Ceremonies: A Guide for Caregivers.** Alan D. Wolfelt. 65p. (Orig.). 1994. pap. 12.95 (*1-879651-08-4*) Ctr Loss Life.

Creating Meaningful Performance Assessments: Fundamental Concepts. Stephen N. Elliott. LC 94-17715. (CEC Mini-Library Performance Assessment). 1994. 8.90 (*0-86586-249-4*, P5059) Coun Exc Child.

Creating Media Culture. Robert P. Snow. LC 83-3125. (Sage Library of Social Research: No. 149). 263p. reprint ed. pap. 75.00 (*0-8357-4857-X*, 2037789) Bks Demand.

Creating Melodies: A Songwriter's Guide to Understanding, Writing & Polishing Melodies. Dick Weissman. 1994. 18.95 (*0-89879-602-4*) Writers Digest.

Creating Memory Quilts. Madonna A. Ferguson. 80p. (Orig.). 1985. pap. 13.00 (*0-9612608-6-6*) B Boyink.

Creating Minds. Howard Gardner. 1994. pap. 15.00 (*0-465-01454-2*) Basic.

Creating Minds: An Anatomy of Creativity Seen Through the Lives of Freud, Einstein, Picasso, Stravinsky, Eliot, Graham & Gandhi. Howard Gardner. LC 92-56172. (Illus.). 608p. 1993. 30.00 (*0-465-01455-0*) Basic.

***Creating Miracles: Understanding the Experience of Divine Intervention.** Carolyn G. Miller. Ed. by Nancy Carleton. LC 94-48620. 312p. 1995. pap. 12.95 (*0-915811-62-6*) H J Kramer Inc.

Creating Modern Probability: Its Mathematics, Physics & Philosophy in Historical Perspective. Jan Von Plato. (Cambridge Studies in Probability, Induction & Decision Theory). 336p. (C). 1994. 59.95 (*0-521-44403-9*) Cambridge U Pr.

Creating Money: Keys to Abundance. Sanaya Roman & Duane Packer. Ed. by Elaine Ratner. (Life Mastery Ser.). 288p. 1988. pap. 12.95 (*0-915811-09-X*) H J Kramer Inc.

Creating Multimedia Applications with CD. Doug Wolfgram. 1994. pap. 39.95 (*1-56529-667-2*) Que.

Creating Multimedia on Your PC. Tom Badgett & Corey Sandler. LC 93-5422. 1993. pap. text ed. 29.95 (*0-471-58928-4*) Wiley.

***Creating New Educational Communities.** Ed. by Jeannie Oakes & Karen H. Quartz. 275p. 1995. 29.00 (*0-226-60166-8*) U Ch Pr.

Creating New Hospital-Physician Collaboration: Integrating Hospitals & Medical Groups. Todd S. Wirth & Seth Allcorn. LC 93-12245. 185p. 1993. Alk. paper. 37.00 (*0-910701-96-2*, 0931) Health Admin Pr.

Creating New Jersey Learning Stations. 1981. pap. write for info. (*0-89359-005-3*) Afton Pub.

***Creating New Native Woodlands.** John Rodwell & Gordon Patterson. (Forestry Commission Bulletin Ser.: No. 112). 85p. 1994. pap. 17.00 (*0-11-710320-9*, HM03209, Pub. by HMSO UK) UNIPUB.

Creating Newsletters, Brochures, & Pamphlets: A How-to-Do-It Manual for School & Public Librarians. Barbara R. Radke & Barbara L. Stein. (How-to-Do-It Ser.). 144p. 1992. 32.50 (*1-55570-107-8*) Neal-Schuman.

***Creating Nongraded K-3 Primary Classrooms: Teachers' Stories & Lessons Learned.** 2nd ed. Ed. by Ric A. Hovda et al. LC 94-29654. (Illus.). 264p. 1995. 24.95 (*0-590-49503-8*) Scholastic Inc.

***Creating OLE 2.x Applications.** John Toohey. (Illus.). (Orig.). 1994. pap. 49.99 (*1-56529-991-4*) Que.

Creating Oncidinae Intergenerics. W. W. Moir & May A. Moir. LC 81-16182. (Illus.). 120p. 1982. pap. text ed. 12.00 (*0-8248-0784-7*) UH Pr.

Creating Opportunity: Strategies for Reducing Poverty Through Economic Development. Hugh O'Neill. LC 85-5931. 207p. 1985. 16.95 (*0-934842-41-8*) CSPA.

***Creating Original Hand Knitted Lace.** Margaret Stove. 192p. 1995. pap. 29.00 (*0-916896-63-3*) Lacis Pubns.

Creating Original Porcelain Dolls. Hildegard Gunzel. (Illus.). 112p. (C). 1994. 29.95 (*0-87588-339-7*, 3729) Hobby Hse.

***Creating Paradox for Windows Applications.** Vince Kellen & Bill Todd. 550p. (Orig.). 1994. 45.00 (*0-615-00150-5*); pap. 45.00 (*1-56205-404-X*) New Riders Pub.

An Asterisk (*) at the beginning of an entry indicates that the title is appearing in BIP for the first time.

C

An Asterisk (*) at the beginning of an entry indicates that the title is appearing in BIP for the first time.

Creating Writers: Linking Assessment & Writing Instruction. Vicki Spandel & Richard J. Stiggins. 256p. (Orig.). (C). 1990. pap. text ed. 27.95 (0-8013-0055-X, 75719) Longman.

***Creating Your Christian Engagement.** John B. Ryan & Francis J. Lodato. LC 94-76020. 144p. (Orig.). 1994. pap. 6.95 (0-89243-575-5) Liguori Pubns.

Creating Your Future: Level 1. Mary J. Cera & Judith Bisignano. (Illus.). 72p. 1982. 6.95 (0-910141-00-2, KP107) Kino Pubns.

Creating Your Future: Level 2. Marilyn Robinson & Judith Bisignano. (Illus.). 72p. 1982. 6.95 (0-9607366-8-9, KP108) Kino Pubns.

Creating Your Future: Level 3. Joseph Bisignano et al. (Illus.). 72p. 1982. student ed 6.95 (0-9607366-9-7, KP109) Kino Pubns.

Creating Your Future: Level 4. Joseph Bisignano & Judith Bisignano. (Illus.). 64p. 1983. student ed 6.95 (0-910141-01-0, KP115) Kino Pubns.

Creating Your Future: Personal Strategic Planning for Professionals. George L. Morrisey. LC 92-19057. 216p. (Orig.). 1992. pap. 15.95 (1-881052-06-0) Berrett-Koehler.

Creating Your Giant Self. Robert Rose. LC 89-81557. 224p. (Orig.). 1990. pap. 12.95 (0-941404-61-7) New Falcon Pubns.

Creating Your Herbal Profile: How & Where to Find the Herbs That Match Your Personality Traits & Health Needs. Dorothy Hall. 327p. (Orig.). 1990. pap. 10.95 (0-87983-496-X) Keats.

Creating Your Home Office. Contrib by Marie V. Scher. (Illus.). 208p. (Orig.). 1994. pap. text ed. 14.95 (0-9641450-0-6) MVS Home Ofc.

Creating Your Life: A Guide for Transformation. Richard J. Van Donk. LC 89-50213. 144p. 1989. pap. 9.95 (0-924755-00-8) Vision CA.

Creating Your Own Career for Job Satisfaction. Marilynn M. Angers & William P. Angers. LC 82-61718. 170p. (Orig.). 1983. pap. 9.95 (0-910793-00-X) Marlborough Pr.

***Creating Your Own Cosmetics - Naturally: The Alternative to Today's Harmful Cosmetic Products.** Nikolaus J. Smeh. (Illus.). 233p. (Orig.). 1995. pap. 22.95 (0-9637755-1-0) Alliance VA.

Creating Your Own Future: A Woman's Guide to Retirement Planning. Judith A. Martindale & Mary J. Moses. LC 90-46484. 244p. 1991. 28.95 (0-942061-08-X, Sourcebooks Trade); pap. 14.95 (0-942061-09-8, Sourcebooks Trade) Sourcebks.

Creating Your Own Marketing Makes Good Dollars & Sense. Ira S. Kalb. Ed. by Helen Rosenberg. (Illus.). 200p. (C). 1989. 39.95 (0-924050-01-2) K & A Pr.

Creating Your Own Success: College Study Skills. V. Rose Kitchen & MaryAnn Moore. LC 93-30556. 1994. pap. 10.95 (0-538-70924-3) S-W Pub.

Creating Your Own Water Garden. Charles B. Thomas. 1998. pap. 2.95 (0-88266-656-8, Garden Way Pub) Storey Comm Inc.

Creating Your Own Woodshop. Charles Self. (Illus.). 128p. (Orig.). 1994. pap. 18.95 (1-55870-326-8) Betterway Bks.

Creating Your Own Work. Micheline Mason. 108p. 1980. 35.00 (0-905418-80-8, Pub. by Gresham Bks UK) St Mut.

Creating Your Own Work. Micheline Mason. 108p. 1983. 25.00 (0-946095-04-3, Pub. by Gresham Bks UK) St Mut.

***Creating Your Personal Journey: A Primer: To Discover Who You Are & to Uncover Your True Desires.** Roger L. Paradis. Ed. by Carol White. LC 94-69155. 200p. 1995. 9.95 (0-9643604-0-3) Concord Pr MA.

Creating Your Personal Plan for Financial Success. William C. Crews. 167p. (Orig.). pap. text ed. 19.95 (0-9615787-0-X) Creative Intl.

***Creating Your Personal Vision: A Mind-Body Guide for Better Eyesight.** Samuel A. Berne. LC 94-72147. (Illus.). 170p. (Orig.). 1994. pap. write for info. (0-9641599-3-7) Color Stone.

Creating Your Success Reality: Practical Application of the Future Self Concept. Jeff King. LC 87-51054. 192p. (Orig.). 1988. pap. 6.95 (0-944756-00-X) Jeffco.

***Creatio Ex Nihilo: The Doctrine of 'Creation Out of Nothing' in Early Christian Thought.** Gerhard May. Tr. by A. S. Worral. 216p. 1994. text ed. 39.95 (0-567-09695-5, Pub. by T & T Clark UK) Bks Intl VA.

Creation. (Burl Ives Bible-Time Stories). (J). (ps-2). 1976. audio 5.99 (0-89191-804-3, 98046, Chariot Bks) Chariot Family.

Creation. Bruce Beasley. LC 93-33496. 64p. 1994. 16.95 (0-8142-0623-9); pap. 10.95 (0-8142-0624-7) Ohio St U Pr.

Creation. Carol Greene. (PassAlong Arch Book Ser.). (Illus.). 32p. (Orig.). (J). (ps-3). 1994. pap. 2.99 (0-570-09040-7) Concordia.

Creation. Susan T. Hall. (Tickle Giggle Bks.). (Illus.). 10p. (J). (ps). 1991. bds. 7.49 (1-55513-482-3, 63230, Chariot Bks) Chariot Family.

Creation. Frank Jakubowsky. (Illus.). 106p. (Orig.). 1978. pap. 5.95 (0-932588-00-X) Jesus Bks.

***Creation.** James W. Johnson. (Illus.). 1995. pap. 6.95 (0-8234-1207-5) Holiday.

Creation. James Weldon Johnson. LC 93-3207. (Illus.). 32p. (J). (ps-3). 1994. lib. bdg. 15.95 (0-8234-1069-2) Holiday.

Creation. Gordon Lindsay. (Old Testament Ser.: Vol. 1). 1964. 1.95 (0-89985-123-1) Christ for the Nations.

Creation. Stephen Mitchell. LC 89-39726. (Illus.). 40p. (J). 1990. 15.95 (0-8037-0617-0) Dial Bks Young.

Creation. Gordon Onslow-Ford. (Illus.). 123p. 1978. text ed. 35.00 (0-9612760-0-2) Bishop Pine.

***Creation.** Rabbit. Date not set. pap. 19.95 (0-689-80238-2) Macmillan.

Creation. Gore Vidal. 560p. 1986. mass mkt. 5.95 (0-345-34020-5) Ballantine.

Creation, No. 5. Yasaku Kamekura. (Illus.). 168p. 1993. pap. 24.95 (4-89737-101-5, Pub. by Rikuyo-Sha JA) Bks Nippan.

Creation, No. 6. Yasaku Kamekura. (Illus.). 168p. 1993. pap. 24.95 (4-89737-102-3, Pub. by Rikuyo-Sha JA) Bks Nippan.

Creation, No. 7. Yasaku Kamekura. (Illus.). 168p. 1993. pap. 24.95 (4-89737-103-1, Pub. by Rikuyo-Sha JA) Bks Nippan.

Creation, No. 08. Yasaku Kamekura. (Illus.). 168p. 1993. pap. 24.95 (4-89737-126-0, Pub. by Rikuyo-Sha JA) Bks Nippan.

Creation, No. 9. Yasaku Kamekura. (Illus.). 168p. 1993. pap. 24.95 (4-89737-127-9, Pub. by Rikuyo-Sha JA) Bks Nippan.

Creation, No. 10. Yasaku Kamekura. (Illus.). 168p. 1993. pap. 24.95 (4-89737-128-7, Pub. by Rikuyo-Sha JA) Bks Nippan.

Creation, No. 11. Yasaku Kamekura. (Illus.). 168p. 1993. pap. 24.95 (4-89737-147-3, Pub. by Rikuyo-Sha JA) Bks Nippan.

Creation, No. 12. Yasaku Kamekura. (Illus.). 168p. 1993. pap. 24.95 (4-89737-148-1, Pub. by Rikuyo-Sha JA) Bks Nippan.

Creation, No. 13. Yasaku Kamekura. (Illus.). 168p. 1993. pap. 24.95 (4-89737-152-X, Pub. by Rikuyo-Sha JA) Bks Nippan.

Creation, No. 15. Yasaku Kamekura. (Illus.). 168p. 1993. pap. 24.95 (4-89737-154-6, Pub. by Rikuyo-Sha JA) Bks Nippan.

Creation, No. 16. Yasaku Kamekura. (Illus.). 168p. 1993. pap. 24.95 (4-89737-173-2, Pub. by Rikuyo-Sha JA) Bks Nippan.

Creation, No. 17. Yasaku Kamekura. (Illus.). 168p. 1993. pap. 24.95 (4-89737-174-0, Pub. by Rikuyo-Sha JA) Bks Nippan.

Creation, No. 18. Yasaku Kamekura. (Illus.). 168p. 1994. pap. 24.95 (4-89737-175-9, Pub. by Recruit JA) Bks Nippan.

Creation, No. 19. Yasaku Kamekura. (Illus.). 168p. 1994. pap. 24.95 (4-89737-189-9, Pub. by Recruit JA) Bks Nippan.

Creation, No. 20. Yasaku Kamekura. (Illus.). 168p. 1994. pap. 24.95 (4-89737-190-2, Pub. by Recruit JA) Bks Nippan.

Creation: A Poem. James Weldon Johnson. LC 92-24304. (Illus.). (J). 1993. 15.95 (0-316-46744-8) Little.

Creation: Cosmic Radiation in Florida. Hilton Hotema. 129p. 1962. spiral bd. 7.70 (0-7873-0432-8) Mokelumne.

Creation: The Beginning. Oliver C. Grube. LC 92-97525. 108p. 1993. pap. write for info. (0-9640371-0-6) John Oliver Pubng.

Creation: The Story of the Origin & Evolution of the Universe. Barry Parker. LC 88-17893. (Illus.). 312p. 1988. 22.95 (0-306-42952-7, Plenum Pr) Plenum.

Creation: What Does the Bible Teach? large type ed. Bessie R. Foster. LC 92-96977. 60p. (Orig.). 1992. pap. 4.64 (0-9633898-0-7, 1-92) Triple Label.

Creation: You Can't Beat the Bible - the Book & Game about the Bible, Incl. game. Freda Oelbaum. 224p. 1990. 10.95 (0-944007-15-5) Sure Sellers.

Creation see Summa Contra Gentiles

Creation - An Ecumenical Challenge: Reflections Issuing from a Study by the Institute for Ecumenical Research, Strasbourg. Per Lonning. LC 89-35703. viii, 272p. (C). 1989. 31.95 (0-86554-356-9, MUP/H285) Mercer Univ Pr.

Creation - Genesis, Big Bang, Evolution. 2nd ed. John Wend. 45p. 1991. pap. 12.00 (0-932223-11-7) Churchill PC.

***Creation Accounts in the Ancient Near East & the Bible.** Richard J. Clifford. LC 94-26565. (Catholic Bible Quarterly Monographs: No. 26). 1994. 9.00 (0-915170-25-6) Catholic Bibl Assn.

Creation & Abortion: A Study in Moral & Legal Philosophy. Frances M. Kamm. 240p. 1992. pap. 15.95 (0-19-507284-7) OUP.

Creation & Blessing: A Guide to the Study & Exposition of Genesis. Allen P. Ross. LC 88-6173. 784p. 1988. 29.99 (0-8010-7748-6) Baker Bk.

Creation & Control of Money. 1991. lib. bdg. 69.95 (0-8490-4403-0) Gordon Pr.

Creation & Criticism: A Passage to India. June P. Levine. LC 78-134772. 218p. reprint ed. pap. 62.20 (0-317-27831-2, 2055945) Bks Demand.

Creation & Detection of the Excited State. Ed. by William R. Ware. LC 76-134785. 240p. Vol. 2, 240p. pap. 68.40 (0-7837-0037-7, 2034574); Vol. 3, 205p. pap. 58.50 (0-7837-0038-5) Bks Demand.

Creation & Detection of the Excited State, 2 pts. Ed. by Angelo A. Lamola. LC 76-134785. (Illus.). 391p. reprint ed. Vol. 1, Pt. A, 391p. pap. 111.50 (0-7837-0943-9, 2041248); reprint ed. Vol. 1, Pt. B, 301p. pap. 85.80 (0-7837-0944-7, 2041248) Bks Demand.

Creation & Detection of the Excited State, Vol. 4. Ed. by William R. Ware. LC 76-134785. 334p. pap. 95.20 (0-8357-6080-4, 2034574) Bks Demand.

Creation & Discovery: Essays in Criticism & Aesthetics. Eliseo Vivas. LC 72-3365. (Essay Index Reprint Ser.). 1977. reprint ed. 20.95 (0-8369-2931-4) Ayer.

Creation & Evolution: Myth or Reality. Norman D. Newell. Ed. by Ruth N. Anshen. LC 84-17858. (Convergence Ser.). 266p. 1984. pap. text ed. 12.95 (0-275-91792-4, B1792, Praeger Pubs) Greenwood.

Creation & Evolution in Primitive Cosmogonies & Other Pieces. James G. Frazer. LC 67-26742. (Essay Index Reprint Ser.). 1977. 18.95 (0-8369-0456-7) Ayer.

***Creation & Evolution in the Early American Scientific Affiliation.** Ed. by Mark A. Kalthoff. LC 94-45528. (Creationism in Twentieth-Century America Ser.: Vol. 10). 512p. 1995. 83.00 (0-8153-1811-1) Garland.

Creation & Fall. Dietrich Bonhoeffer. Bd. with Temptation. 128p. 1965. Set pap. 5.95 (0-02-083890-5) Macmillan.

Creation & Fall. Lazar Puhalo. 36p. (Orig.). 1986. pap. text ed. 4.00 (0-913026-97-2) Synaxis Pr.

Creation & Fall: Temptation. Dietrich Bonhoeffer. 1983. 18.50 (0-8446-5962-2) Peter Smith.

Creation & Fall & Temptation. Dietrich Bonhoeffer. 1965. 4.95 (0-685-46253-6, Collier S&S) S&S Trade.

Creation & Gospel: The New Situation of European Theology. Gustaf Wingren. LC 78-78183. (Toronto Studies in Theology: Vol. 2). 189p. 1979. lib. bdg. 79.95 (0-88946-994-6) E Mellen.

Creation & Imitation. James D. Farquhar. LC 76-29199. 1976. 27.50 (0-917736-02-8) Nova U Pr.

Creation & Interpretation. Denis Donoghue et al. 300p. 1984. pap. 65.00 (0-930586-20-4) Haven Pubns.

Creation & Liturgy: Studies in Honor of H. Boone Porter. Ed. by Ralph N. McMichael, Jr. (Orig.). 1993. pap. text ed. 24.95 (1-56929-001-6) Pastoral Pr.

Creation & Procreation: Feminist Reflections on Mythologies of Cosmogony & Parturition. Marta Weigle. LC 89-40401. (Publications of the American Folklore Society, Bibliographical & Special Ser.). (Illus.). 310p. (C). 1989. pap. text ed. 20.95 (0-8122-1264-9) U of Pa Pr.

Creation & Re-Creation of Music. David M. Key. LC 93-33536. 1994. write for info. (0-13-138622-0) P-H Gen Ref & Trav.

Creation & Re-Creation of Music: A New Approach to Music Fundamentals. David Key. 240p. 1994. pap. text ed. 25.00 (0-13-189622-9) P-H.

Creation & Recreation. Northrop Frye. 80p. 1980. pap. 12.95 (0-8020-6422-1) U of Toronto Pr.

Creation & Recreation Experiments in Literary Form in Early Modern Spain: Studies in Honor of Stephen Gilman. Ed. by Ronald Surtz & Nora Weinerth. (Homenajes Ser.: No. 2). 126p. 1983. 14.75 (0-936388-19-6); pap. 9.75 (0-936388-16-1) Juan de la Cuesta.

Creation & Redemption. Gabriel Daly. LC 88-24622. (Theology & Life Ser.: Vol. 25). 229p. (Orig.). 1988. pap. 17.95 (0-8146-5748-6) Liturgical Pr.

Creation & Restoration of Coastal Plant Communities. Ed. by Roy R. Lewis, III. 232p. 1982. 156.00 (0-8493-6573-2, QK938, CRC Reprint) Franklin.

Creation & Scientific Creativity: A Study in the Thought of S. L. Jaki. Paul Haffner. 206p. (Orig.). 1991. pap. 8.95 (0-931888-41-7) Christendom Pr.

Creation & the Character of God. Ronald Storer. 204p. 1986. 40.00 (0-7223-1973-8, Pub. by A H S Ltd UK) St Mut.

Creation & the End of Days - Judaism & Scientific Cosmology: Proceedings of the 1984 Meeting of the Academy for Jewish Philosophy. Ed. by David Novak & Norbert Samuelson. LC 86-19062. 336p. (Orig.). 1986. 52.00 (0-8191-5524-1, Studies in Judaism) U Pr of Amer.

***Creation & the History of Science.** fac. ed. Christopher B. Kaiser. LC 91-123. (History of Christian Theology Ser.: No. 3). 324p. (Orig.). 1991. reprint ed. pap. 92.40 (0-7837-7961-5, 2047717) Bks Demand.

Creation & the Modern Christian. Henry M. Morris. 298p. 1985. pap. 8.95 (0-89051-111-X) Master Bks.

***Creation & the Persistence of Evil: The Jewish Prama of Divine Omnipotence.** Jon D. Levenson. LC 94-31950. 1994. pap. 12.95 (0-691-02950-4) Princeton U Pr.

Creation & the Second Coming. Henry M. Morris. 194p. 1991. 12.95 (0-89051-163-2) Master Bks.

Creation & Time: A Biblical & Scientific Perspective on the Creation-Date Controversy. Hugh Ross. LC 94-4308. 192p. 1994. pap. 10.00 (0-89109-776-7) NavPress.

***Creation & Time, a Report on the Progressive Creationist Book by Hugh Ross.** 2nd ed. Mark Van Bebber & Paul S. Taylor. Ed. by Dale T. Mason & Marian Taylor. 128p. (Orig.). 1994. reprint ed. pap. 6.99 (1-877775-02-9, Eden Communs) Films Christ.

Creation: Artistic & Spiritual. Omraam M. Aivanhov. (Izvor Collection: Vol. 223). 203p. (Orig.). 1987. pap. 8.95 (2-85566-402-0, Pub. by Prosveta FR) Prosveta USA.

Creation Book. William F. Dakenbing. LC 75-39840. (Illus.). 70p. (J). (gr. 3 up). 1976. 5.95 (0-685-68397-4); pap. 3.95 (0-685-68398-2) Triumph Pub.

Creation, Christ & Culture. Ed. by Richard W. McKinney. 336p. 39.95 (0-567-01019-8, Pub. by T & T Clark UK) Bks Intl VA.

Creation Crafts. Darlene Hoffa. (Illus.). 64p. (Orig.). (J). 1993. pap. 5.99 (0-570-04758-7) Concordia.

Creation, Dissemination, & Disposition of Juvenile & Family Court Records: 1981 Statutes Analysis. Thomas S. Vereb. 212p. 1980. With state statutes, 212 pgs. 40.00 (0-318-36226-0); Without state statutes, 49 pgs. 10.00 (0-318-36227-9) Natl Juv & Family Ct Judges.

Creation, Eschaton, & Ethics: The Ethical Significance of the Creation - Eschaton Relation in the Thought of Emil Brunner & Jurgen Moltmann. Douglas J. Schuurman. LC 90-23092. (American University Studies: Theology & Religion: Ser. VII, Vol. 86). 200p. (C). 1991. text ed. 35.95 (0-8204-1423-9) P Lang Pubs.

Creation-Evolution Controversy. 1976. 15.95 (0-918112-01-X); kivar, pap. 9.95 (0-918112-02-8) Inquiry Pr.

***Creation-Evolution Debates.** Ed. by Ronald L. Numbers. LC 94-45074. (Creationism in Twentieth-Century America Ser.: Vol. 2). 520p. 1995. 95.00 (0-8153-1803-0) Garland.

***Creation Fire: A Cafra Anthology of Caribbean Women's Poetry.** Ed. by Espinet. Date not set. per. 19.95 (0-920813-02-X, Pub. by Sister Vision CN) InBook.

Creation, Genesis, the Big Bang, & Evolution. John Wend. 35p. 1989. pap. 9.00 (0-932223-07-9) Churchill PC.

Creation Hypothesis: Scientific Evidence for an Intelligent Designer. Ed. by J. P. Moreland. LC 93-42724. 240p. (Orig.). 1994. pap. 12.99 (0-8308-1698-4, 1698) InterVarsity.

Creation in Crisis: Responding to God's Covenant. Shantilal P. Bhagat. LC 90-45512. 173p. (Orig.). 1991. pap. 9.95 (0-87178-164-6) Brethren.

Creation in Full Score. Joseph Haydn. 1990. pap. 12.95 (0-486-26411-4) Dover.

Creation in Space, Vol. 2: Interim Edition. Jonathan B. Friedman. 448p. 1993. per. 45.95 (0-8403-8449-1) Kendall-Hunt.

Creation in the Biblical Traditions. Ed. by Richard J. Clifford et al. LC 92-20268. (Catholic Biblical Quarterly Monographs: No. 24). vi, 151p. 1992. pap. 7.00 (0-915170-23-X) Catholic Bibl Assn.

Creation, Its Laws & You. June K. Burke. (Illus.). (Orig.). 1993. pap. 9.95 (0-929377-01-X) Burke-Srour Pubns Inc.

Creation Liturgy see Celebrating the Earth: An Earth-Centered Theology of Worship with Blessings, Prayers, & Rituals

***Creation Myths.** Marie-Louise Von Franz. 1995. pap. 17.00 (0-87773-528-X) Shambhala Pubns.

Creation Myths: Man's Introduction to the World. David Maclagan. (Art & Imagination Ser.). (Illus.). 1977. pap. 14.95 (0-500-81010-9) Thames Hudson.

Creation Myths of Primitive America. Jeremiah Curtin. 1980. 34.95 (0-405-13697-8, 1710) Ayer.

Creation Myths of Primitive America. Jeremiah Curtin. (Works of Jeremiah Curtin Ser.). 1990. reprint ed. lib. bdg. 79.00 (0-7812-2501-9) Rprt Serv.

Creation, Nature, & Political Order in the Philosophy of Michael Foster (1903-1959) The Classic Mind Articles & Others, with Modern Critical Essays. Ed. by Cameron Wybrow. LC 92-43017. (Illus.). 376p. 1993. text ed. 79.95 (0-7734-9207-0) E Mellen.

Creation of a Barrier-Free Interior. Patricia M. Johnson. (Illus.). 140p. 1988. pap. text ed. 15.00 (0-317-91057-4) Positive NJ.

Creation of a California Tribe: Grandfather's Maidu Indian Tale. Clifford E. Trafzer & Lee A. Smith-Trafzer. LC 88-61007. (Illus.). 45p. (Orig.). (J). (gr. 3-6). 1988. pap. 6.95 (0-940113-18-X) Sierra Oaks Pub.

Creation of a Community: The City of Wells in the Middle Ages. David G. Shaw. LC 92-42694. (Oxford Historical Monographs). (C). 1993. 60.00 (0-19-820401-9, Clarendon Pr) OUP.

Creation of a Community Setting. Seymor B. Sarason et al. LC 76-38796. (Segregated Settings & the Problems of Change Ser.). 100p. (C). 1972. text ed. 17.95x (0-8156-8077-5) Syracuse U Pr.

Creation of a European Banking System: A Study of Its Legal & Technical Aspects. Richard Cordero. LC 89-13890. (American University Studies: Political Science: Ser. X, Vol. 27). 390p. (C). 1990. text ed. 67.50 (0-8204-1315-1) P Lang Pubs.

Creation of a Medical Profession in Egypt, 1800-1922. Amira E. Sonbol. LC 91-7640. (Contemporary Issues in the Middle East Ser.). 256p. 1991. text ed. 39.95x (0-8156-2541-3) Syracuse U Pr.

Creation of a Mexican Landscape: Territorial Organization & Settlement in the Eastern Puebla Basin, 1520-1605. Jack A. Licate. LC 81-12941. (Research Papers Ser.: No. 201). (Illus.). 143p. 1981. pap. text ed. 12.00 (0-89065-107-8) U Chicago Comm Geo.

Creation of a National Air Force: The Official History of the Royal Canadian Air Force, Vol. II. W. A. Douglas. 49.95 (0-8020-2584-6) U of Toronto Pr.

Creation of American Team Sports: Baseball & Cricket, 1838-72. George B. Kirsch. LC 88-14209. (Sport & Society Ser.). (Illus.). 304p. 1989. 27.50 (0-252-01560-6) U of Ill Pr.

Creation of an Ensemble: The First Years of the American Conservatory Theatre. John R. Wilk. LC 85-1698. 232p. (Orig.). (C). 1986. pap. text ed. 10.95 (0-8093-1213-1) S Ill U Pr.

Creation of Bangladesh. Gerald Kurland. (Events of Our Times Ser.: No. 12). 32p. (Orig.). (gr. 7-12). 1973. lib. bdg. 4.95 (0-87157-713-5) SamHar Pr.

Creation of Brittany: A Late Medieval State. Michael Jones. 435p. 1988. text ed. 65.00 (0-907628-80-X) Hambledon Press.

Creation of Chaos: William James & the Stylistic Making of a Disorderly World. Frederick J. Ruf. LC 90-44858. (SUNY Series in Rhetoric & Theology). 185p. 1991. 59.50 (0-7914-0701-2); pap. 19.95 (0-7914-0702-0) State U NY Pr.

Creation of Confederate Nationalism: Ideology & Identity in the Civil War South. Drew G. Faust. LC 88-9036. (Walter Lynwood Fleming Lecture Ser.). (Illus.). 110p. 1988. pap. text ed. 8.95 (0-8071-1606-8) La State U Pr.

***Creation of Consciousness.** Edinger. 1995. pap. 15.00 (0-919123-13-9) Atrium Pubs.

Creation of Dangerous Violent Criminals. Lonnie H. Athens. 120p. (C). 1992. 22.95 (0-252-01939-3); pap. 11.95 (0-252-06262-0) U of Ill Pr.

Creation of Feminist Consciousness: From the Middle Ages to 1870. Gerda Lerner. 416p. 1994. reprint ed. pap. 11.95 (0-19-509060-8) OUP.

Creation of Full Human Personality. Joseph W. Drew & W. Hague. pap. 1.95 (0-8199-0383-3, L38115, Frncscn Herld) Franciscan Pr.

Creation of Health: The Emotional, Psychological, & Spiritual Responses That Promote Health. rev. ed. C. Norman Shealy & Caroline M. Myss. 416p. 1993. reprint ed. pap. 14.95 (0-913299-94-4) Stillpoint.

An Asterisk (*) at the beginning of an entry indicates that the title is appearing in BIP for the first time.

An Asterisk (*) at the beginning of an entry indicates that the title is appearing in BIP for the first time.

1681

Creative Arts for the Severely Handicapped. 2nd fac. ed. Claudine Sherrill. (Illus.). 304p. 1979. Photocopy ed. 46.95 (*0-398-03908-9*) C C Thomas.

Creative Arts with Older Adults: A Sourcebook. Naida Weisberg & Rosilyn Wilder. 252p. 1984. 42.95 (*0-89885-161-0*); pap. 20.95 (*0-89885-163-7*) Human Sci Pr.

Creative Arts with Older People. Intro. by Janice McMurray. LC 89-20049. (Activities, Adaptation & Aging Ser.: Vol. 14, Nos. 1 & 2). (Illus.). 138p. 1989. text ed. 29.95 (*0-86656-929-4*) Haworth Pr.

Creative Astrology: Experiential Understanding of the Horoscope. Ed. by Prudence Jones. 176p. 1991. pap. 12.95 (*1-85538-110-9*, Pub. by Mandala UK) Thorsons SF.

Creative Awakening: The Jewish Presence in Twentieth-Century American Literature, 1900-1940s-Published in Cooperation with the American Jewish Archives. Louis Harap. LC 86-14986. (Contributions in Ethnic Studies: No. 17). 214p. 1987. text ed. 49.95 (*0-313-25386-2*, HFI/) Greenwood.

Creative BasketMaking. Lois Walpole. (Illus.). 160p. 1989. 24.95 (*0-89134-299-0*, 30164) North Light Bks.

Creative Bass Technique. Henry Portnoi. 12.00 (*0-318-18108-8*) Am String Tchrs.

Creative Batik. Vijaya Hiremath. 1986. 32.00 (*0-685-14202-7*, Pub. by Abhinav II) S Asia.

***Creative Bead Jewelry: Weaving, Looming, Stringing, Wiring, Making Beads.** Carol Taylor. LC 95-4595. (Illus.). 144p. 1995. pap. 18.95 (*0-8069-1306-1*, Lark Bks) Sterling.

***Creative Bedroom Decorating.** (Illus.). 128p. (Orig.). 1995. pap. 14.99 (*1-55870-402-7*) Betterway Bks.

Creative Being: How to Raise Loving, Creative Children & Bring Out the Greatness in Us All. Judith Kurka Nagel. LC 90-83088. (Illus.). 295p. (Orig.). 1991. 29.95 (*0-9627342-0-9*); pap. 15.95 (*0-9627342-1-7*) Creativity Hse.

Creative Being: The Crafting of Person & World. Eliot Deutsch. 288p. 1992. text ed. 38.00 (*0-8248-1423-1*) UH Pr.

Creative Bible Games. Judy Dorsett. Ed. by Judy Sparks. 48p. 1990. student ed 6.99 (*0-87403-656-9*, 14-03061) Standard Pub.

Creative Bible Learning for Adults. Monroe Marlowe & Bobbie Reed. LC 77-76206. (International Center for Learning Handbooks Ser.). 192p. 1977. pap. 6.99 (*0-8307-0480-9*, 9900152) Regal.

***Creative Bible Lessons on the Life of Christ.** Doug Fields. 96p. 1994. pap. 12.99 (*0-310-40251-4*) Zondervan.

Creative Bible Studies for Young Adults. Denny Rydberg. 204p. (Orig.). 1990. pap. 12.99 (*0-931529-99-9*) Group Pub.

Creative Bible Teaching. Lawrence O. Richards. LC 74-104830. (C). 1970. 18.99 (*0-8024-1640-3*) Moody.

Creative Biology Teaching. Delma E. Harding et al. LC 68-17496. 350p. reprint ed. pap. 99.80 (*0-685-15898-5*, 2027066) Bks Demand.

***Creative Bird Carving.** William I. Tawes. LC 79-107781. (Illus.). reprint ed. pap. 63.60 (*0-7837-9075-9*, 2049824) Bks Demand.

Creative Black Book: 1992 Portfolio Edition. Creative Black Book Staff. (Illus.). 925p. 1992. 80.00 (*0-916098-68-0*) Black Bk.

Creative Black Book Portfolio Edition 1993. 1000p. Date not set. 100.00 (*0-916098-75-3*); write for info. (*0-916098-86-9*) Black Bk.

Creative Black Book, 1992, 2 vols., Set. Creative Black Book Staff. (Illus.). 1275p. 1992. boxed 110.00 (*0-916098-60-5*) Black Bk.

Creative Black Book 1993, 2 vols., Set. 1100p. Date not set. 110.00 (*0-916098-72-9*) Black Bk.

Creative Black Book 1994, 3 vols., Set. 1300p. Date not set. write for info. (*0-916098-83-4*) Black Bk.

Creative Book of Decorative Painting. Juliet Bawden. (Creative Book Ser.). (Illus.). 124p. 1989. pap. 9.95 (*0-937769-09-6*) Mark Inc CA.

Creative Book of Pressed Flowers. Mary Lawrence. (Creative Book Ser.). (Illus.). 124p. 1989. pap. 9.95 (*0-937769-12-6*) Mark Inc CA.

Creative Bookbinding. Pauline Johnson. 1990. pap. 10.95 (*0-486-26307-X*) Dover.

Creative Brain. rev. ed. Ned Herrmann. LC 87-72980. (Illus.). 456p. 1991. pap. 26.95 (*0-944850-02-2*) Brain Bks.

Creative Brain. 2nd ed. Ned Herrmann. LC 87-72980. (Illus.). 456p. 1990. 49.95 (*0-944850-01-4*) Brain Bks.

Creative Brainstorms: The Relationship Between Madness & Genius. Ruseell R. Monroe. (Frontiers of Consciousness Ser.). 312p. 1992. 27.95 (*0-8290-1769-0*) Irvington.

Creative Bread Baking: How to Bake Bread Without Recipes. John Blake. LC 91-91847. 55p. 1990. pap. 7.95 (*0-9628966-0-8*) J & D Blake Assocs.

Creative Bread Baking Two: Specialty Breads & the Rule of Two. John Blake. 1991. pap. 7.95 (*0-9628966-1-6*) J & D Blake Assocs.

Creative Breakthroughs: Tap the Power of Your Unconscious Mind. Jill Morris. 272p. (Orig.). 1992. pap. 12.99 (*0-446-39217-0*) Warner Bks.

Creative Bulletin Boards for Sunday Schools. Nancy S. Williamson. 96p. 1992. pap. 9.99 (*0-8010-9717-7*) Baker Bk.

Creative Business Financing: How to Make Your Best Deal When Negotiating Equipment, Leases & Business Loans. James Simmons. (Illus.). 310p. 1982. pap. 12.95 (*0-685-05662-7*) P-H.

Creative Business Letters for Employee Leasing. T. Joe Willey. LC 88-80567. 140p. (Orig.). 1988. pap. 87.50 (*0-944308-03-1*); disk 40.00 (*0-317-91153-8*) Aegis Consulting.

Creative Calligraphy. Marie Lynskey. (Illus.). 192p. (Orig.). 1984. pap. 12.95 (*0-7225-1509-X*) Thorsons SF.

***Creative Calligraphy: A Do-It-Yourself Guide to Decorative Lettering.** Peter Halliday. (Illus.). 40p. (J). (gr. 2-6). 1995. pap. 5.95 (*1-85697-539-8*, Kingfisher LKC) LKC.

Creative Campaigning. TSR Staff. (Advanced Dungeons & Dragons, Second Edition; Al-Qadim Ser.). (Illus.). 1993. pap. 15.00 (*1-56076-561-5*) TSR Inc.

Creative Campaigning: PACS & the Presidential Selection Process. Anthony Corrado. 286p. 1992. text ed. 39.00 (*0-8133-1450-X*) Westview.

Creative Canada: A Biographical Dictionary of Twentieth-Century Creative & Performing Artists, 2 vols., 2. McPherson Library - Reference Division - University of Victoria Staff. LC 73-80898. 1972. 35.00 (*0-8020-3285-0*) U of Toronto Pr.

Creative Canada: A Biographical Dictionary of Twentieth-Century Creative & Performing Artists, Vol. 2. University of Victoria (B. C.), Library, Reference Division Staff. LC 71-151387. 320p. reprint ed. pap. 91.20 (*0-8357-3975-9*, 2036516) Bks Demand.

Creative Canada, Vol. 1: A Biographical Dictionary of Twentieth-Century Creative & Performing Artists. University of Victoria (BC), Library, Reference Division Staff. LC 71-151387. 324p. reprint ed. pap. 92.40 (*0-8357-3786-1*, 2036516) Bks Demand.

Creative Candlewicking for the Home. Sue Millard. 96p. (C). 1988. 100.00 (*1-85368-069-9*, Pub. by New Holland Pubs UK) St Mut.

***Creative Canes & Walking Sticks: Carving with Tom Wolfe.** Tom Wolfe. (Illus.). 64p. (Orig.). 1995. pap. 12.95 (*0-88740-885-0*) Schiffer.

Creative Capers. L. Schwartz. (Enrichment & Gifted Ser.). (J). (gr. 4-6). 1985. 5.95 (*0-88160-117-9*, LW 251) Learning Wks.

Creative Card Magic of William P. Miesel. William P. Miesel. LC 80-80275. (Illus.). 178p. 1980. 20.00 (*0-9604016-0-1*) Unikorn Magik.

Creative Card Play. James S. Kauder. LC 89-80898. 240p. 1989. pap. 11.95 (*1-877908-00-2*) Lawrence & Leong Pub.

Creative Cards: Wrap a Message with a Personal Touch. Yoshiko Kitagawa. Ed. by Tsuizaki & Barry. (Illus.). 76p. 1990. reprint ed. pap. 15.95 (*0-87011-964-8*) Kodansha.

Creative Care for the Person with Alzheimer's. Marie A. Fasano. (Illus.). 80p. 1987. pap. text ed. 14.00 (*0-89303-369-3*) P-H.

Creative Careers: Minorities in the Arts. Paul Bullock. 220p. 1977. 5.50 (*0-89215-063-7*) U Cal LA Indus Rel.

Creative Careers: Real Jobs in Glamour Fields. Gary Blake & Robert W. Bly. LC 84-29093. 335p. 1985. pap. text ed. 17.95 (*0-471-81560-8*) Wiley.

Creative Caregiving. James R. Sherman. (Illus.). 80p. (Orig.). 1994. pap. 7.95 (*0-935538-17-8*) Pathway Bks.

***Creative Caring: Support & Encouragement Ideas to Help Others Through Life's Challenges.** Linda D. Rockey & Beth Kitzinger. LC 95-68237. 160p. 1995. pap. 6.95 (*0-9646115-0-3*) Support Pubns.

Creative Cartoonist. Dick Gautier. (Illus.). 128p. (Orig.). 1989. pap. 11.00 (*0-399-51434-1*, Perigree Bks) Berkley Pub.

Creative Carving. Stephen Yan. (Illus.). 96p. (Orig.). 1989. pap. 11.95 (*0-921053-03-7*) Gordon Soules Bk.

Creative Cash: How to Sell Your Crafts, Needlework, Designs & Know-How. 5th rev. ed. Barbara Brabec. LC 96-93448. 200p. 1993. reprint ed. pap. 14.95 (*0-9613909-3-X*) B Brabec Prods.

Creative Casseroles. Anne Willan. LC 93-3086. (Anne Willan's Look & Cook Ser.). (Illus.). 128p. 1994. 19.95 (*1-56458-299-X*) Dorling Kindersley.

Creative Casting: Jewelry, Silverware, Sculpture. Sharr Choate. (Illus.). 1986. pap. 15.00 (*0-517-56174-3*, Crown) Crown Pub Group.

Creative Catechist. rev. ed. Janaan Manternach & Carl Pfeifer. LC 91-90951. 160p. (Orig.). 1991. pap. 9.95 (*0-89622-490-2*) Twenty-Third.

Creative Century: Selections from the Twentieth-Century Collections. Ed. by Andreas Brown. (Illus.). 1970. pap. 8.00 (*0-87959-004-1*) U of Tex H Ransom Ctr.

Creative Chalkboard Activities. Les Landin & Frank Thibault. (J). (gr. 1-6). 1986. pap. 5.99 (*0-8224-1636-0*) Fearon Teach Aids.

***Creative Challenge Projects.** Michael T. Ganci. 1992. pap. text ed. 10.97 (*0-937659-47-9*) GCT.

Creative Change: A Cognitive-Humanistic Approach to Social Work Practice. Howard Goldstein. 280p. 1985. pap. 14.95 (*0-422-78650-0*, NO. 9169, Pub. by Tavistock UK) Routledge Chapman & Hall.

Creative Characters. Elisabeth Young-Bruehl. 272p. 1991. 25.00 (*0-415-90369-6*, A5186, Routledge NY) Routledge.

Creative Chef Two. Ed. by Ellen Greene et al. LC 93-61058. 260p. 1993. 16.95 (*0-9638628-0-4*) Tourette Syndrome.

Creative Chess. A Avni. 149p. 1991. pap. 15.95 (*0-08-037800-5*, Pub. by CHES UK) Macmillan.

Creative Chicago: From the Chap-Book to the University. Henry Regnery. LC 93-11130. 1993. 25.00 (*0-924772-24-7*) CH Bookworks.

Creative Chicken. Rachel Blackmore. 1993. 12.98 (*1-55521-849-0*) Bk Sales Inc.

Creative Chicken Cookbook. Family Circle Editors. 1977. 12.95 (*0-405-11397-8*) Ayer.

Creative Child Care: You Can Make a Difference. Janet Spaulding. (Illus.). 140p. (Orig.). 1992. spiral bd., pap. 18.00 (*0-9634214-0-9*) MARV Pubns.

Creative Childbirth: The Leclaire Method of Easy Birthing Through Hypnosis & Rational-Intuitive Thought. Michelle L. O'Neill. LC 92-81691. (Illus.). 105p. (Orig.). 1993. pap. 11.95 (*0-9633087-3-4*) Papyrus Pr.

Creative Chip Carving. rev. ed. Frank Manning. (Illus.). 48p. 1984. pap. 2.95 (*0-486-23735-4*) Dover.

Creative Choice in Hypnosis. Milton H. Erickson. Ed. by Ernest L. Rossi & Margaret O. Ryan. (Seminars, Workshops & Lectures of Milton H. Erickson: Vol. IV). 288p. 1992. 19.95 (*0-8290-3152-9*); audio, text ed. 42.50 (*0-8290-2418-2*); Hypnosis: Creative Choice or Manipulation?. audio 20.00 (*0-8290-3158-8*) Irvington.

***Creative Chords.** Marilynn M. Moe. 88p. 1994. student ed 15.50 (*1-884816-00-2*) M M Moe.

***Creative Chords Answer Key.** Marilynn M. Moe. 88p. 1994. pap. text ed. 7.95 (*1-884816-01-0*) M M Moe.

Creative Christian Education: Teaching the Bible Through the Church Year. Howard Hanchey. LC 85-63571. 224p. (Orig.). 1986. pap. 10.95 (*0-8192-1380-2*) Morehouse Pub.

***Creative Christian Leadership: Skills for More Effective Ministry.** Kevin Treston. LC 94-62050. 120p. (Orig.). 1995. pap. 9.95 (*0-89622-648-4*) Twenty-Third.

Creative Christmas: Simple Crafts from Many Lands. Kathryn Shoemaker. 1978. pap. 7.95 (*0-03-045716-5*) Harper SF.

Creative Christmas Crafts. Alison Wormleighton. LC 93-83531. (Illus.). 144p. 1993. 24.95 (*1-56138-294-9*) Running Pr.

Creative Christmas Kitchen. 1992. 19.95 (*0-942237-18-8*) Leisure AR.

Creative Christmas Programs: For Sunday Schools & Church Groups. Jerry Koetje. 160p. (Orig.). 1991. pap. 9.99 (*0-8010-5297-1*) Baker Bk.

Creative Circuit. K. G. Subramanyan. (C). 1992. 24.00 (*81-7046-096-4*, Pub. by Seagull Bks II) S Asia.

Creative Classroom: A Guide for Using Drama in the Classroom, Pre-K-6. Lenore Kelner. LC 93-29149. (Illus.). 174p. (J). (gr. 1-6). 1993. pap. text ed. 17.50 (*0-435-08628-6*, 08628) Heinemann.

Creative Classroom Testing: Ten Designs for Assessment & Instruction. 192p. 1988. 14.95 (*0-317-67890-6*) Educ Testing Serv.

Creative Clay Jewelry: Extraordinary, Colorful, Fun Designs to Make from Polymer Clay. Leslie Dierks. LC 93-37188. (Illus.). 144p. 1994. 18.95 (*0-937274-74-7*) Lark Books.

***Creative Clay Jewelry Book & Kit.** (Illus.). 1995. pap. 40.00 (*0-8069-0920-X*) Sterling.

Creative Clays: American Art Pottery from the New Orleans Museum of Art. John W. Keefe. LC 92-80409. (Illus.). 32p. 1992. 9.95 (*0-89494-037-6*) New Orleans Mus Art.

Creative Clowning. 2nd ed. Bruce Fife et al. LC 91-24284. (Illus.). 224p. (Orig.). 1992. pap. 24.00 (*0-941599-16-7*) Piccadilly Bks.

Creative Cognition: Theory, Research & Applications. Ronald A. Finke et al. (Illus.). 240p. 1992. 27.50 (*0-262-06150-3*, Bradford Bks) MIT Pr.

***Creative Cognition Approach.** Ed. by Steven M. Smith et al. LC 94-21947. 320p. 1995. 39.95x (*0-262-19354-X*, Bradford Bks) MIT Pr.

***Creative Collage.** Date not set. 29.99 (*0-614-01911-7*) Rockport Pubs.

Creative Collage Techniques. Nita Leland & Virginia L. Williams. 144p. 1994. 27.95 (*0-89134-563-9*) North Light Bks.

Creative College Student: An Unmet Challenge. Ed. by Paul Heist. LC 68-21316. (Jossey-Bass Higher Education Ser.). 272p. reprint ed. pap. 77.60 (*0-317-08594-8*, 2013937) Bks Demand.

Creative Color. Faber Birren. LC 87-60000. (Illus.). 128p. 1987. pap. 14.95 (*0-88740-096-5*) Schiffer.

Creative Color: An Analysis & Synthesis of Useful Color Knowledge. Essene Fellowship of Peace Staff. LC 88-81957. (Illus.). 204p. (Orig.). 1989. pap. 24.95 (*0-9620292-0-3*) Essene Fellowship.

***Creative Color Schemes for Your Home.** (Illus.). 128p. (Orig.). 1995. pap. 14.99 (*1-55870-401-9*) Betterway Bks.

***Creative Colored Pencil: The Step-by-Step Guide & Showcase.** Vera Curnow. 1995. 29.99 (*1-56496-141-9*) Rockport Pubs.

Creative Communication. 4th ed. Fran A. Tanner. 1991. pap. 19.33 (*0-931054-24-9*) Clark Pub.

Creative Communication: How to Develop & Apply Your Skills to Communicate Persuasively, Professionally & Productively. Victor Annigian. Ed. by Diane Parker. LC 92-50173. 200p. 1993. text ed. 21.95 (*0-88247-933-4*); pap. 15.95 (*0-88247-932-6*) R & E Pubs.

***Creative Communication: Principles & Applications.** Craig E. Johnson & Michael Z. Hackman. (Illus.). 245p. (Orig.). (C). 1995. pap. text ed. 14.95x (*0-88133-828-1*) Waveland Pr.

Creative Communication & Discussion Activities. Wayne Rice & Mike Yaconelli. Ed. by Robert P. Stamschror. (Creative Resources for Youth Ministry Ser.). (Illus.). 96p. (YA). (gr. 7-12). 1991. pap. 12.95 (*0-88489-266-2*) St Marys.

Creative Communicative Activities for the French Class: For All Students of French. Linda Skaife. 112p. (FRE.). 1992. pap. 23.95 (*0-8442-1371-3*, Natl Textbk) NTC Pub Grp.

Creative Communicator: 399 Goals to Communicate Commitment Without Boring People to Death! Barbara A. Glanz. LC 93-12106. 192p. 1993. text ed. 20.00 (*1-55623-832-0*) Irwin Prof Pubng.

Creative Communion: African Folk Models of Fertility & the Regeneration of Life. Ed. by Anita Jacobson-Widding & Walter E. Van Beek. (Uppsala Studies in Cultural Anthropology: No. 15). 351p. (Orig.). 1990. pap. 65.50x (*91-554-2660-3*, Pub. by Almqv & Wiksell SW) Coronet Bks.

Creative Companion. Sark. (Illus.). 160p. (Orig.). 1991. pap. 11.95 (*0-89087-651-7*) Celestial Arts.

***Creative Compartments: A Design for Future Organization.** Gerard Fairtlough. LC 94-28285. (Praeger Studies on the 21st Century). 264p. 1994. text ed. 59.95 (*0-275-95089-1*, Praeger Pubs) Greenwood.

***Creative Compartments: A Design of Future Organization.** Gerard Faiartlough. LC 94-28285. (Praeger Studies on the Twenty-First Century). 264p. 1994. pap. text ed. 19.95 (*0-275-95090-5*, Praeger Pubs) Greenwood.

Creative Compromise: The Macbride Commission: a Firsthand Report & Reflection on the Workings of UNESCO's International Commission for the Study of Communication Problems. William G. Harley. LC 92-27092. 272p. 1993. lib. bdg. 39.50 (*0-8191-8906-5*) U Pr of Amer.

***Creative Computer Graphics.** Date not set. 29.99 (*1-56496-177-X*) Rockport Pubs.

Creative Computer Graphics. Annabel Jankel et al. (Illus.). 176p. 1984. 44.95 (*0-521-26251-8*) Cambridge U Pr.

Creative Computer Imaging. Joan Truckenbrod. 208p. 1988. pap. text ed. 42.00 (*0-13-189309-2*) P-H.

Creative Computer Software for Strategic Thinking & Decision Making: A Guide for Senior Management & MIS Professionals. Robert J. Thierauf. LC 92-18930. 344p. 1993. text ed. 55.00 (*0-89930-758-2*, TCK, Quorum Bks) Greenwood.

Creative, Confident Children: Making the Most of the Preschool Years. Maxine Hancock. 256p. (Orig.). 1992. pap. 9.99 (*0-87788-146-4*) Shaw Pubs.

Creative Conflict: Secret of Heart to Heart Communion. Christopher Hills. Ed. by Deborah Rozman & Ann Ray. LC 80-5562. (Illus.). 324p. (Orig.). 1980. pap. 7.95 (*0-916438-36-8*) Univ of Trees.

Creative Conflict Resolution: More Than 200 Activities for Keeping Peace in the Classroom. William Kreidler. 216p. (Orig.). 1983. pap. 12.95 (*0-673-15642-7*) GdYrBks.

Creative Conflict Solving for Kids. 2nd ed. Fran Schmidt & Alice Friedman. (Illus.). 80p. 1985. 19.95 (*0-685-29154-5*); pap. 13.95 (*0-685-29153-7*) Peace Educ.

Creative Conflict Solving for Kids: Grades 3-4. 2nd ed. Fran Schmidt & Alice Friedman. 90p. (Orig.). (J). (gr. 3-4). 1993. Wkbk. student ed 11.95 (*0-685-64734-X*) Peace Educ.

Creative Conflict Solving for Kids: Grades 3-4, Incl. poster. Fran Schmidt & Alice Friedman. 90p. (Orig.). (J). (gr. 3-4). 1991. 21.95 (*1-878227-10-6*) Peace Educ.

Creative Conflict Solving for Kids: Grades 3-4, Incl. poster. 2nd ed. Fran Schmidt & Alice Friedman. 90p. (Orig.). (J). (gr. 3-4). 1993. Tchr's ed., incl. poster. teacher ed 21.95 (*1-878227-17-3*) Peace Educ.

Creative Conflict Solving for Kids: Grades 3-4, Set. Fran Schmidt & Alice Friedman. 24p. (Orig.). (J). (gr. 3-4). 1991. 11.95 (*1-878227-11-4*) Peace Educ.

Creative Conflict Solving for Kids: Grades 5-9, Incl. poster. 2nd rev. ed. Fran Schmidt & Alice Friedman. (Illus.). 80p. (J). (gr. 4-9). 1985. pap. text ed. 21.95 (*1-878227-00-9*) Peace Educ.

Creative Connection. Natalie Rogers. LC 93-83958. 1993. 29.95 (*0-8314-0080-3*) Sci & Behavior.

Creative Connection: Advertising Copy & Idea Visualization. Shirley F. Milton & Arthur A. Winters. (Illus.). 200p. (C). 1981. text ed. 20.00 (*0-87005-316-7*) Fairchild.

Creative Connection Instructors Guide. Arthur Winters & Shirley Milton. 71p. (C). 1982. 2.50 (*0-87005-330-2*) Fairchild.

Creative Connections: Literature & the Reading Program, Grades 1-3. Mary L. Olsen. LC 87-29665. xix, 250p. 1987. pap. 23.50 (*0-87287-651-9*) Libs Unl.

Creative Conservation: Interactive Management of Wild & Captive Animals. Ed. by P. J. Olney et al. LC 93-33949. 1993. 94.95 (*0-412-49570-8*, Chap & Hall NY) Chapman & Hall.

Creative Constitution of the Universe. R. J. Fajardo. 41p. (C). 1988. student ed 10.00 (*0-940774-03-8*) Pulsante Assn News.

***Creative Container Gardening.** Elaine Stevens & Dagmar Hungerford. 224p. (Orig.). 1995. pap. 14.95 (*0-89815-697-1*) Ten Speed Pr.

Creative Container Gardening: One Hundred Fifty Recipes for Window Boxes, Tubs, & Baskets. Kathleen Brown & Effie Romain. (Illus.). 192p. 1988. pap. 17.00 (*0-7181-3034-0*, Mermaid) Viking Penguin.

Creative Cookie. James D. Rudoff. LC 87-72388. (Allergy Kitchen Ser.: Vol. 2). (Illus.). 112p. (Orig.). 1988. pap. 7.95 (*0-9616708-8-6*) Allergy Pubns.

Creative Cooking - FAST: Reproducible Master. (YA). (gr. 7-12). 1989. Package of 10. 15.95 (*1-877844-01-2*, 2221M) Meridian Educ.

Creative Cooking - The Low Fat Way: A Lifetime Approach to Delicious Healthy Living. Yvonne Jacob. Ed. by Jo Girard. (Illus.). 283p. (Orig.). 1989. pap. 19.95 (*0-9618415-3-2*) AZ Bariatric Phy.

***Creative Cooking Library, 4 bks., Set.** 1994. pap. 27.96 (*0-376-00904-7*) Sunset Menlo Pk.

Creative Cooking Low-Sodium. Caroline Weiss et al. (Illus.). 1994. pap. 5.50 (*0-686-47049-4*) Budlong.

Creative Cooking Recipes from the Authors You Love. Writers Group of the Triad Staff. Ed. by Nancy G. Gates. LC 94-68684. (Illus.). 176p. 1994. pap. 13.95 (*1-878086-30-8*) Down Home NC.

C

An Asterisk (*) at the beginning of an entry indicates that the title is appearing in BIP for the first time.

C

An Asterisk (*) at the beginning of an entry indicates that the title is appearing in BIP for the first time.

1683

An Asterisk (*) at the beginning of an entry indicates that the title is appearing in BIP for the first time.

C

An Asterisk (*) at the beginning of an entry indicates that the title is appearing in BIP for the first time.

1685

Creative Resources for ECE Classroom. 2nd ed. Judy Herr & Yvonne Libby. LC 94-19870. 672p. 1994. pap. text ed. 39.95 (*0-8273-5871-7*) Delmar.

Creative Resources for Teaching General Business, Consumer Education, & Private Enterprise. Gwendolyn S. Watson. 431p. (C). 1980. pap. text ed. 33.25 (*0-15-515812-0*) HB Coll Pubs.

***Creative Resources for the Ear.** Herr. Date not set. 35.95 (*0-8273-3603-9*) Delmar.

Creative Responsibility. C. Thomas Sikking & John D. Bischel. 92p. (Orig.). 1980. pap. 5.95 (*0-87516-389-0*) DeVorss.

***Creative Restaurant Graphics.** (Illus.). 224p. 1995. 75.00 (*4-938812-06-1*, Pub. by Meisei Co Ltd JA) Bks Nippan.

***Creative Retirement: Shifting Gears from a Life of Work to a World of Options.** Frieda Porat. LC 94-69745. 198p. (Orig.). 1994. pap. 9.95 (*0-9643745-0-1*) NewLife CA.

Creative Revolt: A Study of Wright, Ellison, & Dostoevsky. Michael F. Lynch. (American University Studies: American Literature: Ser. XXIV, Vol. 12). 200p. (C). 1989. text ed. 42.95 (*0-8204-1018-7*) P Lang Pubs.

Creative Rhetoric. Francine Hardaway. 304p. 1976. 15.95 (*0-685-03812-2*) P-H.

Creative Rhythmic Movement: Boys & Girls Dancing. Gladys A. Fleming. (Illus.). 432p. (C). 1976. pap. write for info. (*0-13-191106-6*) P-H.

***Creative Ribbon Embroidery.** Heather Joynes. (Illus.). 72p. (Orig.). 1994. pap. 12.95 (*0-86417-625-2*) Seven Hills Bk.

***Creative Ribbon Embroidery.** Salli Van Rensburg. 90p. 1995. 20.00 (*0-614-04344-1*) Quilters Res.

***Creative Ribbon Embroidery.** Sally Van Rensburg. 1995. 20.00 (*0-9629056-2-3*) Quilters Res.

Creative Ritual. Thomas Healki. LC 85-51400. (Illus.). 80p. 1986. pap. 4.95 (*0-87728-625-6*) Weiser.

Creative Romance. Doug Fields. 1991. pap. 6.99 (*0-89081-880-0*) Harvest Hse.

Creative Sceptics: In Defense of the Liberal Temper. Thomas V. Smith. LC 75-177967. (Essay Index Reprint Ser.). 1977. reprint ed. 21.95 (*0-8369-2572-6*) Ayer.

Creative Science Experiences for the Young Child. rev. ed. Imogene Forte & Joy MacKenzie. (Illus.). 176p. (gr. k-2). 1983. pap. text ed. 9.95 (*0-86530-056-9*, IP-056) Incentive Pubns.

Creative Sciencing: Ideas & Activities for Teachers & Children. 2nd ed. Alfred DeVito & Gerald H. Krockover. (C). 1987. pap. text ed. 17.75 (*0-673-39149-3*) HarpCollege.

Creative Sciencing: Ideas & Activities for Teachers & Children Grades K to Eight. Alfred De Vito & Gerald H. Krockover. 1991. pap. 19.95 (*0-673-52008-0*) GdYrBks.

Creative Screwing: A Woman's Guide to Becoming an Erotic Enchantress of Superlustful Sex. rev. ed. Nannette L. Hernandez. (Illus.). 135p. 1994. pap. 21.95 (*0-9641299-8-1*) Brilliant Creations.

Creative Scripts for Hypnotherapy. Marlene E. Hunter. LC 94-6138. 232p. 1994. pap. 25.95 (*0-87630-742-X*) Brunner-Mazel.

***Creative Sculpture.** William I. Tawes. LC 76-10862. (Illus.). reprint ed. pap. 75.30 (*0-7837-9076-7*, 2049825) Bks Demand.

Creative Secrets to a Successful Band: A Step by Step Guide for Bands to Survive & Come Out on Top in the Music Industry. Brian Hamm & Jamie W. Borden. (Orig.). 1993. pap. 12.95 (*0-9637900-0-5*) B Hamm.

Creative Selectivity in Apollonius' Argonautica. Steven Jackson. 82p. 1994. pap. 22.00 (*90-256-1066-8*, Pub. by A M Hakkert NE) Benjamins North Am.

Creative Self-Communication. Venetia McKenzie. 1978. pap. 1.25 (*0-87516-254-1*) DeVorss.

Creative Self-Promotion on a Limited Budget. Sally P. Davis. (Illus.). 128p. (Orig.). 1992. pap. 19.95 (*0-89134-438-1*, 30422) North Light Bks.

Creative Selling. 4th ed. H. Webster Johnson & Anthony J. Faria. 416p. (C). 1986. pap. text ed. write for info. (*0-538-19930-X*, S93) S-W Pub.

Creative Selling. 5th rev. ed. Anthony J. Faria & H. Webster Johnson. LC 92-31584. 1993. text ed. 33.95 (*0-538-81834-4*) S-W Pub.

Creative Selling for the 1990's. rev. ed. Ben Feldman. 198p. 1988. 18.95 (*0-88462-117-0*, 2401-04) Dearborn Finan.

Creative Selling Today. 3rd ed. Stan Kossen. 496p. (C). 1990. text ed. 63.50 (*0-06-043762-6*) HarpCollege.

***Creative Serging.** Pati Palmer et al. 1995. pap. 8.95 (*0-935278-12-5*) Palmer-Pletsch.

Creative Sewing Ideas. Cy DeCosse Incorporated Staff. LC 90-42685. (Singer Sewing Reference Library). (Illus.). 128p. 1990. 16.95 (*0-86573-258-2*); pap. 14.95 (*0-86573-259-0*) Cy De Cosse.

Creative Sex. G. E. Poesnecker. 62p. (Orig.). 1976. pap. 2.00 (*0-916285-26-X*) Humanitarian.

Creative Side of Experimentation: Personal Perspective from Leading Researchers in Motor Control, Motor Development, & Sport Psychology. Ed. by Conrad W. Snyder & Bruce Abernethy. LC 92-6234. (Illus.). 280p. 1992. text ed. 38.00x (*0-87322-376-4*, BSNY0376) Human Kinetics.

Creative Silence. Ed. by Denis Duncan. (C). 1990. pap. 24.00 (*0-85305-222-0*, Pub. by J Arthur Ltd UK) St Mut.

Creative Silence. Rohit Mehta. 1986. 9.95 (*81-7059-017-5*) Theos Pub Hse.

***Creative Silk Painting.** Diane Tuckman & Jan Janas. LC 95-176. 1995. write for info. (*0-89134-610-4*) North Light Bks.

***Creative Silk Screening.** Date not set. 29.99 (*0-614-01913-3*) Rockport Pubs.

Creative Singlehood & Pastoral Care. John R. Landgraf. LC 82-7439. (Creative Pastoral Care & Counseling Ser.). 95p. reprint ed. pap. 27.10 (*0-685-23502-5*, 2029098) Bks Demand.

Creative Skits for Youth Groups 2. Randy Fishell & Greg Dunn. (Good Things for Youth Leaders Ser.). 1989. pap. 9.99 (*0-8010-3553-8*) Baker Bk.

Creative Slide-Tape Programs. Lee Green. LC 86-10462. 141p. 1986. pap. 22.50 (*0-87287-444-3*) Libs Unl.

Creative Socials & Specials Events. Mike Yaconelli & Wayne Rice. 192p. 1986. pap. 10.99 (*0-310-35131-6*, 10827P) Zondervan.

Creative Solutions to Ecological Issues. Gail E. Gelburd. LC 93-71859. (Illus.). 80p. (Orig.). 1993. pap. 19.95 (*0-8122-1531-1*) U of Pa Pr.

Creative Sound Recording on a Budget. Delton T. Horn. (Illus.). 224p. 1987. pap. 11.95 (*0-8306-2635-2*) TAB Bks.

Creative Source Book. Ed. by Rosemary Rawson & Zoa Trent. 216p. (Orig.). 1986. pap. 7.95 (*0-936633-01-8*) Gnsis Pubns Tucson.

***Creative Source Canada Fifteen.** Wilcord Publications Staff. 300p. 1994. 52.50 (*0-8230-6350-X*) Watsn-Guptill.

Creative Sources for the Music of Toru Takemitsu. Noriko Ohtake. LC 92-28294. 160p. 1993. 44.95 (*0-85967-954-3*, Pub. by Scolar Pr UK) Ashgate Pub Co.

Creative Speech: The Nature of Speech Formation. Rudolf Steiner & Marie Steiner Von Sivers. Tr. by Winifred Budgett et al. 240p. 1978. 20.00 (*0-85440-322-1*, Steinerbks) Anthroposophic.

Creative Spiral: PS-6 to PS-12. Marla McCabe. LC 91-71011. 208p. 1991. teacher ed 24.95 (*0-932881-14-9*) Greenpl Bks.

Creative Spirit. Daniel Goleman et al. LC 92-21352. (Illus.). 192p. 1993. pap. 12.95 (*0-452-26879-6*, Plume) NAL-Dutton.

Creative Spirits of the Nineteenth Century. George M. Brandes. Tr. by R. B. Anderson. LC 67-26719. (Essay Index Reprint Ser.). 1977. 30.95 (*0-8369-0245-9*) Ayer.

Creative Stitching. Jeannie Walker. 72p. (C). 1989. 100.00 (*1-85368-070-2*, Pub. by New Holland Pubs UK) St Mut.

Creative Storytelling: Choosing, Inventing, & Sharing Tales for Children. Jack Maguire. (Illus.). 192p. 1985. text ed. write for info. (*0-07-039513-6*) McGraw.

Creative Storytelling: Choosing, Inventing & Sharing Tales for Children. Jack Maguire. (Illus.). 200p. 1992. reprint ed. pap. 10.95 (*0-938756-35-4*) Yellow Moon.

Creative Strategic Change: Designing the Flexible, High-performing Organization. William A. Pasmore. LC 93-39202. 1994. text ed. 29.95 (*0-471-59729-5*) Wiley.

***Creative Strategies for School Problems: Solutions for Psychologists & Teachers.** Michael Durrant. 192p. (C). 1995. 23.00 (*0-393-70190-5*) Norton.

Creative Strategy for Assuring Success. Alfred H. McPherson. 1991. 18.95 (*0-533-09443-7*) Vantage.

Creative Strategy in Advertising. 4th ed. A. Jerome Jewler. 418p. (C). 1992. pap. 38.95 (*0-534-16290-8*) Intl Thomson.

***Creative Strategy in Advertising.** 5th ed. A. Jerome Jewler. LC 94-34874. 389p. 1995. pap. 38.95 (*0-534-25260-5*) Intl Thomson.

Creative Strategy in Direct Marketing. Susan K. Jones. LC 90-41587. (Illus.). 448p. 1991. 39.95 (*0-8442-3179-7*, NTC Busn Bks) NTC Pub Grp.

Creative Stress Management: The 1-2-3 Cope System. Jonathan C. Smith. LC 92-10771. 288p. 1992. pap. text ed. 23.00 (*0-13-155805-6*) P-H.

Creative Stroke: Communication with Brush & Pen in Graphic Design. Richard Emery. (Illus.). 192p. 1992. 39.99 (*0-935603-61-1*, 30393) Rockport Pubs.

Creative Stroke 2. 192p. 1994. 39.99 (*1-56496-078-1*) Rockport Pubs.

Creative Suffering of God. Paul S. Fiddes. 296p. 1992. pap. 19.95 (*0-19-826347-3*) OUP.

Creative Suggestions on Obtaining Company Benefits for a Small Business: A Workbook. rev. ed. Center for Self-Sufficiency Staff. 117p. 1992. 23.95 (*0-910811-21-0*) Ctr Self Suff.

Creative Supervision. 2nd ed. Karen R. Gillespie. 486p. (C). 1988. pap. text ed. 27.00 (*0-15-515825-2*) Dryden Pr.

Creative Survival: A Narrative History of Azel Adams, The Forks, Maine. Azel Adams. Ed. by Sally K. Butcher. LC 91-68485. (Illus.). 201p. (Orig.). 1992. pap. 12.95 (*0-9631912-1-7*) Old Bess Pub.

Creative Survival: The Providence Black Community in the 19th Century. Rowena Stewart et al. (Illus.). 73p. (Orig.). 1984. pap. 8.00 (*0-917012-71-2*) RI Pubns Soc.

Creative Synchronized Swimming. Beula O. Gundling & Jill E. White. LC 87-17049. (Illus.). 176p. (Orig.). (C). 1988. pap. 22.00 (*0-88011-299-9*, PGUN0299) Human Kinetics.

Creative T-Shirts & Sweats. Consumer Guide Editors. (Creative Ideas Ser.). (Illus.). 128p. (Orig.). 1994. pap. 6.99 (*0-451-82288-9*, Sig) NAL-Dutton.

Creative Talents: Their Nature, Uses & Development. J. P. Guilford. 139p. (Orig.). 1986. pap. 12.95 (*0-943456-15-0*) Bearly Ltd.

Creative Teacher: An Instructor's Guide for Milady's Standard. Darla D. Delduca. 112p. 1991. pap. 16.00 (*1-56253-015-1*) Milady Pub.

Creative Teaching: A Practical Approach. Alfred De Vito et al. LC 92-31797. (C). 1992. text ed. 40.00 (*0-06-500320-9*) HarpCollege.

***Creative Teaching Ideas.** 176p. 1993. 20.00 (*0-933964-40-4*) Natl Busn Ed Assoc.

Creative Teaching in Health. 3rd ed. Donald A. Read & Walter H. Greene. (Illus.). 436p. (C). 1989. reprint ed. pap. text ed. 23.95x (*0-88133-394-8*) Waveland Pr.

***Creative Teaching in Primary Schools: Strategies & Adaptations.** Peter Woods. LC 94-23036. 1995. pap. text ed. write for info. (*0-335-19313-7*, Open Univ Pr) Taylor & Francis.

Creative Teaching Methods: Helps You Be a Better Teacher. Marlene D. LeFever. 320p. 1985. 21.95 (*0-89191-760-8*, 25254) Cook.

Creative Teaching of the Gifted. D. Sisk. (Special Education Ser.). 384p. 1987. text ed. write for info. (*0-07-057701-3*) McGraw.

Creative Teaching of U. S. History & Government with Ready to Use Lessons in 18 Subject Units: Time Saving Techniques for Classroom Business. Patsy L. Brock. (Illus.). 144p. 1992. pap. 22.00 (*0-9633606-6-3*) Brocks Bks.

Creative Teaching Techniques for All Teachers: An Inspirational, Information-Packed Seminar, Set, incl. video. Chuck Edwards. Ed. by Cindy G. Spear. (Illus.). 50p. 1994. ring bd. 99.95 (*1-57052-017-8*) Chrch Grwth VA.

Creative Techniques for Photographing Children. Vik Orenstein. 144p. 1993. pap. 24.95 (*0-89879-543-5*, 10358) Writers Digest.

Creative Tension: Key Issues of Socialist Feminism. Ed. by Anja Meulenbelt et al. 152p. (Orig.). 1984. 30.00 (*0-89608-237-7*); pap. 8.50 (*0-89608-236-9*) South End Pr.

Creative Theory of the Universe. Frank Jakubowsky. 201p. (Orig.). 1983. pap. 8.95 (*0-932588-04-2*) Jesus Bks.

Creative Therapy: Fifty-Two Exercises for Groups. Jane Dossick & Eugene Shea. LC 88-42577. (Illus.). 124p. 1988. pap. 25.20 (*0-943158-50-8*, CTBP) Pro Resource.

Creative Therapy II: Fifty-Two More Exercises for Groups. Jane Dossick & Eugene Shea. LC 88-42577. (Illus.). 118p. 1990. pap. 25.20 (*0-943158-60-5*, CT2BP) Pro Resource.

***Creative Therapy III: 52 More Exercises for Groups.** Jane Dossick & Eugene Shea. LC 94-35064. (Illus.). 116p. 1995. pap. text ed. 21.95 (*1-56887-008-6*, CT3BP, Prof Resc Pr) Pro Resource.

Creative Thinking. 3rd ed. John G. Bennett. 1989. reprint ed. pap. 10.95 (*0-934254-30-3*) Claymont Comm.

Creative Thinking: Problem Solving Skills & the Arts Orientation. John F. Wakefield. Ed. by Mark Runco. (Creativity Research Ser.). 144p. (C). 1992. text ed. 39.50 (*0-89391-808-3*); pap. text ed. 22.50 (*0-89391-984-5*) Ablex Pub.

Creative Thinking Activities. rev. ed. Garry C. Myers. 32p. (J). (gr. 2-6). 1980. pap. 2.95 (*0-87534-113-6*) Highlights.

Creative Thinking & Problem Solving. John Fabian. (Illus.). 200p. 1990. 54.95 (*0-87371-153-X*, Q172) Lewis Pubs.

***Creative Thinking for Leaders & Teams.** Lee Towe. Ed. by Dave Kirchner. (AMI How-to Ser.). 100p. 1995. 9.95 (*1-884926-37-1*) Amer Media.

Creative Thinking in Warfare. Brig J. Nazareth. 1987. 34.00 (*81-7062-035-X*, Pub. by Lancer II) S Asia.

Creative Thinking Through Art, Vol. 1: Mixed Media. Joy Evans. (Illus.). 64p. (J). (gr. 2-5). 1993. pap. text ed. 11.95 (*1-55799-263-0*) Evan-Moor Corp.

Creative Thinking Through Art, Vol. 2: Drawing. Joy Evans. (Illus.). 64p. (J). (gr. 2-5). 1993. pap. text ed. 11.95 (*1-55799-264-9*) Evan-Moor Corp.

Creative Thinking Through Language Arts, 2 bks. Annette Geitsfeld et al. (Illus.). 125p. 1984. Bk. 1. pap. 12.50 (*0-912773-07-3*); Bk. 2. pap. 12.50 (*0-912773-06-5*) One Hund Twenty Creat.

Creative Thought Remedies. rev. ed. Alex Jones. (Illus.). 144p. 1986. pap. 12.50 (*0-87516-566-4*) DeVorss.

Creative Thoughts for Inner Peace. William H. Thompson. 96p. (Orig.). 1994. pap. 9.95 (*0-87516-667-9*) DeVorss.

Creative Timed Writings. M. Axelrod. 1975. text ed. 13.56 (*0-07-002610-6*) McGraw.

Creative Touch, No. 1. Faythelma Bechtel. 1973. 5.50 (*0-87813-909-5*) Christian Light.

Creative Touch, No. 2. Faythelma Bechtel. 1982. 5.50 (*0-87813-919-2*) Christian Light.

Creative Touch, No. 3. Faythelma Bechtel. 1988. 5.50 (*0-87813-923-0*) Christian Light.

Creative Touches. 1992. 19.95 (*0-942237-16-1*) Leisure AR.

Creative Training Techniques Handbook. Robert Pike. 175p. 1989. 45.50 (*0-943210-06-2*) Lakewood Pubns.

Creative Transformation. John D. Garcia. 192p. 1991. 15.00 (*0-87426-056-6*) Whitmore.

Creative Transformation: A Practical Guide for Maximizing Creativity. John D. Garcia. LC 89-38211. (Illus.). 480p. (Orig.). 1991. pap. 15.00 (*1-878260-01-4*) Noetic Pr.

Creative Transformation: The Healing Power of the Arts. Penny Lewis. (Illus.). 200p. (Orig.). 1993. pap. 19.95 (*0-933029-66-7*) Chiron Pubns.

Creative Triangles for Quilters. Janet Elwin. 144p. 1995. pap. 21.95 (*0-8019-8477-7*) Chilton.

Creative Troubleshooting in the Chemical Process Industries. David I. Saletan. LC 94-9082. 1994. 54.95 (*0-412-98441-5*) Chapman & Hall.

Creative Typography. Marion March. (Illus.). 144p. 1988. 27.95 (*0-89134-258-3*, 30079) North Light Bks.

Creative Understanding: Philosophical Reflections on Physics. Roberto Torretti. 456p. 1990. lib. bdg. 79.95 (*0-226-80834-3*); pap. text ed. 32.50 (*0-226-80835-1*) U Ch Pr.

Creative Underwater Photography. 1988. 4.95 (*0-89816-108-8*) Embee Pr.

Creative Union of Person & Community: A Geo-Humanist Ethic. Joseph Grau. (Tolbert Pubns). 1990. 3.50 (*0-89012-060-9*) Anima Pubns.

Creative Unity. Rabindranath Tagore. 1973. 300.00 (*0-87968-959-5*) Gordon Pr.

Creative Universities. Frederick Mayer. 1961. pap. 13.95 (*0-8084-0094-0*) NCUP.

Creative Urban Youth Ministry: A Resource for Youth Workers. rev. ed. Glandion Carney. 144p. 1991. reprint ed. pap. 7.99 (*0-87403-798-0*, 18-03168) Standard Pub.

Creative Use of Bearing Steels. Ed. by Joseph J. Hoo. LC 92-45677. (ASTM Special Technical Publication Ser.: No. 1195). (Illus.). 317p. 1993. 87.00 (*0-8031-1850-3*, 04-011950-02) ASTM.

Creative Use of Emotion. Swami Rama & Swami Ajaya. LC 86-223. Orig. Title: Emotion to Enlightenment. 162p. 1976. pap. 9.95 (*0-89389-093-6*) Himalayan Pubs.

Creative Use of Music in Group Therapy. Tom Plach. (Illus.). 90p. 1980. 27.95 (*0-398-04156-3*) C C Thomas.

***Creative Use of Music in Group Therapy.** Tom Plach. (Illus.). 90p. 1980. pap. 15.95 (*0-398-06323-0*) C C Thomas.

Creative Uses of Children's Literature. Mary A. Paulin. LC 81-12405. 730p. 1986. 55.00 (*0-208-01861-1*, Lib Prof Pubns); pap. 47.50 (*0-208-01862-X*, Lib Prof Pubns) Shoe String.

Creative Ventures. Paul Weiss. LC 91-7731. (Philosophical Explorations Ser.). 496p. (C). 1992. 45.00 (*0-8093-1729-X*) S Ill U Pr.

***Creative Victory: Reflections on the Process of Power from the Collected Works of Carlos Castanada.** Tomas. 244p. (Orig.). 1995. pap. 12.95 (*0-87728-853-4*) Weiser.

Creative Vision of Guillaume Apollinaire: A Study in Imagination. David Berry. (Stanford French & Italian Studies: Vol. 25). vi, 165p. 1982. pap. 46.50 (*0-915838-14-1*) Anma Libri.

Creative Visual Thinking. Morton Garchik. LC 81-66880. (Illus.). 100p. (C). 1982. 22.50 (*0-910158-80-0*); pap. 16.95 (*0-88108-070-5*) Art Dir.

Creative Visualization. Shakti Gawain. 144p. 1983. mass mkt. 5.50 (*0-553-27044-3*) Bantam.

Creative Visualization. Shakti Gawain. LC 79-13760. (Illus.). 160p. 1978. pap. 9.95 (*0-931432-02-2*) New Wrld Lib.

Creative Visualization: How to Use Imagery & Imagination for Self-Improvement. Ronald Shone. 160p. (Orig.). 1984. pap. 9.95 (*0-89281-214-1*) Inner Tradit.

***Creative Visualization: Use the Power of Your Imagination to Create What You Want in Your Life.** 2nd rev. ed. Shakti Gawain. LC 94-40704. 160p. 1995. pap. 9.95 (*1-880032-62-7*) New Wrld Lib.

Creative Visualization with Children: A Practical Guide. Jennifer Day. 1994. pap. 10.95 (*1-85230-469-3*) Element MA.

Creative Visualization Workbook. Shakti Gawain. 144p. (Orig.). 1982. pap. 11.95 (*0-931432-12-X*) New Wrld Lib.

***Creative Visualization Workbook.** rev. ed. Shakti Gawain. 144p. (Orig.). 1995. student ed, pap. 11.95 (*1-880032-75-9*) New Wrld Lib.

***Creative Water Gardener.** Andrew Wilson. (Illus.). 128p. 1995. 24.95 (*0-7063-7290-5*, Pub. by Ward Lock UK) Sterling.

***Creative Watercolor.** Date not set. 29.99 (*1-56496-172-9*) Rockport Pubs.

Creative Watercolor. Jose M. Parramon. LC 92-34437. (Artist's Library). (Illus.). 112p. 1993. pap. 14.95 (*0-8230-5683-X*, Watsn-Guptill) Watsn-Guptill.

Creative Watercolour Techniques. (Leisure Arts Ser.: No. 7). (Illus.). 32p. pap. 4.95 (*0-85532-406-6*, Pub. by Search Pr UK) A Schwartz & Co.

Creative Wax Carving: For the Hobbyist, Sculptor & Serious Jewelry Designer. Ruth Barnette Pierce. Ed. by Susan Guymon. LC 89-50846. (Illus.). 109p. (Orig.). 1989. pap. 19.50 (*0-9624729-0-5*) Mancuso Pub.

Creative Ways to Ask for a Date. Barbara B. Seegmiller. 129p. 1986. pap. write for info. (*0-318-60876-6*) Creatv Pubns UT.

Creative Ways to Improve Reading & Language Skills in Gifted Students: An Innovative Perception Building Approach for Elementary & Secondary Levels. Win Wenger. (Creative Thinking for the Gifted Ser.). 52p. (Orig.). 1986. pap. text ed. 12.00 (*0-910609-12-8*) Gifted Educ Pr.

Creative Ways to Offer Praise: One Hundred Ideas for Sunday Worship. Lisa Flinn & Barbara Younger. LC 92-36733. 80p. (Orig.). 1993. pap. 6.95 (*0-687-09845-9*) Abingdon.

***Creative Wedding Idea Book.** Jacqueline Smith. 1994. pap. 12.00 (*1-55850-425-7*) Adams Pubng.

Creative Weddings: An Up-to-Date Guide to Making Your Wedding As Unique As You Are. Laurie Levin & Laura G. Bellotti. LC 93-31490. 192p. (Orig.). 1994. pap. 9.95 (*0-452-27203-3*, Plume) NAL-Dutton.

***Creative Weekends: 29 1-2 Ready-to-Use Ideas for Your Single Adult Ministry.** 1995. write for info. (*0-7814-5060-8*, 87858) Cook.

Creative Wellness: The Power of the Personality to Heal Self. rev. ed. Michelle Lusson. LC 94-2787. 360p. 1994. pap. 11.95 (*0-9637891-2-0*) Printed Voice.

Creative Wellsprings for Science Teaching. Alfred De Vito. (Illus.). 348p. (Orig.). 1989. pap. 17.95 (*0-942034-06-6*) Creat Ventures IN.

Creative Whack Pack. Roger Von Oech. 12p. 1989. 12.95 (*0-88079-358-9*) US Games Syst.

Creative Whack Pack Deck-Book Set, Success Edition: Includes A Whack on the Side of the Head. Roger Von Oech. 196p. 1989. 21.95 (*0-88079-543-3*) US Games Syst.

Creative Will: An Exhibition of Works by Thirty-One Artists with Multiple Sclerosis. National MS Society Staff. LC 93-84778. (Illus.). 96p. (Orig.). 1993. pap. 19.95 (*1-56640-597-1*) Pomegranate Calif.

Creative Window Treatments. Cy DeCosse Incorporated Staff. LC 91-42084. (Arts & Crafts for Home Decorating Ser.). 128p. 1992. 18.95 (*0-86573-352-X*); 15.95 (*0-86573-355-4*) Cy De Cosse.

An Asterisk (*) at the beginning of an entry indicates that the title is appearing in BIP for the first time.

Creative Winemaking. Ed. by Robert A. Fowler. 1972. pap. 12.95 (*0-317-11984-2*) WWWWW Info Serv.

***Creative with Words Christmas: It's a Matter of Love.** Ed. by Brigitta Geltrich. (Thematic Anthology Ser.). (Illus.). 40p. (Orig.). 1987. pap. text ed. 8.00 (*0-936945-15-X*) Creat with Wds.

Creative Woman's Getting It All Together at Home Handbook. 2nd ed. Jean R. Laury. (Illus.). reprint ed. pap. 8.95 (*0-9614804-0-8*) Hot Fudge Pr.

Creative Women in Medieval & Early Modern Italy: A Religious & Artistic Renaissance. Ed. by E. Ann Matter & John Coakley. (Middle Ages Ser.). (Illus.). 376p. (C). 1994. text ed. 36.95 (*0-8122-3236-4*) U of Pa Pr.

Creative Woodturning. Dale L. Nish. LC 75-6952. (Illus.). 280p. 1975. text ed. 15.95 (*0-8425-0469-9*); pap. text ed. 12.95 (*0-8425-1557-7*) BYU Scholarly.

Creative Word. Charles S. Price. LC 93-72394. 110p. 1994. reprint ed. pap. 5.95 (*0-88270-676-4*) Bridge Pub.

Creative Word: Canon As a Model for Biblical Education. Walter Brueggemann. LC 81-71387. 176p. 1982. pap. 13.00 (*0-8006-1626-X*, 1-1626, Fortress Pr) Augsburg Fortress.

Creative Word Processing. Janice Silverman. 1988. pap. 9.99 (*0-89824-247-9*) Trillium Pr.

Creative Work: Karma Yoga. Edmond B. Szekely. (Illus.). 32p. 1973. pap. 3.50 (*0-89564-066-X*) IBS Intl.

***Creative Worklife.** fac. ed. Donald N. Scobel. LC 80-25970. (Building Blocks of Human Potential Ser.). 262p. Date not set. pap. 74.70 (*0-7837-7423-0*, 2047218) Bks Demand.

Creative World of Conjuring. John Booth. (Illus.). 284p. 1990. text ed. 38.00 (*0-943230-65-5*) Ridgeway Pr.

Creative Worship. Faye Schwartz & David Mohr. 1982. 4.75 (*0-89536-567-7*, 0376) CSS OH.

Creative Writer's Handbook. 2nd ed. Philip K. Jason & Allan B. Lefcowitz. LC 93-7757. 1993. pap. text ed. 26.00 (*0-13-709099-4*) P-H Gen Ref & Trav.

Creative Writer's Phrase-Finder. Edward Prestwood. LC 83-5617. 384p. 1984. 23.95 (*0-88280-104-X*) ETC Pubns.

Creative Writes, Bk. B. Evelyn Rothstein et al. 34p. (J). (gr. 5-12). 1984. pap. 14.95 (*0-913935-26-3*) ERA-CCR.

Creative Writing. Kristen Anderson. 324p. (C). 1984. pap. text ed. 15.75 (*0-911337-00-8*) Intell Pr CA.

Creative Writing. Charles I. Glicksberg. 604p. 1961. pap. 6.95 (*0-87532-169-0*) Hendricks House.

Creative Writing. Flora Joy. (Illus.). 64p. (J). (gr. 1-6). 1992. student ed 7.95 (*0-86653-679-5*, 1413) Good Apple.

Creative Writing. Kathleen Phillips. 1985. 23.50 (*0-87287-488-5*) Libs Unl.

Creative Writing. Mark Sonnenfeld. 32p. Date not set. pap. 3.00 (*0-9632820-5-0*) M Sonnenfeld.

***Creative Writing: A Handbook for Workshop Leaders.** Comp. by Sue Thomas. 192p. 1995. pap. 17.95 (*1-85041-078-X*, Pub. by U Nottingham UK) Paul & Co Pubs.

Creative Writing: A Log-Book of Teaching 1st Graders. Mary L. Murphy. (Illus.). 104p. 1966. 6.35 (*0-87825-254-1*) Ed Solutions.

Creative Writing: For People Who Can't Not Write. Kathryn Lindskoog. 288p. 1989. pap. 18.99 (*0-310-25321-7*) Zondervan.

Creative Writing: Forms & Techniques. Lavonne Mueller & Jerry D. Reynolds. 256p. 1990. 15.95 (*0-8442-5379-0*, Natl Textbk); pap. 10.95 (*0-8442-5365-0*, Natl Textbk) NTC Pub Grp.

Creative Writing see **Disney Practice Workbooks**

Creative Writing Activities, 2-6. Constance McAllister. 32p. (J). (gr. 2-6). 1980. pap. 2.95 (*0-87534-176-4*) Highlights.

Creative Writing Booklets. Flora Joy. 64p. (J). (gr. k-6). 1985. 7.95 (*0-86653-274-9*, GA626) Good Apple.

Creative Writing Booklets, No. 2. Flora Joy. 64p. (J). (gr. k-6). 1985. 7.95 (*0-86653-284-6*, GA629) Good Apple.

Creative Writing for Beginners. Constance McAllister. 32p. (Orig.). (J). (gr. 1-3). 1976. pap. 2.95 (*0-87534-165-9*) Highlights.

Creative Writing for Lawyers. Michael H. Cohen. 1991. pap. 7.95 (*0-8065-1213-X*, Citadel Pr) Carol Pub Group.

Creative Writing Handbook. Jay Amberg & Mark Larson. (Illus.). 144p. (Orig.). (J). (gr. 6-10). 1991. pap. 7.95 (*0-673-36013-X*) GdYrBks.

Creative Writing I: A Handbook for Teaching Classes Wherever Adults Gather. Pat Quigley. (Illus.). 98p. (Orig.). 1982. pap. 6.95 (*0-932910-40-8*) Potentials Development.

Creative Writing Ideas. Jo E. Moore & Joy Evans. (Creative Writing Ser.). (Illus.). 80p. (J). (gr. 1-6). 1987. pap. 9.95 (*1-55799-060-3*, EMC206) Evan-Moor Corp.

Creative Writing II: A Handbook of Techniques for Effective Writing, Vol. II. Pat Quigley. 145p. (Orig.). 1983. pap. text ed. 7.95 (*0-932910-45-9*) Potentials Development.

Creative Writing Motivators. Thomas J. Palumbo. (Illus.). 144p. (J). (gr. 2-7). 1994. 12.95 (*0-86653-819-4*, GA1511) Good Apple.

Creative Writing Patterns. Mary D. Smith & Brad Smith. (Illus.). 48p. (J). (gr. k-4). 1983. student ed 6.95 (*1-55734-130-3*) Tchr Create Mat.

Creative Writing Rocket. Linda Schwartz. (Learning Works Creative Writing Ser.). 48p. (J). (gr. 1-4). 1976. 5.95 (*0-88160-003-2*, LW 104) Learning Wks.

Creative Writing Roundup. Linda Schwartz. (Learning Works Creative Writing Ser.). 48p. (J). (gr. 4-7). 1976. 5.95 (*0-88160-017-2*, LW 201) Learning Wks.

Creative Writing Workbook: Instructor's Manual. Carol A. Osley. 180p. (Orig.). (C). 1983. 15.00 (*0-910119-10-4*) SOCO Pubns.

Creative Writing Workbook: Student's Manual. Carol A. Osley. 180p. (Orig.). (C). 1983. 15.00 (*0-910119-09-0*) SOCO Pubns.

Creative Writings by W. E. B. Du Bois: A Pageant, Poems, Short Stories & Playlets. W. E. B. Du Bois. LC 84-17121. (Complete Published Works of W. E. B. Du Bois). 1985. lib. bdg. 42.00 (*0-527-25346-4*) Kraus Intl.

Creative Written Expression for Children. Phyllis Kaplan et al. 1988. pap. 5.95 (*0-89108-149-6*, 8705) Love Pub Co.

Creatively Designing Your Future. Courtney Price & Dianne Baker. 124p. pap. 14.95 (*0-944303-05-6*) Creat Mgmt Unltd.

Creativite et Mystification Dans l'Oeuvre Romanesque de Marguerite Yourcenar: Cinq Lectures Genetiques. Beatrice Ness. LC 93-85869. (North Carolina Studies in the Romance Languages & Literatures). 210p. (C). 1994. pap. text ed. 25.00 (*0-8078-9251-3*) U of NC Pr.

Creativities! Art Activities Across the Elementary Curriculum. Charles Szeglin & Adrienne K. Holtje. 224p. 1991. pap. 24.95 (*0-13-189804-3*, 710403) P-H.

Creativities: One Hundred One Creative Activities for Children to Celebrate God's Love. Patricia Mathson. LC 92-71631. (Illus.). 152p. (Orig.). 1992. pap. 9.95 (*0-87793-485-1*) Ave Maria.

Creativity. Ed. by Don Barron. LC 59-14827. (Creativity Ser.: Vol. 7). (Illus.). 1978. 20.00 (*0-910158-35-5*) Art Dir.

Creativity. Ed. by John Brockman. 256p. (Orig.). 1993. 12.00 (*0-671-78926-0*, Touchstone Bks) S&S Trade.

Creativity. D. Jones. (C). 1988. text ed. 35.00 (*0-685-44253-5*, Pub. by Univ Nottingham UK) St Mut.

Creativity. Helene Lerner-Robbins. LC 92-56433. 96p. 1993. pap. 7.00 (*0-06-255289-9*, Hazelden SF) Harper SF.

Creativity. Ed. by A. Dale Timpe. (Art & Science of Business Management Ser.). (Illus.). 400p. 1986. 29.95 (*0-8160-1463-9*) Facts on File.

Creativity. David Jones. (C). 1985. reprint ed. 35.00 (*0-902031-95-3*, Pub. by Univ Nottingham UK) St Mut.

Creativity, Eight. Ed. by Don Barron & Art Direction Staff. LC 59-14827. (Creativity Ser.: No. 8). (Illus.). 1979. 20.00 (*0-910158-54-1*) Art Dir.

Creativity, Eleven. Ed. by Don Barron. LC 74-168254. (Creativity Annuals Ser.). (Illus.). 368p. 1982. 25.00 (*0-910158-93-2*) Art Dir.

Creativity, Five. LC 59-14827. (Creativity Ser.: Vol. 5). (Illus.). 1976. 20.00 (*0-910158-07-X*) Art Dir.

Creativity, Four. LC 59-14827. (Creativity Ser.: Vol. 4). (Illus.). 1975. 20.00 (*0-910158-06-1*) Art Dir.

Creativity, No. 15. Ed. by Don Barron. LC 74-168254. 450p. 1986. 37.50 (*0-88108-025-X*) Art Dir.

Creativity, No. 16. Ed. by Don Barron. LC 87-71252. 472p. 1987. 49.50 (*0-88108-040-3*) Art Dir.

Creativity, One. Intro. by Art Direction Magazine Editors. LC 59-14827. (Creativity Ser.: Vol. 1). (Illus.). 288p. 1972. 20.00 (*0-910158-02-9*) Art Dir.

Creativity, Reading Level 2. Petrucelli. (Learn the Value Ser.: Set II). (Illus.). 32p. (J). (gr. 1-4). 1989. lib. bdg. 15.94 (*0-86592-444-9*) Rourke Corp.

Creativity, Ten. Ed. by Don Barron. LC 74-168254. (Illus.). 368p. 1982. 25.00 (*0-910158-77-0*) Art Dir.

Creativity, Vol. 22. Don Barron. LC 74-168254. (Illus.). 364p. 1993. text ed. 59.95 (*0-88108-111-6*) Art Dir.

***Creativity, Vol. 24.** Ed. by Don Barron. LC 74-168254. 364p. 1995. text ed. 59.95 (*0-88108-152-3*) Art Dir.

Creativity: An Examination of the Creative Process, 3rd Communications Conference, Art Directors Club, New York Staff. Ed. by Paul Smith. LC 77-167306. (Essay Index Reprint Ser.). 1977. reprint ed. 35.95 (*0-8369-2578-5*) Ayer.

Creativity: Beyond the Myth of Genius. Robert Weisberg. LC 92-36442. (C). 1995. text ed. 25.95 (*0-7167-2365-4*); pap. text ed. write for info. (*0-7167-2119-8*); pap. text ed. 15.95 (*0-7167-2367-0*) W H Freeman.

Creativity: Concept & Findings. Shamshad Hussain. (C). 1988. 11.00 (*81-208-0391-4*, Pub. by Motilal Banarsidass II) S Asia.

Creativity: Conversations with 28 Who Excel. Ed. by Susan Charlotte et al. (Illus.). 412p. 1993. 24.95 (*1-879094-11-8*) Momentum Bks.

Creativity: The Magic Synthesis. Silvano Arieti. LC 75-36374. (Illus.). 448p. 1980. pap. text ed. 21.00 (*0-465-01442-9*) Basic.

Creativity: Theory & Research. Ed. by Morton Bloomberg. 1973. 24.95 (*0-8084-0347-8*); pap. 16.95 (*0-8084-0348-6*) NCUP.

Creativity - Anthropology. Ed. by Smadar Lavie et al. LC 92-52765. (Anthropology of Contemporary Issues Ser.). (Illus.). 368p. 1993. 43.50 (*0-8014-2255-8*); pap. 15.95 (*0-8014-9542-3*) Cornell U Pr.

Creativity & Collaborative Learning: A Practical Guide to Empowering Students & Teachers. Ed. by Jacqueline S. Thousand et al. LC 93-43006. 448p. 1994. reprint ed. pap. 35.00 (*1-55766-158-8*, 1588) P H Brookes.

Creativity & Conformity: A Problem for Organizations. Foundation for Research on Human Behavior Staff. LC 58-13555. 55p. reprint ed. pap. 25.00 (*0-317-10339-3*, 2001734) Bks Demand.

Creativity & Constraint in the British Film Industry. Duncan J. Petrie. LC 90-48652. 240p. 1991. text ed. 39.95 (*0-312-05700-8*) St Martin.

Creativity & Culture: A Psychoanalytic Study of the Creative Process in the Arts, Sciences & Culture. Daniel Dervin. LC 88-46150. (Illus.). 408p. 1990. 55.00 (*0-8386-3366-8*) Fairleigh Dickinson.

Creativity & Disease: How Illness Affects Literature, Art & Music. enl. rev. ed. Philip Sandblom. (Illus.). 224p. 1995. pap. 19.95 (*0-7145-2941-9*) M Boyars Pubs.

Creativity & Disease: How Illness Affects Literature, Art & Music. 5th ed. Philip Sandblom. (Illus.). 143p. 1989. text ed. 34.95 (*0-397-58314-1*) Lippincott.

Creativity & Divergent Thinking: A Task-Specific Approach. John Baer. 144p. 1993. text ed. 29.95 (*0-8058-1295-4*) L Erlbaum Assocs.

Creativity & Effect. Ed. by Melvin P. Shaw & Mark A. Runco. LC 94-1959. (Creativity Research Ser.). 298p. 1994. 45.00 (*0-89391-977-2*); pap. 22.50 (*1-56750-012-9*) Ablex Pub.

***Creativity & God: A Challenge to Process Theology.** Robert C. Neville. 163p. (C). 1995. text ed. 49.50x (*0-7914-2821-4*); pap. text ed. 16.95x (*0-7914-2822-2*) State U NY Pr.

Creativity & Innovation. Harry Nystrom. LC 78-8594. (Illus.). 135p. reprint ed. pap. 38.50 (*0-8357-6636-5*, 2035289) Bks Demand.

***Creativity & Innovation in Information Systems Organizations.** J. Daniel Couger. LC 90-12876. 1995. write for info. (*0-7895-0109-0*) Boyd & Fraser.

Creativity & Learning. Beth A. Hennessey & Teresa M. Amabile. 32p. 1987. 3.95 (*0-8106-1078-7*) NEA.

Creativity & Liberal Learning. Ed. by David L. Tuerck. LC 87-11404. 336p. 1988. text ed. 45.00 (*0-89391-415-0*) Ablex Pub.

Creativity & Madness: New Findings & Old Stereotypes. Albert Rothenberg. LC 90-30770. 200p. 1990. 32.50x (*0-8018-4011-2*) Johns Hopkins.

Creativity & Madness: New Findings & Old Stereotypes. Albert Rothenberg. 208p. 1994. reprint ed. pap. text ed. 13.95x (*0-8018-4977-2*) Johns Hopkins.

***Creativity & Madness: Psychological Studies of Art & Artists, Vol. I.** Barry M. Panter et al. LC 94-94521. (Illus.). 320p. 1995. 24.95 (*0-9641185-1-3*) AIMED.

Creativity & Method: Studies in Honor of Rev. Bernard Lonergan, S.J. Ed. by Matthew L. Lamb. LC 81-80327. 600p. 1981. pap. 20.00 (*0-685-03299-X*) Marquette.

Creativity & Perversion. Janine Chasseguet-Smirgel. 172p. 1984. 22.50 (*0-393-01938-1*) Norton.

Creativity & Pop Culture. David Holbrook. LC 93-58947. 1994. write for info. (*0-8386-3473-7*) Fairleigh Dickinson.

***Creativity & Problem Solving: The McGraw-Hill One-Day Workshop.** Lowe. 1995. text ed. 99.95 (*0-07-912091-1*) McGraw.

Creativity & Problem Solving at Work. Tudor Rickards. 256p. 1990. pap. text ed. 25.95 (*0-566-02891-3*, Pub. by Gower UK) Ashgate Pub Co.

Creativity & Psychological Health. Frank Barron. 292p. (C). 1990. reprint ed. pap. text ed. 16.95 (*0-930222-90-3*) Creative Ed.

Creativity & Psychopathology: A Neurocognitive Perspective. Robert A. Prentky. LC 80-15856. 282p. 1980. text ed. 41.95 (*0-275-90540-3*, C0540, Praeger Pubs) Greenwood.

Creativity & Reception: Toward a Theory of Third World Criticism. Syed Amanuddin. (American University Studies: General Literature: Ser. XIX, Vol. 12). 202p. (C). 1988. text ed. 32.60 (*0-8204-0623-6*) P Lang Pubs.

Creativity & Risk in the Workplace. Terence Duniho. 1993. pap. text ed. 9.95 (*1-878287-36-2*, BDAJ) Type & Temperament.

Creativity & the Art Therapist's Identity. Ed. by Roberta H. Shoemaker. (Conference Proceedings Ser.). 118p. (Orig.). 1976. pap. 7.00 (*1-882147-04-9*) Am Art Therapy.

Creativity & the Imagination: Case Studies from the Classical Age to the Twentieth Century. Ed. by Mark Amsler. LC 85-41031. (Studies in Science & Culture: Vol. 3). 224p. 1987. 35.00 (*0-87413-296-7*) U Delaware Pr.

***Creativity & the Mind: Discovering the Genius Within.** Thomas B. Ward et al. (Illus.). 275p. 1995. 24.95 (*0-306-45086-0*, Plenum Pr) Plenum.

Creativity & the Philosophy of C. S. Peirce. Douglas R. Anderson. (C). 1987. lib. bdg. 77.50 (*90-247-3574-2*) Kluwer Ac.

***Creativity & the Roots of Liturgy.** John B. Foley. 320p. (Orig.). (C). 1994. pap. text ed. 19.95 (*1-56929-015-6*) Pastoral Pr.

Creativity & the Writing Process. Ed. by Olivia Bertagnolli & Jeff Rackham. (C). 1982. pap. text ed. 14.75 (*0-673-15732-6*) HarpCollege.

Creativity & Tradition in Folklore: New Directions. Intro. by Simon J. Bronner. (Publications of the American Folklore Society, Bibliographical & Special Ser.). (Illus.). 384p. 1992. text ed. 42.50 (*0-87421-158-1*) Utah St U Pr.

Creativity & Work. Elliott Jaques. (Emotions & Behavior Monographs: No. 9). 445p. 1990. text ed. 52.50 (*0-8236-1135-3*, BN 01088) Intl Univs Pr.

***Creativity: Around the World.** Patricia Lakin. LC 94-41207. (We All Share Ser.). (J). 1995. lib. bdg. 13.95 (*1-56711-142-4*) Blackbirch.

***Creativity Around Us.** OM Association, Inc. Staff. 1995. vdisk 64.95 (*0-7872-0972-4*) Kendall-Hunt.

Creativity As an Educational Objective for Disadvantaged Students. Mark A. Runco. (Illus.). 105p. (Orig.). (C). 1994. pap. text ed. 35.00 (*0-7881-0440-3*) Diane Pub.

Creativity As an Exact Science. G. S. Altshuller. (Studies in Cybernetics: Vol. 5). 332p. 1984. text ed. 111.00 (*0-677-21230-5*) Gordon & Breach.

Creativity at Work. Dorothy S. M. Yep. LC 93-38859. 104p. 1994. pap. 10.00 (*0-7863-0223-2*) Irwin Prof Pubng.

***Creativity Challenge: Management of Innovation & Technology, 2 pts.** Martin E. Ginn. Incl. Pt. A. Creativity Challenge Pt. B: Management of Innovation & Technology. LC 95-11836. 1995. (*1-55938-950-8*); Pt. B. Creativity Challenge: Management of Innovation & Technology. LC 95-11836. 1995. (*1-55938-951-6*); LC 95-11836. (Monographs in Organizational Behavior & Industrial Relations: Vol. 20). write for info. (*1-55938-944-3*) Jai Pr.

Creativity, Culture, & Values: Comparative Essays in Literary Aesthetics. Shirley J. Paolini. LC 90-5873. (New Studies in Aesthetics: Vol. 5). 239p. (C). 1991. text ed. 47.95 (*0-8204-1341-0*) P Lang Pubs.

Creativity Doesn't Die. Joan Parry & Marie Freudenberg. Ed. by Gwen Costa. 1990. pap. 13.95 (*0-87949-337-2*) Ashley Bks.

Creativity Eighteen. Ed. by Don Barron. LC 74-168254. (Illus.). 412p. 1989. text ed. 55.00 (*0-88108-064-0*) Art Dir.

Creativity Factor: Unlocking the Potential of Your Team. Edward Glassman. LC 91-645149. 92p. 1991. pap. text ed. 14.95 (*0-88390-292-3*) Pfeiffer & Co.

***Creativity for Graphic Designers.** Mark Oldach. (Illus.). 144p. 1995. 29.99 (*0-89134-583-3*) North Light Bks.

Creativity for Kids Through Writing. Bob Stanish. (Illus.). 64p. (J). (gr. 1 up). 1983. student ed 7.95 (*0-86653-118-1*, GA 486) Good Apple.

***Creativity for Leaders.** Gary Fellers. 88p. 1995. 14.95 (*1-56554-162-6*) Pelican.

Creativity Fourteen. Ed. by Don Barron. LC 74-168254. (Illus.). 1985. 34.50 (*0-88108-022-5*) Art Dir.

Creativity Game. Cynthia D. Bayern & Diane E. Kramer. 99p. (Orig.). 1986. pap. 9.50 (*0-943456-17-7*) Bearly Ltd.

Creativity Handbook: Shift Paradigms & Harvest Creative Thinking at Work. Edward Glassman. (Illus.). (Orig.). 1991. pap. 78.00 (*0-9625684-4-9*) LCS Pr.

Creativity, Holocaust, Reconstruction: Jewish Life in Wuertemberg, Past & Present. Herman Dicker. (Illus.). 1984. 18.50 (*0-87203-118-7*) Hermon.

Creativity Illustrated. Ed. by Charles M. Helmken. 1983. 43.00 (*0-89964-216-0*) Coun Adv & Supp Ed.

Creativity, Imagination, Logic: Meditations for the Eleventh Hour. Horace M. Kallen. LC 73-81073. (Current Topics of Contemporary Thought Ser.). 222p. 1973. text ed. 96.00 (*0-677-04940-4*) Gordon & Breach.

Creativity in American Philosophy. Charles Hartshorne. LC 83-15562. 299p. 1985. 49.50 (*0-87395-816-0*); pap. 16.95 (*0-87395-817-9*) State U NY Pr.

Creativity in Business. Carol Goman. Ed. by Michael G. Crisp. LC 88-72254. (Fifty-Minute Ser.). (Illus.). 96p. (Orig.). 1989. pap. 9.95 (*0-931961-67-X*) Crisp Pubns.

Creativity in Business. Michael L. Ray & Rochelle Meyers. 1989. pap. 12.00 (*0-385-24851-2*) Doubleday.

Creativity in Death Education & Counseling. Ed. by Charles A. Corr et al. v, 170p. 1983. pap. 12.95 (*0-9607394-2-4*) Assn Death Educ.

Creativity in Early Childhood Classrooms. Deborah W. Tegano et al. 136p. 1991. 14.95 (*0-8106-0358-6*) NEA.

Creativity in Education: The Waldorf Approach. Rene Quendo. 1982. pap. 9.95 (*0-930420-05-5*) H S Dakin.

Creativity in Film: Conversations with 14 Who Excel. Ed. by Susan Charlotte et al. (Projected Ser.). (Illus.). 189p. (Orig.). 1993. pap. 14.95 (*1-879094-28-2*) Momentum Bks.

Creativity in George Herbert Mead. Ed. by Pete A. Gunter. 126p. (C). 1990. lib. bdg. 31.00 (*0-8191-7916-7*) Foun Phil Creat.

Creativity in Invention & Design: Computational & Cognitive Explorations of Technological Originality. Subrata Dasgupta. LC 93-28650. (Illus.). 370p. (C). 1994. 39.95 (*0-521-43068-2*) Cambridge U Pr.

Creativity in Motion: An Early Childhood Program. Janet M. Grant. 1992. 19.95 (*1-55691-070-3*, 703) Learning Pubns.

***Creativity in Organizations: Ivory Tower Visions & Real World Voices.** Ed. by Cameron M. Ford & Dennis A. Gioia. LC 95-8240. 360p. (C). 1995. 45.00 (*0-8039-5349-6*); pap. 21.95 (*0-8039-5350-X*) Sage.

Creativity in Paper. M. Hanamura & W. Jones. (Illus.). 128p. 1994. pap. 27.95 (*4-7661-0722-5*, Pub. by Graphic Sha JA) Bks Nippan.

Creativity in Services Marketing: Whats New, What Works, What's Developing. M. Venkatesan et al. LC 85-26785. (Proceedings Ser.). (Illus.). 175p. (Orig.). 1986. pap. text ed. 16.00 (*0-87757-179-1*) Am Mktg.

Creativity in Small Groups. Alexander P. Hare. LC 81-13583. 199p. reprint ed. pap. 56.80 (*0-7837-4573-7*, 2044102) Bks Demand.

Creativity in the Arts & Science. Ed. by William R. Shea & Antonio Spadafora. LC 90-8697. (Illus.). 240p. 1990. 40.00 (*0-88135-064-8*, Sci Hist) Watson Pub Intl.

Creativity in the Classroom: Schools of Curious Delight. Alane J. Starko. LC 94-8555. 320p. (C). 1995. pap. text ed. 24.95 (*0-8013-1230-2*) Longman.

Creativity in the Communicative Arts: A Selected Bibliography, 1960-1970. Ed. by Marvin E. Ceynar et al. LC 74-18202. vii, 120p. 1975. 8.50 (*0-87875-062-2*) Whitston Pub.

Creativity in the Later Years: An Annotated Bibliography. John A. McLeish. LC 91-32398. 155p. 1992. 23.00 (*0-8240-4645-5*, SS552) Garland.

Creativity in the Life Cycle, 2 vols. A. R. Arasteh. Incl. Vol. 1. Annotated Bibliography. 1968. (*0-318-53268-9*); Vol. 2. Interpretative Account of Creativity in Childhood, Adolescence & Adulthood. 1968. (*0-318-53269-7*); 1968. Set. 75.00 (*90-04-00103-4*) E J Brill.

Creativity in the Music Classroom. Ed. by Donald L. Hamann. (Best of MEJ Ser.). (Illus.). 104p. (C). 1992. teacher ed write for info. (*1-56545-001-9*) Music Ed Natl.

Creativity in the R&D Laboratory. Theresa M. Amabile & Stanley S. Gryskiewicz. (Technical Report Ser.: No. 130G). 34p. 1987. pap. 12.00 (*0-912879-28-9*) Ctr Creat Leader.

Creativity, Innovation & Entrepreneurship in Libraries. Intro. by Donald E. Riggs. LC 89-33071. (Journal of Library Administration: Vol. 10, Nos. 2-3). (Illus.). 233p. 1989. text ed. 39.95 (*0-86656-940-5*) Haworth Pr.

C

An Asterisk (*) at the beginning of an entry indicates that the title is appearing in BIP for the first time. 1687

*Creativity Inside Out: Learning Through Multiple Intelligences. Terry Marks-Tarlow. Ed. by Mali Apple. 400p. (Orig.). (YA). 1995. teacher ed. pap. 31.20 (0-201-49044-7) Altrntv Pub Grp.

Creativity Is Forever. 3rd ed. Gary A. Davis. 352p. 1991. per. 19.95 (0-8403-6691-4) Kendall-Hunt.

Creativity Is Our Tradition: Three Decades of Contemporary Indian Art at the Institute of American Indian Arts. Rick Hill. 176p. (C). 1992. 45.00 (1-881396-04-5); pap. 34.00 (1-881396-05-3) IOA Indian Arts.

Creativity Nine. Ed. by Don Barron. LC 74-168254. (Illus.). 370p. 1980. text ed. 20.00 (0-910158-55-X) Art Dir.

Creativity of Perception: Essays in the Genesis of Literature & Art. Philip Brockbank. 208p. 1991. 54.95 (0-631-14648-2) Blackwell Pubs.

Creativity of Power: Cosmology & Action in African Societies. Ed. by William Arens & Ivan Karp. LC 88-38200. 400p. 1989. pap. 24.95 (0-87474-617-5) Smithsonian.

Creativity One, Two, Three: Fostering the Creative Potential of Young Children. Susan E. Baum & Martha Cray-Andrews. 1992. pap. 9.99 (0-89824-076-X) Trillium Pr.

Creativity, Productivity & Positivity: A Poetry Book. Center for Self Sufficiency, Research Division Staff. 50p. 1993. pap. text ed. 4.95 (0-910811-15-6) Ctr Self Suff.

Creativity Question. Albert Rothenberg & Carl R. Hausman. LC 75-30132. xiv, 366p. 1976. 41.95 (0-8223-0353-1); pap. 18.95 (0-8223-0354-X) Duke.

Creativity Research: International Perspective. Ed. by M. K. Raina. 332p. 1980. 18.95 (0-318-37231-2) Asia Bk Corp.

Creativity Seventeen. Ed. by Don Barron. LC 74-168254. (Illus.). 428p. 1988. text ed. 55.00 (0-88108-057-8) Art Dir.

Creativity, Talent & Personality. Emanual F. Hammer. LC 84-3883. 182p. (C). 1985. pap. text ed. 10.50 (0-89874-742-2) Krieger.

Creativity Thirteen. Ed. by Don Barron. LC 74-168254. (Illus.). 1984. 25.00 (0-88108-008-X) Art Dir.

*Creativity Toolbox. Jordan Ayan. Date not set. write for info. (0-517-88400-3) Random.

Creativity Twelve. Ed. by Don Barron. LC 74-168254. (Illus.). 1983. 25.00 (0-910158-99-1) Art Dir.

Creativity Twenty-One. Ed. by Don Barron. LC 74-168254. 370p. 1992. text ed. 59.95 (0-88108-101-9) Art Dir.

*Creativity Twenty-Three No. 23. Ed. by Don Barron. LC 74-168254. 370p. 1994. text ed. 59.95 (0-88108-133-7) Art Dir.

Creativity with Gourds. Esther V. Hamel & M. Sparkman. 1977. pap. 5.80 (0-317-03362-X) Ponderosa.

Creator. Cliffor Simak. 288p. 1994. 20.00 (0-7278-4569-1) Severn Hse.

Creator. Clifford D. Simak. 1981. 10.00 (0-9616629-0-5) Locus Pr.

Creator & Creation: Nature in the Worldview of Ancient Israel. Ronald A. Simkins. LC 94-21262. 220p. 1994. pap. 14.95 (1-56563-042-4) Hendrickson MA.

Creator & Creature. Frederick W. Faber. LC 78-66301. 1978. reprint ed. pap. 13.50 (0-89555-076-8) TAN Bks Pubs.

Creator & Man. Warren B. Blumenthal. LC 80-5843. 139p. 1980. pap. text ed. 18.00 (0-8191-1341-7) U Pr of Amer.

Creator & the Cosmos: An Astrophysicist Reconciles Science & Scripture. Hugh Ross. LC 92-64094. 192p. (Orig.). 1993. pap. 10.00 (0-89109-700-7) NavPress.

Creator of Nikho. Benjamin Digo. 201p. (Orig.). 1993. pap. 10.25 (971-10-0513-1, Pub. by New Day Pub PH) Cellar.

Creator or Almighty Always Has an Answer. Bibliotheca Press Staff. Date not set. 7.95 (0-317-00012-8); pap. text ed. 2.95 (0-939476-23-1) Prosperity & Profits.

*Creator or Liar. Tr. by CRM Staff. 22p. (CHI.). 1983. 0.25 (1-56582-072-X) Christ Renew Min.

Creators: A History of Heroes of the Imagination. Daniel J. Boorstin. LC 91-3994. 1992. 29.50 (0-394-54395-5) Random.

Creators: A History of Heroes of the Imagination. Daniel J. Boorstin. LC 93-15502. 1993. reprint ed. pap. 16.00 (0-679-74375-8, Vin) Random.

Creators & Disturbers: Reminiscences by Jewish Intellectuals of New York. Bernard Rosenberg & Ernest Goldstein. LC 82-4281. 432p. 1982. text ed. 37.00 (0-231-04712-6) Col U Pr.

Creator's Healing Star: The Five-Pointed Star: A Workbook for Psychic Development & Self Healing. Milton H. Schwartz. LC 91-71413. (Illus.). 96p. 1991. spiral bd. 14.95 (0-9629802-0-X) Clear Lght.

Creators of the Jewish Experience in Ancient & Medieval Times. Simon Noveck. 1985. 20.00 (0-910250-02-2) Bnai Brith Intl.

Creators of the Jewish Experience in Ancient & Medieval Times. Ed. by Simon Noveck. (B'nai B'rith History of the Jewish People Ser.: Vol. I). 368p. (C). 1985. 20.00 (0-685-67346-4); pap. 12.00 (0-685-67347-2, 01-120013) Bnai Brith Intl.

Creators of the Jewish Experience in the Modern World. Ed. by Simon Noveck. (B'nai B'rith History of the Jewish People Ser.: Vol. II). 384p. (C). 1985. 20.00 (0-910250-04-9); pap. 12.00 (0-685-67345-6, 01-120014) Bnai Brith Intl.

Creators of the Jewish Experience in the Modern World: B'nai B'rith History of the Jewish. Simon Noveck. 1985. pap. 12.00 (0-910250-05-7) Bnai Brith Intl.

Creativia. Joseph W. Gastman. 112p. (J). (gr. 4-8). 1989. 10.95 (0-86653-482-2, GA1087) Good Apple.

Creatura. Paolo E. Serpieri. Ed. by Julie Simmons. Tr. by Michela Nonis. (Illus.). 64p. 1993. reprint ed. 14.95 (1-879450-97-6) Tundra MA.

Creatura Di Creature, Poesie, 1949-1978 see Creature of Creatures: Selected Poems

Creature. Drake Douglas. 400p. (Orig.). 1988. pap. 3.95 (0-8439-2634-1) Dorchester Pub Co.

Creature. John Saul. 1990. mass mkt. 5.99 (0-553-28411-8) Bantam.

Creature: Personal Experiences with Bigfoot. Jan Klement. LC 75-44591. 1976. pap. 3.00 (0-910042-27-6) Allegheny.

Creature & Creator: Myth-Making & the English Romanticism. Paul A. Cantor. 250p. 1985. pap. 19.95 (0-521-31362-7) Cambridge U Pr.

Creature Catalog. John Nephew. (Dungeons & Dragons Ser.). (Illus.). 1993. pap. 15.00 (1-56076-593-3) TSR Inc.

Creature Comforts. Grace Cavalieri. LC 82-51068. 56p. 1982. pap. text ed. 8.00 (0-915380-16-1) Word Works.

*Creature Comforts. Lisa A. Shano. (Illus.). 28p. (Orig.). (J). (gr. k-6). 1994. pap. 9.95 (0-9642972-0-5) LAS Designs.

Creature Features. Ed. by Chicago Zoological Society Staff. (Brookfield Zoo Connections Ser.). (Orig.). (J). (gr. 2-3). 1986. pap. text ed. 30.00 (0-913934-05-4) Chicago Zoo.

Creature Features Movie Guide Strikes Again: An A-Z Encyclopedia to the Cinema of the Fantastic. 4th rev. ed. John Stanley. LC 93-74251. (Creature Features Movie Guide Ser.). (Illus.). 464p. 1994. 50.00 (0-940064-10-3); pap. 20.00 (0-940064-09-X) Creatures at Large.

*Creature From Jekyll Island: A Second Look at the Federal Reserve. G. Edward Griffin. (Illus.). 624p. (Orig.). (C). 1994. 28.50 (0-912986-16-6); pap. 19.50 (0-614-00419-5) Am Media.

Creature from the Black Lagoon. LC 92-61225. (Universal Filmscripts Series: Classic Science Fiction Films: Vol. 2). pap. 19.95 (1-882127-30-7) Magicimage Filmbooks.

Creature from the Black Lagoon. Ian Thorne. LC 81-12468. (Monsters Ser.). (Illus.). 48p. (Orig.). (J). (gr. 3-5). 1981. text ed. 11.95 (0-89686-187-2, Crstwood Hse) Silver Burdett Pr.

Creature of Creatures: Selected Poems. Danilo Dolci. Ed. by Justin Vitiello. (Stanford French & Italian Studies: No. 22). Orig. Title: Creatura Di Creature, Poesie, 1949-1978. xxviii, 104p. 1980. pap. 46.50 (0-915838-17-6) Anma Libri.

*Creature of the Mists. Sigmund Brouwer. 132p. (YA). (gr. 8-12). 1995. pap. text ed. 4.99 (1-56476-375-7, 6-3375, Victor Books) SP Pubns.

Creature to Creature. Nancy Cardozo. (Illus.). 82p. (Orig.). 1987. pap. 7.00 (0-913057-37-1) L I U Press.

Creature to Creature. deluxe limited ed. Nancy Cardozo. (Illus.). 82p. (Orig.). 1987. 20.00 (0-913057-38-X) L I U Press.

Creature Totems: Nature Teacher Medicine. Twylah H. Nitsch. Ed. by Albert F. Rinebold. (Illus.). 130p. (Orig.). 1991. pap. 16.00 (0-9626135-1-7) Aware Tribe.

Creatures. (Ripley's Believe It or Not! Mind Teasers Ser.). 48p. (J). (gr. 5-6). 1991. lib. bdg. 11.95 (1-56065-061-3) Capstone Pr.

Creatures. Ed. by Lee B. Hopkins. LC 84-15698. (Illus.). 32p. (J). (ps-3). 1985. 14.95 (0-15-220875-5, HB Juv Bks) HarBrace.

Creatures. Howard Nelson. 47p. (Orig.). 1983. pap. 4.50 (0-914946-40-4) Cleveland St Univ Poetry Ctr.

Creatures. Leonid Tishkow. (Illus.). 175p. 1994. pap. 20.00 (0-8223-1565-3) Duke.

Creatures. Beth Van Hosen. (BookCard Ser.). 1993. pap. 4.95 (0-8118-0330-9) Chronicle Bks.

Creatures: Poems. Ed. by Lee B. Hopkins. (Illus.). 32p. (J). (ps-3). 1990. pap. 3.95 (0-15-220876-3, Voyager Bks) HarBrace.

Creatures: The Art of Seeing Animals. Beth Van Hoesen. LC 86-23595. (Illus.). 104p. 1987. 35.00 (0-87701-470-1); pap. 16.95 (0-87701-464-7) Chronicle Bks.

Creatures & Chronicles from Cross Creek. W. Horace Carter. LC 80-68460. (Illus.). 286p. (Orig.). 1981. pap. text ed. 9.95 (0-937866-02-4) Atlantic Pub Co.

Creatures & Treasures. S. Coleman Charlton. (Illus.). 96p. (YA). (gr. 10-12). 1985. 12.00 (0-915795-30-2, 1400) Iron Crown Ent Inc.

Creatures & Treasures, No. II. Monte J. Cook. Ed. by Kevin Barrett. (Rolemaster Ser.). (Illus.). 96p. (Orig.). (C). 1989. pap. 13.00 (1-55806-079-0) Iron Crown Ent Inc.

Creature's Choir. Carmen B. De Gasztold. (Illus.). (FRE.). (J). (gr. 3-8). 29.95 (0-8288-9331-4, F140841) Fr & Eur.

Creatures, Corals, & Colors in America's Seas. Ann Scarborough-Bull. (Illus.). 134p. 1990. 35.95 (0-9616452-1-0) Audubon Park.

Creatures Great & Small. Michael Gabb. LC 79-64386. (Lerner Question & Answer Bks.). (Illus.). 36p. (J). (gr. 3-6). 1980. lib. bdg. 13.50 (0-8225-1178-9, Lerner Publctns); pap. 4.95 (0-8225-9540-0, Lerner Publctns) Lerner Publctns.

Creatures, Large & Small. Charles Schulz. LC 94-15493. (Snoopy's World Ser.). (Illus.). (J). 1994. 9.99 (0-517-11902-1, Derrydale Bks) Random Hse Value.

Creatures Nobody Loves. Everett W. Newcomb, Jr. LC 91-66375. (Illus.). 48p. (J). (gr. 4-6). 1991. pap. 3.95 (0-9627974-3-X) Tabby Hse Bks.

Creatures of an Exceptional Kind. Dorothy A. Whitney. LC 88-34736. (Illus.). 32p. (J). (ps up). 1990. 14.95 (0-89334-127-4) Humanics Ltd.

Creatures of Barsaive. Fasa Corporation Staff. (EarthDawn Ser.). (Illus.). 160p. 1994. pap. 18.00 (1-55560-250-9) FASA Corp.

Creatures of Circumstance. W. Somerset Maugham. LC 75-26130. (Works of W. Somerset Maugham Ser.). 1977. reprint ed. 23.95 (0-405-07853-6) Ayer.

Creatures of Earth, Sea, & Sky. Georgia Heard. LC 91-65978. (Illus.). 32p. (J). (gr. 1-4). 1992. 15.95 (1-56397-013-9, Wordsong) Boyds Mills Pr.

*Creatures of Habit. Julie Baumgold. 1994. pap. 3.99 (0-517-13051-3) Random.

Creatures of Habit. Thelma S. Robinson. 28p. (Orig.). 1989. pap. text ed. 5.00 (0-685-28348-8) In Tradition Pub.

Creatures of Habit: A Novel. Julie Baumgold. LC 92-54801. 1993. 22.00 (0-679-41805-9) Knopf.

Creatures of Habit & Creatures of Change: Essays on Art, Literature & Society, 1914-1956. Wyndham Lewis. Ed. & Intro. by Paul Edwards. LC 89-14999. (Illus.). 430p. (Orig.). (C). 1989. pap. 15.00 (0-87685-769-1) Black Sparrow.

Creatures of Light & Darkness. Roger Zelazny. 192p. (YA). (gr. 7 up). 1982. pap. 3.50 (0-380-01122-0) Avon.

Creatures of Long Ago: Dinosaurs, Vol. 1. Illus. by John Sibbick. (Pop-Up Bks.: No. 3). (J). (ps-3). 1993. 16.00 (0-87044-723-8) Natl Geog.

Creatures of Middle Earth. Ruth S. Pitt et al. (Middle Earth Ser.). (Illus.). 64p. (Orig.). (C). 1988. pap. 10.00 (1-55806-019-7, 8005) Iron Crown Ent Inc.

Creatures of Mystery. Jan Fortman. LC 77-24705. (Great Unsolved Mysteries Ser.). (Illus.). 48p. (J). (gr. 4 up). 1983. reprint ed. lib. bdg. 21.36 (0-8172-1063-6) Raintree Steck-V.

Creatures of Orrorsh. 128p. 1992. per., pap. 18.00 (0-87431-336-8, 20574) West End Games.

Creatures of the Deep. (Hidden Pictures Coloring Bks.). (Illus.). 48p. (Orig.). (J). (ps-2). 1989. pap. 2.95 (0-8431-2726-0) Price Stern.

*Creatures of the Desert World. 1995. 16.00 (0-87044-687-8) Natl Geog.

Creatures of the Desert World & Strange Animals of the Sea, 2 bks., Set. Barbara Gibson & Jerry Pinkney. Ed. by Donald J. Crump. (Pop-Up Bks.: No. 2). (Illus.). 20p. (J). (gr. 3-8). 1987. 21.95 (0-87044-688-6) Natl Geog.

*Creatures of the Kingdom. James A. Michener. 1995. pap. write for info. (0-449-22092-3) Fawcett.

Creatures of the Kingdom. large type ed. James A. Michener. LC 93-44109. 1994. 25.95 (1-56895-054-3) Wheeler Pub.

Creatures of the Kingdom: Stories of Animals & Nature. James A. Michener. 1993. 22.00 (0-679-41367-7) Random.

Creatures of the Night: The Rocky Horror Picture Show Experience. Sal Piro. Ed. by Merylene Schneider. (Illus.). 160p. (Orig.). 1990. pap. 15.95 (0-941613-12-7) Stabur Pr.

Creatures of the Sea. John C. Fine. LC 89-34. (Illus.). 32p. (J). (ps-3). 1989. text ed. 14.95 (0-689-31420-5, Atheneum Bks Young) S&S Childrens.

Creatures of the Sea: Sea Birds, Beasts, & Fishes. Frank T. Bullen. 1977. lib. bdg. 69.95 (0-8490-1682-7) Gordon Pr.

Creatures of the Woods see Books for Young Explorers

Creatures That Time Forgot: Photography & Disability Imagery. David Hevey. 1992. pap. 19.95 (0-415-07019-8, Pub. by Tavistock UK) Routledge Chapman & Hall.

Creatures Underneath. Jennifer O. Dewey. LC 93-33847. (Illus.). 72p. (J). (gr. 1-7). 1994. 16.95 (1-878610-39-2); pap. 10.95 (1-878610-48-1) Red Crane Bks.

Crebillon fils Economie Erotique & Narrative. Jean R. Joseph. LC 84-80767. (French Forum Monographs: No. 52). 176p. (Orig.). 1984. pap. 14.45 (0-917058-52-6) French Forum.

Creche of Krakow: A Christmas Story. Harvey A. Hirsch. LC 91-34115. (Illus.). 46p. 1992. 9.95 (1-879094-07-X) Momentum Bks.

Crecimiento de la Iglesia: Church Growth. Pedro Larson. 272p. (Orig.). (SPA.). 1990. pap. 7.50 (0-311-17031-5) Casa Bautista.

Crecimiento de la Iglesia por Medio de la Escuela Dominical. John T. Sisemore. Tr. by Sonia S. De Modroff. 160p. (Orig.). (SPA.). 1992. pap. 4.95 (0-311-11054-1) Casa Bautista.

Crecimiento de las Empresas en los Estados Unidos y en la America Latina: Un Estudio Comparativo. G. Hugo Vivo. LC 81-70693. 121p. (Orig.). (SPA.). (C). 1982. pap. 9.95 (0-89729-306-1) Ediciones.

Crecimiento de un Nino. (SPA.). 1993. 3.75 (0-88336-554-5) New Readers.

Crecimiento Dinamico (Three Stages of the Christian Life) L. Palau. (SPA.). Date not set. 1.79 (1-56063-007-8, 498009) Editorial Unilit.

Crecimiento En Cristo: Growing in Christ. Andrew Murray. (SPA.). 3.25 (84-7228-595-2, 220197, Pub. by Edit Clie SP) TSELF.

Crecimiento Reforma y Ajuste: Las Politicas Comerciales y Macroeconomicas De America Latina En los Decenios De 1970 y 1980. Sebastian Edwards & Simon Teitel. 1991. write for info. (950-557-108-9) IADB.

Crecy War: A Military History of the Hundred Years' War from 1337 to the Peace of Bretigny, 1360. Alfred H. Burne. LC 75-17195. (Illus.). 366p. 1976. reprint ed. text ed. 65.00 (0-8371-8301-4, BUCW, Greenwood Pr) Greenwood.

Crecy War: A Military History of the 100 Years War from 1337-1360. Alfred H. Burne. 368p. 1991. 37.50 (1-85367-081-2, 5484) Stackpole.

Credential Society: A Historical Sociology of Education & Stratification. Randall Collins. LC 78-20042. 1979. text ed. 49.95 (0-12-181360-6) Acad Pr.

*Credentialing in Counseling. Bradley. 110p. 1991. 12.95 (1-55620-087-0) Am Coun Assn.

*Credentialing in the Managed Care Environment: A Guide for MCOs & Health Care Networks. Hugh P. Greeley & Kristen A. Woods. 226p. 1994. ring bd. 127.00 (1-885829-13-2) Opus Communs.

*Credentialing Process - Tips, Tools, & Techniques. Eric Joseph & Brenda Winters. Ed. by Ellen Crowhurst & Elizabeth Hild. 193p. (Orig.). 1994. pap. text ed. write for info. (0-916499-53-7) Care Educ Grp.

Credentials for Employment, Connections: School & Work Transitions - Employment File. National Center for Research in Vocational Education Staff. 1987. write for info. (0-318-67162-X, SP100EA01) Ctr Educ Trng Employ.

Credibility: How Leaders Gain & Lose It, Why People Demand It. James M. Kouzes & Barry Z. Posner. LC 93-15388. (Jossey-Bass Management Ser.). 1993. 28.00 (1-55542-550-X) Jossey-Bass.

*Credibility: How Leaders Gain & Lose It, Why People Demand It. James S. Kouzes & Barry Z. Posner. LC 93-15388. (Management Ser.). 368p. 1995. pap. 16.50 (0-7879-0056-7) Jossey-Bass.

Credibility & Cross Examination. Irving Younger. 1981. student ed 15.00 (1-55917-087-5, 154); audio 125.00 (1-55917-085-9); vhs 450.00 (1-55917-086-7) Natl Prac Inst.

Credibility Assessment. Ed. by John C. Yuille. (C). 1989. lib. bdg. 105.50 (0-7923-0195-1) Kluwer Ac.

Credibility Factor: Putting Ethics to Work in Public Relations. Lee W. Baker. LC 92-20630. 320p. 1992. 35.00 (1-55623-885-1) Irwin Prof Pubng.

Credibility of Herodotus' Account of Egypt in the Light of Egyptian Monuments. Wilhelm Spiegelberg. (African Studies). reprint ed. 12.00 (0-938818-41-4) ECA Assoc.

Credibility Principle & Teacher Attitudes Toward Science. Ralph E. Martin, Jr. LC 83-49429. (American University Studies: Education: Ser. XIV, Vol. 3). 191p. (Orig.). (C). 1984. pap. text ed. 20.55 (0-8204-0101-3) P Lang Pubs.

Credible & Timely Word: Preaching in the Light of Process Theology. Clark M. Williamson & Ronald J. Allen. 168p. (Orig.). 1991. pap. 14.99 (0-8272-0457-4) Chalice Pr.

Credible Christianity: The Gospel in Contemporary Society. Hugh Montefiore. LC 94-16689. xii, 287p. 1994. 19.99 (0-8028-3768-9) Eerdmans.

Credit: The Complete Guide to Consumer Credit. Timothy J. Smith. (Illus.). 100p. 1991. 14.95 (0-9625456-8-6) SJT Enterprises.

Credit: The Cutting Edge. Scott French. LC 92-36716. 1993. 14.95 (0-942637-70-4) Barricade Bks.

Credit - Get It! How to Get the Credit You Deserve, Handle Debt Wisely & Build a Secure Financial Future. Carl E. Bock. 320p. (Orig.). 1994. pap. 29.95 (1-884000-01-0) Action Pubng.

Credit Acts Handbook for Victoria, N. S. W., A. C. T. & W. A. Anna Sharpe. xviii, 163p. 1985. pap. 43.00 (0-455-20622-8, Pub. by Law Bk Co) W W Gaunt.

Credit Analysis, Vol. 1. Ed. by Charlotte Weisman. LC 86-28628. (Special Collection from the Journal of Commercial Bank Lending). 148p. 1986. pap. 39.00 (0-936742-38-0) Robt Morris Assocs.

Credit Analysis: A Complete Guide. Roger H. Hale. LC 83-10217. (Professional Banking & Finance Ser.: No. 1588). 302p. 1983. text ed. 85.00 (0-471-88725-0) Wiley.

Credit Analysis Method. Credit Research Foundation Staff. 1989. 40.00 (0-939050-58-7) Credit Res NYS.

Credit Analysis, Vol. 2: A Special Collection from the Journal of Commercial Bank Lending. Ed. by Joan H. Behr. 88p. (Orig.). 1990. pap. 39.00 (0-936742-79-8, 36043) Robt Morris Assocs.

Credit & Borrowing in Texas: Consumers' Rights & Duties. William R. Wishard & Frederick E. Felder. LC 78-15355. 1978. pap. 6.95 (0-89666-001-X) Cragmont Pubns.

Credit & Charge Cards: The International Market. Euromonitor Staff. 20p. (C). 1989. 2,925.00 (0-685-30329-2, Pub. by Euromonitor Pubns UK) Gale.

Credit & Collection. Associated Equipment Distributors Staff. 86p. 1985. 25.00 (0-318-19174-1) Assn Equip Distrs.

Credit & Collection Coordinator. Jack Rudman. (Career Examination Ser.: C-3107). 1994. pap. 34.95 (0-8373-3107-2) Nat Learn.

Credit & Collection Letters That Get Results. Harold E. Meyer. 1994. pap. 14.95 (0-13-123704-7) P-H.

Credit & Collection Manager's Guides, 1993-94. Bureau of Business Practice Staff. 1993. pap. 59.95 (0-13-189953-8) P-H.

Credit & Collections. James J. Jurinski. (Business Library). 1994. pap. 16.95 (0-8120-4877-6) Barron.

Credit & Collections for Your Small Business. Cecil J. Bond. 224p. (Orig.). 1989. 29.95 (0-8306-9035-2, Liberty Hse); pap. 18.95 (0-8306-3035-X, Liberty Hse) TAB Bks.

Credit & Debit Cards: New Applications, New Technologies, No. G-132. Business Communications Co., Inc. Staff. 283p. 1991. 2,450.00 (0-89336-834-2) BCC.

Credit & Debt the Consumer Interest. Judith Wilcox. 192p. 1990. pap. 15.00 (0-11-701215-7, HM2157) UNIPUB.

Credit & Lending Dictionary. Ed. by Daphne Smith & Shelley W. Geehr. 140p. (Orig.). 1994. pap. text ed. 25.00 (0-936742-97-6) Robt Morris Assocs.

*Credit & Sales: The Winning Team. Lynn Tylczak. Ed. by Teresa Donohue. 90p. 1994. pap. 19.50 (0-934914-89-3) NACM.

Credit & Savings for Development: A Practical Guide. Stephen Devereux et al. 80p. (C). 1990. text ed. 80.00 (0-85598-159-8, Pub. by Oxfam Pubns UK); pap. text ed. 24.00 (0-85598-160-1, Pub. by Oxfam Pubns UK) St Mut.

Credit-Anstalt Crisis of 1931. Aurel Schubert. (Studies in Monetary & Financial History). (Illus.). 224p. (C). 1992. 64.95 (0-521-36537-6) Cambridge U Pr.

Credit Approved. Kevin Pilot. 144p. 1992. pap. 5.95 (1-55850-111-8) Adams Pubng.

An Asterisk (*) at the beginning of an entry indicates that the title is appearing in BIP for the first time.

Credit, Bankruptcy & Living Well. rev. ed. Jay Kimmel. 200p. 1994. pap. write for info. (*0-685-50314-3*) Corey-Stevens Pub.

***Credit Based Systems As Vehicles for Change in Universities & Colleges.** Robert Allen et al. (Managing Innovation & Change Ser.). 192p. 1995. pap. 35.00x (*0-7494-1244-5*, Pub. by Kogan Page Educ UK) Taylor & Francis.

Credit Bible: Everything You Ever Want to Know about Credit. Phil Turner, Jr. LC 89-51961. (Illus.). 120p. (Orig.). 1989. pap. 19.95 (*0-9622996-1-8*) Unique Memphis.

Credit Card Analysis. John J. Williams. 1990. pap. 29.00 (*0-934274-30-4*) Consumertronics.

Credit Card & Check Fraud: A Stop-Loss Manual. 11th ed. Larry Schwartz & Pearl Sax. 330p. 1993. 199.95 (*0-914801-00-7*) Nat Assn Credit.

***Credit Card Catastrophe.** Matty Simons. LC 94-44571. 1995. 22.00 (*1-56980-038-3*) Barricade Bks.

Credit Card Collection Sourcebook. Ed. by John Stewart. 206p. 1993. 175.00 (*0-685-70649-4*) Faulkner & Gray.

Credit Card Collections Sourcebook. Ed. by John Stewart & Kevin Higgins. 200p. (Orig.). 1993. pap. 175.00 (*1-881393-13-5*) Faulkner & Gray.

Credit Card Fraud. Burt Rapp. LC 90-63591. 136p. (Orig.). 1991. pap. 13.95 (*1-55950-055-7*, 49024) Loompanics.

Credit Card Game. Beau R. Davis. 100p. 1986. 14.95 (*0-9603644-3-9*) Beau R D Prof Ent.

Credit Card Industry: A History. Lewis Mandell. (Twayne's Evolution of American Business Ser.: No. 4). 200p. (C). 1990. text ed. 26.95 (*0-8057-9810-2*, Twayne); pap. 14.95 (*0-8057-9816-1*, Twayne) Macmillan.

Credit Card Industry: Emerging Trends. Business Communications Co., Inc. Staff. 225p. 1988. 2,150.00 (*0-89336-626-9*, G-108) BCC.

Credit Card Industry Dynamics. Janet L. Brandes. 200p. 1991. 1,950.00 (*0-945235-45-3*) Lead Edge Reports.

Credit Card Management: Card Industry Directory: 1993 Edition. Ed. by Kevin T. Higgins. 750p. 1992. 345.00 (*1-881393-05-4*) Faulkner & Gray.

Credit Card Management - Card Industry Directory: The Blue Book of Credit & Debit Card in the United States, 1990. Kurt Peters. 1989. pap. 295.00 (*0-685-29402-1*) Faulkner & Gray.

Credit Card Management, Card Industry Directory: The Blue Book of Credit & Debit Card in the United States, 1990. Kurt Peters. 1989. pap. 295.00 (*0-9624775-0-8*) Faulkner & Gray.

Credit Card Management Card Industry Directory: 1994 Edition. Ed. by Kevin Higgins. 760p. 1993. pap. 345.00 (*1-881393-15-1*) Faulkner & Gray.

***Credit Card Market.** 400p. (Orig.). 1994. pap. 2,295.00 (*1-57205-988-5*) Rector Pr.

Credit Card Marketing. Bill Grady. 176p. 1992. 24.95 (*0-9633182-1-7*) A&S Pubs.

***Credit Card Marketing.** Bill Grady. (Small Business Editions Ser.). 1995. text ed. 55.00 (*0-471-10662-3*) Wiley.

Credit Card Safety for Every Cardholder. Larry Schwartz & Pearl Sax. 200p. 1991. 9.95 (*0-914801-18-X*) Nat Assn Credit.

Credit Card Safety for Every VISA-MasterCard Merchant. Larry Schwartz & Pearl Sax. 50p. 1993. 25.00 (*0-914801-16-3*) Nat Assn Credit.

Credit Card Scams. John J. Williams. Ed. by Laurie Williams. (Illus.). 50p. 1992. pap. 29.00 (*0-934274-32-0*) Consumertronics.

Credit Card Secrets: You Will Surely Profit From. Ed. by Howard Strong. 208p. (Orig.). 1989. pap. 29.95 (*0-944077-51-X*) Boswell Corp.

Credit Card Services: A Report on the Supply of Credit Card Services in the United Kingdom. 237p. 1989. pap. 35.00 (*0-10-107182-5*, HM6825, Pub. by HMSO UK) UNIPUB.

Credit Card Use in the United States. Lewis Mandell. LC 72-86124. 120p. 1972. pap. 8.00 (*0-87944-129-1*) Inst Soc Res.

Credit Card Use in the United States. Lewis Mandell. LC 72-86124. (Illus.). 121p. reprint ed. pap. 34.50 (*0-7837-5275-X*, 2045013) Bks Demand.

Credit Cards. A. C. Drury & Charles W. Ferrier. 1984. U.K. pap. 34.00 (*0-406-25940-2*) Butterworth Legal Pubs.

***Credit Cards & the Law.** Mavis Fowler. (Oceana's Legal Almanac Ser.). 108p. (YA). (gr. 9-12). Date not set. text ed. 17.50 (*0-379-11190-X*) Oceana.

Credit Cards & the Law: An Introduction. Peter E. Sayer. 152p. (C). 1988. 65.00 (*1-85190-046-2*, Pub. by Tolley Pubng UK) St Mut.

Credit Cards in the Payment System. Business Communications Co., Inc. Staff. 159p. 1983. 1,000.00 (*0-89336-379-0*, G-066-C) BCC.

Credit, Cash & Co-Dependency. Yvonne Kaye. 1991. pap. 9.95 (*1-55874-133-X*) Health Comm.

Credit Committee: Duties & Responsibilities (V200) Competency Test. 3rd ed. CUNA Staff & Ewing. (VAP Ser.). 6p. 1994. 9.00 (*0-8403-9328-8*) Kendall-Hunt.

***Credit Concentrations: The Management Process.** Arthur H. Stampleman. Ed. by Joan Behr. 44p. (Orig.). 1994. pap. text ed. 32.00 (*1-57070-006-0*, 31101) Robt Morris Assocs.

Credit Considerations, Vol. I. 352p. 1986. 99.00 (*0-317-47030-2*) Robt Morris Assocs.

Credit Considerations, Vol. II. Ed. by Daphne Smith. LC 89-13778. 424p. 1990. ring bd. 116.00 (*0-936742-71-2*) Robt Morris Assocs.

Credit Considerations, Vol. III. Ed. by Daphne Smith & Joan Behr. LC 89-13778. 160p. 1992. text ed. 116.00 (*0-936742-92-5*, 32183) Robt Morris Assocs.

Credit Control in Boom & Recession. T. H. Donaldson. LC 93-31231. 1994. text ed. 69.95 (*0-312-10642-4*) St Martin.

Credit Crisis: A Step by Step Survival Guide. Jennifer L. Yeates. Ed. by Marcia Christman. (Illus.). 94p. (Orig.). 1994. pap. 7.95 (*0-9612310-6-8*) Harsand Pr.

***Credit Culture.** Ed. by Charlotte Weisman. (Special Collection from the Journal of Commercial Lending). 108p. 1994. pap. text ed. 37.00 (*1-57070-005-2*, 36052) Robt Morris Assocs.

***Credit, Debit-Cards.** 1994. 26.50 (*0-614-03438-8*, G132N) BCC.

Credit Department: Its Role in Training. 2nd ed. Charles S. Dickerson. LC 84-2009. 48p. (Orig.). 1984. pap. text ed. 10.00 (*0-936742-15-1*) Robt Morris Assocs.

Credit Department Management. 2nd ed. D. Laurence Blackstone. Ed. by Daphne Smith & Shelley Geehr. (Illus.). 258p. 1992. pap. text ed. 65.00 (*0-936742-94-1*, 32061) Robt Morris Assocs.

Credit Department Primer for Small Business. Credit Research Foundation Staff. 34p. 1985. 40.00 (*0-939050-12-9*) Credit Res NYS.

Credit Discrimination. National Consumer Law Center, Inc. Staff. LC 93-86621. (Consumer Credit & Sales Legal Practice Ser.). 360p. 1993. pap. 60.00 (*1-881793-10-9*) Nat Consumer Law.

Credit Executive Profiles. (Credit Research Foundation Ser.). 29p. 1987. 40.00 (*0-939050-55-2*) Credit Res NYS.

Credit Executives Handbook. Credit Research Foundation Staff. 650p. 1986. 49.50 (*0-939050-01-3*) Credit Res NYS.

Credit File Storage & Retrieval. Credit Research Foundation Staff. 15p. 1983. 40.00 (*0-939050-13-7*) Credit Res NYS.

Credit Files Manual. William G. Dearhammer et al. LC 86-5257. (Illus.). 64p. (Orig.). 1986. pap. text ed. 41.00 (*0-936742-30-5*) Robt Morris Assocs.

Credit for the Poor. 60p. 1990. 14.95 (*92-1-126015-9*) UN.

Credit Guarantee Schemes for Small & Medium Enterprises. Jacob Levitsky & Ranga N. Prasad. (Technical Paper Ser.: No. 58). 98p. 1987. 7.95 (*0-8213-0866-1*, 10866) World Bank.

Credit Improvement & Protection Hbk. Oscar Rodriguez. LC 93-70051. (Illus.). 132p. (Orig.). 1993. pap. 19.95 (*0-918751-32-2*) J O Flores.

Credit Improvement Handbook. James Bandy. 1986. pap. 6.95 (*0-9615425-0-0*) Coastline Assocs.

Credit Institutions for Local Authorities in Latin America. S. L. Descartes. LC 73-75403. 81p. 1973. pap. 1.50 (*0-913480-16-9*) Inter Am U Pr.

Credit Insurance. R. H. Briggs. (C). 1988. 400.00 (*0-685-32836-8*, Pub. by Witherby & Co UK) St Mut.

Credit Insurance Loss Ratios for 1988-1990. 85p. (C). 1992. 100.00 (*0-89382-189-6*) Nat Assn Insu Comm.

***Credit Insurance Loss Ratios for 1989-1991.** annuals 50p. (C). 1993. 100.00 (*0-89382-225-6*) Nat Assn Insu Comm.

***Credit Jungle: Consumer's Guide to Credit.** Robert Dietz & Michael Langer. 112p. (Orig.). 1995. pap. 10.00 (*0-87573-069-8*) Jain Pub Co.

Credit, Law Enforcement & Taxation see Jewish Law & Jewish Life

***Credit Life, Accident & Health Experience by State: 1990-1992.** annuals 20p. (C). 1995. 25.00 (*0-89382-315-5*) Nat Assn Insu Comm.

***Credit Life, Accident & Health Insurance Loss Ratios for 1990-1992.** annuals 84p. (C). 1995. ring bd. 100.00 (*0-89382-316-3*) Nat Assn Insu Comm.

Credit Life & Accident & Health Insurance Loss Ratios for 1990-1992. 54p. 1993. ring bd. 100.00 (*0-89382-257-4*) Nat Assn Insu Comm.

Credit Management. B. Bass. (C). 1989. 130.00 (*0-09-182280-7*, Pub. by S Thornes Pubs UK) St Mut.

***Credit Management.** R. M. Bass. 320p. (C). 1991. 75.00x (*0-7487-1374-3*, Pub. by S Thornes Pubs UK) St Mut.

Credit Management. Robert Bartela. LC 67-11256. (Illus.). 496p. reprint ed. pap. 141.40 (*0-317-10062-9*, 2012391) Bks Demand.

***Credit Management: Policies & Procedures Manual.** Charles D. Salbin. 352p. 1994. 125.00 (*0-7913-1947-4*) Warren Gorham & Lamont.

***Credit Management: Principles & Practices.** Charles L. Gahala. Ed. by Teresa Donohue. 221p. 1994. pap. 30.95 (*0-934914-91-5*) NACM.

***Credit Management & Policy: Strategic Approach.** Sam N. Basu & Harold L. Rolfes. Date not set. text ed. 60.00 (*0-471-58343-X*) Wiley.

***Credit Management Handbook.** 400p. (Orig.). 1994. pap. 225.00 (*0-7605-0831-3*) Rector Pr.

***Credit Management Handbook.** 2nd ed. Credit Research Staff. (C). 1965. 20.00 (*0-256-00085-9*) Irwin.

Credit Management Handbook. 3rd ed. Burt Edwards. 640p. 1990. text ed. 99.95 (*0-566-02856-5*, Pub. by Gower UK) Ashgate Pub Co.

Credit Management Handbook: A Complete Guide to Credit & Accounts Receivable Operations. Cecil J. Bond. LC 92-28307. 1992. text ed. 69.50 (*0-07-006564-0*) McGraw.

Credit Management Reports. Credit Research Foundation. 18p. 1975. 40.00 (*0-939050-14-5*) Credit Res NYS.

***Credit Manager.** Ed. by Sondra Servais. 256p. (Orig.). 1994. pap. 24.95 (*1-56382-303-9*) E-Z Legal.

Credit, Markets, & the Agrarian Economy of Colonial India. Ed. by Sugata Bose. (India Readings: Themes in Indian History Ser.). 320p. 1994. 19.95 (*0-19-563308-3*) OUP.

Credit Markets & the Distribution of Income. Anup Shah. (Illus.). 192p. 1992. pap. text ed. 44.95 (*0-12-638130-5*) Acad Pr.

Credit Markets with Asymmetric Information. G. Clemenz. (Lecture Notes in Economics & Mathematical Systems Ser.: Vol. 272). viii, 212p. 1986. pap. 37.50 (*0-387-16778-1*) Spr-Verlag.

Credit Mechanic: The Poor Man's Guide to Credit Repair. Juliette A. White. (Illus.). 68p. 1991. pap. 10.00 (*0-87364-593-6*) Paladin Pr.

Credit Mobilier. Logan D. Trent. Ed. by Stuart Bruchey. LC 80-1292. (Railroads Ser.). 1981. lib. bdg. 15.95 (*0-405-13762-1*) Ayer.

Credit Mobilier of America. Jay B. Crawford. LC 75-155099. reprint ed. 37.50 (*0-404-01837-8*) AMS Pr.

Credit-Money Blue Book: How to Beat the Recession & Unemployment & Avoid a Great Depression. 1992. lib. bdg. 88.95 (*0-8490-8735-X*) Gordon Pr.

Credit Needs of Small Business. U. S. Senate Committee on Banking & Currency. Ed. by Stuart Bruchey & Vincent P. Carosso. LC 78-18982. (Small Business Enterprise in America Ser.). (Illus.). 1979. reprint ed. lib. bdg. 40.95 (*0-405-11484-2*) Ayer.

***Credit Policies & the Industrialization of Korea.** Yoon-Je Cho & Joon-Kyung Kim. LC 95-2870. (Discussion Papers: Vol. 286). 1995. write for info. (*0-8213-3246-5*) World Bank.

Credit Policies of the Federal Reserve System. Federal Reserve System, Board of Governors Staff & Charles O. Hardy. Bd. with Annual Report of the Federal Reserve Board, 1923. LC 82-48185. LC 82-48185. (Gold, Money, Inflation & Deflation Ser.). 452p. 1983. 61.00 (*0-8240-5238-2*) Garland.

Credit Policy & Economic Activity in Developing Countries with IMF Stablization Programs. Thorvaldur Gylfason. LC 87-3389. (Studies in International Finance: No. 60). 1987. pap. text ed. 11.00 (*0-88165-232-6*) Princeton U Int Finan Econ.

Credit Policy of the Firm & Issues in Cost of Financing Accounts Receivable - Another Look. Credit Research Foundation Staff. 11p. 1986. 40.00 (*0-939050-45-5*) Credit Res NYS.

***Credit pour Petites et Miro Enterprises: Recommendations et Etudes des Cas Presentes au Cours de l'Atelier "Meilleurres Pratiques"** Ed. by Jim Cotter. 156p. (Orig.). 1994. pap. text ed. 25.00 (*0-9637044-6-X*) PACT Pubns.

Credit Power & Democracy. C. H. Douglas. 1972. 59.95 (*0-87968-960-9*) Gordon Pr.

Credit Problems You Can Fix, Those You Can't, Those You Take to Small Claims Court. Samuel E. Hunt. LC 89-92173. 416p. (Orig.). (gr. 11). 1990. 59.95 (*0-9623446-1-3*); pap. 29.95 (*0-9623446-0-5*) M J McCorkle.

***Credit Ratings U. S. A., 12 vols., Set.** (Orig.). 1995. pap. 1,895.00 (*0-7605-1864-5*) Rector Pr.

Credit Rationing & Asymmetric Information. Stefania Cosci. (Luiss Ser.). 144p. 1993. 54.95 (*1-85521-095-9*, Pub. by Dartmth Pub UK) Ashgate Pub Co.

***Credit Repair.** (E-Z Legal Guide Ser.). 128p. (Orig.). 1995. pap. text ed. 12.95 (*1-56382-403-5*) E-Z Legal.

***Credit Repair & Debt Collection Practices.** John Carter. LC 95-67534. 120p. 1995. pap. 9.95 (*0-9637515-4-9*) Dageforde Pub.

Credit Repair Handbook. rev. ed. Bonnie M. Lawrence. Ed. by Deborah F. Harris. 60p. 1989. 29.95 (*0-685-29184-7*); pap. 19.95 (*0-9624059-0-6*) MoneyTree Enterprises.

Credit Repair Kit. Arnold Goldstein. 90p. 1991. student ed 16.95 (*1-56382-138-9*) E-Z Legal.

Credit Repair Kit. John Ventura. 215p. (Orig.). 1993. pap. 19.95 (*0-7931-0518-8*, 5608-76) Dearborn Finan.

Credit Repair Kit: Do-It-Yourself. T. J. Smith. 32p. (Orig.). 1993. pap. 9.95 (*1-880398-11-7*) SJT Enterprises.

Credit Repair Made Easy! 93. Mervin L. Evans. 90p. 1995. spiral bd. 29.99 (*0-914391-15-1*) Comm People Pr.

Credit Repair Rip-Off: How to Avoid the Scams & Do It Yourself. Bob Hammond. 208p. 1993. pap. 16.00 (*0-87364-752-1*) Paladin Pr.

***Credit Report Made Simple.** Steven Chabotte. LC 94-68639. 124p. (Orig.). 1994. pap. 19.95 (*0-9642939-0-0*) Rapport Tech.

Credit Reporting Entities. John J. Williams. 1990. pap. 29.00 (*0-934274-29-0*) Consumertronics.

***Credit Reporting System Gazette: Quarterly Report on Individual Aid Commitments Oct. 1994-Feb. 1995.** OECD Staff. 50p. (Orig.). 1995. pap. 12.00x (*0-614-04183-X*) OECD.

Credit Risk & Exposure in Securitization & Transactions. T. H. Donaldson. LC 88-35566. 150p. 1989. text ed. 49.95 (*0-312-03094-0*) St Martin.

Credit Risk-Rating System. Ed. by Nancy Welsh & Joan Behr. (Illus.). 52p. (Orig.). 1994. pap. text ed. 45.00 (*1-57070-004-4*, 31206) Robt Morris Assocs.

Credit River Valley. Credit Valley Conservation Foundation Staff & John DeVisser. Ed. by Noel Hudson. (Illus.). 120p. 40.00 (*1-55046-072-2*, Pub. by Boston Mills Pr CN) Genl Dist Srvs.

Credit Role in Organizations. 12p. 1981. 40.00 (*0-939050-15-3*) Credit Res NYS.

Credit Saver: How to Protect Yourself from the Credit Bureaus. Ed Marti & Michael F. Spano. 108p. 1993. 69.95 (*1-883685-00-1*) Pincushion Pr.

Credit Secrets: How to Erase Bad Credit. Bob Hammond. 80p. 1989. pap. 14.00 (*0-87364-529-4*) Paladin Pr.

Credit Sense: How to Borrow Money & Manage Debt. Kevin E. Ready. 250p. 1989. pap. 12.60 (*0-8306-3025-2*, 30025, Liberty Hse) TAB Bks.

Credit Solutions. John F. Kratz. 124p. 1993. pap. text ed. 16.95 (*0-9636799-0-2*); audio 29.95 (*0-9636799-1-0*) Credit Solutions.

Credit Survival Guide. Ed. by Robert W. Johnson. LC 93-70647. (Illus.). 164p. (Orig.). 1994. pap. 14.95 (*0-9635779-9-9*) Am Bureau Info.

***Credit Survival Guide Instructor's Manual.** Gregory Marcus et al. Ed. by Robert W. Johnson. 162p. (Orig.). 1995. teacher ed, pap. 14.95 (*0-9635779-8-0*) Am Bureau Info.

Credit System in Early Medieval India, C. 650 A. D. - 1200 A. D. Arbind Kumar. (C). 1992. 18.00 (*81-7169-185-4*, Commonwealth) S Asia.

Credit to Their Community: Jewish Loan Societies in the United States, 1880-1945. Shelly Tenenbaum. LC 92-47377. 204p. 1993. text ed. 29.95 (*0-8143-2287-5*) Wayne St U Pr.

Credit Union: Its Position in the Consumer Financial Marketplace. Peter K. Bros. 186p. (C). 1989. 29.95 (*0-9627769-0-4*) Fin Bk Partners.

Credit Union Development in Wisconsin. Eli Shapiro. LC 70-76652. (Columbia University. Studies in the Social Sciences: No. 525). 1969. reprint ed. 20.00 (*0-404-51525-8*) AMS Pr.

Credit Union Director: Roles, Duties & Responsibilities. Wendell V. Fountain. (Illus.). 180p. (C). 1994. 69.00 (*1-885475-00-4*) FAI Pubng.

Credit Union Extended Rate: Payment Factor Tables. Financial Publishing Co. Staff. 66p. 1980. pap. 15.00 (*0-87600-890-2*) Finan Pub.

Credit Union Law Service, 4 vols. Bender's Editorial Staff & Credit Union National Associaton Staff. 1985. Updates. ring bd. write for info. (*0-8205-1161-7*) Bender.

Credit Union Loan Tables. Financial Publishing Co. Staff. 276p. 1980. pap. 25.00 (*0-87600-882-1*) Finan Pub.

Credit Union Management: Past, Present & Future. Olin S. Pugh & Gerald Ingram. LC 84-186431. (C). 1984. 43.50 (*0-8359-1173-X*) P-H.

Credit Union Payment Factor Tables. Financial Publishing Co. Staff. 238p. 1980. pap. 25.00 (*0-87600-880-5*) Finan Pub.

Credit Union Teller Handbook. Rees. 128p. (C). 1994. per., pap. text ed. 3.79 (*0-8403-5858-X*) Kendall-Hunt.

Credit Unions in a Changing World: The Tanzania-Kenya Experience. Jack Dublin & Selma M. Dublin. LC 83-1353. 302p. 1983. reprint ed. pap. 86.10 (*0-7837-3647-9*, 2043518) Bks Demand.

Credit Where It's Due: Development Banking for Communities. Julia A. Parzen & Michael H. Kieschnick. 288p. (C). 1992. 49.95 (*0-87722-811-6*) Temple U Pr.

Credit Where It's Due: Development Banking for Communities. Julia A. Parzen & Michael H. Kieschnick. 288p. (C). 1994. pap. 22.95 (*1-56639-185-7*) Temple U Pr.

***Credit You Deserve.** Milo Georgeff. Ed. by Alfa Mdg. Corp. Staff. (Illus.). 92p. (Orig.). 1995. pap. text ed. 7.95 (*0-9644502-0-8*) Alfa MDG.

Creditable Warriors: 1830-1876, Vol. 3. Ed. by Michael Cotsell. LC 88-7489. (English Literature & the Wider World Ser.). (Illus.). 328p. (C). 1990. text ed. 55.00 (*0-948660-10-4*, Pub. by Ashfield Pr UK) Humanities.

Credited Institute of Post. 2nd ed. American Council Staff. 1988. pap. 27.50 (*0-02-913980-5*) Macmillan.

Credito Facil Para una Vida Mejor: How to Establish & Repair Credit in the U. S., Avoid Scams & Make Money. Martin St. John. LC 91-73246. 168p. 1991. text ed. 19.95 (*1-56467-146-1*); pap. text ed. 12.95 (*1-56467-147-X*) Elan Pubns.

Credito Moneda y Bancos en Puerto Rico Durante el Siglo XIX. Annie Santiago De Curet. LC 89-32168. 238p. (Orig.). 1989. pap. 9.50 (*0-8477-2644-4*) U of PR Pr.

***Creditor Reporting System Gazette: Individual Aid Commitments Reports July to October 1994.** OECD Staff. 128p. (Orig.). 1994. pap. 12.00x (*92-64-04268-7*) OECD.

***Creditors' & Debtors' Practice in Florida.** Florida Bar Staff. LC 94-71303. 536p. 1994. disk, ring bd. 90.00 (*0-945979-59-2*) FL Bar Legal Ed.

Creditors' Committee Manual. Andrew DeNatale et al. 1992. ring bd. 140.00 (*0-685-69637-5*, CRCM) Warren Gorham & Lamont.

***Creditors Committee Manual.** Denatale H. Jones et al. 560p. 1992. 165.00 (*0-614-06645-X*) Warren Gorham & Lamont.

Creditors' Remedies & Debtors' Protection: Cases & Materials. 4th ed. Stefan A. Riesenfeld. (American Casebook Ser.). 514p. 1992. reprint ed. text ed. 43.50 (*0-314-30130-5*) West Pub.

Creditors' Remedies & Debtors' Protection, 1990 Supplement. 4th ed. Stefan A. Riesenfeld. (American Casebook Ser.). 92p. 1990. pap. text ed. 10.50 (*0-314-76484-4*) West Pub.

Creditors' Remedies Forms, 1990. Arlen W. Langvardt. (Nebraska Legal Forms Ser.). 140p. disk, ring bd. 85.00 (*0-685-49522-1*) Butterworth Legal Pubs.

Creditors' Remedies Forms, 1990. Arlen W. Langvardt. (Nebraska Legal Forms Ser.). 140p. ring bd. 50.00 (*0-86678-026-2*) Michie Butterworth.

Creditors' Remedies Forms, 1990. suppl. ed. Arlen W. Langvardt. (Nebraska Legal Forms Ser.). 140p. 1993. 34.50 (*0-685-74348-9*) Butterworth Legal Pubs.

***Creditors' Remedies in New Zealand.** R. J. Sutton. 342p. 1981. pap. 54.00 (*0-409-60111-X*, NZ) Butterworth Legal Pubs.

Creditors' Rights: Adaptable to Courses Utilizing Riesenfeld's Casebook on Creditors' Remedies & Debtors' Protection. Casenotes Publishing Co., Inc. Staff. Ed. by Norman S. Goldenberg et al. (Legal Briefs Ser.). 1987. pap. write for info. (*0-87457-052-2*, 1300) Casenotes Pub.

Creditors' Rights & Bankruptcy. Steve H. Nickles & David G. Epstein. (Black Letter Ser.). 576p. 1990. reprint ed. pap. text ed. 20.00 (*0-314-48841-3*) West Pub.

Creditors' Rights & Remedies. 2nd ed. Ed. by John P. Davenport & Jerome B. Shank. 586p. 1989. write for info. (*0-318-68349-0*) OR Bar CLE.

Creditors' Rights, Debtors' Protection & Bankruptcy. 2nd ed. King & Cook. 1989. write for info. (*0-8205-0046-1*); teacher ed write for info. (*0-8205-0047-X*) Bender.

C

Creditors' Rights Handbook. Don M. Campbell et al. Date not set. pap. 115.00 (0-87632-785-4) Clark Boardman Callaghan.
Creditors' Rights in Bankruptcy. Patrick A. Murphy. LC 79-25731. 784p. 1980. text ed. 90.00 (0-07-044060-3) Shepards-McGraw.
Creditors' Rights in Bankruptcy. 2nd ed. Patrick A. Murphy. 1058p. 1988. text ed. 90.00 (0-07-172186-X) Shepards-McGraw.
Creditors Workout Strategies. Milbank, Tweed, Hadley & McCloy Law Firm Staff. 152.00 (0-685-69622-7, BBWR) Warren Gorham & Lamont.
Credits, 3 Vols., Set. Debbie Brenner & Gary Hill. (Orig.). 1985. pap. 75.00 (0-935469-00-1) Magpie Pr.
Credits & Collections. Candace Mondello. Ed. by Elaine Brett. LC 90-84234. (Fifty-Minute Ser.). (Illus.). (Orig.). 1991. pap. 8.95 (1-56052-080-9) Crisp Pubns.
Creditworthiness & Reform in Poland: Western & Polish Perspectives. Ed. by Paul Marer & Wlodzimierz Siwinski. LC 87-26962. 372p. 1988. 40.00 (0-253-31472-0); pap. 25.00 (0-253-20477-1, MB-477) Ind U Pr.
Credo: A Catholic Catechism. 296p. (J). (gr. 7-12). 1984. pap. 8.95 (0-225-66343-0) Harper SF.
Credo: A Catholic Catechism. Benedict Davies. 300p. (J). 1984. pap. 12.00 (0-86683-901-1) Harper SF.
Credo: The Apostle's Creed Explained for Today. Hans Kung. Tr. by John Bowden. LC 93-915. 1993. 20.00 (0-385-47181-5) Doubleday.
Credo! The Game of Dueling Dogmas. Gidlow. Ed. by Greg Stafford. (Illus.). 400p. (Orig.). 1993. pap. 14.95 (1-56882-008-9, 1011) Chaosium.
Credo of Christendom & Other Addresses & Essays on Esoteric Christianity. Anna B. Kingsford & Edward Maitland. 260p. 1994. reprint ed. pap. 18.95 (1-56459-446-7) Kessinger Pub.
Credo of the People of God. Pope Paul VI. 1989. 0.50 (0-911988-93-9) AMI Pr.
Credos y Confesiones I-bL-Alumno. Guillermo Renkema. (SPA.). 1989. 1.10 (1-55955-014-7) CITE MI.
Credos y Confesiones I-C-Alumno. Guillermo Renkema. (SPA.). 1992. 1.50 (1-55955-142-9) CITE MI.
Credos y Confesiones I-C-Maestro. Guillermo Renkema. (SPA.). 1992. 1.30 (1-55955-143-7) CITE MI.
Credos y Confesiones I-Db-Alumno. Guillermo Renkema. (SPA.). 1989. 1.30 (1-55955-012-0) CITE MI.
Credos y Confesiones I-Db-Maestro. Guillermo Renkema. (SPA.). 1989. 1.80 (1-55955-013-9) CITE MI.
Credos y Confesiones II: C-Alumno. Guillermo Renkema. (SPA.). 1993. write for info. (1-55955-165-8) CITE MI.
Credos y Confesiones II: C-Maestro. Guillermo Renkema. (SPA.). 1993. write for info. (1-55955-166-6) CITE MI.
Credos y Confesiones II-bL-Alumno. Guillermo Renkema. (SPA.). 1993. 1.50 (1-55955-158-5) CITE MI.
Credos y Confesiones II-bL-Maestro. Guillermo Renkema. (SPA.). 1993. 1.10 (1-55955-159-3) CITE MI.
Credos y Confesiones II-Db-Alumno. Guillermo Renkema. (SPA.). 1993. 1.50 (1-55955-156-9) CITE MI.
Credos y Confesiones II-Db-Maestro. Guillermo Renkema. (SPA.). 1993. 1.10 (1-55955-157-7) CITE MI.
Credos y Confesions I-bL-Maestro. Guillermo Renkema. (SPA.). 1989. 1.30 (1-55955-015-5) CITE MI.
Cree-English Lexicon, 2 vols., Set. Leonard Bloomfield. (Language & Literature Ser.). 1984. 44.00 (0-317-37051-0) HRAFP.
Creed. Bryce Hart. 1991. pap. 3.95 (0-425-12562-9) Berkley Pub.
Creed. William C. Jones. Ed. by Ronald A. Dennis. (Illus.). (Orig.). pap. write for info. (0-939614-00-6) Day Star NV.
Creed: The Apostolic Faith in Contemporary Theology. rev. ed. Berard Marthaler. LC 92-82595. 480p. (C). 1993. pap. 19.95 (0-89622-537-2) Twenty-Third.
Creed & Culture: The Place of English-Speaking Catholics in Canadian Society, 1750-1930. Ed. by Terrence Murphy & Gerald Stortz. (Illus.). 304p. 1993. 44.95 (0-7735-0954-2, Pub. by McGill CN) U of Toronto Pr.
Creed & Deed: A Series of Discourses. Felix Alder. LC 76-38430. (Religion in America, Ser.: 2). 254p. 1972. reprint ed. 19.95 (0-405-04051-2) Ayer.
Creed & Drama: An Essay in Religious Drama. William M. Merchant. LC 66-23222. 127p. reprint ed. pap. 36.20 (0-685-17063-2, 2027867) Bks Demand.
Creed & Personal Identity: The Meaning of the Apostles' Creed. David B. Harned. LC 80-8056. 120p. reprint ed. pap. 34.20 (0-685-23503-3, 2029099) Bks Demand.
Creed & the Christian: A Twelve-Part Study of the Apostles' Creed. Marni S. McKenzie. 56p. 1993. student ed 2.95 (1-882630-02-5); audio 24.95 (1-882630-01-7) Mercy Pr.
Creed As Symbol. Nicholas Ayo. LC 88-40321. (C). 1989. text ed. 21.95 (0-268-00769-1) U of Notre Dame Pr.
Creed as Symbol. Nicholas Ayo. LC 88-40321. 196p. (C). 1990. reprint ed. pap. text ed. 11.95 (0-268-00771-3) U of Notre Dame Pr.
Creed for Children. H. J. Richards. 28p. (Orig.). (YA). 1991. pap. 2.95 (0-8146-2037-X) Liturgical Pr.
Creed for Sceptics. Charles A. Strong. LC 75-3400. reprint ed. 11.00 (0-404-59396-8) AMS Pr.
Creed for the Third Millennium. Colleen McCullough. 464p. 1986. mass mkt. 5.99 (0-380-70134-0) Avon.
Creed, No. 2: Wanted. Bryce Harte. 1991. pap. 3.95 (0-425-12727-3) Berkley Pub.
Creed, No. 5: Missouri Guns. Bryce Harte. (Creed Ser.: No. 5). 1992. pap. 3.99 (0-425-13179-3) Berkley Pub.
Creed, No. 9: Cheyenne Justice. Bryce Harte. 224p. (Orig.). 1993. pap. 3.99 (0-425-13760-0) Berkley Pub.
Creed of a Schoolmaster. Claude M. Fuess. LC 76-99636. (Essay Index Reprint Ser.). 1977. 20.95 (0-8369-1608-5) Ayer.
Creed of Buddha. Edmond Holmes. LC 72-9918. 260p. 1973. reprint ed. text ed. 55.00 (0-8371-6606-3, HOCB, Greenwood Pr) Greenwood.
Creed of Half Japan: Historical Sketches of Japanese Buddhism. Arthur Lloyd. LC 78-70095. reprint ed. 40.50 (0-404-17344-6) AMS Pr.
Creed of the Old South. B. L. Gildersleeve. 1971. 59.95 (0-87968-961-7) Gordon Pr.
Creed of the Old South, 1865-1915. Basil L. Gildersleeve. 1979. 17.95 (0-405-10602-5) Ayer.
Creed of the Thelemites. Aleister Crowley. 1973. lib. bdg. 250.00 (0-87968-500-X) Krishna Pr.
***Creed or Chaos?** Dorothy L. Sayers. LC 95-8261. 135p. 1995. write for info. (0-918477-27-1) Sophia Inst Pr.
Creede, Colorado Boom Town. rev. ed. Leland Feitz. pap. 3.50 (0-936564-03-2) Little London.
***Creedence Clearwater Comp.** Cpp Belwin Staff. 1993. pap. 18.95 (0-89898-156-5) CPP Belwin.
***Creedence Clearwater Comp.** Cpp Belwin Staff. 1993. pap. 18.95 (0-89898-636-2) CPP Belwin.
***Creedence Clearwater Greatest Anthology.** Cpp Belwin Staff. 1993. pap. 16.95 (0-89898-671-0) CPP Belwin.
Creeds & Platforms of Congregationalism. Ed. by Williston Walker. LC 91-12049. 656p. 1990. reprint ed. pap. 25.95 (0-8298-0854-X) Pilgrim OH.
Creeds in Contrast. Dale M. Yocum. 1986. pap. 9.99 (0-88019-183-X) Schmul Pub Co.
Creeds of Christendom, 3 vols., Set. Schaff. 1931. text ed. 95.00 (0-8010-8232-3) Baker Bk.
Creeds of Faith & Inspiration. Ed. by Robin Andrews. LC 90-83142. (Illus.). 64p. 1990. pap. 7.95 (0-88396-283-7) Blue Mtn Pr CO.
Creeds of the Churches: A Reader in Christian Doctrine from the Bible to the Present. 3rd ed. Ed. by John H. Leith. LC 82-48029. 1982. pap. 18.99 (0-8042-0526-4, John Knox) Westminster John Knox.
Creeds to Live By, Dreams to Follow. Susan P. Schutz. LC 86-7318. (Illus.). 64p. (Orig.). 1987. pap. 7.95 (0-88396-248-9) Blue Mtn Pr CO.
***Cre(egg)tivity Plus: Extraordinary Learning Eggsperiences.** Kathy Frazier & Elaine Reynolds. (Illus.). 80p. (Orig.). (J). (gr. 3-8). 1988. pap. 15.95 (1-878347-08-X) NL Assocs.
Creek. James T. Glisson. LC 92-32537. (Illus.). 288p. 1993. 29.95 (0-8130-1184-1); pap. 16.95 (0-8130-1185-X) U Press Fla.
Creek Called Wounded Knee. Douglas C. Jones. 1984. pap. 7.95 (0-684-18257-2, Scribners) S&S Trade.
Creek Captives: And Other Alabama Stories. Helen F. Blackshear. (Illus.). 112p. (Orig.). (J). (gr. 4-9). 1990. pap. 9.95 (0-9622815-2-2) Black Belt Pr.
Creek Indian History: A Historical Narrative of the Genealogies, Traditions & Downfall of the Ispocoga or Creek Indian Tribe of Indians by One of the Tribe. George Stiggins. Ed. by Virginia P. Brown. LC 89-1035. (Illus.). 160p. 1989. lib. bdg. 24.95 (0-942301-15-3) Birm Pub Lib.
Creek Indians. Ellen Scordato. LC 92-35972. (Junior Library of American Indians). (Illus.). 80p. (J). (gr. 3-7). 1993. lib. bdg. 14.95 (0-7910-1660-9); pap. 6.95 (0-7910-1974-8) Chelsea Hse.
Creek (Muscogee) New Testament Concordance. Lee Chupco et al. 167p. 1982. 8.00 (0-940392-10-0) Indian U Pr OK.
Creek Verb. Henry O. Harwell & Delores T. Harwell. 57p. 1981. 6.00 (0-940392-03-8) Indian U Pr OK.
***Creek War of 1813 & 1814.** H. S. Halbert & T. H. Ball. Ed. by Frank L. Owsley, Jr. (Library of Alabama Classics). (Illus.). 400p. 1995. pap. 29.95 (0-8173-0775-3) U of Ala Pr.
Creek Warrior for the Confederacy: The Autobiography of Chief G. W. Grayson. G. W. Grayson. LC 87-27617. (Civilization of the American Indian Ser.: Vol. 189). (Illus.). 200p. 1991. pap. 14.95 (0-8061-2322-2) U of Okla Pr.
Creekers. Edward Lee. 416p. 1994. mass mkt. 4.50 (0-8217-4568-9) Zebra.
Creeks. Michael D. Green. (Indians of North America Ser.). (Illus.). 128p. (J). (gr. 5 up). 1990. lib. bdg. 17.95 (1-55546-703-2) Chelsea Hse.
Creeks & Seminoles: The Destruction & Regeneration of the Muscogulge People. J. Leitch Wright, Jr. LC 86-11281. (Indians of the Southeast Ser.). (Illus.). xvi, 383p. 1987. reprint ed. pap. 12.95 (0-8032-9728-9) U of Nebr Pr.
Creekside to Gourmet Cooking: Ozark Hills to Texas Society. Arch Reid & C. H. Kaiser. (Illus.). (Orig.). 1986. pap. 8.95 (0-9616178-0-2) K & R Pub.
Creel & Angler Surveys in Fisheries Management. Ed. by D. Guthrie et al. LC 91-77875. (Symposium Ser.: No. 12). 540p. 1991. text ed. 84.50 (0-913235-75-X) Am Fisheries Soc.
Creel of Irish Stories. Jane Barlow. LC 70-116934. (Short Story Index Reprint Ser.). 1977. 21.95 (0-8369-3436-9) Ayer.
Creel Report. U. S. Committee on Public Information. LC 75-37319. (Civil Liberties in American History Ser.). 290p. 1972. reprint ed. lib. bdg. 37.50 (0-306-70241-X) Da Capo.
Creemos En Maria: We Believe in Mary. Helgue Berntsson. (SPA.). 3.25 (84-7645-087-7, 220195, Pub. by Edit Clie SP) TSELF.
Creep. B. Battin. 1987. pap. 3.50 (0-449-13061-4) Fawcett.
Creep Analysis. Harry Kraus. LC 80-15242. 270p. reprint ed. pap. 77.00 (0-317-55588-X, 2056342) Bks Demand.
Creep & Fatigue in High Temperature Alloys: Proceedings of a Course Held at the Joint Research Centre of the Commission of the European Communities Petten Establishment, the Netherlands. Ed. by J. Bressers. (Illus.). 190p. 1981. 74.00 (0-85334-947-9, Pub. by Elsevier Applied Sci UK) Elsevier.
Creep & Fracture of Engineering Materials & Structures: Proceedings of the Fifth International Conference. Ed. by B. Wilshire & R. W. Evans. (Illus.). 815p. 1993. 145.00 (0-901716-43-X, Pub. by Inst Materials UK) Ashgate Pub Co.
Creep & Fracture of Engineering Materials & Structures: Proceedings of the First International Conference. Ed. by B. Wilshire & D. R. Owen. 670p. 1981. text ed. 94.50 (0-906674-10-7, Pub. by Inst Materials UK) Ashgate Pub Co.
Creep & Fracture of Engineering Materials & Structures: Proceedings of the Second International Conference, 2 vols., Set. Ed. by B. Wilshire & D. R. Owen. 1370p. 1984. text ed. 136.50 (0-906674-37-9, Pub. by Inst Materials UK) Ashgate Pub Co.
Creep & Shrinkage: Their Effect on the Behavior of Concrete Structures. H. Ruesch et al. (Illus.). 284p. 1983. 124.00 (0-387-90669-X) Spr-Verlag.
Creep & Shrinkage Characterization for Analyzing Prestressed Concrete Structures. (PCI Journal Reprints Ser.). 37p. 1980. pap. 8.00 (0-686-40129-8, JR225) P-PCI.
Creep & Shrinkage in Concrete Structures. Ed. by Z. P. Bazant & F. H. Wittmann. LC 82-4766. (Wiley Series in Numerical Methods in Engineering). 373p. reprint ed. pap. 106.40 (0-685-15453-X, 2026686) Bks Demand.
Creep & Shrinkage of Concrete: Effect of Materials & Environment. 100p. 1992. 44.50 (0-685-62950-3) ACI.
Creep Behaviour of Crystalline Solids. Ed. by B. Wilshire & R. W. Evans. 362p. 1985. text ed. 75.60 (0-906674-42-5, Pub. by Inst Materials UK) Ashgate Pub Co.
Creep-Fatigue-Environment Interactions: Proceedings of a Symposium. Metallurgical Society of AIME Staff. Ed. by R. M. Pelloux & N. S. Stoloff. LC 80-82904. (Conference Proceedings Ser.). (Illus.). 202p. reprint ed. pap. 57.60 (0-8357-5605-X, 2056845) Bks Demand.
Creep, Fatigue, Flaw Evaluation, & Leak-Before-Break Assessment. Ed. by Y. S. Garud. 304p. 1993. 60.00 (0-7918-0993-5, H00825) ASME.
Creep-fatigue Interaction, 1976 ASME-EPC Symposium: Presented at the Winter Meeting of the ASME, New York, N. Y. December 5-10, 1976. Ed. by R. M. Curran. LC 76-28849. 438p. reprint ed. pap. 124.90 (0-317-08007-5, 2016816) Bks Demand.
Creep in Structures: Fourth Symposium, Cracow, Poland September 10-14, 1990. Michal Zyczkowski. (International Union of Theoretical & Applied Mechanics Symposia Ser.). (Illus.). 736p. 1991. 169.00 (0-387-53786-4) Spr-Verlag.
Creep of Crystals. Jean-Paul Poirier. (Cambridge Earth Science Ser.). (Illus.). 275p. 1985. 69.95 (0-521-26177-5); pap. 34.95 (0-521-27851-1) Cambridge U Pr.
Creep of Engineering Materials & Structures. G. Bernasconi. 420p. 1980. 117.00 (0-85334-878-2, Pub. by Elsevier Applied Sci UK) Elsevier.
Creep of Metals & Alloys. R. W. Evans & B. Wilshire. 314p. 1985. text ed. 73.50 (0-904357-59-7, Pub. by Inst Materials UK) Ashgate Pub Co.
Creep of Zirconium Alloys in Nuclear Reactors- STP 815. Ed. by Franklin et al. 284p. 1983. 42.00 (0-8031-0259-3, 04-815000-35) ASTM.
Creep-Rupture Data for the Refractory Metals to High Temperatures. J. B. Conway & P. N. Flagella. 798p. 1971. text ed. 449.00 (0-677-02660-9) Gordon & Breach.
Creep, Shadow, Creep! A. Merritt. 1991. reprint ed. lib. bdg. 21.95 (1-56849-033-X) Buccaneer Bks.
Creep, Viscoelasticity & Creep Fracture in Solids. John H. Gittus. (Illus.). 725p. 1975. 169.25 (0-85334-597-X, Pub. by Elsevier Applied Sci UK) Elsevier.
Creeper. Mary Roberts. LC 93-134. (J). 1994. write for info. (0-383-03684-4) SRA Schl Grp.
Creepers: British Horror & Fantasy in the Twentieth Century. Ed. by Clive Bloom. LC 92-36706. 190p. (C). 1993. pap. text ed. 18.95 (0-7453-0665-9) Westview.
Creepers: British Horror & Fantasy in the Twentieth Century. Ed. by Clive Bloom. LC 92-36706. 190p. (C). 1993. text ed. 55.50 (0-7453-0664-0) Westview.
Creepies. Rose Impey. Incl. Flat Man. 1988. 8.95 (0-8120-5975-1); Scare Yourself to Sleep. 1988. 8.95 (0-8120-5974-3); (Illus.). 48p. (J). (gr. 1-4). 1988. write for info. (0-318-62939-9) Barron.
Creeping Fingers. large type ed. Mary Williams. (Dales Ser.). 262p. 1994. pap. 16.95 (1-85389-408-7, Dales) Ulverscroft.
Creeping Jenny: A Celia Grant Mystery. John Sherwood. 256p. 1993. text ed. 20.00 (0-684-19613-1, Scribners) S&S Trade.
Creeping Shadows. Gary Amo. 352p. 1992. mass mkt. 4.50 (1-55817-633-0, Pinnacle NY) Windsor NY.
Creeping Shadows. Lois W. Johnson. 144p. (Orig.). (YA). (gr. 2-8). 1990. pap. 5.99 (1-55661-102-1) Bethany Hse.
Creeps. Shelly Fredman. LC 89-50957. 208p. (YA). (gr. 7-12). 1989. 16.95 (0-943864-55-0) Davenport.
Creeps. Tim Schoch. 1985. pap. 2.50 (0-380-89852-7, Camelot) Avon.
Creeps. David Freeman. LC 72-191690. (Canadian Play Ser.). 54p. reprint ed. pap. 25.00 (0-317-27049-4, 2023618) Bks Demand.
Creepshow. Stephen King. 1982. pap. text ed. 12.00 (0-452-25380-2, 25380, Plume) NAL-Dutton.
Creepy Carousel. Lorraine Avery. LC 89-20279. (Apple Park Adventures Ser.). (Illus.). 96p. (J). (gr. 4-6). 1990. lib. bdg. 9.89 (0-8167-1712-5); pap. text ed. 2.95 (0-8167-1713-3) Troll Assocs.
Creepy Castle. (Hidden Pictures Ser.). (Illus.). 24p. (J). 1992. 4.98 (0-8317-4679-3) Smithmark.
Creepy Castles. Christine S. Rom. LC 89-28986. (Incredible Histories Ser.). (Illus.). 48p. (J). (gr. 5-6). 1990. text ed. 11.95 (0-89686-505-3, Crstwood Hse) Silver Burdett Pr.
Creepy Classics. Ed. by Mary Hill. LC 94-5079. (Illus.). 128p. (J). (gr. 4-8). 1994. pap. 4.99 (0-679-86692-2) Random Bks Yng Read.
***Creepy Company: Ten Tales of Terror.** Joan Aiken. (J). (gr. 4-7). 1995. pap. 3.99 (0-440-40993-4) Dell.
Creepy Crawlies. Kathie Atkinson. LC 92-31908. (Voyages Ser.). (J). 1993. 3.75 (0-383-03562-7) SRA Schl Grp.
Creepy Crawlies. Michael Benton. LC 93-50177. (Illus.). 32p. (J). 1994. 3.95 (1-85697-502-9, Kingfisher LKC) LKC.
Creepy Crawlies. Kilpatrick. (First Nature Bks.). (J). (gr. 2-5). 1982. lib. bdg. 11.96 (0-88110-076-5, Usborne); pap. 3.95 (0-86020-630-0, Usborne) EDC.
Creepy Crawlies. Ruth Thomson. LC 91-7482. (Aladdin Basics Ser.). (Illus.). 32p. (J). (gr. k-3). 1991. pap. 5.95 (0-689-71489-0, Aladdin Paperbacks) S&S Childrens.
Creepy Crawlies: A Thematic Unit. Mary E. Sterling. (Thematic Units Ser.). (Illus.). 80p. (gr. k-3). 1990. student ed 8.95 (1-55734-268-7) Tchr Create Mat.
Creepy Crawlies: Ladybugs, Lobsters, & Other Amazing Arthropods. Comp. by Natural History Museum, London, England Staff. LC 90-27531. (Illus.). 108p. (J). 1991. 14.95 (0-8069-8336-1) Sterling.
Creepy Crawlies: Ladybugs, Lobsters & Other Amazing Arthropods. Comp. by Natural History Museum Staff. LC 90-27531. (Illus.). 108p. (J). (gr. 4-10). 1992. pap. 9.95 (0-8069-8337-X) Sterling.
Creepy Crawlies & the Scientific Method: Over 100 Hands-on Science Experiments for Children. Sally S. Kneidel. LC 92-53033. (Illus.). 238p. (Orig.). (J). 1993. pap. 15.95 (1-55591-118-8) Fulcrum Pub.
Creepy Crawlies for Curious Kids. Lynn Ransford. (Illus.). 48p. (J). (gr. k-3). 1987. student ed 6.95 (1-55734-217-2) Tchr Create Mat.
***Creepy Crawlies in 3-D!** Rick Sammon & Susan Sammon. (Illus.). 28p. 1995. 9.95 (1-57359-006-1) Elliott & Clark.
Creepy-Crawly Birthday. James Howe. 48p. (J). 1992. pap. 5.99 (0-380-75984-5, Camelot) Avon.
Creepy-Crawly Birthday. James Howe. LC 90-35370. (Illus.). 48p. (J). (gr. k up). 1991. 13.95 (0-688-09687-5); lib. bdg. 13.88 (0-688-09688-3) Morrow Jr Bks.
***Creepy Crawly Caterpillar.** Kara May. LC 94-32713. (Illus.). (J). 1995. write for info. (0-385-32166-X) Doubleday.
Creepy, Crawly Caterpillars. Margery Facklam. LC 93-41443. (Illus.). (J). 1995. 14.95 (0-316-27391-0) Little.
Creepy, Crawly, Critter Riddles. Joanne Bernstein & Paul Cohen. Ed. by Kathleen Tucker. LC 86-15911. (Illus.). 32p. (J). (gr. 1-5). 1986. lib. bdg. 8.95 (0-8075-1345-8) A Whitman.
Creepy Crawly Critters & Other Halloween Tongue Twisters. Nola Buck. LC 94-15405. (I Can Read Ser.). (Illus.). 32p. (J). (gr. k-3). 1995. 14.95 (0-06-024808-4); lib. bdg. 14.89 (0-06-024809-2) HarpC Child Bks.
***Creepy, Crawly Halloween Fright.** Thomas Beach. (J). (ps-3). 1994. pap. 9.95 (0-8167-3395-3) Troll Assocs.
Creepy Crawly Song Book. Hiawyn Oram. (J). (ps-3). 1993. 17.00 (0-374-31639-2) FS&G.
Creepy Crawly Stickers. Frank Daniel. (Illus.). (J). (gr. k-3). 1993. pap. 1.00 (0-486-27455-1) Dover.
Creepy Crawly Things see Books for Young Explorers
Creepy Creatures. (Funny Face Sticker Bks.). (Illus.). 16p. (J). 1990. pap. 3.99 (0-517-03347-X) Random Hse Value.
Creepy Creatures, 8 vols. Steve Parker. (J). (gr. 4-7). 1994. lib. bdg. 111.84 (0-8114-0711-X) Raintree Steck-V.
Creepy Cuisine. Lucy Monroe. LC 92-41654. (Illus.). 80p. (J). (gr. 4-7). 1993. pap. 4.99 (0-679-84402-3) Random Bks Yng Read.
***Creepy Halloween Sticker Fun.** (Sticker Bks.). 16p. (J). Date not set. 4.95 (0-7894-0322-6, 5-70674) Dorling Kindersley.
Creepy Poems. Comp. by H. Amery. (Poetry Bks.). (Illus.). 32p. (J). (gr. 2-6). 1990. pap. 5.95 (0-7460-0440-0, Usborne) EDC.
***Creepy Sleepaway.** Butcher. (Camp At Your Own Risk Ser.: No. 3). (J). 1995. pap. 3.50 (0-553-48253-X) Bantam.
Creezy. Felicien Marceau. (FRE.). 1972. pap. 10.95 (0-7859-3995-4) Fr & Eur.
Creifelds' Law Dictionary: Creifelds' Rechtswoerterbuch. 8th ed. Carl Creifelds. 1413p. (GER.). 1986. 95.00 (0-8288-1522-4, M6529) Fr & Eur.
***Creifelds Rechtsworterbuch: Legal Dictionary.** 12th ed. Ca Creifelds. 1491p. 1994. write for info. (0-7859-8754-1) Fr & Eur.
***Creifelds Rechtsworterbuch Legal Dictionary.** 12th ed. Carl Creifelds. 1491p. (GER.). 1994. 70.00x (3-406-38190-1, Pub. by BCH Verlag GW) IBD Ltd.
Creighton Law Review: 1968-1992, 26 vols., Set. 1,172.50 (0-8377-9049-2) Rothman.
Creighton University. Photos by Don Doll. (Illus.). 112p. 1991. 39.00 (0-916509-68-0) Harmony Hse Pub LO.
***Cremaster 4.** (Illus.). 100p. Date not set. pap. 40.00 (2-86925-051-7) Dist Art Pubs.
Cremation. Paul E. Irion. LC 68-10291. 160p. reprint ed. pap. 45.60 (0-685-16046-7, 2026951) Bks Demand.
Cremation: A Christian Perspective. John Davis. 10.99 (0-88469-226-4) BMH Bks.
Cremation: Is It Christian? James W. Fraser. 1965. Pkg. of 5. pap. 12.50 (0-87213-551-9); pap. 2.50 (0-87213-180-7) Loizeaux.
***Cremation & the Funeral Director: Successfully Meeting the Challenge.** Michael W. Kubasak. 156p. 1990. pap. 19.95 (0-9627692-0-7) Avalon Pr CA.
Cremation Concerns. William E. Phipps. (Illus.). 114p. (C). 1989. text ed. 34.95x (0-398-05532-7) C C Thomas.

An Asterisk (*) at the beginning of an entry indicates that the title is appearing in BIP for the first time.

An Asterisk (*) at the beginning of an entry indicates that the title is appearing in BIP for the first time.

1691

C

Crick Crack Monkey. Merle Hodge. (Caribbean Writers Ser.). (C). 1981. reprint ed. pap. 7.95 (*0-435-98401-2*) Heinemann.

Crickdam. Roscoe Howells. 264p. (C). 1990. 36.00x (*0-86383-643-7*, Pub. by Gomer Pr UK) St Mut.

Cricket. Yo Hasegawa. Ed. by Kathy Pohl. LC 85-28201. (Nature Close-Ups Ser.). (Illus.). 32p. (J). (gr. 3-7). 1986. text ed. 10.95 (*0-8172-2532-3*) Raintree Steck-V.

Cricket: Techniques, Tactics, Training. Doug Ferguson. (Crowood Sports Guides Ser.). (Illus.). 96p. 1993. pap. 22.95 (*1-85223-600-0*, Pub. by Crowood Pr UK) Trafalgar.

Cricket & the Crackerbox Kid. Alane Ferguson. 192p. (J). (gr. 5). 1992. pap. 3.50 (*0-380-71341-1*, Camelot) Avon.

Cricket & the Crackerbox Kid. Alane Ferguson. LC 89-39291. 192p. (J). (gr. 3-7). 1990. text ed. 14.95 (*0-02-734525-4*, Bradbury S&S) S&S Childrens.

Cricket & the Victorians. Keith A. Sandiford. (Illus.). 220p. 1994. 59.95 (*1-85928-089-7*, Pub. by Scolar Pr UK) Ashgate Pub Co.

Cricket Behavior & Neurobiology. Ed. by Franz Huber et al. LC 88-43256. (Comstock Book Ser.). (Illus.). 536p. 1989. 69.95 (*0-8014-2272-8*) Cornell U Pr.

Cricket Conspiracy. Derek Humphrey. 1975. 20.00 (*0-901108-40-5*, Pub. by NCCL UK) St Mut.

Cricket Explained. Robert Eastaway. LC 93-9664. (Illus.). 144p. (Orig.). 1993. pap. 10.95 (*0-312-09411-6*) St Martin.

Cricket for Americans: Playing & Understanding the Game. Tom Melville. LC 92-7488. 214p. 1993. 25.95 (*0-87972-606-7*) Bowling Green Univ.

***Cricket Goes to the Dogs.** Susan Meyers. LC 94-19829. (Always Friends Ser.). 128p. (J). (gr. 3-6). 1995. pap. text ed. 2.95 (*0-8167-3577-8*, Little Rainbow) Troll Assocs.

Cricket in Many Lands. Tony Lewis. 256p. 1992. 34.95 (*0-340-50889-2*, Pub. by H & S UK) Trafalgar.

Cricket in My Heart. rev. ed. Eddie Doherty. (Illus.). 290p. 1990. pap. 10.50 (*0-9628295-0-1*) Blue Hse TX.

Cricket in the Road. Michael Anthony. (Caribbean Writers Ser.). 1973. pap. 7.95 (*0-435-98032-7*) Heinemann.

Cricket in the Thorn Tree: Helen Suzman & the Progressive Party of South Africa. Joanna Strangwayes-Booth. LC 76-486. reprint ed. pap. 80.00 (*0-317-27881-9*, 2056067) Bks Demand.

Cricket in Times Square. George Selden. (Illus.). (J). (gr. 2-7). 1970. mass mkt. 3.99 (*0-440-41563-2*, YB) Dell.

Cricket in Times Square. George Selden. LC 60-12640. (Illus.). 160p. (J). (gr. 4 up). 1960. 15.00 (*0-374-31650-3*) FS&G.

Cricket in Times Square: A Literature Unit. Susan Onion. (Literature Units Ser.). (Illus.). 48p. (Orig.). 1993. student ed, pap. 6.95 (*1-55734-419-1*) Tchr Create Mat.

Cricket in Times Square: A Study Guide. Gloria Levine. (Novel-Ties Ser.). (J). (gr. 4-7). 1987. student ed, teacher ed 15.95 (*0-88122-073-6*) Lrn Links.

Cricket Moon. Elizabeth Revere. LC 92-5472. (Illus.). 80p. 1992. 7.95 (*0-918606-09-8*) Heidelberg Graph.

Cricket on the Hearth. Charles Dickens. (BCL1-PR English Literature Ser.). 171p. 1992. reprint ed. lib. bdg. 69.00 (*0-7812-7510-5*) Rprt Serv.

Cricket on the Hearth. Marian Jonson. 62p. 1957. reprint ed. pap. 3.45 (*0-87129-048-0*, C75) Dramatic Pub.

Cricket on the Hearth & Other Christmas Stories. Charles Dickens. 128p. (Orig.). 1994. pap. 1.00 (*0-486-28039-X*) Dover.

Cricket Quotations. Ed. by Helen Exley. (Quotations Bks.). (Illus.). 60p. 1992. 6.99 (*1-85015-319-1*) Exley Giftbooks.

Cricket Sings. Federico G. Lorca. Tr. by Will Kirkland. LC 80-15560. (Illus.). 64p. (Orig.). 1980. pap. 6.95 (*0-8112-0734-X*, NDP506) New Directions.

Cricket Sings: A Novel of Pre-Columbian Cahokia. Kathleen King. LC 82-8046. x, 162p. 1983. pap. 12.95 (*0-8214-0705-8*) Ohio U Pr.

Cricket Stumps & Sticlebacks. Don Smith. (C). 1989. pap. 39.00 (*0-947934-23-5*, Pub. by Bridge Pubns UK) St Mut.

Cricket Umpiring & Scoring. Tom Smith. (Illus.). 192p. 1994. pap. 11.95 (*0-297-81359-5*) Trafalgar.

Cricket Warrior. Margaret Chang & Raymond Chang. LC 93-35395. (Illus.). 32p. (J). (gr. 3 up). 1994. text ed. 14.95 (*0-689-50605-8*, Atheneum Bks Young) S&S Childrens.

***Cricket Weather.** Anthony Walton. 32p. (Orig.). 1995. pap. 8.95 (*0-942396-71-5*) Blackberry ME.

Cricketing Bygones. Stephen Green. 1989. pap. 25.00 (*0-85263-605-9*, Pub. by Shire UK) St Mut.

Crickets & Corn. Peg Back. 1985. 3.50 (*0-377-00152-X*) Friendship Pr.

Crickets & Katydids, Concerts & Solos. Vincent G. Dethier. (Illus.). 140p. 1992. text ed. 18.95 (*0-674-17577-8*) HUP.

Crickets in a Hobo's Pocket. Perry Chandler. 96p. (Orig.). 1992. pap. write for info. (*0-915214-28-8*, Wrds Worth Pr) Current.

***Crickets of Hawaii: Origin, Systematics & Evolution.** Daniel Otte. (Publications on Orthopteran Diversity). (Illus.). 396p. (Orig.). 1994. pap. text ed. 75.00 (*0-9640101-0-0*) Orthopterists.

***Cricket's Song.** Muff Singer. (Illus.). 20p. (J). (ps). 1995. bds. 3.99 (*0-89577-672-3*) RD Assn.

Cricklade. Diana Holmes. (Towns & Villages of England Ser.). (Illus.). 1993. pap. 12.50 (*0-7509-0494-1*) A Sutton Pub.

Crickle-Crack. Stephen Cosgrove. (Serendipity Bks.). (Illus.). 32p. (J). (gr. 1-4). 1987. pap. 2.95 (*0-8431-1909-8*) Price Stern.

Crictor. Tomi Ungerer. LC 58-5288. (Illus.). 32p. (J). (ps-3). 1958. lib. bdg. 14.89 (*0-06-026181-1*) HarpC Child Bks.

Crictor. Tomi Ungerer. LC 58-5288. (Illus.). 32p. (J). (ps-3). 1958. 14.95 (*0-06-026180-3*) HarpC Child Bks.

Crictor. Tomi Ungerer. LC 58-5288. (Trophy Picture Bk.). (Illus.). 32p. (J). (ps-3). 1983. pap. 4.95 (*0-06-443044-8*, Trophy) HarpC Child Bks.

Cried & Measured. Karl Young. LC 77-70788. 1977. pap. 5.00 (*0-686-19543-4*) Tree Bks.

Criemos Ninos Seguros de Si. James Dobson. (SPA.). Date not set. pap. 7.99 (*0-88113-136-9*) Edit Betania.

Criers & Hawkers of London: Engravings & Drawings by Marcellus Laroon. Ed. by Sean Shesgreen. (Illus.). 264p. 1990. 47.50 (*0-8047-1506-8*) Stanford U Pr.

Criers of the Shops. Sherlock B. Gass. LC 74-142633. (Essay Index Reprint Ser.). 1977. 23.95 (*0-8369-2049-X*) Ayer.

Cries & Claws: Poetry by Joyce Mansour. Joyce Mansour. Tr. by Jan Pallister. 31p. 1987. 5.00 (*0-934477-00-0*) Edits Autrui.

Cries for Democracy: Writings & Speeches from the 1989 Chinese Democracy Movement. Ed. by Han Minzhu. (Illus.). 300p. (Orig.). 1990. text ed. 55.00 (*0-691-03146-0*); pap. text ed. 16.95 (*0-691-00857-4*) Princeton U Pr.

Cries from a Wounded Madrid: Poetry of the Spanish Civil War. Ed. by Carlos Bauer. LC 83-18304. xviii, 158p. 1984. pap. 12.95 (*0-8040-0376-9*, Swallow) Ohio U Pr.

Cries from the Cross: Sermons on the Seven Last Words of Jesus. Leighton Ferrell. LC 93-41820. (Protestant Pulpit Exchange Ser.). 96p. (Orig.). 1994. pap. 7.95 (*0-687-13296-7*) Abingdon.

Cries from the Eagle's Nest, Vol. 1. Nancy Solomon. 300p. (Orig.). 1992. pap. 9.95 (*0-9631932-0-1*) Lobe Pub.

Cries from the Heart: Prayers for Bereaved Parents. Margaret B. Spiess. 64p. (Orig.). 1991. pap. 5.99 (*0-8010-8317-6*) Baker Bk.

Cries from the Mammal House. Terry Johnson. (Royal Court Writers Ser.). 31p. 1988. pap. 5.95 (*0-413-56250-6*, A0067) Heinemann.

Cries of Flesh & Stone. Richard O'Connell. 1962. pap. 10.00 (*0-685-62608-3*) Atlantis Edns.

Cries of Swimmers. 2nd ed. Maura Stanton. (Classic Contemporaries Ser.). 72p. (Orig.). 1991. reprint ed. pap. 10.95 (*0-88748-124-8*) Carnegie-Mellon.

Cries of the Children. Clare McNally. 320p. (Orig.). 1992. pap. 4.99 (*0-451-40320-7*, Onyx) NAL-Dutton.

***Cries of the Heart: Praying Our Losses.** Wayne Simsic. Ed. by Carl Koch. (Illus.). 87p. (Orig.). 1994. pap. 4.95 (*0-88489-335-9*) St Marys.

Cries of the People: Ministry Matters Mostly Personal. 2nd ed. Lawrence M. Ventline. 96p. 1993. pap. 7.95 (*1-883520-00-2*) Jeremiah Pr.

Cries of the Spirit: A Celebration of Women's Spirituality. Ed. by Marilyn Sewell. LC 90-52581. 340p. 1991. pap. 18.95 (*0-8070-6813-6*) Beacon Pr.

Cries of the Wolf Man. Patrick Mahony. Ed. by Chicago Institute for Psychoanalysis Staff. LC 83-26525. (History of Psychoanalysis Ser.: No. 1). xiii, 188p. (C). 1984. text ed. 30.00 (*0-8236-1090-X*) Intl Univs Pr.

Crime. Georges Bernanos. 8.95 (*0-7859-0635-5*, F87830) Fr & Eur.

Crime. Marianne LeVert. Ed. by Gerald Leinwand. (American Issues Ser.). 160p. (YA). (gr. 9-12). 1991. 16.95 (*0-8160-2102-3*) Facts on File.

***Crime.** James Q. Wilson & Joan Petersilia. LC 94-33070. 1995. 69.95 (*1-55815-427-2*); pap. 34.95 (*1-55815-417-5*) ICS Pr.

Crime, Vol. 5. Ed. by Eleanor C. Goldstein. (Resources Ser.). 1995. 38.00 (*0-89777-180-X*) Sirs Inc.

***Crime: A Serious American Problem.** rev. ed. Ed. by Mark A. Siegel et al. (Reference Ser.). (Illus.). 168p. 1994. pap. text ed. 22.95 (*1-878623-80-X*) Info Plus TX.

Crime: A Spatial Perspective. Ed. by Daniel E. George-Abey & Keith D. Harries. LC 80-14640. 320p. 1980. text ed. 50.00 (*0-231-04734-7*) Col U Pr.

Crime: Al Jar'imah. Nagib Mahfouz. (ARA.). 1985. pap. 8.95 (*0-86685-147-X*) Intl Bk Ctr.

***Crime: An Encyclopedia.** Oliver Cyriax. (Illus.). 468p. 1995. 29.95 (*0-233-98821-1*, Pub. by A Deutsch UK) Trafalgar.

Crime: Index of Modern Information. Anthony I. Quaine. LC 88-47548. 150p. 1988. 39.50 (*0-88164-820-5*); pap. 34.50 (*0-88164-821-3*) ABBE Pubs Assn.

***Crime: Is It Out of Control?** Ed. by Shari Binford et al. (Compact Reference Ser.). 72p. (YA). 1994. pap. text ed. 11.95 (*1-878623-87-7*) Info Plus TX.

Crime: Its Cause & Treatment. Clarence Darrow. (C). 1990. 100.00 (*0-89771-161-0*) St Mut.

Crime a La Carte. Ed. by Cynthia Manson. 256p. (Orig.). 1994. pap. 4.99 (*0-451-18052-6*, Sig) NAL-Dutton.

Crime, Abnormal Minds & the Law. Ernest B. Hoag & Edward H. Williams. (Historical Foundations of Forensic Psychiatry & Psychology Ser.). 405p. 1980. reprint ed. lib. bdg. 39.50 (*0-306-76060-6*) Da Capo.

Crime Against Humanity. W. C. Deb. (C). 1992. 18.50 (*81-85565-20-1*, Pub. by Uppal Pub Hse II) S Asia.

Crime Against Kansas, the Apologies for the Crime, the True Remedy. Charles Sumner. LC 78-82226. (Anti-Slavery Crusade in America Ser.). 1970. reprint ed. 17.95 (*0-405-00665-9*) Ayer.

Crime Against Marcella. large type ed. George Milner. (Linford Mystery Library). 288p. 1988. pap. 11.95 (*0-7089-6622-5*, Linford) Ulverscroft.

Crime Against Nature. Minnie B. Pratt. LC 90-2778. 128p. (Orig.). 1990. 18.95 (*0-932379-73-7*); pap. 8.95 (*0-932379-72-9*) Firebrand Bks.

Crime Against Puerto Rico. W. D. Washburn, Jr. (Studies in Puerto Rican History, Literature & Culture). 1980. lib. bdg. 59.95 (*0-8490-3202-4*) Gordon Pr.

Crime Against the Elderly: Implications for Policy-Makers & Practitioners. Robert J. Smith. 61p. 1979. pap. text ed. 5.00 (*0-910473-07-2*) Intl Fed Ageing.

Crime Against Women. Ram Ahuja. 216p. 1987. 29.95 (*81-7033-022-X*) Asia Bk Corp.

Crime Against Women. Ed. by O. C. Sharma. (Illus.). 248p. 1994. 25.00 (*81-7024-624-5*, Pub. by Ashish Pub Hse II) Nataraj Bks.

***Crime Analysis--with Medical, Forensic, Political, & Social Involvement: Index of New Information & Research.** Pierre W. Petrosonne. LC 94-34921. 189p. 1995. 44.50 (*0-7883-0450-X*); pap. 39.50 (*0-7883-0451-8*) ABBE Pubs Assn.

Crime Analysis Charting. Jack Morris. (Illus.). 116p. 1994. pap. 16.00 (*0-912479-01-9*) Palmer Pr.

***Crime Analysis Through Computer Mapping, Vol. 1.** rev. ed. Ed. by Carolyn R. Block et al. 312p. 1995. write for info. (*1-878734-34-2*) Police Exec Res.

Crime & Campus Police: A Handbook for Police Officers & Administrators. 2nd ed. Michael C. Smith. Ed. by Donald D. Gehring & Parker Young. (Higher Education Administration Ser.). 120p. 1994. pap. 16.95 (*0-912557-10-9*) Coll Admin Pubns.

Crime & Capitalism: Readings in Marxist Criminology. Ed. by David F. Greenberg. LC 92-34763. 568p. 1993. 49.95 (*1-56639-025-7*); pap. 22.95 (*1-56639-026-5*) Temple U Pr.

Crime & Conflict in English Communities, Thirteen Hundred to Thirteen Forty-Eight. Barbara A. Hanawalt. LC 79-1211. 371p. 1979. 32.00 (*0-674-17580-8*) HUP.

Crime & Control in Comparative Perspectives. Ed. by Hans-Gunther Heiland et al. xiv, 290p. (C). 1991. lib. bdg. 59.95 (*3-11-012614-1*, 230-91) De Gruyter.

Crime & Correction: An Islamic Perspective. Sidney R. Sharif. Tr. by Claude Field. 98p. (Orig.). 1988. 12.95 (*1-56744-248-X*); pap. 8.50 (*1-56744-257-9*) Kazi Pubns.

Crime & Crime Again: Unexpected Mystery Stories by the World's Great Writers. 1990. 6.99 (*0-517-01758-X*) Random Hse Value.

Crime & Crime Prevention for Insurance Practice. Roger A. Litton. (Illus.). 198p. 1990. text ed. 63.95 (*0-566-07076-6*, Pub. by Avebury Pub UK) Ashgate Pub Co.

Crime & Criminal Justice. Ed. by John Gardiner & Michael Mulkey. (C). 1974. pap. 12.00 (*0-918592-08-9*) Pol Studies.

***Crime & Criminal Justice: Essays in the History of Canadian Law, Vol. 5.** Ed. by Jim Phillips et al. (Osgoode Society for Canadian Legal History Ser.). 584p. 1994. 70.00 (*0-8020-0633-7*) U of Toronto Pr.

Crime & Criminal Justice Since 1945. Terence Morris. (Making Contemporary Britain Ser.). (Illus.). 160p. 1989. pap. 16.95 (*0-631-16109-0*) Blackwell Pubs.

Crime & Criminal Justice System in India. Mir Mehraj-Ud-Din. 338p. 1984. 44.95 (*0-318-36848-X*) Asia Bk Corp.

Crime & Criminal Justice System in India. Mir Mehraj-Ud-Din. (C). 1990. 110.00 (*0-89771-179-3*) St Mut.

Crime & Criminal Justice under the Third Republic: The Shame of Marianne. Benjamin F. Martin. LC 89-27334. 392p. 1990. text ed. 45.00 (*0-8071-1572-X*) La State U Pr.

Crime & Criminal Law. Ed. by Kermit L. Hall. (United States Constitutional & Legal History Ser.). 707p. 1987. lib. bdg. 35.00 (*0-8240-0141-9*) Garland.

***Crime & Criminal Notions - Can the Perfect Murder Be Planned & Possibly Executed? Essay Varieties & Debates from Around the World!** John C. Bartone. (Illus.). 270p. Date not set. 51.50 (*0-7883-0416-X*); pap. 45.50 (*0-7883-0417-8*) ABBE Pubs Assn.

Crime & Criminal Policy in Japan: Analysis & Evaluation of the Showa Era, 1928-1988. M. Shikita & S. Tsuchiya. (Research in Criminology Ser.). 448p. 1991. 65.00 (*0-387-97647-7*) Spr-Verlag.

***Crime & Criminal Psychology: Index of New Information with Authors, Subjects, Research Categories & References.** Clement K. Zaine. 160p. 1995. 49.50 (*0-7883-0742-8*); pap. 39.50 (*0-7883-0743-6*) ABBE Pubs Assn.

Crime & Criminal Statistics in Boston. Sam B. Warner. LC 74-3863. (Criminal Justice in America Ser.). 1974. reprint ed. 18.95 (*0-405-06178-1*) Ayer.

Crime & Criminals: An Address Delivered to the Prisoners in the Chicago County Jail. Clarence Darrow. LC 73-77548. 48p. 1975. pap. 5.00 (*0-88286-025-9*) C H Kerr.

Crime & Criminals: Opposing Viewpoints. Ed. by Paul A. Winters. LC 94-4976. (Opposing Viewpoints Ser.). (Illus.). 264p. (YA). (gr. 10 up). 1995. lib. bdg. 19.95 (*1-56510-176-6*); pap. text ed. 11.55 (*1-56510-177-4*) Greenhaven.

Crime & Criminology. Jay Livingston. 624p. (C). 1991. text ed. write for info. (*0-13-192782-5*) P-H.

Crime & Criminology. Sue T. Reid. LC 90-5168. (Illus.). 590p. (C). 1991. text ed. 46.75 (*0-03-035302-5*, HV6025.R515) HB Coll Pubs.

***Crime & Criminology.** 7th ed. Sue T. Reid. (C). 1994. boxed write for info. (*0-697-27463-2*) Brown & Benchmark.

Crime & Culture in America: A Comparative Perspective. Parviz Saney. LC 86-3594. (Contributions in Criminology & Penology Ser.: No. 11). 215p. 1986. text ed. 55.00 (*0-313-24340-9*, SAN/, Greenwood Pr) Greenwood.

Crime & Custom in Savage Society. Bronislaw Malinowski. LC 84-19807. (Illus.). xii, 132p. 1984. reprint ed. text ed. 45.00 (*0-313-24686-6*, MCRC, Greenwood Pr) Greenwood.

Crime & Custom in Savage Society. Bronislaw Malinowski. (Quality Paperback Ser.: No. 210). 1976. reprint ed. pap. 19.00 (*0-8226-0210-5*) Littlefield.

Crime & Defoe: A New Kind of Writing. Lincoln B. Faller. LC 92-17642. (Cambridge Studies in Eighteenth-Century English Literature & Thought: No. 16). 286p. (C). 1993. 59.95 (*0-521-42086-5*) Cambridge U Pr.

Crime & Delinquency. Ed. by Dae H. Chang. LC 77-24066. 179p. 1977. pap. text ed. 19.95 (*0-87073-398-2*) Transaction Pubs.

Crime & Delinquency Prevention Specialist. Jack Rudman. (Career Examination Ser.: C-3212). 1994. pap. 34.95 (*0-8373-3212-5*) Nat Learn.

Crime & Destiny. Johannes Lange. Tr. by Charlotte Haldane. (Historical Foundations of Forensic Psychiatry & Psychology Ser.). 250p. 1983. reprint ed. lib. bdg. 25.00 (*0-306-76209-9*) Da Capo.

Crime & Deviance: A Comparative Perspective. Ed. by Graeme R. Newman. LC 80-11629. (Sage Annual Reviews of Studies in Deviance: No. 4). 335p. reprint ed. pap. 95.50 (*0-8357-8501-7*, 2034777) Bks Demand.

Crime & Diet: The Macrobiotic Approach. Michio Kushi et al. Ed. by Edward Esko et al. LC 86-62959. (Illus.). 212p. 1987. 17.95 (*0-87040-682-5*) Japan Pubns USA.

Crime & Disrepute. John Hagan. 128p. 1994. pap. 15.95 (*0-8039-9039-1*) Pine Forge.

Crime & Everyday Life: Insights & Implications for Society. Marcus Felson. 240p. 1993. pap. 13.95 (*0-8039-9029-4*) Pine Forge.

Crime & God's Judgment in Shakespeare. Robert R. Reed. LC 83-19701. 231p. reprint ed. pap. 65.90 (*0-685-44499-6*, 2031524) Bks Demand.

Crime & Human Nature. James Q. Wilson & Richard J. Herrnstein. 640p. 1986. pap. 15.95 (*0-671-62810-0*, Touchstone Bks) S&S Trade.

Crime & Inequality. Ed. by John Hagan & Ruth Peterson. LC 94-17742. 1995. 49.50 (*0-8047-2404-0*); pap. 16.95 (*0-8047-2477-6*) Stanford U Pr.

Crime & Insanity in England. Nigel Walker. 299p. 1979. Vol. 1, 299 p. 20.00 (*0-85224-017-1*, Pub. by Edinburgh U Pr UK) Col U Pr.

Crime & Its Modification: A Social Learning Perspective. Michael Nietzel. LC 78-23984. (General Psychology Ser.: Vol. 77). (Illus.). 1979. pap. 24.00 (*0-08-023877-7*, Pergamon Pr) Elsevier.

Crime & Its Repression. Gustav Aschaffenburg. Tr. by Adalbert Albrecht. LC 68-55767. (Criminology, Law Enforcement, & Social Problems Ser.: No. 11). 1968. reprint ed. 26.00 (*0-87585-011-1*) Patterson Smith.

Crime & Its Social Context: Toward an Integrated Theory of Offenders, Victims, & Situations. Terance D. Miethe & Robert F. Meier. LC 93-24503. (SUNY Series in Deviance & Social Control). 209p. 1994. 57.50x (*0-7914-1901-0*); pap. 18.95x (*0-7914-1902-9*) State U NY Pr.

Crime & Its Treatment. 2nd ed. John B. Mays. LC 76-357144. (Aspects of Modern Sociology: the Social Structure of Modern Britain Ser.). 183p. reprint ed. pap. 52.20 (*0-685-43699-3*, 2027708) Bks Demand.

Crime & Its Victims: International Research & Public Policy Issues. Emilio C. Viano. 317p. 1989. 60.00 (*0-89116-950-4*) Hemisp Pub.

Crime & Its Victims: What We Can Do. Daniel W. Van Ness. LC 86-10467. 240p. 1986. 10.99 (*0-87784-512-3*, 512) InterVarsity.

Crime & Justice. 2nd ed. Howard Abadinsky & L. Thomas Winfree. (Law, Crime, & Justice Ser.). 400p. (C). 1992. text ed. 41.95 (*0-8304-1252-2*); write for info. (*0-8304-1332-4*) Nelson-Hall.

Crime & Justice, 2 vols., 1. Ed. by Jackwell Susman. LC 78-38401. (AMS Anthology Ser.). 1974. lib. bdg. 47.50 (*0-404-10201-8*) AMS Pr.

Crime & Justice, 2 vols., 2. Ed. by Jackwell Susman. LC 78-38401. (AMS Anthology Ser.). 1974. lib. bdg. 47.50 (*0-404-10202-6*); pap. 11.95 (*0-404-10252-2*) AMS Pr.

Crime & Justice, 2 vols., Set. Ed. by Jackwell Susman. LC 78-38401. (AMS Anthology Ser.). 1974. lib. bdg. 95.00 (*0-404-19512-1*) AMS Pr.

Crime & Justice, Vol. 14. Ed. by Michael H. Tonry. 376p. 1991. lib. bdg. 39.95 (*0-226-80812-2*) U Ch Pr.

Crime & Justice: A Biannual Review of Research, Vol. 10. Ed. by Michael H. Tonry & Norval Morris. LC 80-642217. x, 344p. (C). 1988. lib. bdg. 27.50 (*0-226-80804-1*) U Ch Pr.

Crime & Justice: A Biannual Review of Research,, Vol. 12. Ed. by Michael H. Tonry & Norval Morris. LC 80-642217. 350p. 1989. lib. bdg. 34.95 (*0-226-80808-4*) U Ch Pr.

Crime & Justice: An AMS Anthology, 2 vols., Set. Intro. by Jackwell Susman. 95.00 (*0-404-10200-X*) AMS Pr.

Crime & Justice: An Annual Review of Research, Vol. 1. Ed. by Norval Morris & Michael H. Tonry. 1979. lib. bdg. 14.00 (*0-226-53955-5*, P903) U Ch Pr.

Crime & Justice: An Annual Review of Research, Vol. 1. Ed. by Norval Morris & Michael H. Tonry. 1980. pap. text ed. 6.95 (*0-226-53956-3*, P903) U Ch Pr.

Crime & Justice: An Annual Review of Research, Vol. 3. Michael H. Tonry & Norval Morris. (Studies in Crime & Justice Ser.). 362p. (C). 1981. lib. bdg. 22.50 (*0-226-80795-9*) U Ch Pr.

Crime & Justice: An Annual Review of Research, Vol. 3. Michael H. Tonry & Norval Morris. (Studies in Crime & Justice Ser.). 362p. (C). 1982. pap. text ed. 5.95 (*0-226-80796-7*) U Ch Pr.

Crime & Justice: An Annual Review of Research, Vol. 4. Ed. by Michael H. Tonry & Norval Morris. LC 82-13435. 344p. 1983. lib. bdg. 25.00 (*0-226-80797-5*) U Ch Pr.

Crime & Justice: An Annual Review of Research,, Vol. 5. Ed. by Michael H. Tonry & Norval Morris. LC 80-642217. 320p. 1983. lib. bdg. 28.50 (*0-226-80799-1*) U Ch Pr.

An Asterisk (*) at the beginning of an entry indicates that the title is appearing in BIP for the first time.

An Asterisk (*) at the beginning of an entry indicates that the title is appearing in BIP for the first time.

1693

1995. pap. 14.95 (*0-929497-94-5*) Ariadne CA.

Crime Classics: The Mystery Story from Poe to the Present. Ed. by Rex Burns & Mary R. Sullivan. 416p. 1991. reprint ed. pap. 11.95 (*0-14-013128-0*, Penguin Bks) Viking Penguin.

Crime Classification Manual. John E. Douglas et al. 352p. 1992. text ed. 49.95 (*0-669-24638-7*) Free Pr.

Crime Comics: The Illustrated History. Mike Benton. LC 92-37159. (Library of Comic Book Histories: No. 5). (Illus.). 176p. 1993. 24.95 (*0-87833-814-4*) Taylor Pub.

Crime, Community & Police. V. K. Mohanan. 1987. 27.50 (*81-212-0107-1*, Pub. by Gian Publng Hse II) S Asia.

Crime, Community & Police. V. K. Mohanan. (C). 1990. 90.00 (*0-89771-159-9*) St Mut.

Crime Control: The Use & Misuse of Police Resources. David J. Farmer. LC 84-11470. (Criminal Justice & Public Safety Ser.). 254p. 1984. 42.50 (*0-306-41688-3*, Plenum Pr) Plenum.

***Crime Control & Justice in America: Searching for Facts & Answers.** Paul W. Keve. (Last Quarter Century Ser.: No. 3). 370p. (Orig.). 1995. pap. text ed. 38.00x (*0-8389-0644-3*) ALA.

***Crime Control As Industry.** 2nd ed. Nils Christie. 192p. 1995. pap. 17.95 (*0-415-12539-1*, B7227) Routledge.

Crime Control As Industry: Towards Gulags, Western Style. Nils Christie. LC 92-38179. (Illus.). 192p. 1993. pap. 17.95 (*0-415-09478-X*, B0614) Routledge.

Crime Control by the National Government. Arthur Chester Millspaugh. LC 70-168678. (American Constitutional & Legal History Ser). 306p. 1972. reprint ed. lib. bdg. 37.50 (*0-306-70418-8*) Da Capo.

***Crime Control in Public Housing: A Guide for a Safer Community.** Donna K. Wells et al. (Illus.). 107p. (Orig.). (C). (gr. 12 up). 1994. pap. text ed. 45.00 (*0-7881-0864-6*) Diane Pub.

Crime, Correction, & Society: An Introduction to Criminology. Elmer H. Johnson. LC 77-88300. (Dorsey Series in Sociology). (Illus.). 629p. reprint ed. pap. 179. 30 (*0-317-09066-6*, 2055671) Bks Demand.

Crime, Criminal Justice & the Probation Service. Robert Harris. 224p. 1991. 69.95 (*0-415-05034-0*, A5949); pap. 19.95 (*0-415-05035-9*, A5953) Routledge.

Crime, Criminals & Corrections. Donal E. MacNamara & Llyod McCorkle. LC 81-84361. 304p. 1982. lib. bdg. 17. 00 (*0-89444-032-2*); pap. text ed. 15.00 (*0-89444-033-0*) John Jay Pr.

Crime, Criminology & Public Policy: Essays in Honour of Sir Leon Radzinowicz. Roger G. Hood. LC 75-2813. 1975. reprint ed. 39.95 (*0-02-914920-7*) Free Pr.

Crime, Crusades & Corruption: Prohibitions in the United States, 1900-1987. Michael Woodiwiss. 260p. 1988. 56. 00 (*0-389-20796-9*, N8354) B&N Imports.

Crime, Culpability & Remedy. Ed. by Ellen F. Paul et al. x, 248p. (Orig.). 1990. pap. text ed. 22.95 (*0-631-17304-8*) Blackwell Pubs.

Crime de Sylvestre Bonnard. Anatole France. 249p. (FRE.). 1970. 13.95 (*0-8288-9813-8*, F104500) Fr & Eur.

Crime de Sylvestre Bonnard see Romans et Contes

Crime de Village see Oeuvres

Crime, Detective, Espionage, Mystery, & Thriller Fiction & Film: A Comprehensive Bibliography of Critical Writing Through 1979. David Skene Melvin & Ann Skene Melvin. LC 80-1194. xx, 367p. 1980. text ed. 49.95 (*0-313-22062-X*, MCD/) Greenwood.

Crime, Disorder, & the Risorgimento: The Politics of Policing in Bologna. Steven C. Hughes. LC 93-9579. (Studies in Italian History & Culture). (Illus.). 320p. (C). 1994. 54.95 (*0-521-44450-0*) Cambridge U Pr.

Crime et Chatiment, Tome I. Fyodor Dostoyevsky. 512p. (FRE.). 1975. pap. 11.95 (*0-7859-1798-5*, 2070366529) Fr & Eur.

Crime et Chatiment, Tome II. Fyodor Dostoyevsky. 512p. (FRE.). 1975. pap. 11.95 (*0-7859-1799-3*, 2070366537) Fr & Eur.

Crime et Chatiment: Maison des Morts, Etc. Fyodor Dostoyevsky. (FRE.). 1978. 99.50 (*0-8288-3436-9*, F79860) Fr & Eur.

Crime et Chatiment, Journal de Raskolnikov, Souvenirs de la Maison des Morts. Fyodor Dostoyevsky. 1280p. 39. 95 (*0-686-56501-0*) Fr & Eur.

Crime, Fear, & the New York City Subways: The Role of Citizen Action. Dennis J. Kenney. LC 86-25305. 148p. 1986. text ed. 49.95 (*0-275-92322-3*, C2322, Praeger Pubs) Greenwood.

Crime Fiction II: A Comprehensive Bibliography, 1749-1990. rev. ed. Allen J. Hubin. LC 93-41230. (Reference Library of the Humanities: Vol. 1353). 1608p. 1994. 195. 00 (*0-8240-6891-2*, H1353) Garland.

Crime-Fighting. Ian Graham. LC 94-13839. (Science Spotlight Ser.). (J). 1995. lib. bdg. write for info. (*0-8114-3840-6*) Raintree Steck-V.

Crime for Christmas. Ed. by Richard Dalby. 288p. 1992. 18.95 (*0-312-08170-7*, Pub. by Thomas Dunne Bks) St Martin.

Crime for Christmas. Richard Dalby. 1993. mass mkt. 4.99 (*0-312-95148-5*) St Martin.

Crime for Christmas. Carolyn Keene. (Nancy Drew & Hardy Boys Supermystery Ser.). (YA). (gr. 7 up). 1991. mass mkt. 3.99 (*0-671-74617-0*, Archway) PB.

***Crime-Free America.** Royce M. Hilliard. 104p. 1995. text ed. 11.00 (*0-8059-3674-2*) Dorrance.

Crime Free Housing. Barry Poyner & Barry Webb. (Illus.). 128p. 1991. 52.95 (*0-7506-1273-8*, Butterwrth Archit) Buttrwrth-Heinemann.

Crime, Guilt, & Punishment: A Philosophical Introduction. C. L. Ten. LC 87-5571. 186p. 1987. pap. 19.95 (*0-19-875081-1*) OUP.

***Crime History & Histories of Crime: Studies in the Historiography of Crime & Criminal Justice in Modern History.** Ed. by Clive Emsley & Louis A. Knafla. LC 95-6654. (Contributions in Criminology & Penology Ser.: No. 48). 1995. text ed. write for info. (*0-313-28722-8*, Greenwood Pr) Greenwood.

Crime in a Rural Community. Michael O'Conner & David Gray. 150p. 1989. pap. 26.00 (*0-685-51048-4*, Pub. by Federation Pr AU) W W Gaunt.

Crime in America. Milton Meltzer. LC 90-5698. 176p. (YA). (gr. 7 up). 1990. 12.95 (*0-688-08513-X*) Morrow Jr Bks.

Crime in America. Estes Kefauver. Ed. by Sidney Shalett. LC 68-8062. (Illus.). 333p. 1969. reprint ed. text ed. 38. 50 (*0-8371-0126-3*, KECA, Greenwood Pr) Greenwood.

Crime in America: Some Existing & Emerging Problems. Jay S. Albanese & Robert D. Pursley. LC 92-9904. 416p. 1992. pap. text ed. 33.00 (*0-13-191446-4*) P-H.

Crime in America: The War at Home. Ed. by Oliver Trager. LC 88-11259. (Editorials on File Book Ser.). 221p. reprint ed. pap. 63.00 (*0-7837-1368-1*, 2041517) Bks Demand.

Crime in American Society. 2nd ed. Charles H. McCaghy & Stephen A. Cernkovich. 496p. (C). 1987. text ed. write for info. (*0-02-378340-0*) Macmillan.

***Crime in America's Top-Rated Cities: A Statistical Profile.** Ed. by Rhoda Garoogian & Andrew Garoogian. 730p. 1995. pap. 69.95 (*1-881220-28-1*) Univ Ref Pubns.

Crime in Biological, Social & Moral Contexts. Ed. by Lee Ellis & Harry Hoffman. LC 90-31184. 344p. 1990. text ed. 59.95 (*0-275-93003-3*, C3003, Praeger Pubs) Greenwood.

Crime in Corn Weather. 2nd ed. Mary M. Atwater. Ed. by Linda C. Ligon. 160p. reprint ed. pap. 6.95 (*0-934026-84-X*) Interweave.

Crime in Developing Countries: A Comparative Perspective. Marshall B. Clinard & Daniel J. Abbott. LC 73-4031. 334p. reprint ed. pap. 95.20 (*0-7837-3435-2*, 2057757) Bks Demand.

Crime in Early Modern England 1550-1750. J. A. Sharpe. (Themes in British Social History Ser.). (Illus.). 256p. (C). 1984. pap. text ed. 23.95 (*0-582-48994-6*, 73438) Longman.

Crime in England: Its Relation, Character & Extent As Developed from 1801-1848. Thomas Plint. LC 73-14175. (Perspectives in Social Inquiry Ser.). 192p. 1974. reprint ed. 13.95 (*0-405-05518-8*) Ayer.

Crime in England, 1550-1800. Ed. by J. S. Cockburn. LC 77-2867. 378p. reprint ed. pap. 107.80 (*0-8357-2773-4*, 2039898) Bks Demand.

Crime in Europe. Ed. by Frances Heidensohn & Martin Farrell. 224p. (C). 1991. text ed. 55.00 (*0-415-05072-3*, A5129) Routledge.

Crime in Its Relations to Social Progress. Arthur C. Hall. LC 68-56660. (Columbia University. Studies in the Social Sciences: No. 40). reprint ed. 27.50 (*0-404-51040-X*) AMS Pr.

Crime in Motion Pictures. 56p. (Orig.). (C). 1993. pap. text ed. 25.00 (*1-56806-855-7*) Diane Pub.

Crime in Nineteenth-Century Wales. David J. V. Jones. 295p. 50.00 (*0-7083-1142-3*, Pub. by U of Wales UK) Bks Intl VA.

Crime in Question. Margaret Yorke. 240p. 1990. pap. 3.95 (*0-14-012435-7*, Penguin Bks) Viking Penguin.

Crime in Texas. Morgan O. Reynolds. 1991. pap. 10.00 (*0-943802-61-X*, 158) Natl Ctr Pol.

Crime in the District of Columbia: Reports & Hearings. U. S. House of Representatives, Committee on the District of Columbia. (Police in America Ser.). 1971. 65.95 (*0-405-03368-0*, 16930) Ayer.

Crime in the Making: Pathways & Turning Points Through Life. Robert J. Sampson & John H. Laub. LC 92-35723. (Illus.). 319p. (C). 1993. 34.00 (*0-674-17604-9*) HUP.

***Crime in the Making: Pathways & Turning Points Through Life.** Robert J. Sampson & John H. Laub. (Illus.). 319p. 1995. pap. text ed. 17.95 (*0-674-17605-7*, SAMCRX) HUP.

***Crime in the Public Mind.** Kathlyn T. Gaubatz. LC 94-25221. 1995. 34.50 (*0-472-10582-5*) U of Mich Pr.

Crime in the Queen's Court. Carolyn Keene. Ed. by Ellen Winkler. (Nancy Drew Ser.: No. 112). 160p. (Orig.). (J). 1993. pap. 3.99 (*0-671-79298-9*, Minstrel Bks) PB.

Crime in the Streets & Crime in the Suites: Perspectives on Crime & Criminal Justice. Ed. by Doug A. Timmer & D. Stanley Eitzen. 468p. 1989. pap. text ed. 30.00 (*0-205-11977-8*, H19771) Allyn.

Crime in the United States. Ed. by J. P. Shalloo. LC 74-3814. (Criminal Justice in America Ser.). 1974. reprint ed. 23.95 (*0-405-06169-2*) Ayer.

Crime in Trinidad: Conflict & Control in a Plantation Society, 1838-1900. David V. Trotman. LC 86-7092. 320p. 1986. text ed. 36.00x (*0-87049-491-0*) U of Tenn Pr.

Crime in Victorian Britain: An Annotated Bibliography from Nineteenth-Century British Magazines. Comp. by E. M. Palmegiano. LC 92-44640. (Bibliographies & Indexes in World History Ser.: No. 31). 192p. 1993. text ed. 59.95 (*0-313-26523-2*, PCM, Greenwood Pr) Greenwood.

Crime, Inc. The Inside Story of the Mafia's First 100 Years. William Balsamo & George Carpozi, Jr. Ed. by Joan S. Dunphy. Orig. Title: Under the Clock. 391p. 1991. pap. 13.95 (*0-88282-073-7*) New Horizon NJ.

Crime Investigation. 2nd ed. Paul L. Kirk & John I. Thornton. LC 85-5208. 528p. (C). 1985. reprint ed. lib. bdg. 53.00 (*0-89874-854-2*) Krieger.

Crime Investigation Quizzer. D. DelBagno & R. Spina. 1994. pap. 21.95 (*0-87526-407-7*) Gould.

Crime Investigations with Forensic Sciences: Index of New Information with Authors & Subjects. American Health Research Institute Staff. 180p. 1992. 44.50 (*1-55914-684-2*); pap. 39.50 (*1-55914-685-0*) ABBE Pubs Assn.

Crime Is a Five Letter Word: A Detective Puzzle. John Escott. (Illus.). 64p. (J). (gr. 2-5). 1994. 5.95 (*0-340-56910-7*, Pub. by H & S UK) Trafalgar.

Crime, Its Cause & Treatment. Clarence Darrow. LC 70-172562. (Criminology, Law Enforcement, & Social Problems Ser.: No. 148). 320p. 1972. reprint ed. 26.00 (*0-87585-143-6*) Patterson Smith.

Crime, Its Causes & Remedies. Cesare Lombroso. Tr. by Henry P. Horton. LC 68-55776. (Criminology, Law Enforcement, & Social Problems Ser.: No. 14). 1968. reprint ed. 35.00 (*0-87585-014-6*) Patterson Smith.

Crime, Justice & Protecting the Public. 50p. 1990. pap. 14. 00 (*0-10-109652-6*, HM6526) UNIPUB.

Crime, Justice & Society in Colonial Sri Lanka. John Rogers. (University of London, School of Oriental & African Studies, Centre of South Asian Studies, London Studies on South Asia Ser.: No. 5). 271p. (C). 1987. 42. 00 (*0-913215-24-4*) Riverdale Co.

Crime Lab Chemistry. rev. ed. Jacqueline Barber. Ed. by Lincoln Bergman & Kay Fairwell. (Great Explorations in Math & Science (GEMS) Ser.). (Illus.). 10p. (Orig.). (J). (gr. 4-8). 1989. pap. 8.50 (*0-912511-16-8*) Lawrence Science.

Crime Lab. 101: Experimenting with Crime Detection. Robert Gardner. 123p. (YA). (gr. 6-9). 1992. 13.95 (*0-8027-8158-6*); lib. bdg. 14.85 (*0-8027-8159-4*) Walker & Co.

Crime Lab 101: Experimenting with Crime Detection. Robert Gardner. 96p. (Orig.). (YA). (gr. 7 up). 1994. pap. 5.95 (*0-8027-7420-2*) Walker & Co.

Crime Laboratory: Case Studies of Scientific Investigation. 2nd ed. James W. Osterburg. LC 81-7694. 1982. pap. 19. 95 (*0-87632-364-6*) Clark Boardman Callaghan.

Crime Law & Social Science. Jerome Michael & Mortimer J. Adler. LC 77-108235. (Criminology, Law Enforcement, & Social Problems Ser.: No. 118). 1971. reprint ed. 30.00 (*0-87585-118-5*) Patterson Smith.

Crime, Law & Society. Jeffrey H. Goldstein & A. Goldstein. LC 77-136009. 1971. pap. 18.95 (*0-02-912260-0*) Free Pr.

Crime, Law & Society. Frank E. Hartung. LC 65-13410. 320p. reprint ed. pap. 91.20 (*0-685-20902-4*, 2032020) Bks Demand.

Crime, Madness & Politics in Modern France: The Medical Concept of National Decline. Robert A. Nye. LC 83-43087. 1984. 52.50 (*0-691-05414-2*) Princeton U Pr.

***Crime, Mental Health & Poverty: Japan & America.** Robert J. Yoder. 61p. (Orig.). (C). 1994. pap. text ed. 15.00 (*1-880596-11-3*) Allegan Educ.

Crime News & the Public. Doris A. Graber. LC 80-16032. 256p. 1980. text ed. 79.50 (*0-275-90491-1*, C0491, Praeger Pubs) Greenwood.

Crime Novel: A Deviant Genre. Tony Hilfer. (Illus.) 192p. 1990. text ed. 30.00 (*0-292-71131-X*); pap. 13.95 (*0-292-71136-0*) U of Tex Pr.

Crime of Caste in Our Country: Bullets, 1861-Ballots 1892. Benjamin R. Davenport. 1977. text ed. 27.95 (*0-8369-9248-2*, 9102) Ayer.

***Crime of Christendom.** Fred G. Bratton. 256p. 1994. pap. 12.95 (*1-56474-122-2*) Fithian Pr.

Crime of Claudius Ptolemy. Robert R. Newton. LC 77-4211. 1977. text ed. 50.00 (*0-8018-1990-3*) Johns Hopkins.

Crime of Coy Bell. Sam Brown. 192p. 1992. 19.95 (*0-8027-4115-0*) Walker & Co.

Crime of Coy Bell. large type ed. Sam Brown. 238p. 1992. reprint ed. lib. bdg. 17.95 (*1-56054-491-0*) Thorndike Pr.

Crime of Coy Bell. Sam Brown. 192p. 1993. reprint ed. mass mkt. 3.99 (*0-671-78543-5*) PB.

Crime of Cuba. Carleton Beals. LC 76-111709. (American Imperialism: Viewpoints of United States Foreign Policy, 1898-1941 Ser.). 1970. reprint ed. 29.95 (*0-405-02003-1*) Ayer.

Crime of Galileo. Giorgio De Santillana. LC 55-7400. (Midway Reprint Ser.). (Illus.). xvi, 339p. 1978. reprint ed. pap. text ed. 18.95 (*0-226-73481-1*) U Ch Pr.

Crime of Imprisonment. George Bernard Shaw. LC 71-90708. (Illus.). 125p. 1970. reprint ed. text ed. 35.00 (*0-8371-2288-0*, SHCI, Greenwood Pr) Greenwood.

Crime of Innocence in the Fiction of Toni Morrison. Terry Otten. LC 89-4851. 104p. 1991. pap. 9.95 (*0-8262-0711-1*) U of Mo Pr.

Crime of Magnitude: The Murder of Little Annie. Mark Lemberger. LC 93-6866. (Illus.). 320p. 1993. 23.95 (*1-879483-12-2*); pap. 14.95 (*1-879483-13-0*) Prairie Oak Pr.

Crime of Passion. Kay Hooper. 240p. 1991. pap. 3.50 (*0-380-76197-1*) Avon.

***Crime of Passion.** Idanna Pucci. 1995. 18.95 (*1-56858-034-7*) FWEW.

Crime of Passion: Murder & the Murderer. David Lester & Gene Lester. LC 74-20788. 308p. 1975. 27.95 (*0-88229-139-4*) Nelson-Hall.

***Crime of Passion (Legal Thriller)** Maggie Ferguson. 1995. mass mkt. 3.50 (*0-373-22347-1*) Harlequin Bks.

Crime of Ruby McCollum. William Bradford. 1976. 18.95 (*0-8488-1377-4*) Amereon Ltd.

Crime of Ruby McCollum. William B. Huie. 210p. 1990. reprint ed. lib. bdg. 25.95 (*0-89966-755-4*) Buccaneer Bks.

Crime of Self-Defense: Bernhard Goetz & the Law on Trial. George P. Fletcher. 288p. 1988. text ed. 29.95 (*0-02-910311-8*) Free Pr.

Crime of Self-Defense: Bernhard Goetz & the Law on Trial. George P. Fletcher. LC 90-35781. 272p. 1990. pap. text ed. 13.95 (*0-226-25334-1*) U Ch Pr.

Crime of the Boulevard. Jules Claretie. Tr. by Carlton A. Kingsbury. LC 75-32739. (Literature of Mystery & Detection Ser.). 1976. reprint ed. 21.95 (*0-405-07867-6*) Ayer.

Crime of the Century. Kingsley Amis. 1989. 16.95 (*0-89296-398-0*) Mysterious Pr.

Crime of the Century. John Bennett. 112p. (Orig.). 1987. pap. 10.00 (*0-915016-37-0*) Second Coming.

Crime of the Century: Richard Speck & the Murder of Eight Nurses. Dennis L. Breo. 1993. 5.99 (*0-553-56025-5*) Bantam.

Crime of the Century: The Kennedy Assassination from a Historian's Perspective. 2nd ed. Michael L. Kurtz. LC 93-21272. 1993. pap. 14.95 (*0-87049-824-X*) U of Tenn Pr.

Crime of the Century: The Lindbergh Kidnapping Hoax. Greg Ahlgren & Stephen R. Monier. (Illus.). 300p. 1993. 21.95 (*0-8283-1971-5*) Branden Pub Co.

Crime of the Century - Insurance: Everything You Need to Know Before You Buy Insurance. Ron Alford. 114p. (Orig.). 1989. pap. 19.95 (*0-924893-00-1*) Plan Pub.

Crime of Vengeance: An Armenian Struggle for Justice. Edward Alexander. 1991. text ed. 24.95 (*0-02-900475-6*) Free Pr.

Crime on Her Mind: Fifteen Stories of Female Sleuths form the Victorian Era to the Forties. Ed. by Michele B. Slung. 25.95 (*0-89190-716-5*, Am Repr) Amereon Ltd.

Crime on My Hands. George Sanders. LC 90-80761. 199p. 1990. reprint ed. pap. 7.95 (*1-55882-070-1*) Intl Polygonics.

***Crime on the Tracks.** Virginia Deayton-Groom. (Illus.). 60p. (J). 1995. text ed. 14.50 (*0-930329-89-9*) KABEL Pubs.

Crime Partners. Donald Goines. (Orig.). 1974. pap. 3.50 (*0-87067-183-9*) Holloway.

Crime Pays, but So Does Imprisonment. Morgan O. Reynolds. 1990. pap. 10.00 (*0-943802-52-0*, 149) Natl Ctr Pol.

Crime, Police & the Courts in British History, No. 1: Readings from Criminal Justice History. Ed. by Louis A. Knafla. LC 89-14043. 368p. 1990. text ed. 79.50 (*0-313-28073-8*, KPT/, Greenwood Pr) Greenwood.

Crime, Policing & Place: Essays in Environmental Criminology. Ed. by David J. Evans et al. LC 91-24980. 320p. 1992. 87.50 (*0-415-04990-3*, A6664) Routledge.

Crime Prevention. Arthur Woods. LC 77-38677. (Foundations of Criminal Justice Ser.). reprint ed. 32.50 (*0-404-09193-8*) AMS Pr.

Crime Prevention. Arthur Woods. LC 78-154597. (Police in America Ser.). 1979. reprint ed. 19.95 (*0-405-03390-7*) Ayer.

Crime Prevention: Approaches, Practices & Evaluations. 2nd ed. Steven P. Lab. LC 91-76928. 327p. (C). 1992. pap. 24.95 (*0-87084-401-6*) Anderson Pub Co.

Crime Prevention & Control. (Terminology Bulletin Ser.: No. 340). 325p. 36.00 (*92-1-002052-9*) UN.

Crime Prevention & Control. United Nations Staff. (Terminology Bulletin Ser.: No. 340). 325p. 1990. 69.95 (*0-8288-7363-1*, 9210020529) Fr & Eur.

Crime Prevention & Control: Index & Analysis of Activity, Success & Services. Sonny S. Springer. LC 90-56238. 190p. 1991. 44.50 (*1-55914-254-5*); pap. 39.50 (*1-55914-255-3*) ABBE Pubs Assn.

Crime Prevention & Control: Index & Analysis of Activity, Success & Services. rev. ed. Sonny S. Springer. 150p. 1992. 44.50 (*1-55914-954-X*); pap. 39.50 (*1-55914-955-8*) ABBE Pubs Assn.

Crime Prevention & Intervention: Legal & Ethical Problems. Peter A. Albrecht & Otto Backes. viii, 286p. (C). 1989. lib. bdg. 65.95 (*0-89925-497-7*) De Gruyter.

Crime Prevention for Pathfinders: A Basic Youth Enrichment Skill Honor Packet. L. S. Gattis, III. (Illus.). 20p. (Orig.). (J). (gr. 5 up). 1987. teacher ed, pap. 5.00 (*0-936241-27-6*) Cheetah Pub.

Crime Prevention for Small Businesses. (Illus.). 52p. (Orig.). (C). 1994. pap. text ed. 19.95 (*1-56806-238-9*) Diane Pub.

Crime Prevention Handbook. Koepsell-Girard & Assoc Inc. 1976. pap. 2.95 (*0-685-91650-2*, MTI Film & Video) Coronet.

Crime Prevention in America: A British Perspective. Jon Bright. LC 91-51072. 126p. (C). 1992. 20.00 (*0-942511-52-2*) OICJ.

Crime Prevention in Schools. 51p. (Orig.). 1987. pap. text ed. 12.00 (*0-11-270637-1*, HM1632, Pub. by HMSO UK) UNIPUB.

Crime Prevention in Schools: Specification, Installation & Maintenance of Intruder Alarm Systems. 85p. 1989. pap. 19.00 (*0-11-270677-0*, HM6770, Pub. by HMSO UK) UNIPUB.

***Crime Prevention in the 90s.** Esther P. Davis. 76p. (YA). (gr. 7-12). 1993. pap. write for info. (*1-57515-057-3*) PPI Pubng.

Crime Prevention Studies, Vol. 1. Ed. by Ronald V. Clarke. 180p. 1993. 47.50 (*1-881798-00-3*, Crimnal Justce) Willow Tree NY.

Crime Prevention Studies, Vol. 2. Ed. by Ronald V. Clarke. 240p. 1994. text ed. 47.50 (*1-881798-01-1*, Crimnal Justce) Willow Tree NY.

Crime Prevention Through Environmental Design. Timothy D. Crowe. 256p. 1991. text ed. 37.95 (*0-7506-9058-5*) Buttrwrth-Heinemann.

Crime Prevention Through Housing Design. P. Stollard. (Illus.). 120p. 1991. pap. 29.95 (*0-442-31317-9*) Chapman & Hall.

Crime Prevention Through Physical Security. W. Strobl. (Occupational Safety & Health Ser.: Vol. 2). 448p. 1978. 99.75 (*0-8247-6722-5*) Dekker.

C

1694

An Asterisk (*) at the beginning of an entry indicates that the title is appearing in BIP for the first time.

An Asterisk (*) at the beginning of an entry indicates that the title is appearing in BIP for the first time.

1695

C

Criminal Behaviour: A Psychological Analysis. Maurice P. Feldman. LC 76-13229. 346p. reprint ed. pap. 98.70 (*0-317-26340-4*, 2025198) Bks Demand.

Criminal Behaviour: Explanation & Prevention. Clive R. Hollin. (Contemporary Psychology Ser.). 224p. 1992. 75.00 (*1-85000-951-1*, Falmer Pr); pap. 29.00 (*1-85000-955-4*, Falmer Pr) Taylor & Francis.

***Criminal Behavoir: Psychosocial Approach.** 4th ed. Curt R. Bartol. LC 94-29305. 480p. 1994. text ed. write for info. (*0-13-327990-1*) P-H.

Criminal Career Continuity: Its Social Context. Lyle W. Shannon. 239p. (C). 1988. 35.95 (*0-89885-387-7*) Human Sci Pr.

Criminal Careers, 3 vols. Nettler. Incl. Vol. 1. Explaining Criminals. 220p. 1982. 16.95 (*0-87084-600-0*); Vol. 3. Lying, Cheating, Stealing. 143p. 1982. pap. 15.95 (*0-87084-602-7*); Vol. 4. Responding to Crime. 191p. 1982. 16.95 (*0-87084-603-5*); 1982. write for info. (*0-685-10468-0*) Anderson Pub Co.

Criminal Careers & "Career Criminals", Vol. I. National Research Council. Ed. by Alfred Blumstein et al. 458p. 1986. text ed. 34.95 (*0-309-03684-4*) Natl Acad Pr.

Criminal Careers & "Career Criminals", Vol II. National Research Council. Ed. by Jacqueline Cohen et al. 404p. 1986. text ed. 49.95 (*0-309-03683-6*) Natl Acad Pr.

Criminal C.O.D. braille ed. Phoebe A. Taylor. 327p. 1992. Braille. vinyl bd. 26.16 (*1-56956-348-9*, BR8489) W A T Braille.

Criminal C.O.D. Phoebe A. Taylor. (Asey Mayo Cape Cod Mystery Ser.). 288p. 1988. reprint ed. pap. 6.00 (*0-88150-106-9*, Foul Play) Countryman.

Criminal Complaints & Indictments. 3rd rev. ed. 326p. 1988. pap. text ed. 26.95 (*0-87084-656-6*) Anderson Pub Co.

***Criminal Confessions & Admissions: California Cases.** Gerald E. Flanagan. (National Compendium Ser.). 700p. 1995. ring bd. 140.00 (*1-887019-01-4*) Preced Pubns.

***Criminal Confessions & Admissions: Federal Cases, 2 vols., Set.** Gerald E. Flanagan. (National Compendium Ser.). 1363p. 1995. ring bd. 180.00 (*1-887019-00-6*) Preced Pubns.

Criminal Conspiracy. 2nd ed. Peter Gillies. 300p. 1989. 53.00 (*1-86287-019-5*, Pub. by Federation Pr AU) W W Gaunt.

Criminal Constitutional Law, 3 vols., Set. David Rudstein et al. 1990. write for info. (*0-8205-1098-X*, 098) Bender.

Criminal Conversation. Evan Hunter. 400p. 1994. 21.95 (*0-446-51755-0*) Warner Bks.

Criminal Conversation. Evan Hunter. 384p. 1995. pap. 6.50 (*0-446-36513-0*, Warner Vision) Warner Bks.

Criminal Conversation. large type ed. Evan Hunter. LC 94-20263. (Basic Ser.). 603p. 1994. 22.95 (*0-7862-0268-8*) Thorndike Pr.

Criminal Convictions: Errant Essays on Perpetrators of Literary License. Nicolas Freeling. 1994. 22.95 (*0-87923-973-5*) Godine.

Criminal Court Consultation. Ed. by Richard Rosner & R. B. Harmon. (Critical Issues in American Psychiatry & the Law Ser.: Vol. 5). (Illus.). 344p. 1989. 65.00 (*0-306-43061-4*, Plenum Pr) Plenum.

Criminal Court Handbook: (Three Major Acts) 15th ed. P. L. Malik. (C). 1991. 95.00 (*0-685-39748-3*) St Mut.

Criminal Court Handbook: Three Major Acts. P. L. Malik. 808p. 1982. 270.00 (*0-317-54865-4*) St Mut.

Criminal Court Handbook (Minor Acts), 4 vols. 1985. 65.00 (*0-317-56710-1*) St Mut.

Criminal Court Handbook (Minor Acts), 4 vols., Set. P. L. Malik. (C). 1991. 150.00 (*0-685-39749-1*) St Mut.

Criminal Court Handbook (Three Major Acts) 18th ed. P. L. Malik. (C). 1992. 150.00 (*81-7012-489-1*, Pub. by Eastern Book II) St Mut.

Criminal Court in Action. 3rd ed. David Barnard. 1988. 71.00 (*0-406-55614-8*); pap. 44.00 (*0-406-55615-6*, U.K.) Butterworth Legal Pubs.

***Criminal Court Plea Bargain.** David W. Felder. 44p. 1995. pap. text ed. 5.00 (*0-910959-95-1*, B&G 19A) Felder Bks.

Criminal Courts: Structure, Personnel, & Processes. N. Gary Holten. 1991. pap. text ed. write for info. (*0-07-029636-7*) McGraw.

Criminal Courts in New York State. LC 74-3841. (Criminal Justice in America Ser.). 1974. reprint ed. 53.95 (*0-405-06141-2*) Ayer.

Criminal Damage. Margaret Yorke. 256p. 1993. 17.95 (*0-89296-499-5*) Mysterious Pr.

Criminal Damage. Margaret Yorke. 256p. 1994. mass mkt. 4.99 (*0-446-40197-8*, Mysterious Paperbk) Warner Bks.

Criminal Damage. large type ed. Margaret Yorke. (Popular Ser.). 396p. 1993. reprint ed. pap. 17.95 (*1-56054-629-8*) Thorndike Pr.

Criminal Defences. 2nd ed. D. O'Connor & P. A. Fairall. 1988. Australia. 76.00 (*0-409-49276-0*) Butterworth Legal Pubs.

Criminal Defendants with Trial Disabilities: The Theory & Practice of Competency Assistance - Final Report. 139p. 1987. 9.00 (*0-685-19938-X*, NCSC-056) Natl Ctr St Courts.

Criminal Defense: Jury Instructions. Harry Ackley. 318p. 1981. ring bd. 135.00 (*1-878337-15-7*) Knowles Law.

Criminal Defense Ethics: Law & Liability. John M. Burkoff. LC 86-6092. 1986. ring bd. 140.00 (*0-87632-498-7*) Clark Boardman Callaghan.

Criminal Defense Services for the Poor: Methods & Programs for Providing Legal Representation & the Need for Adequate Financing. 440p. 1982. pap. write for info. (*0-685-07151-0*, 419-0001) Amer Bar Assn.

Criminal Defense Techniques, 8 vols. Michael Eisenstein & Robert M. Cipes. 1969. Updates. ring bd. write for info. (*0-8205-1202-8*) Bender.

Criminal Elite: Professional & Organized Crime. Howard Abadinsky. LC 83-1445. (Contributions to Criminology & Penology Ser.: No. 1). (Illus.). xv, 190p. 1983. text ed. 37.50 (*0-313-23833-2*, ACE/, Greenwood Pr) Greenwood.

***Criminal Elite: The Sociology of White Collar Crime.** 3rd ed. James W. Coleman. 272p. 1993. pap. text ed. 16.00 (*0-312-08657-1*) St Martin.

Criminal Evidence. J. A. Andrews & M. Hirst. (Criminal Law Library). 512p. 1987. 75.00 (*0-08-039237-7*, Pergamon Pr) Elsevier.

Criminal Evidence. Edward J. Imwinkelried et al. (Criminal Justice Ser.). 408p. 1979. pap. text ed. 40.50 (*0-8299-0221-X*) West Pub.

***Criminal Evidence.** 3rd ed. Judy H. Kaci. 360p. 1995. pap. 29.95 (*0-942728-67-X*) Copperhouse.

Criminal Evidence. 5th ed. John Klotter. LC 91-70556. (Justice Administration Legal Ser.). 752p. (C). 1991. 34.95 (*0-87084-505-5*) Anderson Pub Co.

Criminal Evidence: Principles, Cases & Readings. 2nd ed. Thomas J. Gardner. LC 87-13367. 583p. 1988. text ed. 55.25 (*0-314-34735-6*) West Pub.

***Criminal Evidence: Principles, Cases & Readings.** 3rd ed. Thomas J. Gardner & Terry M. Anderson. LC 94-37747. 650p. 1995. text ed. 56.50 (*0-314-04460-4*) West Pub.

Criminal Evidence: Statutes & Materials. J. A. Andrews. 256p. 1990. pap. 39.95 (*0-08-036900-6*, Waterlow) Macmillan.

Criminal Evidence for Police. 2nd ed. Kenneth M. Wells & Paul B. Weston. (Criminal Justice Ser.). (Illus.). 352p. 1976. 27.95 (*0-685-03815-7*) P-H.

***Criminal Evidence for Police.** 4th ed. Paul B. Weston et al. LC 94-33197. 235p. 1994. text ed. 48.00 (*0-13-304635-4*) P-H.

Criminal Evidence in Hong Kong. 2nd ed. Andrew Bruce & Gerard McCoy. 530p. 1992. 136.00 (*0-409-99609-2*) Butterworth Legal Pubs.

Criminal Evidence Laboratory: An Introduction to the Crime Laboratory. 2nd ed. L. S. Miller & A. M. Brown. LC 89-81937. (Illus.). 256p. (C). 1990. pap. text ed. 24.95 (*0-87084-564-0*) Anderson Pub Co.

Criminal Evidence Trial Manual for Texas Lawyers. 2nd ed. Murl A. Larkin. 1300p. 1994. ring bd. 170.00 (*1-56257-958-4*) Michie Butterworth.

Criminal Evidence Trial Manual for Texas Lawyers. 2nd suppl. ed. Murl A. Larkin. 1300p. 1994. 50.00 (*0-685-70861-6*) Butterworth Legal Pubs.

Criminal Experiments on Human Beings in Auschwitz & War Research Laboratories: Twenty Women Prisoners' Accounts. Ed. by Lore Shelley. LC 91-40557. (Illus.). 420p. 1992. lib. bdg. 109.95 (*0-7734-9884-2*) E Mellen.

Criminal Fraud. David Lanham et al. xli, 629p. 1987. 96.00 (*0-455-20745-3*, Pub. by Law Bk Co) W W Gaunt.

Criminal Gods & Demon Devotees: Essays on the Guardians of Popular Hinduism. Ed. by Alf Hiltebeitel. LC 88-24960. 491p. 1989. 74.50 (*0-88706-981-9*); pap. 24.95 (*0-88706-982-7*) State U NY Pr.

Criminal Hands. Jennifer Welch. (Orig.). 1985. pap. 3.50 (*0-318-20626-9*) Pudding Hse Pubns.

Criminal, His Personnel & Environment: A Scientific Study. August Drahms. LC 72-108231. (Criminology, Law Enforcement, & Social Problems Ser.: No. 114). (Illus.). 1971. reprint ed. lib. bdg. 25.00 (*0-87585-114-2*) Patterson Smith.

Criminal History of Mankind. Colin Wilson. 702p. 1990. pap. 13.95 (*0-88184-646-5*) Carroll & Graf.

Criminal History Record Information: Compendium of State Privacy & Security Legislation. 153p. (Orig.). (C). 1993. pap. text ed. 20.00 (*1-56806-206-0*) Diane Pub.

Criminal Identification Technician. Jack Rudman. (Career Examination Ser.: C-3105). 1994. pap. 29.95 (*0-8373-3105-6*) Nat Learn.

Criminal Imbecile: An Analysis of Three Remarkable Murder Cases. Henry H. Goddard. (Illus.). ix, 157p. 1986. reprint ed. lib. bdg. 22.50 (*0-8377-2204-7*) Rothman.

Criminal Incapacitation. W. Spelman. (Crime & Justice Ser.). (Illus.). 290p. (C). 1994. 39.50 (*0-306-44383-X*, Plenum Pr) Plenum.

Criminal Injuries Compensation. Peter Duff. 1991. U.K. pap. 32.00 (*0-406-12131-1*) Butterworth Legal Pubs.

Criminal Injuries Compensation. 2nd ed. Burns. 480p. 1991. 100.00 (*0-409-80907-1*) Butterworth Legal Pubs.

Criminal Injuries Compensation. 2nd ed. D. B. Williams. (Waterlow Practitioner's Library). (Illus.). 144p. 1986. pap. 26.00 (*0-08-039244-X*, K130, Waterlow) Macmillan.

Criminal Injuries Compensation Board Report & Accounts for the Year Ended 31 March 1987, 23rd Report. 35p. (Orig.). 1987. pap. text ed. 11.00 (*0-10-102652-8*, HM1540, Pub. by HMSO UK) UNIPUB.

Criminal Injustice: Violence Against Women in Brazil. Ed. by Human Rights Watch Staff. 80p. (Orig.). 1991. pap. 7.00 (*1-56432-048-0*) Hum Rts Watch.

Criminal Intelligence. Carl Murchison. (Historical Foundations of Forensic Psychiatry & Psychology Ser.). 291p. 1983. reprint ed. lib. bdg. 29.50 (*0-306-76183-1*) Da Capo.

Criminal Intelligence Analysis. Ed. by Paul Andrews, Jr. & Marilyn Peterson. (Illus.). 215p. 1990. 20.00 (*0-912479-07-8*) Palmer Pr.

Criminal Intelligence File. Jack Morris. (Illus.). 100p. 1992. 20.00 (*0-912479-00-0*) Palmer Pr.

Criminal Intelligence Program for Smaller Agencies. 51p. (Orig.). (C). 1993. pap. text ed. 20.00 (*1-56806-836-0*) Diane Pub.

Criminal Intent. Michael L. Monhollon. 288p. (Orig.). 1992. pap. 4.99 (*0-451-17330-9*, Sig) NAL-Dutton.

Criminal Interrogation. enl. rev. ed. John M. Macdonald & David L. Michaud. LC 92-70604. Orig. Title: The Confession: Interrogation & Criminal Profiles for Police Officers. 232p. (C). 1992. pap. text ed. 9.95 (*0-9618230-2-X*) Apache Pr.

***Criminal Interrogation.** 3rd ed. Arthur S. Aubry, Jr. & Rudolph R. Caputo. 464p. 1980. pap. 38.95 (*0-398-06010-X*) C C Thomas.

Criminal Interrogation. 3rd ed. Arthur S. Aubry, Jr. & Rudolph R. Caputo. 464p. 1980. 69.95x (*0-398-03978-X*) C C Thomas.

***Criminal Interrogation: Law & Tactics.** 3rd ed. Devallis Rutledge. (Illus.). 171p. (Orig.). 1994. pap. 19.95 (*0-942728-62-9*) Copperhouse.

Criminal Interrogation & Confessions. 3rd ed. Fred E. Inbau et al. 356p. 1986. 49.00 (*0-683-04305-6*) Williams & Wilkins.

Criminal Investigation. Charles M. Bozza. LC 77-9876. (Justice Administration Ser.). 435p. 1977. 38.95 (*0-88229-183-1*) Nelson-Hall.

Criminal Investigation. IACP Staff. 560p. 1992. boxed 20.00 (*0-8403-7933-1*) Kendall-Hunt.

Criminal Investigation. John M. Macdonald & Thomas P. Haney. LC 90-82052. 320p. (Orig.). (C). 1990. pap. text ed. 9.95 (*0-9618230-1-1*) Apache Pr.

Criminal Investigation. Michael J. Palmiotto. LC 92-14264. 425p. 1994. 38.95 (*0-8304-1180-1*); teacher ed write for info. (*0-8304-1404-5*); write for info. (*0-8304-1399-5*) Nelson-Hall.

Criminal Investigation. Jack Rudman. (College Proficiency Examination Ser.: CPEP-30). 1994. pap. 23.95 (*0-8373-5430-7*) Nat Learn.

Criminal Investigation. Jack Rudman. (ACT Proficiency Examination Program Ser.: PEP-9). 1994. pap. 23.95 (*0-8373-5509-5*) Nat Learn.

Criminal Investigation. 2nd ed. J. J. Horgan. 1979. text ed. 43.95 (*0-07-030334-7*) McGraw.

Criminal Investigation. 3rd ed. Wayne Bennett & Karen M. Hess. Ed. by Hannan. 653p. (C). 1991. text ed. 50.75 (*0-314-79788-2*) West Pub.

Criminal Investigation. 3rd ed. James N. Gilbert. (Illus.). 528p. (C). 1993. text ed. write for info. (*0-02-342901-1*) Macmillan.

Criminal Investigation. 4th ed. Wayne W. Bennett & Karen M. Hess. Ed. by Jucha. LC 93-45031. 650p. (C). 1994. text ed. 54.00 (*0-314-02862-5*) West Pub.

Criminal Investigation. 4th ed. Charles R. Swanson, Jr. & Neil C. Chamelin. write for info. (*0-318-61974-1*) Random.

Criminal Investigation. 5th ed. Charles R. Swanson, Jr. 1992. text ed. write for info. (*0-07-062618-9*) McGraw.

Criminal Investigation: A Guide to Techniques & Solutions. James V. Vandiver. LC 82-10554. 408p. 1983. 32.50 (*0-8108-1576-1*) Scarecrow.

Criminal Investigation: A Method for Reconstructing the Past. James W. Osterburg & Richard H. Ward. LC 90-84735. (Illus.). 875p. (C). 1992. text ed. 44.95 (*0-87084-671-X*) Anderson Pub Co.

Criminal Investigation: Basic Perspectives. 5th ed. Paul B. Weston & Kenneth M. Wells. 400p. 1989. text ed. 58.00 (*0-13-193244-6*) P-H.

Criminal Investigation: Basic Perspectives. 6th ed. Paul B. Weston & Kenneth M. Wells. LC 93-3652. 1993. text ed. 66.00 (*0-13-106337-5*) P-H.

Criminal Investigation: Essays, Readings & Cases. 3rd ed. James N. Gilbert. 224p. (C). 1990. pap. write for info. (*0-675-21200-6*, Merrill Pub Co) Macmillan.

Criminal Investigation: Managing for Results. John Bizzack. 200p. 1991. pap. 28.95 (*0-9630878-9-4*) Autumn Hse KY.

Criminal Investigation: The Art & the Science. Michael D. Lyman. 464p. 1993. text ed. 66.00 (*0-13-151929-8*) P-H.

Criminal Investigation & Interrogation: Police Techniques. (Criminology Ser.). 1992. lib. bdg. 111.95 (*0-8490-5303-X*) Gordon Pr.

***Criminal Investigation of Drug Offenses: The Narcs' Manual.** John M. Macdonald & Jerry Kennedy. 422p. 1983. pap. 37.95 (*0-398-06253-6*) C C Thomas.

Criminal Investigation of Drug Offenses: The Narcs' Manual. John M. Macdonald & Jerry Kennedy. 422p. (C). 1983. 67.95x (*0-398-04915-7*) C C Thomas.

Criminal Investigation, Practical. 3rd rev. ed. Manuel S. Pena. LC 82-70470. (Illus.). 400p. 1993. pap. 29.95 (*0-942728-57-2*) Copperhouse.

Criminal Investigation Procedures. Ray K. Robbins. LC 93-77666. 350p. (C). 1993. text ed. 38.00 (*0-8211-1752-1*) McCutchan.

Criminal Investigation Study Guide: Based on the Text by Swanson, Territo & Chamelin. 5th ed. Davis Publishing Company Staff. 272p. (C). 1991. 21.95 (*1-56325-001-2*, DS098) Davis Pub Law.

***Criminal Investigation Study Guide: Based on the Text by Swanson, Territo & Chamelin.** 5th ed. Davis Publishing Company Staff. 1994. 21.95 (*1-56325-056-X*) Davis Pub Law.

Criminal Investigations: A Behavioral Approach. John B. Wilson. (Illus.). 420p. (Orig.). (C). 1993. pap. text ed. 19.95 (*0-88133-731-5*) Waveland Pr.

Criminal Investigator. Jack Rudman. (Career Examination Ser.: C-1229). 1994. pap. 29.95 (*0-8373-1229-9*) Nat Learn.

Criminal Investigator's Guide. Steven T. Kernes & Lowell L. Kuehn. (Illus.). 170p. 1987. pap. 24.95 (*0-937935-03-4*) Justice Syst Pr.

Criminal Journey. Don Hendrie, Jr. LC 90-19488. 216p. (C). 1990. 16.95 (*0-89924-072-0*); pap. 9.95 (*0-89924-071-2*) Lynx Hse.

Criminal Jurisprudence of the Jews. Samuel Mendelsohn. (Studies in Jewish Jurisprudence: Vol. 6). 280p. (C). 1991. 25.00 (*0-87203-122-5*) Hermon.

Criminal Justice. Freda Adler et al. LC 93-28243. 1993. text ed. write for info. (*0-07-000457-9*) McGraw.

Criminal Justice. Freda Adler et al. LC 93-28243. 1994. Study guide. student ed, pap. text ed. write for info. (*0-07-000477-3*) McGraw.

***Criminal Justice.** Davies et al. LC 95-13898. 1995. pap. write for info. (*0-582-24768-3*) Longman.

***Criminal Justice.** Davies et al. LC 95-13898. 1995. boxed write for info. (*0-582-24769-1*) Longman.

***Criminal Justice.** James Inciardi. 800p. (C). 1995. text ed. write for info. (*0-15-502099-4*) HarBrace.

Criminal Justice. Ed. by J. Roland Pennock & John W. Chapman. LC 84-14776. (Nomos Ser.: Vol. 27). 384p. 1985. 45.00 (*0-8147-6588-2*) NYU Pr.

Criminal Justice. Robert M. Regoli. (Illus.). 696p. 1994. text ed. write for info. (*0-02-399181-X*) Macmillan.

Criminal Justice. Sanders. 1993. U.K. pap. 31.00 (*0-406-51660-X*) Butterworth Legal Pubs.

Criminal Justice. large type ed. Rene Weis. (Non-Fiction Ser.). 560p. 1992. 23.95 (*0-7089-8668-4*) Ulverscroft.

Criminal Justice. 2nd ed. Joel Samaha. Ed. by Schiller. 644p. (C). 1991. text ed. 51.50 (*0-314-77105-0*) West Pub.

Criminal Justice. 3rd ed. James A. Inciardi. 815p. (C). 1990. text ed. 46.75 (*0-15-516107-5*) HB Coll Pubs.

Criminal Justice. 3rd ed. Sue T. Reid. (Illus.). 752p. (C). 1993. text ed. write for info. (*0-02-399173-9*) Macmillan.

Criminal Justice. 3rd ed. Joel Samaha. Ed. by Schiller. LC 93-24691. 675p. (C). 1994. text ed. 56.00 (*0-314-02541-3*) West Pub.

Criminal Justice. 4th ed. James Inciardi. Ed. by Steve Welch. 766p. (C). 1993. text ed. 51.00 (*0-15-500128-0*) HB Coll Pubs.

Criminal Justice: A Brief Introduction. Frank Schmalleger. LC 93-17153. 1993. pap. text ed. 33.40 (*0-13-014649-8*) P-H.

Criminal Justice: A Community Relations Approach. Charles P. McDowell. 462p. 1984. pap. 18.95 (*0-685-42744-7*) Pilgrimage Inc.

Criminal Justice: Adaptable to Courses Utilizing Weinreb's Casebook on Criminal Justice. Casenotes Publishing Co., Inc. Staff. Ed. by Norman S. Goldenberg et al. (Legal Briefs Ser.). 1993. pap. write for info. (*0-87457-053-0*, 1550) Casenotes Pub.

Criminal Justice: An Overview. 3rd ed. Alexander B. Smith & Harriet Pollack. Ed. by Hannan. 312p. (C). 1991. pap. text ed. 31.75 (*0-314-77063-1*) West Pub.

Criminal Justice: Aspects of Britain. 80p. 1992. pap. 12.00 (*0-11-701692-6*, HM16926, Pub. by HMSO UK) UNIPUB.

Criminal Justice: Concepts & Issues. Chris W. Eskridge. LC 92-37331. (Illus.). 325p. (Orig.). (C). 1993. pap. text ed. write for info. (*0-935732-44-6*) Roxbury Pub Co.

***Criminal Justice: Concepts & Issues (An Anthology)** 2nd ed. Ed. by Chris W. Eskridge. 350p. (C). 1995. pap. text ed. write for info. (*0-935732-70-5*) Roxbury Pub Co.

Criminal Justice: Constitutional Provisions, Criminal Code with Comment, Juvenile Court Statutes, Controlled Substances, Rules of Criminal Procedure, Rules of Juvenile Procedure, Ohio Rules of Evidence, with Annotations & Complete Analysis of Elements of Crimes in Ohio. Ohio Staff & Case Western Reserve University. Center for Criminal Justice Staff. LC 83-174489. 1985. 35.00 (*0-317-00848-X*) Case Western.

Criminal Justice: Introductory Cases & Materials. 5th ed. John Kaplan et al. 647p. 1991. text ed. 38.50 (*0-88277-873-0*) Foundation Pr.

Criminal Justice: Law & Politics. 6th ed. George F. Cole. 528p. (C). 1993. pap. 22.95 (*0-534-19686-1*) Intl Thomson.

Criminal Justice: New Technologies & the Constitution. (Illus.). 55p. (C). 1993. pap. text ed. 30.00 (*1-56806-853-0*) Diane Pub.

Criminal Justice: New Technologies & the Constitution. 1991. lib. bdg. 250.00 (*0-8490-4764-1*) Gordon Pr.

Criminal Justice: Opposing Viewpoints. Ed. by Michael D. Biskup. (Opposing Viewpoints Ser.). (Illus.). 264p. (YA). (gr. 10 up). 1993. lib. bdg. 19.95 (*0-89908-624-1*); pap. text ed. 11.55 (*0-89908-623-3*) Greenhaven.

Criminal Justice: Problems & Perspectives in India. S. Venugopal Rao. xiv, 310p. 1991. 35.00 (*81-220-0233-1*) Advent Bks Div.

Criminal Justice: Situations & Decisions. Howard Daudistel et al. (C). 1979. write for info. (*0-318-53476-2*); write for info. (*0-03-039426-0*) HB Coll Pubs.

Criminal Justice: Study Guide. 3rd ed. Roger H. Voltz. (Illus.). 240p. (C). 1993. pap. write for info. (*0-02-399176-3*) Macmillan.

Criminal Justice: Supplement. Helen Silving & Paul K. Ryu. LC 75-145583. iv, 174p. 1977. pap. 32.00 (*0-930342-71-2*, 301450) W S Hein.

***Criminal Justice? The Legal System Versus Individual Responsibility.** 2nd ed. Ed. by Robert J. Bidinotto. (Illus.). 318p. 1995. 24.95 (*1-57246-016-4*); pap. 15.95 (*1-57246-017-2*) Foun Econ Ed.

***Criminal Justice? The Legal System vs. Individual Responsibility.** Ed. by Robert J. Bidinotto. 304p. (Orig.). 1994. 29.95 (*0-614-04262-3*) Foun Econ Ed.

***Criminal Justice? The Legal System vs. Individual Responsibility.** Ed. by Robert J. Bidinotto. (Orig.). 1994. pap. 19.95 (*0-614-04263-1*) Foun Econ Ed.

Criminal Justice Abstracts: Cumulative Index, 1968-1985. 1988. write for info. (*0-9606960-5-9*) Criminal Justice.

Criminal Justice Act, 1987: A Commentary. J. Morton. (Criminal Law Guides Ser.). 128p. 1988. pap. 34.00 (*0-08-033088-6*, Pergamon Pr) Elsevier.

Criminal Justice Act, 1988. Christopher Emmins & Gary Scanlan. 432p. (C). 1988. 156.00 (*1-85431-022-4*, Pub. by Blackstone Pr UK) St Mut.

1696

An Asterisk (*) at the beginning of an entry indicates that the title is appearing in BIP for the first time.

Criminal Justice Act, 1988, Chapter 33. 1988. pap. 30.00 (0-10-543388-8, HM3987, Pub. by HMSO UK) UNIPUB.

Criminal Justice Administration: Cases & Materials On. 4th ed. Frank W. Miller et al. (University Casebook Ser.). 1265p. 1991. text ed. 44.50 (0-88277-860-9) Foundation Pr.

***Criminal Justice Administration: Cases & Materials, 1994 Supplement.** 4th ed. Frank W. Miller et al. (University Casebook Ser.). 129p. 1994. pap. text ed. 7.95 (1-56662-209-3) Foundation Pr.

***Criminal Justice Administration: Linking Practice & Research.** Ed. by William A. Jones, Jr. LC 82-23561. (Annals of Public Administration Ser.: No. 5). 161p. 1983. reprint ed. pap. 45.90 (0-7837-8329-9, 2049116) Bks Demand.

Criminal Justice Administration, 1993 Supplement to Cases & Materials On. 4th ed. Frank W. Miller et al. (University Casebook Ser.). 91p. 1993. pap. text ed. 7.95 (1-56662-091-0) Foundation Pr.

Criminal Justice & Civil & Political Liberties, Report 2, No. RC2. 1983. pap. 20.00 (0-946088-42-X, Pub. by NCCL UK) St Mut.

Criminal Justice & Crime in Late Renaissance Florence, 1537-1609. John K. Brackett. (Illus.). 192p. (C). 1992. 44.95 (0-521-40405-3) Cambridge U Pr.

***Criminal Justice & Latino Communities.** Ed. & Intro. by Antoinette S. Lopez. LC 94-36051. (Latinos in the United States Ser.: Vol. 3). 312p. 1994. 60.00 (0-8153-1772-7) Garland.

Criminal Justice & the Pursuit of Decency. Andrew Rutherford. LC 92-1686. 224p. 1993. pap. 15.95 (0-19-285275-2) OUP.

***Criminal Justice & the Supreme Court.** Lafave. 375p. 1990. pap. 12.95 (0-02-897215-5) Macmillan.

Criminal Justice & the Victim. Ed. by William F. McDonald. LC 75-42754. (Sage Criminal Justice System Annuals Ser.: No. 6). 288p. reprint ed. pap. 82.10 (0-8357-8496-7, 2034771) Bks Demand.

Criminal Justice & Violations of Your Civil Rights. 2nd ed. Joseph Bogan. 172p. (C). 1994. pap. text ed. 18.50 (0-8403-9134-X) Kendall-Hunt.

***Criminal Justice at the Crossroads.** Ed. by Sloan T. Letman. 195p. (Orig.). (C). 1994. pap. text ed. 20.00 (1-884028-09-8) SL Pubs.

Criminal Justice Careers Guidebook. 1991. lib. bdg. 300.00 (0-8490-5029-4) Gordon Pr.

Criminal Justice Careers Guidebook. 184p. 1982. pap. 7.00 (0-16-003877-4, S/N 029-014-00200-3) USGPO.

Criminal Justice Citations. Shepard's Citation, Inc. Staff. 172.00 (0-685-58368-6) Shepards-McGraw.

Criminal Justice Dictionary. rev. ed. Erik Beckman. LC 78-72049. 1983. pap. 25.00 (0-87650-152-8) Pierian.

Criminal Justice Documents: A Selective, Annotated Bibliography of U. S. Government Publications since 1975. Ed. by John F. Berens. LC 87-158. (Bibliographies & Indexes in Law & Political Science Ser.: No. 7). 251p. 1987. text ed. 69.50 (0-313-25183-5, BCS/) Greenwood.

***Criminal Justice Education: The End of the Beginning.** Richard Pearson et al. 1980. pap. text ed. 5.50 (0-614-07045-7) John Jay Pr.

Criminal Justice Ethics: Annotated Bibliography & Guide to Sources. Ed. by Robert McKenrick. LC 90-29186. (Research & Bibliographical Guides in Criminal Justice Ser.: No. 2). 136p. 1991. text ed. 47.95 (0-313-26791-X, SCK, Greenwood Pr) Greenwood.

Criminal Justice History, Vol. I: An International Annual, 1980. Ed. by Henry Cohen. 288p. 1980. text ed. 75.00 (0-313-28058-4, CJ80, Greenwood Pr) Greenwood.

Criminal Justice History, Vol. II: An International Annual, 1981, Vol. 2. Ed. by Henry Cohen. 203p. 1981. text ed. 75.00 (0-313-28059-2, CJ81, Greenwood Pr) Greenwood.

Criminal Justice History, Vol. III: An International Annual, 1982, Vol. 3. Ed. by Henry Cohen. 359p. 1983. text ed. 75.00 (0-313-28060-6, CJ82, Greenwood Pr) Greenwood.

Criminal Justice History, Vol. IV: An International Annual, 1983, Vol. 4. Ed. by Henry Cohen. 350p. 1984. text ed. 75.00 (0-313-28061-4, CJ83, Greenwood Pr) Greenwood.

Criminal Justice History, Vol. IX: An International Annual, 1988, Vol. 9. Louis A. Knafla. 257p. 1988. text ed. 75.00 (0-313-28066-5, CJ88, Greenwood Pr) Greenwood.

Criminal Justice History, Vol. V: An International Annual, 1984, Vol. 5. Ed. by Louis A. Knafla. 220p. 1985. text ed. 75.00 (0-313-28062-2, CJ84, Greenwood Pr) Greenwood.

Criminal Justice History, Vol. VI: An International Annual, 1985, Vol. 7. Ed. by Louis A. Knafla. 272p. 1987. text ed. 75.00 (0-313-28063-0, CJ85, Greenwood Pr) Greenwood.

Criminal Justice History, Vol. VII: An International Annual, 1986, Vol. 6. Ed. by Louis A. Knafla. 224p. 1986. text ed. 75.00 (0-313-28064-9, CJ86, Greenwood Pr) Greenwood.

Criminal Justice History, Vol. VIII: An International Annual, 1988, Vol. 8. Ed. by Louis A. Knafla. 250p. 1988. text ed. 75.00 (0-313-28065-7, CJ87, Greenwood Pr) Greenwood.

Criminal Justice History, Vol. X: An International Annual, 1989, Vol. 10. Ed. by Louis A. Knafla. 250p. 1989. text ed. 75.00 (0-313-28067-3, CJ89, Greenwood Pr) Greenwood.

Criminal Justice History, Vol. XI: An International Annual, 1990, Vol. 11. Ed. by Louis A. Knafla. 250p. 1990. text ed. 75.00 (0-313-28068-1, Greenwood Pr) Greenwood.

Criminal Justice History, Vol. XII: An International Annual, 1991, Vol. 12. Louis A. Knafla. (Bibliographies of the History of Crime & Criminal Justice Ser.). 296p. 1993. text ed. 75.00 (0-313-28318-4, CJ91, Greenwood Pr) Greenwood.

Criminal Justice History, Vol. XIII: An International Annual, 1992. Louis A. Knafla. 288p. 1993. text ed. 75.00 (0-313-28319-2, CJ92, Greenwood Pr) Greenwood.

Criminal Justice History, Vol. XIV: An International Annual, 1993, Vol. 14. Louis A. Knafla. (International Criminal Justice History Annual Ser.: Vol. 14). 231p. 1994. text ed. 79.50 (0-313-28736-8, Greenwood Pr) Greenwood.

Criminal Justice in America. (Illus.). 212p. 1983. 7.95 (0-318-02224-9) Constitutional Rights Found.

***Criminal Justice in America.** George F. Cole & Christopher Smith. LC 95-12626. 1997. pap. 33.95 (0-534-24420-3) Intl Thomson.

Criminal Justice in America. Roscoe Pound. LC 79-37841. (American Constitutional & Legal History Ser). 224p. 1972. reprint ed. lib. bdg. 27.50 (0-306-70435-8) Da Capo.

Criminal Justice in America. Roscoe Pound. LC 74-22045. (Quality Paperbacks Ser.). xiv, 226p. 1975. reprint ed. pap. 7.95 (0-306-80007-1) Da Capo.

Criminal Justice in America, 46 vols., Set. 1974. 1,266.00 (0-405-06135-8) Ayer.

***Criminal Justice in America: Theory, Practice, & Policy.** Barry W. Hancock & Paul M. Sharp. LC 95-10675. 1995. pap. text ed. 28.00 (0-13-433871-5) P-H.

Criminal Justice in Cleveland. Cleveland Foundation Staff. Ed. by Roscoe Pound & Felix Frankfurter. LC 68-55769. (Criminology, Law Enforcement, & Social Problems Ser.: No. 8). (Illus.). 1968. reprint ed. 35.00 (0-87585-008-1) Patterson Smith.

Criminal Justice in Crisis. Ed. by Michael McConville & Lee Bridges. LC 94-5165. (Law in Its Social Setting Ser.). 1994. 59.95 (1-85898-003-8, Pub. by E Elgar Pub UK) Ashgate Pub Co.

Criminal Justice in England: A Study in Law Administration. Pendleton Howard. xv, 436p. 1981. reprint ed. lib. bdg. 35.00 (0-8377-0634-3) Rothman.

Criminal Justice in England: A Study in Law Administration. Howard Pendleton. LC 87-81959. xv, 436p. 1987. reprint ed. lib. bdg. 42.00 (0-89941-579-2, 305340) W S Hein.

***Criminal Justice in England & the United States.** J. David Hirschel & William Wakefield. LC 95-3337. (Criminology & Crime Control Policy Ser.). 248p. 1995. text ed. 65.00 (0-275-94133-7, Praeger Pubs) Greenwood.

Criminal Justice in Europe: A Comparative Study. Ed. by Christopher Harding. 400p. 1995. 75.00 (0-19-825807-0) OUP.

***Criminal Justice in Israel: An Annotated Bibliography of English Language Publications, 1948-1993.** Robert R. Friedmann. LC 94-39770. (Research & Bibliographical Guides in Justice Ser.: Vol. 4). 224p. 1995. text ed. 75.00 (0-313-29439-9, Greenwood Pr) Greenwood.

***Criminal Justice in Louisiana.** 3rd ed. Ed. by Burk Foster et al. 384p. (C). Date not set. 22.50 (0-940984-89-X) U of SW LA Ctr LA Studies.

Criminal Justice in Metropolitan Court. Harry I. Subin. LC 72-172177. (American Constitutional & Legal History Ser). 234p. 1973. reprint ed. lib. bdg. 29.50 (0-306-70239-8) Da Capo.

Criminal Justice in Post-Mao China: Analysis & Documents. Shao-Chuan Leng & Hungdah Chiu. LC 84-16362. 330p. 1985. pap. 24.95 (0-87395-950-7) State U NY Pr.

Criminal Justice in Post-Mao China: Analysis & Documents. Shao-Chuan Leng & Hunqdah Chiu. LC 84-16362. 330p. 1985. 74.50 (0-87395-949-3) State U NY Pr.

Criminal Justice in Rural America. Ed. by Shanler D. Cronk et al. 255p. 1982. 3.00 (0-89695-006-9) U Tenn CSW.

Criminal Justice in the Community. 2nd ed. Charles P. McDowell. LC 92-70235. (Illus.). 482p. (C). 1993. pap. text ed. write for info. (0-87084-559-4) Anderson Pub Co.

Criminal Justice in the United States. Dean J. Champion. 624p. (C). 1990. text ed. write for info. (0-675-20672-3, Merrill Pub Co); pap. write for info. (0-675-21197-2, Merrill Pub Co) Macmillan.

Criminal Justice in the 1990's: Future of Information Management. 58p. (Orig.). (C). 1993. pap. text ed. 25.00 (1-56806-878-6) Diane Pub.

Criminal Justice Induction Training: The Field Training Concept. Ed. by Peter C. Unsinger & Harry W. More. (Illus.). 184p. (C). 1990. text ed. 38.95x (0-398-05677-3) C C Thomas.

***Criminal Justice Induction Training: The Field Training Concept.** Ed. by Peter C. Unsinger & Harry W. More. (Illus.). 184p. 1990. pap. 24.95 (0-398-06470-9) C C Thomas.

Criminal Justice Information Policy. 1991. lib. bdg. 74.95 (0-8490-4481-2) Gordon Pr.

Criminal Justice Internships. 2nd ed. Gary R. Gordon & R. Bruce McBride. LC 89-81936. 130p. (C). 1990. pap. text ed. 18.95 (0-87084-326-5) Anderson Pub Co.

Criminal Justice, Introduction to. Cliff Roberson. 500p. 1993. pap. 34.95 (0-942728-58-0) Copperhouse.

Criminal Justice Network: An Introduction. 2nd ed. Steven M. Cox & John Wade. 368p. (C). 1989. pap. write for info. (0-697-03177-2) Brown & Benchmark.

Criminal Justice, New Developments (1988) 88p. 1988. pap. text ed. 10.00 (1-56986-060-2) Federal Bar.

Criminal Justice, New Technologies & the Constitution. 54p. (Orig.). 1989. reprint ed. pap. text ed. 7.95 (1-55950-016-6) Loompanics.

Criminal Justice Organizations: Administration & Management. John Klofas et al. LC 89-15918. 420p. (C). 1990. text ed. 43.95 (0-534-11952-2) Intl Thomson.

Criminal Justice, Politics & Women: The Aftermath of Legally Mandated Change. Ed. by Claudine Schweber & Clarice Feinman. LC 84-25213. (Women & Politics Ser., Fall 1984: Vol. 4, No. 3). 133p. 1985. text ed. 39.95 (0-86656-364-4) Haworth Pr.

Criminal Justice Procedure. 4th ed. Ronald L. Carlson. LC 91-70611. 417p. (C). 1992. pap. text ed. 28.95 (0-87084-131-9) Anderson Pub Co.

Criminal Justice Processes & Procedures. Julian R. Hanley. LC 82-62035. (Illus.). 264p. 1983. pap. text ed. 19.00 (0-8211-0765-8) McCutchan.

Criminal Justice Research in Libraries: Strategies & Resources. Marilyn Lutzker. LC 85-17765. (Illus.). 183p. 1986. text ed. 55.00 (0-313-24490-1, LCJ/, Greenwood Pr) Greenwood.

Criminal Justice Research Sources. 3rd ed. Robert L. O'Block. LC 92-70236. 189p. (C). 1992. pap. text ed. write for info. (0-87084-665-5) Anderson Pub Co.

Criminal Justice Resource Manual. 51p. (Orig.). (C). 1993. pap. text ed. 20.00 (1-56806-848-4) Diane Pub.

Criminal Justice Resource Manual: Data Processsing Terms & Concepts for Criminal Investigators & Prosecutors. (Law Enforcement Ser.). 1986. lib. bdg. 250.00 (0-8490-3776-X) Gordon Pr.

Criminal Justice, Restitution & Reconciliation. Ed. by Burt Galaway & Joe Hudson. 250p. 1990. pap. text ed. 25.00 (0-9606960-6-7) Willow Tree NY.

Criminal Justice Standards Bench Book for Special Court Judges. American Bar Association Staff et al. LC 82-72587. v, 66p. 1982. pap. 5.00 (0-89707-085-2, 482-0002) Amer Bar Assn.

***Criminal Justice Statistics: A Practical Approach.** Seng et al. 1999. write for info. (0-7506-9672-9, Focal) Buttrwrth-Heinemann.

Criminal Justice System: An Introduction. 4th ed. Ronald J. Waldron et al. LC 88-23226. 555p. reprint ed. pap. 158.20 (0-7837-3954-0, 2043783) Bks Demand.

Criminal Justice System: Materials on the Administration & Reform of the Criminal Law. Franklin E. Zimring & Richard S. Frase. 1038p. 1980. 45.00 (0-316-98795-6) Little.

Criminal Justice System & Blacks. Daniel E. Georges-Abeyie. LC 84-9437. 1984. pap. 29.95 (0-87632-438-3) Clark Boardman Callaghan.

Criminal Justice System & Mental Retardation: Defendants & Victims. Ed. by Ronald W. Conley et al. 336p. (C). 1991. pap. text ed. 29.00 (1-55766-070-0) P H Brookes.

Criminal Justice System & Women: Offenders, Victims & Workers. 2nd ed. Ed. by Natalie J. Sokoloff. LC 94-21320. 1994. write for info. (0-07-050779-1) McGraw.

Criminal Justice System of Argentina: (An Overview for American Readers) Alejandro D. Carrio. 216p. (Orig.). 1989. pap. 9.00 (0-940448-18-1) LSU Law Pubns.

Criminal Justice System of Kentucky. Perry T. Ryan. (Illus.). 50p. (YA). (gr. 9). 1990. reprint ed. pap. 4.95 (0-9625504-1-8) P T Ryan.

Criminal Justice System Study Guide. David R. Struckhoff. 56p. (C). 1993. pap. text ed. 10.00 (1-884028-02-0) SL Pubs.

Criminal Justice Systems in Other Jurisdictions. HMSO Staff. 236p. 1993. pap. 50.00 (0-11-341082-4, HM10824, Pub. by HMSO UK) UNIPUB.

Criminal Justice Systems of the Latin-American Nations: A Bibliography of the Primary & Secondary Literature. Richard Rank. (New York University Criminal Law Education & Research Center Monograph: Vol. 11). xxxiii, 576p. 1974. text ed. 45.00 (0-8377-1026-X) Rothman.

Criminal Justice Systems Review, 2 vols., 1972-1974. Ed. by Jon S. Schultz & Jon P. Thames. LC 74-29386. 1974. 95.00 (0-930342-33-X); Set, 95.00. write for info. (0-318-56355-X) W S Hein.

Criminal Justice Systems Review, 2 vols., 1972-1974, 2. Ed. by Jon S. Schultz & Jon P. Thames. LC 74-29386. 1974. 95.00 (0-930342-34-8, 108610) W S Hein.

Criminal Justice Systems Review, 2 vols., 1972-1974, I. Ed. by Jon S. Schultz & Jon P. Thames. 1974. write for info. (0-318-56354-1) W S Hein.

Criminal Justice Today: An Introductory Text for the Twenty-First Century. Frank Schmalleger. 752p. write for info. (0-318-68289-3) P-H.

Criminal Justice Today: An Introductory Text for the Twenty-First Century. 3rd ed. Frank Schmalleger. LC 94-6699. 752p. 1994. text ed. 55.00 (0-13-302895-X) P-H Gen Ref & Trav.

Criminal Justice under Stress. E. Stockdale & S. Casale. 1992. 38.00 (1-85431-222-7, Pub. by Blackstone Pr UK) W W Gaunt.

Criminal Justice with Chinese Characteristics: China's Criminal Process & Violations of Human Rights. Timothy Gelatt. Ed. by James D. Ross. 90p. (Orig.). 1993. pap. text ed. 10.00 (0-934143-63-3) Lawyers Comm Human.

***Criminal Law.** Katherine Delsack. (Education Ser.). 250p. (C). 1992. pap. text ed. 10.95 (0-614-04991-1) Lawprep Pr.

Criminal Law. Joshua Dressler. Ed. by Robert J. Switzer. (Law Outlines Ser.). 210p. (Orig.). pap. text ed. 14.95 (0-87457-178-2, 5020) Casenotes Pub.

Criminal Law. Ed. by Lieven Dupont & Cyrillus Fijnaut. 1991. ring bd. write for info. (0-318-68489-6) Kluwer Law Tax Pubs.

Criminal Law. Steven Emanuel. 302p. 1992. pap. text ed. 14.95 (1-56542-040-3) E Law Outlines.

Criminal Law. Peter Gilles. 1993. write for info. (0-455-21207-4, CRC Reprint); pap. write for info. (0-455-21208-2, CRC Reprint) Franklin.

Criminal Law. Michael T. Molan. 230p. (C). 1991. 65.00 (1-85352-697-5, Pub. by HLT Pubns UK) St Mut.

Criminal Law. Ed. by Michael T. Molan. 230p. (C). 1991. pap. 65.00 (1-85352-833-1, Pub. by HLT Pubns UK) St Mut.

Criminal Law. Ed. by Thomas Morawetz. (International Library of Essays in Law & Legal Theory). 520p. 1991. text ed. 150.00 (0-8147-5464-3) NYU Pr.

Criminal Law. Ed. by F. R. Sampson. 226p. (C). 1990. pap. 65.00 (1-85352-745-9, Pub. by HLT Pubns UK) St Mut.

Criminal Law. Gary Scanlan & Jennifer Trigger. (C). 1990. 125.00 (1-85431-083-6, Pub. by Blackstone Pr UK) St Mut.

***Criminal Law.** Gary Scanlan. (Student Statutes Ser.). 224p. 1993. pap. text ed. 18.00 (0-406-02301-8, UK) Butterworth Legal Pubs.

Criminal Law. Jennifer Trigger. (C). 1991. text ed. 22.00 (1-85431-131-X, Pub. by Blackstone Pr UK) W W Gaunt.

Criminal Law. rev. ed. Peter W. Low. (Black Letter Ser.). 443p. 1993. reprint ed. pap. text ed. 24.50 (0-314-73494-5) West Pub.

Criminal Law. 2nd ed. Cook & Marcus. 1988. write for info. (0-8205-0066-6, 139); teacher ed write for info. (0-8205-0067-4) Bender.

Criminal Law. 2nd ed. Peter Gillies. lxi, 795p. 1990. pap. 75.00 (0-455-20931-6, Pub. by Law Bk Co) W W Gaunt.

Criminal Law. 2nd ed. Wayne R. LaFave & Austin W. Scott, Jr. (Hornbook Ser.). 918p. 1991. reprint ed. text ed. 37.00 (0-314-26045-5) West Pub.

Criminal Law. 2nd ed. Mewett & Manning. 816p. 1985. 120.00 (0-409-84922-7) Butterworth Legal Pubs.

Criminal Law. 2nd ed. Sue T. Reid. (Illus.). 464p. (C). 1992. text ed. write for info. (0-02-399171-2) Macmillan.

***Criminal Law.** 2nd ed. C. R. Snyman. 595p. 1989. boxed 151.00 (0-409-05621-9, SA) Butterworth Legal Pubs.

***Criminal Law.** 2nd ed. C. R. Snyman. 595p. 1989. pap. 108.00 (0-409-05622-7, SA) Butterworth Legal Pubs.

Criminal Law. 2nd ed. R. B. Wilson & B. H. Donovan. (LBC Nutshell Ser.). xv, 112p. 1990. pap. 11.95 (0-455-20980-4, Pub. by Law Bk Co) W W Gaunt.

Criminal Law. 3rd ed. John C. Klotter. LC 89-86001. 741p. (C). 1990. text ed. 34.95 (0-87084-525-X) Anderson Pub Co.

Criminal Law. 3rd ed. Rollin M. Perkins & Ronald N. Boyce. LC 82-15976. (University Textbook Ser.). 1269p. (C). 1991. reprint ed. text ed. 34.50 (0-88277-067-5) Foundation Pr.

Criminal Law. 3rd ed. Sue T. Reid. LC 94-12638. 560p. 1994. text ed. 57.00 (0-02-399211-5) P-H.

Criminal Law. 3rd ed. Joel Samaha. Ed. by Schiller. 579p. (C). 1990. text ed. 48.75 (0-314-56394-6) West Pub.

Criminal Law. 4th ed. John C. Klotter. LC 93-71749. (Justice Administration Legal Ser.). 805p. (C). 1993. text ed. write for info. (0-87084-526-8) Anderson Pub Co.

Criminal Law. 4th ed. Joel Samaha. Ed. by Schiller. LC 92-16021. 600p. (C). 1993. reprint ed. text ed. 54.75 (0-314-00774-1) West Pub.

Criminal Law. 7th ed. J. C. Smith & Brian Hogan. 1004p. 1992. U. K. 99.00 (0-406-00314-9); pap. 54.00 (0-406-00313-0) Butterworth Legal Pubs.

Criminal Law: A Problem Solving Approach. John Delaney. (Delaney Ser.). (Illus.). 442p. (Orig.). 1987. pap. text ed. 17.95 (0-9608514-2-9) J Delaney Pubns.

Criminal Law: Adaptable to Courses Utilizing Boyce & Perkin's Casebook on Criminal Law. Casenotes Publishing Co., Inc. Staff. Ed. by Norman S. Goldenberg et al. (Legal Briefs Ser.). 1989. pap. write for info. (0-87457-058-1, 1020) Casenotes Pub.

Criminal Law: Adaptable to Courses Utilizing Dix & Sharlot's Casebook on Criminal Law. Casenotes Publishing Co., Inc. Staff. Ed. by Norman S. Goldenberg et al. (Legal Briefs Ser.). 1987. pap. write for info. (0-87457-054-9, 1024) Casenotes Pub.

Criminal Law: Adaptable to Courses Utilizing Foote & Levy's Casebook on Criminal Law. Casenotes Publishing Co., Inc. Staff. Ed. by Norman S. Goldenberg et al. (Legal Briefs Ser.). 1982. pap. write for info. (0-87457-055-7, 1025) Casenotes Pub.

Criminal Law: Adaptable to Courses Utilizing Johnson's Casebook on Criminal Law. Casenotes Publishing Co., Inc. Staff. Ed. by Norman Goldenberg et al. (Legal Briefs Ser.). 1990. pap. write for info. (0-87457-156-1, 1027) Casenotes Pub.

Criminal Law: Adaptable to Courses Utilizing Kadish & Schulhofer's Casebook on Criminal Law & Its Processes. Casenotes Publishing Co., Inc. Staff. Ed. by Norman S. Goldenberg et al. (Legal Briefs Ser.). 1989. pap. write for info. (0-87457-056-5, 1021) Casenotes Pub.

Criminal Law: Adaptable to Courses Utilizing LaFave's Casebook of Modern Criminal Law. Casenotes Publishing Co., Inc. Staff. Ed. by Norman S. Goldenberg et al. (Legal Briefs Ser.). 1988. pap. write for info. (0-87457-057-3, 1023) Casenotes Pub.

Criminal Law: Adaptable to Courses Utilizing Materials by Dix. George E. Dix & Richard I. Aaron. LC 87-116615. (Legalines Ser.). 100p. 9.95 (0-685-18526-5) HarBrace.

Criminal Law: Adaptable to Courses Utilizing Materials by Kadish. Sanford H. Kadish. LC 87-115693. (Legalines Ser.). 197p. 12.95 (0-685-18648-2) HarBrace.

Criminal Law: Adaptable to Courses Utilizing Materials by Perkins. Rollin M. Perkins. LC 87-118871. (Legalines Ser.). 317p. 12.95 (0-685-18527-3) HarBrace.

Criminal Law: Adaptable to Courses Utilizing Weinreb's Casebook on Criminal Law. Casenotes Publishing Co., Inc. Staff. Ed. by Norman S. Goldenberg et al. (Legal Briefs Ser.). 1993. pap. write for info. (0-87457-059-X, 1022) Casenotes Pub.

C

An Asterisk (*) at the beginning of an entry indicates that the title is appearing in BIP for the first time.

Criminal Law: Adaptable to Kaplan & Weisberg's Casebook on Criminal Law. Casenotes Publishing Co., Inc. Staff. Ed. by Norman S. Goldenberg et al. (Legal Briefs Ser.). (Orig.). 1991. pap. text ed. write for info. (*0-87457-146-4*, 1026) Casenotes Pub.

Criminal Law: An Indictment. Richard J. Orloski. LC 76-28995. 1977. 26.95 (*0-88229-211-0*) Nelson-Hall.

Criminal Law: Cases & Materials. Caleb Foote & Robert J. Levy. 950p. (C). 1981. 50.00 (*0-316-28853-5*) Little.

Criminal Law: Cases & Materials. 2nd ed. Kaplan. 1991. 52.00 (*0-316-48283-8*) Little.

Criminal Law: Cases & Materials. 2nd ed. Peter W. Low et al. (University Casebook Ser.). 1089p. 1990. reprint ed. text ed. 40.95 (*0-88277-325-9*) Foundation Pr.

Criminal Law: Cases & Materials. 3rd ed. George E. Dix & M. Michael Sharlot. (American Casebook Ser.). 837p. 1988. reprint ed. text ed. 43.00 (*0-314-35159-0*) West Pub.

Criminal Law: Cases & Readings. 4th ed. Jerome Hall et al. 834p. 1983. 35.00 (*0-87215-705-9*) Michie Butterworth.

Criminal Law: Cases, Comment, Questions. 5th ed. Lloyd L. Weinraub. LC 93-2774. (University Casebook Ser.). 1450p. (C). 1993. text ed. 40.95 (*1-56662-055-4*) Foundation Pr.

Criminal Law: Cases, Materials & Texts. 4th ed. Phillip E. Johnson. (American Casebook Ser.). 759p. 1991. reprint ed. text ed. 44.00 (*0-314-72635-7*) West Pub.

Criminal Law: Principles & Cases. 4th ed. Thomas J. Gardner. Ed. by Tubb. 538p. (C). 1989. text ed. 48.00 (*0-314-47351-3*) West Pub.

Criminal Law: Principles & Cases. 5th ed. Thomas J. Gardner & Terry Anderson. Ed. by Jucha. 657p. (C). 1991. text ed. 55.25 (*0-314-92953-3*) West Pub.

Criminal Law: Teacher's Manual to Accompany Cases, Materials & Text. 4th ed. Phillip E. Johnson. (American Casebook Ser.). 113p. 1990. pap. text ed. write for info. (*0-314-80197-9*) West Pub.

***Criminal Law: Text & Materials.** 3rd ed. C. Clarkson & H. Keating. 1994. pap. 47.00 (*0-421-48210-9*, Pub. by Sweet & Maxwell) W W Gaunt.

Criminal Law - Binding Over: The Issues. (Law Commission Working Paper Ser.: No. 103). 113p. (Orig.). 1987. pap. text ed. 10.00 (*0-11-730185-X*, HM1152, Pub. by HMSO UK) UNIPUB.

Criminal Law - Cases & Materials. 5th ed. J. C. Smith & Brian Hogan. 768p. 1993. pap. 52.00 (*0-406-01480-9*, U.K.) Butterworth Legal Pubs.

Criminal Law - Cases, Comments & Questions. 4th ed. Lloyd L. Weinreb. (University Casebook Ser.). 1032p. 1991. reprint ed. text ed. 35.00 (*0-88277-328-3*) Foundation Pr.

Criminal Law - Essays in Honour of J. C. Smith. Ed. by P. Smith. 1987. 66.00 (*0-406-50110-6*, U.K.) Butterworth Legal Pubs.

Criminal Law - United States see Treatise on the Criminal Law As Now Administered in the United States

Criminal Law Advocacy, 7 vols. M. Kadish. 1982. write for info. (*0-8205-1198-6*) Bender.

Criminal Law & Approaches to the Study of Law, Cases & Materials. 2nd ed. John M. Brumbaugh. (University Casebook Ser.). 1002p. 1991. text ed. 41.50 (*0-88277-866-8*) Foundation Pr.

Criminal Law & Approaches to the Study of Law, Manual for Teachers to Accompany Cases & Materials On. 2nd ed. John M. Brumbaugh. (University Casebook Ser.). 175p. 1991. pap. text ed. write for info. (*0-88277-894-3*) Foundation Pr.

Criminal Law & Colonial Subject: New South Wales, 1810-1830. Paula J. Byrne. LC 92-11457. (Studies in Australian History). (Illus.). 320p. (C). 1993. 69.95 (*0-521-40379-0*) Cambridge U Pr.

Criminal Law & Its Administration. 5th ed. Fred E. Inbau et al. (Miscellaneous Ser.). 1472p. 1989. text ed. 43.95 (*0-88277-724-6*) Foundation Pr.

Criminal Law & Its Administration: Instructor's Manual. Fred E. Inbau et al. 111p. 1990. pap. text ed. write for info. (*0-88277-846-3*) Foundation Pr.

Criminal Law & Its Administration: The Ditchley Papers. W. C. Warren et al. LC 70-152650. (Symposia on Law & Society Ser.). 1971. reprint ed. lib. bdg. 17.50 (*0-306-70130-8*) Da Capo.

Criminal Law & Its Processes: Cases & Materials. 4th ed. Sanford H. Kadish et al. 1985. 37.95 (*0-316-47812-1*); Supplement, 1985. mass mkt. 7.95 (*0-316-47814-8*) Little.

Criminal Law & Justice Dictionary. John N. Ferdico. Ed. by Lippert. 476p. (C). 1992. pap. text ed. 21.75 (*0-314-93310-7*) West Pub.

Criminal Law & Juvenile Justice. D. J. McQuoid-Mason et al. (Human Rights for All Ser.: Bk. 2). 104p. 1987. student ed, pap. write for info. (*0-7021-2465-6*, Pub. by Juta SA); teacher ed, pap. write for info. (*0-7021-2466-4*, Pub. by Juta SA) W W Gaunt.

Criminal Law & Practice of Papua New Guinea. 2nd ed. Donald R. Chalmers et al. xxxiv, 807p. 1985. 67.00 (*0-455-20398-9*, Pub. by Law Bk Co) W W Gaunt.

Criminal Law & Procedure. Stephen C. Mancini & Shellie Rich. (Lex Paralegal Ser.). 249p. (C). 1992. pap. 39.95 (*1-881643-08-5*) Carleston Pub.

Criminal Law & Procedure. 2nd ed. John M. Scheb & John M. Scheb, II. Ed. by Gill. LC 93-34757. 675p. (C). 1994. text ed. 55.50 (*0-314-02765-3*) West Pub.

Criminal Law & Procedure: Cases & Materials. 7th ed. Ronald N. Boyce & Rollin M. Perkins. (University Casebook Ser.). 1263p. 1991. reprint ed. text ed. 42.75 (*0-88277-706-8*) Foundation Pr.

Criminal Law & Procedure: Text & Cases. George T. Felkenes. LC 75-5735. 480p. (C). 1976. text ed. 27.95 (*0-685-03816-5*) P-H.

Criminal Law & Procedure: The Counter Revolution. Charles H. Whitebread. 1987. 15.00 (*1-55917-090-5*, 7325); audio 115.00 (*1-55917-088-3*) Natl Prac Inst.

Criminal Law & Procedure, Cases & Materials. 2nd ed. James Vorenberg. LC 81-11625. (American Casebook Ser.). 1088p. (C). 1993. reprint ed. text ed. 47.00 (*0-314-59850-2*) West Pub.

Criminal Law & Procedure, Cases & Materials. James Vorenberg. LC 81-11625. (American Casebook Ser.). 58p. (C). 1993. reprint ed. Tchr's. guide, 58p. teacher ed, pap. text ed. write for info. (*0-314-62842-8*) West Pub.

***Criminal Law & Procedure for Illinois Police.** Albert M. Johnston, Jr. 786p. 1995. pap. 34.80 (*0-87563-561-X*) Stipes.

Criminal Law & Procedure for Paralegals. Daneil Hall. 1992. text ed. 40.95 (*0-8273-4559-3*) Delmar.

Criminal Law & Procedure for the Paralegal: A Systems Approach. James W. H. McCord & Sandra L. McCord. LC 94-13488. 600p. 1994. text ed. 45.25 (*0-314-03917-1*) West Pub.

Criminal Law & Procedure, Manual for Teachers to Accompany Cases & Materials. 7th ed. Ronald N. Boyce. (University Casebook Ser.). 483p. 1989. pap. text ed. write for info. (*0-88277-762-9*) Foundation Pr.

Criminal Law Anthology. Ed. by Arnold H. Loewy. LC 92-20849. 1992. write for info. (*0-87084-182-3*) Anderson Pub Co.

Criminal Law (Australia) Text & Cases. 7th ed. L. Waller & C. R. Williams. 1020p. (C). 1993. pap. 99.00 (*0-409-30741-6*, Austral); boxed 132.00 (*0-409-30761-0*, Austral) Butterworth Legal Pubs.

Criminal Law Bulletin. Ed. by Fred Cohen. 125.00 (*0-685-69657-X*, CLB) Warren Gorham & Lamont.

Criminal Law Bulletin: 1965-1992, 29 vols., Set. 2,537.50 (*0-8377-9050-6*) Rothman.

Criminal Law, California. 3rd rev. ed. Cliff Roberson. LC 88-72096. 175p. 1993. pap. 24.95 (*0-942728-56-4*) Copperhouse.

***Criminal Law Casebook: A Selection of Summaries.** E. J. Coertzen. 246p. 1990. pap. 37.00 (*0-409-05645-6*, SA) Butterworth Legal Pubs.

***Criminal Law Cases & Materials.** Peter Charleton. 1992. pap. text ed. 88.00 (*1-85475-169-7*, IE) Butterworth Legal Pubs.

Criminal Law, Cases & Materials On. Joshua Dressler. LC 94-15665. (American Casebook Ser.). 968p. 1994. text ed. 47.00 (*0-314-03791-8*) West Pub.

***Criminal Law, Cases & Materials On.** Joshua Dressler. LC 94-15665. (American Casebook Ser.). 1994. pap. text ed. write for info. (*0-314-04201-6*) West Pub.

***Criminal Law, Cases & Materials On.** 5th ed. Phillip E. Johnson. (American Casebook Ser.). 757p. (C). Date not set. text ed. write for info. (*0-314-06410-9*) West Pub.

Criminal Law, Criminology & Criminal Justice: A Casebook. William J. Chambliss & Thomas F. Courtless. LC 91-12828. 304p. (C). 1992. text ed. 46.95 (*0-534-13266-9*) Intl Thomson.

Criminal Law Defenses, Vol 1 & 2. Paul H. Robinson. 784p. 1984. Vol. 2, 784 pgs. write for info. (*0-318-57626-0*); Vol. 1, 585 pgs. text ed. 115.00 (*0-314-81513-9*) West Pub.

Criminal Law Deskbook. Patrick McCloskey & Ronald Schoenberg. 1984. Looseleaf Updates Avail. write for info. (*0-8205-1217-6*) Bender.

Criminal Law Digest, 2 vol. set. 3rd ed. Ed. by James A. Douglas & Donald S. Benton. (General Law Ser.). 1983. Supplemented semi-annually. 120.00 (*0-88262-904-2*, 78-56429) Warren Gorham & Lamont.

Criminal Law Digest, 2 vol. set, No. 1. 3rd suppl. ed. Ed. by James A. Douglas & Donald S. Benton. (General Law Ser.). 1992. 70.00 (*0-7913-1187-2*) Warren Gorham & Lamont.

Criminal Law Digest, 2 vol. set, No. 2. 3rd suppl. ed. Ed. by James A. Douglas & Donald S. Benton. (General Law Ser.). 1992. 72.00 (*0-685-05290-7*) Warren Gorham & Lamont.

Criminal Law for California Peace Officers. 3rd ed. Daniel L. Dramer. LC 84-72353. 464p. 1988. pap. 21.95 (*0-9613903-2-8*) Aviary Pub Co.

Criminal Law for Paralegals. Daniel J. Markey, Jr. & Mary Q. Donnelly. LC 93-17337. 1994. text ed. 28.95 (*0-538-70861-1*) S-W Pub.

Criminal Law for Peace Officers. Jesse R. Pistole. 480p. 1976. 31.00 (*0-87909-163-0*, Reston) P-H.

Criminal Law for Police Officers. 5th ed. Neil C. Chamelin & Kenneth R. Evens. 320p. 1990. text ed. 59.00 (*0-13-193384-1*) P-H.

***Criminal Law for Police Officers.** 6th ed. Neil C. Chamelin & Kenneth R. Evans. LC 94-38364. 1995. text ed. 59.00 (*0-13-308578-3*) P-H.

Criminal Law Forms, 1982. Donald B. Fiedler & Deborah R. Pred. (Nebraska Legal Forms Ser.). 240p. ring bd. 50.00 (*0-86678-064-5*); disk, ring bd. 85.00 (*0-685-49525-6*) Butterworth Legal Pubs.

Criminal Law Forms, 1982. suppl. ed. Donald B. Fiedler & Deborah R. Pred. (Nebraska Legal Forms Ser.). 240p. 1992. 30.00 (*0-86678-021-1*) Butterworth Legal Pubs.

Criminal Law in a Nutshell. 2nd ed. Arnold H. Loewy. (Nutshell Ser.). 321p. 1993. reprint ed. pap. text ed. 16.00 (*0-314-58529-X*) West Pub.

Criminal Law in Action. Ed. by Jan J. Van Dijk et al. 448p. 1986. pap. 72.00 (*90-6544-360-6*) Kluwer Law Tax Pubs.

Criminal Law in Action. John B. Waite. LC 74-3862. (Criminal Justice in America Ser.). 1974. reprint ed. 26.95 (*0-405-06177-3*) Ayer.

Criminal Law in Hong Kong - Cases & Commentary. Findlay & Howarth. 1992. 128.00 (*0-409-99619-X*) Butterworth Legal Pubs.

***Criminal Law in Queensland & Western Australia: Cases & Commentary.** E. Colvin & S. Linden-Laufer. 700p. 1994. pap. 138.00 (*0-409-30650-9*, Austral) Butterworth Legal Pubs.

Criminal Law in Singapore & Malaysia - Text & Materials. Koh et al. 1989. 158.00 (*9971-70-069-7*) Butterworth Legal Pubs.

***Criminal Law in the Company Context.** Janet Dine. 240p. 1995. text ed. 59.95 (*1-85521-342-7*) Ashgate Pub Co.

Criminal Law in the United States. Eugene Smith. (Russell Sage Foundation Reprint Ser.). reprint ed. lib. bdg. 39.50 (*0-697-00208-X*) Irvington.

Criminal Law Instructors Guide. Daniel Hall. 1992. teacher ed 8.00 (*0-8273-4560-7*) Delmar.

Criminal Law, Instructor's Manual for Cases & Comments. 5th ed. Andre A. Moenssens et al. (University Casebook Ser.). 201p. 1992. pap. text ed. write for info. (*0-88277-989-3*) Foundation Pr.

Criminal Law Investigator. Jack Rudman. (Career Examination Ser.: C-969). 1994. pap. 29.95 (*0-8373-0969-7*) Nat Learn.

Criminal Law Journal (Nineteen Sixty-One to Nineteen Eighty-Five) Eastern Book Co. Staff. (C). 1987. 7,500.00 (*0-685-25175-6*) St Mut.

Criminal Law Library, 9 vols., Set. Ed. by Lord Elwyn-Jones. (Waterlow Criminal Law Library). 1991. 750.00 (*0-08-040857-5*, Waterlow) Macmillan.

Criminal Law of Botswana. K. Frimpong & A. McCall Smith. 170p. 1992. pap. 36.00 (*0-7021-2670-5*, Pub. by Juta SA) W W Gaunt.

Criminal Law of Islam. Abdul Qader Shaheed. 375p. (Orig.). 1987. pap. 14.95 (*1-56744-258-7*) Kazi Pubns.

***Criminal Law of Kentucky Annotated, 1992-1993.** 1152p. 1994. pap. 77.00 (*0-8322-0516-8*) Banks-Baldwin.

Criminal Law of New York, 2 Vols. Henry B. Rothblatt. LC 78-151142. 1386p. 1971. 150.00 (*0-317-00473-5*); Suppl. 1993. 80.00 (*0-317-03181-3*) Lawyers Cooperative.

Criminal Law of New York State: Principles, Cases & Readings. Elliott R. Cohen. 300p. 1994. ring bd. 24.95 (*0-930137-72-8*); 5.95 (*0-930137-21-3*) Looseleaf Law.

Criminal Law of South Carolina. 2nd ed. William S. McAninch & W. Gaston Fairey. 1989. text ed. 75.00 (*0-943856-06-X*, 414) SC Bar CLE.

Criminal Law Outline. William A. Grimes. 150p. 1985. pap. 18.00 (*0-686-08768-2*) Natl Judicial Coll.

***Criminal Law Procedures for Private Security.** 2nd ed. Arthur C. Weinstock, Jr. LC 95-2366. 192p. (C). 1995. text ed. 47.95x (*0-398-05997-7*); pap. text ed. 29.95x (*0-398-05998-5*) C C Thomas.

Criminal Law Reporter Cumulative Digest & Index, 2 vols. Criminal Law Reporter Editorial Staff. 3325p. 1982. 150.00 (*0-317-10346-6*) BNA.

Criminal Law Statutes. P. Glazebrook. (C). 1991. 80.00 (*1-85431-175-1*, Pub. by Blackstone Pr UK) W W Gaunt.

Criminal Law Statutes. D. M. Hirst. (Waterlow Criminal Law Guides Ser.). 400p. (Orig.). 1990. pap. 59.95 (*0-08-033106-8*, Waterlow) Macmillan.

Criminal Law System of Medieval & Renaissance Florence. Laura I. Stern. LC 93-14557. (Studies in Historical & Political Science: 112th Series, No. 1). 1994. text ed. 49.50 (*0-8018-4672-2*) Johns Hopkins.

Criminal Law, 1986 & Supplement, 1990. Ed. by Bill Snouffer. write for info. (*0-318-61742-0*) OR Bar CLE.

Criminal Law, 1993: Pocket Part. 2nd ed. Wayne R. LaFave & Austin W. Scott, Jr. (Hornbook Ser.). 60p. 1993. pap. text ed. 5.00 (*0-314-02242-2*) West Pub.

Criminal Law, 1994: Pocket Part. 2nd ed. Wayne R. LaFave. (Hornbook Ser.). 65p. 1994. pap. text ed. 6.50 (*0-314-04363-2*) West Pub.

Criminal Laws: Materials & Commentary on Criminal Law & Process in New South Wales. David Brown et al. 1464p. 1990. pap. 98.00 (*1-86287-024-1*, Pub. by Federation Pr AU) W W Gaunt.

Criminal Lawyer. Arthur L. Wood. 1967. 19.95x (*0-8084-0095-9*); pap. 11.95 (*0-8084-0096-7*) NCUP.

Criminal Lawyers: An Endangered Species. Paul B. Wice. LC 78-14478. (Sage Library of Social Research: Vol. 67). 233p. reprint ed. pap. 66.50 (*0-317-55497-2*, 2056324) Bks Demand.

Criminal Lifestyle: Understanding Patterns of Criminal Conduct. Glenn D. Walters. 320p. (C). 1990. text ed. 42.00 (*0-8039-3840-3*); pap. text ed. 18.95 (*0-8039-5340-2*) Sage.

Criminal Litigation. M. S. Iller & G. A. Goodwin. 1985. 86.00 (*0-406-25813-9*); pap. 50.00 (*0-406-50000-2*, U.K.) Butterworth Legal Pubs.

Criminal Litigation. Craig Osborne & Maria Tighe. 200p. 1993. 34.00 (*1-85431-294-4*, Pub. by Blackstone Pr UK) W W Gaunt.

Criminal Litigation & Remedies. (Legal Skills for the 1990s Ser.). 1990. pap. 40.00 (*1-85431-096-8*, Pub. by Blackstone Pr UK) W W Gaunt.

Criminal Litigation & Sentencing. Blackstone Press Ltd. Staff. (C). 1991. text ed. 150.00 (*1-85431-158-1*, Pub. by Blackstone Pr UK) W W Gaunt.

Criminal Man: According to the Classification of Cesare Lombroso. Gina Lombroso-Ferrero & Leonard D. Savitz. LC 70-129338. (Criminology, Law Enforcement, & Social Problems Ser.: No. 134). (Illus.). 395p. (C). 1972. reprint ed. lib. bdg. 25.00 (*0-87585-134-7*) Patterson Smith.

Criminal Manual. Vijay Malik. 550p. 1983. 125.00 (*0-317-54611-2*) St Mut.

Criminal Manual: (Three Major Acts, CRP.C., I.P.C. & Evidence in English) Ed. by Vijay Malik. (C). 1990. 90.00 (*0-685-39747-5*) St Mut.

Criminal Mentality. Gerald Locklin. 1976. pap. 2.50 (*0-88031-031-6*) Invisible-Red Hill.

Criminal Mind: A Study of Communication Between the Criminal Law & Psychiatry. Philip Roche. LC 76-28524. 299p. 1976. reprint ed. text ed. 38.50 (*0-8371-9056-8*, ROCM, Greenwood Pr) Greenwood.

Criminal Minor Acts, 2 vols. W. Bhatnagar. (C). 1988. 300.00 (*0-685-25700-2*) St Mut.

Criminal Minor Acts: Amended up-to-Date with Short Notes. R. C. Khera. (C). 1988. 180.00 (*0-685-36521-2*) St Mut.

Criminal Organizations: Vice, Racketeering, & Politics in an American City. Gary W. Potter. (Illus.). 213p. (Orig.). (C). 1993. pap. text ed. 12.95 (*0-88133-770-6*) Waveland Pr.

***Criminal Personality Volume II: The Change Process.** Samuel Yochelson & Stanton E. Samenow. LC 75-13507. 592p. 1994. reprint ed. pap. text ed. 45.00 (*1-56821-349-2*) Aronson.

Criminal Personality, Vol. I: A Profile for Change. Samuel Yochelson & Stanton E. Samenow. LC 75-13507. 552p. 1976. 60.00 (*0-87668-218-2*) Aronson.

Criminal Personality, Vol. I: A Profile for Change. Samuel Yochelson & Stanton E. Samenow. LC 75-13507. 552p. 1993. pap. 45.00x (*1-56821-105-8*) Aronson.

Criminal Personality, Vol. III: The Drug User. Samuel Yochelson & Stanton E. Samenow. LC 75-13507. 384p. 1994. reprint ed. pap. 35.00 (*1-56821-244-5*) Aronson.

Criminal Pleading, Law, Practice & Procedure with Model Forms. 3rd ed. B. Banerjee. (C). 1990. 160.00 (*0-89771-190-4*) St Mut.

***Criminal Polit Buros & Other Plagues.** Gyeorgos C. Hatonn. (Phoenix Journals). 209p. 1994. pap. 6.00 (*1-56935-041-8*) Phoenix Source.

Criminal Practice, 7 vols. T. Prem. (C). 1988. 1,000.00 (*0-685-25687-1*) St Mut.

Criminal Practice & Procedure, Set, Vols. 1 & 2. Richard B. McNamara. (New Hampshire Practice Ser.). 1050p. 1987. Set. 72.00 (*0-685-19441-8*) Equity Pubng NH.

Criminal Practice & Procedure, 3 vols., Vols. 1, 2 & 2A. 2nd ed. Richard B. McNamara. (New Hampshire Practice Ser.: Vols. 1-2A). 1530p. 1994. boxed 210.00 (*0-88063-485-5*) Michie Butterworth.

Criminal Practice, Eighteen Sixty-Four to Nineteen Eighty. 7th ed. Daulat R. Prem. (C). 1983. 130.00 (*0-685-36518-2*) St Mut.

***Criminal Practice Handbook.** Stephen Hrones & Catherine C. Czar. 710p. 1995. 95.00 (*0-614-05799-X*) Michie Butterworth.

***Criminal Practice Law Review.** annuals 1993. ring bd. 100.00 (*0-87473-452-5*) Michie Butterworth.

Criminal Pretrial & Trial Procedure: Cases & Materials. Charles A. Pulaski. (Contemporary Legal Education Ser.). 886p. 1982. 28.00 (*0-87215-546-3*) Michie Butterworth.

Criminal Prisons of London: And Scenes of Prison Life. Henry Mayhew & John Binny. LC 68-18227. (Illus.). xii, 634p. 1968. reprint ed. 49.50 (*0-678-05072-4*) Kelley.

Criminal Prisons of London & Scenes of Prison Life. Henry Mayhew & John Binny. (Illus.). 634p. 1968. 35.00 (*0-7146-1411-4*, Pub. by F Cass Pubs UK) Intl Spec Bk.

Criminal Procedure. J. B. Bishop. 1983. Australia. 50.00 (*0-409-49460-7*, Australia); Australia. pap. 33.00 (*0-409-49201-9*, Australia) Butterworth Legal Pubs.

Criminal Procedure. Steven Emanuel. 310p. 1993. pap. text ed. 14.95 (*1-56542-051-9*) E Law Outlines.

Criminal Procedure. Scott Harr & Karen M. Hess. Ed. by Tubb. 416p. (C). 1990. text ed. 55.25 (*0-314-57495-6*) West Pub.

***Criminal Procedure.** Judy H. Kaci. 300p. (Orig.). 1995. pap. 29.95 (*0-942728-66-1*) Copperhouse.

Criminal Procedure. Alan Raphael. 508p. (C). 1993. 46.00 (*1-879581-09-4*) Lupus Pubns.

Criminal Procedure. Albert V. Sheehan et al. 1990. U.K. pap. 53.00 (*0-406-12126-5*) Butterworth Legal Pubs.

Criminal Procedure. Marvin Zalman & Larry J. Siegel. Ed. by Schiller. 678p. (C). 1991. text ed. 53.25 (*0-314-78708-9*) West Pub.

***Criminal Procedure.** rev. ed. Alan Raphael. 542p. (C). 1995. ring bd. 46.50 (*1-879581-20-5*) Lupus Pubns.

Criminal Procedure. 2nd ed. Cook & Marcus. 1982. write for info. (*0-8205-0161-1*, 266); teacher ed write for info. (*0-8205-0162-X*); Supplement 1990. write for info. (*0-8205-0164-6*) Bender.

Criminal Procedure. 2nd ed. Wayne R. LaFave & Jerold H. Israel. (Hornbook Ser.). 1309p. (C). 1993. reprint ed. text ed. 41.00 (*0-314-79327-5*) West Pub.

Criminal Procedure. 2nd ed. Joel Samaha. Ed. by Schiller. LC 92-24728. 600p. (C). 1993. text ed. 50.75 (*0-314-01101-3*) West Pub.

Criminal Procedure. 3rd enl. rev. ed. R. V. Kelkar. (C). 1993. 100.00 (*81-7012-507-3*, Pub. by Eastern Book II) St Mut.

Criminal Procedure, 4 vols. Ed. by Paul L. Murphy. (Bill of Rights & American Legal History Ser.). 2768p. 1990. reprint ed. 440.00 (*0-8240-5865-8*) Garland.

Criminal Procedure, Vol. 3. 2nd ed. Wayne La Fave & Jerold Israel. (Criminal Practice Ser.). 912p. Date not set. text ed. write for info. (*0-314-87381-3*) West Pub.

Criminal Procedure, Vols. 1-5. Wayne R. LaFave & Jerold H. Israel. LC 84-10391. (Criminal Practice Ser.). 2283p. 1993. reprint ed. text ed. write for info. (*0-314-79279-1*) West Pub.

***Criminal Procedure: A Case Approach.** 2nd ed. Judy H. Kaci. 536p. (Orig.). 1994. pap. 34.95 (*0-942728-61-0*) Copperhouse.

Criminal Procedure: Adaptable to Courses Utilizing Haddad, Zagel, Starkman, & Bauer's Casebook on Criminal Procedure. Casenotes Publishing Co., Inc. Staff. Ed. by Norman Goldenberg et al. 1992. pap. write for info. (*0-87457-060-3*, 1202) Casenotes Pub.

C

An Asterisk (*) at the beginning of an entry indicates that the title is appearing in BIP for the first time.

C

An Asterisk (*) at the beginning of an entry indicates that the title is appearing in BIP for the first time.

1699

Criminology: An Introduction Through MicroCase. 2nd ed. Rodney Stark. (Illus.). 181p. (C). 1992. pap. text ed. 15.00 (0-922914-04-4) MicroCase.

*Criminology: An Introduction Using MicroCase. 3rd ed. Rodney Stark. Ed. by David Smetters. (Illus.). (C). 1995. student ed, pap. text ed. 16.00 (0-922914-17-6) MicroCase.

Criminology: Applying Theory. John Holman & James Quinn. Ed. by LaMarre. 338p. (C). 1992. text ed. 54.75 (0-314-92142-7) West Pub.

Criminology: Crime & Criminality. 4th ed. Lewis Yablonsky. 640p. (C). 1990. text ed. 60.50 (0-06-047292-8) HarpCollege.

Criminology: Explaining Crime & Its Context. Stephen E. Brown et al. LC 90-81068. 800p. (C). 1991. text ed. 38.95 (0-87084-111-4) Anderson Pub Co.

Criminology: Perspectives on Crime & Criminality. Peter Wickman et al. 628p. (C). 1980. text ed. 27.50 (0-669-01600-4) Heath.

Criminology: Power, Crime, & Criminal Law. John E. Galliher. Ed. by James L. McCartney. LC 76-47733. (Dorsey Series in Sociology). 562p. reprint ed. pap. 160.20 (0-317-09072-0, 2021672) Bks Demand.

Criminology: Problems & Perspectives. Ahmed Siddique. (C). 1993. 87.50 (81-7012-488-3); pap. 60.00 (81-7012-522-7, Pub. by Eastern Book II) St Mut.

Criminology: Problems & Perspectives. Ahmed Siddiqui. (C). 1990. 30.00 (0-685-39351-8) St Mut.

Criminology: Theories, Patterns, & Typologies. Larry J. Siegel. Ed. by Schiller. 482p. (C). 1992. text ed. 51.50 (0-314-92321-7) West Pub.

*Criminology: Theories, Patterns & Typologies. 5th ed. Larry J. Siegel. LC 94-34059. 550p. 1994. text ed. 52.00 (0-314-04567-8) West Pub.

Criminology: Theory, Research & Policy. Gennaro F. Vito & Ronald M. Holmes. 431p. 1994. text ed. 48.95 (0-534-14886-7) Intl Thomson.

Criminology & Crime. Harold J. Vetter & Ira Silverman. 656p. (C). 1990. text ed. 60.50 (0-06-046833-5) HarpCollege.

Criminology & Forensic Sciences: An International Bibliography 1950-1980, 3 vols. Ed. by Rudolf Vom Ende. xv, 2389p. 1982. lib. bdg. 175.00 (3-598-10374-3) K G Saur.

Criminology & Justice. Lydia Voigt et al. LC 93-23273. 1993. pap. text ed. write for info. (0-07-064528-0) McGraw.

Criminology & Penology. 3rd ed. John L. Gillin. LC 71-138238. (Illus.). 615p. 1971. reprint ed. text ed. 46.00 (0-8371-5595-9, GICP, Greenwood Pr) Greenwood.

Criminology & Public Policy: An Introduction. James Gilsinan. 448p. (C). 1990. Casebound. text ed. write for info. (0-13-193665-4) P-H.

Criminology & the Administration of Criminal Justice: A Bibliography. Leon Radzinowicz & Roger G. Hood. LC 76-24998. 400p. (Orig.). 1977. text ed. 49.95 (0-8371-9068-1, RCA/, Greenwood Pr) Greenwood.

Criminology As Peacemaking. Ed. by Harold E. Pepinsky & Richard Quinney. LC 90-42361. (Illus.). 350p. 1991. 39.95 (0-253-34357-7); pap. 17.50 (0-253-20659-6, MB-659) Ind U Pr.

Criminology in the Making: An Oral History. John H. Laub. LC 83-8147. 287p. 1983. text ed. 32.50 (0-930350-46-4); pap. 12.95 (0-930350-53-7) NE U Pr.

Criminology Lessons: Arguments about Crime, Punishment, & the Interpretation of Conduct, with Advice for Individuals & Prescriptions for Public Policy. Gwynn Nettler. LC 88-71498. (Illus.). 342p. (Orig.). (C). 1988. pap. text ed. 26.95 (0-87084-604-3) Anderson Pub Co.

Criminology of Edwin Sutherland. Mark S. Gaylord & John F. Galliher. 184p. 1988. 32.95 (0-88738-181-2) Transaction Pubs.

Criminology-Problems & Perspectives. 2nd ed. Ahmed Siddique. 483p. 1983. 160.00 (0-317-54754-2) St Mut.

Criminology Problems & Perspectives, 1983: With Supplement. 2nd ed. Ed. by Ahmed Siddique. (C). 1990. 50.00 (0-685-39742-4) St Mut.

Criminology Review Yearbook, Vol. 1. Criminology Review Yearbook Staff. Ed. by Sheldon L. Messinger & Egon Bittner. LC 79-642873. 767p. pap. 180.00 (0-8357-8497-5, 2034773) Bks Demand.

Criminology Theory: Selected Classic Readings. Frank P. Williams, III & Marilyn D. McShane. LC 92-73229. 317p. (C). 1992. pap. text ed. write for info. (0-87084-199-8) Anderson Pub Co.

*Criminology Today: An Introductory Text for 21st Century. Frank Schmalleger. LC 95-15801. 1995. text ed. 58.00 (0-13-291824-2) P-H.

Crims in Grass Castles: The Trimbole Affair. Keith Moor. 224p. (C). 1990. 45.00 (0-947087-17-6, Pub. by Pascoe Pub AT) St Mut.

Crimson. large type ed. Shirley Conran. LC 92-23106. 1993. 23.95 (0-7927-1402-4, Eagle Lrg Print); pap. write for info. (0-7927-1401-6, Eagle Lrg Print) Chivers N Amer.

Crimson. Shirley Conran. Ed. by Julie Rubenstein. 576p. 1992. reprint ed. mass mkt. 5.99 (0-671-79161-3) PB.

Crimson & Blue Handbook: Stories, Stats & Stuff about KU Basketball. Eric Nelson & Lauretta McMillen. (Illus.). 160p. (Orig.). 1993. pap. 9.95 (1-880652-31-5) Wichita Eagle.

Crimson & the Gray: One Hundred Years with the WSU Cougars. Richard B. Fry. (WSU Press Centennial Histories Ser.). 368p. 1989. 24.95 (0-87422-057-2) Wash St U Pr.

Crimson Angel. Penelope Neri. 1986. pap. 3.95 (0-317-39257-3) Zebra.

Crimson Bears, Pt. 1. Tom La Farge. (New American Fiction Ser.: No. 26). 272p. (Orig.). 1993. pap. 12.95 (1-55713-074-4) Sun & Moon CA.

*Crimson Blue. Leonard Reid. 1995. 23.95 (0-8062-5081-X) Carlton.

Crimson Chalice. large type ed. Victor Canning. 380p. 1980. 12.00 (0-7089-0543-9) Ulverscroft.

Crimson Conquest. Sandra DuBay. 320p. 1984. pap. 3.50 (0-8439-2153-6) Dorchester Pub Co.

*Crimson Cookery. 144p. 1995. 19.95 (1-881548-15-5) Crane Hill AL.

Crimson Deception. Therese Alderton. 320p. 1986. pap. 2.95 (0-8217-1913-0) Zebra.

Crimson Deception. Therese Alderton. 1991. pap. 3.95 (0-8217-3325-7) Zebra.

Crimson Desire. Katherine Kincaid. (Orig.). 1983. pap. 3.75 (0-8217-1190-3) Zebra.

Crimson Embrace. Katharine Kincaid. 1984. pap. 3.75 (0-8217-1326-4) Zebra.

Crimson Fairy Book. Ed. by Andrew Lang. LC 67-17988. (Illus.). 371p. (J). (gr. 4-6). 1966. pap. 6.95 (0-486-21799-X) Dover.

Crimson Fairy Book. Andrew Lang. LC 67-17988. (Illus.). (J). (gr. 4-8). 19.25 (0-8446-0753-3) Peter Smith.

Crimson Fish. Neal Robbins. (Illus.). 58p. (Orig.). (J). (gr. 1 up). Date not set. pap. 4.00 (1-884993-02-8) Koldarana.

Crimson Fountain for Harlingscourt. John D. Duncan, Jr. Ed. by Sylvia Ashton. LC 75-774. 1976. 22.95 (0-87949-038-1) Ashley Bks.

Crimson Gardenia. Rex Beach. 1975. lib. bdg. 16.70 (0-89966-015-0) Buccaneer Bks.

Crimson Green: A Quinn Parker Novel of Suspense. Bruce Zimmerman. LC 94-14751. 1994. 20.00 (0-06-017069-7) HarpC.

Crimson Ice, Sugar & Spice: A Novel of Suspense. J. Bruce Monson. 224p. (Orig.). 1994. pap. 10.95 (1-56474-083-8) Fithian Pr.

Crimson Jester: Zapata of Mexico. H. H. Dunn. 1976. lib. bdg. 59.95 (0-87968-964-1) Gordon Pr.

Crimson Joy. Robert B. Parker, Jr. 1989. mass mkt. 4.99 (0-440-20343-0) Dell.

*Crimson Kind of Evil. Ed. by S. G. Johnson. 56p. 1995. pap. 7.00 (1-887666-10-9) Obelesk Bks.

Crimson Legion. Troy Denning. (Dark Sun Novel, Prism Pentad Ser.: Bk. 2). 1992. 4.95 (1-56076-260-8) TSR Inc.

*Crimson Moon. Bryant Benton. 1995. 19.95 (0-533-11194-3) Vantage.

Crimson Mountain. Grace L. Hill. 1976. reprint ed. 21.95 (0-89190-006-3, Rivercity Pr) Amereon Ltd.

Crimson Nightmare. Patricia Rosemoor. (Intrigue Ser.). 1994. mass mkt. 2.99 (0-373-22291-2, 1-22291-8) Harlequin Bks.

Crimson Obsession. Deana James. 1989. pap. 3.95 (0-8217-2272-7) Zebra.

Crimson Patch. Phoebe A. Taylor. (Asey Mayo Cape Cod Mystery Ser.). 240p. 1986. reprint ed. pap. 6.00 (0-88150-064-X, Foul Play) Countryman.

Crimson Rain. Stephen Chan. Ed. by Patricia Schultz. LC 91-34988. (Poetry Ser.: Vol. 18). 72p. 1991. pap. 12.95 (0-7734-9658-0) E Mellen.

Crimson Ribbon. Hilary H. Hippely. LC 92-43066. (Illus.). 32p. (J). (ps-3). 1994. lib. bdg. 15.95 (0-399-22542-0, Putnam) Putnam Pub Group.

Crimson Rice. limited ed. Serge Lecomte. 14.95 (0-685-40173-1) Librado Pr.

Crimson Ring. Paul A. Barra. Ed. by Stanley C. Coy. 170p. (Orig.). 1994. pap. 11.95 (1-881459-12-8) Eagle Pr SC.

Crimson River. Lamont B. Steptoe. (Illus.). 150p. (Orig.). (C). 1989. 9.00 (0-685-23082-1) Whirlwind Pr.

Crimson River. 3rd ed. Lamont B. Steptoe. 24p. (Orig.). (YA). (gr. 11 up). 1991. reprint ed. pap. text ed. 7.00 (0-922827-07-9) Whirlwind Pr.

Crimson Roses. Grace L. Hill. 256p. 1992. pap. text ed. 4.99 (0-8423-0481-9) Tyndale.

Crimson Roses of Fountain Court. Peggy Darty. 1991. pap. 3.95 (0-8217-3450-4) Zebra.

Crimson Skies: The History of a Twentieth Century English Working Man. Charlie Framp. 284p. (C). 1989. text ed. 50.00 (0-902662-82-1, Pub. by R K Pubns UK); pap. text ed. 21.00 (0-902662-83-X, Pub. by R K Pubns UK) St Mut.

*Crimson Tapestry. Joens. 1995. pap. 10.99 (0-8024-1693-4) Moody.

*Crimson Tide. Henrick. 1995. mass mkt. (0-380-78323-1) Avon.

Crimson Tide: The Story of Alabama Football. rev. ed. Clyde Bolton. (College Sports Book Ser.). (Illus.). 328p. 1987. pap. 10.95 (0-87397-301-1) Strode.

Crimsoned Prairie: The Indian Wars. S. L. Marshall. (Quality Paperbacks Ser.). (Illus.). 270p. (C). 1984. reprint ed. pap. 11.95 (0-306-80226-0) Da Capo.

Crinan Canal. Picton Publishing Staff. (Illus.). 40p. 1987. 35.00 (0-317-90394-2, Pub. by Picton UK) St Mut.

Crinkleroot's Book of Animal Tracking. Jim Arnosky. LC 88-15353. (Illus.). 48p. (J). (gr. k-5). 1989. text ed. 14.95 (0-02-705851-4, Bradbury S&S) S&S Childrens.

Crinkleroot's Guide to Knowing the Birds. Jim Arnosky. LC 91-38234. (Illus.). 32p. (J). (gr. k-5). 1992. text ed. 14.95 (0-02-705857-3, Bradbury S&S) S&S Childrens.

Crinkleroot's Guide to Knowing the Trees. Jim Arnosky. LC 91-18651. (Crinkleroot Ser.). (Illus.). 40p. (J). (ps-5). 1992. text ed. 14.95 (0-02-705855-7, Bradbury S&S) S&S Childrens.

Crinkleroot's Guide to Walking in Wild Places. Jim Arnosky. LC 89-38427. (Illus.). 32p. (J). (gr. k-5). 1990. text ed. 14.95 (0-02-705842-5, Bradbury S&S) S&S Childrens.

Crinkleroot's Guide to Walking in Wild Places. Jim Arnosky. LC 92-45775. (Illus.). 32p. (J). (gr. k-5). 1993. pap. 4.95 (0-689-71753-9, Aladdin Paperbacks) S&S Childrens.

Crinkleroot's Twenty-Five Mammals Every Child Should Know. Jim Arnosky. LC 93-7585. (Illus.). 32p. (J). (ps-3). 1994. text ed. 12.95 (0-02-705845-X, Bradbury S&S) S&S Childrens.

Crinkleroot's Twenty-Five More Animals Every Child Should Know. Jim Arnosky. LC 93-7584. (Illus.). 32p. (J). (ps-3). 1994. text ed. 12.95 (0-02-705846-8, Bradbury S&S) S&S Childrens.

Crinkleroot's 25 Birds Every Child Should Know. Jim Arnosky. LC 92-36059. (Illus.). 32p. (J). (ps-3). 1993. text ed. 12.95 (0-02-705859-X, Bradbury S&S) S&S Childrens.

Crinkleroot's 25 Fish Every Child Should Know. Jim Arnosky. LC 92-39381. (Illus.). 32p. (J). (ps-3). 1993. text ed. 12.95 (0-02-705844-1, Bradbury S&S) S&S Childrens.

Crinoids Rom the Girardeau Limestone see Palaeontographica Americana: No. 2

Crinoline to Calico. Nan Heacock. LC 87-3346. (Iowa Heritage Collection). 254p. 1987. reprint ed. pap. 6.95 (0-8138-0067-6) Iowa St U Pr.

Crinolines & Crimping Irons: Victorian Clothes: How they Were Cleaned & Cared for. Christina Walkley & Vanda Foster. (Illus.). 199p. 1978. 28.00 (0-685-33536-4, Pub. by P Owen Ltd UK) Dufour.

Cripple Creek! Leland Feitz. (Illus.). pap. 3.50 (0-936564-02-4) Little London.

*Cripple Creek & Victor Book. (Illus.). 24p. Date not set. pap. 2.95 (0-614-04443-X, 23) Mntn Automation.

Cripple Creek & Victor Book. Claude Wiatrowski & Margaret Wiatrowski. (Illus.). 24p. 1990. pap. 2.95 (0-936206-23-3) Mntn Automation.

Cripple Creek Conflagrations. Lester L. Williams. (Illus.). 52p. 1994. pap. 4.00 (0-86541-028-3) Filter.

Cripple Creek Days. Mabel B. Lee. LC 84-5204. xviii, 286p. 1984. reprint ed. pap. 8.95 (0-8032-7912-4, Bison Books) U of Nebr Pr.

Cripple Creek Dulcimer. Bud Ford & Donna Ford. 1993. 7.95 (0-87166-506-9, 93445) Mel Bay.

Cripple Creek, Nineteen Hundred. Francis Lynde. Ed. by William R. Jones. (Illus.). 20p. 1976. reprint ed. pap. 3.95 (0-89646-001-0) Vistabooks.

Cripple Creek Railroads. Leland Feitz. (Illus.). pap. 2.95 (0-936564-15-6) Little London.

*Cripple Creek Songbird. Kit Dalton. (Buckskin Giant Special Edition Ser.). 368p. (Orig.). 1995. mass mkt., pap. 5.99 (0-8439-3873-0) Dorchester Pub Co.

Cripple Creek Strike: A History of Industrial Wars in Colorado 1903-4-5. Emma F. Langdon. LC 75-90402. (Mass Violence in America Ser.). (Illus.). 1975. reprint ed. 46.95 (0-405-01322-1) Ayer.

Cripple Liberation Front Marching Band Blues. Lorenzo W. Milam. 222p. 1992. 14.95 (0-917320-10-7); pap. 9.95 (0-917320-09-3) Mho & Mho.

Cripple Nation. Alan Vega. (Illus.). 128p. (Orig.). 1994. pap. 15.00 (1-880985-16-0) Two Thirteen Sixty-one.

Crippled & the Disabled: Rehabilitation of the Physically Handicapped in the United States. Henry H. Kessler. Ed. by William R. Phillips & Janet Rosenberg. LC 79-6908. (Physically Handicapped in Society Ser.). (Illus.). 1980. reprint ed. lib. bdg. 35.95 (0-405-13118-6) Ayer.

Crippled Dancer. T. Obinkaram Echewa. (African Writers Ser.). 228p. (Orig.). 1986. pap. 8.95 (0-435-90666-6) Heinemann.

Crippled Giant: A Literary Relationship with Louis-Ferdinand Celine, with Selections from the Celine-Hindus Correspondence. Milton Hindus. LC 85-40934. 171p. 1986. 20.00 (0-87451-367-7) U Pr of New Eng.

Crippled Lamb. Max Lucado. LC 94-19865. (Illus.). (J). 1994. 12.99 (0-8499-1005-6) Word Inc.

Crippled Lion: Letters to Mark. Richard L. Fulgham. LC 87-80963. (Illus.). 110p. 1988. pap. 3.50 (0-9618857-0-X) R L Fulgham.

Crippled Pockets. Albany S. Devers. 102p. 1994. 9.95 (1-885110-00-6) Devers Pubng.

Crips: The Story of a South Central L.A. Street Gang. Donald Bakeer. 195p. 1992. reprint ed. 19.95 (0-9634969-0-5) Precocious.

CripZen: A Manual for Survival. Lorenzo W. Milam. 254p. 1993. 17.95 (0-917320-02-6); pap. 12.95 (0-917320-03-4) Mho & Mho.

CRIR Index. rev. ed. 120p. (C). 1994. 79.95 (0-916812-54-5) Weil Pub.

Cris de Paris, 1529 see Florilege du Concert Vocal de la Renaissance

*Cris de Tonnerre: Thunder Cry. Afrikadzata Deku (Afrikan Culture Institute) Staff. LC 91-72691. (Afrikan Poetry in French Ser.). 100p. 1995. write for info. (1-56454-029-4) Cont Afrikan.

Crisco Cookies & Pies: Favorite Brand Name. 1992. pap. 6.99 (0-517-06677-7) Random Hse Value.

Crisco Cookies Galore. (Favorite All Time Recipes Ser.). (Illus.). 96p. 1993. spiral bd. 3.50 (1-56173-062-9, 2103600) Pubns Intl Ltd.

Crise de la Conscience Europeenne, 2 vols. Paul Hazard. 318p. 1961. Vol. 1, 318p. 10.95 (0-8288-7487-5); Vol. 2, 312p. 10.95 (0-8288-7488-3) Fr & Eur.

Crise Montaniste: Bibliotheque de la Fondation Thiers, fasc. XXXI. Piere C. De Labriolle. LC 82-45816. (Orthodoxies & Heresies in the Early Church Ser.). reprint ed. 57.50 (0-404-62389-1) AMS Pr.

Crise Religieuse du Fifteenth Siecle: Le Pape et la Concile, 1418-1450, 2 vols. Noel Valois. xxxiii, 834p. reprint ed. write for info. (0-318-71438-8, Pub. by Georg Olms GW) Lubrecht & Cramer.

Crises & Commitments: The Politics & Diplomacy of Australia's Involvement in Southeast Asian Conflicts 1948-1965. Peter Edwards. Ed. by Gregory Pemberton. 528p. 1992. 45.00 (1-86373-184-9, Pub. by Allen Unwin AT) Paul & Co Pubs.

Crises & Panics. James L. Fraser. 32p. (C). 1993. pap. text ed. 6.00 (0-87034-109-X) Fraser Pub Co.

Crises & Perspectives: Studies in Ancient Near Easter Polytheism, Biblical Theology, Palestinian Archaeology & Intertestamental Literature: Papers read at the Joint British-Dutch Old Testament Conference Held at Cambridge, U. K., 1985. (Oudtestamentische Studien Ser.: No. 24). (Illus.). 154p. 1986. 50.50 (90-04-07873-8) E J Brill.

Crises & Sequences in Political Development. Leonard Binder et al. LC 79-141952. (Studies in Political Development: No. 7). 337p. reprint ed. pap. 96.10 (0-8357-6081-2, 2034294) Bks Demand.

*Crises & Special Problems in Psychoanalysis & Psychotherapy. Leopold Bellak. LC 94-72438. 264p. 1994. pap. text ed. 25.00 (1-56821-351-4) Aronson.

Crises at the Crossroads: Ruth-Esther. (New Horizons Bible Study Ser.). 48p. (Orig.). 1982. teacher ed, pap. 2.35 (0-89367-074-X); student ed 2.95 (0-89367-075-8) Light & Life.

*Crises Communications: A Casebook Approach. Kathleen Fearn-Banks. (LEA's Communication Ser.). 100p. 1995. student ed 12.00 (0-8058-2082-5); teacher ed 18.00 (0-8058-2083-3); text ed. 70.00 (0-8058-1921-5); pap. 35.00 (0-8058-1922-3) L Erlbaum Assocs.

Crises in Continental Philosophy. Ed. by Arleen B. Dallery et al. LC 90-34077. 283p. (C). 1990. 59.50 (0-7914-0419-6); pap. 19.95 (0-7914-0420-X) State U NY Pr.

Crises in Foreign Policy: A Simulation Analysis. Charles F. Hermann. LC 69-11534. (C). 1969. write for info. (0-672-51134-7, Bobbs) Macmillan.

Crises in Midwifery. James R. O'Dell. 50p. (Orig.). 1989. pap. write for info. (0-933865-17-1) Doris Pubns.

Crises in Midwifery. James R. O'Dell. LC 88-82207. 33p. (Orig.). 1988. pap. text ed. 5.00 (0-933856-17-2) Green Rvr Writers.

Crises in Modern Thought: Solutions to the Problem of Meaninglessness. J. Donald Walters. LC 88-154857. (Illus.). 280p. (Orig.). 1988. pap. 11.95 (0-916124-47-9, CCP10) Crystal Clarity.

Crises in the Caribbean Basin. Ed. by Richard Tardanico. LC 86-1852. (Political Economy of the World-System Annuals Ser.: No. 9). 263p. reprint ed. pap. 75.00 (0-7837-1132-8, 2041662) Bks Demand.

Crises in the History of the Papacy. Joseph McCabe. 1977. lib. bdg. 59.95 (0-8490-1684-3) Gordon Pr.

Crises in the Twentieth Century, 2 vols., Set. Michael Brecher et al. 900p. 1988. 220.00 (0-08-034981-1, Pergamon Pr) Elsevier.

Crises in the World-System. Ed. by Albert Bergesen. LC 82-21474. (Political Economy of the World-System Annuals Ser.: No. 6). 311p. reprint ed. pap. 88.70 (0-8357-8470-3, 2034738) Bks Demand.

Crises of Conscience: Journalism Ethics. Hausman. (C). 1991. text ed. 34.50 (0-06-500365-9) HarpCollege.

Crises of Political Development in Europe & the United States. Ed. by Raymond Grew. LC 78-51166. (Studies in Political Development: No. 9). 447p. reprint ed. pap. 127.40 (0-8357-4669-0, 2037615) Bks Demand.

Crises of the African-American Male: Dangers & Opportunities. Ed. by Lawrence E. Carter. 410p. 1995. pap. 24.95 (0-931761-34-4) Beckham House.

Crises of the Christ. G. Campbell Morgan. LC 89-8429. 1989. pap. 9.99 (0-8007-5307-0) Revell.

Crises of the Christ: The Seven Greatest Events of His Life. G. Campbell Morgan. LC 89-2565. 344p. 1989. reprint ed. pap. 12.99 (0-8254-3258-8) Kregel.

Crises of the Christ see Crisis de Cristo

Crises of the European Regions. Ed. by Dudley Seers & Kjell Ostrom. LC 82-23086. 200p. 1983. text ed. 29.95 (0-312-17396-2) St Martin.

Crises of the House Divided: An Interpretation of the Issues in the Lincoln-Douglas Debates with a New Preface. Harry V. Jaffa. (Phoenix Paperback Ser.). 452p. (C). 1982. pap. text ed. 19.95 (0-226-39112-4) U Ch Pr.

Crises of the Republic. Hannah Arendt. LC 72-187703. 240p. 1972. pap. 10.95 (0-15-623200-6, Harvest Bks) HarBrace.

Crises of the Self: Further Essays on Psychoanalysis & Politics. Ed. by Barry Richards. 278p. 1989. 45.00 (1-85343-095-1) Col U Pr.

Crises of the Self: Further Essays on Psychoanalysis & Politics. Ed. by Barry Richards. 278p. 1989. pap. 19.50 (1-85343-094-3) Col U Pr.

Crisis. Winston Churchill. 432p. 1984. reprint ed. lib. bdg. 32.95 (0-89966-510-1) Buccaneer Bks.

Crisis: A Commentary on the Book of Revelation, 2 vols. Desmond Ford. 207p. (Orig.). (C). 1982. Vol. 1, 207p. pap. 9.00 (1-883619-02-5); Vol. 2, 620p. pap. 16.00 (1-883619-03-3) D Ford Pubns.

Crisis: Crucible of Praise. Latayne C. Scott. 144p. 1992. pap. 7.95 (1-878990-22-5) Howard Pub LA.

Crisis: In the Third World. Andre G. Frank. LC 80-239444. 375p. (C). 1981. text ed. 36.95 (0-8419-0584-3) Holmes & Meier.

Crisis: In the World Economy. Andre G. Frank. LC 80-14540. 382p. (C). 1980. 36.95 (0-8419-0583-5); pap. 18.95 (0-8419-0596-7) Holmes & Meier.

Crisis: Psychological First Aid. Ann S. Kliman. LC 93-74811. 236p. 1994. reprint ed. pap. 27.50 (1-56821-208-9) Aronson.

Crisis: The Japanese Attack on Pearl Harbor & Southeast Asia. Allan Beekman. (Illus.). 456p. 1992. 25.95 (0-9609132-3-8) Heritage Pac.

Crisis: The True Story about How the World Almost Ended. John Somerville. LC 90-45711. 64p. 1990. reprint ed. pap. text ed. 9.95 (0-89341-632-0, Longwood Academic) Hollowbrook.

1700 An Asterisk (*) at the beginning of an entry indicates that the title is appearing in BIP for the first time.

An Asterisk (*) at the beginning of an entry indicates that the title is appearing in BIP for the first time.

Crisis in International News: Policies & Prospects. Ed. by Jim Richstad & Michael H. Anderson. LC 81-677. 480p. 1981. text ed. 53.50 (*0-231-05254-5*); pap. text ed. 22.50 (*0-231-05255-3*) Col U Pr.

Crisis in Intimacy. Jacquelyn B. Carr. LC 87-32560. 187p. (C). 1988. pap. 14.95 (*0-534-09006-0*) Brooks-Cole.

***Crisis in Iranian National Security.** Ahmed S. Hashim. (Adelphi Papers). 1995. pap. text ed. 16.95 (*0-19-828023-8*) OUP.

Crisis in Israel: A Peace Plan to Resist. Yechiel Leiter. 1994. pap. 4.99 (*1-56171-338-4*) Sure Sellers.

Crisis in Japanese Buddhism: Case of the Otani Sect. David A. Suzuki. 285p. 1985. 21.50 (*0-914910-51-5*) Buddhist Bks.

Crisis in Korea. Ed. by Gavan McCormack & John Gittings. 190p. 1977. pap. 22.50 (*0-85124-187-5*, Pub. by Spokesman Bks UK) Coronet Bks.

Crisis in Korea: The Emergence of a New & Dangerous Nuclear Power. Yossef Bodansky. 1994. pap. 5.99 (*1-56171-332-5*) Sure Sellers.

Crisis in Miami: Community Context & Institutional Response in the Adaptation of 1980 Mariel Boatlift Cubans & Undocumented Haitian Entrants in South Florida. Yohel Camayd-Freixas. LC 88-72214. 186p. (Orig.). 1988. pap. 25.00 (*0-923206-00-0*) Boston UR & DG.

Crisis in Modern Social Psychology: How to End It. Ian Parker. 176p. 1989. 45.00 (*0-685-26090-9*, A1668); pap. 12.95 (*0-415-01494-8*, A3373) Routledge Chapman & Hall.

Crisis in Modernism: Bergson & the Vitalist Controversy. Ed. by Frederick Burwick & Paul Douglass. (Illus.). 420p. (C). 1992. 74.95 (*0-521-41294-3*) Cambridge U Pr.

Crisis in Moral Teaching in the Episcopal Church. Ed. by Timothy Sedgwick & Philip Turner. LC 92-21582. 176p. (Orig.). 1992. pap. 13.95 (*0-8192-1592-9*) Morehouse Pub.

Crisis in Organizations: Managing & Communicating in the Heat of Chaos. Laurence Barton. LC 92-12552. 1993. text ed. 23.95 (*0-538-81818-2*) S-W Pub.

Crisis in Our Courts. Steve Bertsch. 252p. 1993. pap. 12.99 (*0-914839-30-6*) Gollehon Pr.

Crisis in Print: Desegregation & the Press in Tennessee. Hugh D. Graham. LC 67-21654. (Illus.). 1967. 19.95 (*0-8265-1105-8*) Vanderbilt U Pr.

Crisis in Science Education: A Source Guide. 1991. lib. bdg. 75.00 (*0-8490-4826-5*) Gordon Pr.

Crisis in Secondary Education: Rebuilding America's High Schools. B. Frank Brown. LC 84-6923. 163p. 1984. 16.95 (*0-13-193517-8*, Busn) P-H.

Crisis in Social Security: Problems & Prospects. Ed. by Michael J. Boskin. 214p. 1977. pap. text ed. 21.95 (*0-917616-16-2*) Transaction Pubs.

Crisis in Sociology. Raymond Boudon. 1980. text ed. 46.50 (*0-231-05178-6*) Col U Pr.

Crisis in South Africa. I. Griffiths. (Flashpoints Ser.). (Illus.). 80p. (J). (gr. 7 up). 1988. lib. bdg. 18.60 (*0-86592-035-4*) Rourke Corp.

Crisis in Swiss Pluralism: The Romanisch & Their Relations with the German & the Italian-Swiss in the Perpective of a Millenium. Robert H. Billigmeier. (Contributions to the Sociology of Language Ser.: No. 26). 1979. 96.15 (*90-279-7577-9*) Mouton.

***Crisis in Teacher Education: A European Concern?** Anthony Adams & Witold Tulasiewicz. LC 94-46158. 160p. 1995. 75.00x (*0-7507-0284-2*, Falmer Pr); pap. 26.00x (*0-7507-0285-0*, Falmer Pr) Taylor & Francis.

Crisis in Teaching: Perspectives on Current Reforms. Ed. by Lois Weis et al. LC 87-33634. (SUNY Series, Frontiers in Education). 289p. 1989. 59.50 (*0-88706-819-7*); pap. 19.95 (*0-88706-820-0*) State U NY Pr.

Crisis in the Arabian Gulf: An Independent Iraqi View. Omar Ali. LC 92-39281. 184p. 1993. text ed. 49.95 (*0-275-94158-2*, C4158, Praeger Pubs) Greenwood.

Crisis in the Atmosphere: The Greenhouse Factor. Ed Phillips. (Illus.). (Orig.). 1990. pap. 6.95 (*0-9625245-0-6*) D B Clark & Co Pub.

Crisis in the Budget Process: Exercising Political Choice. Allen Schick. LC 85-28788. (AEI Studies: 438). 88p. 1986. pap. 10.75 (*0-8447-3596-5*) Am Enterprise.

Crisis in the Catskills. Mary Bogardus. 1976. reprint ed. 15.95 (*0-910746-62-1*, CIT01) Hope Farm.

Crisis in the Christian Science Church. Ann Beals. 145p. 1978. pap. 6.95 (*0-930227-08-5*) Bookmark CA.

Crisis in the French Labor Movement: A Grassroots Perspective. W. Rand Smith. 256p. 1987. text ed. 39.95 (*0-312-17316-4*) St Martin.

Crisis in the Great Republic: Essays Presented to Ross J.S. Hoffman. Ed. by Gaetano L. Vincitorio et al. LC 70-79567. 346p. reprint ed. pap. 98.70 (*0-7837-0478-X*, 2040801) Bks Demand.

Crisis in the Gulf: Enforcing the Rule of Law. John N. Moore. (Terrorism, Documents of International & Local Control, Second Ser.: Vol. 1). 677p. 1992. 60.00 (*0-379-20166-6*) Oceana.

Crisis in the Life of the Artist. 2nd ed. Albert Steffen. 40p. 1987. pap. 4.25 (*0-932776-12-4*) Adonis Pr.

Crisis in the Muslim Mind. AbdulHamid AbuSulayman. Tr. by Yusuf T. DeLorenzo. LC 93-24088. (Islamic Methodology Ser.: Vol. 1). 160p. (Orig.). 1993. 20.00 (*1-56564-137-X*); pap. 10.00 (*1-56564-138-8*) IIIT VA.

Crisis in the Oil Patch: How America's Energy Industry Is Being Destroyed & What Must Be Done to Save It. Donald P. Hodel & Robert Deitz. LC 93-5882. 185p. 1993. 20.00 (*0-89526-502-8*) Regnery Pub.

Crisis in the Philippines: A Threat to U. S. Interests. Frwd. by A. James Gregor & Howard H. Baker. LC 84-21124. 128p. (Orig.). 1984. pap. 13.75 (*0-89633-087-7*) Ethics & Public Policy.

Crisis in the Philippines: The Making of a Revolution. E. San Juan, Jr. LC 85-22980. (Illus.). 288p. 1986. text ed. 55.00 (*0-89789-085-X*, Bergin & Garvey) Greenwood.

Crisis in the Philippines: The Marcos Era & Beyond. Ed. by John Bresnan. 290p. 1986. text ed. 55.00 (*0-691-05490-8*); pap. 15.95 (*0-691-00810-8*) Princeton U Pr.

Crisis in the Primary Classroom. Maurice Galton. 160p. 1994. pap. 27.50 (*1-85346-245-4*, Pub. by D Fulton UK) Taylor & Francis.

Crisis in the Public Sector--Challenge to the Public Health: American Public Health Association 1980 Meeting in Detroit, Michigan. Ed. by O. Gish. 48p. 1982. pap. 18.25 (*0-08-028948-7*, Pergamon Pr) Elsevier.

Crisis in the Sudan: Re-Thinking the Future. Bona Malwal & Peter N. Kok. 1994. pap. 15.95 (*0-936508-35-3*) Barber Pr.

Crisis in the Sudan: Re-Thinking the Future. Bona Malwal & Peter N. Kok. 1995. 29.95 (*0-936508-34-5*) Barber Pr.

Crisis in the West: American Leadership & the Global Balance. Lionel Gelber. LC 75-857. 250p. (C). 1975. text ed. 29.95 (*0-312-17395-4*) St Martin.

Crisis in the Working Class: Some Arguments for Creating a New Labor Movement. John McDermott. LC 80-51437. 255p. (Orig.). 1980. pap. 6.00 (*0-89608-014-5*) South End Pr.

Crisis in the Workplace: Occupational Disease & Injury - (A Report to the Ford Foundation) Nicholas A. Ashford. LC 75-28424. 1976. 45.00 (*0-262-01045-3*) MIT Pr.

Crisis in the World's Fisheries: People, Problems, & Policies. James R. McGoodwin. LC 90-37484. 247p. 1991. 39.50 (*0-8047-1790-7*) Stanford U Pr.

***Crisis in the World's Fisheries: People, Problems, & Policies.** James R. McGoodwin. 1994. pap. 13.95 (*0-8047-2371-0*) Stanford U Pr.

Crisis in Uganda: The Breakdown of Health Services. Ed. by Cole P. Dodge & Paul D. Wiebe. (Illus.). 240p. 1985. text ed. 117.00 (*0-08-032682-X*, Pub. by Aberdeen U Pr) Macmillan.

Crisis in Urban Education. Ed. by Lawrence A. Fink & Raymond A. Ducharme. LC 73-141258. 350p. (C). reprint ed. pap. 99.80 (*0-8357-9869-0*, 2012541) Bks Demand.

Crisis in Urban Public Finance: A Case Study of Thirty-Eight Cities. Pearl M. Kamer. 336p. 1983. text ed. 59.95 (*0-275-91019-9*, C1019, Praeger Pubs) Greenwood.

Crisis in Urban Recreational Services. Jay S. Shivers & Joseph W. Halper. LC 79-17414. 384p. 1970. 45.00 (*0-8386-3006-5*) Fairleigh Dickinson.

Crisis in Western Security. Lawrence S. Hagen. LC 81-14340. 1982. text ed. 32.50 (*0-312-17397-0*) St Martin.

Crisis in World Politics: Theory & Reality. Michael Brecher. LC 92-29898. 1993. 112.00 (*0-08-041376-5*, Pergamon Pr); pap. 48.00 (*0-08-041377-3*, Pergamon Pr) Elsevier.

Crisis in Zaire. Nzongola-Ntalaja. (C). 1988. 32.00 (*0-86543-023-3*); pap. 11.95 (*0-86543-024-1*) Africa World.

***Crisis Intervention.** Eric Lindemann. LC 94-47404. 1995. pap. 30.00 (*1-56821-468-5*) Aronson.

Crisis Intervention. 2nd ed. Ed. by Lawrence Cohen et al. (Community Psychology Ser.: Vol. IV). (Illus.). 222p. 1982. 38.95 (*0-89885-107-6*); pap. 20.95 (*0-89885-108-4*) Human Sci Pr.

Crisis Intervention. 7th ed. Aguilera. 384p. 1994. pap. 22.95 (*0-8016-6936-7*) Mosby Yr Bk.

Crisis Intervention: A Handbook for Practice & Research. 2nd ed. Karl A. Slaikeu. 360p. 1990. text ed. 48.95 (*0-205-12342-2*, H23427) Allyn.

***Crisis Intervention: A Handbook of Immediate Person-to-Person Help.** 2nd ed. Kenneth France. (Illus.). 276p. 1990. pap. 32.95 (*0-398-06129-7*) C C Thomas.

Crisis Intervention: A Handbook of Immediate Person-to-Person Help. 2nd ed. Kenneth France. (Illus.). 276p. (C). 1990. text ed. 54.95x (*0-398-05630-7*) C C Thomas.

Crisis Intervention: A Manual for Education & Action. John P. Eddy et al. LC 83-6499. 134p. (Orig.). (C). 1983. pap. text ed. 18.00 (*0-8191-3231-4*) U Pr of Amer.

Crisis Intervention: Case Histories. J. K. Morrice. Ed. by J. H. Kahn. 117p. 1976. 51.00 (*0-08-019742-6*, Pub. by Pergamon Repr UK) Franklin.

***Crisis Intervention: Contemporary Issues for On-Site Interveners.** 2nd ed. James E. Hendricks & Jerome B. McKean. LC 94-24040. (Illus.). 302p. (C). 1995. pap. text ed. 35.95x (*0-398-05973-X*) C C Thomas.

***Crisis Intervention: Contemporary Issues on On-Site Interveners.** 2nd ed. James E. Hendricks & Jerome B. McKean. LC 94-24040. (Illus.). 302p. (C). 1995. text ed. 63.95x (*0-398-05972-1*) C C Thomas.

Crisis Intervention: Index of Modern Authors & Subjects with Guide for Rapid Research. Sally Z. Hollinder. LC 90-56264. 200p. 1991. 44.50 (*1-55914-314-2*); pap. 39.50 (*1-55914-315-0*) ABBE Pubs Assn.

Crisis Intervention: Selected Readings. Ed. by Howard J. Parad. LC 65-20273. 384p. reprint ed. pap. 109.50 (*0-7837-1630-3*, 2041923) Bks Demand.

Crisis Intervention: Theory & Methodology. 6th ed. Aguilera. 320p. 1989. pap. 24.95 (*0-8016-0063-4*) Mosby Yr Bk.

Crisis Intervention & Counseling by Telephone. David Lester & Gene W. Brockopp. (Illus.). 336p. 1976. 47.95x (*0-398-02641-6*) C C Thomas.

***Crisis Intervention & Counseling by Telephone.** David Lester & Gene W. Brockopp. (Illus.). 336p. 1976. pap. 29.95 (*0-398-06230-7*) C C Thomas.

Crisis Intervention & Prevention. Ed. by Harold L. Pruett & Vivian B. Brown. LC 85-644751. (New Directions for Student Services Ser.: No. 49). 1990. 16.95 (*1-55542-836-3*) Jossey-Bass.

Crisis Intervention, Bk. 2: The Practitioner's Sourcebook for Brief Therapy. Ed. by Howard J. Parad & Libbie G. Parad. LC 89-17151. x, 402p. 1990. pap. 27.95 (*0-87304-237-9*) Families Intl.

Crisis Intervention Handbook. Stewart Ehly. 80p. 1986. pap. text ed. 10.00 (*0-614-07254-9*) Natl Assn Psych.

Crisis Intervention Handbook: Assessment, Treatment & Research. Albert R. Roberts. 341p. (C). 1990. text ed. 49.95 (*0-534-12510-7*) Brooks-Cole.

Crisis Intervention in Criminal Justice - Social Service. Ed. by James E. Hendricks. 284p. (C). 1991. text ed. 55.95 (*0-398-05745-1*) C C Thomas.

***Crisis Intervention in Criminal Justice - Social Service.** Ed. by James E. Hendricks. 284p. 1991. pap. 33.95 (*0-398-06386-9*) C C Thomas.

Crisis Intervention in Practice: The Multidisciplinary Team & the Mental Health Social Worker. Richard Mitchell. (Studies of Care in the Community). 150p. 1993. 58.95 (*1-85628-452-2*, Pub. by Avebury Pub UK) Ashgate Pub Co.

Crisis Intervention in Residential Treatment: The Clinical Innovations of Fritz Redl. William C. Morse. LC 91-25834. (Residential Treatment for Children & Youth Ser.). (Illus.). 107p. 1991. lib. bdg. 29.95 (*1-56024-215-9*) Haworth Pr.

Crisis Intervention in the Schools. Gayle D. Pitcher & A. Scott Poland. LC 92-1417. (Guilford School Practitioner Ser.). 246p. 1992. lib. bdg. 25.00 (*0-89862-364-2*) Guilford Pr.

Crisis Intervention Strategies. 2nd ed. Burl Gilliland & Richard James. LC 92-10291. 512p. (C). 1993. text ed. 38.95 (*0-534-19494-X*) Brooks-Cole.

Crisis Intervention Strategies for School-Based Helpers. Ed. by Thomas N. Fairchild. (Illus.). 574p. (C). 1986. 88.95x (*0-398-05209-3*) C C Thomas.

***Crisis Intervention Strategies for School-Based Helpers.** Ed. by Thomas N. Fairchild. (Illus.). 547p. 1986. pap. 45.95 (*0-398-06113-0*) C C Thomas.

Crisis Intervention Verbatim. Nira Kfir. 175p. 1989. 28.00 (*0-89116-837-0*) Hemisp Pub.

Crisis Intervention Worker. Jack Rudman. (Career Examination Ser.: Series 1). 1991. pap. 27.95 (*0-8373-3708-9*) Nat Learn.

Crisis Into Chaos: Political India 1981. E. M. Namboodiripad. 172p. 1981. pap. text ed. 4.25 (*0-86131-279-1*, Pub. by Orient Longman Ltd II) Apt Bks.

Crisis Investing for the Rest of the '90s. Douglas Casey. LC 92-35971. 1993. 22.50 (*1-55972-177-4*, Birch Ln Pr) Carol Pub Group.

***Crisis Investing for the Rest of the 90's.** enl. ed. Douglas Casey. 456p. (Orig.). 1995. pap. 14.95 (*0-8065-1612-7*, Citadel Pr) Carol Pub Group.

***Crisis Management: A Casebook.** Ed. by Michael T. Charles & John C. Kim. 1988. pap. 33.95 (*0-398-06054-1*) C C Thomas.

Crisis Management: A Casebook. Ed. by Michael T. Charles & John C. Kim. (Illus.). 310p. (C). 1988. text ed. 55.95 (*0-398-05408-8*) C C Thomas.

Crisis Management: A Diagnostic Guide for Improving Your Organization's Crisis-Preparedness. Alan I. Mitroff & Christine Pearson. LC 96-16039. (Management Ser.). 160p. 1993. 24.95 (*1-55542-563-1*) Jossey-Bass.

Crisis Management: A Guide to School Crises & Actions Taken. Jerry J. Herman. Ed. by Janice L. Herman. (Roadmaps to Success Ser.). 64p. 1994. pap. 15.00 (*0-8039-6159-6*) Corwin Pr.

Crisis Management: A Guide to School Crises & Actions Taken. Jerry J. Herman. Ed. by Janice L. Herman. (Roadmaps to Success (RTS) Ser.). 64p. 1994. pap. 15.00 (*0-8039-6133-2*) Corwin Pr.

***Crisis Management: A Model for Managers.** Wheeler L. Baker. (Illus.). 112p. (Orig.). (C). 1994. pap. write for info. (*0-9641182-0-3*) Foot Hill Pr.

Crisis Management: A Model for Managers. Wheeler L. Baker. 80p. (Orig.). 1993. pap. write for info. (*0-9627114-5-4*) Legacy CA.

***Crisis Management: A Work Book for Managers.** Richardson & Smith. Date not set. text ed. 45.00 (*0-471-95356-3*) Wiley.

Crisis Management: Planning for the Inevitable. Steven Fink. 256p. 1989. 19.95 (*0-8144-5859-9*) AMACOM.

Crisis Management & Decision Making: Simulation Oriented Scenarios. Ed. by Uriel Rosenthal. 168p. (C). 1991. lib. bdg. 69.00 (*0-7923-1177-9*) Kluwer Ac.

***Crisis Management & the Politics of Reconciliation in Somalia.** Ed. by M. A. Salih & L. Wohlgemuth. (Scandinavian Institute of African Studies). 176p. 1994. pap. 44.50 (*91-7106-356-0*, Pub. by Almqv & Wiksell SW) Coronet Bks.

Crisis Management in a Cross-Cultural Setting. Patricia Burak. 58p. 1987. pap. text ed. 12.00 (*0-912207-18-3*) NAFSA Washington.

Crisis Management in American Higher Education. Barbara A. Scott. LC 82-24615. 368p. 1983. text ed. 65.00 (*0-275-91077-6*, C1077, Praeger Pubs) Greenwood.

Crisis Management in Anesthesiology. Ed. by David M. Gaba et al. LC 93-39076. (Illus.). 294p. (Orig.). 1994. pap. text ed. 39.95 (*0-443-08910-8*) Churchill.

***Crisis Management in Catholic Schools.** Thomas M. Batsis. 279p. (Orig.). 1994. pap. 11.00 (*1-55833-140-9*) Natl Cath Educ.

***Crisis Management in the Food & Drinks Industry: A Practical Approach.** Colin Doeg. LC 94-72658. 250p. 1995. 59.95 (*0-412-57110-2*) Chapman & Hall.

Crisis Management in the Power Industry: An Inside Story. Frank Ledger & Howard Sallis. LC 94-12501. (Illus.). 360p. 1995. 65.00x (*0-415-11876-X*, C0109) Routledge.

Crisis Management in the Schools: The Legal Implications. Ed. by National School Boards Association Staff. 717p. 1992. ring bd. 200.00 (*0-88364-149-6*) Natl Sch Boards.

Crisis Management Strategy: Competition & Change in Modern Industries. Simon A. Booth. LC 92-42828. 1939. write for info. (*0-415-06230-6*) Routledge.

Crisis Marketing: When Bad Things Happen to Good Companies. Joe Marconi. 225p. 1992. 22.95 (*1-55738-246-8*) Probus Pub Co.

Crisis Meters: Business Response to Social Crises. Irving S. Michelman. LC 73-4914. (Illus.). xviii, 418p. 1973. lib. bdg. 45.00 (*0-678-01320-9*) Kelley.

Crisis Ministries. Thomas C. Oden. (Classical Pastoral Care Ser.). 278p. 1994. reprint ed. pap. 12.99 (*0-8010-6766-9*) Baker Bk.

Crisis of Abstraction in Canada: The 1950s. Ed. by Denise Leclerc. (Illus.). 272p. 1993. pap. 39.95 (*0-88884-624-X*, Pub. by Natl Gallery CN) U Ch Pr.

***Crisis of an Idea: Some Implications for the Philippines of Europe's Anti-Communist Revolution.** Douglas J. Elwood. (Illus.). 53p. (Orig.). 1994. pap. 6.00x (*971-10-0547-6*, Pub. by New Day Pub PH) Cellar.

Crisis of Argentine Capitalism. Paul H. Lewis. LC 89-31350. xxviii, 573p. 1992. pap. 19.95 (*0-8078-4356-3*) U of NC Pr.

***Crisis of Biblical Authority: The Setting & Range of the Current Evangelical Controversy.** Robert M. Price. LC 95-3865. (Studies in Philosophy & Religion: No. 3). 1995. lib. bdg. write for info. (*0-912134-16-X*, St Willibrords Pr); pap. write for info. (*0-912134-17-8*, St Willibrords Pr) Borgo Pr.

Crisis of Care: Affirming & Restoring Caring Practices in the Helping Professions. Ed. by Susan S. Phillips & Patricia Benner. 256p. 1994. 55.00 (*0-87840-558-5*) Georgetown U Pr.

Crisis of Caring: Recovering the Meaning of True Fellowship. Jerry Bridges. LC 92-14842. 1992. pap. 7.99 (*0-87552-110-X*) Presby & Reformed.

Crisis of Chinese Consciousness: Radical Antitraditionalism in the May Fourth Era. Lin Yu-Sheng. LC 77-91057. 216p. 1979. 32.50 (*0-299-07410-2*) U of Wis Pr.

Crisis of Church & State, 1050-1300. Brian Tierney. 224p. 1988. pap. text ed. 10.95 (*0-8020-6701-8*) U of Toronto Pr.

Crisis of Civilization. Hilaire Belloc. LC 73-114465. 245p. 1973. reprint ed. text ed. 35.00 (*0-8371-4761-1*, BECC, Greenwood Pr) Greenwood.

Crisis of Civilization. Hilaire Belloc. LC 92-60965. 208p. 1992. reprint ed. pap. 10.00 (*0-89555-462-3*) TAN Bks Pubs.

Crisis of Color & Democracy: Essays on Race, Class & Power. Manning Marable. (Orig.). 1992. 29.95 (*0-9628838-3-2*); pap. 14.95 (*0-9628838-2-4*) Common Courage.

Crisis of Competence: Transitional Stress & the Displaced Worker. Carl A. Maida et al. LC 89-15825. (Psychosocial Stress Ser.: No. 16). 224p. 1990. 29.95 (*0-87630-559-1*) Brunner-Mazel.

***Crisis of Confidence in American Education: A Blueprint for Fixing What Is Wrong & Restoring America's Confidence in the Public Schools.** Robert Hagerty. 226p. (C). 1994. text ed. 48.95x (*0-398-05965-9*); pap. text ed. 29.95x (*0-398-05966-7*) C C Thomas.

***Crisis of Conscience.** H. Barber. 1994. pap. 4.99 (*0-517-13189-7*) Random.

Crisis of Conscience: A Catholic Doctor Speaks Out. Hugh R. Barber. LC 92-39827. 1993. 17.95 (*1-55972-162-6*, Birch Ln Pr) Carol Pub Group.

Crisis of Conscience: Moral Ambivalence & Education in Northern Ireland. T. P. Burgess. 123p. 1992. 55.95 (*1-85628-420-4*, Pub. by Avebury Pub UK) Ashgate Pub Co.

Crisis of Conscience: The Struggle Between Loyalty to God & Loyalty to One's Religion. enl. rev. ed. Raymond Franz. (Illus.). 400p. 1992. 13.95 (*0-914675-01-X*) Comment Pr.

Crisis of Conscience: The Struggle Between Loyalty to God & Loyalty to One's Religion. enl. rev. ed. Raymond Franz. (Illus.). 418p. 1994. pap. 10.95 (*0-914675-04-4*) Comment Pr.

Crisis of Consciousness in Contemporary Philosophy. Adras Gedo. 290p. 1982. 30.00 (*0-685-17100-0*, Pub. by Collets UK) Pro-Am Music.

Crisis of Conservatism: The Politics, Economics, & Ideology of Conservative Party, 1880-1914. Ewen H. Green. LC 94-10882. 256p. 1994. 69.95x (*0-415-01255-4*, A6020) Routledge.

Crisis of Conservative Virginia: The Byrd Organization & the Politics of Massive Resistance. James W. Elv. LC 75-43742. (Twentieth-Century America Ser.). 234p. reprint ed. pap. 66.70 (*0-317-28041-4*, 2025560) Bks Demand.

Crisis of Contemporary Culture: An Inaugural Lecture Delivered Before the University of Oxford on 27 November 1992. Terry Eagleton. LC 93-18201. 1993. pap. 4.50 (*0-19-951360-0*, Clarendon Pr) OUP.

Crisis of Courtesy: Studies in the Conduct Book in Britain, 1600-1900. Ed. by Jacques Carre. LC 94-5758. (Studies in Intellectual History: Vol. 51). 1994. 71.50 (*90-04-10005-9*) E J Brill.

Crisis of Culture: Steps to Re-Open the Phenomenological Investigation of Man. Ed. by Anna-Teresa Tymieniecka. (Analecta Husserliana Ser.: No. 5). 400p. 1976. lib. bdg. 117.00 (*90-277-0632-8*) Kluwer Ac.

Crisis of Democracy. Michel Crozier et al. (Triangle Papers: No. 8). 1975. 15.00 (*0-8147-1305-X*); pap. 6.00 (*0-318-02781-X*) Trilateral Comm.

Crisis of Democracy: Report on the Governability of Democracies to the Trilateral Commission. Michel Crozier et al. LC 75-27167. 1975. 12.50 (*0-8147-1364-5*); pap. 12.50x (*0-8147-1365-3*) NYU Pr.

An Asterisk (*) at the beginning of an entry indicates that the title is appearing in BIP for the first time.

An Asterisk (*) at the beginning of an entry indicates that the title is appearing in BIP for the first time.

1703

Cristianismo Es Religion? Christianity: Is It a Religion? Arno C. Gaebelein. (SPA.). 4.95 (84-7645-012-5, 223076, Pub. by Edit Clie SP) TSELF.
Cristianismo Evangelico a Traves de los Siglos: Evangelical Christianity Through. Samuel Vila. (SPA.). 8.95 (84-7228-687-8, 220229, Pub. by Edit Clie SP) TSELF.
Cristianismo Frente a las Sectas: Christianity vs. the Cults. Enrique Gomez. (SPA.). 3.25 (84-7645-422-8, 223329, Pub. by Edit Clie SP) TSELF.
Cristianismo Practico: Practical Christianity. A. B. Simpson. (SPA.). 3.25 (84-7228-932-X, 223007, Pub. by Edit Clie SP) TSELF.
Cristianismo y Otras Religiones. E. L. Copeland. Tr. by Abdias A. Mora. (Christianity & World Religions Ser.). Orig. Title: Christianity & World Religious. (Illus.). 192p. (SPA.). 1981. reprint ed. pap. 3.95 (0-311-05760-8, Edit Mundo) Casa Bautista.
Cristianismo y Psicologia En la Educa: Christianity & Psychology in Ed. J. Bellostas. (SPA.). 5.25 (84-7645-507-0, 223587, Pub. by Edit Clie SP) TSELF.
Cristiano De Rodillas: The Kneeling Christian. (SPA.). 4.95 (84-7228-521-9, 220204, Pub. by Edit Clie SP) TSELF.
Cristiano Intercesor. Kenneth E. Hagin. 1985. pap. 1.95 (0-89276-118-0) Hagin Ministries.
Cristiano Visto Por Si Mismo: The Christian Looks at Himself. Antonny Hoekema. (SPA.). 4.95 (84-7228-508-1, 220203, Pub. by Edit Clie SP) TSELF.
Cristiano y las Ideologias - When Kingdoms Clash: The Christian & Ideologies. Clavin E. Shenk. Tr. by Rafael C. De Bustamante. 96p. (Orig.). (SPA.). 1991. pap. 3.50 (0-311-05044-1) Casa Bautista.
Cristianos Ante la Pobreza: A Christian Approach to Poverty. Juan Simarro. (SPA.). 5.95 (84-7645-396-5, 223515, Pub. by Edit Clie SP) TSELF.
Cristianos En el Mundo Hoy: Christians in the Contemporary. J. M. Martinez. (SPA.). 6.95 (84-7645-244-6, 223283, Pub. by Edit Clie SP) TSELF.
Cristification: And la Hermanidad de la Rosa Cruz. 2nd ed. R. Swinburne Clymer & George Lippard. Tr. by J. E. Bucheli. 206p. (SPA.). 1980. pap. 6.95 (0-932785-52-2) Philos Pub.
Cristo a las Naciones (Christ to the Nations) L. Palau. (SPA.). Date not set. 5.99 (0-945792-22-0, 498023) Editorial Unilit.
Cristo De la Historia: Christ Throughout History. Juan Young. (SPA.). 6.95 (84-7645-008-7, 223077, Pub. by Edit Clie SP) TSELF.
Cristo E O Sofrimento Humano. E. Stanley Jones. 156p. (POR.). 1991. pap. 7.95 (0-8297-1660-2) Life Pubs Intl.
Cristo el Camino: Christ the Way. David M. McIntyre. (SPA.). 4.95 (84-7645-141-5, 223182, Pub. by Edit Clie SP) TSELF.
Cristo En el Credo: Christ in the Creed. W. Scroggie. (SPA.). 4.25 (84-7228-997-4, 223060, Pub. by Edit Clie SP) TSELF.
Cristo En el Tabernaculo: Christ in the Tabernacle. A. B. Simpson. (SPA.). 3.25 (84-7228-706-8, 220231, Pub. by Edit Clie SP) TSELF.
Cristo En Isaias: Christ in Isaiah. F. B. Meyer. (SPA.). 6.50 (84-7228-676-2, 220205, Pub. by Edit Clie SP) TSELF.
Cristo En las Prisiones Comunistas: In God's Underground. R. Wurmbrand. (SPA.). 6.50 (84-7228-479-4, 220206, Pub. by Edit Clie SP) TSELF.
Cristo En los Salmos: Finding the Living Christ in Psalms. John Hunter. (SPA.). 4.95 (84-7228-053-5, 220207, Pub. by Edit Clie SP) TSELF.
Cristo En Mallorca: Christ in Mallorca. Jose Flores. (SPA.). 5.50 (84-7228-066-7, 220209, Pub. by Edit Clie SP) TSELF.
Cristo Es el Senor-bL-Alumno. Tomas Soerens. (SPA.). 1989. 1.10 (1-55955-020-1) CITE MI.
Cristo Es el Senor-bL-Maestro. Tomas Soerens. (SPA.). 1990. 2.50 (1-55955-021-X) CITE MI.
Cristo Es el Senor-C-Alumno. Tomas Soerens. (SPA.). 1989. 1.20 (1-55955-016-3) CITE MI.
Cristo Es el Senor-C-Maestro. Tomas Soerens. (SPA.). 1990. 2.00 (1-55955-017-1) CITE MI.
Cristo es el Senor-Db-Alumno. Tomas Soerens. (SPA.). 1989. 1.20 (1-55955-018-X) CITE MI.
Cristo Es el Senor-Db-Maestro. Tomas Soerens. (SPA.). 1989. 2.50 (1-55955-019-8) CITE MI.
Cristo Nuestro Camino Hacia el Padre. (ENG & SPA.). (J). (gr. 3). 1983. pap. text ed. 2.00 (0-8198-1428-8); 1.00 (0-8198-1429-6) Pauline Bks.
Cristo Vive en Me. (ENG & SPA.). (J). (gr. 2). 1983. pap. text ed. 2.00 (0-8198-1426-1); 1.00 (0-8198-1427-X) Pauline Bks.
Cristo Viviente: The Living Christ. Will H. Houghton. (SPA.). 4.25 (84-7645-038-9, 223101, Pub. by Edit Clie SP) TSELF.
Cristo y Los Poderes. Hendrikus Berkhof. 89p. (SPA.). 1985. pap. 4.25 (0-939125-01-3) Evangelical Lit.
Cristo y Su Ley de Amor. (ENG & SPA.). (J). (gr. 4). 1984. pap. text ed. 2.00 (0-8198-1437-7); 1.80 (0-8198-1438-5) Pauline Bks.
Cristo Yanqui. Mauricio De Begona. LC 82-84263. 777p. (Orig.). (SPA.). 1984. pap. 19.00 (0-89729-323-1) Ediciones.
Cristobal Balenciaga. Lesley Miller. (Fashion Designers Ser.). (Illus.). 96p. (Orig.). 1994. pap. 25.95 (0-8419-1344-7) Holmes & Meier.
Cristobal Colon. (SPA.). 9.95 (84-241-5406-1) E Torres & Sons.
Cristobal Colon. Antonio Gala. (Nueva Austral Ser.: Vol. 138). (SPA.). 1991. pap. text ed. 24.95x (84-239-1938-2) Elliots Bks.
***Cristobal Colon: El Capricho de la Reina.** Julio P. Andujar. LC 94-71768. (Coleccion Hispanica - Narrativa). 144p. (Orig.). (SPA.). 1994. pap. 16.00 (0-89729-742-3) Ediciones.
Cristobal Colon: Su Vida y Descubrimiento a la Luz de Sus Profecias. Kay Brigham. LC 91-128168. (Illus.). 178p. (SPA.). 1991. 16.95 (84-7645-404-X, 223537, Pub. by Edit Clie SP) TSELF.
Cristobical. Federico Garcia Lorca. 30p. (SPA.). 1986. pap. 12.00 (0-89295-050-1) Society Sp & Sp-Am.
Cristoforo Colombo: God's Navigator. Douglas T. Peck. (Illus.). 148p. (Orig.). 1994. 18.95 (0-9641798-2-2); lib. bdg. 18.95 (0-9641798-1-4); pap. 12.95 (0-9641798-0-6) Columbian Pubs.
Cristologia De Juan: Christology of John. Jose Flores. (SPA.). 6.95 (84-7228-216-3, 220212, Pub. by Edit Clie SP) TSELF.
Cristologia De Pedro: Christology of Peter. Jose Flores. (SPA.). 5.25 (84-7228-398-4, 220214, Pub. by Edit Clie SP) TSELF.
Cristologia desde America Latina see Christology at the Crossroads: A Latin American Approach
***Cristy Lane: One Day at a Time.** Ed. by Carol Cuellar. 48p. (Orig.). (YA). 1994. pap. text ed. 12.95 (0-7604-0010-5) CPP Belwin.
Cristy Lane: One Day at a Time. Leeie Stroller. 1992. mass mkt. 4.99 (0-312-95121-3) St Martin.
Criswell's Guidebook for Pastors. W. A. Criswell. LC 79-7735. 1992. 19.99 (0-8054-2536-5) Broadman.
Criteria & Guidelines for Evaluation of Associate Degree Programs in Nursing. rev. ed. National League for Nursing Staff. 46p. 1991. pap. text ed. 5.95 (0-88737-535-9, 23-2439) Natl League Nurse.
Criteria & Guidelines for Evaluation of Baccalaureate & Higher Degree Programs in Nursing. rev. ed. National League for Nursing Staff. 74p. 1992. pap. text ed. 6.95 (0-88737-552-9, 15-2474) Natl League Nurse.
Criteria & Guidelines for Evaluation of Diploma Programs in Nursing. rev. ed. National League for Nursing Staff. 50p. 1992. pap. text ed. 5.95 (0-88737-538-3, 16-2444) Natl League Nurse.
Criteria & Guidelines for Evaluation of Practical Nursing Programs. rev. ed. National League for Nursing Staff. 64p. 1992. pap. text ed. 5.95 (0-88737-539-1, 38-2445) Natl League Nurse.
Criteria & Standards of Quality. Avedis Donabedian. LC 81-6873. (Explorations in Quality Assessment & Monitoring Ser.: Vol. II). (Illus.). 522p. 1981. text ed. 40.00 (0-914904-67-1, 0837); pap. text ed. 38.00 (0-914904-68-X, 0837) Health Admin Pr.
Criteria (Dose-Effect Relationships) for Cadmium. Commission of the European Communities. LC 77-30193. 1978. pap. 89.00 (0-08-022024-X, Pub. by Pergamon Repr UK) Franklin.
Criteria (Dose Effect Relationships) for Organichlorine Pesticides: Report of a Working Group of Experts Prepared for the Commission of the European Communities. Ed. by M. Mercier. 400p. 1981. pap. 171.00 (0-08-023441-0, Pub. by Pergamon Repr UK) Franklin.
Criteria for a Recommended Standard: Occupational Exposure to Radon Progeny in Underground Mines. (DHHS Publication NIOSH Ser.: No. 88-101). 223p. (Orig.). 1987. pap. 12.00 (0-16-002532-X, S/N 017-033-00433-1) USGPO.
Criteria for a Recommended Standard: Welding, Brazing, & Thermal Cutting. (DHHS Publication Ser.: No. 88-110). (Illus.). 246p. 1988. pap. 12.00 (0-16-002535-4, S/N 017-033-00438-2) USGPO.
Criteria for & Approaches to Water Quality Management in Developing Countries. 388p. 1991. 49.00 (92-1-104357-3, 91.II.A.1) UN.
Criteria for Awarding School Leaving Certificates, an International Discussion: Proceedings of the International Association for Education Assessment of the 3rd Annual Conference, Narrobi, May 23, 1977. International Association for Educational Assessment Staff. Ed. by Frances M. Ottobre. LC 79-40175. 1979. 97.00 (0-08-024685-0, Pub. by Pergamon Repr UK) Franklin.
Criteria for Competence: Controversies in the Conceptualization & Assessment of Children's Abilities. Ed. by Michael Chandler & David Chapman. 296p. (C). 1991. text ed. 59.95 (0-8058-0606-7) L Erlbaum Assocs.
***Criteria for Comprehensive Health Education Curricula.** 1990. 2.50 (0-917160-22-3) Am Sch Health.
Criteria for Design of Bearing Pads. Prestressed Concrete Institute Staff. 118p. 1985. ring bd. 35.00 (0-318-19829-0, TR-4-85) P-PCI.
Criteria for Design of Elevated Temperature Class 1 Components in Section III, Division 1 of the ASME Boiler & Pressure Vessel Code. 84p. 1976. pap. text ed. 20.00 (0-685-72341-0, E00097) ASME.
Criteria for Developing - Evaluating Records Management Software. 10p. 1990. pap. 27.00 (0-933887-37-X, A4518) Assn Recs Mgrs & Admin.
Criteria for Divisibility. N. N. Vorobyov. Tr. by Daniel A. Levine & Timothy McLarnan. LC 74-11634. (Popular Lectures in Mathematics). 1980. pap. text ed. 10.00 (0-226-86516-9) U Ch Pr.
Criteria for Drug Use Evaluation, Vol. 1. 137p. 1989. pap. 63.00 (0-930530-95-0) Am Soc Hlth-Syst.
Criteria for Drug Use Evaluation, Vol. 2. 113p. 1990. pap. 63.00 (0-930530-99-3) Am Soc Hlth-Syst.
Criteria for Drug Use Evaluation, Vol. 3. ASHP Staff. 176p. (Orig.). 1992. pap. 50.00 (1-879907-19-4) Am Soc Hlth-Syst.
Criteria for Drug Use Evaluation, Vol. 4. 96p. 1993. pap. text ed. 50.00 (1-879907-37-2) Am Soc Hlth-Syst.
Criteria for Evaluating Advancement Programs. 2nd ed. Ed. by P. Warren Heemann. 26p. (Orig.). 1989. 16.00 (0-89964-264-0) Coun Adv & Supp Ed.
Criteria for Evaluating an AIDS Curriculum. rev. ed. National Coalition of Advocates for Students Staff. 23p. 1992. reprint ed. pap. 4.00 (1-880002-02-7) Natl Coal Advocates.
Criteria for Evaluating Business & Office Education, 1969. (Yearbook Ser.). 324p. 5.00 (0-933964-07-2) Natl Busn Ed Assoc.
Criteria for Evaluation of Truck Weight Enforcement Programs. (National Cooperative Highway Research Program Report Ser.: No. 82). 74p. 1981. 7.20 (0-309-03271-7) Transport Res Bd.
***Criteria for Excellence.** rev. ed. 42p. 1990. pap. text ed. 5.00 (0-87355-094-3) Natl Sci Tchrs.
Criteria for Improving the Professional Status of Librarianship. Dale E. Shaffer. 49p. 1980. pap. text ed. 4.25 (0-915060-15-9) D E Shaffer.
Criteria for Maintenance of Multilane Highways. (Manual & Report on Engineering Practice Ser.: No. 53). 23p. 1971. pap. 3.00 (0-87262-227-4) Am Soc Civil Eng.
Criteria for Measurement of Stream Channels As an Indicator of Peak Flow History. Thomas R. Hammer. (Discussion Paper Ser.: No. 36). 1970. pap. 10.00 (1-55869-020-4) Regional Sci Res Inst.
Criteria for Moisture Control. G. Brundrett. (Illus.). 128p. 1990. text ed. 84.95 (0-408-02374-0) Buttrwrth-Heinemann.
Criteria for Open Space System Planning: An Exploratory Survey & Synthesis. Robert E. Coughlin. (Discussion Paper Ser.: No. 83). 1975. pap. 10.00 (1-55869-021-2) Regional Sci Res Inst.
Criteria for Preceptors of Administrators-in-Training Programs. Robert W. Haacker. 262p. (C). 1987. 44.50 (0-929442-03-2) Publicare Pr.
Criteria for Price Indexes for Library Materials. (National Information Standards Ser.). 1983. 10.00 (0-88738-982-1, Z39.20) Transaction Pubs.
Criteria for Quality of Petroleum Products. Institute of Petroleum Staff. Ed. by J. P. Allison. 286p. 1973. 72.00 (0-85334-469-8, Pub. by Elsevier Applied Sci UK) Elsevier.
Criteria for Selecting Appropriate Technologies Under Different Cultural, Technical & Social Conditions: Proceedings of the IFAC Symposium, Bari, Italy, May, 1979. IFAC Symposium Staff. Ed. by A. De Giorgio & C. Roveda. (IFAC Proceedings Ser.). (Illus.). 320p. 1980. 140.00 (0-08-024455-6, Pub. by Pergamon Repr UK) Franklin.
Criteria for Skill Attainment. rev. ed. 1986. 5.00 (0-939418-07-X) Ferguson-Florissant.
Criteria for the Catholic Protection of Reinforced Bridge Elements. Jack Bennett & Thomas Turk. 14p. (Orig.). (C). 1994. pap. text ed. 5.00 (0-309-05615-2, SHRP-S-359) SHRP.
Criteria for the Depths of Dredged Navigational Channels. National Research Council (U. S.), Marine Board Staff. 177p. reprint ed. pap. 50.50 (0-8357-7710-3, 2036066) Bks Demand.
Criteria for the Life History, with Analyses of Six Notable Documents. John Dollard. (Select Bibliographies Reprint Ser.). 1977. reprint ed. 23.95 (0-8369-6685-6) Ayer.
Criteria for the Renovation or Replacement of Water Treatment Plants. 280p. 1991. pap. 36.50 (0-89867-498-0, 90563) Am Water Wks Assn.
Criteria for the Selection & Use of Visuals in Instruction. George L. Gropper et al. LC 70-158736. 971p. 1971. student ed 42.95 (0-87778-021-8) Educ Tech Pubns.
Criteria for Use of Asphalt Friction Surfaces. (National Cooperative Highway Research Program Report Ser.: No. 104). 41p. 1983. 6.80 (0-309-03565-1) Transport Res Bd.
Criteria for Writers. Daniel Brown & Bill Burnette. 308p. (C). 1987. pap. text ed. 21.50 (0-03-006173-3) HB Coll Pubs.
Criteria, Guidelines, Practices, Procedures & Standards of the Ground Water Industry. Ed. by K. McCray. 40p. 1988. 6.25 (1-56034-065-7, K454) Natl Water Well.
Criteria of Certainty: Truth & Judgment in the English Enlightenment. Kevin L. Cope. LC 90-12264. 232p. 1990. text ed. 28.00 (0-8131-1750-X) U Pr of Ky.
Criteria of Social Scientific Knowledge: Interpretation, Prediction, Praxes. Terrence E. Cook. 208p. (C). 1994. lib. bdg. 59.50 (0-8476-7884-9); pap. text ed. 21.95 (0-8476-7883-0) Rowman.
Criteria of Truth. Ralph Doty. LC 90-21079. (American University Studies: Philosophy: Ser. V, Vol. 108). 127p. (C). 1991. text ed. 35.95 (0-8204-1424-7) P Lang Pubs.
***Criterion for Tune: Collections of Poems by Writers in Delaware, Maryland, Virginia, & the District of Columbia.** Comp. by Joseph D. Adams. (Poet's Domain Ser.: Vol. 11). 160p. (Orig.). 1995. pap. text ed. 8.00 (1-880016-19-2) Road Pubs.
Criterion-Referenced Articulation Profile. Larry J. Mattes. 1986. pap. text ed. 45.00 (0-930951-06-9) Acad Comm.
Criterion-Referenced Measurement. W. James Popham. (Illus.). 1978. pap. 19.95 (0-685-03817-3) P-H.
Criterion-Referenced Measurement: The State of the Art. Ronald A. Berk. LC 79-18194. 1980. 32.00 (0-8018-2264-5) Johns Hopkins.
Criterion Referenced Test Kit: Math. Linda Craig & Phyllis Praytor. (Criterion Reference Tests Ser.). (Illus.). 54p. (J). (gr. 4). 1978. write for info. (0-936394-01-3) Education Serv.
Criterion Test of Basic Skills. Kerth Lundell et al. (J). (gr. 1 up). 1974. pap. 55.00 (0-87879-154-X) Acad Therapy.
Critic. Richard B. Sheridan. (C). 1993. pap. text ed. 6.95 (0-393-90058-4) Norton.
Critic Agonistes: Psychology, Myth, & the Art of Fiction. Daniel Weiss. Ed. by Stephen Arkin & Eric Solomon. LC 84-21953. (Illus.). 288p. 1985. pap. text ed. 25.00 (0-295-96161-9) U of Wash Pr.
Critic & Society: From Matthew Arnold to the New Historicism. Morris Dickstein. 256p. 1992. 25.00 (0-19-507399-1) OUP.
Critic & the Drama. George J. Nathan. LC 75-120099. 152p. 1975. 20.00 (0-8386-7964-1) Fairleigh Dickinson.
Critic As Artist: Essays on Books 1920-1970. Ed. by Gilbert A. Harrison. 464p. 1972. 12.00 (0-87140-544-X) Liveright.
Critic As Artist: Essays on Books 1920-1970. Ed. by Gilbert A. Harrison. 464p. 1972. pap. 3.95 (0-87140-260-2) Liveright.
Critic As Artist: The Intentionality of Art. Donald Kuspit. LC 83-24099. (Contemporary American Art Critics Ser.: No. 2). 418p. reprint ed. 119.20 (0-8357-1532-9, 2070729); reprint ed. pap. 19.95 (0-8357-1927-8) Bks Demand.
Critic As Conservator: Essays in Literature, Society, & Culture. George A. Panichas. LC 91-32217. 262p. 1992. text ed. 49.95 (0-8132-0762-2) Cath U Pr.
Critic at the Opera: Contemporary Comments on Opera in London Over Three Centuries. Dennis Arundell. LC 79-25062. (Music Reprint Ser.: 1980). (Illus.). 1980. reprint ed. lib. bdg. 45.00 (0-306-76026-6) Da Capo.
Critic into Anti-Critic. James Hepburn. LC 84-70174. (Studies in English & American Literature, Linguistics & Culture: Vol. 3). 250p. (C). 1984. 34.50 (0-938100-33-5) Camden Hse.
Critic of Crisis: A Study of Frank Kermode. Jan Gorak. LC 86-30792. 120p. 1987. pap. 9.95 (0-8262-0634-4) U of Mo Pr.
Critic, Power, & the Performing Arts. John E. Booth. 1991. 27.95 (0-231-07460-3) Col U Pr.
Critic Sees: A Guide to Art Criticism. Sarah Gill. 192p. (C). 1993. per., pap. text ed. 24.95 (0-8403-8590-0) Kendall-Hunt.
***Critica: Untersuchungen zur Gerchichte der Literaturkritik Zwischen Quintilian und Thomasius.** Herbert Jaumann. (Brill's Studies in Intellectual History: No. 62). 448p. 1995. 129.25 (90-04-10276-0) E J Brill.
Critica - Criticizing: Como Vencer la Autocritica - How to Overcome Self-Criticism. William J. Diehm. Tr. by Josie Smith. 112p. (Orig.). (SPA.). 1992. pap. 4.20 (0-311-46130-1) Casa Bautista.
Critica al Poder Politico. Carlos M. Mendez. LC 81-67847. (Illus.). 269p. (Orig.). (SPA.). 1981. pap. 14.95 (0-89729-298-7) Ediciones.
Critica de Hombre de Luz de Odon Betanzos Palacios. Ernesto F. Jaldon. (SPA.). 1974. pap. 3.50 (84-399-2786-X) Edit Mensaje.
Critica de la Razon Poetica. Hector O. Ciarlo. 170p. (Orig.). (C). 1982. pap. 3.50 (0-8477-2824-2) U of PR Pr.
Critica del Juicio. Immanuel Kant. Ed. & Tr. by Manuel Garcia Morente. (Nueva Austral Ser.: Vol. 167). (SPA.). 1991. pap. text ed. 24.95x (84-239-1967-6) Elliots Bks.
Critica Del Nuevo Testamento (The New Testament & Criticism) George E. Ladd. Tr. by Moises Chavez. 176p. (Orig.). (SPA.). 1991. pap. 5.95 (0-311-04365-8) Casa Bautista.
Critica Literaria Como Defensa de los Derechos Humanos: Cuestion Teorica. Hernan Vidal. Ed. by Thomas Lathrop et al. (U. Cal Irvine, Hispanic Studies: No. 2). 124p. (SPA.). Date not set. 16.50 (0-936388-63-3) Juan de la Cuesta.
Critica Literaria en la Obra de Gabriela Mistral. Onilda A. Jimenez. LC 82-70206. (Coleccion Polymita Ser.). (Illus.). 303p. (Orig.). (SPA.). 1983. pap. 19.95 (0-89729-308-8) Ediciones.
Critica Sacra. Edward Leigh. reprint ed. write for info. (0-318-72037-X, Pub. by Georg Olms GW) Lubrecht & Cramer.
Critica Teatral en ABC: 1918-1936. Vance R. Holloway. LC 91-22975. (American University Studies: Romance Languages & Literature: Ser. II, Vol. 181). 196p. (SPA.). (C). 1992. text ed. 38.95 (0-8204-1677-0) P Lang Pubs.
Critical Act: Criticism & Community. Evan Watkins. LC 78-3426. 1978. 35.00 (0-300-02221-2) Yale U Pr.
Critical Aesthetics & Postmodernism. Paul Crowther. LC 92-29734. (Illus.). 236p. 1993. 39.95 (0-19-824037-6) OUP.
Critical Analyses in English Renaissance Drama: A Bibliographic Guide. 3rd rev. ed. Brownell Salomon. LC 90-45814. 282p. 1990. 38.00 (0-8240-7183-2, 1370) Garland.
Critical Analyses in Renaissance Drama: A Bibliographic Guide. Brownell Salomon. 1979. 14.00 (0-87972-127-8); pap. 7.95 (0-87972-125-1) Bowling Green Univ.
Critical Analysis: Language & Its Functions. Pasqual S. Schievella. LC 68-22331. (Illus.). 125p. 1987. 12.95 (0-9616731-1-7) Sebastian LI.
Critical Analysis-Monochonal Therapy in Transplantation. William J. Burlingham. 304p. 1991. 121.00 (0-8493-6821-9, RC1235) CRC Pr.
Critical Analysis of De La Fayette's "La Princesse De Cleves" As a Royal Novel: Kings, Queens, & Splendor. Michael G. Paulson. LC 91-31495. (Studies in French Literature: Vol. 13). 116p. 1991. lib. bdg. 59.95 (0-7734-9740-4) E Mellen.
Critical Analysis of the Fuel Management Program for Schools: Selected New Jersey Cities Compared with Nation-Wide Practice. Ashley M. McCullough. LC 72-177019. (Columbia University. Teachers College. Contributions to Education Ser.: No. 713). reprint ed. 22.50 (0-404-55713-9) AMS Pr.
Critical Analysis of the Philosophy of Emile Meyerson. George Boas. LC 70-109616. (Select Bibliographies Reprint Ser.). 1977. 19.95 (0-8369-5224-3) Ayer.
Critical Analysis of Valle-Inclan's Ruedo Iberico. Linda S. Glaze. LC 84-81669. (Coleccion de Estudios Hispanicos - Hispanic Studies Collection). 206p. (Orig.). 1985. pap. 12.95 (0-89729-357-6) Ediciones.

C

An Asterisk (*) at the beginning of an entry indicates that the title is appearing in BIP for the first time.

C

An Asterisk (*) at the beginning of an entry indicates that the title is appearing in BIP for the first time.

1705

Critical Concordance to the Letter of Paul to the Colossians. A. Q. Morton et al. Ed. by J. Arthur Baird & David Freedman. (Computer Bible Ser.: Vol. XXIV). (Orig.). 1981. pap. text ed. 20.00 (0-935106-19-7) Biblical Res Assocs.

Critical Concordance to the Letter of Paul to the Ephesians. A. Q. Morton et al. Ed. by J. Arthur Baird & David Freedman. (Computer Bible Ser.: Vol. XXII). (Orig.). 1980. pap. text ed. 20.00 (0-935106-17-0) Biblical Res Assocs.

Critical Concordance to the Letter of Paul to the Philippians. A. Q. Morton et al. Ed. by J. Arthur Baird & David Freedman. (Computer Bible Ser.: Vol. XXIII). (Orig.). 1980. pap. text ed. 20.00 (0-935106-18-9) Biblical Res Assocs.

Critical Concordance to the Letter of Paul to the Romans. A. Q. Morton et al. Ed. by J. Arthur Baird & David Noel Freedman. (Computer Bible Ser.: Vol. XIII). 1977. pap. 27.50 (0-935106-08-1) Biblical Res Assocs.

Critical Concordance to the Letter to the Hebrews. J. David Thompson et al. (Computer Bible Ser.: Vol. 29). 300p. 1988. 50.00 (0-935106-25-1) Biblical Res Assocs.

Critical Concordance to the Letters of First, Second, Third John & Jude. J. Arthur Baird & J. David Thompson. (Computer Bible Ser.: Vol. XXXIII). 1991. 54.00 (0-935106-29-4) Biblical Res Assocs.

Critical Concordance to the Pastoral Epistles, I, II Timothy, Titus, Philemon. A. Q. Morton et al. Ed. by J. Arthur Baird & David N. Freedman. (Computer Bible Ser.: Vol. XXV). 1982. pap. 35.00 (0-935106-20-0) Biblical Res Assocs.

Critical Concordance to the Synoptic Gospels, Vol. I. J. Arthur Baird. (Computer Bible Ser.). 1971. 15.00 (0-685-43088-X) Biblical Res Assocs.

Critical Condition. Martha Stearn. 368p. (Orig.). 1993. pap. 4.99 (0-451-17585-9, Sig) NAL-Dutton.

Critical Condition: Human Health & the Environment. Ed. by Eric Chivian et al. (Illus.). 240p. 1993. 29.95 (0-262-03212-0); pap. 15.95 (0-262-53118-6) MIT Pr.

Critical Condition: Women on the Edge of Violence. Ed. by Amy Scholder. (Illus.). 200p. (Orig.). 1993. pap. text ed. 10.95 (0-87286-285-2) City Lights.

Critical Conditions: Postmodernity & the Question of Foundations. Horace L. Fairlamb. (Literature, Culture, Theory Ser.: No. 8). 288p. (C). 1994. 59.95 (0-521-45047-0); pap. 17.95 (0-521-45665-7) Cambridge U Pr.

Critical Conditions: Regarding the Historical Moment. Ed. by Michael Hays. 224p. (C). 1992. text ed. 39.95 (0-8166-2021-0); text ed. 16.95 (0-8166-2022-9) U of Minn Pr.

Critical Connection: The Motorola Service Station Story. Kathi A. Brown. LC 91-73592. 250p. (C). 1992. pap. write for info. (1-56946-003-5) Motorola Univ.

Critical Connections: Communication for the Future. (Illus.). 403p. 1990. per., pap. 17.00 (0-16-018464-9, S/N 052-003-011) USGPO.

***Critical Connections: Communication for the Future, New Technologies for Business, Politics, Culture, & Individuals, 2 vols., Set.** 1995. lib. bdg. 603.95 (0-8490-6747-2) Gordon Pr.

Critical Control Systems: Theory, Design, & Applications. J. F. Whidborne & G. P. Lui. LC 93-11314. (Engineering Systems Modelling & Control Ser.: Vol. 2). 1993. text ed. 79.95 (0-471-94183-2) Wiley.

Critical Conventions: Interpretation in the Literary Arts & Sciences. John O'Neill. LC 91-50868. (Project for Discourse & Theory Ser.: Vol. 8). (Illus.). 352p. 1992. 34.95 (0-8061-2378-8) U of Okla Pr.

Critical Conventions: Interpretation in the Literary Arts & Sciences. John O'Neill. LC 91-50868. (Project for Discourse & Theory Ser.: Vol. 8). (Illus.). 354p. 1992. pap. text ed. 14.95 (0-8061-2445-8) U of Okla Pr.

***Critical Conversations in Philosophy of Education.** Ed. by Wendy Kohli. 416p. 1994. 59.95 (0-415-90693-8, A9757) Routledge.

***Critical Conversations in Philosophy of Education.** Ed. by Wendy Kohli. 416p. 1994. pap. 19.95 (0-415-90694-6, A9761) Routledge.

Critical Cosmos, 15 vols., Set. Ed. by Harold Bloom. 1989. 589.50 (0-87754-950-8) Chelsea Hse.

Critical Crosscurrents in Education. Michael Collins. 1995. write for info. (0-89464-755-5) Krieger.

Critical Crossings: The New York Intellectuals in Postwar America. Neil Jumonville. LC 89-20517. (Illus.). 320p. 1990. 30.00 (0-520-06858-0) U CA Pr.

Critical Current Limitation in High Temperature Superconductors. Ed. by M. Barah et al. (Progress in High Temperature Superconductivity: Vol. 30). 500p. (C). 1992. text ed. 121.00 (981-02-0803-0) World Scientific Pub.

Critical Currents: Proceedings of the 6th International Workshop, Cambridge, 8-11 July 1991. Ed. by J. Evetts. 522p. 1992. 146.00 (0-7503-0177-5) IOP Pub.

Critical Currents in Superconductors: Proceedings of the 7th International Workshop. H. W. Weber. 700p. 1994. text ed. 118.00 (981-02-1809-5) World Scientific Pub.

Critical Data of Pure Substances, 2 pts., Set, Vol. 2, Pts. 1 & 2. K. H. Simrock et al. (Dechema Chemistry Data Ser.). 1500p. 1986. Set. lib. bdg. 503.00 (3-921567-77-7, Pub. by Dechema GW) Scholium Intl.

Critical Decisions in Following Jesus. George S. Johnson. 1992. pap. 9.50 (1-55673-427-1, 9230) CSS OH.

Critical Defense Choices. Sam Nunn. Ed. by Hal Gulliver. LC 82-63197. (Papers on International Issues: No. 4). 19p. (Orig.). 1983. pap. text ed. 5.00 (0-935082-03-4) Southern Ctr Intl Stud.

***Critical Desire: Psychoanalysis & the Literary Subject.** Linda R. Williams. (Interrogating Texts Ser.). 224p. 1995. 59.50 (0-340-64557-1, Pub. by E Arnld UK); pap. 16.95 (0-340-56816-X, Pub. by E Arnld UK) St Martin.

Critical Development of David Pugh. Deborah Godin. 48p. 1984. 4.95 (0-920806-65-1, Pub. by Penumbra Pr CN) U of Toronto Pr.

Critical Dictionary of Composers & Their Music. Percy M. Young. LC 78-66927. (Encore Music Editions Ser.). 1982. reprint ed. 31.35 (0-88355-771-1) Hyperion Conn.

Critical Dictionary of Educational Concepts: An Appraisal of Selected Ideas & Issues in Educational Theory & Practice. Robin Barrow & Geoffrey Milburn. LC 86-21953. 240p. 1986. text ed. 39.95 (0-312-00229-7) St Martin.

Critical Dictionary of Educational Concepts: An Appraisal of Selected Ideas & Issues in Educational Theory & Practice. 2nd ed. Robin Barrow & Geoffrey Milburn. 384p. (C). 1990. text ed. 43.95 (0-8077-3058-0) Tchrs Coll.

Critical Dictionary of English Literature & British & American Authors, 3 vols. Samuel Allibone. 1972. 300.00 (0-87968-965-X) Gordon Pr.

Critical Dictionary of English Literature & British & American Authors. Samuel A. Allibone. (Principle Works of Samuel Austin Allibone). 1989. reprint ed. lib. bdg. 690.00 (0-7812-1784-9) Rprt Serv.

Critical Dictionary of Jungian Analysis. Andrew Samuels et al. 224p. 1986. text ed. 39.50 (0-7102-0410-8, 04108, RKP); pap. 16.95 (0-7102-0915-0, 09150, RKP) Routledge.

Critical Dictionary of Jungian Anaylsis. Andrew Samuels. 1991. pap. 16.95 (0-415-05910-0) Routledge.

Critical Dictionary of Marxism: Dictionnaire Critique de Marxisme. G. Labica & G. Bensussan. 1256p. (FRE.). 1985. 150.00 (0-8288-2252-2, F70761) Fr & Eur.

***Critical Dictionary of Psychoanalysis.** Charles Rycroft. 256p. 1995. pap. 13.95 (0-14-051310-8, Penguin Bks) Viking Penguin.

Critical Dictionary of Psychology: Dictionnaire Critique De Psychiatrie. Barthold Berens de Haan. 304p. (FRE.). 1986. 39.95 (0-8288-1788-X, M2335) Fr & Eur.

Critical Dictionary of Sociology. Raymond Boudon & Francois Bourricaud. Tr. & Sel. by Peter Hamilton. LC 89-4868. 624p. 1989. 49.95 (0-226-06728-9) U Ch Pr.

Critical Dictionary of Sociology: Dictionnaire Critique De la Sociologie. 4th rev. ed. Raymond Boudon & R. Bourricaud. 736p. (FRE.). 1994. 175.00 (0-8288-2357-X, M14125) Fr & Eur.

Critical Dictionary of the French Revolution. Ed. by Francois Furet & Mona Ozouf. Tr. by Arthur Goldhammer. LC 89-30656. (Illus.). 1168p. 1989. text ed. 97.50 (0-674-17728-2) HUP.

Critical Difference: Essays in the Contemporary Rhetoric of Reading. Barbara Johnson. LC 80-21533. 168p. (C). 1985. reprint ed. pap. text ed. 12.95x (0-8018-2728-0) Johns Hopkins.

***Critical Discography of Readings in Old English.** N. J. Marples & O. D. Macrae-Gibson. 1988. 5.00 (0-614-01293-7) Medieval Inst.

Critical Discourse: A Survey of Literary Theorists. Robert De Beaugrande. LC 87-19462. 496p. 1988. text ed. 65.00 (0-89391-441-X); pap. text ed. 35.00 (0-89391-453-3) Ablex Pub.

***Critical Discourses on Teacher Development.** John Smyth. LC 94-45426. (Teacher Development Ser.). 208p. 1995. 65.00 (0-304-33401-4); pap. 20.00 (0-304-33402-2) Cassell.

***Critical Documents of Jewish History: A Sourcebook.** Ed. by Ronald H. Isaacs & Kerry M. Olitzky. LC 94-44933. 1995. text ed. write for info. (1-56821-392-1) Aronson.

Critical Double: Figurative Meaning in Aesthetic Discourse. Paul Gordon. 200p. 1995. text ed. 29.95 (0-8173-0710-9) U of Ala Pr.

Critical Dreams. Jess. 36p. 1986. 75.00 (0-918395-03-8) Poltroon Pr.

Critical Edge: Critical Thinking for Reading & Writing. Vincent E. Barry. 528p. (C). 1992. pap. text ed. 29.50 (0-03-047522-8) HB Coll Pubs.

Critical Edition of Cheuelere Assigne: Text, Glossary, & Critical Analyses. R. E. Stratton. LC 91-4986. (Studies in Mediaeval Literature: Vol. 11). 96p. 1991. lib. bdg. 49.95 (0-7734-9743-9) E Mellen.

Critical Edition of Endymion. Stephen Steinhoff. LC 82-50410. 300p. 1987. 25.00 (0-87875-236-6) Whitston Pub.

Critical Edition of George Buchanan's Baptistes & of Its Anonymous Seventeenth-Century Translation Tyrannicall-Government Anatomized. rev. ed. Ed. by Steven Berkowitz. LC 91-34201. (Renaissance Imagination Ser.). (Illus.). 624p. 1992. 132.00 (0-8153-0450-1) Garland.

Critical Edition of Juan Bautista Diamante's "La Reina Maria Estuarda" Michael G. Paulson & Tamara Alvarez-Detrell. 1990. 44.50 (0-916379-64-7) Scripta.

Critical Edition of Midmay Fane's Vertues Triumph (1644) Gerald W. Morton. (American University Studies: English Language & Literature: Ser. IV, Vol. 75). 222p. (C). 1989. text ed. 32.50 (0-8204-0809-3) P Lang Pubs.

Critical Edition of Mira De Amescua's "La Fe De Hungria" & "El Monte De la Piedad", Vol. 7. James C. Maloney. 149p. 1975. pap. 7.00 (0-912788-06-2) Tulane Romance Lang.

Critical Edition of Sir Thomas Elyot's "The Boke Named the Governour" Ed. by Donald W. Rude. LC 92-3303. (Renaissance Imagination Ser.). 472p. 1992. 100.00 (0-8153-0458-7) Garland.

Critical Edition of the Coptic (Bohairic) Pentateuch, Vol. 5. Melvin K. Peters. LC 83-3260. (Society of Biblical Literature Septuagint & Cognate Studies Ser.). 126p. (C). 1983. pap. 16.95 (0-89130-617-X, 06 04 15) Scholars Pr GA.

Critical Edition of the Coptic (Bohairic) Pentateuch: Genesis, Vol. 1. Ed. by Melvin K. Peters. (C). 1985. pap. 11.95 (0-89130-924-1) Scholars Pr GA.

Critical Edition of the Coptic (Bohairic) Pentateuch: Society of Biblical Literature. Melvin K. Peters. LC 83-3260. (Septugaint & Cognate Studies, Exodus: Vol. 2). 122p. (C). 1986. 20.95 (1-55540-030-2, 06-04-22); pap. 15.95 (1-55540-031-0) Scholars Pr GA.

***Critical Edition of the Medieval Play Mankind.** Frank Knittel & Grosvenor Fattic. LC 94-24216. 136p. 1995. text ed. 69.95 (0-7734-8994-0) E Mellen.

Critical Edition of "The True Chronicle History of King Lear & His Three Daughters, Gonorill, Ragan & Cordella" Ed. by Donald M. Michie. LC 91-31663. (Renaissance Imagination Ser.). 256p. 1992. 72.00 (0-8153-0456-0) Garland.

Critical Edition of "The War of the Worlds" H. G. Well's Scientific Romance. Ed. by David Y. Hughes & Harry M. Geduld. 1993. 35.00 (0-253-32853-5) Ind U Pr.

Critical Edition of Thomas Middleton's "The Witch" Ed. by Edward J. Esche. LC 92-45122. (Illus.). 328p. 1993. 70.00 (0-8153-1090-0) Garland.

***Critical Education for Work: Multidisciplinary Approaches.** Richard D. Lakes. 224p. (Orig.). 1994. pap. text ed. 19.95 (1-56750-110-9) Ablex Pub.

***Critical Education for Work: Multidisciplinary Approaches.** Ed. by Richard D. Lakes. 224p. (Orig.). 1994. 37.50 (1-56750-109-5) Ablex Pub.

Critical Elections & Congressional Policy Making. David W. Brady. LC 87-18068. (Studies in the New Political History: Vol. 1). 232p. 1988. 35.00 (0-8047-1442-8); pap. 11.95 (0-8047-1840-7) Stanford U Pr.

Critical Employment Issues Facing the Southeast. Ed. by Bruce Kaufman & William T. Rutherford. 239p. 1986. pap. 19.95 (0-88406-191-4, RM98) GA St U Busn Pr.

Critical Encounters: Between Philosophy & Politics. Fred R. Dallmayr. LC 86-40240. 288p. (C). 1989. text ed. 31.95 (0-268-00760-8); pap. text ed. 12.95 (0-268-00774-8) U of Notre Dame Pr.

Critical Encounters: Reference & Responsibility in Deconstructive Writing. Ed. by Cathy Caruth & Deborah Esch. LC 93-39309. (Center for the Critical Analysis of Contemporary Culture Ser.). 340p. (C). 1994. text ed. 50.00 (0-8135-2085-1); pap. text ed. 20.00 (0-8135-2086-X) Rutgers U Pr.

Critical English Translation of Vijnaptimatratatrimsika Treatise in 30 Verses on Mere Consciousness. Swati Ganguly. (C). 1992. 16.00 (0-8364-2801-3, Pub. by Motilal Banarsidass II) S Asia.

Critical Essay on Donald Barthelme. Richard F. Patteson. (Critical Essays on American Literature Ser.). 190p. (C). 1991. text ed. 45.00 (0-8161-7305-2, Hall Reference) G K Hall.

Critical Essay on George Bernard Shaw. Elsie B. Adams. (Critical Essays on British Literature Ser.). 200p. (C). 1991. text ed. 45.00 (0-8161-8858-0, Hall Reference) Macmillan.

Critical Essay on Oscar Wilde. Reginia Gagnier. (Twayne's Critical Essays on British Literature Ser.). 200p. (C). 1991. text ed. 45.00 (0-8161-8860-2, Hall Reference) Macmillan.

Critical Essays. Roland Barthes. Tr. by Richard Howard. xxi, 279p. 1972. pap. 14.95 (0-8101-0589-6) Northwestern U Pr.

Critical Essays. Osbert Burdett. LC 79-99685. (Essay Index Reprint Ser.). 1977. 20.95 (0-8369-1346-9) Ayer.

Critical Essays. Hans M. Enzensberger. Ed. by Reinhold Grimm. LC 81-19612. (German Library: Vol. 98). 320p. 1982. 29.50 (0-8264-0258-5); pap. text ed. 14.95 (0-8264-0268-2) Continuum.

Critical Essays. W. W. Robson. 240p. 1993. text ed. 39.95 (0-312-09612-7) St Martin.

Critical Essays. Erik Stenius. (Acta Philosophica Fennica Ser.: Vol. 25). Date not set. pap. 31.00 (0-444-10360-0) Elsevier.

Critical Essays, Vol. 1. Dionysius of Halicarnassus. Tr. by Stephen Usher. (Loeb Classical Library: No. 465). 670p. 1974. text ed. 18.95 (0-674-99512-0) HUP.

Critical Essays: Gay & Lesbian Writers of Color. Intro. by Emmanuel S. Nelson. LC 93-30614. (Journal of Homosexuality: Vol. 26, Nos. 2-3). 250p. 1993. lib. bdg. 39.95 (1-56024-482-8) Haworth Pr.

Critical Essays: Gay & Lesbian Writers of Color. Intro. by Emmanuel S. Nelson. LC 93-30614. (Journal of Homosexuality: Vol. 26, Nos. 2-3). 250p. 1994. pap. 14.95 (1-56023-048-7) Haworth Pr.

Critical Essays & Literary Fragments. J. Churton Collins. LC 64-16745. (Arber's an English Garner Ser.). 1964. reprint ed. 57.00 (0-8154-0052-7) Cooper Sq.

Critical Essays in American Literature: Romanticism Cloth Edition. Quirk Barbour. LC 85-20649. 354p. 1986. 35.00 (0-8240-9348-8); pap. 18.95 (0-8240-9349-6) Garland.

Critical Essays of Nadine Gordimer. Rowland Smith. (Critical Essays on World Literature Ser.). 232p. (C). 1990. text ed. 45.00 (0-8161-8847-5) G K Hall.

Critical Essays of the Eighteenth Century, 1700-1725. Williar H. Durham. (BCL1-PR English Literature Ser.). 445p. 1992. reprint ed. lib. bdg. 99.00 (0-7812-7000-6) Rprt Serv.

Critical Essays of the Seventeenth Century. Ed. by J. E. Spingarn. Incl. Vol. III. LC 57-10727. 384p. 1957. 12.95 (0-253-31553-0); LC 57-10727. 1957. Vol. III, 384p. write for info. (0-318-53521-1) Ind U Pr.

***Critical Essays of Thornton Wilder.** Blank. 1995. text ed. 42.00 (0-8161-7323-0) G K Hall.

Critical Essays of Washington Irving. Ralph M. Aderman. (Critical Essays on American Literature Ser.). 280p. (C). 1990. text ed. 45.00 (0-8161-8896-3) G K Hall.

Critical Essays on African & Third World Economic Development, Vol. 1: Africa, the Awakening Giant. Wilfred A. Ndongko & Franklin Vivekananda. 218p. (Orig.). 1989. pap. 84.50x (91-86702-05-X, Pub. by Almqv & Wiksell SW) Coronet Bks.

Critical Essays on Albert Camus. Bettina L. Knapp. (Critical Essays Ser.). 176p. 1988. text ed. 45.00 (0-8161-8838-6) G K Hall.

***Critical Essays on Aldous Huxley.** Ed. by Jerome Meckier. LC 95-12209. (Critical Essays on British Literature Ser.). 1995. write for info. (0-8161-8873-4) G K Hall.

Critical Essays on Alexander Pope. Ed. by Wallace Jackson & R. Paul Yoder. LC 93-7761. (Critical Essays on British Literature Ser.). 200p. 1993. text ed. 45.00 (0-8161-8862-9) G K Hall.

Critical Essays on Alfred Lord Tennyson. Herbert F. Tucker. (Critical Essays on British Literature Ser.). 280p. 1993. text ed. 45.00 (0-8161-8864-5, Twayne) Macmillan.

Critical Essays on American Modernism. Michael J. Hoffman. (Critical Essays on American Literature Ser.). 190p. (C). 1992. text ed. 45.00 (0-8161-7307-9) G K Hall.

***Critical Essays on American Postmodernism.** Stanley Trachtenberg. LC 94-26333. (Critical Essays on American Literature Ser.). 240p. 1994. text ed. 45.00 (0-8161-7324-9, Twayne) Macmillan.

Critical Essays on Anne Sexton. Linda Wagner-Martin. (Critical Essays on American Literature Ser.). 272p. 1989. text ed. 45.00 (0-8161-8891-2) G K Hall.

Critical Essays on Anne Tyler. Alice H. Petry. (Critical Essays on American Literature Ser.). 250p. 1992. text ed. 45.00 (0-8161-7308-7, Hall Reference) G K Hall.

Critical Essays on Anthony Burgess. Ed. by Geoffrey Aggeler. 240p. 1986. lib. bdg. 40.00 (0-8161-8757-6) G K Hall.

Critical Essays on Anton Chekov. Thomas Eekman. (Critical Essays Ser.). 216p. 1989. text ed. 45.00 (0-8161-8843-2) G K Hall.

Critical Essays on Arthur Miller. James J. Martine. (Critical Essays on American Literature Ser.). 240p. 1979. text ed. 45.00 (0-8161-8258-2, Hall Reference) Macmillan.

Critical Essays on Benjamin Franklin. Melvin H. Buxbaum. (Critical Essays on American Literature Ser.). 208p. 1987. text ed. 45.00 (0-8161-8699-5) G K Hall.

Critical Essays on Bernard Malamud. Ed. by Joel Salzberg. (Critical Essays on American Literature Ser.). 256p. 1987. lib. bdg. 40.00 (0-8161-8881-5) G K Hall.

Critical Essays on Bertolt Brecht. Siegfried Mews. (Critical Essays on World Literature Ser.). 280p. 1989. text ed. 45.00 (0-8161-8844-0) G K Hall.

Critical Essays on C. F. Woolson. C. Torsney. (Critical Essays on American Literature Ser.). 250p. 1992. text ed. 45.00 (0-8161-7309-5, Hall Reference) Macmillan.

Critical Essays on C. P. Gilman. Joanne B. Karpinsky. (Critical Essays on American Literature Ser.). 200p. 1992. text ed. 45.00 (0-8161-7315-X, Hall Reference) Macmillan.

Critical Essays on C. S. Lewis. Ed. by George Watson. (Critical Thoughts Ser.: Vol. 1). 294p. 1993. 35.00 (0-85967-853-9, Pub. by Scolar Pr UK) Ashgate Pub Co.

Critical Essays on Cervantes. Ruth E. Saffar. (Critical Essays on World Literature Ser.). 240p. (C). 1986. text ed. 45.00 (0-8161-8825-4) G K Hall.

Critical Essays on Charles Dickens' Bleak House. Elliot L. Gilbert. (Critical Essays on British Literature Ser.). 216p. 1989. text ed. 45.00 (0-8161-8771-1) G K Hall.

Critical Essays on Charles Dickens' "Great Expectations" Michael Cotsell. Ed. by Zack R. Bowen. (Critical Essays on British Literature Ser.). 248p. (C). 1990. text ed. 45.00 (0-8161-8852-1) G K Hall.

Critical Essays on Charlotte Bronte. Barbara T. Gates. (Critical Essays on British Literature Ser.). 304p. 1989. text ed. 45.00 (0-8161-8772-X, Twayne) Macmillan.

Critical Essays on Chaucer's Canterbury Tales. Ed. by Malcolm Andrew. 256p. 1991. 65.00 (0-8020-5005-0); pap. 18.95 (0-8020-6936-3) U of Toronto Pr.

Critical Essays on Chaucer's Troilus & Criseyde & His Major Early Poems. Ed. by C. David Benson. 256p. 1991. 65.00 (0-8020-5006-9); pap. 18.95 (0-8020-6937-1) U of Toronto Pr.

Critical Essays on Chinese Literature. Ed. by W. H. Nienhauser, Jr. et al. x, 207p. 1976. text ed. 33.50 (962-201-019-9, Pub. by Chinese Univ HK) Coronet Bks.

Critical Essays on Clifford Odets. Gabriel Miller. (Critical Essays on American Literature Ser.). 288p. (C). 1991. text ed. 45.00 (0-8161-7300-1, Hall Reference) Macmillan.

Critical Essays on Coleridge. Leonard Orr. (Critical Essays on British Literature Ser.). 208p. 1994. text ed. 45.00 (0-8161-8867-X, Twayne) Macmillan.

Critical Essays on D. H. Lawrence. Dennis Jackson & Fleda B. Jackson. (Critical Essays on British Literature Ser.). 240p. 1988. text ed. 45.00 (0-8161-8765-7) G K Hall.

***Critical Essays on Daniel Defoe.** Lund. 1997. 42.00 (0-7838-0007-X) G K Hall.

Critical Essays on Dante. Giuseppe Mazzotta. (Critical Essays in World Literature Ser.). 232p. 1991. text ed. 45.00 (0-8161-8849-1, Hall Reference) Macmillan.

Critical Essays on Denise Levertov. Linda Wagner-Martin. (Critical Essays on American Literature Ser.). 304p. (C). 1990. text ed. 45.00 (0-8161-8899-8) G K Hall.

Critical Essays on Doris Lessing. Claire Sprague & Virginia Tiger. (Critical Essays on British Literature Ser.). 225p. (C). 1986. lib. bdg. 40.00 (0-8161-8756-8) G K Hall.

Critical Essays on Dylan Thomas. George M. Gaston. (Critical Essays on British Literature Ser.). 216p. 1989. text ed. 45.00 (0-8161-8770-3) G K Hall.

Critical Essays on E. B. White. Robert Root. (Critical Essays on American Literature Ser.). 224p. 1994. text ed. 45.00 (0-8161-7321-4, Twayne) Macmillan.

C

1706

An Asterisk (*) at the beginning of an entry indicates that the title is appearing in BIP for the first time.

Critical Essays on e. e. cummings. Guy Rotella. (Critical Essays on American Literature Ser.). 352p. (C). 1984. text ed. 45.00 (*0-8161-8677-4*) G K Hall.

Critical Essays on E. M. Forster. Alan Wilde. (British Literature Ser.). 192p. 1985. text ed. 45.00 (*0-8161-8754-1*) G K Hall.

Critical Essays on Edna St. Vincent Millay. William B. Thesing. (Critical Essays on American Literature Ser.). 200p. 1993. text ed. 45.00 (*0-8161-7310-9*, Twayne) Macmillan.

Critical Essays on Education, Modernity, & the Recovery of the Ecological Imperative. C. A. Bowers. LC 93-18527. 240p. (C). 1993. text ed. 45.00 (*0-8077-3245-1*); pap. text ed. 18.95 (*0-8077-3244-3*) Tchrs Coll.

Critical Essays on Edward Albee. Ed. by Philip C. Kolin & James M. Davis, Jr. (Critical Essays on American Literature Ser.). 240p. 1986. text ed. 45.00 (*0-8161-8875-0*) G K Hall.

Critical Essays on Emily Dickinson. Paul J. Ferlazzo. (Critical Essays on American Literature Ser.). 291p. 1984. text ed. 45.00 (*0-8161-8463-1*) G K Hall.

Critical Essays on Eudora Welty. W. Craig Turner & Lee E. Harding. (Critical Essays on American Literature Ser.). 288p. 1989. text ed. 45.00 (*0-8161-8888-2*) G K Hall.

Critical Essays on Eugene O'Neill. James J. Martins. (Critical Essays on American Literature Ser.). 224p. 1984. text ed. 45.00 (*0-8161-8683-9*) G K Hall.

Critical Essays on Evelyn Waugh. Ed. by James F. Carens. (Critical Essays on British Literature Ser.). 216p. 1987. text ed. 45.00 (*0-8161-8762-2*) G K Hall.

Critical Essays on F. Scott Fitzgerald's "Tender Is the Night" Milton R. Stern. (Critical Essays on American Literature Ser.). 280p. 1986. text ed. 45.00 (*0-8161-8444-5*) G K Hall.

Critical Essays on F. Scott Fitzgerald's "The Great Gatsby" Ed. by Scott Donaldson. (Critical Essays on American Literature Ser.). 304p. 1984. text ed. 45.00 (*0-8161-8679-0*) G K Hall.

Critical Essays on Federico Fellini. Ed. by Peter E. Bondanella & Cristina Degli-Esposti. LC 92-43472. (Critical Essays on Film Ser.). 326p. 1993. text ed. 50.00 (*0-8161-7330-3*) G K Hall.

Critical Essays on Flannery O'Connor. Melvin J. Friedman & Beverly L. Clark. (Critical Essays on American Literature Ser.). 240p. 1985. text ed. 45.00 (*0-8161-8693-6*) G K Hall.

Critical Essays on Ford Madox Ford. Ed. by Richard A. Cassell. (Critical Essays Ser.). 208p. 1987. text ed. 45.00 (*0-8161-8761-4*, Hall Reference) Macmillan.

Critical Essays on Franz Kafka. Ruth V. Gross. (Critical Essays on World Literature Ser.). (C). 1990. text ed. 45.00 (*0-8161-8848-3*) G K Hall.

Critical Essays on Frederick Douglass. William L. Andrews. (Critical Essays on American Literature Ser.). 256p. (C). 1991. text ed. 45.00 (*0-8161-7301-X*, Hall Reference) Macmillan.

Critical Essays on Gabriel Garcia Marquez. Ed. by George R. McMurray. (Critical Essays Ser.). 224p. 1987. text ed. 45.00 (*0-8161-8834-3*, Hall Reference) Macmillan.

Critical Essays on Gabriel Rossetti. D. Riede. (Critical Essays on British Literature Ser.). 250p. 1992. text ed. 45.00 (*0-8161-8863-7*, Hall Reference) Macmillan.

***Critical Essays on Galway Kinnell.** Tuten. 1996. 40.00 (*0-7838-0030-4*) G K Hall.

Critical Essays on George Santayana. Kenneth M. Price & Robert C. Leitz, III. (Critical Essays on American Literature Ser.). 288p. 1991. text ed. 45.00 (*0-8161-7303-6*, Hall Reference) Macmillan.

Critical Essays on Gerard Manley Hopkins. Alison G. Sulloway. (Critical Essays on British Literature Ser.). 208p. 1989. text ed. 45.00 (*0-8161-8773-8*) G K Hall.

Critical Essays on Gertrude Stein. Ed. by Michael J. Hoffman. (Critical Essays on American Literature Ser.). 280p. (C). 1986. lib. bdg. 40.00 (*0-8161-8696-0*) G K Hall.

Critical Essays on Gunter Grass. Ed. by Patrick O'Neill. (Critical Essays on World Literature Ser.). 208p. 1987. text ed. 45.00 (*0-8161-8830-0*) G K Hall.

Critical Essays on Gustave Flaubert. Ed. by Laurence M. Porter. (Critical Essays on World Literature Ser.). 248p. 1986. lib. bdg. 40.00 (*0-8161-8831-9*) G K Hall.

Critical Essays on H. G. Wells. John Huntington. (Critical Essays on British Literature Ser.). 208p. 1991. text ed. 45.00 (*0-8161-8856-4*, Hall Reference) Macmillan.

Critical Essays on H. L. Mencken. Douglas C. Stenerson. (Critical Essays on American Literature Ser.). 228p. 1987. text ed. 45.00 (*0-8161-8694-4*) G K Hall.

Critical Essays on Harold Pinter. Steven H. Gale. (Critical Essays on British Literature Ser.). 360p. 1990. text ed. 45.00 (*0-8161-8853-X*) G K Hall.

Critical Essays on Hawthorne's Short Stories. Albert J. Von Frank. (Critical Essays on American Literature Ser.). 242p. (C). 1990. text ed. 45.00 (*0-8161-1843-4*) G K Hall.

Critical Essays on Hawthorne's "The Scarlet Letter" David B. Kesterton. (Critical Essays Ser.). 216p. 1988. text ed. 45.00 (*0-8161-8883-1*) G K Hall.

Critical Essays on Hemingway's Farewell to Arms. George Monteiro. LC 94-19102. (Critical Essays on American Literature Ser.). 208p. 1994. text ed. 45.00x (*0-7838-0011-8*, Twayne) Macmillan.

***Critical Essays on Hemingway's The Sun Also Rises.** James Nagel. LC 94-34994. (Critical Essays on American Literature Ser.). 1995. lib. bdg. 45.00x (*0-8161-7312-5*, Twayne) Macmillan.

Critical Essays on Henrik Ibsen. Charles R. Lyons. (Critical Essays on World Literature Ser.). 264p. 1987. text ed. 45.00 (*0-8161-8835-1*) G K Hall.

Critical Essays on Henry David Thoreau's Walden. Joel Myerson. (Critical Essays Ser.). 240p. 1988. text ed. 45.00 (*0-8161-8885-8*) G K Hall.

Critical Essays on Henry James. Ed. by Peter Rawlings. (Critical Thoughts Ser.: Vol. 5). 460p. 1993. 55.95 (*0-85967-953-5*, Pub. by Scolar Pr UK) Ashgate Pub Co.

Critical Essays on Henry James: The Early Novels. Ed. by James W. Gargano. (Critical Essays on American Literature Ser.). 224p. 1987. text ed. 45.00 (*0-8161-8876-9*) G K Hall.

Critical Essays on Henry James: The Late Novels. Ed. by James W. Gargano. (Critical Essays on American Literature Ser.). 200p. 1987. text ed. 45.00 (*0-8161-8877-7*) G K Hall.

Critical Essays on Henry Miller. Ronald Gottesman. LC 92-16873. (Critical Essays on American Literature Ser.). 200p. 1992. text ed. 45.00 (*0-8161-7319-2*, Hall Reference) Macmillan.

Critical Essays on Herman Melville's Benito Cereno. Ed. by Robert E. Burkholder. LC 92-10831. (Critical Essays on American Literature Ser.). 250p. 1992. text ed. 45.00 (*0-8161-7317-6*, Hall Reference) Macmillan.

Critical Essays on Herman Melville's Moby Dick. Ed. by Brian Higgins & Hershel Parker. LC 92-16874. (Critical Essays on American Literature Ser.). 200p. 1992. text ed. 45.00 (*0-8161-7318-4*, Hall Reference) Macmillan.

Critical Essays on Honore de Balzac. Martin Kanes. (Critical Essays on World Literature Ser.). 248p. (C). 1990. text ed. 45.00 (*0-8161-8845-9*) G K Hall.

Critical Essays on Indo-Anglian Themes. Murli D. Melwani. (Greybird Ser.). 1976. 5.00 (*0-89253-128-2*) Ind-US Inc.

Critical Essays on Iris Murdoch. Lindsey Tucker. (Critical Essays on British Literature Ser.). 200p. 1992. text ed. 45.00 (*0-8161-8871-8*, Hall Reference) Macmillan.

Critical Essays on Israeli Social Issues & Scholarship: Books on Israel, Vol. III. Ed. by Russell A. Stone & Walter P. Zenner. LC 93-39862. (SUNY Series in Israeli Studies). 268p. (C). 1994. 57.50x (*0-7914-1959-2*); pap. 18.95x (*0-7914-1960-6*) State U NY Pr.

Critical Essays on Israeli Society, Politics, & Culture: Books on Israel, Vol. II. Ed. by Ian S. Lustick & Barry Rubin. LC 90-10055. (SUNY Series in Israeli Studies). 205p. 1991. 49.50 (*0-7914-0646-6*); pap. 16.95 (*0-7914-0647-4*) State U NY Pr.

***Critical Essays on Issac Bashevis.** Farrell. 1995. 40.00 (*0-7838-0028-2*) G K Hall.

Critical Essays on Ivan Turgenev. Ed. by David A. Lowe. (Critical Essays Ser.). 176p. 1988. text ed. 45.00 (*0-8161-8842-4*) G K Hall.

Critical Essays on James Baldwin. Fred L. Standley & Nancy V. Burt. (Critical Essays Ser.). 288p. 1988. text ed. 45.00 (*0-8161-8879-3*) G K Hall.

Critical Essays on James Dickey. Robert Kirschten. (Critical Essays on American Literature Ser.). 264p. 1994. text ed. 42.00 (*0-8161-7311-7*, Twayne) Macmillan.

Critical Essays on James Joyce. Ed. by Bernard Benstock. (Critical Essays on American Literature Ser.). 248p. (C). 1985. text ed. 45.00 (*0-8161-8751-7*) G K Hall.

Critical Essays on James Joyce's "Finnegans Wake." P. McCarthy. (Critical Essays on British Literature Ser.). 250p. 1992. text ed. 45.00 (*0-8161-8870-X*, Hall Reference) Macmillan.

Critical Essays on James Joyce's "Ulysses" Bernard Benstock. (Critical Essays on British Literature Ser.). 344p. 1989. text ed. 45.00 (*0-8161-8766-5*) G K Hall.

***Critical Essays on James Merrill.** Rotella. 1996. 40.00 (*0-7838-0031-2*) G K Hall.

Critical Essays on Jean-Paul Sartre. Ed. by Robert Wilcocks. (Critical Essays on World Literature Ser.). 278p. 1988. text ed. 45.00 (*0-8161-8839-4*) G K Hall.

***Critical Essays on Jean Toomer.** Jones. 1995. 40.00 (*0-7838-0025-8*) G K Hall.

Critical Essays on John Cheever. Robert G. Collins. (Critical Essays on American Literature Ser.). 1982. lib. bdg. 40.00 (*0-8161-8623-5*) G K Hall.

***Critical Essays on John Donne.** Arthur F. Marotti. (Critical Essays on British Literature Ser.). 1994. lib. bdg. 42.00x (*0-8161-8769-X*, Twayne) Macmillan.

Critical Essays on John Fowles. Ed. by Ellen Pifer. (Critical Essays on British Literature Ser.). 192p. 1986. lib. bdg. 40.00 (*0-8161-8759-2*) G K Hall.

Critical Essays on John Hawkes. Stanley Trachtenberg. (Critical Essays on American Literature Ser.). 200p. 1991. text ed. 45.00 (*0-8161-7304-4*, Hall Reference) Macmillan.

Critical Essays on John Keats. Hermione De Almeida. (Critical Essays on British Literature Ser.). 352p. 1990. text ed. 45.00 (*0-8161-8851-3*) G K Hall.

Critical Essays on John Millington Synge. Daniel J. Casey. (Critical Essays on British Literature Ser.). 200p. 1994. text ed. 45.00 (*0-7838-0006-1*, Twayne) Macmillan.

***Critical Essays on John Milton.** Christopher Kendrick. LC 94-36080. (Critical Essays on British Literature Ser.). 1995. lib. bdg. 45.00x (*0-8161-8874-2*, Twayne) Macmillan.

Critical Essays on John O'Hara. Ed. by Philip B. Eppard. LC 94-6642. (Critical Essays on American Literature Ser.). 280p. 1994. text ed. 42.00 (*0-7838-0026-6*) G K Hall.

Critical Essays on Jonathan Swift. Ed. by Frank Palmeri. LC 92-42993. (Critical Essays on British Literature Ser.). 288p. 1993. text ed. 45.00 (*0-7838-0003-7*) G K Hall.

Critical Essays on Jonathan Swift. Frank Palmeri. (Critical Essays on British Literature Ser.). 200p. 1993. lib. bdg. 40.00 (*0-685-60864-6*, Twayne) Macmillan.

Critical Essays on Jorge Luis Borges. Ed. by Jaime Alazraki. (Critical Essays on World Literature Ser.). 208p. 1987. text ed. 45.00 (*0-8161-8829-7*) G K Hall.

Critical Essays on Joseph Conrad. Ted Billy. (Critical Essays on British Literature Ser.). 208p. (C). 1987. text ed. 45.00 (*0-8161-8763-0*) G K Hall.

***Critical Essays on Kate Chopin.** Petry. 1996. 42.00 (*0-7838-0032-0*) G K Hall.

***Critical Essays on Katherine Anne Porter.** Unrue. 1997. 45.00 (*0-7838-0022-3*) G K Hall.

Critical Essays on Katherine Mansfield. Ed. by Rhoda B. Nathan. LC 93-2963. (Critical Essays on British Literature Ser.). 300p. 1993. text ed. 45.00 (*0-8161-8868-8*, Hall Reference) Macmillan.

***Critical Essays on Kay Boyle: <.** Elkins. 1997. 42.00 (*0-7838-0012-6*) G K Hall.

Critical Essays on Kurt Vonnegut. Robert Merrill. (Critical Essays on American Literature Ser.). 248p. 1989. text ed. 45.00 (*0-8161-8893-9*) G K Hall.

Critical Essays on Langston Hughes. Edward J. Mullen. (Critical Essays on American Literature Ser.). 211p. (C). 1986. text ed. 45.00 (*0-8161-8697-9*) G K Hall.

Critical Essays on Language Use & Psychology. D. C. O'Connell. xx, 351p. 1988. pap. 41.00 (*0-387-96703-6*) Spr-Verlag.

Critical Essays on Lillian Hellman. Mark W. Estrin. (Critical Essays on American Literature Ser.). 288p. 1989. text ed. 45.00 (*0-8161-8890-4*) G K Hall.

Critical Essays on Lionel Trilling. John Rodden. (Critical Thoughts Ser.: Vol. 6). 400p. 1994. 35.00 (*0-85967-890-3*, Pub. by Scolar Pr UK) Ashgate Pub Co.

Critical Essays on Lord Byron. Robert F. Gleckner. (Critical Essays on British Literature Ser.). 200p. (C). 1991. text ed. 45.00 (*0-8161-8859-9*, Hall Reference) Macmillan.

Critical Essays on Louis-Ferdinand Celine. Ed. by William K. Buckley. (Critical Essays on World Literature Ser.). 272p. 1988. text ed. 45.00 (*0-8161-8841-6*) G K Hall.

Critical Essays on Margaret Atwood. Ed. by Judith McCombs. (Critical Essays on World Literature Ser.). 312p. 1988. text ed. 45.00 (*0-8161-8840-8*) G K Hall.

Critical Essays on Mark Twain, 1910-1980. Louis J. Budd. (Critical Essays on American Literature Ser.). 256p. 1983. text ed. 45.00 (*0-8161-8652-9*) G K Hall.

Critical Essays on Mary Wilkins Freeman. Shirley Marchalonis. (Critical Essays on American Literature Ser.). 200p. 1991. text ed. 45.00 (*0-8161-7306-0*, Hall Reference) Macmillan.

Critical Essays on Melville's "Billy Budd" Robert Milder. (Critical Essays on American Literature Ser.). 264p. (C). 1989. text ed. 45.00 (*0-8161-8889-0*) G K Hall.

Critical Essays on Michel Foucault. Ed. by Peter Burke. (Critical Thoughts Ser.: Vol. 2). 242p. 1992. 55.95 (*0-85967-854-7*, Pub. by Scolar Pr UK) Ashgate Pub Co.

Critical Essays on Milton from ELH. ELH Staff et al. LC 71-93296. (English Literary History Ser.). 290p. (C). 1969. pap. 12.95 (*0-8018-1094-9*) Johns Hopkins.

Critical Essays on Muriel Spark. Ed. by Joseph Hynes. LC 92-19137. (Critical Essays on British Literature Ser.). 200p. 1992. text ed. 45.00 (*0-8161-8869-6*, Hall Reference) Macmillan.

Critical Essays on Nathanael West. Ben Siegel. LC 94-14474. (Critical Essays on American Literature Ser.). 248p. 1994. text ed. 45.00 (*0-7838-0027-4*) G K Hall.

Critical Essays on Native American Literature. Andrew O. Wiget. (Critical Essays on American Literature Ser.). (C). 1985. lib. bdg. 40.00 (*0-8161-8687-1*) G K Hall.

***Critical Essays on Native Son.** Kinnamon. 1996. 42.00 (*0-7838-0013-4*) G K Hall.

Critical Essays on Patrick White. Peter Wolfe. (Critical Essays on World Literature Ser.). 280p. (C). 1990. text ed. 45.00 (*0-8161-8846-7*) G K Hall.

Critical Essays on Peter Taylor. Hubert H. McAlexander. (Critical Essays on American Literature Ser.). 200p. 1993. text ed. 45.00 (*0-8161-7322-2*, Twayne) Macmillan.

Critical Essays on Post Impressionism. Carl Donnell-Kotrozo. LC 81-65879. (Illus.). 176p. 1983. 37.50 (*0-87982-041-1*) Art Alliance.

Critical Essays on Robert Bly. William V. Davis. (Critical Essays on American Literature Ser.). 200p. 1992. text ed. 45.00 (*0-8161-7316-8*, Twayne) Macmillan.

Critical Essays on Robert Browning. Mary E. Gibson. (Critical Essays on British Literature Ser.). 250p. 1992. text ed. 45.00 (*0-8161-8861-0*, Hall Reference) Macmillan.

Critical Essays on Robert Frost. Ed. by Philip L. Gerber. (Critical Essays on American Literature Ser.). 264p. 1982. text ed. 45.00 (*0-8161-8442-9*) G K Hall.

Critical Essays on Robinson Jeffers. James Karman. (Critical Essays on American Literature Ser.). 288p. 1990. text ed. 45.00 (*0-8161-8897-1*) G K Hall.

Critical Essays on Rudyard Kipling. Ed. by Harold Orel. (Critical Essays on British Literature Ser.). 248p. 1989. text ed. 45.00 (*0-8161-8767-3*) G K Hall.

Critical Essays on Salinger's "The Catcher in the Rye" Joel Salzberg. (Critical Essays on American Literature Ser.). 248p. 1989. text ed. 45.00 (*0-8161-8894-7*) G K Hall.

Critical Essays on Samuel Beckett. Lance S. Butler. LC 93-18344. (Critical Thoughts Ser.: Vol. 4). 345p. 1993. 59.95 (*0-85967-871-7*, Pub. by Scolar Pr UK) Ashgate Pub Co.

Critical Essays on Samuel Beckett. Patrick A. McCarthy. (Critical Essays on British Literature Ser.). 240p. 1986. lib. bdg. 40.00 (*0-8161-8760-6*) G K Hall.

***Critical Essays on Samuel Johnson.** Vance. 1997. 45.00 (*0-7838-0023-1*) G K Hall.

Critical Essays on Sarah Orne Jewett. Gwen L. Nagel. (Critical Essays on American Literature Ser.). 264p. 1984. lib. bdg. 40.00 (*0-8161-8422-4*) G K Hall.

***Critical Essays on Seamus Heaney.** Robert F. Garratt. LC 94-48144. (Critical Essays on British Literature Ser.). 1995. write for info. (*0-7838-0004-5*) G K Hall.

***Critical Essays on Shakespeare's Hamlet.** David S. Kastan. LC 94-46650. (Critical Essays on British Literature Ser.). 1995. write for info. (*0-7838-0001-0*) G K Hall.

Critical Essays on Shakespeare's Othello. Anthony Barthelemy. (Critical Essays on British Literature Ser.). 256p. 1994. text ed. 45.00x (*0-8161-8866-1*, Twayne) Macmillan.

Critical Essays on Simone de Beauvoir. Elaine Marks. (Critical Essays Ser.). 280p. 1987. text ed. 45.00 (*0-8161-8836-X*) G K Hall.

Critical Essays on Sinclair Lewis. Ed. by Martin Bucco. (Critical Essays on American Literature Ser.). 256p. 1986. lib. bdg. 40.00 (*0-8161-8698-7*) G K Hall.

Critical Essays on Sir Arthur Conan Doyle. Harold Orel. (Critical Essays on British Literature Ser.). 250p. 1992. text ed. 45.00 (*0-8161-8865-3*, Hall Reference) Macmillan.

***Critical Essays on Sir Walter Scott.** Shaw. 1996. 40.00 (*0-7838-0005-3*) G K Hall.

Critical Essays on Spenser from ELH. ELH Staff. LC 76-123199. (English Literary History Ser.). 257p. (Orig.). 1970. pap. 12.95 (*0-8018-1199-6*) Johns Hopkins.

Critical Essays on Steinbeck's "The Grapes of Wrath" John Ditsky. (Critical Essays on American Literature Ser.). 216p. 1989. text ed. 45.00 (*0-8161-8887-4*) G K Hall.

Critical Essays on Stephen Crane's "The Red Badge of Courage" Donald Pizer. Ed. by James Nagel. (Critical Essays on American Literature Ser.). 264p. (C). 1990. text ed. 45.00 (*0-8161-8898-X*) G K Hall.

***Critical Essays on Susan Glaspell.** Ed. by Linda Ben-Zui. 320p. 1995. text ed. 39.50x (*0-472-10549-3*) U of Mich Pr.

Critical Essays on Sylvia Plath. Ed. by Linda Wagner. (Critical Essays on American Literature Ser.). 240p. 1984. text ed. 45.00 (*0-8161-8682-0*) G K Hall.

Critical Essays on T. S. Eliot's "The Waste Land." Lois A. Cuddy & David Hirsch. (Critical Essays on American Literature Ser.). 288p. (C). 1991. text ed. 45.00 (*0-8161-7302-8*, Hall Reference) Macmillan.

Critical Essays on Ted Hughes. Leonard Scigaj. (Critical Essays on British Literature Ser.). 200p. 1992. text ed. 45.00 (*0-8161-8872-6*, Hall Reference) Macmillan.

Critical Essays on "The Adventures of Tom Sawyer" Ed. by Gary Scharnhorst. LC 92-43993. (Critical Essays on American Literature Ser.). 264p. 1993. text ed. 45.00 (*0-8161-7320-6*) G K Hall.

Critical Essays on the Literatures of Spain & Spanish America. Ed. by L. T. Gonzalez-del-Valle & Julio Baena. LC 91-62081. 1992. pap. 50.00 (*0-89295-064-1*) Society Sp & Sp-Am.

***Critical Essays on Thomas Berger.** David W. Madden. (Critical Essays on American Literature Ser.). 1995. lib. bdg. 45.00x (*0-7838-0029-0*, Twayne) Macmillan.

Critical Essays on Thomas Hardy: The Novels. Dale Kramer. (Critical Essays on British Literature Ser.). 286p. (C). 1990. text ed. 45.00 (*0-8161-8850-5*) G K Hall.

***Critical Essays on Thomas Hardy's Poetry.** Harold Orel. LC 94-27561. (Critical Essays on British Literature Ser.). 208p. 1994. lib. bdg. 42.00x (*0-8161-8768-1*, Twayne) Macmillan.

Critical Essays on Thomas Mann. Inta Ezergailis. (Critical Essays on World Literature Ser.). 264p. 1988. text ed. 45.00 (*0-8161-8837-8*) G K Hall.

***Critical Essays on Thornton Wilder.** Ed. by Martin Blank. LC 95-2274. (Critical Essays on American Literature Ser.). 1995. write for info. (*0-7838-0020-7*) G K Hall.

Critical Essays on Tom Stoppard. Anthony Jenkins. (Critical Essays on British Literature Ser.). 224p. 1990. lib. bdg. 36.00 (*0-685-46296-X*) G K Hall.

Critical Essays on Toni Morrison. Nellie Y. McKay. (Critical Essays Ser.). 216p. 1988. text ed. 45.00 (*0-8161-8884-X*) G K Hall.

Critical Essays on Virginia Woolf. Ed. by Morris Beja. (Critical Essays on British Literature Ser.). 264p. 1985. text ed. 45.00 (*0-8161-8753-3*) G K Hall.

Critical Essays on W. B. Yeats. Richard J. Finneran. (Critical Essays on British Literature Ser.). 264p. 1986. text ed. 45.00 (*0-8161-8758-4*) G K Hall.

Critical Essays on W. H. Auden. George W. Bahlke. (Critical Essays on British Literature Ser.). 200p. (C). 1991. text ed. 45.00 (*0-8161-8855-6*, Hall Reference) Macmillan.

Critical Essays on Walker Percy. J. Donald Crowley. (Critical Essays on American Literature Ser.). 264p. (C). 1989. text ed. 45.00 (*0-8161-8880-7*) G K Hall.

Critical Essays on Wallace Stevens. Ed. by Steven G. Axelrod & Helen Deese. (Critical Essays Ser.). 272p. 1988. text ed. 45.00 (*0-8161-8886-6*) G K Hall.

Critical Essays on Walt Whitman. Ed. by James Woodress. (Critical Essays on American Literature Ser.). 352p. 1983. text ed. 45.00 (*0-8161-8632-4*) G K Hall.

Critical Essays on Willa Cather. Ed. by John J. Murphy. (Critical Essays on American Literature Ser.). 344p. (C). 1984. text ed. 45.00 (*0-8161-8676-6*) G K Hall.

Critical Essays on William Blake. Hazard Adams et al. (Critical Essays on British Literature Ser.). 256p. 1991. text ed. 45.00 (*0-8161-8857-2*, Hall Reference) Macmillan.

***Critical Essays on William Carlos Williams.** Helen Deese & Steven G. Axelrod. (Critical Essays on American Literature Ser.). 1995. lib. bdg. 42.00x (*0-7838-0015-0*, Twayne) Macmillan.

Critical Essays on William Empson. Ed. by John Constable. (Critical Thoughts Ser.: Vol. 3). 400p. 1993. 35.00 (*0-85967-884-9*, Pub. by Scolar Pr UK) Ashgate Pub Co.

Critical Essays on William Faulkner: The McCaslin Family. Arthur F. Kinney. (Critical Essays on American Literature Ser.). 288p. 1990. text ed. 45.00 (*0-8161-8895-5*) G K Hall.

C

An Asterisk (*) at the beginning of an entry indicates that the title is appearing in BIP for the first time.

Critical Essays on William Faulkner: The Sartoris Family. Ed. by Arthur F. Kinney. (Critical Essays on American Literature Ser.). 1985. text ed. 45.00 (0-8161-8690-1) G K Hall.

***Critical Essays on William Faulkner: The Sutpen Family.** Ed. by Arthur F. Kinney. LC 94-44656. (Critical Essays on American Literature Ser.). 1995. write for info. (0-8161-7314-1) G K Hall.

Critical Essays on William Golding. Ed. by James R. Baker. (Critical Essays on British Literature Ser.). 216p. 1988. text ed. 45.00 (0-8161-8764-9) G K Hall.

***Critical Essays on William Saroyan.** Ed. by Harry Keyishian. LC 94-48129. (Critical Essays on American Literature Ser.). 1995. write for info. (0-7838-0018-5) G K Hall.

Critical Essays on William Wordsworth. George H. Gilpin, Jr. Ed. by Zack R. Bowen. (Critical Essays on British Literature Ser.). 360p. (C). 1990. text ed. 45.00 (0-8161-8774-6) G K Hall.

***Critical Essays on Zora Neale Hurston.** Cronin. 1997. 45.00 (0-7838-0021-5) G K Hall.

Critical Essays, Vol. II. Dionysius of Halicarnassus. (Loeb Classical Library: No. 466). 454p. 1985. text ed. 18.95 (0-674-99513-9) HUP.

Critical Etymological Dictionary of the Spanish Language (Diccionario Critico Etimologico de la Lengua Espanala), 6 vols., Set. 2nd ed. J. Corominas & J. A. Pascual. 6000p. (SPA.). 1991. 695.00 (0-7859-3343-3, S11937) Fr & Eur.

Critical Evaluation of Albert Henry Newman (1852-1933), Church Historian. William G. Jonas, Jr. LC 92-19310. 212p. 1992. lib. bdg. 89.95 (0-7734-9798-6) E Mellen.

Critical Evaluation of Alternatives to Acute Ocular Irritation Testing. Ed. by Alan M. Goldberg. (Alternative Methods in Toxicology Ser.: Vol. 4). 138p. 1987. 148.00 (0-913113-09-3) M Liebert.

Critical Evaluation of Cardiac Rehabilitation, Tel-Aviv, Nov.-Dec. 1975: Proceedings of the Meeting on Critical Evaluation of Cardiac Rehabilitation, Tel-Aviv, Nov.-Dec. 1975. Meeting on Critical Evaluation of Cardiac Rehabilitation Staff. Ed. by J. J. Kellerman. (Bibliotheca Cardiologica Ser.: No. 36). (Illus.). 1977. 49.75 (3-8055-2373-4) S Karger.

Critical Evaluation of Comparative Financial Accounting Thought in America: 1900-1920. Gary J. Previts. Ed. by Richard P. Brief. LC 80-1517. (Dimensions of Accounting Theory & Practice Ser.). 1980. lib. bdg. 28.95 (0-405-13496-7) Ayer.

Critical Evaluation of Equilibrium Constants Involving Hydroxyquinoline & Its Metal Chelates: Critical Evaluation of Equilibrium Constants in Solutions: Pt. A: Stability Constants of Metal Complexes. Ed. by J. Stary et al. (Chemical Data Ser.: Vol. 24). (Illus.). 1979. pap. 27.00 (0-08-023929-3, Pub. by Pergamon Repr UK) Franklin.

Critical Evaluation of the Chicago School of Antitrust Analysis. Ingo L. Schmidt & Jan B. Rittaler. (C). 1989. lib. bdg. 77.50 (90-247-3792-3) Kluwer Ac.

Critical Evaluation of the Suitability of Karl Rahner's Sacramental Ecclesiology for a World Church. James J. Woolever. LC 91-43791. 684p. 1992. lib. bdg. 129.95 (0-7734-9941-5) E Mellen.

***Critical Events: An Anthropological Approach to Contemporary India.** Veena Das. 275p. 1995. text ed. 22.00 (0-19-563540-X) OUP.

Critical Events in Teaching & Learning. Peter Woods. LC 93-9071. 76p. 1993. 75.00 (0-7507-0232-X, Falmer Pr); pap. 27.50 (0-7507-0233-8, Falmer Pr) Taylor & Francis.

Critical Examination of Socialism. William H. Hallock. 328p. 1989. 39.95 (0-88738-264-9) Transaction Pubs.

Critical Examination of the Dual Ladder Approach to Career Advancement. Laurie M. Roth. 1982. pap. 12.00 (0-317-11510-3) CU Ctr Career Res.

Critical Examination of the First Principles of Geology. George B. Greenough. Ed. by Claude C. Albritton, Jr. LC 77-6520. (History of Geology Ser.). 1978. reprint ed. lib. bdg. 30.95 (0-405-10442-1) Ayer.

Critical Examination of the Orientation Postulate in Accounting with Particular Attention to Its Historical Development. Stephen A. Zeff. Ed. by Richard P. Brief. LC 77-87306. (Development of Contemporary Accounting Thought Ser.). 1978. lib. bdg. 24.95 (0-405-10945-8) Ayer.

Critical Examination of the Peshitta Version of the Book of Ezra. Charles A. Hawley. LC 24-1925. (Columbia University. Contributions to Oriental History & Philology Ser.: No. 8). reprint ed. 12.50 (0-404-50538-4) AMS Pr.

***Critical Experience.** David Cowles et al. 368p. (C). 1994. per., pap. text ed. 13.56 (0-7872-0012-3) Kendall-Hunt.

Critical Eye: An Introduction to Looking at Movies. Kasdan & Saxton. 240p. 1993. per. 20.50 (0-8403-8593-5) Kendall-Hunt.

Critical Eye: Thematic Readings for Writers. Sally T. Taylor. (Illus.). 711p. (Orig.). (C). 1990. pap. text ed. 20.00 (0-03-025458-2) HB Coll Pubs.

Critical Eye: Thematic Readings for Writers. 2nd ed. Sally T. Taylor. (Illus.). 736p. (Orig.). (C). 1993. pap. text ed. write for info. (0-15-500589-8) HB Coll Pubs.

Critical Eye I. John T. Paoletti. LC 83-51290. (Illus.). 87p. 1984. 12.95 (0-930606-46-9) Yale Ctr Brit Art.

Critical Fable. Amy Lowell. LC 78-64043. (Des Imagistes: Literature of the Imagist Movement Ser.). 112p. reprint ed. 17.50 (0-404-17126-5) AMS Pr.

Critical Factors in Localized Corrosion. Ed. by G. S. Frankel & R. C. Newman. LC 92-71335. (Proceedings Ser.: Vol. 92-9). 550p. 1992. 54.00 (1-56677-009-2) Electrochem Soc.

Critical Factors in Why Disadvantaged Students Succeed or Fail in School. Reginald M. Clark. 19p. 1988. pap. 2.00 (0-685-59933-7) Acad Educ Dev.

Critical Factors in Why Disadvantaged Students Succeed or Fail in School. Reginald M. Clark. 19p. 1988. 2.00 (0-86510-059-4) Natl Inst Work.

Critical Fall & Rise of John Marston. Fred Wharton. (LCENG Ser.). xiv, 134p. 1994. 55.95 (1-879751-89-5) Camden Hse.

Critical Features of Piaget's Theory of the Development of Thought. Ed. by Frank B. Murray. LC 72-6359. 196p. 1972. pap. text ed. 9.95 (0-8422-0244-7) Irvington.

Critical Feminism Argument in the Disciplines. Kate Campbell. (Ideas & Production Ser.). 192p. 1992. pap. 29.00 (0-335-09757-X, Open Univ Pr) Taylor & Francis.

Critical Fictions: The Politics of Imaginative Writing. Ed. by Philomena Mariani. LC 89-650815. (Discussions in Contemporary Culture Ser.: No. 7). 304p. (Orig.). 1991. pap. 15.95 (0-941920-24-0) Bay Pr.

Critical Focus: The Black & White Photographs of Harvey Wilson Richards. Paul D. Richards. 104p. (Orig.). 1987. pap. 12.95 (0-9618725-0-0) Estuary Pr.

Critical Fortunes of a Romantic Novel: Novalis's Heinrich von Ofterdingen. Dennis F. Mahoney. LC 94-11094. (Studies in German Literature, Linguistics, & Culture). 175p. 1994. 54.95 (1-879751-58-5) Camden Hse.

Critical Genealogies: Historical Situations for Postmodern Literary Studies. Jonathan Arac. LC 86-26984. (Social Foundations of Aesthetic Forms Ser.). 288p. 1989. text ed. 47.50 (0-231-06254-0); pap. text ed. 16.50 (0-231-06255-9) Col U Pr.

Critical Guide to Catholic Reference Books. 3rd rev. ed. James P. McCabe. (Research Studies in Library Science: No. 20). 323p. 1989. lib. bdg. 47.00 (0-87287-621-7) Libs Unl.

Critical Guide to Horror Film Series. Ken Hanke. LC 91-19952. 388p. 1991. 51.00 (0-8240-5545-4, H1214) Garland.

Critical Guide to the Kwangtung Provincial Archives Deposited at the Public Record Office, London. David Pong. (East Asian Monographs: No. 63). 400p. 1975. pap. 14.00 (0-674-17722-3) HUP.

Critical Handbook of Children's Literature. 4th ed. Rebecca J. Lukens. (C). 1989. pap. text ed. 16.25 (0-673-38773-9) HarpCollege.

Critical Handbook of Children's Literature. 5th ed. Ed. by Rebecca J. Lukens & Cline. LC 93-42826. 352p. (C). 1994. text ed. 17.25 (0-673-46937-9) HarpCollege.

Critical Handbook of Young Adult & Children's Literature. 5th ed. Ed. by Rebecca J. Lukens & Cline. (C). 1994. text ed. 20.00 (0-06-501108-2) HarpCollege.

Critical Hermeneutics: A Study in the Thought of Paul Ricoeur & Jurgen Habermas. John B. Thompson. LC 80-41935. 257p. 1984. pap. 25.95 (0-521-27666-7) Cambridge U Pr.

Critical Hermeneutics & Social Research. 160p. 1993. pap. text ed. 9.00 (1-879771-09-8) Global Pub NJ.

Critical Hermeneutics & Shakespeare's History Plays. William M. Hawley. LC 91-27576. (American University Studies: English Language & Literature: Ser. IV, Vol. 138). 227p. (C). 1992. text ed. 39.95 (0-8204-1682-7) P Lang Pubs.

Critical Historian. G. Kitson Clark. Ed. by Robin W. Winks. Bd. with Guide for Research Students Working on Historical Subjects. LC 83-49175. LC 83-49175. (History & Historiography Ser.). 267p. 1985. Set lib. bdg. 35.00 (0-8240-6354-6) Garland.

Critical Historians of Art. Michael Podro. LC 82-4934. (Illus.). 260p. 1982. 45.00 (0-300-02862-8) Yale U Pr.

Critical Historians of Art. Michael Podro. LC 82-4934. (Illus.). 260p. 1984. reprint ed. pap. 15.00 (0-300-03240-4, Y-499) Yale U Pr.

Critical History of Children's Literature. Meigs. 1987. 19.95 (0-02-583900-4) Macmillan.

Critical History of French Poetry. Michael Bishop. (Twayne's Critical History of Poetry Ser.). 384p. 1993. text ed. 29.95 (0-8057-8453-5, Twayne) Macmillan.

Critical History of Modern Aesthetics. Earl of Listowell. LC 75-1009. (Studies in Comparative Literature: No. 35). 1974. lib. bdg. 75.00 (0-8383-1958-0) M S G Haskell Hse.

Critical History of Modern Aesthetics. W. A. Listowel. 1972. 59.95 (0-87968-966-8) Gordon Pr.

Critical History of Nepal. Dhundy R. Bhandari. 120p. 1950. 15.00 (0-318-12870-5, 24) Am-Nepal Ed.

Critical History of the Doctrine of a Future Life, in Israel, in Judaism, & in Christianity. Robert H. Charles. LC 79-8600. reprint ed. 38.50 (0-404-18455-3) AMS Pr.

Critical History of Western Philosophy. Ed. by D. J. O'Connor. (C). 1985. pap. 17.95 (0-02-923840-4) Free Pr.

Critical Humanism As a Philosophy of Culture: The Case of E. P. Papanoutos. John Anton. (Modern Greek History & Culture Ser.). 1981. 10.00 (0-935476-07-5) Nostos Bks.

Critical I. Norman N. Holland. 224p. 1992. text ed. 35.00 (0-231-07650-9) Col U Pr.

Critical I. Norman N. Holland. 288p. 1993. pap. 15.50 (0-231-07651-7) Col U Pr.

Critical Idyll: Traditional Values & the French Revolution in Goethe's Hermann und Dorothea. Peter Morgan. (Studies in German Literature, Linguistics & Culture: Vol. 59). 186p. 1991. 43.00 (0-938100-85-8) Camden Hse.

Critical Image: Essays on Contemporary Photography. Ed. by Carol Squiers. LC 89-81357. (Illus.). 240p. (C). 1990. 18.95 (0-941920-14-3); pap. 14.95 (0-941920-15-1) Bay Pr.

Critical Incident Management. Rod Paschall. (Illus.). 104p. (Orig.). 1992. pap. 9.50 (0-942511-54-9) OICJ.

Critical Incident Stress & Trauma in the Workplace. Gerald Lewis. 134p. (Orig.). 1994. pap. text ed. 18.95 (1-55959-054-8) Accel Devel.

***Critical Incident Stress Debriefing: An Operations Manual for the Prevention of Traumatic Stress among Emergency Services & Disaster Workers.** 2nd ed. Jeffrey T. Mitchell & George S. Everly, Jr. (Illus.). 304p. (Orig.). 1995. pap. text ed. 30.00 (1-883581-02-8) Chevron Pub.

***Critical Incident Stress Debriefing: The Basic Course Workbook.** Jeffrey T. Mitchell & George S. Everly, Jr. (Illus.). 78p. 1995. 7.00 (0-9646356-0-7) ICISF.

Critical Incident Stress Debriefing - Three-Fourths Inch. ASVP Staff. 1991. 159.95 (1-56200-401-8) Mosby Yr Bk.

Critical Incident Stress Debriefing-PAL. ASVP Staff. 1991. 149.95 (1-56200-402-6) Mosby Yr Bk.

Critical Incident Technique: A Bibliography. 2nd ed. Ed. by Grace Fivars. 1980. pap. 7.50 (0-89785-662-7) Am Inst Res.

Critical Incidents in Group Therapy. Jeremiah Donigian & Richard Malnati. LC 86-1011. (Psychology Ser.). 239p. (C). 1987. pap. 27.95 (0-534-06282-2) Brooks-Cole.

Critical Incidents in Management. 6th ed. John M. Champion & John J. James. 352p. (C). 1988. pap. text ed. 32.50 (0-256-06825-9) Irwin.

Critical Incidents in Teaching: Developing Professional Judgment. David Tripp. LC 93-13435. 1994. write for info. (0-415-09542-5) Routledge.

Critical Index: A Bibliography of Articles on Film in English, 1946-1973, Arranged by Names & Topics. John C. Gerlach & Lana Gerlach. LC 74-1959. (New Humanistic Research Ser.). 774p. reprint ed. pap. 180.00 (0-685-12280-8, 2026015) Bks Demand.

Critical Influences on Child Language Acquisition & Development. Ed. by David J. Messer & Geoffrey J. Turner. LC 92-18461. 1993. text ed. 59.95 (0-312-08474-9) St Martin.

Critical Information Network: The Next Generation of Executive Information Systems. Thomas P. McAuliffe & Carolyn S. Shamlin. (Illus.). 130p. 1992. pap. 29.95 (0-9633121-7-0) McAuliffe & Co.

***Critical Inquiry into American Politics.** Larry Tomlinson & Alan Balboni. 432p. (C). 1994. per., pap. text ed. 41.95 (0-8403-9579-5) Kendall-Hunt.

Critical Inquiry into American Politics. 3rd ed. K. Larry Tomlinson. 432p. 1993. per. 39.95 (0-8403-8319-3) Kendall-Hunt.

Critical Interventions in Psychotherapy. Haim Omer. 192p. 1994. 23.00 (0-393-70182-4) Norton.

Critical Introduction to Don Quixote. L. A. Murillo. 270p. (C). 1988. pap. 29.95 (0-685-44145-8) P Lang Pubs.

Critical Introduction to Henry Green's Novels: The Living Vision. Oddvar Holmesland. LC 85-18485. 260p. 1986. text ed. 35.00 (0-312-17471-3) St Martin.

Critical Introduction to Twentieth-Century American Drama: 1900-1940, Vol. 1. C. W. Bigsby. LC 81-18000. 352p. reprint ed. pap. 100.40 (0-685-15546-3, 2026333) Bks Demand.

Critical Introduction to Twentieth Century American Drama, Vol. 1: 1900-1940. C. W. Bigsby. LC 81-18000. (Illus.). 340p. 1982. pap. 22.95 (0-521-27116-9) Cambridge U Pr.

Critical Introduction to Twentieth-Century American Drama, Vol. 2: Tennessee Williams, Arthur Miller, Edward Albee. C. W. Bigsby. (Illus.). 369p. 1985. pap. 22.95 (0-521-27717-5) Cambridge U Pr.

Critical Introduction to Twentieth-Century American Drama, Vol. 3: Beyond Broadway. C. W. Bigsby. (Illus.). 400p. 1985. pap. 22.95 (0-521-27896-1) Cambridge U Pr.

Critical Inventory of Ramayana Studies in the World, Vol. I. Ed. by K. Krishnamoorthy. (C). 1991. text ed. 29.00 (81-7201-100-8, Pub. by Sahitya Akademi II) S Asia.

Critical Inventory of Ramayana Studies in the World, Vol. 2: Foreign Languages. Ed. by K. Krishnamoorthy. (C). 1993. 16.00 (81-7201-507-0, Pub. by Sahitya Akademi II) S Asia.

Critical Issues. Elizabeth Warner & Richard Alden. 319p. (C). 1991. pap. text ed. 28.30 (1-56226-049-9) CT Pub.

Critical Issues: Drunk Driving Prosecutions. LC 90-61615. 1990. 105.00 (0-317-02933-9); Suppl. 1993. 37.00 (0-317-03965-2) Lawyers Cooperative.

Critical Issues: Freedom of Information Acts. LC 90-61614. 1990. 105.00 (0-317-02934-7); Suppl. 1993. 37.00 (0-317-03966-0) Lawyers Cooperative.

Critical Issues & Answers: Issues That Must Be Resolved If We Are to Survive. Eli V. Gaiani. LC 94-17499. 129p. (Orig.). 1994. pap. 20.00 (0-912526-72-6) Lib Res.

Critical Issues, Critical Choices: Special Topics in Child Support Guidelines Development. Intro. by Women's Legal Defense Fund Staff. 160p. (Orig.). 1987. pap. 17.00 (0-932689-18-3) Women's Legal Defense.

Critical Issues, Developments, & Trends in Professional Psychology, Vol. 1. Ed. by Regis McNamara & Allan G. Barclay. LC 81-15863. 336p. 1982. text ed. 65.00 (0-275-90860-7, C08601, Praeger Pubs) Greenwood.

Critical Issues, Developments & Trends in Professional Psychology, Vol. 2. Ed. by J. Regis McNamara. LC 81-15863. 320p. 1984. text ed. 59.95 (0-275-91227-2, C12272, Praeger Pubs) Greenwood.

Critical Issues, Developments & Trends in Professional Psychology, Vol. 3. Ed. by J. Regis McNamara & Margaret A. Appel. LC 81-15863. 262p. 1986. text ed. 55.00 (0-275-92250-2, C22503, Praeger Pubs) Greenwood.

Critical Issues for Clinton's Domestic Agenda. Ed. by Demetrios Caraley. LC 93-74869. 224p. 1994. reprint ed. pap. 19.95 (1-884853-00-5) Acad Poli Sci.

Critical Issues in American Education: Toward the 21st Century. H. Svi Shapiro & David E. Purpel. 608p. (C). 1993. pap. text ed. 33.95 (0-8013-0950-6, 79233) Longman.

***Critical Issues in American Nursing in the Twentieth Century: Perspectives & Case Studies.** Ed. by Darwin H. Stapleton & Cathryne A. Welch. 152p. (Orig.). (C). 1994. pap. 20.00 (1-886511-02-0) Fnd NY St Nurses.

Critical Issues in American Psychiatry & the Law, Vol. 2. Ed. by Richard Rosner. LC 81-9059. 324p. 1985. 70.00 (0-306-41954-8, Plenum Pr) Plenum.

***Critical Issues in Asian Development: Theories, Experiences & Policies.** Ed. by M. G. Quibria. 261p. 1995. text ed. 49.00 (0-19-586606-1) OUP.

Critical Issues in Business Conduct: Legal, Ethical, & Social Challenges for the 1990s. Walter Manley, II & William A. Shrode. LC 90-30009. 336p. 1990. text ed. 55.00 (0-89930-570-9, MCZ/, Quorum Bks) Greenwood.

Critical Issues in Child Welfare. Nora S. Gustavsson & Elizabeth A. Segal. LC 93-46436. 312p. (C). 1994. text ed. 42.00 (0-8039-4504-3); pap. text ed. 18.95 (0-8039-4505-1) Sage.

Critical Issues in Contemporary Health Care: Proceedings of the Eighth Bishops' Workshop. Ed. by Russell E. Smith. 354p. 1989. pap. 17.95 (0-935372-27-X) Pope John Ctr.

Critical Issues in Corrections: Problems, Trends, & Prospects. Roy R. Roberg & Vincent J. Webb. 380p. (C). 1981. pap. text ed. 48.75 (0-8299-0405-0) West Pub.

Critical Issues in Crime & Justice. Ed. by Albert R. Roberts. 328p. (C). 1994. text ed. 48.00 (0-8039-5497-2); pap. text ed. 22.95 (0-8039-5498-0) Sage.

Critical Issues in Criminal Investigation. Michael J. Palmiotto. 130p. 1984. pap. 9.95 (0-932930-64-6) Pilgrimage Inc.

Critical Issues in Criminal Investigation. 2nd ed. Michael J. Palmiotto. 280p. 1988. pap. 19.95 (0-932930-81-6) Anderson Pub Co.

Critical Issues in Criminal Justice: Proceedings of the Illinois Academy of Criminology, 1985-1986 Program. Ed. by G. J. Bensinger. 55p. (C). 1988. pap. text ed. 8.00 (0-933757-17-4) Ill Academy.

Critical Issues in Curriculum. Laurel N. Tanner. (National Society for the Study of Education Publication Ser.: No. 87, Pt. 1). x, 290p. 1988. 26.00 (0-226-60146-3, Natl Soc Stud Educ) U Ch Pr.

Critical Issues in Defense Conversion: A Report of the CSIS Executive Committee on Defense Conversion. Daniel Goure & Debra Van Opstal. LC 94-7942. (CSIS Panel Report Ser.). 51p. (Orig.). 1994. pap. 19.95 (0-89206-266-5) CSI Studies.

***Critical Issues in Dying & Death: Reflections on Death Studies.** Vanderlyn R. Pine. (Death, Value & Meaning Ser.). 1995. text ed. write for info. (0-614-02668-7); pap. write for info. (0-614-02669-5) Baywood Pub.

***Critical Issues in Editing Exploration Texts.** Ed. by Germaine Warkentin. (Conference on Editorial Problems Ser.). 160p. 1995. 40.00 (0-8020-0694-9) U of Toronto Pr.

Critical Issues in Educating African-American Children. Norris M. Haynes. 220p. 1993. 29.95 (1-879893-02-9) IAAS Pubs.

Critical Issues in Education: A Dialectic Approach. 2nd ed. Jack L. Nelson et al. LC 92-19341. 1992. pap. text ed. write for info. (0-07-046211-9) McGraw.

Critical Issues in Educational Policy. Ed. by Samuel Gove & Frederick Wirt. (C). 1976. pap. 12.00 (0-918592-15-1) Pol Studies.

Critical Issues in Electronic Media. Ed. by Simon Penny. (SUNY Series in Film History & Theory). 336p. 1995. text ed. 59.50 (0-7914-2317-4); pap. 19.95 (0-7914-2318-2) State U NY Pr.

Critical Issues in Facilities Management: Capital Renewal & Deferred Maintenance. 200p. 1989. pap. 30.00 (0-913359-42-4); pap. 22.00 (0-685-19203-2) APPA VA.

Critical Issues in Facilities Management: Computer Applications. Intro. by Howard J. Cihak. 137p. 1987. pap. 30.00 (0-913359-40-8); pap. 22.00 (0-685-19200-8) APPA VA.

Critical Issues in Facilities Management: Energy Management. 147p. 1990. 22.00 (0-685-37886-1); pap. 30.00 (0-913359-43-2) APPA VA.

Critical Issues in Facilities Management: Management Basics. 140p. 1990. 22.00 (0-685-37885-3); pap. 30.00 (0-913359-45-9) APPA VA.

Critical Issues in Facilities Management: Personnel Management & Development. Intro. by James R. Thiry. 131p. 1988. 22.00 (0-685-19202-4); pap. 30.00 (0-913359-41-6) APPA VA.

Critical Issues in Foreign Language Instruction. Ellen Silber. LC 90-47987. (Source Books on Education: Vol. 22). 304p. 1991. 40.00 (0-8240-4432-0) Garland.

Critical Issues in Gifted Education, Vol. I: Defensible Programs for the Gifted. Ed. by C. June Maker. LC 86-17345. 357p. 1986. 37.00 (0-89079-194-5, 2069) PRO-ED.

Critical Issues in Gifted Education, Vol. II: Defensible Programs for Cultural & Ethnic Minorities. Ed. by C. June Maker. LC 88-992. (Critical Issues in Gifted Education Ser.). 347p. 1989. text ed. 35.00 (0-89079-184-8, 2072) PRO-ED.

Critical Issues in Gifted Education, Vol. 3, Vol. III. Ed. by June C. Maker. LC 92-39. 480p. (C). 1992. text ed. 39.00 (0-89079-549-5, 2071) PRO-ED.

Critical Issues in Information Systems Research. Ed. by Richard J. Boland & Rudy A. Hirschheim. (Series in Information Systems). 1987. text ed. 135.95 (0-471-91281-6) Wiley.

Critical Issues in Information Systems Research. Richard J. Boland & Rudy A. Hirschheim. (Information Systems Ser.). 394p. 1992. pap. text ed. 49.95 (0-471-93085-7) Wiley.

An Asterisk (*) at the beginning of an entry indicates that the title is appearing in BIP for the first time.

An Asterisk (*) at the beginning of an entry indicates that the title is appearing in BIP for the first time.

1709

Critical Perspective: Edmund Spenser & William Shakespeare, Vol. 2. Ed. by Harold Bloom. 650p. 1986. 70.00 (*0-87754-791-2*) Chelsea Hse.

Critical Perspective: Izaak Walton to Henry Fielding, Vol. 4. Ed. by Harold Bloom. 650p. 1987. 70.00 (*0-87754-793-9*) Chelsea Hse.

Critical Perspective: Jonathan Edwards to Edmund Burke, Vol. 5. Ed. by Harold Bloom. 650p. 1987. 70.00 (*0-87754-794-7*) Chelsea Hse.

Critical Perspective: Twentieth-Century Criticism of British & American Literature to 1904, 11 vols., Set. Ed. by Harold Bloom. 1988. 745.00 (*0-87754-789-0*) Chelsea Hse.

***Critical Perspective on J. M. Coetzee.** Ed. by Graham Huggan & Stephen Watson. LC 94-24879. 1994. write for info. (*0-312-12312-4*) St Martin.

Critical Perspective, Vol. 10: John Ruskin to William Dean Howells. Ed. by Harold Bloom. 1989. 70.00 (*0-87754-799-8*) Chelsea Hse.

Critical Perspective, Vol. 11: Bibliographical Supplement & Index. Ed. by Harold Bloom & S. T. Joshi. (Chelsea House Library of Literary Criticism). 200p. 1989. text ed. 45.00 (*1-55546-774-1*) Chelsea Hse.

Critical Perspective, Vol. 6: Mary Wollstonecraft to William Godwin. Ed. by Harold Bloom. 650p. 1988. 70.00 (*0-87754-795-5*) Chelsea Hse.

Critical Perspective, Vol. 7: Fanny Burney to Walter Savage Landor. Ed. by Harold Bloom. 650p. 1988. 70.00 (*0-87754-796-3*) Chelsea Hse.

Critical Perspective, Vol. 8: Nathaniel Hawthorne to Edward FitzGerald. Ed. by Harold Bloom. 650p. 1989. 70.00 (*0-87754-797-1*) Chelsea Hse.

Critical Perspective, Vol. 9: Emily Dickinson to Lewis Carroll. Ed. by Harold Bloom. 650p. 1989. 70.00 (*0-87754-798-X*) Chelsea Hse.

Critical Perspectives. R. K. Narayan. Ed. by A. L. McLeod. (C). 1994. 21.00x (*81-207-1623-X*, Pub. by Sterling Plns Pvt II) S Asia.

Critical Perspectives & Issues in Health Policy. Ed. by Ralph Straetz et al. (Orig.). 1980. pap. 12.00 (*0-918592-42-9*) Pol Studies.

***Critical Perspectives for Christian Education.** Jeff Astley & Leslie Francis. 1994. pap. 22.95 (*0-85244-254-8*, Pub. by Gracewing UK) Morehouse Pub.

Critical Perspectives in Sociology: A Reader. 2nd ed. Berch Berberoglu. 320p. 1993. per. 24.95 (*0-8403-8468-8*) Kendall-Hunt.

Critical Perspectives on Aging: The Political & Moral Economy of Growing Old. Ed. by Meredith Minkler & Carroll Estes. (Policy, Politics, Health & Medicine Ser.). 372p. 1991. text ed. 38.00 (*0-89503-076-4*); pap. text ed. 28.50 (*0-89503-075-6*) Baywood Pub.

***Critical Perspectives on Algerian Literature.** Ed. by Mildred Mortimer. 320p. 1996. 36.00 (*0-89410-797-6*); pap. 18.00 (*0-89410-798-4*) Three Continents.

Critical Perspectives on Amos Tutuola. Ed. by Bernth Lindfors. LC 75-13706. (Illus.). 318p. (Orig.). 1975. 25.00 (*0-914478-05-2*); pap. 15.00 (*0-914478-06-0*) Three Continents.

Critical Perspectives on Ayi Kwei Armah. Ed. by D. L. Wright. LC 91-28952. 340p. 1992. pap. 16.00 (*0-89410-641-4*) Three Continents.

Critical Perspectives on Bilingual Education Research. Ed. by Raymond V. Padilla & Alfredo H. Benavides. LC 91-21873. 432p. 1992. pap. 22.00 (*0-927534-20-7*) Biling Rev-Pr.

Critical Perspectives on Calderon de la Barca. Ed. by Frederick A. De Armas et al. LC 80-53823. 183p. (Orig.). reprint ed. pap. 52.20 (*0-317-41817-3*, 2025571) Bks Demand.

Critical Perspectives on Christopher Okigbo. Ed. by Donatus I. Nwoga. LC 80-53349. (Critical Perspectives Ser.). (Illus.). 367p. (C). 1985. 25.00 (*0-89410-258-3*); pap. 16.00 (*0-89410-259-1*) Three Continents.

Critical Perspectives on Computers & Composition Instruction. Ed. by Gail E. Hawisher & Cynthia L. Selfe. (Computers & Education Ser.: No. 7). 248p. (C). 1989. text ed. 26.95 (*0-8077-2948-5*) Tchrs Coll.

Critical Perspectives on Democracy. Mathew Kramer. 320p. (C). 1994. pap. text ed. 22.95 (*0-8476-7888-1*) Rowman.

Critical Perspectives on Democracy. Ed. by Lyman H. Legters et al. 188p. (C). 1994. pap. text ed. 23.95 (*0-8476-7889-X*) Rowman.

Critical Perspectives on Dennis Brutus. Ed. by Craig M. McLuckie & Patrick J. Colbert. 224p. 1995. pap. 16.00 (*0-89410-770-4*) Three Continents.

Critical Perspectives on Dennis Brutus. Ed. by Craig M. McLuckie & Patrick J. Colbert. 224p. 1995. 28.00 (*0-89410-769-0*) Three Continents.

Critical Perspectives on Derek Walcott. Ed. by Robert V. Hamner. 490p. 1993. pap. 20.00 (*0-89410-142-0*) Three Continents.

Critical Perspectives on Early Childhood Education. Ed. by Lois Weis et al. LC 90-43396. (SUNY Series, Frontiers in Education). 282p. (C). 1991. 59.50 (*0-7914-0697-0*); pap. 19.95 (*0-7914-0698-9*) State U NY Pr.

Critical Perspectives on Educational Leadership. Ed. by John Smyth. 200p. 1989. 65.00 (*1-85000-524-9*, Falmer Pr); pap. 33.00 (*1-85000-525-7*, Falmer Pr) Taylor & Francis.

Critical Perspectives on Gabriel Garcia Marquez. Ed. by Bradley A. Shaw & Nova Vera-Godwin. LC 83-51008. 159p. reprint ed. pap. 45.40 (*0-318-34732-6*, 2031987) Bks Demand.

Critical Perspectives on Housing. Ed. by Rachel G. Bratt et al. LC 85-17274. 646p. 1986. 44.95 (*0-87722-395-5*); pap. 24.95 (*0-87722-396-3*) Temple U Pr.

Critical Perspectives on Imperialism & Social Class in the Third World. James F. Petras. LC 78-13915. 324p. reprint ed. pap. 92.40 (*0-7837-3901-X*, 2043749) Bks Demand.

Critical Perspectives on Jean Rhys. Ed. by Pierrette Frickey. LC 90-11062. 250p. 1991. 25.00 (*0-89410-058-0*); pap. 15.00 (*0-89410-059-9*) Three Continents.

Critical Perspectives on Leon Gontran Damas. Ed. by Keith Warner. LC 80-53347. (Critical Perspectives Ser.). 180p. 1988. 25.00 (*0-914478-57-5*); pap. 15.00 (*0-914478-58-3*) Three Continents.

Critical Perspectives on Leopold Sedar Senghor. Ed. by Janice Spleth. 192p. 1994. 30.00 (*0-89410-548-5*); pap. 18.00 (*0-89410-549-3*) Three Continents.

Critical Perspectives on Lusophone Literature from Africa. Comp. by Donald Burness. LC 80-53348. (Illus.). 307p. 1981. 25.00 (*0-89410-015-7*); pap. 12.00 (*0-89410-016-5*) Three Continents.

Critical Perspectives on Media & Society. Ed. by Robert K. Avery & David Eason. LC 91-22126. (Guilford Communication Ser.). 417p. 1991. lib. bdg. 45.00 (*0-89862-315-4*); pap. text ed. 20.95 (*0-89862-289-1*) Guilford Pr.

Critical Perspectives on Modern Arabic Literature. Ed. by Issa Boullata. LC 78-13850. 384p. (Orig.). 1980. reprint ed. 26.00 (*0-89410-007-6*) Three Continents.

Critical Perspectives on Modern Persian Literature. Ed. by Thomas M. Ricks. LC 81-51656. (Critical Perspectives Ser.). (Illus.). 540p. 1984. 40.00 (*0-914478-95-8*) Three Continents.

***Critical Perspectives on Mongo Beti.** Ed. by Stephen Arnold. 380p. 1996. 40.00 (*0-89410-586-8*); pap. 20.00 (*0-89410-587-6*) Three Continents.

Critical Perspectives on Naguib Mahfouz. Ed. by Trevor Le Gassick. LC 90-48890. 192p. 1991. 25.00 (*0-89410-659-7*); pap. 15.00 (*0-89410-660-0*) Three Continents.

Critical Perspectives on Native American Fiction. Ed. by Richard F. Fleck. 420p. 1993. pap. 16.00 (*0-89410-701-1*) Three Continents.

Critical Perspectives on Ngugi wa Thiong'o. Ed. by G. D. Killam. LC 81-51673. (Critical Perspectives Ser.). (Illus.). 321p. (C). 1984. 25.00 (*0-89410-064-5*) Three Continents.

Critical Perspectives on Nigerian Literatures. Ed. by Bernth Lindfors. LC 75-27391. 1976. boxed 25.00 (*0-914478-27-3*) Three Continents.

Critical Perspectives on Nonacademic Science & Engineering. Ed. by Paul T. Durbin. LC 89-64066. (Research in Technology Studies: Vol. 4). 304p. 1991. 45.00 (*0-934223-15-7*) Lehigh Univ Pr.

Critical Perspectives on Sam Selvon. Ed. by Susheila Nasta. LC 81-51645. (Critical Perspectives Ser.). 280p. 1988. 25.00 (*0-89410-238-9*); pap. 15.00 (*0-89410-239-7*) Three Continents.

Critical Perspectives on the Organization & Improvement of Schooling. Ed. by Kenneth A. Sirotnik & Jeannie Oakes. 1986. lib. bdg. 56.00 (*0-89838-212-2*) Kluwer Ac.

Critical Perspectives on V. S. Naipaul. Robert D. Hamner. LC 77-71683. (Illus.). (Orig.). 1977. 25.00 (*0-914478-17-6*); pap. 15.00 (*0-914478-18-4*) Three Continents.

Critical Perspectives on Wole Soyinka. Ed. by James Gibbs. LC 79-89931. (Critical Perspectives Ser.). (Illus.). 274p. (Orig.). 1980. 25.00 (*0-914478-49-4*); pap. 15.00 (*0-914478-50-8*) Three Continents.

Critical Perspectives on Yusuf Idris. Ed. by Roger Allen. LC 92-35320. (Critical Perspectives Ser.: Vol. 43). 224p. 1994. 25.00 (*0-89410-671-6*); pap. 16.00 (*0-89410-672-4*) Three Continents.

Critical Phase in Tanzania, 1945-1968: Nyerere & the Emergence of a Socialist Strategy. Cranford Pratt. LC 75-22979. 327p. reprint ed. pap. 93.20 (*0-317-27579-8*, 2024516) Bks Demand.

Critical Phenomena at Surfaces & Interfaces: Evanescent X-Ray & Neutron Scattering. H. Dosch. (Tracts in Modern Physics Ser.: Vol. 126). (Illus.). x, 145p. 1992. 80.00 (*0-387-54534-4*) Spr-Verlag.

Critical Phenomena in Liquid Crystals: A Special Issue of the Journal Molecular Crystals & Liquid Crystals. M. A. Anisimov. viii, 96p. 1988. pap. text ed. 48.00 (*2-88124-268-5*) Gordon & Breach.

Critical Phenomena, Random Systems, Gauge Theories, 2 Vols., 1. Ed. by K. Osterwalder & R. Stora. 1240p. 1986. 195.00 (*0-444-87006-7*, North Holland) Elsevier.

Critical Phenomena, Random Systems, Gauge Theories, 2 Vols., 2. Ed. by K. Osterwalder & R. Stora. 1240p. 1986. 231.00 (*0-444-87007-5*, North Holland) Elsevier.

Critical Phenomena, Random Systems, Gauge Theories, 2 Vols., Set. Ed. by K. Osterwalder & R. Stora. 1240p. 1986. 364.00 (*0-444-86980-8*, North Holland) Elsevier.

Critical Pluralism, Democratic Performance, & Community Power. Paul Schumaker. LC 90-12621. (Studies in Government & Public Policy). 256p. 1990. 29.95 (*0-7006-0439-1*) U Pr of KS.

Critical Point Theory & Hamiltonian Systems. J. L. Mawhin & M. Willem. (Applied Mathematical Sciences Ser.: Vol. 74). (Illus.). xiv, 277p. 1989. 59.00 (*0-387-96908-X*) Spr-Verlag.

Critical Practice. Catherine Belsey. 176p. 1980. pap. 13.95 (*0-416-72950-9*, NO.2021) Routledge Chapman & Hall.

Critical Practices in Post-Franco Spain. Ed. by Silvia L. Lopez et al. LC 94-1236. (Hispanic Issues Ser.: Vol. 11). 1994. text ed. 49.95 (*0-8166-2473-9*) U of Minn Pr.

Critical Practices in Post-Franco Spain. Ed. by Silvia L. Lopez et al. LC 94-1236. (Hispanic Issues Ser.: Vol. 11). 1994. pap. text ed. 19.95 (*0-8166-2474-7*) U of Minn Pr.

Critical Prefaces of the French Renaissance. Bernard Weinberg. LC 76-129377. (Northwestern University. Humanities Ser.: No. 20). reprint ed. 25.00 (*0-404-50720-4*) AMS Pr.

Critical Press & the New Deal: The Press Versus Presidential Power, 1933-38. Gary D. Best. LC 92-31715. 216p. 1993. text ed. 52.95 (*0-275-94350-X*, C4350, Praeger Pubs) Greenwood.

Critical Probings: Essays in European Literature. Hermann J. Weigand. Ed. by Ulrich K. Goldsmith. (Utah Studies: Vol. 22). (Illus.). 310p. 1983. 46.15 (*3-261-04921-9*) P Lang Pubs.

Critical Problems in Children & Youth. Grant L. Martin. (Contemporary Christian Counseling Ser.: Vol. 5). 1992. 15.99 (*0-8499-0886-8*) Word Inc.

Critical Problems in Software Measurement. Capers Jones. 102p. 1993. ring bd. 180.00 (*1-56909-000-9*) Info Systs Mgmt.

Critical Problems in the History of Science. Ed. by Marshall Clagett. LC 59-5304. 569p. reprint ed. pap. 162.20 (*0-8357-9773-2*, 2015357) Bks Demand.

Critical Prose & Letters. 2nd ed. Osip Mandelstam. Ed. by Jane G. Harris & C. Anthony. (Illus.). 725p. (C). 1990. pap. 19.95 (*0-88233-164-7*) Ardis Pubs.

Critical Psychological Issues: Judaic Perspectives. Reuven P. Bulka. 162p. (Orig.). (C). 1992. lib. bdg. 31.00 (*0-8191-8476-4*); pap. text ed. 16.50 (*0-8191-8477-2*) U Pr of Amer.

Critical Psychology: Contributions to an Historical Science of the Subject. Ed. by Charles W. Tolman & Wolfgang Maiers. 400p. (C). 1991. 49.95 (*0-521-39344-2*) Cambridge U Pr.

Critical Psychology: Interpretation of the Personal World. Edmund V. Sullivan. LC 83-20184. (PATH in Psychology Ser.). 212p. 1984. 55.00 (*0-306-41434-1*, Plenum Pr) Plenum.

Critical Psychology & Critical Pedagogy: Interpretation of the Personal World. Edmund V. Sullivan. LC 89-18635. (Critical Studies in Education). 320p. 1990. reprint ed. pap. text ed. 16.95 (*0-89789-213-5*, G213, Bergin & Garvey) Greenwood.

Critical Psychophysical Passages in the Life of a Woman. Ed. by J. Offerman-Zuckerberg. LC 88-12615. (Illus.). 310p. 1988. 45.00 (*0-306-42639-0*, Plenum Med Bk) Plenum.

Critical Questions: Invention, Creativity, & the Criticism of Discourse & Media. Ed. by William L. Nothstine et al. 448p. 1994. text ed. 39.95 (*0-312-09140-0*) St Martin.

***Critical Questions: Invention, Creativity, & the Criticism of Discourse & Media.** William L. Nothstine et al. 464p. 1994. pap. text ed. 21.00 (*0-312-08971-6*) St Martin.

Critical Questions: On Music & Letters, Culture & Biography, 1940-1980. Jacques Barzun. Ed. by Bea Friedland. LC 81-22023. 1982. lib. bdg. 22.50 (*0-226-03863-7*) U Ch Pr.

Critical Questions: On Music & Letters, Culture & Biography, 1940-1980. Jacques Barzun. Ed. by Bea Friedland. LC 81-22023. 1984. pap. 8.95 (*0-226-03864-5*) U Ch Pr.

***Critical Race Theory: The Cutting Edge.** Ed. by Richard Delgado. (Orig.). (C). 1995. pap. text ed. 22.95 (*1-56639-348-5*) Temple U Pr.

***Critical Race Theory: The Cutting Edge.** Ed. by Richard Delgado. 664p. (Orig.). (C). 1995. lib. bdg. 59.95 (*1-56639-347-7*) Temple U Pr.

***Critical Race Theory: The Key Writings that Formed the Movement.** Ed. by Kimberle Crenshaw et al. 608p. 1995. pap. 30.00 (*1-56584-271-5*) New Press NY.

***Critical Race Theory: The Key Writings that Formed the Movement.** Ed. by Kimberle Crenshaw et al. 1995. 45.00 (*1-56584-270-7*) New Press NY.

Critical Rationalism: A Restatement & Defence. David Miller. 275p. 1994. 44.95 (*0-8126-9197-0*); pap. 19.95 (*0-8126-9198-9*) Open Court.

Critical Rationalism: Essays for Joseph Agassi, 2 vols., II. Ed. by I. C. Jarvie & Nathaniel Laor. LC 94-19889. (Boston Studies in the Philosophy of Science: Vol. 161-162). 1995. lib. bdg. 130.00 (*0-7923-2961-9*) Kluwer Ac.

Critical Rationalism: Essays for Joseph Agassi, 2 vols., Vol. I. Ed. by I. C. Jarvie. LC 94-19889. (Boston Studies in the Philosophy of Science: Vol. 161-162). 272p. (C). 1995. lib. bdg. 118.00 (*0-7923-2960-0*) Kluwer Ac.

Critical Reader. William D. Lutz & Harry Brent. 528p. (C). 1990. pap. text ed. 28.00 (*0-06-044111-9*) HarpCollege.

Critical Reader, Thinker & Writer. W. Ross Winterowd & Geoffrey R. Winterowd. 641p. (C). 1992. teacher ed write for info. (*0-87484-929-2*); pap. text ed. 25.95 (*0-87484-926-8*) Mayfield Pub.

Critical Reading: Primers A-D. Janette M. Scandura. Ed. by Alice M. Scandura. (Critical Reading Primer Ser.). (Illus.). 48p. (gr. 1-3). 1978. Level A, 48p. 9.00 (*0-87879-714-9*, Ann Arbor Div); Level B, 48p. 9.00 (*0-87879-715-7*, Ann Arbor Div); Level C, 48p. 9.00 (*0-87879-716-5*, Ann Arbor Div); Level D. 9.00 (*0-87879-717-3*, Ann Arbor Div) Acad Therapy.

Critical Reading: Workbook A: Reusable Edition. George F. Lowerre & Alice M. Scandura. 54p. (J). (gr. 3-8). 1973. 10.00 (*0-87879-719-X*, Ann Arbor Div); teacher ed 5.00 (*0-87879-723-8*, Ann Arbor Div) Acad Therapy.

Critical Reading: Workbook B: Reusable Edition. George F. Lowerre. 70p. (J). (gr. 3-8). 1973. student ed 10.00 (*0-87879-720-3*, Ann Arbor Div) Acad Therapy.

Critical Reading: Workbook C: Reusable Edition. George F. Lowerre. 78p. (J). (gr. 3-8). 1973. student ed 10.00 (*0-87879-721-1*, Ann Arbor Div) Acad Therapy.

Critical Reading: Workbook D: Reusable Edition. George F. Lowerre & Alice M. Scandure. 68p. (J). (gr. 3-8). 1973. student ed 10.00 (*0-87879-722-X*, Ann Arbor Div) Acad Therapy.

Critical Reading & Writing for Advanced ESL Students. Sharon Scull. (Illus.). 384p. (C). 1987. pap. text ed. 22.25 (*0-13-194010-4*) P-H.

***Critical Reading for Primary Care.** Ed. by Roger Jones & Ann-Louise Kinmonth. (Oxford General Practice Ser.: No. 28). (Illus.). 248p. 1995. pap. 49.95 (*0-19-262381-8*) OUP.

Critical Reading of the Selected Poems of T. S. Eliot. Manju Jain. 260p. 1992. 18.95 (*0-19-562546-3*) OUP.

Critical Reading Series, 8 bks., Set. write for info. (*0-89061-749-X*) Jamestown Pubs.

Critical Readings for Hospital Trustees. Ed. by Richard J. Umbdenstock & Winifred M. Hageman. LC 91-18266. 143p. (Orig.). 1991. 32.95 (*1-55648-074-1*, 196200) AHPI.

Critical Readings in Planning Theory. Ed. by C. Paris. (Urban & Regional Planning Ser.: Vol. 27). (Illus.). 260p. 1982. text ed. 140.00 (*0-08-024681-8*, Pub. by Pergamon Repr UK) Franklin.

Critical Real Estate Issues in the Nineties. Allen Cymrot. 200p. 1992. 18.95 (*0-9633472-0-9*) C R Pub.

Critical Realism: An Introduction to Roy Bhaskar's Philosophy. Andrew Collier. LC 93-39601. 1994. 59.95 (*0-86091-437-2*, Pub. by Verso UK); pap. 19.95 (*0-86091-602-2*, Pub. by Verso UK) Routledge Chapman & Hall.

Critical Realism in the New Testament. Ben F. Meyer. LC 88-31722. (Princeton Theological Monograph Ser.: No. 17). 225p. (Orig.). 1989. pap. 19.95 (*0-915138-97-2*) Pickwick.

Critical Reasoning: The Fixation of Belief. Robert Boyd. LC 92-73355. 416p. (C). 1992. pap. text ed. 24.95 (*0-938991-94-9*) Colonial Pr AL.

Critical Reasoning: Understanding & Criticizing Arguments & Theories. 3rd ed. Jerry Cederblom & David W. Paulsen. 416p. (C). 1991. pap. 34.95 (*0-534-14688-0*) Intl Thomson.

Critical Reasoning in Contemporary Culture. Ed. by Richard A. Talaska. LC 91-27680. (SUNY Series in the Philosophy of the Social Sciences). 422p. (C). 1992. 59.50 (*0-7914-0979-1*); pap. 19.95 (*0-7914-0980-5*) State U NY Pr.

Critical Reception of Andre Malraux's l'Espoir in the French Press: December 1937-June 1940. John B. Romeiser. LC 79-19837. (Romance Monographs: No. 37). 176p. 1980. 24.00 (*84-499-3368-4*) Romance.

Critical Reception of Charles Dickens, 1833-1841. Kathryn Chittick. LC 88-33644. 294p. 1989. 40.00 (*0-8240-5620-5*, 900) Garland.

Critical Reception of Hamlin Garland, 1891-1978. Charles L. Silet et al. LC 83-61039. 462p. 1985. 30.00 (*0-87875-274-9*) Whitston Pub.

Critical Reception of Shakespeare's Antony & Cleopatra from 1607 to 1905. Michael Steppat. (Bochum Studies in English Ser.: No. 9). xvi, 619p. (Orig.). 1980. pap. 47.00x (*90-6032-188-X*, Pub. by B R Gruener NE) Benjamins North Am.

Critical Reconstructions: The Relationship of Fiction & Life. Ed. by Robert M. Polhemus & Roger B. Henkle. 370p. (C). 1994. 42.50 (*0-8047-2243-9*) Stanford U Pr.

Critical Reflection & the Culture of Schooling: Empowering Teachers. Landon E. Beyer. (C). 1989. 45.00 (*0-685-59371-1*, Pub. by Deakin Univ AT) St Mut.

Critical Reflections on Distance Education. Ed. by Terry Evans & Daryl Nation. (Deakin Studies in Education Ser.). 275p. 1989. 70.00 (*1-85000-462-5*, Falmer Pr); pap. 33.00 (*1-85000-463-3*, Falmer Pr) Taylor & Francis.

Critical Reflections on Generative Grammar. rev. ed. Claude Hagege. Tr. by Robert A. Hall, Jr. LC 82-21297. (Edward Sapir Monograph Ser. in Language Culture & Cognition: 10). Orig. Title: La Grammaire Generative: Reflexions Critiques. viii, 196p. (C). 1981. pap. 12.00 (*0-933104-09-X*) Jupiter Pr.

Critical Reflections on Poetry, Painting & Music, 3 vols., Set. Jean B. Dubos. LC 78-3659. (Music & Theatre in France in the 17th & 18th Centuries Ser.). reprint ed. 195.00 (*0-404-60170-7*) AMS Pr.

Critical Reflections on the Fiction of Ernest J. Gaines. Ed. by David C. Estes. LC 93-5333. 296p. 1994. 45.00 (*0-8203-1607-5*) U of Ga Pr.

Critical Reformulation of Educational Policy Analysis. John J. Prunty. 113p. (C). 1984. 56.00 (*0-7300-0113-X*, Pub. by Deakin Univ AT) St Mut.

Critical Resource Management: A Control Perspective. Fred A. Jacobs & Larry H. Beard. 250p. 1993. 28.95 (*0-88406-252-X*) GA St U Busn Pr.

Critical Response to Ann Beattie. Ed. by Jaye B. Montresor. LC 92-46531. (Critical Responses in Arts & Letters Ser.: No. 4). 296p. 1993. text ed. 49.95 (*0-313-28358-3*, MTW, Greenwood Pr) Greenwood.

Critical Response to Ann Radcliffe. Ed. by Deborah D. Rogers. LC 93-28048. (Critical Responses in Arts & Letters Ser.: No. 7). 320p. 1993. text ed. 59.95 (*0-313-28031-2*, Greenwood Pr) Greenwood.

Critical Response to Bram Stoker. Ed. by Carol A. Senf. LC 93-28055. (Critical Responses in Arts & Letters Ser.: No. 9). 216p. 1993. text ed. 55.00 (*0-313-28527-6*, Greenwood Pr) Greenwood.

***Critical Response to Dashiell Hammett.** Ed. by Christopher Metress. LC 94-28713. (Critical Responses in Arts & Letters Ser.: No. 15). 304p. 1994. text ed. 59.95 (*0-313-28938-7*) Greenwood.

Critical Response to Eudora Welty's Fiction. Ed. by Laurie Champion. LC 93-43709. (Critical Responses in Arts & Letters Ser.: No. 12). 312p. 1994. text ed. 55.00 (*0-313-28596-9*, Greenwood Pr) Greenwood.

Critical Response to Eugene O'Neill. Ed. by John H. Houchin. LC 93-6562. (Critical Responses in Arts & Letters Ser.: No. 5). 344p. 1993. Alk. paper. text ed. 59.95 (*0-313-27617-X*, HEL/, Greenwood Pr) Greenwood.

An Asterisk (*) at the beginning of an entry indicates that the title is appearing in BIP for the first time.

An Asterisk (*) at the beginning of an entry indicates that the title is appearing in BIP for the first time.

1711

C

Critical Theory & Philosophy. David Ingram. (Issues in Philosophy Ser.). 240p. 1990. pap. text ed. 12.95 (*1-55778-201-6*) Paragon Hse.

***Critical Theory & Political Possibilities: Conceptions of Emancipatory Politics in the Works of Horkheimer, Adorno, Marcuse & Habermas.** Joan Alway. LC 94-29849. (Contributions in Society Ser.). 184p. 1995. text ed. 49.95 (*0-313-29317-1*, Greenwood Pr) Greenwood.

Critical Theory & Poststructuralism: In Search of a Context: Including 7 charts. Mark Poster. LC 89-7262. (Illus.). 200p. 1989. pap. 12.95 (*0-8014-9588-1*) Cornell U Pr.

***Critical Theory & Practice.** Keith Green & Jill LeBihan. LC 95-3558. 1995. write for info. (*0-415-11438-1*); pap. write for info. (*0-415-11439-X*) Routledge.

Critical Theory & Public Life. Ed. by John Forester. (Studies in Contemporary German Social Thought). 360p. 1987. reprint ed. pap. 15.00 (*0-262-56042-9*) MIT Pr.

Critical Theory & Society: A Reader. Ed. by Stephen E. Bronner & Douglas M. Kellner. 304p. 1989. 49.50 (*0-415-90040-9*, A2329, Routledge NY); pap. 16.95 (*0-415-90041-7*, A2333, Routledge NY) Routledge.

Critical Theory & the English Teacher: Transforming the Subject. Nick Peim. LC 93-9850. (Teaching Secondary English Ser.). 208p. 1993. 59.95 (*0-415-05751-5*, B0800); pap. 16.95 (*0-415-05752-3*, B0804) Routledge.

Critical Theory & the Novel: Mass Society & Cultural Criticism in Dickens, Melville, & Kafka. David Suchoff. LC 93-21116. 232p. (C). 1994. 43.00 (*0-299-14080-6*); pap. 19.95 (*0-299-14084-9*) U of Wis Pr.

Critical Theory & the Sociology of Knowledge: A Comparative Study in the Theory of Ideology. Leon Bailey. LC 93-6953. (American University Studies, XI, Anthropology: Vol. 62). 232p. (C). 1994. text ed. 39.95 (*0-8204-1988-5*) P Lang Pubs.

Critical Theory, Cultural Politics, & Latin American Narrative. Ed. by Steven M. Bell et al. LC 92-53744. (C). 1993. text ed. 29.95 (*0-268-00795-0*) U of Notre Dame Pr.

Critical Theory in Political Practice. Stephen T. Leonard. 318p. 1990. text ed. 42.50 (*0-691-07840-8*) Princeton U Pr.

Critical Theory, Marxism, & Modernity. Douglas Kellner. LC 89-32113. (Parallax). 280p. 1989. text ed. 45.00x (*0-8018-3913-0*); pap. text ed. 14.95 (*0-8018-3914-9*) Johns Hopkins.

Critical Theory Now. Ed. by Philip Wexler. (Knowledge & Society Ser.). 256p. 1991. 65.00 (*1-85000-753-5*, Falmer Pr); pap. 29.00 (*1-85000-754-3*, Falmer Pr) Taylor & Francis.

Critical Theory of Art History. Vernon H. Minor. 250p. 1993. pap. text ed. write for info. (*0-13-194606-4*) P-H.

Critical Theory of Education: Habermas & Our Children's Future. R. E. Young. (Advances in Contemporary Educational Thought Ser.). 192p. (C). 1989. text ed. 20.95 (*0-8077-3018-1*) Tchrs Coll.

Critical Theory of Jurgen Habermas. Thomas McCarthy. 1978. pap. 20.00 (*0-262-63073-7*) MIT Pr.

Critical Theory of Literature. Costanzo Di Girolamo. 122p. (C). 1981. 22.50 (*0-299-08120-6*) U of Wis Pr.

Critical Theory of Public Life: Knowledge, Discourse & Politics in an Age of Decline. Ben Agger. (Critical Perspectives on Literacy & Education Ser.). 240p. 1991. 80.00 (*1-85000-966-X*, Falmer Pr); pap. 29.00 (*1-85000-967-8*, Falmer Pr) Taylor & Francis.

***Critical Theory of Religion: A Feminist Analysis.** Marsha A. Hewitt. LC 94-32897. 1995. pap. 17.00 (*0-8006-2612-5*, Fortress Pr) Augsburg Fortress.

Critical Theory of Religion: The Frankfurt School from Universal Pragmatic to Political Theology. Rudolf J. Siebert. (Religion & Reason Ser.: Vol. 29). xvi, 722p. 1985. 180.80 (*0-89925-119-6*) Mouton.

Critical Theory of Technology. Andrew Feenberg. 256p. 1991. pap. 17.95 (*0-19-506855-6*) OUP.

Critical Theory, Public Policy, & Planning Practice. John Forester. LC 92-1633. 214p. 1993. 49.50 (*0-7914-1445-0*); pap. 16.95 (*0-7914-1446-9*) State U NY Pr.

Critical Theory since Plato. Ed. by Adams & Hazard. 1267p. (C). 1971. text ed. 48.00 (*0-15-516142-3*) HB Coll Pubs.

Critical Theory since Plato. Hazard Adams. 1350p. (C). 1992. text ed. 48.00 (*0-15-516143-1*) HB Coll Pubs.

Critical Theory since 1965. Ed. by Hazard Adams & Leroy Searle. LC 86-13216. 904p. (C). 1986. pap. 39.95 (*0-8130-0844-1*) U Press Fla.

***Critical Thinker t/a Psychology.** 2nd ed. Lester M. Sdorow et al. 80p. (C). 1994. write for info. (*0-697-26685-0*) Brown & Benchmark.

***Critical Thinking.** Robert H. Ennis. LC 95-6243. 1995. pap. text ed. write for info. (*0-13-374711-5*) P-H.

***Critical Thinking, Testbank.** Brooke N. Moore et al. (C). 1994. teacher ed, disk write for info. (*1-55934-340-0*) Mayfield Pub.

Critical Thinking. rev. ed. Brooke N. Moore & Richard Parker. 528p. (C). 1992. teacher ed, pap. text ed. write for info. (*0-318-68888-3*) Mayfield Pub.

Critical Thinking. 3rd rev. ed. Brooke N. Moore & Richard Parker. 528p. (C). 1992. pap. text ed. 35.95 (*1-55934-072-X*) Mayfield Pub.

Critical Thinking. 4th ed. Brooke N. Moore et al. LC 94-12647. 544p. (C). 1994. pap. text ed. 34.95 (*1-55934-339-7*) Mayfield Pub.

Critical Thinking, Bk. I. Anita Harnader. 1976. teacher ed 5.95 (*0-910974-90-X*); pap. 14.95 (*0-910974-75-6*) Crit Think Soft.

Critical Thinking: A Collection of Readings. David J. Stroup & Robert D. Allen. 140p. (C). 1991. pap. write for info. (*0-697-14556-5*) Wm C Brown Pubs.

Critical Thinking: A Functional Approach. Eugene B. Zechmeister & James E. Johnson. LC 91-18045. 320p. (C). 1992. pap. 27.95 (*0-534-16596-6*) Brooks-Cole.

Critical Thinking: A Guide to Interpreting Literary Texts. Colin Manlove. LC 89-30824. 180p. 1989. text ed. 35.00 (*0-312-03166-1*) St Martin.

Critical Thinking: An Annotated Bibliography. Jeris F. Cassel & Robert J. Congleton. LC 92-35306. 461p. 1992. 47.50 (*0-8108-2635-6*) Scarecrow.

Critical Thinking: An Introduction to Reasoning. Francis W. Dauer. (Illus.). 560p. (C). 1989. text ed. 39.95 (*0-19-504884-9*); Instr's. manual. teacher ed write for info. (*0-19-505853-4*) OUP.

Critical Thinking: An Introductory Text. William Hughes. 352p. 1992. pap. 16.95 (*0-921149-83-2*) Broadview Pr.

Critical Thinking: Consider the Verdict. 2nd ed. Bruce N. Waller. LC 93-29615. 387p. 1993. pap. text ed. write for info. (*0-13-177635-5*) P-H.

Critical Thinking: Defining & Assessing It. Michael Scriven & Alec Fisher. 1993. 25.00 (*0-8039-6127-8*); pap. 12.50 (*0-8039-6128-6*) Corwin Pr.

Critical Thinking: Educational Imperative. Ed. by Cynthia A. Barnes. LC 85-644753. (New Directions for Community Colleges Ser.: No. CC 77). 140p. 1992. 16.95 (*1-55542-749-9*) Jossey-Bass.

Critical Thinking: Helping Students Learn Reflectively. S. Samuel Shermis. LC 91-44698. 80p. (C). 1991. pap. 14.95 (*0-927516-28-4*) ERIC-REC.

Critical Thinking: Reading & Writing Across the Curriculum. Anne B. Grinols. 365p. (C). 1988. pap. 23.95 (*0-534-08838-4*) Intl Thomson.

Critical Thinking: Reading & Writing in a Diverse World. Joan Rasool et al. 311p. (C). 1993. pap. 29.95 (*0-534-12818-1*) Intl Thomson.

***Critical Thinking: Semiotic Perspective.** Majorie Siegel & Robert F. Carey. Ed. & Intro. by Jerome Harste. LC 89-1354. (Monographs on Teaching Critical Thinking). (Illus.). 55p. (C). 1989. pap. 8.95 (*0-927516-00-4*) ERIC-REC.

Critical Thinking: The Analysis of Arguments. James A. Herrick. 275p. (C). 1991. pap. text ed. 32.00 (*0-89787-342-4*) Gorsuch Scarisbrick.

Critical Thinking: Theory, Research, Practice, & Possibilities. Joanne G. Kurfiss. LC 88-71519. (ASHE-ERIC Higher Education Report Ser.: No. 2, 1988). 148p. (Orig.). (C). 1988. pap. text ed. 15.00 (*0-913317-44-6*) GWU Schl E&HD.

Critical Thinking: What Every Person Needs to Survive in a Rapidly Changing World. Richard W. Paul. Ed. by A. J. Binker. LC 90-80195. 704p. 1992. pap. text ed. 19.95 (*0-944583-07-5*) Ctr Critical Thinking.

Critical Thinking Across the Curriculum: Building the Analytical Classroom. Victor P. Maiorana. LC 92-20683. 180p. (Orig.). (C). 1992. pap. text ed. 14.95 (*0-927516-35-7*) ERIC-REC.

Critical Thinking & Communication: The Use of Reason in Argument. Barbara Warnick & Edward S. Inch. 597p. (C). 1988. pap. write for info. (*0-02-424550-X*) Macmillan.

Critical Thinking & Communication: The Use of Reason in Argument. 2nd ed. Barbara Warnick & Edward S. Inch. (Illus.). 400p. (C). 1993. pap. write for info. (*0-02-424742-1*) Macmillan.

Critical Thinking & Effective Expression. Larry A. Christiansen. 96p. (C). 1994. per., pap. text ed. 10.95 (*0-8403-9477-2*) Kendall-Hunt.

Critical Thinking & Logic. Don S. Levi. 449p. (C). 1991. pap. text ed. 27.95 (*1-879215-01-2*) Sheffield WI.

***Critical Thinking & Reading: Empowering Learners to Think & Act.** Allan R. Neilsen. (Monographs on Teaching Critical Thinking). (Illus.). 54p. (C). 1989. pap. 8.95 (*0-927516-02-0*) ERIC-REC.

Critical Thinking & Thinking Skills: State-of-the-Art Definitions & Practice in Public Schools. Barbara Z. Presseisen. 57p. 1986. pap. 13.95 (*1-56602-011-5*) Research Better.

***Critical Thinking & Writing: A Developing Writer's Guide with Readings.** Kristan Cavina. 1995. pap. 27.95 (*0-534-24294-4*) Intl Thomson.

***Critical Thinking & Writing: Reclaiming the Essay.** Thomas Newkirk. Ed. & Intro. by Jerome Harste. LC 89-23515. (Monographs on Teaching Critical Thinking). 56p. (C). 1989. pap. 8.95 (*0-927516-04-7*) ERIC-REC.

Critical Thinking & Writing for Science & Technology. Thomas H. Miles. 345p. (C). 1990. pap. text ed. 25.50 (*0-15-516156-3*); pap. text ed. 1.50 (*0-15-516157-1*) HB Coll Pubs.

Critical Thinking as a Philosophical Movement. Seale Doss et al. 140p. (Orig.). (C). 1989. pap. text ed. 6.95 (*0-929331-02-8*) Ripon Coll Pr.

***Critical Thinking Companion for Introductory Psychology.** Jane Halonen. 130p. 1995. pap. text ed. 7.95x (*1-57259-018-1*) Worth.

Critical Thinking, Critical Choices: Listening & Speaking, Bk. 2. JoAnn Aebersold et al. (Illus.). 256p. (C). 1985. pap. text ed. 13.75 (*0-13-194127-5*) P-H.

Critical Thinking, Discussion, & the Learning Process. D. Allen Goedeke. 152p. 1990. per. 14.95 (*0-8403-6255-2*) Kendall-Hunt.

Critical Thinking Exercises for Western Civilization Courses. Arthur Auten. 352p. (C). 1993. pap. text ed. 18.95 (*0-8403-8404-1*) Kendall-Hunt.

Critical Thinking for the Professions of Health, Sport & Physical Eduation, Recreation & Dance. Earle F. Zeigler. 76p. (Orig.). (C). 1994. pap. text ed. 6.00 (*0-87563-503-2*) Stipes.

***Critical Thinking Handbook.** 350p. (Orig.). 1994. pap. text ed. write for info. (*0-02-309660-8*, Merrill Pub Co) Macmillan.

Critical Thinking Handbook - 4th-6th Grades: A Guide for Remodelling Lesson Plans in Language Arts, Social Studies, & Science. Richard Paul et al. LC 87-72836. (Orig.). (C). 1987. pap. text ed. 18.00 (*0-944583-01-6*) Ctr Critical Thinking.

Critical Thinking Handbook--High School: A Guide for Re-Designing Instruction. Richard Paul & A. J. Binker. LC 89-62293. (Orig.). 1989. pap. text ed. 18.00 (*0-944583-03-2*) Ctr Critical Thinking.

Critical Thinking Handbook--K-3: A Guide for Remodelling Lesson Plans in Language Arts, Social Studies, & Science. Richard Paul et al. LC 87-71979. (Orig.). (C). 1987. pap. text ed. 18.00 (*0-944583-00-8*) Ctr Critical Thinking.

Critical Thinking Handbook--6th-9th Grades: A Guide for Remodelling Lesson Plans in Language Arts, Social Studies, & Science. Richard Paul et al. LC 88-64125. (Orig.). 1989. pap. text ed. 18.00 (*0-944583-02-4*) Ctr Critical Thinking.

Critical Thinking Handbook: K-Three: A Guide for Remodelling Lesson Plans in Language Arts, Social Studies & Science. 2nd ed. Richard W. Paul et al. LC 90-82938. (Illus.). 410p. 1990. pap. text ed. 18.00 (*0-944583-05-9*) Ctr Critical Thinking.

Critical Thinking in an Image World: Alfred Korzybski's Theoretical Principles Extended to Critical Television Evaluation. Geraldine E. Forsberg. 220p. (C). 1993. pap. text ed. 18.50 (*0-8191-8971-5*) U Pr of Amer.

Critical Thinking in an Image World: Alfred Korzybski's Theoretical Principles Extended to Critical Television Evaluation. Geraldine E. Forsberg. 220p. (C). 1993. lib. bdg. 46.50 (*0-8191-8970-7*) U Pr of Amer.

Critical Thinking in Clinical Practice: Improving the Accuracy of Judgments & Decisions about Clients. Eileen Gambrill. LC 89-24660. (Nonprofit Sector-Public Administration Ser.). 454p. 1990. 33.95x (*1-55542-198-9*) Jossey-Bass.

***Critical Thinking in Nursing.** 2nd ed. Elsie L. Bandman. LC 94-29377. 1994. 32.50 (*0-8385-1374-3*) Appleton & Lange.

***Critical Thinking in Nursing: A Practical Approach.** Rosalinda Alfaro-LeFevre. LC 94-25233. 1995. pap. text ed. 19.95 (*0-7216-5897-0*) Saunders.

Critical Thinking in Nursing: An Interactive Approach. Rubenfeld. 336p. 1995. write for info. (*0-397-55099-5*) Lippincott.

Critical Thinking, Reading & Writing. Mary Morgan & Michael Shermis. LC 89-49156. (Teaching Resources in the ERIC Database (TRIED) Ser.). 1989. pap. 14.95 (*0-927516-08-X*) ERIC-REC.

Critical Thinking, Reading, & Writing: A Brief Guide to Argument. Sylvan Barnet & Hugo A. Bedau. LC 92-72225. 230p. (C). 1992. pap. text ed. 10.00 (*0-312-08613-X*, Bedford Bks) St Martin.

Critical Thinking Skills. Marcia Heiman & Joshua Slomianko. 48p. 1986. 7.95 (*0-8106-0690-9*) NEA.

***Critical Thinking Workbook for Radiographers.** Doreen Towsley. 150p. (Orig.). (C). 1995. pap. text ed. 15.95 (*1-881795-09-8*) Eastwind Pub.

Critical Thought: An Anthology of 20th Century Indian English Essays. S. K. Desai & G. N. Devy. 256p. 1987. text ed. 30.00 (*81-207-0663-3*, Pub. by Sterling Pubs II) Apt Bks.

Critical Thoughts & Notions. Duane L. Whitlock. LC 87-63353. (Illus.). 284p. (C). 1988. 24.95 (*0-945077-00-9*) Omega CA.

Critical Tradition: Classic Texts & Contemporary Trends. Ed. by David H. Richter. LC 88-70423. 1436p. (C). 1989. pap. text ed. 42.00 (*0-312-00344-7*, Bedford Bks) St Martin.

***Critical Traditions in Contemporary Archaeology: Essays in the Philosophy, History, & Socio-Politics of Archaeology.** Ed. by Valerie Pinsky & Alison Wylie. LC 94-45894. 180p. 1995. reprint ed. pap. 19.95 (*0-8263-1599-2*) U of NM Pr.

Critical Trends in HTC Superconductivity. B. K. Chakraverty. 300p. (C). 1995. text ed. 73.00 (*981-02-0195-8*) World Scientific Pub.

Critical Turn: Rhetoric & Philosophy in Postmodern Discourse. Ed. by Ian Angus & Lenore Langsdorf. LC 92-9398. 240p. (C). 1992. 34.95 (*0-8093-1843-1*); pap. 14.95 (*0-8093-1844-X*) S Ill U Pr.

Critical Turn: Studies in Kant, Herder, Wittgenstein, & Contemporary Theory. Michael Morton. LC 92-13153. (Kritik: German Literary Theory & Cultural Studies). 346p. (C). 1992. 39.95 (*0-8143-2376-6*) Wayne St U Pr.

Critical Understanding: The Powers & Limits of Pluralism. Wayne C. Booth. LC 78-15107. 1982. pap. text ed. 10.95 (*0-226-06555-3*) U Ch Pr.

Critical Ventures in Modern French Literature. Arnold Whitridge. LC 67-22066. (Essay Index Reprint Ser.). 1977. 15.95 (*0-8369-0993-3*) Ayer.

Critical Victimology: International Perspectives. R. I. Mawby & Sandra Walklate. 240p. (C). 1994. text ed. 65.00 (*0-8039-8511-8*); pap. text ed. 19.95 (*0-8039-8512-6*) Sage.

Critical Viewing of Television: A Book for Parents & Teachers. Ibrahim M. Hefzallah. 218p. (Orig.). 1987. lib. bdg. 47.50 (*0-8191-6107-1*); pap. text ed. 22.50 (*0-8191-6108-X*) U Pr of Amer.

Critical Views on Vicente Aleixandre's Poetry. Ed. by Vicente Cabrera & Harriet Boyer. LC 79-65008. 185p. reprint ed. pap. 52.80 (*0-317-41823-8*, 2025614) Bks Demand.

Critical Villager: Beyond Community Participation. Eric Dudley. (Illus.). 197p. 1993. 59.95 (*0-415-07343-X*, B2406); pap. 17.95 (*0-415-07344-8*, B2410) Routledge.

***Critical Vision: Random Essay & Tracts Concerning Sex Religion Death.** Ed. by David Kerekes & David Slater. (Illus.). 200p. (Orig.). 1994. pap. 19.95 (*0-9523288-0-1*, Pub. by Head Pr UK) AK Pr Dist.

Critical Voices in American Catholic Economic Thought. Ed. by John J. Mitchel, Jr. 1989. pap. 10.95 (*0-8091-3029-7*) Paulist Pr.

Critical Voices on Special Education: Problems & Progress Concerning the Mildly Handicapped. Ed. by Scott B. Sigmon. LC 89-38707. 265p. 1990. 64.50 (*0-7914-0319-X*); pap. 21.95 (*0-7914-0320-3*) State U NY Pr.

Critical Wager: Essays on Criticism & the Architecture of Ideology. William D. Gairdner. 200p. (C). 1982. pap. text ed. 6.50 (*0-920802-41-9*, Pub. by ECW Press CN) Genl Dist Srvs.

Critical Water Issues & Computer Applications. Ed. by Mike Strech. (Conference Proceedings Ser.). 408p. 1988. 38.00 (*0-87262-660-1*) Am Soc Civil Eng.

Critical Way in Religion. Duncan Howlett. LC 80-7460. 360p. 1984. reprint ed. pap. 22.95 (*0-87975-266-1*) Prometheus Bks.

Critical Word Book of Leviticus, Numbers, Deuteronomy. Peter M. Morris & Edward James. (Computer Bible Ser.: Vol. VIII). 1975. pap. 20.00 (*0-935106-13-8*) Biblical Res Assocs.

Critical Word Book of the Pentateuch. Peter M. Morris & Edward James. (Computer Bible Ser.: Vol. XVII). 1980. pap. 25.00 (*0-935106-03-0*) Biblical Res Assocs.

Critical Work III: Illustrations. Robert G. Cohn. (Stanford French & Italian Studies: No. 81). 176p. 1994. pap. 46.50 (*0-915838-97-4*) Anma Libri.

Critical Works of John Dennis. John Dennis. Ed. by Edward N. Hooker. LC 39-5971. reprint ed. Vol. 1: 1692-1711. pap. 137.30 (*0-317-28816-4*, 2020537); reprint ed. Vol. 2: 1711-1729. pap. 160.00 (*0-317-28817-2*) Bks Demand.

Critical Writing Workshop: Designing Writing Assignments to Foster Critical Thinking. Ed. by Toni-Lee Capossela. LC 93-9449. 225p. (C). 1993. pap. text ed. 20.00 (*0-86709-319-6*, 0319) Boynton Cook Pubs.

Critical Writings. Ford Madox Ford. Ed. by Frank MacShane. LC 64-11356. 182p. reprint ed. pap. 51.90 (*0-7837-1893-4*, 2042097) Bks Demand.

Critical Writings of James Joyce. James Joyce. Ed. by Ellsworth Mason & Richard Ellmann. LC 88-43400. 288p. 1989. pap. 12.95 (*0-8014-9587-3*) Cornell U Pr.

Critical Writings on R. S. Thomas. rev. ed. Ed. by Sandra Anstey. 235p. 1993. 35.00 (*1-85411-062-4*, Pub. by Seren Bks UK) Dufour.

Critical Writings, 1953-1978. Paul De Man. (Theory & History of Literature Ser.: Vol. 66). 320p. (Orig.). 1989. pap. 15.95 (*0-8166-1696-5*) U of Minn Pr.

Critical Years: Birth to Two. rev. ed. Judith K. Schneider et al. (Competent Caregiver Ser.). (Illus.). 58p. (C). 1986. student ed 3.95 (*0-944454-15-1*); pap. text ed. 6.95 (*0-944454-04-6*); 2.95 (*0-318-23738-5*) CAPE Center.

Critical Years: Relations Between Elizabeth & the Papacy 1558-1572. John M. Pafford. LC 88-71468. 196p. (Orig.). (C). 1987. pap. 5.95 (*0-9620878-0-7*) Anglican Heritage Pubns.

Critical Years in Immigration: Canada & Australia Compared. 2nd ed. Freda Hawkins. (McGill-Queen's Studies in Ethnic History). 392p. (C). 1991. reprint ed. pap. text ed. 24.95 (*0-7735-0852-X*, Pub. by McGill CN) U of Toronto Pr.

Critical Years in Immigration: Canada & Australia Compared. Freda Hawkins. LC 91-90407. (McGill-Queen's Studies in Ethnic History: No. 2). 406p. reprint ed. pap. 115.80 (*0-7837-2625-2*, 2042975) Bks Demand.

***Critically Evaluating the Role of Experiments.** Ed. by Kendon J. Conrad. LC 85-644749. (New Directions for Program Evaluation Ser.: No. 63). 111p. (Orig.). 1994. pap. 17.95 (*0-7879-9992-X*) Jossey-Bass.

Criticas Constructivas del Sistema Politico Mexicano: Critiques of the Mexican Political System: Conference Papers. Ed. by William P. Glade & Stanley R. Ross. LC 72-510. (Encuesta Politica, Mexico Ser.: No. 2). 252p. reprint ed. pap. 71.90 (*0-685-17103-5*, 2027322) Bks Demand.

Criticism. Desmond Maccarthy. LC 78-97710. (Essay Index Reprint Ser.). 1977. 23.95 (*0-8369-1360-4*) Ayer.

Criticism: An Unpublished Essay. Walt Whitman. 1973. 69.95 (*0-87968-967-6*) Gordon Pr.

Criticism: Its Philosophical Structure. David Collingridge. LC 87-2089. 178p. (Orig.). 1988. pap. text ed. 19.00 (*0-8191-6282-5*) U Pr of Amer.

Criticism: Major Statements. 3rd ed. Ed. by Charles Kaplan & William Anderson. LC 89-63905. 896p. (C). 1991. pap. text ed. 24.50 (*0-312-03502-0*) St Martin.

Criticism: Speculative & Analytical Essays. Ed. by L. S. Dembo. 160p. 1968. pap. 4.00x (*0-299-04974-4*) U of Wis Pr.

Criticism: The Major Texts. enl. ed. Walter J. Bate. 719p. (C). 1970. text ed. 45.25 (*0-15-516148-2*) HB Coll Pubs.

Criticism & Compliment: The Politics of Literature in the England of Charles I. Kevin Sharpe. (Cambridge Studies in Early Modern British History). (Illus.). 320p. 1987. 69.95 (*0-521-34239-2*) Cambridge U Pr.

Criticism & Compliment: The Politics of Literature in the England of Charles I. Kevin Sharpe. (Cambridge Studies in Early Modern British History). (Illus.). 310p. (C). 1990. pap. 22.95 (*0-521-38661-6*) Cambridge U Pr.

Criticism & Convention: Midgard, Vol. 1. Contrib by Mildred Friedman et al. (Illus.). 176p. 1991. pap. 14.95 (*1-878271-53-9*) Princeton Arch.

Criticism & Creation. (Yale French Studies: No. 3). 1949. pap. 15.00 (*0-527-01711-6*) Periodicals Srv.

Criticism & Creation. Herbert J. Grierson. LC 78-58259. (Essay Index in Reprint Ser.). 1978. 17.50 (*0-8486-3021-1*) Roth Pub Inc.

Criticism & Creativity. P. J. Robertson. 84p. (C). 1989. 60.00 (*0-907839-22-3*, Pub. by Brynmill Pr Ltd UK) St Mut.

C

An Asterisk (*) at the beginning of an entry indicates that the title is appearing in BIP for the first time.

Criticism & Culture. Ed. by Sherman Paul. (Papers of the Midwest Modern Language Association: No. 2). x, 123p. (Orig.). 1972. pap. 19.00 (*0-87352-171-4*, MM69) Modern Lang.

Criticism & Culture: The Role of Critique in Modern Literary Theory. Robert C. Davis & Ronald Schleifer. 259p. (C). 1992. pap. text ed. 28.50 (*0-582-05082-0*, 79203) Longman.

Criticism & Fiction. William Dean Howells. (Notable American Authors Ser.). 1992. reprint ed. lib. bdg. 75.00 (*0-7812-3272-4*) Rprt Serv.

Criticism & Ideology: A Study in Marxist Theory. Terry Eagleton. 191p. (Orig.). 1978. pap. text ed. 13.95 (*0-86091-707-X*, Pub. by Verso UK) Routledge Chapman & Hall.

Criticism & Ideology: Second African Writers' Conference, Stockholm, 1986. Ed. by Kirsten H. Petersen. (Scandinavian Institute of African Studies: No. 20). 223p. 1988. 58.00x (*91-7106-276-9*, Pub. by Nordisk Afrikainstitutet SW) Coronet Bks.

Criticism & Lacan: Essays & Dialogue on Language, Structure & the Unconscious. Ed. by Patrick C. Hogan & Lalita Pandit. LC 89-20323. 296p. 1990. 38.00 (*0-8203-1209-6*); pap. 18.50 (*0-8203-1210-X*) U of Ga Pr.

Criticism & Other Addresses. Josiah C. Stamp. LC 67-22119. (Essay Index Reprint Ser.). 1977. 23.95 (*0-8369-0900-3*) Ayer.

Criticism & Public Rationality: Professional Rigidity & the Search for Caring Government. Harry Smart. 240p. (C). 1991. text ed. 74.00 (*0-415-03072-2*, A5116) Routledge.

Criticism & Self-Criticism: A Sign of Love & Concern. Ann Tompkins. (Illus.). Date not set. 6.95 (*0-394-42278-3*); pap. 4.95 (*0-394-73478-5*) Random.

Criticism & Social Change. Frank Lentricchia. LC 83-9299. viii, 176p. 1984. 15.00 (*0-226-47199-3*) U Ch Pr.

Criticism & Social Change. Frank Lentricchia. LC 83-9299. viii, 176p. 1985. pap. text ed. 12.95 (*0-226-47200-0*) U Ch Pr.

***Criticism & the History of Science: Kuhn's, Lakato's, & Feyrabend's Criticisms of Critical Rationalism.** Gunnar Andersson. LC 94-26308. (Philosophy of History & Culture Ser.: Vol. 13). 1994. 63.00 (*90-04-10050-4*) E J Brill.

Criticism & Truth. Roland Barthes. Ed. & Tr. by Katrine P. Keunemen. LC 86-27264. 119p. (Orig.). 1987. text ed. 29.95 (*0-8166-1608-6*); pap. text ed. 11.95 (*0-8166-1609-4*) U of Minn Pr.

Criticism, History, & Intertextuality, Vol. 31, No. 1. Ed. by Richard Fleming & Michael Payne. LC 86-47998. (Illus.). 184p. 1988. 22.00 (*0-8387-5118-0*) Bucknell U Pr.

Criticism in Action: Enlightenment Experiments in Political Writing. Dena Goodman. LC 88-47915. 256p. 1989. 36.50 (*0-8014-2201-9*) Cornell U Pr.

Criticism in America. T. S. Eliot. 1973. lib. bdg. 250.00 (*0-87968-045-8*) Gordon Pr.

Criticism in America: Its Functions & Status. T. S. Eliot. LC 68-57456. (Studies in T. S. Eliot: No. 11). 1972. reprint ed. lib. bdg. 75.00 (*0-8383-0541-5*) M S G Haskell Hse.

Criticism in America, Its Functions & Status. (BCL1-PS American Literature Ser.). 30p. 1992. reprint ed. lib. bdg. 59.00 (*0-7812-6601-7*) Rprt Serv.

Criticism in Society: Interviews wth Jacques Derrida, Northrop Frye, Harold Bloom & Geoffrey Hartman, Etc. Imre Salusinszky. (New Accents Ser.). 256p. 1989. pap. 14.95 (*0-416-92270-8*, 1100) Routledge Chapman & Hall.

Criticism in the Borderlands: Studies in Chicano Literature, Culture, & Ideology. Ed. by Hector Calderon & Jose D. Saldivar. LC 90-25853. (Post-Contemporary Interventions Ser.). 312p. 1991. lib. bdg. 50.50 (*0-8223-1137-2*); pap. text ed. 19.95 (*0-8223-1143-7*) Duke.

Criticism in the Twilight Zone: Postmodern Perspectives on Literature & Politics. Ed. by D. Zadworna-Fjellestad & Lennart Bjork. (Stockholm Studies in English: No. LXXVII). 153p. (Orig.). 1990. pap. 42.50x (*91-22-01314-8*, Pub. by Almqv & Wiksell SW) Coronet Bks.

Criticism in the Wilderness: The Study of Literature Today. Geoffrey H. Hartman. LC 80-13491. 336p. 1982. pap. 15.00 (*0-300-02839-3*) Yale U Pr.

Criticism of Fiction: A Study of Trends in the Atlantic Monthly. Helen McMahon. LC 74-148278. reprint ed. 18.00 (*0-404-04144-2*) AMS Pr.

Criticism of Milton's Paradise Lost, from the Spectator, 1711-12. large type ed. Joseph Addison. Ed. by Edward Arber. 152p. 1983. pap. 15.00 (*0-87556-550-6*) Saifer.

Criticism of Photography As Art: The Photographs of Jerry Uelsmann. John L. Ward. LC 71-630252. (University of Florida Humanities Monographs: No. 32). (Illus.). 1970. pap. 12.95 (*0-8130-0303-2*) U Press Fla.

Criticism of the Crusade: A Study of Public Opinion & Crusade Propaganda. P. A. Throop. 1972. 59.95 (*0-87968-968-4*) Gordon Pr.

Criticism of Theological Reason: Time & Timelessness as Primordial Presuppositions. Fernando L. Canale. (Andrews University Seminary Doctoral Dissertation Ser.: Vol. 10). 479p. 1987. pap. 19.99 (*0-943872-43-X*) Andrews Univ Pr.

Criticism, Theory & Children's Literature. Peter Hunt. 276p. 1991. pap. 21.95 (*0-631-16231-3*) Blackwell Pubs.

Criticism Without Boundaries: Directions & Crosscurrents in Postmodern Critical Theory. Ed. by Joseph A. Buttigieg. LC 86-40593. (Ward-Phillips Lecture Ser.: Vol. 12). 1987. text ed. 31.95 (*0-268-00762-4*) U of Notre Dame Pr.

Criticisms of Life. Horace J. Bridges. LC 75-99684. (Essay Index Reprint Ser.). 1977. 23.95 (*0-8369-1342-6*) Ayer.

Criticisms on Contemporary Thought & Thinkers: Selected from the Spectator, 2 vols., Set. Richard H. Hutton. LC 75-30030. reprint ed. 115.00 (*0-404-14070-X*) AMS Pr.

Criticizing. William J. Diehm. LC 86-17372. (Christian Growth Bks.). 128p. (Orig.). 1986. pap. 9.99 (*0-8066-2211-3*, 10-1722, Augsburg) Augsburg Fortress.

Criticizing Art: Understanding the Contemporary. Terry Barrett. LC 93-27241. 200p. (C). 1994. pap. 17.95 (*1-55934-147-5*) Mayfield Pub.

Criticizing Photographs: An Introduction to Understanding Images. Terry Barrett. LC 90-6292. 180p. 1990. pap. text ed. 17.95 (*0-87484-906-3*) Mayfield Pub.

Criticizing the Media: Empirical Approaches. James B. Lemert. (CommText Ser.: Vol. 21). 160p. (C). 1989. text ed. 37.00 (*0-8039-2636-7*); pap. text ed. 16.95 (*0-8039-2637-5*) Sage.

Criticon, 3 vols. in 2, Set. Baltasar Gracian. xiv, 1293p. 1978. reprint ed. write for info. (*3-487-06511-8*, Pub. by Georg Olms GW) Lubrecht & Cramer.

Critic's Alchemy. Ruth Z. Temple. (Orig.). 1953. pap. 11.95 (*0-8084-0097-5*) NCUP.

Critics & Customers: The Control of Social Policy Research. Ed. by Jill Vincent & Stephen Brown. 133p. 1992. 55.95 (*1-85628-192-2*, Pub. by Avebury Pub UK) Ashgate Pub Co.

***Critics Bear It Away.** Crews. 1994. pap. 3.99 (*0-517-13027-0*) Random.

Critics' Canon: Standards of Theatrical Reviewing in America. Richard H. Palmer. LC 88-5671. (Contributions in Drama & Theatre Studies: No. 26). 195p. 1988. text ed. 49.95 (*0-313-26211-X*, PAO/, Greenwood Pr) Greenwood.

Critic's Choice. Ira Levin. 1962. pap. 4.75 (*0-8222-0252-2*) Dramatists Play.

Critic's Choice. Kathleen Yapp. 224p. (Orig.). 1992. pap. 2.95 (*1-878702-80-7*, Kismet) Meteor Pub.

Critics' Choice: New York Drama Critics' Circle Prize Plays, 1935-55. Ed. by Jack Gaver. LC 70-173622. (Play Anthology Reprint Ser.). 1980. reprint ed. 47.95 (*0-8369-8221-5*) Ayer.

Critic's Choice Recipe Collection: 145 Recipes from Monterey Peninsula's Best Restaurants. Janice Block & David Rankine. Ed. by Ticien Carlson & Barbara Kantro. (Illus.). 168p. (Orig.). 1992. pap. 15.95 (*0-9632181-0-7*) Crits Choice.

Critics Favorites. D. K. Jackson. Ed. by Lee Stanley et al. (Illus.). 96p. (C). 1988. reprint ed. pap. 4.95 (*0-9621891-0-3*) D & A Pub CA.

Critic's Notebook. Irving Howe. 1994. 27.95 (*0-15-119949-3*) HarBrace.

***Critic's Notebook.** Irving Howe. Ed. & Intro. by Nicholas Howe. LC 95-17560. 1995. write for info. (*0-15-600257-4*, Harvest Bks) HarBrace.

Critic's Notebook. Ed. by Robert W. Stallman. LC 76-48931. 303p. 1977. reprint ed. 59.75 (*0-8371-9324-9*, STCN, Greenwood Pr) Greenwood.

Critics of Abstract Expressionism. Stephen C. Foster. LC 80-17239. (Studies in the Fine Arts: No. 2). 146p. reprint ed. pap. 41.70 (*0-8357-1088-2*, 2070634) Bks Demand.

Critics of Capitalism: Victorian Criticism of Political Economy. Ed. by Elizabeth Jay & Richard Jay. (Cambridge English Prose Texts Ser.). 278p. 1987. 59.95 (*0-521-26588-6*) Cambridge U Pr.

Critics of Consciousness: The Existential Structures of Literature. Sarah N. Lawall. LC 68-25614. 295p. reprint ed. pap. 84.10 (*0-7837-1519-6*, 2041796) Bks Demand.

Critics of Edmund Spenser. Herbert E. Cory. LC 65-15901. (Studies in Spenser: No. 26). 1969. reprint ed. lib. bdg. 75.00 (*0-8383-0532-6*) M S G Haskell Hse.

Critics of Keynesian Economics. Intro. by Henry Hazlitt. LC 83-21781. 438p. 1984. pap. text ed. 27.00 (*0-8191-3667-0*) U Pr of Amer.

***Critics of Keynesian Economics.** Ed. by Henry Hazlitt. 427p. 1995. reprint ed. 24.95 (*1-57246-013-X*); reprint ed. pap. 19.95 (*1-57246-012-1*) Foun Econ Ed.

Critics of Marxism. David Gordon. 164p. 1986. pap. 19.95x (*0-912051-12-4*) Transaction Pubs.

Critics of Society: Radical Thought in North America. 2nd ed. Thomas B. Bottomore. LC 86-29451. 153p. 1987. text ed. 52.50 (*0-313-25695-0*, BOCS, Greenwood Pr) Greenwood.

Critics of the Bible: 1724-1873. Ed. by John Drury. (Cambridge English Prose Texts Ser.). (C). 1989. 59.95 (*0-521-32992-2*); pap. 18.95 (*0-521-33870-0*) Cambridge U Pr.

Critics of the Italian Parliamentary System, 1860-1915. Armand Patrucco. LC 91-44343. (Modern European History Ser.). 336p. 1992. 75.00 (*0-8153-0738-1*) Garland.

Critics of the Italian World, Fifteen Thirty to Fifteen Sixty: Anton Francesco Doni, Nicolo Franco & Ortensio Lando. Paul F. Grendler. LC 69-16112. (Illus.). 296p. 1969. 30.00 (*0-299-05220-6*) U of Wis Pr.

Critics on Blake. Ed. by Judith O'Neill. LC 75-142198. (Readings in Literary Criticism Ser.: No. 7). 1970. 10.95 (*0-87024-189-3*) U of Miami Pr.

Critics on Charlotte & Emily Bronte. Ed. by Judith O'Neill. LC 68-54477. (Readings in Literary Criticism Ser.: No. 2). 1979. pap. 10.95 (*0-87024-098-6*) U of Miami Pr.

Critics on Chaucer. Ed. by Sheila Sullivan. LC 70-124654. (Readings in Literary Criticism Ser.: No. 6). 1979. pap. 10.95 (*0-87024-169-9*) U of Miami Pr.

Critics on D. H. Lawrence. Ed. by W. T. Andrews. LC 77-159294. (Readings in Literary Criticism Ser.: No. 9). 1979. pap. 10.95 (*0-87024-207-5*) U of Miami Pr.

Critics on Emerson. Ed. by Thomas J. Rountree. LC 73-77552. (Readings in Literary Criticism Ser.: No. 20). 128p. 1973. 10.95 (*0-87024-237-7*) U of Miami Pr.

Critics on Emily Dickinson. Ed. by Richard H. Rupp. LC 77-143454. (Readings in Literary Criticism Ser.: No. 14). (Orig.). 1986. pap. 10.95 (*0-685-25021-0*) U of Miami Pr.

Critics on Ezra Pound. Ed. by Epifanio San Juan, Jr. LC 70-143455. (Readings in Literary Criticism Ser.: No. 15). 1972. 10.95 (*0-87024-196-6*) U of Miami Pr.

Critics on Hawthorne. Ed. by Thomas J. Rountree. LC 78-159297. (Readings in Literary Criticism Ser.: No. 16). 1972. 10.95 (*0-87024-209-1*) U of Miami Pr.

Critics on Henry James. Ed. by J. Don Vann. LC 74-159296. (Readings in Literary Criticism Ser.: No. 18). 1972. 10.95 (*0-87024-211-3*) U of Miami Pr.

Critics on Jane Austen. Ed. by Judith O'Neill. LC 69-15928. (Readings in Literary Criticism Ser.: No. 5). 1970. 10.95 (*0-87024-117-6*) U of Miami Pr.

Critics on Mark Twain. Ed. by David B. Kesterson. LC 73-77553. (Readings in Literary Criticism Ser.: No. 21). 128p. 1979. pap. 10.95 (*0-87024-251-2*) U of Miami Pr.

Critics on Marlowe. Ed. by Judith O'Neill. LC 69-15927. (Readings in Literary Criticism Ser.: No. 4). 1970. 10.95 (*0-87024-121-4*) U of Miami Pr.

Critics on Melville. Ed. by Thomas J. Rountree. LC 74-143456. (Readings in Literary Criticism Ser.: No. 12). 1972. 10.95 (*0-87024-193-1*) U of Miami Pr.

Critics on Poe. Ed. by David B. Kesterson. LC 73-77554. (Readings in Literary Criticism Ser.: No. 22). 1973. pap. 10.95 (*0-685-25022-9*) U of Miami Pr.

Critics on Pope. Ed. by Judith O'Neill. LC 68-54478. (Readings in Literary Criticism Ser.: No. 3). (C). 1968. 10.95 (*0-87024-099-4*) U of Miami Pr.

Critics on Robert Lowell. Ed. by Jonathan Price. LC 78-161435. (Readings in Literary Criticism Ser.: No. 17). 1972. 10.95 (*0-87024-210-5*) U of Miami Pr.

Critics on Trial: An Introduction to the Catholic Modernist Crisis. Marvin R. O'Connell. LC 93-41850. 464p. 1994. 59.95 (*0-8132-0799-1*) Cath U Pr.

Critics on Trial: An Introduction to the Catholic Modernist Crisis. Marvin R. O'Connell. LC 93-41850. 464p. 1995. pap. write for info. (*0-8132-0800-9*) Cath U Pr.

Critics on Upton Sinclair. Ed. by Abraham Blinderman. LC 74-11470. (Readings in Literary Criticism Ser.: No. 24). 1975. 10.95 (*0-87024-263-6*) U of Miami Pr.

Critics on Virginia Woolf. Ed. by Jacqueline E. Latham. LC 77-124653. (Readings in Literary Criticism Ser.: No. 8). 1979. pap. 10.95 (*0-87024-170-2*) U of Miami Pr.

Critics on Wallace Stevens. Ed. by Peter L. McNamara. LC 78-173694. (Readings in Literary Criticism Ser.: No. 19). 1972. 10.95 (*0-87024-232-6*) U of Miami Pr.

Critics on Whitman. Ed. by Richard H. Rupp. LC 78-143457. (Readings in Literary Criticism Ser.: No. 13). 1972. 10.95 (*0-87024-195-8*) U of Miami Pr.

Critics on Willian Dean Howells. Ed. by Paul A. Eschholz. LC 74-11430. (Readings in Literary Criticism Ser.: No. 23). 128p. 1975. 10.95 (*0-87024-271-7*) U of Miami Pr.

Critics on Yeats. Ed. by Raymond Cowell. LC 78-148725. (Readings in Literary Criticism Ser.: No. 10). 1979. pap. 10.95 (*0-87024-200-8*) U of Miami Pr.

Critics, Values, & Restoration Comedy. John T. Harwood. LC 81-18397. 196p. 1982. 18.95 (*0-8093-1049-X*) S Ill U Pr.

Critics Who Made Us: Essays from Sewanee Review. Ed. by George Core. LC 93-4857. 328p. 1993. text ed. 39.95 (*0-8262-0916-5*) U of Mo Pr.

Critifiction: Postmodern Essays. Raymond Federman. LC 92-44360. (SUNY Series in Postmodern Culture). 133p. (C). 1993. 49.50 (*0-7914-1679-8*); pap. 16.95 (*0-7914-1680-1*) State U NY Pr.

Critique: A Review of the Department of State's Country Reports on Human Rights Practices for 1985. LC 86-202462. 126p. 1986. 8.00 (*0-938579-54-1*, Fund Free Exp) Hum Rts Watch.

Critique: Review of the Department of State's Country. Ed. by Patricia Armstrong. (Reports on Human Rights Practices for 1992 Ser.). 445p. (Orig.). 1993. pap. text ed. 15.00 (*0-934143-60-9*, U of Pa Pr) Lawyers Comm Human.

Critique: Review of the Department of State's Country. Ed. by George Black. (Reports on Human Rights Conditions for 1993 Ser.). 426p. (Orig.). 1994. pap. text ed. 18.00 (*0-934143-68-4*) Lawyers Comm Human.

Critique: Review of the Department of State's Country Reports on Human Rights Practice for 1989. Lawyers Committee for Human Rights Staff. 267p. 1990. pap. text ed. 15.00 (*0-934143-34-X*) Lawyers Comm Human.

Critique: Review of the Department of State's Country Reports on Human Rights Practice for 1989. Lawyers Committee for Human Rights Staff. 335p. 1991. pap. 15.00 (*0-934143-43-9*) Lawyers Comm Human.

Critique: Review of the Department of State's Country Reports on Human Rights Practices for 1983. Americas Watch Staff et al. 84p. 1984. 6.00 (*0-938579-53-3*, Fund Free Exp) Hum Rts Watch.

Critique: Review of the Department of State's Country Reports on Human Rights Practices for 1984. Americas Watch Committee (U.S.) et al. LC 86-151574. 1985. 6.00 (*0-938579-50-9*, Fund Free Exp) Hum Rts Watch.

Critique: Review of the Department of State's Country Reports on Human Rights Practices for 1988. Human Rights Watch Staff & Lawyers Committee for Human Rights Staff. 216p. 1989. pap. 15.00 (*0-929692-25-X*) Hum Rts Watch.

Critique: Review of the U. S. Department of State's Country Reports on Human Rights Practices for 1991. Lawyers Committee for Human Rights. Ed. by Patricia Armstrong. 460p. (Orig.). 1992. pap. text ed. 19.95 (*0-934143-55-2*) Lawyers Comm Human.

Critique, Action, & Liberation. James L. Marsh. LC 93-48999. (SUNY Series in the Philosophy of the Social Sciences). 352p. (C). 1994. text ed. 59.50 (*0-7914-2169-4*); pap. text ed. 19.95 (*0-7914-2170-8*) State U NY Pr.

Critique & Anti-Critique: Essays on Dependence & Reformism. Andre Gunder Frank. LC 83-13683. 320p. 1984. text ed. 42.95 (*0-275-91158-6*, C1158, Praeger Pubs) Greenwood.

Critique & Crisis: Enlightenment & the Pathogenesis of Modern Society. Reinhart Koselleck. (Studies in Contemporary German Social Thought). 212p. 1988. 30.00 (*0-262-11127-6*) MIT Pr.

Critique & Explanation: Essays in Honor of Gwynne Nettler. Ed. by Robert A. Silverman & Timothy F. Hartnagel. 225p. (C). 1986. 34.95x (*0-88738-070-0*) Transaction Pubs.

Critique & Power: Recasting the Foucault - Habermas Debate. Ed. by Michael Kelly. (Studies in Contemporary German Social Thought). (Illus.). 415p. 1994. pap. 20.00 (*0-262-61093-0*) MIT Pr.

Critique & Power: Recasting the Foucault-Habermas Debate. Ed. by Michael Kelly. (Studies in Contemporary German Social Thought). (Illus.). 415p. 1994. 39.00 (*0-262-11182-9*) MIT Pr.

Critique de la Dialectique et de la Philosophie de Hegel (D'Apres les Manuscrits Parisiens de 1844 see Cahiers de l'Institut de Science Economique Appliquee: Bibliographie Marxologique. Liste Complementaire

Critique De la Raison Dialectique, 2 Tomes, 1. Jean-Paul Sartre. (Gallimard Ser.). (FRE.). 1960. pap. 76.95 (*2-07-070493-9*) Schoenhof.

Critique De la Raison Dialectique, 2 Tomes, 2. Jean-Paul Sartre. (Gallimard Ser.). (FRE.). 1960. 49.95 (*2-07-070525-0*) Schoenhof.

Critique de l'Ecole des Femmes. Moliere. (FRE.). 1985. pap. 8.95 (*0-7859-4648-9*) Fr & Eur.

Critique des Critiques. Marcel Pagnol. (Coll. Litterature). 168p. (FRE.). 1987. pap. 19.95 (*0-7859-1548-6*, 2826308173) Fr & Eur.

Critique et Verite. Roland Barthes. 80p. (FRE.). 1966. pap. 24.95 (*0-7859-0929-X*, F80540) Fr & Eur.

Critique for Ecology. Robert H. Peters. (Illus.). 400p. (C). 1991. 89.95 (*0-521-40017-1*); pap. 32.95 (*0-521-39588-7*) Cambridge U Pr.

Critique, Norm, & Utopia: A Study of the Foundations of Critical Theory. Seyla Benhabib. LC 85-13323. 424p. 1987. pap. text ed. 18.00 (*0-231-06165-X*) Col U Pr.

***Critique of Accounting: Examination of the Foundations & Normative Structure of an Applied Discipline.** Richard V. Mattessich. LC 95-3776. 296p. 1995. text ed. 65.00 (*0-89930-863-5*, Quorum Bks) Greenwood.

Critique of Applied Ethics: Reflections & Recommendations. Abraham Edel et al. LC 93-26981. 264p. 1994. 49.95 (*1-56639-157-1*); pap. 24.95 (*1-56639-158-X*) Temple U Pr.

Critique of Artificial Intelligence: The Enchanted Loom. Israel Rosenfield. 400p. 1990. 60.00 (*0-685-47601-4*) OUP.

Critique of Beckett Criticism: A Guide to Research in English, French, & German. P. J. Murphy et al. (Literary Criticism in Perspective Ser.). 200p. 1994. 57.95 (*1-879751-93-3*) Camden Hse.

Critique of Civilization in Modern Times. 1991. lib. bdg. 79.95 (*0-8490-4620-3*) Gordon Pr.

Critique of Commodity Aesthetics: Appearance, Sexuality & Advertising in Capitalist Society. Wolfang F. Haug. Tr. by Robert Bock. LC 86-6917. 192p. 1986. text ed. 39.95 (*0-8166-1531-4*); pap. text ed. 15.95 (*0-8166-1532-2*) U of Minn Pr.

Critique of Contemporary American Sociology. Ed. by Ted R. Vaughan et al. LC 92-75608. 350p. (Orig.). 1993. text ed. 42.95 (*1-882289-03-X*); pap. text ed. 24.94 (*1-882289-02-1*) Gen Hall.

Critique of Cynical Reason. Peter Sloterdijk. Tr. & Illus. by Michael Eldred. LC 86-24918. (Theory & History of Literature Ser.: Vol. 40). 598p. 1988. text ed. 49.95 (*0-8166-1585-3*); pap. text ed. 19.95 (*0-8166-1586-1*) U of Minn Pr.

Critique of Dialectical Reason, Vol. II. Jean-Paul Sartre. Tr. by Quintin Hoare. 500p. 1991. 49.95 (*0-86091-311-2*, A4984, Pub. by Verso UK) Routledge Chapman & Hall.

Critique of Dialectical Reason: Theory of Practice Ensembles, Vol. 1. Jean-Paul Sartre. Ed. by Jonathan Ree. Tr. by Alan Sheridan. 836p. 1984. pap. text ed. 18.95 (*0-86091-757-6*, Pub. by Verso UK) Routledge Chapman & Hall.

Critique of Economic Reason. Andre Gorz. Tr. by Gillian Hardyside & Chris Turner. 300p. 1989. 50.00 (*0-86091-253-1*, A3741); pap. 17.95 (*0-86091-968-4*, A3745) Routledge Chapman & Hall.

Critique of Everyday Life. Henri Lefebvre. 1991. 39.95 (*0-86091-340-6*, Pub. by Verso UK) Routledge Chapman & Hall.

Critique of Everyday Life, Vol. 1. Henri Lefebvre. Tr. by John Moore. 336p. 1991. 39.95 (*0-86091-331-7*, A6393, Pub. by Verso UK) Routledge Chapman & Hall.

Critique of Everyday Life, Vol. 1. Henri Lefebvre. Tr. by John Moore. 312p. 1992. pap. 18.95 (*0-86091-587-5*, A9726, Pub. by Verso UK) Routledge Chapman & Hall.

Critique of Humanism: A Symposium. Ed. by Clinton H. Grattan. LC 68-20303. (Essay Index Reprint Ser.). 1977. 23.95 (*0-8369-0493-1*) Ayer.

Critique of Indian Dualism. Ed. by Shivnarayan Joshi. (C). 1992. text ed. 125.00 (*81-7233-022-7*, Pub. by Scientific Pubs II) St Mut.

Critique of Instrumental Reason. Max Horkheimer et al. LC 74-8450. 160p. 1974. pap. text ed. 16.95 (*0-8264-0088-4*) Continuum.

C

An Asterisk (*) at the beginning of an entry indicates that the title is appearing in BIP for the first time.

Critique of Jean-Paul Sartre's Ontology. Maurice
Natanson. LC 72-8367. (Studies in Philosophy: No. 40).
136p. 1972. reprint ed. lib. bdg. 75.00 (0-8383-1412-0)
M S G Haskell Hse.
Critique of Judgement. Immanuel Kant. 384p. 1970. pap.
13.95 (0-02-847500-3) Macmillan.
Critique of Judgement. Immanuel Kant. Tr. by J. C.
Meredith. 1978. pap. 19.95 (0-19-824589-0) OUP.
Critique of Judgment. Immanuel Kant. 342p. 1970. pap. 10.
95 (0-685-10978-X) Free Pr.
Critique of Judgment. Immanuel Kant. Tr. by Werner S.
Pluhar. LC 86-14852. (HPC Classics Ser.). 684p. (C).
1987. lib. bdg. 37.95 (0-87220-026-4); pap. text ed. 13.
95 (0-87220-025-6) Hackett Pub.
Critique of Judgment. Immanuel Kant. Tr. by J. H. Bernard.
(Library of Classics: No. 14). pap. text ed. 12.95
(0-685-02036-3) Hafner.
Critique of Keynesian Economics. Ed. by Walter Allan. LC
92-18932. 1993. text ed. 69.95 (0-312-08554-0) St
Martin.
Critique of Marxist & Nonmarxist Thought. Ed. by Ajit
Jain & Alexander J. Matejko. LC 85-19393. 305p. 1985.
text ed. 55.00 (0-275-92109-3, C2109, Praeger Pubs)
Greenwood.
Critique of Modern Textual Criticism. Jerome J. McGann.
LC 92-14702. 160p. (C). 1992. reprint ed. pap. text ed.
12.95 (0-8139-1418-3) U Pr of Va.
Critique of Modernity. Alain Touraine. Tr. by David
Macey. 416p. 1995. 54.95 (1-55786-530-2); pap. 21.95
(1-55786-531-0) Blackwell Pubs.
Critique of Modernity: Theological Reflections on
Contemporary Culture. Julian N. Hartt et al. LC 86-
13251. 113p. reprint ed. pap. 32.30 (0-7837-4356-4,
2044066) Bks Demand.
Critique of Monetary Policy: Theory & British Experience.
J. C. Dow & I. D. Saville. 288p. 1990. reprint ed. pap.
21.00 (0-19-828319-9) OUP.
Critique of Musicology: Clarifying the Scope, Limits &
Purposes of Musicology. John A. Kimmey, Jr. LC 88-
9355. (Studies in the History & Interpretation of Music:
Vol. 12). 330p. 1989. lib. bdg. 99.95 (0-88946-437-5) E
Mellen.
Critique of Pastoral Care. Stephen Pattison. 224p. (C).
1988. 16.95 (0-334-00280-X, SCM Pr) TPI PA.
Critique of Power: Reflective Stages in a Critical Social
Theory. Axel Honneth. Tr. by Kenneth Baynes. (Studies
in Contemporary German Social Thought). 350p. 1991.
40.00 (0-262-08202-0) MIT Pr.
Critique of Power: Reflective Stages in a Critical Social
Theory. Axel Honneth. Tr. by Kenneth Baynes. (Studies
in Contemporary German Social Thought). (Illus.). 350p.
1993. pap. 18.50 (0-262-58128-0) MIT Pr.
Critique of Practical Reason: Kant. 3rd ed. Immanuel Kant.
(Philosophical Library of Liberal Arts). (Illus.). 208p.
(C). 1993. pap. write for info. (0-02-307753-0)
Macmillan.
Critique of Psychoanalytic Reason: Hypnosis as a Scientific
Problem from Lavoisier to Lacan. Leon Chertok &
Isabelle Stengers. Tr. by Martha N. Evans. LC 91-
22388. 356p. (C). 1992. 37.50 (0-8047-1950-0) Stanford
U Pr.
Critique of Pure English see Fate of French-E in English:
The Plural of Nouns Ending in-th
Critique of Pure Modernity: Hegel, Heidegger, & After.
David Kolb. LC 85-24510. 334p. 1987. 25.00
(0-226-45031-7) U Ch Pr.
Critique of Pure Modernity: Hegel, Heidegger, & After.
David Kolb. LC 85-24510. 334p. 1988. pap. text ed. 15.
95 (0-226-45029-5) U Ch Pr.
Critique of Pure Reason. Immanuel Kant. Ed. by Vasilis
Politis. 555p. 1993. pap. 12.95 (0-460-87358-X,
Everyman's Classic Lib) C E Tuttle.
Critique of Pure Reason. Immanuel Kant. Ed. by Norman
K. Smith. 1969. pap. text ed. 13.00 (0-312-45010-9) St
Martin.
Critique of Pure Reason. Immanuel Kant. Tr. by J. M.
Meiklejohn. (Great Books in Philosophy). 480p. (C).
1990. reprint ed. pap. 9.95x (0-87975-596-2) Prometheus
Bks.
Critique of Pure Verbiage. Ronald Englefield. 1990. 36.95
(0-8126-9107-5); pap. 16.95 (0-8126-9108-3) Open
Court.
Critique of Religion & Philosophy. Walter Kaufmann. 1979.
pap. 18.95 (0-691-02001-9) Princeton U Pr.
Critique of Revolutionary Humanism: Frantz Fanon.
Richard C. Onwuanibe. 168p. 1983. 15.50
(0-87527-296-7) Green.
Critique of Scientific Reason. Kurt Hubner. Tr. by Paul R.
Dixon, Jr. & Hollis M. Dixon. LC 82-23690. 296p. 1983.
lib. bdg. 27.50 (0-226-35708-2) U Ch Pr.
Critique of Scientific Reason. Kurt Hubner. Tr. by Paul R.
Dixon, Jr. & Hollis M. Dixon. LC 82-23690. 296p. 1985.
pap. text ed. 12.95 (0-226-35709-0) U Ch Pr.
Critique of Slavery: Antislavery Thought. Ed. by Paul
Finkelman. (Articles on American Slavery Ser.). 560p.
1990. reprint ed. 48.00 (0-8240-6794-0) Garland.
*Critique of Soviet Economics. Mao Tse-Tung. Tr. by Moss
Roberts. LC 77-70971. reprint ed. pap. 44.80
(0-7837-9611-0, 2060368) Bks Demand.
Critique of Stammler. Max M. Weber. Tr. by Guy Oakes.
LC 77-72682. 1977. text ed. 22.95 (0-02-934100-0) Free
Pr.
Critique of Taste. Galvano Della Volpe. Tr. by Michael
Caesar. (Verso Modern Classics Ser.). 272p. 1991. pap.
18.95 (0-86091-565-4, A6421, Pub. by Verso UK)
Routledge Chapman & Hall.
Critique of Taste. Galvano D. Volpe. Tr. by Michael
Caesar. 272p. 1985. text ed. 34.95 (0-902308-48-3, Pub.
by Verso NLB UK) Routledge Chapman & Hall.

Critique of Teachers' Ratings of High School Boys As an
Indication of Later Neuropsychiatric Rejection for the
Armed Services. Olive L. Ives. LC 71-176898.
(Columbia University. Teachers College. Contributions
to Education Ser.: No. 950). reprint ed. 37.50
(0-404-55950-6) AMS Pr.
Critique of the Cost of Capital Theory: A Study of Flawed
Proofs of the M-M Theorm. William Sher & Rudy
Pinola. 1992. 22.50 (1-883428-00-9) Econ Res Srv.
Critique of the Foundations of Psychology: The Psychology
of Psychoanalysis. Georges Politzer. Tr. by Maurice
Apprey. LC 94-4139. 250p. (C). 1994. pap. text ed. 22.
50 (0-8207-0257-9) Duquesne.
Critique of the Foundations of Psychology: The Psychology
of Psychoanalysis. Georges Politzer. Tr. by Maurice
Apprey. LC 94-4139. 250p. (C). 1994. text ed. 54.00
(0-8207-0256-0) Duquesne.
Critique of the German Intelligentsia. Hugo Ball. Tr. by
Brian L. Harris. LC 93-7111. 273p. 1993. 55.00
(0-231-07526-X) Col U Pr.
Critique of the Gotha Program. Karl Marx. LC 69-20357.
116p. (Orig.). 1938. pap. text ed. 3.45 (0-7178-0043-1)
Intl Pubs Co.
Critique of the Human Potential Movement. Lawrence
Plumb. LC 92-40360. (Cults & Nonconventional
Religious Groups Ser.). 272p. 1993. 60.00
(0-8153-0777-2) Garland.
Critique of the New Natural Law Theory. Russell Hittinger.
LC 87-40344. (C). 1989. pap. text ed. 12.95
(0-268-00775-6) U of Notre Dame Pr.
*Critique of the Origins of Islamic Economic Thought.
Mohammed Y. Essid. (Islamic History & Civilization
Ser.). 275p. 1995. text ed. pap. 91.50 (90-04-10079-2) E J
Brill.
Critique of the Psycho-Physical Identity Theory: A
Refutation of Scientific Materialism & an
Establishment of Mind-Matter Dualism by Means of
Philosophy & Scientific Method. Eric P. Polten. LC
72-94504. (Studies in the Social Sciences: No. 14). 290p.
1973. text ed. 44.65 (90-279-7224-9) Mouton.
Critique of the Reagan Administration: First Year 1981,
Vol. 1. Tracy Voigt. 1982. 25.00 (0-686-37769-9) T
Voigt.
Critique of the Study of Kinship. David M. Schneider. LC
84-5246. 352p. (C). 1984. pap. text ed. 19.95x
(0-472-08051-2) U of Mich Pr.
Critique of the United States Income & Product Accounts.
(Studies in Income & Wealth: No. 22). 599p. 1958.
reprint ed. 155.80 (0-87014-178-3) Natl Bur Econ Res.
Critique of Thought: A Re-Examination of Hegel's Science
of Logic. 1989. text ed. 55.95 (0-566-05765-4, Pub. by
Avebury Pub UK) Ashgate Pub Co.
Critique of Ultra-Leftism in China, 1958-1981. William A.
Joseph. LC 83-42832. 328p. 1984. 39.50
(0-8047-1208-5) Stanford U Pr.
Critique of Urban Modelling see Progress in Planning
Critique of Vedanta. L. V. Rajagopal. (C). 1993. text ed. 27.
00 (81-215-0592-5, Pub. by Munshiram Manoharial II) S
Asia.
Critique, Resistance, & Action: Working Papers in the
Politics of Nursing. Ed. by David G. Allen et al. LC
92-48677. 208p. (Orig.). (C). 1992. pap. text ed. 38.95
(0-88737-563-4) Natl League Nurse.
Critique Stendhalienne de Balzac a Zola. Emile J. Talbot.
LC 78-73998. 279p. (FRE.). 1979. 17.95
(0-917786-14-9) Summa Pubns.
Critiques. Augustus J. Ralli. LC 67-22114. (Essay Index
Reprint Ser.). 1977. 20.95 (0-8369-0808-2) Ayer.
Critiques & Addresses. Thomas H. Huxley. LC 72-3358.
(Essay Index Reprint Ser.). 1977. reprint ed. 17.95
(0-8369-2908-X) Ayer.
Critiques de Notre Temps et Camus. Levi-Valensi. (FRE.).
13.95 (0-7859-0036-5, F91100) Fr & Eur.
Critiques Litteraires. Jean-Paul Sartre. (FRE.). 1975. pap.
12.95 (0-7859-2845-6) Fr & Eur.
Critiques of Contemporary Rhetoric. Karlyn K. Campbell.
217p. (C). 1972. pap. 18.95 (0-534-00135-1) Intl
Thomson.
Critiques of God. Ed. by Peter A. Angeles. LC 76-43520.
(Skeptic's Bookshelf Ser.). 371p. (C). 1976. pap. 21.95
(0-87975-078-2) Prometheus Bks.
*Critiques of Pure Abstraction. Mark Rosenthal. 72p. 1995.
pap. 20.00 (0-916365-43-3) Ind Curators.
Critiques of Research in the Social Sciences: An Appraisal
of Thomas & Znaniecki's "The Polish Peasant in Europe
& America" Herbert Blumer. (Social Science Classics
Ser.). 210p. (C). 1979. text ed. 39.95x (0-87855-312-6);
pap. text ed. 21.95 (0-87855-694-X) Transaction Pubs.
Critiques of the NRC Study, A Common Destiny: Blacks &
American Society. Ed. by Wornie L. Reed. (Assessment
of the Status of African-Americans Ser.). 96p. (Orig.).
(C). 1990. pap. 3.95 (1-878358-06-5) U MA W M
Trotter Inst.
Critiques on Sanskrit Dramas. Sadashiv A. Dange &
Sindhu S. Dange. (C). 1994. text ed. 30.00
(81-7305-033-3, Pub. by Aryan Bks Intl IA) S Asia.
Critiquing Approach to Expert Computer Advice: Attending.
Perry Miller. (Research Notes in Artificial Intelligence
Ser.). 1984. 29.95 (0-273-08665-0) Morgan Kauf.
Critiquing Human Error: A Knowledge Based Human-
Computer Collaboration Approach. Barry Silverman.
(Knowledge Based Systems Ser.). (Illus.). 317p. 1992.
text ed. 80.00 (0-12-643740-8) Acad Pr.
Critiquing Moral Arguments. Robert G. Pielke. 56p. (C).
1992. chap. text ed. 8.75 (0-8191-8643-0) U Pr of Amer.
Critiquing Moral Arguments. Robert G. Pielke. 56p. 1992.
lib. bdg. 26.50 (0-8191-8642-2) U Pr of Amer.
Crito see Last Days of Socrates
Crito see Euthyphro
Crito see Euthyphro, Apology Crito: With the Death Scene
from Phaedo

Crito see Republic & Other Works
Crittenden: A Kentucky Story of Love & War. John Fox.
1976. lib. bdg. 12.95 (0-89968-035-6, Lghtyr Pr)
Buccaneer Bks.
Crittenden Report: Report of the Board Appointed to
Prepare & Submit Recommendations to the Secretary
of the Navy for the Revision of Policies, Procedures &
Directives Dealing with Homosexuals. 67p. (Orig.).
(C). 1993. pap. text ed. 17.95x (1-56806-283-4) Diane
Pub.
Criter: The Class Cat. Colleen S. Bare. (Illus.). 32p. (J).
(ps-2). 1993. pap. 3.99 (0-14-055266-9, Puff Unicorn)
Puffin Bks.
Criter: The Hunt of the Century. Rainy Knight. (Orig.).
1991. pap. 7.95 (0-9631780-0-8) R Knight.
Critter Cakes & Frog Tea: Tales & Treats from the Emerald
River. Marie Rudisill. LC 94-9086. (J). (gr. 1). 1994.
spiral bd. 12.95 (1-881548-09-0) Crane Hill AL.
Critter Chronicles. Jim Dunlap. (Illus.). 168p. (Orig.). 1993.
pap. 12.95 (1-55622-312-9) Wordware Pub.
*Critter County Camping Trip. Paula Bussard & Christine
Wyrtzen. (1993 50-Day Spiritual Adventure Ser.).
(Illus.). 64p. (Orig.). (J). (ps-2). 1992. student ed. pap.
text ed. 4.99 (1-879050-10-2) Chapel of Air.
*Critter County Dream Team: Coming Soon to a Town
Near You Activity Book. Paula Bussard & Christine
Wyrtzen. (1994 50-Day Spiritual Adventure Ser.).
(Illus.). 64p. (Orig.). (J). (ps-2). 1993. student ed. pap.
text ed. 4.99 (1-879050-17-X) Chapel of Air.
*Critter Crackers: The ABC Book of Limericks. Kathryn
Barron. Ed. by Nancy R. Thatch. LC 95-8700. (Books
for Students by Students Ser.). (Illus.). 29p. (J). (gr. k-3).
1995. lib. bdg. 14.95 (0-933849-58-3) Landmark Edns.
Critter Crafts. Elaine Grant. (Illus.). 30p. (J). (gr. 4-7).
1991. spiral bd., pap. 9.95 (0-9632722-0-9) Arteg
Creations.
Critter Cuisine. Al Clayton & Mary A. Clayton. LC 92-
71787. (Illus.). 64p. 1992. 15.95 (1-56352-023-0)
Longstreet Pr Inc.
Critter of the Cracks. Freddie L. Butler. (Illus.). 64p. (J).
1994. pap. 8.00 (0-9639-3572-X) Dorrance.
Critter Race. Bob Reese. LC 81-3874. (Critterland Desert
Adventures Ser.). (Illus.). 24p. (J). (ps-2). 1981. pap.
2.95 (0-516-42302-9) Childrens.
Critter Sitters. Constance Hiser. LC 91-23002. (Illus.). 96p.
(J). (gr. 3-7). 1992. 13.95 (0-8234-0928-7) Holiday.
Critter Sitters. Constance Hiser. Ed. by Patricia
MacDonald. 96p. (YA). 1993. reprint ed. pap. 2.99
(0-671-86521-8, Minstrel Bks) PB.
Critter Sitters Board Books. Incl. Seasons. 1984. 3.50
(0-528-82342-6); Rainy Day Play. 1984. 3.50
(0-528-82343-4); Nursery Rhymes. 1984. 3.50
(0-528-82344-2); Our Friends. 1984. 3.50
(0-528-82345-0); Busy Day. 1984. 3.50 (0-528-82346-9);
Toys. 1984. 3.50 (0-528-82347-7); (J). (ps-4). 1984. write
for info. (0-318-58537-5) Checkerboard.
Critter Sitters Cloth Books. Incl. Playtime. 1983.
(0-528-87080-7); Mother Goose. (0-528-87081-5); On
the Farm. 1983. (0-528-87083-1); (J). (ps-4). 1983. write
for info. (0-318-57687-2) Checkerboard.
Critters. R. A. Noonan. LC 90-45819. (Tales of Terror
Ser.). (Illus.). 48p. (J). (gr. 5-6). 1991. text ed. 13.95
(0-89686-575-4, Crstwood Hse) Silver Burdett Pr.
Critters: Adventures in Wildest Suburbia. A. B. C.
Whipple. (Illus.). 256p. 1994. 18.95 (0-312-10445-6,
Pub. by Thomas Dunne Bks) St Martin.
Critters of Gazink. Grace R. Hicks. (Illus.). 64p. (J). (gr.
4-7). 1992. 11.95 (0-89015-816-9) Sunbelt Media.
Crkva i Hrvatsko Iseljenistvo (The Church & Croatian
Immigration) Croatian Ch. 214p. 1982. 9.00
(0-918660-29-7) Ragusan Pr.
*CRM Study Bible: New Testament. Ed. by John Pao.
848p. (CHI.). 1992. 20.00 (1-56582-000-2) Christ Renew
Min.
*CRM Study Bible (Simplified Script) New Testament.
deluxe ed. Ed. by John Pao. 712p. (CHI.). 1994. 16.00
(1-56582-050-9) Christ Renew Min.
Cro-Gu-Phant Mini Flip Book. (Illus.). (J). (ps-2). 1992.
4.20 (1-56021-022-7) W J Fantasy.
Croat Question: Partisan Politics in the Formation of the
Yugoslav Socialist State. Jill A. Irvine. 318p. (C). 1992.
text ed. 59.95 (0-8133-8542-3) Westview.
*Croatan Song: Graphic Novel. (Werewolf). Date not set.
12.00 (1-56504-311-1) White Wolf.
*Croatia: Human Rights & Democracy. (Illus.). 60p.
(Orig.). 1994. pap. 125.00 (0-7605-0018-5) Rector Pr.
Croatia: Land, People & Culture, 2 vols., 1. Ed. by Francis
H. Eterovich & Christopher Spalatin. LC 65-2286.
(Illus.). 1964. 35.00 (0-8020-3122-6) U of Toronto Pr.
Croatia: Myth & Reality. C. Michael McAdams. 89p. 1992.
pap. 10.00 (0-9633625-1-8) CIS Monographs.
Croatia: Myth & Reality. 2nd ed. C. Michael McAdams.
(Illus.). 93p. 1994. pap. 12.95 (0-9633625-2-6) CIS
Monographs.
Croatia & the Croatians: An Annotated Bibliography.
George J. Prpic. LC 80-66277. (Illus.). 315p. 1982. 16.95
(0-910164-05-3); pap. 9.95 (0-910164-02-9) Assoc Bk
Pubs.
*Croatia Rediviva. Ivo Omrcanin. 72p. (CRO.). 1995.
10.00 (0-614-06281-0) Ivor Pr.
Croatian Americans. Ellen Shapiro & Daniel P. Moynihan.
(Peoples of North America Ser.). 112p. (J). (gr. 5 up).
1989. 17.95 (0-87754-891-9) Chelsea Hse.
Croatian & Dalmatian Coats of Arms. Adam S. Eterovich.
LC 74-95024. (Illus.). 260p. 1978. pap. 15.00
(0-918660-05-X) Ragusan Pr.
Croatian & the Croatians: An English-Language
Bibliography & Resource Guide. rev. ed. George J.
Prpic. Ed. by Ruzica Kapetanovic. (Illus.). 450p. 1993.
pap. 17.95 (0-910164-24-X) Assoc Bk Pubs.

Croatian & the Croatians: An English-Language
Bibliography & Resource Guide. 2nd rev. ed. George J.
Prpic. Ed. by Ruzica Kapetanovic. (Illus.). 450p. 1993.
24.95 (0-910164-23-1) Assoc Bk Pubs.
Croatian Composer. William H. Hadow. LC 72-4147.
(Select Bibliographies Reprint Ser.). 1977. reprint ed. 15.
95 (0-8369-6881-6) Ayer.
Croatian Cuisine. Alojzije Kapetanovic & Ruzica
Kapetanovic. LC 78-62684. (Illus.). 1978. 11.95
(0-910164-00-2) Assoc Bk Pubs.
Croatian Cuisine. 2nd ed. Alojzije Kapetanovic & Ruzica
Kapetanovic. (Illus.). 224p. 1992. 29.95 (0-910164-18-5)
Assoc Bk Pubs.
Croatian-English - English-Croatian Dictionary of
Mechanical Engineering: Power Engineering with Basic
Mechanical Terms. L. Bartolic. 250p. (CRO & ENG.).
1991. 20.00 (86-03-00103-0, Pub. by Skolska Knjiga)
IBD Ltd.
Croatian-English - English-Croatian Dictionary of Naval
Architecture, Mechanical & Nuclear Engineering
Terms. 4th ed. L. Bartolic. 275p. (CRO & ENG.). 1991.
20.00 (86-03-99995-3, Pub. by Skolska Knjiga) IBD Ltd.
*Croatian-English--English-Croatian Dictionary of Naval
Architecture Mechanical & Nuclear Engineering Terms.
4th ed. L. Bartolic. (CRO & ENG.). 1991. 20.00
(0-7859-8926-9) Fr & Eur.
*Croatian-English--English-Croatian Dictionary of
Mechanical Engineering: Power Engineering with Basic
Mechanical Terms. L. Bartolic. (CRO & ENG.). 1991.
20.00 (0-7859-8925-0) Fr & Eur.
*Croatian-English--English-Croatian Dictionary of
Electronics. A. Stambuk. (CRO & ENG.). 1991. 60.00
(0-7859-8927-7) Fr & Eur.
*Croatian-English--English-Croatian Pocket Dictionary. B.
Brozovic. (CRO & ENG.). 1992. pap. 16.00
(0-7859-8832-7) Fr & Eur.
*Croatian-English Dictionary of Business & Government.
3rd ed. V. Ivir. 235p. (CRO & ENG.). 1993. write for
info. (0-7859-8798-3) Fr & Eur.
*Croatian-English, English-Croatian Pocket Dictionary.
Brozovic. 428p. (CRO & ENG.). 1992. pap. 15.95
(0-7859-7471-7, 860300725X) Fr & Eur.
Croatian Immigrants in America. George J. Prpic. (Illus.).
1971. 12.00 (0-686-61038-5) Ragusan Pr.
Croatian Migration to & from the United States, 1900-
1914. Frances Kraljic. LC 77-93262. 1978. per. 8.00
(0-918660-04-1) Ragusan Pr.
Croatian Musical Folklore: An Introduction. Walter W.
Kolar. (Illus.). 85p. (Orig.). 1981. pap. 5.00
(0-936922-02-8) Tamburitza.
Croatian National Movement, 1966-1972. Ante Cuvalo.
(East European Monographs). 256p. 1990. text ed. 32.50
(0-88033-179-8) Col U Pr.
Croatian Newspapers & Calendars in the U. S. Nada
Kestercanek. LC 79-146896. 1951. pap. 8.00
(0-88247-116-3) Ragusan Pr.
Croatian or Serbian-English Dictionary. Milan Drvodelic.
847p. 1983. 20.00 (0-918660-32-7) Ragusan Pr.
Croatian Pioneers in America, 1685-1900. Adam S.
Eterovich. LC 78-1109. 1979. per. 10.00
(0-918660-10-6) Ragusan Pr.
Croatian Renaissance Music Theorists. Stanislav Tuksar.
152p. 1980. pap. 10.00 (0-918660-51-3) Ragusan Pr.
Croatian Sourcebook: A Comprehensive Guide to
Information about Croatia & Croatians. Ivan
Kapetanovic. (Illus.). 300p. 1993. pap. 17.95
(0-910164-20-7) Assoc Bk Pubs.
Croation-English - English-Croation Dictionary of
Electronics. A. Stambuk et al. 777p. 1991. 88.00
(86-359-0060-X) IBD Ltd.
Croation-English Dictionary of Business & Government.
3rd enl. rev. ed. V. Ivir et al. 235p. 1993. 70.00
(0-88431-151-1, Pub. by Skolska Knjiga) IBD Ltd.
Croatoan. Ed. by Carole M. Longmeyer. (Lost Colony
Collection). (Illus.). 76p. (gr. 4-12). 1994. pap. 14.95
(0-935326-36-7) Gallopade Pub Group.
Croc & the Baby Tree. Hirokazu Miyazaki. LC 91-41719.
(Illus.). 28p. (J). (gr. k up). 1993. reprint ed. 14.95
(0-88708-224-6, Picture Book Studio) S&S Childrens.
Croccodile Smile. Jerome Lawrence & Robert E. Lee. 1972.
pap. 4.75 (0-8222-0253-0) Dramatists Play.
Croce As Shakespearean Critic. John M. Robertson.
(Studies in Shakespeare: No. 24). 1978. lib. bdg. 23.95
(0-8383-1810-X) M S G Haskell Hse.
Croce D'Oro. Patricia D'Alessandro. (Illus.). 32p. (Orig.).
1991. pap. 3.00 (1-880575-10-8) Hot Pepper.
Croce, the King & the Allies. Benedetto Croce. LC 78-
63660. (Studies in Fascism: Ideology & Practice). reprint
ed. 22.50 (0-404-16916-3) AMS Pr.
Croce Versus Gentile: A Dialogue on Contemporary Italian
Philosophy. Patrick Romanell. LC 78-63709. (Studies in
Fascism: Ideology & Practice). (Illus.). 80p. reprint ed.
20.00 (0-404-16979-1) AMS Pr.
Croce's Aesthetic. Bernard Bosanquet. 1974. lib. bdg. 59.95
(0-87968-969-2) Gordon Pr.
Crochet. Pauline Turner. 1989. pap. 25.00 (0-7478-0068-5,
Pub. by Shire UK) St Mut.
Crochet: A Fresh Approach to Traditional Art. Karey
Solomon. (Illus.). 160p. 1986. text ed. 19.95
(0-668-06279-7) P-H.
*Crochet: History & Technique. Lis Paludan. Tr. by Jean
Olsen & Kristine Fredricksson. 320p. 1995. 35.00
(1-883010-09-8) Interweave.
*Crochet Collection. Oxmoor House Staff. 1995. pap. 14.95
(0-942237-55-2) Leisure Art.
Crochet Designs for the Home: Full-Size Templates for
Twelve Patchwork Projects. 1990. pap. 2.95
(0-486-26168-9) Dover.
Crochet Designs from Hungary. Juliana Ray & Madeleine
Bokoli. Ed. by Jean Kinmond. 71p. 1973. reprint ed.
pap. 3.50 (0-486-20391-3) Dover.

An Asterisk (*) at the beginning of an entry indicates that the title is appearing in BIP for the first time.

C

Crochet Designs of Anne Orr. Anne Orr. LC 77-92502. (Needlework Ser.). (Illus.). 1978. pap. 2.75 (0-486-23621-8) Dover.

Crochet Lace with Complete Diagrams. Ondori Publishing Company Staff. (Ondori Needlecraft Ser.). (Illus.). 1979. pap. 14.95 (0-87040-415-6) Japan Pubns USA.

Crochet Workbook. Sylvia Cosh. 1990. pap. 15.95 (0-312-04032-6) St Martin.

*__Crocheted Gifts in a Weekend: 70 Quick & Lively Projects to Make.__ Nola Theiss. LC 94-23838. (Illus.). 144p. 1995. 24.95 (0-8069-0970-6) Sterling.

Crocheted Toys & Dolls: Complete Instructions for 12 Easy-to-Do Projects. Susan Verkest. (Illus.). 48p. 1978. pap. 2.25 (0-486-23637-4) Dover.

Crocheting Afgans. Rita Weiss. (Illus.). 1979. pap. 2.95 (0-486-23883-0) Dover.

Crocheting Baby Blankets & Carriage Covers. Annette Lep. (Illus.). 48p. (Orig.). 1983. pap. 2.95 (0-486-24480-6) Dover.

Crocheting Bedspreads. Ed. by Rita Weiss. LC 77-88742. (Needlework Ser.). (Illus.). 1978. pap. 2.95 (0-486-23610-2) Dover.

Crocheting Christmas Ornaments: Complete Instructions for 13 Projects. Susan Verkest. (Knitting, Crocheting, Tatting Ser.). (Illus.). 32p. (Orig.). 1982. pap. 2.95 (0-486-24351-6) Dover.

Crocheting Collars, Cuffs & Yokes. Mary C. Waldrep. (Illus.). 48p. (Orig.). 1987. pap. 2.95 (0-486-25516-6) Dover.

Crocheting Doilies. Ed. by Rita Weiss. LC 76-24565. (Illus.). 48p. 1976. pap. 3.50 (0-486-23424-X) Dover.

Crocheting Edgings. Rita Weiss. (Illus.). 48p. 1980. pap. 2.95 (0-486-24031-2) Dover.

Crocheting Fashion Sweaters for Women: Directions for 12 Cardigans, Pullovers & Vests. Annette Lep. 48p. 1986. pap. 2.95 (0-486-24957-3) Dover.

Crocheting in Plain English. Maggie Righetti. (Illus.). 258p. 1988. pap. 14.95 (0-312-01412-0) St Martin.

Crocheting Patchwork Patterns. Annette Lep. 48p. (Orig.). 1981. pap. 3.50 (0-486-23967-5) Dover.

Crocheting Placemats. Ed. by Rita Weiss. (Needlework Ser.). (Illus.). 1978. pap. 2.50 (0-486-23700-1) Dover.

Crocheting Ruffled Doilies. Linda Macho. (Knitting, Crocheting, Tatting Ser.). (Illus.). 48p. (Orig.). 1983. pap. 2.95 (0-486-24400-8) Dover.

Crocheting Storybook Hand Puppets. Susan Verkest. 1980. pap. 2.95 (0-486-23887-3) Dover.

Crocheting Tablecloths & Placemats. Ed. & Intro. by Florence Weinstein. LC 74-21221. (Illus.). 160p. 1975. pap. 5.95 (0-486-20659-9) Dover.

Crocheting Teddy Bears. Illus. by Ruth Jacksier & Barbara Jacksier. (Knitting, Crocheting, Tatting Ser.). 48p. 1984. pap. 2.95 (0-486-24639-6) Dover.

Crocheting with Anne Orr. Anne Orr. (Illus.). 48p. (Orig.). 1988. pap. 3.50 (0-486-25672-3) Dover.

Crochets & Quavers: Or Revelations of an Opera Manager in America. 2nd ed. Max Maretzek. LC 65-23397. (Music Ser.). 1966. reprint ed. lib. bdg. 39.50 (0-306-70915-5) Da Capo.

Crock, No. 4. Brant Parker et al. 128p. (Orig.). 1979. pap. 1.25 (0-449-13868-2, GM) Fawcett.

Crock-It. Barbara Neslen. (Illus.). 176p. 1991. pap. 12.95 (0-9629290-9-3) Star Feather.

Crock of Gold. James Stephens. 19.95 (0-89190-616-9, Am Repr) Amereon Ltd.

Crock of Gold. large type ed. Angela Devine. 306p. 1993. 21.95 (0-7505-0578-8) Ulverscroft.

Crock of Gold. large type ed. James Stephens. (Large-Print Ser.). 273p. 1992. reprint ed. lib. bdg. 20.00 (0-939495-34-1) North Bks.

*__Crock of Gold.__ James Stephens. (Illus.). 228p. 1995. reprint ed. pap. 15.95 (0-7171-2297-2, Pub. by Gill & MacMill IE) Irish Bks Media.

Crocker. Michael Gaskey. Ed. by Judy Hilvosky. 1989. 13.95 (0-87949-284-8) Ashley Bks.

*__Crocker Genealogy.__ Andrea Leonard. 311p. (Orig.). 1995. pap. text ed. 23.00 (0-7884-0197-1) Heritage Bk.

*__Crocker Genealogy: Descendants of Wm. Crocker of Barnstable MA, 1612-1692.__ J. R. Crocker et al. (Illus.). 321p. 1994. reprint ed. lib. bdg. 59.00 (0-8328-4269-9); reprint ed. pap. 49.00 (0-8328-4270-2) Higginson Bk Co.

Crockery Cook Book. Sunset Editors. (Cooking Ser.). 96p. (Orig.). 1992. pap. 9.99 (0-376-02224-8) Sunset Menlo Pk.

Crockery Cookbook. 1994. 14.95 (0-696-20365-0) Meredith Bks.

Crockery Cookbook. Marie R. Hamm. 1981. pap. 2.50 (0-449-14292-2, GM) Fawcett.

Crockery Cookery. Mabel Hoffman. 288p. 1983. mass mkt. 5.50 (0-553-25604-1) Bantam.

Crockery Cookery. Mable Hoffman. LC 74-30823. 176p. 1975. pap. 12.95 (0-912656-43-3) Price Stern.

Crockery Cookery see Mable Hoffman's Crockery Cookery

Crockery Favorites. Mabel Hoffman. (Orig.). 1993. mass mkt. 4.99 (0-553-56058-1) Bantam.

Crockery Favorites. Mable Hoffman & Gar Hoffman. LC 91-20000. (Illus.). 160p. (Orig.). 1991. pap. 9.95 (1-55561-046-3) Fisher Bks.

Crockett: A Bio-Bibliography. Richard B. Hauck. LC 82-6109. (Popular Culture Bio-Bibliographies Ser.). (Illus.). 169p. 1982. text ed. 47.95 (0-313-22272-X, HCR/, Greenwood Pr) Greenwood.

Crockett: The True Story of a Cowboy. Soren Roegdke & Kay Busse. 300p. (Orig.). 1993. pap. 20.00 (0-9629242-1-0) WKB Enterp.

*__Crockett Almanacs: Nashville Series, 1835-1838.__ Ed. by Franklin J. Meine. 1955. 25.00 (0-614-04638-6) Caxton Club.

Crockett at Two Hundred: New Perspectives on the Man & the Myth. Ed. by Michael A. Lofaro & Joe Cummings. LC 88-29369. 280p. 1989. 30.00x (0-87049-592-5) U of Tenn Pr.

Crockett of Tennessee. Judd Cameron. 1994. mass mkt. 5.99 (0-553-56856-6) Bantam.

Crockett's Flower Garden. James U. Crockett. 1981. pap. 22.95 (0-316-16133-0) Little.

Crockett's Indoor Garden. James U. Crockett. LC 78-8939. 1978. pap. 19.95 (0-316-16126-8) Little.

Crockett's Victory Garden. James U. Crockett. (Illus.). 1977. pap. 19.95 (0-316-16121-7) Little.

Crocodile. (YA). 1989. 3.50 (1-878657-26-7) Blue Q.

Crocodile. David Hawcock. (Egg Pop-ups Ser.). (Illus.). 12p. (J). (ps). 1994. 3.95 (0-307-17301-1, Artsts Writrs) Western Pub.

Crocodile. Paula Z. Hogan. LC 79-13699. (Life Cycles Bks.). (Illus.). 32p. (J). (gr. 1-4). 1979. lib. bdg. 19.97 (0-8172-1503-4) Raintree Steck-V.

Crocodile. Paula Z. Hogan. LC 79-13699. (Life Cycles Clippers Ser.). (Illus.). 32p. (J). (gr. 1-4). 1981. audio, lib. bdg. 29.28 (0-8172-1842-4) Raintree Steck-V.

Crocodile! Mick Inkpen. (Illus.). (J). (gr. 4-7). 1993. 4.99 (1-878685-73-2, Bedrock Press) Turner Pub GA.

Crocodile. Alison Tibbitts & Alan Roocroft. (Animals, Animals, Animals Ser.). (Illus.). 24p. (J). (ps-2). 1992. lib. bdg. 12.95 (1-56065-102-4) Capstone Pr.

Crocodile, an Extraordinary Event. Fyodor Dostoyevsky. Tr. by Samuel D. Cioran. Orig. Title: Krokodil. 1984. pap. 9.50 (0-88233-588-X) Ardis Pubs.

Crocodile & Alligator. Vincent Serventy. LC 84-15890. (Animals in the Wild Ser.). (Illus.). 24p. (J). (gr. k-5). 1985. lib. bdg. 9.95 (0-8172-2404-1); pap. 3.95 (0-8114-6873-9) Raintree Steck-V.

Crocodile & Alligator. Vincent Serventy. (Animals in the Wild Ser.). (Illus.). 24p. (J). (gr. k-3). 1986. reprint ed. pap. 2.50 (0-590-44722-X) Scholastic Inc.

Crocodile & Cassowary. Douglas Newton. 1994. pap. 9.95 (0-8109-6455-4) Abrams.

Crocodile & Cassowary. Douglas Newton. (Illus.). 112p. 1971. pap. 9.95 (0-912294-42-6) Metro Mus Art.

Crocodile & the Crane: Surviving in a Crowded World. Judy Cutchins & Ginny Johnston. LC 86-5339. (Illus.). 64p. (J). (gr. 2-5). 1986. 12.95 (0-688-06304-7); lib. bdg. 12.88 (0-688-06305-5) Morrow Jr Bks.

Crocodile & the Dentist. Taro Gomi. LC 94-20306. (Illus.). 32p. (J). (ps-2). 1994. lib. bdg. 13.90 (1-56294-555-6) Millbrook Pr.

*__Crocodile & the Elephant.__ F. I. Rejab. (Illus.). 40p. (J). 1995. 9.95 (983-9808-25-7, Pub. by Delta Edits II) Weatherhill.

Crocodile Attack. Hugh Edwards. 272p. 1990. mass mkt. 4.95 (0-380-71189-3) Avon.

Crocodile Beat. Gail Jorgensen. LC 89-578. (Illus.). 32p. (J). (ps-1). 1989. text ed. 14.95 (0-02-748010-0, Bradbury S&S) S&S Childrens.

Crocodile Beat. Gail Jorgensen. LC 94-7135. (Illus.). 32p. (J). (gr. 2 up). 1994. pap. 4.95 (0-689-71881-0, Aladdin Paperbacks) S&S Childrens.

Crocodile Bind. large type ed. Rendell. 1994. write for info. (0-318-72285-2) Thorndike Pr.

Crocodile Bird. Ruth Rendell. LC 93-14734. 1993. 20.00 (0-517-59576-1, Crown) Crown Pub Group.

*__Crocodile Bird.__ Ruth Rendell. 1994. pap. 5.99 (0-440-21865-9) Dell.

Crocodile Bird. large type ed. Ruth Rendell. LC 93-37403. 1994. 20.95 (0-7862-0091-X); pap. 13.95 (0-7862-0092-8) Thorndike Pr.

Crocodile Burning. Michael Williams. 192p. (YA). (gr. 7 up). 1992. 15.00 (0-525-67401-2, Lodestar Bks) Dutton Child Bks.

Crocodile Burning. Michael Williams. 208p. (J). (gr. 7 up). 1994. pap. 3.99 (0-14-036793-4) Puffin Bks.

Crocodile Club. Kaz Cooke. (Illus.). 230p. (Orig.). 1993. pap. 10.95 (1-86373-000-1, Pub. by Allen & Unwin Aust Pty AT) IPG Chicago.

Crocodile, Crocodile. Peter Nickl. Tr. by Ebbitt Cutler. Orig. Title: Krokodil, Krokodil. (Illus.). 32p. (J). 1989. 11.95 (0-940793-33-4, Crocodile Bks); pap. 3.95 (0-940793-32-6, Crocodile Bks) Interlink Pub.

Crocodile! Crocodile! And Other Folktales. Barbara Baumgartner. LC 93-28027. (Illus.). 48p. (J). (gr. k-3). 1994. 13.95 (1-56458-463-1) Dorling Kindersley.

*__Crocodile Dentist, No. 1.__ Milton Bradley Company Staff. Date not set. write for info. (0-679-87411-9) Random.

Crocodile Family Book. Mark Deeble & Victoria Stone. LC 94-17262. (Animal Family Ser.). (J). 1994. 16.95 (1-55858-263-0); lib. bdg. 16.88 (1-55858-264-9) North-South Bks NYC.

Crocodile Fury. Beth Yahp. 329p. (Orig.). 1993. pap. 12.00 (0-207-17055-X, Pub. by Angus & Robertson AT) HarpC.

Crocodile Gene & His Friends. Eduard Uspensky. Tr. by Nina Ignatowicz. (Illus.). 144p. (J). (gr. 1-5). 1994. 15.00 (0-679-82062-0) Knopf Bks Yng Read.

Crocodile-Hunting in Central America. Karl P. Schmidt. LC 52-9236. (Chicago Natural History Museum. Popular Series: Zoology: No. 15). 23p. reprint ed. pap. 25.00 (0-685-17844-7, 2029196) Bks Demand.

Crocodile Man. deluxe limited ed. Bradley Strahan. LC 88-62709. (Illus.). 44p. (Orig.). 1989. pap. 40.00 (0-912292-81-4) The Smith.

Crocodile Meatloaf. Nancy S. Levene. LC 92-32615. (J). (ps-6). 1993. pap. 4.99 (0-7814-0000-7, Chariot Bks) Chariot Family.

Crocodile on the Sandbank. Elizabeth Peters. 288p. 1988. mass mkt. 5.99 (0-445-40651-8, Mysterious Paperbk) Warner Bks.

Crocodile on the Sandbank. limited ed. Elizabeth Peters. LC 90-613. 272p. 1990. reprint ed. 75.00 (0-922890-38-2) Armchair Detective.

Crocodile on the Sandbank. Elizabeth Peters. LC 90-613. 272p. 1990. reprint ed. 18.95 (0-922890-36-6); reprint ed. 25.00 (0-922890-37-4) Armchair Detective.

Crocodile, Ou la Guerre Du Bien et Du Mal, Arrivee Sous le Regne De Louis the Fifteenth, Vol. IX. Louis-Claude De Saint-Martin. Ed. by Robert Amadou. 460p. reprint ed. write for info. (0-318-71420-5, Pub. by Georg Olms GW) Lubrecht & Cramer.

Crocodile Smile. Sarah Weeks. LC 94-3210. (Laura Geringer Bk.). (Illus.). 48p. (J). (ps-3). 1994. audio 24.95 (0-06-022867-9) HarpC Child Bks.

Crocodile Snaps - Kangaroo Jumps. Daniel Lehan. LC 92-50842. (Illus.). 32p. (J). (ps-k). 1993. 13.95 (0-531-05484-5) Orchard Bks Watts.

Crocodile Tears. Douglas Huebler. 44p. 1984. pap. 12.00 (0-939784-13-0) CEPA Gall.

Crocodiles. Lynn Stone. (Australian Animals Discovery Library). (Illus.). 24p. (J). (gr. k-5). 1990. lib. bdg. 11.94 (0-86593-060-0); lib. bdg. 8.95 (0-685-36369-4) Rourke Corp.

Crocodiles: An Action Plan for Their Conservation. Ed. by Harry Messel et al. 136p. 20.00 (2-8317-0060-4, Pub. by IUCN SZ) Island Pr.

Crocodiles & Alligators. Norman S. Barrett. LC 88-51517. (Picture Library). (Illus.). 32p. (J). (gr. k-6). 1990. lib. bdg. 12.53 (0-531-10705-1) Watts.

Crocodiles & Alligators. Marie Farre. Tr. by Sarah Matthews. LC 87-31804. (Illus.). 38p. (J). (gr. k-5). 1988. 5.95 (0-944589-01-4, 014) Young Discovery Lib.

Crocodiles & Alligators. Charles Levy. 1991. 9.98 (1-55521-714-1) Bk Sales Inc.

Crocodiles & Alligators. Kate Petty. (First Library Bks.). (Illus.). (J). 1990. pap. 3.95 (0-531-15153-0) Watts.

Crocodiles & Alligators. Ed. by Charles Ross. 1989. 35.00 (0-8160-2174-0) Facts on File.

Crocodiles & Alligators of the World. David Alderton. (Of the World Ser.). (Illus.). 192p. 1991. lib. bdg. 25.95 (0-8160-2297-6) Facts on File.

Crocodile's Masterpiece. Max Velthuijs. (Illus.). 32p. (J). (ps-1). 1992. bds. 14.00 (0-374-31658-9) FS&G.

Crocodilian, Tuatara, & Turtle Species of the World: A Taxonomic & Geographic Reference. F. Wayne King & Russell L. Burke. 216p. 1989. pap. 29.00 (0-942924-15-0) Assn Syst Coll.

Crocodylia. R. Steel. (Encyclopedia of Paleoherpetology Ser.: Pt. 16). (Illus.). 116p. 1973. pap. text ed. 60.25 (3-437-30141-1) Lubrecht & Cramer.

*__Croco'nile.__ Roy Gerrard. (Illus.). 32p. (J). (ps-3). 1994. 15.00 (0-374-31659-7) FS&G.

*__Croco's Pond.__ Illus. by Marie-Anne Didierjean. 6p. (J). (ps). 1995. write for info. (1-881445-49-6) Sandvik Pub.

Crocs 'n' Cairns. Carol Stetser. (Illus.). 26p. (Orig.). 1989. reprint ed. pap. 10.00 (0-917960-14-9) Padma.

Crocus & Colchicum. E. A. Bowles. (Illus.). 222p. 1985. reprint ed. 27.00 (0-947752-26-9) Sagapr.

*__Crocus Coulee in Bloom.__ Betty Kilgour. (Illus.). 160p. (Orig.). 1993. pap. 12.95 (1-55059-073-1) Temeron Bks.

Crocus in the Snow: A Book of Poems. Joan W. Anglund. (Illus.). 64p. 1990. 8.95 (0-394-58436-8) Random.

Crocus List. large type ed. Gavin Lyall. 512p. 1986. 23.95 (0-7089-8327-8, Charnwood) Ulverscroft.

Croesus & the Witch - Hansel & Gretel in the 1980's. Vinette Carroll & Micki Grant. 200p. (Orig.). 1984. pap. 9.95 (0-88145-024-3) Broadway Play.

Croesus Conspiracy. Benjamin J. Stein. 1979. pap. 2.25 (0-345-28159-4) Ballantine.

Croft & Creel: A Hundred Years of Coastal Memories. Anna Blair. LC 87-60970. (Illus.). 240p. 1992. pap. 7.95 (0-85683-096-8, Pub. by Shepheard-Walwyn Pubs UK) Paul & Co Pubs.

Croft Borehole in the Lilleshall Inlier of North Shropshire. A. Rushton et al. (British Geological Survey - BGS Reports). 1988. pap. 5.00 (0-11-884463-6, HM4636, Pub. by HMSO UK) UNIPUB.

Croft in the Hills. Katherine Stewart. 185p. (C). 1960. 40.00 (0-9505884-6-6, Pub. by Mercat Pr Bks UK) St Mut.

Crofter & the Laird. John McPhee. LC 77-113774. (Illus.). 160p. 1970. 18.95 (0-374-13192-9) FS&G.

Crofter & the Laird. John McPhee. LC 77-113774. (Illus.). 160p. 1992. pap. 10.00 (0-374-51465-8) FS&G.

Crofters & Habitants: Settler Society, Economy, & Culture in a Quebec Township, 1848-1881. J. I. Little. 1991. 49.95 (0-7735-0807-4, Pub. by McGill CN) U of Toronto Pr.

Crofter's Cottage. large type ed. Jeanette Richards. (Dales Romance Ser.). 201p. 1993. pap. 16.95 (1-85389-404-4, Medcom-Trainex) Ulverscroft.

Crofters War. I. M. Macphail. 250p. (C). 1992. text ed. 90.00 (0-86152-860-3, Pub. by Acair Ltd UK) St Mut.

Crofting Law. MacCuish & Flyn. U.K. text ed. 112.00 (0-406-17912-3) Butterworth Legal Pubs.

Crofting Years. Francis Thompson. 1989. pap. 45.00 (0-946487-06-5, Pub. by Luath Pr UK) St Mut.

Crohn's Disease: Treatment & Pathogenesis. 1987. 110.00 (0-8493-6736-0, RC862, CRC Reprint) Franklin.

Crohn's Disease & Ulcerative Colitis Fact Book. National Foundation for Ileitis & Colitis Staff. Ed. by Peter A. Banks et al. (Illus.). 208p. 1983. text ed. 18.95 (0-684-17967-9, Scribners) S&S Trade.

Croisade: Essai sur la Formation d'une Theorie Juridique. Michel Villey. LC 78-63373. (Crusades Ser.). reprint ed. 57.50 (0-404-17046-3) AMS Pr.

Croisades et Etats Latins d'Orient. Jean Richard. 336p. 1992. 95.00 (0-86078-340-5, Pub. by Variorum UK) Ashgate Pub Co.

Croisements Culturels. Ed. by Andre Tournon. LC 81-50963. (Michigan Romance Studies: Vol. 7). 135p. (Orig.). 1987. pap. 9.00 (0-939730-06-5) Mich Romance.

Croises, Missionaires et Voyageurs: Perspectives Orientales du Monde Latin Medieval. Jean Richard. (Collected Studies: No. CS182). 340p. (FRE.). (C). 1983. reprint ed. lib. bdg. 99.50 (0-86078-130-5, Pub. by Variorum UK) Ashgate Pub Co.

Croisic to les Sables d'Olonne. Imray Laurie Norie & Wilson Ltd. Staff. (Illus.). (C). 1989. text ed. 60.00 (0-685-40216-9, Pub. by Imray Laurie Norie & Wilson UK) St Mut.

Croissance. (FRE.). 1989. 3.95 (0-86508-380-0) BCM Pubn.

Croissance Agricole En France et En Bourgogne De 1850 a Nos Jours. Jean-Baptiste Viallon. Ed. by Stuart Bruchey. LC 77-77186. (Dissertations in European Economic History Ser.). (Illus.). (FRE.). 1978. lib. bdg. 50.95 (0-405-10799-4) Ayer.

Croissants at Croydon: The Memoirs of Jack Bamford. London Borough of Sutton Staff. (C). 1985. 45.00 (0-907335-15-2, Pub. by Sutton Libs & Arts) St Mut.

Croker Papers, 3 Vols, 1. 2nd rev. ed. John W. Croker. Ed. by L. J. Jennings. LC 77-154125. reprint ed. write for info. (0-404-01881-5) AMS Pr.

Croker Papers, 3 Vols, 2. 2nd rev. ed. John W. Croker. Ed. by L. J. Jennings. LC 77-154125. reprint ed. write for info. (0-404-01882-3) AMS Pr.

Croker Papers, 3 Vols, 3. 2nd rev. ed. John W. Croker. Ed. by L. J. Jennings. LC 77-154125. reprint ed. write for info. (0-404-01883-1) AMS Pr.

Croker Papers, 3 Vols, Set. 2nd rev. ed. John W. Croker. Ed. by L. J. Jennings. LC 77-154125. reprint ed. 225.00 (0-404-01880-7) AMS Pr.

Cromartie: Highland Life 1650-1914. E. Richards & Monica Clough. 672p. 1989. text ed. 59.00 (0-08-037732-7, Pub. by Aberdeen U Pr) Macmillan.

Cromatografia de Gases. Harold M. McNair. Tr. by Xorge A. Dominguez. (Serie de Quimica: Monografia No. 23). 90p. (C). 1981. pap. 3.50 (0-8270-1360-4) OAS.

Cromatografia Liquida Alta Presion: Monografia, No. 10. OAS, General Secretariat. (Serie de Quimica). (Illus.). 72p. (SPA.). (C). 1980. reprint ed. pap. 3.50 (0-8270-1229-2) OAS.

Crombergers of Seville: The History of a Printing & Merchant Dynasty. Clive Griffin. (Illus.). 296p. 1989. 125.00 (0-19-815831-9) OUP.

Crome Yellow. Aldous Huxley. 1976. 21.95 (0-8488-1378-2) Amereon Ltd.

Crome Yellow. Aldous Huxley. 307p. 1990. pap. 10.95 (0-88184-588-4) Carroll & Graf.

Crome Yellow. Aldous Huxley. 300p. 1991. reprint ed. lib. bdg. 22.95 (0-89966-847-X) Buccaneer Bks.

Cromedeyre le Vieil. Jules Romains. 172p. (FRE.). 1926. pap. 11.95 (0-7859-1392-0, 2080255093) Fr & Eur.

Crommelin's Thunderbirds: Air Group 12 Strikes the Heart of Japan. Roy W. Bruce & Charles R. Leonard. LC 94-16277. (Illus.). 308p. 1994. 29.95 (1-55750-509-8) Naval Inst Pr.

Cromoterapia. Thomas Aguero. LC 85-52367. (Illus.). 80p. (SPA.). 1986. pap. 10.95 (0-918454-56-5) Senda Nueva.

Cromwell. Victor Hugo. Ed. by Annie Ubersfeld. 10.95 (0-8288-9999-1, F63840) Fr & Eur.

Cromwell. Brendan Kennelly. LC 88-70233. 160p. 1988. pap. 17.95 (1-85224-026-1, Pub. by Bloodaxe Bks UK) Dufour.

Cromwell. Jessica Sarage. (Reputations Ser.). (Illus.). 64p. (YA). (gr. 7-10). 1989. 19.95 (0-7134-6033-4, Pub. by Batsford UK) Trafalgar.

Cromwell: The Lord Protector. Antonia Fraser. LC 73-7270. (Illus.). 826p. 1986. reprint ed. pap. 14.95 (0-917657-90-X, Primus Lib Contemp) D I Fine.

Cromwell Connecticut, 1650-1990: The History of a River Port Town. Robert O. Decker & Margaret A. Harris. LC 91-6465. (Illus.). 560p. 1991. 35.00 (0-914659-51-0) Phoenix Pub.

Cromwell Family. John Cooper & Susan Morris. 52p. (YA). (gr. 6 up). 1987. pap. 7.95 (0-85950-546-4, Pub. by S Thornes UK) Dufour.

*__Cromwellian Foreign Policy.__ Timothy Venning. LC 94-34686. 1995. write for info. (0-312-12499-6) St Martin.

Cromwellian Gazetteer: An Illustrated Guide to Britain in the Civil War & Commonwealth. Peter Gaunt. (Illus.). 320p. 1992. pap. 20.00 (0-7509-0063-6) A Sutton Pub.

Cromwell's Army: A History of the English Soldier During the Civil Wars. C. H. Firth. 464p. 1992. 37.50 (1-85367-120-7) Stackpole.

Cromwell's Boy. Erik C. Haugaard. (J). (gr. 4-7). 1990. pap. 6.95 (0-395-54975-2) HM.

Cromwell's Captains. Cecil E. Phillips. LC 73-37908. (Select Bibliographies Reprint Ser.). 1977. reprint ed. 27.95 (0-8369-6746-1) Ayer.

Cromwell's Glasses. Holly Keller. LC 81-6644. (Illus.). 32p. (J). (gr. k-3). 1982. 14.95 (0-688-00834-8) Greenwillow.

Cromwell's Navy: The Fleet & the English Revolution, 1648-1660. Bernard Capp. 432p. 1992. reprint ed. pap. 29.95 (0-19-820393-4) OUP.

Cromwell's Place in History. Samuel R. Gardiner. LC 76-94270. (Select Bibliographies Reprint Ser.). 1977. 18.95 (0-8369-5044-5) Ayer.

Cronaca Familiare see Family Chronicle

Cronache Italiane Nel Medio Evo. Ugo Balzani. xiv, 333p. 1973. reprint ed. write for info. (3-487-04671-7, Pub. by Georg Olms GW) Lubrecht & Cramer.

Cronartium Ribicola: Its Growth & Reproduction in the Tissues of the Eastern White Pine, No. 86. 1964. 1.50 (0-686-20698-3) SUNY Environ.

Crone: History of the Crone, Pence, Switzer, Weaver, Heatwole, Stout, Steel & Fissell Families, from Which Are Descended John S. Crone & Ella Weaver Crone. F. L. Crone. (Illus.). 50p. 1991. reprint ed. pap. 10.00 (0-8328-1877-1) Higginson Bk Co.

Crone: Women of Age, Wisdom & Power. Barbara G. Walker. 1988. pap. 10.00 (0-06-250934-9) Harper SF.

C

An Asterisk (*) at the beginning of an entry indicates that the title is appearing in BIP for the first time.

Crone Oracles: Initiate's Guide to the Ancient Mysteries. Victoria Ransom & Henrietta Bernstein. 176p. (Orig.). 1994. pap. 12.95 (0-87728-800-3) Weiser.

Cronenberg on Cronenberg. David Cronenberg. Ed. by Chris Rodley. (Illus.). 260p. 1992. 19.95 (0-571-14436-5) Faber & Faber.

Cronenberg on Cronenberg. Ed. by Chris Rodley. (Directors on Directors Ser.). (Illus.). 256p. 1994. pap. 10.95 (0-571-16993-7) Faber & Faber.

Crone's Book of Wisdom. Valerie Worth. LC 88-45194. (Practical Magick Ser.). (Illus.). 192p. (Orig.). 1988. pap. 6.95 (0-87542-892-4) Llewellyn Pubns.

Crone's Book of Words. Valerie Worth. LC 85-82364. 160p. 1971. pap. 6.95 (0-87542-891-6) Llewellyn Pubns.

Cronica da Casa Assasinada. Lucio Cardoso. Ed. by Marlo Carelli. (Coleccion Archivos). 848p. (SPA.). 1991. 41.95 (84-00-07127-1) U of Pittsburgh Pr.

Cronica de Morea. Juan F. De Heredia. (Dialect Ser.). 1991. write for info. (0-942260-49-X) Hispanic Seminary.

Cronica de tres Decadas: Poesia Puertorriquena Actual. Ruben Gonzalez. LC 89-5386. 230p. (Orig.). 1989. pap. 8.75 (0-8477-3639-3) U of PR Pr.

Cronica De una Muerte Anunciada. Gabriel G. Marquez. 250p. (SPA.). 1983. pap. 10.95 (0-7859-4985-2) Fr & Eur.

Cronica Sarracina: Estudio de los Elementos Novelescos y Caballerescos. Gloria Alvarez-Hesse. LC 89-32490. (American University Studies: Romance Languages & Literature: Ser. II, Vol. 124). 200p. (C). 1989. text ed. 39.50 (0-8204-0984-7) P Lang Pubs.

Cronica y Relacion Copiosa y Verdadera De los Reynos De Chile, Vol. 2. Geronimo De Bibar. Ed. by Irving A. Leonard & Guillermo F. Cruz. (Illus.). 1966. pap. 25.00 (0-911028-09-9) Newberry.

Cronicas Brasileiras: A Portuguese Reader. Ed. by Alfred Hower & Richard A. Preto-Rodas. LC 77-634081. 1971. pap. 19.95 (0-8130-0325-3) U Press Fla.

Cronicas Brasileiras: Nova Fase. Ed. by Richard A. Preto-Rodas et al. (Center for Latin American Studies, University of Florida). (Illus.). 352p. (C). 1994. pap. text ed. 24.95 (0-8130-1246-5) U Press Fla.

Cronicas De Puerto Rico: Desde la Conquista Hasta Nuestros Dias, 1493-1955. 2nd ed. Eugenio F. Mendez. (C). reprint ed. pap. 8.00 (0-8477-0811-X) U of PR Pr.

Cronicas del Mariel. Fernando Villaverde. LC 92-73982. (Coleccion Caniqui Ser.). 201p. (Orig.). (SPA.). 1992. pap. 15.00 (0-89729-657-5) Ediciones.

Cronicas Diabolicas. Jorge Ulica, pseud. Ed. by Juan Rodriguez. LC 82-80256. 176p. (Orig.). 1982. pap. text ed. 6.95 (0-939558-02-5) Maize Pr.

Cronicas Francesas de los Indios Caribes. Ed. & Tr. by Manuel Cardenas-Ruiz. LC 79-11655. (Illus.). xii, 624p. (Orig.). (SPA.). 1981. pap. 15.00 (0-8477-0852-7) U of PR Pr.

Cronies. Brenda Sorci. LC 86-72865. 64p. (Orig.). 1987. pap. 5.00 (0-916383-17-2) Aegina Pr.

Cronologia Biblica Portavoz. David Payne. Orig. Title: The Student Bible Timeline. (Illus.). 16p. (SPA.). 1994. pap. 9.99 (0-8254-1552-7) Kregel.

Cronometria: Consideraciones: Cronometry, Critic Considerations. (SPA.). 7.50 (84-7645-204-7, 223327, Pub. by Edit Clie SP) TSELF.

Cronus' Children. Yves Navarre. Tr. by Howard Girven. 320p. 1990. pap. 14.95 (0-7145-4014-5) Riverrun NY.

Crooked Adam. large type ed. D. E. Stevenson. LC 92-41148. 446p. 1993. reprint ed. lib. bdg. 19.95 (1-56054-487-2) Thorndike Pr.

Crooked Adam. large type ed. D. E. Stevenson. 1976. 12.00 (0-85456-464-0) Ulverscroft.

Crooked Hearts. Robert Boswell. 1987. 17.95 (0-394-55706-9) Knopf.

Crooked Hearts. Patricia Gaffney. 384p. (Orig.). 1994. pap. 4.99 (0-451-40459-9, Topaz) NAL-Dutton.

Crooked Hearts. Robert Boswell. LC 93-26948. 352p. 1994. reprint ed. pap. 12.00 (0-06-097586-5, PL) HarpC.

Crooked Hinge. John Dickson Carr. LC 76-56880. 283p. 1976. 18.95 (0-89163-026-0) Boulevard.

Crooked House. Agatha Christie. 1991. mass mkt. 4.99 (0-06-100277-1, Harp PBks) HarpC.

Crooked Island. Victoria McKernan. 288p. 1994. 18.95 (0-88184-998-7) Carroll & Graf.

Crooked Journey: The Story of a Woman's Fight against Scoliosis. Louise F. Sohrabi. (Illus.). 256p. (Orig.). 1985. pap. 11.12 (0-9613941-3-7) Rima Pr.

Crooked Ladder: Gangsters, Ethnicity, & the American Dream. James M. O'Kane. 185p. (C). 1992. 34.95 (1-56000-021-X) Transaction Pubs.

Crooked Letter. large type ed. Linda A. Dubreuil. (Linford Mystery Library). 368p. 1992. pap. 14.95 (0-7089-7235-7, Trailtree Bookshop) Ulverscroft.

Crooked Letter: Linford Mystery Library. large type ed. Linda Dubreuil. 1993. pap. 14.95 (0-685-67905-5, Linford) Ulverscroft.

***Crooked Line.** Ismat Chugtai. (Asian Writers Ser.). 1995. pap. 10.95 (0-435-95089-4) Heinemann.

Crooked Lines. Neal Sorber. LC 91-73497. 1993. 8.95 (0-8158-0475-X) Chris Mass.

Crooked Man. Tony Dunbar. LC 94-5072. 240p. 1995. 19.95 (0-399-13973-7, Putnam) Putnam Pub Group.

***Crooked Man.** Christopher Lehman-Haupt. 351p. 1995. 23.00 (0-671-73444-X) S&S Trade.

***Crooked Mirror: And Other Stories.** Anton Chekhov. 240p. 1995. pap. 11.00 (0-8217-5031-3) Zebra.

Crooked Mirror: And Other Stories. Anton Chekov. 1992. pap. 9.00 (0-8217-3733-3) Zebra.

Crooked Past: The History of a Frontier Mining Camp: Fairbanks, Alaska. Terrence Cole. LC 91-4024. (Illus.). 164p. 1991. 8.95 (0-912006-53-6) U of Alaska Pr.

Crooked Pictures: A Book of Stories. Timothy Petrocchi. LC 92-91199. 180p. (Orig.). 1994. pap. 9.00 (1-56002-292-2, Univ Edtns) Aegina Pr.

Crooked Pitch: An Account of the Curveball in American Baseball History. Martin Quigley. (Illus.). 212p. 1984. 16.95 (0-912697-08-3) Algonquin Bks.

Crooked Pitch: The Curveball in American Baseball History. Martin Quigley. (Illus.). 212p. 1988. reprint ed. pap. 9.95 (0-912697-82-2) Algonquin Bks.

***Crooked Scythe: An Anthology of Oral History.** George E. Evans. Ed. & Illus. by David Gentleman. 240p. (Orig.). 1995. pap. 10.95 (0-571-17194-X) Faber & Faber.

Crooked Stovepipe: Athapaskan Fiddle Music & Square Dancing in Northeast Alaska & Northwest Canada. Craig Mishler. LC 92-36827. (Music in American Life Ser.). (Illus.). 248p. 1993. 29.95 (0-252-01996-2) U of Ill Pr.

Crooked Timber of Humanity. Isaiah Berlin. 1992. pap. 12.00 (0-679-73576-3) McKay.

Crooked Timber of Humanity: Chapters in the History of Ideas. Isaiah Berlin. Ed. by Henry Hardy. 1991. 22.00 (0-679-40131-8) Knopf.

Crooked Trail. Fred Donaldson. 208p. (Orig.). 1983. pap. 2.25 (0-8439-2008-4) Dorchester Pub Co.

Crooked Trails. Frederic Remington. LC 74-101820. (Short Story Index Reprint Ser.). 1898. 3.95 (0-8369-3208-0) Ayer.

Crooked Trails. Frederic Remington. (Illus.). 226p. 1992. reprint ed. pap. 18.00 (1-55613-566-1) Heritage Bk.

Crooked Trails. Frederic Remington. LC 72-104547. (Illus.). 1979. reprint ed. lib. bdg. 17.00 (0-8398-1753-3) Irvington.

Crooked Tree. Joe W. Cates. (Illus.). 48p. (Orig.). (J). (gr. k-6). 1986. lib. bdg. 9.95 (0-942403-02-9); pap. 6.00 (0-942403-00-2) J Barnaby Dist.

Crooked Way. Loren D. Estleman. 1993. pap. 7.95 (1-56060-192-2) Eclipse Bks.

Crooked Wood. large type ed. Michael Underwood. 335p. 1980. 12.00 (0-7089-0464-5) Ulverscroft.

Crookes of Epping. Barry Dickins. 156p. (C). 1990. 35.00 (0-9592104-3-1, Pub. by Pascoe Pub AT) St Mut.

Crooks. Peter Whalley. 192p. 1990. pap. 3.50 (0-380-70617-2) Avon.

Crooks. Peter Whalley. 1988. 15.95 (0-8027-1038-7) Walker & Co.

Crooks & Squares: Lifestyles of Thieves & Addicts in Comparison to Conventional People. Malin Akerstrom. 254p. (C). 1993. pap. text ed. 19.95 (1-56000-653-6) Transaction Pubs.

***Crooning.** J. Dunne. (Orig.). 1994. pap. 3.99 (0-517-13295-8) Random.

Crooning. John G. Dunne. 1991. pap. 9.95 (0-671-74031-8, Touchstone Bks) S&S Trade.

Crop & Soil Management in Dryland Agroecosystems. (Illus.). 59p. (Orig.). (C). 1993. pap. text ed. 30.00 (0-7881-0138-2) Diane Pub.

Crop Art & Other Earthworks. Stanley J. Herd. LC 93-26839. 1994. 19.95 (0-8109-2575-3) Abrams.

Crop Breeding. Ed. by D. R. Wood. (Foundation for Modern Crop Science Ser.: Vol. 4). (Illus.). 294p. 1983. 18.00 (0-89118-036-2) Am Soc Agron.

Crop Circle Enigma: A Range of Viewpoints from the Centre of Crop Circle Studies. Ralph Noyes. (Illus.). 192p. 1995. 19.95 (0-946551-66-9, Pub. by Gateway Bks UK) Atrium Pubs.

***Crop Circle Meanings: Understanding the Symbols: The Returning Goddess & Coming Transformations.** Steve Canada. (Illus.). 70p. (Orig.). 1995. pap. 6.95x (1-883424-37-2) S Canada.

Crop Circle Origins: Ancient Symbols Used Reveal Where Circlemakers Are From. rev. ed. Steve Canada. 70p. 1993. pap. 5.95 (1-883424-10-0) S Canada.

Crop Circle Reading Manual: How to Decode Linear, Multi-Image Pictograms. Steve Canada. 51p. 1992. pap. 5.95x (1-883424-01-1) S Canada.

Crop Circle Translation Guide: How to Apply Fourteen Original Decipherment Methodologies. Steve Canada. 61p. 1992. pap. 5.95x (1-883424-02-X) S Canada.

Crop Circles: Deception - Methods & Implications. Steve Canada. (No. 3: Vol. 3). 76p. 1994. pap. 5.95 (1-883424-30-5) S Canada.

Crop Circles: Hoax or Happening. Carolyn North. Ed. by Sara Glaser. (Fringe Ser.: Vol. 1). (Illus.). 32p. (Orig.). 1992. pap. 3.95 (0-916147-22-3) Regent Pr.

Crop Circles - Cracking the Code: Analysis of National Interest Implications. Steve Canada. (National Security Ser.: No. 2). 68p. 1994. pap. 5.95x (1-883424-27-5) S Canada.

Crop Circles - Harbingers of World Change. Ed. by Alick Bartholomew. 192p. 1995. pap. 17.95 (0-946551-89-8, Pub. by Gateway Bks UK) Atrium Pubs.

***Crop Circles--Goddess Language: Archaeology of Imagery & Symbolism.** Steve Canada. (Inanna Book Ser.: No. 5). 86p. 1994. pap. 7.95x (1-883424-36-4) S Canada.

***Crop Circles--Language of the Goddess: Meanings of Crop-Inscribed Ancient Symbols.** Steve Canada. (Inanna Book Ser.: No. 4). 84p. 1994. pap. 7.95x (1-883424-35-6) S Canada.

***Crop Circles: A Convergence of Narrative: Making Sense of the Symbols.** Steve Canada. (Illus.). 75p. (Orig.). 1995. pap. 7.95x (1-883424-40-2) S Canada.

Crop Circles: Ancient Symbols, Portents of the Future: The Past As Prologue. Steve Canada. 56p. 1993. pap. 5.95 (0-88342-415-0) S Canada.

Crop Circles & Coming Changes: Implications for Human History. rev. ed. Ed. by Steve Canada. 74p. 1993. pap. 5.95 (1-883424-06-2) S Canada.

Crop Circles & Genetics: Reproduction, Bioengineering & Immortality. rev. ed. Steve Canada. 88p. 1993. pap. 7.95x (1-883424-07-0) S Canada.

Crop Circles & Mars: New Mathematical Constants Reveal NASA-Detected 10th Planet Connection. rev. ed. Steve Canada. 74p. 1993. pap. 5.95x (1-883424-08-9) S Canada.

Crop Circles & Mining: Gold & the Returning Ancient Rulers. rev. ed. Steve Canada. 62p. 1993. pap. 5.95x (1-883424-09-7) S Canada.

Crop Circles & National Security. Steve Canada. (National Security Ser.: No. 1). 72p. 1993. pap. 5.95 (1-883424-23-2) S Canada.

Crop Circles & Quantum Physics: Hydrogen Atom Electron States. Steve Canada. 52p. 1993. pap. 4.95x (1-883424-22-4) S Canada.

Crop Circles & Religion. rev. ed. Steve Canada. 67p. 1993. pap. 5.95x (1-883424-11-9) S Canada.

Crop Circles & the Returning Goddess Inanna, Queen of Heaven & Earth. Steve Canada. (Inanna Book Ser.: No. 1). 64p. 1994. pap. 5.95x (1-883424-25-9) S Canada.

Crop Circles & the Returning Ruler Inanna, Great Lady of Heaven. Steve Canada. (Inanna Book Ser.: No. 2). 72p. 1994. pap. 6.95x (1-883424-28-3) S Canada.

Crop Circles & UFOs: Eyewitnesses, Photos, Videos of Discs & Crop Formations. rev. ed. Steve Canada. 58p. 1993. pap. 5.95x (1-883424-12-7) S Canada.

Crop Circles As Communication Artifacts: The Medium Is the Message. Steve Canada. (Communication Book Ser.: No. 1). 56p. 1993. pap. 4.95 (1-883424-18-6) S Canada.

Crop Circles As Interplanetary Communication: Media Technology & Consciousness. Steve Canada. (Communication Book Ser.: No. 2). 56p. 1993. pap. 4.95 (1-883424-19-4) S Canada.

Crop Circles: Decrypting, Deciphering, Decoding: Understanding This Neighboring Planet's Communication System. Steve Canada. (Communication Book Ser.: No. 4). 58p. 1993. pap. 4.95 (1-883424-21-6) S Canada.

Crop Circles: Media, Metaphor, Meaning: Understanding These Communication Artifacts. Steve Canada. (Communication Book Ser.: No. 3). 56p. 1993. pap. 4.95 (1-883424-20-8) S Canada.

Crop Circles, UFOs, & Music: The Diatonic Scale Discovered in Crop Circles, UFO Notes Heard, Ancient Ratio Uncovered. Steve Canada. 100p. (Orig.). 1994. pap. 10.95x (0-88342-433-9) S Canada.

Crop Circles: Who Will Return to Earth, When, & Why? Successful Crop Formation Prediction, Based on Ancient Knowledge, Included. rev. ed. Steve Canada. 74p. 1993. pap. 5.95 (1-883424-13-5) S Canada.

***Crop Circles 1994: Provisional, Interim Report on the English 1994 Summer Season: The 1990 Warnings Repeated.** Steve Canada. (Illus.). 40p. (Orig.). 1995. pap. 4.95x (1-883424-38-0) S Canada.

***Crop Circles 1994: The Returning "Bull of Heaven" New Weapon Displayed.** Steve Canada. (Illus.). 65p. (Orig.). 1995. pap. write for info. (1-883424-39-9) S Canada.

Crop Ecology: Productivity & Management in Agricultural Systems. R. S. Loomis & D. J. Connor. (Illus.). 600p. (C). 1992. 105.00 (0-521-38379-X); pap. 39.95 (0-521-38776-0) Cambridge U Pr.

Crop Evolution, Adaptation & Yield. L. T. Evans. (Illus.). 275p. (C). 1993. 95.00 (0-521-22571-X) Cambridge U Pr.

Crop Genetic Resources: Conservation & Evaluation. Ed. by John H. Holden & J. T. Williams. (Illus.). 300p. 1985. pap. text ed. 34.95 (0-04-581018-4) Routledge Chapman & Hall.

Crop Improvement: Physiological Attributes, Vol. 1. U. S. Gupta. 267p. (C). 1992. text ed. 45.00 (0-8133-1380-5) Westview.

Crop Improvement for Sustainable Agriculture. M. Brett Callaway et al. LC 93-18567. (Our Sustainable Future Ser.: Vol. 4). (Illus.). xiv, 262p. 1993. 35.00 (0-8032-1462-6) U of Nebr Pr.

Crop Improvement Utilizing Biotechnology. Ed. by R. M. Lal & Sukayna Lal. 368p. 1989. 270.00 (0-8493-5082-4, SB123) CRC Pr.

Crop Insurance for Agricultural Development: Issues & Experience. Ed. by Peter Hazell et al. LC 85-9810. 344p. 1986. text ed. 34.50 (0-8018-2673-X) Johns Hopkins.

Crop-Livestock Interaction in Sub-Sarahan Africa. John McIntire et al. LC 92-23012. (Regional & Sectoral Studies). 260p. 1992. 14.95 (0-8213-2166-8, 12166) World Bank.

Crop Loss Assessment & Pest Management. Ed. by P. S. Teng. LC 87-70150. (Illus.). 270p. (Orig.). 1987. 30.00 (0-89054-079-9) Am Phytopathol Soc.

***Crop Modeling & Related Environmental Data: A Focus on Application for Arid & Semiarid Regions in Developing Countries.** Ed. by Paul F. Uhlir & Gelsomina C. Carter. LC 94-70099. (CODATA Monograph Ser.: No. 1). (Illus.). xix, 240p. (Orig.). 1994. 69.00 (1-884893-00-7) CODATA.

***Crop Modeling & Related Environmental Data: A Focus on Application for Arid & Semiarid Regions in Developing Countries.** Ed. by Paul F. Uhlir & Gelsomina C. Carter. LC 94-70099. (CODATA Monograph Ser.: No. 1). (Illus.). xix, 240p. (Orig.). 1994. pap. 34.00 (1-884893-01-5) CODATA.

Crop Nutrition: Science & Practice Before Liebig. G. E. Fussell. 236p. 1971. 8.50 (0-87291-026-1) Coronado Pr.

Crop Nutrition & Fertilizer Use. 2nd ed. John Archer. 278p. 1988. 29.95 (0-85236-175-0, Pub. by Farming Pr UK) Diamond Farm Bk.

Crop Photosynthesis: Spatial & Temporal Determinants. Ed. by N. R. Baker & H. Thomas. LC 92-18712. (Topics in Photosynthesis Ser.: Vol. 12). xviii, 452p. 1992. write for info. (0-444-41596-3) Elsevier.

Crop Physiology. (BIOTOL Ser.). 300p. 1993. pap. 41.95 (0-7506-0560-X) Buttrwrth-Heinemann.

Crop Physiology & Cereal Breeding. J. H. Spietz. (C). 1991. text ed. 210.00 (0-89771-657-4, Pub. by Intl Bk Distr II) St Mut.

Crop Production. Kevin J. Donnelly. 288p. (C). 1994. per., pap. text ed. 25.56 (0-8403-9205-2) Kendall-Hunt.

***Crop Production.** Smith. Date not set. text ed. 59.95 (0-471-07972-3) Wiley.

Crop Production. J. J. Vorst. (Illus.). 350p. 1993. pap. 24.95 (0-87563-405-2) Stipes.

Crop Production. 4th ed. Richard Delorit et al. 1973. text ed. 31.52 (0-13-194761-3) P-H.

Crop Productivity. H. C. Srivastava et al. 1987. 20.00 (81-204-0257-X, Pub. by Oxford IBH II) S Asia.

Crop Protection & Sustainable Agriculture. Ed. by Derek J. Chadwick & Joan Marsh. LC 93-22791. (CIBA Foundation Symposia Ser.: Vol. 177). 1993. text ed. 72.00 (0-471-93944-7) Wiley.

Crop Protection Chemicals. B. G. Lever. (Applied Science & Industrial Technology Ser.). 1991. 81.00 (0-13-194242-5, 520504) P-H.

Crop Protection Chemicals Reference, 1994. 10th ed. C & P Press, Inc. Staff. LC 85-642883. 2200p. 1994. 130.00 (1-57009-003-3) Chem & Pharmac.

Crop Protection Information: An International Perspective. Ed. by K. M. Harris & P. R. Scott. 310p. 1990. 69.00 (0-85198-636-6) CAB Intl.

Crop Protection Strategies for Subsistence Farmers. Ed. by Miguel A. Altieri. LC 93-14990. (Studies in Insect Biology). 197p. (C). 1993. text ed. 55.85 (0-8133-8635-7) Westview.

Crop Quality, Storage, & Utilization. Ed. by C. S. Hoveland. (Foundation for Modern Crop Science Ser.: Vol. 3). (Illus.). 276p. 1980. 15.00 (0-89118-035-4) Am Soc Agron.

Crop Residue Management for Conservation. Pref. by Verlon K. Vrana. 52p. (C). 1991. pap. text ed. 12.50 (0-935734-26-0) Soil & Water Conserv.

Crop Residue Management Systems. Ed. by W. R. Oschwald. 248p. 1978. pap. 9.00 (0-89118-050-8) Am Soc Agron.

Crop Response to Abiotic Stresses. D. Kumar. (C). 1991. text ed. 375.00 (81-7233-021-9, Pub. by Scientific Pubs II) St Mut.

Crop Safeners for Herbicides: Development, Uses & Mechanisms of Action. Ed. by Kriton K. Hatzios & Robert E. Hoagland. 500p. 1988. text ed. 106.00 (0-12-332910-8) Acad Pr.

Crop Science. 65.00 (0-686-40174-3); 13.00 (0-317-05968-8); 3.00 (0-686-40175-1) Crop Sci Soc Am.

Crop Science: A Laboratory Manual. Gail S. Drallmeier et al. (Illus.). 300p. (C). 1988. spiral bd., pap. 20.00 (0-9620569-0-1) U IL Voc Agric Serv.

Crop Science & Food Production. Douglas D. Bishop et al. 416p. 1983. text ed. 25.96 (0-07-005431-2) McGraw.

Crop Science Laboratory Studies. Donald M. Elkins. LC 89-82775. (Illus.). 184p. 1990. pap. text ed. 19.95 (0-8138-0549-X) Iowa St U Pr.

Crop Tolerance to Suboptimal Land Conditions. Ed. by Gerald A. Jung. 343p. 1978. 11.00 (0-89118-051-6) Am Soc Agron.

Crop Water Management Research. Thomas J. Bredero. (C). 1991. 31.00 (81-204-0489-0, Pub. by Oxford IBH II) S Asia.

Crop Weeds. J. L. Wilding et al. (Illus.). 160p. 1986. pap. 45.00 (0-909605-38-6, Pub. by Inkata Pr AT) Intl Spec Bk.

Crop Yields & Climate Change to the Year 2000. 1991. lib. bdg. 79.95 (0-8490-4479-0) Gordon Pr.

Crop Yields & Climate Change to the Year 2000: Report on the Second Phase of a Climate Impact Assessment, Vol. 2, Climate Model & Technical Appendixes. LC 83-600529. 238p. (Orig.). 1986. pap. 11.00 (0-16-001595-2, S/N 008-020-009) USGPO.

Cropland Crisis: Myth or Reality? Ed. by Pierre R. Crosson. LC 81-48216. 250p. 1982. 27.50 (0-8018-2816-3); pap. 15.95 (0-8018-2817-1) Resources Future.

Cropper's Cabin. Jim Thompson. 1992. 9.00 (0-679-73315-9, Vin) Random.

Croppers Cabin. Jim Thompson. LC 87-72260. 160p. 1987. reprint ed. pap. 3.95 (0-88739-047-1, Blk Lizard) Creat Arts Bk.

Cropping Strategies for Efficient Use of Water & Nitrogen. W. L. Hargrove. 218p. 1988. 15.00 (0-89118-097-4) Am Soc Agron.

Cropping System: Theory & Practice. Chatterjee et al. (C). 1989. pap. 10.00 (81-204-0419-X, Pub. by Oxford IBH II) S Asia.

Cropping Systems in Intensive Agriculture. Ed. by D. Djumalieva & Anton Vassilev. 214p. (C). 1993. 83.00 (81-85880-07-7, Pub. by Print Hse II) St Mut.

Cropping Systems in the Tropics: Principles & Management. S. P. Palaniappan. (C). 1986. pap. 11.50 (0-85226-712-6, Pub. by Wiley Eastern II) S Asia.

Croppy: A Tale of 1798, 3 vols. in 2, Set. John Banim. LC 79-8230. reprint ed. 84.50 (0-404-61765-4) AMS Pr.

Crops & Man. Jack R. Harlan. (Foundation for Modern Crop Science Ser.: Vol. 1). (Illus.). 295p. 1975. 11.25 (0-89118-032-X) Am Soc Agron.

Crops As Enhancers of Nutrient Use. Ed. by V. C. Baliger & R. R. Duncan. 574p. 1990. text ed. 142.00 (0-12-077125-X) Acad Pr.

Crops As Sources of Nutrients for Humans. Ed. by R. M. Welch & W. H. Gabelman. 89p. 1984. 12.00 (0-89118-079-6) Am Soc Agron.

Crops I. Ed. by Y. P. Bajaj. (Biotechnology in Agriculture & Forestry Ser.: Vol. 2). (Illus.). 625p. 1986. 278.00 (0-387-15842-1) Spr-Verlag.

C

An Asterisk (*) at the beginning of an entry indicates that the title is appearing in BIP for the first time.

Cross Cultural Design. K. Haas. (Design & Graphic Design Ser.). 1990. text ed. 49.95 (*0-442-00407-9*) Van Nos Reinhold.

*__Cross-Cultural Design: Communicating in the Global Marketplace.__ Henry Steiner & Ken Haas. LC 95-62071. (Illus.). 240p. 1995. 40.00 (*0-500-97423-3*) Thames Hudson.

Cross-Cultural Dialogues: Seventy-Four Brief Encounters with Cultural Difference. Craig Storti. LC 93-38121. 145p. (Orig.). 1993. pap. 15.95 (*1-877864-28-5*) Intercult Pr.

Cross-Cultural Encounter: West Meets East. Paul M. Stuart. (Illus.). 104p. (Orig.). (C). 1994. pap. text ed. 15.00 (*1-880596-09-1*) Allegan Educ.

Cross Cultural Encounters. Brislin. (Practitioner Guidebook Ser.). (C). 1981. 50.95 (*0-205-14295-8*, H4295, Longwood Div) Allyn.

Cross Cultural Encounters. Brislin. (Practitioner Guidebook Ser.). (C). 1992. pap. text ed. 32.95 (*0-205-14294-X*, H4294, Longwood Div) Allyn.

*__Cross-Cultural Human Development.__ rev. ed. Robert L. Munroe & Ruth H. Munroe. (Illus.). 181p. (C). 1994. pap. text ed. 9.95x (*0-88133-804-4*) Waveland Pr.

Cross-Cultural Interaction in Indian-English Fiction. Ramesh Chadha. (C). 1988. 24.00 (*81-85135-32-0*, Pub. by Natl Bk Org II) S Asia.

Cross-Cultural Interpersonal Communication. Ed. by Stella Ting-Toomey & Felipe Korzenny. (International & Intercultural Communication Ser.: Vol. 15). (Illus.). 310p. 1991. 52.00 (*0-8039-4047-5*); pap. 24.00 (*0-8039-4048-3*) Sage.

Cross-Cultural Issues in Alaskan Education, Vol. 2, 1982. Ed. by Ray Barnhardt. 206p. 9.95 (*1-877962-10-4*) Univ AK Ctr CCS.

Cross Cultural Literacy. Fraida Dubin & Natalie Kuhlman. 256p. (C). 1992. pap. text ed. write for info. (*0-13-194408-8*) P-H.

Cross-Cultural Literacy: Ethnographies of Communication in Multiethnic Classrooms. Ed. by Arvizu Saravia-Shore. LC 91-11781. (Studies in Education & Culture: Vol. 3). 566p. 1992. 70.00 (*0-8240-4293-X*, SS566); pap. 18.95 (*0-8153-0465-X*) Garland.

*__Cross-Cultural Look at Death, Dying, & Religion.__ Ed. by Joan K. Parry & Angela S. Ryan. LC 94-42941. (Social Work Ser). 1995. write for info. (*0-8304-1333-2*) Nelson-Hall.

*__Cross Cultural Management.__ Terence Jackson. (Management Reader Ser.). 250p. 1995. pap. 29.95 (*0-7506-1933-3*) Buttrwrth-Heinemann.

Cross-Cultural Management Communication. Richard Mead. 273p. 1992. text ed. 65.95 (*0-471-92660-4*); pap. text ed. 48.95 (*0-471-93718-5*) Wiley.

*__Cross-Cultural Marriages & the Church: Living the Global Neighborhood.__ Comp. by J. Lawrence Driskill. LC 94-41144. 1995. 15.95 (*0-932727-81-6*); pap. 9.95 (*0-932727-80-8*) Hope Pub Hse.

*__Cross Cultural Model for Learning Teaching & Working: A Central America & Caribbean Perspective.__ 104p. (C). 1994. teacher ed write for info. (*0-9643101-5-5*) Editora Educ.

Cross-Cultural Models of Teaching: Latin American Examples. J. Doyle Casteel et al. LC 76-13369. 173p. reprint ed. pap. 49.40 (*0-7837-4915-5*, 2044580) Bks Demand.

Cross-Cultural Musical Analysis. Ed. by Kaye Shelemay. LC 90-3541. (Ethnomusicology Ser.: Vol. 5). 370p. 1990. reprint ed. 86.00 (*0-8240-6473-9*) Garland.

Cross-Cultural Nursing: Anthropological Approaches to Nursing. Ed. by J. M. Morse. vi, 144p. 1989. pap. text ed. 21.00 (*2-88124-383-5*) Gordon & Breach.

Cross-Cultural Orientation: A Guide for Leaders & Educators. rev. ed. Mary V. McCoy et al. Ed. by Alvino F. Fantini. (International Exchange Ser.). 230p. 1984. pap. text ed. 10.00 (*0-936141-01-8*) Experiment Pr.

Cross Cultural Orientation: New Conceptualizations & Applications. Ed. by R. Michael Paige. LC 86-15999. (Orig.). (C). 1986. pap. 31.00 (*0-8191-5608-6*, CIEE) U Pr of Amer.

Cross-Cultural Performances: Differences in Women's Re-visions of Shakespeare. Ed. by Marianne Novy. LC 92-44535. 280p. 1993. 49.95 (*0-252-02017-0*); pap. 18.95 (*0-252-06323-6*) U of Ill Pr.

Cross-Cultural Perspectives in Language: Assessment & Intervention. Ed. by Katharine G. Butler. 238p. 1994. 30.00 (*0-8342-0594-7*) Aspen Pub.

Cross Cultural Perspectives in Medical Ethics: Readings. Veatch. 1989. pap. text ed. 33.75 (*0-86720-075-8*) Jones & Bartlett.

Cross-Cultural Perspectives in Nonverbal Communication. F. Poyatos. LC 87-7485. 354p. (C). 1988. 56.00 (*0-88937-018-4*) Hogrefe & Huber Pubs.

Cross-Cultural Perspectives of Mate-Selection & Marriage. Ed. by George Kurian. LC 78-19306. (Contributions in Family Studies: No. 3). 462p. 1979. text ed. 42.95 (*0-313-20624-4*, KCC/, Greenwood Pr) Greenwood.

Cross-Cultural Perspectives on Families, Work & Change. Ed. by Boh et al. LC 89-20092. (Marriage & Family Review Ser.: Vol. 14, Nos. 1-2). 292p. 1990. text ed. 49.95 (*0-86656-961-8*) Haworth Pr.

Cross-Cultural Perspectives on Learning. Ed. by Richard W. Brislin et al. LC 73-91353. (Cross-Cultural Research & Methodology Ser.). 346p. reprint ed. pap. 98.70 (*0-317-09954-X*, 2021875) Bks Demand.

Cross-Cultural Perspectives on Reading & Reading Research: Includes Selected Papers from the Sixth IRA World Congress on Reading, Singapore, August 17-19, 1976. World Congress on Reading (6th: 1976: Singapore) Staff. Ed. by Dina Feitelson. LC 78-5850. 211p. reprint ed. pap. 60.20 (*0-685-23505-X*, 2027950) Bks Demand.

*__Cross-Cultural Practice of Clinical Case Management in Mental Health.__ Ed. by Peter Manoleas. LC 94-47017. 1995. text ed. 24.95 (*1-56024-874-2*) Haworth Pr.

Cross-Cultural Pragmatics: Requests & Apologies. Ed. by Shoshana Blum-Kulka et al. LC 88-22176. (Advances in Discourse Processes Ser.: Vol. 31). 320p. (C). 1989. text ed. 75.00 (*0-89391-513-0*) Ablex Pub.

Cross-Cultural Pragmatics: The Semantics of Human Interaction. Anna Wierzbicka. (Trends in Linguistics, Studies & Monographs: No. 53). (Illus.). xiv, 502p. (C). pap. text ed. 34.95 (*3-11-013787-9*) Mouton.

Cross-Cultural Pragmatics: The Semantics of Human Interaction. Anna Wierzbicka. (Trends in Linguistics, Studies & Monographs: No. 53). (Illus.). xiv, 502p. (C). 1991. lib. bdg. 144.65 (*3-11-012538-2*) Mouton.

Cross-Cultural Problems in International Business: The Role of the Cultural Integration Function. Robert C. Maddox. LC 92-43086. 160p. 1993. text ed. 45.00 (*0-89930-581-4*, MOK, Quorum Bks) Greenwood.

Cross-Cultural Psychology: Research & Applications. John W. Berry et al. (Illus.). 480p. (C). 1992. 79.95 (*0-521-37387-5*); pap. 34.95 (*0-521-37761-7*) Cambridge U Pr.

Cross-Cultural Reader. 2nd ed. Tajpertab Rajkumar. 240p. 1993. per. 25.95 (*0-8403-8969-8*) Kendall-Hunt.

Cross-Cultural Reckonings: A Triptych of Russian, American, & Canadian Texts. Blanche H. Gelfant. LC 94-9763. (Studies in American Literature & Culture: No. 84). 224p. (C). 1995. 49.95 (*0-521-44038-6*) Cambridge U Pr.

Cross-Cultural Reentry: A Book of Readings. Clyde N. Austin. LC 85-73568. 320p. 1986. pap. 13.95 (*0-915547-74-0*) Abilene Christ U.

Cross-Cultural Research in Human Development: A Life-Span Perspective. Ed. by Leonore L. Adler. LC 88-15536. (Illus.). 312p. 1989. text ed. 62.95 (*0-275-93048-3*, C3048, Praeger Pubs) Greenwood.

Cross-Cultural Review Chapbook Anthology: Volume 1 (Chapbooks 1-10) Ed. by Stanley H. Barkan. 252p. 1983. 50.00 (*0-89304-925-5*) Cross-Cultrl NY.

Cross-Cultural Review Chapbooks, Vol. 1. Ed. by Stanley H. Barkan. 1991. pap. write for info. (*0-318-65333-8*); boxed 40.00 (*0-89304-901-8*) Cross-Cultrl NY.

Cross-Cultural Review Minichapbooks, Vol. 1. Ed. by Stanley H. Barkan. 1991. boxed 40.00 (*0-89304-900-X*) Cross-Cultrl NY.

Cross-Cultural Roots of Minority Child Development. Ed. by Patricia M. Greenfield & Rodney R. Cocking. 440p. 1994. text ed. 89.95 (*0-8058-1223-7*); pap. 29.95 (*0-8058-1224-5*) L Erlbaum Assocs.

Cross-Cultural Social Work: An Existential Approach. Karen Harper & Jim Lantz. 320p. 1996. pap. text ed. 20.95 (*0-925065-20-X*) Lyceum IL.

Cross-Cultural Sourcebook for Business. Catlin & White. (C). 1994. text ed. 16.95 (*0-538-83518-4*, GN71AA) S-W Pub.

Cross-Cultural Studies & Urban Form. Amos Rapoport. (Urban Studies Monograph Ser.: No. 10). 64p. 7.50 (*0-913749-20-6*) U MD Urban Stud.

Cross-Cultural Studies in Cognition & Mathematics. David Lancy. (Developmental Psychology Ser.). 220p. 1983. text ed. 59.00 (*0-12-435620-6*) Acad Pr.

Cross-Cultural Studies of Factors Related to Differential Food Consumption. James R. Leary et al. (Cross-Cultural Research Ser.). 1984. 22.00 (*0-317-37054-5*) HRAFP.

Cross-Cultural Studies of Personality, Attitudes & Cognition. Ed. by Gajendra K. Verma & Christopher Bagley. LC 88-14857. 256p. 1988. text ed. 45.00 (*0-312-02376-6*) St Martin.

Cross-Cultural Study of Perception. rev. ed. Melville Herskovits et al. LC 67-21404. 1969. spiral bd. 20.00 (*0-672-60811-1*) Irvington.

Cross-Cultural Study of Women: A Comprehensive Guide. Ed. by Margot I. Duley & Mary I. Edwards. LC 84-14209. 464p. (Orig.). (C). 1986. 35.00 (*0-935312-45-5*) Feminist Pr.

Cross-Cultural Summary. Comp. by Robert B. Textor. LC 67-18560. (Comparative Studies). 2828p. 1967. 12.00 (*0-87536-105-6*) HRAFP.

Cross-Cultural Teaching Tales. Ed. by Judith Kleinfeld. (Teaching Cases in Cross-Cultural Education Ser.). 38p. (Orig.). (C). 1989. pap. text ed. 5.00 (*1-877962-03-1*) Univ AK Ctr CCS.

Cross-Cultural Topics in Psychology. Lenore Loeb Adler & Uwe P. Gielen. LC 93-40574. 272p. 1994. text ed. 69.50 (*0-275-94524-3*, Praeger Pubs) Greenwood.

Cross-Cultural Trade in World History. Philip D. Curtin. LC 83-23202. (Cambridge Studies in Comparative World History). 352p. 1984. pap. 16.95 (*0-521-26931-8*) Cambridge U Pr.

Cross-Cultural Training for Mental Health Professionals. Ed. by Harriet P. Lefley & Paul B. Pedersen. (Illus.). 360p. (C). 1986. 53.95 (*0-398-05257-3*) C C Thomas.

*__Cross-Cultural Training for Mental Health Professionals.__ Ed. by Harriet P. Lefley & Paul B. Pedersen. (Illus.). 360p. 1986. pap. 32.95 (*0-398-06226-9*) C C Thomas.

Cross-Cultural Training Programs. Darlene E. York. LC 93-37846. 208p. 1994. text ed. 49.95 (*0-89789-375-1*, Bergin & Garvey) Greenwood.

Cross-Cultural Universals of Affective Meaning. Charles E. Osgood et al. LC 73-85570. (Illus.). 520p. 1975. 44.95 (*0-252-00426-4*); pap. 17.50 (*0-252-00550-3*) U of Ill Pr.

Cross Culture Communications Readings. Weaver. 1987. 20.20 (*0-536-05904-7*) Ginn Pr.

Cross Currency Swaps. Ed. by Carl R. Beidleman. 750p. 1991. text ed. 80.00 (*1-55623-316-7*) Irwin Prof Pubng.

Cross Current. C. Terry Cline, Jr. 1980. pap. 2.50 (*0-449-24289-7*, Crest) Fawcett.

Cross Currents. Lee G. Cantwell. LC 93-12389. x, 244p. (Orig.). (YA). (gr. 8-12). 1993. pap. 9.95 (*0-87579-672-9*) Deseret Bk.

Cross Currents, No. 3. Ed. by Ladislav Matejka & B. A. Stolz. (Michigan Slavic Materials Ser.: No. 24). 1984. pap. 15.00 (*0-930042-60-3*) Mich Slavic Pubns.

Cross Currents, No. 7. Ed. by Ladislav Matejka. (Michigan Slavic Materials Ser.: No. 29). 1988. pap. 15.00 (*0-930042-66-2*) Mich Slavic Pubns.

Cross Currents, No. 8. Ed. by Ladislav Matejka. (Michigan Slavic Materials Ser.: No. 30). 1989. pap. 15.00 (*0-930042-67-0*) Mich Slavic Pubns.

Cross Currents, No. 11. Ed. by Ladislav Matejka. (Illus.). 296p. (C). 1992. pap. 25.00 (*0-300-05242-1*) Yale U Pr.

Cross Currents: A Yearbook of Central European Culture, No. 10. Ed. by Ladislav Matejka (Cross Current Yearbooks of Central European Culture Ser.). 272p. (Orig.). 1991. pap. 25.00 (*0-300-04326-0*) Yale U Pr.

Cross Currents: Exploring the Implications of Christianity for Our Time; An Anthology of Forty Years of Cross Currents. Ed. by William Birmingham. 288p. 1990. pap. 19.95 (*0-8245-0956-0*) Crossroad NY.

Cross-Currents: Interactions Between Science & Faith. Colin A. Russell. LC 85-10199. 272p. reprint ed. pap. 77.60 (*0-685-23460-6*, 2032745) Bks Demand.

Cross Currents: The Perils of Electropollution, the Promise of Electromedicine. Robert O. Becker. (Illus.). 352p. 1991. pap. 13.95 (*0-87477-609-0*) J P Tarcher.

Cross Currents in Early Buddhism. S. N. Dube. 1981. 22.50 (*0-8364-0686-9*, Pub. by Manohar II) S Asia.

Cross Currents in Israeli Culture & Politics. Ed. by Myron J. Aronoff. (Political Anthropology Ser.: Vol. IV). 115p. (C). 1984. text ed. 34.95 (*0-88738-010-7*); pap. text ed. 21.95 (*0-87855-811-X*) Transaction Pubs.

Cross Currents in Second Language Acquisition & Linguistic Theory. Ed. by Thom Huebner & Charles A. Ferguson. LC 91-17382. (Language Acquisition & Language Disorders (LALD) Ser.: Vol. 2). viii, 435p. 1991. 130.00 (*1-55619-235-5*); pap. 29.95 (*1-55619-238-X*) Benjamins North Am.

Cross Currents, No. 1. Ed. by Ladislav Matejka & Benjamin A. Stolz. (Michigan Slavic Materials Ser.: No. 20). 1982. pap. 15.00 (*0-930042-43-3*) Mich Slavic Pubns.

Cross Currents, No. 6. Ed. by Ladislav Matejka. (Michigan Slavic Materials Ser.: No. 28). 1987. 15.00 (*0-930042-65-4*) Mich Slavic Pubns.

Cross Currents of American Architecture. Frank Gehry. (Academy Architecture Ser.). (Illus.). 88p. 1985. pap. 21.95 (*0-312-17670-8*, Pub. by Marek) St Martin.

Cross Currents 12. Ed. by Ladislav Matejka. (Slavic Studies - Literature). (Illus.). 240p. (C). 1993. 25.00 (*0-300-05838-1*) Yale U Pr.

Cross-Curricular Contexts, Themes & Dimensions in Primary Schools. Ed. by G. K. Verma & P. D. Pumfrey. LC 93-47540. (Cultural Diversity & the Curriculum Ser.: Vol. 4). 1994. write for info. (*0-7507-0145-5*, Falmer Pr) Taylor & Francis.

Cross Curricular Themes in Secondary Schools. Ed. by Gajendra K. Verma & Peter D. Pumfrey. (Cultural Diversity & the Curriculum Ser.: Vol. 2). 300p. 1993. 90.00 (*0-7507-0141-2*, Falmer Pr); pap. 34.00 (*0-7507-0142-0*, Falmer Pr) Taylor & Francis.

Cross Design Synthesis: A New Strategy for Medical Effectiveness Research. (Illus.). 121p. (Orig.). (C). 1994. pap. text ed. 50.00 (*0-7881-0590-6*) Diane Pub.

Cross-Disciplinary Study of the European Immigrants of 1870 to 1925. Loretta K. Matulich. Ed. by Francesco Corasco. LC 80-878. (American Ethnic Groups Ser.). 1981. lib. bdg. 30.95 (*0-405-13439-8*) Ayer.

Cross Dressing, Sex, & Gender. Vern L. Bullough & Bonnie Bullough. LC 92-32030. 400p. (Orig.). (C). 1993. text ed. 52.95 (*0-8122-3163-5*); pap. text ed. 17.95 (*0-8122-1431-5*) U of Pa Pr.

Cross-Examination. G. Colman. 168p. 1970. 29.00 (*0-7021-0305-5*, Pub. by Juta SA) W W Gaunt.

*__Cross-Examination: Science & Techniques.__ Larry S. Pozner & Roger J. Dodd. 763p. 1993. 105.00 (*1-55834-071-8*) Michie Butterworth.

Cross-Examination: The Art of the Advocate. rev. ed. Salhany. 176p. 1991. 43.00 (*0-409-89786-8*) Butterworth Legal Pubs.

Cross Examination: The Mosaic Art. John N. Ianuzzi. 270p. 1981. text ed. 59.95 (*0-13-194704-4*) P-H.

Cross Examination in Criminal Trials. F. Lee Bailey & Henry B. Rothblatt. LC 78-18628. 1978. 98.00 (*0-685-59830-6*) Clark Boardman Callaghan.

Cross-Examination in Criminal Trials. Marcus Stone. 1988. pap. 34.00 (*0-406-10505-7*) Butterworth Legal Pubs.

Cross Examination of Lay Witnesses, Looseleaf updates available. Durst & Queller. (Art of Advocacy Ser.). 1988. write for info. (*0-8205-1048-3*) Bender.

Cross-Examination of Medical Experts, Looseleaf Updates Avail. Marshall Houts. 1982. write for info. (*0-8205-1031-9*) Bender.

Cross-Examination of Non-Medical Experts, Looseleaf Updates Avail. Robert L. Habush. 1981. write for info. (*0-8205-1042-4*) Bender.

Cross-Examination of Witnesses: The Litigator's Puzzle. Aron et al. 1989. text ed. 95.00 (*0-07-053623-6*) Shepards-McGraw.

Cross-Examination on Trial. Arnold J. Wolf. 500p. 1988. boxed 60.00 (*0-88063-229-1*) Michie Butterworth.

*__Cross Examination Practice & Procedure.__ 2nd ed. J. L. Glissan. 248p. 1990. 72.00 (*0-409-30815-3*, Austral) Butterworth Legal Pubs.

Cross-Examinations of Law & Literature: Cooper, Hawthorne, Stowe & Melville. Brook Thomas. LC 86-20756. (Cambridge Studies in American Literature & Culture: No. 21). 320p. 1987. 59.95 (*0-521-33081-5*) Cambridge U Pr.

Cross Examinations of Law & Literature: Cooper, Hawthorne, Stowe & Melville. Brook Thomas. (Cambridge Studies in American Literature & Culture: No. 21). 312p. (C). 1991. pap. 19.95 (*0-521-40970-5*) Cambridge U Pr.

Cross-Eyed Ghost. Zeno Zeplin. (Illus.). 154p. (J). (gr. 3-6). 1991. pap. text ed. 7.95 (*1-877740-06-3*); boxed 14.95 (*1-877740-05-5*) Nel-Mar Pub.

Cross-Fertilization: The Human Spirit As Place. Intro. by Morty Sklar. LC 81-215660. (Contemporary Anthology Ser.: No. 3). (Illus.). 64p. (C). 1980. pap. 2.50 (*0-930370-10-4*) Spirit That Moves.

Cross Flow Filtration: Theory & Practice. J. Murkes & C. G. Carlsson. 133p. 1989. text ed. 195.00 (*0-471-92097-5*) Wiley.

Cross-Functional Management. Ed. by Kenji Kurogane. 272p. 1993. text ed. 41.00 (*92-833-1117-5*, 311175, Pub. by APO JA); pap. text ed. 35.00 (*92-833-1118-3*, 311183, Pub. by APO JA) Qual Resc.

*__Cross-Functional Sourcing Team Effectiveness.__ Robert M. Monczka & Robert J. Trent. Ed. by Carol Ketchum. 72p. (Orig.). (C). 1993. pap. text ed. 20.00 (*0-945968-15-9*) Ctr Advanced Purchasing.

Cross-Functional Teams: Working with Allies, Enemies, & Other Strangers. Glenn M. Parker. LC 93-48674. (Business-Management Ser.). 225p. 1994. 24.00 (*1-55542-609-3*) Jossey-Bass.

Cross-GUI Handbook for Multiplatform User Interface Design. Nick Smilonich et al. LC 93-39692. (C). 1995. pap. text ed. 39.75 (*0-201-57592-2*) Addison-Wesley.

Cross in China: The Story of My Mission. M. Servatia. Ed. by Robert E. Connolly. 350p. (Orig.). 1989. pap. 10.00 (*0-9614659-4-8*) Cuchullain Pubns.

Cross in the Life & Literature of the Anglo-Saxons. William O. Stevens. 1972. 69.95 (*0-87968-970-6*) Gordon Pr.

*__Cross in the Middle of Nowhere: A History of the Catholic Church in Eastern Oregon.__ William S. Stone. (Illus.). 376p. 1993. pap. 19.95 (*0-9642016-0-7*) W S Stone.

Cross in the Normal Christian Life see Cruz en la Vida Cristiana Normal

Cross in the Sand: The Early Catholic Church in Florida, 1513-1870. Michael V. Gannon. LC 83-10498. 1983. reprint ed. pap. 19.95 (*0-8130-0776-3*) U Press Fla.

Cross Index. Robert J. Peshek. 1982. 10.00 (*0-9605902-5-0*) Color Coded Charting.

Cross-Index of Indices of Books on Thanatology. Martin L. Kutscher. 1979. 20.95 (*0-405-12509-7*) Ayer.

Cross Index of Synonyms & Trade Names in Volumes 1 to 26. International Agency for Research on Cancer Staff. (IARC Monographs on the Evaluation of the Carcinogenic Risk of Chemicals to Humans: No. 3). 205p. reprint ed. pap. 58.50 (*0-8357-6466-4*, 2035837) Bks Demand.

Cross Index of Synonyms & Trade Names in Volumes 1 to 36. (IARC Monographs on the Evaluation of the Carcinogenic Risk of Chemicals to Humans: Supplement No. 5). 259p. 1985. pap. 27.60 (*92-832-1312-2*) World Health.

Cross Index Title Guide to Classical Music. Comp. by Steven G. Pallay. LC 86-25723. (Music Reference Collection Ser.: No. 12). 215p. 1987. text ed. 59.95 (*0-313-25531-8*, PCR/, Greenwood Pr) Greenwood.

Cross Index Title Guide to Opera & Operetta. Ed. by Steven G. Pallay. LC 89-2131. (Music Reference Collection Ser.: No. 19). 222p. 1989. text ed. 49.95 (*0-313-25622-5*, PCX, Greenwood Pr) Greenwood.

Cross-Industry Analysis of Financial Ratios: Comparabilities & Corporate Performance. J. Edward Ketz et al. LC 90-8439. 232p. 1990. text ed. 59.95 (*0-89930-463-X*, KCI, Quorum Bks) Greenwood.

Cross Infection Control in General Dental Practice. Croser & Chipping. 1989. text ed. 32.00 (*0-86715-210-9*) Quint Pub Co.

*__Cross-Level Inference.__ Christopher H. Achen & Shively W. Phillips. LC 94-22590. 1995. pap. text ed. 18.95 (*0-226-00220-9*) U Ch Pr.

*__Cross-Level Inference.__ Christopher H. Achen & Shively W. Phillips. LC 94-22590. 1995. lib. bdg. 55.00 (*0-226-00219-5*) U Ch Pr.

*__Cross-Linguistic Study of Bilingual Development.__ Ed. by G. Extra & L. Verhoeven. 288p. 1994. pap. 48.50 (*0-444-85778-8*) Elsevier.

Cross-Linguistic Study of Sentence Processing. Ed. by Brian MacWhinney & Elizabeth Bates. (Illus.). (C). 1990. 44.95 (*0-521-26196-1*) Cambridge U Pr.

Cross-Linked Polymers: Chemistry, Properties, & Applications. Ed. by Ray A. Dickie et al. LC 88-3327. (Symposium Ser.: No. 367). (Illus.). ix, 494p. 1988. 99.95 (*0-8412-1471-9*) Am Chemical.

*__Cross Merchandising Sticker Rolls.__ 1994. pap. 14.00 (*0-517-11340-6*) Random.

Cross My Heart & Hope to Die: An Inspector Quantrill Mystery. Sheila Radley. (Quantrill Ser.: No. 8). 288p. 1992. text ed. 19.00 (*0-684-19410-4*, Scribners) S&S Trade.

Cross-National Comparative Survey Research: Theory & Practice - Papers & Proceedings of a Round Table Conference, Budapest, 1972. Ed. by A. Szalai & R. Petrelia. LC 76-8272. 1977. 208.00 (*0-08-020979-3*, Pub. by Pergamon Repr UK) Franklin.

Cross-National Innovation in Social Policy: European Perspectives on the Evaluation of Action-Research. Graham Room. LC 85-18302. 189p. 1986. text ed. 29.95 (*0-312-17676-7*) St Martin.

Cross-National Longitudinal Research on Human Development & Criminal Behavior. Ed. by Elmar G. M. Weitekamp & Hans-Jergen Kerner. LC 93-41424. 1993. lib. bdg. 167.00 (*0-7923-2620-2*) Kluwer Ac.

C

An Asterisk (*) at the beginning of an entry indicates that the title is appearing in BIP for the first time.

An Asterisk (*) at the beginning of an entry indicates that the title is appearing in BIP for the first time.

1719

Crossed Silver: Poems in Poetry, Drawing, & Geometry. R. H. Crane. 252p. 1993. 16.95 (*0-9631041-0-1*) M M & C.

***Crossed Stars: Artistic Sources & Social Conflict in the Ballet 'Romeo & Juliet'** Ed. by Rita Felciano & Eric Hellman. (Orig.). 1995. pap. 12.00 (*1-881106-04-7*) SF Perf Arts Lib.

Crossed Swords. M. Gyi. (Illus.). 44p. (Orig.). 1982. pap. write for info. (*0-318-56879-9*) Am Bando Assn.

Crossed Wires - Cable Television in New Jersey. 100p. 1972. 12.50 (*0-943136-04-0*) Ctr Analysis Public Issues.

Crosses. Shelley Stoehr. 1993. pap. 3.50 (*0-440-21561-7*) Dell.

Crosses & Culture of Ireland. Arthur K. Porter. LC 68-56480. (Illus.). 1979. reprint ed. 36.95 (*0-405-08860-4*, Pub. by Blom Pubns UK) Ayer.

***Crosses, Domes & Crescents: From Byzantium to Victorian.** Eleanor Lehner. (Illus.). 168p. Date not set. per. 15.00 (*0-934616-43-4*) Valkyrie Pub Hse.

Crosses of Lent. 1987. pap. 7.95 (*0-570-04478-2*, 12-3094) Concordia.

Crosses of the Isle of Man. A. M. Cubbon. pap. 7.50 (*0-89979-068-2*) British Am Bks.

Crosses on the Ballot: Patterns of British Voter Alignment since 1885. Kenneth D. Wald. LC 82-61392. 290p. 1983. 42.50 (*0-691-07652-9*) Princeton U Pr.

Crossfire. David Hagberg. 1992. mass mkt. 5.99 (*0-8125-1358-4*) Tor Bks.

Crossfire. J. C. Pollock. 1992. reprint ed. mass mkt. 4.99 (*0-440-11602-3*) Dell.

Crossfire: A Video Reader. Myron C. Tuman. LC 93-32718. 1993. pap. text ed. write for info. (*0-205-14903-0*) Allyn.

Crossfire: An Argument Rhetoric & Reader. Ed. by Gary Goshgarian & Kathleen Krueger. LC 93-23536. (C). 1993. 19.25 (*0-06-501513-4*) HarpCollege.

Crossfire: Faith & Doubt in an Age of Certainty. Richard Holloway. LC 88-19120. 175p. reprint ed. pap. 49.90 (*0-7837-0516-6*, 2040840) Bks Demand.

Crossfire: Philosophy & the Novel in Spain, 1900-1934. Roberta Johnson. LC 92-38875. (Studies in Romance Languages: Vol. 35). 248p. 1993. text ed. 26.00 (*0-8131-1824-7*) U Pr of Ky.

Crossfire: The Plot That Killed Kennedy. Jim Marrs. (Illus.). 620p. 1990. pap. 13.95 (*0-88184-648-1*) Carroll & Graf.

***Crossfire at Dawn: The Real Awakening.** Frank Fracasso. (Illus.). (C). 1995. 17.95 (*0-9630034-1-0*) FMS.

Crossfire in Professional Education. Bruno A. Boley. LC 76-47033. 1977. 48.00 (*0-08-021429-0*, Pub. by Pergamon Repr UK) Franklin.

Crossfire Killings. large type ed. Bill Knox. 400p. 1988. 16.95 (*0-7089-1849-2*) Ulverscroft.

Crossfire Trail. Louis L'Amour. 176p. 1985. pap. 3.99 (*0-553-28099-6*) Bantam.

Crossfire Trail. large type ed. Louis L'Amour. LC 92-41743. (General Ser.). 1993. pap. 16.95 (*0-8161-5724-3*, Large Print Bks) Hall.

Crosshatch Men. large type ed. Ray Hogan. (Nightingale Series Large Print Bks.). 245p. 1992. pap. 14.95 (*0-8161-5275-6*, Nightingale) Hall.

Crossin' the Line. Phil Bosakowski. 36p. (Orig.). 1988. pap. 2.75 (*0-8222-0254-9*) Dramatists Play.

Crossing. Winston Churchill. 1976. 32.95 (*0-8488-0964-5*) Amereon Ltd.

Crossing. John Clive & Nicolas Head. 304p. 1988. pap. 3.95 (*0-380-70473-0*) Avon.

***Crossing.** Erica Magnus. LC 94-42372. (J). 1996. write for info. (*0-688-13927-2*); lib. bdg. write for info. (*0-688-13928-0*) Lothrop.

Crossing. Cormac McCarthy. 1994. 23.00 (*0-394-57475-3*) Knopf.

Crossing. Cormac McCarthy. 1995. pap. 5.99 (*0-679-76434-8*, Vin) Random.

***Crossing.** Cormac McCarthy. 1995. pap. 13.00 (*0-679-76084-9*, Vin) Random.

***Crossing.** Cormac McCarthy. 1995. pap. 7.00 (*0-679-76086-5*) Random.

***Crossing.** Rae McCartney. Ed. by J. Friedland & R. Kessler. (Novel-Ties Ser.). (J). (gr. 5-7). 1994. student ed, pap. text ed. 15.95 (*1-56982-066-X*) Lrn Links.

Crossing. Gary Paulsen. (J). (gr. k up). 1990. mass mkt. 3.99 (*0-440-20582-4*, LFL) Dell.

Crossing. Gary Paulsen. LC 87-7738. 128p. (J). (gr. 6-8). 1987. 14.95 (*0-531-05709-7*); lib. bdg. 14.99 (*0-531-08309-8*) Orchard Bks Watts.

Crossing. large type ed. Cormac McCarthy. 1994. pap. 22.00 (*0-679-75434-2*) Random.

Crossing. Howard Fast. LC 84-60569. (Illus.). 213p. 1985. reprint ed. pap. 12.95 (*0-911020-10-1*) NJ Hist Soc.

Crossing: A Journal of Survival & Resistance in World War Two. Jan Yoors. (Illus.). 224p. 1988. reprint ed. pap. text ed. 9.95 (*0-88133-364-6*) Waveland Pr.

***Crossing: Language & Ethnicity among Adolescents.** Ben Rampton. LC 94-29266. (Real Language Ser.). 400p. (C). 1995. text ed. 57.95 (*0-582-21790-3*, 77024, Pub. by Longman UK); pap. text ed. 27.95 (*0-582-21791-1*, 77023, Pub. by Longman UK) Longman.

Crossing--Adano to Catonsville: Leland Hayward's Producing Career. Sonia Berman. LC 94-2325. 1995. write for info. (*0-8108-2848-0*) Scarecrow.

Crossing America. (Insight Guides Ser.). 1993. pap. 21.95 (*0-395-66254-0*) HM.

Crossing America. deluxe ed. Leo Connellan. (Illus.). 48p. 1976. 25.00 (*0-915778-11-4*) Penmaen Pr.

Crossing America: National Geographic's Guide to the Interstates. Book Division Staff. LC 94-16464. 1994. pap. 29.95 (*0-87044-984-2*) Natl Geog.

Crossing America: National Geographic's Guide to the Interstates. National Geographic Society Book Division Staff. LC 94-16464. 1994. pap. 21.95 (*0-87044-985-0*) Natl Geog.

Crossing & Cruising: From the Decline of Yesterday's Ocean Liners to the Rise of the Cruise Ships of Today. John Maxtone-Graham. (Illus.). 320p. 1992. text ed. 30.00 (*0-684-19154-7*, Scribners) S&S Trade.

Crossing Antarctica. Will Steger & Jon Bowermaster. 1991. 25.00 (*0-394-58714-6*) Knopf.

Crossing Antarctica. Will Steger. 1993. mass mkt. 5.99 (*0-440-21460-2*) Dell.

Crossing Antarctica. Will Steger. 1993. pap. 4.99 (*0-517-10974-3*) Random Hse Value.

Crossing at Ivalo. Rod MacLeish. 320p. 1992. reprint ed. mass mkt. 4.99 (*0-8217-3961-1*) Zebra.

Crossing Barriers: People Who Overcame. Mary E. Snodgrass. 250p. 1993. lib. bdg. 32.50 (*0-87287-992-5*) Libs Unl.

Crossing Blood. Nanci Kincaid. 288p. 1994. pap. 10.00 (*0-380-72111-2*) Avon.

Crossing Blood. Nancy Kincaid. 320p. 1992. 21.95 (*0-399-13719-X*, Putnam) Putnam Pub Group.

Crossing Borders. Thomas E. Kennedy. 240p. 1990. pap. 7.50 (*0-922820-09-0*) Watermark Pr.

Crossing-Borders. Thomas Lavazzi. LC 93-6536. 64p. 1993. pap. 12.95 (*0-7734-2784-8*, Mellen Poetry Pr) E Mellen.

Crossing Borders. Peter D. Scott. LC 94-20526. 144p. (Orig.). 1994. pap. 11.95 (*0-8112-1284-X*, NDP796) New Directions.

Crossing Borders: From Revolutionary Russia to China to America. Helen Yakobson. LC 94-15590. (Illus.). 212p. (Orig.). 1994. pap. 12.00 (*1-55779-071-X*) Hermitage.

Crossing Borders: Reception Theory, Poststructuralism, Deconstruction. Robert C. Holub. LC 91-40251. 256p. (Orig.). (C). 1992. lib. bdg. 42.00 (*0-299-13270-6*); pap. 16.95 (*0-299-13274-9*) U of Wis Pr.

***Crossing Boundaries.** Roberta Wright & Lynda William. LC 94-34479. 1994. pap. text ed. write for info. (*0-07-072073-8*) McGraw.

Crossing Boundaries: A Theory & History of Essay Writing in German, 1680-1815. John A. McCarthy. LC 88-26834. 360p. (C). 1989. text ed. 43.95 (*0-8122-8148-9*) U of Pa Pr.

***Crossing Boundaries: Mine Migrancy in a Democratic South Africa.** James Wilmot & Jonathan Crush. (Illus.). 233p. 1995. pap. 25.00 (*0-88936-764-7*, IDRC7647, Pub. by IDRC CN) UNIPUB.

***Crossing Boundary Waters: A Spiritual Journey in Canoe Country.** Andrew Rogness. 1994. pap. 9.99 (*0-8066-2730-1*, Augsburg) Augsburg Fortress.

Crossing Boundries. Ed. by Caine & Grosz. 1988. pap. text ed. 16.95 (*0-04-305004-2*, Pub. by Allen Unwin AT) Paul & Co Pubs.

Crossing by Night. David Aaron. 416p. 1994. mass mkt. 5.99 (*0-380-72191-0*) Avon.

Crossing by Night. David Aaron. LC 92-34200. 1993. 22.00 (*0-688-09296-9*) Morrow.

Crossing by Night. large type ed. David Aaron. LC 93-11442. 711p. 1993. reprint ed. lib. bdg. 21.95 (*0-7862-0008-1*) Thorndike Pr.

Crossing Canal Street. John Yau. 4.00 (*0-686-21116-2*) Bellevue Pr.

Crossing Cultural Borders: Education for Immigrant Families in America. Concha Delgado-Gaitan & Henry T. Trueba. 224p. 1991. 55.00 (*1-85000-885-X*, Falmer Pr); pap. 26.00 (*1-85000-886-8*, Falmer Pr) Taylor & Francis.

Crossing Cultures: Essays in the Displacement of Western Civilization. Ed. by Daniel Segal. LC 91-35113. (Illus.). 270p. 1992. 39.95 (*0-8165-1277-9*) U of Ariz Pr.

Crossing Cultures: Readings for Composition. 4th ed. Henry Knepler & Myrna Knepler. (Illus.). 452p. (C). 1994. pap. write for info. (*0-02-365250-0*) Macmillan.

Crossing Cultures Through Film. Ellen Summerfield. LC 93-10456. 184p. (Orig.). 1993. pap. 15.95 (*1-877864-21-8*) Intercult Pr.

Crossing Eden. Emma Gordon. 416p. (Orig.). 1992. mass mkt. 5.99 (*0-446-35406-6*) Warner Bks.

Crossing Eden. Emma Gordon. 416p. (Orig.). 1992. reprint ed. 22.00 (*0-7278-4363-X*) Severn Hse.

Crossing Frontiers: Explorations in International Political Economy. Benjamin J. Cohen. (Political Economy of Global Interdependence Ser.). 336p. 1990. text ed. 77.50 (*0-8133-7990-3*) Westview.

***Crossing Frontiers: Gerontology Emerges As a Science.** W. Andrew Achenbaum. 288p. (C). 1995. pap. 18.95 (*0-521-55880-8*) Cambridge U Pr.

***Crossing Frontiers: Gerontology Emerges As a Science.** W. Andrew Achenbaum. 288p. (C). 1995. 59.95 (*0-521-48194-5*) Cambridge U Pr.

Crossing Guard. David Rabe. 320p. 1995. 22.95 (*0-7868-6119-3*) Hyperion.

Crossing Home: The Spiritual Lessons of Baseball. James Penrice. LC 93-4222. 118p. (Orig.). 1993. pap. 5.95 (*0-8189-0675-8*) Alba.

Crossing Many Bridges: Memoirs of a Pharmacist in Poland, the Soviet Union, the Middle East, Italy, the United Kingdom, & Nebraska. Witold Saski. (Illus.). 256p. 1988. pap. 15.95 (*0-89745-110-4*) Sunflower U Pr.

Crossing Map. Liliane Lijn. (Illus.). (Orig.). 1983. pap. 14.95 (*0-500-97310-5*) Thames Hudson.

Crossing Ocean Parkway: Readings by an Italian American Daughter. Marianna D. Torgovnick. LC 94-14355. 1994. 22.50 (*0-226-80829-7*) U Ch Pr.

Crossing of Borders & the Creation of Worlds: The Art of Howard Jones. Udo Kultermann. Ed. by Jane N. Franklin. LC 93-60789. (Illus.). 28p. (Orig.). 1993. pap. 5.00 (*0-936316-17-9*) Wash U Gallery.

Crossing of the Suez. Saad El Shazly. Ed. by Susan Benson. (Illus.). 333p. 1980. pap. 20.00 (*0-9604562-0-1*, 80-67107) Am Mideast.

Crossing of the Ways: William Faulkner, the South, & the Modern World. Karl F. Zender. 220p. (Orig.). 1990. text ed. 16.00 (*0-8135-1376-6*) Rutgers U Pr.

Crossing Open Ground. Barry H. Lopez. 1989. pap. 9.00 (*0-679-72183-5*, Vin) Random.

Crossing Open Ground. Barry H. Lopez. 1988. write for info. (*0-333-46943-7*, Scribners) S&S Trade.

Crossing Over. Jesse Maguire. 1990. mass mkt. 3.99 (*0-8041-0446-8*) Ivy Books.

Crossing Over: Feminism & Art of Social Concern. Arlene Raven. Ed. & Pref. by Donald Kuspit. LC 87-25545. (Contemporary American Art Critics Ser.: No. 10). (Illus.). 242p. reprint ed. pap. 64.80 (*0-8357-2017-9*) Bks Demand.

Crossing Over: The Vietnam Stories. Richard Currey. LC 92-32124. (Illus.). 104p. 1993. pap. 11.00 (*0-944439-21-7*) Clark City Pr.

Crossing Over: Whole Languages for Secondary English Teachers. Harold M. Foster. (Illus.). 256p. (Orig.). (C). Date not set. pap. write for info. (*0-318-69920-6*) HB Coll Pubs.

Crossing over Jordan. Linda B. Brown. 290p. Date not set. pap. 22.00 (*0-345-37857-1*) Ballantine.

Crossing over the Line: Legislating Morality & the Mann Act. David J. Langum. LC 94-13292. (Chicago Series in Sexuality, History, & Society). (Illus.). 264p. 1994. 24.95 (*0-226-46880-1*) U Ch Pr.

Crossing Paths. Laurence Steinberg. 1994. 23.00 (*0-671-79758-1*) S&S Trade.

***Crossing Paths: How Your Child's Adolescence Can Be an Opportunity for Your Own Personal Growth.** Laurence Steinberg & Wendy Steinberg. 1995. pap. 12.00 (*0-684-80405-0*, Fireside) S&S Trade.

Crossing Pedagogical Oceans: International Teaching Assistants in U. S. Undergraduate Education. Rosslyn M. Smith et al. Ed. by Jonathan D. Fife. LC 93-83926. (ASHE-ERIC Higher Education Report Ser.: No. 92-8). 110p. (Orig.). 1993. pap. text ed. 17.00 (*1-878380-21-4*) GWU Schl E&HD.

Crossing Place: A Journey among the Armenians. Philip Marsden. 272p. (Orig.). 1994. pap. 13.00 (*1-56836-052-5*) Kodansha.

Crossing Point: Selected Talks & Writings. Mary C. Richards. LC 73-6010. (Illus.). 256p. 1973. pap. 15.95 (*0-8195-6029-4*, Wesleyan Univ Pr) U Pr of New Eng.

Crossing the Border. Russell Hart. 1993. pap. 14.95 (*0-87243-197-5*) Templegate.

Crossing the Border. Joyce Carol Oates. 1978. pap. 2.50 (*0-449-23751-6*, Crest) Fawcett.

Crossing the Border. Richard Rooke. (Illus.). 48p. 1992. 25.00 (*0-930126-37-8*) Typographeum.

Crossing the Border: An Erotic Journey. Kim Chernin. LC 93-22131. 352p. 1994. 22.00 (*0-449-90522-5*, Columbine) Fawcett.

***Crossing the Border: An Erotic Journey.** Kim Chernin. 1995. pap. write for info. (*0-449-90988-3*) Fawcett.

***Crossing the Border: The Canada-United States Boundary.** Chris Merrit. (Borderlands Monograph Ser.: No. 5). 19-55p. (C). 1991. pap. text ed. 5.00 (*0-614-04707-2*) Canadian-Amer Ctr.

Crossing the Border: The Social & Engineering Design in Computer Integrated Manufacturing Systems. M. J. Corbett et al. Ed. by K. S. Gill. (Artificial Intelligence & Society Ser.). (Illus.). 136p. 1991. pap. 44.00 (*0-387-19613-7*) Spr-Verlag.

Crossing the Border (Colossians) Guy H. King. 1988. pap. 4.95 (*0-87508-274-2*) Chr Lit.

Crossing the Border Fast & Easy: How to Get in - & Out! - of Baja, Mexico, Without the Hassle. Paula McDonald et al. LC 92-90310. (Illus.). 208p. (Orig.). 1992. pap. 6.95 (*0-9633517-0-2*) Borderline Assocs.

Crossing the Boundaries: Christian Piety & the Arts in Italian Medieval Renaissance Confraternities. Ed. by Konrad Eisenbichler. (Early Drama, Art & Music Monograph: No. 15). 1990. 26.95 (*0-918720-45-1*); 16.95 (*0-918720-46-X*) Medieval Inst.

***Crossing the Boundaries: Essays in Biblical Interpretation in Honor of Michael D. Goulder.** Ed. by Stanley E. Porter et al. LC 94-26021. (Biblical Interpretation Ser.: 8). 1994. 83.00 (*90-04-10131-4*) E J Brill.

Crossing the Boundaries in Linguistics. Willem J. Levelt. Ed. by Wolfgang Klein. 1981. lib. bdg. 84.00 (*90-277-1259-X*) Kluwer Ac.

Crossing the Boundary: Black Women Survive Incest. Melba Wilson. LC 93-41813. 238p. 1994. reprint ed. pap. 12.95 (*1-878067-42-7*) Seal Pr Feminist.

Crossing the Bridge. Sydney Metrick. 144p. (Orig.). 1994. pap. 11.95 (*0-89087-738-6*) Celestial Arts.

Crossing the Bridge: A Jungian Approach to Adolescence. Kaspar Kiepenheuer. LC 90-26888. 250p. 1991. 37.95 (*0-8126-9136-9*); pap. 16.95 (*0-8126-9137-7*) Open Court.

Crossing the Bridge Between You & Me. Susan Lenzkes. 1994. pap. 7.99 (*0-929239-83-0*) Discovery Hse Pubs.

***Crossing the Chasm.** Geoffrey Moore. 256p. 1995. pap. 13.00 (*0-88730-717-5*) Harper Busn.

Crossing the Chasm: Marketing & Selling Smart Products to Apprehensive Customers. Jeffrey A. Moore. LC 17-3183. 224p. 1991. 25.00 (*0-88730-519-9*) Harper Busn.

Crossing the Circle at the Holy Wells of Ireland. Walter L. Brenneman, Jr. & Mary G. Brenneman. LC 94-18909. 1995. 27.95 (*0-8139-1548-1*) U Pr of Va.

Crossing the Color Line: Race, Parenting & Culture. Maureen T. Reddy. LC 94-535. 215p. (C). 1994. 22.95 (*0-8135-2105-X*) Rutgers U Pr.

Crossing the Danger Water: Four Hundred Years of African-American Writing. Intro. by Deirdre Mullane. LC 93-17194. 1993. 16.00 (*0-385-42243-1*, Anchor NY) Doubleday.

Crossing the Deadly Ground: United States Army Tactics, 1865-1899. Perry D. Jamieson. LC 93-45318. (Illus.). 256p. (C). 1994. text ed. 29.95 (*0-8173-0720-6*) U of Ala Pr.

Crossing the Delaware: The Story of the Delaware Memorial Bridge. William J. Miller, Jr. 114p. 1990. reprint ed. 9.95 (*0-685-33045-1*); reprint ed. pap. 5.95 (*0-911293-06-X*) Guage Corp.

Crossing the Delaware: The Story of the Delaware Memorial Bridge, the Longest Twin Suspension Bridge in the World. William J. Miller, Jr. Ed. by Kathy K. Demerast. LC 83-71879. (Illus.). 114p. 1983. 9.95 (*0-911293-02-7*); pap. 5.95 (*0-911293-01-9*) Guage Corp.

Crossing the Double-Cross: The Practice of Feminist Criticism. Elizabeth A. Meese. LC 85-20920. xiii, 180p. 1986. 27.50 (*0-8078-1683-3*); pap. 11.95 (*0-8078-4149-8*) U of NC Pr.

Crossing the Field. Kate Barnes. (Illus.). 48p. 1992. pap. 7.95 (*0-942396-67-7*) Blackberry ME.

Crossing the Great Divide. Jean Feraca. 64p. (Orig.). 1992. pap. 9.95 (*1-882280-00-8*) WI Acad Sci.

Crossing the Great River: A Glimpse into the Funeral Rites of African-Americans. Skobi Matunde. (Illus.). 72p. (Orig.). (C). 1990. pap. 7.00 (*0-936868-20-1*) Freeland Pubns.

Crossing the Hackensack. Bart Edelman. Ed. by Lee Mallory. 61p. Date not set. pap. 8.95 (*0-9626168-4-2*) Prometh Pr CA.

Crossing the Heartland: Chicago to Denver. John C. Hudson. LC 92-10535. (Touring North America Ser.). (Illus.). 150p. 1992. 25.00 (*0-8135-1880-6*); pap. 9.95 (*0-8135-1881-4*) Rutgers U Pr.

Crossing the Industrial Divide. Alisdair Bowie. 1991. text ed. 42.00 (*0-231-07212-0*) Col U Pr.

Crossing the Internet Threshold: An Instructional Handbook. Roy Tennant et al. LC 93-159140. viii, 134p. (Orig.). 1993. pap. 45.00 (*1-882208-01-3*) Library Solns.

***Crossing the Internet Threshold: An Instructional Handbook.** 2nd ed. Roy Tennant et al. (Illus.). 175p. (Orig.). 1994. spiral bd. 45.00 (*1-882208-07-2*) Library Solns.

***Crossing the Jabbok: Illness & Death in Ashkenazi Judaism in Sixteenth- Through Nineteenth-Century Prague.** Sylvie-Anne Goldberg. Tr. by Carol Cosman. LC 95-2035. (Contraversions: Critical Studies in Jewish Literature, Culture, & Society Ser.: Vol. 3). (Illus.). 260p. 1995. 45.00 (*0-520-08149-8*) U CA Pr.

***Crossing the Key Stages of History: Effective History Teaching 5-16 & Beyond.** Ruth Watts & Ian Grosvenor. 160p. 1995. pap. 27.95x (*1-85346-324-8*, Pub. by D Fulton UK) Taylor & Francis.

Crossing the Line: A Bluejacket's World War II Odyssey. Alvin Kernan. LC 94-16547. (Illus.). 192p. 1994. 24.95 (*1-55750-455-5*) Naval Inst Pr.

Crossing the Line: A Year in the Land of Apartheid. William Finnegan. LC 94-7521. 1994. pap. 13.00 (*0-520-08872-7*) U CA Pr.

Crossing the Line: Black Major Leaguers, 1947-1959. Larry Moffi & Jonathan Kronstadt. 251p. 1994. lib. bdg. 35.00 (*0-89950-930-4*) McFarland & Co.

Crossing the Line: From Editor to Activist to Inmate - A Writer's Journey. Samuel H. Day, Jr. LC 90-84431. (Illus.). 280p. (Orig.). 1991. 19.95 (*1-879175-00-2*); pap. 15.95 (*1-879175-01-0*) Fortkamp.

Crossing the Line: Immigrants, Economic Integration, & Drug Enforcement on the U. S.-Mexico Border. Tom Barry. 146p. 1994. 9.95 (*0-911213-46-5*) Interhemisp Res Ctr.

Crossing the Line: The Final Conspiracy. Mike Rozsa. LC 92-62015. 126p. (Orig.). 1994. pap. 8.95 (*1-56002-229-9*, Univ Edtns) Aegina Pr.

***Crossing the Line: The Joel Rifkin Serial Murder Case.** Lisa B. Pulitzer. Ed. by Joan Swirsky. (Orig.). 1994. pap. text ed. 5.99 (*0-425-14441-0*) Berkley Pub.

Crossing the Line: Word & Image in Art, 1960-1990. Mary D. MacNaughton. (Illus.). 14p. 1990. 3.00 (*0-685-51609-1*) Galleries Coll.

Crossing the Mainstream: Multicultural Perspectives in Teaching Literature. Eileen Iscoff Oliver. 235p. (Orig.). 1994. pap. 19.95 (*0-8141-0972-1*) NCTE.

***Crossing the Mangrove.** Maryse Conde. Tr. by Richard Philcox. LC 94-35504. 1995. 10.95 (*0-385-47633-7*, Anchor NY) Doubleday.

***Crossing the Minefield: Tactics for Overcoming Today's Toughest Management Challenges.** 2nd ed. Robert W. Barner. LC 94-25592. 256p. 1994. 24.95 (*0-8144-0241-0*) AMACOM.

Crossing the Narrow Bridge: A Practical Guide to Rebbe Nachman's Teachings. Chaim Kramer. Ed. by Moshe Mykoff. 452p. 1990. 16.00 (*0-930213-40-8*) Breslov Res Inst.

Crossing the New Bridge. Emily A. McCully. LC 93-16047. (Illus.). 32p. (J). (ps-3). 1994. lib. bdg. 15.95 (*0-399-22618-4*, Putnam) Putnam Pub Group.

Crossing the Next Meridian: Land, Water, & the Future of the West. Charles F. Wilkinson. LC 92-16869. 377p. 1992. 27.50 (*1-55963-150-3*); pap. 17.95 (*1-55963-149-X*) Island Pr.

Crossing the Plains. Origen Thomson. 1983. 14.95 (*0-87770-292-6*) Ye Galleon.

Crossing the Plains to California in 1849 & Crossing the Plains to California in 1850. Samuel R. Dundass & George Keller. 170p. 1983. 14.95 (*0-87770-291-8*) Ye Galleon.

Crossing the Plains to Oregon in 1853. Maria P. Belshaw. 50p. Date not set. write for info. (*0-318-68184-6*) Ye Galleon.

Crossing the Postmodern Divide. Albert Borgmann. LC 91-31971. 168p. 1992. 19.95 (*0-226-06626-6*) U Ch Pr.

Crossing the Postmodern Divide. Albert Borgmann. LC 91-31971. viii, 174p. (C). 1993. pap. 9.95 (*0-226-06627-4*) U Ch Pr.

Crossing the River. Ray Gonzalez. LC 87-60783. 208p. 1987. pap. 16.00 (*0-932966-80-2*) Permanent Pr.

1720

An Asterisk (*) at the beginning of an entry indicates that the title is appearing in BIP for the first time.

***Crossword Puzzles.** Corinne Stockley. (Hotshots Ser.). (Illus.). 32p. (J). (gr. 1 up). 1995. pap. 2.95 (*0-7460-2278-6*, Usborne) EDC.

Crossword Puzzles, No. 14. Dell Puzzle Magazine Staff. 1993. mass mkt. 7.99 (*0-440-50515-1*) Dell.

Crossword Puzzles, No. 18. large type ed. Charles Preston. 96p. 1994. pap. 6.95 (*0-399-52119-4*, Perigree Bks) Berkley Pub.

Crossword Puzzles: For Fun & Pleasure!, Bks. 1-10. large type ed. pap. 2.21 (*0-685-74148-6*) Briggs Corp.

***Crossword Puzzles No. 19.** large type ed. Charles Preston. 96p. 1995. pap. 6.95 (*0-399-51912-2*, Perigree Bks) Berkley Pub.

Crossword Puzzles No. 19. large type ed. Ed. by Charles Preston. (Perigee Crossword Puzzles Ser.: No. 16). 96p. 1992. pap. 6.95 (*0-399-52108-9*) Putnam Pub Group.

Crossword Puzzles No. 19, No. 13. Charles Preston. 1989. pap. 6.95 (*0-399-52085-6*, Perigree Bks) Berkley Pub.

Crossword Puzzles No. 19, No. 14. large type ed. Ed. by Charles Preston. (Perigee Crossword Puzzles Ser.). 96p. 1990. pap. 6.95 (*0-399-52094-5*) Putnam Pub Group.

Crossword Puzzles No. 19, No. 15. large type ed. Charles Preston. 96p. 1991. pap. 6.95 (*0-399-52101-1*) Putnam Pub Group.

Crossword Puzzles Extraordinaires, Vol. I. Studium Press Staff. 64p. (Orig.). 1990. pap. 5.95 (*0-940099-00-4*) Studium Pr.

Crossword Puzzles Extraordinaires, Vol. II. Studium Press Staff. 64p. (Orig.). 1990. pap. 5.95 (*0-940099-01-2*) Studium Pr.

Crossword Puzzles Extraordinaires, Vol. III. Studium Press Staff. 64p. (Orig.). 1990. pap. 5.95 (*0-940099-02-0*) Studium Pr.

Crossword Puzzles Extraordinaires, Vol. IV. Studium Press Staff. 64p. (Orig.). 1990. pap. 5.95 (*0-940099-03-9*) Studium Pr.

Crossword Puzzles for Fun. Keith Folse. (Illus.). 180p. 1990. pap. 11.95 (*0-933704-88-7*) Dawn Pr.

Crossword Puzzles for U. S. History, Vol. 1. Duane Gage. 40p. (C). 1993. 4.27 (*1-56870-060-1*) RonJon Pub.

Crossword Puzzles for U. S. History, Vol. 2. Duane Gage. 400p. (C). 1993. 3.96 (*1-56870-061-X*) RonJon Pub.

Crossword Puzzles in Large Print, No. 17. large type ed. Charles Preston. 1993. pap. 6.95 (*0-399-52112-7*) Putnam Pub Group.

***Crossword Puzzles in Large Type Omnibus No. 6.** Charles Preston. 176p. (Orig.). 1994. pap. 8.95 (*0-399-52143-7*, Perigree Bks) Berkley Pub.

Crossword Puzzles in Large Type Omnibus. Ed. by Charles Preston. (Perigee Crossword Puzzle Ser.: No. 5). 176p. 1993. pap. 8.95 (*0-399-52109-7*, Perigree Bks) Berkley Pub.

Crossword Puzzles in Large Type Omnibus, No. 4. large type ed. Ed. by Charles Preston. (Perigee Crossword Puzzle Ser.). 176p. 1991. pap. 8.95 (*0-399-52099-6*) Putnam Pub Group.

***Crossword Puzzles to Help You Learn to Spell.** Virginia F. Allen. 64p. 1991. 4.95 (*0-940723-07-7*) SIIS.

Crossword Puzzles Using Rhyming Words. Fred Justus. (Puzzles Ser.). 24p. (gr. 5-7). 1980. student ed 5.00 (*0-8209-0299-3*, PU-13) ESP.

Crossword Puzzles, Wordsearches & Codes. Darlene Spivak. (Illus.). 48p. (J). (gr. 2-5). 1986. student ed 6.95 (*1-55734-067-6*) Tchr Create Mat.

Crossword Quick-List: Three Thousand Words They Use All the Time, Plus One Thousand Names & Phrases Other Dictionaries Don't Include. Kathryn Callahan. 128p. (Orig.). 1988. pap. 8.95 (*0-9620018-9-9*) Newpenny Pr.

***Crossword Review of Anatomy & Physiology.** Dan Riddle. (Illus.). 348p. (C). 1995. student ed 15.00 (*1-886855-03-X*) Tavenner Pub.

Crossword Series, Vol. 161. Eugene T. Maleska. 1991. pap. 6.95 (*0-671-74047-4*, Fireside) S&S Trade.

CrossWord Sticklers Basic Pack. Dorothee Baker. (CrossWord Sticklers Ser.). 1993. 14.50 (*1-883459-00-1*) Adv Methodologies.

CrossWord Sticklers Class Pack. Dorothee Baker. (CrossWord Sticklers Ser.). 1993. 34.50 (*1-883459-01-X*) Adv Methodologies.

CrossWord Sticklers Parental Involvement Program. Dorothee Baker. (CrossWord Sticklers Ser.). 1993. 250.00 (*1-883459-04-4*) Adv Methodologies.

CrossWord Sticklers School Pack. Dorothee Baker. (CrossWord Sticklers Ser.). 1993. 335.00 (*1-883459-02-8*) Adv Methodologies.

Crossword Study Guide for Medical Personnel. Linda K. Dutchess. (Illus.). 56p. 1993. pap. 7.95 (*0-8059-3318-2*) Dorrance.

Crossword Treasury, No. 29. Ed. by Margaret P. Farrar & Eugene T. Maleska. 1986. pap. 6.95 (*0-671-62105-X*, Fireside) S&S Trade.

Crossword Treasury, Nos. 1-16. Ed. by Margaret P. Farrar. Incl. No. 6. pap. 3.95 (*0-671-10393-8*); Set pap. write for info. (*0-318-55619-7*, Fireside) S&S Trade.

Crosswords. (J). (gr. 4-7). 1994. pap. 1.00 (*0-486-28139-6*) Dover.

Crosswords, No. 16. Ed. by Mel Rosen. 96p. (Orig.). 1990. pap. 5.95 (*0-89471-865-7*) Running Pr.

Crosswords, No. 17. Ed. by Mel Rosen. 96p. (Orig.). 1991. pap. 5.95 (*0-89471-987-4*) Running Pr.

Crosswords, No. 19. Ed. by Mel Rosen. 96p. (Orig.). 1992. pap. 6.95 (*1-56138-084-9*) Running Pr.

Crosswords, No. 20. Ed. by Mel Rosen. 96p. (Orig.). 1992. pap. 6.95 (*1-56138-136-5*) Running Pr.

Crosswords, No. 21. Ed. by Mel Rosen. 96p. (Orig.). 1993. spiral bd. 6.95 (*1-56138-203-5*) Running Pr.

Crosswords, No. 22. Ed. by Mel Rosen. (Illus.). 96p. (Orig.). 1993. spiral bd., pap. 6.95 (*1-56138-283-3*) Running Pr.

Crosswords, No. 23. Ed. by Mel Rosen. 96p. (Orig.). 1994. spiral bd. 6.95 (*1-56138-397-X*) Running Pr.

Crosswords, No. 24. Ed. by Mel Rosen. 96p. (Orig.). 1994. 6.95 (*1-56138-424-0*) Running Pr.

Crosswords: A Victoria Cross Mystery. Penny Sumner. LC 93-47346. 256p. 1994. pap. 9.95 (*1-56280-064-7*) Naiad Pr.

Crosswords: Language, Education, & Ethnicity in French Ontario. Monica Heller. LC 94-15992. (Contributions to the Society of Language Ser.: No. 66). x, 252p. (C). 1994. lib. bdg. 113.85 (*3-11-014111-6*) Mouton.

***Crosswords Challenge No. 1.** Ed. by Daniel Stark & Roslyn Stark. 96p. 1995. spiral bd. 6.95 (*1-56138-512-3*) Running Pr.

Crosswords Club. Will Weng. (Crosswords Club Ser.: Vol. 10). 1993. mass mkt. 9.99 (*0-440-50257-8*) Dell.

Crosswords Club, No. 8. Will Weng. 1991. mass mkt. 8.99 (*0-440-50292-6*) Dell.

Crosswords Club, Vol. 7. Ed. by Will Weng. (Orig.). 1990. mass mkt. 8.95 (*0-440-50254-3*) Dell.

Crosswords Club, Vol. 9. Ed. by Weng Will. 1992. mass mkt. 8.99 (*0-440-50256-X*, Dell Trade Pbks) Dell.

Crosswords for Kids. (J). 1991. pap. 1.95 (*0-8167-0882-7*) Troll Assocs.

Crosswords for Language Arts. Joy B. Glicksburg. (J). (gr. 1-5). 1985. pap. 9.99 (*0-8224-2353-7*) Fearon Teach Aids.

Crosswords for Spelling. Christine Thornton. (J). (gr. 4-6). 1985. pap. 8.99 (*0-8224-2354-5*) Fearon Teach Aids.

Crosswords for the Connoisseur. Ed. by Charles Preston. (Perigee Crossword Puzzles Ser.: No. 47). 80p. 1992. pap. 6.95 (*0-399-52107-0*, Perigree Bks) Berkley Pub.

Crosswords for the Connoisseur. Ed. by Charles Preston. (Perigee Crossword Puzzles Ser.: No. 48). 80p. 1993. pap. 6.95 (*0-399-52110-0*, Perigree Bks) Berkley Pub.

Crosswords for the Connoisseur, No. 36. Ed. by Charles Preston. 96p. 1986. pap. 4.95 (*0-399-52052-X*, Perigree Bks) Berkley Pub.

Crosswords for the Connoisseur, No. 43. Charles Preston. 80p. 1990. pap. 6.95 (*0-399-52089-9*, Perigree Bks) Berkley Pub.

Crosswords for the Connoisseur, No. 44. Ed. by Charles Preston. (Perigee Crossword Puzzles Ser.). 80p. 1990. pap. 6.95 (*0-399-52093-7*, Perigree Bks) Berkley Pub.

Crosswords for the Connoisseur, No. 46. Charles Preston. 80p. 1991. pap. 6.95 (*0-399-52102-X*, Perigree Bks) Berkley Pub.

Crosswords for the Connoisseur, No. 50. Charles Preston. LC 93-30008. 80p. 1994. pap. 6.95 (*0-399-52116-X*, Perigree Bks) Berkley Pub.

***Crosswords for the Connoisseur No. 51.** Charles Preston. 80p. (Orig.). 1994. pap. 6.95 (*0-399-52140-2*, Perigree Bks) Berkley Pub.

***Crosswords for the Connoisseur No. 52, No. 52.** Charles Preston. 80p. (Orig.). 1995. pap. 6.95 (*0-399-51951-3*, Perigree Bks) Berkley Pub.

Crosswords for the Connoisseur Omnibus. Ed. by Charles Preston. (Perigee Crossword Puzzles Ser.: No. 5). 128p. 1992. pap. 8.95 (*0-399-52104-6*, Perigree Bks) Berkley Pub.

Crosswords for the Connoisseur Omnibus, No. 6. Charles Preston. 128p. 1994. pap. 8.95 (*0-399-52118-6*, Perigree Bks) Berkley Pub.

***Crosswords for the Connoisseur Omnibus No. 47.** Charles Preston. 128p. (Orig.). 1995. pap. 8.95 (*0-399-51945-9*, Perigree Bks) Berkley Pub.

Crosswords from the National Observe. Ed. by Charles Preston. (Perigee Crossword Puzzles Ser.: No. 13). 64p. (Orig.). 1992. pap. 7.95 (*0-399-52105-4*, Perigree Bks) Berkley Pub.

Crosswords from the Nineteen Twenties. (Illus.). 160p. (Orig.). 1990. pap. 6.95 (*0-88687-456-4*, Pharos) Wrld Almnc.

Crosswords, No. 11. Ed. by Mel Rosen. 96p. (Orig.). 1988. spiral bd. 5.95 (*0-89471-594-1*) Running Pr.

Crosswords, No. 4. Ed. by Mel Rosen. 96p. (Orig.). 1984. spiral bd., pap. 5.95 (*0-89471-277-2*) Running Pr.

Crosswords, No. 8. Ed. by Mel Rosen. 96p. 1986. spiral bd., pap. 5.95 (*0-89471-451-1*) Running Pr.

Crosswords No. 9. Ed. by Mel Rosen. 96p. (Orig.). 1987. spiral bd., pap. 5.95 (*0-89471-497-X*) Running Pr.

Crostics, No. 104. Thomas H. Middleton. 1990. pap. 6.95 (*0-671-72354-5*) S&S Trade.

Crotalaria in Africa & Madagascar. R. M. Polhill. 400p. (C). 1982. text ed. 140.00 (*90-6191-090-0*, Pub. by A A Balkema NE) Ashgate Pub Co.

Crotchets: A Few Short Musical Notes. Percy A. Scholes. LC 67-22115. (Essay Index Reprint Ser.). 1977. 20.95 (*0-8369-0855-4*) Ayer.

Crotchets: A Few Short Musical Notes. Percy A. Scholes. 292p. 1990. reprint ed. lib. bdg. 69.00 (*0-685-45703-6*) Rprt Serv.

Crotchets & Quavers: On Revelations of an Opera Manager in America. Max Maretzek. (American Biography Ser.). 346p. 1991. reprint ed. lib. bdg. 79.00 (*0-7812-8266-7*) Rprt Serv.

Croton Elegies. Antonio Barolini. Tr. by Helen Barolini. 100p. (ENG & ITA.). 1991. pap. 12.00 (*0-920717-39-X*) SPD-Small Pr Dist.

***Croutons.** Kate Carothers. Date not set. pap. 10.95 (*0-9639528-2-X*) Blue Beginnings.

Croutons on a Cow Pie. Baxter Black. (Illus.). 64p. 1988. 10.50 (*0-939343-03-7*) R Stockman & Coyote.

Croutons on a Cow Pie, Vol. 2. Baxter Black. (Illus.). 208p. 1992. 24.95 (*0-939343-12-6*) R Stockman & Coyote.

Crow. Katherine M. Doherty & Craig A. Doherty. LC 93-35660. (Native American People Ser.). (J). 1994. write for info. (*0-86625-529-X*) Rourke Pubns.

Crow. Ruth Hagman. LC 90-37679. (New True Bks.). (Illus.). 48p. (J). (gr. k-4). 1990. lib. bdg. 12.90 (*0-516-01103-0*); pap. 4.95 (*0-516-41103-9*) Childrens.

Crow. Frederick E. Hoxie. (Indians of North America Ser.). (Illus.). 128p. (J). (gr. 5 up). 1989. 17.95 (*1-55546-704-0*); pap. 9.95 (*0-7910-0379-5*) Chelsea Hse.

Crow. James O'Barr. 224p. 1993. pap. 15.95 (*0-87816-221-6*) Kitchen Sink.

Crow. Mary Y. Sampson & Harry Bertschmann. Ed. by Mary Bertschmann. (Illus.). 48p. (J). 1989. pap. 8.00 (*0-935505-05-9*) Bank St Pr.

Crow: The Movie. Jeff Conner. Ed. by Phil Amara & Michael Eastman. (Illus.). 112p. (YA). 1994. pap. 14.95 (*0-87816-285-2*) Kitchen Sink.

***Crow & Hawk: A Traditional Pueblo Indian Story.** Ed. & Ret. by Michael Rosen. LC 94-15176. (Illus.). (J). 1995. 15.00 (*0-15-200257-X*) HarBrace.

Crow & the Eagle: A Tribal History from Lewis & Clark to Custer. Keith Algier. LC 93-8008. (Illus.). 326p. 1993. pap. 14.95 (*0-87004-357-9*) Caxton.

Crow & Weasel. Barry Lopez. LC 90-31500. (Illus.). 64p. (J). (gr. 5 up). 1990. 16.95 (*0-86547-439-7*, North Pt Pr) FS&G.

Crow & Weasel. Barry Lopez. LC 92-54858. 1993. pap. 12.00 (*0-06-097528-8*, PL) HarpC.

Crow Bait. Joseph Meek. (Mountain Jack Pike Ser.: No. 4). 1989. pap. 2.95 (*1-55817-282-3*, Pinnacle NY) Windsor NY.

Crow Boy. Taro Yashima. (Picture Puffins Ser.). (Illus.). (J). (gr. k-3). 1976. pap. 4.99 (*0-14-050172-X*, Puffin) Puffin Bks.

Crow Boy. Taro Yashima. (Illus.). (J). (gr. k-3). 1955. pap. 15.99 (*0-670-24931-9*) Viking Child Bks.

***Crow Chief.** Illus. & Ret. by Paul Goble. LC 90-28457. 32p. (J). (ps-2). 1995. pap. 5.95 (*0-531-07064-6*) Orchard Bks Watts.

Crow Chief: A Plains Indian Story. Paul Goble. LC 90-28457. (Illus.). 32p. (J). (ps-2). 1992. 15.95 (*0-531-05947-2*); lib. bdg. 15.99 (*0-531-08547-3*) Orchard Bks Watts.

Crow Doesn't Need a Shadow: A Guide to Writing Poetry from Nature. Lorraine Ferra. LC 93-34991. 128p. (J). 1994. pap. 9.95 (*0-87905-600-2*) Gibbs Smith Pub.

Crow Dog: Sioux Family Saga. R. Erdos. 1995. 25.00 (*0-06-016861-7*, HarpT) HarpC.

Crow Dog's Case: American Indian Sovereignty, Tribal Law, & United States Law in the Nineteenth Century. Sidney L. Harring. (Cambridge Studies in North American Indian History). (Illus.). 304p. (C). 1994. 54.95 (*0-521-41563-2*) Cambridge U Pr.

Crow Dog's Case: American Indian Sovereignty, Tribal Law, & United States Law in the Nineteenth Century. Sidney L. Harring. (Cambridge Studies in North American Indian History). (Illus.). 304p. (C). 1994. pap. 17.95 (*0-521-46715-2*) Cambridge U Pr.

Crow Eaters: A Novel. Bapsi Sidhwa. LC 92-3509. (Alive Again Ser.). 268p. 1992. reprint ed. pap. 13.00 (*0-915943-78-6*) Milkweed Ed.

***Crow Feather.** Paul A. Hawkins. 352p. (Orig.). 1995. mass mkt. 4.50 (*0-451-18449-1*, Sig) NAL-Dutton.

Crow Horse. large type ed. Buck Lyon. (Linford Western Library). 320p. 1993. pap. 14.95 (*0-7089-7361-2*, Trailtree Bookshop) Ulverscroft.

Crow in the Snow & Other Bedtime Stories. Erwin Moser. Tr. by Joel Agee. LC 86-10740. (Illus.). 48p. (J). (ps up). 1986. 10.95 (*0-915361-49-3*) Modan-Adama Bks.

Crow Indian Beadwork: A Descriptive & Historical Study. rev. ed. John C. Ewers. Ed. by Monte Smith & E. K. Burnett. LC 84-73388. (Illus.). 108p. 1985. reprint ed. per., pap. text ed. 8.95 (*0-943604-06-0*) Eagles View.

Crow Indians. Incl. Crow Tribe of Indians. Norman B. Plummer. 1974. (*0-318-52439-2*); Findings of Fact, & Opinion. Indian Claims Commission. 1974. (*0-318-52440-6*); (American Indian Ethnohistory Series: Plains Indians). (Illus.). 1974. Set lib. bdg. 51.00 (*0-8240-0756-5*) Garland.

Crow Indians. (Junior Library of American Indians). (Illus.). 80p. (J). (gr. 3-7). 1993. lib. bdg. 14.95 (*0-7910-1661-7*); pap. 6.95 (*0-7910-1964-0*) Chelsea Hse.

Crow Indians. Robert H. Lowie. LC 35-9409. (Illus.). 350p. 1982. reprint ed. pap. 9.95 (*0-8290-0409-2*) Irvington.

Crow Indians. Robert H. Lowie. LC 82-20103. (Illus.). xxii, 350p. 1983. reprint ed. pap. 12.00 (*0-8032-7909-4*, Bison Books) U of Nebr Pr.

Crow Killer. Raymond W. Thorp & Robert Bunker. reprint ed. lib. bdg. 20.95 (*0-88411-078-8*, Aeonian Pr) Amereon Ltd.

Crow Killer: The Saga of Liver-Eating Johnson. rev. ed. Raymond W. Thorp & Robert Bunker. LC 58-8120. (Illus.). 192p. 1969. 24.95 (*0-253-11425-X*); pap. 8.95 (*0-253-20312-0*, MB-312) Ind U Pr.

Crow Moon, Worm Moon. James Skofield. LC 89-1370. (Illus.). 32p. (J). (gr. k-3). 1990. text ed. 13.95 (*0-02-782915-4*, Four Winds Pr) S&S Childrens.

Crow Portfolio. James O'Barr. (Illus.). 64p. 1993. 24.95 (*1-879450-90-9*) Tundra MA.

***Crow Time.** Sheila Cudahy. (New American Fiction Ser.: No. 32). 250p. (Orig.). 1995. pap. 11.95 (*1-55713-202-X*) Sun & Moon CA.

Crow with No Mouth: Ikkyu Fifteenth Century Zen Master. Stephen Berg. LC 88-63223. 80p. (Orig.). 1989. pap. 10.00 (*1-55659-022-9*) Copper Canyon.

***Crowd.** rev. ed. Gustav Le Bon. 224p. (C). 1994. pap. 19.95 (*1-56000-788-5*) Transaction Pubs.

Crowd. Gustave LeBon. LC 82-14042. 240p. 1982. reprint ed. pap. 12.95 (*0-87797-168-4*) Cherokee.

Crowd & Not Evening or Light. Leslie Scalapino. 110p. 1992. pap. 9.00 (*1-55713-141-4*) Sun & Moon CA.

Crowd Culture. Bernard I. Bell. LC 74-117758. (Essay Index Reprint Ser.). 1977. 19.95 (*0-8369-1742-1*) Ayer.

Crowd for Christ. Joe Brice. 1993. reprint ed. pap. 8.99 (*0-88019-303-4*) Schmul Pub Co.

Crowd in American Literature. Nicolaus Mills. LC 86-3014. ix, 146p. 1986. text ed. 25.00 (*0-8071-1286-0*) La State U Pr.

Crowd in the French Revolution. George Rude. (Illus.). 1967. reprint ed. pap. text ed. 14.95 (*0-19-500370-5*) OUP.

Crowd in the French Revolution. George Rude. LC 86-3166. 295p. 1986. reprint ed. text ed. 89.50 (*0-313-25168-1*, RUCR, Greenwood Pr) Greenwood.

Crowd Inside. Elizabeth Libby. LC 79-59801. (Poetry Ser.). 1978. 16.95 (*0-915604-52-3*); pap. 9.95 (*0-915604-53-1*) Carnegie-Mellon.

Crowd of Witnesses: Interviews with Famous New Testament Men & Women. Enzo Crocetti & Mario Giordano. Tr. by Lisa Maroni. LC 94-20697. (Illus.). (J). 1994. pap. 9.95 (*0-8198-1531-4*) Pauline Bks.

***Crowd of Witnesses: Interviews with Famous Old Testament Men & Women.** Enzo Crocetti & Mario Giordano. Tr. by Lisa Maroni. LC 94-17857. (Illus.). 133p. (Orig.). (J). (gr. 4-8). 1995. pap. 9.95 (*0-8198-1530-6*) Pauline Bks.

Crowd Pleasers. Rosemary Rogers. 528p. 1980. mass mkt. 4.95 (*0-380-75622-6*) Avon.

Crowd Theory as a Psychology of the Leader & the Led. Erika G. King. (Mellen Studies in Sociology: Vol. 7). 248p. 1990. lib. bdg. 89.95 (*0-88946-624-6*) E Mellen.

Crowd Your Luck on Death. Harry Kapustin. LC 75-160937. (Short Story Index Reprint Ser.). 1977. reprint ed. 19.95 (*0-8369-3916-6*) Ayer.

Crowded Hours. Alice R. Longworth. Ed. by Annette K. Baxter. LC 79-8799. (Signal Lives Ser.). (Illus.). 1980. reprint ed. lib. bdg. 41.95 (*0-405-12846-0*) Ayer.

Crowded with Ghosts. Lani Steele. (Illus.). 26p. (Orig.). 1986. pap. 5.00 (*0-9616635-0-2*) Oblong Pr.

Crowder Tales. Nixon Smiley. LC 73-80589. (Illus.). 169p. 1973. 5.95 (*0-912458-22-4*) Banyan Bks.

Crowding & Behavior. Chalsa M. Loo. LC 74-8362. 246p. 1974. 29.50 (*0-8422-5180-4*); pap. text ed. 6.95 (*0-8422-0415-6*) Irvington.

Crowding in Real Environments. Ed. by Susan Saegert. LC 75-42756. (Sage Contemporary Social Science Issues Ser.: No. 25). 128p. reprint ed. pap. 36.50 (*0-317-08125-X*, 2021954) Bks Demand.

Crowding out the Future: World Population Growth: U. S. Immigration & Pressures on Natural Resources. Robert W. Fox & Ira H. Mehlman. (Illus.). 64p. (Orig.). (C). 1992. pap. 10.00 (*0-935776-12-5*) F A I R.

Crowds & History: Mass Phenomena in English Towns, 1790-1835. Mark Harrison. (Past & Present Publications). 300p. 1989. 64.95 (*0-521-30210-2*) Cambridge U Pr.

Crowds & Power. Elias Canetti. Tr. by Carol Stewart. 496p. (C). 1984. pap. 17.00 (*0-374-51820-3*) FS&G.

Crowds, Psychology, & Politics, 1871-1899. Jaap Van Ginneken. (Studies in the History of Psychology). (Illus.). 200p. (C). 1992. 59.95 (*0-521-40418-5*) Cambridge U Pr.

Crowe: John Crowe & His Descendants. L. Crowell. (Illus.). 109p. 1991. reprint ed. pap. 19.00 (*0-8328-1808-9*) Higginson Bk Co.

Crowell's Handbook of World Opera. Frank L. Moore. LC 73-3025. (Illus.). 683p. 1974. reprint ed. text ed. 43.00 (*0-8371-6822-8*, MOCH, Greenwood Pr) Greenwood.

Crowfoot: Chief of the Blackfeet. Hugh A. Dempsey. LC 72-865. (Civilization of the American Indian Ser.: Vol. 122). (Illus.). 248p. 1989. pap. 13.95 (*0-8061-1596-3*) U of Okla Pr.

Crowheart's Revenge. Jon Sharpe. (Trailsman Ser.: No. 151). 176p. (Orig.). 1994. pap. 3.50 (*0-451-17887-4*) NAL-Dutton.

Crowland Chronicle Continuations 1459-1486. Ed. by Nicholas Pronay & John Cox. (Illus.). 2072p. 1993. text ed. 55.00 (*0-948993-00-6*) A Sutton Pub.

Crowley, Aleister, Thoth Tarot. James Wasserman. 52p. 1983. 16.00 (*0-913866-15-6*) US Games Syst.

Crowley Deck, Small. Hermit. 46p. 1986. 14.00 (*0-88079-308-2*) US Games Syst.

Crowley Gift Set: Includes Tarot: Mirror of the Soul. Gerd Ziegler. 144p. 1989. 27.95 (*0-88079-322-8*) US Games Syst.

Crowley Swiss Tarot. Stuart R. Kaplan. 10p. 1970. 17.95 (*0-88079-469-0*) US Games Syst.

Crowley's Apprentice: The Life & Ideas of Israel Regardie. Gerald Suster. 192p. (Orig.). 1990. pap. 9.95 (*0-87728-700-7*) Weiser.

***Crown: A Tale of Sir Gawein & King Arthur's Court.** Heinrich Von dem Turlin. Tr. & Intro. by J. W. Thomas. LC 88-20661. 363p. 1989. reprint ed. pap. 103.50 (*0-7837-8885-1*, 2049596) Bks Demand.

Crown & Calumet: British-Indian Relations, 1783-1815. Colin G. Calloway. LC 86-16151. (Illus.). 360p. 1987. 32.95 (*0-8061-2033-9*) U of Okla Pr.

Crown & Cortes: Government, Institutions & Representation in Early Modern Castile. I. A. Thompson. (Collected Studies: No. CS 427). 350p. 1993. 89.95 (*0-86078-393-6*, Pub. by Variorum UK) Ashgate Pub Co.

Crown & Jewel. Jeri Massi. (Pennant Ser.). (Illus.). 160p. (Orig.). (J). (gr. 5). 1987. pap. 5.95 (*0-89084-390-2*) Bob Jones Univ Pr.

Crown & Mitre: Religion & Society in Northern Europe since the Reformation. Ed. by W. M. Jacob & Nigel Yates. (Illus.). 320p. (C). 1993. text ed. 81.00 (*0-85115-346-1*, Boydell Pr) Boydell & Brewer.

Crown & Sword: The Milesian-Celtic Heritage of Ireland & Britain. George A. Jones. LC 76-44145. 1977. pap. 4.00 (*0-917610-00-8*) Peacehaven.

Crown & the Crucible. Michael Phillips & Judith Pella. (Russians Ser.: Bk. 1). 448p. (Orig.). 1991. pap. 9.99 (*1-55661-172-2*) Bethany Hse.

C

An Asterisk (*) at the beginning of an entry indicates that the title is appearing in BIP for the first time.

C

An Asterisk (*) at the beginning of an entry indicates that the title is appearing in BIP for the first time.

1723

Crucifixion & the Resurrection of Jesus. Louise Morris. 94p. 1993. spiral bd. 5.50 (0-7873-0626-6) Mokelumne.

Crucifixion in American Painting. Robert Henkes. 1978. lib. bdg. 300.00 (0-8490-1370-4) Gordon Pr.

Crucifixion of Esmerelda Sweetwater: A Parable for All Ages. Don Elkins & Carla L. Rueckert. 200p. (Orig.). (C). 1986. pap. 9.95 (0-945007-06-X) L-L Resrch.

*Crucifixion of Jesus: History, Myth, Faith. Gerard S. Sloyan. LC 95-2480. 1995. write for info. (0-8006-2931-0, Fortress Pr); pap. write for info. (0-8006-2886-1, Fortress Pr) Augsburg Fortress.

Crucifixion of the Jews. Franklin H. Littell. (Reprints of Scholarly Excellence (ROSE) Ser.: No. 12). 160p. (C). 1986. reprint ed. pap. 10.95 (0-86554-227-9, P31) Mercer Univ Pr.

Crucifixion of the Phoenix. Gyeorgos C. Hatonn. (Phoenix Journals). 320p. (Orig.). (C). 1990. pap. 10.00 (0-922356-14-9) Amer West Pubs.

Crucifixion Viewed from a Jewish Standpoint (1908) see My Religion

Crucifixions. Sujatha Modayil. (Redbird Ser.). 1975. 8.00 (0-88253-725-3); 4.80 (0-89253-543-1) Ind-US Inc.

*Cruciform Character - 1967, Vol. 31. Eugen Rosenstock-Huessy. (Eugen Rosenstock-Huessy Lectures). 65p. Date not set. audio, pap. 35.00 (0-614-05408-7); pap. 15.00 (0-912148-50-0); audio 25.00 (0-614-05407-9) Argo Bks.

Cruciform Church: Becoming a Cross-Shaped People in a Secular World. 2nd ed. C. Leonard Allen. LC 89-82537. 191p. 1990. pap. 11.95 (0-89112-098-X) Abilene Christ U.

Cruciformed: Images of the Cross Since 1980. David S. Rubin. (Illus.). 64p. 1991. pap. text ed. 15.00 (1-880353-00-8) Cleveland Ctr.

*Cruciformed: The Literary Impact of Mark's Story of Jesus & His Disciples. Mark I. Wegener. 286p. (C). 1995. lib. bdg. 36.50 (0-8191-9831-5) U Pr of Amer.

Crucify Him: A Lawyer Looks at the Trial of Jesus. Dale Foreman. 224p. 1990. 9.99 (0-310-51211-5) Zondervan.

Crucifying the Savior of France: Petain. Harry E. Barnes. 1971. 250.00 (0-87700-281-9) Revisionist Pr.

Crucigramas Biblicos Y Otras Actividades. Ed. by Nola Granberry. 80p. (Orig.). 1989. reprint ed. pap. 4.25 (0-311-26609-6) Casa Bautista.

Crucigramas Para Estudiantes. Jane Burnett. (Illus.). 64p. (SPA.). 1983. pap. 14.60 (0-8442-7229-9, Natl Textbk) NTC Pub Grp.

Crude Black Molasses. Cyril Scott & John Lust. 1980. pap. 2.95 (0-87904-010-6) Lust.

Crude Oil & Natural Gas Production in Nebraska. James R. Schmidt. 1981. 7.50 (0-318-42807-5) Bur Busn Res U Nebr.

Crude Oil Pipe Lines & Competition in the Oil Industry & Costs of Operating Crude Oil Pipe Lines. Leslie Cookenboo, Jr. Ed. by Stuart Bruchey. LC 78-22669. (Rice Institute Pamphlet: Energy in the American Economy Ser.: Vol. 41, No. 1). (Illus.). 1979. reprint ed. lib. bdg. 28.95 (0-405-11973-9) Ayer.

Crude Oil Washing Systems. International Maritime Organization Staff. 1983. text ed. 75.00 (0-89771-969-7, Pub. by Intl Maritime Org UK) St Mut.

Cruden's Compact Concordance. abr. ed. Alexander Cruden. 576p. 1968. 14.99 (0-310-22910-3, 9440) Zondervan.

Cruden's Compact Concordance. abr. ed. Alexander Cruden. 1988. 14.99 (0-310-22919-7) Zondervan.

Cruden's Complete Concordance. Alexander Cruden. 796p. 1988. 15.95 (0-917006-31-3) Hendrickson MA.

Cruden's Complete Concordance. Alexander Cruden. 800p. 1991. pap. 9.95 (0-943575-82-6) Hendrickson MA.

Cruden's Complete Concordance. Alexander Cruden. 1967. 19.99 (0-310-22920-0, 9441) Zondervan.

Cruden's Complete Concordance. Alexander Cruden. 1976. pap. 14.99 (0-310-22921-9) Zondervan.

Cruden's Complete Concordance to the Old & New Testaments. Ed. by Alexander Cruden. (Reference Library Edition). 15.99 (0-529-06675-0) World Bible.

Cruden's Concordance. (Bible Reference Library). 400p. 1988. pap. 7.95 (1-55748-015-X) Barbour & Co.

Cruden's Concordance. 1992. 9.95 (1-55748-273-X) Barbour & Co.

*Cruden's Condensed Concordance. Cruden. 1990. pap. text ed. 7.95 (1-55674-143-X) Dugan Pubs Inc.

Cruden's Handy Concordance. Alexander Cruden. 1988. pap. 9.99 (0-310-22911-1, 6769P) Zondervan.

Cruel & Inhuman Treatment: The Use of Four-Point Restraint in the Onondaga County Public Safety Building, Advance press. Physicians for Human Rights Staff. LC 93-84902. (Illus.). 90p. 1993. pap. 7.00 (1-879707-15-2) Phy Human Rights.

Cruel & Inhuman Treatment: The Use of Four-Point Restraint in the Onondaga County Public Safety Building, Final copy. Physicians for Human Rights Staff. LC 93-84902. (Illus.). 90p. 1993. pap. 7.00 (1-879707-16-0) Phy Human Rights.

*Cruel & Unusal: A Fusco Brothers Collection. Joe Duffy. (Illus.). 128p. 1995. pap. 8.95 (0-8362-0421-2) Andrews & McMeel.

Cruel & Unusual. Patricia D. Cornwell. 416p. 1995. mass mkt. 6.50 (0-380-71834-0) Avon.

Cruel & Unusual. Patricia D. Cornwell. Date not set. 21.00 (0-684-19599-2, Scribners) S&S Trade.

Cruel & Unusual. large type ed. Patricia D. Cornwell. LC 92-38203. (General Ser.). 1993. 23.00 (0-8161-5727-8, Large Print Bks) Hall.

Cruel & Unusual: A Novel. Patricia D. Cornwell. 384p. 1993. text ed. 21.00 (0-684-19530-5, Scribners) S&S Trade.

Cruel & Unusual: A Novel. large type ed. Patricia D. Cornwell. 448p. 1993. text ed. 23.00 (0-684-19612-3, Scribners) S&S Trade.

Cruel & Unusual Punishment. Duane Magnani. 1986. 13.95 (1-883858-05-4) Witness CA.

*Cruel & Unusual Punishment: The U. S. Blockade of Cuba. Mary Murray. 117p. 1993. pap. 9.95 (1-875284-78-8, Pub. by Ocean Pr AT) Talman.

Cruel & Unusual Puns. Don Hauptman. 1991. mass mkt. 5.99 (0-440-20850-5) Dell.

*Cruel April: A Dave Garrett Mystery. Neil Albert. LC 94-32328. 256p. 1995. 19.95 (0-525-93719-6, Dutton) NAL-Dutton.

Cruel April: The Fall of Saigon. Oliver Todd. 1990. 24.95 (0-393-02787-2) Norton.

Cruel As the Grave. large type ed. Helen McCloy. 1979. 12.00 (0-7089-0260-X) Ulverscroft.

Cruel Awakening: Sweden & the Killing of Olof Palme. Chris Mosey. LC 91-15981. 208p. 1991. text ed. 49.95 (0-312-06711-9) St Martin.

Cruel Choice: A New Concept in the Theory of Development. Denis Goulet. LC 85-3313. 384p. (C). 1985. reprint ed. pap. text ed. 27.50 (0-8191-4612-9) U Pr of Amer.

Cruel City. Marianne Ruth & Raymond F. Locke. LC 90-52813. (Illus.). 240p. (J). 1991. 19.95 (0-915677-48-2) Roundtable Pub.

Cruel City & Other Korean Short Stories. So Chong-in et al. Ed. by Korean National Commission for UNESCO The. Tr. by Yi Chang-guk et al. (Best Korean Short Stories Ser.: No. 1). xviii, 210p. 1983. 20.00 (0-89209-212-2) Pace Intl Res.

Cruel Compassion: Psychiatric Control of Society's Unwanted. Thomas Szasz. LC 93-31600. 1994. text ed. 19.95 (0-471-01012-X) Wiley.

Cruel Deception. Cathryn H. Chadwick. 1990. pap. 3.95 (0-8217-3246-3) Zebra.

Cruel Doubt. Joe McGinniss. Ed. by Julie Rubenstein. 512p. 1992. reprint ed. mass mkt. 5.99 (0-671-77539-1) PB.

*Cruel Duet. Julia Mishkin. (QRL Poetry Book Ser.: Vol. XXVI). 20.00 (0-614-06416-3) Quarterly Rev.

Cruel Fate: One Man's Triumph over Injustice. Hugh Callaghan. 207p. 1993. 30.00 (1-85371-258-2, Pub. by Poolbeg Pr IE) Dufour.

*Cruel Fate: One Man's Triumph over Injustice. Hugh Callaghan & Sally Mulready. (Illus.). 1995. pap. 13.95 (0-87023-987-2) U of Mass Pr.

*Cruel Fate: One Man's Triumph over Injustice. 2nd ed. Hugh Callaghan & Sally Mulready. 272p. (C). 1995. text ed. 35.00 (0-87023-986-4) U of Mass Pr.

Cruel in the Shadow. large type ed. Lorn Macintyre. 576p. 1982. 15.95 (0-7089-0867-5) Ulverscroft.

*Cruel Justice. William Bernhardt. LC 95-14697. 1996. write for info. (0-345-38684-1) Ballantine.

*Cruel Legacy. Penny Jordan. 1995. pap. 5.99 (1-55166-075-X, 1-66075-2, Mira Bks) Harlequin Bks.

Cruel Lord Cranham. Sandra Heath. (Regency Romance Ser.). 224p. (Orig.). 1993. pap. 3.99 (0-451-17736-3, Sig) NAL-Dutton.

Cruel Miracles. Orson S. Card. (Maps in a Mirror Ser.: No. 3). 256p. 1992. reprint ed. mass mkt. 4.99 (0-8125-2304-0) Tor Bks.

Cruel Month. Osbert Sitwell. 4.95 (0-7043-3155-1, Pub. by Quartet UK) Charles River Bks.

Cruel Mother. Janet Lapierre. 1991. reprint ed. mass mkt. 3.95 (0-373-26078-4) Harlequin Bks.

Cruel Peace: Everyday Life & the Cold War. Fred Inglis. LC 91-70059. (Illus.). 512p. 1993. reprint ed. pap. 15.00 (0-465-01495-X) Basic.

Cruel Radiance: Notes of a Prosewriter in a Visual Age. Ron Powers. LC 94-20541. 288p. 1994. 25.00 (0-87451-690-0) U Pr of New Eng.

Cruel Sacrifice. Aphrodite Jones. 320p. 1994. mass mkt. 4.99 (1-55817-884-8, Pinnacle NY) Windsor NY.

Cruel Sea. Nicholas Monsarrat. 1951. 25.00 (0-394-42090-X) Knopf.

Cruel Sea. Nicholas Monsarrat. Ed. by Jack Sweetman. LC 88-15126. (Classics of Naval Literature Ser.). (Illus.). 400p. 1988. 32.95 (0-87021-055-6) Naval Inst Pr.

Cruel Trade. Fergus Finlay. 281p. 1991. 22.95 (0-233-98586-7, Pub. by A Deutsch UK) Trafalgar.

Cruel Tricks for Dear Friends. Penn & Teller. 1989. 23.00 (0-394-75351-8, Villard Bks) Random.

Cruelest Death: The Enigma of Adolescent Suicide. David Lester. LC 92-34448. 178p. (Orig.). 1993. pap. 16.95 (0-914783-64-5) Charles.

Cruellest Lie. Susan Napier. (Presents Ser.). 1994. mass mkt. 2.99 (0-373-11674-8, 1-11674-8) Harlequin Bks.

*Cruellest Lie. large type ed. Susan Napier. (Traditional Romance Ser.). 1994. 17.95 (0-263-13823-2, Pub. by Mills & Boon Ltd UK) Chivers N Amer.

Cruellest Month. Hazel Holt. 224p. 1992. 4.50 (0-451-40313-4, Onyx) NAL-Dutton.

Cruelty & Silence: War, Tyranny, Uprising, & the Arab World. Kanan Makiya. 1994. pap. 10.95 (0-393-31141-4) Norton.

Cruelty & Silence: War, Tyranny, Uprising in the Arab World. Kanan Makiya. (Illus.). 256p. 1993. 22.95 (0-393-03108-X) Norton.

Cruelty of Heresy: An Affirmation of Christian Orthodoxy. C. FitzSimons Allison. LC 93-39541. 200p. (Orig.). 1994. pap. 15.95 (0-8192-1513-9) Morehouse Pub.

Cruelty of the Desert. Michael Wurster. 48p. (Orig.). 1989. pap. 8.00 (0-685-29146-4) Cottage Wordsmiths.

*Cruets Cruets Cruets Vol. II. Elaine Ezell & George Newhouse. 238p. 1994. pap. 32.95 (0-915410-49-4) Antique Pubns.

Cruets Cruets Cruets Vol. II, Vol. 1. Elaine Ezell & George Newhouse. (Illus.). 200p. (YA). 1991. 37.95 (0-915410-73-7, 4004); pap. 29.92 (0-915410-72-9, 4003) Antique Pubns.

Cruickshank's Photographs of Birds of America. Allan D. Cruickshank. LC 77-70078. (Illus.). 1977. pap. 10.95 (0-486-23497-5) Dover.

*Cruise. Dennis Eichhorn. (Illus.). 75p. (Orig.). (YA). (gr. 7-12). 1987. pap. 3.95 (0-89872-207-1) Turman Pub.

*Cruise: The Unauthorized Biography. Frank Sanello. 256p. 1995. 19.95 (0-87833-913-2) Taylor Pub.

Cruise Books of the U. S. Navy in World War II: A Bibliography. 1994. lib. bdg. 250.00 (0-8490-5711-6) Gordon Pr.

Cruise Books of the United States Navy in World War II: A Bibliography. Dean L. Mawdsley. LC 92-41498. 162p. 1993. 6.00 (0-945274-13-0) Naval Hist Ctr.

Cruise Bridge. Don Von Elsner. LC 84-223817. 187p. 1980. pap. 5.95 (0-939460-09-2) Devyn Pr.

Cruise Control: So, You Want to Be Led by God's Spirit. 2nd ed. W. Howard Adams. Ed. by Mary J. Adams. 200p. 1989. write for info. (0-318-65921-2) Sound Abundance.

Cruise for Cinderella. large type ed. Alex Stuart. 352p. 1992. 21.95 (0-7089-2650-9) Ulverscroft.

Cruise Hosting. Brooke Bravos. 225p. (C). 1992. pap. text ed. 19.95 (0-9630614-9-6) Trvl Time.

Cruise Missile: Bargaining Chip or Defense Bargain? Robert L. Pfaltzgraff, Jr. & Jacquelyn K. Davis. LC 76-51854. (Special Report Ser.). 53p. 1977. 11.95 (0-89549-001-3) Inst Foreign Policy Anal.

Cruise Missile Proliferation in the 1990s. W. Seth Carus. LC 92-26115. (Washington Papers: No. 159). 176p. 1992. text ed. 45.00 (0-275-94519-7, C4519, Praeger Pubs); pap. text ed. 14.95 (0-275-94520-0, B4520, Praeger Pubs) Greenwood.

Cruise Missiles: A Drama about Nuclear First Strike Planning. Mot Remeis & Thomas K. Siemer. 142p. (Orig.). (C). 1989. pap. 14.95 (0-685-30774-3) Abbeyhills O C.

Cruise Missiles: Technology, Strategy, Politics. Ed. by Richard K. Betts. LC 81-18149. 612p. 1981. 38.95 (0-8157-0932-3); pap. 16.95 (0-8157-0931-5) Brookings.

Cruise Missiles & U. S. Policy. Richard K. Betts. LC 82-72704. 612p. 1982. pap. 7.95 (0-8157-0933-1) Brookings.

Cruise of the Aardvark. Ogden Nash. LC 67-27296. (Illus.). 48p. (J). (ps up). 1989. pap. 5.95 (0-87131-570-X) M Evans.

Cruise of the Alerte. E. F. Knight. 224p. (Orig.). 1984. pap. 14.95 (0-246-12312-5, Pub. by Granada UK) Sheridan.

Cruise of the Blue Flujin. Ken C. Wise. LC 87-50082. (Illus.). 218p. 1987. boxed 12.95 (0-9611596-6-9) Wilderness Adventure Bks.

Cruise of the Cachalot. Frank T. Bullen. (Illus.). 1980. pap. 4.95 (0-918172-06-3) Leetes Isl.

Cruise of the Corwin. John Muir. LC 92-25139. (John Muir Library). (Illus.). 240p. (Orig.). 1993. pap. 10.00 (0-87156-523-4) Sierra.

Cruise of the Dancer. McCarty & Young. 1994. pap. 15.95 (1-881116-29-8) Black Forrest Pr.

Cruise of the Dazzler. Jack London. (Illus.). 250p. 1981. pap. 6.95 (0-932458-06-8) Star Rover.

Cruise of the Dazzler. Jack London. reprint ed. lib. bdg. 15.95 (0-89190-652-5, Rivercity Pr) Amereon Ltd.

Cruise of the "Gipsy" the Journal of John Wilson, Surgeon on a Whaling Voyage in the Pacific Ocean. John Wilson. 500p. 1991. 32.50 (0-87770-488-0) Ye Galleon.

Cruise of the Pnyx. Robert Kelly. LC 79-64918. 50p. 1979. pap. 10.00 (0-930794-08-7) Station Hill Pr.

Cruise of the Raider Wolf. Roy Alexander. (War & Warriors Ser.). 270p. 1991. 15.95 (0-939482-36-3) Noontide.

Cruise of the Rolling Junk. F. Scott Fitzgerald. 1976. 30.00 (0-89723-008-6) Bruccoli.

Cruise of the Santa Maria. Eilis Dillon. (Illus.). (J). (gr. 3-7). 1991. pap. 9.95 (0-86278-263-5, Pub. by OBrien Pr IE) Dufour.

Cruise of the Skuld. Marguerite Pedersen. LC 87-61085. 160p. (Orig.). 1987. pap. 7.00 (0-914752-25-1) Sovereign Pr.

Cruise of the Snark. Jack London. (Illus.). 340p. 1984. 22.50 (0-85036-152-4, Pub. by Seafarer Bks UK) Sheridan.

Cruise of the Snark. Jack London. 340p. 1971. reprint ed. pap. 25.00 (0-87556-437-2) Saifer.

Cruise of the Snark. Jack London. 1992. reprint ed. lib. bdg. 18.95 (0-89966-954-9) Buccaneer Bks.

Cruise of the Snark. Jack London. (Illus.). 340p. 1993. reprint ed. pap. 14.95 (0-924486-46-5) Sheridan.

Cruise of the Snark: A Pacific Voyage. Jack London. 300p. 1986. 14.95 (0-7103-0139-1, Pub. by Kegan Paul Intl UK) Routledge Chapman & Hall.

Cruise, Pershing & SS-20: The Search for Consensus: Nuclear Weapons in Europe. J. Cartwright & J. Critchley. 188p. 1985. text ed. 45.00 (0-08-031201-2, Pergamon Pr); pap. text ed. 23.75 (0-08-031202-0, Pergamon Pr) Elsevier.

*Cruise Secrets Exposed: The How-to Resource Guide to the Best Values in Cruise Travel. Sharon Tyler & Matthew Wunder. LC 94-76367. Date not set. 16.95 (0-614-05178-9) Univ Info Corp.

Cruise Ship Cookbook. Connie Von Hundertmark. 120p. (Orig.). 1986. pap. 6.95 (0-915765-33-0) Natl Pr Bks.

*Cruise Ships - Riverboats - Casinos: The New Job Manual. 6th rev. ed. Richard M. Zink. (Illus.). 64p. 1995. pap. 14.95x (0-939446-46-4) Zinks Career Guide.

*Cruise Ships-Riverboats-Casinos: The New Job Manual. 6th rev. ed. Richard M. Zink. (Illus.). 64p. 1995. pap. text ed. 14.95 (0-939469-46-4) Zinks Career Guide.

*Cruise Staffing: Fred Divel's Guide to Jobs & Working on Cruise Ships. Fred Divel. (Fred Divel's Guide to Jobs & Working on Cruise Ships). 250p. (Orig.). 1995. pap. text ed. 24.95 (0-9644334-0-0) F Divel Pub.

Cruiser Bartolomeo Colleoni. Franco Gay & Valerio Gay. LC 87-61493. (Anatomy of the Ship Ser.). (Illus.). 120p. 1988. 36.95 (0-87021-900-6) Naval Inst Pr.

Cruiser Belfast. Ross Watton. LC 85-60097. (Anatomy of the Ship Ser.). (Illus.). 120p. 1985. 36.95 (0-87021-138-2) Naval Inst Pr.

Cruisers. J. Rawlinson. (Sea Power Library). (Illus.). 48p. (J). (gr. 3-8). 1989. lib. bdg. 18.60 (0-86625-085-9) Rourke Corp.

Cruiser's Guide to Spearfishing: Tips & Techniques for the Use of Pole Spears & Hawaiian Slings in the Bahamas & Florida Keys. Pat DeGroodt. LC 90-70580. (Illus.). 56p. (Orig.). 1990. pap. 10.95 (0-9626713-0-4) Triangle Bks Intl.

Cruisers of the Royal & Commonwealth Navies. Maritime Books Staff. (C). 1986. text ed. 100.00 (0-907771-35-1, Pub. by Maritime Bks UK) St Mut.

Cruisers of the U. S. Navy, 1922-1962. Stefan Terzibaschitsch. (Illus.). 320p. 1988. 41.95 (0-87021-974-X) Naval Inst Pr.

Cruises. Chris Hoosen & Francis Dix. (Travel Agent Training Ser.). (Illus.). (Orig.). 1989. student ed, pap. 20.00 (0-917063-14-7) Travel Text.

Cruises: Selecting, Sailing, & Booking. 2nd ed. Juls Zvoncheck. LC 93-7594. 1993. pap. text ed. 34.20 (0-13-192691-8) Prentice ESL.

Cruises: Selecting, Selling & Booking. Juls Zvoncheck. (Illus.). 235p. 1988. pap. text ed. 13.95 (0-935920-46-3, Ntl Pubs Blck) P-H.

Cruises & Ports of Call, 1995: Choosing the Perfect Ship & Enjoying Your Time Ashore. Fodor's Travel Staff. (Illus.). 1994. pap. 18.00 (0-679-02710-6) Fodors Travel.

Cruisin' & Choosin'. J. Brent Bill & Bill J. Brent. LC 88-39416. (Orig.). (YA). 1989. pap. 6.99 (0-8007-5298-8) Revell.

Cruisin' at the Limit: Selected Poems 1968-78. D. R. Wagner. Ed. by Kirk Robertson. LC 82-72997. (Windriver Ser.). 120p. (Orig.). 1982. pap. 7.95 (0-916918-20-3) Duck Down.

Cruisin' at the Limit: Selected Poems 1968-78. deluxe ed. D. R. Wagner. Ed. by Kirk Robertson. LC 82-72997. (Windriver Ser.). 120p. (Orig.). 1982. pap. 25.00 (0-916918-21-1) Duck Down.

Cruisin' the Dry Tortugas Archives. Jon Holtzworth & Susan Holtzworth. Ed. by Susan M. Holtzworth. LC 90-93247. (Illus.). 130p. (Orig.). 1990. pap. 9.95 (0-9627233-0-4) J Holtzworth.

Cruising: A Manual for Small Cruiser Sailing. 4th ed. J. D. Sleightholme. (Illus.). 256p. 1986. pap. 22.50 (0-7136-3477-4, Adlard Coles) Sheridan.

Cruising Altitude. Bob Reiss. 1994. 23.00 (0-671-77650-9) S&S Trade.

*Cruising America Online Vol. 1. David C. Gardner. 1994. pap. 19.95 (1-55958-597-8) Prima Pub.

Cruising Among the Caribbees: Summer Days in Winter Months. C. A. Stoddard. 1976. lib. bdg. 69.95 (0-8490-1686-X) Gordon Pr.

Cruising & Ocean Racing: A Complete Manual on Yachting. E. G. Martin & John Irving. 1977. lib. bdg. 99.95 (0-8490-1687-8) Gordon Pr.

Cruising Association Handbook. Imray, Laurie, Norie & Wilson Ltd. Staff. 400p. (C). 1989. 210.00 (0-685-54762-0, Pub. by Imray Laurie Norie & Wilson UK) St Mut.

Cruising Association Handbook. Wilson Ltd. Staff & Imray L. Norie. 400p. (C). 1989. 280.00 (0-685-40418-8, Pub. by Imray Laurie Norie & Wilson UK) St Mut.

Cruising Beyond Desolation Sound. rev. ed. John Chappell. (Illus.). 211p. 1987. pap. 24.95 (0-9692825-0-8) Gordon Soules Bk.

Cruising Boat Sailing: The Basic Guide. Bob Bond & Steve Sleight. LC 82-48882. (Illus.). 1983. 14.95 (0-394-52447-0) Knopf.

Cruising Catamaran Advantage: For Every Sailor Who Wants More Comfort, More Space, & More Speed! Rod Gibbons & Derek Bronte. (Illus.). 330p. (Orig.). 1988. pap. 24.95 (0-929458-11-7) Isl Educ Pub.

Cruising Chef Cookbook. rev. ed. Michael Greenwald. (Illus.). 420p. 1984. pap. 14.98 (0-931297-00-1) Blue San Diego.

*Cruising Compuserve. David C. Gardner. 1994. pap. 19.95 (1-55958-598-6) Prima Pub.

Cruising Cook. Shirley H. Deal. LC 77-78074. 288p. 1977. ring bd., vinyl bd. 15.95 (0-930006-00-3) S Deal Assoc.

Cruising Crew: How to Be Welcome on Board. Malcolm McKeag. 96p. (C). 1990. text ed. 59.00 (0-906754-63-1, Pub. by Fernhurst Bks UK) St Mut.

Cruising Designs-Power & Sail. Andrew R. Setzer. (Illus.). 1979. pap. 2.00 (0-915160-16-1) Seven Seas.

Cruising Diary & Log Book. Joy A. Wassell. 128p. 1992. 24.95 (1-883037-02-6) HANDSON Pub.

*Cruising for a Living: How to Find Your Dream Job on a Luxury Cruise Ship. Andy Heath. 96p. (Orig.). Date not set. pap. 13.95 (0-9646640-5-4) INFACT Pub.

*Cruising French Waterways. 2nd ed. Hugh McKnight. (Illus.). 318p. Date not set. 50.00 (0-7136-3282-8) Sheridan.

Cruising Fundamentals. American Sailing Association. 1992. pap. 17.95 (0-685-71204-4) TAB Bks.

Cruising Fundamentals. American Sailing Association Staff. 160p. 1992. pap. 17.95 (0-87742-334-2) Intl Marine.

Cruising Guide from Acapulco to the Panama Canal. Charles Goodman & Nancy Goodman. (Illus.). 112p. (Orig.). 1993. pap. 29.95 (0-939837-13-7) Paradise Cay Pubns.

Cruising Guide to Abaco, Bahamas: 1995. Steve Dodge. 96p. 1994. pap. text ed. 8.95 (0-932265-33-2) White Sound.

Cruising Guide to Anglesey & Menai Strait. R. Kemp. (C). 1987. 66.00 (0-85174-546-6, Pub. by Brwn Son Ferg) St Mut.

An Asterisk (*) at the beginning of an entry indicates that the title is appearing in BIP for the first time.

C

An Asterisk (*) at the beginning of an entry indicates that the title is appearing in BIP for the first time.

1725

Crusader Castles. T. E. Lawrence. (Insider's Guides Ser.). 1992. pap. 16.95 (*0-7818-0038-2*) Hippocrene Bks.

Crusader Castles. T. E. Lawrence. 224p. (C). 1990. 150.00 (*0-907151-68-X*, Pub. by IMMEL Pubng UK); pap. 125. 00 (*0-907151-67-1*, Pub. by IMMEL Pubng UK) St Mut.

Crusader Castles. 2nd ed. T. E. Lawrence. (Illus.). 224p. 1992. pap. 24.95 (*0-87052-290-6*) Hippocrene Bks.

***Crusader Cruiser Tank 1939-43.** David Fletcher. (New Vanguard Ser.). (Illus.). 48p. 1995. pap. 11.95 (*1-85532-512-8*, Pub. by Osprey UK) Stackpole.

Crusader for Christ (Billy Graham) Jean Wilson. (J). (gr. 6-9). 1979. pap. 3.95 (*0-87508-602-0*) Chr Lit.

Crusader for Freedom: A Life of Lydia Maria Child. Deborah P. Clifford. LC 91-33106. 384p. 1992. 30.00 (*0-8070-7050-5*) Beacon Pr.

Crusader for the Future: A Portrait of Aurelio Peccei, Founder of the Club of Rome. Gunter A. Pauli. (Illus.). 110p. 1987. 53.00 (*0-08-034861-0*, Pergamon Pr) Elsevier.

Crusader in Babylon: W. T. Stead & the Pall Mall Gazette. Raymond L. Schults. LC 71-109603. 303p. reprint ed. pap. 86.40 (*0-8357-2948-6*, 2039204) Bks Demand.

Crusader in Crinoline: The Life of Harriet Beecher Stowe. Robert F. Wilson. LC 70-159717. (Illus.). 706p. 1972. reprint ed. text ed. 45.50 (*0-8371-6191-6*, WIHS, Greenwood Pr) Greenwood.

Crusader Manuscript Illumination at Saint-Jean D'Acre, 1275-1291. Jaroslav Folda. LC 75-2991. (Illus.). 646p. 1975. 99.50 (*0-691-03907-0*) Princeton U Pr.

Crusaders. 2nd ed. Ann Williams. Ed. by Marjorie Reeves. (Then & There Ser.). (Illus.). 95p. (YA). (gr. 7-12). 1975. reprint ed. pap. text ed. 8.60 (*0-582-31096-2*, 78069) Longman.

Crusaders: The Radical Legacy of Marian & Arthur Lesueur. Meridel Le Sueur. LC 84-14696. (Illus.). 109p. 1984. reprint ed. 11.95 (*0-87351-174-3*, Borealis Book); reprint ed. pap. 6.95 (*0-87351-178-6*, Borealis Book) Minn Hist.

Crusaders: Voices from the Abortion Front. Marian Faux. 320p. 1990. 19.95 (*1-55972-020-4*, Birch Ln Pr) Carol Pub Group.

***Crusaders Against Opium: Protestant Missionaries in China, 1847-1917.** Kathleen L. Lodwick. (Illus.). 208p. 1996. text ed. 29.95 (*0-8131-1924-3*) U Pr of Ky.

Crusaders & Compromisers: Essays on the Relationship of the Antislavery Struggle to the Antebellum Party System. Ed. by Alan M. Kraut. LC 82-21085. (Contributions in American History Ser.: No. 104). xii, 286p. 1983. text ed. 55.00 (*0-313-22537-0*, KRA/) Greenwood.

***Crusaders and Heretics, Twelfth to Fourteenth Centuries.** Malcolm Barber. (Variorum Collected Studies Ser.: Vol. 498). 1995. 82.50 (*0-86078-476-2*, Pub. by Variorum UK) Ashgate Pub Co.

Crusaders & Muslims in Twelfth-Century Syria. Ed. by Maya Shatzmiller. LC 93-21764. (Medieval Mediterranean Ser.). 1993. 63.00 (*90-04-09777-5*); pap. 37.25 (*90-04-09829-1*) E J Brill.

Crusaders & Pragmatists: Movers of Modern American Foreign Policy. 2nd ed. John G. Stoessinger. (C). 1985. pap. text ed. 10.95 (*0-393-95506-0*) Norton.

Crusaders, Aztecs & Samurai. Millard. (Picture History Ser.). (Illus.). (J). (gr. 4-6). 1978. lib. bdg. 13.96 (*0-88110-110-9*, Usborne); pap. 6.95 (*0-86020-194-5*, Usborne) EDC.

Crusaders for Fitness: The History of American Health Reformers. James C. Whorton. LC 82-47621. (Illus.). 300p. 1984. pap. 15.95x (*0-691-00594-X*) Princeton U Pr.

Crusaders in the Courts: How a Dedicated Band of Lawyers Fought for the Civil Rights Revolution. Jack Greenberg. LC 93-45972. 448p. 1994. 30.00 (*0-465-01518-2*) Basic.

***Crusaders in the Courts: How a Dedicated Band of Lawyers Fought for the Civil Rights Revolution.** Jack Greenberg. (Illus.). 656p. 1995. pap. 15.00 (*0-465-01519-0*) Basic.

***Crusaders in the Courts: How a Dedicated Band of Lawyers Fought for the Civil Rights Revolution.** Jack Greenberg. 1995. pap. 15.00 (*0-465-01509-3*) Basic.

Crusaders in the East. W. B. Stevenson. 1982. 20.00 (*0-86685-035-X*) Intl Bk Ctr.

Crusaders in the East. W. B. Stevenson. (C). 1988. 135.00 (*1-85077-203-7*, Darf Pubs Ltd) St Mut.

Crusaders of Chemistry. Jonathan N. Leonard. LC 72-8533. (Essay Index Reprint Ser.). 1977. reprint ed. 26.95 (*0-8369-7320-8*) Ayer.

Crusaders of New France: A Chronicle of the Fleur-de-Lis in the Wilderness. William B. Munro. (BCL1 - History - Canada Ser.). 237p. 1991. reprint ed. lib. bdg. 79.00 (*0-7812-6352-2*) Rprt Serv.

Crusader's Tomb. large type ed. A. J. Cronin. 622p. 1982. 23.95 (*0-7089-8042-2*, Trail West Pubs) Ulverscroft.

Crusades. Timothy L. Biel. (World History Ser.). (Illus.). 128p. (J). (gr. 5-9). 1995. 16.95 (*1-56006-245-2*) Lucent Bks.

Crusades. Ken Hills. (Wars That Changed the World Ser.: Group 2). (Illus.). 32p. (J). (gr. 3-9). 1991. lib. bdg. 10. 95 (*1-85435-260-1*) Marshall Cavendish.

***Crusades.** Terry Jones & Alan Ereira. LC 94-31746. (Illus.). 256p. 1995. 24.95 (*0-8160-3275-0*) Facts on File.

Crusades. Steven Kurtz. (Advanced Dungeons & Dragons 2nd Ed. Accessory Ser.: HR7). 1994. pap. 18.00 (*1-56076-858-4*) TSR Inc.

Crusades. David Nicole. (Paper Soldiers of the Middle Ages Ser.: Bk. 1). (J). (gr. 1-9). 1992. pap. 3.95 (*0-88388-096-2*) Bellerophon Bks.

Crusades. David Nicolle. (Elite Ser.: No. 19). (Illus.). 64p. pap. 12.95 (*0-85045-854-4*, 9419, Pub. by Osprey UK) Stackpole.

Crusades. rev. ed. Richard Newhall. (Illus.). 64p. (C). 1991. pap. text ed. 2.25 (*1-877891-03-7*) Paperbook Pr Inc.

Crusades. 2nd ed. Hans E. Mayer. Tr. by John Gillingham. (Illus.). 368p. 1988. pap. text ed. 19.95 (*0-19-873097-7*) OUP.

Crusades. Ernest Barker. LC 76-160956. (Select Bibliographies Reprint Ser.). 1977. reprint ed. 15.95 (*0-8369-5823-3*) Ayer.

Crusades: A Short History. Jonathan Riley-Smith. 332p. (C). 1990. reprint ed. pap. 14.95 (*0-300-04700-2*) Yale U Pr.

Crusades: Cultures in Conflict. Pamela Kernaghan & Tony McAleavy. (History Programme Ser.). (Illus.). 48p. (C). 1993. pap. 9.95 (*0-521-44617-1*) Cambridge U Pr.

Crusades: Cultures in Conflict. Pamela Kernaghan. LC 93-27297. (History Programme Ser. Key Stage: No. 3). (J). 1993. pap. 9.25 (*0-521-42846-7*) Cambridge U Pr.

Crusades: The Story of the Latin Kingdom of Jerusalem. Thomas A. Archer & Charles L. Kingsford. LC 76-29833. reprint ed. 39.50 (*0-404-15409-3*) AMS Pr.

Crusades: The World's Debate. Hilaire Belloc. LC 92-60960. 250p. 1992. reprint ed. pap. 11.00 (*0-89555-467-4*) TAN Bks Pubs.

Crusades & Other Historical Essays, Presented to Dana C. Munro by His Former Students. Ed. by Louis J. Paetow. LC 68-14902. (Essay Index Reprint Ser.). 1977. 23.95 (*0-8369-0354-4*) Ayer.

Crusades, Holy War & Canon Law. James A. Brundage. (Collected Studies: No. CS338). 300p. 1991. text ed. 82. 50 (*0-86078-291-3*, Pub. by Variorum UK) Ashgate Pub Co.

Crusades Through Arab Eyes. Amin Maalouf. 1989. pap. 16.00 (*0-8052-0898-4*) Schocken.

Crusading Doctor: My Fight for Cooperative Medicine. Michael A. Shadid. LC 90-50696. 256p. 1992. 18.95 (*0-8061-2344-3*) U of Okla Pr.

Crusading for Chemistry: The Professional Career of Charles Holmes Herty. Germaine M. Reed. LC 94-25816. (Illus.). 496p. 1995. 45.00 (*0-8203-1671-7*) U of Ga Pr.

***Crusading Warfare 1097-1193.** R. C. Small. (Cambridge Studies in Medieval Life & Thought). (Illus.). 328p. (C). 1995. pap. 18.95 (*0-521-45838-2*) Cambridge U Pr.

Crush. Jo Gibson. (Scream Ser.: No. 8). 224p. 1994. pap. 3.50 (*0-8217-4513-1*) Zebra.

Crush. 3rd ed. Jane Futcher. 248p. (YA). (gr. 7 up). 1995. pap. 5.95 (*1-55583-602-X*, AlyCat) Alyson Pubns.

Crush, No. II. Jo Gibson. 224p. 1994. mass mkt. 3.50 (*0-8217-4704-5*) Zebra.

Crushed Blossom. (Red Stripe Ser.). 1989. pap. 4.50 (*0-8216-5062-9*, Univ Books) Carol Pub Group.

Crushed but Not Destroyed. Sharon Longenecker. 232p. (Orig.). 1984. pap. 7.95 (*0-9614244-0-0*) Sun Ray Pub.

Crushed for Better Wine. Sara Robbins. 1979. reprint ed. 7.00 (*0-87516-373-4*) DeVorss.

***Crushed into Glory: And Other Dramas for Preaching & Teaching.** Joseph J. Juknialis & James Heimerl. 104p. (Orig.). 1995. pap. 16.95 (*0-89390-340-X*) Resource Pubns.

Crushed into Honey. Jean Hollander. LC 86-26112. (Eileen W. Barnes Award Ser.). (Illus.). 72p. (Orig.). 1986. pap. 6.50 (*0-938158-08-2*) Saturday Pr.

Crushed Stone. (Metals & Minerals Ser.). 1993. lib. bdg. 250.95 (*0-8490-8969-7*) Gordon Pr.

Crusher Strike. David Robbins. (Blade Ser.: No. 6). 192p. (Orig.). 1990. pap. 2.95 (*0-8439-2909-X*) Dorchester Pub Co.

Crushing & Grinding Process Handbook. C. L. Prasher. LC 85-26434. 474p. 1987. text ed. 315.00 (*0-471-10535-X*) Wiley.

***Crushing & Milling.** Multimedia Development Services Staff. (Plant Fundamentals Ser.). (Illus.). (Orig.). 1995. student ed 30.00 (*1-57431-018-6*) Tech Trng Systs.

***Crushing & Milling, Vol VI, Module I.** Multimedia Development Services Staff. (Plant Fundamentals Ser.). (Illus.). (Orig.). 1995. teacher ed 45.00 (*1-57431-058-5*) Tech Trng Systs.

Crusoe in New York & Other Tales. Edward E. Hale. 1972. reprint ed. 22.50 (*0-8422-8066-9*) Irvington.

Crusoe's Footprints: Cultural Studies in Britain & America. Patrick Brantlinger. 200p. 1990. 39.50 (*0-415-90146-4*, A1564, Routledge NY); pap. 13.95 (*0-415-90284-3*, A1568, Routledge NY) Routledge.

Crust & Upper Mantle of the Pacific Area. Ed. by L. Knopoff et al. LC 68-61439. (Geophysical Monograph Ser.: Vol. 12). (Illus.). 522p. 1968. 31.00 (*0-87590-012-7*) Am Geophysical.

Crust-Mantle Recycling at Convergence Zones: Proceedings of the NATO Advanced Research Workshop Held in Antalya, Turkey, 25-29, May, 1987. Ed. by Stanley R. Hart & Levent Gulen. (C). 1988. lib. bdg. 111.50 (*0-7923-0066-1*) Kluwer Ac.

Crust on Its Uppers. Derek Raymond. 1993. pap. 11.99 (*1-85242-268-8*) Serpents Tail.

Crustacea. Frederick R. Schram. (Illus.). 620p. 1986. 65.00 (*0-19-503742-1*) OUP.

Crustacea. James D. Dana. (Notable American Authors Ser.). 1992. reprint ed. lib. bdg. 90.00 (*0-7812-2606-6*) Rprt Serv.

Crustacea, Vol. 9. Frederick W. Harrison et al. (Microscopic Anatomy of Invertebrates Ser.). 616p. 1992. text ed. 225.00 (*0-471-56116-9*, Wiley-Liss) Wiley.

Crustacea, Copepoda, Calanoida und Cyclopoida. A. Bruner. Ed. by Schwoerbel Zwick & P. Zwick. (Suesswasserfauna von Mitteleuropa Ser.: Vol. 8/4-1). (Illus.). 209p. 1993. pap. 125.00 (*3-447-30631-9*, Pub. by G Fischer Verlag GW) Lubrecht & Cramer.

Crustacea from Palmyra & Fanning Islands. C. H. Edmondson & Mary J. Rathbun. (BMB Ser.). 1972. reprint ed. pap. 15.00 (*0-527-02108-3*) Periodicals Srv.

Crustacea of Bermuda: Schizopoda, Cumacea, Stomatopoda, & Phyllocarida. Addison E. Verrill. (Connecticut Academy of Arts & Sciences Ser., Trans.: Vol. 26). 1923. pap. 69.50 (*0-685-22822-3*) Elliots Bks.

Crustacean & Mollusk Aquaculture in the United States. Jay V. Huner & E. Evan Brown. (Illus.). 1985. text ed. 95.95 (*0-87055-468-9*) AVI.

Crustacean Biogeography. Ed. by Robert H. Gore & Kenneth L. Heck. 303p. (C). 1986. text ed. 120.00 (*90-6191-593-7*, Pub. by A A Balkema NE) Ashgate Pub Co.

Crustacean Egg Production. Ed. by Adrian Wenner & Armand Kuris. (Crustacean Issues Ser.: No. 7). (Illus.). 408p. (C). 1991. text ed. 115.00 (*90-6191-098-6*, Pub. by A A Balkema NE) Ashgate Pub Co.

Crustacean Farming. Daniel O. Lee & John F. Wickins. 392p. 1992. text ed. 95.00 (*0-470-21850-9*) Halsted Pr.

Crustacean Growth: Factors in Adult Growth. Ed. by Adrian Wenner. 375p. 1985. text ed. 115.00 (*90-6191-535-X*, Pub. by A A Balkema NE) Ashgate Pub Co.

Crustacean Growth: Larval Growth. Ed. by Adrian Wenner. 247p. (C). 1985. text ed. 120.00 (*90-6191-294-6*, Pub. by A A Balkema NE) Ashgate Pub Co.

Crustacean Integument: Morphology & Biochemistry. Michael N. Horst. 1993. 149.95 (*0-8493-4986-9*, QL445) CRC Pr.

Crustacean Sexual Biology. Raymond T. Bauer & Joel W. Martin. 1991. text ed. 73.50 (*0-231-06880-8*) Col U Pr.

Crustaceans. Edward Ricciuti. (Our Living World Ser.). (Illus.). 64p. (J). (gr. 4-8). 1994. lib. bdg. 16.95 (*1-56711-046-0*) Blackbirch.

Crustaces Copepodes Calanoides des Eaux Interieures Africaines. Bernard Dussart. LC 89-10017. (Crustaceana Supplements Ser.: No. 15). (Illus.). 205p. (Orig.). (FRE.). 1989. pap. text ed. 68.75 (*90-04-09053-3*) E J Brill.

Crustal Evolution & Orogeny. Ed. by S. P. Sychanthavong. (Illus.). 339p. (C). 1990. text ed. 70.00 (*90-6191-222-9*, Pub. by A A Balkema NE) Ashgate Pub Co.

***Crustal Structure of the Bohemian Massif & the West Carpathians.** Ed. by H. J. Behr & C. B. Raleigh. 372p. 1994. 143.00 (*0-387-57986-9*) Spr-Verlag.

Crutch & I. Edyth Harrell. (Illus.). 80p. 1983. 9.90 (*0-911843-01-9*) Myriad.

Crutches. Peter Hartling. Tr. by Elizabeth D. Crawford. LC 88-80400. 160p. (J). (gr. 5 up). 1988. 12.95 (*0-688-07991-1*) Lothrop.

Crutches of Dusk. Mirko Tuma. LC 74-10928. 1974. 4.25 (*0-686-05786-4*) Community Pub.

Crux. Richard Aellen. 400p. 1991. mass mkt. 4.95 (*0-380-71200-8*) Avon.

Crux. Richard Aellen. 352p. 1989. 18.95 (*1-55611-135-5*) D I Fine.

Crux & Controversy in Middle English Textual Criticism. Ed. by A. J. Minnis & Charlotte Brewer. 224p. (C). 1992. text ed. 63.00 (*0-85991-321-X*, DS Brewer) Boydell & Brewer.

Crux Ansata: An Indictment of the Roman Catholic Church. 2nd ed. H. G. Wells. 160p. 1989. pap. 7.50 (*0-911826-21-1*, 5512) Am Atheist.

Crux Ansata: An Indictment of the Roman Catholic Church. H. G. Wells. LC 73-161344. (Atheist Viewpoint Ser.). (Illus.). 114p. 1976. reprint ed. 16.95 (*0-405-03798-8*) Ayer.

Crux Imperatorum Philosophia: Imperial Horizons of the Cluniac Confraternitas, 964-1109. Robert G. Heath. LC 76-56099. (Pittsburgh Theological Monographs: No. 13). 1977. pap. 10.00 (*0-915138-17-4*) Pickwick.

Cruz Chronicle: A Novel. Henry H. Roth. (Fiction Ser.). 200p. 1988. 18.95 (*0-8135-1404-5*) Rutgers U Pr.

Cruz Chronicle: A Novel. Henry H. Roth. (Fiction Ser.). 184p. (C). 1991. reprint ed. pap. 10.95 (*0-8135-1750-8*) Rutgers U Pr.

Cruz De Cristo. John Stott. 360p. (POR.). 1991. 12.95 (*0-8297-1630-0*) Life Pubs Intl.

Cruz De Cristo: The Cross of Christ. A. B. Simpson. (SPA.). 3.95 (*84-7228-905-2*, 222314, Pub. by Edit Clie SP) TSELF.

Cruz Del Calvario y Su Mensaje: The Message of the Cross. Jessie Penn-Lewis. (SPA.). 4.25 (*84-7228-731-9*, 220250, Pub. by Edit Clie SP) TSELF.

Cruz en la Vida Cristiana Normal. T. S. Nee. Orig. Title: The Cross in the Normal Christian Life. 144p. (SPA.). 1993. pap. 4.99 (*0-8254-1501-2*) Kregel.

Cruz Es Nuestra Espada: The Cross Is Our Sword. Antonio Almudevar. (SPA.). 6.95 (*84-7228-021-7*, 220216, Pub. by Edit Clie SP) TSELF.

Cruz, Piedra De Toque De la Fe: The Cross Touchstone of Faith. Jessie Penn-Lewis. (SPA.). 3.25 (*84-7228-850-1*, 220248, Pub. by Edit Clie SP) TSELF.

Cruz y el Punal (The Cross & the Switchblade) A. Hartley. (Historietas Peq. (Small Comics Ser.)). (SPA.). Date not set. 0.49 (*0-685-74924-X*, 496012) Editorial Unilit.

Cruzada Educativa Cubana. Dia de la Cultura Cubana Premio Juan J. Remos. Minibiografias de los Que Recibieron ese Galardon de 1971 a 1983. Ed. by Alberto G. De la Solana. LC 84-51473. (Senda de Estudios y Ensayos Ser.). (Illus.). 400p. (Orig.). (SPA.). 1984. pap. 24.95 (*0-918454-42-5*) Senda Nueva.

***Cruzando el Embral de la Esperanza.** Pope John Paul II. 1994. 20.00 (*0-679-44082-8*) Knopf.

Cruzando las Fronteras: Across the Borders. Vera F. Barnes. (SPA.). 4.95 (*84-7645-373-6*, 223522, Pub. by Edit Clie SP) TSELF.

Cry. Jay Klemon. 170p. (Orig.). 1992. pap. text ed. 11.95 (*0-9632129-2-3*, PS3561.L3864.C78) Les Livres.

Cry: A New Dramatic Fable. Sarah Fielding. LC 86-11887. 1986. reprint ed. 60.00 (*0-8201-1416-2*) Schol Facsimiles.

Cry: The Johnnie Ray Story. Jonny Whiteside. 1994. 22.99 (*1-56980-013-8*) Barricade Bks.

Cry Amandla! South African Women & the Question of Power. June Goodwin. (Illus.). 252p. 1984. text ed. 24. 95 (*0-8419-0899-0*, Africana) Holmes & Meier.

Cry & the Covenant. Morton Thompson. 31.95 (*0-8488-1488-6*) Amereon Ltd.

Cry & the Covenant. Morton Thompson. 480p. 1991. reprint ed. lib. bdg. 32.95 (*0-89966-758-9*) Buccaneer Bks.

***Cry & the Dedication.** Carlos Bulosan. Ed. & Intro. by E. San Juan, Jr. LC 94-29767. (Asian American History & Culture Ser.). (C). 1995. lib. bdg. 49.95 (*1-56639-295-0*); pap. text ed. 16.95 (*1-56639-296-9*) Temple U Pr.

Cry & You Cry Alone: Poetry of Tracy Voigt. Tracy Voigt. 8p. (Orig.). 1987. 1.50 (*0-317-01381-5*) T Voigt.

Cry at Salem. Jeffrey J. Richards. 80p. (Orig.). (C). 1992. pap. text ed. 8.50 (*0-88252-153-5*) Paladin Hse.

Cry, Baby, Cry. G. F. Bale. 1992. mass mkt. 4.99 (*1-55773-643-X*) Diamond.

Cry Bunny. (Rabbit Tales Ser.: No. S899-5). (J). 1989. boxed 3.95 (*0-7214-5234-5*) Ladybird Bks.

***Cry, Coyote.** Steve Frazee. 1994. 15.95 (*0-7451-4617-1*, Gunsmoke) Chivers N Amer.

Cry Cry My Beloved People. Paul M. Eko. Ed. by Paula Scalist. 286p. (YA). 1990. 18.95 (*0-685-28130-2*) Backwards & Backwards.

***Cry for a Deliverer.** Earlene Wallace. 96p. 1995. pap. text ed. 3.95 (*0-9646474-0-0*) Harvestfield Minist.

Cry for Action. LC 89-110890. (Moments in American History Ser.). (Illus.). 80p. (J). (gr. 4-10). 1990. lib. bdg. 19.97 (*0-8114-2671-8*) Raintree Steck-V.

Cry for Help. Gigi Burke & Friday. (Illus.). 60p. (Orig.). 1994. 4.99 (*0-9641234-0-1*) Crossfire Across.

Cry for Help: The Professional Response. J. Kahn & E. Earle. LC 81-21110. (Pergamon International Library Science Technology Engineering & Social Studies). 130p. 1982. text ed. 66.00 (*0-08-027438-2*, Pub. by Pergamon Repr UK); pap. text ed. 19.25 (*0-08-027437-4*, Pub. by Pergamon Repr UK) Franklin.

Cry for Justice. Joy Swift. LC 93-50604. (Illus.). 240p. 1994. 17.95 (*1-56790-084-4*) Cool Hand Comms.

Cry for Luck: Sacred Song & Speech among the Yurok, Hupa, & Karok Indians of Northwestern California. Richard Keeling. (C). 1992. 40.00 (*0-520-07560-9*) U CA Pr.

Cry for Mercy: Prayers from the Genesee. Henri J. Nouwen. LC 93-38555. 125p. (Orig.). 1994. reprint ed. pap. 9.95 (*0-88344-961-7*) Orbis Bks.

Cry for Miracles. write for info. (*1-56441-001-3*) M Hickey Min.

Cry for Myth. Rollo May. 1992. pap. 12.95 (*0-385-30685-7*, Delta) Dell.

Cry for Peace. Jean Springer. 200p. (Orig.). 1982. pap. 5.99 (*0-934998-07-8*) Bethel Pub.

Cry for the Dead. Judith Wright. (Illus.). 1982. 32.50 (*0-19-554296-7*) OUP.

Cry for the Strangers. John Saul. 416p. 1986. mass mkt. 5.99 (*0-440-11870-0*) Dell.

Cry for War: The Story of Suzan & Michael Carson. Richard D. Reynolds. 368p. (Orig.). 1987. pap. 7.95 (*0-9618577-2-2*) Squibob Pr.

Cry from the Cotton: The Southern Tenant Farmers' Union & the New Deal. Donald H. Grubbs. LC 72-109464. 242p. reprint ed. pap. 69.00 (*0-7837-0321-X*, 2040641) Bks Demand.

Cry from the Earth: Music of the North American Indians. John Bierhorst. LC 91-59002. (Illus.). 113p. (J). 1992. reprint ed. pap. 14.95 (*0-941270-53-X*) Ancient City Pr.

Cry from the Heart: The Baha'is in Iran. William Sears. (Illus.). 224p. 1982. pap. 4.50 (*0-85398-134-5*) G Ronald Pub.

Cry from the Mountain. Daniel L. Quick & Thomas A. Noton. 159p. 1986. pap. 5.95 (*0-89066-064-6*) World Wide Pubs.

Cry Hard & Swim: The Story of an Incest Survivor. Jacqueline Spring. 179p. 1991. pap. 11.95 (*0-86068-813-5*, Pub. by Virago Pr UK) Trafalgar.

Cry in the Desert. Jed A. Bryan. 240p. (Orig.). 1987. pap. 9.95 (*0-934411-04-2*, Banned Bks) Edward-William Austin.

Cry in the Night. Kat Brosnan. 1978. pap. 1.50 (*0-8439-0518-2*) Dorchester Pub Co.

Cry in the Night. Mary Higgens Clark. 1993. pap. 6.50 (*0-685-71985-5*) S&S Trade.

Cry in the Night. Mary Higgins Clark. 1993. pap. 6.99 (*0-671-88666-5*) PB.

Cry in the Night. Judi Miller. 224p. 1990. pap. 3.95 (*0-380-75699-4*) Avon.

***Cry in the Night.** Sharon Vincent-Lum. LC 91-67917. 64p. (Orig.). 1994. pap. 8.00 (*1-56002-176-4*, Univ Edtns) Aegina Pr.

Cry in the Night. Mary Higgins Clark. 1993. reprint ed. lib. bdg. 25.95 (*0-89968-447-5*, Lghtyr Pr) Buccaneer Bks.

Cry in the Wilderness. Melody Green. 1992. 12.95 (*0-917143-14-0*) Sparrow TN.

Cry Insanity. Richard Petz. Ed. by John Welburn. 85p. 1988. pap. write for info. (*0-318-62237-8*) RAPCOM Enter.

***Cry Is War, War, War: The Civil War Correspondence of Lts. Burwell T. Cotton & George J. Huntley, 34th Regiment North Carolina.** Michael Taylor. 1994. 30.00 (*0-89029-321-X*) Morningside Bkshop.

Cry Justice! Prayers, Meditations & Readings from South Africa. John W. De Gruchy. LC 86-667. (Illus.). 264p. (Orig.). 1986. pap. 9.95 (*0-88344-223-X*) Orbis Bks.

Cry, Liberia, Cry! G. Henry Andrews. 1993. 16.95 (*0-533-10254-5*) Vantage.

Cry Like a Bell. Madeleine L'Engle. LC 87-26940. (Wheaton Literary Ser.). 128p. (Orig.). 1987. pap. 8.99 (*0-87788-148-0*) Shaw Pubs.

C

An Asterisk (*) at the beginning of an entry indicates that the title is appearing in BIP for the first time.

An Asterisk (*) at the beginning of an entry indicates that the title is appearing in BIP for the first time.

1727

Cryogenic Optical Systems & Instruments IV, Vol. 1340. R. K. Melugin & G. R. Pruitt. 1990. 62.00 (*0-8194-0401-2*) SPIE.

Cryogenic Process Engineering. Thomas M. Flynn & Klaus D. Timmerhaus. (International Cryogenics Monograph). (Illus.). 620p. 1989. 120.00 (*0-306-43283-8*, Plenum Pr) Plenum.

Cryogenic Processes & Equipment - 1993. Ed. by F. J. Kadi et al. 72p. 1993. 30.00 (*0-7918-0944-7*, H00776) ASME.

Cryogenic Processes & Equipment in Energy Systems: Presented at the Cryogenic Processes & Equipment Conference, Century 2-Emerging Technology Conference, San Francisco, CA, August 19-21, 1980. Cryogenic Processes & Equipment Conference Staff. Ed. by W. M. Toscano et al. LC 80-66045. 201p. reprint ed. pap. 57.30 (*0-685-23448-7*, 2032703) Bks Demand.

Cryogenic Processes & Machinery. Ed. by Leonard A. Wenzel. LC 93-13491. (Symposium Ser.: No. 294). 1993. 75.00 (*0-8169-0613-0*) Am Inst Chem Eng.

Cryogenic Properties of Polymers: Papers. Ed. by Tito T. Serafini & Jack L. Koenig. LC 68-28775. 312p. reprint ed. pap. 89.00 (*0-317-08389-9*, 2055020) Bks Demand.

Cryogenic Recycling & Processing. Norman R. Braton. 256p. 1980. 135.00 (*0-8493-5779-9*, TP482, CRC Reprint) Franklin.

Cryogenic Systems. 2nd ed. Randall F. Barron. (Monographs on Cryogenics). (Illus.). 1985. 65.00 (*0-19-503567-4*) OUP.

Cryogenics & Refrigeration: Proceedings of International Conference. Ed. by Guobang Chen & Thomas M. Flynn. (International Academic Publishers Ser.). 394p. 1989. 115.00 (*0-08-037534-0*, 1107; 1712; 1708, Pub. by IAP UK) Elsevier.

Cryogenics Safety Manual. 3rd ed. Ed. by BCC Staff. 1991. 57.95 (*0-7506-0225-2*) Buttrwrth-Heinemann.

Cryonics: A Sociology of Death & Bereavement. Arlene Sheskin. LC 79-13402. 216p. 1980. text ed. 29.95 (*0-470-26786-0*) Irvington.

Cryonics: Reaching for Tomorrow. Brian Wowk & Michael Darwin. 104p. 1991. pap. 8.95 (*1-880209-00-4*) Alcor Life Ext.

Cryopreparation of Thin Biological Specimens for Electron Microscopy: Methods & Applications. Norbert Roos & A. John Morgan. (Royal Microscopical Society Microscopy Handbooks Ser.: No. 21). (Illus.). 120p. 1990. pap. 19.95 (*0-19-856424-4*) OUP.

***Cryopreservation & Freeze-Drying Protocols.** Ed. by John G. Day & Mark R. McLellan. LC 94-44732. (Methods in Molecular Biology Ser.: Vol. 38). (Illus.). 264p. 1995. 79.50 (*0-89603-296-5*) Humana.

Cryopreservation & Low Temperature Biology in Blood Transfusion. Ed. by C. T. Sibinga et al. (C). 1990. lib. bdg. 61.00 (*0-7923-0908-1*) Kluwer Ac.

Cryopreservation of Plant Cells & Organs. Ed. by K. K. Kartha. 288p. 1985. 191.00 (*0-8493-6102-8*, QK725) CRC Pr.

***Cryopreservative of Plant Germplasm I.** Ed. by Y. P. Bajaj. LC 94-46550. (Biotechnology in Agriculture & Forestry: Vol. 32). 1995. write for info. (*3-540-57451-4*); pap. text ed. write for info. (*0-387-57451-4*) Spr-Verlag.

Cryopumping: Theory & Practice. R. A. Haefer. Tr. by J. Shipwright. (Monographs on Cryogenics: No. 4). (Illus.). 456p. 1989. 125.00 (*0-19-854812-5*) OUP.

Cryosurgery of Maxillofacial Region: General Principles & Clinical Applications to Benign Lesions. P. Bradley. LC 85-22421. 1986. 107.00 (*0-8493-5219-3*, CRC Reprint) Franklin.

Cryosurgery of Maxillofacial Region, Vol. 2: Clinical Application Malignant Lesions & Comparison Lasers. P. Bradley. LC 85-22421. 1986. 96.00 (*0-8493-5220-7*, CRC Reprint) Franklin.

Cryosurgery of the Maxillofacial Region, 2 vols., Set, Vols. I-II. Paul F. Bradley. 1986. Set. 248.00 (*0-8493-5218-5*, RD523) CRC Pr.

Cryosurgery of the Maxillofacial Region, Vol. I. Paul F. Bradley. 200p. 1986. write for info. (*0-318-61365-4*) CRC Pr.

Cryosurgery of the Maxillofacial Region, 2 vols., Vols. I-II. Paul F. Bradley. 1986. Vol. 2, 176 pgs. write for info. (*0-318-61366-2*) CRC Pr.

Cryosurgical Treatment for Skin Cancer. Emanuel Kuflik & Andrew Gage. LC 88-34782. (Illus.). 218p. 1990. 98.50 (*0-89640-157-X*) Igaku-Shoin.

Cryotherapy in Chest Medicine. J. P. Homasson & N. Bell. (Illus.). 122p. 1993. 98.00 (*0-387-59570-8*) Spr-Verlag.

Crypt of the Shadowking. Mark Anthony. (Harpers Ser.: No. 6). 320p. (Orig.). 1993. pap. 4.95 (*1-56076-594-1*) TSR Inc.

Crypt 33: The Saga of Marilyn Monroe - the Final Word. Milo Speriglio & Adela Gregory. (Illus.). 380p. 1993. 21.95 (*1-55972-125-1*, Birch Ln Pr) Carol Pub Group.

Cryptanalysis: A Study of Ciphers & Their Solutions. Helen F. Gaines. (Illus.). 1939. pap. text ed. 4.95 (*0-486-20097-3*) Dover.

Cryptanalysis of an Enciphered Code Problem: Where an "Additive" Method of Encipherement Has Been Used. Wayne G. Barker. 182p. (Orig.). 1979. pap. 24.80 (*0-89412-037-9*) Aegean Park Pr.

Cryptanalysis of Shift-Register Generated Stream Cipher Systems. Wayne G. Barker. (Orig.). (C). 1984. lib. bdg. 58.30 (*0-89412-087-5*); pap. 48.80 (*0-89412-062-X*) Aegean Park Pr.

Cryptanalysis of the Hagelin Cryptograph. Wayne G. Barker. 223p. 1978. pap. 32.80 (*0-89412-022-0*) Aegean Park Pr.

Cryptanalysis of the Simple Substitution Cipher with Word Divisions. Wayne G. Barker. LC 75-18083. 132p. 1975. lib. bdg. 26.30 (*0-89412-089-1*); pap. 16.80 (*0-89412-000-X*) Aegean Park Pr.

Cryptanalysis of the Single Columnar Transposition Cipher - with Added Computer Program Written in Basic. rev. ed. Wayne G. Barker. 150p. (C). 1992. lib. bdg. 38.30 (*0-89412-193-6*); pap. 28.80 (*0-89412-192-8*) Aegean Park Pr.

Cryptanalysis Techniques. John J. Williams. Ed. by Laurie Williams. (Illus.). (Orig.). 1990. pap. 29.00 (*0-934274-11-8*) Consumertronics.

Cryptarithms. Josephine Andree & Richard Andree. 1978. teacher ed 2.00 (*0-686-28564-6*); pap. 2.95 (*0-686-23790-0*) Mu Alpha Theta.

Cryptarithms & Other Arithmetical Pastimes. N. J. Kuenzi & Bob Prielipp. (Topics for Teachers Ser.). 58p. (Orig.). 1979. pap. 2.50 (*0-912047-01-1*) Sch Sci Math.

Cryptic Clue. Rebecca P. Janney. (Heather Reed Mystery Ser.). (J). 1993. pap. 3.99 (*0-8499-3834-1*) Word Inc.

Cryptic Masonry. Jackson H. Chase. 94p. 1990. reprint ed. pap. 5.00 (*0-88053-014-6*, M060) Macoy Pub.

Crypto-amnesia Club. Michael Bracewell. 112p. 1991. pap. 8.50 (*1-85242-115-0*) Serpents Tail.

Crypto Man. large type ed. Kenneth Royce. 528p. 1988. 15.95 (*0-7089-1841-7*) Ulverscroft.

Crypto Users' Handbook: A Guide for Implementors of Cryptographic Protection in Computer Systems. P. Christofferson et al. 94p. 1988. 38.50 (*0-444-70484-1*, North Holland) Elsevier.

***CRYPTO '94: Advances in Cryptography.** Ed. by Y. G. Desmedt et al. (Lecture Notes in Computer Science: Vol. 839). 439p. 1994. pap. text ed. 62.00 (*0-387-58333-5*) Spr-Verlag.

Cryptogram. Jules Verne. 14.95 (*0-8488-0654-9*) Amereon Ltd.

***Cryptogram & Other Plays.** David Mamet. 1995. pap. 9.00 (*0-679-74653-6*) Random.

Cryptograms & Spygrams. Norma Gleason. 128p. (Orig.). 1981. pap. 3.95 (*0-486-24036-3*) Dover.

Cryptograms in Portuguese. Stewart Todd. 128p. (Orig.). 1986. lib. bdg. 19.30 (*0-89412-132-4*); pap. 9.80 (*0-89412-131-6*) Aegean Park Pr.

Cryptograms in Spanish. Wayne G. Barker. 128p. (Orig.). 1987. lib. bdg. 19.30 (*0-89412-128-6*); pap. 9.80 (*0-89412-058-1*) Aegean Park Pr.

Cryptograms, One Hundred Ten Cryptograms to Be Solved. Wayne G. Barker. 119p. (J). (gr. 9 up). 1980. lib. bdg. 14.45 (*0-89412-090-5*); pap. 4.95 (*0-89412-043-3*) Aegean Park Pr.

Cryptographic Significance of the Knapsack Problem: Plus Exercises & Solutions. Luke J. O'Connor & Jennifer Seberry. 186p. (Orig.). (C). 1988. lib. bdg. 42.30 (*0-89412-151-0*); pap. 32.80 (*0-89412-150-2*) Aegean Park Pr.

Cryptography: Burg Feuerstein, FRG 1982. Ed. by T. Beth. (Lecture Notes in Computer Science Ser.: Vol. 149). 402p. 1986. pap. 37.00 (*0-387-11993-0*) Spr-Verlag.

Cryptography: The Science of Secret Writing. Laurence D. Smith. 1955. pap. 4.95 (*0-486-20247-X*) Dover.

***Cryptography: Theory & Practice.** Douglas R. Stinson. (Discrete Mathematics & Its Applications Ser.). 500p. 1995. 59.95 (*0-8493-8521-0*, 8521) CRC Pr.

Cryptography: A New Dimension in Computer Data Security: A Guide for the Design & Implementation of Secure Systems. Carl H. Meyer & Stephen M. Matyas. LC 82-2831. 755p. 1982. text ed. 124.00 (*0-471-04892-5*) Wiley.

Cryptography, a Primer. Alan G. Konheim. LC 80-24978. 432p. 1981. text ed. 144.00 (*0-471-08132-9*, Wiley-Interscience) Wiley.

Cryptography & Coding. Ed. by Henry J. Beker & F. C. Piper. (Institute of Mathematics & Its Applications Conference Series, New Ser.: New Series 20). (Illus.). 312p. 1989. 77.50 (*0-19-853623-2*) OUP.

Cryptography & Coding. Ed. by M. J. Ganley. LC 93-31646. (Institute of Mathematics & Its Applications Conference Series, New Ser.). (Illus.). 389p. 1994. 82.50 (*0-19-853691-7*, Clarendon Pr) OUP.

Cryptography & Coding, No. 2. Ed. by Chris Mitchell. (Institute of Mathematics & Its Applications Conference Series, New Ser.: New Series 33). (Illus.). 320p. 1992. 87.00 (*0-19-853393-4*) OUP.

Cryptography & Cryptanalysis Articles, 2 vols., 1. rev. ed. Ed. by William F. Friedman. 1976. reprint ed. pap. 20.80 (*0-89412-003-4*) Aegean Park Pr.

Cryptography & Cryptanalysis Articles, Vol. 2. rev. ed. Ed. by William F. Friedman. 1976. reprint ed. pap. 20.80 (*0-89412-004-2*) Aegean Park Pr.

Cryptography & Data Security. Dorothy E. Denning. LC 81-15012. (Computer Science Ser.). (Illus.). 500p. (C). 1982. text ed. 50.50 (*0-201-10150-5*) Addison-Wesley.

***Cryptography & Privacy Sourcebook: The 3rd CPSR Conference, 1993.** Ed. by David Banisar & Marc Rotenberg. (Illus.). 325p. (Orig.). (C). 1994. pap. text ed. 75.00 (*0-7881-0836-0*) Diane Pub.

***Cryptography & Privacy Sourcebook, 1994: Primary Documents on U. S. Encryption Policy, the Clipper Chip, the Digital Telephony Proposal & Export Controls.** Ed. by David Banisar. (Illus.). 360p. (Orig.). (C). 1994. pap. text ed. 75.00 (*0-7881-0837-9*) Diane Pub.

Cryptography & Secure Communications. Man Y. Rhee. 1993. text ed. 50.00 (*0-07-112502-7*) McGraw.

Cryptography & Security. Ed. by Shigeo Tsujii. 156p. (Orig.). 1992. pap. text ed. 55.00 (*2-88124-869-1*) Gordon & Breach.

Cryptology. Albrecht Beutelspacher. 176p. 1994. pap. 31.00 (*0-88385-504-6*) Math Assn.

Cryptology: Machines, History & Methods. Ed. by B. Winkel et al. (Artech House Cryptology Ser.). 518p. 1990. text ed. 33.00 (*0-89006-399-0*) Artech Hse.

Cryptology & Computational Number Theory. Pomerance. LC 90-1248. (PSAPM Ser.: Vol. 42). 171p. 1990. 59.00 (*0-8218-0155-4*, PSAPM-42) Am Math.

Cryptology Yesterday, Today & Tomorrow. C. Deavours et al. 450p. 1987. text ed. 33.00 (*0-89006-253-6*) Artech Hse.

CryptoPrivacy: A Cryptographer's Manual. Clayton C. Pierce. LC 89-91620. (Illus.). 139p. 1989. lib. bdg. 19.95 (*0-9601564-4-5*); pap. 16.95 (*0-9601564-5-3*) C C Pierce.

CryptoPrivacy: A Cryptographer's Manual. 2nd rev. ed. Clayton C. Pierce. (Illus.). 128p. (C). 1992. lib. bdg. 34.95 (*0-9601564-6-1*) C C Pierce.

CryptoPrivacy: A Cryptographer's Manual on Classic Ciphers. 3rd rev. ed. Clayton C. Pierce. LC 89-91620. (Illus.). 130p. 1994. lib. bdg. 39.95 (*0-9601564-9-6*) C C Pierce.

Cryptorchid Testis. Ed. by Tom O. Abney & Brooks A. Keel. 192p. 1989. 121.00 (*0-8493-4751-3*, RJ477) CRC Pr.

Cryptorchidism. Ed. by J. C. Job. (Pediatric & Adolescent Endocrinology Ser.: Vol. 6). 1979. pap. 79.25 (*3-8055-2998-8*) S Karger.

Cryptorchidism: Management & Implications. F. Hadziselimovic. (Illus.). 135p. 1982. 81.50 (*0-387-11881-0*) Spr-Verlag.

Cryptorchidism & Related Anomalies. Fray F. Marshall. Ed. by Jack S. Elder. LC 82-11302. 128p. 1982. text ed. 55.00 (*0-275-91374-0*, C1374, Praeger Pubs) Greenwood.

Cryptorhynchinae of Rapa. E. C. Zimmerman. (BMB Ser.). 1972. reprint ed. 20.00 (*0-527-02259-4*) Periodicals Srv.

Cryptosporidiosis in Man & Animals. Ed. by Pubey. 1990. 144.00 (*0-8493-6401-9*, RC136) CRC Pr.

***Cryptoverse!** Jan Renfrow. 16p. (Orig.). 1994. 4.95 (*0-9613072-8-5*) JANART-LOVE.

Cryptozoology. Greenwell. Date not set. 19.95 (*0-06-016774-2*, HarpT) HarpC.

Cryptych. Melissa Bell. Ed. by Bradley R. Strahan. (Illustrated Poetry Chapbook Ser.: No. XIII). (Illus.). 24p. (Orig.). 1994. pap. 4.50 (*0-938872-17-6*) Black Buzzard.

Crystal. Donna Baker. (Glassmakers Trilogy Ser.). 496p. 1990. pap. 8.95 (*0-7472-3150-8*, Pub. by Headline UK) Trafalgar.

Crystal, Bk. VII. Helen Luster. 1980. pap. 5.00 (*0-686-28713-4*) Man-Root.

***Crystal: Spectrums of Chinese Culture Through Poetry.** Sandra A. Wawrytko & Catherine Y. Woo. LC 94-5297. (Asian Thought & Culture: Vol. 14). 248p. (C). 1995. text ed. 45.95 (*0-8204-2286-X*) P Lang Pubs.

Crystal: The Sacred Stone. Miriam Kaplan. (Illus.). 114p. (Orig.). 1988. pap. 8.95 (*0-9620233-0-2*) Crystal Heart Pr.

Crystal: The Story of a Real Baby Whale. Karen Smyth. LC 85-52440. (Illus.). 96p. (J). (gr. 2 up). 1986. pap. 8.95 (*0-89272-327-0*) Down East.

Crystal Age. William H. Hudson. reprint ed. 64.50 (*0-404-03392-X*) AMS Pr.

Crystal & Dragon: The Cosmic Dance of Symmetry & Chaos in Nature, Art, & Consciousness. David Wade. (Illus.). 288p. (Orig.). 1993. pap. 19.95 (*0-89281-404-7*, Destiny Bks) Inner Tradit.

Crystal & Gem. R. F. Symes & Roger Harding. LC 90-4930. (Eyewitness Bks.: No. 25). (Illus.). 64p. (J). (gr. 5 up). 1991. 16.00 (*0-679-80781-0*) Knopf Bks Yng Read.

Crystal & Gem. R. F. Symes & Roger Harding. LC 90-4930. (Eyewitness Bks.: No. 25). (Illus.). 64p. (J). (gr. 5 up). 1991. lib. bdg. 18.99 (*0-679-90781-5*) Knopf Bks Yng Read.

***Crystal & the Amulet.** Micheal Moorcock. (Illus.). 100p. (Orig.). 1981. pap. 12.95 (*0-86130-044-0*, Pub. by Savoy Bks UK) AK Pr Dist.

Crystal & The Way of Light. Namkhai Norbu. 1988. pap. 13.00 (*0-14-019314-6*, Penguin Bks) Viking Penguin.

Crystal Awareness. Catherine Bowman. LC 87-46112. (New Age Ser.). (Illus.). 224p. (Orig.). 1987. pap. 3.95 (*0-87542-058-3*) Llewellyn Pubns.

Crystal Ball. Sibyl Ferguson. 16p. 1980. pap. 2.95 (*0-87728-483-0*) Weiser.

Crystal Ball. Gerda M. Scheidl. Tr. by Rosemary Lanning. LC 92-44762. (Illus.). 32p. (J). (gr. k-3). 1993. 14.95 (*1-55858-197-9*); lib. bdg. 14.88 (*1-55858-198-7*) North-South Bks NYC.

***Crystal Balls & Crystal Bowls: Tools for Ancient Scrying & Modern Seership.** Ted Andrews. LC 94-44921. (Illus.). 256p. 1995. pap. 12.95 (*1-56718-026-4*) Llewellyn Pubns.

***Crystal-Barkley Career Design Handbook.** Nella Barkley & Eric Sandburg. LC 95-105. 1995. 9.95 (*1-56305-495-7*) Workman Pub.

***Crystal Book.** Loretta Kurban. (Orig.). 1991. pap. text ed. 4.00 (*0-938863-41-X*) Libra Press Chi.

Crystal Boys. Pai Hsien-yung. Tr. by Howard Goldblatt. 336p. (CHI.). 1995. lib. bdg. 25.00 (*0-940567-10-5*); pap. 14.95 (*0-940567-11-3*) Gay Sunshine.

***Crystal Bucephalus.** Craig Hinton. (Dr. Who Ser.). (Illus.). Date not set. pap. 5.95 (*0-426-20429-8*, London Bridge) Genl Dist Srvs.

Crystal Cage. Sandy Bayer. 216p. (Orig.). 1991. pap. 8.95 (*1-55583-158-3*) Alyson Pubns.

Crystal Cage: Adventures of the Imagination in the Fiction of Henry James. Daniel J. Schneider. LC 77-26894. viii, 192p. 1978. 25.00 (*0-7006-0177-5*) U Pr of KS.

Crystal Carousel. Ross Hagen. 1990. pap. 6.95 (*0-927444-07-0*) Lilly & Belote.

Crystal Carousel. 2nd rev. ed. Ross Hagen. Ed. by Julie Lilly & Claire Hagen. LC 89-2591. (Illus.). 66p. (C). reprint ed. 6.95 (*0-927444-29-1*) Lilly & Belote.

Crystal Cave. Mary Stewart. 1984. mass mkt. 5.95 (*0-449-20644-0*, Crest) Fawcett.

Crystal Chain Letters: Architectural Fantasies by Bruno Taut & His Circle, 1919-1920. Ed. by Iain B. Whyte. (Illus.). 1985. 42.50x (*0-262-23121-2*) MIT Pr.

Crystal Chemistry & Properties of Materials with Quasi-One-Dimensional Structures. Jean Rouxel. 1986. lib. bdg. 136.50 (*90-277-2057-6*) Kluwer Ac.

Crystal Chemistry & Refractivity. Howard W. Jaffe. (Illus.). 448p. 1988. 84.95 (*0-521-25505-8*) Cambridge U Pr.

***Crystal Chemistry of Condensed Phosphates.** A. Durif. LC 95-2312. 420p. 1995. 115.00 (*0-306-44878-5*) Plenum.

Crystal Chemistry of High Tc Superconducting Copper Oxides. Bernard Raveau et al. Ed. by U. Gonser et al. (Materials Science Ser.: Vol. 15). (Illus.). 352p. 1991. 106.00 (*0-387-51545-3*) Spr-Verlag.

Crystal Chemistry of Large-Cation Silicates. Nikolai V. Belov. LC 63-17642. 168p. reprint ed. pap. 47.90 (*0-317-08935-8*, 2003357) Bks Demand.

Crystal Chemistry of Simple Compounds of Uranium, Thorium, Plutonium, Neptunium. Evgeniis S. Makarov. Tr. by E. B. Uvarov. LC 59-14486. 153p. reprint ed. pap. 43.70 (*0-317-08925-0*, 2003366) Bks Demand.

Crystal Chemistry of Tetrahedral Structures. Erwin Parthe. 186p. 1964. text ed. 169.00 (*0-677-00700-0*) Gordon & Breach.

Crystal Christianity: A Vital Guide to Personal Revival. Charles G. Finney. Orig. Title: Lectures to Professing Christians. 330p. 1986. pap. 5.99 (*0-88368-171-4*) Whitaker Hse.

Crystal Clarinets: A Coffee Table Book of Nice. Don Best & Jim Freeman. LC 80-83629. (Illus.). 96p. (Orig.). (C). 1980. pap. 6.66 (*0-938104-00-4*) Cosmic Concerns.

Crystal Clear. Connie Church. LC 87-40225. 112p. 1987. pap. 8.95 (*0-394-75642-8*, Villard Bks) Random.

Crystal Clear. Cay David. 224p. (Orig.). 1991. pap. 2.95 (*1-878702-67-X*, Kismet) Meteor Pub.

***Crystal Clear.** Joan Randell. 176p. 1995. 34.95 (*0-7872-1001-3*) Kendall-Hunt.

***Crystal Clear: A Guide to Quartz Crystal.** Jennifer Dent. 1994. pap. 15.95 (*1-898307-30-X*) Holmes Pub.

***Crystal Clear Vol. 1: Vintage American Crystal Sets, Crystal Detectors, & Crystals.** Maurice L. Sievers. LC 94-41185. 282p. 1995. pap. 29.95 (*1-886606-01-3*) Sonoran Pub.

Crystal Clear Access for Windows. Que Development Group Staff. (Illus.). 352p. (Orig.). 1993. pap. 24.95 (*1-56529-509-9*) Que.

Crystal Clear Cobol, Vol. II: Advanced Cobol & Database Concepts. William H. Trotter. 800p. 1990. pap. text ed. write for info. (*0-13-194192-5*) P-H.

Crystal Clear DOS. Que Development Group Staff. (Illus.). 352p. (Orig.). 1993. pap. 24.95 (*1-56529-358-4*) Que.

Crystal Clear Excel. Que Development Group Staff. (Illus.). 352p. (Orig.). 1993. pap. 24.95 (*1-56529-536-6*) Que.

***Crystal Clear Guide to Sight for Life: A Complete Manual of Eye.** Johnny L. Gayton & Jan R. Ledford. (Illus.). 352p. (Orig.). 1995. pap. 14.95 (*0-914984-68-3*) Starburst.

Crystal Clear One Two Three Release 4 for Windows. 1994. pap. 24.95 (*1-56529-716-4*) Que.

Crystal Clear Windows. Que Development Group Staff. (Illus.). 352p. (Orig.). 1993. pap. 24.95 (*1-56529-357-6*) Que.

Crystal Clear Word for Windows. 1993. pap. 24.95 (*1-56529-510-2*) Que.

Crystal Clear WordPerfect. Que Development Group Staff. (Illus.). 352p. (Orig.). 1993. pap. 24.95 (*1-56529-359-2*) Que.

Crystal Clear Wordperfect 6 for Windows. Que Development Group Staff. (Illus.). 352p. (Orig.). 1993. pap. 24.95 (*1-56529-508-0*) Que.

***Crystal Co-Creators.** Dorothy Roeder. 288p. 1994. pap. 14.95 (*0-929385-40-3*) Light Tech Comns Servs.

Crystal Cohesion & Conformal Energies. Ed. by R. M. Metzger. (Topics in Current Physics Ser.: Vol. 26). (Illus.). 160p. 1981. 37.00 (*0-387-10520-4*) Spr-Verlag.

Crystal Communion: Lovelight Meditations. Sri Akhenaton. LC 90-61184. (Illus.). 354p. (Orig.). 1994. pap. 21.95 (*0-9621839-4-6*) Portal MD.

Crystal Curtain. Sandy Bayer. LC 87-72877. 214p. (Orig.). 1988. pap. 7.95 (*1-55583-123-0*) Alyson Pubns.

Crystal Desert: Summers in Antarctica. David G. Campbell. LC 92-10583. 288p. 1992. 21.95 (*0-395-58969-X*) HM.

Crystal Desert: Summers in Antarctica. David G. Campbell. 1994. pap. 10.95 (*0-395-68082-4*) HM.

Crystal Destiny. Christina Blair. 400p. 1984. pap. 2.95 (*0-8217-1394-9*) Zebra.

***Crystal Divination for Today's Woman.** Cassandra Eason. 1994. pap. 9.95 (*0-572-01998-X*, Pub. by W Foulsham UK) Trans-Atl Phila.

Crystal Dragon. Richard A. Knaak. 304p. 1993. mass mkt. 4.99 (*0-446-36432-0*, Aspect) Warner Bks.

Crystal Dragon. P. Wayne Stauffer. Ed. by Gary Tunmore. (Illus.). 47p. (J). (gr. 3-5). 1991. 12.95 (*0-924649-04-6*); lib. bdg. 15.95 (*0-924649-05-4*); pap. 7.95 (*0-924649-06-2*) Scribblers Pub.

Crystal Empire. L. Neil Smith. 464p. 1989. mass mkt. 4.50 (*0-8125-5425-6*) Tor Bks.

***Crystal Enchantment.** Ed. by Saranne Dawson. 448p. (Orig.). 1995. mass mkt., pap. 5.99 (*0-505-52058-3*) Dorchester Pub Co.

Crystal Energy. M. Hackl. 1994. pap. 10.95 (*1-85230-590-8*) Element MA.

Crystal Engineering: The Design of Organic Solids. G. R. Desiraju. (Materials Science Monographs: No. 54). 312p. 1989. 113.00 (*0-444-87457-7*) Elsevier.

Crystal Enlightenment: The Transforming Properties of Crystals & Healing Stones. 175p. 1985. pap. 10.95 (*0-943358-27-2*) Aurora Press.

Crystal Express. Bruce Sterling. 1990. mass mkt. 4.99 (*0-441-12423-2*) Ace Bks.

***Crystal Factory! The World's Craziest Crystal Kit Ever.** Irene Trimble. (Planet Dexter's Ser.). (J). 1995. pap. 15.99 (*0-201-40934-8*) Addison-Wesley.

An Asterisk (*) at the beginning of an entry indicates that the title is appearing in BIP for the first time.

C

An Asterisk (*) at the beginning of an entry indicates that the title is appearing in BIP for the first time.

1729

Crystallography & Crystal Chemistry - An Introduction. F. Donald Bloss. (Illus.). 360p. (C). 1989. reprint ed. text ed. 60.00 (*1-878907-02-6*, RAN) TechBooks.

Crystallography & Crystal Chemistry of Materials with a Layered Structure. Ed. by Francis A. Levy. (Physics & Chemistry of Materials with Layered Structures Ser.: No. 2). 380p. 1976. lib. bdg. 131.50 (*90-277-0586-0*) Kluwer Ac.

Crystallography & Crystal Defects. Anthony Kelly & G. W. Groves. (Illus.). 428p. (C). reprint ed. 45.00 (*1-878907-36-0*) TechBooks.

Crystallography in Modern Chemistry: A Resource Book of Crystal Structures. Thomas C. Mak & Zhou Gongdu. 1344p. 1992. text ed. 195.00 (*0-471-54702-6*) Wiley.

Crystallography in Molecular Biology. Ed. by Dino Moras et al. LC 87-2509. (NATO ASI Series A, Life Sciences: Vol. 126). 454p. 1987. 125.00 (*0-306-42497-5*, Plenum Pr) Plenum.

Crystallography in North America. Ed. by Dan McLachlan et al. LC 81-71539. 479p. 1985. reprint ed. 25.00 (*0-937140-07-4*) Polycrystal Bk Serv.

Crystallography Made Crystal Clear: A Guide for Users of Macromolecular Models. Gale Rhodes. (Illus.). 202p. 1993. pap. text ed. 34.95 (*0-12-587075-2*) Acad Pr.

Crystallography Reviews: A Special Issue of the Journal Crystallography Reviews, Issue 1. Ed. by M. Moore. 84p. 1987. pap. text ed. 66.00 (*2-88124-218-9*) Gordon & Breach.

Crystallography Reviews: A Special Issue of the Journal Crystallography Reviews, Vol. 2. Ed. by M. Moore. 106p. 1987. Issue 2, 1987, 106p. pap. text ed. 66.00 (*2-88124-217-0*) Gordon & Breach.

Crystals. Robert A. Bell. (Golden Science Close-up Ser.). (Illus.). 24p. (J). (gr. k-5). 1992. pap. write for info. (*0-307-12856-3*, 12856, Golden Pr) Western Pub.

Crystals. Ian Mercer. (British Museum of Natural History Ser.). (Illus.). 60p. 1990. pap. text ed. 9.95 (*0-674-17914-5*) HUP.

Crystals: The Science, the Lore & the Mysteries. Douglas Bullis. 1990. 14.99 (*0-517-68929-4*) Random Hse Value.

Crystals & Consciousness: A Shamanic Primer. Aja Thomas. (Illus.). 50p. (Orig.). 1987. pap. text ed. 5.00 (*0-9620108-1-2*) ATMA.

Crystals & Crystal Gardens You Can Grow. Jean Stang. (First Bks.). (Illus.). (J). (ps-3). 1990. lib. bdg. 13.93 (*0-531-10889-9*) Watts.

Crystals & Crystal Growing. Alan Holden & Phylis S. Morrison. (Illus.). 352p. 1982. reprint ed. pap. 12.95 (*0-262-58050-0*) MIT Pr.

Crystals & Gemstones: Windows of the Self. Miriam Kaplan. 88p. 1987. 7.95 (*0-9615875-3-9*) Cassandra Pr.

Crystals & Light: An Introduction to Optical Crystallography. Elizabeth A. Wood. LC 76-27458. (Illus.). 156p. 1977. pap. text ed. 5.95 (*0-486-23431-2*) Dover.

Crystals & Their Use. Page Bryant. 64p. 1984. pap. 7.50 (*0-89540-151-7*, SB-151) Sun Pub.

Crystals, Colors & You. Jeanette Hudson. (Illus.). (Orig.). 1989. pap. write for info. (*0-318-65729-5*) Franklin-Belle.

Crystals, Electrons & Transistors. Michael Eckert & Helmut Schubert. Tr. by Thomas E. Hughes. (Illus.). 256p. 1989. 20.00 (*0-88318-719-1*) Am Inst Physics.

Crystals, Electrons & Transistors. Michael Eckert & Helmut Schubert. Tr. by Thomas E. Hughes. (AIP Translation Ser.). (Illus.). 256p. 1989. 40.00 (*0-88318-622-5*) Am Inst Physics.

Crystals, Fabrics, & Fields: Metaphors of Organicism in the Twentieth-Century Developmental Biology. Donna J. Haraway. LC 75-18174. 240p. 1976. 40.00x (*0-300-01864-9*) Yale U Pr.

Crystal's Fight. Rosie M. Shaw. 80p. 1994. pap. 8.95 (*0-8059-3468-5*) Dorrance.

Crystals for Pathfinders: A Basic Youth Enrichment Skill Honor Packet. L. S. Gattis, III. (Illus.). 20p. (Orig.). (J). (gr. 5 up). 1987. teacher ed, pap. 5.00 (*0-936241-22-5*) Cheetah Pub.

Crystals, Gems & Minerals of the Bible. Ruth V. Wright. 1988. pap. 9.95 (*0-87983-469-2*) Keats.

Crystals Gemstones-7 Rays. C. Nelson Stewart. 1989. pap. 5.95 (*0-938294-69-5*) Glob Comm-Inner Lght.

Crystals Growth, Properties, & Applications, Vol. 13: Organic Crystals I: Characterization Ser. Ed. by N. Karl. (Illus.). 176p. 1991. 110.00 (*0-387-53394-X*) Spr-Verlag.

Crystals in Gels & Liesegang Rings. Heinz K. Henisch. 180p. 1988. 74.95 (*0-521-34503-0*) Cambridge U Pr.

Crystals in the Sky: An Intellectual Odyssey Involving Chumash Astronomy, Cosmology & Rock Art. Travis Hudson & Ernest Underhay. Ed. by Lowell J. Bean & Thomas Blackburn. (Anthropological Papers: No. 10). (Illus.). 163p. (Orig.). 1978. pap. 18.95 (*0-87919-074-4*) Ballena Pr.

Crystals of Life. Walter I. Allen. 80p. 1989. 9.00 (*0-8233-0461-2*) Golden Quill.

*__Crystals of Light.__ Robert L. Neumann. 56p. 1995. pap. 8.00 (*0-8059-3776-5*) Dorrance.

Crystals R for Kids. Leia A. Greene. (Little Angel Books Ser.). (Illus.). 40p. (J). (gr. k-12). 1991. student ed, pap. text ed. 4.95 (*1-880737-04-3*) Crystal Jrns.

Crystals Stones & Chakras. David Pond et al. 1988. 15.95 (*0-915395-28-2*); pap. text ed. 3.95 (*0-915395-31-2*) Reflecting Pond.

Crystal's Vision. Frank Holmes, Jr. & K. C. Montgomery. Ed. by Gail Wedel. (Illus.). 28p. (J). (ps-3). 1992. 16.95 (*1-883005-00-0*) Holmes & Mont.

Crystalworld. Isidore Haiblum. 224p. (Orig.). 1992. mass mkt. 4.50 (*0-380-75859-8*, AvoNova) Avon.

CS 1 Skillbooklet. Barbara J. Crane. (Crane Reading System-English Ser.). (Illus.). (gr. k-2). 1982. pap. text ed. 2.49 (*0-89075-033-5*) Bilingual Ed Serv.

*__CSA Archive Book.__ Charles S. Anderson. (Illus.). 500p. Date not set. 50.00 (*0-9622431-1-6*) C S Anderson.

Csallokozi Hattyu. Cecile Tormay. 1977. reprint ed. 11.00 (*0-918570-03-4*) Karpat.

Csardas. Diane Pearson. 608p. 1984. pap. 3.50 (*0-449-20615-7*, Crest) Fawcett.

CSC, '90: Cooperation: Eighteenth Annual Computer Science Conference, Held in Washington, DC, Feb. 20-22, 1990. (Illus.). xxv, 475p. 1990. pap. text ed. 34.00 (*0-89791-348-5*, 404900) Assn Compu Machinery.

CSCE & the New Blueprint for Europe. Ed. by Marilyn Wyatt. LC 91-75833. 86p. (Orig.). (C). 1991. pap. text ed. 5.00 (*0-934742-64-2*, GU Schl Foreign) Geo U Inst Dplmcy.

CSCE Decision-Making: The Madrid Experience. Jan Sizoo & Rudolph T. Jurrjens. 1984. lib. bdg. 114.50 (*90-247-2989-0*) Kluwer Ac.

CSCE Helsinki Document, 1992 - The Challenges of Change. HMSO Staff. (Command Paper Ser.: No. 2092). 61p. 1992. pap. 17.00 (*0-10-120922-3*, HM09223, Pub. by HMSO UK) UNIPUB.

CSCSI, 1990: Proceedings of the Eighth Biennial Conference of the Canadian Society for Computational Studies of Intelligence. 267p. 1990. pap. 35.00 (*0-9694596-0-2*) Morgan Kaufmann.

CSCSI, 1992: Proceedings of the Ninth Biennial Conference of Canadian Society for Computational Studies of Intelligence. 1992. 35.00 (*0-9694596-1-0*) Morgan Kaufmann.

CSCW: Cooperation or Conflict? Ed. by S. M. Easterbrook. LC 92-20405. (Computer Supported Cooperative Work Ser.). 1993. 59.00 (*0-387-19755-9*) Spr-Verlag.

*__CSCW & Artificial Intelligence.__ Ed. by J. H. Connolly et al. (Computer Supported Cooperative Work Ser.). 216p. 1994. pap. text ed. 48.00 (*0-387-19816-4*) Spr-Verlag.

CSCW in Practice: An Introduction & Case Studies. Ed. by Dan Diaper & Colston Sanger. LC 92-39255. (Computer Supported Cooperative Work Ser.). 1993. 59.00 (*0-387-19784-2*) Spr-Verlag.

CSF Proteins: A Biochemical Approach. E. J. Thompson. 172p. 1988. 74.50 (*0-444-80946-5*) Elsevier.

*__Csh & Tcsh.__ Paul DuBois. 150p. 1995. 24.95 (*1-56592-132-1*) OReilly & Assocs.

CSH Reference Guide. Anatole Olczak. (Orig.). 1986. pap. 7.95 (*0-935739-06-8*) A System Pubns.

CSIRO Atlas of Hardwoods. J. Ilic. (Illus.). 600p. 1991. 244.00 (*0-387-53242-0*) Spr-Verlag.

CSIS Strengthening of America Commission First Report. Sam Nunn et al. 182p. (gr. 13). 1992. pap. text ed. 20.00 (*0-89206-211-8*) CSI Studies.

CSL 'Eighty-Eight. Ed. by E. Borger et al. (Lecture Notes in Computer Science Ser.: Vol. 385). vi, 399p. 1989. pap. 47.00 (*0-387-51659-X*, 3505) Spr-Verlag.

CSL 'Eighty-Nine: Third Workshop on Computer Science Logic Kaiserslautern, FRG, October 2-6, 1989 Proceedings. Ed. by E. Borger et al. (Lecture Notes in Computer Science Ser.: Vol. 440). vi, 437p. 1990. pap. 43.00 (*0-387-52753-2*) Spr-Verlag.

CSL 'Eighty-Seven. Ed. by E. Borger et al. (Lecture Notes in Computer Science Ser.: Vol. 329). vi, 346p. 1988. pap. 39.00 (*0-387-50241-6*) Spr-Verlag.

CSP: A Developer's Guide. Shashi Malik. 1992. text ed. write for info. (*0-07-039780-5*) McGraw.

CSP: A Developer's Guide. Shashi Malik & Henry Yamauchi. LC 92-11092. 1992. text ed. 45.00 (*0-07-039825-9*) McGraw.

CSS Alabama: Builder, Captain, & Plans. Charles G. Summersell. LC 83-17952. (Illus.). xii, 152p. 1985. 39.50 (*0-8173-0209-3*) U of Ala Pr.

C.S.S. Florida: Her Building & Operations. Frank L. Owsley, Jr. LC 86-19362. 224p. 1987. 19.50 (*0-8173-0336-7*) U of Ala Pr.

*__CSSR Directory of Departments & Programs of Religious Studies in North America: 1994 Edition.__ Ed. by David G. Truemper. xvi, 529p. 1994. 34.95 (*1-883135-02-8*) Coun Societies.

*__CSSR Directory of Departments & Programs of Religious Studies in North America: 1994 Edition.__ Ed. by David G. Truemper. 1994. pap. 27.95 (*1-883135-03-6*) Coun Societies.

*__CSSR Directory of Departments & Programs of Religious Studies in North America-1993 Edition.__ Ed. by David G. Truemper. xvii, 546p. 1993. 28.95x (*1-883135-00-1*) Coun Societies.

*__CSSR Directory of Departments & Programs of Religious Studies in North America-1993 Edition.__ Ed. by David G. Truemper. 1993. pap. 22.95x (*1-883135-01-X*) Coun Societies.

CT & MRI of the Genitourinary Tract. Ed. by Stanford M. Goldman & Olga M. Gatewood. (Contemporary Issues in Computed Tomography Ser.: Vol. 13). (Illus.). 323p. 1990. text ed. 95.00 (*0-443-08657-5*) Churchill.

CT & MRI of the Liver & Biliary System. Ed. by Paul M. Silverman & Robert K. Zeman. LC 89-22258. (Contemporary Issues in Computed Tomography Ser.: Vol. 12). 341p. reprint ed. pap. 97.20 (*0-7837-1369-X*, 2041518) Bks Demand.

CT & MRI of the Thorax. Ed. by Elias A. Zerhouni. (Contemporary Issues in Computed Tomography Ser.: Vol. 11). (Illus.). 222p. 1990. text ed. 73.00 (*0-443-08602-8*) Churchill.

CT & MRI Radioanatomy. S. Merran. (Illus.). 320p. 1991. 140.00 (*0-7506-1060-3*) Buttrwrth-Heinemann.

CT & Sonography of the Acute Abdomen. R. Brooke Jeffrey, Jr. 314p. 1989. 115.00 (*0-88167-506-7*, 1977) Raven.

CT Densitometry in Osteoporosis: The Impact on Management of the Patient. L. E. Lampmann et al. (Series in Radiology). 124p. 1984. lib. bdg. 80.50 (*0-89838-633-0*) Kluwer Ac.

CT G-U. Resnick. 592p. 1991. 92.00 (*1-55664-350-0*) Mosby Yr Bk.

CT of the Abdomen. Y. Wang. LC 85-4243. 1986. 221.00 (*0-8493-6448-5*, CRC Reprint); 214.00 (*0-8493-6449-3*, CRC Reprint) Franklin.

CT of the Abdomen, 2 vols., Set. Ed. by Yen Wang. 1986. 178.00 (*0-8493-6447-7*, RC944) CRC Pr.

CT of the Abdomen, Vol. I. Ed. by Yen Wang. 424p. 1986. write for info. (*0-318-60786-7*) CRC Pr.

CT of the Abdomen, Vol. II. Ed. by Yen Wang. 408p. 1986. write for info. (*0-318-60787-5*) CRC Pr.

CT of the Immunocompromised Host. Ed. by Janet E. Kuhlman. (Contemporary Issues in Computed Tomography Ser.: Vol. 14). (Illus.). 194p. 1991. text ed. 63.95 (*0-443-08721-0*) Churchill.

CT-RI Automotive Directory: (Connecticut-Rhode Island) Ed. by T. L. Spelman. 1985. 24.95 (*1-55527-005-0*) Auto Contact Inc.

CT Simulation Proceedings. Shirish K. Jani. 185p. 1993. 45.00 (*0-944838-32-4*) Med Physics Pub.

*__CT Technique Guide.__ James J. Hickman, Jr. 75p. 1994. write for info. (*0-9642926-0-2*) J & L Prods.

CTA. Jim McCurry. 1976. pap. 1.50 (*0-686-20607-X*) Ghost Dance.

CTA at Forty Five: A History of the First 45 Years of the Chicago Transit Authority. George Krambles & Arthur H. Peterson. LC 93-91685. (Illus.). 144p. 1993. 49.95 (*0-9637965-4-2*) G Krambles TSF.

CTFA Cosmetic Ingredient Handbook. 2nd ed. CTFA Staff. LC 92-74497. 680p. 1992. 240.00 (*1-882621-00-X*) Cosmetic T&FA.

*__CTFA Cosmetic Ingredient Handbook.__ 3rd ed. CTFA Staff. Ed. by John A. Wenninger & Gerald N. McEwen. LC 95-67175. 800p. 1995. text ed. 375.00 (*1-882621-10-7*) Cosmetic T&FA.

CTFA Environmental Manual: A Guide to Environmental Laws Affecting Consumer Product Companies. CTFA Staff. LC 93-71752. (Illus.). 280p. 1994. pap. text ed. 225.00 (*1-882621-07-7*) Cosmetic T&FA.

CTFA International Color Handbook. 2nd ed. CTFA Staff. 325p. 1992. 200.00 (*1-882621-03-4*) Cosmetic T&FA.

CTFA International Cosmetic Ingredient Dictionary, 2 vols., Set. 5th ed. CTFA Staff. Ed. by John A. Wenninger & Gerald N. McEwen. LC 93-71756. 1301p. 1993. text ed. 475.00 (*1-882621-06-9*) Cosmetic T&FA.

CTFA International Resource Manual. 3rd ed. CTFA Staff. 336p. 1991. pap. 95.00 (*1-882621-04-2*) Cosmetic T&FA.

CTFA Labeling Manual. CTFA Staff. 194p. 1990. pap. 195.00 (*1-882621-05-0*) Cosmetic T&FA.

CTFA List of Japanese Cosmetic Ingredients. 2nd ed. CTFA Staff. LC 92-74585. 160p. 1992. pap. 195.00 (*1-882621-01-8*) Cosmetic T&FA.

CTG Capacitance Theory of Gravity. Morton F. Spears. LC 91-90526. (Illus.). 87p. 1991. 19.70 (*0-9629933-0-1*) M F Spears.

CTG Capacitance Theory of Gravity, Bk. 2. Morton F. Spears. LC 91-90526. (Illus.). 103p. 1993. 19.70 (*0-9629933-1-X*) M F Spears.

CTG in Practice. Adam Balen & John Smith. (Illus.). 203p. (Orig.). 1992. pap. text ed. 32.50 (*0-443-04675-1*) Churchill.

CTG Made Easy. Susan M. Gauge & Christine Henderson. (Illus.). 276p. (Orig.). 1992. pap. text ed. 19.95 (*0-443-04439-2*) Churchill.

Cthulhu: The Mythos & Kindred Horrors. Robert E. Howard. Ed. by David Drake. 256p. (Orig.). 1987. mass mkt. 4.99 (*0-671-65641-4*) Baen Bks.

Cthulhu by Gaslight: Horror Roleplaying in the 1890's. 2nd ed. William A. Barton. Ed. by Sandy Petersen & Lynn Willis. (Call of Cthulhu Roleplaying Game System Ser.). (Illus.). 128p. 1988. pap. 18.95 (*0-933635-55-9*, 3303) Chaosium.

Cthulhu Casebook: Adventures & Atmosphere for Call of Cthulhu. Hargrave et al. Ed. by Sandy Petersen et al. (Call of Cthulhu Roleplaying Game System Ser.). (Illus.). 130p. (Orig.). (YA). (gr. 12 up). 1990. pap. 18.95 (*0-933635-67-2*, 3305) Chaosium.

Cthulhu Classics: A Full-Length Campaign & Five Adventures. Sandy Petersen et al. Ed. by Willam G. Dunn et al. (Call of Cthulhu Roleplaying Game System Ser.). (Illus.). 152p. (Orig.). 1989. pap. 18.95 (*0-933635-61-3*, 3301) Chaosium.

Cthulhu for President Kit. Ed. by Charlie Krank. (Call of Cthulhu Accessories Ser.). (Illus.). 1992. 14.95 (*0-933635-89-3*, 5109) Chaosium.

Cthulhu Now. 2nd ed. William A. Barton et al. Ed. by Sam Shirley. (Call of Cthulhu Roleplaying Game System Ser.). (Illus.). 1992. pap. 14.95 (*0-933635-51-6*, 3307) Chaosium.

*__Cthulhu 2000: A Lovecraftian Anthology.__ Ed. & Intro. by Jim Turner. (Illus.). 420p. 1995. 24.95 (*0-87054-169-2*) Arkham.

Cthulhu's Heirs. S. Aniolowski et al. Ed. & Intro. by Thomas M. Stratman. (Cthulhu Cycle Bks.). (Illus.). 270p. (Orig.). 1994. pap. 9.95 (*1-56882-013-5*, 6003) Chaosium.

CTOS - Open Application Programming Interface Specification: Networking Services. 1992. pap. text ed. 45.00 (*0-13-194655-2*) P-H.

CTOS Open Programming Practices & Standards. UniSys Corp. Staff. 544p. 1991. pap. text ed. 53.00 (*0-13-194382-0*, 260503) P-H.

Ctt Reference Card. Specialized Systems Consultants, Inc. Staff. 16p. (Orig.). (C). 1991. pap. 4.50 (*0-916151-49-2*) Specialized Sys.

CTTS CDL Study Manual. CTTS-Safety Prod. Staff. 400p. 1994. per., pap. text ed. 27.95 (*0-8403-9440-3*) Kendall-Hunt.

*__CU Financial Analysis.__ CUNA Staff. 83p. 1995. teacher ed 20.00 (*0-7872-0321-1*, S320); per., pap. text ed. 21.14 (*0-7872-0322-X*, S320) Kendall-Hunt.

CUA Census Report, No. 3: Indian Population in Douglas County. C. J. Lunbeck. 23p. (Orig.). 1972. pap. 2.50 (*1-55719-054-2*) U NE CPAR.

Cua, Cua, Gra, Gra! (Quack & Honk) Allan Fowler. LC 92-35056. (Rookie Read-about Science Ser.). (Illus.). 32p. (SPA.). (J). (ps-2). 1993. lib. bdg. 11.10 (*0-516-36012-4*); pap. 3.95 (*0-516-56012-3*) Childrens.

*__Cuaderno De Trabajo Del Esfodiante.__ Dennis Graver. 21p. 1994. pap. 4.50 (*0-916974-57-X*, 093SP) NAUI.

*__Cuaderno Do Trabajo Para Padres, Maestros y Ninos Sobre el Trasterno de Bajo Nivel de Atencion (ADD) O Hiperactividad.__ Harvey C. Parker. (Illus.). 142p. 1994. student ed, pap. 16.00 (*0-9621629-5-7*) Spec Pr FL.

Cuaderno Espiritual. Paul Twitchell. Tr. by Mario Proano & Maria A. De Mercado. 256p. (Orig.). (SPA.). 1979. pap. 5.00 (*0-914766-48-1*, 0928) Illum Way Pub.

Cuaderno Espiritual. Paul Twitchell. 244p. 1991. pap. 5.00 (*1-57043-097-7*) ECKANKAR.

Cuaderno para la Tecnologia de las Unas de Milady. 125p. (SPA.). 1993. student ed 15.50 (*1-56253-207-3*) Milady Pub.

Cuaderno Practico Para Texto De Cosmetologia Milady - Milady's Standard Practical Workbook. 281p. (SPA.). 1992. 15.50 (*1-56253-097-6*) Milady Pub.

Cuaderno Sobre el Arte y la Ciencia de la Manicura. Cimaglia. 96p. (SPA.). pap. 15.50 (*0-87350-380-5*) Milady Pub.

Cuaderno Sobre Practica de la Bellicultura: (Practical Beauty Culture Workbook) (SPA.). 1985. 16.00 (*0-87350-379-1*); 24.95 (*0-685-74319-5*) Milady Pub.

Cuaderno Sobre Teoria de la Bellicultura: (Workbook for Beauty Culture Theory) (SPA.). 1985. 17.50 (*0-87350-426-7*); 25.95 (*0-87350-435-6*) Milady Pub.

Cuaderno Teorico Para Texto De Cosmetologia Milady - Milady's Standard Theory Workbook. 136p. (SPA.). 1992. 14.95 (*1-56253-094-1*) Milady Pub.

Cuaderno y Algo Mas: A Notebook & Something More. 2nd ed. (Textbook Ser.). (Illus.). 160p. (Orig.). (ENG & SPA.). 1991. reprint ed. pap. text ed. 7.95 (*1-56328-000-0*) Edit Plaza Mayor.

Cuadro Biblico Del Predicador: The Preacher's Portrait. John Stott. (SPA.). 4.25 (*84-7228-165-5*, 220219, Pub. by Edit Clie SP) TSELF.

Cuadro Lam (Lam. Plaque) Cuando Peleamos (When We Argue) (SPA.). Date not set. 25.99 (*0-685-74925-8*, 490796) Editorial Unilit.

Cuadros. Noemi Escandell. Ed. by SLUSA Staff. LC 81-85665. (Illus.). 56p. (SPA.). (C). 1982. pap. 5.00 (*0-9606758-0-9*) SLUSA.

Cual Es la Diferencia? William MacDonald. Orig. Title: What Is the Difference?. 112p. (SPA.). 1981. pap. 3.99 (*0-8254-1450-4*) Kregel.

Cual Es la Diferencia? So What's the Difference? Fritz Ridenour. (SPA.). 5.50 (*84-7228-307-0*, 220222, Pub. by Edit Clie SP) TSELF.

Cual Es la Verdad? (What's the Point) M. Warren. (SPA.). Date not set. 1.50 (*0-8423-6478-1*, 490246) Editorial Unilit.

Cual Es Su Color? Frank Calderon. 80p. (Orig.). (SPA.). 1985. pap. 2.25 (*0-939193-09-4*, Southeast Periodical & Bk Sales) Edit Concepts.

Cual es Tu Flor Favorita? - What's Your Favorite Flower? Allan Fowler. LC 92-7404. (Rookie Read-about Science - Spanish Ser.). (Illus.). 32p. (SPA.). (J). (ps-2). 1993. 23.48 (*0-516-59634-9*); lib. bdg. 11.10 (*0-516-36007-8*); pap. 3.95 (*0-516-56007-7*) Childrens.

Cuando Dios Llama: When God Calls You. Edward Deratany. (SPA.). 6.95 (*84-7228-392-5*, 220223, Pub. by Edit Clie SP) TSELF.

Cuando el Dinero Causa Problemas. Jose L. Martinez. (Serie de la Familia). 96p. (SPA.). 1986. pap. 4.90 (*0-311-46265-0*) Casa Bautista.

Cuando el Dinero Falla: When Your Money Fails. Mary S. Relfe. (SPA.). 5.50 (*84-7228-732-7*, 360121, Pub. by Edit Clie SP) TSELF.

Cuando el Embarazo es un Problema: When Pregnancy is a Problem. Josie H. De Smith. (Serie de la Familia - Series on the Family). 112p. (Orig.). 1992. pap. 4.90 (*0-311-46269-3*) Casa Bautista.

Cuando el Medico Dice: Es Cancer (When the Doctor Says It's Cancer) M. B. Noster. (SPA.). Date not set. 2.49 (*0-8423-6515-X*, 498042) Editorial Unilit.

Cuando el Padre Cuida de la Familia. Wilson Grant. Tr. by Laura E. Paredes. (Serie de la Familia). 110p. 1987. pap. 4.90 (*0-311-46268-5*) Casa Bautista.

Cuando el Sexo-Vuelve-Adiccion (Addicted to Love) S. Arterburn. (SPA.). Date not set. 1.79 (*1-56063-435-9*, 497441) Editorial Unilit.

Cuando el Sida Llega a la Iglesia. William E. Amos, Jr. Tr. by Jose L. Martinez. 128p. (Orig.). (SPA.). 1990. pap. text ed. 4.90 (*0-311-42080-X*) Casa Bautista.

Cuando el Venga: The Second Coming. Samuel Vila. (SPA.). 5.95 (*84-7228-014-4*, 220225, Pub. by Edit Clie SP) TSELF.

Cuando El Verde Olivo Se Torna Rojo. Ricardo R. Sarinas. LC 81-69542. (Coleccion Caniqui Ser.). 360p. (Orig.). 1982. pap. 14.95 (*0-89729-301-0*) Ediciones.

Cuando en Casa No Nos Comprenden - When We Are Not Understood at Home. Jose S. Velez. (Serie de la Familia - Series on the Family). 112p. (Orig.). (SPA.). (YA). (gr. 9 up). 1991. pap. 4.90 (*0-311-46263-4*) Casa Bautista.

Cuando en la Iglesia Hay Pecado. J. Carl Laney. 176p. (Orig.). (SPA.). 1991. pap. 4.95 (*0-88113-050-8*) Edit Betania.

Cuando Hay Que Decidirse: When You Have to Make a Decision. Arnoldo Canclini. (SPA.). 3.25 (*84-7228-242-2*, 220228, Pub. by Edit Clie SP) TSELF.

An Asterisk (*) at the beginning of an entry indicates that the title is appearing in BIP for the first time.

C

An Asterisk (*) at the beginning of an entry indicates that the title is appearing in BIP for the first time.

1731

Cuba at a Crossroads: Politics & Economics after the Fourth Party Congress. Ed. by Jorge Perez-Lopez. LC 94-16203. 288p. 1994. lib. bdg. 39.95 (*0-8130-1310-0*) U Press Fla.

***Cuba at the Crossroads.** Ron Ridenour. 193p. 1994. pap. 9.95 (*0-9624975-7-6*) Infoservicios.

Cuba Before Columbus, 2 vols., Set. Mark R. Harrington. LC 76-44731. reprint ed. 55.00 (*0-404-15990-7*) AMS Pr.

Cuba Between Empires, Eighteen Seventy-Eight to Nineteen Two. Louis A. Perez, Jr. LC 82-11059. (Latin American Ser.). 510p. 1983. 49.95 (*0-8229-3472-8*) U of Pittsburgh Pr.

***Cuba Business Executive Outlook.** 70p. (Orig.). 1994. pap. 295.00 (*0-7605-1346-5*) Rector Pr.

***Cuba Business Intelligence Handbook.** (Illus.). 70p. (Orig.). 1994. pap. 295.00 (*0-7605-1076-8*) Rector Pr.

Cuba Cocina! The Tantalizing World of Cuban Cooking--Yesterday, Today, & Tomorrow. Joyce LaFray. LC 94-1594. 1994. 25.00 (*0-688-11067-3*) Hearst Bks.

***Cuba Commercial Tax.** 150p. (C). 1994. pap. 295.00 (*0-7605-0103-3*) Rector Pr.

Cuba Commission Report: A Hidden History of the Chinese in Cuba: the Original English-Language Text of 1876. Intro. by Denise Helly. LC 92-38926. (Studies in Atlantic History & Culture). (Illus.). 176p. (C). 1993. pap. text ed. 21.95 (*0-8018-4641-2*) Johns Hopkins.

Cuba, Cubans, & Cuban Americans: A Bibliography. Jesse J. Dossick. 116p. (C). 1992. pap. 19.95 (*0-935501-49-5*) U Miami N-S Ctr.

Cuba, Dominican Republic, Haiti, Puerto Rico: Business Risk Overview. Ed. by Lewis B. Sckolnick. 125p. (Orig.). (C). 1994. pap. text ed. 495.00 (*1-57205-570-7*) Rector Pr.

Cuba Economia y Sociedad, 15 vols., Vol. I. Levi Marrero. (Illus.). 1979. Vol. 1. 30.00 (*84-359-0128-9*) Ediciones.

***Cuba Economia y Sociedad, 15 vols., Vol. I.** 2nd ed. Levi Marrero. (Illus.). 1992. 30.00 (*84-399-8831-1*) Ediciones.

Cuba Economia y Sociedad, Vols. II-VII. Levi Marrero. (Illus.). 1979. 20.00 (*0-685-73234-7*) Ediciones.

Cuba Economia y Sociedad, Vols. VIII-XIII. Levi Marrero. (Illus.). 1979. 30.00 (*0-685-73235-5*) Ediciones.

Cuba Economia y Sociedad, Vols. XIV-XV. Levi Marrero. (Illus.). 1979. 35.00 (*0-685-73236-3*) Ediciones.

Cuba en Guerra: Historia de la Oposicion Anticastrista 1959-1993. Enrique Encinosa. 300p. (SPA.). 1993. pap. 12.00 (*1-884619-00-2*) Endowment CAS.

Cuba en Mis Versos. Luis Mario. LC 92-74962. (Coleccion Espejo de Paciencia Ser.). 140p. (Orig.). (SPA.). 1993. pap. 12.00 (*0-89729-662-1*) Ediciones.

***Cuba Entre la Independencia y la Libertad.** Armando P. Ribas. LC 94-71842. (Coleccion Cuba y sus Jueces). 91p. (Orig.). (SPA.). 1994. pap. 12.00 (*0-89729-745-8*) Ediciones.

Cuba Fomento de la Isla 1749: Primer Estudio Geo-Economico de la Isla. 2nd ed. Bernardo J. De Urrutia y Matos. 111p. (SPA.). 1993. pap. 13.00 (*0-89729-636-2*) Ediciones.

Cuba for Beginners. Rius. (Documentary Comic Bks.). (Illus.). 1981. 6.95 (*0-906495-29-6*) Writers & Readers.

Cuba for Beginners. RIUS Staff & Eduardo Del Rio. LC 70-108717. 1993. reprint ed. lib. bdg. 40.00 (*0-87348-193-3*); reprint ed. pap. 12.95 (*0-87348-128-3*) Pathfinder NY.

Cuba in a Changing World. Ed. by Antonio Jorge et al. 130p. (C). 1991. 12.95 (*0-685-63344-6*, CP336) U Miami N-S Ctr.

***Cuba in Focus: A Guide to the People, Politics, & Culture.** (Illus.). 80p. 1995. pap. 10.00 (*0-85345-958-4*, PB9584) Monthly Rev.

Cuba in Pictures. Nathan A. Haverstock. (Visual Geography Ser.). (Illus.). 64p. (YA). (gr. 5 up). 1987. lib. bdg. 18.95 (*0-8225-1811-2*, Lerner Publctns) Lerner Group.

***Cuba in the International System: Normalization & Integration.** Ed. by Archibald R. Ritter & John M. Kirk. LC 95-1328. (International Political Economy Ser.). 1995. write for info. (*0-312-12653-0*) St Martin.

Cuba in the 1850's: Through the Lens of Charles DeForest Fredricks. Robert M. Levine. 86p. 1990. 24.95 (*0-8130-1010-1*) U Press Fla.

Cuba in Transition: Crisis & Transformation. Ed. by Sandor Halebsky et al. 244p. (C). 1992. text ed. 66.00 (*0-8133-8094-4*); pap. text ed. 21.50 (*0-8133-8095-2*) Westview.

Cuba in Transition: Options for U.S. Policy. Gillian Gunn. LC 93-16054. 1993. 9.95 (*0-87078-347-5*) TCFP-PPP.

Cuba in Transition: Papers & Proceedings of the First Annual Meeting of the Association for the Study of the Cuban Economy. Association for the Study of the Cuban Economy Staff. (Study of the Cuban Economy Ser.). 336p. 1992. pap. text ed. 20.00 (*1-879862-03-4*) FL Intl U Latin.

Cuba in Transition, Vol. II: Papers & Proceedings of the Second Annual Meeting of the Association for the Study of the Cuban Economy. Association for the Study of the Cuban Economy Staff. 372p. 1993. pap. text ed. 20.00 (*1-879862-04-2*) FL Intl U Latin.

Cuba Is My Home. Photos by Mercedes Lopez. LC 92-17725. (My Home Country Ser.). (Illus.). (J). 1992. lib. bdg. 18.60 (*0-8368-0848-7*) Gareth Stevens Inc.

***Cuba Justicia y Terror.** Luis F. Caubi. LC 94-70487. (Coleccion Cuba y Sus Jueces). 124p. 1994. pap. 13.00 (*0-89729-730-X*) Ediciones.

Cuba Le Toco Perder. Justo Carrillo. LC 93-73083. (Coleccion Cuba y Sus Jueces Ser.). (Illus.). 208p. (Orig.). (SPA.). 1993. pap. 19.00 (*0-89729-689-3*) Ediciones.

Cuba Looks to the Year Two Thousand. Marc Frank. Ed. by Gail Reed. LC 92-39652. (Illus.). xiv, 258p. (Orig.). 1993. pap. 9.95 (*0-7178-0704-5*) Intl Pubs Co.

Cuba Night: Poetry. Dave Smith. LC 89-12880. 96p. 1990. 18.95 (*0-688-08991-7*, Quill); pap. 9.95 (*0-688-09578-X*, Quill) Morrow.

Cuba Nineteen Thirty-Three: Estudiantes, Yankis & Soldados. Justo Carrillo. (Illus.). 485p. (SPA.). 1985. pap. 11.95 (*0-935501-00-2*) U Miami N-S Ctr.

Cuba on the Brink: Castro, the Missile Crisis, & the Soviet Collapse. James G. Blight et al. LC 93-19177. 1993. 30.00 (*0-679-42149-1*) Pantheon.

***Cuba Por Dentro: El Minint.** Juan A. Menier. LC 93-74509. (Coleccion Cuba y sus Jueces). 173p. (Orig.). (SPA.). 1994. pap. 18.00 (*0-89729-718-0*) Ediciones.

Cuba Si! - Bringing It All Back Home - Last Gasps. Terrence McNally. 1970. pap. 4.75 (*0-8222-0257-3*) Dramatists Play.

***Cuba Stands Firm - Cuba Sigue Firme.** Fidel Castro. 1992. pap. 2.50 (*0-89567-112-3*) World View Forum.

***Cuba: Talking about Revolution: Conversations with Juan Antonio Blanco.** Medea Benjamin. 108p. 1994. 11.95 (*1-875284-79-6*, Pub. by Ocean Pr AT) Talman.

Cuba, the Economic & Social Revolution. Ed. by Dudley Seers. LC 73-15400. 432p. 1975. reprint ed. text ed. 35.00 (*0-8371-7198-9*, SECU, Greenwood Pr) Greenwood.

Cuba the Revolution in Peril. Janette Habel. 1991. 34.95 (*0-86091-308-2*, A5345, Pub. by Verso UK) Routledge Chapman & Hall.

***Cuba Trade & Investment Handbook.** (Illus.). 100p. (Orig.). 1995. pap. 595.00 (*0-7605-1684-7*) Rector Pr.

Cuba: 25 Years of Revolution: 1959-1984. Ed. by Sandor Halebsky & John M. Kirk. 480p. 1985. text ed. 69.50 (*0-275-90114-9*, C0114); pap. text ed. 19.95 (*0-275-91648-0*, B1648, Praeger Pubs) Greenwood.

Cuba under the Platt Amendment: 1902-1934. Louis A. Perez, Jr. LC 85-26451. (Latin American Ser.). 430p. 1986. 49.95 (*0-8229-3533-3*) U of Pittsburgh Pr.

Cuba under the Platt Amendment, 1902-1934. Louis A. Perez, Jr. LC 85-26451. (Latin American Ser.). 430p. (C). 1991. pap. 19.95 (*0-8229-5446-X*) U of Pittsburgh Pr.

Cuba vs. United States: The Politics of Hostility. rev. ed. Lynn-Darrell Bender. LC 74-78314. 108p. (C). 1981. 12.50 (*0-913480-51-7*); pap. 5.75 (*0-913480-52-5*) Inter Am U Pr.

Cuba Will Never Adopt Capitalist Methods. Fidel Castro. 30p. 1990. reprint ed. 3.00 (*0-87348-538-6*) Pathfinder NY.

Cuba y Espana: Perscepciones y Relaciones. Joaquin Roy. (Biblioteca Cubana Contemporanea Ser.). 100p. (Orig.). (SPA.). 1988. pap. 9.95 (*84-359-0542-X*, Pub. by Editorial Playor SP) Ediciones.

Cuba y su Cultura. Raul M. Shelton. LC 93-71466. (Coleccion Cuba y Sus Jueces Ser.). (Illus.). 500p. (Orig.). (SPA.). 1993. pap. 29.95 (*0-89729-690-7*) Ediciones.

Cuba y Su Destino Historico. Ernesto Ardura. LC 88-83552. (Coleccion Cuba y Sus Jueces Ser.). (Illus.). 291p. (Orig.). (SPA.). 1989. pap. 15.00 (*0-89729-518-8*) Ediciones.

Cuba, 1753-1815: Crown, Military & Society. Allan J. Kuethe. LC 85-17844. (Illus.). 232p. 1986. text ed. 28.00x (*0-87049-487-2*) U of Tenn Pr.

Cuba, 1933: Students, Yankees, & Soldiers. Justo Carillo. (University of Miami North-South Center Ser.). 497p. (C). 1993. pap. text ed. 24.95 (*1-56000-690-0*) Transaction Pubs.

Cubal Analysis: A Post Sexist Model of the Psyche. Karin Blair. 1983. 14.50 (*0-913660-17-5*); pap. 10.50 (*0-913660-18-3*) Magic Cir Pr CT.

Cuban-American Experience: Culture, Images & Perspectives. Thomas D. Boswell & James R. Curtis. LC 83-16042. 214p. 1984. text ed. 57.00 (*0-86598-116-7*, R3912) Rowman.

***Cuban American Family Album.** Dorothy Hoobler & Thomas Hoobler. (Illus.). 128p. (J). 1995. 19.95 (*0-19-510340-8*); lib. bdg. 22.95 (*0-19-508132-3*) OUP.

Cuban-American Radio Wars. Howard H. Frederick. Ed. by Melvin J. Voigt. LC 85-22883. (Communication & Information Science Ser.). 208p. 1986. text ed. 39.50 (*0-89391-264-6*) Ablex Pub.

Cuban American Theatre. Matias M. Huidobro et al. Ed. by Miguel Pando et al. LC 91-9898. 280p. (Orig.). 1994. pap. 11.00 (*1-55885-020-1*) Arte Publico.

Cuban American Writers: Los Atrevidos. Roberto Fernandez et al. (Illus.). 198p. (Orig.). (C). 1989. pap. 12.00 (*0-913827-01-0*, Ediciones ELLAS) Linden Ln Pr.

Cuban Americans. Renee Gernand. (Peoples of North America Ser.). (Illus.). 112p. (J). (gr. 5 up). 1989. lib. bdg. 17.95 (*0-87754-869-2*) Chelsea Hse.

***Cuban Americans.** Renee Gernand. LC 94-42011. (Immigrant Experience Ser.). (J). 1995. write for info. (*0-7910-3354-6*); pap. text ed. write for info. (*0-7910-3376-7*) Chelsea Hse.

***Cuban Americans.** James S. Olson & Judith E. Olson. LC 94-34365. (Immigrant Heritage of America Ser.). 1995. lib. bdg. 26.95x (*0-8057-8430-6*, Twayne); pap. 15.95 (*0-8057-8439-X*, Twayne) Macmillan.

Cuban & North American Marxism. Ed. by Edward D'Angelo. iv, 214p. 1984. pap. 24.00 (*90-6032-265-7*, Pub. by B R Gruener NE) Benjamins North Am.

Cuban & Puerto Rican Campaigns. Richard H. Davis. (Select Bibliographies Reprint Ser.). (Illus.). 1977. 31.95 (*0-8369-5278-2*) Ayer.

Cuban Art & National Identity: The Vanguardia Painters, 1927-1950. Juan A. Martinez. LC 94-7649. (Illus.). 216p. 1994. 34.95 (*0-8130-1306-2*) U Press Fla.

Cuban Communism. 4th ed. Irving L. Horowitz. LC 80-21821. 690p. (C). 1981. pap. 19.95 (*0-87855-838-1*) Transaction Pubs.

Cuban Communism. 7th rev. ed. Ed. by Irving L. Horowitz. 873p. 1991. pap. 22.95 (*0-88738-794-2*) Transaction Pubs.

***Cuban Communism.** 8th ed. Ed. by Irving L. Horowitz. 787p. (C). 1995. pap. 29.95 (*1-56000-758-3*) Transaction Pubs.

Cuban Condition: Translation & Identity in Modern Cuban Literature. Gustavo P. Firmat. (Cambridge Studies in Latin American & Iberian Literature). 196p. (C). 1989. 49.95 (*0-521-32747-4*) Cambridge U Pr.

Cuban Consciousness in Literature: 1923-1974. Jose R. De Armas & Charles W. Steele. LC 78-53265. (Coleccion Antologias Ser.). 1978. pap. 12.00 (*0-89729-166-2*) Ediciones.

***Cuban Counterpoint: Tobacco & Sugar.** Fernando Ortiz. Tr. by Harriet De Onis. LC 94-38200. (Illus.). 408p. 1995. pap. text ed. 18.95 (*0-8223-1616-1*) Duke.

Cuban Dilemma. R. Hart Phillips. 1962. 19.95 (*0-8392-1018-3*) Astor-Honor.

Cuban Economy: Dependency & Development. Ed. by Antonio Jorge & Jaime Suchlicki. 120p. 1989. pap. 16.95 (*0-935501-16-9*, CP310) U Miami N-S Ctr.

Cuban Economy: Measurement & Analysis of Socialist Performance. Andrew Zimbalist & Claes Brundenius. LC 89-32029. (Studies in Development). 240p. 1989. text ed. 38.00 (*0-8018-3846-0*) Johns Hopkins.

Cuban Exile. Patrick L. Gallagher. Ed. by Carlos E. Cortes. LC 79-6207. (Hispanics in the United States Ser.). (Illus.). 1981. lib. bdg. 28.95 (*0-405-13157-7*) Ayer.

Cuban Exiles in Florida: Their Presence & Contributions. Ed. by Antonio Jorge et al. 370p. (C). 1991. pap. 21.95 (*0-935501-24-X*, CP333) U Miami N-S Ctr.

Cuban Exiles in the United States: An Original Anthology. Ed. by Carlos E. Cortes. LC 79-6236. (Hispanics in the United States Ser.). (Illus.). 1981. lib. bdg. 19.95 (*0-405-13183-6*) Ayer.

Cuban Experience in the United States: An Original Anthology. Ed. by Carlos E. Cortes. LC 79-6230. (Hispanics in the United States Ser.). 1981. lib. bdg. 56.95 (*0-405-13177-1*) Ayer.

Cuban Festivals: An Illustrated Anthology, Alk. paper. Ed. by Judith Bettelheim. LC 93-18140. (Reference Library of the Humanities, Vol. 1410; Books of the Bible Ser.: Vol. 3). (Illus.). 272p. 1993. 40.00 (*0-8153-0310-6*, H1444) Garland.

Cuban Flavor: A Cookbook. 2nd ed. Ed. by Raquel M. Rabade. 230p. 1981. pap. 8.95 (*0-941010-00-7*) Downtown Bk.

Cuban Foreign Policy: Caribbean Tempest. Pamela S. Falk. LC 81-47890. 352p. 1986. text ed. 42.95 (*0-669-05127-6*) Free Pr.

Cuban Foreign Policy: The New Internationalism. Ed. by Jaime Suchlicki & Damian J. Fernandez. 174p. 1988. pap. 18.95 (*0-935501-10-X*, CP315) U Miami N-S Ctr.

Cuban Foreign Policy Confronts a New International Order. Ed. by H. Michael Erisman & John M. Kirk. LC 91-8351. 244p. 1991. lib. bdg. 40.00 (*1-55587-239-5*) Lynne Rienner.

Cuban Home Cooking. Jane Cossio & J. Young. 1989. pap. 9.95 (*0-942084-37-3*) SeaSide Pub.

Cuban Image: Cinema & Cultural Politics in Cuba. Michael Chanan. LC 85-45505. (Illus.). 320p. 1986. 35.00 (*0-253-31587-5*) Ind U Pr.

Cuban Insurrection, 1952-1959. Ramon L. Bonachea & Marta S. Martin. LC 72-94546. (Social History Ser.). 450p. 1974. pap. 21.95 (*0-87855-576-5*) Transaction Pubs.

Cuban Internationalism in Sub-Saharan Africa. Ed. by Sergio Diaz-Briquets. LC 89-16974. 250p. 1989. pap. text ed. 18.95 (*0-8207-0226-9*) Duquesne.

Cuban Leadership after Castro: Biographies of Cuba's Top Generals. Rafael Fermoselle. 203p. (C). 1992. pap. 16.95 (*0-935501-35-5*, CP327) U Miami N-S Ctr.

Cuban Leadership after Castro: Biographies of Cuba's Top Military Commanders. Rafael Fermoselle. LC 87-82711. (Coleccion Cuba y Sus Jueces Ser.). 128p. (Orig.). 1987. pap. 9.95 (*0-89729-466-1*) Ediciones.

Cuban Medicine. Roswell S. Danielson. LC 76-1768. 247p. 1978. 37.95x (*0-87855-114-X*) Transaction Pubs.

Cuban Military: Under Castro. Ed. by Jaime Suchlicki. 200p. 1989. pap. 18.95 (*0-935501-15-0*, CP311) U Miami N-S Ctr.

Cuban Minority in the U. S. The Preliminary & Final Reports on Need Identification & Program Evaluation, 2 vols., Set. Cuban National Planning Council et al. 1981. 82.95 (*0-405-13199-2*) Ayer.

Cuban Minority in the United States, 2 vols., Set. Ed. by Carlos E. Cortes. LC 79-17461. (Hispanics in the United States Ser.). (Illus.). 1981. lib. bdg. 41.95 (*0-405-13174-7*) Ayer.

Cuban Missile Crisis. Susan M. Clinton. LC 93-12689. (Cornerstones of Freedom Ser.). (Illus.). 32p. (J). (gr. 3-6). 1993. lib. bdg. 12.98 (*0-516-06667-6*); pap. 4.95 (*0-516-46667-4*) Childrens.

***Cuban Missile Crisis.** Eubank. (Anvil Ser.). 1997. pap. write for info. (*0-89464-890-X*) Krieger.

***Cuban Missile Crisis.** Mark J. White. 256p. 1995. 45.00 (*0-333-63052-1*) NYU Pr.

Cuban Missile Crisis. rev. ed. Ed. by Robert A. Divine. (Illus.). 364p. (C). 1988. pap. text ed. 11.95 (*0-910129-86-X*) Wiener Pubs Inc.

Cuban Missile Crisis. 2nd rev. ed. Ed. by Robert A. Divine. (Illus.). 364p. (C). 1988. text ed. 29.95 (*0-910129-15-0*) Wiener Pubs Inc.

Cuban Missile Crisis: President Kennedy's Address to the Nation, October 22, 1962. Ed. by National Archives Staff. LC 88-600062. (Milestone Documents Ser.). (Illus.). 38p. 1988. pap. text ed. 3.50 (*0-911333-59-2*, 200113) National Archives & Recs.

Cuban Missile Crisis: U. S. Deliberations & Negotiations at the Edge of the Precipice. Gabrielle S. Brussel. (Pew Case Studies in International Affairs). 50p. (C). 1992. pap. text ed. 2.50 (*1-56927-334-0*) Geo U Inst Dplmcy.

Cuban Missile Crisis of Nineteen Sixty-Two: Needless or Necessary? William J. Medland. LC 87-36025. 175p. 1988. text ed. 49.95 (*0-275-92844-6*, C2844, Praeger Pubs) Greenwood.

Cuban Missile Crisis Revisited. James A. Nathan. LC 91-47951. 304p. 1992. text ed. 39.95 (*0-312-06069-6*) St Martin.

Cuban Missile Crisis Revisited. Ed. by James A. Nathan. 304p. 1993. text ed. 17.95 (*0-312-09725-5*) St Martin.

Cuban Missile Crisis, 1962. 356p. (Orig.). (C). 1993. pap. text ed. 75.00 (*1-56806-514-0*) Diane Pub.

Cuban Missile Crisis, 1962: A National Security Archive Documents Reader. Ed. by Laurence Chang & Peter Kornbluh. LC 92-53734. (Illus.). 448p. 1992. 25.00 (*1-56584-019-4*) New Press NY.

Cuban Missile Crisis, 1962: Canadian Involvement Reconsidered. Peter T. Haydon. (Illus.). 200p. (Orig.). (C). 1993. pap. text ed. 40.00x (*1-56806-413-6*) Diane Pub.

Cuban Missile Crisis, 1962: The Making of U. S. Policy, 1962, Guide & Index, Set: Vol. 1, & 2. National Security Archive Staff & Chadwyck-Healey Staff. Ed. by Laurence Chang et al. (Making of U. S. Policy Ser.). (Illus.). (C). 1990. Set: Vol. 1, 940p.; Vol. 2, 1220p. 900.00 (*0-89887-071-2*) Chadwyck-Healey.

Cuban Missle Crisis: An Analysis of Soviet Calculations & Behavior. Arnold L. Horelick. (Reprint Series in Social Sciences). (C). 1993. reprint ed. pap. text ed. 1.00 (*0-8290-3755-1*, PS-393) Irvington.

Cuban Nationalization: The Demise of Foreign Private Property. Michael W. Gordon. LC 76-17458. 239p. 1976. lib. bdg. 42.00 (*0-930342-13-5*, 300440) W S Hein.

Cuban Politics: The Revolutionary Experiment. Rhoda P. Rabking. LC 90-38808. (Politics in Latin America Ser.). 256p. 1990. text ed. 49.95 (*0-275-93739-9*, C3739, Praeger Pubs) Greenwood.

***Cuban Refugee Program: The Early Years, 1959 - 1965.** Ricardo Nunez-Portuondo. LC 94-92122. 135p. (Orig.). 1995. pap. 16.50 (*0-9641879-7-3*) Cultural Pub.

Cuban Refugee Programs: An Original Anthology. Ed. by Carlos E. Cortes. LC 79-6237. (Hispanics in the United States Ser.). (Orig.). 1981. lib. bdg. 91.95 (*0-405-13184-4*) Ayer.

Cuban Revolution. Earle Rice, Jr. (World History Ser.). (Illus.). 128p. (J). (gr. 5-9). 1995. lib. bdg. 16.95 (*1-56006-275-4*, 2754) Lucent Bks.

Cuban Revolution: Origins, Course, & Legacy. Marifeli Perez-Stable. LC 93-19990. 256p. (C). 1993. 23.00 (*0-19-508406-3*) OUP.

Cuban Revolution: Origins, Course, & Legacy. Marifeli Perez-Stable. LC 93-19990. 256p. (C). 1993. pap. 14.95 (*0-19-508407-1*) OUP.

Cuban Revolution & the United States: A Chronological History. Jane Franklin. (Illus.). 316p. 1992. 34.95 (*1-875284-42-7*, Pub. by Ocean Pr AT); pap. 15.95 (*1-875284-26-5*, Pub. by Ocean Pr AT) Talman.

Cuban Revolution at Thirty: A Conference by the Cuban American National Foundation. Cuban American National Foundation Staff. 1989. 4.00 (*0-685-37919-1*) Cuban Amer Natl Fndtn.

Cuban Revolution in Crisis: From Managing Socialism to Managing Survival. Frank T. Fitzgerald. 288p. 1994. 34.00 (*0-85345-889-8*); pap. 16.00 (*0-85345-890-1*) Monthly Rev.

Cuban Revolution into the 1990s: Cuban Perspectives. Ed. by Centro De Estudios Sobre America Staff. 197p. (C). 1992. text ed. 61.00 (*0-8133-1186-1*); pap. text ed. 19.95 (*0-8133-1187-X*) Westview.

Cuban Rural Society in the Nineteenth Century: The Social & Economic History of Monoculture in Matanzas. Laird W. Bergad. (Illus.). 507p. 1990. text ed. 69.50 (*0-691-07816-5*) Princeton U Pr.

***Cuban Slave Market, 1790-1880.** Laird W. Bergad et al. (Cambridge Latin American Studies: No. 79). (Illus.). 272p. (C). 1995. 59.95 (*0-521-48059-0*) Cambridge U Pr.

Cuban State Budget: Concepts & Measurement. Jorge F. Perez-Lopez. 51p. pap. 10.95 (*0-935501-38-X*) U Miami N-S Ctr.

Cuban Studies. Ed. by Jorge I. Dominguez. LC 75-649635. (Latin American Ser.: Vol. 22). 328p. (C). 1992. text ed. 39.95 (*0-8229-3723-9*) U of Pittsburgh Pr.

Cuban Studies, Vol. 16. Ed. by Carmelo Mesa-Lago. LC 75-649635. 302p. 1986. 39.95 (*0-8229-3540-6*) U of Pittsburgh Pr.

Cuban Studies, Vol. 17. Ed. by Carmelo Mesa-Lago et al. LC 75-649635. 255p. 1987. 39.95 (*0-8229-3562-7*) U of Pittsburgh Pr.

Cuban Studies, Vol. 18. Ed. by Carmelo Mesa-Lago. LC 75-649635. (Latin American Ser.). 261p. (C). 1988. 39.95 (*0-8229-3593-7*) U of Pittsburgh Pr.

Cuban Studies, Vol. 19. Ed. by Carmelo Mesa-Lago. LC 75-649635. (Latin American Ser.). 384p. 1990. 39.95 (*0-8229-3626-7*) U of Pittsburgh Pr.

Cuban Studies, Vol. 20. Ed. by Carmelo Mesa-Lago. LC 75-649635. (Latin American Ser.). 256p. 1990. 39.95 (*0-8229-3649-6*) U of Pittsburgh Pr.

Cuban Studies, Vol. 21. Ed. by Louis A. Perez, Jr. LC 75-64935. (Latin American Ser.). 320p. 1992. 39.95 (*0-8229-3691-7*) U of Pittsburgh Pr.

Cuban Studies since the Revolution. Ed. by Damian J. Fernandez. 352p. (C). 1992. lib. bdg. 42.95 (*0-8130-1124-8*) U Press Fla.

Cuban Studies XXIII. Jorge Perez-Lopez. 288p. (C). 1994. text ed. 39.95 (*0-8229-3765-4*) U of Pittsburgh Pr.

Cuban Studies XXIV. Ed. by Enrico M. Santi. 256p. (C). 1995. 39.95 (*0-8229-3866-9*) U of Pittsburgh Pr.

***Cuban Studies XXV.** Ed. by Louis A. Perez, Jr. (Latin American Ser.). 296p. (C). 1996. 39.95x (*0-8229-3911-8*) U of Pittsburgh Pr.

C

An Asterisk (*) at the beginning of an entry indicates that the title is appearing in BIP for the first time.

C

An Asterisk (*) at the beginning of an entry indicates that the title is appearing in BIP for the first time.

1733

Cuento de un Pez Grande. Joanne Wylie. Tr. by Lada Kratky. LC 83-7449. (Spanish Fishy Fish Stories Ser.). (Illus.). 32p. (SPA.). (J). (ps-2). 1984. pap. 3.95 (*0-516-52982-X*) Childrens.

Cuento del Conejito Benjamin. Beatrix Potter. (Original Peter Rabbit Bks.). (Illus.). 64p. (SPA.). (J). 1988. 5.95 (*0-7232-3558-9*) Warne.

***Cuento Del Conejito Benjamin: Libro De Cuentos En Colores - Por Beatrix Potter, Ilustrado Por Anna Pomaska.** Beatrix Potter & Anna Pomaska. Tr. by Paul F. DeZardain. LC 94-43851. (Dover Little Activity Bks.). (Illus.). 32p. (SPA.). (J). 1995. pap. text ed. 1.00 (*0-486-28536-7*) Dover.

Cuento Del Conejo Pedrin (The Tale of Peter Rabbit) Beatrix Potter. (Pudgy Pal Board Bks.). (Illus.). 18p. (SPA.). (J). (ps). 1995. bds. 3.95 (*0-448-40847-3*, G&D) Putnam Pub Group.

Cuento del Gato Tomas. Beatrix Potter. (Original Peter Rabbit Bks.). (Illus.). 64p. (SPA.). (J). 1988. 4.95 (*0-7232-3565-1*) Warne.

Cuento Del Gato y Otras Poesias Favoritas: Blue Set. (Dias y Dias de Poesia Ser.). (Illus.). 40p. (Orig.). (SPA.). (J). (ps-2). 1992. pap. text ed. 7.00 (*1-56334-155-7*) Hampton-Brown.

Cuento Del Gato y Otras Poesias Favoritas: Shared Reading Charts, Blue Set. (Dias y Dias de Poesia Ser.). (Illus.). 36p. (SPA.). 1992. 99.95 (*1-56334-153-0*); teacher ed (*1-56334-154-9*) Hampton-Brown.

Cuento Del Manzano, Vol. 9: Pasitos Spanish Language Development Books. Darlyne F. Schott. (Pasitos Hacia la Lectura Ser.). 16p. (J). (gr. k-1). 1990. pap. text ed. 11.00 (*1-56537-058-9*) D F Schott Educ.

Cuento Del Rey Pancho y el Primer Reloj. Norbert Lopez. LC 70-108730. (Illus.). 32p. (J). (gr. 2-7). 1970. lib. bdg. 9.95 (*0-87783-010-X*); audio 7.94 (*0-685-03700-2*) Oddo.

Cuento Del Rey Pancho y el Primer Reloj. deluxe ed. Norbert Lopez. LC 70-108730. (Illus.). 32p. (J). (gr. 2-7). 1970. pap. 3.94 (*0-87783-104-1*) Oddo.

Cuento Gracioso de Peces (A Funny Fish Story) Joanne Wylie & David Wylie. LC 83-24058. (Fishy Fish Stories Concept Bks.). (Illus.). 32p. (ENG & SPA.). (J). (ps-2). 1989. lib. bdg. 11.55 (*0-516-32986-3*); pap. 3.95 (*0-516-52986-2*) Childrens.

Cuento Hispanico: A Graded Literary Anthology. 4th ed. Ed. by Edward J. Mullen & John F. Garganigo. 1993. pap. text ed. write for info. (*0-07-043955-9*) McGraw.

Cuento Mas - Just One More: Combination Big Book Set. (Illus.). (ENG & SPA.). 1991. 337.00 (*1-56334-131-X*) Hampton-Brown.

Cuento Mexicano Index. Comp. by Herbert H. Hoffman. LC 79-127156. 600p. 1978. 32.00 (*0-89537-007-7*) Headway Pubns.

Cuento Para la Hora De Dormir De Big Bird. Rick Wetzel & Maggie Swanson. Tr. by Rita Guibert. LC 92-3815. (Illus.). 32p. (SPA.). (J). (ps-3). 1992. pap. 2.25 (*0-679-83500-8*) Random Bks Yng Read.

Cuento Verdadero de los Tres Cerditos. A. Wolf. (J). (ps-3). 1991. 14.95 (*0-670-84162-5*) Viking Child Bks.

Cuentos. Maruxa De Nunez de Villavicencio. 237p. (Orig.). (SPA.). 1987. pap. 9.00 (*84-359-0519-5*, Pub. by Editorial Playor SP) Ediciones.

Cuentos. Myrna Nieves. 100p. (Orig.). (SPA.). 1991. pap. 8.00 (*0-685-26448-3*) Atabex Collection.

Cuentos: An Anthology of Short Stories. Lina E. Moore. iii, 131p. (Orig.). 1985. pap. text ed. 7.50 (*971-10-0173-X*, Pub. by New Day Pub PH) Cellar.

Cuentos: Stories by Latinas. Ed. by Alma Gomez et al. 241p. (Orig.). 1983. pap. 9.95 (*0-913175-01-3*) Kitchen Table.

Cuentos: Tales from the Hispanic Southwest. Jose Griego & Maestas. Tr. by Rudolfo Anaya. (Illus.). 1981. pap. 11.95 (*0-89013-111-2*) Museum NM Pr.

Cuentos Alegres. 3rd ed. M. B. Rodriguez. LC 78-153486. (C). 1972. pap. text ed. 22.75 (*0-03-080276-8*) HB Coll Pubs.

Cuentos Americanos. 3rd ed. Ed. by Donald D. Walsh & Lawrence B. Kiddle. (SPA.). (C). 1970. pap. text ed. 14.95 (*0-393-09907-5*) Norton.

Cuentos Argentinos de Misterio. Ed. by E. Dale Carter, Jr. & Joe Bas. LC 68-13434. (Orig.). (gr. 9 up). 1968. pap. text ed. 8.95 (*0-89197-119-X*) Irvington.

Cuentos Blancos y Negros. Jose Sanchez-Boudy. LC 82-83768. (Coleccion Caniqui Ser.). 107p. (Orig.). (SPA.). 1983. pap. 6.00 (*0-89729-321-5*) Ediciones.

Cuentos Chicanos: A Short Story Anthology. Ed. by Rudolfo A. Anaya & Antonio Marquez. LC 84-13066. 194p. 1984. reprint ed. pap. 13.95 (*0-8263-0772-8*) U of NM Pr.

Cuentos Completos. Alejo Carpentier. 219p. (SPA.). 1980. 8.95 (*0-8288-7078-0*) Fr & Eur.

Cuentos Completos. Oscar Wilde. (Nueva Austral Ser.: No. 60). (SPA.). 1991. pap. text ed. 24.95x (*84-239-1860-2*) Elliots Bks.

Cuentos Contemporaneos Espanoles: Advanced Intermediate Through Advanced. Juana A. Hernandez & Edenia Guillermo. 176p. (SPA.). (YA). 1993. pap. 19.95 (*0-8442-7313-9*, Natl Textbk) NTC Pub Grp.

Cuentos Cubanos. Frank Rivera. LC 92-73682. (Coleccion Caniqui Ser.). (Illus.). 75p. (Orig.). (SPA.). 1992. pap. 9.95 (*0-89729-653-2*) Ediciones.

Cuentos de Ambos Mundos. Mario B. Rodriguez et al. Ed. by Sherman H. Eoff. (Graded Spanish Readers Ser.: Bk. 2). (C). 1972. pap. 15.56 (*0-395-04125-2*) HM.

Cuentos de Andersen. (SPA.). 9.95 (*84-241-5629-3*) E Torres & Sons.

Cuentos de Apolo. 3rd ed. Hilda Perera. (Illus.). 103p. (SPA.). (YA). (gr. 6 up). 1975. pap. 5.00 (*0-89729-438-6*) Ediciones.

***Cuentos de Eva Luna.** Isabel Allende. (SPA.). 1995. pap. 8.95 (*0-06-095131-1*, Harp PBks) HarpC.

Cuentos de Eva Luna. 4th ed. Isabel Allende. 256p. (SPA.). 1991. pap. 24.95 (*0-7859-5019-2*) Fr & Eur.

Cuentos De la Abeja Encinta. Marigloria Palma. LC 76-6153. (UPREX, Ficcion Ser.: No. 48). (Orig.). (SPA.). 1976. pap. 1.50 (*0-8477-0048-8*) U of PR Pr.

Cuentos de la Alhambra. Washington Irving. Ed. by Antonio Gallego Morell. (Nueva Austral Ser.: Vol. 209). (SPA.). 1991. pap. text ed. 24.95x (*84-239-7209-7*) Elliots Bks.

Cuentos de la Ninez. Jose Sanchez-Boudy. LC 83-81036. (Coleccion Caniqui Ser.). 79p. (Orig.). (SPA.). 1983. pap. 6.00 (*0-89729-331-2*) Ediciones.

Cuentos de Lucha y Alegria. (SPA.). 1993. 5.25 (*0-88336-629-0*); audio 16.00 (*0-88336-668-1*) New Readers.

Cuentos de Mario Benedetti. Corina S. Mathieu. LC 83-48144. (American University Studies: Romance Languages & Literature: Ser. II, Vol. 3). 112p. 1983. pap. text ed. 12.65 (*0-8204-0015-7*) P Lang Pubs.

***Cuentos De Mary y Tierra.** Ed. by Carmen R. Izcoa. (Illus.). 96p. (SPA.). (J). 1995. write for info. (*0-929157-30-3*) Ediciones Huracan.

Cuentos De Nueva York. Angel Castro. 1973. pap. 2.50 (*84-399-0644-7*) Ediciones.

Cuentos Del Caribe. Anita Arroyo. LC 91-77116. (Coleccion Caniqui Ser.). 64p. (Orig.). (SPA.). 1992. pap. 9.95 (*0-89729-630-3*) Ediciones.

Cuentos del Pobre Diablo. Natalie Babbitt. (J). (gr. 4-7). 1994. pap. 4.95 (*0-374-41624-9*, Mirasol) FS&G.

Cuentos del Pobre Diablo. Natalie Babbitt. (J). (gr. 4-7). 1994. 13.00 (*0-374-31769-0*, Mirasol) FS&G.

Cuentos Espanoles De Colorado y Nuevo Mejico: Spanish Tales from Colorado & New Mexico, 2 vols., 1. Juan B. Rael. Ed. by Richard M. Dorson. LC 77-70617. (International Folklore Ser.). 1977. lib. bdg. 58.95 (*0-405-10120-1*) Ayer.

Cuentos Espanoles De Colorado y Nuevo Mejico: Spanish Tales from Colorado & New Mexico, 2 vols., 2. Juan B. Rael. Ed. by Richard M. Dorson. LC 77-70617. (International Folklore Ser.). 1977. lib. bdg. 58.95 (*0-405-10121-X*) Ayer.

Cuentos Espanoles De Colorado y Nuevo Mejico: Spanish Tales from Colorado & New Mexico, 2 vols., Set. Juan B. Rael. Ed. by Richard M. Dorson. LC 77-70617. (International Folklore Ser.). 1977. lib. bdg. 116.95 (*0-405-10119-8*) Ayer.

Cuentos Faciles de Hoy y de Ayer. Pittaro. 1973. pap. text ed. 7.95 (*0-88334-059-3*, 76059) Longman.

Cuentos Fantasticos. Jaime Martinez Tolentino. LC 81-10292. (UPREX, Estudios Literarios Ser.: No. 62). 70p. 1983. pap. 2.00 (*0-8477-0062-3*) U of PR Pr.

Cuentos from My Childhood, New Mexico. Paulette Atencio. 1991. 19.95 (*0-89013-225-9*); pap. 11.95 (*0-89013-226-7*) Museum NM Pr.

***Cuentos-Granados-Piano.** 1994. 9.95 (*0-614-01277-5*, UM20943) Omnibus NY.

Cuentos Hispanos de los Estado Unidos. Ed. by Julian Olivares. LC 92-21056. 350p. 1993. pap. 15.00 (*1-55885-045-7*) Arte Publico.

Cuentos Infantiles Mas Famosos Del Mundo. Editorial America, S. A. Staff. Ed. by Maria E. Del Real. (Illus.). 464p. (Orig.). (SPA.). (J). (ps-8). 1990. pap. write for info. (*0-944499-93-7*) Editorial Amer.

Cuentos Negros De Cuba. 3rd ed. Lydia Cabrera. (Coleccion del Chichereku). 175p. (SPA.). 1993. pap. 16.00 (*0-89729-671-0*) Ediciones.

Cuentos Negros de Lydia Cabrera: Un Estudio Morfologico. Mariela Gutierrez. LC 86-80151. (Coleccion Ebano y Canela Ser.). 148p. (Orig.). (SPA.). 1986. pap. 12.00 (*0-89729-389-4*) Ediciones.

Cuentos Olidados De Alfonso Hernandez Cata. Jorge Febles. LC 81-52007. (Senda Antological Ser.). 250p. (Orig.). (SPA.). (C). 1981. pap. 10.95 (*0-918454-27-1*) Senda Nueva.

Cuentos Panamenos: Stories of Struggle & Hope in Rural Panama. Richard A. Bower. LC 92-20850. 1993. pap. 11.95 (*0-377-00249-6*) Friendship Pr.

Cuentos Para la Medianoche. Luis A. Casas. LC 91-78013. (Coleccion Caniqui Ser.). (Illus.). 189p. (Orig.). (SPA.). 1992. pap. 18.00 (*0-89729-632-X*) Ediciones.

Cuentos para Lectores Complices. Antonio Pereira. (Nueva Austral Ser.: Vol. 101). (SPA.). 1991. pap. text ed. 24.95x (*84-239-1901-3*) Elliots Bks.

Cuentos Ticos: Short Stories of Costa Rica. 3rd ed. Ricardo Fernandez Guardia. Tr. by Gray Casement. LC 78-121540. (Short Story Index Reprint Ser.). 1977. 26.95 (*0-8369-3496-2*) Ayer.

Cuentos y Cronicas Cubanas. Jose M. Alvarez. LC 89-84624. (Coleccion Caniqui Ser.). 157p. (Orig.). (SPA.). 1991. pap. 15.00 (*0-89729-539-0*) Ediciones.

Cuentos y Leyendas de Mexico. Alfredo Ibarra. LC 78-67722. (Folktale Ser.). reprint ed. 28.00 (*0-404-16097-2*) AMS Pr.

Cuentos y Microcuentos. Guillermo I. Castillo-Feliu. LC 77-12972. 227p. (C). 1978. pap. text ed. 20.75 (*0-03-021796-2*) HB Coll Pubs.

Cuentos y Patranas. Juan A. Zunzunegui. Ed. by Rex E. Ballinger. LC 66-15549. (SPA.). 1966. pap. text ed. 6.95 (*0-89197-120-3*) Irvington.

Cuentos Yanquis. Angel Castro. 1972. pap. 2.50 (*0-89729-137-9*) Ediciones.

Cuerda Tensa. Luis Romero. LC 79-66063. 62p. 1979. pap. 12.00 (*0-89295-012-9*) Society Sp & Sp-Am.

Cuerpo De Cristo. Gary Teja. (SPA.). 1985. 5.60 (*1-55955-058-9*) CITE MI.

Cuerpo De Cristo: La Realidad: The Body of Crist: A Reality. Watchman Nee. (SPA.). 3.25 (*84-7645-269-1*, 223303, Pub. by Edit Clie SP) TSELF.

Cuerpo Herido de Cristo. Earl Paulk. Orig. Title: Wounded Body of Christ. 144p. (Orig.). (SPA.). 1985. pap. 3.50 (*0-917595-05-X*) Kingdom Pubs.

Cuerpo Humano - The Human Body. Ed. by Maria Puncel & Juan J. Basquez. Tr. by Jose M. Secanell. (Diccionarios Visuales Altea Ser. - Visual Dictionary Ser.). (Illus.). 63p. (SPA.). (YA). (gr. 5-12). 1992. write for info. (*84-372-4528-1*) Santillana.

Cuervo Tales. Robert Roper. LC 93-145. 256p. 1993. 19.95 (*0-89919-988-7*) Ticknor & Fields.

Cues & Comprehension: Level 1. Kitty Wehrli. (Ann Arbor Tracking Program Ser.). (J). (gr. 2). 1976. student ed 10.00 (*0-87879-743-2*, Ann Arbor Div) Acad Therapy.

Cues & Comprehension: Level 2. Kitty Wehrli. (Ann Arbor Tracking Program Ser.). (J). (gr. 2). 1976. student ed 10.00 (*0-87879-744-0*, Ann Arbor Div) Acad Therapy.

Cues & Comprehension: Level 3. Kitty Wehrli. (Ann Arbor Tracking Program Ser.). (J). (gr. 2). 1976. student ed 10.00 (*0-87879-745-9*, Ann Arbor Div) Acad Therapy.

Cues & Comprehension: Level 4. Kitty Wehrli. (J). (gr. 2). 1976. student ed 10.00 (*0-87879-746-7*, Ann Arbor Div) Acad Therapy.

Cues & Signals in Math, Book One: Number Tracking, Reusable Edition. Kitty Wehrli. 48p. (J). (gr. 1 up). 1971. 10.00 (*0-87879-757-2*, Ann Arbor Div) Acad Therapy.

Cues & Signals 1: A Self-Instruction Workbook for Visual Accuracy. Ed. by B. Steele. (J). (gr. 3). 1971. student ed 10.00 (*0-87879-752-1*, Ann Arbor Div) Acad Therapy.

Cues & Signals 2: A Self-Instruction Workbook for Visual Accuracy. Ed. by B. Steele & K. Wehrli. (J). (gr. 3). 1971. student ed 10.00 (*0-87879-753-X*, Ann Arbor Div) Acad Therapy.

Cues & Signals 3: A Self-Instruction Workbook for Visual Accuracy. Ed. by B. Steele & K. Wehrli. (J). (gr. 3). 1971. student ed 10.00 (*0-87879-754-8*, Ann Arbor Div) Acad Therapy.

Cues & Signals 4: A Self-Instruction Workbook for Visual Accuracy. Ed. by B. Steele & K. Wehrli. (J). (gr. 3). 1971. student ed 10.00 (*0-87879-755-6*, Ann Arbor Div) Acad Therapy.

Cuestion Cubana en la OEA y la Crisis del Sistema Interamericano. F. V. Garcia-Amador. 139p. (SPA.). 1987. 11.95 (*0-935501-08-8*, CP305) U Miami N-S Ctr.

***Cuestion De los Animales (The Animals Issue) Teoria De la Moral Aplicada (Moral Theory in Practice)** Peter Carruthers. Tr. by Jose M. Perzaao. 272p. (SPA.). (C). 1995. pap. write for info. (*0-521-47834-0*) Cambridge U Pr.

Cuestion de Tiempo: Relatos. Carlos Mellizo. LC 90-86071. (Coleccion Hispanica - Narrativa Ser.: No. 1). 93p. (Orig.). (SPA.). 1991. pap. 9.95 (*0-89729-591-9*) Ediciones.

***Cuestiones Relativas al Desarrollo - Development Issues: Exposiciones Presentadas en la XLVIII Reunion del Comite Para el Desarrollo, Celebrada en la Ciudad de Washington, el 26 de Abril de 1994 - Presentations to the 48th Meeting of the Development Committee, Washington, D.C., April 26, 1994.** World Bank Staff. 184p. (SPA.). 1994. 9.95 (*0-8213-2875-1*) World Bank.

Cueva de la Pala Chica: A Burial Cave in the Guaymas Region of Coastal Sonora, Mexico. Keith A. Dixon. Ed. by Ronald Spores et al. (Publications in Anthropology: No. 38). 97p. (Orig.). 1990. pap. 12.50 (*0-935462-29-5*) Vanderbilt Pubns.

Cueva Pintada: Documenting the Rock Paintings at National Register Site CA-MNT-256. Gary S. Breschini & Trudy Haversat. vi, 32p. (Orig.). (C). 1980. pap. text ed. 2.50 (*1-55567-012-1*) Coyote Press.

***Cuff Jewelry: A Historical Account for Collectors & Dealers. Howard L. Bell, Jr. (Illus.). 115p. (Orig.). 1995. pap. text ed. 35.00 (*0-9646080-0-6*) Bells MO. Like most hobbies, Cuff Link collecting is addictive. Fortunately, it is an affordable hobby to date. CUFF JEWELRY: A HISTORICAL ACCOUNT FOR COLLECTORS & DEALERS is the ONLY price guide for Cuff Jewelry. It is heartily endorsed by the National Cuff Link Society. The book contains 1,225 historic EXAMPLES, United States & Foreign in 61 PAGES OF COLOR photographs of virtually every type of link & closure ever manufactured. Included are cuff buttons, cuff links, bachelor's buttons, collar buttons, shirt studs, tie bars & pins, stick pins, hair jewelry & Arts & Crafts examples. This is a thoroughly researched reference for the novice or the knowledgeable - making each reader an expert. The commentary about metals used in manufacturing & the sketches about gemstones are well organized & easily interpreted. The earliest illustrated pair in CUFF JEWELRY dates to 1820 & was found in England. The most recent style is called "wrap-around" & is available at a nominal cost at flea markets & garage sales. A brief discussion gives highlights of the Georgian, Victorian, Art Nouveau, Art Deco & Contemporary periods. The Appendix gives the chronology of Cuff Jewelry by illustration & a listing of U.S. & Foreign manufacturers who produced examples. A large segment of the population will be interested in this publication because Cuff Jewelry has mirrored the economy, lifestyle & fashion of the past 175 years. To order contact: Bell's Books, 6500 Claremont, Raytown, MO 64133. 816-358-1412.**
Publisher Provided Annotation.

Cuff Links. Susan Jonas & Marilyn Nissenson. (Illus.). 112p. 1991. 35.00 (*0-8109-3168-0*) Abrams.

Cuidade del Hombre Desnudo Que Te Ofrece Su Camisa. Harvey MacKay. 1987. pap. text ed. 17.95 (*0-07-104030-7*) McGraw.

Cuidado con los Falaces! John F. MacArthur. Orig. Title: Beware the Pretenders. 102p. (SPA.). pap. 2.99 (*0-8254-1453-9*) Kregel.

Cuidado de Dios. Edna C. Horton & Roberta Hadley. Tr. by Emma Z. Villasenor. (Illus.). (J). (gr. 1-3). 1989. reprint ed. pap. 1.40 (*0-311-38555-9*) Casa Bautista.

Cuidado Pastoral: El Desde la Cuna Hasta la Tumba. J. A. Hightower, Jr. Tr. by Edgar Morales. 192p. (Orig.). (SPA.). 1986. pap. 5.95 (*0-311-11045-2*) Casa Bautista.

Cuidado Pastoral de la Iglesia. C. W. Brister. Tr. by D. Tinao et al. Orig. Title: Pastoral Care in the Church. 226p. (SPA.). 1988. reprint ed. pap. 6.75 (*0-311-42040-0*) Casa Bautista.

Cuidado! Patos Cruzando. Uriel Ofek. Tr. by C. C. Writer & Lisa C. Nielsen. (Hippy Ser.). (Illus.). 24p. (Orig.). (SPA.). (J). (ps). 1992. pap. text ed. 3.00 (*1-56134-155-X*) Dushkin Pub.

Cuidado Prenatal y Preparacion. National Association for Childbirth Education Staff. (Avery's Childbirth Education Ser.). (Illus.). 104p. (SPA.). 1984. spiral bd. 7.95 (*0-89529-238-6*) Avery Pub.

Cuidando a Rosita. Lynn Salem & Josie Stewart. Tr. by Mariana Robles. (Illus.). 8p. (J). (gr. 1). Date not set. pap. 3.50 (*1-880612-23-2*) Seedling Pubns.

Cuidate: The Consumer's Guide to Medical Care. 3rd ed. Donald M. Vickery & James F. Fries. 1988. pap. 16.30 (*0-201-08292-6*) Addison-Wesley.

Cuisenaire Alphabet Book. Maria Marolda. 64p. (J). (gr. k-4). 1980. pap. text ed. 8.95 (*0-914040-78-2*) Cuisenaire.

Cuisenaire Roddles: Games & Puzzles to Measure Thinking Skills. Estelle Dickens & Jeffrey Sellon. (Illus.). 28p. (J). (gr. 3-12). 1981. pap. text ed. 10.95 (*0-914040-90-1*) Cuisenaire.

***Cuisine a la Valeur: The Art of Steam Cooking.** Jacques Maniere. Tr. & Adapt. by Stephanie Lyness. LC 94-32732. 1995. write for info. (*0-688-10507-6*) Morrow.

Cuisine Actuelle. Victor Gielisse. 208p. 1992. 21.95 (*0-87833-786-5*) Taylor Pub.

Cuisine & Forte: Scottish Cases in Materials in Commercial Law, U.K. D. J. Cuisine & A. Forte. 1987. pap. 67.00 (*0-406-10870-6*) Butterworth Legal Pubs.

Cuisine Cajun. Jude Theriot. LC 86-774. 249p. (Orig.). 1986. 15.95 (*0-88289-806-X*); spiral bd. 14.95 (*0-88289-489-7*) Pelican.

Cuisine Courante. Bruno Loubet. (Illus.). 160p. 1992. 39.95 (*1-85165-652-9*, Pub. by Pavilion UK) Trafalgar.

***Cuisine Courante.** Bruno Loubet. (Illus.). 160p. 1995. 29.95 (*1-85145-819-0*, Pub. by Pavilion UK) Trafalgar.

Cuisine Creole. Lafcadio Hearn. (Notable American Authors Ser.). 1992. reprint ed. lib. bdg. 75.00 (*0-7812-3070-5*) Rprt Serv.

Cuisine Die Chine see Oriental Express: Chinese Menus for the Food Processor

Cuisine Economique. Jacques Pepin. 1992. 22.00 (*0-688-11145-9*) Morrow.

Cuisine Francaise des Premieres Annees de l'Amerique du Nord. Patricia B. Mitchell. Tr. by Mary L. Black. 1992. pap. 4.00 (*0-925117-59-5*) Mitchells.

Cuisine Grandmere: From Brittany, Normandy, Picardy & Flanders. Jenny Baker. (Illus.). 262p. 1994. 22.95 (*0-571-16877-9*) Faber & Faber.

***Cuisine Grandmere: From Brittany, Normandy, Picardy & Flanders.** Jenny Baker. (Illus.). 262p. 1995. pap. 12.95 (*0-571-16878-7*) Faber & Faber.

Cuisine Imaginaire: Delicious Menus for Vegetarian Entertaining. Roselyne Masselin. (Illus.). 224p. 1994. 27.95 (*0-563-36413-0*, BBC-Parkwest) Parkwest Pubns.

Cuisine Is Poetry. Pat'rick N. Pugh. LC 93-92597. 1995. pap. 7.95 (*1-883184-12-6*) PNP.

Cuisine le Marvin. Marvin M. Chomain. 148p. (C). 1992. pap. 11.99 (*1-85594-031-0*, Pub. by Attic IE) InBook.

***Cuisine of Armenia.** (Hippocrene International Cookbooks Ser.). 400p. 1995. pap. 11.95 (*0-7818-0417-5*) Hippocrene Bks.

Cuisine of California. California Restaurant Association Staff. LC 92-19110. 1992. 10.95 (*0-88289-936-8*) Pelican.

Cuisine of California. Diane R. Worthington. LC 83-8491. (Illus.). 336p. (Orig.). 1983. pap. 13.95 (*0-87477-287-7*) J P Tarcher.

Cuisine of China. Sharon W. Hoy. LC 80-70735. (Illus.). 310p. 1982. 15.95 (*0-9607508-1-9*) Benshaw Pub.

Cuisine of Sacrifice among the Greeks. Marcel Detienne & Jean-Pierre Vernant. Tr. by Paula Wissing. LC 88-39143. (Illus.). 304p. 1989. lib. bdg. 39.95 (*0-226-14351-1*); pap. text ed. 15.95 (*0-226-14353-8*) U Ch Pr.

Cuisine of the Rain: Oregon's Extraordinary Foods & Recipes. Karen Brooks. LC 92-34431. 1993. pap. 14.38 (*0-201-63282-9*) Addison-Wesley.

Cuisine of the Sun: Classical French Cooking from Nice & Provence. Mireille Johnston. LC 78-21922. (Illus.). 1979. pap. 8.95 (*0-394-72824-6*, Vin) Random.

An Asterisk (*) at the beginning of an entry indicates that the title is appearing in BIP for the first time.

Cuisine of the Water Gods: Mexican Seafood & Vegetable Cookery. Quintana. 1994. 25.00 (0-671-74898-X) S&S Trade.

Cuisine of Venice. Hedy Giusti-Lanham & Andrea Dodi. LC 78-8539. 1978. 21.95 (0-8120-5138-6) Barron.

***Cuisine on the Nile: Vegetarian Lunch Hour Favorites, 2.** Menkh-t UrTa. 104p. 1993. pap. write for info. (0-9639594-1-7) Few Books.

***Cuisine on the Nile: Vegetarian Meal Favorites.** rev. ed. Menkh-t UrTa. 100p. 1994. pap. write for info. (0-9639594-0-9) Few Books.

Cuisine Rapid. Pierre Franey & Bryan Miller. (Illus.). 416p. 1989. 22.50 (0-8129-1746-4, Times Bks) Random.

Cuisine Sante: The New French Cooking for Healthy Gourmet Eating. Christophe Buey. (Illus.). 192p. 1991. 9.99 (0-517-02633-3) Random Hse Value.

***Cuisine, Texas: A Multiethnic Feast.** Joanne Smith. LC 94-34312. 1995. 29.95 (0-292-77682-9) U of Tex Pr.

Cuisines of Asia: Nine Great Oriental Cuisines by Technique. Jennifer Brennan. (Illus.). 560p. 1989. pap. 15.95 (0-312-03977-8) St Martin.

Cuisines of Germany. Horst Scharfenberg. 1989. 24.95 (0-671-63197-7) S&S Trade.

Cuisines of Mexico. rev. ed. Diana Kennedy. LC 85-45035. (Illus.). 320p. 1989. reprint ed. pap. 18.00 (0-06-091561-7, PL) HarpC.

Cuisines of Southeast Asia: A Culinary Journey Through Thailand, Myanmar, Laos, Vietnam, Malaysia, Singapore, Indonesia, & the Philippines. Gwenda L. Hyman. 208p. 1993. pap. text ed. 14.95 (0-471-58249-2) Wiley.

Cuisines of Southeast Asia: Thai, Vietnamese, Indonesian, Burmese & More. Jay Harlow. LC 93-37929. (California Culinary Academy Ser.). 128p. 1994. pap. 11. 95 (1-56426-042-9) Cole Group.

Cujo. Stephen King. 272p. 1994. pap. 14.95 (0-452-27328-5, Plume) NAL-Dutton.

Cujo. Stephen King. LC 81-50265. 324p. 1981. pap. 27.50 (0-670-45193-2) Viking Penguin.

Cujo. large type ed. Stephen King. LC 93-17717. 1993. 22. 95 (0-8161-5667-0) Hall.

Cujo. Stephen King. 320p. 1982. reprint ed. pap. 6.99 (0-451-16135-1, Sig) NAL-Dutton.

Culavamsa, 2 vols. Tr. by C. Mabel Richmers & Wilhelm Geiger. (C). 1930. 38.00 (0-86013-013-4, Pub. by Pali Text) Wisdom MA.

Culavamsa: Being the More Recent Part of Mahavamsa, 2 vols., Set. Tr. by C. Mabel Rickmers. (C). 1992. reprint ed. text ed. 42.00 (81-206-0430-X, Pub. by Asian Educ Servs II) S Asia.

***Culebra Cut.** Judith Head. LC 94-32023. (Adventures in Time Ser.). (J). 1995. write for info. (0-87614-878-X, Carolrhoda) Lerner Group.

***Culegere de Probleme de Analiza Matematica.** C. Dumitrescu & F. Smarandache. Ed. by R. Muller. (Illus.). 200p. (C). 1994. pap. 9.99 (1-879585-38-3) Xiquan Pubng.

Culhwch & Olwen: An Edition & Study of the Oldest Arthurian Tale. Ed. by Rachel Bromwich & D. Simon Evans. 226p. 1992. 50.00 (0-7083-1127-X, Pub. by U of Wales UK) Bks Intl VA.

Culicine Mosquitoes of the Philippines. Mercedes Delfinado. (Memoir Ser.: No. 7). (Illus.). 252p. 1966. 35. 00 (1-56665-005-4) Assoc Pubs FL.

Culicoides of Southeast Asia (Diptera: Ceratopogonidae) Willis W. Wirth & Alexander A. Hubert. (Memoir Ser.: No. 44). (Illus.). 508p. 1989. 65.00 (1-56665-043-7) Assoc Pubs FL.

Culinary & Salad Herbs. Eleanour S. Rohde. (Illus.). 128p. 1972. pap. 3.50 (0-486-22865-7) Dover.

***Culinary Art: Recipes from Great Chicago Restaurants.** Thomas Fredrickson. (Illus.). 120p. 1995. 29.95 (0-86559-131-8) Art Inst Chi.

Culinary Arts & Crafts, a Cookbook for Moms, Dads & Kids. Ed. by Myrna Ossin. (Illus.). 1984. pap. 12.00 (0-9613532-0-1) Park Maitland.

Culinary Arts Institute Encyclopedic Cookbook. rev. ed. Ed. by Culinary Arts Institute Staff & Ruth Berolzheimer. (Illus.). 1040p. 1988. pap. 18.00 (0-399-51388-4, Perigree Bks) Berkley Pub.

Culinary Arts, Pt. 1: Testbook. California Department of Education Staff. (Apprenticeship Instructional Materials Ser.). 76p. 1972. pap. 3.50 (0-8011-0533-1) Calif Education.

Culinary Arts, Pt. 1: Workbook. California Department of Education Staff. (Apprenticeship Instructional Materials Ser.). (Illus.). 168p. 1972. pap. 5.50 (0-8011-0532-3) Calif Education.

Culinary Arts, Pt. 2: Testbook. California Department of Education Staff. (Apprenticeship Instructional Materials Ser.). 72p. 1975. pap. 3.50 (0-8011-0536-6) Calif Education.

Culinary Arts, Pt. 2: Workbook. California Department of Education Staff. (Apprenticeship Instructional Materials Ser.). (Illus.). 144p. 1975. pap. 5.55 (0-8011-0535-8) Calif Education.

***Culinary Arts 1.** 2nd ed. Johnson & Wales. (Illus.). 352p. (C). 1988. text ed. write for info. (0-256-10558-8) Irwin.

***Culinary Arts 2.** 2nd ed. Johnson & Wales. (Illus.). 496p. (C). 1988. text ed. write for info. (0-256-10559-6) Irwin.

***Culinary Arts 3.** 2nd ed. Johnson & Wales. (Illus.). 464p. (C). 1988. text ed. write for info. (0-256-10560-X) Irwin.

***Culinary Arts 4.** 2nd ed. Johnson & Wales. (Illus.). 352p. (C). 1988. text ed. write for info. (0-256-10561-8) Irwin.

Culinary Careers. Mary D. Donovan. (Opportunities in Career Ser.). 1990. 13.95 (0-8442-8619-2, VGM Career Bks); pap. 10.95 (0-8442-8620-6, VGM Career Bks) NTC Pub Grp.

Culinary Classics & Improvisations. Michael Field. 256p. 1989. pap. 14.95 (0-88001-016-9) Ecco Pr.

Culinary Classics & Improvisations. Michael Field. LC 83-11542. (Cookbook Ser.). 270p. 1983. reprint ed. 18.50 (0-88001-015-0) Ecco Pr.

Culinary Counterpoint: Detroit Symphony Orchestra Cookbook. Ed. by Brenda J. Pangborn. LC 83-71434. (Illus.). 432p. (Orig.). 1983. pap. 12.00 (0-9611348-0-1) Detroit Symphony.

Culinary Cultures of the Middle East. Ed. by Richard Tapper & Sami Zubaida. 320p. 1994. text ed. 59.50 (1-85043-742-4, Pub. by I B Tauris UK) St Martin.

Culinary Herbs. Mary Page & William T. Stearn. (Wisley Handbooks: The Royal Horticultural Society Ser.). (Illus.). 64p. 1992. pap. 5.95 (0-304-32031-5, Pub. by Cassell UK) Sterling.

Culinary Herbs. Ed. by Elizabeth R. Van Brunt. (Plants & Gardens Ser.). (Illus.). 1989. per., pap. 6.95 (0-945352-06-9) Bklyn Botanic.

Culinary Herbs - Basil: A Sprig of Basil. John Midgley. (Illus.). 48p. 1994. 8.95 (0-8212-2097-7) Bulfinch Pr.

Culinary Herbs - Coriander: A Sprig of Coriander. John Midgley. (Illus.). 48p. 1994. 8.95 (0-8212-2098-5) Bulfinch Pr.

Culinary Herbs - Mint: A Sprig of Mint. John Midgley. (Illus.). 48p. 1994. 8.95 (0-8212-2099-3) Bulfinch Pr.

Culinary Herbs - Parsley: A Sprig of Parsley. John Midgley. (Illus.). 48p. 1994. 8.95 (0-8212-2096-9) Bulfinch Pr.

Culinary Herbs & Condiments. M. Grieve. 1954. pap. 5.95 (0-486-21513-X) Dover.

Culinary Jottings: Anglo-Indian Cookery. Wyvern, pseud. 551p. 1985. reprint ed. 25.00 (0-87556-999-4) Saifer.

Culinary Kid: A Nutrition Guide & Cookbook for Parents & Kids. St. Joseph Hospital Staff et al. Ed. by Mecca B. Carpenter. (Illus.). 160p. (Orig.). 1986. pap. 9.95 (0-9616857-0-0); audio 19.95 (0-9616857-1-9) St Joseph Hosp.

Culinary Nutrition for the Food Professional. 2nd ed. Carol A. Hughes. (Illus.). 272p. 1994. text ed. 34.95 (0-442-01763-4) Van Nos Reinhold.

***Culinary Professional's International Directory.** 320p. (Orig.). 1994. pap. 225.00 (0-7605-0640-X) Rector Pr.

***Culinary Secrets from the Virginia Chefs Association.** Ed. by Martha H. Robinson. 272p. 1995. 18.95 (1-55853-335-4) Rutledge Hill Pr.

Culinary Treasures of Japan: The Art of Making & Using Traditional Japanese Foods. John Belleme & Jan Belleme. LC 92-17982. (Illus.). 248p. (Orig.). 1992. pap. 17.95 (0-89529-509-1) Avery Pub.

Culinary Visit to Historic Sonoma. Sonoma League for Historic Preservation Staff. (Illus.). 140p. 1981. 6.95 (0-9616547-0-8) Sonoma Lea Hist.

Culloden & the Forty-Five. Jeremy Black. 256p. 1991. text ed. 39.95 (0-312-05197-2) St Martin.

Culloden & the 'Forty-Five. Jeremy Black. 231p. 1993. pap. 19.95 (0-312-10326-3) St Martin.

Culloden & the '45. Jeremy Black. (Orig.). 1993. pap. 19.99 (0-7509-0375-9) A Sutton Pub.

Culloden 1746: The Highland Clans' Last Charge. Peter Harrington. (Campaign Ser.: No. 12). (Illus.). 96p. pap. 14.95 (1-85532-158-0, 9511, Pub. by Osprey UK) Stackpole.

Cully Cully & the Bear. Wilson Gage. LC 82-11715. (Read with Me Ser.). (Illus.). (J). (ps-3). 1983. lib. bdg. 14.93 (0-688-01769-X); pap. 3.95 (0-688-07043-4) Greenwillow.

Culmination, Cubism & Love. Antonios Knight. (Illus.). 35p. (Orig.). (C). 1989. pap. text ed. 6.95 (0-9625706-2-1) ECLAT Bks.

Culotte. Jean Anouilh. 183p. (FRE.). 1985. pap. 12.95 (0-7859-2228-8, 207037680X) Fr & Eur.

Culpable Homicide & Legal Defence. K. C. Mehrotra. 438p. 1967. 60.00 (0-317-54874-3) St Mut.

Culpable Homicide & Legal Defence. Ed. by K. C. Mehrotra. (C). 1967. 65.00 (0-685-39680-0) St Mut.

Culpables Acusan: The Guilty Accuse. Salvador Iserte. (SPA.). 3.95 (84-7228-989-3, 223070, Pub. by Edit Clie SP) TSELF.

***Culpeper County: Virginia Publick Claims.** Janice L. Abercrombie & Richard Slatten. (Virginia Publick Claims Ser.). ix, 82p. 1991. pap. 11.00x (0-8095-8551-0) Borgo Pr.

Culpeper County: Virginia Publick Claims. Janice L. Abercrombie & Richard Slatten. (Virginia Publick Claims Ser.). ix, 82p. (C). 1991. reprint ed. lib. bdg. 29. 00x (0-8095-8315-1) Borgo Pr.

Culpeper County Marriages, Seventeen Eighty to Eighteen Fifty-Three. John Vogt & T. William Kethley, Jr. LC 88-34672. (Virginia Historic Marriage Register Ser.). (Illus.). ix, 257p. (Orig.). 1986. pap. 15.00x (0-935931-24-4) Borgo Pr.

Culpeper County Marriages, Seventeen Eighty to Eighteen Fifty-Three. John Vogt & T. William Kethley, Jr. LC 88-34672. (Virginia Historic Marriage Register Ser.). ix, 257p. (Orig.). (C). 1986. reprint ed. lib. bdg. 37.00x (0-8095-8213-9) Borgo Pr.

Culpeper's Color Herbal. Nicholas Culpeper. LC 91-39271. 224p. (Orig.). 1992. pap. 17.95 (0-8069-8568-2) Sterling.

Culpeper's Complete Herbal & English Physician. enl. ed. Nicholas Culpeper. (Illus.). 420p. 1987. reprint ed. 25.00 (0-916638-38-3); reprint ed. pap. 12.50 (0-916638-20-0) Meyerbooks.

Culpeper's Herbal Remedies. Nicholas Culpeper. 1980. pap. 5.00 (0-87980-025-9) Wilshire.

Culpepper Adventures: Dunc & Amos Meet the Slasher, No. 20. Gary Paulsen. 1994. pap. 3.50 (0-440-40939-X) Dell.

Culpepper Adventures: Dunc & the Greased Sticks of Doom, No. 21. Gary Paulsen. 1994. pap. 3.50 (0-440-40940-3) Dell.

Culpepper County Marriages, Seventeen Eighty-One to Eighteen Fifteen. Catherine L. Knorr. 136p. 1982. reprint ed. 18.50 (0-89308-253-8, VA 16) Southern Hist Pr.

Culpepper's Cannon. Gary Paulsen. (Culpepper Mystery Adventure Ser.: No. 3). 96p. (J). (gr. 3-7). 1992. pap. 3.50 (0-440-40617-X, YB) Dell.

***Culpepper's Complete Herbal.** Nicholas Culpepper. 1994. 13.95 (0-572-00203-3, Pub. by W Foulsham UK) Trans-Atl Phila.

Culprit Fay & Other Poems. Joseph R. Drake. (Notable American Authors Ser.). 1992. reprint ed. lib. bdg. 75.00 (0-7812-2693-7) Rprt Serv.

Cult - Anti-Cult: How a National Mindset & Government Incompetence Aided & Abetted the Waco Disaster. James R. Lewis. (Illus.). 300p. 1994. 25.00 (1-883322-03-0) Agamemnon Pr.

Cult & Controversy: The Worship of the Eucharist Outside Mass. Nathan Mitchell. 460p. 1992. pap. 19.95 (0-8146-6050-9, Pueblo Bks) Liturgical Pr.

Cult & Countercult: A Study of a Spiritual Growth Group & a Witchcraft Order. Gini G. Scott. LC 79-54057. (Contributions in Sociology Ser.: No. 38). (Illus.). 213p. 1980. text ed. 49.95 (0-313-22074-3, SCC/, Greenwood Pr) Greenwood.

***Cult & Ritual Abuse: Its History, Anthropology, & Recent Discovery.** James R. Noblitt & Pamela S. Perskin. LC 95-2492. 240p. 1995. text ed. 55.00 (0-275-95281-9, Praeger Pubs) Greenwood.

Cult Archaeology & Creationism: Understanding Pseudoscientific Beliefs about the Past. Ed. by Francis B. Harrold & Raymond A. Eve. LC 87-15892. (Illus.). 175p. 1987. text ed. 24.95 (0-87745-176-1) U of Iowa Pr.

***Cult Archaeology & Creationism: Understanding Pseudoscientific Beliefs about the Past.** Ed. by Francis B. Harrold & Raymond A. Eve. LC 95-8515. (Illus.). 204p. 1995. pap. 13.95 (0-87745-513-9) U of Iowa Pr.

Cult Controversy: A Guide to Sources. J. Gordon Melton. (Religious Information Systems Ser.: Vol. 6). 325p. 1992. 45.00 (0-8153-0860-4, H1601) Garland.

Cult Experience. Andrew J. Pavlos. LC 81-13175. (Contributions to the Study of Religion Ser.: No. 6). xvi, 209p. 1982. text ed. 55.00 (0-313-23164-8, PEX/, Greenwood Pr) Greenwood.

***Cult Experience: An Overview of Cults, Their Traditions & Why People Join Them.** John J. Collins. 142p. 1991. pap. 19.95 (0-398-06071-1) C C Thomas.

Cult Experience: An Overview of Cults, Their Traditions & Why People Join Them. John J. Collins. 142p. (C). 1991. text ed. 34.95 (0-398-05721-4) C C Thomas.

***Cult Explosion.** Dave Hunt. 1996. pap. write for info. (1-56507-269-3) Harvest Hse.

Cult Film Experience: Beyond All Reason. Ed. by J. P. Telotte. (Film Studies). (Illus.). 236p. 1991. text ed. 36. 00 (0-292-71135-2); pap. 15.95 (0-292-71144-1) U of Tex Pr.

Cult, Ghetto & State: The Persistance of the Jewish Question. M. Rodinson. 240p. 1993. pap. 11.95 (0-86356-020-2, Pub. by Saqi Books UK) Interlink Pub.

Cult, Ghetto, & State: The Persistence of the Jewish Question. Maxime Rodinson. Tr. by Jon Rothschild. 239p. (Orig.). 1984. pap. 10.95 (0-685-08870-7) Evergreen Dist.

Cult Heros: How to Be Famous More Than Fifteen Minutes: Seen from Within. Deyan Sudjic. 1990. pap. 10.95 (0-393-30656-9) Norton.

Cult Horror Films: Offbeat Thrillers from "Attack of the Fifty Foot Woman" to "Zombies of Mora Tau" Welch Everman. (Illus.). 256p. 1993. pap. 17.95 (0-8065-1425-6, Citadel Pr) Carol Pub Group.

Cult Killers. Rose G. Mandelsberg. 1991. mass mkt. 4.95 (1-55817-528-8, Pinnacle NY) Windsor NY.

Cult of Cannibals. John R. Bohlen. (Illus.). 314p. 1987. pap. 5.95 (0-9607702-1-6) Kingdom God.

Cult of Childhood. George Boas. LC 90-33312. (Dunquin Ser.: No. 18). 120p. 1966. reprint ed. pap. 13.50 (0-88214-218-6) Spring Pubns.

Cult of Crime. Franklin W. Dixon. (Hardy Boys Casefiles Ser.: No. 3). (YA). (gr. 7 up). 1989. mass mkt. 3.99 (0-671-68726-3, Archway) PB.

Cult of Crime: Casefiles Three. large type ed. Franklin W. Dixon. LC 88-21493. (Hardy Boys Ser.). 151p. (YA). (gr. 5-10). 1988. reprint ed. 9.50 (0-942545-44-3); reprint ed. lib. bdg. 10.50 (0-942545-54-0) Grey Castle.

Cult of Draupadi Vol. 1: Mythologies: From Gingee to Kuruksetra. Alf Hiltebeitel. (Illus.). xxviii, 488p. 1988. lib. bdg. 74.95 (0-226-34045-7); pap. text ed. 24.95 (0-226-34046-5) U Ch Pr.

Cult of Draupadi Vol. 2: On Hindu Ritual & the Goddess. Alf Hiltebeitel. (Illus.). 472p. 1991. lib. bdg. 74.95 (0-226-34047-3); pap. text ed. 27.50 (0-226-34048-1) U Ch Pr.

Cult of Elizabeth: Elizabethan Portraiture & Pageantry. Roy Strong. 1986. 52.00 (0-520-05840-2); pap. 18.00 (0-520-05841-0) U CA Pr.

Cult of Enthusiasm in French Romanticism. M. Ursula Clark. LC 70-94179. (Catholic University of America. Studies in Romance Languages & Literatures: No. 37). reprint ed. 37.50 (0-404-50337-3) AMS Pr.

***Cult of Goddess Sitala in Bengal: An Enquiry into Folk Culture.** Subrata K. Mukhopadhyay. (C). 1994. text ed. 19.50 (81-7102-001-1, Pub. by Firma KLM) S Asia.

Cult of Information: A Neo-Luddite Treatise on High Tech, Artificial Intelligence, & the True Art of Thinking. Theodore Roszak. LC 93-37189. 1994. pap. 10.00 (0-520-08584-1) U CA Pr.

Cult of Kasuga Seen Through Its Art. Susan C. Tyler. LC 90-47166. (Michigan Monograph Series in Japanese Studies: No. 8). (Illus.). xvi, 215p. 1992. 39.95 (0-939512-47-5) U MI Japan.

Cult of Kiho-Tumu. J. F. Stimson. (BMB Ser.). 1972. reprint ed. 40.00 (0-527-02217-9) Periodicals Srv.

Cult of Loving Kindness. Paul Park. 320p. 1992. mass mkt. 4.50 (0-380-71819-7, AvoNova) Avon.

Cult of Loving Kindness. Paul Park. (Starbridge Chronicles Ser.). 1991. 20.00 (0-688-10574-2) Morrow.

Cult of Pan in Ancient Greece. Philippe Borgeaud. Tr. by Kathleen Atlass & James Redfield. (Illus.). 312p. 1988. lib. bdg. 42.50 (0-226-06595-2) U Ch Pr.

Cult of Remembrance & the Black Death: Six Renaissance Cities of Central Italy. Samuel K. Cohn, Jr. 416p. 1992. text ed. 49.95x (0-8018-4303-0) Johns Hopkins.

Cult of Silvanus: A Study in Roman Folk Religion. Peter F. Dorcey. LC 91-45622. (Columbia Studies in the Classical Tradition: Vol. 20). (Illus.). 193p. 1992. 63.00 (90-04-09601-9) E J Brill.

Cult of Tara: Magic & Ritual in Tibet. Stephen Beyer. LC 74-186109. (Hermeneutics: Studies in the History of Religions: No. 2). (Illus.). 1974. pap. 18.00 (0-520-03635-2) U CA Pr.

Cult of the Avant-Garde Artist. Donald Kuspit. 192p. (C). 1994. pap. 15.95 (0-521-46922-8) Cambridge U Pr.

***Cult of the Big Bang.** W. C. Mitchell. LC 94-78655. 240p. 1994. write for info. (0-9643188-0-6) W C Mitchell.

Cult of the Black Virgin. Ean Begg. (Illus.). 304p. 1989. 12. 00 (0-14-019012-0, Penguin Bks) Viking Penguin.

Cult of the Cat. Nicholas J. Saunders. LC 90-70360. (Art & Imagination Ser.). (Illus.). 96p. 1991. pap. 14.95 (0-500-81036-2) Thames Hudson.

Cult of the Court. John Brigham. LC 86-30179. 248p. 1987. 37.95 (0-87722-486-2) Temple U Pr.

Cult of the Court. John Brigham. 248p. 1991. pap. 19.95 (0-87722-828-0) Temple U Pr.

Cult of the Dead in a Chinese Village. Emily M. Ahern. LC 72-97202. (Illus.). 296p. 1973. 32.50 (0-8047-0835-5) Stanford U Pr.

Cult of the Goddess: Social & Religious Change in a Hindu Temple. James J. Preston. (Illus.). 109p. (C). 1985. reprint ed. pap. text ed. 8.50 (0-88133-135-X) Waveland Pr.

Cult of the Goddess Pattini. Gananath Obeyesekere. LC 83-5884. (Illus.). 629p. (C). 1984. lib. bdg. 42.50 (0-226-61602-9) U Ch Pr.

Cult of the Koi. Michugo Tamadachi. 1993. 39.95 (0-86622-440-8, TS-132) TFH Pubns.

Cult of the Peacock Angel: A Short Account of the Yezidi Tribes of Kurdistan. Ralph H. Empson. LC 77-87646. reprint ed. 21.00 (0-404-16416-1) AMS Pr.

Cult of the Sacred Fired & the Formula. Vicente Segrelles. (Mercenary Ser.). 96p. 1986. pap. 14.95x (0-918348-27-7) NBM.

Cult of the Saints: Its Rise & Function in Latin Christianity. Peter Brown. LC 80-11210. xvi, 188p. 1982. pap. 9.95 (0-226-07622-9) U Ch Pr.

Cult of the Seer in the Ancient Middle East: A Contribution to Current Research on Hallucinations Drawn from Coptic & Other Texts. Violet MacDermot. LC 79-152047. 841p. reprint ed. pap. 180.00 (0-7837-4674-1, 2044420) Bks Demand.

Cult of the Serpent: An Interdisciplinary Survey of Its Manifestations & Origins. Balaji Mundkur. LC 82-19394. (Illus.). 363p. 1983. 69.50 (0-87395-631-1); pap. 24.95 (0-87395-632-X) State U NY Pr.

Cult of the Superman. Eric Bentley. Orig. Title: A Century of Hero Worship. 11.50 (0-8446-0486-0) Peter Smith.

Cult of the Virgin: Catholic Mariology & the Apparitions of Mary. Elliot Miller & Kenneth B. Samples. LC 92-4273. (Christian Research Institute Ser.). 192p. 1992. pap. 9.99 (0-8010-6291-8) Baker Bk.

Cult of the Virgin Mary: Psychological Origins. Michael P. Carroll. (Illus.). 270p. 1992. text ed. 39.50 (0-691-09420-9); pap. text ed. 15.95 (0-691-02867-2) Princeton U Pr.

Cult of the Virgin Mary in Anglo-Saxon England. Mary Clayton. (Cambridge Studies in Anglo-Saxon England: No. 2). (Illus.). 300p. (C). 1990. 69.95 (0-521-34101-9) Cambridge U Pr.

***Cult of Thinness.** Sharlene Hesse-Biber. (Illus.). 256p. 1996. 25.00 (0-19-508241-9) OUP.

Cult of Uncertainty. Isaac L. Kandel. LC 72-165718. (American Education Ser, No. 2). 1972. reprint ed. 11. 95 (0-405-03707-4) Ayer.

Cult of Vinayaka. Shanti L. Nagar. (Illus.). 270p. (C). 1992. 59.00 (81-7076-044-5) Nataraj Bks.

Cult Places in the Aegean. Bogdan Rutkowski. LC 85-40469. 320p. 1986. text ed. 55.00 (0-300-02962-4) Yale U Pr.

***Cult Rapture: Revelations of the Apocalyptic Mind.** Adam Parfrey. 1994. pap. 14.95 (0-922915-22-9) Feral Hse.

***Cult Science Fiction Films: From the Amazing Colossal Man to Yog: the Monster from Space.** Welch Everman. (Citadel Film Series Library). (Illus.). 256p. (Orig.). 1995. pap. 17.95 (0-8065-1602-X, Citadel Pr) Carol Pub Group.

Cult TV: A Viewer's Guide to the Shows America Can't Live Without. John Javna. (Illus.). 256p. 1986. pap. 14.95 (0-312-17848-4) St Martin.

Cult TV: The Essential Critical Guide. Jon E. Lewis & Penny Stempel. (Illus.). 256p. 1994. pap. 19.95 (1-85793-053-3, Pub. by Pavilion UK) Trafalgar.

Cult Watch: What You Need to Know about Spiritual Deception. John Ankerberg & John Weldon. LC 90-23715. 1991. pap. 12.99 (0-89081-851-7) Harvest Hse.

Culte de la Generation et l'Evolution Religieuse et Sociale en Guinee. C. Le Coeur. (B. E. Ser.: No. 150). (FRE.). 1932. 18.00 (0-8115-3070-1) Periodicals Srv.

Culte Des Heros et Ses Conditions Sociales. Stefan Czarnowski. LC 74-25745. (European Sociology Ser.). 472p. 1975. reprint ed. 39.95 (0-405-06500-0) Ayer.

An Asterisk (*) at the beginning of an entry indicates that the title is appearing in BIP for the first time.

1735

Culte Imperial. Emile Beurlier. vi, 357p. reprint ed. write for info. (*0-318-71321-7*, Pub. by Georg Olms GW) Lubrecht & Cramer.

Cultic Calendars of the Ancient Near East. Mark E. Cohen. LC 93-6751. 1993. 37.50 (*1-883053-00-5*) CDL Pr.

Cultic Motif in the Spirituality of the Book of Hebrews. Darrell J. Pursiful. LC 93-21560. 208p. 1993. text ed. 89.95 (*0-7734-2376-1*, Mellen Biblical Pr) E Mellen.

Culting of America. Ron Rhodes. LC 94-6868. 1994. pap. 11.99 (*1-56507-186-7*) Harvest Hse.

Cultivars, Anthropic Soils & Stability: A Preliminary Report of Archaeological Research in Araracuara, Colombian Amazonia. Santiago Mora et al. (University of Pittsburgh Latin American Archaeology Reports: No. 2). (Illus.). 1991. pap. 13.00 (*1-877812-05-6*) UPLAAP.

***Cultivated Gardener: Fruits.** Joyce Kristin. Date not set. 17.00 (*0-00-225055-1*, HarpT) HarpC.

Cultivated Hemlocks. John Swartley. Ed. by Humphrey Welch & T. R. Dudley. (Illus.). 270p. 1984. 24.95 (*0-917304-74-8*) Timber.

Cultivated Life: A Year in a California Vineyard. Joy Sterling. LC 93-10035. (Illus.). 1993. 22.00 (*0-679-41989-6*, Villard Bks) Random.

***Cultivated Life: A Year in a California Vineyard, Vol. 1.** Joy Sterling. 1994. pap. 11.95 (*0-316-81298-6*) Little.

Cultivated Mind: Essays on J. S. Mill Presented to John M. Robson. Ed. by Michael Laine. 192p. 1991. 60.00 (*0-8020-5915-5*) U of Toronto Pr.

Cultivated Plants & Domesticated Animals in Their Migration from Asia to Europe: Historico-Linguistic Studies (1870) Victor Hehn. (Amsterdam Classics in Linguistics Ser.: No. 7). lxxv, 523p. 1976. 113.00x (*90-272-0878-6*) Benjamins North Am.

Cultivating a Landscape of Peace: Iroquois-European Encounters in Seventeenth-Century America. Matthew Dennis. LC 92-56771. (Illus.). 296p. 1993. 37.95 (*0-8014-2171-3*) Cornell U Pr.

***Cultivating a Landscape of Peace: Iroquois-European Encounters in Seventeenth-Century America.** Matthew Dennis. (Illus.). 336p. 1995. pap. 15.95 (*0-8014-8301-8*) Cornell U Pr.

Cultivating an Awareness: America & the Holy Land, Vol. 1. Aaron Klieman. LC 90-13802. (American Zionism Ser.). 528p. 1991. reprint ed. 170.00 (*0-8240-7346-0*) Garland.

***Cultivating Congress: Constituents, Issues, & Interests in Agricultural Policymaking.** William P. Browne. (Studies in Government & Public Policy). 216p. 1995. 29.95 (*0-7006-0700-5*); pap. 14.95x (*0-7006-0701-3*) U Pr of KS.

Cultivating Consciousness: Enhancing Human Potential, Wellness, & Healing. Ed. by K. Ramakrishna Rao. LC 92-43428. 248p. 1993. text ed. 55.00 (*0-275-94515-4*, C4515, Praeger Pubs) Greenwood.

***Cultivating Cooperation: A History of the Missouri Farmers Association.** Raymond A. Young. (Illus.). 232p. 1995. 25.00 (*0-8262-0999-8*); pap. 11.95 (*0-8262-1000-7*) U of Mo Pr.

***Cultivating Crisis: The Human Cost of Pesticides.** 3rd ed. Douglas L. Murray. (Illus.). 208p. (C). 1995. text ed. 35.00x (*0-292-75168-0*); pap. 12.95 (*0-292-75169-9*) U of Tex Pr.

Cultivating Customers: Market Women in Harare, Zimbabwe. Nancy E. Horn. LC 94-4426. (Women & Change in the Developing World Ser.). 186p. 1994. lib. bdg. 40.00 (*1-55587-472-X*) Lynne Rienner.

Cultivating Differences: Symbolic Boundaries & the Making of Inequality. Ed. by Michele Lamont & Marcel Fournier. LC 92-15204. 344p. (C). 1992. lib. bdg. 49.95 (*0-226-46813-5*); pap. text ed. 17.95 (*0-226-46814-3*) U Ch Pr.

Cultivating Edible Fungi. Ed. by P. J. Wuest et al. 692p. 1987. 146.25 (*0-444-42747-3*) Elsevier.

Cultivating Excess. Lori Anderson. LC 92-3104. 128p. 1992. lib. bdg. 18.95 (*0-933377-19-3*); pap. 9.95 (*0-933377-18-5*) Eighth Mount Pr.

Cultivating Foundation Support for Education. Ed. by Mary K. Murphy. 210p. 1989. 37.00 (*0-89964-263-2*) Coun Adv & Supp Ed.

Cultivating Freud's Garden in France. Marion M. Oliner. LC 87-31908. 332p. 1988. 40.00 (*0-87668-995-0*) Aronson.

Cultivating Gentlemen: The Meaning of Country Life among the Boston Elite 1785-1860. Tamara P. Thornton. LC 89-30108. 256p. (C). 1989. 32.00 (*0-300-04256-6*) Yale U Pr.

***Cultivating Green Businesses.** Allyn F. Finegold & Barbara B. Wells. Ed. by Karen Glass. 40p. (Orig.). 1994. pap. text ed. 20.00 (*1-55877-191-3*) Natl Governor.

***Cultivating Intelligence: Power, Law, & the Politics of Teaching.** Louise Harmon & Deborah W. Post. (Critical America Ser.). 180p. 1996. 45.00 (*0-8147-6628-5*); pap. 15.95 (*0-8147-6629-3*) NYU Pr.

Cultivating Intuition: An Introduction to Psychotherapy. Peter Lomas. LC 93-9517. 232p. 1993. 30.00x (*0-87668-528-9*) Aronson.

Cultivating Spiritual Fruit. Robert C. Gage. LC 86-20395. 144p. (Orig.). 1986. reprint ed. pap. 5.25 (*0-87227-114-5*) Reg Baptist.

Cultivating Stillness: A Taoist Manual for Transforming Body & Mind. Tr. by Eva Wong. LC 92-50120. (Illus.). 136p. (Orig.). 1992. pap. 11.00 (*0-87773-687-1*) Shambhala Pubns.

***Cultivating Sunday's Word.** Jay Cormier. (Orig.). 1995. pap. write for info. (*1-55612-801-0*) Sheed & Ward MO.

Cultivating the Chi. 2nd ed. Stuart A. Olson. (Chen Kung Ser.: Vol. 1). (Illus.). 164p. (CHI.). 1992. pap. 16.95 (*0-938045-08-3*) Dragon Door.

Cultivating the Ch'i: The Secrets of Energy & Vitality. 3rd ed. Stuart A. Olson. (Chen Kung Ser.). (Illus.). 164p. (Orig.). 1993. pap. 12.95 (*0-938045-11-3*) Dragon Door.

Cultivating the Empty Field: The Silent Illumination of Zen Master Hongzhi. Tr. by Taigen D. Leighton & Yi Wu. (Illus.). 128p. 1991. 24.95 (*0-86547-474-5*, North Pt Pr); pap. 11.95 (*0-86547-475-3*, North Pt Pr) FS&G.

Cultivating the Mind of Love: Looking Deeply in the Mahayana Tradition. Thich N. Hanh. 140p. (Orig.). 1995. pap. 10.00 (*0-938077-70-8*) Parallax Pr.

Cultivating the Rosebuds: The Education of Women at the Cherokee Female Seminary, 1851-1909. Devon A. Mihesuah. LC 92-5845. (Illus.). 240p. (C). 1993. 35.95 (*0-252-01953-9*) U of Ill Pr.

Cultivating the Wasteland: Can Cable Put the Vision Back in TV. Kirsten Beck. LC 83-12257. 249p. 1983. 10.00 (*0-915400-34-0*, ACA Bks) Am Council Arts.

Cultivating Thinking in English & the Language Arts. Robert J. Marzano. (Illus.). 89p. 1991. pap. 9.95 (*0-8141-0991-8*) NCTE.

Cultivating Workers. Victoria Bernal. 1991. text ed. 42.00 (*0-231-07172-8*) Col U Pr.

Cultivation Analysis: New Directions in Media Effects Research. Ed. by Nancy Signorielli & Michael Morgan. (Focus Editions Ser.: Vol. 108). 320p. (C). 1989. text ed. 49.95 (*0-8039-3295-2*); pap. text ed. 24.95 (*0-8039-3296-0*) Sage.

Cultivation & Culture: Labor & the Shaping of Slave Life in the Americas. Ed. by Ira Berlin & Philip D. Morgan. LC 92-31010. (Carter G. Woodson Institute Series in Black Studies). 416p. (C). 1993. text ed. 49.50 (*0-8139-1421-3*); pap. text ed. 17.95 (*0-8139-1424-8*) U Pr of Va.

Cultivation & Processing of Medicinal Plants. Ed. by L. Hornok. 394p. 1993. text ed. 106.95 (*0-471-92383-4*) Wiley.

Cultivation & Utilization of Aromatic Plants. C. K. Atal. (C). 1984. 100.00 (*0-317-92340-4*, Scientific) St Mut.

Cultivation & Utilization of Medicinal Plants. C. K. Atal. (C). 1984. 100.00 (*0-317-92339-0*, Scientific) St Mut.

Cultivation of Ferns. Andrew McHugh. (Illus.). 168p. 1992. 55.00 (*0-7134-6492-5*, Pub. by Batsford UK) Trafalgar.

Cultivation of Hardy Perennials. Richard Bird. (Illus.). 200p. 1994. 39.95 (*0-7134-7061-5*, Pub. by Batsford UK) Trafalgar.

Cultivation of Hatred. Peter Gay. (Illus.). 752p. 1993. 30.00 (*0-393-03398-8*) Norton.

Cultivation of Hatred. Peter Gay. (Illus.). 712p. 1994. pap. 15.00 (*0-393-31224-0*) Norton.

Cultivation of Ivy: A Saga of the College in America. John R. Thelin. LC 76-9682. 96p. 1976. text ed. 18.95 (*0-87073-376-1*) Schenkman Bks Inc.

Cultivation of Marine Organisms & Its Importance for Marine Biology. O. Kinne & H. P. Bulnheim. (International Symposium Helgoland 1969 Ser.). (Illus.). 722p. 1973. reprint ed. pap. text ed. 160.00 (*3-87429-059-X*) Koeltz Sci Bks.

Cultivation of Neglected Tropical Fruits with Promise. Franklin W. Martin et al. (Studies in Tropical Agriculture). 1980. lib. bdg. 59.95 (*0-8490-3074-9*) Gordon Pr.

Cultivation of Reading: Teaching in a Language - Communication Context. Horst G. Taschow. LC 84-29383. 255p. reprint ed. pap. 72.70 (*0-7837-2177-3*, 2042515) Bks Demand.

Cultivation of Reading: Teaching in a Language-Communication Context. Horst G. Taschow. (C). 1985. text ed. 25.95 (*0-8077-2775-X*); pap. text ed. 17.95 (*0-8077-2710-5*) Tchrs Coll.

Cultivation of Rhododendrons. Peter Cox. (Illus.). 288p. 1994. 60.00 (*0-7134-5630-2*, Pub. by Batsford UK) Trafalgar.

Cultivator's Handbook of Marijuana. 6th rev. ed. William Drake. (Illus.). 224p. 1992. reprint ed. pap. 19.95 (*0-914171-53-4*) Ronin Pub.

Cultivemos una Huerta. Guillermo Woggon. Tr. by Nola Granberry. (Libros Para Colorear Ser.). (Illus.). 16p. (SPA.). (J). (gr. 1-3). 1987. reprint ed. pap. 1.40 (*0-311-38564-8*) Casa Bautista.

***Cultivo de la Soya.** Juan C. Rosas & Roberto Young. 60p. (C). 1993. pap. text ed. 3.50 (*1-885995-10-5*) Escuela Agricola.

***Cultivo de las Amarilidaceas: Cebolla, Ajo y Puerro.** Alfredo Montes & M. Holle. 47p. (C). 1987. pap. 4.00 (*1-885995-00-8*) Escuela Agricola.

Cultivo y la Utilizacion del Tarwi: Lupinus Mutabilis Sweet. (Plant Production & Protection Papers: No. 36). 248p. (SPA.). 1982. pap. 30.00 (*92-5-301197-1*, F2479) UNIPUB.

Culto Privato di Roma Antica, 2 vols. in 1. Attilio De Marchi. LC 75-10641. (Ancient Religion & Mythology Ser.). (Illus.). (ITA.). 1976. reprint ed. 57.95 (*0-405-07011-X*) Ayer.

Cultos, Religiones del Mundo y Usted: Un Analisis de Cultos Religiosos a la Luz del Christianismo. Kenneth Boa. Tr. by Pedro Bravo-Guzman. 350p. (SPA.). 1988. reprint ed. write for info. (*0-318-64256-5*) His Pub Works.

Cults. Daniel Cohen. LC 94-966. (Illus.). 128p. (YA). (gr. 7 up). 1994. lib. bdg. 15.90 (*1-56294-324-3*) Millbrook Pr.

Cults. George Papademetriou. 20p. 1985. pap. 1.00 (*0-917651-20-0*) Holy Cross Orthodox.

Cults. Terry Ross. (Troubled Society Ser.). (Illus.). 64p. (YA). (gr. 7 up). 1990. lib. bdg. 17.27 (*0-86593-070-8*); lib. bdg. 12.95 (*0-685-36323-6*) Rourke Corp.

Cults. Sarah Stevens. LC 91-17774. (Facts About Ser.). (Illus.). 48p. (J). (gr. 5-6). 1992. text ed. 12.95 (*0-89686-723-4*, Crstwood Hse) Silver Burdett Pr.

***Cults.** rev. ed. Hubert F. Beck. LC 95-10751. (How to Respond Ser.). Orig. Title: How to Respond to...the Cults. 1995. write for info. (*0-570-04668-8*) Concordia.

Cults: Faith, Healing, & Coercion. Marc Galanter. 240p. 1989. 30.00 (*0-19-505631-0*) OUP.

Cults: Faith, Healing & Coercion. Marc Galanter. 240p. 1990. reprint ed. pap. 12.95 (*0-19-506658-8*) OUP.

***Cults: How & Where to Find Facts & Get Help.** Robert D. Reed & Danek Kaus. Ed. by Diane Parker. LC 94-68699. (Abuse Ser.). 50p. (Orig.). 1994. 4.50 (*1-56875-083-8*, 083-8) R & E Pubs.

Cults: What Parents Should Know. Joan C. Ross & Michael D. Langone. 1989. pap. 5.95 (*0-8184-0511-2*, L Stuart) Carol Pub Group.

Cults & Cons: The Exploitation of the Emotional Growth Consumer. Kenneth Cinnamon & Dave Farson. LC 79-1174. 128p. 1979. 23.95 (*0-88229-456-3*) Nelson-Hall.

Cults & Consequences: The Definitive Handbook. Ed. by Rachel Andres & James R. Lane. 288p. (Orig.). (C). 1988. pap. 14.95 (*0-9621478-7-7*) JFC GLA.

Cults & Creeds in Graeco-Roman Egypt. H. I. Bell. 1975. pap. 12.50 (*0-89005-088-0*) Ares.

Cults & New Religions: Sources for the Study of Nonconventional Religious Groups in Nineteenth & Twentieth-Century America, 22 vols., Set. Ed. by J. Gordon Melton. 1992. 2,420.00 (*0-8153-0000-X*) Garland.

Cults & New Religious Movements: A Report of the Committee on Psychiatry & Religion of the American Psychiatric Association. Ed. by Marc Galanter. LC 88-7817. 346p. 1989. 43.50 (*0-89042-212-5*, 2212) Am Psychiatric.

***Cults & Personality.** Frank J. MacHovec. 210p. 1989. pap. 29.95 (*0-398-06255-2*) C C Thomas.

Cults & Personality. Frank J. MacHovec. 210p. (C). 1989. text ed. 44.95x (*0-398-05607-2*) C C Thomas.

Cults & the Family. Ed. by Florence Kaslow & Marvin B. Sussman. LC 81-20264. (Marriage & Family Review Ser.: Vol. 4, Nos. 3-4). 192p. 1982. text ed. 49.95 (*0-917724-55-0*) Haworth Pr.

Cults & the Occult. 3rd rev. ed. Edmond C. Gruss. 224p. 1994. pap. 8.99 (*0-87552-298-X*) Presby & Reformed.

Cults, Converts, & Charisma: The Sociology of New Religious Movements. Thomas Robbins. 288p. (C). 1988. text ed. 45.00 (*0-8039-8158-9*); pap. text ed. 22.50 (*0-8039-8159-7*) Sage.

Cults, Culture & the Law: Perspectives on New Religious Movements. Ed. by Thomas Robbins et al. (American Academy of Religion, Studies in Religion: No. 36). (C). 1985. pap. 14.95 (*0-89130-833-4*, 01 00 36) Scholars Pr GA.

Cults, Customs, & Superstitions of India: Being a Revised & Enlarged Edition of Indian Life, Religious & Social. John C. Oman. LC 70-179232. (Illus.). reprint ed. 36.00 (*0-404-54859-8*) AMS Pr.

Cults in America: Programmed for Paradise. Willa Appel. LC 82-15538. 216p. 1985. pap. 9.95 (*0-8050-0524-2*, Owl) H Holt & Co.

***Cults in Our Midst: The Hidden Menace in Our Everyday Lives.** Margaret T. Singer & Janja Lalich. LC 94-33598. (Social & Behavioral Sciences Ser.). 416p. 1995. 25.00 (*0-7879-0051-6*) Jossey-Bass.

***Cults in 19th Century Britain.** Robert Cecil. 20p. 1988. pap. 7.00 (*0-904674-15-0*, Pub. by Octagon Pr UK) ISHK Bk Service.

Cults of Campania. Roy M. Peterson. LC 23-13673. (American Academy in Rome, Papers & Monographs: Vol. 1). 413p. reprint ed. pap. 117.80 (*0-685-15582-X*, 2026716) Bks Demand.

Cults of Ostia. L. Ross Taylor. 1985. reprint ed. pap. 15.00 (*0-89005-114-3*) Ares.

Cults of the Dead in Ancient Israel & Ugarit. Theodore J. Lewis. (Harvard Semitic Monographs). 1989. 21.95 (*1-55540-325-5*, 04 00 39) Scholars Pr GA.

Cults of the Greek States, 5 vols., Set. Lewis R. Farnell. Incl. Vol. 4. Poseidon, Apollo. 1977. 75.00 (*0-89241-032-9*); (Illus.). 1977. reprint ed. 300.00 (*0-89241-049-3*) Caratzas.

Cults of the Sabine Territory. Elizabeth C. Evans. LC 39-25699. (American Academy in Rome. Papers & Monographs: Vol. 11). 284p. reprint ed. pap. 81.00 (*0-685-15607-9*, 2026727) Bks Demand.

***Cults of the Shadow, Vol. 1.** Grant. 1995. 34.95 (*1-871438-67-5*) Atrium Pubs.

Cults on Campus: Continuing Challenge. Ed. by Marcia R. Rudin. 126p. (Orig.). 1991. pap. 12.00 (*0-931337-02-X*, Intl Cult Ed Pgm) Am Family Foun.

Cults, Sects, & the New Age. James J. LeBar. LC 88-63530. (Orig.). 1989. pap. 7.95 (*0-87973-431-0*, 431) Our Sunday Visitor.

***Cults, Territory & the Origins of the Greek City-State.** Francois de Polignac. Tr. by Janet Lloyd. LC 94-46009. (ENG & FRE.). 1993. lib. bdg. 39.95 (*0-226-67333-2*) U Ch Pr.

***Cults, Territory & the Origins of the Greek City-State.** Francois de Polignac. LC 94-46009. 176p. 1994. pap. text ed. 14.95 (*0-226-67334-0*) U Ch Pr.

Cults That Kill: Probing the Underworld of Occult Crime. Larry Kahaner. LC 87-40403. 1989. mass mkt. 5.99 (*0-446-35637-9*) Warner Bks.

Cults: What Parents Should Know: A Practical Guide to Help Parents with Children in Destructive Groups. Joan C. Ross & Michael D. Langone. 133p. (Orig.). 1988. pap. text ed. 9.95 (*0-931337-00-3*) Am Family Foun.

Cults, World Religions, & the Occult. Kenneth Boa. 240p. 1990. pap. 9.99 (*0-89693-823-9*) SP Pubns.

Cultura Afrocubana, No. 1: El Negro en Cuba, 1492-1844. Jorge Castellanos & Isabel Castellanos. LC 87-83071. (Coleccion Ebano y Canela Ser.). 369p. (Orig.). (SPA.). 1989. pap. 39.00 (*0-89729-463-7*) Ediciones.

Cultura Afrocubana, No. 3: Las Religiones y las Lenguas. Jorge Castellanos & Isabel Castellanos. LC 87-83071. (Coleccion Ebano y Canela Ser.). (Illus.). 456p. (Orig.). (SPA.). 1992. pap. 39.00 (*0-89729-507-2*) Ediciones.

Cultura Afrocubana 2: El Negro en Cuba, 1845-1959. Jorge Castellanos & Isabel Castellanos. LC 87-83071. (Coleccion Ebano y Canela Ser.). 482p. (Orig.). (SPA.). 1990. pap. 39.00 (*0-89729-506-4*) Ediciones.

Cultura Afrocubana 4: Letras - Musica - Arte. Jorge Castellanos & Isabel Castellanos. LC 87-83071. (Coleccion Ebano y Canela Ser.). 511p. (Orig.). (SPA.). 1994. pap. 39.00 (*0-89729-618-4*) Ediciones.

Cultura Hispanica: Dentro y Fuera de los Estados Unidos. Michael H. Handelsman & William H. Heslin, Jr. 128p. (C). 1981. pap. text ed. write for info. (*0-07-554291-9*) McGraw.

Cultura Nacional Chilena, Critica Literaria y Derechos Humanos. Hernan Vidal. (Literature & Human Rights Ser.: Vol. 5). 495p. (Orig.). (SPA.). 1989. pap. 11.95 (*1-877660-02-7*) IFTSOIL.

Cultura Prenatal: Coma Crear el Hijo Perfecto por la Influencia Prenatal. R. Swinburne Clymer. Tr. by Fina Aparis. 173p. (Orig.). (SPA.). 1950. pap. 4.95 (*0-932785-53-0*) Philos Pub.

Cultural Action for Freedom. Paulo Freire. LC 77-34560. (Monograph Ser.: No. 1). 1970. pap. 6.95 (*0-916690-11-3*) Harvard Educ Rev.

Cultural Adaptation & Resistance on St. John: Three Centuries of Afro-Caribbean Life. Karen F. Olwig. LC 85-13414. (Illus.). 240p. (Orig.). 1985. pap. 24.95 (*0-8130-0818-2*) U Press Fla.

Cultural Adaptation of Asian Immigrants. C. T. Kannan. 246p. 1978. 24.95 (*0-318-36964-8*) Asia Bk Corp.

Cultural Adaptation Within Modern Africa. Ed. by S. H. Irvine & J. T. Sanders. LC 79-171692. (Columbia University, Center for Education in Asia, Publications). 172p. reprint ed. pap. 49.10 (*0-317-41934-X*, 2026025) Bks Demand.

***Cultural Advancement of Orissa under the Gangas of Kalinga.** D. Ratnagiri Rao. (C). 1995. 34.00x (*81-85094-80-2*, Pub. by Punthi Pus II) S Asia.

Cultural Aesthetics: Renaissance Literature & the Practice of Social Ornament. Patricia Fumerton. (Illus.). 256p. 1991. 34.00 (*0-226-26952-3*) U Ch Pr.

Cultural Aesthetics: Renaissance Literature & the Practice of Social Ornament. Patricia Fumerton. (Illus.). xii, 280p. 1993. pap. text ed. 17.95 (*0-226-26953-1*) U Ch Pr.

Cultural Affairs & Foreign Relations. rev. ed. Ed. by Robert Blum. LC 68-20455. 1968. reprint ed. 3.95 (*0-317-02952-5*, C-19557); reprint ed. pap. 2.95 (*0-317-02953-3*) Am Assembly.

Cultural Affairs & Foreign Relations. American Assembly Staff. LC 63-10670. (Spectrum Book Ser.). 192p. reprint ed. pap. 54.80 (*0-685-23506-8*, 2027976) Bks Demand.

Cultural Affairs in Boston: Poetry & Prose, 1956-1985. John Wieners. Ed. by Raymond Foye. LC 88-21550. 214p. (Orig.). 1988. 20.00 (*0-87685-739-X*); pap. 10.00 (*0-87685-738-1*) Black Sparrow.

Cultural Affairs in Boston: Poetry & Prose, 1956-1985, signed ed. deluxe ed. John Wieners. Ed. by Raymond Foye. LC 88-21550. 214p. (Orig.). 1988. 30.00 (*0-87685-740-3*) Black Sparrow.

Cultural Affairs Supervisor. Jack Rudman. (Career Examination Ser.: C-2860). 1991. pap. 22.00 (*0-8373-2860-8*) Nat Learn.

Cultural Alternatives & a Feminist Anthropology: An Analysis of Culturally Constructed Gender Interests in Papua New Guinea. Frederick K. Errington & Deborah B. Gewertz. (Illus.). 288p. (C). 1989. pap. 16.95 (*0-521-37591-6*) Cambridge U Pr.

Cultural Analysis of Student Life at a Liberal Arts College. Maribeth Durst & E. Marilyn Schaeffer. 140p. 1992. lib. bdg. 69.95 (*0-7734-9634-3*) E Mellen.

Cultural & Economic Factors in the Fertility of Thai Women. Dennis P. Hogan et al. LC 87-21459. (Papers of the East-West Population Institute: No. 107). (Illus.). xiii, 32p. (Orig.). 1987. pap. 3.00 (*0-86638-103-1*) EW Ctr HI.

***Cultural & Educational Continuity of Greece.** Constantine Cavarnos. LC 94-93908. (Illus.). 80p. 1995. pap. 5.95 (*1-884729-03-7*) Inst Byzantine.

Cultural & Educational Rights of the Minorities under Indian Constitution. A. Kumar. 290p. 1986. 28.50 (*0-8364-1799-2*, Pub. by Deep) S Asia.

Cultural & Environmental History of Cienega Valley, Southeastern Arizona. Frank W. Eddy & Maurice E. Cooley. LC 83-17942. (Anthropological Papers: No. 43). 62p. 1983. 7.95 (*0-8165-0830-5*) U of Ariz Pr.

Cultural & Historical Context of Hallucinogens: Religion, Ritual, Magic, & Curing. 1991. lib. bdg. 76.95 (*0-8490-4655-6*) Gordon Pr.

Cultural & Historical Grounding for Hispanic & Luso-Brazilian Feminist Literary Criticism. Intro. by Hernan Vidal. (Literature & Human Rights Ser.: Vol. 4). 650p. (Orig.). (POR & SPA.). 1989. pap. 14.95 (*1-877660-01-9*) IFTSOIL.

Cultural & Language Learning in Higher Education. Ed. by Michael Byram. LC 93-50831. 108p. 1994. 29.95 (*1-85359-228-5*, Pub. by Multilingual Matters UK) Taylor & Francis.

Cultural & Political Environment of International Business: A Guide for Business Professionals. Don A. Evans. LC 91-52754. 368p. 1991. lib. bdg. 43.50x (*0-89950-639-9*) McFarland & Co.

Cultural & Social Anthropology. 3rd ed. Robert F. Murphy. 256p. (C). 1988. pap. text ed. write for info. (*0-13-195273-0*) P-H.

C

 An Asterisk (*) at the beginning of an entry indicates that the title is appearing in BIP for the first time.

An Asterisk (*) at the beginning of an entry indicates that the title is appearing in BIP for the first time.

1737

***Cultural Diversity: Challenges & Opportunities (Package of 10)** Catherine D. Fyock. 32p. 1993. 80.00 (0-7863-0173-2) Irwin Prof Pubng.

Cultural Diversity among Aboriginal Cultures of Coastal Virginia & North Carolina. Lewis R. Binford. LC 90-24493. (Evolution of North American Indians Ser.: Vol. 1). 304p. 1991. reprint ed. 64.00 (0-8240-6109-8) Garland.

Cultural Diversity & Adaptation: The Archaic, Anasazi, & Navajo Occupation of the San Juan Basin. Ed. by Lori S. Reed & Paul F. Reed. (Cultural Resources Ser.: No. 9). (Illus.). 182p. (Orig.). 1992. 8.00 (1-878178-10-5) Bureau of Land Mgmt NM.

Cultural Diversity & Economic Education. Elias H. Tuma & Barry Haworth. LC 93-24504. 72p. (Orig.). (C). 1993. pap. text ed. 6.95 (0-87015-264-5) Pacific Bks.

Cultural Diversity & Families. Karen G. Arms et al. 224p. (C). 1992. pap. text ed. write for info. (0-697-16410-1) Brown & Benchmark.

***Cultural Diversity & Geriatric Care: Challenges to the Health Professions.** Ed. by Darryl Wieland et al. (Gerontology & Geriatrics Education Ser.). (Illus.). 130p. 1995. lib. bdg. 24.95 (1-56024-710-X) Haworth Pr.

Cultural Diversity & Learning Efficency. Ed. by Rajinder M. Gupta & Peter Coxhead. LC 87-12925. 256p. 1988. text ed. 45.00 (0-312-00988-7) St Martin.

Cultural Diversity & Social Work Practice. Ed. by Dianne F. Harrison et al. 262p. (C). 1992. text ed. 46.95x (0-398-05755-9) C C Thomas.

***Cultural Diversity & Social Work Practice.** Ed. by Dianne F. Harrison et al. 262p. 1992. pap. 29.95 (0-398-06378-8) C C Thomas.

Cultural Diversity & the Schools, 4 vols., Set. Ed. by James Lynch et al. 1992. 336.00 (0-7507-0149-8, Falmer Pr) Taylor & Francis.

Cultural Diversity & the Special Education System: Communication & Empowerment. Beth Harry. (Special Education Ser.: No. 9). 296p. (C). 1991. text ed. 45.00 (0-8077-3120-X); pap. text ed. 22.95 (0-8077-3119-6) Tchrs Coll.

Cultural Diversity in Health & Illness. 3rd ed. Rachel Spector. (Illus.). 345p. (C). 1991. pap. text ed. 29.95 (0-8385-1396-4, A1396-9) Appleton & Lange.

Cultural Diversity in Latin American Literature. David W. Foster. LC 93-2459. 192p. 1994. 32.50x (0-8263-1490-2) U of NM Pr.

Cultural Diversity in Libraries. Donald E. Riggs & Patricia A. Tarin. 200p. 1993. 39.95 (1-55570-139-6) Neal-Schuman.

Cultural Diversity in Organizations: Theory, Research & Practice. Taylor Cox, Jr. LC 93-17920. 312p. 1993. 29.95 (1-881052-19-2) Berrett-Koehler.

Cultural Diversity in Organizations: Theory, Research, & Practice. Taylor Cox, Jr. LC 93-17920. 312p. 1994. pap. 19.95 (1-881052-43-5) Berrett-Koehler.

Cultural Diversity in Schools: From Rhetoric to Practice. Ed. by Robert A. DeVillar et al. LC 93-24309. 384p. (C). 1993. 74.50 (0-7914-1673-9); pap. 24.95 (0-7914-1674-7) State U NY Pr.

Cultural Diversity in the Primary School. David Houlton. (Education in a Multicultural Society Ser.). 160p. 1987. pap. 29.95 (0-7134-4865-2, Pub. by Batsford UK) Trafalgar.

Cultural Diversity in the Workplace. Sally J. Walton. LC 93-33174. (Business Skills Express Ser.). (Illus.). 96p. 1994. pap. 10.00 (0-7863-0125-2) Irwin Prof Pubng.

Cultural Diversity in the Workplace: Issues & Strategies. George Henderson. LC 94-2991. 288p. 1994. text ed. 65.00 (0-89930-888-0, Quorum Bks) Greenwood.

***Cultural Diversity in the Workplace: Issues & Strategies.** George Henderson. LC 94-2991. 288p. 1994. pap. text ed. 19.95 (0-275-95095-6, Praeger Pubs) Greenwood.

Cultural Diversity Manual. Irving Buchen. 88p. (C). 1991. pap. text ed. 24.00 (0-940017-15-6) Info Tec OH.

Cultural Diversity, Module III: Challenges & Opportunities: Participant's Workbook. Catherine D. Fyock. 32p. 1993. pap. 10.00 (1-55623-827-4) Irwin Prof Pubng.

***Cultural Diversity Without Prejudice: A Guide for Critical Thinking in the 21st Century. Kenneth Brooks. LC 95-75515. 110p. (Orig.). 1995. pap. 16.95 (0-9639042-2-1) Amper Pubng.**

"Do you use fair & accurate images when you think about race & ethnic issues?" Few people understand their thinking well enough to answer this question honestly. They can't screen their thoughts for the necessary information. Having these skills is mandatory for those trying to succeed in a culturally diverse society. Here we show you how to develop these skills. This book is your personal workshop for ethnic awareness. It does not tell you what to think. It reveals what you already believe about race & ethnic issues. Then, it helps you decide if you wish to change or continue your present beliefs. First, it explains the elements that we all use when thinking. You think with more precision & accuracy when you understand how these elements fit together. Secondly, it questions you to reveal self-image & your beliefs about ethnic groups. Finally, it analyzes answers typically given to these questions. It discusses some personal & business consequences that come from the beliefs suggested by those answers. Use this book for personal or business ethnic awareness programs. Order: Bookpeople, Baker & Taylor, Amper Publishing, P.O. Box 882, Vallejo, CA 94590, 707-554- 3515.

Publisher Provided Annotation.

Cultural Divide: A Study of African-American College-Level Writers. Valerie Balester. LC 93-18826. 184p. (C). 1993. pap. text ed. 18.50 (0-86709-325-0, 0325) Boynton Cook Pubs.

Cultural Ecology. 2nd ed. Robert M. Netting. (Illus.). 131p. (Orig.). 1986. pap. text ed. 9.50 (0-88133-204-6) Waveland Pr.

Cultural Ecology of a Chinese Village: Cameron Highlands, Malaysa. James D. Clarkson. LC 67-28490. (University of Chicago, Department of Geography, Research Paper Ser.: No. 114). (Illus.). 191p. reprint ed. pap. 54.50 (0-685-44467-8, 2032992) Bks Demand.

Cultural Ecology of a Chinese Village: Cameron Highlands, Malaysia. James D. Clarkson. LC 67-28490. (Research Papers Ser.: No. 114). 174p. 1968. pap. 12.00 (0-89065-022-5) U Chicago Comm Geo.

Cultural Economics. Ed. by Ruth Towse & A. Khakee. (Illus.). 293p. 1992. 89.00 (0-387-55199-9) Spr-Verlag.

Cultural Economics & Cultural Policies. Ed. by Alan Peacock & Ilde Rizzo. LC 94-15817. 196p. (C). 1994. lib. bdg. 87.00 (0-7923-2868-X) Kluwer Ac.

Cultural Economies Past & Present. Rhoda H. Halperin. LC 94-15762. (Texas Press Sourcebooks in Anthropology Ser.: No. 18). (Illus.). 280p. (C). 1994. text ed. 40.00x (0-292-73089-6); pap. 17.95 (0-292-73090-X) U of Tex Pr.

Cultural Encounters. Ed. by Robert Cecil & David Wade. 241p. 1990. 30.00 (0-86304-050-0, Pub. by Octagon Pr UK) ISHK Bk Service.

Cultural Encounters: The Impact of the Inquisition in Spain & the New World. Ed. by Mary E. Perry & Anne J. Cruz. LC 90-22450. (Publications of the Center for Medieval & Renaissance Studies: No. 24). (Illus.). 320p. 1991. 35.00 (0-520-07098-4) U CA Pr.

***Cultural Encounters in the Early South: Indians & Europeans in Arkansas.** Comp. by Jeannie M. Whayyne. LC 95-20274. (Illus.). 240p. 1995. 24.00 (1-55728-394-X) U of Ark Pr.

Cultural Encounters in the U. S. A. Cross-Cultural Dialogues & Mini-Dramas. Andrew Murphy. 128p. 1991. pap. 9.95 (0-8442-0715-2, Natl Textbk) NTC Pub Grp.

Cultural Encounters on China's Ethnic Frontiers. Ed. by Stevan Harrell. LC 94-15697. (Studies on Ethnic Groups in China). 388p. 1994. text ed. 35.00x (0-295-97380-3) U of Wash Pr.

Cultural Encyclopedia of the Eighteen Fifties in America. Robert L. Gale. LC 93-13016. 472p. 1993. text ed. 95.00 (0-313-28524-1, GEY/, Greenwood Pr) Greenwood.

Cultural Environment of International Business. 3rd ed. Vern Terpstra & Kenneth David. 250p. (C). 1991. text ed. 32.95 (0-538-80003-8, SI87CA) S-W Pub.

Cultural Episcopacy & Ecumenism: Representative Ministry in Church History from the Age of Ignatius of Antioch to the Reformation. Allen Brent. LC 92-190. (Studies in Christian Mission: Vol. 6). xiv, 250p. 1992. 63.00 (90-04-09432-6) E J Brill.

Cultural Exchange: American & Chinese Weddings: a High Tea & Linen Shower for Miss Mary Lynn. Robbie R. De Vries. LC 93-90931. (Illus.). (Orig.). 1993. pap. write for info. (0-9627886-1-9) R R P de Vries.

***Cultural Exchange Between European Nations During the Renaissance: Proceedings of the Symposium for Renaissance Studies, June 1993.** Ed. by Gunnar Sorelius & Michael Srigley. (Illus.). 244p. (Orig.). 1994. pap. 44.50x (91-554-3316-2, Pub. by Almqv & Wiksell SW) Coronet Bks.

Cultural Excursions: Marketing Appetites & Cultural Tastes in Modern America. Neil Harris. (Illus.). 424p. 1990. pap. text ed. 24.95 (0-226-31758-7) U Ch Pr.

Cultural Experience: Ethnography in Complex Society. James P. Spradley & David W. McCurdy. 246p. (C). 1988. reprint ed. pap. text ed. 14.95 (0-88133-349-2) Waveland Pr.

Cultural Expression & Grassroots Development: Cases from Latin America & the Caribbean. Ed. by Charles D. Kleymeyer. 293p. 1994. lib. bdg. 42.00 (1-55587-461-4); pap. text ed. 16.95 (1-55587-499-1) Lynne Rienner.

Cultural Expression in the Global Village. 188p. 1993. pap. 25.00 (0-88936-702-7, IDRC7027, Pub. by IDRC CN) UNIPUB.

Cultural Facilities in Mixed-Use Development. Harold R. Snedcof. LC 85-51033. 255p. (C). 1985. pap. 45.95 (0-87420-636-7, C27) Urban Land.

Cultural Factors in Alcohol Research & Treatment of Drinking Problems. Ed. by D. W. Heath et al. (Journal of Studies on Alcohol: Suppl. No. 9). 1981. 15.00 (0-911290-08-7) Rutgers Ctr Alcohol.

Cultural Factors in International Relations. R. P. Anand. 1981. 20.00 (0-8364-0727-X, Pub. by Abhinav II) S Asia.

Cultural Feast: An Introduction to Food Society & Change. Carol A. Bryant et al. (Illus.). 481p. 1985. pap. text ed. 48.00 (0-314-85222-0) West Pub.

***Cultural Foods & Renal Diets: Section I: For the Clinical Dietitian; Section II: A Multilingual Guide for Renal Patients, 2 vols., Set.** Chhaya Patel & Mary Denny. 565p. (C). 1988. pap. text ed. 40.00 (1-883146-53-4) Coun Renal Nutrit.

Cultural Forces in World Politics. Ali A. Mazrui. 262p. (C). 1990. pap. 24.95 (0-435-08047-4, 08047) Heinemann.

Cultural Foundations of Education. Young Pai. 272p. (C). 1990. pap. write for info. (0-675-20934-X, Merrill Pub Co) Macmillan.

Cultural Foundations of Education. Theodore B. Brameld. LC 73-7070. 330p. 1973. reprint ed. text ed. 59.75 (0-8371-6904-6, BRFE, Greenwood Pr) Greenwood.

Cultural Foundations of Education: A Biographical Intro. Gerald L. Gutek. 480p. (C). 1991. pap. write for info. (0-02-348371-7) Macmillan.

Cultural Foundations of Iranian Politics. M. Reza Behnam. LC 86-15871. 198p. reprint ed. pap. 56.50 (0-8357-6843-0, 2035538) Bks Demand.

Cultural Foundations of Iranian Politics. M. Reza Behnam. LC 86-15871. 188p. (C). 1991. reprint ed. pap. 14.95 (0-87480-380-2) U of Utah Pr.

Cultural Front: Power & Culture in Revolutionary Russia. Sheila Fitzpatrick. LC 92-52752. (Cornell Studies in Soviet History & Science). 296p. 1992. 42.50 (0-8014-2196-9); pap. 14.95 (0-8014-9516-4) Cornell U Pr.

Cultural Frontiers in the Upper Cache Valley, Illinois. Veletta Canouts et al. LC 82-72482. (Center for Archaeological Investigations Research Paper Ser.: No. 16). (Illus.). xviii, 240p. 1984. pap. 14.00 (0-88104-004-5) Center Archaeo.

Cultural Gaps: East & West. 2nd ed. John R. Terry. 190p. 1987. pap. 7.50 (0-933704-61-5) Dawn Pr.

Cultural Genocide in the Black & African Studies Curriculum. Yosef Ben-Jochannan. LC 89-81780. 176p. 1989. pap. 14.95 (0-938818-19-8) ECA Assoc.

Cultural Geography: The Global Discipline. Richard H. Jackson & Lloyd E. Hudman. Ed. by LaMarre. 546p. (C). 1990. text ed. 58.25 (0-314-66316-9) West Pub.

Cultural Geography of Health Care. Wilbert M. Gesler. LC 90-44299. 256p. (C). 1991. pap. text ed. 19.95 (0-8229-5490-7) U of Pittsburgh Pr.

Cultural Geography of the United States. rev. ed. Wilbur Zelinsky. 224p. 1992. pap. text ed. 28.00 (0-13-194424-X) P-H.

Cultural Geometry. (Illus.). 92p. 1989. pap. 24.95 (0-9627767-1-8, Pub. by Deste Found GR) Dist Art Pubs.

Cultural Graded Readers: Beethoven. 1959. 9.95 (0-442-22040-5) Heinle & Heinle.

Cultural Graded Readers: Carl Schurz. 1962. 9.95 (0-442-22027-8) Heinle & Heinle.

Cultural Graded Readers: Durer. 1965. 9.95 (0-442-22035-9) Heinle & Heinle.

Cultural Graded Readers: Heine. 1958. 9.95 (0-442-22038-3) Heinle & Heinle.

Cultural Graded Readers: Mozart. 1965. 9.95 (0-442-22037-5) Heinle & Heinle.

Cultural Graded Readers: Schweitzer. 1966. 9.95 (0-442-22034-0) Heinle & Heinle.

Cultural Graded Readers: Sutter. 1963. 9.95 (0-442-22025-1) Heinle & Heinle.

Cultural Graded Readers: Thomas Mann. 1957. 9.95 (0-442-22036-7) Heinle & Heinle.

Cultural Groups & Human Relations: Conference on Educational Problems of Special Cultural Groups--Teachers College, Columbia University, 1949. Ed. by Gordon W. Allport et al. LC 77-117772. (Essay Index Reprint Ser.). 1977. 20.95 (0-8369-1792-8) Ayer.

Cultural Guide to African-American Heritage in New England: A Cultural Guide Map of African-American Heritage in New England. Linda Cline & Robert C. Hayden. LC 92-90178. (Illus.). 112p. (Orig.). 1992. pap. 10.95 (1-881224-00-7) Cline Transport.

Cultural Guide to Doing Business in Europe. 2nd ed. Robert T. Moran & Michael Johnson. 156p. 1992. pap. 24.95 (0-7506-0831-5) Buttrwrth-Heinemann.

***Cultural Handbook to the New Independent States.** American Council of Teachers of Russian Staff. 54p. 1994. pap. text ed. 8.95 (0-9643332-1-X) ACTR.

Cultural Hegemony & African American Development. Clovis E. Semmes. LC 92-16205. 288p. 1992. text ed. 55.00 (0-275-93923-5, C3923, Praeger Pubs) Greenwood.

Cultural Heritage Conservation in the American South. Ed. by Benita J. Howell. LC 89-4848. (Southern Anthropological Society Proceedings Ser.: No. 23). 152p. 1990. pap. 12.00 (0-8203-1165-0) U of Ga Pr.

Cultural Heritage in Asia & the Pacific: Proceedings of a Symposium Held in Honolulu, Hawaii, September 8-13, 1991. Ed. by Margaret G. H. MacLean. LC 93-25491. (Illus.). 131p. 1993. 25.00 (0-89236-248-0) J P Getty Trust.

Cultural Heritage of India, Set. Incl. Vol. 1. Early Phases. Ed. by Bhattacharyya et al. 1937. 25.00 (0-87481-560-6); Vol. 2. Itihasas, Puranas, Dharma & Other Shastras. Ed. by Bhattacharyya et al. 1937. 25.00 (0-87481-561-4); Vol. 3. Philosophies. Ed. by Bhattacharyya et al. 1937. 25.00 (0-87481-562-2); Vol. 4. Religions. Ed. by Bhattacharyya et al. 1937. 25.00 (0-87481-563-0); Vol. 5. Languages & Literatures. Ed. by Bhattacharyya et al. 1937. 25.00 (0-87481-564-9); (Illus.). 1937. 270.00 (0-87481-558-4) Vedanta Pr.

Cultural Heritage of India: Aspects of Buddhist Culture. V. Subramaniam. 1982. 9.00 (0-8364-0845-4, Pub. by Ashish II) S Asia.

Cultural Heritage of Ladakh, Vol. 1: Central Ladakh. Snellgrove. 1977. 75.00 (0-85668-058-3, Pub. by Aris & Phillips UK) David Brown.

Cultural Heritage of Ladakh, Vol. 2: Zangskar & Cave Temples of Ladakh. Snellgrove. 1980. 75.00 (0-85668-148-2, Pub. by Aris & Phillips UK) David Brown.

Cultural Heritage of Nepal Terai. Ram D. Rakesh. xiv, 221p. 1994. 20.00 (81-85693-26-9, Pub. by Nirala Pubns II) Nataraj Bks.

Cultural Heritage of Punjab, 3000 B. C. to 1947 A. D. K. C. Aryan. (Illus.). 149p. 1983. 37.00 (81-900002-9-2, Rekha Prakashan) Nataraj Bks.

Cultural Heritage of the Italian Renaissance: Essays in Honour of T. G. Griffith. Ed. by C. E. Griffiths & R. Hastings. LC 93-36165. (Illus.). 375p. 1993. text ed. 99.95 (0-7734-9396-4) E Mellen.

Cultural Heritage of the Swedish Immigrant. O. Fritiof Ander. Ed. by Franklyn D. Scott. LC 78-15203. (Scandinavians in America Ser.). 1979. reprint ed. lib. bdg. 18.95 (0-405-11629-2) Ayer.

Cultural Heritage Tourism. S. Prohaska. 1992. text ed. write for info. (0-442-00721-3) Van Nos Reinhold.

Cultural-Historical Development of Verbal Thinking: A Psychological Study. Ed. by P. Tulviste. 208p. (C). 1991. pap. text ed. 59.00 (1-56072-006-9) Nova Sci Pubs.

Cultural History: Between Practices & Representations. Roger Chartier. Tr. by Lydia G. Cochrane. LC 88-3823. 230p. 1988. 37.50 (0-8014-2223-X) Cornell U Pr.

Cultural History & Material Culture: Everyday Life, Landscapes, Museums. Thomas J. Schlereth. (Illus.). (C). 1992. pap. text ed. 19.95 (0-8139-1396-9) U Pr of Va.

Cultural History & Material Culture: Everyday Life, Landscapes, Museums. Thomas J. Schlereth. Ed. by Simon Bronner. LC 89-37323. (American Material Culture & Folklife Ser.). 472p. reprint ed. 132.30 (0-8357-1899-9, 2070677) Bks Demand.

Cultural History of Early Medieval Orissa. Sarol K. Patel. (C). 1991. text ed. 78.00 (81-85067-71-6, Pub. by Sundeep Prakashan II) S Asia.

Cultural History of Gesture. Jan Bremmer. Ed. by Herman Roodenburg. LC 91-57953. (Illus.). 1992. 46.95 (0-8014-2744-4); pap. 15.95 (0-8014-8023-X) Cornell U Pr.

Cultural History of India. Ed. by A. L. Basham. (Illus.). 1984. 34.50 (0-19-561520-4) OUP.

Cultural History of India During the British Period. Abdullah Yusuf Ali. LC 75-41006. reprint ed. 25.50 (0-404-14723-2) AMS Pr.

Cultural History of Kashmir & Kishtawar. F. M. Hassnain. (C). 1992. 52.00 (0-8364-2795-5, Pub. by Rima) S Asia.

Cultural History of Modern India. Vishwanath S. Naravane. (C). 1991. 23.00 (81-85119-92-9, Pub. by Northern Bk Ctr II) S Asia.

***Cultural History of Nepal.** Ed. by B. R. Bajracharya. (C). 1993. 44.00x (81-7041-840-2, Pub. by Anmol II) S Asia.

Cultural History of Postwar Japan, 1945-1980. Shunsuke Tsurumi. (Japanese Studies). 174p. (C). 1994. 76.50 (0-7103-0259-2, Pub. by Kegan Paul Intl UK) Routledge Chapman & Hall.

Cultural History of Religion in America. James G. Moseley. LC 80-23609. (Contributions to the Study of Religion Ser.: No. 2). 216p. 1981. text ed. 49.95 (0-313-22479-X, MRA/, Greenwood Pr) Greenwood.

Cultural History of Russia. A. Borg. (Great Civilizations Ser.). 90p. 1988. 60.00 (0-317-40629-9, Pub. by Collets UK) St Mut.

Cultural History of Spanish America: From Conquest to Independence. Mariano Picon-Salas. Tr. by Irving A. Leonard. LC 82-951. xvii, 192p. 1982. reprint ed. text ed. 38.50 (0-313-23454-X, PSCH, Greenwood Pr) Greenwood.

Cultural History of the American Novel: Henry James to William Faulkner. David Minter. 304p. (C). 1994. 47.95 (0-521-45285-6) Cambridge U Pr.

Cultural History of the American Revolution. rev. ed. Kenneth Silverman. LC 85-25541. (Illus.). 699p. 1987. pap. text ed. 19.50 (0-231-06295-8) Col U Pr.

Cultural History of the French Revolution. Emmet Kennedy. LC 88-39966. 448p. (C). 1989. 47.00 (0-300-04426-7) Yale U Pr.

Cultural History of the French Revolution. Emmet Kennedy. (Illus.). 448p. (C). 1991. reprint ed. pap. 20.00 (0-300-05013-5) Yale U Pr.

Cultural History of the Theatre. Jack Watson & Grant McKernie. LC 92-11258. 624p. (C). 1993. pap. text ed. 56.95 (0-8013-0618-3, 78556) Longman.

***Cultural History of Tibet.** rev. ed. Hugh Richardson & David Snellgrove. 1995. pap. 20.00 (1-57062-102-0) Shambhala Pubns.

***Cultural Horizons of India.** Lokesh Chandra. (C). 1995. 105.00x (81-85689-44-X, Pub. by Aditya Prakashan II) S Asia.

Cultural Horizons of India, Vol. 1. Lokesh Chandra. (C). 1990. 94.00 (81-85179-52-2, Pub. by Aditya Prakashan II) S Asia.

Cultural Horizons of India, Vol. II: Studies in Tantra & Buddhism, Art & Archeology, Language & Literature. (Sata-Pitaka Ser.: Vol. 366). (C). 1992. 78.00 (81-85689-00-8, Pub. by Aditya Prakashan II) S Asia.

Cultural Horizons of India, Vol. 3: Studies in Tantra & Buddhism, Art & Archaeology, Language & Literature. Lokesh Chandra. (C). 1993. text ed. 84.00 (81-85689-25-3, Pub. by Aditya Prakashan II) S Asia.

***Cultural Identity & Archeology: The Construction of European Communities.** P. Graves-Brown et al. LC 95-9086. (Theoretical Archeology Group (TAG) Ser.). 1995. write for info. (0-415-10676-1) Routledge.

Cultural Identity & Educational Policy. Ed. by Colin Brock & Witold Tulasiewicz. LC 85-14359. 368p. 1985. text ed. 35.00 (0-312-17849-2) St Martin.

An Asterisk (*) at the beginning of an entry indicates that the title is appearing in BIP for the first time.

C

An Asterisk (*) at the beginning of an entry indicates that the title is appearing in BIP for the first time.

1739

Cultural Resources Assessment of the Hansen Dam Flood Control Basin, City of Los Angeles, California. James Brock et al. (Technical Ser.: No. 5). (Illus.). v, 66p. 1993. pap. 12.95 (*1-881844-00-5*) Archaeol Adv.

Cultural Resources Inventory in Spanish Spring Valley, Washoe County, Nevada. Alvin McLane. (Illus.). 23p. 1980. 4.00 (*0-945920-16-4*) Desert Rsch Inst.

Cultural Resources Inventory of Eight Titan Missile Silos in the Greater Tucson Area, Pima County, Arizona. Jeffrey H. Altschul & Steven D. Shelley. (Statistical Research Technical Ser.: No. 12). 18p. 1987. spiral bd. 2.00 (*1-879442-49-3*) Stats Res.

Cultural Resources Investigations in the Mojave River Forks Reservoir, San Bernadino County, California. Jeffrey Altschul et al. (Statistical Research Technical Ser.: No. 2). (Illus.). 94p. 1985. spiral bd. 7.50 (*1-879442-01-9*) Stats Res.

Cultural Resources Investigations of the Yuma Quartermaster Depot, AZ X: 6: 12 (ASM), Yuma, Arizona. Mark T. Swanson & Jeffrey H. Altschul. (Statistical Research Technical Ser.: No. 21). (Illus.). 207p. 1991. per. 15.00 (*1-879442-19-1*) Stats Res.

Cultural Resources Literature Search & Survey of Portions of Nogales Wash & Potrero Creek, Southern Arizona. Steven D. Shelley & Jeffrey H. Altschul. (Statistical Research Technical Ser.: No. 6). 42p. 1987. spiral bd. 5.00 (*1-879442-12-4*) Stats Res.

Cultural Resources Management. Ronald W. Johnson & Michael G. Schene. LC 85-27024. 270p. (C). 1987. text ed. 31.50 (*0-89874-880-1*) Krieger.

Cultural Resources of Boston. American Federation of Arts Staff. (Orig.). 1965. 10.00 (*0-8079-0030-3*); pap. 5.00 (*0-8079-0031-1*) October.

Cultural Resources Overview for the Nuclear Waste Storage Investigations, Nevada Test Site, Nye County, Nevada. Lonnie Pippin & Donald Zerga. (Social Sciences Center Technical Report Ser.: No. 24). (Illus.). 117p. (C). 1981. spiral bd. 10.00 (*0-945920-24-5*) Desert Rsch Inst.

Cultural Resources Sample Survey of Operations Zones, Barry M. Goldwater Range, Marine Corps Air Station, Yuma, Arizona. Jeffrey H. Altschul & Bruce A. Jones. (Statistical Research Technical Ser.: No. 24). (Illus.). 70p. 1989. spiral bd. 10.00 (*1-879442-23-X*) Stats Res.

Cultural Resources Testing Program, Holbrook, Arizona. Richard S. Ciolek-Torrello. (Statistical Research Technical Ser.: No. 18). 151p. 1989. spiral bd. 12.50 (*1-879442-16-7*) Stats Res.

Cultural Revolution. Norman Wong. 192p. 1994. 21.00 (*0-89255-197-6*) Persea Bks.

***Cultural Revolution.** Norman Wong. 192p. 1995. pap. 10.00 (*0-345-39648-0*) Ballantine.

Cultural Revolution: A Marxist Analysis. Irwin Silber. 64p. (Orig.). 1970. pap. 2.95 (*0-87810-005-9*) Times Change.

Cultural Revolution? The Challenge of the Arts in the 1960s. Ed. by Bart Moore-Gilbert & John Seed. 256p. 1992. 69.95 (*0-415-07824-5*, A7455) Routledge.

Cultural Revolution & Post-Mao Reforms: A Historical Perspective. Tang Tsou. LC 85-8608. xlvi, 352p. 1986. 32.50 (*0-226-81513-7*) U Ch Pr.

Cultural Revolution & Post-Mao Reforms: A Historical Perspective. Tang Tsou. LC 85-8608. xlvi, 352p. 1988. pap. text ed. 14.95 (*0-226-81514-5*) U Ch Pr.

Cultural Revolution at Peking University. Victor Nee. LC 77-81790. 91p. reprint ed. pap. 26.00 (*0-318-34967-1*, 2030765) Bks Demand.

Cultural Revolution in China. Lev Deliusin. 1976. lib. bdg. 59.95 (*0-8490-1693-2*) Gordon Pr.

Cultural Revolution in China's Schools, May 1966 - April 1969. Julia Kwong. (Publication Series: Education & Society: No. 364). 200p. 1988. pap. 16.95 (*0-8179-8642-1*) Hoover Inst Pr.

Cultural Revolution in Russia, 1928-1931. Ed. by Sheila Fitzpatrick. LC 77-74439. (Studies of the Russian Institute, Columbia University & Harvard Series in Ukrainian Studies). 320p. 1978. 35.00 (*0-253-31591-3*); pap. 12.95 (*0-253-20337-6*, MB-337) Ind U Pr.

Cultural Revolution in the Provinces. L. Culman. LC 77-162858. (East Asian Monographs: No. 42). 224p. 1971. pap. 11.00 (*0-674-17985-4*) HUP.

Cultural Rights: Technology, Legality, & Personality. Celia Lury. LC 92-37656. (International Library of Sociology). 1993. write for info. (*0-415-03155-9*, Routledge NY); pap. write for info. (*0-415-09578-6*, Routledge NY) Routledge.

Cultural Schizophrenia: Islamic Societies Confronting the West. Daryush Shayegan. 1993. 39.95 (*0-86356-162-4*, Pub. by Saqi Bks UK) Interlink Pub.

Cultural Sciences: Their Origin & Development. Florian Znaniecki. LC 79-62690. (Social Science Classics Ser.). 438p. 1980. reprint ed. 39.95 (*0-87855-307-X*); reprint ed. pap. text ed. 19.95 (*0-87855-689-3*) Transaction Pubs.

***Cultural Semiotics, Spenser, & the Captive Woman.** Louise Schleiner. LC 94-24491. 280p. 1995. 43.50 (*0-934223-36-X*) Lehigh Univ Pr.

***Cultural Shaping of Accounting.** Ahmed Riahi-Belkaoui. LC 94-45274. 176p. 1995. text ed. 55.00 (*0-89930-953-4*, Quorum Bks) Greenwood.

Cultural Shareability of Edutainment Media in Global Africa. Tama L. Hamilton-Wray. 25p. (C). 1992. pap. text ed. 5.00 (*0-936731-30-3*) Devel Self Rel.

Cultural Shocks of Rudyard Kipling. W. J. Lohmann, Jr. LC 89-13330. (American University Studies: English Language & Literature: Ser. IV, Vol. 73). 309p. (C). 1990. text ed. 46.95 (*0-8204-0649-X*) P Lang Pubs.

Cultural Side of Islam. M. M. Pickthal. 202p. 1981. 14.95 (*0-318-36958-3*) Asia Bk Corp.

Cultural Side of Islam. M. Pickthall. 12.75 (*0-935782-66-4*) Kazi Pubns.

Cultural Significance of Accounts. Scott. LC 73-84524. 1973. reprint ed. text ed. 20.00 (*0-914348-08-6*) Scholars Bk.

***Cultural Sniping: The Art of Transgression.** Jo Spence. Ed. by Jo Stanley. LC 94-41227. (Comedia Ser.). (Illus.). 192p. 1995. 49.95x (*0-415-08883-6*, C0300); pap. 19.95 (*0-415-08884-4*, C0301) Routledge.

Cultural Spaces in a Philadelphia Restaurant. Christopher D. Dore. (Illus.). 1986. reprint ed. pap. text ed. 15.65 (*1-55567-055-5*) Coyote Press.

Cultural Stability & Cultural Change: American Ethnological Society Proceedings, 1957. Ed. by Verne F. Ray. LC 84-45544. 1988. reprint ed. pap. 35.00 (*0-404-62651-3*) AMS Pr.

Cultural, Structural & Strategic Change in Management Buyouts. Sebastian Green & Dean F. Berry. LC 89-70328. 208p. 1991. text ed. 55.00 (*0-312-04615-4*) St Martin.

Cultural Struggle & Development in Southern Africa. Ed. by Preben Kaarsholm. 258p. 1992. pap. 24.95 (*0-435-08062-8*, 08062) Heinemann.

Cultural Studies. Ed. by Lawrence Grossberg et al. (Illus.). 800p. 1991. 59.50 (*0-415-90351-3*, A5891, Routledge NY); pap. 24.95 (*0-415-90345-9*, A4873, Routledge NY) Routledge.

Cultural Studies. Fred Inglis. LC 93-22635. 280p. 1994. text ed. 52.95 (*0-631-18453-8*); pap. text ed. 21.95 (*0-631-18454-6*) Blackwell Pubs.

***Cultural Studies: Journal, Vol. 8, Issue 2.** Ed. by Lawrence Grossberg & Janice Radway. 144p. 1994. pap. 12.95 (*0-415-11095-5*, B3751) Routledge.

***Cultural Studies: Journal, Vol. 8 Issue 3.** Ed. by Lawrence Grossberg & Janice Radway. 144p. 1994. pap. 12.95 (*0-415-11096-3*, B3755) Routledge.

***Cultural Studies & Beyond: Fragments of Empire.** Ioan Davies. LC 94-42065. 1995. 50.00 (*0-415-03836-7*); pap. 18.95 (*0-415-03837-5*) Routledge.

***Cultural Studies & Cultural Value.** John Frow. 170p. 1995. 39.95 (*0-19-871127-1*); pap. 17.95 (*0-19-871128-X*) OUP.

Cultural Studies & Identification of Wood-inhabiting Corticiaceae & Selected Hymenomycetes from North America. K. K. Nakasone. (Mycologia Memoirs Ser.: No. 15). (Illus.). 412p. 1990. lib. bdg. 105.00 (*3-443-76005-8*, Pub. by Cramer-Borntraeger GW) Lubrecht & Cramer.

Cultural Studies & Language Learning: A Research Report. Michael Byram & Susan Taylor. (Multilingual Matters Ser.: No. 63). 350p. 1991. 99.00 (*1-85359-089-4*, Pub. by Multilingual Matters UK) Taylor & Francis.

Cultural Studies As Critical Theory. Ben Agger. 224p. 1992. 80.00 (*1-85000-964-3*, Falmer Pr); pap. 27.00 (*1-85000-965-1*, Falmer Pr) Taylor & Francis.

***Cultural Studies Goes to School: Reading & Teaching Popular Media.** David Buckingham & Julian Sefton-Green. LC 94-26388. (Critical Perspectives on Literacy & Education Ser.). 240p. 1994. 85.00x (*0-7484-0199-7*, Pub. by Tay Francis Ltd UK); pap. 29.00x (*0-7484-0200-4*, Pub. by Tay Francis Ltd UK) Taylor & Francis.

Cultural Studies in Foreign Language Education. Michael Byram. 176p. 1988. 59.00 (*1-85359-018-5*, Pub. by Multilingual Matters UK); pap. 19.95 (*1-85359-017-7*, Pub. by Multilingual Matters UK) Taylor & Francis.

Cultural Studies in the English Classroom. Ed. by James A. Berlin & Michael Vivion. LC 93-7509. 344p. (C). 1993. pap. text ed. 25.00 (*0-86709-320-X*, 0320) Boynton Cook Pubs.

Cultural Studies of Modern Germany: History, Representation, & Nationhood. Russell A. Berman. LC 93-9987. 240p. (Orig.). (C). 1993. 49.50 (*0-299-14010-5*); pap. 14.95 (*0-299-14014-8*) U of Wis Pr.

Cultural Studies Reader. Ed. by Simon During. 496p. 1993. 49.95 (*0-415-07708-7*, A9991); pap. 16.95 (*0-415-07709-5*, A9995) Routledge.

Cultural Studies Reader: Texts & Textuality. Ed. by Anthony Easthope & Kate McGowan. 278p. 1992. 60.00 (*0-8020-2912-4*); pap. 18.95 (*0-8020-7416-2*) U of Toronto Pr.

Cultural Stuttgart 1992-1993. (Illus.). 224p. 1991. 35.00 (*3-89322-386-X*, Pub. by Edition Cantz GW) Dist Art Pubs.

Cultural Tapestry: Readings for a Pluralistic Society. Evans et al. (C). 1991. text ed. 28.50 (*0-673-46428-8*) HarpCollege.

Cultural Theory. Michael Thompson et al. 296p. (C). 1990. pap. text ed. 23.50 (*0-8133-7864-8*) Westview.

Cultural Theory & Cultural Change. Mike Featherstone. (Theory, Culture & Society Ser.). 288p. (C). 1992. text ed. 55.00 (*0-8039-8743-9*); pap. text ed. 21.95 (*0-8039-8744-7*) Sage.

Cultural Theory & Psychoanalytic Tradition. David J. Fisher. 276p. (C). 1991. 34.95 (*0-88738-387-4*) Transaction Pubs.

Cultural Ties As Determinants of Immigrant Settlement in Urban Areas: A Case Study of the Growth of an Italian Neighborhood in Worcester, Massachusetts, 1875-1922. Bryan Thompson. Ed. by Francesco Cordasco. LC 80-901. (American Ethnic Groups Ser.). 1981. lib. bdg. 24.95 (*0-405-13461-4*) Ayer.

Cultural Tourism: How the Arts Can Help Market Tourism Products; How Tourism Can Help Provide Markets for the Arts. Bridget B. McCarthy. (Illus.). 200p. (Orig.). 1992. pap. 59.00 (*0-9616696-7-5*) B B McCarthy.

***Cultural Tourism & Heritage Management.** Shalini Singh. (C). 1995. 20.00x (*81-7033-233-8*, Pub. by Rawat II) S Asia.

Cultural Tradition & Other Essays. Francis Neilson. LC 69-18935. (Essay Index Reprint Ser.). 1977. 20.95 (*0-8369-1046-X*) Ayer.

Cultural Tradition & Other Essays. Francis Neilson. 228p. 1957. 2.00 (*0-911312-82-X*) Schalkenbach.

***Cultural Transactions: Nature, Self, Society.** Paul Hernadi. LC 95-6968. (Illus.). 144p. 1995. 27.50 (*0-8014-3113-1*) Cornell U Pr.

Cultural Transformations & Interactions in Eastern Europe. Ed. by Pavel Dolukhanov & John Chapman. (Worldwide Archaeology Ser.: Vol. 5). 200p. 1993. 59.95 (*1-85628-704-1*, Pub. by Avebury Pub UK) Ashgate Pub Co.

Cultural Transformations in the New Germany: American & German Perspectives. Ed. by Friederike Eigler & Peter C. Pfeiffer. LC 93-12348. (Studies in German Literature, Linguistics & Culture). 220p. 1993. 59.95 (*1-879751-56-9*) Camden Hse.

Cultural Transition: Human Experience & Social Transformation in the Third World & Japan. Ed. by Merry I. White & Susan Pollak. (Project on Human Potential Ser.). 256p. 1986. text ed. 39.50 (*0-7102-0572-4*, RKP) Routledge.

Cultural Transmission & Evolution: A Quantitative Approach. L. L. Cavalli-Sforza & M. W. Feldman. Ed. by M. Robert. LC 80-8539. (Monographs in Population Biology: No. 16). (Illus.). 368p. 1981. 60.00 (*0-691-08280-4*); pap. 22.50 (*0-691-08283-9*) Princeton U Pr.

Cultural Transmissions & Receptions: American Culture in Europe. Ed. by D. Bosscher et al. (European Contributions to American Studies: No. 25). 350p. (Orig.). 1993. pap. 42.50 (*90-5383-207-6*, Pub. by VU Univ Pr NE) Paul & Co Pubs.

Cultural Treasures of Korea, 8 vols., Set. Hong-Sop Chin et al. LC 91-73742. (Illus.). 1993. lib. bdg. 775.50 (*1-56591-100-8*) Hollym Intl. "The first two volumes are devoted to the most highly esteemed of Korea's cultural treasures, designated as National Treasures. Each book consists of a catalog & a list of treasures...the catalogs are preceded by color plates & followed by introductory essays, each by a different specialist, which provide contextual reference for the treasures in each group. In Volume 1, buildings--palace, temple & shrine--in wood construction are grouped together as are pagodas, Buddhist images & monuments carved from stone... Volume 2, groups... tomb deposits...ceramic containers & incense burners, metal work, paintings & ancient books & documents... Every entry (has) a terse explanatory essay... This constitutes the most important feature of the publication. The captions offer, in every case, additional information about each artifact... The remaining volumes are devoted to General Treasures... Each volume has 150-250 splendid color photographs... with details--again, the most important feature of the series... Both the National Treasures & the General Treasures volumes are extraordinary because of the high quality & number of the color plates... the series as a whole is recommended for all libraries with an interest in the cultures of East Asia. Advanced undergraduate; graduate; faculty; professional."--CHOICE 6/94. Direct orders: Hollym International Corp., 18 Donald Pl., Elizabeth, NJ 07208,. Phone: 908-353-1655, FAX: 908353-0255. ***Publisher Provided Annotation.***

***Cultural Treasures of the Internet: Everything a Literate Reader Needs to Find & Access the Internet.** Michael Clark. LC 95-3379. 1995. pap. text ed. 22.95 (*0-13-209669-2*) P-H.

Cultural Turn: Scene-Setting Essays on Contemporary Cultural Theory. David C. Chaney. LC 93-46091. 272p. 1994. 59.95x (*0-415-10297-9*, B4084, Routledge NY); pap. write for info. (*0-415-10298-7*, B4088, Routledge NY) Routledge.

Cultural Unity of Black Africa. 2nd ed. Cheikh A. Diop. LC 77-12276. 1987. reprint ed. pap. 14.95 (*0-88378-049-6*) Third World.

Cultural Uses of Print in Early Modern France. Roger Chartier. Tr. by Lydia G. Cochrane. (Illus.). 384p. 1988. text ed. 49.50 (*0-691-05499-1*) Princeton U Pr.

Cultural Values & Human Ecology in Southeast Asia. Ed. by Karl L. Hutterer et al. LC 84-45711. (Michigan Papers on South & Southeast Asia: No. 27). (Illus.). 416p. (C). 1985. 31.95 (*0-89148-039-0*); pap. 17.95 (*0-89148-040-4*) Ctr S&SE Asian.

Cultural Variability in Context: Woodland Settlements of the Mid-Ohio Valley. Ed. by Mark F. Seeman. LC 91-14831. (Illus.). 96p. (Orig.). 1992. pap. text ed. 14.50 (*0-87338-452-0*) Kent St U Pr.

Cultural Ways: A Concise Introduction to Cultural Anthropology. 3rd ed. Robert B. Taylor. Orig. Title: Cultural Ways: A Concise Edition of Introduction to Cultural Anthropology. (Illus.). 339p. (C). 1988. reprint ed. pap. 15.95 (*0-88133-335-2*) Waveland Pr.

Cultural Ways: A Concise Edition of Introduction to Cultural Anthropology see Cultural Ways: A Concise Introduction to Cultural Anthropology

Cultural Wellsprings of Folktales. Vytautas Bagdanavicius. Tr. by Jeronimas Zemkalnis. Orig. Title: Kulturines Gelmes Pasakose. 1970. 6.00 (*0-87141-030-3*) Manyland.

***Cultural World of Jesus: Sunday by Sunday, Cycle A.** John Pilch. 200p. (Orig.). 1995. pap. text ed. write for info. (*0-8146-2286-0*, Liturg Pr Bks) Liturgical Pr.

***Cultural World of Jesus: Sunday by Sunday, Cycle C.** John J. Pilch. 200p. (Orig.). 1995. pap. text ed. write for info. (*0-8146-2288-7*, Liturg Pr Bks) Liturgical Pr.

Culturally Disadvantaged: A Bibliography & Keyword out-of-Context (KWOC) Index. Robert E. Booth et al. LC 66-27901. 813p. reprint ed. pap. 180.00 (*0-685-15719-9*, 2027666) Bks Demand.

Culturally Diverse Children & Adolescents: Assessment, Diagnosis & Treatment. Ian A. Canino & Jeanne Spurlock. LC 93-50824. 196p. 1994. lib. bdg. 25.00 (*0-89862-409-6*, C2409) Guilford Pr.

Culturally Diverse Library Collections for Children. Herman L. Totten & Risa W. Brown. 200p. 1994. 35.00 (*1-55570-140-X*) Neal-Schuman.

Culturally Diverse Library Collections for Youth. Herman L. Totten & Risa W. Brown. 200p. 1994. 35.00 (*1-55570-141-8*) Neal-Schuman.

Culturally Responsive Teaching & Supervision: A Handbook for Staff Development. C. A. Bowers & David J. Flinders. 64p. (C). 1991. pap. text ed. 9.95 (*0-8077-3078-5*) Tchrs Coll.

Culturally Sensitive Caregiving & Childbearing Families. Leah Ramer. Ed. by Beverly S. Raff & Ellen Fiore. LC 92-13293. (Nursing Issues for the Twenty-First Century Ser.: No. 4, Module 1). 1992. pap. write for info. (*0-86525-054-5*) March of Dimes.

Culturally Speaking: A Conversation & Culture Text. 2nd ed. Rhona B. Genzel & Martha G. Cummings. LC 93-38189. 1994. 20.00 (*0-8384-4212-9*) Heinle & Heinle.

Culture. Chris Jenks. LC 93-3489. (Key Ideas Ser.). 1993. write for info. (*0-415-07278-6*) Routledge.

***Culture.** Ed. by Jeremy Mitchell & Richard Maidment. (The U. S. in the Twentieth Century Ser.). 256p. 1994. pap. 14.95 (*0-340-59687-2*, Pub. by E Arnld UK) St Martin.

Culture: Sociological Perspectives. John R. Hall & Mary J. Nietz. LC 92-26352. 304p. (C). 1993. pap. text ed. write for info. (*0-13-816471-1*) P-H.

Culture: The Tapestry of Life. Cal Easterling. 200p. (Orig.). (C). 1994. pap. text ed. 21.00 (*1-878045-37-7*) Whittier Pubns.

Culture - Contexture: Explorations in Anthropology & Literary Studies. Jeffrey M. Peck. Ed. by E. Valentine Daniel. LC 94-3997. 1995. 50.00 (*0-520-08463-2*) U CA Pr.

***Culture - Contexture: Explorations in Anthropology & Literary Studies.** Jeffrey M. Peck. Ed. by E. Valentine Daniel. 405p. 1995. pap. 16.00 (*0-520-08464-0*) U CA Pr.

***Culture - Flesh: Explorations of Post-Civilized Modernity.** Michael A. Weinstein. (Social Philosophy Research Institute Ser.). 144p. (C). 1995. text ed. 48.50 (*0-8476-8083-5*); pap. text ed. 19.95 (*0-8476-8084-3*) Rowman.

Culture Acquisition: A Holistic Approach to Human Learning. Mary A. Pitman et al. LC 88-27507. 252p. 1989. text ed. 52.95 (*0-275-93031-9*, C3031, Praeger Pubs) Greenwood.

Culture Acquisition: A Holistic Approach to Human Learning. Mary A. Pitman et al. LC 88-27507. (Illus.). 252p. 1989. lib. bdg. 42.95 (*0-318-41925-4*, C3031, Greenwood Pr) Greenwood.

Culture Against Man. Jules Henry. 1965. pap. text ed. 9.95 (*0-07-553685-4*) McGraw.

Culture & African American Politics. Charles P. Henry. LC 88-46100. (Blacks in the Diaspora Ser.). 160p. 1990. 27.50 (*0-253-32754-7*); pap. 9.95 (*0-253-20730-4*, MB-730) Ind U Pr.

Culture & Agency: The Place of Culture in Social Theory. Margaret S. Archer. (Illus.). 384p. (C). 1990. pap. 24.95 (*0-521-38736-1*) Cambridge U Pr.

Culture & Aging. Margaret Clark & Barbara G. Anderson. Ed. by Leon Stein. LC 79-8827. (Growing Old Ser.). (Illus.). 1980. reprint ed. lib. bdg. 48.95 (*0-405-12781-2*) Ayer.

Culture & Agriculture: An Ecological Introduction to Traditional & Modern Farming Systems. Ernest L. Schusky. LC 89-17676. 224p. 1989. text ed. 47.95 (*0-89789-185-6*, Bergin & Garvey) Greenwood.

Culture & AIDS. Ed. by Douglas A. Feldman. LC 90-30003. 224p. 1990. text ed. 47.95 (*0-275-93189-7*, C3189, Praeger Pubs) Greenwood.

Culture & Anarchy. Matthew Arnold. (C). 1932. pap. 15.95 (*0-521-09103-9*) Cambridge U Pr.

Culture & Anarchy. Matthew Arnold. Ed. by Samuel Lipman. LC 93-2427. (Rethinking the Western Tradition Ser.). 289p. 1993. reprint ed. 32.00 (*0-300-05866-7*); reprint ed. pap. 12.00 (*0-300-05867-5*) Yale U Pr.

Culture & Anarchy see Complete Prose Works of Matthew Arnold

Culture & Anarchy & Other Writings. Matthew Arnold. Ed. by Stefan Collini. (Cambridge Texts in the History of Political Thought Ser.). 280p. (C). 1993. 39.95 (*0-521-37440-5*); pap. 10.95 (*0-521-37796-X*) Cambridge U Pr.

Culture & Anomie: Ethnographic Imagination in the Nineteenth Century. Christopher Herbert. LC 91-4366. 312p. 1991. lib. bdg. 48.00 (*0-226-32738-8*); pap. text ed. 16.95 (*0-226-32739-6*) U Ch Pr.

Culture & Art of India. R. Mukherjee. (Illus.). 1984. text ed. 48.00 (*0-685-13648-5*) Coronet Bks.

An Asterisk (*) at the beginning of an entry indicates that the title is appearing in BIP for the first time.

C

An Asterisk (*) at the beginning of an entry indicates that the title is appearing in BIP for the first time.

1741

Culture & Practical Reason. Marshall D. Sahlins. LC 75-27899. (Illus.). 1978. pap. text ed. 11.95 (0-226-73361-0, P773) U Ch Pr.

Culture & Processes of Adult Learning. Ed. by Richard Edwards et al. (Learning Through Life Ser.). 304p. 1993. pap. 19.95 (0-415-08981-6, B0162) Routledge.

Culture & Propagation of Striped Bass & Its Hybrids. R. M. Harrell et al. LC 90-83071. 323p. 1990. pap. text ed. 36.50 (0-913235-66-0) Am Fisheries Soc.

***Culture & Psychology Reader.** Ed. by Nancy R. Goldberger & Jody Veroff. 760p. 1995. 65.00 (0-8147-3080-9); pap. 29.95 (0-8147-3081-7) NYU Pr.

Culture & Psychopathology. Ed. by Juan E. Mezzich & Carlos E. Berganza. 512p. 1984. text ed. 68.50 (0-231-04874-2) Col U Pr.

Culture & Psychotherapy. Theodora M. Abel & Rhoda Metreaux. 1974. 24.95 (0-8084-0368-0); pap. 17.95x (0-8084-0369-9) NCUP.

***Culture & Religion in Japanese-American Relations: Essays on Uchimura Kanzo, No. 5.** Ed. by Ray A. Moore. x, 142p. 1981. pap. 8.95 (0-939512-10-6) U MI Japan.

***Culture & Religion in Merovingian Gaul, A.D. 481-751.** Yitzhak Hen. (Cultures, Beliefs & Traditions Ser.: No. 1). (Illus.). 420p. 1995. 103.25 (90-04-10347-3) E J Brill.

Culture & Retardation. Ed. by Lewis L. Langness & Harold Levine. 1986. lib. bdg. 99.50 (90-277-2177-7) Kluwer Ac.

Culture & Retardation. Ed. by Lewis L. Langness & Harold Levine. 1987. pap. text ed. 41.50 (90-277-2178-5) Kluwer Ac.

Culture & Revolution: Cultural Ramifications of the French Revolution. George Levitine. Ed. by Susan Libby & Pam Hall. (Illus.). 336p. (C). 1989. write for info. (0-9625932-0-6) Univ MD Dept Art Hist.

Culture & Sericulture: Social Anthropology & Development in a South Indian Livestock Industry. Simon Charsley. (Studies in Anthropology). 1982. text ed. 85.00 (0-12-169380-5) Acad Pr.

Culture & Social Institutions of Ancient Iran. Muhammad A. Dandamaev & Vladimir G. Lukonin. 400p. 1989. 115.00 (0-521-32107-7) Cambridge U Pr.

Culture & Society: Contemporary Debates. Ed. by Jeffrey C. Alexander & Steven Seidman. 362p. (C). 1990. 64.95 (0-521-35086-7); pap. 18.95 (0-521-35939-2) Cambridge U Pr.

Culture & Society in Eighteenth Century Hungary. D. Kosary. 250p. (C). 1987. 80.00 (0-569-09042-3, Pub. by Collets UK) Pro-Am Music.

Culture & Society in Lucian. C. P. Jones. LC 86-3099. 224p. 1986. 39.95 (0-674-17974-9) HUP.

Culture & Society in New Order Indonesia. Ed. by Virginia M. Hooker. LC 93-19994. (South-East Asian Social Science Monographs). 360p. 1993. 48.00 (0-19-588618-6) OUP.

***Culture & Society in the Stuart Restoration: Literature, Drama, History.** Ed. by Gerald Maclean. (Illus.). 288p. (C). 1995. 59.95 (0-521-41605-1) Cambridge U Pr.

***Culture & Society in the Stuart Restoration: Literature, Drama, History.** Ed. by Gerald Maclean. (Illus.). 288p. (C). 1995. pap. 19.95 (0-521-47566-X) Cambridge U Pr.

Culture & Society, Seventeen-Eighty to Nineteen-Fifty. 2nd ed. Raymond Williams. LC 85-5195. (Morningside Bk.). 365p. 1983. reprint ed. text ed. 82.00 (0-231-02287-5); reprint ed. pap. text ed. 17.50 (0-231-05701-6) Col U Pr.

Culture & Technology. David S. Bertolotti, Jr. LC 84-71555. 154p. 1984. pap. 8.95 (0-87972-308-4) Bowling Green Univ.

Culture & the Ad: Exploring Otherness in the World of Advertising. William M. O'Barr. LC 93-44451. (Institutional Structures of Feeling Ser.). (C). 1994. text ed. 62.00 (0-8133-2196-4); pap. text ed. 17.95 (0-8133-2197-2) Westview.

Culture & the Anthropological Tradition: Essays in Honor of Robert F. Spencer. Ed. by Robert H. Winthrop. 368p. (Orig.). (C). 1990. lib. bdg. 53.00 (0-8191-7791-1) U Pr of Amer.

Culture & the City: Cultural Philanthropy in Chicago from the 1880s to 1917. Helen L. Horowitz. LC 88-27722. xvi, 288p. 1989. pap. text ed. 13.95 (0-226-35374-5) U Ch Pr.

Culture & the Development of Children's Action: A Cultural-Historical Theory of Developmental Psychology. Jaan Valsiner. LC 86-18925. (Wiley Series in Development Psychology). (Illus.). 276p. reprint ed. pap. 78.70 (0-7837-6165-1, 2045887) Bks Demand.

Culture & the Direction of Human Evolution. Symposium on Culture & the Direction of Human Evolution Staff. Ed. by Stanley M. Garn. LC 64-16088. (Illus.). 103p. reprint ed. pap. 29.40 (0-7837-3792-0, 2043612) Bks Demand.

Culture & the Evolutionary Process. Robert Boyd & Peter J. Richerson. LC 84-24125. (Illus.). viii, 332p. 1988. pap. text ed. 15.95 (0-226-06933-8) U Ch Pr.

Culture & the King: The Social Implications of the Arthurian Legend. Ed. by Martin B. Shichtman & James P. Carley. LC 93-10552. (SUNY Series in Medieval Studies). 324p. (C). 1994. text ed. 59.50 (0-7914-1863-4); pap. text ed. 19.95 (0-7914-1864-2) State U NY Pr.

Culture & the Literary Text: The Case of Flaubert's Madam Bovary. Anna V. Lambros. LC 94-1889. (American University Studies, Series II, Romance Languages & Literatures: Vol. 162). 1995. write for info. (0-8204-2588-5) P Lang Pubs.

Culture & the People. Maxim Gorky. LC 79-119930. (Select Bibliographies Reprint Ser.). 1977. 21.95 (0-8369-5373-8) Ayer.

Culture & the Politics of Third World Nationalism. Dawa Norbu. LC 91-46016. 304p. 1992. 49.95 (0-415-08003-7, A7555) Routledge.

Culture & the Radical Conscience. Eugene Goodheart. LC 72-91910. 191p. 1973. 23.00 (0-674-17966-8) HUP.

Culture & the Radical Conscience. Eugene Goodheart. LC 72-91910. 191p. 1975. pap. 12.95 (0-674-17968-4) HUP.

Culture & the Restructuring of Community Mental Health. William A. Vega & John W. Murphy. LC 90-3158. (Contributions in Psychology Ser.: No. 16). 176p. 1990. text ed. 45.00 (0-313-26887-8, VEA/, Greenwood Pr) Greenwood.

Culture & the Revolution. Paul Dukes. 256p. 1990. text ed. 49.00 (0-86187-788-8, Pub. by Pinter Pubs UK) St Martin.

Culture & Thought in the Transformation of the World. Anisuzzaman & Anouar Abdel-Malek. LC 84-40079. 105p. 1984. text ed. 24.95 (0-312-17865-4) St Martin.

Culture & Truth: The Remaking of Social Analysis. Renato Rosaldo. LC 93-18158. 288p. 1993. pap. 14.00 (0-8070-4623-X) Beacon Pr.

Culture & Urbanization. S. M. Michael. (C). 1989. 60.00 (81-210-0231-1, Pub. by Inter-India Pubns) S Asia.

Culture & Value. Ludwig Wittgenstein. Ed. by George H. Von Wright. Tr. by Peter Winch. LC 80-15234. 1984. pap. 9.95 (0-226-90435-0); pap. 7.95 (0-685-04980-9) U Ch Pr.

Culture & Values Alt, Vol. 3E. 3rd ed. Cunningham. 1993. pap. text ed. 44.25 (0-15-500195-7) HarBrace.

***Culture Anthropology.** 4th ed. Duvall. (C). 1995. student ed, text ed. 10.00 (0-673-46976-X) HarpCollege.

Culture As History: The Transformation of American Society in the Twentieth Century. Warren I. Susman. LC 84-19014. 1985. 22.95 (0-394-53364-X); pap. 15.16 (0-394-72161-6) Pantheon.

Culture As Polyphony: An Essay on the Nature of Paradigms. James M. Curtis. LC 77-25242. 208p. reprint ed. pap. 59.30 (0-7837-2360-1, AU00425) Bks Demand.

Culture Bound: Language Teaching from a Cultural Perspective. Ed. by Joyce M. Valdes. (Cambridge Language Teaching Library). (Illus.). 256p. 1986. pap. 16.95 (0-521-31045-8) Cambridge U Pr.

Culture-Bound Syndromes. Ed. by Ronald C. Simons & Charles C. Hughes. 1985. lib. bdg. 145.50 (90-277-1858-X) Kluwer Ac.

Culture Builders: A Historical & Anthropology of Middle-Class Life. Jonas Frykman & Orvar Lofgren. Tr. by Alan Crozier. 308p. (SWE.). 1987. pap. text ed. 16.00 (0-8135-1239-5) Rutgers U Pr.

Culture Care Diversity & Universality: A Theory of Nursing. Ed. by Madeleine Leininger. LC 15-2402. (Illus.). 448p. (Orig.). (C). 1991. pap. text ed. 34.95 (0-88737-519-7) Natl League Nurse.

Culture-Centered Counseling & Interviewing Skills: A Practical Guide. Paul Pedersen & Allen E. Ivey. LC 93-15372. 224p. 1993. text ed. 59.95 (0-275-94668-1, C4668, Praeger Pubs); pap. text ed. 19.95 (0-275-94669-X, B4669, Praeger Pubs) Greenwood.

Culture, Change & Leadership in a Modern Indian Community: The Colorado River Indian Reservation. Katherine E. Blossom. 101p. 1979. pap. 6.00 (0-935741-12-7) Cherokee Pubns.

Culture Change & Modernization: Mini Models & Case Studies. Louise Spindler. (Illus.). 177p. (C). 1984. reprint ed. pap. text ed. 9.95 (0-88133-089-2) Waveland Pr.

Culture Change & Shifting Populations in Central Northern Mexico. William B. Griffen. LC 69-16327. (Anthropological Papers: No. 13). 196p. 1969. pap. 21.95 (0-8165-0140-8) U of Ariz Pr.

***Culture Clash.** 2nd ed. Ellyn Bache. LC 94-79776. 131p. 1995. pap. 11.95 (0-9635967-0-5) Banks Channel.

Culture Clash: Law & Science in America. Steven Goldberg. 272p. 1994. 29.95 (0-8147-3057-4) NYU Pr.

Culture Clash: Managing in a Multicultural World. H. Ned Seelye & Alan Seelye-James. Ed. by Anne Knudsen. LC 94-16177. 1994. 27.95 (0-8442-3304-8, NTC Busn Bks) NTC Pub Grp.

Culture Clash: The Making of Gay Sensibility. Michael Bronski. LC 84-50941. 249p. (Orig.). 1984. 30.00 (0-89608-218-0); pap. 12.00 (0-89608-217-2) South End Pr.

Culture, Class & Development in Pakistan: The Emergence of an Industrial Bourgeoisie in Punjab. Anita M. Weiss. 207p. (C). 1991. pap. text ed. 39.00 (0-8133-7910-5) Westview.

Culture Collection & Breeding of Edible Mushrooms. Ed. by Shu-Ting Chang et al. LC 92-16952. 324p. 1993. text ed. 55.00 (2-88124-561-7) Gordon & Breach.

Culture, Communication, & Cognition: Vygotskian Perspectives. Ed. by James V. Wertsch. LC 83-14444. 400p. 1986. pap. 24.95 (0-521-33830-1) Cambridge U Pr.

Culture, Communication, & Dependency: The Tradition of H. A. Innis. Ed. by William H. Melody et al. LC 80-21189. (Communication & Information Science Ser.). 264p. (C). 1981. text ed. 55.00 (0-89391-065-1); pap. 29.50 (0-89391-079-1) Ablex Pub.

Culture, Communication, & National Identity: The Case of Canadian Television. Richard Collins. 368p. 1990. 55.00 (0-8020-2733-4); pap. 21.95 (0-8020-6772-7) U of Toronto Pr.

Culture, Communication & Social Change. Ed. by P. C. Joshi. 400p. 1989. text ed. 35.00 (0-7069-4439-9, Pub. by Vikas II) S Asia.

Culture, Conflict, & Communication in the Wildland - Urban Interface. Ed. by Alan W. Ewert et al. (Social Behavior & Natural Resources Ser.). 410p. (C). 1993. pap. text ed. 52.50 (0-8133-8440-0) Westview.

Culture Conflict in Texas, 1821-1835. Samuel H. Lowrie. LC 32-34638. (Columbia University. Studies in the Social Sciences: No. 376). reprint ed. 12.50 (0-404-51376-X) AMS Pr.

Culture Conflict in Texas, 1821-1835. Samuel H. Lowrie. 1993. reprint ed. lib. bdg. 75.00 (0-7812-5943-6) Rprt Serv.

Culture Contact in the Pacific. Ed. by Max Quanchi. LC 92-17851. (Illus.). 200p. (C). 1993. pap. 25.00 (0-521-42284-1) Cambridge U Pr.

Culture, Control & Commitment: A Study of Work Organization & Work Attitudes in the United States & Japan. James R. Lincoln & Arne L. Kalleberg. (Illus.). 264p. (C). 1992. pap. 21.95 (0-521-42866-1) Cambridge U Pr.

Culture, Crisis & Creativity. Dane Rudhyar. LC 76-43008. (Orig.). 1977. pap. 4.25 (0-8356-0487-X, Quest) Theos Pub Hse.

Culture-Criticism-Ideology. Ed. by Stuart Peterfreund. (Proceedings of the Northeastern University Center for Literary Studies: Vol. 4). 75p. 1986. pap. text ed. 6.95 (0-930350-97-9) NE U Pr.

Culture Critique: Fernand Dumont & the New Quebec Sociology. Michael A. Weinstein. (New World Perspectives Ser.). 125p. (Orig.). 1985. text ed. 19.95 (0-312-17883-2); pap. 7.95 (0-312-17884-0) St Martin.

Culture, Curers, & Contagion. Ed. by Norman Klein. LC 79-10888. (Anthropology Ser.). 256p. 1979. pap. text ed. 14.95 (0-88316-531-7) Chandler & Sharp.

Culture des Pommes de Terre. Michel-Guillaume Jean De Crevecoeur. (Works of Michel-Guillaume Jean De Crevecoeur Ser.). 1990. reprint ed. lib. bdg. 79.00 (0-7812-2454-3) Rprt Serv.

Culture-Development Interface. Ed. by Yogesh Atal. 1991. 25.00 (0-7069-5829-2) Advent Bks Div.

***Culture, Difference & the Arts: Multiculturalism & the Arts.** Ed. by Sneja Gunew & Fazal Rizvi. 224p. 1995. pap. 24.95 (1-86373-742-1, Pub. by Allen Unwin AT) Paul & Co Pubs.

Culture et Spiritualite en Espagne du IVe au VIIe Siecle. Jaques Fontaine. (Collected Studies: No. CS234). 352p. (ENG, FRE, ITA & SPA.). (C). 1986. reprint ed. lib. bdg. 97.95 (0-86078-182-8, Pub. by Variorum UK) Ashgate Pub Co.

Culture, Ethnicity, & Identity: Current Issues in Research. Ed. by William C. McCready. LC 82-22651. 1983. text ed. 72.00 (0-12-482920-1) Acad Pr.

Culture, Ethnicity, & Mental Illness. Ed. by Albert C. Gaw. LC 92-10686. 624p. 1992. text ed. 72.00 (0-88048-359-8) Am Psychiatric.

Culture, Excitement & Relevance of Mathematics. V. Krishnamurthy. 1990. 30.00 (81-224-0272-0, Pub. by Wiley Eastern II) S Asia.

Culture, Experience & Pluralism: Essays on African Ideas of Illness & Healing. Ed. by A. Jacobson-Widding & David Westerlund. (Uppsala Studies in Cultural Anthropology: No. 13). 308p. (Orig.). 1989. pap. 58.50x (91-554-2325-6, Pub. by Almqv & Wiksell SW) Coronet Bks.

Culture Facade: Art, Science, & Politics in the Work of Oscar Lewis. Susan M. Rigdon. LC 87-19063. (Illus.). 352p. 1988. 27.95 (0-252-01495-2) U of Ill Pr.

***Culture Factor.** Corporate & International Perspectives Staff. 94p. (C). 1994. pap. 105.00x (0-85292-564-6, Pub. by IPM Hse UK) St Mut.

Culture for Democracy: Mass Communication & the Cultivated Mind in Britain Between the Wars. D. L. LeMahieu. (Illus.). 408p. 1988. 79.00 (0-19-820137-0) OUP.

Culture, Form & Place. Ed. by Kent Mathewson. LC 93-37168. (Geoscience & Man Ser.: Vol. 32). (Illus.). 356p. (C). 1994. pap. text ed. 24.95 (0-938909-55-X) Geosci Pubns LSU.

Culture-Free Self-Esteem Inventories for Children & Adults Complete Battery. 2nd ed. James Battle. Ed. by J. B. Preston. 1981. pap. 115.00 (0-87562-067-1) Spec Child.

Culture, Gender, Race, & U. S. Labor History. Ed. by Ronald C. Kent et al. LC 92-35921. (Contributions in Labor Studies: No. 39). 232p. 1993. text ed. 49.95 (0-313-28828-3, GM8828) Greenwood.

***Culture, Geography, & Environment.** Eric Fournier. 144p. (C). 1995. pap. text ed. 13.95 (0-7872-0806-X) Kendall-Hunt.

***Culture, Health & Illness.** 3rd ed. Helman. 396p. 1995. pap. write for info. (0-7506-1919-8, Focal) Buttrwrth-Heinemann.

Culture, Health & Illness. 3rd ed. C. Helman. 344p. 1991. pap. text ed. 29.95 (0-7506-0478-6, Pub. by John Wright UK) Buttrwrth-Heinemann.

Culture Historical Method of Ethnology. Wilhelm Schmidt. LC 73-10761. 383p. 1974. reprint ed. text ed. 65.00 (0-8371-7036-2, SCET, Greenwood Pr) Greenwood.

Culture, History & Ideology in the Formation of Ba'thist Iraq, 1968-1989. Amatzia Baram. (Illus.). 196p. 1991. 35.00 (0-312-04805-X) St Martin.

Culture, Human Rights & Peace in Central America. Ed. by George F. McLean et al. LC 88-37136. (Cultural Heritage & Contemporary Change Series VI: Foundations of Moral Education,: Vol. 2). 220p. (Orig.). 1989. 45.00 (0-8191-7356-8); pap. 14.00 (0-8191-7357-6) Coun Res Values.

Culture, Ideology & Politics: Essays for Eric Hobsbawm. Ed. by Raphael Samuel & Gareth Stedman-Jones. (History Workshop Ser.). 320p. (Orig.). 1983. pap. 14.95 (0-7100-9433-7, RKP) Routledge.

Culture, Ideology & Social Process. Ed. by Tony Bennett et al. (Illus.). 320p. 1981. pap. 29.95 (0-7134-4314-6, Pub. by Batsford UK) Trafalgar.

***Culture, Ideology & Socialism.** Nick Stevenson. 234p. 1995. 59.95 (1-85972-174-5, Pub. by Avebury Pub UK) Ashgate Pub Co.

***Culture in Action: A Public Art Program of Sculpture Chicago.** Michael Brenson et al. LC 94-78551. (Illus.). 144p. (Orig.). 1995. pap. 20.00 (0-941920-31-3) Bay Pr.

Culture in Action: Family Life, Emotion, & Male Dominance in Banaras, India. Steve Derne. 224p. 1995. text ed. 54.50x (0-7914-2425-1); pap. 17.95x (0-7914-2426-X) State U NY Pr.

***Culture in Africa: An Appeal for Pluralism.** Ed. by Raoul Granqvist. (Scandinavian Institute of African Studies: No. 29). 204p. (Orig.). 1993. pap. 52.50x (91-7106-330-7, Pub. by Almqv & Wiksell SW) Coronet Bks.

Culture in an Age of Money: The Legacy of the 1980s in America. Ed. by Nicolaus Mills. (Illus.). 256p. 1990. 22.50 (0-929587-35-9) I R Dee.

Culture in an Age of Money: The Legacy of the 1980s in America. Ed. by Nicolaus Mills. (Illus.). 256p. 1991. reprint ed. pap. 12.95 (0-929587-71-5, Elephant Paperbacks) I R Dee.

Culture in Another South Africa. Ed. by Willem Campschreur & Joost Divendal. LC 89-3243. (Illus.). 288p. 1989. 24.95 (0-940793-35-0, Olive Branch Pr); pap. 14.95 (0-940793-36-9, Olive Branch Pr) Interlink Pub.

Culture in Britain since Nineteen Forty-Five. Arthur Marwick. 192p. 1991. pap. 12.95 (0-631-17191-6) Blackwell Pubs.

Culture in Conflict: Skilled Workers & Industrial Capitalism in Hamilton, Ontario 1860-1914. Bryan D. Palmer. LC 80-481234. 361p. reprint ed. pap. 102.90 (0-7837-1024-0, 2041335) Bks Demand.

***Culture in Context.** Weston La Barre. (C). 1994. text ed. 40.00 (1-885809-00-X); pap. text ed. 19.95 (1-885809-01-8) Psyche Pr NY.

Culture in Early Anglo-Saxon England. Daisy E. Martin-Clarke. 1979. 18.95 (0-405-10615-7) Ayer.

Culture in Language & Learning. Incl. Anthropological Concept of Culture. Ernestine Friedl. 1960. (0-318-54565-9); Language As Culture. William E. Welmers. 1960. (0-318-54566-7); Teaching of Classical Cultures. Doris E. Kibbe. 1960. (0-318-54567-5); Teaching of Western European Cultures. Ira Wade. 1960. (0-318-54568-3); Teaching of Slavic Cultures. Leon I. Twarog. 1960. (0-318-54569-1); 1960. Set pap. 10.95 (0-915432-60-9) NE Conf Teach Foreign.

***Culture in Mind: Meaning Construction & Culturel Cognition.** Bradd Shore. (Illus.). 416p. 1996. 35.00 (0-19-509597-9) OUP.

Culture in Retrospect: An Introduction to Archaeology. S. J. Knudson. (Illus.). 555p. (C). 1985. reprint ed. pap. text ed. 24.95x (0-88133-168-6) Waveland Pr.

Culture in Search of Survival: The Phuan of Thailand & Laos. Snit Smuckarn & Kennon Breazeale. LC 87-51333. (Monograph Ser.: No. 31). x, 279p. (C). 1988. pap. 17.00 (0-938692-33-X) Yale U SE Asia.

Culture, Inc. The Corporate Takeover of Public Expression. Herbert I. Schiller. (Illus.). 200p. 1989. 25.00 (0-19-505005-3) OUP.

Culture, Inc. The Corporate Takeover of Public Expression. Herbert I. Schiller. (Illus.). 200p. 1991. pap. 10.95 (0-19-506783-5) OUP.

***Culture Incarnate: Native Anthropology from Russia.** Ed. by Marjorie M. Balzer. LC 94-33956. 280p. 1995. 60.00 (1-56324-534-5) M E Sharpe.

***Culture Incarnate: Native Anthropology from Russia.** Intro. by Marjorie M. Balzer. LC 94-33956. 280p. 1995. pap. 22.95 (1-56324-535-3) M E Sharpe.

Culture Industry. Derek Wynne. 144p. 1992. 59.95 (1-85628-287-2, Pub. by Avebury Pub UK) Ashgate Pub Co.

***Culture, Inequality & Self.** Cheryl Childers et al. 128p. (C). 1994. 19.96 (0-7872-0382-3) Kendall-Hunt.

Culture Keepers: Enlightening & Empowering Our Communities: Proceedings of the First National Conference of African American Librarians. Ed. by Stanton F. Biddle. 364p. (Orig.). 1993. pap. 19.95 (0-9640292-0-0) Black Caucus Am Lib.

Culture, Kin, & Cognition in Oceania: Essays in Honor of Ward H. Goodenough. 1989. write for info. (0-913167-31-2) Am Anthro Assn.

Culture Lab. Brian Boigon. (Illus.). 256p. (Orig.). 1993. pap. 17.95 (1-878271-77-6) Princeton Arch.

***Culture Lab 2.** Brian Boigon. 1995. pap. 19.95 (1-56898-036-1) Princeton Arch.

Culture Learning: Concepts, Applications, & Research. Ed. by Richard W. Brislin. LC 77-5111. (East-West Center Book Ser.). 369p. reprint ed. pap. 105.20 (0-7837-3988-5, 2043819) Bks Demand.

Culture Learning: The Fifth Dimension. Louise Damen. (L2 Professional Library). 432p. (C). 1987. pap. text ed. 32.94 (0-201-11478-X) Addison-Wesley.

Culture, Learning, & the Disciplines: Theory & Practice in Cross-Cultural Orientation. Ed. by Josef A. Mestenhauser et al. 184p. 1988. 18.00 (0-912207-23-X) NAFSA Washington.

C

An Asterisk (*) at the beginning of an entry indicates that the title is appearing in BIP for the first time.

An Asterisk (*) at the beginning of an entry indicates that the title is appearing in BIP for the first time.

1743

Culture Relations & U. S. Foreign Policy. Charles A. Thomson & Walter H. Laves. LC 63-7167. 227p. reprint ed. pap. 64.70 (*0-317-09996-5*, 2055199) Bks Demand.

Culture, Religion, & the Sacred Self: A Critical Introduction to the Anthropological Study of Religion. Jacob Pandian. 352p. (C). 1990. pap. text ed. write for info. (*0-13-194226-3*) P-H.

Culture, Schooling, & Psychological Development. Ed. by Liliana T. Landsmann & Sidney Strauss. (Human Development Ser.: Vol. 4). 224p. (C). 1991. text ed. 49.50 (*0-89391-529-7*) Ablex Pub.

Culture, Self-Identity, & Work. Miriam Erez & P. Christopher Earley. LC 92-28734. (Illus.). 280p. 1993. 39.95 (*0-19-507580-3*) OUP.

***Culture Shift: The Employee Handbook for Changing Corporate Culture.** Price Pritchett. 35p. 1993. pap. 5.95 (*0-944002-12-9*) Pritchett Assocs.

Culture Shift in Advanced Industrial Society. Ronald Inglehart. (Illus.). 464p. (C). 1989. text ed. 65.00 (*0-691-07786-X*); pap. 18.95 (*0-691-02296-8*) Princeton U Pr.

Culture Shock! Japan. Rex Shelley & Reiko Makiuchi. (Illus.). 250p. 1992. 10.95 (*1-55868-071-3*) Gr Arts Ctr Pub.

Culture Shock! Korea. 1992. pap. 10.95 (*1-55868-107-8*) Gr Arts Ctr Pub.

Culture Shock: Malaysia. Heidi Munan. (Illus.). 1991. pap. 10.95 (*1-55868-070-5*) Gr Arts Ctr Pub.

Culture Shock! Singapore. 1992. pap. 10.95 (*1-55868-108-6*) Gr Arts Ctr Pub.

***Culture Shock: Soviet Jews in Philadelphia.** Lenora E. Berson. (Illus.). Date not set. 5.00 (*0-615-00717-1*) Balch IES Pr.

Culture Shock! Spain. 1992. pap. 10.95 (*1-55868-106-X*) Gr Arts Ctr Pub.

Culture Shock! Successful Living Abroad - A Wife's Guide. Robin Pascoe. 250p. 1993. pap. 10.95 (*1-55868-123-X*) Gr Arts Ctr Pub.

***Culture Shock, a Traveller's Guide: Successful Globe Trotting.** Fisher. 1995. pap. text ed. 12.95 (*1-55868-238-4*) Gr Arts Ctr Pub.

Culture Shock! Australia. Ilsa Sharp. (Illus.). 256p. 1992. 10.95 (*1-55868-094-2*) Gr Arts Ctr Pub.

Culture Shock! Borneo. Ed. by Heidi Munn. (Illus.). 250p. 1991. pap. 10.95 (*1-55868-075-6*) Gr Arts Ctr Pub.

Culture Shock! Britain. Terry Tan. (Illus.). 250p. 1991. 10.95 (*1-55868-061-6*) Gr Arts Ctr Pub.

Culture Shock! Canada. Pang Guek Cheng-Chen & Robert Barlas. (Illus.). 256p. 1992. 10.95 (*1-55868-087-X*) Gr Arts Ctr Pub.

Culture Shock China. Ed. by Kevin Sinclair. (Illus.). 270p. 1991. pap. 10.95 (*1-55868-060-8*) Gr Arts Ctr Pub.

Culture Shock France. Ed. by Sally A. Taylor. (Illus.). 240p. 1991. pap. 10.95 (*1-55868-056-X*) Gr Arts Ctr Pub.

Culture Shock! Hong Kong. Betty Wei. 280p. 1994. pap. 10.95 (*1-55868-167-1*) Gr Arts Ctr Pub.

Culture Shock Indonesia. Ed. by Cathie Draine & Barbara Hall. (Illus.). 280p. 1991. pap. 10.95 (*1-55868-057-8*) Gr Arts Ctr Pub.

Culture Shock! Israel. Dick Winter. (Illus.). 248p. 1992. 10.95 (*1-55868-088-8*) Gr Arts Ctr Pub.

Culture Shock! Italy. Alessandro Falassi & Raymond Flower. 280p. 1994. pap. 10.95 (*1-55868-165-5*) Gr Arts Ctr Pub.

Culture Shock! Nepal. Ed. by Jon Burbank. (Illus.). 250p. 1991. pap. 10.95 (*1-55868-076-4*) Gr Arts Ctr Pub.

Culture Shock! Norway. Elizabeth Su-Dale. 280p. 1994. pap. 10.95 (*1-55868-166-3*) Gr Arts Ctr Pub.

Culture Shock Pakistan. Ed. by Karin Mittman & Zatar Ihsan. (Illus.). 1991. pap. 10.95 (*1-55868-059-4*) Gr Arts Ctr Pub.

Culture Shock! Philippines. Alfredo Roces & Grace Roces. (Illus.). 248p. 1992. 10.95 (*1-55868-089-6*) Gr Arts Ctr Pub.

Culture Shock: Psychological Reactions to Unfamiliar Environments. Adrian F. Furnham & Stephen Bochner. 300p. 1986. pap. 14.95 (*0-415-04523-1*, 4071) Routledge Chapman & Hall.

Culture Shock! Sri Lanka. Nanda Wanasundera. (Illus.). 250p. 1991. 10.95 (*1-55868-069-1*) Gr Arts Ctr Pub.

Culture Shock! Taiwan. Christopher Bates. 280p. 1994. pap. 10.95 (*1-55868-175-2*) Gr Arts Ctr Pub.

Culture Shock Thailand. Ed. by Robert Cooper & Nanthapa Cooper. (Illus.). 256p. 1991. pap. 10.95 (*1-55868-058-6*) Gr Arts Ctr Pub.

Culture Shock U. S. A. Esther Wanning. (Illus.). 1991. pap. 10.95 (*1-55868-055-1*) Gr Arts Ctr Pub.

Culture Sketches: Case Studies in Anthropology. Holly Peters-Golden. 1993. pap. text ed. write for info. (*0-07-035954-7*) McGraw.

Culture, Society & Menstruation. Ed. by Virginia Olesen & Nancy F. Woods. LC 66-55252. 186p. 1986. 41.00 (*0-89116-557-6*) Hemisp Pub.

Culture, Society & the Media. Ed. by Michael Gurevitch et al. (Illus.). 1982. pap. 15.95 (*0-416-73510-X*, NO. 3585) Routledge.

Culture, Structure or Choice? Essays in the Interpretation of the British Experience. Paul V. Warwick. LC 89-17714. 268p. 1990. 36.00 (*0-87586-087-7*) Agathon.

***Culture, Style & the Educative Process.** Barbara J. Shade. (Illus.). 380p. 1989. pap. 35.95 (*0-398-06418-0*) C C Thomas.

Culture, Style & the Educative Process. Barbara J. Shade. (Illus.). 380p. (C). 1989. text ed. 62.95 (*0-398-05609-9*) C C Thomas.

Culture, the Status of Women, & Demographic Behaviour: Illustrated with the Case of India. Alaka M. Basu. (Illus.). 288p. 1993. 49.95 (*0-19-828360-1*) OUP.

Culture Theory. David Kaplan & Robert Manners. 224p. 1972. pap. 16.95 (*0-685-03820-3*) P-H.

Culture Theory. David Kaplan & Robert A. Manners. 212p. (C). 1986. reprint ed. pap. text ed. 11.50x (*0-88133-222-4*) Waveland Pr.

Culture, Thought, & Social Action: An Anthropological Perspective. Stanley J. Tambiah. (Illus.). 432p. 1985. 42.50 (*0-674-17969-2*) HUP.

Culture Through Time: Anthropological Approaches. Emiko Ohnuki-Tierney. LC 90-36662. 344p. 1991. 45.00 (*0-8047-1792-3*); pap. 14.95 (*0-8047-1791-5*) Stanford U Pr.

Culture Town: Life in Raleigh's African American Communities. Linda Simmons-Henry & Linda H. Edmisten. LC 92-81999. (Illus.). 200p. 1993. 35.00 (*0-9635677-0-5*) Raleigh Hist.

Culture Trek. Dennis Graham et al. (BrainBooster Ser.). (Illus.). 32p. (J). (gr. 3 up). 1989. 5.95 (*0-88679-572-9*) Educ Insights.

Culture under Canvas: The Story of Tent Chautauqua. Harry P. Harrison. LC 78-5333. (Illus.). xxviii, 287p. 1978. reprint ed. text ed. 59.75 (*0-313-20380-6*, HACU, Greenwood Pr) Greenwood.

Culture, Unit Three: Field Notebook. Nan McNutt. (Project Archeology Series: Saving Traditions). (J). (gr. 5-8). 1987. student ed 1.25 (*0-944584-03-9*) Sopris.

Culture Vigilance. Susan L. Mizruchi. (C). 1992. pap. 14.00 (*0-691-01506-6*) Princeton U Pr.

Culture Vulture's Guide to Style, Period, & Ism. Carol Dunlap. LC 93-1394. (Illus.). 320p. 1994. pap. 19.95 (*0-89133-216-2*) Preservation Pr.

Culture Wars. Ira Shor. LC 85-3405. 1992. pap. text ed. 12.95 (*0-226-75360-3*) U Ch Pr.

Culture Wars. Ed. by Fred Whitehand. LC 93-8512. 1994. lib. bdg. 19.95 (*1-56510-101-4*); pap. 11.55 (*1-56510-100-6*) Greenhaven.

Culture Wars: Documents from the Recent Controversies in the Arts. Richard Bolton. 1992. pap. 19.95 (*1-56584-011-9*) New Press NY.

Culture Wars: School & Society in the Conservative Restoration 1969-1984. Ira Shor. 1986. 37.50 (*0-7102-0637-2*, RKP); pap. 12.95 (*0-7102-0649-6*, RKP) Routledge.

Culture Wars: The Struggle to Control the Family, Art, Education, Law, & Politics in America. James D. Hunter. LC 91-70065. 1992. pap. 15.00 (*0-465-01534-4*) Basic.

Culture We Deserve. Jacques Barzun. Ed. by Arthur Krystal. LC 88-33927. 197p. 1990. pap. 13.95 (*0-8195-6237-8*, Wesleyan Univ Pr) U Pr of New Eng.

Culture Without Pain or Money. 2nd ed. Milli Janz. (Best Things Ser.). (C). 1984. reprint ed. pap. 4.00 (*0-9614619-0-X*) Am Community Cultural.

***Culture 2.0 Workbook: Interdisciplinary Lessons.** rev. ed. Walter W. Reinhold. 310p. 1992. pap. 45.00 (*0-9624372-4-7*) Cultural Rescs.

Cultured Foods. Wendy Zeffertt. (Illus.). 160p. (Orig.). 1990. pap. text ed. 16.95 (*0-9628016-1-5*) Gentian Servs.

Cultured Mexico. Michael D. Collins. 297p. 1974. lib. bdg. 69.95 (*0-87968-973-0*) Gordon Pr.

Cultures: Diversity in Reading & Writing. Emily Thiroux. LC 92-27905. 384p. 1992. pap. text ed. write for info. (*0-13-194614-5*) P-H.

Cultures & Civilizations. Struan Reid. (Silk & Spice Routes Ser.). (Illus.). 48p. (J). (gr. 6 up). 1994. text ed. 15.95 (*0-02-726315-0*, New Dscvry Bks) Silver Burdett Pr.

Cultures & Organizations: Software of the Mind - Intercultural Cooperation & Its Importance for Survival. Geert Hofstede. 328p. 1992. text ed. 39.95 (*0-07-707474-2*) McGraw.

Cultures & Societies in a Changing World. Wendy Griswold. 128p. 1994. pap. 15.95 (*0-8039-9018-9*) Pine Forge.

Cultures Around the World. (Encyclopaedia Britannica Fascinating Facts Ser.). (Illus.). 32p. (J). 1993. 8.98 (*1-56173-318-0*) Pubns Intl Ltd.

Cultures Around the World, Vol. 2. George D. Spindler & Louise S. Spindler. LC 76-20447. (C). 1978. pap. text ed. 20.00 (*0-03-039726-X*) HB Coll Pubs.

Culture's Consequences: International Differences in Work-Related Values. Geert Hofstede. LC 80-16327. (Cross-Cultural Research & Methodology Ser.: Vol. 5). (Illus.). 475p. 1980. 59.95 (*0-8039-1444-X*); pap. 24.00 (*0-8039-1306-0*) Sage.

Cultures D'Organes D'Invertebres. Ed. by H. Lutz. 280p. 1969. text ed. 255.00 (*0-677-50100-5*) Gordon & Breach.

Culture's Garland. Eugene Field. (Notable American Authors Ser.). 1992. reprint ed. lib. bdg. 75.00 (*0-7812-2641-4*) Rprt Serv.

Cultures in Collision: The Interaction of Canadian & U. S. Broadcasting Policies. Canadian-U. S. Conference on Communications Policy Staff. LC 83-19232. 224p. 1984. lib. bdg. 49.95 (*0-275-91136-5*, C1136, Praeger Pubs) Greenwood.

***Cultures in Conflict: A Documentary History of the Mormon War in Illinois.** Ed. by Roger E. Lanius & John E. Hallwas. (Illus.). 1995. 37.95x (*0-87421-186-7*) Utah St U Pr.

Cultures in Conflict: A Global Survey of Ethnic, Racial, Linguistic, Religious & Nationalist Factors. Eschel M. Rhoodie. LC 92-50946. 976p. 1995. lib. bdg. 95.00 (*0-89950-830-8*) McFarland & Co.

Cultures in Conflict: Christians, Muslims, & Jews in the Age of Discovery. Bernard Lewis. (Illus.). 128p. 1995. 16.95 (*0-19-509026-8*) OUP.

***Cultures in Conflict: Christians, Muslims, & Jews in the Age of Discovery.** Bernard Lewis. (Illus.). 120p. 1996. reprint ed. pap. 9.95 (*0-19-510283-5*) OUP.

Cultures in Conflict: Encounters Between European & Non-European Cultures, 1492-1800. Urs Bitterli. Tr. by Ritchie Robertson. LC 88-64050. 215p. 1989. 37.50 (*0-8047-1737-0*) Stanford U Pr.

Cultures in Conflict: Social Movements & the State in Peru. Susan C. Stokes. LC 94-11496. 1995. 45.00 (*0-520-08617-1*); pap. 17.00 (*0-520-20023-3*) U CA Pr.

Cultures in Contention. Ed. by Douglas Kahn & Diane Neumaier. LC 84-16074. (Illus.). 288p. (Orig.). 1986. pap. 19.95 (*0-941104-06-0*) Real Comet.

Cultures in Flux: Lower-Class Values, Practices, & Resistance in Late Imperial Russia. Ed. by Stephen P. Frank & Mark D. Steinberg. LC 93-43708. 1994. 49.50 (*0-691-03435-4*); pap. 14.95 (*0-691-00106-5*) Princeton U Pr.

***Cultures in Iowa: A Brief Study.** Lynn M. Alex & R. Clark Mallam. (Illus.). 20p. (Orig.). 1995. pap. 1.50 (*0-915992-81-7*) Eastern Acorn.

Cultures in Organizations: Three Perspectives. Joanne M. Martin. (Illus.). 256p. (C). 1992. pap. text ed. 19.95 (*0-19-507164-6*) OUP.

Cultures in Transition, Issue 119. Photos by Marc Garanger et al. (Illus.). 18.50 (*0-89381-446-6*) Aperture.

***Cultures of America, 5 vols., Set.** (J). (gr. 3-5). 1995. lib. bdg. write for info. (*0-7614-0159-8*, Benchmark NY) Marshall Cavendish.

Cultures of America Series, Set. (J). (gr. 4-7). 1994. 99.75 (*1-85435-780-8*) Marshall Cavendish.

***Cultures of America, 5 bks., Set.** (J). (gr. 3-5). 1995. lib. bdg. write for info. (*0-7614-0150-4*) Marshall Cavendish.

Cultures of Celebrations. Ed. by Ray B. Browne & Michael T. Marsden. LC 93-74428. (Outdoor Entertainment Ser.). (Illus.). 244p. (C). 1994. lib. bdg. 35.95 (*0-87972-651-2*); pap. text ed. 15.95 (*0-87972-652-0*) Bowling Green Univ.

Cultures of Change: Recovery & Relapse Prevention for Dually Diagnosed & Addicted Adolescents. Janice Gabe. 175p. (Orig.). 1993. pap. text ed. 12.95 (*0-9639023-0-X*) Prof Resource.

***Cultures of Collecting.** Ed. by John Elsner & Roger Cardinal. (Illus.). 320p. 1994. text ed. 39.95 (*0-674-17992-7*, ELSCUS); pap. text ed. 18.95 (*0-674-17993-5*, ELSCUX) HUP.

Cultures of Collecting. Ed. by John Elsner & Roger Cardinal. 320p. 1994. 34.95 (*0-522-84630-0*) Intl Spec Bk.

***Cultures of Computing.** Ed. by Susan L. Star. (Sociological Review Monograph Ser.). (Illus.). 288p. (Orig.). 1995. pap. write for info. (*0-631-19282-4*) Blackwell Pubs.

Cultures of Early Western Man. (Illus.). 32p. 1966. 1.00 (*0-915478-06-4*) Galleries Coll.

***Cultures of Healing: Correcting the Image of American Mental Health Care.** Robert T. Fancher. LC 94-41495. 1995. text ed. write for info. (*0-7167-2383-2*) W H Freeman.

Cultures of Letters: Scenes of Reading & Writing in Nineteenth-Century America. Richard H. Brodhead. LC 92-30967. (Illus.). 256p. (C). 1993. 24.95 (*0-226-07525-7*) U Ch Pr.

Cultures of Letters: Scenes of Reading & Writing in Nineteenth-Century America. Richard H. Brodhead. LC 92-30967. (Illus.). 256p. (C). 1994. pap. text ed. 15.95 (*0-226-07526-5*) U Ch Pr.

Cultures of Management. Robert H. Roy. LC 76-47385. (Illus.). 448p. 1977. 60.00x (*0-8018-1875-3*); pap. text ed. 16.95x (*0-8018-2524-5*) Johns Hopkins.

***Cultures of Natural History.** Ed. by N. Jardine et al. (Illus.). 300p. (C). Date not set. write for info. (*0-521-45394-1*) Cambridge U Pr.

***Cultures of Power: Lordship, Status, & Process in Twelfth-Century Europe.** Ed. by Thomas N. Bisson. LC 95-12349. (Middle Ages Ser.). (Illus.). 400p. 1995. text ed. 46.95 (*0-8122-3290-9*) U of Pa Pr.

***Cultures of Power: Lordship, Status, & Process in Twelfth-Century Europe.** Ed. by Thomas N. Bisson. (Middle Ages Ser.). (Illus.). 400p. 1995. pap. text ed. 19.95 (*0-8122-1555-9*) U of Pa Pr.

Cultures of Prehistoric Egypt, 2 vols. in 1. Elise J. Baumgartel. LC 80-24186. (Illus.). xxiii, 286p. 1981. reprint ed. text ed. 72.50 (*0-313-22524-9*, BACU, Greenwood Pr) Greenwood.

Cultures of Prehistoric Egypt Two: Petrie's Naqada Excavation. Baumgartel. 60.00 (*0-85388-055-7*, Pub. by Aris & Phillips UK) David Brown.

Cultures of Schooling: Pedagogies for Cultural Difference & Social Access. Ed. by Mary Kalantzis et al. 220p. 1990. 70.00 (*1-85000-784-5*, Falmer Pr); pap. 30.00 (*1-85000-785-3*, Falmer Pr) Taylor & Francis.

Cultures of Solidarity: Consciousness, Action & Contemporary American Workers. Rick Fantasia. (Illus.). 315p. 1988. pap. 14.00 (*0-520-06795-9*) U CA Pr.

Cultures of the Aztecs, Mayas, & Incas: French & Dutch Discoveries of America. Justin Winsor & C. B. Markham. 250p. 1996. pap. 25.00 (*0-918680-50-6*) Bagehot Council.

Cultures of the Future. Ed. by Magoroh Maruyama & Arthur M. Harkins. (World Anthropology Ser.). xxii, 668p. 1978. 100.00 (*90-279-7979-0*) Mouton.

Cultures of the Hindukush: Selected Papers from the Hindu-Kush Cultural Conference, 1970. Karl Jettmar. xiv, 146p. (Orig.). 1974. pap. text ed. 28.50 (*3-515-01217-6*) Coronet Bks.

Cultures of the Pacific. Thomas G. Harding & Ben J. Wallace. LC 70-91883. 1970. pap. 16.95 (*0-02-913800-0*) Free Pr.

***Cultures of the Past, 5 bks., Set.** (J). (gr. 5-8). 1995. lib. bdg. write for info. (*0-7614-0069-9*, Benchmark NY) Marshall Cavendish.

Cultures of the World, 6 vols., Set. (Cultures of the World Ser.). (Illus.). 128p. (J). (gr. 5-10). 1992. lib. bdg. 131.70 (*1-85435-543-0*) Marshall Cavendish.

Cultures of the World: Austria. (Illus.). 128p. (J). (gr. 5-9). lib. bdg. 21.95 (*1-85435-454-X*) Marshall Cavendish.

Cultures of the World: Europe, 6 vols., Set. (Illus.). (J). (gr. 5-9). lib. bdg. 131.70 (*1-85435-448-5*) Marshall Cavendish.

Cultures of the World: France. (Illus.). 128p. (J). (gr. 5-9). lib. bdg. 21.95 (*1-85435-449-3*) Marshall Cavendish.

Cultures of the World: Greece. (Illus.). 128p. (J). (gr. 5-9). lib. bdg. 21.95 (*1-85435-450-7*) Marshall Cavendish.

Cultures of the World: Italy. (Illus.). 128p. (J). (gr. 5-9). lib. bdg. 21.95 (*1-85435-453-1*) Marshall Cavendish.

Cultures of the World: Spain. (Illus.). 128p. (J). (gr. 5-9). lib. bdg. 21.95 (*1-85435-451-5*) Marshall Cavendish.

Cultures of the World: Sweden. (Illus.). 128p. (J). (gr. 5-9). lib. bdg. 21.95 (*1-85435-452-3*) Marshall Cavendish.

***Cultures of the World Series, 6 vols., Set.** (J). (gr. 3-5). 1995. lib. bdg. write for info. (*0-7614-0167-9*) Marshall Cavendish.

***Cultures of the World Series, 6 Bks., Set.** Sakina Kagda et al. 768p. (J). (gr. 3-5). 1995. lib. bdg. write for info. (*0-7614-0175-X*) Marshall Cavendish.

Cultures of Unemployment: A Comparative Look at Long-Term Unemployment & Urban Poverty. Godfried Engbersen et al. LC 93-3010. (Political Cultures Ser.). 277p. (C). 1993. text ed. 56.50 (*0-8133-8603-9*) Westview.

Cultures of United States Imperialism. Ed. by Amy Kaplan & Donald E. Pease. LC 93-19817. (New Americanists Ser.). (Illus.). 680p. 1994. lib. bdg. 59.95 (*0-8223-1400-2*); pap. text ed. 18.95 (*0-8223-1413-4*) Duke.

Cultures of Work Organizations. Harrison M. Trice & Janice M. Beyer. 528p. 1992. text ed. 50.67 (*0-13-191438-3*) P-H.

Cultures Outside the United States in Fiction: A Guide to 2,875 Books for Librarians & Teachers, K-9. Vicki Anderson. 424p. 1994. lib. bdg. 35.00 (*0-89950-905-3*) McFarland & Co.

Cultures, Politics & Research Programs: An International Assessment of Practical Problems in Field Research. Ed. by Uma Narula & W. Barnett Pearce. 264p. (C). 1990. text ed. 59.95 (*0-8058-0134-0*) L Erlbaum Assocs.

Culture's Sleeping Beauty: Essays on Poetry, Prejudice & Belief. Michael J. Bugeja. LC 91-67974. 126p. 1992. 18.50 (*0-87875-425-3*); pap. 12.00 (*0-87875-429-6*) Whitston Pub.

Culturescope: The Princeton Review Guide to an Informed Mind, College. Samantha Martin. 1995. pap. 15.00 (*0-679-75367-2*, Villard Bks) Random.

Culturescope: The Princeton Review Guide to an Informed Mind, High School. Michael Freedman. 1995. pap. 20.00 (*0-679-75366-4*, Villard Bks) Random.

***CultureWatch (ABC News Intermediate ESL Video Library)** Tomalin & ABC Staff. (Illus.). 160p. 1994. pap. text ed. 15.50 (*0-13-137621-7*) P-H.

Culturgrams: The Nations Around Us, 2 vols. Brigham Young University, David Kennedy International Center Staff. LC 93-29643. (Illus.). 224p. (Orig.). (C). 1994. Vol. I: The Americas & Europe, 224p. pap. 30.00 (*0-912048-86-7*); Vol. II: Africa, Asia, & Oceania, 260p. pap. 30.00 (*0-912048-87-5*) Garrett Pk.

Culturing Nerve Cells. Ed. by Gary Banker & Kimberly Goslin. (Cellular & Molecular Ser.). 428p. 1991. 62.50 (*0-262-02320-2*, Bradford Bks) MIT Pr.

Culver Bill Nelson: A Memoir by the Reverend Culver H. Bill Nelson, D.D., L.H.D. Ed. by Gordon A. Sabine. 176p. (Orig.). 1992. write for info. (*1-879286-03-3*) AZ Bd Regents.

***Culvert Distress & Failure Case Histories & Trenchless Technology (TRR 1431)** Ed. by Norman Solomon. (Transportation Research Record Ser.). (Illus.). 88p. 1994. pap. text ed. 24.00 (*0-309-05509-1*) Transport Res Bd.

Cum: True Homosexual Experiences from S. T. H. Writers, Vol. 4. Ed. by Boyd McDonald. (Illus.). 192p. (Orig.). 1983. pap. 12.00 (*0-917342-30-5*) Gay Sunshine.

Cumbe Reborn: An Andean Ethnography of History. Joanne Rappaport. LC 93-4909. (Illus.). 256p. 1993. pap. text ed. 15.95 (*0-226-70526-9*) U Ch Pr.

Cumbe Reborn: An Andean Ethnography of History. Joanne Rappaport. LC 93-4909. (Illus.). 256p. 1993. lib. bdg. 41.95 (*0-226-70525-0*) U Ch Pr.

Cumberland & Pennsylvania. Harold H. Carstens & Deane Mellander. (Illus.). 64p. 1989. pap. 9.95 (*0-911868-63-1*, C63) Carstens Pubns.

Cumberland Caverns. Larry E. Matthews. 316p. 1989. pap. 9.95 (*0-9615093-4-1*) Natl Speleological.

Cumberland County: A Brief History. Roy Parker, Jr. (Illus.). xi, 158p. (Orig.). 1990. pap. 8.00 (*0-86526-243-8*) NC Archives.

***Cumberland County: Virginia Publick Claims.** Janice L. Abercrombie & Richard Slatten. (Virginia Publick Claims Ser.). ix, 71p. 1991. pap. 9.00x (*0-8095-8553-7*) Borgo Pr.

Cumberland County: Virginia Publick Claims. Janice L. Abercrombie & Richard Slatten. (Virginia Publick Claims Ser.). ix, 71p. (C). 1991. reprint ed. lib. bdg. 25.00x (*0-8095-8316-X*) Borgo Pr.

***Cumberland County, North Carolina Marriage Bonds & Certificates, 1803-1878.** Francis T. Ingmire. 214p. 1994. lib. bdg. 49.00 (*0-8095-8026-8*); pap. 22.50 (*0-8095-8552-9*) Borgo Pr.

***Cumberland County, PA: Divorces, 1789-1860.** Eugene F. Throop. 406p. (Orig.). 1994. pap. text ed. 31.00 (*1-55613-999-3*) Heritage Bk.

***Cumberland County, PA, Cemetery Records Collected by Jeremiah Zeamer.** Wilbur J. McElwain. 266p. (Orig.). 1994. pap. text ed. 36.00 (*0-7884-0075-4*) Heritage Bk.

***Cumberland County, Pennsylvania, Marriages, 1761-1800.** (Special Publication Ser.: No. 3). 40p. 1990. reprint ed. pap. 4.00 (*1-887099-02-6*) Geneal Soc Pa.

C

An Asterisk (*) at the beginning of an entry indicates that the title is appearing in BIP for the first time.

C

An Asterisk (*) at the beginning of an entry indicates that the title is appearing in BIP for the first time.

Cumulative Personal Author Indexes for the Monthly Catalog of U. S. Government Publications, 1941-1975, 5 vols., Set. Ed. by Edward Przebienda. Incl. Decennial Cumulative Personal Author Index, 1941-50. LC 04-18088. 1971. 49.50 (*0-87650-007-6*); Decennial Cumulative Personal Author Index, 1951-60. LC 04-18088. 1971. 49.50 (*0-87650-008-4*); Quinquennial Cumulative Personal Author Index, 1961-65. LC 04-18088. 1971. 49.50 (*0-87650-009-2*); Quinquennial Cumulative Personal Author Index, 1966-70. LC 04-18088. 1971. 49.50 (*0-87650-016-5*); Quinquennial Cumulative Personal Author Index, 1971-75. LC 04-18088. 1979. 49.50 (*0-87650-097-1*); LC 04-18088. (Cumulative Author Index Ser.: No. 2). 1979. 225.00 (*0-686-76934-1*) Pierian.

Cumulative Record of Speech Skill Acquisition. Daniel Ling. LC 77-93949. 1977. pap. text ed. 10.50 (*0-88200-115-9*, A1983) Alexander Graham.

***Cumulative Subject & Author Indexes of Dr. Dobb's Journal, 1982-1994.** Stephen E. Bach. 160p. (Orig.). 1994. pap. 23.95 (*1-882850-07-6*) Springtree Partners.

Cumulative Subject Index: 1959-1972 Cumulative Subject Index. LC 42-4221. 2516p. 1985. 1,454.00 (*0-8218-0095-7*, MREVIN/59/72) Am Math.

Cumulative Subject Index of Mathematical Reviews 1940-58, Vols. 1-19. Ed. by J. L. Selfridge. 413p. 1983. pap. 401.00 (*0-8218-0081-7*, MREVIN-40-58) Am Math.

Cumulative Subject Index to Vols. 1-30 see Methods in Enzymology

Cumulative Subject Indexes, Combination Offer: Cumulative Subject Index, 1940-1958; Cumulative Subject Index, 1959-1972, 2 vols., Set. pap. 1,557.00 (*0-8218-0149-X*, MRCIN/40/72C) Am Math.

Cumulative Sum Tests, Theory & Practice. C. S. Van Dobben de Bruyn. (Griffin's Statistical Monographs: No. 24). (Illus.). 82p. 1968. pap. text ed. 17.95 (*0-85264-085-4*) Lubrecht & Cramer.

Cumulative Supplement - Labor & Employment Law Desk Book, 1989. Gordon E. Jackson. 224p. 1989. pap. text ed. 40.00 (*0-13-517780-4*) P-H.

Cumulative Supplement, Connecticut Evidence, 1990, Vol. I. Benedict M. Holden, Jr. & John J. Daly. 186p. 1990. pap. text ed. 60.00 (*1-878698-06-0*) Atlantic Law.

Cumulative Supplement, Connecticut Evidence, 1990, Vol. II. Benedict M. Holden, Jr. & John J. Daly. 112p. 1990. pap. text ed. 60.00 (*1-878698-05-2*) Atlantic Law.

Cumulative Supplement Connecticut Evidence, 1991, Set, Vols. I-II. Benedict M. Holden & John J. Daly. 377p. 1991. Set. pap. text ed. 65.00 (*1-878698-10-9*) Atlantic Law.

Cumulative Supplement Connecticut Evidence, 1991, Vol. I. Benedict M. Holden & John J. Daly. 235p. 1991. pap. text ed. 65.00 (*1-878698-08-7*) Atlantic Law.

Cumulative Supplement Connecticut Evidence, 1991, Vol. II. Benedict M. Holden & John J. Daly. 142p. 1991. pap. text ed. 65.00 (*1-878698-09-5*) Atlantic Law.

Cumulative Supplement to Administrative & Financial Laws for Local Government in North Carolina, 1993. Comp. by Institute of Government Faculty Members. 133p. (C). 1994. text ed. 15.00 (*1-56011-270-0*, 92.04A) Institute Government.

Cumulative Supplement to Nonprofit Corporations, Organizations & Associations. 5th ed. Howard L. Oleck. 250p. 1990. pap. 39.95 (*0-13-626946-X*) P-H.

Cumulative Surname Index & Soundex to Monographs 1 through 12 of the German-American Genealogical Research Series. (German-American Genealogical Research Monograph: No. 13). 66p. 1983. pap. 17.00 (*0-915162-17-2*) Westland Pubns.

Cumulative Surname Soundex to German-American Genealogical Research Monographs 14 Through 19 & 21 Through 25. Clifford N. Smith. (German-American Genealogical Research Monograph: No. 26). i, 41p. (Orig.). 1990. pap. 17.00 (*0-915162-91-1*) Westland Pubns.

Cumulative Ten-Year Index for the American Journal of Physics, 1953-1962. 266p. 1963. 20.00 (*0-318-41407-4*, OP-3) Am Assn Physics.

Cumulative Ten-Year Index for the American Journal of Physics, 1963-1972. 208p. 1974. 20.00 (*0-318-41408-2*, OP-4) Am Assn Physics.

Cumulative Ten-Year Index for the American Journal of Physics, 1973-1982. 209p. 1984. 20.00 (*0-318-41409-0*, OP-49) Am Assn Physics.

Cumulative Trauma Disorder: A Legal Guide to CTD Prevention, Regulation & Liability. Ed. by CTDNews Staff. LC 93-25971. 1993. 115.00 (*0-9636246-2-8*) Andrews Pubns.

Cumulative Trauma Disorders. O. Bruce Dickerson. 1993. text ed. write for info. (*0-442-01074-5*) Van Nos Reinhold.

Cumulative Trauma Disorders: A Manual for Musculoskeletal Diseases of the Upper Limbs. Ed. by Vern Putz-Anderson. 112p. 1988. 26.00 (*0-85066-405-5*) Taylor & Francis.

Cumulative Trauma Disorders: Current Issues & Ergonomic. Parker. 1992. 62.95 (*0-87371-322-2*, RD97) Lewis Pubs.

Cumulative Trauma Disorders in the Workplace: Costs, Prevention, & Progress. LC 91-23087. 1991. 95.00 (*1-55871-220-8*) BNA.

***Cumulative Trauma Disorders of the Hand & Wrist: An Ergonomics Guide.** Thomas J. Armstrong & Ellen A. Lackey. (Ergonomics Guide Ser.). (Illus.). 24p. (Orig.). 1994. pap. text ed. 8.00 (*0-932627-56-0*, 181-ER-94) Am Indus Hygiene.

Cumunicando: A First Course in Spanish. 2nd ed. David M. Stillman & Ronni L. Gordon. LC 83-80925. 521p. (ENG & SPA.). (C). 1985. text ed. 29.50 (*0-669-06756-3*); Wkbk./Lab. manaul. student ed 14.50 (*0-669-06757-1*); Instr.'s guide. teacher ed 2.00 (*0-669-06758-X*); Cassettes. audio 35.00 (*0-669-06755-5*); Tapescript. 2.00 (*0-669-06761-X*); Demo. tape. 2.00 (*0-669-06760-1*) Heath.

Cunard Line. P. Woolley & T. Moore. 1990. 59.00 (*0-9516038-0-9*, Pub. by Ship Pictorial Pubng UK) St Mut.

Cuncina Del Mare: Fish & Seafood, Italian Style. Evan Kleiman. LC 92-31205. 1993. 23.00 (*0-688-09916-5*) Morrow.

CUNCUR 'Ninety-Two: International Conference on Concurrency Theory, 3rd, Stony Brook, NY, U. S. A., August 1992: Proceedings. Ed. by W. R. Cleaveland. LC 92-26385. (Lecture Notes in Computer Science Ser.: Vol. 630). x, 580p. 1992. pap. 80.00 (*0-387-55822-5*) Spr-Verlag.

***Cune: A New Approach to Publishing.** Scott C. Davis. 12p. (Orig.). 1995. pap. 3.95 (*1-885942-54-0*) Cune.

Cuneiform. C. B. Walker. LC 87-5879. (Reading the Past Ser.: Vol. 3). 64p. 1987. Reading the Past. pap. 11.00 (*0-520-06115-2*) U CA Pr.

***Cuneiform Archives & Libraries: Papers Read at the 30e Rencontre Assyriologique Internationale, Leiden, 4-8 1983.** Ed. by Klaas R. Veenhof. x, 307p. 1986. pap. text ed. 64.00 (*90-6258-057-2*, Pub. by Netherlands Inst NE) Eisenbrauns.

Cuneiform Bullae of the Third Millenium B.C. Clarence E. Keiser. LC 78-63518. (Babylonian Records in the Library of J. Pierpont Morgan: 3). reprint ed. 30.00 (*0-404-60123-5*) AMS Pr.

Cuneiform Documents from the Chaldean & Persian Periods. Comp. by Ronald H. Sack. LC 93-49672. 1994. write for info. (*0-945636-67-9*) Susquehanna U Pr.

Cuneiform Documents in the Smith College Library. Elihu Grant. 49p. 1991. pap. text ed. 4.00 (*0-916157-67-9*) African Islam Miss Pubns.

Cuneiform Parallels to the Old Testament. Ed. by Robert W. Rogers. 1977. lib. bdg. 250.00 (*0-8490-1695-9*) Gordon Pr.

Cuneiform Texts in the Metropolitan Museum of Art. Ira Spar. 1994. 60.00 (*0-8109-6456-2*) Abrams.

Cuneiform Texts in the Metropolitan Museum of Art, Vol. 1. Ed. by Ira Spar. (Illus.). 408p. 1988. 60.00 (*0-87099-495-6*) Metro Mus Art.

Cuneiform Texts of Ras Shamra-Ugarit. C. F. Schaeffer. (British Academy, London, Schweich Lectures on Biblical Archaeology Series, 1930). 1972. reprint ed. pap. 20.00 (*0-8115-1278-9*) Periodicals Srv.

Cunliffe on Cruising. Tom Cunliffe. (Illus.). 128p. (Orig.). 1992. pap. 17.95 (*0-924486-25-2*) Sheridan.

***Cunnabell: Pictorial Genealogy of the Cunnabell, Connable, Canable Family, 1886-1935, Vol. II.** Ralph Connable. (Illus.). 190p. 1994. reprint ed. lib. bdg. 39.50 (*0-8328-4311-3*); reprint ed. pap. 29.50 (*0-8328-4312-1*) Higginson Bk Co.

Cunning. Robert Bloch. 1981. pap. 2.50 (*0-89083-825-9*) Zebra.

Cunning Carnivores. Steve Parker. LC 93-27256. (Creepy Creatures Ser.). (Illus.). (J). 1993. 21.36 (*0-8114-2347-6*) Raintree Steck-V.

Cunning Craft: Original Essays on Detective Fiction & Contemporary Literary Theory. Ed. by Ronald G. Walker & June M. Frazer. LC 90-70583. (Essays in Literature Book Ser.). 203p. (Orig.). 1990. pap. 12.00 (*0-934312-08-7*) WIU Essays Lit.

Cunning Craft: Original Essays on Detective Fiction & Contemporary Literary Theory. Ed. by Ronald G. Walker et al. (Essays in Literature Book Ser.). vii, 204p. (Orig.). 1990. pap. 12.00 (*0-934312-07-9*) WIU Essays Lit.

Cunning Intelligence in Greek Culture & Society. Marcel Detienne & Jean-Pierre Vernant. Tr. by Janet Lloyd. 342p. 1991. pap. text ed. 16.95 (*0-226-14347-3*) U Ch Pr.

***Cunning Man.** Robertson Davies. 480p. 1995. pap. 23.95 (*0-670-85911-7*, Viking) Viking Penguin.

***Cunning Man.** large type ed. Robertson Davies. 1995. pap. 23.95 (*1-56895-230-9*) Wheeler Pub.

Cunning of History. Richard Rubenstein. 1987. pap. text ed. 11.00 (*0-06-132068-4*, TB2068, Torch) HarpC.

Cunning of Reason. Martin Hollis. 232p. 1988. 59.95 (*0-521-24879-5*); pap. 18.95 (*0-521-27039-1*) Cambridge U Pr.

Cunning of the Mountain Man. William W. Johnstone. 320p. 1994. mass mkt. 3.99 (*0-8217-4723-1*) Zebra.

***Cunning Passages.** Rebecca Templeman. (Sally O'Sullivan Ser.). (Illus.). 216p. (Orig.). (YA). (gr. 4-6). 1994. pap. 11.95 (*0-9642889-0-7*) Bookends Pubng.

Cunning Seeds. Cecil Sinnamon. 158p. (C). 1990. pap. 42.00 (*0-908175-54-X*, Pub. by Boolarong Pubns AT) St Mut.

Cunningham: The Cars of Briggs Swift Cunningham. Dean Baatchelor. 1993. pap. 39.95 (*0-87938-795-5*) Motorbooks Intl.

Cunningham Automobiles 1951-1955. R. M. Clarke. (Illus.). 100p. 1993. pap. 16.95 (*1-85520-204-2*, Pub. by Brooklands Bks UK) Motorbooks Intl.

Cunningham Gambit. W. John Lutes. 236p. (Orig.). 1990. pap. 12.95 (*0-945470-00-2*) Chess Ent Inc.

Cunningham Rags-to-Riches Financial Recovery System. Peter Cunningham. LC 83-70248. 75p. 1983. pap. 29.50 (*0-911659-02-1*) Cunningham Pub Co.

Cunninghame Graham: A Critical Biography. Cedric T. Watts & Laurence Davies. LC 78-18107. 347p. reprint ed. pap. 98.90 (*0-685-16226-5*, 2027267) Bks Demand.

Cunningham's Encyclopedia of Crystal, Gem & Metal Magic. Scott Cunningham. LC 87-46256. (Illus.). 248p. 1987. pap. 14.95 (*0-87542-126-1*) Llewellyn Pubns.

Cunningham's Encyclopedia of Magical Herbs. Scott Cunningham. LC 84-48091. (Illus.). 336p. (Orig.). 1985. pap. 12.95 (*0-87542-122-9*) Llewellyn Pubns.

Cunningham's Manual of Practical Anatomy: Vol. 1, Upper & Lower Limbs, 3 vols. 15th ed. Cunningham. Ed. by G. J. Romanes. (Illus.). (C). 1986. pap. text ed. 19.95 (*0-19-263138-1*) OUP.

Cunningham's Manual of Practical Anatomy: Vol. 2 Thorax & Abdomen. 15th ed. Cunningham. Ed. by G. J. Romanes. (Illus.). (C). 1986. pap. text ed. 19.95 (*0-19-263139-X*) OUP.

Cunningham's Manual of Practical Anatomy: Vol. 3 Head & Neck & Brain. 15th ed. Cunningham. Ed. by G. J. Romanes. (Illus.). 1986. pap. text ed. 19.95 (*0-19-263140-3*) OUP.

Cunningham's Textbook of Anatomy. 12th ed. Cunningham. Ed. by G. J. Romanes. (Illus.). (C). 1981. text ed. 75.00 (*0-19-263134-9*) OUP.

Cuno Government & Reparations, 1922-1923. Herman J. Rupieper. (Studies in Contemporary History: No. 1). 1979. pap. text ed. 103.00 (*90-247-2114-8*) Kluwer Ac.

***Cunt Coloring Book.** Dee Corinne. 48p. 1989. 7.95 (*0-86719-371-9*) Last Gasp.

***Cuoc Doi Chua Giesu: Tuyen Tap Tho.** Tien Van Pham. 156p. (Orig.). (VIE.). 1994. pap. 10.00 (*0-9645739-0-3*) Van Pham Found.

Cuomo Factor: Assessing the Political Appeal of New York's Governor. Lee M. Miringoff & Barbara L. Carvalho. LC 86-62229. 126p. (Orig.). 1987. pap. 12.95 (*0-939319-00-4*) Marist Inst.

Cuoto Snatch. large type ed. Jack Shelynn. 274p. 1980. 15.95 (*0-7089-0501-3*) Ulverscroft.

Cup & Saucer Chemistry. Nathan Shalit. 96p. 1989. pap. 3.95 (*0-486-25997-8*) Dover.

Cup Cooking: Individual Child-Portion Picture Recipes. 12th ed. Barbara Johnson. (Illus.). (J). (ps up). 1990. pap. 3.95 (*0-317-99815-3*) Early Educators.

Cup Cooking Starter Set: Single Step Charts for Child-Portion Picture Recipes. Barbara Johnson. (Illus.). 1985. pap. 7.95 (*0-9604390-2-1*) Early Educators.

Cup of Christmas Tea. Tom Hegg. (Illus.). 48p. (J). 1982. 10.95 (*0-931674-08-5*) Waldman Hse Pr.

***Cup of Christmas Tea Ornament Book.** Tom Hegg. (Illus.). 48p. Date not set. 4.95 (*0-931674-21-2*) Waldman Hse Pr.

Cup of Clay. Carole N. Douglas. 416p. 1992. mass mkt. 4.99 (*0-8125-1248-0*) Tor Bks.

Cup of Coffee: From Plantation to Pot, a Coffee Lover's Guide to the Perfect Brew. Norman Kolpas. 1993. 19.95 (*0-8021-1476-8*) Grove-Atltic.

Cup of Coffee with My Interrogator. Ludvik Vaculik. Tr. by George Theiner. (Readers International Ser.). (Illus.). 140p. (Orig.). 1987. 14.95 (*0-930523-34-2*); pap. 7.95 (*0-930523-35-0*) Readers Intl.

Cup of Cold Water. Vivian Guthrie. (Illus.). 96p. (Orig.). 1985. pap. 3.00 (*0-89114-150-2*) Baptist Pub Hse.

Cup of Controversy: The Intrigue Behind the Strangest America's Cup Ever. Tom Coat. (Illus.). 120p. (Orig.). (C). 1988. pap. 16.95 (*0-9621245-0-8*) T Coat.

Cup of Death. Gene Thompson. 1988. pap. 3.50 (*0-345-35881-3*) Ballantine.

Cup of Death. Gene Thompson. LC 87-9610. 288p. 1987. 16.95 (*0-394-56140-6*) Random.

Cup of Fortune. Marjorie A. Fontana & Jean L. Larson. LC 78-67289. (Illus.). 61p. (Orig.). 1979. pap. 3.95 (*0-9603596-2-1*) Fontastic.

Cup of Gold. John Steinbeck. 256p. 1976. mass mkt. 7.00 (*0-14-004234-2*, Penguin Bks) Viking Penguin.

***Cup of Gold.** John Steinbeck. 272p. 1995. 9.95 (*0-14-018743-X*, Penguin Classics) Viking Penguin.

Cup of Gold. large type ed. John Steinbeck. 1973. 23.95 (*0-85456-200-1*) Ulverscroft.

Cup of Sorrow, Cup of Sorrow. Frank D. Janzow & James M. Bickel. 1994. pap. write for info. (*1-55673-925-7*) CSS OH.

Cup of Starshine: Poems & Pictures for Children. J. Bennett. 57p. (J). (ps-1). 1991. 16.95 (*0-15-220982-4*, HB Juv Bks) HarBrace.

Cup of Sugar, Neighbor. Jeanette Lockerbie. (Quiet Time Books for Women). 128p. 1974. pap. 3.99 (*0-8024-1681-0*) Moody.

Cup of Tea. 2nd ed. Osho Rajneesh. Ed. by Swami Anand Somendra. LC 83-43215. (Early Discourses & Writings Ser.). 272p. 1983. pap. 4.95 (*0-88050-538-9*) Osho Chidvilas.

Cup of Tea in Pamplona. Robert Laxalt. LC 85-16371. (Basque Ser.). (Illus.). 96p. (C). 1993. pap. 12.00 (*0-87417-192-X*) U of Nev Pr.

Cup of Tears: A Diary of the Warsaw Ghetto. Abraham Lewin. Ed. by Antony Polonsky. Tr. by Chris Hutton. (Illus.). 224p. 1988. 29.95 (*0-631-16215-1*) Blackwell Pubs.

***Cup of Trembling: Jerusalem & Bible Prophecy.** Dave Hunt. (Orig.). 1995. pap. 9.99 (*1-56507-334-7*) Harvest Hse.

Cup of Trembling & Other Stories. Mary H. Foote. LC 74-110189. (Short Story Index Reprint Ser.). 1977. 20.95 (*0-8369-3340-0*) Ayer.

Cup of Water, Bread of Life: Inspiring Stories about Overcoming Lopsided Christianity. Ronald J. Sider. 176p. 1994. pap. 9.99 (*0-310-40601-3*) Zondervan.

***Cup of Wrath: A Novel Based on Dietrich Bonhoeffer's Resistance to Hitler.** Mary Glazener. 448p. 1995. pap. 18.95 (*1-57312-019-7*) Smyth & Helwys.

Cup of Wrath: A Novel Based on Dietrich Bonhoeffer's Resistance to Hitler. Mary Glazener. (Illus.). 448p. 1993. reprint ed. 29.95 (*1-880837-93-5*) Smyth & Helwys.

Cup of Wrath: The Story of Dietrich Bonhoeffer's Resistance to Hitler. Mary Glazener. LC 90-941. 576p. 1992. 29.95 (*0-913720-71-2*) Beil.

Cup Running Over. James Robinson. (Orig.). 1987. pap. 6.55 (*0-89536-873-0*, 7859) CSS OH.

Cup That I Drink. Gerald O'Mahony. (C). 1988. 39.00 (*0-85439-240-8*, Pub. by St Paul Pubns UK) St Mut.

Cup Which My Father Hath Given Me: A Biblical Revelation of Personal Spiritual Warfare. Jimmy Swaggart. 352p. (Orig.). 1991. 19.98 (*0-935113-11-8*); pap. 14.98 (*0-935113-12-6*) Swaggart Ministries.

***CUPA Membership Directory, 1994-95.** 1993. 150.00 (*1-878240-39-0*) Coll & U Personnel.

Cupboard Cookbook. Donna Brinkerhoff & Susan Rippy. (Illus.). 155p. (Orig.). (C). 1981. pap. 11.95 (*0-9613676-0-1*) Cupbd Cookbk.

Cupboard Kisses. Barbara Metzger. 224p. 1989. pap. 3.50 (*0-449-21760-4*, Crest) Fawcett.

Cupcake Cookbook: More Than Seventy Recipes for Easy, Delicious Cupcakes & Frostings. Laurence Sombke & Catherine Herman. LC 93-900. (Illus.). 144p. (Orig.). 1993. pap. 6.95 (*0-312-09265-2*) St Martin.

***Cupcakes.** Ceri Hadda. 1995. 18.95 (*0-671-86436-X*) S&S Trade.

Cupdeer. Barbara Birenbaum. LC 92-33093. (Illus.). (J). Date not set. lib. bdg. write for info. (*0-935343-04-0*); pap. write for info. (*0-935343-02-4*) Peartree.

Cupid & Commonsense. Arnold Bennett. LC 74-6015. (Collected Works of Arnold Bennett: Vol. 13). 1977. reprint ed. 20.95 (*0-518-19094-3*) Ayer.

Cupid & Psyche. Lucius Apuleius. Ed. by Edwin J. Kenney. (Greek & Latin Classics - Imperial Library). (Illus.). 300p. (C). 1991. 59.95 (*0-521-26038-8*); pap. 21.95 (*0-521-27813-9*) Cambridge U Pr.

Cupid & Psyche. Lucius Apuleius. Ed. by Maurice G. Balme & J. H. Morwood. (Illus.). 1976. pap. 10.95 (*0-19-912047-1*) OUP.

***Cupid & Psyche.** Marie Craft. (Illus.). 1996. write for info. (*0-688-13163-8*) Morrow Jr Bks.

***Cupid & Psyche.** Marie Craft. (Illus.). 1996. lib. bdg. write for info. (*0-688-13164-6*) Morrow Jr Bks.

***Cupid & the King.** Michael Pri. 1995. 20.00 (*0-00-223911-6*, Pub. by HarpC UK) HarpC.

Cupid Computer. Margie Milcsik. LC 91-46152. 128p. (J). (gr. 3-7). 1992. reprint ed. pap. 3.95 (*0-689-71569-2*, Aladdin Paperbacks) S&S Childrens.

Cupid, Couples & Contracts: A Guide to Living Together, Prenuptial Agreements, & Divorce. Lester Wallman & Sharon McDonnell. LC 94-843. 1994. pap. 12.95 (*1-57101-000-9*) MasterMedia Ltd.

***Cupid Doesn't Flip Hamburgers.** Debbie Dadey. (J). (gr. 4-7). 1995. pap. 2.99 (*0-590-48114-2*) Scholastic Inc.

Cupid is Stupid! How to Fall in Love Without Falling on Your Face. William L. Coleman. LC 91-21852. 164p. (Orig.). (YA). (gr. 9 up). 1991. pap. 7.99 (*0-8308-1335-7*, 1335) InterVarsity.

Cupid, Satyr & the Golden Age: Pastoral Dramatic Scences of the Late Renaissance. Gabriel Niccoli. 249p. (C). 1989. text ed. 36.95 (*0-8204-0783-6*) P Lang Pubs.

Cupid with Red Hair. Diana Wynne. (Rainbow Romances Ser.: No. 904). 160p. 1994. 14.95 (*0-7090-4999-4*, Hale-Parkwest) Parkwest Pubns.

Cupid's Arrow. large type ed. Janet Beaton. LC 93-137. (Nightingale Ser.). 1993. 14.95 (*0-8161-5777-4*) G K Hall.

Cupid's Cuisine, the Foods of Love. Susan A. McCreary. LC 85-22279. (Illus.). 160p. 1985. pap. 6.00 (*0-9608428-4-5*) Straw Patchwork.

Cupid's Dagger. Leona Karr. (Intrigue Ser.). 1994. mass mkt. 2.99 (*0-373-22262-9*, 1-22262-9) Harlequin Bks.

Cupid's Touch. Valerie King. 1992. mass mkt. 3.99 (*0-8217-3728-7*) Zebra.

Cupid's Yokes. Ezra H. Heywood. 1974. 59.95 (*0-87968-975-7*) Gordon Pr.

Cuple (1900-1936) Serge Salaun. (Nueva Austral Ser.: Vol. 107). (SPA.). 1991. pap. text ed. 29.95x (*84-239-1907-2*) Elliots Bks.

Cupola Hand Book. 5th ed. American Foundrymen Society Staff. 688p. 1984. 100.00 (*0-317-32613-9*, FC7506) Am Foundrymen.

Cupola Handbook. 404p. 80.00 (*0-87433-025-4*, FC8401) Am Foundrymen.

Cupola Melting, Vol. 1. 104p. 1987. pap. 30.00 (*0-317-59847-3*, TE7505) Am Foundrymen.

Cupola Melting, Vol. 2. 128p. 1987. pap. 30.00 (*0-317-59848-1*, TE7512) Am Foundrymen.

Cupola Operation Guide. American Foundrymen Society Staff. 73p. 12.00 (*0-317-32615-5*, OS7804) Am Foundrymen.

Cupola Practice & Mixing Iron. 1983. reprint ed. pap. 7.50 (*0-917914-12-0*) Lindsay Pubns.

Cuprous Oxide Photovoltaic Cells for Solar Energy Conversion. 113p. 1982. write for info. (*0-318-60084-6*, 273B) Intl Copper.

Cups: Poems by Candice Favilla. Candice Favilla. LC 92-9304. 112p. 1992. 20.00 (*0-8203-1478-1*); pap. 9.95 (*0-8203-1479-X*) U of Ga Pr.

Cups, Cans & Paper Plate Fans. Phyllis Fiarotta & Noel Fiarotta. LC 91-41825. (Illus.). 192p. (YA). (gr. 9-12). 1992. 19.95 (*0-8069-8528-3*) Sterling.

***Cups of Comfort Coffee: Our Daily Cup.** Susanne Kotz & Ed Marquand. (Illus.). 64p. 1996. 6.95 (*0-446-91138-0*) Warner Bks.

***Cups of Comfort Hot Drinks: Cocoas, Toddies, Punches, & Grogs.** Susanne Kotz & Ed Marquand. (Illus.). 64p. 1996. 6.95 (*0-446-91139-9*) Warner Bks.

Cups of Illusion. Henry Bellaman. 1972. 59.95 (*0-87968-976-5*) Gordon Pr.

Cups of Light. . . & Other Illustrations. Clarence W. Cranford. 160p. (Orig.). 1988. pap. 10.00 (*0-8170-1142-0*) Judson.

C

An Asterisk (*) at the beginning of an entry indicates that the title is appearing in BIP for the first time.

C

***Curiosity & Exploration.** K. Schneider et al. 1994. pap. text ed. 98.00 (0-387-54867-X) Spr-Verlag.
Curiosity Club: Kids' Nature Activity Book. Allene Roberts. 192p. (J). 1992. pap. text ed. 14.95 (0-471-55589-4) Wiley.
Curiosity, Imagination & Play: On the Development of Spontaneous Cognitive & Motivational Processes. Ed. by Dietmar Gorlitz & Joachim Wohlwill. 416p. (C). 1987. text ed. 89.95 (0-89859-683-1) L Erlbaum Assocs.
Curiosity Killed the Cop. large type ed. Alan Sewart. (Linford Mystery Library). 320p. 1993. pap. 14.95 (0-7089-7348-5, Trailtree Bookshop) Ulverscroft.
Curiosity of Mr. Treadgold. Valentine Williams. LC 76-37571. (Short Story Index Reprint Ser.). 1977. reprint ed. 20.95 (0-8369-4130-6) Ayer.
Curious about HDTV? Martin Levine. 1994. pap. 15.95 (0-672-30506-2) Sams.
Curious about the Internet? Ned Snell. 272p. 1994. 14.99 (0-672-30459-7) Sams.
Curious Act of Poetry. limited ed. Dorothy Hatch. (Chapbook Ser.: No. 6). (Illus.). 29p. 1991. 45.00 (0-937035-18-1); pap. 30.00 (0-937035-15-7) Stone Hse NY.
Curious Adventures of Jimmy McGee. Eleanor Estes. LC 86-31793. (Illus.). 160p. (J). (gr. 3-7). 1987. 14.95 (0-15-221075-X, HB Juv Bks) HarBrace.
Curious Affair of the Third Dog. Patricia Moyes. LC 85-17610. 224p. 1986. pap. 4.95 (0-8050-0503-X, Owl) H Holt & Co.
Curious & Creative: Critical Thinking & Language Development. Nancy S. Green. pap. 32.00 (0-201-55420-8) Addison-Wesley.
***Curious & Fantastic Creatures.** LC 94-42781. (Dover Pictorial Archives Ser.). (ENG & FRE.). 1995. pap. text ed. write for info. (0-486-28463-8) Dover.
Curious Annals: New Documents Relating to Browning's Roman Murder Story. Beatrice Corrigan. LC 76-3780. (Scholarly Reprint Ser.). 202p. reprint ed. pap. 57.60 (0-685-15336-3, 2026518) Bks Demand.
Curious Architecture: Views from America's Past. National Trust for Historic Preservation Staff. (National Trust for Historic Preservation, Past-Age Postcard Ser.). (Illus.). 20p. (Orig.). 1991. 7.95 (0-89133-165-4) Preservation Pr.
Curious Avenue. Tom Toles. (Illus.). 128p. (Orig.). 1993. pap. 8.95 (0-8362-1733-0) Andrews & McMeel.
Curious Builder. Paul Violi. 1993. pap. 10.00 (1-882413-00-8); boxed 18.00 (1-882413-01-6) Hanging Loose.
Curious Calling: Unconscious Motivations for Practicing Psychotherapy. Michael S. Sussman. LC 91-25913. 320p. 1992. 40.00 (0-87668-516-5) Aronson.
Curious Cape Cod Oddities, No. 25. Noel W. Beyle. (Illus.). 48p. (Orig.). 1985. pap. 0.95 (0-912609-08-7) First Encounter.
***Curious Cape Cod Skull.** Marie Lee. LC 94-96731. 213p. 1995. 17.95 (0-8034-9109-3) Avalon Bks.
Curious Carnival Caper. Diane Woo. (Hidden Picture Hunt Ser.). 64p. (Orig.). (J). (gr. 2-6). 1992. pap. 3.95 (1-56288-217-1) Checkerboard.
Curious Case of Sidd Finch. George Plimpton. 1987. 14.95 (0-02-597650-8) Macmillan.
Curious Cases: A Collection of American & English Decisions Selected for Their Readability. B. A. Milburn. (Illus.). xvi, 441p. 1985. reprint ed. lib. bdg. 37.50 (0-8377-0819-2) Rothman.
Curious Cook. Harold J. McGee. (Illus.). 336p. 1992. reprint ed. pap. 13.00 (0-02-009801-4, Collier S&S) S&S Trade.
Curious Cook: More Kitchen Science & Lore. Harold McGee. LC 90-7087. (Illus.). 352p. 1990. 21.00 (0-86547-452-4, North Pt Pr) FS&G.
Curious Courting. large type ed. Laura Matthews. LC 93-37450. 1994. 18.95 (0-7862-0095-2) Thorndike Pr.
Curious Courtship of Women's Liberation & Socialism. Batya Weinbaum. LC 77-9240. 169p. 1978. pap. 10.00 (0-89608-045-5) South End Pr.
Curious Customs: The Stories Behind More than 300 Popular American Rituals. Thaddeus F. Tuleja. 244p. 1987. 8.95 (0-517-56653-2, Harmony); 10.00 (0-517-56654-0, Harmony) Crown Pub Group.
Curious Eat Themselves: An Alaskan Mystery. John Straley. LC 93-8883. 264p. 1993. 19.95 (0-939149-94-X) Soho Press.
Curious Emily. Robert L. Merriam. (Illus.). 29p. 1980. pap. 2.00 (0-686-32487-0) R L Merriam.
Curious Encounters: Phantom Trains, Spooky Spots & Other Mysterious Wonders. Loren Coleman. LC 85-10132. (Illus.). 170p. (Orig.). 1989. pap. 12.95 (0-571-12542-5) Faber & Faber.
Curious Facts, Myths, Legends & Superstitions Concerning Jesus. J. W. Wright. 1991. lib. bdg. 79.95 (0-8490-4137-6) Gordon Pr.
Curious Facts, Myths, Legends, & Superstitions Concerning Jesus. John W. Wright. 130p. 1967. reprint ed. spiral bd. 4.40 (0-7873-0982-6) Mokelumne.
Curious Fawn. Raija Siekkinen. (Illus.). 32p. (J). (ps-3). 1990. lib. bdg. 18.95 (0-87614-379-6, Carolrhoda) Lerner Group.
Curious Frame: Seven Poems in Text & Context. John E. Hardy. LC 62-12465. 210p. reprint ed. pap. 59.90 (0-317-29691-4, 2022067) Bks Demand.
***Curious George.** Garrett Christopher. Ed. by J. Friedland & R. Kessler. (Novel-Ties Ser.). (J). (gr. k-1). 1993. student ed, pap. text ed. 14.95 (0-88122-945-8) Lrn Links.
Curious George. H. A. Rey. (Illus.). 56p. (J). (gr. k-3). 1973. 13.95 (0-395-15993-8) HM.
Curious George. H. A. Rey. LC 93-40088. (J). 1994. pap. 19.95 (0-395-69803-0) HM.
Curious George. H. A. Rey. (Illus.). 48p. (J). (gr. k-3). 1973. reprint ed. pap. 4.95 (0-395-15023-X, Sandpiper) HM.
Curious George & the Dinosaur. Margaret Rey & Allan J. Shalleck. (Illus.). 32p. (J). (ps-2). 1989. pap. 3.95 (0-395-51936-5) HM.
Curious George & the Dinosaur. Margaret Rey & Allan J. Shalleck. (Illus.). (J). (ps-3). 1990. audio, pap. 7.95 (0-395-56484-0, Clarion Bks) HM.
Curious George & the Dinosaur. Margret Rey. (J). (ps-3). 1989. 9.95 (0-395-51942-X) HM.
Curious George & the Dump Truck. Ed. by Margaret Rey. (Illus.). 32p. (J). (ps-2). 1984. pap. 3.95 (0-395-36629-1) HM.
Curious George & the Pizza. Margaret Rey. LC 85-2434. 32p. (J). (ps-2). 1985. 9.95 (0-395-39039-7); pap. 3.95 (0-395-39033-8) HM.
Curious George & the Pizza. Margaret Rey & Allan J. Shalleck. (Book & Cassette Favorites Ser.). (J). 1988. audio, pap. 7.95 (0-395-48874-5) HM.
Curious George at the Airport. Ed. by Margaret Rey & Allan J. Shalleck. (Illus.). 32p. (J). (ps-2). 1987. pap. 2.95 (0-395-45368-2) HM.
Curious George at the Fire Station. Ed. by Margaret Rey. LC 85-2471. 32p. (J). (ps-2). 1985. 9.95 (0-395-39037-0); pap. 3.95 (0-395-39031-1) HM.
Curious George at the Fire Station. Margaret Rey & Allan J. Shalleck. (Book & Cassette Favorites Ser.). (J). 1988. audio, pap. 7.95 (0-395-48875-3) HM.
Curious George at the Railroad Station. Margaret Rey & Allan J. Shalleck. (Illus.). 32p. (J). (ps-2). 1988. pap. 2.95 (0-395-48657-2) HM.
Curious George Flies a Kite. Margaret Rey & H. A. Rey. (Illus.). 80p. (J). (gr. k-3). 1973. 13.95 (0-395-16965-8) HM.
Curious George Flies a Kite. Margaret Rey & H. A. Rey. (Illus.). (J). (gr. k-3). 1977. pap. 4.95 (0-395-25937-1) HM.
Curious George Gets a Medal. H. A. Rey. (Illus.). 48p. (J). (gr. k-3). 1957. 13.95 (0-395-16973-9) HM.
Curious George Gets a Medal. H. A. Rey. LC 57-7206. (Illus.). 48p. (J). (gr. k-3). 1974. reprint ed. pap. 4.95 (0-395-18559-9, Sandpiper) HM.
Curious George Goes to an Ice Cream Shop. Margaret Ray & Allan J. Shalleck. (Illus.). 32p. (J). (ps-2). 1989. pap. 3.95 (0-395-51937-3) HM.
Curious George Goes to School. Margaret Rey & Allan J. Shalleck. (Illus.). 32p. (J). (ps-2). 1989. 9.95 (0-395-51944-6); pap. 3.95 (0-395-51939-X) HM.
Curious George Goes to School, Incl. cass. Margaret Rey & Allan J. Shalleck. (Illus.). (J). (ps-3). 1990. Bk. & cass. audio, pap. 7.95 (0-395-56483-2) HM.
Curious George Goes to the Aquarium. Ed. by Margaret Rey. (Illus.). 32p. (J). (ps-2). 1984. 9.95 (0-395-36634-8); pap. 3.95 (0-395-36628-3) HM.
Curious George Goes to the Dentist. Margaret Rey & Allan J. Shalleck. (Illus.). 32p. (J). (ps-2). 1989. 9.95 (0-685-26499-8) HM.
Curious George Goes to the Hospital. H. A. Rey & Margaret Rey. (Illus.). 48p. (J). (gr. 1-5). 1973. 14.95 (0-395-18158-5); pap. 4.95 (0-395-07062-7) HM.
Curious George Learns the Alphabet. H. A. Rey. (Illus.). 72p. (J). (gr. k-3). 1963. 14.95 (0-395-16031-6) HM.
Curious George Learns the Alphabet. H. A. Rey. LC 62-12261. (Illus.). 72p. (J). (gr. k-3). 1973. pap. 4.95 (0-395-13718-7, Sandpiper) HM.
Curious George Paper Doll. H. A. Rey. (J). 1982. pap. 3.95 (0-486-24386-9) Dover.
Curious George Plays Baseball. Ed. by Margaret Rey & Allan J. Shalleck. LC 86-10609. (Illus.). 32p. (J). (ps-2). 1986. 8.95 (0-395-39041-9); pap. 3.95 (0-395-39035-4) HM.
Curious George Rides a Bike. H. A. Rey. (Illus.). 48p. (J). (gr. k-3). 1952. 13.95 (0-395-16964-X) HM.
Curious George Rides a Bike. H. A. Rey. 48p. (J). (gr. k-3). pap. 1.95 (0-590-02045-5) Scholastic Inc.
Curious George Rides a Bike. H. A. Rey. (Illus.). 48p. (J). (gr. k-3). 1973. reprint ed. pap. 4.95 (0-395-17444-9, Sandpiper) HM.
Curious George Takes a Job. H. A. Rey. (Illus.). 48p. (J). (gr. k-3). 1973. 13.95 (0-395-15086-8) HM.
Curious George Takes a Job. H. A. Rey. (Illus.). 48p. (J). (gr. k-3). 1974. pap. 4.95 (0-395-18649-8, Sandpiper) HM.
Curious George Visits the Zoo. Ed. by Margaret Rey. LC 85-2415. 32p. (J). (ps-2). 1985. 9.95 (0-395-39036-2); pap. 3.95 (0-395-39030-3) HM.
Curious George Visits the Zoo. Margaret Rey & Allan J. Shalleck. (Book & Cassette Package Ser.). (J). 1988. audio, pap. 7.95 (0-395-48876-1) HM.
Curious History of "Bartholomew Fair" Frances Teague. LC 84-45006. 176p. 1985. 32.50 (0-8387-5072-9) Bucknell U Pr.
Curious Investigation Concerning the Nature of the Sun & Moon. Michael Scotus. (Alchemical Treatise Ser.: No. 5). 1983. pap. 2.95 (0-916411-94-X) Holmes Pub.
Curious Kakariki. David M. Slater. (C). 1989. pap. text ed. write for info. (0-318-66537-9) Starbird Pubns.
Curious Kimo. Malia Maness. LC 93-86143. (Illus.). 32p. (J). (ps-3). 1993. 9.95 (0-9633493-0-9) Pacific Greetings.
Curious Land: Jesuit Accommodation & the Origins of Sinology. David E. Mungello. LC 88-27874. (Illus.). 408p. 1989. reprint ed. pap. text ed. 17.00 (0-8248-1219-0) UH Pr.
Curious Learner: Help Your Child Develop Academic & Creative Skills. Margorie R. Simic et al. Ed. by Carl B. Smith. (Successful Learner Ser.). (Illus.). (Orig.). 1992. pap. 9.95 (0-9628556-8-5) Grayson Bernard Pubs.
Curious Little Dolphin. Ariane Chottin. LC 91-46500. (Little Animal Adventures Ser.). (Illus.). 22p. (J). (ps-3). 1992. 5.98 (0-89577-425-9, Readers Digest Kids) RD Assn.
Curious Lore of Precious Stones. George F. Kunz. 1970. pap. 7.95 (0-486-22227-6) Dover.
Curious Lottery & Other Tales of Russian Justice. Walter Duranty. LC 78-101805. (Short Story Index Reprint Ser.). 1977. 19.95 (0-8369-3193-9) Ayer.
Curious Mechanical Movements. Gardner D. Hiscox. 1986. reprint ed. pap. 14.95 (0-917914-40-6) Lindsay Pubns.
Curious Mishap see Comedies of Goldoni
Curious Myths of the Middle Ages. Sabine Baring-Gould. 1972. 250.00 (0-87968-261-2) Gordon Pr.
Curious Myths of the Middle Ages. S. Baring-Gould. 255p. 1976. reprint ed. spiral bd. 9.90 (0-7873-0071-3) Mokelumne.
Curious Myths of the Middle Ages. Sabine Baring-Gould. 1976. reprint ed. 55.00 (0-403-06309-4, Regency) Scholarly.
Curious Naturalist. Ed. by Jennifer G. Ackerman. LC 91-27559. (Illus.). 1991. 29.95 (0-87044-861-7); 41.95 (0-87044-862-5) Natl Geog.
Curious Naturalists. rev. ed. Niko Tinbergen. LC 84-8504. (Illus.). 272p. 1984. reprint ed. pap. 16.95 (0-87023-456-0) U of Mass Pr.
Curious Perspective: Literary & Pictorial Wit in the Seventeenth Century. Ernest B. Gilman. LC 78-6075. 279p. reprint ed. pap. 79.60 (0-8357-8084-8, 2033729) Bks Demand.
Curious Proposal. Freda Michel. LC 68-21699. 224p. 1980. pap. 1.75 (0-449-50071-3, Coventry) Fawcett.
***Curious Punishments of Bygone Days.** Alice M. Earle. LC 94-43285. 176p. 1995. pap. 10.95 (1-55709-249-4) Applewood.
Curious Punishments of Bygone Days. Alice M. Earle. LC 69-14922. (Criminology, Law Enforcement, & Social Problems Ser.: No. 33). (Illus.). 1969. 12.00 (0-87585-033-2) Patterson Smith.
Curious Punishments of Bygone Days. Alice Earle. 1988. reprint ed. lib. bdg. 59.00 (0-7812-0020-2) Rprt Serv.
Curious Punishments of Bygone Days. Alice Earle. 1977. reprint ed. 29.00 (0-403-08591-8) Scholarly.
Curious Punishments of Bygone Days. Alice M. Earle. LC 86-82640. 160p. 1986. reprint ed. pap. text ed. 8.95 (0-915179-54-7) Loompanics.
Curious Punishments of Bygone Days. Alice M. Earle. LC 89-43345. (Illus.). 149p. 1990. reprint ed. lib. bdg. 38.00 (1-55888-872-1) Omnigraphics Inc.
Curious Questions in History, Literature, Art & Social Life, 3 vols, Set. S. H. Killikelly. 1972. 300.00 (0-87968-979-X) Gordon Pr.
Curious Questions in History, Literature, Art & Social Life, 3 vols., Set. Sarah H. Killikelly. 1968. reprint ed. 90.00 (1-55888-948-5) Omnigraphics Inc.
Curious Quests of Brigadier Fellowes. Sterling E. Lanier. (Illus.). 1986. 30.00 (0-937986-89-5) D M Grant.
Curious Republic of Gondour. Samuel L. Clemens. LC 74-3396. (Mark Twain Ser.: No. 76). 1974. lib. bdg. 75.00 (0-8383-2070-8) M S G Haskell Hse.
Curious Researcher. Bruce Ballenger. LC 93-11200. 1993. pap. text ed. 12.95 (0-205-13905-1) Allyn.
Curious Savage. John Patrick. 1950. pap. 4.75 (0-8222-0260-3) Dramatists Play.
***Curious Sea Horse.** Stewart Cowley. LC 94-67212. (Magic Window Bks.). (Illus.). 20p. (J). (gr. 3). 1994. bds. 6.99 (0-89577-639-1) RD Assn.
Curious Sofa. Edward Gorey. LC 61-12368. (Illus.). 64p. 1986. reprint ed. 11.95 (0-926637-04-5) P Weed Bks.
Curious Sofa, Ogdred Weary. Edward Gorey. (Illus.). 1961. pap. 5.95 (0-8392-1020-5) Astor-Honor.
Curious What You Might Find When You Go Out to Look for Elephants. Mary Macur. LC 48-29. pap. 5.00 (0-686-28865-3) First Amend.
Curious Wine: Tenth Anniversary Edition. Katherine V. Forrest. LC 82-24663. 176p. (Orig.). 1993. pap. 10.95 (1-56280-053-1) Naiad Pr.
Curious Woodcuts of Fanciful & Real Beasts. Conrad Gesner. Ed. by Edmund V. Gillon, Jr. (Pictorial Archive Ser.). Orig. Title: Selection of 16th & 17th-Century Woodcuts from Gesner & Topsell's Natural Histories. (Illus.). (Orig.). 1971. pap. 6.95 (0-486-22701-4) Dover.
Curiouser & Curiouser Cats. Martin Lemans. (Illus.). 32p. (J). (ps-2). 1993. 16.95 (0-575-04707-0, Pub. by V Gollancz UK) Trafalgar.
Curlew. Gerry Cotter. 1989. pap. 25.00 (0-7478-0090-1, Pub. by Shire UK) St Mut.
Curlew's Cry. Mildred Walker. LC 93-43768. v, 382p. 1994. pap. 10.95 (0-8032-9757-2, Bison Books) U of Nebr Pr.
Curling Handbook. Roy D. Thiessen. (Illus.). 88p. pap. 5.95 (0-919654-71-1) Hancock House.
***Curlique Caterpillar & Friends Say Thank You.** Diane Stortz. (Illus.). 10p. (J). (ps). 1995. bds. 4.99 (0-7847-0298-5, 24-03438) Standard Pub.
Curly: An Illustrated Biography of the Superstooge. Joan H. Maurer. (Illus.). 256p. 1985. 19.95 (0-8065-0979-1, Citadel Pr) Carol Pub Group.
CURLY: An Illustrated Biography of the Superstooge. Joan H. Maurer. (Illus.). 224p. 1988. pap. 14.95 (0-8065-1086-2, Citadel Pr) Carol Pub Group.
Curly Coated Retriever Champions, 1952-1987. Camino E. E. & B. Co. Staff. 86p. 1988. pap. 36.95 (0-940808-87-0) Camino E E & Bk.
Curly-Coated Retriever Champions, 1988-1993. Camino Book Co. Staff. (Illus.). 60p. 1995. pap. 32.95 (1-55893-033-7) Camino E E & Bk.
Curly Pig, Vol. 2: Tails with a Moral. Sandi Z. Griffin. (YEA US Ser.). (Illus.). 28p. (J). (ps-2). 1993. write for info. (1-883838-02-9) S Z Griffin.
Curly Top Disease of Sugarbeet & Other Plants. C. W. Bennett. (Phytopathological Monograph Ser.). 81p. 1971. 15.00 (0-89054-039-X) Am Phytopathol Soc.
Curme Volume of Linguistic Studies. Ed. by James T. Hatfield. (LM Ser.: No. 7). 1930. 16.00 (0-527-00811-7) Periodicals Srv.
Curmudgeon's Garden of Love. Comp. by Jon Winokur. (Illus.). 224p. 1991. pap. 8.00 (0-452-26551-7, Plume) NAL-Dutton.
Curo Practico Espanol Para Mayores. M. Wilden-Hart. (C). 1986. 55.00 (0-85950-524-3, Pub. by S Thornes Pubs UK) St Mut.
Curran vs. Catholic University: A Study of Authority & Freedom in Conflict. Larry Witham. LC 91-70531. 340p. 1991. pap. 12.95 (0-9628685-0-7) Edington-Rand.
Currencies & Crises. Paul R. Krugman. 1992. 27.50 (0-262-11165-9) MIT Pr.
***Currencies & Crises.** Paul R. Krugman. 250p. 1995. pap. 15.95x (0-262-61109-0) MIT Pr.
Currencies & Politics in the United States, Germany, & Japan. C. Randall Henning. 406p. 1994. pap. 25.00 (0-88132-127-3) Inst Intl Eco.
Currencies of China. Edward Kann. (Illus.). 1978. reprint ed. lib. bdg. 45.00 (0-915262-22-3) S J Durst.
Currencies of China: An Investigation of Silver & Gold Transactions Affecting China, with a Section on Copper. 2nd ed. Edward Kann. LC 77-38074. (China Classic & Contemporary Works in Reprint Ser.). reprint ed. 110.00 (0-404-56936-6) AMS Pr.
Currencies of the Anglo Norman Isles. A. L. McCammon. (Illus.). 1984. lib. bdg. 45.00 (0-907605-13-3) S J Durst.
Currency & Banking in the Province of the Massachusetts-Bay, 2 vols., Set, Vols. 1-2. Andrew M. Davis. LC 68-55700. (Library of Money & Banking History). (Illus.). 1970. reprint ed. 87.50 (0-678-00637-7) Kelley.
***Currency & Coercion: The Political Economy of International Monetary Power.** Jonathan Kirshner. LC 95-13294. 1995. write for info. (0-691-03768-X) Princeton U Pr.
Currency & Credit. Ralph G. Hawtrey. Ed. by Mira Wilkins. LC 78-3923. (International Finance Ser.). 1979. reprint ed. lib. bdg. 36.95 (0-405-11226-2) Ayer.
Currency & Financial System of Mainland China. Tadao Miyashita. (China in the 20th Century Ser.). 1976. reprint ed. lib. bdg. 32.50 (0-306-70758-6) Da Capo.
Currency & Inflation in Fourth Century Egypt. Roger S. Bagnall. (BASP Supplements Ser.). (C). 1985. pap. 17.75 (0-89130-790-7, 31-11-05) Scholars Pr GA.
Currency & Interest-Rate Hedging: A User's Guide to Options, Futures, Swaps, & Forward Contracts. Torben J. Andersen. (Illus.). 256p. 1987. 35.00 (0-13-195645-0) NY Inst Finance.
Currency & Interest Rate Hedging: A User's Guide to Options, Futures, Swaps, & Forward Contracts. 2nd ed. Toirben J. Andersen. 1993. 49.95 (0-13-226101-4) NY Inst Finance.
Currency & Interest Rate Swaps. 2nd ed. Schuyler K. Henderson & John A. Price. 200p. 1988. boxed 45.00 (0-88063-254-2) Michie Butterworth.
Currency Boards for Developing Countries: A Handbook. Steve H. Hanke & Kurt Schuler. LC 93-45701. (Sector Studies: No. 9). 1994. pap. 12.95 (1-55815-309-8) ICS Pr.
Currency Competition & Monetary Union. Pascal Salin. (Financial & Monetary Policy Studies). 308p. 1984. lib. bdg. 106.50 (90-247-2817-7) Kluwer Ac.
Currency Convertibility in Eastern Europe. Ed. by John Williamson. LC 91-29947. (Illus.). 461p. 1991. pap. 25.00 (0-88132-128-1) Inst Intl Eco.
Currency Convertibility in the Economic Community of West African States. John B. McLenaghan et al. (Occasional Paper Ser.: No. 13). 46p. 1982. pap. 5.00 (1-55775-059-9) Intl Monetary.
Currency Depreciation & Monetary Policy. Milton Gilbert. Ed. by Mira Wilkins. LC 78-3914. (International Finance Ser.). (Illus.). 1979. reprint ed. lib. bdg. 19.95 (0-405-11218-1) Ayer.
***Currency Derivatives: The Handbook of Instruments, Strategies, & Applications.** David Derosa. 350p. 1995. 65.00 (1-55738-876-8) Probus Pub Co.
***Currency Features for Visually Impaired People.** National Research Council, Commission on PHysical Sciences, Mathematics, & Applications Staff. 100p. (Orig.). (C). 1995. pap. text ed. 27.00 (0-309-05194-0) Natl Acad Pr.
Currency Fluctuations & International Double Taxation. (Cahiers de Droit Fiscal International Ser.: Vol. LXXIb). 570p. 1986. pap. 100.00 (90-6544-259-6) Kluwer Law Tax Pubs.
Currency Fluctuations & the Perception of Corporate Performance: A Communications Approach to Financial Accounting & Reporting. Loretta Graziano. LC 86-612. 191p. 1986. text ed. 55.00 (0-89930-136-3, GCM/, Quorum Bks) Greenwood.
Currency Held by the Public, the Banks, & the Treasury, Monthly, December 1917-December 1944. Anna J. Schwartz & Elma Oliver. (Technical Papers: No. 4). 72p. 1947. reprint ed. 20.00 (0-87014-449-9); reprint ed. mic. film 20.00 (0-685-61270-8) Natl Bur Econ Res.
Currency in Roman & Byzantine Egypt. L. C. West & A. C. Johnson. 195p. reprint ed. lib. bdg. 37.50 (0-685-13328-1, Pub. by A M Hakkert SP) Coronet Bks.
Currency of Eros: Women's Love Lyric in Europe, 1540-1620. Ann R. Jones. LC 89-45412. (Women of Letters Ser.). (Illus.). 253p. 1990. 29.95 (0-253-33149-8) Ind U Pr.
Currency of Fame: Portrait Medals of the Rennaissance. Ed. by Stephen K. Scher. LC 93-26690. 1994. 95.00 (0-8109-3191-5); pap. 40.00 (0-8109-2572-9) Abrams.
Currency of the American Colonies, Seventeen Hundred to Seventeen Sixty-Four: A Study in Colonial Finance & Imperial Relations. Leslie V. Brock. LC 75-2576. (Dissertations in American Economic History Ser.). (Illus.). 1978. 63.95 (0-405-07257-0) Ayer.
Currency of the British Colonies. James Pennington. LC 67-18578. (Library of Money & Banking History). 1967. reprint ed. 35.00 (0-678-00260-6) Kelley.

Currency Options: Hedging & Trading Strategies. Henry Clasing, Jr. 260p. 1992. 70.00 (*1-55623-170-9*) Irwin Prof Pubng.

Currency Risk & Business Management. Alfred Kenyon. (Illus.). 350p. 1990. text ed. 79.95 (*0-631-17749-3*) Blackwell Pubs.

Currency Risk & the Corporation. Ed. by Euromoney Staff. 1985. 110.00 (*0-686-79175-4*, Pub. by Euromoney UK) St Mut.

Currency Risk Management. Alfred Kenyon. 191p. 1981. text ed. 73.50 (*0-471-10003-X*, Wiley-Interscience) Wiley.

Currency Substitution & Liberalization: The Case of Argentina. U. Fassano-Filho. Orig. Title: Currency Substitution, Interest Rate & Exchange Rate Policy. 200p. 1986. text ed. 59.95 (*0-566-05234-2*, Pub. by Avebury Pub UK) Ashgate Pub Co.

Currency Substitution, Interest Rate & Exchange Rate Policy see Currency Substitution & Liberalization: The Case of Argentina

Currency Swaps: A Self-Study Guide to Mastering & Applying Currency Swaps. Coopers & Lybrand Staff. 1994. pap. 55.00 (*1-55738-590-4*) Probus Pub Co.

Currency Units. (Terminology Bulletin Ser.: No. 343). 113p. 1992. 10.00 (*92-1-002056-1*) UN.

***Current Account & Foreign Debt.** John Pitchford. LC 94-46487. 1995. write for info. (*0-415-09401-1*) Routledge.

Current-Account Balance & the Dollar: 1977-78 and 1983-84. Stephen S. Golub. LC 86-21056. (Studies in International Finance: No. 57). 1986. pap. text ed. 11.00 (*0-88165-229-6*) Princeton U Int Finan Econ.

Current Accounting Trends. Adolf A. Fitzgerald. Ed. by Richard P. Brief. LC 77-87271. (Development of Contemporary Accounting Thought Ser.). 1978. reprint ed. lib. bdg. 31.95 (*0-405-10899-0*) Ayer.

Current Acoustic Research in Subsea Technology. Ian Bryden. 1989. 125.00 (*90-6314-591-8*, Pub. by Lorne & MacLean Marine) St Mut.

Current Acoustic Research in Subsea Technology. Ian Bryden. (C). 1989. 100.00 (*0-89771-738-4*, Pub. by Lorne & MacLean Marine) St Mut.

Current Action Table. Joseph A. Uphoff, Jr. 54p. 1990. pap. text ed. 3.00 (*0-943123-21-6*) Arjuna Lib Pr.

Current Advances in Ace Inhibition. Ed. by Graham A. MacGregor & Peter S. Sever. (Illus.). 320p. 1989. text ed. 72.00 (*0-443-04235-7*) Churchill.

Current Advances in Ace Inhibition. 3rd ed. Graham A. MacGregor. 1994. 98.00 (*4-89370-071-5*) Churchill.

Current Advances in Ace Inhibition 2. Ed. by Graham A. MacGregor & Peter S. Sever. (Illus.). 320p. 1991. text ed. write for info. (*0-443-04600-X*) Churchill.

Current Advances in Basic & Clinical Microcirculatory Research. Ed. by G. Wolf-Heidegger. (Bibliotheca Anatomica Ser.: No. 18). (Illus.). 1979. 125.00 (*3-8055-3042-0*) S Karger.

Current Advances in Inpatient Psychiatric Care: A Handbook. Ed. by Douglas H. Ruben et al. LC 92-49214. 384p. 1993. text ed. 79.50 (*0-313-28046-0*, RCP/, Greenwood Pr) Greenwood.

Current Advances in LANs, MANs, & ISDN. B. G. Kim. LC 89-17502. (Illus.). 377p. reprint ed. pap. 107.50 (*0-7837-6295-X*, 2046010) Bks Demand.

Current Advances in Mechanical Design & Production: Proceedings. Ed. by G. S. Shawki & S. M. Metwalli. LC 80-41666. (Illus.). 496p. 1981. 211.00 (*0-08-027294-0*, Pub. by Pergamon Repr UK) Franklin.

Current Advances in Mechanical Design & Production: Proceedings of the 4th Cairo University MDP Conference, Cairo, 27-29 December 1988. Ed. by Y. H. Kabil & M. E. Said. (Illus.). 696p. 1988. pap. 20.00 (*0-08-037200-7*, Pergamon Pr) Elsevier.

Current Advances in Mechanical Design & Production 3: Proceedings of the 3rd Cairo University MPD Conference, Cairo, 28-30 December, 1985. Ed. by S. E. Bayoumi & M. Y. Younan. 1986. 200.00 (*0-08-033440-7*, Pub. by Pergamon Repr UK) Franklin.

Current Advances in Semantic Theory. Ed. by Maxim Stamenov. LC 91-39925. (Current Issues in Linguistic Theory Ser.: No. 73). xii, 565p. 1992. 144.00 (*1-55619-129-4*) Benjamins North Am.

Current Advances in Skeletogenesis: Induction, Biomineralization, Bone Seeking Hormones, Congenital & Metabolic Bone Diseases: Proceedings of the International Workshop on Calcified Tissue, 6th, Kiryat-Anavim, Israel, 18-23 March, 1984. Ed. by A. Ornoy et al. (International Congress Ser.: No. 643). 500p. 1985. 168.75 (*0-444-80659-8*, Excerpta Medica) Elsevier.

Current Aeronautical Fatigue Problems: Proceedings of Symposium, Rome, April 1963. J. Schijve & J. Health-Smith. LC 64-23209. (International Series Mono in Aeronautics & Astronautics: Vol. 19). 1965. 204.00 (*0-08-010952-7*, Pub. by Pergamon Repr UK) Franklin.

Current Affairs. Barbara Raskin. 336p. 1991. mass mkt. 5.95 (*0-8041-0537-5*) Ivy Books.

Current Affairs. Barbara Raskin. 288p. 1990. 19.95 (*0-394-57994-1*) Random.

Current Algebra & Anomalies. R. Jackiw et al. 520p. 1985. text ed. 100.00 (*9971-966-96-4*); pap. text ed. 48.00 (*9971-966-97-2*) World Scientific Pub.

Current Algebra & Anomalies. S. B. Treiman et al. 1986. 69.50 (*0-691-08397-5*); pap. 29.95 (*0-691-08398-3*) Princeton U Pr.

Current Algebra & Phenomenological Lagrange Functions: Proceedings of the International Summer School for Theoretical Physics, University of Karlsruhe, 1968. International Summer School for Theoretical Physics Staff. Ed. by G. Hoehler. (Tracts in Modern Physics Ser.: Vol. 50). (Illus.). v, 156p. 1969. 39.00 (*0-387-04713-1*) Spr-Verlag.

Current & Emerging Issues in Cancer Pain Research & Practice. Ed. by C. Richard Chapman & Kathleen M. Foley. LC 93-3669. (Bristol-Myers - Squibb Symposium on Pain Research Ser.). 480p. 1993. 147.00 (*0-7817-0007-8*) Raven.

Current & Future Modalities of Cardiac Imaging. A. James Liedtke. 250p. 1988. 50.00 (*0-89335-308-6*) PMA Pub Corp.

Current & Future Use of Registers in Health Information Systems. Eileen M. Brooke. (Offset Publication Ser.: No. 8). 1974. pap. 5.60 (*92-4-170008-4*) World Health.

Current & Historical Perspectives on the Borderline Patient. Ed. by Reuben Fine & Herbert S. Strean. LC 89-7312. (Current Issues in Psychoanalytic Practice Ser.: No. 1). 434p. 1989. 42.95 (*0-87630-506-0*) Brunner-Mazel.

Current & New Vaccines Market. (Market Research Reports: No. 360). (Illus.). 122p. 1992. 795.00 (*0-317-05034-6*) Theta Corp.

Current & Potential Applications for Erythropoietin. Ed. by B. G. Durie. (Journal: Acta Haematologica: Vol. 87, Suppl. 1, 1992). (Illus.). vi, 34p. 1992. pap. 16.00 (*3-8055-5617-9*) S Karger.

Current & Potential Future Industrial Practices for Reducing & Controlling Volatile Organic Compounds. LC 93-12704. 85p. 1993. 40.00 (*0-8169-0592-4*) Am Inst Chem Eng.

Current & Tide Tables for Puget Sound, Deception Pass, the San Juans, Gulf Islands & Strait of Juan de Fuca, 1990. abr. ed. National Oceanographic & Atmospheric Administration Staff. Ed. by Island Canoe, Inc. Staff. 96p. 1989. pap. 5.95 (*0-918439-11-6*) Island Canoe.

Current & Tide Tables (1991) for Puget Sound, Deception Pass, the San Juans, Gulf Islands & Strait of Juan de Fuca. abr. ed. NOAA (Nat'l Oceanaographic & Atmospheric Administration) Staff. Ed. by Island Canoe, Inc. Staff. 96p. 1990. pap. write for info. (*0-918439-12-4*) Island Canoe.

Current & Tide Tables, 1992: For Puget Sound, Deception Pass, the San Juans, Gulf Islands & Strait of Juan de Fuca. abr. ed. National Oceanographic & Atmospheric Administration Staff. Ed. by Island Canoe Staff. 96p. 1991. pap. 5.95 (*0-918439-15-9*) Island Canoe.

Current & Tide Tables (1994) for Puget Sound, Deception Pass, the San Juans, Gulf Islands & Strait of Juan De Fuca. National Oceanographic & Atmospheric Administration Staff. Ed. by Island Canoe Staff. 1993. pap. 6.95 (*0-918439-17-5*) Island Canoe.

Current Antique Furniture. George Grotz. 1979. pap. 19.95 (*0-385-47052-5*) Doubleday.

Current Applications & Interpretations of the DAT. Ed. by Margaret E. Wallace & Judy Levitt. LC 88-19405. 1988. 7.00 (*0-915355-56-6*) Am Assn Blood.

Current Appraisal of the Behavioral Sciences. 2nd rev. ed. Rollo Handy & E. C. Harwood. LC 73-79255. (C). 1973. 15.00 (*0-913610-01-1*) Behavioral Mass.

Current Approaches to African Linguistics, Vol. 1. Ed. by G. R. Dihoff. (Publications in African Languages & Linguistics). viii, 360p. 1983. pap. 90.80 (*90-70176-57-2*) Mouton.

Current Approaches to African Linguistics, Vol. 2. Ed. by J. Kaye et al. (Publications in African Languages & Linguistics). viii, 389p. 1983. pap. 88.50 (*90-70176-95-5*) Mouton.

Current Approaches to African Linguistics, Vol. 3. Ed. by Gerrit J. Dimmendaal. ix, 297p. (C). 1986. pap. text ed. 75.40 (*3-11-013285-0*) Mouton.

Current Approaches to African Linguistics, Vol. 4. Ed. by D. Odden. (Publications in African Languages & Linguistics). x, 428p. 1987. pap. 113.85 (*3-11-013103-X*) Mouton.

Current Approaches to African Linguistics, Vol. 5. Paul Newman & Robert D. Botre. (Publications in African Languages & Linguistics: No. 8). viii, 266p. 1989. pap. 83.10 (*90-6765-324-1*) Mouton.

Current Approaches to African Linguistics, Vol. 6. Ed. by Isabelle Haiik & Laurice Tuller. (PALL Ser.: No. 9). xiii, 336p. (C). 1989. pap. 106.15 (*90-6765-419-1*) Mouton.

Current Approaches to African Linguistics, Vol. 7. Victor Manfred & John Glutchison. (Publications in African Languages & Linguistics: No. 11). 235p. 1990. pap. 77. 15 (*90-6765-498-1*) Mouton.

Current Approaches to Bone Marrow Histopathology. Ed. by S. Roath & M. Corn. (Hematology Reviews & Communications Ser.: Vol. 3, Nos. 2-3). 114p. 1989. pap. text ed. 158.00 (*3-7186-4974-8*) Gordon & Breach.

Current Approaches to Collective Bargaining: An ILO Symposium on Collective Bargaining in Industrialised Market Economy Countries, Geneva, 2-6 November 1987. (Labour-Management Relations Ser.: No. 71). vii, 184p. (Orig.). 1989. pap. 18.00 (*92-2-106503-0*) Intl Labour Office.

Current Approaches to Down's Syndrome. Ed. by David Lane & Brian Stratford. LC 85-8842. 447p. 1985. text ed. 75.00 (*0-275-90212-9*, C0212, Praeger Pubs) Greenwood.

Current Approaches to Grading Commercial Loans. Charles S. Dickerson. Ed. by Joan H. Behr. LC 87-18458. (Illus.). 44p. 1987. pap. text ed. 39.00 (*0-936742-43-7*) Robt Morris Assocs.

Current Approaches to Improving Access to Government Documents. C. Turner & A. Latta. 1987. pap. 25.00 (*0-918006-54-6*, OP#12) ARL.

Current Approaches to Phonological Theory. Ed. by Daniel A. Dinnsen. LC 78-3241. 348p. reprint ed. pap. 99.20 (*0-8357-6674-8*, 2056852) Bks Demand.

Current Approaches to Shakespeare: Language, Text, Theatre, & Ideology. Ed. by Stanley Wells. (Shakespeare Survey Ser.: No. 40). 200p. 1988. 64.95 (*0-521-34442-5*) Cambridge U Pr.

Current Approaches to Syntax see Syntax & Semantics

Current Approaches to the Prediction of Violence. Ed. by David A. Brizer & Martha L. Crowner. LC 88-7443. (Progress in Psychiatry Ser.). 208p. 1989. 27.50 (*0-88048-289-3*, 8289) Am Psychiatric.

***Current Architecture.** Xavier Guell. (Current Architecture Catalog Ser.). (Illus.). 144p. (ENG & SPA.). 1995. pap. 40.00 (*84-252-1636-2*, Pub. by Gustavo Gili SP) Rizzoli Intl.

Current Argument on Early Man: Nobel Symposium "Current Argument on Early Man" Royal Swedish Academy of Sciences & the Nobel Foundation, Karlskoga, Sweden, May 21-27, 1978. Ed. by Lars-Konig Konigsson & Stephan Sundstrom. (Illus.). 1980. 126.00 (*0-08-024956-6*, Pub. by Pergamon Repr UK) Franklin.

Current Aspects in Ophthalmology: Proceedings of the XIII Congress of the Asia-Pacific Academy of Ophthalmology, Kyoto, Japan, May 12-17, 1991. Ed. by K. Shimizu. LC 92-49965. (International Congress Ser.: No. 982). 1992. write for info. (*0-444-89141-2*, Excerpta Medica) Elsevier.

Current Aspects of Blood Coagulation, Fibrinolysis, & Platelets. Ed. by Ming-Ching Shen et al. LC 93-23882. (Illus.). x, 190p. 1993. pap. 55.00 (*0-387-70123-0*) Spr-Verlag.

Current Aspects of Pancreatic Diseases: Digestion, Supplement 1, 1987, Vol. 37. Ed. by H. G. Worning. (Illus.). iv, 68p. 1987. pap. 21.00 (*3-8055-4618-1*) S Karger.

Current Attitudes & Reactions to Soviet Policies in the Asia-Pacific Region. Ed. by Guy J. Pauker. 155p. (C). 1986. ring bd. 12.50 (*0-317-91350-6*) Pac Forum.

Current Auditing Developments U. K. 3rd ed. Woolf. 1983. pap. 29.95 (*0-85258-229-3*) Chapman & Hall.

Current Australian Trends in Corrections. David Biles. 1988. pap. 30.00 (*1-86287-003-9*, Pub. by Federation Pr AU) W W Gaunt.

***Current Awareness, Current Techniques.** Feona Hamilton. 1995. 50.95 (*0-566-07626-8*) Ashgate Pub Co.

Current Awareness Services in Sci-Tech Libraries. Ed. by Ellis Mount. (Science & Technology Libraries: Vol. 2, No. 1). 80p. 1982. pap. 22.95 (*0-86656-113-7*) Haworth Pr.

Current Biography Cumulated Index, 1940-1990. LC 40-27432. 133p. 1991. 27.00 (*0-8242-0819-6*) Wilson.

Current Biography Yearbook 1994. (Illus.). 700p. 1994. 62. 00x (*0-317-18545-4*) Wilson.

Current Biography, Yearbooks 1940-1985. 54.00 (*0-685-30953-3*) Wilson.

Current British Directories. 12th ed. Anderson. 1993. 235. 00 (*0-900246-60-X*, 070152, Pub. by CN Almanac & Dir CN) Gale.

Current Budgeting Practices in U. S. Industry: The State of the Art. Srinivasan Umapathy. LC 87-5969. (Illus.). 215p. 1987. text ed. 59.95 (*0-89930-250-5*, UCB/, Quorum Bks) Greenwood.

Current Cancer Immunology. Ed. by V. Richards. (Progress in Experimental Tumor Research Ser.: Vol. 25). (Illus.). 1980. 116.00 (*3-8055-3033-1*) S Karger.

Current Cancer Therapeutics. John M. Kirkwood et al. (Illus.). 352p. 1994. pap. text ed. 49.95 (*1-878132-12-1*) Current Med.

***Current Cardiovascular Drug Therapy.** 2nd ed. Ed. by Franz H. Messerli. LC 95-1013. 1995. text ed. write for info. (*0-7216-4814-2*) Saunders.

Current Cardiovascular Drugs. William Frishman. (Illus.). 304p. 1993. text ed. 39.95 (*1-878132-11-3*) Current Med.

***Current Cardiovascular Drugs.** 2nd ed. William H. Frishman. (Illus.). 328p. 1994. pap. text ed. 39.95 (*1-878132-60-1*) Current Science.

Current Central American-U. S. Relations. Ed. by Joan Nordquist. (Contemporary Social Issues: A Bibliographic Ser.: No. 5). 50p. 1987. pap. 15.00 (*0-937855-09-X*) Ref Rsch Serv.

Current Central Legislation. (C). 1989. 252.00 (*0-685-54752-3*) St Mut.

Current Central Legislation. Eastern Book Co. Staff. (C). 1990. 170.00 (*0-685-38604-X*) St Mut.

Current Central Legislation, 12 vols., set. deluxe ed. Eastern Book Co. Staff. (C). 1986. Set. ring bd. 1,250.00 (*0-685-25167-5*) St Mut.

Current Central Legislation, 1975-1988, 14 vols. deluxe ed. Eastern Book Co. Staff. (C). 1988. ring bd. 2,100.00 (*0-685-25677-4*) St Mut.

Current Central Legislation, 1990. B. B. C. Staff. (C). 1991. ring bd. 180.00 (*0-89771-464-4*) St Mut.

Current Child & Family Policy in the United States. Ed. by Francine H. Jacobs & Margery W. Davies. LC 93-37492. 328p. 1994. text ed. 55.00 (*0-86569-223-8*, Auburn Hse); pap. text ed. 19.95 (*0-86569-224-6*, Auburn Hse) Greenwood.

Current Christian Books, 1990. CBA Service Corp. Staff. 1990. 79.95 (*0-317-03836-2*) Chr Bksellers.

Current Climate. Bruce J. Friedman. 1990. pap. 8.95 (*0-87113-388-1*) Grove-Atltic.

Current Clinical Practice. Franz H. Messerli. (Illus.). 1000p. 1987. text ed. 73.50 (*0-7216-1460-4*) Saunders.

Current Clinical Strategies: Critical Care Medicine. Paul D. Chan. 100p. 1992. pap. 8.75 (*0-9626030-4-X*) Current Clin Strat.

Current Clinical Strategies: Family Medicine. Current Clinical Strategies Medical Group Staff & Paul D. Chan. 175p. 1992. pap. 19.00 (*0-9626030-9-0*) Current Clin Strat.

Current Clinical Strategies: Outpatient Medicine. Paul D. Chan. 100p. 1992. pap. 7.75 (*0-9626030-3-1*) Current Clin Strat.

***Current Clinical Strategies, Critical Care Medicine.** 3rd ed. Paul D. Chan et al. 110p. 1995. pap. 12.75 (*1-881528-21-9*) Current Clin Strat.

Current Clinical Strategies, Diagnostic History & Physical Examination in Medicine. Current Clinical Strategies Medical Group Staff & Paul D. Chan. 75p. 1992. pap. 8.75 (*0-9626030-8-2*) Current Clin Strat.

***Current Clinical Strategies, Family Medicine.** 2nd ed. Paul D. Chan. 260p. Date not set. pap. 26.25 (*1-881528-16-2*) Current Clin Strat.

Current Clinical Strategies, Gynecology & Obstetrics. Paul D. Chan. 85p. (Orig.). 1991. pap. 7.75 (*0-9626030-1-5*) Current Clin Strat.

***Current Clinical Strategies, Gynecology & Obstetrics.** 3rd ed. Paul D. Chan & Christopher R. Winkle. 90p. (Orig.). 1995. pap. 10.75 (*1-881528-27-8*) Current Clin Strat.

Current Clinical Strategies, Handbook of Anesthesiology. Mark Ezekiel. Ed. by Paul D. Chan. (Current Clinical Strategies Ser.). 130p. (Orig.). (C). 1993. pap. 6.50 (*1-881528-08-1*) Current Clin Strat.

Current Clinical Strategies, Handbook of HIV-AIDS Therapy. Laurence Pieperl. Ed. by Paul D. Chan. (Current Clinical Strategies Ser.). 83p. (Orig.). 1992. pap. text ed. 6.50 (*1-881528-01-4*) Current Clin Strat.

***Current Clinical Strategies, Manual of HIV-AIDS Therapy: Current Clinical Strategies.** 2nd ed. Laurence Peiperl. 85p. 1995. pap. 8.75 (*1-881528-09-X*) Current Clin Strat.

***Current Clinical Strategies, Medicine.** 3rd ed. Paul D. Chan et al. 102p. 1995. pap. 8.75 (*1-881528-32-4*) Current Clin Strat.

Current Clinical Strategies, Medicine: Admitting Orders & Protocols. 2nd ed. Paul D. Chan et al. (Current Clinical Strategies Ser.). 75p. 1992. pap. 7.75 (*1-881528-00-6*) Current Clin Strat.

***Current Clinical Strategies, Outpatient Medicine.** 2nd ed. Paul D. Chan & Michael Safani. 104p. 1995. pap. 8.75 (*1-881528-13-8*) Current Clin Strat.

***Current Clinical Strategies Pediatric Physician's Drug Resource.** Chan. 1995. pap. text ed. 8.75 (*1-881528-22-7*) Current Clin Strat.

Current Clinical Strategies, Pediatrics. Paul D. Chan. 100p. (Orig.). 1991. pap. 7.75 (*0-9626030-2-3*) Current Clin Strat.

***Current Clinical Strategies, Pediatrics.** 2nd ed. Paul D. Chan & Donald Maldonado. 100p. 1995. pap. 8.75 (*1-881528-02-2*) Current Clin Strat.

Current Clinical Strategies, Physician's Drug Reference. Paul D. Chan et al. 80p. 1993. 6.50 (*1-881528-04-9*) Current Clin Strat.

Current Clinical Strategies, Practice Parameters in Medicine. Paul D. Chan. (Current Clinical Strategies Ser.). 150p. 1994. pap. 7.75 (*1-881528-20-0*) Current Clin Strat.

Current Clinical Strategies, Prescription Writer Computer Software: Prescription Writer. Paul D. Chan & Michael Safani. Ed. by Barbara A. Benjamin. (Current Clinical Strategies Ser.). 45p. 1993. 55.00 (*1-881528-03-0*) Current Clin Strat.

Current Clinical Strategies, Psychiatry. Lisa Burwell. (Current Clinical Strategies Ser.). 90p. 1994. 8.75 (*1-881528-14-6*) Current Clin Strat.

***Current Clinical Strategies, Psychiatry.** 3rd ed. Rhoda K. Hahn. 97p. 1995. pap. 8.75 (*1-881528-19-7*) Current Clin Strat.

Current Clinical Strategies, Surgery. Paul D. Chan. (Current Clinical Strategies Ser.). (Illus.). 92p. (Orig.). 1993. pap. 8.75 (*0-9626030-5-8*) Current Clin Strat.

Current Clinical Topics in Infectious Diseases, Vol. 10. Ed. by Jack S. Remington & Morton N. Swartz. (Illus.). 384p. (C). 1990. 75.00 (*0-86542-058-0*) Blackwell Sci.

Current Clinical Topics in Infectious Diseases, Vol. 11. Ed. by Jack S. Remington & Morton N. Swartz. (Illus.). 384p. (C). 1991. 75.00 (*0-86542-109-9*) Blackwell Sci.

Current Clinical Topics in Infectious Diseases, Vol. 12. Ed. by Jack S. Remington & Morton N. Swartz. (Illus.). 384p. (C). 1992. 75.00 (*0-86542-207-9*) Blackwell Sci.

Current Clinical Topics in Infectious Diseases, Vol. 13. J. S. Remington. 1993. 75.00 (*0-86542-278-8*) Blackwell Sci.

Current Clinical Topics in Infectious Diseases, Vol. 14. Ed. by J. S. Remington & M. N. Swartz. (Illus.). 320p. 1994. 75.00 (*0-86542-359-8*) Blackwell Sci.

Current Clinical Topics in Orthopedics. Ed. by Michael S. Zeide & Sam W. Wiesel. (Illus.). 400p. 1987. text ed. 50. 00 (*0-07-072814-3*) McGraw.

Current Coins of the World. 8th ed. R. S. Yeoman. (Illus.). 1987. 9.95 (*0-87184-801-5*) Coin & Curr.

Current Comparator. W. J. Moore & P. N. Miljanic. 120p. 1987. boxed 64.00 (*0-86341-112-6*, EL004) Inst Elect Eng.

Current Concept in the Therapy of Hypertension with Beta-Blockers. S. Chaithiraphan. (Journal: Cardiology: Vol. 66, Suppl. 1). (Illus.). vi, 62p. 1980. pap. 26.00 (*3-8055-0912-X*) S Karger.

Current Conceptions of Sex Roles & Sex Typing: Theory & Research. Ed. by D. Bruce Carter. LC 87-13157. 213p. 1987. text ed. 65.00 (*0-275-92430-0*, C2430, Praeger Pubs) Greenwood.

Current Concepts in Cardiovascular Physiology. Ed. by Oscar B. Garfein. 554p. 1990. text ed. 193.00 (*0-12-275820-X*) Acad Pr.

Current Concepts in Carnitine Research. A. Lee Carter. 1991. 99.95 (*0-8493-0186-6*, QP772) CRC Pr.

Current Concepts in Childhood Spinal Muscular Atrophy. Ed. by L. Merlini et al. (Illus.). 227p. 1989. 101.00 (*0-387-82131-7*) Spr-Verlag.

Current Concepts in Clinical Cardiology. Ed. by J. H. Vogel. (Advances in Cardiology Ser.: Vol. 27). (Illus.). viii, 360p. 1980. 158.50 (*3-8055-0098-X*) S Karger.

Current Concepts in Contract Dermatitis. Ed. by J. L. Verbov. (New Clinical Applications Dermatology Ser.). (C). 1987. lib. bdg. 70.00 (*0-85200-687-X*) Kluwer Ac.

An Asterisk (*) at the beginning of an entry indicates that the title is appearing in BIP for the first time. 1749

Current Concepts in Diagnosis & Treatment of Vitreoretinal Diseases. Ed. by G. Blankenship et al. (Developments in Ophthalmology Ser.: Vol. 2). (Illus.). xxviii, 408p. 1981. 236.00 (*3-8055-1672-X*) S Karger.

Current Concepts in Endovascular Surgery. Samuel S. Ahn et al. (Medical Intelligence Unit Ser.). 103p. 1994. 89.95 (*1-57059-000-1*, LN9000) R G Landes.

Current Concepts in Erythropoiesis. Ed. by C. D. Dunn. LC 82-13389. (Illus.). 429p. reprint ed. pap. 122.30 (*0-685-18237-1*, 2029634) Bks Demand.

Current Concepts in Hand Surgery. Ed. by John A. Boswick. LC 82-24897. (Illus.). 298p. reprint ed. pap. 85.00 (*0-8357-7640-9*, 2056964) Bks Demand.

Current Concepts in Human Immunology & Cancer Immunomodulation: Proceedings of the International Symposium, Montpellier, France, January 18-20, 1982. Ed. by B. Serrou et al. (Developments in Immunology Ser.: Vol. 17). 664p. 1982. 128.25 (*0-444-80426-9*) Elsevier.

Current Concepts in Kinin Research: Proceedings of the Satellite Symposium, 7th International Congress of Pharmacology. Ed. by G. L. Haberland & U. Hamberg. LC 78-41213. (Advances in the Biosciences Ser.). (Illus.). 285p. 1979. 65.00 (*0-08-023761-4*, Pergamon Pr) Elsevier.

***Current Concepts in Migraine Research.** fac. ed. Ed. by Raymond Greene. LC 77-83690. (Illus.). 181p. Date not set. pap. 51.60 (*0-7837-7276-9*, 2047030) Bks Demand.

Current Concepts in Multiple Sclerosis: Proc. of the 6th Congress of the European Committee for Treatment & Research, Tubingen, Germany, 11-13 Oct., 1990. Ed. by H. Wietholter et al. (International Congress Ser.: No. 960). 390p. 1991. 168.75 (*0-444-81416-7*, Excerpta Medica) Elsevier.

Current Concepts in Obsessive Compulsive Disorder. Ed. by Eric Hollander et al. LC 94-16823. 1994. write for info. (*0-471-95142-0*) Wiley.

Current Concepts in Ophthalmic Surgery. Easty. 1990. text ed. 155.00 (*0-7020-1363-3*) Saunders.

Current Concepts in Parasitology. Ronald C. Ko. 280p. (C). 1989. pap. text ed. 77.00 (*962-209-236-5*, Pub. by Hong Kong U Pr HK) St Mut.

Current Concepts in Parkinson's Disease Research. Ed. by J. S. Schneider & M. Gupta. LC 91-35314. (Illus.). 462p. 1993. text ed. 89.00 (*0-920887-72-4*); write for info. (*3-456-81828-9*) Hogrefe & Huber Pubs.

***Current Concepts in Pediatrics.** Maureen O'Reilly. (Newsletter Ser.: No. 2). 4p. (Orig.). 1994. write for info. (*0-944036-99-6*) Medicine Grp USA.

Current Concepts in Pediatrics, Vol. 1, No. 1. Maureen O'Reilly. 4p. (Orig.). 1994. write for info. (*0-944036-97-X*) Medicine Grp USA.

Current Concepts in Peritoneal Dialysis: Proceedings of the Fifth Congress of the International Society for Peritoneal Dialysis, Kyoto, July 21-24, 1990. Ed. by K. Ota et al. LC 92-14693. (International Congress Ser.: No. 947). 1992. 295.75 (*0-444-81389-6*, Excerpta Medica) Elsevier.

Current Concepts in Positive Mental Health. Marie Jahoda. Ed. by Gerald N. Grob. LC 78-22567. (Historical Issues in Mental Health Ser.). 1980. reprint ed. lib. bdg. 17.95 (*0-405-11921-6*) Ayer.

Current Concepts in Radiology Management. Howard W. Schwartz. 144p. 1992. pap. 20.00 (*0-9634176-0-6*) Amer Hlthcare Radiol.

Current Concepts in Regional Anaesthesia. J. W. Van Kleef et al. (Developments in Critical Care, Medicine, & Anesthesiology Ser.). 1984. lib. bdg. 98.00 (*0-89838-644-6*) Kluwer Ac.

Current Concepts in Research of Gastrointestinal Motility: Selected Papers from an International Symposium in Aarhus, Denmark, July 1991 - Digestive Diseases Journal, Vol. 9, No. 6. Ed. by H. Gregersen et al. (Journal: Digestive Diseases). (Illus.). iv, 130p. 1992. pap. 32.00 (*3-8055-5537-7*) S Karger.

Current Concepts in Respiratory Cell & Molecular Biology. Ed. by Jerome S. Brody et al. (Current Concepts Ser.). 144p. 1991. 39.95 (*0-915116-18-9*) Am Lung Assn.

Current Concepts in Spina Bifida & Hydrocephalus. Ed. by Carys M. Bannister & Brian Tew. (Clinics in Developmental Medicine Ser.: No. 122). 250p. (C). 1992. 54.95 (*0-521-41279-X*) Cambridge U Pr.

Current Concepts in Surfactant Research. Ed. by P. Von Wichert. (Progress in Respiration Research Ser.: Vol. 18). (Illus.). x, 310p. 1984. 197.75 (*3-8055-3916-9*) S Karger.

Current Concepts in the Management of Pain in Cancer Patients. Ed. by Raymond J. Trudnowsky. 1982. 35.00 (*0-915340-10-0*) PJD Pubns.

Current Concepts in the Pharmaceutical Sciences: Biopharmaceutics. Ed. by James Swarbrick. LC 78-123415. (Illus.). 316p. reprint ed. pap. 90.10 (*0-8357-9400-8*, 2014584) Bks Demand.

Current Concepts in Virology: From Ivanofsky to the Present. Ed. by Brian W. Mahy & Dmitri K. Lvov. LC 93-3449. 438p. 1993. text ed. 90.00 (*3-7186-0568-6*) Gordon & Breach.

Current Concepts of a New Animal Model: The NON Mouse. Ed. by N. Sakamoto et al. LC 92-14878. 1992. write for info. (*0-444-89554-X*) Elsevier.

Current Concepts of CAPD: Journal: Blood Purification, Vol. 7, No. 2-3, 1989. Ed. by R. A. Mactier & K. D. Nolph. (Illus.). 120p. 1989. pap. 68.00 (*3-8055-5009-X*) S Karger.

Current Concepts of Diagnosis & Treatment of Bone & Soft Tissue Tumors. Ed. by H. K. Uhthoff. (Illus.). 430p. 1984. 98.00 (*0-387-12570-1*) Spr-Verlag.

Current Concepts of Multifocal Intraocular Lenses. Ed. by W. Andrew Maxwell & Lee Nordan. LC 90-53271. 239p. 1990. 85.00 (*1-55642-167-2*) SLACK Inc.

Current Concepts of Somatization: Research & Clinical Perspectives. Ed. by Laurence J. Kirmayer & James M. Robbins. LC 90-14492. (Progress in Psychiatry Ser.: No. 33). 270p. 1991. text ed. 33.00 (*0-88048-198-6*) Am Psychiatric.

Current Concepts of Suicide. Ed. by David Lester. LC 90-1600. 236p. (Orig.). 1990. pap. 16.95 (*0-914783-45-9*) Charles.

Current Concepts on Fungal Diseases of Rice. S. Gangopadhyay. 349p. 1983. 39.00 (*1-55528-025-0*, Pub. by Today & Tomorrows P & P II) Scholarly Pubns.

Current Concerns in Occupational Stress. Ed. by Cary L. Cooper et al. LC 79-40641. (Wiley Series on Studies in Occupational Stress). (Illus.). 353p. reprint ed. pap. 100.70 (*0-317-09649-4*, 2020971) Bks Demand.

Current Concerns of Anthropologists & Missionaries. Ed. & Intro. by Karl Franklin. LC 86-81558. (International Museum of Cultures Publications: No. 22). 174p. (Orig.). 1987. pap. text ed. 14.00 (*0-88312-176-X*); fiche 12.00 (*0-88312-259-6*) Summer Instit Ling.

Current Confusion. Kitty Grey. (Beyond-Time Romance of Regency England Ser.). 192p. 1989. 19.95 (*0-8027-1060-3*) Walker & Co.

Current Constitutional Issues: A Symposium. C. J. Antieau et al. LC 77-153885. (Symposia on Law & Society Ser.). 1971. reprint ed. lib. bdg. 25.00 (*0-306-70154-5*) Da Capo.

Current Construction Costs, 1990. 27th ed. Lee Saylor. Ed. by Paul Felber. 337p. (Orig.). 1990. pap. 49.95 (*0-931708-21-4*) Saylor.

Current Construction Costs, 1992. Ed. by Stanley J. Strychaz. (Illus.). 350p. (Orig.). 1992. pap. 54.95 (*0-931708-27-3*) Saylor.

Current Construction Costs 1994. Ed. by Stanley J. Strychaz. (Illus.). 440p. 1994. pap. 54.95 (*0-931708-37-0*) Saylor.

***Current Construction Costs, 1995.** Ed. by Stanley J. Strychaz. (Illus.). 1995. pap. 54.95 (*0-931708-45-1*) Saylor.

Current Controversies & Issues in Personality. 2nd ed. Lawrence A. Pervin. LC 83-23246. 357p. (C). 1984. Net. pap. text ed. write for info. (*0-471-88086-8*) Wiley.

Current Controversies & Issues in Personality. Lawrence A. Pervin. LC 78-15361. 323p. reprint ed. pap. 92.10 (*0-7837-3499-9*, 2057832) Bks Demand.

Current Controversies in Alcoholism. Ed. by Barry Stimmel. LC 83-207. (Advances in Alcohol & Substance Abuse Ser.: Vol. 2, No. 2). 82p. 1983. text ed. 32.95 (*0-86656-225-7*) Haworth Pr.

Current Controversies in Biliary Atresia. Mark Hoffman. (Medical Intelligence Unit Ser.). 125p. 1992. 89.95 (*1-879702-21-5*) R G Landes.

Current Controversies in Macroeconomics. Howard Vane & John Thompson. 176p. 1992. text ed. 69.95 (*1-85278-089-4*, Pub. by E Elgar Pub UK) Ashgate Pub Co.

Current Controversies in Marriage & Family. Ed. by Harold Feldman & Margaret Feldman. LC 85-1934. 368p. reprint ed. pap. 104.90 (*0-8357-4788-3*, 2037725) Bks Demand.

Current Controversies in Orthodontics. Ed. by Birte Melsen. (Illus.). 368p. 1991. text ed. 98.00 (*0-86715-174-9*) Quint Pub Co.

Current Controversies in Temporomandibular Disorders: Proceedings of the 10th Annual Squaw Valley Winter Seminar, Squaw Valley, California, January 23-27, 1991. Ed. by Charles McNeill. LC 92-49813. 1992. text ed. 58.00 (*0-86715-252-4*) Quint Pub Co.

Current Controversies in Thoracic Surgery. Frederick C. Kittle. (Illus.). 285p. 1986. text ed. 75.50 (*0-7216-5461-4*) Saunders.

Current Controversies on Family Violence. Ed. by Richard J. Gelles & Donileen Loseke. (Illus.). 360p. (C). 1993. text ed. 55.00 (*0-8039-4673-2*); pap. text ed. 34.95 (*0-8039-4674-0*) Sage.

Current Controversy in Parathyroid Operation & Reoperation. G. Akerstrom. (Medical Intelligence Unit Ser.). 236p. 1994. 89.95 (*1-57059-086-9*) R G Landes.

Current Cost Accounting: Identifying the Issues, A Book of Readings, Vol. 1. G. W. Dean & M. C. Wells. (Illus.). 214p. (Orig.). 1979. pap. text ed. 13.95 (*0-909203-81-4*) Dame Pubns.

Current Cost-Constant Dollar Accounting & Its Uses in the Managerial Decision-Making Process. Philip W. Bell. LC 86-13528. (McQueen Accounting Monograph Ser.: Vol. 3). 73p. (Orig.). 1986. pap. text ed. 10.00 (*0-935951-02-4*) U AR Acc Dept.

Current Crisis in American Politics. Walter D. Burnham. (Illus.). 1983. 35.00 (*0-19-503219-5*) OUP.

Current Crisis in International Lending. Jack M. Guttentag & Richard J. Herring. LC 84-45846. (Studies in International Economics). 55p. 1985. pap. 7.95 (*0-8157-3325-9*) Brookings.

Current Crisis in Sri Lanka. Rajiva Wijesinha. 150p. 1986. 17.50 (*81-7013-039-5*, Pub. by Navrang) S Asia.

Current Critical Care Diagnosis & Treatment. Ed. by Frederic S. Bongard & Darryl Y. Sue. (Illus.). 912p. 1993. pap. text ed. 41.95 (*0-8385-1443-X*, A1443-9) Appleton & Lange.

Current Critical Concepts of Hydrocephalus, Vol. 1. Leech & Brumback. 224p. 1991. 59.00 (*0-8151-5555-7*, Yr Bk Med Pubs) Mosby Yr Bk.

Current Critical Problems in Vascular Surgery, Vol. 4. Ed. by Frank J. Veith. 1992. 85.00 (*0-942219-39-2*) Quality Med Pub.

Current Critical Problems in Vascular Surgery, Vol. 5. Ed. by Frank J. Veith. 1993. 85.00 (*0-942219-54-6*) Quality Med Pub.

Current Critical Problems in Vascular Surgery, Vol. 6. Veith. 1994. 85.00 (*0-942219-42-2*) Quality Med Pub.

***Current Critical Problems in Vascular Surgery Vol. 7.** Frank J. Veith. 1995. 85.00 (*0-614-03621-6*) Quality Med Pub.

Current Dermatologic Therapy. 2nd ed. Madden. 1991. text ed. 61.50 (*0-7216-1053-6*) Saunders.

Current Developments in Anthropological Genetics, Vol. 2: Ecology & Population Structure. Ed. by Michael H. Crawford & James H. Mielke. LC 79-24900. (Illus.). 542p. 1982. 95.00 (*0-306-40842-2*, Plenum Pr) Plenum.

Current Developments in Anthropological Genetics, Vol. 3: Black Caribs: A Case Study in Biocultural Adaptation. Ed. by Michael H. Crawford. 412p. 1984. 95.00 (*0-306-41308-6*, Plenum Pr) Plenum.

Current Developments in Bankruptcy & Reorganization, 1989. (Commercial Law & Practice Ser.). 1837p. 1989. 25.00 (*0-318-42391-X*, A4-4253) PLI.

Current Developments in Bankruptcy & Reorganization 1993. (Commercial Law & Practice Course Handbook Ser.: Vols. 655 & 656). 1423p. 1993. 80.00 (*0-685-69704-5*, A4-4414) PLI.

Current Developments in Broker-Dealer Regulation. (Corporate Law & Practice Course Handbook, 1985-86 Ser.: Vol. 788). 237p. 1992. 70.00 (*0-685-65490-7*, B4-7014) PLI.

Current Developments in Copyright Law, 1988: A Course Handbook. Morton D. Goldberg. 431p. 1988. pap. 17.50 (*0-685-69409-7*) PLI.

Current Developments in International & Comparative Corporate Insolvency Law. Ed. by Jacob S. Ziegel. 700p. 1995. 145.00 (*0-19-825896-8*) OUP.

Current Developments in International Banking & Corporate Financial Operations. Koh et al. 1989. 225.00 (*0-409-99572-X*) Butterworth Legal Pubs.

Current Developments in International Investment Law. Ho et al. 1992. 141.00 (*0-409-99613-0*) Butterworth Legal Pubs.

Current Developments in International Taxation. (Tax Law & Estate Planning Course Handbook Ser.: Vol. 338). 669p. 1993. 70.00 (*0-685-69744-4*, J4-3663) PLI.

***Current Developments in International Transfers of Goods & Services.** Ed. by L. Rao Penna et al. (Singapore Conferences on International Business Law Ser.: Vol. 7). liii, 621p. 1994. text ed. write for info. (*0-409-99667-X*) Butterworth Legal Pubs.

Current Developments in Knowledge Acquisition: ELAW'92: 6th European Knowledge Acquisition Workshop, Heidelberg & Kaiserslautern, Germany, May 18-22, 1992, Proceedings, Vol. 599. Ed. by Thomas Wetter et al. LC 92-11121. xiii, 444p. 1992. pap. 61.00 (*0-387-55546-3*) Spr-Verlag.

Current Developments in Language Testing. Ed. by Arthur Hughes & Don Porter. (Applied Language Studies). 1983. text ed. 82.00 (*0-12-360880-5*) Acad Pr.

Current Developments in Numerical Simulation of Flow & Heat Transfer. (HTD Ser.: Vol. 275). 168p. 1994. 45.00 (*0-7918-1274-X*, H00906) ASME.

Current Developments in Optical Design & Optical Engineering. R. E. Fischer. 1992. 77.00 (*0-8194-0655-4*, 1527) SPIE.

Current Developments in Optical Engineering, No. II. Ed. by Fischer & Smith. 469p. 1987. 65.00 (*0-89252-853-2*, 818) SPIE.

Current Developments in Optical Engineering, Vol. 965, No. 3. Ed. by R. E. Fischer & W. J. Smith. 1988. 59.00 (*0-8194-0000-9*) SPIE.

Current Developments in Optical Engineering & Commercial Optics. Ed. by Robert E. Fischer et al. 445p. 1989. 70.00 (*0-8194-0204-4*, VOL. 1168) SPIE.

Current Developments in Optical Engineering IV, Vol. 1334. R. E. Fischer & W. J. Smith. 1990. 53.00 (*0-8194-0395-4*) SPIE.

Current Developments in Psychopharmacology, Vol. VI. Ed. by W. Essman & L. Valzelli. LC 75-642512. (Illus.). 339p. 1981. text ed. 75.00 (*0-88331-128-3*) Luce.

Current Developments in RCRA: 1993 Report. Ed. by Kenneth M. Kastner. 219p. 1993. pap. text ed. 59.00 (*0-86587-339-9*) Gov Insts.

***Current Developments in Real Estate Law: Annual Survey - 1994.** 320p. pap. 49.95 (*1-57073-010-5*, 543-0353) Amer Bar Assn.

***Current Developments in the Definition of Solid Waste.** Kenneth M. Kastner. (Environmental Management Guides Ser.). 15p. 1994. pap. text ed. 17.50 (*0-86587-430-1*) Gov Insts.

Current Developments in Title Insurance 1992. (Real Estate Law & Practice Course Handbook Ser.: Vol. 384). 770p. 1992. 70.00 (*0-685-65547-4*, N4-4568) PLI.

Current Developments in Trademark Law & Unfair Competition, 1988. Arthur J. Greenbaum. LC 82-82056. (Patents, Copyrights, Trademarks, & Literary Property Ser.). 469p. 1988. 17.50 (*0-685-69410-0*) PLI.

Current Diabetology. F. Belfiore. (Frontiers in Diabetes Ser.: Vol. 6). viii, 284p. 1985. 141.75 (*3-8055-4029-9*) S Karger.

***Current Diagnosis & Treatment in Addiction Psychiatry.** Norman S. Miller. LC 94-32386. 1995. text ed. 54.95 (*0-471-56201-7*) Wiley.

***Current Diagnosis & Treatment in Cardiology.** Michael H. Crawford. (C). 1994. pap. text ed. 41.95 (*0-8385-1444-8*, Medical Exam) Appleton & Lange.

***Current Diagnosis & Treatment in Orthopaedics.** Skinner. (C). 1995. pap. text ed. 41.95 (*0-8385-1009-4*) Appleton & Lange.

Current Diagnosis Eight. 8th ed. Conn. (Illus.). 1648p. 1991. text ed. 105.00 (*0-7216-2816-8*) Saunders.

Current Diagnosis in Neurology. Edward Feldman. 325p. 1993. 69.00 (*0-8016-6963-4*) Mosby Yr Bk.

Current Directions in Computer Music Research. Ed. by Max V. Mathews & John R. Pierce. (System Development Foundation, Benchmark Ser.). 400p. 1991. pap. 21.95 (*0-262-63139-3*) MIT Pr.

Current Directions in Insulin-Like Growth Factor Research. Ed. by Mohan K. Raizada & Derek LeRoith. LC 93-46649. (Advances in Experimental Medicine & Biology Ser.: Vol. 343). (Illus.). 417p. 1994. 110.00 (*0-306-44622-7*, Plenum Pr) Plenum.

Current Distribution & Electrode Shape Changes in Electrochemical Systems. J. Deconinck et al. Ed. by Carlos A. Brebbia & S. A. Orszag. (Lecture Notes in Engineering Ser.: Vol. 75). (Illus.). 281p. 1992. pap. 62.00 (*0-387-55104-2*) Spr-Verlag.

Current Drug Handbook 1984-1986. H. Robert Patterson et al. 1984. text ed. 34.50 (*0-7216-1223-7*) Saunders.

Current Economics & Politics of (Ex-) Czechoslovakia. J. Krovak. (Illus.). 272p. (C). 1994. lib. bdg. 69.00 (*1-56072-147-2*) Nova Sci Pubs.

Current Emergency Diagnosis & Treatment. 4th ed. Charles E. Saunders & Mary T. Ho. (Illus.). 1015p. (C). 1992. pap. text ed. 41.95 (*0-8385-1347-6*, A1347-2) Appleton & Lange.

Current Employment Law Issues 1993. Wake Forest University School of Law Continuing Legal Education Staff. 831p. 1993. pap. 125.00 (*0-942225-68-6*) Wake Forest Law.

Current English: A Study of Present-Day Usages & Tendencies, Including Pronunciation, Spelling, Grammatical Practice, Word-Coining, & the Shifting of Meanings. Arthur G. Kennedy. LC 76-106719. 737p. 1970. reprint ed. text ed. 37.50 (*0-8371-3543-5*, KECE) Greenwood.

Current English Linguistics in Japan. Ed. by Heizo Nakajima. LC 91-22180. (Trends in Linguistics, State-of-the-Art Reports: No. 16). vi, 544p. (C). 1991. lib. bdg. 198.50 (*3-11-011781-9*, 151-91) Mouton.

Current Environmental Engineering Summaries: 1993 Edition. Engineering Information, Inc. Staff. 1110p. 1993. pap. text ed. 89.00 (*0-86587-346-1*) Gov Insts.

Current Environmental Research in Transportation. (Transportation Research Record Ser.: No. 1240). 54p. 1989. 9.00 (*0-309-04951-2*) Transport Res Bd.

***Current Estimates from the National Health Interview Survey.** 1994. lib. bdg. 255.00 (*0-8490-5820-1*) Gordon Pr.

Current Estimates from the National Health Interview Survey, 1989: PHS 90-1504. (Vital & Health Statistics Ser. 10: Data from the National Health Interview Survey: No. 176). 221p. 11.00 (*0-685-61583-9*, 017-022-01122-1) Natl Ctr Health Stats.

***Current Estimates from the National Health Interview Survey, 1992.** National Center for Health Statistics Staff. LC 94-1517. (Series Reports: Series 10, No. 189). 269p. Date not set. 17.00 (*0-614-02907-4*, PB94 135811) Natl Ctr Health Stats.

Current European Anaesthesiology: The Yearbook of the European Academy of Anaesthesiology, Vol. 1, 1985. Current European Anaesthesiology Staff. LC 85-7409. (Illus.). reprint ed. pap. 83.00 (*0-8357-5564-9*, 2035193) Bks Demand.

Current European Anaesthesiology: The Yearbook of the European Academy of Anaesthesiology, Vol. 2, 1986. Current European Anaesthesiology Staff. LC 85-7409. (Illus.). 336p. reprint ed. pap. 95.80 (*0-8357-5565-7*) Bks Demand.

Current European Anaesthesiology: The Yearbook of the European Academy of Anaesthesiology, Vol. 3, 1987. Current European Anaesthesiology Staff. LC 85-7409. (Illus.). 266p. reprint ed. pap. 75.90 (*0-8357-5566-5*) Bks Demand.

***Current European Directories.** 3rd ed. 400p. 1995. 275.00 (*0-900246-64-2*) CBD Res.

Current Feline Practice. Gary D. Norsworthy. (Illus.). 725p. 1993. text ed. 98.00 (*0-397-51204-X*) Lippincott.

Current Feminist Issues in Psychotherapy. Ed. by New England Association for Women in Psychology Staff. LC 82-15721. (Women & Therapy Ser.: Vol. 1, No. 3). 115p. 1983. text ed. 29.95 (*0-86656-206-0*) Haworth Pr.

Current French Security Policy: The Gaullist Legacy. Theodore R. Posner. LC 91-21195. (Contributions in Military Studies: No. 118). 184p. 1991. text ed. 49.95 (*0-313-27934-9*, PCK, Greenwood Pr) Greenwood.

Current Gastroenterology, Vol. 10. Gary Gitnick. 352p. 1990. 69.95 (*0-8151-3511-4*, Yr Bk Med Pubs) Mosby Yr Bk.

Current Gastroenterology, Vol. 11. Gary Gitnick. 386p. 1991. 69.95 (*0-8151-3512-2*, Yr Bk Med Pubs) Mosby Yr Bk.

Current Gastroenterology, Vol. 12. Gitnick. 416p. 1992. 69.95 (*0-8151-3513-0*) Mosby Yr Bk.

Current Gastroenterology, Vol. 13. Gitnick. 352p. 1993. 69.95 (*0-8151-3514-9*) Mosby Yr Bk.

Current Gastroenterology, Vol. 14. Gitnick. 416p. 1994. 69.95 (*0-8151-3515-7*, Yr Bk Med Pubs) Mosby Yr Bk.

Current Gastroenterology, Vol. 15. Gitnick. 416p. 1995. 69.95 (*0-8151-3650-1*, Yr Bk Med Pubs) Mosby Yr Bk.

Current Gastroenterology, Vol. 16. Gitnick. 416p. 1996. 69.95 (*0-8151-3651-X*, Yr Bk Med Pubs) Mosby Yr Bk.

Current Genetic, Clinical & Morphological Problems. Ed. by W. Straub. (Developments in Ophthalmology Ser.: Vol. 3). (Illus.). vi, 218p. 1981. pap. 125.75 (*3-8055-2000-X*) S Karger.

Current Geotechnical Practice in Mine Waste Disposal: Papers Collected by the Committee on Embankment Dams & Slopes of the Geotechnical Engineering Division. American Society of Civil Engineers Staff. LC 79-106963. 266p. reprint ed. pap. 75.90 (*0-317-11260-0*, 2019542) Bks Demand.

Current Geriatric Therapy. Timothy R. Covington & J. Ingram Walker. (Illus.). 463p. 1984. text ed. 87.50 (*0-7216-2743-9*) Saunders.

Current Good Manufacturing Practices: Food Plant Sanitation. 2nd ed. Wilbur A. Gould. LC 93-41592. (Illus.). 416p. 1994. 67.00 (*0-930027-21-3*) CTI Pubns.

C

An Asterisk (*) at the beginning of an entry indicates that the title is appearing in BIP for the first time.

An Asterisk (*) at the beginning of an entry indicates that the title is appearing in BIP for the first time.

Current Issues in Monetary Economics. Ed. by Taradas Bandyopadhyay & Subrata Ghatek. 352p. (C). 1990. lib. bdg. 59.50 (0-389-20911-2) B&N Imports.

Current Issues in Monetary Policy in the United States & Japan: The Predictability of Money Demand. Elias C. Grivoyannis. LC 90-31181. 224p. 1991. text ed. 49.95 (0-275-93563-9, C3563, Praeger Pubs) Greenwood.

Current Issues in Monetary Theory & Policy. 2nd ed. Ed. by Thomas M. Havrilesky & John T. Boorman. LC 79-55733. (Illus.). (C). 1980. pap. text ed. write for info. (0-88295-406-7) Harlan Davidson.

Current Issues in Natural Resource Policy. Ed. by Paul R. Portney & Ruth B. Haas. LC 87-47982. 300p. 1982. 20.00 (0-8018-2916-X); pap. 9.95 (0-8018-2917-8) Resources Future.

Current Issues in Nursing. 3rd ed. McCloskey. (Illus.). 672p. 1989. pap. 35.95 (0-8016-5525-0) Mosby Yr Bk.

Current Issues in Nursing. 4th ed. McCloskey. 744p. 1994. pap. write for info. (0-8016-6954-5) Mosby Yr Bk.

Current Issues in Open Economy Macroeconomics: Paradoxes, Policies & Problems. J. L. Ford. (Illus.). 272p. 1990. text ed. 63.95 (1-85278-185-8, Pub. by E Elgar Pub UK) Ashgate Pub Co.

Current Issues in Pediatric Cardiac Surgery. Marshall L. Jacobs & William I. Norwood. (Illus.). 264p. 1992. 99.95 (0-7506-9061-5) Buttrwrth-Heinemann.

Current Issues in Planning. Sylvia Trench & Taner Oc. (Illus.). 230p. 1990. text ed. 59.95 (0-566-05794-8) Ashgate Pub Co.

*Current Issues in Planning, Vol. 2. Ed. by Sylvia Trench & Taner Oc. 313p. 1995. 51.95 (1-85628-495-6, Pub. by Avebury Pub UK) Ashgate Pub Co.

*Current Issues in Plant Molecular & Cellular Biology: Proceedings of the VIIIth International Congress on Plant Tissue & Cell Culture, Firenze, Italy, 12-17 June, 1994. Ed. by M. Terzi et al. LC 94-46543. (Current Plant Science & Biotechnology in Agriculture Ser.: Vol. 22). 1995. lib. bdg. 198.00 (0-7923-3322-5) Kluwer Ac.

*Current Issues in Public Administration. 5th ed. Fredrick S. Lane. 496p. 1993. pap. text ed. 21.00 (0-312-08413-7) St Martin.

*Current Issues in Public Choice. Ed. by Jose C. Pardo & Friedrich Schneider. 1996. write for info. (1-85898-134-4, Pub. by E Elgar Pub UK) Ashgate Pub Co.

Current Issues in Public Sector Economics. Ed. by Peter M. Jackson & David Greenaway. LC 92-6930. (Current Issues in Economics Ser.). 288p. 1992. text ed. 45.00 (0-312-07995-8) St Martin.

Current Issues in Rational-Emotive Therapy. Wendy Dryden. 220p. 1987. lib. bdg. 42.50 (0-7099-4557-4, Pub. by Croom Helm UK) Routledge Chapman & Hall.

*Current Issues in Research & Treatment of Kaposi's Sarcoma: The KS Project Report. Michael Marco & Martin Majchrowicz. 85p. (Orig.). (C). 1994. pap. text ed. 30.00 (0-7881-1386-0) Diane Pub.

Current Issues in Second Language Acquisition & Development. Carol A. Blackshire-Belay. 210p. (Orig.). (C). 1993. lib. bdg. 49.50 (0-8191-9181-7); pap. text ed. 28.50 (0-8191-9182-5) U Pr of Amer.

Current Issues in Second Language Research & Methodology: Applications to Italian as a Second Language. Ed. by Leonard G. Sbrocchi et al. (Biblioteca di Quaderni d'Italianistica Ser.). 236p. (Orig.). (C). 1989. pap. write for info. (0-9691979-7-7, Pub. by Can Soc Ital Stu CN) Speedimpex.

Current Issues in Semiconductor Physics. A. M. Stoneham. (Illus.). 180p. 1986. pap. 34.00 (0-85274-588-5) IOP Pub.

Current Issues in Social Security: Proceedings of the Social Security Conference, 8th. Social Security Conference Staff. Ed. by William B. Neenan. 1976. 5.00 (0-87736-325-0) U of Mich Inst Labor.

Current Issues in Statistical Inference: Essays in Honor of D. Basu. Ed. by M. Ghosh & P. K. Pathak. LC 91-53163. (IMS Lecture Notes - Monograph Ser.: Vol. 17). iv, 264p. 1992. pap. 25.00 (0-940600-24-2) Inst Math.

Current Issues in Swedish Arbitration. Lars Heuman. 288p. 1990. pap. 98.00 (90-6544-489-0) Kluwer Law Tax Pubs.

Current Issues in Teaching English As a Second Language to Adults. Sandra Nicholls & Elizabeth Hoadley-Maidment. 160p. 1988. pap. text ed. 14.95 (0-7131-8450-7, Pub. by E Arnold UK) Routledge Chapman & Hall.

Current Issues in the Economics of Welfare. Ed. by Nicholas Barr & David K. Whynes. LC 92-28596. (Current Issues in Economics Ser.). 256p. 1993. text ed. 49.95 (0-312-08651-2) St Martin.

Current Issues in the Phonetic Sciences: Proceedings of the IPS-77 Congress, Miami Beach Fla., 17-19 December 1977, 2 vols. Ed. by Harry Hollien & Patricia Hollien. (Current Issues in Linguistic Theory Ser.: No. 9). (Illus.). xxxv, 1196p. 1979. 221.00x (90-272-0910-3) Benjamins North Am.

Current Issues in Theoretical Psychology: Proceedings of the Biannual Conference of the International Society for Theoretical Psychology, 1st, Plymouth, U. K., 30 August-2 September, 1985. International Society for Theoretical Psychology Staff. Ed. by W. J. Baker et al. (Advances in Psychology Ser.: No. 40). 424p. 1986. 93.50 (0-444-70120-6, North Holland) Elsevier.

Current Issues in U. S. Environmental Policy. Ed. by Paul R. Portney et al. LC 78-4328. 207p. 1978. pap. 9.95 (0-8018-2118-5) Resources Future.

Current Issues in Urban Economics. Ed. by Peter Mieszkowski & Mahlon Straszheim. LC 78-14947. 605p. reprint ed. pap. 172.50 (0-7837-4780-2, 2044535) Bks Demand.

Current Issues in Vocational Education & Training in New Zealand. Derek E. Wood. 1988. 3.00 (0-318-40011-1, OC 127) Ctr Educ Trng Employ.

Current Issues in Women's Health: An FDA Consumer Special Report. (Illus.). 63p. (Orig.). (C). 1993. pap. text ed. 25.00 (1-56806-936-7) Diane Pub.

*Current Issues in Women's Health: An FDA Consumer Special Report. 2nd rev. ed. (Illus.). 111p. (YA). (gr. 12 up). 1994. pap. text ed. 35.00 (0-7881-0780-1) Diane Pub.

Current Issues in Women's History. Ed. by Arina Angerman et al. 256p. 1989. 45.00 (0-415-00361-X, A1696); pap. 14.95 (0-415-00362-8, A1700) Routledge.

Current Issues in Workers' Compensation. Ed. by James Chelius. LC 86-9267. 372p. (C). 1986. text ed. 25.00 (0-88099-037-6); pap. text ed. 15.00 (0-88099-036-8) W E Upjohn.

Current Issues Resource Builder: Free & Inexpensive Materials for Librarians & Teachers. Carol Smallwood. LC 88-43487. 414p. 1989. pap. 24.95 (0-89950-388-8) McFarland & Co.

Current Issues, 1995: Critical Issues Facing the Nation & the World. rev. ed. Tim Walker & Amy Edwards. Ed. by Charles Sass. (Illus.). 352p. (YA). (gr. 9-12). 1994. pap. text ed. 12.95 (0-685-57438-5, 1142-93) Close Up.

Current Issues, 1995: Critical Issues Facing the Nation & the World. rev. suppl. ed. Tim Walker & Amy Edwards. Ed. by Charles Sass. (Illus.). 352p. (YA). (gr. 9-12). 1995. teacher ed 14.95 (0-685-57439-3) Close Up.

Current Labour Law, 1993. H. Cheadle et al. 1993. pap. 38.00 (0-7021-2989-5, Pub. by Juta SA) W W Gaunt.

Current Latin American Environmental Journals: A Selective Bibliography, 1993. SALALM Subcommittee for Serials Staff. (Latin American Information Ser.: No. 3). 21p. (Orig.). 1993. pap. 14.00 (0-917617-37-1) SALALM.

Current Law Forms with Tax Analysis, Looseleaf Updates Avail. Jacob Rabkin. 1948. write for info. (0-8205-1240-0) Bender.

Current Leaders of Nations. Ed. by David C. Kurkowski. LC 89-81456. (Illus.). 190p. (YA). (gr. 9-12). 1990. ring bd. 119.00 (0-9624900-0-8) Current Leaders Pub.

Current Leasing Law & Techniques: Forms, 4 vols., Updates available. Patrick J. Rohan & Caroline Donovan. (Real Estate Transactions Ser.). 1982. ring bd. write for info. (0-8205-1401-2) Bender.

Current Legal Aspects of Doing Business in Latin America. 180p. 1981. pap. 20.00 (0-685-07133-2, 521-0031) Amer Bar Assn.

Current Legal Aspects of International Trade Law. LC 82-70935. 255p. 1982. pap. 20.00 (0-89707-069-0, 521-0032) Amer Bar Assn.

Current Legal Aspects of Licensing & Intellectual Property. 603p. 1980. pap. 20.00 (0-685-07130-8, 521-0029) Amer Bar Assn.

Current Legal Issues Affecting Central Banks, Vol. 1. Ed. by Robert C. Effros. LC 92-16996. xvi, 642p. 1992. pap. 42.50 (1-55775-142-0) Intl Monetary.

Current Legal Issues Affecting Central Banks, Vol. II. Ed. by Robert C. Effros. xx, 465p. 1994. 42.50 (1-55775-306-7) Intl Monetary.

Current Legal Problems: 1945-1991, 44 vols., Set. 2,112.00 (0-8377-9053-0) Rothman.

*Current Legal Problems Vol. 47, Pt. 2: Collected Papers. Ed. by M. D. Freeman & Dawn Oliver. 300p. 1995. 55.00 (0-19-826000-8) OUP.

*Current Legal Problems Vol. 48, Pt. 1: Annual Review. Ed. by Andrew Lewis. 224p. 1995. pap. 39.95 (0-19-826041-5) OUP.

Current Legal Problems, 1992 Vol. 45, Pt. 1: Annual Review, Vol. 45, Pt. I. Ed. by Ben Pettet. 244p. 1992. pap. 34.00 (0-19-825721-X) OUP.

Current Legal Problems 1992 Vol. 45, Pt. 2: Collected Papers. R. W. Rideout & Bob A. Hepple. 304p. 1993. 49.95 (0-19-825722-8) OUP.

Current Legal Problems 1993 Vol. 46, Pt. 1: Annual Review. Ben Pettet. 208p. 1993. pap. 25.00 (0-19-825860-7) OUP.

Current Legal Problems 1993 Vol. 46, Pt. 2: Collected Papers. Ed. by Michael D. Freeman & Bob A. Hepple. 320p. (C). 1994. 45.00 (0-19-825870-4) OUP.

Current Legal Problems 1994 Vol. 47, Pt. 1: Annual Review. Ed. by Ben Pettet. 248p. 1994. pap. 27.00 (0-19-825904-2) OUP.

Current Literature on Job Hunting: An Annotated & Classified Bibliography. Rama K. Rao. (Social Science Resource Guides Ser.: No. 2). 35p. (C). 1991. pap. text ed. 8.95 (0-9628998-1-X) Ramdil.

Current Literature on Starting & Staying Successful in Business: An Annotated & Classified Bibliography. Rama K. Rao. (Social Science Resource Guides Ser.: No. 3). 30p. (C). 1991. pap. text ed. 8.95 (0-9628998-2-8) Ramdil.

Current Maharashtra Politics. V. M. Sirsikar. 1993. text ed. 30.00 (0-86311-263-3, Pub. by Orient Longman Ltd II) Apt Bks.

Current Mammalogy, Vol. 1. Ed. by Hugh H. Genoways. LC 86-30384. 540p. 1987. 110.00 (0-306-42430-4, Plenum Pr) Plenum.

Current Mammalogy, Vol. 2. Ed. by Hugh H. Genoways. LC 88-648659. (Illus.). 596p. 1990. 110.00 (0-306-43304-4, Plenum Pr) Plenum.

Current Management Inflammatory Bowel Disease. 2nd ed. Bayless. 432p. write for info. (1-55664-364-0) Mosby Yr Bk.

Current Management of Arrhythmias. Horowitz. 456p. (C). 1990. 79.00 (1-55664-154-0) Mosby Yr Bk.

Current Management of Cerebral Aneurysms. Ed. by Issam Awad. (Neurosurgical Topics Ser.). 200p. 1993. 90.00 (1-879284-13-8) Am Assn Neuro.

Current Management of Hypertensive & Vascular Diseases. Cooke & Frohlich. 380p. 1991. 79.00 (1-55664-356-X) Mosby Yr Bk.

*Current Market Outlook, 1994: World Air Travel Demand & Airplane Supply Requirements. (Illus.). 52p. (Orig.). (C). 1994. pap. text ed. 75.00x (0-7881-1015-2) Diane Pub.

Current Marks on Firm Mud Bottoms. Stanislaw Dzulynski & John E. Sanders. (Connecticut Academy of Arts & Sciences Ser., Trans.: Vol. 42). 1962. pap. 49.50 (0-685-22890-8) Elliots Bks.

Current Mathematical Problems of Mechanics & Their Applications. Ed. by A. A. Barmin. LC 91-17128. (Proceedings of the Steklov Institute of Mathematics Ser.: Vol. 186). 267p. 1991. reprint ed. 159.00 (0-8218-3138-0, STEKLO/186C) Am Math.

*Current Medical Diagnosis & Treatment. 5th ed. Tierney. (C). 1995. pap. text ed. 41.95 (0-8385-1465-0) Appleton & Lange.

*Current Medical Diagnosis & Treatment 1995. 34th ed. Lawrence M. Tierney. (C). 1994. pap. text ed. 41.95 (0-8385-1449-9, Medical Exam) Appleton & Lange.

Current Medical Research in Eastern Africa. P. M. Tukei & A. R. Njogu. 292p. 1983. pap. 65.00 (0-86346-040-2, Tycooly Pub) Weidner & Sons.

Current Medical Terminology. 5th ed. Vera Pyle. 506p. 1994. 36.00 (0-934385-56-4) Hlth Prof Inst.

Current Medical Therapy. 2nd ed. Ed. by Robert W. Schrier. 696p. 1989. pap. text ed. 28.00 (0-88167-467-2) Raven.

Current Medical Treatment. 5th ed. C. W. Havard. (Illus.). 576p. 1983. text ed. 60.95 (0-7020-0989-X, Bailliere-Tindall) Saunders.

Current Medicine Three. Ed. by David A. Lawson. (Illus.). 300p. (Orig.). 1991. pap. text ed. 36.00 (0-443-04598-4) Churchill.

Current Methodology for the Control of Algae in Surface Reservoirs. 200p. 1987. pap. 22.00 (0-89867-397-6, 90522) Am Water Wks Assn.

Current Methodology in Experimental Hematology. Ed. by S. J. Baum. (Bibliotheca Haematologica Ser.: No. 48). (Illus.). vi, 418p. 1985. 198.50 (3-8055-3722-0) S Karger.

Current Methods in Cellular Neurobiology. Ed. by Jeffery L. Barker & Jeffrey F. McKelvy. LC 83-1282. (Wiley-Interscience Publication Ser.: Vol. 1). 339p. reprint ed. pap. 96.70 (0-7837-2384-9, 2040070) Bks Demand.

Current Monetary Issues. Leo Pasvolsky & Jacob Viner. Bd. with Balanced Deflation, Inflation or More Depression. LC 82-48212. LC 82-48212. (Gold, Money, Inflation & Deflation Ser.). 235p. 1983. Set lib. bdg. 28.00 (0-8240-5250-1) Garland.

Current Morphology. Andrew Carstairs-McCarthy. (Linguistic Theory Guides Ser.). 304p. 1992. 77.50 (0-415-00998-7, A6651); pap. 22.50 (0-415-07118-6, A6655) Routledge.

Current Municipal Problems: 1974-1990, 15 vols., Set. Ed. by Byron Matthews. 160.00 (0-317-12012-3) Clark Boardman Callaghan.

Current National Bibliographies. U. S. Library of Congress, General Reference & Bibliography Division Staff. LC 68-55128. (Illus.). 1969. reprint ed. text ed. 69.50 (0-8371-0716-4, CUNB, Greenwood Pr) Greenwood.

Current Nephrology, Vol. 14. Harvey C. Gonick. 480p. 1990. 79.95 (0-8151-3734-6, Yr Bk Med Pubs) Mosby Yr Bk.

Current Nephrology, Vol. 15. Gonick. 470p. 1991. 79.95 (0-8151-3735-4) Mosby Yr Bk.

Current Nephrology, Vol. 16. Gonick. 435p. 1992. 79.95 (0-8151-3742-7) Mosby Yr Bk.

Current Nephrology, Vol. 17. Gonick. 470p. 1993. 79.95 (0-8151-3743-5, Yr Bk Med Pubs) Mosby Yr Bk.

Current Nephrology, Vol. 18. Gonick. 470p. 1994. 79.95 (0-8151-3744-3, Yr Bk Med Pubs) Mosby Yr Bk.

Current Nephrology, Vol. 19. Gonick. 470p. 1995. 79.95 (0-8151-3745-1, Yr Bk Med Pubs) Mosby Yr Bk.

Current Nephrology, Vol. 20. Gonick. 470p. 1996. 79.95 (0-8151-3746-X, Yr Bk Med Pubs) Mosby Yr Bk.

Current Neuro-Ophthalmology. Ed. by Simmons Lessell. 420p. 1991. 89.95 (0-8151-5390-2, Yr Bk Med Pubs) Mosby Yr Bk.

Current Neuro-Ophthalmology, Vol. 2. Lessell. 432p. 1989. 89.95 (0-8151-5389-9, Yr Bk Med Pubs) Mosby Yr Bk.

Current Neurology, Vol. 1. Ed. by H. Richard Tyler. LC 78-68042. 499p. reprint ed. pap. 142.30 (0-7837-3530-8, 2057866) Bks Demand.

Current Neurology, Vol. 8. Appel. 376p. 1988. 69.95 (0-8151-0231-3, Yr Bk Med Pubs) Mosby Yr Bk.

Current Neurology, Vol. 9. Appel. 304p. 1989. 69.95 (0-8151-0232-1, Yr Bk Med Pubs) Mosby Yr Bk.

Current Neurology, Vol. 10. Stanley H. Appel. 408p. 1990. 69.95 (0-8151-0233-X, Yr Bk Med Pubs) Mosby Yr Bk.

Current Neurology, Vol. 11. Appel. 321p. 1991. 69.95 (0-8151-0234-8, Yr Bk Med Pubs) Mosby Yr Bk.

Current Neurology, Vol. 12. Appel. 251p. 1992. 69.95 (0-8151-0235-6) Mosby Yr Bk.

Current Neurology, Vol. 13. Appel. 328p. 1993. 69.95 (0-8151-0236-4, Yr Bk Med Pubs) Mosby Yr Bk.

Current Neurology, Vol. 14. Appel. 320p. 1994. 69.95 (0-8151-0237-2, Yr Bk Med Pubs) Mosby Yr Bk.

Current Neurology, Vol. 15. Appel. 320p. 1995. 69.95 (0-8151-0238-0, Yr Bk Med Pubs) Mosby Yr Bk.

Current Neurology, Vol. 16. Appel. 320p. 1996. 69.95 (0-8151-0239-9, Yr Bk Med Pubs) Mosby Yr Bk.

Current Neurosurgery. Ed. by G. M. Teasdale & J. D. Miller. (Illus.). 351p. 1992. text ed. 115.00 (0-443-04447-3) Churchill.

Current Noninvasive Vascular Diagnosis. A. F. AbuRama. (Illus.). 408p. 1988. 59.00 (0-88416-500-0, Yr Bk Med Pubs) Mosby Yr Bk.

Current Nutritional Therapy: A Clinical Reference. Ronald J. Grabowski. 360p. 1994. ring bd. 79.00 (0-9640099-0-0) Image Pr TX.

Current Obstetric & Gynecologic Diagnosis & Treatment. 8th ed. De Cherney. (C). 1994. pap. text ed. 41.95 (0-8385-1447-2) Appleton & Lange.

Current Obstetric Medicine, Vol. 2. Lee. 380p. 1993. 64.95 (0-8151-5550-6, Yr Bk Med Pubs) Mosby Yr Bk.

Current Obstetric Medicine, Vol. 3. Lee. 380p. 1995. 64.95 (0-8151-5551-4, Yr Bk Med Pubs) Mosby Yr Bk.

Current Obstetric Medicine, Vol. 4. Lee. 270p. 1997. 64.95 (0-8151-5552-2, Yr Bk Med Pubs) Mosby Yr Bk.

Current Obstetric Medicine, Vol. 5. Lee. 270p. 1999. 64.95 (0-8151-5553-0, Yr Bk Med Pubs) Mosby Yr Bk.

Current Obstetrics Medicine. Lee. 380p. 1991. 59.95 (0-8151-5647-2, Yr Bk Med Pubs) Mosby Yr Bk.

Current of Romantic Passion. Jeffrey C. Robinson. LC 91-6580. 214p. (Orig.). (C). 1991. lib. bdg. 40.75 (0-299-12960-8); pap. 16.95 (0-299-12964-0) U of Wis Pr.

Current of Spirituality. Hubert Van Zeller. 1970. pap. 6.95 (0-87243-048-0) Templegate.

Current Operative Surgery: Urology. A. R. Mundy. (Current Operative Surgery Ser.). (Illus.). 255p. 1988. text ed. 115.00 (0-7020-1141-X) Saunders.

Current Operative Surgery: General Surgery. Alfred Cuschieri & Thomas P. Hennessy. (Illus.). 256p. 1989. text ed. 59.95 (0-7020-1072-3, Bailliere-Tindall) Saunders.

Current Operative Urology, 1989. E. Douglas Whitehead. LC 65-10325. 1988. text ed. 79.50 (0-397-50867-0) Lippincott.

Current Operative Urology 1990. E. Douglas Whitehead. (Illus.). 432p. 1989. text ed. 79.50 (0-397-50991-X) Lippincott.

Current Operative Urology 1991. E. Douglas Whitehead. (Illus.). 448p. 1990. text ed. 99.00 (0-397-50992-8) Lippincott.

Current Operative Urology 1992. E. Douglas Whitehead. (Illus.). 448p. 1992. text ed. 99.00 (0-397-51076-4) Lippincott.

Current Opinion in Cosmetic Dentistry. Gary Goldstein et al. (Illus.). 108p. (Orig.). 1993. pap. 59.95 (1-870485-57-2) Current Science.

*Current Opinion in Cosmetic Dentistry. Jeffrey Golub-Evans. (Illus.). 120p. 1995. pap. text ed. 79.95 (1-85922-682-5) Current Science.

Current Opinion in Cosmetic Dentistry. 2nd ed. Jeffrey Golub-Evans. (Illus.). 152p. 1994. pap. text ed. 69.95 (1-85922-670-1) Current Science.

Current Opinion in Dermatology. Mark V. Dahl & Peter J. Lynch. (Illus.). 328p. 1994. text ed. 99.95 (1-85922-672-8) Current Med.

Current Opinion in Dermatology. Mark V. Dahl & Peter J. Lynch. (Illus.). 328p. 1994. text ed. 99.95 (1-870485-77-7) Current Science.

*Current Opinion in Dermatology. 2nd ed. Mark V. Dahl & Peter J. Lynch. (Illus.). 300p. 1994. text ed. 99.95 (1-85922-686-8) Current Science.

Current Opinion in Endocrinology & Diabetes. Peter O. Kohler. (Illus.). 308p. 1993. pap. text ed. 79.95 (1-85922-673-6) Current Science.

Current Opinion in General Surgery. John M. Daly. (Illus.). 346p. (Orig.). 1993. 124.95 (1-870485-60-2) Current Science.

Current Opinion in General Surgery. 2nd ed. John M. Daly. (Illus.). 288p. (Orig.). 1994. text ed. 129.95 (1-85922-671-X) Current Science.

Current Opinion in Hematology. John W. Adamson. (Illus.). 348p. (Orig.). 1993. pap. 79.95 (1-870485-59-9) Current Science.

Current Opinion in Periodontology. Raymond A. Yukna et al. (Illus.). 196p. (Orig.). 1993. pap. 59.95 (1-870485-58-0) Current Science.

Current Opinion in Periodontology. 2nd ed. Ray Williams et al. (Illus.). 220p. 1994. pap. text ed. 69.95 (1-85922-669-8) Current Science.

Current Opinions of the Ethical & Judical Council, 1991 Edition. 1991. 15.00 (0-89970-406-9) AMA.

Current Options for Cereal Improvement: Doubled Haploids, Mutants & Heterosis. Ed. by M. Maluszynski. (Advances in Agricultural Biotechnology Ser.). (C). 1988. lib. bdg. 71.50 (0-7923-0064-5) Kluwer Ac.

Current Ornithology, Vol. 1. Ed. by Richard F. Johnston. LC 84-640616. 442p. 1983. 79.50 (0-306-41339-6, Plenum Pr) Plenum.

Current Ornithology, Vol. 2. Ed. by Richard F. Johnston. LC 84-640616. 378p. 1985. 79.50 (0-306-41780-4, Plenum Pr) Plenum.

Current Ornithology, Vol. 4. Ed. by Richard F. Johnston. LC 84-640616. 338p. 1986. 79.50 (0-306-42352-9, Plenum Pr) Plenum.

Current Ornithology, Vol. 5. Ed. by Richard Johnston. LC 84-640616. (Illus.). 436p. 1988. 85.00 (0-306-42722-2, Plenum Pr) Plenum.

Current Ornithology, Vol. 6. Ed. by D. M. Power. LC 84-640616. (Illus.). 344p. 1989. 85.00 (0-306-43056-8, Plenum Pr) Plenum.

Current Ornithology, Vol. 7. Ed. by D. M. Power. LC 84-640616. (Illus.). 402p. 1990. 85.00 (0-306-43307-9, Plenum Pr) Plenum.

Current Ornithology, Vol. 8. Ed. by D. M. Power. LC 84-640616. (Illus.). 305p. 1990. 85.00 (0-306-43640-X, Plenum Pr) Plenum.

Current Ornithology, Vol. 9. Ed. by D. M. Power. (Illus.). 250p. 1991. 69.50 (0-306-43990-5, Plenum Pr) Plenum.

Current Ornithology, Vol. 10. Ed. by D. M. Power. (Illus.). 390p. (C). 1992. 85.00 (0-306-44282-5, Plenum Pr) Plenum.

Current Ornithology, Vol. 11. Ed. by D. M. Power. 1994. 79.50 (0-306-44550-6, Plenum Pr) Plenum.

*Current Ornithology, Vol. 12. Ed. by Dennis M. Power. 280p. 1995. 79.50 (0-306-44978-1) Plenum.

Current Ornithology, Vol. 3. Ed. by Richard F. Johnston. LC 84-640616. 538p. 1986. 89.50 (*0-306-42051-1*, Plenum Pr) Plenum.

Current Orthopaedic Management. Ed. by William J. Kane. LC 80-25989. 360p. reprint ed. pap. 102.60 (*0-7837-3149-3*, 2042836) Bks Demand.

***Current Orthopedic Practice.** Ed. by P. M. Yeoman & D. M. Spengler. LC 94-44573. 1995. write for info. (*0-7506-1624-5*) Buttrwrth-Heinemann.

Current Overviews in Optical Science & Engineering, No. II. Ed. by Richard Feinberg. 548p. 1991. 56.00 (*0-8194-0575-2*, VOL. AT02) SPIE.

Current Overviews in Optical Science & Engineering I: Advent Technology. Ed. by R. Feinberg. 600p. 1990. 71.00 (*0-8194-0459-4*, VOL. AT01/HC); pap. 56.00 (*0-8194-0460-8*, VOL. AT01) SPIE.

Current Paleoethnobotany: Analytical Methods & Cultural Interpretations of Archaeological Plant Remains. Ed. by Christine A. Hastorf & Virginia S. Popper. LC 88-20467. (Prehistoric Archeology & Ecology Ser.). (Illus.). 248p. 1989. lib. bdg. 24.95 (*0-226-31892-3*); pap. text ed. 10.95 (*0-226-31893-1*) U Ch Pr.

Current Patent Interference Practice. Bruce M. Collins. 538p. 1987. 95.00 (*0-13-288184-5*) Aspen Law.

Current Pediatric Drugs. Fredric D. Burg & Jeffrey A. Bourret. (Illus.). 224p. 1993. pap. text ed. 26.50 (*0-7216-4574-7*) Saunders.

Current Pediatric Therapy 13. 13th ed. Syndey S. Gellis & Benjamin M. Kagan. (Illus.). 832p. 1990. text ed. 73.50 (*0-7216-2334-4*) Saunders.

Current Perinatology. Ed. by Manohar L. Rathi. (Illus.). 290p. 1988. 93.00 (*0-387-96758-3*) Spr-Verlag.

Current Perinatology Two. Ed. by Manohar L. Rathi. (Illus.). xii, 230p. 1990. 93.00 (*0-387-97214-5*) Spr-Verlag.

Current Perspective in Nitrogen Fixation. Ed. by A. H. Gibson & W. E. Newton. 534p. 1981. 114.00 (*0-444-80291-6*) Elsevier.

Current Perspectives in Banking: Operations, Management & Regulation. 2nd ed. Thomas M. Havrilesky & John T. Boorman. LC 79-55734. (Illus.). (C). 1980. pap. text ed. write for info. (*0-88295-405-9*) Harlan Davidson.

Current Perspectives in Hepatology: Festschrift for Hyman J. Zimmerman, M.D. Ed. by L. B. Seeff & J. H. Lewis. (Illus.). 426p. 1989. 95.00 (*0-306-43063-0*, Plenum Med Bk) Plenum.

Current Perspectives in High Pressure Biology. Ed. by H. W. Jannasch et al. 1987. text ed. 93.00 (*0-12-380385-3*) Acad Pr.

Current Perspectives in Lithium Prophylaxis. Ed. by P. Berner et al. (Bibliotheca Psychiatrica Ser.: Vol. 161). (Illus.). viii, 248p. 1981. pap. 70.50 (*3-8055-1753-X*) S Karger.

Current Perspectives in Mass Communication Research. Ed. by F. Gerald Kline & Phillip J. Tichenor. LC 72-84051. (Sage Annual Reviews of Communication Research Ser.: No. 1). 320p. reprint ed. pap. 91.20 (*0-8357-8440-1*, 2034704) Bks Demand.

Current Perspectives in Microbial Ecology: Proceedings of the Third International Symposium on Microbial Ecology, Michigan State University, 7-12 August 1983. International Symposium on Microbial Ecology (3rd: 1983: Michigan State University) Staff. Ed. by M. J. Klug & C. A. Reddy. LC 84-489. (Illus.). 722p. reprint ed. pap. 180.00 (*0-8357-7512-7*, 2036004) Bks Demand.

Current Perspectives in Palynological Research. Ed. by Sunirmal Chanda. (Illus.). 440p. 1991. 70.00 (*1-55528-247-4*, Pub. by Today & Tomorrows P & P II) Scholarly Pubns.

Current Perspectives in Psychological, Legal & Ethical Issues, Vol. 1: Children & Families, Pt. A-Children & Families: Abuse & Endangerment. Ed. by Sandra A. Garcia & Robert Batey. 1991. Pt. A - Children & Families: Abuse & Endangerment. 88.00 (*1-85302-083-4*, Pub. by J Kingsley Pubs UK) Taylor & Francis.

Current Perspectives in Psychological, Legal & Ethical Issues, Vol. 1: Children & Families, Pt. B - Children & Families: Creation & Conflict. Ed. by Sandra A. Garcia & Robert Batey. 1991. 88.00 (*1-85302-084-2*, Pub. by J Kingsley Pubs UK) Taylor & Francis.

Current Perspectives in Psychological, Legal & Ethical Issues, Vol. 1: Children & Families, 2 pts., Set. Ed. by Sandra A. Garcia & Robert Batey. 1991. 175.00 (*1-85302-082-6*, Pub. by J Kingsley Pubs UK) Taylor & Francis.

Current Perspectives in Social Psychology. 4th ed. Ed. by Edwin P. Hollander & Raymond G. Hunt. (Illus.). (C). 1976. teacher ed write for info. (*0-19-502018-8*); pap. text ed. 21.95 (*0-19-501998-9*) OUP.

Current Perspectives in Social Theory, Vol. 1. Ed. by Scott G. McNall & Gary N. Howe. 394p. 1980. 73.25 (*0-89232-154-7*) Jai Pr.

Current Perspectives in Social Theory, Vol. 2. Scott G. McNall & Gary N. Howe. 375p. 1981. 73.25 (*0-89232-190-3*) Jai Pr.

Current Perspectives in Social Theory, Vol. 3. Ed. by Scott G. McNall & John Wilson. 295p. 1982. 73.25 (*0-89232-297-7*) Jai Pr.

Current Perspectives in Social Theory, Vol. 4. Ed. by Scott G. McNall & John Wilson. 358p. 1983. 73.25 (*0-89232-379-5*) Jai Pr.

Current Perspectives in Social Theory, Vol. 5. Scott G. McNall. 1985. 73.25 (*0-89232-511-9*) Jai Pr.

Current Perspectives in Social Theory, Vol. 6. Ed. by Scott G. McNall. 1985. 73.25 (*0-89232-531-3*) Jai Pr.

Current Perspectives in Social Theory, Vol. 7. Ed. by Scott G. McNall & John Wilson. 196p. 1986. 73.25 (*0-89232-713-8*) Jai Pr.

Current Perspectives in Social Theory, Vol. 8. Ed. by John Wilson & Scott G. McNall. 1987. 73.25 (*0-89232-738-3*) Jai Pr.

Current Perspectives in the Use of Nonaversive & Aversive Interventions for Persons with Developmental Disabilities. Ed. by Alan C. Repp & Nirbhay N. Singh. (Illus.). 300p. (C). 1990. write for info. (*0-318-66893-9*) Sycamore Pub.

***Current Perspectives on Administration of Adult Education Programs.** Ed. by Patricia Mulcrone. LC 85-644750. (New Directions for Adult & Continuing Education Ser.: No. 60). 115p. (Orig.). 1993. pap. 16.95 (*1-55542-714-6*) Jossey-Bass.

Current Perspectives on Aging & the Life Cycle, Vol. 3. Ed. by Zena S. Blau. 1988. 73.25 (*0-89232-739-1*) Jai Pr.

Current Perspectives on Criminal Behavior. 2nd ed. Abraham S. Blumberg. 442p. (C). 1981. pap. text ed. 10.00 (*0-394-32156-1*, KnopfC) Knopf.

Current Perspectives on Implantable Devices, Vol. 1. Ed. by David F. Williams. 317p. 1989. 90.25 (*0-89232-885-1*) Jai Pr.

Current Perspectives on Implantable Devices, Vol. 2. Ed. by David F. Williams. 291p. 1990. 90.25 (*1-55938-015-2*) Jai Pr.

Current Perspectives on Implantable Devices, Vol. 3. Ed. by David F. Williams. 1992. 90.25 (*1-55938-358-5*) Jai Pr.

Current Perspectives on International Terrorism. Ed. by Robert O. Slater & Michael Stohl. 240p. 1988. text ed. 49.95 (*0-312-01379-5*) St Martin.

Current Perspectives on Major Depressive Disorders in Children. Ed. by Elizabeth B. Weller & Ronald A. Weller. LC 84-6231. (Clinical Insights Ser.). 105p. reprint ed. pap. 30.00 (*0-8357-7821-5*, 2036193) Bks Demand.

Current Perspectives on Molecular & Cellular Oncology, Vol. 1. Ed. by Demetrios Spandidos. 1991. 90.25 (*1-55938-355-0*) Jai Pr.

Current Perspectives on Personality Disorders. Ed. by James P. Forsch. LC 83-8782. (Clinical Insights Ser.). 124p. reprint ed. pap. 35.40 (*0-8357-7804-5*, 2036174) Bks Demand.

Current Perspectives on Pronunciation: Practices Anchored in Theory. Ed. by Joan Morley. 121p. 1987. pap. 14.00 (*0-939791-28-5*) Tchrs Eng Spkrs.

Current Perspectives on R & D Productivity. Ed. by Herbert I. Fusfeld & Richard N. Langlois. (Technology Policy & Economic Growth Ser.). (Illus.). 168p. 1982. 44.00 (*0-08-028836-7*, K110, Pergamon Pr) Elsevier.

Current Perspectives on the Culture of Schools. Nancy B. Wyner. (School & Community Psychology Ser.). 264p. (Orig.). (C). 1991. pap. text ed. 27.95 (*0-914797-61-1*) Brookline Bks.

Current Perspectives on the History of the Social Sciences. Ed. by Lowell L. Hargens et al. (Knowledge & Society Studies in the Sociology of Science, Past & Present: Vol. 4). 291p. 1983. 73.25 (*0-89232-298-5*) Jai Pr.

Current Physical Therapy. Peat. 296p. (C). 1988. 49.50 (*1-55664-025-0*) Mosby Yr Bk.

***Current Pocket Reference: Pharmacopoeia & Medical Notes, 1994.** Larry T. Shepherd & Thomas J. Whalen. (Illus.). 80p. (Orig.). (C). 1994. text ed. 8.75 (*0-9642193-0-1*) Specialty Cards.

Current Practice in Anesthesiology. 2nd ed. Rogers. 536p. (C). 1991. 82.00 (*1-55664-269-5*) Mosby Yr Bk.

Current Practice in Cost Estimating & Cost Control. Victor F. Spruill & Calin Popescu. LC 83-70399. 256p. 1983. pap. 28.00 (*0-87262-357-2*) Am Soc Civil Eng.

Current Practice in Dryland Resources & Technology, Vols. 1-3. Alam Singh. (C). 1987. 250.00 (*0-317-62059-2*, Scientific) St Mut.

Current Practice in Emergency Medicine. 2nd ed. Callahm. 1360p. 1991. 129.00 (*1-55664-267-9*) Mosby Yr Bk.

Current Practice in Foot & Ankle Surgery, Vol. 1. Ed. by Glenn B. Pfeffer & Carol C. Frey. LC 92-49130. (Current Practice in Foot & Ankle Surgery). 304p. 1993. 49.00 (*0-07-049732-X*) Hlth Prof Div.

Current Practice in Foot & Ankle Surgery, Vol. 2. Glenn B. Pfeffer & Carol C. Frey. (Illus.). 208p. 1994. text ed. 55.00 (*0-07-049799-0*) Hlth Prof Div.

Current Practice in Interventional Radiology. Kadir. (Illus.). 808p. (C). 1991. 160.00 (*1-55664-130-3*) Mosby Yr Bk.

Current Practice in Ophthalmology. Ed. by Andrew P. Schachat et al. LC 92-16342. 403p. 1992. 85.00 (*0-8016-6611-2*) Mosby Yr Bk.

Current Practice in Therapeutic Plasmapheresis. Ed. by Y. Shiokawa & N. Inoue. (International Congress Ser.: No. 694). 228p. 1986. 117.50 (*0-444-80714-4*, Excerpta Medica) Elsevier.

Current Practice of Breast, Skin & Soft Tissue Surgery. Ed. by Barry A. Levine. LC 93-50590. 1994. pap. 29.95 (*0-443-08974-4*) Churchill.

Current Practice of Cardiothoracic Surgery. Barry Levine. LC 93-49075. 1994. pap. 34.95 (*0-443-08976-0*) Churchill.

Current Practice of Clinical Electroencephalography. 2nd ed. David D. Daly & Timothy A. Pedley. 848p. 1990. 115.50 (*0-88167-635-7*) Raven.

Current Practice of Clinical Electromyography. Ed. by S. L. Notermans. 568p. 1984. 224.75 (*0-444-80567-2*, I-482-84) Elsevier.

***Current Practice of Dermatology.** Jeffrey P. Callen. (Illus.). 200p. 1995. text ed. 95.00 (*1-85922-801-1*) Current Med.

Current Practice of Equine Surgery. White & Moore. (Illus.). 736p. 1990. text ed. 110.00 (*0-397-50937-5*) Lippincott.

Current Practice of Fracture Treatment: New Concepts & Common Problems. Ed. by Ping-Chung Leung. 1994. 165.00 (*0-387-57367-4*) Spr-Verlag.

Current Practice of Gastrointestinal & Abdominal Surgery. Barry A. Levine. LC 93-50705. 1994. pap. 49.95 (*0-443-08975-2*) Churchill.

***Current Practice of Medicine: Dermatology.** Jeffrey P. Callen. (Illus.). 200p. 1995. text ed. 39.95 (*1-85922-688-4*) Current Med.

Current Practice of Pediatric Surgery. Barry A. Levine. LC 93-49044. 1994. pap. 29.95 (*0-443-08978-7*) Churchill.

Current Practice of Radiology. Ed. by James H. Thrall. LC 93-10273. (Current Therapy Ser.). 1104p. 1993. 129.00 (*1-55664-385-3*) Mosby Yr Bk.

Current Practice of Surgery, 3 vols., Set. Ed. by Barry A. Levine et al. (Illus.). 2848p. 1993. ring bd. 315.00 (*0-443-08767-9*) Churchill.

Current Practice of Surgery Essentials. Ed. by Barry A. Levine et al. LC 93-48804. 1994. pap. 39.95 (*0-443-08972-8*) Churchill.

Current Practice of Surgical Stapling. Mark M. Ravitch et al. LC 90-5932. (Illus.). 324p. 1991. text ed. 95.00 (*0-8121-1328-4*) Williams & Wilkins.

Current Practice of Trauma Surgery. Barry A. Levine et al. LC 93-48362. 1994. pap. 29.95 (*0-443-08973-6*) Churchill.

Current Practice of Vascular Surgery. Ed. by Barry A. Levine. LC 93-50706. 1994. pap. 34.95 (*0-443-08977-9*) Churchill.

Current Practices & Future Developments in the Pharmacotherapy of Mental Disorders. H. Y. Meltzer & D. Nerozzi. (International Congress Ser.: Vol. 941). 1991. 134.50 (*0-444-81402-7*) Elsevier.

***Current Practices for Interpreting Engineering Drawings.** Edward A. Maruggi. 320p. 1995. spiral bd. 26.75 (*0-314-04576-7*) West Pub.

Current Practices in Ground Water & Vabose Zone Investigations. Ed. by David M. Nielson & Martin N. Sapa. (Special Technical Publication Ser.: STP 1118). (Illus.). 435p. 1992. text ed. 49.00 (*0-8031-1462-1*, 04-011180-38) ASTM.

Current Practices in Modelling the Management of Stormwater Impacts. Ed. by William James. LC 93-48332. 1994. write for info. (*1-56670-052-3*) Lewis Pubs.

Current Problems & New Trends in Cystic Fibrosis. Ed. by M. Schoeni & R. Kraemer. (Monographs in Pediatrics: Vol. 14). (Illus.). xii, 216p. 1981. pap. 119.25 (*3-8055-3417-5*) S Karger.

Current Problems in Congenital Heart Disease. Ed. by W. Jay Eldredge et al. LC 78-15311. 220p. 1979. text ed. 42.50 (*0-88331-129-1*) Luce.

Current Problems in Dermatology, Vol. 3. Ed. by J. W. Mali. 1970. 66.50 (*3-8055-0484-5*) S Karger.

Current Problems in Dermatology, Vol. 4. Ed. by J. W. Mali. 1972. 77.00 (*3-8055-1248-1*) S Karger.

Current Problems in Dermatology, Vol. 5. Ed. by J. W. Mali. 1973. 71.25 (*3-8055-1380-1*) S Karger.

Current Problems in Dermatology: Complete Set, Vol. 16 & 17. Ed. by Tobias Gedde-Dahl, Jr. & K. D. Wuepper. (Illus.). xvi, 472p. 1987. 333.00 (*3-8055-4407-3*) S Karger.

Current Problems in Federal Civil Practice, 2 vols., Set. (Litigation & Administrative Practice Ser.). 1523p. 1992. pap. text ed. 80.00 (*0-685-56925-X*, H4-5124) PLI.

Current Problems in Germ Cell Differentiation. Ed. by Anne McLaren & C. C. Wylie. LC 83-1845. (British Society for Developmental Biology Symposium Ser.: No. 7). 350p. 1983. 100.00 (*0-521-25329-2*) Cambridge U Pr.

Current Problems in Neurocybernetics. Ed. by A. B. Kogan. 156p. 1975. text ed. 41.00 (*0-7065-1486-6*, Pub. by Keter Pub IS) Coronet Bks.

Current Problems in Obstetric Anesthesia. Ed. by Sanjay Datta & Gerard W. Ostheimer. (Illus.). 400p. 1986. 59.95 (*0-8151-6576-5*, ZJO-1, Yr Bk Med Pubs) Mosby Yr Bk.

Current Problems in Pain. Ferrer. 344p. 1990. 62.00 (*0-8151-3347-2*, Yr Bk Med Pubs) Mosby Yr Bk.

Current Problems in Pediatric Otolaryngology. Healy. 496p. 1990. 65.00 (*0-8151-4375-3*, Yr Bk Med Pubs) Mosby Yr Bk.

Current Problems in Pediatric Urology. Gonzales. 488p. 1990. 69.00 (*0-8151-3616-1*, Yr Bk Med Pubs) Mosby Yr Bk.

Current Problems in Policy Theory. Ed. by Phillip Gregg. (C). 1975. pap. 12.00 (*0-918592-10-0*) Pol Studies.

Current Problems in Reference Service. Thomas J. Galvin. LC 77-162527. (Bowker Series in Problem-Centered Approaches to Librianship). 180p. reprint ed. 51.30 (*0-8357-9040-1*, 2017587) Bks Demand.

Current Problems in Sociobiology. Ed. by King's College Sociobiology Group Staff. LC 81-10129. 400p. 1982. 79.95 (*0-521-24203-7*) Cambridge U Pr.

Current Problems in Vocational Education in Switzerland: Report on a National Research Program. Gerhard Steiner. 22p. 1983. 2.75 (*0-318-22071-7*, OC93) Ctr Educ Trng Employ.

***Current Problems of Cardiovascular Surgery.** Z. Szabo. 196p. (C). 1986. 60.00x (*963-05-4435-0*) St Mut.

Current Problems of Indian Economy. Mohammad S. Khan. (Illus.). xii, 262p. 1994. 29.00 (*81-7024-631-8*, Pub. by Ashish Pub Hse II) Nataraj Bks.

Current Problems of International Trade Financing. 2nd ed. Ho et al. 1990. 162.00 (*0-409-99574-6*) Butterworth Legal Pubs.

Current Problems of Mathematics: Differential Equations, Mathematical Analysis & Their Applications. Ed. by A. Logunov. LC 86-10929. (STEKLO Ser.: Vol. 166). 271p. 1986. pap. text ed. 128.00 (*0-8218-3093-7*, STEKLO-166) Am Math.

Current Problems of Mathematics: Mathematical Analysis, Algebra, Topology. Ed. by A. Logunov. LC 86-20640. (STEKLO Ser.: Vol. 167). 304p. 1986. pap. text ed. 137.00 (*0-8218-3095-3*, STEKLOV-167) Am Math.

Current Progress in Afro-Asiatic Linguistics: Papers from the Third International Hamito-Semitic Congress. Ed. by James Bynon. (Current Issues in Linguistic Theory Ser.: Vol. 28). xi, 505p. 1984. 103.00x (*90-272-3520-1*) Benjamins North Am.

Current Progress in Chadic Linguistics: Proceedings of the International Symposium on Chadic Linguistics Boulder, Colorado, 1-2 May, 1987. Ed. by Zygmunt Frajzyngier. LC 88-36036. (Current Issues in Linguistic Theory Ser.: Vol. 62). vi, 312p. (C). 1989. 71.00x (*90-272-3559-7*) Benjamins North Am.

Current Progress in Hyperbolic Systems: Riemann Problems & Computations. W. Lindquist. LC 89-17780. 367p. 1989. pap. 49.00 (*0-8218-5106-3*, CONM-100) Am Math.

***Current Progress in Perinatal Medicine: Proceedings of the World Congress of Perinatal Medicine, 1993, Rome & Florence, Italy.** 2nd ed. Ed. by E. V. Cosmi & G. C. Di Renzo. (Illus.). 902p. (C). 1994. text ed. 95.00 (*1-85070-560-7*) Prthnon Pub.

Current Protocols in Human Genetics, Vol. 1. Ed. by Nicholas C. Dracopoli et al. LC 94-14135. 1994. 295.00 (*0-471-03420-7*) Wiley.

Current Protocols in Immunology. Ed. by John E. Coligan et al. LC 09-15726. 1991. text ed. 295.00 (*0-471-52276-7*) Wiley.

***Current Protocols in Molecular Biology.** Ed. by Frederick M. Ausubel et al. pap. text ed. 450.00 (*0-471-30661-4*) Wiley.

Current Protocols in Molecular Biology, 2 vols., Vol. 2. Frederick M. Ausubel. 1988. Set. text ed. 350.00 (*0-471-50338-X*) Wiley.

***Current Protocols in Protein Science Vol. 1.** Wiley, John & Sons, Inc., Editorial Board Staff et al. LC 95-1030. 1995. 295.00 (*0-471-11184-8*) Wiley.

Current Psychiatric Therapies, Vols. I & II-XII. Ed. by J. H. Masserman. Incl. Vol. I. LC 61-9411. (Illus.). 256p. 1961. 47.00 (*0-8089-0280-6*); Vol V. LC 61-9411. 320p. 1965. text ed. 76.00 (*0-8089-0284-9*, 792705); Vol VI. LC 61-9411. 400p. 1966. text ed. 81.00 (*0-8089-0285-7*, 792706); Vol VII. LC 61-9411. (Illus.). 266p. 1967. text ed. 87.00 (*0-8089-0286-5*, 792707); Vol. VIII. LC 61-9411. 272p. 1968. text ed. 87.00 (*0-8089-0287-3*, 792708); Vol IX. LC 61-9411. (Illus.). 320p. 1969. text ed. 91.00 (*0-8089-0288-1*, 792709); LC 61-9411. write for info. (*0-318-52856-8*, Grune) Saunders.

Current Psychiatric Therapy. David L. Dunner. (Illus.). 608p. 1992. text ed. 60.95 (*0-7216-3973-9*) Saunders.

Current Psychotherapies. 4th ed. Ed. by Raymond J. Corsini & Danny Wedding. LC 88-6351. 623p. 1989. pap. 37.50 (*0-87581-332-1*) Peacock Pubs.

Current Psychotherapies. 5th ed. Ed. by Raymond J. Corsini & Danny Wedding. 1995. pap. text ed. write for info. (*0-87581-392-5*) Peacock Pubs.

Current Publications by Member Societies. 3rd ed. (C). 1987. 30.00 (*0-317-89881-7*, Pub. by Birmingham Midland Soc UK) St Mut.

Current Publications in Legal & Related Fields. pap. 25.00 (*0-8377-9273-8*); pap. 75.00 (*0-685-07513-3*) Rothman.

Current Pulmonology, Vol. 10. Simmons. 484p. 1989. 69.95 (*0-8151-7747-X*, Yr Bk Med Pubs) Mosby Yr Bk.

Current Pulmonology, Vol. 12. Simmons. 328p. 1991. 69.95 (*0-8151-7749-6*, Yr Bk Med Pubs) Mosby Yr Bk.

Current Pulmonology, Vol. 13. Simmons. 356p. 1992. 69.95 (*0-8151-7743-7*) Mosby Yr Bk.

Current Pulmonology, Vol. 14. Tierney. 352p. 1993. 69.95 (*0-8151-7741-0*, Yr Bk Med Pubs) Mosby Yr Bk.

Current Pulmonology, Vol. 15. Tierney. 425p. 1994. 69.95 (*0-8151-7742-9*, Yr Bk Med Pubs) Mosby Yr Bk.

Current Pulmonology, Vol. 16. Tierney. 425p. 1995. 69.95 (*0-8151-7735-6*, Yr Bk Med Pubs) Mosby Yr Bk.

Current Pulmonology, Vol. 17. Tierney. 425p. 1996. 69.95 (*0-8151-7736-4*, Yr Bk Med Pubs) Mosby Yr Bk.

Current Readings on Money, Banking, & Financial Markets, 1989. James A. Wilcox. (C). 1989. pap. text ed. 21.00 (*0-673-39923-0*) HarpCollege.

Current Reform Responsa. Solomon B. Freehof. LC 68-57979. 269p. reprint ed. pap. 76.70 (*0-7837-3002-0*, 2042939) Bks Demand.

Current Regional Issues: Alabama, Arkansas, Georgia, Kentucky, Louisiana, Mississippi, Tennessee, West Virginia. Joy L. Clark et al. 61p. (C). 1994. pap. text ed. 8.00 (*0-03-002049-2*) Dryden Pr.

Current Regional Issues: CT, DE, ME, MA, NH, RI, VT. John M. Halstead et al. 54p. (C). 1993. pap. text ed. 8.00 (*0-03-001954-0*) Dryden Pr.

Current Regional Issues: District of Columbia, Maryland, New Jersey, New York, North Carolina, Pennsylvania, South Carolina, Virginia. V. Glenn Chappell et al. 64p. (C). 1994. pap. text ed. 8.00 (*0-03-002048-4*) Dryden Pr.

Current Regional Issues: Florida. Fadi Asraoui et al. 62p. (C). 1994. pap. text ed. 8.00 (*0-03-001953-2*) Dryden Pr.

Current Regional Issues: Illinois-Indiana-Michigan-Minnesota-Ohio-Wisconsin. John P. Blair et al. 72p. (C). 1993. pap. text ed. 8.00 (*0-03-002052-2*) Dryden Pr.

Current Regional Issues: Iowa, Kansas, Missouri, Nebraska, North Dakota, South Dakota. Scott W. Fausti et al. 68p. (C). 1994. pap. text ed. 8.00 (*0-03-002047-6*) Dryden Pr.

Current Regulation of Money Market Funds Including Rule 2a-7. (Corporate Law & Practice Ser.). 405p. 1992. pap. text ed. 70.00 (*0-685-56891-1*, B4-6988) PLI.

Current Regulatory Issues in Medical Physics: Proceedings of an American College of Medical Physics Symposium, April 1992. Melissa Martin & James Smathers. 350p. 1992. pap. text ed. 55.00 (*0-944838-29-4*) Med Physics Pub.

Current Research Activities in Support of USEPA's Regulatory Agenda. 146p. 1990. pap. 20.50 (*0-89867-549-9*, 20260) Am Water Wks Assn.

C

An Asterisk (*) at the beginning of an entry indicates that the title is appearing in BIP for the first time.

Current Research & Applications in Personality Theories. Larry A. Hjelle & Zeigler. (C). 1992. pap. text ed. write for info. (*0-07-029084-9*) McGraw.

Current Research & Clinical Management of Melanoma, Alk. paper. Ed. by Larry Nathanson. LC 93-9325. (Cancer Treatment & Research Ser.: Vol. 65). 400p. (C). 1993. lib. bdg. 195.00 (*0-7923-2152-9*) Kluwer Ac.

Current Research & Research Needs in Deep Foundations. Ed. by Peter K. Taylor. 46p. 1985. 13.00 (*0-87262-478-1*) Am Soc Civil Eng.

***Current Research by the Geological Survey of Canada: 1993 Canadian Shield, Pt. C.** 366p. (Orig.). 1993. pap. 35.05x (*0-660-57950-2*, Pub. by Canada Commun Grp CN) Accents Pubns.

***Current Research by the Geological Survey of Canada: 1993 Cordillera & Pacific Margin, Pt. A.** Department of Energy, Mines & Resources Staff. 287p. (Orig.). 1993. pap. 29.25x (*0-660-57948-0*, Pub. by Canada Commun Grp CN) Accents Pubns.

***Current Research by the Geological Survey of Canada: 1993 Cordillera & Pacific Margin Interior Plains & Arctic Canada, Canadian Shield, Eastern Canada, & National & General Programs, Pt. E.** 369p. (Orig.). 1993. pap. 46.15x (*0-660-58871-4*, Pub. by Canada Commun Grp CN) Accents Pubns.

***Current Research by the Geological Survey of Canada: 1993 Eastern Canada & National & General Programs, Pt. D.** 213p. (Orig.). 1993. pap. 22.40 (*0-660-57951-0*, Pub. by Canada Commun Grp CN) Accents Pubns.

***Current Research by the Geological Survey of Canada: 1993 Interior Plains & Artic Canada, Pt. B.** 70p. (Orig.). 1993. pap. 10.40x (*0-660-57949-9*, Pub. by Canada Commun Grp CN) Accents Pubns.

***Current Research by the Geological Survey of Canada: 1994 Canadian Shield, Pt. C.** 377p. (Orig.). 1994. pap. 36.40x (*0-660-58987-7*, Pub. by Canada Commun Grp CN) Accents Pubns.

***Current Research by the Geological Survey of Canada: 1994 Cordillera & Pacific Margin, Pt. A.** 243p. 1994. pap. 25.35x (*0-660-58982-6*, Pub. by Canada Commun Grp CN) Accents Pubns.

***Current Research by the Geological Survey of Canada: 1994 Eastern Canada & National & General Programs, Pt. D.** 189p. (Orig.). 1994. pap. 20.80x (*0-660-58988-5*, Pub. by Canada Commun Grp CN) Accents Pubns.

***Current Research by the Geological Survey of Canada: 1994 Interior Plains & Artic Canada, Pt. B.** 91p. (Orig.). 1994. pap. 13.00x (*0-660-58986-9*, Pub. by Canada Commun Grp CN) Accents Pubns.

Current Research for the Information Profession 1991. 258p. 1992. 140.00 (*0-86291-649-6*) Bowker-Saur.

Current Research in African Earth Sciences: Extended Abstracts of the 14th Colloquium on African Geology, Berlin, 18-22 August 1987. Ed. by G. Matheis & H. Schandelmeier. 504p. (C). 1987. text ed. 105.00 (*90-6191-709-3*, Pub. by A A Balkema NE); pap. text ed. 60.00 (*90-6191-710-7*, Pub. by A A Balkema NE) Ashgate Pub Co.

Current Research in Alzheimer Therapy. Ed. by Ezio Giacobini & Robert E. Becker. (Illus.). 366p. (C). 1988. text ed. 63.00 (*0-8448-1555-1*) Taylor & Francis.

Current Research in Arts Medicine. Ed. by Fadi J. Bejjani. LC 93-20251. (Illus.). 512p. (Orig.). 1993. pap. text ed. 29.95 (*1-55652-187-1*) A cappella Bks.

Current Research in Biopsychology. John P. Pinel. 200p. 1991. pap. text ed. 19.00 (*0-205-13000-3*, H3000-0) Allyn.

Current Research in Britain, 4 vols., 6 books, Set. 1993. 580.00 (*0-582-20920-X*, 072455, Pub. by Longman Grp UK) Gale.

***Current Research in Britain, 4 Vol., Set.** 9th ed. 3914p. 1994. pap. 650.00 (*1-56159-123-8*, Stockton Pr) Groves Dictionaries.

***Current Research in Britain Vol. 1: Physical Sciences.** 9th ed. 1994. pap. 250.00 (*1-56159-124-6*, Stockton Pr) Groves Dictionaries.

***Current Research in Britain Vol. 2: Biological Sciences.** 9th ed. 1994. pap. 250.00 (*1-56159-075-4*, Stockton Pr) Groves Dictionaries.

***Current Research in Britain Vol. 3: Social Sciences.** 9th ed. 1994. pap. 250.00 (*1-56159-076-2*, Stockton Pr) Groves Dictionaries.

***Current Research in Britain Vol. 4: Humanities.** 9th ed. 1994. pap. 250.00 (*1-56159-077-0*, Stockton Pr) Groves Dictionaries.

Current Research in British Studies. 7th ed. Phyllis Bultmann. Ed. by William Bultmann. 165p. 1975. pap. text ed. 24.00 (*0-89126-017-X*) MA-AH Pub.

Current Research in British Studies. 8th ed. Ed. by Robert K. Donovan. 82p. (Orig.). 1980. pap. 19.00 (*0-89126-084-6*) MA-AH Pub.

Current Research in British Studies. 9th ed. Patricia Clark. Ed. by Robert K. Donovan. 106p. (Orig.). 1988. pap. 20.95 (*0-89126-167-2*) MA-AH Pub.

Current Research in Decision Support Technology. Robert Blanning & David King. LC 92-41031. 256p. 1993. text ed. 45.00 (*0-8186-2807-3*, 2807) IEEE Comp Soc.

Current Research in Earthquake Prediction, Vol. 1. Ed. by Tsuneji Rikitake. (Developments in Earth & Planetary Sciences Ser.: No. 2). 400p. 1981. lib. bdg. 90.00 (*90-277-1133-X*) Kluwer Ac.

Current Research in Film, Vol. 1. Ed. by Bruce Austin. 232p. (C). 1985. text ed. 55.00 (*0-89391-269-7*) Ablex Pub.

Current Research in Film, Vol. 2. Ed. by Bruce Austin. 268p. 1986. text ed. 55.00 (*0-89391-315-4*) Ablex Pub.

Current Research in Film, Vol. 3. Ed. by Bruce Austin. 240p. (C). 1987. text ed. 55.00 (*0-89391-319-7*) Ablex Pub.

Current Research in Film, Vol. 4. Ed. by Bruce A. Austin. 304p. 1988. text ed. 55.00 (*0-89391-414-2*) Ablex Pub.

Current Research in Film, Vol. 5: Audiences, Economics & Law. Ed. by Bruce A. Austin. 224p. 1991. text ed. 49.50 (*0-89391-552-1*) Ablex Pub.

Current Research in Heat & Mass Transfer: A Copendiem & Festschrift for Professor Arcot Ramachandran. Ed. by M. V. Murthy et al. 283p. 1988. 89.00 (*0-89116-578-9*) Hemisp Pub.

Current Research in Labor Economics. Ed. by Walter Fogel. (Monograph & Research Ser.: No. 38). 159p. 1984. pap. 8.00 (*0-89215-122-6*) U Cal LA Indus Rel.

Current Research in Management. Hammond. (C). 1992. text ed. 49.00 (*0-86187-546-X*, Pub. by Pinter Pubs UK) St Martin.

Current Research in Natural Language Generation. Ed. by Robert E. Dale et al. (Cognitive Science Ser.: Vol. 4). 356p. 1990. text ed. 61.00 (*0-12-200735-2*) Acad Pr.

Current Research in Nephrology in Japan. Ed. by Y. Ueda. (Contributions to Nephrology Ser.: Vol. 4). 1976. 39.25 (*3-8055-2383-1*) S Karger.

Current Research in Neurosciences: Topical Problem in Psychiatry & Neurology. Ed. by E. Gruenthal et al. (Bibliotheca Psychiatrica Ser.: No. 143). 1970. pap. 57.00 (*3-8055-0331-8*) S Karger.

Current Research in Photosynthesis: Proceedings of the VIIIth International Congress on Photosynthesis, Stockholm, Sweden, August 6-11, 1989, 4 vols., Set. Ed. by M. Baltscheffsky. (C). 1990. lib. bdg. 0.01 (*0-7923-0587-6*) Kluwer Ac.

Current Research in Protein Chemistry: Techniques, Structure & Function. Ed. by Joseph J. Villafranca. 606p. 1990. text ed. 140.00 (*0-12-721955-2*); pap. text ed. 61.00 (*0-12-721956-0*) Acad Pr.

Current Research in Sports Biomechanics. Ed. by b. Van Ghelowe. (Medicine & Sport Science Ser.: Vol. 25). (Illus.). viii, 204p. 1988. 137.00 (*3-8055-4546-0*) S Karger.

***Current Research in the Pleistocene.** Ed. by Bradley T. Lepper. (Illus.). 140p. (Orig.). (C). 1994. pap. text ed. 20.00 (*0-614-00503-5*) Ctr Study First Am.

Current Research on Anti-Semitism, Vol. 3-2: Hostages of Modernization. Ed. by Herbert A. Strauss. (Studies on Modern Anti-Semitism 1870-1933-39 Austria - Hungary - Poland - Russia). xii, 1416p. (C). 1993. lib. bdg. 206.15 (*3-11-013715-1*) De Gruyter.

***Current Research on Antisemitism Vol. 1: The Persisting Question: Sociological Perspectives & Social Contexts of Modern Antisemitism.** Ed. by Helen Fein. xiv, 430p. 1987. lib. bdg. 126.95 (*3-11-010170-X*) De Gruyter.

Current Research on Antisemitism, Vol. 1: The Persisting Question: Sociological Perspectives & Social Contexts of Modern Antisemitism. Ed. by Helen Fein. xiv, 430p. 1987. lib. bdg. 126.95 (*0-89925-320-2*) De Gruyter.

Current Research on Fatigue Cracks. Ed. by T. M. Tanaka & K. Komai. 318p. 1987. 90.00 (*1-85166-091-7*, Pub. by Elsevier Applied Sci UK) Elsevier.

Current Research on Fusion, Laboratory & Astrophysical Plasma. S. Kuhn et al. 320p. 1993. text ed. 81.00 (*981-02-1433-2*) World Scientific Pub.

Current Research on Occupations & Professions, Vol. 4. Ed. by Helena Z. Lopata. 1988. 73.25 (*0-89232-561-5*) Jai Pr.

Current Research on Suicide & Parasuicide: Selected Proceedings of the Second European Symposium on Suicidal Behavior. Ed. by Norman Kreitman & Stephen D. Platt. 384p. 1989. 50.00 (*0-85224-629-3*, Pub. by Edinburgh U Pr UK) Col U Pr.

***Current Resources in Cooperative Learning.** Anne Wade et al. 336p. (C). 1995. lib. bdg. 39.50 (*0-8191-9816-1*) U Pr of Amer.

Current Respiratory Care. Kacmarek. 340p. 1988. 49.50 (*1-55664-049-8*) Mosby Yr Bk.

Current Respiratory Care. Kenneth F. MacDonnell & Maurice S. Segal. 489p. 1977. pap. text ed. 15.95 (*0-316-54191-5*, Little Med Div) Little.

Current Restructuring of the Japanese Economy under Yen Appreciation. Masaru Yoshitomi. (Illus.). 35p. 1988. pap. 4.00 (*0-87641-304-1*) Carnegie Ethics & Intl Affairs.

Current Review of Cerebrovascular Disease. Ed. by Marc Fisher & Julien Bogousslavsky. (Illus.). 196p. 1993. text ed. 99.95 (*1-878132-14-8*) Current Med.

***Current Review of Cerebrovascular Disease.** Marc Fisher & Julien Bogousslavsky. (Illus.). 248p. 1995. text ed. 99.95 (*1-878132-62-8*) Current Med.

Current Review of Interventional Cardiology. Eric J. Topol & Patrick W. Serruys. (Illus.). 288p. 1993. text ed. 149.95 (*1-878132-03-2*) Current Med.

***Current Review of Laparoscopy.** 2nd ed. David C. Brooks. (Illus.). 248p. 1995. text ed. 149.95 (*1-878132-61-X*) Current Science.

***Current Review of Magnetic Resonance Imaging.** Javier Beltran. (Illus.). 416p. 1995. text ed. 99.95 (*1-878132-09-1*) Current Med.

Current Review of Pain. P. Prithvi Raj. (Illus.). 272p. 1994. text ed. 109.95 (*1-878132-06-7*) Current Med.

Current Review of Sports Medicine. Robert J. Johnson & John Lombardo. (Illus.). 328p. 1994. text ed. 129.95 (*1-878132-07-5*) Current Med.

***Current Reviews.** fac. ed. Ed. by Walter J. Friedlander. LC 75-14572. (Advances in Neurology Ser.: No. 13). (Illus.). 400p. Date not set. pap. 114.00 (*0-7837-7222-X*, 2047076) Bks Demand.

Current Reviews of Higher Nervous System Dysfunction. Ed. by Walter J. Friedlander. LC 74-15667. (Advances in Neurology Ser.: No. 7). 205p. reprint ed. pap. 58.50 (*0-7837-7109-6*, 2046938) Bks Demand.

Current Russian Phonemic Theory 1952-1962. Dragan D. Milivojevic. LC 75-108142. (Janua Linguarum, Ser. Minor: No. 78). (Orig.). 1970. pap. text ed. 16.15 (*3-10-800273-2*) Mouton.

Current (Safety) Issues in the Screening of Donor Blood & the Preparation of Pure Blood Components. Ed. by S. Seidl et al. (Journal: Vox Sanguinis: Vol. 51, Suppl. 1, 1986). (Illus.). iv, 72p. 1986. pap. 26.50 (*3-8055-4346-8*) S Karger.

Current Situation Evolution & Future Prospects for Agriculture in Yugoslavia. 204p. 1992. pap. 17.00 (*92-826-3485-X*, CM-72-91-899-EN-C, Pub. by Europ Com) UNIPUB.

Current Solutions to Hydrogen Problems in Steels: Proceedings of the Conference, Washington, DC, November 1-5, 1982. International Conference on Current Solutions to Hydrogen Problems in Steels Staff. Ed. by C. G. Interrante & G. M. Pressouyre. LC 82-73166. (Illus.). 495p. reprint ed. pap. 141.10 (*0-8357-6084-7*, 2034326) Bks Demand.

Current Soviet Policies, Vol. V: The Documentary Record of the Twenty-Third Congress of the Communist Party of the Soviet Union. Ed. by Robert Ehlers & Richard Bessel. Tr. by Current Staff of the Soviet Press Staff The. 175p. (Orig.). 1973. pap. 12.50 (*0-913601-05-5*) Current Digest.

Current Soviet Policies, Vol. VI: The Documentary Record of the Twenty-Fourth Congress of the Communist Party of the Soviet Union. Ed. by Robert Ehlers & Richard Bessel. Tr. by Current Digest of the Soviet Press Staff The. 202p. (Orig.). 1973. pap. 12.50 (*0-913601-06-3*) Current Digest.

Current Soviet Policies, Vol. VIII: The Documentary Record of the 26th Congress of the Communist Party of the Soviet Union. Ed. by Robert Ehlers & Malinda Goodrich. Tr. by Current Digest of the Soviet Press Staff. 152p. (Orig.). 1981. pap. 12.50 (*0-913601-08-X*) Current Digest.

Current Soviet Policies, Vol. X: The Proceedings of the 19th CPSU Conference. Current Digest of the Soviet Press Staff. (Current Soviet Policies Ser.). (Orig.). 1988. pap. 25.00 (*0-913601-10-1*) Current Digest.

Current Soviet Policies, Vol. 11: Documents from the 28th Congress of the Communist Party. Ed. by Ann C. Bigelow. Tr. by Current Digest of the Soviet Press Staff. 128p. (Orig.). (C). 1991. pap. 27.00 (*0-913601-11-X*) Current Digest.

Current Standards for the Evaluation of Pharmacological Care of BPH, Proceedings of a Symposium, Genoa, July 1992. Ed. by A. Jardin & F. Di Silverio. (Journal: European Urology: Vol. 24, Suppl. 1, 1993). (Illus.). vi, 50p. 1993. pap. 22.50 (*3-8055-5827-9*) S Karger.

Current State of Knowledge of Lifeline Earthquake Engineering. Comp. by American Society of Civil Engineers Staff. 486p. 1977. pap. 25.00 (*0-87262-086-7*) Am Soc Civil Eng.

Current State of Technology in Hydraulic Machinery: Papers Presented at the Inaugral Meeting of the International Committee for Book Series on Hydraulic Machinery, Held in Beijing, China in July, 1986. Ed. by A. P. Boldy. (Illus.). 340p. 1989. text ed. 93.95 (*0-566-09027-9*, Pub. by Avebury Pub UK) Ashgate Pub Co.

Current State of the Art in Prison Classification Models. 7.00 (*0-318-20300-6*) Natl Coun Crime.

Current State of the Art on Multidisciplinary Design Optimization (MDO) 50p. 1991. pap. 14.95 (*1-56347-021-7*, 21-7) AIAA.

Current State of the Coherence Theory: Critical Essays on the Epistemic Theories of Keith Lehrer & Lawrence BonJour, with Replies. Ed. by John W. Bender. (C). 1989. lib. bdg. 91.50 (*0-7923-0220-6*) Kluwer Ac.

Current Status & Future of Parasitology: Report of a Conference. Sponsored Jointly by the Rockefeller Foundation & the Josiah Macy, Jr., Foundation. Ed. by Kenneth S. Warren & Elizabeth F. Purcell. LC 81-84673. 306p. reprint ed. pap. 87.30 (*0-685-15470-X*, 2026693) Bks Demand.

Current Status of Anthropological Research in the Great Basin: 1964. Ed. by W. L. D'Azevedo et al. 379p. 1966. pap. 2.00 (*0-945920-86-5*) Desert Rsch Inst.

Current Status of Centrally Acting Peptides: Proceedings of the Satellite Symposium of the International Congress of Pharmacology, Lucknow, India, July 8th, 1981, Vol. 38. International Congress of Pharmacology Staff. Ed. by B. N. Dhawan. LC 82-3825. (Illus.). 288p. 1982. 81.00 (*0-08-028008-0*, Pergamon Pr) Elsevier.

Current Status of Clinical Cardiology, 1990. Ed. by Desmond G. Julian. (C). 1990. lib. bdg. 77.50 (*0-7923-8936-0*) Kluwer Ac.

Current Status of Clinical Organ Transplantation. Ed. by George M. Abouna. LC 84-1553. (Developments in Surgery Ser.). 1984. lib. bdg. 136.50 (*0-89838-635-7*) Kluwer Ac.

Current Status of Diabetes Mellitus in East Asian: Proceedings of the 4th Japan-China Symposium on Diabetes Mellitus, Yokohama, 7-8 October, 1993. Ed. by Goro Mimura et al. LC 94-15343. (International Congress Ser.: No. 1053). 1994. write for info. (*0-444-81758-1*) Elsevier.

Current Status of Diagnostic Cytology. Ed. by Peter Pfitzer & Ekkehard Grundmann. (Recent Results in Cancer Research Ser.: Vol. 133). (Illus.). 175p. 1993. write for info. (*3-540-56618-X*) Spr-Verlag.

Current Status of Diagnostic Cytology. Ed. by Peter Pfitzer & Ekkehard Grundmann. LC 93-11295. (Recent Results in Cancer Research Ser.: Vol. 133). 1993. 89.00 (*0-387-56618-X*) Spr-Verlag.

Current Status of Endometriosis: Research & Management: Proceedings of the 3rd World Congress of Endometriosis, Brussels, 1992. Ed. by I. Brosens & J. Donnez. LC 93-18078. (Illus.). 1993. 85.00 (*1-85070-454-6*) Prthnon Pub.

Current Status of EPH Gestosis. Ed. by A. Kurjak et al. (International Congress Ser.: Vol. 534). 524p. 1981. 137.50 (*0-444-90171-X*, Excerpta Medica) Elsevier.

Current Status of Fetal Medicine & Its Future, 1989: Journal: Fetal Therapy, Vol. 4, Suppl. 1. Ed. by S. Mancuso. (Illus.). vi, 134p. 1990. pap. 39.25 (*3-8055-5284-X*) S Karger.

Current Status of GnRH Analogues, Vol. 1. Ed. by B. Lunenfeld. (Advances in the Study of GnRH Analogues Ser.). (Illus.). 100p. (C). 1991. text ed. 55.00 (*1-85070-325-6*) Prthnon Pub.

Current Status of Gynecology & Obstetrics Series, Complete Set in presentation box. Ed. by E. S. Teoh et al. 1993. Complete set in presentation box. boxed 425.00 (*1-85070-400-7*) Prthnon Pub.

Current Status of Health Aspects of Fibrous Glass & Other Man-Made Vitreous Fiber. 4th rev. ed. (Medical Ser.: No. 21). 49p. 1982. 10.00 (*0-911890-05-X*) Indus Health Inc.

Current Status of Hemapheresis: Indications, Technology & Complications. Ed. by Robert G. Westphal & Duke O. Kasprisin. LC 87-14420. 1987. text ed. 7.00 (*0-915355-45-0*) Am Assn Blood.

Current Status of Plastic Recycling, No. P-216. 2,650.00 (*1-56965-256-2*) BCC.

Current Status of Prevention & Treatment of Diabetic Complications: Proceedings of the 3rd International Symposium on Treatment of Diabetes Mellitus, Nagoya, 13-15 July, 1988. Ed. by N. Sakamoto et al. (International Congress Ser.: No. 821). 784p. 1990. 220.50 (*0-444-81160-5*, Excerpta Medica) Elsevier.

Current Strategies for Containing Health Care Expenditures. Jon B. Christianson & Kenneth R. Smith. LC 85-11948. 156p. 1985. text ed. 24.95 (*0-88331-130-5*) Luce.

Current Studies in Nephrology: Dialysis & Transplantation. Ed. by G. D'Amico & G. Colasanti. (Contributions to Nephrology Ser.: Vol. 48). (Illus.). vi, 206p. 1985. 110.50 (*3-8055-4141-4*) S Karger.

Current Studies in Otoneurology: Proceedings of the Barany Society Meeting, Toronto, Aug. 1971. Barany Society Meeting Staff. Ed. by H. O. Barber & J. M. Frederickson. (Advances in Oto-Rhino-Laryngology Ser.: Vol. 19). (Illus.). 1973. 123.25 (*3-8055-1448-4*) S Karger.

Current Studies in Spanish Linguistics. Ed. by Hector Campos & Fernando Martinez-Gil. LC 91-25304. 656p. (C). 1992. pap. text ed. 30.00 (*0-87840-234-9*) Georgetown U Pr.

Current Studies of Hypothalamic Function 1978. Ed. by K. Lederis & W. L. Veale. Incl. Part I: Hormones. 1978. 78.50 (*3-8055-2860-4*); Part II: Metabolism & Behaviour. 1978. 78.50 (*3-8055-2861-2*); (Illus.). 1978. 141.00 (*3-8055-2969-4*) S Karger.

Current Sufi Activity: Work, Literature, Groups & Techniques. Chawan Thurlnas. (Sufi Research Ser.). 40p. 1982. pap. 7.00 (*0-86304-004-7*, Pub. by Octagon Pr UK) ISHK Bk Service.

Current Superstitions, Collected from the Oral Tradition of English Speaking Folk. Ed. by Fanny D. Bergen. LC 04-4052. (AFS Memoirs Ser.). 1972. reprint ed. 25.00 (*0-527-01056-1*) Periodicals Srv.

Current Surgical Diagnosis & Treatment. 10th ed. Lawrence W. Way. (Illus.). 1440p. 1994. pap. 41.95 (*0-8385-1439-1*, A1439-7) Appleton & Lange.

Current Surgical Management of Neurologic Disease. Ed. by Charles B. Wilson & Julian T. Hoff. LC 80-14580. (Illus.). 367p. reprint ed. pap. 104.60 (*0-7837-2588-4*, 2042750) Bks Demand.

Current Surgical Pathology. Warhol. 200p. (C). 1990. 55.00 (*1-55664-157-5*) Mosby Yr Bk.

Current Surgical Therapy. 4th ed. Cameron. 1102p. 1992. 110.00 (*1-55664-358-6*) Mosby Yr Bk.

Current Techniques in Arthroscopy. J. Serge Parisien. (Illus.). 256p. 1994. text ed. 149.95 (*1-878132-04-0*) Current Med.

***Current Techniques in Arthroscopy.** 2nd ed. J. Serge Parisien. (Illus.). 240p. 1995. text ed. 149.95 (*1-878132-63-6*) Current Med.

***Current Techniques in Interventional Cardiology.** 2nd ed. Eric J. Topol & Patrick W. Serruys. (Illus.). 312p. (Orig.). 1995. text ed. 149.95 (*1-878132-56-3*) Current Med.

Current Techniques in Interventional Radiology. Constantin Cope. (Illus.). 216p. 1993. text ed. 99.95 (*1-878132-02-4*) Current Med.

***Current Techniques in Interventional Radiology.** 2nd ed. Constantin Cope. (Illus.). 208p. 1994. text ed. 109.95 (*1-878132-59-8*) Current Med.

Current Techniques in Laparoscopy. David Brooks. (Illus.). 224p. 1993. text ed. 149.95 (*1-878132-05-9*) Current Med.

Current Techniques in Neurosurgery. Illus. by Lori Manzardo. 240p. 1993. text ed. 175.00 (*1-878132-01-6*) Current Med.

***Current Techniques in Neurosurgery.** 2nd ed. Michael Salcman. (Illus.). 248p. 1995. text ed. 174.95 (*1-878132-58-X*) Current Science.

Current Techniques in Opthalmic Laser Surgery. 2nd ed. William E. Benson et al. (Illus.). 224p. 1994. text ed. 139.95 (*1-878132-57-1*) Current Med.

Current Techniques in Small Animal Surgery. 3rd ed. M. Joseph Bojrab et al. LC 89-13005. (Illus.). 950p. 1990. text ed. 105.00 (*0-8121-1193-1*) Williams & Wilkins.

Current Technologies in Flexible Packaging STP 912. Ed. by Michael L. Troedel. LC 86-17490. (Special Technical Publication (STP) Ser.). (Illus.). 115p. 1986. pap. text ed. 26.00 (*0-8031-0478-2*, 04-912000-11) ASTM.

An Asterisk (*) at the beginning of an entry indicates that the title is appearing in BIP for the first time.

C

An Asterisk (*) at the beginning of an entry indicates that the title is appearing in BIP for the first time.

1755

Current Topics in Membrane & Transport, Vol. 34: Cellular & Molecular Biology of Sodium Transport. Ed. by Stanley G. Schultz et al. 379p. 1989. text ed. 126.00 (0-12-153334-4) Acad Pr.

Current Topics in Membranes, Vol. 40. Ed. by Dick Hoekstra. (Illus.). 638p. 1994. text ed. 145.00 (0-12-153340-9) Acad Pr.

Current Topics in Membranes Vol. 42: Chloride Channels. Ed. by William B. Guggino et al. (Illus.). 354p. 1994. text ed. 99.00 (0-12-153342-5) Acad Pr.

Current Topics in Membranes & Transport, Vol. 26. Ed. by Peter S. Aronson & Walter F. Boron. (Serial Publication Ser.). 1986. text ed. 138.00 (0-12-153326-3) Acad Pr.

Current Topics in Membranes & Transport, Vol. 27. Ed. by Lazaro J. Mandel & Dale J. Benos. (Serial Publication Ser.). 320p. 1986. text ed. 143.00 (0-12-153327-1) Acad Pr.

Current Topics in Membranes & Transport, Vol. 29. Ed. by Gerhard H. Giebisch. (Serial Publication Ser.). 1987. text ed. 138.00 (0-12-153329-8) Acad Pr.

Current Topics in Membranes & Transport, Vols. 1-9, 11. Incl. Vol. 1. 1970. 47.50 (0-12-153301-8); Vol. 2. 1971. 47.50 (0-12-153302-6); Vol. 5. 1974. 69.00 (0-12-153305-0); Vol. 6. 1975. 65.00 (0-12-153306-9); Vol. 7. 1975. 65.00 (0-12-153307-7); Vol. 9. 1977. 69.50 (0-12-153309-3); Vol. 11. 1978. 70.00 (0-12-153311-5); (Serial Publication Ser.). write for info. (0-318-50255-0) Acad Pr.

Current Topics in Membranes & Transport: Cell Volume Control - Fundamental & Comparative Aspects in Animal Cells, Vol. 30. Ed. by Arnost Kleinzeller et al. 274p. 1987. text ed. 138.00 (0-12-153330-1) Acad Pr.

Current Topics in Membranes & Transport: Potassium Transport: Physiology & Pathophysiology, Vol. 28. Ed. by Gerhard H. Giebisch. 494p. 1987. text ed. 138.00 (0-12-153328-X) Acad Pr.

Current Topics in Membranes & Transport, Vol. 31: Molecular Neurobiology: Endocrine Approaches. Ed. by Arnost Kleinzeller et al. 350p. 1987. text ed. 138.00 (0-12-153331-X) Acad Pr.

Current Topics in Membranes & Transport, Vol. 32: Membrane Fusion in Fertilization, Cellular Transport, & Viral Infection. Ed. by Nejat Duzgunes & Felix Bronner. 384p. 1988. text ed. 136.00 (0-12-153332-8) Acad Pr.

Current Topics in Membranes & Transport, Vol. 33: Molecular Biology of Ionic Channels. Ed. by William S. Agnew et al. 475p. 1988. text ed. 136.00 (0-12-153333-6) Acad Pr.

Current Topics in Membranes & Transport, Vol. 35: Mechanisms of Leukocyte Activation. Ed. by Sergio Grinstein et al. 628p. 1990. text ed. 176.00 (0-12-153335-2) Acad Pr.

Current Topics in Membranes & Transport, Vol. 36: Protein-Membrane Interactions. Ed. by Joseph H. Hoffman et al. 184p. 1990. text ed. 73.00 (0-12-153336-0) Acad Pr.

Current Topics in Membranes & Transport, Vol. 37: Channels & Noise in Epithelial Tissues. Ed. by Sandy I. Helman & Willy Van Driessche. 318p. 1990. text ed. 121.00 (0-12-153337-9) Acad Pr.

Current Topics in Membranes, Vol. 38: Ordering the Membrane-Cytoskeleton Trilayer. Ed. by Joseph F. Hoffman et al. (Illus.). 255p. 1991. text ed. 88.00 (0-12-153338-7) Acad Pr.

Current Topics in Membranes, Vol. 39: Developmental Biology of Membrane Transport Systems. Ed. by Arnost Kleinzeller et al. (Illus.). 456p. 1991. text ed. 121.00 (0-12-153339-5) Acad Pr.

Current Topics in Membranes, Vol. 41: Cell Biology & Membrane Transport Processes. Ed. by Joseph F. Hoffman et al. (Illus.). 172p. 1994. text ed. 80.00 (0-12-153341-7) Acad Pr.

***Current Topics in Microbiology & Immunology.** Ed. by A. Capron et al. (Molecular & Cellular Mechanisms: Vol. 189). 210p. 1994. text ed. 120.00 (0-387-57259-7) Spr-Verlag.

Current Topics in Microbiology & Immunology, Vol. 66. Ed. by W. Arber et al. LC 15-12910. (Illus.). 130p. 1974. 45.00 (3-540-06831-7) Spr-Verlag.

Current Topics in Microbiology & Immunology, Vol. 67. Ed. by W. Arber et al. LC 15-12910. (Illus.). iv, 162p. 1974. 55.00 (3-540-06838-4) Spr-Verlag.

Current Topics in Microbiology & Immunology, Vol. 75. W. Arber et al. LC 15-12910. (Illus.). 1976. 54.00 (3-540-08013-9) Spr-Verlag.

Current Topics in Microbiology & Immunology, Vol. 76. Ed. by W. Arber et al. LC 15-12910. (Illus.). 1977. 54.00 (3-540-08238-7) Spr-Verlag.

Current Topics in Microbiology & Immunology, Vol. 90. Ed. by W. Arber et al. (Illus.). 147p. 1980. 72.00 (0-387-10181-0) Spr-Verlag.

Current Topics in Microbiology & Immunology, Vol. 91. Ed. by W. Arber et al. (Illus.). 250p. 1981. 89.00 (0-387-10722-3) Spr-Verlag.

Current Topics in Microbiology & Immunology, Vol. 97. Ed. by W. Henle et al. (Illus.). 220p. 1981. 73.00 (0-387-11118-2) Spr-Verlag.

Current Topics in Microbiology & Immunology, Vols. 40-50 & 52-55. Incl. Vol. 41. (Illus.). iv, 183p. 1967. 60.30 (0-387-03755-1); Illus.). (ENG & GER.). write for info. (0-318-55773-8) Spr-Verlag.

Current Topics in Microbiology & Immunology: Rotaviruses. Ed. by R. F. Ramig. 330p. 1994. 129.00 (0-387-56761-5) Spr-Verlag.

***Current Topics in Microbiology & Immunology No. 187.** C. E. Rupprecht et al. 360p. 1994. 114.00 (0-387-57194-9) Spr-Verlag.

Current Topics in Microbiology & Immunology, Vol. 157: Retroviruses, Strategies of Replication. Ed. by R. Swanstrom & P. K. Vogt. (Illus.). 264p. 1990. 59.00 (0-387-51895-9) Spr-Verlag.

Current Topics in Microbiology & Immunology, Vol. 158: Viral Expression Vectors. Ed. by Richard W. Compans et al. (Illus.). 192p. 1992. 117.00 (0-387-52431-2) Spr-Verlag.

Current Topics in Microbiology & Immunology, Vol. 161: Picornaviruses. Ed. by Richard W. Compans et al. 228p. 1990. 96.00 (0-387-52429-0) Spr-Verlag.

Current Topics in Microbiology & Immunology, Vol. 163: Poxviruses. Ed. by Richard W. Compans et al. 256p. 1990. 96.00 (0-387-52430-4) Spr-Verlag.

Current Topics in Microbiology & Immunology, Vol. 164: Human Diabetes: Genetics, Environmental & Autoimmune Etiology. Ed. by Richard W. Compans et al. (Illus.). 216p. 1990. 101.00 (0-387-52652-8) Spr-Verlag.

Current Topics in Microbiology & Immunology, Vol. 165: Neuronal Growth Factors. Ed. by Richard W. Compans et al. (Illus.). 192p. 1991. 88.00 (0-387-52654-4) Spr-Verlag.

Current Topics in Microbiology & Immunology, Vol. 166: Mechanisms in B-Cell Neoplasia 1990: Workshop at the National Cancer Institute, National Institutes of Health, Bethesda, MD, U.S.A., March 28-30, 1990. Ed. by Richard W. Compans et al. (Illus.). xix, 380p. 1990. 109.00 (0-387-52886-5) Spr-Verlag.

Current Topics in Microbiology & Immunology, Vol. 172: Transmissible Spongiform Encephalopathies, Scrapie, BSE & Related Human Disorders. Ed. by Richard W. Compans et al. (Illus.). ix, 288p. 1991. 119.00 (0-387-53883-6) Spr-Verlag.

Current Topics in Microbiology & Immunology, Vol. 174: Superantigens. B. Fleischer et al. Ed. by H. O. Sjogren et al. (Illus.). 160p. 1991. 98.00 (0-387-54205-1) Spr-Verlag.

Current Topics in Microbiology & Immunology, Vol. 175: ADP-Ribosylating Toxins. Ed. by Richard W. Compans et al. (Illus.). 160p. 1992. 110.00 (0-387-54598-0) Spr-Verlag.

Current Topics in Microbiology & Immunology, Vol. 177: Hematopoietic Stem Cells: Animal Models & Human Transplantation. Ed. by Richard W. Compans et al. (Illus.). 256p. 1992. 125.00 (0-387-54531-X) Spr-Verlag.

Current Topics in Microbiology & Immunology, Vol. 178: Membrane Defenses Against Attack by Complement & Perforins. Ed. by Richard W. Compans et al. (Illus.). 192p. 1992. 114.00 (0-387-54653-7) Spr-Verlag.

Current Topics in Microbiology & Immunology, Vol. 180: Pathogenesis of Shigellosis. Ed. by P. J. Sansonetti et al. (Illus.). 160p. 1992. 110.00 (0-387-55058-5) Spr-Verlag.

Current Topics in Microbiology & Immunology, Vol. 183: Neutralization of Animal Viruses. Ed. by Richard W. Compans et al. (Illus.). 160p. 1993. 109.00 (0-387-56030-0) Spr-Verlag.

Current Topics in Mucosal Immunology 1993: Proceedings of the Tokyo International Symposium on Mucosal Immunology, Keidanren Kaikan. Ed. by Masharu Tsuchiya et al. LC 93-49045. (International Congress Ser.: No. 1047). 1994. 185.75 (0-444-81586-4, Excerpta Medica) Elsevier.

Current Topics in Operator Algebras: Satellite Conference of ICM-90, Japan, 16-20 August 1990. Ed. by H. Araki et al. 448p. (C). 1991. text ed. 104.00 (981-02-0651-8) World Scientific Pub.

Current Topics in Organizational Behavior Management. Ed. by Phillip K. Duncan. LC 82-11685. (Journal of Organizational Behavior Management: Vol. 3, No. 3). 111p. 1982. text ed. 39.95 (0-86656-198-6) Haworth Pr.

Current Topics in Pain Research & Therapy: Proceedings of the International Symposium on Pain, Kyoto, Dec. 12-13, 1983. Ed. by T. Yokota & R. Dubner. (International Congress Ser.: No. 613). 324p. 1983. 98.50 (0-444-90310-0, I-347-83, Excerpta Medica) Elsevier.

Current Topics in Photosynthesis. Ed. by J. Amesz et al. 1986. lib. bdg. 120.00 (90-247-3344-8) Kluwer Ac.

Current Topics in Photovoltaics, Vol. 1. Ed. by T. J. Coutts & J. O. Meakin. 1985. text ed. 136.00 (0-12-193860-3) Acad Pr.

Current Topics in Photovoltaics, Vol. 2. Ed. by T. J. Coutts & J. O. Meakin. 208p. 1987. text ed. 124.00 (0-12-153412-X) Acad Pr.

Current Topics in Photovoltaics, Vol. 3. Ed. by T. J. Coutts & J. O. Meakin. 350p. 1988. text ed. 124.00 (0-12-153413-8) Acad Pr.

Current Topics in Photovoltaics, Vol. 4. Ed. by J. Coutts & J. O. Meskin. 191p. 1990. text ed. 94.00 (0-12-153414-6) Acad Pr.

Current Topics in Piping & Pipe Support Design. Ed. by E. Van Stijgeren. (PVP Ser.: Vol. 53). 192p. 34.00 (0-686-34513-4, H00189) ASME.

Current Topics in Plant Biochemistry & Physiology, Vol. 6. Ed. by D. D. Randall et al. (Illus.). 190p. (Orig.). 1987. 12.00 (0-936463-05-8) U MO Plant Bio.

Current Topics in Plant Biochemistry & Physiology, Vol. 7. Ed. by D. D. Randall et al. (Illus.). 258p. (Orig.). 1988. 12.00 (0-685-35120-3) U MO Plant Bio.

Current Topics in Plant Biochemistry & Physiology, Vol. 8. Ed. by D. D. Randall et al. (Illus.). 316p. (Orig.). 1989. 15.00 (0-936463-07-4) U MO Plant Bio.

Current Topics in Plant Biochemistry & Physiology, Vol. 9. Ed. by D. D. Randall et al. (Illus.). (Orig.). 1990. 17.50 (0-936463-08-2) U MO Plant Bio.

Current Topics in Plant Biochemistry & Physiology: Symposium Proceedings, Vol. 5. Ed. by D. D. Randall et al. (Illus.). 216p. (Orig.). 1986. 12.00 (0-936463-04-X) U MO Plant Bio.

Current Topics in Plant Biochemistry & Physiology, Vol. 10: UV-B, Aluminum Stress & Boron. write for info. (0-936463-09-0) U MO Plant Bio.

Current Topics in Polymer Science, Vol. 1: Polymer Chemistry & Polymer Physics. Raphael M. Ottenbrite et al. 343p. (C). 1987. text ed. 119.50 (1-56990-070-1) Hanser-Gardner.

Current Topics in Polymer Science, Vol. 2: Rheology & Polymer Processing - Multiphase Systems. Raphael M. Ottenbrite et al. 376p. (C). 1987. text ed. 119.50 (1-56990-071-X) Hanser-Gardner.

***Current Topics in Primate Vocal Communication: Proceedings of the XIV Congress of the International Primatological Society Held in Strasbourg, France, August 16-21, 1992 & the XV Congress of the International Primatological Society, Held in Kuta-Bali Indonesia, August 3-8, 1994.** Ed. by Elke Zimmerman et al. 280p. 1995. 89.50 (0-306-45064-X) Plenum.

Current Topics in Primatology, Vol. 1: Human Origins. Ed. by Toshisada Nishida et al. 350p. 1992. 72.50 (0-86008-483-3, Pub. by U of Tokyo JA) Col U Pr.

Current Topics in Primatology, Vol. 2: Behavior, Ecology, & Conservation. Ed. by Naosuke Itoigawa et al. 300p. 1992. 57.50 (0-86008-484-1, Pub. by U of Tokyo JA) Col U Pr.

Current Topics in Primatology, Vol. 3: Evolutionary Biology, Reproductive Endocrinology, & Virology. Ed. by Hidemi Ishida & Russell H. Tuttle. 250p. 1992. 57.50 (0-685-54688-8, Pub. by U of Tokyo JA) Col U Pr.

Current Topics in Pulmonary Pharmacology & Toxicology, Vol. 1. Ed. by Mannfred A. Hollinger. 281p. 1986. 59.00 (0-444-01160-9) Elsevier.

Current Topics in Pulmonary Pharmacology & Toxicology, Vol. 2. Ed. by Mannfred A. Hollinger. 190p. 1987. 57.75 (0-444-01175-7) Elsevier.

Current Topics in Pulmonary Pharmacology & Toxicology, Vol. 3. Ed. by Mannfred A. Hollinger. 336p. 1987. 79.00 (0-444-01253-2) Elsevier.

Current Topics in Radiation Research, Vol. 11. Ed. by M. Ebert & A. Howard. 1979. 102.75 (0-444-85183-6, North Holland) Elsevier.

Current Topics in Radiation Research, Vol. 13. Ed. by M. Ebert & A. Howard. 1978. 66.75 (0-444-85164-X, North Holland) Elsevier.

Current Topics in Shock Waves. Ed. by Yong W. Kim. LC 90-55617. (Conference Proceeding Ser.: No. 208). 1000p. 1990. lib. bdg. 105.00 (0-88318-776-0) Am Inst Physics.

Current Topics in Structural Geology. Ed. by Paul L. Hancock & S. H. Treagus. (Journal of Structural Geology Ser.: No. 11). (Illus.). 230p. 1989. 60.00 (0-08-037241-4, Pergamon Pr) Elsevier.

***Current Topics in the Chemistry of Boron.** Ed. by George W. Kabalka. 1994. 110.00 (0-85186-535-6, R6535) CRC Pr.

Current Topics in the Management of Respiratory Diseases, Vol. 1. Ed. by Jerome S. Brody & Gordon L. Snider. LC 81-10264. (Illus.). 192p. reprint ed. pap. 54.80 (0-7837-2559-0, 2042718) Bks Demand.

Current Topics in Vector Research, Vol. 1. Ed. by Kerry F. Harris. 336p. 1983. text ed. 59.95 (0-275-90999-9, C09991, Praeger Pubs) Greenwood.

Current Topics in Vector Research, Vol. 2. Ed. by Kerry F. Harris. 290p. 1984. text ed. 44.95 (0-275-91433-X, C14332, Praeger Pubs) Greenwood.

Current Topics in Vector Research, Vol. 3. Ed. by K. F. Harris. (Illus.). 270p. 1987. 119.00 (0-387-96438-X) Spr-Verlag.

Current Topics in Vector Research, Vol. 4. Ed. by K. F. Harris. (Illus.). 240p. 1987. 109.00 (0-387-96464-9) Spr-Verlag.

Current Topics on Non-Crystalline Solids: Proceedings of the First International Workshop on Non-Crystalline Solids San Feliu De Guixois, Spain May 26-30, 1986. Ed. by M. Baro & N. Clavaguera. 476p. 1987. pap. 40.00 (9971-5-0174-0) World Scientific Pub.

Current Treatment in Dental Practice. Norman S. Levine. (Illus.). 533p. 1986. text ed. 75.50 (0-7216-1198-2) Saunders.

Current Treatment of Ambulatory Asthma. Pref. by Guy A. Settipane. (Illus.). 250p. 1986. text ed. 49.00 (0-936587-01-6) Oceanside Pubns.

Current Treatment of Anorexia Nervosa & Bulimia. Ed. by Pauline S. Powers & R. C. Fernandez. (Biobehavioral Medicine Ser.: Vol. 4). xvi, 348p. 1984. 78.50 (3-8055-3879-0) S Karger.

Current Treatments of Obsessive-Compulsive Disorder. Ed. by Michele A. Pato & Joseph Zohar. LC 90-14497. (Clinical Practice Ser.: No. 18). 270p. 1991. text ed. 30.00 (0-88048-351-2) Am Psychiatric.

***Current Treaty Index.** 14th ed. Ed. by Igor I. Kavass. x, 466p. 1994. pap. 80.00 (0-614-03049-8, 301940) W S Hein.

Current Trends & Issues in Hispanic Linguistics. Kitty Pride. (Publications in Linguistics: No. 80). 136p. 1987. pap. 22.00 (0-88312-012-7); fiche 8.00 (0-88312-419-X) Summer Instit Ling.

Current Trends in AI Planning. C. Backstrom & Sandewall. LC 93-81159. (Frontiers in Artifical Intelligence Ser.: Vol. 20). 316p. 1994. pap. 79.00 (90-5199-153-3, Pub. by IOS Pr NE) IOS Press.

Current Trends in Algebraic Topology. Ed. by Paul Selick et al. LC 82-13789. (Canadian Mathematical Society Conference Proceedings Ser.: Vol. 2). 513p. 1987. reprint ed. Pt. 1, 513p. pap. 42.00 (0-8218-6001-1, CMSAMS-2.1); reprint ed. Pt. 2, 484p. pap. 40.00 (0-8218-6002-X, CMSAMS-2.2) Am Math.

Current Trends in Algebraic Topology, Set. Ed. by Paul Selick et al. LC 82-13789. (Canadian Mathematical Society Conference Proceedings Ser.: Vol. 2). 987p. 1987. reprint ed. pap. 67.00 (0-8218-6003-8, CMSAMS-2) Am Math.

Current Trends in Arithmetical Algebraic Geometry. K. Ribet. LC 87-11506. (CONM Ser.: Vol. 67). 293p. 1990. reprint ed. pap. text ed. 38.00 (0-8218-5074-1, CONM-67) Am Math.

***Current Trends in Biology.** Anne Riggs & Bev Farmer. Ed. by Irena Olejnik. 128p. (C). 1994. 150.00x (0-7478-1580-1, Pub. by S Thornes Pubs UK) St Mut.

Current Trends in Bone Grafting. Peter C. Leung. (Illus.). 130p. 1988. pap. 71.00 (0-387-50139-8) Spr-Verlag.

Current Trends in Comparative Endocrinology. Ed. by B. Lofts & W. N. Holmes. 1318p. (C). 1985. pap. text ed. 300.00 (962-209-039-7, Pub. by Hong Kong U Pr HK) St Mut.

Current Trends in Concrete Fracture Research. Ed. by Zdenek P. Bazant. (C). 1991. lib. bdg. 112.50 (0-7923-1366-6) Kluwer Ac.

Current Trends in Concurrency. Ed. by J. W. De Bakker et al. (Lecture Notes in Computer Science Ser.: Vol. 224). xii, 716p. 1986. pap. 74.00 (0-387-16488-X) Spr-Verlag.

Current Trends in Condensed Matter, Particle Physics & Cosmology. Ed. by J. C. Pati et al. 400p. (C). 1990. text ed. 86.00 (981-02-0114-1); pap. text ed. 43.00 (981-02-0115-X) World Scientific Pub.

***Current Trends in Connectionism.** Ed. by Lars Niklasson & Mikael B. Boden. 392p. 1995. text ed. 69.95 (0-8058-1997-5) L Erlbaum Assocs.

Current Trends in Correctional Education: Theory & Practice. Ed. by Sol Chaneles. LC 83-18542. (Journal of Offender Counseling, Services & Rehabilitation: Vol. 7, Nos. 3-4). 117p. 1983. text ed. 32.95 (0-86656-268-0) Haworth Pr.

Current Trends in Cost of Quality: Linking the Cost of Quality & Continuous Improvement. John H. Atkinson et al. Ed. by Claire Barth. (Bold Step Ser.). (Illus.). 136p. (Orig.). 1991. pap. 34.95 (0-86641-197-6, 91259) Inst Mgmt Account.

Current Trends in Environmental Biology. Ed. by R. R. Mishra. (C). 1990. 18.00 (81-224-0184-8, Pub. by Wiley Eastern II) S Asia.

Current Trends in European Second Language Acquisition Research. Ed. by Hans W. Dechert. 200p. 1989. 89.00 (1-85359-024-X, Pub. by Multilingual Matters UK); pap. 36.00 (1-85359-023-1, Pub. by Multilingual Matters UK) Taylor & Francis.

Current Trends in European Sign Language Research. Ed. by Siegmund Prillwitz & Tomas Vollhaber. (International Studies on Sign Language & the Communication of the Deaf: Vol. 9). 406p. 1993. pap. 37.95 (3-927731-03-X, Pub. by Signum-Verlag GW) Gallaudet Univ Pr.

Current Trends in Event-Related Potential Research. Ed. by R. Johnson, Jr. et al. (Supplements to Electroencephalography & Clinical Neurophysiology Ser.: Vol. 40). 772p. 1988. 243.75 (0-444-80907-4) Elsevier.

Current Trends in Geology, Vol. 11. 1988. 65.00 (0-685-59947-7, Messers Today & Tomorrow) Scholarly Pubns.

Current Trends in Geomathematics. Ed. by Daniel F. Merriam. (Computer Applications in the Earth Sciences Ser.). (Illus.). 334p. 1988. 75.00 (0-306-43087-8, Plenum Pr) Plenum.

Current Trends in Grades & Grading Practices in Undergraduate Higher Education: The Results of the 1992 AACRAO Survey. Herbert J. Riley et al. 76p. (C). 1994. pap. text ed. 18.00 (0-929851-20-X) Am Assn Coll Registrars.

***Current Trends in Hand Surgery: Proceedings of the Sixth Congress of the International Federation of Societies for Surgery of the Hand, Held at Helsinki, 3-7 July 1995.** Sixth Congress of the International Federation of Societies for Surgery of the Hand Staff. Ed. by M. Vastamaki. (International Congress Ser.: Vol. 1083). 680p. 1995. 270.50 (0-444-81914-2, Excerpta Medica) Elsevier.

Current Trends in Hardware Verification & Automated Theorem Proving. Ed. by G. M. Birtwistle & P. A. Subrahmanyam. (Illus.). x, 489p. 1989. 54.00 (0-387-96988-8) Spr-Verlag.

***Current Trends in Hetero Junction Bipolar Devices.** M. F. Chang. (Current Topics in Electronics & System Ser.). 200p. 1995. text ed. 61.00 (981-02-2097-9) World Scientific Pub.

Current Trends in Histocompatability, 2 vols. Ed. by Ralph A. Reisfeld & Soldano Ferrone. Incl. Vol. 1. Immunogenetic & Molecular Profiles. LC 80-18211. 570p. 1981. 110.00 (0-306-40480-X); Vol. 2. Biological & Clinical Concepts. LC 80-18211. 326p. 1981. 85.00 (0-306-40481-8); LC 80-18211. 1981. write for info. (0-318-55317-1, Plenum Pr) Plenum.

Current Trends in Indian Environment. Ed. by Desh Bandhu et al. 240p. 1990. reprint ed. 25.00 (0-685-59948-5, Messers Today & Tomorrow) Scholarly Pubns.

Current Trends in Indian Trade Union Movement. H. P. Khare. (C). 1987. 35.00 (81-85076-31-6, Pub. by Chugh Pubns II) S Asia.

Current Trends in Information Research & Theory. Ed. by Bill Katz & Robin Kinder. LC 87-17724. (Reference Librarian Ser.: No. 18). 305p. 1987. text ed. 49.95 (0-86656-574-4) Haworth Pr.

Current Trends in Integrated Optoelectronics. T. P. Lee. (Current Topics in Electronics & Systems). 200p. 1994. text ed. 61.00 (981-02-1862-1) World Scientific Pub.

An Asterisk (*) at the beginning of an entry indicates that the title is appearing in BIP for the first time.

Current Trends in Knowledge Acquisition. Ed. by B. J. Wielinga et al. (Frontiers in Artificial Intelligence & Applications Ser.: Vol. 8). x, 375p. 1990. pap. 89.00 (*90-5199-036-7*, Pub. by IOS Pr NE) IOS Press.

Current Trends in Language Teaching. S. R. Ganguly. 1987. 12.50 (*0-317-90511-2*, Pub. by Indian Doc Serv II) S Asia.

Current Trends in Life Sciences. Ed. by S. K. Chauhan. (Current Trends in Life Sciences Ser.: Vol. 9). xvii, 392p. 1982. 39.00 (*0-88065-230-6*, Messers Today & Tomorrow) Scholarly Pubns.

Current Trends in Life Sciences, Vol. 7. 1979. 50.00 (*0-685-59949-3*, Messers Today & Tomorrow) Scholarly Pubns.

Current Trends in Life Sciences, Vol. 12. 1985. 79.00 (*0-685-59950-7*, Messers Today & Tomorrow) Scholarly Pubns.

Current Trends in Life Sciences, Vol. 16. 1990. 49.00 (*0-685-59951-5*, Messers Today & Tomorrow) Scholarly Pubns.

Current Trends in Life Sciences, Vol. 17. 1990. 59.00 (*0-685-59952-3*, Messers Today & Tomorrow) Scholarly Pubns.

Current Trends in Linguistics, 14 vols. Incl. Vol. 1. Soviet & East European Linguistics. Ed. by Thomas A. Sebeok. 1963. text ed. 132.35 (*90-279-1242-4*); Vol. 2. Linguistics in East Asia & Southeast Asia. Ed. by Thomas A. Sebeok. 1967. text ed. 203.10 (*90-279-0023-X*); Vol. 3. Theoretical Foundations. Ed. by Charles A. Ferguson et al. 1966. text ed. 116.95 (*90-279-1243-2*); Vol. 4. Ibero-American Caribbean Linguistics. Ed. by Thomas A. Sebeok. 1968. text ed. 144.65 (*90-279-0024-8*); Vol. 5. Linguistics in South Asia. Ed. by Thomas A. Sebeok. 1969. text ed. 178.50 (*90-279-0435-9*); Vol. 6. Linguistics in South West Asia & North Africa. Ed. by Thomas A. Sebeok. 1971. text ed. 175.40 (*90-279-1627-6*); Vol. 8. Linguistics in Oceania, 2 pts. Ed. by Thomas A. Sebeok. 1971. text ed. 269.25 (*90-279-1914-3*); Vol. 9/1, Pt. 1. Linguistics in Western Europe, Pts. 1-2. Ed. by Thomas A. Sebeok. 1972. text ed. 192.35 (*90-279-2337-X*); Vol. 10/1. Linguistics in North America, 2 pts. Ed. by Thomas A. Sebeok. 1973. Set. text ed. 173.85 (*90-279-2518-6*); Vol. 11. Diachronic, Areal & Typological Linguistics. Ed. by Thomas A. Sebeok. text ed. 133.85 (*90-279-2521-6*); Vol. 12/1. Linguistics & Adjacent Arts & Sciences, 4 pts. Ed. by Thomas A. Sebeok. 1974. Pt. 1. text ed. 161.55 (*90-279-3172-0*); Vol. 12/3. Linguistics & Adjacent Arts & Sciences, 4 pts. Ed. by Thomas A. Sebeok. 1974. Pt. 3. text ed. 178.50 (*90-279-3192-5*); write for info. (*0-318-54399-0*) Mouton.

Current Trends in Morphological Techniques. Ed. by John E Johnson, Jr. 272p. 1981. Vol. II, 272p. 134.00 (*0-8493-5826-4*, CRC Reprint); Vol. III, 296p. 134.00 (*0-8493-5828-0*, CRC Reprint) Franklin.

Current Trends in Morphological Techniques, I. Ed. by John E Johnson, Jr. 272p. 1981. 134.00 (*0-8493-5825-6*, QL927, CRC Reprint) Franklin.

***Current Trends in Optics.** Ed. by Chris Dainty. (Lasers & Optics Engineering Ser.). (Illus.). 352p. 1994. text ed. 75.00 (*0-12-200720-4*) Acad Pr.

Current Trends in Organic Synthesis: Proceedings of the Fourth International Conference on Organic Synthesis, Tokyo, Japan, August 22-27, 1982. Ed. by H. Nozaki. LC 82-22445. (IUPAC Symposium Ser.). (Illus.). 442p. 1983. 185.00 (*0-08-029217-8*, Pub. by Pergamon Repr UK) Franklin.

Current Trends in Orthopaedic Surgery. Ed. by C. S. Galasko & J. Noble. LC 88-1308. 272p. 1988. text ed. 85.00 (*0-7190-2535-4*, Pub. by Manchester Univ Pr UK) St Martin.

Current Trends in Plant Virology: Proceedings of Group Discussions on Plant Virology, National Botanical Research Institute, Lucknow. Ed. by B. P. Singh & S. P. Raychaudhuri. xvi, 224p. (C). 1982. 19.00 (*0-88065-220-9*, Pub. by Today & Tomorrows P & P II) Scholarly Pubns.

***Current Trends in Polymer Photochemistry.** Ed. by Norman S. Allen et al. LC 95-14233. 1995. write for info. (*0-13-138785-5*) Routledge Chapman & Hall.

Current Trends in Programming Methodology: Data Structuring, Vol. 4. Ed. by Raymond T. Yeh. (Illus.). 1978. pap. text ed. 48.00 (*0-13-195735-X*) P-H.

Current Trends in Programming Methodology: Software Modeling, Vol. 3. Ed. by K. Chandy & Raymond T. Yeh. (Illus.). 1978. 41.67 (*0-13-195727-9*) P-H.

Current Trends in Protective Packaging of Computers & Electronic Components. Ed. by Robert J. Peache & Denis O'Sullivan. LC 88-3289. (Special Technical Publication Ser.: No. 994). 80p. 1988. pap. text ed. 19.00 (*0-8031-1171-1*, 04-994000-11) ASTM.

Current Trends in PSI Research. Ed. by Betty Shapin & Lisette Coly. LC 85-63348. (International Conference Proceedings Ser.). 282p. 1986. 18.00 (*0-912328-39-8*) Parapsych Foun.

Current Trends in SNePS - Semantic Network Processing System: SNePS Workshop, Buffalo, NY, November 1989 Proceedings. Ed. by Devinder Kumar & Joerg H. Siekmann. (Lecture Notes in Artificial Intelligence Ser.: Vol. 437). vii, 162p. 1990. pap. 27.40 (*0-387-52626-9*) Spr-Verlag.

Current Trends in Surgery, Vol. I. Ed. by J. C. Pal. (C). 1989. 75.00 (*0-89771-368-0*, Current Dist) St Mut.

Current Trends in Surgery, Vol. II. Ed. by J. C. Pal. (C). 1989. 150.00 (*0-89771-369-9*, Current Dist) St Mut.

Current Trends in Textlinguistics. Ed. by Wolfgang U. Dressler. (Research in Text Theory Ser.: Vol. 2). (C). 1978. 65.40 (*3-11-006518-5*) De Gruyter.

Current Trends in the Management of Breast Cancer. Ed. by Ralph R. Baker. LC 76-49094. 175p. reprint ed. pap. 49.90 (*0-317-42247-2*, 2023079) Bks Demand.

Current Trends in the Physics of Materials: Proceedings of the International School of Physics, "Enrico Fermi," Course CVI, 20 June-8 July, 1988. Ed. by G. F. Chiarotti et al. (Enrico Fermi International Summer School of Physics Ser.: Vol. 106). 900p. 1991. 251.50 (*0-444-88333-9*, North Holland) Elsevier.

Current Trends in the Theory of Fields: Tallahassee, 1979. Ed. by J. E. Lannutti & P. K. Williams. (AIP Conference Proceedings Ser.: No. 48). (Illus.). 1978. lib. bdg. 16.25 (*0-88318-147-9*) Am Inst Physics.

Current Trends in Theoretical. Grzegorz Rozenberg & Arto Salomaa. (Series in Computer Science). 630p. 1993. text ed. 109.00 (*981-02-1462-6*) World Scientific Pub.

Current Trends in West Germanic Etymological Lexicography: Proceedings of the Symposium Held in Amsterdam, 12-13 June 1989. Ed. by Rolf H. Bremmer, Jr. & Jan H. Van Den Berg. LC 92-31895. x, 163p. 1993. pap. 45.75 (*90-04-09708-2*) E J Brill.

Current Ultrasonic Doppler Flowmetry in Japan: A Special Issue of the Journal Automedica. Ed. by A. Kitabatake & K. Chihara. 82p. 1989. pap. text ed. 129.00 (*0-677-25950-6*) Gordon & Breach.

Current Urologic Therapy Three. 3rd ed. E. James Seidmon & Philop M. Hanno. LC 94-6845. (Illus.). 608p. 1994. text ed. 94.50 (*0-7216-5033-3*) Saunders.

Current Value Accounting: A Practical Guide for Business. Ed. by Warren Chippindale & Philip L. Defliese. LC 77-21422. 192p. reprint ed. pap. 54.80 (*0-317-26722-1*, 2023522) Bks Demand.

***Current Vascular Surgical Diagnosis & Treatment.** Dean et al. (C). 1995. pap. text ed. 41.95 (*0-8385-1351-4*) Appleton & Lange.

Current Veterinary Practice: Small Animal Practice. Griffin et al. (Illus.). 378p. 1992. 95.00 (*0-8016-3384-2*) Mosby Yr Bk.

Current Veterinary Therapy: Food Animal Practice Two. 2nd ed. Jimmy L. Howard. (Illus.). 1008p. 1986. text ed. 121.00 (*0-7216-1526-0*) Saunders.

Current Veterinary Therapy Nine. Robert W. Kirk. (Illus.). 1346p. 1986. text ed. 99.00 (*0-7216-1500-7*) Saunders.

Current Veterinary Therapy Ten. Robert W. Kirk. 1344p. 1989. text ed. 99.00 (*0-7216-2858-3*) Saunders.

Current Veterinary Therapy 3: Food Animal Practice. 3rd ed. Jimmy L. Howard. (Illus.). 1002p. 1992. text ed. 160.00 (*0-7216-3633-0*) Saunders.

Current Viewpoints on the Use of Soil Nitrate Tests in the South: Proceedings of a Symposium Conducted by the Southern Branch, American Society of Agronomy, February 4, 1992, Lexington Center Heritage Hall, Lexington, KY. Ed. by K. L. Wells et al. LC 92-45592. 1992. write for info. (*0-89118-114-8*) Am Soc Agron.

Current Views on Hypoglycemia & Glucagon: Proceedings. Ed. by Dominico Andreani et al. LC 79-41558. (Serono Symposia Ser.: No. 30). 1980. text ed. 184.00 (*0-12-058680-0*) Acad Pr.

Current Views on Thalassaemia: With Special Reference to Its Mediterranean Presence. Ed. by Stuart Roath & Titus H. Huisman. LC 92-1571. 1992. text ed. 58.00 (*3-7186-5262-5*) Gordon & Breach.

Current, Voltage, Resistance. Johannes G. Lang. (Siemens Programmed Instruction Ser.: 9). 71p. reprint ed. pap. 25.00 (*0-317-27766-9*, 2052086) Bks Demand.

Currents. Carol Stetser. (Illus.). 32p. (Orig.). 1992. pap. 35.00 (*0-917960-10-6*) Padma.

Currents. 2nd ed. Howard J. Smagula. 352p. 1989. pap. text ed. 46.67 (*0-13-195595-0*) P-H.

Currents & Eddies in the English Romantic Generation. Frederick E. Pierce. LC 68-56470. 1972. reprint ed. 26.95 (*0-405-08857-4*) Ayer.

Currents & Mesons. J. J. Sakurai. LC 69-15230. (Chicago Lectures in Physics Ser.). 1969. pap. text ed. 7.00 (*0-226-73383-1*) U Ch Pr.

Currents from the Dancing River: Contemporary Latino Fiction, Nonfiction, & Poetry. Ray Gonzalez. 1994. pap. 15.95 (*0-15-600130-6*) HarBrace.

Currents from the Dancing River: Contemporary Latino Writing. Ed. by Ray Gonzalez. LC 94-4327. 1994. 26.95 (*0-15-123654-2*) HarBrace.

Currents in American Medicine: A Developmental View of Medical Care & Education. Julius B. Richmond. LC 69-12733. (Commonwealth Fund Publications). 150p. 1969. 18.00 (*0-674-18015-1*) HUP.

Currents in Anthropology: Essays in Honor of Sol Tax. Ed. by Robert Hinshaw. 1979. text ed. 161.55 (*90-279-7758-5*) Mouton.

Currents in Astrophysics & Cosmology: Papers in Honor of Maurice M. Shapiro. Ed. by Giovanni G. Fazio & Rein Silberberg. LC 92-40598. (Illus.). 288p. (C). 1993. 69.95 (*0-521-41439-3*) Cambridge U Pr.

***Currents in High-Energy Astrophysics.** Ed. by Maurice M. Shapiro et al. LC 94-46913. (NATO ASI, Series C, Mathematical & Physical Sciences: Vol. 458). 1995. lib. bdg. 150.00 (*0-7923-3354-3*) Kluwer Ac.

Currents in Submarine Canyons & Other Seavalleys. Francis P. Shepard et al. LC 79-53686. (AAPG Studies in Geology: No. 8). (Illus.). 181p. reprint ed. pap. 51.60 (*0-8357-8538-6*, 2034842) Bks Demand.

***Currents of Change.** C. J. Schneider. 380p. 1995. pap. 9.95 (*1-56901-669-0*) NW Pub.

Currents of Lethal Violence: An Integrated Model of Suicide & Homicide. N. Prabha Unnithan et al. LC 93-39934. (SUNY Series in Violence). 230p. 1994. 64.50 (*0-7914-2051-5*); pap. 21.95 (*0-7914-2052-3*) State U NY Pr.

Currents of Malice: Mary Towne Esty & Her Family in Salem Witchcraft. Persis W. McMillen. (Illus.). 650p. 1990. 35.00 (*0-914339-31-1*) P E Randall Pub.

Currents of Radicalism: Popular Radicalism, Organised Labour & Party Politics in Britain, 1850-1914. Ed. by Eugenio F. Biagini & Alastair J. Reid. 350p. (C). 1991. 64.95 (*0-521-39455-4*) Cambridge U Pr.

Currents of Space. Isaac Asimov. 1985. mass mkt. 4.95 (*0-345-33544-9*, Del Rey) Ballantine.

Currents of Space. Isaac Asimov. 1992. mass mkt. 5.99 (*0-553-29341-9*) Bantam.

Currents of Thought in American Social Psychology. Gary Collier et al. (Illus.). 352p. 1991. 39.95 (*0-19-506129-2*) OUP.

Curricula for Diversity in Education. Tony Booth et al. (Learning for All Ser.). 1991. pap. 18.95 (*0-415-07184-4*, A6818) Routledge.

Curricula for the Twenty-First Century: Proceedings of an Interinstitutional Symposium. Ed. by Denise M. Harmening & Margaret J. King. (Illus.). 90p. 1992. 14.95 (*0-943903-01-7*) DH Pub PA.

***Curricula in the Atmospheric, Oceanic & Related Sciences.** 1994. 40.00 (*1-878220-14-4*) Am Meteorological.

Curricular & Instructional Approaches for Persons with Severe Disabilities. Ennio Cipani & Fred Spooner. LC 93-38165. 1993. text ed. write for info. (*0-205-14090-4*) Allyn.

***Curricular Conversations: Themes in Multilingual & Monolingual Classrooms.** Stephen B. Kucer et al. LC 95-14599. 1995. write for info. (*1-57110-016-4*) Stenhse Pubs.

Curricular Decisions in Their Administrative Contexts. P. W. Musgrave. 122p. (C). 1985. 48.00 (*0-7300-0187-3*, Pub. by Deakin Univ AT) St Mut.

Curricular Issues for the Nineteen Nineties. W. J. Morgan. (C). 1989. 50.00 (*1-85041-059-3*, Pub. by Univ Nottingham UK) St Mut.

Curricular Landscapes, Democratic Vistas: Transformative Leadership in Higher Education. William G. Tierney. LC 89-33972. 191p. 1989. text ed. 47.95 (*0-275-93371-7*, C3371, Praeger Pubs) Greenwood.

Curriculum. Franklin Bobbitt. LC 78-165706. (American Education, Ser.). 1979. reprint ed. 30.95 (*0-405-03695-7*) Ayer.

Curriculum: A Comparative Perspective. Brian Holmes & Martin McLean. LC 92-19351. 1992. write for info. (*0-415-08492-X*) Routledge.

Curriculum: A Comprehensive Introduction. 4th ed. John D. McNeil. (C). 1990. text ed. 61.00 (*0-673-52021-8*) HarpCollege.

***Curriculum: A Comprehensive Introduction.** 5th ed. John D. McNeil. LC 95-14586. 1995. write for info. (*0-673-52352-7*) HarpCollege.

Curriculum: A History of the American Undergraduate Course of Study Since 1636. Frederick Rudolph. LC 77-84319. (Higher Education Ser.). 377p. 1977. 36.95 (*0-87589-358-9*) Jossey-Bass.

***Curriculum: A History of the American Undergraduate Course of Study since 1636.** fac. ed. Frederick Rudolph. LC 77-84319. (Carnegie Council Ser.). 380p. 1977. reprint ed. pap. 108.30 (*0-7837-8050-8*, 2047803) Bks Demand.

Curriculum: A History of the American Undergraduate Course of Study Since 1636. Frederick Rudolph. LC 77-84319. (Higher & Adult Education Ser.). 392p. (C). 1993. reprint ed. pap. 24.00 (*1-55542-535-6*) Jossey-Bass.

Curriculum: Alternative Approaches, Ongoing Issues. Colin Marsh & George Willis. LC 94-15871. 400p. (C). 1994. write for info. (*0-02-428113-1*, Merrill Pub Co) Macmillan.

Curriculum: An Introduction to the Field. 2nd ed. Ed. by James Gress & David Purpel. LC 88-60451. 654p. (C). 1988. 38.25 (*0-8211-0617-1*); text ed. write for info. (*0-685-45508-4*) McCutchan.

Curriculum: Design & Development. David Pratt. 503p. (C). 1980. text ed. 37.25 (*0-15-516735-9*) HB Coll Pubs.

Curriculum: Foundations, Principles & Issues. Allan C. Ornstein & Francis P. Hunkins. (Illus.). 448p. (C). 1988. text ed. write for info. (*0-13-195777-5*) P-H.

Curriculum: Perspective, Paradigm, & Possibility. William H. Schubert. xii, 851p. (C). 1986. text ed. write for info. (*0-02-407760-7*) Macmillan.

Curriculum: Principles & Foundations. Robert S. Zais. (C). 1990. pap. text ed. 33.00 (*0-690-00857-0*) HarpCollege.

Curriculum: Problems, Politics, & Possibilities. Ed. by Landon E. Beyer & Michael W. Apple. LC 87-33556. (SUNY Series, Frontiers in Education). 368p. 1988. 64.50 (*0-88706-817-0*); pap. 21.95 (*0-88706-818-9*) State U NY Pr.

Curriculum: Product or Praxis. Shirley J. Grundy. 225p. 1987. pap. 30.00 (*1-85000-205-3*, Falmer Pr) Taylor & Francis.

Curriculum: The Strategic Key to Schooling. Billie G. Blair. 228p. 1992. per. 24.95 (*0-8403-8109-3*) Kendall-Hunt.

Curriculum: The Teacher's Initiative. John McNeil. LC 94-6194. 288p. (C). 1994. pap. write for info. (*0-02-379761-4*, Merrill Pub Co) Macmillan.

Curriculum: Theory & Practice. A. V. Kelly. 286p. (C). 1982. pap. 40.00 (*0-06-318218-1*, Pub. by P Chapman Pub UK) St Mut.

Curriculum - Foundations, Principles, & Issues. 2nd ed. Allan C. Ornstein & Francis P. Hunkins. LC 92-20517. 1993. text ed. write for info. (*0-205-14145-5*) Allyn.

Curriculum Action Research: A Handbook of Methods & Resources for the Reflective Practitioner. James McKernan. LC 91-21321. 288p. 1991. text ed. 49.95 (*0-312-06761-5*) St Martin.

Curriculum Activities for Gifted & Motivated Elementary Students. Arthur Kamiya. 272p. 1987. pap. 19.95 (*0-13-000937-7*, Busn) P-H.

Curriculum Adaptation for Students with Learning & Behavior Problems: Principles & Practices. John J. Hoover. LC 88-81255. 89p. 1988. pap. text ed. 9.00 (*0-940059-04-5*) Hamilton Pubns.

Curriculum Alternatives: Experiments in School Library Media Education. American Library Association Staff. LC 74-12070. 253p. reprint ed. pap. 72.20 (*0-317-26285-8*, 2024261) Bks Demand.

Curriculum & Aims. 2nd ed. Decker Walker & Jonas F. Soltis. (Thinking about Education Ser.). 144p. (C). 1992. pap. text ed. 11.95 (*0-8077-3142-0*) Tchrs Coll.

Curriculum & Assessment Reform. Andy Hargreaves. (Modern Educational Thought Ser.). 176p. 1989. 90.00 (*0-335-09551-8*, Open Univ Pr); pap. 32.00 (*0-335-09550-X*, Open Univ Pr) Taylor & Francis.

Curriculum & Evaluation Standards for School Mathematics. Commission on Standards for School Mathematics of the National Council of Teachers of Mathematics Staff. LC 89-9421. (Illus.). 258p. 1989. pap. 25.00 (*0-87353-273-2*) NCTM.

Curriculum & Instruction: Alternatives in Education. Ed. by Henry A. Giroux et al. LC 80-84142. (C). 1981. 35.50 (*0-8211-0615-5*); text ed. write for info. (*0-685-03198-5*) McCutchan.

Curriculum & Instruction: The Secondary School Physical Education Experience. Wuest et al. (Illus.). 450p. 1990. 29.95 (*0-8016-5729-6*) Mosby Yr Bk.

Curriculum & Instruction after Desegregation. James B. Boyer & Joe L. Boyer. 1975. pap. 5.00 (*0-686-00371-3*) AG Pr.

Curriculum & Instructional Methods for the Elementary & Middle School. 3rd rev. ed. Johanna K. Lemlech. LC 93-14778. (Illus.). 464p. (C). 1994. text ed. write for info. (*0-02-369742-3*) Macmillan.

Curriculum & Methods for the Mentally Retarded. A. U. Iriarte. 1972. pap. text ed. 9.95 (*0-8422-0194-7*) Irvington.

Curriculum & Schooling: A Practitioners Guide. Arthur Shapiro et al. LC 94-16775. xv, 337p. 1995. 29.95 (*0-88280-124-4*) ETC Pubns.

***Curriculum Architecture: Creating a Place of Our Own.** Mary L. Hawkins & M. Dolores Graham. 124p. (C). 1994. pap. text ed. 19.00 (*1-56090-081-4*) Natl Middle Schl.

Curriculum As a Political Problem: Changing Educational Conceptions with Special Reference to Citizenship Education. Thomas Englund. 384p. (Orig.). 1986. pap. text ed. 52.50x (*91-22-00807-1*, Pub. by Almqv & Wiksell SW) Coronet Bks.

***Curriculum As Everything Students Learn in School Module 2: Creating a Classroom Community.** York et al. (A Staff Development Series for General & Special Educators). 64p. 1995. student ed 16.00 (*1-55766-208-8*); teacher ed, spiral bd. 34.00 (*1-55766-207-X*) P H Brookes.

***Curriculum As Everything Students Learn in School Module 3a: Planning for Transitions, 2 Modules, Set.** York et al. (A Staff Development Series for General & Special Educators). 144p. 1995. teacher ed, spiral bd. 79.00 (*0-614-06528-3*, MOD3) P H Brookes.

***Curriculum As Everything Students Learn in School Module 3b: Individualizing Learning Outcomes.** York et al. (A Staff Development Series for General & Special Educators). 128p. 1995. student ed 25.00 (*1-55766-212-6*) P H Brookes.

***Curriculum As Everything Students Learn in School Module 3b: Individualizing Learning Outcomes, 2 Modules, Set.** York et al. (A Staff Development Series for General & Special Educators). 272p. 1995. teacher ed, spiral bd. 79.00 (*0-614-06529-1*, MOD3) P H Brookes.

***Curriculum As Everything Sutdents Learn in School Module 3a: Planning for Transitions.** York et al. (A Staff Development Series for General & Special Educators). 64p. 1995. student ed 16.00 (*1-55766-210-X*) P H Brookes.

Curriculum As Social Psychoanalysis: The Significance of Place. Ed. by Joe L. Kincheloe & William F. Pinar. LC 90-31584. (SUNY Series, Teacher Empowerment & School Reform). 239p. (C). 1991. 64.50 (*0-7914-0477-3*); pap. 21.95 (*0-7914-0478-1*) State U NY Pr.

Curriculum Auditing. Fenwick W. English. LC 88-50463. 376p. 1988. 39.00 (*0-87762-592-1*) Technomic.

***Curriculum Based Assessment: A Primer.** 2nd ed. Charles H. Hargis. LC 94-36230. 190p. (C). 1995. pap. 31.95 (*0-398-05942-X*) C C Thomas.

Curriculum-Based Assessment: Testing What Is Taught. John Salvia & Charles C. Hughes. (Illus.). 422p. (C). 1989. pap. write for info. (*0-02-405371-6*) Macmillan.

***Curriculum-Based Assessment & Programming.** 3rd ed. Joyce S. Choate et al. LC 94-28845. 1994. text ed. write for info. (*0-205-16174-X*) Allyn.

Curriculum-Based Assessment in Special Education. Margaret E. King-Sears. LC 93-43364. (Illus.). 256p. (Orig.). (C). 1994. pap. text ed. 29.95 (*1-56593-099-1*, 0402) Singular Publishing.

Curriculum-Based Education: Teaching & Decision Making. 2nd ed. Kenneth W. Howell et al. LC 92-43402. 1993. pap. 43.95 (*0-534-16428-5*) Brooks-Cole.

Curriculum-Based Measurement: Assessing Special Children. Ed. by Mark R. Shinn. LC 88-24599. (Guilford School Practitioner Ser.). 246p. 1989. lib. bdg. 45.00 (*0-89862-352-9*); pap. text ed. 19.95 (*0-89862-231-X*) Guilford Pr.

Curriculum-Based Vocational Assessment: A Guide for Addressing Youth with Special Needs. Robert A. Stodden et al. 358p. (Orig.). (C). 1987. pap. text ed. 32.00 (*0-943693-01-2*, 1519) TRI Pubns.

Curriculum Building for Adult Learning. John R. Verduin, Jr. LC 79-23111. 187p. 1980. 17.95 (*0-8093-0960-2*) S Ill U Pr.

Curriculum Building in Nursing: A Process. 3rd ed. Em O. Bevis. 304p. 1989. 29.95 (*0-88737-439-5*) Natl League Nurse.

C

An Asterisk (*) at the beginning of an entry indicates that the title is appearing in BIP for the first time.

1757

Curriculum Challenge: Access to the National Curriculum for Pupils with Learning Difficulties. Ed. by Rob Ashdown et al. 224p. 1991. 80.00 (*1-85000-880-9*, Falmer Pr); pap. 31.00 (*1-85000-881-7*, Falmer Pr) Taylor & Francis.

Curriculum Change & Physical Education: Towards a Micro Political Understanding. Andrew C. Sparkes. 132p. (C). 1990. pap. 72.00 (*0-7300-0708-1*, ECT458, Pub. by Deakin Univ AT) St Mut.

Curriculum Change in the Primary School since 1945: Dissemination of the Progressive Ideal. Peter Cunningham. Orig. Title: Tradition & Innovation: Progressivism in Primary Education since 1945'. 255p. 1988. 65.00 (*1-85000-194-4*, Falmer Pr); pap. 33.00 (*1-85000-195-2*, Falmer Pr) Taylor & Francis.

Curriculum, Community, Commitment: Views on the American Jewish Day School in Memory of Bennett I. Solomon. Ed. by Daniel J. Margolis & Elliot S. Schoenberg. LC 93-2812. 1993. 24.95 (*0-87441-545-4*) Behrman.

***Curriculum Compacting: The Complete Guide to Modifying the Regular Curriculum for High Ability Students.** Sally M. Reis et al. 1992. pap. 24.95 (*0-936386-63-0*) Creative Learning.

Curriculum Concentration in Gerontology for Graduate Social Work Education. Ed. by Robert L. Schneider et al. 1984. 5.00 (*0-685-21292-0*, 84-400-13) Coun Soc Wk Ed.

Curriculum Considerations in Inclusive Classrooms: Facilitating Learning for All Students. Ed. by Susan Stainback & William Stainback. 304p. (Orig.). (C). 1991. pap. text ed. 25.00 (*1-55766-078-6*, 0786) P H Brookes.

Curriculum Construction. W. W. Charters. LC 74-165713. (American Education, Ser, No. 2). 1979. reprint ed. 33.95 (*0-405-03702-3*) Ayer.

Curriculum Construction for Youth Development. R. M. Kalra & R. R. Singh. 99p. 1987. text ed. 17.95 (*81-207-0674-9*, Pub. by Sterling Pubs II) Market St Pr.

***Curriculum Content for Students with Moderate & Severe Disabilities in Inclusive Settings.** Diane L. Ryndak & Sandra Alper. LC 95-6135. 1995. write for info. (*0-205-14667-8*) Allyn.

Curriculum Continuity in English & the National Curriculum: Working Together at Transition. Daniel C. Tabor. 260p. 1991. 65.00 (*1-85000-934-1*, Falmer Pr); pap. 31.00 (*1-85000-930-9*, Falmer Pr) Taylor & Francis.

Curriculum Decision Making for Students with Severe Handicaps: Policy & Practice. Dianne L. Ferguson. (Special Education Ser.). 192p. 1987. text ed. 31.00 (*0-8077-2862-4*); pap. text ed. 17.95 (*0-8077-2861-6*) Tchrs Coll.

Curriculum Design Part 1: The Trainers Guide, Pt. 1. Sullivan. 75p. 1990. 31.95 (*0-8342-0158-5*, 20158) Aspen Pub.

Curriculum Design & Development for Graduate Social Work Education. Patricia L. Ewalt. 1983. 8.75 (*0-87293-007-6*, 83-32016) Coun Soc Wk Ed.

Curriculum Design & Innovation. Deakin University Press Staff. 168p. (C). 1985. 44.00 (*0-7300-0311-6*, Pub. by Deakin Univ AT) St Mut.

Curriculum Design for Parenthood Education. California Department of Education Staff. 54p. 1982. pap. 4.00 (*0-8011-0399-1*) Calif Education.

Curriculum Design for Severely & Profoundly Handicapped. Paul H. Wehman. LC 78-23704. 256p. 1979. 37.95 (*0-87705-365-0*) Human Sci Pr.

Curriculum Design in a Changing Society. Ed. by Richard W. Burns & Gary D. Brooks. LC 75-122811. 366p. 1970. 33.95 (*0-87778-003-X*) Educ Tech Pubns.

Curriculum Design Manual for Theological Education. LeRoy Ford. (C). 1991. 29.99 (*0-8054-6042-X*) Broadman.

Curriculum Development: A Guide to Practice. 4th ed. Jon Wiles, Jr. & Joseph Bondi. LC 92-11461. 400p. (C). 1992. write for info. (*0-02-427631-6*, Merrill Pub Co) Macmillan.

Curriculum Development: A Reflection of Programmatic Trends. S. Audean Allman et al. (Illus.). 231p. 1980. pap. text ed. 16.95x (*0-89641-049-8*) American Pr.

Curriculum Development: Problems, Processes, & Progress. rev. ed. Glenys G. Unruh & Adolph Unruh. LC 83-62032. 1984. 32.00 (*0-8211-2003-4*); text ed. 28.50 (*0-685-08705-0*) McCutchan.

Curriculum Development: Theory into Practice. 2nd ed. Daniel Tanner & Laurel N. Tanner. (Illus.). 800p. (C). 1980. text ed. write for info. (*0-02-418960-X*) Macmillan.

Curriculum Development: Theory into Practice. 3rd ed. Daniel Tanner & Laurel Tanner. LC 94-18285. 800p. (C). 1994. write for info. (*0-02-418931-6*) Macmillan.

***Curriculum Development & Alignment.** National School Services Staff. (C). Date not set. teacher ed 95.00 (*0-932957-82-X*) Natl School.

***Curriculum Development & Alignment: Guidebook.** National School Services Staff. (C). Date not set. 25.00 (*0-932957-95-1*) Natl School.

Curriculum Development & Evaluation: A Design for Improvement. Jerry Bellon & Janet R. Handler. 96p. 1982. per. 23.95 (*0-8403-2720-X*) Kendall-Hunt.

***Curriculum Development for Education Reform.** Henson. (C). 1995. text ed. 40.50 (*0-673-99222-5*) HarpCollege.

Curriculum Development for the Gifted. C. June Maker. LC 81-14985. (Illus.). 392p. 1982. 38.00 (*0-89079-130-9*, 2061) PRO-ED.

Curriculum Development in East Asia. Ed. by Colin J. Marsh & Paul Morris. 250p. 1991. 65.00 (*1-85000-685-7*, Falmer Pr); pap. 29.00 (*1-85000-686-5*, Falmer Pr) Taylor & Francis.

Curriculum Development in Education for Business, 1977. (Yearbook Ser.). 248p. 5.00 (*0-933964-14-5*) Natl Busn Ed Assoc.

Curriculum Development in Further Education. 3rd ed. FESC. 1986. 75.00 (*0-9502574-4-3*) St Mut.

***Curriculum Development in the Postmodern Era.** Patrick Slattery. LC 94-33596. (Critical Education Practice Ser.). 328p. 1995. 46.00 (*0-8153-1509-0*, SS929); pap. 18.95 (*0-8153-1926-6*, SS929) Garland.

Curriculum Development in Vocational & Technical Education. 3rd ed. Curtis R. Finch & John R. Crunkilton. 336p. 1989. boxed 40.95 (*0-205-11689-2*, H1689-2) Allyn.

Curriculum Development in Vocational & Technical Education: Planning, Content, & Implementation. 4th ed. Curtis R. Finch & John R. Crunkilton. LC 92-25888. 352p. 1992. text ed. 55.67 (*0-205-14616-3*) Allyn.

Curriculum Differentiation: Interpretive Studies in U. S. Secondary Schools. Ed. by Reba Page & Linda Valli. LC 90-31585. (SUNY Series, Frontiers in Education). 261p. (C). 1990. 64.50 (*0-7914-0469-2*); pap. 21.95 (*0-7914-0470-6*) State U NY Pr.

Curriculum Disclosure As Postmodernist Critical Practice. Henry R. Giroux. 151p. (C). 1990. pap. 50.00x (*0-7300-0734-0*, ESC802, Pub. by Deakin Univ AT) St Mut.

Curriculum Evaluation. Ralph G. Straton. 86p. (C). 1985. 38.00 (*0-7300-0312-4*, Pub. by Deakin Univ AT) St Mut.

Curriculum Exposed. John Mathews. 144p. (Orig.). 1990. pap. 26.95 (*0-8464-1486-4*) Beekman Pubs.

Curriculum for a New Millennium. Wilma S. Longstreet & Harold G. Shane. LC 92-31356. 1992. text ed. 57.00 (*0-205-13966-3*) Allyn.

Curriculum for American Students: James Madison Elementary School. William J. Bennett. 61p. (Orig.). (C). 1993. pap. text ed. 30.00 (*0-7881-0020-3*) Diane Pub.

Curriculum for Better Schools: The Great Ideological Debate. Michael Schiro. LC 77-17794. (Illus.). 308p. 1978. 34.95 (*0-87778-100-1*) Educ Tech Pubns.

Curriculum for Citizenship: A Total School Approach to Citizenship Education. Arnold R. Meier et al. LC 52-13495. 425p. reprint ed. pap. 121.20 (*0-7837-3673-8*, 2043547) Bks Demand.

Curriculum for Early Childhood Education. California College for Health Sciences Staff. 142p. (C). 1992. ring bd. Not Set by Publisher (*0-933195-05-2*) Allied Hlth Pubns.

Curriculum for English, Units 82-84: Student Manual: The Hero. Nebraska Curriculum Development Center Staff. 197p. reprint ed. pap. 56.20 (*0-8357-3819-1*, 2052332) Bks Demand.

Curriculum for Multiply Handicapped Deaf Students. Doris Naiman. 196p. (C). 1982. pap. 4.95 (*0-913072-47-8*) Natl Assn Deaf.

Curriculum for Negotiation & Conflict Management: Instructor's Manual. Elaine M. Landry et al. 524p. (C). 1991. 35.00 (*1-880711-01-X*) Prog Negot HLS.

Curriculum for Special Needs. Wilfred K. Brennan. 192p. 1984. 60.00 (*0-335-10575-0*, Open Univ Pr); pap. 27.00 (*0-335-10421-5*, Open Univ Pr) Taylor & Francis.

Curriculum for Teaching Optacon Music Reading. Sandra Levinson & Kenneth Bruscia. (Illus.). 140p. (Orig.). 1984. teacher ed 30.00 (*0-9614080-7-3*) Tembrook Pr.

Curriculum for the Senior Secondary Years. Terri Seddon & Christine Deer. (C). 1990. 75.00 (*0-86431-095-1*, Pub. by Aust Council Educ Res AT) St Mut.

Curriculum for Tomorrow's Schools. Lois Weis et al. 108p. (Orig.). 1990. pap. 8.50 (*0-937033-18-9*) SUNY GSE Pubns.

Curriculum for Training Protective Services Staff. 352p. 15.00 (*0-318-16351-9*, B7) Regional Inst Social Welfare.

Curriculum for Utopia: Social Reconstructionism & Critical Pedagogy in the Postmodern Era. William B. Stanley. LC 91-15152. (SUNY Series, Teacher Empowerment & School Reform). 266p. 1992. 59.50 (*0-7914-0971-6*); pap. 19.95 (*0-7914-0972-4*) State U NY Pr.

Curriculum from A to Z. Linda A. Good. (Teacher Aid Ser.). 185p. 1984. spiral bd. 17.95 (*0-513-01775-5*) Denison.

Curriculum Gone Astray: When Push Came to Shove. Carol M. Hoffman. LC 86-51065. 224p. 1987. pap. 19.50 (*0-87762-489-5*) Technomic.

Curriculum Guide: Hearing-Impaired Children, Birth to Three Years, & Their Parents. Ed. by Winifred H. Northcott. LC 76-56634. 1977. pap. text ed. 14.95 (*0-88200-077-2*, D1998) Alexander Graham.

Curriculum Guide for Nuclear Medicine Technologists. 2nd ed. Ed. by Wanda M. Mundy & Gregory Passmore. 200p. 1993. 19.95 (*0-932004-42-3*) Soc Nuclear Med.

Curriculum Guide for Plastics Education. Plastics Education Foundation Staff. LC 77-4080. 1977. pap. write for info. (*0-672-97113-5*) Macmillan.

***Curriculum Guide for Public Safety & Emergency Response Workers: Prevention of Transmission of HIV & Hepatitis B Virus.** 1995. lib. bdg. 250.95 (*0-8490-7527-0*) Gordon Pr.

Curriculum Guide for Public-Safety & Emergency-Response Workers: Prevention of Transmission of Human Immunodeficiency Virus & Hepatitis B Virus. (Illus.). 185p. (Orig.). (C). 1994. pap. text ed. 60.00 (*0-7881-0322-9*) Diane Pub.

Curriculum Guide for the Instruction of Oral Interpreting. Anna Witter-Merithew. Ed. by Linda A. Siple. 260p. (C). 1985. pap. text ed. 15.95 (*0-88200-159-0*) Alexander Graham.

Curriculum Guide on Argentina. Ed. & Intro. by Daniel J. Mugan. (Curriculum Guides on Latin America Ser.: No. 4). (Illus.). 225p. 1986. teacher ed 14.50 (*0-938305-03-4*) Assn Tchrs Latin Amer.

Curriculum Guide on Brazil. Ed. & Intro. by Daniel J. Mugan. (Curriculum Guides on Latin America Ser.: No. 3). (Illus.). 230p. 1986. teacher ed 14.50 (*0-938305-02-6*) Assn Tchrs Latin Amer.

Curriculum Guide on Chile. Ed. & Intro. by Daniel J. Mugan. (Curriculum Guides on Latin America Ser.: No. 1). (Illus.). 195p. 1981. reprint ed. teacher ed 12.95 (*0-317-46209-1*) Assn Tchrs Latin Amer.

Curriculum Guide on Ecuador. Ed. & Intro. by Daniel J. Mugan. (Curriculum Guides on Latin America Ser.: No. 2). (Illus.). 350p. 1984. reprint ed. teacher ed 14.95 (*0-938305-01-8*) Assn Tchrs Latin Amer.

Curriculum Guide to Venezuela, No. 5. Ed. by Daniel J. Mugan. 185p. (Orig.). 1989. teacher ed 15.95 (*0-938305-04-2*) Assn Tchrs Latin Amer.

Curriculum Guidelines for Multiethnic Education. 49p. 2.50 (*0-88464-058-2*) ADL.

***Curriculum Handbook for Parents & Teachers: What We Ought to Find Happening in the Public School Classrooms of America.** Betty O. Carpenter. (Illus.). 198p. 1991. pap. 19.95 (*0-398-06046-0*) C C Thomas.

Curriculum Handbook for Parents & Teachers: What We Ought to Find Happening in the Public School Classrooms of America. Betty O. Carpenter. (Illus.). 198p. (C). 1991. text ed. 34.95x (*0-398-05719-2*) C C Thomas.

Curriculum History. David Hamilton. 103p. (C). 1990. pap. 44.00x (*0-7300-0737-5*, ECS802, Pub. by Deakin Univ AT) St Mut.

Curriculum Improvement: Decision Making & Process. 7th rev. ed. Ronald C. Doll. 550p. 1989. boxed 45.00 (*0-205-11851-8*, H1851-8) Allyn.

Curriculum Improvement: Decision Making & Process. 8th ed. Ronald C. Doll. 531p. (C). 1991. text ed. 49.00 (*0-205-13171-9*) Allyn.

***Curriculum Improvement: Decision Making & Process.** 9th ed. Ronald C. Doll. LC 94-48644. 1995. text ed. 40.50 (*0-205-16457-9*) Allyn.

Curriculum in Context. Catherine Cornbleth. 225p. 1990. 65.00 (*1-85000-452-8*, Falmer Pr); pap. 29.00 (*1-85000-453-6*, Falmer Pr) Taylor & Francis.

***Curriculum in Hong Kong: Development, Issues & Policies.** Paul Morris. 160p. 1995. pap. 26.50 (*962-209-370-1*, Pub. by Hong Kong Univ Pr HK) Coronet Bks.

Curriculum in Nursing Education. Ed. by Peta Allan & Moya Jolley. 208p. (C). 1987. 25.00 (*0-7099-1462-8*, Pub. by Croom Helm UK) Routledge Chapman & Hall.

Curriculum in Physical Education. 4th ed. Carl E. Willgoose. 300p. (C). 1983. text ed. write for info. (*0-13-196072-5*) P-H.

Curriculum in the Catholic School. Brother Robert J. Kealey. 61p. 1986. 6.60 (*0-318-20568-8*) Natl Cath Educ.

Curriculum in the Early Years. Margaret Heritage. Ed. by Jonathan Solity. (Introduction to Education Ser.). 144p. 1994. text ed. 55.00 (*0-304-32405-1*); pap. text ed. 18.95 (*0-304-32410-8*) Cassell.

Curriculum in the Making: Teacher Choice & the Classroom Experience. Rebecca K. Hawthorne. 192p. (C). 1992. text ed. 38.00 (*0-8077-3151-X*); pap. text ed. 17.95 (*0-8077-3150-1*) Tchrs Coll.

Curriculum Initiative: An Agenda & Strategy for Library Media Programs. Michael Eisenberg & Robert Berkowitz. Ed. by Charles McClure & Peter Hernon. LC 88-1598. (Information Management, Policies & Services Ser.: Vol. 2). 200p. 1988. text ed. 35.00 (*0-89391-486-X*) Ablex Pub.

Curriculum Innovations for 2000 A.D. Ed. by N. Venkataiah. (Illus.). x, 160p. 1993. 16.00 (*81-7024-551-6*, Pub. by Ashish Pub Hse II) Nataraj Bks.

Curriculum Leadership. Allan A. Glatthorn. (C). 1987. text ed. 49.00 (*0-673-18267-3*) HarpCollege.

Curriculum Leadership: Case Studies for Program Practitioners. David S. Martin et al. 89p. (Orig.). 1989. pap. 12.95 (*0-87120-155-0*, 611-89013) Assn Supervision.

Curriculum Leadership & Development Handbook: Effective Techniques for School Administrators. Leo H. Bradley. 1985. text ed. 29.95 (*0-13-196056-3*, Parker Publishing Co) P-H.

Curriculum-Making: Past & Present. Harold Rugg et al. LC 71-89228. (American Education: Its Men, Institutions & Ideas, Ser. 1). 1974. reprint ed. 24.95 (*0-405-01464-3*) Ayer.

***Curriculum Management Audit: Improving School Quality.** Ed. by Fenwick W. English et al. LC 94-60853. 310p. 1994. text ed. 42.50 (*1-56676-146-8*) Technomic.

***Curriculum Management for Schools, Colleges, Business.** Fenwick W. English. 1987. pap. 34.95 (*0-398-06109-2*) C C Thomas.

Curriculum Management for Schools, Colleges, Business. Fenwick W. English. (Illus.). 322p. 1987. 56.95 (*0-398-05335-9*) C C Thomas.

Curriculum Materials Center Collection Development Policy. 2nd ed. Beth G. Anderson et al. 46p. 1993. 16.95 (*0-8389-7707-3*); 14.95 (*0-685-72680-0*) Assn Coll & Res Libs.

Curriculum Materials Digest. 304p. 1986. 8.00 (*0-685-16518-3*, 611-86020) Assn Supervision.

Curriculum Models & Early Childhood Education: Appraising the Relationship. Stacie G. Goffin. 320p. (C). 1994. pap. write for info. (*0-675-21154-9*) Macmillan.

Curriculum Models in Adult Education. Michael Langenbach. 240p. 1993. 24.00 (*0-89464-784-9*) Krieger.

Curriculum or Craftmanship: Elementary School Teacher in a Bureaucratic System. Harry L. Gracey. LC 71-188235. 1972. lib. bdg. 17.00 (*0-226-30595-3*) U Ch Pr.

Curriculum Package for Essentials of Fire Fighting. 3rd ed. Susan S. Walker. Ed. by Lynne C. Murnane. (Illus.). 2516p. 1993. 33.00 (*0-87939-101-4*); teacher ed 150.00 (*0-87939-104-9*); student ed 55.00 (*0-87939-105-7*); trans. 1,200.00 (*0-87939-106-5*) IFSTA.

Curriculum Package for Essentials of Fire Fighting, Curriculum pkg. 3rd ed. Susan S. Walker. Ed. by Lynne C. Murnane. (Illus.). 2516p. 1993. 1,250.00 (*0-87939-103-0*) IFSTA.

Curriculum Planning: A Handbook for Professionals. David Pratt. 480p. 1993. write for info. (*0-15-501098-0*) HB Coll Pubs.

Curriculum Planning: A New Approach. 5th ed. Glen Hass. 1986. pap. text ed. 45.00 (*0-205-10457-6*, H04575) Allyn.

Curriculum Planning: A New Approach. 6th ed. Ed. by Forrest W. Parkay. LC 92-26341. 1992. pap. text ed. write for info. (*0-205-14620-1*) Allyn.

Curriculum Planning: A Ten Step Process. Sharon K. Zenger & Weldon Zenger. LC 82-60521. 150p. (Orig.). 1983. spiral bd. 15.95 (*0-88247-675-0*) R & E Pubs.

Curriculum Planning: Outcome-Based Accountability. Weldon Zenger & Sharon Zenger. LC 91-50688. 210p. (C). 1992. pap. text ed. 29.95 (*0-88247-954-7*) R & E Pubs.

Curriculum Planning: The Dynamics of Theory & Practice. Dale L. Brubaker. (C). 1982. text ed. 26.50 (*0-673-16031-9*) HarpCollege.

Curriculum Planning & Teaching Using the Library Media Center. Mary K. Urbanik. LC 89-31683. 172p. 1989. 22.50 (*0-8108-2148-6*) Scarecrow.

Curriculum Planning & the Primary School. Keith Morrison & Ken Ridley. 208p. (C). 1988. 45.00 (*1-85396-009-8*, Pub. by P Chapman Pub UK) St Mut.

Curriculum Planning for Better Teaching & Learning. 4th ed. J. Galen Saylor et al. LC 80-20764. 416p. (C). 1981. text ed. 42.75 (*0-03-048761-7*) HB Coll Pubs.

Curriculum Planning for Young Children. Ed. by Janet F. Brown. LC 82-61723. 268p. 1982. pap. text ed. 6.50 (*0-912674-83-0*, NAEYC #113) Natl Assn Child Ed.

***Curriculum Planning on the Local School or District Level: A Guide for Committees or Individuals.** Paul Westmeyer. (Illus.). 196p. 1981. pap. 24.95 (*0-614-02455-2*) C C Thomas.

Curriculum Planning on the Local School or District Level: A Guide for Committees or Individuals. Paul Westmeyer. (Illus.). 196p. (C). 1981. 38.95 (*0-398-04496-1*) C C Thomas.

Curriculum Policy. Ed. by Rob Moore & Jenny Ozga. 160p. 1990. text ed. 33.00 (*0-08-041022-7*, Pergamon Pr); pap. text ed. 16.25 (*0-08-040818-4*, Pergamon Pr) Elsevier.

Curriculum Process in Physical Education. Ann E. Jewett & Linda L. Bain. 416p. (C). 1985. write for info. (*0-697-00132-6*) Brown & Benchmark.

Curriculum Process in Physical Education. 2nd ed. Ann E. Jewett et al. 416p. (C). 1995. pap. text ed. write for info. (*0-697-16825-5*) Brown & Benchmark.

Curriculum Professors' Specialized Knowledge. Carmen L. Rosales-Dordelly & Edmund C. Short. (Illus.). 124p. (Orig.). 1985. pap. text ed. 13.50 (*0-8191-4639-0*) U Pr of Amer.

Curriculum Progress 5-16: School Subject & the National Curriculum. Ed. by Patrick Wiegand & Michael Rayner. 250p. 1989. 70.00 (*1-85000-532-X*, Falmer Pr); pap. 35.00 (*1-85000-533-8*, Falmer Pr) Taylor & Francis.

Curriculum Provision in the Small Primary School. Ed. by Maurice Galton et al. 240p. 1990. 42.50 (*0-415-03628-3*, A4198) Routledge.

***Curriculum Redefined: Schooling for the Twenty-First Century.** 232p. (Orig.). 1994. pap. 30.00 (*92-64-14183-9*) OECD.

Curriculum Reform: An Overview of Trends. Malcolm Skilbeck. Ed. by OECD Staff. 96p. (Orig.). 1990. pap. 17.00 (*92-64-13311-9*) OECD.

Curriculum Reform: Assessment in Question. OECD Staff. 148p. (Orig.). (ENG & FRE.). 1993. pap. 19.00 (*92-64-03863-9*) OECD.

Curriculum Reform & At-Risk Youth. Thomas B. Corcoran. 17p. 1985. pap. 5.95 (*1-56602-007-7*) Research Better.

Curriculum Reform in the Elementary School: Creating Your Own Agenda. M. Frances Klein. 208p. (C). 1989. pap. text ed. 18.95 (*0-8077-2939-6*) Tchrs Coll.

Curriculum Renewal. Allan A. Glatthorn. LC 86-72998. 126p. 1987. pap. text ed. 8.75 (*0-87120-143-7*, 611-86060) Assn Supervision.

Curriculum Research in Europe. Ed. by U. Hameijer et al. 240p. 1986. 27.50 (*90-265-0713-5*, Pub. by Swets Pub Serv NE) Taylor & Francis.

***Curriculum Resource Guide on Drug & Alcohol Abuse.** 1995. lib. bdg. 251.95 (*0-8490-6789-8*) Gordon Pr.

Curriculum Resources for the Alaskan Environment. Judy Diamondstone & Ray Barnhardt. 130p. (Orig.). (C). 1980. pap. 5.00 (*1-877962-12-0*) Univ AK Ctr CCS.

Curriculum Resources for the Alaskan Environment: Review of Secondary Level ANCSA Educational Materials. Richard Gumm. 34p. 1983. 3.00 (*0-685-52896-0*) Univ AK Ctr CCS.

Curriculum Resources for the Alaskan Environment: Energy Options: A Curriculum Guide University of Alaska Fairbanks. 47p. 1982. 3.00 (*0-685-52895-2*) Univ AK Ctr CCS.

Curriculum Resources in Chicano Studies: Undergraduate & Graduate. Ed. by Gary D. Keller et al. LC 89-62205. 346p. 1989. pap. 25.00 (*0-927534-00-2*) Biling Rev-Pr.

Curriculum Revisited: An Update of Curriculum Design. Ed. by Elisabeth Pennington. 48p. 1986. 14.95 (*0-88737-338-0*, 15-2165) Natl League Nurse.

Curriculum Revolution: Community Building & Activism. 160p. 1991. 25.95 (*0-88737-517-0*) Natl League Nurse.

Curriculum Revolution: Mandate for Change. 256p. 1988. pap. 29.95 (*0-88737-404-2*, 15-224) Natl League Nurse.

An Asterisk (*) at the beginning of an entry indicates that the title is appearing in BIP for the first time.

C

Curso de Obligaciones y Contratos: Doctrina General de los Contratos, Vol. II. 3rd enl. ed. Alberto Blanco. LC 77-4251. (SPA.). 1979. 12.00 (*0-8477-3008-5*) U of PR Pr.

Curso de Preguntas Sobre la Teoria Atomica. Joaquin Garcia de La Noceda. LC 80-26696. 242p. 1982. pap. 6.50 (*0-8477-2326-7*) U of PR Pr.

Curso Individualizado de Matematicas Basicas: Aritmetica, Algebra Elemental & Algebra Intermedia. Gladys Aponte et al. LC 84-20838. 356p. (SPA.). (C). 1984. pap. text ed. 15.00 (*0-8477-2638-X*) U of PR Pr.

Cursor Mundi, Pt. VII: Essays on the Manuscripts, Their Dialects, Etc. H. Hupe. (EETS, OS Ser.: Vol. 101). 1972. reprint ed. pap. 34.00 (*0-8115-3367-0*) Periodicals Srv.

Cursory Criticism on the Edition of Shakespeare: Published by Edmond Malone Together with a Letter to the Rev. Richard Farmer, D.D. Relative to the Edition of Shakespeare, Published in 1790. Joseph Ritson. 156p. 1970. reprint ed. 25.00 (*0-7146-2516-7*, Pub. by F Cass Pubs UK) Intl Spec Bk.

Cursory Criticisms on the Edition of Shakespeare. Joseph Ritson. Bd. with Letter to the Rev. Richard Farmer, D.D. Master of Emanuel College, Cambridge. LC 76-174322. LC 76-174322. reprint ed. 34.50 (*0-404-05338-6*) AMS Pr.

Cursory Criticisms on the Edition of Shakespeare Published by Edmond Malone, & a Letter to the Rev. Richard Farmer. Joseph Ritson & Edmond Malone. LC 70-96366. (Eighteenth Century Shakespeare Ser.: No. 20). 1970. reprint ed. 29.50 (*0-678-05132-1*) Kelley.

Cursory Memoranda on Shakespeare's Tragedy of Macbeth. James O. Halliwell-Phillipps. LC 70-144629. reprint ed. 20.00 (*0-404-03054-8*) AMS Pr.

Cursory Observations on the Poems Attributed to Thomas Rowley: The Second Edition, Revised & Augmented. 2nd rev. ed. Edmond Malone. LC 92-2372. (Augustan Reprints Ser.: No. 123 (1966)). reprint ed. 12.00 (*0-404-70123-X*, PR3344) AMS Pr.

Curt Prufer: German Diplomat from the Kaiser to Hitler. Donald M. McKale. LC 87-4114. 290p. 1987. 25.00 (*0-87338-345-1*) Kent St U Pr.

Curtailing Usage of De-Icing Agents in Winter Maintenance. OECD Staff. (Road Transport Research Ser.). 124p. (Orig.). 1989. pap. 24.00 (*92-64-13280-5*) OECD.

C

Curtain. Agatha Christie. 1976. 20.95 (*0-88411-386-8*, Aeonian Pr) Amereon Ltd.

*__Curtain.__ Agatha Christie. LC 94-22681. 1995. write for info. (*0-399-14016-6*) Putnam Pub Group.

Curtain. Michael Korda. 1992. mass mkt. 5.99 (*0-446-36227-1*) Warner Bks.

Curtain. large type ed. Agatha Christie. (General Ser.). 289p. 1992. 19.95 (*0-8161-4539-3*, Large Print Bks) Hall.

Curtain. large type ed. Jennifer Jordan. 336p. 1986. 21.95 (*0-7089-1514-0*) Ulverscroft.

Curtain: A Hercule Poirot Mystery. Agatha Christie. 1993. mass mkt. 4.99 (*0-06-100366-2*, Harp PBks) HarpC.

*__Curtain Book: A Sourcebook for Distinctive Curtains, Drapes, & Shades for Your Home.__ Caroline Clifton-Mogg & Melanie Paine. (Illus.). 180p. 1995. 22.50 (*0-8212-2194-9*) Bulfinch Pr.

Curtain Call. Elizabeth Koehler-Pentacoff. (Illus.). 80p. (J). (gr. k-6). 1989. pap. text ed. 7.95 (*0-86530-065-8*, IP 166-4) Incentive Pubns.

Curtain Call. large type ed. Rona Randall. (Romance Ser.). 720p. 1993. 21.95 (*0-7089-2960-5*) Ulverscroft.

Curtain Calls: British & American Women & the Theater. Ed. by Mary A. Schofield & Cecilia Macheski. LC 90-44396. (Illus.). 426p. (C). 1990. text ed. 39.95 (*0-8214-0957-3*) Ohio U Pr.

Curtain Fall. large type ed. Jean Ure. 308p. 1981. 12.00 (*0-7089-0608-7*) Ulverscroft.

Curtain for a Jester. large type ed. Frances Lockridge & Richard Lockridge. 316p. 1992. reprint ed. lib. bdg. 19.95 (*1-56054-238-1*) Thorndike Pr.

Curtain for a Jester. Frances Lockridge & Richard Lockridge. (Mr. & Mrs. North Ser.). 222p. 1975. reprint ed. lib. bdg. 19.95 (*0-89190-904-4*, Rivercity Pr) Amereon Ltd.

*__Curtain Going Up!__ Elizabeth S. Hill. 160p. (J). (gr. 5-9). 1995. 14.99 (*0-670-85919-2*) Viking Child Bks.

*__Curtain Going Up.__ Jill Parsons. (Voices Romance Ser.: No. 6). 224p. (J). (gr. 4-7). 1995. mass mkt. 3.99 (*0-8217-4819-X*) Zebra.

Curtain I: A Guide to Creative Drama for Children 5-8 Years Old. Sue Thomas & Susan Dinges. (J). (gr. k-3). 1985. pap. 15.00 (*0-89824-148-0*) Trillium Pr.

Curtain II: Creative Drama for Children 9-12. Susan Dinges & Sue Thomas. (J). (ps-7). 1986. pap. 15.00 (*0-89824-168-5*) Trillium Pr.

Curtain of Darkness. large type ed. Nina Shaldon. 1989. 17.95 (*0-7089-2079-9*) Ulverscroft.

Curtain of Green. Welty. 1991. 15.95 (*0-15-123671-2*) HarBrace.

Curtain of Green. Eudora Welty. 22.95 (*0-8488-0658-1*) Amereon Ltd.

Curtain of Green: And Other Stories. Welty. (Modern Classic Ser.). 1991. write for info. (*0-15-123670-4*) HarBrace.

Curtain of Green & Other Stories. Eudora Welty. LC 79-10389. 289p. 1979. pap. 8.95 (*0-15-623492-0*, Harvest Bks) HarBrace.

Curtain of Stars. large type ed. Patricia Wilson. 1991. reprint ed. lib. bdg. 18.95 (*0-263-12568-8*, Pub. by Mills & Boon UK) Thorndike Pr.

Curtain Rises: Rethinking Culture, Ideology, & the State in Eastern Europe. Ed. by Hermine G. De Soto & David G. Anderson. LC 92-13577. 368p. (C). 1993. pap. 19.95 (*0-391-03810-9*) Humanities.

Curtain Rises, Vol. II: A History of European Theater from the Eighteenth Century to the Present. Paula G. Sitarz. (Illus.). 144p. (Orig.). (YA). (gr. 7 up). 1993. pap. 12.95 (*1-55870-293-8*) Betterway Bks.

Curtain Rises, Vol. I: Early Origins & Eastern Theater. Paula Gaj Sitarz. LC 90-21953. (Illus.). 144p. (J). (gr. 5-9). 1991. 14.95 (*1-55870-198-2*) Shoe Tree Pr.

*__Curtain Sketchbook.__ Wendy Baker. LC 94-30789. 1994. 24.95 (*0-8230-1131-3*, Whitney Lib) Watsn-Guptill.

Curtain Time: Plays, Readings, Sketches, Cantatas, & Poems for Jewish Programs. Comp. by Zara Shakow. 1985. pap. 9.95 (*0-8246-0310-9*) Jonathan David.

Curtain Times: The New York Theatre, 1965-1987. Otis L. Guernsey, Jr. (Illus.). 620p. 1987. 32.95 (*0-936839-24-4*) Applause Theatre Bk Pubs.

Curtain Wall Construction. Ed. by Konrad Gatz et al. Tr. by David Stern & Felix Winkler. LC 67-29398. (Illus.). 1965. 89.50 (*0-89197-718-X*) Irvington.

Curtaine-Drawer of the World: Or, Chamberlaine of That Inne of Iniquity. William Parkes. LC 79-84130. (English Experience Ser.: No. 948). 76p. 1979. reprint ed. lib. bdg. 9.00 (*90-221-0948-8*) Walter J Johnson.

Curtains. Gloria Gonzalez. 1976. pap. 2.75 (*0-8222-0263-8*) Dramatists Play.

Curtains. James McManus. LC 85-72236. 130p. (Orig.). 1985. pap. 8.95 (*0-9614644-0-2*) Another Chicago Pr.

Curtains. R. L. Stine. Ed. by Patricia MacDonald. 160p. (Orig.). (YA). (gr. 7 up). 1990. pap. 3.50 (*0-671-69498-7*, Archway) PB.

*__Curtains & Blinds.__ Yvonne Rees. (Quick & Easy Ser.). (Illus.). 96p. 1995. 14.95 (*0-7063-7346-4*, Pub. by Ward Lock UK) Sterling.

Curtains & Draperies: History, Design & Inspiration. Jenny Gibbs. (Illus.). 224p. 1994. 40.00 (*0-87951-539-2*) Overlook Pr.

Curtains, Draperies & Shades. LC 92-62829. 128p. 1993. pap. 9.99 (*0-376-01735-X*) Sunset Menlo Pk.

Curtains, Draperies & Shades. Ed. by Southern Living Staff. (Southern Living Home Improvement Ser.). 128p. 1993. pap. 9.99 (*0-376-09048-0*) Oxmoor Hse.

*__Curtains for the Cardinal.__ Elizabeth Eyre. 256p. 1994. pap. text ed. 4.99 (*0-425-14126-8*) Berkley Pub.

Curtains for the Cardinal. Elizabeth Eyre. LC 92-28375. 1993. 19.95 (*0-15-123682-8*) HarBrace.

*__Curtains for the President.__ Proctor Jones. LC 94-78063. 218p. (Orig.). 1995. pap. write for info. (*0-9608860-9-5*) Proctor Jones.

*__Curtains for Three.__ Rex Stout. 1994. 4.99 (*0-553-24498-1*) Bantam.

Curtains for You. Harrison Fisher. LC 79-65656. (Orig.). 1980. per., pap. 8.00 (*0-915380-10-2*) Word Works.

*__Curtains, Shades & Top Treatments.__ Home Decorating Institute Staff. LC 95-17089. (Arts & Crafts for Home Decorating Ser.). 128p. 1996. 18.95 (*0-86573-380-5*); pap. 15.95 (*0-86573-381-3*) Cy De Cosse.

Curtis. Ray Billingsley. 1993. mass mkt. 3.99 (*0-345-90234-3*) Ballantine.

Curtis: Twist & Shout. Ray Billingsley. 1993. mass mkt. 3.99 (*0-345-90235-1*) Ballantine.

Curtis Aikens' Guide to the Harvest. rev. ed. Curtis G. Aikens. LC 92-45028. 1993. pap. 13.95 (*1-56145-083-9*) Peachtree Pubs.

*__Curtis Arnold's PPS Trading System: A Proven Method for Consistently Beating the Market.__ Curtis M. Arnold. 225p. 1995. 45.00 (*1-55738-877-6*) Probus Pub Co.

Curtis Bernhardt. Mary Kiersch. LC 85-27523. (Directors Guild of America Oral History Ser.: No. 3). (Illus.). 200p. 1986. 22.50 (*0-8108-1870-1*) Scarecrow.

Curtis Creek Manifesto. Sheridan Anderson. (Illus.). 48p. (Orig.). 1978. pap. 7.95 (*0-936608-06-4*) F Amato Pubns.

Curtis Jenkins Cornwell & Company: A Study in Professional Origins, 1816-1966. S. V. Cornwell. LC 90-14043. (New Works in Accounting History). 200p. 1991. 20.00 (*0-8153-0004-2*) Garland.

Curtis Magazine. James P. Wood. LC 78-137774. 309p. reprint ed. pap. 88.10 (*0-317-10525-6*, 2012483) Bks Demand.

Curtis Nebraska - First Hundred Years. Centennial Book Committee Staff. (Illus.). 336p. 1986. 42.00 (*0-88107-059-9*) Curtis Media.

Curtis No. 3. Ray Billingsley. Date not set. pap. write for info. (*0-345-38355-9*) Ballantine.

*__Curtis Piperfield's Biggest Fan.__ Lisa Fiedler. LC 95-11702. (J). 1995. write for info. (*0-395-70728-5*, Clarion Bks) HM.

Curtiss Aircraft, 1907-1947. Peter M. Bowers. LC 87-62882. (Illus.). 450p. 1988. 44.95 (*0-87021-152-8*) Naval Inst Pr.

Curtiss Army Hawks in Action. Larry Davis. (Aircraft in Action Ser.). (Illus.). 50p. 1992. pap. 8.95 (*0-89747-286-1*, 1128) Squad Sig Pubns.

*__Curtiss HS Flying Boats.__ K. M. Molson & A. J. Shortt. (Illus.). 156p. 1995. pap. 29.95 (*1-55750-142-4*) Naval Inst Pr.

*__Curtiss Navy Hawks in Action.__ Peter Bowers. (Aircraft in Action Ser.). (Illus.). 50p. 1995. pap. 9.95 (*0-89747-342-6*) Squad Sig Pubns.

Curtiss OX-5 Aeronautical Engine. (Illus.). 20p. 1973. pap. 3.00 (*0-87994-039-5*) Aviat Pub.

Curtiss P-40 in Action. (Aircraft in Action Ser.). (Illus.). 50p. 1984. pap. 8.95 (*0-89747-025-7*, 1026) Squad Sig Pubns.

Curtiss Standard JN-4D Military Tractor (Aircraft) Handbook. Curtiss Aeroplane & Motor Corp. Ed. by M. S. Rice. (Illus.). 72p. 1974. reprint ed. pap. 8.25 (*0-87994-013-1*) Aviat Pub.

Curtius Rufus, Quintus: Quintus Curtius Rufus, Index Verborum - Releves Lexicaux et Grammaticaux. Quintus Curtius Rufus. Ed. by Jean Therasse. (Alpha-Omega, Reihe A Ser.: Bd. XXIX). 628p. 1976. write for info. (*3-487-05977-0*, Pub. by Georg Olms GW) Lubrecht & Cramer.

Curtsy to the Lady. Zoe Ward. 136p. 1994. pap. 24.00 (*0-86138-041-X*, Pub. by T Dalton UK) St Mut.

Curvature & Homology. Samuel I. Goldberg. (Illus.). xviii, 315p. (C). reprint ed. pap. 8.95 (*0-486-64314-X*) Dover.

Curvature & Topology of Riemannian Manifolds. Ed. by Katsuhiro Shiohama et al. (Lecture Notes in Mathematics Ser.: Vol. 1201). vii, 336p. 1986. pap. 48.30 (*0-387-16770-6*) Spr-Verlag.

Curvature in Japanese Blades. Hawley. 1991. pap. 4.95 (*0-910704-20-1*) Hawley.

*__Curve.__ Bob Judd. 288p. 1994. pap. 4.99 (*0-425-14466-6*, Prime Crime) Berkley Pub.

Curve. Andrew Levy. 80p. 1994. 10.00 (*1-882022-20-3*) O Bks.

Curve & Surface Fitting. Peter Lancaster & Kestutis Salkauskas. (Computational Mathematics & Applications Ser.). 1986. text ed. 125.00 (*0-12-436060-2*); pap. text ed. 45.00 (*0-12-436061-0*) Acad Pr.

*__Curve & Surface Fitting with Splines.__ Paul Dierckx. (Monographs on Numerical Analysis). (Illus.). 304p. 1995. reprint ed. pap. 48.00 (*0-19-853440-X*) OUP.

Curve Away from Stillness: Science Poems. John Allman. LC 88-22791. 96p. (Orig.). 1989. pap. 7.95 (*0-8112-1081-2*, NDP667) New Directions.

*__Curve Ball.__ John Danakas. (J). (gr. 3-8). 1995. pap. 8.95 (*1-55028-433-9*); bds. 16.95 (*1-55028-423-1*) Formac Dist Ltd.

Curve Fitting for Programmable Calculators. 3rd ed. William M. Kolb. LC 83-51845. (Illus.). 158p. 1984. 12.95 (*0-943494-02-8*) SYNTEC Inc.

Curve of Binding Energy. John McPhee. 224p. 1974. 19.95 (*0-374-13373-5*) FS&G.

Curve of Binding Energy. John McPhee. 224p. 1980. pap. 10.00 (*0-374-51598-0*) FS&G.

Curve of Binding Energy: A Journey into the Awesome & Alarming World of Theodore B. Taylor. John McPhee. 160p. 1979. pap. 2.25 (*0-345-28000-8*) Ballantine.

Curve of Fate: From Man-Ape to the Man-God. J. Lonsdale Bryans. 1977. lib. bdg. 59.95 (*0-8490-1696-7*) Gordon Pr.

Curve of Life: The Correspondence of Heinz Kohut, 1923-1981. Ed. by Geoffrey Cocks. LC 93-40922. 1994. 39.95 (*0-226-11170-9*) U Ch Pr.

Curve of the Arch: The Story of Louis Sullivan's Owatonna Bank. Larry Millett. LC 84-25528. (Illus.). 205p. 1985. pap. 14.95 (*0-87351-182-4*) Minn Hist.

Curve of the Future: Food-Trees, Solar Cars, War-Math, the Fun Economy, & Other Essential Knowledge for a... Edward Passerini. 320p. 1992. pap. text ed. 8.00 (*0-8403-7381-3*) Kendall-Hunt.

Curve of Time. M. Wylie Blanchet. LC 92-43650. 170p. 1993. reprint ed. pap. 12.95 (*1-878067-27-3*) Seal Pr Feminist.

Curve Stitching. Jon Millington. (Illus.). 96p. (Orig.). 1990. pap. 17.95 (*0-906212-65-0*, Pub. by Tarquin UK) Parkwest Pubns.

Curveballs Strikes Again: More Wacky Facts to Bat Around. John Rolfe. (Illus.). 32p. (J). (gr. 3-7). 1992. mass mkt. 4.95 (*0-316-75460-9*, Spts Illus Kids) Little.

Curved Like an Eye. George Perreault. Ed. by Tom Trusky. LC 87-14656. (Ahsahta Press Modern & Contemporary Poets of the West Ser.). 59p. (Orig.). 1988. pap. 6.95 (*0-916272-35-4*) Ahsahta Pr.

Curved-Side Cars. Richard Wagner & Birdella Wagner. 120p. 1965. vinyl bd. 10.00 (*0-914196-02-2*) Trolley Talk.

Curved Thought & Textual Wandering: Gertrude Stein's Postmodernism. Ellen E. Berry. 212p. (C). 1992. text ed. 34.50 (*0-472-10300-8*) U of Mich Pr.

Curved Two-Patch System: A Quilter's Exciting Discovery for Creating Pieced Flowers, Foliage & Other Patterns. Joyce M. Schlotzhauer. LC 82-9666. (Illus.). 133p. 1982. pap. 18.95 (*0-914440-56-X*) EPM Pubns.

Curves. Ed. by Gerald Jenkins. (Illus.). 32p. (Orig.). 1988. text ed. 19.95 (*0-905531-29-9*, Pub. by Tarquin UK) Parkwest Pubns.

Curves. Frank Nichols. (J). 1989. pap. 3.95 (*0-85953-049-3*) Childs Play.

Curves & Fractal Dimension. Claude Tricot. LC 93-4690. 1993. write for info. (*0-387-94095-2*) Spr-Verlag.

Curves & Singularities. 2nd ed. J. W. Bruce & P. J. Giblin. (Illus.). 240p. (C). 1993. 69.95 (*0-521-41985-9*); pap. 29.95 (*0-521-42999-4*) Cambridge U Pr.

Curves & Surface Modeling. H. Hagen. (Miscellaneous Ser.: No. 29). ix, 205p. 1992. pap. 47.25 (*0-89871-281-5*) Soc Indus-Appl Math.

Curves & Surfaces. Ed. by P. J. Laurent et al. (Illus.). 514p. 1991. text ed. 59.95 (*0-12-438660-1*) Acad Pr.

Curves & Surfaces for Computer Aided Geometric Design: A Practical Guide. 3rd ed. Gerald Farin. (Computer Science & Scientific Computing Ser.). (Illus.). 473p. 1992. text ed. 49.95 (*0-12-249052-5*) Acad Pr.

Curves & Surfaces in CAGD, '89: Proceedings of the 4th Conference on Surfaces in Computer Aided Geometric Design, Oberwolfach, FRG, 16-22 April, 1989. Ed. by Robert E. Barnhill et al. 374p. 1990. 102.50 (*0-444-88629-X*, North Holland) Elsevier.

Curves & Surfaces in Computer Aided Geometric Design. F. Yamaguchi. (Illus.). 390p. 1988. 111.00 (*0-387-17449-4*) Spr-Verlag.

Curves & Surfaces in Computer Vision & Graphics. Ed. by L. Ferrari & R. J. DeFigueiredo. 1990. 62.00 (*0-8194-0298-2*, VOL. 1251) SPIE.

Curves & Surfaces in Computer Vision & Graphics II. Ed. by M. J. Silbermann & H. D. Tagare. 1992. 62.00 (*0-8194-0747-X*, 1610) SPIE.

Curves & Surfaces in Geometric Design. P. J. Laurent et al. Ed. by Larry Schumaker. 500p. 1994. text ed. 69.95 (*1-56881-039-3*) AK Peters.

Curves, Jacobians, & Abelian Varieties: (Proceedings of a Summer Research Workshop on the Schottky Problem) Ed. by Ron Donagi. LC 92-20586. (Contemporary Mathematics Ser.: Vol. 136). 342p. 1992. 62.00 (*0-8218-5143-8*) Am Math.

Curves of Life. Theodore A. Cook. 1979. pap. 10.95 (*0-486-23701-X*) Dover.

Curves Unlimited: Expanding the Curved Two-Patch System to Soften Shapes & Create New Pattern. Joyce M. Schlotzhauer. LC 84-13617. 155p. (Orig.). 1984. pap. 24.95 (*0-914440-78-0*) EPM Pubns.

Curye on Inglysch. Ed. by Constance B. Hieatt & Sharon Butler. (Early English Text Society Ser.: No. 8). 1985. 24.95 (*0-19-722409-1*) OUP.

Curzio Malaparte: The Skin. Tr. by David Moore. LC 87-63048. 344p. 1988. pap. 12.95 (*0-685-22436-8*) Marlboro Pr.

Cushing at Zuni: The Correspondence & Journals of Frank Hamilton Cushing, 1879-1884. Ed. by Jesse Green. LC 89-70751. (Illus.). 450p. 1990. 45.00 (*0-8263-1172-5*) U of NM Pr.

Cushing of Gettysburg: The Story of a Union Artillery Commander. Kent Masterson Brown. LC 93-19602. (Illus.). 368p. 1993. 32.00 (*0-8131-1837-9*) U Pr of Ky.

Cushioning Against Insurance Cycles: The Role of Risk Retention & Purchasing Groups. 64p. 1989. pap. 34.95 (*0-89707-468-8*, 519-0093) Amer Bar Assn.

*__Cushions & Covers.__ Jill Blake. (Quick & Easy Ser.). (Illus.). 96p. 1995. 14.95 (*0-7063-7377-4*, Pub. by Ward Lock UK) Sterling.

Cushite: or The Children of Ham. Rufus L. Perry. 49p. (Orig.). 1887. pap. 4.00 (*0-916157-20-2*) African Islam Miss Pubns.

Cushite: Or the Children of Ham (the Negro Race) Rufus L. Perry. Ed. by Al I. Obaba. 49p. (Orig.). (YA). 1991. pap. text ed. 4.00 (*0-916157-32-6*) African Islam Miss Pubns.

Cushman Genealogy & General History. A. W. Burt. (Illus.). 432p. 1991. reprint ed. lib. bdg. 77.00 (*0-8328-2045-8*); reprint ed. pap. 67.00 (*0-8328-2046-6*) Higginson Bk Co.

Cusine: Standard Securities. Douglas J. Cusine. 1991. pap. 48.00 (*0-406-10587-1*) Butterworth Legal Pubs.

Custard & Company. Ogden Nash. (Illus.). 128p. (J). (gr. 2-6). 1985. mass mkt. 6.95 (*0-316-59855-0*) Little.

Custard the Dragon. Ogden Nash. (Illus.). (J). (gr. k-3). 1973. lib. bdg. 14.95 (*0-316-59841-0*) Little.

*__Custard the Dragon & the Wicked Knight.__ Ogden Nash. LC 95-9719. (Illus.). (J). 1996. write for info. (*0-316-59882-8*) Little.

Custer: Favor the Bold, a Soldier's Story. D. A. Kinsley. 1989. 9.98 (*0-88394-074-4*) Promntory Pr.

Custer: Frederick Whittaker's Complete Life of General George A. Custer, Major General of Volunteers, Brevet Major U. S. Army & Lieutenant-Colonel Seventh U. S. Cavalry. Intro. by Don H. Tolzmann. (Illus.). 724p. 1993. pap. text ed. 41.50 (*1-55613-860-1*) Heritage Bk.

Custer: The Life of General George Armstrong Custer. Jay Monaghan. LC 59-5937. (Illus.). xii, 479p. 1971. reprint ed. pap. 15.95 (*0-8032-5732-5*) U of Nebr Pr.

Custer: The Story of a Horse. Deborah King. (Illus.). 32p. (J). (ps-3). 1992. lib. bdg. 14.95 (*0-399-22147-6*, Philomel Bks) Putnam Pub Group.

Custer Adventure. Richard Upton. LC 90-170274. (Echoes of the Little Big Horn Ser.: Vol. 4). (Illus.). 119p. 1990. reprint ed. 30.00 (*0-912783-20-6*); reprint ed. pap. 5.00 (*0-912783-19-2*) Upton Sons.

Custer Album. Frost. 1976. 40.95 (*0-8488-1553-X*) Amereon Ltd.

Custer Album: A Pictorial Biography of General George A. Custer. Lawrence A. Frost. LC 89-40783. (Illus.). 192p. 1990. pap. 17.95 (*0-8061-2282-X*) U of Okla Pr.

Custer & His Times, Bk. III. Intro. by Gregory J. Urwin. (Little Big Horn Associates Ser.). (Illus.). 305p. 1988. lib. bdg. 28.95 (*0-9615143-6-1*) Univ Central AR Pr.

Custer & the Great Controversy: The Origin & Development of a Legend. Robert M. Utley. LC 62-19153. (Illus.). 24.95 (*0-87026-053-7*) Westernlore.

Custer & the Little Bighorn: A Psychobiographical Inquiry. Charles K. Hofling. LC 80-23312. 130p. 1986. reprint ed. pap. 14.95 (*0-8143-1814-2*) Wayne St U Pr.

Custer Autograph Album. John M. Carroll. (Illus.). 206p. 1993. 24.95 (*0-932702-97-X*) Creative Texas.

Custer Battle Casualties: Burials, Exhumations, & Reinterments. Richard G. Hardorff. LC 89-50065. (Montana & the West Ser.: Vol. 7). (Illus.). 181p. (C). 1990. 30.00 (*0-912783-14-1*) Upton Sons.

Custer Battlefield. Robert M. Utley. LC 86-600325. (Handbook Ser.: No. 132). (Illus.). 112p. (Orig.). 1988. pap. 4.75 (*0-912627-34-4*) Natl Park Serv.

Custer Battlefield, a History & Guide to the Battle of the Little Bighorn. Robert M. Utley. LC 87-600325. (Illus.). 112p. 1988. pap. 4.75 (*0-16-003544-9*, S/N 024-005-01022-0) USGPO.

Custer, Cavalry & Crows. Thomas B. Marquis. (Source Custeriana Ser.: No. 6). (Illus.). 1975. 20.00 (*0-88342-041-4*) Old Army.

Custer, Cody & the Last Indian Wars. rev. ed. Jay Kimmel. 240p. 1992. pap. 25.00 (*0-685-50315-1*) Corey-Stevens Pub.

Custer, Cody & the Last Indian Wars: A Pictorial History. Jay Kimmel. (Illus.). 240p. (Orig.). 1994. pap. 25.00 (*0-942893-01-8*) Corey-Stevens Pub.

An Asterisk (*) at the beginning of an entry indicates that the title is appearing in BIP for the first time.

An Asterisk (*) at the beginning of an entry indicates that the title is appearing in BIP for the first time.

1761

C

Customary of the Benedictine Abbey of Bury St Edmunds in Suffolk. Ed. by Antonia Gransen. (Henry Bradshaw Society Publication Ser.: No. XCIC (99)). 1970. 30.00 (*0-907077-16-1*) Boydell & Brewer.

Customer - Directed Quality: Logical Sustainable Growth for People & Organizations. Bill Siefkin. 64p. (Orig.). 1994. pap. 13.95 (*0-926365-17-7*) Montchanin.

***Customer - Supplier Evaluations: The Development of Standards for the Objective Measurement of Both, Set, incl. disk.** William J. Tobin. (Illus.). 68p. (Orig.). 1994. pap. text ed. 35.00 (*0-936994-12-6*) W J T Assocs.

Customer & Market-Driven Quality Management. Johnson A. Edosomwan. LC 93-5513. 250p. 1993. 29.95 (*0-87389-137-6*) ASQC Qual Pr.

Customer Bonding: Pathway to Customer Loyalty. Richard Cross & Janet Smith. LC 94-11504. 1994. 25.95 (*0-8442-3318-8*, NTC Busn Bks) NTC Pub Grp.

Customer Care. Ed. by Mac Anderson. 77p. (Orig.). 1989. pap. 7.50 (*1-880461-19-6*) Celebrat Excell.

***Customer Care: Strategy for the 90's.** M. Cardwell. (C). 1994. 150.00x (*0-946655-45-6*, Pub. by S Thornes Pubs UK) St Mut.

Customer Care: The Personnel Implications. Incomes Data Services Staff & Institute of Personnel Management Staff. 100p. (C). 1989. 80.00 (*0-85292-428-3*, Pub. by IPM Hse UK) St Mut.

Customer Centered Reengineering. Edwin Crego, Jr. & Peter D. Schiffrin. 200p. 1994. text ed. 25.00 (*0-7863-0298-4*) Irwin Prof Pubng.

Customer Comes Second: And Other Secrets. Hal Rosenbluth. 1992. 20.00 (*0-688-11466-0*) Morrow.

Customer Comes Second: And Other Secrets of Exceptional Service. Hal F. Rosenbluth. 1994. pap. 12.00 (*0-688-13246-4*, Quill) Morrow.

***Customer Communications: The New Marketing Discipline.** John R. Klug & Thad D. Peterson. 96p. (Orig.). 1993. pap. 11.95 (*0-9639491-2-8*) Customer Commun.

Customer Connection: Quality for the Rest of Us. John Guaspari. 224p. 1991. pap. 16.95 (*0-8144-7758-5*) AMACOM.

Customer Crisis: Turning an Unhappy Customer into a Life-Long Client. Phillip E. Mahfood. 200p. 1993. 24.95 (*1-55738-421-5*) Probus Pub Co.

Customer Deductions Impact on Receivables. Credit Research Foundation Staff. 1988. 40.00 (*0-939050-56-0*) Credit Res NYS.

Customer-Driven Company: Managerial Perspectives on QFD. 2nd ed. William E. Eureka & Nancy E. Ryan. LC 88-22174. (Illus.). 124p. 1994. 25.00 (*0-941243-03-6*) ASI Pr.

Customer-Driven Company: Managerial Perspectives on Quality Function Deployment. 2nd ed. William E. Eureka & Nancy E. Ryan. LC 93-38371. 175p. 1994. text ed. 25.00 (*0-7863-0141-4*) Irwin Prof Pubng.

Customer-Driven Company: Moving from Talk to Action. Richard C. Whiteley. (Illus.). 320p. 1993. pap. 15.38 (*0-201-60813-8*) Addison-Wesley.

Customer-Driven Marketing: Lessons from Entrepreneurial Technology Companies. Ed. by Raymond W. Smilor. 192p. 1989. text ed. 39.95 (*0-669-21128-1*) Free Pr.

Customer-Driven Project Management: A New Paradigm in Managing Total Quality Implementation. Bruce T. Barkley. 1994. text ed. 53.00 (*0-07-003739-6*) McGraw.

Customer Driven Strategy: Winning Through Operational Excellence. Thomas F. Wallace. LC 92-60661. 283p. 1992. 32.50 (*0-939246-26-0*) Oliver Wight.

Customer Education. Claudia G. Meer. LC 84-6938. 168p. 1985. lib. bdg. 34.95 (*0-8304-1049-X*) Nelson-Hall.

Customer Engineering: A Measurement-Based Sales System Designed to Increase Marketing Profitability. Market Intelligence Staff. 336p. 1993. 95.00 (*1-56753-492-9*) Frost & Sullivan.

***Customer Engineering: Cutting Edge Selling Strategies.** David B. Frigstad. (PSI Successful Business Library Ser.). 250p. (Orig.). 1995. ring bd. 39.95 (*1-55571-360-2*) Oasis Pr OR.

***Customer Engineering: Cutting Edge Selling Strategies.** David B. Frigstad. LC 95-8769. (PSI Successful Business Library). 250p. (Orig.). 1995. pap. 19.95 (*1-55571-359-9*) Oasis Pr OR.

Customer First: A Strategy for Quality Service. Denis Walker. 200p. 1990. text ed. 64.95 (*0-566-02860-3*, Pub. by Gower UK) Ashgate Pub Co.

Customer-Focused Marketing. Ian Chaston. LC 92-26506. (Marketing for Professionals Ser.). 1992. write for info. (*0-07-707698-2*) McGraw.

Customer-Focused Quality: What to Do on Monday Morning. Thomas Hinton. 1993. 19.95 (*0-13-189630-X*) P-H.

***Customer Integration: The QFD Leader's Guide for Decision Making.** William Barnard et al. 256p. 1994. 37.50 (*0-939246-67-8*) Oliver Wight.

Customer is Boss. John Tschohl. LC 92-76103. 219p. 1993. 19.95 (*0-9636268-0-9*) Best Sell Pub.

Customer Is Key: Gaining an Unbeaten Advantage Through Customer Satisfaction. Milind M. Lele & Jagdish N. Sheth. LC 87-21549. 260p. 1987. text ed. 24.95 (*0-471-82859-9*) Wiley.

Customer Is Key: Gaining an Unbeaten Advantage Through Customer Satisfaction. Milind M. Lele & Jagdish N. Sheth. LC 87-21549. 260p. 1991. pap. text ed. 14.95 (*0-471-54917-7*) Wiley.

Customer is King. R. Lee Harris. 144p. 1991. pap. 14.95 (*0-87389-122-8*) ASQC Qual Pr.

Customer Is Usually Wrong! Contrary to What You've Been Told What You Know to Be True about Customer Service. Fred Jandt. 211p. (Orig.). 1994. pap. 12.95 (*1-57112-067-X*, CUW, Park Avenue) Park Ave Prods.

***Customer Loyalty: How to Earn It, How to Keep It.** Jill Griffin. 1995. 23.00 (*0-02-912977-X*) Free Pr.

Customer Metering Practices. 80p. 1985. pap. 16.00 (*0-89867-335-6*, 20188) Am Water Wks Assn.

***Customer Networking.** Date not set. write for info. (*0-614-04306-9*) Busn Toolbox.

Customer One Hundred-One: One Hundred-One Ways to Win & Keep Customers. JoAnn Goble & John M. Vraniak. (Illus.). 101p. (Orig.). 1994. pap. 4.95 (*0-9641030-0-1*) Questics.

***Customer Only Rings Once: Managing Telephone Contacts.** Pat Cochrane. (Institute of Management Ser.). 250p. 1995. pap. 47.50 (*0-273-61174-7*, Pub. by Pitman Pub Ltd UK) Trans-Atl Phila.

***Customer or Employer? Vendor or Employee? A Guide to Knowing Who You Are & Why You Should Care.** Ed. by Pamela J. Roth. (Business Management Ser.). 200p. (Orig.). Date not set. pap. 44.95 (*1-57109-004-5*) Spiral Communs.

Customer Oriented Laboratory. William O. Umiker. LC 90-14562. 190p. 1991. 35.00 (*0-89189-310-5*, 45-9-032-00) Am Soc Clinical.

Customer Perceptions of Resettlement Units. N. Smith et al. (DDS Research Report Ser.: No. 11). 110p. 1992. pap. 30.00 (*0-11-761976-0*, HM19760, Pub. by HMSO UK) UNIPUB.

Customer Profitability Analysis. 2nd ed. LC 72-97055. 104p. 1985. pap. text ed. 25.00 (*0-317-47032-9*) Robt Morris Assocs.

Customer Relations: The Road to Greater Profits. rev. ed. Lloyd W. Moseley. LC 72-85929. (Illus.). 1990. pap. 36.95 (*0-912016-79-5*) Lebhar Friedman.

***Customer Relations & the Diversity Challenge: A Trainer's Guide.** Selma Myers & Jonamay Lambert. 55p. 1995. 69.95 (*1-883998-16-6*) Amherst Educ.

Customer Relations for Technicians. Edwin G. Davis. 128p. 1990. teacher ed. (*0-318-65457-1*); pap. write for info. (*0-07-015832-0*) McGraw.

***Customer Retention.** Michael W. Lowenstein. 1994. 25.00 (*0-87389-257-7*) ASQC Qual Pr.

Customer Retention Through Quality Leadership: The Baxter Approach. David D. Auld & Deborah G. Fliehman. (Illus.). 233p. 1993. pap. 19.95 (*0-87389-167-8*) ASQC Qual Pr.

Customer Satisfaction: How to Maximize, Measure, & Market Your Company's "Ultimate Product". Mack Hanan & Peter Karp. LC 88-48026. 194p. 1991. pap. 15.95 (*0-8144-7772-0*) AMACOM.

Customer Satisfaction: The Other Half of Your Job. rev. ed. Dru Scott. Ed. by Michael G. Crisp. LC 91-72764. (Fifty-Minute Ser.). (Illus.). 115p. 1991. pap. 9.95 (*1-56052-084-1*) Crisp Pubns.

Customer-Satisfaction Audit: A Management Perspective. R. N. Lemieux et al. Ed. by Richard Holman. (IIA Monograph). (Illus.). 61p. 1985. pap. text ed. 15.00 (*0-89413-142-7*) Inst Inter Aud.

Customer Satisfaction, Focus on the Customer: Second Congress on, May 17-20, 1992, Lake Buena Vista, Florida. LC 92-18775. (Proceedings Ser.). 1992. write for info. (*0-87757-225-9*) Am Mktg.

Customer Satisfaction Guaranteed. Customer Service Institute Staff. 1988. 27.97 (*0-87280-191-8*, 3393, Asher-Gallant) Caddylak Systs.

Customer Satisfaction Guaranteed: A New Approach to Customer Service, Bedside Manner, & Relationship Ease. Robert Kausen. LC 88-82334. (Illus.). 144p. (Orig.). 1989. pap. 7.95 (*0-945787-55-3*) Life Education.

***Customer Satisfaction Measurement & Management: Using the Voice of the Customer.** Naumann. (SB-Marketing Education Ser.). 1995. text ed. 27.95 (*0-538-84439-6*) S-W Pub.

Customer Satisfaction Through Total Quality Assurance. Robert Grenier. 290p. 1988. 39.95 (*0-933931-08-5*) Hitchcock Pub.

Customer Service. Wendy Carter. LC 94-13298. (McGraw-Hill One-Day Workshop Ser.). 1994. text ed. 99.95 (*0-07-011197-9*) McGraw.

Customer Service: A How-to-Do-It Manual for Librarians. Suzanne Walters. (How-to-Do-It Ser.). 150p. 1994. 39.95 (*1-55570-137-X*) Neal-Schuman.

Customer Service: A Management Perspective. 1988. 60.00 (*0-318-33300-7*) Coun Logistics Mgt.

Customer Service: Employee Study Guide. Educational Foundation of the National Restaurant Association Staff. 84p. (Orig.). 1991. pap. 7.95 (*0-915452-68-5*) Educ Found.

Customer Service: Leader's Guide. Educational Foundation of the National Restaurant Association Staff. 64p. (Orig.). 1991. pap. 25.00 (*0-915452-69-3*) Educ Found.

Customer Service: Manager Handbook. Educational Foundation of the National Restaurant Association Staff. 108p. (Orig.). 1991. pap. 30.00 (*0-915452-67-7*) Educ Found.

Customer Service & Innovation in Libraries. Glenn Miller. 90p. 1995. pap. 12.00 (*0-917846-39-7*, 95614) Highsmith Pr.

***Customer Service & the Phone.** Dennis Becker & Paula B. Becker. (AMI How-to Ser.). 100p. 1995. 9.95 (*1-884926-41-X*) Amer Media.

Customer Service & the Telephone. Dennis Becker & Paula B. Becker. LC 94-340. (Business Skills Express Ser.). 112p. 1994. pap. 10.95 (*0-7863-0224-0*) Irwin Prof Pubng.

Customer Service Excellence. Debra J. MacNeill. LC 93-6. 112p. 1993. pap. 10.00 (*1-55623-969-6*) Irwin Prof Pubng.

Customer Service Excellence. Debra J. MacNeill. LC 94-72158. (Illus.). 93p. (Orig.). 1994. pap. 9.95 (*1-884926-26-6*) Amer Media.

Customer Service for Home Builders. 2nd ed. Carol Smith & William Young. LC 90-19664. 88p. (Orig.). 1990. pap. 15.00 (*0-86718-355-1*) Home Builder.

Customer Service in Corporate America: Implementing the Change. Executive KnowledgeWorks Staff. (Illus.). 160p. 1989. ring bd. 345.00 (*0-943353-08-4*) Exec Knowledge.

Customer Service in Finance. Caren Siehl & David Bowen. LC 94-70915. 100p. (Orig.). 1994. pap. 15.00 (*0-910586-96-9*) Finan Exec.

Customer Service in Health Care. Wendy Leebov. 32p. 1990. 24.95 (*0-318-69719-X*, 049254) AHPI.

Customer Service in Insurance: Improving Your Skills. Richard Bailey et al. (Associate, Customer Service Program Ser.). 252p. (C). 1991. pap. text ed. 24.00 (*0-939921-27-8*) LOMA.

Customer Service in Insurance: Principles & Practices. Kenneth Huggins. (Associate, Customer Service Program Ser.). 240p. (C). 1991. text ed. 41.00 (*0-939921-02-2*) LOMA.

Customer Service in Local Government: Challenges for Planners & City Managers. Bruce McClendon. LC 91-75139. 250p. (Orig.). 1992. lib. bdg. 45.95 (*0-918286-76-X*); pap. 34.95 (*0-918286-75-1*) Planners Pr.

Customer Service in the Information Environment. Guy St. Clair. LC 93-34396. (Information Services Management Ser.). 144p. 1993. 34.95 (*1-85739-004-0*) Bowker-Saur.

***Customer Service Management in a Telemarketing Environment: The Key to Corporate Survival.** J. J. Lauderbaugh. 160p. 1994. write for info. (*0-936840-15-3*) Tech Marketing.

Customer Service Operations: The Complete Guide. Warren Blanding. 240p. 1991. 75.00 (*0-8144-5004-0*) AMACOM.

Customer Service over the Phone. 2nd ed. Stephen Coscia. 1993. 12.95 (*0-685-69336-8*) Telecom Lib.

Customer Service Planner. Martin Christopher. 160p. 1992. pap. 47.95 (*0-7506-0149-3*) Buttrwrth-Heinemann.

Customer Service Planner. Martin Christopher. (Marketing Practitioner Ser.). 136p. 1993. pap. 19.95 (*0-7506-1710-1*) Buttrwrth-Heinemann.

Customer Service Renaissance: Lessons from the Banking Wars. M. Ray Grubbs & R. Eric Reidenbach. 1990. 39.00 (*1-55520-147-4*) Probus Pub Co.

Customer Service Representative. Jack Rudman. (Career Examination Ser.: C-3605). 1994. 29.95 (*0-8373-3605-8*) Nat Learn.

Customer Service Rep's Survival Guide. David Dee. 112p. 1989. pap. 6.95 (*0-85013-164-2*) Dartnell Corp.

***Customer Service the Nordstrom Way: An Inside Look at How It's Done.** Robert Spector & Patrick McCarthy. LC 94-39182. 1995. text ed. 24.95 (*0-471-58496-7*) Wiley.

Customer Services. Leroy M. Buckner. (Occupational Manuals & Projects in Marketing Ser.). (Illus.). 1978. student ed, text ed. 12.28 (*0-07-008823-3*) McGraw.

Customer Services: Marketing & the Competitive Environment Revision Card Pack. Ed. by T. Taylor. (C). 1989. 40.00 (*0-85297-237-7*, Pub. by Inst Bankers UK) St Mut.

Customer Services & User Training. Stephanie C. Ardito. Ed. by Ann M. Cunningham & Wendy Wicks. 150p. (Orig.). (C). 1992. pap. 50.00 (*0-942308-33-6*) NFAIS.

Customer Visits: Tools to Build Market Focus. Edward F. McQuarrie. (Illus.). 176p. (C). 1993. text ed. 46.00 (*0-8039-4669-4*); pap. text ed. 21.50 (*0-8039-4670-8*) Sage.

Customers: How to Get Them, How to Serve Them, How to Keep Them. Ray Dreyfack. 300p. 1983. ring bd. 91.50 (*0-85013-140-5*) Dartnell Corp.

Customers & Products Reprints. American Production & Inventory Control Society Staff. 138p. 1992. 20.00 (*1-55822-032-1*) Am Prod & Inventory.

Customers & Thieves. D. J. Murphy. 200p. 1985. text ed. 75.00 (*0-566-00882-3*) Ashgate Pub Co.

Customers As Partners: Building Relationships That Last. Chip R. Bell. LC 94-16999. 250p. 1994. 24.95 (*1-881052-54-0*) Berrett-Koehler.

Customers Flock to Business That Are in the News: A Step by Step Guide to How a Small Business Can Get Free Press Coverage. Sheila Danzig. Ed. by William Danzig. LC 89-92232. (Marketing Without a Budget Ser.). 130p. (Orig.). 1989. spiral bd. 20.00 (*0-9624333-1-4*) Natl Success.

Customers for Keeps: The Network System to Smash Your Profit Barrier. Pete Lisoskie & Shelly Lisoskie. LC 93-90414. (Illus.). 352p. (Orig.). 1994. pap. 19.95 (*1-879141-10-8*) Busn Toolbox.

Customers for Life. Carl Sewell & Paul B. Brown. 1991. pap. 12.00 (*0-671-74795-9*) PB.

Customhouse Brokers License Examination. Jack Rudman. (Admission Test Ser.: ATS-7). 1994. pap. 39.95 (*0-8373-5007-7*) Nat Learn.

Customising Your Electric Guitar. Adrian Legg. (Illus.). 64p. 1983. pap. 9.95 (*0-8256-2262-X*, AM40973) Music Sales.

Customize Your Phone: Fifteen Electronics Projects. Steve Sokolowski. (Illus.). 180p. 1988. 19.95 (*0-8306-9054-9*, 3054) TAB Bks.

Customized Job Training & Economic Development. Charles Bartsch. Ed. by Jenny Murphy & Andrea Kailo. 24p. (Orig.). 1985. pap. 16.00 (*0-317-04859-7*) Natl Coun Econ Dev.

Customizing AutoCAD. Jeff Allen et al. 154p. (C). 1991. 20.80 (*1-56870-006-7*) RonJon Pub.

Customizing AutoCAD. Sham L. Tickoo. 352p. 1992. pap. 36.95 (*0-8273-5041-4*) Delmar.

Customizing Autocad Release Twelve. Sham Tickoo. 94p. 1994. teacher ed. 15.00 (*0-8273-5915-2*) Delmar.

Customizing AutoCAD Release 12. Sham Tickoo. LC 93-25595. 656p. 1994. pap. text ed. 38.95 (*0-8273-5895-4*) Delmar.

Customizing the Body. Clinton R. Sanders. (Illus.). 224p. 1990. pap. 18.95 (*0-87722-764-0*) Temple U Pr.

Customizing Your Harley. Carl Caiati. (Illus.). 304p. 1992. 29.95 (*0-8306-4118-1*, 4223); pap. 19.95 (*0-8306-4117-3*, 4223) TAB Bks.

Customizing Your Harley. Caiati Carl. 1992. pap. text ed. 19.95 (*0-07-009506-X*) McGraw.

Customizing Your Macintosh for Productivity & for Fun, Incl. disk. Bob Levitus. 1993. disk, pap. 39.95 (*1-56686-087-3*) Brady Compu Bks.

Customizing Your Resume for Teaching Positions. Edward G. Pultorak. LC 92-34092. 52p. (Orig.). (C). 1993. pap. text ed. 16.50 (*0-8191-8938-3*) U Pr of Amer.

Customizing Your Van. 3rd ed. Allan Girdler & Carl Caiati. 1986. pap. text ed. 14.95 (*0-07-157182-5*) McGraw.

Customizing Your Van. 3rd ed. Allan Girdler. (Illus.). 320p. 1986. 18.95 (*0-8306-0242-9*, 2142); pap. 14.95 (*0-8306-2142-3*, 2142P) TAB Bks.

Customs. Joseph Duemer. LC 87-13791. (Contemporary Poetry Ser.). 104p. 1987. pap. 7.95 (*0-8203-0967-2*) U of Ga Pr.

Customs Act Nineteen Sixty-Two. P. L. Malik. 649p. 1982. 255.00 (*0-317-54862-X*) St Mut.

Customs Act, Nineteen Sixty-Two. P. L. Malik. (C). 1990. 60.00 (*0-685-39355-0*) St Mut.

Customs Act, 1962. 3rd ed. Ed. by P. L. Malik. (C). 1990. 105.00 (*0-685-39741-6*) St Mut.

Customs Aide. Jack Rudman. (Career Examination Ser.: C-3442). 1994. pap. 19.95 (*0-8373-3442-X*) Nat Learn.

Customs & Commercial Policy in Europe, U.K. Leonard Hawkes & Francis Snyder. 1992. text ed. write for info. (*0-406-16701-X*) Butterworth Legal Pubs.

***Customs & Controversies: Intertestamental Jewish Backgrounds of the New Testament.** J. Julius Scott, Jr. 336p. (Orig.). 1995. pap. 19.99 (*0-8010-2001-8*) Baker Bk.

Customs & Excise Cases. G. McFarlane. (Criminal Law Library). 384p. 1988. 100.00 (*0-08-039245-8*, Pergamon Pr) Elsevier.

Customs & Fashions in Old New England. Alice M. Earle. 387p. 1969. reprint ed. 22.50 (*0-87928-007-7*) Corner Hse.

Customs & Fashions in Old New England. Alice M. Earle. 394p. 1992. reprint ed. pap. 20.00 (*1-55613-579-3*) Heritage Bk.

Customs & Fashions in Old New England. Alice M. Earle. LC 89-63008. 387p. 1990. reprint ed. lib. bdg. 36.00 (*1-55888-845-4*) Omnigraphics Inc.

Customs & Habits of the Sicilian Peasants. Salvatore Salomone-Marino. Ed. & Tr. by Rosalie N. Norris. LC 80-65583. (Illus.). 256p. 1981. 35.00 (*0-8386-3010-3*) Fairleigh Dickinson.

Customs & Superstitions. J. A. Buckley. (C). 1990. pap. 30.00 (*0-85025-328-4*, Pub. by Tor Mark Pr UK) St Mut.

Customs & Traditions. Bobbie Kalman & Tammy Everts. LC 93-39882. (Historic Communities Ser.). (Illus.). 32p. (Orig.). (J). (gr. k-9). 1994. lib. bdg. 15.95 (*0-86505-495-9*); pap. 7.95 (*0-86505-515-7*) Crabtree Pub Co.

Customs & Traditions of Wales. Trefor M. Owen. (Pocket Guides Ser.). 104p. 1991. pap. 9.95 (*0-7083-1118-0*, Pub. by U of Wales UK) Bks Intl VA.

Customs Areas of the World. 5.00 (*92-1-161309-4*) UN.

Customs Bulletin: Treasury Decisions under Customs & Other Laws, V. 19, January-December 1985. 642p. 1986. 27.00 (*0-16-004593-2*, S/N 048-000-00389-3) USGPO.

Customs in Common: Studies in Traditional Popular Culture. E. P. Thompson. 560p. 1992. 29.95 (*1-56584-003-8*) New Press NY.

Customs in Common: Studies in Traditional Popular Culture. E. P. Thompson. LC 92-13039. 560p. 1993. pap. 15.95 (*1-56584-074-7*) New Press NY.

Customs in Conflict: The Anthropology of a Changing World. Ed. by Frank Manning & J. M. Philibert. 320p. 1990. pap. text ed. 19.95 (*0-921149-34-4*) Broadview Pr.

Customs Inspector. Jack Rudman. (Career Examination Ser.: C-177). 1994. pap. 23.95 (*0-8373-0177-7*) Nat Learn.

Customs Law & Administration. 3rd ed. Ed. by Ruth F. Sturm & Eugene M. Wypyski. 1983. Incl. Customs Service Decisions. ring bd. 695.00 (*0-379-20802-4*) Oceana.

Customs Law & Administration, Annual release. 3rd ed. Ruth F. Sturm. 1983. write for info. (*0-318-65995-6*) Oceana.

Customs Law & Administration: Customs Service Decisions. 3rd ed. Ed. by Eugene M. Wypyski. LC 85-28483. 1985. ring bd. 175.00 (*0-379-20880-6*) Oceana.

Customs Law & Administration: Customs Service Decisions, Annual release. 3rd ed. Ruth L. Sturm. Ed. by Eugene M. Wypyski. LC 85-28483. 1985. write for info. (*0-318-60222-9*) Oceana.

Customs Law Handbook: Annual Edition. Gould Editorial Staff. 1140p. 1989. ring bd. 28.00 (*0-87526-343-7*) Gould.

Customs Law of the European Economic Community. 2nd ed. Dominik Lasok. 300p. 1991. pap. 108.00 (*90-6544-483-1*) Kluwer Law Tax Pubs.

Customs of the Arabian Gulf: Drawings & Paintings by School Children in Bahrain & Dubai. Ann Walko & B. Fakhro. (Illus.). 49p. (J). (ps-8). 1978. 10.95 (*1-882443-01-2*) Bosphorus Bks.

Customs of the Baganda. A. Kagwa. Tr. by Earnest B. Kalibala. LC 70-82346. (Columbia Univ. Contributions to Anthropology Ser.: Vol. 22). reprint ed. 27.00 (*0-404-50572-4*) AMS Pr.

Customs of the Peak District & Derbyshire. John N. Merrill. 48p. 1987. 25.00 (*0-907496-34-2*, Pub. by JNM Pubns UK) St Mut.

An Asterisk (*) at the beginning of an entry indicates that the title is appearing in BIP for the first time.

C

An Asterisk (*) at the beginning of an entry indicates that the title is appearing in BIP for the first time.

1763

Cut-ups Carry On. James Marshall. LC 92-40721. (Illus.). 32p. (J). (ps-3). 1993. pap. 4.99 (*0-14-050726-4*, Puffin) Puffin Bks.
Cut-ups Carry On. James Marshall. (Illus.). 32p. (J). (ps-2). 1990. pap. 12.95 (*0-670-81645-0*) Viking Child Bks.
Cut-ups Crack Up. James Marshall. (Illus.). 32p. (J). (ps-3). 1992. 14.00 (*0-670-84486-1*) Viking Child Bks.
Cut-Ups Crack Up. James Marshall. (Illus.). 32p. (J). (ps-3). 1994. pap. 4.99 (*0-14-055318-5*) Puffin Bks.
Cut-ups Cut Loose. James Marshall. (Illus.). 32p. (J). (ps-3). 1989. pap. 4.99 (*0-14-050672-1*, Puffin) Puffin Bks.
Cut-ups Cut Loose. James Marshall. (Illus.). 32p. (J). (ps-3). 1987. pap. 12.95 (*0-670-80740-0*) Viking Child Bks.
***Cut Waste, Not Trees: How to Save Forests, Cut Pollution & Create Jobs.** Ed. by Atossa Soltani & Penelope Whitney. (Illus.). 68p. (Orig.). 1995. pap. 7.50 (*0-9628033-3-2*) Rainforest Act.
Cut with the Kitchen Knife: The Weimar Photomontages of Hannah Hoch. Maud Lavin. (Illus.). 280p. 1994. pap. 22.50 (*0-300-06164-1*) Yale U Pr.
Cut with the Kitchen Knife: The Weimer Photomontages of Hannah Hoch. Maud Lavin. LC 92-14332. (Illus.). 256p. (C). 1993. text ed. 45.00x (*0-300-04766-5*) Yale U Pr.
Cut-Work Embroidery & How to Do It. Oenoen Cave. (Illus.). 96p. 1982. pap. 3.95 (*0-486-24267-6*) Dover.
Cut Your Bills in Half. Rodale Press Editors. (Illus.). 400p. 1993. 7.98 (*0-8317-1892-7*) Smithmark.
Cut Your Mortgage Down to Size: How to Save Tens of Thousands of Dollars While Building More Equity in Your Home. Arthur Kramer. 175p. 1992. pap. 12.95 (*1-55738-259-X*) Probus Pub Co.
Cut Your Real Estate Taxes Down to Size: How to Win the Battle Against Spiraling Property Taxes. Brett J. Sinclair. 200p. 1992. 16.95 (*1-55738-404-5*) Probus Pub Co.
Cut Your Spending in Half, Without Settling for Less! How to Pay the Lowest Price for Everything. Rodale Press Editors. (Illus.). 480p. 1994. 27.95 (*0-87596-188-6*) Rodale Pr Inc.
Cutaneous Adnexal Tumors. Mark R. Wick et al. LC 91-17214. (Illus.). 238p. 1991. 135.00 (*0-89189-288-5*, 16-1-050-00) Am Soc Clinical.
Cutaneous Aging. Ed. by A. M. Kligman et al. 650p. 1989. 187.50 (*0-86008-435-3*, Pub. by U of Tokyo JA) Col U Pr.
Cutaneous Amyloidoses. Ed. by C. K. Wong & S. M. Breathnach. (Clinics in Dermatology Ser.: Vol. 8, No. 2). 111p. 1990. 40.00 (*0-444-01537-X*) Elsevier.
Cutaneous Antifungal Agents: Selected Compounds in Clinical Practice & Development. Ed. by Rippon & Fromtling. (Basic & Clinical Dermatology Ser.: Vol. 7). 488p. 1993. 185.00 (*0-8247-9055-3*) Dekker.
Cutaneous Arteries of the Human Body. C. Manchot. (Illus.). 149p. 1983. 145.00 (*0-387-90792-0*) Spr-Verlag.
Cutaneous Aspects of Internal Disease. Ed. by Jeffrey P. Callen. LC 80-14099. (Illus.). 697p. reprint ed. pap. 180.00 (*0-8357-7609-3*, 2056932) Bks Demand.
***Cutaneous Cryosurgery: Principles & Clinical Practice.** Rodney Dawber et al. 1992. 70.00 (*1-85317-082-8*) Scovill Paterson.
Cutaneous Development, Aging & Repair. Ed. by G. Abatangelo & J. M. Davidson. (FIDIA Research Ser.: Vol. 18). 360p. 1989. 102.00 (*0-387-96995-0*, 2801) Spr-Verlag.
Cutaneous Drug Reactions: An Integral Synopsis of Today's Systemic Drugs. 2nd rev. ed. K. Zuercher & A. Krebs. (Illus.). viii, 570p. 1992. 397.00 (*3-8055-4939-3*) S Karger.
Cutaneous Electrosurgery. Jack E. Sebben. 222p. 1988. 65.00 (*0-8151-7804-2*, Yr Bk Med Pubs) Mosby Yr Bk.
Cutaneous Facial Surgery. Ed. by J. R. Thomas & Roller. (Illus.). 224p. 1992. pap. text ed. 97.00 (*0-86577-398-X*) Thieme Med Pubs.
Cutaneous Fungal Infections. Ed. by Boni E. Elewski. LC 92-1430. (Topics in Clinical Dermatology Ser.). (Illus.). 272p. 1992. 72.00 (*0-89640-219-3*) Igaku-Shoin.
Cutaneous Head & Neck Melanoma: Diagnosis & Treatment. Ed. by A. J. Balm & B. B. Kroon. (Journal: Diagnostic Oncology: Vol. 3, No. 5, 1994). (Illus.). 58p. 1994. pap. 21.75 (*3-8055-6000-1*) S Karger.
Cutaneous Infestations & Insect Bites. Orkin & Maibach. LC 84-22977. (Dermatology Ser.: Vol. 4). 368p. 1985. 140.00 (*0-8247-7273-3*) Dekker.
Cutaneous Infestations of Man & Animal. Ed. by Lawrence C. Parish et al. LC 82-18946. 408p. 1983. text ed. 75.00 (*0-275-91407-0*, C1407, Praeger Pubs) Greenwood.
Cutaneous Innervation: Proceedings of the Brown University Symposium on the Biology of Skin, 1959. W. Montagna. LC 60-10839. (Advances in Biology of Skin Ser.: Vol. 1). 1960. 96.00 (*0-08-009385-X*, Pub. by Pergamon Repr UK) Franklin.
Cutaneous Investigation in Health & Disease: Noninvasive Methods & Instrumentation. Leveque. (Basic & Clinical Dermatology Ser.: Vol. 1). 464p. 1989. 175.00 (*0-8247-7967-3*) Dekker.
Cutaneous Laser Surgery. David. (Illus.). 400p. 1990. 99.00 (*0-8016-2789-3*) Mosby Yr Bk.
Cutaneous Laser Therapy: Principles & Methods. Ed. by Kenneth A. Arndt et al. LC 82-17379. (Wiley-Medical Publication Ser.). (Illus.). 255p. reprint ed. pap. 72.70 (*0-8357-8630-7*, 2035054) Bks Demand.
Cutaneous Lymphoma. Ed. by W. A. Van Vloten. (Current Problems in Dermatology Ser.: Vol. 19). (Illus.). viii, 270p. 1989. 198.50 (*3-8055-5058-8*) S Karger.
Cutaneous Lymphomas, Pseudolymphomas & Related Disorders. G. Burg & O. Braun-Falco. (Illus.). 550p. 1983. 306.00 (*0-387-10467-4*) Spr-Verlag.

C

***Cutaneous Manifestations of Infection in the Immunocompromised Host.** Marc E. Grossman. LC 94-11480. 196p. 1995. 99.00 (*0-683-03642-4*) Williams & Wilkins.
***Cutaneous Manifestations of Rheumatic Diseases.** Ed. by Richard D. Sontheimer & Thomas T. Provost. LC 95-3774. 1995. write for info. (*0-683-07852-6*) Williams & Wilkins.
Cutaneous Medicine & Surgery: An Integrated Program in Dermatology, 2 vols., Set. Kenneth A. Arndt et al. LC 94-6429. (Illus.). 1600p. 1995. text ed. write for info. (*0-7216-4852-5*) Saunders.
Cutaneous Melanoma. 2nd ed. Balch et al. (Illus.). 608p. 1991. text ed. 130.00 (*0-397-51052-7*) Lippincott.
Cutaneous Melanoma: Status of Knowledge & Future Perspectives. Ed. by Umberto Veronesi et al. 709p. 1987. text ed. 125.00 (*0-12-718855-X*) Acad Pr.
Cutaneous Melanoma & Precursor Lesions. Ed. by Dirk J. Ruiter et al. (Developments in Oncology Ser.). 1984. lib. bdg. 122.50 (*0-89838-689-6*) Kluwer Ac.
Cutaneous Surgery. Ronald G. Wheeland. (Illus.). 1104p. 1993. text ed. 185.00 (*0-7216-3523-7*) Saunders.
Cutaneous Surgical Anatomy of the Head & Neck. Eric A. Breisch & Hubert T. Greenway. (Practical Manuals in Dermatologic Surgery Ser.). (Illus.). 133p. 1991. pap. text ed. 32.00 (*0-443-08744-X*) Churchill.
Cutaneous Toxicity. Ed. by Victor A. Drill & Paul Lazar. (Target Organ Toxicology Ser.). 288p. 1984. text ed. 104.50 (*0-89004-933-5*) Raven.
***Cutaway Cars.** C. Gifford. (Cutaways Ser.). (Illus.). 32p. (YA). (gr. 4 up). 1995. lib. bdg. 14.96 (*0-88110-733-6*, Usborne); pap. 6.95 (*0-7460-1717-0*, Usborne) EDC.
Cutaway Cars: Ten Classics for You to Assemble. David Juniper. (Illus.). 60p. 1991. 19.95 (*1-56138-002-4*) Running Pr.
Cutback Management. George G. Wynne. (Learning from Abroad Ser.: Vol. 6). 150p. 1983. pap. text ed. 18.95 (*0-87855-930-2*) Transaction Pubs.
Cutback Management: A Trinational Perspective. Ed. by George G. Wynne. (Learning from Abroad Ser.). (Illus.). 160p. 1983. 12.95 (*0-932328-04-0*) Intl Ctr Academy.
Cutback Management in Public Bureaucracies: Popular Theories & Observed Outcomes in Whitehall. Andrew Dunsire & Christopher Hood. (Illus.). (C). 1989. 79.95 (*0-521-37240-2*) Cambridge U Pr.
Cute & Other Poems. Jim Everhard. 80p. (Orig.). 1982. pap. 4.95 (*0-917342-93-3*) Gay Sunshine.
Cute & Other Poems. deluxe limited ed. Jim Everhard. 80p. (Orig.). 1982. ring bd. 35.00 (*0-917342-92-5*) Gay Sunshine.
Cute Is a Four-Letter Word. Stella Pevsner. 176p. (J). (gr. 7 up). 1989. pap. 2.75 (*0-671-68845-6*, Archway) PB.
Cuthbert Mills Letters. Ed. by James Willert. (Illus.). 70p. (Orig.). 1984. pap. 20.00 (*0-930798-06-6*) J Willert.
Cuthberts, Barons of Castle Hill & Their Descendants in South Carolina & Georgia. J. G. Bulloch. (Illus.). 1993. reprint ed. lib. bdg. 29.00 (*0-8328-1394-X*); reprint ed. pap. 19.00 (*0-8328-1395-8*) Higginson Bk Co.
Cuthbertson's Little Mountain Bike Book. Leo Wolf. (Illus.). 144p. (Orig.). 1991. pap. 6.95 (*0-89815-438-3*) Ten Speed Pr.
Cuticle Techniques in Arthropods. T. A. Miller. (Experimental Entomology Ser.). (Illus.). 410p. 1980. 152.00 (*0-387-90475-1*) Spr-Verlag.
Cutlass in the Snow. Elizabeth Shub. LC 85-5442. (Illus.). 48p. (J). (gr. 1-4). 1986. 11.95 (*0-688-05927-9*); lib. bdg. 11.88 (*0-688-05928-7*) Greenwillow.
Cutler: Mustang. large type ed. H. V. Elkin. (Linford Mystery Library). 320p. 1992. pap. 14.95 (*0-7089-7178-4*, Trailtree Bookshop) Ulverscroft.
Cutler Memorial & Genealogical History. N. S. Cutler. (Illus.). 665p. 1989. reprint ed. lib. bdg. 109.50 (*0-8328-0450-9*); reprint ed. pap. 99.50 (*0-8328-0451-7*) Higginson Bk Co.
***Cutler's Brigade at Gettysburg.** 2nd rev. ed. James L. McLean, Jr. (Illus.). 264p. (C). 1995. 35.00x (*0-935523-42-1*) Butternut & Blue.
Cutlery Industry. Peter Smithurst. 1989. pap. 25.00 (*0-85263-870-1*, Pub. by Shire UK) St Mut.
Cutlery Trades. George I. Lloyd. (Illus.). 493p. 1968. reprint ed. 37.50 (*0-7146-1403-3*, Pub. by F Cass Pubs UK) Intl Spec Bk.
Cutlip's Quotem Pole. Harley V. Cutlip. 80p. 1992. pap. write for info. (*0-9632843-0-4*) H V Cutlip.
***Cutoff.** Jay Rogoff. 72p. (Orig.). 1995. pap. 10.00 (*0-915380-31-5*) Word Works.
***Cutoffs: How Family Members Who Sever Relationships Can Reconnect.** Carol Netzer. 256p. 1995. pap. 13.95 (*0-88282-138-5*) New Horizon NJ.
Cutout Moons. LeRoy Gorman. 24p. 1980. pap. 2.00 (*0-913719-41-2*) High-Coo Pr.
Cutover Country: Jolie's Story. Jolie Paylin. LC 76-10245. (Illus.). 174p. reprint ed. pap. 49.60 (*0-317-58162-7*, 2029696) Bks Demand.
Cuts. Malcolm Bradbury. 160p. 1988. mass mkt. 5.95 (*0-14-010846-7*, Penguin Bks) Viking Penguin.
Cuts! Robert Kennedy. (Illus.). 192p. 1989. pap. 15.95 (*0-399-51477-5*, Perigee Bks) Berkley Pub.
Cuts. Carter Scholz. (Drumm Booklet Ser.: No. 20). 55p. (Orig.). 1985. pap. 2.50 (*0-936055-19-7*) C Drumm Bks.
Cuts. deluxe limited ed. Carter Scholz. (Drumm Booklet Ser.: No. 20). 55p. (Orig.). 1985. 6.00 (*0-936055-20-0*) C Drumm Bks.
Cuts. Malcolm Bradbury. 240p. 1988. reprint ed. pap. 9.95 (*0-14-023154-4*, Penguin Bks) Viking Penguin.
Cuts Both Ways: (American Heroes) Dee Holmes. (Silhouette Intimate Moments Ser.). 1994. mass mkt. 3.50 (*0-373-07541-3*, 5-07541-1) Silhouette.

Cuts, Breaks, Bruises, & Burns: How Your Body Heals. Joanna Cole. LC 84-45335. (Illus.). 48p. (J). (gr. 2-6). 1985. lib. bdg. 14.89 (*0-690-04438-0*, Crowell Jr Bks) HarpC Child Bks.
Cutter. Laura Crum. 208p. 1994. 18.95 (*0-312-10960-1*, Pub. by Thomas Dunne Bks) St Martin.
Cutter: Panhandle Payback. Duff Mccoy. 1990. pap. 3.50 (*1-55817-378-1*, Pinnacle NY) Windsor NY.
Cutter-Sanborn Three-Figure Author Table: Swanson-Swift Revision. C. A. Cutter & Sanborn. 34p. 1969. 18.00 (*0-87287-210-6*) Libs Unl.
Cutters. large type ed. Bess S. Aldrich. 220p. 1992. reprint ed. lib. bdg. 19.95 (*1-56054-501-1*) Thorndike Pr.
Cutters. Bess S. Aldrich. 275p. 1975. reprint ed. lib. bdg. 21.95 (*0-88411-254-3*, Aeonian Pr) Amereon Ltd.
Cutters. Bess S. Aldrich. LC 88-13864. vi, 276p. 1989. reprint ed. pap. 8.95 (*0-8032-5916-6*, Bison Books) U of Nebr Pr.
Cutter's Official Guide to Hot Springs, Arkansas: 1917. John M. Cutter. (Illus.). 1979. reprint ed. pap. 6.95 (*0-89646-057-6*) Vistabooks.
Cutthroat. Jason Frost. (Warlord Ser.: No. 2). 1984. pap. 2.50 (*0-8217-1308-6*) Zebra.
Cutthroat. Michael Slade. 348p. (Orig.). 1992. pap. 4.99 (*0-451-17452-6*, Sig) NAL-Dutton.
Cutthroat: Native Trout of the West. Patrick C. Trotter. 1987. pap. 17.50 (*0-87081-166-5*) Univ Pr Colo.
Cutthroat Blues. Blacky Hix. 35p. (Orig.). 1991. pap. 5.00 (*1-885466-05-6*) Smoke The Soul.
Cutthroat Blues - Blood Rain. Blacky Hix & Bill Shields. (Illus.). 80p. (Orig.). 1992. pap. 8.00 (*1-885466-08-0*) Smoke The Soul.
Cutthroat Soldiers. Lawrence B. Sulc. Ed. by Nathan Hale Institute Staff. 1987. pap. write for info. (*0-318-61847-8*) Nathan Hale Inst.
Cutthroat Teammates: Achieving Effective Teamwork among Professionals. Donald E. Heany. 1992. pap. 17.00 (*1-55623-882-7*) Irwin Prof Pubng.
***Cutthroats of Lankhmar.** 9.95 (*0-7869-0103-9*) TSR Inc.
***Cuttin' the Body Loose: Historical, Biological & Personal Approaches to Death & Dying.** William J. Gavin. 272p. (Orig.). (C). 1995. lib. bdg. 49.95 (*1-56639-297-7*); pap. text ed. 16.95 (*1-56639-298-5*) Temple U Pr.
Cutting. Leon Harrell. 1990. pap. 12.95 (*0-911647-15-5*) Western Horseman.
Cutting: A Guide for the Non-Pro Competitor. Sally Harrison. Ed. by Madelyn Larsen. (Illus.). 224p. 1992. 29.95 (*0-87605-845-4*) Howell Bk.
Cutting: Training the Horse & Rider. Bill Freeman & Gala Nettles. LC 93-36986. (EquiMedia's Masters Ser.). 1994. 29.95 (*0-9625898-0-2*) EquiMedia.
Cutting & Grinding Fluids: Selection & Application. 2nd ed. Ed. by J. Silliman. LC 92-809773. 212p. 1992. pap. text ed. 39.00 (*0-87263-423-X*) SME.
Cutting & Grinding Fluids: Selection & Application. Ed. by R. K. Springborn. LC 67-17007. (Manufacturing Data Ser.). 180p. reprint ed. pap. 51.30 (*0-685-15527-7*, 2026700) Bks Demand.
Cutting & Packing in Production & Distribution: A Typology & Bibliography. H. Dyckhoff & U. Finke. (Contributions to Management Science Ser.). (Illus.). x, 248p. 1992. 79.00 (*0-387-91426-9*) Spr-Verlag.
Cutting & Polishing Optical & Electronic Materials. 2nd ed. G. W. Fynn. (Optics & Optoelectronics Ser.). (Illus.). 272p. 1988. 138.00 (*0-85274-373-4*) IOP Pub.
Cutting & Welding Processes. National Fire Protection Association Staff. 1994. 16.75 (*0-317-63200-0*, 51B-94) Natl Fire Prot.
Cutting Back: Retrenchment & Redevelopment in Human & Community Services. Larry Hirschhorn et al. LC 82-49038. (Jossey-Bass Social & Behavioral Science Ser.). (Illus.). 415p. reprint ed. pap. 118.30 (*0-8357-4888-X*, 2037820) Bks Demand.
Cutting Carbon Emissions: Burden or Benefit? Pt. 1: The Economics of Energy-Tax & Non-Price Policies. Florentin Krause et al. (Energy Policy in the Greenhouse: Vol. 2). 175p. (Orig.). 1993. pap. 50.00 (*1-883774-01-2*) IPSEP.
Cutting Chemical Wastes: What Twenty-Nine Organic Chemical Plants Are Doing to Reduce Hazardous Waste. David J. Sarokin. LC 85-23896. 548p. 1986. pap. 47.50 (*0-918780-32-2*) INFORM NY.
Cutting Costs: An Executive's Guide to Increased Profits. Harry E. Figgie, Jr. LC 89-17763. 256p. 1990. pap. 17.95 (*0-8144-7720-8*) AMACOM.
Cutting down an Ancient Tree: Seventeenth Century. Ed. & Tr. by Malachi McCormick. (Miniatures Ser.). 24p. Date not set. pap. 7.00 (*0-943984-47-5*) Stone St Pr.
Cutting Down an Ancient Tree: Seventeenth Century. Ed. & Tr. by Malachi McCormick. 24p. 1989. 7.00 (*0-943984-36-X*) Stone St Pr.
Cutting Down the Trees: Agricultural Change, Anthropology & History in Zambia 1890-1990. Megan Vaughan & Henrietta Moore. LC 93-5650. (Social History of Africa Ser.). (C). 1993. text ed. 50.00 (*0-435-08088-1*, 08090) Heinemann.
Cutting Down the Trees: Agricultural Change, Anthropology & History in Zambia 1890-1990. Megan Vaughan & Henrietta Moore. LC 93-5650. (Social History of Africa Ser.). 304p. (C). 1994. pap. 22.95 (*0-435-08090-3*) Heinemann.
Cutting Edge. Caroline Burnes. (Intrigue Ser.). 1994. mass mkt. 2.99 (*0-373-22267-X*, 1-22267-8) Harlequin Bks.
Cutting Edge. Ace Collins. (Springfield Ser.). 128p. (Orig.). 1993. pap. text ed. 4.99 (*0-9628579-5-5*) Vision WY.
Cutting Edge. David Duncan. (Handful of Men Ser.: Pt. 1). 1993. mass mkt. 4.99 (*0-345-38167-X*, Del Rey) Ballantine.
Cutting Edge. John Harvey. 352p. 1992. mass mkt. 4.99 (*0-380-71615-1*) Avon.

Cutting Edge. Photos & Intro. by C. J. Heatley, III. LC 85-52216. (Illus.). 152p. 1991. 19.98 (*0-934738-17-3*); pap. 12.98 (*0-934738-63-7*) Thomasson-Grant.
***Cutting Edge.** Linda Howard. 1995. mass mkt. 4.99 (*1-55166-033-4*, 1-66033-1, Mira Bks) Harlequin Bks.
Cutting Edge. Carolyn Keene. Ed. by Anne Greenberg. (Nancy Drew Files Ser.: No. 70). 160p. (Orig.). (J). 1992. mass mkt. 3.99 (*0-671-73074-6*) PB.
Cutting Edge. Lonnie C. Wormley. (Illus.). 100p. Date not set. pap. 9.95 (*1-883866-04-9*) Clarion Pub.
Cutting Edge, Vol. 2. David A. Clemens. LC 79-52420. (Steps to Maturity Ser.). 1975. teacher ed 17.95 (*0-86508-004-6*); student ed 15.95 (*0-86508-003-8*) BCM Pubn.
***Cutting Edge: A Human Prosection Guide.** Mark B. Frasier & F. D. Giddings. (Illus.). 160p. (Orig.). (C). 1994. student ed, pap. 25.00 (*0-9615226-3-1*) Giddings Studio Pub.
Cutting Edge: For the Man, Woman & Child Who Has Everything - but Wants More. Jim Beckel & Andy Mayer. (Illus.). 64p. 1993. pap. 9.95 (*0-02-040291-0*, Collier S&S) S&S Trade.
Cutting Edge: How Churches Speak on Social & Ethical Issues. Mark Ellingsen. 400p. (Orig.). 1993. pap. text ed. 34.99 (*0-8028-0710-0*) Eerdmans.
Cutting Edge: Military History of Antiquity & Early Feudal Times. Paul F. Gavaghan. LC 89-12200. (American University Studies: History: Ser. IX, Vol. 85). 510p. 1990. text ed. 72.95 (*0-8204-1190-6*) P Lang Pubs.
Cutting Edge: Women & the Pit Strike. Ed. by Vicky Seddon. (Illus.). 288p. (C). 1986. pap. 19.95 (*0-85315-637-9*, Pub. by Lawrence & Wishart UK) Humanities.
***Cutting Edge: 1996 Calendar.** (Illus.). 1995. 11.95 (*1-56566-081-1*) Thomasson-Grant.
Cutting Edge Cases in the Legal Environment of Business. Constance E. Bagley & Christi A. Haubegger. Ed. by Clyde Perlee & Lamar. 250p. (C). 1993. pap. text ed. 17.75 (*0-314-01622-8*) West Pub.
Cutting Edge II. Craig C. Callen. 238p. 1993. 49.95 (*0-318-72977-6*, D7067) PennWell Bks.
Cutting Edge in Physical Education & Exercise Science Research: The Academy Papers. 136p. (Orig.). 1987. pap. text ed. 22.00x (*0-87322-098-6*, BSAF0098) Human Kinetics.
Cutting Edge of Audio Production & Post Production: Theory, Equipment & Techniques. Mico Nelson. 265p. 1994. 39.95 (*0-86729-304-7*) Knowledge Indus.
Cutting Edge of Socialism: Working People Against Transnational Capital. Stephen Bodington. 87p. (Orig.). 1982. pap. 19.95 (*0-85124-332-0*, Pub. by Spokesman Bks UK) Coronet Bks.
Cutting Edge Technologies. 192p. 1984. pap. text ed. 18.95 (*0-309-03489-2*) Natl Acad Pr.
Cutting Edge Technologies. Ed. by Ervin L. Harlacher. 116p. 1988. 5.00 (*0-87117-187-2*) Am Assn Comm Coll.
***Cutting Edges: Postmodern Critical Essays on Eighteenth-Century Satire.** Ed. by James E. Gill. LC 95-4362. (Tennessee Studies in Literature: Vol. 37). 1995. write for info. (*0-615-00664-7*) U of Tenn Pr.
Cutting Edges: Young American Action for the 70's. Jack Hicks. LC 72-86412. (C). 1973. pap. text ed. 14.00 (*0-03-088517-5*) HB Coll Pubs.
Cutting Energy Costs. Richard Dick-Larkham. 1977. 24.95 (*0-8464-0309-9*) Beekman Pubs.
***Cutting Fluids & Industrial Lubricants: A Selection from the Tool & Manufacturing Engineers Handbook.** Ed. by Thomas J. Drozda. LC 82-60312. (Illus.). 66p. 1988. reprint ed. pap. 25.00 (*0-7837-8191-1*, 2047896) Bks Demand.
***Cutting for Sign.** Langewiesche. 1995. pap. 12.00 (*0-679-75963-8*) Random.
Cutting for Sign. William Langewiesche. LC 93-9040. 288p. 1994. 23.00 (*0-679-41113-5*) Pantheon.
Cutting Garden for California. Pat Kite & Betty Mackey. (Illus.). 104p. (Orig.). 1989. pap. 8.00 (*0-9616338-1-6*) B B Mackey Bks.
Cutting Garden for Florida. 2nd ed. Betty B. Mackey & Monica M. Brandies. (Illus.). 96p. (Orig.). 1992. pap. 8.95 (*0-9616338-2-4*) B B Mackey Bks.
Cutting Gardens. Chet Davis. LC 92-41054. (Burpee American Gardening Ser.). (Illus.). 1994. pap. 9.00 (*0-671-85043-1*) P-H.
Cutting Gardens: The Complete Guide to Growing Flowers & Creating Spectacular Arrangements from Your Garden - for Every Season & Every Region. Anne M. Halpin & Betty B. Mackey. (Illus.). 144p. 1993. 27.50 (*0-671-74441-0*) S&S Trade.
Cutting Hair at Home: Step-by-Step Home Hair-Cutting for the Entire Family. Lee Pola & Patricia Bozic. (Illus.). 128p. (Orig.). 1986. pap. 9.95 (*0-452-25830-8*, Plume) NAL-Dutton.
Cutting Hill. Alan Pistorius. 1990. 19.95 (*0-394-57439-7*) Knopf.
Cutting Hill. Alan Pistorius. 1992. pap. 3.99 (*0-517-09184-4*) Random Hse Value.
Cutting Horse. Tom McGuane. 1991. 29.95 (*0-9627181-7-3*) NCHA.
Cutting Hours. Julia Grice. 288p. 1993. 19.95 (*0-312-85677-6*) Forge NYC.
Cutting Hours. Julia Grice. 304p. 1995. pap. (*0-8125-1092-5*) Forge NYC.
Cutting Library Costs: Increasing Productivity & Raising Revenues. Eleanor F. Brown. LC 79-19448. 274p. 1979. 22.50 (*0-8108-1250-9*) Scarecrow.
Cutting Loose. Howard M. Halpern. 1990. pap. 12.00 (*0-671-69604-1*, Fireside) S&S Trade.
Cutting Loose. Jesse Maguire. (Nowhere High Ser.: No. 8). (Orig.). 1992. mass mkt. 3.99 (*0-8041-0850-1*) Ivy Books.

An Asterisk (*) at the beginning of an entry indicates that the title is appearing in BIP for the first time.

An Asterisk (*) at the beginning of an entry indicates that the title is appearing in BIP for the first time.

1765

C

Cybernetics & Systems Eighty-Six. Ed. by Robert Trappl. 1986. lib. bdg. 239.00 (*90-277-2213-7*) Kluwer Ac.

Cybernetics & Systems Research: Proceedings of the Sixth European Meeting, Organized by the Austrian Society for Cybernetic Studies, University of Vienna, 1982. Ed. by Robert Trappl. 984p. 1982. 169.25 (*0-444-86488-1*, North Holland) Elsevier.

Cybernetics & Systems Research, 2. Robert Trappl. 1984. 161.75 (*0-444-86898-4*, I-243-84) Elsevier.

Cybernetics & Systems Research 2000: Proceedings of the 12th European Meeting, 2 vols. R. Trappl. 972p. 1994. text ed. 235.00 (*981-02-1761-7*) World Scientific Pub.

Cybernetics & Systems 1988, 2 pts., Set, Pts. 1-2. Ed. by Robert Trappl. (C). 1988. Set. lib. bdg. 466.50 (*90-277-2728-7*) Kluwer Ac.

Cybernetics & Systems '92: Proceedings of the 11th European Mtg, 2 vols., Set. Robert Trappl. 1700p. 1992. text ed. 235.00 (*981-02-0918-5*) World Scientific Pub.

Cybernetics Group, 1946-1953. Steve J. Heims. 352p. 1991. 27.50 (*0-262-08200-4*) MIT Pr.

Cybernetics in Water Resources Management. Branislav Djordjevic. 641p. 1993. text ed. 85.00 (*0-918334-82-9*) WRP.

Cybernetics of Art: Reason & the Rainbow. M. J. Rosenberg. (Studies in Cybernetics: Vol. 4). (Illus.). 236p. 1983. text ed. 76.00 (*0-677-05970-1*) Gordon & Breach.

Cybernetics of Prejudices in the Practice of Psychotherapy. Gianfranco Cecchin et al. 96p. 1994. pap. 19.95 (*1-85575-056-2*, Pub. by Karnac Bks UK) Brunner-Mazel.

Cybernetics or Control & Communication in the Animal & the Machine. 2nd ed. Norbert Wiener. (Illus.). 212p. (Orig.). 1961. pap. 13.95 (*0-262-73009-X*) MIT Pr.

***Cyberotica Tour of the Internet.** 1995. pap. write for info. (*0-7821-1692-2*) Sybex.

Cyberpapacy. 128p. 1991. 18.00 (*0-87431-307-4*, 20508) West End Games.

Cyberpunk: Outlaws & Hackers on the Computer Frontier. Katie Hafner & John Markoff. 368p. 1992. pap. 12.00 (*0-671-77879-X*, Touchstone Bks) S&S Trade.

***Cyberpunk Handbook.** Goffman. write for info. (*0-679-76345-7*) Random.

***Cyberpunk Handbook.** Goffman. 1995. 9.95 (*0-679-76230-2*) Random Hse Value.

Cyberpunk 2020. 2nd ed. Michael Pondsmith et al. Ed. by Derek Quintanar. (Cyberpunk Ser.). (Illus.). 260p. (C). 1990. pap. 20.00 (*0-937279-13-7*, CP3002) R Talsorian.

***CyberQuest: Problem Solving & Innovation Support System, Conceptual Background & Experiences.** John W. Dickey. (Creativity Research Ser.). (Illus.). 328p. 1995. 55.00 (*1-56750-113-3*); pap. 24.50 (*1-56750-117-6*) Ablex Pub.

Cyberscapes: Computer Graphics from the Yagi Studio. Yasuhiro Asano. (Illus.). 84p. 1994. 36.95 (*4-8381-0126-0*, Pub. by Mitsumura JA) Bks Nippan.

***Cybersex: Making Love Online.** Joshua Bagby. 250p. (Orig.). 1996. pap. 17.95 (*1-56866-069-3*) Index Pub Grp.

Cyberskelter. Adam Fairbairn. Ed. by Kevin Barrett. (Cyberspace Ser.). (Illus.). 64p. (Orig.). (C). 1991. pap. 10.00 (*1-55806-142-8*, 5107) Iron Crown Ent Inc.

Cybersociety: Computer-Mediated Communication & Community. Ed. by Steven G. Jones. 272p. 1994. 46.00 (*0-8039-5676-2*); pap. 22.95 (*0-8039-5677-0*) Sage.

***Cybersource '95.** Frederic E. Davis. 1995. pap. 19.95 (*1-56276-284-2*) Ziff-Davis.

Cyberspace. Tod Foley. Ed. by Kevin Barrett. (Illus.). 208p. (Orig.). (C). 1989. pap. 18.00 (*1-55806-045-6*, 5100) Iron Crown Ent Inc.

Cyberspace: First Steps. Michael L. Benedikt. (Illus.). 304p. 1992. reprint ed. pap. 21.50x (*0-262-52177-6*) MIT Pr.

***Cyberspace Adventure.** Terrance Dicks. LC 94-44715. (Chronicles of a Computer Game Addict Ser.). (Illus.). (J). 1994. write for info. (*0-8120-9421-2*) Barron.

Cyberspace & the Law: Your Rights & Duties in the On-Line World. Edward A. Cavazos & Gavino Morin. LC 94-12356. 215p. 1994. pap. 19.95 (*0-262-53123-2*) MIT Pr.

***Cyberspace Cowboy.** Ted Pedersen & Mel Gilden. LC 95-7898. (Cybersurfers Ser.). (J). 1995. write for info. (*0-8431-3934-X*) Price Stern.

Cyberspace Lexicon: An Illustrated Dictionary of Terms from Multimedia to Virtual Reality. Bob Cotton & Richard Oliver. (Illus.). 224p. (C). 1994. 29.95 (*0-7148-3267-7*, Pub. by Phaidon Press UK) Chronicle Bks.

Cyberspace Warrior. Edward Packard. (Choose Your Own Adventure Ser.: No. 154). (J). (gr. 4-7). 1994. pap. 3.50 (*0-553-56400-5*) Bantam.

***Cyberstorm.** Gloria Skurzynski. LC 94-45722. (J). 1995. 15.00 (*0-02-782926-X*, Mac Bks Young Read) S&S Childrens.

***Cyberstrategies: How to Build an Internet-Based Information System.** Michael Carroll & W. Scott Downs. (Communications Ser.). 300p. 1995. pap. 29.95 (*0-442-01988-2*) Van Nos Reinhold.

Cybertech Killing. John Sievert. (C.A.D.S. Ser.: No. 8). 1989. pap. 2.95 (*0-8217-2818-0*) Zebra.

Cybertexts. Bruce Boston. (Illus.). 40p. (Orig.). 1992. pap. text ed. 5.00 (*0-9626708-4-7*) Talisman IN.

***Cyberweb.** Lisa Mason. LC 94-32026. 1995. 20.00 (*0-688-13987-6*) Morrow.

Cybil War. Betsy C. Byars. (Illus.). 144p. (J). (gr. 3 up). 1990. pap. 3.99 (*0-14-034356-3*, Puffin) Puffin Bks.

Cybil War. Betsy C. Byars. LC 80-26912. (Illus.). 144p. (J). (gr. 8-12). 1981. pap. 13.99 (*0-670-25248-4*) Viking Child Bks.

***Cyborg Handbook.** Chris H. Gray. Ed. by Heidi J. Figueroa & Steven Mentor. (Illus.). 480p. 1995. pap. 19.95 (*0-415-90849-3*, B2872, Routledge NY) Routledge.

***Cyborg Handbook.** Chris H. Gray. Ed. by Heidi J. Figueroa & Steven Mentor. (Illus.). 480p. 1995. 59.95x (*0-415-90848-5*, B2868, Routledge NY) Routledge.

Cyborg Kickboxer. Victor Appleton. Ed. by Ann Greenberg. (Tom Swift Ser.: No. 3). 160p. (Orig.). (J). 1991. pap. 2.95 (*0-671-67825-6*, Archway) PB.

Cycads of the World. David L. Jones. (Illus.). 296p. 1993. 45.00 (*1-56098-220-9*) Smithsonian.

Cyclades Computer Network: Toward Layered Network Architectures. Pouzin. (International Council for Computer Communications Ser.: Vol. 2). 388p. 1982. 72.00 (*0-444-86482-2*, North Holland) Elsevier.

Cyclades in the Bronze Age. R. L. Barber. LC 86-51182. (Illus.). 301p. (C). 1987. text ed. 45.00 (*0-87745-168-0*) U of Iowa Pr.

Cycladic Art. J. Lesley Fitton. (British Museum Paperbacks Ser.). (Illus.). 72p. 1990. pap. 12.50 (*0-674-18035-6*) HUP.

Cycladic Spirit: Masterpieces from the Nicholas P. Goulandris Collection. Colin Renfrew. (Illus.). 207p. 1991. 49.50 (*0-8109-3169-9*) Abrams.

Cyclams & Aza Crowns, Vol. 51. Jerald S. Bradshaw et al. LC 92-35450. (Chemistry of Heterocyclic Compounds Ser.). 550p. 1993. text ed. 299.00 (*0-471-52485-9*) Wiley.

Cycle America Resource Directory Wine Country: Bicycle Routes & Information for San Francisco to Wine Country Region. Sally Vantress & Martin Krieg. (Illus.). 96p. (Orig.). 1991. pap. 4.95 (*0-9611490-4-3*) Cycle Amer.

Cycle C - Decorating for Sundays & Holy Days: Themes, Homily Suggestions, Activities. Bernadette Snyder & Hazelmai Terry. LC 88-72014. 136p. (Orig.). 1988. pap. 9.95 (*0-89622-372-8*) Twenty-Third.

Cycle Chase. C. J. Naden. LC 79-64638. (Illus.). 32p. (J). (gr. 4-9). 1980. lib. bdg. 10.79 (*0-89375-249-5*); pap. 2.95 (*0-89375-263-0*) Troll Assocs.

Cycle Counting for Record Accuracy. rev. ed. 96p. (SPA.). 1994. 30.00 (*1-55822-108-5*) Am Prod & Inventory.

Cycle Counting for Record Accuracy Training Aid. rev. ed. Henry H. Jordan. LC 83-72792. 96p. 1994. 25.00 (*0-935406-60-3*) Am Prod & Inventory.

Cycle Food: A Guide to Satisfying Your Inner Tube. Lauren Hefferon. LC 83-40023. (Illus.). 96p. 1983. pap. 4.95 (*0-89815-099-X*) Ten Speed Pr.

Cycle Linkage: Planetary-Solar-Terrestrial. Ed. by Diane Epperson. 110p. 1988. pap. 70.00 (*1-879192-04-7*) Fndtn Study Cycles.

Cycle Log: Diary & Guide for the Cyclist. Jan Bass & Tim Houts. (Illus.). 176p. 1993. reprint ed. pap. 9.95 (*0-9624232-7-0*) Sports Log Pubs.

Cycle Log: The Comprehensive Diary & Guide for Cyclists. Jan Bass. (Illus.). 256p. (Orig.). 1990. pap. 14.95 (*0-9624232-1-1*) Sports Log Pubs.

Cycle of Adams Letters, 1861-1865, 2 vols., Set. Worthington C. Ford. (History - United States Ser.). 1992. reprint ed. lib. bdg. 150.00 (*0-7812-6187-2*) Rprt Serv.

Cycle of American Literature. Robert E. Spiller. LC 68-7396. 1967. pap. 16.95 (*0-02-930420-2*) Free Pr.

Cycle of Day & Night: Where One Proceeds Along the Path of the Primordial Yoga; A Basic Tibetan Text on the Practice of Dzogchen. Namkhai Norbu. Ed. & Tr. by John Reynolds. LC 87-9953. (Illus.). 128p. 1987. reprint ed. pap. 9.95 (*0-88268-040-4*) Station Hill Pr.

Cycle of Juvenile Justice. Thomas J. Bernard. (Illus.). 208p. (C). 1991. pap. text ed. 14.95 (*0-19-507183-2*) OUP.

Cycle of Marketing. A. C. Spence. 1967. 19.00 (*0-8464-0311-0*) Beekman Pubs.

Cycle of Myths: Native Legends from Southeast Alaska. Ed. by John E. Smelcer. (Illus.). 116p. (Orig.). (YA). (gr. 7 up). 1993. pap. 12.95 (*0-9634000-2-9*) Salmon Run.

Cycle of Outrage: America's Reaction to the Juvenile Delinquent in the 1950's. James B. Gilbert. (Illus.). 266p. 1986. 30.00 (*0-19-503721-9*) OUP.

Cycle of Outrage: America's Reaction to the Juvenile Delinquent in the 1950's. James B. Gilbert. (Illus.). 266p. 1988. pap. 18.95 (*0-19-505641-8*) OUP.

Cycle of Seasons: Spiral of Life. Judy K. Porter. 68p. 1993. pap. write for info. (*0-9636230-0-1*) Transport Pub.

Cycle of Seasons in Corrales. Ruth W. Armstrong. LC 88-12232. (Illus.). 96p. (Orig.). 1988. pap. 8.95 (*0-86534-124-9*) Sunstone Pr.

Cycle of the Werewolf. Stephen King. 1985. pap. 12.95 (*0-451-82219-6*, Sig) NAL-Dutton.

Cycle of the West: Golden Anniversary Edition. John G. Neihardt. LC 91-38033. (Illus.). xiv, 524p. 1992. 100.00 (*0-8032-3323-X*) U of Nebr Pr.

Cycle of the Year. 2nd ed. Rudolf Steiner. Tr. by Margaret Dawson & Barbara Betteridge. 115p. 1984. pap. 8.95 (*0-88010-081-8*) Anthroposophic.

***Cycle Representations of Markov Processes.** Sophia L. Kalpazidou. LC 94-28223. (Applications of Mathematics Ser.: Vol. 28). 1995. write for info. (*0-387-94363-3*) Spr-Verlag.

***Cycle Sport.** Peter Konopka. (Illus.). 160p. 1995. pap. 22.95 (*1-85223-846-1*, Pub. by Crowood Pr UK) Trafalgar.

Cycle Synchronies. Edward R. Dewey et al. 90p. 1990. pap. 70.00 (*1-879192-06-3*) Fndtn Study Cycles.

Cycle Time Management: The Fast Track to Time-Based Productivity Improvement. Patrick Northey & Nigel Southway. LC 92-32449. 1993. 35.00 (*1-56327-015-3*) Prod Press.

Cycle Touring in New Zealand. Bruce Ringer. LC 89-38348. (Illus.). 320p. (Orig.). 1989. pap. 14.95 (*0-89886-182-9*) Mountaineers.

Cycles. Richard G. Nilges. LC 80-12889. 1983. pap. 14.95 (*0-87949-182-5*) Ashley Bks.

Cycles. Samuel A. Schreiner, Jr. 1990. 19.95 (*1-55611-162-2*) D I Fine.

Cycles: A Decade of Photographs. Judith Golden. Ed. by David Featherstone. LC 86-82516. (Untitled Ser.: No. 45). (Illus.). 52p. (Orig.). 1988. pap. 10.95 (*0-933286-47-3*) Frnds Photography.

Cycles: In Universe & Man. rev. ed. Lydia Ross. Ed. by W. Emmett Small & Helen Todd. (Theosophical Manual Ser.: No. 8). 92p. 1975. reprint ed. pap. 3.95 (*0-913004-19-7*) Point Loma Pub.

Cycles: Selected Writings. Edward R. Dewey. 810p. 1970. 65.00 (*1-879192-03-9*) Fndtn Study Cycles.

Cycles & Bridges in Graphs. Heinz-Jurgen Voss. (C). 1991. lib. bdg. 122.50 (*0-7923-0899-9*) Kluwer Ac.

Cycles & Chaos in Economic Equilibrium. Ed. by Jess Benhabib. (Illus.). 466p. 1992. text ed. 80.00 (*0-691-04249-7*); pap. text ed. 27.95 (*0-691-00392-0*) Princeton U Pr.

Cycles & Crises in Property-Casualty Insurance: Causes & Implications for Public Policy. Lawrence A. Berger et al. (Illus.). 412p. (C). 1991. 150.00 (*0-89382-180-2*) Nat Assn Insu Comm.

Cycles & Events in Stratigraphy. Ed. by G. Einsele et al. (Illus.). 1040p. 1991. 83.00 (*0-387-52784-2*) Spr-Verlag.

Cycles & Rays: Proceedings of the NATO Advanced Research Workshop on "Cycles & Rays: Basic Structures in Finite & Infinite Graphs" Held in Montreal, Canada, May 3-9, 1987. Ed. by Gena Hahn et al. (C). 1990. lib. bdg. 109.50 (*0-7923-0597-3*) Kluwer Ac.

Cycles & Stagnation in Socialist Economies: A Mathematical Analysis. Andras Simonovits. (Illus.). 224p. 1991. text ed. 59.95 (*0-631-17679-9*) Blackwell Pubs.

Cycles Classic Library Collection, 4 vols., Set. Edward R. Dewey et al. 1698p. 1987. 125.00 (*1-879192-08-X*) Fndtn Study Cycles.

Cycles, Cycles, Cycles. Michael E. Ross. (Illus.). 88p. (J). (gr. 1-3). 1979. pap. 3.95 (*0-939666-01-4*) Yosemite Assn.

Cycles in Graphs. Ed. by B. R. Alspach & C. D. Godsil. LC 85-13612. (Mathematics Studies: Vol. 115). 468p. 1985. 87.25 (*0-444-87803-3*, North Holland) Elsevier.

***Cycles in Humans & Nature.** John T. Burns. 300p. 1994. 37.50 (*0-8108-2831-6*) Scarecrow.

Cycles of American History. Arthur M. Schlesinger, Jr. 1987. pap. 13.95 (*0-395-45400-X*) HM.

***Cycles of Change: A History of the University of Kansas Division of Continuing Education, 1891-1992.** Theodore A. Wilson. Ed. by Lynn Roberts. (Illus.). 236p. (Orig.). (C). 1994. pap. 20.00 (*0-614-03300-4*) U of KS Cont Ed.

Cycles of Conquest: The Impact of Spain, Mexico & the United States on Indians of the Southwest, 1533-1960. Edward H. Spicer. LC 61-14500. (Illus.). 609p. 1962. pap. 19.95 (*0-8165-0021-5*) U of Ariz Pr.

Cycles of Destiny: Understanding Return Charts. Ronald C. Davison. 1990. pap. 16.95 (*0-85030-768-6*) Thorsons SF.

Cycles of Fire: Stars, Galaxies & the Wonder of Deep Space. William K. Hartmann et al. LC 87-42742. (Illus.). 192p. 1988. 27.50 (*0-89480-510-X*, 1510); pap. 15.95 (*0-89480-502-9*, 1502) Workman Pub.

Cycles of Heaven. Steve Levine. (Morning Coffee Chapbook Ser.). (Illus.). 11p. (Orig.). 1988. pap. 7.50 (*0-918273-38-2*) Coffee Hse.

Cycles of Inflation & Deflation: Money, Debt, & the 1990s. G. Leigh Skene. LC 92-15991. 178p. 1992. text ed. 49.95 (*0-275-94425-5*, C4425, Praeger Pubs) Greenwood.

Cycles of Life. (American Indians Ser.). (Illus.). 184p. 1994. 16.99 (*0-8094-9583-X*); lib. bdg. write for info. (*0-8094-9584-8*) Time-Life.

Cycles of Meaning: Exploring the Potential of Talk in Learning Communities. Ed. by Kathryn Pierce & Carol Gilles. LC 93-5968. (Illus.). 352p. (C). 1993. pap. text ed. 25.00 (*0-435-08797-5*, 08797) Heinemann.

Cycles of Nature: An Introduction to Biological Rhythms. Andrew Ahlgren & Franz Halberg. 96p. 1990. pap. 13.95 (*0-87355-089-7*) Natl Sci Tchrs.

Cycles of Rock & Water: Upheaval of the Pacific Edge. Kenneth A. Brown. 336p. 1994. pap. 12.00 (*0-06-258533-9*) HarpC West.

Cycles of Soils: Carbon, Nitrogen, Phosphorus, Sulfur, Micronutrients. F. J. Stevenson. LC 85-12042. 380p. 1986. text ed. 79.95 (*0-471-82218-3*) Wiley.

Cycles of Time: Charting the Mood Swings of America. Jacqueline C. Whyte. LC 89-62798. (Illus.). 168p. (Orig.). 1989. pap. 11.95 (*0-9624026-7-2*) Manifest Pr.

***Cycles of Time & Scientific Learning in Medieval Europe.** Wesley Stevens. (Collected Studies: Vol. CS482). 350p. 1995. 83.95 (*0-86078-471-1*, Pub. by Variorum UK) Ashgate Pub Co.

Cycles, the Mysterious Forces That Trigger Events. Edward R. Dewey & Og Mandino. 211p. 1987. reprint ed. pap. 15.00 (*1-879192-00-4*) Fndtn Study Cycles.

Cycles, the Science of Prediction. Edward R. Dewey & Edwin F. Dakin. 255p. 1964. pap. 15.00 (*1-879192-01-2*) Fndtn Study Cycles.

Cyclic Analysis in Futures Trading: Contemporary Methods & Procedures. Jacob I. Bernstein. LC 87-26350. 295p. 1988. text ed. 85.00 (*0-471-01185-1*) Wiley.

***Cyclic Cabinet Corrosion Testing, STP 1238.** Ed. by Gardner S. Hayes. LC 95-4205. (Special Technical Publication Ser.: Vol. 1186). 137p. 1995. text ed. 54.00 (*0-8031-2014-1*, 04-012380-27) ASTM.

Cyclic Deformation & Fatigue of Metals. Ed. by Matej Bily. LC 92-31855. (Materials Science Monographs: No. 78). xiv, 372p. 1993. write for info. (*0-444-98790-8*) Elsevier.

Cyclic Deformation, Fracture, & Nondestructive Evaluation of Advanced Materials. Ed. by M. R. Mitchell & Otto Buck. LC 92-16045. (Special Technical Publication Ser.: No. 1157). (Illus.). 350p. 1992. text ed. 87.00 (*0-8031-1444-3*, 04-011570-30) ASTM.

***Cyclic Deformation, Fracture, & Nondestructive Evaluation of Advanced Materials, Vol. 2, STP 1184.** Ed. by M. R. Mitchell & Otto Buck. LC 94-32123. (Special Technical Publication Ser.: Vol. 1184). (Illus.). 400p. 1994. text ed. 115.00 (*0-8031-1989-5*, 04-011840-30) ASTM.

***Cyclic Fatigue in Ceramics.** Ed. by Hidehiro Kishimoto et al. LC 94-44664. (Current Japanese Materials Research: No. 14). 296p. 1995. 154.25 (*0-444-82154-6*) Elsevier.

Cyclic Galois Extensions of Commutative Rings. Cornelius Greither. LC 92-41118. (Lecture Notes in Mathematics Ser.: Vol. 1534). 1993. 28.00 (*0-387-56350-4*) Spr-Verlag.

Cyclic GMP. T. M. Lincoln. (Molecular Biology Intelligence Unit Ser.). 119p. 1994. 89.95 (*1-57059-146-6*, LN9146) R G Landes.

Cyclic Homology. Jean-Louis Loday. LC 92-34146. (Grundlehren der Mathematischen Wissenschaften Ser.: Vol. 301). 1992. 149.00 (*0-387-53339-7*) Spr-Verlag.

Cyclic Homology of Algebras. P. Seibt. 172p. (C). 1987. text ed. 54.00 (*9971-5-0468-5*); pap. text ed. 29.00 (*9971-5-0470-7*) World Scientific Pub.

Cyclic Hope, Cyclic Pain. Uma Parameswaran. (Writers Workshop Redbird Ser.). 23p. 1975. 8.00 (*0-88253-520-X*); pap. text ed. 4.00 (*0-88253-519-6*) Ind-US Inc.

Cyclic Nucleotide Phosphodiesterases. Ed. by Samuel J. Strada & W. Joseph Thompson. (Advances in Cyclic Nucleotide & Protein Phosphorylation Research Ser.: Vol.16). (Illus.). 460p. 1984. 104.00 (*0-89004-779-0*) Raven.

Cyclic Nucleotide Phosphodiesterases: Structure, Regulation, & Drug Action. Ed. by Joe Beavo & Miles D. Houslay. (Molecular Pharmacology Ser.). 1990. text ed. 149.95 (*0-471-92707-4*) Wiley.

Cyclic Nucleotides & Protein Phosphorylation in Cell Regulation: Proceedings of the 12th FEBS Meeting, Dresden, 1978. Ed. by E. G. Krause et al. (Federation of European Biochemical Societies Ser.: Vol. 54). (Illus.). 1979. 136.00 (*0-08-023178-0*, Pub. by Pergamon Repr UK) Franklin.

Cyclic Nucleotides & Therapeutic Perspectives. G. Cehovic & G. A. Robison. 1979. 57.00 (*0-08-023760-6*, Pergamon Pr) Elsevier.

Cyclic Nucleotides, Calcium, & Protein Phosphorylation: Proceedings of the Sixth International Conference. Ed. by Robert S. Adelstein et al. (Advances in Second Messenger & Phosphoprotein Research Ser.: Vol. 21). (Illus.). 240p. 1988. text ed. 107.50 (*0-88167-407-9*) Raven.

***Cyclic Nucleotides in the Nervous System.** George I. Drummond. LC 84-40127. reprint ed. pap. 38.50 (*0-7837-9567-X*, 2060316) Bks Demand.

Cyclic Nucleotides, Part I: Biochemistry. Ed. by J. A. Nathanson & J. W. Kobabian. (Handbook of Experimental Pharmacology Ser.: Vol. 58, Pt. I). (Illus.). 736p. 1982. 287.00 (*0-387-10786-X*) Spr-Verlag.

Cyclic Nucleotides Part II: Physiology & Pharmacology. Ed. by J. W. Kebabian. (Handbook of Experimental Pharmacology Ser.: Vol. 58). 1000p. 1982. 414.00 (*0-387-11239-1*) Spr-Verlag.

***Cyclic Nucleotides, Phosphorylated Proteins, & Neuronal Function.** fac. ed. Paul Greengard. LC 78-66349. (Distinguished Lecture Series of the Society of General Physiologists: No. 1). (Illus.). 134p. Date not set. pap. 38.20 (*0-7837-7285-8*, 2047021) Bks Demand.

Cyclic Organonitrogen Stereodynamics. Joseph B. Lambert & Yoshito Takeuchi. (Methods in Stereochemical Analysis Ser.). 304p. 1991. text ed. 125.00 (*0-89573-773-6*) VCH Pubs.

Cyclic Phenomena in Marine Plants & Animals. Ed. by E. Naylor & E. G. Hartnoll. 1979. 203.00 (*0-08-023217-5*, Pub. by Pergamon Repr UK) Franklin.

Cyclic Plasticity & Low Cycle Fatigue Life of Metals. J. Polak. (Materials Science Monographs: No. 63). 316p. 1991. 128.75 (*0-444-98839-4*) Elsevier.

Cyclic Polymers. Ed. by J. A. Semlyen. 404p. 1986. 119.00 (*0-85334-388-8*, Pub. by Elsevier Applied Sci UK) Elsevier.

Cyclic Stress-Strain & Plastic Deformation Aspects of Fatigue Crack Growth - STP 637. 231p. 1977. 25.00 (*0-8031-0319-0*, 04-637000-30) ASTM.

Cyclic Stress-Strain Behavior: Analysis, Experimentation & Failure Prediction Symposium Sponsored by ASTM Committee E-9 Bal Harbour, FL. American Society for Testing & Materials Staff. (ASTM Special Technical Publication Ser.: 519). 289p. reprint ed. pap. 82.40 (*0-317-55531-6*, 2056332) Bks Demand.

***Cyclic 3', 5'-Nucleotides: Mechanisms of Action.** fac. ed. Ed. by Hinrich Cramer & Joachim Schultz. LC 76-45361. (Illus.). 568p. Date not set. pap. 161.90 (*0-7837-7360-9*, 2047169) Bks Demand.

Cyclic Three Prime, Five Prime -Nucleotides: Mechanisms of Action. Hinrich Cramer & Joachim Schultz. LC 76-45361. 554p. 1977. text ed. 175.00 (*0-471-99456-1*, Wiley-Interscience) Wiley.

Cyclic Voltammetry: Simulation & Analysis of Reaction Mechanisms. David K. Gosser, Jr. LC 93-24400. 154p. 1993. 65.00 (*1-56081-026-2*) VCH Pubs.

Cyclical Analysis of Time Series: Selected Procedures & Computer Programs. Gerhard Bry & Charlotte Boschan. LC 70-123122. 230p. reprint ed. pap. 65.60 (*0-8357-7569-0*, 2056890) Bks Demand.

C

An Asterisk (*) at the beginning of an entry indicates that the title is appearing in BIP for the first time.

An Asterisk (*) at the beginning of an entry indicates that the title is appearing in BIP for the first time.

1767

Cyclops, Alcestis, Medea. Euripides. Ed. & Tr. by David Kovacs. LC 93-821. (Loeb Classical Library: No. L12). 436p. 1994. text ed. 18.95 (0-674-99560-0) HUP.

Cyclops Vale & Other Tales. Tim Taylor. Ed. by John D. Ruemmler. (Shadow World Ser.). (Illus.). 32p. (Orig.). (YA). (gr. 12). 1989. pap. 6.00 (1-55806-042-1, 6009) Iron Crown Ent Inc.

Cyclorama of Gen. Custer's Last Fight: A Reproduction of the Original Document Complete in All Respects. Intro. by John M. Carroll. LC 88-50600. (Echoes of the Little Big Horn Ser.: Vol. 3). (Illus.). 104p. 1988. reprint ed. 30.00 (0-912783-17-6) Upton Sons.

Cyclosporin: Mode of Action & Clinical Application. Ed. by Angus W. Thomson. (C). 1989. lib. bdg. 124.50 (0-7462-0124-9) Kluwer Ac.

Cyclosporin A: Proceedings of the International Symposium, Cambridge, U. K., September 1981. Ed. by D. J. White. 350p. 1982. 55.50 (0-444-80410-2, I-296-82) Elsevier.

Cyclosporin for Severe Psoriasis: The Italian Experience. Ed. by A. F. Finzi. (Journal: Dermatologica: Vol. 187, Suppl. 1, 1993). (Illus.). iv, 44p. 1993. pap. 19.25 (3-8055-5845-7) S Karger.

***Cyclosporin in the Therapy of Renal Disease.** Ed. by A. Tejani. (Contributions to Nephrology Ser.: Vol. 114). (Illus.). x, 150p. 1995. 126.50 (3-8055-6076-1) S Karger.

Cyclosporine, Vol. III. Ed. by Alfred Kahan. 320p. 1985. text ed. 110.00 (0-8089-1783-8, 792225, Grune) Saunders.

Cyclosporine: Biological Activity & Clinical Applications, Vol. I. Ed. by Barry D. Kahan. 928p. 1984. text ed. 265.00 (0-8089-1651-3, 792223X, Grune) Saunders.

Cyclosporine: Nursing & Paraprofessional Aspects, Vol. II. Ed. by Barry D. Kahan. 128p. 1984. text ed. 79.95 (0-8089-1652-1, 792224, Grune) Saunders.

***Cyclosporine: The Ten Year Experience.** Barry D. Kahan. LC 94-45286. 1994. 85.00 (0-8385-1463-4) Appleton & Lange.

Cyclostationarity in Communications & Signal Processing. Ed. by William A. Gardner. LC 93-21059. (Illus.). 520p. 1994. text ed. 69.95 (0-7803-1023-3, PC03731) Inst Electrical.

Cyclostomata: An Annotated Bibliography. Ed. by L. J. Selley & F. W. Beamish. 1977. lib. bdg. 261.00 (90-6193-562-8) Kluwer Ac.

Cyclostomata: An Annotated Bibliography Supplement 1973-1978. Ed. by G. Tandler et al. 1979. lib. bdg. 154.50 (90-6193-597-0) Kluwer Ac.

Cyclostratigraphy & the Milakovich Theory. W. S. Schwarzacher. LC 93-5242. (Developments in Sedimentology Ser.: Vol. 52). 1993. write for info. (0-444-89623-6) Elsevier.

Cyclotomic Fields First & Second. Serge A. Lang. (Graduate Texts in Mathematics Ser.: Vol. 121). (Illus.). 432p. 1989. 49.90 (0-387-96671-4, 1209) Spr-Verlag.

Cyclotonic Fields: Two. Serge A. Lang. (Graduate Texts in Mathematics Ser.: Vol. 69). 288p. 1980. 36.00 (0-387-90447-6) Spr-Verlag.

Cyclotron Waves in Plasma. D. G. Lominadze. Ed. by S. M. Hamberger. Tr. by A. N. Dellis. (International Series of Natural Philosophy: Vol. 102). (Illus.). 220p. 1981. 88.00 (0-08-021680-3, Pub. by Pergamon Repr UK) Franklin.

Cyclotrons & Their Application. K. Ziegler & B. Martin. 792p. (C). 1991. text ed. 159.00 (981-02-0086-2) World Scientific Pub.

Cyclotrons & Their Applications: Proceedings of the 13th International Conference. G. Dutto & M. K. Craddock. 972p. 1993. text ed. 178.00 (981-02-1130-9) World Scientific Pub.

Cyclotrons 1972: Proceedings of the AIP Conference, Univ. of British Columbia, Vancouver, 1972, No. 9. American Institute of Physics. Ed. by J. J. Burgerson & A. Strathdee. LC 72-92798. 836p. 1972. 19.00 (0-88318-108-8) Am Inst Physics.

Cygnes. Marcel Ayme. (Folio - Cadet Bleu Ser.: No. 235). (Illus.). 72p. (FRE.). (J). (gr. 1-5). 1990. pap. 9.95 (2-07-031235-6) Schoenhof.

Cygnet. Marianne Willman. (Historical Ser.). 1993. mass mkt. 3.99 (0-373-28781-X, 1-28781-2) Harlequin Bks.

Cygnet & the Firebird. Patricia A. McKillip. LC 92-21149. 240p. (Orig.). 1993. pap. 17.95 (0-441-12628-6) Ace Bks.

***Cygnet & the Firebird.** Patricia A. McKillip. 320p. Date not set. pap. text ed. 5.99 (0-441-00237-4) Ace Bks.

Cygnus Conspiracy. A. Brook Lindsay, III. Ed. by Terry Amthor. (Space Master Ser.). 32p. (Orig.). (YA). (gr. 10-12). 1987. pap. 12.00 (0-915795-92-2, 9102) Iron Crown Ent Inc.

Cylinder Musical Box Design & Repair. H. A. Bulleid. LC 87-1779. (Illus.). 234p. (Orig.). 1987. pap. 14.95 (0-930256-16-6) Almar.

Cylinder Musical Box Technology: Including Makers, Types, Dating, & Music. H. A. Bulleid. LC 93-46171. (Illus.). 292p. 1994. pap. 21.95 (0-930256-22-0) Almar.

Cylinder of Vision: The Fiction & Journalistic Writings of Steven Crane. Milne Holton. LC 79-181358. 366p. reprint ed. pap. 104.40 (0-317-29863-1, 2019563) Bks Demand.

Cylindric Algebras, Pt. I. Leon Henkin et al. (Studies in Logic: Vol. 64). 1971. 95.00 (0-7204-2043-1, North Holland) Elsevier.

Cylindric Algebras, Pt. II. J. D. Monk et al. (Studies in Logic & the Foundations of Mathematics: Vol. 115). 302p. 1985. 66.75 (0-444-87679-0, North Holland) Elsevier.

Cylindrical Shell Roof Design. Z. M. Elias. 1972. pap. 11.95 (0-8156-6036-7, Am U Beirut) Syracuse U Pr.

Cylobutadienoids see Organic Synthesis

CYMA Bookkeeper. CYMA-McGraw Hill Staff. 1988. 49.00 (0-07-830800-3) McGraw.

Cymbal Book. Hugo Pinksterboer. Ed. by Rick Mattingly. 200p. 1993. pap. 24.95 (0-7935-1920-9, 06621763) H Leonard.

Cymbals. Evelyn Coleman. LC 93-8690. (Illus.). (J). 1995. text ed. 15.95 (0-02-722817-7) Macmillan.

Cymbalum Mundi: Four Very Ancient Joyous & Facetious Poetic Dialogues. Bonaventure des Periers. Tr. by Bettina L. Knapp. LC 65-14414. 1965. lib. bdg. 24.50 (0-8057-5631-0) Irvington.

Cymbeline. Arden. 1985. pap. 8.95 (0-416-27830-2) Routledge Chapman & Hall.

Cymbeline. William Shakespeare. Ed. by Robert H. Heilman. (Pelican Shakespeare Ser.). 1965. mass mkt. 5.95 (0-14-071428-6, Pelican Bks) Viking Penguin.

Cymbeline. Roger Warren. Ed. by J. R. Mulryne et al. LC 88-27376. (Shakespeare in Performance Ser.). 160p. 1989. text ed. 39.95 (0-7190-2717-9, Pub. by Manchester Univ Pr UK) St Martin.

Cymbeline. 2nd ed. William Shakespeare. Ed. by J. M. Nosworthy. (Arden Shakespeare Ser.). 1955. 49.95 (0-416-47350-4, NO.2450); pap. 8.95 (0-415-02689-X, NO.2451) Routledge Chapman & Hall.

Cymbeline. William Shakespeare. Ed. by Arthur Quiller-Couch et al. (New Shakespeare Ser.). (C). 1969. reprint ed. pap. 4.95 (0-521-09473-9) Cambridge U Pr.

***Cymbeline: Granville Barker's Prefaces to Shakespeare.** Granville Barker. 160p. 1995. pap. 6.95 (0-435-08647-2) Heinemann.

Cymbeline: Modern Text with Introduction. Ed. by A. L. Rowse. LC 86-23381. 140p. (Orig.). (C). 1987. pap. text ed. 3.45 (0-8191-3938-6) U Pr of Amer.

Cymbeline (R) William Shakespeare. 1988. pap. 2.95 (0-671-66925-7) Folger.

Cymberline. Shakespeare. (BBC Television Plays Ser.). 1983. pap. 4.95 (0-563-20114-2, Pub. by BBC UK) Parkwest Pubns.

Cymothoidae from Fishes of Kuwait (Arabian Gulf) (Crustacea: Isopoda) Thomas E. Bowman & Inam U. Tareen. LC 83-600096. (Smithsonian Contributions to Zoology Ser.: No. 382). 34p. reprint ed. pap. 25.00 (0-317-29613-2, 2021865) Bks Demand.

Cymry of Seventy-Six: or Welshmen & Their Descendants of the American Revolution. 2nd ed. Alexander Jones. 132p. 1989. reprint ed. 20.00 (0-685-60350-4, 3065) Clearfield Co.

Cyndi Lauper. Chris Crocker. Ed. by Diane Arico. (Illus.). 64p. (J). (gr. 3-7). 1985. 9.29 (0-685-09958-X) S&S Trade.

Cyndy Szekeres' Baby Animals. Cyndy Szekeres. (Golden Sturdy Shape Bks.). (Illus.). 14p. (J). 1994. write for info. (0-307-12479-7, Golden Bks) Western Pub.

Cyndy Szekeres' Colors. Cyndy Szekeres. (Illus.). 24p. (J). (ps-00). 1992. bds. write for info. (0-307-12167-4, 12167, Golden Pr) Western Pub.

Cyndy Szekeres' Favorite Mother Goose Rhymes. Cyndy Szekeres. (Big Golden Book Ser.). (Illus.). 24p. (J). (ps-2). 1992. write for info. (0-307-12347-2, 12347) Western Pub.

Cyndy Szekeres' Hugs. Cyndy Szekeres. (Board Bks.). (J). 1990. bds. write for info. (0-307-06108-6, Golden Pr) Western Pub.

Cyndy Szekeres' I Am a Puppy. Cyndy Szekeres. (J). (ps). 1994. 3.95 (0-307-12457-6, Golden Pr) Western Pub.

Cyndy Szekere's Kisses. Cyndy Szeker. (J). (ps). 1993. 2.25 (0-307-06121-3, Golden Pr) Western Pub.

Cyndy Szekeres' Nice Animals. Cyndy Szekeres. (Golden Board Bks.). (J). 1990. pap. write for info. (0-307-06109-4, Golden Pr) Western Pub.

Cyndy Szekeres' Teeny Mouse Counts Herself. Cyndy Szekeres. (Golden Board Bks.). (Illus.). 12p. (J). (ps). 1992. bds. write for info. (0-307-06118-3, 6118, Golden Pr) Western Pub.

Cyndy Szekeres' Teeny Mouse Plays Learns Her. Cyndy Szekeres. (Golden Board Bks.). (Illus.). 12p. (J). 1994. write for info. (0-307-06088-8, Golden Bks) Western Pub.

Cynegeticon Quae Supersunt, 2 vols in 1. Grattius Faliscus. 255p. 1976. reprint ed. write for info. (3-487-06046-9, Pub. by Georg Olms GW) Lubrecht & Cramer.

Cynewulf: Structure, Style, & Theme in His Poetry. Earl R. Anderson. LC 81-65464. 248p. 1983. 39.50 (0-8386-3091-X) Fairleigh Dickinson.

Cynewulf & the Cynewulf Canon. S. K. Das. 1971. 59.95 (0-87968-987-0) Gordon Pr.

Cynewulf's Part in Our Beowulf. Albert S. Cook. (Connecticut Academy of Arts & Sciences Ser., Trans.: Vol. 27). 1925. pap. 39.50 (0-685-22816-9) Elliots Bks.

Cynewulf's Poems. Tr. by C. W. Kennedy. 1988. 11.25 (0-8446-1143-3) Peter Smith.

Cynic Epistles: A Study Edition. Abraham J. Malherbe. LC 77-21619. (Society for Biblical Literature. Sources for Biblical Study Ser.: No. 12). 342p. reprint ed. pap. 97.50 (0-7837-5447-7, 2045212) Bks Demand.

***Cynic, Sage, or Son of God?** Gregory A. Boyd. LC 95-8773. 1995. write for info. (1-56476-448-6, Victor Books) SP Pubns.

Cynical Americans: Living & Working in an Age of Discontent & Disillusion. Donald L. Kanter & Philip H. Mirvis. LC 88-46087. (Management Ser.). 352p. 1989. 28.95 (1-55542-150-4) Jossey-Bass.

Cynical Society: The Culture of Politics & the Politics of Culture in American Life. Jeffrey C. Goldfarb. LC 90-11187. 212p. 1991. 22.50 (0-226-30106-0) U Ch Pr.

Cynical Society: The Culture of Politics & the Politics of Culture in American Life. Jeffrey C. Goldfarb. LC 90-11187. xii, 200p. 1992. pap. text ed. 13.95 (0-226-30107-9) U Ch Pr.

Cynicalman: The Paperback. Matt Feazell. LC 87-71191. (Showcase Comic Ser.: No. 1). (Illus.). 190p. (Orig.). 1987. pap. 7.95 (0-917976-75-4, White Ewe Pr) Thunder Baas Pr.

Cynicism & Passion. Andre Glucksmann. Tr. by Claudia Royal. (Stanford French & Italian Studies: Vol. 76). 300p. Date not set. pap. 46.50 (0-915838-92-3) Anma Libri.

Cynics & Christian Origins. Gerald F. Downing. 352p. 1992. text ed. 39.95 (0-567-09613-0, Pub. by T & T Clark UK) Bks Intl VA.

Cynic's Dictionary. Rick Bayan. LC 94-5472. 1994. 12.00 (0-688-12922-6) Hearst Bks.

Cynic's Dictionary of Modern American Terms. Richard Reciniello. 1992. 10.00 (0-533-10253-7) Vantage.

***Cynic's Guide to Love.** Texas B. Bender & Gladiola Montana. (Illus.). 144p. 1995. pap. 5.95 (0-87905-696-7) Gibbs Smith Pub.

Cynic's Lexion. Jonathon Green. 240p. 1986. pap. 9.95 (0-312-18056-X) St Martin.

Cynisme et Passion. Alfred Glucksmann. (FRE.). 1982. pap. 16.95 (0-7859-2667-4) Fr & Eur.

Cynthia. Marilyn Bird. Ed. by James B. Van Treese. 268p. (Orig.). 1994. pap. 8.95 (1-880416-42-5) NW Pub.

Cynthia: Springsong. Leila P. Golding. (YA). 1994. pap. 3.99 (1-55661-524-8) Bethany Hse.

***Cynthia & the Runaway Gazeb.** Marston. 1994. pap. 4.99 (0-517-13489-6) Random Hse Value.

Cynthia & the Runaway Gazebo. Elsa Marston. LC 91-32548. (Illus.). 32p. (J). (gr. k-4). 1992. 14.00 (0-688-10282-4, Tambourine Bks); lib. bdg. 13.93 (0-688-10283-2, Tambourine Bks) Morrow.

Cynthia Ann Parker: Indian Captive. Catherine T. Gonzalez. (Stories for Young Americans Ser.). 1980. 10.95 (0-89015-244-6) Sunbelt Media.

Cynthia Ann Parker: Reprint of James T. DeShields 1886 Account. limited ed. Frwd. by John Graves. (Illus.). 60p. 1991. reprint ed. 90.00 (0-9626336-2-3) Chama Pr.

Cynthia Ann Parker: Reprint of James T. DeShields 1886 Account. Frwd. by John Graves. (Illus.). 60p. 1991. reprint ed. 35.00 (0-9626336-1-5) Chama Pr.

Cynthia Ann Parker: The Life & Legend. Margaret S. Hacker. LC 89-52073. (Southwestern Studies: No. 92). 52p. (Orig.). 1990. pap. 12.50 (0-87404-187-2) Tex Western.

Cynthia Carlson: Installations, 1979-1989 (A Decade, More or Less) David S. Rubin. (Illus.). 40p. (Orig.). 1989. pap. text ed. 10.00 (0-941972-08-9) Freedman.

Cynthia Gregory Dances Swan Lake. Cynthia Gregory. (Illus.). 48p. (J). (gr. 3-7). 1990. pap. 14.95 (0-671-68786-7, S&S Bks Young Read) S&S Childrens.

Cynthia Ozick. Joseph Lowin. 208p. 1988. text ed. 21.95 (0-8057-7526-9, TUSAS 545, Twayne) Macmillan.

Cynthia Ozick's Comic Art: From Levity to Liturgy. Sarah Blacher Cohen. LC 93-13994. 1994. 25.00 (0-253-31398-8) Ind U Pr.

Cynthia Ozick's Fiction: Tradition & Invention. Elaine M. Kauvar. LC 92-19603. (Jewish Literature & Culture Ser.). 288p. 1993. 29.95 (0-253-33129-3) Ind U Pr.

Cynthia Schira: New Work. Nancy A. Corwin. (Illus.). 16p. (Orig.). 1987. pap. 5.00 (0-913689-14-9) Spencer Muse Art.

Cyotechniques in Biological Electron Microscopy. Ed. by R. A. Steinbrecht & K. Zierold. (Illus.). 305p. 1987. 166.00 (0-387-18046-X) Spr-Verlag.

Cyphomandra (Solanaceae) Lynn Bohs. (Flora Neotropical Ser.: Vol. 63). (Illus.). 1994. pap. text ed. 24.50 (0-89327-385-6) NY Botanical.

Cypress Gardens: A Pictorial Guide Book. (Illus.). (Orig.). Date not set. pap. write for info. (1-56944-034-4) Terrell Missouri.

Cypress Land: A Late Archaic-Early Woodland Site in the Lower Illinois River Floodplain. Michael D. Conner. LC 86-21567. (Kampsville Archeological Center Technical Reports). (Illus.). 79p. (Orig.). 1986. pap. 5.95 (0-942118-23-5) Ctr Amer Arche.

Cypress Rangers in the Civil War: The Experiences of 85 Confederate Cavalrymen from Texas. James H. Davis. LC 91-73512. 157p. 1992. lib. bdg. 15.00 (0-9630768-4-1) Heritage Oak.

Cypress Swamps. Ed. by Katherine Carter Ewel & Howard T. Odum. LC 84-5230. (Center for Wetlands Research, University of Florida Ser.). (Illus.). 490p. 1985. 49.95 (0-8130-0714-3) U Press Fla.

Cyprian: The Churchman. John A. Faulkner. 1977. lib. bdg. 59.95 (0-8490-1698-3) Gordon Pr.

Cyprian & the Bible: A Study of Third-Century Exegesis. Michael A. Fahey. 701p. 1971. lib. bdg. 80.00 (3-16-132222-3, Pub. by J C B Mohr GW) Coronet Bks.

Cyprian Orations. Isocrates. Ed. by R. W. Connor & Edward S. Forster. LC 78-18574. (Greek Text & Commentaries Ser.). 1979. lib. bdg. 25.95 (0-405-11418-4) Ayer.

Cyprian's Sister. large type ed. Paula Marshall. 1994. 18.95 (0-263-14005-9, Pub. by Mills & Boon Ltd UK) Chivers N Amer.

Cyprianus - Cyprien, Traites, Concordance, 2 vols., Set. Ed. by P. Bouet et al. (Alpha-Omega, Reihe A Ser.: Vol. LXVII). xlvi, 1399p. (GER.). 1986. write for info. (3-487-07698-5, Pub. by Georg Olms GW) Lubrecht & Cramer.

Cypridinidae of the Continental Shelves of Southeastern North America, the Northern Gulf of Mexico, & the West Indies (Ostracoda: Mygdocopina) Louis S. Kornicker. LC 84-600002. (Smithsonian Contributions to Zoology Ser.: No. 401). 41p. reprint ed. pap. 25.00 (0-317-42243-X, 2023161) Bks Demand.

Cyprinid Fishes: Systematics, Biology & Exploitation. I. J. Winfield & J. S. Nelson. (Fish & Fisheries Ser.). (Illus.). 696p. 1991. write for info. (0-412-34920-5) Chapman & Hall.

Cypriot Ceramics: Reading the Prehistoric Record. Ed. by Jane A. Barlow et al. (University Museum Monographs: University Museum Symposium Ser.: Nos. 74 & II). (Illus.). 278p. (C). 1992. text ed. 50.00 (0-924171-10-3) U PA Mus Pubns.

Cypriot Women in the Labour Market: An Exploration of Myths & Reality. William J. House. (Women, Work & Development Ser.: No. 10). xiii, 141p. (Orig.). 1985. pap. 14.00 (92-2-105108-0) Intl Labour Office.

Cyprus. Thomas Cook. (Passport's Illustrated Travel Guides from Thomas Cook Ser.). (Illus.). 192p. 1993. pap. 12.95 (0-8442-9045-9, Passport Bks) NTC Pub Grp.

Cyprus. Mary V. Fox. LC 93-755. (Enchantment of the World Ser.). (Illus.). 128p. (J). (gr. 5-9). 1993. lib. bdg. 21.53 (0-516-02617-8) Childrens.

Cyprus. Comp. by Paschalis M. Kitromilides & Marios L. Evirviades. (World Bibliographical Ser.: No. 28). 195p. 1982. lib. bdg. 50.00 (0-903450-40-2) ABC-CLIO.

Cyprus. Garry Lyle. (Let's Visit Places & Peoples of the World Ser.). (Illus.). 96p. (J). (gr. 5 up). 1988. 14.95 (0-222-00942-X) Chelsea Hse.

Cyprus. Barnaby Rogerson. LC 93-5568. (Cadogan Guides Ser.). (Illus.). 220p. (Orig.). 1993. pap. 14.95 (1-56440-177-4) Globe Pequot.

Cyprus. Lewis B. Sckolnick. (Civil Rights Reporter Ser.). (Illus.). 60p. (Orig.). (C). 1994. pap. 45.00 (1-57205-139-6) Rector Pr.

Cyprus: A Regional Conflict & Its Resolution. Ed. by Norma Salem. LC 91-32523. 260p. 1992. text ed. 49.95 (0-312-07256-2) St Martin.

***Cyprus: Commercial Law.** 300p. (Orig.). 1994. pap. 295.00 (0-7605-1242-6) Rector Pr.

Cyprus: Conflict & Negotiation 1960-1980. Polyvios G. Polyviou. LC 80-25942. 246p. 1981. 49.50 (0-8419-0683-1) Holmes & Meier.

Cyprus: Domestic Dynamics, External Constraints. Ed. by Christos P. Ioannides. (Hellenism: Ancient, Mediaeval, Modern Ser.: No. 6). 150p. 1992. lib. bdg. 35.00 (0-89241-519-3) Caratzas.

Cyprus: Nationalism & International Politics. Michael A. Attalides. LC 79-1388. 1979. text ed. 18.95 (0-312-18057-8) St Martin.

***Cyprus: Nelles Guide.** rev. ed. Comp. by Nelles Verlag. (Nelles Guides Ser.). (Illus.). 256p. (GER.). 1995. pap. 14.95 (3-88618-040-9, Pub. by Nelles Verlag GW) Seven Hills Bk.

Cyprus - War & Adaptation: A Psychoanalytic History of Two Ethnic Groups in Conflict. Vamik D. Volkan. LC 78-57512. 220p. reprint ed. pap. 62.70 (0-7837-3565-0, 2043421) Bks Demand.

Cyprus, a Country Study. 4th ed. Library of Congress, Federal Research Division Staff. Ed. by Eric Solsten. LC 92-36090. (Area Handbook Ser.). 1993. write for info. (0-8444-0752-6) Lib Congress.

Cyprus & Beyond. Fred B. Cook, Jr. LC 84-90790. (Orig.). 1984. pap. write for info. (0-9614001-0-2, 24A) Cook MO.

Cyprus & the International Economy. Rodney Wilson. LC 91-31687. 128p. 1992. text ed. 59.95 (0-312-07510-3) St Martin.

Cyprus Before the Bronze Age: Art of the Chalcolithic Period. Vassos Karageorghis. LC 89-24543. (Illus.). 52p. 1990. pap. 12.50 (0-89236-168-9) J P Getty Trust.

Cyprus Between East & West. Thomas W. Adams & Alvin J. Cottrell. LC 68-19429. (Washington Center of Foreign Policy Research. Studies in International Affairs: No. 7). 104p. reprint ed. pap. 29.70 (0-317-20475-0, 2022998) Bks Demand.

Cyprus Business Forecaster. Ed. by Lewis B. Sckolnick. 70p. (Orig.). (C). 1994. pap. 675.00 (1-57205-349-6) Rector Pr.

***Cyprus Commercial Law.** 150p. (C). 1994. pap. 295.00 (0-7605-0105-X) Rector Pr.

Cyprus in International Tax Planning 1980: A Practical Guide for Foreign Firms & Individuals. Chrysses Demetriades. 464p. 72.00 (0-686-41011-4) Kluwer Ac.

Cyprus in Pictures. Ed. by Lerner Geography Department Staff. (Visual Geography Ser.). (Illus.). 64p. (J). (gr. 5-12). 1992. lib. bdg. 18.95 (0-8225-1910-0, Lerner Publctns) Lerner Group.

Cyprus Pocket Guide. Berlitz Editors. (Pocket Guides Ser.). (Illus.). 128p. 1989. pap. 7.95 (2-8315-0656-5) Berlitz.

Cyprus Postal Stationery, 1880-1992. Alexander C. Ioannides & Christopher J. Podger. (Illus.). 185p. 1993. 45.00 (0-9638547-0-4) A Ioannides.

Cyprus Question & the Turkish Position in International Law. 2nd ed. Zaim M. Necatigil. LC 92-28431. 542p. 1993. 69.00 (0-19-825846-1) OUP.

***Cyprus Tax Law.** 150p. (C). 1994. pap. 295.00 (0-7605-0104-1) Rector Pr.

Cyrano de Bergerac. Edmond Rostand. (Orig.). 19.95 (0-8488-0621-2) Amereon Ltd.

Cyrano de Bergerac. Edmond Rostand. Tr. by Brian Hooker. 208p. (Orig.). 1950. 3.95 (0-553-21360-1, Bantam Classics) Bantam.

Cyrano de Bergerac. Edmond Rostand et al. (Classics Illustrated Ser.). (Illus.). 52p. (Orig.). (YA). Date not set. pap. 4.95 (1-57209-019-7) Classics Int Ent.

Cyrano de Bergerac. Edmond Rostand. Tr. by Jose O. Via Luis Marti. (Nueva Austral Ser.: Vol. 206). (Orig.). (SPA.). 1991. pap. text ed. 24.95x (84-239-7206-2) Elliots Bks.

Cyrano de Bergerac. Edmond Rostand. (Illus.). 216p. (Orig.). (FRE.). 1990. pap. 10.95 (0-685-74009-9, 2080705261) Fr & Eur.

Cyrano de Bergerac. Edmond Rostand. Tr. by Lowell Blair. 240p. (Orig.). 1972. pap. 3.95 (0-451-52548-5, Sig Classics) NAL-Dutton.

Cyrano de Bergerac. Edmond Rostand. (Folio Ser.: No. 1487). (Illus.). (Orig.). (FRE.). 1962. pap. 10.95 (2-07-037487-4) Schoenhof.

An Asterisk (*) at the beginning of an entry indicates that the title is appearing in BIP for the first time.

C

An Asterisk (*) at the beginning of an entry indicates that the title is appearing in BIP for the first time.

1769

Cytomegalovirus & Immunity. J. D. Hamilton. (Monographs in Virology: Vol. 12). (Illus.). viii, 108p. 1982. 60.00 (*3-8055-3495-7*) S Karger.

Cytomegalovirus Infections of Man. U. Krech et al. (Illus.). 124p. 1971. 25.75 (*3-8055-1261-9*) S Karger.

Cytomegloviruses. James B. Hanshaw. Bd. with Rinderpest Virus. W. Plowright.; Lumpy Skin Disease. K. E. Weiss. (Virology Monographs: Vol. 3). (Illus.). iv, 131p. 1968. 36.00 (*0-387-80891-4*) Spr-Verlag.

Cytomorphogenesis in Plants. Ed. by O. Kiermayer. (Cell Biology Monographs: Vol. 8). (Illus.). 470p. 1981. 144.00 (*0-387-81613-5*) Spr-Verlag.

***Cytopathology.** 4th ed. Zuher M. Naib. LC 95-2408. 1995. 79.75 (*0-316-59674-4*) Little.

Cytopathology Annual Nineteen Ninety-Two. Ed. by Waldemar A. Schmidt. (Illus.). 272p. 1992. 75.00 (*0-683-07618-3*) Williams & Wilkins.

Cytopathology Annual, 1993. Waldemar A. Schmidt & Theodore R. Miller. (Illus.). 328p. 1993. 80.00 (*0-683-07619-1*) Williams & Wilkins.

Cytopathology Annual, 1994. Waldemar A. Schmidt. (Illus.). 1994. 100.00 (*0-89189-374-1*) Am Soc Clinical.

***Cytopathology Annual, 1995.** Waldemar A. Schmidt. 1995. 115.00 (*0-89189-377-6*) Am Soc Clinical.

Cytopathology in Pediatrics. J. J. Buchino. (Monographs in Clinical Cytology: Vol. 13). (Illus.). x, 156p. 1991. 160.00 (*3-8055-5299-8*) S Karger.

Cytopathology of Breast Cancer. Yi-Jing Shu & Peter Spieler. (Illus.). 550p. 1988. text ed. 98.00 (*0-07-057213-5*) Hlth Prof Div.

Cytopathology of Pulmonary Disease. Dorothy L. Rosenthal. (Monographs in Clinical Cytology: Vol. 11). (Illus.). x, 238p. 1988. 107.25 (*3-8055-4740-4*) S Karger.

Cytopathology of Soft Tissue & Bone Tumors. S. I. Hajdu & Eva O. Hajdu. (Monographs in Clinical Cytology: Vol. 12). (Illus.). xvi, 348p. 1989. 192.00 (*3-8055-4814-1*) S Karger.

Cytopathology of the Breast. Shahla Masood. (Illus.). 1995. write for info. (*0-89189-380-6*) Am Soc Clinical.

Cytopathology of the Central Nervous System. Sandra H. Bigner. 190p. 1994. 145.00 (*0-89189-362-8*) Am Soc Clinical.

Cytopathology of the Endometrium. Liang-Che Tao. LC 93-4916. (Illus.). 144p. 1994. 115.00 (*0-89189-363-6*) Am Soc Clinical.

***Cytopathology of the Endometrium, Set.** Liang-Che Tao. 1994. sl. 150.00 (*0-89189-369-5*) Am Soc Clinical.

Cytopathology of the Endometrium: Correlation with Histopathology. Yi-Jing Shu & Franz A. Ikle. (Illus.). 332p. 1992. text ed. 98.00 (*0-07-057214-3*) Hlth Prof Div.

Cytopathology of the Lower Female Genital Tract: An Integrated Approach. Gerard J. Nuovo. LC 93-9608. (Illus.). 464p. 1994. 165.00 (*0-683-06595-5*) Williams & Wilkins.

***Cytopathology of the Uterine Cervix, Set.** Alexander Meisels. 1991. sl. 200.00 (*0-89189-341-5*) Am Soc Clinical.

Cytopathology of the Uterine Cervix. Alexander Meisels. LC 90-309. (Illus.). 1991. 145.00 (*0-89189-299-0*) Am Soc Clinical.

Cytopathology of Tumours of the Nervous System. G. Andrioli & L. Rigobello. 100p. 1986. text ed. 34.00 (*1-57235-030-X*) Piccin NY.

***Cytopharmacology of Secretion: Proceedings of the NATO Advanced Study Institute, Venice & Milan, June 16-23, 1973.** fac. ed. NATO Advanced Study Institute Staff. Ed. by B. Ceccarelli et al. LC 74-76090. (Advances in Cytopharmacology Ser.: No. 2). (Illus.). 398p. Date not set. pap. 113.50 (*0-7837-7287-4*, 2047019) Bks Demand.

Cytoplasmic Genetics & Evolution. Paul Grun. LC 75-43987. (Illus.). 435p. 1976. text ed. 83.50 (*0-231-03975-1*) Col U Pr.

Cytoplasmic Organization Systems. George M. Malacinski. (Primers in Developmental Biology Ser.). 448p. 1990. text ed. 65.00 (*0-07-039749-X*) McGraw.

Cytoprotection & Biology: Proceedings of the Symposium on Cytoprotection & Biology, 1st, Kyoto, Japan, February 26, 1983. Ed. by T. Miyake et al. (Current Clinical Practice Ser.: Vol. 24). 200p. 1985. 94.75 (*0-444-90388-7*) Elsevier.

Cytoprotection & Cytobiology, Vol. 3. Ed. by M. Tsuchiya. 324p. 1986. 138.00 (*4-900392-79-0*) Elsevier.

Cytoprotection & Cytobiology: Proceedings, 10th Symposium, Kyoto, Japan, February 1992, Vol. 10. Ed. by M. Kitajima et al. xiv, 290p. 1993. 142.75 (*0-444-89914-6*, Excerpta Medica) Elsevier.

Cytoskeletal & Extracellular Proteins. Ed. by U. Aebi & J. Engel. (Biophysics Ser.: Vol. 3). (Illus.). 360p. 1989. 139.00 (*0-387-50067-7*) Spr-Verlag.

Cytoskeletal Basis of Plant Growth & Form. Ed. by Clive W. Lloyd. (Illus.). 330p. 1991. text ed. 109.00 (*0-12-453770-7*) Acad Pr.

Cytoskeletal Elements. George Poste & G. Nicholson. (Cell Surface Reviews Ser.: Vol. 7). 350p. 1982. 151.50 (*0-444-80335-1*) Elsevier.

Cytoskeletal Proteins in Tumor Diagnosis. Ed. by M. Osborn & K. Weber. (Current Communications in Molecular Biology Ser.). (Illus.). 244p. (C). 1989. pap. text ed. 24.00 (*0-87969-325-8*) Cold Spring Harbor.

Cytoskeleton. Alexander D. Bershadsky & Juri M. Vasiliev. LC 87-38489. (Cellular Organelles Ser.). (Illus.). 310p. 1988. 55.00 (*0-306-42508-4*, Plenum Pr) Plenum.

Cytoskeleton. M. Schliwa. (Cell Biology Monographs: Vol. 13). (Illus.). 340p. 1986. 111.00 (*0-387-81884-7*) Spr-Verlag.

Cytoskeleton: A Practical Approach. Ed. by Kermit L. Carraway & Coralie A. Carraway. (Practical Approach Ser.). (Illus.). 320p. 1992. 79.00 (*0-19-963257-X*); pap. 44.00 (*0-19-963256-1*) OUP.

Cytoskeleton: A Target for Toxic Agents. Ed. by Thomas W. Clarkson et al. LC 85-24470. (Rochester Series on Environmental Toxicity). 276p. 1986. 65.00 (*0-306-42205-0*, Plenum Pr) Plenum.

***Cytoskeleton: Forty-Fifth Colloquium der Gesellschaft fur Biologische Chemie Held at Mosbach, Baden-Wurttemberg, Germany, 14-16 April 1994.** Forty-Fifth Colloquium der Gesellschaft fur Biologische Chemie Staff. Ed. by B. M. Jockusch et al. LC 94-47371. 1995. write for info. (*3-540-58817-5*) Spr-Verlag.

Cytoskeleton & Cell Motility. T. M. Preston et al. (Tertiary Level Biology Ser.). (Illus.). 200p. 1990. text ed. 69.95 (*0-412-02041-6*, A3603, Chap & Hall NY); pap. text ed. 32.00 (*0-412-02051-3*, A3607, Chap & Hall NY) Chapman & Hall.

Cytoskeleton in Normal & Pathologic Processes: Cell Biology. Ed. by Giulio Gabbiani. (Methods & Achievements in Experimental Pathology Ser.: Vol. 8). (Illus.). 1978. 78.50 (*3-8055-2917-1*) S Karger.

Cytoskeleton in Normal & Pathologic Processes: Cell Physiopathology. Ed. by Giulio Gabbiani. (Methods & Achievements in Experimental Pathology Ser.: Vol. 9). (Illus.). 1978. 119.25 (*3-8055-2919-8*) S Karger.

Cytoskeleton of Flagellate & Ciliate Protists. Ed. by Michael Melkonian et al. (Illus.). v, 167p. 1992. 128.00 (*0-387-82294-1*) Spr-Verlag.

Cytoskeleton of the Algae. Menzel. 1992. 199.95 (*0-8493-6679-8*, QK565) CRC Pr.

Cytosolic Calcium Measurements, Regulation & Biologic Significance in Epithelial Tissue. Ed. by Z. S. Agus & E. Kelepouris. (Journal: Mineral & Electrolyte Metabolism: Vol. 14, No. 1, 1988). (Illus.). 96p. 1988. pap. 64.00 (*3-8055-4658-0*) S Karger.

Cytotaxonimical Atlas of the Pteridophyta, Vol. 3. A. Love. (Cytotaxonomical Atlases Ser.: Vol. 3). 1977. 98.00 (*3-7682-1103-7*) Lubrecht & Cramer.

Cytotaxonomical Atlas of the Arctic Flora. A. Love & D. Love. (Cytotaxonimical Atlases Ser.: Vol. 2). (Illus.). 598p. 1975. lib. bdg. 130.00 (*3-7682-0976-8*) Lubrecht & Cramer.

Cytotaxonomical Atlas of the Balkan Flora. J. C. Van Loon. (Cytotaxonimical Atlases Ser.: Vol. IV). 390p. 1987. pap. 105.00 (*3-443-63001-4*) Lubrecht & Cramer.

Cytotaxonomical Atlas of the Slovenian Flora. A. Love & D. Love. (Cytotaxonimical Atlases Ser.: Vol. 1). (Illus.). 1242p. 1974. lib. bdg. 130.00 (*3-7682-0932-6*) Lubrecht & Cramer.

Cytotec: Preclinical & Clinical Review. Illus. by Tim Phelps. LC 89-62978. 160p. 1989. text ed. 28.95 (*0-924428-01-5*) Phys Sci Pub.

Cytotest Two, 1992, 120-35mm Slides. 1992. sl. 265.00 (*0-89189-345-8*) Am Soc Clinical.

Cytotoxic & Anti-Imnflammatory Therapy in Dermatology. Jerome L. Shupack et al. 1992. text ed. 65.00 (*0-07-057549-5*) McGraw.

Cytotoxic & Complement Mediated Reactions. Ed. by P. Dukor et al. (Par Pseudo-Allergic Reactions, Involvement of Drugs & Chemicals Ser.: Vol. 2). (Illus.). viii, 144p. 1980. 52.00 (*3-8055-0666-X*) S Karger.

Cytotoxic Anticancer Drugs: Models & Concepts for Drug Discovery & Development: Proceedings of the 22nd Annual Cancer Symposium, Detroit, Michigan, April 26-28, 1990. Ed. by Frederick A. Valeriote. (Developments in Oncology Ser.). 432p. (C). 1992. lib. bdg. 135.00 (*0-7923-1629-0*) Kluwer Ac.

Cytotoxic Cells: Recognition, Effector Function, Generation, & Methods. Ed. by M. V. Sitkovsky & P. A. Henkart. LC 93-6929. (Illus.). xiv, 650p. 1993. 99.00 (*0-8176-3608-0*) Birkhauser.

Cytotoxic Conjugates. S. Ramakrishnan. LC 93-4767. (Medical Intelligence Unit Ser.). 1993. 89.95 (*1-879702-60-6*) R G Landes.

Cytotoxic Drugs & the Granulopoietic System. Ed. by H. P. Lohrmann & W. Schreml. (Recent Results in Cancer Research Ser.: Vol. 81). (Illus.). 235p. 1981. 65.00 (*0-387-10962-5*) Spr-Verlag.

Cytotoxic Mediators of Inflammation & Host Defense. Ed. by M. L. Shin. (Progress in Allergy Ser.: Vol. 40). (Illus.). xii, 216p. 1988. 118.50 (*3-8055-4636-X*) S Karger.

Cytotoxic T Cells in HIV & Other Retroviral Infections. Ed. by P. Racz et al. (Illus.). 178p. 1992. 153.75 (*3-8055-5469-9*) S Karger.

***Cytotoxics Handbook.** 2nd ed. Ed. by Michael Allwood & Patricia Wright. 1993. 74.95 (*1-870905-04-0*) Scovill Paterson.

CZ-75 Family: The Ultimate Combat Handgun. J. M. Ramos. (Illus.). 1990. 16.00 (*0-87364-566-9*) Paladin Pr.

Czar Ferdinand & His People. John D. MacDonald. LC 74-135815. (Eastern Europe Collection Ser.). 1971. reprint ed. 26.95 (*0-405-02757-5*) Ayer.

Czar Is Dead. Elizabeth Bartlett. 64p. (C). 1986. pap. 38.00 (*0-947612-22-X*, Pub. by Rivelin Grapheme Pr) St Mut.

***Czars: Russia's Rulers for More Than One Thousand Years.** James P. Duffy & Vincent L. Ricci. LC 94-44654. 1995. 29.95 (*0-8160-2873-7*) Facts on File.

Czar's Germans. Hattie P. Williams. LC 75-32862. 1975. 14.00 (*0-914222-01-5*) Am Hist Soc Ger.

Czar's Madman. Joan Kross. Tr. by Anselm Holla. 1994. pap. 13.95 (*1-56584-121-2*) New Press NY.

Czar's Madman: A Novel. Jaan Kross. LC 92-50464. 368p. 1992. 25.00 (*0-394-58437-6*) Pantheon.

Czbel. E. Janos & M. Kratochwill. 176p. (C). 1983. 215.00 (*0-685-34447-9*, Pub. by Collets) St Mut.

***Czech: A Rough Guides Phrasebook.** 224p. (Orig.). 1995. 5.00 (*1-85828-148-2*, Penguin Bks) Viking Penguin.

Czech: Contemporary Language Course. Michael Heim. 271p. (CZE.). audio 65.00 (*0-88432-445-1*, AFCZ10); 24.50 (*0-685-74484-1*) Audio-Forum.

Czech: Country Reporter. Lewis B. Sckolnick. (Illus.). 60p. 1994. pap. 895.00 (*1-57205-209-0*) Rector Pr.

Czech Americans. Stephanie Sakson-Ford. (Peoples of North America Ser.). (Illus.). 112p. (J). (gr. 5 up). 1989. lib. bdg. 17.95 (*0-87754-870-6*) Chelsea Hse.

***Czech & Slovak: Business Financing Handbook.** (Illus.). 70p. (Orig.). 1994. pap. 295.00 (*0-7605-1188-8*) Rector Pr.

Czech & Slovak Experience. Ed. by John Morison. LC 92-4308. 256p. 1992. text ed. 65.00 (*0-312-07992-3*) St Martin.

Czech & Slovak Federal Republic: An Economy in Transition. Jim Prust et al. LC 90-47707. (Occasional Paper Ser.: No. 72). vii, 70p. 1990. pap. 10.00 (*1-55775-169-2*) Intl Monetary.

***Czech & Slovak Ideas of Nationality.** 260p. (C). 1994. 175.00 (*0-7605-0423-7*) Rector Pr.

***Czech & Slovak Republics: Travel Survival Kit.** John King & Richard Nebesky. (Illus.). 504p. 1995. pap. 15.95 (*0-86442-245-8*) Lonely Planet.

***Czech Avantgardists.** Ed. by Alfred French. (Illus.). 106p. (C). 1995. text ed. 34.50 (*0-930329-80-5*); text ed. 34.50 (*0-614-05291-2*) KABEL Pubs.

***Czech Book.** Irene T. Turk & N. C. Tognazzini. LC 90-81718. (Illus.). 96p. 1990. pap. 5.95 (*0-9626591-0-X*) Energeia Pub.

Czech Book: Recipes & Traditions. Comp. by Pat Martin. LC 81-80852. (Illus.). 60p. 1981. pap. 7.95 (*0-9603858-6-X*) Penfield.

Czech Business Forecaster. Ed. by Lewis B. Sckolnick. 70p. (Orig.). (C). 1994. pap. 675.00 (*1-57205-356-9*) Rector Pr.

***Czech Business Intelligence Handbook.** (Illus.). 70p. (Orig.). 1994. pap. 295.00 (*0-7605-1043-1*) Rector Pr.

***Czech Business Risk Outlook.** 70p. (Orig.). 1994. pap. 495.00 (*0-7605-1425-9*) Rector Pr.

Czech Complete Course. 1994. audio 25.95 (*0-8442-3855-4*, NTC Busn Bks) NTC Pub Grp.

Czech Cubism: Architecture, Furniture, Decorative Arts. Ed. by Alexander Von Vegesack. LC 92-16158. (Illus.). 344p. 1992. 65.00 (*1-878271-65-2*); pap. 39.95 (*1-878271-66-0*) Princeton Arch.

Czech Dictionary - Poldaup: English-Czech - Czech-English. 8th ed. 1232p. (CZE & ENG.). 1987. 37.50 (*0-89918-253-4*, C253) Vanous.

Czech Drama Since World War II. Paul Trensky. LC 78-64436. 262p. reprint ed. pap. 74.70 (*0-8357-9434-2*, 2016133) Bks Demand.

Czech-English - English-Czech Dictionary of Electrical Engineering & Electronics. L. Malinova. 924p. 1982. 44.00 (*0-88431-256-9*) IBD Ltd.

Czech-English - English-Czech Dictionary of Nuclear Physics. Z. Bezdek. 343p. 1985. 28.00 (*0-88431-786-2*) IBD Ltd.

Czech-English - English-Czech (Pocket) K. Hais. 509p. 1991. 18.00 (*80-04-26086-1*) IBD Ltd.

Czech-English Chemical Dictionary. B. Kutinova. 515p. 1989. 30.00 (*0-88431-551-7*) IBD Ltd.

Czech-English-Czech Pocket Dictionary: Cesko-Anglicko-Cesky Kapesni Slovnik. K. Hais. 572p. (CZE & ENG.). 1991. 17.95 (*0-8288-0535-0*, M14018) Fr & Eur.

***Czech-English Dictionary of Chemical Engineering.** Kutinova. 519p. (CZE & ENG.). 1989. 35.00 (*0-7859-7510-1*) Fr & Eur.

Czech-English Dictionary of Computer Science. Minihofer. (CZE & ENG.). 1990. 49.95 (*0-8288-7199-X*) Fr & Eur.

Czech-English Dictionary of Computer Science. 2nd ed. D. Minihofer. 334p. 1990. 29.00 (*80-03-00169-2*) IBD Ltd.

Czech-English, English-Czech Dictionary. 8th ed. Ed. by I. Poldauf. 1223p. (CZE & ENG.). 1990. 39.50 (*80-04-25987-1*) IBD Ltd.

***Czech-English, English-Czech Dictionary of Nuclearing Physics.** Bezdek. 343p. (CZE & ENG.). 1985. 29.95 (*0-7859-7462-8*) Fr & Eur.

Czech-English, English-Czech Medical Dictionary. Paroubkova. (CZE & ENG.). 1991. 95.00 (*0-8288-7198-1*, F26310) Fr & Eur.

Czech-English, English-Czech Pocket Dictionary. K. Hais. 568p. (CZE & ENG.). 1991. 20.00 (*80-04-25682-1*, C148) Vanous.

Czech-English Technical Dictionary: Cesko-Anglicky Technicky Slovnik. 4th ed. Malinova. 945p. (CZE & ENG.). 1986. 95.00 (*0-8288-0679-9*, F42070) Fr & Eur.

Czech-English Technical Textile Dictionary. T. Leskova & V. Plisek. 468p. (CZE & ENG.). 1980. 60.00 (*0-686-72090-3*, Pub. by Collets UK) St Mut.

Czech for English Speaking Students. Sara Milan. 600p. 1988. 100.00 (*0-569-06362-0*, Pub. by Collets UK) Pro-Am Music.

Czech Handy Extra Dictionary. Nina Trnka. (Handy Extra Dictionaries Ser.). 186p. (Orig.). 1993. pap. 8.95 (*0-7818-0138-9*) Hippocrene Bks.

***Czech, Hungary, Poland & Privatization (Retail)** (Illus.). 260p. (C). 1994. 165.00 (*0-7605-0433-4*) Rector Pr.

***Czech, Hungary, Poland & Privatization (Retail)** (Illus.). 260p. (Orig.). (C). 1994. pap. 125.00 (*0-7605-0434-2*) Rector Pr.

Czech in Three Months. (Hugo Ser.). 200p. (Orig.). 1995. pap. 7.95 (*0-85285-209-6*); audio, pap. 39.95 (*0-85285-210-X*) Hunter NJ.

Czech-Italian-Czech Dictionary for Travelers. Benesova. 416p. (CZE & ENG.). 1983. 13.95 (*0-8288-1697-2*, M14852) Fr & Eur.

Czech Literature. A. Novak. Ed. by W. E. Harkins. Tr. by P. Kussi. (Joint Committee on Eastern Europe Publication Ser.: No. 4). 1986. 15.00 (*0-930042-64-6*) Mich Slavic Pubns.

Czech Nationalism in the 19th Century. John F. Bradley. 153p. 1984. text ed. 40.00 (*0-88033-049-X*) East Eur Quarterly.

Czech Opera. John Tyrrell. (Natoonal Tradition of Opera Ser.). (Illus.). 368p. 1988. 69.95 (*0-521-23531-6*) Cambridge U Pr.

Czech-Out Cajun Cooking. 2nd ed. Ina Potmesil & Katherine Guillot. (Illus.). 1991. pap. text ed. 15.95 (*0-9627496-0-5*) Czech Out Cajun.

Czech Philosophy in the Twentieth Century. Ed. by Lubomir Novy & Jiri Gabriel. LC 93-5986. (Cultural Heritage & Contemporary Change Series VI: Foundations of Moral Education,: Vol. 4). 1993. 45.00 (*1-56518-028-3*); pap. 17.50 (*1-56518-029-1*) Coun Res Values.

Czech Phrase Book. (Hugo Ser.). (Illus.). 128p. (Orig.). 1991. pap. 4.95 (*0-85285-164-2*); audio, pap. 14.95 (*0-85285-167-7*) Hunter NJ.

Czech Phrasebook. Nina Trnka. 220p. (Orig.). (CZE.). 1991. pap. 9.95 (*0-87052-967-6*) Hippocrene Bks.

Czech Prose: An Anthology. Ed. by William E. Harkins. LC 83-50054. (Michigan Slavic Translations Ser.: No. 6). 1983. 15.00 (*0-930042-51-4*) Mich Slavic Pubns.

Czech Proverbs. 63p. 1994. pap. 10.95 (*1-57216-010-1*) Penfield.

Czech Red Unions, Nineteen Eighteen to Nineteen Twenty-Nine. Kevin McDermott. (East European Monographs: No. 239). 384p. 1988. text ed. 54.00 (*0-88033-136-4*) East Eur Quarterly.

Czech Renascence of the Nineteenth Century: Essays Presented to Otakar Odlozilik in Honour of His Seventieth Birthday. Ed. by Peter Brock & H. Gordon Skilling. LC 76-18281. 359p. reprint ed. pap. 102.40 (*0-317-29883-6*, 2019447) Bks Demand.

***Czech Republic.** (American Geographical Society Around the World Program Ser.). 1995. lib. bdg. 17.95 (*0-614-04862-1*) Am Geographical.

***Czech Republic.** (American Geographical Society Around the World Program Ser.). 1995. pap. 9.95 (*0-614-04863-X*) Am Geographical.

Czech Republic: Commercial & Investment Law. Marta Knappova. 1994. ring bd. 165.00 (*1-56425-050-4*) Transnatl Juris Pubns.

Czech Republic: OECD Economic Survey. Ed. by Lewis B. Sckolnick. (Illus.). 200p. (Orig.). (C). 1994. pap. text ed. 165.00 (*1-57205-653-3*) Rector Pr.

***Czech Republic--in Pictures.** Lerner Publications Company, Geography Department Staff. LC 94-37432. (Visual Geography Ser.). 1995. write for info. (*0-8225-1879-1*) Lerner Group.

***Czech Republic & Economic Transition in Eastern Europe.** Ed. by Jan Svejnar. (Illus.). 461p. 1995. boxed write for info. (*0-12-678180-X*) Acad Pr.

Czech Republic & Slovakia. (Insight Guides, Windows on the World Ser.). (Illus.). 350p. 1993. pap. 21.95 (*0-395-65987-6*) HM.

Czech Republic & Slovakia. 2nd ed. 1994. pap. 12.00 (*0-679-02572-3*) Fodors Travel.

Czech Republic Budget Guide: The Czech Republic. Ed. by Richard Cox. (Thoroughbred Ser.). (Illus.). 280p. (Orig.). 1994. pap. 16.95 (*0-7818-0228-8*) Hippocrene Bks.

Czech-Russian Dictionary of Geology. N. A. Pascenkova et al. 248p. (CZE & RUS.). 1960. 39.95 (*0-8288-6833-6*, M-9067) Fr & Eur.

Czech, Slovakia: Business Risk Overview. Ed. by Lewis B. Sckolnick. 125p. (Orig.). (C). 1994. pap. text ed. 495.00 (*1-57205-605-3*) Rector Pr.

Czech-Slovakia, Hungary, Bulgaria: People to People. Ed. by Jim Haynes. 240p. 1993. pap. 10.95 (*0-939010-33-X*) Zephyr Pr.

Czech-Spanish Dictionary: Cesko-Spanelsky Slovnik. Dubsky-Rejsek. 1240p. (CZE & SPA.). 1980. 35.00 (*0-8288-1083-4*, S39711) Fr & Eur.

Czech-Swedish Dictionary: Cesko-Svedsky Slovnik. Furstova. 1000p. (CZE & SWE.). 1981. 29.95 (*0-8288-1084-2*, M14008) Fr & Eur.

Czech Through Russian. Charles E. Townsend. viii, 263p. (Orig.). (C). 1981. pap. text ed. 17.95 (*0-89357-089-3*) Slavica.

Czech Voices: Stories from Texas in the Amerikan Narodni Kalendar. Ed. by Clinton Machann & James W. Mendl, Jr. LC 91-43294. (Centennial Series of the Association of Former Students: No. 39). 184p. 1991. 18.95 (*0-89096-471-8*) Tex A&M Univ Pr.

Czechoslovak Contribution to World Culture. Ed. by Miloslav Rechcigl, Jr. 1964. text ed. 115.40 (*90-279-1032-4*) Mouton.

Czechoslovak Cookbook. Joza Brizova et al. Ed. by C. Adams. Tr. by A. Vahalla. (International Cookbook Ser.). 1965. 12.00 (*0-517-50547-9*, Crown) Crown Pub Group.

Czechoslovak Corporation Law: Commentary & Forms. Martin F. Klingenberg. 120p. 1992. pap. write for info. (*0-318-68482-9*) Kluwer Law Tax Pubs.

Czechoslovak Culture: Recipes, History & Folk Arts. Pat Martin. Ed. by Joan Liffring-Zug & John Zug. 176p. pap. 12.95 (*0-941016-61-7*) Penfield.

Czechoslovak Economy, Nineteen Eighteen to Nineteen Eighty. Alice Teichova. (Contemporary Economic History of Europe Ser.). 192p. 1988. lib. bdg. 67.00 (*0-415-00376-8*) Routledge.

Czechoslovak Educational System. Pavel Jenik. 78p. 1980. 23.00 (*0-317-53749-0*, Pub. by Collets UK) St Mut.

Czechoslovak Fairy Tales. Parker H. Fillmore. LC 78-67709. (Folktale Ser.). (Illus.). 1980. reprint ed. 31.50 (*0-404-16086-7*) AMS Pr.

Czechoslovak Functionalism, 1918-1939. L. Strizhenova. (C). 1990. 250.00 (*0-685-34368-5*) St Mut.

Czechoslovak Legion in Russia, 1914-1920. John F. Bradley. 200p. 1992. text ed. 28.00 (*0-88033-218-2*) Col U Pr.

Czechoslovak Literature: An Outline. Paul Selver. 1973. 175.00 (*0-87968-988-9*) Gordon Pr.

An Asterisk (*) at the beginning of an entry indicates that the title is appearing in BIP for the first time.

D

D

An Asterisk (*) at the beginning of an entry indicates that the title is appearing in BIP for the first time.

1771

D. Gottlieb & Co. Solid State Pinball Games, 1978: Service Manual. 2nd rev. ed. Ed. by Frank Adams. (Illus.). 94p. reprint ed. spiral bd. 32.50 (*1-56642-158-6*, R-34) AMR Pub Co.

D. H. Lawrence. Intro. by Harold Bloom. (Modern Critical Views Ser.). 321p. 1986. 34.95 (*0-87754-655-X*) Chelsea Hse.

D. H. Lawrence. Ronald P. Draper. (English Authors Ser.: No. 7). 192p. 1964. text ed. 22.95 (*0-8057-1320-4*, Twayne) Macmillan.

D. H. Lawrence. G. M. Hyde. LC 89-70032. (Modern Novelists Ser.). 144p. 1990. text ed. 29.95 (*0-312-04038-5*) St Martin.

D. H. Lawrence. Harry T. Moore & Warren Roberts. LC 87-51298. (Literary Lives Ser.). (Illus.). 144p. 1988. pap. 9.95 (*0-500-26030-3*) Thames Hudson.

D. H. Lawrence. Weldon Thornton. LC 93-25540. (Twayne's Studies in Short Fiction). 174p. 1993. text ed. 23.95 (*0-8057-0862-6*, Twayne) Macmillan.

D. H. Lawrence. Peter Widdowson. (Critical Readers Ser.). 249p. (C). 1992. text ed. 46.25 (*0-582-06156-3*, 79282); pap. text ed. 25.95 (*0-582-06155-5*, 79283) Longman.

D. H. Lawrence. John Worthen. (Modern Fiction Ser.). 128p. 1991. pap. 10.95 (*0-340-51372-1*, A6098, Pub. by E Arnold UK) Routledge Chapman & Hall.

D. H. Lawrence. Frank R. Leavis. LC 72-3172. (Studies in D. H. Lawrence: No. 20). 1972. reprint ed. lib. bdg. 75.00 (*0-8383-1541-0*) M S G Haskell Hse.

D. H. Lawrence. Stephen Potter. LC 78-64051. (Des Imagistes: Literature of the Imagist Movement Ser.). 168p. reprint ed. 32.50 (*0-404-17091-9*) AMS Pr.

D. H. Lawrence: A Biography. Jeffrey Meyers. 445p. 24.95 (*0-685-39477-8*) Knopf.

D. H. Lawrence: A Biography. Jeffrey Meyers. 1992. pap. 14.00 (*0-679-73065-6*, Vin) Random.

D. H. Lawrence: A Centenary Consideration. Ed. by Peter Balbert & Philip L. Marcus. LC 84-45800. 256p. (C). 1985. 33.95 (*0-8014-1596-9*) Cornell U Pr.

D. H. Lawrence: A Collection of Critical Essays. Ed. by Mark Spilka. 1963. 12.95 (*0-13-526855-9*, Spectrum Bks); pap. 2.45 (*0-13-526848-6*) P-H.

D. H. Lawrence: A Composite Biography, 3 vols. Ed. by Edward H. Nehls. 1959. write for info. (*0-318-56169-7*) U of Wis Pr.

D. H. Lawrence: A Composite Biography, 3 vols, 1. Ed. by Edward H. Nehls. 1959. 35.00 (*0-299-81501-3*) U of Wis Pr.

D. H. Lawrence: A Composite Biography, 3 vols, 2. Ed. by Edward H. Nehls. 1959. 35.00 (*0-299-81502-1*) U of Wis Pr.

D. H. Lawrence: A Literary Life. James Worthen. (Literary Lives Ser.). 222p. (C). 1993. pap. text ed. 14.95 (*0-312-08752-7*) St Martin.

D. H. Lawrence: An American Interpretation. Herbert J. Seligmann. LC 73-163113. (Studies in D. H. Lawrence: No. 20). 1971. reprint ed. lib. bdg. 75.00 (*0-8383-1306-X*) M S G Haskell Hse.

D. H. Lawrence: An Annotated Bibliography. J. M. Phillips. 1992. lib. bdg. 79.95 (*0-8490-1372-0*) Gordon Pr.

D. H. Lawrence: An Annotated Bibliography of Writings about Him, Vol. I. Ed. by James C. Cowan. LC 80-8664. (Annotated Secondary Bibliography Series on English Literature in Transition, 1880-1920). 612p. 1982. 45.00 (*0-87580-077-7*) N Ill U Pr.

D. H. Lawrence: An Annotated Bibliography of Writings about Him, Vol. II. Ed. by James C. Cowan. LC 80-8664. (Annotated Secondary Bibliography Series on English Literature in Transition, 1880-1920). 768p. 1985. 45.00 (*0-87580-105-6*) N Ill U Pr.

D. H. Lawrence: An Anthology of Recent Criticism. Ed. by Aruna Sitesh. (New Orientations Ser.). 232p. 1990. text ed. 27.95 (*81-85433-00-3*, Pub. by Pencraft International II) Advent Bks Div.

D. H. Lawrence: An Unprofessional Study. Anais Nin. LC 64-16109. 110p. (Orig.). 1964. pap. 8.95 (*0-8040-0067-0*) Swallow.

D. H. Lawrence: Centenary Essays. Ed. by Mara Kalnins. 1986. 32.50 (*0-8453-4510-9*, Pub. by Brist Class Pr UK) Assoc Univ Prs.

D. H. Lawrence: Critical Assessments, 4 vol. set. Ed. by David Ellis & Ornella De Zorda. (Writers in English Ser.). 1993. 499.00 (*1-873403-03-8*, A9789, Routledge NY) Routledge.

D. H. Lawrence: His First Editions. G. Fabes. 1973. 59.95 (*0-87968-989-7*) Gordon Pr.

D. H. Lawrence: Language & Being. Michael Bell. 256p. (C). 1992. 64.95 (*0-521-39200-4*) Cambridge U Pr.

D. H. Lawrence: Modes of Fictional Style. Bibhu Padhi. LC 87-50832. Orig. Title: Modes of Style in Lawrence's Fiction. 225p. 1989. 22.50 (*0-87875-354-0*) Whitston Pub.

D. H. Lawrence: Myth & Metaphysic in "The Rainbow" & "Women in Love" P. T. Whelan. Ed. by A. Walton Litz. LC 87-38098. (Studies in Modern Literature: No. 88). 232p. reprint ed. 66.20 (*0-8357-1853-0*, 2070778) Bks Demand.

D. H. Lawrence: New Studies. Ed. by Christopher Heywood. LC 85-14618. 192p. 1987. text ed. 39.95 (*0-312-19872-8*) St Martin.

D. H. Lawrence: Pilgrim of the Apocalypse. Horace Gregory. LC 70-140355. (Select Bibliographies Reprint Ser.). 1977. 18.95 (*0-8369-5598-6*) Ayer.

D. H. Lawrence: Selected Poetry & Non-Fictional Prose. John Lucas. (English Texts Ser.). 288p. 1991. pap. 12.95 (*0-415-01429-8*, A6137) Routledge.

D. H. Lawrence: Sexual Crisis. Nigel Kelsey. LC 91-7264. 224p. 1991. text ed. 49.95 (*0-312-06111-0*) St Martin.

D. H. Lawrence: The Artist As Psychologist. Daniel J. Schneider. LC 83-21361. xx, 318p. 1984. 29.95 (*0-7006-0241-0*) U Pr of KS.

D. H. Lawrence: The Critical Heritage. Ed. by Ronald P. Draper. (Critical Heritage Ser.). 1970. text ed. 69.50 (*0-7100-6591-4*, RKP) Routledge.

D. H. Lawrence: The Early Fiction. Michael Black. 320p. 1986. 54.95 (*0-521-32293-6*) Cambridge U Pr.

D. H. Lawrence: The Early Philosophical Works. Michael H. Black. 488p. (C). 1992. 49.95 (*0-521-41584-5*) Cambridge U Pr.

D. H. Lawrence: The Failure & the Triumph of Art. Eliseo Vivas. LC 60-10049. 320p. reprint ed. pap. 91.20 (*0-8357-9452-0*, 2015466) Bks Demand.

D. H. Lawrence: The Married Man. Maddox. LC 94-28960. 621p. 1994. 30.00 (*0-671-68712-3*) S&S Trade.

D. H. Lawrence: The Poet Who Was Not Wrong. Douglas A. Mackey. LC 84-291. (Milford Series: Popular Writers of Today: Vol. 42). 149p. (Orig.). 1986. lib. bdg. 27.00x (*0-89370-171-8*); pap. 17.00x (*0-89370-271-4*) Borgo Pr.

D. H. Lawrence: The True Redeemers? Gladys Lebolt. 1985. 7.50 (*0-912620-63-8*) Portals Pr.

D. H. Lawrence see Henry James

D. H. Lawrence & Feminism. Hilary Simpson. LC 82-14446. 174p. 1982. 22.50 (*0-87580-090-4*) N Ill U Pr.

D. H. Lawrence & Human Existence. 2nd ed. Martin Jarrett-Kerr. 160p. 1971. 24.50 (*0-912378-03-4*) Chips.

D. H. Lawrence & Italy. D. H. Lawrence. (Nonfiction Ser.). 512p. 1985. pap. 13.99 (*0-14-009520-9*, Penguin Bks) Viking Penguin.

D. H. Lawrence & Maurice Magnus. Norman Douglas. LC 72-8663. (Studies in D. H. Lawrence: No. 20). 1973. reprint ed. lib. bdg. 75.00 (*0-8383-1673-5*) M S G Haskell Hse.

D. H. Lawrence & Modernism. Tony Pinkney. LC 90-70151. 190p. (Orig.). (C). 1990. text ed. 26.00 (*0-87745-294-6*); pap. 13.95 (*0-87745-295-4*) U of Iowa Pr.

D. H. Lawrence & Susan His Cow. William Y. Tindall. LC 72-85664. xiv, 231p. 1973. reprint ed. 32.50 (*0-8154-0436-0*) Cooper Sq.

D. H. Lawrence & the Authoritarian Personality. Barbara Mensch. LC 90-45272. 284p. 1991. text ed. 39.95 (*0-312-05558-7*) St Martin.

D. H. Lawrence & the Body Mystical. F. Carter. LC 68-910. (Studies in D. H. Lawrence: No. 20). 1969. reprint ed. lib. bdg. 59.95 (*0-8383-0653-5*) M S G Haskell Hse.

D. H. Lawrence & the Child. Carol Sklenicka. (Illus.). 208p. (C). 1991. text ed. 27.50 (*0-8262-0778-2*) U of Mo Pr.

D. H. Lawrence & the Devouring Mother: The Search for a Patriarchal Ideal of Leadership. Judith Ruderman. LC 84-7987. xi, 211p. 1984. text ed. 39.50 (*0-8223-0598-4*) Duke.

D. H. Lawrence & the Experience of Italy. Jeffrey Meyers. LC 82-60261. 207p. reprint ed. pap. 59.00 (*0-7837-3006-3*, 2042935) Bks Demand.

D. H. Lawrence & the Idea of the Novel. John Worthen. 198p. 1979. 33.00 (*0-8476-6175-X*) Rowman.

D. H. Lawrence & the Phallic Imagination: Essays on Sexual Identity & Feminist Misreading. Peter Balbert. LC 87-20561. 176p. 1989. text ed. 39.95 (*0-312-01357-4*) St Martin.

D. H. Lawrence & the Psychology of Rhythm: The Meaning of Form in the Rainbow. Peter Balbert. (Studies in English Literature: No. 99). 1974. pap. 33.85 (*90-279-3032-5*) Mouton.

D. H. Lawrence & the Trembling Balance. James C. Cowan. 312p. 1990. lib. bdg. 35.00 (*0-271-00692-7*) Pa St U Pr.

D. H. Lawrence & Tradition. Ed. by Jeffrey Meyers. LC 84-16175. 176p. 1985. lib. bdg. 25.00 (*0-87023-464-1*) U of Mass Pr.

D. H. Lawrence at Work: The Emergence of the Prussian Officer Stories. Keith Cushman. LC 77-22149. 255p. reprint ed. pap. 72.70 (*0-8357-6995-X*, 2039048) Bks Demand.

D. H. Lawrence Chronology. Peter Preston. LC 93-43707. 1994. 45.00 (*0-312-12114-8*) St Martin.

D. H. Lawrence Companion: Life, Thought & Works. F. B. Pinion. LC 78-12348. (Illus.). 316p. 1979. text ed. 45.00 (*0-06-495574-5*, N6849) B&N Imports.

D. H. Lawrence Handbook. Ed. by Keith Sagar. LC 82-11569. (Illus.). 460p. (C). 1982. text ed. 53.00 (*0-389-20312-2*) B&N Imports.

D. H. Lawrence in His Time. Kim A. Herzinger. LC 81-65863. 240p. 1982. 35.00 (*0-8387-5028-1*) Bucknell U Pr.

D. H. Lawrence in Oaxaca: A Quest for the Novelist in Mexico. Ross Parmenter. (Illus.). 384p. 1984. 22.95 (*0-318-35420-9*) Hawkshead Bk.

D. H. Lawrence in the Modern World. Ed. by Peter Preston & Peter Hoare. 192p. (C). 1989. 42.95 (*0-521-37169-4*) Cambridge U Pr.

D. H. Lawrence, The Man Who Lived. Papers. Ed. by Robert B. Partlow, Jr. & Harry T. Moore. LC 80-15262. 320p. 1980. 18.95 (*0-8093-0981-5*) S Ill U Pr.

D. H. Lawrence, Vol. 1: The Early Years, 1885-1912. John Worthen. (Illus.). 688p. (C). 1991. 49.95 (*0-521-25419-1*) Cambridge U Pr.

D. H. Lawrence, Vol. 1: The Early Years, 1885-1912. John Worthen. (Illus.). 656p. (C). 1992. pap. 22.95 (*0-521-43772-5*) Cambridge U Pr.

D. H. Lawrence's Bestiary: A Study of His Animal Trope & Symbol. Kenneth Inniss. LC 70-165144. (De Proprietatibus Litterarum, Ser. Practica: No. 30). 207p. (Orig.). 1971. pap. text ed. 47.70 (*90-279-1950-X*) Mouton.

D. H. Lawrence's Literary Inheritors. Ed. by Keith Cushman & Dennis Jackson. LC 90-44895. 270p. 1991. text ed. 45.00 (*0-312-05577-3*) St Martin.

D. H. Lawrence's Non-Fiction: Art, Thought, & Genre. David Ellis & Howard Mills. 200p. 1988. 59.95 (*0-521-32739-3*) Cambridge U Pr.

***D. H. Lawrence's Response to Plato: A Bloomian Interpretation.** Barry J. Scherr. LC 94-28222. (American University Studies, Series IV, English Language & Literature: Vol. 179). 1995. write for info. (*0-8204-2605-9*) P Lang Pubs.

D. H. Lawrence's Sons & Lovers. Intro. by Harold Bloom. (Modern Critical Interpretations Ser.). 1987. 29.95 (*1-55546-024-0*) Chelsea Hse.

D. H. Lawrence's The Rainbow. Intro. by Harold Bloom. (Modern Critical Interpretations Ser.). 160p. 1988. lib. bdg. 29.95 (*1-55546-023-2*) Chelsea Hse.

D. H. Lawrence's Women In Love. Intro. by Harold Bloom. (Modern Critical Interpretations Ser.). 1987. 29.95 (*1-55546-025-9*) Chelsea Hse.

D. Howard Hitchcock. Helen Maxon. 1986. 39.95 (*0-914916-63-7*) Ku Paa.

D. I. E. T. During Pregnancy: The Complete Guide & Calendar. rev. ed. Miriam Erick. Ed. by Dianne Friend. LC 86-81951. Orig. Title: Pregnancy & Nutrition: The Complete D.I.E.T. Guide. (Illus.). 243p. 1987. pap. 11.95 (*0-9613063-4-3*) Grinnen-Barrett Pub Co.

D-I-V-O-R-C-E-S Spell Discover: A Kit to Help Children Express Their Feelings about Divorce. Bonnie Crown & Susan Atlas. (Illus.). 52p. (Orig.). (J). (gr. 1-8). 1992. spiral bd., pap. 15.95 (*0-9633626-0-7*) Courageous Kids.

***D Is for Dani's Baby.** Lisa Jackson. 1995. mass mkt. 3.75 (*0-373-09985-1*, 1-09985-2) Silhouette.

D Is for Deadbeat. Sue Grafton. LC 86-25843. (Kinsey-Millhone Mystery Ser.). 240p. 1987. 21.95 (*0-8050-0248-0*) H Holt & Co.

D Is for Deadbeat. Sue Grafton. 208p. 1988. reprint ed. pap. 5.99 (*0-553-27163-6*) Bantam.

D Is for Dolphin. Cami Berg. (Special Species Ser.). (Illus.). 64p. (J). 1991. 18.95 (*1-879244-01-2*) Windom Bks.

D Is for Dutch: A Last Regional Novel. Thomas R. Williamson. 1993. reprint ed. lib. bdg. 89.00 (*0-7812-5858-8*) Rprt Serv.

D. Iuni Iuvenalis: Satvrae. Ed. by J. R. Martyn. xxxii, 179p. (LAT.). 1987. pap. 42.00 (*90-256-0923-6*, Pub. by A M Hakkert NE) Benjamins North Am.

D. J. Allan Jeffreys et al. LC 73-167723. 1971. 24.95 (*0-87949-001-2*) Ashley Bks.

D. J. Hall: Selected Works 1974-1985. Robert McDonald. Ed. by Marie De Alcuaz & Josine Ianco-Starrels. LC 85-82100. (Illus.). 32p. (Orig.). 1986. pap. 12.00 (*0-936429-00-3*) LA Municipal Art.

D. J. Lawrence: Aesthetics & Ideology. Anne Fernihough. LC 92-46669. 1993. 39.95 (*0-19-811235-1*, Clarendon Pr) OUP.

D. J. Mitrokhin: Original Engravings & Drawings, 1883-1973. 1977. 395.00 (*0-317-14309-3*, Pub. by Collets UK) St Mut.

***D. J.-Stephanie Flipover Book.** Devra Speregen. (J). (gr. 4-7). 1995. pap. 3.25 (*0-590-20257-X*) Scholastic Inc.

D. J.'s Worst Enemy: A Novel by Robert Burch. Robert Burch. LC 92-44783. (Brown Thrasher Bks.). (Illus.). 144p. (J). (gr. 4-6). 1993. reprint ed. 19.95 (*0-8203-1554-0*) U of Ga Pr.

D. L. Moody. Faith C. Bailey. (Golden Oldies Ser.). 1959. pap. 4.99 (*0-8024-0039-6*) Moody.

D. L. Moody. David Bennett. 1994. pap. 4.99 (*1-55661-304-0*) Bethany Hse.

D. L. Moody, Vol. 7 of 7. Gordon Lindsay. (Men Who Changed the World Ser.: Vol. 7). 1972. 1.50 (*0-89985-260-2*) Christ for the Nations.

D. L. Moody: God's Salesman. Sandy Dengler. (Preteen Biography Ser.). (Orig.). 1986. pap. 4.50 (*0-8024-1786-8*) Moody.

D. M. Armstrong. Ed. by Radu J. Bogdan. 1984. lib. bdg. 55.00 (*0-318-00888-2*) Kluwer Ac.

D. M. Z. Downtown Militarized Zone. FASA Staff. (Illus.). 1990. boxed, pap. 30.00 (*1-55560-132-4*, 7111) FASA Corp.

D-Modules & Microlocal Geometry: Proceedings of the International Conference on D- Modules & Microlocal Geometry, Held at the University of Lisbon (Portugal), October 29-November 2, 1990. Ed. by M. Kashiwara et al. LC 92-35610. x, 199p. (C). 1992. lib. bdg. 99.95 (*3-11-012959-0*) De Gruyter.

D-Modules & Spherical Representations. Frederic Bien. (Mathematical Notes Ser.: No. 39). 144p. 1991. pap. text ed. 22.50 (*0-691-02517-7*) Princeton U Pr.

D-Modules, Representation Theory & Quantum Groups: Lectures Given at the 2nd Session of the Centro Internazionale Matematico Estivo (C.I.M.E.) Held in Venezia, Italy, June 12-20, 1992. L. Boutet de Monvel. LC 93-41202. (Lecture Notes in Mathematics Ser.: Vol. 1565). 1994. 35.00 (*0-387-57498-0*) Spr-Verlag.

D, My Name Is Danita. Norma F. Mazer. (J). (gr. 7 up). 1991. 13.95 (*0-590-43655-4*) Scholastic Inc.

D. P. G. Five Hundred: A Way to Cut Down the Cost on Marginal Oilfield Development. Pierre A. Thomas. 1989. 125.00 (*90-6314-523-3*, Pub. by Lorne & MacLean Marine) St Mut.

D. P. R. Korea: Politics, Economics & Society. John Merrill. (Marxist Regimes Ser.). 220p. 1987. 47.50 (*0-86187-424-2*, Pub. by Pinter Pubs UK); pap. 17.50 (*0-86187-425-0*, Pub. by Pinter Pubs UK) St Martin.

D-Plus Forever. Dave Davenport. LC 93-32217. (Illus.). 280p. 1994. 18.95 (*0-944957-42-0*) Rivercross Pub.

D-Poems of Jeremy Bloom. Gordon Korman & Bernice Korman. (J). 1992. pap. 2.95 (*0-590-44819-6*, 059, Apple Paperbacks) Scholastic Inc.

D. S. Merezhkovsky in Exile: The Master of the Genre of Biographie Romancee. Temira Pachmuss. LC 89-13253. (American University Studies: Slavic Languages & Literature: Ser. XII, Vol. 12). 338p. (C). 1990. text ed. 64.00 (*0-8204-1254-6*) P Lang Pubs.

D-Stem in Western Semitic. Stuart A. Ryder. (Janua Linguarum, Ser. Practica: No. 131). 173p. 1974. pap. text ed. 93.10 (*90-279-2669-7*) Mouton.

D Train. 1988. 20.00 (*0-317-90521-X*) Inkblot Pubns.

D Train. Terry Wilson. 153p. (C). 1985. 39.00 (*0-946459-03-7*, Pub. by Rivelin Grapheme Pr) St Mut.

D-Tree: Clinical Decision Analysis for the IBM. Thomas Abendroth et al. 128p. 1989. disk, spiral bd. 180.00 (*0-89189-280-X*) Am Soc Clinical.

D-Two: The Mighty Ducks Are Back! Adapt. by Jordan Horowitz. (Junior Novel Ser.). (Illus.). 144p. (J). (gr. 1-6). 1994. pap. 3.95 (*1-56282-692-1*) Disney Pr.

D. V. O. Models. Dorothy V. Owens. LC 93-90794. (Illus.). 100p. 1993. write for info. (*1-884308-11-2*); pap. write for info. (*1-884308-12-0*) Enlisted Ldrship.

D. W. All Wet. Marc T. Brown. (Illus.). (J). (ps-3). 1988. 10.95 (*0-316-11077-9*, Joy St Bks) Little.

D. W. All Wet. Marc T. Brown. (J). (ps-3). 1991. mass mkt. 4.95 (*0-316-11268-2*) Little.

D. W. Flips. Marc T. Brown. (Illus.). (J). (ps-2). 1987. 12.95 (*0-316-11239-9*, Joy St Bks) Little.

D. W. Flips. Marc T. Brown. (J). (ps-3). 1991. write for info. (*0-318-68259-1*); mass mkt. 4.95 (*0-316-11269-0*) Little.

***D. W. Griffith: His Biograph Films in Perspective.** Kemp R. Niver. (Illus.). 190p. Date not set. 15.00 (*0-614-07427-4*) Historical Films.

D. W. Griffith: His Biograph Films in Perspective. Kemp R. Niver. LC 74-81838. (Illus.). 190p. 1974. 15.00 (*0-913986-06-2*) Renovare Co.

D. W. Griffith & His Films. Jill Phillips & Leona Phillips. 490p. 1975. lib. bdg. 250.00 (*0-87968-334-1*) Gordon Pr.

D. W. Griffith & the Biograph Company. Cooper C. Graham et al. LC 85-2170. (Filmmakers Ser.: No. 10). 343p. 1985. 32.50 (*0-8108-1806-X*) Scarecrow.

D. W. Griffith & the Origins of American Narrative Film: The Early Years at Biograph. Tom Gunning. (Illus.). 328p. 1991. 42.50 (*0-252-01754-4*); pap. 16.95 (*0-252-06366-X*) U of Ill Pr.

D. W. Griffith's Intolerance: Its Genesis & Its Vision. William M. Drew. LC 84-43200. (Illus.). 207p. 1986. lib. bdg. 29.95x (*0-89950-171-0*) McFarland & Co.

D. W. Griffith's "The Battle at Elderbush Gulch" Kemp R. Niver. LC 72-85599. (Illus.). 1972. 7.50 (*0-913986-04-6*) Renovare Co.

***D. W. Griffith's the Battle at Elderbush Gulch.** Kemp R. Niver. Date not set. 7.50 (*0-614-07428-2*) Historical Films.

D. W. Griffith's the Birth of a Nation: Controversy, Suppression, & the First Amendment As It Applies to Filmic Expression, 1915-1973. Nickieann Fleener-Marzec. Ed. by Garth S. Joewtt. LC 79-6675. (Dissertations on Film Ser.). 564p. 1980. lib. bdg. 38.95 (*0-405-12909-2*) Ayer.

D. W. Just Big Enough. Marc T. Brown. LC 92-19947. (J). 1993. 12.95 (*0-316-11305-0*, Joy St Bks) Little.

D. W. Rides Again! Marc T. Brown. LC 93-7192. (J). 1993. 12.95 (*0-316-11356-5*) Little.

***D. W., the Picky Eater.** Marc Brown. LC 94-25674. (J). (gr. 1-8). 1995. 13.95 (*0-316-10957-6*) Little.

D. X. V. Prophecy-Dante & the Sabbatum Fidelium. Rose N. Ferrall. (Studies in Dante: No. 9). 1970. reprint ed. pap. 22.95 (*0-8383-0090-1*) M S G Haskell Hse.

D-2 Digital Video Recorder. John Watkinson. 284p. 1990. 59.95 (*0-240-51302-9*) Buttrwrth-Heinemann.

D-3 Digital Video Recorder. John Watkinson. (Illus.). 288p. 1992. 89.95 (*0-240-51330-4*, Focal) Buttrwrth-Heinemann.

***Da Avatar.** Adi Da. Ed. by Michael Costabile. 500p. Date not set. pap. 19.95 (*1-57097-017-3*) Dawn Horse Pr.

Da 'Boys Are Back: How the Dallas Cowboys Returned to the Super Bowl. Kevin J. Shay. LC 93-92599. 84p. 1993. pap. 4.95 (*1-881365-74-3*) Shay Pubns.

Da Bull: Life over the Edge. Greg Noll & Andrea Gabbard. (Illus.). 200p. 1992. reprint ed. pap. 16.95 (*1-55643-143-0*) North Atlantic.

***Da Capo.** 4th ed. Graziana Lazzarino & Annamaria Moneti. (C). Date not set. pap. write for info. (*0-03-009522-0*) HR&W Schl Div.

Da Capo: An Italian Review Grammar. 3rd ed. Graziana Lazzarino & Annamaria Moneti. 404p. (ITA.). (C). 1990. 173.75 (*0-03-053792-4*) HB Coll Pubs.

Da Capo: An Italian Review Grammar. 3rd ed. Graziana Lazzarino & Annamaria Moneti. 404p. (ITA.). (C). 1991. pap. text ed. 29.50 (*0-03-072232-2*); pap. text ed. 17.00 (*0-03-053898-X*) HB Coll Pubs.

Da Capo: An Italian Review Grammar. 3rd ed. Graziana Lazzarino & Annamaria Moneti. 404p. (ITA.). (C). 1992. pap. text ed. 21.75 (*0-03-072234-9*); audio 28.50 (*0-03-072312-4*); 28.50 (*0-03-072233-0*) HB Coll Pubs.

Da Capo: An Italian Review Grammar, Level II. 3rd ed. Graziana Lazzarino & Annamaria Moneti. 404p. (ITA.). (C). 1991. write for info. (*0-318-69164-7*) HB Coll Pubs.

Da Capo Guide to Contemporary African Music. Ronnie Graham. (Quality Paperbacks Ser.). (Illus.). 352p. (Orig.). 1988. pap. 13.95 (*0-306-80325-9*) Da Capo.

Da Epicuro a Lucrezio: I Maestro ed il Poeta nei Proemi del "de Rerum Natura" C. Graca. (Classical & Byzantine Monographs: No. 14). viii, 126p. (Orig.). 1989. pap. 32.00 (*90-256-0945-7*, Pub. by A M Hakkert NE) Benjamins North Am.

Da Kine Sound: Conversations with People Who Create Hawaiian Music. Burl Burlingame & Robert K. Kasher. Ed. by Mary Poole-Burlingame. LC 78-17556. 1978. pap. 5.95 (*0-916630-08-0*) Pr Pacifica.

Da Nang Diary: A Forward Air Controller's Year of Combat in Vietnam. Tom Yarborough. (Illus.). 304p. 1991. mass mkt. 4.99 (*0-312-92616-2*) St Martin.

Da Ponte Operas. Ed. by Ernest Warburton. LC 92-33289. (Librettos of Mozart's Operas Ser.: Vol. 3). 304p. 1993. 60.00 (*0-8153-0110-3*) Garland.

***Da Qiang Ji: Power Striking.** Hei Long. (Illus.). 176p. 1994. pap. 15.00 (*0-87364-803-X*) Paladin Pr.

D

An Asterisk (*) at the beginning of an entry indicates that the title is appearing in BIP for the first time.

D

An Asterisk (*) at the beginning of an entry indicates that the title is appearing in BIP for the first time.

1773

from three opposing forces. From within, Rockfish & his team passionately strive for the destruction of this horrific technology. From the American Midwest, Noetic Laboratories & federal authorities develop this discovery into a first generation weapon -- the Limbic Inhibitor. From the Far East, Red China's shadow kingdom of TEWU (Chinese Secret Service) receives an edict from her sovereign state: seize the American mind-altering technology at all costs. From the streets of Shanghai ... to the suburbs of Chicago, Illinois ... Eastern warriors confront Midwestern technologists. Heart-pounding. Relentless. Riveting. DADDY ROCKFISH is a whirlwind techno-thriller challenging the very core of american business ethics & scientific casuistry. ***Publisher Provided Annotation.***

Daddy, There's a Hippo in the Grapes. Lucy M. Dobkins. LC 92-20321. (Illus.). 64p. (J). (gr. 3-7). 1992. 12.95 (*0-88289-889-2*) Pelican.

Daddy to the Rescue. Cathy G. Thacker. (American Romance Ser.). 1994. mass mkt. 3.50 (*0-373-16526-9*, 1-16526-5) Harlequin Bks.

Daddy Trouble. Gayle Kaye. 1994. pap. 2.75 (*0-373-91014-2*, 5-91014-6); pap. 2.75 (*0-373-19014-X*, 5-19014-5) Harlequin Bks.

***Daddy Was a Cowboy: (Stetsons & Lace)** Jodi O'Donnell. (Sil Romance Ser.). 1995. mass mkt. 2.99 (*0-373-19080-8*, 1-19080-0) Silhouette.

Daddy Was a Number Runner. Louise Meriwether. LC 86-9019. 240p. 1986. pap. 10.95 (*0-935312-57-9*) Feminist Pr.

Daddy We Hardly Knew You. Germaine Greer. 1991. pap. 12.95 (*0-449-90561-6*) Fawcett.

Daddy, What Did You Do to Me? Vickie Theobald. LC 82-6822. 1989. pap. 13.95 (*0-87949-221-X*) Ashley Bks.

Daddy, Where Are You? large type ed. Shirley McGlade. (Illus.). 400p. 1993. 23.95 (*0-7089-8701-X*, Trail West Pubs) Ulverscroft.

Daddy, Where Were You? Healing for the Father-Deprived Daughter. Heather Harpham. (Heart Issues Ser.). 150p. 1991. pap. 9.95 (*0-932305-88-1*, 535009) Aglow Communs.

Daddy, Why Are You Going to Jail? The True Story of a Father's Descent into White-Collar Crime & His Amazing Restoration. Stephen P. Lawson. LC 92-23261. 1992. 8.99 (*0-87788-161-8*) Shaw Pubs.

Daddy, Why Was I Excommunicated? An Examination of Leonard J. Coppes, "Daddy, May I Take Communion?" Peter J. Leithart. 81p. 1992. pap. 7.00 (*1-883690-00-5*) Transfig Pr.

Daddyboy: A Memoir. Carol W. Konek. 161p. 1992. 18.00 (*1-55597-153-9*); pap. 12.00 (*1-55597-170-9*) Graywolf.

Daddy's Angel: Fabulous Father, under the Mistletoe. Annette Broadrick. (Silhouette Romance Ser.). 1993. pap. 2.75 (*0-373-08976-7*, 5-08976-8) Silhouette.

Daddy's Back. Val Whisenand. 1993. pap. 2.69 (*0-373-08926-0*, 5-08926-3) Silhouette.

Daddy's Chair. Sandy Lanton. LC 90-44908. (Illus.). 32p. (J). (gr. k-4). 1991. 12.95 (*0-929371-51-8*) Kar Ben.

Daddy's Climbing Tree. C. S. Adler. 144p. (J). (gr. 4-7). 1993. 13.95 (*0-395-63032-0*, Clarion Bks) HM.

Daddy's Duchess: An Unauthorized Biography of Doris Duke. Tom Valentine & Patrick Mahn. (Illus.). 256p. 1987. 17.95 (*0-8184-0443-4*) Carol Pub Group.

Daddy's Girl. Charlotte V. Allen. 272p. 1984. mass mkt. 5.99 (*0-425-11367-1*) Berkley Pub.

Daddy's Girl. Janice Kaiser. 224p. (Orig.). 1991. pap. 2.75 (*1-878702-35-1*, Kismet) Meteor Pub.

Daddy's Girl: The Campbell Murder Case. Clifford Irving. 1990. mass mkt. 4.95 (*0-8217-2955-1*) Zebra.

Daddy's Girls. Zoe Fairbairns. 544p. 1992. 24.95 (*0-312-06942-1*) St Martin.

Daddy's Gone to War: The Second World War in the Lives of America's Children. William M. Tuttle, Jr. LC 92-12445. 384p. 1993. 30.00 (*0-19-504905-5*) OUP.

***Daddy's Gone to War: The Second World War in the Lives of America's Children.** William M. Tuttle, Jr. 384p. 1995. pap. 15.95 (*0-19-509649-5*) OUP.

Daddy's Good Ideas. Keith Chatfield. 1990. pap. 1.95 (*0-907018-47-5*, Pub. by Tabb Hse Pubs UK) Seven Hills Bk.

Daddy's Home. Paul D. Anderson. 1990. pap. 3.95 (*1-55817-412-5*, Pinnacle NY) Windsor NY.

Daddy's Home. 2nd ed. Mike Clary. 240p. 1989. pap. 12.95 (*0-940495-23-6*) Pickering Pr.

Daddy's Home: A Practical Guide for Maximizing the Most Important Hours of the Day. Greg Johnson & Mike Yorkey. LC 92-12243. 254p. 1992. 9.99 (*0-8423-1093-2*) Tyndale.

***Daddy's in the Navy.** Rachel Gleason. (J). (ps-3). pap. text ed. 8.95 (*1-881116-69-7*) Black Forrest Pr.

Daddy's Little Dividend. Elda Minger. (American Romance Ser.). 1993. mass mkt. 3.50 (*0-373-16489-0*, 1-16489-6) Harlequin Bks.

***Daddy's Little Girl.** Geeta Kingsley. (Romance Ser.). 1995. pap. 2.99 (*0-373-19062-X*, 1-19062-8) Silhouette.

Daddy's Little Girl. Daniel Ransom. 1985. pap. 3.50 (*0-8217-1606-9*) Zebra.

***Daddy's Little Girl: For Dad's & Little Girls of All Ages.** Donna Reed. (Illus.). 34p. (Orig.). 1994. pap. 8.00 (*0-9641434-1-0*) Westbury Pubng.

***Daddy's Little Helper.** Debbie Macomber. 1995. pap. 2.99 (*0-373-03387-7*, 1-03387-7) Harlequin Bks.

***Daddy's Little Matchmaker.** Nikki Rivers. (American Romance Ser.). 1995. mass mkt. 3.50 (*0-373-16592-7*, 1-16592-7) Harlequin Bks.

***Daddy's Not-So-Little Girl.** Linda Thomas. Ed. by Lisa Clancy. (Full House Stephanie Ser.: No. 7). 128p. (Orig.). (J). 1995. mass mkt. 3.99 (*0-671-89860-4*) PB.

***Daddy's Old Robe.** Shawn Strannigan. (I Can Understand Ser.). (Illus.). 24p. (J). (ps-2). 1995. pap. 2.99 (*0-7847-0292-6*, 24-03459) Standard Pub.

Daddy's Roommate. Michael Willhoite. (Illus.). 32p. (J). (ps). 1990. 14.95 (*1-55583-178-8*) Alyson Pubns.

Daddy's Roommate. Michael Willhoite. (Illus.). 32p. (J). (ps-2). 1991. reprint ed. pap. 8.95 (*1-55583-118-4*) Alyson Pubns.

Daddy's Ties. Shirley Botsford. 96p. 1994. pap. 16.95 (*0-8019-8521-8*) Chilton.

Dade County Pine. Evelyn W. Mayerson. 464p. 1994. 22.95 (*0-525-93646-7*, Dutton) NAL-Dutton.

***Dade's Last Command.** Frank Laumer. LC 94-26086. (Illus.). 312p. 1995. 29.95 (*0-8130-1324-0*) U Press Fla.

Dads. Comp. by Bruce Velick. LC 93-14523. 1994. 17.00 (*0-517-59585-0*, Harmony) Crown Pub Group.

***Dads & Daughters, Fathers & Sons.** Lee. 1994. pap. text ed. 16.95 (*1-879323-12-5*) Sound Horizons AV.

Dads Are Such Fun. Jakki Wood. LC 91-21517. (Illus.). 32p. (J). (ps). 1992. pap. 12.00 (*0-671-75342-8*, S&S Bks Young Read) S&S Childrens.

Dad's Back. Jan Ormerod. LC 84-12614. (Illus.). 24p. (J). (ps). 1985. 4.95 (*0-688-04126-4*) Lothrop.

Dad's Car Wash. Harry A. Sutherland. LC 93-28734. (Illus.). 32p. (J). (ps-00). 1994. reprint ed. pap. 4.95 (*0-689-71807-1*, Aladdin Paperbacks) S&S Childrens.

Dads, Catholic Style. Bill Dodds. 180p. (Orig.). 1990. pap. 7.99 (*0-89283-692-X*) Servant.

Dad's Christmas Miracle. Pat Cook. 1993. 4.95 (*0-87129-212-2*, D55) Dramatic Pub.

***Dad's Daily Book of Memories.** Dean Vaughn & Stephen McCann. (Daily Power Ser.). 384p. 1994. 10.00 (*1-885952-01-5*) Vision Mktng.

Dad's Diary: 30 Days to Being a Better Dad. Ron Rose. 180p. 1994. 10.95 (*1-878990-29-2*) Howard Pub LA.

Dad's Dinosaur Day. Diane D. Hearn. LC 92-22549. (Illus.). 32p. (J). (gr. k-3). 1993. text ed. 14.95 (*0-02-743485-0*, Mac Bks Young Read) S&S Childrens.

Dad's Don't Die: In the Valley of the Shadow of Death. Rod Buzzard. 115p. 1993. pap. 5.95 (*0-9638378-0-X*) Lght for Life.

Dad's Doodle-Bug. Eleanor Parker. (Stories We Tell Ser.). 27p. 1993. pap. 4.00 (*1-884983-05-7*) Homegrown Bks.

Dad's Dying: A Family's Journey Through Death. John D. Suk. (Issues in Christian Living Ser.). 90p. (Orig.). 1991. pap. text ed. 5.95 (*1-56212-010-7*, 1344-0400) CRC Pubns.

***Dad's Little Instruction Book.** Pigeon. 1995. mass mkt. (*0-7860-0150-X*, Pinnacle NY) Windsor NY.

***Dad's Little Instruction Book.** Annie Pigeon. 96p. 1995. pap. 4.99 (*0-8217-0150-9*) Zebra.

Dad's Nuke. Marc Laidlaw. LC 85-80882. 251p. 1986. 15.95 (*0-917657-52-7*) D I Fine.

Dads Only! Bill Howse & Betty Howse. (Friendship Ser.). (Illus.). 48p. (Orig.). 1993. reprint ed. pap. write for info. (*1-882536-09-6*, A100-0032) Bible League.

Dad's Own Cookbook: Everything Your Mother Never Taught You. Bob Sloan. LC 92-50926. 1993. 21.95 (*1-56305-479-5*, 3479); pap. 12.95 (*0-89480-766-8*, 1766) Workman Pub.

Dads Say the Dumbest Things. Bruce Lansky & K. L. Jones. LC 89-29067. 112p. 1989. pap. 6.00 (*0-88166-131-7*) Meadowbrook.

D.A.E Project: Instructional Materials for Dental Health Professions. D.A.E. Project University of Washington. Incl. Self-Care One. 1982. 8.95 (*0-8077-6042-0*); Self-Care Two. 1982. 8.95 (*0-8077-6043-9*); Coronal Polish. 1982. 10.95 (*0-8077-6044-7*); Topical Fluoride. 1982. 6.95 (*0-8077-6045-5*); Normal Radiographic Landmarks. 1982. 9.95 (*0-8077-6046-3*); Oral Inspection. 1982. 6.95 (*0-8077-6047-1*); Oral Inspection Two. 1982. 4.95 (*0-8077-6048-X*); Margination: Overhang Removal. 1982. 8.95 (*0-8077-6049-8*); Trim & Finish Models. 1982. 5.95 (*0-8077-6053-6*); Rubber Dam. 1982. 9.95 (*0-8077-6060-9*); Sterilization & Disinfection. 1982. 9.95 (*0-8077-6062-5*); 1982. write for info. (*0-318-56787-3*) Tchrs Coll.

Daedalus in the Belly of the Beast - Dedalo en el Vientre de la Bestia. Marco A. De La Para. (InterAmericas Ser.: No. 1). 16p. (Orig.). 1992. 5.00 (*0-9633741-1-7*) RI Study of Man.

Daeg-Mael: Times of the Day. Miyoko Tanahashi. (Illus.). 1975. pap. 2.00 (*0-905019-00-8*) Soc New Lang Study.

Daemon in Lithuania. Henri Guigonnat. Tr. by Barbara Wright. LC 84-22707. (Illus.). 160p. 1985. 14.00 (*0-8112-0930-X*); pap. 7.95 (*0-8112-0939-3*, NDP592) New Directions.

Daemonic Figures: Shakespeare & the Question of Conscience. Ned Lukacher. (Illus.). 240p. 1994. 37.50 (*0-8014-3052-6*); pap. 15.95 (*0-8014-8223-2*) Cornell U Pr.

Daemonic in the Poetry of John Keats. Charles I. Patterson, Jr. LC 71-94399. 1970. 20.00 (*0-252-00079-X*) Lib Soc Sci.

***Daemonious.** David F. Camerlin. 300p. 1995. pap. 8.95 (*1-56901-830-8*) NW Pub.

Daemons. 1993. pap. 5.95 (*0-426-11332-2*, Dr Who) Carol Pub Group.

***Daemon's Angel.** Sherrilyn Kenyon. 400p. (Orig.). 1995. mass mkt., pap. text ed. 4.99 (*0-505-52026-5*) Dorchester Pub Co.

Daffodil Affair. Michael Innes. (Crime Ser.). 208p. 1990. mass mkt. 5.00 (*0-14-011498-X*, Penguin Bks) Viking Penguin.

Daffodil Affair see Michael Innes Omnibus

Daffodil & Golden Eagle. John Yeatman. LC 73-83158. (Illus.). 165p. reprint ed. 19.95 (*0-89388-110-4*) Okpaku Communications.

Daffodil Anne. large type ed. Catherine A. Darby. (Dales General Fiction Ser.). 278p. 1993. pap. 16.95 (*1-85389-391-9*, Dales) Ulverscroft.

Daffodil Farmer. Catherine O'Neill. LC 79-63168. (Series Four). 44p. 1979. pap. 7.00 (*0-931846-09-9*) Wash Writers Pub.

Daffodil Poetry Book. Ed. by Ethel L. Fowler. LC 70-128153. (Granger Index Reprint Ser.). 1977. 18.95 (*0-8369-6180-3*) Ayer.

Daffodil Wind. large type ed. Jean Graham. 368p. 1987. 16.95 (*0-7089-1667-8*) Ulverscroft.

Daffodils. Christi Killien. 144p. (J). 1992. 13.95 (*0-590-44241-4*, Scholastic Hardcover) Scholastic Inc.

Daffodils. Christi Killien. (J). (gr. 4-7). 1993. pap. 2.95 (*0-590-44242-2*) Scholastic Inc.

Daffodils: For Home, Garden & Show. Don Barnes. (Illus.). 176p. 1987. 23.95 (*0-88192-044-4*) Timber.

Daffodils & Dragonflies. Hank Dunlap. (Illus.). 40p. (Orig.). 1992. pap. text ed. 7.95 (*0-922484-01-5*) Poligion Pub.

***Daffodils for American Gardens.** Brent Heath & Becky Heath. LC 95-7247. (Illus.). 144p. 1995. 24.95 (*1-880216-33-7*) Elliott & Clark.

***Daffodils for Home & Garden.** Don Barnes. 1987. 9.98 (*0-7153-8853-3*, Pub. by D & C Pub UK) Sterling.

Daffodils in Winter. Pegi N. Macleod. Ed. by Joan Murray. 346p. 1984. 27.50 (*0-920806-48-1*, Pub. by Penumbra Pr CN) U of Toronto Pr.

Daffodils on Fire & Other Stories. Mridula Garg. (C). 1990. 17.50 (*81-214-0306-5*, National Bk Ctr) S Asia.

Daffodils or the Death of Love: Short Fiction. Corinne D. Bliss. LC 82-11048. (Breakthrough Bks.: No.39). 112p. (Orig.). 1983. pap. 10.95 (*0-8262-0385-X*) U of Mo Pr.

Daffy Dinosaurs Sticker Pad. Illus. by M. J. Studios Staff. 32p. (Orig.). (J). (gr. k-6). 1993. pap. 2.95 (*1-879424-48-7*) Nickel Pr.

Daffy Down Dillies: Silly Limericks. Edward Lear. LC 91-72986. (Illus.). 32p. (J). 1992. 14.95 (*1-56397-007-4*) Boyds Mills Pr.

Dafydd ap Gwilym: The Poems. Tr. by Richard M. Loomis. LC 81-16968. (Medieval & Renaissance Texts & Studies: Vol. 9). (Illus.). 352p. 1982. 18.00 (*0-86698-015-6*) MRTS.

***Dafydd Ap Gwilym Vol. 1: Poems.** Ed. by Rachel Bromwich. 207p. 1982. 38.00 (*1-85902-091-7*, Pub. by Gomer Pr UK) St Mut.

Dafydd ap Gwilym & the European Context. Helen Fulton. xiii, 274p. 1989. 45.00 (*0-7083-1030-3*, Pub. by U of Wales UK) Bks Intl VA.

Dag Hammarskjold. Richard Sheldon. (World Leaders - Past & Present Ser.). (Illus.). 112p. (YA). (gr. 5 up). 1987. lib. bdg. 17.95 (*0-87754-529-4*) Chelsea Hse.

Dag Hammarskjold: A Giant in Diplomacy. Robert Lichello. Ed. by D. Steve Rahmas. LC 73-185657. (Outstanding Personalities Ser.: No. 1). 32p. (Orig.). (gr. 7-12). 1972. lib. bdg. 4.95 (*0-87157-501-9*) SamHar Pr.

Dag Hammarskjold, Custodian of the Brushfire Peace. Joseph P. Lash. LC 73-22637. 304p. (C). 1974. reprint ed. text ed. 59.75 (*0-8371-6995-X*, LADJ, Greenwood Pr) Greenwood.

Dag Hammarskjold's United Nations. Mark W. Zacher. LC 71-101593. (International Organization Ser.: No. 7). 1970. text ed. 52.00 (*0-231-03275-7*) Col U Pr.

Dag Hammarskjold's White Book: An Analysis of Markings. Gustaf Aulen. LC 75-84608. 162p. reprint ed. pap. 46.20 (*0-685-16232-X*, 2026974) Bks Demand.

Dagger. William Mason. 352p. 1984. pap. 3.50 (*0-8217-1399-X*) Zebra.

Dagger: On Butch Women. Lily Burana et al. LC 94-2717. 1994. 29.95 (*0-939416-81-6*); pap. 14.95 (*0-939416-82-4*) Cleis Pr.

Daggers & Edged Weapons of Hitler's Germany. 3rd ed. James P. Atwood. LC 64-16165. 240p. 1970. 95.00 (*0-318-40081-2*) Johnson Ref Bks.

Daggers Drawn. large type ed. Margaret Carr. (Linford Mystery Library). 256p. 1987. pap. 11.95 (*0-7089-6356-0*, Linford) Ulverscroft.

Dagger's Edge. Anne Logston. 240p. (Orig.). 1994. pap. text ed. 4.99 (*0-441-00036-3*) Ace Bks.

Daggers of Faith: Thirteenth-Century Christian Missionizing & Jewish Response. Robert Chazan. 256p. (C). 1988. 45.00 (*0-520-06297-3*) U CA Pr.

Daggers of Gold. Katherine Deauxville. 1993. mass mkt. 4.99 (*0-312-92857-2*) St Martin.

Daggers of the Mind: The Russian Literary Imagination. E. C. Barksdale. 212p. 1979. 15.00 (*0-87291-099-7*) Coronado Pr.

***Dagger's Point.** Anne Logston. 272p. (Orig.). 1995. pap. text ed. 4.99 (*0-441-00134-3*) Ace Bks.

Daggerspell. Katharine Kerr. 1993. mass mkt. 5.99 (*0-553-56521-4*, Spectra) Bantam.

Daggie Dogfoot. large type ed. Dick King-Smith. 192p. (J). (gr. 1-7). 1990. 14.95 (*0-7451-1229-3*) G K Hall.

***DAGMAR: Defining Advertising Goals for Measured Advertising Results.** rev. ed. Russell Colley. 1995. 34.95 (*0-8442-3422-2*, NTC Busn Bks) NTC Pub Grp.

Dagmar Freuchen's Cookbook of the Seven Seas. Dagmar Freuchen & William Clifford. LC 68-30504. (Illus.). 256p. 1988. 14.95 (*0-87131-016-3*) M Evans.

Dagmar Schultz & the Angel Edna. Lynn Hall. LC 88-36862. (Dagmar Schultz Ser.). 96p. (J). (gr. 5-8). 1989. text ed. 13.95 (*0-684-19097-4*, C Scribner Sons Young) S&S Childrens.

Dagmar Schultz & the Angel Edna. Lynn Hall. LC 91-39608. 96p. (J). (gr. 3-7). 1992. reprint ed. pap. 3.95 (*0-689-71615-X*, Aladdin Paperbacks) S&S Childrens.

Dagmar Schultz & the Green-Eyed Monster. Lynn Hall. LC 90-43524. 80p. (J). (gr. 5-8). 1991. text ed. 13.95 (*0-684-19254-3*, C Scribner Sons Young) S&S Childrens.

Dagmar Schultz & the Powers of Darkness. Lynn Hall. LC 88-30806. (Dagmar Schultz Ser.). 80p. (J). (gr. 5-8). 1989. text ed. 13.95 (*0-684-19037-0*, C Scribner Sons Young) S&S Childrens.

Dagmar Schultz & the Powers of Darkness. Lynn Hall. LC 91-27939. 80p. (J). (gr. 3-7). 1992. reprint ed. pap. 3.95 (*0-689-71547-1*, Aladdin Paperbacks) S&S Childrens.

Dagny: Dagny Juel Przybyszewska, the Woman & the Myth. Mary K. Norseng. LC 90-30147. (Samuel & Althea Stroum Book Ser.). (Illus.). 240p. 1991. 24.95 (*0-295-96999-7*) U of Wash Pr.

***Dagoes Read: Tradition & the Italian-American Writer.** Fred L. Gardophe. (Essay Ser.: No. 25). 300p. 1995. 20.00 (*1-55071-031-1*) Guernica Editions.

Dagon & Other Macabre Tales. rev. ed. H. P. Lovecraft. Ed. by S. T. Joshi. LC 86-14105. (Collected Lovecraft Fiction Ser.: Vol. 3). (Illus.). 475p. 1987. 19.95 (*0-87054-039-4*) Arkham.

Dagorlad & the Dead Marshes. Ruth Sochard. (Illus.). 36p. (YA). (gr. 10-12). 1984. pap. 7.00 (*0-915795-20-5*, 8020) Iron Crown Ent Inc.

Dagra Perkistan Dynasty: The Teaching. Starhawk. 64p. 1994. pap. 7.95 (*0-8059-3520-7*) Dorrance.

Dags. Debra Oswald. 57p. 1990. pap. 4.25 (*0-87129-012-X*, D48) Dramatic Pub.

Dague: The History & Genealogy of the Dague Family. Carrie M. Dague. (Illus.). 253p. 1992. reprint ed. lib. bdg. 49.00 (*0-8328-2400-3*); reprint ed. pap. 39.00 (*0-8328-2401-1*) Higginson Bk Co.

Daguerreian Annual, 1991. Ed. by Peter E. Palmquist. 264p. 1991. pap. 30.00 (*1-881186-91-1*) Daguerreian.

Daguerreian Annual, 1992. Ed. by Peter Palmquist. 264p. 1992. pap. 30.00 (*1-881186-92-X*) Daguerreian.

Daguerreian Annual 1993. Ed. by Peter E. Palmquist. (Illus.). 288p. (Orig.). 1993. pap. 30.00 (*1-881186-93-8*) Daguerreian.

***Daguerreian Annual, 1994.** Ed. by Laurie A. Baty et al. (Illus.). (Orig.). 1994. pap. 30.00 (*1-881186-00-8*) Daguerreian.

***Daguerreian Annual 1995.** Ed. by Laurie A. Baty et al. (Illus.). (Orig.). 1995. pap. 45.00 (*1-881186-01-6*) Daguerreian.

Daguerreotype: A Sesquicentennial Celebration. Ed. by John Wood. LC 88-27904. (Illus.). 228p. 1989. 69.95 (*0-87745-224-5*) U of Iowa Pr.

Daguerreotype: Nineteenth-Century Technology & Modern Science. M. Susan Barger & William B. White. LC 90-39533. (Illus.). 320p. (C). 1991. text ed. 60.00 (*0-87474-348-6*) Smithsonian.

Daguerreotype in America. Beaumont Newhall. (Illus.). 176p. 1976. reprint ed. pap. 14.95 (*0-486-23322-7*) Dover.

Daguerreotype in Germany: Original Anthology, 3 acts. Ed. by Robert A. Sobieszek. LC 76-23344. (Sources of Modern Photography Ser.). (Illus.). (GER.). 1979. lib. bdg. 27.95 (*0-405-09598-8*) Ayer.

Daguerreotype Process: Three Treatises, 1840-1849. Ed. by Robert A. Sobieszek. LC 72-9192. (Literature of Photography Ser.). 1978. 10.95 (*0-405-04902-1*) Ayer.

Daguerreotypes & Other Essays. Isak Dinesen. Tr. by P. M. Mitchell & W. D. Paden. LC 78-27543. 230p. 1979. 12.95 (*0-226-15305-3*) U Ch Pr.

Daguerreotypes & Other Essays. Isak Dinesen. Tr. by P. M. Mitchell & W. D. Paden. LC 78-27543. 230p. 1984. pap. 12.95 (*0-226-15306-1*) U Ch Pr.

Daguerreotypes of Southworth & Hawes. Robert A. Sobieszek & Odette M. Appel. (Illus.). 1980. pap. text ed. 10.95 (*0-486-23841-5*) Dover.

Daguerreotypie. J. Thierry. Ed. by Peter C. Bunnell & Robert A. Sobieszek. LC 76-23039. (Sources of Modern Photography Ser.). (FRE.). 1979. reprint ed. lib. bdg. 15.95 (*0-405-09601-1*) Ayer.

Dagues Du III Reich. 2nd ed. Charles Mermet & Jean Marfault. (Illus.). 212p. 35.00 (*2-86551-003-4*) Johnson Ref Bks.

Dah Ming. Deak Moon. (Dah Ming Ser.). (Orig.). pap. write for info. (*0-940560-10-0*) Custom Hse.

***Dahcotah: Life & Legends of the Sioux.** Mary H. Eastman. (Illus.). 240p. 1995. reprint ed. 45.00 (*0-9639338-5-X*) Afton Hist Soc.

Dahcotah: Or, Life & Legends of the Sioux Around Fort Snelling. Mary Eastman. LC 75-95. (Mid-American Frontier Ser.). (Illus.). 1975. reprint ed. 26.95 (*0-405-06861-1*) Ayer.

Daheshism & the Journey of Life. Mounir Murad. LC 93-91483. (Illus.). 128p. 1993. 20.00 (*0-9633519-1-5*); pap. 10.00 (*0-9633519-2-3*) Murad Pub.

Dahl Co. Cookbook. Ed. by Marge Kovarik & Mollie O. Krafka. (Illus.). 150p. (Orig.). 1986. pap. 16.50 (*0-317-52975-7*) ARCI Assocs.

***Dahlia.** Gilroy. Date not set. pap. write for info. (*0-09-936651-7*); pap. 4.99 (*0-09-949810-3*) Random Hse Value.

Dahlia. Michael Rothenberg. (Illus.). 36p. 1989. 85.00 (*0-685-31054-X*) Big Bridge Pr.

Dahlia Primer. Eleanor Welling. (Illus.). 104p. (Orig.). 1992. pap. 5.95 (*0-685-59547-1*) Norawell Pubs.

Dahlias. Philip Damp. LC 87-32548. (Classic Garden Plants Ser.). (Illus.). 96p. 1988. 19.95 (*0-87106-733-1*) Globe Pequot.

***Dahlias: The Complete Guide.** (Illus.). 160p. 1995. pap. 19.95 (*1-85223-889-5*, Pub. by Crowood Pr UK) Trafalgar.

Dahlov Ipcar, Artist. Pat D. Reef. (Maine Artists for Young Readers Ser.: No. 2). (Illus.). 48p. (J). (gr. 3-7). 1987. pap. 12.95 (*0-933858-20-5*) Kennebec River.

D

1774

An Asterisk (*) at the beginning of an entry indicates that the title is appearing in BIP for the first time.

An Asterisk (*) at the beginning of an entry indicates that the title is appearing in BIP for the first time.

1775

D

Daily Meditations: The Great Virtues. James Alberione. 1985. 3.95 (*0-8198-1810-0*); pap. 2.95 (*0-8198-1811-9*) Pauline Bks.

Daily Meditations for Dieters: How to Think Thin 365 Days a Year. Anne Colby. LC 94-17784. 1994. 7.95 (*0-8065-1580-5*) Carol Pub Group.

Daily Meditations of John Paul II. Pope John Paul II. 1988. pap. 8.00 (*2-89039-066-7*, EP0275) Pauline Bks.

Daily Meditations (with Scripture) for Busy Moms. Patricia Robertson. (Illus.). 368p. (Orig.). 1993. pap. 8.95 (*0-87946-085-7*) ACTA Pubns.

*__Daily Meditations, 1995.__ Omraam M Aivanhov. 370p. 1994. pap. 12.95 (*1-895978-04-1*) Prosveta USA.

Daily Motivations for African-American Success. Dennis Kimbro. 416p. 1993. pap. 18.00 (*0-449-90786-4*, Columbine) Fawcett.

*__Daily Motivations for African-American Success.__ Dennis Kimbro. 1994. mass mkt. 5.99 (*0-449-22325-6*, Crest) Fawcett.

Daily News' History of Buchanan County & St. Joseph, Missouri. (Illus.). 567p. 1993. reprint ed. lib. bdg. 59.00 (*0-8328-3446-7*) Higginson Bk Co.

Daily Notes on a Trip Around the World. E. W. Howe. (Collected Works of E. W. Howe). 1988. reprint ed. lib. bdg. 59.00 (*0-7812-1291-X*) Rprt Serv.

Daily Notes on a Trip Around the World see Collected Works of E. W. Howe

Daily Notes to God. Noel Palmer. 112p. 1991. 7.00 (*0-9631717-0-4*) N Palmer.

Daily Number One Hits, 1940-1992. Joel Whitburg. (Record Research Ser.). 380p. 1993. pap. text ed. 24.95 (*0-89820-095-4*) Record Research.

Daily Office (Study Guide) Clifford W. Atkinson. LC 77-72493. 126p. 1977. pap. 2.95 (*0-8192-4076-1*) Morehouse Pub.

Daily Office, Vol. 2: A Book of Hours for Daily Prayer, Lent. Ed. by Dwight W. Vogel. (Daily Office Ser.). 160p. (Orig.). 1993. pap. 7.95 (*1-878009-13-3*) Order St Luke Pubns.

Daily Office, Vol. 3: A Book of Hours for Daily Prayer, the Great Fifty Days. Ed. by Dwight W. Vogel. (Daily Office Ser.). (Illus.). 168p. (Orig.). 1994. pap. text ed. 7.95 (*1-878009-19-2*) Order St Luke Pubns.

Daily Pathways. Helen S. Rice. 96p. 1989. 13.99 (*0-8007-1625-6*) Revell.

Daily Physical Education: Collected Paper on Health Based Physical Education in Australia. Richard Tinning & David Kirk. 113p. (C). 1991. pap. 60.00x (*0-949823-15-5*, Pub. by Deakin Univ AT) St Mut.

Daily Plan-It R. Bruce Braunstein. 180p. (Orig.). 1980. pap. 19.95 (*0-686-27615-9*) Tetragrammaton.

Daily Planner, 1995. Emilie Barnes. 1994. spiral bd. 6.99 (*1-56507-211-1*) Harvest Hse.

Daily Plans for Active Preschoolers: 80 Ready-to-Use Daily Activity Plans for Children Ages 3-5. Judy Galloway et al. 250p. 1990. pap. 27.95 (*0-87628-250-8*) Ctr Appl Res.

Daily Play. Jean Ward-Jones. 368p. 1991. pap. 7.95 (*1-882626-01-X*) Impress Ink.

Daily Poem. Ellen Farley. 1991. 15.00 (*0-533-08659-0*) Vantage.

Daily Poetry. Carol Simpson. 224p. (Orig.). (J). (gr. k-3). 1995. pap. 12.95 (*0-673-36172-1*) GdYrBks.

Daily Position Ephemeris of Chiron 1891-2000. Eve S. Gregory et al. Ed. by Al H. Morrison. Tr. by Reinhardt Stiehle. (Illus.). 121p. (Orig.). (ENG & GER.). 1985. pap. text ed. 20.00 (*0-917573-03-X*) CAO Times.

Daily Power for Joyful Living. Donald Curtis. 1975. pap. 7.00 (*0-87980-300-2*) Wilshire.

Daily Power Game. Mauk Mulder. (Quality of Working Life Ser.: No. 6). 1977. lib. bdg. 33.00 (*90-207-0707-8*) Kluwer Ac.

Daily Power Thoughts. Robert H. Schuller. 384p. 1984. pap. text ed. 4.99 (*0-515-08164-7*) Jove Pubns.

*__Daily Practice of Painting: Writings 1960-1993.__ Gerhard Richter. Ed. by Hans-Ulrich Obrist. Tr. by David Britt. LC 95-9818. 272p. (ENG & GER.). 1995. pap. 19.95 (*0-262-68084-X*) MIT Pr.

Daily Practice of the Hindus. Srisa C. Vasu. (C). 1991. 18.50 (*0-685-59600-1*, Pub. by Munshiram Manoharial II) S Asia.

Daily Practice of the Hindus Containing the Morning & Midday Duties. 3rd enl. rev. ed. Srisa Chandra Vasu. Tr. by Srisa Chandra Vidyarnava. LC 73-3812. (Sacred Books of the Hindus: No. 20). 198p. reprint ed. 18.00 (*0-404-57820-9*) AMS Pr.

Daily Praise. Ed Lyman, Jr. 308p. 1990. 8.99 (*1-56043-701-4*) Destiny Image.

Daily Praise from the Bible. 1989. pap. 3.97 (*1-55748-026-5*) Barbour & Co.

*__Daily Praise from the Bible: Inspiration from the Psalms.__ Dick. 1994. pap. text ed. 3.97 (*1-55748-600-X*) Barbour & Co.

Daily Prayer, 2 vols., Set. Robert Sauer. Bd. with Vol. 1. The Time of Christmas & Easter. 544p.; Vol. 2. Time of the Church. 544p. 1986. Set boxed 34.95 (*0-570-04228-3*, 15-2187) Concordia.

Daily Prayer: The Worship of God. Worship for the Presbyterian Church (U.S.A.) Office & Cumberland Presbyterian Church The. LC 87-14781. (Supplemental Liturgical Resource Ser.: Vol. 5). 434p. (Orig.). 1987. pap. 15.99 (*0-664-24089-5*, Westminster) Westminster John Knox.

Daily Prayers. Pandurangarao Malyala. (Illus.). (Orig.). 1984. pap. 2.00 (*0-938924-24-9*) Sri Shirdi Sai.

*__Daily Prayers: A Classic Collection.__ Frederick B. Meyer. LC 95-7979. Orig. Title: My Daily Prayer. 144p. 1995. 12.99 (*0-87788-169-3*) Shaw Pubs.

Daily Prayers for Busy People. William J. O'Malley. Ed. by Carl Koch. (Illus.). 192p. (Orig.). 1990. pap. 7.95 (*0-88489-242-5*); spiral bd. 9.95 (*0-88489-248-4*) St Marys.

Daily Prayers for Orthodox Christians. Ed. by N. Michael Vaporis. vi, 202p. 1986. 7.95 (*0-917651-03-0*) Holy Cross Orthodox.

Daily Problem Solving Activities: Transitioning to Independence. Andrew K. Gruen & Lynn S. Guren. LC 93-46014. 1994. 35.00 (*0-930599-94-2*) Thinking Pubns.

Daily Public School in the United States. Frederic A. Packard. LC 73-89215. (American Education: Its Men, Institutions & Ideas, Ser. 1). 1974. reprint ed. 16.95 (*0-405-01454-6*) Ayer.

Daily Rate. Grace L. Hill. 1976. reprint ed. lib. bdg. 23.95 (*0-89190-020-9*, Rivercity Pr) Amereon Ltd.

Daily Rate. Grace L. Hill. 1990. reprint ed. lib. bdg. 21.95 (*0-89968-523-4*) Buccaneer Bks.

Daily Readings from J. C. Ryle Vol. 1: Matthew, Mark, Luke. J. C. Ryle. 352p. 1982. pap. 11.95 (*0-85234-164-4*) Ballantine.

Daily Readings from J. C. Ryle, Vol. 1: Matthew, Mark, Luke. J. C. Ryle. 1982. pap. 11.99 (*0-87552-940-2*, Pub. by Evangel Pr UK) Presby & Reformed.

Daily Readings from J. C. Ryle, Vol. 2: John. J. C. Ryle. 1985. pap. 11.99 (*0-85234-214-4*, Pub. by Evangel Pr UK) Presby & Reformed.

Daily Readings from Luther's Writings. Martin Luther. LC 93-14902. 336p. 1993. pap. 19.99 (*0-8066-2639-9*, 9-2639) Augsburg Fortress.

Daily Readings from Prayers & Praises in the Celtic Tradition. Ed. by A. M. Allchin & Esther De Waal. 1987. pap. 4.95 (*0-87243-151-7*) Templegate.

Daily Readings from Quaker Writings Ancient & Modern, 2 Vol. Set. Ed. & Pref. by Linda H. Renfer. 400p. 1995. 31.95 (*0-9620869-0-8*) Serenity Pr.

*__Daily Readings from Quaker Writings Ancient & Modern, Vol. II.__ Ed. by Linda H. Renfer. 384p. 1995. 31.95 (*0-9620869-1-6*) Serenity Pr.

Daily Readings from Spiritual Classics. Paul Ofstedal. LC 89-30976. 408p. 1990. pap. 21.99 (*0-8066-2424-8*, 9-2424) Augsburg Fortress.

Daily Readings from the Cloud of Unknowing. Ed. by Robert Llewelyn. (Daily Readings Ser.). 1986. pap. 4.95 (*0-87243-149-5*) Templegate.

Daily Readings from the Prayers of Samuel Johnson. Samuel Johnson. Ed. by Elton Trueblood. (Daily Readings Ser.). 96p. 1987. pap. 4.95 (*0-87243-159-2*) Templegate.

Daily Readings from the Writings of St. John Chrysostom. Ed. by Anthony M. Coniaris. 1988. pap. 8.95 (*0-937032-51-4*) Light&Life Pub Co MN.

Daily Readings in Catholic Classics. Rawley Meyers. LC 92-71959. 332p. (Orig.). 1992. pap. 14.95 (*0-89870-389-1*) Ignatius Pr.

Daily Readings in Quaker Spirituality. Ed. by Edward Cell. 1987. pap. 4.95 (*0-87243-160-6*) Templegate.

Daily Readings with a Modern Mystic: Selections from the Writings of Evelyn Underhill. Comp. by Delroy Oberg. LC 93-60276. 176p. (Orig.). 1993. pap. 9.95 (*0-89622-566-6*) Twenty-Third.

*__Daily Readings with Blaise Pascal.__ Blaise Pascal. Ed. by Robert Van de Weyer. LC 95-60057. 1995. pap. 4.95 (*0-87243-212-2*) Templegate.

Daily Readings with Brother Lawrence. Brother Lawrence. Ed. by Robert Llewelyn. (Daily Readings Ser.). 1986. pap. 4.95 (*0-87243-144-4*) Templegate.

Daily Readings with Jean-Pierre de Caussade. Jean-Pierre De Caussade. Ed. by Robert LLewelyn. (Daily Readings Ser.). 1986. pap. 4.95 (*0-87243-145-2*) Templegate.

Daily Readings with John Wesley. Ed. by Arthur S. Wood. 96p. 1987. pap. 4.95 (*0-87243-158-4*) Templegate.

Daily Readings with Julian of Norwich, 2 vols., 1. Julian of Norwich. Ed. by Robert LLewelyn. (Daily Readings Ser.). 1986. pap. 4.95 (*0-87243-142-8*) Templegate.

Daily Readings with Julian of Norwich, 2 vols., 2. Julian of Norwich. Ed. by Robert LLewelyn. (Daily Readings Ser.). 1986. pap. 4.95 (*0-87243-143-6*) Templegate.

Daily Readings with Martin Luther. Martin Luther. Ed. by James Atkinson. 1987. pap. 4.95 (*0-87243-157-6*) Templegate.

Daily Readings with Mother Teresa. Teresa De Bertodan. 1994. pap. 9.00 (*0-00-627810-8*) Harper SF.

*__Daily Readings with Soren Kierkegaard.__ Ed. by Robert Van de Weyer. LC 95-60056. 1995. pap. 4.95 (*0-8274-3211-9*) Templegate.

Daily Readings with St. Augustine. St. Augustine. Ed. by Robert Llewelyn. (Daily Readings Ser.). 96p. 1986. pap. 4.95 (*0-87243-152-5*) Templegate.

Daily Readings with St. Francis de Sales. St. Francis de Sales. Ed. by Robert LLewelyn. (Daily Readings Ser.). 1986. pap. 4.95 (*0-87243-147-9*) Templegate.

Daily Readings with St. Francis of Assisi. St. Francis of Assisi. Ed. by Robert Llewelyn. (Daily Readings Ser.). 96p. 1988. pap. 4.95 (*0-87243-170-3*) Templegate.

Daily Readings with St. Isaac of Syria. St. Isaac of Syria. Ed. by A. M. Allchin. (Daily Readings Ser.). 96p. 1990. pap. 4.95 (*0-87243-173-8*) Templegate.

Daily Readings with St. John of the Cross. St. John of the Cross. Ed. by Robert Llewelyn. (Daily Readings Ser.). 1986. pap. 4.95 (*0-87243-148-7*) Templegate.

Daily Readings with St. Teresa of Avila. St. Teresa of Avila. Ed. by Robert LLewelyn. (Daily Readings Ser.). 1986. pap. 4.95 (*0-87243-146-0*) Templegate.

Daily Readings with St. Therese of Lisieux. St. Therese of Lisieux. Ed. by Robert Llewelyn. (Daily Readings Ser.). 96p. 1988. pap. 4.95 (*0-87243-154-1*) Templegate.

Daily Readings with the Desert Fathers. Desert Fathers. Ed. by Benedicta Ward. 96p. 1990. pap. 4.95 (*0-87243-185-1*) Templegate.

Daily Readings with William Law. William Law. Ed. by Robert Llewelyn. (Daily Readings Ser.). 96p. 1987. pap. 4.95 (*0-87243-153-3*) Templegate.

*__Daily Reflections.__ (LIT.). 1994. write for info. (*0-916856-55-0*) AAWS.

Daily Reflections. Helen S. Rice. 1990. 13.99 (*0-8007-1642-6*) Revell.

Daily Reflections. braille ed. Helen Steiner Rice & Virginia J. Ruehlman. 109p. 1992. vinyl bd. 8.72 (*1-56956-050-1*, BR8872) W A T Braille.

Daily Reflections: A Book of Reflections by AA Members. 382p. (SPA.). 1991. pap. 6.00 (*0-916856-43-7*) AAWS.

Daily Reflections: A Book of Reflections by AA Members for AA Members. Alcoholics Anonymous World Services, Inc. Staff. 382p. 1990. pap. 5.25 (*0-916856-37-2*) AAWS.

Daily Reflections with Mary. Ed. by Rawleyq Myers. (Illus.). 95p. 1988. pap. 3.95 (*0-89942-372-8*, 372-04) Catholic Bk Pub.

*__Daily Reports on All Legislation.__ Date not set. ring bd. 2,000.00 (*0-614-05803-1*) Michie Butterworth.

Daily Roman Missal: Daily & Sunday Masses. rev. ed. Ed. by James Socias. 2144p. (ENG & LAT.). 1992. 59.95 (*0-933932-58-8*) Scepter Pubs.

Daily Secrets of the Christian Life. rev. ed. Hannah W. Smith. Ed. by Ann Spangler. 232p. 1992. pap. 8.99 (*0-89283-228-2*, Vine Bks) Servant.

Daily Sensorimotor Training Activities. William T. Braly et al. 1968. teacher ed 5.95 (*0-914296-02-7*) Ed Activities.

Daily Sight Playing Exercises, Bk. 1. Cora Ahrens. 1993. 4.95 (*1-56222-542-1*, 94842) Mel Bay.

Daily Sight Playing Exercises, Bk. 2. Cora Ahrens. 1993. 4.95 (*0-685-64692-0*, 94843) Mel Bay.

Daily Sight Playing Exercises, Bk. 3. Cora Ahrens. 1993. 4.95 (*0-685-64693-9*, 94844) Mel Bay.

Daily Sikh Prayer (Nitnem) Shumsher Singh. 438p. 1990. 9.00 (*81-7116-086-7*, National Bk Shop) Nataraj Bks.

Daily Steppingstones. Helen S. Rice. LC 89-32210. 1989. 13.99 (*0-8007-1616-7*) Revell.

*__Daily Strength: One Year of Experiencing the Psalms.__ Victor M. Parachin. 384p. 1995. pap. 12.95 (*0-89243-677-8*) Liguori Pubns.

*__Daily Strength for Daily Needs.__ Smithmark Staff. 1995. 6.98 (*0-8317-2393-9*) Smithmark.

Daily Strength for Daily Needs. Ed. by Mary Tileston. 7.99 (*1-55748-144-X*, Christian Lib) Barbour & Co.

Daily Strength for Daily Needs. Mary W. Tileston. LC 73-80030. (Kregel Large Print Inspirational Classics Ser.). 392p. 10.99 (*0-8254-5324-0*) Kregel.

Daily Strength for Daily Needs. Mary W. Tileston. 1942. 10.95 (*0-316-84592-2*) Little.

Daily Strength for Daily Needs. Mary W. Tileston. 378p. 1993. reprint ed. 5.98 (*0-8317-2100-6*) Smithmark.

Daily Strength for Daily Needs: An Illuminated Selection. Ed. by Peg Streep. LC 93-39923. (Illus.). 96p. 1994. 12.95 (*0-8212-2073-X*) Bulfinch Pr.

Daily Study Bible: New Testament, 18 vols., Set.

Daily Study Bible - Old Testament, 24 vols., Set.

Daily Telegraph Guide to Living & Retiring Abroad. 6th rev. ed. Michael Furnell. pap. text ed. write for info. (*0-7494-0727-1*, Pub. by Kogan Page Educ UK) Taylor & Francis.

*__Daily Things of Christian Living.__ Carlton Coon. (Orig.). 1994. pap. 7.00 (*0-9642348-0-7*) Truth Pubns.

*__Daily Thoughts for Disciples.__ Oswald Chambers. 384p. 1994. 14.99 (*0-929239-47-4*) Discovery Hse Pubs.

Daily Thoughts on Bible Characters. 2nd ed. Harry Foster. (CHI.). 1982. write for info. (*0-941598-99-3*); pap. write for info. (*0-941598-00-4*) Living Spring Pubns.

Daily Thoughts on Living Free. Neva Coyle. LC 82-4495. 174p. (Orig.). 1982. pap. 6.99 (*0-87123-286-3*) Bethany Hse.

Daily Use of the Ephemeris. Elizabeth Aldrich. LC 84-72294. 86p. 1971. 7.00 (*0-86690-286-4*, A2406-014) Am Fed Astrologers.

Daily Vespers: With Complete Rubrics. (New Sarov Service Bks.). 52p. 1988. pap. 6.00 (*1-880364-00-X*) New Sarov.

*__Daily Vitamins for Spiritual Growth.__ Anthony M. Coniaris. 1994. pap. 12.95 (*0-614-06921-1*) Light&Life Pub Co MN.

*__Daily Vitamins for Spiritual Growth Vol. 2.__ Anthony A. Coniaris. 377p. (Orig.). 1995. pap. 12.95 (*1-880971-03-8*) Light&Life Pub Co MN.

Daily Walk Bible. 1987. kivar, pap. 16.99 (*0-8423-7915-0*); kivar, pap. 16.99 (*0-8423-0504-1*) Tyndale.

Daily Walk Bible. Ed. by Bruce H. Wilkinson et al. LC 92-14190. 1992. 22.99 (*0-8423-1062-2*); pap. 16.99 (*0-8423-1063-0*) Tyndale.

Daily Walk Bible, King James Version. 1987. 22.99 (*0-8423-0505-X*) Tyndale.

Daily Walk Bible, The Living Bible. 1987. 22.99 (*0-8423-7916-9*) Tyndale.

Daily Walk Bible (NRSV Version) Ed. by Bruce H. Wilkinson et al. LC 92-14190. 1992. 22.99 (*0-529-07260-2*); pap. 16.99 (*0-529-07259-9*) World Bible.

Daily Wesley. Donald Demaray. 448p. (Orig.). 1994. pap. 12.95 (*0-917851-80-3*) Bristol Hse.

Daily with the King: A Devotional for Self-Discipleship. W. Glyn Evans. 12.99 (*0-8024-1725-6*) Moody.

*__Daily Words of Comfort.__ Julie Yamaguchi. 160p. (Orig.). Date not set. pap. 8.95 (*0-7610-0275-8*) NW Pub.

*__Daimon.__ Date not set. 10.00 (*0-8317-5834-1*) Smithmark.

Daimon. Abel Posse. 288p. 1992. text ed. 20.00 (*0-689-12123-7*, Atheneum S&S) S&S Trade.

Daimon: An Adventure Story for First Year Latin Students. (Illus.). (J). (gr. 7-10). 1977. pap. text ed. 4.95 (*0-88334-095-X*) Longman.

Daimon Life: Heidegger & Life-Philosophy. David F. Krell. LC 91-47493. (Studies in Continental Thought). 320p. 1992. 39.95 (*0-253-33147-1*); pap. 18.95 (*0-253-20739-8*, MB-739) Ind U Pr.

*__Daimonic Reality: A Field Guide to the Otherworld.__ Patrick Harpur. 352p. 1995. 29.95 (*0-670-85569-3*, Arkana) Viking Penguin.

*__Dain Curse.__ Dashiell Hammet. 736p. 1991. Not sold separately (*0-615-00020-7*) Random Hse Value.

Dain Curse. Dashiell Hammett. 1989. pap. 6.95 (*0-679-72260-2*, Vin) Random.

Dain Curse. Dashiell Hammett. 1976. 19.95 (*0-8488-1039-2*) Amereon Ltd.

Dairies & Daydreams. Robyn Burrows. 149p. (C). 1990. 45.00 (*0-7316-8226-2*, Pub. by Boolarong Pubns AT) St Mut.

Dairies, 1995. American Business Directories Staff. 1995. spiral bd., pap. 240.00 (*1-56105-613-8*) Am Busn Direct.

Dairy Aid & Development: India's Operation Flood. Martin Doornbos et al. (Illus.). 344p. (C). 1990. text ed. 35.00 (*0-8039-9641-1*) Sage.

Dairy Cattle: Feeding & Management, Net. 7th ed. William M. Etgen et al. 608p. (C). 1987. text ed. write for info. (*0-471-80891-1*) Wiley.

Dairy Cattle Feeding & Nutrition. W. J. Miller. LC 78-51234. (Animal Feeding & Nutrition Ser.). 1979. text ed. 80.00 (*0-12-497650-6*) Acad Pr.

Dairy Cattle Fertility & Sterility. Hoard's Dairyman Staff. Tr. by Tri-State Breeders Staff. (Illus.). 92p. (SPA.). (C). 1992. pap. text ed. write for info. (*0-932147-14-3*, Hoards Dairyman) Hoard & Sons Co.

Dairy Cattle Fertility & Sterility. rev. ed. Hoard's Dairyman & Sons Co. Staff. Ed. by Elvira B. Kau. (Illus.). 72p. 1989. pap. text ed. 3.50 (*0-932147-05-4*, Hoards Dairyman) Hoard & Sons Co.

Dairy Cattle Judging Techniques. 4th ed. G. Trimberger et al. (Illus.). 356p. (C). 1992. reprint ed. text ed. 39.95 (*0-88133-678-5*) Waveland Pr.

Dairy-Cattle Production. Ed. by H. O. Gravert. (World Animal Science Ser.: Vol. C3). 322p. 1988. 151.50 (*0-444-42680-9*) Elsevier.

Dairy Cattle Science. 3rd ed. M. E. Ensminger. (Illus.). 568p. 1993. 59.95 (*0-8134-2930-7*); text ed. 44.95 (*0-685-61693-2*) Interstate.

Dairy Chemistry & Physics. Pieter Walstra & Robert Jenness. LC 83-16902. 467p. 1984. text ed. 138.00 (*0-471-09779-9*) Wiley.

Dairy Co Operativization: An Instrument of Social Change. Dilip R. Shah. (C). 1992. 16.00 (*81-7033-122-6*, Pub. by Rawat II) S Asia.

Dairy Country. Lynn M. Stone. LC 93-13503. (Back Roads Ser.). (J). 1993. write for info. (*0-86593-302-2*) Rourke Corp.

Dairy Cow Today: U. S. Trends, Breeding & Progress since 1960. Sidney L. Spahr & Bernard M. Heisner. LC 87-83593. (Illus.). 224p. (C). 1988. pap. text ed. 12.95 (*0-932147-04-6*) Hoard & Sons Co.

Dairy Cows. Kathy Henderson. LC 88-11123. (New True Bks.). 48p. (J). (gr. k-4). 1988. lib. bdg. 12.90 (*0-516-01152-9*); pap. 4.95 (*0-516-41152-7*) Childrens.

Dairy Development in Sub-Saharan Africa: A Study of Issues & Options. Michael J. Walshe et al. (Technical Paper Ser.). 114p. 1991. pap. 7.95 (*0-8213-1781-4*, 11781) World Bank.

Dairy Farm Business Management. 2nd ed. Ken Slater & Gordon Throup. 218p. 1983. 27.95 (*0-85236-141-6*, Pub. by Farming Pr UK) Diamond Farm Bk.

Dairy Farm Management: Business Summary New York State 1991. (Illus.). 74p. (Orig.). (C). 1993. pap. text ed. 35.00 (*1-56806-731-3*) Diane Pub.

Dairy Farmer. Susan C. Poskanzer. LC 88-10040. (What's It Like to Be a...Ser.). (Illus.). 32p. (J). (gr. k-3). 1989. lib. bdg. 10.89 (*0-8167-1426-6*); pap. text ed. 2.95 (*0-8167-1427-4*) Troll Assocs.

Dairy Farming in Asia. 380p. 1993. pap. 15.00 (*92-833-2132-4*, APO1324, Pub. by Asian Prod Organ) UNIPUB.

Dairy-Free Cookbook. Jane Zukin. 300p. 1991. reprint ed. pap. 14.95 (*1-55958-088-7*) Prima Pub.

*__Dairy Freestall Housing & Equipment.__ 5th rev. ed. W. G. Bickert & Midwest Plan Service Staff. LC 94-37169. 1995. 20.00 (*0-89373-086-6*, MWPS-7) MidWest Plan Serv.

Dairy Goats, Breeding, Feeding & Management. 77p. 1972. reprint ed. 2.00 (*0-317-05979-3*) Am Dairy Goat.

Dairy Hollow House Cookbook. Crescent Dragonwagon. 1992. pap. 12.95 (*0-9632569-0-4*) Cato & Martin.

Dairy Hollow House Soup & Bread Cookbook. Crescent Dragonwagon. LC 91-50956. (Illus.). 416p. 1992. 21.95 (*1-56305-243-1*); pap. 12.95 (*0-89480-751-X*, 1751) Workman Pub.

Dairy Industry: An International Comparison. Wyn Grant. 134p. 1991. text ed. 52.95 (*1-85521-117-3*, Pub. by Dartmth Pub UK) Ashgate Pub Co.

*__Dairy Industry: Potential for & Barriers to Market Development.__ (Illus.). 68p. (Orig.). (C). 1995. pap. text ed. 40.00x (*0-7881-1717-3*) Diane Pub.

*__Dairy Market.__ 400p. (Orig.). 1994. pap. 1,495.00 (*1-57205-949-4*) Rector Pr.

Dairy Production. 4th ed. Clarence C. Bundy et al. 1977. 31.52 (*0-13-197079-8*) P-H.

*__Dairy Production-Health Records & Binder.__ 1995. 12.95 (*0-614-04405-7*) Lessiter Pubns.

Dairy Products: The International Market. Euromonitor Staff. 120p. (C). 1988. 2,925.00 (*0-685-30332-2*, Pub. by Euromonitor Pubns UK) Gale.

Dairy Products in Human Health & Nutrition: Proceedings of the First World Congress, Madrid, Spain, June 1993. Ed. by M. S. Rios & A. Sastre. (Illus.). 700p. (C). 1993. text ed. 99.00 (*90-5410-359-0*, Pub. by A A Balkema NE) Ashgate Pub Co.

D

An Asterisk (*) at the beginning of an entry indicates that the title is appearing in BIP for the first time.

***Dairy Products International Market.** 325p. (Orig.). 1995. pap. 3,195.00 (0-7605-2213-8) Rector Pr.

***Dairy Products International Market Handbook, 2 vols., Set.** (Illus.). 700p. (Orig.). 1994. pap. 8,900.00 (0-7605-0940-9) Rector Pr.

Dairy Products Specialist. Jack Rudman. (Career Examination Ser.: C-3117). 1994. pap. 29.95 (0-8373-3117-X) Nat Learn.

Dairy Rheology: A Concise Guide. J. H. Prentice. LC 92-34877. (Food Science & Technology Ser.). 165p. 1992. 95.00 (1-56081-505-1) VCH Pubs.

Dairy Science & Technology Handbook, 3 vols., Set. Ed. by Y. H. Hui. LC 92-30191. 1274p. 1993. 275.00 (1-56081-078-5) VCH Pubs.

***Dairy Sector Indicators.** OECD Staff. 228p. (Orig.). (ENG & FRE.). 1994. pap. 36.00x (92-64-04264-4) OECD.

Dairy Systems for the Twenty-First Century. LC 93-74814. 872p. 1994. 59.50 (0-929355-45-8, P0294) Am Soc Ag Eng.

Dairying Bygones. Arthur Ingram. 1989. pap. 25.00 (0-85263-866-3, Pub. by Shire UK) St Mut.

Dairying with Improved Breeds in Warm Climates. R. E. McDowell. LC 93-81317. (Illus.). 10p. (C). 1994. pap. text ed. 19.00 (1-880762-05-6) Kinnic Pubs.

***Daisie's Ark.** Grace Thompson. 1994. lib. bdg. 22.00 (0-7278-4651-5) Severn Hse.

Daisies in the Wind. Jill Gregory. 1994. mass mkt. 5.50 (0-440-21618-4) Dell.

***Daisy.** Leigh Greenwood. (Seven Brides Ser.). 448p. (Orig.). 1995. mass mkt. 5.99 (0-8439-3833-1) Dorchester Pub Co.

Daisy. E. Sandy Powell. (Contemporary Concerns Ser.). (Illus.). 40p. (J). (gr. 1-4). 1991. lib. bdg. 14.95 (0-87614-449-0, Carolrhoda) Lerner Group.

Daisy. large type ed. Jennie Tremaine. (Nightingale Ser.). 266p. 1990. pap. 14.50 (0-8161-4988-7) G K Hall.

Daisy: A Book about Child Abuse. E. Sandy Powell. (J). (gr. 1-4). 1991. pap. 4.95 (0-87614-543-8, Carolrhoda) Lerner Group.

Daisy & Dobbin. Gladys Taber. 20.95 (0-8488-1187-9) Amereon Ltd.

Daisy Bates in the Desert. Julia Blackburn. 1994. pap. 22.00 (0-679-42001-0) Random.

***Daisy Bedroom.** (Paintability Ser.). (Illus.). 12p. Date not set. pap. 12.95 (1-85410-133-1, London Bridge) Genl Dist Srvs.

Daisy Bunny's Teatime. Linda Karl & Seth M. Siegel. (Tea Bunnies Ser.). (Illus.). 12p. (J). (ps-00). 1994. 3.99 (0-679-84001-X) Random Bks Yng Read.

Daisy Chain War. Joan O'Neill. (Bright Sparks Ser.). 256p. (Orig.). (YA). 1990. pap. 9.99 (1-85594-004-3, Pub. by Attic IE) InBook.

Daisy Cup. Keith M. Vlasak. 1974. 1.50 (0-936814-01-2) New Collage.

***Daisy Dare.** Anita Jeram. LC 95-6305. (J). 1995. write for info. (1-56402-645-0) Candlewick Pr.

Daisy Dopp's Vermont. Ed. by Elka Schumann. (Illus.). 122p. (Orig.). 1983. pap. 4.00 (0-9610860-1-7) Orleans.

Daisy Ducks. Rick Boyer. 288p. 1988. reprint ed. mass mkt. 3.50 (0-8041-0293-7) Ivy Books.

Daisy Fay & the Miracle Man. Fannie Flagg. 320p. 1992. mass mkt. 7.99 (0-446-39452-1) Warner Bks.

Daisy Fay & the Miracle Man. large type ed. Fannie Flagg. 1993. pap. 16.00 (0-679-74947-0) Random.

Daisy-Head Mayzie. Dr. Seuss. LC 94-11349. (Illus.). (J). 1994. 15.00 (0-679-86712-0) Random.

***Daisy-Head Mayzie.** Dr. Seuss. LC 94-11349. (Illus.). 48p. (J). (ps-3). 1995. lib. bdg. 15.99 (0-679-96712-5) Random Bks Yng Read.

***Daisy is Lost.** Sue Camm. (Read to Me Ser.). 10p. (J). Date not set. bds. 3.98 (1-85854-136-0) Brimax Bks.

***Daisy Miller.** James. (Thrift Editions Ser.). 1995. pap. 1.00 (0-486-28773-4) Dover.

Daisy Miller. Henry James. 14.95 (0-89190-129-9, Am Repr) Amereon Ltd.

Daisy Miller. Henry James. 1991. pap. 2.50 (0-8125-0440-2) Tor Bks.

Daisy Miller. Henry James. 128p. 1987. pap. 3.95 (0-14-043262-0, Penguin Classics) Viking Penguin.

Daisy Miller. Henry James. (Chicago Studies in the History of Judaism). 1989. reprint ed. lib. bdg. 18.95 (0-89966-639-6) Buccaneer Bks.

Daisy Miller. Henry James, Jr. (Notable American Authors Ser.). 1992. reprint ed. lib. bdg. 75.00 (0-7812-3371-2); reprint ed. lib. bdg. 75.00 (0-7812-3445-X) Rprt Serv.

Daisy Miller. Henry James. Bd. with Pandora. LC 78-158797.; Patagonia. LC 78-158797.; Marriages. LC 78-158797.; Real Thing. LC 78-158797.; Brooksmith. LC 78-158797.; Beldonald Holbein. LC 78-158797.; Story in It. LC 78-158797.; Flickerbridge. LC 78-158797.; Mrs. Medwin. LC 78-158797. LC 78-158797. (Novels & Tales of Henry James Ser.: Vol. 18). xxiii, 505p. 1971. reprint ed. 45.00 (0-678-02818-4) Kelley.

Daisy Miller: A Dark Comedy of Manners. Henry James. Ed. by Daniel M. Fogel. (Masterwork Studies). 136p. 1989. text ed. 21.95 (0-8057-7975-2, MWS-35, Twayne); pap. 12.95 (0-8057-8025-4, Twayne) Macmillan.

Daisy Miller see Turn of the Screw

Daisy Miller & Other Stories. Henry James. LC 84-29480. (Airmont Classics Ser.). (J). (gr. 9 up). 1968. pap. 1.75 (0-8049-0178-3, CL-178) Airmont.

Daisy Miller & Other Stories. Henry James. Ed. by Jean Gooder. (World's Classics Ser.). 320p. 1985. pap. 3.95 (0-19-281618-7) OUP.

Daisy Miller & Other Stories. Henry James. Ed. by Michael Swan. 192p. (C). 1984. pap. 3.95 (0-14-006721-3, Penguin Bks) Viking Penguin.

Daisy Miller & the Turn of the Screw Notes. James L. Roberts. 1965. pap. 4.25 (0-8220-0355-4) Cliffs.

Daisy Miller & Turn of the Screw. (Book Notes Ser.). 1986. pap. 2.50 (0-8120-3508-9) Barron.

Daisy Punkin: Meet Daisy Punkin. Hilda Stahl. LC 91-4693. (Daisy Punkin Ser.: No. 1). 128p. (J). (gr. 2-5). 1991. pap. 4.95 (0-89107-617-4) Crossway Bks.

Daisy Punkin: The Bratty Brother. Hilda Stahl. LC 91-38476. (Daisy Punkin Ser.: No. 2). 128p. (J). (gr. 2-5). 1992. pap. 4.99 (0-89107-662-X) Crossway Bks.

***Daisy Rabbit's Tree House.** Penny Dale. LC 95-16171. (J). 1995. write for info. (1-56402-641-8) Candlewick Pr.

Daisy the Dress-Up Teddy Bear Paper Dolls. Ming-Ju Sun. (Illus.). (J). (gr. k-3). 1990. pap. 2.95 (0-486-26536-6) Dover.

Daisy Thinks She's a Baby. Lisa Kopper. LC 92-44539. (J). (gr. 1-8). 1994. 10.00 (0-679-84723-5); lib. bdg. 10.99 (0-679-94723-X) Knopf Bks Yng Read.

Daisy Thornton. Mary J. Holmes. (Notable American Authors Ser.). 1992. reprint ed. lib. bdg. 75.00 (0-7812-3147-7) Rprt Serv.

***Daisychain: A Collection of Short Stories.** Mikey J. Halliday. (Orig.). Date not set. pap. 10.95 (0-9645092-9-6) Queer Assoc.

Daisy's Christmas. Martin Waddell. (J). 1993. mass mkt. 3.99 (0-440-40876-8) Dell.

Daisy's Crazy Thanksgiving. Margery Cuyler. LC 90-4323. (Illus.). 32p. (J). (ps-2). 1990. 14.95 (0-8050-0559-5, Owlet BYR) H Holt & Co.

Daisy's Crazy Thanksgiving. Margery Cuyler. LC 90-4323. (Illus.). 32p. (J). (ps-2). 1992. pap. 4.95 (0-8050-2348-8, Owlet BYR) H Holt & Co.

Daisys Don't Lie. Sally Knight. LC 91-67770. 113p. 1993. pap. 8.00 (1-56002-167-5, Univ Edtns) Aegina Pr.

Daisy's Garden. Mordecai Gerstein. (J). Date not set. 15.00 (0-06-021141-5, HarpT); lib. bdg. 14.89 (0-06-021142-3, HarpT) HarpC.

***Daisy's Garden.** large type ed. Mordicai Gerstein & Susan Y. Harris. LC 94-22123. (Illus.). 32p. (J). (ps-3). 1995. 14.95 (0-7868-0096-8); lib. bdg. 14.89 (0-7868-2080-2) Hyprn Child.

Daisy's Taxi. Ruth Young. LC 90-7735. (Illus.). 32p. (J). (ps-1). 1991. 14.95 (0-531-05921-9); lib. bdg. 14.99 (0-531-08521-X) Orchard Bks Watts.

***Dajjal: Superpower U. S. A.** Kaukab Siddique. 50p. (C). 1991. pap. 3.00 (0-942978-15-3) Am Soc Ed & Rel.

Dak To: The 173d Airborne Brigade in South Vietnam's Central Highlands, June-November 1967. Edward F. Murphy. LC 93-4142. 355p. 1993. 24.95 (0-89141-429-0) Presidio Pr.

Dakan ("Deccan") under the Sultans 1296-1724: A Bibliography of Monographic & Periodical Literature. Omar Khalidi. xxiv, 121p. 1987. 16.00 (0-930811-01-1) Haydarabad Hist Soc.

***Dakar, A Wolf's Adventure.** Louis Dorfman. 165p. (Orig.). 1995. pap. 7.95 (0-7610-0074-7) NW Pub.

Dake's Annotated Reference Bible. Finis J. Dake, Sr. 1140p. 1989. 55.95 (1-55829-013-3); 55.95 (1-55829-014-1); 55.95 (1-55829-015-X); write for info. (1-55829-016-8); write for info. (1-55829-017-6); 76.95 (1-55829-018-4); 76.95 (1-55829-019-2); 76.95 (1-55829-020-6); 92.95 (1-55829-021-4); 92.95 (1-55829-022-2); 92.95 (1-55829-023-0); 92.95 (1-55829-024-9); pap. 37.95 (1-55829-025-7); pap. 31.95 (1-55829-012-5) Dake Bible.

Dake's Annotated Reference Bible. Finis J. Dake, Sr. 1440p. 1992. write for info. (1-55829-045-1) Dake Bible.

Dake's Annotated Reference Bible. deluxe ed. Finis J. Dake, Sr. 1440p. Date not set. write for info. (1-55829-046-X) Dake Bible.

Dake's Annotated Reference Bible. deluxe ed. Finis J. Dake, Sr. 1440p. 1989. 48.95 (1-55829-000-1); 48.95 (1-55829-001-X); 48.95 (1-55829-002-8); 48.95 (1-55829-003-6); 68.95 (1-55829-004-4); 68.95 (1-55829-005-2); 68.95 (1-55829-006-0); 68.95 (1-55829-007-9); 81.95 (1-55829-008-7); 81.95 (1-55829-009-5); 81.95 (1-55829-010-9); 81.95 (1-55829-011-7) Dake Bible.

Dakin: Descendants of Thomas Dakin of Concord, MA. A. H. Dakin. (Illus.). 716p. 1991. reprint ed. lib. bdg. 109.00 (0-8328-1736-8); reprint ed. pap. 99.00 (0-8328-1737-6) Higginson Bk Co.

Dakini Teachings: Padmasambhava's Oral Instructions to Lady Tsogyal. Padmasambhava. Tr. by Erik P. Kunsang. LC 89-43403. (Dragon Editions Ser.). 200p. (Orig.). 1990. pap. 18.00 (0-87773-546-8, Sham Dragon Edits) Shambhala Pubns.

Dakmonies, Bk. 5. IGOOS Staff. (Illus.). 245p. 1994. 25.00 (1-57179-032-2) Intern Guild ASRS.

Dakota: A Spiritual Geography. Kathleen Norris. 224p. 1994. pap. 9.95 (0-395-71091-X) HM.

Dakota: A Spiritual Geography. Kathleen Norris. LC 92-30820. 192p. 1993. 19.95 (0-395-63320-6) Ticknor & Fields.

***Dakota: A Spiritual Geography.** braille ed. Kathleen Norris. 326p. 1994. text ed. 26.08 (1-56956-414-0, BR9316) W A T Braille.

Dakota: The Literary Heritage of the Northern Prairie State. Kathie R. Anderson. (North Dakota Centennial Heritage Ser.). (Illus.). 186p. 1990. 18.95 (0-9608700-4-0) U NDak Pres.

Dakota & the Wolf Pack. Jan Morns. (Friends of the Forest Adventure Bks.). (Illus.). (J). (ps-8). 1994. 16.95 (0-9641742-0-0) Pequot Pubng.

Dakota Bones. Linda Hasselstrom. 176p. 1992. pap. 9.95 (0-944024-23-8) Spoon Riv Poetry.

Dakota Cookin' B. Carlson. (Illus.). 160p. 1994. 5.95 (1-878488-97-X) Quixote Pr IA.

Dakota Cowboy: My Life in the Old Days. Ike Blasingame. LC 58-11667. (Illus.). 317p. 1964. pap. 10.95 (0-8032-5015-0) U of Nebr Pr.

Dakota Dawn. Dana Ransom. 1991. mass mkt. 4.50 (0-8217-3597-7) Zebra.

Dakota Death Trap. large type ed. Marshall Grover. (Linford Western Library). 272p. 1993. pap. 14.95 (0-7089-7358-2, Trailtree Bookshop) Ulverscroft.

Dakota Desire. Dana Ransom. 1992. mass mkt. 4.50 (0-8217-3768-6) Zebra.

Dakota Destiny. Dana Ransom. 448p. 1993. mass mkt. 4.50 (0-8217-4060-1) Zebra.

Dakota Diaspora: Memoirs of a Jewish Homesteader. Sophie Trupin. LC 84-14325. xii, 160p. 1988. pap. 6.95 (0-8032-9414-X, Bison Books) U of Nebr Pr.

Dakota Doxy. Dirk Fletcher. (Spur Ser.: No. 22). 208p. (Orig.). 1987. pap. 2.50 (0-8439-2496-9) Dorchester Pub Co.

Dakota Doxy - San Diego Sirens, 2 vols. in 1. Kit Dalton. (Spur Double Edition Ser.). 432p. 1992. pap. 4.50 (0-8439-3311-9) Dorchester Pub Co.

Dakota Dream. James Bennett. LC 93-17854. 144p. (YA). (gr. 7 up). 1994. 13.95 (0-590-46680-1) Scholastic Inc.

Dakota Dreams. Constance O'Banyon. 512p. 1991. mass mkt. 4.99 (0-8217-3677-9) Zebra.

Dakota Dugout. Ann Turner. LC 85-3084. (Illus.). 32p. (J). (gr. k-3). 1985. text ed. 13.95 (0-02-789700-1, Mac Bks Young Read) S&S Childrens.

Dakota Dugout. Ann Turner. (Illus.). 32p. (J). (ps-3). 1989. reprint ed. pap. 3.95 (0-689-71296-0, Aladdin Paperbacks) S&S Childrens.

Dakota-English Dictionary. 2nd ed. Stephen R. Riggs. 680p. 1992. reprint ed. pap. 24.95 (0-87351-282-0, Borealis Book) Minn Hist.

Dakota Flame. Sonya T. Pelton. 1989. pap. 3.95 (0-8217-2700-1) Zebra.

Dakota Gold. large type ed. Tim Champlin. LC 94-5129. 1994. 20.00 (0-7862-0199-1) Thorndike Pr.

Dakota Grammar. Franz Boas & Ella Deloria. LC 74-7942. reprint ed. write for info. (0-404-11829-1) AMS Pr.

Dakota Grammar, Texts & Ethnography. Stephen R. Riggs. LC 74-7998. reprint ed. 49.50 (0-404-11891-7) AMS Pr.

***Dakota Guns.** J. R. Roberts. (Gunsmith Ser.: No. 136). 192p. (Orig.). 1994. pap. text ed. 3.99 (0-515-11507-X) Jove Pubns.

Dakota Love. Suzanne Hellman. 1992. pap. 6.99 (0-7814-0945-4, LifeJourney) Chariot Family.

Dakota Maverick. Agnes Geelan. (Illus.). 186p. (J). (gr. 9-12). 1983. reprint ed. pap. 7.95 (0-911007-03-2) Prairie Hse.

Dakota or Sioux in Minnesota As They Were in 1834. Samuel W. Pond. LC 85-31039. xxi, 192p. 1986. reprint ed. pap. 8.95 (0-87351-193-X, Borealis Book) Minn Hist.

Dakota Oratory. Illus. & Comp. by Mark Diedrich. LC 88-71264. 102p. (Orig.). 1989. pap. 16.95 (0-9616901-3-5) Coyote Bks MN.

Dakota Panorama. Boorman Jennewein. (Illus.). 463p. 1973. reprint ed. 14.95 (0-88498-012-X) Brevet Pr.

Dakota Preposition: Panacea or Nightmare for South Dakota? Loren M. Carlson. 1980. 1.00 (1-55614-032-0) U of SD Gov Res Bur.

Dakota Promises. Dana Ransom. 480p. 1993. mass mkt. 4.50 (0-8217-4255-8) Zebra.

Dakota Road. Nick Ward. (Illus.). 160p. (Orig.). 1991. pap. 12.95 (0-571-16302-5) Faber & Faber.

Dakota Run. David Robbins. (Endworld Ser.: No. 5). 256p. (Orig.). 1987. pap. 2.95 (0-8439-2473-X) Dorchester Pub Co.

Dakota Scouts. Flynn J. Ell. 192p. 1992. 18.95 (0-8027-4130-4) Walker & Co.

***Dakota Spring.** D. Anne Love. LC 94-46354. (Illus.). 144p. (J). 1995. pap. 14.95 (0-8234-1189-3) Holiday.

Dakota Squeeze. E. J. Hunter. (White Squaw Ser.: No. 6). 224p. 1984. pap. 2.50 (0-8217-1479-1) Zebra.

Dakota Territory. John Benteen. (Sundance Ser.: No. 3). 1979. pap. 1.75 (0-8439-0708-8) Dorchester Pub Co.

Dakota Territory Federal Census Index 1850 Pembina District (Part of Minnesota Territory) (Every Name) (Illus.). 1982. lib. bdg. 38.00 (0-89593-254-7) Accelerated Index.

Dakota Territory Federal Census Index, 1860 (Every Name) (Illus.). 1980. lib. bdg. 38.00 (0-89593-255-5) Accelerated Index.

Dakota Territory Federal Census Index, 1870. (Illus.). 1979. lib. bdg. 38.00 (0-89593-256-3) Accelerated Index.

Dakota Territory Federal Census Index, 1880. (Illus.). 1979. lib. bdg. 79.00 (0-89593-257-1) Accelerated Index.

Dakota Territory Mortality Schedule, 1880. 1980. 30.00 (0-89593-631-3) Accelerated Index.

Dakota Texts. Ella Deloria. LC 73-3550. (American Ethnological Society Publications: No. 14). reprint ed. 34.50 (0-404-58164-1) AMS Pr.

Dakota Visions: A County Approach. David Holden. LC 82-72870. 391p. 1982. 12.95 (0-931170-21-4); pap. 9.95 (0-931170-19-2) Ctr Western Studies.

Dakotah Sioux Dictionary. 4th ed. Paul WarCloud. 1989. write for info. (0-9626423-0-4) Tekawitha Fine.

Dakotas: At the Wind's Edge. Kathryn L. Davis. 1990. pap. 3.95 (1-55817-330-7, Pinnacle NY) Windsor NY.

Dakota's, No. 2: Endless Sky. Kathryn Davis. 1990. pap. 3.95 (1-55817-352-8, Pinnacle NY) Windsor NY.

Dakota's Parks Guide. Barbara McCaig. Ed. by Chris Boyce. (Illus.). 120p. (Orig.). 1989. pap. text ed. 5.95 (0-935201-82-3) Affordable Adven.

Dakotas' Vanishing Outhouse: A Collection of Illustrations & Stories about a Rapidly Vanishing Institution in the Dakotas, the Little Outhouse Out Back. Bruce Carlson. (Illus.). 175p. (Orig.). 1990. pap. 9.95 (1-878488-23-6) Quixote Pr IA.

Dakshin: Vegetarian Dishes from South India. Chandra Padmanabhan. (Illus.). 1994. 26.00 (0-207-18477-1) Thorsons SF.

Dakshinamurti Stotra of Sri Sankaracharya: And Dakshinamurty Upanishad with Sri Sureswaracharya's Manasollasa & Pranava Vartika. Sri Sankaracharya. Tr. by Alladi M. Sastri. 223p. 1989. 16.95 (0-910261-05-9, Pub. by Samata Bks II) Lotus Light.

Daktar. Lockerbie & Olson. (SPA.). Date not set. 1.95 (0-685-74926-6, 540099) Editorial Unilit.

***Dakto: 173d Airborne Brigade in South Vietnam's Central Highlands, June-November 1967.** Edward Murphy. Ed. by Doug Grad. 400p. (Orig.). 1995. pap. 6.99 (0-671-52268-X) PB.

Dalai Lama. Louis G. Perez. LC 92-38325. (Biographies: World Leaders Ser.). (J). 1993. 19.93 (0-86625-480-3); 14.95 (0-685-67761-3) Rourke Pubns.

Dalai Lama: A Policy of Kindness. Sidney Piburn. 1993. pap. 10.95 (1-55939-022-0) Snow Lion Pubns.

***Dalai Lama: The Institution.** Ram Rahul. (C). 1995. 17.00 (0-7069-8788-8, Pub. by Vikas II) S Asia.

Dalai Lama: The Leader of the Exiled People of Tibet & Tireless Worker for World Peace. Christopher Gibb. LC 89-43119. (People Who Have Helped the World Ser.). (Illus.). 68p. (J). (gr. 5-6). 1990. lib. bdg. 21.26 (0-8368-0224-1) Gareth Stevens Inc.

Dalai Lama at Harvard: Lectures on the Buddhist Path to Peace. Dalai Lama & Jeffrey Hopkins. LC 88-39486. 265p. (Orig.). 1989. pap. 14.95 (0-937938-71-8) Snow Lion Pubns.

Dalawang Dula Ni Clarissa Sa Ecolohiya. Emelina G. Regis. 77p. (Orig.). (TAG.). 1993. pap. 5.75 (971-10-0504-2, Pub. by New Day Pub PH) Cellar.

Dalbergia Sissoo. annot. ed. Kevin J. White. 120p. 1990. 10.00 (974-7315-33-5) Winrock Intl.

D'Albert S'Expose: Aubrey Beardsley's Drawings for Mademoiselle de Maupin. David March. LC 85-90379. (Illus.). 48p. 1985. pap. 20.00 (0-9615493-0-0) D March.

Dale & Applebe's Pharmacy, Law & Ethics. 5th ed. Dale. 624p. 1993. pap. 31.00 (0-85369-285-8, Pub. by Pharmaceutical Pr UK) Rittenhouse.

Dale Archibald's Using Computers. Dale Archibald. (Illus.). 160p. (Orig.). 1986. pap. 8.95 (0-937819-00-X) Archibald Pub.

Dale Carnegie's Biographical Roundup. Dale Carnegie. LC 77-117764. (Essay Index Reprint Ser.). 1977. 24.95 (0-8369-1788-X) Ayer.

Dale Chihuly: Installations: 1964-1992. Patterson Sims. Ed. by Helen Abbott. (Illus.). 64p. (Orig.). 1992. pap. 19.95 (0-932216-41-2) Seattle Art.

Dale Loves Sophie to Death. Robb F. Dew. LC 92-54260. 224p. 1993. pap. 10.00 (0-06-097539-3, PL) HarpC.

Dale Morgan on Early Mormonism: Correspondence & a New History. Dale L. Morgan. Ed. by John P. Walker. LC 86-60251. 413p. 1986. 25.95 (0-941214-36-2) Prometheus Bks.

Dale Murphy: Baseball's Gentle Giant. Patricia S. Martin. (Reaching Your Goal Bks.). (Illus.). 24p. (J). (gr. 1-4). 1987. 10.95 (0-685-67567-X); lib. bdg. 14.60 (0-86592-167-9) Rourke Corp.

Dale Valor a Tu Vida - Make Your Life Worthwhile. Emmet Fox. 180p. 1993. 9.50 (0-06-633703-8, HarpC Latin Am) HarpC.

Daleae Imagines. Rupert C. Barneby. LC 66-6394. (Memoirs Ser.: Vol. 27). (Illus.). 891p. 1977. pap. 50.00 (0-89327-002-4) NY Botanical.

Dalelands. L. Richard Baker. (Advanced Dungeons & Dragons, Second Edition; Al-Qadim Ser.). (Illus.). 1993. pap. 9.95 (1-56076-667-0) TSR Inc.

D'Alembert & Frederick the Great: A Study of Their Relationship. Glenn J. Van Treese. Ed. by Sebastian A. Matczak. LC 73-82788. (Philosophical Questions Ser.: No. 9). 191p. 1974. 18.00 (0-912116-11-0) Learned Pubns.

Dale's Principle & Communication Between Neurons: Proceedings of a Colloquim of the Biochemical Society, University of Oxford, England, July 1982. Ed. by N. Osborne. 190p. 1983. 94.00 (0-08-029789-7, Pub. by Pergamon Repr UK) Franklin.

Dalesmen of the Mississippi. David Morris. (C). 1990. 90.00 (1-85072-062-2, Pub. by W Sessions UK) St Mut.

D'Alessandro. Nicolo D'Alessandro. (Illus.). 54p. 1987. 50.00 (0-685-49065-3); pap. 25.00 (0-685-49066-1) Cross-Cultrl NY.

Daley B.! see You're a Hero, Daley B.!

D'Algues d'Eau Douce des Mares de "La Siberia" en Bolivie. Y. Therezien. (Bibliotheca Phycologica Ser.: Vol. 88). (Illus.). 130p. (FRE.). 1991. pap. 53.50 (0-685-40461-7, Pub. by Cramer-Borntraeger GW) Lubrecht & Cramer.

Dalhousie University. Photos by Brian Smith. (Illus.). 112p. 1990. 49.00 (0-916509-56-7) Harmony Hse Pub LO.

Dali. Dawn Ades. LC 89-50537. (World of Art Ser.). (Illus.). 1989. pap. 14.95 (0-500-20188-9) Thames Hudson.

Dali. Ignacio G. De Liano. LC 83-61925. (Illus.). 128p. 1984. pap. 24.95 (0-8478-0522-0) Rizzoli Intl.

Dali. Robert Descharnes. LC 74-4257. (Library of Great Painters). (Illus.). 176p. 1976. 49.50 (0-8109-0222-2) Abrams.

Dali. Robert Descharnes. (Masters of Art Ser.). (Illus.). 128p. 1985. 22.95 (0-8109-0830-1) Abrams.

***Dali.** Ed. by Jose M. Faerna. (Great Modern Masters Ser.). (Illus.). 64p. 1995. 11.98 (0-8109-4679-3) Abrams.

Dali. Ramon G. La Serna. 1990. 29.98 (1-55521-342-1) Bk Sales Inc.

***Dali.** Christopher Masters. (Color Library). (Illus.). 128p. (C). 1995. pap. 14.95 (0-7148-3338-X, Pub. by Phaidon Press UK) Chronicle Bks.

***Dali.** Christopher Masters. (Color Library). (Illus.). 128p. (C). 1995. 19.95 (0-7148-3339-8, Pub. by Phaidon Press UK) Chronicle Bks.

Dali. Eric Shanes. 1990. 19.99 (0-517-01507-2) Random Hse Value.

D

An Asterisk (*) at the beginning of an entry indicates that the title is appearing in BIP for the first time. 1777

Dali. Meredith E. Smith. 1993. 35.00 (0-679-40061-3) McKay.
***Dali.** rev. ed. Dawn Ades. LC 94-61060. (World of Art Ser.). (Illus.). 216p. 1995. pap. 14.95 (0-500-20280-X) Thames Hudson.
Dali. 3rd ed. Ramon Gomez de la Serna. (Illus.). 254p. (SPA.). 1992. 295.00x (84-239-4274-0) Elliots Bks.
Dali: The Salvador Dali Museum Collection. Dali, Salvador, Foundation, Inc. Staff. (Illus.). 176p. 1994. pap. 25.00 (0-8212-2086-1) Bulfinch Pr.
Dali: The Salvador Dali Museum Collection. Salvador Dali Foundation, Inc., Staff. (Illus.). 184p. 1991. 50.00 (0-8212-1810-7) Bulfinch Pr.
Daligator. Cliff Sahlin. LC 88-83575. (Illus.). 28p. (Orig.). (J). (ps-3). 1988. pap. text ed. 4.95 (0-9621714-0-9) Gamin Pr.
Dalil Al Tabikh (How to Cook) Al Sheikh. (ARA.). 1978. 25.00 (0-86685-516-5) Intl Bk Ctr.
Dalil Maktabat al Usrah al Muslimah: (Guide for the Muslim Family Book Collection) rev. ed. Ed. by 'AbdulHamid AbuSulayman. (Silsilat Islamiyat al Thaqafah Ser.: No. 1). 735p. (ARA.). 1991. pap. text ed. 12.50 (0-912463-82-1) IIIT VA.
Dalil Maktabat al Usrah al Muslimah: (Guide for the Muslim Family Book Collection) 2nd rev. ed. Ed. by 'AbdulHamid AbuSulayman. (Silsilat Islamiyat al Thaqafah Ser.: No. 1). 735p. (ARA.). 1991. text ed. 20.00 (0-912463-81-3) IIIT VA.
Dali's Mustache. Philippe Halsman & Salvador Dali. (Illus.). 126p. Date not set. 12.00 (2-08-013560-0) Abbeville Pr.
Dali's Universal Tarot. Juan Llarch. 44p. 90.00 (0-88079-090-3) US Games Syst.
Dalit: The Black Untouchables of India. V. T. Rajshekar & Y. N. Kly. LC 87-71663. 100p. (Orig.). 1987. pap. 7.95 (0-932863-05-1) Clarity Pr.
***Dalit Movement in India & Its Leaders.** R. K. Kshirsagar. 459p. (C). 1994. 120.00x (81-85880-43-3, Pub. by Print Hse II) St Mut.
Dalit Movements & the Meanings of Labour in India. Ed. by Peter Robb. (SOAS Studies on South Asia). 375p. 1994. 21.00 (0-19-563213-3) OUP.
Dalit Panther Movement in Magarashtra: A Sociological Appraisal. Lata Murugkar. (C). 1990. 32.00 (0-86132-246-0, Pub. by Popular Prakashan II) S Asia.
***Dalita Betrayed.** B. D. Sharma. (C). 1995. 22.00x (81-241-0233-3, Pub. by Har-Anand Pubns II) S Asia.
***Dalits: A Sub-Human Society.** Rebati B. Tripathy. xx, 226p. (C). 1994. 22.00 (81-7024-645-8, Pub. by Ashish Pub Hse II) Nataraj Bks.
Dalits & the Democratic Revolution: Dr. Ambedkar & the Dalit Movement in Colonial India. Gail Omvedt. LC 93-11778. 352p. (C). 1994. text ed. 36.00 (0-8039-9139-8) Sage.
Dalkey Archive. Flann O'Brien. LC 92-30923. 204p. 1993. reprint ed. pap. 9.95 (1-56478-019-8) Dalkey Arch.
Dalkulla Anna. 2nd ed. Sylvia A. Cleeland. 288p. 1984. reprint ed. pap. 7.95 (0-944996-03-5) Carlsons.
Dalla Novellas Alla Commedia Pirandelliana. Domenico Maceri. LC 90-26478. (American University Studies: Romance Languages & Literature: Ser. II, Vol. 165). 179p. (C). 1991. text ed. 34.95 (0-8204-1483-2) P Lang Pubs.
Dallas. 2nd ed. Judith M. Garrett & Erika Sanchez. (Texas Monthly Guidebooks Ser.). 256p. 1992. pap. 14.95 (0-87719-208-1) Gulf Pub.
Dallas: Shining Star of Texas. Jim Donovan. LC 93-47312. (Illus.). 1994. 11.95 (0-89658-239-6) Voyageur Pr.
Dallas: The Deciding Years - a Historical Portrait. A. C. Greene. (Illus.). 192p. 1974. 25.00 (0-88426-034-8) Encino Pr.
Dallas: The History of the Family of Dallas & Their Connections & Descendants from the Twelfth Century. James Dallas. (Illus.). 611p. 1992. reprint ed. lib. bdg. 99.50 (0-8328-2478-X); reprint ed. pap. 89.50 (0-8328-2479-8) Higginson Bk Co.
Dallas: The Rise of the Family Dynasty. N. Gerson. 1990. text ed. write for info. (0-07-053888-3) McGraw.
***Dallas - Fort Worth Jobbank, 1995.** Adams Staff. 1994. pap. 15.95 (1-55850-450-8) Adams Pubng.
***Dallas - Fort Worth Metroplex Jobs.** Steve Hines & Michael Goldberg. 432p. 1994. pap. 15.95 (0-929255-17-8) CareerSource.
Dallas - Fort Worth Souvenir Book: A Full Color Guide. (Illus.). (Orig.). Date not set. pap. write for info. (1-56944-046-8) Terrell Missouri.
Dallas - Fort Worth Underground Shopper, '93. Sue Goldstein. (Underground Shopper Ser.). (Illus.). (Orig.). 1992. pap. 6.99 (1-879524-02-3) Great Buys.
Dallas - Fort Worth Weddings. 5th rev. ed. Gerri Samuels. (Coopwood & Fields Consumer Planning Guide Ser.). 300p. 1994. pap. 14.95 (1-878991-11-6) I Do Pub.
***Dallas - Ft. Worth, TX.** (Streetfinder Ser.). (Illus.). 1994. pap. 24.95 (0-528-91313-1) Rand McNally.
Dallas & the South West Job Seeker's Source Book. Donald D. Walker & Valerie A. Shipe. LC 93-24726. (Illus.). 368p. (Orig.). 1993. pap. 14.95 (1-882499-08-5) Net Research.
Dallas Chefs Book. William Struns. Ed. by R. McMinn. 120p. (Orig.). 1989. pap. text ed. 6.95 (0-935201-91-2) Affordable Adven.
Dallas Cowboys. Brenda Calmera. (NFL Today Ser.). (J). (gr. 4 up). 1991. lib. bdg. 14.95 (0-88682-364-1) Creative Ed.
Dallas Cowboys. Leonard Shapiro. LC 93-14368. (Illus.). 112p. (Orig.). 1993. pap. 8.99 (0-312-09796-4) St Martin.
***Dallas Cowboys Wives' Cookbook: Southwestern Cuisine.** Date not set. pap. 12.95 (0-9634855-2-0) Happy Hill Farm.
Dallas Cuisine. Ed. by Dottie Griffith. (Orig.). 1993. pap. 14.95 (1-878686-06-2) Two Lane Pr.
Dallas Datebook. rev. ed. Kurt W. Kretsinger. 136p. 1991. 4.77 (0-685-74014-5) Datebook Pub.
Dallas Datebook & Austin Datebook. rev. ed. Kurt W. Kretsinger. 136p. 1991. 4.77 (0-685-74044-7) Datebook Pub.
Dallas Datebook & Austin Datebook, Austin Datebook. rev. ed. Kurt W. Kretsinger. 136p. 1991. write for info. (0-929821-01-7) Datebook Pub.
Dallas Datebook & Austin Datebook, Dallas Datebook. rev. ed. Kurt W. Kretsinger. 136p. 1991. write for info. (0-929821-00-9) Datebook Pub.
Dallas Deception: A Jack Kyle Mystery. Richard Abshire. 1992. 20.00 (0-688-10799-0) Morrow.
Dallas Entrees: A Restaurant Guide & Celebrity Cookbook (with a Primer to California Wines) Jan L. Naxon & Beth E. Rosenthal. 144p. (Orig.). 1982. pap. 5.95 (0-910163-00-6) Artichoke Pub.
Dallas-Fort Worth Art Review. Les Krantz. (Illus.). 80p. 1983. pap. 8.95 (0-88415-021-6) Krantz Co.
***Dallas-Fort Worth Business Directory.** CJS, Inc. Staff. 320p. (Orig.). 1995. pap. write for info. (1-882538-51-X) CJS.
Dallas Fort Worth Technology Almanac. Dallas Fort Worth Technology Staff. 200p. 1993. pap. 14.95 (0-9637657-0-1) Dallas-Ft Worth Tech.
Dallas from a Different Perspective. Robert Prince. 15.95 (0-89015-930-0) Sunbelt Media.
Dallas-Ft. Worth Underground Shopper. 1983. pap. 5.95 (0-934180-12-1) Money Business.
Dallas Is Cooking! Renie Steves. 120p. 1992. pap. 15.95 (0-9635470-0-3) Cuisine Concepts.
Dallas Is Cooking! Cookbook from Dallas Restaurants & Chefs. Renie Steves & Linda McDonald. (Illus.). 112p. (Orig.). 1992. pap. write for info. (0-9613643-9-4) Houston Gourmet.
Dallas Lunchbreak. Ramoal Agostini. Ed. by Frank Zimmerman. 108p. (Orig.). 1992. 3.95 (0-9634192-0-X) Dallas Lunchbreak.
Dallas Mavericks. Michael Goodman. (NBA Today Ser.). (Illus.). 32p. (J). (gr. 4 up). 1993. lib. bdg. 14.95 (0-88682-528-8) Creative Ed.
***Dallas Metroplex Child Care Guide.** Ed. by Lisa Jones & Jude Morton. 208p. (Orig.). 1994. 4.95 (0-9643627-0-8) Dallas Child.
Dallas Museum of Art: Selected Works. Anne R. Bromberg. (Illus.). 223p. 1984. pap. 17.50 (0-9609622-3-9) U of Tex Pr.
Dallas on the Go Car Phone Directory. Directories on the Go Inc. Staff. 110p. 1994. pap. 9.95 (0-9640493-0-9) Dirs On The Go.
Dallas O'Neil & the Baker Street Sports Club Series, 8 bks., Set. Jerry B. Jenkins. (J). (gr. 2-7). pap. 39.92 (0-8024-2164-4) Moody.
Dallas O'Neil Mysteries Ser., 8 bks., Set. Jerry B. Jenkins. (J). (gr. 2-7). pap. 39.92 (0-8024-8389-5) Moody.
Dallas Party & Event Planners Sourcebook: To Throw an Unforgettable Party or Special Event, Here's What You Need, & Where To Find It! Lisa C. McElya. Ed. by Shirley McElya. (Orig.). 1988. 19.95 (0-929708-02-4) Applause TX.
Dallas Rediscovered. William L. McDonald. 1988. 14.95 (0-932018-01-7) Dallas His Soc.
Dallas Run. David Robbins. (Endworld Ser.: No. 20). 192p. (Orig.). 1990. pap. 2.95 (0-8439-2938-3) Dorchester Pub Co.
Dallas Stars. John Gilbert. LC 93-48448. (NHL Today Ser.). 32p. (J). 1995. 14.95 (0-88682-673-X) Creative Ed.
Dallas Stoudenmire: El Paso Marshal. Leon C. Metz. LC 70-79109. (C). 1993. pap. 9.95 (0-8061-2487-3) U of Okla Pr.
Dallas Titans Get Ready for Bed. Karla Kuskin. LC 83-49470. (Charlotte Zolotow Bk.). (Illus.). 48p. (J). (gr. k-3). 1986. lib. bdg. 12.89 (0-06-023563-2) HarpC Child Bks.
Dallas Titans Get Ready for Bed. Karla Kuskin. LC 83-49470. (Trophy Picture Bk.). (Illus.). 48p. (J). (ps-3). 1988. pap. 4.95 (0-06-443180-0, Trophy) HarpC Child Bks.
Dallas, U. S. A. A. C. Greene. LC 83-24317. (Illus.). 264p. (Orig.). 1984. pap. 9.95 (0-87719-025-9, Lone Star Bks) Gulf Pub.
Dallas Uncovered. Larenda Roberts. LC 94-11345. 1994. 12.95 (1-55622-378-1, Rep of TX Pr) Wordware Pub.
Dallas Underground Shoppers. 1984. pap. 5.95 (0-934180-09-1) Money Business.
Dallenbach: The Dallenbach Family in America, 1710-1935. A. L. Dillenbeck & K. M. Dallenbach. (Illus.). 439p. 1993. reprint ed. lib. bdg. 77.50 (0-8328-3290-1); reprint ed. pap. 67.50 (0-8328-3291-X) Higginson Bk Co.
Dalles: A Photographic Remembrance. Gladys Seifert. (Illus.). 250p. 1994. 19.95 (0-87595-244-5) Oregon Hist.
***Dalliance & Deception.** Sylvia Andrew & Gail Mallin. 1995. mass mkt. 4.99 (0-373-31220-2) Harlequin Bks.
Dalliance & Undiscovered Country. Tom Stoppard. 160p. 1987. 8.95 (0-571-14750-X); pap. 7.95 (0-571-14739-9) Faber & Faber.
Dalmanellidae of the Cincinnatian see Palaeontographica Americana: No. 2
Dalmatia: A Guide. D. Horvatic. (Illus.). 164p. (C). 1986. pap. 60.00 (0-685-37478-5, Pub. by Collets) St Mut.
Dalmatia & Montenegro: With a Journey to Mostar in Herzegovino, 2 vols., Set. J. Gardner Wilkinson. LC 72-135836. (Eastern Europe Collection Ser.). 1971. reprint ed. 65.95 (0-405-02778-8) Ayer.
Dalmatian. Anna K. Nicholas. (Illus.). 320p. 1986. 19.95 (0-86622-157-3, PS-823) TFH Pubns.
Dalmatian. Bill Sanford & Carl Green. LC 89-31107. (Top Dog Ser.). (Illus.). 48p. (J). (gr. 4-5). 1989. text ed. 12.95 (0-89686-449-9, Crstwood Hse) Silver Burdett Pr.
Dalmatian Champions, 1952-1982. Jan L. Freund. (Illus.). 213p. 1987. pap. 36.95 (0-940808-36-6) Camino E E & Bk.
Dalmatian Champions, 1983-1986. Camino E. E. & B. Co. Staff. (Illus.). 104p. 1988. pap. 28.95 (0-940808-68-4) Camino E E & Bk.
Dalmatian Painting of the Fifteenth & Sixteenth Centuries. Kruno Prijatelj. 125p. 1983. 30.00 (0-918660-44-0) Ragusan Pr.
Dalmatian Painting of the 15th & 16th Centuries. Prijatel Kruno. 127p. 1983. 450.00 (0-317-61248-4, Pub. by Collets UK) Pro-Am Music.
***Dalmatians.** Stuart A. Kallen. LC 95-4019. (Dogs Ser.). (J). 1995. lib. bdg. 9.95 (1-56239-455-X) Abdo & Dghtrs.
Dalmatians. Ed. by Beverly Pisano. (Illus.). 128p. 1980. 11.95 (0-86622-501-3, KW-090) TFH Pubns.
Dalmatians from Croatia & Montenegrin Serbs in the West & South, 1800-1900. Adam S. Eterovich. LC 74-155333. 1971. pap. 8.00 (0-88247-103-1) Ragusan Pr.
***Dalmation.** Patti Strand & Rod Strand. (Owner's Guide to a Happy, Healthy Pet Ser.). 160p. Date not set. 12.95 (0-87605-384-3) Howell Bk.
Dalmations: A Complete Pet Owners Manual. Tanya B. Ditto. (Barron's Pet Owner's Manuals Ser.). (Illus.). 64p. 1991. pap. 5.95 (0-8120-4605-6) Barron.
***Dalton Gang.** Carl R. Green & William R. Sanford. LC 94-32509. (Outlaws & Lawmen of the Wild West Ser.). (Illus.). 48p. (J). (gr. 4-10). 1995. lib. bdg. 14.95 (0-89490-588-0) Enslow Pubs.

Dalton Gang Story: Lawmen to Outlaws. Nancy B. Samuelson. (Illus.). (Orig.). 1992. pap. 25.00 (0-9633362-0-7) Shoot Star CT.
The name DALTON powerfully evokes the popular image of the Wild West Outlaw. The Dalton Gang made history with a bold attempt to rob two banks at once in Coffeyville, Kansas on October 5, 1892. There has been an avalanche of Dalton literature, most of it downright fictitious. THE DALTON GANG STORY, however, is a masterful effort to set the record straight & to tell the real story of this frontier family. Several Dalton brothers were first U.S. Deputy Marshals before turning to crime. The book is copiously illustrated with many fine photographs as well as reproductions of source documents, family Bible & court records, newspaper articles, etc. "The book is nearly dazzling. It is highly recommended as the premier source for Dalton Gang researchers."--Paul Meredith--VIOLENT KIN. "THE DALTON GANG STORY ranks as the new high standard for accurate & primary information on this famous lawman-outlaw family."--Doug Ellison--WESTERN OUTLAW-LAWMAN HISTORY ASSOCIATION JOURNAL. "...Compelling saga... profusely illustrated, well documented, attractively presented &, perhaps above all, enjoyable to read."--Joanne L. Nance--THE VIRGINIA GENEALOGICAL NEWSLETTER. "Samuelson did her homework well & made a good story about outlaws into a good work of history."--Chuck Parsons--TRUE WEST. "An excellent job of presenting the facts...writing style is terrific."--Marley Brant, author of THE OUTLAW YOUNGERS. Shooting Star Press, Box 359, Eastford, CT 06242.
Publisher Provided Annotation.

Dalton, Occupation of the Ozark Border. James E. Price & James J. Krakker. Ed. by L. H. Feldman. LC 75-327206. (Museum Briefs Ser.: No. 20). (Illus.). vii, 41p. 1975. pap. 3.00 (0-913134-20-1) Mus Anthro MO.
Dalton's Back. Keith Curran. 1990. pap. 4.75 (0-8222-0266-2) Dramatists Play.
Dalton's Tables of Houses. Dalton. 80p. 1975. 10.00 (0-88053-750-7, D2010-054) Am Fed Astrologers.
***DAM Architectural Annual 1995.** Ed. by Deutsches Architektur-Museum Staff et al. 200p. 1995. pap. 45.00 (3-7913-1498-X) Pegasus.
DAM Architecture Annual, 1992. Ed. by Deutsches Architektur Museum Staff et al. (Illus.). 192p. (Orig.). (GER.). 1992. pap. 40.00 (3-7913-1152-2, Pub. by Prestel) TeNeues.
DAM Architecture Annual 1993. Ed. by Vittorio M. Lampugnani et al. (Illus.). 200p. 1993. pap. 40.00 (3-7913-1295-2, Pub. by Prestel) TeNeues.
Dam Break in Georgia. K. Neill Foster. (Orig.). 1989. pap. 5.99 (0-88965-023-3, Pub. by Horizon Books CN) Chr Pubns.
Dam-Burst of Dreams. Christopher Nolan. LC 81-9669. 96p. 1988. pap. 9.95 (0-8214-0912-3) Ohio U Pr.
Dam Busters. large type ed. Ed. by Paul Brickhill. 376p. 1992. 24.95 (1-85089-523-6, Pub. by ISIS UK) Transaction Pubs.
Dam Foundation Grouting. Ken D. Weaver. LC 91-34635. 190p. 1991. pap. text ed. 36.00 (0-87262-792-6) Am Soc Civil Eng.
Dam Fracture & Damage: Proceedings of the International Workshop, Chambery, France, March 1994. Ed. by E. Bourdarot et al. (Illus.). (C). 1994. text ed. 99.00 (90-5410-369-8, Pub. by A A Balkema NE) Ashgate Pub Co.
***Dam Lies & Other Statistics: Taking the Measure of Irrigation in China, 1931-1991.** James E. Nickum. LC 94-44338. (East-West Center Occasional Papers: Environment Ser.: Vol. 18). 1995. write for info. (0-86638-168-6) EW Ctr HI.
Dam Safety & the Environment. Ed. by Guy J. Le Moigne et al. (Technical Paper Ser.: No. 115). 196p. 1990. 11.95 (0-8213-1438-6, 11438) World Bank.
Dam That Could Not Break. Marie K. Nuschke. (Illus.). 50p. 1961. pap. 3.75 (0-939542-05-6) Leader Pub Co Inc.
Dam That River! Ecology & Mormon Settlement in the Little Colorado River Basin. William S. Abruzzi. LC 93-17051. 236p. (C). 1993. lib. bdg. 39.50 (0-8191-9126-4) U Pr of Amer.
Dama Boba. Lope de Vega. Ed. by Alonso Zamora Vicente. (Nueva Austral Ser.: No. 177). (SPA.). 1991. pap. text ed. 10.95x (84-239-1977-3) Elliots Bks.
***Dama Boba - Nina de Plata.** 10th ed. Lope De Vega. 176p. 1990. pap. 10.95 (0-7859-5185-7) Fr & Eur.
Dama del Alba. Alejandro Casona & Juan R. Castellano. 207p. (C). 1972. pap. text ed. 17.25 (0-13-521642-7) P-H.
***Dama y el Vagabundo.** (Spanish Classic Ser.). 96p. 1995. 6.98 (1-57082-224-7) Mouse Works.
Damage. Josephine Hart. 1991. 18.00 (0-679-40135-0) Knopf.
Damage. Josephine Hart. 1992. mass mkt. 5.99 (0-8041-0841-2) Ivy Books.
Damage Detection in Composite Materials. Ed. by John E. Masters. LC 92-24755. (Special Technical Publication Ser.: No. 1128). (Illus.). 290p. 1992. text ed. 83.00 (0-8031-1474-5, 04-011280-33) ASTM.
Damage Evaluation & Repair Methods for Prestressed Concrete Bridge Members. (National Cooperative Highway Research Program Report Ser.: No. 226). 66p. 1980. 7.20 (0-309-03032-3) Transport Res Bd.
Damage in Composite Materials. Ed. by George Z. Voyiadjis. LC 92-47475. (Studies in Applied Mechanics: Vol. 34). 1993. write for info. (0-444-89348-2) Elsevier.
Damage in Composite Materials - STP 775. Ed. by K. Reifsnider. 282p. 1982. 33.50 (0-8031-0696-3, 04-775000-30) ASTM.
Damage Limitation or Crisis? Russia & the Outside World. Ed. by Robert D. Blackwill & Sergei A. Karaganov. (CSIA Studies in International Security: No. 5). 352p. 1994. pap. 18.50 (0-02-881119-4) Brasseys Inc.
Damage Mechanics & Continuum Modeling. Ed. by Norris Stubbs & Dusan Krajcinovic. 130p. 1985. 18.00 (0-87262-495-1) Am Soc Civil Eng.
Damage Mechanics & Localization. Ed. by J. W. Ju & K. C. Valanis. (AMD Series, Vol. 142: MD: Vol. 34). 176p. 1992. 50.00 (0-7918-1086-0, G00730) ASME.
Damage Mechanics in Composites. Ed. by D. H. Allen & D. C. Lagoudas. (AMD Series, Vol. 150: AD: Vol. 32). 336p. 1992. 65.00 (0-7918-1108-5, G00752) ASME.
***Damage Mechanics in Composites: 1994 International Mechanical Engineering Congress & Exposition, Chicago, Illinois - November 6-11, 1994.** (AMD Ser.: Vol. 185). 208p. 1994. 74.00 (0-7918-1423-8, G00918) ASME.
Damage Mechanics of Composite Materials. Ed. by R. Talreja. LC 93-47988. (Composite Materials Ser.: No. 9). 1994. 162.75 (0-444-88852-7) Elsevier.
Damage, Mechanisms & Life Assessment of High-Temperature Components. ASM Intl. Staff. 440p. 1989. 139.00 (0-87170-358-0) NACE Intl.
Damage Tolerance in Aircraft Structures - STP 486. 254p. 1971. 19.50 (0-8031-0031-0, 04-486000-30) ASTM.
Damage Tolerance of Metallic Structures: Analysis Methods & Applications - STP 842. 145p. 1984. 30.00 (0-8031-0407-3, 04-842000-30) ASTM.
Damage Within the Community. Edward Mycue. (Illus.). 72p. 1973. pap. 6.00 (0-915572-11-7) Panjandrum.
***Damaged Brain of Iodine Deficiency: Neuromotor, Cognitive, Behavioral & Educative Aspects.** Ed. & Intro. by John B. Stanbury. LC 94-22998. (Illus.). 350p. (C). 1994. lib. bdg. 105.00 (1-882345-03-7) Cognizant Comm.
Damaged Goods. Thomas Friedmann. LC 83-83075. 280p. (Orig.). 1985. 22.00 (0-932966-39-X) Permanent Pr.
Damaged Goods. John Leslie. Ed. by Doug Grad. 320p. (Orig.). 1993. mass mkt. 5.50 (0-671-72479-7) PB.
***Damaged Life.** Tod Sloan. LC 95-16046. (Critical Psychology Ser.). 1995. pap. write for info. (0-415-04352-2) Routledge.
***Damaged Life.** Tod S. Sloan. LC 95-16046. (Critical Psychology Ser.). 1995. write for info. (0-415-04351-4) Routledge.
Damaged Pallet Scr. Scribner Staff. 1986. pap. write for info. (0-318-67214-6, Scribners) S&S Trade.
Damaged Parents: An Anatomy of Child Neglect. Norman Polansky et al. LC 80-22793. (Illus.). xii, 272p. 1983. pap. 9.95 (0-226-67222-0) U Ch Pr.
Damaged Souls. Gamaliel Bradford. (BCL1 - U. S. History Ser.). 284p. 1991. reprint ed. lib. bdg. 79.00 (0-7812-6029-9) Rprt Serv.
Damagers. Donald Hamilton. 1993. mass mkt. 4.99 (0-449-14847-5, GM) Fawcett.

Damages. James L. Branton & Jim D. Lovett. (Trial Lawyer's Ser.: Vol. 4). (Illus.). 475p. 1987. ring bd. 135.00 (1-878337-03-3) Knowles Law.
***Damages.** Elaine Terranova. 84p. (Orig.). 1996. pap. 12.00 (1-55659-105-5) Copper Canyon.
Damages. 2nd ed. McCormick & Fritz. 1952. text ed. 27.00 (0-88277-356-9) Foundation Pr.
Damages, 2 vols., Set. 3rd ed. Ed. by Sid Brockley & Jan K. Kitchel. 850p. 1990. write for info. (0-318-68348-2) OR Bar CLE.
Damages & Loses from Future New Madrid Earthquakes: A Central U. S. Earthquake Intensity Scale (CUSEIS) for Pre-Earthquake Planning. rev. ed. David Stewart. Ed. by Mike Coe & Linda Dillman. LC 92-75134. (Midwest Earthquake Ser.: No. 6). 84p. 1994. reprint ed. pap. 9.95 (0-934426-53-8, Gutenberg-Richter) NAPSAC Reprods.
Damages & Losses from Future New Madrid Earthquakes. (Illus.). 50p. (Orig.). (C). 1993. pap. text ed. 35.00 (1-56806-768-2) Diane Pub.
Damages & Remedies. (Legal Research Guides Ser.). 148p. 1989. 49.00 (0-8352-2867-3) Bowker.
Damages for Personal Injuries & Death. 9th ed. John Munkman. 304p. 1993. boxed 80.00 (0-406-01481-7, U.K.) Butterworth Legal Pubs.
Damages for Personal Injuries & Death in Singapore & Malaysia. Michael F. Rutter. 1000p. 1988. 233.00 (9971-70-060-3) Butterworth Legal Pubs.
Damages for Personal Injury & Death. D. Kemp. (C). 1986. 200.00 (0-685-32835-X, Pub. by Witherby & Co UK) St Mut.
Damages in Massachusetts Litigation. James F. McHugh. LC 93-77116. 404p. 1993. ring bd. 95.00 (0-944490-37-9) Mass CLE.
Damages in Tort Actions, 10 vols., Set. Updates. Marilyn K. Minzer et al. 1982. ring bd. write for info. (0-8205-1309-1) Bender.
Damages Recoverable in Maritime Matters. American Bar Association, Tort & Insurance Practice Section Staff. LC 83-73103. 153p. 1984. pap. 37.00 (0-89707-126-3, 519-0037) Amer Bar Assn.
Damages under the UCC, 2 vols. Roy R. Anderson. 1992. 230.00 (0-685-28162-0) Clark Boardman Callaghan.
Damages under the UCC, 2 vols. annuals suppl. ed. Roy R. Anderson. 1992. (0-318-65582-9) Clark Boardman Callaghan.
***Daman & Diu, Vol. XIX.** (C). 1994. text ed. 18.50x (81-7154-761-3, Pub. by Popular Prakashan II) S Asia.
Damascus & Its People: Sketches of Modern Life in Syria. Mackintosh. LC 77-87617. reprint ed. 25.00 (0-404-16444-7) AMS Pr.
Damascus & Palmyra, 2 vols. in 1. Charles G. Addison. LC 73-6265. (Middle East Ser.). 1973. reprint ed. 39.95 (0-405-05319-3) Ayer.
Damascus Bible. Ed. by Martin Edelmann & Menahem Schmelzer. Incl. Damascus Bible. (ENG & HEB.). 250p. 1979. pap. 495.00 (0-8018-1349-2); Damascus Bible. (ENG & HEB.). 248p. 1982. 485.00 (0-8018-2903-8); write for info. (0-318-56692-3) Johns Hopkins.
Damascus Bible see Damascus Bible
Damascus Chronicle of the Crusades. Ibn Al-Qalanisi. Tr. by H. A. Gibb. LC 78-63342. (Crusades & Military Orders Ser.: Second Series). reprint ed. 32.50 (0-404-17019-6) AMS Pr.
Damascus Nights. Rafik Schami. 1993. 20.00 (0-374-13446-4) FS&G.
***Damascus Nights.** Rafik Schami. 1995. pap. 11.00 (0-684-80265-1, Scribners) S&S Trade.
Damascus under the Mamluks. Nicola A. Ziadeh. LC 64-11330. (Centers of Civilization Ser.: No. 12). 160p. reprint ed. pap. 45.60 (0-317-08342-2, 2005064) Bks Demand.
Damask Days. large type ed. Evelyn Hood. 592p. 1992. 21.95 (0-7089-2578-2) Ulverscroft.
Damaso Alonso. Andrew P. Debicki. LC 74-75876. (Twayne's World Authors Ser.). 1970. lib. bdg. 17.95 (0-685-42216-X) Irvington.
Damballah. John E. Wideman. 1988. pap. 11.00 (0-679-72028-6, Vin) Random.
Dambos: Small Channelless Valleys in the Tropics, Characteristics, Formation, Utilization. Ed. by Michael F. Thomas & Andrew S. Goudie. (Annals of Gemorphology Supplement Ser.: No. 52). (Illus.). 228p. (Orig.). 1985. pap. text ed. 87.50 (3-443-21052-X, Pub. by Gebruder Borntraeger GW) Lubrecht & Cramer.
Dambudzo Marechera: A Source Book on His Life & Work. Flora Veit-Wild. Ed. by Bernth Lindfors. (Documentary Research in African Written Literatures Ser.: Vol. 2). 432p. 1992. lib. bdg. 100.00 (0-905450-97-3, Pub. by H Zell Pubs UK) Bowker-Saur.
Dambusters Raid. John Sweetman. (Illus.). 218p. 1990. 19.95 (0-87938-475-1) Motorbooks Intl.
Dame. H. Greeley Thornhill. 271p. 1985. 15.95 (0-9615343-0-3) Coolidge Pr.
Dame a la Louve see Woman of the Wolf & Other Stories
Dame aux Camelias. Alexandre Dumas. Ed. & Tr. by David Coward. (World's Classics Ser.). 288p. 1986. pap. 7.95 (0-19-281736-1) OUP.
Dame aux Camelias. Alexandre Dumas & Bernard Raffalli. (Folio Ser.: No. 704). (FRE.). 1975. 9.95 (2-07-036704-5) Schoenhof.
Dame Aux Camelias. Alexandre Dumas & Bernard Raffalli. 1975. write for info. (0-318-63468-6) Fr & Eur.
Dame Dans l'Auto Avec des Lunettes et un Fusil. Sebastien Japrisot. 320p. (FRE.). 1980. pap. 11.95 (0-7859-2435-3, 2070372235) Fr & Eur.
Dame De Coeur. Daniel Boulanger. 160p. (FRE.). 1989. pap. 10.95 (0-7859-2129-X, 2070381986) Fr & Eur.
Dame de Monsoreau. Alexandre Dumas. (Illus.). 256p. (FRE.). 1972. 17.95 (0-8288-9975-4, F60346) Fr & Eur.
Dame de Pique, Recist de Feu Ivan Petrovich, Bielkine, Doubrovski. Alexandre Pouchkine. 288p. (FRE.). 1974. pap. 10.95 (0-7859-4027-8) Fr & Eur.
Dame Du Cirque. Guy Des Cars. 256p. 1962. 9.95 (0-686-55623-2) Fr & Eur.
Dame Du Cirque. Guy Des Cars. 320p. (FRE.). 1968. pap. 6.95 (0-8288-9555-4, M5722) Fr & Eur.
Dame Du Lac. Raymond Chandler. 258p. (FRE.). 1988. pap. 10.95 (0-7859-2088-9, 2070379434) Fr & Eur.
Dame Edna Everage & the Rise of Western Civilization: Backstage with Barry Humphries. John Lahr. LC 92-2261. 1992. 22.00 (0-374-13456-1) FS&G.
Dame in the Kimono: Hollywood, Censorship & the Production Code from the 1920's to the 1960's. 1991. 13.00 (0-385-41722-5, Anchor NY) Doubleday.
Dame of Sark: An Autobiography. Dame of Sark. Ed. by Hathaway. (Jersey Heritage Editions Ser.). 1991. write for info. (0-86120-013-6, Pub. by Aris & Phillips UK) David Brown.
Dame Renard et Dame Cigogne - Mrs. Fox & Mrs. Stork. 2nd ed. Jean De la Fontaine. (Interlingo Ser.). (Illus.). 19p. (FRE.). (J). (gr. k-12). 1993. reprint ed. pap. 2.95 (0-922852-20-0) Another Lang Pr.
Dame School of Experience: And Other Papers. Samuel M. Crothers. LC 77-156635. (Essay Index Reprint Ser.). 1977. reprint ed. 21.95 (0-8369-2351-0) Ayer.
Dame Shirley & the Gold Rush. Jim Rawls. LC 92-18083. (Stories of America Ser.). (Illus.). (J). (gr. 2-5). 1992. lib. bdg. 21.36 (0-8114-7222-1) Raintree Steck-V.
Dames & Daughters of Colonial Days. Geraldine Brooks. LC 74-3979. (Women in America Ser.). (Illus.). 308p. 1977. reprint ed. 29.95 (0-405-06080-7) Ayer.
Dames & Daughters of Colonial Days. Geraldine Brooks. 284p. 1982. reprint ed. 22.50 (0-87928-109-X) Corner Hse.
Dames & Daughters of the French Court. Geraldine Brooks. LC 68-8443. (Essay Index Reprint Ser.). 1977. 21.95 (0-8369-0256-4) Ayer.
Dames Can Be Deadly. large type ed. Peter A. Chambers. (Dales General Fiction Ser.). 291p. 1993. pap. 16.95 (1-85389-427-3, Dales) Ulverscroft.
Dames de France. Angelo Rinaldi. (FRE.). 1980. pap. 11.95 (0-7859-4131-2) Fr & Eur.
Dames Du Fauborg. Jean Diwo. (FRE.). 1987. pap. 16.95 (0-7859-2064-1, 2070378349) Fr & Eur.
Dames Employees: The Feminization of Postal Workers in Nineteenth-Century France. Susan Bachrach. LC 83-22879. (Women & History Ser.: No. 8). 134p. 1984. text ed. 32.95 (0-86656-205-2) Haworth Pr.
Dames Galantes. Pierre De Brantome. 704p. (FRE.). 1981. pap. 13.95 (0-7859-2219-9, 207037260X) Fr & Eur.
Damfino. Herb Lorenz. 1992. 21.95 (0-9633256-0-4) Prairie House.
Damia. Anne McCaffrey. 352p. 1993. mass mkt. 5.99 (0-441-13556-0) Ace Bks.
***Damian Parer: Cameraman.** Niall Brennan. 200p. Date not set. pap. 29.95 (0-522-84420-0) Intl Spec Bk.
Damiano's at the Tarrimore House. LC 93-73745. 1993. write for info. (0-87197-393-6) Favorite Recipes.
Damia's Children. Anne McCaffrey. 336p. 1994. 5.99 (0-441-00007-X) Ace Bks.
Damia's Children. Anne McCaffrey. LC 92-31601. 272p. 1993. 22.95 (0-399-13817-X, Ace-Putnam) Putnam Pub Group.
Damia's Children. limited ed. Anne McCaffrey. LC 92-31601. 272p. 1993. 100.00 (0-399-13836-6, Ace-Putnam) Putnam Pub Group.
Damien. Aldyth Morris. LC 79-22915. 44p. 1980. pap. text ed. 7.00 (0-8248-1323-5) UH Pr.
Damien, Hero of Molokai. 3rd rev. ed. Omer Englebert. Tr. by Benjamin T. Crawford. LC 94-4408. (Illus.). 272p. 1994. pap. 5.25 (0-8198-1870-4) Pauline Bks.
Damien the Dragon. Gaby Ross. 1990. pap. 6.95 (1-85371-078-4, Pub. by Poolbeg Pr IE) Dufour.
Damiens Affair & the Unraveling of the Ancien Regime: Church, State, & Society in France, 1750-1770. Dale K. Van Kley. LC 83-42583. (Illus.). 320p. 1984. 57.50x (0-691-05402-9) Princeton U Pr.
***Damiens Affair & the Unraveling of the Ancient Regime, 1750-1770.** Dale K. Van Kley. LC 83-42583. (Illus.). Date not set. reprint ed. pap. 110.10 (0-7837-9466-5, 2060208) Bks Demand.
***D'Ammassa's Guide to Modern Horror Fiction: An Annotated Bibliography of Works in English.** Don D'Ammassa. LC 95-5331. (Borgo Literary Guides: No. 4). 1995. lib. bdg. write for info. (0-8095-0201-1) Borgo Pr.
***Dammed Indians: The Pick-Sloan Plan & the Missouri River Sioux, 1944-1980.** Michael Lawson. LC 81-19721. (Illus.). 300p. (Orig.). 1994. pap. 14.95 (0-8061-2672-8) U of Okla Pr.
***Dammed Strong Love: The True Story of Willi G. & Stephan K.** Lutz Van Dijk. Tr. by Elizabeth D. Crawford. LC 94-42075. (ENG & GER.). (J). 1995. 15.95 (0-8050-3770-5) H Holt & Co.
Dammed Yard & Other Stories. Ivo Andric. 198p. 1993. pap. 21.00 (1-85610-022-7, Pub. by Forest Bks UK) Dufour.
Damming the Colorado: The Rise of the Lower Colorado River Authority, 1933-1939. John A. Adams, Jr. LC 90-32795. (Centennial Series of the Association of Former Students: No. 35). (Illus.). 184p. 1990. 32.50 (0-89096-426-2) Tex A&M Univ Pr.
***Damming the Danube: Gabcikovo.** John Fitzmaurice. (C). 1995. text ed. 49.00 (0-8133-2164-6) Westview.
Damming the Delaware: The Rise & Fall of Tocks Island Dam. Richard C. Albert. LC 86-43197. (Illus.). 224p. 1988. 30.00 (0-271-00481-9) Pa St U Pr.
Damn Good Resume Guide. rev. ed. Yana Parker. 1989. pap. 6.95 (0-89815-348-4) Ten Speed Pr.
Damn Right I've Got the Blues: Buddy Guy & the Blues Roots of Rock & Roll. Donald E. Wilcock. LC 91-75201. 160p. (Orig.). 1993. pap. 19.95 (0-942627-13-X) Woodford Pub.
Damn, Sam, I Want to Share My Life but I Need to Live Alone. Irene Bles. (Minority Poet Ser.). 42p. (ENG & SPA.). 1987. pap. 4.00 (1-880046-00-8) Baculite Pub.
Damn the Dardanelles! The Agony of Gallipoli. John Laffin. (Illus.). 224p. 1990. 22.00 (0-86299-590-6) A Sutton Pub.
Damn the Disabilities: Full Speed Ahead. Jack Cavanaugh. (Illus.). 228p. 1994. pap. 13.95 (1-56796-057-X) WRS Group.
Damn the Torpedoes: A Short History of U. S. Naval Mine Countermeasures, 1777-1991. Tamara M. Melia. (Contributions to Naval History Ser.: No. 4). (Illus.). 209p. (C). 1991. pap. 10.00 (0-945274-07-6) Naval Hist Ctr.
Damn the Torpedoes: Naval Incidents of the Civil War. A. A. Hoehling. LC 89-17630. (Illus.). 207p. 1989. 12.95 (0-89587-073-8) Blair.
***Damn the Torpedos: A History of the United States Naval Mine Countermeasures, 1771-1991.** 1995. lib. bdg. 250.95 (0-8490-6435-X) Gordon Pr.
***Damn Yankees.** (Best of Broadway Ser.). 1993. pap. 11.95 (0-89724-499-0, XW1658) Astor Bks.
Damn Yankees. Douglass Wallop. 250p. 1994. pap. 10.00 (0-393-31266-6) Norton.
Damn Yankees - Selections from Damn Yankees & Don't Thread on Me. 80p. (Orig.). 1993. pap. 19.95 (0-89724-043-X) Warner Brothers.
***Damn You England: Collected Prose.** John Osborne. (Illus.). 268p. 1995. 22.95 (0-571-16921-X) Faber & Faber.
Damnation of Newton: Goethe's Color Theory & Romantic Perception. Frederick Burwick. (Quellen und Forschungen zur Sprach und Kulturgeschichte der Germanischen Voelker Ser.: NF Band 86 210). vi, 308p. 1986. lib. bdg. 119.25 (0-89925-207-9) De Gruyter.
Damnation of Pentheus. Eric Felderman. LC 92-40927. (Illus.). 1993. 49.95 (0-945942-38-9); pap. 36.95 (0-945942-39-7) Portmanteau Editions.
Damnation of Theron Ware. Harold Frederic. Ed. by John H. Raleigh. LC 60-13818. (Rinehart Editions Ser.). 378p. (C). 1960. pap. text ed. 18.50 (0-03-010200-6) HB Coll Pubs.
Damnation of Theron Ware. Harold Frederick. (Classics Ser.). 512p. 1986. pap. 9.95 (0-14-039025-1, Penguin Classics) Viking Penguin.
Damnation of Theron Ware. Harold Frederic. Ed. by Everett Carter. LC 60-11553. (John Harvard Library). 379p. 1960. reprint ed. pap. 14.95 (0-674-19001-7) HUP.
Damnation of Theron Ware. Harold Frederic. (Collected Works of Harold Frederic). 1988. reprint ed. lib. bdg. 79.00 (0-7812-1192-1) Rprt Serv.
Damnation of Theron Ware see Collected Works of Harold Frederic
Damnation of Theron Ware; or, Illumination. Harold Frederic. Ed. by Charlyne Dodge & Stanton Garner. LC 84-25790. (Harold Frederic Edition Ser.: Vol. 3). x, 506p. 1985. 40.00 (0-8032-1967-9) U of Nebr Pr.
Damnation Reef. Jill Tattersall. 288p. 1980. pap. 2.25 (0-449-24325-7, Crest) Fawcett.
Damndest Radical: The Life & World of Ben Reitman, Chicago's Celebrated Social Reformer, Hobo King, & Whorehouse Physician. Roger A. Bruns. LC 86-4364. (Illus.). 350p. 1987. 29.95 (0-252-00984-3) U of Ill Pr.
Damned: Rivers, Dams, & the Coming World Water Crisis. Fred Pearce. (Illus.). 400p. 1994. 39.95 (0-370-31609-6, Pub. by Bodley Head UK) Trafalgar.
Damned: The Light at the End of the Tunnel. (Illus.). 88p. 1987. pap. 11.95 (0-8256-2500-9, AM66622) Music Sales.
Damned & the Beautiful: American Youth in the 1920's. Paula S. Fass. LC 76-42644. 1979. pap. 14.95 (0-19-502492-3) OUP.
Damned & the Elect: Guilt in Western Culture. Friedrich Ohly. Tr. by Linda Archibald. (Illus.). 215p. (C). 1992. 54.95 (0-521-38250-5) Cambridge U Pr.
Damned Don't Die. Jim Nisbet. LC 85-73607. Orig. Title: The Gourmet. 144p. 1986. reprint ed. pap. 3.95 (0-88739-004-8, Blk Lizard) Creat Arts Bk.
Damned for Despair. De Molina. Ed. by Round. (Hispanic Classics Ser.). 1986. 49.95 (0-85668-329-9, Pub. by Aris & Phillips UK); pap. 22.00 (0-85668-330-2, Pub. by Aris & Phillips UK) David Brown.
Damned If We Do. FASA Staff. (Renegade Legion Ser.). 1990. pap. 7.95 (1-55560-099-9, 5602) FASA Corp.
Damned If We Do: Contradictions in Women's Health Care. Dorothy H. Broom. 208p. (Orig.). 1992. pap. text ed. 19.95 (1-86373-054-0, Pub. by Allen Unwin AT) Paul & Co Pubs.
Damned If You Do. Pat Leonard. LC 93-90854. 260p. 1994. lib. bdg. 20.00 (0-9632933-2-X) Leonard Pubns.
Damned in Hell. A. A. Wilson. (Illus.). 42p. 1985. pap. 3.50 (0-938245-03-1) Inverted-A.
Damned Inheritance: The Soviet Union & the Manchurian Crises, 1924-1935. George A. Lensen. LC 74-186318. (Illus.). 533p. 1974. 19.80 (0-910512-17-5) Diplomatic IN.
Damned of the Taiga. large type ed. Heinz G. Konsalik. 421p. 1982. 15.95 (0-7089-0797-0) Ulverscroft.
Damned Old Crank: A Self-Portrait of E. W. Scripps Drawn from His Unpublished Writings. Edward W. Scripps. Ed. by Charles R. McCabe. (Illus.). (C). 1971. reprint ed. text ed. 65.00 (0-8371-6159-2, SCDO, Greenwood Pr) Greenwood.
***Damned Reg Flags of the Rebellion: The Confederate Battle Flag at Gettysburg.** Ed. by Richard Rollins. 1995. write for info. (0-9638993-3-3) Rank & File.
Damned Right: A Novel. Bayard Johnson. (Black Ice Books Ser.). 128p. 1994. pap. 7.00 (0-932511-84-8) Fiction Coll.
Damned Serious Business. large type ed. Rex Harrison. 342p. 1992. 24.95 (1-85089-586-4, Pub. by ISIS UK) Transaction Pubs.
Damned Upcountryman: William Watts Ball: Study in American Conservatism. John D. Stark. LC 68-57269. (Duke Historical Publications). 256p. reprint ed. pap. 73.00 (0-317-26853-8, 2023453) Bks Demand.
Damned Welcome: Aesthetic Realism Maxims. 2nd ed. Eli Siegel. LC 71-171394. (Illus.). 159p. 1972. 6.95 (0-910492-17-4); pap. 4.95 (0-910492-18-2) Definition.
Damned Well Do's & Don'ts for a Perfect Lifestyle. Carlo DiNapoli. Ed. by R. Constantine. (Illus.). 185p. (Orig.). 1994. pap. 9.95 (0-9627946-9-4) Hawk FL.
Damned Yankee: The Life of General Nathaniel Lyon. Christopher Phillips. Ed. by William E. Foley. (Missouri Biography Ser.). (Illus.). 312p. 1990. text ed. 25.95 (0-8262-0731-6) U of Mo Pr.
Damned Yankees: A No-Holds-Barred Account of Life with Boss Steinbrenner. Bill Madden. 1991. mass mkt. 5.95 (0-446-36089-9) Warner Bks.
Damnee Manon, Sacree Sandra. Tr. by Tremblay & John Van Burek. (NFS Canada Ser.). 1999. pap. 8.95 (0-88922-184-7, Pub. by Talonbooks CN) InBook.
Damnes de la Terre. Frantz Fanon. (Petite Coll. Maspero Ser.). (FRE.). pap. 19.95 (0-8288-9737-9, 2070326551) Fr & Eur.
Damning the Innocent. Pierre Darmon. 1999. pap. write for info. (0-14-008529-7, Penguin Bks) Viking Penguin.
Damodar & the Pioneers of the Theosophical Movement. Sven Eek. 1978. 25.95 (0-8356-7003-1) Theos Pub Hse.
Damodaran on Valuation: Security Analysis for Investment & Corporate Finance. Aswath Damodaran. LC 93-21405. 1994. text ed. 65.00 (0-471-30465-4) Wiley.
***Damodaran on Valuation: Security Analysis for Investment & Corporate Finance.** Aswath Damodaran. 1994. text ed. 69.95 (0-471-12015-4) Wiley.
Damodaran on Valuation: Security Analysis for Investment & Corporate Finance. Aswath Damodaran. LC 93-21405. 1994. disk write for info. (0-471-01450-8) Wiley.
***Damodaran on Valuation: Security Analysis for Investment & Corporate Finance.** Aswath Damodaran. 1994. pap. text ed. 29.95 (0-471-10897-9) Wiley.
Damon & Delia. William Godwin. Ed. by Peter Marshall. xx, 182p. 1988. 27.00 (0-9511069-1-0, Pub. by U of Wales UK) Bks Intl VA.
Damon & Pithias. Richard Edwards. LC 76-136388. (Tudor Facsimile Texts. Old English Plays Ser.: No. 45). reprint ed. 49.50 (0-404-53345-0) AMS Pr.
***Damon Hill - from Zero to Hero.** Alan Henry. (Illus.). 208p. 1995. pap. 21.95 (1-85260-517-0, Pub. by J H Haynes & Co UK) Motorbooks Intl.
Damon Hill from Zero to Hero. Alan Henry. (Illus.). 192p. 1994. 21.95 (1-85260-484-0, Pub. by J H Haynes & Co UK) Motorbooks Intl.
***Damon Hill Legacy of Speed.** David Tremayne. (Illus.). 96p. 1994. 19.95 (0-297-83480-0, Pub. by Orion Pubng Grp UK) Motorbooks Intl.
Damon Runyon Favorites. Damon Runyon. reprint ed. lib. bdg. 20.95 (0-89190-440-9, Rivercity Pr) Amereon Ltd.
Damon Runyon Imnibus. Damon Runyon. 1993. reprint ed. lib. bdg. 28.95 (1-56849-217-0) Buccaneer Bks.
Damon Runyon Omnibus. Damon Runyon. 1976. reprint ed. lib. bdg. 30.95 (0-89190-441-7, Rivercity Pr) Amereon Ltd.
Damon Runyon Reader. D. Runyon. 23.95 (0-89190-781-5, Am Repr) Amereon Ltd.
Damos Gracias: Libro de la Eucaristia para Ninos. Corinne Hart. Tr. by P. Fidencio Silva & P. Domenico Di Raimondo. (Illus.). 32p. (SPA.). (J). (ps-2). 1991. pap. 1.90 (1-55944-006-6) Franciscan Comns.
Damp Woods Greening: Poems. Robert E. Carter. LC 92-6671. (Illus.). 64p. 1992. pap. 12.95 (0-7734-9659-9) E Mellen.
Damping of Materials & Members in Structural Mechanics. B. Lazan. LC 66-27370. 1968. 134.00 (0-08-013221-9, Pub. by Pergamon Repr UK) Franklin.
Dampness in Buildings: Diagnosis, Treatment, Instruments. T. Oxley & E. Gobert. (Illus.). 132p. 1983. text ed. 16.95 (0-408-01463-6) Buttrwrth-Heinemann.
Dampness in Buildings: The Professional's & Home Owner's Guide. 2nd ed. T. A. Oxley & E. G. Gobert. LC 94-7413. (Illus.). 136p. 1994. pap. 19.95 (0-7506-2059-5) Buttrwrth-Heinemann.
Dams. Neil Ardley. Ed. by Rebecca Stefoff. LC 90-40360. (How We Build Ser.). (Illus.). 48p. (J). (gr. 4-7). 1990. lib. bdg. 17.26 (0-944483-75-5) Garrett Ed Corp.
Dams. J. Cooper. (Man-Made Wonders Ser.). (J). 1991. 8.95 (0-86592-627-1) Rourke Enter.
Dams. Andrew Dunn. LC 93-6835. (Structures Ser.). 32p. (J). (gr. 5-8). 1993. 13.95 (1-56847-029-0) Thomson Lrning.
Dams & Earthquakes. H. Gupta & B. Rastogi. (Developments in Geotechnical Engineering Ser.: Vol. 11). 230p. 1976. 102.75 (0-444-41330-8) Elsevier.
Dams & Other Disasters: A Century of the Army Corps of Engineers in Civil Works. Arthur E. Morgan. LC 74-172688. (Extending Horizons Ser.). 448p. (C). 1971. 7.50 (0-87558-066-1); pap. 3.95 (0-87558-094-7) Porter Sargent.
Dams & the Environment: Considerations in World Bank Projects. John A. Dixon et al. (Technical Paper Ser.: No. 110). 74p. 1989. 7.95 (0-8213-1363-0, 11363) World Bank.
Dams of National Hunt Winners, 1963-64. E. Buckle. 1990. pap. 25.00 (0-85131-077-X, Pub. by J A Allen & Co UK) St Mut.

D

An Asterisk (*) at the beginning of an entry indicates that the title is appearing in BIP for the first time. 1779

Dams of National Hunt Winners, 1966-73. E. Buckle. 1990. pap. 21.00 (*0-85131-237-3*, Pub. by J A Allen & Co UK) St Mut.

Dams of National Hunt Winners, 1973-75. E. Buckle. 1990. pap. 21.00 (*0-85131-340-X*, Pub. by J A Allen & Co UK) St Mut.

Dams of National Hunt Winners, 1975-77. E. Buckle. 1990. pap. 21.00 (*0-85131-342-6*, Pub. by J A Allen & Co UK) St Mut.

Dams of National Hunt Winners, 1977-78. Comp. by E. Buckle. 1990. pap. 21.00 (*0-85131-347-7*, Pub. by J A Allen & Co UK) St Mut.

Damsel in Distress. Shannon Drake. 416p. 1992. mass mkt. 4.99 (*0-380-76352-4*) Avon.

***Damsel in Distress.** Joan Smith. (Regency Romance Ser.). 1995. mass mkt. 3.99 (*0-449-22278-0*) Fawcett.

Damsel in Distress. P. G. Wodehouse. 256p. 1991. mass mkt. 8.95 (*0-14-001599-X*) Viking Penguin.

Damselflies of Florida, Bermuda, & the Bahamas. Sidney W. Dunkle. (Scientific Publishers Nature Guides Ser.: No. 3). (Illus.). 148p. (YA). 1990. 19.95 (*0-945417-86-1*); pap. 14.95 (*0-945417-85-3*) Sci Pubs.

Damsels from Derbyshire. Ellen Fitzgerald. 224p. 1992. 19.95 (*0-8027-1183-9*) Walker & Co.

Dan. Barbara Fisher. (Illus.). 20p. (Orig.). (J). (gr. k-5). 1981. pap. 2.00 (*0-934830-19-3*) Ten Penny.

***Dan & Gramps.** Scripture Union Staff. 32p. (J). 1995. 5.99 (*1-56476-364-1*, 6-3364, Victor Books) SP Pubns.

Dan Barry's Daughter. Max Brand. 1976. reprint ed. lib. bdg. 23.95 (*0-88411-516-X*, Aeonian Pr) Amereon Ltd.

Dan Busters. P. Brickhill. (Bulls-Eye Ser.). (C). 1977. 30.00 (*0-09-119641-8*, Pub. by S Thornes Pubs UK) St Mut.

***Dan Cassidy's Worldwide College Scholarship Directory.** 4th ed. Daniel J. Cassidy. 400p. 1995. pap. 19.99 (*1-56414-208-6*) Career Pr Inc.

***Dan Cassidy's Worldwide Graduate Scholarship Directory.** 4th ed. Daniel J. Cassidy. 400p. 1995. pap. 26.99 (*1-56414-209-4*) Career Pr Inc.

Dan Chaucer. Henry D. Sedgwick. LC 73-155610. reprint ed. 45.00 (*0-404-05669-5*) AMS Pr.

***Dan Coates Country Music: Made Easy for Piano.** Ed. by Carol Cuellar. 52p. (Orig.). (YA). 1995. pap. text ed. 8.95 (*0-614-06704-9*) Warner Brothers.

***Dan Coates Golden Collection of Broadway Blockbusters.** 224p. (Orig.). 1994. pap. 17.95 (*0-89724-307-2*) Warner Brothers.

***Dan Coates Golden Collection of Movie Themes.** 200p. (Orig.). 1994. pap. 17.95 (*0-89724-305-6*) Warner Brothers.

***Dan Coates Movie Music: Made Easy for Piano.** Ed. by Carol Cuellar. 56p. (Orig.). (YA). 1995. pap. text ed. 8.95 (*0-89724-617-9*) Warner Brothers.

***Dan Coates Plays Selections from "Fiddler on the Roof"** 32p. (Orig.). 1994. pap. 10.95 (*0-89724-198-3*) Warner Brothers.

***Dan Coates Popular Music: Made Easy for Piano.** Ed. by Carol Cuellar. 60p. (Orig.). (YA). 1995. pap. text ed. 8.95 (*0-89724-616-0*) Warner Brothers.

Dan Crary, the Flatpickers Method: With Cassette Tape. Dan Crary. 112p. 1986. pap. text ed. 17.95 (*0-931759-12-9*) Centerstream Pub.

Dan Cushman's Cow-Country Cook Book. Dan Cushman. LC 67-21434. (Illus.). 1967. 15.95 (*0-911436-02-2*) Stay Away.

Dan Dailey: Simple Complexities in Drawings & Glass, 1972-1987. William Warmus & Henry Geldzahler. (Illus.). 64p. 1989. pap. 25.00 (*0-295-96663-7*) U of Wash Pr.

Dan De Quille, The Washoe Giant: A Biography & Anthology. Ed. by Richard E. Lingenfelter. LC 89-16584. (Western Literature Ser.). 464p. (Orig.). 1990. pap. 19.95 (*0-87417-152-0*) U of Nev Pr.

Dan Emergency Handbook: A Guide to the Identification of & First Aid for Scuba (Air) Diving Injuries. 2nd ed. John Lippmann & Stan Bugg. 1991. spiral bd. 12.95 (*0-9590306-1-1*) Aqua Quest.

Dan Fogelberg: The Wild Places. (Piano-Vocal-Guitar Ser.). (Illus.). 64p. 1991. pap. 12.95 (*0-7935-0266-7*, 00490564) H Leonard.

Dan Freeman. Dan Jaffe. LC 67-13150. 95p. reprint ed. pap. 27.10 (*0-7837-0272-8*, 2040581) Bks Demand.

Dan Friedman: Radical Modernism. Dan Friedman. LC 93-21035. (C). 1994. 65.00 (*0-300-05848-9*); pap. write for info. (*0-300-05849-7*) Yale U Pr.

Dan Goes to First Grade. Gila M. Fleisher. Tr. by David Kriss. (Hippy Ser.). (Illus.). 24p. (Orig.). (J). (ps). 1992. pap. text ed. 3.00 (*1-56134-166-5*) Dushkin Pub.

Dan Gookin's Guide to Underground DOS. Dan Gookin. 1993. pap. 24.95 (*0-679-79115-9*) Random.

Dan Gookins Optimizing Windows. Dan Gookin. 1992. pap. 14.95 (*1-55615-506-9*) Microsoft.

***Dan Graham.** Alain Charre et al. 128p. 1995. pap. 23.50 (*2-906571-42-3*) Dist Art Pubs.

***Dan Jansen: Olympic Champion.** Bob Italia. LC 94-35020. (Reaching for the Stars Ser.). 1994. lib. bdg. 12.94 (*1-56239-340-5*) Abdo & Dghtrs.

Dan Kiley: Landscape Design Two. M. Yamada. (Process Architecture Ser.: No. 108). (Illus.). 155p. 1993. pap. 46.95 (*4-89331-108-5*, Pub. by Process Archit JA) Bks Nippan.

Dan Magill's Bull-Doggerel: Fifty Years of Anecdotes from the Greatest Bulldog Ever. Dan Magill. LC 93-79659. (Illus.). 192p. 1993. 16.95 (*1-56352-089-3*) Longstreet Pr Inc.

Dan McGrew, Sam McGee & Other Great Service. Robert W. Service. LC 90-72376. (Illus.). 190p. 1990. pap. 12.95 (*0-923568-12-3*) Wilderness Adventure Bks.

Dan Ostermiller. 1990. write for info. (*0-9626881-0-X*) Actian Pr.

Dan Ostermiller, les Animalier. Donna Fleischer. Ed. by Kathy Verplank. (Illus.). 81p. (Orig.). 1993. pap. 15.00 (*0-9617882-4-0*) FFCA Pub.

Dan, Pioneer Tribe of Israel. J. C. Gawler. (Illus.). 40p. (C). 1985. reprint ed. pap. 2.50 (*0-934666-14-8*) Artisan Sales.

Dan Quayle Meets the Last Judgement: Why It Happened. Lawrence W. Lyons. LC 90-85362. 238p. (Orig.). 1992. pap. 11.88 (*0-942121-33-3*) Grammar Pub.

Dan Rather. Norman King. 1981. pap. 2.25 (*0-8439-0927-7*) Dorchester Pub Co.

Dan Rather & Other Rough Drafts. Martha A. Turner. 160p. 1987. 12.95 (*0-89015-501-1*) Sunbelt Media.

Dan Riley School for a Girl: An Adventure in Home Schooling. Dan Riley. 1994. 21.95 (*0-395-68719-5*) HM.

Dan River Anthology, 1985. Ed. by Richard S. Danbury, III. 1985. 19.95 (*0-89754-040-9*); pap. 9.95 (*0-89754-039-5*) Dan River Pr.

Dan River Anthology, 1986. Ed. by Richard S. Danbury, III. 180p. 1986. 19.95 (*0-89754-046-8*); pap. 9.95 (*0-89754-045-X*) Dan River Pr.

Dan River Anthology, 1987. Ed. by Richard S. Danbury, III. 200p. (Orig.). 1987. 19.95 (*0-89754-061-1*); pap. 9.95 (*0-89754-060-3*) Dan River Pr.

Dan River Anthology, 1988. Ed. by Richard S. Danbury, III. 104p. (Orig.). 1988. 19.95 (*0-89754-067-0*); pap. 9.95 (*0-89754-066-2*) Dan River Pr.

Dan River Anthology, 1989. Ed. by Richard S. Danbury, III. 140p. (Orig.). 1989. 19.95 (*0-89754-069-7*); pap. 9.95 (*0-89754-068-9*) Dan River Pr.

Dan River Anthology, 1991. Ed. by Richard S. Danbury, III. 148p. 1991. 19.95 (*0-89754-079-4*); pap. 9.95 (*0-89754-078-6*) Dan River Pr.

Dan River Anthology, 1993. Ed. by Richard S. Danbury, III. 160p. 1992. 19.95 (*0-89754-081-6*); pap. 9.95 (*0-89754-080-8*) Dan River Pr.

Dan River Anthology, 1994. Ed. by Richard S. Danbury. 104p. 1993. 29.95 (*0-89754-087-5*); pap. 9.95 (*0-685-66250-0*) Dan River Pr.

Dan Sample's Glacier National Park, Montana. (Illus.). 32p. 1994. reprint ed. 3.50 (*1-879485-10-9*) D Sample Postcards.

***Dan Screams.** Andrew Reed & Jeffrey Herron. (Illus.). 64p. (Orig.). 1994. pap. 10.95 (*0-9633307-3-X*) Poets Farm Pr.

Dan Shafer Presents the Power of Prograph. Dan Shafer. 1992. pap. text ed. write for info. (*1-881513-02-5*) Reader Netwk.

Dan Shafer's First Book of Frontier: Twenty-Five Things You Can Do with Frontier That Would Be Hard or Impossible Without It! Dan Shafer & Edward J. Smith. 250p. 1992. pap. 24.95 (*1-881513-00-9*) Reader Netwk.

Dan Shafer's Second Book of Frontier. Dan Shafer & Edward J. Smith. 1992. pap. write for info. (*1-881513-01-7*) Reader Netwk.

Dan Stuart's Fistic Carnival. Leo N. Miletich. (Illus.). 280p. 1994. 29.50 (*0-89096-614-1*); pap. 14.95 (*0-89096-615-X*) Tex A&M Univ Pr.

Dan the Newsboy. Horatio Alger, Jr. (Works of Horatio Alger Jr.). 1989. reprint ed. lib. bdg. 79.00 (*0-7812-3560-X*) Rprt Serv.

Dan Thuy's New Life in America. Karen O'Connor. (In My Shoes Ser.). (Illus.). 40p. (J). (gr. 4-8). 1992. lib. bdg. 18.95 (*0-8225-2555-0*, Lerner Publctns) Lerner Group.

Dan Turner, Hollywood Detective: Lights! Camera! Murder! Robert L. Bellem. Ed. by Tom Mason. (Illus.). 62p. (YA). 1990. pap. 7.95 (*0-944735-65-7*) Malibu Graphics.

Dan Walker: The Glory & the Tragedy. Taylor Peneneau. 1993. 29.95 (*0-9623414-7-9*); pap. 15.95 (*0-9623414-6-0*) Smith Collins.

Dan Yack. Blaise Cendrars. Tr. by Nina Rootes. LC 87-76670. 144p. 1987. 16.95 (*0-935576-22-3*) Kesend Pub Ltd.

Dana Doesn't Like Guns Anymore. Carole Moore-Slater. (Illus.). (Orig.). (J). 1991. 10.95 (*0-377-00246-1*) Friendship Pr.

Dana: Gift System in Ancient India: A Socio-economic Perspective. Vijay Nath. 1988. 33.50 (*81-215-0054-0*, Pub. by Munshiram Manoharial II) S Asia.

Dana Meets the Cow Who Lost Its Moo. Desmond A. Reid. 32p. 1985. 5.95 (*0-912444-29-0*) DARE Bks.

Dana Point Harbor - Capistrano Bay: Home Port for Romance. 2nd ed. Doris Walker. LC 80-53180. (Illus.). 272p. 1987. 45.00 (*0-9606476-3-5*) To-the-Point.

Danagla Traders of Northern Sudan. Elhaj B. Omer. (Sudan Studies: No. 10). 105p. 1985. 25.00 (*0-685-14919-6*, Pub. by Ithaca UK) Evergreen Dist.

Danaides. Antonio Salieri. Ed. by Gustave Lefevre. (Chefs-d'oeuvre classiques de l'opera francaise Ser.: Vol. 39). (Illus.). 280p. (FRE.). 1970. reprint ed. pap. 35.00 (*0-8450-1139-1*) Broude.

***Dana's Cookbook.** 2nd ed. Dana Thornock. (Illus.). 387p. 1995. pap. 19.95 (*1-56684-079-1*) Pubs Dist Ctr Inc.

Danbury Curve. Ruth Mason & Gregory Mason. 13.95 (*0-8084-0370-2*) NCUP.

Danbury Scandals. large type ed. Mary Nichols. 1993. 18.95 (*0-263-13551-9*, Pub. by Mills & Boon Ltd UK) Chivers N Amer.

Dance. P. Bessant & L. Smith. (Dance Guides Ser.). (Illus.). 48p. (J). (gr. 5 up). 1987. lib. bdg. 14.96 (*0-88110-245-8*); pap. 7.95 (*0-7460-0087-1*) EDC.

Dance! Etienne Delessert. 32p. (J). (gr. 2 up). 1994. 16.95 (*1-56846-088-0*) Creative Ed.

Dance! Etienne Delessert. (Yok-Yok Ser.). (Illus.). 32p. (J). (gr. 1-8). 1994. 16.95 (*0-88682-627-6*, 97938-098) Creative Ed.

***Dance.** Ashish Khokar. (C). 1994. 7.50 (*81-7167-207-8*, Pub. by Rupa II) S Asia.

Dance. Ocallahan. audio 18.00 (*1-877954-22-5*) Artana Prodns.

Dance. Christopher Pike. (Final Friends Ser.: No. 2). 1991. mass mkt. 3.99 (*0-671-73679-5*, Archway) PB.

***Dance!** Ward Schumaker. LC 95-13697. (J). 1996. write for info. (*0-15-200046-1*) HarBrace.

***Dance.** Louise Tythacott. (Traditions Around the World Ser.). (Illus.). 48p. (J). (gr. 5-7). 1995. 16.95 (*1-56847-275-7*) Thomson Lrning.

Dance. Eleanor Van Zandt. LC 89-21723. (Arts Ser.). (Illus.). 48p. (J). (gr. 6-11). 1990. lib. bdg. 11.95 (*0-8114-2357-3*) Raintree Steck-V.

Dance. John Martin. LC 79-7776. (Dance Ser.). (Illus.). 1980. reprint ed. lib. bdg. 42.95 (*0-8369-9303-9*) Ayer.

Dance, Vol. 3. Ed. by Lynette Y. Overby & James H. Humphrey. LC 87-47814. (Illus.). 310p. 1992. 37.50 (*0-404-63853-8*) AMS Pr.

Dance: A Creative Art Experience. 2nd ed. Margaret N. H'Doubler. LC 57-7820. 196p. reprint ed. pap. 55.90 (*0-7837-2644-9*, 2042998) Bks Demand.

Dance: A Creative Art Experience. 2nd ed. Margaret N. H'Doubler. (Illus.). 200p. 1959. pap. 8.95 (*0-299-01524-6*) U of Wis Pr.

Dance: A Short History of Classic Theatrical Dancing. Lincoln Kirstein. LC 79-98846. 369p. 1970. reprint ed. text ed. 35.00 (*0-8371-3972-4*, KIDA, Greenwood Pr) Greenwood.

Dance: A Short History of Classic Theatrical Dancing. Lincoln Kirstein. LC 70-77179. (Illus.). 423p. 1987. reprint ed. pap. 17.95 (*0-87127-019-6*) Princeton Bk Co.

Dance: An Annotated Bibliography. Fred R. Forbes. LC 85-45150. (Reference Library of the Humanities). 280p. 1986. lib. bdg. 47.00 (*0-8240-8676-7*) Garland.

Dance: Current Selected Research, 4 vols., Vols. 1-4. Ed. by Lynette Y. Overby & James H. Humphrey. LC 87-47814. 1993. 37.50 (*0-404-63850-3*) AMS Pr.

Dance: Rituals of Experience. 3rd ed. Jamake Highwater. (Illus.). 288p. 1992. pap. 19.95 (*0-87127-174-5*, Dance Horizons) Princeton Bk Co.

Dance: The Art of Production. 2nd ed. Joan Schlaich & Betty DuPont. LC 87-63490. (Illus.). 192p. 1988. pap. 14.95 (*0-916622-68-1*, Dance Horizons) Princeton Bk Co.

Dance - Movement Therapy Abstracts, Vol. I: Doctoral Dissertations, Masters' Theses, & Special Projects. Ed. by Anne C. Fisher & Arlynne Stark. LC 92-72987. 300p. (Orig.). (C). 1992. pap. write for info. (*1-881766-01-2*) M Chace Mem Fund.

Dance! A Complete Guide to Social, Folk, & Square Dancing. J. T. Hall. LC 79-7766. (Dance Ser.). (Illus.). 1980. reprint ed. lib. bdg. 44.95 (*0-8369-9294-6*) Ayer.

Dance a Little Longer. Jane R. Wood. LC 93-9527. 1993. 19.95 (*0-385-30521-4*) Delacorte.

***Dance a Little Longer.** Jane R. Wood. LC 93-9527. 1995. pap. 11.95 (*0-385-31320-9*, Delta) Dell.

Dance a Little Longer. large type ed. Jane R. Wood. LC 93-38620. 1994. 19.95 (*0-7862-0108-8*) Thorndike Pr.

Dance a While. J. A. Harris. (Ballroom Dance Ser.). 1986. lib. bdg. 79.95 (*0-8490-3349-7*) Gordon Pr.

Dance a While. J. A. Harris. (Ballroom Dance Ser.). 1985. lib. bdg. 79.95 (*0-87700-676-8*) Revisionist Pr.

Dance a While. 6th ed. Jane A. Harris et al. 882p. (C). 1988. pap. write for info. (*0-02-350550-8*) Macmillan.

Dance a While: Handbook for Folk, Square, Contra & Social Dance. 7th ed. Jane A. Harriss et al. 576p. (C). 1994. pap. write for info. (*0-02-350581-8*) Macmillan.

Dance across Texas. Betty Casey. (Illus.). 144p. 1985. pap. 11.95 (*0-292-71551-X*) U of Tex Pr.

Dance Aerobics. Maxine Polley. LC 80-23906. (Illus.). 160p. (Orig.). 1980. pap. 5.95 (*0-89037-186-5*) Anderson World.

Dance Aerobics: Two. Maxine Polley. 160p. 1983. pap. 6.95 (*0-89037-256-X*) Anderson World.

Dance Against Time. Diane Solway. Ed. by Tom Miller. 1994. 23.00 (*0-671-78894-9*) PB.

Dance Analysis: Theory & Practice. Valerie Briginshaw et al. Ed. by Janet Adshead. 200p. (Orig.). 1995. pap. 24.95 (*1-85273-003-X*, Dance Horizons) Princeton Bk Co.

Dance & Be Charming. R. Dengel. (Ballroom Dance Ser.). 1986. lib. bdg. 79.95 (*0-8490-3321-7*) Gordon Pr.

Dance & Be Charming. R. Dengel. (Ballroom Dance Ser.). 1985. lib. bdg. 74.50 (*0-87700-765-9*) Revisionist Pr.

Dance & Brothers: Texas Gunmakers of the Confederacy. Gary Wiggins. Ed. by Stephen W. Sylvia. (Illus.). 152p. 1986. 29.95 (*0-943522-12-9*) Moss Pubns VA.

Dance & Grow: Developmental Dance Activities for Three-Through Eight-Year-Olds. Betty Rowen. LC 93-46039. (Illus.). 122p. (C). 1994. pap. 12.95 (*0-87127-196-6*) Princeton Bk Co.

Dance & Instrumental Diferencias in Spain During the 17th & 18th Centuries Vol. 3: The Notes in Spanish. Maurice Esses. (Dance & Music Ser.: No. 2). 1994. pap. 48.00 (*0-945193-54-8*) Pendragon NY.

Dance & Instrumental Diferencias in Spain During the 17th & 18th Centuries, Vol. 1: History & Background. Maurice Esses. LC 90-6935. (Dance & Music Ser.: No. 2). (Illus.). 900p. (ENG & SPA.). 1993. lib. bdg. 72.00 (*0-945193-08-4*) Pendragon NY.

Dance & Instrumental Diferencias in Spain During the 17th & 18th Centuries, Vol. 2: Musical Transcriptions. Maurice Esses. (Dance & Music Ser.: No. 2). 1994. 64.00 (*0-945193-53-X*) Pendragon NY.

Dance & Movement in the Primary School. S. Slater. 1990. pap. 24.00 (*0-7463-0622-9*, Pub. by Northcote UK) St Mut.

Dance & Music in the Temple Architecture. Choodamani Nandgopal. 1990. 135.00 (*81-7186-000-1*, Pub. by Agam II) S Asia.

Dance & Ritual Play in Greek Religion. Steven H. Lonsdale. LC 93-2787. (Ancient Society & History Ser.). (Illus.). 368p. (C). 1993. text ed. 39.95 (*0-8018-4594-7*) Johns Hopkins.

Dance & Stress: Resistance, Reduction & Euphoria. Judith L. Hanna. Ed. by James H. Humprey. LC 86-82028. (Stress in Modern Society Ser.: No. 13). 1988. 32.50 (*0-404-63264-5*) AMS Pr.

Dance & Technology One: Moving Toward the Future. Ed. by A. William Smith. 67p. (C). 1993. pap. text ed. 11.95 (*1-883034-00-0*) Fullhouse.

Dance & the Body Politic in Northern Greece. Ed. by Jane K. Cowan. (Modern Greek Studies). (Illus.). 310p. (C). 1990. text ed. 49.50 (*0-691-09449-7*); pap. text ed. 15.95 (*0-691-02854-0*) Princeton U Pr.

Dance & the Lived Body. Sondra H. Fraleigh. LC 86-19288. (Illus.). 328p. 1987. 29.95 (*0-8229-3548-1*) U of Pittsburgh Pr.

***Dance & the Lived Body.** Sondra H. Fraleigh. (Illus.). 328p. (C). 1995. pap. 19.95x (*0-8229-5579-2*) U of Pittsburgh Pr.

Dance & the Music of J. S. Bach. Meredith Little & Natalie Jenne. LC 90-42362. (Music: Scholarship & Performance Ser.). (Illus.). 270p. 1991. 39.95 (*0-253-33514-0*) Ind U Pr.

Dance & the Railroad & Family Devotions. David H. Hwang. 1983. pap. 4.75 (*0-8222-0265-4*) Dramatists Play.

Dance & the Specific Image: Improvisation. Daniel Nagrin. (Illus.). 256p. (C). 1993. text ed. 49.95 (*0-8229-3776-X*); pap. text ed. 19.95 (*0-8229-5520-2*) U of Pittsburgh Pr.

Dance Anthology. Ed. by Cobbett Steinberg. (Orig.). 1980. pap. 10.95 (*0-452-25702-6*, Z5233, Plume) NAL-Dutton.

Dance As a Theatre Art: Source Readings in Dance History from 1581 to the Present. 2nd ed. Ed. by Selma J. Cohen & Katy Matheson. (Illus.). 288p. (C). 1991. pap. text ed. 16.95 (*0-87127-173-7*, Dance Horizons) Princeton Bk Co.

Dance As an Element of Life. Barbara Mettler. 1985. 15.00 (*0-912536-12-8*) Mettler Studios.

Dance As Education. Peter Brinson. 1991. 65.00 (*1-85000-716-0*, Falmer Pr); pap. 28.00 (*1-85000-717-9*, Falmer Pr) Taylor & Francis.

Dance As Religious Studies. Ed. by Doug Adams & Diane Apostolos-Cappadona. (Illus.). 256p. (Orig.). 1990. pap. 19.95 (*0-8245-0988-9*) Crossroad NY.

Dance As Text: Ideologies of the Baroque Body. Mark Franko. LC 92-23437. (RES Monographs on Anthropology & Aesthetics). (Illus.). 256p. (C). 1993. 65.00 (*0-521-43392-4*) Cambridge U Pr.

Dance at Grandpa's. Laura Ingalls Wilder. LC 93-24535. (My First Little House Bks.). (Illus.). 40p. (J). (ps-3). 1994. 12.00 (*0-06-023878-X*) HarpC Child Bks.

Dance at Grandpa's. Laura Ingalls Wilder. LC 93-24535. (My First Little House Bks.). (Illus.). 40p. (J). (ps-3). 1994. lib. bdg. 11.89 (*0-06-023879-8*) HarpC Child Bks.

***Dance at St. Gabriel's.** Felix Stefanile. 140p. (Orig.). 1995. pap. text ed. 12.95 (*1-885266-08-1*) Story Line.

Dance at the Slaughterhouse. Lawrence Block. 320p. 1992. mass mkt. 4.99 (*0-380-71374-8*) Avon.

Dance at the Slaughterhouse. Lawrence Block. (Matthew Scudder Mystery Ser.). 304p. 1991. 19.00 (*0-688-10349-9*) Morrow.

Dance Away! George Shannon. LC 81-6391. (Illus.). 32p. (J). (gr. k-3). 1982. 13.95 (*0-688-00838-0*); lib. bdg. 13.88 (*0-688-00839-9*) Greenwillow.

Dance Away. George Shannon. LC 81-6391. (Illus.). 32p. (J). (ps up). 1991. reprint ed. pap. 3.95 (*0-688-10483-5*, Mulberry) Morrow.

Dance-Away Lover. Daniel Goldstine et al. 1986. mass mkt. 4.95 (*0-345-33853-7*) Ballantine.

Dance-Based Theory: From Borrowed Models to Dance-Based Experience. Judith B. Alter. LC 90-23458. (New Studies in Aesthetics: Vol. 7). 196p. (C). 1991. text ed. 38.95 (*0-8204-1532-4*) P Lang Pubs.

Dance Beat: Selected Views & Reviews, 1967-1976. Deborah Jowitt. LC 76-44564. 222p. reprint ed. pap. 63.30 (*0-317-28434-7*, 2017854) Bks Demand.

Dance Choreography for Competitive Gymnastics. Denise A. Gula. LC 89-12685. (Illus.). 176p. 1990. pap. text ed. 19.95x (*0-88011-364-2*, PGUL0364) Human Kinetics.

Dance, Civet Cat: Tonga Children & Labour in the Zambezi Valley. Pamela Reynolds. LC 89-22860. 208p. 1990. text ed. 24.95 (*0-8214-0946-8*) Ohio U Pr.

Dance Class: Ballroom Dance Instruction. Betty Beck. LC 90-91855. (Illus.). 271p. 1991. pap. 20.09 (*0-9627020-0-5*) Dambach Bks.

Dance Classics. Nancy Reynolds & Susan Reimer-Torn. LC 90-27665. (Illus.). 164p. 1991. pap. 14.95 (*1-55652-106-5*) A cappella Bks.

Dance Composition & Production. 2nd ed. Elizabeth R. Hayes. 1993. pap. 16.95 (*0-87127-188-5*, Dance Horizons) Princeton Bk Co.

Dance Curricula Guidelines K-12. Sue Stinson et al. 36p. (Orig.). (C). 1988. pap. text ed. 2.50 (*0-88314-484-0*) Natl Dance Assn.

***Dance Dance Dance.** Haruki Murakami. 1995. pap. 13.00 (*0-679-75379-6*, Vin) Random.

Dance Dance Dance: A Novel. Haruki Murakami. Ed. by Elmer Luke. Tr. by Alfred Birnbaum. LC 93-14098. 384p. 1994. 22.00 (*4-7700-1683-2*) Kodansha.

Dance, Daphne, Dance. rev. ed. Ginny McCusker. 1995. 7.95 (*0-8062-4916-1*) Carlton.

Dance Dialects of India. Ragini Devi. (C). 1990. reprint ed. 75.00 (*81-208-0674-3*, Pub. by Motilal Banarsidass II) S Asia.

Dance, Dialogue & Despair: Existentialist Philosophy & Education for Peace in Israel. Haim Gordon. LC 85-1113. (Judaic Studies). 272p. 1986. 29.50 (*0-8173-0270-0*) U of Ala Pr.

1780 An Asterisk (*) at the beginning of an entry indicates that the title is appearing in BIP for the first time.

An Asterisk (*) at the beginning of an entry indicates that the title is appearing in BIP for the first time.

1781

D

Dance of the Seven Veals: And Other Cartoons. Kevin Pope. 1991. pap. 7.95 (*0-312-05828-4*) St Martin.

Dance of the Sleepwalkers: The Dance Marathon Fad. Frank M. Calabria. LC 92-73976. 1993. lib. bdg. 39.95 (*0-87972-569-9*) Bowling Green Univ.

Dance of the Spirit: The Seven Steps of Women's Spirituality. Maria Harris. 1991. pap. 11.95 (*0-553-35306-3*) Bantam.

***Dance of the Tiger: A Novel of the Ice Age.** Bjorn Kurten. LC 95-2292. (ENG & SWE.). 1995. pap. 10.95 (*0-520-20277-5*) U CA Pr.

Dance of the Twelve Apostles. Ed. by A. Caso. (Illus.). 274p. 1991. text ed. 17.95 (*0-8283-1935-9*) Branden Pub Co.

Dance of the Wild Mouse. Daniel Panger. LC 79-51409. 240p. (C). 1979. 9.95 (*0-9601428-4-3*); pap. 7.95 (*0-9601428-5-1*) Entwhistle Bks.

Dance of the Wolves. Roger Peters. 208p. 1986. pap. 3.95 (*0-345-32870-1*) Ballantine.

***Dance on a Sealskin.** Winslow. 1995. 15.95 (*0-88240-443-1*) Alaska Northwest.

***Dance on My Grave.** Aidan Chambers. LC 82-48258. 256p. (YA). (gr. 7 up). 1995. pap. 5.95 (*0-06-440579-6*, Trophy) HarpC Child Bks.

Dance on the Ancient Greek Theatre. Lillian B. Lawler. LC 64-65259. (University of Iowa Monographs). 143p. reprint ed. pap. 40.80 (*0-317-42125-5*, 2025942) Bks Demand.

***Dance on the Wind.** Terry C. Johnston. LC 95-7558. 528p. 1995. 21.95 (*0-553-09071-2*) Bantam.

Dance Out the Answer: An Autobiography. Russell M. Hughes. LC 77-20139. (Dance Program Ser.: No. 7). (Illus.). 224p. reprint ed. pap. 63.90 (*0-7837-0630-8*, 2040974) Bks Demand.

Dance Poems. Lyn Lifshin. (Dialogues on Dance Ser.: No. 7). 1986. pap. 6.00 (*0-941240-05-3*) Ommation Pr.

Dance Quest in Celebes. Claire Holt. LC 77-86962. (Illus.). reprint ed. 28.00 (*0-404-16727-6*) AMS Pr.

Dance Rhythms of the French Baroque: A Handbook for Performance. Betty B. Mather & Dean M. Karns. LC 86-45991. (Music: Scholarship & Performance Ser.). (Illus.). 352p. 1988. 39.95 (*0-253-31606-5*) Ind U Pr.

Dance Series, 20 bks., Set. 1980. lib. bdg. 634.00 (*0-8369-9275-X*) Ayer.

Dance, Sex, & Gender: Signs of Identity, Dominance, Defiance, & Desire. Judith L. Hanna. (Illus.). xx, 312p. 1988. pap. text ed. 15.95 (*0-226-31551-7*) U Ch Pr.

Dance, Snake! Dance! Pampatti. Tr. by David C. Buck. 12.00 (*0-89253-797-3*); 8.00 (*0-89253-798-1*) Ind-US Inc.

Dance Studio: Business Managing for Aerobics, Dance, & Gymnastics Teachers. Marie Zima. LC 87-42526. 148p. 1987. pap. 21.95x (*0-89950-263-6*) McFarland & Co.

Dance, Tanya. Patricia L. Gauch. (Illus.). 32p. (J). (ps-3). 1989. 13.95 (*0-399-21521-2*, Philomel Bks) Putnam Pub Group.

Dance, Tanya: Mini Book & Doll Set. Patricia L. Gauch. (Illus.). 32p. (J). (ps). 1994. pap. 20.95 (*0-399-22795-4*, Philomel Bks) Putnam Pub Group.

Dance Technique & Injury Prevention. Justin Howse et al. 216p. 1988. 29.95 (*0-87830-985-3*, Theatre Arts Bks) Routledge Chapman & Hall.

Dance Technique for Children. Mary Joyce. (Illus.). 191p. (Orig.). 1984. pap. text ed. 20.95 (*0-87484-581-5*) Mayfield Pub.

Dance Technique of Doris Humphrey & Its Creative Potential. 2nd ed. Ernestine Stodelle. LC 90-53349. 272p. 1990. pap. 21.95 (*0-87127-154-0*, Dance Horizons) Princeton Bk Co.

Dance Technique of Lester Horton. Marjorie Perces et al. (Illus.). 256p. (Orig.). 1992. pap. 24.95 (*0-87127-164-8*, Dance Horizons) Princeton Bk Co.

Dance Techniques & Injury Prevention. rev. ed. Justin Howse. 1992. 35.00 (*0-87830-022-8*, Theatre Arts Bks) Routledge Chapman & Hall.

Dance Technology. 1989. 24.00 (*0-88314-429-8*) AAHPERD.

***Dance Terminology Notebook: Advancing Communication in the 90's.** Skippy Blair. (Illus.). 113p. (Orig.). 1994. ring bd. 35.00 (*0-932980-11-2*) Golden St Dance Teach Assn.

Dance the Eagle to Sleep. Marge Piercy. 224p. 1982. pap. 3.95 (*0-449-20114-7*, Crest) Fawcett.

Dance Theatre of Jean Cocteau. Frank W. Ries. LC 85-19078. (Theater & Dramatic Studies: No. 33). 260p. reprint ed. pap. 74.10 (*0-8357-1994-4*, 2070661) Bks Demand.

Dance Therapy: Narrative Case Histories of Therapy Sessions with Six Patients. Helene Lefco. LC 73-88511. 158p. 1974. 28.95 (*0-911012-93-1*) Nelson-Hall.

Dance Therapy: Theory & Application. Liljan Espenak. (Illus.). 210p. 1981. 34.95x (*0-398-04110-5*) C C Thomas.

Dance Therapy & Depth Psychology: The Moving Imagination. Joan Chodorow. 192p. 1991. 55.00 (*0-415-05301-3*, A5107); pap. 16.95 (*0-415-04113-9*, A5111) Routledge.

Dance Therapy Redefined: A Body Approach to Therapeutic Dance. Johanna Exiner & Denis Kelynak. LC 94-8556. (Illus.). 130p. (C). 1994. text ed. 35.95x (*0-398-05913-6*) C C Thomas.

Dance Till You Die. Carolyn Keene. Ed. by Ruth Ashby. (Nancy Drew Files Ser.: No. 100). 160p. (Orig.). (J). 1994. mass mkt. 3.99 (*0-671-79492-2*, Archway) PB.

Dance to a Dolphin's Song. Horace Dobbs. (Illus.). 192p. 1992. pap. 17.95 (*0-224-03076-0*, Pub. by Jonathan Cape UK) Trafalgar.

Dance to the Fiddle-March to the Fife: Instrumental Folk Tunes in Pennsylvania. Samuel P. Bayard. LC 81-83146. 656p. (C). 1982. 32.50 (*0-271-00299-9*) Pa St U Pr.

***Dance to the Music of Time: All Four Movements, 4 vols.** Anthony Powell. Incl. Second Movement. 724p. 1995. pap. 17.95 (*0-226-67716-8*); Third Movement. 734p. 1995. pap. 17.95 (*0-226-67717-6*); Fourth Movement. 792p. 1995. pap. 18.95 (*0-226-67718-4*); First Movement. LC 94-47228. 728p. 1995. pap. 17.95 (*0-226-67714-1*); 1995. Set pap. 72.80 (*0-226-67719-2*) U Ch Pr.

Dance to the Music of Time: First Movement. Anthony Powell. Incl. Question of Upbringing. 1962. (*0-318-54087-8*); Buyer's Market. 1962. (*0-318-54088-6*); Acceptance World. 1962. (*0-318-54089-4*); 1962. 24.95 (*0-316-71535-2*) Little.

Dance to the Music of Time: Third Movement. Anthony Powell. Incl. Valley of Bones. 1971. (*0-318-54093-2*); Soldier's Art. 1971. (*0-318-54094-0*); Military Philosophers. 1971. (*0-318-54095-9*); 1971. 24.95 (*0-316-71546-8*) Little.

***Dance to the Piper.** Nora Roberts. 1994. pap. 4.99 (*1-55166-007-5*, 1-66007-5, Mira Bks) Harlequin Bks.

Dance to the Piper. Anne Stuart et al. 1995. mass mkt. 4.99 (*0-373-48312-0*, 1-48312-2) Harlequin Bks.

Dance to the Piper. Intro. by Agnes De Mille & Cynthia Gregory. LC 79-28689. (Series in Dance). (Illus.). 342p. 1980. reprint ed. lib. bdg. 29.50 (*0-306-79613-9*) Da Capo.

Dance to the Piper, Set. Intro. by Agnes De Mille & Cynthia Gregory. LC 79-28689. (Series in Dance). (Illus.). 342p. 1980. reprint ed. 49.50 (*0-306-79615-5*) Da Capo.

Dance to the Piper & Promenade Home: A Two-Part Autobiography. Agnes De Mille. (Quality Paperbacks Ser.). (Illus.). xii, 643p. 1982. reprint ed. pap. 10.95 (*0-306-80161-2*) Da Capo.

Dance Training for Gymnastics. Rae Pica. LC 87-31862. (Illus.). 160p. (C). 1988. text ed. 25.00x (*0-88011-306-5*, PPIC0306) Human Kinetics.

Dance We Must. Ted Shawn. LC 74-28011. (Studies in Music: No. 42). 1974. lib. bdg. 75.00 (*0-8383-2032-5*) M S G Haskell Hse.

Dance While You Can. Susan Lewis. 1991. mass mkt. 4.99 (*0-06-109933-3*, Harp PBks) HarpC.

Dance While You Can. Shirley MacLaine. 1992. mass mkt. 5.99 (*0-553-29786-4*) Bantam.

Dance While You Can. large type ed. Shirley MacLaine. LC 92-34910. (General Ser.). 386p. 1993. pap. 16.95 (*0-8161-5638-7*) G K Hall.

Dance with a Shadow. Irina Ratushinskaya. Tr. by David McDuff. 77p. 1993. 25.00 (*1-85224-232-9*, Pub. by Bloodaxe Bks UK); pap. 13.95 (*1-85224-233-7*, Pub. by Bloodaxe Bks UK) Dufour.

Dance with Community: The Contemporary Debate in American Political Thought. Robert B. Fowler. LC 90-23001. (American Political Thought Ser.). xii, 212p. 1991. 22.50 (*0-7006-0493-6*); pap. 12.95 (*0-7006-0623-8*) U Pr of KS.

Dance with Death: Soviet Airwomen in World War II. Anne Noggle. LC 94-1301. (Illus.). 400p. 1994. 29.95 (*0-89096-601-X*) Tex A&M Univ Pr.

Dance with Deception: Reading Between the Headlines. Charles W. Colson & Nancy R. Pearcey. LC 93-5322. 1993. 15.99 (*0-8499-1057-9*) Word Inc.

Dance with God. W. Norman Cooper. LC 81-69932. 128p. (Orig.). 1982. 7.50 (*0-87516-491-9*); pap. 4.50 (*0-87516-468-4*) DeVorss.

Dance with Me. Barbara J. Esbensen. LC 93-48442. (Illus.). 32p. (J). (gr. 2-5). 1995. 14.95 (*0-06-022793-1*, HarpT); lib. bdg. 14.89 (*0-06-022823-7*, HarpT) HarpC Child Bks.

***Dance with Me.** Ron Hirschi. LC 94-48531. (Illus.). (J). 1995. 14.99 (*0-525-65204-3*, Cobblehill Bks) Dutton Child Bks.

Dance with Me. large type ed. Sophie Weston. 1993. 17.95 (*0-263-13416-4*, Pub. by Mills & Boon Ltd UK) Chivers N Amer.

Dance with the Devil. Kirk Douglas. LC 94-13168. 554p. 1994. 21.95 (*0-8161-7464-4*) Hall.

Dance with the Devil. Kirk Douglas. LC 89-43423. 320p. 1990. 19.95 (*0-394-58237-3*) Random.

Dance with the Devil. Kirk Douglas. 384p. 1991. mass mkt. 5.99 (*0-446-36191-7*) Warner Bks.

***Dance with the Devil.** Hall. 1994. pap. 3.67 (*0-8161-2082-X*) G K Hall.

Dance with the Devil. Aleece Jacques. 320p. (Orig.). 1981. pap. 2.50 (*0-8439-0981-1*) Dorchester Pub Co.

Dance Workshop: A Guide to the Fundamentals of Movement. Robert Cohan. 192p. 1986. pap. 10.95 (*0-671-61280-8*, Fireside) S&S Trade.

Dance Writing for Classical Ballet. Valerie J. Sutton. (Illus.). 153p. (C). 1979. audio 75.00 (*0-914336-05-3*) Ctr Sutton Movement.

Dance Writing for Modern & Jazz Dance. Valerie J. Sutton. (Illus.). 244p. 1979. 20.00 (*0-914336-10-X*) Ctr Sutton Movement.

Dance Writing Shorthand for Classical Ballet. Valerie J. Sutton. 58p. 1981. pap. text ed. 10.00 (*0-914336-08-8*) Ctr Sutton Movement.

Dance Writing Shorthand for Modern & Jazz Dance. Valerie J. Sutton. 1982. pap. text ed. 10.00 (*0-914336-09-6*) Ctr Sutton Movement.

Dance Writings. Edwin Denby. Ed. by Robert Cornfield & William Mackay. 1986. 40.00 (*0-394-54416-1*) Knopf.

Dancehall. Conners. 1983. 14.95 (*0-02-527490-2*) Macmillan.

Dancehall. Bernard F. Conners. pap. 5.95 (*0-945167-49-0*) British Amer Pub.

Dancer. Fred Burstein. LC 91-41429. (Illus.). 40p. (J). (ps-3). 1993. text ed. 14.95 (*0-02-715625-7*, Bradbury S&S) S&S Childrens.

***Dancer.** Thomas Woolfolk, Jr. Ed. by Jancie B. Hughes. (Orig.). (YA). (gr. 8-12). 1994. pap. 12.00 (*1-886089-00-0*) Woolfolk Pubns.

Dancer: One Woman's Journey from Tragedy to Triumph. Susan Lee. 128p. (Orig.). 1991. pap. 7.99 (*0-8010-5671-3*) Baker Bk.

Dancer & the Dance: Merce Cunningham in Conversation with Jacqueline Lesschaeve. Merce Cunningham. (Illus.). 256p. 1991. reprint ed. pap. 18.00 (*0-7145-2931-1*) M Boyars Pubs.

Dancer & the Ring. M. P. Bhaskaran. 8.00 (*0-89253-459-1*); 4.00 (*0-89253-460-5*) Ind-US Inc.

Dancer as Athlete. Ed. by Caroline G. Shell. LC 85-18119. 256p. (C). 1986. text ed. 36.00x (*0-87322-016-1*, BSHE0016) Human Kinetics.

***Dancer at the Waterfall.** Jonathan London. LC 94-24575. 1995. write for info. (*0-688-13929-9*); lib. bdg. write for info. (*0-688-13930-2*) Lothrop.

Dancer Dawkins & the California Kid. Willyce Kim. 140p. (Orig.). 1985. pap. 5.95 (*0-932870-59-7*) Alyson Pubns.

Dancer from the Dance. Andrew Holleran. 252p. 1986. pap. 10.95 (*0-452-26129-5*, Plume) NAL-Dutton.

Dancer in Relief: Works by Malvina Hoffman. Janis C. Conner. (Illus.). 40p. (Orig.). 1984. pap. 2.00 (*0-943651-15-8*) Hudson Riv.

Dancer Prepares: Modern Dance for Beginners. 3rd ed. James Penrod & Janice G. Plastino. 94p. (C). 1990. pap. text ed. 11.95 (*0-87484-924-1*) Mayfield Pub.

Dancer Quartet. Lacey Dancer. 224p. (Orig.). 1992. pap. 11.80 (*1-56597-750-5*, Kismet) Meteor Pub.

Dancer Takes Flight: Psychological Concerns in the Development of the American Male Dancer. William L. Earl. LC 88-5445. 180p. (Orig.). (C). 1988. pap. text ed. 19.00 (*0-8191-6948-X*) U Pr of Amer.

Dancer to God: Tributes to T. S. Eliot. Ted Hughes. 1993. 16.00 (*0-374-13462-6*) FS&G.

Dancer with Bruised Knees. Lynne McFall. 224p. 1994. 18.95 (*0-8118-0787-8*) Chronicle Bks.

Danceries, Premier Volume see Maitres Musiciens de la Renaissance Francaise

Dancers. Laura Conlon. LC 94-12387. (Performers Discovery Library). (J). 1994. write for info. (*1-57103-064-6*) Rourke Pr.

Dancers. Mark Dunster. (Rin Ser.: Pt. 18). 36p. (Orig.). 1986. pap. 4.00 (*0-89642-133-3*) Linden Pubs.

Dancers. Peggy Roalf. LC 91-73827. (Looking at Paintings Ser.). (Illus.). 48p. (J). (gr. 3-7). 1992. lib. bdg. 14.89 (*1-56282-090-7*); pap. 6.95 (*1-56282-089-3*) Hyprn Child.

Dancers: Eight Stories about the Dance. Ed. by Effie Mihopoulos. 1986. 4.00 (*0-941240-08-8*) Ommation Pr.

Dancers: Photographs by Annie Leibovitz. Ed. by Constance Sullivan. LC 92-12046. (Photographers at Work Ser.). (Illus.). 60p. (Orig.). 1992. pap. 15.95 (*1-56098-208-X*) Smithsonian.

Dancers: Photographs by Philip Trager. Philip Trager. (Illus.). 160p. 1992. 75.00 (*0-8212-1894-8*) Bulfinch Pr.

Dancers & Choreographers: A Selected Bibliography. Leslie Getz. LC 94-12129. 320p. 1995. 29.95 (*1-55921-108-3*); pap. 14.95 (*1-55921-109-1*) Moyer Bell.

Dancers & the Dance. Summer Brenner. LC 90-30312. 144p. (Orig.). (YA). 1990. pap. 9.95 (*0-918273-75-7*) Coffee Hse.

Dancers' Body Book. Allegra Kent et al. LC 83-17732. (Illus.). 1984. pap. 12.00 (*0-688-01539-5*, Quill) Morrow.

Dancer's Book of Health. Larry M. Vincent. LC 78-7523. (Illus.). 152p. (C). 1988. reprint ed. pap. 12.95 (*0-916622-67-3*) Princeton Bk Co.

Dancer's Complete Guide to Healthcare & a Long Career. Allan Ryan & Robert E. Stephens. 224p. 1988. pap. 9.95 (*0-933893-76-0*) Bonus Books.

Dancer's Foot Book. Terry L. Spilken. LC 89-64299. (Illus.). 152p. 1990. pap. 14.95 (*0-916622-96-7*) Princeton Bk Co.

Dancer's Glancer: A Quick Guide to Labanotation (the Method of Recording All Movement) Ann H. Guest. LC 92-7682. 1992. pap. text ed. 12.00 (*2-88124-863-2*) Gordon & Breach.

Dancer's Guide to Injuries of the Lower Extremity: Diagnosis, Treatment, & Care. Stuart Wright. LC 84-45008. (Illus.). 224p. 1985. 18.95 (*0-8453-4782-9*, Cornwall Bks) Assoc Univ Prs.

Dancers Guide to the Nineteen Eighties. F. Borrows. (Ballroom Dance Ser.). 1985. lib. bdg. 250.00 (*0-87700-862-0*) Revisionist Pr.

Dancer's Guide to the Nineteen Eighties. F. Borrows. (Ballroom Dance Ser.). 1986. lib. bdg. 250.00 (*0-8490-3300-4*) Gordon Pr.

Dancers II: Eight Stories about the Dance. Ed. by Effie Mihopoulos. (Dialogues on Dance Ser.: No. 8). 70p. 1987. 6.00 (*0-941240-10-X*) Ommation Pr.

Dancers in Mourning. Margery Allingham. 20.95 (*1-56723-006-7*) Yestermorrow.

Dancers in Mourning. Margery Allingham. 240p. 1993. reprint ed. lib. bdg. 19.95 (*0-89190-189-2*, Am Repr) Amereon Ltd.

Dancers in the Garden. Joanne Ryder. LC 89-10555. (Illus.). 32p. (J). (gr. k-4). 1992. 15.95 (*0-87156-578-1*) Sierra.

Dancers in the Garden. Joanne Ryder. (Illus.). 32p. (J). (gr. k-4). 1994. pap. 5.95 (*0-87156-410-6*) Sierra.

Dancers in the Scalp House. William Eastlake. 245p. reprint ed. pap. 10.00 (*0-917453-19-0*) Bamberger.

***Dancers in the Scalp House: A Novel.** William Eastlake. 245p. 1994. lib. bdg. 27.00 (*0-8095-6513-7*) Borgo Pr.

Dancer's Muse. Karren L. Alenier. (Dialogues on Dance Ser.: No. 2). (Illus.). 25p. (Orig.). 1981. pap. 5.95 (*0-915380-12-9*) Ommation Pr.

Dancers of Don. Ewan Forbes. 80p. 1990. pap. 9.95 (*0-08-037959-1*, 6202, Pub. by Aberdeen U Pr) Macmillan.

Dancers on Horseback: The Perry-Mansfield Story. Lucile Bogue. (Illus.). 256p. (Orig.). 1984. pap. 9.95 (*0-89407-058-4*) Strawberry Hill.

Dancers on the Shore. William M. Kelley. (Howard University Press Library of Contemporary Literature). 201p. 1984. pap. 9.95 (*0-88258-114-7*) Howard U Pr.

Dancer's Progress & Schrodinger's Cat. Marvin Albert. 93p. 1993. 20.00 (*0-9634859-0-3*); pap. 11.95 (*0-9634859-1-1*) Alex Pr & Print.

Dancer's Rise. Jo Clayton. (Dancer Trilogy Ser.: Bk. 1). 368p. (Orig.). 1993. mass mkt. 4.99 (*0-88677-567-1*) DAW Bks.

Dancer's Scrapbook. Serge Leslie. (Illus.). 256p. 1987. 34.95 (*1-85273-001-3*) Princeton Bk Co.

Dances & Stories of the American Indian. Bernard S. Mason. LC 44-516. (Illus.). 280p. reprint ed. pap. 79.80 (*0-8357-9871-2*, 2013407) Bks Demand.

Dances by Mark Morris. Tom Brazil. (Orig.). 1993. pap. 15.00 (*0-685-67272-7*) Dance Res Found.

Dances for Piano Solo: Sonatas and Other Works for Four-Hands and Two Pianos. J. N. Hummel. Ed. by Joel Sachs. (J. N. Hummel: The Complete Works for Piano Ser.). 384p. 1989. reprint ed. 135.00 (*0-8240-3790-1*) Garland.

Dances from Norway. Daniel E. Beal. (Illus.). 192p. (Orig.). 1988. pap. text ed. 14.95 (*0-317-91222-4*) D E Beal.

Dances of Asia. Kiitsu Sakakibara. (Illus.). 218p. 1992. 59.00 (*0-685-63255-5*, Pub. by Abhishek Pubns II) Nataraj Bks.

Dances of England & France from 1450-1600: With Their Music & Authentic Manner of Performance. Mabel Dolmetsch. LC 74-34449. (Series in Dance). (Illus.). xii, 163p. 1975. reprint ed. lib. bdg. 25.00 (*0-306-70725-X*); reprint ed. pap. 11.95 (*0-306-80025-X*) Da Capo.

Dances of Haiti. Katherine Dunham. (Special Publications: Vol. 2). (Illus.). 78p. 1983. pap. 10.50 (*0-934934-11-8*) UCLA CAAS.

Dances of India. Ragini Devi. LC 79-7751. (Dance Ser.). 1980. reprint ed. lib. bdg. 18.95 (*0-8369-9282-2*) Ayer.

Dances of India: A General Guide & a Users' Handbook. Reginald Massey & Jamila Massey. (Illus.). xix, 164p. 1992. 20.00 (*0-317-05152-0*); pap. 13.00 (*0-948725-05-2*) Asia Pub Hse.

Dances of Spain & Italy from 1400 to 1600. Mabel Dolmetsch. LC 74-28450. (Series in Dance). (Illus.). xii, 174p. 1975. reprint ed. lib. bdg. 25.00 (*0-306-70726-8*) Da Capo.

Dances of the Hungarians. Elizabeth C. Rearick. LC 72-177181. (Columbia University. Teachers College. Contributions to Education Ser.: No. 770). reprint ed. 37.50 (*0-404-55770-8*) AMS Pr.

Dances That Come Alive! Jerry D. Poppen. (Illus.). 213p. (Orig.). (C). 1993. pap. 21.50 (*0-9608868-5-0*) Action Prods.

***Dances with Blackflies: Funny Stories about Life in Maine & Life in General.** Stephen R. Bull. 150p. 1994. pap. text ed. 9.95 (*0-9644753-0-8*) Mt Blue Pub.

Dances with Dali. Paul Mariah. Date not set. 6.00 (*0-317-05628-X*) Man-Root.

Dances with Deception. Charles Colson. 1993. pap. 12.99 (*0-8499-3521-0*) Word Inc.

Dances with Trout. John Geirach. 1994. 21.00 (*0-671-77924-9*) S&S Trade.

***Dances with Trout.** John Gierach. 1995. pap. 11.00 (*0-671-77920-6*) S&S Trade.

Dances with Wolves. Michael Blake. 1988. mass mkt. 5.95 (*0-449-13448-2*, GM) Fawcett.

Dances with Wolves. Michael Blake. LC 90-27061. 336p. 1991. 18.95 (*1-55704-091-5*) Newmarket.

Dances with Wolves: (Original Motion Picture Soundtrack) (Piano Solos Ser.). (Illus.). 56p. (Orig.). 1991. pap. 14.95 (*0-7935-0376-0*, 00308093) H Leonard.

Dances with Wolves: The Illustrated Story of the Epic Film. Kevin Costner et al. LC 91-20284. (Illus.). 160p. (Orig.). 1990. 29.95 (*1-55704-101-6*); pap. 16.95 (*1-55704-088-5*) Newmarket.

Dances with Wolves: The Illustrated Story of the Epic Film. abr. ed. Kevin Costner. (Orig.). 1991. pap. 4.95 (*1-55704-105-9*) Newmarket.

Dances with Wolves Storybook: A Story for Children. Adapt. by James Howe. LC 91-20283. (Illus.). 64p. (J). (ps-2). 1991. bds. 14.95 (*1-55704-104-0*) Newmarket.

Dancin' Machine. Greg Scelsa & Steve Millang. (Greg & Steve Ser.). (Illus.). 24p. (J). (ps-1). 1992. audio 9.95 (*0-679-82378-6*) Random Bks Yng Read.

Dancin' Nekkid with the Angels. Howard Cruse. Ed. by Michael Denenny. LC 87-13040. (Illus.). 104p. 1987. 25.00 (*0-87816-028-0*) Kitchen Sink.

Dancin' Nekkid with the Angels. Howard Cruse. (Illus.). 112p. 1987. pap. 9.95 (*0-312-01104-0*) St Martin.

Dancin' with Country. Ed. by Milton Okun. 1994. pap. 9.95 (*0-89524-818-2*) Cherry Lane.

Dancing. Donna Bailey. LC 90-23057. (Sports World Ser.). (Illus.). 32p. (J). (gr. 1-4). 1991. lib. bdg. 19.97 (*0-8114-2902-4*); pap. 3.95 (*0-8114-4707-3*) Raintree Steck-V.

***Dancing.** Denys Cazet. LC 94-45920. (Illus.). 32p. (J). (ps-1). 1995. 15.95 (*0-531-09466-9*); lib. bdg. 15.99 (*0-531-08766-2*) Orchard Bks Watts.

Dancing. Gerald Jonas. (Illus.). 256p. 1992. 45.00 (*0-8109-3212-1*) Abrams.

Dancing. M. Wilson. (Ballroom Dance Ser.). 1986. lib. bdg. 79.95 (*0-8490-3378-0*) Gordon Pr.

Dancing. M. Wilson. (Ballroom Dance Ser.). 1985. lib. bdg. 65.00 (*0-87700-710-1*) Revisionist Pr.

Dancing: A Guide for the Dancer You Can Be. 5th ed. Ellen Jacob. (Illus.). 350p. reprint ed. pap. 15.95 (*0-937180-00-9*) Variety Arts.

An Asterisk (*) at the beginning of an entry indicates that the title is appearing in BIP for the first time.

An Asterisk (*) at the beginning of an entry indicates that the title is appearing in BIP for the first time.

Dancing Tales. D. Allen. (Shorey Historical Ser.). 95p. reprint ed. pap. 3.95 (*0-8466-0287-3*, S287) Shorey.

Dancing Teepees: Poems of American Indian Youth. Ed. by Virginia H. Sneve. LC 88-11075. (Illus.). 32p. (J). (ps-4). 1989. lib. bdg. 15.95 (*0-8234-0724-1*) Holiday.

Dancing Teepees: Poems of American Indian Youth. Illus. by Stephen Gammell. LC 88-11075. 32p. (J). (ps-4). 1991. reprint ed. pap. 5.95 (*0-8234-0879-5*) Holiday.

Dancing the Box Step. Kent R. Brown. 1994. 4.95 (*0-87129-333-1*, D58) Dramatic Pub.

***Dancing the Breeze.** Shannon. Date not set. pap. 4.99 (*0-517-13339-3*) Random.

***Dancing the Code.** Paul Leonard. (Dr. Who Ser.). (Illus.). Date not set. pap. 5.95 (*0-426-20441-7*, London Bridge) Genl Dist Srvs.

Dancing the Fault. Judith Minty. (University of Central Florida Contemporary Poetry Ser.). 86p. 1991. lib. bdg. 18.95 (*0-8130-1079-9*); pap. 10.95 (*0-8130-1080-2*) U Press Fla.

Dancing the New Testament: A Guide to Texts. Hal Taussig. 1977. 3.00 (*0-941500-06-3*) Sharing Co.

Dancing the Old Testament: Christian Celebrations of Israelite Heritage for Worship & Education. Constance L. Fisher. Ed. by Doug Adams. (Illus.). 1980. pap. 8.95 (*0-941500-07-1*) Sharing Co.

Dancing the Wheel of Psychological Types. Mary E. Loomis. (Illus.). 128p. (Orig.). 1991. pap. 14.95 (*0-933029-49-7*) Chiron Pubns.

Dancing Through Airth. Leif Anderson. (Illus.). 50p. 1986. pap. 15.00 (*0-9616720-0-5*) Airth Pubns.

Dancing Through History. Joan Cass. 368p. 1993. pap. text ed. 29.00 (*0-13-204389-0*) P-H.

***Dancing Through Life.** Theresa Hoskin. Ed. by Debra L. Nesbit. (Illus.). 78p. 1994. pap. 9.95 (*1-878398-06-7*) Blue Note Pubns.

Dancing Through Life in a Pair of Broken Heels. Mickey Guisewite. 1994. pap. 9.95 (*0-553-37377-3*) Bantam.

Dancing Through Pentecost: Dance Language for Worship from Pentecost to Thanksgiving. Marian B. MacLeod. Ed. by Doug Adams. (Orig.). 1981. pap. 3.00 (*0-941500-23-3*) Sharing Co.

Dancing Through the Defense. S. S. Gorman. Ed. by Patricia MacDonald. (High-Fives Ser.). 144p. (J). 1992. pap. 2.99 (*0-671-74504-2*, Minstrel Bks) PB.

Dancing till Dawn: A Century of Exhibition Ballroom Dance. Julie Malnig. LC 91-33482. (Contributions to the Study of Music & Dance Ser.: No. 25). 192p. 1992. text ed. 45.00 (*0-313-27647-1*, MND, Greenwood Pr) Greenwood.

***Dancing Till Dawn: A Century of Exhibition Ballroom Dance.** Julie Malnig. (Illus.). 174p. 1995. pap. 15.95 (*0-8147-5528-3*) NYU Pr.

Dancing to a Black Man's Tune: A Life of Scott Joplin. Susan Curtis. LC 93-46116. (Missouri Biography Ser.). (Illus.). 288p. (C). 1994. 26.95 (*0-8262-0949-1*) U of Mo Pr.

Dancing to America. Ann Morris. (Illus.). 40p. (J). (gr. 2-7). 1994. 15.99 (*0-525-45128-5*) Dutton Child Bks.

Dancing to Learn, Learning to Dance. M. Lowden. 1989. 70.00 (*1-85000-618-0*); pap. 33.00 (*1-85000-619-9*) Taylor & Francis.

Dancing to Pay the Light Bill: Essays on New Mexico & the Southwest. Jim Sagel. LC 91-61531. (Illus.). 160p. 1992. pap. 9.95 (*1-878610-10-4*) Red Crane Bks.

Dancing to the End of the Shining Bar. Whitney Scott. LC 93-86798. 160p. (Orig.). 1994. pap. 9.95 (*0-9621039-2-6*) Outrider Pr.

***Dancing Tree.** Ramon R. Ross. LC 95-2124. (J). 1995. 15.00 (*0-689-80072-X*, Atheneum S&S) S&S Trade.

***Dancing up the Moon: A Woman's Guide to Creating Traditions That Bring Sacredness to Daily Life.** Robin H. Lysne. 256p. (Orig.). 1995. pap. 12.95 (*0-943233-85-2*) Conari Press.

***Dancing up the Moon: A Woman's Guide to Creating Traditions That Bring Sacredness to Daily Life.** Robin H. Lysne. 256p. 1995. lib. bdg. 33.00 (*0-8095-5890-4*) Borgo Pr.

Dancing Voices: Wisdom of the American Indian. Ed. by Rex L. Jim. (Gift Editions Ser.). (Illus.). 64p. 1994. 7.99 (*0-88088-447-9*) Peter Pauper.

***Dancing Willows.** large type ed. Nan Maynard. 384p. 1995. 23.95 (*0-7089-3360-2*) Ulverscroft.

Dancing with a Ghost: Exploring Indian Reality. Rupert Ross. 1992. 22.95 (*0-409-90648-4*, Pub. by Buttrwrth Can Acad CN) Buttrwrth-Heinemann.

***Dancing with a Shadow: Making Sense of God's Silence.** Dan A. Schaeffer. LC 94-43711. 160p. (Orig.). 1995. pap. 10.99 (*0-929239-73-3*) Discovery Hse Pubs.

***Dancing with Cancer: A Healing Through Visualization.** Robert E. Elliott. 140p. 1995. pap. 9.95 (*1-886597-01-4*) Noteman Pr.

Dancing with Clara. Mary Balogh. (Regency Romance Ser.). 224p. (Orig.). 1994. pap. 3.99 (*0-451-17873-4*, Sig) NAL-Dutton.

Dancing with Clara. Mary Balogh. 224p. (Orig.). 1993. 20.00 (*0-7278-4543-8*) Severn Hse.

Dancing with Creation. Martha A. Kirk. LC 83-6145. 1983. pap. 7.95 (*0-89390-042-7*) Resource Pubns.

Dancing with Death: Life & Death in Southern Crete C. 3000-2000 BC. Keith Branigan. x, 159p. 1993. pap. 36.00 (*90-256-1032-3*, Pub. by A M Hakkert NE) Benjamins North Am.

Dancing with Demons: The Music's Real Master. Jeff Godwin. LC 88-90860. (Illus.). 352p. (Orig.). (YA). (gr. 7-12). 1988. pap. 11.50 (*0-937958-28-X*) Chick Pubns.

Dancing with Dinosaurs: Ministry in a Hostile & Hurting Church. William M. Easum. LC 93-4029. 144p. (Orig.). 1993. pap. 11.95 (*0-687-31679-0*) Abingdon.

Dancing with Dragons: Invoke Their Ageless Wisdom & Power. D. J. Conway. LC 94-28370. (Illus.). 288p. 1994. pap. 14.95 (*1-56718-165-1*) Llewellyn Pubns.

Dancing with Early Christians. Constance Fisher & Doug Adams. (Illus.). 176p. 1983. pap. 9.95 (*0-941500-30-6*) Sharing Co.

Dancing with Goddesses: Archetypes, Poetry, & Empowerment. Annis Pratt. LC 93-28442. 1994. 39.95 (*0-253-34586-3*); pap. 17.95 (*0-253-20865-3*) Ind U Pr.

Dancing with Lawyers: How to Take Charge & Get Results. Nicholas Carroll. LC 90-64419. 192p. 1992. 19.95 (*1-879435-03-9*) Royce-Baker Pub.

Dancing with Manatees. Faith McNulty. LC 93-7593. (Hello Reader! Ser.: Level 4). (Illus.). 48p. (J). (ps-4). 1994. pap. 2.95 (*0-590-46401-9*) Scholastic Inc.

***Dancing with My Soul.** Claude O. Budhoo. Ed. by Rodney Charles. 200p. (Orig.). 1995. pap. 16.95 (*0-9638502-8-8*) Sunstar Pubng.

Dancing with Myself. Charles Sheffield. 320p. (Orig.). 1993. mass mkt. 4.99 (*0-671-72185-2*) Baen Bks.

Dancing with Myself: Sensuous Exercises for Body, Mind & Spirit. Katia DePeyer. Ed. by Vimala McClure. (Illus.). 176p. (Orig.). 1991. pap. 10.95 (*0-945934-04-1*) New Wrld Lib.

Dancing with Siva: Hinduism's Contemporary Catechism. rev. ed. Satguru S. Subramuniyaswami. (Rishi Collection Ser.). 1008p. 1993. 29.95 (*0-945497-48-2*); pap. 19.95 (*0-945497-47-4*) Himalayan Acad. Library Journal, October, 1993: "This almost encyclopedic SOURCEBOOK of Hinduism presents Hinduism, particularly Salvite Hinduism, from the point of view of contemporary Hindus. It uses the traditional four-line presentation, followed by 21-line commentary, to explain 155 points of history, doctrine, ritual & practice. These explanations are supplemented by verses of scripture, extensive illustrations, a Hindu timeline, a children's primer, & charts. More than triple the length of the preceding edition, this work is accessible to non-Hindus. Highly recommended." K.L. Seshagiri Rao, Professor of Religious Studies & Chief Editor, Encyclopedia of Hinduism: "DANCING WITH SIVA elucidates with exceptional ability the self-understanding of the Hindus about their complex tradition, in the contemporary context. It sets the record of Hinduism straight in the form of questions & answers. It enables the students & teachers to correct misconceptions & misinterpretations to which the Hindu tradition has been subjected by unsympathetic critics...The beautiful illustrations, a copious lexicon (190 pages of Sandskrit, Tamil & English terms) & an exhaustive index (40 pages) make the book especially attractive & useful." ***Publisher Provided Annotation.***

***Dancing with Strangers.** Sandra F. Asher. 1994. 5.00 (*0-87129-408-7*, D59) Dramatic Pub.

Dancing with the Bears. Joycelyn Elders. LC 93-33340. 1993. 12.95 (*0-687-00246-X*) Abingdon.

Dancing with the Devil: Society & Cultural Poetics in Mexican-American South Texas. Jose E. Limon. LC 93-39968. (New Directions in Anthropological Writing Ser.). 256p. 1994. 42.00 (*0-299-14220-5*); pap. 15.95 (*0-299-14224-8*) U of Wis Pr.

Dancing with the Dinosaur. William Lareau. LC 93-33922. 256p. 1993. 14.95 (*0-8329-0505-4*) New Win Pub.

Dancing with the Doe: New & Selected Poems, 1986-91. Margaret Randall. 74p. (Orig.). 1992. pap. 9.95 (*0-931122-70-8*) West End.

Dancing with the Family: A Symbolic-Experiential Approach. Carl A. Whitaker & William M. Bumberry. LC 87-36843. 256p. 1988. 29.95 (*0-87630-496-X*) Brunner-Mazel.

Dancing with the Indians. Angela S. Medearis. LC 90-28666. (Illus.). 32p. (J). (ps-3). 1991. lib. bdg. 15.95 (*0-8234-0893-0*) Holiday.

***Dancing with the Indians.** Angela S. Medearis. (Illus.). (J). (gr. k-3). 1994. audio 22.95 (*0-87499-333-4*); audio, pap. 14.95 (*0-87499-332-6*) Live Oak Media.

***Dancing with the Indians, 4 bks., Set.** Angela S. Medearis. (Illus.). (J). (gr. k-3). 1994. audio, pap. 33.95 (*0-87499-334-2*) Live Oak Media.

Dancing with the Indians: A Reading Rainbow Review Book. Angela S. Medearis. (Illus.). (J). (ps-3). 1993. reprint ed. pap. 5.95 (*0-8234-1023-4*) Holiday.

Dancing with the Pen. Ministry of Education, New Zealand Staff. 152p. 1992. pap. text ed. 25.00 (*0-478-05560-9*) R Owen Pubs.

Dancing with the Shadows in My Room. Lou Alpert. (Illus.). 32p. (J). (ps-3). 1991. 12.95 (*1-879085-06-2*) Whsprng Coyote Pr.

***Dancing with the Skeleton: Meditations for Suicide Survivors.** Kristen Derrek. Ed. by Joy Johnson. (Illus.). 32p. (Orig.). Date not set. pap. 3.95 (*1-56123-081-2*) Centering Corp.

Dancing with the Times: What's a Young Adult to Believe! Pearl Evans. LC 93-92656. 160p. (Orig.). (YA). (gr. 8 up). 1993. pap. 4.99 (*0-938453-05-X*) Small Helm Pr.

Dancing with the Wheel. Sun Bear. 1991. pap. 15.00 (*0-671-76732-1*) S&S Trade.

Dancing with Tigers. Janet Lapp. 123p. 1994. pap. 10.95 (*1-885365-01-2*) Demeter Pr.

***Dancing with Tigers.** Janet Lapp. 224p. 1995. boxed 22.95 (*1-885365-02-0*) Demeter Pr.

Dancing with Your Books: The Zen Way of Studying. J. J. Gibbs. 192p. 1990. pap. 9.95 (*0-452-26496-0*, Plume) NAL-Dutton.

Dancing with Your Horse. Mary E. Campbell. LC 89-24490. (Illus.). 132p. 1989. 20.95 (*0-939481-17-0*) Half Halt Pr.

Dancing Without Music. Beryl Lieff Benderly. LC 90-41334. 302p. 1990. pap. 13.95 (*0-930323-59-9*) Gallaudet Univ Pr.

Dancing Wu Li Masters: An Overview of the New Physics. Gary Zukav. (Bantam New Age Bks.). 384p. 1984. 6.99 (*0-553-26382-X*) Bantam.

Dancing Wu Li Masters: An Overview of the New Physics. Gary Zukav. LC 78-25827. (Illus.). 1979. pap. 13.45 (*0-688-08402-8*, Quill) Morrow.

Dancer's Woman. Mary L. Baxter. (Silhouette Desire Ser.). 1993. mass mkt. 2.99 (*0-373-05822-5*, 5-05822-7) Silhouette.

Dand Prakriya Vyakhyan (Code of Criminal Procedure in Hindi) Murli Manohar. 212p. 1981. 45.00 (*0-317-54574-4*) St Mut.

Dand Vidhi Nirdeshika. Vijay Malik. 561p. 1985. 90.00 (*0-317-54607-4*) St Mut.

Dand Vidhi Nirdeshika: (Three Major Acts in Hindi) Pocket Edition. Vijay Malik. (HIN.). (C). 1990. 42.00 (*0-685-39745-9*) St Mut.

Dand Vidhi Nirdeshika (Three Major Acts in Hindi) Vijay Malik. (C). 1992. 55.00 (*0-89771-777-5*, Pub. by Eastern Book II) St Mut.

***Dandelion.** Garrett Christopher. Ed. by J. Friedland & R. Kessler. (Novel-Ties Ser.). (J). (gr. k-1). 1994. student ed, pap. text ed. 14.95 (*1-56982-077-5*) Lrn Links.

Dandelion. Don Freeman. (Illus.). (J). (gr. k-3). 1982. audio 22.95 (*0-941078-11-6*); audio, pap. 14.95 (*0-941078-09-4*) Live Oak Media.

Dandelion. Don Freeman. LC 64-21472. (Illus.). (J). (ps-2). 1977. pap. 4.99 (*0-14-050218-1*, VS4, Puffin) Puffin Bks.

Dandelion. Don Freeman. LC 64-21472. (Illus.). 48p. (J). (ps-2). 1964. pap. 14.99 (*0-670-25532-7*) Viking Child Bks.

Dandelion. Paula Z. Hogan. LC 78-21155. (Life Cycles Bks.). (Illus.). 32p. (J). (gr. 1-4). 1979. lib. bdg. 19.97 (*0-8172-1250-7*); pap. 4.95 (*0-8114-8182-4*); audio, pap. 9.95 (*0-8114-8190-5*) Raintree Steck-V.

Dandelion. Paula Z. Hogan. LC 78-21155. (Life Cycles Clippers Ser.). (Illus.). 32p. (J). (gr. 1-4). 1984. audio, lib. bdg. 29.28 (*0-8172-2227-8*) Raintree Steck-V.

Dandelion. Judith Martin. (Illus.). (Orig.). (J). (gr. 1-5). 1978. pap. 4.50 (*0-9606662-0-6*) Paper Bag.

Dandelion. Barrie Watts. (Stopwatch Ser.). (Illus.). 25p. (J). (gr. k-4). 1991. 6.95 (*0-382-09442-5*); lib. bdg. 9.95 (*0-382-09438-7*); pap. 3.95 (*0-382-24016-2*) Silver Burdett Pr.

Dandelion, 4 bks., Set. Don Freeman. (Illus.). (J). (gr. k-3). 1982. audio, pap. 31.95 (*0-941078-10-8*) Live Oak Media.

Dandelion: The Triumphant Life of a Misfit, a Story for All Ages. Sheelagh M. Mawe. 165p. (Orig.). (J). (gr. 4). 1994. pap. 6.95 (*0-9642168-0-9*) Totally Unique.

Dandelion Celebration: A Guide to Unexpected Cuisine. Peter A. Gail. LC 94-2408. (Illus.). 160p. (Orig.). 1994. pap. 10.95 (*1-879863-51-0*) Goosefoot Acres.

***Dandelion Clocks.** Nicholas Campbell. Date not set. pap. 7.95 (*0-9633481-2-4*) Blue Beginnings.

Dandelion Cottage. 4th ed. Carroll W. Rankin. 1982. reprint ed. 8.95 (*0-938746-00-6*) Marquette Cnty.

***Dandelion Crumbs: Growing up Catholic.** Steven Denny. Ed. by David Mackenzie. (Illus.). 189p. Date not set. pap. write for info. (*0-9640652-0-7*) Innovate Pub.

***Dandelion Garden & Other Stories.** Budge Wilson. LC 94-26641. (J). 1995. 15.95 (*0-399-22768-7*, Philomel Bks) Putnam Pub Group.

Dandelion Murders. Rebecca Rothenberg. 304p. 1994. 18.95 (*0-89296-561-4*) Mysterious Pr.

***Dandelion Murders.** Rebecca Rothenberg. 256p. 1995. mass mkt. 5.50 (*0-446-40378-4*, Mysterious Paperbk) Warner Bks.

Dandelion on the Acropolis. Jesse Stuart. LC 78-1322. (Illus.). 1978. 10.00 (*0-89097-011-4*) Archer Edns.

Dandelion on the Acropolis. limited ed. Jesse Stuart. LC 78-1322. (Illus.). 1978. 37.50 (*0-89097-012-2*) Archer Edns.

Dandelion Queen. Olivia Long. (Our Precious Planet Ser.). (Illus.). 32p. (J). (ps-4). Date not set. 9.95 (*1-880042-08-8*, SL12461) Shelf-Life Bks.

***Dandelion Soul.** Dona Goldman. Ed. by Carol Spelius & Wayne Spelius. 87p. (Orig.). 1994. pap. text ed. 9.95 (*0-941363-30-9*) Lake Shore Pub.

Dandelion Soul. Terry Persun. Ed. by Roy Zarucchi & Carolyn Page. (Chapbook Ser.). (Illus.). 28p. (Orig.). 1990. pap. 5.00 (*0-9623862-6-X*) Nightshade Pr.

Dandelion Uses: Uses for the Dandelion. rev. ed. Recycling Consortium Staff. 1992. pap. text ed. 14.95 (*0-317-04793-0*, Recycling Consort) Prosperity & Profits.

Dandelion Wine. Ray Bradbury. 1975. 24.95 (*0-394-49605-1*) Knopf.

Dandelion Wine. Ray Bradbury. (J). (gr. 6 up). 1985. mass mkt. 5.50 (*0-553-27753-7*) Bantam.

***Dandelion Wine.** Ray Bradbury. 1994. lib. bdg. 24.95x (*1-56849-448-3*) Buccaneer Bks.

***Dandelion Wine.** Ray Bradbury. 1988. 5.00 (*0-87129-554-7*, D43) Dramatic Pub.

***Dandelions.** Eve Bunting. LC 94-27104. (Illus.). (J). 1995. write for info. (*0-15-200050-X*) HarBrace.

Dandelions. Adapt. by Kathleen Pohl. (Nature Close-Ups Ser.). (Illus.). 32p. (J). (gr. 3-7). 1986. pap. text ed. 10.95 (*0-8172-2708-3*) Raintree Steck-V.

Dandelions in the Castle: Subjectivity, Science, & Theology. Larry A. Sansoucie. LC 89-81064. 90p. (Orig.). 1989. pap. 9.50 (*0-937505-03-X*) Glyndwr Resc.

Dandelion's Vanishing Vegetable Garden. Genevieve Huriet. LC 90-4857. (Beechwood Bunny Tales Ser.). (Illus.). 32p. (J). (gr. k-2). 1991. lib. bdg. 17.27 (*0-8368-0526-7*) Gareth Stevens Inc.

***Dandies & Desert Saints: Styles of Victorian Manhood.** James E. Adams. 264p. 1995. 39.95 (*0-8014-3017-8*); pap. 15.95 (*0-8014-8208-9*) Cornell U Pr.

Dandin's Dasha-Kumara-Charita: The Ten Princes. Dandin. Tr. by Arthur W. Ryder. 248p. reprint ed. pap. 70.70 (*0-317-09902-7*, 2012032) Bks Demand.

Dandniya Manual: (Three Major Acts, Cr.P.C., I.P.C. & Evidence in Hindi) Vijay Malik. (HIN.). (C). 1990. 90.00 (*0-685-39746-7*) St Mut.

Dandniya Manual: Three Major Acts in Hindi. Vijay Malik. 550p. 1983. 135.00 (*0-317-54608-2*) St Mut.

D&S, F-16 A&B Fighting Falcon. Bert Kinzey. 1991. 10.95 (*0-8306-7053-X*) TAB Bks.

Dandy & the Herald. Richard Pine. 200p. 1988. text ed. 39.95 (*0-312-00521-0*) St Martin.

Dandy & the Senorito: Eros & Social Class in the Nineteenth-Century Novel. Gloria Ortiz. LC 91-31679. (Harvard Dissertations in the Romance Languages Ser.). 136p. 1991. 39.00 (*0-8153-0651-2*) Garland.

Dandy, Day & the Devil. Riley. (Orig.). 50.00 (*0-8488-1580-7*); pap. 15.95 (*0-8488-1595-5*) Amereon Ltd.

Dandy, Day & the Devil. James A. Riley. LC 87-90021. (Illus.). 153p. (Orig.). 1987. 49.95 (*0-9614023-3-4*); pap. 12.95 (*0-9614023-2-6*) TK Pubs.

Dandy Dictionary Skills. Ginger Wentrcek. (J). (gr. 2-4). 1986. pap. 5.99 (*0-8224-1830-4*) Fearon Teach Aids.

***Dandy Dollhouse: Twenty Years Later.** Lucina B. Moxley. 92p. 1994. write for info. (*1-878208-51-9*) Guild Pr IN.

Dandy Dollhouse Stories. Lucina B. Moxley. (Illus.). 74p. 1993. 16.95 (*1-878208-30-6*) Guild Pr IN.

Dandy Dutch Recipes. 160p. 1991. spiral bd. 5.50 (*0-941016-84-6*) Penfield.

Dandy of Johns Hopkins. Edward R. Laws, Jr. & William L. Fox. (Illus.). 291p. 1984. lib. bdg. 21.00 (*0-683-04903-8*) Williams & Wilkins.

Dandy-Walker Syndrome. Anthony J. Raimondi et al. (Illus.). viii, 84p. 1983. 46.50 (*3-8055-1722-X*) S Karger.

Dandyism. Jules Barbey d'Aurevilly. Tr. by Douglas Ainslie. (Illus.). 96p. (C). 1988. reprint ed. 22.00 (*1-55554-032-5*); reprint ed. pap. 8.95x (*1-55554-035-X*) PAJ Pubns.

***Dane & Thomas: How to Use a Law Library Vol. 1: An Introduction to Research Skills.** 3rd ed. C. Cope & P. A. Thomas. 1994. pap. text ed. 28.00 (*0-421-46090-3*, Pub. by Sweet & Maxwll) W W Gaunt.

Dane Gray Hansen: Titan of Northwest Kansas. Billy M. Jones. (Illus.). 270p. 10.00 (*0-685-08424-8*) Wichita Ctr Entrep SBM.

Danegeld in France. Einar Joranson. LC 24-23301. (Augustana College Library Publication Ser.: No. 10). 247p. 1924. pap. 1.25 (*0-910182-07-8*) Augustana Coll.

Danes & Their Politicians: A Summary of the Findings of a Research Project on Political Credibility in Denmark. Gunnar V. Morgensen. (Voters in Scandinavia Ser.: No. 2). 85p. (Orig.). 1993. pap. 26.50 (*87-7288-451-7*, Pub. by Aarhus Univ Pr DK) Coronet Bks.

Danes in America. Peter L. Petersen. (In America Bks.). (Illus.). 96p. (YA). (gr. 5 up). 1987. lib. bdg. 17.50 (*0-8225-0233-X*, Lerner Publctns); pap. 5.95 (*0-8225-1031-6*, Lerner Publctns) Lerner Group.

Danes in North America. Ed. by Frederick Hale. LC 83-17077. 256p. 1984. 30.00 (*0-295-96089-2*) U of Wash Pr.

Danes in Wisconsin. Frederick Hale. LC 80-26088. (Illus.). 31p. (Orig.). 1981. pap. 1.50 (*0-87020-205-7*) State Hist Soc Wis.

Daneshvar's Playhouse: A Collection of Stories. Simin Daneshvar. Tr. & Aft. by Maryam Mafi. LC 89-2527. (Illus.). 184p. 1989. 22.00 (*0-934211-19-1*) Mage Pubs Inc.

Danfhocail: Irish Epigrams in Verse. Thomas F. O'Rahilly. LC 75-28834. reprint ed. 29.50 (*0-404-13824-1*) AMS Pr.

Danforth Genealogy: Nicholas Danforth of Framingham, England & Cambridge, Mass. (1589-1638) & William of Newbury, Mass. (1640-1771) & Their Descendants. J. J. May. 492p. 1989. reprint ed. lib. bdg. 72.00 (*0-8328-0452-5*); reprint ed. pap. 62.00 (*0-8328-0453-3*) Higginson Bk Co.

Danforth's Handbook of Obstetrics & Gynecology. James Scott et al. (Illus.). 400p. 1994. pap. 24.95 (*0-397-51281-3*) Lippincott.

Danforth's Obstetrics & Gynecology. 7th ed. Scott. 1994. Text & review. 137.50 (*0-397-51407-7*) Lippincott.

Danforth's Obstetrics & Gynecology. 7th ed. Ed. by James R. Scott et al. LC 93-29365. 1994. 125.00 (*0-397-51353-4*) Lippincott.

Dangar. Patricia Warren. Ed. by Dave Horton. 240p. (Orig.). Date not set. pap. 7.99 (*0-7814-0132-1*, LifeJourney) Chariot Family.

Danger. Dick Francis. 1986. mass mkt. 5.95 (*0-449-21037-5*, Crest) Fawcett.

Danger. Dave Parsons. 1991. pap. 12.98 (*0-87938-517-0*) Motorbooks Intl.

***Danger: Dinky Diplodocus.** (Adventures of Dinosaur Dog Ser.: No. 2). (J). (gr. 3-7). 1994. 6.95 (*1-883649-01-3*) Sutton Pubns.

An Asterisk (*) at the beginning of an entry indicates that the title is appearing in BIP for the first time.

Danger: Marketing Researcher at Work. Terry Haller. LC 82-13261. (Illus.). 312p. 1983. text ed. 55.00 (*0-89930-026-X*, HMK/, Quorum Bks) Greenwood.

Danger: Memory! Two Plays: I Can't Remember Anything; Clara. Arthur Miller. LC 86-29402. 96p. 1987. pap. 5.95 (*0-8021-5176-0*) Grove-Atltic.

Danger: Present Tense Theater. David Savran. 24p. (Orig.). (C). 1989. pap. 4.00 (*0-945926-07-3*) Paradigm RI.

***Danger - the Dogyard Cat.** Libby Riddles & Shelley Gill. (Illus.). 36p. (J). (gr. 1-6). Date not set. 13.95 (*0-934007-09-8*); pap. 8.95 (*0-934007-20-9*) Paws Four Pub.

Danger--Icebergs! Revised Edition of Icebergs. Roma Gans. LC 87-45143. (Trophy Let's-Read-&-Find-Out Bk.). (Illus.). 32p. (J). (ps-3). 1987. pap. 4.50 (*0-06-445066-X*, Trophy) HarpC Child Bks.

Danger All Around: Waste Storage Crisis on the Texas & Louisiana Gulf Coast. Joel B. Goldsteen. LC 92-23903. (Illus.). 279p. (C). 1993. text ed. 35.00 (*0-292-71565-X*) U of Tex Pr.

Danger & Beauty: Dangerous Music, Pet Food & Tropical Apparitions & New Writings. Jessica Hagedorn. LC 92-23245. 1993. pap. 14.00 (*0-14-017340-4*, Penguin Bks) Viking Penguin.

***Danger & Defense: Close Process Attention Analysis.** Ed. by Marianne Goldberger. 1996. 40.00 (*1-56821-583-5*) Aronson.

***Danger & Opportunity: Explaining International Crisis Outcomes.** Eric Herring. LC 95-3507. 1995. text ed. write for info. (*0-7190-4292-5*); text ed. write for info. (*0-7190-4293-3*, Pub. by Manchester Univ Pr UK) St Martin.

Danger & Survival. McGeorge Bundy. 1990. pap. 12.95 (*0-679-72568-7*, Vin) Random.

Danger & Survival: The Political History of the Nuclear Weapon. McGeorge Bundy. LC 88-42824. 880p. 1988. 24.95 (*0-394-52278-8*) Random.

Danger & the Enemy. Jos Vandeloo. Tr. by Dirk H. Van Nouhuys. LC 86-13500. 119p. 1986. 14.95 (*0-937584-09-6*) Sachem Pr.

Danger! Artists at Work: A Guide to Occupational Hazards for Australian Art Workers & Teachers. Monona Rossol & Ben Bartlett. 200p. 1991. pap. 45.00 (*0-909532-98-2*) D W Thorpe.

Danger at Black Dyke. Winifred Finlay. (Illus.). (YA). (gr. 7-12). 1968. 22.95 (*0-87599-150-5*) S G Phillips.

Danger at Demon's Cove. K. Dolb. (Puzzle Adventure Ser.). (Illus.). 48p. (J). (gr. 4-9). 1988. lib. bdg. 11.96 (*0-88110-333-0*); pap. 4.95 (*0-7460-0179-7*) EDC.

***Danger at Dinosaur Camp.** Jerry D. Thomas. LC 94-48882. (Detective Zack Ser.: Vol. 6). (J). 1995. 5.95 (*0-8163-1258-3*) Pacific Pr Pub Assn.

Danger at Half-Moon Lake. Joan R. Biggar. (Adventure Quest Ser.). (Illus.). 128p. (J). (gr. 5-8). 1991. pap. 3.99 (*0-570-04194-5*) Concordia.

Danger at Hanging Rock. Kristi Holl. LC 89-460. (YA). (gr. 7-9). 1989. pap. 3.99 (*1-55513-067-4*, Chariot Bks) Chariot Family.

***Danger at Outlaw Cr, No. 4.** Jerry Jerman. 132p. 1995. pap. 4.99 (*1-56476-465-6*, 6-3465, Victor Books) SP Pubns.

Danger at the Breaker. Catherine A. Welch. (On My Own Ser.). (Illus.). 48p. (J). (gr. k-3). 1991. lib. bdg. 15.95 (*0-87614-693-0*, Carolrhoda) Lerner Group.

Danger at the Breaker. Catherine A. Welch. (J). (gr. k-3). 1992. pap. 5.95 (*0-87614-564-0*, Carolrhoda) Lerner Group.

***Danger at the Fair.** Peg Kehret. LC 94-16873. (J). 1995. 14.99 (*0-525-65182-9*, Cobblehill Bks) Dutton Child Bks.

Danger at Your Door. Duane Magnani. 1987. 13.95 (*1-883858-06-2*, 687) Witness CA.

Danger Beneath the Waves: History of the Confederate Submarine. H. L. Hunley & Jame Kloeppel. 118p. 1922. pap. 9.95 (*0-87844-105-0*) Sandlapper Pub Co.

Danger Beneath the Waves: History of the Confederate Submarine. H. L. Hunley & James E. Kloeppel. 118p. 1992. reprint ed. 18.95 (*0-87844-096-8*) Sandlapper Pub Co.

Danger Cave. Jesse D. Jennings. LC 62-63182. (Utah Anthropological Papers: No. 27). reprint ed. 24.50 (*0-404-60627-X*) AMS Pr.

Danger! Cross Currents: An Alix Nicholson Mystery. Sharon Gilligan. (Orig.). 1994. pap. 9.99 (*1-883061-01-6*) Rising NY.

Danger de Mort. E. P. Davoust. (C). 1984. 30.00 (*0-7175-1227-4*, Pub. by S Thornes Pubs UK) St Mut.

Danger, Dinosaurs! A Musical Comedy about the Evolution & Extinction of the Dinosaurs, Incl. audio tape. Tobin J. Mueller. (Illus.). (J). (ps-8). 1990. Audio tape incl. audio, pap. 14.95 (*1-56213-003-X*) Ctr Stage Prodns.

Danger Dog. Lynn Hall. LC 86-13914. 112p. (J). (gr. 4-7). 1986. text ed. 13.95 (*0-684-18680-2*, C Scribner Sons Young) S&S Childrens.

Danger, Dolphins, & Ginger Beer. John Vigor. LC 92-26182. (Illus.). 192p. (J). (gr. 3-7). 1993. text ed. 14.95 (*0-689-31817-0*, Atheneum Bks Young) S&S Childrens.

***Danger down Under.** Carolyn Keene. Ed. by Anne Greenberg. (Nancy Drew Boxed Gift Set Ser.). 224p. (Orig.). (J). 1995. mass mkt. 3.99 (*0-671-88460-3*, Archway) PB.

Danger for Breakfast. large type ed. John McPartland. (Linford Mystery Library). 288p. 1992. pap. 14.95 (*0-7089-7304-3*, Trailtree Bookshop) Ulverscroft.

Danger for Old Ruff. Vesta Seek. LC 89-25240. (On My Own Bks.). (Illus.). 32p. (J). (ps-2). 1991. pap. 4.99 (*1-55513-360-6*, 33605, Chariot Bks) Chariot Family.

Danger Forward: The Story of the First Division in World War II. S. B. Mason. (Divisional Ser.: No. 14). (Illus.). 479p. 1980. reprint ed. 29.95 (*0-89839-033-8*) Battery Pr.

Danger from Strangers: Confronting the Threat of Assault. J. D. Brewer. (Illus.). 1994. 22.95 (*0-685-70889-6*, Plenum Insight) Plenum.

Danger from Strangers: Confronting the Threat of Assault. James D. Brewer. LC 93-50220. 1994. 22.95 (*0-306-44642-1*, Plenum Insight) Plenum.

Danger from the Dead. large type ed. E. X. Ferrars. (Magna Mystery Ser.). 283p. 1992. 21.95 (*0-7505-0358-0*) Ulverscroft.

Danger Guys: Hollywood Halloween. Tony Abbott. LC 93-29799. (Trophy Bk.). (Illus.). 80p. (J). (gr. 2-5). 1994. pap. 3.95 (*0-06-440519-2*, Trophy) HarpC Child Bks.

Danger Guys: Hollywood Halloween. Tony Abbott. LC 93-29799. (Trophy Book). (Illus.). 96p. (J). (gr. 2-5). 1994. pap. 3.95 (*0-06-440522-2*, Trophy) HarpC Child Bks.

Danger Guys Blast Off. Tony Abbott. LC 93-31806. (Trophy Bk.). (Illus.). 80p. (J). (gr. 2-5). 1994. pap. 3.95 (*0-06-440520-6*, Trophy) HarpC Child Bks.

***Danger Guys Hit the Beach.** Tony Abbott. LC 94-27519. (Trophy Book). (Illus.). 80p. (J). (gr. 2-5). 1995. pap. 3.95 (*0-06-440521-4*, Trophy) HarpC Child Bks.

Danger, Iceberg Ahead. Lynn Poole & Gray Poole. (Illus.). (J). (gr. 1-4). 1961. lib. bdg. 4.39 (*0-394-90121-5*) Random Bks Yng Read.

Danger in D. C. Cat Crimes in the Nation's Capital. Ed. by Martin H. Greenberg & Ed Gorman. LC 93-70900. 256p. 1993. 20.00 (*1-55611-374-9*) D I Fine.

***Danger in D. C. Cat Crimes in the Nation's Capital.** Ed. by Martin H. Greenberg & Ed Gorman. 1995. pap. 5.99 (*0-8041-1277-0*) Ivy Books.

Danger in High Places. Sharon Gilligan. 192p. 1993. pap. 9.95 (*0-9628938-7-0*) Rising NY.

Danger in Kashmir. rev. ed. Josef Korbel. LC 54-9022. 419p. reprint ed. pap. 119.50 (*0-8357-6553-9*, 2035917) Bks Demand.

***Danger in Paradise.** Myra Rankin. 144p. 1994. pap. 6.95 (*1-57087-102-7*) Prof Pr NC.

Danger in Quicksand Swamp. Bill Wallace. LC 89-83485. 196p. (J). (gr. 3-7). 1989. 14.95 (*0-8234-0786-1*) Holiday.

Danger in Quicksand Swamp. Bill Wallace. Ed. by Patricia MacDonald. 192p. (J). 1991. reprint ed. pap. 3.50 (*0-671-70898-8*, Minstrel Bks) PB.

Danger in the Ashes. William W. Johnstone. 1988. pap. 3.50 (*0-8217-2311-1*) Zebra.

Danger in the Comfort Zone: From Boardroom to Mailroom-How to Break the Entitlement Habit That's Killing American Business. Judith M. Bardwick. 200p. 1995. 21.95 (*0-8144-5059-8*, 040531) AMACOM.

***Danger in the Comfort Zone: From Boardroom to Mailroom-How to Break the Entitlement Habit That's Killing American Business.** Judith M. Bardwick. LC 94-24020. 256p. 1995. pap. 16.95 (*0-8144-7886-7*) AMACOM.

Danger in the Dark. Mignon G. Eberhart. 307p. 1975. reprint ed. lib. bdg. 22.95 (*0-88411-753-7*, Aeonian Pr) Amereon Ltd.

Danger in the Fourth Dimension. Franklin W. Dixon. Ed. by Ellen Winkler. (Hardy Boys Ser.: No. 118). 160p. (Orig.). (J). 1993. pap. 3.99 (*0-671-79308-X*, Minstrel Bks) PB.

***Danger in the Land of Mavericks.** Nelson A. Ossorio. (Orig.). 1995. pap. 11.95 (*1-56721-124-0*) Twnty-Fifth Cent Pr.

Danger in Tibet: A Miss Mallard Mystery. Robert Quackenbush. (Illus.). 32p. (J). (gr. 1-4). 1989. 15.95 (*0-945912-03-X*) Pippin Pr.

Danger Insurance Fraud in Progress: How to Avoid Becoming A Victim. Albert B. Lewis. LC 87-71527. 381p. (Orig.). 1987. pap. text ed., spiral bd. 80.00 (*0-939713-02-0*) Carriage House.

Danger Is My Business! Lee Server. LC 92-13391. 1993. 27.50 (*0-8118-0355-4*); pap. 17.95 (*0-8118-0112-8*) Chronicle Bks.

Danger Kid. Gianni Padoan. LC 90-48381. (J). 1989. 11.95 (*0-85953-312-3*) Childs Play.

***Danger Lies Ahead.** Paul McCusker. LC 95-7714. (Adventures in Odyssey Ser.: No. 7). (J). 1995. write for info. (*1-56179-369-8*) Focus Family.

***Danger Line.** large type ed. George Goodchild. (Linford Mystery Large Pr. Ser.). 1994. pap. 14.95 (*0-7089-7631-X*) Ulverscroft.

Danger Lines in the Deeper Life. A. B. Simpson. LC 90-84957. 102p. 1991. 6.99 (*0-87509-440-6*) Chr Pubns.

Danger: Memory! I Can't Remember Anything, & Clara: Two Related One-Act Plays. Arthur Miller. 1987. pap. 4.75 (*0-8222-0268-9*) Dramatists Play.

Danger Money. Mignon G. Eberhart. 224p. 1989. mass mkt. 3.95 (*0-446-35565-8*) Warner Bks.

Danger of Being a Gentleman: And Other Essays. Harold J. Laski. LC 72-1154. (Essay Index Reprint Ser.). 1977. reprint ed. 20.95 (*0-8369-2849-0*) Ayer.

***Danger of Equality & Other Essays.** Geoffrey Gorer. 264p. 1966. 69.50 (*0-614-00058-0*) Elliots Bks.

***Danger of Equality & Other Essays.** Geoffrey Gorer. 264p. 1966. 69.50 (*0-614-00164-1*) Elliots Bks.

Danger of Masquerades & Raree-Shows: As Being the Ground & Occasion of the Late Decay of Wit in the Island of Great-Britain. Bd. with Dancing Devils or the Roaring Dragon: A Dumb Farce.; Letter to My Lord... on the Present Diversions of the Town. (English Stage Ser.: Vol. 46). 1974. Set lib. bdg. 61.00 (*0-8240-0629-1*) Garland.

Danger of Premature Interment. Joseph Taylor. LC 87-60462. (Classics in Death & Burial Ser.). (Illus.). 163p. 1988. reprint ed. pap. 10.95 (*0-915431-07-6*) N American Archives.

Danger of Walking on Water: And Other Cartoons. Chuck Mathias & Bhaskar Puri. (Illus.). 102p. (Orig.). 1992. pap. 4.95 (*0-910303-36-3*) Writers Pub Serv.

Danger on Apollo Thirteen. D. Baker. (Great Adventure Ser.). (Illus.). 32p. (J). (gr. 4 up). 1988. 12.95 (*0-685-58289-2*); lib. bdg. 17.27 (*0-86592-871-1*) Rourke Corp.

***Danger on Midnight River: Gary Paulsen World of Adventure.** Paulsen. 1995. pap. 3.50 (*0-440-41028-2*) Dell.

Danger on Midnight Trail. Mark Littleton. LC 94-11458. 1994. mass mkt. 3.99 (*1-56507-246-4*) Harvest Hse.

Danger on Panther Peak. Bill Wallace. Orig. Title: Shadow on the Snow. (J). 1989. pap. 3.50 (*0-671-70271-8*, Minstrel Bks) PB.

Danger on Parade. Carolyn Keene. Ed. by Anne Greenberg. (Nancy Drew Files Ser.: No. 77). 160p. (Orig.). (YA). (gr. 7 up). 1992. pap. 3.75 (*0-671-73081-9*, Archway) PB.

Danger on the African Grassland. Elisabeth Sackett. (J). (ps-3). 1991. 12.95 (*0-316-76596-1*) Little.

Danger on the Air. Franklin W. Dixon. (Hardy Boys Ser.: No. 95). (Orig.). (J). (gr. 3-7). 1989. pap. 3.50 (*0-671-66305-4*, Minstrel Bks) PB.

Danger on the Diamond. Franklin W. Dixon. Ed. by Anne Greenberg. (Hardy Boys Ser.: No. 90). 160p. (J). (gr. 3-6). 1988. mass mkt. 3.99 (*0-671-63425-9*, Minstrel Bks) PB.

Danger on the Homestead. rev. ed. Bessie H. Heck. LC 93-71892. (Illus.). 160p. (J). (gr. 3-6). 1993. reprint ed. 14.95 (*0-9637259-0-4*) Dinosaur Pr.

Danger on the Right. Arnold Forster & Benjamin R. Epstein. LC 76-10992. 294p. 1976. reprint ed. text ed. 59.75 (*0-8371-8147-X*, FODR, Greenwood Pr) Greenwood.

Danger on the Sunita. G. Lehmann. 1987. pap. 4.95 (*0-87508-438-9*) Chr Lit.

Danger on Thunder Mountain. Lee Roddy. (American Adventure Ser.). 176p. (Orig.). (J). (gr. 3 up). 1989. pap. 5.99 (*1-55661-028-9*) Bethany Hse.

Danger Rode Drag. large type ed. Marshall Grover. (Linford Western Library). 224p. 1987. pap. 11.95 (*0-7089-6344-7*, Linford) Ulverscroft.

Danger Signs & Symptoms: (Clinical SkillBuilder) SPC Staff. 1991. 24.95 (*0-87434-310-0*) Springhouse Pub.

Danger to Self or Others Exception to Confidentiality. C. Emmanuel Ahia & Dan Martin. LC 93-7971. (Legal Ser.: Vol. 8). 1993. 12.95 (*1-55620-123-0*) Am Coun Assn.

Danger Trail. Lee Martin. 192p. 1994. 17.95 (*0-8034-9058-5*, Avalon Bks) Bouregy.

Danger Trail. Max Brand. 1976. reprint ed. lib. bdg. 21.95 (*0-88411-517-8*, Aeonian Pr) Amereon Ltd.

***Danger Trail: Knife Thrower's Journey West.** Boyd Richardson. LC 95-4126. (J). 1995. write for info. (*1-55503-777-1*) Covenant Comms.

Danger Unlimited. Franklin W. Dixon. Ed. by Anne Greenberg. (Hardy Boys Casefiles Ser.: No. 79). 160p. (Orig.). (J). (gr. 6 up). 1993. mass mkt. 3.99 (*0-671-79463-9*, Archway) PB.

***Danger Unlimited, Bk. 1.** John Byrne. (Illus.). 108p. 1995. pap. 14.95 (*1-56971-058-9*) Dark Horse Comics.

***Danger Unlimited, Bk. 1.** limited ed. John Byrne. (Illus.). 108p. 1995. 59.95 (*1-56971-111-9*) Dark Horse Comics.

Danger-Watch Out! Jeanne Sears. (Illus.). 12p. (J). (ps-3). 1988. pap. 1.95 (*0-9621086-0-X*) J Sears.

Danger We All Face: The Radioactive Peril. rev. ed. Raymond W. Bernard. 62p. 1960. reprint ed. spiral bd. 5.50 (*0-7873-1159-6*) Mokelumne.

Danger Wherein the Kingdome Now Standeth, & the Remedie, No. 721. Robert B. Cotton. LC 74-28839. 1975. reprint ed. 15.00 (*90-221-0721-3*) Walter J Johnson.

Danger! White Water. Otto Penzler. LC 75-21844. (Illus.). 32p. (J). (gr. 5-10). 1976. lib. bdg. 10.79 (*0-89375-004-2*) Troll Assocs.

Danger Within: The New Age has Already Invaded Your Life & Home - Do You Know Where It's Lurking? Manuel Vasquez. LC 92-44206. 1993. 8.95 (*0-8163-1152-8*) Pacific Pr Pub Assn.

Danger Zone. Franklin W. Dixon. (Hardy Boys Ser.: No. 37). 1991. pap. 3.75 (*0-671-73751-1*) PB.

***Danger Zone.** David Klass. LC 94-20234. (J). 1995. 13.95 (*0-590-48590-3*) Scholastic Inc.

Danger Zone. J. M. Flynn. (Inflation Fighter Ser.). 192p. 1982. reprint ed. pap. 1.50 (*0-8439-1139-5*) Dorchester Pub Co.

Danger Zones: Defending Yourself Against Surprise Attack. Hei Long. (Illus.). 128p. 1991. pap. 14.00 (*0-87364-590-1*) Paladin Pr.

Dangerous. Caroline Cross. (Silhouette Desire Ser.). 1993. mass mkt. 2.99 (*0-373-05810-1*, 5-05810-2) Silhouette.

Dangerous. Amanda Quick. 1993. mass mkt. 5.99 (*0-553-29317-6*) Bantam.

Dangerous. large type ed. Amanda Quick. LC 93-13495. 1993. Alk. paper. 21.95 (*1-56054-726-X*) Thorndike Pr.

***Dangerous: Savannah's Story.** Jude Watson. LC 95-15702. (Brides of Wildcat County Ser.). (J). 1995. pap. write for info. (*0-689-80626-4*, Aladdin Paperbacks) S&S Childrens.

Dangerous Acquaintances. Pierre A. Laclos. Tr. by Richard Aldington. LC 83-45443. reprint ed. 37.50 (*0-404-20149-0*) AMS Pr.

Dangerous Age. Martin Sylvester. 1990. pap. 3.95 (*1-55817-367-6*, Pinnacle NY) Windsor NY.

Dangerous Age. Karin Michaelis. 215p. 1991. reprint ed. 25.95 (*0-8101-1015-6*); reprint ed. pap. 10.95 (*0-8101-1040-7*) Northwestern U Pr.

Dangerous Ages. Rose Macaulay. 270p. 1986. pap. 8.95 (*0-88184-226-5*) Carroll & Graf.

Dangerous Alibis. Carolyn C. Clark. Ed. by Mary A. Liotta. 160p. 1994. pap. 9.95 (*1-880254-16-6*) Vista.

***Dangerous Alliance.** Helen Bianchin. (Presents Ser.). 1995. pap. 3.25 (*0-373-11741-8*, 1-11741-5) Harlequin Bks.

Dangerous Alliance. Lindsay McKenna. 1994. 3.50 (*0-373-09884-7*) Silhouette.

***Dangerous Alliance.** large type ed. Helen Bianchin. (Harlequin Romance Ser.). 1995. 18.95 (*0-263-14100-4*, Pub. by Mills & Boon UK) Thorndike Pr.

Dangerous Amusements. Jon Davis. LC 87-20388. (Poetry Ser.). 75p. (Orig.). 1987. pap. 8.95 (*0-86538-061-9*) Ontario Rev NJ.

Dangerous Angel. Deborah Martin. 384p. (Orig.). 1994. pap. 4.99 (*0-451-40528-5*, Topaz) NAL-Dutton.

Dangerous Angels. Len Roberts. LC 93-12261. 64p. (Orig.). 1993. pap. 9.95 (*0-914278-61-4*) Copper Beech.

***Dangerous Animals.** Ed. by John Seidensticker & Susan Lumpkin. LC 95-12937. (Discoveries Ser.). (Illus.). 64p. (J). (gr. 4-7). 1995. write for info. (*0-7835-4762-5*) Time-Life.

***Dangerous Animals.** Richard Stoneman. Ed. by Damian Kelleher. (Info Adventure Ser.). (Illus.). 32p. (J). (gr. 4-6). 1995. 12.95 (*1-56847-411-3*); pap. 5.95 (*1-56847-318-4*) Thomson Lrning.

Dangerous Aquatic Animals of the World. Halstead. 264p. 1992. 59.95 (*0-8016-6981-2*) Mosby Yr Bk.

Dangerous Aquatic Animals of the World: A Color Atlas: With Prevention, First Aid & Emergency Treatment Procedures. Bruce W. Halstead. LC 91-13746. (Illus.). xx, 288p. 1992. 60.00 (*0-87850-045-6*) Darwin Pr.

Dangerous Assignments Study Guide. Committee to Protect Journalists Staff. Ed. by Peter Tarr. 29p. (C). 1991. pap. text ed. 8.00 (*0-944823-06-8*) Comm to Protect Jrnlists.

Dangerous at Heart. Elise Title. 1994. mass mkt. 2.99 (*0-373-25609-4*, 1-25609-8) Harlequin Bks.

***Dangerous Attachments.** Sarah Lovett. 1995. 22.00 (*0-679-43559-X*, Villard Bks) Random.

Dangerous Bandit. Vivian D. Gunderson. 1989. pap. 2.95 (*0-915374-06-4*) Rapids Christian.

Dangerous Beauties: Poems New & Selected. Suzanne J. Doyle. (Illus.). 48p. (Orig.). 1992. 15.00 (*0-9620640-1-7*) M Cantor.

Dangerous Behaviour, the Law & Mental Disorder. Herschel Prins. 240p. 1986. pap. 18.95 (*0-422-79220-9*, 9931, Pub. by Tavistock UK) Routledge Chapman & Hall.

Dangerous Birds. Janet Lembke. 192p. 1992. 21.95 (*1-55821-190-X*) Lyons & Burford.

***Dangerous Boys.** Ed. by J. Patrick. 512p. (Orig.). 1995. pap. text ed. 14.95 (*1-877978-53-1*, STARbks Pr) Woldt.

Dangerous Business. large type ed. Michael Underwood. (Mystery Ser.). 368p. 1993. 21.95 (*0-7089-2923-0*) Ulverscroft.

Dangerous by Degrees: Women at Oxford & the Somerville College Novelists. Susan J. Leonardi. (Illus.). 260p. 1989. text ed. 45.00 (*0-8135-1365-0*); pap. text ed. 12.95 (*0-8135-1366-9*) Rutgers U Pr.

Dangerous Call. large type ed. Elizabeth Harrison. 272p. 1984. 15.95 (*0-7089-1087-4*) Ulverscroft.

Dangerous Candy: A True Story about Drug Addiction. Raffaella Fletcher & Peter Mayle. 88p. 1991. 19.95 (*1-85619-020-X*, Sinclair-Stevenson) Trafalgar.

Dangerous Canoe Race. Lee Roddy. (Ladd Family Adventure Ser.: No. 4). (Orig.). (J). (gr. 3-6). 1990. pap. 4.99 (*0-929608-62-3*) Focus Family.

***Dangerous Charade.** Anne Barbour. (Regency Romance Ser.). 224p. (Orig.). 1995. pap. 3.99 (*0-451-17844-0*, Sig) NAL-Dutton.

***Dangerous Chemical Reactions.** Pollution Engineering Staff. 94p. 1994. 34.95 (*0-934165-46-7*) Gulf Pub.

Dangerous Classes: The Underclass & Social Citizenship. Lydia Morris. LC 93-24569. 1993. 45.00 (*0-415-05013-8*, Routledge NY); pap. 14.95 (*0-415-05014-6*, Routledge NY) Routledge.

Dangerous Cliffs of Severon. Vickie Britton. 352p. 1993. mass mkt. 3.99 (*0-8217-4373-2*) Zebra.

Dangerous Conceits. Margaret Moore. 204p. 1989. 17.95 (*0-8027-5727-8*) Walker & Co.

***Dangerous Crossroads: Popular Music, Postmodernism & the Poetics of Place.** George Lipsitz. LC 94-20455. 320p. 1994. 27.95 (*1-85984-935-0*, B4542, Pub. by Verso UK) Routledge Chapman & Hall.

Dangerous Dandy. Barbara Cartland. 1976. 18.95 (*0-685-10861-9*, Am Repr) Amereon Ltd.

***Dangerous Dandy.** Pat Cody. 1994. pap. 3.99 (*0-06-108291-0*, Harp PBks) HarpC.

Dangerous Dandy. Carol Proctor. (Regency Romance Ser.). 224p. (Orig.). 1993. pap. 3.99 (*0-451-17359-7*, Sig) NAL-Dutton.

***Dangerous Dandy.** large type ed. Rachelle Edwards. (Romance Library). 304p. 1995. pap. 14.95 (*0-7089-7667-0*, Linford) Ulverscroft.

***Dangerous Day.** Charlotte Rose. (Orig.). 1995. pap. text ed. 5.95 (*1-56333-293-0*) Masquerade.

Dangerous Days. Mary R. Rinehart. 25.95 (*0-8488-0312-4*) Amereon Ltd.

Dangerous Deceits. Barbara Hazard. (Coventry Romance Ser.: No. 184). 224p. 1982. pap. 1.50 (*0-449-50286-4*, Coventry) Fawcett.

***Dangerous Deceits.** Barbara Hazard. (Regency Romance Ser.). 224p. 1995. pap. 3.99 (*0-451-18202-2*, Sig) NAL-Dutton.

***Dangerous Delusions: America on the Brink: A Critical Solution to America's Political & Economic Dilemma.** Michael F. Spath. LC 94-75992. 295p. 1995. 21.95 (*0-944435-26-2*) Glenbridge Pub.

Dangerous Desire. Ashley Snow. 1990. mass mkt. 4.50 (*0-8217-2984-5*) Zebra.

***Dangerous Desire.** large type ed. Sarah Holland. 1995. 18.95 (*0-263-13937-9*) Thorndike Pr.

Dangerous Desires. Louise Clark. 400p. (Orig.). 1993. pap. 4.99 (*0-505-51910-0*, Love Spell) Dorchester Pub Co.

Dangerous Desires. Peter Wells. 240p. 1994. 20.95 (*0-670-85012-8*, Viking) Viking Penguin.

An Asterisk (*) at the beginning of an entry indicates that the title is appearing in BIP for the first time.

Dangerous Devices. T. Davis Bunn. Ed. by Brian Reck. 128p. (J). (gr. 7-10). Date not set. pap. 4.99 (0-7814-0115-1, Chariot Bks) Chariot Family.

*Dangerous Devotion. Barbara Kyle. 480p. (Orig.). 1995. mass mkt. 5.99 (0-451-17933-1, Onyx) NAL-Dutton.

Dangerous Diagnostics: The Social Power of Biological Information. Dorothy Nelkin & Laurence Tancredi. LC 93-32571. 1994. pap. text ed. 12.95 (0-226-57129-7) U Ch Pr.

*Dangerous Dig. Weinrich. 1995. pap. text ed. 4.99 (0-88965-112-4, Pub. by Horizon Books CN) Chr Pubns.

Dangerous Dimensions Project, No. 1. Gary Gygax. 1992. pap. 4.99 (0-451-45214-3, ROC) NAL-Dutton.

Dangerous Diversions. Margaret E. Porter. (Signet Regency Romance Ser.). 224p. (Orig.). 1994. pap. 3.99 (0-451-18069-0) NAL-Dutton.

Dangerous Doctrine: National Security & U. S. Foreign Policy. Saul Landau. (Pacca Book). 201p. (C). 1988. pap. text ed. 19.95 (0-8133-7508-8) Westview.

Dangerous Dossiers: Exposing the Secret War Against America's Greatest Authors. Herbert Mitgang. LC 87-46257. 1988. 18.95 (1-55611-077-4) D I Fine.

Dangerous Dreamers: The Financial Innovators from Charles Merrill to Michael Milken. Robert Sobel. LC 92-40748. 272p. 1993. Alk. paper. text ed. 27.95 (0-471-57734-0) Wiley.

*Dangerous Drugs Laws in Malaysia. Mimi K. Majid. Date not set. write for info. (0-614-05482-6) Butterworth Legal Pubs.

Dangerous Edge. Gavin Lambert. LC 76-2377. 272p. 1976. 18.95 (0-670-25581-5) Boulevard.

Dangerous Edge. large type ed. Ted Allbeury. LC 92-18450. 1992. 18.95 (0-7927-1400-8, Eagle Lrg Print) Chivers N Amer.

Dangerous Edge. large type ed. Ted Allbeury. 1993. pap. 16.95 (0-7927-1374-5, Paragon Lrg Print) Chivers N Amer.

*Dangerous Edge: A Novel. Robert Daley. 480p. 1995. mass mkt. 5.99 (0-446-60278-7) Warner Bks.

Dangerous Edge: The Psychology of Excitement. Michael J. Apter. LC 92-9030. 192p. 1992. text ed. 22.95 (0-02-900765-8) Free Pr.

Dangerous Encounter. Ernst Junger. Tr. by Hilary Barr. LC 92-62372. 208p. 1993. 21.00 (0-941419-37-1, Eridanos Library) Marsilio Pubs.

Dangerous Encounters: Meanings of Violence in a Brazilian City. Daniel T. Linger. LC 91-28599. (Illus.). 300p. (C). 1993. 45.00x (0-8047-1926-8) Stanford U Pr.

*Dangerous Encounters: Meanings of Violence in a Brazilian City. Daniel T. Linger. (Illus.). 300p. 1995. pap. 14.95 (0-8047-2589-6) Stanford U Pr.

Dangerous Enthusiasm: William Blake & the Culture of Radicalism in the 1790s. Jon Mee. (Illus.). 280p. 1994. reprint ed. pap. 21.00 (0-19-818329-1) OUP.

Dangerous Environments. Michel Peissel & Missy Allen. (Encyclopedia of Danger Ser.). (Illus.). 112p. (J). (gr. 5 up). 1993. lib. bdg. 19.95 (0-7910-1793-1, Am Art Analog) Chelsea Hse.

*Dangerous Evidence. Ellis A. Cohen. Ed. by Milton J. Shapiro. 384p. (Orig.). 1995. pap. text ed. 5.99 (0-425-14725-8) Berkley Pub.

Dangerous Familiars: Representations of Domestic Crime in England, 1550-1700. Frances E. Dolan. LC 93-40060. (Illus.). 272p. 1994. 37.95 (0-8014-2901-3); pap. 15.95 (0-8014-8134-1) Cornell U Pr.

D

Dangerous Families: Assessment & Treatment of Child Abuse. Peter Dale. 280p. 1987. 47.50 (0-422-60140-3, 1129, Pub. by Tavistock UK); pap. 14.95 (0-317-56157-X, 1152, Pub. by Tavistock UK) Routledge Chapman & Hall.

*Dangerous Fieldwork. Raymond M. Lee. (Qualitative Research Methods Ser.: Vol. 34). 96p. 1994. 21.50 (0-8039-5660-6); pap. 9.50 (0-8039-5661-4) Sage.

Dangerous Fish. Ray Broekel. LC 82-4464. (New True Bks.). (J). (gr. k-4). 1982. lib. bdg. 13.50 (0-516-01635-0); pap. 5.50 (0-516-41635-9) Childrens.

Dangerous Flora. Michel Peissel & Missy Allen. (Encyclopedia of Danger Ser.). (Illus.). 112p. (J). (gr. 5 up). 1993. lib. bdg. 19.95 (0-7910-1786-9, Am Art Analog) Chelsea Hse.

Dangerous Food: I Corinthians 8-10 in Its Context. Peter D. Gooch. (Studies in Christianity & Judaism: Vol. 5). 184p. (C). 1993. pap. 25.00 (0-88920-219-2, Pub. by Wilfrid Laurier CN) Humanities.

Dangerous Fortune. Ken Follett. 1993. pap. 23.95 (0-385-31121-4) Delacorte.

*Dangerous Fortune. Ken Follett. 1994. mass mkt. 6.99 (0-440-21749-0) Dell.

Dangerous Game. Jeri Massi. (Light Line Ser.). 121p. (Orig.). (J). (gr. 4-6). 1986. pap. 5.95 (0-89084-347-3) Bob Jones Univ Pr.

*Dangerous Games. Ed. by Lesley Grant-Adamson. LC 94-36027. 1995. 19.95 (0-312-11766-3) St Martin.

Dangerous Games. Warren Murphy. (Destroyer Ser.: No. 40). 192p. (Orig.). 1991. pap. 3.50 (1-55817-468-0, Pinnacle NY) Windsor NY.

Dangerous Games: The True Story of a Convicted Murderer on Death Row Who Changed His Sex & Won Her Freedom. Robert L. Bentley. LC 92-39499. 1993. 19.95 (1-55972-180-4, Birch Ln Pr) Carol Pub Group.

Dangerous Goods at Sea, 2 vols. International Maritime Organization Staff. 1991. Pt. I, Mark 111. write for info. (0-318-69594-4, Pub. by Intl Maritime Org UK); Pt. II, Mark 111. write for info. (0-318-69595-2, Pub. by Intl Maritime Org UK) St Mut.

Dangerous Goods at Sea, 2 vols., Set. International Maritime Organization Staff. 1991. text ed. 5,000.00 (0-89771-884-4, Pub. by Intl Maritime Org UK) St Mut.

*Dangerous Grace: Daily Readings. Charles Colson. 1994. 19.99 (0-8499-1171-0) Word Pub.

Dangerous Ground. Gloria Skurzynski. LC 88-31394. 128p. (J). (gr. 3-7). 1989. text ed. 14.95 (0-02-782731-3, Bradbury S&S) S&S Childrens.

Dangerous Ground: The Rival Detectives. Lawrence L. Lynch. LC 75-32764. (Literature of Mystery & Detection Ser.). (Illus.). 1976. reprint ed. 39.95 (0-405-07885-4) Ayer.

Dangerous Ground: The World of Hazardous Waste Crime. Donald J. Rebovich. 168p. (C). 1992. text ed. 34.95 (1-56000-014-7) Transaction Pubs.

Dangerous Guy. Jaqueline Diamond. (American Romance Ser.). 1993. mass mkt. 3.50 (0-373-16491-2, 1-16491-2) Harlequin Bks.

Dangerous Ideas: A Mystery. Janet L. Graham. 235p. (Orig.). 1994. pap. 10.95 (1-878533-13-4) Clothespin Fever Pr.

Dangerous Ideas of Science. Morris Goran. (American University Studies: Philosophy: Ser. V, Vol. 48). 221p. (C). 1989. text ed. 34.00 (0-8204-0611-2) P Lang Pubs.

Dangerous Illusion. large type ed. Mandy Brown. 1990. 21.95 (0-7089-2149-3) Ulverscroft.

Dangerous Illusions. Amanda Scott. (Denise Little Presents ser.). 512p. 1994. pap. 4.99 (0-7860-0018-X, Pinnacle NY) Windsor NY.

Dangerous Infatuation. large type ed. Stephanie Howard. (Harlequin Ser.). 1992. reprint ed. lib. bdg. 18.95 (0-263-12979-9, Pub. by Mills & Boon UK) Thorndike Pr.

Dangerous Inheritance. large type ed. Stephanie Howard. 1993. 17.95 (0-263-13354-0, Pub. by Mills & Boon Ltd UK) Chivers N Amer.

Dangerous Innocence. Cheryl Morgan. 137p. (Orig.). 1988. pap. 7.50 (0-943487-09-9) Sevgo Pr.

Dangerous Insects. Michel Peissel & Missy Allen. (Encyclopedia of Danger Ser.). (Illus.). 112p. (J). (gr. 5 up). 1993. lib. bdg. 19.95 (0-7910-1785-0, Am Art Analog); pap. 9.95 (0-7910-1933-0, Am Art Analog) Chelsea Hse.

Dangerous Interloper. Penny Jordan. (Presents Ser.). 1993. pap. 2.89 (0-373-11544-X, 1-11544-3) Harlequin Bks.

Dangerous Interloper. large type ed. Penny Jordan. 1992. reprint ed. lib. bdg. 18.95 (0-263-12891-1, Pub. by Mills & Boon UK) Thorndike Pr.

Dangerous Intrigue. Janice Bennett. 320p. 1992. mass mkt. 3.99 (0-8217-4001-6) Zebra.

Dangerous Journey. large type ed. Margaret Mayo. 1991. pap. 8.95 (0-7451-9483-4, 265, Atlantic Lrg Print) Chivers N Amer.

Dangerous Journey: Symbolic Aspects of Boys' Initiation Among the Wagenia of Kisangani, Zaire. Andre Droogers. (Change & Continuity in Africa Ser.). 1979. pap. text ed. 56.95 (90-279-3357-X) Mouton.

Dangerous Journey: The Story of Pilgrim's Progress. Oliver Hunkin. (Illus.). 1985. 21.99 (0-8028-3619-4) Eerdmans.

Dangerous Journey see Heinemann Guided Readers

Dangerous Journeys: 1757. Parish Wells. Ed. by Robert B. Igoe. (Illus.). 112p. (Orig.). pap. 5.95 (0-9629159-0-4) Pine Tree NY.

Dangerous Journeys Mythus Gamemasters Screen. Gary Gygax. 1992. pap. 9.00 (1-55878-142-0) Game Designers.

*Dangerous Knowledge: The JFK Assassination in Art & Film. Art Simon. (Culture & Moving Image Ser.). (Illus.). 288p. (Orig.). (C). 1995. lib. bdg. 49.95 (1-56639-378-7); pap. 18.95 (1-56639-379-5) Temple U Pr.

Dangerous Lady. Barbara Hazard. 224p. (Orig.). 1980. pap. 1.75 (0-449-50120-5, Coventry) Fawcett.

Dangerous Lady. Barbara Hazard. (Orig.). 1988. pap. 2.95 (0-449-21655-1, Crest) Fawcett.

*Dangerous Legacy. Gordon Ryan. LC 94-26638. iv, 379p. 1994. 14.95 (0-87579-905-1) Deseret Bk.

Dangerous Legacy: The Babies of Drug-Taking Parents. Ben Sonder. LC 94-15076. (Illus.). 112p. (YA). (gr. 9-12). 1994. lib. bdg. 14.77 (0-531-11195-4) Watts.

Dangerous Legal Drugs. William C. Douglas. Ed. by Robert K. Kroening. 96p. (Orig.). (C). 1994. pap. 8.95 (0-9626646-6-9) Second Opinion.

Dangerous Lessons. 2nd ed. Paul Little. 176p. 1994. reprint ed. pap. 4.95 (1-878320-32-7) Masquerade.

Dangerous Liaison. Jocelyn Davey. 1987. 16.95 (0-8027-5689-1) Walker & Co.

Dangerous Liaison. Sheri De Borchgrave. (Illus.). 336p. 1994. reprint ed. pap. 4.99 (0-451-40509-9, Onyx) NAL-Dutton.

Dangerous Liaison: The Inside Story of the U. S.-Israeli Covert Relationship. Andrew Cockburn & Leslie Cockburn. LC 90-55949. 432p. 1992. reprint ed. pap. 13.00 (0-06-092145-5, PL) HarpC.

Dangerous Liaisons: The Film. Christopher Hampton. (Illus.). 112p. 1989. pap. 14.95 (0-571-15447-6) Faber & Faber.

Dangerous Life. Lucia M. Perillo. 61p. 1989. pap. text ed. 9.95 (1-55553-059-1) NE U Pr.

Dangerous Life. Ben B. Lindsey & Rube Borough. LC 73-11938. (Metropolitan America Ser.). 468p. 1974. reprint ed. 33.95 (0-405-05400-9) Ayer.

Dangerous Life of the Sea Horse. Miriam Schlein. LC 85-26857. (Illus.). 48p. (J). (gr. 3-6). 1986. text ed. 13.95 (0-689-31180-X, Atheneum Bks Young) S&S Childrens.

Dangerous Lives of Altar Boys: A Novel. Chris Fuhrman. LC 93-41113. 176p. 1994. 19.95 (0-8203-1632-6) U of Ga Pr.

Dangerous Longing. Veronica Sattler. 1990. mass mkt. 4.95 (0-312-92337-6) St Martin.

Dangerous Love. Francine Pascal. (Sweet Valley High Ser.: No. 6). (J). (gr. 7 up). 1984. 3.50 (0-553-27741-3) Bantam.

Dangerous Love. large type ed. Katrina Wright. (Linford Romance Library). 208p. 1992. pap. 14.95 (0-7089-7202-0, Trailtree Bookshop) Ulverscroft.

Dangerous Lover. Lindsay Armstrong. (Presents Ser.). 1993. pap. 2.89 (0-373-11546-6, 1-11546-8) Harlequin Bks.

Dangerous Lover. large type ed. Lindsay Armstrong. (Harlequin Ser.). 18.95 (0-263-13402-4) Thorndike Pr.

Dangerous Loyalties. large type ed. Virginia Coffman. LC 93-13196. 1993. 20.95 (1-56054-332-9) Thorndike Pr.

Dangerous Mammals. Michel Peissel. (J). (gr. 4-7). 1992. pap. 9.95 (0-7910-1935-7, Am Art Analog) Chelsea Hse.

Dangerous Mammals. Michel Peissel & Missy Allen. (Encyclopedia of Danger Ser.). (Illus.). 112p. (J). (gr. 5 up). 1993. lib. bdg. 19.95 (0-7910-1790-7, Am Art Analog) Chelsea Hse.

Dangerous Man. large type ed. Anne Goring. (Linford Romance Library). 272p. 1988. pap. 11.95 (0-7089-6547-4, Linford) Ulverscroft.

*Dangerous Marine Animals: That Bite, Sting, Shock, Are Non-Edible. 3rd ed. Bruce W. Halstead. (Illus.). 256p. 1995. pap. 24.95 (0-87033-474-3) Cornell Maritime.

Dangerous Marine Animals of the Pacific Coast. Christina Parsons. LC 85-81586. (Illus.). 96p. 1986. pap. 4.95 (0-936940-03-4) Helm Pub.

Dangerous Marine Animals of the Pacific Coast. Christina Parsons. LC 85-81586. (Illus.). 96p. 1985. text ed. 5.95 (0-930118-11-1) Sea Chall.

Dangerous Marquis. Barbara Reeves. 240p. (Orig.). 1994. mass mkt. 3.99 (0-380-77672-3) Avon.

Dangerous Marriage. Barbara Cartland. (Camfield Ser.: No. 123). 1993. pap. 3.99 (0-515-11241-0) Jove Pubns.

Dangerous Matter: English Drama & Politics in 1623-24. Jerzy Limon. (Illus.). 174p. 1986. 69.95 (0-521-30664-7) Cambridge U Pr.

Dangerous Memories: House Churches & Our American Story. Bernard J. Lee & Michael Cowan. LC 86-62123. 208p. (Orig.). 1986. pap. 9.95 (0-934134-70-7) Sheed & Ward MO.

Dangerous Memories: Invasion & Resistance Since 1492. Renny Golden et al. LC 91-76224. (Illus.). 272p. 1992. 19.50 (0-9631026-0-5) Chi Rel Task.

*Dangerous Men. Geoffrey Becker. 168p. (C). 1995. 22.50 (0-8229-3899-5) U of Pittsburgh Pr.

Dangerous Men & Adventurous Women: Romance Writers on the Appeal of the Romance. Ed. by Jayne A. Krentz. LC 92-22665. (New Cultural Studies). 200p. (Orig.). (C). 1992. lib. bdg. 26.95 (0-8122-3192-9); pap. 13.95 (0-8122-1411-0) U of Pa Pr.

*Dangerous Minds. Johnson. 1995. mass mkt. 4.99 (0-312-95620-7) St Martin.

Dangerous Mourning. Anne Perry. 1992. mass mkt. 5.99 (0-8041-1037-9) Ivy Books.

Dangerous Natural Phenomena. Michel Peissel & Missy Allen. (Encyclopedia of Danger Ser.). (Illus.). 112p. (J). (gr. 5 up). 1993. lib. bdg. 19.95 (0-7910-1794-X, Am Art Analog) Chelsea Hse.

Dangerous Nature. T. J. Kirby. 352p. 1993. mass mkt. 4.50 (0-8217-4034-2) Zebra.

*Dangerous Neighborhoods. Marnie Prange. LC 93-71913. 57p. (Orig.). 1994. pap. 10.00 (1-880834-70-7) Cleveland St Univ Poetry Ctr.

*Dangerous Obsessions. Tracy Lewis. 740p. Date not set. pap. 12.95 (0-7610-0307-X) NW Pub.

Dangerous Offenders: The Elusive Target of Justice. Mark H. Moore et al. (Illus.). 264p. 1985. 28.50 (0-674-19065-3) HUP.

Dangerous Passage: The Santa Fe Trail & the Mexican War. William Y. Chalfant. LC 93-38605. (Illus.). 336p. 1994. 29.95 (0-8061-2613-2) U of Okla Pr.

Dangerous Passage: The Social Control of Sexuality in Women's Adolescence. Constance Nathanson. (Health, Society, & Policy Ser.). 350p. 1991. 44.95 (0-87722-824-8) Temple U Pr.

Dangerous Passage: The Social Control of Sexuality in Women's Adolescence. Constance A. Nathanson. 304p. 1993. pap. 18.95 (1-56639-077-X) Temple U Pr.

*Dangerous Peace: Security. Alpo M. Rusi. 1995. text ed. 39.95 (0-8133-2258-8) Westview.

Dangerous Plants & Mushrooms. Michel Peissel & Missy Allen. (Encyclopedia of Danger Ser.). (Illus.). 112p. (J). (gr. 5 up). 1993. lib. bdg. 19.95 (0-7910-1787-7, Am Art Analog) Chelsea Hse.

*Dangerous Positions: Mixed Government, the Estates of the Realm & the Making of the Answer to the XIX Propositions. Michael Mendle. LC 83-4798. 269p. 1985. pap. 76.70 (0-7837-8395-7, 2059206) Bks Demand.

Dangerous Positions & Proceedings. Richard Bancroft. LC 74-38147. (English Experience Ser.: No. 427). 192p. 1972. reprint ed. 35.00 (90-221-0427-3) Walter J Johnson.

Dangerous Practices. Francis Roe. 416p. 1993. pap. 5.99 (0-451-17790-8, Sig) NAL-Dutton.

*Dangerous Prayer: Being Vulnerable to God. William J. O'Malley. 160p. 1995. pap. 6.95 (0-89243-787-1) Liguori Pubns.

Dangerous Premises: An Insider's View of OSHA Enforcement. Don J. Lofgren. 256p. 1989. pap. 15.95 (0-87546-150-6) ILR Pr.

Dangerous Professions. Michel Peissel & Missy Allen. (Encyclopedia of Danger Ser.). (Illus.). 112p. (J). (gr. 5 up). 1993. lib. bdg. 19.95 (0-7910-1792-3, Am Art Analog) Chelsea Hse.

Dangerous Promise. Joan L. Nixon. LC 94-464. (Orphan Train Adventures Ser.). (J). 1994. 15.95 (0-385-32073-6) Delacorte.

*Dangerous Properties of Industrial & Consumer Chemicals. Nicholas P. Cheremisinoff et al. LC 94-14912. 816p. 1994. 195.00 (0-8247-9183-5) Dekker.

Dangerous Properties of Industrial Materials, 3 vols., 1. 9th ed. N. Irving Sax & Richard J. Lewis. 1993. text ed. write for info. (0-442-01276-4) Van Nos Reinhold.

Dangerous Properties of Industrial Materials, 3 vols., 2. 9th ed. N. Irving Sax & Richard J. Lewis. 1993. text ed. write for info. (0-442-01277-2) Van Nos Reinhold.

Dangerous Properties of Industrial Materials, 3 vols., 3. 9th ed. N. Irving Sax & Richard J. Lewis. 1993. text ed. write for info. (0-442-01278-0) Van Nos Reinhold.

Dangerous Relations. Carolyn Keene. Ed. by Anne Greenberg. (Nancy Drew Files Ser.: No. 82). 160p. (Orig.). (J). 1993. mass mkt. 3.99 (0-671-73086-X, Archway) PB.

Dangerous Relations: The Soviet Union in World Politics, 1970-1982. Adam B. Ulam. 1983. 29.95 (0-19-503237-3) OUP.

Dangerous Relations: The Soviet Union in World Politics, 1970-1982. Adam B. Ulam. 1984. pap. 9.95 (0-19-503424-4) OUP.

Dangerous Reptilian Creatures. Michel Peissel. (Encyclopedia of Danger Ser.). (J). (gr. 4-7). 1992. pap. 9.95 (0-7910-1934-9, Am Art Analog) Chelsea Hse.

Dangerous Reptilian Creatures. Michel Peissel & Missy Allen. (Encyclopedia of Danger Ser.). (Illus.). 112p. (J). (gr. 5 up). 1993. lib. bdg. 19.95 (0-7910-1789-3, Am Art Analog) Chelsea Hse.

Dangerous River. R. M. Paterson. LC 89-71264. (Illus.). 240p. (Orig.). 1990. reprint ed. pap. 12.95 (0-930031-26-1) Chelsea Green Pub.

Dangerous Sanctuary. Anne Mather. (Presents Ser.). 1993. pap. 2.89 (0-373-11553-9, 1-11553-4) Harlequin Bks.

Dangerous Sanctuary. large type ed. Anne Mather. 1993. reprint ed. lib. bdg. 18.95 (0-263-13183-1, Pub. by Mills & Boon UK) Thorndike Pr.

Dangerous Skies. Suzanne F. Staples. Date not set. write for info. (0-679-86197-1) Random.

Dangerous Skies. A. E. Clouston. Ed. by James B. Gilbert. LC 79-7240. (Flight: Its First Seventy-Five Years Ser.). (Illus.). 1980. reprint ed. 19.95 (0-405-12155-5) Ayer.

Dangerous Sky: A History of Aviation Medicine. Douglas H. Robinson. LC 68-11049. (Illus.). 316p. 1974. 25.00 (0-295-95304-7) U of Wash Pr.

Dangerous Sky: A Resource Guide to the Battle of Britain. Eunice Wilson. LC 94-46943. (Bibliographies of Battles & Leaders Ser.: No. 12). 160p. 1995. text ed. 65.00 (0-313-28216-1, WBR/, Greenwood Pr) Greenwood.

*Dangerous Snakes of Africa: Natural History - Species Directory - Venoms & Snakebite. Stephen Spawls & Bill Branch. LC 94-73975. (Illus.). 192p. 1995. 39.50 (0-88359-029-8) R Curtis Pubng.

Dangerous Society. Carl S. Taylor. LC 89-43115. 160p. (C). 1990. pap. 13.00 (0-87013-287-3) Mich St U Pr.

Dangerous Spaces. Margaret Mahy. 160p. (J). (gr. 5 up). 1993. pap. 3.99 (0-14-036362-9, Puffin) Puffin Bks.

Dangerous Spaces. Margaret Mahy. (YA). 1991. 12.95 (0-670-83734-2) Viking Child Bks.

Dangerous Sports. Michel Peissel & Missy Allen. (Encyclopedia of Danger Ser.). (Illus.). 112p. (J). (gr. 5 up). 1993. lib. bdg. 19.95 (0-7910-1791-5, Am Art Analog) Chelsea Hse.

Dangerous Sports. Michel Peissel & Missy Allen. LC 92-23546. (Encyclopedia of Danger Ser.). (J). 1993. pap. write for info. (0-7910-1942-X) Chelsea Hse.

Dangerous Spring. Margot Benary-Isbert. (YA). (gr. 6-12). 1991. 19.50 (0-8446-6476-6) Peter Smith.

Dangerous Steps: Vernon Tejas & the Solo Winter Ascent of Mount McKinley. Lewis Freedman. LC 90-35027. (Illus.). 208p. (Orig.). 1990. pap. 14.95 (0-8117-2341-0) Stackpole.

Dangerous Stranger. Marian Martin. 1981. pap. 1.75 (0-8439-8024-9) Dorchester Pub Co.

Dangerous Stranger. large type ed. Lucy Gillen. 304p. 1992. 21.95 (0-7089-2574-X) Ulverscroft.

Dangerous Substances: Chameleons in Water Policy. J. Vennekens-Capkova. 20p. 1990. pap. 6.00 (92-826-1085-3, CD-NA-12547-EN-) UNIPUB.

Dangerous Summer. Ernest Hemingway. (Illus.). 208p. 1985. pap. 9.95 (0-685-09991-1, Scribners) S&S Trade.

Dangerous Summer. Ernest Hemingway & James S. Michener. 240p. 1986. pap. 11.95 (0-684-18720-5, Scribners) S&S Trade.

Dangerous Supplements: Resistance & Renewal in Jurisprudence. Ed. by Peter Fitzpatrick. LC 90-28393. (Post-Contemporary Interventions Ser.). 224p. 1991. lib. bdg. 39.50 (0-8223-1140-2); pap. text ed. 19.95 (0-8223-1121-6) Duke.

Dangerous Symptoms. large type ed. Frances Crowne. 272p. 1993. 21.95 (0-7505-0472-2) Ulverscroft.

Dangerous Temptation. Barbara Kyle. 448p. (Orig.). 1994. pap. 4.99 (0-451-17932-3, Onyx) NAL-Dutton.

Dangerous Theatre: The Federal Theatre Project. George Kazacoff. (American University Studies: Ser. XXIV, Vol. 3). 377p. (C). 1989. text ed. 56.95 (0-8204-0752-6) P Lang Pubs.

Dangerous Thing: A Carl Burns Mystery. Bill Crider. 200p. 1994. 19.95 (0-8027-3187-2) Walker & Co.

*Dangerous Things. large type ed. Claire Rayner. (Charnwood Large Print Ser.). 1994. 25.95 (0-7089-8801-6) Ulverscroft.

Dangerous Thoughts. large type ed. Celia Fremlin. (Mystery Ser.). 352p. 1993. 21.95 (0-7089-2953-2) Ulverscroft.

*Dangerous to Kiss. Thornton. 1995. mass mkt. 5.50 (0-553-57372-1) Bantam.

*Dangerous to Know. Barbara T. Bradford. 1995. 24.00 (0-06-017722-5) HarpC.

Dangerous to Know. Margaret Yorke. 272p. 1994. 17.95 (0-89296-500-2) Mysterious Pr.

Dangerous to Know. Margaret Yorke. 256p. 1995. mass mkt. 5.50 (0-446-40198-6, Mysterious Paperbk) Warner Bks.

An Asterisk (*) at the beginning of an entry indicates that the title is appearing in BIP for the first time.

D

Daniel Defoe's Scotland. Moubray House Publishing Ltd. Staff. (Illus.). (C). 1991. pap. 90.00 (*0-948473-19-3* St Mut.

Daniel Deronda. George Eliot. Ed. by Graham Handley. (World's Classics Ser.). 758p. 1988. pap. 6.95 (*0-19-281787-6*) OUP.

Daniel Deronda. George Eliot. Ed. by Barbara Hardy. (English Library). 903p. 1967. mass mkt. 7.95 (*0-14-043020-2*, Penguin Classics) Viking Penguin.

Daniel Dion: Paths. Jean Gagnon et al. 95p. 1994. pap. 19.95 (*0-88884-621-5*) U Ch Pr.

Daniel Discovers Daniel. John Barrett. LC 79-17897. (Illus.). 32p. (J). (gr. k-5). 1980. 16.95 (*0-87705-423-1*) Human Sci Pr.

Daniel Dobyns of Colonial VA: His English Ancestry & American Descendants. Kenneth W. Dobyns & Margaret S. Thorpe. LC 85-71713. 182p. reprint ed. 90.00 (*0-916497-13-5*); reprint ed. fiche 6.00 (*0-916497-03-8*) Burnett Micro.

Daniel Dobyns of Colonial Virginia: His English Ancestry & American Descendants. Kenneth W. Dobyns & Margaret S. Thorpe. LC 73-20318. 188p. reprint ed. pap. 53.60 (*0-317-08867-X*, 2005247) Bks Demand.

Daniel En el Foso De los Leones (Daniel in Lion's Den) P. Frank. (SPA.). Date not set. 1.50 (*0-945792-59-X*, 490327) Editorial Unilit.

Daniel Entra Al Primer Grado. Gila M. Fleisher. Tr. by C. C. Writer & Lisa C. Nielsen. (Hippy Ser.). (Illus.). 24p. (Orig.). (SPA.). (J). (ps). 1992. pap. text ed. 3.00 (*1-56134-176-2*) Dushkin Pub.

Daniel, Esther, & Jeremiah: The Additions. Carey A. Moore. LC 76-42376. (Anchor Bible Ser.: Vol. 44). (Illus.). 1977. 34.00 (*0-385-04702-9*, Anchor NY) Doubleday.

Daniel (Everyman's Bible Commentary) see Daniel (Comentario Biblico Portavoz)

Daniel, Ezra, & Nehemiah - Hebrew Text & Commentary with English Translation: Hebrew Text, English Translation & Commentary Digest. Tr. by A. J. Rosenberg. 1992. 17.95 (*0-910818-94-0*) Judaica Pr.

Daniel, Ezra, Nehemiah: Hebrew Text & English Translation & Commentary Digest. 2nd rev. ed. Ed. by Shalom Shahar. LC 92-32782. (Books of the Bible Ser.). 1995. 14.95 (*1-871055-75-X*) Soncino Pr.

Daniel, First Maccabees, Second Maccabees with an Excursus on Apocalyptic Genre. John Collins. LC 81-80825. (Old Testament Message Ser.: Vol. 15). 372p. 1982. 19.95 (*0-8146-5415-0*); pap. 16.95 (*0-8146-5250-6*) Liturgical Pr.

Daniel Forbes: A Pioneer Boy. Dorothy Hamilton. (Illus.). (Orig.). (J). (ps-4). 1980. pap. 3.95 (*0-686-32860-4*) Barnwood Pr.

Daniel, Gabriel, & Michael: Our Creator. Arlie E. Petty. 1992. 11.95 (*0-533-10070-4*) Vantage.

Daniel, God's Man in a Secular Society. Donald K. Campbell. 1988. 8.99 (*0-929239-05-9*) Discovery Hse Pubs.

Daniel Gregory & His Wife Sarah Lamont: Their Ancestors & Descendants. Ed. by Richard B. Walker. LC 92-61381. 160p. 1992. 23.00 (*0-9622938-2-2*) R B Walker.

Daniel H. Burnham: Architect Planner of Cities. Charles Moore. LC 68-27726. (Architecture & Decorative Art Ser.). (Illus.). 1968. reprint ed. lib. bdg. 75.00 (*0-306-71151-6*) Da Capo.

Daniel Hale Williams: Surgeon. Flossie E. Thompson-Peters. (Illus.). 32p. (Orig.). (J). (gr. 3-9). 1988. pap. 4.70 (*1-880784-05-X*) Atlas Pr.

Daniel: Historia y Profecia: Daniel: History & Prophecy. Kittim Silva. (SPA.). 6.95 (*84-7228-975-3*, 223038, Pub. by Edit Clie SP) TSELF.

Daniel in His Time. Andre LaCocque. Ed. by James Crenshaw. (Studies on Personalities of the Old Testament). 257p. 1987. text ed. 34.95 (*0-87249-481-0*) U of SC Pr.

Daniel in the Critics' Den: A Defense of the Historicity of the Book of Daniel. 3rd ed. Robert Anderson. LC 90-4683. 186p. 1990. reprint ed. pap. 7.99 (*0-8254-2133-0*) Kregel.

***Daniel in the Dangerous Den.** Concordia Staff. 1995. pap. 2.99 (*0-570-07504-1*) Concordia.

Daniel in the Lions' Den. (Children's Bible Stories Ser.). (Illus.). 24p. (J). 1993. 4.98 (*1-56173-722-4*) Pubns Intl Ltd.

***Daniel in the Lions' Den.** (Now You Can Read Bible Stories Ser.). 24p. (J). 1994. 3.98 (*0-86112-786-2*) Brimax Bks.

Daniel in the Lions' Den. Illus. by Susan Crowder. 36p. (Orig.). (J). 1984. pap. 3.00 (*0-912927-08-9*, X008) St John Kronstadt.

Daniel in the Lions' Den. Anne Gill. (Tiny Bible Tales Ser.). (J). (ps-3). 1994. 4.95 (*0-8167-3320-1*) BrdgeWater.

Daniel in the Lion's Den. M. Good. 1993. 2.00 (*0-317-05261-6*) Rod & Staff.

Daniel in the Lions' Den. Jane Latourette & Mathews. (Arch Bks.: Set 3). 1966. 1.99 (*0-570-06018-4*, 59-1127) Concordia.

***Daniel in the Lion's Den.** Rabbit. (J). Date not set. pap. 19.95 (*0-689-80239-0*, Aladdin Paperbacks) S&S Childrens.

***Daniel in the Lion's Den.** Illus. by Kay Widdowson. (Mini Pop-Ups Ser.). (J). (ps-1). 1995. 4.99 (*1-884628-11-7*) Flying Frog.

***Daniel J. Boorstin Reader.** Daniel J. Boorstin. 1995. 18.00 (*0-679-60165-1*) Random.

Daniel Ladd: Merchant Prince of Frontier Florida. Jerrell H. Shofner. LC 77-21789. 1978. 17.95 (*0-8130-0546-9*) U Press Fla.

Daniel Libeskind: Countersign. Daniel Libeskind. LC 91-62802. (Illus.). 144p. 1992. 45.00 (*0-8478-1478-5*) Rizzoli Intl.

Daniel Mannix: Builder of the Australian Church. John O'Brien. 1989. pap. 22.00 (*1-85390-042-7*, Pub. by Veritas IE) St Mut.

Daniel Mannix: The Quality of Leadership. B. A. Santamaria. (Illus.). xi, 282p. 1990. pap. 17.95 (*0-522-84405-7*) Intl Spec Bk.

Daniel Martin. John Fowles. 1977. 19.95 (*0-316-28959-0*) Little.

Daniel Martin. John Fowles. 1978. pap. 4.50 (*0-451-12210-0*, AE2210, Sig) NAL-Dutton.

Daniel McNaughton: His Trial & the Aftermath. Alexander Walk. Ed. by Donald F. West. 185p. 1979. write for info. (*0-902241-01-X*, Pub. by Royal Coll Psych UK) Am Psychiatric.

Daniel Meets a Lion. Cleona Morgan. 1993. pap. 2.95 (*0-88494-885-4*) Bookcraft Inc.

Daniel Morgan: Ranger of the Revolution. North Callahan. LC 71-161759. reprint ed. 29.50 (*0-404-09017-6*) AMS Pr.

Daniel Morgan: Revolutionary Rifleman. Don Higginbotham. LC 61-17062. (Institute of Early American History & Culture Ser.). xvi, 239p. 1979. pap. 11.95 (*0-8078-1386-9*) U of NC Pr.

***Daniel My Son.** Ruthie Perlman. LC 94-70750. 200p. Date not set. write for info. (*1-56062-193-1*) CIS Comm.

Daniel Nash - Prevailing Prince of Prayer. J. Paul Reno. 1989. pap. 1.99 (*1-56632-089-5*) Revival Lit.

Daniel O'Connell: Nationalism Without Violence. Raymond Moley. LC 73-93142. xxiv, 246p. 1974. 30.00 (*0-8232-0977-6*) Fordham.

Daniel O'Connell: Portrait of a Radical. Ed. by Kevin B. Nowlan & Maurice R. O'Connell. LC 85-80412. 120p. 1885. 24.95 (*0-8232-1140-1*) Fordham.

Daniel O'Connell: The Man & His Politics. Maurice O'Connell. 160p. (C). 1990. 29.50 (*0-7165-2446-5*, Pub. by Irish Acad Pr IE) Intl Spec Bk.

Daniel of Babylon. Bob Jones. (Illus.). 216p. (Orig.). 1984. pap. 6.95 (*0-89084-270-1*) Bob Jones Univ Pr.

Daniel O'Rourke. Gerald McDermott. LC 85-20188. (Viking Kestrel Picture Bks.). (Illus.). 32p. (J). (ps-3). 1986. pap. 12.95 (*0-670-80924-1*) Viking Child Bks.

Daniel O'Rourke: An Irish Tale. Gerald McDermott. (J). 1988. pap. 4.99 (*0-14-050673-X*, Puffin) Puffin Bks.

Daniel Ortega. John Stockwell. (World Leaders - Past & Present Ser.). (Illus.). 112p. (J). (gr. 5 up). 1991. 17.95 (*1-55546-846-2*) Chelsea Hse.

Daniel Perrin, "the Huguenot", & His Descendants in America of the Surnames Perrine, Perine, & Prine, 1665-1910. H. D. Perrine. (Illus.). 553p. 1989. reprint ed. lib. bdg. 79.00 (*0-8328-0956-X*); reprint ed. pap. 69.00 (*0-8328-0957-8*) Higginson Bk Co.

Daniel Pinkham: A Bio-Bibliography. Kee DeBoer & John B. Ahouse. LC 88-157. (Bio-Bibliographies in Music Ser.: No. 12). 256p. 1988. text ed. 49.95 (*0-313-25503-2*, DDP/, Greenwood Pr) Greenwood.

Daniel: Prophecies. Lehman Strauss. LC 70-85293. Orig. Title: Prophecies of Daniel. 1969. 16.99 (*0-87213-812-7*) Loizeaux.

Daniel Ricketson & His Friends: Letter, Poems, Sketches, Etc. Ed. by Anna Ricketson & Walton Ricketson. LC 80-2513. (Thoreau Ser.). (Illus.). 440p. reprint ed. 67.50 (*0-404-19061-8*) AMS Pr.

Daniel Rowland & the Great Evangelical Awakening in Wales. Eifion Evans. 383p. 1985. 35.95 (*0-85151-446-4*) Banner of Truth.

Daniel S. Dickinson: Defender of the Constitution. (Illus.). 221p. 1987. 10.00 (*0-317-03777-3*) M B Hinman.

***Daniel Sanders: Aufgeklarte Germanistik Im 19. Jahrhundert.** Ulrike Hass-Zumkehr. (Studia Linguistica Germanica: Bd. 35). 656p. (GER.). (C). 1995. lib. bdg. 190.75 (*3-11-014331-3*) De Gruyter.

Daniel Scott & the Monster. Evelyn-Marie. LC 85-13369. (Illus.). 32p. (J). (gr. k-3). 1985. 7.95 (*0-9614746-1-0*); audio 11.95 (*0-9614746-0-2*); lib. bdg. 9.95 (*0-9614746-2-9*); pap. 3.00 (*0-9614746-4-5*) Berry Bks.

Daniel Shanks, Dedication. (Mathematics of Computation Ser.: Vol. 48, No. 177, Jan. 1987). 448p. 1987. pap. 60.00 (*0-685-70674-5*, SHANKSC) Am Math.

Daniel, Strong in the Lord. Katherine Hershey. (Illus.). (J). (gr. k-6). 1992. pap. text ed. 9.45 (*1-55976-035-4*) CEF Press.

Daniel: Su Vida y Sus Tiempos: The Life & Times of Daniel. William J. Deane. (SPA.). 6.95 (*84-7645-166-0*, 223205, Pub. by Edit Clie SP) TSELF.

Daniel, the Kingdom of the Lord. Charles L. Feinberg. 1984. 14.99 (*0-88469-157-8*) BMH Bks.

***Daniel the Prophet.** M. R. DeHaan. 336p. 1995. pap. 10.99 (*0-8254-2475-5*) Kregel.

Daniel the Prophet. H. A. Ironside. 1911. 14.99 (*0-87213-357-5*); 0.25 (*0-87213-358-3*) Loizeaux.

Daniel the Prophet. Edward B. Pusey. 592p. lib. bdg. 20.99 (*0-8254-5219-8*) Kregel.

Daniel Urrabieta Vierge in the Collection of the Hispanic Society of America, 2 vols., Set. (Illus.). 1936. 12.00 (*0-87535-040-2*) Hispanic Soc.

Daniel Wadsworth: Patron of the Arts. Richard Saunders & Helen Raye. (Illus.). 109p. 1981. pap. 8.50 (*0-317-13591-0*) Wadsworth Atheneum.

Daniel Walravens: Serie Noire. (Illus.). 128p. 1989. pap. 30.00 (*90-72191-16-1*, Pub. by Imschoot BE) Dist Art Pubs.

Daniel Webster. Irving H. Bartlett. (Illus.). 352p. 1981. pap. 8.95 (*0-393-00996-3*) Norton.

Daniel Webster. Henry C. Lodge. Ed. by John T. Morse, Jr. LC 71-128960. (American Statesmen Ser.: No. 21). reprint ed. 35.00 (*0-404-50871-5*) AMS Pr.

Daniel Webster, 2 Vols, Set. 2nd ed. Claude M. Fuess. LC 68-8722. (American Scene Ser.). (Illus.). 1968. reprint ed. lib. bdg. 85.00 (*0-306-71186-9*) Da Capo.

Daniel Webster: Defender of the Union. Robert Allen. (Sower Ser.). (Illus.). (J). (gr. 3-6). 1989. pap. 6.95 (*0-88062-156-7*) Mott Media.

Daniel Webster & Jacksonian Democracy. Sydney Nathans. LC 72-10779. (Johns Hopkins University Studies in Historical & Political Science: Series 91, No. 1). 263p. reprint ed. pap. 75.00 (*0-685-23508-4*, 2027899) Bks Demand.

Daniel Webster & the Blacksmith's Fee. Ted Gibbons. (Keepsake Bookcards Ser.). 8p. (Orig.). (YA). 1988. pap. 1.95 (*0-929985-03-6*) Jackman Pubng.

Daniel Webster & the Rise of National Conservatism. Richard Current. (Illus.). 215p. (C). 1992. reprint ed. pap. text ed. 9.95 (*0-88133-653-X*) Waveland Pr.

Daniel Webster & the Supreme Court. Maurice G. Baxter. LC 66-28116. 280p. 1966. 30.00 (*0-87023-008-5*) U of Mass Pr.

Daniel Webster As an Economist. Robert L. Carey. LC 29-15020. (Columbia University. Studies in the Social Sciences: No. 313). reprint ed. 20.00 (*0-404-51313-1*) AMS Pr.

Daniel Webster, "The Completest Man" Ed. by Kenneth E. Shewmaker. LC 90-13057. 351p. (C). 1990. 39.50 (*0-87451-528-9*); pap. 16.95 (*0-87451-628-5*) U Pr of New Eng.

Daniel Webster, the Expounder of the Constitution. Everett P. Wheeler. ix, 188p. 1986. reprint ed. lib. bdg. 25.00 (*0-8377-1339-0*) Rothman.

Daniel Willard & Progressive Management on the Baltimore & Ohio Railroad. David M. Vrooman. (Historical Perspectives on Business Enterprise Ser.). (Illus.). 288p. 1991. 42.50 (*0-8142-0552-6*) Ohio St U Pr.

Daniel Willard Rides the Line. Edward Hungerford. LC 72-1281. (Select Bibliographies Reprint Ser.). 1977. reprint ed. 32.95 (*0-8369-6828-X*) Ayer.

Daniel y el Reino Mesianico. Evis L. Carballosa. 320p. 1979. pap. 9.99 (*0-8254-1101-7*) Kregel.

Daniel y Juanita. Effie M. Williams. (SPA.). 1982. pap. 1.25 (*0-318-01332-0*) Rod & Staff.

Daniel 8: 14: The Day of Atonement & the Investigative Judgment. Desmond Ford. 700p. (Orig.). 1980. pap. text ed. 9.95 (*1-883619-08-4*) D Ford Pubns.

Daniele Manin & the Venetian Revolution of 1848-1849. Paul Ginsborg. LC 78-56180. 435p. reprint ed. pap. 124.00 (*0-685-17877-3*, 2029219) Bks Demand.

Danielito y el Dinosauria. Syd Hoff. Tr. by Teresa Mlawer. Orig. Title: Danny & the Dinosaur. (Illus.). 64p. (J). (gr. 5-7). 1991. lib. bdg. 11.95 (*0-9625162-2-8*) Lectorum Pubns.

Danielle Ross Mystery Series, 3 vols., Set. Gilbert Morris. 1992. pap. 24.00 (*0-8007-5454-9*) Revell.

Danielle Steel. Incl. Passion's Promise. 1983. (*0-318-57255-9*); Now & Forever. 1983. (*0-318-57256-7*); Seasons of Passion. 1983. boxed (*0-318-57257-5*); 1983. Set boxed 12.60 (*0-440-11652-X*) Dell.

Danielle Steel. Nicole Hoyt. 400p. 1994. mass mkt. 4.99 (*0-7860-0032-5*) Windsor NY.

Danielle Steel, 3 vols. Danielle Steel. 1990. boxed, pap. 17.85 (*0-440-36008-0*) Dell.

Danielle Steel, 3 vols., No. 2. Danielle Steel. 1990. boxed, pap. 17.85 (*0-440-36022-6*) Dell.

Danielle Steel: Family Album; Remembrance; Thurston House, Set. Incl. Family Album. (*0-318-62394-3*); Remembrance. (*0-318-62395-1*); 1986. Set boxed 15.00 (*0-440-11694-5*) Dell.

Daniels: Plays One. Sarah Daniels. (Methuen World Dramatists Ser.). 420p. (Orig.). (C). 1991. pap. 14.95 (*0-413-64930-X*, A0537, Pub. by Methuen UK) Heinemann.

Daniels: The Daniels Family. James H. Daniels, Jr. (Illus.). 264p. 1991. reprint ed. lib. bdg. 51.50 (*0-8328-2217-5*); reprint ed. pap. 41.50 (*0-8328-2218-3*) Higginson Bk Co.

Daniel's Adventure with the Lions. Peter Mills. (Bible Flap Bks.). 24p. (J). 1994. 7.95 (*0-687-10084-4*) Abingdon.

***Daniels & Worthingham's Muscle Testing: Techniques of Manual Examination.** 6th ed. Helen J. Hislop & Jacqueline Montgomery. (Illus.). 400p. 1995. text ed. write for info. (*0-7216-4305-1*) Saunders.

Daniel's Bride. Linda L. Miller. Ed. by Linda Marrow. 400p. (Orig.). 1992. mass mkt. 5.99 (*0-671-73166-1*) PB.

Daniel's Bride. large type ed. Linda L. Miller. LC 92-41556. (Popular Ser.). 504p. (Orig.). 1993. reprint ed. pap. 17.95 (*1-56054-619-0*) Thorndike Pr.

Daniel's Deception. Marie Dewitt. (Stolen Moments Ser.). 1993. pap. 1.99 (*0-373-83284-2*, 1-83284-9) Harlequin Bks.

Daniel's Dog. Jo-Ellen Bogart. (Illus.). (J). 1992. pap. 3.95 (*0-590-43401-2*, Blue Ribbon Bks) Scholastic Inc.

Daniel's Duck. Clyde R. Bulla. LC 77-25647. (I Can Read Bk.). (Illus.). 64p. (J). (gr. k-3). 1979. lib. bdg. 14.89 (*0-06-020909-7*) HarpC Child Bks.

Daniel's Duck. Clyde R. Bulla. LC 78-22156. (Trophy I Can Read Bk.). (Illus.). 64p. (J). (gr. k-3). 1982. pap. 3.50 (*0-06-444031-1*, Trophy) HarpC Child Bks.

Daniel's First Bus Ride. Mary Rogers. (Cityscapes Ser.). 30p. (J). (gr. k). 1992. pap. text ed. 23.00 (*1-56843-008-6*); pap. text ed. 4.50 (*1-56843-058-2*) BGR Pub.

Daniel's Gift. M. C. Helldorfer. LC 87-5160. (Illus.). 32p. (J). (ps-3). 1987. text ed. 14.95 (*0-02-743511-3*, Bradbury S&S) S&S Childrens.

Daniel's Gift. M. C. Helldorfer. LC 90-186. (Illus.). 32p. (J). (gr. k-3). 1990. reprint ed. pap. 4.95 (*0-689-71440-8*, Aladdin Paperbacks) S&S Childrens.

Daniel's Prophecy of the Seventy Weeks. Alva J. McClain. pap. 5.99 (*0-88469-076-8*) BMH Bks.

Daniel's Prophecy of the Seventy Weeks. Alva J. McClain. 1985. pap. 6.99 (*0-310-29011-2*, 10177P) Zondervan.

Daniel's Story. Carol Matas. 144p. (J). (gr. 4-7). 1993. pap. 3.95 (*0-590-46588-0*) Scholastic Inc.

Daniel's Story. Carol Matas. LC 92-27537. 144p. (J). (gr. 4-9). 1993. 13.95 (*0-590-46920-7*) Scholastic Inc.

Daniels, Vol. II: The Daniels Family. James H. Daniels, Jr. (Illus.). 484p. 1991. reprint ed. lib. bdg. 83.00 (*0-8328-2219-1*); reprint ed. pap. 73.00 (*0-8328-2220-5*) Higginson Bk Co.

***Daniels:Plays Two.** Sarah Daniels. 256p. 1995. pap. 15.95 (*0-413-69040-7*) Heinemann.

Danilo the Fruit Man. Amy Valens. LC 91-46893. (Illus.). 32p. (J). (ps-3). 1993. lib. bdg. 12.89 (*0-8037-1152-2*) Dial Bks Young.

Danish. (Hugo's Phrasebks.). 128p. (Orig.). 1989. pap. 4.95 (*0-85285-139-1*) Hunter NJ.

***Danish: A Comprehensive Grammar.** Philip Holmes et al. (Grammars Ser.). 576p. 1995. pap. 29.95 (*0-415-08206-4*, B4090) Routledge.

***Danish: A Grammar.** W. G. Jones. 170p. 1990. 40.00 (*87-01-95481-4*) IBD Ltd.

Danish: An Elementary Grammar & Reader. Elias Bredsdorff. 1984. pap. 29.95 (*0-521-09821-1*) Cambridge U Pr.

Danish: Learn to Speak. Aage Salling. 200p. 1989. audio 135.00 (*0-88432-243-2*, AFDA40); 19.95 (*0-88432-530-X*, AFDA49) Audio-Forum.

***Danish - English - English - Danish Medical Dictionary.** M. Pilegaard & H. Baden. 913p. (DAN.). 1994. 120.00 (*87-12-02240-3*) IBD Ltd.

Danish-American Journey. Erling Duus. 1971. pap. 2.75 (*0-686-00051-X*) Gauntlet Bks.

Danish American Journey. Erling Duus. 134p. 1971. pap. 10.00 (*1-881946-01-0*) Gauntlet Bks.

Danish-American Life & Letters: A Bibliography. Enok Mortensen. Ed. by Franklyn D. Scott. LC 78-15200. (Scandinavians in America Ser.). 1979. reprint ed. lib. bdg. 15.95 (*0-405-11652-7*) Ayer.

Danish Americans. Mark Mussari. (Peoples of North America Ser.). (Illus.). 112p. (J). (gr. 5 up). 1988. lib. bdg. 17.95 (*0-87754-871-4*) Chelsea Hse.

Danish Cassette Pack. Berlitz Editors. (Cassettepaks Ser.). 1993. audio 15.95 (*2-8315-1091-0*) Berlitz.

Danish Cinema Before Dreyer. Ron Mottram. LC 87-16125. 315p. 1988. 29.50 (*0-8108-2035-8*) Scarecrow.

Danish Complete Course. 2nd ed. 1994. 12.95 (*0-8442-3759-0*, NTC Busn Bks) NTC Pub Grp.

Danish Cross-Stitch. Ondori Publishing Company Staff. (Illus.). 112p. 1985. pap. 14.95 (*0-87040-627-2*) Japan Pubns USA.

Danish Cross-Stitch Zodiac Samplers: Charted Designs for the Astrological Year. Jana Hauschild. (Illus.). 1980. pap. 3.50 (*0-486-24032-0*) Dover.

Danish Design or British Disease? Danish Economic Crisis Policy 1974-1979 in a Comparative Perspective. Peter Nannestad. (Acta Jutlandica LXVII: 2 Humanities Ser.). 285p. (Orig.). 1991. pap. 37.50 (*87-7288-399-5*, Pub. by Aarhus Univ Pr DK) Coronet Bks.

***Danish Dictionary: Rode Ordbog-Gyldendals, Danish-English.** 9th ed. J. Axelson. 1991. text ed. 47.00 (*87-00-73972-3*, D705) IBD Ltd.

Danish Dictionary: Rode Ordbog-Gyldendals, English-Danish. 11th ed. H. Vinterberg et al. (C). 1993. text ed. 43.50x (*87-00-69312-X*, D704) Vanous.

Danish Dictionary Deluxe, 2 vols. H. Vinterberg & Sen A. Bodel. (DAN & ENG.). (C). 1976. Vol. 1, 1989. text ed. 50.00x (*0-89918-726-9*, D726) Vanous.

Danish Economy in the Twentieth Century. Hans C. Johansen. LC 86-22574. 240p. 1986. text ed. 45.00 (*0-312-00373-0*) St Martin.

Danish Embroidery see Danish Pulled Thread Embroidery

Danish Emigrant Ballads & Songs. Ed. by Rochelle Wright & Robert L. Wright. LC 82-24230. (Illus.). 240p. 1983. 30.00 (*0-8093-1064-3*) S Ill U Pr.

Danish-English - English-Danish (Pocket) Dictionary. 4th ed. 601p. 1991. reprint ed. 21.00 (*87-14-61188-0*) IBD Ltd.

***Danish-English Comprehensive Dictionary.** H. Vinterberg. 1473p. (DAN & ENG.). 1993. write for info. (*0-7859-8799-1*) Fr & Eur.

***Danish-English Comprehensive Dictionary.** H. Vinterberg & C. A. Bodelsen. 1473p. (DAN & ENG.). 1993. 210.00x (*87-00-25801-6*) IBD Ltd.

Danish-English Dictionary. Berlitz Editors. (Bilingual Pocket Dictionary Ser.). 360p. (DAN & ENG.). 1994. pap. 7.95 (*2-8315-0994-7*) Berlitz.

Danish-English Dictionary. rev. ed. K. Schibsbye & H. Kossmann. Ed. by G. Rona & R. Raylor. (DAN & ENG.). 39.50 (*0-87559-006-3*); 44.50 (*0-87559-007-1*) Shalom.

***Danish-English Dictionary.** 9th ed. J. Axelson. (DAN & ENG.). 1991. 47.00 (*0-7859-8928-5*) Fr & Eur.

Danish-English Dictionary: Dansk-Engelsk Ordbog. 3rd ed. H. Vinterberg & C. A. Bodelsen. 1846p. (DAN & ENG.). 1991. 250.00 (*0-8288-4429-1*, M1281) Fr & Eur.

Danish-English, English-Danish Dictionary. 1989. pap. 14.95 (*0-87052-823-8*) Hippocrene Bks.

***Danish-English Technical Dictionary.** A. O. Christensen. (DAN & ENG.). 1990. 120.00 (*0-7859-8948-X*) Fr & Eur.

Danish-English Technical Dictionary. A. O. Christensen. 379p. (DAN & ENG.). 1990. 120.00 (*87-11-04455-1*) IBD Ltd.

Danish-English Technical Dictionary. A. O. Christiansen. 379p. (DAN & ENG.). 1990. 110.00 (*0-8288-4035-0*, F101210) Fr & Eur.

Danish-English Technical Dictionary: Dansk-Engelsk Teknisk Ordbog. Ed. by A. Warren. 393p. (DAN & ENG.). 1981. 95.00 (*0-88469-430-5*, M1289) Fr & Eur.

Danish Exercises. A. Jones & B. Gade. 1992. pap. 22.50 (*87-00-68091-5*, D761) Vanous.

D

An Asterisk (*) at the beginning of an entry indicates that the title is appearing in BIP for the first time.

An Asterisk (*) at the beginning of an entry indicates that the title is appearing in BIP for the first time.

1789

D

Dante & His Early Biographers. E. Moore. LC 70-122459. (Studies in Dante: No. 9). (C). 1970. reprint ed. lib. bdg. 59.95 (*0-8383-1002-8*) M S G Haskell Hse.

Dante & His Italy. Lonsdale Ragg. LC 72-2129. (Studies in Dante: No. 9). (Illus.). 1972. lib. bdg. 75.00 (*0-8383-1462-7*) M S G Haskell Hse.

Dante & His Time. Karl Federn. LC 78-132439. (Studies in Dante: No. 9). 1970. reprint ed. lib. bdg. 75.00 (*0-8383-1192-X*) M S G Haskell Hse.

Dante & Medieval Latin Traditions. Peter Dronke. 170p. 1986. 49.95 (*0-521-32152-2*) Cambridge U Pr.

Dante & Medieval Latin Traditions. Peter Dronke. 170p. 1989. pap. 19.95 (*0-521-37960-1*) Cambridge U Pr.

Dante & Ovid: Essays in Intertextuality. Ed. by Madison U. Sowell. (Medieval & Renaissance Texts & Studies: Vol. 82). 208p. 1991. 20.00 (*0-86698-094-6*, MR82) MRTS.

Dante & Paul's "Five Words with Understanding" Robert Hollander. LC 92-16372. (CEMERS Occasional Papers, No. 1, Medieval & Renaissance Texts & Studies: Vol. CM1). 1992. pap. 6.00 (*0-86698-121-7*) MRTS.

Dante & Philosophy. Etienne Gilson. Tr. by David Moore. 12.75 (*0-8446-0645-6*) Peter Smith.

Dante & Pound: The Epic of Judgement. James J. Wilhelm. LC 74-22708. (Ezra Pound Scholarship Ser.). (Illus.). 200p. 1974. 18.00 (*0-685-50659-2*) Natl Poet Foun.

Dante & the Book of the Cosmos. John G. Demaray. LC 86-72887. (Transactions Ser.: Vol. 77, Pt. 5). (Illus.). 115p. (Orig.). (C). 1987. pap. 18.00 (*0-87169-775-0*, T775-DEJ) Am Philos.

Dante & the Empire. Donna Mancusi-Ungaro. (American University Studies: Romance Languages & Literature: Ser. II, Vol. 49). 201p. 1987. text ed. 73.95 (*0-8204-0337-7*) P Lang Pubs.

Dante & the English Poets from Chaucer to Tennyson. Oscar Kuhns. 1972. 59.95 (*0-87968-993-5*) Gordon Pr.

Dante & the Medieval Other World. Alison Morgan. (Studies in Medieval Literature: No. 8). (Illus.). 288p. (C). 1990. 59.95 (*0-521-36069-2*) Cambridge U Pr.

Dante & the Mystical Tradition: Bernard of Clairvaux in the "Commedia" Steven Botterill. (Cambridge Studies in Medieval Literature: No. 22). 256p. (C). 1994. 59.95 (*0-521-43454-8*) Cambridge U Pr.

Dante & the Mystics: A Study of the Mystical Aspect of the Divina Commedia. Edward G. Gardner. LC 68-24952. (Studies in Italian Literature: No. 46). 1969. reprint ed. lib. bdg. 75.00 (*0-8383-0271-8*) M S G Haskell Hse.

Dante & the "Quest for Eloquence" in India's Vernacular Languages. Anne Paolucci & Henry Paolucci. 78p. 1984. pap. 10.45 (*0-918680-28-X*) Bagehot Council.

Dante As Dramatist: The Myth of the Earthly Paradise & Tragic Vision in the "Divine Comedy" Franco Masciandaro. LC 91-2536. 224p. (C). 1991. text ed. 29.95 (*0-8122-3069-8*) U of Pa Pr.

Dante, Boris Godunov, D. Merezhkovsky & Z. Hippius: Kinostsenariy, Predislovie T. Pachmuss. D. S. Merezhkhovsky & Z. H. Hippius. (Alternate Currents Ser.). 210p. (Orig.). (RUS.). 1991. pap. 20.00 (*0-922792-50-X*) Gnosis Pr.

Dante, Chaucer & the Currency of the Word: Money, Images & Reference in Late Medieval Poetry. Richard A. Shoaf. LC 83-12095. 312p. 1983. 29.95 (*0-937664-62-6*) Pilgrim Bks OK.

D

Dante Gabriel Rossetti. Helen R. Angeli. LC 76-184272. 1949. 22.00 (*0-405-08206-1*) Ayer.

***Dante Gabriel Rossetti.** Russell Ash. LC 95-12907. 1995. write for info. (*0-8109-3784-0*) Abrams.

Dante Gabriel Rossetti. Alicia Craig Faxon. (Illus.). 256p. 1989. 125.00 (*0-89659-928-0*) Abbeville Pr.

Dante Gabriel Rossetti. Duke University Library Staff. Ed. by Paull F. Baum. LC 31-11769. reprint ed. 21.50 (*0-404-05414-5*) AMS Pr.

Dante Gabriel Rossetti. William Sharp. LC 71-115006. 1970. reprint ed. 31.50 (*0-404-05955-4*) AMS Pr.

Dante Gabriel Rossetti: His Family Letters, 2 Vols, Set. Dante G. Rossetti. LC 70-130231. reprint ed. 72.50 (*0-404-05434-X*) AMS Pr.

Dante Gabriel Rossetti: His Family-Letters, 2 vols., Set. Dante G. Rossetti. (BCL1-PR English Literature Ser.). 1992. reprint ed. lib. bdg. 150.00 (*0-7812-7629-2*) Rprt Serv.

Dante Gabriel Rossetti: Painter & Man of Letters. Frank V. Rutter. LC 78-148295. (Illus.). reprint ed. 31.50 (*0-404-05468-4*) AMS Pr.

Dante Gabriel Rossetti: Painter, Poet of Heaven in Earth. Rodolphe Megroz. LC 74-173851. (English Biography Ser.: No. 31). 1971. reprint ed. lib. bdg. 75.00 (*0-8383-1336-1*) M S G Haskell Hse.

Dante Gabriel Rossetti: Poet & Painter. Eben E. Bass. 362p. (C). 1989. text ed. 64.95 (*0-8204-1028-4*) P Lang Pubs.

Dante Gabriel Rossetti & the Limits of Victorian Vision. David G. Riede. LC 82-22099. (Illus.). 288p. 1983. 36.95 (*0-8014-1552-7*) Cornell U Pr.

Dante Gabriel Rossetti As Designer & Writer. William M. Rossetti. LC 73-144678. reprint ed. 36.00 (*0-404-05429-3*) AMS Pr.

Dante Gabriel Rossetti, Painter Poet of Heaven in Earth. Rodolphe L. Megroz. (BCL1-PR English Literature Ser.). 339p. 1992. reprint ed. lib. bdg. 89.00 (*0-7812-7631-4*) Rprt Serv.

Dante Gabriel Rossetti, Painter Poet of Heaven in Earth. Rodolphe L. Megroz. LC 75-145173. (Illus.). 1971. reprint ed. 39.00 (*0-403-01101-9*) Scholarly.

Dante Gabriel Rossetti Revisited. David Riede. (Twayne's English Author Ser.). 160p. 1992. text ed. 24.95 (*0-8057-7027-5*, Twayne) Macmillan.

Dante Gabriel Rossetti's Versecraft. Joseph F. Vogel. LC 76-150655. (University of Florida Humanities Monographs: No. 34). 120p. reprint ed. pap. 34.20 (*0-7837-5081-1*, 2044779) Bks Demand.

Dante Game. Jane Langton. (Homer Kelly Mystery Ser.). (Illus.). 336p. 1992. mass mkt. 5.95 (*0-14-013887-0*, Penguin Bks) Viking Penguin.

Dante in America: The First Two Centuries. Ed. by A. Bartlett Giamatti. LC 83-2350. (Medieval & Renaissance Texts & Studies: Vol. 23). (Illus.). 432p. 1983. 30.00 (*0-86698-059-8*) MRTS.

Dante, Michelangelo, & Milton. Pref. by John Arthos. LC 78-32053. 124p. 1979. reprint ed. text ed. 45.00 (*0-313-20979-0*, ARDA, Greenwood Pr) Greenwood.

***Dante Now: Current Trends in Dante Studies.** Ed. by Theodore J. Cachey, Jr. LC 94-39220. (William & Katherine Devers Series in Dante Studies: Vol. 1). (C). 1995. pap. text ed. 21.95x (*0-268-00875-2*) U of Notre Dame Pr.

Dante of Our Time: Primo Levi & Auschwitz. Risa B. Sodi. (American University Studies: Romance Languages & Literature: Ser. II, Vol. 134). 150p. (C). 1990. text ed. 36.95 (*0-8204-1219-8*) P Lang Pubs.

Dante, Petrarch, Boccaccio: Studies in the Italian Trecento In Honor of Charles S. Singleton. Ed. by Aldo S. Bernardo & Anthony L. Pellegrini. LC 83-717. (Medieval & Renaissance Texts & Studies: Vol. 22). (Illus.). 400p. 1983. 30.00 (*0-86698-061-X*) MRTS.

Dante, Poet of the Desert: History & Allegory in the Divine Comedy. Giuseppe Mazzotta. LC 78-27468. 360p. 1987. pap. text ed. 18.95 (*0-691-10233-3*) Princeton U Pr.

Dante Rossetti & the Pre-Raphaelite Movement. Esther Wood. LC 72-91205. (Illus.). xii, 323p. 1972. reprint ed. lib. bdg. 52.00 (*0-8154-0445-X*) Cooper Sq.

Dante Studies: With the Annual Report of the Dante Society. Incl. Vol. 85. Dante Society of America, Inc. Ed. by Anthony L. Pellegrini. LC 15-2183. vii, 144p. 1967. 15.00 (*0-685-55610-7*); Vol. 86. Dante Society of America, Inc. Ed. by Anthony L. Pellegrini. LC 15-2183. viii, 196p. 1968. 15.00 (*0-685-55611-5*); Vol. 87. Dante Society of America, Inc. Ed. by Anthony L. Pellegrini. LC 15-2183. viii, 205p. 1969. 15.00 (*0-685-55612-3*); Vol. 89. Contrib by Emerson Brown, Jr. et al. LC 15-2183. viii, 148p. 1971. 15.00 (*0-685-55613-1*); Vol. 90. Dante Society of America, Inc. Ed. by Anthony L. Pellegrini. LC 15-2183. viii, 216p. 1972. 15.00 (*0-685-55614-X*); Vol. 91. Dante Society of America, Inc. Ed. by Anthony L. Pellegrini. LC 15-2183. 1973. 15.00 (*0-685-55615-8*); Vol. 92. Dante Society of America, Inc. Ed. by Anthony L. Pellegrini. LC 15-2183. 1974. 15.00 (*0-685-55616-6*); Vol. 93. Dante Society of America, Inc. Ed. by Anthony L. Pellegrini. LC 15-2183. 1975. 15.00 (*0-685-55617-4*); Vol. 94. Dante Society of America, Inc. Ed. by Anthony L. Pellegrini. LC 15-2183. 1976. 15.00 (*0-685-55618-2*); Vol. 95. Dante Society of America, Inc. Ed. by Anthony L. Pellegrini. LC 15-2183. 1977. 15.00 (*0-685-55619-0*); Vol. 101. Dante Society of America, Inc. Ed. by Anthony L. Pellegrini. LC 15-2183. 1988. 15.00 (*0-685-53881-8*); Vol. 102. Dante Society of America, Inc. Ed. by Anthony L. Pellegrini. LC 15-2183. 1988. 16.50 (*0-685-53882-6*); Vol. 103. Dante Society of America, Inc. Ed. by Anthony L. Pellegrini. LC 15-2183. 1989. 17.50 (*0-685-42364-6*); Vol. 104. Dante Society of America, Inc. Ed. by Anthony L. Pellegrini. LC 15-2183. 1989. 18.50 (*0-685-42365-4*); Vol. 105. Dante Society of America, Inc. Ed. by Anthony L. Pellegrini. LC 15-2183. 1990. 18.95 (*0-685-42366-2*); Vol. 106. Dante Society of America, Inc. Ed. by Anthony L. Pellegrini. LC 15-2183. 1990. 19.95 (*0-685-42367-0*); Vol. 107. Dante Society of America, Inc. Ed. by Anthony L. Pellegrini. LC 15-2183. 1991. 19.95 (*0-685-42368-9*); Vol. 108. Dante Society of America, Inc. Ed. by Anthony L. Pellegrini. LC 15-2183. 1991. 19.95 (*0-685-57783-X*); Vol. 109. Dante Society of America, Inc. Ed. by Anthony L. Pellegrini. LC 15-2183. 1991. 19.95 (*0-685-57784-8*); Vol. 110. Dante Society of America, Inc. Ed. by Anthony L. Pellegrini. LC 15-2183. 1993. 19.95 (*0-685-73443-9*); Vol. 111. Dante Society of America, Inc. Ed. by Anthony L. Pellegrini. LC 15-2183. 1994. 19.95 (*0-685-73444-7*); LC 15-2183. Set pap. write for info. (*0-318-55869-6*) State U NY Pr.

Dante Studies Vol. I: Dante in the Twentieth Century. deluxe limited ed. Jorge L. Borges et al. Ed. by A. Caso. 1982. 50.00 (*0-937832-17-0*) Dante U Am.

Dante Studies Vol. I: Dante in the Twentieth Century, Vol. I. Jorge L. Borges et al. Ed. by A. Caso. 1982. 15.00 (*0-937832-16-2*) Dante U Am.

Dante Studies in the Age of Vico. Domenico Pietropaolo. 400p. 1989. 12.00 (*0-919473-91-1*, DH77, Pub. by Dovehouse CN) MRTS.

Dante the Maker. William Anderson. (Illus.). 1981. 39.50 (*0-7100-0322-6*, RKP) Routledge.

Dante's Beatrice: Priest of an Androgynous God. Joan M. Ferrante. LC 92-17376. (CEMERS Occasional Papers, No. 2, Medieval & Renaissance Texts & Studies: Vol. CM2). 40p. 1992. pap. 6.00 (*0-86698-122-5*) MRTS.

Dante's Burning Sands: Some New Perspectives. Francesca G. D'Antoni. LC 91-34971. (Studies in Italian Culture: Vol. 4). 181p. (C). 1992. text ed. 40.95 (*0-8204-1473-5*) P Lang Pubs.

Dante's Christian Astrology. Richard Kay. LC 93-33923. (Middle Ages Ser.). 416p. (C). 1994. text ed. 46.95 (*0-8122-3233-X*) U of Pa Pr.

Dante's Commedia: Elements of Structure. Charles S. Singleton. LC 77-5267. 110p. reprint ed. pap. 31.40 (*0-8357-8085-6*, 2034136) Bks Demand.

Dante's Conception of Justice. A. H. Gilbert. 1973. 59.95 (*0-87968-995-1*) Gordon Pr.

Dante's Conception of Justice. Allan H. Gilbert. LC 76-166199. (BCL Ser.: I). reprint ed. 22.50 (*0-404-02757-1*) AMS Pr.

Dante's Craft: Studies in Language & Style. Glauco Cambon. LC 70-88564. 225p. reprint ed. pap. 64.20 (*0-318-39798-6*, 2033209) Bks Demand.

Dante's Drama of the Mind: A Modern Reading of the Purgatorio. Francis Fergusson. LC 81-4190. x, 231p. 1981. reprint ed. text ed. 55.00 (*0-313-23034-X*, FEDD, Greenwood Pr) Greenwood.

Dante's Drum-Kit. Douglas Dunn. 128p. 1994. 19.95 (*0-571-16963-5*); pap. 9.95 (*0-571-17055-2*) Faber & Faber.

Dante's Epistle to Cangrande. Robert Hollander. (Recentiores: Later Latin Texts & Contexts Ser.). 150p. (C). 1993. text ed. 32.50 (*0-472-10476-4*) U of Mich Pr.

Dante's Fame Abroad, 1350-1850. Werner P. Friederich. (Studies in Comparative Literature: No. 2). 582p. (Orig.). (C). 1966. pap. 22.50 (*0-8078-7002-1*) U of NC Pr.

Dante's Inferno. Dante Alighieri. Tr. by Nicholas Kilmer. (Illus.). (C). 1985. pap. 9.95 (*0-8283-1884-0*) Branden Pub Co.

Dante's Inferno. Dante Alighieri. Tr. by Nicholas Kilmer. (Illus.). 1985. 19.50 (*0-937832-28-6*) Dante U Am.

Dante's Inferno. Dante Alighieri. Tr. by Mark Musa. LC 70-126214. (Illus.). 320p. 1971. 29.95 (*0-253-14184-2*) Ind U Pr.

Dante's Inferno. Tom Phillips. LC 84-52865. (Illus.). 1985. 19.98 (*0-500-01362-4*) Thames Hudson.

Dante's Inferno. Joseph Tusiani. (Illus.). (J). (gr. 5 up). 1965. 9.95 (*0-8392-3046-X*) Astor-Honor.

***Dante's Inferno: The Indiana Critical Edition.** Dante Alighieri. Ed. & Tr. by Mark Musa. LC 94-20237. (Indiana Masterpiece Editions Ser.). 432p. 1995. pap. 12.95 (*0-253-20930-7*) Ind U Pr.

***Dante's Inferno: The Indiana Critical Edition.** Dantee Alighieri. Ed. & Tr. by Mark Musa. LC 94-20237. (Indiana Masterpiece Editions Ser.). 432p. 1995. text ed. 29.95 (*0-253-33943-X*) Ind U Pr.

Dante's Inferno: Translations by 20 Contemporary Poets. Daniel Halpern. 1994. pap. 13.00 (*0-88001-373-7*) Ecco Pr.

Dante's Influence on American Writers 1776-1976: Proceedings of the Bicentennial Meeting of the Dante Society of America. 1976. pap. 3.95 (*0-918680-02-6*) Bagehot Council.

Dante's Journey of Sanctification. Antonio C. Mastrobuono. LC 90-35108. 260p. 1990. pap. 14.95 (*0-89526-741-1*) Regnery Pub.

Dante's Joynte. K. Gaburo. (Illus.). 12p. 1983. reprint ed. 6.85 (*0-939044-09-9*) Lingua Pr.

Dante's Paradise. Dante Alighieri. LC 83-48828. (Illus.). 416p. 1984. 35.00 (*0-253-31619-7*) Ind U Pr.

Dante's Paradiso. Joseph Tusiani. (Illus.). (J). (gr. 7 up). 1969. 9.95 (*0-685-00563-1*) Astor-Honor.

Dante's Paradiso & the Limitations of Modern Criticism: A Study of Style & Poetic Theory. Robin Kirkpatrick. LC 77-80839. 239p. reprint ed. pap. 68.20 (*0-318-34814-4*, 2031677) Bks Demand.

Dante's Paradiso: The Flowering of the Self: An Interpretation of the Anagogical Meaning. John Saly. LC 88-22499. 244p. (C). 1989. lib. bdg. 45.50 (*0-944473-00-8*) Pace Univ Pr.

Dante's Poets: Textuality & Truth in the Comedy. Teodolinda Barolini. LC 84-42586. 320p. 1984. text ed. 47.50 (*0-691-06609-4*) Princeton U Pr.

Dante's Purgatorio. Joseph Tusiani. (Illus.). (J). (gr. 5 up). 1968. 9.95 (*0-8392-3053-2*) Astor-Honor.

Dante's Purgatory. Dante Alighieri. Tr. by Mark Musa. LC 80-8098. (Illus.). 384p. 1981. 29.95 (*0-253-17926-2*) Ind U Pr.

Dante's Ratchet. Natalie S. Reciputi. 74p. (Orig.). 1993. pap. 7.00 (*0-944920-06-3*) Bellowing Ark Pr.

Dante's Rime. Dante Alighieri. Tr. by Patrick S. Diehl. LC 79-83984. (Lockert Library of Poetry in Translation). 1979. 49.50x (*0-691-06409-1*) Princeton U Pr.

Dante's Style in His Lyric Poetry. Patrick Boyde. LC 74-130906. 371p. reprint ed. pap. 105.80 (*0-685-16351-2*, 2027287) Bks Demand.

Dante's Swift & Strong: Essays on "Inferno XV" Richard Kay. LC 77-6795. xx, 448p. 1978. 40.00 (*0-7006-0158-9*) U Pr of KS.

Dante's Ten Heavens. Edmund G. Gardner. LC 76-132441. (Studies in Dante: No. 9). 1970. reprint ed. lib. bdg. 75.00 (*0-8383-1195-4*) M S G Haskell Hse.

Dante's Ten Heavens: A Study of the Paradiso. 2nd ed. Edmund G. Gardner. LC 74-37880. (Select Bibliographies Reprint Ser.). 1977. reprint ed. 23.95 (*0-8369-6717-8*) Ayer.

Dantes the Divine Comedy. Intro. by Harold Bloom. (Modern Critical Interpretations Ser.). 176p. 1987. 34.95 (*0-87754-908-7*) Chelsea Hse.

Dante's Thought & Poetry. Rocco Montano. (Orig.). 1988. pap. 14.95 (*0-89526-771-3*) Regnery Pub.

Dante's Vision & the Circle of Knowledge. Giuseppe Mazzotta. 352p. 1993. text ed. 39.50 (*0-691-06966-2*) Princeton U Pr.

Dante's Vision of the Artist: Four Modern Illustrators of the Commedia. Jean-Pierre Barricelli. LC 92-10820. 154p. (C). 1993. text ed. 68.95 (*0-8204-1558-8*) P Lang Pubs.

Dante's Vita Nuova: A Translation & an Essay. Dante Alighieri. Tr. by Mark Musa. LC 72-79905. 224p. 1973. pap. 8.95 (*0-253-20162-4*, MB-162) Ind U Pr.

Danteum. rev. ed. Thomas Schumacher. LC 93-29727. (Illus.). 166p. 1993. reprint ed. pap. 17.95 (*1-878271-82-2*) Princeton Arch.

Danto & His Critics. Ed. by Mark Rollins. LC 93-6590. (Philosophers & Their Critics Ser.: No. 4). 256p. 1993. 49.95 (*0-631-18337-X*); pap. 19.95 (*0-631-18338-8*) Blackwell Pubs.

Danton. Norman Hampson. (Illus.). 192p. 1988. pap. text ed. 18.95 (*0-631-16116-3*) Blackwell Pubs.

Danton: A Study. Hilaire Belloc. LC 70-100534. (Illus.). reprint ed. 46.50 (*0-404-00737-6*) AMS Pr.

Danton Case & Thermidor. Stanislawa Przybyszewska. 297p. 1989. pap. 14.95 (*0-8101-0806-2*) Northwestern U Pr.

Danton's Death. Georg Buchner. Tr. by Hedwig Rappolt. LC 82-51254. 96p. (Orig.). (C). 1983. pap. text ed. 4.50 (*0-939858-02-9*) T S L Pr.

Danton's Death. George Buchner. Tr. by Howard Brenton. (Orig.). 1983. pap. 9.95 (*0-413-51260-6*, A0069, Pub. by Methuen UK) Heinemann.

Danton's Death, Leonce & Lena, Woyzeck. Georg Buchner. Tr. & Intro. by Victor Price. (World's Classics Ser.). 176p. 1988. pap. 5.95 (*0-19-281827-9*) OUP.

Dantons Tod & Woyeck. Georg Buchner. Ed. by M. Jacobs. 1988. text ed. 13.95 (*0-7190-0456-X*, Pub. by Manchester Univ Pr UK) St Martin.

Danube. Claudio Magris. Tr. by Patrick Creagh. 1990. pap. 11.95 (*0-374-52245-6*, Noonday) FS&G.

***Danube Voyage.** Adam Wolfarth. 124p. Date not set. pap. 9.95 (*1-887420-04-5*) A Wolfarth.

Danubian Region. Ed. by L. Kadar & Z. Borsy. 100p. (C). 1975. pap. 24.00 (*0-08-019669-1*, Pergamon Pr) Elsevier.

Danville: A Pictorial History. Bob Wright. (Illus.). 200p. 1987. 30.00 (*0-685-20015-9*) G Bradley.

Danville, Eighth Star New Market & Dixie Artillery. Robert H. Moore, II. (Virginia Regimental Histories Ser.). (Illus.). 110p. 1989. 19.95 (*0-930919-72-6*) H E Howard.

Danville, New Hampshire Residents, 1760-1992. Gus Collins. 208p. (Orig.). 1993. pap. text ed. 21.00 (*1-55613-837-7*) Heritage Bk.

***Danvis Tales: Selected Stories.** Rowland E. Robinson. Ed. by David Budbill. LC 95-13841. (Hardscrabble Bks.). (Illus.). 320p. (C). 1995. 24.95 (*0-87451-718-4*) U Pr of New Eng.

***Danyon de Chelly: The Story of It's Ruins & People.** 1995. lib. bdg. 250.00 (*0-8490-6519-4*) Gordon Pr.

Danza! Lynn Hall. LC 88-8047. 192p. (J). (gr. 5-7). 1989. reprint ed. pap. 3.95 (*0-689-71289-8*, Aladdin Paperbacks) S&S Childrens.

Danzantes of Monte Alban, 2 vols. John F. Scott. LC 79-63725. (Studies in Pre-Columbian Art & Archaeology: No. 19). (Illus.). 238p. 1978. pap. 30.00 (*0-88402-079-7*) Dumbarton Oaks.

Danzig: Between East & West. Ed. by Isadore Twersky. (Harvard Judaic Texts & Studies: Vol. 4). 185p. 1985. 21.00 (*0-674-19255-9*) HUP.

Danzig: Between East & West. Ed. by Isadore Twersky. (Harvard Judaic Texts & Studies: Vol. 4). 185p. 1985. pap. 14.00 (*0-674-19256-7*) HUP.

Danzig Nineteen Thirty-Nine: Treasures of a Destroyed Community, the Jewish Museum of New York. Pref. by Joy Ungerleider-Mayerson. LC 79-926430. (Illus.). 144p. 1980. pap. 19.95 (*0-8143-1662-X*) Wayne St U Pr.

Danzig Passage. Bodie Thoene. (Zion Covenant Ser.). 400p. (Orig.). 1991. pap. 10.99 (*1-55661-081-5*) Bethany Hse.

Danzig Trilogy: The Tin Drum, Cat & Mouse, & Dog Years. Gunter Grass. 1987. 29.95 (*0-15-123816-2*) Pantheon.

Danzig Trilogy of Gunter Grass: A Study of the Tin Drum, Cat & Mouse, & Dog Years. John Reddick. LC 74-11027. 290p. 1975. pap. 5.95 (*0-15-623829-2*, Harvest Bks) HarBrace.

Danziger's Adventures: From Miami to Kabul. Nick Danziger. (Illus.). 290p. (Orig.). 1993. pap. 12.00 (*0-586-09081-9*, Pub. by HarpC UK) HarpC.

Danziger's Classic Vermont Cartoons. rev. ed. Jeff Danziger. 64p. 1980. reprint ed. pap. 3.95 (*0-9603900-1-4*) Lanser Pr.

Danziger's Travels: Beyond Forbidden Frontiers. Nick Danziger. (Vintage Departures Ser.). 1988. pap. 14.00 (*0-679-73994-7*, Vin) Random.

Dao de Jing: The Old Sage's Classic of the Way of Virtue. Lao-zi. Tr. by Patrick M. Byrne. 162p. 1991. pap. 15.00 (*0-89540-160-6*, SB-160) Sun Pub.

Dao of Increasing Longevity & Conserving One's Life: A Handbook of Traditional Chinese Geriatrics & Chinese Herbal Patent Formulae. Tr. by Bob Flaws & Anna Lin. LC 91-72616. 165p. (C). 1991. pap. text ed. 16.95 (*0-936185-24-4*) Blue Poppy.

Daoist Theory of Chinese Thought: A Philosophical Interpretation. Chad Hansen. 464p. 1992. 72.00 (*0-19-506729-0*) OUP.

Daphnaida & Other Poems. Edmund Spenser. (BCL1-PR English Literature Ser.). 243p. 1992. reprint ed. lib. bdg. 79.00 (*0-7812-7223-8*) Rprt Serv.

Daphne. Sarah Carlisle. (Coventry Romance Ser.: No. 67). 224p. 1980. pap. 1.75 (*0-449-50098-5*, Coventry) Fawcett.

Daphne. Marilyn Kaye. LC 86-29420. (Sisters Ser.: Bk. 2). (Illus.). 160p. (J). (gr. 3-7). 1987. 13.95 (*0-15-200434-3*, Gulliver Bks); pap. 4.95 (*0-15-200433-5*, Gulliver Bks) HarBrace.

Daphne see Stello

Daphne Deane. G. L. Hill. 19.95 (*0-88411-347-7*, Aeonian Pr) Amereon Ltd.

Daphne Deane, No. 19. Grace L. Hill. 1991. pap. 4.99 (*0-8423-0529-7*) Tyndale.

Daphne Dragon. Annie Kubler. (J). 1985. 4.95 (*0-85953-260-7*) Childs Play.

Daphne du Maurier. Richard Kelly. (Twayne's English Authors Ser.: No. 437). 176p. 1987. text ed. 21.95 (*0-8057-6931-5*, Twayne) Macmillan.

1790

An Asterisk (*) at the beginning of an entry indicates that the title is appearing in BIP for the first time.

*Darin: A Soulprint. Travis A. Haskins. 224p. 1994. 14.95 (0-9641576-0-8) Soulprint Pubng.
"Never judge another person's pain," Travis Haskins advised his sons. It's important advice but difficult to remember when your 21-year-old youngest son allows his Jeep to drift off the freeway & ends up pinned beneath the roll bar. At that point, losing a child seems to fall into a category all its own - the ultimate pain! This is the story of the last two months of the life of Darin Haskins & of his death & the after-death experience that changed his father's life. It's the story of a father/son relationship - often awkward & difficult, often uniquely loving - that died & was reborn in a parent's pain. It is also the love story of Darin & Kellie, the leprechaun of a girl who was one of those whom Darin left behind. Every parent who has struggled to communicate with a son or daughter should read this book. Every parent who has lost a child will find in this story a record of their own anger & despair, but, beyond this, they will find faith that the life of their son or daughter had a purpose. The soulprint of each one of us lives on. This book may be ordered

D

An Asterisk (*) at the beginning of an entry indicates that the title is appearing in BIP for the first time.

1791

from Soulprint Publishing Co., 9801 Ludwig St., Villa Park, CA 92667; 714-998-9217. Quantity discounts available.
Publisher Provided Annotation.

Daring. Patricia Hagan. 304p. 1993. lib. bdg. 20.00 (0-7278-4461-X) Severn Hse.
Daring Adventures of Kit Carson & Fremont. John C. Fremont. (Notable American Authors Ser.). 1992. reprint ed. lib. bdg. 75.00 (0-7812-2900-6) Rprt Serv.
Daring, Darling Dolly. Nellie McCaslin. LC 93-14392. 20p. 1993. pap. 4.00 (0-88734-435-6) Players Pr.
Daring Deceit. Claudette Williams. 256p. 1994. mass mkt. 3.99 (0-8217-4443-7) Zebra.
Daring Deception. Brenda Hiatt. (Regency Romance Ser.). 1993. mass mkt. 2.99 (0-373-31202-4, 1-31202-4) Harlequin Bks.
Daring Deception. Cindy Holbrook. 384p. 1993. mass mkt. 3.99 (0-8217-4231-0) Zebra.
Daring Deeds. Terry Kelly et al. (Hayes Adventure Ser.). (Illus.). 48p. (J). (gr. 5-9). 1985. pap. 5.95 (0-88625-092-7) Durkin Hayes Pub.
***Daring Disciples: Embark on an Exciting Journey of Discovery Children's Journal.** Anne Russell. (1994 50-Day Spiritual Adventure Ser.). (Illus.). 64p. (Orig.). (J). (gr. 3-6). 1993. student ed, pap. text ed. 4.99 (1-879050-16-1) Chapel of Air.
Daring Donald McKay: Or Last War Trail of the Modocs. Ed. by Keith Clark & Donna Clark. LC 74-184573. (Illus.). 1971. pap. 2.95 (0-87595-032-9) Oregon Hist.
***Daring Hearts & Spirits Free: History of the United Methodist Women of the South Carolina Conference.** Harriet A. Mays. 256p. 1995. 16.95 (1-881576-53-1) Providence Hse.
Daring Illusion. Christina Cordaire. 208p. (Orig.). 1994. pap. 3.99 (0-515-11362-X) Jove Pubns.
Daring Masquerade. Mary Balogh. 1989. pap. 4.50 (0-451-15886-5, Sig) NAL-Dutton.
Daring Masquerade. Olivia Sumner. 1991. pap. 3.50 (0-8217-3580-2) Zebra.
Daring Muse: Augustan Poetry Reconsidered. Margaret A. Doody. (Illus.). 320p. 1985. 74.95 (0-521-25825-1); pap. 22.95 (0-521-27723-X) Cambridge U Pr.
Daring Proposition. Miranda Lee. (Presents Ser.). 1994. mass mkt. 2.99 (0-373-11664-0, 1-11664-9) Harlequin Bks.
Daring Rescue of Marlon the Swimming Pig. Susan Saunders. LC 87-4633. (Stepping Stone Bks.). (Illus.). 64p. (J). (gr. 2-4). 1987. lib. bdg. 6.99 (0-394-98293-2) Random Bks Yng Read.
Daring the Unknown: A History of N. A. S. A. Howard E. Smith, Jr. LC 86-33617. (Illus.). 128p. (J). (gr. 3-7). 1987. 16.95 (0-15-200435-1, Gulliver Bks) HarBrace.
Daring to Be Bad: Radical Feminism in America, 1967-75 (AC) Alice Echols. 430p. 1989. pap. text ed. 14.95 (0-8166-1787-2) U of Minn Pr.
Daring to Be Myself: A Case Study in Rational-Emotive Therapy. Wendy Dryden & Joseph Yankura. 224p. 1992. pap. 32.00 (0-335-09341-8, Open Univ Pr) Taylor & Francis.
Daring to Be Yourself. Alexandra Stoddard. 320p. 1992. pap. 14.00 (0-380-71578-3) Avon.
Daring to Dissent: Lesbian Culture from Margin to Mainstream. Liz Gibbs. (Women on Women Ser.). 320p. 1994. pap. 15.95 (0-304-32796-4, Pub. by Cassell Pubng UK) InBook.
***Daring to Dissent: Lesbian Culture from Margin to Mainstream.** Ed. by Liz Gibbs. (Women on Women Ser.). 320p. 1994. 55.00 (0-304-32794-8, Pub. by Cassell Pubng UK) InBook.
Daring to Draw Near: People in Prayer. John White. LC 77-6554. (Orig.). 1977. pap. 8.99 (0-87784-788-6, 788) InterVarsity.
Daring to Dream: Law & the Humanities for Elementary Schools. LC 80-67087. 312p. 1980. pap. 3.00 (0-89707-028-3, 497-0023) Amer Bar Assn.
Daring to Dream: The Life of Hazel Wood Waterman. Sally B. Thornton. LC 87-26507. (Illus.). 118p. 1987. 17.95 (0-918740-06-1); pap. 9.95 (0-918740-07-X) San Diego Hist.
***Daring to Dream: Utopian Fiction by United States Women Before 1950.** 2nd ed. Ed. by Carol F. Kessler. (Utopianism & Communitarianism Ser.). 320p. 1995. text ed. 49.95 (0-8156-2654-1) Syracuse U Pr.
***Daring to Dream: Utopian Fiction by United States Women Before 1950.** 2nd ed. Ed. by Carol F. Kessler. (Utopianism & Communitarianism Ser.). 320p. 1995. pap. text ed. 17.95 (0-8156-2655-X) Syracuse U Pr.
***Daring to Dream Again: Breaking Through Barriers That Hold Us Back.** Chapel of the Air Ministries Staff. (1994 50-Day Spiritual Adventure Ser.). (Illus.). 64p. (Orig.). 1993. pap. text ed. 4.99 (1-879050-14-5) Chapel of Air.
***Daring to Dream Again: Breaking Through Barriers That Hold Us Back, Church Leader's Manual.** Chapel of the Air Ministries Staff. (1994 50-Day Spiritual Adventure Ser.). (Illus.). 188p. 1993. ring bd. 49.99 (1-879050-19-6) Chapel of Air.
***Daring to Dream Again: Breaking Through Barriers That Hold Us Back, Small Group Leader's Guide.** David New. (1994 50-Day Spiritual Adventure Ser.). (Illus.). 52p. (Orig.). 1993. student ed, pap. text ed. 9.99 (1-879050-18-8) Chapel of Air.
***Daring to Dream Again: Choral Collection.** Christine Wyrtzen et al. (1994 50-Day Spiritual Adventure Ser.). 24p. 1993. 3.96 (1-879050-43-9) Chapel of Air.
Daring to Excel: The Story of the National Youth Orchestra of Great Britain. Ruth King. (Illus.). 384p. 1993. 45.00 (0-436-23359-2, Pub. by W Heinemann Ltd) Trafalgar.
Daring to Follow Jesus. Stephen D. Eyre & Jacalyn Eyre. (Spiritual Encounter Guides Ser.). 96p. (Orig.). 1993. pap. 4.99 (0-8308-1179-6, 1179) InterVarsity.
Daring to Hope: Sermons for Pentecost First Lesson, Cycle B. John P. Rossing. LC 93-2759. 1993. pap. 6.50 (1-55673-615-0) CSS OH.
Daring to Live on the Edge: Dealing with Faith & Your Finances. Loren Cunningham. 200p. 1991. pap. 7.99 (0-927545-06-3) YWAM Pub.
Daring to Speak Love's Name: A Gay & Lesbian Prayer Book. Elizabeth Stuart. 192p. 1993. pap. 10.00 (0-241-13335-1, Penguin Bks) Viking Penguin.
***Daring to Win: Special Forces at War.** David Eshel. (Illus.). 218p. 1995. pap. 14.95 (1-85409-283-9, Pub. by Arms & Armour UK) Sterling.
Daring Vow. Sherryl Woods. (Silhouette Special Edition Ser.). 1993. mass mkt. 3.50 (0-373-09855-3, 5-09855-3) Silhouette.
Daring Wager. Valerie King. 352p. 1989. pap. 3.95 (0-8217-2558-0) Zebra.
Daring Young Men: The Story of the American Pre-Raphaelites. David H. Dickason. LC 69-13235. (Illus.). 1972. 24.95 (0-405-08444-7, Pub. by Blom Pubns UK) Ayer.
***Darings of the Red Rose.** Margery Allingham. 150p. (Orig.). 1995. pap. 15.00 (1-885941-01-3) Crippen & Landru.
Dario Fo: People's Court Jester. 2nd ed. Tony Mitchell. 1988. pap. 9.95 (0-413-60250-8, A0070, Pub. by Methuen UK) Heinemann.
Dario Fo & Franca Rame. David Hirst. LC 88-11412. (Modern Dramatists Ser.). 160p. 1989. text ed. 29.95 (0-312-02335-9) St Martin.
Darius, 2 vols. in 1. LC 70-133691. (Tudor Facsimile Texts. Old English Plays Ser.: No. 34). reprint ed. 49.50 (0-404-53334-5) AMS Pr.
***Darius Discovers Derivatives: An Introduction to Calculus for Kids.** Nolan Chen. LC 95-92093. 40p. (Orig.). (J). (gr. 5-8). 1995. 4.95x (0-9645233-0-2) Nolan Learn.
Darius Milhaud. Paul Collaer. Ed. & Tr. by Jane Galante. (Illus.). 1988. 35.00 (0-911302-62-X) San Francisco Pr.
Darjeeling Tea? Asif Currimbhoy. (Writers Workshop Bluebird Ser.). 64p. 1975. 8.00 (0-88253-522-6); pap. text ed. 4.80 (0-88253-521-8) Ind-US Inc.
Dark. Lynn Beach. Ed. by Patricia MacDonald. (Phantom Valley Ser.). 128p. (Orig.). (J). 1991. pap. 3.50 (0-671-74089-X, Minstrel Bks) PB.
***Dark.** Carrie Brown. LC 94-45767. 1995. 21.00 (0-312-11769-8) St Martin.
Dark. Girad Clacy. 1994. 12.95 (0-533-10714-8) Vantage.
Dark. Robert Munsch. 32p. (J). (gr. k-3). 1984. pap. 4.95 (0-920236-85-5, Pub. by Annick CN) Firefly Bks Ltd.
Dark. Robert Munsch. (Annikin Ser.: Series 5). (Illus.). 24p. (J). (ps-1). 1987. pap. 0.99 (0-920303-47-1, Pub. by Annick CN) Firefly Bks Ltd.
Dark. M. C. Sumner. (YA). 1994. pap. 3.50 (0-06-106275-8) HarpC.
Dark above Mad River. Joseph Thackery. LC 92-157. 72p. (Orig.). 1992. pap. 10.00 (0-931846-40-4) Wash Writers Pub.
Dark Abyss of Time: The History of the Earth & the History of Nations from Hooke to Vico. Paolo Rossi. Tr. by Lydia G. Cochrane. LC 84-8481. 352p. 1985. 35.00 (0-226-72835-8) U Ch Pr.
Dark Abyss of Time: The History of the Earth & the History of Nations from Hooke to Vico. Paolo Rossi. Tr. by Lydia G. Cochrane. LC 84-8481. 352p. 1987. pap. text ed. 14.95 (0-226-72832-3) U Ch Pr.
Dark-Adapted Eye. Barbara Vine, pseud. 304p. 1993. mass mkt. 6.00 (0-452-27064-2, Plume) NAL-Dutton.
Dark Advent. Brian Hodge. 448p. 1988. pap. 3.95 (1-55817-088-X, Pinnacle NY) Windsor NY.
Dark Age. Wes Magee. 56p. 1982. pap. 11.95 (0-85640-256-7, Pub. by Blackstaff Pr IE) Dufour.
Dark Age Britain. Henry Marsh. 1987. 22.50 (0-88029-156-7) Dorset Pr.
Dark Ages. Tony Gregory. LC 91-43093. (Illustrated History of the World Ser.: Vol. 24, No. 17). (Illus.). 80p. (J). (gr. 2-6). 1993. 17.95 (0-8160-2787-0) Facts on File.
***Dark Ages.** Sturmen Krieg. 350p. 1994. pap. 8.95 (1-56901-459-0) NW Pub.
Dark Ages. William P. Ker. LC 78-27533. 361p. 1979. reprint ed. text ed. 47.50 (0-313-20933-2, KEDA, Greenwood Pr) Greenwood.
Dark Ages: Life in the U. S. 1945-1960. Marty Jezer. LC 81-51391. 335p. 1982. 25.00 (0-89608-128-1); pap. 15.00 (0-89608-127-3) South End Pr.
***Dark Alchemy: The Films of Jan Svankmajer.** Ed. by Peter Hames. LC 95-4011. 208p. 1995. pap. text ed. 19.95 (0-275-95299-1, Praeger Pubs) Greenwood.
***Dark Alchemy: The Films of Jan Svankmajer.** Ed. by Peter Hames. LC 95-4011. (Contributions to the Study of Popular Culture: Vol. 46). 208p. 1995. text ed. 59.95 (0-313-29698-7, Greenwood Pr) Greenwood.
***Dark Alliance: Vancouver.** (Werewolf). Date not set. 15.00 (1-56504-059-7) White Wolf.
Dark Ancestor: The Literature of the Black Man in the Caribbean. O. R. Dathorne. LC 80-22581. xii, 292p. 1981. text ed. 37.50 (0-8071-0757-3) La State U Pr.
Dark & Bloody Ground. Darcy O'Brien. 1994. mass mkt. 5.99 (0-06-109972-4, Harp PBks) HarpC.
Dark & Bloody Ground. large type ed. Walt A. Coburn. (Linford Western Library). 272p. 1992. pap. 14.95 (0-7089-7257-8, Trailtree Bookshop) Ulverscroft.
***Dark & Bloody Ground: The Hurtgen Forest & the Roer River Dams, 1944-1945.** Edward G. Miller. LC 94-45333. (Texas A&M University Military History Ser.: No. 42). (Illus.). 260p. (C). 1995. 29.95 (0-89096-626-5) Tex A&M Univ Pr.
Dark & Bloody Ground: Outlaw Love, a Miser's Hoard: Lust, Greed, & Killing from the Beaches of Florida to the Mountains of Kentucky. Darcy O'Brien. LC 92-54451. (Illus.). 368p. 1993. 20.00 (0-06-017958-9, HarpT) HarpC.
Dark & Bright Continent: Africa in the Changing World. Richard O. Nwachukwu. LC 89-80209. 344p. 1989. 17.95 (0-941823-02-4); pap. 9.25 (0-941823-01-6) Good Hope Enterp.
Dark & Cruel War. Dan Lowry. (Illus.). 450p. 1993. 29.50 (0-7818-0168-0) Hippocrene Bks.
Dark & Dangerous. rev. ed. Marsha M. Canham. (Temptation Ser.: No. 386). 1992. mass mkt. 2.99 (0-373-25486-5, 1-25486-1) Harlequin Bks.
Dark & Deadly Pool. Joan L. Nixon. 196p. (J). (gr. 6 up). 1989. mass mkt. 3.99 (0-440-20348-1, LFL) Dell.
Dark & Feeling. Clarence Major. LC 73-83162. 196p. 1974. 19.95 (0-89388-118-X) Okpaku Communications.
Dark & Hungry God Arises: The Gap into Power. Stephen R. Donaldson. 1993. mass mkt. 5.99 (0-553-56260-6) Bantam.
Dark & Light. Carroll F. Terrell. (Collected Poems Ser.). 85p. 1986. 8.95 (0-915032-86-4); pap. 5.00 (0-915032-87-2) Natl Poet Foun.
Dark & Light Gods: Essays on the Self in Extremity in Selected Fiction & Non-Fiction Prose. Donald Gutierrez. LC 87-50091. 220p. 1987. 22.50 (0-87875-339-7) Whitston Pub.
Dark & Perfect Angels. Benjamin A. Saenz. LC 93-71567. 128p. (Orig.). 1994. pap. 12.95 (0-913089-39-7) Broken Moon.
***Dark & Perfect Angels: A Collection of Poems.** Benjamin A. Saenz. 144p. 1995. pap. 11.95 (0-938317-23-7) Cinco Puntos.
Dark & Splendid Mass. Mari Evans. 100p. (Orig.). 1992. 16.00 (0-86316-313-0); pap. 8.00 (0-86316-312-2) Writers & Readers.
Dark & Stormy Night. Gail Hamilton. (Road to Avonlea Ser.: No. 25). (J). (gr. 4-7). 1994. mass mkt. 3.99 (0-553-48124-X) Bantam.
Dark & the Feeling. Clarence Major. LC 73-83162. 12.95 (0-89388-119-8) Okpaku Communications.
Dark Angel. V. C. Andrews. Ed. by Linda Marrow. 1990. pap. 6.50 (0-671-72939-X) PB.
Dark Angel. V. C. Andrews. 440p. 1986. 16.45 (0-685-43726-4) S&S Trade.
Dark Angel. Mary Balogh. 224p. (Orig.). 1994. pap. 3.99 (0-451-17953-6, Sig) NAL-Dutton.
Dark Angel. Anna Grant. 448p. 1994. mass mkt. 4.50 (0-8217-4494-1) Zebra.
Dark Angel: Gothic Elements in Shelley's Works. John V. Murphy. LC 73-8304. 199p. 1975. 32.50 (0-8387-1407-2) Bucknell U Pr.
***Dark Angels: Lesbian Vampire Stories.** Ed. by Pam Keesey. 200p. 1995. 24.95 (1-57344-015-9); pap. 10.95 (1-57344-014-0) Cleis Pr.
Dark Angels of Light. David A. Lewis. LC 84-61915. 138p. (Orig.). 1985. pap. 5.95 (0-89221-117-2) New Leaf.
***Dark Apollo.** large type ed. Sara Craven. (Harlequin Romance Ser.). 1995. 18.95 (0-263-14073-3, Pub. by Mills & Boon UK) Thorndike Pr.
Dark Apprentice. Kevin J. Anderson. (Star Wars: Jedi Academy Ser.: No. 2). 1994. 5.99 (0-553-29799-6) Bantam.
Dark Arena. Mario Puzo. 1977. pap. 1.95 (0-449-23295-6, Crest) Fawcett.
***Dark Arrow.** Lucille Mulcahy. LC 94-39582. (Illus.). 224p. (J). 1995. pap. 7.95 (0-8032-8220-6, Bison Books) U of Nebr Pr.
Dark at Heart. Ed. by Karen Lansdale & Joe R. Lansdale. 350p. 1992. 21.95 (0-913165-64-6) Dark Harvest.
Dark at the End of the Tunnel: Federal Clean-up Standards for Nuclear Power Plants. Critical Mass Energy Project Staff. (Illus.). 32p. (C). 1993. pap. text ed. 30.00 (0-937188-46-8) Pub Citizen Inc.
Dark at the Top of the Stairs. William Inge. 1960. pap. 4.75 (0-8222-0271-9) Dramatists Play.
***Dark at the Top of the Stairs.** Sam McBratney. LC 94-48921. (Illus.). 1995. write for info. (1-56402-640-X) Candlewick Pr.
Dark at the Top of the Stairs see Four Plays
Dark Avenues & Other Stories. Ivan A. Bunin. Tr. by R. Hare. LC 76-23875. (Classics of Russian Literature Ser.). 1987. reprint ed. 21.00 (0-88355-479-8) Hyperion Conn.
***Dark Backward.** Gregory Hall. (Illus.). 416p. 1995. 22.95 (0-670-86185-5, Viking) Viking Penguin.
Dark Barbarian: The Writings of Robert E. Howard, a Critical Anthology. Ed. by Don Herron. LC 83-18501. (Contributions to the Study of Science Fiction & Fantasy Ser.: No. 9). xviii, 242p. 1984. text ed. 55.00 (0-313-23281-4, HEB/, Greenwood Pr) Greenwood.
Dark Before the Rising Sun. Laurie McBain. 528p. 1982. mass mkt. 4.50 (0-380-79848-4) Avon.
Dark Behind the Curtain. Gillian Cross. (Illus.). 160p. (Orig.). (J). (gr. 1-5). 1987. 12.95 (0-19-271457-0) OUP.
Dark Beyond the Stars. Frank M. Robinson. 1992. mass mkt. 4.99 (0-8125-1383-5) Tor Bks.
Dark Bible. Albert J. Manachino. (Willie Button Stories Ser.). 12p. (Orig.). 1985. pap. 2.25 (0-9634181-1-4) Argo Pr.
***Dark Blade Falling.** Ciencin. (Jim Lee's WildC.A.T.s Ser.: No. 01). 1995. pap. 3.99 (0-679-87480-1) Random.
***Dark Blood Moon.** Cole Riley. 256p. 1995. 5.95 (0-87067-746-2) Holloway.
Dark Blue, Jacquard. 80p. 1990. 3.00 (0-9620519-2-6) Iris Bks.
Dark Brain of Piranesi: And Other Essays. Marguerite Yourcenar. Tr. by Richard Howard. LC 84-13809. 231p. 1984. 16.95 (0-374-17709-0) FS&G.
Dark Brain of Piranesi: And Other Essays. Marguerite Yourcenar. LC 84-13809. 231p. 1985. pap. 8.95 (0-374-51919-6, Noonday) FS&G.
Dark Bridwell. Vardis Fisher. 1979. write for info. (0-918522-58-7); pap. 5.95 (0-686-60831-3) O L Holmes.
Dark Canyon. Louis L'Amour. (Illus.). 1985. 3.99 (0-553-25324-7) Bantam.
Dark Canyon - Natural Bridges, UT. rev. ed. Ed. by Trails Illustrated Staff. (Illus.). 1993. 7.95 (0-925873-67-5) Trails Illustrated.
Dark Captor. Lindsay Armstrong. (Presents Ser.). 1993. mass mkt. 2.99 (0-373-11569-5, 1-11569-0) Harlequin Bks.
Dark Captor. large type ed. Lindsay Armstrong. 285p. 1992. reprint ed. lib. bdg. 18.95 (0-263-12835-0, Pub. by Mills & Boon UK) Thorndike Pr.
Dark Card. Amy Ehrlich. 180p. (YA). (gr. 7 up). 1993. pap. 3.99 (0-14-036332-7) Puffin Bks.
Dark Carnival. Ray Bradbury. 1994. reprint ed. lib. bdg. 29.95 (1-56849-257-X) Buccaneer Bks.
***Dark Carnival: The Secret World of Tod Browning--Hollywood's Master of the Macabre.** David J. Skal & Elias Savada. LC 95-14870. 1995. write for info. (0-385-47406-7) Doubleday.
Dark Castle. Sally Netzel. (Illus.). 27p. (Orig.). 1993. pap. 4.00 (0-88680-379-9); 40.00 (0-685-66606-9) I E Clark.
Dark Certainty. Dorothy B. Flanagan. LC 79-144737. (Yale Series of Younger Poets: No. 30). reprint ed. 18.00 (0-404-53830-4) AMS Pr.
Dark Champion. Jo Beverley. 400p. (Orig.). 1993. mass mkt. 4.50 (0-380-76786-4) Avon.
Dark Chant in a Crimson Key. George C. Chesbro. 224p. 1992. 18.95 (0-89296-463-4) Mysterious Pr.
Dark Chant in a Crimson Key. George C. Chesbro. 224p. 1993. mass mkt. 4.99 (0-446-40333-4, Mysterious Paperbk) Warner Bks.
Dark Charade. Gyeorgos C. Hatonn. Tr. by Dharma. 171p. (Orig.). (C). 1991. pap. 10.00 (0-922356-53-X) Amer West Pubs.
***Dark Chronicles.** Barbara Steiner. Incl. Dance Bk. 1. 240p. (Orig.). (YA). 1995. mass mkt. 3.99 (0-380-77441-0, Flare); Gallery Bk. 2. 224p. (Orig.). (YA). 1995. mass mkt. 3.99 (0-380-77689-8, Flare); Calling Bk. 3. 224p. (Orig.). (YA). 1995. mass mkt. 3.99 (0-380-77994-3, Flare); write for info. (0-615-00741-4) Avon.
Dark Chronicles Vol. I: The Beginning, Vol. I. Cynthia Soroka. (Illus.). 337p. (Orig.). 1994. pap. 5.99 (1-881374-70-X) Flash Blasters.
Dark Chronicles Vol. II: Red Blood, Vol. II. Cynthia Soroka. (Illus.). 337p. 1994. pap. 5.99 (1-881374-71-8) Flash Blasters.
Dark Chronicles Vol. III: Triumph, Vol. III. Cynthia Soroka. (Illus.). 337p. 1994. pap. 5.99 (1-881374-72-6) Flash Blasters.
Dark Cinema: American Film Noir in Cultural Perspective. Jon Tuska. LC 84-710. (Contributions to the Study of Popular Culture Ser.: No. 9). xxiv, 305p. 1984. text ed. 65.00 (0-313-23045-5, TIC/, Greenwood Pr) Greenwood.
Dark City. Charles Bernstein. (Sun & Moon Classics Ser.: No. 48). 120p. (Orig.). 1994. pap. 11.95 (1-55713-162-7) Sun & Moon CA.
Dark City: The Film Noir. Spencer Selby. LC 84-42732. (Illus.). 263p. 1984. lib. bdg. 32.50x (0-89950-103-6) McFarland & Co.
Dark Cliffs. large type ed. Frederick E. Smith. 1989. 17.95 (0-7089-2096-9) Ulverscroft.
Dark Cloister. Sharon Wagner. 352p. 1994. mass mkt. 3.99 (0-8217-4438-0) Zebra.
Dark Closets & Noises in the Night. Penny Colman. (J). 1991. pap. 3.95 (0-8091-6600-3) Paulist Pr.
Dark Cloud Strong Breeze. Susan Patron. LC 93-4873. (Illus.). 32p. (J). (ps-1). 1994. 15.95 (0-531-06815-3); lib. bdg. 15.99 (0-531-08665-8) Orchard Bks Watts.
***Dark Clouds & Silver Linings: A Story of Love, Families & WWII.** Dorothy S. Fibush. 265p. (Orig.). (C). 1995. pap. 18.00 (0-88739-108-7) Creat Arts Bk.
Dark Clouds, Silver Linings. Archibald D. Hart. 1993. write for info. (1-56179-091-5) Focus Family.
Dark Clouds, Silver Linings. Archibald D. Hart. 1994. pap. write for info. (1-56179-248-9) Focus Family.
***Dark Colony.** (Vampire). Date not set. 15.00 (1-56504-056-2) White Wolf.
Dark Comedies of Shakespeare. H. B. Charlton. 1973. 59.95 (0-87968-996-X) Gordon Pr.
Dark Comedies of Shakespeare. Henry Charlton. LC 74-100728. (Studies in Shakespeare: No. 24). 1970. reprint ed. lib. bdg. 49.95 (0-8383-0340-4) M S G Haskell Hse.
Dark Companions. Campbell. 1982. 3.95 (0-02-521090-4) Macmillan.
Dark Companions of Stars, Vol. 43. Peter Van de Kamp. 1986. lib. bdg. 73.00 (90-277-2270-6) Kluwer Ac.
Dark Conceit: The Making of an Allegory. Edwin Honig. LC 72-2452. 224p. reprint ed. pap. 63.90 (0-8357-6524-5, 2035895) Bks Demand.
Dark Conspiracy. Lester Smith. 336p. (Orig.). (YA). 1991. pap. 22.00 (1-55878-076-9) Game Designers.
Dark Continent: Africa As Seen by Americans. Michael McCarthy. LC 83-8878. (Contributions in Afro-American & African Studies: No. 75). (Illus.). xxx, 192p. 1983. text ed. 55.00 (0-313-23828-6, MDK/, Greenwood Pr) Greenwood.
Dark Corridor. Jay Bennett. (J). (gr. 6 up). 1990. pap. 3.99 (0-449-70337-1, Juniper) Fawcett.
Dark Cries of Gray Oaks. Lee Karr. 1989. pap. 3.95 (0-8217-2736-2) Zebra.
Dark Cries of Grey Oaks. Lee Karr. 1992. mass mkt. 3.99 (0-8217-3759-7) Zebra.

An Asterisk (*) at the beginning of an entry indicates that the title is appearing in BIP for the first time.

An Asterisk (*) at the beginning of an entry indicates that the title is appearing in BIP for the first time.

1793

Dark Money. Arthur Rosenfeld. 256p. (Orig.). 1992. mass mkt. 4.99 (*0-380-76486-5*) Avon.

***Dark Moon.** Lindsay Longford. (Shadows Ser.). 1995. mass mkt. 3.50 (*0-373-27053-4*, 1-27053-7) Silhouette.

Dark Moon. Meredith A. Pierce. 256p. (YA). (gr. 7 up). 1992. 15.95 (*0-685-59346-0*, Joy St Bks) Little.

Dark Moon, Lost Lady. Elsie Lee. 224p. 1986. pap. 2.95 (*0-8217-1918-1*) Zebra.

Dark Moon Rising. Eugenia Moore. Ed. by Esther M. Leiper. 32p. (Orig.). 1989. pap. 3.95 (*0-9617284-7-7*) Sand & Silk.

Dark Moon, Vol. II: Firebringer Trilogy. Meredith A. Pierce. (Illus.). (YA). (gr. 7 up). 1992. 16.95 (*0-316-70744-9*, Joy St Bks) Little.

Dark Moon-White Pine. Gary Lawless & S. Fox. 4.00 (*0-686-15298-0*) Great Raven Pr.

Dark Mother. Waldo D. Frank. LC 78-63986. (Gay Experience Ser.). reprint ed. 29.50 (*0-404-61505-8*) AMS Pr.

Dark Mountain. large type ed. Elisabeth Mayhew. 352p. 1985. 15.95 (*0-7089-1285-0*) Ulverscroft.

Dark Mountains & Blue Valleys, Pt. 2. Samuel Lewin. Tr. by Joseph Leftwich. LC 85-22377. (Trilogy Ser.). 160p. 1988. 12.95 (*0-8453-4804-3*, Cornwall Bks) Assoc Univ Prs.

Dark Music. Patrick Grizzell. (Illus.). 75p. (Orig.). 1989. pap. 7.95 (*0-914485-13-X*) Trill Pr.

Dark Music. Charlotte Lamb. (Presents Ser.: No. 1410). 1991. pap. 2.79 (*0-373-11410-9*) Harlequin Bks.

Dark Music, No. 2. Ann Hodgman. 224p. (YA). (gr. 7 up). 1994. pap. 3.50 (*0-14-036375-0*) Puffin Bks.

Dark Nantucket Noon. Jane Langton. (Black Dagger Crime Ser.). (Illus.). 304p. 1993. 16.50 (*0-7451-8604-1*, Black Dagger) Chivers N Amer.

Dark Nantucket Noon. Jane Langton. (Fiction Ser.). 304p. 1981. mass mkt. 5.95 (*0-14-005836-2*, Penguin Bks) Viking Penguin.

Dark Nebulae, Globules, & Protostars. Ed. by Beverly T. Lynds. LC 73-152040. 160p. reprint ed. pap. 45.60 (*0-318-35032-7*, 2030981) Bks Demand.

Dark Night. Susan Muto. LC 94-71727. (John of the Cross for Today Ser.). 360p. (Orig.). 1994. pap. 9.95 (*0-87793-532-7*) Ave Maria.

Dark Night Journey: Inward Re-Patterning Toward a Life Centered in God. Sandra Cronk. 179p. (Orig.). 1991. pap. 12.50 (*0-87574-914-3*) Pendle Hill.

Dark Night of the Soul. Manly P. Hall. pap. 4.00 (*0-89314-311-1*) Philos Res.

Dark Night of the Soul. St. John of the Cross. 1959. mass mkt. 7.95 (*0-385-02930-6*, D78, Image Bks) Doubleday.

Dark Night, Sleepy Night. Harriet Ziefert. LC 87-25759. (Hello Reading! Ser.). (Illus.). 32p. (J). (ps-3). 1988. pap. 3.50 (*0-14-050812-0*, Puffin) Puffin Bks.

Dark Night, Sleepy Night. Harriet Ziefert. (Easy to Read Ser.: Level 1). (Illus.). (J). (ps-2). 1993. pap. 3.25 (*0-14-036538-9*, Puffin) Puffin Bks.

Dark Night's Passing. Naoya Shiga. Ed. by Shaw. Tr. by Edwin McClellan. LC 76-9351. (Japan's Modern Writers Ser.). 408p. 1993. pap. 14.95 (*0-87011-362-3*) Kodansha.

Dark Night's Work & Other Stories. Elizabeth C. Gaskell. Ed. by Suzanne Lewis. (World's Classics Ser.). 336p. 1992. pap. 10.95 (*0-19-282807-X*) OUP.

Dark Obession. Shelley Sessions. 1990. mass mkt. 5.50 (*0-425-12296-4*) Berkley Pub.

Dark Obsession. Fiona Harrowe. 416p. 1987. pap. 3.95 (*0-449-12899-7*, GM) Fawcett.

Dark Ocean. Jack Vance. Incl. Strange Notions. 1986. (*0-318-60143-5*); 334p. 1986. Set boxed 60.00 (*0-317-38986-6*) Underwood-Miller.

Dark Ocean see Strange Notions & the Dark Ocean

Dark of Night. Richard Nehrbass. 1994. mass mkt. 4.50 (*0-06-109163-4*, Harp PBks) HarpC.

Dark of the Eye. Douglas Clegg. 1994. mass mkt. 5.99 (*0-671-73539-X*) PB.

Dark of the Moon. John D. Carr. 1987. pap. 3.50 (*0-88184-304-0*) Carroll & Graf.

***Dark of the Moon.** John D. Carr. 256p. 1995. mass mkt. 4.95 (*0-7867-0222-2*) Carroll & Graf.

Dark of the Moon. Janice Daugharty. Ed. by Jane Howle. 275p. 1994. 19.00 (*1-880909-17-0*) Baskerville.

Dark of the Moon. Ed. by August W. Derleth. LC 73-80374. (Granger Index Reprint Ser.). 1977. 24.95 (*0-8369-6056-4*) Ayer.

Dark of the Moon. Howard Richardson & William Berney. LC 56-9611. (Orig.). 1966. pap. 6.95 (*0-87830-517-3*, Theatre Arts Bks) Routledge Chapman & Hall.

Dark of the Moon. Karen Robards. 416p. 1988. mass mkt. 5.99 (*0-380-75437-1*) Avon.

Dark of the Moon. TSR Staff. (Advanced Dungeons & Dragons, Second Edition; Al-Qadim Ser.). (Illus.). 1994. pap. 9.95 (*1-56076-688-3*) TSR Inc.

***Dark of the Moon: A Novel.** Janice Daugharty. 288p. 1995. pap. 12.00 (*0-06-097655-1*, PL) HarpC.

Dark of the Sun. Wilbur Smith. 1989. mass mkt. 5.99 (*0-449-21555-5*) Fawcett.

Dark of the Sun: Selected Poems of Umberto Saba. Tr. by Christopher Millis. 126p. (C). 1994. lib. bdg. 34.50 (*0-8191-9330-5*) U Pr of Amer.

Dark of the Tunnel. Phyllis R. Naylor. LC 84-20441. 216p. (YA). (gr. 8 up). 1985. lib. bdg. 14.95 (*0-689-31098-6*, Atheneum Bks Young) S&S Childrens.

Dark on the Other Side. Barbara Michaels. 1988. mass mkt. 6.50 (*0-425-10928-3*) Berkley Pub.

Dark on the Other Side. large type ed. Barbara Michaels. LC 92-40548. 1993. 19.95 (*0-7927-1526-8*, Eagle Lrg Print); pap. write for info. (*0-7927-1525-X*, Eagle Lrg Print) Chivers N Amer.

***Dark One.** Guy N. Smith. 256p. 1995. mass mkt. 4.50 (*0-8217-4941-2*) Windsor NY.

Dark One. large type ed. Vanessa James. (Nightingale Ser.). 358p. 1991. pap. 14.95 (*0-8161-5152-0*, Nightingale) Hall.

Dark Opals of Harrow Island. Beverly C. Warren. 320p. 1993. mass mkt. 3.99 (*0-8217-4102-0*) Zebra.

Dark Orchid: Anthology of Erotica. Ed. by Kelly Richstein & Nan Sachsel. (Illus.). 80p. (Orig.). 1993. pap. 8.75 (*1-882300-02-5*) Willo Trees.

Dark Other Adam Dreaming. Len Fulton. (American Dust Ser.: No. 4). 1975. 8.95 (*0-913218-48-0*); pap. 2.95 (*0-913218-49-9*) Dustbooks.

Dark Paradise. Catherine Brophy. 222p. (Orig.). 1991. pap. 10.95 (*0-86327-291-6*, Pub. by Wolfhound Pr IE) Dufour.

Dark Paradise. Tami Hoag. 1994. mass mkt. 5.99 (*0-553-56161-8*) Bantam.

Dark Paradise: Opiate Addiction in America before 1940. David T. Courtwright. LC 81-6958. (Illus.). 280p. 1982. 32.00 (*0-674-19261-3*) HUP.

Dark Passage. David Goodis. 256p. 1988. pap. 3.50 (*0-8217-2417-7*) Zebra.

Dark Passages. Elizabeth Hall. 16p. (Orig.). 1988. pap. 5.95 (*0-9616572-8-6*) Clothespin Fever Pr.

Dark Path of Our Names. Joan Swift. LC 85-1465. 64p. 1985. 14.00 (*0-937872-26-1*); pap. 7.00 (*0-937872-27-X*) Dragon Gate.

Dark Patrick. Seumas Macmanus. LC 70-178447. (Short Story Index Reprint Ser.). 1977. reprint ed. 15.95 (*0-8369-4048-2*) Ayer.

Dark Peoples of the Land of Sunshine. George T. Bettany. LC 73-89424. (Black Heritage Library Collection). 1977. 23.95 (*0-8369-8510-9*) Ayer.

***Dark Phoenix.** Kamida. 1995. 3.50 (*0-679-87072-5*) Random.

Dark Place. Aaron Elkins. 208p. 1994. mass mkt. 5.50 (*0-446-40403-9*, Mysterious Paperbk) Warner Bks.

***Dark Places.** Kate Grenville. 375p. 1994. 37.50 (*0-330-33549-9*, Pub. by Picador UK) Trans-Atl Phila.

Dark Playground: Poems, 1970-1978. Lawrence P. Spingarn. LC 78-70667. 95p. 1979. pap. 7.95 (*0-911288-15-9*) Perivale Pr.

***Dark Plums.** Maria Espinosa. LC 94-36718. 220p. (Orig.). 1995. pap. 9.95 (*1-55885-128-3*) Arte Publico.

Dark Powers. Jack McKinney. 1988. mass mkt. 4.99 (*0-345-35301-3*, Del Rey) Ballantine.

Dark Prince. David Gemmell. 592p. 1993. pap. write for info. (*0-345-37910-1*, Del Rey) Ballantine.

Dark Prince. Elizabeth Krueger. (Silhouette Romance Ser.). 1993. pap. 2.75 (*0-373-08960-0*, 5-08960-2) Silhouette.

***Dark Prince: The World of Darkness: Vampire.** Keith Herber. 1994. pap. 4.99 (*0-06-105422-4*, Prism Bks) P-H.

***Dark Princess.** W. E. B. Du Bois. (A Banner Book). 312p. Date not set. lib. bdg. 40.00 (*0-87805-764-1*) U Pr of Miss.

***Dark Princess.** W. E. B. Du Bois. (A Banner Book Ser.). Date not set. pap. 16.95 (*0-87805-765-X*) U Pr of Miss.

Dark Princess. W. E. B. Du Bois. reprint ed. write for info. (*0-404-00150-5*) AMS Pr.

Dark Princess: A Romance. W. E. B. Du Bois. LC 28-11319. 340p. 1975. reprint ed. lib. bdg. 18.00 (*0-527-25295-6*) Kraus Intl.

***Dark Prisms: Occultism in Hispanic Drama.** Robert Lima. 208p. 1995. text ed. 29.95 (*0-8131-1909-X*) U Pr of Ky.

Dark Prophecies: George Orwell & Technology. Steven Edelheit. (George Orwell Ser.). 1979. lib. bdg. 250.00 (*0-87700-261-4*) Revisionist Pr.

***Dark Provenance.** Michael D. Anthony. LC 94-45898. 256p. 1995. 21.00 (*0-312-11767-1*) St Martin.

Dark Pursuit. Charlotte Lamb. (Presents Ser.: No. 1370). 1991. pap. 2.75 (*0-373-11370-6*) Harlequin Bks.

Dark Queen. Michael Williams & Teri Williams. (Dragonlance Villians Ser.). 320p. (Orig.). Date not set. pap. 4.95 (*1-56076-925-4*) TSR Inc.

Dark Races, Vol. 1. Lester Smith. (Dark Conspiracy Ser.). 104p. (Orig.). (YA). 1992. pap. 12.00 (*1-55878-105-6*) Game Designers.

Dark Ransom. Sara Craven. (Presents Ser.). 1993. pap. 2.89 (*0-373-11549-0*, 1-11549-2) Harlequin Bks.

Dark Ransom. large type ed. Sara Craven. 1992. reprint ed. lib. bdg. 18.95 (*0-263-13129-7*, Pub. by Mills & Boon UK) Thorndike Pr.

***Dark Rapture.** Michele Hauf. 256p. 1995. mass mkt. 4.99 (*0-7860-0092-9*, Pinnacle NY) Windsor NY.

***Dark Rapture.** Michele Hauf. 480p. 1995. pap. 4.99 (*0-8217-0092-8*) Zebra.

Dark Rapture: The Sex Life of the African Negro. Felix Bryk. Tr. by Arthur J. Norton. LC 72-9712. reprint ed. 39.50 (*0-404-57421-1*) AMS Pr.

Dark Realm. 352p. 1991. pap. 4.95 (*0-87431-302-3*, 20602) West End Games.

***Dark Reflections: Spectres.** Steve Brown. (Black Dog Ser.). 1995. per., pap. 10.00 (*1-56504-650-1*, 6902) White Wolf.

***Dark Refuge: A Story of Cults & Their Seductive Appeal.** Andrew Demsky. LC 94-35484. 1995. pap. 11.95 (*0-8163-1241-9*) Pacific Pr Pub Assn.

Dark Rendezvous at Dungariff. Lois Stewart. 1989. pap. 3.95 (*0-8217-2767-2*) Zebra.

Dark Renegade. Theresa Scott. (Hunters of the Ice Age Ser.). 448p. (Orig.). 1994. pap. 4.99 (*0-505-51952-6*, Love Spell) Dorchester Pub Co.

Dark Reunion. Stephen R. George. 1990. pap. 3.95 (*0-8217-2963-2*) Zebra.

Dark Reunion. L. J. Smith. (Vampire Diaries Ser.: Vol. IV). (YA). 1992. mass mkt. 3.99 (*0-06-106775-X*, Harp PBks) HarpC.

Dark Ride. Len Jenkin. 1982. pap. 4.75 (*0-8222-0273-5*) Dramatists Play.

Dark Ride & Other Plays. Len Jenkin. (Sun & Moon Classics Ser.: No. 22). 300p. (Orig.). 1993. pap. 13.95 (*1-55713-073-6*) Sun & Moon CA.

***Dark Rider.** Johansen. 1995. mass mkt. (*0-553-29947-6*) Bantam.

Dark River Legacy. B. J. Hoff. LC 88-70756. (Orig.). 1990. pap. 6.99 (*0-7814-0479-7*, LifeJourney) Chariot Family.

Dark Rivers of the Heart. Dean Koontz. 1994. pap. 23.00 (*0-679-75649-3*) Random.

Dark Rivers of the Heart: A Novel. Dean R. Koontz. LC 94-12090. 1994. 24.00 (*0-679-42524-1*) Knopf.

Dark Romance: Sexuality in the Horror Film. David J. Hogan. LC 86-161. (Illus.). 350p. 1986. lib. bdg. 32.50x (*0-89950-190-7*) McFarland & Co.

Dark Room. R. K. Narayan. LC 80-39930. iv, 210p. (C). 1981. pap. 10.95 (*0-226-56837-7*) U Ch Pr.

***Dark Room.** Minette Walters. LC 95-10616. 1995. write for info. (*0-399-14078-6*, Putnam) Putnam Pub Group.

Dark Room. Junnosuke Yoshiyuki. Tr. by John Bester. LC 75-11390. 172p. 1994. reprint ed. pap. 10.00 (*0-87011-361-5*, L16) Kodansha.

Dark Room & Other Poems. Enrique Lihn. Ed. by Patricio C. Lerzundi. Tr. by Jonathan Cohen et al. LC 77-12927. 1978. 8.95 (*0-8112-0676-9*); pap. 2.45 (*0-8112-0677-7*, NDP452) New Directions.

***Dark Root.** Archer Mayor. 1995. write for info. (*0-89296-558-4*) Mysterious Pr.

Dark Roses: Poems by Michael Thomas Kelly. Michael T. Kelly. Ed. by Melinda A. Gohn. (Illus.). 64p. (Orig.). 1991. pap. 4.50 (*0-9620793-1-6*) Michael Kelly.

Dark Safari: The Life Behind the Legend of Henry Morton Stanley. John Bierman. LC 92-31514. (Illus.). 412p. 1993. reprint ed. pap. 16.95 (*0-292-70802-5*) U of Tex Pr.

Dark Seas of Maltern Manor. Kay Vernon. (Orig.). 1981. pap. 2.50 (*0-89083-832-1*) Zebra.

Dark Secret. W. Wesley Miller. Ed. by Betty L. Kratoville. (Meridian Bks.). (Illus.). 64p. (J). (gr. 3-9). 1989. lib. bdg. 4.95 (*0-87879-620-7*) High Noon Bks.

Dark Secret of Hunters Hall. Lee Karr. 304p. 1993. mass mkt. 3.99 (*0-8217-4164-0*) Zebra.

Dark Secret of the Ouija. Terry A. Modica. (Young Reader's Christian Library). (Illus.). 224p. (YA). (gr. 9-12). 1990. reprint ed. pap. text ed. 2.50 (*1-55748-138-5*) Barbour & Co.

Dark Secrets: Cooking with Stout - Porter. Malachi McCormick. 40p. 1988. 8.00 (*0-943984-34-3*) Stone St Pr.

Dark Secrets of Greystone Manor. F. Jacquelyn Hallquist. 288p. 1993. mass mkt. 3.99 (*0-8217-4040-7*) Zebra.

Dark Secrets of the New Age: Satan's Plan for a One-World Religion. Texe Marrs. LC 86-72066. 256p. (Orig.). 1987. pap. 9.99 (*0-89107-421-X*) Crossway Bks.

Dark Secrets of Villa Montelano. Anne Knoll. 288p. 1993. mass mkt. 3.99 (*0-8217-4297-3*) Zebra.

Dark Seductions. Ed. by Alice Alfonsi & John Scognamiglio. 352p. 1993. mass mkt. 4.50 (*0-8217-4331-7*) Zebra.

***Dark Seed.** Ingeborg Glasser. 300p. Date not set. pap. 9.95 (*0-7610-0409-2*) NW Pub.

Dark Shadows - The First Year. Ed. by Dark Shadows Fan Club Staff. (Dark Shadows Television Show Ser.). (Illus.). 100p. (Orig.). 1986. pap. 11.00 (*0-317-05623-9*) Fan Club.

Dark Shadows - The Last Year. Ed. by Dark Shadows Fan Club Staff. (Dark Shadows Television Show Ser.). (Illus.). 80p. (Orig.). 1986. pap. 11.00 (*0-317-05624-7*) Fan Club.

***Dark Shadows Almanac: A 30th Anniversary Tribute.** Kathryn L. Scott. Ed. by Jim Pierson. (Illus.). 208p. 1995. 24.95 (*0-938817-40-X*); pap. 17.95 (*0-938817-41-8*) Pomegranate Pr.

***Dark Shadows Announcement.** Ed. by Fan Club Staff. (Dark Shadows Tel Show Ser.). (Illus.). 50p. 1986. pap. 20.00 (*0-614-04386-7*) Fan Club.

Dark Shadows Companion: Twenty-Fifth Anniversary Collection. Ed. by Kathryn L. Scott. (Illus.). 208p. 1990. 24.95 (*0-938817-26-4*); pap. 15.95 (*0-938817-25-6*) Pomegranate Pr.

Dark Shadows Episode Guide. Ed. by Dark Shadows Fan Club Staff. (Dark Shadows Television Show Ser.). (Illus.). 80p. (Orig.). 1986. pap. 11.00 (*0-317-05622-0*) Fan Club.

Dark Shadows in the Afternoon. Kathleen Resch & Marcy Robin. (Illus.). 112p. (Orig.). 1991. pap. 12.95 (*0-685-50337-2*) Image NY.

Dark Shadows Resurrected. Jim Pierson. (Illus.). 176p. (Orig.). 1992. 24.95 (*0-938817-24-8*) Pomegranate Pr.

Dark Shadows Resurrected. Jim Pierson. (Orig.). 1993. pap. 15.95 (*0-938817-23-X*) Pomegranate Pr.

Dark Shadows Tribute Book. Edward Gross. 1990. pap. 14.95 (*1-55698-234-8*) Movie Pubs Servs.

Dark Ship Exclipse. David H. Stone. 179p. 1995. pap. 13.00 (*1-884185-06-1*) Winterbrook.

Dark Ships. Townsend. 112p. (J). (gr. 6-8). 1988. 10.95 (*0-89015-579-8*); pap. 5.95 (*0-89015-590-9*) Sunbelt Media.

Dark Side. William C. Tremmel. 160p. (Orig.). 1987. pap. 10.99 (*0-8272-0614-3*) Chalice Pr.

Dark Side: Tales of Terror & the Supernatural. Guy De Maupassant. Ed. & Tr. by Arnold Kellett. 252p. 1990. pap. 8.95 (*0-88184-596-5*) Carroll & Graf.

Dark Side: Thoughts on the Futility of Life from Ancient Greeks to the Present. Alan R. Pratt. LC 93-45556. 1994. 10.95 (*0-8065-1481-7*) Carol Pub Group.

Dark Side of Adoption. Marsha Riben. 1988. 12.95 (*0-8187-0105-6*) Harlo Press.

***Dark Side of Christian History.** Helen Ellerbe. LC 95-60339. (Illus.). 236p. (Orig.). 1995. pap. 12.95 (*0-9644873-4-9*) Morningstr Bks.

***Dark Side of Civil Rights.** C. M. Rhodes. 1995. 13.95 (*0-8062-5191-3*) Carlton.

Dark Side of Conservatism. abr. ed. George Warren. 216p. 1994. pap. 8.95 (*1-56901-460-4*) NW Pub.

Dark Side of Creativity: Blocks, Unfinished Works & the Urge to Destroy. Cecile Nebel. 175p. 1988. 18.50 (*0-87875-346-X*) Whitston Pub.

Dark Side of Desire. Michelle Reid. (Presents Ser.). 1993. pap. 2.89 (*0-373-11533-4*, 1-11533-6) Harlequin Bks.

Dark Side of Europe: The Extreme Right Today. Geoffrey Harris. 205p. (C). 1990. text ed. 64.50 (*0-389-20924-4*) B&N Imports.

Dark Side of Europe: The Extreme Right Today. Geoffrey Harris. 1994. pap. 25.00 (*0-7486-0466-9*, Pub. by Edinburgh U Pr UK) Col U Pr.

Dark Side of Families: Current Family Violence Research. Ed. by David Finkelhor et al. 384p. 1983. 49.95 (*0-8039-1934-4*); pap. 24.00 (*0-8039-1935-2*) Sage.

Dark Side of Freemasonry. Ed Decker. LC 94-77033. 224p. 1994. 9.99 (*1-56384-061-8*) Huntington Hse.

Dark Side of Genius: The Life of Alfred Hitchcock. Donald Spoto. 1984. mass mkt. 5.95 (*0-345-31462-X*) Ballantine.

Dark Side of Genius: The Life of Alfred Hitchcock, Vol. 1. Donald Spoto. 1993. pap. 14.95 (*0-316-80815-6*) Little.

Dark Side of Hopkinsville: Stories by Ted Poston. Ted Poston. Ed. by Kathleen A. Hauke. LC 90-11251. 144p. 1991. 25.00 (*0-8203-1302-5*); pap. 12.95 (*0-8203-1303-3*) U of Ga Pr.

Dark Side of Interpersonal Communication. Ed. by William R. Cupach & Brian H. Spitzberg. (Communication Ser.). 344p. 1994. text ed. 69.95 (*0-8058-1167-2*) L Erlbaum Assocs.

***Dark Side of Japanese Business: Three "Industry Novels"** Ikko Shimizu. Ed. & Tr. by Tamae K. Prindle. 256p. 1995. 50.00 (*1-56324-616-3*, East Gate Bk); pap. 19.95 (*1-56324-617-1*, East Gate Bk) M E Sharpe.

Dark Side of Love: The Positive Role of Our Negative Feelings - Anger, Jealousy, & Hate. Jane G. Goldberg. 320p. 1993. 21.95 (*0-87477-716-X*) J P Tarcher.

Dark Side of Love: The Positive Role of Our Negative Feelings - Anger, Jealousy, & Hate. Jane G. Goldberg. LC 94-6166. 1994. 12.95 (*0-87477-776-3*, J P T-Putnam) Putnam Pub Group.

***Dark Side of My Heart.** Melody Chesney. 1995. 8.95 (*0-8062-5187-5*) Carlton.

Dark Side of Paradise. large type ed. Alma Blair. 238p. 1992. reprint ed. lib. bdg. 13.95 (*1-56054-537-2*) Thorndike Pr.

***Dark Side of Paradise: Political Violence in Bali.** Geoffrey B. Robinson. (Asia East by South Ser.). (Illus.). 376p. 1995. 35.00x (*0-8014-2965-X*) Cornell U Pr.

Dark Side of Reason: Fictionality & Power. Luiz C. Lima. Tr. by Paulo H. Britto. LC 91-24853. 360p. (C). 1992. 37.50 (*0-8047-1976-4*) Stanford U Pr.

Dark Side of the Brain. Roger Coghill & Harry Oldfield. (Illus.). 208p. 1988. pap. 16.95 (*1-85230-025-6*) Element MA.

***Dark Side of the Dream.** Alejandro Grattan-Dominguez. LC 95-9769. 1995. write for info. (*0-15-588514-6*) Arte Publico.

Dark Side of the Dream: Australian Literature & the Postcolonial Mind. Bob Hodge & Vijay Mishra. 272p. (Orig.). (C). 1992. pap. text ed. 19.95 (*0-04-442346-2*, Pub. by Allen Unwin AT) Paul & Co Pubs.

Dark Side of the Hill. large type ed. Rodney Stone. (Ulverscroft Ser.). 448p. 1994. 20.95 (*0-7089-3051-4*) Ulverscroft.

Dark Side of the Inner Child: The Next Step. Stephen Wolinsky. LC 93-41991. (Illus.). 188p. (Orig.). 1994. pap. 14.95 (*1-883647-00-2*, Bramble Bks) Bramble Co.

Dark Side of the Island. Jack Higgins. 1980. pap. 1.95 (*0-449-13826-7*, GM) Fawcett.

Dark Side of the Landscape: The Rural Poor in English Painting 1730-1840. John Barrel. LC 78-72334. 180p. 1983. pap. 22.95 (*0-521-27655-1*) Cambridge U Pr.

Dark Side of the Moon. Biddle. 1995. 29.95 (*0-8050-2235-X*) H Holt & Co.

Dark Side of the Moon. Hap Gilliland & Tom Kovach. (Indian Culture Ser.). (Illus.). 32p. (J). (gr. 1-4). 1984. pap. 4.95 (*0-89992-086-1*) Coun India Ed.

Dark Side of the Moon. Don Gray. 1970. pap. 6.00 (*0-685-01071-6*) Twowindows Pr.

***Dark Side of the Moon.** Ed. by Diana Zeiger. 730p. 1995. 69.95 (*1-56167-257-2*) Nat Lib Poetry.

Dark Side of the Moon. Pref. by T. S. Eliot. LC 74-26099. reprint ed. 24.50 (*0-404-58526-4*) AMS Pr.

Dark Side of the Screen: Film Noir. Foster Hirsch. LC 83-7559. (Quality Paperbacks Ser.). (Illus.). 229p. 1983. reprint ed. pap. 14.95 (*0-306-80203-1*) Da Capo.

Dark Side of the Street. Jack Higgins. 208p. 1984. pap. 3.95 (*0-451-16451-2*, Sig); pap. 4.99 (*0-451-14980-7*, Sig) NAL-Dutton.

Dark Side of the Universe. James S. Trefil. 1989. mass mkt. 9.95 (*0-385-26212-4*, Anchor NY) Doubleday.

Dark Side of the Universe - Experimental Efforts & Theoretical Framework: Proceedings of the International Workshop. R. Bernabei & C. Tao. 316p. 1994. text ed. 95.00 (*981-02-1600-9*) World Scientific Pub.

Dark Silence. Rick Hautala. 480p. 1992. mass mkt. 5.99 (*0-8217-3923-9*) Zebra.

Dark Silence. Maureen Wartski. (Orig.). (YA). (gr. 9-12). 1993. mass mkt. 3.99 (*0-449-70418-1*, Juniper) Fawcett.

Dark Sister. Rebecca Goldstein. 288p. 1993. pap. 11.95 (*0-14-017247-5*, Penguin Bks) Viking Penguin.

Dark Sky Legacy: Astronomy's Impact on the History of Culture. George Reed. 199p. 1989. 28.95 (*0-87975-541-5*) Prometheus Bks.

Dark Smoke. Pancho Aguila. LC 77-76904. 1977. pap. 5.00 (*0-915016-14-1*) Second Coming.

1794 An Asterisk (*) at the beginning of an entry indicates that the title is appearing in BIP for the first time.

An Asterisk (*) at the beginning of an entry indicates that the title is appearing in BIP for the first time.

Darkness at Dawn: Appalachian Kentucky & the Future. Harry M. Caudill. LC 74-7871. (Kentucky Bicentennial Bookshelf Ser.). 88p. reprint ed. pap. 25.10 (0-8357-4293-8, 2037091) Bks Demand.

Darkness at Each Elbow. Harley Elliott. 1981. pap. 7.00 (0-914610-21-X) Hanging Loose.

Darkness at Fair Winds. Charlotte Douglas. 352p. 1993. pap. 4.50 (0-8439-3356-9) Dorchester Pub Co.

Darkness at Heart: Fathers & Sons in Conrad. Catharine Rising. LC 89-29432. (Contributions to the Study of World Literature Ser.: No. 37). 224p. 1990. text ed. 55.00 (0-313-26880-0, RDH/, Greenwood Pr) Greenwood.

Darkness at Morning Star. Joyce C. Ware. 320p. 1992. mass mkt. 3.99 (0-8217-3938-7) Zebra.

Darkness at Night: A Riddle of the Universe. Edward Harrison. LC 87-32701. (Illus.). 264p. 1987. text ed. 36.00 (0-674-19270-2) HUP.

Darkness at Night: A Riddle of the Universe. Edward Harrison. (Illus.). 264p. 1989. reprint ed. pap. text ed. 12.95 (0-674-19271-0) HUP.

Darkness at Noon. Arthur Koestler. (gr. 9 up). 1984. mass mkt. 5.99 (0-553-26595-4) Bantam.

Darkness at Noon. Arthur Koestler. 1984. 19.95 (0-02-565200-1) Macmillan.

Darkness at Noon. Arthur Koestler. 288p. 1987. text ed. 35.00 (0-02-565210-9, Scribners) S&S Trade.

Darkness at Sethanon. Raymond E. Feist. 1987. mass mkt. 5.99 (0-553-26328-5, Spectra) Bantam.

Darkness Beckons: The History & Development of Cave Diving. 2nd ed. Martyn Farr. LC 81-4075. (Illus.). 280p. 1991. 35.00 (0-939748-32-0) Cave Bks MO.

Darkness Before Dawn. Ace Collins. (Springfield Ser.). 128p. (Orig.). 1992. pap. text ed. 4.99 (0-9628579-4-7) Vision WY.

***Darkness Before the Dawn.** Ryan Hughes. (Children of Athas Ser.). 320p. (Orig.). 1995. pap. 4.95 (0-7869-0104-7) TSR Inc.

Darkness Blossoming. Conleth Ellis. (C). 1990. 30.00 (0-948268-54-9, Pub. by Dedalus Pr IE); pap. 15.00 (0-948268-53-0, Pub. by Dedalus Pr IE) St Mut.

Darkness Casts No Shadow. Arnold Lustig. 173p. 1985. pap. 9.95 (0-8101-0704-X) Northwestern U Pr.

Darkness Creeping: Tales to Trouble Your Sleep. Neal Shusterman. LC 93-13792. (Illus.). 128p. (J). 1993. pap. 4.95 (1-56565-069-7) Lowell Hse.

Darkness Crumbles: Dispatches from the Barricades. John Simpson. (Illus.). 368p. 1993. 39.95 (0-09-177252-4, Pub. by Hutchinson UK) Trafalgar.

Darkness Defined. Gary W. Kioeker. 92p. (Orig.). 1992. pap. text ed. 9.95 (1-881168-14-X) Red Danceflr.

Darkness Descends. Ryder Syvertsen. (Mystic Rebel Ser.: No. 3). 1988. pap. 3.95 (1-55817-141-X, Pinnacle NY) Windsor NY.

Darkness Discovered (Satans Stratagems) Giacomo Aconcio. LC 78-9490. 1978. reprint ed. 50.00 (0-8201-1313-1) Schol Facsimiles.

Darkness Falls. Franklin W. Dixon. Ed. by Ruth Ashby. (Hardy Boys Casefiles Series, Operation Phoenix Trilogy: No. 84). 160p. (Orig.). (YA). 1994. mass mkt. 3.99 (0-671-79473-6, Archway) PB.

Darkness Falls. Joyce A. Schneider. Ed. by Bill Grose. 384p. 1991. reprint ed. mass mkt. 4.95 (0-671-67318-1) PB.

Darkness in St. Louis, Bearheart see Bearheart: The Heirship Chronicles

D

Darkness in Summer. Takeshi Kaiko. Tr. by Cecilia S. Seigle. 210p. 1988. 26.00 (0-7206-0725-6, Pub. by P Owen Ltd UK) Dufour.

Darkness in Summer. Takeshi Kaiko. Tr. by Cecilia S. Seigle. 212p. 1972. reprint ed. pap. 12.95 (0-8048-1375-2) C E Tuttle.

Darkness in the Marketplace: The Christian at Prayer in the World. Thomas H. Green. LC 81-67559. 128p. (Orig.). 1981. pap. 4.95 (0-87793-230-1) Ave Maria.

Darkness into Light. large type ed. Carole Mortimer. (Nightingale Series Large Print Bks.). 233p. 1991. pap. 14.95 (0-8161-5179-2, Nightingale) Hall.

Darkness Is Light Enough: The Field Journal of a Night Naturalist. Chris Ferris. (Illus.). 368p. 1988. reprint ed. pap. 12.95 (0-88001-168-8) Ecco Pr.

Darkness Moves: An Henri Michaux Anthology, 1927-1984. Henri Michaux. Tr. by David Ball. LC 92-12925. 1994. 30.00 (0-520-07231-6) U CA Pr.

Darkness of Corn. large type ed. Caroline Stickland. (General Ser.). 448p. 1993. 21.95 (0-7089-2738-6) Ulverscroft.

***Darkness of God: Negativity in Christian Mysticism.** Denys Turner. 300p. (C). 1995. write for info. (0-521-45317-8) Cambridge U Pr.

Darkness of God: Theology after Hiroshima. James Garrison. LC 83-1415. 248p. reprint ed. pap. 70.70 (0-317-30139-X, 2025322) Bks Demand.

Darkness on the Ice. Lois Tilton. 288p. 1993. mass mkt. 4.50 (1-55817-687-X, Pinnacle NY) Windsor NY.

***Darkness over Covenant.** William J. Eyer. (Orig.). 1995. pap. 9.95 (0-88270-722-1) Bridge Pub.

Darkness over Tibet. Theodore Illion. (Mystic Travellers Ser.). (Illus.). 210p. 1991. reprint ed. pap. 15.95 (0-932813-14-3) Adventures Unltd.

Darkness Starts up Where You Stand. Arthur W. Knight. 124p. (Orig.). 1995. pap. 9.95 (1-884097-31-6) Depth Charge.

Darkness under the Trees: Walking Behind the Spanish. Luis O. Salinas. (Chicano Studies Library Publications: No. 6). 120p. (Orig.). (C). 1982. pap. 6.50 (0-918520-04-5) Chicano Stud Lib.

***Darkness Visible.** William Golding. 1994. lib. bdg. 21.95x (1-56849-470-X) Buccaneer Bks.

Darkness Visible. William Golding. 265p. 1979. 14.95 (0-374-13502-9) FS&G.

Darkness Visible. William G. Golding. LC 84-22397. 276p. 1985. pap. 8.95 (0-15-623931-0, Harvest Bks) HarBrace.

Darkness Visible: A Memoir of Madness. William Styron. 84p. 1990. 15.95 (0-394-58888-6) Random.

Darkness Visible: A Memoir of Madness. large type ed. William Styron. 176p. 1991. 18.00 (0-679-40402-3) Random.

Darkness Visible: A Memoir of Madness. William Styron. 1991. reprint ed. pap. 8.00 (0-679-73639-5, Vin) Random.

Darkness We Carry: The Drama of the Holocaust. Robert Skloot. LC 87-40376. 192p. (C). 1988. text ed. 35.00 (0-299-11660-3); pap. text ed. 12.95 (0-299-11664-6) U of Wis Pr.

Darkness Within. Shawn Macdonald. 320p. 1993. mass mkt. 4.50 (0-8217-4163-2) Zebra.

Darkroom. Kathryn Harrison. LC 92-22130. 1993. 20.00 (0-679-40942-4) Random.

Darkroom. Ed. by Eleanor Lewis. LC 76-57201. (Illus.). 184p. (Orig.). 1979. pap. 17.50 (0-912810-19-X) Lustrum Pr.

Darkroom Cookbook. Stephen G. Anchell. (Illus.). 192p. 1994. spiral bd. 19.95 (0-240-80196-2, Focal) Buttrwrth-Heinemann.

Darkroom Dynamics: A Guide to Creative Darkroom Techniques. Jim Stone. (Illus.). 208p. 1979. pap. text ed. 25.00 (0-240-51767-9, Focal) Buttrwrth-Heinemann.

Darkroom Handbook. Michael Langford. LC 83-49188. 120p. 1984. pap. 26.00 (0-394-72468-2) Knopf.

Darkroom Handbook: A Complete Guide to the Best Design, Construction & Equipment. rev. ed. Dennis Curtin & Joe DeMaio. (Illus.). 192p. 1982. pap. text ed. 14.95 (0-240-51764-4, Focal) Buttrwrth-Heinemann.

Darkroom Logbook for Photographers. Fred M. Roberts. 94p. 1973. pap. 9.50 (0-912746-04-1) F M Roberts.

Darkroom Two. Jain Kelley. LC 78-69948. (Illus.). 160p. (Orig.). 1979. pap. 17.95 (0-912810-21-1) Lustrum Pr.

Darkscope. Margaret Falk. 1990. mass mkt. 4.50 (1-55817-364-1, Pinnacle NY) Windsor NY.

***Darkseid vs. Galactus: The Hunger.** Burne. Ed. by Simpson. (Illus.). 48p. 1995. pap. 4.95 (1-56389-182-4) DC Comics.

***Darkside: Chronicling the Young Black Experience.** Jackson. 1995. pap. text ed. 12.95 (1-879360-40-3) Noble Pr.

Darkside Exile. abr. ed. K. Terrell Fried. 240p. 1995. pap. 8.95 (1-56901-397-7) NW Pub.

Darksong. Jean Simon. 1990. pap. 3.95 (0-8217-2893-8) Zebra.

***Darkspell.** Katharine Kerr. 1994. mass mkt. 5.50 (0-553-56888-4, Spectra) Bantam.

Darksword Adventures. Margaret Weis & Tracy Hickman. 384p. 1988. mass mkt. 4.99 (0-553-27600-X, Spectra) Bantam.

Darksword Trilogy, 3 vols. Margaret Weis. 1988. boxed, pap. 13.50 (0-553-33777-7) Bantam.

Darktek Equipment Handbook. Charles E. Gannon. (Dark Conspiracy Ser.). 104p. (Orig.). (YA). 1991. pap. 12.00 (1-55878-084-X) Game Designers.

Darkthunder's Way. Tom Deitz. 352p. 1989. pap. 3.95 (0-380-75508-4) Avon.

Darktown Strutters. Wesley Brown. LC 93-72463. 225p. (Orig.). (C). 1994. pap. text ed. 11.95 (0-943433-11-8) Cane Hill Pr.

Darktraders. Eluki Bes Shahar. (Hellflower Ser.: Bk. 2). 256p. (Orig.). 1992. mass mkt. 4.50 (0-88677-507-8) DAW Bks.

Darkwalker on Moonshae. Douglas Niles. LC 86-51270. (Forgotten Realms Moonshae Trilogy Ser.: Bk. 1). 352p. (Orig.). 1987. pap. 4.95 (0-88038-451-4) TSR Inc.

Darkwater: Voices from Within the Veil. W. E. B. Du Bois. LC 70-91785. reprint ed. 37.50 (0-404-00151-3) AMS Pr.

Darkwater: Voices from Within the Veil. W. E. B. Du Bois. LC 75-1429. 1975. reprint ed. 17.00 (0-527-25300-6) Kraus Intl.

Darkwater: Voices from Within the Veil. W. E. B. DuBois. (BCL1 - U. S. History Ser.). 276p. 1991. reprint ed. lib. bdg. 79.00 (0-7812-6084-1) Rprt Serv.

Darkwell. Douglas Niles. LC 88-50057. (Forgotten Realms Moonshae Trilogy Ser.: Bk. 3). 1989. pap. 4.95 (0-88038-717-3) TSR Inc.

Darkwing Duck: Just Us Justice Duck. (Illus.). 48p. (J). (gr. 3-7). 1992. pap. 2.95 (1-56115-268-4, 21809, Golden Pr) Western Pub.

Darl. Fred Clifton. (Illus.). 104p. (J). (gr. 2-6). 1973. 12.00 (0-89388-098-1) Okpaku Communications.

Darla: Faith over Fire. Bev Larsen. 130p. (Orig.). 1991. pap. 12.00 (0-929690-13-3) Herit Pubs AZ.

Darlehen im Konkurs. Walter Luther. 144p. 1990. pap. 36.00 (3-7890-1938-0, Pub. by Nomos Verlags GW) Intl Bk Import.

Darlin' Bill. Jerome Charyn. LC 85-70635. 304p. 1985. pap. 8.95 (0-917657-40-3, Primus Lib Contemp) D I Fine.

Darling: An Original Screenplay, Directed by Richard Lester. Frederick Raphael. Ed. by George P. Garrett et al. LC 71-135273. (Film Scripts Ser.). 1989. pap. text ed. 19.95 (0-89197-719-8) Irvington.

Darling Annie. Raine Cantrell. 384p. (Orig.). 1994. pap. 4.99 (0-451-40514-5, Topaz) NAL-Dutton.

Darling Babies. Ernest Nister. (Tiny Pull-the-Tab Bks.). (Illus.). 10p. (YA). 1994. 4.95 (0-399-22722-9, Philomel Bks) Putnam Pub Group.

Darling Buds of May: The Pop Larkin Chronicles. H. E. Bates. LC 92-20439. 1993. 20.00 (0-688-11960-3) Morrow.

Darling Buds of May: The Pop Larkin Chronicles. large type ed. H. E. Bates. LC 93-15035. 1993. 21.95 (1-56054-730-8) Thorndike Pr.

Darling Buds of May: The Pop Larkin Chronicles, 3 vols. in one. H. E. Bates. 352p. 1993. reprint ed. pap. 11.00 (0-06-097596-2, PL) HarpC.

Darling Clementine. Andrew Klavan. LC 87-61103. 160p. 1988. 22.00 (0-932966-81-0) Permanent Pr.

Darling Corey's Dead. Martha G. Webb. 192p. 1994. pap. 3.95 (0-7867-0109-9) Carroll & Graf.

Darling Dinosaurs - Charted for Counted Thread, Embroidery & Applique. Jean D. Crowther. 1988. pap. 5.98 (0-88290-324-1) Horizon Utah.

Darling, I'm Still Alive & Recovering from Love. Carol B. Lyon. 38p. (Orig.). 1993. pap. 3.95 (1-879559-07-2) Galaxy WV.

Darling Innocence. 2nd ed. 1992. pap. 4.95 (1-56333-047-4) Masquerade.

Darling Jenny. Janet Dailey. (Americana Ser.). 1993. mass mkt. 3.59 (0-373-89900-9, 1-89900-4) Harlequin Bks.

Darling Lady. large type ed. Frances A. Bond. 656p. 1993. 21.95 (0-7505-0485-4) Ulverscroft.

Darling of Misfortune: Edwin Booth. Richard Lockridge. LC 79-91908. 1972. 30.95 (0-405-08753-5, Pub. by Blom Pubns UK) Ayer.

***Darling of My Heart: 2000 Years of Irish Love Writing.** Ed. by Laurence Flanagan. 256p. (Orig.). 1994. pap. 19.95 (0-7171-2082-1, Pub. by Gill & MacMill IE) Irish Bks Media.

Darling Twins. Robert L. Merriam. (Illus.). 25p. (Orig.). 1976. pap. 2.00 (0-686-32493-5) R L Merriam.

Darlinghissima: Letters to a Friend. Janet Flanner & Natalia D. Murray. (Illus.). 544p. 1986. pap. 10.95 (0-15-623937-X, Harvest Bks) HarBrace.

Darmstadt Orchids. Stuart Friebert. LC 92-7138. 64p. 1992. 9.25 (0-933532-88-1) BkMk.

Darn Right It's Butch: Memories of Our Gang. Tommy Bond & Ron Genini. LC 93-86222. (Illus.). 224p. 1994. 19.98 (0-9630976-5-2) Morgin Pr.

Darn the Torpedoes, I Have a Boo-Boo. Joe Workman. Ed. by R. Schell & Mary Meador. LC 93-79911. 144p. (Orig.). 1993. pap. 7.95 (0-87208-302-0) Island Pr Pubs.

Darnell Rock Reporting. Walter D. Myers. LC 94-8666. (J). 1994. 14.95 (0-385-32096-5) Delacorte.

DARPA Neural Network Study. Ed. by Lupo et al. LC 88-31655. (Illus.). 625p. (C). 1988. text ed. 49.95 (0-916159-17-5) AFCEA Intl Pr.

Darrow-Lewis Debate on the Theory of Non-Resistance to Evil. Clarence Darrow & Arthur M. Lewis. 37p. 1989. 5.00 (0-911826-48-3, 5076) Am Atheist.

Darrow on Capital Punishment: His Closing Argument in the Loeb-Leopold Trial & His Debate on Capital Punishment. Clarence Darrow. (Illus.). 180p. 1991. reprint ed. pap. 11.95 (0-685-49004-1) CH Bookworks.

Darryl F. Zanuck: "Don't Say Yes Until I Finish Talking" Mel Gussow. (Illus.). 323p. 1980. reprint ed. pap. 7.95 (0-306-80132-9) Da Capo.

Darsan: Seeing the Divine Image in India. 2nd enl. ed. Diana L. Eck. LC 85-22972. 97p. (C). 1985. pap. 8.95 (0-89012-042-0) Anima Pubns.

Darsham's Folly. large type ed. Harriet Esmond. 416p. 1992. 21.95 (0-7089-2606-1) Ulverscroft.

Darshan Hours. Meher Baba. Ed. by Eruch Jessawala & Rick Chapman. 80p. 1973. 8.95 (0-940700-06-9); pap. 4.95 (0-940700-05-0) Meher Baba Info.

Darshan of the Divine World - Teacher, Sri Da Avabhasa (the "Bright) Da Avabhasa. Da Avabhasa. (Illus.). 64p. (Orig.). 1992. 19.95 (0-918801-55-9) Dawn Horse Pr.

Darstellung der Kreuzabnahme und der Beweinung Christi in der Ersten Halfte des 16. Jahrhunderts. Claudia Bertling. Bd. 77. 264p. (GER.). 1992. write for info. (0-318-70551-6, Pub. by Georg Olms GW) Lubrecht & Cramer.

Darstellung der Landschaft in der griechischen Dichtung: Untersuchungen Zur Antiken Literatur und Geschichte, Vol.15. Wilfried Elliger. LC 73-91160. (GER.). (C). 1975. 207.70 (3-11-004794-2) De Gruyter.

Darstellung der Spanischen Literatur Im Mittelalter. Ludwig Clarus. xlii, 1001p. 1970. reprint ed. write for info. (0-318-71632-1, Pub. by Georg Olms GW) Lubrecht & Cramer.

Darstellung und Reaktionen Von Thiooxalsauren und Thiooxalsaurederivaten. W. Thiel & R. Mayer. Ed. by A. Senning. (Sulfer Report Ser.: Vol. 8, No. 1). 58p. (GER.). 1988. pap. text ed. 55.00 (3-7186-4807-5) Gordon & Breach.

Dart Book. Ed. by Dave Prokop. LC 77-85322. (Illus.). 109p. 1978. pap. 4.95 (0-89037-124-5) Anderson World.

D'Artagnan the King Maker. Alexandre Dumas. 1976. 22.95 (0-8488-0358-2) Amereon Ltd.

Dartford-Thurrock Crossing Act, 1988, Chapter 20. 1988. pap. 16.00 (0-10-542088-3, HM3758, Pub. by HMSO UK) UNIPUB.

Dartmoor: The Threatened Wilderness. Brian Carter & Brian Skilton. (Illus.). 160p. 1988. 39.95 (0-7126-1756-6, Pub. by Century UK) Trafalgar.

Dartmoor Burial. Audrey Peterson. Ed. by Dana Isaacson. 256p. (Orig.). 1992. mass mkt. 5.50 (0-671-72970-5) PB.

Dartmoor National Park. 91p. 1983. pap. 5.00 (0-11-700478-2, HM144, Pub. by HMSO UK) UNIPUB.

Dartmoor Reaves. Andrew Fleming. (Illus.). 135p. 1990. reprint ed. pap. 34.95 (0-7134-5666-3, Pub. by Batsford UK) Trafalgar.

***Dartmoor Themes: A Walker's Guide.** J. H. Powell. (Illus.). 224p. 1995. pap. 22.95 (1-85223-915-8, Pub. by Crowood Pr UK) Trafalgar.

Dartmoor Walks. (Ordnance Survey Pathfinder Guides Ser.). (Illus.). 80p. 1993. pap. 12.95 (0-7117-0515-1) Seven Hills Bk.

Dartmoor Yankee. Malcolm Lynch. 174p. (Orig.). 1993. 19.95 (0-907018-68-8, Pub. by Tabb Hse Pubs UK); pap. 11.95 (0-907018-98-X, Pub. by Tabb Hse Pubs UK) Seven Hills Bk.

Dartmouth. Ed. by David Bradley & Shelby Grantham. LC 89-28479. (Illus.). 128p. 1990. 35.00 (0-87451-494-0) U Pr of New Eng.

Dartmouth: A Visual Remembrance. David Bradley. Ed. by James B. Patrick. 144p. 1982. 35.00 (0-940078-06-6) Foremost Pubs.

Dartmouth College Case & the Public-Private Penumbra. Henry J. Friendly. LC 71-627370. (Quarterly Ser.). 1969. 10.00 (0-87959-070-X) U of Tex H Ransom Ctr.

Dartmouth College Causes & the Supreme Court of the United States. John. M. Shirley. LC 79-124904. (American Constitutional & Legal History Ser). (Illus.). 1971. reprint ed. lib. bdg. 49.50 (0-306-71995-9) Da Capo.

Dartmouth Medical School: The First One Hundred Seventy-Five Years. Carleton B. Chapman. LC 72-89557. 120p. reprint ed. pap. 34.20 (0-317-41846-7, 2025634) Bks Demand.

Dartmouth Reader. Ed. by Francis Brown. LC 79-108876. 339p. 1969. 35.00 (0-87451-045-7) U Pr of New Eng.

Dartnell Guide to Cost Conscious Advertising. Jim Montice. 209p. 1991. ring bd. 91.50 (0-85013-175-8) Dartnell Corp.

Dartnell's Sales Training Kit, 1986. vinyl bd. 195.00 (0-685-65964-X, 93-1002) Dartnell Corp.

Darts: Fifty Ways to Play the Game. Jabez Gotobed. (Games & Pastimes Ser.: Vol. 2). (Illus.). 1979. 9.95 (0-900891-71-8); pap. 4.95 (0-900891-72-6) Oleander Pr.

Darts: The Complete Book of the Game. Keith Turner. LC 85-42594. (Illus.). 144p. 1985. reprint ed. pap. 9.00 (0-06-097006-5, PL 7006, PL) HarpC.

***Darts American Style.** Fred H. Holmes. (Orig.). 1988. pap. text ed. 10.95 (0-9626241-0-1) Lone Star Dallas.

Darts in Los Angeles. David L. Dyer. LC 83-51647. (Illus.). 177p. (Orig.). 1984. lib. bdg. 11.95 (0-930103-00-9); pap. 4.95 (0-930103-01-7) Travl Guides.

Dartwood's Daughter. braille ed. Rebecca Baldwin. 314p. 1992. vinyl bd. 25.12 (1-56956-220-2, BR8086) W A T Braille.

Dartwood's Daughters. large type ed. Rebecca Baldwin. LC 90-10730. 267p. 1990. lib. bdg. 17.95 (0-89621-969-0) Thorndike Pr.

Darvishes: or Oriental Spiritualism. John P. Brown. Ed. by Horace A. Rose. (Illus.). 496p. 1968. 32.50 (0-7146-1980-9, Pub. by F Cass Pubs UK) Intl Spec Bk.

Darvon-Darvocet & Other Prescription Narcotics. rev. ed. 1990. pap. 0.25 (0-89230-147-3) Do It Now.

Darweesh see Splinters of Bone

Darwin. Ed. by Philip Appleman. (Critical Editions Ser.). (Illus.). (C). 1979. pap. text ed. 12.95 (0-393-95009-3) Norton.

Darwin. Adrian Desmond & James Moore. 832p. 1992. 35.00 (0-446-51589-2) Warner Bks.

Darwin. F. D. Fletcher. 1989. pap. 25.00 (0-85263-523-0, Pub. by Shire UK) St Mut.

Darwin. Jonathan Howard. (Past Masters Ser.). 1983. pap. 7.95 (0-19-287556-6) OUP.

***Darwin.** Piero Ventura et al. Tr. by Kathleen Leverich. LC 94-29989. (J). 1995. 16.95 (0-395-70738-2) HM.

Darwin. 2nd ed. Ed. by Philip Appleman. (Critical Editions Ser.). (Illus.). (C). 1979. text ed. 24.95 (0-393-01192-5) Norton.

Darwin. 3rd ed. Charles Darwin. Ed. by Philip Appleman. (Critical Editions Ser.). (Illus.). (C). 1990. pap. text ed. write for info. (0-393-95849-3) Norton.

Darwin. Edmund O'Connor. Ed. by Malcolm Yapp et al. (World History Ser.). (Illus.). 32p. (YA). (gr. 6-11). 1980. reprint ed. pap. text ed. 3.45 (0-89908-022-7) Greenhaven.

***Darwin: A Life in Science.** Michael White & John Gribbin. 288p. 1995. 24.95 (0-525-94002-2, Dutton) NAL-Dutton.

Darwin: Competition & Cooperation. Ashley Montagu. LC 72-11332. 148p. 1973. reprint ed. text ed. 35.00 (0-8371-6657-8, MODC, Greenwood Pr) Greenwood.

Darwin: On the Trail of Evolution. Clint Twist. LC 93-31789. (Beyond the Horizon Ser.). (J). 1994. lib. bdg. 22.80 (0-8114-7256-6) Raintree Steck-V.

Darwin: The Life of a Tormented Evolutionist. Adrian Desmond. 1994. pap. 17.95 (0-393-31150-3) Norton.

Darwin & Facial Expression: A Century of Research in Review. Paul Ekman. 1973. text ed. 51.00 (0-12-236750-2) Acad Pr.

Darwin & Social Darwinism. Ed. by Rosaleen Love. 69p. (C). 1982. 38.00 (0-86828-132-8, Pub. by Deakin Univ AT) St Mut.

Darwin & the Darwinian Revolution. Gertrude Himmelfarb. 1968. reprint ed. pap. 13.95 (0-393-00455-4) Norton.

Darwin & the Emergence of Evolutionary Theories of Mind & Behavior. Robert J. Richards. LC 87-10891. (Science & Its Conceptual Foundations Ser.). (Illus.). 688p. 1989. pap. text ed. 17.95 (0-226-71200-1) U Ch Pr.

Darwin & the General Reader: The Reception of Darwin's Theory of Evolution in the British Periodical Press, 1859-1872. Alvar Ellegard. 400p. 1990. pap. text ed. 17.95 (0-226-20487-1) U Ch Pr.

Darwin & the Great Beasts. Kin Platt. LC 90-39674. 64p. (J). (gr. 2 up). 1992. 14.00 (0-688-10030-9) Greenwillow.

Darwin & the Humanities. James M. Baldwin. LC 75-3021. reprint ed. 29.50 (0-404-59016-0) AMS Pr.

***Darwin & the Modern World View.** John C. Greene. LC 61-15489. (Rockwell Lectures, Rice University: No. L-64). 153p. 1981. pap. 43.70 (0-7837-8464-3, 2049269) Bks Demand.

Darwin & the Novelists: Patterns of Science in Victorian Fiction. George L. Levine. LC 87-36201. 336p. 1988. 37.00 (0-674-19285-0) HUP.

Darwin & the Novelists: Patterns of Science in Victorian Fiction. George L. Levine. LC 87-36201. 334p. 1991. pap. text ed. 16.95 (0-226-47574-3) U Ch Pr.

An Asterisk (*) at the beginning of an entry indicates that the title is appearing in BIP for the first time.

D

An Asterisk (*) at the beginning of an entry indicates that the title is appearing in BIP for the first time.

1797

Data Analysis: The Key to Data Base Design. Richard C. Perkinson. LC 83-63212. 303p. reprint ed. pap. 86.40 (*0-7837-5887-1*, 2045610) Bks Demand.

Data Analysis: Using IBM PC Computers. Teara Archwamety. 156p. (Orig.). 1991. teacher ed, disk 40.00 (*1-878276-36-0*) Educ Systs Assocs Inc.

***Data Analysis: Using Macintosh Computers.** Teara Archwamety. 329p. (Orig.). (C). 1994. student ed, disk 40.00 (*1-878276-50-6*) Educ Systs Assocs Inc.

Data Analysis & Informatics III. E. Diday et al. 1984. 118.00 (*0-444-87555-7*, I-344-84) Elsevier.

Data Analysis & Informatics, IV. Ed. by E. Diday et al. 738p. 1986. 159.00 (*0-444-70061-7*, North Holland) Elsevier.

Data Analysis & Informatics, V. Proceeding of the 5th International Symposium Organized by the Institut National de Recherche en Informatique it en Automatique, Versailles, France, 29 Sept. - 2 Oct, 1987. Ed. by E. Diday. 526p. 1988. 133.50 (*0-444-70445-0*, North Holland) Elsevier.

Data Analysis & Regression: A Second Course in Statistics. Frederick Mosteller & John W. Tukey. LC 76-15465. (Behavioral Science Ser.). 608p. (C). 1977. text ed. 64.50 (*0-201-04854-X*, Adv Bk Prog) Addison-Wesley.

Data Analysis & Statistics Across the Curriculum. Gail Burrill et al. LC 92-16923. (Curriculum & Evaluation Standards for School Mathematics Addenda Ser.: Grades 9-12). (Illus.). 88p. (Orig.). (YA). (gr. 9-12). 1992. pap. 15.00 (*0-87353-329-1*) NCTM.

Data Analysis & the Social Sciences. Ed. by David McKay et al. LC 83-42529. 291p. 1983. text ed. 35.00 (*0-312-18300-3*) St Martin.

Data Analysis, Data Modeling, & Classification. Martin E. Modell. 1992. text ed. 43.00 (*0-07-042634-1*) McGraw.

***Data Analysis for Chemists: Applications to QSAR & Chemical Product Design.** David Livingstone. (Illus.). 250p. 1995. 56.00 (*0-19-855728-0*) OUP.

Data Analysis for Comparative Social Research: International Perspectives. Ed. by C. Hayashi et al. LC 92-14452. 1992. write for info. (*0-444-89546-9*, North Holland) Elsevier.

Data Analysis for Data Base Design. D. R. Howe. (Illus.). 320p. 1990. pap. 27.50 (*0-7131-3688-X*, A3809, Pub. by E Arnold UK) Routledge Chapman & Hall.

Data Analysis for Managers with MINITAB 7.0. 2nd ed. Harry V. Roberts. 510p. 1991. text ed., 3.5 hd 47.50 (*0-89426-193-2*); boxed, 5.25 hd 47.50 (*0-89426-192-4*) Boyd & Fraser.

Data Analysis for Politics & Policy. Edward R. Tufte. (Illus.). 192p. 1974. pap. text ed. 34.20 (*0-13-197525-0*) P-H.

Data Analysis for Research Designs. Geoffrey Keppel & Sheldon Zedeck. LC 88-32222. (Psychology Ser.). 594p. (C). 1995. text ed. write for info. (*0-7167-1991-6*) W H Freeman.

Data Analysis for Scientists & Engineers. Stuart L. Meyer. 513p. (C). 1992. reprint ed. text ed. 75.00 (*0-9635027-1-9*); reprint ed. pap. text ed. 45.00 (*0-9635027-0-0*) Peer Mgmt Cnslts.

Data Analysis for the Chemical Sciences: A Guide to Statistical Techniques. Richard C. Graham. 340p. (C). 1993. lib. bdg. 65.00 (*1-56081-048-3*) VCH Pubs.

Data Analysis for the Helping Professions: A Practical Guide. Ed. by Donald M. Pilcher. (Sourcebooks for the Human Services Ser.: Vol. 10). 264p. (C). 1990. text ed. 49.95 (*0-8039-3724-5*); pap. text ed. 24.00 (*0-8039-3061-5*) Sage.

Data Analysis for the Social Sciences. Dennis M. Roberts. 352p. (C). 1992. pap. text ed. 41.95 (*0-8403-7583-2*) Kendall-Hunt.

Data Analysis Graphing & Report Writing. Charles E. Hawkins & James H. Niewahner. Ed. by Scott Dennison. (Illus.). 95p. (Orig.). (C). 1987. pap. text ed. 10.00 (*0-923231-05-6*) Mohican Pub.

***Data Analysis Handbook.** Ildiko E. Frank & Roberto Todeschini. LC 94-34773. (Data Handling in Science & Technology Ser.: Vol. 14). 1994. 203.25 (*0-444-81659-3*) Elsevier.

Data Analysis Handbook Using the SPSS System. Michael J. Cleary & Robert T. Amsden. (Illus.). (Orig.). 1979. pap. 9.95 (*0-89894-015-X*) Advocate Pub Group.

Data Analysis in Astronomy, Vol. 2. Ed. by V. Di Gesu et al. LC 86-25456. (Ettore Majorana International Science Series, Life Sciences: Vol. 27). (Illus.). 412p. 1986. 89.50 (*0-306-42473-8*, Plenum Pr) Plenum.

Data Analysis in Astronomy, Vol. 3. V. Di Gesu et al. (Ettore Majorana International Science Series, Life Sciences: Vol. 40). (Illus.). 428p. 1989. 95.00 (*0-306-43158-0*, Plenum Pr) Plenum.

Data Analysis in Astronomy IV. Ed. by V. Di Gesu et al. (Ettore Majorana International Science Series, Life Sciences: Vol. 59). (Illus.). (C). 1992. 95.00 (*0-306-44106-3*, Plenum Pr) Plenum.

***Data Analysis in Community & Landscape Ecology.** Ed. by R. H.G. Jongman et al. (Illus.). 300p. (C). 1995. pap. 24.95 (*0-521-47574-0*) Cambridge U Pr.

Data Analysis in Hotel & Catering Management. S. Cunningham. 200p. 1991. pap. 29.95 (*0-7506-0111-6*) Buttrwrth-Heinemann.

Data Analysis in Real Life Environment. Ed. by J. F. Marcotorchino et al. (Advanced Series in Management: Vol. 8). 1985. 82.00 (*0-444-87692-8*) Elsevier.

Data Analysis, Learning Symbolic & Numeric Knowledge. Ed. by E. Diday. 538p. (C). 1989. text ed. 145.00 (*0-941743-64-0*) Nova Sci Pubs.

Data Analysis Techniques in High Energy Physics Experiments. M. Regler et al. (Illus.). 450p. (C). 1990. 120.00 (*0-521-34195-7*) Cambridge U Pr.

Data Analysis Using Excel 5.0. Michael R. Middleton. 200p. 1995. pap. 15.95 (*0-534-22122-X*) Intl Thomson.

***Data Analysis Using Regression Models: The Business Perspective.** Edward w. Frees. 1996. write for info. (*0-13-219985-8*) P-H.

Data & Algorithms. Lee. (Math-Computers Ser.). (C). 1992. boxed 38.75 (*0-86720-219-X*) Jones & Bartlett.

Data & Columnar Sheets. (Easy-to-Make Photocopies Bks.). (Orig.). 1980. pap. 19.95 (*0-87280-040-7*, 788, Asher-Gallant) Caddylak Systs.

Data & Computer Communications. 4th ed. William Stallings. LC 93-15050. (Illus.). 875p. (C). 1994. text ed. write for info. (*0-02-415441-5*) Macmillan.

Data & Computer Communications: Terms, Definitions & Abbreviations. Gilbert Held. 1989. text ed. 64.95 (*0-471-92066-5*) Wiley.

Data & Data Processing Issues in the Estimation of Requirements for Aircraft Recoverable Spares & Depot Repair. John B. Abell & Frederick W. Finnegan, Jr. LC 93-28343. 1993. write for info. (*0-8330-1434-X*, MR-264-AF) Rand Corp.

Data & Knowledge Base Integration. Ed. by S. M. Deen & G. P. Thomas. 256p. (Orig.). 1990. pap. 58.50 (*0-273-08826-2*, Pub. by Pitman Pub Ltd UK) Trans-Atl Phila.

Data & Policy Change. David Dery. (C). 1989. lib. bdg. 53.50 (*0-7923-9057-1*, Pub. by Graham & Trotman UK) Kluwer Ac.

Data & Reality: Basic Assumptions in Data Processing Reconsidered. W. Kent. 212p. 1978. 66.50 (*0-444-85187-9*, North Holland) Elsevier.

Data & Security. Longley. 1989. 46.95 (*0-8493-7110-4*) CRC Pr.

Data & Voice Premises Cabling & Wiring Apparatus - U. S. Markets, Technologies, & Opportunities: 1994-1999 Analysis & Forecasts. Amadee Bender et al. 100p. 1994. pap. text ed. 2,900.00 (*1-878218-51-4*) World Info Tech.

Data Annex Upgrade. Larry Bond. (Harpoon Ser.). (Illus.). 136p. (Orig.). (YA). 1990. pap. 10.00 (*1-55878-053-X*) Game Designers.

Data Architecture. 2nd ed. W. H. Inmon. 1993. text ed. 49.95 (*0-471-56912-7*) Wiley.

Data Architecture: The Information Paradigm. 2nd ed. William H. Inmon. 1991. 49.95 (*0-89435-358-6*) Wiley.

***Data Assimilation: Tools for Modeling the Ocean in a Global Change Perspective.** P. Brasseur & J. C. Nihoul. (NATO ASI Series I: Global Environmental Change: No. 19). 1994. 98.00 (*0-387-57909-5*) Spr-Verlag.

Data Bank Applications in Archaeology. Sylvia W. Gaines. LC 81-901. 142p. 1981. pap. 14.95 (*0-8165-0686-8*) U of Ariz Pr.

Data Base Administration. Jay-Louise Weldon. LC 80-20467. (Applications of Modern Technology in Business Ser.). 262p. 1981. 37.50 (*0-306-40595-4*, Plenum Pr) Plenum.

Data Base & Computer Systems Security. John M. Carroll. LC 79-113523. (QED Monograph Series. Data Base Management: No. 4). 65p. reprint ed. pap. 25.00 (*0-318-34682-6*, 2031754) Bks Demand.

Data Base Architecture. Ivan Flores. 480p. 1981. text ed. 55.95 (*0-442-22729-9*) Van Nos Reinhold.

Data Base Coordinator. Jack Rudman. (Career Examination Ser.: C-3232). 1994. pap. 34.95 (*0-8373-3232-X*) Nat Learn.

Data Base Design & Implementation. Leszek Maciaszek. 350p. 1990. boxed 41.00 (*0-13-200015-6*) P-H.

Data Base Design Methodology: A Logical Framework. Paul E. Jones. LC 76-375115. (QED Monograph Series. Data Base Management: No. 3). 98p. reprint ed. pap. 28.00 (*0-318-34681-8*, 2031753) Bks Demand.

Data Base Extracts on Economic Issues & Related Israeli Practices in the Occupied Palestinian Territory: West Bank & Gaza Strip, July 1987-December 1988. 57p. 1991. 10.00 (*92-1-112274-0*, E.89.II.D.8) UN.

Data Base Management. Ed. by Jay-Louise Weldon & Deb Rhoades. 1992. ring bd. 425.00 (*0-87769-265-3*) Warren Gorham & Lamont.

Data Base Management: Theory & Applications. Clyde W. Holsapple & Andrew B. Whinston. 1982. lib. bdg. 117.00 (*90-277-1516-5*) Kluwer Ac.

Data Base Management System Design Using dBASE II. Charles W. McNichols. (C). 1984. text ed. 40.60 (*0-8359-1222-1*, Reston) P-H.

Data Base Management Systems for the Eighties. Shaku Atre. LC 83-60769. 609p. reprint ed. pap. 173.60 (*0-318-34676-1*, 2031748) Bks Demand.

Data Base Manager. Jack Rudman. (Career Examination Ser.: C-2873). 1991. pap. 24.00 (*0-8373-2873-X*) Nat Learn.

Data Base Organization for Data Management. 2nd ed. Sakti P. Ghosh. (Computer Science & Applied Mathematics Ser.). 1986. text ed. 117.00 (*0-12-281851-2*) Acad Pr.

Data Base Programmer Analyst. Jack Rudman. (Career Examination Ser.: C-3233). 1994. pap. 29.95 (*0-8373-3233-8*) Nat Learn.

Data Base Selection, Design, & Administration. Jon D. Clark. LC 80-607121. 250p. 1980. text ed. 55.00 (*0-275-91687-1*, C1687, Praeger Pubs) Greenwood.

Data Base: Structured Techniques for Designs, Performance & Management. S. Atre. 442p. 1980. 31.95 (*0-318-17046-9*); 33.95 (*0-318-17047-7*) Data Process Mgmt.

Data-Based Approach to Statistics. Ronald L. Iman. 848p. (C). 1994. text ed. 57.95 (*0-534-93317-3*) Intl Thomson.

***Data-Based Approach to Statistics: Concise Version.** Ronald L. Iman. LC 94-19342. 1994. disk write for info. (*0-614-02485-4*) Intl Thomson.

Data-Based Approach to Statistics: Concise Version. Ronald L. Iman. LC 94-19342. 577p. 1995. text ed., disk 52.95 (*0-534-23496-8*) Intl Thomson.

Data-Bases for Mortality Measurement. 174p. 18.00 (*92-1-151054-6*) UN.

Data Bases for Special Libraries: A Strategic Guide to Information Management. Lynda W. Moulton. LC 91-11338. (Library Management Collection). 176p. 1991. text ed. 47.95 (*0-313-27369-3*, MOI/, Greenwood Pr) Greenwood.

Data Book. 1989. pap. 15.00 (*0-87259-219-7*) Am Radio.

Data Book for Civil Engineers, 2 vols. 3rd ed. Elwyn E. Seeylye. Incl. Vol.1. Design. 3rd ed. 670p. 1959. text ed. 195.00 (*0-471-77286-0*); write for info. (*0-318-59482-X*) Wiley.

Data Book of Thermoset Resins for Composites. Comp. by Trevor F. Starr. 150p. 1993. 216.00 (*1-85617-196-5*, Pub. by Elsevier Applied Sci UK) Elsevier.

Data Book on Hydrocarbons: Application to Process Engineering. J. B. Maxwell. LC 74-30163. 268p. 1975. reprint ed. text ed. 34.50 (*0-88275-257-X*) Krieger.

Data Book on the Viscosity of Liquids. D. S. Viswanath & G. Natarajan. 2000p. 1989. 236.00 (*0-89116-778-1*) Hemisp Pub.

Data Center Automation Handbook. Chantico Publishing Co., Inc. Staff. (Chantico Executive Handbook Ser.). (Illus.). 400p. 1992. 39.95 (*0-8306-7665-1*, 3665, TAB/TPR) TAB Bks.

Data Center Automation Handbook. Chantico Publishing Staff. 1991. text ed. 39.95 (*0-07-156986-3*) McGraw.

Data Center Disaster Consultant. 2nd ed. Kenniston W. Lord. LC 81-52826. 223p. reprint ed. pap. 63.60 (*0-8357-6085-5*, 2034330) Bks Demand.

Data Center Management Planning Report. Computer Technology Research Corp. Staff. (Illus.). 151p. (Orig.). 1992. pap. 185.00 (*0-927695-99-5*) Comput Tech Res.

Data Center Operations: A Guide to Effective Planning, Processing, & Performance. 2nd ed. Howard Schaeffer. (Illus.). 544p. 1986. text ed. 89.00 (*0-13-196064-4*) P-H.

Data Center Operations Management. Ed. by Layne Bradley & Irene Kim. 1992. ring bd. 425.00 (*0-87769-267-X*) Warren Gorham & Lamont.

Data Collection: Individual Rights to Privacy versus Public Program Needs. Ed. by D. Gregory Sanford et al. 56p. 1977. 2.50 (*0-944277-01-2*, D37) U VT Ctr Rsch VT.

Data Collection & Analysis: Basic Principles. Robert M. Thorndike. LC 81-1423. 356p. (C). 1982. text ed. 34.50 (*0-89876-022-4*) Gardner Pr.

Data Collection & Analysis Techniques for a Planned Experimental Harbor Advisory Radar (HAR) System. Geonautics, Inc. Staff. LC 77-135095. 123p. 1969. 19.00 (*0-403-04502-9*) Scholarly.

Data Collection & Analysis, with Recommendations, for the Tennessee Judicial Information System (TJIS), Vol. I. National Center for State Courts. 160p. 1977. 9.60 (*0-685-16631-7*, MAB-122) Natl Ctr St Courts.

***Data Collection & Management: A Practical Guide.** Magda Stouthamer-Loeber & Wilmoet B. Van Kammen. (Applied Social Research Methods Ser.: Vol. 39). 152p. (C). 1995. 37.00 (*0-8039-5656-8*); pap. 16.95 (*0-8039-5657-6*) Sage.

Data Collection Clerk. Jack Rudman. (Career Examination Ser.: C-1233). 1994. pap. 23.95 (*0-8373-1233-7*) Nat Learn.

Data Collection for Child Fatalities: Existing Efforts & Proposed Guidelines. American Academy of Pediatrics Staff & American Bar Association Staff. 67p. 1992. pap. 17.95 (*0-89707-716-4*) Am Acad Pediat.

Data Collection Forms in Clinical Trials. Bert Spilker & John Schoenfelder. 688p. 1991. 99.50 (*0-88167-759-0*) Raven.

Data Collection in Adoption & Foster Care: The State of the Art in Obtaining Organized Information for Policy Analysis, Program Planning & Practice. Stephen J. Finch et al. 71p. 1991. pap. 12.95 (*0-87868-431-X*, 4310) Child Welfare.

Data Collection in Developing Countries. 2nd ed. D. J. Casley & D. A. Lury. 256p. 1987. pap. 22.00 (*0-19-877282-3*) OUP.

Data Collection in Distance Education Research: The Use of Self-Recorded Audiotape. Fred Lockwood. (C). 1991. pap. 24.00x (*0-7300-1351-0*, IDE806, Pub. by Deakin Univ AT) St Mut.

Data Communication & Computer Networks. Ed. by S. Ramani. 310p. 1981. 46.75 (*0-685-01549-1*, North Holland) Elsevier.

Data Communication & Their Performance: Proceedings of the 3rd IFIP TC6 WG7.3 International Conference, Rio de Janeiro, Brazil, 22-25 June, 1987. Ed. by L. F. De Moraes et al. 530p. 1988. 113.00 (*0-444-70363-2*, North Holland) Elsevier.

Data Communication Networks Audit AP-03. MASP Professional Consulting Staff. (Audit Plan Ser.). 200p. 1990. student ed, ring bd. 899.00 (*0-940706-26-1*) Management Advisory Pubns.

Data Communication Pocket Dictionary: Taschenwoerterbuch der Datenkommunikation. Wilhelm H. Carl. 290p. (ENG, FRE & GER.). 1982. 85.00 (*0-8288-0269-6*, M14466) Fr & Eur.

Data Communication Systems & Their Performance: Proceedings of the IFIP TC6 Fourth International Conference, Barcelona, Spain, 20-22 June 1990. Ed. by G. Pujolle & R. Puigjaner. 500p. 1991. 131.50 (*0-444-88756-3*, North Holland) Elsevier.

Data Communications. Lynn A. DeNoia. 288p. (C). 1987. write for info. (*0-675-20368-6*, Merrill Pub Co) Macmillan.

Data Communications. Frederick F. Driscoll. 450p. (C). 1992. text ed. 39.00 (*0-03-026637-8*) SCP.

Data Communications. William L. Schweber. 1987. 32.95 (*0-07-001097-8*) McGraw.

Data Communications. 2nd ed. Gilbert Held. 1989. 47.95 (*0-07-607002-6*) McGraw.

Data Communications: A Beginners Guide to Concepts & Technology. Scott Helmers. 240p. 1989. text ed. 55.00 (*0-13-198870-0*) P-H.

Data Communications: A Comprehensive Approach. 2nd ed. Gilbert Held & Ray Sarch. (Illus.). 576p. 1989. text ed. 50.00 (*0-07-027988-8*) McGraw.

***Data Communications: A Comprehensive Approach.** 3rd ed. Gil Held & Ray Sarch. 1995. text ed. 59.00 (*0-07-028049-5*) McGraw.

Data Communications: An Introduction to Concepts & Design. Robert Techo. (Applications of Modern Technology in Business Ser.). 304p. 1980. 45.00 (*0-306-40398-6*, Plenum Pr) Plenum.

Data Communications: Concepts & Controls. Marshall B. Romney & James V. Hansen. Ed. by Lee A. Campbell. (IIA Monograph). 66p. 1987. pap. text ed. 15.00 (*0-89413-162-1*) Inst Inter Aud.

Data Communications: Concepts & Systems. Martin Arick. LC 84-62291. (Illus.). 279p. (Orig.). reprint ed. pap. 79.60 (*0-7837-0588-3*, 2040932) Bks Demand.

Data Communications: From Fundamentals to Networking. Gilbert Held. 546p. 1991. pap. text ed. 69.95 (*0-471-93051-2*) Wiley.

***Data Communications: With Network Management.** Randy Ratliff. Ed. by Whitney Freeman. (Illus.). 450p. (C). 1994. write for info. (*1-884268-04-8*); teacher ed 29.00 (*1-884268-05-6*); pap. text ed. 54.00 (*1-884268-03-X*) Marcraft Intl.

***Data Communications & Computer Networks: An OSI Approach.** Curt M. White. 1994. write for info. (*0-7895-0053-1*) Boyd & Fraser.

Data Communications & Distributed Networks. 3rd ed. Uyless D. Black. LC 92-28935. 448p. 1992. text ed. 63.00 (*0-13-203464-6*) P-H.

Data Communications & Networking Dictionary. T. D. Pardoe & R. P. Wenig. LC 91-38380. 155p. 1992. pap. 12.00 (*1-878956-06-X*) CBM Bks.

Data Communications & Networking Fundamentals Using Novell Netware. Emilio Ramos et al. (Illus.). 473p. (Orig.). (C). 1992. teacher ed write for info. (*0-318-69336-4*); pap. write for info. (*0-02-407791-7*) Macmillan.

Data Communications & Networking Fundamentals Using Novell NetWare 3.11. Emilio Ramos et al. LC 93-8780. 475p. (C). 1994. pap. write for info. (*0-02-407766-6*) Macmillan.

***Data Communications & Networks.** 3rd ed. Ed. by R. L. Brewster. (Telecommunications Ser.: No. 31). 252p. 1994. boxed 69.00 (*0-85296-804-3*) Inst Elect Eng.

Data Communications & the Systems Designer. Francis G. Smith. LC 80-23500. (Research for Business Decisions Ser.: No. 27). 211p. reprint ed. pap. 60.20 (*0-685-20850-8*, 2070085) Bks Demand.

Data Communications, Computer Networks, & Open Systems. 3rd ed. Fred Halsall. (C). 1992. text ed. 60.25 (*0-201-56506-4*) Addison-Wesley.

Data Communications Computer Networks & OSI. 2nd ed. Fred Halsall. (Illus.). 352p. (C). 1988. text ed. 36.76 (*0-201-18244-0*) Addison-Wesley.

Data Communications Desk Book: A Systems Analysis Approach. William L. Harper & Robert C. Pollard. LC 81-17794. 352p. 1982. text ed. 59.95 (*0-13-196378-3*) P-H.

Data Communications for Business. Stanley Schatt. 1993. text ed. 50.00 (*0-13-203498-0*) P-H.

Data Communications for Business. 2nd ed. Gerald A. Silver & Myrna L. Silver. 480p. 1991. 34.00 (*0-87835-437-9*) Boyd & Fraser.

Data Communications for Business. 3rd ed. Silver. (C). 1994. text ed. 45.95 (*0-87709-142-0*, BF1420) S-W Pub.

Data Communications for Distributed Information Systems. Dimitris N. Chorafas. (Illus.). 300p. text ed. 25.00 (*0-89433-108-6*) Petrocelli.

Data Communications for Engineers. C. G. Guy. 1992. text ed. 30.00 (*0-07-025354-4*) McGraw.

Data Communications for Programmers. Michael Purser. 256p. (C). 1986. pap. text ed. 15.96 (*0-201-12918-3*) Addison-Wesley.

Data Communications: Going Online see Essential Guide to the Library IBM PC

Data Communications in Business. Robert A. Fleck, Jr. 560p. 1996. boxed write for info. (*0-697-20937-7*) Bus & Educ Tech.

Data Communications in the ISDN Era: Proceedings of the IFIP TC6 International Conference on Data Communications in the ISDN Era Tel-Aviv, Israel, 4-5 March, 1985. Ed. by Y. Perry. 188p. 1985. 48.75 (*0-444-87720-7*, North Holland) Elsevier.

Data Communications Management. Ed. by James Conard & Paul Berk. 1992. ring bd. 425.00 (*0-87769-264-5*) Warren Gorham & Lamont.

Data Communications Networking Devices. 3rd ed. Gilbert Held. 653p. 1992. pap. text ed. 49.95 (*0-471-93072-5*) Wiley.

Data Communications, Networks & Systems. Thomas C. Bartee. LC 84-51868. 1985. 39.95 (*0-672-22235-3*) Sams.

Data Communications, Networks & Systems. 2nd ed. Thomas C. Bartee. 1991. 49.95 (*0-672-22790-8*) Sams.

Data Communications One: Foundation Building. rev. ed. H. E. Brooks, Jr. (Illus.). 240p. (C). 1989. teacher ed 39.95 (*0-317-93627-1*); student ed 19.95 (*0-317-93628-X*); pap. text ed. 39.95 (*0-317-93626-3*) Sterling Series.

Data Communications Pocket Book. Tooley. 1989. 20.95 (*0-8493-7135-X*, TX5105) CRC Pr.

Data Communications Practice. rev. ed. Bruce L. Meyer. LC 73-85629. (ABC of the Telephone Ser.: Vol. 11). (Illus.). 68p. (C). 1988. pap. text ed. 21.95 (*1-56016-010-1*) ABC TeleTraining.

An Asterisk (*) at the beginning of an entry indicates that the title is appearing in BIP for the first time.

Data Communications Principles. R. D. Gitlin et al. (Applications of Communications Theory Ser.). (Illus.). 740p. 1992. 95.00 (*0-306-43777-5*, Plenum Pr) Plenum.

Data Communications Specialist. Jack Rudman. (Career Examination Ser.: C-3234). 1994. pap. 29.95 (*0-8373-3234-6*) Nat Learn.

Data Communications Testing & Troubleshooting. 2nd ed. Gilbert Held. (Illus.). 288p. 1992. pap. 39.95 (*0-442-00990-9*) Van Nos Reinhold.

***Data Communications Using Object-Oriented Design & C.** Anil Ananthaswamy. 1995. text ed. 50.00 (*0-07-911857-7*) McGraw.

Data Communications via Fading Channels. Ed. by Kenneth Brayer. LC 74-33060. 520p. 1975. pap. 39.95 (*0-87942-047-2*, PP00430) Inst Electrical.

Data Compression. Ed. by Lee D. Davisson & Robert M. Gray. LC 76-3629. (Benchmark Papers in Electrical Engineering: Vol. 14). 400p. 1976. text ed. 129.00 (*0-12-786326-5*) Acad Pr.

***Data Compression: A C Plus Plus Developers.** Mark Nelson. 1995. pap. 39.99 (*1-56884-323-2*) IDG Bks.

Data Compression: Applications in Communcations, Storage, Imaging, Audio, Video Multimedia. Leonard Laub. (Illus.). 256p. 1992. text ed. 39.95 (*0-442-01393-0*) Van Nos Reinhold.

Data Compression: Techniques & Applications, Hardware & Software Considerations. 3rd ed. Gil Held. 301p. 1991. disk 54.95 (*0-471-93009-1*) Wiley.

Data Compression: Techniques & Applications, Hardware & Software Considerations. 3rd ed. Gil Held. 301p. 1991. text ed. 59.95 (*0-471-92941-7*) Wiley.

Data Compression & Error Control Techniques with Applications. Ed. by Vito Cappellini. 1985. text ed. 82.00 (*0-12-159260-X*) Acad Pr.

Data Compression Book. Mark Nelson. 527p. (Orig.). 1991. pap. 29.95 (*1-55851-214-4*); disk, pap. 39.95 (*1-55851-216-0*) M&T Bks.

***Data Compression Book.** 2nd ed. Mark Nelson. 600p. 1995. disk, pap. 39.95 (*1-55851-434-1*) M&T Bks.

***Data Compression Conference (DCC 1995) (3-95)** 568p. 1995. text ed. 120.00 (*0-8186-7012-6*, PR07012) IEEE Comp Soc.

Data Compression Conference (DCC '94) Proceedings. 549p. 1994. text ed. 120.00 (*0-8186-5637-9*, 5637) IEEE Comp Soc.

Data Compression Conference, 1992 (DCC '92) LC 92-70381. 464p. 1992. 100.00 (*0-8186-2717-4*, 2717) IEEE Comp Soc.

Data Compression Conference, 1993 (DCC '93) 520p. 1993. 100.00 (*0-8493-3392-X*, 3392) IEEE Comp Soc.

Data Compression Techniques & Applications. Thomas J. Lynch. (Illus.). 352p. 1985. text ed. 69.95 (*0-534-03418-7*) Van Nos Reinhold.

Data Control Assistant. Jack Rudman. (Career Examination Ser.: C-2889). 1994. pap. 23.95 (*0-8373-2889-6*) Nat Learn.

Data Control Specialist. Jack Rudman. (Career Examination Ser.: C-901). 1994. pap. 27.95 (*0-8373-0901-8*) Nat Learn.

Data Conversion. Ruth C. Carter & Scott Bruntjen. LC 83-84. (Professional Librarian Ser.). 169p. 1983. Professional. lib. bdg. 37.50 (*0-86729-047-1*) G K Hall.

Data Conversion Integrated Circuits. Ed. by D. J. Dooley. LC 80-10541. 304p. 1980. 49.95 (*0-87942-131-2*, PC01263) Inst Electrical.

***Data Conversion Operator Exam 710-714 & Mark-up Clerk Automated: U. S. Postal Service - Postal Exam Study Guide.** rev. ed. Stephen M. McNally. 120p. 1995. pap. 19.95 (*0-614-04916-4*) PETC.

Data Conversion Operator (USPS) Jack Rudman. (Career Examination Ser.: C-1609). 1994. pap. 29.95 (*0-8373-1609-X*) Nat Learn.

Data Development Analysis: The Assessment of Performance. Michael Norman & Barry Stoker. 262p. 1991. text ed. 79.95 (*0-471-92835-6*) Wiley.

Data Dictionary: Concepts & Uses. 2nd ed. Charles J. Wertz. LC 88-31279. (Illus.). 412p. reprint ed. pap. 117.50 (*0-7837-0587-5*, 2040931) Bks Demand.

Data Dictionary: Concepts & Uses. 2nd ed. Charles J. Wertz. LC 88-31279. 1989. 39.95 (*0-89435-280-6*) Wiley.

Data Dictionary: Concepts & Uses. 2nd ed. Charles J. Wertz. 390p. 1993. text ed. 39.95 (*0-471-60308-2*) Wiley.

Data Dictionary: Implementation, Use, & Maintenance. Rom Narayan. (Illus.). 608p. (C). 1988. text ed. 73.00 (*0-13-197351-7*) P-H.

Data-Directed Systems Design: A Professional's Guide. Martin E. Modell. 1990. text ed. 43.00 (*0-07-042633-3*) McGraw.

Data Display. Lee A. Seymour & Harrison W. Kelly, III. LC 92-43077. (Six Sigma Research Institute Ser.). 1993. write for info. (*0-201-63407-4*) Addison-Wesley.

Data Distribution: Managing the Environment. Ed. by Richard Williams. (BCS Data Management Specialist Group Ser.: Vol. 4). 160p. 1992. pap. 59.95 (*1-85742-032-2*, Pub. by Ashgate UK) Ashgate Pub Co.

Data Distributions. 2nd ed. Ronald Christensen. (Entropy Minimax Sourcebook Ser.: Vol. VIII). (Illus.). x, 364p. 1989. lib. bdg. 36.95 (*0-685-44660-3*) Entropy Ltd.

Data Driven Systems Modelling. Remi Planche. 450p. 1991. 53.33 (*0-13-201179-4*) P-H.

***Data Ease: A Guide to Creating Applications.** Olu Segun. 300p. 1995. pap. 37.95 (*0-7506-2110-9*, Focal) Buttrwrth-Heinemann.

***Data Encryption Standard: An Extensive Documentation & Evaluation.** Mikael J. Simovits. 120p. 1994. pap. 42.80 (*0-89412-248-7*) Aegean Park Pr.

***Data Engineering, 11th International Conference (ICDE '95)** 576p. 1995. pap. text ed. 120.00 (*0-8186-6910-1*, PR06910) IEEE Comp Soc.

Data Engineering, Tenth International Conference (ICDE '94) Proceedings. 568p. 1994. pap. text ed. 120.00 (*0-8186-5400-7*, 5400) IEEE Comp Soc.

Data Engineering, 8th International Conference (ICDE '92) LC 91-76564. 600p. 1992. pap. 100.00 (*0-8186-2545-7*, 2545) IEEE Comp Soc.

Data Engineering, 9th International Conference (ICDE '93) LC 92-75329. 712p. 1993. pap. text ed. 100.00 (*0-8186-3570-3*, 3570) IEEE Comp Soc.

Data Enquiry That Tests Entity & Correlational-Causal Theories. Fred Dansereau et al. LC 86-7426. 365p. (Orig.). 1986. pap. 24.95 (*0-937719-00-5*) Inst Theory Test.

Data Entry: Applications & Procedures. Glenda H. Easter. 380p. 1989. spiral bd. 35.00 (*0-8403-5681-1*) Kendall-Hunt.

***Data Entry: Concepts & Applications.** 2nd ed. Beth M. Buzby. teacher ed 8.00 (*0-574-20081-9*); disk 69.00 (*1-56118-029-7*); disk write for info. (*1-56118-027-0*) Paradigm MN.

Data Entry: Concepts & Applications. 2nd ed. Beth M. Buzby. 418p. (C). pap. text ed. 24.75 (*1-56118-329-6*) Paradigm MN.

***Data Entry: Concepts & Applications.** 3rd ed. Beth M. Buzby & Kathy Locke. LC 94-25812. 1994. teacher ed 8.00 (*1-56118-591-4*); disk 69.00 (*1-56118-592-2*); disk 69.00 (*1-56118-593-0*) Paradigm MN.

Data Entry: Concepts & Applications. 3rd ed. Beth M. Buzby & Kathy Locke. LC 94-25812. 1994. write for info. (*1-56118-590-6*) Paradigm MN.

Data Entry: Short Course. Beth M. Buzby. 128p. 1990. pap. text ed. 14.95 (*1-56118-030-0*); teacher ed, pap. text ed. 8.00 (*1-56118-031-9*) Paradigm MN.

***Data Entry: Short Course.** Beth M. Buzby. 1990. disk 69.00 (*0-614-00421-7*); disk write for info. (*0-614-00422-5*) Paradigm MN.

Data Entry Applications for Microcomputers - 5.25 Version. Fouad T. Nobari & Michael E. Davidson. 176p. 1993. text ed., 5.25 hd write for info. (*0-13-203522-7*); text ed., 3.5 hd write for info. (*0-13-203803-X*) P-H.

Data Entry Clerk. (Career Examination Ser.: C-3339). 1994. pap. 19.95 (*0-8373-3339-3*) Nat Learn.

Data Entry Control & Management Procedures, (C Entry) William J. Yourwith, Jr. & Eugene J. Sullivan. (Illus.). 1978. text ed. 35.00 (*0-917818-02-4*) Exec Stand.

Data Entry for Microcomputers & Terminals: With Business Applications. Iva H. Lee. LC 86-5562. 203p. (C). 1986. pap. text ed. 28.95 (*0-471-82052-0*) P-H.

Data Entry for Microcomputers & Terminals with Business Applications. 2nd ed. Iva H. Lee. 336p. (C). 1991. pap. text ed. 12.00 (*0-13-201138-7*, 250101) P-H.

Data Entry in Business: Concepts & Applications. Mel Hynek. 272p. 1989. pap. text ed. 9.32 (*0-07-031679-1*) McGraw.

Data Entry Machine Operator. Jack Rudman. (Career Examination Ser.: C-2409). 1994. pap. 23.95 (*0-8373-2409-2*) Nat Learn.

Data Entry Skills: Additional Problems. 2nd ed. Gerald Carter. 103p. (gr. 9-12). 1978. pap. text ed. 14.00 (*0-9610582-1-8*) Apollo Com.

Data Entry Skills-Key Disk Machine. 3rd ed. Gerald L. Carter & Douglas D. Minkema. (Data Entry Skills-Key Disk Machine & Additional Problems Ser.). 97p. (gr. 9-12). 1977. pap. text ed. 14.50 (*0-9610582-0-X*) Apollo Com.

Data Entry Skills Teacher's Guide. Gerald L. Carter & Douglas D. Minkema. text ed. 32.00 (*0-9610582-4-2*) Apollo Com.

Data Entry Supervisor. Jack Rudman. (Career Examination Ser.: C-1232). 1994. pap. 29.95 (*0-8373-1232-9*) Nat Learn.

***Data Envelopment Analysis: Theory, Methodology & Application.** Abraham Charnes et al. LC 94-22053. 528p. (C). 1994. pap. text ed. 60.00 (*0-7923-9480-1*) Kluwer Ac.

***Data Envelopment Analysis: Theory, Methodology & Application.** Abraham Charnes et al. LC 94-22053. 528p. (C). 1995. lib. bdg. 150.00 (*0-7923-9479-8*) Kluwer Ac.

Data Exchange Between Computer System in the Construction Industry. Ed. by J. Wix & C. McLelland. 1986. 40.00 (*0-86022-113-X*, Pub. by Build Servs Info Assn UK) St Mut.

Data Exchange Between Computer Systems in the Construction Industry. Ed. by J. Wix & C. McLelland. (C). 1986. 65.00 (*0-86022-134-2*, Pub. by Build Servs Info Assn UK) St Mut.

Data Exchange in the PC & MS-DOS Environment. Steven Ross. 320p. 1990. pap. text ed. 29.95 (*0-07-053923-5*) McGraw.

Data Fitting in the Chemical Sciences by the Method of Least Squares. P. Gans. 258p. 1992. text ed. 110.00 (*0-471-93412-7*) Wiley.

Data Flow Computing: Theory & Practice. Ed. by John A. Sharp. 576p. (C). 1992. text ed. 85.00 (*0-89391-654-4*); pap. text ed. 37.50 (*0-89391-921-7*) Ablex Pub.

Data for a Windy Day. Ben L. Hiatt. LC 77-76902. 1977. pap. 5.00 (*0-915016-12-5*) Second Coming.

Data for Agrarian Development. C. D. Poate & P. F. Daplyn. LC 92-22831. (Wye Studies in Agricultural & Rural Development). (Illus.). 397p. (C). 1993. 84.95 (*0-521-36566-X*); pap. 32.95 (*0-521-36758-1*) Cambridge U Pr.

Data for Biochemical Research. 3rd ed. R. M. Dawson et al. (Illus.). 592p. 1989. pap. 55.00 (*0-19-855299-8*) OUP.

Data for Decision: Statistics in a Dynamic Economy. 2nd ed. Howard L. Balsley & James J. Conway. 480p. 1992. 34.50 (*0-931541-25-5*) Mancorp Pub.

Data for Discovery: Proceedings of the Twelfth International CODATA Conference, 15-19 July 1990, Columbus, Ohio, U. S. A. Ed. by Rosi Larrondo. LC 92-34429. 1993. 95.00 (*1-56700-002-9*) Begell Hse.

***Data for Process Design & Engineering Practice.** Woods. 160p. (C). 1994. text ed. 40.00 (*0-13-318149-9*) P-H.

Data for Protection Against Ionizing Radiation from External Sources: Combined Reprint of ICRP 15 and Supplement, Vol. 21: Report Com 3 International Commission on Radiological Protection 4-71. International Commission on Radiological Protection Staff. Vol. 21. 1973. write for info. (*0-318-69663-0*, Pub. by Pergamon Repr UK) Franklin.

Data for Room Fire Model Comparisons. Richard D. Peacock et al. (Illus.). 52p. (Orig.). (C). 1993. pap. text ed. 40.00 (*0-7881-0058-0*) Diane Pub.

Data for Science & Technology: Proceedings of the International CODATA Conference, Eighth, Jachranka, Poland, 4-7 Oct., 1982. Ed. by P. S. Glaeser. 350p. 1983. 69.25 (*0-444-86668-X*, I-460-83, North Holland) Elsevier.

Data for Science & Technology: Proceedings of the 7th International CODATA Conference, Kyoto, Japan, 8-11 October 1980. Ed. by P. S. Glaeser. (Illus.). 638p. 1981. 254.00 (*0-08-026201-5*, Pub. by Pergamon Repr UK); 46.00 (*0-08-026203-1*, Pub. by Pergamon Repr UK) Franklin.

Data for Validation of CFD Codes. Ed. by D. Goldstein. LC 93-71633. (FED Ser.: Vol. 146). 89p. 1993. pap. 30.00 (*0-7918-0954-4*, H00786) ASME.

***Data Fusion & Sensor Management.** Manyika & Durrant-Whyte. (Illus.). 289p. 1994. write for info. (*0-13-303132-2*) P-H.

Data Fusion Applications: Workshop Proceedings, Brussels, November 25, 1992. Ed. by S. Pfleger et al. (Research Reports ESPRIT Ser.: Vol. 1). 266p. 1993. pap. 45.00 (*0-387-56973-1*) Spr-Verlag.

Data Fusion in Robotics & Machine Intelligence. Ed. by Mongi A. Abidi & Ralph C. Gonzalez. (Illus.). 546p. 1992. text ed. 49.95 (*0-12-042120-8*) Acad Pr.

Data Fusion Symposium (1993) Technical Papers & Abstracts Summary. 94p. (Orig.). (C). 1994. pap. text ed. 75.00 (*0-7881-0321-0*) Diane Pub.

Data Game: Controversies in Social Science Statistics. Mark H. Maier. 264p. (C). 1991. 49.95 (*0-87332-588-5*); pap. text ed. 20.95 (*0-87332-768-3*) M E Sharpe.

***Data Game: Controversies in Social Science Statistics.** 2nd rev. ed. Mark H. Maier. (Illus.). 300p. 1995. 55.00 (*1-56324-481-0*); pap. text ed. 21.95 (*1-56324-482-9*) M E Sharpe.

Data Goods & Data Services in the Socialist Countries of Eastern Europe. (United Nations Centre on Transnational Corporations (CTC) Publications). 103p. 1988. 13.50 (*92-1-104304-2*, E.88.II.A.20) UN.

Data Handbook: A Guide to Understanding the Organization & Visualization of Technical Data. Brand Fortner. 229p. 1992. pap. 39.95 (*0-9635687-0-1*) Spyglass IL.

Data Handbook for Clay Materials & Other Non-Metallic Minerals. Ed. by H. Van Olphen & J. J. Fripiat. (Illus.). 1979. 144.00 (*0-08-022850-X*, Pub. by Pergamon Repr UK) Franklin.

Data in Astronomy. Carlos Jaschek. 160p. 1989. 59.95 (*0-521-34094-2*) Cambridge U Pr.

Data in Medicine. Ed. by Robert S. Reneman & Jan Strackee. (Instrumentation & Techniques in Clinical Medicine Ser.: No. 1). 1979. lib. bdg. 107.50 (*90-247-2150-4*) Kluwer Ac.

Data in Modern Biology: Selected Papers from the 9th International CODATA Conference, Jerusalem, Israel, June 1984. Ed. by CODATA Staff. (Illus.). 63p. 1985. pap. 11.00 (*0-08-032483-5*, Pergamon Pr) Elsevier.

Data, Instruments, & Theory: A Dialectical Approach to Understanding Science. Robert J. Ackermann. LC 84-15938. 224p. 1985. 37.50 (*0-691-07296-5*) Princeton U Pr.

Data Interpretation Questions & Case Histories. H. L. Beynon et al. (Complete MRCP Ser.). (Illus.). 208p. (Orig.). 1991. pap. text ed. 22.00 (*0-443-04310-8*) Churchill.

Data Item Descriptions & Unique Data Item Descriptions Set, 15 vols., Set. 1993. ring bd. 895.00 (*0-685-28352-6*) Global Eng Doc.

Data Knowledge (DS-2) Proceedings of 2nd IFIP TC2 WG2.6 Working Conf. on Database Semantics, Albufeira, Portugal, 3-7 Nov., 1986. Ed. by R. A. Meersman & A. C. Sernadas. 430p. 1988. 102.75 (*0-444-70528-7*, North Holland) Elsevier.

Data Link Protocols. Uyless D. Black. LC 92-21202. 340p. 1993. text ed. 54.00 (*0-13-204918-X*) P-H.

Data Management & Clinical Trials: EORTC Study Group on Data Management. Ed. by N. K. Rotmensz et al. 246p. 1989. 77.00 (*0-444-81077-3*) Elsevier.

Data Management & Data Description. Richard Williams. 371p. 1992. 85.95 (*1-85742-038-1*, Pub. by Ashgate UK) Ashgate Pub Co.

Data Management & Program Development Software Directory for IBM & Compatible DOS Computers. ICP Staff & Larry A. Welke. Ed. by Sheila Cunningham & Marilyn Law. 1990. pap. 19.95 (*0-88094-179-0*) Intl Computer.

***Data Management Guidebook.** 325p. (C). 1994. text ed. 295.00 (*0-7605-0769-4*) Rector Pr.

Data Management on Distributed Databases. Benjamin W. Wah. LC 81-12982. (Computer Science: Distributed Database Systems Ser.: No. 7). (Illus.). 307p. reprint ed. pap. 87.50 (*0-685-20877-X*, 2070209) Bks Demand.

Data Manipulation in Sci-Tech Libraries. Ed. by Ellis Mount. LC 85-5569. (Science & Technology Libraries: Vol. 5, No. 4). 131p. 1985. text ed. 29.95 (*0-86656-441-1*) Haworth Pr.

Data Modeling. Sanders. 148p. (C). 1995. pap. 8.95 (*0-87709-066-1*, BF0661) S-W Pub.

Data Modeling Handbook: A Best Practice Approach to Building Quality Data Models. Michael C. Reingruber. LC 94-12669. 1994. text ed. 49.95 (*0-471-05290-6*) Wiley.

Data Modelling: Conceptual & Philosophical Foundations. Rudy A. Hirschheim et al. (Cambridge Tracts in Theoretical Computer Science Ser.: No. 16). 240p. (C). 1994. write for info. (*0-521-37369-7*) Cambridge U Pr.

Data Modelling & Process Modelling: Using the Most Popular Methods. Rosemary Rock-Evans. 383p. 1992. pap. 64.95 (*0-7506-0739-4*) Buttrwrth-Heinemann.

Data Modelling for Information Systems. Richard Bidgen & Carriede Carteret. 416p. (Orig.). 1994. pap. 67.50 (*0-273-60262-4*, Pub. by Pitman Pub Ltd UK) Trans-Atl Phila.

Data, Models & Statistical Analysis. R. A. Cooper & A. J. Weekes. LC 82-25110. (Illus.). 416p. 1983. text ed. 57.00 (*0-389-20382-3*, N7255); pap. text ed. 30.00 (*0-389-20383-1*, N7256) B&N Imports.

Data Models, Database Languages & Database Management Systems. Gottfried Vossen. (C). 1991. text ed. 46.25 (*0-201-41604-2*) Addison-Wesley.

Data Modem: Selection & Evaluation Guide. Vess V. Vilips. LC 77-189393. (Modern Frontiers in Applied Science Ser.). (Illus.). 99p. reprint ed. pap. 28.30 (*0-317-08738-X*, 2010073) Bks Demand.

Data Needs for Food Policy in Developing Countries: New Directions for Household Surveys. Ed. by Joachim Von Braun & Detlev Puetz. LC 93-48782. (Occasional Papers-International Food Policy Research Institute Ser.). 1993. write for info. (*0-89629-329-7*) Intl Food Policy.

Data Network: Concepts, Theory, & Practice. Uyless D. Black. 650p. 1989. text ed. 73.00 (*0-13-198466-7*) P-H.

Data Network Design: Packet Switching Frame Relay 802.6 - Dqdb Smds, Atm B-Isdn, Sonet. Darren Spohn. (Computer Communications Ser.). 784p. 1993. text ed. 59.00 (*0-07-060360-X*) McGraw.

Data Network Design Strategies, 1990-1991. Data Communications Magazine Staff. 1990. pap. text ed. 39.95 (*0-07-607023-9*) McGraw.

Data Networks. 2nd ed. Dimitri P. Bertsekas & Robert Gallager. 592p. 1991. text ed. 71.00 (*0-13-200916-1*) P-H.

Data Networks with Satellites. Ed. by J. Majus & Otto Spaniol. (Informatik-Fachberichte Ser.: Vol. 67). 251p. 1983. pap. 32.00 (*0-387-12311-3*) Spr-Verlag.

Data of Day Care, 3 vols., Set. Carol Edwards & Jan Carter. 1980. 75.00 (*0-317-05755-3*, Pub. by Natl Inst Soc Work) St Mut.

Data of Euclid: Translated from the Text of Menge. Tr. by George L. McDowell & Merle Sokolik. LC 93-60045. (Illus.). 228p. (C). 1993. 40.00 (*0-9635924-1-6*); pap. 25.00 (*0-9635924-0-8*) Union Square.

Data of Glaciological Studies: Chronicle Discussions, No. 40. Ed. by G. A. Avsyuk. Tr. by Y. V. Kathavate. (Russian Translation Ser.: No. 67). (Illus.). 500p. (C). 1988. text ed. 95.00 (*90-6191-919-3*, Pub. by A A Balkema NE) Ashgate Pub Co.

Data of Jurisprudence. William G. Miller. xiv, 477p. 1980. reprint ed. lib. bdg. 42.50 (*0-8377-0835-4*) Rothman.

Data on Blindness & Visual Impairment in the U. S. A Resource Manual on Social Demographic Characteristics, Education, Employment & Income, & Services Delivery. 2nd rev. ed. Ed. by Corinne Kirchner. LC 88-7763. 412p. 1988. 40.00 (*0-89128-152-5*) Am Foun Blind.

Data on Music Education. (Illus.). 124p. (Orig.). (C). 1990. teacher ed, pap. 19.50 (*0-940796-87-2*, 1011) Music Ed Natl.

Data on Some Virginia Families. Dakota B. Brown. (Illus.). 282p. 1979. 25.00 (*0-686-63646-5*) VA Bk.

Data on the Abnormal Hemoglobins & Glucose-Six-Phosphate Dehydrogenase Deficiency in Human Populations. Frank B. Livingstone. (Technical Reports: No. 3). 1973. pap. 2.00 (*0-932206-12-3*) U Mich Mus Anthro.

Data Organization in Parallel Computers. Harry A. Wijshoff. (C). 1988. lib. bdg. 67.00 (*0-89838-304-8*) Kluwer Ac.

Data over Radio. Geoffrey Varrall & Roger Belcher. LC 92-10174. 1992. 95.00 (*0-930633-14-8*) Quantum Pub.

Data-Parallel Programming on MIMD Computers. Philip J. Hatcher & Michael J. Quinn. (Scientific & Engineering Computation-Kowalik Ser.). (Illus.). 200p. 1991. 31.50 (*0-262-08205-5*) MIT Pr.

Data Power: Using Racecar Data Acquisition. Buddy Fey. LC 93-94. 176p. 1993. 29.50 (*1-881096-01-7*) Towery Pub.

Data Preparation for Electronic Publications. Helgerson. 1994. pap. 39.95 (*0-442-01784-7*) Van Nos Reinhold.

Data Processing. T. F. Fry. 1984. U.K. pap. 14.50 (*0-408-01171-8*, U.K.) Buttrwrth-Heinemann.

Data Processing. Jack Rudman. (Occupational Competency Examination Ser.: OCE-14). 1994. pap. 23.95 (*0-8373-5714-4*) Nat Learn.

Data Processing Agreements, No. 76. 2nd ed. 800p. 1990. ring bd. 115.00 (*0-929576-55-1*) Busn Laws Inc.

Data Processing & Management Information Systems, 2 vols., Set. 6th ed. R. G. Anderson. (Illus.). 736p. 1987. pap. text ed. 47.50 (*0-7121-0696-0*) Trans-Atl Phila.

Data Processing & Related Fields Dictionary. Michel Devivier. 280p. 1989. lib. bdg. 89.95 (*0-8288-2608-0*) Fr & Eur.

Data Processing & the Courts: Guide for Court Managers. National Center for State Courts Staff. (Illus.). 59p. 1977. pap. 1.50 (*0-89656-021-X*, RG-033) Natl Ctr St Courts.

D

An Asterisk (*) at the beginning of an entry indicates that the title is appearing in BIP for the first time.

Data Processing & the Courts: Reference Manual. National Center for State Courts Staff. 539p. 1977. 32.34 (*0-685-16653-8*, RR-0359) Natl Ctr St Courts.

Data Processing Clerk I. Jack Rudman. (Career Examination Ser.: C-536). 1994. pap. 19.95 (*0-8373-0536-5*) Nat Learn.

Data Processing Clerk II. Jack Rudman. (Career Examination Ser.: C-537). 1994. pap. 23.95 (*0-8373-0537-3*) Nat Learn.

Data Processing Clerk III. Jack Rudman. (Career Examination Ser.: C-538). 1994. pap. 27.95 (*0-8373-0538-1*) Nat Learn.

Data Processing Control Clerk. Jack Rudman. (Career Examination Ser.: C-2483). 1994. pap. 19.95 (*0-8373-2483-1*) Nat Learn.

Data Processing Dictionary. 187p. (ENG, FRE, GER & SWE.). 1984. pap. 69.95 (*0-8288-0909-7*, M7781) Fr & Eur.

Data Processing Dictionary: Dictionnaire d'Informatique. 5th ed. Michel Ginguay & A. Lauret. 384p. (FRE.). 1993. pap. 89.95 (*0-8288-1354-X*, M6273) Fr & Eur.

Data Processing Dictionary: Englisch - Deutsch - Franzosisch - Russisch. Erich Burger. 903p. 1989. 195.00 (*0-8288-2479-7*) Fr & Eur.

Data Processing Dictionary: English - French. 11th ed. Michel Ginguay. 296p. (ENG & FRE.). 1992. pap. 79.95 (*0-8288-0233-5*, F137100) Fr & Eur.

Data Processing Dictionary: Woerterbuch der Datentechnik, 1989. 4th rev. ed. K. Brinkmann & R. Schmidt. 904p. (ENG & GER.). 1989. 150.00 (*0-8288-0240-8*, M7117) Fr & Eur.

Data Processing Dictionary of Terms & Siglas: Informatica-Glosario de Terminos y Siglas. Antonio Vaquero. 464p. (ENG & SPA.). 1985. 75.50 (*0-8288-0259-9*, S60291) Fr & Eur.

Data Processing Documentation: Standards, Procedures & Applications. 2nd ed. William L. Harper. 288p. 1980. 60.00 (*0-685-05873-5*) P-H.

Data Processing Equipment Operator. Jack Rudman. (Career Examination Ser.: C-2301). 1994. pap. 23.95 (*0-8373-2301-0*) Nat Learn.

Data Processing Glossary: Glossaire Informatique. Jacques Biensan. (FRE.). 1987. 15.95 (*0-8288-1351-5*, F127530) Fr & Eur.

Data Processing in Biology & Geology. J. L. Cutbill. (Systematics Association Special Ser.: Special Vol. 3). 1971. text ed. 157.00 (*0-12-199750-2*) Acad Pr.

Data Processing in Chemistry. Ed. by Z. Hippe. (Studies in Physical & Theoretical Chemistry: Vol. 16). 288p. 1982. 82.00 (*0-444-99744-X*) Elsevier.

Data Processing in Japan. H. J. Welke. (Information Research & Resource Reports Ser.: Vol. 1). 198p. 1982. 61.75 (*0-444-86379-6*) Elsevier.

Data Processing in Taxation. International Fiscal Association Staff. (IFA Congress Seminar Ser.: Vol. 13a). 120p. 1990. pap. 47.00 (*90-6544-437-8*) Kluwer Law Tax Pubs.

Data Processing in the Social Sciences with OSIRIS. Judith Rattenbury & Paula Pelletier. LC 74-620138. (Illus.). 253p. reprint ed. pap. 72.20 (*0-7837-5273-3*, 2045011) Bks Demand.

Data Processing in the Social Sciences with OSIRIS III. Judith Rattenbury & Paula Pelletier. LC 74-620138. 245p. 1974. 15.00 (*0-87944-163-1*); pap. 10.00 (*0-87944-162-3*) Inst Soc Res.

Data Processing in the UNIX Environment. Ramkrishna S. Tare. 1989. text ed. 45.00 (*0-07-062885-8*) McGraw.

Data Processing Logic. L. Saret. 1984. text ed. write for info. (*0-07-054723-8*) McGraw.

Data Processing Manager's Model Reports & Formats. Ralph L. Kliem & Irwin Ludin. (Illus.). 397p. 1992. text ed. 69.95 (*0-13-203068-3*) P-H.

Data Processing Methods. Stanley Thornes. (C). 1989. 125.00 (*0-09-154971-X*, Pub. by S Thornes Pubs UK) St Mut.

Data Processing Operations Coordinator. Jack Rudman. (Career Examination Ser.: C-2759). 1994. pap. 34.95 (*0-8373-2759-8*) Nat Learn.

Data Processing Operations Supervisor. Jack Rudman. (Career Examination Ser.: C-2347). 1994. pap. 29.95 (*0-8373-2347-9*) Nat Learn.

***Data Processing Opportunities.** 1995. 26.50 (*0-614-03489-2*) BCC.

***Data Processing Opportunities for Health Care.** 1995. 26.50 (*0-614-03457-4*, G155) BCC.

Data Processing Options Assessment, Lehigh County (PA) Final Report. National Center for State Courts. 17p. 1984. 1.02 (*0-685-16655-4*, NERO-141) Natl Ctr St Courts.

Data Processing Policies & Procedures Manual: Supplement. George H. Jenkins. LC 93-8668. 1993. 39.95 (*0-13-219940-8*) P-H.

Data Processing Salvation Jump. Al Blair. 6p. 1988. pap. 3.95 (*0-930366-33-6*) Northcountry Pub.

Data Processing Services Industry. 1986. lib. bdg. 75.50 (*0-8490-3762-X*) Gordon Pr.

Data Processing Specialist. Jack Rudman. (Career Examination Ser.: C-2242). 1994. pap. 29.95 (*0-8373-2242-1*) Nat Learn.

***Data Processing Technology & Economics.** Montgomery Phister, Jr. 1979. 75.00 (*0-917640-04-7*) Santa Monica Pub.

Data Processing Technology & Economics. 2nd ed. Montgomery Phister, Jr. LC 79-25052. (Illus.). 720p. 1979. pap. 50.00 (*0-917640-05-5*) Santa Monica Pub.

Data Processing Technology & Economics: 1975-1978 Supplement. Montgomery Phister, Jr. LC 79-25052. (Illus.). 1979. pap. 10.00 (*0-917640-03-9*) Santa Monica Pub.

Data Processing Tests. Jonathan Hodgson. write for info. (*0-318-59597-4*) S&S Trade.

Data Processing with Applications. abr. ed. Robert J. Condon. (C). 1981. pap. text ed. write for info. (*0-8359-1259-0*, Reston) P-H.

Data Processing Work Kit. 2nd ed. Beryl Robichaud et al. 96p. (gr. 9-12). 1983. text ed. 13.56 (*0-07-053207-9*) McGraw.

Data Protection. Gordon Hughes. 500p. 1991. pap. 85.00 (*0-455-21043-8*, Pub. by Law Bk Co) W W Gaunt.

Data Protection: Putting the Record Straight. Roger Cornwell & Marie Staunton. (C). 1988. 21.00 (*0-946088-16-0*, Pub. by NCCL UK) St Mut.

Data Protection Act: A Guide for Personnel Managers. Ed. by Alastair Evans. 72p. (C). 1984. 45.00 (*0-85292-338-4*) St Mut.

Data Protection Act: A Practical Guide. Richard Sizer & Philip Newman. LC 84-18702. 256p. 1985. text ed. 49.95 (*0-566-02445-4*) Ashgate Pub Co.

Data Protection & Data Access: Reports from Ten Countries on Data Protection & Data Access in Social Research, with an Annotated International Bibliography. Ed. by P. F. De Guchteneire & E. Mochmann. 274p. 1990. pap. 38.50 (*0-444-85714-1*, North Holland) Elsevier.

Data Protection & Social Science Research. Ekkehard Mochmann & Paul J. Muller. 229p. (C). 1982. text ed. 39.50 (*3-593-32604-3*) Irvington.

Data Protection in Health Information Systems. 2nd ed. G. Griesser et al. 1983. 51.50 (*0-444-86713-9*, I-410-83) Elsevier.

Data Protection Policies & Practice. Alastair Evans. (C). 1986. 60.00 (*0-85292-385-6*, Pub. by IPM Hse UK) St Mut.

Data Protection Policies & Practice. Ed. by Alastair Evans. (C). 1986. 60.00 (*0-685-34648-X*) St Mut.

Data Quality Control: Theory & Pragmatics. Liepins & Uppuluri. (Statistics: Vol. 112). 304p. 1991. 110.00 (*0-8247-8354-9*) Dekker.

Data Quality Control & Editing. Joseph I. Naus. LC 74-19804. (Statistics, Textbooks & Monographs: Vol. 10). 216p. reprint ed. pap. 61.60 (*0-685-16052-1*, 2027086) Bks Demand.

Data Quality Foundations. 2nd rev. ed. Anany Levitin. Ed. by Kimberly Snow. (AT&T Quality Library). 50p. 1992. pap. 22.45 (*0-932764-26-6*, 500-490) AT&T Customer Info.

Data Quality in Longitudinal Research. Ed. by David Magnusson & Lars R. Bergman. (Illus.). 288p. (C). 1990. 64.95 (*0-521-38091-X*) Cambridge U Pr.

Data Rearrangement & Real-Time Computation. Philip N. Armstrong. LC 93-18544. 1993. write for info. (*0-8330-1340-8*, MR-113-OSD/AF) Rand Corp.

Data Recovery along Route N-13, Navajo Indian Reservation, Pt. 1: Research Design. Jeffrey H. Altschul & Steven D. Shelley. (Statistical Research Technical Ser.: No. 16). 215p. 1988. spiral bd. 17.50 (*1-879442-14-0*) Stats Res.

Data Recovery at Prehistoric Localities at U19af, Pahute Mesa, Nye County, Nevada. Comp. by Sue A. Monteleone. (Illus.). 31p. 1991. 4.00 (*0-945920-63-6*) Desert Rsch Inst.

Data Recovery Bible: Covers All Versions of DOS since 3.3. Pamela Kane. LC 93-16645. 1993. disk, pap. 49.95 (*1-56686-080-6*) Brady Compu Bks.

Data Recovery from Historical Sites see Final Report of the New Melones Archeological Project, California

Data Reduction: Analyzing & Interpreting Statistical Data. A. S. Ehrenberg. LC 74-3724. (Wiley-Interscience Publication Ser.). 409p. reprint ed. pap. 116.60 (*0-7837-3235-X*, 2043254) Bks Demand.

Data Reduction & Error Analysis for the Physical Sciences. 2nd ed. Philip Bevington & D. Keith Robinson. 1992. text ed. write for info. (*0-07-911243-9*) McGraw.

Data Requirements for Monitoring Truck Safety. (Special Report Ser.: No. 228). 132p. 1990. 21.00 (*0-309-04964-4*) Transport Res Bd.

Data Research: A Guide for Librarians & Systems Managers. Colin Storey & Grace Cheng. LC 93-36483. 320p. 1993. 79.95 (*0-566-07464-8*, Pub. by Gower UK) Ashgate Pub Co.

Data Response Exercises for GCSE Business Studies. G. Smith & A. Graham. (C). 1989. 75.00 (*0-7487-0162-1*, Pub. by S Thornes Pubs UK) St Mut.

Data Response for Economics Examinations. G. Walker. 280p. 1987. 50.00 (*1-85313-005-2*, Pub. by Checkmate Pubns UK) St Mut.

Data Response for GCSE Geography. A. Musgrove. (C). 1988. 60.00 (*0-7487-0190-7*, Pub. by S Thornes Pubs UK) St Mut.

***Data Reverse Engineering: Untying the Legacy Knot.** Aiken. 1995. text ed. 40.00 (*0-07-000748-9*) McGraw.

***Data Security: How to Bulletproof Your Hardware & Software.** Horace LaBadie. 1994. pap. 34.95 (*1-55958-750-4*) Prima Pub.

Data Security Management. Ed. by Hal Tipton & Robert Elliott. 1992. ring bd. 425.00 (*0-87769-287-4*) Warren Gorham & Lamont.

Data Sets: IPS. Moore & McCabe. (C). 1995. text ed. write for info. (*0-7167-2490-1*) W H Freeman.

Data Sharing Using a Common Data Architecture. Michael H. Brackett. LC 93-33544. 1994. pap. text ed. 39.95 (*0-471-30993-1*) Wiley.

Data Source Book. 200p. 1991. 15.00 (*0-685-65742-6*, P-71) Am Phys Therapy Assn.

Data Sourcebook for Food Scientists & Technologists. Y. H. Hui. 976p. 1991. text ed. 125.00 (*1-56081-009-2*); write for info. (*0-685-56441-X*) VCH Pubs.

***Data Sources for Business & Market Analysis.** 4th ed. John V. Ganly. LC 93-23453. 458p. 1994. 55.00 (*0-8108-2758-1*) Scarecrow.

***Data Sources in Asian-Oceanic Countries.** Ed. by Jen-Leih Wu et al. LC 94-72345. (Proceedings Ser.: Vol. 1). (Illus.). 320p. 1994. 74.00 (*1-884893-02-3*) CODATA.

***Data Sources in Asian-Oceanic Countries.** Ed. by Jen-Leih Wu et al. LC 94-72345. (Proceedings Ser.: Vol. 1). (Illus.). 320p. (Orig.). 1994. pap. 39.00 (*1-884893-03-1*) CODATA.

Data Structure: An Advanced Approach Using C. Tom Weiss & Jeffrey Esakov. 336p. 1989. text ed. 58.00 (*0-13-198847-6*) P-H.

Data Structure & Management. 2nd ed. Ivan Flores. 1977. text ed. write for info. (*0-13-197335-5*) P-H.

Data Structure for Business Programming. Knapp. 1989. pap. text ed. write for info. (*0-07-557830-1*) McGraw.

Data Structure Techniques. Thomas A. Standish. LC 78-67454. 1980. teacher ed write for info. (*0-201-07257-2*) Addison-Wesley.

***Data Structure with C++** Topp William & Ford William. (Illus.). 700p. 1994. pap. write for info. (*0-02-420971-6*, Merrill Pub Co) Macmillan.

Data-Structured Software Maintenance: The Warnier-Orr Approach. David A. Higgins. LC 86-72048. (Illus.). 212p. (Orig.). 1986. pap. 23.00 (*0-932633-03-X*) Dorset Hse Pub Co.

Data Structures: An Object-Oriented Approach. William J. Collins & Thomas C. McMillan. (Illus.). 500p. (C). 1992. text ed. 46.25 (*0-201-56953-1*) Addison-Wesley.

Data Structures: Form & Function. Harry F. Smith, Jr. 785p. (C). 1987. text ed. 51.00 (*0-15-516820-7*) SCP.

Data Structures: Form & Function. Harry F. Smith, Jr. 785p. (C). 1987. pap. text ed. 6.00 (*0-15-516821-5*) SCP.

Data Structures: From Recipes to C. Lawrence E. Turner. 640p. (C). 1993. pap. write for info. (*0-697-17286-4*) Wm C Brown Pubs.

Data Structures: Theory & Practice. 2nd ed. A. T. Berztiss. (Computer Science & Applied Mathematics Ser.). 586p. 1975. text ed. 85.00 (*0-12-093552-X*) Acad Pr.

Data Structures: With Abstract Data Types & Pascal. 2nd ed. Daniel F. Stubbs & Neil W. Webre. LC 88-29302. 480p. (C). 1989. text ed. 53.95 (*0-534-09264-0*) PWS Pubs.

Data Structures, Algorithm & Performance. Derick Wood. (Illus.). 688p. (C). 1993. text ed. 50.50 (*0-201-52148-2*) Addison-Wesley.

Data Structures, Algorithms, & Software Principles. Thomas A. Standish. (Illus.). 700p. (C). 1994. text ed. 50.50 (*0-201-52880-0*) Addison-Wesley.

Data Structures, Algorithms & Software Principles in C. Thomas A. Standish. (Illus.). (C). 1995. pap. text ed. 52.75 (*0-201-59118-9*) Addison-Wesley.

Data Structures & Algorithm Analysis. Weiss. Ed. by John Thompson. 500p. (C). 1992. text ed. 53.75 (*0-8053-9052-9*) Benjamin-Cummings.

Data Structures & Algorithm Analysis. 2nd ed. Mark Weiss. 470p. (C). 1995. text ed. 50.50 (*0-8053-9057-X*) Benjamin-Cummings.

Data Structures and Algorithm Analysis in Ada. Mark A. Weiss. LC 92-43553. 455p. (C). 1993. text ed. 53.75 (*0-8053-9055-3*) Benjamin-Cummings.

Data Structures & Algorithm Analysis in C. Mark A. Weiss. LC 92-33294. (C). 1993. text ed. 53.75 (*0-8053-5440-9*) Benjamin-Cummings.

Data Structures & Algorithm Analysis in C. Mark A. Weiss. 475p. (C). 1994. text ed. 53.75 (*0-8053-5443-3*) Benjamin-Cummings.

Data Structures & Algorithms. Alfred V. Aho et al. (C). 1983. text ed. 55.95 (*0-201-00023-7*) Addison-Wesley.

Data Structures & Algorithms One: Sorting & Searching. K. Mehlhorn. (EATCS Monographs on Theoretical Computer Science). (Illus.). xiv, 336p. 1987. 50.00 (*0-387-13302-X*) Spr-Verlag.

Data Structures & Algorithms with Modula-2. Philippe J. Gabrini & Barry L. Kurtz. 640p. (C). 1992. Incl. IBM 5-1/4" disk. 5.25 hd, pap. text ed. write for info. (*0-669-28846-2*); Incl. IBM 3-1/2" disk. 3.5 hd, pap. text ed. write for info. (*0-669-28847-0*); Incl. Macintosh disk. mac hd, pap. text ed. write for info. (*0-669-29425-X*); Instr.'s guide. teacher ed write for info. (*0-669-12305-6*); Test item file. write for info. (*0-669-29424-1*) Heath.

Data Structures & C Programs. Christopher J. Van Wyck. (Computer Science Ser.). (Illus.). 400p. (C). 1988. text ed. 40.95 (*0-201-16116-8*) Addison-Wesley.

***Data Structures & C Programs.** 2nd ed. Christopher J. Van Wyk. (C). 1990. text ed. 44.25 (*0-201-53985-3*) Addison-Wesley.

Data Structures & Efficient Algorithms: Final Report on the DFG Special Joint Initiative. Ed. by B. Monien et al. LC 92-10725. (Lecture Notes in Computer Science Ser.: Vol. 594). vii, 389p. 1992. write for info. (*3-540-55488-2*); pap. 52.00 (*0-387-55488-2*) Spr-Verlag.

Data Structures & Network Algorithms. Robert E. Tarjan. LC 83-61374. (CBMS-NSF Regional Conference Series in Applied Mathematics: No. 44). vii, 131p. 1983. reprint ed. pap. text ed. 22.25 (*0-89871-187-8*) Soc Indus-Appl Math.

Data Structures & Operating Systems. Teodor Rus. LC 77-3262. (Wiley Series in Computing). 376p. reprint ed. pap. 107.20 (*0-317-26154-1*, 2024377) Bks Demand.

Data Structures & Other Objects: A Second Course in Computer Science. Michael Main & Walter Savitch. 800p. (C). 1995. text ed. 50.50 (*0-8053-7086-2*) Benjamin-Cummings.

Data Structures & PL-1 Programming. Moshe J. Augenstein & Aaron M. Tenenbaum. (Illus.). 1979. pap. text ed. write for info. (*0-13-197731-8*) P-H.

Data Structures & Program Design. 2nd ed. Robert L. Kruse. (Illus.). 592p. 1986. text ed. 65.00 (*0-13-195884-4*) P-H.

Data Structures & Program design. 3rd ed. Robert L. Kruse. LC 93-36453. 1994. text ed. 62.00 (*0-13-208182-2*) P-H.

Data Structures & Program Design in C. Robert Kruse. 1990. text ed. 58.33 (*0-13-725649-3*) P-H.

Data Structures & Program Design in Modula-2. Larry Nyhoff & Sanford Leestma. (Illus.). 675p. (C). 1990. Incl. solns. manual. student ed, text ed. write for info. (*0-02-388621-8*) Macmillan.

Data Structures & Program Design in Pascal. 2nd ed. Larry Nyhoff & Sanford Leestma. (Illus.). 752p. (C). 1992. text ed. write for info. (*0-02-369465-3*) Macmillan.

Data Structures & Target Classification, Vol. 1470. V. Libby. 1991. 62.00 (*0-8194-0579-5*) SPIE.

Data Structures & Their Algorithms. Lewis & Denenberg. (C). 1991. pap. text ed. 67.00 (*0-673-39736-X*) HarpCollege.

Data Structures & Their Algorithms: Solutions Manual. Lewis & Denenberg. (C). 1991. teacher ed 10.00 (*0-673-49381-4*) HarpCollege.

Data Structures & Their Representation in Storage. M. D'Imperio. LC 60-12884. (Annual Review in Automatic Programming Ser.: Vol. 5, Pt. 1). 1969. 42.00 (*0-08-015839-0*, Pub. by Pergamon Repr UK) Franklin.

Data Structures, Data Abstractions: A Contemporary Introduction Using C Plus Plus. Mitchell L. Model. LC 93-33118. 1993. text ed. 59.00 (*0-13-088782-X*) P-H.

Data Structures, Files & Databases. Carl Bamford & Paul Curran. (Computer Science Ser.). (Illus.). 231p. (C). 1987. pap. text ed. 32.50 (*0-333-43690-3*, Pub. by Macmillan UK) Scholium Intl.

Data Structures for Business. Judith Knapp. 256p. (C). 1989. text ed. write for info. (*0-394-39076-8*) Knopf.

Data Structures for Engineering Software. Peter P. Silvester. LC 93-71429. 192p. 1993. 58.00 (*1-56252-157-8*) Computational Mech MA.

Data Structures for Particle Physics Experiments: Evolution or Revolution? Proceedings of the 14th Workshop on the INFN Eloisatron Project, Erice, Trapani, Sicily, 11-18 November 1990. Ed. by R. Brun et al. 400p. (C). 1991. text ed. 104.00 (*981-02-0641-0*) World Scientific Pub.

Data Structures for Programmers. Milton Rosenstein. LC 88-262. 224p. 1992. text ed. 39.95 (*0-471-63520-0*) Krieger.

Data Structures for Raster Graphics. Ed. by L. R. Kessener et al. (Eurographic Seminars Ser.). (Illus.). 210p. 1986. 69.00 (*0-387-16310-7*) Spr-Verlag.

Data Structures in ANSI C. Saumyendra Sengupta & Paul Edwards. (Professional & Technical Ser.). 630p. 1990. text ed. 59.95 (*0-12-636655-1*) Acad Pr.

***Data Structures in C.** Adam Drozdek & Donald L. Simon. LC 94-34858. 448p. 1995. text ed. 45.95 (*0-534-93495-1*) PWS Pubs.

***Data Structures in C++ A Laboratory Course.** James Roberge. 285p. (C). 1995. 3.5 hd, pap. text ed. write for info. (*0-669-34947-X*); 5.25 hd, pap. text ed. write for info. (*0-669-34948-8*) Heath.

Data Structures in Pascal. Edward M. Reingold & Wilfred J. Hansen. (C). 1987. text ed. 58.50 (*0-673-39069-1*) HarpCollege.

***Data Structures in Pascal: A Laboratory Course.** James Roberge. 284p. (C). 1994. 3.5 hd, pap. text ed. write for info. (*0-669-29524-8*); 5.25 hd, pap. text ed. write for info. (*0-669-29525-6*) Heath.

Data Structures on the IBM PC. Steve Roski. write for info. (*0-318-59629-6*) S&S Trade.

Data Structures Study Guide. Deakin University Press Staff. 160p. (C). 1986. 57.00 (*0-7300-0580-1*, Pub. by Deakin Univ AT) St Mut.

Data Structures Using C. Aaron M. Tenenbaum et al. 608p. 1989. boxed, pap. text ed. 60.00 (*0-13-199746-7*) P-H.

Data Structures Using Modula-2. Richard F. Sincovec & Richard S. Wiener. 524p. (C). 1986. lib. bdg. 48.50 (*0-471-81489-X*) Krieger.

Data Structures with Abstract & Ada. Daniel F. Stubbs & Neil W. Webre. 1993. text ed. 54.95 (*0-534-14448-9*) PWS Pubs.

Data Structures with ADA. Michael B. Feldman. (Illus.). 313p. (C). 1985. text ed. 47.50 (*0-201-52673-5*) Addison-Wesley.

Data Structures with C Plus Plus. Frank Carrano. (C). 1995. text ed. 53.75 (*0-8053-1226-9*) Benjamin-Cummings.

Data Structuring in Computers. Clancy. (C). 1995. text ed. write for info. (*0-7167-8285-5*) W H Freeman.

Data Structuring in Pascal. 4th ed. Horowitz. (C). 1995. text ed. write for info. (*0-7167-8282-0*) W H Freeman.

Data Systems Dictionary: English-Russian-German. Joachim Schulz. (ENG, GER & RUS.). 1978. pap. 75.00 (*0-8288-4869-6*, M15284) Fr & Eur.

Data Theory & Dimensional Analysis. William G. Jacoby. (Quantitative Applications in the Social Sciences Ser.: Vol. 78). (Illus.). 96p. 1991. pap. 9.95 (*0-8039-4178-1*) Sage.

Data Transcriber. Jack Rudman. (Career Examination Ser.: C-1634). 1994. reprint ed. pap. 23.95 (*0-8373-1634-0*) Nat Learn.

Data Transmission. 2nd ed. Dogan Tugal & Osman Tugal. 512p. 1989. pap. text ed. 29.95 (*0-07-065455-7*) McGraw.

Data Transmission. 2nd rev. ed. Dogan Tugal & Osman Tugal. 496p. 1990. text ed. 45.00 (*0-07-065447-6*) McGraw.

Data Transmission & Privacy. Ed. by Dennis Campbell & Joy Fisher. LC 94-969. 532p. (C). 1994. lib. bdg. 199.00 (*0-7923-2713-6*) Kluwer Ac.

Data Transmission Service Industry. Business Communications Co., Inc. Staff. 191p. 1984. 1,750.00 (*0-89336-417-7*, G-080) BCC.

Data Transportation & Protection. John E. Hershey & R. K. Yarlagadda. LC 86-15065. (Applications of Communications Theory Ser.). 508p. 1986. 110.00 (*0-306-42257-3*, Plenum Pr) Plenum.

An Asterisk (*) at the beginning of an entry indicates that the title is appearing in BIP for the first time.

D

An Asterisk (*) at the beginning of an entry indicates that the title is appearing in BIP for the first time.

Database Systems Engineering. R. P. Whittington. (Oxford Applied Mathematics & Computing Science Ser.). (Illus.). 448p. 1988. 95.00 (*0-19-859666-9*); pap. 32.50 (*0-19-859672-3*) OUP.

Database Systems for Advanced. S. C. Moom & H. I. Keda. (Advanced Database Research & Development Ser.). 468p. 1993. text ed. 121.00 (*981-02-1380-8*) World Scientific Pub.

Database Systems for Advanced Applications '91: Proceedings of the Second International Symposium on Database Systems for Advanced Applications, April 2-4, 1991, Tokyo, Japan. Ed. by Akifumi Makinouchi. LC 92-19671. (Advanced Database Research & Development Ser.: Vol. 2). 568p. 1992. text ed. 121.00 (*981-02-1055-8*) World Scientific Pub.

***Database Systems for Advanced Applications '95: Proceedings of the Fourth International Conference on Database Systems for Advanced Applications, singapore, April 10-13, 1995.** International Conference on Database Systems for Advanced Applications Staff. Ed. by Tok-Wang Ling & Yoshifumi Masunaga. LC 95-10178. (Advanced Database Research & Development Ser.: Vol. 5). 484p. 1995. text ed. 88.00 (*981-02-2220-3*) World Scientific Pub.

Database Systems for Management. 2nd ed. James F. Courtney & David B. Paradice. 592p. (C). 1989. text ed. 68.95 (*0-256-08229-4*) Irwin.

Database Systems for Next-Generation Applications: Principles & Practice. W. Kim et al. (Advanced Database Research & Development Ser.). 324p. 1993. text ed. 105.00 (*981-02-1315-8*) World Scientific Pub.

Database Systems in Science & Engineering. J. R. Rumble & F. J. Smith. (Illus.). 304p. 1990. 85.00 (*0-7503-0048-5*) IOP Pub.

Database Systems of the 90s: International Symposium Muggelsee, Berlin, FRG, November 5-7, 1990 Proceedings. Ed. by A. Blaser et al. (Lecture Notes in Computer Science Ser.: Vol. 466). viii, 334p. 1990. pap. 38.00 (*0-387-53397-4*) Spr-Verlag.

Database Techniques for Librarians: A Primer Using Turbo Pascal. Andrew H. Bullen & Charles H. Davis. LC 92-33524. 256p. 1993. write for info. (*0-8161-1967-8*); pap. 24.50 (*0-8161-1968-6*) G K Hall.

***Database Theory - ICDT '95: Proceedings of the 5th International Conference, Prague, Czech Republic, January 1995.** Ed. by Georg Gottlob & Moshe Y. Vardi. LC 94-44669. (Lecture Notes in Computer Science: No. 893). 1995. pap. 68.00 (*0-387-58907-4*) Spr-Verlag.

Database Theory - ICDT '92: Fourth International Conference, Berlin, Germany, October 1992, Proceedings. Ed. by J. Biskup & R. Hull. LC 92-32100. (Lecture Notes in Computer Science Ser.: Vol. 646). 1992. 67.00 (*0-387-56039-4*) Spr-Verlag.

Database Transaction Models for Advanced Applications. Ed. by Ahmed K. Elmagarmid. LC 92-12504. (Series in Data Management Systems). 1992. 54.95 (*1-55860-214-3*) Morgan Kaufmann.

Database Tuning. Dennis Shasha. 1992. pap. text ed. 37.33 (*0-13-205246-6*) P-H.

Database 2000: "The Last Address Book You'll Ever Need" David Kirksey. Ed. by Kirksey Group Staff. (Illus.). 384p. 1991. 19.95 (*0-9628675-0-0*, DB2000-1B-01-01) Kirksey Grp Pubs.

Databased Marketing. Herman R. Holtz. 320p. 1992. text ed. 37.95 (*0-471-55187-2*) Wiley.

Databases. Ed. by J. Paradaens. (International Lecture Series in Computer Mathematics). 261p. 1987. text ed. 70.00 (*0-12-544962-3*) Acad Pr.

Databases: An Introduction. David Rothwell. LC 92-28123. 1992. write for info. (*0-07-707703-2*, M-H Bk Intl Group) McGraw.

Databases: How to Manage Information on Your Micro. Peter Laurie. (Illus.). 200p. (Orig.). 1985. pap. 19.95 (*0-412-26380-7*, NO. 9317) Chapman & Hall.

Databases & On-Line Data in Astronomy. Ed. by Miguel A. Albrecht & Daniel Egret. (C). 1991. lib. bdg. 77.50 (*0-7923-1247-3*) Kluwer Ac.

Databases Available in the Research Information Center of the National Institute of Standards & Technology. 1994. lib. bdg. 250.00 (*0-8490-8579-9*) Gordon Pr.

Databases for Cardiology. Ed. by Greert T. Meester & Francesco Pinciroli. (Developments in Cardiovascular Medicine Ser.). (C). 1991. lib. bdg. 202.50 (*0-7923-0886-7*) Kluwer Ac.

***Databases for Global Science.** (Illus.). 450p. (C). 1994. text ed. 295.00 (*0-7605-0063-0*) Rector Pr.

Databases for Production Management: Proceedings of the IFIP TC5-WG5.7 Working Conference on Design, Implementation & Operation, Barcelona, Spain, 10-12 May 1989. Ed. by R. Companys et al. 360p. 1990. 87.75 (*0-444-88658-3*, North Holland) Elsevier.

Databases for Software Engineering. C. Godart & F. Charoy. Tr. by Iain A. Craig. LC 93-37247. (BCS Practitioner Ser.). 300p. 1994. pap. text ed. 49.00 (*0-13-030255-4*) P-H Gen Ref & Trav.

Databases in Systematics. Robert Allkin & Frank A. Bisby. (Systematics Association Special Ser.: Vol. 26). 1984. text ed. 120.00 (*0-12-053040-6*) Acad Pr.

Databases in the Humanities & Social Sciences, No. 4: Proceedings of the 4th International Conference on Databases in the Humanities & Social Sciences, Auburn University, July 1987. 718p. 1989. pap. 50.00 (*0-938734-37-7*) Learned Info.

Databases in the 1990s, No. 2. Ed. by B. Srinivasan et al. 440p. (C). 1991. text ed. 89.00 (*981-02-0603-8*) World Scientific Pub.

Databases in Theory & Practice. J. A. Jones. (Computing Ser.). 324p. 1991. pap. 36.95 (*0-412-43250-1*) Chapman & Hall.

Databases in Theory & Practice. J. A. Jones. 280p. 1987. 28.95 (*0-8306-2600-X*, 2600, TAB/TPR) TAB Bks.

Databook of Anaesthesia & Critical Care Medicine. 5th ed. P. A. Foster & J. Roelofse. 215p. 1987. pap. 35.00 (*0-387-17794-9*) Spr-Verlag.

Databook on Employee Benefits. Employee Benefit Research Institute Staff. 1992. 45.95 (*0-86643-077-6*); pap. 35.95 (*0-86643-047-4*) Empl Benefit Res Inst.

Databook on Employee Benefits. 3rd ed. Employee Benefit Research Institute Staff. 1994. write for info. (*0-318-72711-0*) Empl Benefit Res Inst.

Databook on Endangered Tree & Shrub Species & Provenances Paper, No. 77. FAO Staff. 1993. 325.00 (*81-7089-195-7*, Pub. by Intl Bk Distr II) St Mut.

***Databook on Nonfatal Injury: Incidence, Costs, & Consequences.** Ted R. Miller et al. 200p. (C). 1994. lib. bdg. 48.50 (*0-87766-630-X*) Urban Inst.

Databook Two. 92p. 1979. 10.50 (*0-685-43374-9*); pap. 5.50 (*0-318-14931-1*); spiral bd. 6.50 (*0-685-43375-7*) NA Trackless Trolley.

DATABUS Programming Language. Dan Felder & Don Wills. 368p. (Orig.). (C). 1992. pap. 35.00 (*0-9633748-1-8*) Sftwre Science.

***DataCAD for Architects & Designers.** Carol Buehrens. LC 95-3073. 1995. pap. 39.95 (*0-07-008914-0*) McGraw.

DataCAD for the Architect. Carol Buehrens & K. Neubert. 1989. text ed. 34.95 (*0-07-155166-2*) McGraw.

DataCAD for the Architect. Carol Buehrens & Kevin Neubert. (Computer Graphics Technology & Management Ser.). (Illus.). 296p. 1989. 34.95 (*0-8306-9175-8*, 3075) TAB Bks.

DataCAD for the Architect. 2nd ed. Carol Buehrens. 1990. pap. 27.95 (*0-8306-3746-X*, TAB/TPR) TAB Bks.

Dataciones Radiometricas: Critica: Critique of Radiometric Data. Harold Slusher. (SPA.). 4.95 (*84-7228-528-6*, 220249, Pub. by Edit Clie SP) TSELF.

Datacom Basics. Stanley Schatt. LC 89-82314. (Illus.). 64p. (Orig.). 1990. pap. 25.00 (*0-917845-10-2*) Intertec IL.

Dataflow Architecture for Machine Control. Bogdan Lent. 1989. text ed. 124.00 (*0-471-92473-3*) Wiley.

Datalog. Howard. 1992. 2,500.00 (*0-87371-784-8*, TK) Lewis Pubs.

Dataloggers. Richard K. Miller & Marcia E. Rupnow. LC 90-83898. (Survey on Technology & Markets Ser.: No. 194). 50p. 1991. pap. text ed. 200.00 (*1-55865-218-3*) Future Tech Surveys.

DataMania: A Child's Computer Organizer. Clayton Walnum. (Illus.). (Orig.). (J). (gr. k up). 1992. pap. 19.95 (*0-672-30207-1*) Alpha Bks IN.

DataMyte Handbook: A Practical Guide to Computerized Data Collection for Statistical Process Control. 3rd ed. DataMyte Staff. Ed. by Jerry Houston. 656p. 40.00 (*0-930345-02-9*) DataMyte Corp.

DataMyte Handbook: A Practical Guide to Computerized Data Collection for Statistical Process Control. 4th ed. DataMyte Staff. Ed. by Jerry Houston. LC 84-71481. 640p. 1989. write for info. (*0-930345-03-7*) DataMyte Corp.

Dataordbok: Computers, Automatic Control & Data Processing. (ENG & SWE.). 1983. write for info. (*0-8288-0260-2*, M15707) Fr & Eur.

Datapedia of the United States, 1790-2000. George Kurian. (Illus.). 600p. 1994. lib. bdg. 90.00 (*0-89059-012-5*) Bernan Pr.

Datapro-McGraw-Hill Guide to IBM PC Software. 2nd ed. Datapro-McGraw-Hill. 1985. pap. text ed. 23.95 (*0-07-015407-4*) McGraw.

Datatran: A Comprehensive & Practical System for Developing & Maintaining Data Processing Systems. Harvey J. Gonzalez & Lois Fein. (Illus.). 432p. 1984. pap. text ed. 54.00 (*0-13-196493-3*) P-H.

DataWorld, 4 vols. rev. ed. (Illus.). 4440p. 1977. ring bd. 1,133.00 (*0-318-23145-X*) Faulkner Tech Reports.

Date Abuse. Herma Silverstein. LC 93-25011. (Issues in Focus Ser.). (Illus.). 128p. (J). (gr. 6 up). 1994. lib. bdg. 17.95 (*0-89490-474-4*) Enslow Pubs.

***Date Book.** Margaret Sullivan & Jodi Lennon. (Illus.). 176p. (Orig.). 1995. pap. 6.95 (*1-55652-245-2*) Chicago Review.

Date by Proxy. large type ed. Felicity Hayle. 368p. 1987. 16.95 (*0-7089-1595-7*) Ulverscroft.

Date Is a Four-Letter Word. Marilyn Kaye. (Video High Ser.: No. 3). 224p. 1994. pap. 3.50 (*0-8217-4609-X*) Zebra.

Date Nails Complete. Glenn Wiswell & John Evans. LC 76-27156. 352p. 1976. pap. 7.00 (*0-686-28596-4*); spiral bd. 15.00 (*0-686-17796-7*) Wesis Pubns.

Date of "Love's Labour's Lost" Rupert Taylor. LC 32-4355. reprint ed. 27.50 (*0-404-06356-X*) AMS Pr.

Date of the Roman Denarius & Other Landmarks in Early Roman Coinage. H. Mattingly & E. S. Robinson. (Illus.). 59p. 1974. pap. 8.00 (*0-916710-17-3*) Obol Intl.

Date Rape. Alexandra Bandon. LC 93-24063. (Update Ser.). (YA). (gr. 10 up). 1994. text ed. 13.95 (*0-89686-806-0*, Crstwood Hse) Silver Burdett Pr.

Date Rape: A Study. 1991. lib. bdg. 255.95 (*0-8490-5092-8*) Gordon Pr.

Date Recipes. R. I. Heetland. LC 86-29426. 128p. (Orig.). 1986. spiral bd. 6.95 (*0-914846-28-0*) Golden West Pub.

***Date to Win: How to Have More Dates, Find That Lasting Relationship, or Meet Your Ideal Marriage Partner.** Rick Mater & Kathy Wing. LC 94-96386. 256p. (Orig.). 1995. pap. 12.00 (*0-9643444-0-8*) Laurel Canyon.

***Date Tripping with Friends & Lovers: The Fun, Whimsical, Inexpensive, Outrageous, Extravagant, Sensual, Romantic, & Simple Book of Things to Do on a Date.** Elizabeth Nevins. LC 94-92458. (Illus.). 384p. (Orig.). 1995. pap. 9.95 (*0-9643977-0-6*) Sun Tea Bks.

Date with a Dead Doctor. Toni Brill. 1992. mass mkt. 3.99 (*0-373-26109-8*, 1-26109-8) Harlequin Bks.

***Date with a Plummeting Publisher.** Toni Brill. (WWL Mystery Ser.). 1995. pap. 3.99 (*0-373-26161-6*, 1-26161-9) Harlequin Bks.

Date with a Plummeting Publisher. Toni Brill. LC 92-21221. 240p. 1993. 17.95 (*0-312-08753-5*) St Martin.

Date with a Werewolf. Francine Pascal. (Young Adults Ser.: No. 105). (YA). 1994. 3.50 (*0-553-56228-2*) Bantam.

Date with an Outlaw. Lynn Lockhart. (American Romance Ser.). 1993. mass mkt. 3.50 (*0-373-16498-X*, 1-16498-7) Harlequin Bks.

Date with Danger. Mickey Alman. (Orig.). 1991. mass mkt. 3.95 (*0-8041-0602-9*) Ivy Books.

Date with Death. large type ed. Linington. 1991. 17.95 (*0-7451-8096-5*, AH0154, Atlantic Lrg Print); pap. 15.95 (*0-7927-0574-2*, AS0190, Atlantic Lrg Print) Chivers N Amer.

Date with Destiny. Miranda Lee. 1994. 2.99 (*0-373-11651-9*) Harlequin Bks.

Date with Destiny. large type ed. Miranda Lee. 1992. lib. bdg. 18.95 (*0-263-13125-4*, Pub. by Mills & Boon UK) Thorndike Pr.

Date with the Dead. Dorothea E. Hammond. 250p. 1983. pap. 6.95 (*0-942874-00-5*) Hammond Records.

Dated Alexander Coinage of Sidon & Ake. Edward T. Newell. LC 78-63544. (Yale Oriental Series: Researches: No. 2). reprint ed. 24.50 (*0-404-60272-X*) AMS Pr.

Dated Chinese Antiquities, 600-1650: Six Hundred to Sixteen Fifty. Sheila Riddell. (Illus.). 256p. 1979. 39.95 (*0-571-09753-7*) Faber & Faber.

Dated European Coinage Prior to 1501. Albert R. Frey. Ed. by David R. Cervin. LC 76-62838. (Illus.). 1990. reprint ed. lib. bdg. 30.00 (*0-915262-09-6*) S J Durst.

Dated Greek Manuscripts of the Thirteenth & Fourteenth Centuries in the Libraries of Great Britain. Alexander Turyn. LC 80-81547. (Dumbarton Oaks Studies: Vol. 17). (Illus.). 198p. 1981. 65.00 (*0-88402-077-0*) Dumbarton Oaks.

Dated Greek Manuscripts of the Thirteenth & Fourteenth Centuries in the Libraries of Italy, 2 vols. Alexander Turyn. 348p. 1972. Vol. I, 348p. write for info. (*0-318-56085-2*); Vol. II, 300p. write for info. (*0-318-56086-0*) U of Ill Pr.

Dated Greek Manuscripts of the Thirteenth & Fourteenth Centuries in the Libraries of Italy, 2 vols., Set. Alexander Turyn. LC 79-94402. 300p. 1972. 100.00 (*0-252-00083-8*) U of Ill Pr.

Dated Texts from Mari: A Tabulation. Jack M. Sasson. LC 80-53524. (Aids & Research Tools in Ancient Near Eastern Studies: Vol. 4). 154p. (Orig.). 1980. pap. 16.50 (*0-89003-066-9*) Undena Pubns.

Dateline: Reno. Don Dondero & Jean Stoess. (Illus.). 128p. 1991. pap. 12.95 (*0-9631542-0-6*) Dondero-Stoess.

Dateline - Toronto: Hemingway's Complete Toronto Star Dispatches, 1920-1924. Ernest Hemingway. Ed. by William White. 512p. 1987. pap. 10.95 (*0-684-18802-3*, Scribners) S&S Trade.

Dateline Bhopal. Anees Chisti. (C). 1986. 24.95 (*0-317-66154-X*) Asia Bk Corp.

Dateline Bhopal: A Newsman's Diary of the Gas Disaster. Anees Chishti. 1986. 17.50 (*0-8364-2269-4*, Pub. by Concept II) S Asia.

Dateline Canada: Understanding Economics Through Press Reports. P. Kennedy & G. Dorosh. 1978. pap. 9.67 (*0-13-196774-6*) P-H.

Dateline Freedom: Revelations of an Unwilling Exile. Vitali Vitaliev. (Illus.). 224p. 1992. 39.95 (*0-09-174677-9*, Pub. by Hutchinson UK) Trafalgar.

Dateline Hollywood: Sins & Scandals of Yesterday & Today. Mark Drop. LC 94-7778. 1994. write for info. (*1-56799-108-4*, Friedman-Fairfax) M Friedman Pub Grp Inc.

Dateline Istanbul. J. Friedenson. 1993. 18.95 (*0-89906-146-X*); pap. 15.95 (*0-89906-147-8*) Mesorah Pubns.

***Dateline Soweto: Travels with Black South African Reporters.** William Finnegan. LC 94-22805. 1995. pap. 12.00 (*0-520-08979-0*) U CA Pr.

Dateline 2000: The New Higher Education Agenda. Dale Parnell. 300p. 1990. pap. 27.50 (*0-87117-198-8*, 1210) Am Assn Comm Coll.

Datenanalysesysteme fuer Statistische Auswertungen: Eine Eingeugrung in SPSS, BMDP und SAS. H. Kueffner & H. Wittenberg. (GER.). 1985. pap. 21.60 (*3-437-40136-X*) Lubrecht & Cramer.

Datenerfassung Programmierung. Erich Burger. 386p. (ENG, FRE, GER & RUS.). 1976. 99.00 (*0-317-59483-4*, Pub. by Collets UK) Pro-Am Music.

Datenverarbeitung und Datenanalyse mit SAS (Statistical Analysis System) Hans-Martin Uehlinger. 310p. (GER.). 1983. pap. text ed. 25.50 (*3-437-40127-0*) Lubrecht & Cramer.

Dates & Meanings of Religious & Other Festivals: Incorporating a Calendar for the Five Years 1993-1997. 2nd ed. John G. Walshe & Shrikala Warrier. 104p. (Orig.). 1993. pap. 19.95x (*0-572-01819-3*, Pub. by W Foulsham UK) Trans-Atl Phila.

Dates from Hell. Kathy A. Samon. 160p. (Orig.). 1992. pap. 8.95 (*0-452-26778-1*, Plume) NAL-Dutton.

Dates with Destiny: The One Hundred Most Important Dates in Church History. Ken J. Curtis et al. LC 91-3328. (Illus.). 224p. 1991. 17.99 (*0-8007-1661-2*); pap. 12.99 (*0-8007-5412-3*) Revell.

Dating. Patricia R. Quiri. LC 89-5709. (Venture Bks.). (Illus.). 95p. (YA). (gr. 7-12). 1989. lib. bdg. 14.28 (*0-531-10806-6*) Watts.

Dating: (How to Pick & Choose Your Date) John R. Craig. 144p. (Orig.). 1992. pap. text ed. 5.95 (*0-9614423-0-1*) Rite Bks Pub.

***Dating: A Guide to Creating Intimate Relationships.** 2nd rev. ed. Ed. by Heidi Swillinger. 154p. (Orig.). (C). 1992. pap. 13.95 (*0-9639565-0-7*) D Linder.

***Dating: Delights, Discontents & Dilemmas.** 2nd ed. Mary R. Laner. 290p. (C). 1995. pap. text ed. 15.95 (*1-879215-26-8*) Sheffield WI.

Dating: Going out in Style. Barry St. Clair & Bill Jones. 140p. (Orig.). (YA). 1993. pap. 6.99 (*1-56476-189-4*, Victor Books) SP Pubns.

Dating: Guidelines from the Bible. Scott Kirby. 1979. pap. 5.99 (*0-8010-5277-7*) Baker Bk.

Dating: What to Do...What Not to Do. George B. Eager. (Illus.). 29p. (Orig.). (YA). (gr. 6-12). 1993. pap. 3.00 (*1-879224-09-7*) Mailbox.

***Dating a Twentieth-Century Fault, Elk Summit Talus Apron, Big Creek Area, Valley County, Idaho.** Benjamin F. Leonard & Roger Rosentreter. Vol. 2101. 1995. write for info. (*0-615-00057-6*) US Geol Survey.

Dating & Age Determination of Biological Materials. Ed. by Michael R. Zimmerman & J. Lawrence Angel. (Applied Biology Ser.). 304p. 1986. 85.00 (*0-7099-0470-3*, Pub. by Croom Helm UK) Routledge Chapman & Hall.

Dating & Arrangement of the Undated Coins of Rome A.D. 98-148. P. V. Hill. 1970. 35.00 (*0-685-51523-0*) S J Durst.

Dating & Waiting for Marriage. Raymond T. Brock. LC 81-84763. (Radiant Life Ser.). 128p. (YA). (gr. 9-12). 1982. teacher ed 4.50 (*0-88243-192-7*, 32-0192); pap. 2.95 (*0-88243-881-6*, 02-0881) Gospel Pub.

Dating Book. Julie Cahn. Ed. by Meg F. Schneider. (Just for Teens Ser.). 160p. (J). 1983. 9.29 (*0-685-06228-7*) S&S Trade.

***Dating, College Prep, & a Reason to Live.** (Hot Topics Youth Electives Ser.). (YA). (gr. 7-12). Date not set. 16.95 (*1-55513-204-9*, 62364) Cook.

Dating Decisions. David Cassady. (Active Bible Curriculum Ser.). (Illus.). 48p. 1991. pap. 9.99 (*1-55945-215-3*) Group Pub.

Dating Dilemma: Handling Sexual Pressures. Bob Stone & Bob Palmer. 160p. (Orig.). (J). 1990. pap. 9.99 (*0-8010-8314-1*) Baker Bk.

Dating, Dining, Dancing, & Other Teen Dilemmas. Vivian R. Cline. 1994. pap. 6.95 (*0-88494-931-1*) Bookcraft Inc.

Dating Dinosaurs & Other Old Things. Karen Liptak. LC 91-23072. (Illus.). 72p. (YA). (gr. 7 up). 1992. lib. bdg. 14.90 (*1-56294-134-8*) Millbrook Pr.

Dating Etiquette for Christian Teens. MaryAnn L. Diorio. (Illus.). 48p. (Orig.). (J). (gr. 6-12). 1984. pap. 3.95 (*0-930037-00-6*) Daystar Comm.

Dating Game. Francine Pascal. (Sweet Valley High Ser.: No. 78). (YA). 1991. pap. 2.99 (*0-553-29187-4*) Bantam.

Dating Games. Leigh Michaels. (Romance Ser.). 1993. mass mkt. 2.99 (*0-373-03290-0*, 1-03290-3) Harlequin Bks.

Dating in Exposed & Surface Contexts. Ed. by Charlotte Beck. LC 94-7113. 1994. 45.00x (*0-8263-1523-2*) U of NM Pr.

Dating in the Bronze Age with Special Reference to Scandinavia. Oscar Montelius. 148p. (Orig.). 1986. pap. 37.50x (*91-7402-182-6*) Coronet Bks.

Dating Iron John: A Woman's Survival Guide for the '90s. Linda Sunshine. LC 92-39826. 1993. 16.95 (*1-55972-175-8*, Birch Ln Pr) Carol Pub Group.

Dating Iron John & Other Pleasures: A Woman's Survival Guide for the 90's. Linda Sunshine. 1993. pap. 9.95 (*1-55972-188-X*, Birch Ln Pr) Carol Pub Group.

***Dating is About Finding Someone (So You Never Have to Date Again)** Nancy Kelton. LC 94-34680. (Illus.). 1995. write for info. (*0-8362-6249-2*) Andrews & McMeel.

***Dating Is about Finding Someone So You Never Have to Date Again.** Nancy Kelton. (Illus.). 1995. pap. 8.95 (*0-8362-7026-6*) Andrews & McMeel.

***Dating, Is It or Isn't It in God's Vocabulary.** Lyn-Dianne Franco. 128p. 1994. pap. 7.00 (*0-9642719-0-7*) L D Franco.

Dating, Marriage, Sex & Divorce. R. P. Daniel. 75p. pap. 3.95 (*0-88172-147-6*) Believers Bkshelf.

Dating, Mating, & Marriage. Martin K. Whyte. LC 89-17996. (Social Institutions & Social Change Ser.). (Illus.). 335p. (Orig.). 1990. lib. bdg. 51.95 (*0-202-30415-9*); pap. text ed. 29.95 (*0-202-30416-7*) Aldine de Gruyter.

***Dating, Mating, Relating: Hilarious Pick-up Lines, Simmering Career-Coded Sex Guides...** David Westwood. 1995. pap. 7.95 (*0-681-00773-7*) Longmeadow Pr.

Dating, No Guts No Glory. Joni Hilton. 1989. 6.95 (*1-55503-138-2*, 019101) Covenant Comms.

Dating of Beowulf. Ed. by Colin Chase. (Old English Ser.). 1981. 45.00 (*0-8020-5576-1*) U of Toronto Pr.

Dating of Beowulf. Ed. by Colin Chase. LC 82-102433. (Toronto Old English Ser.: No. 6). 229p. reprint ed. pap. 65.30 (*0-685-15942-6*, 2056128) Bks Demand.

Dating of Old Houses. Henry C. Mercer. (Illus.). 28p. 1976. reprint ed. pap. 2.00 (*0-910302-03-0*) Bucks Co Hist.

Dating Postwar Business Cycles: Methods & Their Application to Western Germany, 1950-67. Ilse Mintz. (Occasional Papers: No. 107). 125p. 1970. reprint ed. 32.50 (*0-87014-212-7*) Natl Bur Econ Res.

Dating Quaternary Sediments. Ed. by D. J. Easterbrook. (Special Paper Ser.: No. 227). (Illus.). 172p. 1988. pap. 10.00 (*0-8137-2227-6*) Geol Soc.

***Dating Quilts: A Quick & Easy Reference.** Helen Kelley. Ed. by Louise Townsend. LC 94-38760. 64p. 1995. pap. 9.95 (*0-914881-95-7*, 10113) C & T Pub.

***Dating Service Maze: The Experts Guide to Dating Services.** Lynda M. Johncock. (Illus.). 125p. (Orig.). 1994. pap. 19.95 (*0-9644568-0-X*) Queen Hearts Pub.

Dating, Sex & Friendship. Joyce Huggett. LC 85-19734. 204p. 1985. pap. 9.99 (*0-87784-406-2*, 406) InterVarsity.

An Asterisk (*) at the beginning of an entry indicates that the title is appearing in BIP for the first time.

Dating United States Growth Cycles. Ilse Mintz. (Explorations in Economic Research One Ser.: No. 1). 113p. 1974. reprint ed. 35.00 (*0-685-61369-0*) Natl Bur Econ Res.

Dating Violence: Young Women in Danger. Ed. by Barrie Levy. LC 90-24538. (New Leaf Ser.). 308p. (Orig.). 1991. pap. 16.95 (*1-878067-03-6*) Seal Pr Feminist.

Dating Violence: Youth At-Risk. Joan G. Sculli. (Family Forum Library Ser.). 16p. 1992. 1.95 (*1-56688-047-5*) Bur For At-Risk.

***Dating Vs. Courtship.** 2nd ed. Paul Jehle. 132p. (YA). 1995. pap. 8.00 (*0-942516-14-1*) Plymouth Rock Found.

Dating with Integrity. John Holzmann. 1992. pap. 9.99 (*0-8499-3437-0*) Word Inc.

Dating Your Mate. Rick Bundschuh & Dave Gilbert. LC 87-80286. 144p. (Orig.). 1987. pap. 5.99 (*0-89081-598-4*) Harvest Hse.

Dating Your Mom. Ian Frazier. 128p. 1986. 11.95 (*0-374-13508-8*) FS&G.

Dato Escolar. 3rd ed. Ed. by Maria E. Alvarez del Real. LC 81-72099. (Illus.). 352p. (SPA.). (J). (gr. 2). 1985. pap. 6.00 (*0-944499-11-2*) Editorial Amer.

Datsun - Nissan Pick-Ups & Pathfinder 1970-88. 640p. 1995. pap. 21.95 (*0-8019-8585-4*) Chilton.

Datsun-Nissan Pick-Ups & Pathfinder, 1970-89: Repair & Tune-Up Guide. Chilton Automotives Editorial Staff. LC 88-43174. (Illus.). 576p. 1989. pap. 16.95 (*0-8019-7932-3*) Chilton.

Datsun 200SX, 510, 610, 710, 810-Nissan Maxima, 1973-86. LC 88-48014. 604p. (SPA.). 1989. 16.95 (*0-8019-7880-7*) Chilton.

Datsun 311 1600-2000 Sports Car: Shop Manual. Motorbooks International Staff. (Illus.). 392p. (Orig.). 1988. pap. 29.95 (*0-87938-294-5*) Motorbooks Intl.

Dattatreya: The Song of the Avadhut. S. Abhayananda. (Classics of Mystical Literature Ser.). 180p. (Orig.). 1992. pap. 7.95 (*0-914557-07-6*) Atma Bks.

Dattilam. Mukund Lath. (C). 1988. 48.50 (*81-208-0586-0*, Pub. by Motilal Banarsidass II) S Asia.

Daugherty's Cave: A Stratified Site in Russell County, Virginia, Vol. 18. Wm. Jack Hranicky & Floyd Painter. 99p. 1991. pap. 26.00 (*1-884626-17-3*) Archeolog Soc.

Daughter. Caroline Gray. 320p. 1992. 22.00 (*0-7278-4347-8*) Severn Hse.

Daughter Buffalo. Janet Frame. 224p. 1992. reprint ed. pap. 8.95 (*0-8076-1284-7*) Braziller.

Daughter of a Pioneer: A True Story of Life in Early Colorado. 2nd ed. Atlanta G. Thompson. LC 90-81451. (Illus.). 168p. 1990. pap. 10.00 (*0-8323-0479-4*) Binford Mort.

Daughter of Anderson Crow. George B. McCutcheon. 1976. lib. bdg. 15.75 (*0-89968-060-7*, Lghtyr Pr) Buccaneer Bks.

Daughter of Damascus: A Memoir. Siham Tergeman. Tr. & Intro. by Andrea Rugh. (Modern Middle East Literature in Translation Ser.). 200p. (Orig.). (C). 1994. pap. 10.95 (*0-292-78126-1*) U of Tex Pr.

Daughter of Deceit. Victoria Holt. 1992. mass mkt. 5.99 (*0-449-22058-3*, Crest) Fawcett.

Daughter of Deceit. large type ed. Victoria Holt. LC 93-24728. 560p. 1993. pap. 17.95 (*0-8161-5806-1*) Hall.

Daughter of Deceit: The Walker Spy Case. Laura Walker & Jerry Horner. 237p. 1988. write for info. (*0-8499-0659-8*) Word Inc.

Daughter of Destiny. Jackie Casto. 368p. (Orig.). 1990. pap. 3.95 (*0-8439-3046-2*) Dorchester Pub Co.

***Daughter of Destiny.** Jackie Casto. 368p. 1995. mass mkt. 4.99 (*0-505-52011-7*, Love Spell) Dorchester Pub Co.

Daughter of Destiny: Kathryn Kuhlman...Her Story. Jamie Buckingham. LC 76-12034. 309p. 1976. pap. 4.95 (*0-88270-318-8*) Bridge Pub.

***Daughter of Destiny: Memoirs of Carlene Howell.** Carlene M. Howell. Ed. by W. B. Carraway. (Illus.). 275p. 1995. text ed. 14.95 (*0-9633855-1-8*) BAC Pubns.

Daughter of Earth. Agnes Smedley. LC 86-33514. 432p. (C). 1987. reprint ed. pap. text ed. 11.95 (*0-935312-68-4*) Feminist Pr.

Daughter of Elysium. Joan Slonczewski. 1993. pap. 25.00 (*0-380-97222-0*, AvoNova) Avon.

***Daughter of Elysium.** Joan Slonczewski. 528p. 1994. mass mkt. 5.99 (*0-380-77027-X*, AvoNova) Avon.

Daughter of Elysium. Joan Slonczewski. 1993. 25.00 (*0-688-12509-3*) Morrow.

Daughter of Fire: A Diary of a Spiritual Training with a Sufi Master. Irina Tweedie. LC 86-72368. 832p. 1986. 29.95 (*0-931892-05-8*); pap. 19.95 (*0-931892-04-X*) B Dolphin Pub.

Daughter of Fly in My Eye. Ed. by Steve Niles. (Illus.). 1990. 9.95 (*1-56060-073-X*) Eclipse Bks.

Daughter of Fortune. Carla Kelly. LC 84-73448. 320p. 1985. 16.95 (*0-917657-23-3*) D I Fine.

Daughter of Grace. Michael R. Phillips & Judith Pella. (Journals of Corrie Belle Hollister). 288p. (Orig.). 1990. pap. 8.99 (*1-55661-105-6*) Bethany Hse.

***Daughter of Grace.** large type ed. Michael Phillips & Judith Pella. 1995. 20.95 (*0-7838-1179-9*, Large Print Bks) Hall.

Daughter of Han: The Autobiography of a Chinese Working Woman. Ning L. T'ai-t'ai. Ed. by Ida Pruitt. (Illus.). viii, 254p. 1945. 35.00 (*0-8047-0605-0*); pap. 10.95 (*0-8047-0606-9*) Stanford U Pr.

Daughter of Heth, 3 vols. in 1. William Black. LC 79-8237. reprint ed. 44.50 (*0-404-61781-6*) AMS Pr.

Daughter of Incest. Josefina T. Torres. 1993. 19.95 (*0-533-10577-3*) Vantage.

Daughter of Indra. 255p. 1993. reprint ed. spiral bd. 8.25 (*0-7873-0005-5*) Mokelumne.

Daughter of Isis Ritual. pap. 4.00 (*0-685-19470-1*) Powner.

Daughter of Israel: Laws of Family Purity. Kalman Kahana. Tr. by Leonard Oschry. 12.95 (*0-87306-092-X*) Feldheim.

***Daughter of Jerusalem: A Novel.** Sara Maitland. LC 95-971. 1995. pap. 12.00 (*0-8050-3810-8*, Owl) H Holt & Co.

Daughter of Jorio: A Pastoral Tragedy. Gabriele D'Annunzio. Tr. by Charlotte Porter et al. LC 69-10064. 208p. 1968. reprint ed. text ed. 55.00 (*0-8371-0005-4*, DADJ, Greenwood Pr) Greenwood.

Daughter of Liberty. A. Cole & C. Bunch. Date not set. pap. write for info. (*0-345-38864-X*) Ballantine.

***Daughter of My People: Henrietta Szold & Hadassah.** Hazel Krantz. LC 95-799. 1995. pap. 20.00 (*1-56821-337-9*) Aronson.

Daughter of Neoptolemus: A Biography of Olympias, the Mother of Alexander the Great. Michael A. Dimitri. 400p. (Orig.). 1993. pap. 12.00 (*1-884191-01-0*) Alexandria Pub.

Daughter of Persia: A Woman's Journey from Her Father's Harem Through the Islamic Revolution. Sattareh F. Farmaian. 448p. 1992. 22.00 (*0-517-58697-5*, Crown) Crown Pub Group.

Daughter of Persia: A Woman's Journey from Her Father's Harem Through the Islamic Revolution. Sattareh F. Farmaian & Dona Munker. LC 92-40640. 1993. 12.95 (*0-385-46866-0*, Anchor NY) Doubleday.

Daughter of Peter the Great. Robert N. Bain. 1899. 13.00 (*0-403-00002-5*) Scholarly.

Daughter of Peter the Great. Nisbet R. Bain. 1988. reprint ed. lib. bdg. 79.00 (*0-7812-0465-8*) Rprt Serv.

Daughter of Peter the Great. Robert N. Bain. LC 72-136407. (BCL Ser.: No. II). reprint ed. 29.50 (*0-404-00447-4*) AMS Pr.

Daughter of Prophecy. Anne K. Bush. 368p. (Orig.). 1995. pap. 5.50 (*0-446-60087-3*, Aspect) Warner Bks.

Daughter of Regals. Stephen Donaldson. (Illus.). 1984. 50.00 (*0-937986-63-1*) D M Grant.

Daughter of Regals & Other Tales. Stephen R. Donaldson. 304p. 1985. mass mkt. 5.95 (*0-345-31443-3*, Del Rey) Ballantine.

Daughter of Riches. Janet Tanner. 524p. 1993. 24.95 (*0-312-09266-0*) St Martin.

Daughter of Shanghai. Tsai Chin. (Illus.). 264p. 1994. pap. 10.95 (*0-312-11258-0*) St Martin.

Daughter of the Bear King. Eleanor Arnason. 256p. (Orig.). 1987. pap. 3.50 (*0-380-75109-7*) Avon.

Daughter of the Boyne. Patricia McDowell. 221p. 1993. pap. 13.95 (*0-86327-349-1*, Pub. by Wolfhound Pr IE) Dufour.

Daughter of the Covenants. Anna M. Dahlquist. LC 94-76457. 200p. (Orig.). 1994. pap. 7.95 (*0-9641261-0-9*) Kings River.

Daughter of the Dales. large type ed. H. Hauxwell & B. Cockcroft. 1991. 21.95 (*0-7089-2553-7*) Ulverscroft.

Daughter of the Dawn. Christine Flynn. (Silhouette Intimate Moments Ser.). 1993. mass mkt. 3.50 (*0-373-07537-5*, 5-07537-9) Silhouette.

Daughter of the Dawn. Elizabeth Shaffer. (J). 1992. write for info. (*0-936369-72-8*) Son-Rise Pubns.

Daughter of the Dawn: A Realistic Story of Maori Magic. William R. Hodder. Ed. by R. Reginald & Douglas Melville. LC 77-84239. (Lost Race & Adult Fantasy Ser.). (Illus.). 1978. reprint ed. lib. bdg. 33.95 (*0-405-10986-5*) Ayer.

Daughter of the Desert. Chloe Gartner. 1978. pap. 2.25 (*0-89083-375-3*) Zebra.

Daughter of the Dreadfuls. Barbara Sherrod. 224p. 1994. 3.99 (*0-451-17868-8*, Sig) NAL-Dutton.

***Daughter of the Drow.** Elaine Cunningham. (Forgotten Realms Ser.). 320p. 1995. 16.95 (*0-7869-0165-9*) TSR Inc.

Daughter of the Eagle. Don Coldsmith. (Spanish Bit Saga Ser.: Bk. 6). (Orig.). 1988. 4.50 (*0-553-27209-8*) Bantam.

Daughter of the East. Benazir Bhutto. 394p. 1989. 21.95 (*0-318-40972-0*) S&S Trade.

Daughter of the Empire. Raymond E. Feist & Janny Wurts. 1988. mass mkt. 5.99 (*0-553-27211-X*, Spectra) Bantam.

Daughter of the Forest. Vella Munn. 416p. 1995. mass mkt. 5.99 (*0-8125-3499-9*) Forge NYC.

Daughter of the Goddess: The Sacred Priestess. Naomi Ozaniec. (Illus.). 1993. pap. 14.00 (*1-85538-280-6*, Pub. by Aquarian Pr UK) Thorsons SF.

Daughter of the Hills: A Woman's Part in the Coal Miners' Struggles. Myra Page. LC 86-9866. (Novels of the Thirties Ser.). 304p. 1983. reprint ed. pap. 8.95 (*0-935312-59-5*) Feminist Pr.

Daughter of the Land. Gene Stratton-Porter. reprint ed. lib. bdg. 26.95 (*0-89190-944-3*, Rivercity Pr) Amereon Ltd.

Daughter of the Legend. Jesse Stuart. Ed. by John H. Spurlock. LC 94-628. (Illus.). 256p. (YA). (gr. 8 up). 1994. reprint ed. 20.00 (*0-945084-42-0*) J Stuart Found.

Daughter of the Lion. Jennifer Roberson. (Chronicles of the Cheysuli Ser.: Bk. 6). 384p. (Orig.). 1989. mass mkt. 4.99 (*0-88677-324-5*) DAW Bks.

Daughter of the Medici, & Other Stories. Donn B. Byrne, pseud. LC 73-125207. (Short Story Index Reprint Ser.). 1977. 19.95 (*0-8369-3574-8*) Ayer.

Daughter of the Middle Border. Hamlin Garland. (Collected Works of Hamlin Garland). 1988. reprint ed. lib. bdg. 79.00 (*0-7812-1246-4*) Rprt Serv.

Daughter of the Middle Border see Collected Works of Hamlin Garland

Daughter of the Mountain. Vella Munn. 416p. (Orig.). 1994. mass mkt. 5.99 (*0-8125-2325-3*) Tor Bks.

Daughter of the Mountain: Un Cuento. Edna Escamill. LC 91-9754. 192p. (Orig.). (J). (gr. 5 up). 1991. lib. bdg. 18.95 (*1-879960-08-7*); pap. 8.95 (*1-879960-07-9*) Aunt Lute Bks.

Daughter of the Mountains. Louise Rankin. LC 92-26793. (Newbery Library). (Illus.). 192p. (J). (gr. 5 up). 1993. pap. 4.99 (*0-14-036335-1*) Puffin Bks.

Daughter of the Night. Elaine Bergstrom. 336p. (Orig.). 1994. pap. text ed. 4.99 (*0-441-00110-6*) Ace Bks.

Daughter of the Night. Elaine Bergstrom. 336p. (Orig.). 1992. mass mkt. 4.99 (*0-515-10951-7*) Jove Pubns.

Daughter of the Pacific. Yoko Matsuoka. LC 72-12634. 245p. 1973. reprint ed. text ed. 35.00 (*0-8371-6683-7*, MADP, Greenwood Pr) Greenwood.

Daughter of the Red Deer. Joan Wolf. 480p. 1992. pap. 5.99 (*0-451-40334-7*, Onyx) NAL-Dutton.

Daughter of the Revolution, & Other Stories. John Reed. LC 75-134975. (Short Story Index Reprint Ser.). 1977. 16.95 (*0-8369-3707-4*) Ayer.

Daughter of the Samurai. Etsu I. Sugimoto. LC 66-15849. 314p. (J). (gr. 9 up). 1966. pap. 14.95 (*0-8048-1655-7*) C E Tuttle.

Daughter of the Sanctuary. Carol Hopper. 111p. (Orig.). 1984. pap. 3.95 (*0-88144-022-1*, CPS023) Christian Pub.

Daughter of the Snows. Jack London. (Illus.). 336p. 1987. pap. 6.95 (*0-932458-36-X*) Star Rover.

Daughter of the Soil: Autobiographical Sketches. Lois Barton. LC 85-62993. 60p. (Orig.). 1985. pap. 6.95 (*0-9609420-1-7*) S Butte Pr.

Daughter of the South, & Shorter Stories. Constance C. Harrison. LC 75-90583. (Short Story Index Reprint Ser.). 1977. 20.95 (*0-8369-3066-5*) Ayer.

Daughter of the Stars. Phyllis A. Whitney. 1994. 20.00 (*0-517-59929-5*) Crown Pub Group.

Daughter of the Stars. large type ed. Phyllis A. Whitney. 1994. pap. 19.00 (*0-679-75648-5*) Random.

Daughter of the Storage: Short Stories. William Dean Howells. (Notable American Authors Ser.). 1992. reprint ed. lib. bdg. 75.00 (*0-7812-3263-5*) Rprt Serv.

Daughter of the Storm. Jeanne Williams. 384p. 1994. 20.95 (*0-312-10441-3*) St Martin.

***Daughter of the Storm.** large type ed. Jeanne Williams. LC 95-11462. 487p. 1995. pap. 19.95 (*0-7862-0469-9*) Thorndike Pr.

Daughter of the Sun. large type ed. Mary Wibberley. LC 92-23103. 1992. pap. 16.95 (*0-7927-1387-7*, Atlantic Lrg Print) Chivers N Amer.

Daughter of the Sun: A Tale of Adventure. Jackson Gregory. Ed. by R. Reginald & Douglas Melville. LC 77-842333. (Lost Race & Adult Fantasy Ser.). 1978. reprint ed. lib. bdg. 26.95 (*0-405-10981-4*) Ayer.

Daughter of the Swan: Legacies of Love & Knowledge in Eudora Welty's Fiction. Gail L. Mortimer. LC 93-41117. 264p. 1994. 40.00 (*0-8203-1633-4*) U of Ga Pr.

Daughter of the Tenements. Edward W. Townsend. LC 78-104586. (Illus.). 301p. reprint ed. lib. bdg. 29.00 (*0-8398-1973-0*) Irvington.

Daughter of the Tenements. Edward W. Townsend. (Illus.). 301p. (C). 1986. reprint ed. pap. text ed. 7.95 (*0-8290-1910-3*) Irvington.

Daughter of Tibet. Rinchen D. Taring. (Tibet Book - Yellow Ser.). (Illus.). 324p. (Orig.). 1986. pap. 18.95 (*0-86171-044-4*) Wisdom MA.

Daughter of Time. Josephine Tey. 220p. 1976. lib. bdg. 23.95 (*0-89966-184-X*) Buccaneer Bks.

Daughter of Time. Josephine Tey. (Josephine Tey Mysteries Ser.). 208p. 1988. pap. 6.00 (*0-02-054550-9*, Collier S&S) S&S Trade.

***Daughter of Tintagel.** Fay Sampson. 832p. 1995. pap. 9.95 (*0-7472-3894-4*, Pub. by Headline UK) Trafalgar.

Daughter of Valdoro. large type ed. Evelyn S. Armstrong. 467p. 1976. 12.00 (*0-85456-457-8*) Ulverscroft.

Daughter of Zion. Bodie Thoene. LC 87-8064. (Zion Chronicles Ser.: Bk. II). 352p. (Orig.). 1987. pap. 9.99 (*0-87123-940-X*) Bethany Hse.

***Daughter of Zion: Henrietta Szold & American Jewish Womanhood.** Ed. by Barry Kessler. 104p. 1995. write for info. (*0-614-04271-2*) Jew Hist Soc MD.

Daughtering & Mothering: Female Subjectivity Reanalysed. Ed. by Janneke Van Mens-Verhulst et al. LC 93-14821. 208p. 1993. 59.95 (*0-415-08649-3*, B0895); pap. 16.95 (*0-415-08650-7*, B0899) Routledge.

Daughters. Paule Marshall. LC 92-53558. (Contemporary Fiction Ser.). 416p. 1992. pap. 11.95 (*0-452-26912-1*, Plume) NAL-Dutton.

Daughters. Paule Marshall. 416p. 1991. text ed. 19.95 (*0-689-12139-3*, Atheneum S&S) S&S Trade.

Daughters: On Family & Fatherhood. Gerald Early. (Illus.). 160p. 1994. 16.35 (*0-201-62724-8*) Addison-Wesley.

Daughters: Poems by Stephen Berg. Stephen Berg. LC 77-134465. 1971. pap. 6.55 (*0-672-61153-8*, Bobbs) Macmillan.

Daughter's a Daughter. Mary Westmacott. 18.95 (*0-8488-0963-7*) Amereon Ltd.

Daughter's a Daughter. Mary Westmacott, pseud. 1988. pap. 3.95 (*0-515-09494-3*) Jove Pubns.

Daughter's a Daughter. large type ed. Mary Westmacott. 1978. 21.95 (*0-7089-0217-0*) Ulverscroft.

Daughters & Fathers. Ed. by Lynda E. Boose & Betty S. Flowers. LC 88-45407. 480p. (C). 1989. text ed. 58.00 (*0-8018-3665-4*); pap. text ed. 15.95 (*0-8018-3666-2*) Johns Hopkins.

Daughters & Mothers: Healing the Relationship. Julie Firman & Dorothy Firman. 256p. 1990. pap. 14.95 (*0-8245-1305-3*) Crossroad NY.

Daughters & Rebels: An Autobiography. Jessica Mitford. LC 81-47450. 304p. 1981. pap. 9.95 (*0-8050-1172-2*, Owl) H Holt & Co.

Daughter's Devotion. rev. ed. George MacDonald. Ed. by Michael Phillips. LC 88-19256. (George MacDonald Classics Ser.). 320p. (YA). (gr. 11 up). 1988. pap. 7.99 (*0-87123-906-X*) Bethany Hse.

Daughter's Dilemma. large type ed. Miranda Lee. 1993. 17.95 (*0-263-13316-8*, Pub. by Mills & Boon Ltd UK) Chivers N Amer.

Daughter's Dilemma: Family Process & the Nineteenth-Century Domestic Novel. Paula M. Cohen. 208p. (C). 1991. text ed. 37.50 (*0-472-10234-6*) U of Mich Pr.

Daughter's Dilemma: Family Process & the Nineteenth-Century Domestic Novel. Paula M. Cohen. 240p. (C). 1993. pap. text ed. 19.95 (*0-472-08232-9*) U of Mich Pr.

Daughters, Fathers, & the Novel: The Sentimental Romance of Heterosexuality. Linda Zwinger. LC 90-50656. 184p. 1991. 37.50 (*0-299-12850-4*); pap. text ed. 14.95 (*0-299-12854-7*) U of Wis Pr.

Daughter's Geography. Ntozake Shange. 80p. 1991. pap. 8.95 (*0-312-06327-X*) St Martin.

Daughter's Gift of Love: A Holocaust Memoir. Trudy Birger & Jeffrey M. Green. LC 92-15503. 224p. (J). 1992. 24.95 (*0-8276-0420-3*) JPS Phila.

Daughters in Law. Henry Cecil. 190p. pap. 8.95 (*1-55882-105-8*) Intl Polygonics.

Daughters in the House: Modes of the Gothic in Victorian Fiction. Alison Milbank. LC 91-27231. 256p. 1992. text ed. 45.00 (*0-312-07168-X*) St Martin.

***Daughters of a Coral Dawn.** 10th ed. Katherine V. Forrest. (Orig.). 1994. pap. 10.95 (*1-56280-104-X*) Naiad Pr.

Daughters of Abya Yala: Indigenous Women Regaining Control. Ed. by Meso-American Indian Center Women's Committee. LC 94-2780. (Illus.). 128p. 1994. 8.95 (*0-913990-09-4*) Book Pub Co.

Daughters of Africa: An International Anthology of Words & Writings by Women of African Descent & from the Ancient Egyptian to the Present. Ed. by Margaret Busby. 1152p. 1994. pap. 19.95 (*0-345-38268-4*, One World) Ballantine.

Daughters of Africa: An International Anthology of Words & Writings by Women of African Descent & from the Ancient Egyptian to the Present. Intro. by Margaret Busby. LC 92-54116. 1152p. 1992. 35.00 (*0-679-41634-X*) Pantheon.

Daughters of Albion. A. N. Wilson. 304p. 1993. pap. 10.00 (*0-14-013166-3*, Penguin Bks) Viking Penguin.

***Daughters of Anowa: African Women & Patriarchy.** Mercy A. Oduyoye. 226p. (Orig.). 1995. pap. 16.95 (*0-88344-999-4*) Orbis Bks.

Daughters of Artemis. Lauren W. Douglas. (Caitlin Reece Mystery Ser.). (Orig.). 1991. pap. 9.95 (*0-941483-95-9*) Naiad Pr.

***Daughters of Cain.** Dexter. Date not set. write for info. (*0-517-70153-7*) Random Hse Value.

***Daughters of Cain.** Dexter. Date not set. write for info. (*0-8041-1364-5*) Random Hse Value.

***Daughters of Cain.** Colin Dexter. 1995. 21.00 (*0-517-70067-0*, Crown) Crown Pub Group.

***Daughters of Canaan: A Saga of Southern Women.** Margaret R. Wolfe. LC 94-30150. (New Perspectives on the South Ser.). (Illus.). 312p. 1995. text ed. 37.50 (*0-8131-1902-2*); pap. 14.95 (*0-8131-0837-3*) U Pr of Ky.

Daughters of Captain Cook. Linda Spalding. Ed. by Hillel Black. 240p. 1989. 15.95 (*1-55972-008-5*, Birch Ln Pr) Carol Pub Group.

Daughters of Copper Woman. Anne Cameron. 1988. pap. 9.50 (*0-88974-022-4*) Inland Pub.

***Daughters of Dakota, No. VI.** Ed. by Sally R. Wagner. (Stories from the Black Hills Ser.). 183p. (Orig.). 1994. pap. 12.95 (*1-880589-06-0*) Daughters Dak.

Daughters of Dakota: Schooled in Privation. Intro. by Sally R. Wagner. (South Dakota Pioneer Daughters Collection: Vol. IV). (Illus.). 176p. (Orig.). 1991. pap. 12.95 (*1-880589-04-4*) Daughters Dak.

Daughters of Dakota: Stories from the Attic. Photos by South Dakota Historical Society Staff. (South Dakota Pioneer Daughters Collection: Vol. II). (Illus.). 176p. (Orig.). 1990. pap. 11.95 (*1-880589-02-8*); write for info. (*0-318-68740-2*) Daughters Dak.

Daughters of Dakota: Stories of Friendship Between Settlers & the Dakota Indians. Ed. & Intro. by Sally R. Wagner. (South Dakota Pioneer Daughters Collection: Vol. III). (Illus.). 148p. (Orig.). 1990. pap. 12.95 (*1-880589-03-6*); write for info. (*0-318-68741-0*) Daughters Dak.

Daughters of Dakota, Vol. I: A Sampler. 1989. pap. 11.95 (*1-880589-01-X*) Daughters Dak.

Daughters of Dakota, Vol. 5: The Long Stories. Ed. by Sally R. Wagner. (Illus.). 164p. (Orig.). 1992. pap. 12.95 (*1-880589-05-2*) Daughters Dak.

Daughters of Dallas. Vivian A. Castleberry. 550p. 1994. 35.00 (*0-9623216-8-0*) Odenwald Pr.

Daughters of Danaus. Mona Caird. LC 89-11627. 544p. 1989. 35.00 (*1-55861-014-6*); pap. 13.95 (*1-55861-015-4*) Feminist Pr.

Daughters of Darkness: Lesbian Vampire Stories. Ed. by Pam Keesey. 250p. (Orig.). 1993. 24.95 (*0-939416-77-8*); pap. 9.95 (*0-939416-78-6*) Cleis Pr.

***Daughters of Deborah. Sabrina M. Davidson. LC 94-34513. 1995. 14.95 (*1-885275-52-8*) C J Howie. DAUGHTERS OF DEBORAH, is historical fiction of Deborah, Hebrew prophetess & territorial judge in ancient Israel; Barak, her brilliant military commander; & the women's militia. The times were raw, barbaric & bloody. Hebrews left the wilderness in successive waves, & entered Canaan with soft weapons of bronze. They faced an enemy already in the iron age & suffered heavily under King Jabin & his henchman, General Sisera. The broken treaties, & mounting demands for tribute collected by Sisera in his iron chariots, made some Hebrews want to return to the ancestral wilderness.**

D

An Asterisk (*) at the beginning of an entry indicates that the title is appearing in BIP for the first time.

Deborah's people mainly stayed in the hill country, where the feared chariots could not penetrate. But Sisera also stole Hebrews & sold them into slavery to make up the difference. Deborah found a way to break the Canaanite yoke by stealth, guerilla warfare, & the women's militia that bought time for Barak to position his army & battle Sisera at Mt. Tabor. From Cataloging-in-Publishing Data: 1. Deborah (Biblical judge)--Fiction. 2. Bible. O.T.--History of Biblical events--Fiction. 3. Women in the Bible--Fiction. Order from: C.J. Howie Publishing, P.O. Box 27215, Columbus OH 43227-9998. ***Publisher Provided Annotation.***

Daughters of Decadence: Women Writers of the Fin-de-Siecle. Intro. by Elaine Showalter. LC 93-1571. 342p. (Orig.). (C). 1993. pap. 14.95 (0-8135-2018-5) Rutgers U Pr.

Daughters of Desire. Serita Stevens. 480p. (Orig.). 1987. pap. 3.95 (0-8439-2499-3) Dorchester Pub Co.

Daughters of Destiny: Women Who Revolutionized Jewish Life & Torah Education. Devora Rubin. (ArtScroll History Ser.). (Illus.). 240p. 1988. 14.95 (0-89906-494-9); pap. 11.95 (0-89906-495-7) Mesorah Pubns.

***Daughters of England.** Carr. pap. write for info. (0-449-14955-2) Fawcett.

***Daughters of England.** Philippa Carr. LC 94-33987. 1995. 22.95 (0-399-14023-9) Putnam Pub Group.

***Daughters of England.** large type ed. Philippa Carr. LC 95-13271. 482p. 1995. 24.95 (0-7838-1352-X, Large Print Bks) Hall.

Daughters of Erin. Elizabeth Coxhead. 236p. 1979. pap. 9.95 (0-317-65903-0, Pub. by Colin Smythe Ltd UK) Dufour.

Daughters of Eve. Lois Duncan. (YA). 1990. mass mkt. 3.99 (0-440-91864-2) Dell.

Daughters of Eve: Strength for Today from Women of Yesterday. 22th ed. Lottie B. Hobbs. 235p. 1963. reprint ed. pap. 5.95 (0-913838-04-7) Harvest TX.

Daughters of Eve: The Magical Mysteries of Womanhood. Dolores Ashcroft-Nowicki. 176p. 1993. pap. 15.00 (0-85030-977-8, Pub. by Aquarian Pr UK) Thorsons SF.

***Daughters of Eve: Women of the Bible Speak to Women of Today.** Virginia S. Owens. 200p. 1995. pap. text ed., pap. 10.00 (0-89109-824-0, NavPr); student ed., per. 5.00 (0-89109-825-9, NavPr) NavPress.

Daughters of Eve: Women's Writing from the German Democratic Republic. Ed. by Nancy Lukens & Dorothy Rosenberg. LC 92-31238. (European Women Writers Ser.). xi, 332p. 1993. 40.00 (0-8032-2892-9); pap. 14.95 (0-8032-7942-6) U of Nebr Pr.

Daughters of Feminists: Young Women with Feminist Mothers Talk about Their Lives. Rose L. Glickman. LC 93-24286. 256p. 1993. 19.95 (0-312-09778-6) St Martin.

***Daughters of Feminists: Young Women with Feminist Mothers Talk about Their Lives.** Rose L. Glickman. LC 94-38236. 1995. pap. 12.95 (0-312-11770-1) St Martin.

***Daughters of Grail.** Elizabeth Chadwick. Date not set. pap. write for info. (0-345-38840-2) Ballantine.

Daughters of Independence: Gender, Caste, & Class in India. Joanna Liddle & Rama Joshi. 264p. (C). 1989. text ed. 40.00 (0-8135-1435-5); pap. text ed. 15.00 (0-8135-1436-3) Rutgers U Pr.

Daughters of Isis. Legrand Clegg, II & Karima Y. Ahmed. (Clegg Ser.: Pt. II). 1992. pap. text ed. 12.00 (1-882578-77-5) Clegg Series.

***Daughters of Isis: Women of Ancient Egypt.** Joyce Tyldesley. 352p. 1995. 11.95 (0-14-017596-2, Penguin Bks) Viking Penguin.

Daughters of Jefferson, Daughters of Bootblacks: Racism & American Feminism. Barbara H. Andolsen. LC 86-86. xiv, 130p. (Orig.). 1986. pap. 12.95 (0-86554-205-8, P23) Mercer Univ Pr.

Daughters of Jerusalem. Marla J. Selvidge. LC 87-7437. 176p. (Orig.). 1987. pap. 10.95 (0-8361-3440-0) Herald Pr.

Daughters of Joy, Sisters of Misery: Prostitutes in the American West, 1865-90. Anne M. Butler. LC 84-195. (Illus.). 208p. 1987. pap. 12.95 (0-252-01466-9) U of Ill Pr.

Daughters of Megwyn. large type ed. Antoinette K. Bird. 496p. 1989. 17.95 (0-7089-1924-3) Ulverscroft.

Daughters of Memory. Janis Arnold. 378p. 1991. 16.95 (0-945575-68-8) Algonquin Bks.

Daughters of Memory. Janis Arnold. (Front Porch Paperback Ser.). 1993. pap. 8.95 (1-56512-031-0) Algonquin Bks.

Daughters of Memory. Peter Najarian. LC 85-63859. (Illus.). 176p. (Orig.). 1986. pap. 8.95 (0-933944-13-6) City Miner Bks.

Daughters of Memory. deluxe ed. Peter Najarian. LC 85-63859. (Illus.). 176p. (Orig.). 1986. 20.00 (0-685-12079-1) City Miner Bks.

Daughters of Painted Ladies. Michael Larsen & Elizabeth Pomada. (Illus.). 144p. 1987. 29.95 (0-525-24609-6, Dutton); pap. 15.95 (0-525-48337-3, Dutton) NAL-Dutton.

***Daughters of Palestine: Leading Women of the Palestinian National Movement.** Amal Kawar. 192p. (C). 1996. text ed. 49.50x (0-7914-2845-1); pap. 16.95x (0-7914-2846-X) State U NY Pr.

***Daughters of Ra.** Illus. by Tiffany William. 25p. (Orig.). 1995. pap. 4.00x (1-56411-094-X) Untd Bros & Sis.

***Daughters of Rahab: Prostitution & the Church of Liberation in Brazil.** Margaret E. Guider. LC 95-5122. (Harvard Theological Studies). 1995. write for info. (0-8006-7093-0, Fortress Pr) Augsburg Fortress.

Daughters of Revolution: A History of Women in the U.S.S.R. Barbara E. Clements. Ed. by Keith Eubank. (European History Ser.). (Illus.). 184p. (C). 1994. pap. text ed. write for info. (0-88295-908-5) Harlan Davidson.

Daughters of Sappho. Ed. & Tr. by Rae Dalven. LC 91-58950. 1993. write for info. (0-8386-3470-2) Fairleigh Dickinson.

***Daughters of Saturn: From Father's Daughter to Creative Woman, Vol. 1.** Patricia Reis. 286p. 1995. 24.95 (0-8264-0812-5) Continuum.

***Daughters of Song.** Paula Huston. LC 94-22683. 1995. 23.00 (0-679-41969-1) Random.

Daughters of Sorrow: Attitudes Toward Black Women, 1880-1920. Beverly Guy-Sheftall. LC 90-1398. (Black Women in United States History Ser.: Vol. 11). (Illus.). 264p. 1990. 50.00 (0-926019-17-1) Carlson Pub.

Daughters of Strathannan. large type ed. Anne Vivis. 573p. 1993. 21.95 (0-7505-0532-X) Ulverscroft.

Daughters of the American Colonists in Oklahoma: Our Book of Memories. Veneta B. Arrington. LC 84-61836. (Illus.). 1984. 24.95 (0-913507-02-4) New Forums.

Daughters of the Canton Delta: Marriage Patterns & Economic Strategies in South China, 1860-1930. Janice Stockard. (Illus.). 248p. 1989. 35.00 (0-8047-1392-8); pap. 11.95 (0-8047-2014-2) Stanford U Pr.

Daughters of the Church. Daniel Hannefin. (Illus.). 360p. (Orig.). 1989. pap. 28.00 (0-911782-66-4) New City.

Daughters of the Church: Women & Ministry from New Testament Times to the Present. Ruth A. Tucker & Walter L. Liefeld. 544p. (Orig.). 1987. 24.99 (0-310-45741-6, 12608P) Zondervan.

Daughters of the Conquistadores: Women of the Viceroyalty of Peru. Luis Martin. LC 89-42899. (Illus.). 368p. 1989. reprint ed. pap. text ed. 14.95 (0-87074-297-3) SMU Press.

Daughters of the Covenant: Portraits of Six Jewish Women. Edward Wagenknecht. LC 83-3562. (Illus.). 200p. 1983. lib. bdg. 27.50x (0-87023-396-3) U of Mass Pr.

Daughters of the Dreaming. 2nd ed. Diane Bell. LC 93-14760. 342p. 1993. pap. text ed. 16.95 (0-8166-2398-8) U of Minn Pr.

Daughters of the Dust: The Making of an African American Woman's Film. Julie Dash et al. LC 92-50333. (Illus.). 192p. 1992. 27.95 (1-56584-029-1); pap. 17.95 (1-56584-030-5) New Press NY.

Daughters of the Earth. Carolyn Niethammer. 304p. 1977. pap. 16.00 (0-02-096150-2, Collier S&S) S&S Trade.

Daughters of the Elderly: Building Partnerships in Caregiving. Ed. by Jane Norris. LC 87-46236. 236p. (Orig.). 1988. 29.95 (0-253-31612-X); pap. 9.95 (0-253-20484-4, MB-484) Ind U Pr.

Daughters of the Goddess: The Women Saints of India. Linda Johnsen. 150p. (Orig.). 1994. pap. 12.95 (0-936663-09-X) Yes Intl.

***Daughters of the Great Depression: Women, Work & Fiction in the American 1930s.** Laura Hapke. LC 94-40316. 1995. write for info. (0-8203-1718-7) U of Ga Pr.

Daughters of the Great Star. Diana Rivers. 400p. (Orig.). 1992. pap. 9.95 (1-55583-314-4, Lace MA) Alyson Pubns.

Daughters of the House. Michele Roberts. LC 92-45713. 1993. 18.00 (0-688-04610-X) Morrow.

Daughters of the House. Michele Roberts. 224p. 1994. reprint ed. pap. 10.00 (0-380-72139-2) Avon.

Daughters of the Island: Contemporary Chamorro Women Organizers on Guam. rev. ed. Laura M. Souder. (Monograph Ser.: No. 1). (Illus.). 293p. (C). 1992. 45.00 (1-878453-04-1); pap. 17.50 (0-685-58489-5) Univ Guam MAR Ctr.

Daughters of the Island: Contemporary Chomorro Women Organizers on Guam. 2nd ed. Laura M. Torres Souder. (MARC Monograph Ser.: No. 1). (Illus.). 312p. (C). 1992. lib. bdg. 47.00 (0-8191-8607-4); pap. text ed. 19.50 (0-8191-8608-2) U Pr of Amer.

Daughters of the King. 2nd ed. Pat Brooks. LC 75-22573. 1987. pap. text ed. 5.00 (0-932050-32-8) New Puritan.

Daughters of the King: Women & the Synagogue. Susan Grossman & Rivka Haut. LC 91-31430. 352p. 1993. 29.95 (0-8276-0395-9); pap. 19.95 (0-8276-0441-6) JPS Phila.

Daughters of the Moon: Wish, Will, & Social Constraint in Fiction by Modern Japanese Women. Victoria V. Vernon. LC 86-45977. (Japan Research Monograph: No. 9). 245p. (Orig.). (C). 1988. pap. 12.00 (0-912966-94-7) IEAS.

Daughters of the Moon: Witch Tales from Around the World. Ed. by Shahrukh Husain. (Illus.). 244p. 1994. 22.95 (0-571-19856-2) Faber & Faber.

***Daughters of the Moon: Witch Tales from Around the World.** Ed. by Shahrukh Husain. (Illus.). 244p. 1995. reprint ed. pap. 14.95 (0-571-19874-0) Faber & Faber.

Daughters of the Moon Tarot: Tarot of the Goddess. Ffiona Morgan. Ed. by Cherie Pei. (Illus.). 96p. 1991. reprint ed. pap. 9.95 (1-880130-01-7); reprint ed. 21.95 (1-880130-00-9) Daughters Moon.

Daughters of the New World. Susan R. Shreve. 1994. mass mkt. 5.99 (0-8041-1123-5) Ivy Books.

Daughters of the Prince. large type ed. Noel Barber. 1992. 21.95 (0-7927-1060-6, E0027, Eagle Lrg Print) Chivers N Amer.

Daughters of the Prince. large type ed. Noel Barber. 1992. pap. 17.95 (0-7927-1061-4, Paragon Lrg Print) Chivers N Amer.

Daughters of the Puritans: A Group of Brief Biographies. Seth C. Beach. LC 67-22054. (Essay Index Reprint Ser.). 1977. 21.95 (0-8369-0180-0) Ayer.

Daughters of the Reconquest: Women in Castilian Town Society, 1100-1300. Heath Dillard. (Cambridge Iberian & Latin American Studies). (Illus.). 296p. (C). 1990. pap. 19.95 (0-521-38737-X) Cambridge U Pr.

***Daughters of the Resistance: The Women's War to Free France.** Margaret C. Weitz. LC 95-7632. 1995. text ed. 30.00 (0-471-12676-4) Wiley.

***Daughters of the Revolution: Classic Essays by Women.** Ed. by James D. Lester. LC 95-11910. 1995. pap. write for info. (0-8442-5880-6) NTC Pub Grp.

Daughters of the Rich. Edgar Saltus. LC 75-116004. reprint ed. 37.50 (0-404-05540-0) AMS Pr.

Daughters of the Rich: A Play. Jack London. 1971. Octavo wrappers. 5.00 (0-910740-18-6) Holmes.

Daughters of the Shtetl: Life & Labor in the Immigrant Generation. Susan A. Glenn. LC 90-1557. (Illus.). 328p. 1990. 39.95 (0-8014-1966-2) Cornell U Pr.

Daughters of the Shtetl: Life & Labor in the Immigrant Generation. Susan A. Glenn. LC 90-1557. (Illus.). 328p. 1991. reprint ed. pap. 14.95 (0-8014-9759-0) Cornell U Pr.

Daughters of the Sphinx Ritual. 5.00 (0-685-19471-X) Powner.

Daughters of the State: A Social Portrait of the First Reform School for Girls in North America 1856-1905. Barbara M. Brenzel. (Joint Center for Urban Studies). (Illus.). 206p. 1985. pap. 9.95 (0-262-52104-0) MIT Pr.

Daughters of the Sun. Sally Hayton-Keeva. 400p. (Orig.). 1994. pap. 4.99 (0-451-17678-2, Onyx) NAL-Dutton.

***Daughters of the Sun: Short Stories from Western Australia.** Ed. by Bruce Bennett & Susan Miller. Date not set. pap. 16.95 (1-875560-26-2, Pub. by Univ of West Aust Pr AT) Intl Spec Bk.

Daughters of the Sun, Women of the Moon: An Anthology of Canadian Black Women Poets. Ayanna Black et al. Ed. by Ann Wallace. 107p. (Orig.). 1991. pap. text ed. 11.95 (0-88795-091-4, Pub. by Willms Wallce CN) Distributors.

Daughters of the Sun, Women of the Moon: Poetry by Black Canadian Women. Ed. by Ann Wallace. 1992. 29.95 (0-86543-194-9); pap. 9.95 (0-86543-195-7) Africa World.

Daughters of the Twilight. Farida Karodia. 1990. pap. 8.95 (0-7043-4017-8, Pub. by Womens Pr UK) Interlink Pub.

Daughters of Time: Creating Woman's Voice in Southern Story. Lucinda H. Mackethan. LC 89-4824. (Brown Thrasher Bks.). 144p. 1992. pap. 10.95 (0-8203-1444-7) U of Ga Pr.

Daughters of Time: Women in the Western Tradition. Mary Kinnear. (Women & Culture Ser.). (Illus.). 256p. 1982. pap. text ed. 15.95 (0-472-08029-6) U of Mich Pr.

Daughters of Troy see **Works**

Daughters of Vienna. Karl Adolph. Tr. by Josef Von Sternberg. 1991. lib. bdg. 75.00 (0-87700-976-7) Revisionist Pr.

Daughter's Promise. Julie Ellis. LC 87-30683. 464p. 1988. 19.95 (0-87795-954-4) Morrow.

Daughter's Promise. Julie Ellis. 1989. mass mkt. 4.95 (0-8217-2806-7) Zebra.

Daughter's Seduction: Feminism & Psychoanalysis. Jane Gallop. LC 81-70709. 164p. 1982. 26.95 (0-8014-1493-8); pap. 11.95 (0-8014-9235-1) Cornell U Pr.

Daughters Who Care: Daughters Caring for Mothers at Home. Jane Lewis & Barbara Meredith. 200p. (C). 1988. lib. bdg. 54.00 (0-415-00681-3) Routledge.

Daughters Who Dared: Answering God's Call to Nigeria. Gerald L. Zandstra & Winnabelle Gritter. 104p. (Orig.). 1992. pap. text ed. 8.95 (1-56212-018-2, 1700-8900) CRC Pubns.

Daughters, Wives, & Widows: Writings by Men about Women & Marriage in England, 1500-1640. Ed. by Joan L. Klein. 352p. 1992. 37.50 (0-252-01840-0); pap. 14.95 (0-252-06206-X) U of Ill Pr.

D'Aulaire's Book of Greek Myths. Ingri D'Aulaire. (J). (ps-3). 1992. pap. 15.95 (0-440-40694-3, YB) Dell.

D'Aulaires' Book of Greek Myths. Ingri D'Aulaire & Edgar P. D'Aulaire. LC 62-15877. (Illus.). (J). 1980. 20.00 (0-385-01583-6, Zephyr-BFYR) Doubleday.

D'Aulaires Book of Greek Myths: A Literature Unit. Cynthia Ross. (Literature Units Ser.). (Illus.). 48p. 1993. student ed 6.95 (1-55734-423-X) Tchr Create Mat.

D'Aulaire's Norse Gods & Giants. Ingri D'Aulaire & Edgar P. D'Aulaire. LC 86-11677. (Illus.). 168p. (J). (ps up). 1986. pap. 16.95 (0-385-23692-1, Zephyr-BFYR) Doubleday.

D'Aulaires' Norse Gods & Giants. Ingri D'Aulaire & Edgar D'Aulaire. 1993. 23.75 (0-8446-6692-0) Peter Smith.

D'Aulaire's Trolls. Ingri D'Aulaire. (J). (ps-3). 1993. mass mkt. 8.00 (0-440-40779-6) Dell.

D'Aulaires' Trolls. Ingri D'Aulaire & Edgar D'Aulaire. 1994. 19.25 (0-8446-6783-8) Peter Smith.

Daum. Clotilde Bacri. LC 92-41536. (Illus.). 272p. 1993. 85.00 (0-8478-1668-0) Rizzoli Intl.

Daumier: One Hundred Twenty Great Lithographs. Honore Daumier. Ed. by Charles Ramus. LC 77-83928. (Illus.). 1978. pap. 9.95 (0-486-23512-2) Dover.

Daumier: The Complete Engravings, L'Oeuvre Grave du Maitre, Catalogue Raisonne & Bibliography. Eugene Bouvy. (Illus.). 640p. (FRE.). 1995. reprint ed. 175.00 (1-55660-224-3) A Wofsy Fine Arts.

Daumier & Music. Honore Daumier. (Music Reprint Ser.). 1992. lib. bdg. 35.00 (0-306-76054-1) Da Capo.

Daumier Drawings. Colta Ives et al. LC 92-30905. (Illus.). 280p. 1993. 65.00 (0-685-61641-X); 65.00 (0-8109-6423-6) Abrams.

Daumier, Honore: Catalogue Raisonne of the Paintings, Watercolours & Drawings, 2 vols., Set, Vols. 1-2. K. E. Maison. (Illus.). 1995. reprint ed. Set, Vol. 1: Paintings, 446p. Vol. 2: Watercolours & Drawings, 620p. 350.00 (1-55660-251-0) A Wofsy Fine Arts.

Daumier on War. Ed. by Hans Rothe. LC 77-9349. (Quality Paperbacks Ser.). (Illus.). 1977. pap. 6.95 (0-306-80079-9) Da Capo.

Daumier's Complete Lithographs, 10 vols. Loys Delteil. (Illus.). 2500p. (FRE.). 1969. reprint ed. 2,000.00 (1-55660-030-5) A Wofsy Fine Arts.

Daumier's Financiers & Businessmen. Jean Adhemar. (Illus.). 1974. 25.00 (0-685-02929-8) L Amiel Pub.

Daumier's Hunting & Fishing. Tr. by Howard Brabyn. (Illus.). 140p. 1975. 12.98 (0-8148-0642-2) L Amiel Pub.

Daumier's Lithographs, 1830-37: Catalogue Raisonne. rev. ed. Loys Delteil. (Illus.). 352p. (ENG & FRE.). 1995. 150.00 (1-55660-250-2) A Wofsy Fine Arts.

Dauntless. Alan Evans. 1985. 14.95 (0-8027-0864-1) Walker & Co.

Dauntless. large type ed. Alan Evans. 464p. 1982. 15.95 (0-7089-0851-9) Ulverscroft.

Dauntless Dive Bomber of World War II. Barrett Tillman. LC 76-5200. (Illus.). 232p. 1976. 26.95 (0-87021-569-8) Naval Inst Pr.

Dauntless Durham of the U. S. A. Harry Hershfield. Ed. by Bill Blackbeard. LC 76-53046. (Classic American Comic Strips Ser.). (Illus.). 18.00 (0-88355-647-2); pap. 10.00 (0-88355-646-4) Hyperion Conn.

Dauntless Helldivers. Harold L. Buell. 1992. mass mkt. 5.99 (0-440-21239-1) Dell.

Dauntless Helldivers: A Dive Bomber Pilot's Epic Story of the Carrier Battles. Harold L. Buell. (Illus.). 320p. 1991. 22.00 (0-517-57794-1, Orion Bks) Crown Pub Group.

Dauntless in Mississippi: The Life of Sarah A. Dickey. Helen Griffith. LC 75-35885. 1976. reprint ed. 21.95 (0-89201-006-1) Zenger Pub.

Dauntless Women: Stories of Pioneer Wives. Winifred Mathews. LC 70-126325. (Biography Index Reprint Ser.). (Illus.). 1977. reprint ed. 18.95 (0-8369-8031-X) Ayer.

Dauntless Women in Childhood Education, 1856-1931. Agnes Snyder. LC 72-80018. (Illus.). 405p. 1972. pap. 12.35 (0-87173-021-9) ACEI.

Dauntless Women in Childhood Education, 1856-1931. Agnes Smith. Ed. by Margaret Rasmussen. LC 72-80018. (Illus.). 423p. reprint ed. pap. 120.60 (0-7837-2608-2, 2042772) Bks Demand.

Dauphin County Tombstone Inscriptions, Vol. 3. Oscar H. Stroh. 108p. 1993. pap. text ed. 16.00 (1-55856-123-4) Closson Pr.

Dausien's Grosses Pilzbuch in Farbe. Mirko Svrcek. Tr. by J. Ostmeyer. (Illus.). 313p. (GER.). 1983. lib. bdg. 27.50 (3-7684-2343-3) Lubrecht & Cramer.

Daut Niehe Tastament. Tr. by John J. Neufeld. 483p. (GER.). 1988. 15.95 (0-919797-76-8) Kindred Prods.

D'autres et Moi. Francois Mauriac. (FRE.). 1966. pap. 17.95 (0-7859-5303-5) Fr & Eur.

Dave. Dave Miller. (Illus.). 144p. 1994. pap. 7.95 (0-8092-3626-5) Contemp Bks.

***Dave & Jane in Outer Space.** Bob Knox. LC 95-13346. (Illus.). 32p. (J). 1995. 15.95 (0-8478-1916-7) Rizzoli Intl.

Dave & Jane's Adventures with Lewis & Clark. Bob Knox. LC 94-14446. (Illus.). 32p. (J). (gr. 2-7). 1994. 15.95 (0-8478-1834-9) Rizzoli Intl.

Dave & the Tooth Fairy. Verna Wilkins. (J). (ps-3). 1993. pap. 3.95 (0-85953-133-3) Childs Play.

***Dave & the Tooth Fairy.** Verna A. Wilkins. (Illus.). 24p. (J). 1995. lib. bdg. 12.95 (1-56674-120-3) Forest Hse.

Dave Barry Does Japan. Dave Barry. 224p. 1993. pap. 10.00 (0-449-90810-0, Columbine) Fawcett.

***Dave Barry Does Japan.** Dave Barry. 4.99 (0-517-13723-2) Random Hse Value.

Dave Barry Does Japan. Dave Barry. LC 92-53634. 1992. 18.00 (0-679-40485-6) Random.

Dave Barry Is Not Making This Up. Dave Barry. 1994. 20.00 (0-517-59574-5) Crown Pub Group.

***Dave Barry Is Not Making This Up.** Dave Barry. 256p. 1995. pap. 10.00 (0-449-90973-5) Fawcett.

Dave Barry is Not Making This Up. large type ed. Dave Barry. 1994. pap. 19.00 (0-679-75390-7) Random.

Dave Barry Slept Here: A Sort of History of the United States. Dave Barry. 192p. 1990. pap. 10.00 (0-449-90462-8, Columbine) Fawcett.

Dave Barry Talks Back. Dave Barry. (Illus.). 304p. 1991. 18.00 (0-517-58546-4, Crown) Crown Pub Group.

Dave Barry Talks Back. Dave Barry. (Illus.). 1992. 10.00 (0-517-58868-4, Crown) Crown Pub Group.

Dave Barry Turns Forty. Dave Barry. 1991. pap. 10.00 (0-449-90587-X) Fawcett.

Dave Barry's Bad Habits: A One Hundred Percent Fact-Free Book. Dave Barry. 304p. 1993. pap. 8.95 (0-8050-2964-8) H Holt & Co.

Dave Barry's Greatest Hits. Dave Barry. 1989. pap. 10.00 (0-449-90406-7, Columbine) Fawcett.

***Dave Barry's Guide to Guys: A User's Manual.** Dave Barry. 1995. 21.00 (0-679-40486-4) Random.

Dave Barry's Guide to Life: Dave Barry's Guide to Marriage & - or Sex, Babies & Other Hazards of Sex, Claw Your Way to the Top, Stay Fit & Healthy until You're Dead. Dave Barry. 384p. 1991. reprint ed. 9.99 (0-517-06486-3, Pub. by Wings Bks) Random Hse Value.

Dave Barry's Guide to Marriage & or Sex. Dave Barry. LC 87-18461. (Illus.). 96p. 1987. pap. 6.95 (0-87857-725-4, 20-718-1) Rodale Pr Inc.

***Dave Barry's Homes & Other Black Holes.** Dave Barry. 1995. mass mkt. 5.99 (0-345-39440-2) Ballantine.

Dave Barry's Only Travel Guide You'll Ever Need. Dave Barry. (Illus.). 192p. 1992. pap. 10.00 (*0-449-90759-7*, Columbine) Fawcett.

Dave Burbeck, Improvisations & Compositions: The Idea of Cultural Exchange: with Discography. Ilse Storb & Klaus G. Fischer. LC 92-46477. 336p. (C). 1994. text ed. 45.95 (*0-8204-2003-4*) P Lang Pubs.

Dave Dravecky. Dave Dravecky & Tim Stafford. (Today's Heroes Ser.). 112p. (J). (gr. 3-9). 1993. pap. 4.99 (*0-310-58651-8*) Zondervan.

Dave Godfrey & His Works. Michael Larsen. (Canadian Author Studies). 55p. (C). 1989. pap. text ed. 9.95 (*0-920763-87-1*, Pub. by ECW Press CN) Genl Dist Srvs.

Dave Heeren's Basketball Abstract: 1991-1992 Edition. Dave Heeren. 1991. pap. 14.95 (*0-13-202995-2*) P-H.

Dave Hopfer's Fresh-Water Fish Cookbook, Vol. 1. Dave Hopfer. (Illus.). 1988. spiral bd. write for info. (*0-9621207-0-7*) D Hopfer Enter.

Dave Johnson. Dave Johnson & Verne Becker. (Today's Heroes Ser.). 112p. 1994. pap. 4.99 (*0-310-46181-2*) Zondervan.

***Dave Litfin's Expert Handicapping: Winning Insights into Betting Thoroughbreds.** Dave Litfin. LC 95-8508. 1995. 24.95 (*0-316-52781-5*) Little.

***Dave Miller's New Homebrewing Guide.** Dave Miller. LC 95-13385. 296p. 1995. pap. 14.95 (*0-88266-905-2*) Storey Comm Inc.

***Dave Perry's 100 Best Racing Rules Quizzes.** Dave Perry. 168p. 1994. pap. text ed. 16.95 (*1-882502-19-1*) US Sail Assn.

Dave Scott's Triathalon Training. Dave Scott & Liz Barrett. 1986. pap. 12.95 (*0-671-60473-2*, Fireside) S&S Trade.

Dave Was Right. Chuck Hanners. LC 89-51349. 125p. 1990. pap. 6.95 (*1-55523-263-9*) Winston-Derek.

Dave Whitlock's Guide to Aquatic Trout Foods. (Illus.). 224p. 1992. pap. 22.95 (*1-55821-202-7*) Lyons & Burford.

Dave Winfield. Judy Monroe. LC 87-30503. (Sports Close-Ups 2 Ser.). (Illus.). 48p. (J). (gr. 5-6). 1988. lib. bdg. 11.95 (*0-89686-370-0*, Crstwood Hse) Silver Burdett Pr.

Dave Winfield, Three Thousand & Counting. St. Paul Pioneer Pr. Staff. LC 93-36304. 1993. 9.95 (*0-8362-8046-6*) Andrews & McMeel.

Davenport Conspiracy Revisited. Marshall McKusick. (Illus.). 206p. 1991. 24.95 (*0-8138-0344-6*) Iowa St U Pr.

***Davenport Genealogy: History & Genealogy of the Ancestors & Descendants of the Rev. John Davenport.** Robert R. Davenport. 332p. 1982. text ed. 38.00 (*1-885943-00-8*) Eastwood Pubng.

Davenport Past & Present. Franc B. Wilkie. (Illus.). 333p. 1993. reprint ed. lib. bdg. 39.00 (*0-8328-2917-X*) Higginson Bk Co.

***Davenport-Schinzel Sequences & Their Geogetric Applications.** Micha Sharir & Pankaj K. Agarwal. (Illus.). 375p. (C). 1995. 49.95 (*0-521-47025-0*) Cambridge U Pr.

Davenport's Art Reference & Price Guide: 1994-95, 3 vols. 7th ed. R. J. Davenport. 2200p. 1994. 175.00 (*0-9616110-6-5*) Davenport Pub.

***Davenport's Art Reference & Price Guide, 1996-1997.** 8th rev. ed. Raymond J. Davenport. 2000p. 1995. 165.00 (*0-9616110-7-3*) Davenport Pub.

Davenport's Digest of Digestion. 3rd ed. Travis Solomon. 1991. 14.95 (*0-8151-8059-4*, Yr Bk Med Pubs) Mosby Yr Bk.

***Davera's Timeless Quest.** Brian Brechtel. 100p. 1996. pap. 7.95 (*0-7610-0510-2*) NW Pub.

***Dave's Diary: A Collection of Dave Brubeck Piano Solos.** Ed. by Tom Roed. 56p. (Orig.). (YA). 1995. pap. text ed. 12.95 (*0-89724-613-6*) Warner Brothers.

Dave's Tune: A Novel. June R. Welch. LC 73-84217. 200p. 1973. 15.95 (*0-912854-04-9*) Yellow Rose Pr.

***Dave's World: The Unauthorized Guide to the Late Show with David Letterman.** Michael Cader. (Illus.). 96p. (Orig.). 1995. pap. 8.99 (*0-446-67129-0*) Warner Bks.

Davey's Hanukkah Golem. David Gantz. LC 91-2328. (Illus.). 32p. (J). (gr. k-3). 1991. 14.95 (*0-8276-0380-0*) JPS Phila.

David. Jane Bearman. LC 65-21753. (Illus.). (J). (gr. 3 up). 1975. 3.95 (*0-8246-0085-1*) Jonathan David.

David. Robert D. Cox. 189p. 1989. pap. 5.95 (*0-9621663-0-8*) Robair Pub.

David. Luc De Nanteuil. (Library of Great Painters). (Illus.). 168p. 1985. 49.50 (*0-8109-0833-6*) Abrams.

David. Susan L. Lingo & Melissa C. Downey. (Graded Activity - Resource Bks.). (Illus.). 32p. (J). (ps-7). 1992. student ed 3.99 (*0-87403-918-5*, 23-02528) Standard Pub.

David. F. B. Meyer. 1992. pap. 5.95 (*0-87508-342-0*) Chr Lit.

David. Bernard Noel. (CAL Art Ser.). 1990. 14.95 (*0-517-57317-2*, Crown) Crown Pub Group.

David. Marie Rothenberg & Mel White. (Illus.). 200p. 1984. pap. 3.99 (*0-8007-8589-4*) Revell.

David. Marie Rothenberg. 1986. pap. 4.50 (*0-425-08766-2*) Phoenix Soc.

David, Vol. I. Katherine Hershey. (Illus.). 52p. (J). (gr. k-6). 1972. pap. text ed. 9.45 (*1-55976-020-6*) CEF Press.

David, Vol. II. Katherine Hershey. (Illus.). 55p. (J). (gr. k-6). 1973. pap. text ed. 9.45 (*1-55976-021-4*) CEF Press.

David: A Heart for God. Stuart Briscoe. 180p. 1988. pap. 7.99 (*0-89693-466-7*, Victor Books) SP Pubns.

David: A Heart for God. Jack Kuhatschek. (LifeGuide Bible Studies). 62p. 1990. 4.99 (*0-8308-1063-3*, 1063) InterVarsity.

David: A Play. D. H. Lawrence. LC 74-6380. (Studies in D. H. Lawrence: No. 20). (C). 1974. lib. bdg. 75.00 (*0-8383-1960-2*) M S G Haskell Hse.

David: His Life & Psalms. Jim Jordon. 192p. 1989. pap. 6.99 (*0-89225-354-1*) Gospel Advocate.

David: His Life & Times. Ivor C. Powell. LC 90-36487. 368p. 1990. pap. 12.99 (*0-8254-3532-3*) Kregel.

David: King of Israel. F. W. Krummacher. LC 93-41453. 544p. 1994. pap. 14.99 (*0-8254-3061-5*) Kregel.

David: Man after God's Own Heart, 2 vols. Robbie Castleman. (Fisherman Bible Studyguide Ser.). 70p. 1981. Vol. 1, 70p. 4.99 (*0-87788-164-2*); Vol. 2, 63p. 4.99 (*0-87788-165-0*) Shaw Pubs.

David: Masters of Art. Luc De Nanteuil. 1990. 22.95 (*0-8109-3201-6*) Abrams.

David: Modelo De Liderato (Model of Leadership) K. Silva. (SPA.). Date not set. 4.50 (*1-56063-012-4*, 498459) Editorial Unilit.

***David: Seeking God Faithfully.** Gene A. Getz. LC 94-44608. 1995. 10.99 (*0-8054-6164-7*) Broadman.

David: Sinner & Believer. Carlo-Maria Martini. 187p. (C). 1990. 49.00 (*0-85439-322-6*, Pub. by St Paul Pubns UK) St Mut.

David: Testimony of a Holocaust Survivor. Ezra BenGershom. Tr. by J. A. Underwood. 320p. 1988. 31.50 (*0-85496-222-0*) Berg Pubs.

David see Abahn

***David, a Biography.** Barbara Cohen. (J). (gr. 4-7). 1995. 15.95 (*0-395-58702-6*, Clarion Bks) HM.

David A. Wells & the American Revenue System 1865-1870. Herbert R. Ferleger. LC 77-7106. (Perspectives in American History Ser.: No. 32). vi, 335p. 1977. reprint ed. lib. bdg. 37.50 (*0-87991-356-8*) Porcupine Pr.

David Aldens Daughter & Other Stories. Jane G. Austin. (Works of Jane (Goodin) Austin). 1989. reprint ed. lib. bdg. 79.00 (*0-7812-1836-5*) Rprt Serv.

David Alden's Daughter, & Other Stories of Colonial Times. Jane Austin. LC 71-98556. (Short Story Index Reprint Ser.). 1977. 21.95 (*0-8369-3130-0*) Ayer.

David & Alfred Smart Museum of Art: A Guide to the Collection. Ed. by Sue Taylor & Richard A. Born. (Illus.). 216p. 1990. 40.00 (*0-685-70297-9*); pap. 22.50 (*0-685-70298-7*) D & A Smart Museum.

David & Della. Paul Zindel. LC 93-12719. (Charlotte Zolotow Bk.). 176p. (YA). (gr. 7 up). 1993. lib. bdg. 13.89 (*0-06-023354-0*) HarpC Child Bks.

David & Goliath. (Children's Bible Stories Ser.). (Illus.). 24p. (J). 1993. 4.98 (*1-56173-720-8*) Pubns Intl Ltd.

***David & Goliath.** (Now You Can Read Bible Stories Ser.). 24p. (J). 1994. 3.98 (*0-86112-785-4*) Brimax Bks.

***David & Goliath.** (Bible Big Bks.). (Illus.). 8p. (J). 1994. pap. 14.99 (*1-55945-242-0*) Group Pub.

David & Goliath. Berthe Amoss. (Illus.). 10p. (J). (ps-7). 1989. pap. 2.95 (*0-922589-12-7*) More than Card.

***David & Goliath.** Leon Baxter. (Let's Play Ser.). (Illus.). 24p. (J). (ps-2). 1995. 3.99 (*0-7459-3192-8*) Lion USA.

David & Goliath. Illus. & Adapt. by Leonard E. Fisher. LC 92-24063. 32p. (J). (ps-3). 1993. lib. bdg. 15.95 (*0-8234-0997-X*) Holiday.

David & Goliath. Penny Frank. (Lion Story Bible Ser.). (Illus.). 24p. (J). (gr. 1 up). 1986. 3.99 (*0-85648-743-0*) Lion USA.

***David & Goliath.** Ed. by Henrietta Gambill. (Illus.). 9p. (J). 1995. text ed. 7.99 (*0-7847-0340-X*, 24-03706) Standard Pub.

David & Goliath. Anne Gill. (Tiny Bible Tales Ser.). (J). (ps-3). 1994. 4.95 (*0-8167-3318-X*) BridgeWater.

David & Goliath. M. Good. 1993. 2.00 (*0-317-05262-4*) Rod & Staff.

David & Goliath. Martha S. Jander. (Arch Bks.). (Illus.). 24p. (Orig.). (J). (gr. k-4). 1994. pap. 1.89 (*0-570-09034-2*) Concordia.

David & Goliath. Eric Metaxas. (Greatest Stories Ever Told Ser.). (Illus.). 40p. (J). (gr. k up). 1993. audio 19.95 (*0-88708-295-5*, Rabbit); 14.95 (*0-88708-294-7*, Rabbit) S&S Childrens.

David & Goliath. Illus. by Pat Schories. (Read along with Me Bible Stories Ser.). 24p. (J). (ps-3). 1992. 4.95 (*1-56288-221-X*) Checkerboard.

***David & Goliath.** Illus. by Kay Widdowson. (Mini Pop-ups Ser.). (J). (ps-1). 1995. 4.99 (*1-884628-13-3*) Flying Frog.

David & Goliath. Guy Williams. LC 90-53572. (Orig.). (J). (gr. 3 up). 1991. pap. 5.00 (*0-88734-411-9*) Players Pr.

David & Goliath & Five Other Stories. Peter Enns & Glen Forsberg. (Stories that Live Ser.: Bk. 3). (Illus.). 24p. (J). (ps-5). 1985. audio 4.95 (*0-936215-03-8*) STL Intl.

David & His God: Religious Ideas As Reflected in Biblical Historiography & Literature. Shamai Gelander. (Jerusalem Biblical Studies: Vol. 5). 205p. (ENG & HEB.). 1991. pap. text ed. 30.00 (*0-685-72502-2*, Pub. by Simor Ltd IS) Eisenbrauns.

David & His Mighty Men. R. O. Corvin. LC 74-136646. (Biography Index Reprint Ser.). 1977. 19.95 (*0-8369-8041-7*) Ayer.

David & His Songs see King David & His Songs: A Story of the Psalms

David & I Talk to God Series. Campbell Murphy. (J). (ps-2). 1983. pap. 2.95 (*0-686-45018-3*, Chariot Bks) Chariot Family.

David & Jonathan. Alyce Bergey. (Arch Bks.). (Illus.). 24p. (J). (gr. k-4). 1987. pap. 1.89 (*0-570-09006-7*, 59-1434) Concordia.

David & Jonathan. Cynthia Voight. (YA). 1994. pap. 3.95 (*0-590-45166-9*) Scholastic Inc.

David & Jonathan. Cynthia Voight. 208p. (J). 1992. 14.95 (*0-590-45165-0*, Scholastic Hardcover) Scholastic Inc.

David & Max. Gary Provost & Gail Levine-Provost. 196p. (J). (gr. 5-9). 1991. pap. 9.95 (*0-8276-0392-4*) JPS Phila.

***David & Prince Jonathan.** (Bible Big Bks.). (Illus.). 8p. (J). 1994. pap. 14.99 (*1-55945-244-7*) Group Pub.

David & Susan at the Little Green House. Mary M. Landis. 1975. 6.70 (*0-686-11146-X*) Rod & Staff.

David & Susan at Wild Rose Cottage. Mary M. Landis. 1979. 7.85 (*0-686-22988-6*) Rod & Staff.

David & the Deuteronomist: A Literary Study of the Deuteronomic History, Pt. 3: 2 Samuel. Robert Polzin. LC 93-22056. (Literary Study of the Deuteronomic History Ser.: Pt. 3). 1993. 39.95 (*0-253-34553-7*) Ind U Pr.

***David & the Dummy & Other Stories for Children.** Sarah Neuberger. 1995. 7.95 (*0-533-11425-X*) Vantage.

David & the Giant. Emily Little. LC 86-22079. (Step into Reading Bks.). (Illus.). 48p. (J). (ps-1). 1987. lib. bdg. 7.99 (*0-394-98867-1*); pap. 3.50 (*0-394-88867-7*) Random Bks Yng Read.

David Anhaghte: The "Invincible" Philosopher. Ed. by Avedis Sanjian. LC 86-20443. (UCLA Studies in Near Eastern Culture & Society). 166p. 1987. 20.95 (*1-55540-067-1*, 22-00-07); pap. 15.95 (*1-55540-068-X*) Scholars Pr GA.

David Anton Randall, 1905-1975. Dean H. Keller. (Great Bibliographers Ser.: No. 10). 248p. 1992. 39.50 (*0-8108-2624-0*) Scarecrow.

David Astor & the Observer. Richard Cockett. (Illus.). 320p. 1992. 39.95 (*0-233-98735-5*, Pub. by A Deutsch UK) Trafalgar.

David Austen, No. 43. Ed. by Kyoichi Tsuzuki. (Art Random Ser.). (Illus.). 48p. 1990. 32.95 (*4-7636-8502-3*, Pub. by Kyoto Shoin JA) Bks Nippan.

David Austin's English Roses: Glorious New Roses for American Gardens. David Austin. 1993. 40.00 (*0-316-05975-7*) Little.

***David Baker: Avatars of the Tortoise.** Jerry Saltz. (Illus.). 44p. (Orig.). 1990. pap. text ed. 10.00 (*0-614-00474-8*) Contemp Art Mus.

David Baker's Arranging & Composing, for the Small Ensemble: Jazz - R&B - Jazz & Rock. rev. ed. David Baker. 176p. (C). 1985. pap. text ed. 21.95 (*0-88284-469-5*, 2750) Alfred Pub.

David Balfour: Being Memoirs of the Further Adventures of David Balfour at Home & Abroad. Robert Louis Stevenson. LC 94-6961. (J). 1994. text ed. 25.00 (*0-684-19736-7*, Scribners); text ed. 75.00 (*0-684-19735-9*, Scribners) S&S Trade.

David Barbero Recent Paintings: The Paintings of David Barbero. Ed. by Nancy Pierson. (Illus.). 32p. (C). 1988. write for info. (*0-913763-02-0*) E Mayans Gallery.

David Barbero Recent Paintings: The Paintings of David Barbero. Ed. by Nancy Pierson. (Illus.). 32p. (C). 1989. write for info. (*0-913763-05-5*) E Mayans Gallery.

David Bates: Forty Paintings. Marla Price. Ed. by Jane Sweeney. LC 88-62325. (Illus.). 100p. (Orig.). 1988. pap. 20.00 (*0-929865-00-6*) Mod Art Mus Ft Worth.

David Baumgardt & Ethical Hedonism. Ze'ev Levy. 1989. 39.50 (*0-88125-304-9*) Ktav.

David Belasco: Naturalism in the American Theatre. Lise-Lone Marker. LC 74-2970. 271p. reprint ed. pap. 77.30 (*0-8357-3421-8*, 2039678) Bks Demand.

David Ben-Gurion: Politics & Leadership in Israel. Ronald W. Zweig. 1992. text ed. 37.50 (*0-7146-3423-9*, Pub. by F Cass Pubs UK) Intl Spec Bk.

David Ben Gurion Album. Rivlin. 1987. 24.95 (*0-915361-76-0*) Modan-Adama Bks.

David Ben-Gurion & the American Alignment for a Jewish State. Allon Gal. LC 91-18446. (Modern Jewish Experience Ser.). 1992. 29.95 (*0-253-32534-X*) Ind U Pr.

David Bernard: Prints & Sculptures, A Retrospective 1947-1982. Howard E. Wooden. LC 82-63188. (Illus.). 13p. 1983. pap. 5.00 (*0-939324-09-1*) Wichita Art Mus.

David Black: An American Sculptor. Ruth K. Meyer. (Illus.). (Orig.). 1985. pap. 3.00 (*0-915577-06-2*) Taft Museum.

David Black: Sculpture As Proto-Architecture. 1987. pap. 7.50 (*0-933742-10-X*) Kalamazoo Inst Arts.

David Blackburn: Light & Landscape. Peter Fuller. (Illus.). 48p. (Orig.). 1989. pap. 12.95 (*0-930606-59-0*) Yale Ctr Brit Art.

David Bohm's World: New Physics & New Religion. Kevin J. Sharpe. LC 92-55002. 1993. 32.50 (*0-8387-5239-X*) Bucknell U Pr.

David Bomberg. Richard Cork. LC 86-23402. 352p. 1987. text ed. 110.00 (*0-300-03827-5*) Yale U Pr.

David Bomberg. Richard Cork. LC 86-23402. 352p. 1988. pap. 42.00 (*0-300-04194-2*) Yale U Pr.

David Bowes, No. 3. Ed. by Kyoichi Tsuzuki. (Art Random Ser.). (Illus.). 48p. 1990. 32.95 (*4-7636-8508-2*, Pub. by Kyoto Shoin JA) Bks Nippan.

***David Bowie: An Illustrated Record.** Carr & Murray. (Illus.). Date not set. per. 14.95 (*0-906008-25-5*, Pub. by Plexus Pub UK) InBook.

***David Bowie: Moonage Daydream.** Thomson. Date not set. per. 14.95 (*0-85965-140-1*, Pub. by Plexus Pub UK) InBook.

David Bowie: The Starzone Interviews. Ed. by David Currie. (Illus.). 128p. 1985. pap. 19.95 (*0-7119-0685-8*, OP43355) Omnibus NY.

David Bowie Anthology. David Bowie. (Piano-Vocal-Guitar Personality Folio Ser.). 216p. 1985. pap. 19.95 (*0-88188-360-3*, HL 00356339) H Leonard.

David Bowie Black Book. Miles Charlesworth & Chris Charlesworth. (Illus.). 144p. 1988. pap. 19.95 (*0-7119-1438-9*, OP41029) Omnibus NY.

David Boyle: From Artisan to Archaeologist. Gerald Killan. 288p. 1983. pap. 15.95 (*0-8020-6496-5*) U of Toronto Pr.

David Boyle: From Artisan to Archaeologist. Gerald Killan. LC 84-29842. (Illus.). 302p. reprint ed. pap. 86.10 (*0-8357-8086-4*, 2034046) Bks Demand.

David Brainerd, Vol. 2. Jesse Page. 1979. pap. 4.99 (*0-88019-015-9*) Schmul Pub Co.

***David Braves the Giant.** Little. 2.99 (*0-679-87518-2*) Random.

David Bronstein: Chess Improviser. B. S. Vainstein. Tr. by K. P. Neat. LC 82-22403. (Russian Chess Ser.). 194p. 1983. 27.90 (*0-08-029723-4*, Pergamon Pr) Elsevier.

David Broome's Training Manual. Marcy Pavord. (Illus.). 152p. 1994. 29.95 (*1-57076-008-X*, Trafalgar Sq Pub) Trafalgar.

David Brower: Friend of the Earth. Debby Anker & John De Graff. (Earth Keepers Ser.). (Illus.). 80p. (J). (gr. 4-7). 1993. lib. bdg. 14.95 (*0-8050-2124-8*, TFC Bks NY) H Holt & Co.

David Bruce's "Long Telegram" of July 3, 1951. Martin F. Herz. LC 78-71946. 26p. (Orig.). 1979. pap. 5.00 (*0-934742-24-3*) Geo U Inst Dplmcy.

David Bruce's Long Telegram of July 3, 1951. Martin F. Herz. (Illus.). 30p. (C). 1986. reprint ed. pap. text ed. 9.00 (*0-8191-5051-7*, Inst Study Diplomacy) U Pr of Amer.

David Bumbeck: Prints. Danny Brown & David Bumbeck. (Illus.). (Orig.). 1989. pap. 20.00 (*0-685-31756-0*) Middlebury Coll Mus.

***David Burliuk: Years of Transition, 1910-1931.** Intro. by Helen Harrison. (Illus.). 16p. (C). 1978. pap. 1.00 (*0-614-00849-2*) Parrish Art.

David Bushnell & His Turtle: The Story of America's First Submarine. June Swanson. LC 90-628. (Illus.). 40p. (J). (gr. 2-5). 1991. text ed. 13.95 (*0-689-31628-3*, Atheneum Bks Young) S&S Childrens.

David Butler: Interviewed by Irene Khan Atkins. David Butler. LC 93-29551. (Directors Guild of America Oral History Ser.: No. 5). (Illus.). 337p. 1993. 42.50 (*0-8108-2705-0*) Scarecrow.

David by the Sea, Twenty-Five, Unshaven. T. Richard Williams. (Illus.). 37p. (Orig.). 1993. pap. text ed. 6.95 (*1-56315-074-3*) Sterling Hse.

David Byrne. John Howell. (American Originals Ser.). 160p. 1992. pap. 11.95 (*1-56025-031-3*) Thunders Mouth.

David C. Broderick: A Political Portrait. David A. Williams. LC 79-85342. (Huntington Library Publications). 288p. reprint ed. pap. 82.10 (*0-7837-5289-X*, 2045043) Bks Demand.

David C. Sacco: An American Master. David C. Sacco. Ed. by Rita Goldman. (Illus.). 48p. Date not set. 25.00 (*0-9638842-0-4*) Mstr Touch Gallery.

David Cannon Dashiell: "Queer Mysteries" Nayland Blake et al. LC 93-84527. (Illus.). 32p. (Orig.). 1993. pap. 8.00 (*0-930495-20-9*) San Fran Art Inst.

***David Carradine's Tai Chi Workout: The Beginner's Program for a Healthier Mind & Body.** David Carradine & David Nakahara. (Illus.). 1995. pap. 11.95 (*0-8050-3767-5*, Owl) H Holt & Co.

David Caspar Friedrich. Ed. by B. Asvarishch. (Illus.). (C). 1985. text ed. 90.00 (*0-685-40277-0*, Pub. by Collets) St Mut.

David Chipperfield. Intro. by Kenneth Frampton. (Illus.). 96p. (ENG & SPA.). 1993. pap. 28.95 (*84-252-1555-2*) Rizzoli Intl.

***David Christian Crummey & His Wife Addie Maria Bean; Judson Lysander Gelatt & His Wife Ella Venelia Dow of Santa Clara County, California: Their Forebearers & Their Descendants.** xii, 128p. 1995. per., pap. write for info. (*0-929626-07-9*) Rose Family Assn.

David Claypool Johnston, American Graphic Humorist, 1798-1865. Malcolm Johnson. (Illus.). 1970. 10.00 (*0-89073-028-8*); pap. 4.00 (*0-685-72185-X*) Boston Public Lib.

David Comes into the Kingdom. Gordon Lindsay. (Old Testament Ser.: Vol. 22). 1965. 1.95 (*0-89985-142-8*) Christ for the Nations.

David Copperfield. (Book Notes Ser.). 1985. pap. 2.50 (*0-8120-3509-7*) Barron.

David Copperfield. Ed. by Harold Bloom. (Major Literary Characters Ser.). 272p. 1992. lib. bdg. 29.95 (*0-7910-0937-8*) Chelsea Hse.

David Copperfield: Grandes Esperances. Charles Dickens. (FRE.). 105.00 (*0-8288-3432-6*, M5090) Fr & Eur.

David Copperfield: Interweaving Truth & Fiction. Graham Storey. (Twayne's Masterworks Ser.: No. 68). 120p. 1991. text ed. 21.95 (*0-8057-9415-8*, Twayne); pap. 12.95 (*0-8057-8142-0*, Twayne) Macmillan.

***David Copperfield, Hard Times: Charles Dickens.** Ed. by John Peck. LC 94-35204. (New Casebooks Ser.). 1995. write for info. (*0-312-12492-9*) St Martin.

David Copperfield Notes. J. M. Lybyer. 1980. pap. 3.75 (*0-8220-0364-3*) Cliffs.

David Copperfield's Library. J. Langstaff. 1972. 59.95 (*0-87968-998-6*) Gordon Pr.

***David Coulthard - The Flying Scotsman.** Jim Dunn. (Illus.). 176p. 1995. pap. 21.95 (*1-85260-530-8*, Pub. by J H Haynes & Co UK) Motorbooks Intl.

David Crockett: His Life & Adventures. John Abbott. 1993. reprint ed. lib. bdg. 75.00 (*0-7812-5860-X*) Rprt Serv.

David Crockett: Sure He Was Right. Mary D. Wade. (Illus.). 64p. (J). (gr. 2-3). 1992. 11.95 (*0-89015-854-1*) Sunbelt Media.

David Crockett: The Man & the Legend. Ed. by James A. Shackford. LC 86-40193. 364p. reprint ed. pap. 103.80 (*0-7837-5232-6*, 2044966) Bks Demand.

David Cronenberg: A Delicate Balance. Peter Morris. (Illus.). 160p. 1994. pap. 9.95 (*1-55022-191-4*, Pub. by Jon Pubng UK) InBook.

David d'Angers: Sculptural Communication in the Age of Romanticism. Jacques De Caso. Tr. by Dorothy Johnson. (Illus.). 210p. 1992. text ed. 49.50 (*0-691-04078-8*) Princeton U Pr.

David David. Cynthia Todd & Debbie Ziemann. (Sing Me a Song Ser.). (Illus.). 23p. (J). (gr. k-6). 1990. lib. bdg. 7.95 (*1-879056-01-1*) Alpenhorn Pr.

David Decides: No More Thumb-Sucking - An Interactive Tale for Children & Parents. Susan Heitler. 112p. (Orig.). 1993. pap. 8.00 (*0-380-76852-6*) Avon.

D

David Delafield: A Retrospective of an Iowa Artist 1939-1983. Daniel E. Stetson. Ed. by Kevin Boatright. 12p. (Orig.). 1983. pap. 3.50 (0-932660-09-6) U of NI Dept Art.

David Deutsch. Klaus Ottmann & Ross Bleckner. Ed. by Elizabeth Cunnick. (Illus.). 36p. (Orig.). 1989. pap. 10.00 (0-924008-02-4) Blum Helman.

David Diamond: A Bio-Bibliography. Victoria J. Kimberling. LC 87-16536. (Illus.). 192p. 1987. 20.00 (0-8108-2058-7) Scarecrow.

David Dreaming of Dinosaurs. Keith Faulkner. (Illus.). (J). (ps-3). 1992. 13.00 (1-56021-182-2) W J Fantasy.

David Duke: Evolution of a Klansman. Michael Zatarain. LC 90-7339. 272p. 1990. 22.95 (0-88289-817-5) Pelican.

***David Duke & the Rebirth of Race in Southern Politics.** Ed. by John C. Kuzenski et al. 168p. (Orig.). (C). 1995. write for info. (0-8265-1266-6) Vanderbilt U Pr.

David Eccles: Pioneer Western Industrialist. Leonard J. Arrington. LC 75-2093. (Illus.). 310p. reprint ed. pap. 88.40 (0-7837-6213-5, 2045937) Bks Demand.

David Edgar: Playwright & Politician. Elizabeth Swain. (American University Studies: English Language & Literature: Ser. IV, Vol. 36). 345p. 1986. text ed. 42.00 (0-8204-0288-5) P Lang Pubs.

David Fairchild's the World Was My Garden. LC 82-72427. (Illus.). 494p. 1982. reprint ed. 20.00 (0-916224-82-1) Banyan Bks.

***David Farragut.** Chrisman. (J). 1995. pap. text ed. (0-8114-6754-6) Raintree Steck-V.

David Farragut. Abbott Chrisman. LC 88-37398. (Hispanic Stories Ser.). (Illus.). 32p. (J). (gr. 4-5). 1991. lib. bdg. 19.97 (0-8172-2904-3) Raintree Steck-V.

David Farragut & the Great Naval Blockade. Russell Shorto. (History of the Civil War Ser.). (Illus.). 160p. (J). (gr. 5 up). 1990. lib. bdg. 12.95 (0-382-09941-9); pap. 7.95 (0-382-24050-2) Silver Burdett Pr.

***David Frost.** Frost. 1995. pap. text ed. 13.00 (0-00-638082-4) Basic.

David G. Burnet: From New Jersey to Texas. Ruth J. Carnes. 64p. (J). (gr. 4-7). 1986. 10.95 (0-89015-583-6) Sunbelt Media.

David Garrick. Joseph Knight. LC 74-91904. 1972. 26.95 (0-405-08711-X, Pub. by Blom Pubns UK) Ayer.

David Garrick. A Critical Biography. George W. Stone, Jr. & George M. Kahrl. LC 79-9476. (Illus.). 791p. 1979. 60.00 (0-8093-0931-9) S Ill U Pr.

David Garrick & His French Friends. Frank A. Hedgcock. LC 70-81976. (Illus.). 1972. 31.95 (0-405-08610-5, Pub. by Blom Pubns UK) Ayer.

David Garrick, Dramatist. Elizabeth P. Stein. LC 67-23859. 1972. 22.95 (0-405-08994-5, Pub. by Blom Pubns UK) Ayer.

***David Gentleman's India.** David Gentleman. (Illus.). 192p. 1995. 39.95 (0-340-58160-3, Pub. by H & S UK) Trafalgar.

David Gentleman's Paris. David Gentleman. (Illus.). 192p. 1992. 50.00 (0-312-07694-0) St Martin.

David Gentleman's Paris. David Gentleman. (Illus.). 192p. 1993. pap. 24.95 (0-340-57244-2, Pub. by H & S UK) Trafalgar.

David Gilhooly. Kenneth Baker et al. (Illus.). 150p. 1992. 40.00 (1-881572-99-4) J Natsoulas.

David Glasgow Farragut. Charles L. Lewis. LC 79-6115. (Navies & Men Ser.). (Illus.). 1980. Vol. Repr. Of 1941 Ed. lib. bdg. 38.95 (0-405-13043-0); Vol. 2, Repr. Of 1943 Ed. lib. bdg. 44.95 (0-405-13044-9) Ayer.

David Glasgow Farragut: Courageous Naval Officer. Leila M. Foster. LC 91-8031. (People of Distinction Ser.). (Illus.). 152p. (J). (gr. 4 up). 1991. lib. bdg. 14.48 (0-516-03273-9); pap. 5.95 (0-516-43273-7) Childrens.

David Glasgow Farragut: Our First Admiral. Jean L. Latham. (Discovery Biographies Ser.). (Illus.). 80p. (J). (gr. 2-6). 1991. reprint ed. lib. bdg. 12.95 (0-7910-1438-X) Chelsea Hse.

***David Glendenning Cogan, M. D. The How Laboratory of Ophthalmology at Harvard Medical School, the Massachusetts Eye & Ear Infirmary, & the National Eye Institute.** David G. Cogan. (Ophthalmology Oral History Ser.). (Illus.). xxvii, 256p. 1990. pap. 45.00 (0-926886-05-3) FAAO.

David Goines Poster Book. David Goines. 1994. 19.95 (0-89815-651-3) Ten Speed Pr.

David Graham Phillips. Abe C. Ravitz. (Twayne's United States Authors Ser.). 1966. lib. bdg. 17.95 (0-8290-0006-2); pap. text ed. 4.95 (0-685-42217-8) Irvington.

David Graham Phillips. Abe C. Ravitz. (Twayne's United States Authors Ser.). 1966. pap. 13.95x (0-8084-0098-3, T96) NCUP.

David Graham's Guide to Golf Equipment. David Graham. 160p. 1993. pap. 16.95 (0-8048-1848-7) C E Tuttle.

David Hammons: Rousing the Rubble. Steve Cannon et al. LC 91-61578. (Illus.). 96p. 1991. 27.50x (0-262-03184-1) MIT Pr.

***David Hammons in the Hood.** Robert Sill. LC 94-32133. 1994. write for info. (0-89792-144-5) Ill St Museum.

David Hare. Joan F. Dean. (Twayne's English Authors Ser.: No. 480). 168p. (C). 1990. text ed. 22.95 (0-8057-6997-8, Twayne) Macmillan.

David Hare: A Casebook. Ed. by Hersh Zeifman. LC 94-6740. (Reference Library of the Humanities, Casebooks on Modern Dramatists: Vol. 18). 280p. 1994. 42.00 (0-8240-2579-2, H1240) Garland.

David Hare: Theatricalizing Politics. Judy L. Oliva. LC 89-27751. (Theatre & Dramatic Studies: No. 66). 216p. (C). reprint ed. 61.60 (0-8357-2048-9, 2070747) Bks Demand.

David Harvey's Geography. John Paterson. LC 83-22293. 232p. 1984. 56.00 (0-389-20441-2, N8003) B&N Imports.

David Has AIDS. Doris Sanford. LC 89-3162. (In Our Neighborhood Ser.). (Illus.). 28p. (J). (gr. k-4). 1989. 6.99 (0-88070-299-0, Gold & Honey) Questar Pubs.

David Henry Hwang. Douglas Street. LC 89-60059. (Western Writers Ser.: No. 90). (Illus.). 51p. (Orig.). 1989. pap. 3.95 (0-88430-089-7) Boise St U W Writ Ser.

David Hicks Style & Design. David Hicks. 1988. 29.95 (0-316-36070-8) Little.

David Hockney. (Art & Design Profiles Ser.). (Illus.). 80p. 1988. pap. 21.95 (0-312-01904-1) St Martin.

***David Hockney.** Peter Clothier. LC 94-34739. (Modern Masters Ser.). 1995. pap. 24.95 (0-7892-0036-8) Abbeville Pr.

***David Hockney.** Peter Clothier. LC 94-34739. (Modern Masters Ser.: 17). 1995. 35.00 (1-55859-642-9) Abbeville Pr.

***David Hockney.** Ed. by Paul Melia. LC 94-42848. (Critical Introductions to Art Ser.). 1995. text ed. write for info. (0-7190-4404-9, Pub. by Manchester Univ Pr UK); text ed. write for info. (0-7190-4405-7, Pub. by Manchester Univ Pr UK) St Martin.

David Hockney. Kenneth Silver. LC 94-11123. (Art Ser.). (Illus.). 24p. 1994. pap. 7.95 (0-8478-1820-9) Rizzoli Intl.

David Hockney. rev. ed. Marco Livingstone. LC 87-50185. (World of Art Ser.). (Illus.). 1988. reprint ed. pap. 11.95 (0-500-20224-9) Thames Hudson.

David Hockney: Graphics. David Hockney. (Illus.). 128p. 1992. pap. 39.95 (90-6918-100-2, Pub. by Museum Boymans-van NE) Dist Art Pubs.

***David Hockney: La Isla de Martha's Vineyard y Otros Lugares.** limited ed. Illus. by David Hockney. (Ediciones Especiales y de Bibliofilo Ser.). (SPA.). 1993. 600.00 (84-343-0450-3) Elliots Bks.

David Hockney: Looking at Pictures in a Book. David Hockney. (Illus.). 26p. 1981. pap. 10.00 (0-902825-17-8) Petersburg Pr.

David Hockney: Martha's Vineyard-My Third Sketchbook from the Summer of 1982. David Hockney. (Facsimile Reproduction Sketchbook Ser.). (Illus.). 160p. 1985. 130.00 (0-8109-1086-1) Abrams.

David Hockney: Poster Art. David Hockney. LC 94-25815. 1995. 24.95 (0-8118-0915-3) Chronicle Bks.

David Hockney Faces. Marco Livingstone. LC 86-83167. (Illus.). 96p. 1987. pap. 19.95 (0-500-27464-9) Thames Hudson.

***David Hockney Paintings.** Ulrich Luckhardt. Ed. by Paul Melia. (Illus.). 200p. 1994. 55.00 (3-7913-1381-9) TeNeues.

David Hockney Photographs. David Hockney. Ed. by Alain Sayag. (Illus.). 126p. 1982. 30.00 (0-902825-15-1) Petersburg Pr.

***David Hollowell.** Seymour Howard. (Illus.). 96p. 1995. 35.00 (0-295-97408-7) U of Wash Pr.

David Holzman's Diary: A Screenplay. L. M. Carson. LC 77-125153. (Illus.). 126p. 1970. 16.95 (0-910278-69-5) Boulevard.

David Huddle Reader: Selected Poetry & Prose. David Huddle. LC 93-13607. (Bread Loaf Series of Contemporary Writers). 287p. 1994. text ed. 40.00 (0-87451-652-8); pap. 16.95 (0-87451-644-7) U Pr of New Eng.

David Hume. John V. Price. (Twayne's English Authors Ser.: TEAS No. 77). 160p. 1991. text ed. 24.95 (0-8057-7004-6, Twayne) Macmillan.

David Hume. A. H. Basson. LC 78-26704. 183p. 1981. reprint ed. text ed. 49.75 (0-313-20668-6, BADH, Greenwood Pr) Greenwood.

David Hume. Thomas H. Huxley. Ed. by John Morley. LC 68-58382. (English Men of Letters Ser.). reprint ed. lib. bdg. 29.50 (0-404-51714-5) AMS Pr.

David Hume. Andre L. Leroy. Ed. by J. P. Mayer. LC 78-67413. (European Political Thought Ser.). (FRE.). 1980. reprint ed. lib. bdg. 28.95 (0-405-11713-2) Ayer.

David Hume: An Introduction to His Philosophical System. Terence Penelhum. LC 91-9096. (Series in the History of Philosophy). 240p. (C). 1992. 27.00 (1-55753-012-2); pap. 13.75 (1-55753-013-0) Purdue U Pr.

David Hume: Common-Sense Moralist, Sceptical Metaphysician. David F. Norton. LC 81-47937. 343p. reprint ed. pap. 97.80 (0-7837-6769-2, 2046599) Bks Demand.

David Hume: Critical Assessments, 1. Ed. by Stanley Tweyman. LC 94-7160. 1994. write for info. (0-415-11779-8) Routledge.

David Hume: Critical Assessments, Vols. 1-4, Set. Stanley Tweyman. LC 94-7160. 2000p. 1995. 635.00 (0-415-02012-3, B4161) Routledge.

David Hume: The Natural History of Religion. James Fieser. (Library of Liberal Arts). (Illus.). 112p. (Orig.). (C). 1991. pap. write for info. (0-02-337250-8) Macmillan.

David Hume & the History of England. Victor G. Wexler. LC 78-68423. (American Philosophical Society, Memoirs Ser.: No. 131). 126p. reprint ed. pap. 36.00 (0-8357-7916-5, 2036346) Bks Demand.

David Hume & the Problem of Reason: Recovering the Human Sciences. John W. Danford. LC 89-29104. 240p. (C). 1990. text ed. 28.00 (0-300-04667-7) Yale U Pr.

David Hume (1711-1776) & James Steuart (1712-1780) Mark Blaug. (Pioneers in Economics Ser.: Vol. 11). 320p. 1991. text ed. 119.95 (1-85278-473-3, Pub. by E Elgar Pub UK) Ashgate Pub Co.

David Hume's Argument Against Miracles: A Critical Analysis. Francis J. Beckwith. LC 89-33135. 160p. (C). 1989. lib. bdg. 34.00 (0-8191-7487-4) U Pr of Amer.

David Hume's Dialogues Concerning Natural Religion in Focus. Ed. by Stanley Tweyman. (Philosophers in Focus Ser.). 288p. 1991. 59.95 (0-415-02013-1, A5470); pap. 17.95 (0-415-02014-X, A5474) Routledge.

David Hume's Theory of Mind. Daniel E. Flage. 208p. 1990. 65.00 (0-415-02138-3, A4568) Routledge.

***David Humphrey: Paintings & Drawings, 1987-1994.** Ross Feld & Elaine King. (Illus.). 48p. 1995. pap. 28.95 (0-917562-68-2) Contemp Arts.

David Humphreys' "Life of General Washington," with George Washington's "Remarks" Ed. by Rosemarie Zagarri. LC 90-40542. (Illus.). 216p. 1991. 24.95 (0-8203-1293-2) U of Ga Pr.

***David Ireland: Skellig.** Jane Levy Reed & Andy Grundberg. 60p. 1995. pap. 40.00 (0-933286-65-1) Frnds Photography.

***David Irving: Revisionist Historian.** 1995. lib. bdg. write for info. (0-8490-7434-7) Gordon Pr.

David Irving's Hitler: A Faulty History Dissected. Eberhard Jackel. Tr. by H. David Kirk. LC 93-72355. 64p. (Orig.). 1993. pap. 5.95 (0-914539-08-6) Ben-Simon.

David J. Brewer: The Life of a Supreme Court Justice, 1837-1910. Michael J. Brodhead. LC 93-16866. 262p. (C). 1994. 39.95 (0-8093-1909-8) S Ill U Pr.

***David Janssen: My Fugitive.** Ellie Janssen. Ed. & Told to J. Michael Phelps. LC 94-24713. 1995. 18.95 (0-8119-0797-X) LIFETIME.

David Jayne Hill & the Problem of World Peace. Aubrey L. Parkman. LC 72-3530. 293p. 1975. 39.50 (0-8387-1259-2) Bucknell U Pr.

David Jones. Ed. by Roland Mathias. 144p. (C). 1976. pap. 20.00x (0-85088-372-5, Pub. by Gomer Pr UK) St Mut.

David Jones: A Commentary on Some Poetic Fragments. Christine Pagnoulle. viii, 162p. 1989. 35.00 (0-7083-0962-3, Pub. by U of Wales UK) Bks Intl VA.

David Jones: Man & Poet. Ed. by John Matthias. (Man & Poet Ser.). 580p. 1989. 55.00 (0-943373-03-4); pap. 30.00 (0-943373-04-2) Natl Poet Foun.

David Jones & Other Wonder Voyagers: Essays. Philip Pacey. 134p. 1982. 35.00 (0-907476-14-7) Dufour.

David Joris & Dutch Anabaptism, 1524-1543. Gary K. Waite. 240p. (C). 1990. text ed. 32.50 (0-88920-992-8, Pub. by Wilfrid Laurier CN) Humanities.

David Kimhi: The Man & the Commentaries. Frank E. Talmage. LC 75-1747. (Harvard Judaic Monographs: No. 1). 248p. reprint ed. pap. 70.70 (0-8357-8087-2, 2033941) Bks Demand.

David Knowles Remembered. Christopher N. Brooke et al. (Illus.). 200p. (C). 1991. 44.95 (0-521-37233-X) Cambridge U Pr.

David Kopay Story: An Extraordinary Self-Revelation. David Kopay & Perry D. Young. LC 87-46264. 1988. pap. 8.95 (1-55611-080-4, Primus Lib Contemp) D I Fine.

David L. Hostetler: The Carver. Richard Wootten. Ed. by Terrill Eiler. LC 91-36139. (Illus.). 112p. 1991. 39.95 (0-8214-1024-5) Ohio U Pr.

David Lant: The Vanished Outlaw. Douglas W. Ellison. 232p. (Orig.). (YA). 1988. pap. text ed. write for info. (0-929918-01-0) Midstates Pub.

David Lanz-Bridge of Dreams. (Piano Solos-Vocal Ser.). 64p. (Orig.). 1993. pap. 12.95 (0-7935-2929-8, HL00308212) H Leonard.

David Lanz Collection: New Age Piano Solos. 96p. (Orig.). 1992. pap. 12.95 (0-7935-1218-2, 00308126) H Leonard.

David Lanz Solos for New Age Piano. (Illus.). 80p. 1991. pap. 12.95 (0-7935-0057-5, 00490414) H Leonard.

David Leadbetter's Faults & Fixes: How to Correct the 80 Most Common Mistakes Golfers Make. David Leadbetter. LC 92-56202. (Illus.). 144p. 1993. 25.00 (0-06-016977-X, HarpT) HarpC.

David Lean. Stephen M. Silverman. (Illus.). 216p. 1992. pap. 19.95 (0-8109-2507-9) Abrams.

David Lean & His Films. Alain Silver & James Ursini. (Illus.). 265p. (Orig.). 1991. pap. 14.95 (1-879505-00-2) Silman James Pr.

***David Letterman.** Intro. by Leeza Gibbons. (Pop Culture Legends Ser.). (Illus.). 128p. (YA). (gr. 5 up). 1995. 18.95 (0-7910-3252-3) Chelsea Hse.

David Letterman: On Stage & Rosemarie Lennon. 320p. 1994. pap. 4.99 (0-7860-0084-8, Pinnacle NY) Windsor NY.

David Levine: Caricatures & Watercolours. Intro. by Nicholas Penny. (Illus.). 28p. 1995. pap. 6.96 (0-907849-83-0, 830, Pub. by Ashmolean Mus UK) A Schwartz & Co.

David Levine: Contemporary Master of Caricature. Howard D. Spencer. (Illus.). 8p. 1988. pap. 1.50 (0-939324-36-9) Wichita Art Mus.

***David Levinthal: Dark Light--Photographs 1984-1994.** David Allan Mellor. (Illus.). 48p. 1995. pap. 17.50 (0-907879-43-8) Dist Art Pubs.

***David Levinthal: Die Nibelungen.** Julien Robson. 1994. pap. 15.00 (1-881616-41-X) Dist Art Pubs.

David Lindsay. Gary K. Wolfe. Ed. by Roger C. Schlobin. LC 82-5563. (Starmont Reader's Guide Ser.: Vol. 9). ii, 64p. 1982. lib. bdg. 20.00 (0-916732-29-0); pap. 10.00 (0-916732-26-6) Borgo Pr.

David Lindsay's Vision. David Power. 40p. 1991. reprint ed. lib. bdg. 23.00x (0-8095-6764-4) Borgo Pr.

***David Lindsay's Vision.** David Power. 40p. 1991. reprint ed. pap. 13.00x (0-946650-30-6) Borgo Pr.

David, Lion & Lamb. Michael Mills. Ed. by Michael L. Sherer. (Orig.). 1988. pap. 7.10 (1-55673-029-2, 8814) CSS OH.

***David Livingston.** Ben Alex. 42p. 1995. pap. 7.99 (1-56476-474-5, 6-3474, Victor Books) SP Pubns.

David Livingstone. (SPA.). 4.95 (84-7228-940-0, 223010, Pub. by Edit Clie SP) TSELF.

David Livingstone. Dan Larsen. (Young Reader's Christian Library). (J). (gr. 3 up). 1992. per., pap. 2.50 (1-55748-259-4) Barbour & Co.

David Livingstone. J. H. Worchester, Jr. (Golden Oldies Ser.). 128p. 1980. pap. 4.99 (0-8024-4782-1) Moody.

David Livingstone: Letters & Documents, 1841-1872. Ed. by Timothy Holmes. LC 89-24725. 222p. 1990. 39.95 (0-253-33516-7) Ind U Pr.

David Livingstone: The Truth Behind the Legend. Rob Mackenzie. (Orig.). 1993. pap. 32.50 (0-85476-387-2) Trans-Atl Phila.

David Lloyd, Colonial Lawmaker. Roy N. Lokken. LC 59-13419. (Publications in History Ser.). (Illus.). 319p. 1959. 20.00 (0-295-73762-X) U of Wash Pr.

David Lloyd George. Deirdre Shearman. (World Leaders - Past & Present Ser.). (Illus.). 112p. (YA). (gr. 5 up). 1988. lib. bdg. 17.95 (0-87754-581-2) Chelsea Hse.

David Lloyd George: Welsh Radical As World Statesman. Kenneth O. Morgan. LC 82-2988. 85p. 1982. reprint ed. text ed. 49.75 (0-313-23453-1, MODG, Greenwood Pr) Greenwood.

David Lloyd George, a Political Life, Vol. II: Organizer of Victory, 1912-1916. Bentley B. Gilbert. (Illus.). 1992. lib. bdg. 65.00 (0-8142-0597-6) Ohio St U Pr.

David Lloyd George, a Political Life, Vol. 1: The Architect of Change 1863-1912. Bentley B. Gilbert. LC 86-33211. 544p. 1987. 54.50 (0-8142-0432-5) Ohio St U Pr.

David Lloyd George & the British Labour Movement: Peace & War. Chris Wrigley. (Modern Revivals in Economic & Social History Ser.). 312p. 1992. 61.95 (0-7512-0072-7, Pub. by Gregg Revivals UK) Ashgate Pub Co.

David Lodge: How Far Can You Go? Merritt Moseley. LC 89-29632. (Milford Ser.: Popular Writers of Today: Vol. 16). viii, 112p. 1991. lib. bdg. 25.00x (0-8095-5204-3); pap. 15.00x (0-8095-5229-9) Borgo Pr.

David Low. Colin Seymour-Ure & Jom Schoff. (Illus.). 180p. 1987. pap. 22.95 (0-436-44755-X, Pub. by Seck & Warburg UK) HarpC.

***David Lynch.** Michel Chion. 1994. pap. 21.95 (0-85170-457-3, Pub. by British Film Inst UK) Ind U Pr.

***David Lynch.** Michel Chion. 1994. 45.00 (0-85170-456-5) Ind U Pr.

David Lynch. Kenneth Kaleta. (Twayne's Filmmakers Ser.). 160p. 1992. text ed. 22.95 (0-8057-9317-8, Twayne); pap. 13.95 (0-8057-9323-2, Twayne) Macmillan.

David Mach, No. 74. Ed. by Kyoichi Tsuzuki. (Art Random Ser.). (Illus.). 48p. 1991. 32.95 (4-7636-8576-7, Pub. by Kyoto Shoin JA) Bks Nippan.

David Malouf. Ivor Indyk. (Australian Writers Ser.). 128p. 1993. pap. 17.95 (0-19-553321-6) OUP.

David Malouf: Johnno, Short Stories, Poems, Essays & Interviews. Ed. by James Tulip. 1991. pap. 19.95 (0-7022-2310-7, Pub. by Univ Queensland Pr AT) Intl Spec Bk.

David Malouf: Selected Poems. David Malouf. 120p. (Orig.). 1992. pap. 10.00 (0-207-17280-3, Pub. by Angus & Robertson AT) HarpC.

David Mamet. C. W. Bigsby. (Contemporary Writers Ser.). 96p. 1985. pap. 8.95 (0-416-40980-6, 9597) Routledge Chapman & Hall.

David Mamet. Dennis Carroll. (Modern Dramatists Ser.). 183p. 1992. pap. 11.95 (0-333-41366-0) St Martin.

David Mamet: A Casebook. Leslie Kane. LC 91-18448. (Casebooks on Modern Dramatists Ser.: Vol. 12). 352p. 1991. 47.00 (0-8240-8196-X, H1211) Garland.

David Mamet: Language As Dramatic Action. Anne Dean. LC 89-45405. 248p. 1990. 33.50 (0-8386-3367-6) Fairleigh Dickinson.

David Mamet & Film: Illusion - Disillusion in a Wounded Land. Gay Brewer. LC 92-50951. 221p. 1993. lib. bdg. 27.50 (0-89950-834-0) McFarland & Co.

***David Man after Gods Own Heart.** Swindolls. 1988. pap. text ed. (0-8499-8328-2) Word Pub.

David Marr's Key Papers. Lucia M. Vaina & Tomaso Poggio. 1991. 52.00 (0-8176-3472-X) Birkhauser.

David Matthew Kennedy: Banker, Statesman, Churchman. Martin B. Hickman. LC 87-19898. 403p. 1987. 15.95 (0-87579-093-3) Deseret Bk.

David McCutchion: Shraddanjali. P. Lal. 15.00 (0-89253-671-3); 6.75 (0-89253-672-1) Ind-US Inc.

David McPhail's Animals A to Z. David McPhail. (Illus.). 32p. (J). (ps-1). 1993. 2.50 (0-590-46462-0, Cartwheel) Scholastic Inc.

David Mcphail's Animals A to Z. David Mcphail. (J). 1989. pap. 2.50 (0-590-40347-8) Scholastic Inc.

David Merrick: A Bio-Bibliography. Barbara L. Horn. LC 92-19789. (Bio-Bibliographies in the Performing Arts Ser.: No. 33). 280p. 1992. text ed. 47.95 (0-313-28520-9, HDR, Greenwood Pr) Greenwood.

David Merrick: The Abominable Showman. Howard Kissel. (Illus.). 512p. 1993. 24.95 (1-55783-172-6) Applause Theatre Bk Pubs.

David Merrick & Hal Prince: An Annotated Bibliography. Brenda Coven et al. LC 93-20378. 248p. 1993. 38.00 (0-8240-3041-9, H883) Garland.

David Milne. Ed. by Ian M. Thom. (Illus.). 224p. 1992. 60.00 (0-88894-740-2) U of Wash Pr.

David Moreno: Beneath the Skin. Contrib by Peter F. Spooner. (Illus.). 24p. 1991. 8.00 (0-945558-13-9) ISU Univ Galls.

***David Muench in Texas.** Illus. by David Muench. 128p. 1995. 39.95 (1-56313-757-7) BrownTrout Pubs Inc.

David Myth in Western Literature. Ed. by Raymond-Jean Frontain & Jan Wojcik. LC 78-69904. (Illus.). 224p. 1980. 22.00 (0-911198-55-5) Purdue U Pr.

David Nash: Sixty Seasons. 48p. 1983. 35.00 (0-685-16970-7, Pub. by Third Eye Centre UK) St Mut.

David Nash: Voyages & Vessels. Graham W. Beal. (Illus.). 83p. (Orig.). 1994. pap. 19.95 (0-936364-23-8) Joslyn Art.

David Newman's Movie Quiz Book. David Newman. Ed. by Kelly A. Spradlin & Michael P. Spradlin. 208p. (Orig.). 1993. pap. 12.50 (1-881892-01-8) Spradlin & Assocs.

D

An Asterisk (*) at the beginning of an entry indicates that the title is appearing in BIP for the first time.

D

An Asterisk (*) at the beginning of an entry indicates that the title is appearing in BIP for the first time.

1807

Daviess County, Indiana, Vol. II. L. Rex Myers. LC 88-50352. 336p. 1991. 45.00 (0-685-50370-4) Turner Pub KY.

Daviess County, Indiana History. L. Rex Myers. LC 88-50352. 336p. 1988. 50.00 (0-938021-66-4) Turner Pub KY.

Daviess County, Kentucky, Cemeteries: "Mater Dolorosa", Vol. 4. (Illus.). 381p. 27.50 (0-318-35067-X) West Cent KY Family Re Assoc.

Daviess County, KY, Cemeteries, 3 vols. 111p. 1988. Vol. I, 111 pgs. 12.00 (0-318-23369-X); Vol. II, 110 pgs. 12.00 (0-318-32459-8); Vol. III: Burials in Rose Hill Cemetary of Owensboro, KY 1976, 146 pgs. 16.00 (0-318-32460-1) West Cent KY Family Re Assoc.

Daviess County, KY, Marriages, 1815-1865. Ed. by Emma Dunn Mastin. 268p. 1988. 22.00 (0-318-23372-X) West Cent KY Family Re Assoc.

Daviess County, KY Marriages, 1815-1865: From Marriage in the Davies Co Courthouse. Ed. by Emma D. Mastin. 268p. 22.00 (0-318-24039-4) West Cent KY Family Re Assoc.

Daviess County, KY, Order Book D, 1837-1946. 138p. 1988. 12.00 (0-318-23373-8) West Cent KY Family Re Assoc.

Daviess County, Missouri 1860 Census. Mary Inglis-Sims. 92p. 1985. pap. text ed. 12.50 (0-930595-01-7) Sims Pub.

Daviess County, Missouri 1870 Census. Mary Inglis-Sims. LC 85-62535. 120p. 1987. pap. text ed. 12.50 (0-930595-03-3) Sims Pub.

Davis: Genealogies of the Davis & Goss Families, 2 pts. Henry W. Clark. (Illus.). 141p. 1993. reprint ed. lib. bdg. 69.50 (0-8328-2982-X); reprint ed. pap. 59.50 (0-8328-2983-8) Higginson Bk Co.

Davis: Genealogy of the Clinton H. Davis Family, Short Sketch of the Lost Creek 7th Day Baptist Church. W. M. Davis. 100p. 1994. reprint ed. lib. bdg. 29.00 (0-8328-4147-1); reprint ed. pap. 19.00 (0-8328-4148-X) Higginson Bk Co.

Davis - Woodruff Families of Western Kentucky. Virginia Couchot. (Illus.). 74p. 1993. reprint ed. lib. bdg. 25.00 (0-8328-3069-0); reprint ed. pap. 15.00 (0-8328-3070-4) Higginson Bk Co.

***Davis & Lee at War.** Steven E. Woodworth. (Modern War Studies). (Illus.). 440p. (C). 1995. 29.95 (0-7006-0718-8) U Pr of KS.

***Davis & Russell's Finding Birds in Southeast Arizona.** Tucson Audubon Society Publications Committee. (Illus.). 1995. pap. 16.95 (0-9645031-0-7) Tucson Audubon.

Davis, Baldridge, & Huggins Sites: Three 19th Century Upland South Farmsteads in Perry County, Illinois. Mary R. McCorvie. (Preservation Ser.: No. 4). (Illus.). 323p. 1987. 10.00 (0-913415-03-0) Am Resources.

Davis Book of Medical Abbreviations: A Deciphering Guide. Sara L. Mitchell-Hatton. 1028p. 1991. pap. text ed. 32.95 (0-8036-6268-8) Davis Co.

Davis Catalog of Periodical Articles-Decorative & Fine Arts, 4 vols., Set. Bibliotheque Forney Staff. 1972. lib. bdg. 360.00 (0-8161-0965-6, Hall Library) G K Hall.

Davis Catalog of the Catalogs of Sales of Art, 2 vols., Set. Bibliotheque Forney Staff. 1972. lib. bdg. 220.00 (0-8161-0962-1, Hall Library) G K Hall.

Davis Cup Conspiracy. Jack M. Bickham. 384p. 1994. 22.95 (0-312-85727-6) Forge NYC.

Davis Cup Conspiracy. Jack M. Bickham. 1995. pap. 4.50 (0-8125-5055-2) Forge NYC.

Davis Diary, 2 vols., 1. Ed. by Sheila Hardy. (C). 1987. lib. bdg. 22.00 (0-8095-6950-7) Borgo Pr.

Davis Diary, 2 vols., 2. Ed. by Sheila Hardy. (C). 1987. lib. bdg. 20.00 (0-8095-6951-5) Borgo Pr.

Davis Family: A History of the Descendants of Wm. Davis & His Wife, Mary Means. T. K. Davis. (Illus.). 248p. 1992. reprint ed. lib. bdg. 49.00 (0-8328-2648-0); reprint ed. pap. 39.00 (0-8328-2649-9) Higginson Bk Co.

Davis Family: A Personal Recordkeeping Practice Set. 2nd ed. Merle W. Wood. (Illus.). (gr. 10-12). 1982. text ed. 11.84 (0-07-071623-4) McGraw.

Davis, Mangan, Ferguson. William Butler Yeats & Thomas Kinsella. (Anglo-Irish Studies 2, Tower Ser). 1971. 13.95 (0-85105-166-9) Dufour.

Davis, Mangan, Ferguson? William Butler Yeats et al. 1971. 13.95 (0-8023-9055-2) Dufour.

Davis Museum & Cultural Center: History & Holdings. Lucy Flint-Gohlke. 272p. 1992. pap. text ed. 35.00 (1-881894-00-2) WC Davis Mus & Cult.

Davis-Wood Family of Gadsden County, Florida & Their Forebears. Fenton G. Avant. LC 79-189245. (Illus.). 535p. 35.00 (0-685-57876-3) L'Avant Studios.

Davison County: An Historic Sampler. Bob Karolevitz. LC 93-23708. 1993. write for info. (0-89865-884-5) Donning Co.

Davison's Salesman's Book. 79th ed. 474p. 1991. 50.00 (0-87515-032-2) Davison.

Davison's Salesmans Book. 80th ed. 474p. 1992. 50.00 (0-87515-035-7) Davison.

Davison's Salesman's Book. 81th ed. 460p. 1993. 60.00 (0-87515-041-1) Davison.

Davison's Textile Blue Book. 125th ed. 695p. 1991. 100.00 (0-87515-031-4) Davison.

Davison's Textile Blue Book. 126th ed. 700p. 1992. 100.00 (0-87515-034-9) Davison.

Davison's Textile Blue Book. 127th ed. 700p. 1993. 120.00 (0-87515-040-3) Davison.

Davison's Textile Buyer's Guide. 58th ed. 400p. 1992. 50.00 (0-87515-036-5) Davison.

***Davis's Clinical Guide to Health Assessment.** 2nd ed. Ed. by Patricia G. Morton et al. (Illus.). 340p. (C). 1995. pap. text ed., spiral bd. 26.95 (0-8036-0119-0) Davis Co.

Davis's Drug Guide for IV Medications. 2nd ed. April H. Vallerand & Judith H. Deglin. (Illus.). 650p. (C). 1993. pap. text ed. 25.95 (0-8036-8841-5) Davis Co.

Davis's Drug Guide for Nurses. 4th ed. Judith H. Deglin & April H. Vallerand. LC 93-48230. (Illus.). 1347p. (C). 1994. pap. text ed. 28.95 (0-8036-2458-1) Davis Co.

***Davis's Guide to IV Medications.** 3rd ed. April H. Vallerand & Judith H. Deglin. (Illus.). 1000p. (C). 1995. pap. text ed., spiral bd. 25.95 (0-8036-0092-5) Davis Co.

Davis's Handbook of Applied Hydraulics. 4th rev. ed. Ed. by Vincent J. Ziparro & Hans Hasen. LC 92-28842. 1993. text ed. 92.50 (0-07-073002-4) McGraw.

***Davis's Manual of Critical Care Therapeutics: Therapeutics.** Kathleen M. Baldwin et al. (Illus.). 757p. (C). 1995. pap. text ed. 29.95 (0-8036-0574-9) Davis Co.

Davis's NCLEX-PN Review Book. Ed. by Patricia G. Beare et al. (Illus.). 695p. (C). 1993. pap. text ed. 25.95 (0-8036-0671-0) Davis Co.

Davis's NCLEX-RN Health Assessment Review Cards: Including Lab & Diagnostic Aspects. Patricia G. Beare. (C). 1992. Shrink-wrapped, 320 cards. 21.95 (0-8036-0687-7) Davis Co.

Davis's NCLEX-RN Nutrition Review Cards: The Passing Game. Patricia G. Beare. (C). 1991. Shrink-wrapped, 176 cards. pap. 17.95 (0-8036-0673-7) Davis Co.

Davis's NCLEX-RN Pharmacology Review Cards: The Passing Game, Vol. 1. Patricia G. Beare. (C). 1991. Shrink-wrapped, 288 cards. pap. 19.95 (0-8036-0677-X) Davis Co.

Davis's NCLEX-RN Review. Ed. by Patricia G. Beare et al. LC 90-13838. 833p. 1990. pap. 28.95 (0-8036-0684-2) Davis Co.

***Davis's NCLEX-RN Review.** 2nd ed. Ed. by Patricia G. Beare et al. (Illus.). 950p. 1995. pap. text ed. 29.00 (0-8036-0063-1) Davis Co.

Davis's NCLEX-RN Review Cards: The Passing Game. Patricia G. Beare. 1990. Shrink-wrapped, 240 cards. 18.95 (0-8036-0685-0) Davis Co.

Davita's Harp. Chaim Potok. LC 84-48526. 336p. 1985. 16.95 (0-394-54290-8) Knopf.

Davita's Harp. Chaim Potok. LC 85-17672. 448p. 1986. mass mkt. 5.95 (0-449-20775-7, Crest) Fawcett.

Davitt & Irish Revolution: Eighteen Forty-Six to Eighteen Eighty-Two. T. W. Moody. (Illus.). 1984. pap. 32.00 (0-19-820069-2) OUP.

Davva-Samgaha (Dravya-Samgaha) Devendra Gani. Ed. & Intro. by Sarat C. Goshal. LC 73-3835. reprint ed. 27.50 (0-404-57701-6) AMS Pr.

Davy. Edgar Pangborn. 288p. 1982. pap. 2.75 (0-345-30702-X) Ballantine.

Davy Chadwick. large type ed. James Buchan. 1990. 21.95 (0-7089-2150-7) Ulverscroft.

Davy Crockett. (Story Clippers Ser.). (Illus.). (J). (gr. 2-5). 1989. 29.28 (0-8172-2953-1) Raintree Steck-V.

Davy Crockett. Debra Hess. 1989. 9.95 (0-943718-33-3) Kipling Pr.

***Davy Crockett.** James H. Kunstler. LC 94-48135. (Illus.). (J). 1995. write for info. (0-689-80189-0, Mac Bks Young Read) S&S Childrens.

Davy Crockett. Told by Felicity Trotman & Shirley Greenway. LC 85-16694. (Stories Ser.). (Illus.). 32p. (J). (gr. 2-5). 1985. lib. bdg. 19.97 (0-8172-2504-8) Raintree Steck-V.

***Davy Crockett.** rev. ed. Ret. by Felicity Trotman & Shirley Greenway. LC 94-42878. (First Biographies Ser.). (J). 1995. 19.97 (0-8114-8457-2) Raintree Steck-V.

Davy Crockett: American Comic Legend. Richard Dorson. (BCL1-PS American Literature Ser.). 171p. 1993. reprint ed. lib. bdg. 69.00 (0-7812-6596-7) Rprt Serv.

Davy Crockett: American Comic Legend. Ed. by Richard M. Dorson. LC 77-70590. (International Folklore Ser.). (Illus.). 1977. reprint ed. lib. bdg. 18.95 (0-405-10091-4) Ayer.

Davy Crockett: An American Hero. Tom Townsend. Ed. by Edwin M. Eakin. LC 87-16545. (Illus.). 72p. (J). (gr. 4-7). 1987. 10.95 (0-89015-643-3); pap. 5.95 (0-89015-627-1) Sunbelt Media.

Davy Crockett: Hero of the Wild Frontier. Elizabeth R. Moseley. (Discovery Biographies Ser.). (Illus.). 80p. (J). (gr. 2-6). 1991. reprint ed. lib. bdg. 12.95 (0-7910-1409-6) Chelsea Hse.

Davy Crockett: The Man & the Legend. James A. Shackford. Ed. by John B. Shackford. (Illus.). 362p. 1994. pap. 12.95 (0-8032-9230-9, Bison Books) U of Nebr Pr.

Davy Crockett: The Man, the Legend, the Legacy, 1786-1986. Ed. by Michael A. Lofaro. LC 84-25737. (Illus.). 228p. 1985. 35.00x (0-87049-459-7); pap. 16.00x (0-87049-507-0) U of Tenn Pr.

Davy Crockett: Young Pioneer. Laurence Santrey. LC 82-16040. (Illus.). 48p. (J). (gr. 4-6). 1983. lib. bdg. 10.79 (0-89375-847-7); pap. text ed. 3.50 (0-89375-848-5) Troll Assocs.

Davy Crockett: Young Rifleman. Aileen W. Parks. LC 86-10781. (Childhood of Famous Americans Ser.). (Illus.). 192p. (J). (gr. 2-6). 1986. reprint ed. pap. 3.95 (0-02-041840-X, Aladdin Paperbacks) S&S Childrens.

Davy Crockett & the Creek Indians. Justine Korman. LC 91-71357. (Disney's American Frontier Ser.: Bk. 2). (Illus.). 80p. (J). (gr. 1-4). 1991. lib. bdg. 12.89 (1-56282-004-4); pap. 3.50 (1-56282-005-2) Disney Pr.

Davy Crockett & the Highwaymen. Ron Fontes & Justine Korman. LC 92-52975. (Disney's American Frontier Ser.: Bk. 6). (Illus.). 80p. (J). (gr. 1-4). 1992. lib. bdg. 12.89 (1-56282-261-6); pap. 3.50 (1-56282-260-8) Disney Pr.

Davy Crockett & the King of the River. A. L. Singer. LC 91-71356. (Disney's American Frontier Ser.: Bk. 1). (Illus.). 80p. (J). (gr. 1-4). 1991. lib. bdg. 12.89 (1-56282-006-0); pap. 3.50 (1-56282-007-9) Disney Pr.

Davy Crockett & the Pirates at Cave-in Rock. A. L. Singer. LC 91-71355. (Disney's American Frontier Ser.: Bk. 3). (Illus.). 80p. (J). (gr. 1-4). 1991. lib. bdg. 12.89 (1-56282-002-8); pap. 3.50 (1-56282-003-6) Disney Pr.

Davy Crockett & the Unconstitutional Welfare State. Michael J. Mendenhall. LC 90-81995. 43p. 1990. pap. 4.00 (0-9625954-1-1) Inst Cons Res.

Davy Crockett at the Alamo. Justine Korman. LC 91-71350. (Disney's American Frontier Ser.: Bk. 4). (Illus.). 80p. (J). (gr. 1-4). 1991. lib. bdg. 12.89 (1-56282-008-7); pap. 3.50 (1-56282-009-5) Disney Pr.

Davy Crockett-Daniel Boone. Naunerle C. Farr. (Pendulum Illustrated Biography Ser.). (Illus.). (J). (gr. 4-12). 1979. student ed 1.25 (0-88301-375-4); pap. text ed. 2.95 (0-88301-351-7) Pendulum Pr.

Davy Crockett, Frontier Hero. rev. ed. Walter Blair. (Illus.). 225p. 1985. reprint ed. pap. 7.95 (0-942936-08-6) Lincoln-Herndon Pr.

Davy Crockett Meets Death Hug. Ron Fontes & Justine Korman. LC 93-71032. (American Frontier Ser.: Bk. 12). (Illus.). 80p. (J). (gr. 1-4). 1993. lib. bdg. 12.89 (1-56282-496-1); pap. 3.50 (1-56282-495-3) Disney Pr.

Davy Crockett's Almanacks, 1835-1843: The Nashville Imprints. 1986. 9.95 (0-913150-56-8) Pioneer Pr.

Davy Crockett's Own Story: A Narrative of the Life of David Crockett of the State of Tennessee. Davy Crockett. LC 93-34222. (Illus.). 128p. (J). 1993. pap. 12.95 (1-55709-218-4) Applewood.

Davy Crockett's Own Story as Written by Himself: The Autobiography of America's Great Folk Hero. Illus. by Milton Glaser. LC 92-5553. 1992. 7.98 (0-681-41651-3) Longmeadow Pr.

Davydov's Soliton Revisited: Self-Trapping of Vibrational Energy in Protein. Ed. by Peter L. Christiansen & A. C. Scott. LC 90-20930. (NATO ASI Series B, Physics: Vol. 243). (Illus.). 530p. 1990. 125.00 (0-306-43734-1, Plenum Pr) Plenum.

***Davy's Dawg.** Billie L. Matthews & Virginia E. Hurlburt. Ed. by Karen E. Welch. (Illus.). 64p. (J). (gr. 3-8). 1989. pap. 4.95 (1-885777-02-7) Hendrick-Long.

Davy's Dream. Paul O. Lewis. (Illus.). 64p. (J). (ps-6). 1988. 14.95 (0-941831-32-9); pap. 9.95 (0-941831-28-0) Beyond Words Pub.

***Davy's Lake.** Margaret Rockwell. (Orig.). 1995. pap. text ed. 10.95 (0-9608496-1-0) Caribou Pr.

DAW Science-Fiction Books. Roger Robinson. 20p. (C). 1990. reprint ed. lib. bdg. 17.00x (0-8095-4606-X) Borgo Pr.

***Dawah & Its Objective.** Shamim A. Siddiqi. 1994. write for info. (0-9625301-3-1) Forum Islamic.

***Dawah Program.** Shamim A. Siddiqi. 1993. write for info. (0-9625301-2-3) Forum Islamic.

Dawes - Gates Ancestral Lines: a Memorial Volume Containing the American Ancestry of Rufus R. Dawes, Vol. I: Dawes & Allied Families. M. W. Ferris. (Illus.). 758p. 1991. reprint ed. lib. bdg. 115.00 (0-8328-2011-3); reprint ed. pap. 105.00 (0-8328-2012-1) Higginson Bk Co.

Dawes Act & the Allotment of Indian Lands. Delos S. Otis. LC 72-3597. (Civilization of the American Indian Ser.: No. 123). 226p. reprint ed. pap. 64.50 (0-8357-8088-0, 2033965) Bks Demand.

***Dawg's Tale: The Story of the Salty Dawg Saloon, the Homer Spit & the Town of Homer, Alaska.** Diane F. Wood. (Alaska Landmark Ser.: No. 1). (Illus.). 224p. (Orig.). 1995. pap. 15.95 (1-886921-01-6) Alaska Pr.

Dawlish Season. large type ed. Desmond Rayner. (General Ser.). 656p. 1993. 21.95 (0-7089-2792-0) Ulverscroft.

Dawn. V. C. Andrews. Ed. by Linda Marrow. 416p. (Orig.). 1990. 19.95 (0-685-46977-8); pap. 6.99 (0-671-67068-9) PB.

Dawn. Molly Bang. LC 83-886. (Illus.). 32p. (J). (ps up). 1983. lib. bdg. 14.93 (0-688-02404-1) Morrow Jr Bks.

Dawn. Octavia E. Butler. 256p. 1989. mass mkt. 5.50 (0-445-20779-5) Warner Bks.

Dawn. Molana-al-Moazam Hazrat & Shah M. Pir Oveyssi. LC 89-5834. (Shahmaghsoudi (Angha) Heritage Series on Sufism). 44p. (Orig.). (C). 1989. pap. text ed. 12.00 (0-8191-7429-7) U Pr of Amer.

Dawn. Tania Langley. 224p. 1980. pap. 1.75 (0-449-50049-7, Coventry) Fawcett.

Dawn. Eleanor H. Porter. 23.95 (0-8488-0309-4) Amereon Ltd.

Dawn. Uri Shulevitz. LC 74-9761. (Illus.). 32p. (J). (ps up). 1974. 16.00 (0-374-31707-0) FS&G.

Dawn. Uri Shulevitz. (Sunburst Ser.). (Illus.). 32p. (J). (ps up). 1988. pap. 5.95 (0-374-41689-3) FS&G.

Dawn. Elie Wiesel. 112p. 1982. mass mkt. 4.99 (0-553-22536-7) Bantam.

Dawn. large type ed. V. C. Andrews. (General Ser.). 472p. (Orig.). 1991. text ed. 20.95 (0-8161-5184-9, Large Print Bks); pap. 16.95 (0-8161-5186-5, Large Print Bks) Hall.

Dawn. Molly Bang. LC 83-886. (Illus.). 32p. (J). (ps up). 1983. reprint ed. pap. 3.95 (0-688-10989-6, Mulberry) Morrow Jr Bks.

Dawn: A Charleston Legend. Dawn L. Simmons. (Illus.). 1995. 19.95 (0-941711-16-1) Wyrick & Co.

Dawn: History of the Birth & Consolidation of the Republic of Chile. Agustin Edwards. 1976. lib. bdg. 59.95 (0-8490-1701-7) Gordon Pr.

Dawn: Short Stories & a Novella. Martha T. Dudman. 136p. (Orig.). 1990. pap. 8.95 (0-913006-42-4) Puckerbrush.

Dawn after Dachau. Joel Sack. LC 90-53264. 141p. 1990. 14.95 (0-88400-141-5) Shengold.

Dawn after Danger. Ann W. Strawbridge. 1993. reprint ed. lib. bdg. 89.00 (0-7812-5839-1) Rprt Serv.

Dawn after Dark. Rene Huyghe & Daisaku Ikeda. Tr. by Richard L. Gage. 420p. 1991. 35.00 (0-8348-0238-4) Weatherhill.

Dawn & Devolution of the Indus Civilization. S. R. Rao. (C). 1991. 120.00 (81-85179-74-3, Pub. by Aditya Prakashan II) S Asia.

***Dawn & Her World: Identification & Price Guide.** Joedi Johnson. LC 95-68058. (Illus.). 80p. (Orig.). 1995. pap. 19.95 (0-9646764-0-0) Cattpig Pr.

Dawn & the Big Sleepover. Ann M. Martin. (Baby-Sitters Club Ser.: No. 44). (J). (gr. 4-7). 1991. pap. 3.50 (0-590-43573-6) Scholastic Inc.

Dawn & the Disappearing Dogs. Ann M. Martin. (Baby-Sitters Club Mystery Ser.: No. 07). (J). (gr. 4-7). 1993. pap. 3.50 (0-590-44960-5) Scholastic Inc.

***Dawn & the Halloween Mystery.** Ann M. Martin. (Baby-Sitters Club Mystery Ser.: No. 17). (J). (gr. 4-7). 1994. pap. 3.50 (0-590-48232-7) Scholastic Inc.

Dawn & the Impossible Three. Ann M. Martin. (Baby-Sitters Club Ser.: No. 5). 144p. (Orig.) (J). (gr. 4-6). 1987. pap. 3.50 (0-590-43720-8) Scholastic Inc.

Dawn & the Impossible Three. 2nd ed. Ann M. Martin. (Baby-Sitters Club Ser.: No. 5). (Orig.). 1988. pap. 3.50 (0-590-42232-4) Scholastic Inc.

Dawn & the Older Boy. Ann M. Martin. (Baby-Sitters Club Ser.: No. 37). (J). (gr. 4-7). 1990. pap. 3.25 (0-590-43566-3) Scholastic Inc.

Dawn & the Round-to-It. Irene Smalls-Hector. LC 93-19731. (Illus.). (J). 1994. pap. 15.00 (0-671-87166-8, S&S Bks Young Read) S&S Childrens.

Dawn & the Surfer Ghost. Ann M. Martin. (Baby-Sitters Club Mystery Ser.: No. 12). (J). (gr. 4-7). 1993. pap. 3.50 (0-590-47050-7) Scholastic Inc.

Dawn & the We Kids Club. Ann M. Martin. (Baby-Sitters Club Ser.: No. 72). (J). (gr. 4-7). 1994. pap. 3.50 (0-590-47010-8) Scholastic Inc.

Dawn & Whitney: Friends Forever. Ann M. Martin. (Baby-Sitters Club Ser.: No. 77). (J). (gr. 4-7). 1994. pap. 3.50 (0-590-48221-1) Scholastic Inc.

Dawn Appears. Annie G. Nelson. LC 76-18799. 135p. 1976. reprint ed. 10.00 (0-87152-244-6) Reprint.

Dawn Breaks in the East: One Spiritual Warrior's Thirty-Three Year Struggle in Defense of the Church. Peter Zhou. Ed. by Cynthia Haan & Jim Moeller. LC 92-60393. 225p. (Orig.). (C). 1992. pap. write for info. (1-881614-00-X) Serenity CA.

Dawn Brown's Complete Guide to Step Aerobics. Dawn Brown. (Fitness & Health Ser.). 1992. pap. text ed. 9.95 (0-86720-269-6) Jones & Bartlett.

Dawn Builder. John G. Neihardt. LC 90-21279. (Landmark Edition Ser.). 335p. 1991. reprint ed. 35.00 (0-8032-3330-2) U of Nebr Pr.

Dawn Chorus. Tim Reynolds. LC 80-24377. 42p. 1980. 4.00 (0-87886-111-4, Greenfld Rev Pr) Greenfld Rev Lit.

Dawn Command. Roland K. Jordon. 1978. pap. 1.75 (0-8439-0600-6) Dorchester Pub Co.

Dawn, Dusk & Deer. Arthur Cadman. (Illus.). 136p. 1990. 24.95 (0-948253-41-X, Pub. by Sportsmans Pr UK) Trafalgar.

Dawn Fish. H. Geoffrey Moser. LC 78-56849. 1979. 6.95 (0-87212-109-7) Libra.

Dawn for a Fawn. Albert Trudeau. (Illus.). 16p. 1994. 7.00 (0-8059-3634-3) Dorrance.

Dawn Horse Testament: The Testament of Secrets of the Divine World-Teacher & True Heart-Master, Da Avabhasa (The "Bright") rev. ed. Da Avabhasa. LC 90-25915. (Illus.). 820p. 1991. 48.00 (0-918801-33-8); pap. 24.95 (0-918801-03-6) Dawn Horse Pr.

***Dawn Horse Testament of Adi Da: The Testament of Secrets of the Da Avatar.** rev. ed. Adi Da. LC 90-25915. (Illus.). 850p. Date not set. pap. 48.00 (1-57097-007-6) Dawn Horse Pr.

Dawn in Arctic Alaska. Diamond Jenness. LC 84-16153. (Illus.). viii, 222p. 1985. reprint ed. pap. text ed. 9.95 (0-226-39741-6) U Ch Pr.

Dawn in Darkest Africa. John Harris. (Illus.). 308p. 1968. reprint ed. 35.00 (0-7146-1672-9, Pub. by F Cass Pubs UK) Intl Spec Bk.

Dawn in Russia or Scenes in the Russian Revolution. Henry W. Nevinson. LC 77-115569. (Russia Observed Ser.). (Illus.). 1971. reprint ed. 25.95 (0-405-03088-6) Ayer.

Dawn in the Desert: Sketchbook Diary of a Journey with Archaeologists in Saudi Arabia. Philip Bouchard. 74p. (C). 1990. 150.00 (0-907151-15-9, Pub. by IMMEL Pubng UK) St Mut.

Dawn in the West. Allan Tarshish. Ed. by Sefton D. Temkin. 318p. (Orig.). 1985. lib. bdg. 52.50 (0-8191-4432-0) U Pr of Amer.

Dawn Is Always New: Selected Poetry of Rocco Scotellaro. Rocco Scotellaro. Tr. by Ruth Feldman & Brian Swann. LC 79-3229. (Lockert Library of Poetry in Translation). (ENG & ITA.). 1980. 35.00 (0-691-06423-7); pap. 11.95 (0-691-01370-5) Princeton U Pr.

Dawn Is at Hand: Selected Poems. Kath Walker. 128p. 1990. pap. 15.00 (0-7145-2921-4) M Boyars Pubs.

Dawn Land. Joseph Bruchac. LC 92-54767. 336p. 1993. 19.95 (1-55591-134-X) Fulcrum Pub.

***Dawn Land.** Joseph Bruchac. 336p. 1995. pap. 12.95 (1-55591-215-X) Fulcrum Pub.

Dawn of a Dream. large type ed. Lisa Charles. (Linford Romance Library). 304p. 1993. pap. 14.95 (0-7089-7463-5, Trailtree Bookshop) Ulverscroft.

Dawn of a Kingdom (First Samuel) J. Keddie. 1988. pap. 10.99 (0-85234-248-9, Pub. by Evangel Pr UK) Presby & Reformed.

Dawn of a Magnificent Quest. Thomas Huntley. LC 90-70312. 353p. 1990. 12.95 (1-55523-337-6) Winston-Derek.

Dawn of a New Age: Reflections on Science & Human Affairs. Eugene I. Rabinowitch. LC 63-20898. 340p. reprint ed. pap. 96.90 (0-317-09265-0, 2020150) Bks Demand.

An Asterisk (*) at the beginning of an entry indicates that the title is appearing in BIP for the first time.

D

An Asterisk (*) at the beginning of an entry indicates that the title is appearing in BIP for the first time.

1809

Dawn's Early Light: Daring to Challenge the Deepening Darkness. Joseph M. Stowell. 1990. 14.99 (*0-8024-7171-4*) Moody.

Dawn's Family Feud. Ann M. Martin. (Baby-Sitters Club Ser.: No. 64). (J). (gr. 4-7). 1993. pap. 3.50 (*0-590-45666-0*) Scholastic Inc.

Dawn's Wicked Stepsister. Ann M. Martin. (Baby-Sitters Club Ser.: No. 31). (J). (gr. 4-7). 1990. pap. 3.50 (*0-590-42497-1*) Scholastic Inc.

Dawnwatchers. Hiram Bingham. 365p. 1984. pap. 6.95 (*0-9613602-0-8*) Triune Bks.

Dawr Hurriyat al Ra'y fi al Wahdah al Fikriyah Bayna al Muslimin: (The Role of Freedom of Opinion in the Intellectual Unity Amongst Muslims) Abdul Majid al Najjar. LC 91-44549. (Silsilat Abhath 'Ilmiyah: No. 6). 88p. (Orig.). (ARA.). 1992. pap. 5.00 (*1-56564-024-1*) IIIT VA.

Daws: A Man Who Trusted God. Betty L. Skinner. LC 73-22700. 398p. (Orig.). 1994. pap. 12.00 (*0-89109-796-1*, NavPr) NavPress.

Daws: Some Descendants of Frank Daws of County Sussex, England, with Information on Associate Kiplinger Family. Steve Roth. (Illus.). 89p. 1993. reprint ed. lib. bdg. 27.50 (*0-8328-3294-4*); reprint ed. pap. 17.50 (*0-8328-3293-6*) Higginson Bk Co.

Dawson City. Alaska Geographic Staff et al. LC 72-92087. (Alaska Geographic Ser.: Vol. 15, No. 2). (Illus.). 94p. (Orig.). 1989. pap. 15.95 (*0-88240-185-8*) Alaska Geog Soc.

***Dawson City Seven.** Don Reddick. 1994. pap. 14.95 (*0-86492-158-6*, Pub. by Goose Ln Edits CN) InBook.

Dawson's Government of Canada. 6th ed. Norman Ward. 570p. 1987. 50.00 (*0-8020-5731-4*); pap. 22.95 (*0-8020-6644-5*) U of Toronto Pr.

Dawson's Guide to Colorado's Fourteeners: The Northern Peaks, the Complete Mountaineering Guide to Colorado's High Mountains, Vol. 1. Louis W. Dawson, II. Ed. by Robert Couchman. LC 94-71273. (Illus.). 256p. (Orig.). 1994. pap. 19.95 (*0-9628867-1-8*) Blue Clover.

Dawson's Practical Lawncraft. R. Hawthorne. (Illus.). 313p. 1977. 34.95 (*0-8464-1085-0*) Beekman Pubs.

Dawud ibn Marwan al-Muqammis's Twenty Chapters: Ishrun Maqala. Ed. & Tr. by Sarah Stroumsa. (Etudes sur le Judaisme Medieval Ser.: Vol. 13). 320p. (ENG & HEB.). 1989. 77.25 (*90-04-09216-1*) E J Brill.

Daxel Menu. Edward A. Swanson. 1993. pap. 3.95 (*0-9637773-0-0*) Daxel.

Dax's Case: Essays in Medical Ethics & Human Meaning. Ed. by Lonnie D. Kliever. 252p. 1989. pap. 12.50 (*0-87074-278-7*) SMU Press.

***Day after Midnight: The Effects of Nuclear War.** Mihcael Riordan. LC 82-9538. (Illus.). reprint ed. pap. 40.80 (*0-7837-9010-4*, AU00462) Bks Demand.

***Day After Tomorrow.** Allan Folsom. Date not set. pap. 6.99 (*0-615-00411-3*) Warner Bks.

***Day after Tomorrow.** Allan Folsom. pap. 6.99 (*0-615-00479-2*) Warner Bks.

Day after Tomorrow. Allan R. Folsom. 736p. 1995. mass mkt. 6.99 (*0-446-60041-5*, Warner Vision) Warner Bks.

***Day After Tomorrow.** large type ed. Allan Folsom. LC 94-30490. 1994. write for info. (*1-56895-121-3*) Wheeler Pub.

Day after Tomorrow: A Novel. Allan Folsom. LC 93-30344. 1994. 24.95 (*0-316-28829-2*) Little.

***Day after Yesterday.** Raymond Houston. 332p. (Orig.). 1995. pap. 9.95 (*1-56883-059-9*) Colonial Pr AL.

Day After...Study Nuclear Proliferation in the Post-Cold War, Vol. II: Main Report. Marc D. Millot et al. LC 93-27731. 1993. write for info. (*0-8330-1424-2*, MR-253-AF) Rand Corp.

Day After...Study: Nuclear Proliferation in the Post-Cold War World, Vol. I: Summary Report. Marc D. Millot et al. LC 93-33243. 1993. write for info. (*0-8330-1459-5*, MR-266-AF) Rand Corp.

Day America's Music Went Bye. John L. Wilson. LC 93-71444. 52p. (Orig.). 1993. pap. 12.00 (*0-9637636-3-6*) Americana Pubs.

***Day & Night.** Maria Gordon. (Simple Science Ser.). (Illus.). 32p. (J). (ps-2). 1995. 10.95 (*1-56847-457-1*) Thomson Lrning.

***Day & Night.** Maria Gordon. (Simple Science Ser.). (Illus.). (J). (ps-2). 1995. pap. 4.95 (*1-56847-461-X*) Thomson Lrning.

***Day & Night.** Claire Llewellyn & Anthony Lewis. LC 94-45156. (Why Do We Have? Ser.). (J). 1995. write for info. (*0-8120-6509-3*); pap. write for info. (*0-8120-9280-5*) Barron.

Day & Night. Joy Richardson. LC 92-31302. (Picture Science Ser.). (Illus.). 30p. (J). (gr. k-4). 1992. lib. bdg. 12.25 (*0-531-14139-X*) Watts.

Day & Night. Joachim Roth. (Illus.). 1993. 7.95 (*0-8059-3521-5*) Dorrance.

Day & Night. Lynn M. Stone. (J). 1994. write for info. (*1-55916-022-5*) Rourke Bk Co.

***Day & Night & Other Dreams.** Edens. (J). Date not set. audio 19.95 (*0-671-74906-4*, S&S Bks Young Read) S&S Childrens.

Day & Night & Other Dreams. Cooper Edens. LC 91-3977. (Illus.). (J). 1991. audio 19.95 (*0-671-75590-0*, Green Tiger S&S) S&S Childrens.

Day & Night Stories: Collected Novels & Stories, Vol. 9. Guy De Maupassant. Ed. by Ernest A. Boyd. Tr. by Storm Jameson. LC 70-157787. (Short Story Index Reprint Ser.). 1977. reprint ed. 18.95 (*0-8369-3899-2*) Ayer.

***Day at a Time.** LC 76-55448. 384p. 1976. 10.95 (*1-56838-048-8*); 12.95 (*1-56838-049-6*) Hazelden.

Day at a Time. Ed. by Denis Duncan. (C). 1990. pap. 24.00 (*0-85305-283-2*, Pub. by J Arthur Ltd UK) St Mut.

Day at a Time: A Woman's Look at Perfection. Beppie Harrison. 1994. 9.95 (*0-88494-918-4*) Bookcraft Inc.

Day at a Time: Gamblers Anonymous. Jane T. Noland. 384p. (Orig.). 1989. reprint ed. pap. 8.95 (*1-56838-036-4*) Hazelden.

Day at a Time: The Diary Literature of American Women Writers from 1764 to the Present. Ed. by Margo Culley. LC 85-13140. 368p. 1985. pap. 14.95 (*0-935312-51-X*) Feminist Pr.

Day at Home. Michael Aubin. (Child's World Library). (Illus.). 32p. (J). (gr. 3-5). 1991. lib. bdg. 18.50 (*0-89565-762-7*) Childs World.

Day at the Beach. Robert Grenier. 80p. (Orig.). 1985. pap. 6.00 (*0-937804-14-2*) Segue NYC.

Day at the Beach. Mary Lesley. (Story Puzzle Book Ser.). 4p. (J). (ps-2). 1990. 9.95 (*0-88679-843-4*) Educ Insights.

Day at the Beach. Mircea Vasiliu. LC 76-24169. (Pictureback Library Editions). (J). (ps-2). 1978. 2.25 (*0-394-83475-5*) Random Bks Yng Read.

Day at the Beach. Karen E. Young. (Emergent Reader Ser.). 16p. (J). (ps-1). 1991. pap. text ed. 21.00 (*1-56843-034-5*); pap. text ed. 4.25 (*1-56843-082-5*) BGR Pub.

Day at the Beach: Recollections. Geoffrey Wolff. LC 92-50627. 1993. pap. 12.00 (*0-679-74449-5*, Vin) Random.

Day at the Bookbindery of Lippincott, Grambo & Co. C. T. Hinckley. (Illus.). 16p. 1988. reprint ed. 10.00 (*0-938768-14-X*) Oak Knoll.

***Day at the Fair.** Arleta Richardson. (Grandma's Attic Ser.). (Illus.). 32p. (J). (ps-3). 1995. 14.99 (*0-7814-0249-2*, Chariot Bks) Chariot Family.

***Day at the Farm.** (First Story Board Ser.). 20p. (J). 1994. bds. 3.98 (*0-86112-986-5*) Brimax Bks.

***Day at the Farm.** (First Story Board Ser.). 20p. (J). 1994. 3.98 (*0-86112-985-7*) Brimax Bks.

***Day at the Farm.** 1995. 4.98 (*1-85854-283-9*) Brimax Bks.

Day at the Farm. Mary Lesley. (Story Puzzle Book Ser.). 4p. (J). 1990. 9.95 (*0-88679-842-6*) Educ Insights.

Day at the Mountains. Mary Lesley. (Story Puzzle Book Ser.). 4p. (J). 1990. 9.95 (*0-88679-844-2*) Educ Insights.

Day at the Park. Mary Lasley. (Story Puzzle Book Ser.). 4p. (J). (ps-2). 1990. 9.95 (*0-88679-841-8*) Educ Insights.

Day at the Park: In Celebration of Wrigley Field. William Hartel. (Illus.). 145p. 1994. 29.95 (*0-915611-91-0*) Sagamore Pub.

***Day at the Park: In Celebration of Wrigley Field.** rev. ed. William Hartel. Ed. by Susan Smith. (Illus.). 128p. 1995. 32.00 (*1-885758-03-0*) Quality Sports.

***Day at the Park: In Celebration of Wrigley Field.** rev. ed. William Hartel. (Illus.). 128p. 1995. 32.00 (*0-614-04025-6*) Quality Sports.

Day at the Races. Harold Roth. LC 83-2345. (Illus.). 64p. (J). (gr. 3-6). 1983. 10.95 (*0-394-85814-X*) Pantheon.

Day at the Races. Sidney Burris. LC 89-5295. (University of Utah Press Poetry Ser.). 78p. reprint ed. pap. 25.00 (*0-7837-5539-2*, 2045313) Bks Demand.

Day at the Races with Austin & Kyle Petty. Evelyn C. Mott. LC 92-10947. (Pictureback Ser.). 32p. (J). (ps-3). 1993. pap. 2.25 (*0-679-83258-0*) Random Bks Yng Read.

Day Before. Donald W. Baker. 48p. (Orig.). 1988. pap. 5.95 (*0-935306-43-9*) Barnwood Pr.

Day Before America. William H. MacLeish. LC 94-9504. 1994. 21.95 (*0-395-46882-5*) HM.

Day Before Christmas. Eve Bunting. (Illus.). 32p. (J). (ps-3). 1992. 14.95 (*0-89919-866-X*, Clarion Bks) HM.

Day Before Midnight. Stephen Hunter. 1990. mass mkt. 6.50 (*0-553-28235-2*) Bantam.

Day Before Now. Margaret W. Brown. Ed. by Joan W. Blos. LC 93-12814. (Illus.). (J). 1994. pap. 15.00 (*0-671-79628-3*, S&S Bks Young Read) S&S Childrens.

Day Before the Day After. Dom Martin. (Illus.). 86p. 1985. pap. text ed. 4.95 (*0-9616078-0-7*) Trans Gala Pubns.

Day Before the Downpour: Five One-Acts on Bible Situations. T. M. Williams. 1987. 8.50 (*0-685-68714-7*, MP-645) Lillenas.

Day Before Yesterday. Leon De Winter. Tr. by Scott Rollins. 96p. (Orig.). 1985. pap. 8.00 (*0-931428-15-7*) Vehicle Edns.

Day Before Yesterday see History of the English Novel

***Day Book.** Jane Ray. (J). (ps-3). 1994. 12.99 (*0-525-45259-1*) NAL-Dutton.

Day Book of Daniel Campbell of Shawfield 1767: With Relevant Papers Concerning the Estate of Islay. Anno. by Freda Ramsay. 1991. 39.90 (*0-08-040933-4*, Pub. by Aberdeen U Pr) Macmillan.

Day Breakers, No. 3. Louis L'Amour. 1984. mass mkt. 3.99 (*0-553-27674-3*) Bantam.

Day Breaks. Bethea VerDorn. (Illus.). 32p. (J). (ps-3). 1992. 14.95 (*1-55970-187-0*) Arcade Pub Inc.

Day Brought Back My Night: Ageing & New Vision Loss. Stephen Ainlay. 176p. 1989. 29.95 (*0-415-00764-X*) Routledge.

Day Busy Buzzy Stopped Being. (J). 1989. pap. 1.95 (*0-8167-0029-X*) Troll Assocs.

Day by Day. pap. 9.00 (*0-06-255453-0*, Hazelden SF) Harper SF.

Day by Day. Robert Lowell. LC 77-6799. 138p. 1977. 12.95 (*0-374-13525-8*) FS&G.

Day by Day. Robert Lowell. LC 77-6799. 138p. 1978. pap. 9.00 (*0-374-51471-2*) FS&G.

Day By Day. 2nd ed. Bonnie Bernstein. (J). (gr. k-6). 1989. pap. 17.99 (*0-8224-4253-1*) Fearon Teach Aids.

Day by Day. 365p. 1986. reprint ed. pap. 9.00 (*0-86683-536-9*, 1081A) Hazelden.

Day-by-Day: A Program of Preparation for Christian Marriage. John J. Colligan & Kathleen A. Colligan. 112p. (Orig.). 1994. pap. 12.95 (*0-8091-3457-8*) Paulist Pr.

Day by Day: English for Employment Communication. Steven J. Molinsky & Bill Bliss. LC 93-44412. 1993. pap. 10.67 (*0-13-328238-4*) P-H Intl.

Day-by-Day: Reflection Guide for the Engaged & Newly Married. John J. Colligan & Kathleen A. Colligan. LC 93-31032. 112p. (Orig.). 1994. pap. 8.95 (*0-8091-3458-6*) Paulist Pr.

***Day by Day: The Eighties.** Marc Aronson. LC 94-26632. 1994. 195.00 (*0-8160-1592-9*) Facts on File.

Day by Day: The Fifties. Jeffrey Merrit. (Day by Day Ser.). (Illus.). 1036p. 1979. 125.00 (*0-87196-383-3*) Facts on File.

Day by Day: The Forties. Thomas M. Leonard. (Day by Day Ser). (Illus.). 1072p. 1977. lib. bdg. 125.00 (*0-87196-375-2*) Facts on File.

Day by Day: The Notre Dame Prayerbook for Students. Thomas McNally & William Storey. (Illus.). 208p. 1975. pap. 3.95 (*0-87793-100-3*) Ave Maria.

Day by Day: The Old West. Mike Flanagan. LC 94-4663. (Illus.). 512p. 1995. 60.00x (*0-8160-2689-0*) Facts on File.

Day by Day: The Seventies, 2 vols., Set. Thomas Leonard et al. (Day by Day Ser.). (Illus.). 1328p. 1988. 195.00 (*0-8160-1020-X*) Facts on File.

Day by Day: The Sixties, 2 vols., Set. Thomas Parker & Douglas Nelson. 1136p. 1983. 195.00 (*0-87196-648-4*) Facts on File.

Day by Day see Enfolded by Christ: An Encouragement to Pray

Day-by-Day Baby Care Book: An Owner's Manual for the First Three Years. Miriam Stoppard. 344p. 1984. pap. 10.50 (*0-345-30101-3*, Ballantine Trade) Ballantine.

Day by Day Horoscopes, 1994: Aquarius. 192p. 1993. pap. 3.99 (*0-425-13855-0*) Berkley Pub.

Day by Day Horoscopes, 1994: Aries. 192p. 1993. pap. 3.99 (*0-425-13845-3*) Berkley Pub.

Day by Day Horoscopes, 1994: Cancer. 192p. (Orig.). 1993. pap. 3.99 (*0-425-13848-8*) Berkley Pub.

Day by Day Horoscopes, 1994: Capricorn. 192p. 1993. pap. 3.99 (*0-425-13854-2*) Berkley Pub.

Day by Day Horoscopes, 1994: Gemini. 192p. (Orig.). 1993. pap. 3.99 (*0-425-13847-X*) Berkley Pub.

Day by Day Horoscopes, 1994: Leo. 192p. 1993. pap. 3.99 (*0-425-13849-6*) Berkley Pub.

Day by Day Horoscopes, 1994: Libra. 192p. 1993. pap. 3.99 (*0-425-13851-8*) Berkley Pub.

Day by Day Horoscopes, 1994: Pisces. 192p. (Orig.). 1993. pap. 3.99 (*0-425-13856-9*) Berkley Pub.

Day by Day Horoscopes, 1994: Sagittarius. 192p. 1993. pap. 3.99 (*0-425-13853-4*) Berkley Pub.

Day by Day Horoscopes, 1994: Scorpio. 192p. 1993. pap. 3.99 (*0-425-13852-6*) Berkley Pub.

Day by Day Horoscopes, 1994: Taurus. 192p. (Orig.). 1993. pap. 3.99 (*0-425-13846-1*) Berkley Pub.

Day by Day Horoscopes, 1994: Virgo. 192p. (Orig.). 1993. pap. 3.99 (*0-425-13850-X*) Berkley Pub.

Day by Day in Advent: Devotions for the Season. Christopher G. Milarch. LC 90-29126. (Illus.). 32p. (Orig.). 1991. pap. 4.99 (*0-8066-2556-2*, 10-25562) Augsburg Fortress.

Day-by-Day in Jewish History. Abraham P. Bloch. 1983. 29.50 (*0-87068-736-0*) Ktav.

Day-By-Day Parent Communication: Reproducible Notehead & Forms for Teachers. Ty Tuchscherer & Pam Tuchscherer. (Illus.). 48p. (Orig.). 1989. pap. 9.95 (*0-939705-04-4*) Pinnaroo.

Day by Day Runner's Log. David N. Meyer. (Illus.). 138p. 1990. pap. 6.95 (*0-681-40968-1*) Longmeadow Pr.

Day by Day Through Lent: Reflections, Prayers, Practices. Daniel L. Lowery. LC 83-82033. 142p. 1983. pap. 3.95 (*0-89243-194-6*) Liguori Pubns.

Day by Day Through the Easter Season. Mark Boyer. LC 87-82945. 96p. (Orig.). 1988. pap. 4.95 (*0-89243-278-0*) Liguori Pubns.

Day by Day Through the Gospel of Mark: A Devotional Bible Study. Merrill Gilbertson & Olga Gilbertson. LC 92-32116. 160p. (Orig.). 1992. pap. 11.99 (*0-8066-2614-3*, 9-2614, Augsburg) Augsburg Fortress.

Day-by-Day Way to Spelling Mastery. Raymond E. Laurita. 103p. (Orig.). 1993. pap. 10.50 (*0-914051-33-4*) Leonardo Pr.

Day by Day We Magnify Thee. Martin Luther. LC 82-2481. 448p. 1982. pap. 16.00 (*0-8006-1637-5*, 1-1637, Fortress Pr) Augsburg Fortress.

Day-by-Day with Billy Graham. Comp. by Joan W. Brown. 1976. pap. 6.95 (*0-89066-056-5*) World Wide Pubs.

Day by Day with Billy Graham. deluxe ed. Billy Graham. 1976. 19.95 (*0-89066-220-7*) World Wide Pubs.

Day by Day with Billy Graham see Dia-Tras-Dia Con Billy Graham

Day by Day with C. H. Spurgeon. Comp. by Al Bryant. LC 91-40879. 264p. 1991. pap. 9.99 (*0-8254-3771-7*) Kregel.

***Day by Day with Catherine Marshall.** Catherine Marshall. 382p. 1995. 10.99 (*0-8007-9234-3*) Chosen Bks.

Day by Day with Jesus. John Killinger. LC 93-44082. 320p. (Orig.). 1994. pap. 12.95 (*0-687-12186-8*) Abingdon.

Day by Day with Jesus. Rudolph F. Norden. 400p. (Orig.). 1985. pap. 13.99 (*0-570-03971-1*, 12-3006) Concordia.

Day by Day with Vance Havner: 366 Devotions. Vance Havner. LC 54-5430. 272p. 1984. reprint ed. pap. 7.99 (*0-8010-4279-8*) Baker Bk.

Day by Day with Your Health Coach. Beverly Chesser. LC 93-86324. 192p. (Orig.). 1994. 9.95 (*0-89221-247-0*) New Leaf.

Day Care: Child Psychology & Adult Economics. Intro. by Bryce J. Christensen. (Family in America Research Ser.). 150p. (Orig.). (C). 1989. 15.95 (*0-9619364-3-6*); pap. 9.95 (*0-9619364-2-8*) Rockford Inst.

Day Care: Looking for Answers. Kathlyn Gay. LC 91-18141. (Issues in Focus Ser.). (Illus.). 128p. (J). (gr. 6 up). 1992. lib. bdg. 17.95 (*0-89490-324-1*) Enslow Pubs.

Day Care: Scientific & Social Policy Issues. Ed. by Edward F. Zigler & Edmund W. Gordon. LC 81-12838. 515p. (C). 1981. text ed. 29.95 (*0-86569-098-7*, Auburn Hse); pap. text ed. 16.95 (*0-86569-109-6*, Auburn Hse) Greenwood.

Day Care ABC. Tamara Phillips. Ed. by Abby Levine. LC 88-33911. (Illus.). (J). (ps-2). 1989. lib. bdg. 13.95 (*0-8075-1483-7*) A Whitman.

Day Care & Children's Development: The Relations among Direct Teaching, Communicative Speech, Cognitive Performance, & Social Participation. Knut Sundell. (Studia Psychologica Upsaliensia: No. 13). 149p. (Orig.). 1988. pap. 35.50x (*91-554-2234-9*, Pub. by Uppsala Univ Acta Univ Uppsaliensis SW) Coronet Bks.

Day Care & Its Effects on Early Development: A Study of Group & Home Care in Multi-Ethnic, Working-Class Families. William Fowler. LC 85-151251. (Ontario Institute for Studies in Education, Symposium Ser.: No. 8). 117p. reprint ed. pap. 33.40 (*0-685-20791-9*, 2030098) Bks Demand.

Day Care & Public Policy in Ontario. Michael Krashinsky. LC 78-305398. (Ontario Economic Council Research Studies: No. 11). 149p. reprint ed. pap. 42.50 (*0-8357-3994-5*, 2036694) Bks Demand.

Day Care & the Public Schools. James A. Levine. 140p. 1978. pap. 5.00 (*0-89292-078-5*) Educ Dev Ctr.

Day Care & the Working Poor: The Struggle for Self-Sufficiency. Georgia L. McMurray & Dolores P. Kazanjian. LC 82-199119. 140p. 1982. pap. 10.00 (*0-88156-001-4*) Comm Serv Soc NY.

Day Care Center Aide. Jack Rudman. (Career Examination Ser.: C-1235). 1994. pap. 23.95 (*0-8373-1235-3*) Nat Learn.

Day Care Centers in the U. S. A National Profile, 1976-1977. Craig Coelen et al. (Illus.). 234p. 1984. reprint ed. pap. text ed. 29.00 (*0-8191-4106-2*) U Pr of Amer.

Day Care Dilemma: Critical Concerns for American Families. A. Browne Miller. LC 89-26684. (Illus.). 328p. 1990. 23.95 (*0-306-43435-0*, Plenum Insight) Plenum.

Day Care Dilemma: Who Should Be Responsible for the Children. National Issues Forum Staff. 48p. 1989. 2.95 (*0-8403-5264-6*) Kendall-Hunt.

Day Care Dilemma: Who Should Be Responsible for the Children. National Issues Forum Staff. 48p. 1989. teacher ed, per. 15.00 (*0-8403-5266-2*) Kendall-Hunt.

Day Care Directory: Fairfield County, 1991. Ann H. Maier. 368p. (Orig.). 1991. pap. write for info. (*0-9626513-0-3*) Schl Hse Pubns.

Day Care for Young Children: International Perspectives. Edward Melhuish & Peter Moss. (Illus.). 235p. 1990. 66. 00 (*0-415-01746-7*, A4839); pap. 19.95 (*0-415-01747-5*, A4843) Routledge.

Day Care Kit. Deborah Spaide. 1990. pap. 7.95 (*1-55972-031-X*, Birch Ln Pr) Carol Pub Group.

Day Care Programs for Alzheimer's Disease & Related Disorders. John Panella, Jr. LC 87-71317. 160p. 1987. text ed. 39.95 (*0-939957-05-1*) Demos Vermande.

Day Care Solution in America: The Learning Center. Vera H. Young. LC 86-90980. 45p. (Orig.). 1985. pap. text ed. 14.50 (*0-9619433-0-0*) Operation Super.

***Day Care...an Emerging Crisis.** George Thorman. 138p. 1989. pap. 22.95 (*0-398-06459-8*) C C Thomas.

Day Care...an Emerging Crisis. George Thorman. 138p. (C). 1989. text ed. 37.95x (*0-398-05619-6*) C C Thomas.

Day-Case Anaesthesia & Sedation: Anaesthesia & Sedation for Day-Case Procedures & Ambulatory Surgery. Ed. by J. G. Whitwam. LC 93-34778. (Illus.). 304p. 1994. write for info. (*0-632-03704-0*) Blackwell Sci.

***Day Christ Died.** Bishop. 1995. mass mkt. 5.50 (*0-06-104342-7*, Harp PBks) HarpC.

Day Christ Died. Jim Bishop. 1991. pap. 10.00 (*0-06-060816-1*) Harper SF.

Day Christ Was Born. Jim Bishop. 1989. pap. 9.00 (*0-06-060794-7*) Harper SF.

Day Christ Was Born. large type ed. Jim Bishop. (Large Print Inspirational Ser.). 128p. 1986. pap. 8.95 (*0-8027-2548-1*) Walker & Co.

Day Christ Was Born & the Day Christ Died. Jim Bishop. 1993. 9.98 (*0-88365-830-5*) Galahad Bks.

***Day Congress Remembered: A Parable for Our Times.** Robert Skutch. 96p. 1995. pap. 8.95 (*0-89087-751-3*) Celestial Arts.

Day Dawns in Fire: America's Quest for Meaning. Merrill R. Abbey. LC 75-36439. 128p. reprint ed. pap. 36.50 (*0-685-16194-3*, 2026966) Bks Demand.

Day Dreaming-Night Thinking: Roaming in Two Worlds. Colin P. Osborne, III. LC 81-84497. (Illus.). 80p. 1982. 7.50 (*0-9607332-2-1*) Ololon Pubns.

Day Dreaming on Company Time. Robert Hood. 96p. (C). 1990. 45.00 (*0-9587972-2-6*, Pub. by Pascoe Pub AT) St Mut.

Day Dreams. Illus. by Pam Adams. LC 90-45583. (Imagination Ser.). 32p. (Orig.). (J). (ps-2). 1978. 11.95 (*0-85953-105-8*, Pub. by Childs Play UK); pap. 5.95 (*0-85953-082-5*, Pub. by Childs Play UK) Childs Play.

***Day Dreams.** Ed. by Christina Krayer. (YA). (gr. 7-12). 1994. pap. write for info. (*1-882869-09-5*) Varsity Read Servs.

Day Dreams. Elizabeth Walker. 384p. 1992. 25.95 (*0-7472-0516-7*, Pub. by Headline UK) Trafalgar.

Day Elvis Met Nixon. Egil Krogh. 61p. (Orig.). 1994. pap. 18.95 (*0-9640251-0-8*) Pejama Pr.

Day Estivall: Essays on the Music, Poetry & History of Scotland & England & Poems Previously Unpublished; in Honour of Helena Mennie Shire. Ed. by Alisoun Gardner-Medwin & Janet H. Williams. (Illus.). 192p. 1990. pap. text ed. 29.95 (*0-08-040914-8*, Pub. by Aberdeen U Pr) Macmillan.

Day Face & Night Face. Michael Fraenkel. 74p. 1947. pap. 25.00 (*0-87556-093-8*) Saifer.

An Asterisk (*) at the beginning of an entry indicates that the title is appearing in BIP for the first time.

D

An Asterisk (*) at the beginning of an entry indicates that the title is appearing in BIP for the first time.

1811

Day in the Life of Japan. Rick Smolan & David C. Cohen. 240p. 1985. 45.00 (*0-00-217580-0*) Collins SF.

Day in the Life of Mrs. Murphy: Murphy's Law Ad Infinitum. Zulma Gonzalez-Parker. 1989. 1.00 (*1-878255-00-2*) Heartfelt Pr.

Day in the Life of Spain. David C. Cohen & Rick Smolan. (Illus.). 224p. 1988. 45.00 (*0-318-33330-9*); Spanish Edition. 45.00 (*84-320-6564-1*) Collins SF.

***Day in the Life of Thailand.** Susan Wells & Steve Van Beek. Ed. by David Cohen et al. LC 94-43683. (Illus.). 1995. 45.00 (*0-00-255481-X*) Collins SF.

***Day in the Life of the Amish.** Ed. by Bob Ottum. 100p. Date not set. 14.98 (*0-89821-126-3*) Reiman Pubns.

Day in the Life of the Monarch Butterfly. Liz Zappler. Ed. by Ed Eakin. (Illus.). 48p. (J). (gr. 2-6). 1989. 8.85 (*0-89015-616-6*) Sunbelt Media.

Day in the Life of the New York Times. Ruth Adler. 1981. 24.95 (*0-405-13782-6*) Ayer.

Day in the Life of the Soviet Union. Rick Smolan & David C. Cohen. (Illus.). 1993. 45.00 (*0-00-255333-3*) Collins SF.

Day in the Life of Ziggy. Tom Wilson. (Ziggy Collection Ser.). (Illus.). 104p. 1993. pap. 6.95 (*0-8362-1713-6*) Andrews & McMeel.

Day in the Night of America. Kevin Coyne. LC 90-53139. 320p. 1992. 20.00 (*0-685-48008-9*) Random.

Day in the Night of America. Kevin Coyne. 336p. 1993. pap. 14.95 (*0-8050-2874-9*) H Holt & Co.

Day in the Night of America. Kevin Coyne. 1992. 21.50 (*0-394-57640-3*) Random.

Day in the Park. Marinella Nava. (Wire-O-Board Bks.). (Illus.). 24p. (J). (gr. 2 up). 1994. 7.95 (*1-55550-992-4*) Universe.

Day in the Season of the L. A. Dodgers. Tom Zimmerman. (Illus.). 192p. 1990. 16.95 (*0-944007-89-9*) Sure Sellers.

Day in the Season of the L. A. Dodgers. Tom Zimmerman. 1993. reprint ed. pap. 9.99 (*0-685-67862-8*, S P I Bks) Sure Sellers.

Day in the Strait. Emmanuel Hocquard. Tr. by Maryann DeJulio & Jane Staw. LC 85-70374. 48p. 1985. pap. 4.95 (*0-87376-045-X*) Red Dust.

Day in Thy Courts. Dorothy Ranaghan. LC 84-70866. 144p. (Orig.). 1984. pap. 4.95 (*0-943780-05-5*, 8055) Charismatic Ren Servs.

Day in Your Presence. St. Francis of Assisi. Ed. by David Hazard. (Rekindling the Inner Fire Ser.). 144p. (Orig.). 1992. pap. 6.99 (*1-55661-206-0*) Bethany Hse.

***Day Is Such a Lady.** Tom Cox & G. Kim Franz. Ed. by Reva Cox. 124p. (Orig.). 1994. pap. write for info. (*0-9644276-0-5*) Cox-Franz Pr.

Day Is Waiting. Linda Z. Knab. 1986. pap. 3.50 (*0-14-050395-1*, Penguin Bks) Viking Penguin.

Day Israel Dies! Salem Kirban. (Illus.). 1975. pap. 2.95 (*0-912582-21-9*) Kirban.

Day It Rained Forever: A Story of the Johnstown Flood. Virginia T. Gross. (Once Upon America Ser.). (Illus.). 64p. (J). (gr. 2-6). 1991. 11.95 (*0-670-83552-8*) Viking Child Bks.

Day It Rained Forever: The Story of the Johnstown Flood. Virginia T. Gross. LC 92-44712. (Once Upon America Ser.). (Illus.). 64p. (J). (gr. 2-6). 1993. reprint ed. pap. 3.99 (*0-14-034567-1*, Puffin) Puffin Bks.

Day It Snowed Tortillas: Tales from Spanish New Mexico. Illus. by Lucy Jelinek. 80p. 1981. reprint ed. pap. 9.95 (*0-933553-00-5*) Mariposa Print Pub.

Day J. F. K. Died, Thirty Years Later: The Event That Changed a Generation. Ed. & Photos by Dallas Morning News Staff. (Illus.). 160p. (Orig.). 1993. pap. 10.95 (*0-8362-6247-6*) Andrews & McMeel.

Day-Ja Vu. Bill Day. (Illus.). 195p. 1988. pap. 9.95 (*0-937247-07-3*) Detroit Pr.

Day Japan Bombed Pearl Harbor & Other Stories. Leslie W. Hedley. 148p. 1984. pap. 7.95 (*0-933515-03-0*) Exile Pr.

Day Jimmy's Boa Ate the Wash. Trinka H. Noble. LC 80-15098. (Pied Piper Bks.). (Illus.). 32p. (J). (ps-3). 1980. 14.99 (*0-8037-1723-7*); lib. bdg. 13.89 (*0-8037-1724-5*); pap. 4.95 (*0-8037-0094-6*) Dial Bks Young.

Day Jimmy's Boa Ate the Wash. Trinka H. Noble. (Illus.). 32p. (J). (ps-3). 1992. pap. 4.99 (*0-14-054623-5*, Puff Pied Piper) Puffin Bks.

Day Jimmy's Boa Ate the Wash. enl. ed. Trinka H. Noble. (J). (ps-3). 1991. pap. 17.95 (*0-8037-1073-9*, Puff Pied Piper) Puffin Bks.

Day Jimmy's Boa Ate the Wash: Giant Edition. Trinka H. Noble. (J). (ps-3). 1993. pap. 18.99 (*0-14-054622-7*) Viking Penguin.

***Day John Met Paul: An Hour-by-Hour Account of How the Beatles Began. Jim O'Donnell. LC 99-77840. 164p. (Orig.). 1994. pap. 9.95 (*0-9636905-6-6*) Hall Fame Bks.**

THE DAY JOHN MET PAUL is the remarkable hour-by-hour account of the day the Beatles began: July 6, 1957. On that day in northwest England, teenagers John Lennon & Paul McCartney met & exchanged guitar licks. Jim O'Donnell, a journalist & author of three rock music books, goes further back than the Hamburg of the "Backbeat" movie to unearth this amazing close-up portrait. O'Donnell reconstructs the events of that single July day, from pre-dawn to near-midnight, with each chapter containing a group of hours. During his eight years of research, O'Donnell gained the unprecedented cooperation of many of the day's major figures, including most of Lennon's band, the Quarry Men. Includes extensive bibliography. According to Ray Coleman, best-selling writer of John Lennon's authorized biography, "This is one of the best Beatle books ever written! It's a crucial book to understanding the Beatle story." Colin Hanton, the Quarry Man who played drums behind Lennon that day, said: "THE DAY JOHN MET PAUL is brilliant! I can't fault it." To order direct: send $12.95 ($9.95 plus $3 s&h) to Hall of Fame Books, Box 232, 61 East 8th St., New York, NY 10003.
Publisher Provided Annotation.

Day Kennedy Was Shot. Jim Bishop. 713p. 1992. pap. 13.00 (*0-00-637901-X*, Pub. by HarpC CN) HarpC.

Day Lasts More Than a Hundred Years. Chingiz Aitmatov. Tr. by John French. LC 83-48135. 368p. 1983. 30.00 (*0-253-11595-7*); pap. 12.95 (*0-253-20482-8*, MB 482) Ind U Pr.

***Day Late & a Dollar Short.** McMillan. 1995. (*0-670-86042-5*, Viking) Viking Penguin.

Day Late & a Dollar Short. Spike Van Cleve. LC 81-83817. (Illus.). 298p. 1982. 19.95 (*0-913504-65-3*) Lowell Pr.

Day Light Day Bright. 366p. (Orig.). 1989. spiral bd. 7.00 (*1-882835-05-0*) STA-Kris.

Day Lights, Night Lights. Cecile Schoberle. LC 93-18680. (J). (gr. 4 up). 1994. pap. 14.00 (*0-671-87439-X*, S&S Bks Young Read) S&S Childrens.

Day Lincoln Was Shot. Jim Bishop. 1942. mass mkt. 6.50 (*0-06-080005-4*, P5, PL) HarpC.

Day Mama Got Her Bonus, Set. ETR Associates. (J). (gr. 4 up). 1993. 235.00 (*1-56071-081-0*) ETR Assocs.

Day Man Lost: Hiroshima, 6 August 1945. Pacific War Research Society Staff. LC 80-85386. (Illus.). 312p. 1981. reprint ed. pap. 7.95 (*0-87011-471-9*) Kodansha.

Day Martin Luther King, Jr. Was Shot: A Photo History of the Civil Rights Movement. Jim Haskins. (J). (gr. 4-7). 1992. pap. 5.95 (*0-590-43661-9*) Scholastic Inc.

Day Michael Collins Was Shot. Meda C. Ryan. LC 89-82488. 1989. pap. 13.95 (*1-85371-041-5*, Pub. by Poolbeg Pr IE) Dufour.

Day Miss Bessie Lewis Disappeared. Doris M. Disney. 224p. 1987. pap. 2.95 (*0-8217-2080-5*) Zebra.

Day Mom Stopped the Bus! Ellen Ford. (Illus.). 16p. (Orig.). (J). (gr. 5-8). 1994. pap. 5.95 (*0-9615961-3-9*) Raven Rocks Pr.

Day My Father Died: Women Share Their Stories of Love, Loss, & Life. Ed. by Diana Ajjan. LC 93-85509. (Illus.). 256p. 1994. 19.95 (*1-56138-189-6*) Running Pr.

***Day My Mom Almost Enrolled in Preschool.** Dianne Dannhauss. Ed. by Debbie Bowen. (Professional Mom Ser.). (Illus.). 24p. (J). (gr. 1-4). Date not set. lib. bdg. 11.95 (*1-56763-149-5*); pap. text ed. 5.95 (*1-56763-150-9*) Ozark Pub.

Day No Pigs Would Die. Robert N. Peck. 1972. 20.00 (*0-394-48235-2*) Knopf.

***Day No Pigs Would Die.** Robert N. Peck. LC 72-259. 156p. (J). (gr. 7 up). 1994. pap. 3.99 (*0-679-85306-5*) Random Bks Yng Read.

Day No Pigs Would Die: A Study Guide. Crystal Norris. (Novel-Ties Ser.). (gr. 7-11). 1987. student ed, teacher ed 15.95 (*0-88122-111-2*) Lrn Links.

Day Noah Died: Tales by Francesco Jovine. Francesco Jovine. Tr. by Walter J. Centuori. (Illus.). 100p. (Orig.). 1987. pap. 6.95 (*0-9615937-2-5*) Star City Pubns.

Day Nothing Happened. Terence Clarke. LC 87-28747. 223p. 1988. 16.95 (*0-916515-36-2*) Mercury Hse Inc.

Day Nothing Happened. Terence Clarke. LC 87-28747. 223p. 1990. pap. 8.95 (*0-916515-75-3*) Mercury Hse Inc.

***Day Nurseries at a Crossroads: Meeting the Challenge of Child Care in the Nineties.** Jeni Vernon & Celia Smith. 192p. 1995. pap. 27.50 (*1-874579-36-9*) Paul & Co Pubs.

Day of Ahmed's Secret. Florence P. Heide. 32p. (J). 1990. 16.00 (*0-688-08894-5*); lib. bdg. 15.93 (*0-688-08895-3*) Lothrop.

Day of Ahmed's Secret. Florence Heide & Judith H. Gilliland. Ed. by Amy Cohn. (Illus.). 32p. (J). (ps up). 1995. reprint ed. pap. 4.95 (*0-318-72966-0*, Mulberry) Morrow.

Day of Ahmed's Secret. Florence P. Heide & Judith H. Gilliland. LC 87-33316. (Illus.). 32p. (J). (ps up). 1995. reprint ed. pap. 4.95 (*0-688-14023-8*, Mulberry) Morrow.

Day of Atonement. Faye Kellerman. (Los Angeles Mysteries Ser.). 1992. mass mkt. 5.99 (*0-449-14824-6*, GM) Fawcett.

Day of Atonement. large type ed. Faye Kellerman. (General Ser.). 401p. 1992. text ed. 21.95 (*0-8161-5351-5*, Large Print Bks) Hall.

Day of Brahma. Sri Donato. Ed. by Morningland Publications, Inc. Staff. (Illus.). 377p. 1981. pap. 10.00 (*0-935146-20-2*) Morningland.

Day of Delight: A Jewish Sabbath in Ethiopia. Maxine R. Schur. LC 93-31451. (Illus.). (J). (gr. k-4). 1994. 15.99 (*0-8037-1413-0*); lib. bdg. 15.89 (*0-8037-1414-9*) Dial Bks Young.

Day of Descent. Judith Reeves-Stevens & Garfield Reeves-Stevens. Ed. by Kevin Ryan. (Alien Nation Ser.: No. 1). 416p. (Orig.). 1993. mass mkt. 4.99 (*0-671-73599-3*, Pocket Star Bks) PB.

Day of Disaster. Katie F. Wiebe. LC 75-43057. (Illus.). 225p. 1976. pap. 1.95 (*0-8361-1793-X*) Herald Pr.

Day of Doom. Michael Wigglesworth. 100p. 1991. pap. 5.95 (*0-929408-05-5*) Amer Eagle Pubns Inc.

Day of Glory: The Life of Baha'u'llah. Mary Perkins. (Illus.). 160p. 1992. 24.95 (*0-85398-347-X*); pap. 11.95 (*0-85398-339-9*) G Ronald Pub.

Day of Humiliation: Times of Affliction & Disaster. Cotton Mather. LC 68-24211. 1970. 60.00 (*0-8201-1067-1*) Schol Facsimiles.

Day of Infamy. Walter Lord. (Illus.). (J). (gr. 9 up). 1991. reprint ed. 15.00 (*0-03-027620-9*) Adm Nimitz Foun.

Day of Joy. (ENG & HEB.). 7.50 (*0-87559-103-5*) Shalom.

Day of Judgement. Jack Higgins. 1991. mass mkt. 5.95 (*0-671-74628-6*) PB.

Day of Judgement. Salem Kirban. LC 74-13724. (Musical Cantata Ser.). 1975. pap. 9.95 (*0-912582-19-7*) Kirban.

Day of Judgement. Salatore Satta. Tr. by Patrick Creagh. 298p. 1994. pap. 14.00 (*0-00-271147-8*, IntlDept) HarpC.

Day of Judgment. Frank Rich. (Jake Strait Ser.). 1994. mass mkt. 3.50 (*0-373-63609-1*, 1-63609-1) Harlequin Bks.

***Day of Judgment.** Salvatore Satta. 1995. 23.00 (*0-8446-6868-0*) Peter Smith.

Day of Maysalun: A Page from the Modern History of the Arabs. Abu Khaldun Sati Al Husri. Tr. by Sidney Glazer. LC 66-29228. 1966. pap. 1.50 (*0-916808-06-8*) Mid East Inst.

Day of Pleasant Bread. David Grayson, pseud. (Illus.). 32p. 1988. reprint ed. pap. 5.95 (*1-55838-098-1*) R H Pub.

Day of Pleasure: Stories of a Boy Growing up in Warsaw. Isaac Bashevis Singer. LC 70-95461. (Illus.). 160p. (J). (gr. 3 up). 1986. pap. 5.95 (*0-374-41696-6*, Sunburst Bks) FS&G.

Day of Pleasure & Other Stories. Isaac Bashevis Singer. 1992. 11.98 (*0-88365-798-8*) Galahad Bks.

Day of Prosperity: A Vision of the Century to Come. Paul Devinne. LC 73-154439. (Utopian Literature Ser.). 1976. reprint ed. 23.95 (*0-405-03522-5*) Ayer.

Day of Reckoning. Robert Angel. 79p. 1974. 6.50 (*0-87881-010-2*) Mojave Bks.

Day of Reckoning. Nyle W. Estes. (Illus.). 160p. 1990. pap. 6.95 (*0-910042-58-6*) Allegheny.

Day of Reckoning. Benjamin M. Friedman. 1989. pap. 11.00 (*0-679-72569-5*, Vin) Random.

Day of Reckoning. Ray Hogan. Bd. with Dead Man on a Black Horse. 1982. Set pap. 2.50 (*0-451-11523-6*, AE1523, Sig) NAL-Dutton.

Day of Reckoning. John Katzenbach. 1990. mass mkt. 5.95 (*0-345-36515-1*) Ballantine.

Day of Reckoning. abr. ed. Kurt Arnusch. 90p. 1995. pap. 6.95 (*1-56901-480-9*) NW Pub.

***Day of Reckoning.** large type ed. Ray Hogan. LC 94-44694. 1995. 17.95 (*0-7862-0406-0*) Thorndike Pr.

Day of Reckoning: The Consequences of American Economic Policy in the 1980's. Benjamin M. Friedman. LC 87-43222. 256p. 1988. 19.45 (*0-394-56553-3*) Random.

Day of Redemption. Douglas Orbaker & Robert A. Blake. Ed. by Michael L. Sherer. (Orig.). 1987. pap. 2.35 (*0-89536-848-X*, 7807) CSS OH.

Day of Remembrance. Sandra S. Yamate. LC 93-45792. (J). 1994. 12.95 (*1-879965-12-7*) Polychrome Pub.

Day of Silence & Other Stories. George Gissing. 375p. 1993. pap. 6.95 (*0-460-87242-7*, Everyman's Classic Lib) C E Tuttle.

Day of Surprises. Sylvia R. Tester. LC 78-23263. (Understanding Myself Picture Bks.). (Illus.). (J). (ps-2). 1979. lib. bdg. 21.36 (*0-89565-022-3*) Childs World.

Day of the Beast. Zane Grey. 1992. mass mkt. 3.99 (*0-06-100499-5*, Harp PBks) HarpC.

Day of the Big Dollar. large type ed. Peter Chambers. (Linford Mystery Library). 288p. 1994. pap. 14.95 (*0-7089-7481-3*, Linford) Ulverscroft.

Day of the Black Sun. Jean Van Hamme. Tr. by Jean-Jacques Surbeck. (Code XIII Ser.). (Illus.). (Orig.). 1989. pap. 6.95 (*0-87416-061-8*, Comcat Comics) Catalan Communs.

Day of the Bonanza. Hiram M. Drache. LC 64-65044. (Illus.). 239p. 1964. text ed. 20.95 (*0-8134-1995-6*, 1995) Interstate.

Day of the Cheetah. Dale Brown. 528p. 1990. mass mkt. 5.99 (*0-425-12043-0*) Berkley Pub.

Day of the Comancheros. large type ed. Steven C. Lawrence. (Linford Western Library). 272p. 1985. pap. 11.95 (*0-7089-6080-4*, Trailtree Bookshop) Ulverscroft.

Day of the Confederacy: Chronicle of the Embattled South. Nathaniel W. Stephenson. (History - United States Ser.). 214p. 1992. reprint ed. lib. bdg. 79.00 (*0-7812-6184-8*) Rprt Serv.

Day of the Covenant: A Compilation. Date not set. 14.95 (*0-933770-88-X*) Kalimat.

Day of the Daleks. Terrance Dicks. (Dr. Who Ser.: No. 1). 1989. pap. 3.50 (*1-55817-188-6*, Pinnacle NY) Windsor NY.

***Day of the Dead.** Diane Hoyt-Goldsmith. (Illus.). 1995. pap. 6.95 (*0-8234-1200-8*) Holiday.

Day of the Dead: A Mexican-American Celebration. Diane Hoyt-Goldsmith. LC 93-42106. (Illus.). 32p. (J). (gr. 3-7). 1994. lib. bdg. 15.95 (*0-8234-1094-3*) Holiday.

***Day of the Dead: And Other Mortal Reflections.** F. Gonzalez-Crussi. LC 94-3409. 1994. pap. 8.95 (*0-15-600142-X*, Harvest Bks) HarBrace.

Day of the Dead: And Other Mortal Reflections. Frank Gonzalez-Crussi. LC 93-15459. 1993. 19.95 (*0-15-181192-X*, Harvest Bks) HarBrace.

Day of the Dead: And other Portal Reflections. Crussi F. Gonzalez. 1994. pap. 8.95 (*0-15-600000-8*) HarBrace.

Day of the Delphi. Jon Land. 432p. (Orig.). 1993. mass mkt. 5.99 (*0-8125-3434-4*) Tor Bks.

Day of the Destroyer. Scott Bennie. Ed. by Rob Bell. (Champions Ser.). (Illus.). 32p. (Orig.). (YA). (gr. 12). 1990. pap. 7.00 (*1-55806-101-0*, 408) Iron Crown Ent Inc.

Day of the Dinosaur. Stan Berenstain & Janice Berenstain. LC 87-9828. (First Time Readers Ser.). (Illus.). 32p. (J). (gr. k-3). 1987. lib. bdg. 5.99 (*0-394-99130-3*); pap. 2.25 (*0-394-89130-9*) Random Bks Yng Read.

Day of the Dinosaur. Franklin W. Dixon. Ed. by Ruth Ashby. (Hardy Boys Ser.: No. 128). 160p. (Orig.). (J). 1994. mass mkt. 3.99 (*0-671-87212-5*, Minstrel Bks) PB.

Day of the Dinosaur. David Noffs & Laurie Noffs. (Illus.). 24p. (Orig.). (J). (gr. 4-8). 1989. student ed 2.50 (*0-929875-12-5*) Noffs Assocs.

Day of the Dissonance. Alan D. Foster. 1984. 17.00 (*0-932096-30-1*) Phantasia Pr.

Day of the Dragon: How Current Events Have Set the Stage for America's Destiny: The Great Controversy Vindicated. Clifford Goldstein. LC 92-41909. 1993. 8.95 (*0-8163-1148-X*) Pacific Pr Pub Assn.

Day of the East Wind. Julia Shuken. LC 93-12304. 256p. (Orig.). 1993. pap. 9.99 (*0-89107-743-X*) Crossway Bks.

***Day of the Great Wave: And Other Folktales from Highlights.** Highlights Staff. LC 94-72484. (Illus.). 96p. (J). (gr. 2-5). 1995. 2.95 (*1-56397-442-8*, Wordsong) Boyds Mills Pr.

Day of the Halfbreeds. Peter McCurtin. (Sundance Ser.: No. 29). 1979. pap. 1.75 (*0-8439-0693-6*) Dorchester Pub Co.

Day of the High Climber. Gary Hines. LC 93-12254. (Illus.). 32p. (J). (ps up). 1994. 14.00 (*0-688-11494-6*); lib. bdg. 13.93 (*0-688-11495-4*) Greenwillow.

Day of the Hunter. Ann Ahlswede. 1994. lib. bdg. 15.95 (*0-7451-4604-X*, Gunsmoke) Chivers N Amer.

Day of the Hunter. large type ed. Ann Ahlswede. LC 94-9238. 1994. pap. 15.95 (*0-8161-5981-5*) Hall.

Day of the Jackal. Frederick Forsyth. 1982. mass mkt. 6.99 (*0-553-26630-6*) Bantam.

Day of the Jackal. large type ed. Frederick Forsyth. 1992. 20.95 (*0-7927-1003-7*, E0024, Eagle Lrg Print) Chivers N Amer.

Day of the Jackal. large type ed. Frederick Forsyth. 1992. pap. 17.95 (*0-7927-1004-5*, Paragon Lrg Print) Chivers N Amer.

Day of the Jackal. Frederick Forsyth. 1994. reprint ed. lib. bdg. 32.95 (*1-56849-279-0*) Buccaneer Bks.

Day of the Jubilee: The Civil War Experience of Black Southerners. Intro. by Donald G. Nieman. LC 93-33613. (African American Life in the Post-Emancipation South Ser.: No. 1). (Illus.). 408p. 1994. 63.00 (*0-8153-1438-8*) Garland.

Day of the Leopards: Essays in Defense of Poems. William K. Wimsatt. LC 75-27762. 272p. reprint ed. pap. 77.60 (*0-8357-3761-6*, 2036487) Bks Demand.

Day of the Locust. Nathanael West. 17.95 (*0-88411-871-1*, Aeonian Pr) Amereon Ltd.

Day of the Locust. Nathanael West. 208p. 1983. pap. 5.95 (*0-451-52348-2*, Sig Classics) NAL-Dutton.

Day of the Locust. Nathanael West. 391p. 1992. reprint ed. lib. bdg. 18.95 (*0-89966-302-8*) Buccaneer Bks.

Day of the Lord: Prophecy Revealed. Roy A. Reinhold. LC 86-51559. (Illus.). 216p. (Orig.). 1987. pap. 6.95 (*0-9616306-0-4*) Windstar Bks.

Day of the Minotaur. Thomas B. Swann. 1993. reprint ed. lib. bdg. 18.95 (*0-89968-413-0*, Lghtyr Pr) Buccaneer Bks.

Day of the Moon. Bill Pronzini & Jeffrey Wallmann. 192p. 1993. pap. 3.95 (*0-88184-976-6*) Carroll & Graf.

***Day of the Moon Shadow: Tales with Ancient Answers to Scientific Questions.** Judy Gail & Linda A. Houlding. 135p. 1995. pap. text ed. 22.00 (*1-56308-348-5*) Teacher Ideas Pr.

Day of the Ogre Kachinas. Janet H. Hammond. LC 94-66101. (Council for Indian Education Ser.). (Illus.). 48p. (J). (gr. k-6). 1994. pap. 4.95 (*1-57098-002-0*) R Rinehart.

Day of the Rope. Kevin Hamilton. 1990. 25.00 (*0-932526-28-4*) Nexus Pr.

Day of the Rope. deluxe ed. Kevin Hamilton. 1990. 350.00 (*0-932526-31-4*) Nexus Pr.

Day of the Scorpion. Paul Scott. (Raj Quartet Ser.: Vol. II). 512p. 1979. mass mkt. 4.95 (*0-380-40923-2*) Avon.

Day of the Scorpion. Paul Scott. (Raj Quartet Ser.). 512p. 1992. pap. 11.00 (*0-380-71809-X*) Avon.

Day of the Snake. Matthew J. Costello. (Time Warrior Ser.: No. 3). 320p. (Orig.). 1992. pap. 4.99 (*0-451-45170-8*, ROC) NAL-Dutton.

Day of the Storm. Rosamunde Pilcher. 1989. mass mkt. 4.99 (*0-440-20253-1*) Dell.

Day of the Storm. large type ed. Rosamunde Pilcher. 313p. 1992. reprint ed. lib. bdg. 19.95 (*1-56054-154-7*) Thorndike Pr.

Day of the Triffids. John Wyndham. 224p. 1993. pap. 3.95 (*0-88184-989-8*) Carroll & Graf.

Day of the Triffids. John Wyndham. 192p. 1985. mass mkt. 4.95 (*0-345-32817-5*, Del Rey) Ballantine.

Day of the Triffids. John Wyndham. 1993. reprint ed. lib. bdg. 18.95 (*0-89968-386-X*, Lghtyr Pr) Buccaneer Bks.

***Day of the Twelve-Story Wave.** Diane Swanson. (Illus.). (J). (gr. k-4). 1995. 14.95 (*1-56352-260-8*) Longstreet Pr Inc.

Day of the Tyrant: There Will be War, No. 4. Ed. by Jerry Pournelle. 352p. 1988. pap. 3.95 (*0-8125-0066-0*) Tor Bks.

Day of the Unicorn. Mollie Hunter. LC 91-44763. (Illus.). 96p. (J). (gr. 2-5). 1994. 14.00 (*0-06-021062-1*, HarpT) HarpC.

Day of the Winged Lion & Other Stories. Silo. Tr. by John Incledon. 140p. Date not set. pap. 12.95 (*1-878977-20-2*) Latitude Pr.

1812

An Asterisk (*) at the beginning of an entry indicates that the title is appearing in BIP for the first time.

D

An Asterisk (*) at the beginning of an entry indicates that the title is appearing in BIP for the first time.

1813

Day with Yoga. Elisabeth Haich. 104p. 1987. pap. 4.95 (0-943358-12-4) Aurora Press.

Day Without Cartoons: Poetry for Gifted Students. Kristopher K. Johnson. Ed. by Ellen S. Kester. (Illus.). 50p. (Orig.). (J). (gr. 3-8). 1989. pap. 6.95 (0-685-26282-0) Pickwick Pubs.

Day Without Cartoons: Teacher's Manual: Gifted Education. Ellen S. Kester. (Illus.). 150p. (Orig.). 1989. pap. 35.00 (0-685-26283-9) Pickwick Pubs.

Day Without Sunshine. Les Whitten. 416p. 1986. pap. 4.95 (0-07-079885-0) McGraw.

Day X. Kurt E. Koch. LC 70-160688. 128p. 1970. pap. 4.99 (0-8254-3005-4) Kregel.

Daybook: The Journal of an Artist. Anne Truitt. 240p. 1984. pap. 11.95 (0-14-006963-1, Penguin Bks) Viking Penguin.

Daybook - Division. Robert Crosson et al. 128p. 1991. 12.50 (0-88031-070-7) Invisible-Red Hill.

Daybook from a Kitchen Drawer. Irene Fay. LC 85-13490. (Illus.). 1985. 16.95 (0-915361-25-6) Modan-Adama Bks.

Daybooks of Edward Weston. Edward Weston. 1991. 45.00 (0-89381-450-4); pap. 29.95 (0-89381-445-8) Aperture.

Daybreak. North Callahan. LC 85-442. 264p. 1986. 15.95 (0-8453-4796-9, Cornwall Bks) Assoc Univ Prs.

*Daybreak. Harold Fickett. LC 94-40301. (Of Saints & Sinners Ser.: Bk. 2). 288p. 1995. pap. 8.99 (1-55661-176-5) Bethany Hse.

Daybreak. Jack Hayford. 112p. (Orig.). 1987. 3.99 (0-8423-0524-6) Tyndale.

Daybreak. Burt Hirschfeld. 384p. 1992. 20.00 (0-7278-4386-9) Severn Hse.

Daybreak. Belva Plain. 1994. 22.95 (0-385-31104-4) Delacorte.

*Daybreak. Belva Plain. 1995. mass mkt. 6.99 (0-440-21681-8) Dell.

Daybreak. Mary S. Rain. 1991. pap. 14.95 (1-878901-14-1) Hampton Roads Pub Co.

Daybreak. Arthur Schnitzler. Tr. by William A. Drake. LC 73-175443. reprint ed. 37.50 (0-404-05615-6) AMS Pr.

Daybreak: A Novel. Belva Plain. 1994. 27.95 (0-385-31232-6) Delacorte.

Daybreak: A Romance of an Old World. 2nd ed. James Cowan. LC 72-154436. (Utopian Literature Ser.). (Illus.). 1976. reprint ed. 28.95 (0-405-03519-5) Ayer.

Daybreak: Meditations for Women Survivors of Sexual Abuse. Maureen Brady. 400p. (Orig.). 1991. pap. 10.00 (0-89486-759-8, 5053A) Hazelden.

Daybreak: Thoughts on the Prejudices of Morality. Friedrich Nietzsche. Tr. by R. J. Hollingdale. LC 81-18017. (Texts in German Philosophy Ser.). 220p. 1982. pap. 16.95 (0-521-28662-X) Cambridge U Pr.

Daybreak: Walking Daily in Christ's Presence. Jack W. Hayford. LC 84-80749. (Orig.). 1984. pap. 2.95 (0-916847-05-5) Living Way.

Daybreak Boys: Essays on the Literature of the Beat Generation. Gregory Stephenson. LC 88-27095. 240p. (C). 1990. 24.95 (0-8093-1564-5) S Ill U Pr.

Daybreakers. Jane L. Curry. (Illus.). (J). (gr. 3-7). 1991. 20.50 (0-8446-6474-X) Peter Smith.

*Daybreak's Men of Character. 1995. spiral bd. 7.99 (0-310-96240-4) Zondervan.

*Daybreak's Treasured Inspiration. 1995. spiral bd. 9.99 (0-310-96241-2) Zondervan.

*Daycamp Nightmare. Butcher. (Camp At Your Own Risk Ser.: No. 1). (J). 1995. pap. 3.50 (0-553-48247-5) Bantam.

Daycare. rev. ed. Alison Clarke-Stewart. LC 92-19515. (Developing Child Ser.). 216p. 1993. 24.00 (0-674-19405-5) HUP.

Daycare. rev. ed. Alison Clarke-Stewart. LC 92-19515. (Developing Child Ser.). 216p. 1993. pap. text ed. 9.95 (0-674-19406-3) HUP.

*Daycare: What Can a Mother Do. Loretta Rose. 16p. 1994. per., pap. 6.00 (0-8059-3653-X) Dorrance.

Daycare Mother's Manual: How to Start & Operate a Childcare Service in Your Home. Terri Denis. LC 85-82160. 1986. pap. 7.00 (0-936733-02-0) Fred Robot Factory.

Daydream Believer. Nicole Grey. (Girl Friends Ser.: No. 6). 224p. 1993. pap. 3.50 (0-8217-4420-8) Zebra.

Daydreamer. Ian McEwan. LC 93-44476. (Illus.). 208p. (J). (gr. 3 up). 1994. 14.00 (0-06-024426-7); lib. bdg. 13.89 (0-06-024427-5) HarpC Child Bks.

Daydreamers. Eloise Greenfield. LC 80-27262. (Pied Piper Bks.). (Illus.). (J). (gr. k up). 1985. reprint ed. pap. 4.95 (0-8037-0167-5) Dial Bks Young.

Daydreaming in Humans & Machines: A Computer Model of the Stream of Thought. Erik T. Mueller. LC 89-6483. 416p. 1990. text ed. 65.00 (0-89391-562-9) Ablex Pub.

Daydreams. Marina Palmieri. 224p. (Orig.). 1991. pap. 2.95 (1-878702-53-X, Kismet) Meteor Pub.

Daydreams. Mitchell Smith. 480p. 1988. pap. 5.99 (0-451-40089-5, Onyx) NAL-Dutton.

Daydreams & Nightmares: Czech Communist & Ex-Communist Literature, 1917-1987. Peter Hruby. (East European Monographs: No. 290). 384p. 1990. text ed. 29.50 (0-88033-187-9) Col U Pr.

Daydreams & Nightmares: Reflections of a Harlem Childhood. Irving L. Horowitz. LC 89-25054. 152p. 1990. 20.00 (0-87805-428-6) U Pr of Miss.

Daydreams & Sunbeams: An Album of Framable Word Pictures. Charlotte C. Partin. (Illus.). 18p. (Orig.). (YA). (gr. 7 up). 1987. pap. 4.00 (0-9619816-0-1) C C Partin.

Dayenu - Enough! How Uncle Murray Saved the Seder. Rosalind Schilder. LC 88-1238. (Illus.). (Orig.). (J). (ps-3). 1988. pap. 5.95 (0-930494-76-8) Kar Ben.

Dayhiker. Robert Wood. 144p. (Orig.). 1991. pap. 8.95 (0-89815-406-5) Ten Speed Pr.

Dayhiker's Guide to Southern California. John C. McKinney. Ed. by Cheri Rae. (Illus.). 400p. (Orig.). 1992. pap. 14.95 (0-934161-12-7) Olympus Pr.

Daykeeper: The Life & Discourse of As Ixtil Dviner. Benjamin N. Colby & Lore M. Colby. (Illus.). 345p. (C). 1981. 39.95 (0-674-19409-8) HUP.

Daylight. Jelaluddin Rumi. (Illus.). 1990. 19.00 (0-939660-35-0) Threshold VT.

Daylight Bodies. Taylor Graham. 98p. (Orig.). 1992. pap. 7.50 (1-880575-11-6) Hot Pepper.

Daylight Devotional Bible: NIV. 12.99 (0-88469-223-X) BMH Bks.

Daylight in the Canyon: The Memoirs of Eleanor Lynde. 2nd ed. Eleanor Lynde. (Illus.). 231p. reprint ed. pap. text ed. write for info. (0-9639967-0-3) Daylght MT.

Daylight in the Swamp. Robert W. Wells. LC 77-77666. 240p. 1984. reprint ed. pap. 11.95 (0-942802-07-1) NorthWord.

Daylight Moon & Other Poems. Les Murray. LC 87-7918. 120p. 1988. 17.95 (0-89255-125-9); pap. 9.95 (0-89255-138-0) Persea Bks.

Daylight, 4449's Family Album. Kenneth G. Johnsen. (Illus.). 116p. (Orig.). 1984. pap. 16.95 (0-9613267-0-0) K G Johnsen.

Daylighting. (Recommended Practice Ser.). 50p. 1991. 25.00 (0-87995-052-8, RP-5-1979) Illum Eng.

Daylighting Buildings. B. Norton & H. Lockhart-Ball. (C). 1989. 125.00 (0-685-33097-4, Pub. by Interntl Solar Energy Soc UK) St Mut.

Daylighting in Architecture: A European Reference Book. Ed. by N. V. Baker et al. (Illus.). 420p. (Orig.). (C). 1993. 95.00 (1-873936-21-4, Pub. by J & J Sci Pubs UK) Bks Intl VA.

*Daylighting Performance & Design. Gregg D. Ander. LC 94-45674. 1995. text ed. 59.95 (0-442-01921-1) Van Nos Reinhold.

Daylilies. Arlow B. Stout. (Illus.). 200p. 1986. 29.00 (0-89831-028-8) Sagapr.

Daylilies: The Beginner's Handbook. American Hemerocallis Society Staff. Ed. by Frances L. Gatlin. (Illus.). 80p. 1991. pap. text ed. 6.00 (0-9631072-0-8) Am Hemerocallis.

Daylilies: The Perfect Perennial. Lewis Hill & Nancy Hill. Ed. by Gwen Steege. (Illus.). 208p. (Orig.). 1991. 24.95 (0-88266-652-5, Garden Way Pub); pap. 14.95 (0-88266-651-7, Garden Way Pub) Storey Comm Inc.

*Daylilies - A Fifty Year Affair: The Story of a Society & Its Flower. Frances Gatlin. (Illus.). 1995. 29.95 (0-9631072-1-6) Am Hemerocallis.

Daylily Encyclopedia. Ed. by Steve Webber. LC 87-91714. (Illus.). 176p. (Orig.). 1988. pap. 13.95 (0-9619515-0-8) Webber Gardens.

Daymares. abr. ed. Adrian Harris. 262p. Date not set. pap. 8.95 (1-56901-376-4) NW Pub.

*Dayneford's Library: American Homosexual Literature, 1900-1913. James Gifford. (Illus.). 1995. pap. 13.95 (0-87023-994-5) U of Mass Pr.

*Dayneford's Library: American Homosexual Literature, 1900-1913. James Gifford. (Illus.). 200p. (C). 1995. text ed. 35.00 (0-87023-993-7) U of Mass Pr.

Days. Ralph F. Parkison. Ed. by Marion O. Withrow. (Illus.). 60p. (Orig.). (J). (gr. 2-8). 1988. pap. write for info. (0-318-64003-1) Little Wood Bks.

Days along the Buckwheat & Dandelion. Fred Pugh. 142p. 1984. pap. 20.00 (0-914821-04-0) Worden Pr.

Days & Customs of All Faiths. Howard V. Harper. LC 89-63106. xiv, 399p. 1990. reprint ed. lib. bdg. 48.00 (1-55888-850-0) Omnigraphics Inc.

*Days & Hours of the Life of the Lord Jesus. (Walk with Jesus Ser.). 108p. 1992. pap. 20.00 (1-57277-407-X) Truth Center.

Days & Knights of Camelot Paper Dolls. Charlotte Whatley. (Illus.). 32p. (Orig.). 1990. pap. 4.95 (0-87588-361-3) Hobby Hse.

Days & Memory. Charlotte Delbo. Tr. & Pref. by Rosette Lamont. LC 89-63596. 140p. (Orig.). 1990. pap. 10.95 (0-910395-55-1) Marlboro Pr.

Days & Nights. Alfred Jarry. Tr. by Alexis Lykiard. 140p. (Orig.). 1992. pap. 13.99 (0-947757-19-8) Serpents Tail.

Days & Nights by the Desert. Parker Gillmore. LC 72-3982. (Black Heritage Library Collection). 1977. reprint ed. 24.95 (0-8369-9097-8) Ayer.

*Days & Nights in Calcutta. Clark Blaise & Bharati Mukherjee. 336p. 1995. reprint ed. pap. 14.00 (1-886913-01-3) Hungry Mind.

Days & Nights of Beebee Fenstermaker. William Snyder. 1963. pap. 4.75 (0-8222-0280-8) Dramatists Play.

Days & Nights of Love & War. Eduardo Galeano. Tr. by Judith Brister. LC 82-48034. 192p. 1982. 16.00 (0-85345-620-8); pap. 8.00 (0-85345-621-6) Monthly Rev.

Days & Nights of the Central West End. Suzanne Goell. (Illus.). 166p. (Orig.). 1992. pap. text ed. 8.95 (0-9631448-0-4) VA Pub Corp.

*Days & Nights on the Amazon. Darlene B. Quaife. 1995. pap. 12.95 (0-88801-183-0) InBook.

Days & Routes Through Maps & Scores. Jocy De Oliveira. (Illus.). 176p. 1984. 16.95 (85-7069-001-0) Lingua Pr.

Days & Years. Karl Young. 62p. 1987. pap. 5.00 (0-87924-057-1) Membrane Pr.

Days Are Just Packed: A Calvin & Hobbes Collection. Bill Watterson. (Illus.). 176p. (Orig.). 1993. 19.95 (0-8362-1736-5); pap. 12.95 (0-8362-1735-7) Andrews & McMeel.

Days Are Surely Coming: Sermons for Advent, Christmas & Epiphany - First Lesson. Robert A. Hausman. LC 94-1003. (Orig.). 1994. pap. write for info. (0-7880-0025-X) CSS OH.

Days at Sea. Ralph Gibson. LC 74-13171. 72p. 1974. pap. 12.95 (0-912810-15-7) Lustrum Pr.

Days at the Factories: Or, The Manufacturing Industry of Great Britain Described. George Dodd. (Illus.). 1978. reprint ed. 18.00 (0-7158-1076-6) Charles River Bks.

Days Before. Katherine A. Porter. LC 77-117827. (Essay Index Reprint Ser.). 1977. 21.95 (0-8369-2066-X) Ayer.

*Days Before Christmas. Sandra E. Guzzo. LC 94-92399. (Illus.). 32p. (Orig.). (J). (gr. 1-3). 1994. pap. 6.95 (0-9643692-0-6) Dandelion WY.

Days Before the Tube in Plainfield. Alfred M. Munoz. LC 83-70391. 1983. pap. 9.95 (0-89754-033-6) Dan River Pr.

Day's Burden. Thomas M. Kettle. LC 68-54353. (Essay Index Reprint Ser.). 1977. 19.95 (0-8369-0595-4) Ayer.

Day's End & Other Stories. Herbert E. Bates. 1971. reprint ed. 39.00 (0-403-00504-3) Scholarly.

Day's End for Gunmen. large type ed. Marion Chrisomalis. (Linford Western Library). 240p. 1993. pap. 14.95 (0-7089-7373-6, Traitree Bookshop) Ulverscroft.

Days from a Dream Almanac. Dennis Tedlock. LC 89-31665. (Folklore & Society Ser.). 112p. 1990. pap. 11.95 (0-252-06092-X) U of Ill Pr.

Days Full of Love. Glen N. Herrington-Hall & Barbara Herrington-Hall. 366p. (Orig.). 1991. spiral bd. 8.50 (1-882835-15-8) STA-Kris.

Days Gone By. M. L. Faulkner. 1994. 10.95 (0-533-10855-1) Vantage.

Days Gone By. Sally T. Hayes. (Silhouette Intimate Moments Ser.). 1994. mass mkt. 3.50 (0-373-07549-9, 5-07549-4) Silhouette.

Days Gone By. David K. Thaemert. (Illus.). 120p. 1993. 19.95 (0-9620009-0-6) Pleasant Val Pr.

Days Gone by in Alpharetta & Roswell, Georgia, Vol. I. Caroline M. Dillman. 1992. 49.95 (0-9634253-0-7) Chattahoochee.

Days Grow Short: The Life & Music of Kurt Weill. Ronald Sanders. (Illus.). 469p. 1991. reprint ed. pap. 14.95 (1-879505-06-1) Silman James Pr.

Days I Knew. Lillie Langtry. LC 79-8067. (Illus.). 336p. reprint ed. 29.50 (0-404-18378-6) AMS Pr.

Days I Knew. Lillie Langtry. (Illus.). 338p. 1992. reprint ed. lib. bdg. 24.95 (0-89966-927-1) Buccaneer Bks.

Days in an Indian Monastery. 3rd ed. Devamata. 1975. pap. 5.95 (0-911564-20-9) Vedanta Ctr.

Days in Dickensland. Walter Dexter. LC 72-3610. (Studies in Dickens: No. 52). (Illus.). 1972. reprint ed. lib. bdg. 75.00 (0-8383-1559-3) M S G Haskell Hse.

Days in Dixie. Kathleen Cope. (Illus.). 144p. 1991. 16.50 (0-9622815-5-7) Black Belt Pr.

Days in Old Spain. G. Bone. 1976. lib. bdg. 59.95 (0-8490-1702-5) Gordon Pr.

Days in the Life: Voices from the English Underground, 1961-1971. Jonathon Green. 468p. (C). 1990. reprint ed. pap. 9.95 (0-7493-9012-3, A0474, Pub. by Mandarin UK) Heinemann.

Days in the Life of Atlanta. Norman Shavin. (Illus.). 232p. 1987. 24.95 (0-910719-21-7) Capricorn Corp.

Days Multiplied. Leonard H. Budd. 1984. 4.15 (0-89536-666-5, 0424) CSS OH.

Days of Anger, Days of Hope: A Memoir of the League of American Writers, 1937-1942. Franklin Folsom. LC 94-26. (Illus.). 416p. 1994. 27.50 (0-87081-332-3) Univ Pr Colo.

Days of Atonement. Walter J. Williams. 1991. 19.95 (0-312-85118-9) Tor Bks.

Days of Atonement. Walter J. Williams. 1992. mass mkt. 4.99 (0-8125-0180-2) Tor Bks.

Days of Auld Lang Syne. Ian MacLaren. 1976. 21.95 (0-8488-0291-8) Amereon Ltd.

Days of Auld Lang Syne. John B. Watson. LC 72-113690. (Short Story Index Reprint Ser.). 1977. 24.95 (0-8369-3419-9) Ayer.

Days of Awe. Maurya Simon. LC 88-63224. 96p. (Orig.). 1989. pap. 9.00 (1-55659-023-7) Copper Canyon.

Days of Awe: Stories for Rosh Hashanah & Yom Kippur. Eric A. Kimmel. (J). (gr. 4-7). 1991. 13.95 (0-670-82772-X) Viking Child Bks.

Days of Awe: Stories for Rosh Hashanah & Yom Kippur. Eric A. Kimmel. LC 93-583. (Illus.). 48p. (J). (gr. 3-7). 1993. reprint ed. pap. 4.99 (0-14-050271-8, Puffin) Puffin Bks.

Days of Blood & Fire. Katharine Kerr. 1994. mass mkt. 5.99 (0-553-29012-6) Bantam.

Days of Challenge, Years of Change: A Technical History of the Pacific Missile Test Center. (Illus.). 319p. 1990. per., pap. 21.00 (0-16-002060-3, S/N 008-046-001) USGPO.

*Days of Challenge, Years of Change: A Technical History of the Pacific Missile Test Center. 1994. lib. bdg. 260.95 (0-8490-6434-1) Gordon Pr.

Days of Courage: The Little Rock Story. Richard Kelso. LC 92-12805. (Stories of America Ser.). (Illus.). 88p. (J). (gr. 2-5). 1992. lib. bdg. 22.13 (0-8114-7230-2) Raintree Steck-V.

Days of Creation. Rebecca Daniel. (Big Book - Frieze Ser.). 16p. (J). (ps-3). 1991. 16.95 (0-86653-633-7, SS1877, Shining Star Pubns) Good Apple.

Days of Crime & Roses. Kate Morgan. 192p. (Orig.). 1992. pap. 3.99 (0-425-13471-7) Berkley Pub.

Days of Darkness: The Feuds of Eastern Kentucky. John E. Pearce. LC 94-2773. (Illus.). 240p. 1994. 23.95 (0-8131-1874-3) U Pr of Ky.

Days of Darkness: The Gettysburg Civilians. William G. Williams. 1990. mass mkt. 5.99 (0-425-12353-7) Berkley Pub.

Days of Darkness: The Gettysburg Civilians. 2nd ed. William G. Williams. (Illus.). 268p. (C). 1994. 19.95 (0-942597-59-1) White Mane Pub.

Days of Decision: An Oral History of Conscientious Objectors in the Military during the Vietnam War. Gerald R. Giolio. LC 88-70891. 338p. (Orig.). 1989. pap. 14.95 (0-9620024-0-2) Broken Rifle Pr.

*Days of Decision: An Oral History of Conscientious Objectors in the Military During Vietnam. Icke. 1993. pap. 11.95 (1-897766-01-7, Pub. by Jon Pubng UK) InBook.

Days of Dreams & Laughter: The Story Girl & Other Tales. Lucy M. Montgomery. (J). 1990. 10.99 (0-517-05137-0) Random Hse Value.

Days of Dust. 2nd ed. Halim I. Barakat. Tr. by Trevor Le Gassick. LC 82-74265. (Illus.). 200p. (C). 1983. reprint ed. pap. 11.00 (0-89410-360-1) Three Continents.

Days of Fire. Louella Nelson. (American Romance Ser.). 1993. mass mkt. 3.39 (0-373-16479-3, 1-16479-7) Harlequin Bks.

Days of Forty-One: Pearl Harbor Remembered. Ed Sheehan. (Illus.). 171p. (Orig.). 1987. reprint ed. pap. 3.95 (0-915870-01-0) AZ Mem Mus.

Days of Future Past. adapted ed. Illus. by Aristides Ruiz. (X-Men Digest Novels Ser.). 108p. (Orig.). (J). (gr. 2 up). 1994. pap. 3.50 (0-679-86181-5) Random Bks Yng Read.

Days of Glory, a Gentleman's Chronicle. Marshall Ausburn. (Illus.). 112p. 1992. pap. 14.95 (0-9613287-4-6) Paint Box.

Days of Grace. Arthur Ashe. 1994. pap. write for info. (0-345-38444-X) Ballantine.

Days of Grace: A Memoir. Arthur Ashe & Arnold Rampersad. LC 92-54919. 1993. 24.00 (0-679-42396-6) Knopf.

Days of Grace: A Memoir. large type ed. Arthur Ashe & Arnold Rampersad. LC 93-36046. (General Ser.). 1993. lib. bdg. 24.95 (0-8161-5883-5) Hall.

Days of Grace: A Memoir. large type ed. Arthur Ashe & Arnold Rampersad. LC 93-36046. (General Ser.). 1994. pap. 17.95 (0-8161-5884-3) Hall.

Days of Grace: A Memoir. Arthur Ashe & Arnold Rampersad. (Black History Titles Ser.). 1994. reprint ed. mass mkt. 5.99 (0-345-38681-7) Ballantine.

Days of H. L. Mencken: Three Volumes in One: Happy Days, Newspaper Days, & Heathen Days. H. L. Mencken. 925p. 1990. 29.95 (0-88029-417-5) Dorset Pr.

Days of Halcyon. O. Talmadge Spence. 73p. (Orig.). (C). 1992. pap. 4.50 (1-882542-02-9) Foundations.

Days of Healing, Days of Joy: Daily Meditations for Adult Children. Earnie Larsen & Carol L. Hegarty. 400p. (Orig.). 1989. pap. 9.00 (0-89486-455-6, 5024A) Hazelden.

Days of Healing, Days of Joy: Daily Meditations for Adult Children. Earnie Larsen & Carol L. Hegarty. LC 86-43009. (Orig.). 1987. reprint ed. pap. 10.00 (0-06-255449-2, Hazelden SF) Harper SF.

Days of Heaven. Gloria Gaffney. 100p. 1992. pap. 7.50 (1-56770-252-X) S Scheewe Pubns.

Days of Heaven on Earth. rev. ed. Albert B. Simpson. LC 84-70150. 369p. 1984. pap. 9.99 (0-87509-346-9) Chr Pubns.

Days of Henry Thoreau: A Biography. Walter Harding. LC 92-28836. (Illus.). 518p. (C). 1993. pap. text ed. 17.95 (0-691-02479-0) Princeton U Pr.

Days of Henry Thoreau: A Biography. Walter Harding. (Illus.). 544p. (C). reprint ed. pap. 10.95 (0-486-24263-3) Dover.

Days of Honey, Days of Onion: The Story of a Palestinian Family in Israel. Michael Gorkin. LC 92-30444. 1993. 13.00 (0-520-08186-2) U CA Pr.

Days of Infamy. John Costello. Ed. by Paul McCarthy. (Illus.). 424p. (Orig.). 1994. 24.00 (0-671-76985-5) PB.

Days of Josie. Karen E. Young. (Cityscapes Ser.). 19p. (J). (gr. k). 1992. pap. text ed. 23.00 (1-56843-013-2); pap. text ed. 4.50 (1-56843-063-9) BGR Pub.

Days of Judgment: The World War II War Crimes Trials. Isobel V. Morin. LC 94-11295. (Illus.). 144p. (YA). (gr. 7 up). 1995. 15.90 (1-56294-442-8) Millbrook Pr.

Days of Lorne: Impressions of a Governor-General. William S. MacNutt. LC 77-16170. (Illus.). 272p. 1978. reprint ed. text ed. 59.75 (0-313-20021-1, MADL, Greenwood Pr) Greenwood.

Days of Majesty. Simon Welfare. 1993. 27.50 (1-55859-657-7) Abbeville Pr.

Days of Mars: A Memoir, Nineteen Forty to Nineteen Forty-Six. Winifred Bryher. 160p. 1981. pap. 7.95 (0-7145-2745-9) M Boyars Pubs.

Days of My Life: A Journal for the Teen Years. Betsy M. McMahon. (Illus.). 288p. (Orig.). 1987. 13.95 (0-942257-05-7) New Chapter Pr.

Days of My Years. Earl R. Smith. LC 68-64777. (Illus.). 322p. 1968. pap. 7.95 (0-87595-001-9) Oregon Hist.

Days of Obligation: An Argument with My Mexican Father. Richard Rodriguez. 256p. 1993. reprint ed. pap. 11.00 (0-14-009622-1, Penguin Bks) Viking Penguin.

*Days of Obsidian, Days of Grace: Selected Poetry & Prose by Four Native American Writers. Adrian C. Louis et al. 152p. 1994. pap. 13.95 (0-9641986-0-6) Poetry Harbor.

*Days of Our Lives: A Complete History of the Long-Running Soap Opera. Maureen Russell. 240p. 1995. lib. bdg. 29.95 (0-7864-0112-5) McFarland & Co.

Days of Plenty, Days of Want. Patricia P. Martin. LC 88-71438. x, 76p. 1988. pap. 7.00 (0-916950-88-3) Biling Rev-Pr.

Days of Rondo. Evelyn Fairbanks. LC 90-35352. (Illus.). 182p. 1990. pap. 12.95 (0-87351-256-1); audio 16.95 (0-87351-289-8) Minn Hist.

Days of Sadness, Years of Triumph: The American People, 1939-1945. Geoffrey Perrett. LC 72-87594. 512p. 1985. reprint ed. pap. 17.50 (0-299-10394-3) U of Wis Pr.

*Days of Shame. Danielle Steel. LC 94-45481. 1996. write for info. (0-385-31301-2) Delacorte.

Days of Shoddy: A Novel of the Great Rebellion in 1861. Henry Morford. LC 73-164571. (American Fiction Reprint Ser.). 1977. reprint ed. 35.95 (0-8369-7048-9) Ayer.

An Asterisk (*) at the beginning of an entry indicates that the title is appearing in BIP for the first time.

Days of Sorrow, Years of Glory, 1831-1850: From the Nat Turner Revolt to the Fugitive Slave Law. Timothy J. Paulson. LC 93-40851. 1994. write for info. (*0-7910-2263-3*); pap. write for info. (*0-7910-2552-7*) Chelsea Hse.
Days of Summer Gone. Joe Bolton. 75p. (Orig.). 1990. pap. 9.95 (*0-913123-30-7*) Galileo.
Days of Sunshine: To Commemorate the International Year of Peace. Violet Hanschke. (Illus.). 14p. 1987. 9.95 (*0-9693430-0-0*) V Hanschke.

Days of Temple Houston. Bill Sinclair. 103p. (Orig.). 1994. pap. 5.95x (*0-9642908-0-4*) Sinclair NV. "A gun-toting tough hombre & silver-tongued darling of the frontier courtroom!" That's how the newspapers referred to Temple Houston in the late 1800s. Temple Houston, the youngest son of General Sam Houston, was one of the most eccentric criminal attorneys in American History. As you travel along with Temple & his life-long friend Sheriff Jack Love of Woodward, Oklahoma, you will experience their many adventures together. This is a western story based on true life experiences filled with characters that lived the wild west to its fullest. From courtroom drama to blazing guns in the street. Take pleasure in meeting one of the most overlooked frontier heroes in the American West. Temple still has his courtroom speeches displayed in the halls of Congress. Temple Houston was quick to defend the innocent by using the law, but even quicker to use his hand gun! THE DAYS OF TEMPLE HOUSTON is the first volume of a series. Order from: Sinclair Enterprises, 3342 S. Sandhill #9-418, Las Vegas, NV 89121.** ***Publisher Provided Annotation.

Days of the Ching Pao. rev. ed. Malcolm Rosholt. LC 78-52589. (Illus.). 192p. 1986. 30.00 (*0-910417-07-5*) Rosholt Hse.
Days of the Clyde Steamers. (C). 1989. 23.00 (*1-85098-380-1*, Pub. by Jordanhill College UK) St Mut.
Days of the Consuls. Ivo Andric. Tr. by Celia Hawkesworth & Bogdan Rakic. LC 92-72470. 396p. 1993. pap. 27.00 (*1-85610-024-3*, Pub. by Forest Bks UK) Dufour.
***Days of the Dead.** Agnes Bushell. 290p. 1995. pap. 9.00 (*0-9639050-8-2*) J Brown Bks.
Days of the Dead. Kathryn Lasky. LC 93-47957. (Illus.). 48p. (J). (gr. 3-7). 1994. 15.95 (*0-7868-0022-4*); lib. bdg. 15.89 (*0-7868-2018-7*) Hyprn Child.
Days of the Dead (Los Dias de los Muertos) Sarah Lane & Marilyn Turkovich. 39p. (J). (gr. 6-12). 1991. pap. 10.95 (*0-930141-42-3*) World Eagle.
Days of the Dinosaurs Coloring Book. Matthew Kalmenoff. (Illus.). (J). (gr. k-3). 1989. pap. 2.95 (*0-486-25359-7*) Dover.
Days of the French Revolution: The Day-to-Day Story of the Revolution. Christopher Hibbert. LC 81-9666. (Illus.). 24p. 1981. pap. 13.45 (*0-688-00746-5*, Quill) Morrow.
Days of the King. Bruno Frank. Tr. by Helen T. Lowe-Porter. LC 75-121550. (Short Story Index Reprint Ser.). 1977. 17.95 (*0-8369-3506-3*) Ayer.
Days of the Liberals in Spain. R. M. Smith. 1977. lib. bdg. 59.95 (*0-8490-1703-3*) Gordon Pr.
Days of the Lord: The Liturgical Year, Vol 6. 365p. (Orig.). 1992. pap. text ed. 17.95 (*0-8146-1904-5*) Liturgical Pr.
Days of the Lord: The Liturgical Year: Advent, Christmas, Epiphany, Vol. 1. Brepols. 346p. 1991. pap. text ed. 17.95 (*0-8146-1899-5*) Liturgical Pr.
Days of the Lord, Vol. 2: The Liturgical Year - Lent. Tr. by Thomas Hallsten. 279p. (Orig.). 1993. 17.95 (*0-8146-1900-2*) Liturgical Pr.
Days of the Lord, Vol. 3: The Liturgical Year: Easter Triduum, Easter Season. Tr. by Gregory LaNave. 370p. (Orig.). 1993. pap. text ed. 17.95 (*0-8146-1901-0*) Liturgical Pr.
Days of the Lord, Vol. 4: The Liturgical Year, Ordinary Time, Cycle A. Brepols. 352p. (Orig.). 1992. pap. text ed. 17.95 (*0-8146-1902-9*) Liturgical Pr.
Days of the Lord, Vol. 5: The Liturgical Year, Ordinary Time, Year B. Ed. by Brepols. Tr. by Jours De Seigneur. 384p. (Orig.). 1993. 17.95 (*0-8146-1903-7*) Liturgical Pr.
Days of the Lord, Vol. 7: The Liturgical Year, Solemnities & Fasts. 408p. (Orig.). 1994. pap. text ed. 17.95 (*0-8146-1905-3*) Liturgical Pr.
Days of the North Shore Line. George V. Campbell. (Illus.). 256p. 1986. 38.00 (*0-933449-01-1*) Transport Trails.
Days of the Russian Revolution. V. V. Shulgin. Ed. by Bruce F. Adams. (Illus.). 1990. 25.00 (*0-87569-115-3*) Academic Intl.
Days of the Spirit: Advent to Lent, Vol. 1. J. Massyngbaerde Ford. 216p. (Orig.). 1994. pap. text ed. 14.95 (*0-8146-2217-8*) Liturgical Pr.
Days of the Steamboats. William H. Ewen. (Illus.). 112p. 1988. pap. 14.95 (*0-913372-47-1*) Mystic Seaport.
***Days of the Warlords: A History of the Byzantine Empire: A. D. 969 - 991.** Paul A. Blaum. LC 94-27632. 142p. (Orig.). (C). 1994. lib. bdg. 42.00 (*0-8191-9656-8*) U Pr of Amer.
***Days of the Warlords: A History of the Byzantine Empire: A. D. 969 - 991.** Paul A. Blaum. LC 94-27632. 142p. (Orig.). (C). 1994. pap. text ed. 28.50 (*0-8191-9657-6*) U Pr of Amer.
Days of the Week. Paul Hughes. Ed. by Peter Harris. LC 89-11758. (Illus.). 62p. (J). (gr. 4-7). 1989. lib. bdg. 17.26 (*0-944483-32-1*) Garrett Ed Corp.
Days of the West. Mike Flanagan. LC 87-26542. (Illus.). 225p. (Orig.). 1987. pap. 6.95 (*0-685-18133-2*); write for info. (*0-939650-14-2*) R H Pub.
Days of Thunder. Risa Kirk. (Superromance Ser.). 1994. mass mkt. 3.50 (*0-373-70607-3*, 1-70607-6) Harlequin Bks.
Days of Tragedy: Lebanon Nineteen Seventy-Five to Nineteen Seventy-Six, 2 vols., Set. Joseph G. Chami. Bd. with Vol. II. Days of Wrath: Lebanon Nineteen Seventy-Seven to Nineteen Eighty-Two. (Illus.). 400p. 1983. 125.00 (*0-88738-038-7*) Transaction Pubs.
Days of Tragedy: Lebanon Nineteen Seventy-Five to Nineteen Seventy-Six, Vol. 1. Joseph G. Chami. (Illus.). 400p. (C). 1980. 74.95 (*0-88738-036-0*) Transaction Pubs.
Days of Uncertain Health. Gary Fincke. LC 88-1547. 72p. 1988. 15.95 (*0-89924-058-5*); pap. 8.00 (*0-89924-053-4*) Lynx Hse.
***Days of "Uncertainty & Dread" The Ordeal Endured by the Citizens at Gettysburg.** 130p. 1994. pap. 10.95 (*0-9643599-3-6*) G R Bennett.
***Days of Vengeance.** Joyce E. Black. 405p. 1995. pap. 12.95 (*1-56901-559-7*) NW Pub.
Days of Vengeance: An Exposition of the Book of Revelation. David Chilton. write for info. (*0-930462-09-2*) Am Bur Eco Res.
Days of Vengeance: An Exposition of the Book of Revelation. David Chilton. LC 86-50798. 721p. 1987. text ed. 24.95 (*0-930462-02-5*, Dominion) Am Bur Eco Res.
Days of Visitation: A Practical & Statistical Study of the Parishes of the Diocese of Swansea & Brecon Based on the Returns to the Visitation Questionnaire of Bishop Vaughan from 1977 to 1987. Peter M. Morris. LC 89-48075. (Welsh Studies: Vol. 2). 272p. 1990. lib. bdg. 89.95 (*0-88946-065-5*) E Mellen.
Days of Wine & Roses. J. P. Miller. 1973. pap. 4.75 (*0-8222-0281-6*) Dramatists Play.
Days of Wine & Roses? Christopher Nicole. 1991. 21.95 (*0-7278-4187-4*) Severn Hse.
Days of Wrath. D. W. Baker. 562p. 1985. 44.95 (*0-522-84297-6*) Intl Spec Bk.
Days of Wrath: Lebanon Nineteen Seventy-Seven to Nineteen Eighty-Two, Vol. II. Joseph G. Chami. (Illus.). 400p. 1983. 74.95 (*0-88738-037-9*) Transaction Pubs.
Days of Wrath: Lebanon Nineteen Seventy-Seven to Nineteen Eighty-Two see Days of Tragedy: Lebanon Nineteen Seventy-Five to Nineteen Seventy-Six
Days Off. Paul Nelson. LC 82-20294. (Virginia Commonwealth University Series for Contemporary Poetry). 70p. 1982. 10.95 (*0-8139-0965-1*) U Pr of Va.
Days on Earth: The Dance of Doris Humphrey. Marcia B. Siegel. LC 92-33367. (Illus.). 351p. 1993. pap. 14.95 (*0-8223-1346-4*) Duke.
Days on the Farm with Annette & Samuel. Teresa Morgan. 1987. 7.15 (*0-318-37713-6*) Rod & Staff.
Days on the Wing: Being the War Memoirs of Major the Chevalier Willy Coppens De Houthulst D.S.O., M.C., Etc., Etc. Willy C. De Houthulst. Ed. by James B. Gilbert. Tr. by A. J. Insall. LC 79-7242. (Flight: Its First Seventy-Five Years Ser.). (Illus.). 1980. reprint ed. 28.95 (*0-405-12157-1*) Ayer.
Days Out & Other Papers. Elizabeth Morris. LC 67-26767. (Essay Index Reprint Ser.). 1977. 18.95 (*0-8369-0721-3*) Ayer.
Days Out from London. Automobile Association Staff. (AA - Ordnance Survey Leisure Guide Ser.). (Illus.). 128p. (Orig.). 1992. pap. 15.95 (*1-55650-517-5*) Hunter NJ.
Days Out-In & Around London. Pauline Gorman. 1986. pap. 5.95 (*0-582-23540-5*) Little.
***Days Out in Britain, 1995.** (Illus.). 248p. (Orig.). 1995. pap. 15.95 (*0-7495-0905-8*) Hunter NJ.
Days Out in Dorset. Joy Parsons. (C). 1988. text ed. 29.00 (*0-685-45095-3*, Pub. by Thornhill Pr UK) St Mut.
Days Pleasant & Unpleasant in the Order Sons of Italy: The Problem of Races & Racial Societies in the U. S. - Assimilation or Isolation. Robert Ferrari. LC 73-21967. 1974. reprint ed. 27.50 (*0-678-01363-2*) Kelley.
Day's Portion. Harvey Shapiro. LC 93-30713. 1994. 18.00 (*1-882413-11-3*); pap. 10.00 (*1-882413-10-5*) Hanging Loose.
Days Run Away Like Wild Horses over the Hills. Charles Bukowski. 204p. 1993. reprint ed. 20.00 (*0-87685-006-9*); reprint ed. pap. 11.00 (*0-87685-005-0*) Black Sparrow.
Days, Tangier Journal: 1987-89. Paul Bowles. (Illus.). 128p. 1992. pap. 9.95 (*0-88001-282-X*) Ecco Pr.
Days, Tangier Journal: 1987-1989. Paul Bowles. (Illus.). 128p. (C). 1991. 15.95 (*0-88001-269-2*) Ecco Pr.
Days That Are No More. Elizabeth B. Johnston. LC 75-38655. (Black Heritage Library Collection). 1977. reprint ed. 21.95 (*0-8369-9013-7*) Ayer.
Days to Celebrate. Ruth Miner. (Illus.). 50p. pap. 1.00 (*0-686-30389-X*) WILPF.
Days to Remember. William Lipkind. (Illus.). (J). (gr. 3 up). 1961. 10.95 (*0-8392-3006-0*) Astor-Honor.
Days to Remember. Joshua Nickerson. 304p. 1988. 14.95 (*0-9615051-1-7*) Parnassus Imprints.
Days to Remember. Joshua A. Nickerson. 1988. pap. 14.95 (*0-317-67586-9*) Chatham His Soc.
***Days to Remember: A Birthday Book.** Illus. by Donna Green. 144p. 1995. 9.98 (*0-8317-2176-6*) Smithmark.
Days When the Animals Talked: Black American Folktales & How They Came to Be. William J. Faulkner. LC 93-9905. (Illus.). 210p. 1993. reprint ed. 29.95 (*0-86543-373-9*); reprint ed. pap. 12.95 (*0-86543-374-7*) Africa World.
Days with Chief Joseph: Diary of Erskine Wood. Erskine Wood & Mary Rose. 56p. 1991. pap. 7.95 (*0-9631232-1-1*) Rose Wind Pr.
***Days with Diam: Or Life at Night.** Svend A. Madsen. Tr. by W. Glyn Jones. 246p. 1995. pap. 24.00 (*1-870041-26-7*) Dufour.
Days with Frog & Toad. Arnold Lobel. LC 78-21786. (Harper I Can Read Bk.). (Illus.). 64p. (J). (gr. k-3). 1979. 14.00i (*0-06-023963-8*); lib. bdg. 14.89 (*0-06-023964-6*) HarpC Child Bks.
Days with Frog & Toad. Arnold Lobel. LC 78-21786. (Trophy I Can Read Book & Cassette Set). (Illus.). 64p. (J). (ps-3). 1984. pap. 3.50 (*0-06-444058-3*, Dealer Bank) HarpC Child Bks.
Days with Frog & Toad. unabridged ed. Arnold Lobel. (I Can Read Book Ser.). (Illus.). (J). (ps-3). 1990. audio, pap. 6.95 (*1-55994-227-4*, Caedmon) HarperAudio.
Days with Frog & Toad: (Dios con Sapo y Sepo) Arnold Lobel. (SPA.). (J). (gr. 1-6). 8.95 (*84-204-3743-3*) Santillana.
***Days with Gran.** Catherine Farthing-Knight. (Jam Roll Picture Bks.). 32p. (J). 1995. 19.95 (*0-7022-2828-1*, Pub. by Univ Queensland Pr AT) Intl Spec Bk.
Days with Ulanova. Albert E. Kahn. LC 79-7770. (Dance Ser.). (Illus.). 1980. reprint ed. lib. bdg. 54.95 (*0-8369-9297-0*) Ayer.
***Days with Uncle God-Momma: A Man's Retreat Diary.** Francis L. Gross, Jr. (Illus.). 144p. (Orig.). 1995. pap. 11.95 (*0-8245-1500-5*) Crossroad NY.
Days with Walt Whitman: With Some Notes on His Life & Work. Edward Carpenter. LC 78-22293. (Gay Experience Ser.). reprint ed. 41.50 (*0-404-61522-8*) AMS Pr.
Day's Work. Eve Bunting. (J). 1994. 14.95 (*0-395-67321-6*, Hills Med) HM.
Day's Work. Rudyard Kipling. 1976. 22.95 (*0-8488-0288-8*) Amereon Ltd.
Day's Work. Rudyard Kipling. 544p. 1988. mass mkt. 5.95 (*0-14-043312-0*, Penguin Classics) Viking Penguin.
Day's Work. David Lee. LC 89-81836. 144p. (Orig.). 1990. pap. 10.00 (*1-55659-027-X*) Copper Canyon.
Day's Work. Michael McMahon. 1976. pap. 2.25 (*0-913006-08-4*) Puckerbrush.
Day's Work. Rudyard Kipling. LC 76-37275. (Short Story Index Reprint Ser.). 1977. reprint ed. 25.95 (*0-8369-4086-5*) Ayer.
Daysies. 366p. (Orig.). 1988. spiral bd. 7.00 (*1-882835-02-6*) STA-Kris.
Daysleepers & Other Poems. Bryce Milligan. LC 84-70036. 64p. (Orig.). 1984. pap. 6.95 (*0-931722-29-2*) Corona Pub.
Dayspring. Anne S. White. LC 71-160700. 180p. (Orig.). 1971. pap. 4.95 (*0-9605178-2-0*) Victorious Ministry.
Dayspring: Poetry of the Morning. Ed. by Jackson Wilcox. (Illus.). 24p. 1993. 2.00 (*0-944231-16-0*) Slvr Wings CA.
Dayspring in Darkness: Sacrament in Hopkins. Jeffrey B. Loomis. LC 87-47819. 224p. 1988. 36.50 (*0-8387-5138-5*) Bucknell U Pr.
Dayted Excellence. 366p. (Orig.). 1989. spiral bd. 7.00 (*1-882835-12-3*) STA-Kris.
Daytime Animals. Joanna Cole. LC 85-4301. (Large As Life Ser.). (Illus.). 32p. (J). (ps-2). 1985. lib. bdg. 12.99 (*0-394-97188-4*) Knopf Bks Yng Read.
Daytime Baby: Baby Books. Illus. by Alison Ross. 8p. (J). (ps). 1992. bds. 3.50 (*0-7214-1515-6*, S9212-4) Ladybird Bks.
Daytime School for Adults. Morton Gordon. 1967. write for info. (*0-87060-015-X*, OCP 15) Syracuse U Cont Ed.
Daytime Television Gameshows & the Celebration of Merchandise: The Price Is Right. Morris B. Holbrook. LC 92-75573. 125p. (C). 1993. 21.95 (*0-87972-620-2*); pap. 8.95 (*0-87972-621-0*) Bowling Green Univ.
Daytime Television Programming. Marilyn Matelski. (Electronic Media Guide Ser.). 112p. 1991. pap. 15.95 (*0-240-80087-7*, Focal) Buttrwrth-Heinemann.
Daytime Words. (Panda's House Ser.). (Illus.). (J). 1991. 4.99 (*0-517-05885-5*) Random Hse Value.
Dayton & Troy Electric Railway. Scott D. Trostel. Ed. by Russell Heine. (Ohio Railroad Heritage Ser.). (Illus.). 80p. 1989. pap. text ed. 12.95 (*0-317-93049-4*) Cam-Tech Pub.
Dayton (OH) Municipal Court Automation Requirements Analysis. Robert Lowe et al. 202p. 1990. 12.00 (*0-685-38113-7*, NERO-241) Natl Ctr St Courts.
Dayton Sketchbook. Robert Frame. (Illus.). 200p. (Orig.). 1986. pap. 12.95 (*0-913428-27-2*) Landfall Pr.
***Daytona: Thunder at the Beach!** Jay Schleifer. LC 94-28496. (Out to Win Ser.). (J). 1995. write for info. (*0-89686-818-4*, Crstwood Hse) Silver Burdett Pr.
Daytona Five Hundred: Men & Machines 1991. (Illus.). 160p. 1991. 29.90 (*0-929323-06-8*) Autosport Intl.
Daytona Five Hundred: The Men & Machines of Speed Week '94. Autosport Editors. (Racing Annual Ser.). (Illus.). 160p. 1994. 29.90 (*0-929323-12-2*) Autosport Intl.
***Daytona 200: The History of America's Premier Motorcycle Race.** Don Emde. Ed. by Tracy Emde. (Morotcycle Heritage Press Ser.). (Illus.). 288p. 1991. 29.95 (*0-9627434-0-2*, Motorcycle Heritage Pr) Infosport.
Daytona 500: The Men & Machines of Speed Week 1993. Autosport Editors. (Yearbook Ser.). (Illus.). 160p. 1993. 29.90 (*0-929323-10-6*) Autosport Intl.
Daytona 500: The Men & Machines of Speed Weeks, '90. 1990. 29.90 (*0-929323-04-1*) Autosport Intl.
Daytona 500, Week 92: The Men & Machines of Speed. (Illus.). 160p. 1992. 29.90 (*0-929323-08-4*) Autosport Intl.
Dayton's Revenge. Erle Adkins. 224p. 1987. pap. 2.50 (*0-8217-2016-3*) Zebra.
Dayton's Shopping Glide, a Pocketbook Flattener. Al Blair. 4p. 1990. pap. 3.95 (*0-930366-18-2*) Northcountry Pub.
Daytop Village: A Therapeutic Community. Ed. by Barry Sugarman et al. (Case Studies in Cultural Anthropology). (Illus.). 140p. (C). 1983. reprint ed. pap. 7.95 (*0-8290-0589-7*) Irvington.
Daytripper, No. 2: Fifty Trips in & Around Toronto. Donna Carpenter. Ed. by Noel Hudson. (Illus.). 120p. (Orig.). pap. 17.95 (*1-55046-033-1*, Pub. by Boston Mills Pr CN) Genl Dist Srvs.
Daytripping: An Educator's Guide to Regional Cultural Resources. 120p. (Orig.). 1991. pap. 7.95 (*0-9618539-1-3*) Fed Hist Services.
Daytrips. Jo Carson. 1991. pap. 4.75 (*0-8222-0282-4*) Dramatists Play.
Daytrips. Cleve Twitchell. 87p. 1992. pap. write for info. (*0-9636976-0-9*) Mail Tribune.
***Daytrips France: 45 One Day Adventures by Rail, Bus, or Car.** 4th ed. Earl Steinbicker. 1995. pap. 14.95 (*0-8038-9366-3*) Hastings.
Daytrips from New York. Lida Newberry et al. (Earl Steinbicker Guide Ser.). (Illus.). 350p. (Orig.). 1994. pap. 14.95 (*0-8038-9332-9*) Hastings.
Daytrips from Washington, D. C. Earl Steinbicker. (Daytrips Ser.). (Illus.). 304p. 1993. pap. 12.95 (*0-8038-9349-3*) Hastings.
***Daytrips Germany: 55 One Day Adventures.** 4th ed. Earl Steinbicker. 1995. pap. 14.95 (*0-8038-9369-8*) Hastings.
Daytrips, Getaway Weekends, & Vacations in New England. 4th ed. Patricia Foulke & Robert Foulke. (Voyager Book Ser.). (Illus.). 400p. 1994. pap. 16.95 (*1-56440-366-1*) Globe Pequot.
Daytrips, Getaway Weekends, & Vacations in the Mid-Atlantic States: New York, New Jersey, Pennsylvania, Delaware, Maryland, Virginia, & Washington, D. C. 3rd ed. Patricia Foulke & Robert Foulke. LC 92-34320. (Voyager Book Ser.). 416p. 1993. pap. 16.95 (*1-56440-144-8*) Globe Pequot.
***Daytrips Holland, Belgium, & Luxembourg: 40 One Day Adventures by Rail, Bus, or Car.** 2nd ed. Earl Steinbicker. 1995. pap. 14.95 (*0-8038-9368-X*) Hastings.
Daytrips in Archaeological Mexico: One Hundred One Day Adventures by Car or Bus with Maps & Travel Tips. Robert D. Wood. (Daytrips Ser.). Orig. Title: A Travel Guide to Archaeological Mexico. (Illus.). 150p. 1991. reprint ed. pap. 12.95 (*0-8038-9336-1*) Hastings.
Daytrips in Britain. Earl Steinbicker. (Earl Steinbicker Guide Ser.). (Illus.). 350p. 1991. pap. 12.95 (*0-8038-9301-9*) Hastings.
Daytrips in Europe: One Day Adventures by Rail, Bus or Car. Earl Steinbicker. (Earl Steinbicker Guide Ser.). (Illus.). 416p. (Orig.). 1991. pap. 15.95 (*0-8038-9330-2*) Hastings.
Daytrips Israel. Earl Steinbicker. (Daytrips Ser.). (Illus.). 200p. (Orig.). 1992. pap. 12.95 (*0-8038-9342-6*) Hastings.
***Daytrips Italy: 46 One Day Adventures.** 3rd ed. Steinbicker. 1995. pap. 14.95 (*0-8038-9372-8*) Hastings.
***Daytrips London: Fifty One Day Adventures by Rail or Car, in & Around London & Southern England.** 5th ed. Earl Steinbicker. 1995. pap. 14.95 (*0-8038-9367-1*) Hastings.
***Daytrips New York: 107 One Day Adventures.** 7th ed. Steinbicker. 1995. pap. 14.95 (*0-8038-9371-X*) Hastings.
Dayworld Breakup. Philip Jose Farmer. (Dayworld Ser.: No. 3). 1991. mass mkt. 4.95 (*0-8125-0889-0*) Tor Bks.
***Daze of Whine & Neurosis.** Dick Locher. (Editorial Cartoonists Ser.). (Illus.). 160p. (Orig.). 1995. pap. 8.95 (*1-56554-156-1*) Pelican.
Daze on the Plains: A New Yorker on the Level. Pat Staten. LC 91-55213. 256p. (Orig.). 1992. 19.95 (*1-55591-085-8*) Fulcrum Pub.
Dazed & Confused. Richard Linklater. LC 93-868. (Illus.). 160p. (Orig.). 1993. pap. 13.95 (*0-312-09466-3*) St Martin.
Dazhan. 2nd rev. ed. Douglas Dunn. LC 88-1296. 244p. 1988. pap. 6.95 (*0-944363-00-8*) Word Wizards.
Dazy the Guinea Pig. Jane Burton. LC 89-11397. (Baby Animals Growing up Ser.). (Illus.). 32p. (J). (gr. 2-3). 1989. lib. bdg. 17.27 (*0-8368-0206-3*) Gareth Stevens Inc.
Dazzle. Judith Gould. 768p. (Orig.). 1989. pap. 5.99 (*0-451-40118-2*, Onyx) NAL-Dutton.
Dazzle. Judith Krantz. 1992. mass mkt. 6.99 (*0-553-29376-1*) Bantam.
Dazzle. large type ed. Judith Krantz. 1990. 24.95 (*0-517-58190-6*, Crown) Crown Pub Group.
***Dazzle: Creating Artistic Jewelry & Distinctive Accessories.** Linda F. Kengle. 128p. 1995. pap. 21.95 (*0-8019-8639-7*) Chilton.
***Dazzle: Creating Artistic Jewelry & Distinctive Accessories.** Linda F. Kenzle. LC 95-7315. (Craft Kaleidoscope Ser.). 1995. pap. write for info. (*0-8019-8638-9*) Chilton.
Dazzle 'Em with Style: An Introduction to the Art of Oral Scientific Presentation. Robert R. H. Anholt. LC 93-50603. (C). 1995. pap. text ed. write for info. (*0-7167-2583-5*) W H Freeman.

D

An Asterisk (*) at the beginning of an entry indicates that the title is appearing in BIP for the first time. 1815

*Dazzle of Hummingbirds. Bruce Berger. Ed. by Vicki Leon. (Close up: A Focus on Nature Ser.). (Illus.). 40p. (YA). (gr. 5 up). 1994. lib. bdg. 14.95 (0-382-24893-7); pap. 7.95 (0-382-24894-5) Silver Burdett Pr.

*Dazzle the Dinosaur. Marcus Pfister. Tr. by J. Alison James. LC 94-34840. (Illus.). 32p. (J). (gr. k-3). 1994. 16.95 (1-55858-337-8); lib. bdg. 16.88 (1-55858-338-6) North-South Bks NYC.

Dazzled. Catherine Hart. 400p. (Orig.). 1994. mass mkt. 5.50 (0-380-77730-4) Avon.

Dazzled. Arthur Sze. 60p. (Orig.). 1982. pap. 6.00 (0-912449-07-1) Floating Island.

Dazzler. Shooter et al. 64p. 1984. 9.95 (0-87135-000-9) Marvel Entmnt.

*Dazzling! Jewerly of the Ancient World. Geography Department, Runestone Press. LC 94-21445. (Buried Worlds). (YA). (gr. 6 up). 1995. lib. bdg. 22.95 (0-8225-3203-4, Lerner Publctns) Lerner Group.

Dazzling Brightness. Roberta Gellis. 448p. 1994. pap. 4.99 (0-7860-0023-6, Pinnacle NY) Windsor NY.

Dazzling Desserts: Over 100 Delicious Recipes. Miriam Canter. (Illus.). 40p. 1983. pap. 1.00 (0-941016-08-0) Penfield.

*Dazzling Enigma: The Story of Morgan Edwards. Howard R. Stewart. LC 95-3475. (Illus.). x428p. (C). 1995. lib. bdg. 54.00 (0-8191-9901-X) U Pr of Amer.

Dazzling Images: The Masks of Sir Philip Sidney. Alan Hager. LC 89-40767. 224p. 1991. 39.50 (0-87413-390-4) U Delaware Pr.

Dazzling Mazes: Fifty Inventive Puzzles with Solutions. Ulrich Koch. 80p. (Orig.). 1985. pap. 3.95 (0-486-24986-7) Dover.

DB Technology: Software Engineering Approach. James G. Hughes. 300p. 1988. text ed. 69.00 (0-13-197914-0) P-H.

DB Two: Design & Development Guide. Gabrielle Wiorkowski & David Kull. (Illus.). 352p. (C). 1988. text ed. 36.75 (0-201-16949-5) Addison-Wesley.

DB2 Developer's Guide. 2nd ed. Craig S. Mullins. 1200p. 1994. 49.99 (0-672-30512-7) Sams.

DBA Utilities, 1990-91. Frank Sweet. (Database Engineering Ser.: Vol. 6). (Illus.). 84p. (Orig.). (C). 1991. pap. 47.50 (0-939479-08-7) Boxes & Arrows.

DBAE Handbook: An Overview of Discipline-Based Art Education. Stephen M. Dobbs. 1992. pap. 10.00 (0-89236-214-6) J P Getty Trust.

DBASE - From the Dot Prompt: An Introduction to Structured Programming Using dBASE IV. Warren M. Littlefield. LC 93-18937. 591p. (C). 1993. pap. 24.95 (0-7914-1780-8) State U NY Pr.

DBase Compiled for DOS Developer's Guide. Pierre Lapointe. 1994. 30.00 (0-679-75159-9) Random.

DBASE Compilers: A Programmer's Resource Book. Ken Knecht. (Illus.). 290p. 1988. pap. 18.95 (0-8306-2943-2, 2943) TAB Bks.

DBASE Dialect Software Engineering. T. David Millican. 1994. text ed. write for info. (0-442-00510-5) Van Nos Reinhold.

dBase Dialects Software Engineering. T. David Millican. 1991. text ed. 39.95 (0-442-00254-8) Van Nos Reinhold.

DBASE DOS Version. S. R. Pasewark. (C). pap. text ed. 14.00 (0-13-096959-1) P-H.

*DBase 5 for Windows Programming for Dummies. James Coombs & Ted Coombs. 1994. pap. 19.99 (1-56884-215-5) IDG Bks.

*DBase 5 for Windows Quick & Easy. Audrey Kalman. LC 94-61359. 265p. 1994. pap. 16.99 (0-7821-1464-4) Sybex.

*DBase 5.0 for Windows. Sarah E. Hutchinson et al. (Advantage Series for Computer Education). 200p. 1995. pap. 17.00 (0-7863-0442-1) Irwin Prof Pubng.

DBase for DOS for Dummies. Scott Palmer. 1994. pap. 19.95 (1-56884-188-4) IDG Bks.

DBase for Windows: Amazing Programming Solutions. Steve Davis. (Illus.). 752p. (Orig.). 1992. pap. 39.95 (1-55958-241-3) Prima Pub.

DBase for Windows for Dummies. Scott Palmer. 1994. pap. 19.95 (1-56884-179-5) IDG Bks.

DBASE for Windows Handbook. Cary Prague. 1994. pap. 30.00 (0-679-79131-0) Random.

DBASE for Windows Inside & Out. Edward C. Jones. 656p. 1992. pap. text ed. 27.95 (0-07-881792-7) Osborne-McGraw.

DBASE for Windows Unleashed, Incl. disk. Ernest Escobar & Paul Mahar. 1994. disk, pap. 45.00 (0-672-30503-8) Sams.

DBASE Four. Learn-PC Staff. 400p. (C). 1991. pap. text ed. write for info. (0-13-203142-6) P-H.

DBase Four Smart Start. M. Dalkibic. (SmartStart Ser.). (Illus.). 256p. (Orig.). 1993. pap. 8.95 (1-56529-251-0) Que.

DBase Four 2.0 Quick Reference. Steve Davis. (Quick Reference Ser.). (Illus.). 160p. (Orig.). 1993. pap. 9.95 (1-56529-267-7) Que.

DBASE Handbook. 2nd ed. Mary Campbell. 1993. pap. 29.95 (0-679-79166-3) Random.

DBASE II: A Comprehensive User's Manual. Kerman D. Bharucha. (Illus.). 304p. 1985. 24.95 (0-8306-0884-2, 1884); pap. 18.95 (0-8306-1884-8, 1884P) TAB Bks.

DBASE II & III. Dan Remenyi & James Dalby. 336p. (C). 1986. text ed. 130.00 (0-582-29676-5, Pub. by Pitman Pubng UK) St Mut.

DBASE II & III in English I. (English I Computer Tutorials Ser.). 312p. 19.95 (0-915869-02-0) Eng Comp Tut.

DBASE II for Beginners. Anthony K. Lima. LC 84-22897. (Personal Computing Ser.). (Illus.). 160p. 1986. 16.50 (0-13-196080-6); pap. text ed. 24.33 (0-13-196098-9) P-H.

DBASE II for the IBM PC. Ron Ingalsbe. (C). 1986. pap. write for info. (0-675-20612-X, Merrill Pub Co) Macmillan.

DBASE II in English I. 234p. 29.95 (0-915869-00-4) Eng Comp Tut.

DBASE II Simplified for the IBM Personal Computer. Don Cassel. (Illus.). 176p. 1986. 16.50 (0-13-195934-4); pap. text ed. 24.33 (0-13-195942-5) P-H.

DBase III. Catherine Garrison et al. (Ready Reference Manual Ser.). 128p. (C). 1987. pap. text ed. 12.95 (0-201-11625-1) Addison-Wesley.

DBASE III, III Plus & IV. James E. Potter. Ed. by Alfred J. Garrotto. (FasTrak Jr. Ser.). 110p. 1993. spiral bd. 18.50 (0-9632069-4-X) Bridge Lrn Systs.

DBase III-III Plus Quick Reference Guide. Lynn Underwood & David Segal. (DDC Quick Reference Guides Ser.). (Illus.). 76p. 1989. 8.95 (0-936862-57-2, B-17); trans. 150.00 (0-936862-60-2, BT-19) DDC Pub.

DBASE III Plus. (STAR Ser.). 176p. (C). 1992. pap. text ed. 7.50 (0-87835-725-4) Boyd & Fraser.

DBase III Plus. Ann J. Swafford & Christine M. Haff. 352p. (C). 1990. pap. text ed. 29.50 (0-15-517035-X); teacher ed. pap. text ed. 5.00 (0-15-517037-6) Dryden Pr.

DBASE III Plus. rev. ed. Timothy J. O'Leary & Linda I. O'Leary. 1993. pap. text ed. write for info. (0-07-048898-3) McGraw.

DBASE III Plus: A Practical Approach. Anthony Krehbiel & David Matthews. LC 91-9479. (Illus.). 305p. (C). 1990. pap. text ed. 32.95 (0-938661-06-X) Franklin Beedle.

DBASE III Plus: A Practical Approach with ASSIST. Anthony Krehbiel & David Matthews. LC 90-13813. (Illus.). 372p. (C). 1990. pap. text ed. 32.95 (0-938661-18-3) Franklin Beedle.

DBase III Plus: A Short Course. Dennis P. Curtin. 144p. 1991. pap. text ed. 18.40 (0-13-201641-9) P-H.

DBASE III Plus: Advanced. R. Baker. 1991. 29.95 (0-8306-6639-7) TAB Bks.

DBASE III Plus: The Pocket Reference. Miriam Liskin. 1992. pap. text ed. 9.95 (0-07-881831-1) Osborne-McGraw.

DBase III Plus: Things the Manual Didn't Tell You. Neil Dunlop. 200p. 1987. pap. 21.95 (0-938862-72-3) Weber Systems.

DBASE III Plus - Programmer's Reference Guide. Nathan Goldenthal. 538p. (Orig.). 1988. pap. 26.95 (0-938862-95-2) Weber Systems.

*DBase III Plus DOS Introduction. 150p. 1991. 29.95 (1-57533-048-2) Comput Confidence.

DBase III Plus Handbook. 2nd ed. George T. Chou. 517p. 1992. pap. 29.95 (0-88022-269-7) Que.

dBASE III Plus Made Easy. Miriam Liskin. 350p. 1988. pap. text ed. 19.95 (0-07-881294-1) Osborne-McGraw.

DBase III Plus Multiuser. R. Baker. 1991. 29.95 (0-8306-6646-X) TAB Bks.

Dbase III Plus Procedures Manual. Dennis P. Curtin. 128p. 1989. pap. 21.33 (0-685-26608-7) P-H.

DBase III Plus Programmer Field Guide. R. Doies. 1989. 19.95 (0-13-199365-8) P-H.

dBASE III Plus Programmer's Reference Guide. Alan Simpson. LC 87-82212. (Ready Reference Ser.). 1035p. (Orig.). 1987. pap. 39.95 (0-89588-508-5) Sybex.

DBase III Plus Programming. Wray. 1988. pap. 30.00 (0-87835-293-7) Boyd & Fraser.

DBASE III PLUS Programming. 2nd ed. Wray. 416p. 1991. 29.00 (0-87835-478-6) Boyd & Fraser.

DBase III Plus S. A. V. E. Edition. Dennis P. Curtin. 176p. (C). 1992. pap. text ed. write for info. (0-13-045576-8) P-H.

DBase III Plus Supplement Booklet. Clark Sexton & Doug Clark. 112p. (C). 1993. pap. text ed., spiral bd. 10.95 (0-8403-8660-5) Kendall-Hunt.

DBase III Plus to dBase IV: The Language Bridge Book. Adam B. Green. (Illus.). 400p. 1988. 24.95 (0-13-198680-5) P-H.

DBase III Plus Users Manual (IBM) Kerman D. Bharucha. 1991. 27.95 (0-8306-6633-8) TAB Bks.

DBase III Programming Handbook. Cary N. Prague & James E. Hammitt. (Illus.). 240p. 1986. pap. 16.95 (0-8306-2676-X, 2676P) TAB Bks.

dBASE III Programming Handbook. Cary N. Prague & James E. Hammitt. 1986. pap. text ed. 16.95 (0-07-155669-9) McGraw.

DBase IV. Don Cassel. 1992. write for info. (0-13-045634-9) P-H.

DBase IV: A Comprehensive User's Manual for Nonprogrammers. Kerman D. Bharucha. (Illus.). 512p. (Orig.). 1989. 32.95 (0-8306-1324-2, Windcrest) TAB Bks.

dBASE IV: A Practical Learning Guide. Alan D. Mazursky & Eileen B. Dlugoss. 448p. (C). 1990. teacher ed 8.00 (1-56118-347-4); pap. text ed. 29.95 (1-56118-346-6) Paradigm MN.

dBase IV: A Ready Reference Manual. Catherine Garrison & Mercedes McGowen. (Illus.). 176p. (C). 1990. pap. text ed. 12.95 (0-201-19714-6) Addison-Wesley.

DBase IV: A Short Course. 2nd ed. Dennis P. Curtin. 200p. 1993. pap. text ed. 24.00 (0-13-095928-6) P-H.

DBASE IV: A Tutorial to Accompany Peter Norton's Introduction to Computers. Miguel Pendas. LC 93-23741. 1994. write for info. (0-02-801327-1) Glencoe.

DBase IV: Advanced. Douglas M. Finney & Gary Hanks. 174p. 1991. spiral bd. 29.95 (1-56435-012-6) Finney Lrng Systs.

DBase IV: Advanced Applications for Nonprogrammers. Patricia A. Hartman. (Illus.). 304p. (Orig.). 1989. 29.95 (0-8306-9168-5, Windcrest); pap. 21.95 (0-8306-3168-2, Windcrest) TAB Bks.

DBASE IV: Applications for Nonprogrammers. Patricia A. Hartman. 1989. pap. 21.95 (0-07-156321-0) McGraw.

DBase IV: Beginning. Douglas M. Finney & Gary Hanks. 163p. 1991. spiral bd. 29.95 (1-56435-011-8) Finney Lrng Systs.

DBase IV: Complete User's Manual. Kerman D. Bharucha. 1991. 24.95 (0-8306-5383-X); 24.95 (0-8306-5413-5) TAB Bks.

DBase IV: Easy Reference Guide. Martin Jansen. LC 93-4471. 1994. text ed. 5.95 (0-538-62677-1) S-W Pub.

*DBASE IV: Up to & Including Version 2.0. (Prisma Computer Courses Ser.). (Illus.). 200p. (Orig.). 1995. pap. 12.95 (1-85365-375-6, Pub. by Spectrum UK) Seven Hills Bk.

DBase IV Advanced Programmer's Guide. Ralph Davis et al. 450p. 1988. 29.95 (0-13-198722-4) P-H.

DBase IV Business Applications Programming. Howard Dickler. 1988. 24.95 (0-13-198730-5) P-H.

dBASE IV Developer's Reference Guide. Clifford Phillip. 1989. disk 51.95 (0-318-42846-6) MIS Press.

dBase IV for Nonprogrammers. Kerman D. Bharucha. 1990. pap. 22.95 (0-8306-3570-X) TAB Bks.

DBase IV for the First-Time User. Howard Dickler & Cathy Ledbetter. (Illus.). 300p. 1988. pap. 19.95 (0-318-37393-9) P-H.

DBASE IV for VMS & UNIX: A Technical Support Approach. Sumant Pendharkar & Richard Biegel. (Illus.). 656p. 1992. pap. 49.95 (0-442-00908-9) Van Nos Reinhold.

DBase IV for Windows: A Developer's Resource Book. Jack L. Hursch & Carolyn J. Hursch. (Illus.). 464p. 1993. pap. 32.95 (0-8306-4245-5, 4290, Windcrest) TAB Bks.

DBASE IV Handbook Version 1.5. Mary Campbell. 1992. pap. 29.95 (0-679-79116-7) Random.

DBase IV Hotline Q & A. Richard Biegel & Sumant Pendharkar. LC 92-36131. 1993. pap. 29.95 (0-442-01384-1) Van Nos Reinhold.

DBase IV Inside & Out. Edward C. Jones. 1992. pap. text ed. 27.95 (0-07-881817-6) McGraw.

DBASE IV 1.5 Applied. Larry Smith & James Vaughn. Date not set. pap. text ed. write for info. (0-13-027989-7) P-H.

DBase IV Programming. Sumant S. Pendharkar & Richard A. Biegel. LC 94-1530. 1994. 30.00 (0-02-800424-8) Glencoe.

DBase IV Programming. Cary N. Prague & James E. Hammitt. 1989. 29.95 (0-8306-9466-8, 3066); pap. 26.95 (0-8306-9366-1, 3066P) TAB Bks.

DBase IV Programming. Cary N. Prague. 1990. pap. 32.95 (0-8306-3569-6) TAB Bks.

DBase IV Programming. Cary N. Prague. 1991. 5.25 hd 24.95 (0-8306-6687-7); 3.5 hd 24.95 (0-8306-6688-5) TAB Bks.

dBASE IV Programming: Tips & Techniques. Cary N. Prague & James E. Hammitt. 350p. 1989. pap. 24.95 (0-13-199050-0) P-H.

DBase IV Programming Language. Jeb Long. (Illus.). (Orig.). 1992. pap. 29.95 (0-672-22840-8) Sams.

dBASE IV Programming Language. Jeb J. Long & Alastair W. Dallas. 550p. 1989. 34.95 (0-13-199647-9) P-H.

DBase IV Programming Language: A Building Block Approach. Sumant Pendharkar & Richard Biegel. 560p. 1994. pap. 17.50 (0-13-301870-9) P-H.

Dbase IV Quick Reference Guide. 1990. pap. 19.95 (0-913365-60-2) Microref Educ Systs.

DBase IV Quick Reference Guide. Karl Schwartz. Ed. by Robert Mitilieri. (DDC Quick Reference Guides Ser.). 200p. (Orig.). 1990. spiral bd. 8.95 (0-936862-83-1, B-18); trans. 300.00 (1-56243-019-X, BT-4) DDC Pub.

DBASE IV Quick Reference Guide with Template. 24.95 (1-56351-032-4, S126) Microref Educ Systs.

DBASE IV, Release 1.1. Timothy J. O'Leary et al. 1992. pap. text ed. write for info. (0-07-048814-2) McGraw.

DBase IV S. A. V. E. Edition. Dennis P. Curtin. (C). 1993. pap. text ed. write for info. (0-13-045584-9) P-H.

DBase IV SQL User's Guide. Jack Hursch & Carolyn J. Hursch. (Illus.). 400p. 1988. pap. 24.95 (0-318-37394-7) P-H.

dBASE IV Template Language Reference. Dan Aspenwall. 1989. pap. 29.95 (0-13-197278-2) P-H.

DBase IV 2.0. Alan Boyd & Fraser. (C). Date not set. text ed. write for info. (0-318-70350-5, BF4179) S-W Pub.

DBASE IV Version 1.1. (STAR Ser.). 192p. 1993. 7.50 (0-87835-741-6) Boyd & Fraser.

dBase IV Version 1.1. James A. Senn. (C). 1991. pap. 27.95 (0-201-50662-9) Addison-Wesley.

dBASE IV, Vol. 1: User's Reference. Anatol Gardner. 300p. 1993. pap. text ed. 38.00 (0-13-200338-4) P-H.

dBASE IV, Vol. 2: Programmer's Reference. Anatol Gardner. 300p. 1989. boxed 53.33 (0-13-200353-8) P-H.

*DBase IV V1.5 DOS Introduction. 150p. 1992. 29.95 (1-57533-047-4) Comput Confidence.

DBase IV 1.1 Program. 2nd ed. Cary N. Prague & James E. Hammitt. 1991. 29.95 (0-8306-6757-1); 29.95 (0-8306-8758-0) TAB Bks.

DBase IV, 1.1 y SQL Pragnamacion para Exputo. Philip S. Heydt. 631p. 1993. pap. text ed. write for info. (968-18-4142-5, Pub. by Limusa MX) Computer & Tech.

DBASE IV 1.5 Programming. Cary N. Prague & James E. Hammitt. 1000p. 1992. pap. 36.95 (0-8306-4050-9, 4187, Windcrest) TAB Bks.

DBASE IV 1.5 Programming. 3rd ed. Cary N. Prague & James E. Hammitt. 1992. pap. 36.95 (0-07-050693-0) McGraw.

DBASE IV 2.0 Developers Handbook. 2nd ed. Howard Dickler. LC 93-60628. 737p. 1993. pap. 34.99 (0-7821-1263-3) Sybex.

DBase IV 2.0 for DOS. Sumant Pendharkar & Richard Biegel. LC 93-2263. 1994. pap. 29.95 (0-442-01680-8) Van Nos Reinhold.

DBase IV 2.0 Inside & Out. Edward C. Jones. 1993. pap. text ed. 27.95 (0-07-881944-X) Osborne-McGraw.

DBASE IV 2.0 Programmer's Instant Reference. Virginia Andersen. LC 93-83901. 529p. 1993. 14.95 (0-7821-1176-9) Sybex.

DBase IV 2.0 Programming. Cary N. Prague. 1993. pap. text ed. 34.95 (0-8306-4578-0, Windcrest) TAB Bks.

DBASE IV 2.0 Programming. Gary N. Prague. 1993. pap. text ed. 36.95 (0-07-050699-X) McGraw.

dBASE Language Advisor. Michael S. Bodner. (Illus.). 640p. 1991. 39.95 (0-8306-8644-4, 3644, Windcrest); pap. 27.95 (0-8306-7644-9, Windcrest) TAB Bks.

DBASE Language Handbook. David Kalman. 1000p. (C). 1989. pap. text ed. 310.00 (0-273-03155-4, Pub. by Pitman Pubng UK) St Mut.

DBase Language Reference with Annotations. Michael Masterson. 1993. pap. 40.00 (0-679-79173-6) Random.

Dbase Mac in Business. Jim Heid. 1988. 19.95 (0-13-198797-6) P-H.

DBase Management with dBase IV & & 3Plus. McLaren. (C). 1991. text ed. 16.50 (0-06-500529-5) HarpCollege.

Dbase Power: Building & Using Programming Tools. Peter L. Olympia. 1988. 29.95 (0-13-198805-0) P-H.

DBASE Programming. Wray & Pratt. (Illus.). 432p. 1992. 5.25 hd 29.00 (0-87835-794-7) Boyd & Fraser.

DBase Programming. Robert Wray. 1992. 3.5 hd, pap. 35.95 (0-87835-859-5) Boyd & Fraser.

DBASE Programming for Dummies. Michael Irwin. (For Dummies Ser.). (Illus.). 350p. 1994. pap. 19.95 (1-56884-080-2) IDG Bks.

DBase Symposium Proceedings: Fall, 1988. 1988. 250.00 (0-318-41124-5) Digit Consult MA.

dBASE Systems Development Handbook. Boston Systems Group, Inc. Staff et al. 900p. 1988. 49.95 (0-13-198771-2); pap. 39.95 (0-685-25567-0) P-H.

DBase Three Plus. Learn-PC Staff. 96p. (C). 1991. pap. text ed. write for info. (0-13-203159-0) P-H.

DBase Three Plus: A Short Course. 2nd ed. Dennis P. Curtin. LC 92-8686. (Computer Application Software Ser.). 224p. 1992. pap. text ed. 24.00 (0-13-203712-2) P-H.

DBP Ninety One Worldwide Directory of Protein & Peptide Producers. 1991. 385.00 (0-89336-896-2) BCC.

*DBug: An 8080 Interpretive DeBugger. Christopher A. Titus et al. LC 77-22128. (Techni-Reference Bk.: No. 3). 1977. pap. text ed. 5.00 (0-89704-013-9) E&L Instru.

DB2: Concepts, Design, & Programming. James Martin. 400p. 1989. text ed. 77.00 (0-13-198581-7) P-H.

DB2: Concepts, Programming & Design. Jay Ranade. 1991. text ed. 48.00 (0-07-051265-5) McGraw.

DB2: Design & Development Guide. 2nd ed. Gabrielle Wiorkowski. (Illus.). 416p. (C). 1990. text ed. 45.25 (0-201-50735-8) Addison-Wesley.

DB2: Design & Development Guide. 3rd ed. Gabrielle Wiorkowski & David Kull. (Illus.). 480p. (C). 1992. text ed. 48.50 (0-201-58049-7) Addison-Wesley.

DB2: Maximizing Performance of Online Production Systems. W. H. Inmon. 1993. pap. text ed. 49.95 (0-471-57008-7) Wiley.

DB2: Maximizing Performance of Online Production Systems. William H. Inmon. LC 88-18083. 392p. 1988. pap. 44.95 (0-89435-256-3) Wiley.

DB2: The Complete Guide to Implementation & Use. 2nd ed. Jeff D. Vowell. LC 89-8480. 340p. 1990. 49.95 (0-89435-300-4) Wiley.

DB2: The Complete Guide to Implementation & Use. 2nd ed. Jeff D. Vowell, Jr. 392p. 1993. text ed. 59.95 (0-471-60307-4) Wiley.

DB2 & SQL-DS: A User's Reference. Richard Schasberger & Fritz Wipper. 288p. 1989. pap. text ed. 32.95 (0-07-055170-7) McGraw.

DB2 Applications Development Handbook. CAP GEMINI Consultants. (CAP GEMINI America Ser.). 400p. 1989. text ed. 59.50 (0-07-009783-6) McGraw.

DB2 Design Review Guidelines. W. H. Inmon. 110p. 1988. ring bd. 90.00 (0-471-56773-6) Wiley.

DB2 Design Review Guidelines. William H. Inmon. LC 88-18082. 200p. 1988. 90.00 (0-89435-255-5) Wiley.

DB2 Developer's Guide. Craig S. Mullins. (Illus.). 400p. (Orig.). 1992. pap. 59.95 (0-672-30191-1) Sams.

Db2 for Application Programmers. Pacifico A. Lim. 1989. text ed. 57.00 (0-13-199795-5) P-H.

DB2 for Programmers & Non-Programmers. David I. Gourley. (Illus.). 316p. (Orig.). 1987. pap. 19.95 (0-943621-25-9) TechWest Pubns.

DB2 for the COBOL Programmer: An Advanced Course, Pt. 2. Steve Eckols. LC 91-30359. 393p. 1992. pap. 32.50 (0-911625-64-X) M Murach & Assoc.

DB2 for the COBOL Programmer: An Introductory Course, Pt. 1. Steve Eckols. LC 91-30359. 371p. 1991. pap. 32.50 (0-911625-59-3) M Murach & Assoc.

DB2 Handbook for DBAS. Aaron Werman. 1992. text ed. 49.50 (0-07-069460-5) McGraw.

DB2 Performance: Design, & Implementation. David Silverberg. 512p. 1992. text ed. 48.00 (0-07-057553-3) McGraw.

DB2 Performance & Development Guide. Joseph R. Geller. (Illus.). 300p. 1991. text ed. 49.95 (0-442-00526-1) Van Nos Reinhold.

DB2 System & Database Administration. Charles Hinchey. 1991. 55.50 (0-07-028978-6) McGraw.

DB2 Tools Symposium Proceedings: Spring & Fall, 1988. 1988. 250.00 (0-318-41117-2) Digit Consult MA.

DB2-400 Database Design & Programming. Ken Weimer. 250p. (C). 1996. pap. text ed. write for info. (1-882419-06-5, Duke Pr) Duke Commns Intl.

DC - AC Circuits: Concepts & Applications. Richard Parrett. 600p. 1991. boxed, text ed. 44.00 (0-13-200858-0, 420102) P-H.

DC - AC Circuits: Concepts & Applications. Richard Parrett. 480p. (C). 1992. pap. text ed. write for info. (0-13-042615-6) P-H.

An Asterisk (*) at the beginning of an entry indicates that the title is appearing in BIP for the first time.

D

An Asterisk (*) at the beginning of an entry indicates that the title is appearing in BIP for the first time.

1817

De Dos en Dos (Noe) Marilyn Lashbrook. Orig. Title: Two by Two. 32p. (SPA.). 1994. pap. 3.50 (*0-8254-1429-6*) Kregel.

De Duabus Naturis in Christo see Two Natures in Christ

De Embajadora A Prisionera Politica: Memorias De Albertini O'Farrill. Victor P. Yerovi. LC 90-86070. (Coleccion Cuba y Sus Jueces Ser.). (Illus.). 185p. (Orig.). (SPA.). 1991. pap. 15.00 (*0-89729-589-7*) Ediciones.

De-Escalation of Nuclear Crises. Ed. by Joseph E. Nation. LC 91-20553. 210p. 1992. text ed. 59.95 (*0-312-05245-6*) St Martin.

De Ese Dios de las Totalidades. Odon Betanzos-Palacios. 1989. pap. 5.00 (*0-86515-004-4*) Edit Mensaje.

De Eternidad a Eternidad. Erich Sauer. Orig. Title: From Eternity to Eternity. (SPA.). 1996. pap. 9.99 (*0-8254-1653-1*) Kregel.

De Excidio Brittaniae. Gildas. Tr. by J. A. Giles. pap. 3.95 (*0-89979-014-3*) British Am Bks.

De Facto & Second Marriage Partners: Inter Vivos Claims, Wills & Testamentary Disputes. Ed. by Paul K. Cooper. (C). 1992. pap. 80.00 (*1-875114-30-0*, Blckstone AT) W W Gaunt.

De Fato see De Oratore

De Femmes, Vol. X: Ecritures de Femmes dans la Litterature Francaise du XIX-XIXe Siecles. Claire-Lise Tondeur. 398p. (Orig.). (C). 1990. lib. bdg. 41.50 (*0-8191-7792-X*); pap. text ed. 26.50 (*0-8191-7793-8*) U Pr of Amer.

De Filippo: Four Plays. Eduardo De Filippo. Tr. by Carlo Ardito & Peter Tinniswood. 362p. 1992. pap. 15.95 (*0-413-66620-4*, A0657, Pub. by Methuen UK) Heinemann.

De Fine Versus. Paolo Mastandrea. Bd. CXXXII. Date not set. write for info. (*0-318-71172-9*, Pub. by Georg Olms GW) Lubrecht & Cramer.

De Fine Versus: Repertorio Di Clausole Riccorenti Nella Poesia Dattilica Latina Dalle Origini a Sidonio Apollinare, 2 vols. Paolo Mastandrea. (Alpha-Omega, Reihe A Ser.: Bd. CXXXII). xxiv, 1132p. (GER.). 1993. write for info. (*3-487-09693-5*, Pub. by Georg Olms GW) Lubrecht & Cramer.

De Fine Versus Repertorio Di Clausole Ricorrenti Nella Poesia Dattilica Latina, Dalle Origini a Sidonio Apollinare. Paolo Mastandrea. Bd. CXXXII. Date not set. write for info. (*0-318-70678-4*, Pub. by Georg Olms GW) Lubrecht & Cramer.

De Finibus. Marcus T. Cicero. (Loeb Classical Library: No. 40). 534p. 1914. 15.50 (*0-674-99044-7*) HUP.

De Finibus Bonorum et Malorum, Libri I, II. Cicero. Ed. by J. S. Reid. viii, 239p. 1968. reprint ed. write for info. (*0-318-71092-7*, Pub. by Georg Olms GW) Lubrecht & Cramer.

De Finibus Bonorum et Malorum, Libri V. Cicero. lxx, 869p. 1963. reprint ed. write for info. (*0-318-71093-5*, Pub. by Georg Olms GW) Lubrecht & Cramer.

De Finibus Bonorum et Malorum, Libri V. Cicero. Bd. 18. lxx, 869p. 1963. reprint ed. pap. write for info. (*0-318-71094-3*, Pub. by Georg Olms GW) Lubrecht & Cramer.

De Finibus Bonorum et Malorum Libri I, II. M. Tullius Cicero. Ed. by James S. Reid. 247p. reprint ed. lib. bdg. 36.40 (*0-89563-510-0*, 05101883, Pub. by Georg Olms GW) Lubrecht & Cramer.

De Finibus Bonorum et Malorum Libri V. M. Tullius Cicero. Bd. 18. pap. write for info. (*0-318-70794-2*, Pub. by Georg Olms GW) Lubrecht & Cramer.

De Finibus Bonorum et Malorum Libri V. M. Tullius Cicero. lxx, 869p. 1963. reprint ed. lib. bdg. 157.50 (*0-317-66605-3*) Coronet Bks.

De Forests of Avenes. John W. De Forest. (Collected Works of John W. De Forest). 1988. reprint ed. lib. bdg. 59.00 (*0-7812-1166-2*) Rprt Serv.

De Forests of Avenes (& of New Netherland) A Hugenot Thread in American Colonial History, 1494-1900. J. W. De Forest. 307p. 1989. reprint ed. lib. bdg. 59.00 (*0-8328-0466-5*); reprint ed. pap. 49.00 (*0-8328-0467-3*) Higginson Bk Co.

De Frederias y Otros Poemas. Freddy G. Cajape. 56p. (SPA.). 1984. pap. 5.00 (*0-9606758-7-6*) SLUSA.

De Fructu Qui Ex Doctrina Percipitur (The Benefit of a Liberal Education, 1517) Richard Pace. Ed. by Francis Manley & Richard S. Sylvester. LC 66-21029. (Renaissance Text Ser.: No. 2). xxvi, 190p. 1967. 8.50 (*0-9602696-1-4*) Renaiss Society Am.

De-Gaming Teaching & Learning: How to Motivate Learners & Invite OKness. Richard J. Stapleton. LC 78-73696. (Illus.). (Orig.). 1979. pap. 15.00 (*0-933594-00-3*) Effect Learning GA.

De Gaulle. Francois Mauriac. (FRE.). 1964. 24.95 (*0-8288-9861-8*, F112660) Fr & Eur.

De Gaulle: The Rebel 1890-1944. Jean Lacouture. Tr. by Patrick O'Brian. (Illus.). 640p. 1993. pap. 15.95 (*0-393-30999-1*) Norton.

De Gaulle: The Ruler 1945-1970. Jean Lacouture. Tr. by Alan Sheridan. (Illus.). 668p. 1993. pap. 15.95 (*0-393-31000-0*) Norton.

De Gaulle: The Ruler 1945-1970, Vol. II. Jean Lacouture. Tr. by Alan Sheridan. (Illus.). 700p. (C). 1992. 29.95 (*0-393-03084-9*) Norton.

De Gaulle & Modern France. John N. Horne. Ed. by Hugh Gough. LC 93-2042. 192p. 1993. pap. 19.95 (*0-340-58826-8*, B2316, Pub. by E Arnold UK) Routledge Chapman & Hall.

De Gaulle & the United States: A Centennial Reappraisal. Ed. by Robert O. Paxton & Nicholas Wahl. LC 93-8091. 320p. 1994. 54.95 (*0-85496-998-5*) Berg Pubs.

***De Gaulle & the United States: A Centennial Reappraisal.** Ed. by Robert O. Paxton & Nicholas Wahl. LC 93-8091. 320p. 1994. pap. 19.95 (*1-85973-066-3*) Berg Pubs.

De Gaulle & the World: The Foreign Policy of the Fifth French Republic. Wladyslaw W. Kulski. LC 66-28137. 1966. 34.95 (*0-8156-0052-6*) Syracuse U Pr.

De Gaulle Republic: Quest for Unity. Roy C. Macridis & Bernard E. Brown. LC 76-7417. 400p. 1976. reprint ed. text ed. 55.00 (*0-8371-8848-2*, MADG, Greenwood Pr) Greenwood.

De Gaulle Revolution. Alexander Werth. LC 75-31477. 404p. 1976. reprint ed. text ed. 55.00 (*0-8371-8508-4*, WEDG, Greenwood Pr) Greenwood.

De Gaulle to Mitterrand: Presidential Power in France. Martin Harrison et al. Ed. by Jack Hayward. LC 92-40931. 272p. (C). 1993. text ed. 45.00 (*0-8147-3355-7*); pap. text ed. 15.00 (*0-8147-3356-5*) NYU Pr.

De Gaulle, Vol. 1: The Rebel 1890-1944. Jean Lacouture. 1990. 29.95 (*0-393-02699-X*) Norton.

De Generatione et Corruptione. Aristotle. Ed. by C. S. Williams. (Clarendon Aristotle Ser.). 1982. 32.00 (*0-19-872062-9*); pap. 22.00 (*0-19-872063-7*) OUP.

De Gestis Concilii Basiliensis Commentariorum: Libri II. Ed. by Denys Hay. (Medieval Texts Ser.). 312p. 1992. 59.00 (*0-19-822201-7*) OUP.

De Gheyn-Three Generations, 3 vols. I. Van Regteren Altena. (Illus.). 685p. 1987. lib. bdg. 403.50 (*90-247-2741-3*) Kluwer Ac.

De Gide a Sartre. Andre Maurois. (FRE.). 12.95 (*0-8288-9877-4*, F113550) Fr & Eur.

De Goupil a Margot. Louis Pergaud. (FRE.). 1982. pap. 10.95 (*0-7859-4162-2*) Fr & Eur.

De Goya al Arte Abstracto. 2nd ed. Ricardo Gullon. 211p. 1963. pap. 3.50 (*0-8477-2104-3*) U of PR Pr.

De Graecae Linguae Dialectis, 2 vols. Heinrich L. Ahrens. xxx, 871p. 1971. reprint ed. Bd. I: De Dialectis Aerolicis et Pseudoaeolicis. write for info. (*0-318-70849-3*, Pub. by Georg Olms GW); reprint ed. Bd. II: De Dialecto Dorica. write for info. (*0-318-70850-7*, Pub. by Georg Olms GW) Lubrecht & Cramer.

De Graecae Linguae Dialectis, 2 vols., Set. Heinrich L. Ahrens. xxx, 871p. 1971. reprint ed. write for info. (*3-487-04180-4*, Pub. by Georg Olms GW) Lubrecht & Cramer.

De Grammatico of St. Anselm: The Theory of Paronymy. St. Anselm. LC 64-17066. (Notre Dame, University Publications in Mediaeval Studies Ser.: No. 18). 188p. reprint ed. pap. 53.60 (*0-317-08123-3*, 2022069) Bks Demand.

***De Grammaticus et Rhetoribus: With Translation, Introduction, & Commentary.** Suetonius. Ed. by Robert A. Kaster. 300p. 1995. text ed. 72.00 (*0-19-814091-6*) OUP.

De Gratia: Faustus of Riez's Treatise on Grace & Its Place in the History of Theology. Thomas A. Smith. LC 89-40747. (Christianity & Judaism in Antiquity Ser.: Vol. 4). 276p. (C). 1990. text ed. 29.95 (*0-268-00866-3*) U of Notre Dame Pr.

De Grazia & Mexican Cookery. Illus. by Ted De Grazia. LC 82-80299. 86p. (Orig.). 1982. pap. 12.95 (*0-87358-307-8*) Northland AZ.

De Groot's Wills, Probate & Administration Practice (Victoria) Robert D. Shepherd & Patricia Duke. 366p. (C). 1989. 280.00 (*1-875114-01-7*, Pub. by Blackstone Pr UK) W W Gaunt.

De Guerre Lasse. Francoise Sagan. (FRE.). 1986. pap. 10.95 (*0-8288-3727-9*, F123412) Fr & Eur.

De Guerre Lasse. Francoise Sagan. (Folio Ser.: No. 1759). 219p. (FRE.). 1987. pap. 8.95 (*2-07-037759-8*) Schoenhof.

De Gustibus: Essays for Alain Renoir. Ed. by John M. Foley. LC 92-20833. (Albert Bates Lord Studies in Oral Tradition: Vol. 11). 616p. 1992. 75.00 (*0-8153-0395-5*, H1482) Garland.

***De Gustibus Presents the Great Cooks' Cookbooks: Southwest Cooking.** Arlene Feltman-Sailhac. (Illus.). 89p. 1995. 12.98 (*1-884822-14-2*, 30919) Blck Dog & Leventhal.

De Haeresibus. Aurelius Augustinius. Tr. by Liguori G. Muller. LC 78-63165. (Heresies of the Early Christian & Medieval Era Ser.: Second Ser.). reprint ed. write for info. (*0-404-16178-2*) AMS Pr.

De Harmonia Musicorum Instrumentorum Opus. Franchinus Gafurius. (Monuments of Music & Music Literature in Facsimile: Series II, Vol. 97). 1979. reprint ed. lib. bdg. 60.00 (*0-8450-2297-0*) Broude.

De Havilland Aircraft since 1909. 3rd ed. A. J. Jackson. LC 87-61415. (Illus.). 552p. 1987. 36.95 (*0-87021-896-4*) Naval Inst Pr.

De Havilland DH-4: From Flaming Coffin to Living Legend. Walter J. Boyne. LC 84-1391. (Famous Aircraft of the National Air & Space Museum Ser.: Vol. 7). (Illus.). 120p. 1984. pap. 12.95 (*0-87474-277-3*, BODHP) Smithsonian.

***De-Hegemonizing Language Standards: Learning from (Post) Colonial Englishes about "English"** Arjuna Parakrama. LC 94-25478. 1994. write for info. (*0-312-12316-7*) St Martin.

DE Herculis Laborbvs. D. W. Blanford. (Illus.). (C). 1982. pap. text ed. 39.00 (*0-900269-02-2*, Pub. by Old Vicarage UK) St Mut.

De Historia Piscium & Icthyographia ad Amplisimum Virum Dnum: Samuelem Pepys, Presidem Soc. Reg, 2 vols in one. Francis Willughby. Ed. by Keir B. Sterling. LC 77-81089. (Biologists & Their World Ser.). (Illus.). 1978. reprint ed. lib. bdg. 64.95 (*0-405-10667-X*) Ayer.

De Hito en Hito: Siete Ensayos Sobre Literatura Espanola. Gustavo Agrait. LC 83-8864. 151p. (SPA.). 1983. pap. 5.00 (*0-8477-3508-7*) U of PR Pr.

De-Icing Salt Damage to Trees & Shrubs. HMSO Staff. (Forestry Commission Bulletin Ser.: No. 101). 76p. 1991. pap. 16.00 (*0-11-710302-0*, HM2514) UNIPUB.

De Inspiracion (Of Inspiration) A. H. Mottesi. (SPA.). Date not set. 1.79 (*0-8423-6450-1*, 498508) Editorial Unilit.

De Institutione Oratoria Libri Duodecim, 6 vols., Set. Marcus F. Quintilianus. ccxxxvi, 4175p. 1968. reprint ed. write for info. (*0-318-71207-5*, Pub. by Georg Olms GW) Lubrecht & Cramer.

De Institutione Oratoria Libri Duodecim, Vol. 6: Lexicon Quintilianeum. Marcus F. Quintilianus. Ed. by E. Bonell. lxxxiv, 1044p. 1962. reprint ed. write for info. (*0-318-71208-3*, Pub. by Georg Olms GW) Lubrecht & Cramer.

De Inventione. Marcus T. Cicero. Ed. by E. H. Warmington. Bd. with De Optimo Genere Oratorum; Topica. (Loeb Classical Library: No. 386). (ENG & LAT.). (C). 15.50 (*0-674-99425-6*) HUP.

De Jean Coste. Charles Peguy. 228p. (FRE.). 1937. pap. 10.95 (*0-7859-1294-0*, 2070249832) Fr & Eur.

De Jerusalem a Roma (Neigh Bib Study: Acts) Kunz & Schell. (SPA.). Date not set. 1.50 (*0-945792-53-0*, 490451) Editorial Unilit.

De Jure Personarum: or, a Treatise on the Roman Law of Persons. W. H. Rattingan. LC 93-79723. 362p. 1994. reprint ed. 85.00 (*1-56169-081-3*) W W Gaunt.

De Kansas a Califas & Back to Chicago: Poems & Art. Carlos Cortez. LC 92-60876. (Illus.). 51p. (Orig.). 1992. pap. 6.50 (*1-877636-09-6*) March Abrazo.

***De Kleine Zeemeermin - Little Mermaid.** Adapt. by Sarah Harris. (Comes to Life Bks.). 16p. (DUT & ENG.). (J). (ps-2). 1995. write for info. (*1-57234-032-0*) YES Ent.

De Kock's Industrial Laws of South Africa. 2nd ed. C. Thompson & P. Benjamin. (South African Labour Law Ser.). 1965. ring bd. 120.00 (*0-7021-0067-6*, Pub. by Juta SA) W W Gaunt.

De Kooning & Dubuffet: The Late Works. Text by Peter Schjeldahl. LC 93-85892. 74p. 1993. write for info. (*1-878283-33-2*) PaceWildenstein.

De la Angoisse a la Foi. D. Martyn Lloyd-Jones. 96p. (FRE.). 1986. 3.95 (*0-8297-0694-1*) Life Pubs Intl.

De la Brevedad de la Vida. Lucius Annaeus Seneca. Ed. & Tr. by Vicente Reynal. LC 78-24050. (UPREX, Humanidades Ser.: No. 55). (SPA.). 1987. pap. text ed. 3.75 (*0-8477-0078-X*) U of PR Pr.

De la Brujeria a Cristo: From Witchcraft to Christ. Dooren Irvine. (SPA.). 5.95 (*84-300-1013-0*, 220254, Pub. by Edit Clie SP) TSELF.

De la Bruyere a Proust: Lecture Mon Doux Plaisir. Andre Maurois. (Coll. Les Grands Evenements Litteraires). (FRE.). 11.95 (*0-8288-9878-2*, F113560) Fr & Eur.

De la Corruption du Goust dans la Musique Francaise. Louis Bollioud-Mermet. LC 76-43907. (Music & Theatre in France in the 17th & 18th Centuries Ser.). reprint ed. 31.50 (*0-404-60150-2*) AMS Pr.

De la Decadence de la Peinture Italienne au 16e Siecle. Romain Rolland. (Illus.). 169p. (FRE.). 1957. pap. 9.95 (*0-7859-5446-5*) Fr & Eur.

De la Democratie en Amerique, 2 vols., Vol. 1. Alexis De Tocqueville. (Folio-Histoire Ser.: Nos. 12 & 13). (FRE.). 11.95 (*2-07-032354-4*) Schoenhof.

De la Democratie en Amerique, 2 vols., Vol. 2. Alexis De Tocqueville. (Folio-Histoire Ser.: Nos. 12 & 13). (FRE.). 11.95 (*2-07-032364-1*) Schoenhof.

De la Estabilidad Al Crecimiento. Barbosa et al. 1992. write for info. (*1-55815-169-9*) ICS Pr.

***De la Experiencia Mistica a la Creacion Grotesca: Tres Ensayos de Aprozimacion a los Limites.** Maria N. Fernandez-Garcia. 115p. 1993. lib. bdg. 10.00 (*1-881708-00-4*) Edcnes Mairena.

De la Folie: Considerations Sur Cette Maladie. Etienne-Jean Georget. LC 75-16705. (Classics in Psychiatry Ser.). (FRE.). 1976. reprint ed. 42.95 (*0-405-07431-X*) Ayer.

De la Folie: Consideree Sous le Point de Vue Pathologique, Philosophique, Historique et Judiciai Re, 2 vols. in 1. Louis-Florentin Calmeil. LC 75-16695. (Classics in Psychiatry Ser.). (FRE.). 1976. reprint ed. 87.95 (*0-405-07423-9*) Ayer.

De la Grace et de l'Humanite de Jesus. 2nd ed. Jacques Maritain. 156p. (FRE.). 1967. 15.95 (*0-8288-9848-0*, F111690) Fr & Eur.

De la Langue Parlee a la Langue Litteraire. Emanuelle Wagner. 124p. 1965. 18.95 (*0-8288-7448-4*) Fr & Eur.

De la Litterature des Negres. Henri Gregoire. Tr. by D. B. Warden. (B. E. Ser.: No. 70). 1810. 57.00 (*0-8115-3021-3*) Periodicals Srv.

De la Litterature Francaise. Denis Hollier. (Bordas Ser.). 1091p. (FRE.). 1993. 69.95 (*2-04-018597-6*) Schoenhof.

De la Mano De Jesus (So You Want to Grow?) Luis Palau. (SPA.). 1990. 4.99 (*1-56063-006-X*, 498024) Editorial Unilit.

De la Necesidad y Del Amor: (Poesia, 1967-1979) Miguel A. Loredo. LC 88-80054. (Coleccion Espejo de Paciencia Ser.). (Illus.). 160p. (Orig.). (SPA.). 1990. pap. 15.00 (*0-89729-475-0*) Ediciones.

De la Oracion Simple A la Oracion Compuesta: Curso Superior De Gramatica Espanola. Hector Campos. LC 92-45723. 232p. (Orig.). (SPA.). (C). 1993. pap. text ed. 22.95 (*0-87840-240-3*) Georgetown U Pr.

De la Oracion Simple A la Oracion Compuesta: Curso Superior De Gramatica Espanola: Clave De los Ejercicios. Hector Campos. 94p. (Orig.). (SPA.). (C). 1993. teacher ed. pap. text ed. 7.50 (*0-87840-241-1*) Georgetown U Pr.

De la Palabra. Sam Silva. (Dog River Review Poetry Ser.). 36p. (Orig.). 1992. pap. 4.00 (*0-916155-15-3*) Trout Creek.

De la Paralysie Consideree chez les Alienes. Louis-Florentin Calmeil. LC 75-16696. (Classics in Psychiatry Ser.). (FRE.). 1976. reprint ed. 37.95 (*0-405-07424-7*) Ayer.

De la Penisula Hacia Latinoamerica: El Naturalismo Social en Emlia Pardo-Bazan, Eugenio Cambaceres y Aluisio de Azevedo. Percio B. De Castro. LC 92-39170. (American University Studies: Comparative Literature: Ser. III, Vol. 51). 153p. (C). 1994. text ed. 39.95 (*0-8204-2105-7*) P Lang Pubs.

De La Philosophie Ancienne a la Theologie Patristique. Jean Pepin. (Collected Studies: No. CS233). 348p. (C). 1986. reprint ed. lib. bdg. 99.50 (*0-86078-181-X*, Pub. by Variorum UK) Ashgate Pub Co.

De la Recherche de la Verite & Eclaircissements see Search after Truth & Elucidations of the Search after Truth

De la Revolte a l'Exercice: Essai Sur l'Hedonisme Contemporain. Jean-Michel Heimonet. LC 89-52102. 303p. (FRE.). 1990. lib. bdg. 39.95 (*0-917786-77-7*) Summa Pubns.

De La Seduction. Jean Baudrillard. (Folio Essais Ser.: No. 81). (FRE.). pap. 9.95 (*2-07-032465-6*) Schoenhof.

De la Syntaxe a la Pragmatique: Actes du Colloque de Linguistique de Rennes, Nov. 17-19, 1979. Ed. by Pierre Attal & Claude Muller. LC 84-9329. (Lingvisticae Investigationes Supplementa Ser.: 8). 389p. (FRE.). 1984. 78.00x (*90-272-3118-4*) Benjamins North Am.

De la Terre a la Lune. Jules Verne. pap. 8.95 (*0-685-37132-8*) Fr & Eur.

De la Terre a la Lune. Jules Verne. (Illus.). 246p. (FRE.). 1979. pap. 10.95 (*0-686-55042-0*, 2080703056) Fr & Eur.

De la Terre a la Lune. Jules Verne. (Folio - Junior Ser.: No. 12). 246p. (FRE.). (J). (gr. 5-10). 1977. pap. 9.95 (*2-07-056625-0*) Schoenhof.

De la Toponymie Bretonne, Dictionnaire Etymologique. W. B. Smith. (LM Ser.: Vol. 20). (FRE.). 1972. reprint ed. 16.00 (*0-527-00824-9*) Periodicals Srv.

De la Vanite. Michel E. De Montaigne. 141p. (FRE.). 1989. pap. 18.95 (*0-7859-1556-7*, 2869302282) Fr & Eur.

De la Vida Real: From Real Life - Ideas for Sermons. Roberto Velert. (SPA.). 4.25 (*84-7645-415-5*, 223532, Pub. by Edit Clie SP) TSELF.

De l'administration de la Justice Criminelle en Angleterre, et de l'esprit du Gouvernement Anglais. Charles Cottu. Ed. by J. P. Mayer. LC 78-67348. (European Political Thought Ser.). (FRE.). 1980. reprint ed. lib. bdg. 25.95 (*0-405-11689-6*) Ayer.

De l'Agent Inconnu Au Philosophie Inconnu, Vol. VI. Robert Amadou & Alice Joly. 262p. reprint ed. write for info. (*0-318-71427-2*, Pub. by Georg Olms GW) Lubrecht & Cramer.

De Laicis: Or, the Treatise on Civil Government. Roberto F. Bellarmino. Tr. by Kathleen E. Murphy. LC 78-20450. 1994. reprint ed. 18.75 (*0-88355-927-7*) Hyperion Conn.

De L'Allegorie see Versuch einer Allegorie

De l'Allemagne, 5 vols. de Stael. (Grands Escrivains de France Ser.). 350p. 1967. 15.95 (*0-685-73259-2*) Fr & Eur.

De l'Allemagne, Vol. 1. Germaine de Stael-Holstein. Ed. by Simone Balaye. 350p. (FRE.). 1967. pap. 20.95 (*0-7859-5393-0*) Fr & Eur.

De l'Amour. Stendhal, pseud. Ed. by Henri Martineau. (Coll. Prestige). (FRE.). 1980. pap. 10.95 (*0-7859-1373-4*, 2070371891) Fr & Eur.

De l'Amour. Stendhal. (Folio Ser.: No. 1189). (FRE.). 1959. pap. 12.95 (*2-07-037189-1*) Schoenhof.

De las Garras Del Dragon. Carroll Hunt. 176p. (SPA.). 1991. 4.95 (*0-8297-0664-X*) Life Pubs Intl.

De las Jarchas a la Poesia Negra. Rosa Valdes-Cruz. LC 79-64144. (Senda de Estudios y Ensayos Ser.). (Orig.). (SPA.). 1979. pap. 9.95 (*0-918454-16-6*) Senda Nueva.

De Laudibus Legum Anglia. Stanley B. Chrimes & John Fortescue. LC 85-81802. (Cambridge Studies in English Legal History). 349p. 1986. reprint ed. 82.00 (*0-912004-41-X*) W W Gaunt.

De Laudibus Legum Anglia. John Fortescue. LC 78-62331. 1985. reprint ed. 30.00 (*0-88355-793-2*) Hyperion Conn.

De Lawd: Richard B. Harrison & The Green Pastures. Walter C. Daniel. LC 86-7588. (Contributions in Afro-American & African Studies: No. 99). 188p. 1986. text ed. 45.00 (*0-313-25300-5*, DDL/, Greenwood Pr) Greenwood.

De l'Economie Politique Moderne. Jean F. De Herrenschwand. 1990. reprint ed. 58.00 (*3-601-00157-8*) Periodicals Srv.

De Lector a Escritor: El Desarollo de la Communicacion Escrita. Finnemann & Gorell. 1991. pap. 32.95 (*0-8384-1990-9*); pap. 32.95 (*0-8384-2083-4*) Heinle & Heinle.

De Lege Pactorum: Essays in Honor of R. R. Wilson. David R. Deener. LC 70-101129. 288p. reprint ed. pap. 82.10 (*0-8357-9101-7*, 2017898) Bks Demand.

De Legibus et Consuetudinibus Angliae, 4. Henry De Bracton. Ed. by G. E. Woodbine. 1942. 100.00 (*0-686-51370-3*) Elliots Bks.

De Legibus Libri Tres. Cicero. xxx, 793p. 1977. reprint ed. write for info. (*3-487-04628-8*, Pub. by Georg Olms GW) Lubrecht & Cramer.

De l'Eglise du Christ. Jacques Maritain. 430p. (FRE.). 1970. 15.95 (*0-8288-9847-2*, F111685) Fr & Eur.

De l'Espirit des Lois: Les Grands Themes. Charles-Louis de Montesquieu. 1970. 9.95 (*0-686-54781-0*) Fr & Eur.

De l'Esprit de Conquete. Benjamin Constant. 72p. (FRE.). 1980. pap. write for info. (*0-7859-4585-7*) Fr & Eur.

De l'Esprit des Lois, 2 vols. Charles-Louis de Montesquieu. 566p. 1973. Vol. 1, 566p. 19.95 (*0-8288-7485-9*); Vol. 2, 753p. 19.95 (*0-8288-7486-7*); write for info. (*0-685-74480-9*) Fr & Eur.

An Asterisk (*) at the beginning of an entry indicates that the title is appearing in BIP for the first time.

De l'Esprit des Lois, 2 tomes, Set. Charles-Louis De Montesquieu. (Coll. Prestige). 510p. (FRE.). 1979. pap. 13.95 (*0-7859-4632-2*) Fr & Eur.

De l'Esprit des Lois, 2 tomes, Set. Charles-Louis De Montesquieu. Ed. by Truc. (FRE.). 1962. pap. 7.95 (*0-8288-9966-5*, F48434) Fr & Eur.

De l'Esprit des Lois, Vol. 1. 192p. 1992. reprint ed. pap. write for info. (*0-7859-4640-3*) Fr & Eur.

De l'Esthetique a la Metaphysique. Piguet. (Phaenomenologica Ser.: No. 3). 1960. pap. text ed. 56.50 (*90-247-0236-4*) Kluwer Ac.

De l'Etat Actuel De La Grece et Des Moyens d'Arriver a Sa Restauration, 2 vols. Friedrich Thiersch. (GER.). Date not set. Vol. I, De l'etat politique et de la pacification de la Grece; xxvi, 466p. write for info. (*0-318-70434-X*, Pub. by Georg Olms GW); Vol. II: Des moyens d'arriver a la restauration de la Grece; xx, 327p. write for info. (*0-318-70435-8*, Pub. by Georg Olms GW) Lubrecht & Cramer.

De l'Etat Actuel De La Grece et Des Moyens d'Arriver a Sa Restauration, 2 vols., Set. Friedrich Thiersch. (GER.). Date not set. write for info. (*0-318-70433-1*, Pub. by Georg Olms GW) Lubrecht & Cramer.

De Libanio Socratis Defensore. Hieronymus Markowski. No. 40. viii, 196p. 1970. reprint ed. write for info. (*0-318-70974-0*, Pub. by Georg Olms GW) Lubrecht & Cramer.

De l'Inconvenient d'Etre Ne. E. M. Cioran. (FRE.). 1989. pap. 10.95 (*0-7859-2808-1*) Fr & Eur.

De l'Inconvenient d'Etre Ne. E. M. Cioran. (Folio Essais Ser.: No. 80). 243p. (FRE.). 1973. pap. 8.95 (*2-07-032448-6*) Schoenhof.

De Lingua Latina, 2 vols, 1. Marcus T. Varro. (Loeb Classical Library: No. 333-334). 420p. 1938. 18.95 (*0-674-99367-5*) HUP.

De Lingua Latina, 2 vols, 2. Marcus T. Varro. (Loeb Classical Library: No. 333-334). 676p. 1938. 18.95 (*0-674-99368-3*) HUP.

De Lingua Latina Buch VIII. Varro. Ed. by Hellfried Dahlmann. 194p. 1966. write for info. (*3-296-15850-2*, Pub. by Georg Olms GW) Lubrecht & Cramer.

De Linne A Lamarck: Methodes de la Classification et Idee de Serie en Botanique et En Zoologie. H. Daudin. 264p. 1984. pap. text ed. write for info. (*2-903928-05-3*) Gordon & Breach.

De l'Opera en France, 2 vols., Set. Francois H. Blaze. LC 80-2259. reprint ed. 82.50 (*0-404-18810-9*) AMS Pr.

De l'Ordre Social. Guillaume F. Le Trosne. (Economistes Francais du XVIIIe Siecle Ser.). 1990. reprint ed. pap. 70.00 (*3-601-00155-1*) Periodicals Srv.

De Los Archivos del Trasgo. Rafael Dieste. Tr. by Cesar A. Molina. (Nueva Austral Ser.: Vol. 84). (SPA.). 1991. pap. text ed. 24.95x (*84-239-1884-X*) Elliots Bks.

De los Gallos De Pelea y De Otros Temas. Felix R. Robles. (Illus.). 402p. (Orig.). 1991. pap. 20.00 (*0-685-51538-9*) Saeta.

De Los Nombres de Cristo. Fray L. de Leon. Ed. by Antonio Sanchez Zamarreno. (Nueva Austral Ser.: Vol. 190). (SPA.). 1991. pap. text ed. 32.95x (*84-239-1990-0*) Elliots Bks.

***De los Otros: Intimacy & Homosexuality among Mexican Men.** Joseph Carrier. LC 95-6244. (Between Men-Between Women Ser.). (SPA.). 1995. write for info. (*0-231-09692-5*); pap. write for info. (*0-231-09693-3*) Col U Pr.

De Ludo Globi. Nicholas De Cusa. Tr. by Pauline W. Trinkaus. (Janus Ser.). 136p. 1986. 20.00 (*0-89835-068-9*) Abaris Bks.

De Luna. John Appleyard. 1977. lib. bdg. 5.95 (*0-686-22981-9*) Appleyard Agency.

De Luxe Show. (Illus.). 74p. 1971. pap. 9.95 (*0-939594-11-0*) Inst for the Arts.

De Magnete. William Gilbert. 1991. pap. 8.95 (*0-486-26761-X*) Dover.

De Malaquias a Mateo: Four Hundred Years of Silence. H. A. Ironside. (SPA.). 3.25 (*84-7645-421-X*, 223436, Pub. by Edit Clie SP) TSELF.

De Marie a Genevre see Ronsard Poete de l'Amour

De Mayor of Harlem. David Henderson. 128p. 1985. reprint ed. pap. 12.95 (*0-938190-39-3*) North Atlantic.

***De Meaning of Words, Illustrated.** Jack Hande. (Illus.). 134p. (Orig.). 1994. pap. 9.95 (*1-886090-00-9*) Hande Hus Pubng.

De Medicina, 3 vols., 1. Celsus. (Loeb Classical Library: No. 292, 304, 336). 504p. 1935. 18.95 (*0-674-99322-5*) HUP.

De Medicina, 3 vols., 2. Celsus. (Loeb Classical Library: No. 292, 304, 336). 360p. 1938. 18.95 (*0-674-99335-7*) HUP.

De Medicina, 3 vols., 3. Celsus. (Loeb Classical Library: No. 292, 304, 336). 656p. 1938. 18.95 (*0-674-99370-5*) HUP.

De Minimis Risk. Ed. by C. Whipple. LC 87-27590. (Contemporary Issues in Risk Analysis Ser.: Vol. 2). (Illus.). 224p. 1988. 65.00 (*0-306-42530-0*, Plenum Pr) Plenum.

De Mio Cid a Alfonso Reyes: Perspectivas Criticas. Ignacio R. Galbis. LC 80-53519. (Senda de Estudios y Ensayos Ser.). 139p. (Orig.). (SPA.). 1981. pap. 9.95 (*0-918454-22-0*) Senda Nueva.

De Monarchia. Dante Alighieri. 1973. 59.95 (*0-8490-0000-9*) Gordon Pr.

***De-Monopolization & Competition.** Ed. by Ben Slay. (C). 1995. text ed. 45.95 (*0-8133-8864-3*) Westview.

De Montherlant: Port Royal. Henry De Montherlant. Ed. by Richard Griffiths. (Bristol French Texts Ser.). 200p. (FRE.). 1992. reprint ed. pap. 11.95 (*0-631-00730-X*, Pub. by Brstl Class Pr UK) Focus Info Gr.

De-Moralization of Society: From Victorian Virtues to Modern Values. Gertrude Himmelfarb. LC 94-12365. 314p. 1995. 24.00 (*0-679-43817-3*) Knopf.

De Motu & the Analyst: A Modern Edition, with Introductions & Commentary. G. Berkeley. Ed. & Tr. by Douglas M. Jesseph. (New Synthese Historical Library). 244p. (C). 1991. lib. bdg. 97.00 (*0-7923-1520-0*) Kluwer Ac.

De Motu Cordis: Anatomical Studies on the Motion of the Heart & Blood. 5th ed. William Harvey. Tr. by Chauncey D. Leake. (Illus.). 186p. 1978. 29.95 (*0-398-00793-4*) C C Thomas.

De Muerte a Vida: From Death to Life. Oswald Smith. (SPA.). 3.95 (*84-7645-037-0*, 223108, Pub. by Edit Clie SP) TSELF.

***De Mujer A Mujer.** Gloria Ricardo. 18p. 1992. pap. 1.00 (*1-885630-15-8*) HLM Producciones.

De Mujeres y Perros. Felix R. Morgan. LC 89-81221. (Coleccion Caniqui Ser.). (Illus.). 101p. (Orig.). (SPA.). 1990. pap. 9.95 (*0-89729-555-2*) Ediciones.

De Musica. Alfredo M. Jimeno. 639p. 1992. 38.00 (*0-8477-0179-4*) U of PR Pr.

De Musica Figurata. Marcin Kromer. Ed. by Albert Seay. (Texts-Translations Ser.: No. 3). 35p. 1980. pap. 5.00 (*0-933894-08-2*) Colo Coll Music.

De Musica Mensurata: The Anonymous of St. Emmeram: Complete Critical Edition, Translation, & Commentary. Jeremy Yudkin. LC 87-45435. (Music: Scholarship & Performance Ser.). (Illus.). 398p. 1990. 45.00 (*0-253-30706-6*) Ind U Pr.

De Name Mary: Memoirs of an American Woman in the Austrian Underground. Muriel Gardiner. LC 82-20213. 197p. 1987. pap. 12.00x (*0-300-04033-4*, Y-667) Yale U Pr.

De Natura Deorum. Marcus T. Cicero. Bd. with Academica 1-2 (Loeb Classical Library: No. 268). 15.50 (*0-674-99296-2*) HUP.

De natura et dignitate amoris see Nature & Dignity of Love

De Natura Hominis. Nemesius Emesenus. Ed. by C. F. Matthaei. 538p. 1967. reprint ed. write for info. (*0-318-70983-X*, Pub. by Georg Olms GW) Lubrecht & Cramer.

De Naturae Philosophiae Seu De Platonis Et Aristotelis Consensione Libri V. Sebastian Fox Morzillo. xv, 414p. 1977. reprint ed. write for info. (*3-487-06452-9*, Pub. by Georg Olms GW) Lubrecht & Cramer.

De Naturalium Effectuum Causis Sive De Incantationibus. Petrus Pomponatius, pseud. 328p. 1970. reprint ed. write for info. (*0-318-71607-0*, Pub. by Georg Olms GW) Lubrecht & Cramer.

De Nemethy Method: Modern Techniques for Training the Show Jumper & Its Rider. Bertalan De Nemethy. LC 87-13688. (Illus.). 1988. 24.95 (*0-385-23620-4*) Doubleday.

De Nigromancia. Roger Bacon. Ed. & Tr. by Michael-Albion Macdonald. 96p. 1988. 30.00 (*0-935214-10-0*) Heptangle.

De-NoIR, Mucosal Protection & Peptic Ulcer Disease: Journal, Digestion, Supplement 2, 1987, Vol. 37. Ed. by G. N. Tytgat. (Illus.). iv, 64p. 1987. 19.25 (*3-8055-4617-3*) S Karger.

De Nugis Curialium. Walter Map. Ed. by Montagu R. James. (Anecdota Oxoniensia Ser.: No. 14). 1988. reprint ed. 71.50 (*0-404-63964-X*) AMS Pr.

De Nunca a Siempre: Poemas. Omar Torres. LC 81-71569. (Coleccion Espejo de Paciencia Ser.). 51p. (Orig.). (SPA.). 1982. pap. 5.95 (*0-89729-307-X*) Ediciones.

De Occulta Philosophia, Libri Tres. Henricus C. Agrippa. Ed. by Vittoria P. Compagni. LC 91-31186. (Studies in the History of Christian Thought: No. 48). (Illus.). 656p. 1992. 168.75 (*90-04-09421-0*) E J Brill.

De Officiis. M. Tullius Cicero. Ed. by M. Winterbottom. (Classical Texts Ser.). 192p. (LAT.). 1994. 22.00 (*0-19-814673-6*) OUP.

De Officiis. Marcus T. Cicero. (Loeb Classical Library: No. 30). 442p. 1913. 18.95 (*0-674-99033-1*) HUP.

De Olympionicarum Statuis. Gualtherus Hyde. 80p. 1980. 15.00 (*0-89005-341-3*) Ares.

De Onda: A Gay Guide to Mexico & Its People. Joseph Itiel. (Illus.). 1990. write for info. (*1-878256-01-7*) Intl Wavelength.

De Opkomst der Abbasiden in Chorasan. Gerlof Van Vloten. LC 77-10454. (Studies in Islamic History: No. 16). 154p. 1978. reprint ed. lib. bdg. 29.50 (*0-87991-465-3*) Porcupine Pr.

De Oraculis Chaldaicis. Wilhelm Kroll. (Breslauer Philogische Abhandlungen Ser.: Vol. VII, 1). 83p. 1986. reprint ed. write for info. (*3-487-00229-9*, Pub. by Georg Olms GW) Lubrecht & Cramer.

De Oratore, Vol. 4, Bk. 3. Marcus T. Cicero. Bd. with De Fato.; Paradoxa Stoicorum.; De Partitione Oratoria. (Loeb Classical Library: No. 349). 15.50 (*0-674-99384-5*) HUP.

De Oratore, Bks 1 & 2, Vol. 3. Marcus T. Cicero. (Loeb Classical Library: No. 348). 508p. 1942. 18.95 (*0-674-99383-7*) HUP.

De Oratore Libri Tres. M. Tullius Cicero. Bd. 9. pap. write for info. (*0-318-70792-6*, Pub. by Georg Olms GW) Lubrecht & Cramer.

De Oratore Libri Tres. Cicero. (Olms Paperbacks Ser.: Vol. 9). viii, 573p. 1990. reprint ed. pap. 76.70 (*3-487-05025-0*, Pub. by Georg Olms GW) Lubrecht & Cramer.

De Ore Domini: Preacher & Word in the Middle Ages. Ed. by Thomas L. Amos et al. (Studies in Medieval Culture: Vol. 27). 1989. 32.95 (*0-918720-28-1*); pap. 15.95 (*0-918720-27-3*) Medieval Inst.

De Ortu Grammaticae. Studies in Medieval Grammar & Linguistic Theory in Memory of Jan Pinborg. Ed. by G. L. Bursill-Hall et al. LC 90-44. (Studies in the History of the Language Sciences: Vol. 43). x, 372p. 1990. 112.00x (*90-272-4526-6*) Benjamins North Am.

De Padres a Hijos Acerca del Sexo. Wilson W. Grant. Tr. by Maria T. La Valle et al. (Sexo en la Vida Cristiana Ser.). (Illus.). 192p. (SPA.). 1986. reprint ed. pap. 5.50 (*0-311-46255-3*) Casa Bautista.

De Paganini: The Genoese, 2 vols., Set. G. I. C. Courcy. LC 76-5892. (Music Reprint Ser.). 1977. reprint ed. lib. bdg. 85.00 (*0-306-70872-8*) Da Capo.

De Paroecia Domui Religiosae Commissa. Francis J. Muller. 1956. 3.50 (*0-686-11580-5*) Franciscan Inst.

De Partibus Animalium, Book I, & De Generatione Animalium, Book I with Passages from Book II, 1-3. rev. ed. Aristotle. Ed. by D. M. Balme. (Clarendon Aristotle Ser.). 192p. 1992. pap. 26.00 (*0-19-875128-1*) OUP.

De Partitione Oratoria see De Oratore

***De Paseo.** Long. (College Spanish Ser.). 1995. pap. 124.95 (*0-8384-2583-6*) Heinle & Heinle.

De Pastor a Pastor: Etica Pastoral Practica. James Giles. 218p. (Orig.). 1989. pap. 4.50 (*0-311-42076-1*) Casa Bautista.

De Paula's Auditing. 18th ed. Frank F. Attwood & Neil Stein. Date not set. pap. write for info. (*0-318-72410-3*) Trans-Atl Phila.

De-Persona. Paul Tomidy. LC 90-64185. (Illus.). 104p. 1992. pap. 24.95 (*0-295-97163-0*) U of Wash Pr.

De Peyster Genealogy. Waldron P. Belknap, Jr. LC 56-34875. (Illus.). 1990. text ed. 10.00 (*0-674-19801-8*) HUP.

De Philosophia Ex Oraculis Haurienda Librorum Reliquiae. Porphyrius. Ed. by Gustav Wolff. vi, 253p. 1984. reprint ed. write for info. (*3-487-00202-7*, Pub. by Georg Olms GW) Lubrecht & Cramer.

***De Pina's Technical Dictionary Vol. 1: English-Portuguese.** A. DePina Araujo. 616p. (ENG & POR.). 1975. 125.00 (*0-7859-7138-6*) Fr & Eur.

***De Pina's Technical Dictionary Vol. 2: Portuguese-English.** A. DePina Araujo. 495p. (ENG & POR.). 1975. 125.00 (*0-7859-7139-4*) Fr & Eur.

De Pleins Pourvoirs a sans Pouvoirs. Jean Giraudoux. 272p. (FRE.). 1950. pap. 13.95 (*0-7859-4591-1*) Fr & Eur.

De Pleno Gozo (To Fill You with Joy) A. H. Mottesi. (SPA.). Date not set. 1.79 (*0-8423-6349-1*, 498507) Editorial Unilit.

De Poetica Liber. Aristoteles. (Documenta Semiotica Serie 2). 357p. (GER.). 1976. reprint ed. write for info. (*3-487-05859-6*, Pub. by Georg Olms GW) Lubrecht & Cramer.

De Polemonis Rhetoris Vita Operibus Arte. Hugo Juttner. No. 30. vi, 116p. 1967. reprint ed. write for info. (*0-318-70946-5*, Pub. by Georg Olms GW) Lubrecht & Cramer.

***De Pratica Seu Arte Tripudii: On the Practice Or Art of Dancing.** Guglielmo Ebreo. Ed. & Tr. by Barbara Sparti. Tr. by Michael Sullivan. (Illus.). 288p. 1995. pap. 24.00 (*0-19-816574-9*) OUP.

De Pres et de Loin; Entretiens; Deux Ans Apres. Claude Levi-Strauss. (FRE.). 1991. pap. 16.95 (*0-7859-3935-0*) Fr & Eur.

De Primo Principio of John Duns Scotus: A Revised Text & Translation. Evan Roche. (Philosophy Ser.). 1949. 8.00 (*0-686-11535-X*) Franciscan Inst.

De Principiis Astronomiae & Cosmographiae. Gemma Frisius. LC 92-18498. 1992. 55.00 (*0-8201-1474-X*) Schol Facsimiles.

***De-Privatizing Morality.** Philip J. Ross. (Philosophy Ser.). 125p. 1994. pap. 54.95 (*1-85628-659-2*, Pub. by Avebury Pub UK) Ashgate Pub Co.

De Profundis: Grand Motet for Soloists, Chorus, Woodwinds, Strings, & Continuo. Michel R. Lalande. Ed. by James R. Anthony. LC 79-29740. (Early Musical Masterworks Ser.). 182p. reprint ed. pap. 51.90 (*0-8357-3897-3*, 2036629) Bks Demand.

De Profundis & Other Writings. Oscar Wilde. (English Library). 256p. 1976. mass mkt. 7.95 (*0-14-043089-X*, Penguin Classics) Viking Penguin.

De Prospetiva Pingendi, Facsimile of Parma, Biblioteca Palatina, MS 1576. Piero D. Francesca. (Documents of Art & Architectural History Ser.: Vol. 2). 420p. (LAT.). 1994. lib. bdg. 125.00 (*0-89371-201-9*) Broude Intl Edns.

De Provinciis Consularibus see Pro Caelio

De Que Hablamos? George E. Starnes & Oscar Fernandez. (Orig.). (SPA.). 1981. reprint ed. 19.95 (*0-8290-0504-8*) Irvington.

De Que Trata la Biblia (What the Bible Is All About) H. Mears. (SPA.). Date not set. 14.99 (*1-56063-164-3*, 498490) Editorial Unilit.

De Que Trata la Biblia (What the Bible Is All About) Jovenes Exploradores (Young Explorers) Henrietta Mears. (SPA.). 1992. 12.99 (*1-56063-325-5*, 498491) Editorial Unilit.

De Quincey Memorials, 2 vols. in 1. Ed. by Alexander H. Japp. (Anglistica & Americana Ser.: No. 149). (Illus.). xvi, 563p. 1974. reprint ed. 76.70 (*3-487-04485-4*, Pub. by Georg Olms GW) Lubrecht & Cramer.

De Quincey, Wordsworth & the Art of Prose. D. D. Devlin. LC 82-20443. 132p. 1983. text ed. 35.00 (*0-312-19397-1*) St Martin.

De Quincey's Art of Autobiography. Edmund Baxter. 224p. 1990. 59.00 (*0-389-20919-8*) B&N Imports.

De Quincey's Disciplines. Josephine McDonagh. LC 93-39460. 250p. 1994. 42.00 (*0-19-811285-8*, Clarendon Pr) OUP.

De Re Metallica. Georgius Agricola. (Illus.). 640p. 1912. pap. 18.95 (*0-486-60006-8*) Dover.

De Re Metrica Poetarum Latinorum Praeter Plautum et Terentium, Libri VII. Lucian Mueller. xiv, 651p. (GER.). 1967. reprint ed. write for info. (*0-318-70573-7*, Pub. by Georg Olms GW) Lubrecht & Cramer.

De Re Metrica Poetarum Latinorum Praeter Plautum et Terentium Libri VII. Lucian Mueller. xiv, 651p. 1967. reprint ed. write for info. (*0-318-71182-6*, Pub. by Georg Olms GW) Lubrecht & Cramer.

De Re Poetica: or Remarks upon Poetry. Thomas P. Blount. (Anglistica & Americana Ser.: No. 32, 1). x, 377p. 1969. reprint ed. 128.70 (*0-685-66433-3*, 05102305, Pub. by Georg Olms GW) Lubrecht & Cramer.

De Re Publica. Marcus T. Cicero. Bd. with De Legibus (Loeb Classical Library: No. 213). (ENG & LAT.). (C). 15.50 (*0-674-99235-0*) HUP.

***De re publica: Selections.** Cicero. Ed. by James E.G. Zetzel. (Cambridge Greek & Latin Classics Ser.). 288p. (C). 1995. 59.95 (*0-521-34465-4*); pap. 21.95 (*0-521-34896-X*) Cambridge U Pr.

De Re Rustica, 3 vols., 1. Columella. (Loeb Classical Library: No. 361, 407, 408). 496p. 1941. 18.95 (*0-674-99398-5*) HUP.

De Re Rustica, 3 vols., 2. Columella. (Loeb Classical Library: No. 361, 407, 408). 516p. 1954. 18.95 (*0-674-99448-5*) HUP.

De Re Rustica, 3 vols., 3. Columella. (Loeb Classical Library: No. 361, 407, 408). 444p. 1955. 18.95 (*0-674-99449-3*) HUP.

De Rebus Gestis Alexandri Magni. Quintus Curtius Rufus. Ed. by Julius Mutzell. xc, 972p. 1976. reprint ed. write for info. (*3-487-06003-5*, Pub. by Georg Olms GW) Lubrecht & Cramer.

De-Recognizing Taiwan: The Legal Problems. Victor H. Li. LC 77-78287. 1977. pap. 1.50 (*0-87003-031-0*) Carnegie Endow.

De Reductione Artium Ad Theologiam. Emma T. Healy. (Works of Saint Bonaventure Ser.). 1955. 4.50 (*0-686-11590-2*) Franciscan Inst.

De Regimine Principum: Fifteen Hundred Nine. Baron Stephen. Ed. & Tr. by P. J. Mroczkowski. LC 90-6126. 330p. (C). 1990. text ed. 46.00 (*0-8204-0648-1*) P Lang Pubs.

De Remnant Truth: The Tales of Jake Mitchell & Robert Wilton Burton. Ed. by Kathryn M. Sport & Bert Hitchcock. 256p. 1991. pap. 19.95 (*0-8173-0515-7*) U of Ala Pr.

De Repente-All of a Sudden: Bi-Lingual with English & Spanish on Facing Pages. Teresa De Jesus. Tr. by Maria A. Proser et al. LC 77-15118. 92p. 1978. pap. 7.95 (*0-915306-14-X*) Curbstone.

De Republica Anglorum: Or, History with the Politics Put Back. Patrick Collinson. 1990. pap. 7.95 (*0-521-39895-9*) Cambridge U Pr.

De Republica Anglorum, the Maner of Government of England. Thomas Smith. LC 73-25629. (English Experience Ser.: No. 219). 120p. 1970. reprint ed. 35.00 (*90-221-0219-X*) Walter J Johnson.

De Rerum Natura. 2nd ed. Lucretius. Ed. by Cyril Bailey. (Oxford Classical Texts Ser.). 1922. 19.95 (*0-19-814624-8*) OUP.

De Rerum Natura, Bk. 3. Lucretius. Ed. by Edwin J. Kenney. (Cambridge Greek & Latin Classics Ser.). 1977. pap. 21.95 (*0-521-29177-1*) Cambridge U Pr.

De Rerum Natura, No. VI. Lucretius. Ed. by Godwin. 1991. 49.95 (*0-85668-499-6*, Pub. by Aris & Phillips UK); pap. 24.95 (*0-85668-500-3*, Pub. by Aris & Phillips UK) David Brown.

De Rerum Natura: The Latin Text of Lucretius. Lucretius. Ed. by William E. Leonard & Stanley B. Smith. (Illus.). 896p. 1942. text ed. 29.50 (*0-299-00362-0*) U of Wis Pr.

De Rerum Natura IV. Lucretius. Ed. by Godwin. (Classical Texts Ser.). 1987. 49.95 (*0-85668-308-6*, Pub. by Aris & Phillips UK); pap. 19.95 (*0-85668-309-4*, Pub. by Aris & Phillips UK) David Brown.

De-Romanization of the American Catholic Church. Edward Wakin & Joseph F. Scheuer. LC 78-10157. 318p. 1979. reprint ed. text ed. 59.75 (*0-313-21238-4*, WADE, Greenwood Pr) Greenwood.

De Romanorum Precationibus. Georgius Appel. LC 75-10628. (Ancient Religion & Mythology Ser.). 1976. reprint ed. 22.95 (*0-405-07004-7*) Ayer.

De Rousseau a Lenine. L. Colletti. 318p. 1972. pap. text ed. 68.00 (*0-677-50645-7*) Gordon & Breach.

De Sainte Katerine: An Anonymous Picard Version of the Life of St. Catherine of Alexandria. William MacBain. 232p. (C). 1987. text ed. 47.50 (*0-8026-0010-7*, G Mason Univ Pr) Univ Pub Assocs.

De San Juan a Ponce En el Tren. Jack Delano. LC 90-46114. 123p. (SPA.). 1991. pap. 19.95 (*0-8477-2117-5*) U of PR Pr.

De Sang-Froid. Truman Capote. (FRE.). 1972. pap. 11.95 (*0-7859-1690-3*, 2070360598) Fr & Eur.

De Sapientia Veterum, Repr. Of 1609 Ed. Francis Bacon. Bd. with Wisedome of the Ancients. LC 75-27863. LC 75-27863. (Renaissance & the Gods Ser.: Vol. 20). (Illus.). 1976. Set lib. bdg. 34.00 (*0-8240-2068-5*) Garland.

De Satyrica Graecorum Poesi & Romanorum Satira. Isaac Casaubon. LC 72-13784. 392p. (LAT.). 1973. reprint ed. lib. bdg. 60.00 (*0-8201-1115-5*) Schol Facsimiles.

De-Scribing Empire: Post-Colonialism & Textuality. Ed. by Chris Tiffin & Alan Lawson. LC 93-44378. 240p. 1994. 55.00x (*0-415-10546-3*, B3100, Routledge NY); pap. 19.95 (*0-415-10547-1*, B3104, Routledge NY) Routledge.

***De Scvlptvra.** Pomponio Gaurico. (Documents of Art & Architectural History Ser.: Vol. 2). (Illus.). 1981. lib. bdg. 30.00 (*0-89371-202-7*) Broude Intl Edns.

De Senecae Philosophi Librorum Recensione Et Emendatione. Otto Rossbach. Vol. II, 3. xxxii, 184p. 1969. reprint ed. write for info. (*0-318-71218-0*, Pub. by Georg Olms GW) Lubrecht & Cramer.

De Senectute. Cicero. Ed. by E. S. Shuckburgh. (College Classical Ser.). pap. text ed. 16.00 (*0-89241-348-4*) Caratzas.

D

An Asterisk (*) at the beginning of an entry indicates that the title is appearing in BIP for the first time.

De Senectute. Marcus T. Cicero. Bd. with De Amicitia; De Divinatione. (Loeb Classical Library: No. 154). (ENG & LAT.). (C). 15.50 (*0-674-99170-2*) HUP.

De Senectute: De Amicicia. Marcus T. Cicero. LC 77-6867. (English Experience Ser.: No. 861). 1977. reprint ed. lib. bdg. 45.00 (*90-221-0861-9*) Walter J Johnson.

De Senectute: More Last Words. Frederic Harrison. LC 79-128256. (Essay Index Reprint Ser.). 1977. 19.95 (*0-8369-1834-7*) Ayer.

De-Sensitization by Systematic Steps with Relaxation, Set-D. Russell E. Mason. 1975. Incl. Notes; Clinical Applications (rev. 1979); Tape 9 (ISBN 0-89533-039-3); Tape 1A; Tape 2. pap. 35.00 (*0-89533-005-9*) F I Comm.

De Shootinest Gent'man. 2nd ed. Nash Buckingham. (Nash Buckingham Collection Ser.). (Illus.). 240p. 1986. reprint ed. 20.00 (*1-56416-054-8*) Derrydale Pr.

De Shootinest Gent'man. 2nd ed. Nash Buckingham. (Fifty Greatest Bks.). 239p. 1992. reprint ed. 40.00 (*1-56416-032-7*) Derrydale Pr.

De Shootinest Gent'Man. Nash Buckingham. 336p. 1992. reprint ed. lib. bdg. 32.95 (*0-89968-310-X*, Lghtyr Pr) Buccaneer Bks.

De Si Brave Garcons. Patrick Modiano. (FRE.). 1987. pap. 8.95 (*0-7859-3393-X*, 207037811X) Fr & Eur.

De Si Braves Garcons. Patrick Modiano. (Folio Ser.: No. 1811). (FRE.). pap. 6.95 (*2-07-037811-X*) Schoenhof.

De Sitter & Conformal Groups & Their Applications. Conference on De Sitter & Conformal Groups & Their Applications Staff. Ed. by Asim O. Barut & Wesley E. Brittin. LC 72-179661. (Lectures in Theoretical Physics: No. 13). (Illus.). 450p. reprint ed. pap. 128.30 (*0-8357-5510-X*, 2035125) Bks Demand.

***De Smith, Woolf & Jowell: Judicial Review of Administrative Action.** 5th ed. Lord Woolf of Barnes & Jeffrey Jowell. 1994. 176.00 (*0-420-46620-7*, Pub. by Sweet & Maxwll) W W Gaunt.

De Socrate Iuste Damnato: The Rise of the Socratic Problem in the Eighteenth Century. Mario Montuori. (London Studies in Classical Philology: Vol. 7). 153p. (Orig.). (C). 1981. pap. 27.00 (*90-70265-73-7*, Pub. by Gieben NE) Benjamins North Am.

De Sonata de Otono al Esperpento: Aspectos del Arte de Valle-Inclan. Emma S. Speratti-Pinero. (Serie A: Monagrafias, XI). 341p. (Orig.). (SPA.). (C). 1968. pap. 45.00 (*0-900411-03-1*, Pub. by Tamesis Bks Ltd UK) Boydell & Brewer.

De Soto Chronicles: The Expedition of Hernando de Soto to North America in 1539-1543, 2 vols. Lawrence A. Clayton et al. Ed. by Vernon J. Knight, Jr. & Edward C. Moore. 1993. Vol. II, 568p. write for info. (*0-318-69671-1*) U of Ala Pr.

De Soto Chronicles: The Expedition of Hernando de Soto to North America in 1539-1543, Set, 2 vols. Lawrence A. Clayton et al. Ed. by Vernon J. Knight, Jr. & Edward C. Moore. 1995. Vol. I, 464p. pap. 50.00 (*0-8173-0824-5*) U of Ala Pr.

De Soto Chronicles: The Expedition of Hernando de Soto to North America in 1539-1543, 2 vols., Set. Lawrence A. Clayton et al. Ed. by Vernon J. Knight, Jr. & Edward C. Moore. LC 92-31504. 1993. 50.00 (*0-8173-0593-9*) U of Ala Pr.

De Spectaculis see Apology

De-Stalinisation & the House of Culture: Declining State Control over Leisure in the U. S. S. R., Poland & Hungary, 1953-89. Anne White. 224p. 1990. 52.50 (*0-415-04244-5*, A4193) Routledge.

De Stijl: The Formative Years. Carel Blotkamp et al. Ed. by Hans Esser et al. Tr. by Charlotte I. Loeb & Arthur L. Loeb. (Illus.). 246p. (DUT.). 1990. reprint ed. pap. 24.95 (*0-262-52149-0*) MIT Pr.

De Stijl Nineteen Seventeen to Nineteen Thirty-One. H. L. Jaffe. (Illus.). 352p. 1986. pap. 22.50 (*0-674-19972-3*) Belknap Pr.

***De-Stressing Your Life.** Diane Stout. 96p. 1995. pap. 5.99 (*1-56476-325-0*, 6-3325, Victor Books) SP Pubns.

De-Structing the Novel: Essays in Postmodern Hermeneutics. Leonard Orr. LC 81-52811. 280p. (C). 1982. 22.50 (*0-87875-223-4*) Whitston Pub.

De Summe-Rerum: Metaphysical Papers, 1675-1676. Gottfried W. Leibniz. Tr. by G. H. Parkinson. (Leibniz Ser.). 208p. (C). 1992. text ed. 40.00 (*0-300-05187-5*) Yale U Pr.

***De Sun Do Move: The Sermon of John J. Jasper.** Date not set. pap. 2.50 (*0-87517-025-0*) Dietz.

De Svenska Luterska Forsamlingarnas och Svenska Historia i Amerika see Pioneer Swedish Settlements & Swedish Lutheran Churches in America 1845-1860

De Swiet Medical Disorders in OB Practice. 2nd ed. May. 1989. 134.95 (*0-632-01974-3*, Yr Bk Med Pubs) Mosby Yr Bk.

De Terminologie van het Crediet-Wezen in het Grieksch. Jan Korver. Ed. by Moses Finley. LC 79-4987. (Ancient Economic History Ser.). (DUT.). 1979. reprint ed. lib. bdg. 18.95 (*0-405-12372-8*) Ayer.

De Thessalonica Eiusque Agro Dissertatio Geographica. T. L. Tafel. 688p. 1972. 50.00 (*0-902089-36-6*) St Mut.

De Tierras Lejanas Te Llame: From Distant Lands I Called You. Neel Wijesinghe. (SPA.). 4.25 (*84-7645-317-5*, 223476, Pub. by Edit Clie SP) TSELF.

De Todo Corazon. Thea B. Van Halsema & Aric Leeler. (SPA.). 1989. 1.25 (*1-55955-109-7*) CITE MI.

De Triplici Nodo, Triplex Cuneus James I. Archival Facsimiles Ltd., Staff & James. (Books of the Monarchs of England). 256p. (C). 1989. reprint ed. 135.00 (*1-85297-007-3*, Pub. by Archival Facs UK) St Mut.

De Tristitia Christi: Complete Works of St. Thomas More, Vol. 14, Pts. 1 & 2. Thomas More. Ed. by Clarence H. Miller. LC 63-7949. 1976. 100.00 (*0-300-01793-6*) Yale U Pr.

De Tunis a Kairouan. Guy De Maupassant. (FRE.). 1993. pap. 24.95 (*0-7859-3326-3*, 2870274785) Fr & Eur.

De Valera: The Man & the Myth. T. Ryle Dwyer. 370p. (Orig.). 1992. pap. 14.95 (*1-85371-180-2*, Pub. by Poolbeg Pr IE) Dufour.

De Valera & the Ulster Question, 1917 - 1973. John Bowman. 384p. 1990. pap. 18.95 (*0-19-285216-7*) OUP.

De-Valuing of America. William J. Bennett. 272p. 1994. 17.99 (*1-56179-224-1*) Focus Family.

***De-Valuing of America.** William J. Bennett. 1995. pap. 9.99 (*1-56179-360-4*) Focus Family.

De-Valuing of America: The Fight for Our Culture & Our Children. William J. Bennett. 272p. 1994. pap. 12.00 (*0-671-79719-0*, Touchstone Bks) S&S Trade.

De-Valuing of America: The Fight for Our Culture & Our Children. William J. Bennett. 320p. 1992. 20.00 (*0-671-68305-5*) Summit Bks.

De Verborum Significatione Quae Supersunt Cum Pauli Epitome. Sextus P. Festus. Ed. by Wallace M. Lindsay. xxviii, 573p. 1965. write for info. (*0-318-72021-3*, Pub. by Georg Olms GW) Lubrecht & Cramer.

De Verborum Significatione Quae Supersunt Cum Pauli Epitome. Sextus P. Festus. xliv, 461p. 1975. reprint ed. write for info. (*3-487-05280-6*, Pub. by Georg Olms GW) Lubrecht & Cramer.

De Vere: Or, the Man of Independence, 4 vols. in 2, Set. Robert P. Ward. LC 79-8211. reprint ed. 84.50 (*0-404-62150-3*) AMS Pr.

***De Veres of Castle Hedingham.** Verily Anderson. 272p. 1994. 60.00 (*0-86138-062-2*, Pub. by T Dalton UK) St Mut.

De Virginia Hambook. Ed. by Meredith Dietz. 1949. pap. 2.00 (*0-87517-001-3*) Dietz.

De Vita Agricolae. 2nd ed. Tacitus. Ed. by R. M. Ogilvie et al. (Illus.). 1967. 49.95 (*0-19-814438-5*) OUP.

De Vita et Morte Roberti Rollok. George Robertson & Henry Charteris. Ed. by John Lee. LC 77-172040. (Bannatyne Club, Edinburgh. Publications: No. 16). reprint ed. 30.00 (*0-404-52716-7*) AMS Pr.

De Vita Libri Tres. Marsilius Ficinus. 272p. 1978. reprint ed. write for info. (*3-487-06354-9*, Pub. by Georg Olms GW) Lubrecht & Cramer.

De Vitis, Dogmatis et Apophthegmatis Clarorum Philosophorum, 4 vols., Set. Diogenes Laertius. xxxii, 2587p. (GER.). 1981. reprint ed. write for info. (*3-487-07067-7*, Pub. by Georg Olms GW) Lubrecht & Cramer.

De Voil: Value Added Tax, 3 vols. Ed. by C. Barcroft. 1991. U.K. ring bd. 450.00 (*0-406-51459-3*) Butterworth Legal Pubs.

De Voluptate. Lorenzo Valla. Tr. by Kent Hieatt & Maristella Lorch. LC 77-86234. (Janus Ser.). 418p. 1977. 20.00 (*0-913870-33-1*) Abaris Bks.

De Vulgari Eloquentia: Dante's Book of Exile. Marianne Shapiro. LC 90-31069. (Regents Studies in Medieval Culture). xiv, 277p. 1990. 35.00 (*0-8032-4211-5*) U of Nebr Pr.

De Winckelmann a Heidegger: Ensayos Sobre el Encuentro Griego-Aleman. Ludwig Schajowicz. LC 85-29428. 339p. 1986. pap. 12.00 (*0-8477-2826-9*) U of PR Pr.

De Witt Clinton. Dorothie Bobbe. 308p. 1993. reprint ed. lib. bdg. 89.00 (*0-7812-5168-0*) Rprt Serv.

De Witt Clinton & the American Political Economy: Sectionalism, Politics, & Republican Ideology, 1787-1828. Steven E. Siry. (American University Studies: History: Ser. IX, Vol. 35). 377p. (C). 1989. text ed. 53.95 (*0-8204-1041-1*) P Lang Pubs.

De Witt Clinton & the Origin of the Spoils System in New York. Howard L. McBain. LC 07-36153. (Columbia University. Studies in the Social Sciences: No. 75). reprint ed. 12.50 (*0-404-51075-2*) AMS Pr.

De Witt's War. Hans Koning. 252p. 1989. 7.95 (*0-942986-16-4*) LongRiver Bks.

De Zenodoti Studiis Homericis. Heinrich Duentzer. vii, 218p. 1981. reprint ed. write for info. (*3-487-07051-0*, Pub. by Georg Olms GW) Lubrecht & Cramer.

DEA Classified Intelligence Reports: Inside Tricks of the Smuggling Trade. (Illus.). 120p. 1988. pap. 18.00 (*0-87364-480-8*) Paladin Pr.

DEA Stash & Hideout Handbook. (Illus.). 48p. 1988. pap. 10.00 (*0-87364-469-7*) Paladin Pr.

Deacon. Myron Augsburger & Marcia A. Kincanon. (Illus.). 120p. (Orig.). 1990. pap. 7.95 (*0-919797-94-6*) Kindred Prods.

***Deacon.** Ada E. Crain. 180p. 1995. 13.95 (*0-9643286-0-7*) A E Crain.

Deacon & His Ministry. Richard L. Dresselhaus. LC 77-73518. 1977. pap. 2.95 (*0-88243-493-4*, 02-0493) Gospel Pub.

Deacon at Work. Frederick A. Agar. 1923. pap. 9.00 (*0-8170-0783-0*) Judson.

Deacon in the Church. Lynn C. Sherman. LC 90-27863. 114p. 1991. pap. 7.95 (*0-8189-0607-3*) Alba.

Deacon of Dobbinsville. John A. Morrison. 64p. pap. 1.00 (*0-686-29146-8*) Faith Pub Hse.

***Deaconess Heritage: One Hundred Years of Caring, Healing & Teaching.** Ruth W. Rasche. 350p. 1994. pap. 9.95 (*0-9642849-0-1*) Deaconess Fnd.

Deaconess in the Armenian Church. Abel Oghlukian. Tr. by S. Peter Cowe. LC 94-65849. (Illus.). 68p. 1994. pap. 10.00 (*1-885011-00-8*) St Nersess.

Deacons: Male & Female? A Study for Churches of Christ. J. Stephen Sandifer. LC 88-92783. 246p. (Orig.). (C). 1989. pap. 10.95 (*0-9621965-0-9*) J S Sandifer.

Deacons: Servants of the Church Christ Built & Spiritual Gifts. Karl G. Wilks. LC 86-90143. (Bible Teaching on Church Government & Management Ser.). 66p. (Orig.). 1986. pap. 6.00 (*0-9616912-0-4*) K G Wilks.

Deacons & Deaconesses Through the Centuries: One Ministry - Many Roles. Jeannine E. Olson. LC 92-30071. (Scholarship Today Ser.). 1992. 21.95 (*0-570-04596-7*) Concordia.

Deacons & Their Ministry. Waldo Hiebert & Herb Kopp. (Orig.). 1979. pap. 2.50 (*0-937364-02-9*) Kindred Prods.

Deacon's Book: Records of the First Church, Dedham, Mass., 1677-1737. Ed. by Robert B. Hanson. 336p. (Orig.). 1990. pap. 25.00 (*1-55613-402-9*) Heritage Bk.

***Deacon's Demise.** Dean Hovey. 230p. Date not set. pap. 8.95 (*0-7610-0331-2*) NW Pub.

Deacons for Scotland. Multilateral Church Conversation in Scotland Staff. 88p. 1993. pap. 22.00 (*0-86153-125-6*) St Mut.

Deacon's Handbook. Gerard Berghoef & Lester DeKoster. 269p. 1980. 18.95 (*0-934874-01-8*) Chr Lib Pr.

Deacons in the Liturgy. Ormonde Plater. LC 91-39693. 79p. (Orig.). 1992. pap. 8.95 (*0-8192-1585-6*) Morehouse Pub.

Deacon's Ministry. 1991. pap. 14.95 (*0-85244-182-7*, Pub. by Gracewing UK) Morehouse Pub.

Deacon's Son. Phoebe Hall. (Illus.). 152p. (Orig.). 1994. pap. 9.95 (*1-879201-08-9*) Meyer Enter.

Deacon's Upholding the Pastor's Arms. Alfred J. Smith. 96p. 1983. pap. 4.00 (*0-686-46044-8*) Prog Bapt Pub.

Deacon's Woman & Other Portraits. Jerry B. Jenkins. 1992. pap. 11.99 (*0-8024-1738-8*) Moody.

Deactivation of Catalysis. Ron Hughes. 1984. text ed. 101.00 (*0-12-360870-8*) Acad Pr.

Dead. David Abolofia. 1993. 2.50 (*0-87129-294-7*, D57) Dramatic Pub.

Dead. James Joyce. Ed. by Daniel R. Schwarz. (Case Studies in Contemporary Criticism). 224p. 1993. pap. text ed. 5.00 (*0-312-08073-5*) St Martin.

***Dead.** James Joyce. Ed. by Setlok. (Joyce Ser.). 1993. audio 16.95 (*1-883049-02-4*) Commuters Lib.

***Dead.** James Joyce. 1993. audio, lib. bdg. 18.95 (*1-883049-21-0*) Commuters Lib.

Dead, Vol. I. 3rd ed. Hank Harrison. (Dead Trilogy Ser.: Vol. I). Orig. Title: The Dead Book. (Illus.). 279p. 1992. 21.95 (*0-918501-48-2*); pap. 18.95 (*0-918501-49-0*) Archives Pr.

Dead, Vol. II. rev. ed. Hank Harrison. Ed. by Catriona Watson. (Dead Trilogy Ser.: Vol. II). Orig. Title: The Dead Book. (Illus.). 322p. 1993. reprint ed. 21.95 (*0-918501-12-1*); reprint ed. pap. text ed. 18.95 (*0-918501-13-X*) Archives Pr.

Dead Ahead. Ruby Horansky. 240p. 1992. mass mkt. 4.99 (*0-380-71653-4*) Avon.

Dead Ahead. Bridget McKenna. 208p. (Orig.). 1994. pap. text ed. 4.50 (*0-425-14300-7*, Prime Crime) Berkley Pub.

***Dead & Buried.** Melissa Cleary. 208p. (Orig.). 1994. pap. text ed. 4.50 (*0-425-14547-6*, Prime Crime) Berkley Pub.

***Dead & Buried.** Jean Hager. (Iris House Mystery Ser.). 224p. (Orig.). 1995. mass mkt. 4.99 (*0-380-77210-8*) Avon.

Dead & Buried. Jim Somerville. (Illus.). 133p. 1991. pap. 9.95 (*0-944735-81-9*) Malibu Graphics.

Dead & Gone. Mary Kittredge. 1989. 18.95 (*0-8027-5728-6*) Walker & Co.

Dead & Gone: A Charlotte Kent Mystery. Mary Kittredge. 224p. 1991. reprint ed. mass mkt. 3.95 (*0-373-26075-X*) Harlequin Bks.

Dead & Gone: Classic Crimes of North Carolina. Manly W. Wellman. LC 55-391. xv, 190p. 1955. pap. 18.95 (*0-8078-4072-6*) U of NC Pr.

Dead & the Living. Sharon Olds. LC 83-47780. (Poetry Ser.: No. 12). 96p. 1984. pap. 13.00 (*0-394-71563-2*) Knopf.

Dead Architect. Frank Tedesco. 40p. 1993. pap. 11.95 (*0-9639542-0-2*) Shadow MA.

Dead Are Alive. Harold Sherman. 1986. mass mkt. 5.99 (*0-449-13158-0*) Fawcett.

Dead Are with Us. Rudolf Steiner. Tr. by D. S. Osmond. 32p. 1973. pap. 4.95 (*0-85440-274-8*, Steinerbks) Anthroposophic.

Dead Artists, Live Theories, & Other Cultural Problems. Stanley Aronowitz. 256p. 1993. 49.95 (*0-415-90737-3*, A9970, Routledge NY); pap. 16.95 (*0-415-90738-1*, A9974, Routledge NY) Routledge.

Dead As a Dinosaur. large type ed. Frances Lockridge & Richard Lockridge. 333p. 1991. reprint ed. lib. bdg. 19.95 (*1-56054-129-6*) Thorndike Pr.

Dead As a Dinosaur. Frances Lockridge & Richard Lockridge. (Mr. & Mrs. North Ser.). 185p. 1975. reprint ed. lib. bdg. 19.95 (*0-89190-903-6*, Rivercity Pr) Amereon Ltd.

Dead As a Dinosaur. Frances Lockridge & Richard Lockridge. 1993. reprint ed. lib. bdg. 17.95 (*1-56849-208-1*) Buccaneer Bks.

Dead As Dead Can Be. Ann Crowleigh. 256p. 1993. mass mkt. 3.99 (*0-8217-4099-7*) Zebra.

Dead Asleep. Hillary Wolfe. (You-Solve-It-Mysteries Ser.: No. 2). 224p. 1994. pap. 3.50 (*0-8217-4581-6*) Zebra.

Dead at the Box Office. 2nd rev. ed. John Dandola. LC 93-12266. Orig. Title: West of Orange. (Illus.). 240p. 1993. reprint ed. pap. 10.95 (*1-878452-15-0*, Jersey Yarns) Tory Corner Editions.

Dead Babies. Martin Amis. LC 90-50616. 224p. 1991. 10.00 (*0-679-73449-X*, Vin) Random.

Dead Babies & Other Works. Natalie McKelvy. Ed. by Charles McKelvy. LC 94-94129. 411p. (Orig.). 1994. pap. 5.00 (*0-944771-14-9*) Dunery Pr.

***Dead Before Morning.** Geraldine Evans. (Mystery Ser.). 1995. mass mkt. 3.99 (*0-373-26184-5*, 1-26184-1, Wrldwide Lib) Harlequin Bks.

***Dead Bird.** Margaret W. Brown. LC 84-43124. (Illus.). 48p. (J). (ps-3). 1995. pap. 4.95 (*0-06-443326-9*, Trophy) HarpC Child Bks.

Dead Bird. Margaret W. Brown. LC 84-43124. (Illus.). 48p. (J). (gr. k-3). 1989. reprint ed. lib. bdg. 14.89 (*0-06-020758-2*) HarpC Child Bks.

Dead Birds. John Milne. 208p. 1988. pap. 3.95 (*0-14-009704-X*, Penguin Bks) Viking Penguin.

Dead Book see Dead

Dead by Morning. large type ed. Dorothy Simpson. 1990. 21.95 (*0-7089-2342-9*) Ulverscroft.

***Dead by Sunset: Perfect Husband, Perfect Killer?** Ann Rule. 1995. 23.00 (*0-684-80205-8*) S&S Trade.

Dead Center: A Nikki Trakos Mystery. Ruby Horansky. 224p. 1994. text ed. 20.00 (*0-684-19606-9*, Scribners) S&S Trade.

Dead Cert. Dick Francis. 1987. mass mkt. 5.95 (*0-449-21263-7*) Fawcett.

Dead Cert. large type ed. Dick Francis. LC 93-30430. 1994. 21.95 (*0-8161-5784-7*) Hall.

Dead Cert. limited ed. Dick Francis. LC 88-38211. 216p. 1989. reprint ed. 75.00 (*0-922890-03-X*) Armchair Detective.

Dead Cert. Dick Francis. LC 88-38211. 216p. 1989. reprint ed. 25.00 (*0-922890-01-3*); reprint ed. 18.95 (*0-922890-07-2*) Armchair Detective.

Dead Certain. Claire McNab. (Carol Ashton Mystery Ser.: No. 5). 224p. 1992. pap. 9.95 (*1-56280-027-2*) Naiad Pr.

Dead Certainties: (Unwarranted Speculations) Simon Schama. 1992. pap. 13.00 (*0-679-73613-1*, Vin) Random.

Dead Certainties (Unwarranted Speculations) Simon Schama. 1991. 21.00 (*0-679-40213-6*) Knopf.

Dead City. Shane Stevens. 320p. 1992. pap. 4.95 (*0-88184-892-1*) Carroll & Graf.

Dead Clients Don't Pay: The Bodyguard's Manual. Leroy Thompson. (Illus.). 120p. 1984. pap. 12.00 (*0-87364-287-2*) Paladin Pr.

Dead Clue. D. L. Henning. Tr. by Ingram. 278p. 1994. pap. 8.95 (*0-685-70603-6*) NW Pub.

Dead Color. Charles Wright. (Poetry Ser.). (Illus.). 20p. 1980. 60.00 (*0-931356-04-0*) Seluzicki Fine Bks.

Dead Come Sundown. large type ed. Bill Wade. (Dales Western Ser.). 190p. 1992. pap. 16.95 (*1-85389-338-2*, Medcom-Trainex) Ulverscroft.

Dead Crazy. Nancy Pickard. Ed. by Linda Marrow. 1989. mass mkt. 4.99 (*0-671-73430-X*) PB.

***Dead Days: A Book of Days.** Herb Greene. 140p. 1995. pap. text ed. 17.95 (*0-9643831-1-X*) Global Intrprnt.

Dead Die Young. Jeffrey A. Zable. (Illus.). 25p. (Orig.). 1980. pap. text ed. 1.50 (*1-879594-00-5*) Androgyne Bks.

Dead, Dinner, or Naked. Evan Zimroth. 80p. 1993. 15.00 (*0-916384-10-1*); pap. 8.95 (*0-916384-14-4*) TriQuarterly.

Dead Dinosaurs: A Luis Balam Mystery of the Yucatan. Gary Alexander. LC 94-6496. 1994. 19.95 (*0-385-46896-2*) Doubleday.

Dead Do Not Praise. Pauline Bell. 192p. 1993. 17.95 (*0-312-09780-8*, Pub. by Thomas Dunne Bks) St Martin.

Dead Dog Blues. Neal Barrett, Jr. 368p. 1994. 22.95 (*0-312-10963-6*, Pub. by Thomas Dunne Bks) St Martin.

Dead Don't Care. Jonathan Latimer. (C). 1989. 35.00 (*0-948353-07-4*, Pub. by Oldcastle Bks UK) St Mut.

Dead Don't Care. Jonathan Latimer. LC 90-84278. 261p. 1990. reprint ed. pap. 7.95 (*1-55882-082-5*) Intl Polygonics.

Dead Easy. Arthur F. Nehrbass. 320p. 1993. pap. 4.99 (*0-451-17704-5*, Onyx) NAL-Dutton.

Dead Easy. E. S. Russell. 202p. 1992. 19.95 (*0-8027-3214-3*) Walker & Co.

Dead Easy for Dover. Joyce Porter. (Inspector Dover of Scotland Yard Ser.). 176p. 1991. reprint ed. pap. 6.00 (*0-88150-212-X*, Foul Play) Countryman.

Dead Elvis: A Chronicle of a Cultural Obsession. Greil Marcus. LC 92-17939. 1992. pap. 14.00 (*0-385-41719-5*, Anchor NY) Doubleday.

***Dead End.** Barry Friedman. 246p. (Orig.). 1994. pap. 8.95 (*1-885591-17-9*) Morris Pubng.

Dead End. Gary E. Goldhammer. (Illus.). 200p. (Orig.). 1994. pap. 10.95 (*1-879418-15-0*) Biddle Pub.

Dead End. Jack Gregory. 1994. mass mkt. 4.99 (*0-312-92575-1*) St Martin.

Dead End. John Peel. (Shockers Ser.). (Illus.). 160p. (J). (gr. 5-9). 1994. pap. 3.50 (*0-448-40530-X*, G&D) Putnam Pub Group.

Dead End. Ritchie Perry. 160p. 1983. pap. 2.25 (*0-345-29214-6*) Ballantine.

***Dead End.** R. L. Stine. Ed. by Pat MacDonald. (Fear Street Super Chiller Ser.). 176p. (Orig.). (J). 1995. mass mkt. 3.99 (*0-671-86837-3*, Archway) PB.

Dead End: A Book about Suicide. John J. Langone. LC 85-25620. (J). (gr. 6 up). 1986. 14.95 (*0-316-51432-2*) Little.

***Dead End: Homeless Teenagers: A Multi-Service Approach.** Margaret A. Michaud. (Illus.). 137p. (Orig.). 1988. pap. 14.95 (*0-920490-81-6*) Temeron Bks.

***Dead End Game.** Christopher Newman. 320p. (Orig.). 1995. pap. text ed. 5.99 (*0-425-14564-6*) Berkley Pub.

Dead End Game. Christopher Newman. 256p. (Orig.). 1994. 21.95 (*0-399-13952-4*, Putnam) Putnam Pub Group.

Dead End Trail. Norman A. Fox. 176p. 1988. pap. 2.75 (*0-380-70298-3*) Avon.

Dead End Trail. large type ed. Norman A. Fox. LC 92-17215. 299p. 1992. reprint ed. lib. bdg. 14.95 (*1-56054-348-5*) Thorndike Pr.

Dead Ends. Ann C. Fallon. Ed. by Dana Isaacson. 256p. (Orig.). 1992. mass mkt. 4.99 (*0-671-75134-4*) PB.

Dead Ends. Michael Reynolds. (Illus.). 304p. (Orig.). 1992. mass mkt. 4.99 (*0-446-36282-4*) Warner Bks.

Dead Engine Kids: World War II Diary of John J. Briol, B-17 Turret Gunner. John J. Briol et al. (Illus.). 216p. (Orig.). 1993. pap. write for info. (*0-9637909-0-0*) Silv Wings.

D

An Asterisk (*) at the beginning of an entry indicates that the title is appearing in BIP for the first time.

An Asterisk (*) at the beginning of an entry indicates that the title is appearing in BIP for the first time.

1821

Dead Sea Scrolls: A Personal Account. 2nd ed. John C. Trever. LC 77-10808. (Illus.). 246p. 1988. reprint ed. pap. text ed. 11.95 (*0-9621391-4-9*) Dead Sea Scrolls Proj.

Dead Sea Scrolls: Qumran in Perspective. Geza Vermes. LC 80-2382. 240p. 1981. reprint ed. pap. 14.00 (*0-8006-1435-6*, 1-1435, Fortress Pr) Augsburg Fortress.

***Dead Sea Scrolls: With Slides.** Dan P. Cole. Ed. by Hershel Shanks. 40p. (Orig.). 1993. pap. text ed. 119.50 (*1-880317-33-8*, 5096-AC) Biblical Arch Soc.

Dead Sea Scrolls after Forty Years. Hershel Shanks et al. LC 91-71320. (Illus.). 85p. (C). 1992. reprint ed. pap. 7.95 (*0-9613089-7-4*, 7H40) Biblical Arch Soc.

***Dead Sea Scrolls after Forty Years, Set.** LC 91-71320. audio write for info. (*1-880317-29-X*) Biblical Arch Soc.

Dead Sea Scrolls & Modern Translations of the Old Testament. Harold P. Scanlin. LC 93-3056. 196p. 1993. 19.99 (*0-8423-1010-X*) Tyndale.

Dead Sea Scrolls & Primitive Christianity. Jean Danielou. Tr. by Salvator Attanasio. LC 78-21516. 128p. 1979. reprint ed. text ed. 35.00 (*0-313-21144-2*, DADE, Greenwood Pr) Greenwood.

Dead Sea Scrolls & the Bible. enl. rev. ed. Charles F. Pfeiffer. LC 72-76780. (Baker Studies in Biblical Archaeology). (Illus.). 1969. pap. 7.99 (*0-8010-6898-3*) Baker Bk.

Dead Sea Scrolls & the Christian Myth. rev. ed. John Allegro. (Illus.). 252p. (C). 1992. reprint ed. pap. 19.95 (*0-87975-757-4*) Prometheus Bks.

Dead Sea Scrolls & the Life of the Ancient Essene. Raymond W. Bernard. (Essene-Jesus-Apollonius Ser.: Vol. 1). 29p. 1956. reprint ed. spiral bd. 4.40 (*0-7873-1209-6*) Mokelumne.

***Dead Sea Scrolls Catalogue: Documents, Photographs, & Museum Inventory Numbers.** Ed. by Stephen A. Reed et al. LC 94-29939. (SBL Resources for Biblical Study: No. 32). (Illus.). 606p. 1994. 89.95 (*0-7885-0017-1*, 060332); pap. 64.95 (*0-7885-0018-X*, 060332) Scholars Pr GA.

Dead Sea Scrolls Deception. Michael Baigent & Richard Leigh. (Illus.). 288p. 1993. pap. 13.00 (*0-671-79797-2*, Touchstone Bks) S&S Trade.

Dead Sea Scrolls in English. Geza Vermes. (Orig.). 1962. mass mkt. 4.95 (*0-14-020551-9*, Penguin Bks) Viking Penguin.

Dead Sea Scrolls in English. rev. ed. Geza Vermes. 304p. 1988. pap. 7.95 (*0-14-022779-2*, Penguin Bks) Viking Penguin.

Dead Sea Scrolls in English. 3rd ed. Geza Vermes. 336p. 1990. pap. 12.00 (*0-14-013544-8*, Penguin Bks) Viking Penguin.

***Dead Sea Scrolls in English.** 4th expanded rev. ed. Ed. by Geza Vermes. 448p. 1995. pap. 12.95 (*0-14-023730-5*, Penguin Bks) Viking Penguin.

Dead Sea Scrolls, The Gospel of Barnabas & the New Testament. M. A. Yusseff. LC 85-73210. 154p. (Orig.). 1986. reprint ed. pap. 8.00 (*0-89259-061-0*) Am Trust Pubns.

Dead Sea Scrolls Today. James C. VanderKam. (Illus.). 216p. (Orig.). (C). 1994. pap. text ed. 12.99 (*0-8028-0736-4*) Eerdmans.

Dead Sea Scrolls Translated: The Qumran Texts in English. Ed. & Tr. by Florentino G. Martinez. LC 94-17429. 1994. 80.00 (*90-04-10088-1*); pap. 30.00 (*90-04-10048-2*) E J Brill.

Dead Sea Scrolls Uncovered. Robert Eisenman & Michael Wise. (Illus.). 286p. 1992. 24.95 (*1-85230-368-9*) Element MA.

Dead Sea Scrolls Uncovered: The First Complete Translation & Interpretation of 50 Key Documents Withheld for over 35 Years. Robert Eisenman & Michael Wise. (Illus.). 304p. 1993. reprint ed. pap. 12.95 (*0-14-023250-8*, Penguin Bks) Viking Penguin.

Dead Sea Scrolls, Vol. 1: Rules of the Community & Related Documents. Ed. by James H. Charlesworth. (Princeton Theological Seminary Dead Sea Scrolls Project Ser.). 300p. 1994. text ed. 99.00 (*0-664-21994-2*) Westminster John Knox.

Dead Sea Scrolls, Vol. 2: Rules, Damascus Document, War Scroll, & Related Documents. Ed. by James H. Charlesworth. (Princeton Theological Seminary Dead Sea Scrolls Project Ser.). 300p. 1994. text ed. 99.00 (*0-664-22037-1*) Westminster John Knox.

Dead Seagull. George Barker. 111p. 1985. reprint ed. pap. 10.95 (*0-948166-00-2*, Pub. by Soho Bk Co UK) Dufour.

Dead Season. Franklin W. Dixon. (Hardy Boys Casefiles Ser.: No. 35). 160p. (J). 1991. pap. 3.50 (*0-671-74105-5*, Archway) PB.

Dead Season. J Bradley Owen. 368p. (Orig.). 1988. pap. 3.95 (*0-8439-2593-0*) Dorchester Pub Co.

***Dead Season: A Story of Murder & Revenge on the Philippine Island of Negros.** Alan Berlow. 352p. 1995. 24.00 (*0-679-42664-7*) Pantheon.

Dead Secret. Wilkie Collins. LC 78-74113. (Illus.). 384p. 1979. reprint ed. pap. 7.95 (*0-486-23775-3*) Dover.

Dead Secrets: Wilkie Collins & the Female Gothic. Tamar Heller. 208p. (C). 1992. text ed. 30.00x (*0-300-04574-3*) Yale U Pr.

Dead Serious: A Book for Teenagers about Teenage Suicide. Jane M. Leder. 160p. (YA). (gr. 7 up). 1989. pap. 3.50 (*0-380-70661-X*, Flare) Avon.

Dead Serious: A Book for Teenagers about Teenage Suicide. Jane M. Leder. LC 86-25880. 160p. (YA). (gr. 7 up). 1987. text ed. 14.95 (*0-689-31262-8*, Atheneum Bks Young) S&S Childrens.

***Dead Set.** Jennie Melville. (WWL Mystery Ser.). 1995. mass mkt. 3.99 (*0-373-26174-8*, 1-26174-2) Harlequin Bks.

Dead Silent. Jane Toombs. 288p. 1992. mass mkt. 4.50 (*1-55817-608-X*, Pinnacle NY) Windsor NY.

Dead Sinners. large type ed. Norman A. Lazenby. (Linford Mystery Library). 256p. 1993. pap. 14.95 (*0-7089-7422-8*, Trailtree Bookshop) Ulverscroft.

Dead Skip. Joe Gores. 208p. 1992. reprint ed. mass mkt. 4.99 (*0-446-40312-1*, Mysterious Paperbk) Warner Bks.

Dead Smile. F. Marion Crawford. (H. P. Lovecraft's Favorite Horror Stories Ser.). (Orig.). 1986. pap. 1.95 (*0-940884-15-1*) Necronomicon.

Dead Solid Perfect. Dan Jenkins. (Illus.). 254p. 1974. pap. 8.95 (*0-8431-1568-8*) Putnam Pub Group.

Dead Souls. Nikolai V. Gogol. (Airmont Classics Ser.). (J). (gr. 11 up). 1966. pap. 1.75 (*0-8049-0122-8*, CL-122) Airmont.

Dead Souls. Nikolai V. Gogol. 21.95 (*0-89190-261-9*, Am Repr) Amereon Ltd.

Dead Souls. Nikolai V. Gogol. Tr. by Andrew R. MacAndrew. 1961. pap. 4.50 (*0-451-52308-3*, Sig Classics) NAL-Dutton.

Dead Souls. Nikolai V. Gogol. Tr. by David Magarshack. (Classics Ser.). 1961. mass mkt. 8.95 (*0-14-044113-1*, Penguin Classics) Viking Penguin.

Dead Souls. Nikolai V. Gogol. Ed. by George Gibian. (Critical Editions Ser.). (C). 1986. pap. text ed. 15.95 (*0-393-95292-4*) Norton.

Dead Souls. Laurence Senelick. 128p. 1984. pap. 4.95 (*0-88145-016-2*) Broadway Play.

Dead Souls. Nikolai Gogol. 250p. 1992. reprint ed. lib. bdg. 17.95 (*0-89966-925-5*) Buccaneer Bks.

Dead Souls: Dramatized by the Globe Radio Reperatory. Nikolai V. Gogol. 1987. Five C-60 audio cass. audio 39. 95 (*0-295-75540-7*) U of Wash Pr.

Dead Spit. large type ed. Janet Edmonds. 1990. 21.95 (*0-7089-2311-9*) Ulverscroft.

Dead-Stick. large type ed. L. J. Washburn. 1992. pap. 20.95 (*0-7927-1177-7*, Curley Lrg Print) Chivers N Amer.

Dead Survivor. Neal Pizinger. (Orig.). 1979. pap. 2.50 (*0-89083-470-9*) Zebra.

Dead Tech: A Guide to the Archaeology of Tomorrow. Rolf Steinberg. LC 83-392. (Illus.). 132p. (Orig.). 1983. reprint ed. pap. 14.95 (*0-87156-347-9*) Sierra.

Dead Time. Eleanor T. Bland. 304p. 1993. pap. 4.99 (*0-451-40427-0*, Sig) NAL-Dutton.

Dead Time. Richard L. Byers. 288p. 1992. mass mkt. 3.99 (*0-8217-3963-8*) Zebra.

Dead Time: A Marti MacAlister Mystery. Eleanor T. Bland. 224p. 1992. 17.95 (*0-312-07053-5*) St Martin.

Dead to Rights. Anna Maxes. 256p. 1994. 20.95 (*0-312-10449-9*) St Martin.

Dead to the World. J. N. Williamson. 368p. (Orig.). 1988. pap. 3.95 (*0-8439-2627-9*) Dorchester Pub Co.

Dead to the World. large type ed. Francis Durbridge. 1978. 15.95 (*0-7089-0120-4*) Ulverscroft.

Dead Tour. Alan N. Izumi. Ed. by Toni A. Brown et al. 169p. (Orig.). 1988. pap. 10.00 (*0-945328-00-1*) Relix Mag.

Dead Towns of Alabama. W. Stuart Harris. LC 76-29655. (Illus.). 176p. 1977. 19.50 (*0-8173-5232-5*) U of Ala Pr.

Dead Towns of Georgia. Charles C. Jones, Jr. LC 74-2175. 264p. 1974. reprint ed. pap. 12.95 (*0-87797-212-5*) Cherokee.

Dead Towns of Sunbury & Dorchester. 3rd ed. Paul McIlvaine. LC 75-26008. 1976. 5.95 (*0-9600410-3-6*) P McIlvaine.

Dead Tree, No. 3. Ed. & Photos by Cass Hook. (Illus.). 128p. (Orig.). 1987. pap. 10.00 (*0-918855-03-9*) Aldin Pub.

Dead Tree, No. 4. Ed. by Cass Hook & Judson Petty. (Illus.). 112p. (Orig.). 1988. pap. 10.00 (*0-918855-04-7*) Aldin Pub.

Dead Tree: Metamorphosis. Ed. by Cass Hook. (Illus.). 68p. (Orig.). 1984. pap. 8.00 (*0-918855-00-4*) Aldin Pub.

Dead Trouble. large type ed. Martin Carroll. (Linford Mystery Library). 231p. 1988. pap. 11.95 (*0-7089-6560-1*, Linford) Ulverscroft.

Dead Valley. Ralph A. Cram. (H. P. Lovecraft's Favorite Horror Stories Ser.). 16p. (Orig.). 1984. pap. 1.50 (*0-318-04711-X*) Necronomicon.

Dead Voices. Abigail McDaniels. 256p. 1994. mass mkt. 4.50 (*0-8217-4695-2*) Zebra.

Dead Voices: Natural Agonies in the New World. Gerald Vizenor. LC 91-45649. (American Indian Literature & Critical Studies: Vol. 2). 152p. 1992. 17.95 (*0-8061-2427-X*); pap. 9.95 (*0-8061-2579-9*) U of Okla Pr.

Dead Water. Ngaio Marsh. 1976. reprint ed. lib. bdg. 21.95 (*0-88411-475-9*, Aeonian Pr) Amereon Ltd.

***Dead Water: The Klindt Affair.** Pat Gipple & Matthew Clemens. 280p. 1995. pap. 10.98 (*0-9646637-0-8*) P Gipple.

Dead Water Zone. Kenneth Oppel. LC 92-37282. (J). 1993. 14.95 (*0-316-65102-8*, Joy St Bks) Little.

Dead Will Arise: Nongqawuse & the Great Xhosa Cattle-Killing Movement of 1856-57. J. B. Peires. LC 88-32799. (Illus.). 364p. 1989. 39.95 (*0-253-34338-0*); pap. 17.95 (*0-253-20524-7*, MB-524) Ind U Pr.

Dead Winter. large type ed. William G. Tapply. (General Ser.). 350p. 1991. lib. bdg. 18.95 (*0-8161-5003-6*) G K Hall.

Dead Witness. Dave Pedneau. 208p. 1987. pap. 2.95 (*0-380-75214-X*) Avon.

Dead Woman's Trail. large type ed. Cynthia H. Haseloff. (Linford Western Library). 240p. 1985. pap. 11.95 (*0-7089-6135-5*, Trailtree Bookshop) Ulverscroft.

Dead Wrong. William X. Kienzle. (Midwest Mysteries Ser.). 1994. mass mkt. 5.99 (*0-345-37766-4*) Ballantine.

Dead Wrong. Alida E. Young. 128p. (J). (gr. 5-8). 1992. pap. 2.99 (*0-87406-602-6*) Willowisp Pr.

Dead Years: Surviving the Holocaust. Joseph Schupack. LC 86-81286. 1987. 16.95 (*0-89604-066-6*) Holocaust Pubns.

Dead Zone. Stephen King. 368p. 1994. pap. 14.95 (*0-452-27329-3*, Plume) NAL-Dutton.

Dead Zone. Stephen King. 1979. 27.95 (*0-670-26077-0*) Viking Penguin.

Dead Zone. large type ed. Stephen King. LC 92-36471. (General Ser.). 672p. 1993. 23.95 (*0-8161-5668-9*) G K Hall.

Dead Zone. Stephen King. 416p. 1980. reprint ed. pap. 6.99 (*0-451-15575-0*, Sig) NAL-Dutton.

Dead Zone Strike. David Robbins. (Blade Ser.: No. 10). 192p. (Orig.). 1990. pap. 2.95 (*0-8439-3013-6*) Dorchester Pub Co.

***Deadalus Encounter Official Guide.** Bradygames Staff. (Illus.). 224p. (Orig.). 1995. pap. 19.99 (*1-56686-295-7*) Brady Compu Bks.

***DeadBase '93: The Annual Edition of the Complete Guide to Grateful Dead Songlists.** John W. Scott et al. (Illus.). 240p. (Orig.). 1994. pap. 14.00 (*1-877657-14-X*) DeadBase.

***DeadBase VIII: The Complete Guide to Grateful Dead Songlists.** John W. Scott et al. (Illus.). 576p. (Orig.). 1994. boxed, pap. 40.00 (*1-877657-16-6*); pap. 32.00 (*1-877657-15-8*) DeadBase.

DeadBase '88: Annual Edition of the Complete Guide to Grateful Dead Song Lists. John W. Scott et al. (Illus.). 128p. (Orig.). 1989. pap. 12.00 (*1-877657-02-6*) DeadBase.

DeadBase '89: The Annual Edition of the Complete Guide to Grateful Dead Songlists. John W. Scott et al. (Illus.). 192p. (Orig.). 1990. pap. 14.00 (*1-877657-04-2*) DeadBase.

DeadBase '90: The Annual Edition of the Complete Guide to Grateful Dead Songlists. John W. Scott et al. (Illus.). 224p. (Orig.). 1991. pap. 14.00 (*1-877657-06-9*) DeadBase.

***DeadBase '91: The Annual Edition of the Complete Guide to Grateful Dead Songlists.** John W. Scott et al. (Illus.). 208p. (Orig.). 1992. pap. 14.00 (*1-877657-08-5*) DeadBase.

***DeadBase '92: The Annual Edition of the Complete Guide to Grateful Dead Songlists.** John W. Scott et al. (Illus.). 208p. (Orig.). 1993. pap. 14.00 (*1-877657-11-5*) DeadBase.

Deadbolt. Jay Brandon. Ed. by Dana Isaacson. 288p. 1992. reprint ed. mass mkt. 4.99 (*0-671-70887-2*) PB.

Deader They Fall. Peter Chambers. (Mystery Ser.). 304p. 1994. pap. 14.95 (*0-7089-7560-7*, Trailtree Bookshop) Ulverscroft.

Deadest Thing You Ever Saw. large type ed. Jonathan Ross. 1992. 18.95 (*0-7451-6417-X*, Scarlet Dagger Lrg Print) Chivers N Amer.

Deadest Thing You Ever Saw. large type ed. Jonathan Ross. 1993. pap. 16.95 (*0-7451-6422-6*, Scarlet Dagger Lrg Print) Chivers N Amer.

Deadeye. Sam Llewellyn. Ed. by Jane Chelius. 288p. 1992. reprint ed. mass mkt. 4.99 (*0-671-67044-1*) PB.

Deadeye: How It Was Made in Lunenburg, Nova Scotia, & Some Notes on Its History & Rigging. John M. Kochiss. LC 77-128782. 43p. reprint ed. pap. 25.00 (*0-8357-2793-9*, 2039919) Bks Demand.

Deadeye Dick. Kurt Vonnegut, Jr. 1985. mass mkt. 5.99 (*0-440-11765-8*) Dell.

Deadeyes: The Story of the 96th Infantry Division. Orlando R. Davidson et al. (Divisional Ser.: No. 20). (Illus.). 310p. 1981. reprint ed. 32.50 (*0-89839-051-6*) Battery Pr.

Deadface: Immortality Isn't Forever Collection. Eddie Campbell & Ed Hillyer. Ed. by Diana Schutz. (Illus.). 200p. 1990. pap. 14.95 (*1-878574-15-9*) Dark Horse Comics.

Deadfall. (Super Bolan Ser.). 1993. mass mkt. 4.99 (*0-373-61430-6*, 1-61430-4) Harlequin Bks.

Deadfall. Franklin W. Dixon. (Hardy Boys Casefiles Ser.: No. 60). 160p. (Orig.). (J). 1992. pap. 3.75 (*0-671-73096-7*) PB.

Deadfall. Lewis Orde. 464p. 1984. pap. 3.95 (*0-8217-1400-7*) Zebra.

Deadfall in Berlin. R. D. Zimmerman. 1992. mass mkt. 4.99 (*0-440-21217-0*) Dell.

Deadfall in Berlin. R. D. Zimmerman. 1990. 18.95 (*1-55611-222-X*) D I Fine.

Deadfall in Berlin. large type ed. R. D. Zimmerman. 336p. 1991. text ed. 20.95 (*0-8161-5238-1*, Large Print Bks) Hall.

Deadfalls & Snares. A. R. Harding. (Illus.). 218p. pap. 4.00 (*0-936622-03-2*) A R Harding Pub.

Deadlier Than Death. Carolyn C. Clark. 186p. 1993. pap. 12.95 (*1-880254-06-9*) Vista.

Deadliest Dare. Franklin W. Dixon. (Hardy Boys Casefiles Ser.: No. 30). (Orig.). (YA). (gr. 7 up). 1991. pap. 3.50 (*0-671-74613-8*, Archway) PB.

Deadline. Randy Alcorn. 375p. 1994. pap. 8.99 (*0-88070-660-0*, Multnomah Bks) Questar Pubs.

***Deadline.** Gerry Boyle. 288p. (Orig.). 1995. pap. text ed. 4.99 (*0-425-14637-5*, Prime Crime) Berkley Pub.

Deadline. John H. Dunning. 224p. (Orig.). 1981. pap. 2.50 (*0-449-14398-8*, GM) Fawcett.

Deadline. Martin Russell. (Black Dagger Crime Ser.). 192p. 16.50 (*0-86220-710-X*, Black Dagger) Chivers N Amer.

Deadline. Hilda Stahl. (Amber Ainslie Detective Ser.). (Illus.). 154p. (Orig.). 1989. pap. 5.99 (*0-934998-33-7*) Bethel Pub.

Deadline: A Jack McMorrow Mystery. Gerry Boyle. LC 93-6296. 1993. 17.95 (*0-945980-44-2*) Nrth Country Pr.

Deadline: A Jack McMorrow Mystery. large type ed. Gerry Boyle. LC 93-45435. 1994. 19.95 (*0-7862-0163-0*) Thorndike Pr.

Deadline: A Memoir. James Reston. LC 91-52679. (Illus.). 525p. 1991. 25.00 (*0-394-58558-5*) Random.

Deadline: A Memoir. James Reston. 1992. pap. 14.00 (*0-8129-2071-6*, Times Bks) Random.

Deadline! From News to Newspaper. Gail Gibbons. LC 86-47654. (Illus.). 32p. (J). (gr. 1-4). 1987. lib. bdg. 14.89 (*0-690-04602-2*, Crowell Jr Bks) HarpC Child Bks.

Deadline at Dawn: Film Criticism 1980-1990. Judith Williamson. 368p. 1993. pap. 21.95 (*0-7145-2925-7*) M Boyars Pubs.

Deadline at Dawn: Film Writings, 1980-1990. Judith Williamson. 1992. 39.95 (*0-7145-2964-8*) M Boyars Pubs.

Deadline Every Minute: The Story of the United Press. Joe A. Morris. LC 69-10137. 356p. 1968. reprint ed. text ed. 65.00 (*0-8371-0175-1*, MOUP, Greenwood Pr) Greenwood.

Deadline for a Critic. William X. Kienzle. 352p. 1988. mass mkt. 4.95 (*0-345-33190-7*) Ballantine.

Deadline for a Critic. William X. Kienzle. 1990. pap. 2.99 (*0-517-05975-4*) Random Hse Value.

Deadline for a Dream. large type ed. Bill Knox. 1979. 12.00 (*0-7089-0324-X*) Ulverscroft.

Deadline for Danger. Christine B. Mattera. 1993. 13.95 (*0-8034-8995-1*) Bouregy.

Deadline for Final Art. Jan Adkins. 192p. 1990. 18.95 (*0-8027-5759-6*) Walker & Co.

Deadline for Love. large type ed. Leigh Michaels. 1991. 17. 95 (*0-7451-9994-1*, AH028, Atlantic Lrg Print) Chivers N Amer.

Deadline for Murder. Valerie Frankel. Ed. by Leslie Wells. 304p. (Orig.). 1991. pap. 3.95 (*0-671-73021-5*) PB.

Deadline for the Media: Today's Challenges to Press, TV & Radio. James Aronson. LC 72-179640. 348p. 1975. pap. 2.95 (*0-672-52115-6*, Bobbs) Macmillan.

Deadline Poet. Calvin Trillin. LC 93-42604. 1994. 18.00 (*0-374-13552-5*) FS&G.

***Deadline Poet: My Life As a Doggerelist.** Calvin Trillin. 208p. 1995. pap. 10.99 (*0-446-67130-4*) Warner Bks.

Deadlines, Doxies & Demagogues. Robert L. Hutchison. Ed. by Anne Holliday. LC 87-61289. (Illus.). 172p. (Orig.). 1987. pap. 7.95 (*0-317-64831-4*) Packard Co Carmel.

Deadlock. William Cross. 416p. (Orig.). 1994. pap. text ed. 5.50 (*0-515-11433-2*) Jove Pubns.

***Deadlock.** Colin Forbes. 507p. 1988. pap. 14.95 (*0-330-30311-2*, Pub. by Pan Books UK) Trans-Atl Phila.

Deadlock. Sara Paretsky. 1992. mass mkt. 5.99 (*0-440-21332-0*) Dell.

Deadlock: A V.I. Warshawski Mystery. large type ed. Sara Paretsky. LC 92-38595. (General Ser.). 271p. 1993. 20. 95 (*0-8161-5561-5*); pap. 17.95 (*0-8161-5562-3*) G K Hall.

Deadlock at Walla Walla. G. T. Cartier. 332p. (Orig.). (C). 1986. pap. 9.95 (*0-934129-00-2*) Somerton Pr.

Deadlock Before Moscow: Army Group Center 1942-1943. Franz Kurowski. Tr. by Joseph B. Welsh. LC 92-60362. (Illus.). 450p. 1992. text ed. 34.95 (*0-88740-412-X*) Schiffer.

Deadlock or Decision: The United States Senate and the Rise of National Politics. Fred R. Harris. LC 92-43279. (Twentieth Century Fund Book). 360p. 1993. 27.50 (*0-19-508025-4*) OUP.

Deadlock or Decision: The United States Senate and the Rise of National Politics. Fred R. Harris. LC 92-43279. (Twentieth Century Fund Book). 1993. pap. 14.95 (*0-19-508026-2*) OUP.

Deadly Admirer: A Kate Kindella Mystery. Christine Green. LC 93-8724. 1993. 19.95 (*0-8027-3244-5*) Walker & Co.

Deadly Affair. Karen Thomas. 192p. 1995. pap. 10.95 (*1-882587-06-5*) Paradigm San Diego.

Deadly after Dark. Ed. by Jeff Gelb et al. (Hotblood Ser.). 320p. (Orig.). 1994. mass mkt. 5.50 (*0-671-87087-4*) PB.

***Deadly Agent.** (Stony Man Ser.). 1995. mass mkt. 4.99 (*0-373-61898-0*, 1-61898-2) Harlequin Bks.

Deadly Allies. John Bryden. 320p. 1991. pap. 6.95 (*0-7710-1726-X*, Pub. by McClelland & Stewart CN) Firefly Bks Ltd.

***Deadly Allies II.** Randisi. 1995. mass mkt. 4.99 (*0-553-56317-3*) Bantam.

Deadly Allies II: Private Eye Writers of America-Sisters in Crime Collaborative Anthology. Ed. by Robert J. Randisi & Susan Dunlap. LC 93-31344. 1994. 18.95 (*0-385-42468-X*) Doubleday.

Deadly Amigos. large type ed. Barry Cord. (Linford Western Library). 208p. 1988. pap. 11.95 (*0-7089-6596-2*, Linford) Ulverscroft.

Deadly Attraction. Diane Hoh. (Nightmare Hall Ser.: No. 3). (YA). (gr. 9-12). 1993. pap. 3.50 (*0-590-46015-3*) Scholastic Inc.

Deadly Beloved. large type ed. Alanna Knight. (Mystery Ser.). 336p. 1992. 21.95 (*0-7089-2646-0*) Ulverscroft.

Deadly Blessing. Steve Salerno. 1992. mass mkt. 4.99 (*0-312-92804-1*) St Martin.

Deadly Blessings: Faith Healing on Trial. Richard Brenneman. 390p. (C). 1990. 25.95 (*0-87975-580-6*) Prometheus Bks.

Deadly Bonds. Ellen Ryp. 1989. mass mkt. 4.95 (*0-446-35133-4*) Warner Bks.

Deadly Breed. T. J. Kirby. 1991. mass mkt. 4.50 (*0-8217-3576-4*) Zebra.

Deadly Brew: Advanced Improvised Explosives. Seymour Lecker. (Illus.). 64p. 1987. pap. 10.00 (*0-87364-418-2*) Paladin Pr.

Deadly Business: Legal Deals & Outlaw Weapons: The Arming of Iraq & Iran, 1975 to the Present. Herbert Krosney. LC 93-11637. 320p. (Orig.). 1993. 30.00 (*1-56858-002-9*); pap. 13.95 (*1-56858-006-1*) FWEW.

Deadly Canyon. Jake Page. LC 93-22130. 240p. 1994. 20. 00 (*0-345-37930-6*, Ballantine Trade) Ballantine.

***Deadly Canyon.** Jake Page. 1995. mass mkt., pap. 4.99 (*0-345-37931-4*, House of Collect) Ballantine.

An Asterisk (*) at the beginning of an entry indicates that the title is appearing in BIP for the first time.

What would you do if your former best friend - the one who had eloped with your fiance - asked you to take a DEADLY GAMBLE? Charlie Parker doesn't want to be an investigator - she's a CPA, a partner in her brother's private investigation firm. When Stacy North approaches her to locate a missing watch, Charlie's instincts go on red-alert. Why on earth would she want to get re-involved with Stacy & with her former fiance, Brad North? Charlie

takes pity on Stacy, who is obviously an abused wife, & locates the missing watch for her old friend. In the process, Charlie gets a look at the wealthy lifestyle she might have had with Brad North, glimpses that make her glad she didn't marry him - especially when the case turns to murder! Intrigue Press is pleased to present this new series by award-winning author, Connie Shelton. DEADLY GAMBLE is our lead title this season & we will be supporting it with a multi-state author tour, national advertising campaign, & hand-selling aids to stores. Order through your wholesaler or directly from Intrigue Press, 1-800-99-MYSTERY (1-800-996-9783). Inquire about quantity discounts. *Publisher Provided Annotation.*

"...So many come to this/ spirit inhabited place/ tender fingers reach out/ in holy reverence to touch/ this past so alive/ I press my fingertips to yours/ you do not feel my touch from the other side of the Wall..." (excerpt from the poem Some Mistake). "...a Minnesota woman who has never been to Southeast Asia has won many hearts with DEADLY PRESENTS, a collection of poems which vividly captures the enigma known as Vietnam.. .Bye's ability to make her heartfelt sense of a chaotic subject is remarkable. .."--Bernie Schmitt, Vincennes Sun-Commercial, Vincennes, IN. "Very readable, easily understandable & moving."--Nelson DeMille, best selling author of THE GENERAL'S DAUGHTER. "Bye has stared into the pit of hell & these poems shiver with what she saw."--Laura Palmer, author SHRAPNEL IN THE HEART. "Michael Sargent's rather symbolic artwork shows how he squeezed out his real feeling & terrible memories of Vietnam."--Mlle. Laurence Gebhardt, France. To order contact: Turtle Run Publishing, P.O. Box 267, Circle Pines, MN 55014-0267. (MN residents add $.85 for tax). *Publisher Provided Annotation.*

D

An Asterisk (*) at the beginning of an entry indicates that the title is appearing in BIP for the first time.

Deadly Rendezvous: A Toni Underwood Mystery. Diane Davidson. (Orig.). 1994. pap. 9.99 (*1-883061-02-4*) Rising NY.

***Deadly Research.** Eduardo Ibarguen. 1994. pap. 13.95 (*0-533-11045-9*) Vantage.

***Deadly Resemblance.** Deborah De Shields. 170p. Date not set. pap. 7.95 (*0-7610-0214-6*) NW Pub.

Deadly Resolutions. Anna Ashwood-Collins. 1989. 18.95 (*0-8027-5739-1*) Walker & Co.

Deadly Reunion. Ralph Hayes. 368p. 1984. pap. 3.50 (*0-8439-2115-3*) Dorchester Pub Co.

***Deadly Reunion.** Jackie Manthorne. 1995. pap. 10.95 (*0-921881-32-0*) InBook.

Deadly Reunion. large type ed. Jeffrey Ashford. (Mystery Ser.). 352p. 1993. 21.95 (*0-7089-2945-1*) Ulverscroft.

Deadly Rich. Edward Stewart. 1992. mass mkt. 5.99 (*0-440-21288-X*) Dell.

Deadly Routine. Jack Morris. LC 80-82429. (Illus.). 154p. 1980. pap. 17.00 (*0-912479-04-3*) Palmer Pr.

Deadly Safari. Karin McQuillan. (Boston Mysteries Ser.). 1991. mass mkt. 4.99 (*0-345-37057-0*) Ballantine.

***Deadly Safari.** large type ed. Karin McQuillan. 1994. 23.95 (*0-7089-3189-8*) Ulverscroft.

Deadly Sanction. Roger Elwood. 1993. pap. 8.99 (*0-8499-3387-0*) Word Inc.

***Deadly Sanctuary.** Sylvia Williams. 360p. 1995. pap. 9.95 (*1-56901-685-2*) NW Pub.

Deadly Schedule: An Inspector Roper Mystery. Roy Hart. 224p. 1994. 19.95 (*0-312-10964-4*) St Martin.

Deadly Scholarship: The True Story of Gang Lu & Mass Murder in America's Heartland. Edwin Chen. LC 94-19041. 1994. 19.95 (*1-55972-241-X*, Birch Ln Pr) Carol Pub Group.

Deadly Secret. Martha Johnson. 308p. 1994. mass mkt. 4.50 (*0-8217-4464-X*) Zebra.

Deadly Secrets. David Belbin. (YA). 1994. pap. 3.50 (*0-590-48318-8*) Scholastic Inc.

Deadly Secrets. Hilda Stahl. 284p. 1993. write for info. (*0-932081-33-9*) Victory Hse.

Deadly Secrets: The CIA-Mafia War Against Castro & the Assassination of JFK. Warren Hinckle & Bill Turner. (Illus.). 464p. 1992. pap. 14.95 (*1-56025-053-4*) Thunders Mouth.

Deadly Seed. Warren Murphy. (Destroyer Ser.: No. 21). 1989. pap. 3.50 (*1-55817-237-8*, Pinnacle NY) Windsor NY.

Deadly Shade of Gold. John D. MacDonald. (Travis McGee Mystery Ser.). 288p. 1987. mass mkt. 4.95 (*0-449-13313-3*, GM) Fawcett.

Deadly Side of the Square. Lee Jordan. Ed. by Janet Hutchings. 189p. 1991. 17.95 (*0-8027-5794-4*) Walker & Co.

Deadly Side of the Square. large type ed. Lee Jordan. 1990. 21.95 (*0-7089-2222-8*) Ulverscroft.

Deadly Silence: The Ordeal of Cheryl Pierson: A Case of Incest & Murder. Dena Kleiman. (Illus.). 305p. 1991. 5.99 (*0-517-05803-0*) Random Hse Value.

Deadly Sin of Terrorism: Its Effect on Democracy & Civil Liberty in Six Countries. David A. Charters. LC 93-31604. (Series Contributions in Political Science: Vol. 340). 264p. 1994. text ed. 55.00 (*0-313-28964-6*, Greenwood Pr) Greenwood.

Deadly Sins. Pynchon et al. LC 94-9135. (Illus.). 1994. 17.00 (*0-688-13690-7*) Morrow.

D

Deadly Sins & Saving Virtues. Donald Capps. LC 85-45912. 176p. 1987. pap. text ed. 14.00 (*0-8006-1948-X*, 1-1948) Augsburg Fortress.

Deadly Skies. Lawrence Cortesi. 288p. 1987. pap. 3.50 (*0-8217-2078-3*) Zebra.

Deadly Snare. Sara Mitchell. LC 89-81809. 1990. pap. 6.99 (*0-89636-263-9*, AC 214, LifeJourney) Chariot Family.

***Deadly Spirits.** Phillip Marchand. 224p. 1995. 15.95 (*0-7737-5641-8*, Pub. by Stoddart Publng CN) Pubs Dist MI.

Deadly Stakes. Bruce Richards. (Nightmare Club Ser.: No. 8). 224p. 1994. pap. 3.50 (*0-8217-4450-X*) Zebra.

Deadly Stakes. H. Fred Wiser. 264p. 1989. 17.95 (*0-8027-5732-4*) Walker & Co.

Deadly Storms in Action: An Early Reader Pop-up Book. Marianne Borgardt. (Illus.). 16p. (Orig.). (J). (ps-3). 1993. bds. 8.95 (*0-689-71719-9*, Aladdin Paperbacks) S&S Childrens.

Deadly Stranger. Peg Kehret. 176p. (J). (gr. 2-9). 1988. pap. 2.95 (*0-8167-1308-1*) Troll Assocs.

Deadly Stranger. M. C. Sumner. (YA). (gr. 9-12). 1993. mass mkt. 3.50 (*0-06-106742-3*, Harp PBks) HarpC.

***Deadly Streak.** large type ed. Douglas Enefer. (Linford Mystery Large Pr. Ser.). 1994. pap. 14.95 (*0-7089-7633-6*) Ulverscroft.

Deadly Summer. Francine Pascal. (Sweet Valley High Super Thriller Ser.: No. 4). (YA). 1989. mass mkt. 3.99 (*0-553-28010-4*) Bantam.

Deadly Sunshade. large type ed. Phoebe A. Taylor. 1992. pap. 17.95 (*0-7927-1317-6*, Curley Lrg Print) Chivers N Amer.

Deadly Swarm & Other Stories. LaVerne H. Clark. LC 85-61099. (Illus.). 136p. (Orig.). 1985. pap. 5.00 (*0-9605008-2-0*) Hermes Hse.

***Deadly Sweet.** Watson. 1995. mass mkt. 5.50 (*0-671-87136-6*) PB.

Deadly Sweet. Sterling Watson. Ed. by Bill Grose. 384p. 1994. 22.00 (*0-671-87135-8*) PB.

***Deadly Threats.** Weinrich. 1995. pap. text ed. 4.99 (*0-88965-108-6*, Pub. by Horizon Books CN) Chr Pubns.

***Deadly Thrills: The True Story of Chicago's Most Shocking Killers.** Jaye S. Fletcher. (Illus.). 352p. 1995. pap. 5.99 (*0-451-40625-7*, Onyx) NAL-Dutton.

Deadly Trail. William L. Thon. 1992. 8.95 (*0-533-10044-5*) Vantage.

***Deadly Travellers.** Dorothy Eden. 1994. reprint ed. lib. bdg. 19.00 (*0-7278-4630-2*) Severn Hse.

Deadly Triplets: A Theatre Mystery & Journal. Adrienne Kennedy. (Emergent Literatures Ser.). (Illus.). 130p. 1990. 14.95 (*0-8166-1837-2*) U of Minn Pr.

Deadly Valentine. Carolyn G. Hart. 1991. pap. 4.99 (*0-553-28847-4*) Bantam.

Deadly Vengeance. Stephen R. George. 384p. 1993. mass mkt. 4.50 (*0-8217-4159-4*) Zebra.

Deadly Venom. Pope. (Curious Creatures Ser.). (Illus.). 48p. (J). (gr. 3-4). Date not set. lib. bdg. 22.80 (*0-8114-3154-1*) Raintree Steck-V.

***Deadly Venom.** Joyce Pope. (Curious Creatures Ser.). (J). (gr. 4-7). 1993. pap. 4.95 (*0-8114-6254-4*) Raintree Steck-V.

***Deadly Vintage: A Jack Donne Mystery.** William Relling, Jr. LC 94-45904. 1995. 19.95 (*0-8027-3262-3*) Walker & Co.

Deadly Virtues. Francois Camoin. LC 87-35064. 1988. pap. 10.00 (*0-934847-07-X*) Arrowood Bks.

***Deadly Visions.** Diane Hoh. (Nightmare Hall Ser.: No. 20). (YA). 1995. pap. 3.50 (*0-590-20298-7*) Scholastic Inc.

***Deadly Waters: The Great Flood of '94.** Athology Reprints Staff. Ed. by Howard Elgison & Betsy Reeves. (Illus.). 100p. 1994. pap. 12.95 (*1-882526-03-1*) BD Pub.

Deadly Welcome. John D. MacDonald. 1985. pap. 2.95 (*0-449-12890-3*, GM) Fawcett.

Deadly Whispers. Ted Schwarz. 1992. mass mkt. 4.99 (*0-312-92489-5*) St Martin.

Deadly White Female. Clifford L. Linedecker. 1994. mass mkt. 4.99 (*0-312-95165-5*) St Martin.

Deadman. Jon A. Jackson. LC 93-31521. 272p. 1994. 20.00 (*0-87113-562-0*) Grove-Atltic.

***Deadman: A Detective Sergeant Mulheisen Novel.** Jon A. Jackson. 1995. pap. 4.99 (*0-440-22047-5*) Dell.

***Deadman: Lost Souls.** Baron. Ed. by B. Kahan. (Illus.). 200p. 1995. pap. 19.95 (*1-56389-188-3*) DC Comics.

Deadman Canyon. large type ed. Louis Trimble. 1992. pap. 16.95 (*0-7927-1215-3*, Curley Lrg Print) Chivers N Amer.

Deadman Switch. Timothy Zahn. 384p. (Orig.). 1988. mass mkt. 4.99 (*0-671-69784-6*) Baen Bks.

Deadman's Gold - Powdersmoke Payoff. Al Cody. 416p. 1993. pap. 4.99 (*0-8439-3526-X*) Dorchester Pub Co.

***Deadpan Parables Vol 1, No. 4: Blackwater.** Kirpal Gordon. 35p. 1994. 5.00 (*1-881604-16-0*) Scopcraeft.

Deadpoint. Stephen Cassell. 512p. 1993. mass mkt. 4.99 (*1-55817-690-X*, Pinnacle NY) Windsor NY.

Deadridge Doll. Dirk Fletcher. (Spur Ser.: No. 34). 176p. (Orig.). 1991. pap. 2.95 (*0-8439-3064-0*) Dorchester Pub Co.

Deadshot. Robert Tralins. 320p. 1993. mass mkt. 4.50 (*1-55817-680-2*, Pinnacle NY) Windsor NY.

Deadspawn. Brian Lumley. (Necroscope Ser.: No. V). (Orig.). 1991. mass mkt. 5.99 (*0-8125-0835-1*) Tor Bks.

Deadspeak. Brian Lumley. (Necroscope Ser.: No. 4). 1992. mass mkt. 5.99 (*0-8125-3032-2*) Tor Bks.

***Deadstick.** Terence Faherty. (WWL Mystery Ser.). 1995. mass mkt. 3.99 (*0-373-26167-5*, 1-26167-6) Harlequin Bks.

Deadtime Story. Margaret Bingley. 1990. mass mkt. 4.95 (*0-445-20722-1*, Mysterious Paperbk) Warner Bks.

Deadweight. Robert Devereaux. 1994. mass mkt. 4.99 (*0-440-21482-3*) Dell.

Deadweight: Owning the Ocean Freighter. Max Hardberger. 205p. (Orig.). 1994. pap. 29.95 (*0-9640433-0-0*) Carifreight.

***Deadwood.** Burnett Battiste. 1995. 11.95 (*0-8062-5129-8*) Carlton.

Deadwood. Pete Dexter. LC 85-19635. 384p. 1986. 17.95 (*0-394-53669-X*) Random.

Deadwood. Pete Dexter. 512p. 1987. mass mkt. 4.95 (*0-14-009910-7*, Penguin Bks) Viking Penguin.

Deadwood. Pete Dexter. 1989. pap. 10.00 (*0-14-012729-1*, Penguin Bks) Viking Penguin.

Deadwood: The Golden Years. Watson Parker. LC 80-24100. (Illus.). xiv, 334p. 1981. pap. 12.95 (*0-8032-8702-X*) U of Nebr Pr.

Deadwood Dick. Steven C. Levi. (Orig.). 1988. pap. 2.95 (*0-87067-732-2*) Holloway.

Deadwood Dick & the Code of the West. Bruce H. Thorstad. Ed. by Dana Isaacson. 288p. (Orig.). 1991. pap. 3.95 (*0-671-70656-X*) PB.

Deaf - Blindness: Essential Information for Families, Professionals, & Students. Isabell Florence. (Illus.). 71p. 1994. pap. 10.00 (*0-9630608-4-8*) R Dean Pr.

Deaf Ability, Not Disability. McCracken & Sutherland. 1991. 19.95 (*1-85359-080-0*, Pub. by Multilingual Matters UK); pap. 59.00 (*1-85359-081-9*, Pub. by Multilingual Matters UK) Taylor & Francis.

Deaf Adult Speaks Out. 3rd rev. ed. Leo M. Jacobs. LC 89-11787. 169p. 1989. pap. 12.95 (*0-930323-61-0*) Gallaudet Univ Pr.

Deaf & Dumb. Edwin J. Mann. 1972. 59.95 (*0-8490-0002-5*) Gordon Pr.

Deaf & Dumb. W. R. Scott. 1972. 59.95 (*0-8490-0003-3*) Gordon Pr.

Deaf & Dumb. Samuel Smith. 1972. 59.95 (*0-8490-0004-1*) Gordon Pr.

Deaf & Dumb. Joseph Toynbee. 1972. 34.95 (*0-8490-0005-X*) Gordon Pr.

Deaf & Dumb Child's Picture Defining & Reading Book. John Anderson. 1972. 59.95 (*0-8490-0006-8*) Gordon Pr.

Deaf & Hard of Hearing. Jack Rudman. (Teachers License Examination Ser.: T-11). 1994. pap. 23.95 (*0-8373-8011-1*) Nat Learn.

Deaf Blind Children: Evaluating Their Multiple Handicaps. Ed. by Scott Curtis et al. 180p. reprint ed. pap. 51.30 (*0-685-20542-8*, 2030015) Bks Demand.

Deaf-Blind Infants & Children: A Development Guide. John M. McInnes & J. A. Treffry. LC 82-190483. 302p. reprint ed. pap. 86.10 (*0-7837-2049-1*, 2042324) Bks Demand.

Deaf-Blind Infants & Children: A Developmental Guide. J. M. McInnes & J. A. Treffry. 1994. pap. 17.95 (*0-8020-7787-0*) U of Toronto Pr.

Deaf Boy's Triumph: Working & Winning. William M. Thayer. 1972. 59.95 (*0-8490-0007-6*) Gordon Pr.

Deaf Child in Care. B. Warr. (C). 1989. 45.00 (*0-903534-86-X*, Pub. by Brit Ag for Adopt & Fost UK) St Mut.

Deaf Child Listened: Thomas Gallaudet, Pioneer in American Education. Anne E. Neimark. LC 82-23942. 160p. (J). (gr. 7-p). 1983. 14.00 (*0-688-01719-3*) Morrow Jr Bks.

Deaf Children: Developmental Perspectives. Ed. by Lynn S. Liben. (Developmental Psychology Ser.). 1979. text ed. 63.00 (*0-12-447950-2*) Acad Pr.

***Deaf Children & Their Families.** Susan Gregory. (Illus.). 250p. (C). 1992. pap. write for info. (*0-521-43847-0*) Cambridge U Pr.

Deaf, Dumb, & Black: An Accounting of an Actual Life of a Family. Mary Miller-Hall. 1994. 13.95 (*0-8062-4929-3*) Carlton.

Deaf Experience: An Anthology of Literature by & about the Deaf. 2nd ed. Ed. by Trenton W. Batson & Eugene Bergman. LC 76-27476. 384p. (C). 1976. pap. 9.00 (*0-914562-03-7*) Merriam-Eddy.

Deaf Experience: Classics in Language & Education. Ed. by Harlan Lane. Tr. by Franklin Philip. (Illus.). 384p. 1984. 32.00 (*0-674-19460-8*) HUP.

Deaf Heritage: A Narrative History of Deaf America. Jack Gannon. (Illus.). (C). 1981. pap. 21.95 (*0-913072-39-7*) Natl Assn Deaf.

Deaf Heritage Student Text & Workbook. Felicia M. Alexander & Jack R. Gannon. (Illus.). 115p. (Orig.). 1984. pap. 11.95 (*0-913072-66-4*) Natl Assn Deaf.

Deaf History Unveiled: Interpretations from the New Scholarship. Ed. by John V. Van Cleve. LC 93-12018. (Illus.). 316p. (C). 1993. text ed. 39.95 (*1-56368-021-1*) Gallaudet Univ Pr.

Deaf in America: Voices from a Culture. Carol A. Padden & Tom L. Humphries. LC 88-11769. (Illus.). 160p. 1988. 24.00 (*0-674-19423-3*) HUP.

Deaf in America: Voices from a Culture. Carol A. Padden & Tom L. Humphries. (Illus.). 144p. 1990. pap. text ed. 9.95 (*0-674-19424-1*) HUP.

Deaf Jew in the Modern World. Ed. by Jerome D. Schein & Lester J. Waldman. 1986. pap. text ed. 12.95 (*0-88125-096-1*) Ktav.

Deaf Like Me. James P. Spradley & Thomas S. Spradley. 1978. 16.95 (*0-394-42825-0*) Random.

***Deaf Maggie Lee Sayre: Photographs of a River Life.** Sayre. (Illus.). 1995. pap. text ed. 17.95 (*0-87805-799-4*) U Pr of Miss.

***Deaf Maggie Lee Sayre: Photographs of a River Life.** Maggie L. Sayre. Ed. & Intro. by Tom Rankin. (Illus.). 96p. 1995. 35.00 (*0-87805-788-9*) U Pr of Miss.

***Deaf Persons in the Arts & Sciences: A Biographical Dictionary.** Harry G. Lang & Bonnie Meath-Lang. LC 94-24206. 496p. 1995. text ed. 69.50 (*0-313-29170-5*, Greenwood Pr) Greenwood.

***Deaf Perspectives on Sign Writing Video.** Deaf Action Committee Staff. 1995. pap., vdisk 30.00 (*0-914336-71-1*) Ctr Sutton Movement.

Deaf Population of the United States. Jerome Schein & Marcus Delk. 1974. 4.95 (*0-913072-16-8*); pap. 1.95 (*0-685-03481-X*) Natl Assn Deaf.

***Deaf President Now! The 1988 Revolution at Gallaudet University.** John B. Christiansen & Sharon N. Barnartt. 232p. 1995. text ed. 24.95x (*1-56368-035-1*) Gallaudet Univ Pr.

Deaf Smith: The Eyes & Ears of the Texas Army. Jan Seale. (Texas History Biography Ser.). (Illus.). 30p. (J). (gr. k-3). 1987. pap. 2.95 (*0-936927-20-8*) Knowing Pr.

Deaf Smith Country Cookbook: Natural Foods for Natural Kitchens. Marjorie W. Ford et al. LC 72-12451. (Illus.). 368p. (Orig.). 1991. pap. 11.95 (*0-89529-495-8*) Avery Pub.

Deaf Sport: The Impact of Sports Within the Deaf Community. David A. Stewart. LC 91-2056. 234p. (C). 1991. text ed. 24.95 (*0-930323-74-2*) Gallaudet Univ Pr.

***Deaf Students in Local Public High Schools: Backgrounds, Experiences, & Outcomes.** Thomas N. Kluwin & Michael S. Stinson. LC 93-16870. (Illus.). 174p. 1993. pap. 24.95 (*0-398-06208-0*) C C Thomas.

Deaf Students in Local Public High Schools: Backgrounds, Experiences, & Outcomes. Thomas N. Kluwin & Michael S. Stinson. LC 93-16870. (Illus.). 174p. (C). 1993. text ed. 39.95x (*0-398-05865-2*) C C Thomas.

Deaf Students in Post-Secondary Education. Ed. by Susan B. Foster & Gerard Walter. LC 91-30101. 256p. 1992. 49.95 (*0-415-07128-3*, A6893) Routledge.

Deaf to the City. Marie-Claire Blais. LC 86-43063. 224p. 1987. 18.95 (*0-87951-276-8*) Overlook Pr.

Deaf to the City. Marie-Claire Blais. 224p. 1989. pap. 10.95 (*0-87951-296-2*) Overlook Pr.

Deaf Way: Perspectives from the International Conference on Deaf Culture. Ed. by Carol J. Erting et al. 800p. 1994. 75.00 (*1-56368-026-2*) Gallaudet Univ Pr.

***Deaf Young People & Their Families: Developing Understanding.** Susan Gregory et al. (Illus.). 350p. (C). Date not set. write for info. (*0-521-41977-8*); pap. write for info. (*0-521-42998-6*) Cambridge U Pr.

Deafening Silence: American Jewish Leaders & the Holocaust, 1933-1945. Rafael Medoff. 328p. 1987. 18.95 (*0-933503-63-6*) Sure Sellers.

Deafferentation Pain Syndromes: Pathophysiology & Treatment. Janice Ovelmen-Levitt. Ed. by Blaine S. Nashold, Jr. (Advances in Pain Research & Therapy Ser.: Vol. 19). 368p. 1991. 108.50 (*0-88167-823-6*) Raven.

Deafinitions for Signlets. Kenneth P. Glickman. LC 86-72758. (Illus.). 120p. (Orig.). 1986. pap. 7.95 (*0-9617583-0-9*) DiKen Prod.

Deafmutism. James K. Love. 1976. 250.00 (*0-87968-303-1*) Gordon Pr.

Deafmutism. Holger Mygind. 1976. 300.00 (*0-8490-0008-4*) Gordon Pr.

Deafmutism & the Education of Deafmutes by Lip-Reading & Articulation. Arthur Hartmann. 1976. 250.00 (*0-87968-090-3*) Gordon Pr.

Deafness. Elaine Landau. (Understanding Illness Ser.). (Illus.). 64p. (J). (gr. 5-8). 1994. lib. bdg. 15.98 (*0-8050-2993-1*) TFC Bks NY.

***Deafness.** 5th ed. Ballantyne. 1993. 63.50 (*1-56593-517-9*, 0426) Singular Publishing.

Deafness: A Personal Account. D. Wright. 202p. 1991. pap. 8.95 (*0-571-14195-1*) Faber & Faber.

Deafness: An Autobiography. David Wright. LC 93-46510. 256p. 1994. reprint ed. pap. 12.00 (*0-06-097616-0*, PL) HarpC.

Deafness: The Facts. Andrew P. Freeland. (Facts Ser.). (Illus.). 168p. 1989. 19.95 (*0-19-261741-9*) OUP.

Deafness & Child Development. Kathryn P. Meadow. LC 74-81435. 1980. 32.00 (*0-520-02819-8*) U CA Pr.

Deafness & Mental Health. John C. Denmark. LC 94-181829. 160p. 1993. pap. 24.95 (*1-85302-212-8*, Pub. by J Kingsley Pubs UK) Taylor & Francis.

Deafness & Mental Health: Emerging Responses. Ed. by Eugene W. Peterson. (Readings in Deafness Ser.: No. 12). 152p. (Orig.). 1985. pap. 5.00 (*0-914494-13-9*) Am Deaf & Rehab.

***Deafness, Children & the Family: A Guide to Professional Practice.** Jennifer Densham. 337p. 1995. 42.95 (*1-85742-221-X*, Pub. by Ashgate UK) Ashgate Pub Co.

Deafness, Deprivation & IQ. J. P. Braden. (Perspectives on Individual Differences Ser.). (Illus.). 224p. (C). 1994. 35.00 (*0-306-44686-3*, Plenum Pr) Greenwood.

Deafness, Development & Literacy. Alec Webster. (Illus.). 180p. 1986. text ed. 45.00 (*0-416-92050-0*, 9998); pap. text ed. 17.95 (*0-416-92060-8*, 1010) Routledge Chapman & Hall.

Deafness in Childhood. National Symposium on Deafness in Childhood Staff. Ed. by Freeman McConnell & Paul H. Ward. LC 67-21653. 349p. reprint ed. pap. 99.50 (*0-8357-3260-6*, 2039481) Bks Demand.

Deaig Encyclopedic Dictionary of Arts & Industrial Graphics: Deaig Diccionario Enciclopedico de las Artes e Industrias Graficas. E. Martin & L. Tapiz. 651p. (SPA.). 1981. 75.00 (*0-8288-2227-1*, S39788) Fr & Eur.

Deal. Peter Lefcourt. 1991. 18.50 (*0-679-40152-0*) Random.

Deal. Matthew Witten. 1990. pap. 4.75 (*0-8222-0285-9*) Dramatists Play.

Deal: A Business Gaming Simulation. Precha Thavikulwat. 45p. (C). 1994. 4.75 (*1-885303-00-9*) Towson St Univ.

Deal: A Novel of Hollywood. Peter Lefcourt. LC 92-54927. 304p. 1993. pap. 12.00 (*0-06-097560-1*, PL) HarpC.

***Deal Breaker: A Myron Bolitar Mystery.** Coben. 1995. mass mkt. (*0-440-22044-0*) Dell.

Deal Decade: What Takeovers & Leveraged Buyouts Mean for Corporate Governance. Ed. by Margaret M. Blair. 390p. (C). 1993. 39.95 (*0-8157-0946-3*); pap. 18.95 (*0-8157-0945-5*) Brookings.

Deal Decade Handbook. Margaret M. Blair & Girish Uppal. LC 93-18026. 72p. 1993. pap. 9.95 (*0-8157-0943-9*) Brookings.

Deal in Wheat. Frank Norris. LC 77-173797. (Illus.). reprint ed. 21.50 (*0-404-04788-2*) AMS Pr.

Deal in Wheat: And Other Stories of the New & Old West. Frank Norris. (BCL1-PS American Literature Ser.). 272p. 1992. reprint ed. lib. bdg. 79.00 (*0-7812-6808-7*) Rprt Serv.

Deal in Wheat & Other Stories of the New & Old West. Frank Norris. LC 74-131788. (Illus.). 1971. reprint ed. 16.00 (*0-403-00675-9*) Scholarly.

Deal Maker, All the Negotiating Skills & Secrets You Need. Robert L. Kuhn. 250p. 1990. pap. text ed. 14.95 (*0-471-51201-X*) Wiley.

Deal Me In: Children's Card Games. rev. ed. Margaret Golick. 190p. (J). 1988. 8.95 (*0-88432-253-X*, B53739) Audio-Forum.

Deal Me In! The Use of Playing Cards in Teaching & Learning. Margie Golick. 1985. pap. 8.95 (*0-685-09992-X*, Arco Test) P-H Gen Ref & Trav.

Deal Me Out. Nicole Grey. (Girl Friends Ser.: No. 3). 224p. 1993. pap. 3.50 (*0-8217-4352-X*) Zebra.

Deal of a Lifetime. large type ed. Susan Napier. 1991. reprint ed. lib. bdg. 16.95 (*0-263-12687-0*, Pub. by Mills & Boon UK) Thorndike Pr.

Deal the First Deadly Blow. U. S. Army Staff. (Illus.). 156p. 1972. reprint ed. pap. 18.00 (*0-87364-126-4*) Paladin Pr.

Deal with the Devil. large type ed. Sandra Marton. LC 94-20151. 1995. pap. 15.95 (*0-8161-7454-7*) Hall.

Deal with the Devil. Eden Phillpotts. Ed. by R. Reginald & Douglas Menville. LC 75-46300. (Supernatural & Occult Fiction Ser.). 1976. reprint ed. lib. bdg. 18.95 (*0-405-08160-X*) Ayer.

Dealbreakers & Breakthroughs: The 10 Most Common & Costly Negotiation Mistakes & How to Overcome Them. John Ilich. 1992. text ed. 22.95 (*0-471-53041-7*) Wiley.

Dealer: An Autobiography - The True Story of Jon Kregel. Jon Kregel & Verne Becker. 160p. (Orig.). 1990. pap. 8.99 (*0-8010-5287-4*) Baker Bk.

Dealer's Choice. 2nd ed. Tom Kelly. 100p. 1983. 12.95 (*0-318-39970-9*) Wing Feather Pr.

An Asterisk (*) at the beginning of an entry indicates that the title is appearing in BIP for the first time.

Dealer's Thesaurus: Six Thousand Ways to Describe Books & Historical Paper. Lynn Vigeant. LC 93-91497. 224p. 1993. 24.00 (*0-9636914-0-6*) Maps Antiquity.

Dealership Business Management. LC 75-9416. 17.50 (*0-87359-007-4*, AM 104) Northwood Univ.

Dealership Business Management. Phil A. Lancaster & David I. Wangberg. LC 81-83717. 315p. 1981. write for info. (*0-87359-027-9*) Northwood Univ.

Dealership Organization & Management. LC 73-88867. 22. 75 (*0-87359-002-3*, AM 101) Northwood Univ.

Dealescope Merchandising Goldbook, 1993. Ed. by Michelle Dalton & Donna Witzleben. 500p. 1993. pap. 495.00 (*0-685-66171-7*) North Am Pub Co.

Dealing. Richard Fire & June Shellene. 52p. 1992. pap. 5.95 (*1-56850-005-X*) Chicago Plays.

Dealing Creatively with Death: A Manual of Death Education & Simple Burial. 11th rev. ed. Ernest Morgan. Ed. by Jenifer Morgan. LC 87-32573. (Illus.). 186p. 1988. pap. 9.00 (*0-914064-26-6*) Celo Pr.

Dealing Creatively with Death: A Manual of Death Education & Simple Burial. 12th ed. Ernest Morgan. Ed. by Jenifer Morgan. 167p. 1990. pap. 11.95 (*0-935016-79-1*, Barclay House) Excelsior Music Pub Co.

Dealing Creatively with Death: A Manual of Death Education & Simple Burial. 13th ed. Ernest Morgan. 1994. pap. 12.95 (*0-935016-89-9*, Barclay House) Excelsior Music Pub Co.

Dealing Effectively with Counsel Abroad. John A. Nilsson. (International Business Portfolios Ser.). 1988. write for info. (*0-8205-1955-3*) Bender.

Dealing Effectively with the Media. John Wade. Ed. by Michael G. Crisp. (Fifty-Minute Ser.). 90p. (Orig.). 1992. pap. 9.95 (*1-56052-116-3*) Crisp Pubns.

Dealing, Feeling & Breathing Better with Asthma. P. D. Jordan. LC 89-82764. 96p. (Orig.). 1990. pap. text ed. 10.00 (*0-929885-09-0*) Haypenny Pr.

***Dealing in Diversity: America's Market for Nature Conservation.** Victoria Edwards. (Illus.). 200p. (C). 1995. write for info. (*0-521-46567-2*) Cambridge U Pr.

Dealing in Futures. Joe W. Haldeman. 253p. 1993. pap. 4.99 (*0-451-45258-5*, ROC) NAL-Dutton.

Dealing in Hate. Michael Connors. 40p. 1979. pap. 4.00 (*0-911038-55-8*) Inst Hist Rev.

Dealing in Hate: The Development of Anti-German Propaganda. Michael Connors. 1981. lib. bdg. 59.95 (*0-686-73180-8*) Revisionist Pr.

Dealing Redemptively. John C. Wenger. 29p. (Orig.). 1965. pap. 0.95 (*0-8361-1518-X*) Herald Pr.

Dealing with a Criminal Investigation: An Overview. 1992. 25.00 (*0-685-54786-8*) NYS Bar.

Dealing with AIDS: Breaking the Chain of Infection. Katherine E. Keough. 32p. 1988. pap. text ed. 5.00 (*0-87652-126-X*, 021-00234) Am Assn Sch Admin.

***Dealing with an Angry Public.** Susskind. 1996. 25.00x (*0-02-874055-6*) Free Pr.

Dealing with Anger. Carol Rogne. 51p. 1991. pap. text ed. 4.95 (*1-881565-02-5*) Discov Counsel.

Dealing with Anger Problems: Rational-Emotive Therapeutic Interventions. Windy Dryden. Ed. by Harold H. Smith, Jr. LC 90-52986. (Practitioner's Resource Ser.). 60p. 1990. pap. 14.70 (*0-943158-59-1*, DAPBP) Pro Resource.

Dealing with Art. (Illus.). 60p. 1992. pap. 19.50 (*3-89322-397-5*, Pub. by Edition Cantz GW) Dist Art Pubs.

Dealing with Change in the Connecticut River Valley: A Design Manual for Conservation & Development. Yaro et al. 181p. 1988. pap. 30.00 (*1-55844-083-6*) Lincoln Inst Land.

Dealing with Childhood Depression & Teen Suicide. Marvin Goldstein & Helene Goldstein. (Family Forum Library Ser.). 16p. 1992. 1.95 (*1-56688-018-1*) Bur For At-Risk.

Dealing with Complexity: An Introduction to the Theory & Application of Systems Science. 2nd ed. R. L. Flood & Ewart R. Carson. (Illus.). 320p. (C). 1993. 29.50 (*0-306-44299-X*, Plenum Pr) Plenum.

Dealing with Conflict: Healing Our Hurts. Michael Lawson. LC 90-71752. 152p. (Orig.). 1991. pap. 8.95 (*0-89622-468-6*) Twenty-Third.

***Dealing with Crime and Aggression at Work: A Handbook for Organizational Action.** Peter Reynolds. LC 94-34351. 1994. 18.95 (*0-07-707932-9*) McGraw.

Dealing with Data. A. J. Lyon. LC 76-92111. 1970. text ed. 172.00 (*0-08-006398-5*, Pub. by Pergamon Repr UK) Franklin.

Dealing with Data & Chance. Judith S. Zawojewski et al. Ed. by Frances R. Curcio. LC 91-5036. (Curriculum & Evaluation Standards for School Mathematics Addenda Ser.). (Illus.). 71p. (Orig.). 1991. pap. 15.00 (*0-87353-321-6*) NCTM.

Dealing with Dealers: After All, It's Your Money. Focus Group Staff. 88p. (Orig.). 1992. pap. 14.95 (*0-9633666-0-2*) Focus Group.

Dealing with Death. Norma Gaffron. LC 89-37592. (Overview Ser.). (Illus.). 96p. (YA). (gr. 5 up). 1989. lib. bdg. 16.95 (*1-56006-108-1*) Lucent Bks.

***Dealing with Death.** Green. 1991. 45.95 (*1-56593-001-0*, 0242) Singular Publishing.

Dealing with Death: Strategy for Tragedy. Evelyn B. Kelly. LC 90-62023. (Fastback Ser.: No. 306). (Orig.). (C). 1990. pap. 1.25 (*0-87367-306-9*) Phi Delta Kappa.

***Dealing with Death & Dying: HP560, Health Promotions Version.** California College for Health Sciences Staff. 176p. (C). 1989. spiral bd. write for info. (*0-933195-29-X*) Allied Hlth Pubns.

***Dealing with Death & Dying: SOC 110, Sociology Version.** California College for Health Sciences Staff. 176p. (C). 1990. spiral bd. write for info. (*0-933195-28-1*) Allied Hlth Pubns.

Dealing with Debt: International Financial Negotiations & Adjustment Bargaining. Ed. by Thomas J. Biersteker. 215p. (C). 1993. pap. text ed. 14.95 (*0-8133-1283-3*) Westview.

Dealing with Debt: International Financial Negotiations & Adjustment Bargaining. Ed. by Thomas J. Biersteker. 215p. (C). 1993. text ed. 47.50 (*0-8133-1282-5*) Westview.

Dealing with Delinquency: An Investigation of Juvenile Justice. Jay S. Albanese. (Illus.). 138p. (Orig.). 1985. lib. bdg. 43.50 (*0-8191-4448-7*); pap. text ed. 15.00 (*0-8191-4449-5*) U Pr of Amer.

Dealing with Delinquency: The Future of Juvenile Justice. 2nd ed. Jay S. Albanese. LC 92-14275. 1992. 18.95 (*0-8304-1290-5*); student ed write for info. (*0-8304-1367-7*) Nelson-Hall.

Dealing with Demanding Customers: How to Turn Complaints into Opportunities. David Martin. (Institute of Management Ser.). 192p. (Orig.). 1994. pap. 39.50x (*0-273-60729-4*, Pub. by Pitman Pub Ltd UK) Trans-Atl Phila.

Dealing with Demons: Total Victory in Christ. Ralph E. Woodrow. (Illus.). 64p. 1990. pap. 3.00 (*0-916938-10-7*) R Woodrow.

Dealing with Denial. 32p. (Orig.). 1975. pap. 3.95 (*0-89486-096-8*, 1229B) Hazelden.

***Dealing with Depression: Five Pastoral Interventions.** Dayringer. 1995. pap. text ed. 12.95 (*1-56024-967-6*) Harrington Pk.

***Dealing with Depression: Five Ways to Help.** Richard Dayringer & Byron Eicher. LC 94-33088. 1995. 29.95 (*1-56024-933-1*) Haworth Pr.

Dealing with Depression in Twelve Step Recovery. Jack O. LC 90-14047. (Fellow Travelers Ser.). 72p. (Orig.). 1990. pap. 4.95 (*0-934125-13-9*) Hazelden.

***Dealing with Depression Naturally.** Syd Baumel. 1995. pap. 19.95 (*0-87983-645-8*) Keats.

Dealing with Difference: How Trainers Can Take Account of Cultural Diversity. Teresa Williams & Adrian Green. 216p. 1993. 49.95 (*0-566-07425-7*, Pub. by Gower UK) Ashgate Pub Co.

Dealing with Differences in Marriage. Brent A. Barlow. LC 93-11070. x, 161p. 1993. 12.95 (*0-87579-732-6*) Deseret Bk.

***Dealing with Difficult Men.** Judith Segal. 1994. pap. 5.99 (*0-06-100806-0*, Harp PBks) HarpC.

Dealing with Difficult Men. Judith Segal. 204p. 1993. 22.95 (*1-56565-079-4*, Woman-Woman) Lowell Hse.

***Dealing with Difficult People.** Warren M. Hoffman. 75p. 1995. pap. 9.95 (*0-940916-03-7*) Daybreak Pr.

Dealing with Difficult People. Charles J. Keating. LC 83-82018. 224p. (C). 1984. pap. 10.95 (*0-8091-2596-X*) Paulist Pr.

Dealing with Difficult People: An Understandable Practical Guide. Ben Bissell. 148p. (Orig.). 1992. pap. 7.95 (*0-9612604-1-6*, Shirah Publishing) C Bissell.

Dealing with Difficult Volunteers. Marilyn Mackenzie. (Volunteer Management Ser.). 1988. 7.00 (*0-911029-11-7*) Heritage Arts.

Dealing with Dilemma: A Manual for Genetic Counselors. P. T. Kelly. (Heidelberg Science Library). 1977. pap. 19. 50 (*3-540-90237-6*) Spr-Verlag.

Dealing with Disappointment. Amy Napa. (Active Bible Curriculum Ser.). (Illus.). 48p. 1992. pap. 9.99 (*1-55945-139-4*) Group Pub.

Dealing with Disaster. 50p. 1992. pap. 17.00 (*0-11-341044-1*, HM10441, Pub. by HMSO UK) UNIPUB.

Dealing with Disaster: Hurricane Response in Fiji. John R. Campbell. 209p. 1984. pap. 9.00 (*0-86638-058-2*) EW Ctr HI.

Dealing with Discounting: Refocus on Retail. Kate Halverson. (Orig.). 1993. pap. 19.95 (*0-9623401-2-X*) Weston Comns.

***Dealing with Diversity.** Governors State University Zaborowski Staff. 128p. (C). 1994. pap. text ed., spiral bd. 16.08 (*0-7872-0330-0*) Kendall-Hunt.

Dealing with Diversity: A Guide for Parish Leaders. Greg Dues. LC 87-51565. 128p. (Orig.). 1988. pap. 7.95 (*0-89622-356-6*) Twenty-Third.

Dealing with Diversity Through Multicultural Fiction: Library-Classroom Partnerships. Lauri Johnson & Sally Smith. LC 92-38872. (AASL Focus on Trends & Issues Ser.: No. 12). (Illus.). 106p. 1993. pap. 18.00 (*0-8389-0605-2*) ALA.

Dealing with Divorce. Roger Paige. 1979. pap. 6.50 (*0-8309-0240-6*) Herald Hse.

Dealing with Dragons. Patricia C. Wrede. 212p. (J). (gr. 7 up). 1990. 15.95 (*0-15-222900-0*, J Yolen Bks) HarBrace.

Dealing with Dragons. Patricia C. Wrede. (YA). 1992. pap. 3.25 (*0-590-45722-5*, Point) Scholastic Inc.

Dealing with Dropouts: The Urban Superintendents' Call to Action. Nancy Paulu. (Education Department Publication Ser.: PIP 87-201). 87p. (Orig.). 1987. pap. 3.25 (*0-16-006720-0*, S/N 065-000-00321-0) USGPO.

Dealing with Drugs: Consequences of Government Control. Ed. by Ronald Hamowy. LC 86-46340. 385p. 1987. pap. 14.95 (*0-936488-16-6*) PRIPP.

Dealing with Dyslexia. Ed. by Pat Heaton & Patrick Winterson. (C). 1988. 65.00 (*0-904700-48-8*, Pub. by Bath Educ Pubs UK) St Mut.

Dealing with Ethical Dilemmas on Campus. Marcia L. Whicker & Jennie J. Kronenfeld. LC 94-18899. (Survival Skills for Scholars Ser.: Vol. 14). 128p. 1994. 27.50 (*0-8039-5480-8*); pap. 12.95 (*0-8039-5481-6*) Sage.

Dealing with Feelings. Joanne Richards & Marianne V. Standley. (Values & Feelings Ser.). 72p. (J). (gr. 3-7). 1982. 7.95 (*0-88160-015-6*, LW 118) Learning Wks.

Dealing with Genes: The Language of Heredity. Paul Berg & Maxine Singer. LC 01-75179. (Illus.). 288p. (C). 1992. text ed. 34.00 (*0-935702-69-5*) Univ Sci Bks.

Dealing with Hazardous Waste Sites: A Compendium for Highway Agencies. (National Cooperative Highway Research Program Report Ser.: No. 310). 107p. 1988. 12.00 (*0-309-04607-6*) Transport Res Bd.

Dealing with Individual Differences in the Early Childhood Classroom. Bernard Spodek & Olivia N. Saracho. LC 92-35209. 400p. (C). 1994. pap. text ed. 39.95 (*0-8013-0451-2*, 78264) Longman.

Dealing with Inequality: Analysing Gender Relations in Melanesia & Beyond. Ed. by Marilyn Strathern. (Illus.). 416p. 1987. pap. 22.95 (*0-521-33652-X*) Cambridge U Pr.

Dealing with Legal Issues Module, PACE: A Program for Acquiring Competence in Entrepreneurship, 3 levels. rev. ed. National Center for Research in Vocational Education Staff. 1983. 2.50 (*0-317-06036-8*); Level 1. 2.50 (*0-317-06037-6*, RD240AB9); Level 2. 2.50 (*0-317-06038-4*, RD240BB9); Level 3. 2.50 (*0-318-67163-8*, RD240CB9) Ctr Educ Trng Employ.

Dealing with Life's Pressures. Group Publishing, Inc. Editors. (Active Bible Curriculum Ser.). (Illus.). 48p. 1993. pap. 9.99 (*1-55945-232-3*) Group Pub.

***Dealing with Math Anxiety.** Anna N. Kitchens. LC 94-30121. 224p. (C). 1994. 10.95 (*0-256-15453-8*) Irwin.

***Dealing with Medical Knowledge: Computers in Clinical Decision Making.** Tibor Deutsch et al. LC 94-24011. 300p. 1995. 69.50 (*0-306-44849-1*, Plenum Pr) Plenum.

Dealing with Medical Malpractice: The British & Swedish Experience. Marilynn M. Rosenthal. LC 87-27245. xviii, 270p. (C). 1988. lib. bdg. 48.00 (*0-8223-0830-4*) Duke.

Dealing with Poverty: Self-Employment for Poor, Rural Women. Usha Jumani. (Illus.). 264p. 1992. 29.95 (*0-8039-9691-8*) Sage.

Dealing with Renters. rev. ed. Intro. & Pref. by David Felber. 100p. (C). 1994. pap. 15.95 (*0-941301-26-5*) CAI.

Dealing with Risk: The Courts, the Agencies & Congress. LC 86-70914. 48p. 1986. pap. 8.00 (*0-89707-231-6*, 359-0013-01) Amer Bar Assn.

Dealing with Statutes. James W. Hurst. LC 75-26574. (Carpenter Lecture Ser.). 144p. 1982. text ed. 32.50 (*0-231-05390-8*) Col U Pr.

Dealing with Stress: A Challenge for Educators. William C. Miller. LC 79-89540. (Fastback Ser.: No. 130). (Orig.). (C). 1979. pap. 1.25 (*0-87367-130-9*) Phi Delta Kappa.

Dealing with Students from Dysfunctional Families. Ed. by Robert I. Witchel. LC 85-644751. (New Directions for Student Services Ser.: No. SS 54). 1991. 16.95 (*1-55542-798-7*) Jossey-Bass.

Dealing with the Behavioral & Psychological Problems of Students. Ed. by Ursula Delworth. LC 85-644751. (New Directions for Student Services Ser.: No. 45). 1989. 16.95 (*1-55542-876-2*) Jossey-Bass.

Dealing with the Dad of Your Past. Maureen Rank. 160p. (Orig.). 1990. pap. 7.99 (*0-87123-622-2*) Bethany Hse.

Dealing with the Debt Crisis. Ed. by Ishrat Husain & Ishac Diwan. 322p. 1989. 24.95 (*0-8213-1246-4*, 11246) World Bank.

Dealing with the Devil. C. S. Lovett. 1967. pap. 7.45 (*0-938148-05-2*) Prsnl Christianity.

Dealing with the Idiots in Your Life. Jim Benton. (Illus.). 192p. (Orig.). 1993. pap. 9.00 (*0-671-79158-3*, Fireside) S&S Trade.

Dealing with the IRS. Scott S. Miller & Thomas Guy. (Illus.). 70p. 1992. pap. 8.95 (*0-9631941-0-0*) Creek Bend Pub.

Dealing with the New ACRS Regulations. Mark L. Yecies. (Illus.). 310p. write for info. (*0-318-59320-3*) HarBrace.

***Dealing with the Problem of Low Self-Esteem: Common Characteristics & Treatment in Individual, Marital-Family & Group Psychotherapy.** Robert P. Rugel. LC 94-33872. 228p. (C). 1994. text ed. 45.95x (*0-398-05936-5*) C C Thomas.

***Dealing with the Problem of Low Self-Esteem: Common Characteristics & Treatment in Individual, Marital-Family & Group Psychotherapy.** Robert P. Rugel. LC 94-33872. (Illus.). 228p. (C). 1995. pap. 29.95x (*0-398-05951-9*) C C Thomas.

Dealing with the Therapist's Vulnerability to Depression. Sheldon Heath. LC 90-15591. 192p. 1991. 27.50 (*0-87668-612-9*) Aronson.

Dealing with Tough Times. Marilyn Kielbasa. (Discovering Program Ser.). (Illus.). 75p. (Orig.). 1990. text ed. 2.80 (*0-88489-202-6*); teacher ed 6.00 (*0-88489-203-4*) St Marys.

Dealing with Young Offenders. John Seymour. xxxi, 495p. 1988. pap. 64.50 (*0-455-20793-3*, Pub. by Law Bk Co) W W Gaunt.

***Dealing with Your Child's Feelings.** Diane T. Rubins. (For Parents Only Ser.). 16p. 1994. 1.95 (*1-56688-187-0*) Bur For At-Risk.

***Dealing with Youth Violence: What Schools & Communities Need to Know.** Ed. by Rose Duhon-Sells. 112p. (Orig.). 1995. pap. 15.95 (*1-879639-31-9*) Natl Educ Serv.

Dealings with the Dead: Narratives from "La Legende de la mort en Basse Bretagne" Anatole Le Braz. Tr. by E. A. Whitehead. LC 77-87695. reprint ed. 18.50 (*0-404-16491-9*) AMS Pr.

Dealings with the Dead: The Human Soul, Its Migrations & Its Transmigrations. P. B. Randolph. 156p. 1959. spiral bd. 8.80 (*0-7873-0694-0*) Mokelumne.

Dealings with the Firm of Dombey, & Son, Wholesale, Retail, & for Exploration see Oxford Illustrated Dickens

Dealmaking in the Film & Television Industry: From Negotiations Through Final Contracts. Mark Litwak. LC 94-1939. 405p. (Orig.). 1993. pap. 26.95 (*1-879505-15-0*) Silman James Pr.

***Deals on Wheels.** Tana Reiff. LC 94-79121. (That's Life Ser.: Bk. 5). 1994. pap. 4.95 (*1-56103-780-X*) Lake Pub Co.

***Deals on Wheels.** Tana Reiff. (That's Life Ser.: Bk. 5). 1995. audio 9.90 (*1-56103-790-7*) Lake Pub Co.

Deals on Wheels: How to Buy, Care for & Sell a Car: Complete Buyer's Guide & Expose of the Automotive Jungle. Gordon T. Page. (Illus.). 304p. (Orig.). 1984. pap. 9.95 (*0-9607804-0-8*) Page Pub WI.

Deals with the Devil. Ed. by Mike Resnick et al. 304p. 1994. mass mkt. 4.99 (*0-88677-623-6*) DAW Bks.

Deals with the Devil: And Other Reasons to Riot. Pearl Cleage. LC 92-97479. 304p. 1993. 22.00 (*0-345-38278-1*, One World) Ballantine.

Deals with the Devil: And Other Reasons to Riot. Pearl Cleage. 224p. 1994. reprint ed. pap. 11.00 (*0-345-38871-2*, One World) Ballantine.

Dealt With see Thick As Thieves

Deamidation & Isoapsparate Formation in Peptides - Proteins. Aswad. 272p. 1994. 89.95 (*0-8493-7823-0*, 7823) CRC Pr.

Dean Acheson: The Cold War Years. Douglas Brinkley. (Illus.). 512p. 1994. pap. 18.00 (*0-300-06075-0*) Yale U Pr.

Dean Acheson: The Cold War Years, 1953-71. Douglas Brinkley. (Illus.). 512p. (C). 1992. 40.00 (*0-300-04773-8*) Yale U Pr.

Dean Acheson & the Making of U. S. Foreign Policy. Douglas Brinkley. 1993. text ed. 49.95 (*0-312-05016-X*) St Martin.

Dean & the Anarchist. James Preu. LC 72-888. (Studies in Anarchy & Anarchism Ser.: No. 99). 124p. (C). 1972. reprint ed. lib. bdg. 42.95 (*0-8383-1419-8*) M S G Haskell Hse.

Dean Cuisine: The Liberated Man's Guide to Fine Cooking. Jack Greenberg & James Vorenberg. (Illus.). 168p. (Orig.). (C). 1990. pap. 12.95 (*0-935296-99-9*) Sheep Meadow.

***Dean Duffy.** Randy Powell. LC 94-29037. 176p. 1995. 15. 00 (*0-374-31754-2*) FS&G.

Dean Dunham; or, the Waterford Mystery. Horatio Alger. 275p. 1974. reprint ed. lib. bdg. 21.95 (*0-88411-801-0*, Aeonian Pr) Amereon Ltd.

Dean Fearing's Southwest Cuisine: Blending Asia & the Americas. Dean Fearing. (Illus.). 256p. 1990. 29.95 (*0-8021-1321-4*) Grove-Atltic.

***Dean Gardens.** Larry Dean. LC 93-80133. 148p. 1994. 30. 00 (*1-56352-124-5*) Longstreet Pr Inc.

Dean It Was That Died. Whitehead. 1993. pap. 2.99 (*0-517-11078-4*) Random Hse Value.

Dean Koontz: Three Novels, a New Collection. Dean Koontz. 1992. 11.99 (*0-517-07369-2*) Random Hse Value.

Dean Koontz Companion. Ed. by Martin H. Greenberg et al. 320p. (Orig.). 1994. pap. 13.00 (*0-425-14135-7*, Berkley Trade) Berkley Pub.

Dean Meant Business. Courtney C. Brown. LC 83-20625. 288p. (Orig.). 1985. 17.50 (*0-9612584-0-3*) Grad Sch Bus NY.

Dean Mountain Story. Gloria Dean. LC 81-81878. 80p. 1982. pap. 5.50 (*0-915746-20-4*) Potomac Appalach.

Dean of Education & the Looking-Glass Self. Richard Wisniewski. (Occasional Paper: No. 11). 1979. pap. 3.00 (*0-933669-14-3*) Soc Profs Ed.

Dean of Steam Fire Engine Builders. Ed Hass. (Illus.). 224p. 1986. 40.00 (*0-9611166-2-5*) E Hass.

Dean of the Birdwatchers: A Biography of Ludlow Griscom. William E. Davis, Jr. LC 93-38095. (Illus.). 336p. 1994. 29.95 (*1-56098-310-8*) Smithsonian.

Dean R. Koontz: Three Complete Novels: The Servants of Twilight, Darkfall, Phantoms. Dean R. Koontz. 752p. 1991. reprint ed. 11.99 (*0-517-06487-1*, Pub. by Wings Bks) Random Hse Value.

***Dean Smith: A Biography.** Mumau. 1994. pap. 5.99 (*0-517-13435-7*) Random.

Dean Swift & His Writings. G. P. Moriarty. LC 70-130247. (English Literature Ser.: No. 33). 1970. reprint ed. lib. bdg. 53.95 (*0-8383-1137-7*) M S G Haskell Hse.

Dean Tucker & Eighteenth Century Economic & Political Thought. W. G. Shelton. LC 79-29742. 1981. text ed. 29.95 (*0-312-18538-3*) St Martin.

Dean Witter: Understanding Wall Street. Jeffrey B. Little. 1991. 3.25 (*0-8306-5326-0*) TAB Bks.

Dean Witter Guide to Personal Investing. Robert K. Gardiner. 240p. 1989. pap. 4.99 (*0-451-15918-7*, Sig) NAL-Dutton.

Deane C. Davis: An Autobiography. Deane C. Davis. Ed. by Nancy P. Graff. LC 91-52770. (Illus.). 400p. 1990. 24.95 (*0-933050-91-7*) New Eng Pr VT.

Deaner: Fifty Years of University of Kansas Athletics. Michael P. Fisher. LC 86-15175. 352p. 1986. 19.95 (*0-932845-16-9*) Lowell Pr.

Deaning: Middle Management in Academe. Van C. Morris. LC 80-26119. 192p. 1981. 24.95 (*0-252-00871-5*) U of Ill Pr.

Deanmania: The Man, the Character, the Legend. Robert J. Headrick. 1991. pap. 14.95 (*1-55698-286-0*) Movie Pubs Servs.

Deanna's Desire. Sylvie F. Sommerfield. (Orig.). 1982. pap. 3.50 (*0-89083-906-9*) Zebra.

Dean's December. Saul Bellow. 1985. mass mkt. 4.50 (*0-671-60254-3*, WSP) PB.

Dean's List. Roy Dean. (Illus.). 1980. 12.95 (*0-685-04348-7*) Rho-Delta Pr.

Dean's List: Hawaii. Roy Dean. (Illus.). 1982. 12.95 (*0-685-07159-6*) Rho-Delta Pr.

An Asterisk (*) at the beginning of an entry indicates that the title is appearing in BIP for the first time.

1825

Dean's Role in Fund Raising. Margarete R. Hall. LC 92-23826. 144p. 1993. text ed. 25.95 (*0-8018-4495-9*) Johns Hopkins.

Dean's Watch. Elizabeth Goudge. 1976. 22.95 (*0-8488-0509-7*) Amereon Ltd.

Dean's Watch. Elizabeth Goudge. 392p. 1991. reprint ed. pap. 10.99 (*0-89283-700-4*) Servant.

Dear Abby on Planning Your Wedding. Abigail Van Buren. 1988. pap. 8.95 (*0-8362-7943-3*) Andrews & McMeel.

Dear African Americans (Africans in Bondage in U. S. A.) Osodi E. Echezonam. 1994. 12.95 (*0-8062-4903-X*) Carlton.

Dear Agnos: Letters to an Agnostic. 274p. 1992. reprint ed. pap. text ed. 9.99 (*0-89900-457-1*) College Pr Pub.

Dear Alec: Guiness at Seventy-Five. large type ed. Ronald Harwood. 192p. 1991. 8.97 (*1-85089-396-9*, Pub. by ISIS UK) Transaction Pubs.

Dear All: The Selected Letters of R. H. "Pat" Uhlmann, 1959-1991. R. H. Uhlmann. Ed. by Robert Uhlmann. LC 92-83735. 624p. Date not set. 24.95 (*0-939644-90-8*, Midgrd Press) Media Pub.

Dear America: Letters from Home. Bernard Edelman. Ed. by Paul McCarthy. 384p. 1989. mass mkt. 5.99 (*0-671-69178-3*) PB.

Dear America: Letters Home from Vietnam. New York Vietnam Veterans Memorial Commission. Ed. by Bernard Edelman. 276p. 1985. 13.95 (*0-393-01998-5*) Norton.

***Dear Amy: Thoughts on the Soul's Voyage.** Tom Kay. 208p. (Orig.). 1994. pap. 9.95 (*1-57174-010-4*) Hampton Roads Pub Co.

Dear & Glorious Physician. Ronald Fernand & Taylor Caldwell. 83p. 1963. pap. 4.95 (*0-87129-116-9*, D41) Dramatic Pub.

Dear & Glorious Physician. Taylor Caldwell. 1993. reprint ed. lib. bdg. 37.95x (*1-56849-242-1*) Buccaneer Bks.

Dear & Honoured Lady. Ed. by Hope Dyson & Charles Tennyson. LC 72-151284. 152p. 1975. 20.00 (*0-8386-7922-6*) Fairleigh Dickinson.

Dear Angels. Diantha C. Rau. (Illus.). 61p. (Orig.). 1985. pap. 5.95 (*0-935557-00-8*) D C Rau.

Dear Anne Frank. Marjorie Agosin. Tr. by Richard Schaaf. LC 93-73680. 128p. (Orig.). 1994. pap. 11.95 (*0-9632363-6-9*) Azul Edits.

Dear Annie. Judith Caseley. LC 90-39793. (Illus.). 32p. (J). (ps up). 1991. 13.95 (*0-688-10010-4*); lib. bdg. 13.88 (*0-688-10011-2*) Greenwillow.

Dear Annie. Judith Caseley. Ed. by Amy Cohn. LC 90-39793. (Illus.). 32p. (J). (ps up). 1994. reprint ed. pap. 4.95 (*0-688-13575-7*, Mulberry) Morrow.

***Dear Author: Students Write about the Books That Changed Their Lives.** Comp. by Read Magazine Staff. 150p. (Orig.). (YA). (gr. 6-12). 1995. pap. 9.95 (*1-57324-003-6*) Conari Press.

Dear Babysitter Handbook. Vicki Lansky. 60p. (J). (gr. 7 up). 1990. pap. 4.95 (*0-916773-16-7*) Book Peddlers.

Dear Barbara, Dear Lynne: The True Story of Two Women in Search of Motherhood. Barbara Shulgold & Lynne Sipiora. (Illus.). 370p. 1992. 19.18 (*0-201-60841-3*) Addison-Wesley.

Dear Bart: Washington Views of World War II. Glen C. Perry. LC 81-13418. (Contributions in Military History Ser.: No. 31). xix, 341p. 1982. text ed. 59.95 (*0-313-23265-2*, PED/, Greenwood Pr) Greenwood.

Dear Bear. Joanna Harrison. LC 93-44730. (J). (ps-3). 1994. 18.95 (*0-87614-839-9*, Carolrhoda) Lerner Group.

Dear Benjamin Banneker. Andrea D. Pinkney. LC 93-31162. (Illus.). (J). 1994. 14.95 (*0-15-200417-3*, Gulliver Bks) HarBrace.

Dear Betsy - Dear Gilbert. Emily B. Stothert et al. LC 89-80327. (Illus.). 220p. 1989. lib. bdg. 24.95 (*0-944419-02-X*) Everett Cos Pub.

Dear Bill: The Correspondence of William Arthur Deacon. Ed. by John Lennox & Michele Lacombe. 400p. 1988. 40.00 (*0-8020-2624-9*) U of Toronto Pr.

Dear Birthmother: Thank You for Our Baby. Kathleen Silber & Phylis Speedlin. 194p. (Orig.). 1983. pap. 10.95 (*0-931722-19-5*) Corona Pub.

Dear Bishop: Memoirs of the Author Concerning the History of the Blue Army. John M. Haffert. (Illus.). 352p. 1981. 6.95 (*0-911988-44-0*); pap. 4.95 (*0-911988-42-4*) AMI Pr.

***Dear Boris: The Life of William Henry Pratt a.k.a. Boris Karloff.** Cynthia Lindsay. (Illus.). (Orig.). 1995. pap. 20.00 (*0-614-06773-1*) Limelight Edns.

***Dear Boris: The Life of William Henry Pratt a.k.a. Boris Karloff.** Cynthia Lindsay. (Illus.). 288p. (Orig.). 1995. reprint ed. pap. 20.00 (*0-87910-076-1*) Limelight Edns.

Dear Boss. William B. Werther, Jr. LC 88-37152. 226p. 1989. 14.95 (*0-88166-166-X*) Meadowbrook.

Dear Boys: World War II Letters from a Woman Back Home. Mrs. Keith Somerville. Ed. by Judy B. Litoff & David C. Smith. LC 91-16921. 1991. text ed. 37.50 (*0-87805-521-5*); pap. 15.95 (*0-87805-540-1*) U Pr of Miss.

Dear Bronx Zoo. Joyce Altman & Sue Goldberg. (J). (gr. 4-7). 1992. pap. 3.50 (*0-380-71649-6*, Camelot) Avon.

Dear Bronx Zoo. Joyce Altman & Sue Goldberg. LC 89-28226. (Illus.). 160p. (J). (gr. 3 up). 1990. text ed. 14.95 (*0-02-700640-9*, Mac Bks Young Read) S&S Childrens.

Dear Brother. Frank Asch & Vladimir Vagin. 32p. (J). 1992. 13.95 (*0-590-43107-2*, Scholastic Hardcover) Scholastic Inc.

Dear Brother. Gordon R. Forrer. LC 79-93051. 1980. 10.95 (*0-87212-128-3*) Libra.

Dear Brother, Here Departed. large type ed. Stella Phillips. (Linford Mystery Library). 1990. pap. 12.95 (*0-7089-6847-3*, Trailtree Bookshop) Ulverscroft.

Dear Brother Walt: The Letters of Thomas Jefferson Whitman. Thomas J. Whitman. Ed. by Dennis Berthold & Kenneth M. Price. LC 83-26775. (Illus.). 236p. reprint ed. pap. 67.30 (*0-7837-0507-7*, 2040831) Bks Demand.

***Dear Brotherhood: A Fantasy.** Alex Voyd. 256p. (Orig.). 1995. pap. 14.95 (*0-9645019-0-2*) Sch Life Bks.

Dear Brothers & Sisters in Christ: Five Letters of Comfort. Basilea Schlink. 1978. pap. 0.95 (*3-87209-622-2*) Evang Sisterhood Mary.

Dear Brutus & Other Plays see Works of J. M. Barrie

***Dear Bunkie.** Sally A. Stevens. 43p. 1995. pap. 7.95 (*1-56901-711-5*) NW Pub.

Dear Calamity--Love, Belle. Calamity Wronsky & Belle Bandall. LC 94-8655. 1994. 17.00 (*0-517-59888-4*, Harmony) Crown Pub Group.

Dear Caliban. large type ed. Jane Donnelly. (Linford Romance Library). 360p. 1984. pap. 11.95 (*0-7089-6046-4*, Trailtree Bookshop) Ulverscroft.

Dear Caprice. large type ed. Juliet Gray. 1990. 21.95 (*0-7089-2328-3*) Ulverscroft.

Dear Carnap, Dear Van: The Quine-Carnap Correspondence & Related Work. Willard V. Quine & Rudolf Carnap. 499p. 1990. 45.00 (*0-520-06847-5*) U CA Pr.

Dear Carrie... The Civil War Letters of Thomas N. Stevens. Ed. by George M. Blackburn. LC 84-222354. (Illus.). 1984. 17.50 (*0-916699-10-2*) CMU Clarke Hist Lib.

Dear Chelsea: Letters from Kids. Scholastic Inc Staff. (J). (gr. 5-7). 1994. pap. 4.95 (*0-590-47906-7*) Scholastic Inc.

***Dear Cherry: Questions & Answers on Eating Disorders.** Cherry B. O'Neill. 144p. 1987. pap. 8.95 (*0-8264-0387-5*) Crossroad NY.

***Dear Chief Rabbi: From the Correspondence of Chief Rabbi Immanuel Jakobovits on Matters of Jewish Law, Ethics & Contemporary Issues, 1980-1990.** Ed. by Jeffrey M. Cohen. LC 95-6166. 1995. write for info. (*0-88125-471-1*) Ktav.

Dear Child: Encouragement for the Sexually Abused. Barnabas. LC 89-27679. (Orig.). 1990. pap. 4.00 (*0-915541-53-X*) Star Bks Inc.

Dear Children of the Earth. Schim Schimmel. LC 93-47672. (Illus.). 32p. (J). (gr. k-5). 1994. 11.95 (*1-55971-225-2*) NorthWord.

Dear Chris. Christine Wells. LC 91-73966. 1993. pap. 6.95 (*0-8158-0477-6*) Chris Mass.

Dear Chris: A Letter of Advice on How to Study in College. Erwin Boschmann. (Illus.). 1981. write for info. (*0-930116-04-6*) Sci Ent.

Dear Chris: Advice to a Volunteer Fund Raiser. John D. Verdery. 105p. (Orig.). 1986. pap. 19.95 (*0-914756-17-6*, 600006) Taft Group.

***Dear Chris, Dear Sam: Really Reading!** Mikal Keefer. Ed. by Diane Stortz. LC 94-67876. (Really Reading! Bks.). (Illus.). 48p. (Orig.). (J). (gr. k-2). 1995. pap. 4.49 (*0-7847-0302-7*, 24-03978) Standard Pub.

***Dear Christian Friends: A Revealing Look at Paul's Letters to the Galatians, Ephesians, Philippians, Collosians & to Philemon.** Daisy Tweeddale. 96p. 1994. pap. 6.99 (*1-56322-043-1*); pap. text ed. 16.99 (*1-56322-042-3*) V Hensley.

Dear Christopher: Letters to Christopher Columbus by Contemporary Native Americans. Ed. by Darryl Wilson & Barry Joyce. 211p. (Orig.). (C). 1992. pap. 14.95 (*0-9635573-0-0*) U CA Nat Am Stud.

Dear Client: A Complete Handbook for Divorce Litigation. Ellen Ostman. Ed. by Karen L. Jacob. (Illus.). 560p. 1995. pap. 24.95 (*0-936417-44-7*) Axelrod Pub.

Dear Comrade Editor: Readers' Letters to the Soviet Press under Perestroika. Ed. by James Riordan & Sue Bridger. Tr. by Sue Bridger & Jim Riordan. LC 91-20441. (Illus.). 256p. (Orig.). 1992. text ed. 35.00 (*0-253-34990-7*); pap. text ed. 12.95 (*0-253-20696-0*, MB-696) Ind U Pr.

Dear Comrades: Menshevik Reports on the Bolshevik Revolution & the Civil War. Ed. by Vladimir N. Brovkin & Robert Hessen. (Publication Series: Archival Documentaries: No. 398). 296p. 1991. 29.95 (*0-8179-8981-1*); pap. 21.95 (*0-8179-8982-X*) Hoover Inst Pr.

Dear Corliss: Letters from Eminent Persons. Ed. by Corliss Lamont. 202p. (C). 1990. 21.95 (*0-87975-627-6*) Prometheus Bks.

Dear Corpus Christi. Eve L. Caram. 1992. pap. 11.95 (*0-911051-59-7*) Plain View.

Dear Country: A Quest for England. Harry Reid. (Illus.). 224p. 1992. 29.95 (*1-85158-374-2*, Pub. by Mnstream UK) Trafalgar.

Dear Craig & Brian: A Space Age Grandfather Shares His Faith. Fred Ebersole. 1991. 16.95 (*0-533-09036-9*) Vantage.

Dear Dad. L. Norma Cox. 1988. pap. 2.95 (*0-345-35309-9*) Ballantine.

Dear Dad. Mary Z. Holmes. LC 91-37774. (History's Children Ser.). (Illus.). 48p. (J). (gr. 4-5). 1992. lib. bdg. 20.70 (*0-8114-3503-2*); pap. write for info. (*0-8114-6428-8*) Raintree Steck-V.

Dear Dad: Letters from an Adult Child. Louie Anderson. 240p. 1991. pap. 10.95 (*0-14-014845-0*, Penguin Bks) Viking Penguin.

Dear Dad: Thank You for Being Mine. Scott Matthews & Tamara Nikuradse. LC 92-40270. 1993. pap. 5.99 (*0-553-37198-3*) Bantam.

Dear Daddy. Philippe Dupasquier. (J). (ps-3). 1988. pap. 3.95 (*0-14-050822-8*, Puffin) Puffin Bks.

***Dear Daddy.** John Schindel. LC 94-22006. (Illus.). (J). Date not set. write for info. (*0-8075-1531-0*) A Whitman.

***Dear Daisy.** Geoffrey C. Ward. LC 94-45394. Date not set. write for info. (*0-614-04779-X*) HM.

Dear Dance of Eros. Mary Mackey. LC 86-7612. (International Poetry Ser.: No. 2). 150p. (Orig.). 1987. pap. 7.95 (*0-940242-17-6*) Fjord Pr.

Dear Danish Recipes. Michelle N. Spencer. 160p. 1988. pap. 5.50 (*0-941016-53-6*) Penfield.

Dear Dark Faces: Portraits of a People. Ed. by Helen E. Simcox. LC 79-92240. (Illus.). 104p. (YA). (gr. 7-12). 1980. per., pap. 6.00 (*0-916418-23-5*) Lotus.

Dear David: Prisons & Capital Punishment-A Needed, Balanced Fresh Approach. 2nd ed. Albert DiNicola. (Orig.). 1986. write for info. (*0-318-59204-5*) Lumen Series.

Dear Dead Person: Short Fiction by Benjamin Weissman. Benjamin Weissman. Ed. by Ira Silverberg. (Orig.). 1994. pap. 10.99 (*1-85242-330-7*) Serpents Tail.

Dear, Dear Momma. Todd Barnett. 301p. 1990. 15.95 (*0-685-46308-7*) Vantage.

Dear Deceit. Sylvia E. Kirk. (Rainbow Romances Ser.). 160p. 1993. 14.95 (*0-7090-4899-8*, Hale-Parkwest) Parkwest Pubns.

***Dear Deceiver.** Elizabeth Lynch. 272p. (Orig.). 1995. mass mkt. 3.99 (*0-380-78046-1*) Avon.

Dear Deedee. Ed. by Anne Schaffer. 1978. 10.00 (*0-8184-0271-7*) Carol Pub Group.

Dear Delinquent. Jack Popplewell. 1958. pap. 4.75 (*0-8222-0286-7*) Dramatists Play.

Dear Dentist: Stop Being Your Own Worst Enemy. R. H. Schaper. LC 94-1885. 1994. 39.95 (*0-87814-418-8*, D4309) PennWell Bks.

***Dear Departed.** Enes Smith. 320p. (Orig.). 1994. pap. 5.50 (*0-7865-0063-8*) Diamond.

Dear Departed. Marguerite Yourcenar. Tr. by Maria L. Ascher. (Illus.). 346p. 1992. 25.00 (*0-374-13554-1*) FS&G.

Dear Departed: A Memoir. Marguerite Yourcenar. Tr. by Maria L. Ascher. 1992. 14.00 (*0-374-52367-3*, Noonday) FS&G.

Dear Departed: Poetry for the Occasion. Alpha Pyramis Research Division Staff. 20p. 1984. pap. text ed. 2.95 (*0-913597-67-8*) Prosperity & Profits.

Dear Diary. Pat Baker. (J). (gr. 3-8). 1990. pap. 4.99 (*0-8423-0536-X*) Tyndale.

***Dear Diary.** Lila Fuhriman. 76p. Date not set. pap. 4.95 (*0-87770-542-9*) Ye Galleon.

Dear Diary. Lindy H. Lumbert. 119p. (J). (gr. 4-10). 1981. pap. 4.25 (*0-943280-00-1*) Blossom Bks.

Dear, Dirty Dublin: A City in Distress 1899-1916. Joseph V. O'Brien. LC 79-64662. (Illus.). 416p. 1982. 50.00 (*0-520-03965-3*) U CA Pr.

Dear Doctor. Saul V. Levine & Kathleen Wilcox. LC 86-21335. 256p. (YA). (gr. 7 up). 1987. lib. bdg. 12.93 (*0-688-07094-9*) Lothrop.

Dear Doctor: A Personal Letter to a Physician. Charles E. Odegaard. 172p. (Orig.). 1987. pap. text ed. 3.00 (*0-318-23186-7*) H J Kaiser.

Dear Dolphin: Iskra's Atlantic Adventures. Frank Mulville. (Illus.). 192p. (Orig.). 1992. pap. 14.95 (*0-924486-26-0*) Sheridan.

Dear Dr. Bell - Your Friend, Helen Keller. Judith St. George. 172p. (J). (gr. 5-9). 1992. 15.95 (*0-399-22337-1*, Putnam) Putnam Pub Group.

Dear Dr. Bell...Your Friend, Helen Keller. Judith St. George. LC 93-9304. 96p. (J). (gr. 6 up). 1993. pap. text ed. 4.95 (*0-688-12814-9*, Pub. by Beech Tree Bks) Morrow.

***Dear Dr. Humor: A Collection of Humorous Stories for All Occasions.** Stuart Robertshaw. 155p. (Orig.). 1995. pap. 10.00 (*0-9645793-0-8*) NAHI.

Dear Dr. Psych. Nate Zinsser. (J). (gr. 3-7). 1991. mass mkt. 5.95 (*0-316-98898-7*, Spts Illus Kids) Little.

Dear Dr. Stare: What Should I Eat? Fredrick J. Stare. LC 82-50207. 216p. 1982. 14.95 (*0-397-53077-3*) Lippincott.

Dear Earth... A Love Letter from Spring Hollow. Radine T. Nehring. LC 94-28966. 176p. 1995. 17.95 (*0-9636620-2-3*) Brett Bks. The unforgettable chronicle of a couple who traded secure jobs & the rat race for a life of simplicity & quiet joy. "Read it & dream."--BOOKLIST "Radine reminds us that dreams are meant to be dreamed -- that woods are meant to be walked in -- & the Earth is meant to be cared for. She is a wonderfully warm, descriptive writer who will have you sitting on her bench in the woods -- watching & loving the things around you -- & loving her gentle company as well. You should give this book to everyone you love..."--MIKE FLYNN, Host, FOLK SAMPLER, National Public Radio. "Nehring's book is a must!"--DR. NEIL COMPTON, Conservationist & Pulitzer Prize nominee. National advertising & promotion. Brett Books, Inc., P.O. Box 290-637, Brooklyn, NY 11229-0011. Phone & FAX: 718-376-5470. Distributed by INDEPENDENT PUBLISHERS GROUP: 1-800-888-4741. *Publisher Provided Annotation.*

Dear Editor... Virgie V. Jones. (Illus.). 132p. 1990. 12.00 (*0-9600890-4-7*) Morris-Burt Pr.

***Dear Elijah: A Passover Story.** Miriam Bat-Ami. LC 94-29941. 96p. (J). (gr. 1-8). 1995. 14.00 (*0-374-31755-0*) FS&G.

Dear Ellen: Two Mormon Women & Their Letters. Ed. by S. George Ellsworth. LC 73-91999. 92p. 1974. 11.95 (*0-941214-33-8*) Signature Bks.

***Dear Emily.** Fern Michaels. 512p. 1995. mass mkt. 5.99 (*0-8217-4952-8*) Zebra.

Dear Empire State Building: 13 Tales of Sex & Apocalypse in New York. Kirpal Gordon. (Illus.). 112p. (Orig.). (C). 1990. pap. 9.95 (*0-9623693-1-4*) Heaven Bone Pr.

Dear Enemies: A Dialogue on French & English Canada. Gwethalyn Graham & Solange C. Rolland. 1965. 10.00 (*0-8159-5300-3*) Devin.

Dear Enemy. Jean Webster. 19.95 (*0-8488-0324-8*) Amereon Ltd.

Dear Family. Edith Schaeffer. 428p. 1989. 18.95 (*0-685-29538-9*) Harper SF.

Dear Family. Zig Ziglar. LC 84-3180. 216p. 1984. 15.95 (*0-88289-416-1*) Pelican.

Dear Family. large type ed. Camilla R. Bittle. 388p. 1992. reprint ed. lib. bdg. 18.95 (*1-56054-294-2*) Thorndike Pr.

Dear Fanny: Women's Letters to & from New South Wales, 1788-1857. Helen Heney. 1988. text ed. 32.00 (*0-08-029876-1*, Pergamon Pr) Elsevier.

Dear Father - Dear Son: The Correspondence of John D. Rockefeller & John D. Rockefeller, Jr. Intro. by Joseph W. Ernst. (Illus.). 228p. (C). 1994. 25.00 (*0-8232-1559-8*) Fordham.

Dear Father...Letters to Frederick Douglass from his Children. Ed. by Mark A. Cooper. write for info. (*0-318-68429-2*) Fulmore Pr.

Dear Folks at Home: The Writings of Harold M. Gowin. Harold M. Gowin & Ruby A. Gowin. (Illus.). 216p. (Orig.). 1988. pap. 9.95 (*0-942323-04-1*) N Amer Heritage Pr.

Dear Fred. Susanna Rodell. LC 94-19926. (Illus.). (J). 1995. 13.95 (*0-395-71544-X*) Ticknor & Flds Bks Yng Read.

***Dear Freud.** Fran C. Goodman. 200p. 1995. 10.95 (*0-9643473-2-6*) Francie PR.

Dear Friend. Carol Amen. (Outreach Ser.). 31p. 1986. pap. 0.15 (*0-8163-0662-1*) Pacific Pr Pub Assn.

Dear Friend: Mastering the Art of Direct-Mail Fund Raising. 2nd ed. Ed. by Kay P. Lautman & Henry Goldstein. 378p. 1991. 70.00 (*0-930807-18-9*, 600301) Fund Raising.

Dear Friend Anna: The Civil War Letters of a Common Soldier from Maine. Abial H. Edwards. Ed. by Beverly H. Kallgren & James L. Crouthamel. LC 92-8232. (Illus.). 173p. (C). 1992. 21.95 (*0-89101-079-3*) U Maine Pr.

Dear Friend, I Love You. Mary Katherine MacDougall. 176p. (Orig.). 1986. pap. 9.95 (*0-87707-226-4*) Now Comns.

Dear Friends. Reginald Rose. 1968. pap. 4.75 (*0-8222-0287-5*) Dramatists Play.

***Dear Future People.** Anne Nolting. (Orig.). (YA). (gr. 7 up). 1995. lib. bdg. write for info. (*0-88092-288-5*); pap. write for info. (*0-88092-287-7*) Royal Fireworks.

Dear Gandhi, Now What? Jim Douglass & Shelley Douglass. (Illus.). 108p. (Orig.). 1988. 26.95 (*0-86571-124-0*); pap. 6.95 (*0-86571-125-9*) New Soc Pubs.

Dear General: Eisenhower's Wartime Letters to Marshall. Dwight D. Eisenhower. Ed. by Joseph P. Hobbs. LC 72-123573. 267p. reprint ed. pap. 76.10 (*0-318-34948-5*, 2030745) Bks Demand.

***Dear General: The Private Letters of Annie E. Kennedy & John Bidwell, 1866-1868.** Ed. by Linda Rawlings. LC 93-74235. (Illus.). 212p. 1994. text ed. 19.95 (*0-941925-12-9*) Cal Parks Rec.

Dear Gift of Life: A Man's Encounter with Death. Bradford Smith. LC 65-24496. (Orig.). 1965. pap. 3.00 (*0-87574-142-8*) Pendle Hill.

***Dear Gladys.** Sharp. 1995. pap. 15.00 (*0-919123-36-8*) Atrium Pubs.

Dear God. M. Rogers. (My First Prayers Ser.). 12p. (J). (ps). 1994. bds. 2.98 (*0-86112-218-6*) Brimax Bks.

Dear God: Children's Letters to God. David Heller. LC 94-6938. 160p. 1994. pap. 9.00 (*0-399-52142-9*, Perigree Bks) Berkley Pub.

Dear God, Bless Our Food. Annie Fitzgerald. LC 84-71372. (Dear God Bks.). 16p. (Orig.). (J). (ps-4). 1984. pap. 1.99 (*0-8066-2108-7*, 10-1859, Augsburg) Augsburg Fortress.

Dear God, Good Morning. Annie Fitzgerald. LC 84-71377. (Dear God Bks.). 16p. (Orig.). (J). (ps-4). 1984. pap. 1.99 (*0-8066-2104-4*, 10-1860, Augsburg) Augsburg Fortress.

Dear God, Good Night. Annie Fitzgerald. LC 84-71374. (Dear God Bks.). 16p. (J). (ps-4). 1984. pap. 1.99 (*0-8066-2105-2*, 10-1861, Augsburg) Augsburg Fortress.

Dear God, Help! Love, Earl. Barbara Park. LC 92-20909. 108p. (J). (gr. 3-7). 1994. pap. 3.99 (*0-679-85395-2*) Random Bks Yng Read.

Dear God, I Just Love Birthdays. Annie Fitzgerald. LC 84-71371. (Dear God Bks.). 16p. (Orig.). (J). (ps-4). 1984. pap. 1.99 (*0-8066-2107-9*, 10-1862, Augsburg) Augsburg Fortress.

Dear God, I Like Summer. Illus. by Annie Fitzgerald. LC 87-72252. (Dear God Bks.: Series 3). 16p. (Orig.). 1987. pap. 1.99 (*0-8066-2294-6*, 10-1866, Augsburg) Augsburg Fortress.

Dear God, I Need You. Annie Fitzgerald. LC 87-72250. (Dear God Bks.: Series 3). (Illus.). 16p. (Orig.). 1987. pap. 1.99 (*0-8066-2292-X*, 10-1869, Augsburg) Augsburg Fortress.

Dear God, I Wonder. Illus. by Annie Fitzgerald. LC 87-72248. (Dear God Bks.: Series 3). 16p. (Orig.). 1987. pap. 1.99 (*0-8066-2289-X*, 10-1871, Augsburg) Augsburg Fortress.

Dear God, I'm Divorced! Dialogs with God. Sara A. Thrash. 136p. (Orig.). 1991. pap. 7.99 (*0-8010-8898-4*) Baker Bk.

An Asterisk (*) at the beginning of an entry indicates that the title is appearing in BIP for the first time.

An Asterisk (*) at the beginning of an entry indicates that the title is appearing in BIP for the first time.

1827

Dear Peter Rabbit: Querido Pedrin. Alma F. Ada. Tr. by Rosa Zubizarreta. LC 93-8459. (Illus.). 40p. (J). (ps-3). 1994. English ed. text ed. 14.95 (*0-689-31850-2*, Atheneum Bks Young); Spanish ed. text ed. 14.95 (*0-689-31915-0*, Atheneum Bks Young) S&S Childrens.

Dear, Please...Could You Fix My Vacuum? Florencio O. Garcia. (Illus.). 82p. 1992. pap. 13.00 (*0-929928-13-X*) Fog Pubns.

Dear Princess. Mary M. Landis. 1973. 8.00 (*0-317-00267-8*) Rod & Staff.

Dear Professor. large type ed. Sara Seale. 304p. 1984. 21.95 (*0-7089-1146-3*) Ulverscroft.

Dear Progeny. Michael F. Keleher. 720p. 1992. 40.00 (*0-9632949-0-3*) Value Quest Grp.

Dear Prue's Husband, & Other People. Joseph J. Reilly. LC 68-8487. (Essay Index Reprint Ser.). 1977. 21.95 (*0-8369-0816-3*) Ayer.

Dear Psychic: A New Perspective on Life's Everyday Problems. Pat McAnaney. LC 92-31487. 167p. (Orig.). 1993. 9.95 (*1-878217-07-0*) Victory Press.

***Dear Purchase: A Theme in German Modernism.** J. P. Stern. (Studies in German). 468p. (C). 1995. 64.95 (*0-521-43330-4*) Cambridge U Pr.

***Dear Rachel: The Civil War Letters of Daniel Peck.** Daniel Peck. Ed. by Martha G. Stanford. LC 93-87081. (Illus.). 69p. (Orig.). 1993. pap. 6.00 (*0-9639704-0-2*) Devon Press.

Dear Rafe. Rolando Hinojosa. LC 84-72299. 136p. (Orig.). 1985. pap. 8.50 (*0-934770-38-7*) Arte Publico.

Dear Reader. Haskel Dyer & Norma J. Dyer. 172p. (Orig.). 1993. pap. text ed. 12.95 (*0-930161-00-9*) St of the Art Bk.

Dear Rebecca, Winter Is Here. Jean C. George. LC 92-9515. (Illus.). 32p. (J). (ps-3). 1993. 15.00 (*0-06-021139-3*); lib. bdg. 14.89 (*0-06-021140-7*) HarpC Child Bks.

***Dear Remembered World.** Meta Lilienthal. (American Autobiography Ser.). 248p. 1995. reprint ed. lib. bdg. 79.00 (*0-7812-8577-1*) Rprt Serv.

***Dear Robert, I'll See You at the Crossroads: A Project by Renee Stout.** Marla C. Berns & George Lipstiz. LC 95-15975. 1995. pap. write for info. (*0-942006-27-5*) U of CA Art.

Dear Russ & Rebecca: Letters to Parents & Others Interested in Natural Childbirth. Diana Davies. Ed. by Carrie Teasdale. 320p. (Orig.). 1986. pap. 9.95 (*0-251-93704-6*) Another Way.

Dear Russell-Dear Jourdain: A Commentary on Russall's Logic Based on His Correspondence with Philip Jourdain. Ed. by Ivor Grattan-Guinnes. LC 77-9431. 234p. 1977. text ed. 44.00 (*0-231-04460-7*) Col U Pr.

Dear Ruth. Norman Krasna. 1945. pap. 4.75 (*0-8222-0288-3*) Dramatists Play.

Dear Ruth. Christine Kyle. LC 91-61588. 1992. pap. 12.95 (*0-87212-250-6*) Libra.

Dear Santa. (Illus.). 5p. (J). (gr. k-3). 1991. 9.95 (*0-8167-2455-5*) Troll Assocs.

Dear Santa. Illus. by Patricia D. Ludlow. LC 93-28618. (J). 1993. 11.95 (*0-85953-778-1*) Childs Play.

Dear Santa Chubby Board Book. Alan Benjamin. (J). (ps-6). 1993. pap. 3.95 (*0-671-87068-8*, Litl Simon S&S) S&S Childrens.

Dear Santa Claus. (Play - a - Sound Ser.). (Illus.). 24p. (J). 1993. 12.98 (*0-7853-0136-4*) Pubns Intl Ltd.

Dear Santa, Make Me a Star. Stephen Roos. (Maple Street Kids Ser.). (Illus.). 96p. (J). (gr. 2-6). 1991. per., pap. 1.95 (*0-89486-764-4*, 5174A) Hazelden.

Dear Scott Dear Max: The Fitzgerald-Perkins Correspondence. John Kuehl. (Hudson River Editions Ser.). 288p. 1991. text ed. 65.00 (*0-02-538481-3*) Macmillan.

***Dear Sister.** John Hell. (YA). 1994. pap. 3.99 (*0-06-106282-0*) HarpC Child Bks.

Dear Sister. Francine Pascal. (Sweet Valley High Ser.: No. 7). (J). (gr. 7 up). 1984. pap. 3.50 (*0-553-27672-7*) Bantam.

Dear Sister: Medieval Women & the Epistolary Genre. Ed. by Karen Cherewatuk & Ulrike Wiethaus. (Middle Ages Ser.). 232p. (Orig.). (C). 1993. text ed. 32.95 (*0-8122-3170-8*); pap. text ed. 14.95 (*0-8122-1437-4*) U of Pa Pr.

Dear Son, about Your Wedding: A Guide for the Groom-to-Be. Nancy Robison. 1989. pap. 5.95 (*0-671-67329-7*, Fireside) S&S Trade.

***Dear Sos: Thirty Years of Recipe Requests to the Los Angeles Times.** Rose Dosti. 1994. pap. 18.95 (*1-883792-06-1*) LA Times.

Dear Stephen: A Mother's Letters to Her Teenage Son, Following His Suicide. Anne Downey. (C). 1990. pap. 24.00 (*0-85305-281-6*, Pub. by J Arthur Ltd UK) St Mut.

Dear Stieglitz, Dear Love. Ed. by Ann L. Morgan. LC 87-5030. (American Art Ser.). (Illus.). 536p. 1988. 85.00 (*0-87413-292-4*) U Delaware Pr.

Dear Store: An Affectionate Portrait of Rich's. Celestine Sibley. LC 90-7289. (Illus.). 152p. 1990. reprint ed. 12.95 (*1-56145-000-6*) Peachtree Pubs.

Dear Tabby. B. Carlson. (Illus.). 83p. 1993. pap. 5.95 (*1-878488-78-3*) Quixote Pr IA.

Dear Tabby. Joy Dueland. (Illus.). (J). (gr. 4-8). 1978. pap. 2.50 (*0-931942-02-0*) Phunn Pubs.

***Dear Tabby: Feline Advice on Love, Life, & the Pursuit of Mice.** Leigh W. Rutledge. LC 94-33413. 192p. 1995. 10.95 (*0-525-93944-X*, Dutton) NAL-Dutton.

Dear Tabby: Letters from the Purr-Plexed. Rosalind Welcher. (Illus.). 72p. (Orig.). 1989. pap. 5.95 (*0-685-53752-8*) West Hill Pr.

Dear Teacher. Paul Brownlow. 1993. 4.99 (*1-877719-60-9*) Brownlow Pub Co.

***Dear Ted - Letters to a Senator.** Dorothy M. Benner. 92p. 1994. pap. 9.75 (*0-9636317-0-5*) Natl Fnd Better Wrld.

***Dear Teddy Bear.** Dorothy I. Murray. 12p. 1994. pap. 5.99 (*0-925037-19-2*) Great Lks Poetry.

Dear Terry. Joyce Voelker. (Light Line Ser.). (Illus.). 97p. (Orig.). (J). (gr. 3-6). 1990. pap. 5.95 (*0-89084-526-3*) Bob Jones Univ Pr.

Dear Theo: Autobiography of Vincent van Gogh. Irving Stone. 1969. pap. 5.99 (*0-451-16246-3*) NAL-Dutton.

***Dear Theo: The Autobiography of Vincent Van Gogh.** Ed. by Irving Stone & Jean Stone. 480p. 1995. 13.95 (*0-452-27504-0*, Plume) NAL-Dutton.

Dear Theo: The Autobiography of Vincent Van Gogh. Vincent Van Gogh. Ed. by Irving Stone. 1969. pap. 4.95 (*0-451-14098-2*, E9598, Sig) NAL-Dutton.

Dear Timothy Tibbitts. Judith R. Enderle & Stephanie G. Tessler. LC 94-14412. (Illus.). (J). (gr. 3 up). 1995. text ed. 13.95 (*0-02-733384-1*, Mac Bks Young Read) S&S Childrens.

Dear Tokens. Gomer Pr. Staff. (C). 1987. pap. 20.00x (*0-86383-311-X*, Pub. by Gomer Pr UK) St Mut.

Dear Tom: Letters to an Enquiring Christian. John D. Legg. 1990. pap. 3.99 (*0-85234-275-6*, Pub. by Evangel Pr UK) Presby & Reformed.

Dear Uncle Dave. Yuri E. Norton. (Illus.). 40p. (Orig.). (J). (gr. 1 up). 1993. lib. bdg. 13.95 (*0-9622808-4-4*) S&T Waring.

***Dear Uncle Go: Male Homosexuality in Thailand. rev. ed. Peter A. Jackson. 352p. (Orig.). 1995. pap. text ed. write for info. (*0-942777-11-5*) Bua Luang Pub.**
A revised edition of MALE HOMOSEXUALITY IN THAILAND: AN INTERPRETATION OF CONTEMPORARY THAI SOURCES (1989, Global Academic Publishers). This is the first systematic study of homoeroticism in the nonhomophobic culture of Thailand. Jackson's sources include translated letters from gay men to an advice columnist, UNCLE GO, appearing in a nationally circulated mainstream publication as well as Thai gay & mainstream publications to further analyze the social attitudes toward homoeroticism & the development of Thai gay identity. Introduction by Dr. Gilbert Herdt. To order: International Wavelength Inc., 2215-R Market St., #829, San Francisco, CA 94114, (415) 864-6522 FAX (415) 864-6615. ***Publisher Provided Annotation.***

Dear Wife: Letters of a Civil War Soldier. Ed. by Jack C. Davis. 238p. 1992. pap. 14.95 (*0-9624086-4-6*) Sulgrave Pr.

Dear Willie Rudd. Libba M. Gray. LC 92-25064. (Illus.). (YA). 1993. pap. 14.00 (*0-671-79774-3*, S&S Bks Young Read) S&S Childrens.

Dear Wit. H. Jack Lang. 256p. 1990. 17.95 (*0-685-31178-3*, Websters New Wrld); pap. 9.95 (*0-685-31179-1*, Websters New Wrld) P-H Gen Ref & Trav.

Dear Wit: Letters from the World's Wits. H. Jack Lang. 1990. 17.95 (*0-13-961707-8*) P-H.

Dear World. (Illus.). 1982. 7.95 (*0-88188-070-1*, 00383360) H Leonard.

Dear World: A Message of Hope. . .for Everyday Human Hearts. Pam Trout. LC 91-16003. (Illus.). (Orig.). 1991. pap. 5.00 (*0-915541-82-3*) Star Bks Inc.

Dear World: How Children Around the World Feel about Our Environment. Ed. by Lannis Temple. LC 92-29929. Orig. Title: Where Would We Sleep?. (Illus.). 152p. (J). (gr. k up). 1993. pap. 15.00 (*0-679-84403-1*) Random Bks Yng Read.

Dear You. Donald R. Robertson. 212p. 1989. write for info. (*0-8499-0677-6*) Word Inc.

Dear Zoo. Rod Campbell. 1987. pap. 4.99 (*0-14-050446-X*, Puffin) Puffin Bks.

Dear Zoo. Rod Campbell. LC 82-83224. (Illus.). 22p. (J). (ps-1). 1986. pap. 10.95 (*0-02-716440-3*, Four Winds Pr) S&S Childrens.

Dear Zoo. Rod Campbell. (Illus.). 24p. (J). (ps-1). 1988. bds. 3.95 (*0-689-71230-8*, Aladdin Paperbacks) S&S Childrens.

Dear Zoo. Rod Campbell. (J). (ps-00). 1987. reprint ed. pap. 4.95 (*0-317-62180-7*, Puffin) Puffin Bks.

***Dear Zoradu.** John H. Walker. (Illus.). 120p. 1995. write for info. (*0-9623780-7-0*) Ars Obscura.

Dearborn Investment Companion: A Worldwide Guide to Investment Performance. 2nd ed. Gordon K. Williamson. 208p. 1991. pap. 22.95 (*0-7931-0274-X*, 5608-15) Dearborn Finan.

Dearest Andrew: Letters from Vita Sackville-West to Andrew Reiber. Vita Sackville-West. Ed. by Nancy Macknight. 1984. pap. 7.95 (*0-913006-32-7*) Puckerbrush.

Dearest Baby. Diane Muldrow. (Golden Sturdy Shape Bks.). (Illus.). 14p. (J). (ps). 1993. bds. 3.95 (*0-307-12394-4*, 12394, Golden Pr) Western Pub.

***Dearest Beloved: The Hawthornes & the Making of the Middle-Class Family.** Walter T. Herbert. 1993. 28.00 (*0-520-07587-0*) U CA Pr.

***Dearest Beloved: The Hawthornes & the Making of the Middle-Class Family.** Walter T. Herbert. (The New Historicism: Studies in Cultural Poetics: Vol.24). (Illus.). 331p. 1995. pap. 15.00 (*0-520-20155-8*) U CA Pr.

***Dearest Brothers, Love Awaits, Much Peace, the Sisters: African American Women Talk about Sex, Love & Life.** Courtney Long. LC 94-22167. 1995. 21.95 (*0-553-09702-4*) Bantam.

Dearest Children. Ruchoma Shain. LC 92-13103. 1992. 17.95 (*0-87306-610-3*) Feldheim.

Dearest Chums & Partners: Joel Chandler Harris's Letters to His Children: a Domestic Biography. Joel C. Harris. Ed. by Hugh T. Keenan. LC 92-8235. (Illus.). 576p. 1993. 39.95 (*0-8203-1480-3*) U of Ga Pr.

Dearest Emilie: The Love Letters of Sir Wilfred Laurier to Madame Emilie Lavergne. Intro. by Charles Fisher. 160p. 1989. 24.95 (*1-55021-056-4*, Pub. by NC Press CN) U of Toronto Pr.

***Dearest Enemy.** Alexandra Sellers. (Intimate Moments Ser.). 1995. mass mkt. 3.75 (*0-373-07635-5*, 1-07635-5) Silhouette.

Dearest Enemy. Alfred Shaughnessy. 264p. 1991. 24.95 (*0-907018-81-5*, Pub. by Tabb Hse Pubs UK) Seven Hills Bk.

Dearest Enemy. large type ed. Carol Marsh. 268p. 1989. 17.95 (*0-7089-1934-0*) Ulverscroft.

Dearest Father: The Civil War Letters of Lt. Frank Dickerson, a Son of Belfast, Maine. Frank W. Dickerson. Ed. by H. Draper Hunt. LC 92-28299. (Illus.). (Orig.). 1992. pap. 14.95 (*0-945980-36-1*) Nrth Country Pr.

Dearest Goddess. Eso Benjamins. 128p. (Orig.). 1985. pap. text ed. 7.95 (*0-9615413-1-8*) Current Nine Pub.

Dearest Isa: Robert Browning's Letters to Isabella Blagden. Robert Browning. Ed. by Edward C. McAleer. 440p. reprint ed. pap. 125.40 (*0-8357-7712-X*, 2036069) Bks Demand.

Dearest Isabel: Letters from an Enlisted Man in World War II. Sidney Bowen. (Illus.). 232p. 1992. 18.95 (*0-89745-150-3*) Sunflower U Pr.

Dearest Isabella: The Life & Letters of Isabella Ferguson, 1819-1910. Prue Joske. 1990. pap. 19.95 (*0-85564-262-9*, Pub. by Univ of West Aust Pr AT) Intl Spec Bk.

Dearest It's Time see Beyond My Fear

***Dearest Julie Denise.** Rafael Garcia. 1995. 14.95 (*0-533-11162-5*) Vantage.

***Dearest Love: (Sealed with a Kiss)** Betty Neels. (Romance Ser.). 1995. mass mkt. 2.99 (*0-373-03355-9*, 1-03355-4) Harlequin Bks.

***Dearest Mary Jane.** large type ed. Betty Neals. (Harlequin Romance Ser.). 1995. 18.95 (*0-263-14076-8*, Pub. by Mills & Boon UK) Thorndike Pr.

Dearest Mother: The Letter of F. R. Kendall. F. R. Kendall. Ed. by Brian MacDonald. 173p. (Orig.). 1988. pap. 20.00 (*1-85044-220-7*) Lloyds London Pr.

Dearest Pet: On Bestiality. Midas Dekkers. 1994. 29.95 (*0-86091-462-3*, Pub. by Verso UK) Routledge Chapman & Hall.

***Dearest Phylabe: Letters from Wartime England by Edith Base.** Ed. by Benjamin Byerley & Catherine R. Byerley. 176p. 1996. write for info. (*0-614-06700-6*) Univ Pr Colo.

Dearest Tiger. large type ed. Edna Dawes. (Linford Romance Library). 320p. 1985. pap. 11.95 (*0-7089-6122-3*, Trailtree Bookshop) Ulverscroft.

Dearest Traitor. Patricia Wilson. (Presents Ser.). 1994. mass mkt. 2.99 (*0-373-11685-3*, 1-11685-4) Harlequin Bks.

***Dearest Wilding: A Memoir, with Love Letters from Theodore Dreiser.** Yvette Eastman. Ed. & Anno. by Thomas P. Riggio. LC 95-1821. (Illus.). 176p. 1995. text ed. 21.95 (*0-8122-3311-5*) U of Pa Pr.

Dearie Dot: A Keepsake Book. Illus. by Connie Ross. 32p. (J). (ps up). 1992. pap. 2.75 (*1-878893-25-4*) Telcraft Bks.

***Dearing Tracks Throughout America.** Betty V. Dearing. 400p. 1994. lib. bdg. 60.00 (*0-614-00585-X*) B V Dearing.

Dearly Beloved. Mary J. Putney. 416p. (Orig.). 1990. pap. 4.99 (*0-451-40185-9*) NAL-Dutton.

Dearly Beloved. Anne M. Lindbergh. 202p. 1991. reprint ed. lib. bdg. 28.95x (*0-89966-790-2*) Buccaneer Bks.

Dearly Beloved: The Secrets of Successful Marriage & The Parent Your Parents Were Not. J. Zink. 123p. 1988. Marriage, 123p. 19.95 (*0-942490-06-1*); Parenting, 226p. write for info. (*0-942490-17-7*) J Zink.

***Dearly Beloved Wedding Album.** Illus. by Kathy Orr. 64p. 1994. 20.00 (*0-8378-2243-2*) Gibson.

***Dearly Beloved Wedding Guest Book.** Illus. by Kathy Orr. 48p. 1994. 13.00 (*0-614-04419-7*) Gibson.

***Dearly Beloved Wedding Organizer.** Illus. by Kathy Orr. 1994. 20.00 (*0-8378-2245-9*) Gibson.

Dearly Beloved-Wedding Songs. Ed. by Denes Agay. 1959. pap. 8.95 (*0-8256-4162-4*) Music Sales.

Dearly Departed. David Bottrell & Jessie Jones. 1992. pap. 4.75 (*0-8222-1303-6*) Dramatists Play.

Death. James O'Barr. (Crow Ser.: No. 3). (Illus.). 64p. (Orig.). 1992. pap. 4.95 (*1-879450-75-5*) Tundra MA.

Death. C. H. Spurgeon. 1978. pap. 3.00 (*1-56186-411-0*) Pilgrim Pubns.

Death. Gail Stewart. LC 89-31257. (Facts About Ser.). (Illus.). 48p. (J). (gr. 5-6). 1989. text ed. 12.95 (*0-89686-446-4*, Crstwood Hse) Silver Burdett Pr.

Death. Maurice Maeterlinck. Ed. by Robert Kastenbaum. LC 76-19581. (Death & Dying Ser.). 1977. reprint ed. lib. bdg. 19.95 (*0-405-09577-5*) Ayer.

Death: A Part of Life. rev. ed. George G. Otero & Zoanne Harris. (Illus.). 147p. (gr. 4-12). 1981. pap. 12.00 (*0-943804-10-8*) U of Denver Teach.

Death: A Primer for All Ages. Sandra L. Bertman. (Illus.). 60p. 1990. pap. 6.95 (*0-930194-21-7*) Ctr Thanatology.

Death: Beyond Whole-Brain Criteria. Ed. by Richard M. Zaner. (C). 1988. lib. bdg. 104.00 (*1-55608-053-0*) Kluwer Ac.

Death: Completion & Discovery. Charles A. Corr & Richard Pacholski. ix, 298p. (Orig.). 1987. pap. 14.95 (*0-9607394-4-0*) Assn Death Educ.

Death: Confronting the Reality. William E. Phipps. LC 86-45405. 204p. (Orig.). 1987. pap. 13.99 (*0-8042-0487-X*, John Knox) Westminster John Knox.

Death: Current Perspectives. 3rd ed. Ed. by Edwin S. Shneidman. 1984. pap. text ed. 32.95 (*0-87484-713-3*) Mayfield Pub.

***Death: Current Perspectives.** 4th ed. John B. Williamson & Edwin S. Shneidman. LC 94-25375. 487p. (C). 1994. pap. 30.95 (*1-55934-011-8*) Mayfield Pub.

Death: Graduation to Glory. C. S. Lovett. 1974. pap. 6.25 (*0-938148-20-6*) Prsnl Christianity.

Death: In the Land of the Living Dead. 4th ed. Prentiss Tucker. Ed. by Rosicrucian Fellowship Staff. 168p. 1975. reprint ed. pap. text ed. 5.75 (*0-911274-83-9*) Rosicrucian.

Death: Index of Modern Information. Lillian B. Sheridan. LC 88-47555. 150p. 1988. 39.50 (*0-88164-864-7*); pap. 34.50 (*0-88164-865-5*) ABBE Pubs Assn.

Death: The Beginning of Life. Terry Chitwood. Ed. by Deb Chitwood. 78p. (Orig.). 1988. pap. 9.95 (*0-942044-04-5*) Polestar.

Death: The Causes & Phenomena with Special Reference to Immortality. Hereward Carrington. Ed. by Robert Kastenbaum. LC 76-19563. (Death & Dying Ser.). 1977. lib. bdg. 30.95 (*0-405-09559-7*) Ayer.

Death: The Final Frontier. Dale V. Hardt. (Illus.). 1979. 13.95 (*0-685-03821-1*) P-H.

Death: The Final Stage of Growth. Elisabeth Kubler-Ross. 1986. pap. 9.00 (*0-671-62238-2*, Touchstone Bks) S&S Trade.

Death: The Great Adventure. Alice A. Bailey. 1985. pap. 8.00 (*0-85330-138-7*) Lucis.

Death: The High Cost of Living. Neil Gaiman. Ed. by Bob Kahan. (Illus.). 104p. 1994. pap. 12.95 (*1-56389-133-6*, Vertigo) DC Comics.

Death: The Trip of a Lifetime. Greg Palmer. LC 92-56122. 224p. 1993. 15.00 (*0-06-250802-4*) Harper SF.

Death: The Trip of a Lifetime. Greg Palmer. 1995. pap. 12.00 (*0-06-250803-2*, PL) HarpC.

Death: Volumes 3, 3a, 3b, 3 vols. Marshalll Houts & Irwin H. Haut. (Courtroom Medicine Ser.). 1966. Updates. ring bd. write for info. (*0-8205-1236-2*) Bender.

Death: Words of Comfort. Nancy McCormack. 82p. 1986. 35.00 (*0-7223-2029-9*, Pub. by A H S Ltd UK) St Mut.

Death, After Life, & the Soul. Intro. by Lawrence E. Sullivan. (Readings from the Encyclopedia of Religion Ser.). (Orig.). (C). 1989. pap. 12.95 (*0-02-897403-4*) Macmillan.

Death American Style. Ryder Stacy. (Doomsday Warrior Ser.: No. 12). 1987. pap. 2.50 (*0-8217-2211-5*) Zebra.

Death among Strangers. Deidre S. Laiken. 256p. 1988. pap. 3.95 (*0-380-70521-4*) Avon.

Death among the Artists. J. D. Forbes. 237p. 1993. 35.00 (*0-86332-864-4*, Pub. by Bk Guild Ltd UK) St Mut.

***Death Among the Dons.** Neel. (Illus.). (J). 1995. mass mkt. 5.50 (*0-671-89952-X*) PB.

Death among the Dons. Janet Neel. 240p. 1993. 19.95 (*0-312-10450-2*) St Martin.

Death among the Dons. large type ed. Janet Neel. LC 94-14548. 369p. 1994. 20.95 (*0-8161-7439-3*) Hall.

Death among the Lilacs. Adeline Palen. 218p. (Orig.). 1987. pap. 5.95 (*0-9619488-0-9*) Blue Spruce Pr.

Death & After. Annie Besant. 1972. 7.50 (*81-7059-178-3*) Theos Pub Hse.

Death & After. Manly P. Hall. pap. 4.00 (*0-89314-312-X*) Philos Res.

Death & Afterlife. Ed. by Stephen T. Davis. 240p. 1990. text ed. 39.95 (*0-312-03537-3*) St Martin.

Death & Afterlife: Perspectives of World Religion. Ed. by Hiroshi Obayash. LC 91-3876. (Contributions to the Study of Religion Ser.: No. 33). 240p. 1991. text ed. 55.00 (*0-313-27906-3*, ODE, Greenwood Pr); pap. text ed. 17.95 (*0-275-94104-3*, B4104, Greenwood Pr) Greenwood.

Death & Afterward. H. A. Ironside. LC 89-36835. 1989. Pkg. of 5. pap. 12.50 (*0-87213-552-7*); pap. 2.50 (*0-87213-346-X*) Loizeaux.

Death & Attitudes Towards Death. Stacey B. Day. LC 72-76821. Orig. Title: Proceedings A Symposium of the Bell Museum, Univ. of Minn. Med. School. 94p. (Orig.). 1984. reprint ed. 10.00 (*0-934314-76-4*) Intl Found Biosocial Dev.

Death & Beyond: Answers to Teens' Questions about Death, Reincarnation, Ghosts, & the Afterlife. Jim Watkins. LC 93-9702. 1993. 8.99 (*0-8423-1278-1*) Tyndale.

Death & Beyond in the Eastern Perspective. Jung Y. Lee. LC 73-85065. 112p. 1974. text ed. 62.00 (*0-677-05010-0*) Gordon & Breach.

***Death & Birth, Heaven & Earth.** Katherine B. MacLaurin. 470p. 1995. pap. 12.95 (*0-7610-0128-X*) NW Pub.

Death & Birth of Judaism: The Impact of Christianity, Secularism, & the Holocaust on Jewish Faith. Jacob Neusner. LC 92-41013. (USF Studies in the History of Judaism: No. 66). 380p. 1993. reprint ed. pap. 54.95 (*1-55540-811-7*, 24 00 66) Scholars Pr GA.

Death & Burial in Christian Antiquity. Alfred C. Rush. 1972. 250.00 (*0-8490-0009-2*) Gordon Pr.

***Death & Burial in Medieval Europe.** Michael Muller-Wille. (Illus.). 71p. (Orig.). 1993. pap. 29.00x (*91-22-01575-2*, Pub. by Almqv & Wiksell SW) Coronet Bks.

Death & Celebrity. Ed. by Janet Cave. (True Crime Ser.). (Illus.). 176p. 1993. 14.99 (*0-7835-0025-4*); lib. bdg. 17.45 (*0-7835-0026-2*) Time-Life.

Death & Children: A Guide for Educators, Parents & Caregivers. Ed. by Stephen V. Gullo et al. 210p. 1985. 21.95 (*0-930194-15-2*) Ctr Thanatology.

An Asterisk (*) at the beginning of an entry indicates that the title is appearing in BIP for the first time.

D

Death & Consciousness. David H. Lund. LC 84-43211. 204p. 1985. lib. bdg. 27.50x (*0-89950-140-0*) McFarland & Co.

Death & Creativity: An Interdisciplinary Encounter. Florence M. Hetzler. pap. 6.50 (*0-686-11632-1*) Westmail Pr.

Death & Damnation. Staley Krause et al. 400p. 1994. pap. 4.99 (*1-56504-126-7*, 04126) White Wolf.

***Death & Deconstruction.** Anne Fleming. LC 95-8570. 1995. write for info. (*0-312-13046-5*) St Martin.

***Death & Deliverance: "Euthansasia" in Germany c. 1900-1945.** Michael Burleigh. (Illus.). 398p. (C). 1995. 59.95 (*0-521-41613-2*); pap. 18.95 (*0-521-47769-7*) Cambridge U Pr.

Death & Deliverance: The True Story of an Airplane Crash at the North Pole. Robert M. Lee. LC 92-54763. (Illus.). 288p. (Orig.). 1993. pap. 12.95 (*1-55591-140-4*) Fulcrum Pub.

Death & Desire: Psychoanalytic Theory in Lacan's Return to Freud. Richard Boothby. 281p. 1991. 42.50 (*0-415-90171-5*, A3542, Routledge NY); pap. 15.95 (*0-415-90172-3*, A3546, Routledge NY) Routledge.

Death & Desire: The Rhetoric of Gender in the Apocalypse of John. Tina Pippin. (Literary Currents in Biblical Interpretation Ser.). 144p. (Orig.). 1992. pap. 18.99 (*0-664-25157-9*) Westminster John Knox.

Death & Destiny in the Bible. Michael G. Wensing. 80p. (Orig.). 1993. 5.95 (*0-8146-2093-0*) Liturgical Pr.

Death & Dignity: Making Choices & Taking Charge. Timothy E. Quill. 196p. 1993. 21.95 (*0-393-03448-8*) Norton.

Death & Dignity: Making Choices & Taking Charge. Timothy E. Quill. 1994. pap. 10.95 (*0-393-31140-6*) Norton.

Death & Diplomacy in Persia. Iurri N. Tynianov. Tr. by A. Brown. LC 74-10092. (Illus.). 357p. 1975. reprint ed. 24.75 (*0-88355-178-0*) Hyperion Conn.

Death & Disaster: The Rise of the Warhol Empire & the Race for Andy's Millions. Paul Alexander. 1994. 23.00 (*0-679-43273-6*, Villard Bks) Random.

Death & Discrimination: Racial Disparities in Capital Sentencing. Samuel R. Gross & Robert Mauro. 268p. 1989. 35.00 (*1-55553-040-0*) NE U Pr.

Death & Disease in Southeast Asia: Explorations in Social, Medical & Demographic History. Ed. by Norman G. Owen. (Illus.). 297p. 1987. pap. 25.00 (*0-19-588853-7*) OUP.

Death & Dissymmetry: The Politics of Coherence in the Book of Judges. Mieke Bal. (Chicago Studies in the History of Judaism). (Illus.). 392p. 1988. lib. bdg. 49.95 (*0-226-03554-9*); pap. text ed. 16.95 (*0-226-03555-7*) U Ch Pr.

Death & Duplicity. John B. Carn. LC 88-51028. 200p. 1988. pap. 7.95 (*1-55523-176-4*) Winston-Derek.

Death & Dying. Dickie Hill. 1982. 4.75 (*0-89137-532-5*) Quality Pubns.

Death & Dying. Jean Knox. (Life Cycle Ser.). (Illus.). 112p. (YA). (gr. 6-12). 1989. 18.95 (*0-7910-0037-0*) Chelsea Hse.

Death & Dying, 40 vols., Set. Ed. by Robert Kastenbaum. (Illus.). 1977. lib. bdg. 1,041.50 (*0-405-09550-3*) Ayer.

Death & Dying, Vol. 3 (Incl. 1987-1991 Supplements) Ed. by Eleanor C. Goldstein. (Social Issues Resources Ser.). 1992. 95.00 (*0-89777-091-9*) Sirs Inc.

Death & Dying: A Bibliographical Survey. Comp. by Samuel Southard. LC 91-7222. (Bibliographies & Indexes in Religious Studies: No. 19). 560p. 1991. text ed. 79.50 (*0-313-26465-1*, SOY/, Greenwood Pr) Greenwood.

Death & Dying: Current Issues in the Treatment of the Dying Person. Leonard Pearson. LC 67-11483. 247p. reprint ed. pap. 70.40 (*0-317-10622-8*, 2002266) Bks Demand.

Death & Dying: Opposing Viewpoints. Ed. by William Dudley. LC 92-6667. (Opposing Viewpoints Ser.). (Illus.). 240p. (YA). (gr. 10 up). 1992. lib. bdg. 19.95 (*0-89908-192-4*); pap. text ed. 11.55 (*0-89908-167-3*) Greenhaven.

Death & Dying: Supplement 1974-1978. G Howard Poteet & Joseph C. Santora. 556p. 1989. 38.50 (*0-87875-351-6*) Whitston Pub.

Death & Dying: The Tibetan Tradition. Glenn H. Mullin. 272p. 1988. pap. 11.95 (*0-14-019013-9*, Arkana) Viking Penguin.

Death & Dying: Understanding & Care. 2nd ed. Barbara A. Backer et al. LC 92-42472. 349p. 1993. pap. text ed. 35.95 (*0-8273-4954-8*) Delmar.

Death & Dying: Values, Institutions, & Human Mortality. David W. Moller. (Illus.). 304p. (C). 1995. pap. text ed. 16.95 (*0-19-504296-4*) OUP.

Death & Dying: Values, Institutions, & Human Mortality. David W. Moller. (Illus.). 304p. (C). 1995. 45.00 (*0-19-504295-6*) OUP.

***Death & Dying: Who Decides.** Ed. by Alison Landes et al. (Reference Ser.). 168p. 1994. pap. text ed. 21.95 (*1-878623-81-8*) Info Plus TX.

Death & Dying Vol. 4: (Incl. 1992-94 Supplement) Ed. by Eleanor C. Goldstein. (Social Issues Resources Ser.). 1994. 57.00 (*0-89777-177-X*) Sirs Inc.

Death & Dying Education. Richard O. Ulin. LC 77-12278. (Developments in Classroom Instruction Ser.). 72p. reprint ed. pap. 25.00 (*0-317-55506-5*, 2029542) Bks Demand.

Death & Dying in Central Appalachia: Changing Attitudes & Practices. James K. Crissman. LC 93-23784. (Illus.). 288p. 1994. 39.95 (*0-252-02061-8*); pap. 13.95 (*0-252-06355-4*) U of Ill Pr.

Death & Dying in Children's & Young People's Literature: A Survey & Bibliography. Marian S. Pyles. LC 87-46386. 187p. 1988. lib. bdg. 28.50x (*0-89950-335-7*) McFarland & Co.

Death & Dying, Life & Living. Charles A. Corr et al. LC 93-3208. 1994. pap. 35.95 (*0-534-21138-0*) Brooks-Cole.

Death & Elizabethan Tragedy: A Study of Convention & Opinion in the Elizabethan Drama. Theodore Spencer. 1988. reprint ed. lib. bdg. 79.00 (*0-7812-0014-8*) Rprt Serv.

Death & Elizabethan Tragedy: A Study of Conventions & Opinions in the Elizabethan Drama. Theodore Spencer. 1985. reprint ed. 49.00 (*0-403-02468-4*) Scholarly.

Death & Eternal Life. John Hick. 496p. 1994. pap. 19.99 (*0-664-25509-4*) Westminster John Knox.

Death & Ethnicity: A Psychocultural Study. Ed. by Richard A. Kalish & David K. Reynolds. LC 81-65932. (Perspectives on Death & Dying Ser.: Vol. 4). 230p. (C). 1976. reprint ed. pap. text ed. 19.95x (*0-89503-021-7*) Baywood Pub.

***Death & Euthanasia in Jewish Law: Essays & Responsa.** Ed. by Walter Jacob & Moshe Zemer. Vol. IV. 224p. (Orig.). 1995. pap. 16.50 (*0-614-00605-8*) Rodef Shalom Pr.

***Death & Exile: The Ethnic Cleansing of Ottoman Muslims, 1821-1922.** Justin McCarthy. 384p. 1995. 35.00 (*0-87850-094-4*) Darwin Pr.

Death & Grief: A Guide for Clergy. Alan Wolfelt. LC 88-70009. 216p. 1988. text ed. 19.95 (*0-915202-76-X*) Accel Devel.

***Death & Grief: Poetic Commentary by Sol the Sage.** Sol Finkelman. LC 94-75362. 86p. 1994. pap. 12.95 (*0-9641973-0-8*) Genie Pubng.

Death & Grief: Selected Readings for the Medical Student. Ed. by David Peretz et al. LC 77-6195. 270p. 1977. pap. 6.95 (*0-930194-82-9*) Ctr Thanatology.

Death & Identity. 3rd ed. Ed. by Robert Fulton & Robert Bendiksen. LC 93-26364. 480p. (C). 1994. pap. 24.95 (*0-914783-63-7*) Charles.

Death & Illness. Leslie McGuire. (Family Ser.). (Illus.). 64p. (YA). (gr. 7 up). 1990. lib. bdg. 17.27 (*0-86593-079-1*); lib. bdg. 12.95 (*0-685-46439-3*) Rourke Corp.

Death & Jack Shade. large type ed. William S. Brady. Bd. with Hawk: Sierra Gold. 1984. 12.00 (*0-685-29749-7*) Ulverscroft.

***Death & Judgement.** Donna Leon. 1995. 20.00 (*0-06-017796-9*) HarpC.

Death & Justice Frescoes. David Cumberland. (Illus.). 96p. (Orig.). (C). 1972. 15.00 (*0-912846-26-7*); pap. 10.00 (*0-912846-27-5*) Bookstore Pr.

Death & Letters of Alice James: Selected Correspondence. Ed. by Ruth B. Yeazell. (Illus.). 200p. 1980. pap. 12.00 (*0-520-04963-2*) U CA Pr.

Death & Life. Joseph M. Donatelli. LC 88-62571. (Speculum Anniversary Monographs: No. 15). (Illus.). xii, 136p. 1989. 20.00 (*0-915651-01-7*); pap. 12.00 (*0-915651-02-5*) Medieval Acad.

Death & Life in Morazan: A Priest's Testimony from a War-Zone in El Salvador. Ed. by Maria L. Vigil. Tr. by Dinah Livingstone. 105p. (Orig.). 1989. pap. 8.95 (*1-85287-036-2*) EPICA.

Death & Life in the Tenth Century. Eleanor S. Duckett. (Ann Arbor Paperbacks Ser.). 376p. 1988. reprint ed. pap. text ed. 17.95x (*0-472-06172-0*, Ann Arbor Bks) U of Mich Pr.

Death & Life of Great American Cities. Jane Jacobs. 1963. pap. 10.00 (*0-394-70241-7*, Vin) Random.

Death & Life of Great American Cities. Jane Jacobs. LC 92-5008. 1992. pap. 12.00 (*0-679-74195-X*, Vin) Random.

Death & Life of Great American Cities. Jane Jacobs. LC 92-32407. 1993. 17.50 (*0-679-60047-7*, Modern Lib) Random.

Death & Life of Malcolm X. 2nd ed. Peter L. Goldman. LC 79-18105. (Blacks in the New World Ser.). 476p. 1979. reprint ed. pap. 12.95 (*0-252-00774-3*) U of Ill Pr.

Death & Life of Sherlock Holmes. Suzan L. Zeder. (Orig.). (YA). 1991. Playscript. pap. 6.00 (*0-87602-296-4*) Anchorage.

Death & Life of Sneaky Fitch: A Farcical Tragedy in Three Acts. James L. Rosenberg. 47p. 1987. reprint ed. pap. 4.75 (*0-8222-0289-1*) Dramatists Play.

***Death & Life of Superman.** Roger Stern. 1994. mass mkt. 5.99 (*0-553-56930-9*) Bantam.

Death & Life of Sylvia Plath. Ronald Hayman. 1991. 19.95 (*1-55972-068-9*, Birch Ln Pr) Carol Pub Group.

***Death & Life of the American Quality Movement.** Ed. by Robert E. Cole. (Illus.). 304p. 1995. 25.00 (*0-19-509206-6*) OUP.

***Death & Loss: Compassionate Approaches in the Classroom.** Oliver Leaman. (Cassell Studies in Pastoral Care & PSE). (Illus.). 160p. 1995. 60.00 (*0-304-33087-6*); pap. 19.95 (*0-304-33089-2*) Cassell.

Death & Loss: Reflections & Interventions from the Arts. Ed. by Sandra L. Bertman et al. (Current Thanatology Ser.). 120p. 1991. pap. 16.95 (*0-930194-47-0*) Ctr Thanatology.

***Death & Mourning.** Ed. by Hendrik M. Ruitenbeek. LC 95-3545. 1995. pap. 30.00 (*1-56821-527-4*) Aronson.

Death & Mourning: A Halakhic Guide. Abner Weiss. 1987. 22.50 (*0-88125-127-5*); pap. 14.95 (*0-88125-134-8*) Ktav.

Death & Neurosis. Joachim E. Meyer. Tr. by Margarete Nunberg. LC 73-19951. 147p. (C). 1975. text ed. 25.00 (*0-8236-1130-2*) Intl Univs Pr.

Death & Obituary Notices from the Southern Christian Advocate 1867-1878. Brent H. Holcomb. 1993. 40.00 (*0-913363-12-X*) SCMAR.

Death & Personal Survival: The Evidence for Life after Death. Robert Almeder. 288p. (C). 1992. text ed. 50.00 (*0-8476-7728-1*) Rowman.

Death & Personal Survival: The Evidence for Life after Death. Robert F. Almeder. 1992. pap. 17.95 (*0-8226-3016-8*) Littlefield.

Death & Postmortem Changes-Normal, Rare, Bizarre & Mysterious: Index of New Information. Willis S. Pelton. 150p. 1994. 44.50 (*0-7883-0054-7*); pap. 39.50 (*0-7883-0055-5*) ABBE Pubs Assn.

Death & Property in Siena, Twelve Hundred Five-Eighteen Hundred: Strategies for the Afterlife. Samuel K. Cohn, Jr. LC 88-35249. (Studies in Historical & Political Science: 10th Series, No. 2 (1988)). 352p. 1988. text ed. 49.50 (*0-8018-3594-1*) Johns Hopkins.

Death & Rebirth in Virgil's Arcadia. M. Owen Lee. LC 88-24824. (Classical Studies). 140p. (C). 1989. 59.50 (*0-7914-0016-6*); pap. 19.95 (*0-7914-0017-4*) State U NY Pr.

***Death & Rebirth of Religious Life.** Desmond Murphy. 1995. pap. 14.95 (*0-85574-126-0*, Pub. by E J Dwyer AT) Morehouse Pub.

Death & Rebirth of the Seneca. Anthony F. Wallace. 416p. 1972. pap. 7.16 (*0-394-71699-X*, Vin) Random.

Death & Reincarnation. Swami Jyotir Maya Nanda. (Illus.). 1970. 14.95 (*0-934664-04-8*) Yoga Res Foun.

Death & Reincarnation: Eternity's Voyage. Sri Chinmoy. LC 74-81308. (Illus.). 143p. (Orig.). 1974. pap. 5.95 (*0-88497-038-8*) Aum Pubns.

Death & Representation. Ed. by Sarah W. Goodwin & Elisabeth Bronfen. LC 93-15169. (Parallax). (Illus.). 368p. (C). 1993. text ed. 48.50 (*0-8018-4624-2*); pap. text ed. 14.95 (*0-8018-4627-7*) Johns Hopkins.

Death & Resurrection. Joanne M. Dewart. (Fathers of the Church Ser.: Vol. 22). 198p. 1986. 15.95 (*0-8146-5362-6*); pap. 11.95 (*0-8146-5333-2*) Liturgical Pr.

Death & Resurrection in Guatemala. Fernando Bermudez. Tr. by Robert R. Barr. LC 85-48305. 96p. (Orig.). reprint ed. pap. 27.40 (*0-8357-2667-3*, 2040203) Bks Demand.

Death & Resurrection of Jesus. Donald Goergan. (Theology of Jesus Ser.: Vol. 2). 287p. 1988. pap. 16.95 (*0-8146-5604-8*) Liturgical Pr.

Death & Resurrection of Jesus: A Narrative-Critical Reading of Matthew 26-28. John P. Heil. LC 91-30492. 136p. (Orig.). 1991. pap. 11.00 (*0-8006-2514-5*, 1-2514, Fortress Pr) Augsburg Fortress.

Death & Resurrection of the Beloved Son: The Transformation of Child Sacrifice in Judaism & Christianity. Jon D. Levenson. LC 93-7545. 272p. 1993. 27.50 (*0-300-05532-3*) Yale U Pr.

Death & Return of the Author: Criticism & Subjectivity in Barthes, Foucault, & Derrida. Sean Burke. 240p. 1992. text ed. 49.00 (*0-7486-0361-1*, Pub. by Edinburgh U Pr UK); pap. 19.50 (*0-7486-0355-7*, Pub. by Edinburgh U Pr UK) Col U Pr.

Death & Ritual in Renaissance Florence. Sharon T. Strocchia. (Studies in Historical & Political Science). 336p. 1992. text ed. 45.00x (*0-8018-4364-2*) Johns Hopkins.

Death & Sensuality: A Study of Eroticism & the Taboo. Georges Bataille. Ed. by Robert Kastenbaum. LC 76-19560. (Death & Dying Ser.). 1979. reprint ed. lib. bdg. 31.95 (*0-405-09556-2*) Ayer.

Death & Spirituality. Ed. by Kenneth J. Doka & John D. Morgan. LC 92-31413. (Death, Value, & Meaning Ser.). 416p. 1993. text ed. 38.95 (*0-89503-106-X*); pap. text ed. 29.95 (*0-89503-107-8*) Baywood Pub.

***Death & Taxes.** Pat Cook. 1994. 5.00 (*0-87129-409-5*, D60) Dramatic Pub.

Death & Taxes. Susan Dunlap. 1993. mass mkt. 4.99 (*0-440-21406-8*) Dell.

Death & Taxes. 2nd rev. ed. Hans F. Sennholz. LC 83-167162. iv, 105p. 1982. 5.95 (*0-89195-017-6*) Ctr Futures Ed.

Death & Taxes in the Ancient Near East. Ed. by Sara E. Orel. LC 92-4673. (Illus.). 256p. 1992. lib. bdg. 89.95 (*0-7734-9512-6*) E Mellen.

Death & the after Life. Andrew J. Davis. 210p. 1973. spiral bd. 8.80 (*0-7873-0240-6*) Mokelumne.

Death & the Afterlife. Robert A. Morey. LC 84-15682. 322p. 1984. pap. 16.99 (*0-87123-433-5*) Bethany Hse.

Death & the Afterlife in Modern France. Thomas A. Kselman. (Illus.). 432p. 1992. text ed. 65.00 (*0-691-03190-8*); pap. text ed. 18.95 (*0-691-00889-2*) Princeton U Pr.

Death & the Afterlife in Pre-Columbian America: A Conference at Dumbarton Oaks, October 27, 1973. Ed. by Elizabeth P. Benson. LC 74-22694. (Illus.). 196p. 1975. 18.00 (*0-88402-062-2*) Dumbarton Oaks.

Death & the Art of Dying in Tibetan Buddhism. Bokar Rinpoche. Tr. by Christiane Buchet. LC 93-74661. (Illus.). 144p. (Orig.). 1993. pap. text ed. 14.95 (*0-9630371-2-9*) ClearPoint.

Death & the Chapman. Kate Sedley. 1994. mass mkt. 4.50 (*0-06-104319-2*, Harp PBks) HarpC.

Death & the Chapman. large type ed. Kate Sedley. (Magna Mystery Ser.). 315p. 1992. 21.95 (*0-7505-0420-X*) Ulverscroft.

Death & the Christian Answer. Mary E. Lyman. LC 60-9784. (C). 1960. pap. 3.00 (*0-87574-107-X*) Pendle Hill.

Death & the Circulations of the Cosmos, I. G. De Purucker & W. Emmett Small. (Esoteric Teachings Ser.: Vol. XI). 130p. 1987. pap. 7.00 (*0-913004-62-6*) Point Loma Pub.

Death & the Circulations of the Cosmos, II. G. De Purucker. (Esoteric Teachings Ser.: Vol. XII). 150p. 1987. pap. 7.00 (*0-913004-63-4*) Point Loma Pub.

Death & the Creative Life. Lisl M. Goodman. (Death & Suicide Ser.). 192p. (C). 1981. 24.95 (*0-8261-3500-5*) Springer Pub.

***Death & the Dancing Footman.** Marsh. 1995. mass mkt. (*0-425-14655-3*) Berkley Pub.

Death & the Dancing Footman. Ngaio Marsh. 320p. 1992. pap. 3.99 (*0-515-08610-X*) Jove Pubns.

Death & the Dancing Footman. Ngaio Marsh. 1976. reprint ed. lib. bdg. 25.95 (*0-88411-477-5*, Aeonian Pr) Amereon Ltd.

Death & the Delinquent. B. J. Oliphant. (Southwest Mysteries Ser.). (Orig.). 1992. mass mkt. 4.50 (*0-449-14718-5*, GM) Fawcett.

Death & the Disinterested Spectator: An Inquiry into the Nature of Philosophy. Ann Hartle. LC 86-14447. 263p. (Orig.). 1986. 64.50 (*0-88706-285-7*); pap. 21.95 (*0-88706-284-9*) State U NY Pr.

Death & the Dogwalker. A. J. Orde. 1993. mass mkt. 4.50 (*0-449-22027-3*, Crest) Fawcett.

Death & the Dutch Uncle. Patricia Moyes. LC 82-23259. 256p. 1983. pap. 5.95 (*0-8050-0506-4*, Owl) H Holt & Co.

Death & the Enlightenment: Changing Attitudes to Death among Christians & Unbelievers in Eighteenth-Century France. John McManners. 640p. 1982. 39.95 (*0-19-826440-2*) OUP.

Death & the Epicure. Janet Laurence. 208p. 1993. 18.95 (*0-312-10451-0*, Pub. by Thomas Dunne Bks) St Martin.

Death & the Future Life in Victorian Literature & Theology. Michael Wheeler. (Illus.). 480p. (C). 1990. 64.95 (*0-521-30617-5*) Cambridge U Pr.

Death & the Good Life. Richard Hugo. LC 91-61901. 224p. 1991. reprint ed. pap. 9.95 (*0-944439-41-1*) Clark City Pr.

Death & the Hereafter. Gordon Lindsay. 1972. 1.95 (*0-89985-096-0*) Christ for the Nations.

Death & the Humanities. Sharon Scholl. LC 81-72025. (Illus.). 240p. 1984. 36.50 (*0-8387-5047-8*) Bucknell U Pr.

Death & the Invisible Powers: The World of Kongo Belief. Simon Bockie. LC 92-30614. 1993. 25.00 (*0-253-31564-6*); pap. 12.95 (*0-253-20808-4*) Ind U Pr.

***Death & the Joyful Woman.** Ellis Peters. 224p. 1995. mass mkt. 5.50 (*0-446-40068-8*, Mysterious Paperbk) Warner Bks.

Death & the Joyful Woman. large type ed. Ellis Peters. LC 92-24308. 1992. 18.95 (*0-7927-1404-0*, Eagle Lrg Print) Chivers N Amer.

Death & the Joyful Woman. large type ed. Ellis Peters. 1993. pap. 16.95 (*0-7927-1403-2*, Paragon Lrg Print) Chivers N Amer.

Death & the King's Horseman. Wole Soyinka. 1990. pap. 9.00 (*0-374-52210-3*, Noonday) FS&G.

Death & the Magic Lantern: Thanatology on Film. Sandra L. Bertman. 95p. 1991. pap. 13.95 (*0-930194-19-5*) Ctr Thanatology.

Death & the Maiden. Ariel Dorfman. 64p. (Orig.). 1992. pap. 7.50 (*0-14-048238-5*, Penguin Bks) Viking Penguin.

***Death & the Maiden.** Ariel Dorfman. 96p. 1994. 7.95 (*0-14-024684-3*, Penguin Bks) Viking Penguin.

Death & the Maiden. P. N. Elrod. 256p. (Orig.). 1994. pap. text ed. 4.99 (*0-441-00071-1*) Ace Bks.

Death & the Maiden: Girls' Initiation Rites in Greek Mythology. Ken Dowden. 256p. 1989. 35.00 (*0-415-01263-5*, A2518) Routledge.

Death & the Metropolis: Studies in the Demographic History of London, 1670-1830. John Landers. LC 92-10887. (Studies in Population, Economy & Society in Past Time: No. 20). 368p. (C). 1993. 64.95 (*0-521-35599-0*) Cambridge U Pr.

Death & the Optimistic Prophecy in Vergil's AENEID. James J. O'Hara. 228p. 1990. text ed. 37.50 (*0-691-06815-1*) Princeton U Pr.

Death & the Oxford Box: A Mystery Introducing Kate Ivory. Veronica Stallwood. 224p. 1994. text ed. 20.00 (*0-684-19596-8*, Scribners) S&S Trade.

Death & the Pleasant Voices. Mary Fitt. (Detective Stories Ser.). 224p. 1984. reprint ed. pap. 5.95 (*0-486-24603-5*) Dover.

Death & the Plowman; or, the Bohemian Plowman. Tr. by Ernest A. Kirrmann. LC 58-63297. (North Carolina. University. Studies in the Germanic Languages & Literatures: No. 22). reprint ed. 27.00 (*0-404-50922-3*) AMS Pr.

Death & the Prince: Memorial Preaching Before 1350. David D'Avray. 352p. 1994. 65.00 (*0-19-820396-9*) OUP.

Death & the Regeneration of Life. Ed. by Maurice Bloch & Jonathan Parry. LC 82-9467. 256p. 1982. pap. 16.95 (*0-521-27037-5*) Cambridge U Pr.

Death & the Serpent: Immortality in Science Fiction & Fantasy. Ed. by Carl B. Yoke & Donald M. Hassler. LC 84-6522. (Contributions to the Study of Science Fiction & Fantasy Ser.: No. 13). ix, 235p. 1985. text ed. 59.95 (*0-313-23279-2*, YOD/) Greenwood.

Death & the Sexes: A Differential Examination of Longevity, Attitudes, Behaviors, & Coping Skills. Judith Stillion. LC 84-10801. (Death Education, Aging & Health Care Ser.). (Illus.). 275p. 1985. 37.50 (*0-89116-313-1*) Hemisp Pub.

Death & the Trumpets of Tuscany. large type ed. Hazel W. Jones. (General Ser.). 352p. 1993. 21.95 (*0-7089-2879-X*) Ulverscroft.

Death & the Visual Arts: Original Arno Press Anthology. Ed. by Robert Kastenbaum. LC 76-19565. (Death & Dying Ser.). (Illus.). 1979. reprint ed. lib. bdg. 19.95 (*0-405-09561-9*) Ayer.

Death & Violence on the Reservation: Homicide, Family Violence, & Suicide in American Indian Populations. Ronet Bachman. LC 91-37158. 192p. 1992. text ed. 45.00 (*0-86569-015-4*, T015, Auburn Hse) Greenwood.

Death-Angel. J. N. Williamson. (Orig.). 1982. pap. 2.95 (*0-89083-909-3*) Zebra.

Death Angel: A Vietnam Memoir of a Bearer of Death Messages to Families. Harry Spiller. LC 92-53500. 256p. 1992. pap. 19.95 (*0-89950-728-X*) McFarland & Co.

D

An Asterisk (*) at the beginning of an entry indicates that the title is appearing in BIP for the first time. 1829

Death Anxiety: The Loss of the Self. James B. McCarthy. 1980. text ed. 27.95 (0-89876-069-0) Gardner Pr.

Death Anxiety Handbook. Ed. by Robert A. Neimeyer. (Series in Death Education, Aging, & Health Care). 312p. 1994. 54.50 (1-56032-282-9, Pub. by Paul Chapman UK) Taylor & Francis.

Death As a Fact of Life. David Hendin. 256p. 1984. pap. 8.95 (0-393-30134-6) Norton.

***Death As a Salesman: What's Wrong with Assisted Suicide.** Brian P. Johnston. 208p. 1994. pap. 10.95 (0-9641125-0-7) New Regency.

Death As a Speculative Theme in Religious, Scientific, & Social Thought: An Original Anthology. Ed. by Robert Kastenbaum. LC 76-19566. (Death & Dying Ser.). 1979. reprint ed. lib. bdg. 31.95 (0-405-09562-7) Ayer.

Death As an Enemy According to Ancient Egyptian Conceptions. Jan Zandee. Ed. by Robert Kastenbaum. LC 76-19597. (Death & Dying Ser.). 1977. reprint ed. lib. bdg. 41.95 (0-405-09591-0) Ayer.

Death As Departure: The Johannine Descent-Ascent Schema. Godfrey C. Nicholson. LC 81-18336. (Society of Biblical Literature Dissertation Ser.). 250p. (C). 1982. pap. 15.95 (0-89130-555-6, 060163) Scholars Pr GA.

Death at an Early Age. Jonathan Kozol. 1985. pap. 10.95 (0-452-26292-5, Plume) NAL-Dutton.

Death at Bishop's Keep. Robin Paige. 272p. (Orig.). 1994. mass mkt. 4.99 (0-380-77498-4) Avon.

***Death at Broadcasting House.** large type ed. Val Gielgud & Holt Marvell. 1994. 18.95 (0-7451-6463-3, Scarlet Dagger Lrg Print) Chivers N Amer.

Death at Broadcasting House. Val Gielgud & Holt Marvell. (Black Dagger Crime Ser.). 264p. 1992. reprint ed. 16.50 (0-86220-828-9, Black Dagger) Chivers N Amer.

Death at Chappaquiddick. Richard L. Tedrow & Thomas L. Tedrow. LC 76-3349. (Illus.). 217p. 1976. 17.95 (0-916054-28-4, Jameson Bks) Green Hill.

Death at Chappaquiddick. rev. ed. Richard L. Tedrow & Thomas L. Tedrow. LC 79-21703. 240p. 1980. pap. 5.95 (0-88289-249-5) Pelican.

Death at Cross Plains: An Alabama Reconstruction Tragedy. Gene L. Howard. 1994. pap. 16.95 (0-8173-0749-4) U of Ala Pr.

Death at Deepwood Grange. large type ed. Michael Underwood. 320p. 1987. 16.95 (0-7089-1673-2) Ulverscroft.

***Death at Face Value.** Joyce Christmas. (Orig.). 1995. mass mkt. 4.99 (0-449-14801-7, GM) Fawcett.

***Death at Gallows Green.** Robin Paige. (Victorian Mystery Ser.). 272p. (Orig.). 1995. mass mkt. 4.99 (0-380-77499-2) Avon.

Death at Half-Term. large type ed. Josephine Bell. 1992. 18.95 (0-7451-6412-9, Scarlet Dagger Lrg Print) Chivers N Amer.

Death at Half-Term. large type ed. Josephine Bell. 1993. pap. 16.95 (0-7451-6418-8, Scarlet Dagger Lrg Print) Chivers N Amer.

***Death at la Fenice.** Donna Leon. 1994. pap. 4.50 (0-06-104337-0, Harp PBks) HarpC.

Death at Sea: Issues Arising from the 1989 Explosion Aboard the U. S. S. Iowa. (Illus.). 64p. (Orig.). (C). 1994. pap. text ed. 30.00 (0-7881-0297-4) Diane Pub.

***Death at Sea: A Murder Mystery in 3-D.** Len Oszustowicz. Ed. by Mike Towle. (Illus.). 80p. (YA). (gr. 6 up). 1994. 12.95 (1-56530-165-X) Summit TX.

Death at St Asprey's School. Leo Bruce. (Carolus Deene Mystery Ser.). 221p. 1984. pap. 5.95 (0-89733-094-3) Academy Chi Pubs.

Death at the Bar. Ngaio Marsh. (Ngaio Marsh Mystery Ser.). 272p. 1984. pap. text ed. 3.99 (0-515-07700-3) Jove Pubns.

Death at the Bar. Ngaio Marsh. 1976. reprint ed. lib. bdg. 23.95 (0-88411-476-7, Aeonian Pr) Amereon Ltd.

Death at the Chase. Michael Innes. 192p. 1986. reprint ed. mass mkt. 6.00 (0-14-017242-4, Penguin Bks) Viking Penguin.

Death at the Chateau Noir. large type ed. E. Radford & M. A. Radford. 1975. 12.00 (0-85456-375-X) Ulverscroft.

Death at the Parasite Cafe: Social Science (Fictions) & the Postmodern. Stephen Pfohl. Ed. by Arthur Kroker & Marilouise Kroker. (Culture Texts Ser.). 300p. 1992. pap. 14.95 (0-312-07573-1) St Martin.

Death at the President's Lodging. Michael Innes. 288p. 1992. mass mkt. 6.00 (0-14-010555-7, Penguin Bks) Viking Penguin.

Death at the President's Lodging. large type ed. Michael Innes. 448p. 1989. 17.95 (0-7089-2012-8) Ulverscroft.

Death at the President's Lodging see Michael Innes Omnibus

Death at the Strike. large type ed. Colin Willock. 448p. 1983. 15.95 (0-7089-0981-7) Ulverscroft.

Death at the Wedding. large type ed. Madelaine Duke. (Linford Mystery Library). 249p. 1988. pap. 11.95 (0-7089-6557-1, Linford) Ulverscroft.

Death at Wentwater Court: A Daisy Dalrymple Mystery. Carola Dunn. 240p. 1994. 19.95 (0-312-11030-8) St Martin.

***Death Au Gratin.** Richard Grayson. LC 95-14720. 192p. 1995. 19.95 (0-312-13047-3) St Martin.

Death Be Not Proud. large type ed. John Gunther. LC 92-18710. 1992. reprint ed. pap. 18.95 (0-7927-1336-2, Curley Lrg Print) Chivers N Amer.

Death Be Not Proud. John J. Gunther. LC 88-45953. 224p. 1989. reprint ed. mass mkt. 6.50 (0-06-080973-6, P 973, PL) HarpC.

Death Be Not Proud: A Memoir. John Gunther. 231p. 1991. reprint ed. lib. bdg. 23.00x (0-8095-9101-4) Borgo Pr.

Death Beat: A Colombian Journalist's Life Inside the Cocaine Wars. Maria J. Duzan. Ed. & Tr. by Peter Eisner. LC 93-36048. (Illus.). 288p. 1994. 22.00 (0-06-017057-3, HarpT) HarpC.

Death Bed Miracles. Joy D. Patterson. LC 89-50862. 50p. 1990. pap. 5.95 (1-55523-245-0) Winston-Derek.

Death Before Bedtime. limited ed. Edgar Box, pseud. LC 91-383. 224p. 1991. reprint ed. 75.00 (0-922890-92-7) Armchair Detective.

Death Before Bedtime. Edgar Box, pseud. LC 91-383. 224p. 1991. reprint ed. 18.95 (0-922890-90-0); reprint ed. 25.00 (0-922890-91-9) Armchair Detective.

***Death Before Denial: A Study of the Revelation of Jesus Christ.** 1992. audio 14.99 (1-884553-35-4) Discipleshp.

Death Before Denial: A Study of the Revelation of Jesus Christ. Gordon Ferguson. 34p. 1992. 4.99 (1-884553-07-9) Discipleshp.

***Death Before Dishonor: The Andersonville Diary of Eugene Forbes, 4th NJ Infantry.** Eugene Forbes. Ed. & Intro. by William Styple. (Illus.). 208p. 1995. 25.00 (1-883926-03-3) Belle Grv Pub.

Death Before Dying. Collin Wilcox. 1994. pap. 5.95 (0-8050-3122-7) H Holt & Co.

Death Below Deck. Douglas Kiker. 1991. 17.95 (0-685-39017-9) Random.

Death Beneath the Christmas Tree. Robert Nordan. (Orig.). 1993. mass mkt. 4.50 (0-449-45258-1, GM) Fawcett.

Death Benefit. David Heilbroner. 440p. 1994. mass mkt. 5.50 (0-380-72262-3) Avon.

Death Benefits: A Rachel Gold Mystery. Michael A. Kahn. 320p. 1994. pap. 4.99 (0-451-17687-1, Sig) NAL-Dutton.

Death-Blow to Spiritualism: Being the True Story of the Fox Sisters. Reuben B. Davenport. LC 75-36836. (Occult Ser.). 1976. reprint ed. 21.95 (0-405-07949-4) Ayer.

Death Book. Joseph Amato. 120p. 1985. 13.95 (0-933180-66-7) Ellis Pr.

***Death Book: Terrors, Consolations, Contradictions & Paradoxes.** Joseph A. Amato. 1985. 13.95 (0-9614119-1-0) Crossings Pr.

Death Bringers. large type ed. Dell Shannon. LC 92-41186. 1993. pap. 19.95 (0-7927-1512-8, Curley Lrg Print) Chivers N Amer.

Death Brings Many Surprises. Robert H. Coddington. 304p. (Orig.). 1987. mass mkt. 3.50 (0-8041-0128-0) Ivy Books.

Death, Burial & Afterlife in Ancient Egypt. James F. Romano. LC 89-85822. (Illus.). 48p. (Orig.). (C). 1990. pap. text ed. 7.95 (0-911239-19-7) Carnegie Mus.

Death, Burial & the Individual in Early Modern England. Clare Gittings. 224p. 1988. 17.95 (0-685-26523-4, Pub. by Croom Helm UK) Routledge Chapman & Hall.

Death Business. large type ed. Anthony Graham. 336p. 1988. 21.95 (0-7089-1798-4) Ulverscroft.

Death, but at a Good Price. Chris Semansky. LC 90-52854. (Roerich Poetry Prize Winner Ser.). 76p. (Orig.). 1990. pap. 9.95 (0-934257-46-9) Story Line.

***Death by Association.** large type ed. Richard Lockridge & Frances Lockridge. LC 94-25980. 322p. 1995. pap. 17.95 (1-56054-306-X) Thorndike Pr.

Death by Babysitting. Susan K. Wright. 168p. (Orig.). (J). (gr. 4-8). 1994. pap. 5.95 (0-8361-3694-2) Herald Pr.

***Death by Cheeseburger: High School Journalism in the 1990's & Beyond.** Freedom Forum Staff. Ed. by Alice Bonner & Judy Hines. (Illus.). 181p. (Orig.). Date not set. pap. 14.95 (0-9640284-0-9) Freed Forum.

Death by Chocolate: The Last Word on a Consuming Passion. Marcel Desaulniers. LC 91-45878. (Illus.). 144p. 1992. 27.50 (0-8478-1564-1) Rizzoli Intl.

Death by Crystal. Agnes Bushell. LC 92-41202. (Illus.). 160p. (Orig.). 1993. per., pap. 8.95 (0-9624626-5-9) Astarte Shell Pr.

Death by Deception. Anne Wingate. 1991. mass mkt. 3.95 (0-06-100146-5, PL) HarpC.

Death by Deception. Anne Wingate. 192p. 1988. 17.95 (0-8027-5714-6) Walker & Co.

Death by Deception: Advanced Improvised Booby Traps. JoJo Gonzales. (Illus.). 120p. 1992. pap. 14.00 (0-87364-651-7) Paladin Pr.

***Death by Degrees.** Eric Wright. (WWL Mystery Ser.). 1995. mass mkt. 3.99 (0-373-26169-1, 1-26169-2) Harlequin Bks.

Death by Degrees. Eric Wright. (Inspector Charlie Salter Mystery Ser.). 224p. 1993. text ed. 20.00 (0-684-19648-4, Scribners) S&S Trade.

Death by Degrees. large type ed. Eric Wright. LC 94-2096. 1994. pap. 17.95 (0-7862-0195-9) Thorndike Pr.

Death by Denial: Preventing Suicide in Gay & Lesbian Teenagers. Intro. by Gary Remafedi. 205p. (Orig.). 1993. pap. 9.95 (1-55583-260-1) Alyson Pubns.

Death by Design: A John Blaine Mystery. Vincent Banville. 254p. 1993. pap. 9.95 (0-86327-335-1, Pub. by Wolfhound Pr IE) Dufour.

Death by Dieselization: A Case Study in the Reaction to Technological Change. W. F. Cottrell. (Reprint Series in Social Sciences). (C). 1993. reprint ed. pap. text ed. 1.00 (0-8290-3794-2, S-53) Irvington.

Death by Dressage. Carolyn Banks. 1993. mass mkt. 4.50 (0-449-14843-2, GM) Fawcett.

Death by Ecstasy: Illustrated Adaptation of the Larry Niven Novella. Bill Spangler. (Illus.). 75p. 1991. pap. 9.95 (1-56398-004-5) Malibu Graphics.

Death by Education: An American Autopsy. William Wieser. LC 92-96913. (Illus.). 420p. 1993. 25.00 (0-9634543-5-8) Wiser Ent.

Death by Election. Patricia Hall. LC 94-12922. 256p. 1994. 20.95 (0-312-11461-3, Pub. by Thomas Dunne Bks) St Martin.

Death by Government: Genocide & Mass Murder since 1900. R. J. Rummel. LC 93-21279. 510p. (C). 1994. 49.95 (1-56000-145-3) Transaction Pubs.

Death by Installments: The Ordeal of Willie Francis. Arthur S. Miller & Jeffrey H. Bowman. LC 88-3124. (Contributions in Legal Studies: No. 44). 189p. 1988. text ed. 49.95 (0-313-26009-5, MDN/, Greenwood Pr) Greenwood.

Death by Migration: Europe's Encounter with the Tropical World in the Nineteenth Century. Philip D. Curtin. (Illus.). (C). 1989. pap. 16.95 (0-521-38922-4) Cambridge U Pr.

Death by Narration. Debby Knight. 58p. 1981. 5.95 (0-89962-201-1) Voyager Pub Hse.

***Death by Publication.** J. J. Fiechter. LC 94-43059. 176p. 1995. 19.95 (1-55970-285-0) Arcade Pub Inc.

Death by Rock & Roll: The Untimely Deaths of the Legends of Rock. Gary J. Katz. LC 94-19224. 1994. pap. 9.95 (0-8065-1581-3, Citadel Pr) Carol Pub Group.

***Death by Sheer Torture.** Robert Barnard. LC 94-48136. 192p. 1995. mass mkt. 5.95 (0-14-023787-9, Penguin Bks) Viking Penguin.

***Death by Sheer Torture.** Robert Barnard. 1993. Not sold separately (0-615-00008-8) Random.

Death by Station Wagon. John Katz. (Crime Line Ser.). 1994. mass mkt. 4.99 (0-553-29881-X) Bantam.

Death by Station Wagon: A Suburban Detective Mystery. Jon Katz. LC 92-29809. 1993. 18.50 (0-385-42112-5) Doubleday.

Death by Suicidal Means. Walter Henderson. LC 93-61056. 227p. 1994. 19.95 (0-9638086-0-5); pap. 8.95 (0-9638086-1-3) Inherit Pr.

Death by the Light of the Moon. Joan Hess. (Southern Mysteries Ser.). 1994. mass mkt. 4.99 (0-345-37838-5) Ballantine.

Death by the Light of the Moon: A Claire Malloy Mystery. Joan Hess. 240p. 1992. 18.95 (0-312-06949-9) St Martin.

Death by the Riverside. J. M. Redmann. LC 90-42741. 256p. (Orig.). 1990. pap. 9.95 (0-934678-27-8) New Victoria Pubs.

Death Calls the Shots. large type ed. Bill Knox. (Linford Mystery Library). 1990. pap. 12.95 (0-7089-6852-X, Trailtree Bookshop) Ulverscroft.

Death Came Dressed in White. Michael W. Sherer. (Orig.). 1992. mass mkt. 3.99 (0-06-100429-4, Harp PBks) HarpC.

***Death Camp.** Judd Cole. (Cheyenne Ser.: No. 14). (Orig.). 1995. mass mkt., pap. text ed. 3.99 (0-8439-3800-5) Dorchester Pub Co.

***Death Care Industry in the United States.** Ronald G. Smith. 416p. 1995. lib. bdg. 47.50 (0-7864-0118-4) McFarland & Co.

Death Certificate. P. Sachidanandan. Tr. by Gita Krishnankutty. 112p. 1983. pap. 2.95 (0-86131-288-0, Pub. by Orient Longman Ltd II) Apt Bks.

Death Channels. Robert E. Vardeman. 224p. (Orig.). 1992. mass mkt. 4.50 (0-380-76725-2) Avon.

Death Chant. Judd Cole. (Cheyenne Ser.: No. 2). 176p. (Orig.). 1992. pap. 3.50 (0-8439-3337-2) Dorchester Pub Co.

Death Cheaters. Gordon Lindsay. 1971. 2.95 (0-89985-081-2) Christ for the Nations.

Death Check. Warren Murphy. (Destroyer Ser.: No. 2). 1988. pap. 3.50 (1-55817-037-5, Pinnacle NY) Windsor NY.

Death Claims. Joseph Hansen. LC 80-15548. 176p. 1980. pap. 5.95 (0-8050-0622-2, Owl) H Holt & Co.

Death-Coach. J. N. Williamson. (Orig.). 1981. pap. 2.95 (0-89083-805-4) Zebra.

Death Collection. Gregory Altreuter. (Illus.). 24p. 1982. pap. 3.00 (0-911627-04-9) Neither-Nor Pr.

Death College & Other Poems. Tom Veitch. (Illus.). (Orig.). 1976. 4.50 (0-929844-11-4) Big Sky Bolinas.

***Death Comes As Epiphany.** Sharan Newman. 320p. 1995. mass mkt. 4.99 (0-8125-2293-1) Forge NYC.

Death Comes As Epiphany. Sharan Newman. 320p. 1993. 19.95 (0-312-85419-6) Tor Bks.

Death Comes As the End. Agatha Christie. 1992. mass mkt. 4.99 (0-06-100368-9, Harp PBks) HarpC.

Death Comes As the End. Agatha Christie. (Agatha Christie Ser.). 1982. 9.95 (0-396-08109-6, Putnam) Putnam Pub Group.

Death Comes As the End. large type ed. Agatha Christie. 1970. 17.95 (0-85456-004-1) Ulverscroft.

Death Comes for the Archbishop. Willa Cather. 1927. 19.95 (0-394-42154-X) Knopf.

Death Comes for the Archbishop. Willa Cather. 1992. 15.00 (0-679-41319-7, Everymans Lib) Knopf.

Death Comes for the Archbishop. Willa Cather. 1976. 22.95 (0-8488-0448-1) Amereon Ltd.

Death Comes for the Archbishop. Willa Cather. 1971. pap. 6.95 (0-394-71679-5) Random.

Death Comes for the Archbishop. Willa Cather. 1984. 15.00 (0-394-60503-9) Random.

Death Comes for the Archbishop. Willa Cather. LC 89-40540. 1990. pap. 9.00 (0-679-72889-9, Vin) Random.

Death Comes for the Archbishop. Willa Cather. LC 92-34349. 1993. 13.50 (0-679-60050-7, Modern Lib) Random.

Death Comes for the Chief Justice: The Slough-Rynerson Quarrel & Political Violence in New Mexico. Gary L. Roberts. (Illus.). 288p. 1990. 24.95 (0-87081-212-2) Univ Pr Colo.

***Death Comes to Dinner: Scene of the Crime, No. 1.** Miller. 1995. pap. (0-590-56871-X) Scholastic Inc.

Death Comes to Perigord. John Ferguson. 292p. 1983. reprint ed. pap. 6.95 (0-486-24434-2) Dover.

Death Comes to the Archbishop. Willa Cather. 1992. reprint ed. lib. bdg. 19.95 (0-89966-978-6) Buccaneer Bks.

Death Comes to the Circus. Ed. by Stanley Thornes. (Spirals Ser.). (C). 1989. 40.00 (0-09-152171-8, Pub. by S Thornes Pubs UK) St Mut.

Death Comes to the Maiden: Sex & Execution, 1431-1933. Camille Naish. 304p. 1991. 45.00 (0-415-05585-7, A6227) Routledge.

Death Count. L. A. Graf. Ed. by Dave Stern. (Star Trek Ser.: No. 62). 288p. (Orig.). 1992. mass mkt. 4.99 (0-671-79322-5) PB.

Death Crystal. J. Edward Ames. 400p. (Orig.). 1990. pap. 4.50 (0-8439-3053-5) Dorchester Pub Co.

Death Customs. Lucy Rushton. LC 92-42150. (Comparing Religions Ser.). (Illus.). 32p. (J). (gr. 4-8). 1993. 13.95 (1-56847-031-2) Thomson Lrning.

Death Customs: An Analytical Study of Burial Rites. Effie Bendann. 1972. 59.95 (0-8490-0010-6) Gordon Pr.

Death Customs: An Analytical Study of Burial Rites. Effie Bendann. LC 89-63007. xiii, 304p. 1990. reprint ed. lib. bdg. 44.00 (1-55888-844-6) Omnigraphics Inc.

Death Dance. Peter McCurtin. (Sundance Ser.). 224p. 1984. pap. 2.50 (0-8439-2159-5) Dorchester Pub Co.

Death Dance. Jack McKinney. (Sentinels Ser.). (YA). (gr. 10 up). 1988. mass mkt. 4.95 (0-345-35302-1, Del Rey) Ballantine.

Death Dance. large type ed. Peter McCurtin. 416p. 1983. 21.95 (0-7089-1055-6) Ulverscroft.

Death Danced at the Boulevard Ballroom. Thomas E. Krupowicz. 213p. (Orig.). (C). 1992. pap. 12.95 (1-881690-00-8) Terk Bks & Pubs.

Death Dealer: The Memoirs of the SS Kommandant at Auschwitz. Rudolf Hoss. Ed. by Steven Paskuly. (Illus.). 381p. (C). 1992. 27.95 (0-87975-714-0) Prometheus Bks.

Death Dealer's Manual. Bradley J. Steiner. (Illus.). 112p. 1982. pap. 12.00 (0-87364-247-3) Paladin Pr.

Death, Deeds, & Descendants: Inheritance in Modern America. Remi Clignet. (Social Institutions & Social Change Ser.). 247p. 1992. lib. bdg. 46.95 (0-202-30398-5) Aldine de Gruyter.

Death Deferred: How to Live Long & Happily, Defer Death, & Lose All Fear of It. Hereward Carrington. 262p. 1993. reprint ed. spiral bd. 8.80 (0-7873-0154-X) Mokelumne.

Death Deferred: How to Prolong Life & Postpone Death. H. Carrington. 1991. lib. bdg. 250.00 (0-87700-945-7) Revisionist Pr.

Death Department. large type ed. Bill Knox. 1977. 21.95 (0-7089-0043-7) Ulverscroft.

Death Dictionary: Over Fifty-Five Hundred Clinical, Legal, Literary & Vernacular Terms. Comp. by Christine Quigley. LC 93-28817. 207p. 1994. lib. bdg. 29.95 (0-89950-869-3) McFarland & Co.

Death, Distress, & Solidarity. Ed. by Robert J. Kastenbaum. 100p. 1993. pap. text ed. 16.95 (0-89503-115-9) Baywood Pub.

Death Doctor. J. N. Williamson. (Death Ser.). 1982. pap. 2.95 (0-8217-1108-3) Zebra.

Death Does Not Part Us. Elsie R. Sechrist. Ed. by Mark Thurston. 273p. (Orig.). 1992. pap. 10.95 (0-87604-295-7, 373) ARE Pr.

***Death Doll.** large type ed. Anthea Goddard. (Magna Large Print Ser.). 1994. 21.95 (0-7089-3186-3) Ulverscroft.

Death Down Home. Eve K. Sandstrom. 1993. mass mkt. 3.99 (0-373-26125-X, 1-26125-4) Harlequin Bks.

Death Down Under. Claire McNab. 240p. 1990. pap. 9.95 (0-941483-39-8) Naiad Pr.

Death Draw. Kit Dalton. (Buckskin Ser.: No. 32). 176p. (Orig.). 1992. pap. 3.50 (0-8439-3278-3) Dorchester Pub Co.

Death Dream. Ben Bova. LC 93-46463. 1994. pap. 22.95 (0-553-08234-5) Bantam.

Death Dreams: Unveiling Mysteries of the Unconscious Mind. Kenneth P. Kramer & John Larkin. LC 92-29605. 304p. 1993. pap. 14.95 (0-8091-3349-0) Paulist Pr.

***Death Dressed in White.** Les Purtee. 310p. 1995. 21.50 (0-9644420-0-0) Flag Pub.

Death Drive. George G. Gilman. (Edge Ser.: No. 27). 1991. pap. 3.50 (1-55817-515-6, Pinnacle NY) Windsor NY.

Death Drop. large type ed. B. M. Gill. 1993. 39.95 (0-7066-1025-3, Pub. by Remploy Pr CN) St Mut.

Death Drops the Pilot. large type ed. George Bellairs. 1991. 21.95 (0-7089-2547-2) Ulverscroft.

***Death Du Jour.** Will Hawley. LC 94-90110. 152p. (Orig.). 1995. pap. 10.00 (1-56002-442-9, Univ Edtns) Aegina Pr.

Death, Dying & Bereavement. Ed. by Donna Dickenson & Malcolm Johnson. (Illus.). 252p. (C). 1993. text ed. 65.00 (0-8039-8796-X); pap. text ed. 21.95 (0-8039-8797-8) Sage.

Death, Dying, & Euthanasia. Ed. by Dennis J. Horan & David Mall. LC 77-72189. 860p. 1980. text ed. 85.00 (0-313-27097-X, U7097, Greenwood Pr); pap. text ed. 21.95 (0-313-27092-9, P7092, Greenwood Pr) Greenwood.

Death, Dying & Society: A Special Issue of Psychology & Psychotherapy. Ed. by Craig Newnes. 180p. 1990. text ed. 29.95 (0-86377-177-7) L Erlbaum Assocs.

Death, Dying, & the Biological Revolution: Our Last Quest for Responsibility. rev. ed. Robert M. Veatch. (C). 1989. text ed. 40.00 (0-300-04364-3); pap. 18.00 (0-300-04365-1) Yale U Pr.

***Death Echo.** Kerry Tucker. 1994. pap. 4.50 (0-06-109986-4, Harp PBks) HarpC.

Death, Ecstasy, & Other Worldly Journeys. Ed. by John J. Collins & Michael Fishbane. 352p. (C). 1995. text ed. 74.50x (0-7914-2345-X); pap. text ed. 24.95x (0-7914-2346-8) State U NY Pr.

Death Education: An Annotated Resource Guide. H. Wass et al. 1981. 27.90 (0-07-068439-1) McGraw.

Death Education & Research: Critical Perspectives. Pref. by W. G. Warren. LC 88-37599. (Gerontology & Geriatrics Education Ser.: Vol. 9, Nos. 1 & 2). (Illus.). 212p. 1989. text ed. 39.95 (0-86656-814-X) Haworth Pr.

D

1830 An Asterisk (*) at the beginning of an entry indicates that the title is appearing in BIP for the first time.

An Asterisk (*) at the beginning of an entry indicates that the title is appearing in BIP for the first time.

Death in the Scillies. large type ed. Howard C. Davis. (Linford Mystery Library). 304p. 1989. pap. 11.95 (0-7089-6725-6, Linford) Ulverscroft.

Death in the Silent Places. Peter H. Capstick. 320p. 1981. pap. 18.95 (0-312-18618-5) St Martin.

Death in the Silent Places. Peter H. Capstick. 1989. mass mkt. 4.95 (0-312-91537-3) St Martin.

Death in the Stars. large type ed. Norman A. Lazenby. (Linford Mystery Library). 224p. 1993. pap. 14.95 (0-7089-7419-8, Trailtree Bookshop) Ulverscroft.

*__Death in the Tiwi Islands: Conflict, Ritual & Social Life in an Australian Aboriginal Society.__ Eric Venbrux. (Illus.). 272p. (C). 1995. write for info. (0-521-47351-9) Cambridge U Pr.

Death in the Trenches. (Civil War Ser.). (Illus.). 176p. 1986. 19.93 (0-8094-4776-2); lib. bdg. 25.93 (0-8094-4777-0) Time-Life.

Death in the Woods: And Other Stories. Sherwood Anderson. (Shoreline Bks.). 298p. 1986. pap. 7.95 (0-87140-140-1) Norton.

*__Death in Towns: Urban Responses to the Dying & the Dead, 100-1600.__ Ed. by Steven Bassett. (Illus.). 258p. 1995. pap. 19.95 (0-7185-2280-X, Pub. by Leicester Univ Pr) St Martin.

Death in Venice. Thomas Mann. 1976. 11.95 (0-8488-0574-7) Amereon Ltd.

Death in Venice. Thomas Mann. Tr. by Erich Heller. (Modern Library College Editions). (C). 1970. pap. text ed. write for info. (0-07-553669-2, T99) McGraw.

Death in Venice. Thomas Mann. Ed. & Tr. by Clayton Kolb. (Critical Editions Ser.). (C). 1994. pap. text ed. 6.95 (0-393-96013-7) Norton.

*__Death in Venice.__ Thomas Mann. Tr. & Comment by Stanley Appelbaum. LC 95-2967. (Thrift Editions Ser.). 1995. pap. 1.00 (0-486-28714-9) Dover.

Death in Venice. Thomas Mann. 451p. 1983. reprint ed. lib. bdg. 12.95 (0-89966-455-5) Buccaneer Bks.

Death in Venice: Making & Unmaking a Master. T. J. Reed. LC 94-4252. (Twayne's Masterwork Studies Ser.: No. 140). 125p. 1994. text ed. 23.95x (0-8057-8069-6, Twayne); pap. 12.95 (0-8057-8114-5, Twayne) Macmillan.

Death in Venice & Other Stories. Thomas Mann. 400p. (Orig.). 1991. 17.00 (0-679-40666-2, Everymans Lib) Knopf.

Death in Venice & Other Stories. Thomas Mann. Tr. & Intro. by David Luke. 320p. (Orig.). 1988. mass mkt. 5.95 (0-553-21333-4) Bantam.

Death in Venice & Seven Other Stories. Thomas Mann. 1954. pap. 4.95 (0-394-70003-1) Random.

Death in Venice & Seven Other Stories. Thomas Mann. Tr. by Helen T. Lowe-Porter. (International Ser.). 1989. pap. 10.00 (0-679-72206-8, Vin) Random.

Death in Venice & Seven Other Stories. Thomas Mann. Tr. by Helen T. Lowe-Porter. LC 92-25325. 1992. 15.50 (0-679-60040-X, Modern Lib) Random.

*__Death in Yellowstone: Accidents & Foolhardiness in Our First National Park.__ Lee H. Whittlesey. 240p. (Orig.). 1995. pap. 16.95 (1-57098-021-7) R Rinehart.

Death in Zanzibar. M. M. Kaye. 1984. pap. 3.95 (0-312-90130-5) St Martin.

Death Inheritance. Phyllis Swan. (Anna J. Ser.: No. 3). (Orig.). 1980. pap. 1.75 (0-8439-0731-2) Dorchester Pub Co.

Death Instinct. Phillip Emmons. 336p. (Orig.). 1992. pap. 4.99 (0-451-17284-1, Sig) NAL-Dutton.

Death, Intermediate State & Rebirth. Lati Rinbochay & Jeffrey Hopkins. 86p. 1981. pap. 9.95 (0-937938-00-9) Snow Lion Pubns.

Death Investigation Evidence Manual. (Illus.). 110p. (Orig.). (C). 1994. pap. text ed. 39.95 (0-7881-0286-9) Diane Pub.

Death Investigator's Handbook: A Field Guide to Crime Scene Processing, Forensic Evaluations, & Investigative Techniques. Louis N. Eliopulos. (Illus.). 888p. 1993. pap. 40.00 (0-87364-727-0) Paladin Pr.

Death Is... Rich Hillman & Steven M. Mickle. Ed. by Diane Parker. LC 92-50857. 96p. 1993. pap. 7.95 (0-88247-965-2, 965-2) R & E Pubs.

Death Is a Kind of Love. Christopher Fry. (Illus.). 1979. 15.00 (0-930954-12-2); 75.00 (0-930954-13-0) Tidal Pr.

Death Is a Red Rose. large type ed. Dorothy Eden. (Scarlet Dagger Ser.). 1993. 18.95 (0-7451-6444-7, Scarlet Dagger Lrg Print) Chivers N Amer.

Death Is a Social Disease: Public Health & Political Economy in Early Industrial France. William Coleman. (Wisconsin Publications in the History of Science & Medicine: No. 1). 352p. 1982. text ed. 37.50 (0-299-08950-9) U of Wis Pr.

Death Is a Two Stroke Penalty. James Y. Bartlett. 1991. 16.95 (0-312-04599-9) St Martin.

Death Is & Approaches to the Edge. William J. Higginson. (Xtras Ser.: No. 9). 48p. (Orig.). 1981. pap. 2.50 (0-89120-019-3) From Here.

Death Is Different: Studies in the Morality, Law, & Politics of Capital Punishment. Hugo A. Bedau. 360p. 1987. text ed. 37.50 (1-55553-008-7) NE U Pr.

Death Is for All: Death & Death Related Beliefs of Rural Spanish-Americans. Juli E. Skansie. LC 85-3980. (Immigrant Communities & Ethnic Minorities in the U. S. & Canada Ser.: No. 5). (C). 1985. 39.50 (0-404-19414-1) AMS Pr.

Death Is for Losers. large type ed. William Newton. 1991. pap. 13.95 (0-7089-7003-6) Ulverscroft.

Death Is Forever. John Gardner. 352p. 1993. mass mkt. 5.99 (0-425-13700-7) Berkley Pub.

Death Is Forever. large type ed. John Gardner. LC 93-2159. 1994. 19.95 (0-7927-1751-1, Paragon Lrg Print); pap. 17.95 (0-7927-1750-3, Paragon Lrg Print) Chivers N Amer.

Death Is Hard to Live With: Teenagers & How They Cope with Death. Comp. by Janet Bode. LC 92-32409. 1993. 16.95 (0-385-31041-2) Delacorte.

*__Death Is Hard to Live With: Teenagers Talk about How They Cope with Loss.__ Janet Bode. (YA). 1995. pap. 3.99 (0-440-21929-9) Dell.

*__Death Is Lighter Than a Feather.__ David Westheimer. 431p. 1995. pap. 16.95 (0-929398-90-4) UNTX Pr.

Death Is Natural. Laurence Pringle. LC 90-46402. (Illus.). 64p. (J). (gr. 1 up). 1991. reprint ed. lib. bdg. 12.88 (0-688-10467-3) Morrow Jr Bks.

Death Is Natural. Laurence Pringle. LC 90-46402. (Illus.). 64p. (J). (gr. 1 up). 1991. reprint ed. pap. 5.95 (0-688-10528-9, Pub. by Beech Tree Bks) Morrow.

Death Is Not Saying Goodbye. Rose Perl. 60p. 1987. pap. 6.50 (0-910458-60-X) Select Bks.

Death Is Not the End. Billy J. Daugherty. 32p. (Orig.). 1993. pap. 0.50 (1-56267-095-6) Victory Ctr OK.

Death Is Nothing at All. 1995. 5.95 (0-285-62824-0, Pub. by Souvenir UK) Atrium Pubs.

*__Death Is of Vital Importance: On Life, Death, & Life after Death.__ Elisabeth Kubler-Ross. 1994. pap. 12.95 (0-88268-186-9) Station Hill Pr.

Death Is Only a Horizon: Thoughts in Time of Bereavement. Michael McGreevy. (Illus.). 16p. 1990. reprint ed. pap. text ed. 1.95 (0-89243-446-5) Liguori Pubns.

Death Is So Kind. Liam Redmond. 1959. 9.95 (0-8159-5301-1) Devin.

Death Is the Mother of Beauty: Metaphor, Mind, Criticism. Mark Turner. LC 87-5998. xii, 212p. (C). 1987. 16.95 (0-226-81721-0) U Ch Pr.

Death Kit. Susan Sontag. 1991. mass mkt. 9.95 (0-385-26711-8, Anchor NY) Doubleday.

Death Knell. C. Terry Cline, Jr. 1978. pap. 2.25 (0-449-23639-0, Crest) Fawcett.

Death Knell. large type ed. Terry Cline. 480p. 1981. 15.95 (0-7089-0561-7) Ulverscroft.

Death, Lies & Videotape. 48p. 1991. 10.00 (0-87431-159-4, 12023) West End Games.

Death Lights a Candle. Phoebe A. Taylor. (Asey Mayo Cape Cod Mystery Ser.). 304p. 1989. reprint ed. pap. 6.95 (0-88150-145-X, Foul Play) Countryman.

Death Likes It Hot. limited ed. Edgar Box, pseud. LC 91-12799. 224p. 1991. reprint ed. 75.00 (1-56287-001-7) Armchair Detective.

Death Likes It Hot. Edgar Box, pseud. LC 91-12799. 224p. 1991. reprint ed. 18.95 (1-56287-000-9); reprint ed. 25.00 (1-56287-012-2) Armchair Detective.

Death-Line. large type ed. June Mercer. 304p. 1987. 16.95 (0-7089-1614-7) Ulverscroft.

Death List. Donald Goines. (Orig.). 1974. pap. 3.50 (0-87067-195-2) Holloway.

Death Lives Next Door. large type ed. Gwendoline Butler. (Popular Ser.). 242p. 1993. reprint ed. pap. 17.95 (1-56054-630-1) Thorndike Pr.

Death Load. (Executioner Ser.: No. 150). 1991. mass mkt. 3.50 (0-373-61150-1, Wrldwide Lib) Harlequin Bks.

Death Log. James Romenesko. LC 82-90083. (Orig.). 1982. pap. 7.95 (0-942724-00-3) Police Beat Pr.

Death March: The Survivors of Bataan. Donald Knox. LC 81-47555. (Illus.). 412p. 1983. pap. 11.95 (0-15-625224-4, Harvest Bks) HarBrace.

Death March on Mount Hakkoda. Jiro Nitta. Tr. by James Westerhoven. LC 91-24157. (Rock Spring Collection). 204p. (Orig.). 1991. pap. 10.95 (0-9628137-2-9, Rock Spring Collect) Stone Bridge Pr.

Death Mask. Jane Dentinger. 304p. 1994. reprint ed. mass mkt. 5.95 (0-14-015843-X, Penguin Bks) Viking Penguin.

*__Death Masque.__ P. N. Elrod. 272p. (Orig.). 1995. pap. text ed. 4.99 (0-441-00143-2) Ace Bks.

Death Master Strike. David Robbins. (Blade Ser.: No. 12). 192p. (Orig.). 1991. pap. 3.50 (0-8439-3116-7) Dorchester Pub Co.

Death Mazurka: Poems. rev. ed. Charles Fishman. LC 89-5032. (Illus.). (C). 1989. reprint ed. 15.95 (0-89672-201-5); reprint ed. pap. 8.95 (0-89672-206-6) Tex Tech Univ Pr.

Death Merchants. James H. Readus. 382p. 1991. pap. 3.95 (0-87067-323-8, BH323) Holloway.

*__Death My Generation.__ Michael Fyodrov. (American Autobiography Ser.). 301p. 1995. reprint ed. lib. bdg. 89.00 (0-7812-8526-7) Rprt Serv.

Death Next Door. Gwendoline Butler. (WWL Mystery Ser.). 1994. mass mkt. 3.99 (0-373-26157-8, 1-26157-7) Harlequin Bks.

Death Notes. Ruth Rendell. (Chief Inspector Wexford Ser.). 224p. 1986. mass mkt. 5.99 (0-345-34198-8) Ballantine.

Death Notices, Dutchess & Columbia County, New York 1859-1918. Margaret E. Herrick. 321p. 1991. lib. bdg. 56.00 (1-56012-115-7) Kinship Rhinebeck.

*__Death Notices, Dutchess & Columbia County, New York, 1919-1936: From Red Hook & Rhinebeck Newspapers.__ Ed. by Margaret E. Herrick. 126p. 1992. pap. 23.00 (1-56012-122-X, 116) Kinship Rhinebeck.

Death Notices from Freewill Baptist Publications: 1811-1851. David C. Young & Robert L. Taylor. vi, 453p. (Orig.). 1985. 37.50 (0-917890-51-5) Heritage Bk.

Death Notices from the Canada Christian Advocate, 1858-1872. Donald A. McKenzie. 384p. 1992. lib. bdg. 27.50 (0-912606-35-5) Hunterdon Hse.

Death Notices from The Christian Guardian, 1836-1850. Donald A. McKenzie. 368p. 1982. lib. bdg. 25.00 (0-912606-10-X) Hunterdon Hse.

Death Notices from the Christian Guardian, 1851-1860. Donald A. McKenzie. 365p. 1984. lib. bdg. 25.00 (0-912606-25-8) Hunterdon Hse.

Death Notification: A Practical Guide to the Process. Moroni Leash. (Orig.). 1994. pap. 19.95 (0-942679-08-3) Upper Access.

Death of a Beekeeper. Lars Gustafsson. Tr. by Janet K. Swaffer & Guntram H. Weber. LC 81-11182. 160p. 1981. 7.95 (0-8112-0809-5); pap. 5.95 (0-8112-0810-9, NDP523) New Directions.

*__Death of a Blue Hero.__ A. C. Tassie. 320p. (Orig.). 1995. pap. 9.95 (0-7610-0014-3) NW Pub.

*__Death of a Busy Body.__ Dell Shannon. 192p. 1988. 7.98 (1-56865-082-5, GuildAmerica) Dblday Bk Music.

Death of a Butterfly. large type ed. Margaret Maron. 1991. 21.95 (0-7089-2465-4) Ulverscroft.

Death of a Cad. M. C. Beaton. 1988. mass mkt. 4.99 (0-8041-0225-2) Ivy Books.

Death of a Chancellor. large type ed. Warren Carrier. LC 94-1766. 274p. 1994. lib. bdg. 17.95 (0-7862-0204-1) Thorndike Pr.

Death of a Charming Man. M. C. Beaton. 224p. 1994. 18.95 (0-89296-529-0) Mysterious Pr.

Death of a Charming Man. M. C. Beaton. 176p. 1995. mass mkt. 5.50 (0-446-40338-5, Mysterious Paperbk) Warner Bks.

Death of a Christian: The Order of Christian Funerals. Richard Rutherford. 224p. 1992. pap. 14.95 (0-8146-6040-1, Pueblo Bks) Liturgical Pr.

Death of a Cloudwalker. E. S. Russell. 192p. 1991. 18.95 (0-8027-5784-7) Walker & Co.

Death of a Commuter. Leo Bruce. (Carolus Deene Mystery Ser.). 192p. 1988. pap. 5.95 (0-89733-326-8) Academy Chi Pubs.

Death of a Conman. Bell. (Black Dagger Crime Ser.). 16.50 (0-86220-784-3, Black Dagger) Chivers N Amer.

*__Death of a Critic: An Alex Grismolet Mystery.__ Dean Fuller. LC 95-11766. 1995. write for info. (0-316-29601-5) Little.

Death of a Daimyo. large type ed. James Melville. 256p. 1986. 21.95 (0-7089-1462-4) Ulverscroft.

Death of a Dandie Dinmont. large type ed. Madelaine Duke. (Linford Mystery Library). 240p. 1988. pap. 11.95 (0-7089-6614-4, Linford) Ulverscroft.

*__Death of a Darklord.__ Lavrell K. Hamilton. (Ravenloft Ser.). 320p. (Orig.). 1995. pap. 4.95 (0-7869-0112-8) TSR Inc.

*__Death of a Difficult Woman.__ Carole Berry. 272p. (Orig.). 1994. text ed. 18.95 (0-425-14356-2, Prime Crime) Berkley Pub.

*__Death of a Difficult Woman.__ Carole Berry. 272p. (Orig.). 1995. pap. 4.99 (0-425-15008-9, Prime Crime) Berkley Pub.

Death of a Dissident. Stuart M. Kaminsky. 1989. mass mkt. 5.50 (0-8041-0404-2) Ivy Books.

*__Death of a Dissident.__ Moorhead Kennedy & Martha Keys. Date not set. 89.95 (0-614-02989-9) Amer Forum.

Death of a Dissident. limited ed. Stuart M. Kaminsky. LC 91-12800. 256p. 1991. reprint ed. 75.00 (1-56287-019-X) Armchair Detective.

Death of a Dissident. Stuart M. Kaminsky. LC 91-12800. 256p. 1991. reprint ed. 19.95 (1-56287-017-3); reprint ed. 25.00 (1-56287-018-1) Armchair Detective.

*__Death of a Dissident & Fire in the Forest, 2 bks., Set.__ Moorhead Kennedy & Martha Keys. Date not set. 150.00 (0-614-02990-2) Amer Forum.

Death of a Doctor: And Other Stories. Elspeth Davie. 224p. 1992. 23.95 (1-85619-134-6, Sinclair-Stevenson) Trafalgar.

*__Death of a Dream Maker.__ Gallagher Gray. 1995. mass mkt. 5.50 (0-8041-1247-9) Ivy Books.

Death of a Dude, Vol. 1. Rex Stout. 1994. mass mkt. 4.99 (0-553-24730-1) Bantam.

Death of a Dunwoody Matron. Patricia H. Sprinkle. LC 92-38574. 1993. 17.00 (0-385-42485-X) Doubleday.

Death of a Fool. Ngaio Marsh. 288p. 1994. pap. 4.50 (0-425-14303-1, Prime Crime) Berkley Pub.

Death of a Fool. Ngaio Marsh. 1976. reprint ed. lib. bdg. 21.95 (0-88411-480-5, Aeonian Pr) Amereon Ltd.

Death of a "Gentleman" large type ed. E. Radford & M. A. Radford. (Mystery Ser.). 1976. 15.95 (0-85456-447-0) Ulverscroft.

Death of a Ghost. Margery Allingham. 175p. 1993. 16.95 (0-89190-195-7, Am Repr) Amereon Ltd.

Death of a Ghost. Margery Allingham. 1993. reprint ed. lib. bdg. 15.95 (0-89968-453-X) Buccaneer Bks.

*__Death of a Glutton.__ M. C. Beaton. 1995. mass mkt. 5.50 (0-8041-1212-6) Ivy Books.

Death of a Glutton. M. C. Beaton. LC 92-21220. 1993. 16.95 (0-312-08761-6) St Martin.

Death of a God & Its Fruits in Humanity (Plus) The Gospel of St. Mark. Rudolf Steiner. 20p. 1969. spiral bd. 3.30 (0-7873-0840-4) Mokelumne.

Death of a Good Woman. J. F. Straker. 224p. 1994. 16.95 (0-7451-8635-1, Black Dagger) Chivers N Amer.

Death of a Good Woman. large type ed. Marjorie Eccles. 1991. 21.95 (0-7089-2460-3) Ulverscroft.

Death of a Gossip. M. C. Beaton. 160p. 1988. reprint ed. mass mkt. 4.99 (0-8041-0226-0) Ivy Books.

Death of a Guru. rev. ed. Rabindranath R. Maharaj & Dave Hunt. LC 84-81212. 208p. 1986. reprint ed. pap. 7.99 (0-89081-434-1) Harvest Hse.

*__Death of a Hawker.__ Janwillem Van de Wetering. 221p. 1995. pap. 10.00 (1-56947-079-0) Soho Press.

*__Death of a Hero, Birth of the Soul: Answering the Call of Midlife.__ John C. Robinson. 352p. 1995. pap. 16.95 (0-929999-09-6) Tzedakah Pubns.

Death of a Hollow Man. Caroline Graham. 320p. 1990. mass mkt. 4.99 (0-380-70951-1) Avon.

Death of a Holy Murderer. large type ed. Madelaine Duke. (Linford Mystery Library). 224p. 1988. pap. 11.95 (0-7089-6626-8, Linford) Ulverscroft.

Death of a Hussy. M. C. Beaton. 1991. mass mkt. 4.50 (0-8041-0768-8) Ivy Books.

Death of a Jewish American Princess: The True Story of a Victim on Trial. Shirley Frondorf. LC 87-40576. (Illus.). 320p. 1988. 18.95 (0-394-56854-0, Villard Bks) Random.

Death of a Joyce Scholar. Bartholomew Gill. 256p. 1990. reprint ed. mass mkt. 4.99 (0-380-71129-X) Avon.

Death of a Kaiser. Jain I. Lin. (Illus.). 128p. (Orig.). 1985. pap. 5.95 (0-913428-56-6) Landfall Pr.

Death of a Lake. Arthur W. Upfield. 192p. 1983. pap. 6.00 (0-684-17886-9, Scribners) S&S Trade.

Death of a Language: The History of Judeo-Spanish. Tracy K. Harris. LC 93-39867. 1994. write for info. (0-87413-497-8) U Delaware Pr.

Death of a Left-Handed Woman. large type ed. Cyril Joyce. (Linford Mystery Library). 304p. 1993. pap. 14.95 (0-7089-7379-5, Trailtree Bookshop) Ulverscroft.

*__Death of a Macho Man.__ M. C. Beaton. 1996. write for info. (0-89296-531-2) Mysterious Pr.

Death of a Man. Kay Boyle. LC 88-26799. (Revived Modern Classics Ser.). 336p. 1989. reprint ed. pap. 10.95 (0-8112-1089-8, NPD670) New Directions.

Death of a Man-Tamer. large type ed. Miles Tripp. 1990. 21.95 (0-7089-2145-0) Ulverscroft.

*__Death of a Marionette.__ Frank M. Robinson & Joe Smith. 1995. 22.95 (0-614-03855-3) Forge NYC.

Death of a Marriage. Pauline Bunin. LC 94-71240. 238p. (Orig.). 1995. pap. 14.95 (1-884866-00-X) Cosmos Bks.

Death of a Marriage Law: Epitaph for the Rishis. J. Duncan Derrett. LC 77-93389. 254p. 1978. 18.95 (0-89089-056-0) Carolina Acad Pr.

Death of a Martyr: The Ballad of Rocky Ruiz. Manuel Ramos. 208p. 1993. 17.95 (0-312-09271-7, Pub. by Thomas Dunne Bks) St Martin.

*__Death of a Merry Widow.__ Richard Hunt. 1994. 18.95 (0-312-11773-6) St Martin.

Death of a Metaphor. Desmond Egan. 167p. (C). 1991. text ed. 64.50 (0-389-20952-X) B&N Imports.

*__Death of a Modern Man.__ Date not set. 14.95 (0-9644731-0-0) Appleton & Lange.

*__Death of a Mother.__ Ainley. 1995. pap. 13.00 (0-04-440928-1) Harper SF.

*__Death of a Mother: Daughter's Stories.__ Rosa Ainley. 1995. pap. 12.00 (0-06-440928-7) Harper SF.

*__Death of a Mystery Writer.__ Robert Barnard. 1993. Not sold separately (0-615-00013-4) Random Hse Value.

*__Death of a Mystery Writer.__ Robert Barnard. 224p. 1995. mass mkt. 5.95 (0-14-023786-0, Penguin Bks) Viking Penguin.

Death of a Nag. M. C. Beaton. 1995. 18.95 (0-89296-530-4) Mysterious Pr.

Death of a Nation. John A. Stormer. 1983. pap. 5.95 (0-914053-03-5) Liberty Bell Pr.

Death of a Nation: The Story of Lee & His Men at Gettysburg. Clifford Dowdey. 383p. 1988. reprint ed. 25.00 (0-935523-14-6) Butternut & Blue.

Death of a Nation: The Story of Lee & His Men at Gettysburg. Clifford Dowdey. 383p. 1995. reprint ed. pap. 12.95 (0-935523-15-4) Butternut & Blue.

Death of a Naturalist. Seamus Heaney. LC 85-12908. 58p. 1969. pap. 9.95 (0-571-09024-9) Faber & Faber.

Death of a Navy: Japanese Naval Action in World War II. Andrieu D'Albas. 1957. 14.95 (0-8159-5302-X) Devin.

Death of a Nurse. Ed McBain. 192p. 1991. mass mkt. 4.50 (0-380-71125-7) Avon.

Death of a Nurse. limited ed. Ed McBain. (Armchair Detective Library). 192p. 1994. reprint ed. 75.00 (1-56287-062-9) Armchair Detective.

Death of a Nurse. Ed McBain. (Armchair Detective Library). 192p. reprint ed. 22.00 (1-56287-061-0) Armchair Detective.

Death of a Partner. Janet Neel. 1991. 16.95 (0-312-05411-4) St Martin.

Death of a Partner. Janet Neel. Ed. by Jane Chelius. 256p. 1994. reprint ed. mass mkt. 4.99 (0-671-74839-4) PB.

Death of a Peer. Ngaio Marsh. 320p. 1994. pap. text ed. 4.99 (0-425-14353-8, Prime Crime) Berkley Pub.

Death of a Peer. Ngaio Marsh. 1976. reprint ed. lib. bdg. 24.95 (0-88411-481-3, Aeonian Pr) Amereon Ltd.

*__Death of a Perfect Mother.__ Robert Barnard. 1993. Not sold separately (0-615-00011-8) Random.

Death of a Perfect Wife. M. C. Beaton. 1990. mass mkt. 4.99 (0-8041-0593-6) Ivy Books.

Death of a Poison-Tongue. large type ed. Josephine Bell. 1979. 12.00 (0-7089-0378-9) Ulverscroft.

*__Death of a Postmodernist.__ Janice Steinberg. 256p. (Orig.). 1995. pap. text ed. 4.99 (0-425-14546-8, Prime Crime) Berkley Pub.

Death of a Prankster. M. C. Beaton. 1993. mass mkt. 4.50 (0-8041-1102-2) Ivy Books.

Death of a President: November 1963. William Manchester. LC 88-45174. 752p. 1988. pap. 16.00 (0-06-091531-5, HarpT) HarpC.

Death of a Raven. large type ed. Margaret Duffy. 1990. 21.95 (0-7089-2202-3) Ulverscroft.

Death of a Rebel: A Biography of Phil Ochs. rev. ed. Marc Eliot. LC 94-20257. 1994. 14.95 (0-8065-1555-4, Citadel Pr) Carol Pub Group.

Death of a Riverkeeper. Ernest Schwiebert. LC 80-10824. (Illus.). 312p. 1984. pap. 8.95 (0-916870-72-3) Creat Arts Bk.

Death of a Russian Priest. Stuart M. Kaminsky. 1993. mass mkt. 4.99 (0-8041-0836-6) Ivy Books.

Death of a Sahib. large type ed. Clive Egleton. 1990. 21.95 (0-7089-2204-X) Ulverscroft.

Death of a Salesman. Arthur Miller. 17.95 (0-89190-729-7, Am Repr) Amereon Ltd.

Death of a Salesman. Arthur Miller. 1952. pap. 4.75 (0-8222-0290-5) Dramatists Play.

Death of a Salesman. Arthur Miller. 1976. pap. 7.95 (0-14-048134-6, Penguin Bks) Viking Penguin.

*__Death of a Salesman.__ Yasinski. (Max Notes Ser.). 128p. 1995. pap. text ed. 3.95 (0-87891-995-3) Res & Educ.

Death of a Salesman: A Study Guide. Joy Leavitt. (Novel-Ties Ser.). (YA). (gr. 10-12). 1984. student ed, teacher ed 15.95 (0-88122-113-9) Lrn Links.

1832

An Asterisk (*) at the beginning of an entry indicates that the title is appearing in BIP for the first time.

An Asterisk (*) at the beginning of an entry indicates that the title is appearing in BIP for the first time.

1833

Death of the Playwright? Modern British Drama & Literary Theory. Ed. by Adrian Page & Clive Bloom. (Insights Ser.). 192p. 1992. text ed. 49.95 (0-312-06537-X) St Martin.

Death of the Plover & Trace of the Buckskin: Two Stories. Marianne Gruber. Tr. & Aft. by Margaret T. Peischl. LC 94-6442. (Studies in Austrian Literature, Culture, & Thought. Translation Ser.). 119p. 1994. pap. 12.95 (0-929497-91-0) Ariadne CA.

Death of the Prophet. rev. ed. Jason Leen. LC 88-32021. 1988. reprint ed. pap. 7.95 (0-935699-02-3) Illum Arts.

Death of the Prussian Republican: A Study of Reich-Prussian Relations, 1932-1934. Earl R. Beck. LC 59-9600. (Florida State University Studies: No. 31). 293p. reprint ed. pap. 83.60 (0-7837-5021-8, 2044689) Bks Demand.

Death of the Schooner Integrity. Frank Mulville. (Illus.). 169p. 1981. 12.95 (0-89182-032-9); pap. 7.95 (0-89182-033-7) Charles River Bks.

Death of the Soul: From Descartes to the Computer. William E. Barrett. LC 82-45317. 192p. 1987. pap. 11.95 (0-385-17327-X, Anchor NY) Doubleday.

Death of the Sweet Waters. Donald E. Carr. (Illus.). 1966. 6.95 (0-393-06354-2) Norton.

Death of the Third Nature. Robert J. Pruitt. 1975. pap. 2.50 (0-934942-04-8) White Wing Pub.

Death of the Troubadour: The Late Medieval Resistance to the Renaissance. Gregory B. Stone. LC 93-35923. 232p. (C). 1994. text ed. 32.95 (0-8122-3214-3) U of Pa Pr.

Death of the Woodstock Generation. Paul Carton. LC 94-94453. 80p. (Orig.). 1994. pap. 6.95 (0-9641889-0-2) V Cortlandt Bks.

Death of Titian. Hugo Von Hofmannsthal. 1977. lib. bdg. 59.95 (0-8490-1704-1) Gordon Pr.

Death of Tutankhamen. William Leftschatz. 220p. (Orig.). 1989. pap. 10.95 (0-933753-07-1) Canterbury.

Death of Tyrants. Tyler. 1994. 19.95 (0-8050-2340-2) H Holt & Co.

Death of Understanding. limited ed. Harry Kondoleon. 22p. 1987. 20.00 (0-936897-06-6) Caliban.

Death of Virgil. Hermann Broch. 15.75 (0-8446-1742-3) Peter Smith.

***Death of Virgil.** Hermann Broch. Tr. by Jean S. Untermeyer. LC 94-34712. 1995. pap. 16.00 (0-679-75548-9, Vin) Random.

Death of Virgil. Hermann Broch. Tr. by Jean S. Untermeyer. LC 82-73712. (Broch Novels Ser.). 496p. 1982. reprint ed. pap. 16.95 (0-86547-115-0, North Pt Pr) FS&G.

***Death of William Gooch: A History's Anthropology.** Greg Dening. LC 95-7563. Orig. Title: A History's Anthropology: The Death of William Gooch. 1995. write for info. (0-8248-1754-0) UH Pr.

Death of Woman Wang. Jonathan D. Spence. 1979. pap. 9.95 (0-14-005121-X, Penguin Bks) Viking Penguin.

Death of Zukasky. Richard Strand. 1991. pap. 4.75 (0-8222-0293-X) Dramatists Play.

Death on a Cold, Wild River. Bartholomew Gill. 256p. 1994. mass mkt. 4.99 (0-380-72205-4) Avon.

Death on a Cold, Wild River: A Peter McGarr Mystery. Bartholomew Gill. LC 93-7729. 1993. 20.00 (0-688-12881-5) Morrow.

Death on a Quiet Beach. large type ed. Simon Challis. (Linford Mystery Library). 304p. 1989. pap. 11.95 (0-7089-6724-8, Linford) Ulverscroft.

Death on Allhallowe'en. Leo Bruce. (Carolus Deene Mystery Ser.). 176p. 1988. pap. 5.95 (0-89733-292-X) Academy Chi Pubs.

Death on Demand. Carolyn G. Hart. 1987. mass mkt. 4.99 (0-553-26351-X) Bantam.

Death on Demand. 3rd ed. Kim Hill & Owen Dale. 1994. pap. text ed. 9.95 (0-913878-52-9) T Horton & Dghts.

Death on Doomsday. large type ed. Elizabeth Lemarchand. 1973. 12.00 (0-85456-173-0) Ulverscroft.

Death on Hemodialysis: Preventable or Inevitable? Ed. by E. A. Friedman. LC 93-42588. (Developments in Nephrology Ser.: Vol. 35). 224p. (C). 1994. lib. bdg 86.00 (0-7923-2652-0) Kluwer Ac.

Death on High Mesa. large type ed. Elliot Long. (Linford Western Library). 224p. 1994. pap. 14.95 (0-7089-7492-9, Linford) Ulverscroft.

Death on Remand. large type ed. Michael Underwood. 1992. 18.95 (0-7451-6414-5, Scarlet Dagger Lrg Print) Chivers N Amer.

Death on Remand. large type ed. Michael Underwood. 1993. pap. 16.95 (0-7451-6420-X, Scarlet Dagger Lrg Print) Chivers N Amer.

Death on Site. Janet Neel. Ed. by Jane Chelius. 288p. 1993. reprint ed. mass mkt. 4.99 (0-671-73581-0) PB.

Death on Television: The Best of Henry Slesar's Alfred Hitchcock Stories. Henry Slesar. Ed. by Francis M. Nevins, Jr. & Martin H. Greenberg. LC 88-26342. 270p. (C). 1989. 19.95 (0-8093-1500-9) S Ill U Pr.

Death on the Agenda. Patricia Moyes. LC 84-6750. 192p. 1984. pap. 5.95 (0-8050-0507-2, Owl) H Holt & Co.

Death on the Cards. large type ed. Richard Grayson. 1990. 21.95 (0-7089-2190-6) Ulverscroft.

Death on the Cliff Walk. Mary Kruger. (Gilded Age Mystery Ser.). 1994. 16.95 (0-8217-4769-X) Zebra.

Death on the Dragon's Tongue. Margot Arnold. 224p. 1990. reprint ed. pap. 6.50 (0-88150-158-1, Foul Play) Countryman.

Death on the High C's. large type ed. Robert Barnard. 298p. 1992. 21.95 (0-7505-0341-6) Ulverscroft.

Death on the Installment Plan. Louis-Ferdinand D. Celine. Tr. by Ralph Manheim. LC 48-6410. 1971. reprint ed. pap. 14.95 (0-8112-0017-5, NDP330) New Directions.

Death on the Isles of Scilly: The Grave in California Field. John Purchas. (C). 1989. 35.00 (0-907566-79-0, Pub. by Dyllansow Truran UK) St Mut.

Death on the Late Show. Jan Michaels. (Mystery Puzzler Ser.: No. 14). (Illus.). (Orig.). 1979. pap. 1.95 (0-89083-434-2) Zebra.

Death on the Motorway. large type ed. Christopher Coram. (Linford Mystery Library). 1991. pap. 13.95 (0-7089-7065-6) Ulverscroft.

Death on the Move. Bill Crider. 1990. mass mkt. 3.95 (0-8041-0425-5) Ivy Books.

Death on the Move. Bill Crider. 204p. 1989. 17.95 (0-8027-5730-8) Walker & Co.

Death on the Nile. Agatha Christie. 1992. mass mkt. 4.99 (0-06-100369-7, Harp PBks) HarpC.

***Death on the Pasture.** S. B. Jones-Hendrickson. 304p. 1994. 19.95 (0-932831-13-3) Eastern Caribbean Inst.

Death on the Picket Line: The Story of John McCoy. Jerry White. (Illus.). 70p. (Orig.). (C). 1990. pap. 12.95 (0-929087-52-6) Labor Pubns Inc.

Death on the Prairie: The Thirty Years' Struggle for the Western Plains. Paul I. Wellman. LC 87-10886. (Illus.). xii, 322p. 1987. reprint ed. 33.00 (0-8032-4747-8); reprint ed. pap. 10.95 (0-8032-9721-1) U of Nebr Pr.

***Death on the Rhine.** Charles Whiting. 1995. lib. bdg. 20.00 (0-7278-4693-0) Severn Hse.

Death on the Rocks. large type ed. J. R. Anderson. 1978. 21.95 (0-7089-0121-2) Ulverscroft.

Death on the Run. Intro. by Timothy J. Rogers. LC 86-62497. 99p. 1987. 13.00 (0-938972-11-1) Spanish Lit Pubns.

Death on the Slopes. Norma Schier. (Mystery Puzzler Ser.: No. 11). (Illus.). (Orig.). 1978. pap. 1.95 (0-89083-423-7) Zebra.

Death on the Texas Range. Patrick E. Andrews. 224p. 1992. pap. 3.50 (0-8217-3804-6) Zebra.

***Death on the Verandah.** Ed. by Cynthia Manson. 304p. 1995. pap. text ed. 4.99 (0-425-14836-X, Prime Crime) Berkley Pub.

Death on the Verandah: Mystery Stories of the South. Ed. by Cynthia Manson. 288p. 1994. 19.95 (0-7867-0055-6) Carroll & Graf.

Death on the White Time. Jim Dawson. 272p. (Orig.). 1990. pap. 8.95 (0-88739-143-5) Creat Arts Bk.

***Death on the Wild Side.** Jack Corbett. 465p. (Orig.). 1995. pap. 19.95 (0-9647143-0-2) Nirvana Pubng.

Death on Your Doorstep: One Hundred One Weapons in the Average Home. Rdean Omar. (Illus.). 75p. 1992. pap. 7.95 (0-939427-85-0) Alpha Pubns OH.

Death on 66: A Taggart Roper Mystery. William Sanders. 256p. 1993. 20.95 (0-312-10452-9, Pub. by Thomas Dunne Bks) St Martin.

Death or Dialogue? From the Age of Monologue to the Age of Dialogue. John B. Cobb, Jr. et al. LC 90-31485. 160p. 1991. pap. 15.95 (0-334-02445-5) TPI PA.

***Death or Resurrection: A Story of the Hindus.** J. A. Naik. (C). 1995. 14.00x (0-8364-2909-5, Pub. by Ajanta II) S Asia.

***Death Out of Order.** Cecil L. Bolding. 80p. Date not set. pap. 6.95 (0-7610-0401-7) NW Pub.

Death Pays All Debts. large type ed. Miriam Sharman. (Linford Mystery Library). 384p. 1993. pap. 14.95 (0-7089-7424-4, Trailtree Bookshop) Ulverscroft.

Death Pays the Rose Rent: A Tori Miracle Mystery. Valerie S. Malmont. LC 93-42075. 1994. 20.00 (0-671-86967-1) S&S Trade.

Death Penalties. Paula Gosling. 1991. 17.95 (0-89296-458-8) Mysterious Pr.

Death Penalties. Paula Gosling. 304p. 1992. mass mkt. 4.99 (0-446-40189-7, Mysterious Paperbk) Warner Bks.

Death Penalties. large type ed. Paula Gosling. LC 91-44758. 450p. 1992. reprint ed. lib. bdg. 17.95 (1-56054-349-3) Thorndike Pr.

Death Penalties: The Supreme Court's Obstacle Course. Raoul Berger. 252p. 1982. 29.95 (0-674-19426-8) HUP.

Death Penalty. 64p. 0.10 (0-318-16907-X, CSE2058) Bd Church & Soc.

Death Penalty. Amnesty International Staff. (Illus.). 209p. (Orig.). 1979. pap. 5.00 (0-900058-88-9, Pub. by Amnesty Intl Pubns UK) Amnesty Intl USA.

Death Penalty. William J. Coughlin. 1993. pap. 22.95 (0-7927-1541-1, Paragon Lrg Print) Chivers N Amer.

Death Penalty. William J. Coughlin. 1993. mass mkt. 5.99 (0-06-109053-0, Harp PBks) HarpC.

Death Penalty. Leon Friedman. (Constitutional Issues Ser.). 384p. 29.95x (0-8160-2502-9) Facts on File.

***Death Penalty.** Dennis Hamley. (YA). 1995. pap. 3.50 (0-590-20356-8) Scholastic Inc.

Death Penalty. Don Nardo. LC 92-20366. (Overview Ser.). (Illus.). 112p. (J). (gr. 5-8). 1992. lib. bdg. 16.95 (1-56006-132-4) Lucent Bks.

***Death Penalty.** Mark Tushnet. (Constitutional Issues Ser.). 256p. 1994. 35.00x (0-614-03745-X) Facts on File.

Death Penalty. Peter T. Van Pelt. LC 90-71974. 160p. (Orig.). 1993. pap. 9.00 (1-56002-034-2, Univ Edtns) Aegina Pr.

Death Penalty. Ed. by Carol Wekesser. LC 91-9931. (Opposing Viewpoints Ser.). (Illus.). 264p. (YA). (gr. 10 up). 1991. lib. bdg. 19.95 (0-89908-180-0); pap. text ed. 11.55 (0-89908-155-X) Greenhaven.

Death Penalty. large type ed. William J. Coughlin. LC 93-2955. 1993. 22.95 (0-7927-1542-X, Eagle Lrg Print) Chivers N Amer.

***Death Penalty: A Bibliographic Research.** Ed. by Ugo Leone. 119p. (Orig.). (C). 1995. pap. text ed. 40.00x (0-7881-1573-1) Diane Pub.

Death Penalty: A Bibliographical Research. 25.00 (92-9078-006-1, E. 88. III.N.3) UN.

Death Penalty: A Debate. Ernest Van den Haag & John P. Conrad. LC 83-11079. 320p. 1983. 19.95 (0-306-41416-3, Plenum Pr) Plenum.

Death Penalty: A World-Wide Perspective. Roger G. Hood. 200p. 1991. reprint ed. pap. 18.95 (0-19-825706-6) OUP.

Death Penalty: God's Will or Man's Folly? Robert P. Martin. 87p. (Orig.). (C). 1991. pap. 5.95 (0-9622508-5-6) Simpson NJ.

Death Penalty: Identifying Propaganda Techniques. Carol O'Sullivan. LC 89-11033. (Opposing Viewpoints Juniors Ser.). (Illus.). 32p. (J). (gr. 3-6). 1990. lib. bdg. 11.95 (0-89908-636-5) Greenhaven.

Death Penalty: Is It Justice? Richard Steins. (Issues of Our Time Ser.). (Illus.). 64p. (J). (gr. 5-8). 1993. lib. bdg. 15.98 (0-8050-2571-5) TFC Bks NY.

Death Penalty: Issues & Answers. David Lester. 102p. 1987. 31.95x (0-398-05305-7) C C Thomas.

Death Penalty - A View from the Bench: An Autobiography. Mark Brandler. 1993. 17.95 (0-533-10424-6) Vantage.

Death Penalty & Crime: Empirical Studies. Kilman Shin. LC 77-84025. (C). 1978. text ed. 20.00 (0-686-12042-6) G Mason Econ.

Death Penalty & Racial Bias: Overturning Supreme Court Assumptions. Gregory D. Russell. LC 93-25069. (Contributions in Legal Studies: No. 75). 184p. 1993. text ed. 55.00 (0-313-28889-5, GM8889, Greenwood Pr) Greenwood.

Death Penalty Enquiry see Capital Punishment in the Twentieth Century: With Intro. & Index Added

Death Penalty in America. 3rd ed. Ed. by Hugo A. Bedau. (Illus.). 1982. 30.00 (0-19-502986-0); pap. 12.95 (0-19-502987-9) OUP.

Death Penalty in America: Current Research. Robert M. Bohm. LC 90-82314. (ACJS-Anderson Monograph Ser.). 145p. (C). 1991. pap. text ed. 14.95 (0-87084-013-4) Anderson Pub Co.

Death Penalty in the Eighties: An Examination of the Modern System of Capital Punishment. Welsh S. White. LC 87-5909. 1987. 34.95 (0-472-10088-2) U of Mich Pr.

Death Penalty in the Nineties: An Examination of the Modern System of Capital Punishment. Welsh S. White. LC 90-49339. 280p. (C). 1991. pap. text ed. 19.95 (0-472-06461-4) U of Mich Pr.

Death Prone. Clare Curzon. 224p. 1994. 19.95 (0-312-10453-7) St Martin.

Death, Property, & the Ancestors: A Study of the Mortuary Customs of the LoDagaa of West Africa. Jack Goody. (Illus.). 464p. 1962. 52.50 (0-8047-0068-0) Stanford U Pr.

Death Puppet. Jim Nisbet. LC 88-7905. 192p. 1989. 16.95 (0-88739-136-2, Blk Lizard) Creat Arts Bk.

Death Qualified. Kate Wilhelm. (Northwest Mysteries Ser.). 1992. mass mkt. 5.99 (0-449-22155-5, Crest) Fawcett.

Death Quest. David Alexander. (Phoenix Ser.: No. 3). 224p. (Orig.). 1988. pap. 2.95 (0-8439-2571-X) Dorchester Pub Co.

Death Quest. L. Ron Hubbard. (Mission Earth Ser.: No. 6). 1995. pap. 5.99 (0-88404-287-1) Bridge Pubns Inc.

Death Ranch. Jon Sharpe. (Canyon O'Grady Ser.: No. 15). 176p. (Orig.). 1991. pap. 3.50 (0-451-17049-0, Sig) NAL-Dutton.

Death Records of Earth County, Texas (1903-1917), Vol. 1. Shirley B. Cawyer. LC 92-75273. 50p. (C). 1993. pap. 10.00 (0-9622746-3-1) Datatrace Systems.

***Death Records of Monroe County, MI Vol. 1: 1867-1878, with Index.** Ed. & Intro. by Marie McNair. 346p. 1994. 22.50 (0-614-03320-9) Monroe County Lib.

***Death Rehearsal.** Doug Pokorski. LC 95-60159. 1995. pap. 12.95 (0-87243-215-7) Templegate.

Death, Resurrection, Immortality. Joseph E. Kirk. 111p. 1977. pap. 3.00 (0-910424-67-5) Concordant.

Death Ride. Paul Hofrichter. (Roadblaster Ser.: No. 2). 192p. (Orig.). 1988. pap. 2.95 (0-8439-2594-9) Dorchester Pub Co.

Death Rides in Texas. Clint Hawkins. (Saddle Tramp Ser.: No. 8). 1994. mass mkt. 3.50 (0-06-100765-X, Pub. by Haags Gemeentemuseum) HarpC.

Death Rides the Rockies. Robert Kammen. 288p. 1988. pap. 2.95 (0-8217-2509-2) Zebra.

Death Rides the Thunderhead. large type ed. Ames King. (Dales Western Ser.). 204p. 1992. pap. 16.95 (1-85389-337-4, Medcom-Trainex) Ulverscroft.

Death Rites. pap. write for info. (0-938924-18-4) Sri Shirdi Sai.

Death Rites: Law & Ethics at the End of Life. Ed. by Robert Lee & Derek Morgan. LC 93-6982. (Illus.). 352p. 1993. 59.95 (0-415-06260-8, B2279, Routledge NY) Routledge.

Death, Ritual & Bereavement. Ed. by Ralph Houlbrooke. 240p. 1989. 55.00 (0-415-01165-5) Routledge.

Death-Ritual & Social Structure in Classical Antiquity. Ian Morris. (Key Themes in Ancient History Ser.). (Illus.). 288p. (C). 1992. pap. 21.95 (0-521-37611-4) Cambridge U Pr.

Death Ritual in Late Imperial & Modern China. Ed. by James L. Watson & Evelyn S. Rawski. 349p. 1988. pap. 14.00 (0-520-07129-8) U CA Pr.

Death Ritual in Late Imperial & Modern China. Ed. by James L. Watson & Evelyn S. Rawski. (Studies on China: Vol. 8). 368p. (C). 1988. 47.50 (0-520-06081-4) U CA Pr.

Death Rituals & Life in the Societies of the Kula Ring. Ed. by Roy Wagner. (Illus.). 297p. 1989. text ed. 35.00 (0-87580-151-X); pap. text ed. 16.50 (0-87580-546-9) N Ill U Pr.

Death Rituals of Rural Greece. Loring M. Danforth. LC 82-47589. (Illus.). 248p. 1982. 57.50x (0-691-03132-0); pap. 19.95 (0-691-00027-1) Princeton U Pr.

Death Rode the Wind. Winston Cooke. 1995. 15.95 (0-8062-4983-8) Carlton.

Death Roll. Sam Llewellyn. Ed. by Jane Chelius. 256p. 1991. reprint ed. pap. 3.95 (0-671-67043-3) PB.

Death Row. Ed. by Dan Burger. (Illus.). 254p. (Orig.). 1993. pap. 19.95 (0-9624857-2-1) Glenn Hare Pubns.

Death Row. Bruce Jackson & Diane Christian. (Illus.). 312p. 1980. 34.95 (0-8070-3202-6) Transaction Pubs.

Death Row: Interviews with Inmates, Their Families & Opponents of Capital Punishment. Shirley Dicks. LC 89-13931. 158p. 1990. pap. 20.95x (0-89950-477-9) McFarland & Co.

Death Row Chaplain. Byron E. Eshelman & Frank Riley. LC 82-45876. (Capital Punishment Ser.). reprint ed. write for info. (0-404-62414-6) AMS Pr.

Death Row Dreamers. Keith D. Wilcock. 272p. 1993. 29.95 (0-917939-09-3) Sang Froid.

Death Row U. S. A. Reporter 1975-1988 & 1989-1993. NAACP Legal Defense & Educational Fund Staff. LC 89-81793. 1990. ring bd. 300.00 (0-89941-708-6, 306050) W S Hein.

Death Row Women. Tom Kuncl. Ed. by Dana Issacson. 288p. (Orig.). 1994. mass mkt. 5.99 (0-671-79391-8) PB.

Death Row 1992. Ed. by Dan Burger & Amy Little. (Illus.). 228p. 1989. 19.95 (0-685-52364-0) Glenn Hare Pubns.

Death Run. Mack Tanner. (Stalker Ser.: No. 3). (Orig.). 1992. mass mkt. 3.99 (0-06-100471-5, Harp PBks) HarpC.

Death, Sacrifice, & Tragedy. Martin Foss. LC 66-16513. 135p. reprint ed. pap. 38.50 (0-317-08120-9, 2001980) Bks Demand.

***Death Scene.** Beadle. Date not set. per. 10.95 (0-85449-088-4, Pub. by Gay Mens Pr UK) InBook.

Death-School. J. N. Williamson. 1982. pap. 2.95 (0-89083-981-6) Zebra.

Death Screen. Richard F. Beaird. 1983. pap. 2.95 (0-8217-1253-5) Zebra.

Death Sentence. Maurice Blanchot. Tr. by Lydia Davis. LC 78-59907. Orig. Title: L' Arret De Mort. 88p. 1978. 10.00 (0-930794-05-2); pap. 5.95 (0-930794-04-4) Station Hill Pr.

Death Sentence. Gary Hunter. 336p. (Orig.). 1992. mass mkt. 4.99 (0-446-36014-7) Warner Bks.

Death Sentence: Murder on the Prairie. rev. ed. John Forsythe. Ed. by Richard J. Wesnick. (Illus.). 1984. pap. 7.95 (0-913311-02-2) Unicorn Comm.

Death Sentence of AIDS: A Comprehensive Source Book of Quotes by the World's Leading Physicians, Scientists & Researchers. Troy R. Mader. LC 87-72211. (Orig.). 1987. pap. 9.94 (0-944402-00-3) Cmmn Man Inst.

Death Sentences: Styles of Dying in British Fiction. Garrett Stewart. (Illus.). 352p. 1984. 37.00 (0-674-19428-4) HUP.

***Death Served up Cold.** B. J. Oliphant. (Orig.). 1994. mass mkt. 5.99 (0-449-14896-3, GM) Fawcett.

Death, Sex, & Fertility: Population Regulation in Pre-Industrial & Developing Societies. Marvin Harris & Eric B. Ross. LC 86-18401. 184p. 1990. text ed. 34.00 (0-231-06270-2, King's Crown Paperbacks); pap. text ed. 19.50 (0-231-06271-0, King's Crown Paperbacks) Col U Pr.

Death Shift. Peter Elkind. 1990. pap. 4.95 (0-451-40196-4, Onyx) NAL-Dutton.

Death Ship. 2nd ed. B. Traven. LC 91-25293. 377p. 1991. reprint ed. pap. 12.95 (1-55652-110-3) L Hill Bks.

Death Ship: A Strange Story, 2 vols. in one. William C. Russell. Ed. by R. Reginald. LC 75-46306. (Supernatural & Occult Fiction Ser.). 1976. reprint ed. lib. bdg. 70.95 (0-405-08166-9) Ayer.

Death Shock. Harrison Arnston. 448p. 1988. pap. 3.95 (0-8217-2378-2) Zebra.

Death Shuttle. Dan Streib. 192p. (Orig.). 1983. pap. 2.50 (0-449-12389-8, GM) Fawcett.

Death Signs. H. Edward Hunsburger. 1987. 15.95 (0-8027-5679-4) Walker & Co.

Death, Sin & the Moral Life. Bonnie J. Miller-McLemore. LC 87-28872. (American Academy of Religion Academy Ser.). 357p. 1988. 31.95 (1-55540-202-X, 01 01 59); pap. 20.95 (1-55540-203-8) Scholars Pr GA.

Death, Sleep & the Traveler. John Hawkes. LC 73-89481. 192p. 1974. pap. 9.95 (0-8112-0569-X, NDP393) New Directions.

Death, Society, & Human Experience. 4th ed. Robert Kastenbaum. 368p. (C). 1991. pap. write for info. (0-675-21189-1, Merrill Pub Co) Macmillan.

***Death, Society, & Human Experience.** 5th ed. Robert Kastenbaum. LC 94-26578. 1995. pap. text ed. 27.00 (0-02-362062-5) Allyn.

Death, Society, & Ideology in a Hohokam Community. Randall H. McGuire. 209p. (C). 1992. pap. text ed. 42.50 (0-8133-8350-1) Westview.

Death Song. Drake Douglas & Stephen Kent. 400p. (Orig.). 1987. pap. 3.95 (0-8439-2546-9) Dorchester Pub Co.

Death Song. Bill Dugan. 1994. mass mkt. 3.50 (0-06-100663-7, Harp PBks) HarpC.

Death Song. Thomas McGrath. Ed. by Sam Hamill. LC 90-85091. 128p. (Orig.). 1991. 19.00 (1-55659-035-0); pap. 10.00 (1-55659-036-9) Copper Canyon.

Death Sounds Grand. large type ed. Richard Hunt. 300p. 1994. pap. 16.95 (1-85389-473-7, Dales) Ulverscroft.

Death Speaks Softly. large type ed. Anthea Fraser. 320p. 1988. 15.95 (0-7089-1846-8) Ulverscroft.

Death Spore. Harry A. Knight. 1990. pap. 3.95 (1-55817-348-X, Pinnacle NY) Windsor NY.

Death Squad. Thurman Hoskins. (Orig.). 1991. pap. 2.95 (0-87067-359-9) Holloway.

Death Squad. Peter McCurtin. (Soldier of Fortune Ser.). 224p. 1985. pap. 2.50 (0-8439-2190-0) Dorchester Pub Co.

Death Squad. Tom Willard. (Strike Fighters Ser.: No. 9). (Orig.). 1992. mass mkt. 3.99 (0-06-100401-4, Harp PBks) HarpC.

Death Squad London. large type ed. Jack Gerson. 1991. 21.95 (0-7089-2409-3) Ulverscroft.

Death Squadron. Grover C. Hall, Jr. (World at War Ser.: No. 20). 432p. 1980. pap. 2.95 (0-89083-944-1) Zebra.

An Asterisk (*) at the beginning of an entry indicates that the title is appearing in BIP for the first time.

D

An Asterisk (*) at the beginning of an entry indicates that the title is appearing in BIP for the first time.

1835

Deathbed Observations by Physicians & Nurses. 4th ed. Karlis Osis. LC 61-18247. (Parapsychological Monograph Ser.: No. 3). 1961. pap. 7.00 (*0-912328-06-1*) Parapsych Foun.

Deathbird Stories. Harlan Ellison. 320p. 1993. pap. 9.00 (*0-02-084745-9*) Macmillan.

Deathbird Stories. Harlan Ellison. 352p. 1990. pap. 6.00 (*0-02-028361-X*, Collier S&S) S&S Trade.

Deathblow. John A. McCormack. LC 87-91069. 1988. 18.95 (*0-87212-207-7*) Libra.

Deathblow Hill: An Asey Mayo Cape Cod Mystery. Phoebe A. Taylor. 286p. 1993. pap. 6.00 (*0-88150-262-6*, Foul Play) Countryman.

Deathblow Trail. Jon Sharpe. (Trailsman Ser.: No. 143). 176p. 1993. pap. 3.50 (*0-451-17754-1*, Sig) NAL-Dutton.

Deathbound Subjectivity. Alphonso Lingis. LC 88-45450. (Studies in Phenomenology & Existential Philosophy). 222p. 1989. 34.95 (*0-253-31660-X*) Ind U Pr.

Deathbringer. Dana Reed. 400p. (Orig.). 1987. 3.95 (*0-8439-2562-0*) Dorchester Pub Co.

Deathbroker. Johnathan St. James. 350p. (Orig.). 1989. pap. 3.95 (*0-9623340-1-4*) Johns & Johns.

Deathday. Robert Neville. 400p. (Orig.). 1986. pap. 3.95 (*0-8439-2805-0*) Dorchester Pub Co.

Deathday Cake by Dominique Rollin. Jennifer C. Gage & Dominique Rolin. LC 86-16086. 176p. 1987. pap. 10.95 (*0-8262-0624-7*, 83-36323) U of Mo Pr.

Deathday of Socrates: Living, Dying & Immortality--The Theater of Ideas in Plato's Phaedo. Jerome Eckstein. LC 81-924. 288p. 1981. 18.00 (*0-914366-20-3*) Columbia Pub.

Deathdeal. Garry Disher. 1994. pap. 5.95 (*1-86373-455-4*, Pub. by Allen & Unwin Aust Pty AT) IPG Chicago.

Deathgame. Franklin W. Dixon. (Hardy Boys Casefiles Ser.: No. 7). 160p. (Orig.). (YA). (gr. 7 up). 1991. mass mkt. 3.99 (*0-671-73672-8*, Archway) PB.

Deathgame: Casefiles Seven. large type ed. Franklin W. Dixon. (Hardy Boys Ser.). 151p. (YA). (gr. 7-10). 1988. reprint ed. 9.50 (*0-942545-48-6*); reprint ed. lib. bdg. 10.50 (*0-942545-58-3*) Grey Castle.

Deathhunter. Ian Watson. 1988. pap. 2.95 (*0-317-65519-1*) St Martin.

Deathics: A Margaret Binton Mystery. large type ed. Richard Barth. LC 93-17003. 1993. 17.95 (*1-56054-741-3*) Thorndike Pr.

Deathing: An Intelligent Alternative for the Final Moments of Life. rev. ed. Anya Foos-Graber. LC 87-30884. (Illus.). 430p. 1989. pap. 14.95 (*0-89254-016-8*) Nicolas-Hays.

Deathless. Myles Murchison. 368p. 1989. pap. 3.95 (*0-345-35378-1*) Ballantine.

Deathless White Stallion & Other Tales. Joe Ferguson. Ed. by Edwin M. Eakin. (Illus.). 64p. (J). (gr. 4-6). 1989. 10.95 (*0-89015-702-2*); pap. 3.95 (*0-89015-712-X*) Sunbelt Media.

Deathline. Barbara Steiner. 176p. (Orig.). (J). (gr. 5). 1993. pap. 3.50 (*0-380-77066-0*, Flare) Avon.

Deathlok, No. 1. McDuffie et al. 48p. 1990. 3.95 (*0-87135-668-6*) Marvel Entmnt.

Deathlok, No. 2. McDuffie et al. 48p. 1990. 3.95 (*0-87135-677-5*) Marvel Entmnt.

Deathlok, No. 3. McDuffie et al. 48p. 1990. 3.95 (*0-87135-678-3*) Marvel Entmnt.

Deathlok, No. 4. McDuffie et al. 48p. 1990. 3.95 (*0-87135-679-1*) Marvel Entmnt.

***Deathlord of Ixia, No. 17.** Joe Dever. (Lone Wolf Ser.: No. 17). 208p. 1994. pap. text ed. 3.99 (*0-425-14459-3*) Berkley Pub.

Deathly Pale. Daniel Lynch. 448p. 1988. pap. 3.95 (*0-8217-2379-0*) Zebra.

***Deathly Still: Pictures of Concentration Camps.** Photos by Dirk Reinartz. (Illus.). 1995. 49.95 (*1-881616-44-4*, Pub. by Scalo Pubs) Dist Art Pubs.

Deathly Waters & Hungry Mountains: Agrarian Ritual & Class Formation in an Andean Town. Peter Cose. (Anthropological Horizons Ser.: No. 4). (Illus.). 376p. (C). 1994. 60.00 (*0-8020-0606-X*); pap. 22.95 (*0-8020-7210-0*) U of Toronto Pr.

Deathman Pass Me by: Two Years on Death Row. Philip Brasfield & Jeffrey M. Elliot. LC 82-4126. (Borgo Bioviews Ser.: No. 3). (Illus.). 96p. 1983. lib. bdg. 23.00x (*0-89370-164-5*); pap. 13.00x (*0-89370-264-1*) Borgo Pr.

Deathmaster. William W. Johnstone. 272p. 1987. pap. 3.50 (*0-8217-1971-8*) Zebra.

Deathport. Ed. by Ramsey Campbell & Sally Peters. (Horror Writers of America Ser.). 368p. (Orig.). 1993. mass mkt. 4.99 (*0-671-69575-4*) PB.

Deathright. Dev Stryker. LC 92-33363. 320p. 1992. 21.95 (*0-312-85386-6*) Tor Bks.

Deathright. Dev Stryker. 336p. 1995. mass mkt. 5.99 (*0-8125-2162-5*) Tor Bks.

Deathright: Culture, Medicine, Politics & the Right to Die. James M. Heofler. (C). 1994. pap. text ed. 17.95 (*0-8133-1702-9*) Westview.

Deathright: Culture, Medicine, Politics & the Right to Die. James M. Heofler. (C). 1994. text ed. 58.00 (*0-8133-1701-0*) Westview.

Death's Advantage Little Regarded. Incl. Soules Solace Against Sorrow. William Leigh. LC 92-41759. 1993. (*0-318-69967-2*); Brief Discourse of the Christian Life & Godly Death of Mistris Katherin Brettergh (1602) Intro. by Retha M Warnicke & Bettie Anne Doebler. LC 92-41759. 1993. (*0-318-69968-0*); LC 92-41759. 1993. 50.00 (*0-8201-1466-9*) Schol Facsimiles.

Death's an End & a Beginning Without. B. M. Billon. 1981. 30.00 (*0-7223-1388-8*, Pub. by A H S Ltd UK) St Mut.

***Deaths & Burials in St. Mary's County, Maryland.** Leona Cryer. 447p. (Orig.). 1995. pap. text ed. 33.00 (*0-7884-0173-4*) Heritage Bk.

Deaths & Distances. Richard O'Connell. 1965. pap. 10.00 (*0-685-62613-X*) Atlantis Edns.

Deaths & Miscellaneous from Hudson, NY Newspapers Vol. 1: The Balance & Columbian Repository, 1802-1811; The Rural Repository or Bower of Literature, 1824-1851. Arthur C. Kelly. LC 80-105723. 223p. 1979. lib. bdg. 32.00 (*1-56012-045-2*) Kinship Rhinebeck.

Deaths & Much Miscellaneous from Rhinebeck New York Newspapers, 1846-1899, Vol. 1. Arthur C. Kelly. LC 79-101054. 214p. 1978. lib. bdg. 29.00 (*1-56012-041-X*) Kinship Rhinebeck.

Death's Bounty. George G. Gilman. (Edge Ser.: No. 12). 1990. pap. 3.50 (*1-55817-320-X*, Pinnacle NY) Windsor NY.

Death's Bright Angel. Janet Neel. Ed. by Jane Chelius. 288p. 1991. reprint ed. mass mkt. 4.99 (*0-671-73579-9*) PB.

Death's Darkest Face. large type ed. Julian Symons. (General Ser.). 300p. 1991. text ed. 18.95 (*0-8161-5200-4*, Large Print Bks) Hall.

Death's Epicure. Suresh Kohli. 5.00 (*0-89253-695-0*) Ind-US Inc.

***Deaths from the Delaware Gazette 1854-59, 61-64.** Ed. by Mary F. Richard. (Delaware Genealogical Abstracts from Newspapers Ser.: Vol. 1). 314p. 1995. pap. text ed. 25.00 (*1-887061-06-1*) DE Geneal Soc.

***Death's Garden: Relationships with Graveyards.** Ed. by Loren Rhoads. 180p. 1995. pap. 19.99 (*0-9636794-1-4*) Automatism Pr.

***Death's Gift: Chapters on Resurrection & Bereavement.** Nicholas P. Harvey. 160p. 1995. pap. 12.99 (*0-8028-4085-X*) Eerdmans.

Death's Gray Land. Mike Shupp. 352p. (Orig.). 1991. mass mkt. 4.95 (*0-345-32552-4*, Del Rey) Ballantine.

Death's Head. (Super Bolan Ser.). 1994. mass mkt. 4.99 (*0-373-61435-7*, 1-61435-3) Harlequin Bks.

Death's Head: Body in Question. Simon Furman & Geoff Senior. 64p. 1990. 9.95 (*1-85400-217-1*) Marvel Entmnt.

Death's Head - Life & Times Of. Furman et al. 144p. 1990. pap. 12.95 (*1-85400-238-4*) Marvel Entmnt.

Death's Head Berlin. large type ed. Jack Gerson. 432p. 1992. 21.95 (*0-7089-2573-1*) Ulverscroft.

Death's Head Trail. Jory Sherman. (Gunn Ser.: No. 3). 240p. (Orig.). 1980. pap. 1.95 (*0-89083-648-5*) Zebra.

Deaths in China Due to Communism: Propaganda Vs. Reality. Stephen R. Shalom. LC 82-84463. (Occasional Paper Arizona State Univ., Center for Asian Studies: No. 15). v, 235p. 1984. pap. 10.00 (*0-939252-11-2*) ASU Ctr Asian.

Deaths in Custody: International Perspectives. Alison Liebing & Tony Ward. 196p. 1994. 90.00 (*1-871177-55-3*, Pub. by Whiting & Birch UK); pap. 34.95 (*1-871177-42-1*, Pub. by Whiting & Birch UK) Paul & Co Pubs.

Death's Long Shadow. large type ed. John Penn. (Mystery Ser.). 304p. 1993. 21.95 (*0-7089-2959-1*) Ulverscroft.

Death's Men. Denis Winter. (Nonfiction Ser.). 304p. 1985. pap. 9.95 (*0-14-005215-1*, Penguin Bks) Viking Penguin.

***Death's Men: Soldiers of the Great War.** Denis Winter. 1985. pap. 12.00 (*0-14-016822-2*, Penguin Bks) Viking Penguin.

Deaths of Animals & Lesser Gods. Gerald Barrax. Ed. by Charles H. Rowell. (Callaloo Poetry Ser.: No. 4). (Illus.). 73p. (Orig.). 1984. pap. 9.95 (*0-912759-02-X*) U Pr of Va.

Deaths of Don Bernardo. Barbara Mujica. (Mujer Latina Ser.). 365p. (Orig.). 1990. pap. 19.95 (*0-685-45619-6*) Floricanto Pr.

Deaths of Jocasta. J. M. Redmann. LC 92-14648. 288p. (Orig.). 1992. pap. 9.95 (*0-934678-39-1*) New Victoria Pubs.

Deaths of Louis XVI: Regicide & the French Political Imagination. Susan Dunn. LC 93-39519. 1994. 29.95 (*0-691-03429-X*) Princeton U Pr.

Deaths of Man. Ed. by Edwin S. Shneidman. LC 83-12294. 256p. 1983. reprint ed. 30.00 (*0-87668-642-0*) Aronson.

Deaths of Sybil Bolton: An American History. Dennis McAuliffe. 1994. 23.00 (*0-8129-2150-X*, Times Bks) Random.

Deaths of Various People Bristol & Plymouth Counties, MA. Clizabeth Perkins. Ed. by Charles D. Townsend. 44p. (Orig.). 1993. pap. 10.00 (*0-9607906-9-1*) ACETO Bookmen.

Death's Pale Flag. Edward Wiley. 1981. pap. 1.95 (*0-8439-0859-9*) Dorchester Pub Co.

Deaths Reported by Der Libanon Demokrat: A German-Language Newspaper Published at Lebanon, PA, 1832-1864. Tr. by Robert A. Heilman. 134p. (Orig.). 1991. pap. 12.50 (*1-55613-410-X*) Heritage Bk.

***Death's Revenge.** Marlene Slaton. 1995. 10.95 (*0-8062-5226-X*) Carlton.

Deaths That Travel with the Weather. Louie Skipper. LC 91-26842. 64p. (Orig.). 1992. 25.00 (*0-914061-29-1*); pap. 10.00 (*0-914061-24-0*) Orchises Pr.

Deathsong. Jack Scaparro. 1989. pap. 3.95 (*0-8217-2730-3*) Zebra.

Deathsong of the River: A Reader's Guide to the Chinese TV Series, Heshand. Su Xiaokang & Wang Luxiang. Tr. by Richard W. Bodman & Pin P. Wan. (Cornell East Asia Ser.: No. 54). 15.00 (*0-939657-54-6*) Cornell East Asia Pgm.

Deathspell. Veronica Stallwood. LC 93-50792. 1994. 21.95 (*0-7927-1989-1*, Curley Lrg Print); pap. 19.95 (*0-7927-1988-3*, Curley Lrg Print) Chivers N Amer.

Deathspell. Veronica Stallwood. 224p. 1992. text ed. 20.00 (*0-684-19517-8*, Scribners) S&S Trade.

Deathstalk. Bruce Clark. 192p. 1985. reprint ed. pap. 2.50 (*0-8439-2231-1*) Dorchester Pub Co.

***Deathstalker.** Simon R. Green. 528p. (Orig.). 1995. pap. 5.99 (*0-451-45435-9*, ROC) NAL-Dutton.

Deathstar Companion: S. Wars. 1991. 15.00 (*0-87431-120-9*, 40008) West End Games.

Deathtale of Gustav Uyterhoeven. Brooks Hansen. LC 93-42077. 1994. write for info. (*0-15-124160-0*) HarBrace.

Deathtrap. Ira Levin. 1979. pap. 4.75 (*0-8222-0294-8*) Dramatists Play.

Deathtrap. Ira Levin. 1979. 9.95 (*0-394-50727-4*) Random.

Deathtrap: The Vault. Danny Fingeroth et al. (Avengers Ser.). (Illus.). 64p. 1991. 9.95 (*0-87135-810-7*) Marvel Entmnt.

Deathtrap & Dinosaur. Jane McFann. 224p. (Orig.). 1989. pap. 2.75 (*0-380-75624-2*, Flare) Avon.

Deathtrap Equalizer. Ken St. Andre. 1977. 4.95 (*0-940244-02-0*) Flying Buffalo.

Deathtrap! Improvised Booby-Trap Devices. Jo Jo Gonzales. (Illus.). 176p. 1989. pap. 15.00 (*0-87364-519-7*) Paladin Pr.

Deathtraps: The Postmodern Comedy Thriller. Marvin Carlson. LC 92-45237. 1993. 29.95 (*0-253-31305-8*); 12.95 (*0-253-20826-2*) Ind U Pr.

***Deathwalker.** Gates. 1995. mass mkt. 4.99 (*0-440-21467-X*) Dell.

Deathwalker. Patrick Whalen. Ed. by John Swenamiglio. 320p. (Orig.). 1992. mass mkt. 4.99 (*0-671-74636-7*) PB.

***Deathwatch.** Estelle Kleinman. Ed. by J. Friedland & R. Kessler. (Novel-Ties Ser.). (J). (gr. 6-9). 1994. student ed, pap. text ed. 15.95 (*1-56982-072-4*) Lrn Links.

Deathwatch. Robb White. 224p. (gr. 7 up). 1973. mass mkt. 3.99 (*0-440-91740-9*, G Davis) Dell.

Deathwatch see Maids

Deathwatch Program. Lester W. Smith. (Twenty-Three Hundred AD Ser.). (Illus.). 64p. (Orig.). (YA). 1990. pap. 8.00 (*1-55878-051-3*) Game Designers.

Deathwind. D. R. Bensen. Ed. by Doug Grad. (Tracker Ser.: No. 6). 224p. (Orig.). 1993. mass mkt. 3.99 (*0-671-73839-9*) PB.

Deathwind. abr. ed. Don Force. 210p. 1994. pap. 8.95 (*1-56901-495-7*) NW Pub.

Deathworld: Based on the Novel by Harry Harrison. John Holland. 109p. (Orig.). 1991. pap. 9.95 (*0-944735-46-0*) Malibu Graphics.

Debacle. Emile Zola. 1976. pap. 10.95 (*0-7859-2971-1*) Fr & Eur.

Debacle. Emile Zola. (Folio Ser.: No. 1586). (FRE.). 1976. 13.95 (*2-07-037586-2*) Schoenhof.

Debacle. Emile Zola. Tr. by Leonard W. Tancock. (Classics Ser.). 1973. mass mkt. 9.95 (*0-14-044280-4*, Penguin Classics) Viking Penguin.

Debacle. Emile Zola. 372p. (FRE.). 1984. pap. 14.95 (*0-7859-1635-0*, 2070375862) Fr & Eur.

***Debatable Land.** Candia McWilliam. LC 94-26104. 1995. 23.50 (*0-385-26310-4*) Doubleday.

Debate about the Earth: An Approach to Geophysics Through Analysis of Continental Drift. rev. ed. H. Takeuchi et al. Tr. by K. Kanamori. LC 67-21261. (Illus.). 281p. (C). 1970. text ed. 32.50 (*0-87735-303-4*) Jones & Bartlett.

Debate & Argument: A Systems Approach to Advocacy. Michael W. Pfau et al. (C). 1987. text ed. 20.25 (*0-673-18163-4*) HarpCollege.

***Debate & Argument: A Systems Approach to Advocacy.** Michael Pfau. LC 87-4859. 349p. 1987. reprint ed. pap. 99.50 (*0-7837-8852-5*, 2049529) Bks Demand.

Debate & Critical Analysis: The Harmony of Conflict. Robert J. Branham. 264p. (C). 1991. text ed. 24.95 (*0-8058-0724-1*) L Erlbaum Assocs.

Debate in Tibetan Buddhism. Daniel Perdue. 938p. 1992. 45.00 (*0-937938-84-X*); pap. 38.95 (*0-937938-76-9*) Snow Lion Pubns.

Debate of King Milinda. Bhikkhu Pesala. (C). 1991. 14.00 (*81-208-0893-2*, Pub. by Motilal Banarsidass II) S Asia.

Debate on Classes. Erik O. Wright et al. 256p. 1990. 60.00 (*0-86091-251-5*, A3755, Pub. by Verso UK); pap. 18.95 (*0-86091-966-8*, A3759, Pub. by Verso UK) Routledge Chapman & Hall.

***Debate on Health Care Reform, 1993-1994: Did the Polls Mislead the Policy Makers?** Karlyn Bowman. 32p. 1994. pap. 9.95 (*0-8447-7031-0*) Am Enterprise.

***Debate on Money in Europe.** Alberto Giovannini. LC 95-15934. (Illus.). 352p. (C). 1995. 35.00x (*0-262-07168-1*) MIT Pr.

***Debate on Opportunity-to-Learn Standards.** Susan L. Traiman. Ed. by Gerry Feinstein. 40p. (Orig.). 1993. pap. text ed. 15.00 (*1-55877-175-1*) Natl Governor.

***Debate on Opportunity-to-Learn Standards: Supporting Works.** Ed. by Gerry Feinstein. 363p. (Orig.). 1993. pap. text ed. 28.95 (*1-55877-178-6*) Natl Governor.

Debate on Slavery. Jonathan Blanchard. LC 70-92419. 1845. 18.00 (*0-403-00153-6*) Scholarly.

Debate on Slavery: Is Slavery in Itself Sinful & the Relation Between Master & Slave a Sinful Relation. Jonathan Blanchard & N. L. Rice. LC 72-82175. (Anti-Slavery Crusade in America Ser.). 1970. reprint ed. 37.95 (*0-405-00614-4*) Ayer.

Debate on the American Revolution, 1761-1783. 3rd ed. Ed. by Max Beloff. 316p. (C). 1989. pap. text ed. 13.95 (*0-685-63310-1*) Madison Hse.

Debate on the Constitution, 2 vols. Ed. by Bernard Bailyn. LC 92-25449. 1993. Vol. 1, September 1787 to February 1788. 35.00 (*0-940450-42-9*); Vol. 2, January to August 1788. 35.00 (*0-940450-64-X*) Library of America.

Debate on the Constitution, 2 vols., Set. Ed. by Bernard Bailyn. LC 92-25449. 1993. 70.00 (*0-940450-81-X*) Library of America.

Debate on the English Reformation. Rosemary O'Day. 217p. 1986. pap. text ed. 12.95 (*0-416-72680-1*, 9802) Routledge Chapman & Hall.

Debate on the English Revolution. 2nd ed. R. C. Richardson. (Illus.). 400p. 1989. pap. 25.00 (*0-415-01167-1*) Routledge.

Debate on the Nature, Role & Influence of Woman in Eighteenth-Century Spain. Sally-Ann Kitts. LC 94-8972. (Women's Studies: Vol. 13). 332p. 1994. 99.95 (*0-7734-9088-4*) E Mellen.

Debate over Child Care, 1969-1990: A Sociohistorical Analysis. Abbie G. Klein. LC 91-13640. (SUNY Series, Issues in Child Care). 450p. (C). 1992. 59.50 (*0-7914-0975-9*) State U NY Pr.

Debate over Christian Reconstruction. Gary DeMar. 284p. (Orig.). 1988. pap. 8.95 (*0-930462-33-5*, Dominion) Am Bur Eco Res.

Debate over Jury Performance: Observations from a Recent Asbestos Case. Molly Selvin & Larry Picus. LC 86-33833. 1987. 10.00 (*0-8330-0789-0*, R-3479-ICJ) Rand Corp.

Debate over Slavery: Stanley Elkins & His Critics. Ed. by Ann J. Lane. LC 79-141518. (Illini Book Ser.: No. IB-73). 384p. reprint ed. pap. 109.50 (*0-317-09737-7*, 2022257) Bks Demand.

Debate over Vietnam. David W. Levy. LC 90-49525. (American Moment Ser.). 216p. 1991. text ed. 38.95 (*0-8018-4148-8*); pap. text ed. 12.95 (*0-8018-4149-6*) Johns Hopkins.

***Debate over Vietnam.** 2nd ed. David W. Levy. LC 95-3385. (American Moment Ser.). 230p. 1995. pap. text ed. 13.95x (*0-8018-5114-9*) Johns Hopkins.

***Debate over Vietnam.** 2nd ed. David W. Levy. LC 95-3385. (American Moment Ser.). 230p. 1995. text ed. 38.95x (*0-8018-5113-0*) Johns Hopkins.

***Debate Politico Vol. 8: Modernidad, Poder y Disidencia En Yo el Supremo De Augusto Roa Bastos.** Adriana J. Bergero. (Wor(l)ds of Change Ser.). 285p. (SPA.). (C). 1994. text ed. 57.95 (*0-8204-2583-4*) P Lang Pubs.

Debate Tournament Administrator. Stephen Wood & Joseph B. Miller. 68p. 1991. 150.00 (*0-8403-6870-4*) Kendall-Hunt.

Debate Tournament Administrator: Lincoln - Douglas Version. 2nd ed. Stephen Wood & Joseph B. Miller. 68p. 1992. per. 49.00 (*0-8403-8277-4*) Kendall-Hunt.

Debater's Guide. rev. ed. Jon M. Ericson et al. LC 86-33855. 155p. (Orig.). 1987. pap. text ed. 10.95 (*0-8093-1386-3*) S Ill U Pr.

***Debates & Issues in Feminist Research & Pedagogy: A Reader.** LC 94-29844. (Equality & Difference Ser.). 1995. pap. write for info. (*1-85359-251-X*) Taylor & Francis.

***Debates & Issues in Feminist Research & Pedagogy: A Reader.** Ed. by Janet Holland et al. LC 94-29844. (Equality & Difference Ser.). 1995. write for info. (*1-85359-252-8*) Taylor & Francis.

Debates & Proceedings in the Constitutional Convention of the State of Nevada. Andrew J. Marsh. LC 76-39613. 959p. 1976. reprint ed. lib. bdg. 45.00 (*0-930342-32-1*, 300990) W S Hein.

Debates Commentary. Tr. by B. C. Law. (C). 1940. 12.00 (*0-86013-019-3*, Pub. by Pali Text) Wisdom MA.

Debates in Clinical Surgery, Vol. 1. Ed. by Richard L. Simmons. (Illus.). 344p. 1987. 54.95 (*0-8151-7740-2*, Yr Bk Med Pubs) Mosby Yr Bk.

Debates in Clinical Surgery, Vol. 2. Richard L. Simmons. 256p. 1990. 54.95 (*0-8151-7709-7*, Yr Bk Med Pubs) Mosby Yr Bk.

Debates in Medicine, Vol. 2. Gitnick. 296p. 1989. 54.95 (*0-8151-3601-3*, Yr Bk Med Pubs) Mosby Yr Bk.

Debates in Medicine, Vol. 3. Gitnick. 368p. 1990. 54.95 (*0-8151-3602-1*, Yr Bk Med Pubs) Mosby Yr Bk.

Debates in Medicine, Vol. 4. Gitnick. 343p. 1991. 59.95 (*0-8151-3603-X*, Yr Bk Med Pubs) Mosby Yr Bk.

Debates in Nephrology. Ed. by L. Minetti et al. (Contributions to Nephrology Ser.: Vol. 34). (Illus.). viii, 132p. 1982. pap. 71.25 (*3-8055-3535-X*) S Karger.

Debates in the Federal Convention of 1787, 2 vols., Set. James Madison. LC 86-63352. 677p. 1987. 72.95 (*0-87975-388-9*) Prometheus Bks.

Debates in Value Theory. Ed. by Simon Mohun. LC 93-44298. 1994. text ed. 59.95 (*0-312-12098-2*, Pub. by Macm UK) St Martin.

Debates on Evaluation. Ed. by Marvin C. Alkin. (Illus.). 288p. (C). 1990. 46.00 (*0-8039-3523-4*); pap. 22.95 (*0-8039-3524-2*) Sage.

Debates on God & Experience in the Netherlands, 1965-1989. David G. Murphy. 250p. 1993. 64.95 (*1-883255-09-0*, Cath Scholar Pr); pap. 44.95 (*1-883255-02-3*, Cath Scholar Pr) Intl Scholars.

Debates on the Decline of Science: An Original Anthology. Ed. by Yahuda Elkana et al. LC 74-25148. (History, Philosophy & Sociology of Science Ser.). 1975. reprint ed. 24.95 (*0-405-06632-5*) Ayer.

Debates on the Future of Communism. W. Vladimir Tismaneanu & Judith Shapiro. LC 90-8640. 184p. 1991. text ed. 29.95 (*0-312-05220-0*) St Martin.

Debates on the Meaning of Life, Evolution, & Spiritualism. Frank Harris et al. LC 92-46231. (Freethought Library). 168p. (Orig.). (C). 1993. pap. 14.95 (*0-87975-828-7*) Prometheus Bks.

Debates over Medical Authority & Challenges in Biomedical Experimentation, Vol. II: Emerging Issues in Biomedical Policy: an Annual Review. Ed. by Robert H. Blank & Andrea L. Bonnicksen. 244p. 1993. 45.00 (*0-231-08016-6*) Col U Pr.

Debates, Resolutions, & Other Proceedings in Convention on the Adoption of the Federal Constitution. Jonathan Elliot. (Notable American Authors Ser.). 1992. reprint ed. lib. bdg. 75.00 (*0-7812-2798-4*) Rprt Serv.

Debating Affirmative Action: Race, Gender, Ethnicity, & the Politics of Inclusion. Intro. by Nicolaus Mills. LC 93-23253. 1994. 10.95 (*0-385-31221-0*, Delta) Dell.

Debating American Government. 2nd ed. Peter Woll. (C). 1988. pap. text ed. 20.00 (*0-673-39781-5*) HarpCollege.

Debating Archaeology. Ed. by Lewis R. Binford. 534p. 1989. text ed. 39.95 (*0-12-100045-1*) Acad Pr.

1836

An Asterisk (*) at the beginning of an entry indicates that the title is appearing in BIP for the first time.

D

D

An Asterisk (*) at the beginning of an entry indicates that the title is appearing in BIP for the first time.

1837

Debt of Love. Karen Young. (Superromance Ser.: No. 453). 1991. mass mkt. 3.25 (*0-373-70453-4*) Harlequin Bks.

Debt of Nations: A Twentieth Century Fund Paper. M. S. Mendelsohn. (International Debt Ser.). 67p. (Orig.). (C). 1984. pap. 7.00 (*0-87078-158-8*) TCFP-PPP.

***Debt or Equity? How Firms in Developing Countries Choose.** Jack D. Glen & Brian Pinto. LC 94-26481. 1994. write for info. (*0-8213-2974-X*) World Bank.

Debt Penalty. Richard E. McConnell. LC 91-91155. 120p. 1991. 24.95 (*0-9630852-0-4*) R E McConnell.

Debt Politics after Independence: The Funding Conflict in Bolivia. Thomas Millington. (University of Florida Social Sciences Monographs: No. 79). (Illus.). 200p. 1992. lib. bdg. 29.95 (*0-8130-1140-X*) U Press Fla.

Debt Problem: Acute & Chronic Aspects, No. 16. 258p. 19. 00 (*92-1-104167-8*, E.85.II.A.12) UN.

Debt Problems of Eastern Europe. Iliana Zloch-Christy. (Cambridge Russian, Soviet & Post-Soviet Studies: No. 57). 240p. 1987. 59.95 (*0-521-33542-6*) Cambridge U Pr.

Debt Recovery in Europe. Ed. by James Richardson. 165p. 1993. pap. 34.00 (*1-85431-242-1*, Pub. by Blackstone Pr UK) W W Gaunt.

Debt Reduction & Development: The Case of Mexico. Sudarshan Gooptu. LC 92-3725. 240p. 1993. text ed. 49. 95 (*0-275-94213-9*, C4213, Praeger Pubs) Greenwood.

Debt Reduction & Economic Activity. Michael P. Dooley et al. (Occasional Paper Ser.: No. 68). v, 30p. 1990. pap. 10.00 (*1-55775-135-8*) Intl Monetary.

Debt Reductions & North-South Resource Transfers to the Year 2000. Richard E. Feinberg et al. LC 92-4493. (Policy Essay Ser.: No. 3). 72p. (Orig.). (C). 1992. pap. text ed. 8.00 (*1-56517-002-4*) Overseas Dev Council.

Debt Relief & Growth. 192p. (Orig.). 1994. pap. 24.00 (*92-64-14068-9*) OECD.

Debt Relief & Sustainable Development in Sub-Saharan Africa. George C. Abbott. 256p. 1992. 59.95 (*1-85278-513-6*, Pub. by E Elgar Pub UK) Ashgate Pub Co.

Debt Repayment Capacity: Cash Flow Forecasting for Borrowers & Lenders. Albert R. McMeen, III. 336p. 1992. 59.95 (*0-8144-5956-0*) AMACOM.

Debt Rescheduling Process. Marko Milivojevic. LC 85-18342. 300p. 1986. text ed. 45.00 (*0-312-18898-6*) St Martin.

Debt Securities. 1990. 56.95 (*0-434-90588-7*) Buttrwrth-Heinemann.

Debt Squads: The U. S., the Banks & Latin America. Sue Branford & Bernardo Kucinski. LC 88-17215. 192p. (C). 1988. text ed. 49.95 (*0-86232-790-3*, Pub. by Zed Books UK); pap. 15.00 (*0-86232-791-1*, Pub. by Zed Books UK) Humanities.

Debt, Stabilization & Development Essays in Memory of Carlos Diaz-Alejandro. Ed. by Ronald Calvo et al. (Illus.). 400p. 1989. text ed. 59.95x (*0-631-15685-2*) Blackwell Pubs.

***Debt Stocks, Debt Flows, & the Balance of Payment.** OECD Staff. 156p. (Orig.). 1994. pap. 36.00x (*92-64-14258-4*) OECD.

Debt, Taxes, & Corporate Restructuring. Ed. by John B. Shoven. 210p. 1990. 29.95 (*0-8157-7884-8*); pap. 11.95 (*0-8157-7883-X*) Brookings.

Debt to Shakespeare in Beaumont & Fletcher Plays. Daniel M. McKeithan. LC 73-128189. 240p. (C). 1970. reprint ed. 50.00 (*0-87752-070-4*) Gordian.

Debt to Shakespeare in the Beaumont & Fletcher Plays. Daniel M. McKeithan. LC 70-126691. reprint ed. 9.50 (*0-404-04134-5*) AMS Pr.

Debt Trap: Rethinking the Logic of Development. Richard W. Lombardi. LC 84-18303. 240p. 1985. text ed. 55.00 (*0-275-90137-8*, C0137, Praeger Pubs) Greenwood.

Debt Trap: The IMF & the Third World. Cheryl Payer. LC 74-24794. 256p. 1975. pap. 10.00 (*0-85345-376-4*) Monthly Rev.

Debt Virus: A Compelling Solution to the World's Debt Problems. Jacques S. Jaikaran. LC 91-70030. (Illus.). 247p. 1992. 19.95 (*0-944435-13-0*) Glenbridge Pub.

Debtor-Creditor: Adaptable to Courses Utilizing Eisenberg's Casebook on Debtor-Creditor Law. Ed. by Norman S. Goldenberg et al. (Legal Briefs Ser.). 1985. pap. write for info. (*0-87457-065-4*, 1303) Casenotes Pub.

Debtor-Creditor: Adaptable to Courses Utilizing Epstein, Landers & Nickel's Casebook on Debtors & Creditors. Casenotes Publishing Co., Inc. Staff. Ed. by Norman S. Goldenberg et al. 1987. pap. write for info. (*0-87457-066-2*, 1302) Casenotes Pub.

Debtor-Creditor: Adaptable to Courses Utilizing Warren & Hogan's Casebook on Debtor-Creditor Law. Casenotes Publishing Co., Inc. Staff. Ed. by Norman S. Goldenberg et al. (Legal Briefs Ser.). 1982. pap. write for info. (*0-87457-067-0*, 1301) Casenotes Pub.

Debtor-Creditor: Adaptable to Courses Utilizing Warren & Westbrook's Casebook on the Law of Debtors & Creditors. Casenotes Publishing Co., Inc. Staff. Ed. by Norman S. Goldenberg et al. (Legal Briefs Ser.). (Orig.). 1991. pap. text ed. write for info. (*0-87457-151-0*, 1304) Casenotes Pub.

Debtor-Creditor Law, 10 vols. Theodore Eisenberg. 1982. Updates. ring bd. write for info. (*0-8205-1216-8*) Bender.

Debtor-Creditor Law: A Treatise. Howard L. Oleck. (Business Enterprises Reprint Ser.). xi, 474p. 1986. reprint ed. lib. bdg. 47.50 (*0-89941-480-X*, 304080) W S Hein.

Debtor-Creditor Law in a Nutshell. 4th ed. David G. Epstein. (Nutshell Ser.). 401p. 1990. pap. text ed. 16.50 (*0-314-80711-X*) West Pub.

Debtor-Creditor Litigation Handbook. 2nd rev. ed. Stuart J. Faber. 400p. 1983. pap. text ed. 36.50 (*0-89074-081-X*) Lega Bks.

***Debtor-Creditor Relations: Manual & Forms.** Leo O. Myers. (Business Practice Library). 1994. text ed. 118.00 (*0-471-11225-9*) Wiley.

Debtor-Creditor Relations: Manual & Forms. Leo O. Myers. LC 86-7179. 734p. 1986. text ed. 95.00 (*0-07-044266-5*) Shepards-McGraw.

Debtor in Possession Financing: What Debtors & Lenders Need to Know. (Commercial Law & Practice Ser.). 598p. 1992. pap. text ed., vhs 550.00 (*0-685-56873-3*, A4-4372) PLI.

***Debtor Unashamed: The Road to Mission Is a Two-Way Street.** L. Arden Almquist. (Orig.). 1993. pap. 12.95 (*0-910452-76-8*) Covenant.

Debtors & Creditors - A Socio-Legal Perspective. Iain Ramsey. 1986. U.K. text ed. 56.00 (*0-86205-101-0*) Butterworth Legal Pubs.

Debtors & Creditors, Cases & Materials. 3rd ed. David G. Epstein et al. LC 87-10739. (American Casebook Ser.). 1059p. 1989. reprint ed. 34.95 (*0-685-18697-0*) West Pub.

Debtors & Creditors, Cases & Materials. David G. Epstein et al. LC 87-10739. (American Casebook Ser.). 1059p. 1989. reprint ed. text ed. 45.00 (*0-314-44102-6*) West Pub.

Debtors & Creditors in America: Insolvency, Imprisonment for Debt, & Bankruptcy 1607-1900. Peter J. Coleman. LC 74-502. 375p. 1974. 17.50 (*0-87020-141-7*) State Hist Soc Wis.

Debtor's Handbook: How to Stay Cool in Hot Water. Dick Bloomfield. Ed. by Sheila Peer & Sue Menow. (Illus.). 270p. (Orig.). 1992. pap. 20.00 (*0-9632046-0-2*) No-Stress Pr.

Debtors or Bill Payer's Reference: How to Find or Locate Information on Debt Repayment. Ed. by Data Notes Research Staff. 75p. 1992. 15.95 (*0-911569-03-0*) Prosperity & Profits.

Debtor's Planet. W. R. Thompson. Ed. by John Ordover. (Star Trek: The Next Generation Ser.: No. 30). 288p. (Orig.). 1994. mass mkt. 5.50 (*0-671-88341-0*) PB.

Debtors' Rights: Self-Help Legal Guide. Gudrun M. Nickel. LC 91-66962. 158p. 1992. pap. 12.95 (*0-913825-43-3*) Sphinx Pub FL.

Debts & Deficits. Hans F. Sennholz. 189p. 1987. pap. 7.95 (*0-910884-18-8*) Libertarian Press.

Debts, Deficits & Exchange Rates. Helmut Reisen. 256p. 1994. 59.95 (*1-85278-930-1*, Pub. by E Elgar Pub UK) Ashgate Pub Co.

Debugging: Creative Techniques & Tools for Software Repair. Martin Stitt. 432p. 1992. disk, pap. 70.00 (*0-471-55829-X*); pap. text ed. 32.95 (*0-471-55831-1*); disk 32.95 (*0-471-57537-2*) Wiley.

Debugging & Maintaining FoxPro Applications. Michael Antonvich. Ed. by Lance A. Leventhal. LC 92-32253. (Lance A. Leventhal Microtrend Ser.). 500p. (Orig.). 1992. pap. 34.95 (*0-915391-73-2*, Microtrend) Slawson Comm.

Debugging Assembly Language on the IBM PC. Jerome R. Corsi & William F. Hills. 1986. pap. 21.95 (*0-89303-627-7*) P-H.

Debugging MacIntosh Software & MacsBug Includes MacsBug 6.2 with Disk. Konstantin Othmer. 1991. pap. 34.95 (*0-201-57049-1*) Addison-Wesley.

Debugging Techniques for IBM PC BASIC. Jerome R. Corsi & William F. Hills. 176p. 1985. pap. 17.95 (*0-317-37794-9*) S&S Trade.

Debugging the Development Process. Steve Maguire. 1994. pap. 24.95 (*1-55615-650-2*) Microsoft.

DeBugging with GDB Manual. Richard M. Stallman & Roland H. Pesch. 182p. (C). 1992. pap. 20.00 (*1-882114-11-6*) Free Software.

Deburring & Surface Conditioning '85: Conference Proceedings, September 23-26, 1985, Chicago, IL. Society of Manufacturing Engineers Staff. LC 85-61968. (Illus.). 480p. reprint ed. pap. 136.80 (*0-8357-6471-0*, 2035842) Bks Demand.

Deburring Capabilities & Limitations. LaRoux K. Gillespie. LC 76-47179. (Illus.). 435p. reprint ed. pap. 124.00 (*0-685-23509-2*, 2029124) Bks Demand.

Debussy. Paul Holmes. (Illustrated Lives of the Great Composers Ser.). (Illus.). 136p. 1989. pap. 14.95 (*0-7119-1626-8*, OP45244) Omnibus NY.

Debussy. Rollo H. Myers. LC 78-66912. (Encore Music Editions Ser.). (Illus.). 1985. reprint ed. 16.50 (*0-88355-752-5*) Hyperion Conn.

Debussy: La Mer. Simon Trezise. LC 93-42789. (Cambridge Music Handbooks Ser.). 132p. (C). 1995. 29.95 (*0-521-44100-5*); pap. 10.95 (*0-521-44656-2*) Cambridge U Pr.

Debussy: Music Book Index. Rollo H. Myers. 125p. 1993. reprint ed. lib. bdg. 89.00 (*0-7812-9592-0*) Rprt Serv.

Debussy: Musician of France. Victor I. Seroff. LC 73-126326. (Biography Index Reprint Ser.). 1977. reprint ed. 24.95 (*0-8369-8032-8*) Ayer.

Debussy & Ravel. Frank H. Shera. 58p. 1990. reprint ed. lib. bdg. 59.00 (*0-7812-0086-5*) Rprt Serv.

Debussy & Ravel. Frank H. Shera. LC 74-181259. 58p. 1925. reprint ed. 25.00 (*0-403-01682-7*) Scholarly.

Debussy & Wagner. Robin Holloway. (Eulenburg Music Ser.). (Illus.). 235p. 1982. reprint ed. pap. text ed. 19.50 (*0-903873-55-9*) Da Capo.

Debussy Letters. Claude Debussy. Ed. by Francois Lesure & Roger Nichols. Tr. by Roger Nichols. LC 87-385. (Illus.). 384p. 1987. 37.00 (*0-674-19429-2*) HUP.

Debussy on Music. Claude Debussy. Ed. by Francois Lesure & Richard L. Smith. 1988. pap. 15.95 (*0-8014-9420-6*) Cornell U Pr.

Debussy, Prelude to the Afternoon of a Faun. Claude Debussy. Ed. by William W. Austin. (Critical Scores Ser.). (C). 1970. pap. text ed. 9.95 (*0-393-09939-3*) Norton.

Debussy Remembered. Roger Nichols. (Illus.). 282p. 1992. 24.95 (*0-931340-41-1*, Amadeus Pr); pap. 12.95 (*0-931340-42-X*, Amadeus Pr) Timber.

Debut. Anita Brookner. (Vintage Contemporaries Ser.). 1990. pap. 10.00 (*0-679-72712-4*, Vin) Random.

Debut. Anita Brookner. 1985. pap. 5.95 (*0-394-72856-4*) Random.

Debut Dans la Vie. Honore De Balzac. 251p. (FRE.). 1991. pap. 10.95 (*0-7859-3480-4*) Fr & Eur.

Debut Dans la Vie: Avec: un Homme d'Affairs, Un Prince de la Boheme. Honore De Balzac. pap. 14.95 (*0-686-53862-5*) Fr & Eur.

***Debutamts Anglais-French, Level 1.** (ENG & FRE.). Date not set. 10.95 (*1-56015-475-6*) Penton Overseas.

***Debutamts Anglais-French, Level 2.** (ENG & FRE.). Date not set. 10.95 (*1-56015-479-9*) Penton Overseas.

Debutante Ball. deluxe limited ed. Beth Henley. LC 91-23878. (Author & Artist Ser.). 1991. boxed 85.00 (*0-87805-518-5*) U Pr of Miss.

Debutante Nation: Feminism Rewrites History of the 1890's. Ed. by Susan Magarey et al. 224p. 1993. pap. 19.95 (*1-86373-296-9*, Pub. by Allen Unwin AT) Paul & Co Pubs.

Debuts Litteraires. Phyllis R. Block. LC 76-58856. (C). 1977. pap. text ed. 22.75 (*0-03-015011-6*) HB Coll Pubs.

Dec Alpha Environment: Architecture, Design, Implementation & Migration. Jay Shay. 1994. pap. text ed. 50.00 (*0-07-056409-4*) McGraw.

Decade: A Collection of Poems from the First Ten Years of The Wesleyan Poetry Program. Norman H. Pearson. LC 72-82542. 302p. reprint ed. pap. 86.10 (*0-7837-0218-3*, 2040526) Bks Demand.

Decade Dance. Michael Lassell. LC 90-43181. 144p. (Orig.). 1990. pap. 7.95 (*1-55583-179-6*) Alyson Pubns.

Decade II: A Twentieth Anniversary Anthology. Ed. by Julian Olivares. LC 92-35458. 256p. (Orig.). 1993. pap. 12.00 (*1-55885-062-7*) Arte Publico.

Decade Matrix. James O. Gollub. (Illus.). 368p. 1992. pap. 14.38 (*0-201-60824-3*) Addison-Wesley.

Decade of Achievement, 1977-1987: A Report of a Survey Based on the National Plan of Action for Women. Susanna Downie et al. 72p. (Orig.). 1988. pap. text ed. 5.00 (*0-9620208-2-6*) NWCC.

Decade of American Foreign Policy: Basic Documents 1941-1949, 2 vols. 1992. lib. bdg. 995.99 (*0-8490-5491-5*) Gordon Pr.

Decade of American Foreign Policy, Basic Documents, 1941-1949. Foreign Relations Committee Staff. 1968. 65.00 (*0-403-00008-4*) Scholarly.

Decade of American Realism: 1975-1985. Howard D. Spencer. LC 85-52228. (Illus.). 52p. 1985. pap. 4.00 (*0-939324-23-7*) Wichita Art Mus.

Decade of Anarchy: An Anthology of Anarchist Writings. 1991. lib. bdg. 75.00 (*0-8490-4628-9*) Gordon Pr.

Decade of Anarchy: 1961-1970: Selections from the Monthly Journal Anarchy. Intro. by Colin Ward. (Freedom Press Centenary Ser.). 283p. 1987. pap. 12.00 (*0-900384-37-9*) Left Bank.

***Decade of Archaeology in Israel: 1948-1958.** S. Yeiven. xiii, 61p. 1960. pap. text ed. 23.25 (*0-614-04006-X*, Pub. by Netherlands Inst NE) Eisenbrauns.

***Decade of Betrayal: Mexican Repatriation in the 1930s.** Francisco E. Balderrama & Raymond Rodriguez. LC 94-48682. (Illus.). 320p. 1995. 39.95 (*0-8263-1628-X*) U of NM Pr.

Decade of Champions: Super Bowls XVI-XXIV. Nathan Aaseng. (Great Sports Events Ser.). (Illus.). 64p. (J). (gr. 5 up). 1991. lib. bdg. 15.95 (*0-8225-1504-0*, Lerner Publctns) Lerner Group.

Decade of Change: Public Education Reform in Texas 1981-1992. (Special Project Report Ser.). 82p. 1993. pap. 9.45 (*0-89940-874-5*) LBJ Sch Pub Aff.

Decade of Change: The Remaking of Forest Service Statutory Authority During the 1970s. Frwd. by Dennis C. Le Master & William E. Towell. LC 83-22641. (Contributions in Political Science Ser.: No. 113). (Illus.). xv, 290p. 1984. text ed. 37.50 (*0-313-24341-7*, LDC/) Greenwood.

Decade of Change & Future Trends in Roofing: Proceedings of the 1985 International Symposium on Roofing Technology. (Illus.). 500p. 1985. 150.00 (*0-934809-00-3*) Natl Roofing Cont.

Decade of China's Economic Reform: Challenges for the Future. Penelope Hartland-Thunberg. LC 89-70818. (Significant Issues Ser.: Vol. 11, No. 12). 75p. (Orig.). reprint ed. pap. 25.00 (*0-7837-6141-4*, 2043249) Bks Demand.

***Decade of Classic Crime.** large type ed. Martin H. Greenberg. (Magna Large Print Ser.). 1994. 24.95 (*0-7505-0722-5*) Ulverscroft.

Decade of Collecting, 1984-1993: Friends of Asian Art Gifts. Judith Smith. (Illus.). 64p. 1993. 9.95 (*0-685-71014-9*) Metro Mus Art.

Decade of Concurrency: Reflections & Perspectives. Ed. by J. W. De Bakker et al. LC 94-15490. (Lecture Notes in Computer Science: Vol. 803). 1994. 88.00 (*0-387-58043-3*) Spr-Verlag.

***Decade of Debate & Division: Georgia Baptists & the Formation of the Southern Baptist Convention.** Robert G. Gardner. LC 95-6240. 1995. write for info. (*0-86554-484-0*) Mercer Univ Pr.

Decade of Decision: A Physician Remembers the American College of Physicians 1977-1986. Robert H. Moser. 336p. 1991. 38.00 (*0-943126-17-7*, DDS91) Amer Coll Phys.

Decade of Decision: A Physician Remembers the American College of Physicians 1977-1986. limited ed. Robert H. Moser. 336p. 1991. 49.00 (*0-685-49577-9*, DDH91) Amer Coll Phys.

Decade of Decisions: American Policy Toward the Arab-Israeli Conflict, 1967-1976. William B. Quandt. LC 77-73499. 1977. pap. 14.00 (*0-520-03536-4*) U CA Pr.

Decade of Decline: Civil Liberties in the Thatcher Years. Peter Thornton. (C). 1988. 30.00 (*0-946088-30-6*, Pub. by NCCL UK) St Mut.

Decade of Deficits: Congressional Thought & Fiscal Action. Steven E. Schier. LC 91-13464. 195p. 1992. 57.50 (*0-7914-0955-4*); pap. 18.95 (*0-7914-0956-2*) State U NY Pr.

Decade of Design, Bk. 2. Flying Models Staff & Robert Buragas. (Hobby Bks.). (Illus.). 100p. 1970. pap. 3.00 (*0-911868-09-7*, C19) Carstens Pubns.

***Decade of Destiny: A Season of Harvest & a Time of Gathering.** Scott Wallis. LC 94-75456. 128p. 1994. pap. write for info. (*0-9642211-9-5*) Lghthouse Pubns.

Decade of Detente: Shifting Definitions & Denouement. Louisa S. Hulett. LC 82-40155. 200p. (Orig.). (C). 1982. pap. text ed. 21.50 (*0-8191-2519-9*) U Pr of Amer.

Decade of Devolution: Perspectives of State & Local Relations. Ed. by E. Blaine Liner. LC 89-31871. (Illus.). 260p. (Orig.). 1989. lib. bdg. 57.00 (*0-87766-464-1*); pap. text ed. 31.50 (*0-87766-463-3*) Urban Inst.

Decade of Digital Computing in the Mineral Industry. LC 72-91452. 952p. 1969. 5.00 (*0-89520-010-4*) SMM&E Inc.

***Decade of Digital Computing in the Mineral Industry: A Review of the State-of-the-Art.** fac. ed. International Symposium on Computer Applications & Operations Research in the Mineral Industry Staff. Ed. by Alfred Weiss. LC 72-91452. (Illus.). 962p. 1969. reprint ed. pap. 180.00 (*0-7837-7866-X*, 2047624) Bks Demand.

Decade of Discontent: An Index to Fighting Talk, 1954-1963. Dorothy C. Woodson. LC 92-40641. 1992. 25.00 (*0-942615-15-8*) U Wis African Stud.

Decade of Discovery: Selected Acquisitions, 1970-1980. Julia K. Murray. LC 79-55426. (Illus.). 1979. pap. 18.50 (*0-934686-36-X*) Freer.

Decade of Discovery in Astronomy & Astrophysics. National Research Council, Astronomy & Astrophysics Survey Committee Staff. 200p. (C). 1991. pap. text ed. 24.95 (*0-309-04381-6*) Natl Acad Pr.

Decade of Disillusion: Britain in the Sixties. David McKie & Christopher Cook. LC 72-83416. 1972. text ed. 29.95 (*0-312-18900-1*) St Martin.

Decade of Disillusionment: The Kennedy-Johnson Years. Jim F. Heath. LC 74-18871. (America since World War II Ser.). 352p. 1975. 29.95 (*0-253-31670-7*); pap. 9.95 (*0-253-20201-9*, MB-201) Ind U Pr.

Decade of Dissent: Impact of the Sixties. Ed. by Thelma McCormack. (Studies in Communications Ser.: Vol. 1). 200p. 1980. lib. bdg. 73.25 (*0-89232-146-6*) Jai Pr.

Decade of Dreams. Mary P. Lillie. LC 79-53015. (Living Poets' Library Ser.: Vol. 23). 1979. pap. 3.50 (*0-686-81663-3*) Dragons Teeth.

Decade of Duffy's. Brian Duffy. LC 94-750. 152p. (C). 1994. pap. 10.95 (*0-8138-2667-5*) Iowa St U Pr.

Decade of Energy Policy: Policy Analysis in Oil Importing Countries. Paul Kemezis, III & Ernest J. Wilson. LC 84-15936. 288p. 1984. text ed. 45.00 (*0-275-91205-1*, C1205, Praeger Pubs) Greenwood.

Decade of Federal Antipoverty Programs: Achievements, Failures & Lessons. Ed. by Robert H. Haveman. 1977. pap. text ed. 30.00 (*0-12-333256-7*) Acad Pr.

Decade of Health Services: Social Survey Trends in Use & Expenditure. Ronald Anderson & Odin W. Anderson. LC 67-30125. (University of Chicago, Graduate School of Business, Studies in Business & Society). 264p. reprint ed. pap. 75.30 (*0-317-26636-5*, 2024081) Bks Demand.

Decade of LMR-Progress & Promise Conference, Washington, DC, Nov. 11-16, 1990. 356p. 1990. 40.00 (*0-89448-157-6*, 700157) Am Nuclear Soc.

Decade of Lupus: Selections from Lupus News. Henrietta Aladjem. 288p. (Orig.). 1991. pap. text ed. 12.00 (*0-9608660-9-4*) Lupus Found Am.

Decade of Novels: Fiction of the 1970s: Form & Challenge. Charles Berryman. LC 89-51479. 140p. 1990. 18.50 (*0-87875-390-7*) Whitston Pub.

Decade of Pattern: Prints, Pieces & Prototypes From The Fabric Workshop. Marion Stroud. Ed. by Elizabeth F. Spungen. (Illus.). (Orig.). 1988. pap. text ed. 8.95 (*0-9619760-0-4*) Fabric Workshop Inc.

Decade of Probation, a Study & Report. Irving W. Halpern. LC 69-14930. (Criminology, Law Enforcement, & Social Problems Ser.: No. 66). 1969. reprint ed. 24.00 (*0-87585-066-9*) Patterson Smith.

Decade of Progress. Ed. by Arnold Goldberg. (Progress in Self Psychology Ser.: Vol. 10). 328p. 1994. text ed. write for info. (*0-88163-179-5*) Analytic Pr.

Decade of Progress in Teacher Training. Clyde M. Hill. LC 71-176863. (Columbia University. Teachers College. Contributions to Education Ser.: No. 233). reprint ed. 37.50 (*0-404-55233-1*) AMS Pr.

Decade of Radio Advertising. Herman S. Hettinger. LC 70-161150. (History of Broadcasting: Radio to Television Ser.). 1976. reprint ed. 29.95 (*0-405-03569-1*) Ayer.

Decade of Revolution, 1789-1799. Clarence C. Brinton. LC 83-10715. (Rise of Modern Europe Ser.). (Illus.). x, 330p. (C). 1983. reprint ed. text ed. 69.50 (*0-313-24077-9*, BRDE, Greenwood Pr) Greenwood.

Decade of Riba Student Competitions: UIA Journal. (Illus.). 124p. (Orig.). 1993. pap. 25.00 (*0-312-07894-3*, Academy Edits) St Martin.

Decade of Robotics: Analysis of the Diffusion of Industrial Robots in the 1980s by Countries, Application Areas, Industrial Branches & Types of Robots. Jan M. Karlsson. 214p. (Orig.). 1991. pap. 143.50x (*91-524-1115-X*, Pub. by Almqv & Wiksell SW) Coronet Bks.

Decade of Sales Clinic. Howard Feiertag. LC 93-70559. 1993. pap. 39.95 (*0-929870-13-1*) Advanstar Commns.

Decade of Sculpture. Julia Busch. (Illus.). 1974. 50.00 (*0-87982-007-1*) Art Alliance.

D

An Asterisk (*) at the beginning of an entry indicates that the title is appearing in BIP for the first time.

An Asterisk (*) at the beginning of an entry indicates that the title is appearing in BIP for the first time.

1839

Decennial Supplements Mortality & Geography: A Review in the Mid-1980's England & Wales, No. 9. M. Britton. 246p. 1990. pap. 37.00 (*0-11-691294-4*, HM9244) UNIPUB.

Decent Cup of Tea. Malachi McCormick. 80p. 1991. 12.00 (*0-517-58462-X*, C P Pubs) Crown Pub Group.

Decent Housing: A Promise to Keep. Thomas F. Lord. 176p. 1976. boxed 22.95 (*0-87073-491-1*) Transaction Pubs.

Decent Intentions. Judy Simmons. 60p. 1983. pap. 5.95 (*0-940738-03-1*) Blind Beggar.

*Decent Killer.** large type ed. Jeanne Hart. 1995. pap. 16.95 (*0-7838-1139-X*) Hall.

Decentered Universe of Finnegans Wake: A Structuralist Analysis. Margot Norris. LC 76-25507. 159p. reprint ed. pap. 45.40 (*0-8357-8089-9*, 2034116) Bks Demand.

Decentralisation & Educational Building Management: The Impact of Recent Reforms. 88p. (Orig.). 1992. pap. 28.00 (*92-64-13660-6*) OECD.

Decentralisation & the Curriculum. Andrew Sturman. (C). 1992. 70.00 (*0-86431-051-X*, Pub. by Aust Council Educ Res AT) St Mut.

Decentralised Energy Planning. Pramod Deo et al. (C). 1991. text ed. 17.50 (*81-204-0629-X*, Pub. by Oxford IBH II) S Asia.

Decentralised Planning: The Karnataka Experiment. Abdul Aziz. LC 93-6861. 146p. (C). 1993. 26.00 (*0-8039-9113-4*) Sage.

Decentralising for Participatory Planning: Comparing the Experience of Zimbabwe & Other Anglophone Countries in Eastern & Southern Africa. P. De Valk & K. H. Wekwete. (Illus.). 304p. 1990. text ed. 76.95 (*0-566-07113-4*, Pub. by Avebury Pub UK) Ashgate Pub Co.

Decentralization: The Administrator's Guidebook to School District Change. Daniel J. Brown. 150p. 1991. 25.00 (*0-685-75355-7*, 60050) Corwin Pr.

Decentralization: The Administrator's Guidebook to School District Change. Daniel J. Brown. (Illus.). 128p. 1994. 32.00 (*0-8039-6005-0*); pap. 16.00 (*0-8039-6187-1*) Corwin Pr.

Decentralization: The Territorial Dimensions of the State. B. C. Smith. 250p. 1985. pap. text ed. 24.95 (*0-04-352114-2*) Routledge Chapman & Hall.

Decentralization & Its Implications for Urban Service Delivery. William Dillinger. LC 94-5013. (Urban Management Programme Ser.: Vol. 16). 50p. 1994. write for info. (*0-8213-2792-5*) World Bank.

Decentralization & Local Government: A Danish-Polish Comparative Study in Political Systems. Ed. by Jerzy Regulski et al. 200p. 1989. pap. 34.95 (*0-88738-730-6*) Transaction Pubs.

Decentralization & School-Based Management. Daniel J. Brown. 250p. 1989. pap. 35.00 (*1-85000-601-6*, Falmer Pr) Taylor & Francis.

Decentralization & School Improvement: Can We Fulfill the Promise? Ed. by Jane Hannaway & Martin Carnoy. LC 92-29938. (Jossey-Bass Education Ser.). 268p. 1993. 32.95 (*1-55542-505-4*) Jossey-Bass.

Decentralization & the Implementation of Rural Development in Senegal: The View from Below. Richard Vengroff & Alan Johnston. LC 87-34949. (African Studies). 250p. 1989. lib. bdg. 89.95 (*0-88946-183-X*) E Mellen.

D

Decentralization in Indonesia as a Political Problem. Gerald S. Maryanov. (Cornell University, Modern Indonesia Project, Monograph Ser.). 126p. reprint ed. pap. 36.00 (*0-317-09553-6*, 2010637) Bks Demand.

Decentralization in Infinite Horizon Economies. Ed. by Mukul Majumdar. 193p. (C). 1992. text ed. 54.50 (*0-8133-8090-1*) Westview.

Decentralization in Latin America: An Evaluation. Ed. by Arthur Morris & Stella Lowder. LC 91-17806. 240p. 1992. text ed. 55.00 (*0-275-94021-7*, C4021, Praeger Pubs) Greenwood.

Decentralization, Local Governments & Markets: Towards a Post-Welfare Agenda. Ed. by R. J. Bennett. (Illus.). 432p. 1990. 74.00 (*0-19-828687-2*) OUP.

Decentralization of Collective Bargaining: An Analysis of Recent Experience in the U. K. Michael P. Jackson et al. LC 93-18907. 256p. 1993. text ed. 69.95 (*0-312-09634-8*) St Martin.

*Decentralization of the Socialist State.** Ed. by Richard M. Bird et al. LC 95-2528. (Regional & Sectoral Studies). 1995. write for info. (*0-8213-3186-8*) World Bank.

Decentralized A. I. 3: Proceedings of the Third European Workshop on Modelling Autonomous Agents in a Multi-Agent World, Kaiserlauten, Germany, August 5-7, 1991. Ed. by Eric Werner & Yves Demazeau. LC 92-2276. 1992. write for info. (*0-444-89661-9*, North Holland) Elsevier.

Decentralized & Distributed Systems: Proceedings of the IFIP WG10.3 International Conference on Decentralized & Distributed Systems, Palma de Mallorca, Spain, 13-17 September 1993. Ed. by Michel Cosnard & Ramon Puigjaner. LC 93-46651. (IFIP Transactions A: Computer Science & Technology Ser.: Vol. A-39). 1994. write for info. (*0-444-81791-3*, North Holland) Elsevier.

Decentralized Artificial Intelligence: Proceedings of the European Workshop on Modelling Autonomous Agents in a Multi-Agent World, 1st, Cambridge, UK, 16-18 Aug., 1989. Ed. by Yves Demazeau & J. P. Muller. 280p. 1990. 82.00 (*0-444-88705-9*, North Holland) Elsevier.

Decentralized Camping. Lois Goodrich. 183p. 1982. pap. 14.00 (*0-87603-069-X*) Am Camping.

Decentralized Control. Madan G. Singh. (Systems & Control Ser.: Vol. 1). 1981. 95.00 (*0-444-86198-X*, North Holland) Elsevier.

Decentralized Control of Complex Systems. Dragoslav D. Siljak. (Mathematics in Science & Engineering Ser.: Vol. 184). 527p. 1990. text ed. 97.00 (*0-12-643430-1*) Acad Pr.

*Decentralized Industrialization & Urban Dynamics: The Case of Jetpur in West India.** Veronique Dupont. LC 95-926. 532p. 1995. 36.00 (*0-8039-9236-X*) Sage.

Decentralized Production Management Systems. Ed. by S. Augustin et al. 220p. 1986. reprint ed. pap. 41.00 (*0-444-87963-3*, North Holland) Elsevier.

Decentralized Systems: Proceedings of the IFIP WG 10.3 Working Conference, Lyon, France, 11-13, Dec., 1989. Ed. by M. Cosnard & C. Girault. 452p. 1990. 102.50 (*0-444-88898-5*, North Holland) Elsevier.

Decentralizing City Government: A Practical Study of a Radical Proposal for New York City. Walter G. Farr, Jr. et al. LC 72-83567. (Special Studies in U. S. Economic, Social & Political Issues). 1972. 36.00 (*0-275-06330-5*) Irvington.

Decentralizing Urban Policy: Case Studies in Community Development. Paul R. Dommel et al. LC 81-70465. 271p. 1982. 32.95 (*0-8157-1888-8*); pap. 12.95 (*0-8157-1887-X*) Brookings.

*Decentring Leisure.** Chris Rojeck. (Theory, Culture & Society Ser.). 240p. 1995. text ed. 65.00 (*0-8039-8812-5*); pap. text ed. 21.95 (*0-8039-8813-3*) Sage.

Deceptio, Falsum et Dissimulatio: A Critique. Edward M. Matthews. 96p. 1984. reprint ed. pap. 5.00 (*0-935461-09-4*) St Alban Pr CA.

Deception. Ruth Langan. (Historical Ser.). 1993. mass mkt. 3.99 (*0-373-28796-8*, 1-28796-0) Harlequin Bks.

Deception. Amanda Quick. 1994. mass mkt. 5.99 (*0-553-56506-0*) Bantam.

*Deception.** Reed. write for info. (*0-517-70156-1*) Random Hse Value.

Deception. Philip Roth. Date not set. pap. write for info. (*0-679-75294-3*) Random.

Deception. Philip Roth. 208p. 1991. 18.95 (*0-685-37883-7*, Touchstone Bks) S&S Trade.

Deception. large type ed. Amanda Quick. LC 93-28767. (Romance Ser.). 1993. 22.95 (*1-56054-770-7*) Thorndike Pr.

Deception. Eleanor Cooney & Daniel Altieri. 640p. 1994. reprint ed. mass mkt. 5.99 (*0-380-70872-8*) Avon.

Deception: A Novel of Murder & Madness in Tang China. Eleanor Cooney & Daniel Altieri. 1993. 22.00 (*0-688-08938-0*) Morrow.

Deception: A Tool of Soviet Foreign Policy. Natalie Grant. (Orig.). 1987. pap. 8.00 (*0-935067-12-4*) Nathan Hale Inst.

Deception: Perspectives on Human & Nonhuman Deceit. Ed. by Robert W. Mitchell & Nicholas S. Thompson. LC 85-2703. (SUNY Series on Animal Behavior). 388p. 1985. 64.50 (*0-88706-107-9*); pap. 24.95 (*0-88706-108-7*) State U NY Pr.

Deception & Desire. Saranne Dawson. (American Romance Ser.). 1993. mass mkt. 3.39 (*0-373-16480-7*, 1-16480-5) Harlequin Bks.

Deception & Desire. Janet Tanner. 464p. 1995. 24.95 (*0-312-11261-0*) St Martin.

*Deception & Deterrence: In "Wars of National Liberation," State-Sponsored Terrorism, & Other Forms of Secret Warfare.** Ed. by John N. Moore. LC 95-68696. (C). 1995. text ed. write for info. (*0-89089-858-8*) Carolina Acad Pr.

Deception As an Art. 1991. lib. bdg. 77.75 (*0-8490-4641-6*) Gordon Pr.

Deception at Midnight. Corey McFadden. 368p. (Orig.). 1993. pap. 4.50 (*0-8439-3520-0*) Dorchester Pub Co.

Deception Detection: Winning the Polygraph Game. Charles Clifton. 152p. 1991. 15.00 (*0-87364-621-5*) Paladin Pr.

Deception of the Thrush. David Parrott. 1986. 50.00 (*0-7223-2049-3*, Pub. by A H S Ltd UK) St Mut.

Deception Operations: Studies in the East-West Context. Ed. by David A. Charters & Maurice Tugwell. 432p. 1990. 68.00 (*0-08-036706-2*, 3004, Pub. by Brasseys UK) Brasseys Inc.

Deception Pass. Sue Standing. LC 84-70354. 71p. 1984. 15.95 (*0-914086-50-2*); pap. 9.95 (*0-914086-51-0*) Alicejamesbooks.

Deceptions. Michael Weaver. 464p. 1995. 21.95 (*0-446-51749-6*) Warner Bks.

*Deceptions.** Michael Weaver. 1996. mass mkt. write for info. (*0-446-60295-7*) Warner Bks.

Deceptions: Editor's Choice. Janice Kaiser. (Temptation Ser.). 1993. mass mkt. 2.99 (*0-373-25566-7*, 1-25566-0) Harlequin Bks.

Deceptions & Dreams. Debra Dier. 448p. (Orig.). 1994. mass mkt., pap. text ed. 4.99 (*0-8439-3674-6*) Dorchester Pub Co.

Deceptions & Myths of the Bible. Lloyd M. Graham. 1989. pap. 12.95 (*0-8065-1124-9*, Citadel Pr) Carol Pub Group.

Deception's Bride. Jaclyn Reding. 336p. (Orig.). 1993. mass mkt. 4.99 (*1-55773-966-8*) Diamond.

Deceptions Embrace. Jeanne E. Hansen. 1989. pap. 3.75 (*0-8217-2720-6*) Zebra.

Deceptions of the Heart. Patricia Pellicane. 512p. 1988. pap. 3.95 (*0-8217-2427-4*) Zebra.

Deceptions of the New Theology. Colin D. Standish & Russell R. Standish. 188p. (Orig.). (C). 1989. pap. 5.95 (*0-923309-18-7*) Hartland Pubns.

Deception's Sweet Kiss. Gina Robins. 1990. mass mkt. 4.50 (*0-8217-2960-8*) Zebra.

Deceptive Advertising: Behavioral Study of a Legal Concept. Jef I. Richards. (Communication Ser.). 264p. (C). 1990. text ed. 49.95 (*0-8058-0649-0*) L Erlbaum Assocs.

Deceptive Appearance. John Malcolm. (Tim Simpson Mystery Ser.). 224p. 1992. text ed. 20.00 (*0-684-19508-9*, Scribners) S&S Trade.

Deceptive Appearance. large type ed. John Malcolm. LC 93-9001. (Nightingale Ser.). 1993. pap. 14.95 (*0-8161-5780-4*) Hall.

Deceptive Clarity. Aaron J. Elkins. 1993. mass mkt. 4.99 (*0-449-14900-5*, GM) Fawcett.

Deceptive Communication: Many Questions & a Few Answers. Gerald R. Miller & James B. Stiff. (Series in Interpersonal Communication: Vol. 14). (Illus.). 160p. 1993. 49.95 (*0-8039-3484-X*); pap. 24.00 (*0-8039-3485-8*) Sage.

Deceptive Desires. Wanda Owen. 1990. mass mkt. 4.50 (*0-8217-2887-3*) Zebra.

Deceptive Desires. Shira Stevens. 288p. (Orig.). 1987. pap. 3.50 (*0-8439-2535-3*) Dorchester Pub Co.

Deceptive Distinctions: Sex, Gender & the Social Order. Cynthia F. Epstein. 315p. (C). 1990. reprint ed. pap. 16.00x (*0-300-04694-4*) Yale U Pr.

Deceptive Hands of Wing Chun. Douglas L. Wong. LC 76-55613. (Illus.). 112p. 1977. pap. 6.50 (*0-86568-002-7*, 201) Unique Pubns.

Deceptive Heart. Maureen Kurr. 368p. (Orig.). 1988. pap. 3.95 (*0-8439-2623-6*) Dorchester Pub Co.

*Deceptive Images.** Laura C. Guysinger. Ed. by Holly Sowels. (Illus.). 236p. 1994. pap. 12.95 (*0-9637441-3-5*) Kehori.

Deceptive Images: Toward a Redefinition of American Judaism. Charles S. Liebman. 256p. 1988. 34.95 (*0-88738-218-5*) Transaction Pubs.

Deceptive Love - By Love Betrayed. Anne N. Reisser. 368p. 1990. pap. 3.95 (*0-8439-3008-X*) Dorchester Pub Co.

Deceptive Lure of Detente. Marian Leighton. 500p. 1989. text ed. 39.95 (*0-312-02801-6*) St Martin.

DECHEMA Biotechnology Conferences, Vol. 3, Pts. A & B: Lectures Held At the 7th DECHEMA Annual Meeting of Biotechnologists May 30-31, 1989, Frankfurt Am Main, FRG. (DECHEMA Monographs). 1151p. 1990. pap. text ed. 390.00 (*0-89573-960-7*) VCH Pubs.

DECHEMA Biotechnology Conferences, Vol. 4: Lectures Held at the Eighth DECHEMA Annual Meeting of Biotechnologists May 28-30, 1990, Frankfurt Am Main. Ed. by Dieter Behrens. 1238p. (Orig.). 1991. text ed. 425.00 (*0-89573-924-0*); 360.00 (*0-685-54387-0*) VCH Pubs.

DECHEMA Corrosion Handbook: Corrosive Agents & Their Interaction with Materials: Cumulative Index for Vols. 1-6. Ed. by Dieter Behrens. 147p. 1991. lib. bdg. 125.00 (*0-89573-640-3*); 105.00 (*0-685-56322-7*) VCH Pubs.

DECHEMA Corrosion Handbook: Corrosive Agents & Their Interaction with Materials: Cumulative Index for Vols. 1-6, Set. Ed. by Dieter Behrens. 147p. 1991. write for info. (*1-56081-604-X*) VCH Pubs.

DECHEMA Corrosion Handbook, Corrosive Agents & Their Interaction with Materials, Vol. 6: Acetic Acid, Alkanols, Benzene & Benzene Homologues, Hydrogen Chloride. LC 87-28025. (Corrosion Handbook Ser.). 368p. 1989. lib. bdg. 575.00 (*0-89573-627-6*); 480.00 (*0-685-47653-7*) VCH Pubs.

Dechema Corrosion Handbook, Vol. 1: Acetates, Aluminium Chloride, Chlorine & Chlorinated Water, Fluorides, Potassium Hydroxide, Steam, Sulfonic Acids. Ed. by Dieter Behrens. LC 87-28025. 334p. 1987. 575.00 (*0-89573-622-5*); 480.00 (*0-685-44504-6*) VCH Pubs.

DECHEMA Corrosion Handbook, Vol. 10: Corrosive Agents & Their Interaction with Materials. Ed. by Dieter Behrens et al. 220p. 1992. 575.00 (*0-89573-631-4*); 480.00 (*0-685-61426-3*) VCH Pubs.

Dechema Corrosion Handbook, Vol. 2: Aliphatic Aldehydes, Ammonia & Ammonium Hydroxide, Sodium Hydroxide, Soil (Underground Corrosion) Ed. by Dieter Behrens. LC 87-28025. 340p. 1988. lib. bdg. 575.00 (*0-89573-623-3*); 480.00 (*0-685-44102-4*) VCH Pubs.

Dechema Corrosion Handbook, Vol. 3: Acid Halides, Amine Salts, Bromine & Bromides, Carbonic Acid, Lithium Hydroxide. Ed. by Dieter Behrens. LC 87-28025. 282p. 1988. lib. bdg. 575.00 (*0-89573-624-1*); 480.00 (*0-685-44618-2*) VCH Pubs.

Dechema Corrosion Handbook, Vol. 4: Alkanecarboxylic Acids, Formic Acid, Hot Oxidizing Gases, Polyols. Ed. by Dieter Behrens. LC 87-28025. 392p. 1989. lib. bdg. 575.00 (*0-89573-625-X*); 480.00 (*0-685-44987-4*) VCH Pubs.

DECHEMA Corrosion Handbook, Vol. 5: Aliphatic Amines, Alkaline Earth Chlorides, Alkaline Earth Dydroxides, Fluorine Hydrogen Fluoride & Hydrochloric Acid. (DECHEMA Monographs). 323p. 1989. lib. bdg. 575.00 (*0-89573-626-8*); 480.00 (*0-685-46006-1*) VCH Pubs.

Dechema Corrosion Handbook, Vol. 8: Sulfuric Acid. Ed. by Dieter Behrens. 283p. 1991. text ed. 575.00 (*0-89573-629-2*); 480.00 (*0-685-60608-2*) VCH Pubs.

Dechema Corrosion Handbook, Vol. 9: Methanol, Sulfur Dioxide, Key to Materials Compositions. Ed. by Dieter Behrens. 375p. 1992. text ed. 575.00 (*0-89573-630-6*); 480.00 (*0-685-60607-4*) VCH Pubs.

Dechiffrer la France: LaStatistique Departementale a l'Epoque Napoleonienne. M. N. Bourguet. 476p. (FRE.). 1988. pap. text ed. 99.00 (*2-88124-225-1*) Gordon & Breach.

*Dechilo.** J. D. K. 670p. 1995. pap. 12.95 (*0-7610-0095-X*) NW Pub.

*Dechine of Rural Minnesota.** Joseph Amato & John Meyer. (Illus.). 1994. pap. 8.95 (*0-9614119-6-1*) Crossings Pr.

Dechter Collection of Greek Vases. (Illus.). 86p. 1989. per., pap. 11.00 (*0-945486-06-5*) CSU SBUAG.

Decidability & Boolean Representations. Stanley Burris & Ralph McKenzie. LC 81-7902. (Memoirs of the American Mathematical Society Ser.: No. 32/246). 106p. 1981. pap. 16.00 (*0-8218-2246-2*, MEMO 32/246) Am Math.

Decide! H. J. Ariston. LC 83-80421. (Illus.). 56p. (Orig.). 1983. pap. 5.95 (*0-935344-01-2*) Jupiter Bks.

Decide: A Computer-Based Decision Game Student Manual. Thomas Pray & Daniel Strang. (Business Division Ser.). 120p. (C). 1984. pap. text ed. write for info. (*0-07-554259-5*) McGraw.

Decide for Yourself: A Theological Workbook. Gordon R. Lewis. LC 71-116046. (Orig.). 1970. pap. 12.99 (*0-87784-633-2*, 633) InterVarsity.

Decide for Yourself: Life Support, Living Will, Power of Attorney for Health Care. Carolyn Brown et al. Ed. by Nancy R. Hull. LC 92-19858. (Illus.). 40p. (Orig.). 1993. pap. text ed. 4.80 (*0-939838-34-6*) Pritchett & Hull.

Decide to Love. Gary Smalley et al. 64p. (Orig.). 1985. student ed, pap. 4.99 (*0-310-44331-8*, 18253P) Zondervan.

Decide to Love: Leader's Kit. Gary Smalley et al. 64p. (Orig.). 1985. teacher ed, pap. 29.99 (*0-310-44861-1*, 18249P) Zondervan.

*Decider.** Dick Francis. 352p. (Orig.). 1995. mass mkt. 5.99 (*0-515-11617-3*) Jove Pubns.

Decider. Dick Francis. 320p. (Orig.). 1993. 22.95 (*0-399-13871-4*, Putnam) Putnam Pub Group.

*Decider.** braille ed. Dick Francis. 516p. (Orig.). 1994. text ed., vinyl bd. 41.28 (*1-56956-539-2*, BR9448) W A T Braille.

Decider. large type ed. Dick Francis. LC 93-38618. (Orig.). 1994. 23.95 (*0-8161-5913-0*, Large Print Bks) Hall.

Decider. large type ed. Dick Francis. LC 93-38618. (Orig.). 1995. pap. 17.95 (*0-8161-5914-9*, Large Print Bks) Hall.

*Decider-O. M.** Dick Francis. 1994. pap. 5.99 (*0-449-22348-5*) Fawcett.

Deciding: Self-Deception in Life Choices. Tod S. Sloan. 1987. 19.95 (*0-416-91560-4*) Routledge Chapman & Hall.

Deciding Factors in British Politics: A Case Studies Approach. John Greenaway et al. 256p. 1991. 69.50 (*0-415-02015-8*, A6708) Routledge.

Deciding for Others: The Ethics of Surrogate Decisionmaking. Allen Buchanan & Dan W. Brock. (Studies in Philosophy & Health Policy). 368p. (C). 1990. 69.95 (*0-521-32422-X*); pap. 24.95 (*0-521-31196-9*) Cambridge U Pr.

Deciding Germany's Future, 1943-1945. David S. Painter. (Pew Case Studies in International Affairs). 50p. (C). 1992. pap. text ed. 2.50 (*1-56927-323-5*) Geo U Inst Dplmcy.

Deciding to Be Legal: A Maya Community in Houston. Jacqueline M. Hagan. (Illus.). 224p. (C). 1994. text ed. 44.95 (*1-56639-256-X*); pap. text ed. 16.95 (*1-56639-257-8*) Temple U Pr.

Deciding to Decide: Agenda Setting in the United States Supreme Court. H. W. Perry. 316p. (C). 1992. 45.00 (*0-674-19442-X*) HUP.

Deciding to Decide: Agenda Setting in the United States Supreme Court. H. W. Perry. 316p. 1994. pap. 17.95 (*0-674-19443-8*) HUP.

Deciding to Grow. Evertt W. Huffard. 1983. pap. 4.95 (*0-89137-540-6*) Quality Pubns.

*Deciding Together: Bioethics & Moral Consensus.** Jonathan D. Moreno. 192p. 1995. 29.95 (*0-19-509218-X*) OUP.

Deciding What to Teach & Test: Developing, Aligning, & Auditing the Curriculum. Fenwick W. English. 144p. 1992. 34.95 (*0-8039-6126-X*); pap. 17.95 (*0-8039-6019-0*) Corwin Pr.

Deciding What's News: A Study of CBS Evening News, NBC Nightly News, Newsweek & Time. Herbert J. Gans. LC 79-22849. 1980. pap. 14.00 (*0-394-74354-7*, Vin) Random.

Deciding Who Lives: Fateful Choices in the Intensive-Care Nursery. Renee R. Anspach. 1993. 30.00 (*0-520-05268-4*) U CA Pr.

Deciding Wisely. Bill Syrios. (Christian Character Bible Studies). 64p. (Orig.). 1992. pap. 4.99 (*0-8308-1148-6*, 1148) InterVarsity.

Decima. Pedro Escabi & Elsa Escabi. LC 76-7976. (Estudio Etnografico De la Cultura Popular De Puerto Rico Ser.: Pt. 2). (Illus.). 526p. (Orig.). (SPA.). 1976. pap. text ed. 9.00 (*0-8477-2502-2*) U of PR Pr.

Decima Culta en la Literatura Puertorriquena. Amalia Lluch-Velez. LC 85-22643. 1988. pap. 10.00 (*0-8477-3804-3*) U of PR Pr.

Decima in Puerto Rico: Historical Survey & Analysis of the Ten Line Stanza Composition As an Expression of the Puerto Rican Spirit. Yvette De Lourdes Cabrera. (Puerto Rico Ser.). 1979. lib. bdg. 59.95 (*0-8490-2905-8*) Gordon Pr.

Decimal Computation. Hermann Schmid. LC 80-29514. 280p. (C). 1984. reprint ed. lib. bdg. 29.50 (*0-89874-318-4*) Krieger.

*Decimals & Fractions.** 4th ed. Charuhas. (Essential Mathematics for Life Ser.: No. 2). 1995. pap. text ed. 7.95 (*0-02-802609-8*) Glencoe.

Decimals & Percent. rev. ed. Mervin L. Keedy & Marvin L. Bittinger. (Algebra, a Modern Introduction Ser.). (gr. 7-9). 1981. pap. text ed. write for info. (*0-201-03980-X*) Addison-Wesley.

Decimals & Percentages. Frances F. Loose. (Illus.). 100p. (gr. 4-6). 1977. 10.00 (*0-87879-803-X*, Ann Arbor Div) Acad Therapy.

*Decimals & Statistics.** (Tai Mathematics Ser.). (J). 1995. 5.25 (*0-88106-163-8*, M011) Charlesbridge Pub.

An Asterisk (*) at the beginning of an entry indicates that the title is appearing in BIP for the first time.

An Asterisk (*) at the beginning of an entry indicates that the title is appearing in BIP for the first time.

Decision Making in Emergency Nursing. Mancini. (Illus.). 218p. (C). 1987. 32.95 (*1-55664-003-X*) Mosby Yr Bk.
Decision Making in Endocrinology & Metabolism. Kohler. 1991. 59.00 (*1-55664-078-1*) Mosby Yr Bk.
Decision-Making in Ethiopia: A Study of the Political Process. Peter Schwab. LC 72-419. 201p. 1972. 20.00 (*0-8386-1153-2*) Fairleigh Dickinson.
Decision-Making in Federal Contract Management. Curtis R. Cook. (Monograph Ser.). 100p. (Orig.). 1989. spiral bd. 29.95 (*0-940343-22-3*) Natl Contract Mgmt.
Decision Making in Fertility Disorders. DeCherney et al. 218p. (C). 1988. 49.00 (*1-55664-015-3*) Mosby Yr Bk.
Decision Making in Forest Management. Ed. by R. W. Williams. 133p. (C). 1988. text ed. 270.00 (*0-685-52003-X*, Pub. by Intl Bk Distr II) St Mut.
Decision-Making in Forest Management. 2nd ed. M. R. Williams. 160p. 1988. text ed. 105.00 (*0-471-91908-X*) Wiley.
Decision Making in Gastroenterology, No. 2. Levine. 512p. 1992. 69.00 (*1-55664-323-3*) Mosby Yr Bk.
Decision Making in Gastrointestinal Surgery. Carey. 1991. 69.00 (*1-55664-024-2*) Mosby Yr Bk.
Decision Making in Gerontologic Nursing. Loftis. 352p. 1993. pap. 32.95 (*1-55664-186-9*) Mosby Yr Bk.
Decision Making in Health Sciences: Medical Analysis Index with Reference Bibliography. American Health Research Institute Staff. LC 85-48752. 150p. 1987. 39.50 (*0-88164-378-5*); pap. 34.50 (*0-88164-379-3*) ABBE Pubs Assn.
Decision Making in Hematology. Brain. 1991. 48.00 (*1-55664-155-9*) Mosby Yr Bk.
Decision Making in Imaging. Kuhns. 868p. 1989. 155.00 (*0-8151-5211-6*, Yr Bk Med Pubs) Mosby Yr Bk.
Decision Making in Large Animal Alimentary Tract Surgery. Horney et al. 1991. 48.00 (*0-941158-78-0*) Mosby Yr Bk.
Decision Making in Long-Term Care: Factors in Planning. Ed. by Ruth E. Dunkle & May L. Wykle. 224p. 1988. 24.95 (*0-8261-5970-2*) Springer Pub.
Decision Making in Magistrates' Courts. Kerry Barker & John Sturges. 95p. 1990. 24.00 (*1-85190-017-9*, Pub. by Tolley Pubng UK) St Mut.
Decision Making in Medical-Surgical Nursing. Gorzeman & Bowdoin. (Illus.). 448p. (C). 1990. 40.95 (*1-55664-120-6*) Mosby Yr Bk.
Decision Making in Medicine. Ed. by Harry L. Greene et al. LC 92-49391. (Clinical Decision Making Ser.). 561p. 1992. 65.00 (*1-55664-226-1*) Mosby Yr Bk.
Decision Making in Nephrology. Shapiro. 1991. 49.00 (*1-55664-116-8*) Mosby Yr Bk.
Decision Making in Neurological Surgery. Bucholz. 1991. 52.00 (*0-941158-58-6*) Mosby Yr Bk.
***Decision Making in Nursing.** Ed. by Rebecca A. Jones & Sharon E. Beck. LC 94-42417. 1995. write for info. (*0-8273-5684-6*) Delmar.
Decision Making in Obstetrical Nursing. Knor. (Illus.). 286p. (C). 1987. 32.95 (*1-55009-020-8*) Mosby Yr Bk.
Decision Making in Oncological Nursing. Baird. 228p. (C). 1987. 34.95 (*1-55009-018-6*) Mosby Yr Bk.
Decision Making in Oncology. Schein. 248p. 1989. 55.00 (*1-55664-072-2*) Mosby Yr Bk.
Decision Making in Ophthalmology. Van Heuven & Zwaan. 318p. 1992. 67.00 (*1-55664-052-8*) Mosby Yr Bk.
Decision Making in Pain Management. Ranamurthy. 305p. 1992. 52.00 (*1-55664-370-5*) Mosby Yr Bk.
Decision Making in Pediatric Nursing. Murphy. (Illus.). 216p. (C). 1988. 29.50 (*0-941158-85-3*) Mosby Yr Bk.
Decision Making in Pediatric Nursing, No. 2. 2nd ed. Murphy. Date not set. 44.00 (*1-55664-354-3*) Mosby Yr Bk.
Decision Making in Pediatric Ophthalmology. Cibis et al. 352p. 1992. 69.00 (*1-55664-296-2*) Mosby Yr Bk.
Decision Making in Periodontology. 2nd ed. Ed. by Walter B. Hall. LC 92-48927. (Illus.). 1992. write for info. (*0-8016-7526-X*) Mosby Yr Bk.
Decision Making in Perioperative Nursing. Wells. (Illus.). 212p. (C). 1987. 32.95 (*1-55664-014-5*) Mosby Yr Bk.
Decision Making in Perioperative Nursing. 2nd ed. Wells. Date not set. 44.00 (*1-55664-355-1*) Mosby Yr Bk.
Decision Making in Physical Education & Athletics Administration: A Case Method Approach. Earle F. Zeigler. 181p. 1982. pap. text ed. 12.00x (*0-87563-221-1*) Stipes.
Decision Making in Plastic & Reconstructive Surgery. Colen. 1990. 58.00 (*0-941158-43-8*) Mosby Yr Bk.
Decision Making in Plastic Surgery. Jeffrey L. Marsh. 249p. 1992. 70.00 (*0-8016-6675-9*) Mosby Yr Bk.
Decision Making in Post Anesthesia Nursing. Drain. 320p. 1991. 44.00 (*1-55664-050-1*) Mosby Yr Bk.
Decision Making in Psychiatric & Psychosocial Nursing. Baumann et al. 256p. (C). 1990. 39.95 (*1-55664-158-3*) Mosby Yr Bk.
Decision Making in Psychiatry & the Law. Thomas G. Gutheil et al. 296p. 1991. 36.00 (*0-683-03801-X*) Williams & Wilkins.
Decision Making in Public Education. Ed. by J. A. Kinder. 1978. text ed. 9.95 (*0-931984-02-5*) Mesa Pubns.
Decision Making in Pulmonary Medicine. Karlinsky. 1991. 65.00 (*1-55664-164-8*) Mosby Yr Bk.
Decision-Making in Reproductive Endocrinology. Ed. by John A. Rock & William D. Schlaff. LC 92-21892. (Illus.). 672p. 1993. 135.00 (*0-86542-214-1*) Blackwell Sci.
Decision-Making in Soviet Politics. John Lowenhardt. 1981. text ed. 32.50 (*0-312-19013-1*) St Martin.
Decision Making in Speech-Language Pathology. Yoder & Kent. 210p. (C). 1987. 38.95 (*0-941158-91-8*) Mosby Yr Bk.
Decision Making in Sports Medicine. Balduini. 1991. 42.00 (*1-55664-007-2*) Mosby Yr Bk.
Decision Making in Surgical Sepsis. Ronald L. Nichols et al. 408p. (C). 1990. 62.00 (*1-55664-053-6*) Mosby Yr Bk.
Decision Making in the European Community: The Council Presidency & European Integration. Emil J. Kirchner. LC 91-4332. 208p. 1992. text ed. 59.95 (*0-7190-3173-7*, Pub. by Manchester Univ Pr UK) St Martin.
Decision Making in the European Community: The Council Presidency & European Integration. Emil J. Kirchner. 208p. 1993. pap. 24.95 (*0-7190-3996-7*, Pub. by Manchester Univ Pr UK) St Martin.
Decision Making in the Post Anesthesia Care Unit. Drain. 288p. 1995. 29.95 (*0-8016-7875-7*) Mosby Yr Bk.
Decision Making in the Public Sector. Nigro. (Public Administration & Public Policy Ser.: Vol. 25). 336p. 1984. 59.75 (*0-8247-7155-9*) Dekker.
Decision Making in the Purchasing Process: A Report. Phillip D. White. LC 78-9749. (AMA Management Briefing Ser.). 54p. reprint ed. pap. 25.00 (*0-317-29941-7*, 2051695) Bks Demand.
Decision-making in the Soviet Energy Industry: Selected Papers with Analysis. David Katsman et al. Ed. by Katherine Young. 166p. (Orig.). 1986. pap. text ed. 100.00 (*1-55831-066-5*) Delphic Associates.
Decision Making in the Soviet Microelectronics Industry: The Leningrad Design Bureau: A Case Study. Eric Firdman. Ed. by Andrew Michta. 104p. (Orig.). 1985. pap. text ed. 75.00 (*1-55831-010-X*) Delphic Associates.
Decision-Making in the White House: The Olive Branch or the Olives. Theodore C. Sorensen. LC 63-20465. 1964. pap. text ed. 16.50 (*0-231-08550-8*) Col U Pr.
Decision Making in Timber Production, Harvest, & Marketing. Marion Clawson. LC 77-84930. (Resources for the Future. Research Paper Ser.: No. R-4). 129p. reprint ed. pap. 36.80 (*0-317-29715-5*, 2019816) Bks Demand.
Decision Making in Trauma Management: A Multidisciplinary Approach. Mary E. Mancini. (Illus.). 464p. (C). 1990. 44.00 (*1-55664-227-X*) Mosby Yr Bk.
Decision-Making in Undefined Conditions. Rudolph V. Trukhayev. (Series on Optimization). 500p. 1995. text ed. 109.00 (*981-02-1742-0*) World Scientific Pub.
Decision Making in Urology. 2nd ed. Martin I. Resnick et al. 264p. (C). 1990. 72.00 (*1-55664-266-0*) Mosby Yr Bk.
Decision Making in Vascular Surgery. Goldstone. 220p. Date not set. 36.00 (*0-941158-14-4*) Mosby Yr Bk.
Decision Making, Models & Algorithms: A First Course. Saul I. Gass. 430p. (C). 1991. reprint ed. lib. bdg. 49.95 (*0-89464-596-X*) Krieger.
Decision-Making Models in Production & Operations Management. Michael Ballot. LC 84-29740. 312p. (C). 1986. lib. bdg. 37.50 (*0-89874-825-9*) Krieger.
Decision-Making Process for Library Collections: Case Studies in Four Types of Libraries. Beatrice Kovacs. LC 89-26021. (Contributions in Librarianship & Information Science Ser.: No. 65). 208p. 1990. text ed. 49.95 (*0-313-26042-7*, KDM/, Greenwood Pr) Greenwood.
Decision-Making Process in Journalism. Carl Hausman. 140p. (Orig.). 1990. pap. text ed. 16.95 (*0-8304-1203-4*) Nelson-Hall.
Decision-Making Skills for Middle School Students. Sherrel Bergmann & Gerald J. Rudman. 64p. 1985. 8.95 (*0-8106-1528-2*) NEA.
Decision-Making under Uncertainty. Hans Bleiker & Annemarie Bleiker. 1988. ring bd. write for info. (*0-925368-01-6*) IPMP.
Decision-Making under Uncertainty: An Applied Statistics Approach. George K. Chacko. LC 89-78157. 272p. 1990. text ed. 59.95 (*0-275-93569-8*, C3569, Praeger Pubs) Greenwood.
Decision Making Under Uncertainty: An Artificial Intelligence Approach. Jerry Felsen. LC 75-32712. (Illus.). 150p. 1976. pap. 20.00 (*0-916376-00-1*) CDS Pub.
Decision Making under Uncertainty: Cognitive Decision Research, Social Interaction, Development & Epistemology. Ed. by Roland W. Scholz. (Advances in Psychology Ser.: Vol. 16). 446p. 1983. 89.75 (*0-444-86738-4*, I-254-83, North Holland) Elsevier.
Decision Making under Uncertainty: The Case of State-Dependent Preferences. Edi Karni. (Illus.). 176p. 1985. 32.00 (*0-674-19525-6*) HUP.
Decision Making Using Lotus 1-2-3 for Windows: Building Quality Applications. Donald Amoroso. 1994. pap. text ed. write for info. (*0-07-001578-3*) McGraw.
Decision Making with Lotus 1-2-3. Donald Amoroso. 1993. pap. text ed. write for info. (*0-07-001574-0*) McGraw.
Decision Making with Multiple Objectives. Ed. by Yacov Y. Haimes & V. Chankong. (Lecture Notes in Economics & Mathematical Systems Ser.: Vol. 242). xi, 571p. 1985. 63.50 (*0-387-15223-7*) Spr-Verlag.
Decision Mate. Edward De Bono. 3.95 (*0-9615400-1-X*) Intl Ctr Creat Think.
Decision Methodology: A Formalization of the OR Process. Douglas J. White. LC 74-1754. (Wiley-Interscience Publication Ser.). 286p. reprint ed. pap. 81.60 (*0-7837-3239-2*, 2043258) Bks Demand.
Decision Models for Industrial Systems Engineers & Managers. Ed. by P. Adulbhan & M. T. Tabucanon. (Illus.). 467p. 1981. 201.00 (*0-08-027612-1*, Pub. by Pergamon Repr UK) Franklin.
Decision Models in Stochastic Programming. Jati K. Sengupta. (Systems Science & Engineering Ser.: Vol. 7). 190p. 1982. 77.00 (*0-444-00667-2*, North Holland) Elsevier.
Decision Networks. N. A. Hastings & J. M. Mello. LC 77-7336. 206p. reprint ed. pap. 58.80 (*0-7837-6380-8*, 2046093) Bks Demand.
***Decision of the Executive Directors under Article X of the Articles of Agreement on Questions of Interpretation of the Articles of Agreement: International Development Association.** 4p. Date not set. write for info. (*0-8213-1847-0*, 11847) World Bank.
***Decision of the Executive Directors under Article X of the Articles of Agreement on Questions of Interpretation of the Articles of Agreement: International Development Association.** 4p. (FRE.). Date not set. write for info. (*0-8213-2001-7*, 12001) World Bank.
***Decision of the Executive Directors under Article X of the Articles of Agreement on Questions of Interpretation of the Articles of Agreement: International Development Association.** 4p. (SPA.). Date not set. write for info. (*0-8213-2041-6*, 12041) World Bank.
Decision of the Heart. Alma Blair. 1993. 13.95 (*0-8034-9032-1*) Bouregy.
Decision on the Rules of Golf by the United States Golf Association & the Royal & Ancient Golf Club of St. Andrews, Scotland. 1990. 15.00 (*0-318-03115-9*) US Golf Assn.
Decision-Oriented Educational Research. William Cooley & William Bickel. 1985. lib. bdg. 56.50 (*0-89838-201-7*) Kluwer Ac.
Decision Point. Robert B. Nelson. 224p. 1992. pap. 14.95 (*0-89815-485-5*) Ten Speed Pr.
Decision Power: How to Make Successful Decisions with Confidence. Harvey Kaye. 1992. 24.95 (*0-13-203530-8*); pap. 9.95 (*0-13-203548-0*) P-H.
Decision, Probability & Utility: Selected Readings. Ed. by Peter Gardenfors & Nils-Eric Sahlin. (Illus.). 400p. 1988. 79.95 (*0-521-33391-1*) Cambridge U Pr.
Decision, Probability & Utility: Selected Readings. Ed. by Peter Gardenfors & Nils-Eric Sahlin. (Illus.). 400p. 1988. pap. 24.95 (*0-521-33658-9*) Cambridge U Pr.
Decision Process for the Retrofit of Municipal Buildings with Solar Energy Systems. 200p. 1980. 20.00 (*0-318-16215-6*, DG80 309) Pub Tech Inc.
Decision Processes in Dynamic Probabilistic Systems. Adrian V. Gheorghe. (C). 1990. lib. bdg. 150.00 (*0-7923-0544-2*) Kluwer Ac.
Decision Processes in Economics: Proceedings of the VI Italian Conference on Game Theory Held in Modena, Italy, October 9-10, 1989. Ed. by G. Ricci. (Lecture Notes in Economics & Mathematical Systems Ser.: Vol. 353). (Illus.). iii, 209p. 1991. pap. 37.00 (*0-387-53592-6*) Spr-Verlag.
Decision-Related Research on the Organization of Service Delivery Systems in Metropolitan Areas: Fire Protection. Lois MacGillivray. LC 79-83819. 1979. write for info. (*0-89138-985-7*) ICPSR.
Decision-Related Research on the Organization of Service Delivery Systems in Metropolitan Areas: Police Protection. Elinor Ostrom. LC 79-83821. 1979. write for info. (*0-89138-983-0*) ICPSR.
Decision-Related Research on the Organization of Service Delivery Systems in Metropolitan Areas: Public Health. Patrick O'Donoghue. LC 79-83820. 1979. write for info. (*0-89138-984-9*) ICPSR.
Decision-Related Research on the Organization of Service Delivery Systems in Metropolitan Areas: Solid Waste Management. E. Steven Savas. LC 79-83822. 1979. write for info. (*0-89138-982-2*) ICPSR.
Decision Research: A Field Guide to Studying Decision Behavior. John S. Carroll & Eric J. Johnson. (Applied Social Research Methods Ser.: Vol. 22). (Illus.). 160p. (C). 1990. 37.00 (*0-8039-3268-5*); pap. 16.95 (*0-8039-3269-3*) Sage.
Decision Science & Social Risk Management. Miley W. Merkhofer. (C). 1986. lib. bdg. 97.50 (*90-277-2275-7*) Kluwer Ac.
Decision Sciences: An Integrative Perspective. Paul R. Kleindorfer et al. (Illus.). 400p. (C). 1993. 69.95 (*0-521-32867-5*); pap. 19.95 (*0-521-33812-3*) Cambridge U Pr.
Decision Strategies in Financial Management. Donald H. Schuckett & Edward J. Mock. LC 72-75468. (Illus.). 253p. reprint ed. pap. 72.20 (*0-317-09499-8*, 2013203) Bks Demand.
Decision Structure of Organization. Jule N. Dews. LC 78-53774. (Illus.). 120p. 1978. pap. 15.00 (*0-937300-00-4*) Stoneridge Inst.
Decision Support & Executive Information Systems. Ed. by Paul R. Gray. LC 93-1929. 1993. pap. text ed. 35.00 (*0-13-235789-5*) P-H.
Decision Support & Expert Systems: Management Support Systems. 3rd ed. Efraim Turban. LC 92-39523. (Illus.). 960p. (C). 1993. write for info. (*0-02-421691-7*) Macmillan.
***Decision Support & Expert Systems: Management Support Systems.** 4th ed. Turban Efraim. (Illus.). 984p. 1994. 69.33 (*0-02-421701-8*, Merrill Pub Co) Macmillan.
Decision Support in Public Administration: Proceedings, the Netherlands, May 1993. Ed. by P. W. Bots et al. (IFIP Transactions A: Computer Science & Technology Ser.: Vol. A-26). x, 200p. 1993. pap. 77.25 (*0-444-81485-X*, North Holland) Elsevier.
Decision Support Models for Regional Sustainable Development: An Application of Geographic Information Systems & Evaluation Models to the Greek Sporades Islands. Peter Nijkamp & Maria Giaoutzi. 314p. 1993. 59.95 (*1-85628-496-4*, Pub. by Avebury Pub UK) Ashgate Pub Co.
Decision Support Systems. William C. House. 250p. pap. 20.00 (*0-89433-208-2*) Petrocelli.
Decision Support Systems. Richard K. Miller & Terri C. Walker. LC 88-81884. (Survey on Technology & Markets Ser.: No. 93). 50p. 1989. pap. text ed. 200.00 (*1-55865-092-X*) Future Tech Surveys.
Decision Support Systems. TAB Books Staff. 1983. 25.00 (*0-07-155788-1*) McGraw.
Decision Support Systems. 3rd ed. Ralph H. Sprague, Jr. & Hugh J. Watson. 450p. 1993. text ed. 43.00 (*0-13-036229-8*) P-H.
Decision Support Systems: A Handbook to Design, Development Applications. Stephen J. Andriole. (Illus.). 390p. 1988. text ed. 39.95 (*0-89433-314-3*) Petrocelli.
Decision Support Systems: An Organizational Perspective. Peter F. Keen & Michael S. Scott-Morton. 1978. text ed. 47.50 (*0-201-03667-3*) Addison-Wesley.
Decision Support Systems: Current Practice & Continuing Challenges. Steven L. Alter. LC 78-67960. 1979. text ed. 47.50 (*0-201-00193-4*) Addison-Wesley.
Decision Support Systems: Putting Theory into Practice. Ralph H. Sprague, Jr. & Hugh J. Watson. (Illus.). 384p. 1986. pap. text ed. 29.00 (*0-13-197286-3*) P-H.
Decision Support Systems: Theory & Application. Ed. by C. W. Wolsapple & Andrew B. Whinston. (NATO Asi Series F: Vol. 13). 520p. 1987. 111.00 (*0-387-17774-4*) Spr-Verlag.
***Decision Support Systems: Theory & Practice.** Paul C. Rhodes. 322p. Date not set. pap. 27.50 (*1-872474-07-1*, Pub. by Alfred Waller UK) Paul & Co Pubs.
Decision Support Systems: Water Resources Planning. Ed. by Daniel P. Loucks & J. R. Da Costa. (NATO ASI Series G: Ecological Sciences: Vol. 26). xvi, 600p. 1991. 203.00 (*0-387-53097-5*) Spr-Verlag.
Decision Support Systems - Issues & Challenges: Proceedings of an International Task Force Meeting, June 23-25, 1980. Ed. by G. Fick & Ralph H. Sprague, Jr. (IIASA Proceedings Ser.: Vol. 11). (Illus.). 190p. 1980. 88.00 (*0-08-027321-1*, Pub. by Pergamon Repr UK) Franklin.
Decision Support Systems: A Decade in Perspective: Proceedings of the IFIP WG8.3 Working Conference, Noordwijkerhout, The Netherlands, 16-18 June, 1986. IFIP WG8.3 Working Conference. Ed. by E. McLean & H. G. Sol. 240p. 1986. 54.00 (*0-444-70037-4*, North Holland) Elsevier.
Decision Support Systems & Performance Assessment in Academic Libraries. Roy Adams et al. LC 93-2962. (British Library Research Ser.). 200p. 1993. lib. bdg. 40.00 (*1-85739-047-4*) Bowker-Saur.
Decision Support Systems & Qualitative Reasoning: Proceedings of the IMACS International Workshop, Toulouse France, 13-15 March, 1991. Ed. by Madan G. Singh & L. Trave-Massuyes. 426p. 1991. 110.25 (*0-444-89179-X*, North Holland) Elsevier.
Decision Support Systems Engineering. Andrew P. Sage. (Series in Systems Engineering: No. 1851). 360p. 1991. text ed. 91.95 (*0-471-53000-X*) Wiley.
Decision Support Systems: Experiences & Expectations: Proceedings of the IFIP TC-WG8.3 Working Conference on Decision Support Systems: Experiences & Expectations, Fontainebleau, France, 30 June-3 July 1992. Ed. by Tawfik Jelassi et al. LC 92-16588. (IFIP Transactions A: Computer Science & Technology Ser.: Vol. A-9). 1992. write for info. (*0-444-89673-2*, North Holland) Elsevier.
Decision Support Systems for Effective Planning & Control: A Case Study Approach. Robert J. Thierauf. (Illus.). 672p. (C). 1982. teacher ed write for info. (*0-13-198242-7*) P-H.
Decision Support Systems for Management Accountants. Germain Boer. 56p. 7.95 (*0-86641-136-4*, 85177) Inst Mgmt Account.
Decision Support Systems for Management Science: 3.5 Inch Version & 5.25 Inch Version. 2nd ed. Vahid Lotfi & Carl C. Pegels. 400p. (C). 1992. text ed., 3.5 hd 28.95 (*0-256-09276-1*); text ed., 5.25 hd 28.95 (*0-256-09413-6*) Irwin.
Decision Support Systems for Production & Operations Management for Use with IBM PC. 2nd ed. Vahid Lotfi & C. Carl Pegels. 368p. (C). 1991. pap. text ed. 28.95 (*0-256-09349-0*, 18-2255-02) Irwin.
Decision Support Systems for Production & Operations Management for Use with IBM PC. 2nd ed. Vahid Lotfi & C. Carl Pegels. 368p. (C). 1994. pap. text ed. 28.95 (*0-256-09350-4*, 18-3362-02) Irwin.
Decision Support Systems for the Management of Grazinglands: Emerging Issues. Jerry W. Stuth & Bonnie G. Lyons. (Man & the Biosphere Ser.: Vol. 11). (Illus.). 250p. (C). 1993. text ed. 68.00 (*1-85070-382-5*) Prthnon Pub.
Decision Support Systems in Critical Care. Ed. by M. Michael Shabot & Reed M. Gardner. LC 93-11902. (Computers & Medicine Ser.). (Illus.). 320p. 1993. 59.00 (*0-387-97799-6*) Spr-Verlag.
Decision Support Systems in Finance & Accounting. H. G. Heyman & Robert Bloom. LC 87-32609. 209p. 1988. text ed. 49.95 (*0-89930-269-6*, BDN/, Quorum Bks) Greenwood.
***Decision Support Systems in Mathematica.** Robert J. Korsan. 1995. disk 44.95 (*0-387-94183-5*) Spr-Verlag.
Decision Synthesis: The Principles & Practice of Decision Analysis. Stephen R. Watson & Dennis M. Buede. 300p. 1988. pap. 24.95 (*0-521-31078-4*) Cambridge U Pr.
Decision Systems for Inventory Management & Production Planning. 2nd ed. Edward Silver & Rein Peterson. LC 84-15179. (Management Ser.). 722p. (C). 1985. Net. text ed. write for info. (*0-471-86782-9*) Wiley.
Decision Tables & Computer Programming. Ray Welland. LC 81-28274. 211p. reprint ed. pap. 60.20 (*0-685-23440-1*, 2032693) Bks Demand.
Decision Tables & Flowcharts: DEVA, the Decision Table Evaluation Program for Strategic Logic Design & Development. Wayne P. Lill, Jr. 200p. 1992. 34.95 (*1-882619-08-0*) Binary Triangles.
Decision Theory & Decision Analysis: Trends & Challenges. Ed. by Sixto Rios et al. LC 94-15768. 312p. (C). 1994. lib. bdg. 89.95 (*0-7923-9466-6*) Kluwer Ac.

D

An Asterisk (*) at the beginning of an entry indicates that the title is appearing in BIP for the first time.

Decision Theory & Decision Behaviour. Anatol Rapoport. (C). 1989. lib. bdg. 201.00 (0-7923-0297-4) Kluwer Ac.

Decision Theory & Social Ethics. Hans W. Gottinger & Werner Leinfellner. (Theory & Decision Library: No. 17). 1978. lib. bdg. 103.00 (90-277-0887-8); pap. text ed. 51.50 (90-277-0937-8) Kluwer Ac.

***Decision Theory As Philosophy.** Mark Kaplan. 240p. (C). 1995. write for info. (0-521-47505-8) Cambridge U Pr.

Decision Time: A Guide to Career Enhancement. Michael Shahnassarian. LC 93-37598. 224p. 1994. pap. 19.95 (0-911907-12-2) Psych Assess.

Decision Time in Dapro School District. Allen Englebright. 110p. 1990. 10.00 (0-9627312-0-X) A Englebright.

Decision to Discriminate: A Study of Executive Selection. Robert P. Quinn et al. LC 68-65536. 162p. 1968. pap. 7.00 (0-87944-062-7) Inst Soc Res.

Decision to Discriminate: A Study of Executive Selection. Robert P. Quinn et al. LC 68-65536. 170p. reprint ed. pap. 48.50 (0-7837-5272-5, 2045010) Bks Demand.

Decision to Divest: Major Documents in U. S. vs. AT&T, 1974-1984, 3 vols. Ed. by Christopher H. Sterling et al. 2100p. 1986. lib. bdg. 225.00 (0-89461-045-7) Broadcasting Pubns.

Decision to Divest: The First Review, 1985-1987, No. IV. Ed. by Jill F. Kasle. 768p. 1988. lib. bdg. 90.00 (0-89461-049-X, Comm Pr DC) Broadcasting Pubns.

Decision to Love: A Marriage Preparation Program. John M. Midgley & Susan V. Midgley. LC 92-80388. 144p. (Orig.). 1992. pap. 6.50 (0-89622-514-3) Twenty-Third.

Decision to Publish. Mary Bold. LC 87-30904. 176p. (Orig.). 1989. pap. 14.95 (0-938267-01-9) Bold Prodns.

Decision to Relocate the Japanese Americans. Roger Daniels. LC 85-12678. 150p. (C). 1985. reprint ed. pap. text ed. 10.50 (0-89874-879-8) Krieger.

***Decision to Use the Atomic Bomb & the Architecture of an American Myth.** Gar Alperovitz. LC 95-8778. 1995. write for info. (0-679-44331-2) Knopf.

Decision Tools for Pest Management. G. Norton & J. Mumford. 320p. 1993. 71.25 (0-85198-783-4) CAB Intl.

Decision Traps: The Ten Barriers to Brilliant Decision-Making & How to Overcome Them. J. Edward Russo & Paul J. Schoemaker. 1989. 19.95 (0-385-24835-0) Doubleday.

Decision Vision. Gloria Gaither. 1991. pap. 7.95 (0-87162-607-1, D3565) Warner Pr.

Decision with Inadequate Hydrologic Data: Proceedings of the International Symposium in Hydrology, 2nd, Colorado State University, Sept. 11-13, 1972. International Symposium in Hydrology Staff. Ed. by David A. Woolhiser. LC 73-80677. 1973. 22.00 (0-918334-04-7) WRP.

Decisional Structures in Automated Manufacturing. Ed. by A. Villa & G. Murari. (IFAC Publication Ser.: No. 9003). 1990. 94.00 (0-08-037865-X, Pergamon Pr) Elsevier.

Decisional Thinking of Arbitrators & Judges: National Academy of Arbitrators, 33rd Annual Meeting. Ed. by James L. Stern & Barbara D. Dennis. 502p. 1981. text ed. 35.00 (0-87179-346-6, 0346) BNA.

Decisiones a la Sombra De la Cruz (Decisions in Shadow-Cross) L. Palau. (SPA.). Date not set. 1.79 (0-8423-6477-3, 498005) Editorial Unilit.

Decisiones de Puerto Rico. 1980. 34.00 (0-685-74140-0) Butterworth Legal Pubs.

Decisiones de Puerto Rico. (SPA.). 1987. write for info. (0-318-62480-X) Equity Pubng NH.

Decisiones de Puerto Rico, Set. 1980. boxed 1,870.00 (0-88063-502-9) Michie Butterworth.

Decisiones Equivocadas (Wrong Decisions) Caida Sin Retorno? (Falling Off Without Return?) L. Palau. (SPA.). Date not set. 1.79 (1-56063-540-1, 498027) Editorial Unilit.

Decisionmaking Context in the U. S. Department of the Navy: A Primer for Cost Analysis. Eric V. Larson & Adele R. Palmer. LC 93-48871. (MR-255-PA&E Ser.). 189p. 1994. pap. text ed. 15.00 (0-8330-1502-8) Rand Corp.

Decisionmaking, Incapacity, & the Elderly 1987 (1990 Supplement) Legal Counsel for the Elderly Staff. 186p. 1987. pap. 44.95 (0-933945-00-0) Legal Coun Elderly.

***Decisions.** Concordia Publishing Staff. (Connections Ser.). 1994. pap. 3.99 (0-570-09370-8) Concordia.

Decisions. Francine Pascal. (Sweet Valley High Ser.: No. 46). (YA). (gr. 6 up). 1988. pap. 2.99 (0-553-27278-0) Bantam.

Decisions. Lawrence G. Wrenn. 182p. (Orig.). 1980. pap. 3.50 (0-943616-02-6) Canon Law Soc.

Decisions. 2nd ed. Jack Roeda. (Illus.). 80p. (YA). (gr. 9-12). 1992. teacher ed 8.50 (1-56212-000-X, 1240-4940); pap. text ed. 6.50 (0-930265-96-3, 1240-4920); 4.95 (0-685-60757-7, 1240-4910) CRC Pubns.

Decisions. 2nd rev. ed. Lawrence G. Wrenn. vi, 200p. (Orig.). 1983. pap. 6.50 (0-943616-17-4) Canon Law Soc.

Decisions, 1. Sherlie Rowe. 1983. pap. 4.75 (0-89137-806-5) Quality Pubns.

Decisions, 2. Sherlie Rowe. 1983. pap. 4.75 (0-89137-807-3) Quality Pubns.

Decisions, 5 Vols., Set. Tanja Westfall & Patrick Miles. Ed. by Cheri Karch. (Illus.). 160p. (J). (gr. 4-7). 1989. text ed. 38.95 (1-877618-00-4) APIX Intl.

Decisions: Building Bricks - Crystal, Vol 3. Tanja Westfall & Patrick Miles. Ed. by Cherl Karch. (Illus.). 32p. (J). (gr. 4-7). 1989. text ed. 7.79 (1-877618-03-9) APIX Intl.

Decisions: Struggle in the Willow Tree, Vol. 1. Tanja Westfall & Patrick Miles. Ed. by Cheri Karch. (Illus.). 32p. (J). (gr. 4-7). 1989. text ed. 7.79 (1-877618-01-2) APIX Intl.

Decisions: The Edge - LSD, Vol. 5. Tanja Westfall & Patrick Miles. Ed. by Cheri Karch. (Illus.). 32p. (J). (gr. 4-7). 1989. text ed. 7.79 (1-877618-05-5) APIX Intl.

Decisions: The Pit, Vol. 2. Tanja Westfall & Patrick Miles. Ed. by Cheri Karch. (Illus.). 32p. (J). (gr. 4-7). 1989. text ed. 7.79 (1-877618-02-0) APIX Intl.

Decisions: The Survivor, Vol. 4. Tanja Westfall & Patrick Miles. Ed. by Cheri Karch. (Illus.). 32p. (J). (gr. 4-7). 1989. text ed. 7.84 (1-877618-04-7) APIX Intl.

Decisions & Attitudes As Outcomes of the Discussion of a Social Problem. William M. Timmons. LC 75-177707. (Columbia University. Teachers College. Contributions to Education Ser.: No. 777). reprint ed. 37.50 (0-404-55777-5) AMS Pr.

Decisions & Dilemmas: Case Studies in Presidential Foreign Policy Making. Robert A. Strong. 252p. (C). 1992. pap. text ed. write for info. (0-13-200908-0) P-H.

Decisions & Diplomacy: Essays in Twentieth Century International History. Ed. by Glyn Stone & Dick Richardson. LC 94-6470. (In Memory of George Grun & Esmonde Robertson Ser.). 256p. 1995. 59.95x (0-415-09795-9, B4091) Routledge.

Decisions & Images: The Supreme Court & the Press. Richard Davis. LC 93-11073. 1993. pap. text ed. 23.40 (0-13-034505-9) P-H.

Decisions & Orders of the National Labor Relations Board, V. 275, April 6, 1985 Through August 27, 1985. 1573p. 1986. 48.00 (0-16-004100-7, S/N 031-000-00267-2) USGPO.

Decisions & Orders of the National Labor Relations Board, 1985-86, Vol. 277. 1694p. 1987. 45.00 (0-16-004104-X, S/N 031-000-00272-9) USGPO.

Decisions & Orders of the National Labor Relations Boards, V. 276, August 28, 1985 Through October 29, 1985. 1598p. 45.00 (0-16-004101-5, S/N 031-000-00268-1) USGPO.

Decisions & Organizations. James G. March. 300p. 1988. pap. text ed. 32.95 (0-631-16856-7) Blackwell Pubs.

Decisions & Revisions: Philosophical Essays on Knowledge & Value. Isaac Levi. 310p. 1984. 64.95 (0-521-25457-4) Cambridge U Pr.

Decisions at Yalta: An Appraisal of Summit Diplomacy. Russell D. Buhite. LC 86-13779. 176p. (C). 1986. 35.00 (0-8420-2256-2) Scholarly Res Inc.

Decisions by Consensus: A Study of the Quaker Method. Glenn Bartoo. (Studies in Quakerism: No. 4). 48p. (Orig.). 1978. pap. 3.00 (0-89670-003-8) Progresiv Pub.

Decisions by the Numbers: An Introduction to Quantitative Techniques of Public Policy Analysis. Dipak K. Gupta. LC 93-3898. 1994. write for info. (0-13-474438-1) P-H.

Decisions by the Numbers: An Introduction to Quantitative Techniques Public Poll. Dipak Gupta. 560p. 1994. pap. text ed. 30.00 (0-13-492265-4) P-H.

Decisions, Decisions! A Practical Guide to Problem Solving & Decision Making. Andrew Leigh. 224p. (C). 1983. 63.00 (0-85292-315-5) St Mut.

Decisions! Decisions! Thinking & Problem-Solving Activities for Primary Grades. Imogene Forte & Joy MacKenzie. (Illus.). 80p. (Orig.). 1991. pap. text ed. 7.95 (0-86530-179-4, IP 192-4) Incentive Pubns.

Decisions for Defense. William W. Kaufmann & John D. Steinbruner. 78p. 1991. pap. 9.95 (0-8157-4885-X) Brookings.

Decisions for Health. Ruth Rich & Carol N. D'Onofrio. (Discover Ser.). (Illus.). 520p. (YA). (gr. 9-12). 1993. teacher ed 41.95 (0-7854-0050-8, 15192); text ed. 31.95 (0-7854-0149-0, 15191); audio 113.95 (0-7854-0060-5, 15190); Total tchr. support system. 221.95 (0-7854-0051-6, 15193) Am Guidance.

Decisions for Health. 3rd ed. Clint E. Bruess & Glenn Richardson. 656p. (C). 1992. pap. write for info. (0-697-10300-5) Brown & Benchmark.

Decisions for Health. 4th ed. Clint E. Bruess & Glenn Richardson. 608p. (C). 1995. pap. text ed. write for info. (0-697-15224-3) Brown & Benchmark.

Decisions for Health. 4th ed. Clint E. Bruess & Susan Laing. 608p. (C). 1995. student ed, pap. write for info. (0-697-15227-8) Brown & Benchmark.

Decisions for Health: Black & White Version. 4th ed. Clint E. Bruess & Glenn Richardson. 608p. (C). 1995. pap. write for info. (0-697-25719-3) Brown & Benchmark.

Decisions for Independent Living. Caughey. (gr. 9-12). 1983. text ed. 8.52 (0-02-663190-3) Bennett IL.

Decisions for Today & Tomorrow. Louis A. Iozzi & Peter J. Bastardo. (Preparing for Tomorrow's World Ser.). (YA). (gr. 9-12). 1990. teacher ed 60.00 (0-944584-22-5) Sopris.

Decisions for Your Life: Preventing Teenage Pregnancy. Girl Scouts of the U. S. A. Staff. (Contemporary Issues Ser.). 20p. 1989. pap. 1.75 (0-88441-466-3, 26-826) Girl Scouts USA.

Decisions in Adult Acute Care. Philip H. Goodman & Kenneth J. Kurtz. 208p. 1989. 23.00 (0-88167-472-9) Raven.

Decisions in Doubt: The Environment & Public Policy. Wade L. Robison. LC 94-20549. (Nelson A. Rockefeller Series in Social Science & Public Policy). 288p. 1994. 39.95 (0-87451-695-1) U Pr of New Eng.

Decisions in Maintenance. M. H. Smith. (C). 1992. 110.00 (0-86022-370-1, Pub. by Build Servs Info Assn UK) St Mut.

Decisions in Organizations: A Three-Country Comparative Study. Frank Heller et al. 256p. (C). 1988. text ed. 39.95 (0-8039-8054-X) Sage.

Decisions in Philosophy of Religion. William B. Williamson. LC 85-42846. 407p. (C). 1985. reprint ed. pap. 26.95x (0-87975-295-5) Prometheus Bks.

Decisions in Public & Private Sectors: Theories, Practices, & Processes. Donald Clough. (Illus.). 448p. (C). 1984. text ed. 38.00 (0-13-198226-5) P-H.

Decisions in Syracuse. Roscoe C. Martin et al. LC 68-9709. 368p. 1968. reprint ed. text ed. 65.00 (0-8371-0160-3, MADS, Greenwood Pr) Greenwood.

Decisions in the Penal Process. Keith A. Bottomley. (Law in Society Ser.). 270p. 1973. text ed. 11.75 (0-8377-1935-6) Rothman.

Decisions of International Institutions Before Domestic Courts. Christoph H. Schreuer. LC 80-27503. 407p. 1981. lib. bdg. 45.00 (0-379-20709-5) Oceana.

***Decisions of Pennsylvania Public Utility Commission, Vol. 78.** 722p. 1994. write for info. (0-910325-54-5) Public Util.

***Decisions of Pennsylvania Public Utility Commission, Vol. 79.** 692p. Date not set. write for info. (0-910325-55-3) Public Util.

***Decisions of Pennsylvania Public Utility Commission, Vol. 80.** 844p. 1994. write for info. (0-910325-57-X) Public Util.

Decisions of the Comptroller General of the United States, Vol. 68: Oct. 1, 1988-Sept. 30, 1989. 842p. 1990. text ed. 30.00 (0-16-022241-9, S/N 020-000-00248-4) USGPO.

***Decisions of the European Court of Justice & Their National Implications.** Aidan O'Neill & David Vaughan. 315p. 1994. pap. text ed. 193.00 (0-406-02896-6, UK) Butterworth Legal Pubs.

Decisions of the Federal Labor Relations Authority, Vol. 33: Oct.1, 1988 through Aug.31, 1989. 1020p. 1990. boxed 39.00 (0-16-006694-8, S/N 063-000-000) USGPO.

Decisions of the Highest Order: Perspectives on the National Security Council. Karl F. Inderfurth & Loch K. Johnson. LC 88-5033. 357p. (C). 1988. pap. 23.95 (0-534-09342-6) Intl Thomson.

Decisions of the United States Supreme Court: 1963-64, 1964-65, 1965-66, 1966-67, 1967-68, 1968-69, 1969-70, 1970-71, 1971-72, 1972-73, 1973-74, 1974-75, 1975-76, 1976-77, 1977-78, 1978-79, 1979-80, 1980-81, 1981-82, 1982-83, 1983-84, 1984-85, 1985-86, 1986-87, 1987-88, 1988-89, 1989-90, 1990-91, 29 vols. Lawyers Co-Operative Publishing Company Staff. 1,100.00 (0-317-00149-3) Lawyers Cooperative.

Decisions of the United States Supreme Court: 1963-64, 1964-65, 1965-66, 1966-67, 1967-68, 1968-69, 1969-70, 1970-71, 1971-72, 1972-73, 1973-74, 1974-75, 1975-76, 1976-77, 1977-78, 1978-79, 1979-80, 1980-81, 1981-82, 1982-83, 1983-84, 1984-85, 1985-86, 1986-87, 1987-88, 1988-89, 1989-90, 1990-91, 29 vols., Set. Lawyers Co-Operative Publishing Company Staff. 1,426.50 (0-317-00147-7) Lawyers Cooperative.

***Decisions on the Rules of Golf: Official Rulings on Over 1000 Golf Situations.** 2nd rev. ed. United States Golf Association Staff & Royal & Ancient Golf Club of St. Andrews Staff. 700p. 1995. pap. 16.95 (1-57243-047-8) Triumph Bks.

Decisions: Perspectives for the School Administrator. Robert Maidment. 48p. 1986. pap. 6.00 (0-88210-192-7) Natl Assn Student.

Decisions Under Uncertainty: Drilling Decisions by Oil & Gas Operators. C. Jackson Grayson, Jr. Ed. by Stuart Bruchey. LC 78-22686. (Energy in the American Economy Ser.). (Illus.). 1979. reprint ed. lib. bdg. 35.95 (0-405-11989-5) Ayer.

Decisions, Values & Groups: Proceedings of the Conference Held at the University of New Mexico. Air Force Office of Scientific Staff & N. Washburne. LC 60-12604. 1962. 221.00 (0-08-009705-7, Pub. by Pergamon Repr UK) Franklin.

***Decisions When Retiring: Tax Guide 301.** Holmes F. Crouch. Ed. by Irma J. Crouch. LC 94-78020. (Three Hundred: Retirees & Estates Ser.). (Illus.). 224p. 1995. pap. text ed. 16.95 (0-944817-22-X) Allyear Tax.

Decisions with Multiple Objectives: Preferences & Value Tradeoffs. Ralph L. Keeney & Howard Raiffa. (Illus.). 569p. (C). 1993. 69.95 (0-521-44185-4); pap. 21.95 (0-521-43883-7) Cambridge U Pr.

Decisions Without Hierarchy: Feminist Interventions in Organization Theory & Practice. Kathleen P. Iannello. LC 92-12562. 176p. 1992. 45.00 (0-415-90428-5, A5625, Routledge NY); pap. 14.95 (0-415-90429-3, A5629, Routledge NY) Routledge.

Decisive Battle of Nashville. Stanley F. Horn. LC 56-12173. 181p. 1991. pap. 11.95 (0-8071-1709-9) La State U Pr.

***Decisive Battles of India Through the Ages Vol. I.** H. N. Verma & Amrit Verma. Ed. by Gautam Verma. (Illus.). 208p. (C). 1994. per. 24.95 (1-881155-02-1) GIP Bks.

Decisive Battles of the Civil War. Joseph B. Mitchell. 1980. pap. 2.25 (0-449-30745-X) Fawcett.

Decisive Battles of the Civil War. Joseph B. Mitchell. 1985. mass mkt. 5.99 (0-449-30031-5, Q745, Prem) Fawcett.

Decisive Battles of the Civil War. Joseph B. Mitchell. (Reprints Ser.). (Illus.). 226p. 1990. 19.95 (0-88029-410-8) Dorset Pr.

Decisive Battles of the Civil War. William Swinton. 1989. 9.98 (0-88394-064-7) Promntory Pr.

Decisive Battles of the Korean War. Sherman W. Pratt. 1992. 24.95 (0-533-09584-0) Vantage.

Decisive Battles of the Law: Narrative Studies of Eight Legal Contests Affecting the History of the United States Between the Years 1800 & 1886. Frederick T. Hill. ix, 268p. 1982. reprint ed. lib. bdg. 25.00 (0-8377-0646-7) Rothman.

Decisive Battles of the U. S. A. J. F. Fuller. (Illus.). 428p. 1993. reprint ed. pap. 14.95 (0-306-80532-4) Da Capo.

Decisive Blow Is Struck. Illus. by Edward C. Papenfuse & Gregory A. Stiverson. (Orig.). 1977. pap. 2.00 (0-942370-00-7) MD St Archives.

Decisive Campaigns of the Second World War. Ed. by John Gooch. 206p. 1990. text ed. 35.00 (0-7146-3369-0, Pub. by F Cass Pubs UK); pap. text ed. 18.00 (0-7146-4070-0, Pub. by F Cass Pubs UK) Intl Spec Bk.

Decisive Games in Chess History. Ludek Pachman. viii, 258p. 1987. reprint ed. pap. 7.95 (0-486-25323-6) Dover.

Decisive Issues Facing Christians Today. John Stott. LC 90-39095. 1990. pap. 11.99 (0-8007-5312-7) Revell.

***Decisive Victory & Correct Doctrine: Cults in French Military Thought.** Gideon Akavia. 94p. (Orig.). 1993. pap. 12.00 (0-935371-26-5) CFISAC.

Decisive Warfare: A Study in Military Theory. Reginald Bretnor. LC 84-315. (Stokvis Studies in Historical Chronology & Thought: No. 5). 192p. 1986. reprint ed. pap. 19.00x (0-89370-420-2) Borgo Pr.

***Decisive Warfare: A Study in Military Theory.** Reginald Bretnor. LC 84-315. (Stokvis Studies in Historical Chronology & Thought: No. 5). 192p. 1986. reprint ed. lib. bdg. 29.00x (0-89370-320-6) Borgo Pr.

Decisive Woman. Marion Duckworth. 168p. (Orig.). 1993. pap. 1.80 (1-56476-058-8, Victor Books) SP Pubns.

Decisive Years in France, 1840-1847. David H. Pinkney. LC 85-43304. 248p. reprint ed. pap. 70.70 (0-7837-1425-4, 2041780) Bks Demand.

Decison-Making & Problems of Incompetence. Ed. by Andrew Grubb. LC 93-6187. 170p. 1994. text ed. 65.95 (0-471-94236-7) Wiley.

Deck & Patio Upgrades. Karin Shakery. LC 90-80070. (Illus.). 112p. (Orig.). 1991. pap. 9.95 (0-89721-225-8) Ortho Info.

Deck Chairs. Madeleine Laik. Tr. by Gideon Y. Schein. (Publications Ser.: No. 6). 120p. (Orig.). 1984. pap. text ed. 8.95 (0-913745-05-7) Ubu Repertory.

Deck Designer. Stanley Tools Staff. (Stanley Project Planners Ser.). (Illus.). (Orig.). 1989. pap. 15.95 (0-924648-05-8) Stanley Tools.

Deck of Encounters. TSR, Inc. Staff. (Illus.). Date not set. 20.00 (1-56076-900-9) TSR Inc.

Deck Officer Study Guide. Ed. by Joseph S. Murphy, II. 800p. (C). 1989. teacher ed 85.00 (0-685-32261-0); pap. 125.00 (0-685-32260-2) Academy Pub.

Deck Officer Study Guide, 5 vols., Set. Joseph S. Murphy, II. 1000p. (C). 1990. teacher ed 85.00 (0-685-38551-5); pap. 125.00 (0-685-38550-7) Academy Pub.

Deck Officer Study Guide, 5 vols., Set. 2nd ed. Joseph S. Murphy, II. 1000p. (C). 1990. lib. bdg. 85.00 (0-9625393-0-9) Academy Pub.

Deck Officer Study Guide, Vol. 1: Deck General. 2nd ed. Joseph S. Murphy, II. 200p. (C). 1990. lib. bdg. write for info. (0-9625393-1-7) Academy Pub.

Deck Officer Study Guide, Vol. 2: Navigation General. 2nd ed. Joseph S. Murphy, II. 175p. (C). 1990. lib. bdg. write for info. (0-9625393-2-5) Academy Pub.

Deck Officer Study Guide, Vol. 3: Deck Safety. 2nd ed. Joseph S. Murphy, II. 250p. (C). 1990. lib. bdg. write for info. (0-9625393-3-3) Academy Pub.

Deck Officer Study Guide, Vol. 4: Rules of the Road. 2nd ed. Joseph S. Murphy, II. 175p. (C). 1990. lib. bdg. write for info. (0-9625393-4-1) Academy Pub.

Deck Officer Study Guide, Vol. 5: Navigation Problems. 2nd ed. Joseph S. Murphy, II. 300p. (C). 1990. lib. bdg. write for info. (0-9625393-5-X) Academy Pub.

Deck Planner: Twenty-Five Outstanding Decks You Can Build. (Illus.). 112p. 1990. pap. 7.95 (0-918894-81-6) Home Planners.

Deck Plans. Sunset Editors. LC 90-71531. 96p. 1991. pap. 9.99 (0-376-01066-5) Sunset Menlo Pk.

Deck Plans: Includes Complete Plans for 12 Decks. Bob Beckstrom. Ed. by Anne Coolman. LC 85-60006. (Illus.). 96p. (Orig.). 1985. pap. 9.95 (0-89721-043-3) Ortho Info.

Deck the Halls. (Lights & Music of Christmas Ser.). (Illus.). 16p. (J). 1993. 12.98 (1-56173-709-7) Pubns Intl Ltd.

Deck the Halls. Tom Tozer & Ralph E. Dessem. Ed. by Michael L. Sherer. (Orig.). 1986. pap. 2.35 (0-89536-827-7, 6844) CSS OH.

Deck the Halls. rev. ed. Nancy J. Smith & Lynda S. Milligan. Tr. by Marilyn Robinson & Keri Schneider. (Illus.). 64p. (Orig.). 1989. reprint ed. pap. 15.95 (0-9622477-1-5) Pssblts Denver.

***Deck the Halls: Fifty Beloved Traditional & Contemporary Christmas Favorites.** Ed. by Milton Okun. 143p. (Orig.). (YA). 1994. pap. 12.95 (0-89524-858-1) Cherry Lane.

Deck the Halls: Treasures of Christmas Past. Robert M. Merck. 96p. 1992. 21.95 (1-55859-267-9) Abbeville Pr.

***Deck Us All with Boston Charlie.** Walt Kelly. (Pogo Collector's Edition Ser.). 128p. 1994. 19.95 (1-886460-00-0) Jonas Winter.

Deck Widening & Replacement of the Woodrow Wilson Memorial Bridge. (PCI Journal Reprints Ser.). 20p. 1984. pap. 7.00 (0-318-19818-5, JR305) P-PCI.

Deck with a View: On the Water Vacations in Greece & Turkey. Dale Ward & Dustine Davidson. (Illus.). 352p. (Orig.). 1993. pap. 18.95 (1-880435-17-9) Link Intl.

Deck with a View: Vacation Sailing in the Caribbean. Dale Ward & Dustine Davidson. LC 91-75459. (Illus.). 352p. (Orig.). 1992. pap. 18.95 (1-880435-11-X) Link Intl.

Deckchair Detectives. G. Waters. (Whodunnits Ser.). (Illus.). 48p. (J). (gr. 4 up). 1993. lib. bdg. 11.96 (0-88110-524-4, Usborne); pap. 4.95 (0-7460-0716-7, Usborne) EDC.

***Decked.** braille ed. Carol H. Clark. 350p. 1994. text ed. 28.00 (1-56956-455-8, BR9306) W A T Braille.

Decked. large type ed. Carol H. Clark. LC 93-38923. 1994. bds. 20.95 (0-7862-0129-0) Thorndike Pr.

Decked: A Regan Reilly Mystery. Carol Higgins Clark. (Dove Bk. Ser.). 288p. 1993. mass mkt. 5.50 (0-446-36470-3) Warner Bks.

Decker's Complete Handbook on Mormonism. Ed Decker. LC 93-26329. 1995. 19.99 (1-56507-012-7) Harvest Hse.

***Decker's Complete Handbook on Mormonism.** Ed Decker. 1995. 19.99 (1-56507-821-7) Harvest Hse.

Decker's Patterns of Exposition. 12th ed. Randall E. Decker & Robert A. Schwegler. (C). 1989. pap. text ed. 16.00 (0-673-52016-1) HarpCollege.

D

***Decker's Patterns of Exposition 14.** 14th ed. Ed. by Randall E. Decker & Robert A. Schwegler. LC 94-29863. 1995. pap. text ed. write for info. (*0-673-52338-1*); pap. text ed. write for info. (*0-673-52339-X*) HarpCollege.

Deckhand. Jack Rudman. (Career Examination Ser.: C-190). 1994. pap. 29.95 (*0-8373-0190-4*) Nat Learn.

Decks. Ed. by Southern Living Staff. (Southern Living Bks.). 96p. 1992. pap. 8.99 (*0-376-09045-6*) Oxmoor Hse.

Decks. Sunset Magazine & Book Editors. LC 89-85167. 96p. 1990. pap. 9.99 (*0-376-01078-9*) Sunset Menlo Pk.

Decks: How to Design & Build the Perfect Deck for Your Home. Tim Snyder. LC 90-25479. (Illus.). 256p. 1992. 26.95 (*0-87857-949-4*, 14-133-0); pap. 14.95 (*0-87857-955-9*, 14-133-1) Rodale Pr Inc.

Decks & Patios. LC 80-12177. (Illus.). 160p. 1982. pap. 9.95 (*0-932944-16-7*) Creative Homeowner.

Decks Design & Build. Creative Homeowner Press Editors. LC 89-91776. (Illus.). 160p. 1989. pap. 9.95 (*0-932944-89-2*) Creative Homeowner.

Decks, Porches & Patios. Time-Life Books Editors. (Home Repair & Improvement Ser.). (Illus.). 128p. 1994. 11.99 (*0-7835-3850-2*); lib. bdg. write for info. (*0-7835-3851-0*) Time-Life.

Declamations, 1. Seneca the Elder. Tr. by M. Winterbottom. (Loeb Classical Library: No. 463-464). 558p. 1974. text ed. 18.95 (*0-674-99510-4*) HUP.

Declamations, 2. Seneca the Elder. Tr. by M. Winterbottom. (Loeb Classical Library: No. 463-464). 648p. 1974. text ed. 18.95 (*0-674-99511-2*) HUP.

Declamations et les Declamateurs d'Apres Seneque le Pere. Henri Bornecque. 214p. 1967. reprint ed. write for info. (*0-318-71080-3*, Pub. by Georg Olms GW); reprint ed. write for info. (*0-318-71324-1*, Pub. by Georg Olms GW) Lubrecht & Cramer.

Declamations of Calpurnius Flaccus: Text, Translation, & Commentary. Lewis A. Sussman. LC 94-168. (Mnemosyne, Bibliotheca Classica Batava Ser.: Vol. 133). 1994. 85.75 (*90-04-09983-2*) E J Brill.

Declan's Night. P. C. Robinson. 224p. (Orig.). 1992. pap. 12.95 (*1-881333-01-9*) White Mount Pubns.

Declaracion de Independencia: (The Declaration of Independence) LC 88-11870. (New True Bks.). 48p. (ENG & SPA.). (J). (gr. k-4). 1989. lib. bdg. 13.28 (*0-516-31153-0*); pap. 5.50 (*0-516-51153-X*) Childrens.

***Declaration: Text & Contexts.** Ed. by Michael F. Meister. (Christian Brothers Seminar, 1994 Ser.). 225p. (Orig.). 1995. pap. text ed. 10.00 (*1-884904-05-X*) Christian Brothers.

Declaration of a Heretic. Jeremy Rifkin. 150p. 1985. pap. 8.95 (*0-7102-0710-7*, RKP) Routledge.

Declaration of Conscience. M. C. Smith. LC 77-186044. 501p. 1972. 10.00 (*0-318-03953-2*) Northwood Univ.

Declaration of Ecumenical Commitment: A Policy Statement of the Evangelical Lutheran Church in America. LC 93-47963. (ENG, FRE, GER & SPA.). 1994. 9.99 (*0-8066-2710-7*) Augsburg Fortress.

Declaration of Financial Independence: How to Create Government-Credit Money. 1992. lib. bdg. 79.95 (*0-8490-8728-7*) Gordon Pr.

Declaration of Independence. LC 92-11893. (Milestone Documents in the National Archives Ser.). 1992. 3.50 (*0-911333-96-7*, 200004) National Archives & Recs.

Declaration of Independence. Dennis B. Fradin. LC 88-11870. (New True Bks.). (Illus.). 48p. (J). (gr. k-4). 1988. lib. bdg. 12.90 (*0-516-01153-7*); pap. 4.95 (*0-516-41153-5*) Childrens.

***Declaration of Independence.** R. Conrad Stein. LC 94-24370. (Cornerstones of Freedom Ser.). (Illus.). 32p. (J). (gr. 3-6). 1995. lib. bdg. 12.30 (*0-516-06693-5*) Childrens.

Declaration of Independence: A Study in the History of Political Ideas. Carl L. Becker. 1958. pap. 9.00 (*0-394-70060-0*, V-60, Vin) Random.

Declaration of Independence: An Interpretation & an Analysis. Herbert Friedenwald. LC 77-166325. (American Constitutional & Legal History Ser.). xii, 299p. 1974. reprint ed. lib. bdg. 35.00 (*0-306-70230-4*) Da Capo.

Declaration of Independence: Its History. John H. Hazelton. LC 79-124892. (American Constitutional & Legal History Ser). (Illus.). 1970. reprint ed. lib. bdg. 55.00 (*0-306-71987-8*) Da Capo.

Declaration of Independence & Constitution of the United States. 1987. pap. text ed. 0.97 (*0-685-03058-X*) Lion Bks.

Declaration of Independence & the Constitution. 3rd ed. Ed. by Earl Latham. (Problems in American Civilization Ser.). 288p. (C). 1976. pap. text ed. 8.50 (*0-669-94888-8*) Heath.

Declaration of Independence & the Constitution of the United States of America. LC 84-8116. 76p. (Orig.). (C). 1984. pap. text ed. 2.95 (*0-87840-412-0*) Georgetown U Pr.

Declaration of Independence & the Constitution of the United States of America. 56p. reprint ed. pap. 2.00 (*0-16-006379-5*, S/N 052-071-00596-0) USGPO.

Declaration of Independence & What It Means Today. Edward Dumbauld. 208p. reprint ed. pap. 59.30 (*0-317-27970-X*, 2052153) Bks Demand.

Declaration of Independence-Constitution of the U. S., 2 vols., Set. 1987. 49.50 (*0-686-63049-1*); 34.50 (*0-686-63050-5*) Lion Bks.

Declaration of Legal Faith. Wiley Rutledge. LC 74-114563. (American Constitutional & Legal History Ser). 1970. reprint ed. lib. bdg. 17.95 (*0-306-71921-5*) Da Capo.

Declaration of Rights, Sixteen Eighty-Nine. Lois G. Schwoerer. LC 81-2942. (Illus.). 407p. reprint ed. pap. 116.00 (*0-8357-8090-2*, 2034137) Bks Demand.

Declaration of the Bab: A Compilation. (Illus.). 1992. 12.95 (*0-933770-86-3*) Kalimat.

Declaration of the Causes Mouing the Queenes Maiestie to Send a Navy to the Seas. LC 72-5979. (English Experience Ser.: No. 507). 1973. reprint ed. 25.00 (*90-221-0507-5*) Walter J Johnson.

Declaration of the Demeanor & Cariage of Sir W. Raleigh As Well in His Voyage, As in His Returne. Walter Raleigh. LC 71-25674. (English Experience Ser.: No. 288). 68p. 1970. reprint ed. 9.50 (*90-221-0288-2*) Walter J Johnson.

Declaration of the Estate of Clothing Now Used Within This Realme of England. John May. LC 71-171775. (English Experience Ser.: No. 400). 60p. 1971. reprint ed. 8.00 (*90-221-0400-1*) Walter J Johnson.

Declaration of the Favourable Dealing of Her Maiesties Commissioners Appointed for the Examination of Certaine Traitours. William Cecil. LC 73-25637. (English Experience Ser.: No. 113). 1969. reprint ed. 7.00 (*90-221-0113-4*) Walter J Johnson.

Declaration of the International Conference on Drug Abuse & Illicit Trafficking & Comprehensive Multidisciplinary Outline of Future Activities in Drug Abuse Control. 100p. 1988. 9.00 (*92-1-148075-2*, E.88.XI.1) UN.

Declaration of the People's Natural Right to a Share in the Legislature. Granville Sharp. LC 74-119046. (Era of the American Revolution Ser.). 1971. reprint ed. lib. bdg. 29.50 (*0-306-71955-X*) Da Capo.

Declaration of the Rights of Man & of Citizens: A Contribution to Modern Constitutional History. Georg Jellinek. Tr. by Max Farrand. LC 79-1630. 1985. reprint ed. 15.50 (*0-88355-934-X*) Hyperion Conn.

Declaration of the State of the Colonie & Affaires of Virginia: By His Majesties Counseil for Virginia. LC 72-6037. (English Experience Ser.: No. 563). 1973. reprint ed. 45.00 (*90-221-0563-6*) Walter J Johnson.

Declaration of the State of the Colony in Virginia. Edward Waterhouse. LC 73-25515. (English Experience Ser.: No. 276). 56p. 1970. reprint ed. 45.00 (*90-221-0276-9*) Walter J Johnson.

Declaration of Tokyo. (Western Pacific Reports & Studies: No. 2). 40p. 1986. pap. 1.80 (*92-9061-162-6*) World Health.

Declaration of War: Killing People to Save Animals & the Environment. Screaming Wolf. LC 91-90095. 124p. (Orig.). 1991. pap. 8.95 (*0-9629259-7-7*) Patrick Henry.

Declaration on Certain Questions Concerning Sexual Ethics (Vatican Congregation) 1990. 0.50 (*0-911988-99-8*) AMI Pr.

Declaration on Peace: In God's People the World's Renewal Has Begun. Douglas P. Gwyn et al. 112p. (Orig.). 1991. pap. 4.95 (*0-8361-3541-5*) Herald Pr.

Declaration on the Juridical Personality of Foreign Companies. (Treaty Ser.: No. 26). 16p. (ENG, FRE, POR & SPA.). 1936. pap. 1.00 (*0-8270-0405-2*) OAS.

Declarations. Lalitha Venkateswaran. 4.80 (*0-89253-760-4*); 4.00 (*0-89253-761-2*) Ind-US Inc.

Declarations of Independence: Cross-Examining American Ideology. Howard Zinn. LC 89-46566. 352p. 1991. reprint ed. pap. 13.00 (*0-06-092108-0*, PL) HarpC.

Declarations of Independence: Women & Political Power in Nineteenth-Century American Fiction. Barbara Bardes & Suzanne Gossett. 266p. (C). 1990. text ed. 40.00 (*0-8135-1500-9*); pap. text ed. 14.00 (*0-8135-1501-7*) Rutgers U Pr.

Declarative Programming Sasbachwalden 1991: Phoenix Seminar & Workshop, Black Forest, Germany 18-22 November 1991. Ed. by J. Darlington et al. (Workshops in Computing Ser.). (Illus.). 336p. 1992. pap. 59.00 (*0-387-19735-4*) Spr-Verlag.

Declarative Systems: Proceedings of the IFIP TC10-WG10.1 Workshop on Concepts & Characteristics, Budapest, Hungary, 16-20 October, 1988. Ed. by G. David et al. 324p. 1990. 87.25 (*0-444-88431-9*, North Holland) Elsevier.

Declaratory Judgment. I. Zamir. (Legal Reprint Ser.). (Illus.). xxii, 337p. 1986. reprint ed. lib. bdg. 35.00 (*0-421-35570-0*) Rothman.

Declaratory Orders. 2nd ed. P. W. Young. 1984. 83.00 (*0-409-49353-8*) Butterworth Legal Pubs.

Declare the Glory of God. Yeghia E. Babikian. 168p. 1991. pap. 7.95 (*0-8341-1377-5*) Beacon Hill.

Declare War! Wayne Green. 368p. (Orig.). 1992. pap. 12.95 (*1-882281-00-4*) W Green Inc.

Declare Yourself: Discovering the Me in Relationships. David Burkett & John Narcisco. LC 75-11802. (Illus.). 1975. 11.95 (*0-13-197582-X*, Spectrum Bks) P-H.

Declaring Independence: Jefferson, Natural Language, & the Culture of Performance. Jay Fliegelman. LC 92-17928. 296p. 1993. 39.50 (*0-8047-2075-4*); pap. 12.95 (*0-8047-2076-2*) Stanford U Pr.

Declassified Documents Reference System Retrospective Collection, 3 vols., Set. Ed. by Elizabeth Jones. LC 76-39673. 1977. 460.00 (*0-8408-0029-0*) Res Pubns CT.

Declension & Gradation of Russian Substantives. Edward Stankiewicz. (D A C S R Ser.: No. 4). 1968. text ed. 75.40 (*90-279-0026-4*) Mouton.

Decline & Abolition of Negro Slavery in Venezuela, 1820-1854. John V. Lombardi. LC 74-105976. (Contributions in Afro-American & African Studies: No. 1). (Illus.). 217p. 1971. text ed. 55.00 (*0-8371-3303-3*, LOD/, Greenwood Pr) Greenwood.

Decline & Destruction of the Orion Empire, Vol. 1. Ruth E. Norman. (Illus.). 373p. (Orig.). 1979. pap. 9.95 (*0-932642-50-0*) Unarius Acad Sci.

Decline & Destruction of the Orion Empire, Vol. 2. Ruth E. Norman. 375p. 1981. pap. 9.95 (*0-932642-54-3*) Unarius Acad Sci.

Decline & Destruction of the Orion Empire, Vol. 3. Ruth E. Norman. 375p. 1982. pap. 9.95 (*0-932642-55-1*) Unarius Acad Sci.

Decline & Discontent: Communism & the West Today. Paul Hollander. 300p. (C). 1991. text ed. 34.95 (*0-88738-434-X*) Transaction Pubs.

Decline & Fall. David Cannadine. 1992. 18.00 (*0-385-42103-6*, Anchor NY) Doubleday.

Decline & Fall. Evelyn Waugh. LC 92-54285. 1993. 15.00 (*0-679-42041-X*, Everymans Lib) Knopf.

Decline & Fall. Evelyn Waugh. 1977. 15.45 (*0-316-92619-1*); pap. 10.95i (*0-316-92607-8*) Little.

Decline & Fall. Evelyn Waugh. 1991. reprint ed. lib. bdg. 21.95 (*1-56849-075-5*) Buccaneer Bks.

Decline & Fall of American Education. Carl Salser & Fred West. 308p. 1991. pap. text ed. 19.95 (*0-89420-283-9*, 440050) Natl Book.

Decline & Fall of Byzantium to the Ottoman Turks. annot. ed. Ducas. Tr. & Anno. by Harry J. Magoulias. LC 75-9949. (Illus.). 347p. reprint ed. pap. 98.90 (*0-7837-3611-8*, 2043477) Bks Demand.

***Decline & Fall of Episcopal Church.** Peter Taylor. 1995. audio 16.95 (*1-883049-57-1*); audio, lib. bdg. 18.95 (*1-883049-59-8*) Commuters Lib.

Decline & Fall of Hemispheric Specialization. Robert Efron. 128p. (C). 1990. text ed. 24.95 (*0-8058-0716-0*) L Erlbaum Assocs.

Decline & Fall of Israel & Judah. Gordon Lindsay. (Old Testament Ser.: Vol. 33). 1967. 1.95 (*0-89985-153-3*) Christ for the Nations.

Decline & Fall of Leftism. Colin Wilson. 34p. (C). 1990. reprint ed. lib. bdg. 23.00x (*0-8095-6757-1*) Borgo Pr.

***Decline & Fall of Leftism.** Colin Wilson. 34p. (C). 1990. reprint ed. pap. 13.00 (*0-946650-12-8*) Borgo Pr.

***Decline & Fall of Medieval Sicily: Politics, Religion & Economy in the Reign of Frederick III, 1296-1337.** Clifford R. Backman. 285p. (C). Date not set. write for info. (*0-521-49664-0*) Cambridge U Pr.

Decline & Fall of Mr. Heath: Essays in Criticism of Recent British Politics. Ed. by Ian Robinson & David Sims. 78p. (C). 1989. 40.00 (*0-9502723-4-5*, Pub. by Brynmill Pr Ltd UK) St Mut.

Decline & Fall of Nazi Germany & Imperial Japan. Hans Dollinger. (Illus.). 1968. 5.98 (*0-517-01313-4*) Random Hse Value.

***Decline & Fall of Nazi Germany & Imperial Japan: A Pictorial History of the Final Days...** Dollinger. (Illus.). 1995. 14.99 (*0-517-12399-1*) Random Hse Value.

Decline & Fall of Practically Everybody. Will Cuppy. LC 83-48892. 256p. 1984. pap. 12.95 (*0-87923-514-4*) Godine.

Decline & Fall of Science. Celia Green. 1989. 70.00 (*0-900076-06-2*) St Mut.

Decline & Fall of Sex, with Some Curious Digressions on the Subject of True Love. Robert E. Fitch. LC 72-12555. 114p. 1973. reprint ed. text ed. 55.00 (*0-8371-6722-1*, FIDS, Greenwood Pr) Greenwood.

Decline & Fall of the American Empire. Gore Vidal. (Real Story Ser.). 96p. 1992. pap. 5.00 (*1-878825-00-3*) Odonian Pr.

Decline & Fall of the American Programmer. Edward Yourdon. 320p. 1992. boxed 24.95 (*0-13-203670-3*) P-H.

Decline & Fall of the American Programmer. Edward Yourdon. LC 93-3153. (Yourdon Press Computing Ser.). 352p. 1993. pap. 14.95 (*0-13-191958-X*, Yourdon) P-H.

Decline & Fall of the British Aristocracy. David Cannadine. (Illus.). 832p. (C). 1990. 45.00 (*0-300-04761-4*) Yale U Pr.

Decline & Fall of the Freudian Empire. Hans J. Eysenck. 224p. (C). 1990. lib. bdg. 20.00 (*1-878465-01-5*) Scott-Townsend Pubs.

Decline & Fall of the Freudian Empire. Hans J. Eysenck. 224p. 1992. pap. 10.00 (*0-14-013685-1*, Penguin Bks) Viking Penguin.

Decline & Fall of the Habsburg Empire, 1815-1918. Alan Sked. (Illus.). 295p. (C). 1989. pap. text ed. 22.95 (*0-582-02531-1*, 78196) Longman.

Decline & Fall of the Hapsburg Empire. Alan Sked. (Dorset Classic Reprints Ser.). 312p. 1991. 19.95 (*0-685-60038-6*) Dorset Pr.

Decline & Fall of the Hapsburg Empire. Alan Sked. 1992. pap. 19.95 (*0-88029-708-5*) Marboro Bks.

Decline & Fall of the Hebrew Kingdoms. T. H. Robinson. LC 74-137284. reprint ed. 39.50 (*0-404-05376-9*) AMS Pr.

Decline & Fall of the Liberal Republicans: From 1952 to the Present. Nicol C. Rae. 288p. 1989. 39.95 (*0-19-505605-1*) OUP.

Decline & Fall of the Ottoman Empire. Alan Palmer. LC 93-24525. 1994. 22.50 (*0-87131-754-0*) M Evans.

Decline & Fall of the Roman Empire. Edward Gibbon. LC 93-1857. 1993. 45.00 (*0-679-42308-7*, Everymans Lib) Knopf.

Decline & Fall of the Roman Empire. Edward Gibbon. Ed. by Moses Hadas. 1987. mass mkt. 4.95 (*0-449-30056-0*, Prem) Fawcett.

Decline & Fall of the Roman Empire, 3 Vols. Edward Gibbon. LC 32-28173. 1977. 11.95 (*0-685-03393-7*, Modern Lib) Random.

***Decline & Fall of the Roman Empire, 2 vols., 1.** Ed. by J. B. Bury. LC 94-27080. 1995. 22.00 (*0-679-60148-1*, Modern Lib) Random.

Decline & Fall of the Roman Empire, 3 Vols, 1. Edward Gibbon. LC 32-28173. 1977. 20.00 (*0-394-60401-6*, Modern Lib) Random.

***Decline & Fall of the Roman Empire, 2 vols., 2.** Ed. by J. B. Bury. LC 94-27080. 1995. 22.00 (*0-679-60149-X*, Modern Lib) Random.

Decline & Fall of the Roman Empire, One-Volume Abridgement. Edward Gibbon. Ed. by Dero A. Saunders & Charles A. Robinson, Jr. (English Library). 704p. 1983. pap. 11.95 (*0-14-043189-6*, Penguin Classics) Viking Penguin.

Decline & Fall of the Roman Empire: A One-Volume Abridgement. abr. ed. Edward Gibbon. Ed. by D. M. Low. 944p. Date not set. 39.95 (*0-7011-4010-0*, Pub. by Chatto & Windus UK) Trafalgar.

***Decline & Fall of the Roman Empire Vols. 4-6, 3 vols., Set.** Edward Gibbon. 1994. 45.00 (*0-679-43593-X*, Everymans Lib) Knopf.

Decline & Fall of the Romantic Ideal. Frank L. Lucas. LC 75-30007. 1976. reprint ed. 24.50 (*0-404-14013-0*) AMS Pr.

Decline & Fall of the Soviet Empire. Bernard Gwertzman. 1992. pap. 15.00 (*0-8129-2046-5*, Times Bks) Random.

Decline & Fall of the Supreme Court: Living Out the Nightmare of the Federalists. Christopher C. Faille. LC 94-13733. 224p. 1995. text ed. 52.95 (*0-275-94826-9*, Praeger Pubs) Greenwood.

Decline & Fall of the United States. Anthony M. Masse. 275p. 1985. pap. 8.95 (*0-9608294-0-7*) Bataan Bk Pubs.

***Decline & Fall Roman Empire Vol. 3.** Edward Gibbon. 1995. 22.00 (*0-679-60150-3*, Modern Lib) Random.

Decline & Rebirth: 1933-1962 see Ford

Decline & Resurgence of Congress. James L. Sundquist. LC 81-66191. 500p. 1981. 39.95 (*0-8157-8224-1*); pap. 18.95 (*0-8157-8223-3*) Brookings.

Decline & Rise of the Consumer. Horace M. Kallen. 512p. 1945. 7.95 (*0-87532-150-X*) Hendricks House.

Decline & Rise of the Consumer: A Philosophy of Consumer Cooperation. Horace M. Kallen. LC 75-39251. (Getting & Spending: the Consumer's Dilemma Ser.). 1976. reprint ed. 41.95 (*0-405-08024-7*) Ayer.

***Decline in Marriage among African Americans: Causes, Consequences & Policy Implications.** Ed. by M. Belinda Tucker & Claudia Mitchell-Kernan. (Illus.). 416p. 1995. 49.95x (*0-87154-887-9*) Russell Sage.

***Decline in Marriage among African Americans: Causes, Consequences & Policy Implications.** Ed. by M. Belinda Tucker & Claudia Mitchell-Kernan. (Illus.). 416p. 1995. pap. 19.95x (*0-87154-886-0*) Russell Sage.

Decline of American Capitalism. Lewis Corey. LC 70-38265. (Evolution of Capitalism Ser.). 628p. 1972. reprint ed. 38.95 (*0-405-04116-0*) Ayer.

Decline of American Communism: A History of the Communist Party of the United States Since 1945. David A. Shannon. (Communism in American Life Ser.). 425p. 1971. reprint ed. 25.00 (*0-911860-05-3*) Chatham Bkseller.

Decline of American Gentility. Stow Persons. LC 73-534. 336p. 1976. text ed. 63.00 (*0-231-03015-0*); pap. text ed. 19.50 (*0-231-08347-5*) Col U Pr.

Decline of American Pluralism. Henry S. Kariel. x, 339p. 1961. reprint ed. 42.50 (*0-8047-0034-6*); reprint ed. pap. 14.95 (*0-8047-0035-4*) Stanford U Pr.

Decline of American Political Parties, 1952-1992. Martin P. Wattenberg. LC 93-41952. 239p. 1994. pap. 15.95x (*0-674-19433-0*) HUP.

Decline of American Steel: How Management, Labor, & Government Went Wrong. Paul A. Tiffany. 304p. 1988. 30.00 (*0-19-504382-0*) OUP.

Decline of Annual Hours Worked in the United States Since 1947. Frwd. by Theresa Diss-Greis & Herbert R. Northrup. LC 84-47551. (Manpower & Human Resources Studies: No. 10). 350p. 1984. 30.00 (*0-89546-044-0*) U PA Wharton Ctr Human Resc.

Decline of Aristocracy in the Politics of New York. Dixon R. Fox. LC 70-161764. (Columbia University. Studies in the Social Sciences: No. 198). (Illus.). reprint ed. 24.50 (*0-404-51198-8*) AMS Pr.

Decline of Authority: Public Economic Policy & Political Development in New York State, 1800-1860. L. Ray Gunn. LC 87-47954. 320p. 1988. 39.95 (*0-8014-2101-2*) Cornell U Pr.

***Decline of Belgian Fertility, 1800-1970.** Ron J. Lesthaeghe. LC 77-71991. reprint ed. pap. 79.80 (*0-7837-9374-X*, 2060118) Bks Demand.

Decline of Belgian Fertility, 1870-1970. Ron J. Lesthaeghe. LC 77-71991. (Office of Population Research Ser.). 1978. 47.50x (*0-691-05253-0*) Princeton U Pr.

Decline of Bismarck's European Order: Franco-Russian Relations, 1875-1890. George F. Kennan. LC 79-83997. (Illus.). 1979. 65.00x (*0-691-05282-4*); pap. 19.95 (*0-691-00784-5*) Princeton U Pr.

Decline of British Radicalism, 1847-1860. Miles Taylor. (Illus.). 290p. 1995. 69.00 (*0-19-820482-5*) OUP.

Decline of Civil Law Liability. L. Solyom. 244p. 1981. lib. bdg. 49.50 (*90-286-2181-4*) Kluwer Ac.

Decline of Comity in Congress. Eric M. Uslaner. LC 93-14861. 200p. (C). 1993. text ed. 39.50 (*0-472-10456-X*) U of Mich Pr.

Decline of Communism in China: Legitimacy Crisis, 1977-1989. X. L. Ding. (Illus.). 272p. (C). 1994. 49.95 (*0-521-45138-8*) Cambridge U Pr.

Decline of Community in Zinacantan: Economy, Public Life, & Social Stratification, 1960-1987. Frank Cancian. LC 92-5550. (Illus.). 328p. (C). 1992. 45.00 (*0-8047-2040-1*) Stanford U Pr.

***Decline of Community in Zinacantan: Economy, Public Life, & Social Stratification, 1960-1987.** Frank Cancian. 1994. pap. 14.95 (*0-8047-2362-1*) Stanford U Pr.

Decline of Competition in the Automobile Industry, 1920-1940. Harold Katz. Ed. by Stuart Bruchey. LC 76-39831. (Nineteen Seventy-Seven Dissertations Ser.). (Illus.). 1977. lib. bdg. 41.95 (*0-405-09911-8*) Ayer.

Decline of Constitutional Democracy in Indonesia. Herbert Feith. (Illus.). 638p. 1962. 59.95 (*0-8014-0126-7*) Cornell U Pr.

Decline of Deference. Neil Nevitte. 320p. 1995. pap. 19.95 (*1-55111-031-8*) Broadview Pr.

Decline of Democracy: Essays on an Endangered Political Species. Ralph Buultjens. LC 77-13276. 160p. reprint ed. pap. 45.60 (*0-8357-8856-3*, 2033482) Bks Demand.

An Asterisk (*) at the beginning of an entry indicates that the title is appearing in BIP for the first time.

An Asterisk (*) at the beginning of an entry indicates that the title is appearing in BIP for the first time.

D

Decolonizing the Text: Glissantian Readings in Caribbean & African-American Literatures. Debra L. Anderson. LC 94-11769. (Francophone Cultures & Literatures Ser.: Vol. 1). 1995. write for info. (*0-8204-2521-4*) P Lang Pubs.

Decolonizing Tradition: New Views of Twentieth-Century "British" Literary Canons. Ed. by Karen R. Lawrence. 304p. 1991. 42.50 (*0-252-01821-4*); pap. 15.95 (*0-252-06193-4*) U of Ill Pr.

Decommissioning: Nuclear Power's Missing Link. Cynthia Pollock. LC 86-50307. (Worldwatch Papers). 56p. 1986. pap. 5.00 (*0-916468-70-4*) Worldwatch Inst.

Decommissioning Costs of Light Water Nuclear Power Plants in Germany. J. Adler & P. Petrasch. (EUR Ser.: No. 14798). 102p. 1993. pap. 16.00 (*92-826-6462-7*, CD-NA-14798-EN-C, Pub. by Europ Com) UNIPUB.

Decommissioning of Nuclear Facilities: An Analysis of the Variability of Decommissioning Cost Estimates. OECD Staff. 130p. (Orig.). 1991. pap. 33.00 (*92-64-13552-9*) OECD.

Decommissioning of Nuclear Installations: Proceedings of an International Conference Organized by the Commission of the European Communities, Directorate-General Science, Research & Development, Decommissioning Programme, Held in Brussels, Belgium, 24-27 October, 1989. Ed. by K. Pflugrad et al. 858p. 1990. 176.50 (*1-85166-523-4*) Elsevier.

Decommissioning of Nuclear Power Plants. Commission of the European Communities Staff. 462p. 1984. lib. bdg. 125.00 (*0-86010-558-X*) G & T Inc.

Decommissioning Policies for Nuclear Facilities: Proceedings 2-4 Oct 1991 in Paris. OECD Staff. 398p. (Orig.). (ENG & FRE.). 1992. pap. 82.00 (*92-64-03689-X*) OECD.

DECOMP: An Implementation of Dantzig-Wolfe Decomposition for Linear Programming. J. K. Ho & R. P. Sundarraj. (Lecture Notes in Economics & Mathematical Systems Ser.: Vol. 338). (Illus.). 206p. 1989. pap. 32.00 (*0-387-97154-8*, 3518) Spr-Verlag.

Decomposer Basidiomycetes: Their Biology & Ecology. Juliet C. Frankland et al. LC 81-18145. (British Mycological Society Symposium Ser.: No. 4). (Illus.). 250p. 1982. 115.00 (*0-521-24634-2*) Cambridge U Pr.

Decomposer's Art: Ideas of Music in the Poetry of Wallace Stevens. Barbara Holmes. (Alaska Pacific Studies in Interdisciplinarity). 177p. (C). 1989. text ed. 41.95 (*0-8204-1000-4*) P Lang Pubs.

Decomposing Figures: Rhetorical Readings in the Romantic Tradition. Cynthia Chase. LC 85-45868. 256p. 1986. text ed. 36.00x (*0-8018-3136-9*) Johns Hopkins.

Decomposition & Dimension in Module Catagories. Jonathan S. Golan. (Lecture Notes in Pure & Applied Mathematics Ser.: Vol. 33). 200p. 1977. 110.00 (*0-8247-6643-1*) Dekker.

Decomposition & Invariance of Measures with a View to Statistical Transformation Models. O. E. Barndorff-Nielsen et al. (Lecture Notes in Statistics Ser.: Vol. 58). 191p. 1989. pap. 22.00 (*0-387-97131-9*, 3368) Spr-Verlag.

Decomposition & Isomerization of Organic Compounds see Comprehensive Chemical Kinetics

Decomposition of Alloys: The Early Stages: Proceedings of the 2nd Acta-Scripta Conference, Sonnenberg, 19-23 September 1983. Ed. by P. Haasen et al. (Acta-Scripta Metallurgica Proceedings Ser.). (Illus.). 240p. 1984. 108.00 (*0-08-031651-4*, Pub. by Pergamon Repr UK) Franklin.

Decomposition of Austenite by Diffusional Processes. Ed. by V. F. Zackay & H. I. Aaronson. LC 62-12208. 633p. reprint ed. pap. 180.00 (*0-317-10286-9*, 2000683) Bks Demand.

Decomposition of Figures into Smaller Parts. Vladimir G. Boltyanskii & Izrail T. Gokhberg. Tr. by Henry Christoffers & Thomas P. Branson. LC 79-10382. (Popular Lectures in Mathematics). 1980. pap. text ed. 10.00 (*0-226-06357-7*) U Ch Pr.

Decomposition of Inorganic & Organometallic Compounds see Comprehensive Chemical Kinetics

Decomposition of Random Variables & Vectors. Jurii V. Linnik & Iosif V. Ostrovskii. LC 76-51345. (Translations of Mathematical Monographs: Vol. 48). 380p. 1977. 89.00 (*0-8218-1598-9*, MMONO-48) Am Math.

Decomposition of Sociology. Irving L. Horowitz. LC 92-36400. (Illus.). 288p. (C). 1993. 35.00 (*0-19-507316-9*) OUP.

Decomposition of Sociology. Irving L. Horowitz. (Illus.). 288p. 1994. reprint ed. pap. 14.95 (*0-19-509256-2*) OUP.

Decomposition of Solids. D. Young & F. C. Tompkins. LC 65-29329. (International Encyclopedia of Physical Chemistry & Chemical Physics Ser.: Vol. 1). 1966. 91.00 (*0-08-011645-0*, Pub. by Pergamon Repr UK) Franklin.

Decomposition of Superpositions of Distribution Functions. Pal Medgyessy. LC 59-14874. 228p. reprint ed. pap. 65.00 (*0-685-15698-2*, 2026292) Bks Demand.

Decomposition of Walsh & Fourier Series. I. I. Hirschman. LC 52-42839. (Memoirs Ser.: No. 1/15). 65p. 1983. reprint ed. pap. 21.00 (*0-8218-1215-7*, MEMO 1/15) Am Math.

Decomposition Spectrale et Series d'Eisenstein: Une Paraphase de L'Ecriture. C. Moeglin & J. L. Waldspurger. (Progress in Mathematics Ser.: Vol. 113). 1994. 98.00 (*0-8176-2938-6*) Spr-Verlag.

Decompositions of Graphs. Juraj Bosak. (C). 1990. lib. bdg. 133.00 (*0-7923-0747-X*) Kluwer Ac.

Decompositions of Manifolds. Robert J. Daverman. (Pure & Applied Mathematics Ser.). 1986. text ed. 84.00 (*0-12-204220-4*) Acad Pr.

Decompositions of Operator Algebras, 1 & 2. Irving E. Segal. LC 52-42839. (Memoirs Ser.: No. 1/9). 133p. 1989. reprint ed. pap. 16.00 (*0-8218-1209-2*, MEMO 1/9) Am Math.

Decompression Sickness: The Biophysical Basis of Prevention & Treatment, Vol. 1. Brian A. Hills. LC 76-55806. 332p. reprint ed. pap. 94.70 (*0-317-26150-9*, 2024376) Bks Demand.

Decompression Theory, Dive Tables & Dive Computers. John Lewis & Karl Shreeves. Ed. by Tonya Talley. (Illus.). 100p. (Orig.). (C). 1990. pap. text ed. 14.95 (*1-878663-06-2*) PADI.

Decompression Workbook. George Lewbel. 1990. pap. 9.95 (*1-55992-011-4*, Pisces Bks) Gulf Pub.

Decompressive Lumbar Laminectomy. Oliver D. Grin & Dorothy L. Bouwman. (Patient Education Ser.). (Illus.). 24p. (Orig.). 1993. pap. text ed. 3.50 (*0-929689-60-7*) Ludann Co.

Decon Team Guide. Shirley Ayers. 51p. (Orig.). 1992. pap. write for info. (*0-945790-01-5*) Detrick Lawrence.

Deconstructing America: Representations of the Other. Peter Mason. (Illus.). 240p. 1990. 39.95 (*0-415-05260-2*, A4735) Routledge.

Deconstructing Developmental Psychology. Erica Burman. LC 93-5880. (Critical Psychology Ser.). 1994. write for info. (*0-415-06437-6*, Routledge NY); pap. write for info. (*0-415-06438-4*, Routledge NY) Routledge.

***Deconstructing Durkheim.** Jennifer M. Lehmann. 288p. 1995. pap. 17.95 (*0-415-12374-7*, C0393) Routledge.

Deconstructing Durkheim: A Post-Post Structuralist Critique. Jennifer M. Lehmann. LC 92-28815. 1993. write for info. (*0-415-07039-2*, Routledge NY) Routledge.

Deconstructing Macbeth: The Hyperontological View. H. W. Fawkner. LC 89-45784. 264p. 1990. 38.50 (*0-8386-3393-5*) Fairleigh Dickinson.

Deconstructing Morphology: Word Formation in Syntactic Theory. Rochelle Lieber. (Illus.). 232p. 1992. lib. bdg. 57.50 (*0-226-48062-3*); pap. text ed. 24.95 (*0-226-48063-1*) U Ch Pr.

Deconstructing Social Psychology. Ed. by Ian Parker & John Shotter. 224p. 1990. 49.95 (*0-415-01077-2*, A4030); pap. 14.95 (*0-415-01074-8*, A4034) Routledge.

Deconstructing the Kimbell. Michael Benedikt. (Illus.). 144p. (Orig.). 1991. pap. 14.95 (*0-930829-16-6*) Lumen Inc.

Deconstructing the Left: From Vietnam to the Persian Gulf. Peter Collier & David Horowitz. 212p. (Orig.). 1991. pap. 14.95 (*0-8191-8315-6*) Madison Bks UPA.

Deconstructing the Nation: Immigration, Racism & Citizenship in Modern France. Maxim Silverman. LC 92-2779. (Critical Studies in Racism & Migration). 192p. 1992. 89.95 (*0-415-04483-9*, A7583) Routledge.

Deconstructing the New Testament. David Seeley. LC 97-45452. (Biblical Interpretation Series: Vol. 5). 1994. 68.75 (*90-04-09880-1*) E J Brill.

Deconstructing Theology. Mark C. Taylor. LC 82-5970. (American Academy of Religion, Studies in Religion). 152p. 1982. 23.95 (*0-89130-582-3*, 01-00-28) Scholars Pr GA.

Deconstruction: The Omnibus Volume. Ed. by Andreas Papadakis et al. (Illus.). 264p. 1989. pap. 45.00 (*0-8478-1066-6*) Rizzoli Intl.

Deconstruction: Theory & Practice. Christopher Norris. LC 81-22422. 200p. 1982. pap. 13.95 (*0-416-32070-8*, NO. 3660) Routledge Chapman & Hall.

Deconstruction: Theory & Practice. rev. ed. Christopher Norris. (New Accents Ser.). 216p. 1991. pap. 13.95 (*0-415-06174-1*, A5676) Routledge.

Deconstruction & Criticism. Harold Bloom et al. 250p. 1979. pap. text ed. 14.95 (*0-8264-0010-8*) Continuum.

Deconstruction & Philosophy: The Texts of Jacques Derrida. Ed. by John Sallis. LC 86-19236. 224p. 1989. pap. text ed. 16.95 (*0-226-73439-0*) U Ch Pr.

***Deconstruction & The Ethical Turn.** Peter Baker. LC 95-5313. 1995. write for info. (*0-8130-1365-8*) U Press Fla.

***Deconstruction & the Ethical Turn.** Peter Baker. 184p. 1995. lib. bdg. 34.95 (*0-614-06060-5*) U Press Fla.

Deconstruction & the Interests of Theory. Christopher Norris. LC 88-40546. (Project for Discourse & Theory Ser.: Vol. 4). 256p. (C). 1992. pap. text ed. 14.95x (*0-8061-2388-5*) U of Okla Pr.

Deconstruction & the Possibility of Justice. Ed. by Drucilla Cornell et al. 438p. 1992. 52.50 (*0-415-90303-3*, A4797, Routledge NY); pap. 16.95 (*0-415-90304-1*, A4801, Routledge NY) Routledge.

Deconstruction & the Visual Arts: Art, Media, Architecture. Ed. by Peter Brunette & David Wills. LC 92-44388. (Cambridge Studies in New Art History & Criticism). (Illus.). 336p. (C). 1993. 59.95 (*0-521-44271-0*); pap. 19.95 (*0-521-44781-X*) Cambridge U Pr.

Deconstruction & Theology. Thomas J. Altizer et al. 176p. 1982. pap. 8.95x (*0-8245-0412-7*) Crossroad NY.

Deconstruction II. (Architectural Design Ser.: No. 27). (Illus.). 120p. (Orig.). 1993. pap. 26.95 (*1-85490-242-3*, Academy Edits) St Martin.

Deconstruction in Architecture. (Architectural Design Ser.: No. 72). (Illus.). 120p. (Orig.). 1993. pap. 26.95 (*1-85490-241-5*, Academy Edits) St Martin.

Deconstruction in Context: Literature & Philosophy. Ed. by Mark C. Taylor. viii, 446p. (C). 1986. pap. text ed. 17.95 (*0-226-79140-8*) U Ch Pr.

***Deconstruction Is/in America: A New Sense of the Political.** Ed. by Anselm Haverkamp. LC 94-38318. 272p. 1995. 27.95 (*0-8147-3518-5*) NYU Pr.

***Deconstruction Is/in America: A New Sense of the Political.** Ed. by Anselm Haverkamp. LC 94-38318. 1995. pap. 19.95 (*0-8147-3519-3*) NYU Pr.

Deconstruction of Literature: Criticism after Auschwitz. David H. Hirsch. LC 91-50367. 326p. 1991. text ed. 40.00 (*0-87451-535-1*); pap. 18.95 (*0-87451-566-1*) U Pr of New Eng.

Deconstructionalism. Ed. by Sibel Irzik. LC 90-3642. (Studies in Comparative Literature). 112p. 1990. reprint ed. 15.00 (*0-8240-0145-1*) Garland.

Deconstructionism: A Bibliography. Ed. by Joan Nordquist. (Social Theory: A Bibliographic Ser.: No. 26). 68p. (Orig.). 1992. pap. 15.00 (*0-937855-51-0*) Ref Rsch Serv.

Deconstructive Criticism: An Advanced Introduction & Survey. Vincent B. Leitch. LC 82-1120. 256p. 1982. text ed. 50.50 (*0-231-05472-6*); pap. text ed. 18.50 (*0-231-05473-4*) Col U Pr.

***Deconstructive Subjectivities.** Ed. by Simon Critchley & Peter Dews. (Contemporary Continental Philosophy Ser.). 256p. 1995. text ed. 64.50x (*0-7914-2723-4*) State U NY Pr.

***Deconstructive Subjectivities.** Ed. by Simon Critchley & Peter Dews. (Contemporary Continental Philosophy Ser.). 256p. 1995. pap. 21.95 (*0-7914-2724-2*) State U NY Pr.

Deconstructive Turn: Essays in the Rhetoric of Philosophy. Christopher Norris. LC 83-22141. 201p. 1984. pap. 12.95 (*0-416-36140-4*, NO. 4063) Routledge Chapman & Hall.

***Deconstructive Variations: Music & Reason in Western Society.** Rose R. Subotnik. LC 95-13730. 272p. 1995. text ed. 54.95 (*0-8166-2197-7*); pap. text ed. 21.95 (*0-8166-2198-5*) U of Minn Pr.

Decontamination of Nuclear Installations: Proceedings of the First International Symposium Held at the Atomic Energy Research Establishment, 1966. International Symposium on the Decontamination of Nuclear Installations Staff. Ed. by H. J. Blythe. LC 67-13799. 389p. reprint ed. pap. 110.90 (*0-317-26080-4*, 2024414) Bks Demand.

Decontamination Techniques for Buildings, Structures & Equipment. M. P. Esposito et al. LC 86-31193. (Pollution Technology Review Ser.: No. 142). (Illus.). 252p. 1987. 36.00 (*0-8155-1120-5*, 900112) Noyes.

Deconvolution. Ed. by G. M. Webster. LC 78-55218. (Geophysics Reprint Ser.: No. 1). (Illus.). 480p. 1978. pap. text ed. 20.00 (*0-931830-01-X*, 461) Soc Expl Geophys.

Deconvolution. Anton Ziolkowski. LC 83-12624. (Illus.). 175p. 1983. text ed. 35.00 (*0-934634-62-9*) Intl Human Res.

Deconvolution & Inverse Theory: Application to Geophysical Problems. Vijay Dimri. LC 92-12252. (Methods in Geochemistry & Geophysics Ser.). 1992. write for info. (*0-444-89493-4*) Elsevier.

Deconvolution of Absorption Spectra. William E. Blass & George Halsey. LC 81-12667. 1981. text ed. 71.00 (*0-12-104650-8*) Acad Pr.

Deconvolution of Geophysical Time Series in the Exploration of Oil & Natural Gas. M. T. Silvia & E. A. Robinson. (Developments in Petroleum Science Ser.: Vol. 10). 252p. 1979. 79.50 (*0-444-41679-X*) Elsevier.

Decor. Ed. by Wolfgang Hageney. (Illus.). 208p. (ENG, FRE, GER, ITA & SPA.). 1981. pap. 39.95 (*88-7070-004-6*) Belvedere USA.

Decor, Drama, & Design. Alan Little. 1977. 6.50 (*0-89679-007-X*) Moretus Pr.

Decor et dualisme, L'immoraliste d'Andre Gide. Paul A. Fortier. (Stanford French & Italian Studies: No. 56). 230p. (FRE.). 1988. pap. 46.50 (*0-915838-72-9*) Anma Libri.

Decoracion del Hogar: Decorating with Paint & Wallcovering. (Black & Decker Home Improvement Library). 1994. 14.95 (*0-86573-723-1*) Cy De Cosse.

Decorate a Christmas Tree with 40 Stickers. Cathy Beylon. (Illus.). (J). (gr. k-3). 1994. pap. 1.00 (*0-486-28104-3*) Dover.

Decorate Your Denims. (Illus.). 64p. 1993. spiral bd. 5.98 (*1-56173-069-6*, 3601201) Pubns Intl Ltd.

***Decorate Your Doors.** Edie Stockstill. LC 94-36664. (Illus.). 144p. 1995. 24.95 (*0-8069-0968-4*, Chapelle) Sterling.

Decorate Your Garden: Affordable Ideas & Ornaments for Small Gardens. Mary Keen. (Illus.). 160p. 1994. 29.95 (*0-943955-87-4*, Trafalgar Sq Pub) Trafalgar.

Decorate Your Room. Ed. by F. Everett & P. Woods. (Practical Guides Ser.). (Illus.). 48p. (J). (gr. 6 up). 1989. lib. bdg. 14.96 (*0-88110-392-6*, Usborne); pap. 8.95 (*0-7460-0438-9*, Usborne) EDC.

Decorate Your T Shirts & Sweats. 1991. pap. 5.98 (*1-56173-071-8*) Pubns Intl Ltd.

Decorated Biscuit Tins: American, English & European. Peter Hornsby. LC 84-51188. (Illus.). 200p. 1984. 45.00 (*0-88740-016-7*) Schiffer.

Decorated Breastplate from Hasanlu, Iran: Type, Style, & Context of an Equestrian Ornament. Irene J. Winter. Ed. by Robert H. Dyson, Jr. (University Museum Monographs: Hasanlu Special Studies: Nos. 39 & 1). (Illus.). xiv, 105p. (Orig.). (C). 1980. pap. 30.00 (*0-934718-34-2*) U PA Mus Pubns.

***Decorated Cloth in America: Publishers' Bindings 1840-1910.** Sue Allen & Charles Gullans. (Illus.). 107p. Date not set. 35.00 (*0-614-07225-5*) Oak Knoll Pr.

Decorated Diagram: Harvard Architecture & Failure of Bauhaus Legacy. Klaus Herdeg. (Illus.). 224p. (C). 1983. 25.00 (*0-262-08127-X*) MIT Pr.

Decorated Diagram: Harvard Architecture & the Failure of the Bauhaus Legacy. Klaus Herdeg. (Illus.). 136p. 1985. reprint ed. pap. 10.95x (*0-262-58073-X*) MIT Pr.

Decorated Doll House: How to Design & Create Miniature Interiors. Jessica Ridley. (Illus.). 128p. 1990. 34.95 (*0-8021-1232-3*) Grove-Atltic.

***Decorated Earthenware.** Mike Levy. (Complete Potter Ser.). (Illus.). 96p. 1995. pap. 19.95 (*0-7134-7714-8*) Trafalgar.

Decorated Firearms, 1540-1870, from the Collection of Clay P. Bedford. Wallace B Gusler & James D. Lavin. LC 76-53750. (Illus.). 242p. 1977. 25.95 (*0-87935-041-5*) Colonial Williamsburg.

***Decorated Frames.** (Creative Craft Bks.). 80p. 1995. 19.95 (*0-7894-0336-6*, 6-70522) Dorling Kindersley.

Decorated Letter. Ed. by J. J. Alexander. LC 78-6487. 1978. pap. 12.95 (*0-8076-0895-5*) Braziller.

Decorated Lettering. John Lancaster. LC 90-12036. (Fresh Start Ser.). (Illus.). 48p. (J). (gr. 5-8). 1990. lib. bdg. 12.95 (*0-531-14074-1*) Watts.

***Decorated Style: Architecture & Ornament 1240-1360.** Nicola Coldstream. (Illus.). 210p. 1995. 50.00 (*0-8020-0700-7*) U of Toronto Pr.

Decorated Tumbler. Hazel M. Weatherman. (Illus.). 160p. 1978. pap. 15.00 (*0-913074-11-X*) Glassbooks Mo.

Decorated Tumbler. Hazel M. Weatherman. (Illus.). 160p. 1978. pap. 15.00 (*0-685-05336-9*) Weatherman.

Decorated Tumbler "PriceGuy" Hazel M. Weatherman. 128p. 1983. pap. 4.00 (*0-913074-13-6*) Weatherman.

Decorating Baskets. Dawn Cusick. LC 89-21903. (Illus.). 128p. 1991. pap. 14.95 (*0-8069-5825-1*) Sterling.

Decorating Book. Mary Gilliatt. LC 81-1309. (Illus.). 400p. 1987. pap. 25.00 (*0-394-75243-0*) Pantheon.

Decorating Christmas Trees. W. Eugene Burkhart, Jr. (Illus.). 64p. (Orig.). 1985. pap. 8.95 (*0-9615199-0-8*) Burkharts.

Decorating Easter Eggs. Mara Rogers. (J). (ps-3). 1994. 14.95 (*0-316-75414-5*) Little.

Decorating Eden: A Comprehensive Sourcebook of Classic Garden Details. Ed. by Elizabeth Wilkinson & Marjorie Henderson. (Illus.). 256p. 1992. 40.00 (*0-8118-0124-1*); pap. 19.95 (*0-8118-0118-7*) Chronicle Bks.

Decorating Eggs: In the Style of Faberge. Pamela Purves. Ed. by Rosalind Dace. (Illus.). 96p. (Orig.). (YA). 1989. pap. 16.95 (*0-85532-644-1*, Pub. by Search Pr UK) A Schwartz & Co.

Decorating for Christmas. Cy DeCosse Incorporated Staff. LC 92-5358. (Arts & Crafts for Home Decorating Ser.). (Illus.). 128p. 1992. 18.95 (*0-86573-353-8*) Cy De Cosse.

Decorating for Christmas. Sheila Pickles. LC 94-642. 1994. 22.50 (*0-517-59697-0*, Harmony) Crown Pub Group.

***Decorating for Dining & Entertaining.** Home Decorating Institute Staff. LC 94-32785. (Arts & Crafts for Home Decorating Ser.). 128p. 1994. 18.95 (*0-86573-369-4*); pap. 15.95 (*0-86573-370-8*) Cy De Cosse.

Decorating for Sundays & Holidays, Cycle A: Themes, Homily Suggestions, Activities. Bernadette M. Snyder & Hazelmai M. Terry. LC 89-85346. (Illus.). 120p. 1989. pap. 9.95 (*0-89622-416-3*) Twenty-Third.

Decorating for Sundays & Holy Days, Cycle B. Bernadette M. Snyder & Hazelmai M. Terry. LC 88-72014. (Illus.). 128p. (Orig.). 1990. pap. 9.95 (*0-89622-446-5*) Twenty-Third.

Decorating in the Glass Industry. 2nd ed. Ed. by Alexis G. Pincus & Shung-Huei Chang. LC 84-73283. (Processing in the Glass Industry Ser.). (Illus.). 1985. 39.95 (*0-911993-23-1*) Ashlee Pub Co.

Decorating into the Ninety's: Technical Paper, RETEC, October 24-25, 1989, Hyatt Regency, Dearborn, MI. Society of Plastics Engineers Staff. (Illus.). 91p. reprint ed. pap. 26.00 (*0-8357-3622-9*, 2036323) Bks Demand.

Decorating Magic. John Sutcliffe. LC 91-42667. (Illus.). 192p. 1992. 40.00 (*0-679-41212-3*) Pantheon.

Decorating Magic. John Sutcliffe. 1994. pap. 24.00 (*0-679-74385-5*) Pantheon.

***Decorating Magic.** John Sutcliffe. 1994. pap. 19.99 (*0-517-13103-X*) Random.

Decorating Old House Interiors. Lawrence Schwin, III. LC 93-49719. (Illus.). 144p. 1994. 27.95 (*0-8069-7431-1*, Sterling-Main St) Sterling.

Decorating on a Mini Budget: The "Inside Scoop" Brenda S. Gitlin & Leslea B. Harelick. Ed. by Adolph Caso. (Illus.). 320p. (Orig.). 1993. pap. 12.95 (*0-8283-1980-4*, Pop Technology) Branden Pub Co.

Decorating Our Homes to Please the Lord. 1978. 3.50 (*0-918403-03-0*) Agape Ministries.

Decorating Plastics. James M. Margolis. 135p. (C). 1986. text ed. 39.95 (*1-56990-058-2*) Hanser-Gardner.

Decorating Plastics for Automotive Applications: The Society of Plastics Engineers, Decorating Division RETEC, September 25-26, 1985, Hyatt Regency, Dearborn, Michigan, Technical Papers. Society of Plastics Engineers Staff. 84p. reprint ed. pap. 25.00 (*0-685-16404-7*, 2027697) Bks Demand.

Decorating Plastics RETEC: Proceedings of the Society of Plastics Engineers, the Hamilton, Itesce, Illinois, October 17-18, 1984. Society of Plastics Engineers Staff. 138p. reprint ed. pap. 39.40 (*0-317-42291-X*, 2025799) Bks Demand.

Decorating Plastics RETEC: Technical Papers, Society of Plastics Engineers, Decorating Division, Hyatt Cherry Hill, Cherry Hill, N. J, Oct. 5 & 6, 1983. Society of Plastics Engineers Staff. 154p. reprint ed. pap. 43.90 (*0-317-28101-1*, 2022513); reprint ed. pap. 39.70 (*0-317-29610-8*, 2021696) Bks Demand.

Decorating Pottery. F. Carlton Ball. LC 67-19833. 1967. 3.95 (*0-934706-05-0*) Prof Pubns Ohio.

Decorating Recipe Book. Darla Sims. 80p. 1995. pap. 7.95 (*1-56901-730-1*) NW Pub.

Decorating Rich: How to Achieve a Monied Look Without Spending a Fortune. Teri Seidman & Sherry S. Cohen. 1988. 22.50 (*0-394-56630-0*, Villard Bks) Random.

Decorating Sweaters with Duplicate Stitch: 60 Gorgeous Designs - One Easy Embroidery Technique. Nola Theiss. LC 94-7980. (Illus.). 128p. (Orig.). 1994. 24.95 (*0-8069-0810-6*) Sterling.

***Decorating Sweaters with Duplicate Stitch: 60 Gorgeous Designs - One Easy Embroidery Technique.** Nola Theiss. (Illus.). 128p. (Orig.). 1995. pap. 14.95 (*0-8069-0811-4*) Sterling.

Decorating T-Shirts. R. Gibson. (How to Make Ser.). (Illus.). 32p. (J). (gr. 2-6). 1994. lib. bdg. 12.96 (*0-88110-710-7*, Usborne); pap. 5.95 (*0-7460-1696-4*, Usborne) EDC.

An Asterisk (*) at the beginning of an entry indicates that the title is appearing in BIP for the first time.

An Asterisk (*) at the beginning of an entry indicates that the title is appearing in BIP for the first time.

1847

Decorative Painting for Children's Rooms. Rosie Fisher. (Illus.). 215p. 1990. 29.95 (0-89134-321-0, 30189) North Light Bks.
Decorative Painting for the Home: Creating Exciting Effects with Water-Based Paints. Lee Andre & David Lipe. LC 94-7982. (Illus.). 144p. 1994. 24.95 (0-8069-0804-1) Sterling.
***Decorative Painting for the Home: Creating Exciting Effects with Water-Based Paints.** Lee Andre & David Lipe. (Illus.). 144p. (Orig.). 1995. pap. 14.95 (0-8069-0805-X, Lark Bks) Sterling.
***Decorative Paper: Projects, Techniques, Pull-out Designs.** Andrea Maflin. (Illus.). 108p. 1995. pap. 22.95 (1-57076-027-6, Trafalgar Sq Pub) Trafalgar.
Decorative Paper Crafts: Block Print, Stencil, Marbleize, & Fold & Dye - 12 Easy-to-Make Projects. Vivien Frank. 96p. 1993. pap. 14.95 (0-8050-2382-8, Owl) H Holt & Co.
Decorative Papering. Richard Wiles. (Illus.). 128p. 1991. 29.95 (0-7063-6878-9, Pub. by Ward Lock UK) Sterling.
Decorative Papering. Richard Wiles. (Illus.). 128p. 1993. pap. 14.95 (0-304-34278-5, Pub. by Cassell UK) Sterling.
Decorative Patterns from Historic Sources. Ed. by James Spero. (Pictorial Archive Ser.). 48p. (Orig.). 1986. pap. 3.95 (0-486-25120-9) Dover.
Decorative Patterns of the Ancient World. Flinders Petrie. (Illus.). 104p. 1991. 12.99 (0-517-02217-6) Random Hse Value.
Decorative Patterns of the Ancient World for Craftsmen. Flinders Petrie. LC 73-79745. (Illus.). 1974. reprint ed. 6.95 (0-486-22986-6) Dover.
Decorative Plant & Flower Studies. J . Foord. 1983. 13.75 (0-8446-5956-8) Peter Smith.
Decorative Plant & Flower Studies for Artists & Craftsmen. J. Foord. (Illus.). 144p. (C). 1982. reprint ed. pap. 6.95 (0-486-24276-5) Dover.
Decorative Prints for Children's Rooms: A Portfolio of Six Self-Matted Full Color Prints. Elizabeth K. Brownd. (Illus.). (J). (gr. k-3). 1993. pap. 0.95 (0-486-27711-9) Dover.
Decorative Quilling: Fifty New Designs. Trees Tra & Malinda Johnston. (Illus.). 48p. (Orig.). 1994. pap. 12.95 (0-86417-560-4, Pub. by Kangaroo Pr AT) Seven Hills Bk.
Decorative Silhouettes of the Twenties for Designers & Craftsmen. Ed. by JoAnne C. Day. LC 73-89255. (Pictorial Archive Ser.). (Illus.). 160p. (Orig.). 1975. pap. 5.95 (0-486-23152-6) Dover.
Decorative Soldering for Stained Glass, Jewelry, & Other Crafts. Trudy Thomas. (Illus.). 64p. (Orig.). 1985. pap. 7.95 (0-913417-00-9, T700) Aurora Pubns.
***Decorative Stamping.** Sasha Dorey. LC 95-10532. 1995. write for info. (0-88266-809-9); 18.95 (0-614-06544-5, Garden Way Pub) Storey Comm Inc.
Decorative Stencils for Interior Design: More Than 150 Stencil Motifs, from Classical... Magie M. Maule. 1992. pap. 17.00 (0-207-17095-9, Pub. by Angus & Robertson AT) HarpC.
Decorative Stuffed Toys for the Needle-Worker. Winsome Douglass. (Sewing & Related Miscellaneous Ser.). 224p. 1984. reprint ed. pap. 8.95 (0-486-24638-8) Dover.
Decorative Stuffed Toys for the Needleworker. Winsome Douglass. 15.25 (0-8446-6137-6) Peter Smith.
Decorative Style Most Original. Kevin Mccloud. 1990. 40.00 (0-671-69142-2) S&S Trade.
Decorative Tile Designs in Full Color. Ed. by Carol B. Grafton. (Illus.). 96p. (Orig.). 1992. pap. 14.95 (0-486-26952-3) Dover.
***Decorative Tile in Architecture & Interiors.** Tony Herbert & Kathryn Huggins. (Illus.). 240p. (C). 1995. 59.95 (0-7148-3161-1, Pub. by Phaidon Press UK) Chronicle Bks.
***Decorative Tiling.** Henry. 1995. (0-7858-0321-1) Bk Sales Inc.
Decorative Victorian Needlework. Elizabeth Bradley. 1990. 32.50 (0-517-58127-2, C P Pubs) Crown Pub Group.
Decorative Woodcarving. Jeremy Williams. (Illus.). 152p. 1994. pap. 14.95 (0-946819-47-5, Pub. by Guild Mstr Craftsman UK) Sterling.
Decorative Woodcrafts. (Illus.). 64p. 1993. 5.98 (0-7853-0284-0, 3616600) Pubns Intl Ltd.
***Decorative Workshop: Stenciling.** Katrina Hall & Laurence Llewelyn-Bowen. LC 95-12165. (Illus.). 1995. write for info. (1-56799-214-5, Friedman-Fairfax); pap. write for info. (1-56799-210-2, Friedman-Fairfax) M Friedman Pub Grp Inc.
***Decorative Wreaths & Garlands.** Hilary More & Pamela Westland. (Illus.). 96p. 1995. 19.99 (0-89134-662-7) North Light Bks.
Decoupage. Mila Boutan. (Illus.). (J). (ps-1). 1992. 4.50 (1-56021-194-6) W J Fantasy.
***Decoupage.** Mark Churchus. (Lothian Australian Craft Ser.). (Illus.). 64p. (Orig.). 1995. pap. 14.95 (0-85091-484-1, Pub. by Lothian Pub AT) Seven Hills Bk.
Decoupage. Nerida Singleton. (C). 1990. pap. text ed. 60.00 (0-646-01485-4, Pub. by Boolarong Pubns AT) St Mut.
Decoupage: A History & Practical Guide. Dee Davis. LC 94-60348. (Illus.). 144p. 1995. 19.95 (0-500-01628-3) Thames Hudson.
***Decoupage: A Practical Step-by-Step Guide.** 1995. 17.95 (1-56799-191-2, Friedman-Fairfax) M Friedman Pub Grp Inc.
***Decoupage: A Practical Step-by-Step Guide.** Joanna Jones. LC 94-27978. (Decorative Workshop Ser.). 1995. pap. write for info. (1-56799-152-1, Friedman-Fairfax) M Friedman Pub Grp Inc.
Decoupage: Cut, Glue, Varnish to Make Decoupage. Juliet B. Moxley. (Illus.). 96p. 1994. pap. 14.95 (0-8050-2813-7) H Holt & Co.
Decoupage: The Big Picture Sourcebook. Ed. by Eleanor H. Rawlings. LC 75-11080. (Pictorial Archive Ser.). (Illus.). 176p. 1975. pap. 8.50 (0-486-23182-8) Dover.
Decoupage Book: More Than Sixty Decorative Projects Using Simple Techniques. Holly Boswell. LC 93-36461. 128p. 1994. 24.95 (0-8069-0610-3) Sterling.
***Decoupage Book: More Than 60 Decorative Projects Using Simple Techniques.** Holly Boswell. (Illus.). 128p. 1995. pap. 14.95 (0-8069-0611-1) Sterling.
***Decoupage Quilts.** Barbara Roberts. Ed. by Laura Reinstatler. (Illus.). 48p. (Orig.). 1995. pap. 12.95 (1-56477-111-3, B228) That Patchwork.
***Decoupage Sourcebook.** Jocasta Innes & Stewart Walton. (Illus.). 96p. 1995. pap. 22.95 (1-57076-031-4, Trafalgar Sq Pub) Trafalgar.
Decoupage with Scrapbook Pictures. Vivienne Garforth. (Illus.). 80p. (Orig.). 1993. pap. 12.95 (0-86417-524-8, Pub. by Kangaroo Pr AT) Seven Hills Bk.
Decouverte de la Photographie en 1839. A. Mentienne. Ed. by Peter C. Bunnell & Robert A. Sobieszek. LC 76-23037. (Sources of Modern Photography Ser.). (FRE.). 1979. reprint ed. lib. bdg. 15.95 (0-405-09600-3) Ayer.
Decouverte du Poeme: Introduction a l'Explication de Textes. Micheline Dufau & Ellen D'Alelio. 172p. (Orig.). (FRE.). (C). 1967. pap. text ed. 20.00 (0-15-517290-5) HB Coll Pubs.
Decouverte et Creation. 4th ed. Gerard Jian & Ralph Hester. LC 84-81523. 528p. (C). 1985. 15.96 (0-685-10560-1) HM.
Decouverte et Creation: Les Bases du Francais Moderne, 5 Vols. 5th ed. Gerard Jian & Ralph Hester. (C). 1990. text ed. 51.56 (0-395-36912-6); Tchr's. guide. teacher ed, text ed. 50.36 (0-395-52673-6) HM.
Decouverte et Creation: Les Bases du Francais Moderne, 5 Vols. 5th ed. Gerard Jian & Ralph Hester. (C). 1990. Test bank. pap. 2.76 (0-395-52940-9) HM.
Decouverte et Creation: Les Bases du Francais Moderne, 5 Vols. 5th ed. Gerard Jian & Ralph Hester. (C). 1990. Wkbk. student ed, pap. 25.56 (0-395-52942-5); Cass., Pt. I. audio 25.16 (0-395-52938-7) HM.
Decouverte et Creation: Les Bases du Francais Moderne, 5 Vols. 5th ed. Gerard Jian & Ralph Hester. (C). 1990. Cass., Pt. II. audio 25.16 (0-395-52937-9) HM.
Decouverte et Creation: Les Bases du Francais Moderne, 5 Vols. 5th ed. Gerard Jian & Ralph Hester. (C). 1990. Transparencies. trans. 25.96 (0-395-52939-5) HM.
Decouverte et Creation: Les Bases du Francais Moderne, 5 Vols., Incl. tests. 5th ed. Gerard Jian & Ralph Hester. (C). 1990. Instr's. manual with tests. teacher ed, pap. 2.36 (0-395-52941-7) HM.
Decouverte par mer des bouches du Mississippi et etablissement de Lemoyne d'Iberville sur le golfe du Mexique (1694-1703) see Decouvertes et Establissements des francais dans l'ouest et dans le sud de l'Amerique septentrional: 1614-1754
Decouvertes. Eugene Ionesco. (Illus.). 152p. (FRE.). 24.95 (0-8288-9822-7, F105900) Fr & Eur.
Decouvertes et Establissements des francais dans l'ouest et dans le sud de l'Amerique septentrional: 1614-1754, 6 vols., Set. Ed. by Pierre Margry. Incl. Vol. 1. Voyages des francais sur les Grands Lacs et Decouverte de l'Ohio et du Mississippi (1614-1684) reprint ed. (0-318-50550-9); Vol. 2. Lettres de Cavelier de la Salle et Correspondance Relative a ses Entreprises (1678-1685) reprint ed. (0-318-50551-7); Vol. 3. Recherche des Bouches du Mississippi et Voyage a Travers le Continent Depuis les Cotes du Texas jusqu'a Quebec (1669-1698) reprint ed. (0-318-50552-5); Vol. 4. Decouverte par mer des bouches du Mississippi et etablissement de Lemoyne d'Iberville sur le golfe du Mexique (1694-1703) reprint ed. (0-318-50553-3); Vol. 5. Premiere Formation d'une Chaine de Postes entre le Fleuve Saint-Laurent et le Golfe du Mexique (1683-1724) reprint ed. (0-318-50554-1); Vol. 6. Exploration des Affluents du Mississippi et Decouverte des Montagnes Rocheuses (1679-1754) reprint ed. (0-318-50555-X); 750.00 (0-404-04230-9) AMS Pr.
Decouvrez...Who Stole Granny? Viv Edwards & Nicole Berube. (Gemini Adventures Ser.). 80p. (ENG & FRE.). 1990. pap. 9.95 (1-85658-000-8, Pub. by Multilingual Matters UK) Taylor & Francis.
Decouvrir les Roses Anciennes et Anglaises. David Austin. (Illus.). 220p. (FRE.). 1993. lib. bdg. 59.95 (0-7859-3643-2, 2706617330) Fr & Eur.
Decoy. Elaine Equi. 80p. (Orig.). 1994. pap. 11.95 (1-56689-026-8) Coffee Hse.
Decoy. Stephen Robertson. 1989. pap. 3.95 (1-55817-239-4, Pinnacle NY) Windsor NY.
Decoy. large type ed. Dudley Pope. (Adventure Suspense Ser.). 560p. 1985. 15.95 (0-7089-1271-0) Ulverscroft.
Decoy & Wildfowl Art Trivia. Barry R. Berkey & Velma Berkey. 131p. (Orig.). 1989. pap. text ed. 15.50 (0-9606930-1-7) V A Berkey.
Decoy As Art: Waterfowl in a Wooden Soul. James A. Warner & Margaret J. White. (Illus.). 96p. 1985. 19.95 (0-912608-25-0) Mid Atlantic.
Decoy as Folk Sculpture: An Exhibition of Waterfowl & Fish Decoys from the Collections of Ronald Swanson & Julie & Michael Hall. 58p. 1986. pap. 10.00 (1-880337-04-5) Cranbrook Acad.
Decoy Carving Techniques for the Intermediate Carver. George Barber & Larry Reader. LC 83-51212. (Illus.). 56p. 1984. pap. 6.95 (0-916838-95-1) Schiffer.
Decoy Ops: Fighting Street Crime Undercover. Charles Beene. (Illus.). 120p. 1992. pap. 15.95 (0-87364-669-X) Paladin Pr.
Decoying: St. Clair to St. Lawrence. Barney Crandell. (Illus.). 208p. 39.50 (0-317-05887-8, Pub. by Boston Mills Pr CN) Genl Dist Srvs.
Decoying the Yanks. (Civil War Ser.). (Illus.). 176p. 1984. 19.93 (0-8094-4724-X); lib. bdg. 25.93 (0-8094-4725-8) Time-Life.
***Decoys.** Heather Cadsby. 82p. 1995. lib. bdg. 25.00 (0-8095-4536-5) Borgo Pr.
Decoys. Kangas. 1991. 24.95 (0-89145-484-5) Collector Bks.
Decoys: A Celebration of Contemporary Wildfowl Carving. Laura Aziz. (Illus.). 120p. 1994. 34.95 (0-921820-83-6, Pub. by Camden Hse CN) Firefly Bks Ltd.
Decoys: And Other Stories. Ken Smith. LC 85-71132. (Short Fiction Ser.). 50p. 1985. 12.95 (0-917652-53-3) Confluence Pr.
Decoy's Desire. Kerry S. Keys. 1993. pap. 6.00 (0-938631-14-4) Pennywhistle Pr.
Decoys of Lake Champlain. Loy S. Harrell. LC 86-61296. (Illus.). 133p. 1986. 35.00 (0-88740-075-2) Schiffer.
Decoys of Maritime Canada. Dale Guyette & Gary Guyette. LC 82-62953. (Illus.). 204p. 1983. text ed. 35.00 (0-916838-76-5) Schiffer.
Decoys of the Mid-Atlantic Region. Henry A. Fleckenstein, Jr. LC 79-52438. (Illus.). 256p. (YA). (gr. 9-12). 1989. pap. 19.95 (0-88740-174-0) Schiffer.
Decoys of the Mississippi Flyway. Alan G. Haid. LC 81-51447. (Illus.). 271p. 1981. 45.00 (0-916838-50-1) Schiffer.
Decoys of the Thousand Islands. Jim Stewart & Larry Lunman. Ed. by Noel Hudson. (Illus.). 240p. 75.00 (1-55046-048-X, Pub. by Boston Mills Pr CN) Genl Dist Srvs.
Decoys of the Winnebago Lakes. Ronald M. Koch. Ed. & Illus. by Constance J. Koch. 208p. 1988. 40.00 (0-9620727-0-2) Rivermoor Pubns.
Decoys Simplified. Paul Casson. (Illus.). 132p. 1973. 14.95 (0-88395-016-2) Freshet Pr.
Decreasing Behaviors of Persons with Severe Retardation & Autism. Richard M. Foxx. LC 82-60088. 198p. (Orig.). (C). 1982. pap. text ed. 14.95 (0-87822-264-2, 2642) Res Press.
Decreasing Classroom Behavior Problems: Practical Guidelines for Teachers. John C. Burke. (Illus.). 205p. (Orig.). (C). 1992. pap. text ed. 34.95 (1-879105-37-3, 0221) Singular Publishing.
Decree & Destiny. Shaykh F. Haeri. 176p. 1990. pap. 13.95 (1-85230-178-3) Element MA.
Decree & Establishment of the Kingsmaiestie, Upon a Controversie of Precedence, Betweene the Yonger Sonnes of Viscounts & Barons, & the Baronets. LC 74-28850. (English Experience Ser.: No. 731). 1975. reprint ed. 3.50 (90-221-0731-0) Walter J Johnson.
Decree of Canopus see Decrees of Memphis & Canopus
Decree of Starre-Chamber, Concerning Printing. LC 70-25951. (English Experience Ser.: No. 190). 1969. reprint ed. 25.00 (90-221-0190-8) Walter J Johnson.
Decrees of Demotionidai. Charles W. Hedrick, Jr. 120p. 1990. 24.95 (1-55540-466-9); pap. 14.95 (1-55540-467-7) Scholars Pr GA.
Decrees of Memphis & Canopus, 3 vols., Set. Ernest A. Budge. Incl. 1. Rosetta Stone. LC 73-18842. (0-404-11323-0); 2. Rosetta Stone. LC 73-18842. (0-404-11324-9); Vol. 3. Decree of Canopus. LC 73-18842. (0-404-11325-7); LC 73-18842. reprint ed. 57.50 (0-404-11322-2) AMS Pr.
Decrees of the Ecumenical Councils, 2 vols. Ed. by Norman P. Tanner. LC 90-3209. 2498p. 1990. text ed. 210.00 (0-87840-490-2) Georgetown U Pr.
Decreto de la Alhambra: Novela Historica Sobre la Expulsion de los Judios de Espana en 1492. David Raphael. Tr. by Daniel Santacruz. 357p. (SPA.). 1992. 25.00 (0-9620772-4-0); pap. 15.00 (0-9620772-5-9) Carmi Hse Pr.
Decrucifixion. Maximillian Yesson. LC 91-78129. 142p. (Orig.). 1992. pap. 11.95 (1-55618-095-0) Brunswick Pub.
Decubitus Ulcers of the Pelvic Region: Diagnostics & Surgical Therapy. N. Luscher. (Illus.). 160p. 1992. text ed. 113.00 (0-88937-049-4) Hogrefe & Huber Pubs.
Deculturalization & the Struggle for Equality: A Brief History of the Education of Dominated Cultures in the United States. Joel Spring. LC 93-14506. 1993. pap. text ed. write for info. (0-07-060553-X) McGraw.
Decus Par Dieu. Phil Yancey. 264p. (FRE.). 1991. 10.95 (0-8297-1107-4) Life Pubs Intl.
Dedalus. James Joyce. 384p. (FRE.). 1974. pap. 11.95 (0-7859-2342-X, 2070365700) Fr & Eur.
Dedalus - Ariadne Book of Austrian Fantasy: The Meyrink Years 1890-1930. Ed. & Tr. by Mike Mitchell. 416p. 1993. pap. 17.95 (0-929497-63-5) Ariadne CA.
Dedalus Book of British Fantasy: The Nineteenth Century. Brian Stableford. 1993. pap. 14.95 (0-946626-78-2, Pub. by Dedalus Bks UK) Hippocrene Bks.
Dedalus Book of British Fantasy: The Nineteenth Century. Ed. by Brian Stableford. 416p. 1993. pap. 14.95 (0-7818-0212-1) Hippocrene Bks.
Dedalus Book of Decadence: Moral Ruins. Brian Stableford. 1992. pap. 14.95 (0-7818-0109-5); pap. 14.95 (0-946626-63-4, Pub. by Dedalus Bks UK) Hippocrene Bks.
Dedalus Book of Dutch Fantasy. Ed. by Richard Huijing. (Dedalus Anthology Ser.). 450p. 1994. pap. 14.95 (0-946626-69-3, Pub. by Dedalus Bks UK) Hippocrene Bks.
Dedalus Book of Femmes Fatales. Ed. by Brian Stableford. 228p. (Orig.). 1992. pap. 14.95 (0-7818-0108-7) Hippocrene Bks.
Dedalus Book of German Decadence: Voices of the Abyss. Ed. & Tr. by Ray Furness. Tr. by Mike Mithell. 356p. (Orig.). 1994. pap. 14.95 (0-7818-0294-6) Hippocrene Bks.
Dedalus Book of Polish Fantasy. Ed. & Tr. by Wiesiek Powaga. (Dedalus European Fantasy Anthologies Ser.). 320p. (Orig.). 1995. pap. 14.95 (0-7818-0292-X) Hippocrene Bks.
***Dedalus Book of Portuguese Fantasy.** Ed. by Eugenio Lisboa. (Dedalus Anthology Ser.). 384p. (Orig.). (POR.). 1995. pap. 16.95 (0-7818-0386-1) Hippocrene Bks.
Dedalus Book of Roman Decadence: Emperors of Debaucheries. Ed. by Geoffrey Farrington. (Dedalus Decadence Ser.). 288p. (Orig.). 1994. pap. 14.95 (1-873982-16-X, Pub. by Dedalus Bks UK) Hippocrene Bks.
Dedalus Book of Russian Decadence. Ed. by Natalia Rubenstein. Tr. by Frank Williams. (Dedalus Decadence Ser.). 400p. (Orig.). 1993. pap. 16.95 (0-7818-0107-9) Hippocrene Bks.
***Dedalus Book of Surrealism Pt. I: Identity of Things.** 2nd ed. Ed. by Michael Richardson. (Anthology Ser.). 384p. 1995. pap. 14.95 (0-7818-0347-0, Pub. by Dedalus Bks UK) Hippocrene Bks.
***Dedalus Book of Surrealism Pt. II: Myth of the World.** Ed. by Michael Richardson. (Anthology Ser.). 320p. 1995. pap. 14.95 (0-7818-0367-5, Pub. by Dedalus Bks UK) Hippocrene Bks.
Dede & the Dinosaur. Shirleyann Costigan. (Wonders! Ser.: Level 1). (Illus.). 24p. (Orig.). (J). (gr. 1-3). 1992. pap. text ed. 29.95 (1-56334-174-3); pap. text ed. 6.00 (1-56334-176-X) Hampton-Brown.
Dede & the Dinosaur: Level 1. Ina Cumpiano. (Wonders! Ser.). (Illus.). 24p. (Orig.). 1992. pap. write for info. (1-56334-201-4) Hampton-Brown.
DeDe Takes Charge! Johanna Hurwitz. LC 84-9085. (Illus.). 128p. (J). (gr. 3-7). 1984. 14.00 (0-688-03853-0) Morrow Jr Bks.
DeDe Takes Charge! Johanna Hurwitz. LC 84-9085. (Illus.). 128p. (J). (gr. 3-7). 1984. pap. 3.95 (0-688-11499-7) Morrow Jr Bks.
Dedekind Sums. Emil Grosswald & Hans Rademacher. LC 72-88698. (Carus Monograph: No. 16). 102p. 1972. 12.00 (0-88385-016-8) Math Assn.
Dedicated. large type ed. Alex Stuart. 1989. 17.95 (0-7089-2111-6) Ulverscroft.
Dedicated: A Biography of Nivedita. Lizelle Reymond. 380p. 1985. 10.95 (0-910261-16-4, Pub. by Samata Bks II) Lotus Light.
Dedicated Clean Ballast Tanks. International Maritime Organization Staff. 1982. text ed. 50.00 (0-89771-970-0, Pub. by Intl Maritime Org UK) St Mut.
Dedicated Disciples. Henry W. Stough. LC 86-72552. (Illus.). 176p. 1987. pap. 6.00 (0-934666-22-9) Artisan Sales.
Dedicated Life: Tributes Offered in Memory of Rosalind Moss. James. 1990. 69.00 (0-900416-56-4, Pub. by Aris & Phillips UK) David Brown.
Dedicated Life & Rainer Maria Rilke. Eric Knight. LC 74-7280. (Studies in German Literature: No. 13). 1974. lib. bdg. 49.95 (0-8383-1920-3) M S G Haskell Hse.
Dedicated Lives. Helen O'Connell. (C). 1993. pap. text ed. 35.00 (0-85598-197-0, Pub. by Oxfam Pubns UK) St Mut.
Dedicated Man. Peter Robinson. 272p. 1992. mass mkt. 4.99 (0-380-71645-3) Avon.
Dedicated Man. Peter Robinson. 272p. 1991. text ed. 18.95 (0-684-19265-9, Scribners) S&S Trade.
Dedicated Man & Other Stories. Elizabeth Taylor. (Virago Modern Classic Ser.). 224p. 1993. pap. 10.95 (0-86068-607-8, Pub. by Virago Pr UK) Trafalgar.
Dedicated to That Boy I Love. Linda Lewis. (Linda Story Ser.). 168p. (J). (gr. 6-9). 1990. pap. 2.75 (0-671-68244-X, Archway) PB.
Dedication: Nobody Said It Was Easy. D. J. Watson. 1987. pap. 6.99 (0-88469-181-0) BMH Bks.
Dedication & Leadership. Douglas Hyde. LC 66-19032. 1966. pap. 6.95 (0-268-00073-5) U of Notre Dame Pr.
Dedication, Love & Humour: My Life with Professor Roger Wyburn-Mason. Joan Wyburn-Mason. LC 85-61440. 44p. (Orig.). 1985. pap. 4.50 (0-931150-17-5) Rheumatoid.
Dedication of a Church. J. D. Crichton. 82p. 1989. 60.00 (0-905092-84-8, Pub. by Veritas IE) St Mut.
Dedication of a Church in an Altar. Veritas Publications Staff. 120p. 1989. 75.00 (1-85390-165-2, Pub. by Veritas IE) St Mut.
Dedication of the Library Building May the Seventeenth A. D. 1904 with the Addresses by William Vail Kellen & Frederick Jackson Turner. vi, 69p. 1905. 35.00 (0-916617-19-X) J C Brown.
Dedication Services for Every Occasion. Comp. by Manfred Holck, Jr. 96p. 1984. pap. 9.00 (0-8170-1033-5) Judson.
Dedication to Freedom: MN Roy - The Man & His Times. Sushanto Das. 1986. 14.00 (81-202-0169-8, Pub. by Ajanta II) S Asia.
***Dedication to Hunger: The Anorexic Aesthetic in Modern Culture.** Leslie Heywood. LC 95-729. 1996. write for info. (0-520-20117-5) U CA Pr.
Dedications of Monastic Houses in England & Wales, 1066-1216. Alison Binns. (Studies in Medieval Religion: No. 1). 240p. 1989. 81.00 (0-85115-521-9) Boydell & Brewer.
***Deditating with Children: The Art of Concentration & Centering.** rev. ed. Deborah Rozman. 160p. 1994. lib. bdg. 37.00x (0-8095-5813-0) Borgo Pr.
Deducibility & Decidability. R. R. Gill. 176p. 1990. 47.50 (0-415-00033-5, A4569) Routledge.
Deducing Function from Structure, Vol. 1: Membranes. Fritiof Sjostrand. 473p. 1990. text ed. 132.00 (0-12-647655-1) Acad Pr.
Deducing Function from Structure, Vol. 2: Information Processing in the Retina. Fritiof Sjostrand. 233p. 1990. text ed. 99.00 (0-12-647656-X) Acad Pr.

D

An Asterisk (*) at the beginning of an entry indicates that the title is appearing in BIP for the first time.

***Deduct! Payroll Processing.** Date not set. disk 29.95 (*1-878608-00-2*) Marigold Computer Consultants.

***Deduct! Payroll Processing.** Date not set. disk 29.95 (*1-878608-01-0*) Marigold Computer Consultants.

Deduct This Book! How Not to Pay Taxes While Ronald Reagan Is President. J. Peter Segall. 130p. (Orig.). 1983. pap. 4.95 (*0-9610422-0-6*) Involve Group Pr.

Deductability of State & Local Taxes: Implications of Proposed Policy Changes. 75p. 1985. 15.00 (*0-933729-02-2*) Natl League Cities.

Deduction. P. N. Johnson-Laird & R. M. Byrne. 256p. 1990. 49.95 (*0-86377-148-3*); pap. 22.00 (*0-86377-149-1*) L Erlbaum Assocs.

Deduction: Automated Logic. Wolfgang Bibel. (Illus.). 253p. 1993. text ed. 45.00 (*0-12-095835-X*) Acad Pr.

Deduction: Introductory Symbolic Logic. Daniel Bonevac. LC 86-62995. 458p. (C). 1987. text ed. 47.95 (*0-87484-772-9*) Mayfield Pub.

Deduction Allowed! Challenge the IRS & Win. James D. McCarthy. 1989. pap. 19.95 (*0-13-199134-5*) P-H.

Deduction Codes for Electronic Payments. Credit Research Foundation Staff. 7p. 1977. 40.00 (*0-939050-18-8*) Credit Res NYS.

Deduction for Business Expenses & Losses. William D. Popkin & Oliver Oldman. LC 71-172245. (Tax Technique Handbook Ser.). (Illus.). 112p. (Orig.). 1973. pap. 5.00 (*0-915506-14-9*) Harvard Law Intl Tax.

Deduction Model of Belief. Kurt Konolige. LC 86-7351. (Research Notes in Artificial Intelligence Ser.). (Illus.). 165p. (Orig.). 1986. pap. text ed. 29.95 (*0-934613-08-7*) Morgan Kaufmann.

Deduction of Belief. Kurt Konolige. 176p. (C). 1986. pap. text ed. 180.00 (*0-273-08764-9*, Pub. by Pitman Pubng UK) St Mut.

Deductions Suggested by the Geographical Distribution of Some Post-Columbian Words Used by the Indians of South America. Erland Nordenskiold. LC 75-46058. (Comparative Ethnographical Studies: Vol. 5). 1977. reprint ed. 48.50 (*0-404-15145-0*) AMS Pr.

Deductive & Declarative Programming. P. Padawitz. (Tracts in Theoretical Computer Science Ser.: No. 28). (Illus.). 250p. (C). 1992. 47.95 (*0-521-41723-6*) Cambridge U Pr.

Deductive & Object-Oriented Databases: Proceedings of the 1st International Conference (DOOD '89), Kyoto, Japan, 4-6 Dec., 1989. Won Kim et al. 610p. 1991. 137.50 (*0-444-88433-5*, North Holland) Elsevier.

Deductive & Object-Oriented Databases: Second International Conference, DOOD '91 Munich, Germany, December 16-18, 1991 Proceedings. Ed. by C. Delobel et al. (Lecture Notes in Computer Science Ser.: Vol. 566). xv, 581p. 1991. pap. 73.00 (*0-387-55015-1*) Spr-Verlag.

Deductive & Object-Oriented Databases: Third International Conference, DOOD '93, Phoenix, Arizona, U. S. A., December 6-8, 1993: Proceedings. Ed. by Stefano Ceri & Katsumi Tanaka. LC 93-39552. (Lecture Notes in Computer Science Ser.: Vol. 760). 1993. 65.00 (*0-387-57530-8*) Spr-Verlag.

Deductive Databases & Logic Programming. Subrata K. Das. LC 92-24864. (C). 1992. text ed. 43.25 (*0-201-56897-7*) Addison-Wesley.

Deductive Interpretation of Natal Horoscope. John McCormick. 76p. 1976. 6.50 (*0-86690-126-4*, M1305-014) Am Fed Astrologers.

Deductive Interpretation of Progressed Horoscopes. McCormick & Rushman. LC 77-10369. 120p. 1977. 8.00 (*0-86690-127-2*, M1306-014) Am Fed Astrologers.

Deductive Logic. 3rd ed. Hugues Leblanc & William Wisdom. LC 92-26701. 480p. 1993. text ed. write for info. (*0-13-203852-8*) P-H.

Deductive Logic: An Introduction to Evaluation Technique & Logical Theory. D. S. Clarke, Jr. LC 73-10459. 255p. 1973. pap. 9.95 (*0-8093-0657-3*) S Ill U Pr.

Deductive Models in Policy Analysis. Ed. by Gordon Tullock & Richard Wagner. (C). 1977. pap. 12.00 (*0-918592-20-8*) Pol Studies.

Deductive Systems: Finite & Non-Euclidean Geometries. Garth E. Runion & James R. Lockwood. LC 78-17827. (Illus.). 90p. 1978. pap. 6.00 (*0-87353-129-9*) NCTM.

***Deductor XIII: Thirteenth California Edition.** 12th ed. Stephen Adams & Frederick A. Mandabach. (Illus.). 214p. 1994. student ed 85.00 (*0-932663-74-5*) CA Fam Law.

Dee Brown. Lyman B. Hagen. LC 90-80260. (Western Writers Ser.: No. 95). (Illus.). 52p. (Orig.). 1990. pap. 3.95 (*0-88430-094-3*) Boise St U W Writ Ser.

Dee Brown's Folktales of the Native American Indian: Retold for Our Times. Dee Brown. LC 93-12449. Orig. Title: Tepee Tales of the American Indian. (Illus.). 176p. 1993. reprint ed. pap. 9.95 (*0-8050-2607-X*) H Holt & Co.

***Dee-Dee Chickadee Gets Lost.** S. Bernadine Riske. LC 95-94019. (Illus.). 20p. (Orig.). (J). (gr. 2 up). 1995. pap. 7.95 (*1-885981-05-8*, Brisk Pubng) Brisk Pubng.

***Dee-Dee Chickadee Goes to School.** Bernadine Riske. LC 95-96426. (Illus.). 20p. (Orig.). (J). (gr. 2-9). 1995. pap. 7.95 (*1-885981-04-X*) Brisk Pubng.

***Dee-Dee Chickadee Visits Neighbors.** Bernadine Riske. LC 94-92383. (Illus.). 20p. (Orig.). (J). (gr. 1-9). 1994. pap. 7.95 (*1-885981-01-5*) Brisk Pubng.

Dee Goong An: Three Murder Cases Solved by Judge Dee. Robert H. Van Gulik. LC 75-32788. (Literature of Mystery & Detection Ser.). (Illus.). 1980. reprint ed. 29.95 (*0-405-07875-7*) Ayer.

Deed: Poems by Carole Simmons Oles. Carole S. Oles. LC 91-3931. 72p. 1991. text ed. 14.95 (*0-8071-1701-3*); pap. 7.95 (*0-8071-1702-1*) La State U Pr.

Deed Abstracts of Tryon, Lincoln & Rutherford Counties, N.C., 1769-1786, & Tryon Co. Wills & Estates. Brent Holcomb. (Illus.). 224p. 1979. reprint ed. 27.50 (*0-89308-047-0*) Southern Hist Pr.

Deed Book One, Halifax County, Virginia 1752-1759. Marian D. Chiarito. 64p. 1985. 10.00 (*0-945503-09-1*) Clarkton Pr.

Deed Book Seven, Halifax County, VA 1767-1770. Marian D. Chiarito. 60p. 1990. 12.00 (*0-945503-18-0*) Clarkton Pr.

Deed Books Two, Three, Four, Five & Six, Halifax County, Virginia 1759-1767. Marian D. Chiarito. 225p. 1986. 30.00 (*0-945503-10-5*) Clarkton Pr.

Deed Descriptions I Have Known but Could Have Done Without. Donald A. Wilson. (Illus.). 233p. 1982. 35.00 (*0-910845-06-9*, 935) Landmark Ent.

Deed of Christ & the Opposing Spiritual Powers Lucifer, Ahriman, Mephistopheles, Asuras. Rudolf Steiner. 3.95 (*0-919924-02-6*, Pub. by Steiner Book Centre CN) Anthroposophic.

Deed of Gift: The Putnam Hospital Story. Tyler Resch. (Illus.). 154p. 1991. 24.95 (*0-943741-01-7*) Paradigm VT.

Deed of Glory. large type ed. Alan Evans. 1985. 15.95 (*0-7089-1309-1*) Ulverscroft.

Deed of Paksenarrion. Elizabeth Moon. 1040p. 1992. pap. 15.00 (*0-671-72104-6*) Baen Bks.

Deed, Pots & Nellie. Peter R. Keedwell. 80p. 1994. pap. 11.95 (*0-8059-3477-4*) Dorrance.

***Deed Without a Name: The Witch in Society & History.** Andrew Sanders. 256p. 1995. 45.95 (*1-85973-048-5*); pap. 19.95 (*1-85973-053-1*) Berg Pubs.

***Deedo & Dido.** Robert Lardinois et al. LC 92-20879. (Our Feathered & Furry Friends Ser.). (Illus.). 42p. (J). (ps-2). 1992. audio, lib. bdg. 21.95 (*0-9629715-2-9*); audio 7.95 (*0-9629715-3-7*) Jewel Publishing.

Deedo & Dido: Story. Robert Lardinois et al. LC 92-20879. (Our Feathered & Furry Friends Ser.). (Illus.). 42p. (J). (ps-2). 1992. lib. bdg. 14.95 (*0-9629715-1-0*) Jewel Publishing.

Deeds & Rules in Christian Ethics. Paul Ramsey. LC 83-10257. 256p. (C). 1983. reprint ed. pap. text ed. 23.00 (*0-8191-3355-8*) U Pr of Amer.

***Deeds Book.** 3rd ed. Mary Randolph. LC 94-34110. (Illus.). 1994. pap. 16.95 (*0-87337-279-4*) Nolo Pr.

Deeds Done in Words: Presidential Rhetoric & the Genres of Governance. Karlyn K. Campbell & Kathleen H. Jamieson. LC 89-20579. 288p. 1990. 27.50 (*0-226-09241-0*) U Ch Pr.

Deeds Instituting Bursaries, Scholarships & Other Foundations, in the College & University of Glasgow. Ed. by William Thomson. LC 75-168166. (Maitland Club, Glasgow. Publications: No. 69). reprint ed. 32.50 (*0-404-53083-4*) AMS Pr.

Deeds Not Words. Hilda Kean. (C). 1991. pap. text ed. 19.00 (*0-7453-0413-3*, Pub. by Pluto Pr UK) Westview.

Deeds Not Words: The Lives of Suffragette Teachers. Hilda Kean. 179p. (C). 1990. text ed. 53.50 (*0-7453-0308-0*) Westview.

Deeds of Amherst County, Virginia, 1808-1852, Books L-R, Vol. 2. Bailey F. Davis. 384p. 1985. 35.00 (*0-89308-301-1*) Southern Hist Pr.

Deeds of Amherst County, Virginia, 1808-1852, Books S-2, Vol. 3. Bailey F. Davis. 420p. 1985. 37.50 (*0-89308-363-1*) Southern Hist Pr.

***Deeds of Frederick Barbarossa.** Bishop Otto of Freising. (MART Thirty-One Medieval Academy Reprints for Teaching Ser.: No. 31). 368p. 1994. pap. 16.95 (*0-8020-7574-6*) U of Toronto Pr.

***Deeds of Honor.** Davis Curriuck. 600p. 1995. pap. 12.95 (*1-56901-890-1*) NW Pub.

Deeds of John & Manuel Comnenus. John Kinnamos. Tr. by Charles M. Brand. LC 76-15317. (Records of Civilization, Sources & Studies: No. 85). 177p. 1976. text ed. 46.50 (*0-231-04080-6*) Col U Pr.

Deeds of Louis the Fat. Abbot of St. Denis Suger. Tr. by Richard C. Cusimano & John Moorhead. LC 91-25427. 1992. pap. text ed. 14.95 (*0-8132-0758-4*) Cath U Pr.

Deeds of the Disturber. Elizabeth Peters. 304p. 1989. mass mkt. 5.99 (*0-446-35333-7*) Warner Bks.

***Deeds of the Night.** Max Exander. (Orig.). 1995. pap. text ed. 5.95 (*1-56333-348-1*) Masquerade.

Deeds of the Righteous. Beth Jacob Hebrew Teachers College Staff. (Illus.). 160p. 6.95 (*0-934390-00-2*) B J Hebrew Tchrs.

Deeds of Utmost Kindness. Forrest Gander. LC 93-17845. (Wesleyan Poetry Ser.). 86p. 1994. 22.50 (*0-8195-2209-0*, Wesleyan Univ Pr); pap. 10.95 (*0-8195-1212-5*, Wesleyan Univ Pr) U Pr of New Eng.

Deeds of Valor: How America's Civil War Heroes Won the Congressional Medal of Honor. Ed. by W. F. Beyer & D. F. Keydel. (Illus.). 544p. 1992. 9.98 (*0-681-41567-3*) Longmeadow Pr.

Deeeeelicious Dragon. Hope Slaughter. LC 86-652. (Illus.). 32p. (J). (ps-3). 1986. pap. 4.95 (*0-931093-05-8*) Red Hen Pr.

***Deeley-Motorcycle Millionaire.** Frank Hilliard. (Illus.). 254p. (C). 1994. 24.95 (*1-55143-023-1*); pap. 12.95 (*1-55143-025-8*) Orca Bk Pubs.

Deeltitels Ninety-Five van 1986, Wet Op: Sectional Titles Act 95 of 1986. ring bd. write for info. (*0-7021-2065-0*, Pub. by Juta SA) W W Gaunt.

Deemster. Hall Caine. LC 78-63983. (Gay Experience Ser.). reprint ed. 29.50 (*0-404-61503-1*) AMS Pr.

Deena the Damselfly. Steven S. Rosman. LC 91-43472. (J). (gr. k-3). 1992. 10.95 (*0-8074-0477-2*, 101069) UAHC.

Deenie. Judy Blume. 144p. (YA). (gr. 7 up). 1991. mass mkt. 3.99 (*0-440-93259-9*, LFL) Dell.

Deenie. Judy Blume. LC 73-80197. 192p. (J). (gr. 6-8). 1982. text ed. 14.95 (*0-02-711020-6*, Bradbury S&S) S&S Childrens.

Deep. Stanley Thornes. (Bulls-Eye Ser.). (C). 1989. 35.00 (*0-09-139821-5*, Pub. by S Thornes Pubs UK) St Mut.

Deep. large type ed. Mickey Spillane. LC 92-35989. 1993. 21.95 (*0-7927-1484-9*, Curley Lrg Print); pap. 19.95 (*0-7927-1483-0*, Curley Lrg Print) Chivers N Amer.

***Deep Alert.** (Stony Man Ser.). 1995. mass mkt. 4.99 (*0-373-61900-6*, 1-61900-6) Harlequin Bks.

Deep & Crisp & Even. large type ed. Peter Turnbull. 339p. 1982. 21.95 (*0-7089-0830-6*) Ulverscroft.

Deep Are the Roots. Arnaud D'Usseau & James Gow. 1947. pap. 4.75 (*0-8222-0296-4*) Dramatists Play.

Deep Are the Roots. William Gellin. LC 88-43582. 424p. 1989. 18.95 (*0-88400-135-0*) Shengold.

Deep Are the Roots: Memoirs of a Black Expatriate. Gordon Heath. LC 92-181. (Illus.). 208p. (C). 1992. lib. bdg. 27.50x (*0-87023-778-0*) U of Mass Pr.

Deep Atlantic. Richard Ellis. Date not set. pap. write for info. (*0-679-43324-4*) Random.

Deep Battle: The Brainchild of Marshall Tukhachevskil. Richard E. Simpkin. 281p. 1987. 53.00 (*0-08-031193-8*, Pub. by Brasseys UK) Brasseys Inc.

Deep Black. William E. Burrows. 1988. mass mkt. 5.99 (*0-425-10879-1*) Berkley Pub.

Deep Black: Space Espionage & National Security. William E. Burrows. LC 86-10220. (Illus.). 320p. 1987. 22.50 (*0-394-54124-3*) Random.

Deep Blue. John Bramhall. 132p. (Orig.). 1991. pap. 15.11 (*0-685-54274-2*) Dayspring Pr.

***Deep Blue Funk & Other Stories.** Daniel B. Frank & Arnold Aprill. Date not set. 3.00 (*0-87129-509-1*, D62) Dramatic Pub.

Deep Blue Funk & Other Stories: Portraits of Teenage Parents. Daniel B. Frank. LC 83-3965. 1983. pap. 3.95 (*0-226-25994-3*, 25994-3 ORDER #) U Ch Pr.

***Deep Blue Goodbye.** John MacDonald. 320p. 1995. mass mkt. 6.99 (*0-449-22383-3*) Fawcett.

Deep Blue Goodbye. John D. MacDonald. 1987. mass mkt. 4.95 (*0-449-13252-8*) Fawcett.

***Deep Blue Heart.** Daniel L. Blanchard. 1995. pap. 8.95 (*1-56901-779-4*) NW Pub.

Deep Blue Memory. Monique Urza. LC 92-29029. (Basque Ser.). 176p. 1993. 18.00 (*0-87417-212-8*) U of Nev Pr.

Deep Blue Sea: Pardon the Ocean. Thor Vilhjalmsson. (Illus.). 57p. 1981. pap. 6.00 (*0-910477-01-9*) LoonBooks.

Deep Blue Seize. large type ed. Donald McLarty. 384p. 1992. pap. 14.95 (*0-7089-7157-1*, Trailtree Bookshop) Ulverscroft.

Deep Blues. Robert Palmer. 1982. pap. 11.95 (*0-14-006223-8*, Penguin Bks) Viking Penguin.

Deep Blues: Bill Trayler, Self-Taught Artist. Mary E. Lyons. LC 93-23736. (J). 1994. text ed. 15.95 (*0-684-19458-9*, Scribners) S&S Trade.

Deep Bodywork & Personal Development: Harmonizing Our Bodies, Emotions, & Thoughts. Jack W. Painter. 1987. 19.00 (*0-938405-01-2*) Bodymind Bks.

Deep Boring at Spur (Dickens County, Texas) J. A. Udden. (Scientific Ser.: No. 28). (Illus.). 101p. 1926. reprint ed. 0.75 (*0-318-03299-6*, BULL 363) Bur Econ Geology.

Deep Breathing to Fitness. Melvin L. Beckett. (Illus.). 17p. 1981. pap. 2.95 (*0-686-32543-5*) MLB Pub.

Deep Brine Aquifers in the Palo Duro Basin: Regional Flow & Geochemical Constraints. R. L. Bassett & M. E. Bentley. (Report of Investigations Ser.: RI 130). (Illus.). 59p. 1983. 2.50 (*0-318-03280-5*) Bur Econ Geology.

***Deep Calleth unto Deep.** O. Talmadge Spence. 172p. (Orig.). 1995. pap. 5.95 (*1-882542-09-6*) Foundations.

Deep Calls to Deep: A Christian Spirituality of the Heart. George A. Maloney. 160p. 1993. pap. 11.95 (*0-87193-286-5*) Dimension Bks.

Deep Canyon: A Desert Wilderness for Science. Ed. by I. P. Ting & Bill Jennings. LC 76-12717. 1976. 7.95 (*0-942290-02-X*) Boyd Deep Canyon.

Deep Centers in Semiconductors: A State-of-the-Art Approach. Sokrates T. Pantelides. 783p. 1986. text ed. 179.00 (*2-88124-109-3*) Gordon & Breach.

Deep Centers in Semiconductors: A State of the Art Approach. 2nd ed. Ed. by Sokrates T. Pantelides. LC 92-18744. 1992. text ed. 140.00 (*2-88124-562-5*) Gordon & Breach.

Deep Convictions. Ed. by Tom Jones. 31p. 1991. 3.99 (*1-884553-01-X*) Discipleshp.

Deep Country. Amory Hare. 1993. reprint ed. lib. bdg. 89.00 (*0-7812-5464-7*) Rprt Serv.

Deep Cover. Laurien Berenson. 384p. 1994. mass mkt. 4.50 (*0-8217-4692-8*) Zebra.

Deep Cover: Police Intelligence Operations. Burt Rapp. 136p. 1989. pap. 14.00 (*0-87364-507-3*) Paladin Pr.

Deep Creek Site (CA-SBr-176), a Late Prehistoric Base Camp in the Mojave River Forks Region, San Bernardino County, California. Jeffrey H. Altschul et al. (Statistical Research Technical Ser.: No. 22). (Illus.). 98p. 1989. per. 12.50 (*1-879442-20-5*) Stats Res.

Deep Cuts & the Future of Nuclear Deterrence. Aspen Strategy Group Staff. LC 88-14744. (Aspen Strategy Group Reports). (Illus.). 92p. (Orig.). (C). 1989. lib. bdg. 26.50 (*0-8191-7004-6*, Aspen Strategy Group); pap. text ed. 11.00 (*0-8191-7005-4*, Aspen Strategy Group) U Pr of Amer.

Deep, Deep Down in Your Heart. Brown Landone. 249p. 1971. reprint ed. spiral bd. 8.80 (*0-7873-1251-7*) Mokelumne.

Deep Disagreement in U. S. Agriculture: Making Sense of Policy Conflict. Ed. by Christopher Hamlin & Philip T. Shepard. 319p. (C). 1992. pap. text ed. 52.00 (*0-8133-8703-5*) Westview.

Deep Dive. large type ed. Doug Hornig. (General Ser.). 373p. 1989. lib. bdg. 18.95 (*0-8161-4690-X*) G K Hall.

Deep Divide: Why American Women Resist Equality. Sherrye Henry. LC 93-38876. 480p. 1994. text ed. 25.00 (*0-02-551015-0*) Macmillan.

Deep Diving. Hal Watts & Laurie C. Humpal. (Specialty Diver Ser.). 40p. 1991. teacher ed 6.95 (*1-880229-05-6*); pap. text ed. 10.95 (*1-880229-04-8*); vhs 59.95 (*0-943717-93-0*) Concept Sys.

Deep Diving: An Advanced Guide to Physiology Procedures & Equipment. Bret Gilliam et al. 1992. pap. 16.95 (*0-922769-30-3*) Watersport Pub.

***Deep Down: Getting Beyond Surface Christianity.** Tim Riter. LC 95-13606. 1995. pap. write for info. (*0-8423-1797-X*) Tyndale.

Deep Down: The New Sensual Writing by Women. Intro. by Laura Chester. 348p. 1988. pap. 12.95 (*0-571-12968-4*) Faber & Faber.

Deep Down in the Jungle: Negro Narrative Folklore from the Streets of Philadelphia. rev. ed. Roger D. Abrahams. LC 78-124404. 287p. 1970. pap. text ed. 25.95 (*0-202-01092-9*) Aldine de Gruyter.

Deep Down Things: Poems of the Inland Pacific Northwest. Ed. by Ron McFarland et al. LC 90-24601. 220p. 1991. 20.00 (*0-87422-081-5*); pap. 14.95 (*0-87422-078-5*) Wash St U Pr.

***Deep Down Things: Selected Writing.** Richard McCullen. LC 95-2255. 1995. pap. write for info. (*1-56548-033-3*) New City.

Deep Down Underground. Olivier Dunrea. LC 88-13534. (Illus.). 32p. (J). (ps-2). 1989. text ed. 14.95 (*0-02-732861-9*, Mac Bks Young Read) S&S Childrens.

Deep down Underground. Olivier Dunrea. LC 92-45273. (Illus.). 32p. (J). (gr. k-3). 1993. reprint ed. pap. 4.95 (*0-689-71756-3*, Aladdin Paperbacks) S&S Childrens.

Deep Dream of the Rain Forest. Malcolm Bosse. LC 92-55095. (J). 1993. 15.00 (*0-374-31757-7*) FS&G.

***Deep Dream of the Rain Forest.** Malcolm Bosse. 192p. (YA). (gr. 7 up). 1994. pap. text ed. 4.50 (*0-374-41702-4*, Sunburst Bks) FS&G.

Deep Dream of the Rain Forest. large type ed. Malcolm Bosse. LC 93-42093. (J). 1994. 15.95 (*0-7862-0145-2*) Thorndike Pr.

Deep Drilling. OECD Staff. 135p. (Orig.). 1993. pap. 40.00 (*92-64-13956-7*) OECD.

Deep Drilling in Crystalline Bedrock, Vol. 1. Ed. by A. Boden & K. G. Eriksson. (Exploration of the Deep Continental Crust Ser.). (Illus.). 400p. 1988. 93.00 (*0-387-18995-5*) Spr-Verlag.

Deep Drilling Results in the Atlantic Ocean: Continental Margins & Paleoenvironment. Ed. by Manik Talwani et al. LC 79-88754. (Maurice Ewing Ser.: Vol. 3). (Illus.). 437p. 1979. 23.00 (*0-87590-402-5*, ME0300) Am Geophysical.

Deep Drilling Results in the Atlantic Ocean: Ocean Crust. Ed. by Manik Talwani et al. LC 79-88753. (Maurice Ewing Ser.: Vol. 2). (Illus.). 431p. 1979. 23.00 (*0-87590-401-7*, ME0200) Am Geophysical.

Deep Dyslexis. Ed. by Max Coltheart et al. (International Library of Psychology). 472p. (C). 1988. pap. text ed. 27.50 (*0-7102-1235-6*, RKP) Routledge.

Deep Earth Electrical Conductivity: PAGEOPH Ser., Vol. 134. Wallace H. Campbell. 96p. 1991. pap. 13.50 (*0-8176-2564-X*) Birkhauser.

Deep East Texas. David H. Gibson. LC 93-80139. 56p. 1993. pap. 19.95 (*1-56352-117-2*) Longstreet Pr Inc.

Deep Ecology: Living As If Nature Mattered. Bill Devall & George Sessions. 266p. 1987. pap. 15.95 (*0-87905-247-3*, Peregrine Smith) Gibbs Smith Pub.

Deep Ecology for the Twenty-First Century. Ed. by George Sessions. 448p. 1995. pap. 20.00 (*1-57062-049-0*) Shambhala Pubns.

***Deep Ecology Movement: An Introductory Anthology.** Ed. by Alan Drengson & Yuichi Inoue. 250p. (Orig.). 1995. pap. 14.95 (*1-55643-198-8*) North Atlantic.

Deep Empire. James Axler. (Deathlands Ser.). 1994. mass mkt. 4.99 (*0-373-62519-7*, 1-62519-3) Harlequin Bks.

Deep End. Chris Crutcher. 320p. 1994. mass mkt. 4.99 (*0-8217-4425-9*) Zebra.

Deep End. Joy Fielding. 1987. pap. 4.99 (*0-451-14802-9*, Sig) NAL-Dutton.

Deep End. Geoffrey Norman. LC 93-37748. 1994. 20.00 (*0-688-11655-8*) Morrow.

***Deep End.** Geoffrey Norman. 256p. 1995. mass mkt. 4.99 (*0-380-71912-6*) Avon.

Deep End. large type ed. Geoffrey Norman. LC 94-16394. 431p. 1994. 20.95 (*0-7862-0241-6*) Thorndike Pr.

Deep End: A Novel. Robert Liddell. 187p. 1994. 28.00 (*0-7206-0903-8*, Pub. by P Owen Ltd UK) Dufour.

Deep End: A Novel of Suspense. Chris Crutcher. 224p. 1992. 19.00 (*0-688-09983-1*) Morrow.

Deep Enough: A Working Stiff in the Western Mine Camps. Frank A. Crampton. LC 81-43639. (C). 1993. pap. 13.95 (*0-8061-2529-2*) U of Okla Pr.

Deep Enough: A Working Stiff in the Western Mine Camps. Frank A. Crampton. LC 81-43639. (Illus.). 304p. 1982. reprint ed. 24.95 (*0-8061-1716-8*) U of Okla Pr.

Deep Enough for Ivorybills. James Kilgo. (Illus.). 208p. 1988. 14.95 (*0-912697-71-7*) Algonquin Bks.

***Deep Enough for Ivorybills.** James Kilgo. LC 95-10156. (Illus.). 1995. pap. write for info. (*0-8203-1760-8*) U of Ga Pr.

***Deep Face Lifting Techniques.** Ed. by Jorge Psillakis. (Illus.). 232p. 1994. 119.00 (*0-86577-530-3*) Thieme Med Pubs.

Deep Fall. large type ed. Bill Knox. 1975. 12.00 (*0-85456-357-1*) Ulverscroft.

Deep Flight. Carpenter. 1994. mass mkt. 5.99 (*0-671-75903-5*) PB.

D

An Asterisk (*) at the beginning of an entry indicates that the title is appearing in BIP for the first time.

Deep Foundation Improvements: Design, Construction, & Testing. Ed. by Melvin I. Esrig & Robert C. Bachus. LC 91-12795. (Special Technical Publication Ser.: No. 1089). (Illus.). 337p. 1991. 45.00 (*0-8031-1392-7*, 04-010890-38) ASTM.

Deep Foundations. Frank Fuller. LC 80-69155. 544p. 1980. pap. 28.00 (*0-87262-256-8*) Am Soc Civil Eng.

Deep Foundations on Bored & Auger Piles: Proceedings of the 1st International Geotechnical Seminar on Bored & Auger Piles, Ghent, 7-10 June 1988. Ed. by W. F. Van Impe. 612p. (C). 1988. text ed. 140.00 (*90-6191-814-6*, Pub. by A A Balkema NE) Ashgate Pub Co.

Deep Foundations on Bored & Auger Piles BAP II: Proceedings of the 2nd International Geotechnical Seminar on Deep Foundations on Bored & Auger Piles, Ghent, Belgium 1-4 June 1993. Ed. by W. F. Van Impe. (Illus.). 479p. (C). 1993. text ed. 85.00 (*90-5410-313-2*, Pub. by A A Balkema NE) Ashgate Pub Co.

Deep Freeze. Zach Hughes. 256p. (Orig.). 1992. mass mkt. 4.99 (*0-88677-539-6*) DAW Bks.

***Deep Fried Indulgences.** Tom Katona & Christie Katona. (Illus.). 176p. (Orig.). 1995. pap. 8.95 (*1-55867-116-1*, Nitty Gritty Ckbks) Bristol Pub Ent CA.

Deep Gold. Jay Amberg. 1991. mass mkt. 4.99 (*0-446-36057-0*) Warner Bks.

Deep Implants: Fundamentals & Applications. Ed. by G. G. Bentini et al. 260p. 1989. 92.50 (*0-444-87332-5*, North Holland) Elsevier.

***Deep in a Rainforest.** Gwen Pascoe. 32p. (J). 1995. 12.95 (*1-86374-210-7*, Pub. by ERA Pubns AT) Pubs Dist MI.

Deep in His Heart J. R. Is Laughing at Us. Jane C. Coleman. 28p. (Orig.). 1991. pap. 7.00 (*0-938566-49-0*) Adastra Pr.

Deep in My Heart. Joy Singleton. (Sweet Dreams Ser.: No. 215). (YA). 1994. pap. 3.50 (*0-553-56480-3*) Bantam.

Deep in Piney Woods. J. W. Church. LC 70-39080. (Black Heritage Library Collection). (Illus.). 1977. reprint ed. 19.95 (*0-8369-9018-8*) Ayer.

Deep in the Bayou. Joanna Wayne. (Intrigue Ser.). 1994. mass mkt. 2.99 (*0-373-22288-2*, 1-22288-4) Harlequin Bks.

Deep in the Forest. Brinton Turkle. LC 76-21691. (Unicorn Paperbacks Ser.). (Illus.). 32p. (J). (ps-1). 1976. 13.99 (*0-525-28617-9*, DCB); pap. 3.95 (*0-525-44322-3*, DCB) Dutton Child Bks.

***Deep in the Green: An Exploration of Country Pleasures.** Ann Raver. 1995. 24.00 (*0-679-43483-6*) Knopf.

Deep in the Heart. Elley Crain. (Silhouette Intimate Moments Ser.). 1993. mass mkt. 3.39 (*0-373-07478-6*, 5-07478-6) Silhouette.

Deep in the Heart. Dallas Junior Forum Staff. LC 86-71410. (Illus.). 304p. 1986. 14.95 (*0-9617187-0-6*) Dallas Jr Forum.

Deep in the Heart. Barbara Kaye. (Crystal Creek Ser.). 1993. mass mkt. 3.99 (*0-373-82513-7*, 1-82513-2) Harlequin Bks.

Deep in the Heart: A Remedy for an Ailing Texas. Rob Mosbacher. LC 93-42367. 1993. pap. 9.95 (*1-56530-122-6*) Summit TX.

Deep in the Heart: The Lives & Legends of Texas Jews. Ruthe Winegarten & Cathy Schechter. Ed. by Ed Eakin. (Illus.). 224p. 1990. 29.95 (*0-89015-759-6*) Sunbelt Media.

Deep in the Heart of Texas: Confessions of Dallas Cowboy Cheerleaders. Stephanie Scholz. 1992. mass mkt. 4.99 (*0-312-92889-0*) St Martin.

***Deep in the Heat of... 30 Postcards of Texas.** (Postcard Bks.). (Illus.). Date not set. pap. 7.95 (*1-55859-746-8*) Abbeville Pr.

Deep in the Russian Night. Aron Hazan. LC 90-82186. (C). 1990. 15.95 (*1-56062-030-7*); pap. 12.95 (*1-56062-034-X*) CIS Comm.

Deep in Thought: A Thematic Approach to Thinking & Writing Well. Thomas E. Tyner. 303p. (C). 1992. pap. 22.95 (*0-534-16032-8*) Intl Thomson.

***Deep Inelastic Scattering & Related Subjects: Proceedings of the International Workshop.** A. Levy. 552p. 1995. text ed. 124.00 (*981-02-2053-7*) World Scientific Pub.

***Deep Inner Peace.** Jack Hartman. 159p. 1984. pap. 6.95 (*0-915445-02-6*) Lamplight FL.

Deep Interior of the Earth. Jack A. Jacobs. (Topics in the Earth Sciences Ser.). (Illus.). 160p. (C). 1992. pap. 27.50 (*0-412-36570-7*, A7087) Chapman & Hall.

Deep Is the Hunger. Howard Thurman. LC 73-16023. 212p. 1973. reprint ed. pap. 10.00 (*0-913408-10-7*) Friends United.

Deep Language. limited ed. Thomas R. Crowe. 40p. 1991. pap. 4.50 (*0-685-64799-4*) New Native Pr.

Deep Levels in Semiconductors. M. Jaros. (Illus.). 313p. 1982. 92.00 (*0-85274-516-8*) IOP Pub.

Deep Lie. Stuart Woods. 352p. 1987. mass mkt. 5.99 (*0-380-70266-5*) Avon.

Deep Lie. large type ed. Stuart Woods. 512p. 1987. 23.95 (*0-7089-8413-4*, Charnwood) Ulverscroft.

Deep Like the Rivers: Education in the Slave Quarter Community, 1831-1865. Thomas L. Webber. 1981. pap. 11.95 (*0-393-00998-X*) Norton.

***Deep Magic: Avanced Magic Cards Strategies.** C. Wolfe & George Baxter. 1995. pap. 15.95 (*1-55622-461-3*) Wordware Pub.

Deep Marine Environments: Clastic Sedimentation & Tectonics. K. T. Pickering et al. (Illus.). 352p. 1989. 130.00 (*0-04-551122-5*); pap. 49.95 (*0-04-445201-2*) Routledge Chapman & Hall.

Deep-Marine Sedimentation: Depositional Models & Case Histories in Hydrocarbon Exploration & Development. Ed. by G. C. Brown et al. (Illus.). 326p. (Orig.). 1990. pap. 23.00 (*1-878861-00-X*) Pac Section SEPM.

Deep Models for Medical Knowledge Engineering. Ed. by Elpida T. Keravnou. LC 92-49143. (Medical Artificial Intelligence Ser.: Vol. 1). 1992. write for info. (*0-444-89592-2*) Elsevier.

Deep North. Fanny Howe. (Sun & Moon Classics Ser.: No. 15). 1990. pap. 9.95 (*1-55713-105-8*) Sun & Moon CA.

Deep Objective Prism Survey of the Large Magellanic Cloud for OB & Supergiant Stars. A. G. Davis Philip & N. Sanduleak. 30p. 1983. pap. 12.00 (*0-9607902-3-3*) L Davis Pr.

Deep Ocean Circulation: Physical & Chemical Aspects. Ed. by T. Teramoto. (Oceanography Ser.: Vol. 59). 1993. write for info. (*0-444-88961-2*) Elsevier.

Deep Ocean Mining: Presented at the Winter Annual Meeting of the American Society of Mechanical Engineers, New York, New York, December 2-7, 1979. American Society of Mechanical Engineers Staff. Ed. by John E. Flipse. LC 79-54436. (OED Ser.: Vol. 8). (Illus.). 79p. reprint ed. pap. 25.00 (*0-8357-2859-5*, 2039094) Bks Demand.

Deep Ocean Sediment Transport: Preliminary Results of the High Energy Benthic Boundary Layer Experiment. Ed. by A. R. Nowell & C. D. Hollister. 418p. 1985. reprint ed. 128.25 (*0-444-42519-5*) Elsevier.

Deep-Penetration Eddy-Current Techniques to Detect Corrosion Under Insulation. (MTI Publication Ser.: No. 22). (Illus.). 54p. 1986. 24.00 (*0-685-39504-9*) NACE Intl.

Deep Plowing the Pastures of Heaven: A Collection of Haiku, Tanka & Choka Poetry. Victoria A. Cooper. 44p. 1993. 6.95 (*0-9638767-0-8*) CWR Pubng.

Deep Pockets, Empty Pockets: Who Wins in Cook County Jury Trials. Audrey Chin & Mark A. Peterson. LC 85-9517. 1985. 10.00 (*0-8330-0651-7*, R-3249-ICJ) Rand Corp.

Deep Politics & the Death of JFK. Peter D. Scott. LC 93-3209. 1993. 25.00 (*0-520-08410-1*) U CA Pr.

Deep Powder Snow: Forty-Years of Ecstatic Skiing, Avalanches, & Earth Wisdom. Dolores LaChapelle. (Illus.). 112p. (Orig.). 1993. pap. text ed. 6.95 (*1-882308-21-2*) Kivaki Pr.

Deep Proterozoic Crust in the North Atlantic Provinces. Ed. by Alex C. Tobi & Jacques L. Touret. LC 85-14484. 1985. lib. bdg. 164.50 (*90-277-2101-7*) Kluwer Ac.

Deep Purple. Ted Allbeury. 1990. 18.95 (*0-89296-401-4*) Mysterious Pr.

Deep Purple. Michael Bond. 1982. mass mkt. 5.95 (*0-449-90073-8*) Fawcett.

Deep Purple: Nobody's Perfect. (Illus.). 120p. pap. 17.95 (*0-8256-2558-0*, AM72448) Music Sales.

Deep Purple: Perfect Strangers. (Illus.). 72p. 1988. pap. 12.95 (*0-8256-1194-6*, AM71150) Music Sales.

Deep Purple: The House of Blue Light. (Illus.). 80p. 1987. pap. 12.95 (*0-8256-1115-6*, AM67075) Music Sales.

Deep Red. Donna Hilbert. LC 92-75963. 64p. (Orig.). 1993. pap. 9.95 (*1-880391-04-X*) Event Horizon.

***Deep Red.** Rawdon Tomlinson. (University of Central Florida Contemporary Poetry Ser.). 96p. 1995. pap. 10.95 (*0-8130-1347-X*) U Press Fla.

Deep Red, Vol. 7. Ed. by C. Balun. (Illus.). 128p. (Orig.). 1991. 39.95 (*0-938782-17-7*); pap. 14.95 (*0-938782-16-9*) Fantaco.

***Deep Red: Poems.** Rawdon Tomlinson. LC 94-40998. (University of Central Florida Contemporary Poetry Ser.). 1995. write for info. (*0-8130-1346-1*) U Press Fla.

Deep Rescue. Irving A. Greenfield. (Death Force Ser.: No. 13). 1990. pap. 3.50 (*0-8217-3239-0*) Zebra.

Deep Revision: A Guide for Teachers, Students, & Other Writers. Meredith S. Willis. 192p. (Orig.). 1993. lib. bdg. 23.95 (*0-915924-40-4*); pap. 13.95 (*0-915924-41-2*) Tchrs & Writers Coll.

***Deep River.** Shusaku Endo. Tr. by Van C. Gessel. LC 94-38913. 224p. 1995. 19.95 (*0-8112-1289-0*) New Directions.

Deep River. Elaine Moore. LC 93-23043. (Illus.). (J). 1994. pap. 14.00 (*0-671-86534-X*, S&S Bks Young Read) S&S Childrens.

Deep River. Howard Thurman. Bd. with Negro Spiritual Speaks of Life & Death. LC 75-27041. LC 75-27041. 136p. 1975. reprint ed. Set pap. 9.50 (*0-913408-20-4*) Friends United.

Deep River. Clement Wood. LC 72-4616. (Black Heritage Library Collection). 1977. reprint ed. 28.95 (*0-8369-9132-X*) Ayer.

***Deep River Friends: A Valiant People.** Cecil E. Haworth. 147p. 1985. pap. 7.50 (*0-614-04681-5*) NC Frnds Hist Soc.

Deep River, Lawd. Jean E. Holmes. LC 92-31781. 1993. 9.95 (*0-8163-1119-6*) Pacific Pr Pub Assn.

Deep River Quarterly Meeting: A Valiant People. Cecil B. Haworth. 30p. (Orig.). 1976. pap. 1.50 (*0-942727-00-2*) NC Yrly Pubns Bd.

Deep River Talk: Collected Poems. Hone Tuwhare. (Talanoa: Contemporary Pacific Literature Ser.). 209p. (C). 1994. reprint ed. text ed. 26.00 (*0-8248-1588-2*); reprint ed. pap. 14.95 (*0-8248-1607-2*) UH Pr.

Deep Rivers. Jose M. Arguedas. Tr. by Frances H. Barraclough. LC 77-26243. (Texas Pan American Ser.). 264p. 1978. pap. 12.95 (*0-292-71533-1*) U of Tex Pr.

Deep Roots. Murli D. Melwani. (Writers Workshop Bluebird Ser.). 56p. 1975. 8.00 (*0-88253-524-2*); pap. text ed. 4.80 (*0-88253-523-4*) Ind-US Inc.

Deep Sea Bed: Its Physics, Chemistry & Biology. Ed. by H. Charnock & J. M. Edmond. (Royal Society Discussion Volumes Ser.). 1991. 74.95 (*0-521-39496-1*) Cambridge U Pr.

Deep-Sea Biology. Ed. by Gilbert T. Rowe. (Sea Ser.: No. 8). 569p. reprint ed. pap. 162.20 (*0-7837-2806-9*, 2057666) Bks Demand.

Deep-Sea Biology: A Natural History of Organisms at the Deep-Sea Floor. J. D. Gage & P. A. Tyler. (Illus.). 520p. (C). 1991. 145.00 (*0-521-33431-4*) Cambridge U Pr.

Deep-Sea Biology: A Natural History of Organisms at the Deep-Sea Floor. J. D. Gage & P. A. Tyler. (Illus.). 520p. (C). 1992. pap. 42.95 (*0-521-33665-1*) Cambridge U Pr.

Deep Sea Creatures. Susan Cuthbert. (Coloring Bks.). (Illus.). 16p. (J). (gr. 1-6). 1992. pap. 1.99 (*0-7459-2143-4*) Lion USA.

Deep Sea Diver: Yesterday, Today & Tomorrow. Robert C. Martin. LC 77-19076. (Illus.). 222p. 1979. text ed. 10.00 (*0-87033-238-4*) Cornell Maritime.

Deep Sea Drilling Project: A Decade of Progress. Ed. by John E. Warme et al. (Special Publications Ser.: No. 32). 564p. 1981. 36.50 (*0-918985-12-9*) SEPM.

Deep Sea Explorer: The Story of Robert Ballard, Discoverer of the Titanic. Rick Archbold. LC 93-1983. 160p. (J). (gr. 3-7). 1994. 13.95 (*0-590-47232-1*) Scholastic Inc.

Deep-Sea Fish: An Educational Coloring Book. Spizzirri Publishing Co. Staff & Linda Spizzirri. (Illus.). 32p. (J). (gr. k-5). 1985. pap. 1.75 (*0-86545-064-1*) Spizzirri.

Deep-Sea Food Chains & the Global Carbon Cycle. Ed. by Gilbert T. Rowe & Vita Pariente. (C). 1992. lib. bdg. 137.50 (*0-7923-1608-8*) Kluwer Ac.

Deep Sea Mining & the Law of the Sea. Alexandra M. Post. 1983. lib. bdg. 149.50 (*90-247-3049-X*) Kluwer Ac.

Deep Sea Moorings: Designs & Use with Unmanned Instrument Stations. John Isaacs et al. LC 63-63465. (University of California, Scripps Institution of Oceanography, Bulletin: Vol. 8, No. 3). 46p. reprint ed. pap. 25.00 (*0-317-29134-3*, 2021282) Bks Demand.

Deep-Sea Plunderings. Frank T. Bullen. LC 75-106251. (Short Story Index Reprint Ser.). 1977. 23.95 (*0-8369-3288-9*) Ayer.

***Deep-Sea Pycnogonida from the Temperate West Coast of the U. S.** fac. ed. C. Allan Child. LC 94-15498. (Smithsonian Contributions to Zoology Ser.: No. 556). 27p. 1994. reprint ed. pap. 25.00 (*0-7837-8261-6*, 2049042) Bks Demand.

Deep Sea Sailing. Erroll Bruce. (Illus.). 1978. pap. 5.95 (*0-679-50853-8*) McKay.

Deep-Sea Vents: Living Worlds Without Sun. John F. Waters. LC 92-41111. (Illus.). 48p. (J). (gr. 5 up). 1994. 14.99 (*0-525-65145-4*, Cobblehill Bks) Dutton Child Bks.

Deep Sea's Toll. James B. Connolly. LC 78-37262. (Short Story Index Reprint Ser.). (Illus.). 1977. reprint ed. 23.95 (*0-8369-4073-3*) Ayer.

Deep-Seated Inclusions in Kimberlites & the Problem of the Composition of the Upper Mantle. N. V. Sobolev. Tr. by David A. Brown. LC 76-62627. (Illus.). 279p. (ENG.). 1977. 28.00 (*0-87590-202-2*) Am Geophysical.

Deep Secrets. Carolyn Keene. Ed. by Ann Greenberg. (Nancy Drew Files Ser.: No. 50). 160p. (YA). (gr. 7 up). 1991. reprint ed. pap. 3.50 (*0-671-74525-5*, Archway) PB.

Deep Shadows. Renee L. Brandeis. LC 88-32280. (Illus.). 80p. 1989. 24.95 (*0-8290-2225-2*) Irvington.

Deep Shaker. Les Roberts. 1991. 17.95 (*0-312-05855-1*) St Martin.

Deep Shooter. Buck Gentry. (Scout Ser.: No. 34). 224p. 1992. pap. 3.50 (*0-8217-3937-9*) Zebra.

Deep Six. Clive Cussler. Ed. by Paul McCarthy. 480p. 1990. pap. 6.99 (*0-671-70945-3*) PB.

Deep Six. large type ed. J. M. Flynn. (Linford Mystery Library). 272p. 1993. pap. 14.95 (*0-7089-7428-7*, Trailtree Bookshop) Ulverscroft.

***Deep Sky: An Introduction.** Philip S Harrington. Ed. by Leif J. Robinson. (Sky & Telescope Observer's Guides Ser.). (Illus.). 176p. (Orig.). 1995. pap. 18.95 (*0-933346-80-8*) Sky Pub.

Deep-Sky Field Guide to Uranometria 2000.0. Murray Cragin et al. LC 92-27060. 1993. 49.95 (*0-943396-38-7*) Willmann-Bell.

Deep-Sky Name Index 2000.0. Hugh C. Maddocks. LC 90-84968. 125p. (Orig.). 1991. pap. 16.95 (*0-9628305-0-X*) Foxon-Maddocks.

Deep-Sky Objects for Binoculars. John T. Kozak. (Illus.). 128p. (Orig.). 1988. pap. 10.95 (*0-933346-50-6*) Sky Pub.

Deep-Sky Observing with Small Telescopes. Ed. by David J. Eicher. LC 89-7653. 336p. 1989. pap. 29.95 (*0-89490-075-7*) Enslow Pubs.

Deep Sleep. Frances Fyfield. Ed. by Jane Chelius. 240p. 1993. mass mkt. 4.99 (*0-671-73547-0*) PB.

Deep Sleep. Wright Morris. LC 75-5746. viii, 312p. 1975. reprint ed. pap. 7.95 (*0-8032-5823-2*, Bison Books) U of Nebr Pr.

Deep Sleepers. Charles Leipart. 1989. pap. 4.75 (*0-8222-0297-2*) Dramatists Play.

Deep Snow. Spinelli. (J). 1996. 14.95 (*0-06-023370-2*); lib. bdg. 14.89 (*0-06-023371-0*) HarpC Child Bks.

Deep Song & Other Prose. Federico G. Lorca. Ed. by Christopher Maurer. LC 80-394. 1980. 5.95 (*0-8112-0764-1*) New Directions.

***Deep South.** Richard Manton. (Orig.). 1993. pap. text ed. 5.95 (*1-56201-061-1*) Blue Moon Bks.

Deep South. Caldwell Delaney. (Illus.). 1981. reprint ed. 15.00 (*0-940882-00-0*) HB Pubns.

Deep South: A Social Anthropological Study of Caste & Class. Allison Davis et al. LC 41-23645. (CAAS Community Classics Ser.: Vol. 1). 567p. 1988. 25.95 (*0-934934-26-6*); pap. 17.50 (*0-934934-27-4*) UCLA CAAS.

Deep Space. Ronan. 1982. 24.95 (*0-02-604510-9*) Macmillan.

***Deep Space.** Chris Young & Scott Hedrick. (Cyberpunk Ser.). (Illus.). 120p. (Orig.). 1989. pap. 12.00 (*0-937279-35-8*, CP3211) R Talsorian.

Deep Space Celebration. James Van Hise. 1994. pap. 14.95 (*1-55698-330-1*) Movie Pubs Servs.

***Deep Space Celebrations, No. 2.** Van. 1995. pap. text ed. 16.95 (*1-55698-379-4*) Movie Pubs Servs.

Deep Space CrewBook. James Van Hise. 1994. pap. 14.95 (*1-55698-335-2*) Movie Pubs Servs.

Deep Space Nine. Ed. by Dave Stern. (Star Trek Ser.). 288p. 1993. mass mkt. 5.50 (*0-671-79858-8*) PB.

Deep Space Telecommunications Systems Engineering. Ed. by Joseph H. Yuen. LC 83-17830. (Applications of Communications Theory Ser.). 626p. 1983. 129.50 (*0-306-41489-9*, Plenum Pr) Plenum.

Deep Sting. Charles D. Taylor. Ed. by Paul McCarthy. 384p. 1991. mass mkt. 4.95 (*0-671-67631-8*) PB.

Deep Structure & Past Kinematics of Accreted Terranes, Vol. 50, IUGG 5. Ed. by J. W. Hillhouse. (Geophysical Monograph Ser.). 283p. 1989. 34.00 (*0-87590-454-8*) Am Geophysical.

Deep Structure of the Sentence in Sara-Ngambay Dialogues. James E. Thayer. (Publications in Linguistics & Related Fields: No. 57). 221p. 1978. fiche 12.00 (*0-88312-470-X*) Summer Instit Ling.

Deep Summer. Gwen Bristow. 310p. 1979. reprint ed. lib. bdg. 25.95 (*0-89966-025-8*) Buccaneer Bks.

Deep-Tap Tree. Alexander Hutchison. LC 78-53174. 80p. 1978. 15.00 (*0-87023-254-1*); pap. 9.95 (*0-87023-255-X*) U of Mass Pr.

Deep Thermal Methods Oil Recovery. A. E. Sheindlen. 1990. write for info. (*0-89116-608-4*) CRC Pr.

Deep Thoughts. Jack Handey. 96p. 1992. pap. 6.95 (*0-425-13365-6*, Berkley Trade) Berkley Pub.

***Deep Thoughts: A Book of Postcards.** Jack Handey. (Illus.). 30p. 1994. pap. 8.95 (*0-8362-3206-2*) Andrews & McMeel.

Deep Treasure & Cache Location with the Fisher Gemini-3. Stephen Ryland. 64p. 1993. 7.00 (*1-883170-04-4*) FRL.

Deep Trek. James Axler. (Earthblood Ser.). 1994. mass mkt. 4.99 (*0-373-63808-6*, 1-63808-9) Harlequin Bks.

Deep Trouble. Franklin W. Dixon. Ed. by Anne Greenberg. (Hardy Boys Casefiles Ser.: No. 54). 160p. (Orig.). (J). 1991. mass mkt. 3.99 (*0-671-73090-8*, Archway) PB.

Deep Trouble. R. L. Stine. (Goosebumps Ser.: No. 19). (J). (gr. 4-7). 1994. pap. 3.50 (*0-590-47741-2*) Scholastic Inc.

Deep Trouble. Walt Morey. (Walt Morey Adventure Library). (YA). (gr. 5-9). 1989. reprint ed. pap. 7.95 (*0-936085-15-0*) Blue Heron OR.

***Deep Truth.** A. Havill. 1994. pap. 5.99 (*0-517-13187-0*) Random.

Deep Truth: The Unauthorized Biography of Bob Woodward & Carl Bernstein. Adrian Havill. LC 92-35892. 1993. 21.95 (*1-55972-172-3*, Birch Ln Pr) Carol Pub Group.

***Deep Universe.** A. R. Sandage et al. (Astronomy & Astrophysics Library). 528p. 1995. 59.00 (*3-540-58913-9*) Spr-Verlag.

Deep Water. large type ed. Marjorie Lewty. (Harlequin Ser.). 1992. reprint ed. lib. bdg. 18.95 (*0-263-12981-0*, Pub. by Mills & Boon UK) Thorndike Pr.

***Deep Water Canyons, Fans, & Facies: Models for Stratigraphic Trap Exploration.** Ed. by Roderick W. Tillman & Syed A. Ali. (AAPG Reprint Ser.: No. 26). (Illus.). vi, 596p. 1982. pap. 21.00 (*0-89181-547-3*) AAPG.

Deep-Water Carbonate Environments. Ed. by Harry Cook & Paul Enos. (Special Publications Ser.: No. 25). 336p. 1977. 20.00 (*0-918985-05-6*) SEPM.

Deep-Water Carbonates. Ed. by Paul D. Crevello & Paul M. Harris. (Core Workshop Notes Ser.: No. 6). 527p. 1985. pap. 35.00 (*0-918985-52-8*) SEPM.

Deep-water Clastic Sediments: A Core Workshop No. 2, S. E.P.M. San Francisco, May 30 & 31, 1981. S. E. P. M. Core Workshop, (1981,. Ed. by Charles T. Siemers et al. (Society of Economic Paleontologists & Mineralogists, Special Publication Ser.: No. 2). 419p. reprint ed. pap. 119.50 (*0-685-15590-0*, 2027225) Bks Demand.

Deep Water Exercise for Health & Fitness. J. Glenn McWaters. LC 87-35861. (Illus.). 192p. (Orig.). 1988. 16.95 (*0-913581-07-0*); pap. 11.95 (*0-913581-08-9*) Publitec.

***Deep Water Passage.** Ann Linnea. LC 94-48635. 1995. 22.95 (*0-316-52683-5*) Little.

Deep-Water Sail. Harold A. Underhill. (C). 1987. 125.00 (*0-85174-172-X*, Pub. by Brwn Son Ferg) St Mut.

***Deep Water Training & Aerobics: A New Approach to a Total Physical Fitness.** Alilali G. Mehale. Ed. by Denise Davis et al. (Illus.). 80p. (Orig.). (C). 1994. pap. text ed. 9.00 (*0-9642960-6-3*) Scientific Sports.

Deep Water Turbidite Systems. Ed. by Dorrik Stow. (International Association of Sedimentologists Special Publication Ser.: No. 3). (Illus.). 480p. 1992. pap. 89.95 (*0-632-03262-6*) Blackwell Sci.

***Deep Waters.** Lydia Bennett. 352p. 1995. 27.00 (*0-340-60073-X*, Pub. by H & S UK) Trafalgar.

Deep West. Ernest Haycox. 1989. pap. 2.95 (*1-55817-274-2*, Pinnacle NY) Windsor NY.

Deep West. large type ed. Ernest Haycox. LC 93-13979. 1993. 19.95 (*0-7927-1713-9*, Roundup Lrg Print Westerns); pap. 17.95 (*0-7927-1712-0*, Roundup Lrg Print Westerns) Chivers N Amer.

Deep Woods. Craig Richardson. (Orig.). 1984. pap. 2.95 (*0-87067-825-6*, BH825) Holloway.

Deep Woods Frontier: A History of Logging in Northern Michigan. Theodore J. Karamanski. LC 88-32320. (Great Lakes Bks.). (Illus.). 306p. 1989. 29.95 (*0-8143-2048-1*); pap. 17.95 (*0-8143-2049-X*) Wayne St U Pr.

1850

An Asterisk (*) at the beginning of an entry indicates that the title is appearing in BIP for the first time.

An Asterisk (*) at the beginning of an entry indicates that the title is appearing in BIP for the first time.

1851

***Def Leppard: No Safety Net.** Chris Collingwood. 1994. pap. 14.95 (1-898141-55-X, Pub. by Castle Communs UK) Viking Penguin.

Def Leppard - Hysteria. Ed. by Jeannette DeLisa. 128p. (Orig.). (YA). 1994. reprint ed. pap. text ed. 18.95 (0-89898-768-7) CPP Belwin.

Defaite de la Pensee see Defeat of the Mind: Alain Finkielkraut

Defamation: The Lawyers Guide. David A. Elder. LC 93-71461. (Tort Law Ser.). 1993. ring bd. 135.00 (0-685-68850-X) Clark Boardman Callaghan.

Defamation Law in Louisiana, Eighteen Hundred to Nineteen Eighty-Eight. Michael A. Konczal & Gerald V. Flannery. LC 89-35175. 160p. (C). 1989. lib. bdg. 50.00 (0-8191-7547-1) U Pr of Amer.

Defamiliarization in Language & Literature. R. H. Stacy. 1977. 34.95x (0-8156-2184-1) Syracuse U Pr.

Defamiliarization in the Work of Gabriel Garcia Marquez from 1947-1967. Kenrick Mose. LC 89-9406. (Hispanic Literature Ser.). 350p. 1989. lib. bdg. 99.95 (0-88946-387-5) E Mellen.

Default! John C. Pool & Ross M. LaRoe. LC 87-60562. 139p. (C). 1987. pap. text ed. 10.00 (0-312-00518-0) St Martin.

Default Inheritance Within Unification-Based Approaches to the Lexicon. Ed. by Ted Briscoe et al. (Studies in Natural Language Processing). (Illus.). 300p. (C). 1994. 59.95 (0-521-43027-5) Cambridge U Pr.

Default Reasoning: Causal & Conditional Theories. Hector Geffner. (ACM Doctoral Dissertation Award, 1990 Ser.). (Illus.). 212p. 1991. 27.50 (0-262-07137-1) MIT Pr.

Defcon One. Joe Weber. 1990. mass mkt. 5.99 (0-515-10419-1) Jove Pubns.

Defeat & Disarmament: Allied Diplomacy & the Politics of Military Affairs in Austria, 1918-1922. Joe C. Dixon. LC 82-49193. 168p. 1986. 32.50 (0-87413-221-5) U Delaware Pr.

Defeat, Disgrace, & Dishonor! The Reagan-Bush Regimes: 1981-1993. Stanley J. Marks. 300p. (Orig.). 1993. write for info. (0-938780-28-X); pap. write for info. (0-938780-27-1) Bur Intl Aff.

Defeat into Victory. William Slim. 1991. reprint ed. lib. bdg. 27.95x (1-56849-077-1) Buccaneer Bks.

Defeat of Che Guevara: Military Response to Guerrilla Challenge in Bolivia. Gary P. Salmon. LC 89-29664. 304p. 1990. text ed. 59.95 (0-275-93211-7, C3211, Greenwood Pr) Greenwood.

Defeat of Distance: Qantas 1919-1939. John Gunn. (Illus.). 1989. text ed. 32.95 (0-7022-1707-7, Pub. by Univ Queensland Pr AT); pap. text ed. 19.95 (0-7022-2154-6, Pub. by Univ Queensland Pr AT) Intl Spec Bk.

Defeat of Imperial Germany: 1917-1918. Rod Paschall. Ed. by John S. Eisenhower. LC 88-29356. (Major Battles & Campaigns Ser.: Vol. I). (Illus.). 245p. 1989. 22.95 (0-945575-05-X) Algonquin Bks.

Defeat of Imperial Germany, 1917-1918. Rod Paschall. LC 94-11169. Orig. Title: Major Battles & Campaigns, Vol. 1. (Illus.). 288p. 1994. reprint ed. pap. 13.95 (0-306-80585-5) Da Capo.

Defeat of the Confederacy. Henry S. Commager. LC 78-25755. (Anvil Ser.). 189p. 1964. reprint ed. pap. 10.50 (0-442-00071-5) Krieger.

Defeat of the German Air Force: United States Strategic Bombing Survey, 10 vols. Ed. by David MacIsaac. Incl. Vol. 1. LC 75-26396. 1976. (0-8240-2026-X); Vol. 2. LC 75-26396. 1976. (0-8240-2027-8); Vol. 3. LC 75-26396. 1976. (0-8240-2028-6); Vol. 4. LC 75-26396. 1976. (0-8240-2029-4); Vol. 5. LC 75-26396. 1976. (0-8240-2030-8); Vol. 6. LC 75-26396. 1976. (0-8240-2031-6); Vol. 7. LC 75-26396. 1976. (0-8240-2032-4); Vol. 8. LC 75-26396. 1976. (0-8240-2033-2); Vol. 9. LC 75-26396. 1976. (0-8240-2034-0); Vol. 10. LC 75-26396. 1976. (0-8240-2035-9); LC 75-26396. 1976. Set lib. bdg. 53.00 (0-685-01848-2) Garland.

Defeat of the German U-Boats: The Battle of the Atlantic. David Syrett. LC 93-44333. 330p. (C). 1994. text ed. 39.95 (0-87249-984-7) U of SC Pr.

***Defeat of the Mind: Alain Finkielkraut.** Alan Finkielkraut. Tr. by Judith Friedlander. LC 94-34464. Orig. Title: Defaite de la Pensee. 166p. 1995. 22.95 (0-231-08022-0) Col U Pr.

Defeated Demons. Morris Venden. (Uplook Ser.). 16p. 1982. pap. 0.25 (0-8163-0487-4) Pacific Pr Pub Assn.

Defeated Enemies. Corrie Ten Boom. 1991. pap. 1.95 (0-87508-021-9) Chr Lit.

***Defeating Dark Angels: Breaking Demonic Oppression in the Believer's Life.** Charles H. Kraft. Tr. by Chi-Ming Lee. (Ministry Ser.). 255p. (Orig.). 1994. pap. write for info. (1-885216-02-5) Evan Formosan.

Defeating Dark Angels: Breaking Demonic Oppression in the Believer's Life. Charles H. Kraft. 254p. (Orig.). 1992. pap. 8.99 (0-89283-773-X, Vine Bks) Servant.

Defeating Delay: Developing & Implementing a Court Delay Reduction Program: Based Upon the American Bar Association's Court Delay Reduction Standards. American Bar Association, Lawyers Conference Task Force on Reduction of Litigation Cost & Delay. LC 86-70015. xiv, 200p. 1986. pap. 17.50 (0-89707-218-9, 410-0006) Amer Bar Assn.

Defeating Depression: Lifting Yourself from Sadness into Joy. Dale R. Olen. (Illus.). 60p. (Orig.). 1992. pap. 5.95 (1-56583-011-3) Life Skills WI.

***Defeating Depression: Run It Away!** John Stewart. LC 94-61292. (Illus.). 128p. (Orig.). 1995. pap. 11.95 (0-944482-10-4) Except Bks NM.

Defeating Doubt. Garnett Reid. 1982. pap. 1.95 (0-89265-076-1) Randall Hse.

Defeating Industrial Spies. Duncan Long. LC 91-61944. (Illus.). 144p. 1991. pap. 16.95 (1-55950-073-5, 55086) Loompanics.

Defeating Mau Mau. Louis S. Leakey. LC 74-15061. reprint ed. 27.50 (0-404-12102-0) AMS Pr.

Defeating Pain: The War Against a Silent Epidemic. Patrick D. Wall & Mervyn Jones. (Illus.). 294p. 1991. 24.95 (0-306-43964-6, Plenum Pr) Plenum.

Defeating the Evil Eye. Muhammad Al-Akili. 128p. (Orig.). 1993. pap. 8.95 (1-879405-08-3) Pearl Pub Co.

Defeating the IRS. David C. Skinner & George Wachendorf. (Illus.). 347p. 1993. reprint ed. text ed. write for info. (0-9638119-0-8) Sunbelt FL.

Defeating Those Dragons. David P. Seemuth. (Groupbuilders Series for Adults). 132p. 1991. pap. 5.99 (0-89693-924-3) SP Pubns.

***Defect- & Impurity-Engineered Semiconductors & Devices.** Ed. by S. Ashok et al. (Symposium Proceedings Ser.: Vol. 378). 1995. text ed. 83.00 (1-55899-281-2) Materials Res.

Defect & Fault Tolerance in VLSI Systems, Vol. 1. Ed. by Israel Koren. (Illus.). 378p. 1989. 75.00 (0-306-43224-2, Plenum Pr) Plenum.

Defect & Fault Tolerance in VLSI Systems, Vol. 2. Ed. by C. H. Stapper et al. (Illus.). 300p. 1990. 75.00 (0-306-43531-4, Plenum Pr) Plenum.

Defect & Fault-Tolerance in VLSI Systems, 1992 Workshop. LC 92-70739. 352p. 1992. 76.00 (0-8186-2835-9, 2835) IEEE Comp Soc.

Defect & Fault-Tolerance in VLSI Systems, 1993 Workshop. 320p. 1993. 80.00 (0-8186-3502-9, 3502) IEEE Comp Soc.

Defect Complexes in Semiconductor Structures: Proceedings, Metrafuered, Hungary, 1982. Ed. by J. Giber et al. (Lecture Notes in Physics Ser.: Vol. 175). 308p. 1983. pap. 33.00 (0-387-11986-8) Spr-Verlag.

Defect Control in Semiconductors: Proceedings of the International Conference, Yokohama, Japan, 17-22 Sept., 1989, 2 vols., Set. Ed. by K. Sumino. 1800p. 1990. 436.00 (0-444-88429-7, North Holland) Elsevier.

Defect Correction Methods. Ed. by K. Bohmer & H. J. Stetter. (Computing Ser.: Suppl. 5). (Illus.). 240p. 1985. 49.00 (0-387-81832-4) Spr-Verlag.

Defect Engineering in Semiconductor Growth, Processing & Device Technology. Ed. by S. Ashok et al. (Materials Research Society Symposium Proceedings Ser.: Vol. 262). 1992. text ed. 66.00 (1-55899-157-3) Materials Res.

Defect Induced Failure Mechanisms: Accelerated by Environmental Stress Screening. rev. ed. C. E. Mandel, Jr. & Billy R. Livesay. LC 62-38584. 200p. (Orig.). 1990. pap. text ed. 100.00 (1-877862-04-5) Inst Environ Sci.

Defect-Interface Interactions, Vol. 319: Materials Research Society Symposium Proceedings. Ed. by E. P. Kvam et al. 1994. text ed. 71.00 (1-55899-218-9) Materials Res.

Defect Prevention: Use of Simple Statistical Tools. Kane. (Quality & Reliability Ser.: Vol. 17). 712p. 1989. 125.00 (0-8247-7887-1) Dekker.

Defect Prevention: Use of Simple Statistical Tools Solutions Manual. Kane. (Quality & Reliability Ser.: Vol. 18). 104p. 1989. Solutions Manual. 25.00 (0-8247-8163-5) Dekker.

Defect Processes Induced by Electronic Excitation in Insulators. Ed. by N. Itoh. (Series on Directions in Condensed Matter Physics: Vol. 5). 288p. (C). 1989. text ed. 109.00 (9971-5-0351-4); pap. text ed. 52.00 (9971-5-0352-2) World Scientific Pub.

Defect Recognition & Image Processing in III-V Compounds: Proceedings of the International Symposium on Defect Recognition & Image Processing in III-V Compounds, Montpellier, France, July 2-4, 1985. Ed. by J. P. Fillard. (Materials Science Monographs: No. 31). 302p. 1986. 133.50 (0-444-42558-6) Elsevier.

Defect Recognition & Image Processing in III-V Compounds, II: Proceedings of the Second International Symposium on Defect Recognition & Image Processing in III-V Compounds, (DRIP II), Monterey, CA, 27-29 April,1987. Ed. by E. R. Weber. (Materials Science Monographs: Vol. 44). 320p. 1988. 105.25 (0-444-42892-5) Elsevier.

Defect Recognition & Image Processing in Semiconductors & Devices: Proceedings of the 5th International Conference, 6-10 September 1993, Santander, Spain. J. Jimenez. (Institute of Physics Conference Ser.: No. 135). 356p. 1994. 95.00 (0-7503-0294-1) IOP Pub.

Defect Recognition in Semiconductors Before & after Processing: Proceedings of the 4th International Conference Held 18-22 March 1991. Ed. by M. Brozel & D. J. Stirland. (Illus.). 326p. 1992. 140.00 (0-7503-0188-0) IOP Pub.

Defecting in Place: Women Taking Responsibility for Their Own Spiritual Lives. Miriam T. Winter et al. 360p. 1994. 22.95 (0-8245-1417-3) Crossroad NY.

Defection of Igor Gouzenko, Vol. 1. Royal Canadian Commission Staff. 96p. (Orig.). (C). 1984. lib. bdg. 25.70 (0-89412-094-8); pap. 16.20 (0-89412-066-2) Aegean Park Pr.

Defection of Igor Gouzenko, Vol. 2. Royal Canadian Commission Staff. 447p. (Orig.). (C). 1984. lib. bdg. 25.70 (0-89412-095-6); pap. 16.20 (0-89412-067-0) Aegean Park Pr.

Defection of Igor Gouzenko, Vol. 3. Royal Canadian Commission Staff. 196p. (Orig.). (C). 1984. lib. bdg. 25.70 (0-89412-096-4); pap. 16.20 (0-89412-068-9) Aegean Park Pr.

Defective Colour Vision: Fundamentals, Diagnosis & Management. R. Fletcher & J. Voke. (Illus.). 624p. 1985. 149.00 (0-85274-395-5) IOP Pub.

Defective Delinquent & Insane. Henry A. Cotton. Ed. by Gerald N. Grob. LC 78-22557. (Historical Issues in Mental Health Ser.). (Illus.). 1980. reprint ed. lib. bdg. 19.95 (0-405-11911-9) Ayer.

Defective Detective in the Pulps. Gary Hoppenstand & Ray B. Browne. LC 83-70741. 1983. 16.95 (0-87972-235-5); pap. 8.95 (0-87972-236-3) Bowling Green Univ.

Defective Detectives: Mystery Parodies by the Great Humorists. Ed. by Steve Carper. LC 92-17734. 256p. 1992. pap. 9.95 (0-8065-1367-5, Citadel Pr) Carol Pub Group.

Defective Evangelism. James A. Stewart. 1963. pap. 1.99 (1-56632-031-3) Revival Lit.

***Defective Product: Evidence to Verdict.** Raymond P. Johnson & Lewis S. Eidson, Jr. 820p. 1994. 95.00 (0-614-05805-8) Michie Butterworth.

Defector. Monika Maron. Tr. by David N. Marinelli. 250p. (Orig.). 1988. 16.95 (0-930523-40-7); pap. 8.95 (0-930523-41-5) Readers Intl.

Defector Reports: The Institute of the U. S. A. & Canada. Barbara L. Dash. 229p. (Orig.). 1982. pap. text ed. 100.00 (1-55831-061-4) Delphic Associates.

Defects & Anelasticity in the Characterization of Crystalline Solids. Ed. by L. M. Brock. (AMD Ser.: Vol. 148). 176p. 1992. 50.00 (0-7918-1102-6, G00746) ASME.

Defects & Defect Processes in Nonmetallic Solids. William Hayes & A. M. Stoneham. LC 84-13104. 472p. 1985. text ed. 89.95 (0-471-89791-4, Wiley-Interscience) Wiley.

Defects & Deterioration in Buildings. B. A. Richardson. (Illus.). 220p. 1991. 72.95 (0-442-31302-0) Chapman & Hall.

Defects & Diffusion in Solids: An Introduction. S. Mrowec. (Materials Science Monographs: Vol. 5). 466p. 1980. 105.25 (0-444-99776-8) Elsevier.

Defects & Disorder in Crystalline & Amorphous Solids: Proceedings of the NATO ASI on Defects & Disorder in Crystalline & Amorphous Solids, Madrid, Spain, September 15-28, 1991. Ed. by C. R. Catlow. (NATO Advanced Science Institutes Series C: Mathematical & Physical Sciences). 520p. (C). 1994. lib. bdg. 199.00 (0-7923-2610-5) Kluwer Ac.

Defects & Failures in Pressure Vessels & Piping. Helmut Thielsch. LC 75-15675. 464p. 1977. reprint ed. 52.50 (0-88275-308-8) Krieger.

Defects & Processes in the Solid State: Geoscience Applications, the McLaren Volume. Ed. by James N. Boland & John D. FitzGerald. LC 93-26347. 1993. 175.00 (0-444-81700-X) Elsevier.

Defects & Properties of Semiconductors: Defect Engineering. Ed. by J. Chikawa et al. 1987. lib. bdg. 169.50 (90-277-2352-4) Kluwer Ac.

Defects & Radiation Effects in Semiconductors, 1980: Invited & Contributed Papers from the Eleventh International Conference on Defects & Radiation Effects in Semiconductors Held in Oiso, Japan, 8-11 September 1980. International Conference on Defects & Radiation Effects in Semiconductors Staff. Ed. by R. R. Hasiguti. (Conference Ser.: No. 59). 585p. reprint ed. pap. 166.80 (0-7837-3254-6, 2043273) Bks Demand.

Defects & Structural Phase Transitions. A. P. Levanyuk & A. S. Sigov. 244p. 1988. text ed. 194.00 (2-88124-067-4) Gordon & Breach.

Defects, Fracture & Fatigue. Ed. by G. C. Sih & James W. Provan. 1983. lib. bdg. 149.50 (90-247-2804-5) Kluwer Ac.

***Defects in Electronic Ceramics.** Ed. by S. Pizzini. (Materials Science Forum Ser.: Vol. 116). 260p. 1993. text ed. 80.00 (0-87849-653-X) LPS Dist Ctr.

Defects in Electronic Materials. Ed. by M. Stavola et al. (Materials Research Society Symposium Proceedings Ser.: Vol. 104). 1988. text ed. 52.00 (0-931837-72-3) Materials Res.

Defects in Glasses. Ed. by Frank L. Galeener et al. (Materials Research Society Symposium Proceedings Ser.: Vol. 61). 1986. text ed. 41.00 (0-931837-26-X) Materials Res.

Defects in Insulating Materials: Proceedings of the 12th International Conference, 2 vols., Set. O. Kanert & J. M. Spaeth. 1600p. 1993. text ed. 235.00 (981-02-1282-8) World Scientific Pub.

Defects in Materials: Materials Research Society Symposium Proceedings, Vol. 209. Ed. by P. D. Bristowe et al. 920p. 1991. text ed. 70.00 (1-55899-101-8) Materials Res.

Defects in Semiconductors. Ed. by H. J. Von Bardeleben. (Material Science Forum Ser.: Vols. 10-12). 1400p. (C). 1986. pap. text ed. 260.00 (0-87849-551-7, Pub. by Trans Tech GW) LPS Dist Ctr.

Defects in Semiconductors: Proceedings of the Thirteenth International Conference. International Conference on Defects in Semiconductors Staff. Ed. by L. C. Kimerling & J. M. Parsey, Jr. LC 84-62228. (Illus.). 1276p. reprint ed. pap. 180.00 (0-8357-8662-5, 2052305) Bks Demand.

Defects in Semiconductors I: NCDS-1. Ed. by Nickolay T. Bagraev. (Defect & Diffusion Forum Ser.: Vol. 103-105). (Illus.). 691p. (C). 1993. text ed. 220.00 (0-87849-666-1, Pub. by Trans Tech SZ) LPS Dist Ctr.

Defects in Semiconductors Sixteen. Ed. by Gordon Davies et al. 1634p. 1992. text ed. 346.00 (0-87849-628-9, Pub. by Trans Tech GW) LPS Dist Ctr.

Defects in Semiconductors 15. Ed. by G. Ferenczi. (Materials Science Forum Ser.: Vols. 38-41). 1506p. 1989. text ed. 275.00 (0-87849-584-3, Pub. by Trans Tech GW) LPS Dist Ctr.

***Defects in Semiconductors 17: ICDS-17.** Ed. by Helmut Heinrich & Wolfgang Jantsch. (Materials Science Forum Ser.: Vols. 143-7). 1722p. (C). 1994. text ed. 346.00 (0-87849-671-8, Pub. by Trans Tech SZ) LPS Dist Ctr.

Defects in Solids: Modern Techniques. Ed. by A. V. Chadwick & M. Terenzi. LC 85-25417. (NATO ASI Series B, Physics: Vol. 147). 470p. 1986. 110.00 (0-306-42474-6, Plenum Pr) Plenum.

Defence & Diplomacy: Britain & the Great Powers, 1815-1914. C. J. Bartlett. LC 92-38136. (New Frontiers in History Ser.). (C). 1993. text ed. 39.95 (0-7190-3519-8, Pub. by Manchester Univ Pr UK); pap. write for info. (0-7190-3520-1, Pub. by Manchester Univ Pr UK) St Martin.

Defence & Foreign Policies of India. V. Longer. 390p. 1988. text ed. 40.00 (81-207-0738-9, Pub. by Sterling Pubs II) Apt Bks.

Defence & the Media in Time of Limited War. Ed. by Peter R. Young. 281p. 1992. text ed. 35.00 (0-7146-3478-6, Pub. by F Cass Pubs UK); pap. text ed. 19.50 (0-7146-4085-9, Pub. by F Cass Pubs UK) Intl Spec Bk.

Defence by Ministry: The British Ministry of Defence, 1944-1974. Franklyn Johnson. LC 79-28587. 234p. 1980. 54.50 (0-8419-0598-3) Holmes & Meier.

Defence Electronics - Standards & Quality Assurance. R. L. Tricker. 300p. 1991. 120.00 (0-7506-0095-0) Buttrwrth-Heinemann.

Defence Equation: British Military Systems: Policy Planning & Performance since 1945. Ed. by M. Edmonds. 244p. 1986. 52.00 (0-08-033590-X, Pergamon Pr) Elsevier.

Defence Expenditure, Industrial Conversion & Local Employment. Ed. by Liba Paukert & Peter Richards. ix, 228p. 1991. 32.00 (92-2-107288-6); pap. 24.00 (92-2-107287-8) Intl Labour Office.

Defence in Depth. Martin Hoffman. LC 84-28733. 144p. 1985. pap. 7.95 (0-571-13531-5) Faber & Faber.

Defence Industrial Base & the West. Ed. by David B. Haglund. 272p. 1990. 57.50 (0-415-00923-5, A3948) Routledge.

Defence Industries: A World of Survey. Daniel Todd & Jamie Simpson. 256p. 1988. lib. bdg. 62.50 (0-415-00411-X) Routledge.

Defence of Britain. Basil H. Liddell Hart. LC 79-23041. 444p. 1980. reprint ed. text ed. 65.00 (0-313-22175-8, LHDB, Greenwood Pr) Greenwood.

Defence of Conservatism. A. M. Ludovici. 1972. 59.95 (0-8490-0014-9) Gordon Pr.

Defence of Contraries. Tr. by A. Munday. LC 72-188. (English Experience Ser.: No. 175). 1969. reprint ed. 13.00 (90-221-0175-4) Walter J Johnson.

Defence of Dramatick Poetry. Elkanah Settle. Incl. Farther Defence of Dramatick Poetry. LC 79-170450. 1973. (0-318-52444-9); LC 79-170450. (English Stage Ser.: Vol. 25). 1973. Set lib. bdg. 61.00 (0-8240-0608-9) Garland.

Defence of Duffer's Drift. E. D. Swinton. LC 86-3423. (West Point Art of Command Ser.). 72p. 1986. pap. 6.95 (0-89529-323-4) Avery Pub.

Defence of Greece 490-479 B.C. Lazenby. pap. write for info. (0-85668-591-7, Pub. by Aris & Phillips UK) David Brown.

Defence of Lieut. Col. J. C. Fremont. John C. Fremont. (Notable American Authors Ser.). 1992. reprint ed. lib. bdg. 75.00 (0-7812-2898-0) Rprt Serv.

Defence of Mr. Kenrick's Review of Dr. Johnson's Shakespeare. W. Kenrick. LC 74-144646. reprint ed. 37.50 (0-404-03658-9) AMS Pr.

Defence of Prejudice & Other Essays. John G. Hibben. LC 75-134092. (Essay Index Reprint Ser.). 1977. 19.95 (0-8369-1952-1) Ayer.

Defence of the American Policy As Opposed to the Encroachments of Foreign Influence, & Especially to the Interference of the Papacy in the Political Interests & Affairs of the United States. Thomas R. Whitney. LC 75-145496. (American Immigration Library). 372p. 1971. reprint ed. lib. bdg. 42.95 (0-89198-029-6) Ozer.

Defence of the Constitutions of Government of the United States of America, 3 vols, Set. John Adams. reprint ed. 260.00 (3-511-05000-6) Adlers Foreign Bks.

Defence of the New-England Charters. Jeremiah Dummer. LC 71-141122. (Research Library of Colonial Americana). 1972. reprint ed. 20.95 (0-405-03333-8) Ayer.

Defence of the Undefended Border: Planning for War in North America, 1867-1939. Richard A. Preston. LC 78-313309. 312p. reprint ed. pap. 89.00 (0-7837-1149-2, 2041678) Bks Demand.

Defence of Trade, in a Letter to Sir T. Smith. Dudley Digges. LC 68-54640. (English Experience Ser.: No. 26). 52p. 1968. reprint ed. 9.50 (90-221-0026-X) Walter J Johnson.

Defence of White Power: South African Foreign Policy under Pressure. Robert S. Jaster. 240p. 1989. text ed. 45.00 (0-312-02829-6) St Martin.

Defence Science & Technology: Adjusting to Change. Ed. by Richard Coopey et al. LC 93-1362. (Studies in Defence Economics: Vol. 3). 1993. text ed. 35.00 (3-7186-5400-8) Gordon & Breach.

Defence, Security & Development. Ed. by Saadet Deger & Robert West. LC 87-12129. 233p. 1987. text ed. 39.95 (0-312-01243-8) St Martin.

Defence Spending in Southeast Asia. Ed. by Chin Kin Wah. 326p. 1987. pap. 32.00 (9971-988-70-4, Pub. by Inst SE Asian Studies SI) Ashgate Pub Co.

Defence Terminology. Ed. by R. G. Lee. 200p. 1991. 39.00 (0-08-041320-X, Pub. by Brasseys UK); pap. 18.00 (0-08-041334-X, Pub. by Brasseys UK) Brasseys Inc.

Defence Trade: Demand, Supply, & Control. Ed. by Trevor Taylor & Ryukichi Imai. 176p. (C). Date not set. pap. 15.95 (0-905031-74-1) Brookings.

Defences of Norumbega. E. N. Horsford. 1977. 59.95 (0-8490-1705-X) Gordon Pr.

An Asterisk (*) at the beginning of an entry indicates that the title is appearing in BIP for the first time.

An Asterisk (*) at the beginning of an entry indicates that the title is appearing in BIP for the first time.

1853

D

Defense Counsel Training Manual. Ed. by Kevin J. Dunne & Richard B. Allen. (Illus.). 305p. (Orig.). 1989. pap. 65.00 (*0-9621989-0-0*) IADC IL.

Defense Decision Making: Analytical Support & Crisis Management. Ed. by Rudolf Avenhaus et al. (Illus.). xii, 342p. 1991. 109.00 (*0-387-54022-9*) Spr-Verlag.

Defense Dollars & Sense: A Common Cause Guide to the Defense Budget Process. Mark J. Rovner. (Illus.). 96p. (Orig.). 1983. pap. 4.50 (*0-914389-00-9*) Common Cause.

Defense Economics. Gavin Kennedy. LC 82-25028. 256p. 1983. text ed. 39.95 (*0-312-19103-0*) St Martin.

Defense for a New Era: Lessons of the Persian Gulf War. Les Aspin & Bill Dickinson. (Association of the U. S. Army Book Ser.). 128p. 1992. 16.95 (*0-02-881028-7*) Brasseys Inc.

Defense Game. USAF Staff. 118p. (C). 1993. 5.40 (*0-8403-8427-0*) Kendall-Hunt.

Defense Implications of Europe 92. Michael Moodie. (Significant Issues Ser.: Vol. 12, No. 2). 36p. (Orig.). 1990. pap. text ed. 1.00 (*0-89206-151-0*) CSI Studies.

***Defense in the Late 1990s: Avoiding the Train Wreck: The 1994 CSIS Defense Conference.** Don M. Snider et al. LC 94-49037. (Report Ser.). 31p. (C). 1995. pap. 14.95 (*0-89206-316-5*) CSI Studies.

Defense Industries in Latin American Countries: Argentina, Brazil, & Chile. Jose O. Maldifassi & Pier A. Abetti. LC 93-43070. 280p. 1994. text ed. 59.95 (*0-275-94729-7*, Praeger Pubs) Greenwood.

Defense Industries of the Newly Independent States of Eurasia. (Illus.). 75p. (Orig.). (C). 1993. pap. text ed. 60.00 (*1-56806-513-2*) Diane Pub.

Defense Industry. Jacques S. Gansler. 432p. 1980. pap. 13.95 (*0-262-57059-9*) MIT Pr.

Defense Lawyer's Trial Handbook: Successful Courtroom Strategies for Defending Personal Injury & Malpractice Cases. James B. Rosenblum. LC 84-481. 1984. 99.50 (*0-13-197807-1*) Exec Reports.

***Defense Management: Impediments Jeopardize Logistics Corporate Information Management.** (Illus.). 80p. (Orig.). (C). 1994. pap. text ed. 30.00x (*0-7881-1483-2*) Diane Pub.

Defense Management Challenge: Weapons Acquisition. J. Ronald Fox. 40p. 1988. teacher ed. write for info. (*0-87584-214-3*) Harvard Busn.

Defense Management Challenge: Weapons Acquisition. J. Ronald Fox. 1988. text ed. 27.95 (*0-07-103234-7*); Instr's. manul. teacher ed write for info. (*0-07-103235-5*) McGraw.

Defense Manpower Planning: Issues for the 1980's. Ed. by William J. Taylor, Jr. et al. (Policy Studies on Security Affairs). (Illus.). 250p. 1981. 72.00 (*0-08-027561-3*, Pergamon Pr) Elsevier.

Defense Manpower Policy: A Critical Reappraisal. Alan N. Sabrosky. LC 78-12078. (Foreign Policy Research Institute. Monograph Ser.: No. 22). 115p. reprint ed. pap. 32.80 (*0-7837-1775-X*, 2041973) Bks Demand.

Defense Mechanisms. (BIOTOL Ser.). 300p. 1993. pap. 39.95 (*0-7506-0565-0*) Buttrwrth-Heinemann.

Defense Mechanisms of Woody Plants Against Fungi. Ed. by R. A. Blanchette & A. R. Biggs. (Wood Science Ser.). (Illus.). 468p. 1992. 298.00 (*0-387-54643-X*) Spr-Verlag.

Defense Never Rests. F. Lee Bailey. 1972. pap. 5.99 (*0-451-12640-8*, AE2640, Sig) NAL-Dutton.

Defense Nuclear Waste Processing Facilities: Cost, Schedules & Technical Issues. 62p. (Orig.). (C). 1992. pap. text ed. 45.00 (*1-56806-032-7*) Diane Pub.

Defense of a Legend: Crockett & the De la Pena Diary. Bill Groneman. LC 93-33614. 304p. (Orig.). 1993. pap. 14.95 (*1-55622-322-6*, Rep of TX Pr) Wordware Pub.

Defense of Art. Christine Herter. (Illus.). 192p. 1982. reprint ed. pap. 4.95 (*0-393-30036-6*) Norton.

Defense of Attica: The Dema Wall & the Boiotian War of 378-375 B.C. Mark H. Munn. (C). 1994. 40.00 (*0-520-07685-0*) U CA Pr.

Defense of Berlin. Jean E. Smith. LC 63-17670. 449p. reprint ed. pap. 128.00 (*0-685-15529-3*, 2026329) Bks Demand.

Defense of Biblical Infallibility. Clark H. Pinnock. LC 66-30703. 1967. pap. 2.50 (*0-87552-350-1*) Presby & Reformed.

Defense of Charleston Harbor: Including Fort Sumter & the Adjacent Islands, 1863-1865. John F. Johnson. LC 73-126239. (Select Bibliographies Reprint Ser.). (Illus.). 1977. reprint ed. 42.95 (*0-8369-5466-1*) Ayer.

Defense of Christian Perfection. Daniel Steele. 1984. pap. 7.99 (*0-88019-164-3*) Schmul Pub Co.

Defense of Community in Peru's Central Highlands: Peasant Struggle & Capitalist Transition, 1860-1940. Florencia E. Mallon. LC 83-42565. 400p. 1983. 59.50x (*0-691-07647-2*); pap. 17.95x (*0-691-10140-X*) Princeton U Pr.

Defense of Dr. Thomson's Discourse. Alexander Hamilton. (Notable American Authors Ser.). 1992. reprint ed. lib. bdg. 75.00 (*0-7812-3001-2*) Rprt Serv.

Defense of Drunk Driving Cases: Criminal & Civil, 4 vols. 3rd ed. Richard E. Erwin. 1971. Updates. ring bd. write for info. (*0-8205-1275-3*) Bender.

Defense of Economic Rationalism. Ed. by Chris Jones et al. 224p. 1994. pap. 19.95 (*1-86373-534-8*, Pub. by Allen Unwin AT) Paul & Co Pubs.

Defense of Edgar Allan Poe. John J. Moran. LC 79-171361. reprint ed. 27.50 (*0-404-04399-2*) AMS Pr.

Defense of Equal Employment Claims. William L. Diedrich & William Gaus. LC 81-21339. (Individual Rights Publications). 631p. 1982. text ed. 95.00 (*0-07-016824-5*) Shepards-McGraw.

Defense of Galileo. Thomas Campanella. LC 74-26254. (History, Philosophy & Sociology of Science Ser.). 1978. reprint ed. 17.95 (*0-405-06582-5*) Ayer.

Defense of Galileo of Thomas Campanella. Tommasso Campanella. Tr. by Grant McColley. LC 76-1114. (Smith College Studies in History). 93p. 1976. reprint ed. lib. bdg. 16.00 (*0-915172-20-8*) Richwood Pub.

Defense of Galileo, the Mathematician from Florence. Thomas Campanella. Tr. & Intro. by Richard J. Blackwell. LC 93-8497. (C). 1994. text ed. 27.95 (*0-268-00869-8*) U of Notre Dame Pr.

Defense of Hill Seven Eighty-One: An Allegory of Modern Mechanized Combat. James R. McDonough. 224p. 1993. pap. 12.95 (*0-89141-475-4*) Presidio Pr.

***Defense of Indian Land Rights: William Bollan & the Mohegan Case 1743.** David W. Conroy. 20p. (Orig.). Date not set. reprint ed. pap. write for info. (*0-944026-52-4*) Am Antiquarian.

Defense of Liberty Against Tyrants. Junius Brutus. 1992. lib. bdg. 155.95 (*0-8490-5560-1*) Gordon Pr.

Defense of Narcotic Cases, 3 vols. David Bernheim. 1972. Updates. ring bd. write for info. (*0-8205-1249-4*) Bender.

Defense of Narragansett Bay in WWII. Walter K. Schroder. 128p. 1993. pap. 9.95 (*0-685-70407-6*) Prof Pr NC.

Defense of NATO's Northern Front & U. S. Military Policy. Sherwood S. Cordier. LC 88-33696. 90p. (Orig.). (C). 1989. lib. bdg. 31.00 (*0-8191-7340-1*); pap. text ed. 15.00 (*0-8191-7341-X*) U Pr of Amer.

Defense of Poetry. Philip Sidney. Ed. by Jan A. Van Dorsten. 1971. pap. 9.95 (*0-19-911022-0*) OUP.

***Defense of Poetry: Reflections on the Occasion of Writing.** Paul H. Fry. LC 94-34286. 264p. (C). 1995. pap. 16.95 (*0-8047-2531-4*) Stanford U Pr.

***Defense of Poetry: Reflections on the Occasion of Writing.** Paul H. Fry. LC 94-34286. 1995. 29.50 (*0-8047-2452-0*) Stanford U Pr.

Defense of Saigon: November, 1967-August, 1968. A. W. Thompson. 97p. 1993. reprint ed. pap. 13.00x (*0-923135-73-1*) Dalley Bk Service.

Defense of Shakespeare's Romeo & Juliet Against Modern Criticism. Maximilian Guenther. LC 72-144624. reprint ed. 29.50 (*0-404-02946-9*) AMS Pr.

Defense of Southern Slavery & Other Pamphlets. LC 70-76478. 60p. 1969. reprint ed. text ed. 45.00 (*0-8371-2083-7*, DSS&) Greenwood.

Defense of Speeding, Reckless Driving & Vehicular Homicide, 2 vols., Set. Bender's Editorial Staff & Farragher J. Campbell. LC 84-71307. 1984. ring bd. write for info. (*0-8205-1104-8*) Bender.

Defense of the Constitutions of Government of the United States of America, 3 Vols, Set. John A. Adams. LC 69-11328. (American Constitutional & Legal History Ser). 1971. reprint ed. lib. bdg. 165.00 (*0-306-71176-1*) Da Capo.

Defense of the Faith. Cornelius Van Til. LC 55-7140. 1967. pap. 9.99 (*0-87552-483-4*) Presby & Reformed.

Defense of the Ocular Surface. J. Feher. 200p. Date not set. 35.00 (*963-05-6632-X*, Pub. by A K HU) Intl Spec Bk.

Defense of the Parliament of England in the Case of James II see Lex Parliamentaria: or, a Treatise of the Law & Custom of the Parliaments of England

Defense of the Ruffians: A Dialogue with Conscience. Thomas B. Davis. 14p. 1993. pap. 2.50 (*0-88053-007-3*, M-13) Macoy Pub.

Defense of the Sugar Islands. Turner Cassity. 28p. 1979. 25.00 (*0-936576-01-4*) Symposium Pr.

Defense of Uranian Love. A. L. Raile, pseud. LC 78-22240. (Gay Experience Ser.). reprint ed. 11.50 (*0-404-61531-7*) AMS Pr.

Defense of Wake - Marines at Midway. Robert Heinl. (Elite Unit Ser.: No. 27). (Illus.). 146p. 1990. reprint ed. 32.50 (*0-89839-155-5*) Battery Pr.

Defense of Western Europe. Ed. by Lewis H. Gann. LC 86-22321. 320p. 1987. text ed. 39.95 (*0-86569-159-2*, Auburn Hse) Greenwood.

Defense of Western Europe. Ed. by John C. Garnett. LC 73-88028. 250p. (C). 1974. text ed. 29.95 (*0-312-19110-3*) St Martin.

Defense Officer Personnel Management Act of 1980: A Retrospective Assessment. Bernard Rostker et al. LC 92-42096. 1993. write for info. (*0-8330-1287-8*, R-4246-FMP) Rand Corp.

Defense or Aggression? U. S. Arms Export Control Laws & the Israeli Invasion of Lebanon. Williams Espinosa & Les Janka. (Illus.). 1982. pap. 1.00 (*0-318-01024-0*) Am Educ Trust.

Defense over Offense in Central Europe. George H. Quester. 30p. (Orig.). 1978. pap. text ed. 9.00 (*0-8191-5841-0*, Aspen Inst for Humanistic Studies) U Pr of Amer.

***Defense Planning for the Late 1990's: Beyond the Desert Storm Framework.** Michael O'Hanlon. 150p. (C). 1995. pap. 12.95x (*0-8157-6449-9*) Brookings.

Defense Policies of Nations: A Comparative Study. 3rd ed. Ed. by Douglas J. Murray & Paul R. Viotti. LC 93-20958. (Orig.). 1994. text ed. 65.00 (*0-8018-4793-1*); pap. text ed. 25.95 (*0-8018-4794-X*) Johns Hopkins.

Defense Policies of Nations: A Comparative Study. Ed. by Douglas J. Murray & Paul R. Viotti. LC 81-3790. (Illus.). 541p. (Orig.). reprint ed. pap. 154.20 (*0-8357-7886-X*, 2036305) Bks Demand.

Defense Policies of the Nordic Countries, 1918-1939. Klaus-Richard Bohme. Tr. by H. Peter Krosby. 80p. (Orig.). 1979. pap. 19.00 (*0-89126-073-0*) MA-AH Pub.

Defense Policy Between the Wars, 1919-1938, Culminating in the Munich Agreement of September 1938. R. H. Haigh & P. W. Turner. 196p. (Orig.). 1979. pap. 27.00 (*0-89126-072-2*) MA-AH Pub.

Defense Policy Formation: Towards Comparative Analysis. Ed. & Intro. by James M. Roherty. LC 79-54443. 315p. 1980. lib. bdg. 29.75 (*0-89089-152-4*) Carolina Acad Pr.

Defense Policy in the North Atlantic Alliance: The Case of the Netherlands. Jan W. Honig. LC 92-18840. 280p. 1993. text ed. 52.95 (*0-275-94369-0*, C4369, Praeger Pubs) Greenwood.

Defense Policy in the Reagan Administration. Ed. by William P. Snyder & James Brown. LC 88-9967. 451p. 1988. per., pap. 9.50 (*0-16-001685-1*, S/N 008-020-011) USGPO.

Defense Policy Making: A Comparative Analysis. Ed. by G. M. Dillon. 256p. 1989. text ed. 14.50 (*0-7185-1268-5*, Pub. by Pinter Pubs UK) St Martin.

Defense Positioning & Geometry: Rules for a World with Low Force Levels. Raj Gupta. 294p. (C). 1993. 36.95 (*0-8157-3312-7*) Brookings.

Defense Procurement Mess: A Twentieth Century Fund Essay. William H. Gregory. 240p. 1989. text ed. 22.95 (*0-669-20807-8*) Free Pr.

Defense Procurement Policy for the 1990s: Selected Army & Air Force Systems. Carl Conetta & Charles Knight. (PDA Briefing Report Ser.: No. 1). 43p. 1991. reprint ed. pap. 7.50 (*1-881677-03-6*) Commonwlth Inst.

Defense Reform & Technology: Tactical Aircraft. Serge Herzog. LC 93-37244. 224p. 1994. text ed. 55.00 (*0-275-94628-2*, Praeger Pubs) Greenwood.

Defense Reform Debate: Issues & Analysis. Ed. by Asa A. Clark et al. LC 83-49196. 392p. 1984. 55.00 (*0-8018-3205-5*) Johns Hopkins.

***Defense Research & Development: Mandated Reports on Noncompetitive Awards to Colleges & Universities.** (Illus.). 51p. (Orig.). (C). 1995. pap. text ed. 30.00x (*0-7881-1675-4*) Diane Pub.

Defense Revolution: Intelligent Downsizing of America's Military. Kenneth L. Adelman & Norman R. Augustine. 239p. 1992. pap. 11.95 (*1-55815-075-7*) ICS Pr.

Defense Revolution: Strategy for the Future by an Arms Builder and an Arms Controller. Kenneth L. Adelman & Norman R. Augustine. 239p. 1990. 19.95 (*1-55815-074-9*) ICS Pr.

Defense Services in New Hampshire. National Center for State Courts Staff. 260p. 1976. Manuscript. 15.60 (*0-685-16944-8*, NERO-001) Natl Ctr St Courts.

Defense Spending & Economic Growth. Ed. by James E. Payne & Anandi P. Sahu. LC 93-15757. (C). 1993. pap. text ed. 47.50 (*0-8133-8631-4*) Westview.

Defense Spending in Transition. Julie A. Clark. 68p. (Orig.). (C). 1994. pap. text ed. 25.00 (*1-56806-166-8*) Diane Pub.

Defense Strategy for Women: Be Your Own Risk Manager. David R. Locke & Kent L. Maurer. Ed. by Daniel V. Runyon. (Illus.). 136p. (Orig.). 1991. pap. 9.50 (*1-878559-02-8*) Saltbox Pr.

Defense Strategy in Bridge. Hy Lavinthal. Ed. by George Coffin. 192p. 1974. reprint ed. pap. 4.50 (*0-486-23010-4*) Dover.

Defense Tactics for Law Enforcement: Weaponless Defense & Control & Baton Techniques. rev. ed. Bruce Tegner. LC 77-28136. (Illus.). (C). 1972. pap. 12.00 (*0-87407-028-7*, T-28) Thor.

Defense Technology. Ed. by Asa A. Clark, IV & John F. Lilley. LC 88-27575. 320p. 1989. text ed. 59.95 (*0-275-93078-5*, C3078, Praeger Pubs) Greenwood.

Defense, Technology & International Integration. Trevor Taylor. 290p. 1982. text ed. 35.00 (*0-312-19115-4*) St Martin.

Defense Technology & the Atlantic Alliance: Competition or Collaboration? Frank T. Bray & Michael Moodie. LC 77-80297. (Foreign Policy Reports). 42p. 1977. 11.95 (*0-89549-000-5*) Inst Foreign Policy Anal.

Defense Technology Conversion, Reinvestment, & Transition Assistance: Program Information Package & SBIR Program. Advanced Research Projects Agency (ARPA) Staff. 104p. (Orig.). (C). 1994. pap. text ed. 75.00 (*0-7881-0360-1*) Diane Pub.

Defense that Defends: Blocking Nuclear Attack. Daniel O. Graham & Gregory A. Fossedal. (Illus.). 172p. 1984. 17.50 (*0-8159-5317-8*) Devin.

Defense, Vol. 3 (Incl. 1987-1991 Supplements) Ed. by Eleanor C. Goldstein. (Social Issues Resources Ser.). 1992. 95.00 (*0-89777-088-9*) Sirs Inc.

Defense, Welfare & Growth: Perspectives & Evidence. Ed. by Steve Chan & Alex Mintz. 320p. 1992. 49.95 (*0-04-032402-8*, A8188) Routledge Chapman & Hall.

Defense Wins! A New, Winning Approach to Team Man-to-Man Basketball. Bill Haubrich. LC 92-13315. 1992. write for info. (*0-13-203720-3*, Parker Publishing Co) P-H.

***Defense Without Damage: A Photo-Illustrated Guide to Low Liability Arrest & Control Skills.** Robert Rail. (Illus.). 184p. (Orig.). (C). 1994. pap. 39.95 (*0-7881-1350-X*) Diane Pub.

Defenseless. Nancy Knight. 320p. 1993. mass mkt. 4.50 (*1-55817-713-2*, Pinnacle NY) Windsor NY.

Defenseless Flower: A New Reading of the Bible. Carlos Mesters. Tr. by Francis McDonagh. LC 89-35761. 225p. 1989. pap. 14.95 (*0-88344-596-4*) Orbis Bks.

Defenseless Society. Frank Carrington & William Lambie. LC 76-32544. 160p. (Orig.). 1976. pap. 1.95 (*0-916054-11-X*) Green Hill.

Defenses of Northern New Spain: Hugo O'Conor's Report to Teodoro de Croix, July 22, 1777. Tr. & Intro. by Donald C. Cutter. LC 93-18212. (DeGolyer Library Ser.: No. 4). 184p. 1994. text ed. 47.50 (*0-87074-347-3*) SMU Press.

Defensing the Delaware Wing-T. Bob Kenig. (Illus.). 112p. (Orig.). 1989. pap. 12.00 (*0-685-29419-6*) Harding Pr.

Defensing the Run & Shoot. Bob Kenig. LC 93-44892. (Illus.). 112p. (Orig.). 1994. pap. 12.00 (*0-9624779-5-8*) Harding Pr.

Defensio Ecclesiae Anglicanae. Richard Crakanthorp. LC 72-1027. (Library of Anglo-Catholic Theology: No. 6). reprint ed. 27.50 (*0-404-52087-1*) AMS Pr.

Defensive Art of India. A. P. Singh. 1990. 58.50 (*0-8364-2524-3*, Pub. by Agam Kala Prakashan) S Asia.

***Defensive Baseball.** Rod Delmonico. (Illus.). (Orig.). 1995. pap. 12.95 (*1-57028-029-0*) Masters Pr IN.

Defensive Bidding Quiz Book. Robert Ewen. 105p. (Orig.). 1980. 5.95 (*0-685-08326-8*) Barclay Bridge.

Defensive Bidding Quiz Book. Robert Ewen. 105p. (Orig.). 1980. pap. 5.95 (*0-87643-039-6*) M Lisa Precision.

Defensive Design & Construction in Retreat Buildings. CWL. LC 87-50170. (Urban & Rural Survival Ser.). (Illus.). 100p. (Orig.). (C). 1987. pap. 25.00 (*0-939856-70-0*) Tech Group.

Defensive Driving for Military Police. (Law Enforcement Ser.). 1986. lib. bdg. 79.95 (*0-8490-3826-X*) Gordon Pr.

Defensive Earthworks at Becan, Campeche, Mexico: Implications for Maya Warefare. David L. Webster. (Publication Ser.: No. 41). (Illus.). x, 134p. 1976. 17.50 (*0-939238-46-2*) Tulane MARI.

***Defensive Elevatoring.** D. A. Swerrie. 292p. (Orig.). 1993. pap. text ed. 25.00 (*1-886536-04-X*) Elevator Wrld.

***Defensive Living: When Defensive Driving, Diets, & Exercise Aren't Enough to Keep You Alive & Well!** rev. ed. Bo Hardy. LC 92-90632. (Illus.). 256p. (Orig.). 1995. pap. 12.95 (*0-9633237-9-2*) Defensive Liv.

Defensive Measures Against Hostile Takeovers in the Common Market. Ed. by J. M. Maeijer & K. Geens. 232p. 1991. lib. bdg. 99.50 (*0-7923-0834-4*) Kluwer Ac.

Defensive Mechanisms in the Social Insects. Henry R. Hermann. LC 83-24798. 272p. 1984. text ed. 45.00 (*0-275-91189-6*, C1189, Praeger Pubs) Greenwood.

***Defensive Medicine & Medical Malpractice.** 1995. lib. bdg. 252.75 (*0-8490-7512-2*) Gordon Pr.

Defensive Programming with C Plus Plus: Program Planning, Diagnosis, & Design. Scott R. Ladd. 1993. disk, pap. 49.95 (*0-471-30341-0*); pap. text ed. 29.95 (*0-471-30339-9*) Wiley.

Defensive Rapture. Barbara Guest. (Sun & Moon Classics Ser.: No. 30). 1992. pap. 11.95 (*1-55713-032-9*) Sun & Moon CA.

Defensive Sites of Dinetah: Bureau of Land Management New Mexico State Office. Margaret A. Powers & Byron P. Johnson. (Cultural Resources Ser.: No. 2). (Illus.). 142p. (Orig.). 1991. reprint ed. pap. 8.00 (*1-878178-02-4*) Bureau of Land Mgmt NM.

Defensive Skills for You. Andrew Kambites. 144p. 1994. 24.95 (*0-575-05637-1*, Pub. by V Gollancz UK) Trafalgar.

Defensive Tactics for Law Enforcement, Public Safety & Correction Officers. R. A. Flesch. 130p. 1994. pap. 24.95 (*0-87526-421-2*) Gould.

***Defensive Tips for Bad Card Holders: Over Five-Hundred Hands to Improve Your Defensive Play.** Eddie Kantar. 1994. pap. 12.95 (*1-882180-21-6*) Griffin CA.

Defensor Minor & de Translatione Imperli. Marsiglio of Padua. Ed. by Cary J. Nederman. LC 92-33311. (Cambridge Texts in the History of Political Thought Ser.). 120p. (C). 1993. 44.95 (*0-521-40277-8*); pap. 14.95 (*0-521-40846-6*) Cambridge U Pr.

Defensor Pacis. Marsilius of Padua. Tr. by Alan Gewirth. (Medieval Academy Reprints for Teaching Ser.). 1980. pap. 15.95 (*0-8020-6412-4*) U of Toronto Pr.

Defensor's Liber Scintillarum. E. W. Rhodes. (EETS, OS Ser.: No. 93). 1972. reprint ed. 40.00 (*0-527-00092-2*) Periodicals Srv.

Defer Payment - Let the Next Generation Pay. William P. Bernazzani. LC 80-13862. 1981. 21.95 (*0-87949-145-0*) Ashley Bks.

Deference & Defiance in Nineteenth-Century Japan. William W. Kelly. LC 85-42688. (Illus.). 315p. 1985. text ed. 47.50 (*0-691-09417-9*) Princeton U Pr.

Deference of Iudiciall Astrologie: In Answer to a Treatise Lately Published by M. John Chamber. Christopher Heydon. LC 77-7407. (English Experience Ser.: No. 873). 1977. reprint ed. lib. bdg. 65.00 (*90-221-0873-2*) Walter J Johnson.

Deferred Compensation: Accounting, Taxation, & Funding for Nonqualified Plans. Albert D. Spalding. LC 85-62426. 346p. write for info. (*0-13-199761-0*) P-H.

Deferred Compensation Handbook: A Complete Guide to Non-Qualified Plans. Stephan R. Leimberg & Linda I. Feldman. 240p. 1989. 32.95 (*0-88462-834-5*, 2402-31) Dearborn Finan.

Deferred Cost Recovery for Higher Education: Student Loan Programs in Developing Countries. Douglas Albrecht & Adrian Ziderman. (Discussion Paper Ser.: No. 137). 66p. 1991. pap. 7.95 (*0-8213-1952-3*, 11952) World Bank.

Deferred Gratification Pattern: A Preliminary Study. Louis Schneider & Sanford M. Dornsbusch. (Reprint Series in Social Sciences). (C). 1993. reprint ed. pap. text ed. 1.00 (*0-8290-3975-9*, S-250) Irvington.

Deferred Hopes: Blacks in Contemporary America. Sanjukta Banerji. LC 86-73077. 399p. (C). 1987. text ed. 40.00 (*0-89891-013-7*) Advent Bks Div.

Deferring a Dream: Literary Sub-Versions of the American Columbiad. Ed. by Gert Buelens. LC 94-6566. (International Cooper Series in English Language & Literature). 1994. 29.50 (*0-8176-5022-9*) Birkhauser.

Defiance: The Bielski Partisans. Nechama Tec. (Illus.). 294p. 1994. reprint ed. pap. 13.95 (*0-19-509390-9*) OUP.

Defiance in Manchuria: The Making of Japanese Foreign Policy, 1931-1932. Sadako N. Ogata. LC 84-543. xvi, 259p. (C). 1984. reprint ed. text ed. 41.50 (*0-313-24428-6*, OGDM, Greenwood Pr) Greenwood.

***Defiance, Oklahoma.** Lorraine Andrews & Eugene Andrews. (Illus.). 313p. 1991. 59.50 (*0-88107-192-7*) Curtis Media.

An Asterisk (*) at the beginning of an entry indicates that the title is appearing in BIP for the first time.

Defiant. Tom Early. (Sons of Texas Ser.: No. 6). 272p. (Orig.). 1993. mass mkt. 4.99 (*0-425-13706-6*) Berkley Pub.

*__Defiant.__ Shalom Yoran. 500p. Date not set. pap. 12.95 (*0-7610-0390-8*) NW Pub.

Defiant & Faithful: The Story of a Prussian Family. Cynog H. Von Rauchfuss. 110p. 1984. 30.00 (*0-7212-0649-2*, Pub. by Regency Press) St Mut.

Defiant Angel. Lisann St. Pierre. 400p. 1988. pap. 3.95 (*0-380-75511-4*) Avon.

Defiant Angel. Stephanie Stevens. 400p. (Orig.). 1991. mass mkt. 4.50 (*0-380-76449-0*) Avon.

Defiant Captive. Kathy Jones. (Heartfire Romance Ser.). 1987. pap. 3.75 (*0-8217-2220-4*) Zebra.

Defiant Captive. Roberta Stahlberg & Christina Skye. 1990. mass mkt. 4.99 (*0-440-20626-X*) Dell.

Defiant Celebration: Theological Ethics & Gay Sexuality. J. Michael Clark. LC 90-30837. 200p. (Orig.). 1990. pap. 10.00 (*0-934667-08-X*) Tangelwuld.

Defiant Children: A Clinician's Manual for Parent Training. Russell A. Barkley. LC 86-25796. 195p. 1987. student ed 25.00 (*0-89862-920-9*); spiral bd. 27.95 (*0-89862-700-1*, 2700) Guilford Pubns.

*__Defiant Desire: Gay & Lesbian Lives in South Africa.__ Ed. by Edwin Cameron & Mark Gevisser. LC 94-22150. 376p. 1994. 65.00 (*0-415-91060-9*, B4485, Routledge NY); pap. 17.95 (*0-415-91061-7*, B4489, Routledge NY) Routledge.

Defiant Desire: Some Dialectical Legacies of D. H. Lawrence. Kingsley Widmer. LC 91-28121. 256p. (C). 1992. 29.95 (*0-8093-1763-X*) S Ill U Pr.

Defiant Ecstasy. Janelle Taylor. (Orig.). 1991. mass mkt. 4.95 (*0-8217-3497-0*) Zebra.

Defiant Embrace. Barbara D. Smith. 1985. pap. 3.95 (*0-8217-1540-2*) Zebra.

Defiant Enchantress. Dorothy Powell. (Hologram Romances Ser.). 512p. 1988. pap. 3.95 (*0-8217-2252-2*) Zebra.

Defiant Heart. Anita Gordon. 352p. (Orig.). 1993. pap. 4.99 (*0-425-13825-9*) Berkley Pub.

Defiant Heart. Laurie Grant. 480p. (Orig.). 1989. pap. 3.95 (*0-8439-2432-2*) Dorchester Pub Co.

Defiant Heart. Nancy Moulton. 368p. (Orig.). 1989. pap. 3.95 (*0-380-75730-3*) Avon.

Defiant Hope: Spirituality for Survivors of Family Abuse. James Leehan. 176p. (Orig.). 1993. pap. 11.99 (*0-664-25463-2*) Westminster John Knox.

Defiant Impostor. Miriam Minger. 384p. (Orig.). 1992. mass mkt. 4.50 (*0-380-76312-5*) Avon.

Defiant Mistress. Elaine Barbieri. 1986. pap. 3.95 (*0-8217-1839-8*) Zebra.

Defiant Muse: French Feminist Poems from the Middle Ages to the Present, A Bilingual Anthology. Ed. by Domna C. Stanton. LC 85-16270. 240p. (Orig.). (ENG & FRE.). 1986. text ed. 35.00 (*0-935312-46-3*); pap. text ed. 11.95 (*0-935312-52-8*) Feminist Pr.

Defiant Muse: German Feminist Poems from the Middle Ages to the Present, A Bilingual Anthology. Ed. by Susan L. Cocalis. LC 86-4774. 176p. (Orig.). (ENG & GER.). 1986. text ed. 35.00 (*0-935312-49-8*); pap. text ed. 11.95 (*0-935312-53-6*) Feminist Pr.

Defiant Muse: Hispanic Feminist Poems from the Middle Ages to the Present, a Bilingual Anthology. Ed. by Angel Flores & Kate Flores. LC 85-16294. 176p. (Orig.). (ENG & SPA.). 1986. pap. text ed. 11.95 (*0-935312-54-4*) Feminist Pr.

Defiant Muse: Italian Feminist Poems from the Middle Ages to the Present, a Bilingual Anthology. Ed. by Beverly Allen et al. LC 84-4841. 176p. (Orig.). (ENG & ITA.). 1986. text ed. 35.00 (*0-935312-48-X*); pap. text ed. 11.95 (*0-935312-55-2*) Feminist Pr.

Defiant Ones: A Manual for Raising Kids. Jeffrey M. Bruns. LC 89-82212. 168p. (Orig.). 1990. 23.95 (*1-877758-37-X*); pap. 11.95 (*1-877758-36-1*) Calgre Pr.

Defiant Ones: A Screen Adaptation of the Story of "The Long Road" Nathan Douglas et al. Ed. by George Garrett et al. LC 71-135273. (Film Scripts Ser.). 1989. reprint ed. pap. text ed. 19.95 (*0-89197-725-2*) Irvington.

Defiant Pose. Stewart Home. 144p. 1991. 30.00 (*0-7206-0828-7*, Pub. by P Owen Ltd UK) Dufour.

Defiant Spitfire. Kay Mcmahon. 1988. pap. 3.95 (*0-8217-2326-X*) Zebra.

Defiant Splendor. Michalann Perry. 512p. 1988. pap. 3.95 (*0-8217-2374-X*) Zebra.

Defiant Surrender. Barbara D. Smith. 464p. 1987. pap. 3.95 (*0-8217-1966-1*) Zebra.

Defiant Voices: Hungary 1956-1986. Istvan B. Gereben. LC 86-51347. 168p. per. 10.00 (*0-912404-05-1*) Alpha Pubns.

Defibrillation of the Heart. Tacker. 325p. 1993. 64.95 (*0-8016-7292-9*) Mosby Yr Bk.

Defibrillation of the Heart: ICDs, AEDs, & Manual. Ed. by W. A. Tacker, Jr. 1993. write for info. (*0-318-72428-6*) Mosby Yr Bk.

Defibrillator Markets Report, No. 252. 180p. 1992. 295.00 (*0-317-04226-2*) Theta Corp.

Deficiencia De Hierro en la Infancia y la Ninez. Peter R. Dallman et al. Ed. by Thomas H. Bothwell et al. Tr. by Guillermo Arroyave. (Illus.). 83p. (Orig.). (SPA.). 1985. pap. text ed. 3.50 (*0-318-35288-5*) ILSI.

Deficiencia De Hierro en la Mujer. Thomas H. Bothwell & Robert W. Carlton. Ed. by James D. Cook et al. Tr. by Guillermo Arroyave. (Illus.). 139p. (Orig.). (SPA.). 1985. pap. text ed. 3.50 (*0-318-35289-3*) ILSI.

*__Deficient Cause of Moral Evil According to St. Thomas.__ Edward Cook. LC 94-40760. (Cultural Heritage & Contemporary Change, Ser. I, Culture & Values: Vol. 14). 1995. 45.00 (*1-56518-069-0*); pap. text ed. 17.50 (*1-56518-070-4*) Coun Res Values.

Deficit: Twelve Steps to Ease the Crisis. Helen P. Rogers. LC 87-51350. 465p. 1988. 17.95 (*0-915915-06-5*) Wellington Pubns.

Deficit & the Public Interest: The Search for Responsible Budgeting in the 1980s. Joseph White & Aaron B. Wildavsky. 671p. 1989. 50.00 (*0-520-06533-6*) U CA Pr.

Deficit & the Public Interest: The Search for Responsible Budgeting in the 1980s. Joseph White & Aaron B. Wildavsky. (Russell Sage Foundation Book Ser.). 695p. 1991. reprint ed. pap. 19.00 (*0-520-07650-8*, WHIDEX) U CA Pr.

Deficit Control & the Gramm-Rudman-Hollings Act: History of the Balanced Budget & Emergency Deficit Control Act of 1985 (P.L. 99-177), 5 vols., Set. Bernard D. Reams, Jr. & Margaret H. McDermott. LC 86-80964. 1986. lib. bdg. 250.00 (*0-89941-484-2*, 304110) W S Hein.

*__Deficit Government: Taxing & Spending in Modern America.__ Iwan W. Morgan. LC 94-46129. (American Ways Ser.). 1995. write for info. (*1-56663-081-9*); pap. write for info. (*1-56663-082-7*) I R Dee.

*__Deficit Lie: Exposing the Myth of the National Debt.__ Rick Boettger. Ed. by Mike Towle. LC 94-3644. 398p. 1994. 22.95 (*1-56530-159-5*) Summit TX.

Deficit Politics. Donald F. Kettl. 192p. (Orig.). (C). 1992. pap. write for info. (*0-02-363570-3*) Macmillan.

Deficits: How Big? How Long? How Dangerous? Daniel Bell & Lester Thurow. 100p. 1985. text ed. 12.00 (*0-8147-1083-2*) NYU Pr.

Deficits & Detente: Report of an International Conference on the Balance of Trade in the Comecon Countries. Richard Portes. 92p. (Orig.). (C). 1983. pap. text ed. 6.00 (*0-87078-150-2*) TCFP-PPP.

*__Deficits & the Dollar: The World Economy at Risk.__ fac. ed. Stephan Marris. LC 85-17303. (Policy Analyses in International Economics Ser.: Vol. 14). 384p. 1985. reprint ed. pap. write for info. (*0-7837-7774-4*, 2047530) Bks Demand.

*__Deficits & the Dollar: The World Economy at Risk.__ fac. ed. Stephan Marris. LC 85-17303. (Policy Analyses in International Economics Ser.: Vol. 14). 40p. 1985. reprint ed. pap. 25.00 (*0-7837-7775-2*) Bks Demand.

*__Deficits & the Dollar: The World Economy at Risk.__ Stephen Marris. LC 87-29887. (Policy Analyses in International Economics Ser.: 14). (Illus.). 416p. 1987. reprint ed. pap. 118.60 (*0-7837-7776-0*, 2047531) Bks Demand.

Deficits, Debts, & the Economy: Getting Out of the Financial Maze. Thomas F. Dernburg. (Orig.). 1995. pap. 14.95 (*0-9644810-0-6*) T D Econ. No subject more occupies the attention of the public & the Congress than the federal budget deficit. Indeed deficit reduction is the centerpiece of the Republican CONTRACT WITH AMERICA. This book, written by an economist with a wide range of government & academic experience, attempts to put the issues into perspective in a way intended to be intelligible to the general reader. How serious is the problem? Did Clinton cut the deficit or did the recovering economy do the job for him? Can deficit reduction be accomplished without harm to the economy? What are intelligent ways to deal with runaway health inflation? Can other entitlement programs be reformed to effect economies without harming the programs? What is the relationship between the budget deficit & the ongoing trade deficit? How does our budget deficit affect the deficit problems of other countries? Do deficits necessarily cause inflation? Do deficits place severe burdens on future generations? In what ways might this be true? Is it important to repay the national debt? For further information write to TD Economics, 2150 Michael Drive, Clarksville, TN 37043 or Telephone (615) 648-1098.** ***Publisher Provided Annotation.

*__Defiendete!__ Gershen Kaufman & Lev Raphael. (Illus.). 112p. (SPA.). (J). (gr. 3-7). pap. 9.95 (*968-860-226-4*) Free Spirit Pub.

Defilement. C. L. Morrison. LC 78-64744. (Illus.). 1979. 18.95 (*0-932508-02-2*) Seven Oaks.

Defined Immunoflourescence, Immunoenzyme Studies, & Related Labeling Techniques, 7th International Conference, Vol. 420. Ed. by Ernst H. Beutner et al. 84.00 (*0-89766-238-5*); pap. 84.00 (*0-89766-239-3*) NY Acad Sci.

Defining a Linquistic Area: South Asia. Colin P. Masica. LC 74-16677. 256p. 1976. lib. bdg. 19.00 (*0-226-50944-3*) U Ch Pr.

Defining Acts: Aging As Drama. Robert Kastenbaum. LC 93-30310. (Society & Aging Ser.). 191p. 1993. 25.95 (*0-89503-119-1*); pap. 19.95 (*0-89503-118-3*) Baywood Pub.

Defining America: Christian Critique of the American Dream. Robert Benne & Philip Hefner. LC 73-89062. 160p. reprint ed. pap. 45.60 (*0-685-16038-6*, 2026941) Bks Demand.

Defining American Psychology: The Correspondence Between Adolph Meyer & Edward Brandord Titchener. Ed. by Ruth Leys & Rand B. Evans. LC 89-15315. 296p. 1990. text ed. 45.00x (*0-8018-3865-7*) Johns Hopkins.

Defining & Applying Effective Teaching Strategies for Library Instruction. Ed. by Mary B. Bunge & Teresa B. Mensching. (Library Orientation Ser.: No. 18). 133p. 1989. pap. 35.00 (*0-87650-252-4*) Pierian.

Defining & Assessing Baccalaureate Skills: Ten Case Studies. 80p. (Orig.). 1986. pap. text ed. 24.50 (*0-88044-065-1*) AASCU Press.

Defining & Describing. Marilyn M. Toomey. (Illus.). 140p. (J). (gr. 3-8). 1991. Grades 3-8. pap. 17.95 (*0-923573-14-3*) Circuit Pubns.

*__Defining & Measuring Democracy.__ Ed. by David Beetham. (Sage Modern Politics Ser.: Vol. 35). 224p. 1995. 69.95 (*0-8039-7788-3*) Sage.

*__Defining & Measuring Democracy.__ Ed. by David Beetham. (Sage Modern Politics Ser.: Vol. 35). 224p. 1995. pap. 24.95 (*0-8039-7789-1*) Sage.

*__Defining & Measuring Sustainability: The Biophysical Foundation.__ Ed. by Mohan Munasinghe et al. LC 95-2865. 1995. write for info. (*0-8213-3134-5*) World Bank.

Defining Biology. Ed. by Jane Maienschein. LC 86-307. (Illus.). 352p. 1986. 35.00 (*0-674-19615-5*) HUP.

Defining Child Abuse. Jeanne M. Giovannoni & Rosina Becerra. LC 79-7180. (Illus.). 1982. 27.95 (*0-02-911750-X*); pap. 19.95 (*0-02-911780-1*) Free Pr.

Defining Commercial Timberland: A Position Statement of the Society of American Foresters & Report of the SAF Task Force. Society of American Foresters Staff. 1985. pap. 4.50 (*0-939970-31-7*) Soc Am Foresters.

*__Defining Complex Interdisciplinary Societal Problems: A Theoretical Study for Constructing a Co-Operative Problem Analyzing Method: The Method COMPRAM.__ D. J. DeTombe. 439p. 1994. pap. 36.50 (*90-5170-302-3*, Pub. by Thesis Pubs NE) IBD Ltd.

Defining Critical Mass - The Case in Animal Research. Doug Daniels & Barry Nestel. 61p. 1993. pap. 10.00 (*0-88936-649-7*, IDRC6497, Pub. by IDRC CN) UNIPUB.

*__Defining Cultural Differences in Space: Public Housing As a Microcosm.__ Jacqueline Leavitt. (Urban Studies & Planning Monograph Ser.: No. 11). 84p. 1994. pap. 7.50 (*0-913749-21-4*) U MD Urban Stud.

Defining Dictionary of Business Commerce & Marketing. P. F. Petrochenko. 64p. (C). 1992. text ed. 60.00 (*0-569-07110-0*, Pub. by Collets) St Mut.

Defining Dictionary of Computing. W. Illingworth. 567p. (C). 1989. 100.00 (*0-685-37115-8*, Pub. by Collets) St Mut.

Defining Dictionary of Russian Language, Vol. 1. Ed. by V. Dal. 700p. (C). 1989. 125.00 (*0-685-46808-9*, Pub. by Collets) St Mut.

Defining Dictionary of the Hungarian Language. J. Juhasz. 2424p. (C). 1987. 170.00 (*0-685-54137-1*, Pub. by Collets) St Mut.

*__Defining Disabled Access Claims.__ Gregory F. Hurley. LC 94-48237. (Real Estate Practice Library). 1995. text ed. 125.00 (*0-471-05057-1*, Pub. by Wiley Law Pubns) Wiley.

*__Defining Dominion: The Discourses of Magic & Witchcraft in Early Modern France & Germany.__ Gerhild S. Williams. LC 95-3470. (Studies in Medieval & Early Modern Civilization). 1995. write for info. (*0-472-10619-8*) U of Mich Pr.

*__Defining Environmental Education.__ John F. Disinger & Martha C. Monroe. Ed. by David Cappaert. (EEToolbox-Workshop Resource Manual Ser.). (Illus.). 40p. 1994. 8.00 (*1-884782-03-5*) Natl Consort EET.

Defining Females: The Nature of Women in Society. Ed. by Shirley Ardener. LC 92-39823. (Cross-Cultural Perspectives on Women Ser.). 228p. 1993. pap. 16.50 (*0-85496-727-3*) Berg Pubs.

Defining Infants' Race & Ethnicity in a Study of Very Low Birthweight Infants. Donna O. Farley et al. LC 93-8807. 1993. write for info. (*0-8330-1414-5*, MR-191-AHCPR) Rand Corp.

Defining Literacy Levels. Brenda M. Weaver. 257p. 1992. 19.95 (*0-87157-849-2*) Story Hse Corp.

Defining Media Studies: Reflections on the Future of the Field. Mark R. Levy & Michael Gurevitch. (Illus.). 448p. (C). 1994. text ed. 48.00 (*0-19-508787-9*); pap. text ed. 19.95 (*0-19-508788-7*) OUP.

Defining Modern Art: Selected Writings of Alfred H. Barr. Ed. by Amy Newman. (Illus.). 302p. 1986. 39.95 (*0-8109-0715-1*) Abrams.

Defining Moment: Motivating People to Take Action. Brent Filson. 256p. 1993. 39.50 (*0-9626845-5-4*) Williamstown Pub.

Defining Music Therapy. Kenneth E. Bruscia. LC 89-62706. 188p. (Orig.). (C). 1989. pap. text ed. 16.00 (*0-9624080-0-X*) Barcelona Pubs.

Defining National Security. Joseph J. Romm. (Pew Project Ser.). 96p. 1993. pap. 10.95 (*0-87609-135-4*) Coun Foreign.

Defining Noah Webster: Mind & Morals in the Early Republic. K. Alan Snyder. 430p. (Orig.). (C). 1990. lib. bdg. 55.00 (*0-8191-7862-4*) U Pr of Amer.

Defining Nursing Care in Your Hospital. Joint Commission on Accreditation of Healthcare Staff. 1992. 25.00 (*0-86688-282-0*) Joint Comm Hlthcare.

Defining Peasants: Essays Concerning Rural Societies, Expolary Economies & the Learning from Them in the Contemporary World. Teodor Shanin. 1990. text ed. 52.95 (*0-631-15037-4*) Blackwell Pubs.

Defining Personal Success Through Spiritual Principles. J. Forte. Ed. by S. M. Gardner. 1993. pap. 14.95 (*0-9636676-0-2*) Inner Pathway.

Defining Perspectives in Moral Development. Ed. by Bill Puka. LC 94-462. (Moral Development: a Compendium Ser.: No. 1). (Illus.). 264p. 1994. reprint ed. 47.00 (*0-8153-1548-1*) Garland.

Defining Physical Education: The Social Construction of School Subject in Post-War Britain. David Kirk. 160p. 1992. 70.00 (*0-7507-0024-6*, Falmer Pr) Taylor & Francis.

Defining Power: Influence & Force in the Contemporary International System. John M. Rothgeb, Jr. LC 92-50035. 1993. text ed. 39.95 (*0-312-08682-2*) St Martin.

Defining Power: Influence & Force in the Contemporary System. John M. Rothgeb, Jr. LC 92-50035. (Illus.). 205p. (C). 1992. pap. text ed. 15.00 (*0-312-06105-6*) St Martin.

Defining Rape. Linda B. Bourque. LC 88-30764. (Illus.). xix, 428p. 1989. lib. bdg. 62.95 (*0-8223-0901-7*) Duke.

Defining Relations & Algorithmic Problems for Groups & Semigroups. Steklov Institute of Mathematics, Academy of Sciences, U. S. S. R. Staff. Ed. by S I. Adjan. (Proceedings of the Steklov Institute of Mathematics Ser.: No. 85). 152p. 1967. 50.00 (*0-8218-1885-6*, STEKLO-85) Am Math.

Defining Science: William Whewell, Natural Knowledge & Public Debate in Early Victorian Britain. Richard R. Yeo. LC 92-30620. (Ideas in Context Ser.: No. 28). 272p. (C). 1993. 59.95 (*0-521-43182-4*) Cambridge U Pr.

Defining Soil Quality for a Sustainable Environment: Proceedings of a Symposium Sponsored by Divisions S-3, S-6, & S-2 of the Soil Science Society of America, Division A5 of the American Society of Agronomy, & the North Central Region Committee on Soil Organic Matter (NCR-59) in Minneapolis, MN, 4-5 November, 1992. Ed. by J. W. Doran et al. LC 94-6338. (SSSA Special Publication Ser.: No. 35). 1994. pap. 30.00 (*0-89118-807-X*) Am Soc Agron.

Defining Sustainable Forestry. Ed. by Greg Aplet et al. LC 93-8389. (Illus.). 320p. 1993. text ed. 49.95 (*1-55963-233-X*); pap. 24.95 (*1-55963-234-8*) Island Pr.

Defining the Common Good: Empire, Religion & Philosophy in Eighteenth-Century Britain. Peter N. Miller. (Ideas in Context Ser.: No. 29). 448p. (C). 1994. 69.95 (*0-521-44259-1*) Cambridge U Pr.

Defining the Manager's Job: The AMA Manual of Position Descriptions. C. L. Bennet. LC 58-14306. (American Management Association Research Study Ser.: No. 33). 447p. reprint ed. pap. 127.40 (*0-317-09571-4*, 2051306) Bks Demand.

Defining the New Rhetorics. Theresa Enos & Stuart S. Brown. (Written Communication Annual Ser.: Vol. 7). (Illus.). 320p. (C). 1992. 52.00 (*0-8039-4270-2*); pap. 24.00 (*0-8039-4271-0*) Sage.

Defining the Political. Dick Howard. 340p. (Orig.). 1989. text ed. 44.95 (*0-8166-1716-3*); pap. text ed. 15.95 (*0-8166-1717-1*) U of Minn Pr.

Defining the Role of the Non-Jew in the Synagogue: A Resource for Congregations. 138p. 1990. pap. 10.00 (*0-8074-0453-5*, 280057) UAHC.

Defining the Social Studies. Robert D. Barr et al. LC 77-85192. (National Council for the Social Studies Bulletin: No. 51). 127p. reprint ed. pap. 36.20 (*0-685-16144-7*, 2027731) Bks Demand.

Defining Transportation Requirements: Papers & Discussions of the 1968 Transportation Engineering Conference, Washington, D.C., October 28-30, 1968. Transportation Engineering Conference Staff. LC 66-28397. 385p. reprint ed. pap. 109.80 (*0-317-08393-7*, 2016810) Bks Demand.

Defining Woman: Natural Workout for Body & Mind. Judy Kalvin-Stiefel. (Illus.). 256p. (Orig.). 1993. pap. 19.95 (*0-9628504-1-1*) Bywood.

Defining Women: Television & the Case of Cagney & Lacey. Julie D'Acci. LC 93-32536. (Illus.). xiv, 344p. (C). 1994. lib. bdg. 45.00 (*0-8078-2132-2*); pap. text ed. 16.95 (*0-8078-4441-1*) U of NC Pr.

*__Defining Work & Family Issues: Listening to the Voices of Women of Color.__ Jennifer Tucker & Leslie R. Wolfe. 17p. (Orig.). (C). 1994. 10.00 (*1-877966-18-5*) Ctr Women Policy.

*__Defining Years of the Dutch East Indies, 1942-1949: Survivors' Accounts.__ Jan A. Krancher. (Illus.). 304p. 1995. lib. bdg. 42.50 (*0-7864-0070-6*) McFarland & Co.

Definite: A System to Support Decisions On a Finite Set of Alternatives User Manual. Ron Janssen. 1994. lib. bdg. 1,750.00 (*0-685-75292-5*) Kluwer Ac.

Definite Article in English Transformations. Beverly Robbins. 1968. pap. text ed. 56.95 (*90-279-0082-5*) Mouton.

*__Definite Country: The Ultimate Encyclopedia of Country Music & Its Performers.__ Barry McCloud. LC 94-28400. 1994. pap. 19.00 (*0-399-52144-5*, Perigree Bks); pap. text ed. 40.00 (*0-399-51890-8*, Perigree Bks) Berkley Pub.

Definite Cure of Chronic Constipation. Arnold Ehret. 1983. pap. 2.95 (*0-87904-032-7*) Lust.

Definite Decisions for New Church Members. Jerome O. Williams. 1936. pap. 1.25 (*0-8054-9402-2*) Broadman.

Definite Integral. G. M. Fichtenholz. Tr. by R. A. Silverman. LC 78-149513. (Illus.). 98p. 1973. text ed. 117.00 (*0-677-21090-6*) Gordon & Breach.

Definite Medication. Eli G. Jones. 312p. 1974. reprint ed. spiral bd. 16.50 (*0-7873-0481-6*) Mokelumne.

Definite Nominal Phrase Anaphora: A Pragmatic Approach. Marit R. Westergaard. (Norwegian University Press Publication Ser.). 130p. 1987. 39.95 (*82-00-06950-8*) OUP.

Definite Object. Jeffrey Farnol. 1975. lib. bdg. 16.70 (*0-89966-087-8*) Buccaneer Bks.

D

An Asterisk (*) at the beginning of an entry indicates that the title is appearing in BIP for the first time.

Definite Quantum Measurements. L. S. Schulman. (Lecture Notes in Physics Ser.: No. 45). 250p. 1994. text ed. 38.00 (*981-02-0873-1*) World Scientific Pub.

Definitely Cool. Brenda Wilkinson. LC 92-12112. 176p. (YA). (gr. 3-7). 1993. 13.95 (*0-590-46186-9*) Scholastic Inc.

Definitely Danish History, Culture Recipes. 64p. 1994. pap. 10.95 (*0-941016-94-3*) Penfield.

Definitely Different. Noreen Cotter. LC 93-133. (J). 1994. write for info. (*0-383-03685-2*) SRA Schl Grp.

Definitely from out of Town. (Star Shows Ser.). 48p. (J). (gr. 4-5). 1991. lib. bdg. 11.95 (*1-56065-008-7*) Capstone Pr.

***Definition: Shape Without Bulk in 15 Minutes a Day!** Joyce L. Vedral. (Illus.). 304p. (Orig.). 1995. pap. 14.99 (*0-446-67069-3*) Warner Bks.

***Definition & Induction: A Historical & Comparative Study.** Kisor K. Chakrabarti. LC 95-7339. (Society for Asian & Comparative Philosophy Ser.: No. 13). 248p. (C). 1995. teacher ed 16.00x (*0-8248-1658-7*) UH Pr.

Definition & Payment for Uncompensated Services & Special Problems of a Disproportionate Share. Uncompensated Services Task Force Staff & Richard L. Clarke. 17p. (Orig.). 1987. pap. 10.00 (*0-930228-54-5*) Hlthcare Fin Mgmt.

Definition & Prevalence of Learning Disabilities. National Center for State Courts Staff. 21p. 1978. Manuscript. 1.26 (*0-685-16963-4*, LDJD-013) Natl Ctr St Courts.

Definition of a Peripheral Economy: Turkey 1923-1929. Cagler Keyder. LC 80-41829. (Studies in Modern Capitalism). (Illus.). 180p. 1981. 44.95 (*0-521-23699-1*) Cambridge U Pr.

Definition of a Profession: The Authority of Metaphor in the History of Intelligence Testing, 1890-1930. JoAnne Brown. 216p. 1992. text ed. 32.50 (*0-691-08632-X*) Princeton U Pr.

Definition of Capital Gains in the Various Countries, Vol. LXIb. 436p. pap. 33.00 (*0-686-40996-5*) Kluwer Ac.

Definition of College Quality & Its Impact on Earnings. Lewis C. Solomon. (Explorations in Economic Research Two Ser.: No. 4). 51p. 1975. reprint ed. 35.00 (*0-685-61389-5*) Natl Bur Econ Res.

Definition of Educational Technology. Ed. by Kenneth Silber. LC 79-53125. 1979. pap. 10.95 (*0-89240-006-4*) Assn Ed Comm Tech.

Definition of Good. Alfred C. Ewing. LC 78-59021. 1987. reprint ed. 22.00 (*0-88355-695-2*) Hyperion Conn.

Definition of Intelligence in Relation to Modern Methods of Mental Measurements see Tentative Standardization of a Hard Opposites Test

Definition of Language Competences Through Testing see Language Learner

Definition of Moral Virtue. Yves R. Simon. Ed. by Vukan Kuic. LC 85-80404. xiv, 137p. 1986. 30.00 (*0-8232-1143-6*); pap. 15.00 (*0-8232-1144-4*) Fordham.

Definition of Quality & Approaches to Its Assessment. Avedis Donabedian. LC 80-15173. (Explorations in Quality Assessment & Monitoring Ser.: Vol. I). (Illus.). 178p. 1980. pap. text ed. 28.00 (*0-914904-48-5*, 0824) Health Admin Pr.

Definition of "Small Business" Within Meaning of Small Business Act of 1953, as Amended. U. S. House of Representative Subcommittee No. 2 of the Select Committee on Small Business. Ed. by Stuart Bruchey & Vincent P. Carosso. LC 78-19006. (Small Business Enterprise in America Ser.). (Illus.). 1979. reprint ed. lib. bdg. 23.95 (*0-405-11498-2*) Ayer.

Definition of Standard ML. Robin Milner et al. 100p. 1990. 30.00 (*0-262-13255-9*); pap. 15.00 (*0-262-63132-6*) MIT Pr.

Definition of Suicide. Edwin Shneidman. LC 93-74372. 270p. 1995. pap. 35.00 (*1-56821-196-1*) Aronson.

Definition of the Thing: With Some Notes on Language. John W. Miller. (C). 1980. reprint ed. text ed. 20.00 (*0-393-01377-4*) Norton.

Definition of the Thing: With Some Notes on Language. John W. Miller. 1983. reprint ed. pap. 6.50 (*0-393-30059-5*) Norton.

Definitions. Peter Oresick. LC 90-12346. 72p. (C). 1990. 18.95 (*0-931122-59-7*); pap. 8.95 (*0-931122-58-9*) West End.

Definitions: Essays in Contemporary Criticism. Henry S. Canby. (BCL1-PS American Literature Ser.). 308p. 1992. reprint ed. lib. bdg. 89.00 (*0-7812-6600-9*) Rprt Serv.

Definitions - Conversions - Calculus for Occupational Safety & Health Professions. Edward W. Finucane. 1993. 49.95 (*0-87371-863-1*, RC863) Lewis Pubs.

Definitions & Definability: Philosophical Perspectives. James H. Fetzer. 328p. (C). 1991. lib. bdg. 110.00 (*0-7923-1046-2*) Kluwer Ac.

Definitions & Diagnostic Criteria of Alcoholism. (Illus.). 65p. (Orig.). (C). 1992. pap. text ed. 40.00 (*1-56806-130-7*) Diane Pub.

Definitions & Divisions of Philosophy. David. Tr. by Bridget Kendall & Robert W. Thomson. LC 83-3308. (Armenian Texts & Studies). 216p. (C). 1983. 18.50 (*0-89130-653-6*, 21 02 05); pap. 14.00 (*0-89130-616-1*) Scholars Pr GA.

Definitions & Doctrines of the Military Art. Ed. & Intro. by Thomas Griess. LC 85-18673. (West Point Military History Ser.). (Illus.). 240p. 1985. 25.00 (*0-89529-309-9*); pap. 19.95 (*0-89529-275-0*) Avery Pub.

Definitions & Information Pertaining to Electrical Instruments in Hazardous (Classified) Locations. 1991. 52.00 (*1-55617-321-0*, S12.1) Instru Soc.

Definitions & Realities of Poverty. Francis G. Caro & Patricia Simpson. LC 90-198046. 68p. 1988. 6.50 (*0-88156-097-9*) Comm Serv Soc NY.

Definitions for Asbestos & Other Health-Related Silicates: A Symposium. American Society for Testing & Materials Staff. Ed. by Benjamin Levadie. LC 83-72557. (ASTM Special Technical Publication Ser.: No. 834). (Illus.). 221p. reprint ed. pap. 63.00 (*0-7837-4790-X*, 2044827) Bks Demand.

Definitions in Biomaterials. D. F. Williams. (Biomedical Engineering Ser.: Vol. 4). 72p. 1987. 69.25 (*0-444-42858-5*) Elsevier.

Definitions in Political Economy: Preceded by an Inquiry into the Rules Which Ought to Guide Political Economists in the Definition & Use of Their Terms. Thomas R. Malthus. LC 86-7468. (Reprints of Economic Classics Ser.). 1986. reprint ed. 35.00 (*0-678-00018-2*) Kelley.

Definitions of Art. Stephen Davies. LC 90-55756. 256p. 1991. 35.00 (*0-8014-2568-9*); pap. 13.95 (*0-8014-9794-9*) Cornell U Pr.

Definitions of Nonviolence. Lanza Del Vasto. Tr. by Jean Sidgwick. 27p. (Orig.). 1972. pap. 1.50 (*0-934676-06-2*) Greenlf Bks.

Definitions of Practice of Law Survey. Center for Professional Responsibility Staff. 16p. 1984. pap. 7.95 (*0-685-19029-3*, 561-0067-01) Amer Bar Assn.

Definitions of Quantities & Conventions Related to Blood pH & Gas Analysis. 2nd ed. National Committee for Clinical Laboratory Standards Staff. (Tentative Standard Ser.: Vol. 2). 1991. 40.00 (*1-56238-138-5*, C12-T2) Natl Comm Clin Lab Stds.

***Definitions of Surveying & Associated Terms.** ACSM Staff & ASCE Staff. 210p. 1978. pap. 18.00 (*0-614-06117-2*, S180) Am Congrs Survey.

Definitions of Surveying & Associated Terms. Comp. by American Society of Civil Engineers Staff. (Manual & Report on Engineering Practice Ser.: No. 34). 218p. 1978. pap. 20.00 (*0-87262-211-8*) Am Soc Civil Eng.

Definitions of Surveying & Associated Terms. rev. ed. 210p. 1978. write for info. (*0-317-32452-7*) Am Congrs Survey.

Definitions of Terms for Admissions & Records. American Association of Collegiate Registrars & Admissions Officers Staff. (AACRAO Handbook, 1980: Data & Definitions Ser.). 82p. reprint ed. pap. 25.00 (*0-8357-3112-X*, 2039369) Bks Demand.

Definitions of the Enemy: A Collection of Poems with Jewish Themes. Ben Wilensky. LC 92-28603. 64p. 1992. pap. 12.95 (*0-7734-9600-9*) E Mellen.

Definitions of Time & Recovery in Paralytic Polio Convalescence. Fred Davis. (Reprint Series in Sociology). (C). 1993. reprint ed. pap. text ed. 1.00 (*0-8290-2640-1*, S-366) Irvington.

***Definitive Andy Griffith Show Reference: Episode-by-Episode, with Cast & Production Biographies & a Guide to Collectibles.** Dale Robinson & Dale Fernandes. 344p. 1995. lib. bdg. 39.95 (*0-7864-0136-2*) McFarland & Co.

Definitive Bibliography of Harmonically Sophisticated Tonal Music. Reese Markewich. LC 77-104898. 1970. pap. 4.95 (*0-9600160-2-3*) Markewich.

Definitive Biography of P. D. Q. Bach. Peter Schickele. 1977. pap. 15.00 (*0-394-73409-2*) Random.

Definitive Blues Collection. 288p. 1992. pap. 22.95 (*0-7935-1397-9*, 00311563) H Leonard.

Definitive Book of Tarot. Kathleen McCormack. (Illus.). 177p. 1989. 10.95 (*0-88079-468-2*) US Games Syst.

Definitive Broadway Collection. 480p. 1989. pap. 27.95 (*0-88188-984-9*, 00359570) H Leonard.

Definitive California Bed & Breakfast Touring Guide 93-94. Stephen Gittings & John R. H. Walker. Ed. by Jessie Wood & Melissa Greenblatt. (Illus.). 240p. 1993. pap. 14.95 (*1-882641-00-0*) Travel Print.

Definitive Christmas Collection: 0963683209. (Piano-Vocal-Guitar Ser.). 288p. 1993. pap. 24.95 (*0-7935-1985-3*, 00311602) H Leonard.

***Definitive Country: The Ultimate Encyclopedia of Country Music & Its Performers.** 1995. write for info. (*0-614-03898-7*, Perigee Bks) Berkley Pub.

***Definitive Country: The Ultimate Encyclopedia of Country Music & Its Performers.** (Orig.). 1995. pap. write for info. (*0-614-03899-5*, Perigee Bks) Berkley Pub.

Definitive Country Collection. Hal Leonard Publishing Staff. (Piano-Vocal-Guitar Ser.). 288p. (Orig.). 1992. pap. 24.95 (*0-7935-1226-3*, 00311555) H Leonard.

Definitive Dixieland Collection. 280p. 1993. pap. 22.95 (*0-7935-1509-2*, 00311575) H Leonard.

Definitive Donkey. Betsy Hutchins & Paul Hutchins. (Illus.). 221p. 1982. pap. 10.00 (*0-317-01434-X*) Am Donkey.

***Definitive Guide for the D. O. Trying to Get an M. D. Residency: D. O.'s Eat Their Young.** Jeremy S. Weiss. LC 95-60316. (Illus.). 160p. (Orig.). 1995. pap. 24.95 (*0-9646824-0-0*) Gotta Reach Jam.

Definitive Guide to Futures Trading, Vol. I. Larry Williams. 1988. 50.00 (*0-930233-19-0*) Windsor.

Definitive Guide to Futures Trading, Vol. II. Larry Williams. 1989. 50.00 (*0-930233-36-0*) Windsor.

Definitive Guide to Long Range Planning. Thomas Hatcher & Rosemary Hatcher. 118p. 1981. pap. text ed. 22.00 (*0-940082-00-4*) Futures Unlimited Inc.

Definitive Guide to Long Range Planning Facilitators Handbook. Thomas Hatcher. 90p. 1981. pap. text ed. 89.00 (*0-940082-01-2*) Futures Unlimited Inc.

Definitive Guide to Shot Glasses. Mark Pickvet. (Illus.). 228p. (Orig.). 1993. pap. 19.95 (*0-915410-90-7*) Antique Pubns.

Definitive Index of Aurora ThunderJets & Vibrators. Kevin Timothy. 36p. (Orig.). 1993. pap. 3.95 (*1-883796-01-6*) What It Is.

Definitive Jazz Collection. 288p. 1989. pap. 22.95 (*0-88188-856-7*, 00359571) H Leonard.

Definitive Kobbe's Opera Book. rev. ed. Ed. by Earl of Harewood. 1408p. 1987. 39.95 (*0-399-13180-9*, Putnam) Putnam Pub Group.

Definitive Microwave Cookery. Carolyn Dodson. (Illus.). (Orig.). 1994. pap. write for info. (*1-882330-25-0*) Magni Co.

Definitive Microwave Cookery II. Carolyn Dodson. (Illus.). 220p. (Orig.). 1995. pap. 16.95 (*1-882330-30-7*) Magni Co.

Definitive Middle School Guide: A Handbook for Success. Imogene Forte & Sandra Schurr. Ed. by Jan Keeling. LC 93-77473. (Illus.). 352p. (Orig.). 1993. teacher ed 29.95 (*0-86530-270-7*) Incentive Pubns.

***Definitive Movie Collection.** Hal. (Illus.). 432p. (Orig.). 1995. pap. text ed. 24.95 (*0-7935-3846-7*, HL00311705) H Leonard.

Definitive Nineteen Sixty-Seven to Nineteen Sixty-Eight Camaro Z-28 Book. Jerry MacNeish. (Illus.). 148p. 1990. pap. 21.95 (*0-9626399-0-7*) J MacNeish.

Definitive Performance Writing Guide. Douglas L. Drewry. LC 89-92039. (Illus.). 496p. (Orig.). 1989. pap. 25.95 (*0-9623673-0-3*) Prof Mgmt Spectrum.

Definitive Quotations. John Ferguson. 39p. 1981. pap. 2.95 (*0-930454-09-X*) Verbatim Bks.

Definitive Rock & Roll Collection: 1955-1966. (Piano-Vocal-Guitar Ser.). 304p. (Orig.). 1989. pap. 22.95 (*0-88188-833-8*, 00490195) H Leonard.

Definitive Statements: American Art, 1964-66. Brown University, Department of Art Staff. LC 86-70127. (Illus.). 180p. (Orig.). 1986. pap. text ed. 14.00 (*0-933519-01-X*) D W Bell Gallery.

Definitive System for Analysis of Grizzly Bear Habitat & Other Wilderness Resources Utilizing LANDSAT Multispectral Imagery & Computer Technology. J. J. Craighead et al. Ed. by J. A. Mitchell et al. (Illus.). 279p. (Orig.). (C). 1982. pap. text ed. 27.50 (*0-910439-01-X*) Wildlife-Wildlands.

Definitive Themes in Home Economics & Their Impact on Families, 1909-1984. Ed. by Marjorie East & Joan Thomsom. 188p. 1984. pap. 16.00 (*0-8461-5050-6*) Am Home Eco.

Definitive Work on the Origins of Human Lymphomas. Sergio DeCarvalho. LC 84-72903. 148p. 19.50 (*0-930376-40-4*) Chem-Orbital.

Definitively Unfinished Marcel Duchamp. Ed. by Thierry De Duve. (Illus.). 550p. 1991. 57.50x (*0-262-04117-0*) MIT Pr.

Definitively Unfinished Marcel Duchamp. Ed. by Thierry De Duve. 1993. pap. 30.00 (*0-262-54072-X*) MIT Pr.

***Defis Pour un Tricheur.** Margot Dalton. (OR Ser.). (FRE.). 1994. pap. 4.50 (*0-373-38161-1*, 1-38161-5) Harlequin Bks.

Defis, Projets et Textes dans l'Edition Critique au Canada see Challenges, Projects, Texts: Canadian Editing: Papers Given at the Conference on Editorial Problems, University of Toronto, 17-18, November, 1989

Deflection - Reflection in the Lyric Poetry of Charles D'Orleans. Rouben Cholakian. 1985. 25.00 (*0-916379-21-3*) Scripta.

Deflections of Concrete Structures: Proceedings of the American Concrete Institute Symposium, San Francisco, 1974. American Concrete Institute Deflections of Structures Symposium Staff. LC 73-94365. (American Concrete Institute Publication Ser.: No. SP-43). (Illus.). 643p. reprint ed. pap. 180.00 (*0-317-09994-9*, 2003786) Bks Demand.

Deflections of Concrete Structures, SP-86. 448p. pap. 103.50 (*0-317-39823-7*) ACI.

Defoaming: Theory & Industrial Applications. Ed. by P. R. Garrett. LC 92-29097. (Surfactant Science Ser.: Vol. 45). 344p. 1992. 145.00 (*0-8247-8770-6*) Dekker.

Defoe. Leslie Scalapino. (Sun & Moon Classics Ser.: No. 46). 420p. (Orig.). 1995. pap. 11.95 (*1-55713-163-5*) Sun & Moon CA.

Defoe & Economics: The Fortunes of Roxana in the History of Interpretation. Bram Dijkstra. LC 86-29691. 224p. 1987. text ed. 39.95 (*0-312-00535-0*) St Martin.

Defoe & Spiritual Autobiography. George A. Starr. LC 75-150419. 216p. 1971. reprint ed. 45.00 (*0-87752-138-7*) Gordian.

Defoe & the Idea of Fiction, 1713-1719. Geoffrey M. Sill. LC 82-60073. (Illus.). 185p. 1983. 32.50 (*0-87413-227-4*) U Delaware Pr.

Defoe Companion. J. R. Hammond. LC 92-39387. 192p. (C). 1993. lib. bdg. 54.00 (*0-389-21006-4*) B&N Imports.

***Defoe De-Attributions: A Critique of J. R. Moore's Checklist.** P. N. Furbank & W. R. Owens. LC 95-3671. 1995. write for info. (*1-85285-128-7*) Hambledon Press.

Defoe's Art of Fiction: Robinson Crusoe, Moll Flanders, Colonel Jack & Roxana. David Blewett. LC 79-12827. 188p. reprint ed. pap. 53.60 (*0-317-55636-3*, 2029324) Bks Demand.

Defoes Gesellschaftskonzeption. Klaus Degering. (Bochum Studies in English: No. 5). (Illus.). x, 512p. (Orig.). (GER.). 1977. pap. 37.00 (*90-6032-079-4*) Benjamins North Am.

Defoe's Perpetual Seekers: A Study of the Major Fiction. Virginia O. Birdsall. LC 83-46154. 208p. 1985. 32.50 (*0-8387-5076-1*) Bucknell U Pr.

Defoe's Politics: Parliament, Power, Kingship & Robinson Crusoe. Manuel Schonhorn. (Studies in Eighteenth-Century English Literature & Thought: No. 9). 224p. (C). 1991. 54.95 (*0-521-38452-4*) Cambridge U Pr.

Defoe's Sources for Robert Drury's Journal. John R. Moore. LC 72-6862. (English Literature Ser.: No. 33). 1972. reprint ed. lib. bdg. 46.95 (*0-8383-1656-5*) M S G Haskell Hse.

DeFord. David Shetzline. LC 89-25257. 224p. 1990. reprint ed. pap. 9.95 (*0-932576-76-1*) Breitenbush Bks.

DeFord Bailey: A Black Star in Early Country Music. David C. Morton & Charles K. Wolfe. LC 90-22519. (Illus.). 224p. (C). 1993. pap. 14.95 (*0-87049-792-8*) U of Tenn Pr.

Deforestation: Social Dynamics in Watersheds & Mountain Ecocystems. Ed. by D. C. Pitt. 224p. 1988. lib. bdg. 55.00 (*0-415-00456-X*) Routledge.

Deforestation & Government Policy. Malcolm Gillis & Robert Repetto. 34p. 1988. pap. 5.00 (*1-55815-037-4*) ICS Pr.

Deforestation in the Brazilian Amazon. Emilio F. Moran. Ed. by Dennis Conway. (Series on Environment & Development). 36p. (Orig.). 1992. pap. 2.00 (*1-881157-10-5*) In Ctr Global.

Deforestation in the Postwar Philippines. David M. Kummer. (Geography Research Papers). (Illus.). 216p. 1992. pap. text ed. 17.00 (*0-226-46169-6*) U Ch Pr.

Deforestation of Tropical Rain Forests: Economic Causes & Impact on Development. Torsten Amelung & Markus Diehl. 157p. (Orig.). 1992. pap. 54.00 (*3-16-145918-0*, Pub. by J C B Mohr GW) Coronet Bks.

***Deforestations of Tropical Rain Forests: Economic Causes & Impact on Development.** Torsten Amelung & Markus Diehl. 196p. 1992. pap. 45.00 (*0-472-08287-6*) U of Mich Pr.

Deforests of Avesnes see Collected Works of John W. De Forest

Deformation & Failure of Granular Materials: International Union of Theoretical & Applied Mechanics Symposium on Deformation & Failure of Granular Materials, Delft, 31 August to 3 September 1982. Ed. by P. A. Vermeer & H. J. Luger. 672p. (C). 1982. text ed. 150.00 (*90-6191-224-5*, Pub. by A A Balkema NE) Ashgate Pub Co.

Deformation & Flow of Solids: Proceedings of the International Union of Theoretical & Applied Mechanics Symposium, Madrid, Festokoerpors. International Union of Theoretical & Applied Mechanics Staff. Ed. by Richard Grammel. (Illus.). (ENG, FRE, GER & SPA.). 1956. 39.00 (*0-387-02095-0*) Spr-Verlag.

Deformation & Fracture Mechanics of Engineering Materials. 3rd ed. Richard W. Hertzberg. LC 88-14903. 704p. 1989. Net. text ed. write for info. (*0-471-63589-8*) Wiley.

Deformation & Strength of Ice. V. V. Lavrov. 170p. 1971. text ed. 46.50 (*0-7065-1098-4*, Pub. by Keter Pub IS) Coronet Bks.

Deformation & Strength of Materials. Paul Feltham. LC 67-70596. reprint ed. pap. 35.50 (*0-685-16138-2*, 2056142) Bks Demand.

Deformation Geometry for Material Scientists. C. N. Reid. LC 73-4716. 220p. 1974. 94.00 (*0-08-017237-7*, Pub. by Pergamon Repr UK) Franklin.

Deformation Measurements. Istvan Joo & Akos Detrekoi. 900p. 1983. 289.00 (*0-569-08754-6*, Pub. by Collets UK) Pro-Am Music.

***Deformation Measurements: Proceedings of the Third International Symposium on Deformation Measurements by Geodetic Methods.** Ed. by I. Joo & A. Detrekoi. 900p. (C). 1983. 177.00x (*963-05-3497-5*, Pub. by Akad Kiado HU) St Mut.

Deformation Measurements Workshop. 488p. 1986. 51.60 (*0-318-42976-4*, S290) Am Congrs Survey.

Deformation-Mechanism Maps: The Plasticity & Creep of Metals & Ceramics. H. J. Frost et al. (Illus.). 184p. 1982. 79.00 (*0-08-029338-7*, CRC Reprint) Franklin.

***Deformation Mechanisms, Rheology & Tectonics.** Ed. by R. J. Knipe & E. H. Rutter. (Geological Society Special Publication Classic). 528p. (C). 1994. pap. 40.00 (*1-897799-16-0*, Pub. by Geol Soc Pub Hse UK) AAPG.

Deformation Mechanisms, Testure & Anistrophy in Zirconium & Zircaloy. Ed. by Erich Tenckhoff. (Special Technical Publication Ser.: No. 966). (Illus.). 84p. 1988. pap. text ed. 35.00 (*0-8031-0959-8*, 04-966000-35) ASTM.

Deformation of Concrete Structures. D. Branson. 1977. text ed. 55.00 (*0-07-007240-X*) McGraw.

Deformation of Elastic Solids. Ajit K. Mal & Sarva J. Singh. 352p. 1990. text ed. 81.00 (*0-13-200700-2*) P-H.

Deformation of Metals During Rollings. Y. Tarnovskii & A. Pozdeyev. LC 63-10070. 1965. 138.00 (*0-08-010223-9*, Pub. by Pergamon Repr UK) Franklin.

Deformation of Solids - a Treatise on Strength of Materials. Amitabha Bhattacharyya. (C). 1989. 60.00 (*0-89771-382-6*, Current Dist) St Mut.

Deformation Processes in Minerals, Ceramics & Rocks. Ed. by D. J. Barber et al. (Mineralogical Society Ser.: No. 1). 256p. 1989. 110.00 (*0-04-445088-5*) Routledge Chapman & Hall.

Deformation Processing. Walter A. Backofen. LC 71-132054. (Engineering Science Ser.). (C). 1972. text ed. write for info. (*0-201-00388-0*) Addison-Wesley.

Deformation, Processing, & Structure: Papers Presented at the 1982 ASM Materials Science Seminar. ASM Materials Science Seminar Staff. Ed. by George Krauss. LC 83-48774. (Illus.). 540p. reprint ed. pap. 153.90 (*0-8357-6086-3*, 2034312) Bks Demand.

Deformation Properties of Clad Sheet Metals (Copper-Mild Steel Sandwich Sheet) University of Aston in Birmingham Staff. 188p. 1970. 28.40 (*0-317-34505-2*, 166) Intl Copper.

Deformation Quantization for Actions of Rd. Marc A. Rieffel. LC 93-6114. (Memoirs Ser.: No. 506). 116p. 1993. pap. 29.00 (*0-8218-2575-5*) Am Math.

An Asterisk (*) at the beginning of an entry indicates that the title is appearing in BIP for the first time.

Deformation Theory & Quantum Groups with Applications to Mathematical Physics: (Proceedings of a AMS-IMS-SIAM 1990 Joint Summer Research Conference Held June 14-20 at the University of Massachusetts, Amherst, with Support from the National Science Foundation) Ed. by Murray Gerstenhaber & Jim Stasheff. LC 92-13890. (Contemporary Mathematics Ser.: Vol. 134). 377p. 1992. 55.00 (*0-8218-5141-1*) Am Math.

Deformation Theory of Algebras & Structures & Applications. Ed. by Michiel Hazewinkel & Murray Gerstenhaber. (C). 1988. lib. bdg. 280.00 (*90-277-2804-6*) Kluwer Ac.

Deformation Theory of Pseudogroup Structures. V. W. Guillemin & Shlomo Sternberg. LC 52-42839. (Memoirs Ser.: No. 1/64). 80p. 1966. pap. 16.00 (*0-8218-1264-5*, MEMO 1/64) Am Math.

Deformation Twining: Proceedings, Gainesville, Florida, March 21-22, 1963. Ed. by R. E. Reed-Hill et al. LC 64-8380. (Metallurgical Society Conference Ser.: Vol. 25). 476p. reprint ed. pap. 135.70 (*0-317-10405-5*, 2001513) Bks Demand.

Deformations Infinitesmales des Structures Conformer Plates. J. Gasqui & H. L. Goldschmidt. (Progress in Mathematics Ser.: No. 52). (FRE.). 1985. text ed. 45.00 (*0-8176-3260-3*) Birkhauser.

Deformations of Coherent Analytic Sheaves with Compact Supports. Yum-Tong Siu & Gunther Trautmann. LC 80-26105. (MEMO Ser.: No. 29/238). 155p. 1981. pap. 19.00 (*0-8218-2238-1*, MEMO 29/238) Am Math.

Deformations of Mathematical Structures: Complex Analysis with Physical Applications. Ed. by Julian Lawrynowicz. (C). 1988. lib. bdg. 157.50 (*0-7923-0023-8*) Kluwer Ac.

Deformations of Mathematical Structures II: Hurwitz-Type Structures & Applications to Surface Physics: Selected Papers from the Seminar on Deformations, Lodz'-Malinka 1988-92. Ed. by Julian Lawrinowicz. LC 93-33466. 480p. (C). 1994. lib. bdg. 199.00 (*0-7923-2576-1*) Kluwer Ac.

Deformations of Nilpotent Matrices Over Rings & Reduction of Analytic Families of Meromorphic Differential Equations. D. Babbitt & V. Varadarajan. LC 85-5997. (Memoirs of the AMS Ser. No. 325: No. 55/325). 147p. 1985. pap. text ed. 26.00 (*0-8218-2326-4*, MEMO 55/325) Am Math.

Deformities of Dr. Samuel Johnson: Selected from His Works. 2nd ed. John Callander. LC 92-23649. (Augustan Reprints Ser.: No. 147-148 (1971)). reprint ed. 18.50 (*0-404-70147-7*, PR3534) AMS Pr.

Defrauding America: A Pattern of Related Scandals. 2nd ed. Rodney Stich. LC 93-74654. 650p. 1994. pap. 25.00 (*0-932438-08-3*) Diablo West Pr. A highly documented expose of CIA misconduct within the United States & related scandals written by a government insider with the help of deep-cover CIA operatives. Specifics of CIA drug trafficking & drug-money laundering within the United States, liaison with organized crime, involvement in Arkansas politics; October Surprise; Inslaw; Iran-Contra; Chapter 11 judicial corruption; BCCI; pattern of killings, mysterious deaths & persecution of whistle-blowers by the CIA, Justice Department & federal judges; Mossad's symbiotic role with the CIA; aided & abetted by government & non-government checks & balances; & much more. UNCLASSIFIED: "This extraordinary book...required reading for anyone concerned with national security system abuses...this moving book by a man of integrity...it is a hell of a good read." DICK GREGORY: "Should be on top of every Bible;" JOHN AUSTIN HOLLYWOOD REVIEW: "The most explosive book on the market;" ANN HARP: "A guaranteed can't-put-it-down thriller...a wake-up call to understand & share with each other what's going on behind the scenes." Parallel publication UNFRIENDLY SKIES, by author Rodney Stich, guest on over 2,000 radio & television shows since 1978. Call or write for information to order, Diablo Western Press, P.O. Box 5, Alamo, CA 94507, 510-944-1930, FAX 510-295-1203. ***Publisher Provided Annotation.***

***Defrostings.** Carolyn W. Greenlee. (Illus.). 34p. 1993. pap. 8.50 (*1-887400-02-8*) Earthen Vessel Prodns.

DeFunis vs. Odegaard & the University of Washington - the University Admissions Case, 3 vols., Set. Ed. by Ann F. Ginger. LC 74-13343. 1500p. 1974. lib. bdg. 120.00 (*0-379-00442-9*) Oceana.

***Defusing the Software Crisis Information Systems Flexibility Through Data Independence.** Martin Boogaard. (Tinbergen Institute Research Ser.: No. 79, Series B). 312p. 1994. pap. 26.50 (*90-5170-289-2*, Pub. by Thesis Pubs NE) IBD Ltd.

Defusing the Toxics Threat: Controlling Pesticides & industrial Waste. Sandra Postel. (Worldwatch Papers). 70p. (Orig.). 1987. pap. 5.00 (*0-916468-80-1*) Worldwatch Inst.

***Defy Mediocrity: The Employee's 90-Minute Guide to Excellence.** Derrick W. Welch. 144p. (Orig.). 1995. pap. 10.95 (*1-886262-01-2*) LeeMar Pubng.

Defy Not the Heart. Johanna Lindsey. 416p. (Orig.). 1989. mass mkt. 5.99 (*0-380-75299-9*) Avon.

Defy the Eagle. Lynn Bartlett. (Historical Ser.). 1994. mass mkt. 3.99 (*0-373-28807-7*, 1-28807-5) Harlequin Bks.

Defy the Wind. Kate O'Donnell. 368p. (Orig.). 1987. pap. 3.95 (*0-380-75396-0*) Avon.

Defying Gravity: The Making of Newton. Doug Menuez & Markos Kounalakis. Ed. by Julie Livingston. (Illus.). 224p. 1993. 29.95 (*0-941831-94-9*) Beyond Words Pub.

Defying the Gods: Inside the New Frontiers of Organ Transplants. Scott McCartney. LC 93-38976. 298p. 1994. text ed. 22.00 (*0-02-582820-7*) Macmillan.

Defying the Holocaust: A Diplomat's Report. Aba Gefen. LC 93-9283. (Studies in Judaica & the Holocaust: No. 11). 248p. 1993. lib. bdg. 33.00x (*0-89370-366-4*); pap. 23.00x (*0-89370-466-0*) Borgo Pr.

Defying the Odds. Ed Morales & Mitzi Morales. LC 91-68356. 224p. (Orig.). 1992. pap. 8.95 (*0-89221-219-5*) New Leaf.

Degarmo's Wife & Other Stories. David C. Phillips. (Collected Works of David G. Phillips). 1988. reprint ed. lib. bdg. 59.00 (*0-7812-1345-2*) Rprt Serv.

Degarmo's Wife & Other Stories see Collected Works of David G. Phillips

Degas. (Phidal Art Ser.). (Illus.). 60p. 1990. 9.95 (*2-89393-047-6*, Pub. by Phidal CN) Firefly Bks Ltd.

Degas. Patrick Bade. (Masterworks Ser.). (Illus.). 144p. 1991. 15.99 (*0-517-05378-0*) Random Hse Value.

Degas. Catherine Barry. (Pocket Painters Ser.). (Illus.). 1994. 6.50 (*0-517-59970-8*, Clarkson Potter) Crown Bks Yng Read.

Degas. Robert Gordon & Andrew Forge. 1988. 75.00 (*0-8109-1142-6*) Abrams.

Degas. Robert Gordon & Andrew Forge. Tr. by Richard Howard. (Illus.). 288p. 1991. pap. 34.98 (*0-8109-8107-6*, Abradale Pr) Abrams.

Degas. Eduard Huettinger. (Crown Art Library). (Illus.). 96p. 1988. 14.95 (*0-517-00502-6*, Crown) Crown Pub Group.

***Degas.** Edward Huettinger. 1995. 12.00 (*0-517-88418-6*) Random.

Degas. Sebastian Melmoth. 1993. 5.98 (*1-55521-826-1*) Bk Sales Inc.

Degas. Daniel C. Rich. (Library of Great Painters). (Illus.). (Orig.). 1966. 49.50 (*0-8109-0067-X*) Abrams.

Degas. Daniel C. Rich. (Masters of Art Ser.). (Illus.). (Orig.). 1985. 22.95 (*0-8109-0829-8*) Abrams.

***Degas.** Anne Roquebert. (Grandes Monografias). (Illus.). 200p. (SPA.). 1993. 200.00 (*84-343-0538-0*) Elliots Bks.

Degas. Julius Meier-Graefe. (Fine Art Ser.). (Illus.). 128p. 1988. reprint ed. pap. 4.50 (*0-486-25702-9*) Dover.

Degas. Keith Roberts. (Color Library). (Illus.). 128p. (C). 1994. reprint ed. pap. text ed. 14.95 (*0-7148-2757-6*, Pub. by Phaidon Press UK) Chronicle Bks.

***Degas.** Keith Roberts. (Color Library). (Illus.). 128p. (C). 1994. reprint ed. 19.95 (*0-7148-3212-X*, Pub. by Phaidon Press UK) Chronicle Bks.

Degas: A Postcard Book. (Postcard Book Ser.). (Illus.). 64p. (Orig.). 1989. pap. 7.95 (*0-89471-712-X*) Running Pr.

Degas: An Intimate Portrait. Ambroise Vollard. 96p. 1986. reprint ed. pap. 4.95 (*0-486-25131-4*) Dover.

Degas: Dancers. Pierre Cabanne. (Rhythm & Color One Ser.). 1970. 9.95 (*0-8288-9506-6*) Fr & Eur.

Degas: His Life & Work. Denys Sutton. (Illus.). 344p. 1991. 39.98 (*0-89660-024-6*, Artabras) Abbeville Pr.

Degas: Images of Women. Richard Kendall et al. (Illus.). 72p. 1990. pap. 20.00 (*0-295-96959-8*) U of Wash Pr.

Degas: Impressions of a Great Master. Gerhard Gruitrooy. 1994. 14.98 (*0-8317-5779-5*) Smithmark.

Degas: In Search of His Technique. Denis Rouart. LC 87-36083. (Illus.). 140p. 1988. pap. 25.00 (*0-8478-0949-8*) Rizzoli Intl.

Degas: Paintings. LC 93-3824. (Illus.). 1993. 4.99 (*0-517-09356-1*) Random Hse Value.

Degas: The Artist's Mind. Theodore Reff. LC 87-11827. (Paperbacks in AA History Ser.). (Illus.). 352p. 1987. pap. 22.50 (*0-674-19543-4*) HUP.

Degas: The Man & His Art. Henri Loyrette. Tr. by I. Mark Paris. (Discoveries Ser.). (Illus.). 192p. 1993. pap. 12.95 (*0-8109-2897-3*) Abrams.

Degas: The Painted Gesture. Jacqueline Loumaye. LC 93-33682. (Art for Children Ser.). (Illus.). 64p. (J). (gr. 3 up). 1994. lib. bdg. 14.95 (*0-7910-2809-7*) Chelsea Hse.

Degas & the Business of Art: A Cotton Office in New Orleans. Marilyn R. Brown. LC 92-34466. (College Art Association Monographs on the Fine Arts: Vol. LI). (Illus.). 176p. 1993. 57.50 (*0-271-00944-6*) Pa St U Pr.

Degas Artists & Their Work. Jean J. Leveque. 1990. 12.99 (*0-517-69481-6*) Random Hse Value.

Degas at the Ballet. (PostBox Collections). (Illus.). 1990. Shrinkwrapped. boxed 10.95 (*0-87701-776-X*) Chronicle Bks.

***Degas by Himself.** Richard Kendall. 1994. 32.98 (*0-7858-0166-9*) Bk Sales Inc.

Degas' Complete Graphic Work. Sue W. Reed & Barbara S. Shapiro. (Painter As Printmaker Ser.). (Illus.). 344p. 1984. 125.00 (*1-55660-196-4*); pap. 75.00 (*0-915346-89-3*) A Wofsy Fine Arts.

Degas, Danse, Dessin. Paul Valery. (Idees Ser.). (FRE.). pap. 7.95 (*2-07-035481-4*) Schoenhof.

Degas et Son Oeuvre, 4 Vols. Paul-Andre Lemoisne. LC 83-48625. (Illus.). 1500p. 1984. 473.00 (*0-8240-5526-8*) Garland.

Degas et Son Oeuvre: A Supplement. Comp. by Philippe Brame et al. LC 83-48626. (Illus.). 200p. 1984. 97.00 (*0-8240-5525-X*) Garland.

Degas in the Clark Collection. Rafael Fernandez & Alexandra R. Murphy. LC 87-6115. (Illus.). 79p. (Orig.). 1987. pap. 14.95 (*0-931102-23-5*) S & F Clark Art.

Degas Landscapes. Richard Kendall. (Illus.). 232p. Date not set. 55.00 (*0-300-05837-3*) Yale U Pr.

Degas Monotypes: Essay, Catalogue & Checklist see Exhibition Catalogues from the Fogg Art Museum

Degas Pastels. Jean S. Boggs & Anne Maheux. (Illus.). 200p. 1992. 75.00 (*0-8076-1276-6*) Braziller.

Degas Pastels. Anne F. Maheux. (Illus.). 88p. 1988. pap. 19.95 (*0-88884-547-2*, Pub. by Natl Gallery CN) U Ch Pr.

***Degas Portraits.** Ed. by Marianne Karabelnik & Felix Baumann. (Illus.). 327p. 1995. 60.00 (*1-85894-014-1*) U of Wash Pr.

Degas Sketchbook: The Halevy Sketchbook, 1877-1883. Edgar Degas. (Illus.). 64p. 1989. pap. 5.95 (*0-486-25926-9*) Dover.

Degas, the Ballet, & Me. Tom Van Beek. (Illus.). 48p. (J). (gr. 2-7). 1993. 12.95 (*1-56288-424-7*) Checkerboard.

Degas to Matisse: The Maurice Wertheim Collection. John O'Brian. (Illus.). 176p. 1988. 39.95 (*0-8109-1138-8*) Abrams.

***Degas to Matisse: The Maurice Wertheim Collection.** John O'Brian. (Illus.). 176p. 1995. pap. 19.95 (*0-916724-65-4*, 4654) Harvard Art Mus.

Degas to Picasso: Modern Masters from the Smooke Collection. Carol S. Eliel. LC 86-27435. (Illus.). 144p. (Orig.). 1987. pap. 24.95 (*0-87587-137-2*) LA Co Art Mus.

Degas's Atelier at Auction: Paintings, Pastels & Drawings, Paris, 1918-1919, 2 vols., Set. rev. ed. Edgar Degas. (ENG & FRE.). 1989. 295.00 (*1-55660-025-9*) A Wofsy Fine Arts.

Degas's Complete Sculpture: A Catalogue Raisonne. rev. ed. John Rewald. (Illus.). 216p. 1990. 125.00 (*1-55660-045-3*) A Wofsy Fine Arts.

Degassers: Degassers. Walter Liljestrand & Gordon Lawson. LC 83-161604. (Mud Equipment Manual Ser.: No. 5). (Illus.). 94p. (Orig.). 1985. pap. 25.00 (*0-87201-617-X*) Gulf Pub.

DeGaulle's Foreign Policy: 1944-1946. Anton W. DePorte. LC 67-29624. 340p. 1968. 36.00 (*0-674-19550-7*) HUP.

Degen Discus. Bernd Degen. (Illus.). 112p. 1989. lib. bdg. 24.95 (*0-86622-086-0*, TS-134) TFH Pubns.

Degeneracy Crisis & Victorian Youth. Thomas E. Jordan. LC 91-39941. 335p. (C). 1992. 59.50 (*0-7914-1245-8*); pap. 19.95 (*0-7914-1246-6*) State U NY Pr.

Degeneracy Graphs & Simplex Cycling. P. Zornig. Ed. by Martin J. Beckmann & W. Krelle. (Lecture Notes in Economics & Mathematical Systems Ser.: Vol. 357). (Illus.). xv, 194p. 1991. pap. 35.00 (*0-387-54593-X*) Spr-Verlag.

Degeneracy Graphs & the Neighbourhood Problem. H. J. Kruse. (Lecture Notes in Economics & Mathematical Systems Ser.: Vol. 260). viii, 128p. 1986. pap. 21.60 (*0-387-16049-3*) Spr-Verlag.

Degenerate Art: The Fate of the Avant-Garde in Nazi Germany. Stephanie Barron. (Illus.). 424p. 1991. 75.00 (*0-8109-3653-4*) Abrams.

Degenerate Diffusions: Proceedings of the IMA Workshop "Degenerate Diffusions" Held at the University of Minnesota from May 13-18, 1991. Ed. by Wei-ming Ni et al. LC 93-10431. (IMA Volumes in Mathematics & Its Applications Ser.: Vol. 47). 1993. Acid-free paper. 49.00 (*0-387-94068-5*) Spr-Verlag.

Degenerate Elliptic Equations. Serge Levendorskii. LC 93-13188. (Mathematics & Its Applications Ser.: Vol. 258). 460p. (C). 1993. lib. bdg. 186.50 (*0-7923-2305-X*) Kluwer Ac.

Degenerate Moderns. E. Michael Jones. LC 92-75406. (Illus.). 259p. (Orig.). 1993. pap. 17.95 (*0-89870-447-2*) Ignatius Pr.

Degenerate Parabolic Equations. Emmanuele DiBenedetto. LC 93-285. 1993. 39.00 (*0-387-94020-0*) Spr-Verlag.

Degenerate Principal Series for Sp(2n) Robert Gustafson. LC 81-13033. (Memoirs of the American Mathematical Society Ser.: No. 33/248). 81p. 1981. pap. 16.00 (*0-8218-2248-9*, MEMO 33/248) Am Math.

Degenerate Principal Series for Symplectic Groups. Chris Jantzen. LC 92-42412. (Memoirs of the American Mathematical Society Ser.: No. 488). 111p. 1993. 30.00 (*0-8218-2549-6*) Am Math.

Degenerates. Norman E. Mutka. 175p. (Orig.). 1994. pap. 8.95 (*0-9637082-0-1*) N E Mutka. THE DEGENERATES is the story of family life as it existed in the 1950s & 1960s. It highlights a time when people lived by values, whether they were spiritual, family, etc., or a combination of all of them. The following is a review of the book as seen through the eyes of a book critic. This novel is also under consideration for the possibility of a motion picture. "THE DEGENERATES is a thought-provoking tale that traces Kelly Waterman's spiritual growth as he develops into a responsible young man. The compelling plot also details intimacies regarding the Waterman family & relays the activities concerning the quaint but aged Soapwood Church located in Stapleton, Oregon. The story line deals with the morality taught through religious beliefs, the significance of seeking redemption, & the beauty of love. Colloquial dialogue & vivid descriptions enhance this story's endearing theme while your unique character development adds to the overall quality of this work." To order, write to Norman E. Mutka, 5214 Great View Ave. N., Brooklyn Center, MN 55429. Or call (612) 537-5727 collect. ***Publisher Provided Annotation.***

Degenerates of Lake Tahoe: A Study of Persistence in the Social World of Horse Race Gambling. John Rosecrance. (American University Studies: Anthropology & Science: Ser. XI, Vol. 8). 169p. (C). 1985. text ed. 32.00 (*0-8204-0187-0*) P Lang Pubs.

Degeneration. Max Nordau. LC 93-8474. xxxvi, 566p. 1993. pap. 18.00 (*0-8032-8367-9*, Bison Books) U of Nebr Pr.

Degeneration & the Sanity of Art. Max Nordau & George Bernard Shaw. 1972. 250.00 (*0-8490-0015-7*) Gordon Pr.

Degeneration, Culture & the Novel: 1880-1940. William Greenslade. 388p. (C). 1994. 59.95 (*0-521-41665-5*) Cambridge U Pr.

Degeneration in the Great French Masters. Jean Carrere. Tr. by Joseph McCabe. LC 67-26722. (Essay Index Reprint Ser.). 1977. 23.95 (*0-8369-0277-7*) Ayer.

Degeneration of Abelian Varieties. G. Faltings & C. L. Chai. Ed. by E. Bombieri et al. (Ergebnisse der Mathematik und Ihrer Grenzgebiete Ser.). 320p. 1990. 49.00 (*0-387-52015-5*) Spr-Verlag.

Degenerative Disease of the Cervical Spine. Ed. by Paul R. Cooper. (Neurosurgical Topics Ser.). 175p. 1993. 90.00 (*1-879284-04-9*) Am Assn Neuro.

***Degenerative Diseases: Movement Disorders.** Luigi Amaducci. Ed. by J. Timothy Greenamyre. (Current Opinion in Neurology Ser.). (Illus.). (Orig.). 1994. pap. text ed. 49.95 (*1-85922-677-9*) Current Science.

Degenerative Joint Diseases: Degenerative Joints, Vol. 2. Ed. by G. Verbruggen & E. M. Veys. (International Congress Ser.: No. 668). 398p. 1986. 122.75 (*0-444-80705-5*, Excerpta Medica) Elsevier.

Degenerative Retinopathies: Advances in Clinical & Genetic Research. Peter Humphries et al. 1991. 89.95 (*0-8493-0187-4*, RE661) CRC Pr.

DeGowin & DeGowin's Diagnostic Examination. 6th ed. Richard L. DeGowin. LC 93-38286. 1993. 35.00 (*0-07-016338-3*) Hlth Prof Div.

DeGowin & DeGowin's Diagnostic Examination. 6th ed. Richard L. DeGowin. LC 93-38286. 1072p. 1994. pap. text ed. 35.00 (*0-07-016258-1*) Hlth Prof Div.

Degradable Materials. Ed. by Barenberg. 1990. 72.00 (*0-8493-4274-0*, QP801) CRC Pr.

Degradable Plastics: Impact on Litter & Solid Waste Disposal. 161p. 1992. 2,650.00 (*0-89336-933-0*, P-112R) BCC.

Degradable Polymers. 1992. 1,000.00 (*0-89336-911-X*, TAP-13) BCC.

Degradation & Stabilisation of Polymers. Ed. by G. Geuskens. (Illus.). ix, 203p. 1991. 68.00 (*0-85334-639-9*, Pub. by Elsevier Applied Sci UK) Elsevier.

Degradation & Stabilisation of Polyolefins. Ed. by N. S. Allen. (Illus.). 384p. 1983. 97.25 (*0-85334-194-X*, Pub. by Elsevier Applied Sci UK) Elsevier.

Degradation & Stabilisation of PVC. E. D. Owen. (Illus.). 314p. 1984. 90.00 (*0-85334-265-2*, I-219-84, Pub. by Elsevier Applied Sci UK) Elsevier.

Degradation & Stabilization of Polymers: A Series of Comprehensive Reviews. Ed. by H. H. Jellinek & H. Kachi. 720p. 1989. 228.25 (*0-444-87402-X*) Elsevier.

Degradation & Stabilization of Polymers: Theory & Practice. Ed. by G. E. Zaikov. 205p. 1994. text ed. 82.00 (*1-56072-122-7*) Nova Sci Pubs.

Degradation & Stabilization of Vinylchloride Based Polymers. K. S. Minsker et al. LC 87-36029. 520p. 1988. 216.00 (*0-08-034857-2*, Pub. by Pergamon Repr UK) Franklin.

Degradation Mechanisms in III-V Compound Semiconductor Devices & Structures: Symposium Proceedings Ser., Vol. 184. Ed. by V. Swaminathan et al. 1990. text ed. 35.00 (*1-55899-073-9*) Materials Res.

Degradation of Bioactive Substances: Physiology & Pathophysiology. Jens H. Henriksen. (Illus.). 368p. 1991. 213.00 (*0-8493-6858-8*, QP171) CRC Pr.

Degradation of Chemical Carcinogens. M. W. Slein & E. B. Sansone. LC 79-19671. 184p. (Orig.). 1980. lib. bdg. 32.50 (*0-442-24489-4*) Van Nos Reinhold.

Degradation of Dental Polymers. Jean-Francois Roulet. (Illus.). xiv, 228p. 1986. 158.50 (*3-8055-4320-4*) S Karger.

Degradation of Filled Polymers: High-Temperature & Thermal-Oxidative Processes. M. T. Bryk. 192p. 1991. text ed. write for info. (*0-13-202490-X*) P-H.

Degradation of Herbicides. Ed. by Philip C. Kearney & D. D. Kaufman. LC 68-28981. 406p. reprint ed. pap. 115.80 (*0-318-35005-X*, 2030865) Bks Demand.

Degradation of Lignocellulosics in Ruminants & in Industrial Processes. J. M. Van Der Meer. 1987. 41.50 (*1-85166-165-4*, Pub. by Elsevier Applied Sci UK) Elsevier.

Degradation of Metals in the Atmosphere. Ed. by Sheldon W. Dean & T. S. Lee. (Special Technical Publication Ser.: No. 965). (Illus.). 455p. 1988. text ed. 55.00 (*0-8031-0966-0*, 04-965000-27) ASTM.

D

An Asterisk (*) at the beginning of an entry indicates that the title is appearing in BIP for the first time.

1857

Degradation of Pesticides, Desication & Defoliation, ACh-Receptors as Targets. (Chemistry of Plant Protection Ser.: Vol. 2). (Illus.). 265p. 1989. 129.00 (*0-387-13488-3*, 2867) Spr-Verlag.

Degradation of Polymers see Comprehensive Chemical Kinetics

Degradation of the Democratic Dogma. Henry Adams. 12.00 (*0-8446-1007-0*) Peter Smith.

Degradation of the Democratic Dogma. Henry Adams. (Works of Henry Adams). 1989. reprint ed. lib. bdg. 79.00 (*0-7812-1445-9*) Rprt Serv.

Degradation of the Land. Mark Cherrington. (Earth at Risk Ser.). (Illus.). (YA). (gr. 5 up). 1992. lib. bdg. 19.95 (*0-7910-1589-0*) Chelsea Hse.

Degradation Phenomena on Polymeric Biomaterials: Proceedings of the 4th International ITV Conference on Biomaterials, Denkendorf, September 3-5, 1991. Ed. by H. I. Planck et al. LC 92-14876. (Illus.). x, 197p. 1992. 89.00 (*0-387-55548-X*) Spr-Verlag.

Degradation, Retention & Dispersion of Pollutants in Groundwater: Proceedings of the IAWPRC Seminar Held in Copenhagen, Denmark, 12-14 September 1984. Ed. by E. Arvin. LC 82-645900. 432p. 1985. pap. 48.00 (*0-08-033658-2*, Pub. by PPL UK) Elsevier.

Degradative Processes in Heart & Skeletal Muscle. K. Wildenthal. (Research Monographs in Cell & Tissue Physiology: Vol. 3). 462p. 1980. 153.50 (*0-444-80235-5*) Elsevier.

Degrading the Grading Myths: A Primer of Alternatives to Grades & Marks. Ed. by Sidney B. Simon & James A. Bellanca. LC 76-20413. 160p. 1976. pap. 6.00 (*0-87120-080-5*, 611-76082) Assn Supervision.

DeGraffenried: History of the DeGraffenried Family, from 1191 to 1925. T. P. DeGraffenried. (Illus.). 282p. 1992. reprint ed. lib. bdg. 54.50 (*0-8328-1777-5*); reprint ed. pap. 44.50 (*0-8328-1778-3*) Higginson Bk Co.

Degre Zero de l'Ecriture. Roland Barthes. (FRE.). 1953. 29.95 (*0-686-53930-3*, F1870); pap. 10.95 (*0-8288-9059-5*) Fr & Eur.

Degree Analysis: Chandra Symbols In the Horoscope, Pt. II. John Sandbach. 145p. 1984. 5.00 (*0-930706-14-5*) Seek-It Pubns.

***Degree Book of the Independent Order of Good Templars (1854)** 1995. pap. 7.95 (*1-56459-489-0*) Kessinger Pub.

***Degree of Guilt.** Richard Patterson. 1994. pap. 5.98 (*0-517-13072-6*) Random Hse Value.

Degree of Guilt. Richard N. Patterson. LC 92-54446. 1992. 23.00 (*0-679-42064-9*) Knopf.

Degree of Guilt. Richard N. Patterson. 1993. 25.00 (*0-679-42211-0*) Random.

Degree of Guilt. Richard N. Patterson. 1993. reprint ed. mass mkt. 6.99 (*0-345-38184-X*) Ballantine.

Degree of Order. Timothy DeVinney. (Illus.). 199p. (Orig.). 1993. pap. 12.00 (*960-7459-03-2*, Pub. by Talos Pr GR) Bosphorus Bks.

Degree Planning & Prior Learning. 2nd ed. Robert H. McKenzie. 176p. 1991. per., pap. text ed. 17.95 (*0-8403-7145-4*) Kendall-Hunt.

Degree Theory for Equivariant Maps, the General S1-Action. Jorge Ize et al. LC 92-28573. (Memoirs of the American Mathematical Society Ser.: No. 481). 179p. 1992. 30.00 (*0-8218-2542-9*) Am Math.

Degree Words. Dwight Bolinger. (Janua Linguarum, Series Major: No. 53). 1972. text ed. 59.00 (*90-279-2239-X*) Mouton.

D

Degrees. Vanna Bonta. Ed. by Luisa Lorona. LC 89-51378. (Illus.). 96p. (Orig.). 1990. pap. 12.95 (*0-912339-05-5*) Meridian Hse.

Degrees for Jobs: Employer Expectations of Higher Education. Judith Roizen & Mark Jepson. 225p. 1985. pap. write for info. (*0-335-15617-7*, Open Univ Pr) Taylor & Francis.

Degrees for Jobs: Employer Expectations of Higher Education. Judith Roizen & Mark Jepson. LC 85-15343. 224p. 1985. pap. 38.00 (*1-85059-005-2*, Open Univ Pr) Taylor & Francis.

Degrees of Deviance: Student Accounts of Their Deviant Behavior. Ed. by Stuart Henry. 149p. (C). 1990. reprint ed. pap. text ed. 12.50 (*0-88133-500-2*) Sheffield WI.

Degrees of Deviance: Student Accounts of Their Deviant Behaviour. Stuart Henry. 1989. text ed. 59.95 (*0-566-05674-7*, Pub. by Avebury Pub UK) Ashgate Pub Co.

Degrees of Difference: Higher Education in the 1990s. Patrick Ainley. 256p. (C). 1994. pap. 25.00 (*0-85315-804-5*, Pub. by Lawrence & Wishart UK) Humanities.

Degrees of Difference: Higher Education in the 1990s. Patrick Ainley. 256p. 1994. pap. 25.00 (*0-685-75296-8*, Pub. by Lawrence & Wishart UK) Humanities.

Degrees of Difficulty. Vladimir Shatayev. Tr. by Deborah Piranian. LC 87-14885. (Illus.). 208p. (Orig.). 1987. pap. 10.95 (*0-89886-013-X*) Mountaineers.

Degrees of Disaster. Jeff Wheelwright. 1994. 24.00 (*0-671-70241-6*) S&S Trade.

***Degrees of Equality: The American Association of University Women & The Challenge of Twentieth Century Feminism.** Susan Levine. LC 94-44693. (Critical Perspectives on the Past Ser.). 1995. 29.95 (*1-56639-326-4*) Temple U Pr.

Degrees of Guidance: Essays on Twentieth-Century American Photography. Peter C. Bunnell. (Illus.). 272p. (C). 1993. 59.95 (*0-521-32751-2*) Cambridge U Pr.

***Degrees of Knowledge.** Jacques Maritain. Ed. by Ralph McInerny. Tr. by Gerald B. Phelan. LC 94-45159. (Collected Works of Jacques Maritain: Vol. 7). (ENG & FRE.). (C). 1995. text ed. 34.95x (*0-268-00876-0*) U of Notre Dame Pr.

Degrees of the Zodiac. Donna Henson. LC 81-65534. 80p. 1981. 7.00 (*0-86690-009-8*, W2454-014) Am Fed Astrologers.

Degrees of the Zodiac Symbolised. 2nd ed. Charubel. 136p. 1970. spiral bd. 4.40 (*0-7873-0165-5*) Mokelumne.

Degrees of Unsolvability. Gerald Sacks. (Annals of Mathematics Studies: No. 55). (Orig.). 1963. pap. 35.00 (*0-691-07941-2*) Princeton U Pr.

Degrees of Unsolvability: Local & Global Theory. M. Lerman. (Perspectives in Mathematical Logic Ser.). (Illus.). 307p. 1983. 103.00 (*0-387-12155-2*) Spr-Verlag.

Degrees Offered see College Blue Book

Degrees Offered by Coll. & Sub. see College Blue Book

Degres. Michel Butor. (FRE.). 1978. pap. 19.95 (*0-7859-2748-4*) Fr & Eur.

Degres. Michel Butor. (Imaginaire Ser.). (FRE.). 1960. 18.95 (*2-07-029734-9*) Schoenhof.

***DeGustibus Presents the Great Cooks' Cookbooks: French Cooking for the Home.** Arlene Feltman-Sailhac. 1995. 12.98 (*1-884822-15-0*) Blck Dog & Leventhal.

Dehiscence. John Taggart. 62p. (Orig.). 1984. pap. 5.00 (*0-87924-050-4*) Membrane Pr.

***Dehumanization of Art; & Other Essays on Art, Culture, & Literature.** Jose Ortega y Gasset. LC 68-8963. (Princeton Paperbacks Ser.: Vol. 128). reprint ed. pap. 59.90 (*0-7837-9281-6*, 2060020) Bks Demand.

***Dehumanizing the Vulnerable: Linguistic Oppression & Its Life-Affirming Challenges.** William Brennan. LC 94-41824. (Values & Ethics Ser.: Vol. 11). 305p. 1995. 22.95 (*0-8294-0822-3*, Campion Bks); pap. 13.95 (*0-8294-0821-5*, Campion Bks) Loyola Univ Pr.

Dehumanizing Women: Treating Persons As Sex Objects. Linda LeMoncheck. (New Feminist Perspectives Ser.). 180p. 1985. 45.00 (*0-8476-7331-6*) Rowman.

Dehumanizing Women: Treating Persons As Sex Objects. Linda LeMoncheck. (New Feminist Perspectives Ser.). 184p. 1985. pap. 16.00 (*0-8476-7386-3*) Rowman.

Dehydrator Cookbook. Joanna White. (Illus.). 192p. (Orig.). 1992. pap. 8.95 (*1-55867-067-X*, Nitty Gritty Ckbks) Bristol Pub Ent CA.

***Dehydrator Delights: A Practical Guide to Using Your Food Dehydrator.** Noreen Thomas. (Illus.). 1994. pap. text ed. write for info. (*0-9643087-0-3*) Doubting Thomas.

Dei Gloria Intacta. Jan Van Rijckenborgh. 244p. (SPA.). 1987. pap. 18.00 (*84-87055-09-5*) Rosycross Pr.

Dei Gloria Intacta: The Christian Mystery of Initiation of the Holy Rosycross for the New Era. J. Van Rickenborgh. (Rosicrucian Ser.). Orig. Title: Dutch. 252p. 1988. 23.00 (*90-70053-17-9*) Rosycross Pr.

Deicing Chemicals & Snow Control. (Research Record Ser.: No. 1157). 53p. 1988. 9.00 (*0-309-04669-6*) Transport Res Bd.

Deidad de Cristo. Evis L. Carballosa. 168p. (SPA.). 1982. pap. 4.99 (*0-8254-1102-5*) Kregel.

Deification in Christ: The Nature of the Human Person. Nellas & Panayiotis. LC 86-31479. (Contemporary Greek Theologians Ser.: No. 5). 254p. (Orig.). 1991. pap. 13.95 (*0-88141-030-6*) St Vladimirs.

Deification of Abstract Ideas in Roman Literature & Inscriptions. Harold L. Axtell. 100p. (C). 1987. reprint ed. lib. bdg. 30.00 (*0-89241-159-7*) Caratzas.

Deification of Man: St. Gregory Palamas & the Orthodox Tradition. Georgios I. Mantzaridis. Tr. by Liadain Sherrard. (Contemporary Greek Theologians Ser.: No. 2). 137p. (Orig.). 1984. pap. 9.95 (*0-88141-027-6*) St Vladimirs.

Deina Ta Polla: A Classicist's Checklist of Twenty Literary-Critical Positions. Thomas G. Rosenmeyer. (Arethusa Monographs: No. 12). vii, 74p. (C). 1988. pap. 10.00 (*0-930881-09-5*) Dept Classics.

Deindustrialization & Plant Closure. Ed. by Paul D. Staudohar & Holly E. Brown. 384p. 1986. text ed. 45.00 (*0-669-14037-6*); pap. 24.95 (*0-669-14038-4*) Free Pr.

Deindustrialization & Regional Economic Transformation: The Experience of the United States. Ed. by Lloyd Rodwin & Hidehiko Sazanami. (Illus.). 288p. 1989. 65.00 (*0-04-445538-0*); pap. 27.95 (*0-04-445539-9*) Routledge Chapman & Hall.

Deindustrialization of America. Barry Bluestone & Bennet Harrison. LC 82-70844. 336p. 1984. pap. text ed. 16.00 (*0-465-01592-1*) Basic.

Deinking Seminar, 1992: Atlanta Airport Marriott Hotel, Atlanta, GA, June 22-24. Technical Association of the Pulp & Paper Industry Staff. (TAPPI Notes Ser.). (Illus.). 306p. reprint ed. pap. 82.70 (*0-7837-3077-2*, 2043171) Bks Demand.

Deinonychus. Michael Benton. LC 93-43402. (Dinoworld Ser.). 40p. (J). (gr. 3-7). 1994. pap. 5.95 (*1-85697-991-1*, Kingfisher LKC) LKC.

Deinonychus. Oliver. (Dinosaur Library: Set II). (Illus.). 24p. (J). 1984. lib. bdg. 14.00 (*0-86592-213-6*) Rourke Enter.

***Deinonychus.** Janet Riehecky. (Dinosaur Bks.). (Illus.). 32p. (ENG & SPA.). (J). (ps-2). 1990. lib. bdg. 21.36 (*1-56766-127-0*) Childs World.

Deinonychus. Janet Riehecky. (Dinosaur Bks.). (Illus.). 32p. (ENG & SPA.). (J). (ps-2). 1990. lib. bdg. 21.36 (*0-89565-625-6*) Childs World.

Deinosuchus. White. (Dinosaur Library: Set V). (Illus.). 24p. (J). 1984. lib. bdg. 14.00 (*0-86592-524-0*) Rourke Enter.

Deinstitutionalization: Program & Policy Development. Ed. by James M. Paul et al. (Special Education & Rehabilitation Monograph Ser.: No. 12). (C). 1977. 24.95x (*0-8156-0132-8*) Syracuse U Pr.

Deinstitutionalizing Delinquent Youth. Michael Fabricant. 215p. 1980. 18.95 (*0-87073-866-6*); pap. 11.95 (*0-87073-892-5*) Schenkman Bks Inc.

Deion Sanders. Carl R. Green & M. Roxanne Ford. LC 93-951. (Sports Headliners Ser.). (Illus.). 48p. (J). (gr. 5-6). 1994. text ed. 13.95 (*0-89686-840-0*, Crstwood Hse) Silver Burdett Pr.

***Deion Sanders.** Aaron Klein. (J). (gr. 4-6). 1995. 14.95 (*0-8027-8369-4*) Walker & Co.

***Deion Sanders.** Aaron Klein. (J). (gr. 4-6). 1995. lib. bdg. 15.85 (*0-8027-8370-8*) Walker & Co.

Deion Sanders: Prime Time Player. Stew Thornley. LC 92-45686. (Achievers Ser.). (J). (gr. 4-9). 1993. 13.50 (*0-8225-0523-1*, Lerner Publctns) Lerner Group.

Deion Sanders: Prime Time Player. Stew Thornley. (J). (gr. 4-9). 1993. pap. 4.95 (*0-8225-9648-2*, Lerner Publctns) Lerner Group.

Deipnosophists, 7 vols. Athenaeus. Incl. Vol. 1. Bks. 1-3. 14.50 (*0-674-99224-5*); Vol. 2. Bks. 3-5. 14.50 (*0-674-99229-6*); Vol. 3. Bks. 6 & 7. 14.50 (*0-674-99247-4*); Vol. 4. Bks. 8-10. 14.50 (*0-674-99259-8*); Vol. 5. Bks. 11 & 12. 14.50 (*0-674-99302-0*); Vol. 6. Bks. 13 & 14. 14.50 (*0-674-99361-6*); Vol. 7. Bks. 14 & 15. 14.50 (*0-674-99380-2*); Vol. 1. Bks. 1-3. 14.50 (*0-674-99224-5*); Vol. 2. Bks. 3-5. 14.50 (*0-674-99229-6*); Vol. 3. Bks. 6 & 7. 14.50 (*0-674-99247-4*); Vol. 4. Bks. 8-10. 14.50 (*0-674-99259-8*); Vol. 5. Bks. 11 & 12. 14.50 (*0-674-99302-0*); Vol. 6. Bks. 13 & 14. 14.50 (*0-674-99361-6*); Vol. 7. Bks. 14 & 15. 14.50 (*0-674-99380-2*); (Loeb Classical Library). write for info. (*0-318-53046-5*) HUP.

Deir El-Ballas: Preliminary Report on the Deir el-Ballas Expedition, 1980-1986. Peter Lacovara. (American Research Center in Egypt; Reports: Vol. 12). x, 84p. 1990. text ed. 31.50 (*0-936770-24-4*, Pub. by Amer Res Ctr Egypt UA) Eisenbrauns.

Deirdre: A Celtic Legend. David Guard. LC 80-69774. (Illus.). 120p. (J). (gr. 4 up). 1993. reprint ed. pap. 8.95 (*1-883672-05-8*) Tricycle Pr.

Deirdre & Don Juan. Jo Beverley. 224p. (Orig.). 1993. mass mkt. 3.99 (*0-380-77281-7*) Avon.

Deism, Masonry, & the Enlightenment: Essays Honoring Alfred Owen Aldrige. Ed. by J. A. Lemay. LC 86-40585. (Illus.). 216p. 1987. 32.50 (*0-87413-317-3*) U Delaware Pr.

Deities & Divinities of Tibet. K. S. Tenzin & G. Obshey. 98p. (C). 1988. 80.00 (*0-89771-059-2*, Pub. by Ratna Pustak Bhandar) St Mut.

Deities & Divinities of Tibet. T. Tenzin & O. Olishey. Tr. by Ketih Dowman. 1993. 175.00 (*0-7855-0303-X*, Pub. by Ratna Pustak Bhandar) St Mut.

Deities & Divinities of Tibet: The Nyingma Icons, a Collection of Line Drawing of Deities & Divinities. K. S. Tenzin & O. Obshey. 1993. 50.00 (*0-7855-0253-X*, Pub. by Ratna Pustak Bhandar) St Mut.

Deities, Dolls, & Devices: Neolithic Figurines from Franchthi Cave, Greece. Lauren E. Talalay. LC 92-43060. (Excavations at Franchthi Cave, Greece Ser.: Fasc. 9). 1993. 39.95 (*0-253-31981-1*) Ind U Pr.

Deity & Domination: Images of God & the State in the Nineteenth & Twentieth Centuries. David Nicholls. 336p. 1989. 29.95 (*0-415-01171-X*, A3381) Routledge.

Deity, Cosmos, & Man. G. A. Farthing. 278p. 1993. 12.50 (*0-913004-82-0*); 19.50 (*0-913004-74-X*) Point Loma Pub.

Deity Yoga: In Action & Performance Tantras. Dalai Lama et al. LC 87-16562. 274p. 1987. reprint ed. pap. 18.95 (*0-937938-50-5*) Snow Lion Pubns.

Deixis, Grammar & Culture. Revere D. Perkins. LC 92-33519. (Typological Studies in Language Ser.: No. 24). x, 245p. 1992. 59.00x (*1-55619-412-9*); pap. 24.95x (*1-55619-413-7*) Benjamins North Am.

Deixis in Narrative: A Cognitive Science Perspective. Ed. by Judith F. Duchan et al. 536p. 1995. text ed. 89.95 (*0-8058-1462-0*); pap. 39.95 (*0-8058-1463-9*) L Erlbaum Assocs.

Deja Everything. Adam Hammer. LC 78-68771. 68p. 1979. pap. 7.00 (*0-89924-017-8*) Lynx Hse.

Deja Ir a Mi Pueblo (Let My People Go!) P. Frank. (SPA.). Date not set. 1.50 (*0-8423-6305-X*, 490310) Editorial Unilit.

Deja Que Cristo Se Encargue De Ti: When Christ Takes Over. Simon Blocker. (SPA.). 3.25 (*84-7645-093-1*, 223152, Pub. by Edit Clie SP) TSELF.

Deja Vu. Ann Murphy. 120p. (Orig.). 1994. pap. 10.00 (*1-56002-304-X*, Univ Edtns) Aegina Pr.

Deja-Vu. enl. rev. ed. Sean Woodward. (C). 1989. reprint ed. 35.00 (*1-871058-00-7*, Pub. by Dragonheart Pr UK) St Mut.

Deja-Vu: Second in the Black Trilogy. Ralph Gibson. LC 72-96851. 52p. 1972. 12.95 (*0-912810-06-8*) Lustrum Pr.

***Deja-vu 16.** Photos by Louis Faurer. (Illus.). 144p. 1995. pap. 25.00 (*4-309-90336-3*) Dist Art Pubs.

***Deja-vu 17.** Contrib by August Sander & Furuya Seichi. 130p. 1995. pap. 25.00 (*4-309-90337-1*) Dist Art Pubs.

***Deja-vu 18.** Contrib by New Tokyo Photographers Staff. 130p. 1995. pap. 25.00 (*4-309-90338-X*) Dist Art Pubs.

Deja Vu...with...Flippance...& Flippance. Larry Lyre. 174p. (C). 1989. 39.95 (*0-7212-0774-X*, Pub. by Regency Press) St Mut.

Dejad De Apretarme el Cuello: Get Your Hands off My Throat. David Wilkerson. (SPA.). 3.95 (*84-7228-133-7*, 220269, Pub. by Edit Clie SP) TSELF.

Dejad Que el Amor Presida (Let Love Preside) Rodolfo Loyola. (SPA.). 1993. 6.99 (*1-56063-437-5*, 498579) Editorial Unilit.

Dejadme Ser Mujer: Let Me Be a Woman. Elisabeth Elliot. (SPA.). 4.95 (*84-7228-499-9*, 220270, Pub. by Edit Clie SP) TSELF.

Dejame Estar a Tu Lado: Let Me Stand at Your Side. Basilea Schlink. (SPA.). 4.95 (*84-7645-345-0*, 223458, Pub. by Edit Clie SP) TSELF.

Dejando a un Lado Lo Que Es De Nino: Putting Away Childish Things. David Seamands. (SPA.). 5.50 (*84-7645-136-9*, 223185, Pub. by Edit Clie SP) TSELF.

Dejavu. John Osborne. (Orig.). 1994. 5.45 (*0-87129-237-8*, D56) Dramatic Pub.

Dejavu. John Osborne. 160p. (Orig.). 1991. pap. 8.95 (*0-571-14345-8*) Faber & Faber.

Deje Que la Biblia Hable Sobre las Lenguas. Richard C. Schwab. Orig. Title: Let the Bible Speak about Tongues. 144p. (SPA.). 1993. pap. 6.99 (*0-8254-1659-0*) Kregel.

Dejeuner Du Lundi. Jean Dutourd. 342p. (FRE.). 1986. pap. 12.95 (*0-7859-2042-0*, 2070377563) Fr & Eur.

DeJong's the Neurologic Examination. 5th ed. Armin F. Haerer. (Illus.). 880p. 1992. text ed. 89.95 (*0-397-51104-3*) Lippincott.

Dekadenter Wagnerismus: Studien zur europaeischen Literatur des Fin de siecle. Erwin Koppen. (Komparatistische Studien: Vol. 2, Beihefte zur Zeitschrift 'Arcadia'). (C). 1973. 146.15 (*3-11-004388-2*) De Gruyter.

Deke! Deke Slayton & Michael Cassutt. 368p. 1994. 23.95 (*0-312-85503-6*) Forge NYC.

Deke! Deke Slayton & Michael Cassutt. 1995. pap. 5.99 (*0-8125-2462-4*) Forge NYC.

***Deke!** Deke Slayton & Michael Cassutt. 352p. 1995. pap. 14.95 (*0-312-85918-X*) Forge NYC.

Dekker & Heywood: Professional Dramatists. Kathleen E. McLuskie. LC 93-30472. 160p. 1994. text ed. 39.95 (*0-312-10629-7*) St Martin.

Dekker Perspective. Ed. by D. Overkleeft & L. E. Groosman. (C). 1988. lib. bdg. 34.00 (*1-85333-108-2*, Pub. by Graham & Trotman UK) Kluwer Ac.

Dekodiphukan. Robert Baratta-Lorton. LC 85-70308. (Illus.). 116p. 1985. pap. 24.95 (*0-9614646-0-7*) Ctr Innovation.

Dekok & Death of a Clown. Albert C. Baantjer. Tr. by H. G. Smittenaar. 240p. (Orig.). 1996. pap. 7.95 (*1-881164-20-9*) Intercont VA.

Dekok & Murder by Melody. Albert C. Baantjer. Tr. by H. G. Smittenaar. 240p. (Orig.). 1996. pap. 7.95 (*1-881164-19-5*) Intercont VA.

Dekok & Murder in Ecstasy. Baantjer, pseud. Tr. by H. G. Smittenaar. 200p. (Orig.). 1995. pap. 7.95 (*1-881164-16-0*) Intercont VA.

Dekok & Murder in Seance. Baantjer, pseud. Tr. by H. G. Smittenaar. 200p. (Orig.). 1995. pap. 7.95 (*1-881164-15-2*) Intercont VA.

DeKok & Murder on the Menu. Albert C. Baantjer. Tr. by H. G. Smittenaar. 180p. (Orig.). 1992. pap. 7.95 (*1-881164-31-4*) Intercont VA.

Dekok & the Begging Death. Baantjer, pseud. Tr. by H. G. Smittenaar. 200p. (Orig.). 1995. pap. 7.95 (*1-881164-17-9*) Intercont VA.

Dekok & the Brothers of the Easy Death. Baantjer, pseud. Tr. by H. G. Smittenaar. 196p. (Orig.). 1995. pap. 7.95 (*1-881164-13-6*) Intercont VA.

DeKok & the Careful Killer. Albert C. Baantjer. Tr. by H. G. Smittenaar. 245p. (Orig.). 1993. pap. 7.95 (*1-881164-07-1*) Intercont VA.

DeKok & the Corpse at the Church Wall. Albert C. Baantjer. Tr. by H. G. Smittenaar. 202p. (Orig.). 1994. pap. 7.95 (*1-881164-10-1*) Intercont VA.

DeKok & the Dancing Death. Albert C. Baantjer. Tr. by H. G. Smittenaar. 217p. (Orig.). 1994. pap. 7.95 (*1-881164-11-X*) Intercont VA.

DeKok & the Dead Harlequin. Albert C. Baantjer. Tr. by H. G. Smittenaar. 226p. (Orig.). 1993. pap. 7.95 (*1-881164-04-7*) Intercont VA.

Dekok & the Deadly Accord. Baantjer, pseud. Tr. by H. G. Smittenaar. 200p. (Orig.). 1995. pap. 7.95 (*1-881164-14-4*) Intercont VA.

DeKok & the Disillusioned Corpse. Albert C. Baantjer. Tr. by H. G. Smittenaar. 246p. (Orig.). 1993. pap. 7.95 (*1-881164-06-3*) Intercont VA.

DeKok & the Dying Stroller. Albert C. Baantjer. Tr. by H. G. Smittenaar. 199p. (Orig.). 1994. pap. 7.95 (*1-881164-09-8*) Intercont VA.

Dekok & the Geese of Death. Baantjer, pseud. Tr. by H. G. Smittenaar. 200p. (Orig.). 1995. pap. 7.95 (*1-881164-18-7*) Intercont VA.

DeKok & the Naked Lady. Albert C. Baantjer. Tr. by H. G. Smittenaar. 205p. (Orig.). 1994. pap. 7.95 (*1-881164-12-8*) Intercont VA.

DeKok & the Romantic Murder. Albert C. Baantjer. Tr. by H. G. Smittenaar. 199p. (Orig.). 1994. pap. 7.95 (*1-881164-08-X*) Intercont VA.

DeKok & the Somber Nude. Albert C. Baantjer. Tr. by H. G. Smittenaar. 232p. (Orig.). 1992. pap. 7.95 (*1-881164-01-2*) Intercont VA.

DeKok & the Sorrowing Tomcat. Albert C. Baantjer. Tr. by H. G. Smittenaar. 240p. (Orig.). 1993. 19.95 (*1-881164-61-6*); pap. 7.95 (*1-881164-05-5*) Intercont VA.

Dekok & Variations on Murder. Albert C. Baantjer. Tr. by H. G. Smittenaar. 240p. (Orig.). 1996. pap. 7.95 (*1-881164-21-7*) Intercont VA.

DEKORP-Atlas. Ed. by R. Meissner & R. K. Bortfeld. (Illus.). 390p. 1990. 96.00 (*0-387-52512-2*) Spr-Verlag.

Dektri Horlogoj. James Thurber. Tr. by Ralph A. Lewin. 42p. 1993. pap. text ed. 3.95 (*1-882251-04-0*) Eldonejo Bero.

Del Amor a la Revolucion. Ed. by Anthony G. Lozano & Eduardo Zayas-Bazan. 225p. (C). 1975. pap. text ed. 10.95 (*0-393-09283-6*) Norton.

***Del Amor y Otros Demonios.** Marquez G. Garcia. 1994. pap. 9.95 (*0-14-024559-6*, Penguin Bks) Viking Penguin.

Del Camino. Jose F. Martinez. Ed. by Cima Communications Staff. (Orig.). (SPA.). 1991. write for info. (*0-9628846-0-X*) J F Martinez.

Del Camino. Julio Mercado. 120p. (SPA.). 1923. 1.00 (*0-318-14254-6*) Hispanic Inst.

Del Canaveral a la Fabrica: Cambio Social en Puerto Rico. Eduardo Rivera-Medina & Rafael L. Ramirez. LC 85-80187. (Huracan Academia Ser.). 152p. (SPA.). 1985. pap. 7.25 (*0-940238-78-0*) Ediciones Huracan.

1858

An Asterisk (*) at the beginning of an entry indicates that the title is appearing in BIP for the first time.

An Asterisk (*) at the beginning of an entry indicates that the title is appearing in BIP for the first time.

***Delaware Limited Liability Company Forms & Practice Manual.** Wayne J. Carey & Ellisa O. Habbart. 480p. Date not set. ring bd. 149.95 (*0-9637468-4-7*) Data Trace Legal.

Delaware Loyalists. Harold B. Hancock. LC 72-8730. (American Revolutionary Ser.). reprint ed. lib. bdg. 29.50 (*0-8398-0800-3*) Irvington.

Delaware, Maryland, Virginia, West Virginia. 2nd ed. H. M. Gousha Staff. 1989. pap. 2.25 (*0-671-87922-7*, H M Gousha) P-H Gen Ref & Trav.

Delaware Media Book: A Surprising Guide to the Amazing Print, Broadcast & Online Media of Our State for Students, Teachers, Writers & Publishers - Includes Reproducible Mailing Labels Plus Activities for Young People! Carole Marsh. (Carole Marsh Delaware Bks.). (Illus.). 1994. lib. bdg. 24.95 (*0-7933-3182-X*); pap. 14.95 (*0-7933-3183-8*); disk 29.95 (*0-7933-3184-6*) Gallopade Pub Group.

Delaware, Michigan, Its History. Clarence J. Monette. (Copper Country Local History Ser.: Vol. 28). (Illus.). 120p. (Orig.). 1987. pap. 3.00 (*0-942363-27-2*) C J Monette.

Delaware Mystery Van Takes Off! Book 1: Handicapped Delaware Kids Sneak Off on a Big Adventure. Carole Marsh. (Carole Marsh Delaware Bks.). (Illus.). (J). (gr. 3-12). 1994. 24.95 (*0-7933-4985-0*); pap. 14.95 (*0-7933-4986-9*); disk 29.95 (*0-7933-4987-7*) Gallopade Pub Group.

Delaware Notes, Twenty-First Series. Delaware University Staff. LC 74-38399. (Biography Index Reprint Ser.). 1977. reprint ed. 15.95 (*0-8369-8120-0*) Ayer.

Delaware Photographs by Jake Rajs. Frwd. by Russell W. Peterson. LC 92-23810. (Illus.). 1992. 50.00 (*0-89802-617-2*) Beautiful Am.

Delaware Prehistoric Archaeology: An Ecological Approach. Jay F. Custer. (Illus.). 224p. 1984. 35.00 (*0-87413-233-9*) U Delaware Pr.

Delaware Property & Casualty Course. James J. Smith. Date not set. 50.00 (*1-56461-078-0*, 26973) Rough Notes.

Delaware Public Archives, 5 Vols, Set. Delaware Public Archives Commission. reprint ed. lib. bdg. 382.50 (*0-404-07170-8*) AMS Pr.

Delaware Public Archives, Vol. 1. Delaware Public Archives Commission. reprint ed. lib. bdg. write for info. (*0-404-07171-6*) AMS Pr.

Delaware Public Archives, Vol. 2. Delaware Public Archives Commission. reprint ed. lib. bdg. write for info. (*0-404-07172-4*) AMS Pr.

Delaware Public Archives, Vol. 3. Delaware Public Archives Commission. reprint ed. lib. bdg. write for info. (*0-404-07173-2*) AMS Pr.

Delaware Public Archives, Vol. 4. Delaware Public Archives Commission. reprint ed. lib. bdg. write for info. (*0-404-07174-0*) AMS Pr.

Delaware Public Archives, Vol. 5. Delaware Public Archives Commission. reprint ed. lib. bdg. write for info. (*0-404-07175-9*) AMS Pr.

Delaware Quiz Bowl Crash Course! Carole Marsh. (Carole Marsh Delaware Bks.). (Illus.). (YA). (gr. 3-12). 1994. lib. bdg. 24.95 (*1-55609-556-2*); pap. 14.95 (*1-55609-555-4*); disk 29.95 (*0-7933-1450-X*) Gallopade Pub Group.

***Delaware River & Flow of Time.** James S. Volton. (Illus.). 12p. 1994. pap. 2.25 (*0-915992-68-X*) Eastern Acorn.

Delaware Rollercoasters! Carole Marsh. (Carole Marsh Delaware Bks.). (Illus.). (YA). (gr. 3-12). 1994. lib. bdg. 24.95 (*0-7933-5245-2*); pap. 14.95 (*0-7933-5246-0*); disk 29.95 (*0-7933-5247-9*) Gallopade Pub Group.

***Delaware Rules: 1994 Edition.** annot. ed. Date not set. pap. 45.00 (*1-55834-074-2*) Michie Butterworth.

Delaware School Trivia: An Amazing & Fascinating Look at Our State's Teachers, Schools & Students! Carole Marsh. (Carole Marsh Delaware Bks.). (Illus.). (YA). (gr. 3-12). 1994. lib. bdg. 24.95 (*0-7933-0247-1*); pap. 14.95 (*0-7933-0246-3*); disk 29.95 (*0-7933-0248-X*) Gallopade Pub Group.

Delaware Seashore. Michael Biggs. 1989. 19.50 (*0-89802-523-0*) Beautiful Am.

Delaware Silly Basketball Sportsmysteries, Vol. I. Carole Marsh. (Carole Marsh Delaware Bks.). (Illus.). (YA). (gr. 3-12). 1994. lib. bdg. 24.95 (*0-7933-0244-7*); pap. 14.95 (*0-7933-0243-9*); disk 29.95 (*0-7933-0245-5*) Gallopade Pub Group.

Delaware Silly Basketball Sportsmysteries, Vol. II. Carole Marsh. (Carole Marsh Delaware Bks.). (Illus.). (YA). (gr. 3-12). 1994. lib. bdg. 24.95 (*0-7933-1456-9*); pap. 14.95 (*0-7933-1457-7*); disk 29.95 (*0-7933-1458-5*) Gallopade Pub Group.

Delaware Silly Football Sportsmysteries, Vol. I. Carole Marsh. (Carole Marsh Delaware Bks.). (Illus.). (YA). (gr. 3-12). 1994. lib. bdg. 24.95 (*0-7933-1441-0*); pap. 14.95 (*0-7933-1442-9*); disk 29.95 (*0-7933-1443-7*) Gallopade Pub Group.

Delaware Silly Football Sportsmysteries, Vol. II. Carole Marsh. (Carole Marsh Delaware Bks.). (Illus.). (YA). (gr. 3-12). 1994. lib. bdg. 24.95 (*0-7933-1444-5*); pap. 14.95 (*0-7933-1445-3*); disk 29.95 (*0-7933-1446-1*) Gallopade Pub Group.

Delaware Silly Trivia! Carole Marsh. (Carole Marsh Delaware Bks.). (Illus.). (YA). (gr. 3-12). 1994. lib. bdg. 24.95 (*1-55609-549-X*); pap. 14.95 (*1-55609-548-1*); disk 29.95 (*0-7933-1438-0*) Gallopade Pub Group.

***Delaware State Business Handbook.** 400p. (C). 1995. text ed. 395.00 (*0-7605-1924-2*) Rector Pr.

Delaware, the First State. Pauline P. Citro. (Illus.). (Orig.). 1989. pap. write for info. (*0-924117-02-8*) Delaware HP.

Delaware, the First State. Carol E. Hoffecker. (Illus.). 256p. (Orig.). (J). 1987. pap. 12.95 (*0-912608-47-1*) Mid Atlantic.

Delaware Timeline: A Chronology of Delaware History, Mystery, Trivia, Legend, Lore & More. Carole Marsh. (Carole Marsh Delaware Bks.). (Illus.). (J). (gr. 3-12). 1994. lib. bdg. 24.95 (*0-7933-5896-5*); pap. 14.95 (*0-7933-5897-3*); disk 29.95 (*0-7933-5898-1*) Gallopade Pub Group.

Delaware Tithables Census Index, 1665-1697. Ronald V. Jackson. LC 77-94997. (Illus.). 1977. lib. bdg. 38.00 (*0-89593-166-4*) Accelerated Index.

***Delaware to War.** Historical Briefs, Inc. Staff. Ed. by Thomas Antonucci & Michael Antonucci. 176p. 1990. pap. 14.95 (*0-89677-019-2*) Hist Briefs.

Delaware Two Hundred Years Ago 1780-1800. Harold B. Hancock. (Illus.). 256p. (Orig.). 1987. pap. 9.95 (*0-912608-52-8*) Mid Atlantic.

Delaware Wing-T: An Order of Football. H. R. Raymond. 1986. 21.95 (*0-13-198326-1*) P-H.

***Delaware 1782 Tax Assessment & Census List.** Ed. by Nelson et al. 270p. 1994. text ed. 31.00 (*1-887061-04-5*) DE Geneal Soc.

Delaware 1790 Tax Lists, Vol. 1. Ronald V. Jackson. lib. bdg. 50.00 (*0-89593-716-6*) Accelerated Index.

***Delaware 1950's.** Historical Briefs, Inc. Staff. Ed. by Thomas Antonucci & Michael Antonucci. 176p. 1991. pap. 14.95 (*0-89677-040-0*) Hist Briefs.

Delaware...Close to Home. Comegys. 1988. 29.95 (*0-89802-520-6*) Beautiful Am.

Delaware's Finest. Ed. by Cookbook Committee Staff. 208p. (Orig.). 1990. pap. 10.00 (*0-9626794-0-2*) Amer Red Cross DE.

Delaware's (Most Devastating!) Disasters & (Most Calamitous!) Catastrophies! Carole Marsh. (Carole Marsh Delaware Bks.). (Illus.). (YA). (gr. 3-12). 1994. lib. bdg. 24.95 (*0-7933-0235-8*); pap. 14.95 (*0-7933-0234-X*); disk 29.95 (*0-7933-0236-6*) Gallopade Pub Group.

Delaware's Unsolved Mysteries (& Their "Solutions") Includes Scientific Information & Other Activities for Students. Carole Marsh. (Carole Marsh Delaware Bks.). (Illus.). (J). (gr. 3-12). 1994. lib. bdg. 24.95 (*0-7933-5743-8*); pap. 14.95 (*0-7933-5744-6*); disk 29.95 (*0-7933-5745-4*) Gallopade Pub Group.

Delay & Differential Equations: Proceedings in Honor of George Seifert on His Retirement Ames, Iowa, October 18-19, 1991. Ed. by A. M. Fink et al. LC 92-9107. 184p. 1992. text ed. 98.00 (*981-02-0891-X*) World Scientific Pub.

Delay Differential Equations: With Applications in Population Dynamics. Yang Kuang. (Mathematics in Science & Engineering Ser.). (Illus.). 398p. 1993. text ed. 69.95 (*0-12-427610-5*) Acad Pr.

Delay Differential Equations & Dynamical Systems: Proceedings of a Conference Held in Claremont, California, Jan. 13-16, 1990. Stavros N. Busenberg. Ed. by Maurizio Martelli. (Lecture Notes in Mathematics Ser.: Vol. 1475). viii, 249p. 1991. pap. 36.00 (*0-387-54120-9*) Spr-Verlag.

***Delay Equations: Functional, Complex, & Nonlinear Analysis.** Odo Diekmann et al. LC 94-41858. (Applied Mathematical Sciences Ser.: Vol. 110). 508p. 1995. 49.00 (*0-387-94416-8*) Spr-Verlag.

Delay Equations, Approximation, & Application. Gunter Meinardus & Gunter Nurnberger. (International Series of Numerical Mathematics: No. 74). 356p. 1985. lib. bdg. 105.00 (*0-8176-1733-7*) Birkhauser.

Delay in the Court. 2nd ed. Hans Zeisel et al. LC 77-28194. (Illus.). xxvii, 313p. 1978. reprint ed. text ed. 38.50 (*0-313-20252-4*, ZEDC, Greenwood Pr) Greenwood.

***Delay Is Not Denial.** Bobbie J. Merck. 83p. (Orig.). (C). 1994. pap. text ed. 5.95 (*0-929263-08-1*) Great Love Church Intl.

Delay Learning in Artificial Neural Networks. Catherine Myers. LC 92-19237. (Neural Computing Ser.). 1992. write for info. (*0-442-31627-5*) Chapman & Hall.

Delay Reduction Plan: Kanawha County Circuit Court. National Center for State Courts Staff. 17p. 1985. 1.00 (*0-685-15503-X*, SERO-014) Natl Ctr St Courts.

Delayed: Not Postponed. Fielding Dawson. Ed. by Maureen Owen. LC 77-21162. (Illus.). 1978. pap. 4.00 (*0-916382-17-6*) Telephone Bks.

Delayed Answers: Poems. Albert Cook. LC 92-20422. 164p. 1992. pap. 24.95 (*0-7734-9566-5*) E Mellen.

***Delayed Birth Records at Dearborn County, Indiana.** Lois L. Harper. 67p. 1995. pap. 8.50 (*1-55856-201-X*) Closson Pr.

Delayed Concessions. Mary R. Dees. Ed. by Lana Canon. LC 93-91716. 256p. (Orig.). 1994. pap. 10.95 (*0-9630600-2-3*) Marmor.

Delayed Departures, Overdue Arrivals: Industrial Familialism & the Japanese National Railways. Paul H. Noguchi. LC 89-27924. 248p. 1990. text ed. 31.00 (*0-8248-1234-4*); pap. text ed. 14.95 (*0-8248-1288-3*) UH Pr.

Delayed Hypersensitivity. 3rd ed. J. L. Turk. (Research Monographs in Immunology: Vol. 1). 296p. 1980. 129.75 (*0-444-80163-4*) Elsevier.

Delayed Primary School Enrollment & Childhood Malnutrition in Ghana: An Economic Analysis. Paul Glewwe & Hanan Jacoby. LC 93-36185. (Living Standards Measurement Study Working Paper Ser.: No. 98). 46p. 1993. 6.95 (*0-8213-2665-1*, 12665) World Bank.

Delayed Space. Homa Fardjadi & Mohsen Mostafavi. LC 93-80338. (Illus.). 147p. (Orig.). 1994. pap. 24.95 (*1-878271-89-X*) Princeton Arch.

Delayering Organizations: How to Beat Bureaucracy & Create a Flexible & Responsive Organisation. Ed. by Doede Keuning & Wilfrid Opheij. (Financial Times Management Ser.). 232p. 1994. 75.00x (*0-273-60383-3*, Pub. by Pitman Pubng UK) St Mut.

***Delaying the Onset of Late-Life Dysfunction.** Ed. by Robert N. Butler & Jacob A. Brody. (Illus.). 256p. 1995. 38.95 (*0-8261-8880-X*) Springer Pub.

Delcroz Today: An Education Through & into Music. MArie L. Bachmann. Tr. by David Parlett. (Illus.). 392p. 1993. pap. 19.95 (*0-19-816400-9*) OUP.

Delectable Apple. Kathleen D. Stang. LC 94-5193. 72p. 1994. 9.95 (*0-8118-0524-7*) Chronicle Bks.

Delectable Duchy: Stories, Studies & Sketches. Arthur T. Quiller-Couch. LC 78-125235. (Short Story Index Reprint Ser.). 1977. 19.95 (*0-8369-3602-7*) Ayer.

Delectable Mountains. Arthur W. Colton. LC 71-86139. (Short Story Index Reprint Ser.). 1977. 19.95 (*0-8369-3043-6*) Ayer.

Delectable Mountains. Christopher Gautschi. (Illus.). 1978. pap. 4.00 (*0-918824-11-7*) Turkey Pr.

Delectable Mountains. Maxwell S. Burt. LC 70-144922. 1971. reprint ed. 29.00 (*0-403-00885-9*) Scholarly.

Delectably Danish: Recipes & Reflections. Julie J. McDonald. LC 82-81568. (Illus.). 64p. 1982. pap. 7.95 (*0-941016-04-8*) Penfield.

Delectus ex Iambis et Elegis Graecis. Ed. by M. L. West. (Classical Texts Ser.). (C). 1980. text ed. 27.00 (*0-19-814589-6*) OUP.

Delegated Legislation in Australia & New Zealand. D. C. Pearce. 1977. Australia. 76.00 (*0-409-31820-5*) Butterworth Legal Pubs.

Delegating Authority. Andrew E. Schwartz. (Business Success Ser.). 96p. 1992. pap. 4.95 (*0-8120-4958-6*) Barron.

Delegating for Results. Robert B. Maddux. Ed. by Mike Crisp. LC 89-81246. (Fifty-Minute Ser.). (Illus.). (Orig.). 1990. pap. 9.95 (*1-56052-008-6*) Crisp Pubns.

Delegating Skills see Productive Supervisor: A Program of Practical Managerial Skills

***Delegation Skills.** Bruce B. Tepper. (AMI How-to Ser.). 100p. 1995. 9.95 (*1-884926-45-2*) Amer Media.

Delegation Skills. Bruce B. Tepper. LC 93-29257. (Business Skills Express Ser.). 96p. 1994. pap. 10.00 (*0-7863-0148-1*) Irwin Prof Pubng.

Dele's Child. Ronald Dathorne. LC 84-51445. 158p. (Orig.). 1986. 19.50 (*0-89410-421-7*); pap. 10.50 (*0-89410-422-5*) Three Continents.

DeLesseps S. Morrison & the Image of Reform: New Orleans Politics, 1946-1961. Edward F. Haas. LC 73-90867. xii, 368p. 1986. pap. text ed. 11.95 (*0-8071-1349-2*) La State U Pr.

Deleuze & Guattari. Ronald Bogue. (Critics of the Twentieth Century Ser.). 192p. 1989. 42.50 (*0-415-02017-4*); pap. 13.95 (*0-415-02443-9*) Routledge.

Deleuze et la Litterature. Andre Colombat. LC 89-13966. (American University Studies: Romance Languages & Literature: Ser. II, Vol. 132). 348p. (FRE.). (C). 1990. text ed. 62.95 (*0-8204-1189-2*) P Lang Pubs.

Deleuze Reader. Gilles Deleuze. Ed. by Constantin V. Boundas. 416p. 1993. text ed. 49.50 (*0-231-07268-6*); text ed. 17.50 (*0-231-07269-4*) Col U Pr.

"Delfin" Laser Thermonuclear Installation: Operational Complex & Future Directions. Ed. by G. V. Sklizkov. (Proceedings of the Lebedev Physics Institute Ser.: Vol. 178). 302p. 1988. text ed. 125.00 (*0-941743-22-5*) Nova Sci Pubs.

Delfina Cuero: Her Autobiography, an Account of Her Last Years & Her Ethnobotanic Contributions. Florence C. Shipek. Ed. by Sylvia B. Vane. LC 91-20493. (Anthropological Papers: No. 38). (Illus.). 120p. 1991. 16.00 (*0-87919-123-6*); pap. 12.00 (*0-87919-122-8*) Ballena Pr.

Delfines. Donna Bailey. LC 91-23779. (Animales Ser.). (Illus.). 32p. (SPA.). (J). (gr. 1-4). 1992. lib. bdg. 19.97 (*0-8114-2656-4*) Raintree Steck-V.

Delfines. Norman S. Barrett. LC 90-71418. (Picture Library). (Illus.). 32p. (SPA.). (J). (gr. k-4). 1991. lib. bdg. 12.60 (*0-531-07920-1*) Watts.

Delfines (Dolphins) S. Palmer. (Spanish Language Books, Set 4: Mamifero Marino (Sea Mammals)). (J). 1991. 8.95 (*0-86592-849-5*) Rourke Enter.

Delft. Albert Goldbarth. Ed. by Craig Goad et al. 36p. (Orig.). 1991. pap. 6.50 (*0-9616467-6-4*) GreenTower Pr.

Delhi. Photos by Raghu Rai. (Illus.). 1994. 65.00 (*81-7223-092-3*) Harper SF.

Delhi. Henry W. Norman. (Illus.). 400p. (C). 1987. reprint ed. 44.00 (*0-8364-2142-6*, Pub. by Gian Publng Hse II) S Asia.

Delhi: Its Monuments & History. T. G. Spear. (Illus.). 192p. 1994. 19.95 (*0-19-563460-8*) OUP.

Delhi, Agra, & Jaipur. Louise Nicholson. (Asian Guides Ser.). 208p. 1988. pap. 12.95 (*0-8442-9917-0*, Passport Bks) NTC Pub Grp.

Delhi, Agra & Jaipur. 2nd ed. (Handbooks of the World Ser.). 1994. 16.95 (*0-8442-9680-5*, Passport Bks) NTC Pub Grp.

Delhi Agra Jaipur. Ed. by Khushwant Singh et al. (Illus.). 144p. (C). 1990. 795.00 (*81-7002-041-7*, Pub. by Himalayan Bks II) St Mut.

Delhi Declaration: Cardinal of Indo-Soviet Relations. Shri N. Sahai. 1990. 47.50 (*81-7099-226-5*, Pub. by Mittal II) S Asia.

Delhi Diary: Daily Talks at Prayer Meetings, 1947-1948. M. K. Gandhi. 426p. 1982. 15.00 (*0-934676-56-9*) Greenlf Bks.

Delhi, Jaipur, Agra. (Insight Guides Ser.). 1993. pap. 21.95 (*0-395-66269-9*) HM.

Delhi Meerut Riots. Ed. by Asghar Ali. (C). 1987. 26.00 (*81-202-0198-1*, Pub. by Ajanta II) S Asia.

Delhi Past & Present. H. C. Fanshawe. (C). 1991. 42.50 (*81-85326-44-4*, Pub. by Vintage II) S Asia.

Delhi Six & Soviet Policy. Viktor Samarin & Vladislav Okolov. (C). 1988. 10.50 (*0-8364-2359-3*, Pub. by Allied II) S Asia.

Delhi Through the Ages: Essays in Urban History, Culture, & Society. Ed. by Robert E. Frykenberg. (Illus.). 566p. 1988. 29.95 (*0-19-561728-2*) OUP.

Delhi Through the Ages: Selected Essays in Urban History, Culture Society. Ed. by Robert E. Frykenberg. (Oxford India Paperbacks Ser.). 364p. (C). 1994. pap. 11.95 (*0-19-563023-8*) OUP.

***Delhi's March Towards Statehood.** Purushotam Goyel. (C). 1993. 22.50x (*81-85944-78-4*, Pub. by UBS Pubs Dist II) S Asia.

Deli Trays Around the World with Nora Mitchell. Nora Mitchell. (Illus.). 112p. 1990. 29.95 (*0-9626113-0-1*) N Mitchell.

Delia Ironfoot. Jeane Harris. 224p. 1992. pap. 9.95 (*1-56280-014-0*) Naiad Pr.

***Delia Smith's Summer Collection: One Hundred Forty Recipes for Summer.** Delia Smith. 1995. (*0-670-86152-9*, Viking) Viking Penguin.

Delia, the Bluebird of Mulberry Bend. E. M. Whittemore. (J). 1980. pap. 2.99 (*0-88019-017-5*) Schmul Pub Co.

Delian Book of the Dead. Ben R. Ezzell & Mary Ezzell. (Illus.). 143p. 1986. pap. 11.95 (*0-940918-09-9*, STK 82-009) Dragon Tree.

Delia's Song. Lucha Corpi. LC 88-9401. 224p. (Orig.). (C). 1989. pap. 9.50 (*0-934770-82-4*) Arte Publico.

Deliberate Acts: Changing Hopi Culture Through the Oraibi Split. Peter M. Whiteley. LC 87-30240. 373p. 1988. 45.00 (*0-8165-1037-7*) U of Ariz Pr.

Deliberate Criticism: Toward a Postmodern Humanism. Stephen R. Yarbrough. LC 90-11319. 208p. 1992. 30.00 (*0-8203-1325-4*) U of Ga Pr.

Deliberate Deceptions: Facing the Facts about the U. S. - Israeli Relationship. Paul Findley. LC 92-42294. 343p. 1993. 24.95 (*1-55652-181-2*) L Hill Bks.

***Deliberate Deceptions: Facing the Facts about the U. S. - Israeli Relationship.** 2nd rev. ed. Paul Findley. LC 92-42294. 343p. 1995. pap. 14.95 (*1-55652-239-8*) L Hill Bks.

Deliberate Indifference: A Story of Murder & Racial Injustice. Howard Swindle. (Illus.). 336p. 1994. pap. 11.95 (*0-14-023370-9*, Penguin Bks) Viking Penguin.

Deliberate Provocation. large type ed. Emma Richmond. (Romance Ser.). 1992. 17.95 (*0-263-13101-7*, Pub. by Mills & Boon Ltd UK) Chivers N Amer.

Deliberate Provocation: Presents Plus. Emma Richmond. (Presents Ser.). 1994. mass mkt. 2.99 (*0-373-11624-1*, 1011624-3) Harlequin Bks.

***Deliberate Search for the Subtle Trap.** Ed. by Michael T. Halbouty. (AAPG Memoir Ser.: No. 32). (Illus.). viii, 351p. 1982. 33.00 (*0-89181-309-8*) AAPG.

Deliberate Smoke Operations. (Military Science Ser.). 1989. lib. bdg. 79.95 (*0-8490-3991-6*) Gordon Pr.

Deliberate Speed: The Origins of a Cultural Style in the American 1950's. W. T. Lhamon. 1990. 21.95 (*0-87474-379-6*) Smithsonian.

Deliberate Speed: The Origins of a Cultural Style in the American 1950's. W. T. Lhamon, Jr. LC 89-26197. 304p. 1993. reprint ed. pap. 15.95 (*1-56098-316-7*) Smithsonian.

Deliberation in Education & Society. Ed. by J. T. Dillon. LC 93-46340. 1994. 45.00 (*1-56750-056-0*); pap. 22.50 (*1-56750-057-9*) Ablex Pub.

Deliberations of the Council of Four, March 24-June 28, 1919: Notes of the Official Interpreter, Paul Mantoux, 2 vols., Set. Ed. by Arthur Link. (Papers of Woodrow Wilson). (Illus.). 1283p. 1992. text ed. 99.50 (*0-691-04793-6*) Princeton U Pr.

Delicacy & Strength of Lace: Letters Between Leslie Marmon Silko & James A. Wright. Ed. by Anne Wright. LC 85-80977. 96p. (Orig.). 1986. pap. 8.95 (*0-915308-74-6*) Graywolf.

Delicate & Difficult Question: Documents in the History of Ukrainians in Canada, 1899-1962. Bohdan S. Kordan & Lubomyr Y. Luciuk. Ed. by Richard A. Pierce. (Builders of Canada Ser.: No. 3). 1986. 15.00 (*0-317-56129-4*) Limestone Pr.

Delicate Art of Dancing with Porcupines: Learning to Appreciate the Finer Points of Others. Bob Phillips. Ed. by Ed Stewart. LC 89-31020. 175p. 1989. pap. 7.99 (*0-8307-1333-6*, 5419749) Regal.

Delicate Art of Whale Watching. Joana M. Varawa. LC 90-48285. (Illus.). 144p. 1991. pap. 10.00 (*0-87156-550-1*) Sierra.

***Delicate Art of Whale Watching.** Joana M. Varawa. 1995. 20.00 (*0-8446-6860-5*) Peter Smith.

Delicate Balance. Roberta Gellis. 288p. (Orig.). 1993. pap. 4.50 (*0-8439-3425-5*) Dorchester Pub Co.

Delicate Balance. Irene Hannon. 192p. 1994. 17.95 (*0-8034-9040-2*, Avalon Bks) Bouregy.

Delicate Balance. John Zajac. LC 89-91627. 200p. (Orig.). 1989. pap. 8.99 (*0-910311-57-9*) Huntington Hse.

Delicate Balance: Conservation & Development in Chile & Costa Rica. Jack W. Hopkins. Ed. by Dennis Conway. (Series on Environment & Development). (Illus.). 62p. (Orig.). 1992. pap. 3.00 (*1-881157-13-X*) In Ctr Global.

Delicate Balance: Love & Authority in Torah Parenting. Sara Chana Radcliffe. 292p. 1989. 16.95 (*0-944070-22-1*) Targum Pr.

Delicate Balances: Collaborative Research in Language Education. Ed. by Judith W. Lindfors. LC 93-8097. (Illus.). 148p. (Orig.). 1993. pap. 14.95 (*0-8141-1077-0*) NCTE.

Delicate Creation. Christopher Derrick. 144p. 1972. 9.95 (*0-8159-5304-6*) Devin.

Delicate Dance: Sex, Celibacy, & Relationships Among Catholic Clergy & Religous. Sheila Murphy. 128p. 1992. pap. 14.95 (*0-8245-1159-X*) Crossroad NY.

Delicate Experiment: The Harvard Business School, 1908-1945. Jeffrey L. Cruikshank. 1987. text ed. 110.00 (*0-07-103228-2*) McGraw.

1860

An Asterisk (*) at the beginning of an entry indicates that the title is appearing in BIP for the first time.

An Asterisk (*) at the beginning of an entry indicates that the title is appearing in BIP for the first time.

*Deliver Us from Squid Roe. Dale D. Mills. LC 94-71494. 176p. (Orig.). 1995. pap. 7.50 (1-56002-454-2) Aegina Pr.

Deliver Us from Temptation: The Tragic & Shocking Story of the Temptations & Motown. Tony Turner & Barbara Aria. (Illus.). 368p. 1992. 22.95 (1-56025-034-8) Thunders Mouth.

Deliver Us from the Evil One. Robert G. Bayley. 48p. 1987. pap. 3.00 (0-934421-09-9) Presby Renewal Pubns.

Deliverance. James Dickey. 1976. 23.95 (0-8488-0476-7) Amereon Ltd.

*Deliverance. James Dickey. 1994. pap. 9.95 (0-385-31387-X, Delta) Dell.

Deliverance. Gregory N. Forker. 1977. pap. text ed. 2.50 (0-916556-07-7) Desert First.

Deliverance. limited ed. James Dickey. LC 91-10975. 256p. 1991. reprint ed. 75.00 (0-922890-97-8) Armchair Detective.

Deliverance. James Dickey. LC 91-10975. 256p. 1991. reprint ed. 19.95 (0-922890-96-X); reprint ed. 25.00 (1-56287-010-6) Armchair Detective.

Deliverance: A Romance of the Virginia Tobacco Fields. Ellen A. Glasgow. 1977. 23.95 (0-8369-7161-2, 7993) Ayer.

Deliverance: Face a Face. Phillipe Sollers & Maurice Clavel. 160p. (FRE.). 1977. pap. 13.95 (0-7859-1248-7, 2020045761) Fr & Eur.

*Deliverance: The Story of Six Young Men, A. A. & God. Dick B. 200p. Date not set. pap. text ed. 16.95 (1-881212-10-6) Good Bk Pub.

*Deliverance & Healing Manual. Archie R. Shanks. 1995. reprint ed. 5.95 (0-9646769-1-5) Crown of Life.

Deliverance & Inner Healing: A Comprehensive Guide. John Sandford & Mark Sandford. LC 92-27970. 320p. (Orig.). 1992. pap. 14.99 (0-8007-9206-8) Chosen Bks.

Deliverance & Spiritual Warfare Manual. John Eckhardt. 64p. (Orig.). 1993. 10.00 (0-9630567-7-8) Crusaders Minist.

Deliverance for Children & Teens, Vol. 3. (Power for Deliverance Ser.). (Orig.). 1989. pap. 5.95 (0-89228-034-4) Impact Christian.

Deliverance from Childlessness. Bill Banks. 140p. 1990. pap. 5.95 (0-89228-037-9) Impact Christian.

Deliverance from Drugs. Marvin Yakos. LC 89-5445. (Illus.). 192p. (Orig.). 1989. pap. 6.99 (0-932581-46-3) Word Aflame.

*Deliverance from Error & Mystical Union with the Almighty: Al-Munqid Min Al-Dalal. Al Ghazali. Tr. by Muhammad Abulaylah. LC 95-14438. (Cultural Heritage & Contemporary Change. Series IIA, Islam: Vol.2). 1995. write for info. (1-56518-081-X); pap. write for info. (1-56518-082-8) Coun Res Values.

*Deliverance from Evil Spirits: A Practical Manual. 2nd ed. Francis MacNutt. LC 95-5150. 288p. (Orig.). 1995. pap. 11.99 (0-8007-9232-7) Chosen Bks.

Deliverance from Evil Spirits: A Weapon for Spiritual Warfare. Michael Scanlan & Randall J. Cirner. 125p. (Orig.). 1980. pap. 7.99 (0-89283-091-3) Servant.

Deliverance from Fat, Vol. 2. Bill Banks. (Power for Deliverance Ser.). (Orig.). 1988. pap. 5.95 (0-89228-032-8) Impact Christian.

Deliverance from Fear. Bob Buess. 96p. 1993. pap. 3.99 (0-88368-233-8) Whitaker Hse.

Deliverance from Hunger: The Public Distribution System in India. K. R. Venugopal. (Illus.). 222p. (C). 1992. 29.95 (0-8039-9408-7) Sage.

D

Deliverance from the Bondage of Fear. Bob Buess. 1972. reprint ed. pap. 2.50 (0-934244-03-0) Sweeter Than Honey.

Deliverance Ministry. George Birch. 1989. pap. 11.99 (0-88965-084-5, Pub. by Horizon Books CN) Chr Pubns.

Deliverance to the Captives. Karl Barth. LC 78-12767. 160p. 1979. reprint ed. text ed. 35.00 (0-313-21179-5, BADC, Greenwood Pr) Greenwood.

Delivered from Death Unto Life. Norman McFarland. 70p. 1974. pap. write for info. (1-881909-06-9) Advent Christ Gen Conf.

Delivered from Evil. Billy J. Daugherty. 32p. (Orig.). 1992. pap. 0.50 (1-56267-089-1) Victory Ctr OK.

Delivered from Evil: The Saga of World War II - The First Complete One-Volume History. Robert Leckie. LC 86-46305. 1024p. 1988. reprint ed. pap. 18.00 (0-06-091535-8, PL 1535, PL) HarpC.

Delivered from Torment. 2nd ed. Archie R. Shanks. 139p. 1989. reprint ed. 9.00 (*0-9646769-0-7*) Crown of Life. This book is designed to help a person be an overcomer over doubts, fears, unbelief, occult, frustrations, depression as well as be healed in their bodies of any & all sicknesses. Book designed for all faiths, Protestant, Catholic & Jewish. Adults have trouble with straight facts as they do not want to admit they do not know everything. Deliverance is basically a question of dealing with ownership. You must leave the past behind & go forward in life. This book teaches you HOW to be an OVERCOMER & WIN IN LIFE. Example: IMAGINATIONS: The Bible clearly says in Jeremiah 4:4a to ask the Lord to cut out any thought you should not have & it will leave immediately. You can depend on it to work everytime! HEALINGS & MIRACLES spelled out in the book to give HOPE to people that they can be healed also. Stories of cancer healed, broken bones healed, people lifted out of depression & oppression. This Ministry gives seminars all over the country upon request as well as in Haiti, Nassau, Nigeria, West Africa, Jamaica, Trinidad & India. Please feel free to call 1-313-531-6820 or write to P.O. Box 401016, Redford, MI 48239.** ***Publisher Provided Annotation.

Deliverers of Their Country. Edith Nesbit. LC 85-9389. (Illus.). 32p. (J). (gr. 3-5). 1991. pap. 15.95 (0-88708-005-7, Picture Book Studio) S&S Childrens.

*Delivering a Course: Practical Strategies for Teachers, Lecturers & Trainers. Ian Forsyth et al. 96p. 1995. pap. 28.95 (0-7494-1531-2) Nichols Pub.

*Delivering Customer Service Using Client Server Architecture. J. S. Bate & S. Hope. 300p. 1995. 65.00 (1-872474-20-9, Pub. by Alfred Waller UK) Paul & Co Pubs.

*Delivering Customer Value: It's Everyone's Job. Karl Albrecht. LC 95-12452. (Management Master Ser.: Vol. 16). (Illus.). 64p. 1995. 15.95 (1-56327-095-1) Prod Press.

Delivering Effective Training. Tom W. Goad. LC 82-50125. 189p. 1982. pap. 29.95 (0-88390-173-0) Pfeiffer & Co.

Delivering Effective Training Sessions. Geri McArdle. Ed. by Philip Gerould. (Fifty-Minute Ser.). 100p. (Orig.). 1993. pap. 9.95 (1-56052-193-7) Crisp Pubns.

Delivering Government Services: An Annotated Bibliography. William J. Murin & Judith Pryor. (Public Affairs & Administration Ser.). 352p. 1988. lib. bdg. 51.00 (0-8240-6618-9) Garland.

*Delivering Health Care Comprehensively. R. Brotman et al. LC 89-20966. (Illus.). 180p. (Orig.). 1990. pap. text ed. 10.00 (0-9627072-0-1) Ctr CHP.

Delivering Health Care Comprehensively. Richard Brotman et al. LC 91-1952. 192p. 1991. text ed. 45.00 (0-275-93999-5, C3999, Praeger Pubs) Greenwood.

Delivering Health Care to Homeless Persons: The Diagnosis & Management of Medical & Mental Health Conditions. Ed. by David Wood. LC 91-5074. 304p. 1992. 38.95 (0-8261-7780-8) Springer Pub.

*Delivering Health Care to Refugees: Cross-Cultural Training to Enhance the Delivery of Quality Health Care to Culturally Diverse Persons. David Dunn. 32p. 1992. 5.00 (0-940723-08-5) SIIS.

Delivering High Technology Home Care: Issues for Decisionmakers. Ed. by Maxwell J. Mehlman & Stuart J. Youngner. LC 91-4741. 256p. 1991. 33.95 (0-8261-7610-0) Springer Pub.

Delivering Human Services: A Learning Approach to Practice. 3rd ed. Alexis A. Halley et al. 622p. (C). 1992. pap. text ed. 47.95 (0-8013-0667-1, 78644) Longman.

*Delivering In-House Outplacement: A Practical Handbook for Trainers, Managers, & Personnel Specialists. Alan Jones. LC 94-27727. 1995. pap. text ed. 29.95 (0-07-707895-0) McGraw.

*Delivering Individual & Group Learning. IPM Staff. (Training Delivery Ser.: No. 5). (C). 1994. pap. 93.00x (0-08-042161-X, Pub. by IPM Hse UK) St Mut.

Delivering Knock Your Socks off Service. Kristin Anderson & Ron Zemke. 130p. 1991. pap. 15.95 (0-8144-7777-1, 040533) AMACOM.

Delivering Motherhood: Maternal Ideologies & Practices in the 19th & 20th Centuries. Ed. by Katherine Arnup et al. 352p. 1990. 29.95 (0-415-02018-2, A3992) Routledge.

*Delivering on the Promise: Positive Practices for Immigrant Students. Rachel N. Sing & Vivian W. Lee. 188p. (Orig.). 1994. pap. 18.95 (1-880002-07-8) Natl Coal Advocates.

Delivering Primary Health Care: Nurse Practitioners at Work. Michael Yedidia. LC 81-1946. 152p. (C). 1981. text ed. 45.00 (0-86569-075-8, Auburn Hse) Greenwood.

Delivering Public Services in Western Europe: Sharing Western European Experiences on Para-Government Organization. Ed. by Christopher Hood & Gunner F. Schuppert. (Modern Politics Ser.: Vol. 16). 288p. (C). 1988. text ed. 45.00 (0-8039-8078-7) Sage.

Delivering Quality Service. Valarie A. Zeithaml. 1990. 32.95 (0-02-935701-2) Free Pr.

Delivering the Future Organization, Key Levers for Success: Corporate Sponsor Forum Proceedings, 1991. Ulrich Beer et al. 192p. 1992. pap. 29.95 (1-881115-00-3) Human Res Plan.

Delivering the Goods: Education As Cargo in Papua New Guinea. Colin Swatridge. LC 85-1376. (Illus.). 200p. (C). 1988. text ed. 75.00 (0-7190-1778-5, Pub. by Manchester Univ Pr UK) St Martin.

*Delivering the Goods: Public Works Technologies, Management & Financing. 1994. lib. bdg. 260.95 (0-8490-6428-7) Gordon Pr.

Delivering the Male: Out of the Tough Guy Trap into a Better Marriage. Clayton C. Barbeau. 136p. reprint ed. pap. 12.95 (0-9633157-1-4) Ikon Pr.

*Delivering Welfare: The Governance of the Social Services in the 1990s. Tony Butcher. LC 94-43713. (Public Policy & Management Ser.). 1995. text ed. write for info. (0-335-15711-4, Open Univ Pr); pap. write for info. (0-335-15710-6, Open Univ Pr) Taylor & Francis.

Delivery Alternatives for Residential Television, No. G-147. 171p. 1993. 2,450.00 (0-89336-057-0) BCC.

Delivery of Community Leisure Services: A Holistic Approach. James F. Murphy & Dennis R. Howard. LC 76-41372. 227p. reprint ed. pap. 64.70 (0-317-26690-X, 2056003) Bks Demand.

Delivery of Emergency Medical Services in Disasters: Assumptions & Realities. E. L. Quarantelli. LC 83-13028. 190p. (C). 1985. text ed. 29.50 (0-8290-0531-5) Irvington.

Delivery of Furies. large type ed. Victor Canning. 1992. 18.95 (0-7451-6400-5, Scarlet Dagger Lrg Print) Chivers N Amer.

Delivery of Furies. large type ed. Victor Canning. 1993. pap. 16.95 (0-7451-6406-4, Scarlet Dagger Lrg Print) Chivers N Amer.

Delivery of Health Care & International Medicine: Subject Analysis Index with Reference Bibliography. Alanzo G. Hofmeister. LC 85-47875. 150p. 1987. 39.50 (0-88164-350-5); pap. 34.50 (0-88164-351-3) ABBE Pubs Assn.

Delivery of Psychological Services in the Schools: Concepts, Precesses & Issues. Ed. by Stephen N. Elliot & Joseph C. Witt. 448p. (C). 1986. text ed. 89.95 (0-89859-581-9) L Erlbaum Assocs.

Delivery of Urban Services. Ed. by A. J. Swersey & E. J. Ingall. (TIMS Studies in the Management Sciences: Vol. 22). 408p. 1986. 65.00 (0-444-87824-6, North Holland) Elsevier.

*Delivery Strategies for Antisense Oligonucleotide Therapeutics. Ed. by Saghir Akhtar. 336p. 1995. 199.95 (0-8493-4778-5, 4778) CRC Pr.

Delivery Systems for Cancer Care. Groenwald. 1991. pap. 22.50 (0-86720-306-4) Jones & Bartlett.

Delivery Systems for Peptide Drugs. Ed. by S. S. Davis et al. LC 87-11036. (NATO ASI Series A, Life Sciences: Vol. 125). 380p. 1987. 110.00 (0-306-42496-7, Plenum Pr) Plenum.

Delivery Van: Words for Town & Country. Betsy Maestro. (Illus.). 32p. (J). (ps-2). 1990. 14.95 (0-395-51119-4, Clarion Bks) HM.

Dell & His Dot. Beverly Cory. (Ms. Stories Tell Tales Ser.). (Illus.). 64p. (Orig.). (J). (ps-4). 1993. pap. 9.95 (0-8449-4252-9); 4.95 (0-8449-4281-2); 4.95 (0-8449-4283-9); 4.95 (0-8449-4282-0); 4.95 (0-8449-4280-4) Good Morn Tchr.

Dell Big Book of Crosswords & Pencil Puzzles, No. 6. Ed. by Rosalind Moore. (Orig.). 1987. mass mkt. 9.99 (0-440-51899-7) Dell.

Dell Big Book of Crosswords & Pencil Puzzles, No. 7. Ed. by Rosalind Moore. (Orig.). (J). 1989. mass mkt. 9.99 (0-440-50161-X) Dell.

Dell Big Book of Crosswords & Pencil Puzzles No. 5. Ed. by Rosalind Moore. (Orig.). 1985. mass mkt. 8.95 (0-440-51877-6, Dell Trade Pbks) Dell.

*Dell Book of Anacrostic Puzzles. Dell Magazines Editors. 1995. 9.99 (0-440-50688-3) Dell.

Dell Book of Classic Logic Problems, No. 6. Dell Magazine Pubble Editors. 1994. mass mkt. 8.99 (0-440-50621-2) Dell.

Dell Book of Large Print Crosswords. large type ed. Wayne R. Williams. 1991. mass mkt. 8.95 (0-440-50350-7) Dell.

Dell Book of Logic Problems, No. 1. Ed. by Rosalind Moore. (Orig.). 1984. pap. 10.99 (0-440-51891-1, Dell Trade Pbks) Dell.

Dell Book of Logic Problems, No. 2. Ed. by Rosalind Moore. (Orig.). 1986. pap. 10.99 (0-440-51875-X, Dell Trade Pbks) Dell.

Dell Book of Logic Problems, No. 3. Ed. by Erica L. Rothstein & Renineke. (Orig.). (J). 1988. pap. 10.99 (0-440-50068-0, Dell Trade Pbks) Dell.

Dell Book of Logic Problems, No. 4. Erica L. Rothstein. (Orig.). 1989. mass mkt. 10.00 (0-440-50181-4, Dell Trade Pbks) Dell.

Dell Crossword Dictionary. Ed. by Kathleen Rafferty. (Orig.). 1984. mass mkt. 9.95 (0-440-56318-6, Dell Trade Pbks) Dell.

*Dell Crossword Dictionary. large type ed. Ed. by Kathleen Rafferty & Rosalind Moore. LC 94-44579. 1995. write for info. (0-7838-1227-2); pap. write for info. (0-7838-1228-0) Hall.

Dell Crossword Puzzles, No. 5. Dell Puzzle Magazine Editors. (Orig.). 1990. mass mkt. 5.95 (0-440-50283-7) Dell.

Dell Crossword Puzzles, No. 11. 1992. mass mkt. 5.99 (0-440-50295-0) Dell.

Dell Crossword Puzzles, No. 12. 1992. mass mkt. 6.99 (0-440-50297-7, Dell Trade Pbks) Dell.

Dell Crossword Puzzles, No. 13. Dell Magazine Editors. 1992. mass mkt. 6.99 (0-440-50493-7) Dell.

Dell Crossword Puzzles, No. 15. Dell Puzzle Magazines Editors. 1994. mass mkt. 8.99 (0-440-50519-4) Dell.

Dell Crossword Puzzles, No. 16. Dell Puzzle Magazine Editors. (Orig.). 1994. mass mkt. 8.99 (0-440-50628-X) Dell.

Dell Logic Problems, No. 5. Dell Magazine Editors. 1992. 10.99 (0-440-50298-5, Dell Trade Pbks) Dell.

Dell Paperbacks, Nineteen Forty-Two to Mid-Nineteen Sixty-Two: A Catalog-Index. Comp. by William H. Lyles. LC 82-25505. (Illus.). xxxv, 471p. 1983. text ed. 75.00 (0-313-23668-2, LYE/, Greenwood Pr) Greenwood.

Dell Turner: The Stories of His Life. John T. Meader. Ed. by Edward D. Ives. (Illus.). 150p. (Orig.). 1988. pap. 10.00 (0-943197-19-8) ME Folklife Ctr.

Della Robbia: A Family of Artists. Fiamma Domestici. Tr. by Christopher Evans. (Library of Great Masters). (Illus.). 80p. (Orig.). 1993. pap. 12.99 (1-878351-45-1) Riverside NY.

Delle Statue Antiche, Che Per Tutta Roma, in Diversi Luoghi, e Case si Veggono. Ulisses Aldroandi. xxiv, 315p. 1975. reprint ed. write for info. (3-487-05674-7, Pub. by Georg Olms GW) Lubrecht & Cramer.

Dellen Statistical Software Manual & Software to Accompany Statistics 5th Edition by James T. McClave, Frank Dietrich. 5th rev. ed. Michael Conlon & James T. McClave, II. (Illus.). 304p. (C). 1991. text ed. write for info. (0-02-324255-8) Macmillan.

Dell'Origine E Delle Regole Della Musica Colla Storia Del Suo Progresso, Decadenza E Rinnovazione. Antonio Eximeno. (Illus.). xii, 468p. 1983. reprint ed. write for info. (3-487-07137-1, Pub. by Georg Olms GW) Lubrecht & Cramer.

Delmar's Medical Assisting Video Series: Instructor's Guide. 25p. 1994. 12.00 (0-8273-6111-4) Delmar.

Delmar's Standard Textbook of Electricity. Stephen L. Herman. LC 92-11410. 1002p. 1993. text ed. 49.95 (0-8273-4934-3) Delmar.

Delmar's Standard Textbook of Electricity. rev. ed. Stephen L. Herman. 1002p. 1994. text ed. 49.95 (0-8273-6849-6) Delmar.

Delmar's Standard Textbook of Electricity: Instructor's Guide. Stephen L. Herman. 48p. 1993. 12.00 (0-8273-4935-1) Delmar.

Delmar's Standard Textbook of Electricity Transparency Package. Stephen L. Herman. 1993. 129.95 (0-8273-5608-0) Delmar.

Delmarva Conspiracy. Sharon Miner. LC 92-72680. 136p. (YA). (gr. 7-9). 1993. 14.95 (1-880851-06-7) Greene Bark Pr.

*Delmore Brothers: Truth Is Stranger Than Publicity. Alton Delmore. Ed. by Charles K. Wolfe. LC 95-69025. (Illus.). 256p. Date not set. reprint ed. pap. 14.95 (0-915608-15-4) Country Music Found.

Delo Akademika Vavilova. Mark Popovsky. LC 83-16435. (Illus.). 280p. (Orig.). (RUS.). 1983. pap. 10.00 (0-938920-33-2) Hermitage.

*Delog: Journey to Realms Beyond Death. Delog D. Drolma. Tr. by Richard Barron. LC 94-22389. (Illus.). 184p. (Orig.). 1995. pap. 13.95 (1-881847-05-5) Chagdud Gonpa-Padma.

Deloitte's 1992 Guide. Richard Gleed et al. 125p. 1989. pap. 14.95 (0-406-50480-6) Michie Butterworth.

Deloraine, 3 vols. in 2, Set. William Godwin. LC 79-8271. reprint ed. 84.50 (0-404-61867-7) AMS Pr.

Delpha Green & Company. Vera Cleaver & Bill Cleaver. LC 79-172141. 144p. (J). (gr. 6 up). 1972. pap. 2.95 (0-397-31344-6, LSC-8, Junior Bks) HarpC.

Delphi. Old Vicarage Publications Staff. 96p. (C). 1982. pap. text ed. 33.00 (0-947818-01-4, Pub. by Old Vicarage UK) St Mut.

Delphi. Frederik Poulsen. 38.95 (0-405-19034-4) Ayer.

Delphi: The Official Guide. 2nd rev. ed. Michael A. Banks. Ed. by Chip Matthes. 300p. 1990. reprint ed. pap. text ed. 19.95 (0-9625623-0-0) Genl Videotex.

Delphi: The Official Guide. 3rd rev. ed. General Videotex Corporation Staff. reprint ed. pap. 19.95 (0-9625623-1-9) Genl Videotex.

Delphi: The Official Guide. 4th rev. ed. Delphi Internet Services Corp. Staff. pap. text ed. 19.95 (0-9625623-2-7) Genl Videotex.

Delphi see Greek Museums

*Delphi Developer's Guide. Teixeira & Pacheco. (Illus.). 950p. (Orig.). 1995. pap. 45.00 (0-672-30704-9) Sams.

*Delphi Nuts & Bolts: For Experienced Programmers. Gary Cornell & Troy Strain. 1995. pap. text ed. 24.95 (0-07-882136-3) Osborne-McGraw.

*Delphi Power Toolkit. 800p. 1995. cd-rom 49.95 (1-56604-292-5) Ventana Pr.

*Delphi Program for Dummies. Neil Rubenking. 1995. pap. 19.99 (1-56884-200-7) IDG Bks.

*Delphi Programming Explorer. Duntemann. 1995. pap. text ed. 39.99 (1-883577-25-X) Coriolis Grp.

*Delphi Starter Kit (Box) Coriolis Group Staff. 1995. pap. 99.99 (1-883577-55-1) Coriolis Grp.

Delphic Choice. Norma Johnston. LC 88-24570. 208p. (YA). (gr. 7 up). 1989. text ed. 14.95 (0-02-747711-8, Four Winds Pr) S&S Childrens.

Delphic Maxims in Literature. Eliza G. Wilkins. 281p. 1993. pap. 18.95 (1-56459-423-8) Kessinger Pub.

Delphic Oracle: Its Early History, Influence & Fall. T. Dempsey. LC 69-13234. 1972. reprint ed. 18.95 (0-405-08442-0) Ayer.

Delphine. Molly Bang. LC 87-34958. (Illus.). 32p. (J). (gr. 2 up). 1988. 12.95 (0-688-05636-9); lib. bdg. 12.88 (0-688-05637-7) Morrow Jr Bks.

*Delphine. Germaine De Stael. Tr. by Avriel Goldberger. LC 94-45742. 550p. 1995. lib. bdg. 50.00 (0-87580-200-1); pap. 22.95 (0-87580-567-1) N Ill U Pr.

Delphinium Blossoms. Ed. by Cecile Engel et al. 303p. 1990. 18.95 (1-883285-05-4) Delphinium.

Delphiniums. David Bassett. (Wisley Handbook Ser.). (Illus.). 64p. 1994. pap. 5.95 (0-304-32022-6, Pub. by Cassell UK) Sterling.

*Delphiniums: The Complete Guide. Colin Edwards. (Illus.). 160p. 1995. pap. 19.95 (1-85223-891-7, Pub. by Crowood Pr UK) Trafalgar.

Delsarte Recitation Book. 4th ed. Comp. by Elsie M. Wilbor. LC 77-167487. (Granger Index Reprint Ser.). 1977. reprint ed. 34.95 (0-8369-6292-3) Ayer.

Delson's Dictionary of Cable, Video & Satellite Terms. Donn Delson & Ed Michalove. Ed. by Neil Posner. LC 82-17767. (Entertainment Communication Ser.: Vol. 3). (Orig.). 1982. pap. 6.95 (0-9603574-3-2, A-4) Bradson.

Delson's Dictionary of Motion Picture Marketing Terms. rev. ed. Donn Delson & Stuart Jacob. (Entertainment Communication Ser.). 104p. 1990. pap. 14.95 (0-9603574-7-5, A-2B) Bradson.

Delson's Dictionary of Radio & Record Industry Terms. Donn Delson & Walter E. Hurst. Ed. by Neil Posner. LC 80-24486. (Entertainment Communication Ser.: Vol. 2). 112p. (Orig.). (C). 1981. pap. 9.95 (0-9603574-2-4) Bradson.

1862

An Asterisk (*) at the beginning of an entry indicates that the title is appearing in BIP for the first time.

An Asterisk (*) at the beginning of an entry indicates that the title is appearing in BIP for the first time.

1863

Demand for Money: Some Theoretical & Empirical Results. Milton Friedman. (Occasional Papers: No. 68). 30p. 1959. reprint ed. 20.00 (*0-87014-382-4*) Natl Bur Econ Res.

Demand for Money: Theories, Evidence, & Problems. 3rd ed. David E. Laidler. 178p. (C). 1990. pap. text ed. 19.50 (*0-06-043827-4*) HarpCollege.

Demand for Money: Theories, Evidence, & Problems. 4th ed. David E. Laidler. LC 92-11945. (C). 1992. 38.00 (*0-06-501098-1*) HarpCollege.

Demand for Money by Firms. C. Robert Coates. LC 75-11418. (Business Economics & Finance Ser.: No. 7). 191p. reprint ed. pap. 54.50 (*0-8357-6087-1*, 2034525) Bks Demand.

Demand for Money in Israel, 1955-1967. Lewis Mandell. LC 75-192. (Business Economics & Finance Ser.: No. 3). 132p. reprint ed. pap. 37.70 (*0-7837-0785-1*, 2041099) Bks Demand.

Demand for Primary Health Services in the Third World. John S. Akin et al. LC 84-18153. (Illus.). 272p. 1985. 61.50 (*0-8476-7355-3*, R7355) Rowman.

Demand for Recreation in America. National Recreation & Park Association Staff. (Quest for Quality Ser.: No. 1). 39p. reprint ed. pap. 25.00 (*0-7837-1537-4*, 2041819) Bks Demand.

Demand for Urban Water. P. Darr et al. (Studies in Applied Regional Science: No. 6). 1976. pap. text ed. 33.50 (*90-207-0647-0*) Kluwer Ac.

Demand Forecasting & Financial Risk Assessment. 64p. 1985. pap. 12.50 (*0-89867-339-9*, 20192) Am Water Wks Assn.

Demand Forecasting for Electric Utilities. Clark W. Gellings. (Illus.). 518p. 1991. pap. 95.00 (*0-88173-126-9*, 0264) Fairmont Pr.

Demand Functions & the Slutsky Matrix. S. N. Afriat. LC 79-83973. (Mathematical Economics Studies: No. 7). 1980. 42.50x (*0-691-04222-5*) Princeton U Pr.

Demand Management. Ed. by Herbert Giersch. 258p. 1972. lib. bdg. 34.00 (*3-16-333421-0*, Pub. by J C B Mohr GW) Coronet Bks.

Demand Processing & Performance in Public Service Agencies. Stephen L. Percy & Eric J. Scott. LC 83-9325. (Illus.). xiv, 167p. 1984. 21.50 (*0-8173-0204-2*) U of Ala Pr.

Demand-Side Constraints & Structural Adjustment in Sub-Saharan African Countries. large type ed. U. Koester et al. 90p. 1990. 10.00 (*0-89629-313-0*) Intl Food Policy.

Demand Side Management. Ron L. Highnote. 108p. (C). 1990. 69.95 (*1-880168-03-0*) Inst Applied Sci.

Demand Side Management. Richard K. Miller & Marcia E. Rupnow. (Survey on Technology & Markets Ser.: No. 220). 50p. 1993. pap. text ed. 200.00 (*1-55865-251-5*) Future Tech Surveys.

Demand-Side Management: Concepts & Methods. 2nd ed. Clark W. Gellings & John H. Chamberlin. LC 92-21944. 1992. write for info. (*0-88173-148-X*) Fairmont Pr.

Demand Side Management: Opportunities & Perspectives in the Asia-Pacific Region with Emphasis on the Gas & Electricity Sectors. OECD Staff. 308p. (Orig.). 1994. pap. 42.00 (*0-317-05753-7*) OECD.

Demand-Side Management: Opportunities & Perspectives in the Asia-Pacific Region, with Emphasis on the Gas & Electricity Sectors. OECD Staff. 308p. (Orig.). 1994. pap. text ed. 42.00 (*92-64-14060-3*, 61-94-03-1) OECD.

Demand-Side Management & Electricity End-Use Efficiency. Ed. by Anibal T. De Almeida & Arthur H. Rosenfeld. (C). 1988. lib. bdg. 212.00 (*90-247-3698-6*) Kluwer Ac.

Demand-Side Management Planning. Fairmont Press Staff et al. 1992. text ed. 85.00 (*0-13-204983-X*) P-H.

Demand-Side Management Planning. Clark W. Gellings & John H. Chamberlin. LC 92-14179. 452p. 1992. 85.00 (*0-88173-149-8*) Fairmont Pr.

Demand System Specification & Estimation. Robert A. Pollak & Terence J. Wales. (Illus.). 232p. 1992. 45.00 (*0-19-506941-2*) OUP.

***Demand System Specification & Estimation.** Robert A. Pollak & Terence J. Wales. (Illus.). 256p. 1995. reprint ed. pap. 19.95 (*0-19-510121-9*) OUP.

Demand the Impossible: Science Fiction & the Utopian Imagination. Tom Moylan. 256p. 1987. 39.95 (*0-317-54027-0*, 1125); pap. 14.95 (*0-416-00022-3*, 1154) Routledge Chapman & Hall.

Demande see Oeuvres

Demanding Clean Food & Water: The Fight for a Basic Human Right. Joan Goldstein. (Illus.). 290p. 1990. 25.00 (*0-306-43570-5*, Plenum Pr) Plenum.

Demanding Democracy. Robert Schmuhl. (C). 1994. text ed. 22.95 (*0-268-00872-8*); pap. text ed. 10.95 (*0-268-00873-6*) U of Notre Dame Pr.

Demanding Democracy after Three Mile Island. Raymond L. Goldsteen & John K. Schorr. 304p. (C). 1991. lib. bdg. 37.95 (*0-8130-1073-X*); pap. text ed. 18.95 (*0-8130-1098-5*) U Press Fla.

Demanding Literature: Soviet Literature of the 70s & Early 80s. Boris Pankin. 340p. 1984. 30.00 (*0-317-56655-5*, Pub. by Collets UK) Pro-Am Music.

Demanding Skill: Women & Technology. Pocock. 1989. pap. text ed. 18.95 (*0-04-332137-2*, Pub. by Allen Unwin AT) Paul & Co Pubs.

Demands for Early Closing Hours: 1843. LC 72-2523. (British Labour Struggles Before 1850 Ser.). 1974. reprint ed. 20.95 (*0-405-04416-X*) Ayer.

Demands for Energy & Conservation in the United States. Ed. by Noel D. Uri. LC 82-81205. (Contemporary Studies in Energy Analysis & Policy: Vol. 1). 208p. 1982. 73.25 (*0-89232-278-0*) Jai Pr.

Demands of Art: With an Appendix, Toward an Empirical Theory of Art. Max Raphael. LC 65-10431. (Bollingen Ser.: No. 78). (Illus.). 293p. reprint ed. pap. 83.60 (*0-317-10221-4*, 2051182) Bks Demand.

Demands of Love. Miriam W. Moyer. 1978. 6.15 (*0-686-24048-0*) Rod & Staff.

Demarcating the Disciplines: Philosophy, Art, Literature. Glyph Textual Studies Staff. Ed. by Samuel Weber. LC 84-28057. 263p. 1986. pap. text ed. 11.95 (*0-8166-1398-2*) U of Minn Pr.

Demasiados Globos (Too Many Balloons) Catherine Matthias. LC 81-15520. (Rookie Reader Ser.). (Illus.). 32p. (SPA.). (J). (ps-2). 1990. pap. 2.95 (*0-516-53633-8*) Childrens.

Demass: Transforming the Dinosaur Corporation. M. M. Stuckey. LC 92-28998. (Illus.). 283p. 1993. 25.00 (*1-56327-042-0*) Prod Press.

Demassification: A Cost Comparison of Micro vs. Mini. M. M. Stuckey. Ed. by Susan Kamener & Larry Pape. (Illus.). 150p. (Orig.). 1989. pap. 19.95 (*0-9623283-0-8*) Fourth Shift.

Dematerialization of Karl Marx: Literature & Marxist Theory. Leonard Jackson. LC 93-39201. 352p. (C). 1994. pap. text ed. 28.50 (*0-582-06655-7*, Pub. by Longman UK) Longman.

Dematerialization of Karl Marx: Literature & Marxist Theory. Leonard Jackson. LC 93-39201. 352p. (C). 1995. text ed. 58.95 (*0-582-06654-9*, Pub. by Longman UK) Longman.

Dematiaceous Hyphomycetes. M. B. Ellis. 608p. 1971. pap. text ed. 60.00 (*0-85198-017-1*) CAB Intl.

Dematiaceous Hyphomycetes. M. B. Ellis. 608p. (C). 1971. text ed. 60.00 (*0-85198-618-8*) CAB Intl.

Demaundes of Holy Scripture, with Answers to the Same. Thomas Becon. LC 79-84087. (English Experience Ser.: No. 907). 116p. 1979. reprint ed. lib. bdg. 9.00 (*90-221-0907-0*) Walter J Johnson.

DeMaury Papers. Isabelle Holland. 1978. pap. 1.75 (*0-449-23606-4*, Crest) Fawcett.

***Demele Yon Mo! Unscramble-a-Word.** Oroste Joseph. Ed. by Rita Parisse et al. Tr. & Illus. by Maryse Joseph. 24p. (CRP.). 1995. pap. 3.00 (*1-885566-06-9*) Oresjozef.

Demensions of Energy Economics. Noel D. Uri. Ed. by Edward I. Altman & Ingo Walter. LC 01-81656. (Contemporary Studies in Economic & Financial Analysis: Vol. 32). 275p. 1981. 73.25 (*0-89232-226-8*) Jai Pr.

Dementations on Shank's Mare. Jonathan Williams. 48p. 1988. 7.00 (*0-916562-24-7*) Truck Pr.

Demented Flute: Selected Poems, 1967-1986. Sasaki Mikiro. Ed. by Thomas Fitzsimmons. Tr. by William I. Elliott et al. (Asian Poetry in Translation: Japan Ser.: No. 9). 64p. (Orig.). 1988. lib. bdg. 14.50 (*0-942668-15-4*); pap. 9.50 (*0-942668-14-6*) Katydid Bks.

Dementia. A. J. Edwards. (Perspectives on Individual Differences Ser.). (Illus.). 310p. (C). 1993. 45.00 (*0-306-44286-8*, Plenum Pr) Plenum.

Dementia. Michael A. Stackpole. (Mutant Chronicles Ser.: No. 3). 256p. 1994. pap. 4.99 (*0-451-45417-0*, ROC) NAL-Dutton.

Dementia. Ed. by Peter J. Whitehouse. (Contemporary Neurology Ser.: No. 40). (Illus.). 465p. 1993. 90.00 (*0-8036-9271-4*) Davis Co.

Dementia. 2nd ed. B. Mahendra. 1987. lib. bdg. 78.00 (*0-7462-0044-7*) Kluwer Ac.

Dementia: A Clinical Approach. 2nd ed. Jeffrey L. Cummings & D. Frank Benson. 548p. 1992. text ed. 95.00 (*0-7506-9065-8*) Buttrwrth-Heinemann.

***Dementia: Annotated Bibliography of the Dementia Associated Diseases & Diagnostic Tests.** Jay B. Cohn. 437p. (Orig.). 1992. pap. text ed. 40.00 (*0-935645-03-9*) AJFP.

Dementia: Its Nature & Management. Morris Fraser. 241p. 1987. text ed. 144.95 (*0-471-91548-3*) Wiley.

Dementia: Molecules, Methods & Measures. Ed. by I. Stonier Hindmarch et al. 208p. 1991. text ed. 109.95 (*0-471-92874-7*, Wiley-Liss) Wiley.

Dementia: New Skills for Social Workers. Ed. by Alan Chapman & Mary Marshall. LC 93-38449. (Case Studies for Practice Ser.: No. 5). 160p. 1994. pap. 23.00 (*1-85302-142-3*, Pub. by J Kingsley Pubs UK) Taylor & Francis.

Dementia: Presentations, Differential Diagnosis, & Nosology. Ed. by V. Olga Emery & Thomas E. Oxman. (Johns Hopkins Series in Psychiatry & Neuroscience). 432p. (C). 1993. text ed. 85.00 (*0-8018-4681-1*) Johns Hopkins.

Dementia & Aging: Ethics, Values, & Policy Choices. Ed. by Robert H. Binstock et al. 224p. 1992. text ed. 50.00 (*0-8018-4424-X*); pap. text ed. 18.95 (*0-8018-4545-9*) Johns Hopkins.

Dementia & Communication. Lubinski. 336p. (C). 1990. 55.00 (*1-55664-202-4*) Mosby Yr Bk.

***Dementia & Communication.** Ed. by Rosemary Lubinski. (Illus.). 320p. (C). 1995. pap. text ed. 45.00 (*1-56593-084-3*, 1138) Singular Publishing.

Dementia & Home Care: A Research Report on a Home Support Scheme for Dementia Sufferers. Janet Askham & Catherine Thompson. 176p. (C). 1990. 75.00 (*0-86242-091-1*, Pub. by Age Concern Eng UK) St Mut.

Dementia & Homecare. Janet Askham & Catherine Thompson. (C). 1989. 65.00 (*0-685-50532-4*, Pub. by Age Concern Eng UK) St Mut.

Dementia & Normal Aging. Ed. by Felicia A. Huppert et al. (Illus.). 400p. (C). 1994. 89.95 (*0-521-41393-1*) Cambridge U Pr.

Dementia Care: Patient, Family, & Community. Ed. by Nancy L. Mace. LC 89-8106. 416p. 1991. reprint ed. text ed. 50.00 (*0-8018-3859-2*); reprint ed. pap. text ed. 18.95 (*0-8018-4314-6*) Johns Hopkins.

Dementia Disorders: Advances & Prospects. Ed. by Cornelius Katona. 232p. 1990. 69.95 (*0-412-32860-7*, A3988) Chapman & Hall.

Dementia in Later Life: Research & Action. (Technical Report Ser.: No. 730). 74p. 1986. pap. 6.00 (*92-4-120730-2*) World Health.

Dementia Praecox or the Group of Schizophrenias. Eugen Bleuler. Tr. by Joseph Zinkin. (Monograph Series on Schizophrenia: No. 1). 548p. 1966. text ed. 62.50 (*0-8236-1180-9*) Intl Univs Pr.

Dementia Units in Long-Term Care. Ed. by Philip D. Sloane & Laura J. Mathew. LC 91-7100. (Series in Contemporary Medicine & Public Health). 304p. 1991. text ed. 45.00 (*0-8018-4246-8*) Johns Hopkins.

***Dementia with Dignity.** rev. ed. Barbara Sherman. (Illus.). 219p. 1994. pap. text ed. 29.95 (*0-07-470184-3*) Hlth Prof Div.

Dementias. Ed. by Richard Mayeux & Wilma G. Rosen. (Advances in Neurology Ser.: Vol. 38). 288p. 1983. text ed. 80.00 (*0-89004-696-4*) Raven.

Dementias: A Pathological Sequelae to Glutamate Neurotoxicity. Makram K. Girgis & Katherine Harris. (Illus.). 205p. 1992. 27.50 (*0-87527-350-5*) Green.

***Dementias: Diagnosis, Management, & Research.** 2nd ed. Ed. by Myron F. Weiner. 1995. boxed 68.50 (*0-88048-718-6*, 8718) Am Psychiatric.

Dementielle Hirnerkrankung im Alter. Ed. by W. Meier-Ruge. (Geriatrie fuer die Taegliche Praxis Ser.: Vol. 3). viii, 216p. 1993. pap. 25.75 (*3-8055-4509-6*) S Karger.

Dementing Brain Disease in Old Age. Ed. by W. Meier-Ruge. (Teaching & Training in Geriatric Medicine Ser.: Vol. 3). viii, 216p. 1993. pap. 29.00 (*3-8055-4478-2*) S Karger.

Demerara Martyr: Memoirs of the Reverend John Smith, Missionary to Demerara. Edwin A. Wallbridge. LC 70-79812. (Illus.). 274p. 1970. reprint ed. 52.50 (*0-8371-1511-6*, WAD&, Negro U Pr) Greenwood.

Demes of Attica, 508-7 -ca. 250 B.C.: A Political & Social Study. David Whitehead. LC 85-42709. (Illus.). 485p. 1986. 85.00x (*0-691-09412-8*) Princeton U Pr.

Demesne of the Swans - Lebedinyi Stan. 2nd ed. Marina I. Tsvetaeva. Tr. by Robin Kemball. 211p. (Orig.). Date not set. pap. 15.95 (*0-88233-494-8*) Ardis Pubs.

Demeter & Persephone: The Seasons of Time. I. M. Richardson. LC 82-16023. (Illus.). 32p. (J). (gr. 4-8). 1983. lib. bdg. 11.79 (*0-89375-863-9*); pap. text ed. 2.95 (*0-89375-864-7*) Troll Assocs.

Demeter & Persephone in Ancient Corinth. Nancy Bookidis & Ronald Stroud. (American Excavations in Old Corinth, Corinth Notes Ser.: No. 2). (Illus.). 32p. 1987. pap. 3.00 (*0-87661-671-6*) Am Sch Athens.

Demeter's Manual of Parliamentary Law & Procedure: The Blue Book Edition. George Demeter. 1969. 22.95 (*0-316-18030-0*) Little.

Demetri Porphyrios Selected Buildings & Writings. Demetri Porphyrios. (Architectural Monographs: No. 25). (Illus.). 144p. (Orig.). 1993. 55.00 (*1-85490-174-5*, Academy Edits) St Martin.

Demetrio Aguilera-Malta & Social Justice: The Tertiary Phase of Epic Tradition in Latin American Literature. Clementine C. Rabassa. LC 78-75193. 304p. 1970. 32.50 (*0-8386-2079-5*) Fairleigh Dickinson.

Demetrios Capetanakis. Demetrios Capetanakis. LC 73-148208. (Biography Index Reprint Ser.). 1977. 20.95 (*0-8369-8055-7*) Ayer.

Demetrios Constantine Dounis: His Method in Teaching the Violin. Chris A. Costantakos. (American University Studies: Language: Ser. XIV, Vol. 13). 260p. (C). 1988. text ed. 38.50 (*0-8204-0667-8*) P Lang Pubs.

Demetrius see Bride of Messina

Demetrius Legend & Its Literary Treatment in the Age of the Baroque. Ervin C. Brody. LC 73-141869. 323p. 1975. 37.50 (*0-8386-7969-2*) Fairleigh Dickinson.

Demetrius on Style. Demetrius. Ed. by W. R. Connor. LC 78-18597. (Greek Texts & Commentaries Ser.). (ENG & GRE.). 1979. reprint ed. lib. bdg. 28.95 (*0-405-11438-9*) Ayer.

Demi-Monde. Alexandre Dumas. LC 87-7395. 164p. 1987. reprint ed. lib. bdg. 29.50 (*0-86527-364-2*) Fertig.

Demi-Solde. Jean Dutourd. 192p. (FRE.). 1983. pap. 10.95 (*0-7859-1978-3*, 2070374882) Fr & Eur.

Demian. Hermann Hesse. 1976. 18.95 (*0-8488-1048-1*) Amereon Ltd.

Demian. Hermann Hesse. 1989. reprint ed. lib. bdg. 21.95 (*0-89966-630-2*) Buccaneer Bks.

Demian: A Novel. Hermann Hesse. 192p. (C). 1990. reprint ed. lib. bdg. 27.00x (*0-8095-9003-4*) Borgo Pr.

Demian: A Novel. Hermann Hesse. LC 89-45668. 192p. 1989. reprint ed. pap. 10.00 (*0-06-091652-4*, PL) HarpC.

Demigod. Jeff Putnam. LC 93-70994. 320p. 20.00 (*1-880909-09-X*) Baskerville.

DeMilles Family an American Family. Anne Edwards. 1988. 39.95 (*0-318-33427-5*) Abrams.

Demineralization by Ion Exchange. Samuel B. Applebaum. LC 68-18653. 1968. text ed. 163.00 (*0-12-058950-8*) Acad Pr.

Demineralizers & Polishers. Center for Occupational Research & Development Staff. (EUTEC Power Plant Operator Curriculum Ser.). (Illus.). 34p. (C). 1985. pap. text ed. write for info. (*1-55502-226-X*) CORD Commns.

***Deming: The Way We Knew Him.** Ed. by Frank Voehl. 250p. 1995. text ed. 29.95 (*1-884015-54-9*) St Lucie Pr.

Deming Dimension. Henry R. Neave. 464p. (C). 1990. 40.00 (*0-945320-08-6*); pap. 20.00 (*0-945320-36-1*) SPC Pr.

Deming Guide to Achieving Quality & Competitive Position. Howard Gitlow & Shelly Gitlow. (Illus.). 192p. 1987. 31.95 (*0-13-198441-1*) P-H.

Deming Management at Work. Mary Walton. 256p. 1991. pap. 12.00 (*0-399-51685-9*, Perigee Bks) Berkley Pub.

Deming Management at Work. Mary Walton. 256p. 1991. 21.95 (*0-399-13557-X*, Putnam) Putnam Pub Group.

Deming Management Method. Mary Walton. 256p. 1988. pap. 12.00 (*0-399-55000-3*, Perigee Bks) Berkley Pub.

Deming Management Method. Mary Walton. 1986. 19.95 (*0-399-55001-1*, Putnam) Putnam Pub Group.

Deming Route to Quality & Productivity: Road Maps & Roadblocks. William W. Scherkenbach. LC 87-401099. 154p. 1986. pap. 17.95 (*0-941893-00-6*) CEEPress Bks.

Deming Vision. SPC - TQM for Administrations Staff & Gary Fellers. 209p. 1992. 25.95 (*0-87389-128-7*) ASQC Qual Pr.

Deming's Fourteen Points Applied to Services. A. C. Rosander. (Quality & Reliability Ser.: Vol. 25). 168p. 1991. 55.00 (*0-8247-8517-7*) Dekker.

Deming's Profound Changes: When Will the Sleeping Giant Wake Up? Kenneth T. Delavigne & J. Daniel Robertson. LC 93-42352. 300p. 1994. 24.95 (*0-13-292690-3*) P-H.

Deming's Road to Continual Improvement. William W. Scherkenbach. (Illus.). 360p. 1991. 32.00 (*0-945320-10-8*) SPC Pr.

Demi's Dragons & Fantastic Creatures. Demi. (Illus.). 50p. (J). (ps-2). 1993. 19.95 (*0-8050-2564-2*, Bks Young Read) H Holt & Co.

Demi's Find the Animal A B C. Demi. (Illus.). 48p. (J). 1990. pap. 5.95 (*0-448-19165-2*, G&D) Putnam Pub Group.

Demi's Secret Garden. Illus. & Comp. by Demi. LC 92-27204. 50p. (J). (ps-2). 1993. 19.95 (*0-8050-2553-7*, Bks Young Read) H Holt & Co.

Demise & Regenesis of East Central Europe: Roots of the Political Forces & Their Evolvement. Jouffroy-Lucien Radel. (Illus.). 240p. (Orig.). (C). 1991. pap. text ed. 9.95 (*0-9625359-3-1*) Lakesider Pub.

***Demise of a Dragon: A Work of Fiction.** Harry E. Ewing. LC 95-8085. (Illus.). 80p. (J). (gr. 6-12). 1995. 12.95 (*0-944957-54-4*) Rivercross Pub.

Demise of a Rural Economy: From Subsistence to Capitalism in a Latin American Village. Stephen Gudeman. (International Library of Anthropology). 1978. pap. 14.95 (*0-7100-8836-1*, RKP) Routledge.

Demise of American Nuclear Power: Learning from the Failure of a Politically Unsafe Technology. Joseph Morone & Edward Woodhouse. LC 88-39306. 168p. (C). 1989. text ed. 8.00 (*0-300-04448-8*); pap. 8.00 (*0-300-04449-6*) Yale U Pr.

***Demise of Billy the Kid.** large type ed. Preston Lewis. LC 95-2476. 484p. 1995. 19.95 (*0-7838-1280-9*) Thorndike Pr.

***Demise of Billy the Kid: The Memoirs of H. H. Lomax.** Preston Lewis. 1994. 5.50 (*0-553-56541-9*) Bantam.

Demise of the Author: Autonomy & the German Writer, 1770-1848. Roger F. Cook. LC 92-30153. (Studies in Modern German Literature: Vol. 52). 229p. (C). 1993. text ed. 46.95 (*0-8204-2012-3*) P Lang Pubs.

Demise of the Devil: Magic & the Demonic in Luke's Writings. Susan R. Garrett. LC 89-36046. 192p. (Orig.). 1989. pap. 23.00 (*0-8006-2409-2*, 1-2409) Augsburg Fortress.

Demise of the Reasonable Man: A Cross-Cultural Study of a Legal Concept. Michael Saltman. 224p. (C). 1991. 39.95 (*0-88738-388-2*) Transaction Pubs.

Demise of the Soviet Union: A Bibliographic Survey of English Writings on the Soviet Legal System 1990-1991. Intro. by Igor I. Kavass. LC 92-24865. 288p. 1992. 115.00 (*0-89941-804-X*, 307610) W S Hein.

Demise of the Stars & Stripes. M. Clayton McAffee. 1994. 13.95 (*0-8062-4826-2*) Carlton.

***Demo a Day: A Year of Chemical Demonstrations.** Borislaw Bilash, 2nd et al. Ed. by Mark W. Meszaros. (Illus.). 295p. (Orig.). (YA). (gr. 9-12). 1995. pap. text ed. 33.95 (*1-877991-36-8*) Flinn Scientific.

***Demo Details: Parachute Demonstration Performances.** **2nd ed. Byron T. Dormire. LC 95-92241. 176p. 1995. pap. text ed. 22.95 (*1-887260-07-2*) Dormire Pub.**

DEMO DETAILS - THE INS & OUTS OF PARACHUTE DEMONSTRATION PERFORMANCES is written for Parachute Exhibition jumpers &/or Sponsors who organize promotional affairs for celebrations, special events, or any other occasion. An all-purpose technical reference, it assists parachutists in profiting both financially & professionally within the lucrative discipline of skydiving for shows. Promoters too, can benefit from quintessential publicity elements that go into planning, funding, & organizing a parachuting event. With coordination assistance delineated for anyone who wants to assemble a parachute team for show, masterful skydiving performances can be produced without a hitch. "TEAM elements" help novice to expert jumpers find serious sponsors, complete FAA paperwork, choreograph smoke freefalls & flag parachute work, format show narrations, perform show landings anywhere in safety, contact other professional teams, & more. "SPONSOR elements" help organizers find & recognize a competent parachute team, understand FAA aerial event prerequisites, know that jumper

1864

An Asterisk (*) at the beginning of an entry indicates that the title is appearing in BIP for the first time.

insurance is easily secured, & promote even the smallest, most important affair. Orders $22.95 + $3.50p/h; Dormire Publishing Company, P.O. Box 635, Barksdale AB, LA. 71110-0635. VISA/ MC Cards - (318)949-1763. ***Publisher Provided Annotation.***

DEMO: Dictionnaire Elementaire de Mathematiques Modernes: Elementary Dictionary of Modern Math. Jean-Louis Boursin. 181p. (FRE.). 1987. pap. write for info. (*0-7859-4809-0*) Fr & Eur.

Demo to Ink. Ron Silliman. 180p. (Orig.). 1992. pap. 11.00 (*0-925904-07-4*) Chax Pr.

Demobilization: Our Industrial & Military Demobilization after the Armistice, 1918-1920. Benedict Crowell & Robert F. Wilson. LC 74-75236. (United States in World War I Ser.). (Illus.). xvi, 333p. 1974. reprint ed. lib. bdg. 36.95 (*0-89198-102-0*) Ozer.

***Demobilization & Deintegration after Civil Wars.** Mats R. Berdal. (Adelphi Papers). 1995. pap. text ed. 23.00 (*0-19-828026-2*) OUP.

Demobilization of American Voters: A Comprehensive Theory of Voter Turnout. Michael J. Avey. LC 89-11881. (Contributions in Political Science Ser.: No. 244). 162p. 1989. text ed. 45.00 (*0-313-26600-X*, ADV/, Greenwood Pr) Greenwood.

Democide: Nazi Genocide & Mass Murder. R. J. Rummel. 150p. (C). 1991. text ed. 34.95 (*1-56000-004-X*) Transaction Pubs.

Democracia Integral. Instituto de Solidaridad Cristiana Staff. LC 92-71667. 136p. (Orig.). (SPA.). 1992. pap. 9.95 (*0-89729-648-6*) Ediciones.

***Democracia y Mercado (Democracy & the Market) Reformas Politicas y Economicas en la Europa Del Este y America Latina (Political & Economic Reforms in Eastern Europe & Latin America)** Adam Przeworski. Tr. by Mireia B. Abello. (Illus.). (C). Date not set. pap. write for info. (*0-521-47645-3*) Cambridge U Pr.

Democracies: Patterns of Majoritarian & Consensus Government in Twenty-One Countries. Arend Lijphart. LC 83-14639. 248p. 1984. pap. 12.00 (*0-300-03182-3*, Y 493) Yale U Pr.

Democracies Against Terror: The Western Response to State-Supported Terrorism. Geoffrey M. Levitt. 1988. write for info. (*0-318-63177-6*, Praeger Pubs) Greenwood.

***Democracies & Foreign Policy: Public Participation in the United States & the Netherlands.** Bernard C. Cohen. LC 94-38501. 208p. (Orig.). (C). 1995. lib. bdg. 55.00 (*0-299-14640-5*); pap. text ed. 19.95 (*0-299-14644-8*) U of Wis Pr.

Democracies & Tyrannies of the Caribbean. William Krehm. LC 84-15726. 272p. 1984. pap. 9.95 (*0-88208-169-1*) L Hill Bks.

Democracies at the Turning Point: Britain, France & the End of the Postwar Order, 1928-1933. Maarten L. Pereboom. LC 94-13004. (Studies in Modern European History: Vol. 13). 1995. write for info. (*0-8204-2535-4*) P Lang Pubs.

Democracies in Crisis. Mary M. Slappey. (Illus.). 150p. (J). 1992. pap. 10.95 (*0-930061-27-6*) Interspace Bks.

Democracies in Regions of Crisis: Botswana, Costa Rica & Israel. National Democratic Institute for International Affairs Staff. LC 90-60684. 145p. 1990. pap. 7.95 (*1-880134-03-9*) Natl Demo Inst.

Democractic Liberalism & Social Union. Terry Pinkard. LC 86-23088. 240p. 1987. 32.95 (*0-87722-458-7*) Temple U Pr.

Democracy. Henry Adams. Ed. by Peter Katopes. 1991. 12.95 (*0-8084-0430-X*) NCUP.

Democracy. Anthony Arblaster. LC 87-18130. (Concepts in Social Thought Ser.). 119p. (Orig.). 1988. text ed. 39.95 (*0-8166-1664-7*); pap. text ed. 11.95 (*0-8166-1665-5*) U of Minn Pr.

***Democracy.** Carl Cohen. 315p. (C). 1994. pap. text ed. 17.95 (*1-57074-230-8*) Greyden Pr.

***Democracy.** Joan Didion. 1995. pap. 12.00 (*0-679-75485-7*, Vin) Random.

Democracy. Ed. by John Dunn. 304p. 1994. pap. 15.95 (*0-19-827934-5*) OUP.

Democracy. Ross Harrison. LC 92-30811. (Problems of Philosophy Ser.). 304p. 1993. 49.95 (*0-415-03254-7*, A4763) Routledge.

Democracy. Romulus Linney. 1976. pap. 4.75 (*0-8222-0299-9*) Dramatists Play.

***Democracy.** Ed. by Richard Maidment. (The U. S. in the Twentieth Century Ser.). 288p. 1994. pap. 14.95 (*0-340-59686-4*, Pub. by E Arnld UK) St Martin.

Democracy. Don Nardo. LC 93-4912. (Overview Ser.). (J). (gr. 5-8). 1994. 16.95 (*1-56006-147-2*) Lucent Bks.

Democracy. 2nd ed. Anthony Arblaster. LC 94-9589. (Concepts in Social Thought Ser.). (Orig.). 1994. pap. text ed. 14.95 (*0-8166-2601-4*) U of Minn Pr.

Democracy. Henry Adams. reprint ed. lib. bdg. 20.95 (*0-89190-525-1*, Queens House) Amereon Ltd.

Democracy. Thomas Jefferson. Ed. by Saul K. Padover. LC 69-13952. 291p. 1970. reprint ed. text ed. 35.00 (*0-8371-1985-5*, JEDE, Greenwood Pr) Greenwood.

***Democracy: A Play.** Murrell. 1993. per. 10.95 (*0-921368-28-3*, Pub. by Blizzard Pub CN) InBook.

Democracy: A Project by Group Material. Ed. by Brian Wallis. LC 89-650815. (Discussions in Contemporary Culture Ser.: No. 5). (Illus.). 334p. (Orig.). (C). 1990. pap. 14.95 (*0-941920-17-8*) Bay Pr.

Democracy: A Worldwide Survey. Ed. by Robert Wesson. LC 86-30443. 273p. 1987. text ed. 59.95 (*0-275-92440-8*, C2440, Praeger Pubs) Greenwood.

Democracy: An American Novel. Henry Adams. (Airmont Classics Ser.). (YA). (gr. 9 up). 1968. pap. 1.50 (*0-8049-0164-3*, CL-164) Airmont.

Democracy: An American Novel. Henry Adams. 1983. mass mkt. 9.95 (*0-452-00942-1*, Plume) NAL-Dutton.

Democracy: An American Novel. Henry Adams. 1983. pap. 3.50 (*0-452-00651-1*, Mer) NAL-Dutton.

Democracy: An American Novel. Henry Adams. 1988. reprint ed. lib. bdg. 59.00 (*0-7812-1437-8*) Rprt Serv.

Democracy: An American Novel. Henry Adams. 1976. reprint ed. 59.00 (*0-403-05724-8*, Regency) Scholarly.

Democracy: Can't We Do Better Than That? Bob Avakian. LC 86-3650. 277p. 1986. 29.95 (*0-916650-30-8*); pap. 10.95 (*0-916650-29-4*) Banner Pr.

Democracy: Key Concepts in Critical Theory. Ed. by Philip Green. LC 92-19823. 336p. (C). 1993. pap. 17.50 (*0-391-03779-X*) Humanities.

Democracy: The Unfinished Journey, 508 BC to AD 1993. Ed. by John Dunn. LC 92-8526. 304p. (C). 1992. 30.00 (*0-19-827378-9*) OUP.

Democracy: Theory & Practice. John Arthur. 369p. 1992. pap. 27.95 (*0-534-17148-6*) Intl Thomson.

Democracy see Novels, Mont Saint Michel, the Education

Democracy - The Myth, the Reality: A Primer on the True Nature of Our Democratic Republic. Wallace R. Wirths. Ed. by Florence Lawrence. LC 93-91396. 269p. 1993. lib. bdg. 21.95 (*0-940797-01-1*) Media Spec.

Democracy According to Islam. Niaz F. Kabuli. 216p. 1994. 14.95 (*0-8059-3545-2*) Dorrance.

***Democracy Against Capitalism: Renewing Historical Materialism.** Ellen M. Wood. 336p. (C). 1995. 59.95 (*0-521-47096-X*); pap. 18.95 (*0-521-47682-8*) Cambridge U Pr.

Democracy Against Itself: The Future of the Democratic Impulse. Jean-Francois Revel. 300p. 1993. text ed. 24.95 (*0-02-926387-5*) Free Pr.

Democracy Ancient & Modern. rev. ed. M. I. Finley. 195p. (C). 1985. pap. 15.00 (*0-8135-1127-5*) Rutgers U Pr.

Democracy & American Foreign Policy: Reflections on the Legacy of Tocqueville. Robert Strausz-Hupe. 141p. (C). 1994. 29.95 (*1-56000-175-5*) Transaction Pubs.

Democracy & Arab Political Culture. 2nd rev. ed. Elie Kedourie. LC 93-4779. 118p. (C). 1994. pap. 17.50 (*0-7146-4509-5*, Pub. by F Cass Pubs UK) Intl Spec Bk.

Democracy & Authoritarianism in Peru: Political Coalitions & Social Change. Maxwell A. Cameron. LC 94-9119. 1994. text ed. 39.95 (*0-312-12153-9*) St Martin.

***Democracy & Authoritarianism in South Asia: A Comparative & Historical Perspective.** Ayesha Jalel. (Contemporary South Asia Ser.: 1). (Illus.). 308p. (C). 1995. pap. 19.95 (*0-521-47862-6*) Cambridge U Pr.

***Democracy & Authoritarianism in South Asia: A Comparative & Historical Perspective.** Ayesha Jalel. (Contemporary South Asia Ser.: 1). (Illus.). 308p. (C). 1995. 59.95 (*0-521-47271-7*) Cambridge U Pr.

Democracy & Bureaucracy: Tensions in the Provision of Public Education. Judith D. Chapman & Jeffrey Dunstan. 240p. 1990. 80.00 (*1-85000-790-X*, Falmer Pr); pap. 38.00 (*1-85000-791-8*, Falmer Pr) Taylor & Francis.

Democracy & Capitalism: Property, Community, & the Contradictions of Modern Social Thought. Samuel Bowles & Herbert Gintis. LC 85-47991. 256p. 1987. pap. text ed. 16.00 (*0-465-01601-4*) Basic.

Democracy & Civil Society. John B. Keane. 272p. 1988. text ed. 42.50 (*0-86091-201-9*, Pub. by Verso UK); pap. text ed. 14.95 (*0-86091-917-X*, Pub. by Verso UK) Routledge Chapman & Hall.

Democracy & Civil Society in Eastern Europe. Ed. by Paul G. Lewis. LC 92-1049. (Selected Papers from the Fourth World Congress for Soviet & East European Studies, Harrogate, 1990). 160p. 1992. text ed. 65.00 (*0-312-08042-5*) St Martin.

Democracy & Classical Greece. J. K. Davies. LC 83-45337. (Illus.). 284p. 1978. pap. 12.95 (*0-8047-1226-3*) Stanford U Pr.

Democracy & Classical Greece. 2nd ed. J. K. Davies. LC 93-795. 320p. 1993. pap. 14.50 (*0-674-19607-4*) HUP.

***Democracy & Communication in the New Europe: Change & Continuity in East & West.** Ed. by Farrel Corcoran & Paschal Preston. (IAMCR Book Ser.). 320p. 1995. text ed. 62.50 (*1-881303-88-8*) Hampton Pr NJ.

***Democracy & Communication in the New Europe: Change & Continuity in East & West.** Ed. by Farrel Corcoran & Paschal Preston. (IAMCR Book Ser.). 320p. 1995. pap. text ed. 24.95 (*1-881303-89-6*) Hampton Pr NJ.

Democracy & Complexity: A Realist Approach. Danilo Zolo. 224p. 1992. 35.00 (*0-271-00891-1*); pap. 16.95 (*0-271-00892-X*) Pa St U Pr.

Democracy & Decision: The Pure Theory of Electoral Preference. Ed. by Harold G. Brennan & Loren E. Lomasky. (Illus.). 256p. (C). 1989. 54.95 (*0-521-35043-3*) Cambridge U Pr.

Democracy & Deliberation: New Directions for Democratic Reform. James S. Fishkin. 172p. (C). 1992. text ed. 25.00x (*0-300-05161-1*) Yale U Pr.

Democracy & Deliberation: New Directions for Democratic Reform. James S. Fishkin. (Illus.). 141p. (C). 1993. pap. 12.00 (*0-300-05163-8*) Yale U Pr.

Democracy & Democratization. Ed. by Geraint Parry & Michael Moran. LC 93-725. 256p. 1993. 62.50 (*0-415-09049-0*, B2437, Routledge NY); pap. 17.95 (*0-415-09050-4*, B2441, Routledge NY) Routledge.

Democracy & Democratization: Processes & Prospects in a Changing World. George Sorensen. LC 92-28614. (Dilemmas in World Politics Ser.). 170p. (C). 1992. text ed. 54.50 (*0-8133-1526-3*); pap. text ed. 14.95 (*0-8133-1527-1*) Westview.

Democracy & Deterrence: The History & Future of Nuclear Strategy. Philip Bobbitt. LC 86-33918. 334p. 1988. text ed. 45.00 (*0-312-00522-9*); pap. 14.95 (*0-312-00723-X*) St Martin.

Democracy & Development. Axel Hadenius. (Illus.). 229p. (C). 1992. 47.95 (*0-521-41685-X*) Cambridge U Pr.

Democracy & Development in Latin America: Economics, Politics & Religion in the Postwar Period. David Lehmann. 1990. 49.95 (*0-87722-723-3*) Temple U Pr.

Democracy & Development in Latin America: Economics, Politics & Religion in the Postwar Period. David Lehmann. (C). 1992. pap. 22.95 (*1-56639-011-7*) Temple U Pr.

***Democracy & Development: States, Markets, & Societies in Their Context: Proceedings of the IEA Conference Held in Barcelona, Spain.** Ed. by Amiya Kumar Bagchi. LC 94-44767. (IEA Conference Ser.: Vol. 113). 1995. write for info. (*0-312-12465-1*) St Martin.

Democracy & Dictatorship. Norberto Bobbio. 216p. 1989. text ed. 39.95 (*0-8166-1812-7*); pap. text ed. 15.95 (*0-8166-1813-5*) U of Minn Pr.

***Democracy & Dictatorship: Their Psychology & Patterns of Life.** Zevedei Barbu. 1956. 69.50x (*0-614-01802-1*) Elliots Bks.

Democracy & Difference. Anne Phillips. 176p. 1993. 30.00 (*0-271-01096-7*); pap. 14.95 (*0-271-01097-5*) Pa St U Pr.

***Democracy & Diplomacy: The Impact of Domestic Politics on U. S. Foreign Policy, 1789-1994.** Melvin Small. (American Moment Ser.). 232p. 1995. text ed. 38.95x (*0-8018-5177-7*); pap. text ed. 13.95x (*0-8018-5178-5*) Johns Hopkins.

Democracy & Discontent: India's Growing Crisis of Governability. Atul Kohli. (Illus.). 400p. (C). 1991. 64.95 (*0-521-39161-X*); pap. 18.95 (*0-521-39692-1*) Cambridge U Pr.

Democracy & Discontent: Questions Facing the Political Process of Japan & the United States. Cokie Roberts & Ayako Sono. 140p. write for info. (*0-9635265-0-2*) U MT Mansfld.

Democracy & Disobedience. Peter Singer. (Modern Revivals in Philosophy Ser.). 160p. 1994. 51.95 (*0-7512-0314-9*, Pub. by Gregg Revivals UK) Ashgate Pub Co.

Democracy & Disorder: Protest & Politics in Italy, 1965-1975. Sidney Tarrow. (Illus.). 416p. 1989. 68.00 (*0-19-827561-7*) OUP.

Democracy & Distrust: A Theory of Judicial Review. John H. Ely. LC 79-19859. 268p. 1980. 30.00 (*0-674-19636-8*) HUP.

Democracy & Distrust: A Theory of Judicial Review. John H. Ely. LC 79-19859. (Harvard Paperbacks Ser.). 268p. 1981. pap. text ed. 15.95 (*0-674-19637-6*) HUP.

***Democracy & DNA: The Social Progress of American Medicine.** Gerald Weissmann. 288p. Date not set. 23.00 (*0-8090-9305-7*) FS&G.

Democracy & Economic Power: Extending the ESOP Revolution Through Binary Economics. rev. ed. Louis O. Kelso & Patricia H. Kelso. 202p. (C). 1991. lib. bdg. 47.50 (*0-8191-7908-6*); pap. text ed. 26.25 (*0-8191-7909-4*) U Pr of Amer.

Democracy & Education. James M. Tarrant. 150p. 1989. text ed. 55.95 (*0-566-07031-6*, Pub. by Avebury Pub UK) Ashgate Pub Co.

Democracy & Education: An Introduction to the Philosophy of Education. John Dewey. 1966. pap. 14.95 (*0-02-907370-7*) Free Pr.

***Democracy & Education in India.** Ed. by Krishna Kumar. (C). 1993. 29.00x (*81-7027-205-X*, Pub. by Radiant Pubs II) S Asia.

Democracy & Empire: With Studies of Their Psychological, Economic & Moral Foundations. Franklin H. Giddings. LC 72-5745. (Select Bibliographies Reprint Ser.). 1977. reprint ed. 25.95 (*0-8369-6908-1*) Ayer.

Democracy & Equality: Theories & Programs for the Modern World. Ronald M. Glassman. LC 88-27574. 234p. 1989. text ed. 55.00 (*0-275-93100-5*, C3100, Praeger Pubs) Greenwood.

Democracy & Finance in China. Kinn W. Shaw. LC 73-127445. (Columbia University. Studies in the Social Sciences: No. 282). reprint ed. 29.50 (*0-404-51282-8*) AMS Pr.

Democracy & Foreign Policy. Kjell Goldmann et al. 300p. 1985. text ed. 52.95 (*0-566-05012-9*) Ashgate Pub Co.

Democracy & Foreign Policy. Miroslav Nincic. 1992. text ed. 37.50 (*0-231-07668-1*) Col U Pr.

Democracy & Foreign Policy: Case History of the Sino-Japanese Dispute, 1931-33. Reginald G. Bassett. 680p. 1968. reprint ed. 35.00 (*0-7146-2209-5*, Pub. by F Cass Pubs UK) Intl Spec Bk.

Democracy & Foreign Policy: The Fall of Political Realism. Miroslav Nincic. 200p. 1994. pap. 16.50 (*0-231-07669-X*) Col U Pr.

Democracy & Foreign Policy: The Fallacy of Political Realism. Miroslav Nincic. 224p. 1992. text ed. 37.50 (*0-685-53218-6*) Col U Pr.

Democracy & Free Enterprise As Negative Utopia in America, 1980-1982. (Analysis Ser.: No. 10). 1983. pap. 10.00 (*0-686-42849-8*) Inst Analysis.

Democracy & Halakhan. Eliezer Schweid. LC 93-38732. (Milken Library of Jewish Public Affairs). 186p. Date not set. lib. bdg. 48.00 (*0-8191-9360-7*, Pub. by Jerusalem Ctr Public); pap. text ed. 19.50 (*0-8191-9430-1*, Pub. by Jerusalem Ctr Public) U Pr of Amer.

Democracy & Human Rights in the U. K., Report 4, No. RC4. 1994. pap. 20.00 (*0-685-75338-7*, Pub. by NCCL UK) St Mut.

***Democracy & International Conflict: An Evaluation of the Democratic Peace Proposition.** James Lee Ray. LC 95-4339. (Studies in International Relations). 1995. write for info. (*1-57003-041-3*) U of SC Pr.

Democracy & International Trade: Britain, France, & the United States, 1860-1990. Daniel Verdier. LC 93-34315. 1994. 45.00 (*0-691-03224-6*) Princeton U Pr.

Democracy & Its Critics. Robert A. Dahl. 405p. (C). 1991. reprint ed. pap. 18.00 (*0-300-04938-2*) Yale U Pr.

Democracy & Its Discontents: Reflections on Everyday America. Daniel J. Boorstin. 1974. 5.95 (*0-394-49146-7*) Random.

***Democracy & Judicial Independence: The Federal District Courts of Alabama, 1820-1994.** Tony Freyer & Timothy Dixon. 300p. 1995. 60.00 (*0-926019-86-4*) Carlson Pub.

Democracy & Leadership. Irving Babbitt. LC 78-11418. 1979. reprint ed. 14.00 (*0-913966-54-1*); reprint ed. pap. 7.00 (*0-913966-55-X*) Liberty Fund.

Democracy & Liberty, Set. William E. Lecky. LC 80-82371. 1981. reprint ed. 20.00 (*0-913966-80-0*); reprint ed. pap. 10.00 (*0-913966-81-9*) Liberty Fund.

Democracy & Liberty, Vol. I. William E. Lecky. LC 80-82371. 520p. 1981. reprint ed. 10.00 (*0-913966-82-7*) Liberty Fund.

Democracy & Liberty, Vol. II. William E. Lecky. 528p. 1981. reprint ed. write for info. (*0-913966-83-5*) Liberty Fund.

Democracy & Local Governance: Ten Empirical Studies. Ed. by Betty M. Jacob et al. 1994. write for info. (*0-318-72605-X*) S M Matsunaga.

Democracy & Markets: The Politics of Mixed Economies. John R. Freeman. LC 89-869. (Cornell Studies in Political Economy). (Illus.). 352p. 1989. 45.00 (*0-8014-2326-0*); pap. 13.95 (*0-8014-9601-2*) Cornell U Pr.

Democracy & Mediating Structures: A Theological Inquiry. Ed. by Michael Novak. 119p. 1979. 34.00 (*0-8447-2175-1*); pap. 12.50 (*0-8447-2176-X*) Am Enterprise.

Democracy & Modernity: International Colloquium on the Centenary of David Ben-Gurion. Ed. by S. N. Eisenstadt. LC 91-30460. (Studies in Human Society: No. 4). 184p. 1991. pap. 45.75 (*90-04-09544-6*) E J Brill.

Democracy & Moral Development: A Politics of Virtue. David L. Norton. LC 90-37723. 216p. 1991. 30.00 (*0-520-07067-4*) U CA Pr.

***Democracy & Moral Development: A Politics of Virtue.** David L. Norton. 1995. pap. 13.95 (*0-520-20348-8*) U CA Pr.

Democracy & New Technology. Iain McLean. (Illus.). 220p. 1989. text ed. 49.95 (*0-7456-0447-1*) Blackwell Pubs.

Democracy & Participation in Athens. R. K. Sinclair. 288p. 1988. 69.95 (*0-521-33357-1*) Cambridge U Pr.

Democracy & Participation in Athens. R. K. Sinclair. (Illus.). 270p. (C). 1991. pap. 21.95 (*0-521-42389-9*) Cambridge U Pr.

Democracy & Poetry. Robert Penn Warren. LC 74-31993. 96p. 1976. pap. 10.95 (*0-674-19626-0*) HUP.

***Democracy & Policing.** Trevor Jones et al. 333p. (C). 1995. pap. 19.95 (*0-85374-579-X*, Pub. by Pol Studies Inst UK) Brookings.

Democracy & Political Theory. Claude Lefort. Tr. by David Macey. LC 88-22034. 304p. (Orig.). 1989. text ed. 44.95 (*0-8166-1754-6*); pap. text ed. 17.95 (*0-8166-1755-4*) U of Minn Pr.

Democracy & Possessive Individualism: The Intellectual Legacy of C. B. Macpherson. Ed. by Joseph H. Carens. LC 92-17915. (SUNY Series in Political Theory: Contemporary Issues). 298p. 1993. 59.50 (*0-7914-1457-4*); pap. 19.95 (*0-7914-1458-2*) State U NY Pr.

Democracy & Poverty in Chile. James Petras et al. LC 93-43013. (Series in Political Economy & Economic Development in Latin America). 200p. (C). 1994. pap. text ed. 19.95 (*0-8133-8227-0*) Westview.

Democracy & Poverty in Chile. James Petras et al. LC 93-43013. (Series in Political Economy & Economic Development in Latin America). 200p. (C). 1994. text ed. 58.00 (*0-8133-8217-3*) Westview.

Democracy & Public Policy. Huey L. Perry. LC 85-51337. 75p. (Orig.). (C). 1985. pap. 14.95 (*0-932269-46-X*) Wyndhall Pr.

Democracy & Punishment: Disciplinary Origins of the United States. Thomas L. Dumm. LC 87-40147. (Rhetoric of the Human Sciences Ser.). 224p. (C). 1987. text ed. 40.00 (*0-299-11400-7*); pap. text ed. 15.75 (*0-299-11404-X*) U of Wis Pr.

Democracy & Race: Asian Americans & World War II. Ronald Takaki. LC 94-6175. 1994. write for info. (*0-7910-2184-X*) Chelsea Hse.

Democracy & Race Friction. John M. Mecklin. LC 70-124244. (Select Bibliographies Reprint Ser.). 1977. reprint ed. 20.95 (*0-8369-5432-7*) Ayer.

Democracy & Race Friction: A Study in Social Ethics. John M. Mecklin. LC 78-172717. reprint ed. 24.50 (*0-404-00090-8*) AMS Pr.

Democracy & Revolution. George Novack. LC 74-143807. 286p. 1993. reprint ed. lib. bdg. 50.00 (*0-87348-192-5*); reprint ed. pap. 18.95 (*0-87348-191-7*) Pathfinder NY.

Democracy & Right-Wing Politics in Eastern Europe in the 1990s. Ed. by Joseph Held. LC 93-71934. (East European Monographs: No. 376). 232p. 1993. 35.00 (*0-88033-273-5*, 376) Col U Pr.

Democracy & Scarcity: A Study in Their Historical & Theoretical Patterns of Interconnection. Aryeh Botwinick. 195p. 1986. pap. text ed. 14.95 (*0-932269-80-X*) Wyndhall Pr.

Democracy & Social Ethics: And Other Essays. Jane Addams. reprint ed. 59.00 (*0-403-00824-7*) Scholarly.

Democracy & Social Ethnics. Jane Addams. 1988. reprint ed. lib. bdg. 75.00 (*0-7812-0225-6*) Rprt Serv.

Democracy & Social Growth in America. Bernard Moses. 1977. 59.95 (*0-8490-1706-8*) Gordon Pr.

An Asterisk (*) at the beginning of an entry indicates that the title is appearing in BIP for the first time.

Democracy & Social Injustice: Law, Politics, Politics & Philosophy. Thomas W. Simon. LC 94-16452. (Studies in Social & Political Philosophy). 320p. (C). 1994. lib. bdg. 69.50 (*0-8476-7937-3*); pap. 24.95 (*0-8476-7938-1*) Rowman.

Democracy & Socialism in Africa. Ed. by Robin Cohen & Harry Goulbourne. 272p. 1991. text ed. 53.00 (*0-8133-8052-9*) Westview.

Democracy & Socialism in Sandinista Nicaragua. Harry E. Vanden & Gary Prevost. LC 92-24289. 184p. 1993. lib. bdg. 34.00 (*1-55587-227-1*) Lynne Rienner.

Democracy & the Amendments to the Constitution. Alan P. Grimes. (Illus.). 206p. (C). 1987. reprint ed. pap. text ed. 22.00 (*0-8191-6286-8*) U Pr of Amer.

Democracy & the Arts: The Role of Participation. Terri L. Cornwell. LC 90-30004. 240p. 1990. text ed. 55.00 (*0-275-93070-X*, C3070, Praeger Pubs) Greenwood.

***Democracy & the Arts of Schooling.** Donald Arnstine. LC 95-4243. 352p. (C). 1995. text ed. 74.50x (*0-7914-2721-8*); pap. 24.95x (*0-7914-2722-6*) State U NY Pr.

Democracy & the Athenians: Aspects of Ancient Politics. Ed. by Frank J. Frost. LC 70-81338. (Major Issues in History Ser.). 159p. reprint ed. pap. 45.40 (*0-317-09303-7*, 2051578) Bks Demand.

Democracy & the Capitalist State. Ed. by Graeme Duncan. 330p. 1989. pap. 21.95 (*0-521-28062-1*) Cambridge U Pr.

Democracy & the Case for Amnesty. Alfonso J. Damico. LC 75-12502. (University of Florida Monographs: Social Sciences: No. 55). 86p. reprint ed. pap. 25.00 (*0-7837-4950-3*, 2044616) Bks Demand.

Democracy & the Civic Community: Tradition & Change in an Italian Experiment. Robert D. Putnam. (Illus.). 288p. 1992. text ed. 35.00 (*0-691-07889-0*) Princeton U Pr.

Democracy & the Cost of Politics in Britain. Pref. by William B. Gwyn. LC 79-28340. (Illus.). vii, 256p. 1980. reprint ed. text ed. 59.75 (*0-313-22257-6*, GWDC, Greenwood Pr) Greenwood.

Democracy & the Ethical Life: A Philosophy of Politics & Community. Claes G. Ryn. LC 77-9505. 246p. 1990. pap. 14.95 (*0-8132-0711-8*) Cath U Pr.

Democracy & the Kingdom of God, Vol. 17. Howard P. Kainz. LC 92-40289. 1993. lib. bdg. 115.00 (*0-7923-2106-5*) Kluwer Ac.

Democracy & the Liberal State. Philip K. Lawrence. 213p. 1989. text ed. 55.95 (*1-85521-019-3*, Pub. by Dartmth Pub UK) Ashgate Pub Co.

Democracy & the Limits of Free Speech. Cass R. Sunstein. 300p. 1993. text ed. 22.95 (*0-02-932271-5*) Free Pr.

Democracy & the Market: Political & Economic Reforms in Eastern Europe & Latin America. Adam Przeworski. (Studies in Rationality & Social Change). (Illus.). 200p. (C). 1991. 47.95 (*0-521-41225-0*); pap. 15.95 (*0-521-42335-X*) Cambridge U Pr.

Democracy & the Mass Media. Ed. by Judith Lichtenberg. (Cambridge Studies in Philosophy & Public Policy). 336p. (C). 1990. pap. 21.95 (*0-521-38817-1*) Cambridge U Pr.

Democracy & the Mass Media. Ed. by Judith Lichtenberg. 1990. 44.50 (*0-317-05240-3*); pap. 14.95 (*0-317-05241-1*) IPPP.

D

Democracy & the Nation State: Aliens, Denizens & Citizens in a World of International Migration. Tomas Hammar. (Illus.). 215p. 1990. text ed. 59.95 (*0-566-07100-2*, Pub. by Avebury Pub UK) Ashgate Pub Co.

Democracy & the Novel: Popular Resistance to Classic American Writers. Henry N. Smith. LC 78-1290. 1981. pap. 7.95 (*0-19-502896-1*) OUP.

Democracy & the Organization of Political Parties, 2 vols. abr. ed. Moisei Ostrogorski. LC 81-2862. (Social Science Classics Ser.). 350p. (C). 1982. reprint ed. Vol. 1: England, 350p. pap. 29.95 (*0-87855-877-2*); reprint ed. Vol. 2: United States, 418p. pap. 29.95 (*0-87855-878-0*) Transaction Pubs.

Democracy & the Organization of Political Parties, 2 Vols. Moisei Ostrogorski. LC 72-122620. (World History Ser.: No. 48). 1970. reprint ed. lib. bdg. 150.00 (*0-8383-1003-6*) M S G Haskell Hse.

Democracy & the Organization of Political Parties, 2 vols., Set. abr. ed. Moisei Ostrogorski. LC 81-2862. (Social Science Classics Ser.). (C). 1982. reprint ed. pap. 39.95 (*0-87855-921-3*) Transaction Pubs.

Democracy & the Party System in the United States: A Study in Extra Constitutional Government. Moisei Ostrogorski. LC 73-19166. (Politics & People Ser.). 480p. 1974. reprint ed. 35.95 (*0-405-05888-8*) Ayer.

***Democracy & the Problem of Free Speech.** Sunstein. 1995. pap. 14.95 (*0-02-874000-9*) Free Pr.

Democracy & the Public Library: Essays on Fundamental Issues. Ed. by Arthur W. Hafner. LC 93-13014. (Contributions in Librarianship & Information Science Ser.: No. 78). 344p. 1993. text ed. 57.95 (*0-313-28667-1*, HDX/, Greenwood Pr) Greenwood.

Democracy & the Public Service. Frederick C. Mosher. (Public Administration & Democracy Ser.). 1968. 12.95 (*0-19-500031-5*) OUP.

Democracy & the Public Service. 2nd ed. Frederick C. Mosher. (Public Administration & Democracy Ser.). (Illus.). (C). 1982. pap. text ed. 14.95 (*0-19-503018-4*) OUP.

Democracy & the Renewal of Public Education, Vol. 4. Richard J. Neuhaus. (Encounter Ser.). 184p. (Orig.). 1987. pap. 11.99 (*0-8028-0204-4*) Eerdmans.

Democracy & the State: An Introduction to Politics. J. E. Esberey & L. W. Johnston. 350p. 1994. pap. text ed. 24. 95 (*1-55111-039-3*) Broadview Pr.

Democracy & the State: The Rise of Administrative Politics in Britain & the U. S. Ed. by B. Guy Peters & James F. Hollifield. 288p. (C). 1996. text ed. 65.00 (*0-8133-8319-6*) Westview.

Democracy & the Welfare State. Ed. by Amy Gutmann. (Studies from the Project on the Federal Social Role). 352p. 1988. pap. text ed. 16.95 (*0-691-02275-5*) Princeton U Pr.

***Democracy & Violence in India & Sri Lanka.** Dennis Austin. LC 94-44994. 1995. 14.95 (*0-87609-174-5*) Coun Foreign.

Democracy & Welfare Economics. 2nd ed. Hans Van den Doel & Ben Van Velthoven. LC 92-23167. (Illus.). 220p. (DUT & ENG.). (C). 1993. 49.95 (*0-521-43057-7*); pap. 15.95 (*0-521-43637-0*) Cambridge U Pr.

Democracy As a Planning System. Charles Lachenmeyer. (Analysis Ser.). 33p. (Orig.). 1981. pap. text ed. 18.00 (*0-938526-03-0*) Inst Analysis.

Democracy Assemblages. Andrew Levy. 32p. 1990. 7.50 (*0-911623-08-6*) I Klang.

Democracy at Risk. Kenneth M. Dolbeare. LC 86-9607. (Chatham House Series on Change in American Politics). 255p. reprint ed. pap. 72.70 (*0-7837-2604-X*, 2042768) Bks Demand.

Democracy at War: America's Fight at Home & Abroad in World War II. William L. O'Neill. 400p. (Orig.). 1993. text ed. 24.95 (*0-02-923678-9*) Free Pr.

***Democracy at War: America's Fight at Home & Abroad in World War II.** William L. O'Neill. (Illus.). 496p. (Orig.). (C). 1995. pap. 16.95 (*0-674-19737-2*) HUP.

Democracy at Work. Fred Emery & Elnar Thorsrud. (Studies in the Quality of Working Life: No. 2). 1976. lib. bdg. 44.50 (*90-207-0633-0*) Kluwer Ac.

Democracy at Work: Changing World Markets & the Future of Labor Unions. Lowell Turner. LC 91-55049. (Cornell Studies in Political Economy). 304p. 1991. 29. 95 (*0-8014-2627-8*) Cornell U Pr.

Democracy at Work: Changing World Markets & the Future of Labor Unions. Lowell Turner. LC 91-55049. (Cornell Studies in Political Economy). 304p. 1993. pap. 12.95 (*0-8014-8118-X*) Cornell U Pr.

Democracy (B. Nineteen Eighty-Four) Robert Leon. 1993. 18.95 (*0-533-10586-2*) Vantage.

Democracy, Bureacracy & Public Choice. Patrick Dunleavy. 224p. (C). 1991. pap. text ed. write for info. (*0-13-201146-8*) P-H.

Democracy by Default: Dependency & Clientelism in Jamaica. Carlene J. Edie. LC 90-47119. 170p. 1990. lib. bdg. 33.50 (*1-55587-225-5*) Lynne Rienner.

***Democracy by Other Means: The Politics of Work, Leisure & Environment.** John Buell. LC 94-45940. 1995. write for info. (*0-252-02181-9*); pap. write for info. (*0-252-06471-2*) U of Ill Pr.

***Democracy, Chaos, & the New School Order.** Spencer J. Maxcy. 240p. 1994. 45.95 (*0-8039-6198-7*) Corwin Pr.

***Democracy, Chaos, & the New School Order.** Spencer J. Maxcy. 240p. 1994. pap. 22.95 (*0-8039-6199-5*) Corwin Pr.

Democracy, Clientelism, & Civil Society. Ayse Gunes-Ayata. Ed. by Luis Roniger. LC 94-4469. 223p. 1994. lib. bdg. 40.00 (*1-55587-340-5*) Lynne Rienner.

***Democracy, Competition & Choice: Emerging Local Self-Government in Nepal.** John Martinussen. LC 94-45236. 188p. (C). 1995. 22.95 (*0-8039-9224-6*) Sage.

Democracy, Constructive & Pacific see Popular View of the Doctrines of Charles Fourier

Democracy Delayed: Congressional Reapportionment & Urban-Rural Conflict in the 1920s. Charles W. Eagles. LC 89-5044. 184p. 1990. 25.00 (*0-8203-1185-5*) U of Ga Pr.

Democracy, Development & Distortion: Punjab Politics in National Perspective. A. S. Narang. 1986. 22.00 (*0-8364-1537-X*, Pub. by Gitanjali Prakashan) S Asia.

***Democracy, Development, & the Countryside: Urban-Rural Struggles in India.** Ashutosh Varshney. (Cambridge Studies in Comparative Politics). (Illus.). 224p. (C). 1995. 54.95 (*0-521-44153-6*) Cambridge U Pr.

***Democracy, Dialogue & Environmental Disputes: The Contested Languages of Social Regulation.** Bruce A. Williams & Albert R. Matheny. LC 95-7650. 1995. write for info. (*0-300-06241-9*) Yale U Pr.

Democracy, Dictatorship & Development. George Sorensen. LC 90-30360. 250p. 1991. text ed. 49.95 (*0-312-04642-1*) St Martin.

Democracy Dies in Dallas: Cops, Lies & Videotape. Arthur F. Ide. LC 89-38693. (Illus.). 220p. (Orig.). 1990. pap. 12.00 (*0-934667-07-1*) Tangelwuld.

Democracy East & West: A Philosophical Overview. Howard P. Kainz. LC 84-6881. 200p. 1984. text ed. 29. 95 (*0-312-19220-7*) St Martin.

Democracy, Education, & Governance: A Developmental Conception. Dale T. Snauwaert. LC 92-19819. (SUNY Series, Global Conflict & Peace Education). 145p. (C). 1993. 44.50 (*0-7914-1459-0*); pap. 14.95 (*0-7914-1460-4*) State U NY Pr.

***Democracy, Education, & the Schools.** Ed. by Roger Soder. (Education Ser.). 1995. 29.95 (*0-7879-0166-0*) Jossey-Bass.

***Democracy Empire Britain, 1865-1914.** E. J. Feuchtwanger. (New History of England Ser.). 416p. 1985. pap. 27.95 (*0-7131-6162-0*, Pub. by E Arnld UK) St Martin.

Democracy for Americans: A Real Plan to Reinvent the Government. Vincent Mountjoy-Pepka. 256p. (Orig.). 1994. pap. 12.00 (*0-9639883-8-7*) Kick Pr.

***Democracy for the Few.** Michael Parenti. 384p. 1994. pap. text ed. 14.00 (*0-312-05233-2*) St Martin.

Democracy for the Privileged: Crisis & Transition in Venezuela. Brian S. Hillman. LC 93-42932. 200p. 1994. 38.00 (*1-55587-412-6*) Lynne Rienner.

Democracy for Young Americans. Jerry Aten. 112p. (J). (gr. 4-8). 1989. 10.95 (*0-86653-483-0*, GA1083) Good Apple.

Democracy from Below: New Social Movements & the Political System in West Germany. Ruud Koopmans. (C). 1995. text ed. 60.00 (*0-8133-8721-3*) Westview.

***Democracy from Scratch: Opposition & Regime in the New Russian Revolution.** Steven M. Fish. LC 94-21026. 1994. 39.50 (*0-691-03703-5*) Princeton U Pr.

Democracy from the Heart: Spiritual Values, Decentralism, & Democratic Idealism in the Movement of the 1960s. Gregory N. Calvert. 302p. (Orig.). (C). 1991. lib. bdg. 29.95 (*0-9628800-1-9*); pap. 14.95 (*0-9628800-0-0*) Communitas Oregon.

Democracy Gap: The Politics of Information & Communication Technologies in the United States & Europe. Jill Hills & S. Papathanassopoulos. LC 90-22396. (Contributions to the Study of Mass Media & Communications Ser.: No. 30). 232p. 1991. text ed. 55. 00 (*0-313-26170-9*, HPN, Greenwood Pr) Greenwood.

***Democracy Imposed: U. S. Occupation Policy & the German Public, 1945-1949.** Richard L. Merritt. LC 95-4263. 1995. write for info. (*0-300-06037-8*) Yale U Pr.

Democracy in a Communist Party: Poland's Experience since 1980. Werner G. Hahn. (Illus.). 400p. 1987. text ed. 56.00 (*0-231-06540-X*) Col U Pr.

Democracy in a Technological Society. Ed. by Langdon Winner. LC 92-31873. (Philosophy & Technology Ser.: Vol. 9). 1992. lib. bdg. 89.00 (*0-7923-1995-8*) Kluwer Ac.

Democracy in Action: Political Parties. Samuel J. Eldersveld. 1952. 5.00 (*0-911586-08-3*) Wahr.

Democracy in Alberta: Social Credit & the Party System. C. B. Macpherson. LC 54-4046. (Social Credit in Alberta Ser.). 1953. pap. 13.95 (*0-8020-6009-9*) U of Toronto Pr.

Democracy in America. De Tocqueville. 1976. 49.95 (*0-89190-572-3*) Amereon Ltd.

Democracy in America. Alexis De Tocqueville. 1994. 20.00 (*0-679-43134-9*, Everymans Lib) Knopf.

Democracy in America. Alexis De Tocqueville. Ed. by Thomas Bender et al. Tr. by Henry Reeve et al. LC 80-24544. (Modern Library College Editions). 603p. 1981. pap. text ed. write for info. (*0-07-554273-0*) McGraw.

Democracy in America. Alexis De Tocqueville. Ed. by Andrew Hacker. Tr. by Henry Reeve. 1971. pap. 1.50 (*0-671-48795-7*, WSP) PB.

Democracy in America. abr. ed. Alexis De Tocqueville. Ed. by Richard D. Heffner. 1956. pap. 4.95 (*0-451-62697-4*, Ment) NAL-Dutton.

Democracy in America. Alexis De Tocqueville. Ed. by J. P. Mayer. Tr. by George Lawrence. 792p. 1991. reprint ed. lib. bdg. 37.00x (*0-8095-9076-X*) Borgo Pr.

Democracy in America. Alexis De Tocqueville. Ed. by J. P. Mayer. Tr. by George Lawrence. LC 88-45111. 784p. 1988. reprint ed. pap. 18.00 (*0-06-091522-6*, PL 1522, PL) HarpC.

Democracy in America, 2 vols., 1. Alexis De Tocqueville. Ed. by Phillips Bradley. 1990. pap. 12.00 (*0-679-72825-2*) Random.

Democracy in America, 2 vols., 1. Alexis C. De Tocqueville. 30.95 (*0-89190-262-7*, Am Repr) Amereon Ltd.

Democracy in America, 2 vols., 2. Alexis De Tocqueville. Ed. by Phillips Bradley. 1990. pap. 12.00 (*0-679-72826-0*) Random.

Democracy in America, 2 vols., 2. Alexis C. De Tocqueville. 30.95 (*0-89190-263-5*, Am Repr) Amereon Ltd.

Democracy in America, 2 vols, Set. Alexis De Tocqueville. Ed. by Phillips Bradley. (American Past Ser.). 1945. 50. 00 (*0-394-42186-8*) Knopf.

Democracy in America, 2 vols., Set. Alexis C. De Tocqueville. 49.95 (*0-89190-246-5*, Am Repr) Amereon Ltd.

Democracy in America, Vol. 1. Alexis De Tocqueville. 1954. pap. 7.95 (*0-394-70110-0*) Random.

Democracy in America, Vol. 2. Alexis De Tocqueville. 1954. pap. 7.95 (*0-394-70111-9*) Random.

Democracy in America: Sardonic Speculations. Paul N. Goldstene. 63p. (C). 1989. pap. 8.95 (*0-9623194-0-6*) Bucknell Hse.

Democracy in America see U. S. A. - Total State: Democracy in America - A Political History of the U. S.A., 1789-1980s, from the Founding to the Present: Truman, the Fiction of the Cold War & the National Service State 1940s-1980s

***Democracy in America-Day by Day.** Stanley Mosk. 1995. 19.95 (*0-533-11204-4*) Vantage.

Democracy in an Age of Corporate Colonization: Developments in Communication & the Politics of Everyday Life. Stanley A. Deetz. LC 90-26171. (SUNY Series in Speech Communication). 399p. (C). 1992. 64. 50 (*0-7914-0863-9*); pap. 21.95 (*0-7914-0864-7*) State U NY Pr.

Democracy in Botswana. Ed. by John D. Holm & Patrick P. Molutsi. LC 89-16309. 308p. (Orig.). (C). 1990. pap. text ed. 19.95 (*0-8214-0943-3*) Ohio U Pr.

Democracy in Britain: A Reader. Ed. by Adam Lively & Jack Lively. 360p. 1993. 54.94 (*0-631-18829-0*); pap. 24. 95 (*0-631-18831-2*) Blackwell Pubs.

Democracy in Colombia: Clientelistic Politics & Guerrilla Warfare. Jorge P. Osterling. 350p. 1989. 39.95 (*0-88738-229-0*) Transaction Pubs.

Democracy in Contemporary Japan. Ed. by Gavan McCormack. LC 86-17744. 272p. 1986. pap. text ed. 25. 95 (*0-87332-398-X*) M E Sharpe.

Democracy in Costa Rica. Charles D. Ameringer. LC 82-9065. 154p. 1982. text ed. 31.95 (*0-275-90753-8*, C0753, Praeger Pubs) Greenwood.

Democracy in Crisis. Harold J. Laski. LC 70-97892. reprint ed. 19.25 (*0-404-03882-4*) AMS Pr.

Democracy in Decline: Rhode Island Constitutional Development, 1776-1841. Patrick T. Conley. LC 77-76314. (Illus.). 1977. 17.50 (*0-917012-09-7*) RI Pubns Soc.

Democracy in Decline: Rhode Island's Constitutional Development, 1776-1841. Patrick T. Conley. 1977. 13. 95 (*0-685-67662-5*) RI Hist Soc.

Democracy in Deficit: The Political Legacy of Lord Keynes. James M. Buchanan & Richard E. Wagner. 1977. text ed. 54.00 (*0-12-138850-6*) Acad Pr.

Democracy in Developing Countries: Africa, Vol. 2. Larry Diamond et al. LC 87-23457. 275p. (C). 1987. pap. text ed. 18.95 (*1-55587-040-6*) Lynne Rienner.

Democracy in Developing Countries: Asia, Vol. 3. Larry Diamond et al. LC 87-23457. 489p. (C). 1989. pap. text ed. 18.95 (*1-55587-042-2*) Lynne Rienner.

Democracy in Developing Countries: Latin America, Vol. 4. Larry Diamond et al. LC 87-23457. 518p. (C). 1989. pap. text ed. 18.95 (*1-55587-044-9*) Lynne Rienner.

Democracy in Developing Countries: Persistence, Failure & Renewal, Vol. 1. Larry Diamond et al. 350p. (C). Date not set. lib. bdg. 40.00 (*1-55587-037-6*); pap. text ed. 15. 95 (*1-55587-038-4*) Lynne Rienner.

Democracy in Education: Boyd H. Bode. Robert V. Bullough, Jr. LC 80-84621. 258p. 1981. lib. bdg. 34.95 (*0-930390-37-7*); pap. text ed. 19.95 (*0-685-05825-5*) Gen Hall.

Democracy in Europe: The Evolving Role of Parliaments. Metro Staff. Ed. by Cees Flinterman et al. 111p. 1994. pap. 37.00 (*90-6215-403-4*, Pub. by Maklu Uitgevers BE) W W Gaunt.

Democracy in France. Francois P. Guizot. LC 74-19357. v, 82p. 1974. reprint ed. 29.50 (*0-86527-040-6*) Fertig.

Democracy in India. R. K. Bhardwaj. 346p. 1980. 27.95 (*0-940500-30-2*) Asia Bk Corp.

Democracy in India: A Hollow Shell. Arthur Bonner et al. 300p. (Orig.). 1994. lib. bdg. 59.50 (*1-879383-25-X*); pap. text ed. 24.50 (*1-879383-26-8*) Am Univ Pr.

Democracy in International Law. James Crawford. 20p. (C). 1994. pap. 7.95 (*0-521-46835-3*) Cambridge U Pr.

Democracy in Israel. Norman F. Dacey. 73p. 1976. pap. 4.00 (*0-685-03587-5*, Inst Hist Rev) Noontide.

Democracy in Israel. Norman F. Dacey. 1981. lib. bdg. 59. 95 (*0-686-73182-4*) Revisionist Pr.

Democracy in Japan. Ed. by Takeshi Ishida & Ellis S. Krauss. LC 88-28057. (Series in Policy & Institutional Studies). 364p. 1989. 49.95 (*0-8229-3608-9*); pap. 19.95 (*0-8229-5414-1*) U of Pittsburgh Pr.

Democracy in Japan: The Emerging Global Concern. Frank McNeil. 1994. 25.00 (*0-517-59014-X*, Crown) Crown Pub Group.

Democracy in Kingston: A Social Movement in Urban Politics, 1965-1970. Richard Harris. 250p. 1987. 44.95 (*0-7735-0583-0*, Pub. by McGill CN) U of Toronto Pr.

Democracy in Korea: The Roh Tae Woo Years. Ed. by Christopher J. Sigur. 136p. 1992. pap. (*0-87641-118-9*) Carnegie Ethics & Intl Affairs.

Democracy in Latin America: Colombia & Venezuela. Ed. by Donald L. Herman. LC 87-17852. 352p. 1988. text ed. 65.00 (*0-275-92478-5*, C2478, Praeger Pubs) Greenwood.

Democracy in Latin America: Visions & Realities. Ed. by Susanne Jonas & Nancy Stein. LC 89-27541. 232p. (Orig.). 1990. text ed. 49.95 (*0-89789-165-1*, H165, Bergin & Garvey); pap. text ed. 16.95 (*0-89789-164-3*, G164, Bergin & Garvey) Greenwood.

Democracy in Latin America & the Caribbean: The Promise & the Challenge. (State Department Special Report Ser.: No. 158). (Illus.). 35p. 1987. pap. 2.00 (*0-16-004459-6*, S/N 044-000-02188-9) USGPO.

Democracy in Mainland China: The Myth & the Reality. Don J. Senese. (JSPES Monograph: No. 16). 1986. pap. 15.00 (*0-930690-19-2*) Coun Soc Econ.

***Democracy in Mexico.** Dan La Botz. 250p. 1995. 35.00 (*0-89608-508-2*); pap. 15.00 (*0-89608-507-4*) South End Pr.

Democracy in Plural Societies: A Comparative Exploration. Arend Lijphart. LC 77-76311. 1980. pap. 14.00 (*0-300-02494-0*) Yale U Pr.

***Democracy in Post-War Japan: Maruyama Masao & the Search for Autonomy.** Rikki Kersten. LC 95-7806. (Nissan Institute Japanese Studies Ser.). 1995. write for info. (*0-415-11753-4*) Routledge.

Democracy in Rural India: Problems & Process. H. D. Lakshminarayana. 180p. 1980. 15.95 (*0-940500-42-6*) Asia Bk Corp.

Democracy in Small Groups: Participation, Decision-Making & Communication. John Gastil. 224p. 1993. 39. 95 (*0-86571-273-5*); pap. 14.95 (*0-86571-274-3*) New Soc Pubs.

Democracy in the Administration of Higher Education. Ed. by Harold R. Benjamin. LC 72-3344. (Essay Index Reprint Ser.). 1977. reprint ed. 18.95 (*0-8369-2892-X*) Ayer.

Democracy in the Americas: Stopping the Pendulum. Ed. by Robert A. Pastor & Jimmy Carter. LC 89-1781. 262p. 1989. 49.50 (*0-8419-1182-7*); pap. 24.50 (*0-8419-1183-5*) Holmes & Meier.

Democracy in the Caribbean: Myths & Realities. Carlene J. Edie. LC 93-5397. 320p. 1994. text ed. 65.00 (*0-275-94595-2*, Praeger Pubs) Greenwood.

Democracy in the Caribbean: Political, Economic, & Social Perspectives. Ed. by Jorge I. Dominguez et al. LC 92-28447. (World Peace Foundation Study Ser.). 352p. 1993. text ed. 48.00 (*0-8018-4450-9*); pap. text ed. 14.95 (*0-8018-4451-7*) Johns Hopkins.

Democracy in the Contemporary State. Frank W. Bealey. 302p. 1988. 65.00 (*0-19-827573-0*) OUP.

An Asterisk (*) at the beginning of an entry indicates that the title is appearing in BIP for the first time.

D

An Asterisk (*) at the beginning of an entry indicates that the title is appearing in BIP for the first time.

1867

Democratic Judge Or, the Equal Liberty of the Press. William Cobbett. LC 70-125686. (American Journalists Ser.). 1974. reprint ed. 16.95 (*0-405-01663-8*) Ayer.

Democratic Leadership: The Changing Context of Administrative Preparation. Ed. by Thomas A. Mulkeen et al. LC 93-42751. (Interpretive Perspectives on Education & Policy Ser.). 1993. 49.50 (*0-89391-912-8*); pap. 22.50 (*1-56750-049-8*) Ablex Pub.

Democratic Left in Exile: The Antidictatorial Struggle in the Caribbean, 1945-1959. Charles D. Ameringer. LC 73-77477. (Illus.). 384p. 1974. 19.95 (*0-87024-238-5*) U of Miami Pr.

Democratic Legislative Institutions: A Comparative View. David M. Olson. LC 94-18913. (Comparative Politics Ser.). (Illus.). 200p. 1994. text ed. 47.50 (*1-56324-314-8*); pap. text ed. 19.95 (*1-56324-315-6*) M E Sharpe.

Democratic Liberalism in South Africa: Its History & Prospect. Ed. by Jeffrey Butler et al. LC 87-6071. (Illus.). 440p. 1987. pap. 19.95 (*0-8195-6197-5*, Wesleyan Univ Pr) U Pr of New Eng.

Democratic Machine, 1850-1854. Roy F. Nichols. LC 68-1159. (Columbia University. Studies in the Social Sciences: No. 248). reprint ed. 20.00 (*0-404-51248-8*) AMS Pr.

Democratic Mask: The Consolidation of the Sandinista Revolution. Douglas W. Payne. LC 85-81020. (Perspectives on Freedom Ser.: No. 3). 100p. 1985. pap. 13.75 (*0-932088-06-6*) Freedom Hse.

Democratic Miners: Work & Labor Relations in the Anthracite Coal Industry, 1875-1925. Perry K. Blatz. LC 93-843. (SUNY Series in American Labor History). (Illus.). 368p. 1994. 59.50 (*0-7914-1819-7*); pap. 19.95 (*0-7914-1820-0*) State U NY Pr.

Democratic Movement In Italy, Eighteen Thirty to Eighteen Seventy-Six. Clara M. Lovett. LC 81-6403. 295p. 1982. 39.95 (*0-674-19645-7*) HUP.

Democratic Myth. Maurice Rotstein. 245p. 1983. 15.00 (*0-912598-21-2*); pap. 6.95 (*0-912598-52-2*) Florham.

Democratic Nepal. D. Dharamdasani. (C). 1992. 60.00 (*0-7855-0175-4*, Pub. by Ratna Pustak Bhandar) St Mut.

***Democratic Opposition to the Lincoln Administration in Indiana.** Gilbert R. Tredway. 433p. 1973. 7.50 (*1-885323-25-5*) IN Hist Bureau.

Democratic Organization for Social Change: Latin American Christian Base Communities & Literacy Campaigns. Johannes P. Van Vugt. LC 90-1132. 192p. 1991. text ed. 49.95 (*0-89789-245-3*, H245, Bergin & Garvey) Greenwood.

Democratic Party & California Politics, 1880-1896. R. Hal Williams. LC 73-80626. (Illus.). 304p. 1973. 39.50 (*0-8047-0847-9*) Stanford U Pr.

Democratic Party & the Negro: Northern & National Politics, 1868-92. Lawrence Grossman. LC 75-30546. (Blacks in the New World Ser.). 228p. reprint ed. pap. 65.00 (*0-317-09504-8*, 2020239) Bks Demand.

Democratic Party Primary in Virginia: Tantamount to Election No Longer. Larry Sabato. LC 77-9615. 181p. reprint ed. pap. 51.60 (*0-7837-4364-5*, 2044074) Bks Demand.

Democratic Political Process: A Cross-National Reader. Ed. by Kurt L. Shell. LC 69-18101. (Blaisdell Book in Political Science Ser.). 521p. reprint ed. pap. 148.50 (*0-317-09491-2*, 2012528) Bks Demand.

Democratic Politics & Policy Analysis. Hank C. Jenkins-Smith. LC 89-17426. 208p. (C). 1990. pap. 19.95 (*0-534-12702-9*) Intl Thomson.

Democratic Polity & Social Change in India. R. Kothari. 124p. 1976. 8.95 (*0-318-36573-1*) Asia Bk Corp.

***Democratic Principals in Action: Eight Pioneers.** Joseph Blase et al. 72p. 1995. 38.00 (*0-8039-6131-6*); pap. 18.00 (*0-8039-6132-4*) Corwin Pr.

Democratic Process & Administrative Law. rev. ed. Robert S. Lorch. LC 69-10420. (Waynebooks Ser.: No. 39). 263p. 1969. pap. 14.95 (*0-8143-1513-5*) Wayne St U Pr.

Democratic Processes in a Developing Society. A. H. Somjee. LC 79-4035. 1979. text ed. 29.95 (*0-312-19373-4*) St Martin.

Democratic Promise: The Populist Moment in America. Lawrence Goodwyn. LC 75-25462. (Illus.). 1976. 35.00 (*0-19-501996-2*) OUP.

Democratic Reform & the Position of Women in Transitional Economies. Ed. by Valentine Moghadam. (WIDER Studies in Development Economics). (Illus.). 376p. 1994. 60.00 (*0-19-828820-4*) OUP.

Democratic Reform in Yugoslavia. April Carter. LC 81-47910. 288p. 1982. 49.50 (*0-691-09397-0*) Princeton U Pr.

***Democratic Reform in Yugoslavia: The Changing Role of the Party.** April Carter. LC 81-47910. Date not set. reprint ed. pap. 84.10 (*0-7837-9493-2*, 2060237) Bks Demand.

Democratic Republic of Viet Nam Coins & Currency. Howard A. Daniel, III. LC 76-351167. (Catalog & Guidebook of Southeast Asian Coins & Currency Ser.: Vol. II, Pt. 3). (Illus.). 300p. (Orig.). 1992. pap. 29.95 (*1-879951-03-7*) Southeast Asian.

Democratic Republic, 1801-1815. Marshall Smelser. (Illus.). 369p. (C). 1992. reprint ed. pap. text ed. 13.95 (*0-88133-668-8*) Waveland Pr.

Democratic-Republican Societies, 1790-1800. Eugene P. Link. (History - United States Ser.). 256p. 1993. reprint ed. lib. bdg. 79.00 (*0-7812-4881-7*) Rprt Serv.

Democratic-Republican Societies, 1790-1800: A Documentary Sourcebook. Ed. by Philip S. Foner. LC 76-5260. 484p. (Orig.). 1976. text ed. 59.95 (*0-8371-8907-1*, FLT/, Greenwood Pr) Greenwood.

Democratic-Republicans of Massachusetts: Politics in a Young Republic. Paul Goodman. LC 86-22823. 294p. 1986. reprint ed. text ed. 89.50 (*0-313-23201-6*, GODR, Greenwood Pr) Greenwood.

Democratic Republicans of New York: The Origins, 1763-1797. Alfred F. Young. LC 67-23493. (Illus.). 658p. reprint ed. pap. 180.00 (*0-8357-3920-1*, 2036655) Bks Demand.

Democratic Review 1849-1850. Ed. by G. Julian Harney. (C). 1968. text ed. 19.95 (*0-85036-098-6*, Pub. by Merlin Pr UK) Humanities.

Democratic Revolution. Bryan Magee. LC 64-25509. 1964. 16.95 (*0-8023-1075-3*) Dufour.

Democratic Revolution: Struggles for Freedom & Pluralism in the Developing World. Intro. by Larry Diamond. LC 91-20648. 220p. (C). 1991. 24.95 (*0-932088-69-4*); pap. 12.95 (*0-932088-68-6*) Freedom Hse.

Democratic Revolution in Latin America: History, Politics & U. S. Policy. Howard J. Wiarda. LC 90-31311. (Twentieth Century Fund Book Ser.). 336p. (Orig.). (C). 1990. 39.50 (*0-8419-1276-9*); pap. 19.95 (*0-8419-1277-7*) Holmes & Meier.

Democratic Revolution in the West Indies. Ed. by Wendell Bell. 232p. 1967. 18.95 (*0-87073-018-5*); pap. 18.95 (*0-87073-019-3*) Schenkman Bks Inc.

Democratic Rights for Union Members: A Guide to Internal Union Democracy. H. W. Benson. 245p. 1979. 6.00 (*0-9602244-1-6*) Assn Union Demo.

***Democratic Schools.** Ed. by Michael W. Apple & James A. Beane. LC 95-7784. 1995. write for info. (*0-87120-241-7*) Assn Supervision.

Democratic Socialism: The Challenge of the Eighties & Beyond. Ed. by Donna Wilson. 264p. (Orig.). 1985. pap. 9.95 (*0-919573-45-2*) Left Bank.

Democratic Socialism: The Mass Left in Advanced Industrial Societies. Ed. by Bogdan Denitch. LC 81-65021. 192p. 1981. text ed. 52.50 (*0-86598-015-2*) Rowman.

Democratic Socialism in Jamaica: The Political Movement & Social Transformation in Dependent Capitalism. Evelyne H. Stephens & John D. Stephens. LC 85-16963. 480p. 1986. text ed. 69.50x (*0-691-07697-9*); pap. 17.95x (*0-691-10172-8*) Princeton U Pr.

***Democratic Socialism of Emile Vandervelde: Between Reform & Revolution.** Janet Polasky. LC 94-46196. (Illus.). 288p. 1995. 45.95 (*0-85496-394-4*); pap. 19.95 (*1-85973-033-7*) Berg Pubs.

Democratic Socialist Vision. Gary J. Dorrien. 192p. 1986. 50.00 (*0-8476-7507-6*) Rowman.

Democratic South Africa? Constitutional Engineering in a Divided Society. Donald L. Horowitz. 1992. pap. 13.00 (*0-520-07885-3*) U CA Pr.

***Democratic Spain: Reshaping External Relations in a Changing World.** Ed. by Richard Gillespie et al. LC 95-5717. (European Public Policy Ser.). 1995. write for info. (*0-415-11325-3*); pap. write for info. (*0-415-11326-1*) Routledge.

Democratic State. Ed. by Roger Benjamin & Stephen L. Elkin. LC 84-21963. (Studies in Government & Public Policy). viii, 280p. (C). 1985. pap. 12.95 (*0-7006-0262-3*) U Pr of KS.

Democratic Subjects: The Self & the Social in Nineteenth-Century England. Patrick Joyce. LC 93-37741. (Illus.). 224p. (C). 1994. 54.95 (*0-521-44334-2*); pap. 19.95 (*0-521-44802-6*) Cambridge U Pr.

Democratic Sweden. Ed. by Margaret I. Cole & Charles Smith. LC 70-128224. (Essay Index Reprint Ser.). 1977. 21.95 (*0-8369-1871-1*) Ayer.

Democratic System in the Eastern Caribbean. Donald C. Peters. LC 91-33502. (Contributions in Political Science Ser.: No. 298). 256p. 1992. text ed. 55.00 (*0-313-28428-8*, PDN, Greenwood Pr) Greenwood.

Democratic Teacher Education: Programs, Processes, Problems, & Prospects. Ed. by John Novak. LC 93-26763. (SUNY Series, Democracy & Education). 288p. 1994. 64.50x (*0-7914-1927-4*); pap. 21.95x (*0-7914-1928-2*) State U NY Pr.

Democratic Theories & the Constitution. Martin Edelman. LC 83-18143. (SUNY Series in Political Theory). 399p. 1985. 59.50 (*0-87395-872-1*); pap. 19.95 (*0-87395-873-X*) State U NY Pr.

Democratic Theory. Giovanni Sartori. LC 72-8241. 479p. 1973. reprint ed. text ed. 79.50 (*0-8371-6545-8*, SADT, Greenwood Pr) Greenwood.

Democratic Theory: Essays in Retrieval. C. B. Macpherson. (C). 1973. pap. 16.95 (*0-19-827189-1*) OUP.

Democratic Theory: The Philosophical Foundations. James L. Hyland. LC 94-16673. 1995. text ed. 69.95 (*0-7190-3941-X*, Pub. by Manchester Univ Pr UK); text ed. 19.95 (*0-7190-4517-7*, Pub. by Manchester Univ Pr UK) St Martin.

Democratic Theory & Local Government. Dilys M. Hill. LC 75-322540. (New Local Government Ser.: No. 12). 243p. reprint ed. pap. 69.30 (*0-317-20050-X*, 2023270) Bks Demand.

Democratic Theory & Practice in Africa. Walter Oyugi et al. LC 88-21101. 237p. (Orig.). (C). 1988. pap. text ed. 18.50 (*0-435-08026-1*, 08026) Heinemann.

Democratic Theory & Socialism. Frank Cunningham. 380p. 1987. pap. 22.95 (*0-521-33578-7*) Cambridge U Pr.

Democratic Theory & Technological Society. Ed. by Richard B. Day et al. LC 88-4442. 378p. 1988. 49.95 (*0-87332-448-X*) M E Sharpe.

Democratic Theory. Based on the Author's Translation of Democrazia e Definizione (2nd Edition). Il Mulino, Bologna, 1958. Giovanni Sartori. LC 62-7184. (Waynebook Ser.: No. 6). 496p. reprint ed. pap. 141.40 (*0-7837-3800-5*, 2043620) Bks Demand.

Democratic Tradition: Four German Constitutions. Elmar M. Hucko. LC 86-32711. 265p. 1988. 48.00 (*0-907582-60-5*) Berg Pubs.

Democratic Tradition: Four German Constitutions. Ed. by Elmar M. Hucko. LC 86-32711. 265p. 1990. pap. 24.00 (*0-85496-299-9*) Berg Pubs.

Democratic Tradition & the Evolution of Schooling in Norway. Val D. Rust. LC 89-11847. 347p. 1989. text ed. 59.95 (*0-313-26849-5*, RDD/, Greenwood Pr) Greenwood.

Democratic Transformation of a Social Class. M. P. Chandel. (C). 1991. text ed. 12.50 (*81-7099-314-8*, Pub. by Mittal II) S Asia.

Democratic Transition & Human Rights: A Primer for U. S. Foreign Policy. Sara Steinmetz. LC 92-22424. 284p. (C). 1994. 54.50 (*0-7914-1433-7*); pap. 17.95 (*0-7914-1434-5*) State U NY Pr.

***Democratic Transition in Asia: The Role of the International Community.** Muthiah Alagappa. (Illus.). 51p. (Orig.). (C). 1994. pap. text ed. 25.00x (*0-7881-1364-X*) Diane Pub.

Democratic Values & Technological Choices. Stuart Hill. LC 91-45821. 288p. (C). 1992. 37.50 (*0-8047-1986-1*) Stanford U Pr.

Democratic Vista. Richard V. Chase. LC 72-12325. 180p. 1973. reprint ed. text ed. 52.50 (*0-8371-6732-9*, CHDV, Greenwood Pr) Greenwood.

Democratic Vistas & Other Papers. Walt Whitman. LC 73-131856. 1970. reprint ed. 25.00 (*0-403-00743-7*) Scholarly.

Democratic Vistas, 1860-1880. Ed. by Alan Trachtenberg. LC 75-103170. 386p. 1970. pap. 4.95 (*0-8076-0547-6*) Braziller.

Democratic Way of Life. Thomas V. Smith. (Midway Reprint Ser.). 324p. reprint ed. pap. 92.40 (*0-317-26587-3*, 2024067) Bks Demand.

Democratic Wish: Popular Participation & the Limits of American Government. James A. Morone. LC 90-80250. 402p. 1992. reprint ed. pap. text ed. 16.00 (*0-465-01602-2*) Basic.

Democratic Worker-Owned Firm. David P. Ellerman. 240p. (C). 1990. text ed. 49.95 (*0-04-445743-X*) Routledge Chapman & Hall.

Democratick Editorials: Essays in Jacksonian Political Economy. William Leggett. Ed. by Lawrence H. White. LC 83-24893. 432p. (C). 1984. 12.00 (*0-86597-036-X*); pap. 6.00 (*0-86597-037-8*) Liberty Fund.

***Democratisation of Disempowerment: The Problem of Democracy in the Third World.** Ed. by Jochen Hippler. LC 95-4121. (Transnational Institute Ser.). (C). 1995. text ed. 69.95 (*0-7453-0977-1*, Pub. by Pluto Pr UK); pap. text ed. 19.95 (*0-7453-0978-X*, Pub. by Pluto Pr UK) Westview.

Democratisation of Schooling. Ed. by Hugh Watson. 109p. (C). 1985. 45.00 (*0-7300-0379-5*, Pub. by Deakin Univ AT) St Mut.

***Democratization? Ethiopia (1991-1994), a Personal View.** Tecola W. Hagos. 350p. (Orig.). (C). 1995. pap. 20.00 (*0-9645902-0-4*) Khepera Pub.

***Democratization & Ethnic Nationalism: African & Eastern European Experiences.** Marina Ottaway. LC 94-36131. (Policy Essay Ser.: Vol. 14). 1994. pap. 9.95 (*1-56517-019-9*) Overseas Dev Council.

Democratization & Reform. Su Shaozhi. 181p. 1988. 57.50 (*0-85124-496-3*, Pub. by Spokesman Bks UK); pap. 27.50 (*0-85124-457-2*, Pub. by Spokesman Bks UK) Coronet Bks.

***Democratization & Social Settlements: The Politics of Change in Contemporary Portugal.** Daniel Nataf. LC 94-33690. 288p. 1995. text ed. 64.50x (*0-7914-2589-4*); pap. 21.95x (*0-7914-2590-8*) State U NY Pr.

Democratization & Structural Adjustment in Africa in the 1990s. Ed. by Lual Deng et al. 215p. (Orig.). 1991. pap. 15.00 (*0-942615-12-3*) U Wis African Stud.

***Democratization & the Protection of Human Rights in Africa: Probems & Prospects.** Brendalyn P. Ambrose. LC 95-3335. 248p. 1995. text ed. 57.95 (*0-275-95143-X*, Praeger Pubs) Greenwood.

***Democratization & the State in the Southern Cone: Essays on South American Politics.** Benno Galjari & Patricio Silva. (CEDLA Latin America Studies (CLAS): No. 53). 232p. 1992. pap. 25.00 (*90-70280-51-5*, Pub. by Thesis Pubs NE) IBD Ltd.

Democratization in Africa: African Views, African Voices. National Research Council Staff. (Project on Democratization Ser.). 94p. (Orig.). (C). 1992. pap. text ed. 22.00 (*0-309-04797-8*) Natl Acad Pr.

Democratization in Eastern Europe: Domestic & International Perspectives. Geoffrey Pridham & Tatu Vanhanen. LC 94-7513. 272p. 1994. 65.00x (*0-415-11063-7*, B4709); pap. 18.95 (*0-415-11064-5*, B4713) Routledge.

Democratization in South Africa: The Elusive Social Contract. Timothy D. Sisk. LC 94-16987. 1994. 39.50 (*0-691-03622-5*) Princeton U Pr.

***Democratization, Liberalization, & Human Rights in the Third World.** Mahmood Monshipouri. LC 94-31377. 200p. 1995. lib. bdg. 42.00 (*1-55587-529-7*); pap. text ed. 17.95 (*1-55587-550-5*) Lynne Rienner.

Democratization of American Christianity. Nathan O. Hatch. (Illus.). 320p. (C). 1991. reprint ed. pap. text ed. 16.00x (*0-300-05060-7*) Yale U Pr.

Democratization of Clothing in America: Student Syllabus. Barbara H. Salser. (gr. 10-12). 1979. pap. text ed. 7.95 (*0-89420-062-3*, 165021); audio 89.10 (*0-89420-204-9*, 165000) Natl Book.

Democratization of Knowledge. Scott. (C). 1990. lib. bdg. 34.95 (*0-226-74306-3*) U Ch Pr.

Democratization of Religion in America: A Commonwealth of Religious Freedom by Design. Joseph Forcinelli. LC 90-32856. (Studies in American Religion: Vol. 50). 372p. 1990. lib. bdg. 99.95 (*0-88946-641-6*) E Mellen.

Democratization of the World's Legal Institutions. 19p. 1991. pap. text ed. 15.00 (*1-56986-128-5*) Federal Bar.

Democratizing Brazil: Problems of Transition & Consolidation. Ed. by Alfred Stepan. (Illus.). 424p. 1989. pap. 16.95 (*0-19-505152-1*) OUP.

Democratizing Development: The Role of Voluntary Organizations. John Clark. LC 91-7371. (Library of Management for Development). 226p. 1991. pap. 18.95 (*0-931816-91-2*) Kumarian Pr.

Democratizing France: The Political & Administrative History of Decentralization. Vivien A. Schmidt. (Illus.). 366p. (C). 1991. 64.95 (*0-521-39156-3*) Cambridge U Pr.

Democratizing Information: Online Databases & the Rise of End-User Searching. Bryan Pfaffenberger. (Professional Librarian Ser.). 175p. 1989. text ed. 32.50 (*0-8161-1860-4*, Hall Reference); pap. 24.50 (*0-8161-1872-8*, Hall Reference) Macmillan.

Democratizing Japan: The Allied Occupation. Robert E. Ward & Sakamoto Yoshizaku. LC 86-25023. 496p. 1987. text ed. 31.00 (*0-8248-0883-5*) UH Pr.

Democratizing Republicanism. Vigdor Schreibman. LC 87-6206. (Essays on the Impact of the Constitution & Legal System on American Life & Government Ser.: No. 6). (Illus.). 75p. (Orig.). 1989. pap. 18.00 (*0-942539-12-5*); pap. 13.00 (*0-942539-13-3*) Amicas Pubns.

Democratizing the Development Process. Neal Peirce et al. Ed. by Michael Barker. LC 79-67384. (Studies in State Development Policy: Vol. 6). 49p. 1979. pap. 11.95 (*0-934842-05-1*) CSPA.

Democrats & Labor in Rhode Island, 1952-1962: Changes in the Old Alliance. Jay S. Goodman. LC 67-26817. 166p. reprint ed. 47.40 (*0-685-15647-8*, 2027505) Bks Demand.

Democrats & the American Idea: A Bicentennial Appraisal. Peter B. Kovler. (Illus.). 424p. 1992. 29.95 (*0-944237-36-3*) Ctr National Policy.

Democrats' Dilemma: Walter F. Mondale & the Liberal Legacy. Steven M. Gillon. (Contemporary American History Ser.). (Illus.). 400p. (C). 1992. text ed. 35.00 (*0-231-07630-4*) Col U Pr.

***Democrats' Dilemma: Walter F. Mondale & the Liberal Legacy.** Steven M. Gillon. (Contemporary American History Ser.). (Illus.). 400p. (C). 1992. pap. 17.00 (*0-231-07631-2*) Col U Pr.

Democrats in Exile 1968-1972: Political Confessions of a New England Liberal. R. Bruce Allison. LC 74-78096. 160p. 1974. pap. 6.00 (*0-913370-02-9*, Sol Press) Wisconsin Bks.

Democrats Must Lead: The Case for a Progressive Democratic Party. Ed. by James M. Burns et al. 279p. 1992. text ed. 61.00 (*0-8133-1569-7*) Westview.

Democritus Platonissans: or An Essay upon the Infinity of Worlds Out of Platonick Principles. Henry More. LC 92-24821. reprint ed. 12.00 (*0-404-70130-2*, PR3605) AMS Pr.

***Demodaran on Valuation: Security Analysis for Investment & Corporate Finance.** A. Demodaran. 1994. student ed, text ed. 158.95 (*0-471-11304-2*) Wiley.

Demofoonte (Jommelli) see Italian Opera Librettos, Vol. IV, 1640-1770

Demogorgon. Brian Lumley. 1992. mass mkt. 4.99 (*0-8125-1199-9*) Tor Bks.

Demographic Analysis: A Stochastic Approach. Krishnan Namboodiri. 370p. 1990. text ed. 68.00 (*0-12-513830-X*) Acad Pr.

Demographic Analysis of East Africa: A Sociological Interpretation. Mette Monsted & Walji Parveen. 212p. (Orig.). 1978. pap. 21.50x (*91-7106-126-6*, Pub. by Nordisk Afrikainstitutet SW) Coronet Bks.

Demographic Analysis of Interstate Labor Growth Rate Differentials: United States, 1890-1900 to 1940-1950. Marcel Tenebaum. Ed. by Stuart Bruchey. LC 76-54119. (Nineteen Seventy-Seven Dissertations Ser.). (Illus.). 1977. lib. bdg. 33.95 (*0-405-09930-4*) Ayer.

Demographic & Economic Change in Developed Countries. Universities-National Bureau Staff. (Conference Ser.: No. 11). 547p. 1960. reprint ed. 142.50 (*0-87014-302-6*) Natl Bur Econ Res.

Demographic & Economic Change in Mexico's Northern Frontier: Evidence from the X Censo General de Poblacion y Vivienda. James T. Peach. 47p. (Orig.). (C). 1984. pap. text ed. 5.25 (*0-937795-12-7*) Border Res Inst.

Demographic & Programmatic Consequences of New Contraceptives. Ed. by S. Segal et al. LC 89-23083. (Reproductive Biology Ser.). (Illus.). 335p. 1989. 85.00 (*0-306-43384-2*, Plenum Pr) Plenum.

Demographic Applications of Event History Analysis. Ed. by James Trussell et al. (International Studies in Demography). (Illus.). 288p. 1992. 65.00 (*0-19-828386-5*) OUP.

Demographic Aspects of the Changing Status of Women in Europe. Ed. by M. Niphuis-Nell. (Publications of the Netherlands Inter-University Demographic Institute & the Population & Family Study Centre Ser.: Vol. 7). 1978. pap. text ed. 27.50 (*90-207-0714-0*) Kluwer Ac.

Demographic Atlas of Austin. Claudia Ade & Thomas Erkert. (Special Project Report Ser.). (Illus.). 109p. 1987. 8.00 (*0-89940-858-3*) LBJ Sch Pub Aff.

Demographic Behavior in the Past: A Study of Fourteen German Village Populations in the Eighteenth & Nineteenth Centuries. John E. Knodel. (Cambridge Studies in Population, Economy & Society in Past Time: No. 6). 616p. 1988. 84.95 (*0-521-32715-6*) Cambridge U Pr.

***Demographic Black & Hispanic Population Atlas.** (Illus.). 60p. (Orig.). 1994. pap. 195.00 (*0-7605-0529-2*) Rector Pr.

***Demographic Business Atlas U. S. A.** (Illus.). 200p. (Orig.). 1994. pap. 135.00 (*0-7605-0839-9*) Rector Pr.

***Demographic Buying Power U. S. A. 1994.** 200p. (Orig.). 1995. pap. 295.00 (*0-7605-1556-5*) Rector Pr.

Demographic Change & Economic Development. Ed. by A. Wenig & K. F. Zimmermann. (Studies in Contemporary Economics). (Illus.). xii, 325p. 1989. pap. 48.00 (*0-387-51140-7*, 2984) Spr-Verlag.

An Asterisk (*) at the beginning of an entry indicates that the title is appearing in BIP for the first time.

An Asterisk (*) at the beginning of an entry indicates that the title is appearing in BIP for the first time.

Demon Inside. Barbara Wedgwood. Ed. by Maryanne Sacco. 328p. (Orig.). 1993. mass mkt. 5.50 (*0-671-67417-X*) PB.

Demon Lord of Karanda. David Eddings. 416p. 1989. mass mkt. 5.95 (*0-345-36331-0*, Del Rey) Ballantine.

Demon Lover. Dion Fortune. 286p. 1972. pap. 10.95 (*0-87728-499-7*) Weiser.

Demon Lover. Victoria Holt. 336p. 1983. mass mkt. 5.99 (*0-449-20098-1*, Crest) Fawcett.

Demon Lover. Arthur Wormhoudt. LC 68-29256. (Essay Index Reprint Ser.). 1977. 15.95 (*0-8369-1011-7*) Ayer.

Demon Lover: On the Sexuality of Terrorism. Robin Morgan. 1990. pap. 9.95 (*0-393-30677-1*) Norton.

Demon Lovers. Brad Steiger. (Illus.). 200p. 1986. 17.95 (*0-938294-18-0*); pap. 9.95 (*0-938294-17-2*) Glob Comm-Inner Lght.

Demon-Lovers & Their Victims in British Fiction. Toni Reed. LC 88-18126. 184p. 1988. 20.00 (*0-8131-1663-5*) U Pr of Ky.

Demon Moon. Jack Williamson. 352p. 1994. 22.95 (*0-312-85718-7*) Tor Bks.

Demon Moon. Jack Williamson. 1995. mass mkt. 5.99 (*0-8125-2226-5*) Tor Bks.

Demon Notebook. Steve Richmond. 48p. (Orig.). 1988. pap. 6.95 (*0-934953-21-X*) Water Row Pr.

Demon of Discord: Tensions in the Catholic Church of Victoria, 1853-1864. Margaret M. Pawsey. (Illus.). 200p. 1983. 29.95 (*0-522-84249-6*) Intl Spec Bk.

Demon of Noontide: Ennui in Western Literature. R. Kuhn. 1976. 62.50x (*0-691-06311-7*) Princeton U Pr.

Demon of Noontide: Ennui in Western Literature. Reinhard C. Kuhn. LC 76-3269. 414p. reprint ed. pap. 118.00 (*0-8357-2697-5*, 2040238) Bks Demand.

Demon of the Eiffel Tower. Jacques Tardi. Tr. by R. Lofficier & J. M. Lofficier. (Adventures of Adele Blanc-Sec Ser.: No. 2). 48p. 1990. pap. 9.95 (*1-56163-001-2*) NBM.

Demon Pig. Karen A. Brush. 256p. (Orig.). 1991. mass mkt. 4.50 (*0-380-75760-5*) Avon.

Demon Possession. John W. Montgomery. LC 75-19313. 1976. pap. 13.99 (*0-87123-102-6*) Bethany Hse.

***Demon Possession: A Medical, Historical, Anthropological & Theological Symposium.** Ed. by John W. Montgomery. 384p. (C). 1994. pap. text ed. 14.95 (*1-885914-05-9*) Trinity Bible Coll.

Demon Possession & the Christian: A New Perspective. C. Fred Dickason. LC 88-63692. 355p. 1989. pap. 12.99 (*0-89107-521-6*) Crossway Bks.

Demon Prince. Kathleen Morgan. 448p. (Orig.). 1994. pap. 4.99 (*0-505-51941-0*, Love Spell) Dorchester Pub Co.

Demon Prince: The Dissonant Worlds of Jack Vance. Jack Rawlins. LC 81-21600. (Milford Series: Popular Writers of Today: Popular Writers of Today: Vol. 40). 104p. 1986. lib. bdg. 25.00x (*0-89370-163-7*); pap. 15.00 (*0-89370-263-3*) Borgo Pr.

Demon Slayers & Other Stories: Bengali Folk Tales. Sayantani DasGupta & Shamita D. Dasgupta. LC 94-1706. 1994. 24.95 (*1-56656-164-7*); pap. 12.95 (*1-56656-156-6*) Interlink Pub.

***Demon Spider.** Ian Livingstone. (Adventures of Goldhawk Ser.). (Illus.). 64p. 1995. 4.99 (*0-14-037728-X*) Puffin Bks.

Demon Spofforth. Richard Cashman. 275p. 1990. 34.95 (*0-86840-004-1*, Pub. by New South Wales Univ Pr AT) Intl Spec Bk.

***Demon Sword.** Ken Hood. 1995. pap. 4.99 (*0-06-105410-0*, Prism Bks) P-H.

Demon Tower. large type ed. Virginia Coffman. 400p. 1988. 17.95 (*0-7089-1910-3*) Ulverscroft.

Demon Wine. Thomas Babe. 1989. pap. 4.75 (*0-8222-0300-6*) Dramatists Play.

Demon Within. Dana Reed. 368p. (Orig.). 1993. reprint ed. pap. 4.50 (*0-8439-3382-8*) Dorchester Pub Co.

Demoniacs. John D. Carr. 1989. pap. 3.95 (*0-88184-543-4*) Carroll & Graf.

Demoniacs of Downing Street. John Sampson. (Illus.). 261p. 1992. 8.95 (*0-9613075-4-4*) Thornfield Pr.

Demoniality. Ludovico M. Sinistrari. 1989. pap. 4.95 (*0-486-26147-6*) Dover.

Demoniality. Ludovico M. Sinistrari. LC 72-83751. 1972. reprint ed. lib. bdg. 24.95 (*0-405-08976-7*, Pub. by Blom Pubns UK) Ayer.

Demoniaques dans L'Art. J. M. Charcot & Paul Richter. (Illus.). 116p. reprint ed. lib. bdg. 52.50 (*90-6078-060-4*, Pub. by B M Israel NE) Coronet Bks.

Demonic Imagination: Style & Theme in French Romantic Poetry. John P. Houston. LC 69-15051. xi, 177p. 1969. text ed. 27.50 (*0-8071-0306-3*) La State U Pr.

Demonic Metaphysics of Macbeth. Walter C. Curry. (Studies in Shakespeare: No. 24). 1970. reprint ed. pap. 12.95 (*0-8383-0020-0*) M S G Haskell Hse.

Demonic Mnemonics. Murray Suid. LC 80-82982. (YA). (gr. 5-12). 1981. pap. 9.99 (*0-8224-6464-0*) Fearon Teach Aids.

***Demonic Roots of Globalism: En Route to Spiritual Deception.** 208p. 1995. pap. 10.99 (*0-614-06759-6*) Huntington Hse.

Demonios, Brujeria, Ocultismo (Demons, Witches & the Occult) Stewar McDowell. (SPA.). Date not set. 2.49 (*0-945792-72-7*, 498045) Editorial Unilit.

Demonios, Demonios, Demonios. John P. Newport. Tr. by Arnoldo Canclini. 110p. (Orig.). (SPA.). 1987. pap. 5.50 (*0-311-05765-9*) Casa Bautista.

Demonism Verified & Analyzed. Hugh W. White. 1972. 250.00 (*0-8490-0016-5*) Gordon Pr.

Demonismo (Demonism) El Como Vencer a Satanas (How to Win Against the Devil) C. R. Swindoll. (SPA.). Date not set. 1.79 (*1-56063-027-2*, 498111) Editorial Unilit.

Demonizing the Queen of Sheba: Boundaries of Gender & Culture in Postbiblical Judaism & Medieval Islam. Jacob Lassner. LC 93-7499. (Chicago Studies in the History of Judaism). 360p. 1993. lib. bdg. 49.95 (*0-226-46913-1*); pap. text ed. 19.95 (*0-226-46915-8*) U Ch Pr.

Demonologist: The Extraordinary Career of Ed & Lorraine Warren. Gerald Brittle. (Illus.). 288p. 1991. mass mkt. 4.99 (*0-312-92601-4*) St Martin.

Demonology & Deliverance, No. II. Lester Sumrall. 107p. (C). 1982. pap. text ed. 10.00 (*0-937580-64-3*) LeSEA Pub Co.

Demonology & Deliverance, No. I: Study Guide. Lester Sumrall. 116p. (C). 1981. pap. text ed. 10.00 (*0-937580-54-6*) LeSEA Pub Co.

Demonology & Devil Lore. Moncure D. Conway. (Works of Moncure Daniel Conway Ser.). 1990. reprint ed. lib. bdg. 79.00 (*0-7812-2333-4*) Rprt Serv.

Demonology & Devil-Lore, 2 vols., Set. Moncure D. Conway. 1972. 250.00 (*0-8490-0017-3*) Gordon Pr.

Demonology & Devil Lore, Vol. II. Moncure Conway. Ed. by Thorguard Templar. 435p. 1994. 30.00 (*1-57179-023-3*) Intern Guild ASRS.

***Demonology & Devil Lore Vol. I: Study of Demons.** IGOS Society Staff. Ed. & Intro. by Thor Templar. 430p. Date not set. 25.00 (*1-57179-040-3*) Intern Guild ASRS.

Demonology & Popular Superstitions of Gujarat. Alexander K. Forbes. 1990. 17.00 (*81-85326-20-7*, Pub. by Vintage II) S Asia.

Demonology of the Early Christian World. Everett Ferguson. LC 84-16681. (Symposium Ser.: Vol. 12). 190p. 1984. lib. bdg. 79.95 (*0-88946-703-X*) E Mellen.

Demonology, Past & Present. Kurt E. Koch. LC 72-93353. 162p. 1973. pap. 6.99 (*0-8254-3013-5*) Kregel.

Demons. J. M. Dillard. (Star Trek Ser.: No. 30). 1990. mass mkt. 4.50 (*0-671-70877-5*) PB.

Demons. Fyodor Dostoevsky. 1994. pap. 27.50 (*0-679-42314-1*) Random.

Demons. Heimito Von Doderer. Tr. by Richard Winston & Clara Winston. (Sun & Moon Classics Ser.: No. 13). 1340p. 1992. reprint ed. pap. 29.95 (*1-55713-030-2*) Sun & Moon CA.

Demons: A Biblically Based Perspective. Alex W. Konya. LC 90-33207. 160p. (C). 1990. pap. 10.95 (*0-87227-143-9*) Reg Baptist.

Demons: A "Nameless Detective" Mystery. Bill Pronzini. LC 92-40280. 1993. 19.95 (*0-385-30505-2*) Delacorte.

***Demons: A "Nameless Detective" Mystery.** Bill Pronzini. 1994. pap. 4.99 (*0-440-21118-2*) Dell.

Demons: A Novel in Three Parts. Fyodor Dostoyevsky. Tr. by Richard Pevear & Larissa Volokhonsky. LC 93-33367. (ENG & RUS.). 1995. 25.00 (*0-679-73451-1*) Knopf.

Demons & Deliverance. Frank Hammond. 138p. (Orig.). 1991. pap. 6.00 (*0-89228-001-8*) Impact Christian.

Demons & Deliverance. H. A. Whyte. 176p. 1989. 8.99 (*0-88368-216-8*) Whitaker Hse.

Demons & Demagogues: Political Fanaticism in the Longhorn State. Arthur F. Ide. LC 85-15875. (Illus.). 169p. (Orig.). 1985. pap. 10.00 (*0-934659-00-1*) Liberal Pr.

Demons & Shadows: The Ghostly Best Stories. Robert Westall. (J). (gr. 4-7). 1993. 16.00 (*0-374-31768-2*) FS&G.

Demons & the Devil: Moral Imagination in Modern Greek Culture. Charles Stewart. (Illus.). 338p. 1991. text ed. 55.00 (*0-691-09446-2*); pap. text ed. 17.95 (*0-691-02848-6*) Princeton U Pr.

Demons & the Occult. Gordon Lindsay. (Powers of Darkness Ser.: Vol. 6). 1969. 2.95 (*0-89985-089-8*) Christ for the Nations.

Demons At Your Doorstep. Peter Popoff. Ed. by Don Tanner. LC 82-82842. (Illus.). 56p. 1982. pap. 1.50 (*0-938544-13-6*) Faith Messenger.

Demon's Beach. Nicole Davidson. 160p. (Orig.). (J). (gr. 7-12). 1992. pap. 3.50 (*0-380-76644-2*, Flare) Avon.

Demons by Daylight. Ramsey Campbell. 192p. 1990. pap. 3.95 (*0-88184-610-4*) Carroll & Graf.

***Demons Dancing in My Head: Collected Poems, 1985-95.** Elayne Clift. 110p. (Orig.). 1995. pap. 8.95 (*0-9634827-2-6*) OGN Pubns.

Demons Don't Dream. Piers Anthony. 352p. 1994. mass mkt. 5.99 (*0-8125-3483-2*) Tor Bks.

Demons, Exorcism & the Evangelical. John J. Davis. 1979. pap. 1.50 (*0-88469-043-1*) BMH Bks.

Demons Eye. Stephen Gresham. 1989. pap. 3.95 (*0-8217-2704-4*) Zebra.

Demon's Fright. Penelope B. Kreps. mass mkt. 4.50 (*0-8217-3775-9*) Zebra.

Demons Ghosts & Spectres. Robert Hunt. (C). 1990. pap. text ed. 24.95 (*0-85025-329-2*, Pub. by Tor Mark Pr UK) St Mut.

***Demons, Gods & Holy Men from Indian Myths & Legends.** Shahrukh Husain. LC 94-38057. (World Mythology Ser.). (Illus.). 132p. (J). (gr. 6 up). 1995. 22.50 (*0-87226-923-X*) P Bedrick Bks.

Demons in the Church. Ellis H. Skolfield. 168p. (Orig.). 1993. pap. 8.95 (*0-9628139-2-3*) Fish Hse.

Demons in the World Today. Merrill F. Unger. 1980. pap. 8.99 (*0-8423-0661-7*) Tyndale.

Demons, les Pauvres Gens. Fyodor Dostoyevsky. (FRE.). 1952. 105.00 (*0-8288-3437-7*, F104442) Fr & Eur.

Demons (les Possedes) & les Rauvres Gens. Fyodor Dostoyevsky. 1384p. (FRE.). pap. 17.95 (*0-8288-9741-7*, 2080704206) Fr & Eur.

***Demons, Nausea & Resistance in the Autobiography of Isabel de Jesus (1611-1682)** Sherry M. Velasco. LC 95-4365. 1996. write for info. (*0-8263-1664-6*) U of NM Pr.

Demons of Dancing Gods. Jack L. Chalker. (Orig.). 1984. pap. 3.95 (*0-345-30893-X*, Del Rey) Ballantine.

Demons of the Burning Night. Matthew Power. Ed. by Terry K. Amthor & John D. Ruemmler. (Shadow World Ser.). (Illus.). 64p. (Orig.). (C). 1989. pap. 12.00 (*1-55806-071-5*, 6003) Iron Crown Ent Inc.

***Demons of the Night: Tales of the Fantastic, Madness & the Supernatural from Nineteenth-Century France.** Joan C. Kessler. LC 94-29819. 1995. pap. 14.95 (*0-226-43208-4*) U Ch Pr.

***Demons of the Night: Tales of the Fantastic, Madness & the Supernatural from Nineteeth-Century France.** Ed. & Tr. by Joan C. Kessler. LC 94-29819. (ENG.). 1995. lib. bdg. 45.00 (*0-226-43207-6*) U Ch Pr.

Demons of Zammar. Mike Sirota. (Ro-Lan Ser.: No. 4). (Orig.). 1981. pap. 2.50 (*0-89083-855-0*) Zebra.

Demons Rule. Charles Brown. Ed. by Rob Bell. (Champions Ser.). (Illus.). 32p. (Orig.). (YA). (gr. 12). 1990. pap. 7.00 (*1-55806-110-X*, 412) Iron Crown Ent Inc.

Demons the Answer Book. Lester Sumrall. 146p. 1993. pap. 4.99 (*0-88368-329-6*) Whitaker Hse.

***Demon's Tongue.** Ronald W. Jones. 300p. Date not set. pap. 9.95 (*0-7610-0241-3*) NW Pub.

Demons, Witches & the Occult. abr. ed. Josh McDowell & Don Stewart. (Pocket Guides Ser.). 96p. 1986. 2.99 (*0-8423-0541-6*) Tyndale.

Demons, Yes - but Thank God for Good Angels. Lehman Strauss. LC 75-38804. 1976. pap. 6.99 (*0-87213-831-3*) Loizeaux.

Demonstrating Community-Based Long Term Care in the United States: An Evaluation Research Perspective. Francis G. Caro. 47p. 1980. pap. 3.00 (*0-88156-074-X*) Comm Serv Soc NY.

Demonstrating Philosophy: Novel Ways to Teach Philosophical Concepts. Ed. by Arnold Wilson. LC 88-24849. (Illus.). 240p. (Orig.). (C). 1989. lib. bdg. 53.00 (*0-8191-7198-0*); pap. text ed. 21.00 (*0-8191-7199-9*) U Pr of Amer.

Demonstrating Science with Soap Films. D. Lovett. (Illus.). 200p. 1994. 80.00 (*0-7503-0270-4*); pap. 35.00 (*0-7503-0269-0*) IOP Pub.

Demonstratio Idioma Ungarorum et Lapponum Idem Esse. Joannis Sajnovics & Thomas A. Sebeok. LC 67-66170. (Uralic & Altaic Ser.: Vol. 91). 132p. 1967. reprint ed. pap. text ed. 12.00 (*0-87750-037-1*) Res Inst Inner Asian Studies.

Demonstration. Walter C. Lanyon. reprint ed. 5.00 (*0-685-71646-5*); reprint ed. spiral bd. 5.00 (*0-7873-1000-X*) Mokelumne.

Demonstration Cities Housing & Urban Development & Urban Mass Transit, 2 vols. in one. U. S. House of Representatives Committee on Banking & Currency. LC 77-74955. (American Federalism-the Urban Dimension Ser.). 1978. reprint ed. lib. bdg. 95.95 (*0-405-10499-5*) Ayer.

Demonstration Democracy. Amitai Etzioni. 122p. 1970. text ed. 56.00 (*0-677-02610-2*) Gordon & Breach.

Demonstration Elections: U. S.-Staged Elections in the Dominican Republic, Vietnam & El Salvador. Edward S. Herman & Frank Brodhead. LC 83-51284. 264p. 1984. pap. 11.00 (*0-89608-214-8*) South End Pr.

Demonstration Handbook for Physics. 2nd ed. Ed. by G. D. Freier & F. J. Anderson. (Occasional Publications). (Illus.). 320p. 1981. pap. text ed. 20.00 (*0-917853-32-6*, OP40) Am Assn Physics.

Demonstration of an Advanced Cyclone Coal Combustor, with Internal Sulfur, Nitrogen, & Ash Control for the Conversion of a 23-mm BTU-Hr Oil-Fired Boiler to Pulverized Coal. (Illus.). 175p. (Orig.). (C). 1994. pap. text ed. 95.00 (*0-7881-0485-3*) Diane Pub.

Demonstration of the Gospel. Billy J. Daugherty. 75p. (Orig.). 1991. pap. 4.50 (*1-56267-030-1*) Victory Ctr OK.

Demonstration Policy Evaluation of the Dutch Second Transport Structure Plan (SVV) Warren Walker et al. LC 93-50116. 1994. write for info. (*0-8330-1506-0*, MR-275-EAC) Rand Corp.

Demonstration Techniques. Susan Pottorrf. (C). 1993. 15.52 (*1-56870-093-8*) RonJon Pub.

Demonstration That Current Population De-Concentration Trends Are a Clean Break with Past Trends. Daniel R. Vining & Ann Strauss. (Discussion Paper Ser.: No. 90). 1976. pap. 10.00 (*1-55869-023-9*) Regional Sci Res Inst.

Demonstrative Evidence. Mark A. Dombroff. 1983. 25.00 (*1-55917-115-4*, 991); audio 125.00 (*1-55917-113-8*); vhs 450.00 (*1-55917-114-6*) Natl Prac Inst.

Demonstrative Evidence. Richard A. Givens. 450p. 1989. text ed. 95.00 (*0-07-007230-2*) Shepards-McGraw.

Demonstratives. Ed. by Palle Yourgrau. (Oxford Readings in Philosophy Ser.). 288p. 1990. pap. text ed. 16.95 (*0-19-824868-7*) OUP.

Demoosthenes & the Last Days of Greek Freedom, 384-322 B.C. A. W. Pickard-Cambridge. LC 73-14463. (Heroes of the Nations Ser.). reprint ed. 45.00 (*0-404-58281-8*) AMS Pr.

Demophoon. Maria L. Cherubini. Ed. by Philip Gossett & Charles Rosen. LC 76-49213. (Early Romantic Opera Ser.: Vol. 32). 1979. lib. bdg. 15.00 (*0-8240-2931-3*) Garland.

Demophrenia. Paul Eidelberg. 240p. 1994. pap. 10.99 (*0-933451-27-X*) Prescott Pr.

Demos: A Story of English Socialism. George Gissing. LC 75-148786. reprint ed. 45.00 (*0-404-02778-4*) AMS Pr.

Demos: A Story of English Socialism. George R. Gissing. (BCL1-PR English Literature Ser.). 104p. 1992. reprint ed. lib. bdg. 69.00 (*0-7812-7533-4*) Rprt Serv.

Demos: The Discovery of Classical Attika. Robin Osborne. (Cambridge Classical Studies). (Illus.). 288p. 1985. 64.95 (*0-521-26776-5*) Cambridge U Pr.

Demosclerosis: The Silent Killer of American Government. Jonathan Rauch. 1994. 22.00 (*0-8129-2257-3*, Times Bks) Random.

Demosthenes: De Coronoa. W. W. Goodwin. 304p. 1982. reprint ed. 23.95 (*0-86292-022-1*, Pub. by Brstl Class Pr UK) Focus Info Gr.

Demosthenes Against Andrs0tion & Against Timocrates. 2nd ed. Demosthenes. Ed. by Gregory Vlastos. LC 78-14602. (Morals & Law in Ancient Greece Ser.). (ENG & GRE.). 1979. reprint ed. lib. bdg. 25.95 (*0-405-11581-4*) Ayer.

Demosthenes & His Time: A Study in Defeat. Raphael Sealey. LC 92-18540. (Illus.). 352p. 1993. 59.00 (*0-19-507928-0*) OUP.

Demosthenes & the Last Days of Greek Freedom: 384-322 B. C. A. W. Cambridge-Pickard. Ed. by Gregory Vlastos. LC 78-19377. (Morals & Law in Ancient Greece Ser.). 1979. reprint ed. lib. bdg. 42.95 (*0-405-11566-0*) Ayer.

Demosthenes on the Crown. Demosthenes. Ed. by Gregory Vlastos. LC 78-19354. (Morals & Law in Ancient Greece Ser.). (ENG & GRE.). 1979. reprint ed. lib. bdg. 30.95 (*0-405-11547-4*) Ayer.

Demosthenes' on the Crown: A Critical Case Study of a Masterpiece of Ancient Oratory. Ed. by James J. Murphy. Tr. by John J. Keaney. 209p. (Orig.). (C). 1983. reprint ed. pap. text ed. 9.50 (*0-9611800-1-3*) Hermagoras Pr.

Demosthenes und Seine Zeit, 4 vols. Arnold Schafer. xxxix, 1971p. 1966. reprint ed. Bd. IV. write for info. (*0-318-71021-8*, Pub. by Georg Olms GW) Lubrecht & Cramer.

Demosthenes und Seine Zeit, 3 vols., Set. Arnold Schaefer. Ed. by Gregory Vlastos. LC 78-19374. (Morals & Law in Ancient Greece Ser.). (GER.). 1979. reprint ed. lib. bdg. 132.95 (*0-405-11572-5*) Ayer.

Demosthenes und Seine Zeit, 4 vols., Set. Arnold Schafer. xxxix, 1971p. 1966. reprint ed. write for info. (*0-318-71020-X*, Pub. by Georg Olms GW) Lubrecht & Cramer.

Demosthenes, Volumina 8 et 9: Scholia Graeca ex Codicibus Aucta et Emendata, ex Recensione Gulielmi Dindorfiu, 2 vols., 8. Demosthenes. LC 72-7888. (Greek History Ser.). (GRE & LAT.). 1973. reprint ed. 33.95 (*0-405-04783-5*) Ayer.

Demosthenes, Volumina 8 et 9: Scholia Graeca ex Codicibus Aucta et Emendata, ex Recensione Gulielmi Dindorfiu, 2 vols., 9. Demosthenes. LC 72-7888. (Greek History Ser.). (GRE & LAT.). 1973. reprint ed. 30.95 (*0-405-04784-3*) Ayer.

Demosthenes, Volumina 8 et 9: Scholia Graeca ex Codicibus Aucta et Emendata, ex Recensione Gulielmi Dindorfiu, 2 vols., Set. Demosthenes. LC 72-7888. (Greek History Ser.). (GRE & LAT.). 1973. reprint ed. 59.95 (*0-405-04782-7*) Ayer.

Demotic Greek I. 4th rev. ed. Peter Bien et al. LC 83-40009. (Illus.). 386p. 1983. pap. text ed. 17.95 (*0-87451-262-X*) U Pr of New Eng.

Demotic Greek II: The Flying Telephone Booth. Peter Bien et al. LC 81-51609. (Illus.). 439p. 1982. student ed 15.00 (*0-87451-209-3*); teacher ed 2.95 (*0-87451-980-2*); pap. text ed. 24.00 (*0-87451-208-5*) U Pr of New Eng.

Demotic Mathematical Papyri. Richard A. Parker. LC 77-177501. (Brown Egyptological Studies: No. 7). 142p. reprint ed. pap. 40.50 (*0-8357-5549-5*, 2035168) Bks Demand.

Demotic Verbal System. Janet H. Johnson. LC 76-44966. (Studies in Ancient Oriental Civilization: No. 38). (Illus.). 1976. pap. 15.00 (*0-918986-02-8*) Orientl Inst Pr IT.

Demountable Concrete Structures: A Challenge for Precast Concrete. Ed. by H. W. Reinhardt & J. J. Bouvy. (Illus.). 360p. (Orig.). 1985. pap. text ed. 57.50 (*90-6275-182-2*, Pub. by Delft U Pr NE) Coronet Bks.

***Dempsey.** Anita Hamilton. (J). 1995. 8.95 (*0-8062-5144-1*) Carlton.

Dempsey's Dilemma. large type ed. Christine Adams. 1993. 16.95 (*0-263-13154-8*, MB081, Pub. by Mills & Boon Ltd UK) Chivers N Amer.

***Dempsey's Hot Summer: The July Adventure of a Cape Cod Dog.** Gretchen Markham. LC 95-76153. (Illus.). 30p. (Orig.). (J). (gr. 1-3). 1995. pap. 9.95 (*1-887146-01-6*) Art Works.

Dempsters. Rica Erickson. LC 79-670115. 1979. 30.00 (*0-85564-126-6*, Pub. by Univ of West Aust Pr AT) Intl Spec Bk.

Demurrer; or, Proofs of Error in the Decision of the Supreme Court of the State of New York Requiring Faith in a Particular Religious Doctrine As a Legal Qualification of Witnesses. Thomas Herttell. LC 70-122160. (Civil Liberties in American History Ser.). 154p. 1972. reprint ed. lib. bdg. 19.50 (*0-306-71971-1*) Da Capo.

Demutualization of Life Insurers. (Commercial Law & Practice Course Handbook Ser.: Vol. 648). 559p. 1993. 70.00 (*0-685-70160-3*, A4-4421) PLI.

Demyelinating Diseases: Basic & Clinical Electrophysiology. Ed. by Stephen G. Waxman & J. Murdoch Ritchie. (Advances in Neurology Ser.: Vol. 31). 544p. 1981. 153.00 (*0-89004-625-5*) Raven.

Demystification of Law for Women. Nandita Haksar. 112p. 1986. pap. 6.00 (*0-8364-1638-4*, Pub. by Lancer II) S Asia.

Demystification of Nonformal Education, No. 1. John C. Bock & George J. Papagiannis. (Issue Paper Ser.). 35p. (Orig.). (C). 1976. pap. text ed. 3.00 (*0-932288-37-5*) Ctr Intl Ed U of MA.

Demystifying Baldridge. Donald C. Fisher et al. Orig. Title: World Class Leaders for the 1990s. (Illus.). 160p. 1993. 22.00 (*1-879111-50-0*) Lincoln-Bradley.

Demystifying Compact Discs: A Guide to Digital Audio. Daniel Sweeney. 1986. pap. text ed. 9.95 (*0-07-156328-8*) McGraw.

D

An Asterisk (*) at the beginning of an entry indicates that the title is appearing in BIP for the first time.

Demystifying the Stock Market. John C. Pool & Robert L. Frick. LC 93-72993. (Illus.). 126p. (Orig.). 1995. pap. 9.95 (1-882505-02-6) Durell Inst MSASU. DEMYSTIFYING THE STOCK MARKET provides an introduction to the stock market: its function, its operations, its history. It helps the reader to overcome the mystique of Wall Street by explaining how the markets work, what the advantages & disadvantages might be of various types of investment & how the economy & basic economic principles affect investments & financial markets. Its premise is that knowledge about markets, investments & economics is key to confident & fear-free investing. The reader learns how to deal with a stockbroker, how to make a purchase of stock, how to decipher the stock tables, & how to keep track of investments. The book is a valuable tool for anyone seeking an understanding of this complex subject. Also available from the publisher are companion materials which make the book a complete teaching kit. These materials include workbook, homework exercises, transparency masters, wall charts, & a 30-minute video that explains how the stock market functions. All are available from The Durell Institute, Shenandoah University, 1460 University Drive, Winchester, VA 22601; (703) 665-5428. *Publisher Provided Annotation.*

An Asterisk (*) at the beginning of an entry indicates that the title is appearing in BIP for the first time.

1871

***Denmark Commercial Law.** 150p. (C). 1994. pap. 295.00 (0-7605-0107-6) Rector Pr.

***Denmark FAX Book.** 300p. (Orig.). 1994. pap. 225.00 (0-7605-0568-3) Rector Pr.

Denmark, Iceland: Business Risk Overview. Ed. by Lewis B. Sckolnick. 125p. (Orig.). (C). 1994. pap. text ed. 495.00 (1-57205-606-1) Rector Pr.

Denmark in History. John H. Birch. 1976. lib. bdg. 59.95 (0-8490-1707-6) Gordon Pr.

Denmark in Pictures. Ed. by Lerner Geography Dept. Staff. (Visual Geography Ser.). (Illus.). 64p. (YA). (gr. 5 up). 1991. reprint ed. lib. bdg. 18.95 (0-8225-1880-5, Lerner Publctns) Lerner Group.

***Denmark Tax Law.** 150p. (C). 1994. pap. 295.00 (0-7605-0106-8) Rector Pr.

Denmark Vesey. Lillie Edwards. (Black Americans of Achievement Ser.). (Illus.). (YA). (gr. 5 up). 1990. 17.95 (1-55546-614-1) Chelsea Hse.

***Denmark Vesey.** Robertson. Date not set. pap. write for info. (0-679-44288-X) Random Hse Value.

Denmark Vesey's Revolt: The Slave Plot That Lit a Fuse to Fort Sumter. John Lofton. LC 83-11267. 316p. reprint ed. pap. 90.10 (0-7837-4054-9, 2043885) Bks Demand.

Denmark's Numeral Cancellations 1852-1884. Henry E. Tester & Glenn F. Hansen. (Illus.). xiii, 165p. 1987. pap. 25.00 (0-936493-11-9) Scand Philatelic.

Dennecker Code. J. C. Pollock. 224p. 1982. pap. 2.50 (0-449-14454-2, GM) Fawcett.

Dennen's Forceps Deliveries. 3rd ed. Philip C. Dennen. LC 88-20272. (Illus.). 201p. 1989. 35.00 (0-8036-2511-1) Davis Co.

Denner's Wreck. Lawrence Watt-Evans. 208p. 1988. pap. 2.95 (0-380-75250-6) Avon.

Dennett & His Critics: Demystifying Mind. Ed. by Bo Dahlbom. LC 92-43145. (Philosophers & Their Critics Ser.). 272p. 1993. 44.95 (0-631-18549-6) Blackwell Pubs.

***Dennett & His Critics: Demystifying Mind.** Ed. by Bo Dahlbom. (Philosophers & Their Critics Ser.). 248p. 1995. pap. 21.95 (0-631-19678-1) Blackwell Pubs.

Denning: What Next in the Law. Lord Denning. 1982. 38.00 (0-406-17601-9); pap. 26.00 (0-406-17602-7) Butterworth Legal Pubs.

Denning Report: The Profumo Affair. Lord Denning. 114p. 1993. reprint ed. pap. 17.95 (0-7126-5255-8, Pub. by Pimlico) Trafalgar.

***Dennis Adams: Selling History.** 80p. 1995. pap. 14.95 (0-936080-34-5) Dist Art Pubs.

Dennis Adler's High Country Prints Book. Dennis Adler. (Illus.). 1977. pap. 3.95 (0-918688-01-9) Touchstone Oregon.

Dennis Benson's Creative Bible Studies: Matthew-Acts. Dennis C. Benson. (Illus.). 654p. (Orig.). 1985. pap. 21.99 (0-931529-01-8) Group Pub.

Dennis Benson's Creative Bible Studies: Romans-Revelation. Dennis C. Benson. (Illus.). 276p. (Orig.). 1988. pap. 16.99 (0-931529-52-2) Group Pub.

Dennis Byrd. Dennis Byrd & Michael D'Orso. (Today's Heroes Ser.). 112p. 1995. pap. 4.99 (0-310-41251-X) Zondervan.

Dennis Gould: A Retrospective in Two Parts. Allan Shickman. (Illus.). 12p. (Orig.). 1987. pap. 3.00 (0-932660-13-4) U of NI Dept Art.

Dennis Menace: Short n Snappy. Hank Ketcham. (Illus.). 1984. pap. 2.25 (0-449-12855-5) Fawcett.

Dennis Menace Little Pip Squeek. Hank Ketcham. (Illus.). 1984. pap. 1.95 (0-449-12734-6) Fawcett.

***Dennis Miller Bunker: American Impressionist.** Erica Hirshler. (Illus.). 192p. 1995. 45.00 (0-87846-442-5) Mus Fine Arts Boston.

Dennis Oppenheim: Accelerator for Evil Thoughts. Alain G. Joyaux. 24p. (Orig.). 1985. pap. 5.00 (0-318-18308-0) Ball State Art.

Dennis Oppenheim: Drawings & Selected Sculpture. Peter F. Spooner et al. (Illus.). 56p. 1992. 15.95 (0-945558-16-3) ISU Univ Galls.

Dennis Oppenheim Selected Works, 1967-90: And the Mind Grew Fingers. Alanna Heiss. (Illus.). 200p. 1992. 49.50 (0-8109-3662-3) Abrams.

Dennis Potter. Peter Stead. (Illus.). 152p. 1994. 30.00 (1-85411-071-3, Pub. by Seren Bks UK); pap. 14.95 (1-85411-072-1, Pub. by Seren Bks UK) Dufour.

***Dennis Potter: A Life on Screen.** John R. Cook. LC 95-2169. 1995. text ed. write for info. (0-7190-4601-7, Pub. by Manchester Univ Pr UK); text ed. write for info. (0-7190-4602-5, Pub. by Manchester Univ Pr UK) St Martin.

Dennis Power. Hank Ketcham. (Illus.). 1977. pap. 1.95 (0-449-12760-5) Fawcett.

Dennis Quaid. Gail Birnbaum. 1988. pap. 3.50 (0-312-91247-1) St Martin.

Dennis Ralston's Tennis Workbook. Dennis Ralston et al. (Illus.). 225p. 1991. 12.95 (0-13-198607-4) P-H.

***Dennis Stock: Made in the U. S. A.** Photos by Dennis Stock. (Illus.). 180p. 1995. 49.95 (3-89322-639-7) Dist Art Pubs.

Dennis the Dinosaur Moves to Crystal Pond. Roccy Rotunno & Betsy Rotunno. (Stamptime Stories Ser.). (Illus.). 12p. (J). (gr. 2-6). 1992. Mixed Media Pkg. incls. stamp pad, stamps & box of 4 crayons. 7.00 (1-881980-03-0) Noteworthy.

Dennis the Menace. (J). (ps-3). 1993. pap. 2.95 (0-8167-3147-0) Troll Assocs.

Dennis the Menace. Jordan Horowitz. (Illus.). (J). (gr. k-2). 1993. pap. 2.95 (0-590-47349-2) Scholastic Inc.

Dennis the Menace. Jordan Horowitz. (Illus.). (J). (gr. 4-7). 1993. pap. 3.25 (0-590-47350-6) Scholastic Inc.

Dennis the Menace. Jordan Horowitz. (J). (ps-3). 1993. pap. 2.95 (0-590-47399-9) Scholastic Inc.

Dennis the Menace: Dog's Best Friend. Hank Ketcham. (Dennis the Menace Ser.: No. 43). 128p. (Orig.). 1984. mass mkt. 3.99 (0-449-12801-6, GM) Fawcett.

Dennis the Menace: His First Forty Years. Hank Ketcham. (Illus.). 224p. 1991. 15.95 (1-55859-157-5) Abbeville Pr.

Dennis the Menace: Household Hurricane. Hank Ketcham. (Dennis the Menace Ser.). (Illus.). 1982. pap. 1.75 (0-449-13679-5, GM) Fawcett.

Dennis the Menace: I Done It My Way. Hank Ketcham. (Dennis the Menace Ser.). 1981. pap. 1.95 (0-449-14095-4, GM) Fawcett.

Dennis the Menace: Little Man in a Big Hurry. Hank Ketcham. (Dennis the Menace Cartoon Ser.). (Illus.). 128p. (J). 1984. pap. 1.95 (0-449-12778-8, GM) Fawcett.

Dennis the Menace: Make-Believe Angel. Hank Ketcham. (Dennis the Menace Cartoon Ser.). (Illus.). (J). 1981. pap. 1.95 (0-449-13902-6, GM) Fawcett.

Dennis the Menace: Perpetual Motion. Hank Ketcham. (Dennis the Menace Ser.). (Illus.). 128p. 1979. pap. 1.25 (0-449-13647-7, GM) Fawcett.

Dennis the Menace: Prayers & Graces. Hank Ketcham. LC 92-17186. (Illus.). 64p. (Orig.). (J). 1993. 10.00 (0-664-21993-4); pap. 5.99 (0-664-25252-4) Westminster John Knox.

Dennis the Menace: Teacher's Threat. Hank Ketcham. (Dennis the Menace Cartoon Ser.). (Illus.). (J). 1981. pap. 1.50 (0-449-13643-4, GM) Fawcett.

Dennis the Menace: The Short Swinger. Hank Ketcham. (Dennis the Menace Cartoon Ser.). (Illus.). (J). 1981. pap. 1.50 (0-449-13641-8, GM) Fawcett.

Dennis the Menace: Voted Most Likely. Hank Ketcham. (Dennis the Menace Cartoon Ser.). (Illus.). (J). (gr. 7 up). 1982. pap. 1.75 (0-449-13747-3, GM) Fawcett.

Dennis the Menace: Where the Action Is. Hank Ketcham. (Dennis the Menace Cartoon Ser.). (Illus.). 128p. (J). 1981. pap. 1.50 (0-449-13669-8, GM) Fawcett.

Dennis the Menace: Your Friendly Neighborhood Kid. Hank Ketcham. (Dennis the Menace Cartoon Ser.). (Illus.). (J). 1979. pap. 1.25 (0-449-13778-3, GM) Fawcett.

Dennis the Menace All American Kid. Hank Ketcham. (Illus.). 1986. pap. 3.59 (0-449-13071-1) Fawcett.

Dennis the Menace & Poor Ol' Mr. Wilson. Hank Ketcham. (Dennis the Menace Ser.). (Illus.). 1981. pap. 1.75 (0-449-13837-2, GM) Fawcett.

Dennis the Menace Good Intentions. Hank Ketcham. (Illus.). 1985. pap. 1.95 (0-449-12730-3) Fawcett.

Dennis the Menace Just for Fun. Hank Ketcham. (Illus.). 1987. pap. 1.95 (0-449-12727-3) Fawcett.

Dennis the Menace Ol Droopy. Hank Ketcham. (Illus.). 1984. pap. 1.95 (0-449-12757-5) Fawcett.

Dennis the Menace Perpetual Motion. Hank Ketcham. (Illus.). 1986. pap. 2.95 (0-449-13256-0) Fawcett.

Dennis the Menace the Way I Look at It. Hank Ketcham. (Illus.). 1982. pap. 1.75 (0-449-14451-8) Fawcett.

Dennis the Menace to the Core. Hank Ketcham. (Illus.). 1987. pap. 2.25 (0-449-13257-9) Fawcett.

Dennis the Menace Who Me. Hank Ketcham. (Illus.). 1987. pap. 2.95 (0-449-12790-7) Fawcett.

Dennison's Andersonville Diary. J Klasey. 1987. pap. 7.95 (0-917914-66-X) Lindsay Pubns.

Denny Brauer's Winning Tournament Tactics. Denny Brauer. 1991. write for info. (1-879206-15-3) Outdoor World Pr.

Denny McCulley's Guide to Moving: For Senior Citizens & Anyone Making a Major Move. Denny McCulley. 112p. 1994. write for info. (0-9639628-0-9) Sr Concerns.

Denny McKeown's Complete Guide to Midwest Gardening. Denny McKeown. LC 84-23996. (Illus.). 408p. 1985. 24.95 (0-87833-382-7) Taylor Pub.

Denny Moers: Figments of a Landscape. Diana L. Johnson et al. (Illus.). 48p. (Orig.). 1992. pap. 12.00 (0-933519-23-0) D W Bell Gallery.

Denny Poems, 1985-1986. 60p. (Orig.). 1987. pap. 3.00 (0-935153-05-5) Stormline Pr.

Denny Reading Test. M. J. Nelson et al. 1973. text ed. 22.72 (0-395-17986-6) HM.

Denny Remembered: Dennis Wilson in Words & Pictures. Edward Wincentsen. Ed. by Belinda Subraman. LC 90-71134. (Illus.). 200p. (Orig.). 1990. pap. 19.95 (0-935839-05-4) Vergin Pr.

Denny's Knoll: A History of the Metropolitan Tract of the University of Washington. Neal O. Hines. LC 79-6760. (Illus.). 480p. 1980. 20.00 (0-295-95718-2) U of Wash Pr.

Denominational Doctrines Explained, Examined, Exposed. Samuel G. Dawson. LC 90-33421. 384p. (Orig.). 1990. pap. 11.95 (0-938855-86-7) Gospel Themes Pr.

Denominational Policies in the Support & Supervision of Higher Education. Paul M. Limbert. LC 75-176994. (Columbia University. Teachers College. Contributions to Education Ser.: No. 378). reprint ed. 37.50 (0-404-55378-8) AMS Pr.

Denominations in America, No. 2. 352p. write for info. (0-318-62680-2, Greenwood Pr) Greenwood.

Denominators of the Fur Trade. Arthur Woodward. (Illus.). 1979. 13.95 (0-87026-041-3) Westernlore.

Denotational Semantics: Methodology. David A. Schmidt. 348p. (C). 1988. pap. write for info. (0-697-06849-8) Wm C Brown Pubs.

Denotational Semantics: The Scott-Strachey Approach to Programming Language Theory. Joseph E. Stoy. 1977. pap. 19.50 (0-262-69076-4) MIT Pr.

Denouncement & Reaffirmation of the Afro-Hispanic Identity in Carlos Guillermo Wilson's Works. Ed. by Elba Birmingham-Pokorny. LC 91-78227. (Coleccion Ebano y Canela Ser.). 150p. (Orig.). (SPA.). 1993. pap. 19.95 (0-89729-635-4) Ediciones.

Denry the Audacious. Arnold Bennett. LC 72-6208. (Collected Works of Arnold Bennett: Vol. 14). 1977. reprint ed. 22.95 (0-518-19095-1) Ayer.

Dense Chlorinated Solvents - The Slides. Friedrich Schwille. Tr. by James F. Pankow. (Illus.). 24p. (Orig.). 1991. sl., pap. 79.95 (0-9627452-0-0) Titan Pr OR.

Dense Chlorinated Solvents in Porous & Fractured Media--Model Experiments. Friedrich Schwille. Tr. by James F. Pankow. (Illus.). 146p. 1988. 79.95 (0-87371-121-1, TD426) Lewis Pubs.

Dense Gas Dispersion. R. E. Britter & R. F. Griffiths. (Chemical Engineering Monographs: Vol. 16). 248p. 1982. reprint ed. 105.25 (0-444-42095-9) Elsevier.

Dense Z-Pinches. Ed. by Nino Pereira et al. (AIP Conference Proceedings Ser.: No. 195). 568p. 1989. lib. bdg. 80.00 (0-88318-396-X) Am Inst Physics.

***Dense Z-Pinches: Third International Conference.** Malcolm Haines & Andrew Knight. LC 93-74569. (AIP Conference Proceedings Ser.: No. 299). 728p. 1994. text ed. 710.00x (1-56396-297-7) Am Inst Physics.

Densities of Aqueous Solutions of Inorganic Substances. O. Sohnel & P. Novotny. (Physical Sciences Data Ser.: No. 22). 336p. 1984. 102.75 (0-444-99596-X) Elsevier.

Densities of Binary Aqueous Systems & Heat Capacities of Liquid Systems. J. D'Ans et al. LC 62-53136. (Landolt-Boernstein Ser.: Group IV, Vol. 1, Pt. B). (Illus.). 1977. 406.00 (0-387-08272-7) Spr-Verlag.

Density by Design. Ed. by James W. Wentling & Lloyd W. Bookout. 173p. 1988. 55.95 (0-87420-677-4) Urban Land.

Density Estimation for Statistics & Data Analysis. B. W. Silverman. (Monographs on Statistics & Applied Probability). 200p. 1986. text ed. 35.00 (0-412-24620-1, 9748) Chapman & Hall.

Density Functional Methods in Chemistry. Ed. by J. K. Labanowski & J. W. Andzelm. (Illus.). xv, 443p. 1994. 59.00 (0-387-97512-8) Spr-Verlag.

Density Functional Methods in Physics. Ed. by Reiner M. Dreizler & Joao Da Providencia. LC 85-3563. (NATO ASI Series B, Physics: Vol. 123). 542p. 1985. 110.00 (0-306-41926-2, Plenum Pr) Plenum.

***Density Functional Theory.** Ed. by Eberhard K. Gross & Reiner M. Dreizler. LC 94-48908. (NATO ASI Series B, Physics: Vol. 337). 675p. 1995. 149.50 (0-306-44905-6, Plenum Pr) Plenum.

Density-Functional Theory of Atoms & Molecules. Robert G. Parr & Yang Weitao. (International Series of Monographs on Chemistry: Vol. 16). (Illus.). 352p. 1994. reprint ed. pap. 35.00 (0-19-509276-7) OUP.

***Density Functional Theory of Molecules, Clusters & Solids.** Ed. by D. E. Ellis. LC 94-30303. (Understanding Chemical Reactivity Ser.). 324p. (C). 1994. lib. bdg. 153.50 (0-7923-3083-8) Kluwer Ac.

Density Gradient Centrifugation see Laboratory Techniques in Biochemistry & Molecular Biology

Density Matrices & Density Functionals. Ed. by Robert Erdahl & Vedene H. Smith, Jr. (C). 1987. lib. bdg. 213.50 (90-277-2477-6) Kluwer Ac.

Density Matrix Method & Femtosecond Processes. S. H. Lin et al. 228p. (C). 1991. text ed. 36.00 (981-02-0709-3) World Scientific Pub.

Density Matrix Theory & Applications. Karl Blum. LC 81-268. (Physics of Atoms & Molecules Ser.). 230p. 1981. 65.00 (0-306-40684-5, Plenum Pr) Plenum.

Density Matrix theory & Its Applications in NMR Spectroscopy. Thomas C. Farrar & John E. Harriman. (Illus.). 200p. (C). 1991. text ed. 39.95 (0-917903-03-X); pap. text ed. 24.95 (0-917903-02-1) Farragut Pr.

***Density of Liquids & Solids.** H. A. Neidig & J. N. Spencer. (Modular Series in Solid State Devices). 12p. (C). 1990. pap. text ed. 1.25x (0-87540-383-2) Chem Educ Res.

***Density of Prime Divisors of Linear Recurrences.** Christian Ballot. LC 95-2679. (Memoirs Ser.: No. 551). 1995. write for info. (0-8218-2610-7) Am Math.

Density Waves in Solids. George Gruner. LC 93-32362. (Frontiers in Physics Ser.: Vol. 89). (C). 1994. 55.95 (0-201-62654-3) Addison-Wesley.

***Dent Concertgoer's Companion.** Anthony Hopkins. (Illus.). 672p. 1995. reprint ed. pap. 24.00 (0-460-86112-3) OUP.

***Dent Dictionary of Symbols in Christian Art.** Jennifer Speake. (Illus.). 192p. 1995. 39.95 (0-460-86138-7, Pub. by Orion) Trafalgar.

***Dental Admission Test: The Betz Guide.** Aftab Hassan et al. (Betz Guide Ser.: No. 2). 250p. (Orig.). (YA). (gr. 10 up). 1992. pap. 24.95 (0-941406-33-4) Betz Pub Co Inc.

Dental Admission Test (DAT) Jack Rudman. (Admission Test Ser.: ATS-12). 1994. pap. 23.95 (0-8373-5012-3) Nat Learn.

Dental Amalgam. Arenholt. 144p. 1991. 25.50 (87-16-10328-9) Mosby Yr Bk.

***Dental Analogies: A Collection of Descriptive Dental Analogies Based on Ideas from Practicing Dentists.** Rick Waters & Bill Powell. 136p. (Orig.). 1994. pap. 29.95 (0-9642280-0-9) Dentelligence.

Dental Anatomy. Gerald M. Cathey. (Dental Laboratory Technology Manuals Ser.). viii, 236p. 1972. pap. 25.00 (0-8078-7905-3) U of NC Pr.

Dental Anatomy: Its Relevance to Dentistry. 4th ed. Ed. by Julian B. Woelfel. (Illus.). 438p. 1990. pap. 46.75 (0-8121-1259-8) Williams & Wilkins.

Dental Anatomy & Oral Histology. Arup K. Das. 260p. 1972. 70.00 (0-685-11917-3, Current Dist) St Mut.

Dental Anatomy & Oral Histology Review. A. K. Das. (C). 1991. 70.00 (0-89771-344-3, Current Dist) St Mut.

Dental & Oral Tissues: An Introduction. 3rd ed. Letty Moss-Salentijn & Marlene Hendricks-Klyvert. LC 89-13713. (Illus.). 327p. 1990. pap. text ed. 35.95 (0-8121-1320-9) Williams & Wilkins.

Dental & Otolaryngology Word Book. Littrell. 1992. 16.95 (0-87434-476-X) Springhouse Pub.

Dental Annual 1989. Donald Derrick. (Illus.). 278p. 1989. 98.00 (0-7236-1463-6, Pub. by John Wright UK) Buttrwrth-Heinemann.

Dental Anthropology. Don R. Brothwell. LC 62-22060. (Symposia of the Society for the Study of Human Biology Ser.: Vol. 4). 1963. 127.00 (0-08-009823-1, Pub. by Pergamon Repr UK) Franklin.

Dental Aptitude Test Student Guide. David M. Tarlow & Marc L. Lichtenberg. LC 78-53093. (Illus.). 1993. pap. 12.95 (0-931572-01-0) Datar Pub.

Dental Asepsis: A Self-Instructional Guide, Bk. 5. 3rd rev. ed. Robert J. Whitacre et al. (Illus.). 128p. 1985. pap. 29.95 (0-89939-051-X) Stoma Pr.

Dental Assist. Wilson. 800p. Date not set. 41.95 (0-8016-5594-3) Mosby Yr Bk.

Dental Assistant. Jack Rudman. (Career Examination Ser.: C-205). 1994. pap. 29.95 (0-8373-0205-6) Nat Learn.

Dental Assistant. 6th ed. Pauline C. Anderson & Martha R. Burkard. LC 93-40765. 784p. 1994. pap. text ed. 34.95 (0-8273-5281-6) Delmar.

***Dental Assistant.** 6th ed. Pauline C. Anderson & Martha R. Burkard. 69p. 1994. teacher ed 16.00 (0-8273-5282-4) Delmar.

Dental Assistant. 6th ed. Ed. by Roger E. Barton et al. LC 87-31199. (Illus.). 655p. 1988. text ed. 31.50 (0-8121-1141-9) Williams & Wilkins.

Dental Assistant: Syllabus. E. A. Jacobson & Alma Jacobson. 1978. pap. text ed. 11.95 (0-89420-046-1, 198040); audio 228.60 (0-89420-139-5, 198000) Natl Book.

Dental Assistant Techniques. Betty Lorenzen. LC 74-18674. (Allied Health Ser.). 1976. pap. write for info. (0-672-61395-6) Macmillan.

Dental Assisting. Jack Rudman. (Occupational Competency Examination Ser.: OCE-15). 1994. pap. 23.95 (0-8373-5715-2) Nat Learn.

Dental Assisting: Basic & Dental Sciences. Leimone & Earl. (Illus.). 384p. 1987. pap. text ed. 33.95 (0-8016-2942-X) Mosby Yr Bk.

Dental Assisting Exam Preparation. Hazel O. Torres & Lois Mazzucchi-Ballard. LC 93-19477. 208p. 1993. pap. text ed. 19.95 (0-7216-3295-5) Saunders.

Dental Assisting Manuals, 8 vols. 3rd ed. Ethel M. Earl et al. Incl. No. I. Professionalism, Legal Considerations, & Office Management. LC 79-10801. (Illus.). ix, 85p. 1980. pap. text ed. 10.00 (0-8078-1375-3); LC 79-10801. 1980. Set pap. text ed. write for info. (0-318-56100-X) U of NC Pr.

Dental Auxiliary Education Examination in Dental Materials. Jack Rudman. (College Level Examination Ser.: CLEP-47). 1994. 39.95 (0-8373-5397-1); pap. 23.95 (0-8373-5347-5) Nat Learn.

Dental Auxiliary Education Examination in Head, Neck & Oral Anatomy. Jack Rudman. (College Level Examination Ser.: CLEP-48). 1994. 39.95 (0-8373-5398-X); pap. 23.95 (0-8373-5348-3) Nat Learn.

Dental Auxiliary Education Examination in Oral Radiography. Jack Rudman. (College Level Examination Ser.: CLEP-49). 1994. 39.95 (0-8373-5399-8); pap. 23.95 (0-8373-5349-1) Nat Learn.

Dental Auxiliary Education Examination in Tooth Morphology & Function. Jack Rudman. (College Level Examination Ser.: CLEP-50). 1994. 39.95 (0-8373-5975-9); pap. 23.95 (0-8373-5950-3) Nat Learn.

Dental Bibliography: 1536-1885. C. George Crowley. 1972. 59.95 (0-8490-0018-1) Gordon Pr.

Dental Care & Health Factors: Subject Analysis Index with Research Bibliography. Ilonia Rekany. LC 85-47865. 150p. 1986. 39.50 (0-88164-404-8); pap. 34.50 (0-88164-405-6) ABBE Pubs Assn.

Dental Care for Everyone: Problems & Proposals. James M. Dunning. 240p. 1976. 24.00 (0-674-19790-9) HUP.

Dental Care of the Handicapped Patient. B. Hunter. (Illus.). 112p. 1987. pap. 35.00 (0-7236-0889-X, Pub. by John Wright UK) Buttrwrth-Heinemann.

Dental Care Today. Robert J. Kitson. (Illus.). 50p. (Orig.). 1993. pap. 7.95 (0-9639767-0-2) R J Kitson Pubng.

Dental Caries: A Treatable Infection. rev. ed. Walter J. Loesche. (Illus.). 550p. (C). 1994. pap. 29.50 (0-9639689-0-4) Automat Diag.

Dental Caries As a Cause of Nervous Disorders. Patrick Stortebecker. 235p. 1986. reprint ed. 20.00 (0-941011-00-3) Bio-Probe.

Dental Ceramics: Proceedings of the First International Symposium on Ceramics. Ed. by John W. McLean. (Illus.). 400p. 1983. text ed. 156.00 (0-86715-112-9) Quint Pub Co.

Dental Communication. David W. Chambers & Ronald G. Abrams. 295p. (C). 1992. pap. text ed. 24.00 (0-9632599-0-3) Ohana Grp.

Dental Consultant Looks at Insurance. 3rd rev. ed. Tom M. Limoli. 304p. 1992. 95.00 (0-685-71299-0, D7203) PennWell Bks.

Dental Crowns & Bridges: Design & Preparation. 2nd ed. Bernard G. Smith. (Illus.). 264p. 1990. 72.00 (0-8151-7807-7, Yr Bk Med Pubs) Mosby Yr Bk.

***Dental Education at the Crossroads: Challenges & Changes.** Institute of Medicine Staff. Ed. by Marilyn J. Field. 360p. (Orig.). (C). 1995. text ed. 49.95 (0-309-05195-9) Natl Acad Pr.

Dental Electronics & Equipment Markets: Dentists Look to Esthetics for New Revenues. Market Intelligence Staff. 314p. (Orig.). 1992. 1,695.00 (1-56753-031-1) Frost & Sullivan.

***Dental Enamel: Formation to Destruction.** Ed. by Colin Robinson et al. LC 95-1383. 336p. 1995. 195.00 (0-8493-4589-8, 4589) CRC Pr.

Dental Equipment & Supplies Markets. (Market Research Reports: No. 226). 162p. 1992. 295.00 (0-317-05460-0) Theta Corp.

Dental Ethics. Bruce Weinstein. (Illus.). 250p. 1993. pap. 29.95 (0-8121-1444-2) Williams & Wilkins.

Dental Ethics at Chairside: Professional Principles. Ozar. 250p. 1993. pap. 29.00 (0-8016-7400-X) Mosby Yr Bk.

An Asterisk (*) at the beginning of an entry indicates that the title is appearing in BIP for the first time.

An Asterisk (*) at the beginning of an entry indicates that the title is appearing in BIP for the first time.

1873

Denver Nuggets. rev. ed. Michael E. Goodman. (NBA Today Ser.). (Illus.). 32p. (J). (gr. 4 up). 1993. lib. bdg. 14.95 (*0-88682-546-6*) Creative Ed.

Denver Proficiency & Review Program (PRP) Jack Rudman. (Admission Test Ser.: ATS-66). 1994. pap. 23.95 (*0-8373-5066-2*) Nat Learn.

***Denver Real Estate Guide Denver & Front Range Real Estate Guide.** Global Inc. Staff & James D. Durdy. (Illus.). 180p. (Orig.). 1995. pap. 7.95 (*1-887430-19-9*) Global Inc.

Denver Regional (Close up) Atlas - Street Guide. 1994. pap. 24.95 (*0-914449-33-8*) Pierson Graph.

***Denver Regional, CO.** (Streetfinder Ser.). (Illus.). 1994. pap. 29.95 (*0-528-95271-4*) Rand McNally.

Denver Run. David Robbins. (Endworld Ser.: No. 8). 256p. (Orig.). 1987. pap. 2.95 (*0-8439-2548-5*) Dorchester Pub Co.

Denver Streets: Names, Numbers, Locations, Logic. Phil Goodstein. (Illus.). 226p. (Orig.). 1994. pap. 19.95 (*0-9622169-2-5*) New Social.

Denver the City Beautiful. Thomas S. Noel & Barbara J. Norgren. (Illus.). 256p. 1987. 21.95 (*0-914248-04-9*) Hist Denver.

Denver the City Beautiful. Thomas J. Noel & Barbara S. Norgren. LC 87-80609. (Illus.). 256p. 1993. reprint ed. pap. text ed. 22.95 (*0-914628-22-4*) Graphic Impress.

Denver Weddings. 2nd rev. ed. Gerri Samuels. (Coopwood & Fields Consumer Planning Guide Ser.). 250p. 1995. pap. 14.95 (*1-878991-14-0*) I Do Pub.

Denverides: The Mountain Bike Guide to Denver. Dave Rich. (Fat Tire Guides Ser.). 62p. 1993. pap. 7.95 (*0-9634607-2-2*) Little Rose Pub.

Denver's Capitol Hill: One Hundred Years of a Vibrant Urban Neighborhood. 6th ed. Phil Goodstein, Jr. LC 88-81398. (Illus.). 256p. (Orig.). 1988. 20.00 (*0-317-93362-0*); pap. 12.00 (*0-317-93363-9*) New Social.

Denver's City Park. rev. ed. Bette D. Peters et al. (Illus.). 67p. 1986. pap. 7.95 (*0-937859-01-X*) Univ CO Dept Hist.

Denver's Lady. Jennifer Mikels. (Silhouette Special Edition Ser.). 1994. mass mkt. 3.50 (*0-373-09870-7*, 5-09870-2) Silhouette.

Denver's Larimer Street: Main Street, Skid Row & Urban Renaissance. Thomas J. Noel. LC 81-83395. 1981. pap. 14.95 (*0-914248-02-2*) Hist Denver.

Denver's Railroads. Kenton Forrest & Charles Albi. LC 81-7701. (Illus.). 272p. 1986. 29.95 (*0-918654-31-9*) CO RR Mus.

Denying the Holocaust: The Growing Assault on Truth & Memory. Deborah Lipstadt. LC 93-9952. 300p. 1993. text ed. 22.95 (*0-02-919235-8*) Free Pr.

Denying the Holocaust: The Growing Assault on Truth & Memory. Deborah E. Lipstadt. LC 93-45586. 288p. 1994. pap. 10.95 (*0-452-27274-2*, Plume) NAL-Dutton.

Denying "The Honor of Living" Sudan, a Human Rights Disaster. Africa Watch Staff. 172p. 1990. pap. 15.00 (*0-929692-53-5*, Africa Watch) Hum Rts Watch.

Denys Lasdun: Architecture, City, Landscape. William J. Curtis, Jr. (Illus.). 240p. (C). 1994. 60.00 (*0-7148-2871-8*, Pub. by Phaidon Press UK) Chronicle Bks.

Denys the Areopagite. Andrew Louth. (Outstanding Christian Thinkers Ser.). 145p. 1989. pap. 9.95 (*0-8192-1485-X*) Morehouse Pub.

Denzil Quarrier. George Gissing. LC 79-80634. reprint ed. 52.50 (*0-404-02787-3*) AMS Pr.

Deodorants: Index of New Information & Medical Research Bible. Zelda V. Munk. 150p. 1994. 44.50 (*0-7883-0118-7*); pap. 39.50 (*0-7883-0119-5*) ABBE Pubs Assn.

Deodorants: The International Market. Euromonitor Staff. 90p. (C). 1988. 2,925.00 (*0-685-30319-5*, Pub. by Euromonitor Pubns UK) Gale.

Deontic Logic: Introductory & Systematic Readings. Ed. by Risto Hilpinen. LC 72-135103. (Synthese Library: No. 33). 182p. 1970. lib. bdg. 57.50 (*90-277-0167-9*) Kluwer Ac.

Deontic Logic, Computational Linguistics & Legal Information Systems. Antonio A. Martino. 518p. 1982. 105.25 (*0-444-86415-6*, North Holland) Elsevier.

Deontic Logic in Computer Science: Normative System Specification. J. J. Meyer & R. J. Wieringa. 300p. 1994. text ed. 75.95 (*0-471-93743-6*) Wiley.

Deontische Logik Ohne Paradoxien Semantik Und Logik Des Normativen. Ulrich Nortmann. (Introductiones Ser.). 200p. (GER.). (C). 1989. 50.00 (*3-88405-067-2*) Philosophia Pr.

Deontology: A Table of the Springs of Action on Utilitarianism. Jeremy Bentham. Ed. by Amnon Goldworth. Incl. Table of the Springs of Action & the Article on Utilitarianism. 1983. (*0-318-57041-6*); (Collected Works of Jeremy Bentnam Ser.). (Illus.). 1983. 98.00 (*0-19-822609-8*) OUP.

Deor. Ed. by Kemp Malone. (Old English Ser.). 1966. pap. text ed. 9.95 (*0-89197-566-7*) Irvington.

Deoxyglucose Uptake & Oxygen Consumption: A Metabolic Approach to Cerebral Function. Ed. by M. Le Poncin-Lafitte & J. R. Rapin. (Journal: European Neurology: Vol. 20, No. 3). (Illus.). 170p. 1981. pap. 40.00 (*3-8055-3412-4*) S Karger.

DePalma's the Management of Fractures & Dislocations: An Atlas, 2 vols., 1. 3rd ed. Ed. by John F. Connolly. (Illus.). 2000p. 1981. text ed. 138.00 (*0-7216-2702-1*) Saunders.

DePalma's the Management of Fractures & Dislocations: An Atlas, 2 vols., 2. 3rd ed. Ed. by John F. Connolly. (Illus.). 2000p. 1981. text ed. 138.00 (*0-7216-2703-X*) Saunders.

DePalma's the Management of Fractures & Dislocations: An Atlas, 2 vols., Set. 3rd ed. Ed. by John F. Connolly. (Illus.). 2000p. 1981. text ed. 259.00 (*0-7216-2666-1*) Saunders.

Departed Days. Douglas Tregenza. (C). 1989. 45.00 (*0-907566-98-7*, Pub. by Dyllansow Truran UK) St Mut.

Departed Glory. Peter Danielson. (Children of the Lion Ser.: No. 16). 1993. mass mkt. 4.99 (*0-553-56145-6*) Bantam.

Departement des Hautes-Pyrenees: Cahiers de Doleances de la Senechaussee de Bigorre pour les Etats-generaux de 1789. Ed. by Gaston Balencie. LC 74-29249. (Collection de la Commission d'histoire Economique et sociale de la Revolution Francaise). reprint ed. 45.00 (*0-404-58602-3*) AMS Pr.

Departing Glory: Eight Jeremiads of Increase Mather. Increase Mather. LC 86-31349. 1987. 50.00 (*0-8201-1415-4*) Schol Facsimiles.

Department by Department Implementation for the Certification Audit. Ed. by Jack Kanholm. 168p. (Orig.). (C). 1993. pap. text ed. 98.00 (*0-685-68155-6*) AQA.

Department Chair: New Roles, Responsibilities & Challenges. Alan T. Seagren et al. Ed. by Jonathan D. Fife. (ASHE-ERIC Higher Education Report Ser.: No. 93-1). (Orig.). 1993. pap. text ed. 18.00 (*1-878380-22-2*) GWU Schl E&HD.

Department Chairperson's Role in Enhancing College Teaching. Ed. by Ann F. Lucas. LC 85-644763. (New Directions for Teaching & Learning Ser.: No. TL 37). 1989. 16.95 (*1-55542-878-9*) Jossey-Bass.

***Department de la Meurthe Dictionnaire Historique et Statistique Vol. 1: Communes A-D.** fac. ed. E. Grosse. 364p. (FRE.). 1992. pap. 95.00 (*0-7859-8191-8*, 2877607607) Fr & Eur.

***Department de la Meurthe Dictionnaire Historique et Statistique Vol. 2: Communes E-N.** fac. ed. E. Grosse. 356p. (FRE.). 1992. pap. 95.00 (*0-7859-8192-6*, 2877607615) Fr & Eur.

***Department de la Meurthe Dictionnaire Historique et Statistique Vol. 3: Communes O-Z.** fac. ed. E. Grosse. 326p. (FRE.). 1992. pap. 325.00 (*0-7859-8193-4*, 2877607623) Fr & Eur.

***Department du Pas-de-Calais Dictionnaire des Communes Vol. 2.** fac. ed. M. Harbaville. (FRE.). 1992. pap. 145.00 (*0-7859-8194-2*, 2877608107); pap. 145.00 (*0-7859-8195-0*, 2877608115) Fr & Eur.

Department Head's Survival Guide: Ready-to-Use Techniques & Materials for Effective Leadership. Michael D. Koehler. LC 93-5829. 1993. 34.95 (*0-13-015165-3*) P-H.

Department Librarian. Jack Rudman. (Career Examination Ser.: C-194). 1994. pap. 27.95 (*0-8373-0194-7*) Nat Learn.

Department Library Aide. Jack Rudman. (Career Examination Ser.: C-206). 1994. pap. 23.95 (*0-8373-0206-4*) Nat Learn.

Department of Agriculture. R. Douglas Hurt. (Know Your Government Ser.). (Illus.). 112p. (J). (gr. 5 up). 1989. lib. bdg. 14.95 (*0-87754-833-1*) Chelsea Hse.

Department of Commerce. Robert J. Griffin, Jr. (Know Your Government Ser.). (Illus.). 104p. (J). (gr. 5 up). 1991. 14.95 (*0-87754-836-6*) Chelsea Hse.

Department of Dead Ends: Fourteen Detective Stories. Roy Vickers. 1978. pap. 5.95 (*0-486-23669-2*) Dover.

Department of Defense. Beth Heinsohn & Andrew Cohen. (Know Your Government Ser.). (Illus.). 120p. (J). (gr. 5 up). 1990. 14.95 (*0-87754-837-4*) Chelsea Hse.

Department of Defense Assistance to the Former Soviet Republics: Potential Applications of Existing Army Capabilities. Steedman Hinckley. LC 93-21665. 1993. write for info. (*0-8330-1412-9*, MR-245-A) Rand Corp.

Department of Defense Critical Technologies. 402p. (Orig.). (C). 1993. pap. text ed. 95.00 (*1-56806-519-1*) Diane Pub.

Department of Defense Index of Specifications & Standards, 2 vols., Set. 1993. ring bd. 175.00 (*0-685-28353-4*) Global Eng Doc.

Department of Defense Password Management Guideline. 37p. 1986. pap. 1.75 (*0-16-001479-4*, S/N 008-000-00443-9) USGPO.

Department of Defense Trusted Computer System Evaluation Criteria, 1985. 128p. 1986. pap. 6.00 (*0-16-001483-2*, S/N 008-000-00461-7) USGPO.

Department of Defense Voluntary Disclosure Program: A Description of the Process. 50p. 1988. pap. 7.50 (*0-89707-420-3*, 539-0077) Amer Bar Assn.

Department of Education. Stephen J. Sneigoski. (Know Your Government Ser.). (Illus.). 96p. (J). (gr. 5 up). 1988. lib. bdg. 14.95 (*0-87754-838-2*) Chelsea Hse.

Department of Education & Science. William Pile. 247p. (C). 1979. 90.00 (*0-685-06077-2*) St Mut.

Department of Energy. Catherine Tuggle & Gary Weir. (Know Your Government Ser.). (Illus.). 112p. (J). (gr. 5 up). 1990. 14.95 (*0-87754-839-0*) Chelsea Hse.

Department of Energy New Technology: Sharing New Frontiers. 167p. (Orig.). (C). 1993. pap. text ed. 35.00 (*1-56806-205-2*) Diane Pub.

***Department of Energy Occupational Safety & Health Technical Reference Manual.** U. S. Department of Energy, Office of Assistant Secretary for Environmental, Safety & Health Staff. 206p. (Orig.). 1994. pap. text ed. 69.00 (*0-86587-396-8*) Gov Insts.

Department of Health & Human Services. Merle Broberg. (Know Your Government Ser.). (Illus.). 128p. (J). (gr. 5 up). 1989. lib. bdg. 14.95 (*0-87754-840-4*) Chelsea Hse.

Department of Housing & Urban Development. Bob Bernotas. (Know Your Government Ser.). (Illus.). 104p. (J). (gr. 5 up). 1991. lib. bdg. 14.95 (*0-87754-841-2*) Chelsea Hse.

Department of Justice. Lynne Dunn. (Know Your Government Ser.). (Illus.). 112p. (J). (gr. 5 up). 1990. 14.95 (*0-87754-843-9*) Chelsea Hse.

Department of Justice Manual, 14 vols. 15242p. 1994. ring bd. 1,100.00 (*0-13-300401-5*) Aspen Law.

Department of Justice of the United States. Albert Langeluttig. (Brookings Institution Reprint Ser.). reprint ed. lib. bdg. 39.50 (*0-697-00161-X*) Irvington.

Department of Labor. Cheryl Cutrona. (Know Your Government Ser.). (Illus.). 96p. 1988. lib. bdg. 14.95 (*0-87754-844-7*) Chelsea Hse.

Department of State. Carl Bartz. (Know Your Government Ser.). (Illus.). 120p. (J). (gr. 5 up). 1989. lib. bdg. 14.95 (*0-87754-846-3*) Chelsea Hse.

Department of Surgical Services: Anesthesiology Policy & Procedure Guideline Manual. Judith Smith. 1992. 85.00 (*1-879575-19-1*) Acad Med Sys.

Department of Surgical Services Continuous Quality Improvement: Policy & Procedure Guideline Manual. Lea Johnson. 1992. 110.00 (*1-879575-24-8*) Acad Med Sys.

Department of Surgical Services Hazardous Material Safety Management: Policy & Procedure Guideline Manual. Judith Smith. 1992. 85.00 (*0-685-53683-1*) Acad Med Sys.

Department of Surgical Services Infection Control: Policy & Procedure Guideline Manual. Judith Smith. 1992. 105.00 (*1-879575-22-1*) Acad Med Sys.

Department of Surgical Services Safety Management: Policy & Procedure Guideline Manual. Judith Smith. 1992. 90.00 (*1-879575-21-3*) Acad Med Sys.

Department of Surgical Services Standards - Nursing Care Plans: Policy & Procedure Guideline Manual. Judith Smith. 1992. 85.00 (*1-879575-20-5*) Acad Med Sys.

Department of the Air Force. John Rhea. (Know Your Government Ser.). (Illus.). 104p. (J). (gr. 5 up). 1990. 14.95 (*0-87754-834-X*) Chelsea Hse.

Department of the Army. Arnold G. Fisch, Jr. (Know Your Government Ser.). (Illus.). 96p. (YA). (gr. 5 up). 1988. lib. bdg. 14.95 (*0-87754-835-8*) Chelsea Hse.

Department of the Army Ad Hoc Committee on the Army Need for the Study of Military History: Annex C, Military History Questionnaire-Evaluation of Results, Vol. 4. 1971. reprint ed. pap. text ed. 23.00 (*0-89126-003-X*) MA-AH Pub.

Department of the Army Ad Hoc Committee on the Army Need for the Study of Military History: Annexes A-B, D-H, Vol. 2. 244p. 1971. reprint ed. pap. text ed. 29.00 (*0-89126-001-3*) MA-AH Pub.

Department of the Army Ad Hoc Committee on the Army Need for the Study of Military History: Annexes I-N, Vol. 3. 171p. 1971. reprint ed. pap. text ed. 26.00 (*0-89126-002-1*) MA-AH Pub.

Department of the Army Ad Hoc Committee on the Army Need for the Study of Military History: Report & Recommendations, Vol. 1. 66p. 1971. reprint ed. pap. text ed. 18.00 (*0-89126-000-5*) MA-AH Pub.

Department of the Interior. Fred Clement. (Know Your Government Ser.). (Illus.). 112p. (J). (gr. 5 up). 1989. lib. bdg. 14.95 (*0-87754-842-0*) Chelsea Hse.

Department of the Navy. Theresa Kraus. (Know Your Government Ser.). (Illus.). 112p. (J). (gr. 5 up). 1990. 14.95 (*0-87754-845-5*) Chelsea Hse.

Department of the Treasury. Mark Walston. (Know Your Government Ser.). (Illus.). 128p. (J). (gr. 5 up). 1989. 14.95 (*0-87754-848-X*) Chelsea Hse.

Department of Transportation. Wallace C. Stephany. (Know Your Government Ser.). (Illus.). 96p. 1988. lib. bdg. 14.95 (*0-87754-847-1*) Chelsea Hse.

Department Senior Librarian. Jack Rudman. (Career Examination Ser.: C-1622). 1994. pap. 29.95 (*0-8373-1622-7*) Nat Learn.

***Department Store: A Social History.** William Lancaster. 240p. 1995. 59.95 (*0-7185-1374-6*, Pub. by Leicester Univ Pr); pap. 18.95 (*0-7185-1985-X*, Pub. by Leicester Univ Pr) St Martin.

Department Store: Its Origins Evolution & Economics. Hrant Pasdermadjian. LC 75-39265. (Getting & Spending: the Consumer's Dilemma Ser.). 1976. reprint ed. 20.95 (*0-405-08038-7*) Ayer.

***Department 56 Corporate Report.** 60p. (Orig.). 1995. pap. 295.00 (*0-7605-2103-4*) Rector Pr.

Departmental Guide to Implementation of Student Outcomes Assessment & Institutional Effectiveness. James O. Nichols. (Illus.). 72p. 1991. pap. 6.00 (*0-87586-096-6*) Agathon.

Departure. Melodie M. Davis. LC 90-32027. 200p. (Orig.). 1991. pap. 7.95 (*0-8361-3549-0*) Herald Pr.

Departure from Traditional Roles: Mid-Life Women Break the Daisy Chains. Rosemary A. Segalla. LC 82-20089. (Research in Clinical Psychology Ser.: No. 5). 163p. reprint ed. pap. 46.50 (*0-685-20880-X*, 2070214) Bks Demand.

Departures. Harry Turtledove. (Orig.). 1993. mass mkt. 4.99 (*0-345-38011-8*, Del Rey) Ballantine.

***Departures: A Reader for Developing Writers.** Randall Popken et al. LC 94-29358. 1994. pap. text ed. write for info. (*0-205-16249-5*) Allyn.

Departures: Selected Writings. Isabelle Eberhardt. Ed. by Karim Hamoy & Laura Rice. Tr. by Laura Rice. LC 94-2797. 256p. (Orig.). 1994. pap. 12.95 (*0-87286-288-7*) City Lights.

Departures & Other Stories. Jennifer C. Cornell. (Drue Heinz Literature Prize Ser.). 160p. (C). 1994. 22.50 (*0-8229-3855-3*) U of Pittsburgh Pr.

DePauw: A Pictorial History. Ed. by John J. Baughman. (Illus.). 632p. 1987. 30.00 (*0-936631-12-0*) DePauw Univ.

Depeche Mode. Dave Thomas. (Illus.). 48p. 1986. pap. 9.95 (*0-7119-0804-4*, OP43678) Omnibus NY.

Depeche Mode: Anthology. (Illus.). 208p. 1991. pap. 19.95 (*0-8256-1218-7*, AM73016) Music Sales.

Depeche Mode: Music for the Masses. (Illus.). 40p. 1989. pap. 11.95 (*0-8256-1205-5*, AM73982) Music Sales.

Depeche Mode: Some Great Reward. Dave Thompson. 1994. pap. 13.95 (*0-312-11262-9*) St Martin.

Depeche Mode: Strangers. Anton Corbijn. (Illus.). 120p. 1990. pap. 19.95 (*0-7119-2493-7*, OP46309) Omnibus NY.

Depeche Mode: The Singles 81-85. (Illus.). 48p. 1985. pap. 11.95 (*0-7119-0797-8*, AM61607) Music Sales.

Depeche Mode: Violator. (Illus.). 52p. 1990. pap. 12.95 (*0-8256-1283-7*, AM79880) Music Sales.

Depeche Mode: 101. (Illus.). 80p. 1989. pap. 14.95 (*0-8256-1219-5*, AM72968) Music Sales.

Depeche Mode Collection. (Illus.). 88p. 1991. pap. 15.95 (*0-685-65802-3*, AM73032) Music Sales.

Depend on Katie John. Mary Calhoun. LC 61-7328. (Trophy Bk.). 208p. (J). (gr. 3-7). 1972. pap. 3.95 (*0-06-440029-8*, Trophy) HarpC Child Bks.

Dependability: Basic Concepts & Terminology. Ed. by J. C. Laprie et al. (Dependable Computing & Fault-Tolerant Systems Ser.: Vol. 5). (Illus.). xii, 268p. 1992. 89.00 (*0-387-82296-8*) Spr-Verlag.

Dependability for Systems with a Partitioned State Space: Markov & Semi-Markov Theory & Computational Implementation. Attila Csenki. LC 94-25788. (Lecture Notes in Statistics: Vol. 90). 1994. 39.00 (*0-387-94333-1*) Spr-Verlag.

Dependability of Behavioral Measurements: Theory of Generalizability for Scores & Profiles. Lee J. Cronbach et al. LC 70-180269. (Illus.). 430p. reprint ed. pap. 122.60 (*0-8357-6705-1*, AU00386) Bks Demand.

Dependability of Critical Computer Systems: Guidelines Produced by the European Workshop on Industrial Computer Systems, No. 1. Ed. by F. J. Redmill. 296p. 1989. 75.75 (*1-85166-203-0*) Elsevier.

Dependability of Critical Computer Systems 2: Guidelines Produced by the European Workshop on Industrial Computer Systems Technical Committee, No. 7. Ed. by F. J. Redmill. 288p. 1990. 81.00 (*1-85166-381-9*) Elsevier.

Dependability of Critical Computer Systems 3: Techniques Directory: Guidelines Produced by the European Workshop on Industrial Computer Systems - Technical Committee 7. Ed. by P. G. Bishop. 250p. 1990. 68.50 (*1-85166-544-7*) Elsevier.

Dependability of Mechanical Systems. Matej Bily. (Studies in Mechanical Engineering: No. 8). 390p. 1990. 138.50 (*0-444-98815-7*) Elsevier.

***Dependable Computing--EDCC-1: Proceedings of the First European Dependable Computing Conference, Berlin, Germany, October 4-6, 1994.** Ed. by K. Echtle et al. (Lecture Notes in Computer Science: Vol. 852). xvii, 618p. 1994. 82.00 (*3-540-58426-9*) Spr-Verlag.

***Dependable Computing--EDCC-1: Proceedings of the First European Dependable Computing Conference, Berlin, Germany, October 4-6, 1994.** Ed. by Klaus Echtle et al. LC 94-35445. (Lecture Notes in Computer Science: Vol. 852). 1994. 82.00 (*0-387-58426-9*) Spr-Verlag.

Dependable Computing for Critical Applications 2. Ed. by J. F. Meyer et al. (Dependable Computing & Fault-Tolerant Systems Ser.: Vol. 6). (Illus.). xvi, 442p. 1992. 119.00 (*0-387-82330-1*) Spr-Verlag.

Dependable Computing for Critical Applications 3. Ed. by Carl E. Landwehr et al. LC 93-9046. (Dependable Computing & Fault-Tolerant Systems Ser.: Vol. 8). (Illus.). xii, 382p. 1993. 139.00 (*0-387-82481-2*) Spr-Verlag.

***Dependable Computing for Critical Applications 4.** Ed. by F. Christian et al. LC 95-3217. (Dependable Computing & Fault-Tolerant Systems Ser.: Vol. 9). 1995. write for info. (*3-211-82649-1*) Spr-Verlag.

Dependence Analysis for Supercomputing. Uptal Banerjee. (C). 1988. lib. bdg. 65.50 (*0-89838-289-0*) Kluwer Ac.

Dependence & Autonomy: Women's Employment & Family in Calcutta. Hilary Standing. 192p. 1990. pap. 16.95 (*0-415-04839-7*, A4840) Routledge.

Dependence & Deterrence. G. M. Dillon. 206p. 1983. text ed. 52.95 (*0-566-00588-3*) Ashgate Pub Co.

Dependence & Freedom: The Moral Thought of Horace Bushnell. David W. Haddorff. LC 94-1912. 202p. Date not set. lib. bdg. 42.50 (*0-8191-9484-0*) U Pr of Amer.

***Dependence & Independence.** Jagdish N. Bhagwati. Ed. by Gene M. Grossmen. 1985. 45.00 (*0-262-02230-3*) MIT Pr.

Dependence & Independence in the Third World: An Introduction to Contemporary Algeria. (YA). (gr. 10-12). 1977. 6.00 (*0-317-56403-X*) UM Ctr MENAS.

Dependence & Inequality: A Systems Approach to the Problems of Mexico & Other Developing Countries. Ed. by R. F. Geyer & J. Van der Zouwen. (Systems Science & World Order Library). (Illus.). 336p. 1982. 143.00 (*0-08-027952-X*, Pub. by Pergamon Repr UK) Franklin.

Dependence & Underdevelopment in Colombia. Jon V. Kofas. LC 86-1098. 125p. 1986. text ed. 17.00 (*0-87918-062-5*) ASU Lat Am St.

Dependence, Development, & State Repression. Ed. by George A. Lopez & Michael Stohl. LC 87-32258. (Contributions in Political Science Ser.: No. 209). 286p. 1989. text ed. 59.95 (*0-313-25298-X*, LDV/, Greenwood Pr) Greenwood.

Dependence Dilemma: Gasoline Consumption & America's Security. Ed. by Daniel Yergin. (Harvard Studies in International Affairs: No. 43). 176p. (Orig.). 1984. reprint ed. pap. text ed. 18.00 (*0-8191-4056-2*) U Pr of Amer.

Dependence in Context in Renaissance Florence. Richard C. Trexler. LC 93-25409. 480p. 1994. 30.00 (*0-86698-164-0*, MR111) MRTS.

Dependence in Probability & Statistics. Ernst Eberlein & Murad Taqqu. (Progress in Probability & Statistics Ser.: No. 11). 1986. 63.00 (*0-8176-3323-5*) Birkhauser.

Dependence Phenomenon. Ed. by M. M. Glatt & J. Marks. 1983. lib. bdg. 36.00 (*0-85200-487-7*) Kluwer Ac.

Dependence with Complete Connections & Its Applications. Marius Iosifescu & Serban Grigorescu. (Cambridge Tracts in Mathematics Ser.: No. 96). 350p. (C). 1990. 79.95 (*0-521-33331-8*) Cambridge U Pr.

Dependency: Personal & Social Relations. Beryl Day. 125p. 1992. 55.95 (*1-85628-256-2*, Pub. by Avebury Pub UK) Ashgate Pub Co.

***Dependency & Development: An Introduction to the Third World.** Ted C. Lewellen. LC 94-39193. 288p. 1995. text ed. 65.00 (*0-89789-399-9*, Bergin & Garvey); pap. text ed. 22.95 (*0-89789-400-6*, Bergin & Garvey) Greenwood.

Dependency & Development in Latin America. Fernando E. Cardoso & Enzo Faletto. Tr. by Marjory M. Urquidi. LC 75-46033. 1979. pap. 13.00 (*0-520-03527-5*) U CA Pr.

Dependency & Interdependency in Old Age. Ed. by Chris Phillipson et al. 300p. 1986. 45.00 (*0-7099-3987-6*, Pub. by Croom Helm UK) Routledge Chapman & Hall.

Dependency & Japanese Socialization: Psychoanalytic & Anthropological Investigations into "Amae" Frank A. Johnson. 452p. (C). 1992. text ed. 55.00 (*0-8147-4192-4*); pap. text ed. 22.50 (*0-8147-4222-X*) NYU Pr.

Dependency & Non-Linear Phonology. Ed. by Jacques Durand. LC 85-24265. 352p. 1986. 59.95 (*0-7099-0894-6*, Pub. by Croom Helm UK) Routledge Chapman & Hall.

Dependency & Poverty: Old Problems in a New World. June Axinn & Mark J. Stern. 192p. 1988. text ed. 35.00 (*0-669-14630-7*); pap. 19.95 (*0-669-14631-5*) Free Pr.

Dependency & the Foreign Policy of a Small Power: The Liberian Case. George K. Kieh, Jr. LC 92-34447. 224p. 1992. 89.95 (*0-7734-9813-3*, Mellen Univ Pr) E Mellen.

Dependency Approaches to International Political Economy: A Cross-National Study. Vincent A. Mahler. LC 79-26200. 1980. text ed. 40.50 (*0-231-04836-X*) Col U Pr.

Dependency Movement: Scholarship & Politics in Development Studies. Robert A. Packenham. 362p. (C). 1992. 47.50 (*0-674-19810-7*) HUP.

Dependency, Obligations, & Entitlements. Judah Matras. 256p. (C). 1989. Casebound. text ed. write for info. (*0-13-199316-X*) P-H.

Dependency or Interdependency in Old Age. Joep M. Munnichs et al. 1976. lib. bdg. 51.50 (*90-247-1895-3*) Kluwer Ac.

Dependency Proceedings in California Juvenile Courts. Ted Rubin & Richard Gable. 118p. 1991. 7.00 (*0-685-55336-1*, WRO133) Natl Ctr St Courts.

Dependency Road: Communications, Capitalism, Consciousness & Canada. Dallas W. Smythe. 352p. (C). 1981. text ed. 65.00 (*0-89391-067-8*); pap. 32.50 (*0-89391-088-0*) Ablex Pub.

Dependency Syntax: Theory & Practice. Igor A. Mel'cuk. LC 86-14542. (Suny Series in Linguistics). 428p. 1987. 89.50 (*0-88706-450-7*); pap. 34.95 (*0-88706-451-5*) State U NY Pr.

Dependency Tendency: Returning to Each Other in Modern America. Jay P. Gurian & Julia M. Gurian. LC 82-17569. 176p. (C). 1983. pap. text ed. 19.00 (*0-8191-2782-5*) U Pr of Amer.

Dependency Theory & the Return of High Politics. Ed. by Mary A. Tetreault & Charles F. Abel. LC 85-17745. (Contributions in Political Science Ser.: No. 140). (Illus.). 283p. 1986. text ed. 49.95 (*0-313-24860-5*, TDE/, Greenwood Pr) Greenwood.

Dependency to Enterprise. Ed. by John Hutton et al. (Illus.). 224p. 1991. 74.50 (*0-415-04861-3*, A6141) Routledge.

Dependent Accumulation & Underdevelopment. Andre G. Frank. LC 78-13913. 226p. 1979. 15.00 (*0-85345-468-X*) Monthly Rev.

Dependent Accumulation & Underdevelopment. Andre G. Frank. LC 78-13913. 250p. reprint ed. pap. 71.30 (*0-7837-6988-1*, 2046800) Bks Demand.

Dependent Ally: A Study of Australian Foreign Policy. 2nd ed. Coral Bell. 192p. 1994. pap. 24.95 (*1-86373-400-7*, Pub. by Allen Unwin AT) Paul & Co Pubs.

Dependent Ally: Betrayal of Native German Foreign Policy, 1949-1990. Marcus Stadelman. LC 93-47064. 250p. 1994. pap. 44.95 (*1-883255-44-9*) Intl Scholars.

Dependent Ally: Betrayal of Native German Foreign Policy, 1949-1990. Marcus Stadelman. 250p. 1994. 64.95 (*1-883255-45-7*) Intl Scholars.

Dependent & Neglected Children: Report of the Committee on Socially Handicapped; Dependency & Neglect. White House Conference on Child Health & Protection Staff. LC 74-1714. (Children & Youth Ser.: Vol. 15). 470p. 1974. reprint ed. 39.95 (*0-405-05989-2*) Ayer.

Dependent Arising & Emptiness: A Tibetan Buddhist Interpretation of Madhyamika Philosophy Emphasizing the Compatability of Emptiness & Convential Phenomena. Elizabeth Napper. LC 89-40013. (Advanced Book - Blue Ser.). (Illus.). 848p. (Orig.). 1989. 37.50 (*0-86171-057-6*) Wisdom MA.

Dependent Care & the Employee Benefits Package: Human Resource Strategies for the 1990s. Louellen Crawford. LC 90-32724. 184p. 1990. text ed. 49.95 (*0-89930-465-6*, CNC, Quorum Bks) Greenwood.

Dependent Child: A Story of Changing Aims & Methods in the Care of Dependent Children. Henry W. Thurston. LC 74-1712. (Children & Youth Ser.: Vol. 17). 358p. 1974. reprint ed. 31.95 (*0-405-05986-8*) Ayer.

***Dependent City Revisited.** Paul Kantor. (C). 1995. pap. text ed. 19.95 (*0-8133-1904-8*) Westview.

***Dependent City Revisited: The Political Economy of Urban Development & Social Policy.** Paul Kantor. LC 94-24017. (C). 1995. text ed. 65.00 (*0-8133-1903-X*) Westview.

Dependent Development: The Alliance of Multinational, State, & Local Capital in Brazil. Peter Evans. LC 78-70291. 1979. pap. 16.95 (*0-691-02185-6*) Princeton U Pr.

Dependent Development in United Kingdom Regions with Particular Reference to Wales. Cooke. (Progress in Planning Ser.: Vol. 15, Part 1). 90p. 1980. pap. 16.25 (*0-08-026809-9*, Pergamon Pr) Elsevier.

Dependent Economy: Lesotho & the Southern African Customs Union. 432p. (C). 1991. pap. text ed. 55.50 (*0-8133-8185-1*) Westview.

Dependent Elderly: Autonomy, Justice & Quality of Care. Ed. by Luke Gormally. 160p. (C). 1992. 44.95 (*0-521-41531-4*) Cambridge U Pr.

***Dependent Empire: Colonies, Protectorates & Mandates Select Documents, Vol. 7.** Frederick Madden & John Darwin. LC 84-21213. (Documents in Imperial History Ser.: Vol. 7). 912p. 1994. text ed. 125.00 (*0-313-27318-9*, Greenwood Pr) Greenwood.

Dependent Empire & Ireland, 1840-1900: Advance & Retreat in Representative Self-Government - Select Documents on the Constitutional History of the British Empire & Commonwealth, Vol. V. Ed. by Frederick Madden & David Fieldhouse. (Documents in Imperial History Ser.: No. 5). 864p. 1991. 95.00 (*0-685-54256-4*, MNT/, Greenwood Pr) Greenwood.

Dependent People: Rhode Island in the Revolutionary Era. rev. ed. Elaine F. Crane. LC 92-6806. xii, 196p. 1992. pap. 19.95 (*0-8232-1112-6*) Fordham.

Dependent Personality. Robert F. Bornstein. LC 92-49466. 241p. 1993. lib. bdg. 28.95 (*0-89862-991-8*) Guilford Pr.

Dependent Plant Communities: Proceedings of the 28th International Symposium of the International Association of Veetation Science (IAS), Held at Wageningen, the Netherlands, 16-19 April 1984. Ed. by J. J. Barkman & K. Sykora. (Illus.). x, 174p. 1988. 65.00 (*90-5103-015-0*, Pub. by SPB Acad Pub NE) Koeltz Sci Bks.

Dependent Variables. Melissa Abramovitz. 110p. (Orig.). 1991. pap. 9.99 (*0-945298-05-6*) Curtis Pubns.

Depersonalization of God: A Consideration of Soteriological Difficulties in High Calvinism. Ben M. Carter. 72p. (C). 1989. lib. bdg. 33.00 (*0-8191-7512-9*) U Pr of Amer.

Depeupleur. Samuel Beckett. 58p. (FRE.). 1970. pap. 12.95 (*0-7859-0631-2*, F86020) Fr & Eur.

Depeupleur see Lost Ones

Depicted Deities: Painters' Model Books in Nepal. M. L. Blom. (Groningen Oriental Studies: Vol. IV). vii, 92p. (Orig.). 1989. pap. 46.00 (*90-6980-029-2*, Pub. by Egbert Forsten NE) Benjamins North Am.

Depiction & Interpretation: The Influence of the Holocaust on the Visual Arts. Ziva Amishai-Maisels. (Holocaust Ser.). (Illus.). 1000p. 1993. 190.00 (*0-08-040656-4*, Pergamon Pr) Elsevier.

Depictive Image: Metaphor & Literary Experience. Phillip Stambovsky. LC 87-28802. 168p. 1988. lib. bdg. 22,50 (*0-87023-614-8*) U of Mass Pr.

Deplacement Degagements: Spared, Displaced. Henri Michaux. Tr. by David Constantine & Helen Constantine. (Contemporary French Poets Ser.: No. 3). 192p. (ENG & FRE.). 1993. pap. 21.00 (*1-85224-135-7*, Pub. by Bloodaxe Bks UK) Dufour.

Depleted Self: Sin in a Narcissistic Age. Donald Capps. LC 92-7931. 192p. (Orig.). 1992. pap. 14.00 (*0-8006-2587-0*, 1-2587, Fortress Pr) Augsburg Fortress.

Depletion Myth: A History of Railroad Use of Timber. Sherry H. Olson. LC 70-148940. 246p. 1971. 25.00 (*0-674-19820-4*) HUP.

Deplorable Scarcity: The Failure of Industrialization in the Slave Economy. Fred Bateman & Thomas Weiss. LC 80-13238. 251p. reprint ed. pap. 71.60 (*0-7837-0305-8*, 2040627) Bks Demand.

***Deployed, Not Disconnected.** Ed. by Don Martin, Jr. & Karen Martin. 128p. 1991. pap. 5.50 (*0-913991-01-5*) Off Christian Fellowship.

Deployment: Hiding Behind Power Struggles As a Character Defense. Rena Moses-Hrushovski. LC 94-98. 344p. 1994. 40.00 (*1-56821-042-6*) Aronson.

Depolarization & Related Ratios of Light Scattering by Spheroids. Wilfried Heller et al. LC 74-13816. 121p. reprint ed. pap. 34.50 (*0-7837-3583-9*, 2043443) Bks Demand.

Depopulation Arranged, Convicted & Condemned by the Lawes of God & Man. Robert Powell. LC 76-57407. (English Experience Ser.: No. 823). 1977. reprint ed. lib. bdg. 16.00 (*90-221-0823-6*) Walter J Johnson.

***Deportation & Exile of Poles in the Soviet Union, 1939-48: Siberian Odysseys.** Keith Sword. LC 94-31934. 1995. write for info. (*0-312-12397-3*) St Martin.

Deportation Cases of Nineteen-Nineteen to Nineteen-Twenty. Constantine M. Panunzio. LC 77-109547. (Civil Liberties in American History Ser.). 1970. reprint ed. lib. bdg. 18.50 (*0-306-71901-0*) Da Capo.

Deportation of Aliens from the United States to Europe. Jane P. Clark. LC 69-18766. (American Immigration Collection Ser., No. 1). 1969. reprint ed. 23.95 (*0-405-00514-8*) Ayer.

Deportations Delirium of Nineteen-Twenty. Louis F. Post. LC 73-114343. (Civil Liberties in American History Ser.). 1970. reprint ed. lib. bdg. 42.50 (*0-306-71882-0*) Da Capo.

***Deportes.** Chris Jueggi. (I Know about Ser.). (Illus.). (J). 1995. pap. 2.50 (*0-528-83741-9*) Rand McNally.

Deportes de Invierno. Charles M. Schulz. (Peanuts Ser.). 64p. (SPA.). (J). 1971. 4.95 (*0-8288-4508-5*) Fr & Eur.

Deportes en Puerto Rico. Huyre. 1968. 19.95 (*0-87751-013-X*) E Torres & Sons.

Deposit Account Operations. 1993. pap. 34.95 (*0-912857-57-9*) Inst Finan Educ.

Deposit Accounts & Services. 2nd ed. 369p. 1990. pap. 34.95 (*0-912857-53-6*) Inst Finan Educ.

Deposit Accounts Regulation Manual, 1 vol. Kenneth F. Hall. (Commercial Law Ser.). 1993. 135.00 (*0-685-68836-4*) Clark Boardman Callaghan.

Deposit Insurance: Theory, Policy & Evidence. Rita Carisano. (Luiss Ser.). 212p. 1992. 59.95 (*1-85521-174-2*, Pub. by Dartmth Pub UK) Ashgate Pub Co.

Deposit Operations. David H. Friedman. Ed. by Mary L. Smith. 352p. (C). 1992. text ed. write for info. (*0-89982-333-5*, 050360) Am Bankers.

Deposit-Refund Systems: Theory & Applications to Environmental, Conservation, & Consumer Policy. Peter Bohm. LC 81-47617. 175p. 1981. 22.00 (*0-8018-2706-X*) Resources Future.

Deposit Velocity & Its Significance. George Garvy. LC 78-14435. (Illus.). 88p. 1978. reprint ed. text ed. 59.75 (*0-313-21022-5*, GADV, Greenwood Pr) Greenwood.

Deposition. Pete Green. 88p. 1982. pap. 4.00 (*0-89823-044-6*) New Rivers Pr.

Deposition & Corrosion in Gas Turbines. Ed. by A. B. Hart & A. J. Cutler. (Illus.). 425p. 1973. 102.75 (*0-85334-575-9*, Pub. by Elsevier Applied Sci UK) Elsevier.

Deposition & Growth: Limits for Microelectronics: Proceedings of a Topical Conference on at Anaheim, California in November 1987. Ed. by Gary Rubloff & Gerald Lucovsky. (American Vacuum Society Ser.: No. 4). (Illus.). 402p. 1988. 70.00 (*0-88318-367-6*) Am Inst Physics.

Deposition Both Wet & Dry. Ed. by Bruce B. Hicks & John I. Teasley. (Acid Precipitation Ser.: Vol.4). 224p. 1984. text ed. 54.95 (*0-250-40569-5*) Buttrwrth-Heinemann.

Deposition, Diagenesis, & Weathering of Organic Matter-Rich Sediments. Ralf Littke. LC 93-17490. (Lecture Notes in Earth Sciences Ser.: Vol. 47). (Illus.). ix, 216p. 1993. pap. 61.00 (*0-387-56661-9*) Spr-Verlag.

Deposition Handbook. 2nd ed. Dennis R. Suplee & Diana S. Donaldson. (Trial Practice Library: No. 1676). 320p. 1992. text ed. 118.00 (*0-471-57519-4*) Wiley.

***Deposition Handbook: A Guide to Help You Give a Winning Deposition.** rev. ed. Virginia A. Lathan. LC 93-71190. 100p. 1995. pap. 14.95 (*0-9636195-2-7*) Curry-Co Pubns.

Deposition Manual for Paralegals. 2nd ed. Christine B. Greene. LC 92-34920. (Paralegal Litigation Library). 296p. 1993. text ed. 98.00 (*0-471-58127-5*) Wiley.

Deposition of Organic Facies. Ed. by A. Y. Huc. (Studies in Geology: No. 30). (Illus.). 234p. (Orig.). 1990. pap. 60.00 (*0-89181-038-2*) AAPG.

Deposition Process. Calet. 1992. text ed. write for info. (*0-442-01257-8*) Van Nos Reinhold.

Deposition Strategy, Law, & Forms, 10 vols. Alexander Sann & Steven Bellman. 1981. Updates. ring bd. write for info. (*0-8205-1258-3*) Bender.

Deposition Tactics & Considerations. 2nd ed. Robert E. Oliphant. 186p. 1988. 16.95 (*1-55681-180-2*, FBA0180) Natl Inst Trial Ad.

***Depositional & Diagenetic Facies Patterns & Reservoir Development in Silurian & Devonian Rocks of the Permian Basin.** S. C. Ruppel & M. H. Holtz. (Illus.). 89p. 1994. 6.00 (*0-614-01865-X*) Bur Econ Geology.

Depositional & Diagenetic History of the Sligo & Hosston Formations (Lower Cretaceous) in South Texas. D. G. Bebout et al. (Report of Investigations Ser.: RI 109). (Illus.). 69p. 1981. 4.00 (*0-686-36993-9*) Bur Econ Geology.

Depositional & Ground-Water Flow Systems in the Exploration for Uranium: Syllabus for Research Colloquium Held in Austin, September 1978. W. E. Galloway et al. (Illus.). 267p. 1979. 6.00 (*0-318-03374-7*) Bur Econ Geology.

Depositional & Ground-Water Flow Systems of the Carrizo-Upper Wilcox, South Texas. H. S. Hamlin. (Illus.). 61p. 1988. 3.50 (*0-317-03111-2*, RI 175) Bur Econ Geology.

Depositional & Volcanic Environments of the Middle Tertiary Rocks in the Santa Monica Mountains, Southern California. P. W. Weigand & A. E. Fritsche. 148p. (Orig.). 1993. pap. 15.00 (*1-878861-65-4*) Pac Section SEPM.

Depositional Environments & Paleoecology: Foraminiferal Paleoecology. Society of Economic Paleontologists & Mineralogists Staff. LC 78-101430. (Society of Economic Paleontologists & Mineralogists, Special Publication Ser.: No. 14). (Illus.). 166p. reprint ed. pap. 47.40 (*0-317-58120-1*, 2029673) Bks Demand.

Depositional Environments as Interpreted from Primary Sedimentary Structures & Stratification Sequences. John C. Harms et al. LC 76-350871. (Society of Economic Paleontologists & Mineralogists, Special Publication Ser.: No. 2). 165p. reprint ed. pap. 47.10 (*0-317-27142-3*, 2024748) Bks Demand.

Depositional Environments in Carbonate Rocks: A Symposium. American Association of Petroleum Geologists, Carbonate Rock Subcommittee. Ed. by Gerald M. Friedman. (Society of Economic Paleontologists & Mineralogists, Special Publication Ser.: Special Publication No. 4). 217p. reprint ed. pap. 61.90 (*0-685-15795-4*, 2026655) Bks Demand.

***Depositional Environments of Unstable Shelf-Margin Deltas of the Oligocene Vicksburg Formation, McAllen Ranch Field, South Texas.** R. P. Langford & J. M. Combes. (Illus.). 60p. 1994. 5.00 (*0-614-01868-4*) Bur Econ Geology.

Depositional Framework, Hydrostratigraphy, & Uranium Mineralization of the Oakville Sandstone (Miocene), Texas Coastal Plain. W. E. Galloway et al. (Report of Investigations Ser.: RI 113). (Illus.). 51p. 1982. 2.50 (*0-318-03245-7*) Bur Econ Geology.

Depositional Framework of the Lower Dockum Group (Triassic), Texas Panhandle. J. H. McGowen et al. (Report of Investigations Ser.: RI 97). (Illus.). 60p. 1979. 2.00 (*0-318-03233-3*) Bur Econ Geology.

Depositional Modeling of Detrital Rocks: With Emphasis on Cored Sequences of Petroleum Reservoirs. Robert J. Weimer et al. LC 89-126499. (SEPM Core Workshop Ser.: No. 8). (Illus.). 254p. reprint ed. pap. 72.40 (*0-7837-3879-X*, 2043727) Bks Demand.

Depositional Sedimentary Environments-with Reference to Terrigenous Classics. H. E. Reineck & I. B. Singh. (Illus.). 439p. 1992. 80.00 (*0-387-10189-6*) Spr-Verlag.

Depositional Setting, Structural Style, & Sandstone Distribution in Three Geopressured Geothermal Areas, Texas Gulf Coast. C. D. Winker et al. (Report of Investigations Ser.: RI 134). (Illus.). 60p. 1983. 2.50 (*0-318-03292-9*) Bur Econ Geology.

***Depositional, Structural & Sequence Framework of the Gas-Bearing Cleveland Formation (Upper Pennsylvanian), Western Anadarko Basin, Texas Panhandle.** T. F. Hentz. (Illus.). 73p. 1994. 6.00 (*0-614-01862-5*) Bur Econ Geology.

Depositional Systems. 2nd ed. Richard A. Davis, Jr. 528p. 1992. text ed. 72.00 (*0-13-202912-X*) P-H.

Depositional Systems & Hydrocarbon Resource Potential of the Pennsylvanian System, Palo Duro & Dalhart Basins, Texas Panhandle. S. P. Dutton. (Geological Circular Ser.: GC 80-8). (Illus.). 49p. 1980. 1.50 (*0-318-13665-1*) Bur Econ Geology.

Depositional Systems & Shelf-Slope Relationships in Upper Pennsylvanian Rocks, North-Central Texas. W. E. Galloway & L. F. Brown, Jr. (Report of Investigations Ser.: RI 75). (Illus.). 62p. 1981. reprint ed. 3.00 (*0-318-03182-5*) Bur Econ Geology.

Depositional Systems in Active Margin Basins. Ed. by D. S. Gorsline. (Illus.). 117p. (Orig.). 1987. pap. 13.00 (*1-878861-15-8*) Pac Section SEPM.

Depositional Systems in the Canyon Group (Pennsylvanian System), North-Central Texas. A. W. Erxleben. (Report of Investigations Ser.: RI 82). (Illus.). 76p. 1980. reprint ed. 4.00 (*0-318-03216-3*) Bur Econ Geology.

Depositional Systems in the Nacatoch Formation (Upper Cretaceous), Northeast Texas & Southwest Arkansas. M. K. McGowen & C. M. Lopez. (Report of Investigations Ser.: RI 137). (Illus.). 59p. 1983. 2.00 (*0-318-03297-X*) Bur Econ Geology.

Depositional Systems in the Paluxy Formation (Lower Cretaceous), Northeast Texas--Oil, Gas, & Ground-Water Resources. C. A. Caughey. (Geological Circular Ser.: GC 77-8). (Illus.). 59p. 1985. reprint ed. 2.50 (*0-686-29327-4*) Bur Econ Geology.

Depositional Systems, San Angelo Formation (Permian), North Texas--Facies Control of Red-Bed Copper Mineralization. G. E. Smith. (Report of Investigations Ser.: RI 80). (Illus.). 74p. 1984. reprint ed. 3.00 (*0-318-03206-6*) Bur Econ Geology.

Depositions. James L. Branton & Jim D. Lovett. (Trial Lawyer's Ser.: Vols. 1 & 1A). (Illus.). 1982. Vol. 1, 282 pp., Vol. 1A, 280 pp. ring bd. 185.00 (*1-878337-05-X*) Knowles Law.

Depositions: Procedure, Strategy & Technique. Paul M. Lisnek & Michael J. Kaufman. 255p. 1990. pap. write for info. (*0-314-65444-5*) West Pub.

***Depositions: Procedure, Strategy & Technique.** 2nd ed. Paul Lisnek & Michael Kaufman. 275p. 1994. text ed. write for info. (*0-314-04475-2*) West Pub.

***Depositions: Procedures, Strategy & Technique: Professional Education Edition.** Paul M. Lisnek & Michael J. Kaufman. 230p. (C). 1995. pap. text ed. write for info. (*0-314-06262-9*) West Pub.

***Depository: A Dream Book.** Andrzej Klimowski. (Illus.). 260p. (Orig.). 1995. pap. 12.95 (*0-571-17286-5*) Faber & Faber.

Depository Firm & Industry: Theory, History & Regulation. Lewis Spellman. 1982. text ed. 65.00 (*0-12-656580-5*) Acad Pr.

Depository Institutions: Flexible Accounting Rules Lead to Inflated Financial Reports. 74p. (Orig.). (C). 1993. pap. text ed. 30.00 (*1-56806-959-6*) Diane Pub.

Depository Library Use of Technology: A Practitioner's Perspective. Ed. by Jan Swanbeck & Peter Hernon. LC 92-40351. 320p. 1993. text ed. 54.50 (*0-89391-908-X*); pap. text ed. 24.50 (*0-89391-999-3*) Ablex Pub.

Deposits in Modern Engines. 1987. 19.00 (*0-89883-996-3*, SP725) Soc Auto Engineers.

Deposits of South America. Benjamin S. Miller & Joseph T. Singewald. Ed. by Mira Wilkins. LC 76-29758. (European Business Ser.). (Illus.). 1977. reprint ed. lib. bdg. 51.95 (*0-405-09773-5*) Ayer.

***Depots & Terminals of Boston: An Illustrated History of Boston's Railroad Depots.** Richard C. Barrett. (Illus.). Date not set. write for info. (*1-884650-03-1*) Railroad Res.

Depraved: The Shocking True Story of America's First Serial Killer. Harold Schechter. Ed. by Linda Marrow. LC 93-45648. 392p. (Orig.). 1994. 22.00 (*0-671-73216-1*) PB.

Depraved Angels. (Orig.). 1991. pap. 4.95 (*1-878320-92-0*) Masquerade.

Depraved Indifference. Robert K. Tanenbaum. 400p. 1990. reprint ed. pap. 5.99 (*0-451-16842-9*, Sig) NAL-Dutton.

Depreciation. Alan P. Murray. LC 74-172243. (Tax Technique Handbook Ser.). (Illus.). 138p. (Orig.). 1971. pap. 5.00 (*0-915506-12-2*) Harvard Law Intl Tax.

An Asterisk (*) at the beginning of an entry indicates that the title is appearing in BIP for the first time.

Depreciation: Accounting, Taxes, & Business Decisions. Joseph D. Coughlan & William K. Strand. LC 69-12971. (Illus.). 356p. reprint ed. pap. 101.50 (*0-317-09505-6*, 2012410) Bks Demand.

Depreciation & Capital Planning. 2nd ed. 1987. ring bd. 135.00 (*0-685-69570-0*, DCP) Warren Gorham & Lamont.

Depreciation & Wasting Assets & Their Treatment in Assessing Annual Profit & Loss. Percy D. Leake. LC 75-18474. (History of Accounting Ser.). (Illus.). 1979. 20.95 (*0-405-07556-1*) Ayer.

Depreciation Guide, 1992: Featuring MACRS. 480p. 1992. pap. 15.00 (*0-685-66969-6*, 4723) Commerce.

Depreciation Handbook. Bruce K. Benish & M. Kevin Bryant. (Illus.). 1983. Updates available. ring bd. write for info. (*0-8205-1713-5*) Bender.

Depreciation of Factories, Mines & Industrial Undertakings & Their Valuation. 2nd ed. Ewing Matheson. LC 75-18476. (History of Accounting Ser.). (Illus.). 1979. reprint ed. 18.95 (*0-405-07558-8*) Ayer.

Depreciation Policies & Resultant Problems. William T. Hogan. LC 66-14185. (Studies in Industrial Economics: No. 8). 140p. reprint ed. pap. 39.90 (*0-7837-0451-8*, 2040774) Bks Demand.

Depreciation Practices for Small Gas Distribution Companies. 64p. 1984. 7.00 (*0-317-01662-8*) NARUC.

Depreciation Practices for Small Telephone Utilities. 61p. 1974. 7.50 (*0-317-01648-2*) NARUC.

Depreciation, Reserves, & Reserve Funds. Lawrence R. Dicksee. LC 75-18467. (History of Accounting Ser.). (Illus.). 1979. reprint ed. 17.95 (*0-405-07550-2*) Ayer.

Depreciation Systems. Frank K. Wolf & W. Chester Fitch. LC 93-47634. 352p. (C). 1994. 54.95 (*0-8138-2457-5*) Iowa St U Pr.

Deprenyl: The Anti-Aging Drug. Alastair Dow. LC 92-74929. 280p. (Orig.). 1993. pap. 14.95 (*0-87319-036-X*) Hallberg Pub Corp.

Deprenyl: The Inside Story. Alastair Dow. 220p. (C). reprint ed. 19.95 (*0-9629285-0-X*) Easton CA.

Depresion Espiritual. Martyn Lloyd-Jones. 319p. (SPA.). 1994. pap. 6.95 (*0-939125-61-7*) Evangelical Lit.

Depresion y Su Tratamiento (Depression & Its Treatment) Pablo Polischuk. 154p. (Orig.). (SPA.). 1992. pap. 5.50 (*84-7645-566-6*, 223633, Pub. by Edit Clie SP) TSELF.

***Depressed Child & Adolescent: Developmental & Clinical Perspectives.** Ed. by Ian M. Goodyer. (Cambridge Monographs on Child & Adolescent Psychiatry: 1). (Illus.). 300p. (C). 1995. 79.95 (*0-521-43326-6*) Cambridge U Pr.

Depressed Christian. Gerald F. Mundfrom. 110p. (Orig.). 1983. 2.50 (*0-318-19335-3*) Mercy & Truth.

Depressed Classes in India. Rajendra S. Vatsa. 186p. 1977. 14.95 (*0-318-36812-9*) Asia Bk Corp.

Depressed? Here's a Way Out. Hugh Smith. 206p. (Orig.). 1992. 12.00 (*0-00-627565-6*, Pub. by HarpC UK) HarpC.

Depressed Woman: A Study of Social Relationships. Myrna M. Weissman. LC 73-90944. 309p. reprint ed. pap. 88.10 (*0-685-23832-6*, 2056613) Bks Demand.

***Depression.** Laurie Beckelman. (Hotline Ser.). (Illus.). (YA). (gr. 6 up). 1995. pap. 5.95 (*0-382-24956-9*, Crstwood Hse) Silver Burdett Pr.

Depression. Guy BonGiovanni. 17p. (Orig.). (C). 1983. pap. 2.00 (*0-912981-04-0*) Hse BonGiovanni.

Depression. Cathie Cush. LC 93-14252. (Teen Hotline Ser.). (Illus.). (J). (gr. 6-9). 1993. lib. bdg. 22.80 (*0-8114-3529-6*) Raintree Steck-V.

Depression. Dianne Hales. LC 88-34176. (Encyclopedia of Health Ser.). (Illus.). 104p. (YA). (gr. 6-12). 1989. 18.95 (*0-7910-0046-X*) Chelsea Hse.

***Depression.** Heitler. 1995. 10.95 (*1-884998-09-7*) Listen-to-Lrn.

Depression. B. Mahendra. 1987. lib. bdg. 117.00 (*0-85200-983-6*) Kluwer Ac.

***Depression.** Stephen Merson. (Ward Lock Family Health Guides Ser.). (Illus.). 80p. 1995. pap. 9.95 (*0-7063-7395-2*, Pub. by Ward Lock UK) Sterling.

Depression. Etha E. Powell. LC 90-70220. 195p. 1990. pap. 8.95 (*1-55523-330-9*) Winston-Derek.

Depression. Steven Spotts. 66p. 1991. pap. 2.99 (*0-945276-24-9*) Rapha Pub.

***Depression: A Cognitive Therapy Approach.** Arthur Freeman. (Assessment & Treatment of Psychological Disorders Video Ser.). 1994. vhs write for info. (*1-56784-400-6*) Newbridge Comms.

***Depression: A Cognitive Therapy Approach - a Viewer's Manual.** Arthur Freeman. (Assessment & Treatment of Psychological Disorders, a Video Ser.). 1994. vhs write for info. (*1-56784-401-4*) Newbridge Comms.

***Depression: A Multimedia Sourcebook.** Ed. by John J. Miletich. LC 95-4194. (Bibliographies & Indexes in Medical Studies: Vol. 11). 240p. 1995. text ed. 69.50 (*0-313-29374-0*, Greenwood Pr) Greenwood.

Depression: A Psychobiological Synthesis. Paul Willner. 597p. (Orig.). 1988. pap. text ed. 89.95 (*0-471-61151-4*) Wiley.

Depression: An Integrative Approach. Eugene Paykel. 255p. 1989. text ed. 95.00 (*0-433-00090-2*) Buttrwrth-Heinemann.

Depression: Basic Mechanisms, Diagnosis, & Treatment. Ed. by A. John Rush & Kenneth Altshuler. LC 84-19318. 242p. 1986. lib. bdg. 35.00 (*0-89862-646-3*) Guilford Pr.

Depression: Causes & Treatment. Aaron T. Beck. LC 67-23826. 374p. (C). 1972. reprint ed. pap. text ed. 19.95x (*0-8122-1032-8*) U of Pa Pr.

Depression: Comparative Studies of Normal, Neurotic & Psychotic Conditions. Edith Jacobson. LC 74-162056. 276p. 1971. text ed. 50.00 (*0-8236-1195-7*) Intl Univs Pr.

Depression: Concepts, Controversies & Some New Facts. 2nd ed. Eugene E. Levitt et al. 264p. 1983. text ed. 39.95 (*0-89859-278-X*) L Erlbaum Assocs.

Depression: Finding Hope & Meaning in Life's Darkest Shadow. Don Baker & Emery Nester. LC 82-24609. (Critical Concern Ser.). 1983. pap. 9.99 (*0-88070-186-2*, Multnomah Bks) Questar Pubs.

Depression: Medical Subject Analysis & Research Directory with Bibliography. American Health Research Institute Staff. Ed. by John C. Bartone et al. LC 81-71808. 133p. 1982. 37.50 (*0-941864-30-8*); pap. 29.50 (*0-941864-31-6*) ABBE Pubs Assn.

Depression: Minnesota in the Thirties. D. Jerome Tweton. (Illus.). 89p. 1981. pap. 7.50 (*0-911042-25-3*) N Dak Inst.

Depression: New Trends in Research & Treatment. Kragh. 200p. 1991. 39.95 (*87-16-10798-5*) Mosby Yr Bk.

***Depression: Questions You Have...Answers You Need.** Sandra Salmans. (Illus.). 192p. (Orig.). 1995. pap. 10.95 (*1-882606-14-0*) Peoples Med Soc.

Depression: Recovery & Higher Education. Malcolm W. Wiley. Ed. by Walter P. Metzger. LC 76-55176. (Academic Profession Ser.). (Illus.). 1977. reprint ed. lib. bdg. 46.95 (*0-405-10004-3*) Ayer.

Depression: The Dark Night of the Soul. Raymond E. Runde & Gregory Britton. 100p. 1990. write for info. (*0-9628401-0-6*) Millers Pr.

Depression: The Evolution of Powerlessness. 2nd ed. Paul R. Gilbert. LC 92-1445. 561p. 1992. reprint ed. lib. bdg. 40.00 (*0-89862-884-9*) Guilford Pr.

Depression: The Mood Disease. rev. ed. Francis M. Mondimore. LC 92-40513. 248p. 1993. 22.95 (*0-8018-4592-0*) Johns Hopkins.

Depression: The Way Out of Your Prison. Dorothy Rowe. (Illus.). 242p. 1984. pap. 10.95 (*0-7100-9586-4*, RKP) Routledge.

Depression: What Families Should Know. Elaine F. Shimberg. (Orig.). 1991. mass mkt. 4.99 (*0-345-36961-0*) Ballantine.

Depression - Theories & Treatments: Psychological, Biological, & Social Perspectives. Arthur Schwartz & Ruth M. Schwartz. (Illus.). 528p. (C). 1993. text ed. 37.50 (*0-231-06818-2*) Col U Pr.

Depression after Childbirth: How to Recognize & Treat Postnatal Depression. 2nd ed. Katharina Dalton. (Illus.). 176p. 1989. pap. 10.95 (*0-19-282228-4*) OUP.

Depression & Aggression in Family Interaction: Developmental Perspectives. Gerald R. Patterson. 352p. (C). 1988. text ed. 69.95 (*0-8058-0137-5*) L Erlbaum Assocs.

Depression & Aging: Causes, Care & Consequences. Ed. by Lawrence Breslau & Marie Haug. 352p. 1983. 37.95 (*0-8261-3710-5*) Springer Pub.

Depression & Creativity. Andre Haynal. LC 84-27830. 290p. 1985. text ed. 42.00 (*0-8236-1201-5*, 01201) Intl Univs Pr.

Depression & Expressive Behavior. Jack D. Maser. 128p. (C). 1987. text ed. 29.95 (*0-89859-999-7*) L Erlbaum Assocs.

Depression & Families: Impact & Treatment. Ed. by Gabor I. Keitner. LC 89-15117. (Progress in Psychiatry Ser.). 250p. 1989. text ed. 26.50 (*0-88048-223-0*) Am Psychiatric.

Depression & Human Existence. Ed. by E. James Anthony & Therese Benedek. 568p. 1975. 30.00 (*0-316-04371-0*) Little.

Depression & Its Remedy. Wim Malgo. 1980. 2.95 (*0-937422-03-7*) Midnight Call.

Depression & Its Treatment. John H. Greist & James W. Jefferson. 128p. 1985. mass mkt. 3.95 (*0-446-32718-2*) Warner Bks.

Depression & Its Treatment. rev. ed. John H. Greist & James W. Jefferson. LC 92-9713. 144p. 1992. 17.95 (*0-88048-527-2*) Am Psychiatric.

Depression & Its Treatment. rev. ed. John H. Greist & James W. Jefferson. 176p. 1994. mass mkt. 5.99 (*0-446-60029-6*) Warner Bks.

Depression & Mania: A Comprehensive Textbook. Ed. by Anastasios Georgotas & Robert Cancro. 728p. 1988. 79.50 (*0-8385-1575-4*, A1575-8) Appleton & Lange.

***Depression & Mania: Friends Or Foes.** Ty C. Colbert. LC 94-79289. (Illus.). 240p. (Orig.). 1995. pap. 13.95 (*0-9643635-5-0*) Kevco Pubng.

Depression & Mania: Modern Lithium Therapy. Ed. by F. N. Johnson. 284p. 1987. 80.00 (*1-85221-039-7*, IRL Pr) OUP.

Depression & Mania: Modern Lithium Therapy. Ed. by F. N. Johnson. 284p. 1989. IRL Pr. pap. 49.95 (*1-85221-174-1*, IRL Pr) OUP.

***Depression & Natural Medicine.** Elkins. 1995. pap. text ed. 9.95 (*1-885670-00-1*) Woodland UT.

Depression & New Deal in Virginia: The Enduring Dominion. Ronald L. Heinemann. LC 82-13487. 267p. 1983. 32.50 (*0-8139-0946-5*) U Pr of Va.

***Depression & Other Mental Health Issues: The Filipino American Experience.** Aurora Tompar-Tim & Juliana Sustento-Severicher. LC 94-27879. (Social & Behavioral Sciences Ser.). 208p. (C). 1994. 38.95 (*0-7879-0041-9*) Jossey-Bass.

Depression & Protectionism: Britain Between the Wars. Forrest Capie. (Modern Revivals in Economic & Social History Ser.). 176p. (C). 1993. text ed. 55.95 (*0-7512-0262-2*, Pub. by Gregg Revivals UK) Ashgate Pub Co.

Depression & Recovery. Abraham J. Twenski. 18p. (Orig.). 1990. pap. 2.95 (*0-926028-10-3*) Edgehill Pubns.

Depression & Suicide: Medical, Psychological & Socio-Cultural Aspects, Proceedings of the XI Congress of the International Association for Suicide Prevention, Paris, July 5-9, 1981. Ed. by J. P. Soubrier & J. Vedrinne. (Illus.). 912p. 1983. 363.00 (*0-08-027080-8*, Pub. by Pergamon Repr UK) Franklin.

Depression & Suicide: Special Education Students at Risk. Eleanor C. Gutzloe. (Exceptional Children at Risk Ser.). 45p. 1991. 8.90 (*0-86586-213-3*, P356) Coun Exc Child.

Depression & Suicide in Children & Adolescents. Nina J. Muse. (Child Guidance Mental Health Ser.). 1990. pap. text ed. 8.00 (*0-89079-264-X*, 1508) PRO-ED.

Depression & Suicide in Children & Adolescents. Philip G. Patros. 1988. text ed. 36.95 (*0-205-11670-1*, H16702) Allyn.

Depression & Suicide in Late Life. Ed. by D. De Leo & R. F. Diekstra. LC 90-4428. 264p. 1990. text ed. 49.00 (*0-920887-66-X*) Hogrefe & Huber Pubs.

Depression & the Body. Alexander Lowen. 1993. pap. 12.00 (*0-14-019465-7*, Arkana) Viking Penguin.

Depression & the Integrated Life. Richard Berg. LC 81-7976. 183p. 1981. pap. 9.95 (*0-8189-0412-7*) Alba.

Depression & the Social Environment: Research & Intervention with Neglected Populations. Ed. by Philippe Cappeliez & Robert J. Flynn. 448p. 1993. 49.95 (*0-7735-0960-7*, Pub. by McGill CN) U of Toronto Pr.

Depression & the Urban West Coast, 1929-1933: Los Angeles, San Francisco, Seattle, & Portland. William H. Mullins. LC 90-4752. (American West in the Twentieth Century Ser.). 192p. 1991. 35.00 (*0-253-33935-9*) Ind U Pr.

***Depression & What to Do about It.** rev. ed. Gerald F. Mundfrom. 221p. (YA). 1994. pap. 6.00x (*0-9615494-4-0*) Mercy & Truth.

Depression As a Treatable Illness. 1994. lib. bdg. 250.00 (*0-8490-5702-7*) Gordon Pr.

***Depression Book: Depression As an Opportunity for Spiritual Practice.** Cheri Huber. (Illus.). 123p. 1991. reprint ed. pap. text ed. 7.00 (*0-614-03294-6*) Center Practice Zen.

***Depression Book: Depression As an Opportunity for Spiritual Practices.** Cheri Huber. (Illus.). 123p. Date not set. pap. text ed. 7.00 (*0-9614754-3-9*) Center Practice Zen.

Depression Bums. Ken C. Wise. LC 91-51233. (Illus.). 260p. (Orig.). 1992. pap. 11.95 (*0-923568-26-3*) Wilderness Adventure Bks.

Depression Decade: From New Era Through New Deal, 1929-1941. Broadus Mitchell. LC 89-10693. (Economic History of the United States Ser.). 480p. 1977. pap. text ed. 20.95 (*0-87332-097-2*) M E Sharpe.

Depression-Era Glassware. 3rd ed. Luckey. 220p. 1993. pap. 22.95 (*0-89689-104-6*) Bks Americana.

Depression Era Recipes. Patricia R. Wagner. 1989. 9.95 (*0-934860-55-6*) Adventure Pubns.

Depression in Children & Adolescents. Alfred French & Irving Berlin. LC 79-13481. 298p. 1979. 42.95 (*0-87705-390-1*) Human Sci Pr.

Depression in Children & Adolescents. Ed. by Harold S. Koplewicz & Emily Klass. LC 92-28562. (Monographs in Clinical Pediatrics: Vol. 6). 1993. text ed. 86.00 (*3-7186-5317-6*); pap. text ed. 28.00 (*3-7186-5318-4*) Gordon & Breach.

Depression in Late Life, No. 2. Daniel G. Blazer, II. LC 93-513. 368p. 1993. 32.00 (*0-8016-7434-4*) Mosby Yr Bk.

Depression in Marriage: A Model for Etiology & Treatment. Steven R. Beach et al. LC 90-2775. (Treatment Manuals for Practitioners Ser.). 242p. 1990. lib. bdg. 45.00 (*0-89862-205-0*); pap. text ed. 19.95 (*0-89862-216-6*) Guilford Pr.

Depression in Neurologic Disease. Ed. by Sergio E. Starkstein & Robert G. Robinson. LC 92-49732. (Johns Hopkins Series in Psychiatry & Neuroscience). 256p. 1993. text ed. 55.00 (*0-8018-4567-X*) Johns Hopkins.

Depression in Old Age. Cornelius L. E. Katona. LC 93-46294. 1994. text ed. 36.95 (*0-471-94308-8*) Wiley.

Depression in Primary Care: Detection & Diagnosis. 1994. lib. bdg. 250.95 (*0-8490-5705-1*) Gordon Pr.

Depression in Primary Care: Detection, Diagnosis & Treatment of Major Depression, 2 vols., Set. 1994. lib. bdg. 625.95 (*0-8490-5703-5*) Gordon Pr.

Depression in Primary Care: Detection, Diagnosis, & Treatment Reference Guide for Clinicians. 1994. lib. bdg. 250.00 (*0-8490-5706-X*) Gordon Pr.

Depression in Primary Care: Screening & Detection. Ed. by C. Clifford Attkisson, Jr. & Jane M. Zich. 299p. 1990. 49.95 (*0-415-90125-1*, A3231, Routledge NY) Routledge.

Depression in Primary Care: Treatment of Major Depression. 1994. lib. bdg. 260.75 (*0-8490-5704-3*) Gordon Pr.

Depression in Primary Care, Vol. 1: Detection & Diagnosis. (Illus.). 124p. (Orig.). (C). 1994. pap. text ed. 40.00 (*0-7881-0598-1*) Diane Pub.

Depression in Primary Care, Vol. 2: Treatment of Major Depression. (Illus.). 175p. (Orig.). (C). 1994. pap. text ed. 45.00 (*0-7881-0599-X*) Diane Pub.

Depression in Schizophrenia. Ed. by Lynn E. DeLisi. LC 89-15170. (Progress in Psychiatry Ser.). 160p. 1990. text ed. 22.50 (*0-88048-196-X*) Am Psychiatric.

Depression in Schizophrenics. Ed. by R. Williams & J. T. Dalby. (Illus.). 272p. 1989. 75.00 (*0-306-43240-4*, Plenum Pr) Plenum.

Depression in Texas. Donald W. Whisenhunt. (Texas History Ser.). (Illus.). 43p. 1982. pap. text ed. 3.95x (*0-89641-105-2*) American Pr.

***Depression in the Christian Family.** Herbert M. Carson. 1994. pap. 8.99 (*0-85234-313-2*, Pub. by Evangel Pr UK) Presby & Reformed.

Depression in the Elderly: Clinical Considerations & Therapeutic Approaches. Ed. by S. Kanowski. (Journal: Gerontology: Vol. 40, Suppl. 1, 1994). (Illus.). iv, 30p. 1994. pap. 14.50 (*3-8055-5964-X*) S Karger.

Depression in the Family. Ed. by Arthur Freeman et al. LC 86-22833. (Journal of Psychotherapy & the Family: Vol. 2, Nos. 3-4). 196p. 1987. text ed. 49.95 (*0-86656-624-4*) Haworth Pr.

Depression in the Medically Ill: An Integrated Approach. Gary Rodin et al. LC 90-26064. 384p. 1991. 44.95 (*0-87630-596-6*) Brunner-Mazel.

Depression in Young People: Developmental & Clinical Perspectives. Ed. by Michael Rutter et al. LC 85-870. 568p. reprint ed. pap. 161.90 (*0-7837-1206-5*, 2041738) Bks Demand.

Depression Is a Treatable Illness: A Guide for Patients. 1994. lib. bdg. 256.95 (*0-8490-9056-3*) Gordon Pr.

Depression Kids: Shaping the Character of Our Lives. James E. Alexander. 260p. (Orig.). (YA). 1993. pap. 12.50 (*0-939965-07-0*) Macedon Prod.

Depression of the Dirty Thirties: Howard & Erma's Life. Erma Durheim. LC 92-30365. 1992. 16.95 (*0-87770-516-X*) Ye Galleon.

Depression of the Nineties: An Economic History. Charles Hoffmann. LC 78-90790. (Contributions in Economics & Economic History Ser.: No. 2). 326p. 1970. text ed. 36.95 (*0-8371-1855-7*, HOD/, Greenwood Pr) Greenwood.

Depression Post Office Murals & Southern Culture: A Gentle Reconstruction. Sue B. Beckham. LC 88-22031. (Illus.). 368p. 1989. text ed. 45.00 (*0-8071-1447-2*) La State U Pr.

Depression Prevention: Research Directions. Ed. by Ricardo F. Munoz. 301p. 1987. 68.00 (*0-89116-452-9*) Hemisp Pub.

Depression Recipes: Nineteen Thirties Good Food for Hard Times. Mary Folger. LC 84-29380. (Illus.). 64p. 1985. pap. 6.95 (*0-932769-00-4*) Bumper Crop Pr.

Depression Runs in Families: The Social Context of Risks & Resilience in Children of Depressed Mothers. Constance L. Hammen. (Psychopathology Ser.). (Illus.). 296p. 1991. 54.00 (*0-387-97435-0*) Spr-Verlag.

***Depression, the Mood Disease.** Francis M. Mondimore. (Health Book Ser.). 248p. 1995. reprint ed. pap. 15.95 (*0-8018-5184-X*) Johns Hopkins.

Depression: Theories & Treatments: Psychological, Biological, & Social Perspectives. Arthur Schwartz & Ruth M. Schwartz. 1993. write for info. (*0-318-69718-1*) Col U Pr.

Depression Times Cookbook. B. Carlson. (Illus.). 226p. 1993. 11.95 (*1-878488-84-8*) Quixote Pr IA.

Depression, War, & the New Migration, 1930-1960. Kenneth Kusmer. LC 91-3756. (Black Community & Urban Development in America Ser.: Vol. 6). 360p. 1991. reprint ed. 80.00 (*0-8153-0430-7*) Garland.

Depression Workbook: A Guide for Living with Depression & Manic Depression. Mary E. Copeland. 304p. (Orig.). (C). 1992. 24.95 (*1-879237-33-4*); pap. 13.95 (*1-879237-32-6*) New Harbinger.

Depression Years. Ed. by Arleen Keylin. LC 76-23428. (Individual Publications). 1976. lib. bdg. 18.95 (*0-405-09546-5*) Ayer.

Depression Years As Photographed by Arthur Rothstein. Arthur Rothstein. LC 77-91384. (Illus.). 1978. pap. 10.95 (*0-486-23590-4*) Dover.

Depressive Disorder in Childhood & Adolescence. Ricard Harrington. LC 93-13321. (Series on Studies in Child Psychiatry). 275p. 1994. text ed. 52.95 (*0-471-92917-4*) Wiley.

Depressive Disorders: Facts, Theories, & Treatment Methods. Ed. by Benjamin B. Wolman & George Stricker. (Personality Processes Ser.). 448p. 1990. text ed. 69.95 (*0-471-61819-5*) Wiley.

Depressive Disorders & Immunity. Ed. by Andrew Miller. LC 89-4. (Progress in Psychiatry Ser.). 187p. 1989. text ed. 23.95 (*0-88048-291-5*) Am Psychiatric.

Depressive Illness. Ed. by J. Mendlewicz et al. (Advances in Biological Psychiatry Ser.: Vol. 7). (Illus.). viii, 244p. 1981. pap. 59.25 (*3-8055-2482-X*) S Karger.

Depressive Illness: Prediction of Course & Outcome. Ed. by Tomas Helgason & R. J. Daly. (Illus.). 175p. 1988. 66.00 (*0-387-19090-2*) Spr-Verlag.

Depressive States & Their Treatment. Vamik Volkan. LC 85-6216. 470p. 1994. reprint ed. pap. 45.00 (*1-56821-223-2*) Aronson.

Depressive Stoerungen Erkennen und Behandeln: Leitfaden fuer Aerzte. S. Kasper et al. (Illus.). 64p. 1994. pap. 25.75 (*3-8055-5983-6*) S Karger.

DePrince Master Dream Book. Thessalonia DePrince. 140p. (Orig.). 1985. pap. 4.95 (*0-318-18391-9*) United Spirit.

Deprivation & Delinquency. Donald W. Winnicott. Ed. by Clare Winnicott et al. 304p. 1985. pap. 13.95 (*0-422-79180-6*, 9268, Pub. by Tavistock UK) Routledge Chapman & Hall.

Deprivation & Health in Scotland. Vera Carstairs. 1991. pap. text ed. 39.90 (*0-08-037979-6*, Pub. by Aberdeen U Pr) Macmillan.

Deprived & the Privileged: Personality Development in English Society. B. M. Spinley. LC 72-11337. 1973. text ed. 59.75 (*0-8371-6663-2*, SPDP, Greenwood Pr) Greenwood.

Deprived Children: A Judicial Response: Seventy-Three Recommendations. Metropolitan Court Judges Committee. 48p. 1986. 4.50 (*0-318-23300-2*) Natl Juv & Family Ct Judges.

Deprived Children: The Mersham Experiment; a Social & Clinical Study. Hilda S. Lewis. LC 77-27491. 163p. 1978. reprint ed. text ed. 35.00 (*0-8371-9070-3*, LEDC, Greenwood Pr) Greenwood.

An Asterisk (*) at the beginning of an entry indicates that the title is appearing in BIP for the first time.

An Asterisk (*) at the beginning of an entry indicates that the title is appearing in BIP for the first time.

1877

Derivation of the Laws: Derivation of the Laws of the Symbols of Logic from the Operations of the Human Mind. George Boole. (Illus.). 1991. 250.00 (1-879508-05-2); 350.00 (1-879508-06-0) St Sebastian Pr.

Derivation of the Laws: Derivation of the Laws of the Symbols of Logic from the Operations of the Human Mind. George Boole. (Illus.). 214p. 1991. lib. bdg. 34.95 (1-879508-08-7) St Sebastian Pr.

Derivation of Weighting Factors for Cost & Radiological Impact for Use In, No. EUR 13201. P. T. Allen & T. R. Lee. 150p. 1991. pap. 19.00 (92-826-2237-1, CD-NA-13201-EN-C, Pub. by Europ Com) UNIPUB.

Derivations & Automorphisms of Banach Algebras of Power Series. Sandy Grabiner. LC 74-7124. (Memoirs Ser.: No. 1/146). 124p. 1974. pap. 18.00 (0-8218-1846-5, MEMO 1/146) Am Math.

Derivations, Dissipations & Group Actions on C-Algebras. O. Bratteli. (Lecture Notes in Mathematics Ser.: Vol. 1229). vi, 277p. 1987. pap. 33.00 (0-387-17199-1) Spr-Verlag.

*__Derivations Manual for Formulas Used in Traffic Accident Investigation & Reconstruction.__ Wiley L. Howell. 182p. (C). 1994. pap. text ed. 24.95 (1-884566-16-2) Inst Police Tech.

Derivative Angles. Martha Lang-Wescott. (Illus.). 30p. (Orig.). 1992. pap. text ed. 7.95 (0-9619852-0-8) Treehouse Mtn.

Derivative Financial Products. Susan R. Marki. 224p. 1991. 45.00 (0-88730-455-9) Harper Busn.

*__Derivative Markets.__ Ritchken. (C). 1995. text ed. 63.50 (0-673-46017-7) HarpCollege.

*__Derivative Markets & Investment Management.__ Fox-Andrews. 1995. pap. 34.95 (0-13-343013-8) P-H.

*__Derivative Spectrophotometry.__ Gerhard Talsky. LC 94-34904. 1994. write for info. (3-527-28294-7); 145.00 (1-56081-141-2) VCH Pubs.

*__Derivative Strategies for Managing Portfolio Risk.__ 1993. write for info. (1-879087-28-6) Assn I M&R.

Derivatives: Measuring Growth. Bill Davis et al. 275p. 1993. pap. text ed. write for info. (0-318-72200-3) Addison-Wesley.

*__Derivatives: Strategic Derivatives.__ (Illus.). 125p. (Orig.). 1995. pap. 495.00 (0-7605-1873-4) Rector Pr.

*__Derivatives: Who's Who.__ 200p. (Orig.). 1995. pap. 295.00 (0-7605-1991-9) Rector Pr.

*__Derivatives & the European Securities Market.__ (Illus.). 90p. (Orig.). 1995. pap. 125.00 (0-7605-1665-0) Rector Pr.

*__Derivatives Engineering: A Guide to Structuring, Pricing & Marketing Derivatives.__ Globecon Group Ltd. Staff. 500p. 1995. 75.00 (1-55738-759-1) Probus Pub Co.

*__Derivatives Engineering Workbook: A Step-by-Step Guide to Structuring, Pricing & Marketing Derivatives.__ Globecon Group, Ltd. Staff. 200p. 1995. 50.00 (1-55738-760-5) Probus Pub Co.

*__Derivatives Handbook.__ 125p. (Orig.). 1995. pap. 195.00 (0-7605-1701-0) Rector Pr.

Derivatives of Interval Functions. B. Thomson. LC 91-22745. 186p. 1991. 20.00 (0-8218-2503-8, MEMO 93/452) Am Math.

Derivatives of Links: Milnor's Concordance Invariants & Massey's Products. T. Cochran. LC 89-18593. 73p. 1990. pap. 18.00 (0-8218-2489-9, MEMO 84/427) Am Math.

Derivatives Trading in Europe. David Courtney. 168p. 1992. U.K. text ed. 130.00 (0-406-00143-X) Butterworth Legal Pubs.

Deriving & Testing Rate of Growth & Higher Order Growth Effects in Dynamic Economic Models. K. D. Patterson & J. Ryding. (Bank of England. Discussion Papers: No. 21). 40p. pap. 25.00 (0-317-26765-5, 2024345) Bks Demand.

Deriving Measures of Delinquency from Self-Report Data. National Center for State Courts Staff. 50p. 1980. Manuscript. 3.00 (0-685-16964-2, LDJD-007) Natl Ctr St Courts.

Dermal & Ocular Toxicology: Fundamentals & Methods. Ed. by David W. Hobson. 608p. 1991. 103.95 (0-8493-8811-2, RL803) CRC Pr.

Dermal & Ocular Toxicology: Fundamentals & Methods. David W. Hobson. 550p. 1989. 69.50 (0-936923-20-2) Telford Pr.

Dermal Immune System. Nickoloff. 1992. 161.00 (0-8493-5941-4, RL97) CRC Pr.

Dermaptera. M. Burr. (Illus.). xviii, 238p. 1973. reprint ed. 20.00 (0-88065-074-5, Messers Today & Tomorrow) Scholarly Pubns.

*__Dermatitis in Machinists: Causes & Solutions.__ E. O. Bennett. LC 92-75660. 240p. 1993. pap. 38.00 (1-880319-09-8) Biotech.

Dermatoglyphics: An International Bibliography (World Anthropology) Ed. by Jamshed Mavalwala. xvi, 306p. 1978. text ed. 53.85 (90-279-7999-5) Mouton.

Dermatoglyphics: Science in Transition. Chris C. Plato et al. (Birth Defects: Original Article Ser.: No. 1903). 348p. 1991. text ed. 239.95 (0-471-56104-5, Wiley-Liss) Wiley.

Dermatoglyphics & Functional Lateral Dominance in Mexican Indians (Mayas & Tarahumaras) see Studies in Middle America

Dermatoglyphics Fifty Years Later. Ed. by Wladimir Wertelecki & Chris C. Plato. LC 79-2595. (Alan R. Liss Ser.: Vol. 15, No. 6). 1979. 91.00 (0-685-03284-1) March of Dimes.

Dermatoglyphics in Indians of Southern Mexico & Central America: Santa Eulalia, Tzeltal, Lacondon & Maya Tribes. Harold Cummins. (Middle American Research Series Publication: No. 4). 27p. reprint ed. pap. 25.00 (0-317-28692-7, 2051616) Bks Demand.

Dermatoglypics: An International Perspective. Ed. by Jamshed Mavalwala. (World Anthropology Ser.). (Illus.). xxii, 382p. 1978. text ed. 61.55 (90-279-7580-9) Mouton.

Dermatologic Formulary. Ed. by Jerome L. Shupack et al. 240p. 1989. pap. text ed. 27.50 (0-07-057521-5) Hlth Prof Div.

*__Dermatologic Research Techniques.__ Howard I. Maibach. 240p. 1995. 85.00 (0-8493-8373-0, 8373) CRC Pr.

Dermatologic Surgery: Principles & Practice. Roenigk. 1472p. 1989. 210.00 (0-8247-7926-6) Dekker.

Dermatologic Surgical Suite: Design & Materials. Mary E. Maloney. (Practical Manuals in Dermatologic Surgery Ser.). (Illus.). 105p. 1991. pap. text ed. 32.00 (0-443-08688-5) Churchill.

Dermatological Differential Diagnosis & Pearls. H. Eliot Y. Ghatan. LC 94-9634. 320p. 1994. pap. 29.95 (1-85070-524-0) Prthnon Pub.

Dermatological Formulations: Percutaneous Absorption. Barry. (Drugs & the Pharmaceutical Sciences Ser.: Vol. 18). 496p. 1983. 165.00 (0-8247-1729-5) Dekker.

Dermatological Product Development & Drug Delivery (Seminar Notes - June 1993) ring bd. 85.00 (1-56676-062-3) Technomic.

*__Dermatological Signs of Internal Disease.__ 2nd ed. Jeffrey P. Callen. LC 94-30224. 1994. text ed. 95.00 (0-7216-5454-1) Saunders.

Dermatological Surgery. Ed. by J. L. Verbov. (New Clinical Applications Dermatology Ser.). 1986. lib. bdg. 65.00 (0-85200-934-8) Kluwer Ac.

Dermatologie und Venerologie: Jahresversammlung der Schweizerischen Gesellschaft. (Journal: Dermatologica: Vol. 153, No. 2). 1976. 20.00 (3-8055-2632-6) S Karger.

Dermatology. B. R. Allen. (Brainscan MCQs Ser.). 110p. 1990. pap. text ed. 18.00 (0-387-19607-2) Spr-Verlag.

Dermatology. O. Braun-Falco et al. (Illus.). 1100p. 1991. 220.00 (0-387-16672-6) Spr-Verlag.

Dermatology. Ed. by H. I. Maibach & N. J. Lowe. (Models in Dermatology Ser.: No. 1). (Illus.). x, 374p. 1984. 166.75 (3-8055-3945-2) S Karger.

Dermatology. Milton Orkin et al. (Illus.). 696p. (C). 1991. pap. text ed. 37.95 (0-8385-1288-7, A1288-8) Appleton & Lange.

Dermatology. 2nd ed. Peter Lynch. (House Officer Ser.). 320p. 1986. pap. 20.00 (0-683-05251-9) Williams & Wilkins.

Dermatology. 2nd ed. J. O. Wilkinson et al. (Colour Guide Ser.). (Illus.). 160p. (Orig.). 1993. pap. text ed. 19.95 (0-443-04629-8) Churchill.

Dermatology. 3rd ed. LC 92-49125. (Regents - Prentice-Hall Medical Assistant Kit Ser.). 1993. pap. 10.20 (0-13-105966-1) P-H.

Dermatology. 3rd ed. Peter J. Lynch. LC 92-48556. (House Officer Ser.). 434p. 1994. 20.00 (0-683-05252-7) Williams & Wilkins.

Dermatology, 2 vols., Set. 3rd ed. Samuel L. Moschella & Harry J. Hurley. (Illus.). 2767p. 1992. text ed. 315.00 (0-7216-3263-7) Saunders.

Dermatology: A Text & Colour Atlas. David J. Gawkrodger. (Illus.). 118p. (Orig.). 1992. pap. text ed. 34.95 (0-443-04301-9) Churchill.

Dermatology: An Illustrated Guide. 3rd ed. Lionel Fry. (Illus.). 192p. 1984. text ed. 59.95 (0-407-00335-5) Buttrwrth-Heinemann.

Dermatology: Diagnosis & Therapy. Bondi et al. (Illus.). 432p. (C). 1991. pap. text ed. 26.00 (0-8385-1274-7, A1274-8) Appleton & Lange.

Dermatology & Syphilology of the Nineteenth Century. John T. Crissey & Lawrence C. Parish. LC 81-1954. 488p. 1981. text ed. 110.00 (0-275-91343-0, C1343, Praeger Pubs) Greenwood.

Dermatology & the New Genetics. J. A. Savin & C. Moss. 300p. 1994. 65.00 (0-632-03582-X, Pub. by Blckwell Sci Pubns UK) Blackwell Sci.

Dermatology Education Course. Competence Assurance Systems Staff. (Illus.). 1984. pap. text ed. 75.00 (0-89147-058-1) CAS.

Dermatology for Southern Africa. Heyl. 1990. 65.00 (0-409-10191-5) Buttrwrth-Heinemann.

Dermatology for the Small Animal Practitioner Exotics - Feline - Canine. Gene H. Nesbitt & Lowell J. Ackerman. 1991. pap. 55.00 (1-884254-02-0) Vet Lrn Syst.

Dermatology in General Medicine, Set. 4th ed. Ed. by Thomas B. Fitzpatrick et al. LC 92-48388. 3272p. 1993. 325.00 (0-07-909350-7) Hlth Prof Div.

Dermatology Progress & Perspectives. Ed. by W. H. Burgdorf et al. 1200p. 1993. 148.00 (1-85070-392-2) Prthnon Pub.

*__Dermatology Secrets.__ Ed. by James E. Fitzpatrick & John L. Aeling. (Secrets Ser.). (Illus.). 500p. (Orig.). 1995. pap. text ed. 35.95 (1-56053-124-X) Hanley & Belfus.

Dermatopathology. George Murphy. LC 94-6843. (Illus.). 480p. 1995. text ed. 125.00 (0-7216-2418-9) Saunders.

Dermatopharmacology & Toxicology. Ed. by H. I. Maibach & N. J. Lowe. (Models in Dermatology Ser.: No. 2). (Illus.). x, 370p. 1984. 200.00 (3-8055-3947-9) S Karger.

Dermatophytes: Their Recognition & Identification. 2nd rev. ed. Ed. by Gerbert Rebell & David Taplin. LC 70-130448. (Illus.). 1974. pap. 19.95 (0-87024-185-0) U of Miami Pr.

Dermatosurgery. J. Petres & M. Hundeiker. 1978. 66.00 (0-387-90296-1) Spr-Verlag.

Dermatotoxicology. 4th ed. Ed. by Francis N. Marzulli & Howard I. Maibach. 800p. 1991. 127.00 (1-56032-055-9) Hemisp Pub.

Dermis Probe. Idries Shah. 191p. 1989. 25.00 (0-900860-83-9, Pub. by Octagon Pr UK); pap. 12.50 (0-86304-045-4, Pub. by Octagon Pr UK) ISHK Bk Service.

Dermot Ryan: Archbishop of Dublin 1972-1984. Ed. by Desmond Forristal. 80p. 1989. pap. 22.00 (0-86217-104-0, Pub. by Veritas IE) St Mut.

Dernier Bloc-Notes (V, 1968-1970) Francois Mauriac. 360p. (FRE.). 1971. pap. 34.95 (0-7859-4610-1) Fr & Eur.

Dernier de L'Empire see Last of the Empire

Dernier des Justes. Andre Schwarz-Bart. (FRE.). 1980. pap. 16.95 (0-7859-2678-X, 2020054116) Fr & Eur.

Dernier Des Metiers. Jacques-Laurent Bost. 247p. (FRE.). 1977. pap. 10.95 (0-7859-1850-7, 2070369242) Fr & Eur.

Dernier Elephant. Gerald Hanley. 279p. (FRE.). 1988. pap. 11.95 (0-7859-2653-4, 207037940X) Fr & Eur.

Dernier Jour d'un Condamne & Bug-Jargal. Victor Hugo. (Folio Ser.: No. 919). 434p. (FRE.). 1977. 10.95 (2-07-036919-6) Schoenhof.

Dernier Jour d'un Condamne precede de Bug-Jargal. Victor Hugo. 434p. (FRE.). 1977. pap. 11.95 (0-7859-2388-8, 2070369196) Fr & Eur.

Dernier Nabab. F. Scott Fitzgerald. 246p. (FRE.). 1988. pap. 11.95 (0-7859-2561-9, 2070380912) Fr & Eur.

Dernier Poemes en Vers et un Prose. M. Jacob. (FRE.). 1982. pap. 10.95 (0-8288-3861-5, F106180) Fr & Eur.

Dernier Quete de Gilgamesh, Livre III. Ludmila Zeman. Tr. by Michele Boileau. LC 93-61788. (Illus.). 24p. (FRE.). (J). (gr. 3 up). 1995. 19.95 (0-88776-329-4) Tundra Bks.

Derniere Bande. Samuel Beckett. 76p. (FRE.). 1960. pap. 9.95 (0-7859-0594-4, F85950) Fr & Eur.

Derniere Fee Ou la Nouvelle Lampe Merveilleuse, Paris, 1825. Honore De Balzac. 186p. (FRE.). 1990. pap. 31.95 (0-7859-4583-0) Fr & Eur.

Derniere Fete de l'Empire. Angelo Rinaldi. (FRE.). 1984. pap. 11.95 (0-7859-4212-2) Fr & Eur.

Derniere Illusion de Leconte de Lisle: Lettres Inedites a Emilie LeForestier. Irving Putter. LC 68-65490. 172p. 1983. reprint ed. lib. bdg. 33.00x (0-89370-794-5) Borgo Pr.

Dernieres Pages Inedites. Anatole France. 208p. (FRE.). 1960. pap. 8.95 (0-8288-9756-5, F101190) Fr & Eur.

Derniers Jours: Roman. Raymond Queneau. 232p. (FRE.). 1977. pap. 24.95 (0-7859-1590-7, 207010916X) Fr & Eur.

Derniers Jours de Saint-Exupery. (Illus.). 64p. (FRE.). 1989. pap. 22.50 (3-907509-05-6, Pub. by Parkett Pubs SZ) Dist Art Pubs.

Derniers Poemes d'Amour. Paul Eluard. pap. 8.50 (0-685-34114-3) Fr & Eur.

Derniers Poemes d'Amour. Paul Eluard. 196p. (FRE.). 1989. pap. 26.95 (0-7859-4726-4) Fr & Eur.

*__Dern's Internet Guide for New Users.__ 2nd ed. Daniel P. Dern. 1995. pap. text ed. 27.95 (0-07-016514-9) McGraw.

Deromanticizing Black History: Critical Essays & Reappraisals. Clarence E. Walker. LC 91-11073. 192p. (C). 1991. lib. bdg. 36.00 (0-87049-721-9); pap. 14.00 (0-87049-722-7) U of Tenn Pr.

Derrick Henry Lehmer Dedication: Dedication Issue on His 70th Birthday, Vol. 29, No. 129. 341p. 1989. reprint ed. pap. 35.00 (0-685-00278-0, DHLC) Am Math.

Derrick Sterling: A Story of the Mines. Kirk Munroe. 1993. reprint ed. lib. bdg. 89.00 (0-7812-5496-5) Rprt Serv.

Derrida. Christopher Norris. LC 87-22922. 272p. 1988. pap. 13.95 (0-674-19824-7) HUP.

Derrida: A Critical Reader. Ed. by David Wood. 304p. (C). 1992. pap. 21.95 (0-631-16121-X) Blackwell Pubs.

*__Derrida & Autobiography.__ Robert Smith. (Literature, Culture, Theory Ser.: No. 16). 208p. (C). 1995. 54.95 (0-521-46005-0); pap. 17.95 (0-521-46581-8) Cambridge U Pr.

Derrida & Deconstruction. Hugh J. Silverman. (Continental Philosophy Ser.: Vol. II). 240p. 1989. 40.00 (0-415-03093-5); pap. 13.95 (0-415-03094-3) Routledge.

Derrida & Differance. Ed. by David Wood & Robert Bernasconi. 98p. 1988. 32.95 (0-8101-0785-6); pap. 14.95 (0-8101-0786-4) Northwestern U Pr.

Derrida & Indian Philosophy. Harold Coward. LC 90-32875. 256p. (C). 1990. 49.50 (0-7914-0499-4); pap. 16.95 (0-7914-0500-1) State U NY Pr.

Derrida & Negative Theology. Ed. by Harold Coward & Toby Foshay. LC 91-9956. 349p. (C). 1992. 59.50 (0-7914-0963-5); pap. 19.95 (0-7914-0964-3) State U NY Pr.

Derrida & the Economy of Difference. Irene E. Harvey. LC 84-48249. 300p. reprint ed. pap. 86.40 (0-7837-1754-7, 2057289) Bks Demand.

Derrida & Wittgenstein. Newton Garver & Seung-Chong Lee. LC 93-36225. 240p. 1994. 37.95 (1-56639-172-5) Temple U Pr.

Derrida, Heidegger, Blanchot: Sources of Derrida's Notion & Practice of Literature. Timothy Clark. 264p. (C). 1992. 59.95 (0-521-40539-4) Cambridge U Pr.

Derrida Reader: Between the Blinds. Peggy Kamuf. 632p. 1991. text ed. 68.50 (0-231-06658-9); pap. text ed. 19.50 (0-231-06659-7) Col U Pr.

Derriere Chez Martin. Marcel Ayme. 1973. pap. 7.95 (0-7859-0384-4, M3016) Fr & Eur.

Derriere la Baignoire. Collette Audry. 256p. (FRE.). 1983. pap. 12.95 (0-7859-1979-1, 2070375048) Fr & Eur.

Derriere la Vitre. Robert Merle. (FRE.). 1974. pap. 15.95 (0-7859-4038-3) Fr & Eur.

Derriere la Zizique: Textes de Pochettes de Disquesde de Jazz et de Varietes. Boris Vian. 176p. (FRE.). 1981. pap. 10.95 (0-7859-5496-1) Fr & Eur.

Derringer Danger. Kit Dalton. (Buckskin Ser.: No. 38). 176p. (Orig.). 1994. pap. 3.99 (0-8439-3587-1) Dorchester Pub Co.

Derry: Countdown to Disaster. Frank Curran. 137p. (Orig.). 1986. pap. 9.95 (0-7171-1467-8, Pub. by Gill & MacMill IE) Irish Bks Media.

Derrydale Cook Book of Fish & Game, Vol. I. L. P. DeGouy. (Fifty Greatest Bks.). 308p. (YA). (gr. 10 up). 1992. reprint ed. 40.00 (1-56416-041-6) Derrydale Pr.

Derrydale Cook Book of Fish & Game, Vol. II. L. P. DeGouy. (Fifty Greatest Bks.). 330p. (YA). (gr. 10 up). 1992. reprint ed. 40.00 (1-56416-042-4) Derrydale Pr.

Derrydale Press: A Bibliography. deluxe limited ed. Henry A. Siegel et al. (Illus.). 277p. 1991. boxed 150.00 (0-89032-240-6) Lyons & Burford.

Dervish Lodge: Architecture, Art, & Sufism in Ottoman Turkey. Ed. by Raymond Lifchez. (Comparative Studies on Muslim Societies: No. 10). (C). 1992. 50.00 (0-520-07060-7) U CA Pr.

Dervish Textbook: Kashani's Recension of Suhrawardi's Gifts. Tr. by H. Wilberforce Clarke. 168p. 1990. reprint ed. 27.00 (0-900860-73-1, Pub. by Octagon Pr UK) ISHK Bk Service.

Dervishes of Turkey. Lucy M. Garnett. 202p. 1990. reprint ed. 29.00 (0-86304-052-7) ISHK Bk Service.

Derwood, Inc. Jeri Massi. (English Skills for Christian Schools Ser.). 288p. (Orig.). (J). (gr. 4-6). 1986. pap. 7.72 (0-89084-323-6) Bob Jones Univ Pr.

Deryni Archives. Katherine Kurtz. (Chronicles of the Deryni Ser.). 1986. mass mkt. 4.95 (0-345-32678-4, Del Rey) Ballantine.

Deryni Checkmate. Katherine Kurtz. (Chronicles of the Deryni Ser.: Bk. 2). 1987. mass mkt. 5.99 (0-345-34764-1, Del Rey) Ballantine.

Deryni Magic. Katherine Kurtz. 384p. 1991. mass mkt. 5.95 (0-345-36117-2, Del Rey) Ballantine.

Deryni Rising. Katherine Kurtz. (Chronicles of the Deryni Ser.: Bk. 1). 1987. mass mkt. 4.95 (0-345-34763-3, Del Rey) Ballantine.

Des Armen Teufel: Gesammelte Schriften, 3 vols., Set. Robert Reitzel. 1975. lib. bdg. 600.00 (0-685-57118-1) Revisionist Pr.

Des Associations Religieuses chez les Grecs: Thiases, Eranes, Orgeons. Paul F. Foucart. LC 75-10637. (Ancient Religion & Mythology Ser.). (FRE.). 1976. reprint ed. 23.95 (0-405-07014-4) Ayer.

Des Aveugles. Herve Guibert. 128p. (FRE.). 1986. pap. 10.95 (0-7859-2516-3, 2070377253) Fr & Eur.

Des Aveugles. Herve Guibert. (Folio Ser.: No. 1725). (FRE.). pap. 6.95 (2-07-037725-3) Schoenhof.

Des Bateaux Dans la Nuit. Philippe Labro. (Folio Ser.: No. 1645). (FRE.). pap. 10.95 (2-07-037645-1) Schoenhof.

Des Bleus a l'Ame. Francoise Sagan. 18.95 (0-685-37081-X) Fr & Eur.

Des Causes De la Corruption Du Gout. Anne Dacier. 624p. reprint ed. write for info. (0-318-71335-7, Pub. by Georg Olms GW) Lubrecht & Cramer.

Des Crises Commerciales et De Leur Retour Peri odique En France, En Angleterre, et Aux Etats-Unis. 2nd ed. Clement Juglar. LC 67-27545. (Reprints of Economic Classics Ser.). xx, 560p. 1967. reprint ed. 57.50 (0-678-00315-7) Kelley.

Des Diestilbestrol: New Perspectives. David A. Edelman. 1986. lib. bdg. 108.50 (0-85200-974-7) Kluwer Ac.

Des epingles tremblantes see Signe Ascendant

Des Femmes. Helene Cixous. (FRE.). 1979. pap. 16.95 (0-7859-3302-6, 2721001507) Fr & Eur.

Des Flavius Josephus Schrift Gegen Den Apion. Johann G. Muller. 394p. 1969. reprint ed. write for info. (0-318-70978-3, Pub. by Georg Olms GW) Lubrecht & Cramer.

Des Franzosischen Philosophen Louis-Claude de St. Martin Nachgelessene Werke, Vol. III. Louis-Claude De Saint-Martin. 228p. reprint ed. write for info. (0-318-71431-0, Pub. by Georg Olms GW) Lubrecht & Cramer.

Des Hauts et des Bas. Goscinny Sempe. (FRE.). 1988. pap. 10.95 (0-8288-3785-6, F42170) Fr & Eur.

Des Heilands Letzte Stunden: Des Heilands Letzte Stunden, Vol. 5. Ed. by Clive Brown. (Selected Works of Louis Spohr, 1784-1859). 260p. 1987. lib. bdg. 25.00 (0-8240-1504-5) Garland.

Des Hommes et Des Femmes. Ivy Compton-Burnett. 288p. (FRE.). 1984. pap. 11.95 (0-7859-2004-8, 2070376176) Fr & Eur.

*__Des Identites Culturelles et des Paradigmes de l'Occident dans Leur Relativite.__ Joseph Labat. (FRE.). 1995. write for info. (0-7734-2914-X) E Mellen.

Des Imagistes. LC 78-64017. (Des Imagistes: Literature of the Imagist Movement Ser.). 64p. 1982. reprint ed. 17.50 (0-404-17089-7) AMS Pr.

Des Jardins Extraordinaires, Lyonnais-Dauphine. Isabelle Schliemger. 144p. (FRE.). 1993. lib. bdg. 79.95 (0-7859-3642-4, 2706614161) Fr & Eur.

Des Journees Entieres Dans les Arbres. Marguerite Duras. (Gallimard Ser.). 238p. (FRE.). 1954. 25.95 (2-07-022096-6) Schoenhof.

Des Larmes et des Saints. E. M. Cioran. (FRE.). 1988. pap. 10.95 (0-7859-3143-0, 2253046833) Fr & Eur.

Des Maladies Mentales: Considerees Sous les Rapports Medical Hygienique et Medico-Legal, 3 vols. in 2, 1. Etienne Esquirol. LC 75-16703. (Classics in Psychiatry Ser.). (Illus.). (FRE.). 1976. reprint ed. 66.95 (0-405-07465-4) Ayer.

Des Maladies Mentales: Considerees Sous les Rapports Medical Hygienique et Medico-Legal, 3 vols. in 2, 2-3. Etienne Esquirol. LC 75-16703. (Classics in Psychiatry Ser.). (Illus.). (FRE.). 1976. reprint ed. 66.95 (0-405-07466-2) Ayer.

Des Maladies Mentales: Considerees Sous les Rapports Medical Hygienique et Medico-Legal, 3 vols. in 2, Set. Etienne Esquirol. LC 75-16703. (Classics in Psychiatry Ser.). (Illus.). (FRE.). 1976. reprint ed. 134.95 (0-405-07464-6) Ayer.

D

1878

An Asterisk (*) at the beginning of an entry indicates that the title is appearing in BIP for the first time.

Des Moines & Polk County: Flag on the Prairie. Barbara B. Long. 136p. 1988. 29.95 (*0-89781-273-5*, 5175) Preferred Mktg.

Des Moines Art Center, Selected Paintings, Sculptures & Works on Paper. James T. Demetrion & Louise R. Noun. LC 84-72620. (Illus.). 220p. (Orig.). 1985. pap. 15.00 (*0-9614615-0-0*) Edmundson.

Des Moines Festival of the Avant-Garde Invites You to a Show Without Really Being There. Ed. by Fred Truck. (Orig.). pap. text ed. 7.50 (*0-938236-02-4*) Electric Bank.

***Des Moines Register Cookbook.** Carol McGarvey & Marie McCartan. Ed. by C. R. Mitchell. LC 95-13459. (Bur Oak Original Ser.). (Illus.). 272p. (Orig.). 1995. pap. 14.95 (*0-87745-515-5*) U of Iowa Pr.

Des Moines Visions. Julie Gammack et al. (Urban Tapestry Ser.). 272p. 1993. 39.50 (*1-881096-03-3*) Towery Pub.

Des Nombres, Vol. X. Louis-Claude De Saint-Martin. Ed. by Robert Amadou. 117p. reprint ed. write for info. (*0-318-71421-3*, Pub. by Georg Olms GW) Lubrecht & Cramer.

Des origines a la chretiente medievale (du IIe a la fin du XIIe siecle) see Histoire du Catholicisme en France

Des Origines a la Revolution see Histoire de la Presse Francaise

Des Plaines: Born of the Tall Grass. Donald Johnson. 1984. 19.95 (*0-89781-095-3*, 5092) Preferred Mktg.

Des Roses Blanches pour Danielle, & Autres Histoires. Francine Rigoni et al. (Serie Rouge). (Illus.). 64p. (C). 1994. pap. 5.50 (*0-521-44981-2*) Cambridge U Pr.

Des Salons Victoriens aux Cabanes D'Emigrants: Il y a Cent Ans Erckman-Chatrian. Stephen J. Foster. (American University Studies: Romance Languages & Literature: Ser. II, Vol. 38). 235p. 1986. text ed. 39.45 (*0-8204-0281-8*) P Lang Pubs.

Des Societies Animals: Animal Societies. Alfred V. Espinas. Ed. by Frank N. Egerton, 3rd. LC 77-74219. (History of Ecology Ser.). 1978. reprint ed. lib. bdg. 50.95 (*0-405-10390-5*) Ayer.

Des Vers de Terre Mangent Mes Dechets. Mary Appelhof. Tr. by Loren Card. (Illus.). 1992. pap. 10.95 (*0-942256-06-9*, Flower Pr) Flowerfield Ent.

Des Weltberuhmten Hertzog Wilhelms von Newcastle Neu-Eroffnete Reit-Bahn - Nouvelle Methode Pour Dresser les Chevaux. William Cavendish. (Deutsch-Franzosische Parallelausgabe, Documenta Hippologica Ser.). 301p. 1973. reprint ed. write for info. (*3-487-08052-4*, Pub. by Georg Olms GW) Lubrecht & Cramer.

Des Yeux de Soie; La Diva; La Mort en Espadrille; L'Etang de Solitude et Autres Nouvelles. Francoise Sagan. 240p. 1976. 14.95 (*0-686-55387-X*) Fr & Eur.

Desafio a Servir. Charles R. Swindoll. 210p. 1983. 4.95 (*0-88113-322-1*) Edit Betania.

Desafio de la Mayordomia y las Misiones. N. Aldo Broda. 140p. 1987. pap. 2.95 (*0-311-27023-9*) Casa Bautista.

Desafio Del Islam: Islam's Challenge. Valentin Gonzalez. (SPA.). 5.50 (*84-7645-248-9*, 223279, Pub. by Edit Clie SP) TSELF.

Desafio del Liderazgo. Ted W. Engstrom. Tr. by Adriana P. De Bedoian. 128p. (SPA.). 1987. pap. 3.95 (*0-88113-058-3*) Edit Betania.

Desafio y Solidaridad. Gervasio L. Garcia & A. G. Quintero. LC 82-70525. (Coleccion Semilla Ser.). (Illus.). 176p. 1982. pap. 6.25 (*0-940238-54-3*) Ediciones Huracan.

Desafios Al Sector Privado En los Anos Noventa: Un Seminario Del Bid, Nagoya, Japon, 5 De Abril De 1991. 1991. write for info. (*0-318-69855-2*) IADB.

Desairology: Hairstyling of the Deceased. 4th rev. ed. Noella C. Papagno. LC 91-90370. (Illus.). 105p. 1991. pap. 16.95 (*0-9604610-5-1*) JJ Pub FL.

Desalination: Putting the Technology into Practice. 200p. 1991. 20.00 (*0-317-05671-9*, P93002WAT) Assn Bay Area.

Desalination & Water Re-Use, 4 vols. Institution of Chemical Engineers Staff. (Institution of Chemical Engineers Symposium Ser.: No. 125). 360p. 1991. Vol. 1, 360p. 104.00 (*1-56032-235-7*); Vol. 2, 360p. 104.00 (*1-56032-236-5*); Vol. 3, 360p. 104.00 (*1-56032-237-3*); Vol. 4, 360p. 104.00 (*1-56032-238-1*) Hemisp Pub.

Desalination & Water Re-Use, 4 vols., Set. Institution of Chemical Engineers Staff. (Institution of Chemical Engineers Symposium Ser.: No. 125). 1440p. 1991. 340.00 (*1-56032-234-9*) Hemisp Pub.

Desalination Directory. 5th ed. Ed. by Miriam Balaban. 350p. 1992. lib. bdg. 210.00 (*0-86689-031-9*) Balaban Intl Sci Serv.

Desalination Processes & Multistage Flash Distillation Practice. A. H. Khan. (Desalination & Water Purification Ser.: No. 1). 596p. 1985. 195.00 (*0-444-42563-2*) Elsevier.

Desalination Technology: Developments & Practice. Ed. by Andrew Porteous. (Illus.). 271p. 1983. 74.00 (*0-85334-175-3*, I-453-82, Pub. by Elsevier Applied Sci UK) Elsevier.

Desalting Seawater. M. Clawson & H. H. Landsberg. 286p. 1972. text ed. 156.00 (*0-677-02710-9*) Gordon & Breach.

Desaparicion Misteriosa: Mysterious Disappearance. Jose A. Holowaty. (SPA.). 1.00 (*84-7228-115-9*, 220272, Pub. by Edit Clie SP) TSELF.

Desarraigo En las Novelas De Angel Maria De Lera. Ellen L. Leeder. LC 77-82359. 1978. pap. 8.00 (*0-89729-176-X*) Ediciones.

Desarrollo Agrario y Cambio Demografico en Tres Regiones de Mexico: (Agricultural Development & Demographic Change in Three Regions of Mexico) Agustin Porras. (Research Report Ser.: No. 18). 43p. (Orig.). (SPA.). (C). 1981. pap. 5.00 (*0-935391-17-7*, RR-18) UCSD Ctr US-Mex.

Desarrollo Constitucional De Puerto Rico: Documentos y Casos. 2nd ed. Carmen R. De Santiago. 567p. 1985. pap. 8.00 (*0-8477-2221-X*) U of PR Pr.

Desarrollo De la Filosofia Politica en el Siglo XVI. Pierre Mesnard. 643p. (SPA.). 1956. 3.00 (*0-8477-2805-6*) U of PR Pr.

Desarrollo De Lideres En la Iglesia Que Educa. Jan Chartier. Ed. by Irma V. Cruz. 96p. 1992. pap. 8.00 (*0-8170-1182-X*) Judson.

Desarrollo Economico y Politica Nacional: El Ministerio de Fomento de Guatemala, 1871-1885. David McCreery. LC 82-230313. (CIRMA Serie Monografica: No.1). (Illus.). 177p. (Orig.). (SPA.). 1981. pap. 9.00 (*0-910443-00-9*) CIRMA.

Desarrollo Forestal en America Latina. Ed. by Stephen E. McGaughey & Hans M. Gregersen. 236p. 1983. write for info. (*0-940602-08-3*) IADB.

Desarrollo Rural y Participacion Campesina: La Experiencia de la Fundacion Mexicana para el Desarrollo Rural (Rural Development & Peasant Participation: The Experience of the Mexican Foundation for Rural Development) Miguel A. Ugalde. (Research Report Ser.: No. 25). 28p. (Orig.). (C). 1981. pap. 5.00 (*0-935391-24-X*, RR-25) UCSD Ctr US-Mex.

***Desarrollo y Alineacion del Curriculo: Guia.** National School Services Staff. (SPA.). (C). Date not set. student ed 25.00 (*0-932957-71-4*); teacher ed 125.00 (*0-932957-83-8*) Natl School.

Desastre de Pavie. Jean Giono. 408p. (FRE.). 1963. 29.95 (*0-7859-1138-3*, 2070228347) Fr & Eur.

Desatando la Iglesia (Unleashing the Church) Frank Tillapaugh. (SPA.). 1991. 5.99 (*1-56063-091-4*, 498413) Editorial Unilit.

Descanso: Place of Rest. Molly J. Featheringill et al. (Illus.). 80p. (Orig.). 1993. pap. 8.95 (*0-938711-21-0*) Tecolote Pubns.

Descanso Gardens: Its History & Camellias. Thompson. 1962. pap. 4.00 (*0-87505-144-8*) Borden.

Descant for Gossips. Thea Astley. (Paperbacks Ser.). 259p. (Orig.). 1986. pap. 14.95 (*0-7022-1843-X*, Pub. by Univ Queensland Pr AT) Intl Spec Bk.

Descants: Poems from Hollywood. Mark Dunster. 27p. (Orig.). 1990. pap. 5.00 (*0-89642-179-1*) Linden Pubs.

Descargas De Un Matancero De Pueblo Chiquito: (Contra Esto, Aquello y Lo De Mas Alla) Esteban J. Hoyos. LC 89-83802. (Coleccion Caniqui Ser.). 171p. (SPA.). 1990. pap. 9.95 (*0-89729-533-1*) Ediciones.

Descartes. John G. Cottingham. 224p. 1986. pap. text ed. 19.95 (*0-631-15046-3*) Blackwell Pubs.

Descartes. Marjorie Grene. LC 85-6132. (Philosophers in Context Ser.). 235p. (Orig.). 1985. pap. text ed. 16.95 (*0-8166-1455-5*) U of Minn Pr.

Descartes. John P. Mahaffy. LC 71-94277. (Select Bibliographies Reprint Ser.). 1977. 21.95 (*0-8369-5051-8*) Ayer.

Descartes. Tom Sorell. (Past Masters Ser.). 112p. 1987. pap. 7.95 (*0-19-287635-X*) OUP.

Descartes. Margaret D. Wilson. (Arguments of the Philosophers Ser.). 1978. pap. 15.95 (*0-7100-9208-3*, RKP) Routledge.

Descartes: An Analytical & Historical Introduction. Georges Dicker. (Illus.). 272p. (C). 1993. pap. text ed. 19.95 (*0-19-507590-0*) OUP.

***Descartes: An Intellectual Biography.** Stephen Gaukroger. (Illus.). 608p. 1995. 35.00 (*0-19-823994-7*) OUP.

Descartes Against the Skeptics. E. M. Curley. LC 77-14366. 288p. 1978. 34.50 (*0-674-19826-3*) HUP.

Descartes among the Scholastics. Marjorie Green. LC 90-64234. (Aquinas Lectures). 1991. 10.00 (*0-87462-158-5*) Marquette.

Descartes & Foucault: A Contrastive Introduction to Philosophy. C. G. Prado. 171p. 1992. pap. 17.00 (*0-7766-0275-6*, Pub. by Univ Ottawa Pr CN) Paul & Co Pubs.

***Descartes & His Contemporaries: Objections & Replies.** Roger Ariew & Marjorie Grene. LC 94-6453. 1995. pap. text ed. 18.95 (*0-226-02630-2*) U Ch Pr.

***Descartes & His Contemporaries: Objections & Replies.** Ed. by Roger Ariew & Marjorie Grene. LC 94-6453. 1995. lib. bdg. 49.00 (*0-226-02629-9*) U Ch Pr.

Descartes & Hume: Selected Topics. Stanley Tweyman. LC 89-37322. 1990. 50.00 (*0-88206-071-6*) Caravan Bks.

Descartes & the Autonomy of the Human Understanding. John Carriero. (Harvard Dissertations in Philosophy Ser.). 250p. 1990. reprint ed. 20.00 (*0-8240-3184-9*) Garland.

Descartes & the Dutch: Early Reactions to Cartesian Philosophy, 1637-1650. Theo Verbeek. 256p. 1992. 29.95 (*0-8093-1617-X*) S Ill U Pr.

Descartes & the Enlightenment. Peter A. Schouls. (Studies in the History of Ideas). 216p. (C). 1989. text ed. 47.95 (*0-7735-1014-1*, Pub. by McGill CN) U of Toronto Pr.

Descartes & the Resilience of Rhetoric: Varieties of Cartesian Rhetorical Theory. Thomas M. Carr, Jr. (Studies in Writing & Rhetoric). 224p. (C). 1989. text ed. 22.95 (*0-8093-1557-2*) S Ill U Pr.

Descartes, C'est la France. Alfred Glucksmann. (FRE.). 1989. pap. 14.95 (*0-7859-3149-X*, 2253049735) Fr & Eur.

Descartes: Critical & Interpretive Essays. Ed. by Michael Hooker. LC 78-8419. 333p. reprint ed. pap. 95.00 (*0-317-55760-2*, 2029285) Bks Demand.

Descartes Dictionary. John Cottingham. LC 92-39483. (Blackwell Philosopher Dictionaries Ser.). 200p. 1993. 44.95 (*0-631-17683-7*); pap. 19.95 (*0-631-18538-0*) Blackwell Pubs.

Descartes' Dream: The World According to Mathematics. Philip J. Davis & Reuben Hersh. (Illus.). 400p. 1986. 24.95 (*0-15-125260-2*) HarBrace.

Descartes' Error: Emotion, Reason, & the Human Brain. Antonio Damasio. (Illus.). 320p. 1994. 24.95 (*0-399-13894-3*, Grosset-Putnam) Putnam Pub Group.

Descartes' Metaphysical Physics. Daniel Garber. LC 91-30190. (Science & Its Conceptual Foundations Ser.). (Illus.). 448p. 1992. lib. bdg. 60.00 (*0-226-28217-1*); pap. text ed. 23.95 (*0-226-28219-8*) U Ch Pr.

Descartes on Polyhedra: A Study of the "De Solidorum Elementis" P. J. Federico. (Sources in the History of Mathematics & Physical Sciences Ser.: Vol. 4). (Illus.). 144p. 1982. 76.00 (*0-387-90760-2*) Spr-Verlag.

Descartes on Seeing: Epistemology & Visual Perception. Celia Wolf-Devine. LC 92-12756. (Journal of the History of Philosophy Monograph Ser.). 121p. (C). 1993. pap. 18.95 (*0-8093-1838-5*) S Ill U Pr.

Descartes, Spinoza, Leibniz: The Concept of Substance in Seventeenth Century Metaphysics. Roger S. Woolhouse. LC 92-33547. 232p. 1993. 49.95 (*0-415-09021-0*, B2367, Routledge NY); pap. 15.95 (*0-415-09022-9*, B2371, Routledge NY) Routledge.

Descartes' Theory of the Will. James Petrik. LC 91-3485. 1994. text ed. 35.00 (*0-89341-678-9*, Longwood Academic) Hollowbrook.

Descartes's Rules for the Direction of the Mind. Harold H. Joachim. Ed. by Errol E. Harris & David Ross. LC 79-9958. 122p. 1979. reprint ed. text ed. 35.00 (*0-313-21263-5*, JODE, Greenwood Pr) Greenwood.

Descartes's Theory of Light & Refraction: A Discourse on Method. A. Mark Smith. LC 86-72888. (Transactions Ser.: Vol. 77, Pt. 3). 200p. 1987. pap. 18.00 (*0-87169-773-4*, T773-SMA) Am Philos.

Descendant. Marianne Boruch. LC 88-21117. (Wesleyan Poetry Ser.). 66p. 1989. 12.95 (*0-8195-2160-4*, Wesleyan Univ Pr) U Pr of New Eng.

Descendant. Ellen A. Glasgow. Ed. by Elizabeth Hardwick. LC 76-51667. (Rediscovered Fiction by American Women Ser.). 1977. reprint ed. lib. bdg. 28.95 (*0-405-10046-9*) Ayer.

Descendants & Antecedents of Alfred & Catherine (Dawley) Fellows. Charles M. Otstot. LC 87-80062. 140p. (Orig.). 1987. pap. 15.00 (*0-9603808-1-7*) C M Otstot.

Descendants & Related Families of Kerrs Creek, Rockbridge County, Virginia, Vol. 1. Alfred C. Miller. 1991. lib. bdg. write for info. (*0-9624215-1-0*) A C Miller.

Descendants & Related Families of Kerrs Creek, Rockbridge County, Virginia, Vol. 2. Alfred C. Miller. 1991. lib. bdg. write for info. (*0-9624215-2-9*) A C Miller.

Descendants & Related Families of Kerrs Creek, Rockbridge County, Virginia, Vol. 3. Alfred C. Miller. 1991. lib. bdg. write for info. (*0-9624215-3-7*) A C Miller.

Descendants (by the Female Branches) of Joseph Loomis, Who Came from Braintree, England in 1638, & Settled in Windsor, Connecticut, in 1639, 2 vols. in 1, Vol. 1. E. Loomis. 1132p. 1989. reprint ed. lib. bdg. 159.00 (*0-8328-0785-0*); reprint ed. pap. 149.00 (*0-8328-0786-9*) Higginson Bk Co.

***Descendants of a Shenandoah County German Immigrant: Johann George Wein (Wien)** Thomas M. Spratt. v, 355p. 1993. lib. bdg. 57.00 (*0-8095-8297-X*); pap. 30.00 (*0-8095-8556-1*) Borgo Pr.

Descendants of Abraham Tegarden: Genealogical & Biographical Sketches. 4th ed. LC 67-26911. 800p. 1989. write for info. (*0-9602542-0-X*) H Vogt.

Descendants of Alexander Alvord, of Windsor, Conn., & Northampon, Mass. Samuel M. Alvord. (Illus.). 823p. 1988. reprint ed. lib. bdg. 113.00 (*0-8328-0116-X*); reprint ed. pap. 103.00 (*0-8328-0117-8*) Higginson Bk Co.

Descendants of Andreas Emmerich of Lancaster County, Pa. rev. ed. Oran S. Emrich. LC 82-72105. (Illus.). 1987. spiral bd. 55.00 (*0-941331-12-1*) Ohio Connect.

Descendants of Benjamin & Dorcas Ames of Connecticut: 1786-1979. Kathy DeLong. (Illus.). 205p. 1980. 10.95 (*0-87881-097-8*) Mojave Bks.

Descendants of Captain Thomas Carter of "Lyford", Lancaster County, Virginia, with Allied Families. Joseph Miller. (Illus.). 430p. 1989. reprint ed. lib. bdg. 77.50 (*0-8328-0376-6*); reprint ed. pap. 67.50 (*0-8328-0377-4*) Higginson Bk Co.

Descendants of Conrad Bower, Martin Easterday Sr., John Hoover Sr., & Gabriel Swinehart Sr. Families: From Colonial Maryland to Ohio in the Early 1800's. Arlene F. Mansfield. 490p. 1993. 32.50 (*0-9635981-0-4*) Coyote Tales.

***Descendants of Cornelius W. Loewen & Helena Bartel.** 2nd ed. Melvin J. Loewen. viii, 339p. Date not set. pap. 22.00 (*0-9640876-2-6*) Heritageclassics.

Descendants of Daniel Wolf, 1732-1807. Charles C. Wolf. (Illus.). 374p. (Orig.). 1994. pap. 27.50 (*1-55613-922-5*) Heritage Bk.

Descendants of Edward Colcord of New Hampshire, 1630 to 1908. D. B. Colcord. (Illus.). 166p. 1993. reprint ed. lib. bdg. 34.00 (*0-8328-1366-4*); reprint ed. pap. 24.00 (*0-8328-1367-2*) Higginson Bk Co.

Descendants of Edward Small of New England & Allied Families, & Tracings of English Ancestry, 3 vols., Set. L. A. Underhill. (Illus.). 1835p. 1989. reprint ed. lib. bdg. 275.00 (*0-8328-1082-7*); reprint ed. pap. 259.00 (*0-8328-1083-5*) Higginson Bk Co.

Descendants of Eli S. Miller & Marie Kaufman see Miller Family History: Eighteen Twenty-One to Nineteen Eighty-One

Descendants of Francis LeBaron of Plymouth, Mass. M. Le Baron Stockwell. (Illus.). 521p. reprint ed. lib. bdg. 91.50 (*0-8328-0757-5*); reprint ed. pap. 81.50 (*0-8328-0758-3*) Higginson Bk Co.

***Descendants of Frederick & Caroline Palenske of Wabaunsee County, Kansas.** Hermagene P. Lacy. (Illus.). vii, 225p. Date not set. text ed. 20.00 (*0-938717-50-2*) Shumway Family Hist.

Descendants of George Abbott of Rowley, Mass. & of George Abbott, Sr., of Andover, Mass, 2 vols., Set. Lemuel A. Abbott. (Illus.). 1232p. 1988. reprint ed. lib. bdg. 166.00 (*0-8328-0084-8*); reprint ed. pap. 156.00 (*0-8328-0085-6*) Higginson Bk Co.

Descendants of George Fowle (1610-11? - 1682) of Charlestown, Massachusetts. Eugene C. Fowle. 316p. 1990. 50.00 (*0-88082-028-4*, S3-20250) New Eng Hist.

Descendants of George Holmes of Roxbury, 1594-1908. George A. Gray. x, 432p. 1993. reprint ed. pap. 30.00 (*1-55613-724-9*) Heritage Bk.

Descendants of George Little Who Came to Newbury, Mass., in 1640. G. T. Little. (Illus.). 638p. 1989. reprint ed. lib. bdg. 90.00 (*0-8328-0773-7*); reprint ed. pap. 80.00 (*0-8328-0774-5*) Higginson Bk Co.

Descendants of George Puffer of Braintree, Mass, 1639-1915. C. Nutt. (Illus.). 376p. 1993. reprint ed. lib. bdg. 58.50 (*0-8328-3049-6*); reprint ed. pap. 48.50 (*0-8328-3050-X*) Higginson Bk Co.

Descendants of Gottfried & Wilhelmine Griepp & Their Hintz & Rathke Kinships. Frank R. Griepp & Muriel H. Griepp. (Illus.). 1980. 25.00 (*0-682-49596-4*) Griepp Pub.

Descendants of Henry Doude Who Came from England in 1639. W. W. Dowd. 342p. 1989. reprint ed. lib. bdg. 54.00 (*0-8328-0490-8*); reprint ed. pap. 44.00 (*0-8328-0491-6*) Higginson Bk Co.

Descendants of Henry Hitt of Woodbury, CT Arriving in America 1665 & Including Thomas Hett of Massachusetts & Some Descendants of James Hitt of Rhode Island. Maurice R. Hitt, Jr. LC 93-60998. 635p. 1993. write for info. (*1-55787-106-X*, Windswept Books) Hrt of the Lakes.

Descendants of Henry Wallbridge Who Married Anna Ames, Dec. 25 1688, at Preston, Connecticut, with Notes on Allied Families of Brush, Fassett, Dewey, Fobes, Gager, Lehman, Meech, Stafford, & Scott. W. G. Wallbridge. (Illus.). 369p. 1989. reprint ed. lib. bdg. 68.00 (*0-8328-1220-X*); reprint ed. pap. 58.00 (*0-8328-1221-8*) Higginson Bk Co.

Descendants of Hugh Amory, 1605-1805, British & American. Gertrude E. Meredith. (Illus.). 373p. 1988. reprint ed. lib. bdg. 68.50 (*0-8328-0216-6*); reprint ed. pap. 58.50 (*0-8328-0217-4*) Higginson Bk Co.

Descendants of Hugh Jones of Orange County, VA. Bobbie J. McLane & Richard Steele. 239p. (Orig.). 1991. 35.00 (*0-929604-69-5*); pap. 25.00 (*0-929604-77-6*) Arkansas Ancestors.

Descendants of Isaac S. Miller see Miller Family History: Eighteen Twenty-One to Nineteen Eighty-One

Descendants of Isaac Schneider, 1786-1879. Elizabeth A. Ebbott. LC 88-83598. (Illus.). 512p. 1989. 30.00 (*0-317-02788-3*) E A Ebbott.

Descendants of Jackson M. Yancey & Elizabeth B. Goode His Wife: Descendants of Jackson M. Yancey & Elizabeth B. Goode, His Wife. Lloyd R. Garrison. (Illus.). 134p. 1993. reprint ed. lib. bdg. 32.00 (*0-8328-3103-4*); reprint ed. pap. 22.00 (*0-8328-3104-2*) Higginson Bk Co.

Descendants of Jacob Wilson of Braintree, Massachusetts. Ken Stevens. LC 88-63788. (Wilsons from New England Ser.: Vol. V). 224p. 1988. 20.00 (*0-9621887-0-0*) K Stevens.

Descendants of Jacob Young of Shelby County, Kentucky: Including President Harry S. Truman. Elsie S. Davis. LC 80-70981. (Illus.). 171p. (Orig.). 1980. pap. 11.00 (*0-9605618-0-3*) E S Davis.

Descendants of James & Elizabeth Fleming Ferguson. Herman W. Ferguson. (Illus.). 135p. (Orig.). 1988. pap. write for info. (*0-9620770-0-3*) H W Ferguson.

Descendants of James & William Adams of Londonderry, Now Derry, N. H. Andrew N. Adams. (Illus.). 87p. 1988. reprint ed. lib. bdg. 23.00 (*0-8328-0088-0*); reprint ed. pap. 15.00 (*0-8328-0089-9*) Higginson Bk Co.

Descendants of James Cole of Plymouth, 1633: Record of the Families of Lt. Thomas Burnham, Ipswich, 1635, Lt. Edward Winship, Cambridge, 1634, Simon Huntington; Norwich, England, 1635. E. B. Cole. (Illus.). 449p. 1989. reprint ed. lib. bdg. 65.00 (*0-8328-0414-2*); reprint ed. pap. 55.00 (*0-8328-0415-0*) Higginson Bk Co.

Descendants of Johann Jochim Doose: And Some Related Families. Jazelle D. Fike. 222p. 1992. pap. 20.00 (*0-9634064-0-X*) JDF Fam Geneal.

Descendants of Johannes P. Weinhardt of Wurttemberg: Born about 1670-1686, Died after 1731. Comp. by William R. Shurtleff. (Illus.). 128p. (Orig.). 1994. pap. 39.00 (*0-942515-06-4*) Pine Hill CA.

Descendants of John Ball of Watertown, MA, 1630-1635. F. D. Warren & G. H. Ball. 161p. reprint ed. lib. bdg. 36.00 (*0-8328-1660-4*); reprint ed. pap. 26.00 (*0-8328-1661-2*) Higginson Bk Co.

Descendants of John Brockett of New Haven Colony. Edward J. Brockett et al. (Illus.). 266p. 1988. reprint ed. lib. bdg. 50.00 (*0-8328-0324-3*); reprint ed. pap. 40.00 (*0-8328-0325-1*) Higginson Bk Co.

Descendants of John C. Shrock & Catherine Hochstetler. Ed. by Anna L. Waite. 345p. 1987. lib. bdg. 35.00 (*0-938717-05-7*) Shumway Family Hist.

Descendants of John Keep of Longmeadow, Massachusetts. Margo Keep. (Illus.). 1136p. 1994. lib. bdg. 75.00 (*1-55787-123-X*) Hrt of the Lakes.

***Descendants of John Meridy Turner (1747-1815) of Fauquier Co. VA.** Gwen B. Bjorkman. (Illus.). 163p. 1995. pap. text ed. 15.50 (*0-7884-0145-9*) Heritage Bk.

D

An Asterisk (*) at the beginning of an entry indicates that the title is appearing in BIP for the first time. 1879

Descendants of John Messer Lowell: Revolutionary Soldier Who Changed His Name to John Reed. Laurel K. Chapman. LC 92-74059. (Illus.). 537p. 1992. 50.00 (*1-55787-087-X*, Windswept Books) Hrt of the Lakes.

Descendants of John Rugg. E. R. Rugg. 586p. 1989. reprint ed. lib. bdg. 96.00 (*0-8328-1034-7*); reprint ed. pap. 88.00 (*0-8328-1035-5*) Higginson Bk Co.

Descendants of John Rugg. Ellen R. Rugg. 580p. 1989. reprint ed. lib. bdg. 99.00 (*0-8328-1407-5*); reprint ed. pap. 89.00 (*0-8328-1408-3*) Higginson Bk Co.

Descendants of John Segar of South Kingstown, Rhode Island: Including the Descendants of William Browning & Mary Hoxsie (Lewis) Greene of Charlestown, Rhode Island. William E. Wright. 94p. 1992. 19.00 (*0-9632060-0-1*) W E Wright.

Descendants of John Stubbs of Cappahosic, Gloucester County, Virginia, 1652. William C. Stubbs. 116p. 1991. reprint ed. pap. text ed. 15.00 (*1-55613-429-0*) Heritage Bk.

Descendants of John Teape & Elizabeth Bunce. 304p. 1984. 14.95 (*0-317-68203-2*); pap. 12.95 (*0-317-68204-0*) J H Day Pub.

Descendants of John Whitney, Who Came from London, England to Watertown, Massachusetts, in 1635. F. C. Pierce. (Illus.). 692p. 1989. reprint ed. lib. bdg. 95.00 (*0-8328-1260-9*); reprint ed. pap. 85.00 (*0-8328-1261-7*) Higginson Bk Co.

Descendants of John Wilson of Woburn, Massachusetts, Vol. J. Ken Stevens. 900p. 1990. write for info. (*0-318-66970-6*) K Stevens.

Descendants of Jonathan Towle, 1747-1822, of Hampton & Pittsfield, N. H. A. Towle et al. (Illus.). 312p. 1989. reprint ed. lib. bdg. 59.00 (*0-8328-1174-2*); reprint ed. pap. 49.00 (*0-8328-1175-0*) Higginson Bk Co.

Descendants of Joseph Greene of Westerly, Rhode Island: Including Other Branches of the Greenes of Quidnesset, or Kingston, Rhode Island, & Other Lines of Greenes in America. Frank L. Greene. 500p. 1991. reprint ed. pap. 30.00 (*1-55613-456-8*) Heritage Bk.

Descendants of Joseph Greene of Westerly, R.I. F. L. Greene. 500p. 1989. reprint ed. lib. bdg. 88.00 (*0-8328-0615-3*); reprint ed. pap. 78.00 (*0-8328-0616-1*) Higginson Bk Co.

Descendants of Joshua Ballinger Lippincott & Josephine Craige of Philadelphia: A Line Chart, 1813-1992. Bertram L. O'Neill. 90p. 1992. 45.00 (*0-9631783-0-X*) B L ONeill.

Descendants of Major Samuel Lawrence of Groton, Mass., with Some Mention of Allied Family. R. Lawrence. (Illus.). 355p. reprint ed. lib. bdg. 54.00 (*0-8328-0755-9*); reprint ed. pap. 44.00 (*0-8328-0756-7*) Higginson Bk Co.

Descendants of Martin Benz-Dorothea Schmeller. John D. Bentz. (Illus.). 310p. 1983. pap. 30.00 (*0-9612438-0-5*) J D Bentz.

Descendants of Martin Petry, West Virginia Revolutionary Soldier. 1990. Indexed. write for info. (*0-318-67269-3*) D L Petry.

Descendants of Mathew Battle, England to Virginia, 1647: A Collection of Family Records, Genealogical & Historical. Ed. by Laurie C. Battle et al. LC 92-31939. 1992. 44.95 (*0-87152-459-7*) Reprint.

Descendants of Montilleon Wait & Lydia Douglas. Harlan R. Waite. LC 93-61129. (Illus.). 512p. 1993. 35.00 (*0-9636233-0-3*) H R Waite.

Descendants of Moses & Isabell (Clark) Crawford of Bucks County, Pennsylvania, 2 vols. Allen W. Scholl. xxv, 779p. (Orig.). 1993. pap. text ed. 49.50 (*1-55613-795-8*) Heritage Bk.

Descendants of Nathanial Clarke & His Wife Elizabeth Somerby of Newbury, Mass. A History of Ten Generations, 1642-1902. G. K. Clarke. (Illus.). 468p. 1989. reprint ed. lib. bdg. 83.00 (*0-8328-0404-5*); reprint ed. pap. 73.00 (*0-8328-0405-3*) Higginson Bk Co.

Descendants of Nathaniel Mowry of Rhode Island. W. Mowry. (Illus.). 343p. 1989. reprint ed. lib. bdg. 64.50 (*0-8328-0890-3*); reprint ed. pap. 54.50 (*0-8328-0891-1*) Higginson Bk Co.

Descendants of Nicholas Cady, of Watertown, Mass., 1645-1910. Orrin P. Allen. (Illus.). 546p. 1989. reprint ed. lib. bdg. 79.50 (*0-8328-0360-X*); reprint ed. pap. 69.50 (*0-8328-0361-8*) Higginson Bk Co.

Descendants of Noah & Margaret Crosby Mullin: A Scrapbook Family History. Ann M. Burton. (Illus.). 200p. 1994. pap. 19.00 (*0-937505-10-2*) Glyndwr Resc.

Descendants of Peter Willemse Roome. P. R. Warner. 410p. 1989. reprint ed. lib. bdg. 74.00 (*0-8328-1028-2*); reprint ed. pap. 64.00 (*0-8328-1029-0*) Higginson Bk Co.

Descendants of Rev. Thomas Hooker, Hartford, Conn., 1586-1908. E. Hooker. (Illus.). 558p. reprint ed. lib. bdg. 92.00 (*0-8328-0677-3*); reprint ed. pap. 82.00 (*0-8328-0678-1*) Higginson Bk Co.

Descendants of Richard Beckley of Wethersfield, CT. Caroleen B. Sheppard. 406p. 1948. 10.00 (*0-685-40992-9*) Conn Hist Soc.

Descendants of Richard Billingsley & Elizabeth Pearson of New Carlisle, P.Q., Canada; Second Son, Richard. David S. Billingsley. (Illus.). 298p. 1992. 65.00 (*0-317-04959-3*) D S Billingsley.

Descendants of Richard Church of Plymouth, Mass. J. A. Church. 354p. 1993. reprint ed. lib. bdg. 55.00 (*0-8328-3019-4*); reprint ed. pap. 45.00 (*0-8328-3020-8*) Higginson Bk Co.

Descendants of Richard Everett of Dedham, Massachusetts. E. F. Everett. (Illus.). 389p. 1989. reprint ed. lib. bdg. 71.50 (*0-8328-0530-0*); reprint ed. pap. 61.50 (*0-8328-0531-9*) Higginson Bk Co.

Descendants of Richard Sares (Sears) of Yarmouth, Mass., 1638-1888, with Some Notices of Other Families by the Name of Sears. S. May. 676p. 1989. reprint ed. lib. bdg. 108.00 (*0-685-25064-4*); reprint ed. pap. 98.00 (*0-8328-1053-3*) Higginson Bk Co.

Descendants of Robert Lockwood, Colonial & Revolutionary History of the Lockwood Family in America from A. D. 1630. F. A. Holden & E. D. Lockwood. (Illus.). 909p. 1989. reprint ed. lib. bdg. 134.00 (*0-8328-0781-8*); reprint ed. pap. 134.00 (*0-8328-0782-6*) Higginson Bk Co.

Descendants of Samuel & Hannah Drury: Of Vermont, New York, & Kentucky 1770 to the Present. Linda L. Kmiecik. LC 90-63734. 445p. 1991. 40.00 (*0-9624657-1-2*) L L Kmiecik.

Descendants of the Family of Deacon of Elstowe & London, & Sketches of Allied Families. E. Deacon. (Illus.). 420p. 1989. reprint ed. lib. bdg. 76.00 (*0-8328-0464-9*); reprint ed. pap. 66.00 (*0-8328-0465-7*) Higginson Bk Co.

Descendants of Thomas Carhart. M. Ovsenbury. (Illus.). 142p. 1989. reprint ed. lib. bdg. 35.00 (*0-8328-1310-9*); reprint ed. pap. 25.00 (*0-8328-1311-7*) Higginson Bk Co.

Descendants of Thomas Durfee, Vol. 2. W. F. Reed. (Illus.). 668p. 1989. reprint ed. lib. bdg. 107.00 (*0-8328-0504-1*); reprint ed. pap. 97.00 (*0-8328-0505-X*) Higginson Bk Co.

Descendants of Thomas Durfee of Portsmouth, R. I., Vol. 1. William F. Reed. (Illus.). 593p. 1989. reprint ed. lib. bdg. 99.00 (*0-8328-0502-5*); reprint ed. pap. 89.00 (*0-8328-0503-3*) Higginson Bk Co.

Descendants of Thomas Horton (1602-1640) of Springfield, MA. Carl W. Fischer. 578p. 1976. 25.00 (*0-9622056-1-3*); pap. 20.00 (*0-9622056-2-1*) Interlaken Hist.

Descendants of Thomas Wellman of Lynn, Mass. J. W. Wellman. (Illus.). 596p. 1993. reprint ed. lib. bdg. 99.00 (*0-8328-3063-1*); reprint ed. pap. 89.00 (*0-8328-3064-X*) Higginson Bk Co.

***Descendants of Timothy Jeremiah Harrington, Son of Jeremiah Harrington of County Cork, Ireland.** Richard A. Walkow & Kevin J. O'Brien. Ed. by Cindy Myers. 286p. 1993. lib. bdg. write for info. (*1-55787-126-4*) Hrt of the Lakes.

***Descendants of William Aitchison of Scotland & Nova Scotia, Canada: Born 1794 in Annan Parish, Dumfrieshire, Scotland, died 1 March 1875 in New Annan, Nova Scotia, Canada: Allied Families Bell, Bowron, Byers, Clark, Cooper, Edwards, Kennedy, Langille, Matheson, Miller, Reid, Schrecker, Spencer, Spensley, Tucker.** 2nd ed. Comp. by William R. Shurtleff & Robert G. Aitchison. LC 94-36076. 186p. (Orig.). 1994. pap. 59.00 (*0-942515-08-0*) Pine Hill CA.

Descendants of William & Elizabeth Tuttle, Pts. 1 & 2. George F. Tuttle. (Illus.). 754p. 1992. reprint ed. pap. 45.00 (*1-55613-582-3*) Heritage Bk.

Descendants of William & Elizabeth Tuttle, Who Came from Old to New England in 1635 & Settled in New Haven in 1639, with Numerous Biographical Notes & Sketches. G. F. Tuttle. (Illus.). 814p. 1989. reprint ed. lib. bdg. 105.00 (*0-8328-1188-2*); reprint ed. pap. 95.00 (*0-8328-1189-0*) Higginson Bk Co.

Descendants of William & Margaret McGaughey. Polly R. M. Sutton. LC 84-90165. (Illus.). 271p. 1984. 26.50 (*0-9613693-0-2*) Mc Gaughey Sutton.

***Descendants of William Andrew of Cambridge, Massachusetts.** Craig Partridge. LC 95-4991. 1995. write for info. (*0-89725-226-8*, Penobscot Pr) Picton Pr.

***Descendants of William Henry & Elizabeth Ann (Simmons) Gregory.** Betty C. Gregory. 36p. 1993. pap. text ed. 6.00 (*1-885935-00-5*) Appalchn Log.

Descendants of William Lamson of Ipswich, Massachusetts, 1634-1917. W. Lamson. (Illus.). 414p. 1993. reprint ed. lib. bdg. 75.00 (*0-8328-3043-7*); reprint ed. pap. 65.00 (*0-8328-3044-5*) Higginson Bk Co.

Descendants of William Moore. Carl C. Moore & Dorothy H. Moore. (Illus.). 153p. 1984. 15.00 (*0-87770-322-1*) Ye Galleon.

Descendants of William Russell of Salem, Mass., 1674. George E. Russell. (Illus.). 270p. 1989. pap. 24.00 (*0-914385-06-2*) Catoctin Pr.

Descendants of William Seaman of Washington County Pennsylvania & Allied Families. Hunt et al. (Illus.). 346p. 1981. per. 20.00 (*0-87012-417-X*) H Vogt.

Descendants of William Towne, Who Came to America on or about 1630 & Settled in Salem, Massachusetts. E. E. Towne. (Illus.). 379p. 1989. reprint ed. lib. bdg. 58.50 (*0-8328-1176-9*); reprint ed. pap. 48.50 (*0-8328-1177-7*) Higginson Bk Co.

Descendants of William White of Haverhill, Massachusetts. Daniel A. White. (Illus.). 114p. 1993. reprint ed. pap. text ed. 15.00 (*1-55613-844-X*) Heritage Bk.

Descended & Cryptorchid Testis. Ed. by E. S. Hafez. (Clinics in Andrology Ser.: No. 3). (Illus.). 204p. 1980. lib. bdg. 117.00 (*90-247-2299-3*) Kluwer Ac.

Descending Fire & Other Stories. John Allman. LC 94-6746. 176p. 1994. 19.95 (*0-8112-1274-2*) New Directions.

Descending into Greatness. Bill Hybels & Rob Wilkins. 208p. 1993. audio 12.99 (*0-310-54478-5*) Zondervan.

Descending into Greatness, Incl. discussion guide. Bill Hybels & Rob Wilkins. 240p. 1994. pap. 10.99 (*0-310-54471-8*) Zondervan.

Descent. Diane Carey. (Star Trek: The Next Generation Ser.). 1993. mass mkt. 5.50 (*0-671-88267-8*) PB.

***Descent.** Thomas A. Sylvester. 192p. 1995. pap. 7.99 (*1-57087-135-3*) Prof Pr NC.

Descent: A Selection of Eight Poems. Stephen Stepanchev. (Chapbook Ser.: No. 5). 1988. 30.00 (*0-937035-12-2*) Stone Hse NY.

Descent & Return: The Orphic Theme in Modern Literature. Walter A. Strauss. LC 70-131461. 295p. reprint ed. pap. 84.10 (*0-7837-1730-X*, 2057260) Bks Demand.

Descent Directions & Efficient Solutions in Discretely Distributed Stochastic Programs. K. Marti. (Lecture Notes in Economics & Mathematical Systems Ser.: Vol. 299). 178p. 1988. pap. 32.00 (*0-387-18778-2*) Spr-Verlag.

Descent from Glory: Four Generations of the John Adams Family. Paul C. Nagel. (Galaxy Bks.). (Illus.). 1983. 30.00 (*0-19-503172-5*) OUP.

Descent from Glory: Four Generations of the John Adams Family. Paul C. Nagel. (Galaxy Bks.). (Illus.). 1984. pap. 12.95 (*0-19-503445-7*) OUP.

Descent from Heaven: A Study in Epic Continuity. Thomas H. Greene. LC 63-7934. 444p. reprint ed. pap. 126.60 (*0-317-29582-9*, 2021999) Bks Demand.

Descent from Heaven: Images of Dew in Greek Poetry & Religion. Deborah Boedeker. (American Philological Association, American Classical Studies: No. 13). 154p. (C). 1985. pap. 15.95 (*0-89130-807-5*, 40 04 13) Scholars Pr GA.

Descent from Parnassus. Dilys Powell. LC 75-99720. (Essay Index Reprint Ser.). 1977. 21.95 (*0-8369-1374-4*) Ayer.

Descent from Xanadu. Robbins. 1993. mass mkt. 5.99 (*0-671-87485-3*) PB.

Descent into Chaos: Yugoslavia's Worsening Crisis. Marko Milivojevic. (C). 1989. 35.00 (*0-907967-08-6*, Pub. by Inst Euro Def & Strat UK) St Mut.

Descent into Discourse. Bryan D. Palmer. 312p. 1990. 34.95 (*0-87722-678-4*); pap. 18.95 (*0-87722-720-9*) Temple U Pr.

Descent into Hell see Novels

Descent into Madness. Vernon Frolick. 361p. 1993. pap. 17.95 (*0-88839-300-8*) Hancock House.

Descent into Nightmare. Ed. by Time-Life Books Staff. (Third Reich Ser.). 1992. write for info. (*0-8094-7037-3*); lib. bdg. write for info. (*0-8094-7038-1*) Time-Life.

Descent into Slavery? Des Griffin. (Illus.). 354p. 1980. pap. 10.00 (*0-941380-01-7*) Emissary Pubns.

Descent into Subjectivity: Rawls, Dworkin & Unger in the Context of Modern Thought. Cornelius F. Murphy. LC 90-6005. 1990. 30.00 (*0-89341-620-7*, Longwood Academic); pap. 14.95 (*0-89341-621-5*, Longwood Academic) Hollowbrook.

Descent of Anansi. Larry Niven & Steven Barnes. 1991. pap. 3.95 (*0-8125-1292-8*) Tor Bks.

Descent of Darwin: The Popularization of Darwinism in Germany, 1860-1914. Alfred Kelly. LC 80-19445. xi, 185p. 1981. 22.50 (*0-8078-1460-1*) U of NC Pr.

Descent of Darwin: The Popularization of Darwinism in Germany, 1860-1914. Alfred Kelly. LC 80-19445. 191p. reprint ed. pap. 54.50 (*0-7837-3765-3*, 2043582) Bks Demand.

Descent of God: Divine Suffering in History & Theology. Joseph M. Hallman. LC 91-4086. 176p. (Orig.). 1991. pap. 14.00 (*0-8006-2485-8*, 1-2485, Fortress Pr) Augsburg Fortress.

Descent of Icarus: Science & the Transformation of Contemporary Democracy. Yaron Ezrahi. LC 90-4197. (Illus.). 354p. 1990. 42.50 (*0-674-19828-X*) HUP.

Descent of Language see On Language: Descent from the Tower of Babel

Descent of Man. T. Coraghessan Boyle. 256p. 1990. pap. 10.95 (*0-14-029994-7*, Penguin Bks); mass mkt. 6.95 (*0-14-009286-2*, Penguin Bks) Viking Penguin.

Descent of Man & Selection in Relation to Sex. Charles Darwin. LC 80-8679. (Illus.). 935p. 1981. reprint ed. 95.00 (*0-691-08278-2*); reprint ed. pap. 22.50x (*0-691-02369-7*) Princeton U Pr.

Descent of Political Theory: The Genealogy of an American Vocation. John G. Gunnell. LC 93-519. 312p. 1993. lib. bdg. 47.00 (*0-226-31080-9*); pap. text ed. 17.95 (*0-226-31081-7*) U Ch Pr.

***Descent of the Child.** Elaine Morgan. 208p. 1995. 19.95 (*0-19-509895-1*) OUP.

Descent of the Dove. Ed. by Ann Valentin & Virginia Essene. 193p. (Orig.). 1988. pap. 9.95 (*0-937147-03-6*) SEE Pub Co.

Descent of the God the Continuing Incarnation. Lorna M. Marsden. (C). 1988. 59.00 (*1-85072-093-2*, Pub. by W Sessions UK) St Mut.

Descent of the Gods. George W. Russell. 1988. 75.00 (*0-901072-44-3*) Dufour.

Descent of the Gods: The Mystical Writings of G. W. Russell - A. E. George W. Russell. Ed. by Nandini Iyer. LC 88-51545. 780p. 1989. 75.00 (*0-900675-44-6*, Pub. by Colin Smythe Ltd UK) Dufour.

Descent of the Imagination: Postromantic Culture in the Later Novels of Thomas Hardy. Kevin Z. Moore. 319p. 1993. pap. text ed. 22.50 (*0-8147-5499-6*) NYU Pr.

Descent of the Spirit: Gaining a Relationship to the Dead Through the Language of the Heart (Plus) Supersensible Knowledge, Anthroposophy. Rudolf Steiner. 28p. 1969. spiral bd. 3.30 (*0-7873-0839-0*) Mokelumne.

Descent of Urania: Studies in Milton, 1946-1988. William B. Hunter. LC 88-47943. 288p. 1989. 42.50 (*0-8387-5157-1*) Bucknell U Pr.

***Descent the Official Strategy Guide.** Schwartz. 1995. pap. (*0-7615-0041-3*) Prima Pub.

***Descent to the Chariot: Towards a Description of the Terminology, Place, Function & Nature of the Yeridah in the Hekhalot Literature.** Annelies Kuyt. (Text und Studien Zum Antiken Judentum Ser.). 440p. 1994. text ed. 175.00 (*3-16-146284-X*, Pub. by J C B Mohr GW) Coronet Bks.

***DeSchooling Our Lives: Education That Matters.** Matt Hern. 160p. 1995. pap. 14.95 (*0-86571-342-1*) New Soc Pubs.

***DeSchooling Our Lives: Education That Matters.** Matt Hern. 160p. 1995. lib. bdg. 39.95 (*0-86571-341-3*) New Soc Pubs.

Deschutes. Dave Hughes. (Illus.). 96p. (Orig.). 1990. 29.95 (*0-936608-92-7*); pap. 15.95 (*0-936608-91-9*) F Amato Pubns.

Deschutes River Country: A Guide to the Past & Present. Gregg Kantor. (Orig.). 1993. pap. 6.95 (*0-9637848-0-3*) Advent In Time.

Desconocidos (Strangers) Dorothy Chlad. Tr. by Lada Kratky. LC 81-18109. (Spanish Safety Town Ser.). (Illus.). 32p. (SPA.). (J). (ps-2). 1984. lib. bdg. 12.23 (*0-516-31984-1*) Childrens.

Descorriendo el Velo: The Great Unveiling. W. Scroggie. (SPA.). 4.95 (*84-7228-839-0*, 220273, Pub. by Edit Clie SP) TSELF.

Describer's Dictionary. David Grambs. 352p. 1993. 22.95 (*0-393-03399-6*) Norton.

***Describer's Dictionary.** David Grambs. 416p. 1995. pap. 14.95 (*0-393-31265-8*, Norton Paperbks) Norton.

Describing & Recognizing 3-D Objects Using Surface Properties. T. J. Fan. (Perception Ser.). (Illus.). xii, 142p. 1989. 49.00 (*0-387-97179-3*, 3588) Spr-Verlag.

Describing Archival Materials: The Use of the MARC AMC Format. Ed. & Intro. by Richard P. Smiraglio. LC 90-43012. (Cataloging & Classification Quarterly Ser.). (Illus.). 232p. 1990. text ed. 39.95 (*0-86656-916-2*) Haworth Pr.

Describing Bilingual Education Classrooms: The Role of the Teacher in Evaluation. Andrew D. Cohen. LC 80-80307. 52p. (Orig.). 1980. pap. 4.50 (*0-89763-050-5*) Natl Clearinghse Bilingual Ed.

Describing Early America: Bartram, Jefferson, Crevecoeur, & the Rhetoric of Natural History. Pamela Regis. LC 91-28145. 189p. 1992. lib. bdg. 30.00 (*0-87580-166-8*) N Ill U Pr.

Describing Information Processes: The FIP Technique. 2nd rev. ed. Patricia Janenko. Ed. by Robert Reitman. (AT&T Quality Library). 64p. 1992. pap. 16.95x (*0-932764-27-4*, 500-488) AT&T Customer Info.

Describing Language. David Graddol & Jenny Cheshire. 160p. 1987. 80.00 (*0-335-15980-X*, Open Univ Pr); pap. 24.00 (*0-335-15979-6*, Open Univ Pr) Taylor & Francis.

Describing Language. 2nd ed. David Graddol et al. LC 94-16918. 256p. 1994. pap. 18.95 (*0-335-19315-3*, Open Univ Pr) Taylor & Francis.

Describing Nonstandard Gears: An Alternative to the Rack Shift Coefficient. Donald R. McVittie. (Fall Technical Meeting Papers). (Illus.). 23p. 1986. pap. 30.00 (*1-55589-465-8*, 86-FTM1) AGMA.

Describing Talk: A Taxonomy of Verbal Response Modes. William B. Stiles. (Series in Interpersonal Communication: Vol. 12). 256p. (C). 1992. text ed. 49.95 (*0-8039-4464-0*); pap. text ed. 24.00 (*0-8039-4465-9*) Sage.

Descripcion of Britayne & Also Irlonde Taken Oute of Policronicon. Ranulphus Higden. LC 75-171738. (English Experience Ser.: No. 386). 60p. 1971. reprint ed. 20.00 (*90-221-0386-2*) Walter J Johnson.

Descriptio Publicae Gratulationis Spectaculorum Et Ludorum, in Adventu: Ernesti Archiducis Austriae Antiverpiae. Johannes Bochius & Pieter Van Der Borcht. LC 68-21207. (Illus.). (LAT.). 1972. reprint ed. 54.95 (*0-405-08278-9*, Pub. by Blom Pubns UK) Ayer.

Description. Arkadii Dragomoschenko. Tr. by Lyn Hejinian & Eleana Balashova. (Sun & Moon Classics Ser.: No. 9). 120p. 1989. 11.95 (*1-55713-075-2*) Sun & Moon CA.

***Description.** Monica Wood. 176p. 1995. 15.99 (*0-89879-681-4*) Writers Digest.

Description: Natural History of the Coasts of North America, Vol. 2. Nicolas Denys. Ed. by William F. Ganong. LC 68-28597. 625p. 1968. reprint ed. text ed. 85.00 (*0-8371-3873-6*, DEDH, Greenwood Pr) Greenwood.

Description: Sign, Self, Desire. Marc E. Blanchard. (Approaches to Semiotics Ser.: No. 43). 1979. text ed. 48.60 (*90-279-7778-X*) Mouton.

Description: Sign, Self, Desire: Critical Theory in the Wake of Semiotics. Marc E. Blanchard. (Approaches to Semiotics Ser.: No. 43). 300p. (C). 1980. 46.90 (*90-279-3488-6*); pap. 30.80 (*3-11-000317-1*) Mouton.

Description & an Analysis of a Selected Number of Judicial Councils, with Recommendations. National Center for State Courts Staff. 122p. 1975. Manuscript. 7.32 (*0-685-15152-2*, MAB-041) Natl Ctr St Courts.

Description & Analysis of the Passaic County (NJ) Speedy Trial Demonstration Project. National Center for State Courts Staff & Samuel Conti. 85p. 1980. 5.10 (*0-685-37387-8*, NERO-064) Natl Ctr St Courts.

Description & Analysis of the Passaic County (NJ) Speedy Trial Demonstration Project: Interim Report. National Center for State Courts Staff. 12p. 1980. Manuscript. 0.72 (*0-685-15512-9*, NERO-063) Natl Ctr St Courts.

Description & Comparison in Cultural Anthropology. Ward H. Goodenough. LC 80-67925. (Lewis Henry Morgan Lectures: No. 1968). 185p. reprint ed. pap. 52.80 (*0-318-34796-2*, 2031659) Bks Demand.

Description & History of the Pianoforte & of the Older Keyboard Stringed Instruments. Alfred J. Hipkins. LC 74-24118. (Illus.). reprint ed. 32.50 (*0-404-12971-4*) AMS Pr.

Description & Sampling of Contaminated Soils: A Field Guide. 2nd ed. J. Russell Boulding. LC 93-47072. 1994. write for info. (*1-56670-050-7*) Lewis Pubs.

Description & Use of Globes & the Orrery. Joseph Harris. 1989. reprint ed. pap. 35.00 (*0-87556-759-2*) Saifer.

Description & Use of the Sector, the Crosse-Staffe & Other Instruments, 2 pts. Edmund Gunter. LC 70-38418. (English Experience Ser.: No. 422). 500p. 1971. reprint ed. 65.00 (*90-221-0422-2*) Walter J Johnson.

Description & Use of the Sphere. Edward Wright. LC 71-25883. (English Experience Ser.: No. 136). 104p. 1969. reprint ed. 14.00 (*90-221-0136-3*) Walter J Johnson.

D

An Asterisk (*) at the beginning of an entry indicates that the title is appearing in BIP for the first time.

***Description by Daniel Tilas of Stratigraphy & Petroleum Occurrence at Osmundsberg in the Siljan Region of Central Sweden, 1740.** Hollis D. Hedberg. (Illus.). ix, 96p. 1988. 27.00 (*0-89181-811-1*) AAPG.

Description Generale Des Monnaies Des Rois Wisigoths d'Espagne. Aloiss Heiss. (Illus.). iv, 185p. (FRE.). 1980. reprint ed. 30.00 (*0-916710-64-5*) Obol Intl.

Description of a Journey & Visit to the Pawnee Indians. Dottlieb Oehler & David Z. Smith. 32p. 1974. 7.50 (*0-87770-140-7*); pap. 4.95 (*0-87770-134-2*) Ye Galleon.

Description of a Maske, in Honour of the Lord Hayes. Thomas Campion. LC 75-25214. (English Experience Ser.: No. 153). 20p. 1969. reprint ed. 8.00 (*90-221-0153-3*) Walter J Johnson.

Description of a New Species, Fundulus Julisia, with a Redescription of Fundulus Albolineatus & a Diagnosis of the Subgenius Xenisma (Teleostei: Cyprinodontidae) James D. Williams & David A. Etnier. (Occasional Papers: No. 102). (Illus.). 20p. 1982. 1.00 (*0-317-04836-8*) U of KS Mus Nat Hist.

Description of a Struggle: The Vintage Book of Contemporary Eastern European Writing. Michael March. 1994. pap. 14.00 (*0-679-74514-9*, Vin) Random.

Description of a View of the Great Temple of Karnak. Robert Burford & F. Catherwood. (Illus.). 18p. 1988. reprint ed. pap. 10.00 (*0-933175-16-7*) Van Siclen Bks.

Description of Ancient Greece. J. A. Lauremberg. (Illus.). 140p. 1969. Artificial Vellum. 52.50 (*0-317-54451-9*, Pub. by A M Hakkert SP) Coronet Bks.

Description of Aphrique. William Prat. 1972. 59.95 (*0-8490-0019-X*) Gordon Pr.

Description of British Guiana: Geographical & Statistical Exhibiting Its Resources & Capabilities. Robert H. Schomburgk. LC 67-16358. 1970. reprint ed. 35.00 (*0-678-05002-3*) Kelley.

Description of British Guiana Geographical, Statistical, Etc. Robert H. Schomburgk. 156p. 1970. reprint ed. 45.00 (*0-7146-1949-3*, Pub. by F Cass Pubs UK) Intl Spec Bk.

Description of Chinese Pottery & Porcelain. Chu Yen. LC 77-38058. (China Classic & Contemporary Works in Reprint Ser.). reprint ed. 44.50 (*0-404-56914-5*) AMS Pr.

Description of Cognitive Development: Three Piagetian Themes. Ron Gold. (Illus.). 184p. 1987. pap. 24.95 (*0-19-852151-0*) OUP.

Description of Computer Programs for the Analysis & Presentation of Trade Winds Data. Jerald Schwarz. LC 76-135092. 152p. 1969. 19.00 (*0-403-04537-1*) Scholarly.

Description of Descriptive Bibliography. Thomas Tanselle. LC 92-29815. 1992. write for info. (*0-8444-0766-6*) Lib Congress.

Description of Devices Used in the Study of Wind Erosion of Soils. Ed. by A. P. Bocharov. Tr. by S. C. Dhamija. 98p. (ENG.). (C). 1984. text ed. 90.00 (*90-6191-426-4*, Pub. by A A Balkema NE) Ashgate Pub Co.

***Description of England: The Classic Contemporary Account of Tudor Social Life.** unabridged ed. William Harrison. Ed. by Georges Edelen. LC 94-31219. 512p. 1995. pap. text ed. 12.95 (*0-486-28275-9*) Dover.

Description of Greece, 5 vols., 1. Pausanias. (Loeb Classical Library: No. 93, 188, 272, 297-298). 486p. 1918. 18.95 (*0-674-99104-4*) HUP.

Description of Greece, 5 vols., 2. Pausanias. (Loeb Classical Library: No. 93, 188, 272, 297-298). 560p. 1926. 18.95 (*0-674-99207-5*) HUP.

Description of Greece, 5 vols., 3. Pausanias. (Loeb Classical Library: No. 93, 188, 272, 297-298). 448p. 1926. 18.95 (*0-674-99300-4*) HUP.

Description of Greece, 5 vols., 4. Pausanias. (Loeb Classical Library: No. 93, 188, 272, 297-298). 612p. 1935. 18.95 (*0-674-99328-4*) HUP.

Description of Greece, 5 vols., 5. Pausanias. (Loeb Classical Library: No. 93, 188, 272, 297-298). 290p. 1935. 18.95 (*0-674-99329-2*) HUP.

Description of Greece, 6 vols., Set. 2nd ed. Pausanias. Tr. by J. G. Frazer. LC 65-13634. (Illus.). 1897. 150.00 (*0-8196-0144-6*) Biblo.

Description of Modern Chaldean. Solomon I. Sara. LC 73-91767. (Janua Linguarum, Series Practica: No. 213). 113p. (Orig.). 1974. pap. text ed. 50.80 (*90-279-3013-9*) Mouton.

Description of New Blazing World & Other Writings. Margaret Cavendish. Ed. by Kate Lilley. LC 92-16908. (Women's Classics Ser.). 250p. (C). 1992. text ed. 55.00 (*0-8147-1475-7*) NYU Pr.

Description of Patagonia & the Adjoining Parts of South America. Thomas Falkner. LC 75-41088. reprint ed. 42.50 (*0-404-14747-X*) AMS Pr.

Description of Pennsylvania, Seventeen Hundred. Francis D. Pastorius. 1993. reprint ed. lib. bdg. 89.00 (*0-7812-5816-2*) Rprt Serv.

Description of Pitcairn's Island & Its Inhabitants. John Barrowe. LC 72-302. (World History Ser.: No. 48). 1972. reprint ed. lib. bdg. 75.00 (*0-8383-1409-0*) M S G Haskell Hse.

Description of Rare Indian Plants, 1820. N. Wallich. 1987. 160.00 (*0-317-89549-4*, Scientific) St Mut.

Description of Texas: Its Advantages & Resources. Oran Roberts. 1993. reprint ed. lib. bdg. 75.00 (*0-7812-5898-7*) Rprt Serv.

Description of the Antiquities Discovered in the State of Ohio & Other Western States. Caleb Atwater. LC 72-4997. (Harvard University. Peabody Museum of Archaeology & Ethnology. Antiquities of the New World Ser.: No. 1). (Illus.). reprint ed. 55.00 (*0-404-57301-0*) AMS Pr.

Description of the Burmese Empire: Compiled Chiefly from Burmese Documents. Vicentius Sangermano. Tr. by William Tandy. LC 72-377657. (Illus.). 1966. reprint ed. 45.00 (*0-678-07261-2*) Kelley.

Description of the Canals & Railroads of the United States: Comprehending Notices of All the Works of Internal Improvement Throughout the Several States. Henry S. Tanner. LC 68-27678. (Library of Early American Business & Industry: No. 20). (Illus.). 272p. 1970. reprint ed. 39.50 (*0-678-00595-8*) Kelley.

Description of the Character, Manners, & Customs of the People of India & of Their Institutions, Religious & Civil. Abee J. DuBois. (C). 1989. reprint ed. 25.00 (*81-206-0454-7*, Pub. by Asian Educ Servs II) S Asia.

Description of the Clergy in Rural Russia: The Memoir of a Nineteenth Century Parish Priest. I. S. Belliustin. Ed. by Gregory L. Freeze. LC 85-47699. (Illus.). 214p. (C). 1985. 34.95 (*0-8014-1796-1*); pap. 11.95 (*0-8014-9335-8*) Cornell U Pr.

***Description of the Coasts of East Africa & Malabar in the Beginning of the Sixteenth Century.** Duarte Barbosa. Tr. by Henry E. Stanley. (C). 1995. 42.00x (*81-206-1020-2*, Pub. by Asian Educ Servs II) S Asia.

Description of the Contrey of Aphrique. LC 72-4497. 200p. 1972. reprint ed. 50.00 (*0-8201-1105-8*) Schol Facsimiles.

Description of the Country from Thirty to Forty Miles Round Manchester. J. Aikin. LC 67-19706. (Reprints of Economic Classics Ser.). (Illus.). 1968. reprint ed. 75.00 (*0-678-00340-8*) Kelley.

Description of the English Province of Carolana, by the Spaniards Call'd Florida, & by the French la Louisiane. Daniel Coxe. LC 76-18184. (Floridiana Facsimile & Reprint Ser.). (Illus.). 122p. 1976. reprint ed. 16.95 (*0-8130-0402-0*) U Press Fla.

Description of the Infantry Equipment Model of 1910, 1917. reprint ed. 2.50 (*1-877704-01-6*) Pioneer Pr.

Description of the Lakes. William Wordsworth. LC 91-3940. (Illus.). 170p. 1991. reprint ed. 48.00 (*1-85477-082-9*, Pub. by Woodstock Bks UK) Cassell.

Description of the Low Countreys Gathered into an Epitome. Ludovico Guicciardini. LC 76-57386. (English Experience Ser.: No. 804). 1977. reprint ed. lib. bdg. 25.00 (*90-221-0804-X*) Walter J Johnson.

Description of the Marianas Islands: Manuel Sanz - Manila 1827. Tr. by Marjorie G. Driver. (Educational Ser.: No. 10). (Illus.). 55p. 1991. write for info. (*1-878453-09-2*); pap. 5.95 (*0-685-63293-8*) Univ Guam MAR Ctr.

Description of the New Netherlands. Adriaen Van Der Donck. Ed. by Thomas F. O'Donnell. LC 68-29420. (New York State Bks.). 1968. 34.95x (*0-8156-2127-2*) Syracuse U Pr.

Description of the New York Central Park. Clarence C. Cook. LC 70-174831. (Illus.). 1972. reprint ed. 18.95 (*0-405-08377-7*, Pub. by Blom Pubns UK) Ayer.

Description of the Planes of Fascia of the Human Body, with Special Reference to the Fascia of the Abdomen, Pelvis & Perineum. Bern B. Gallaudet. 83p. reprint ed. pap. 25.00 (*0-685-15313-4*, 2056098) Bks Demand.

Description of the Qualifications Necessary to a Gospel Minister. Samuel Bownas. LC 89-2948. 1989. reprint ed. 8.50 (*0-87574-911-9*) Pendle Hill.

Description of the Site with Short Notes on the Excavations of 1931-32. Linton Satterthwaite. (Piedras Negras Preliminary Papers: No. 1). 36p. reprint ed. pap. 25.00 (*0-317-26210-6*, 2052122) Bks Demand.

Description of the Spanish Islands & Settlements on the Coast of the West Indies. Thomas Jefferys. LC 72-128431. (Illus.). 1973. reprint ed. 46.50 (*0-404-03558-2*) AMS Pr.

Description of the Tax Certiorari. National Center for State Courts Staff. 45p. 1981. Manuscript. 2.70 (*0-685-15017-8*, NERO-093) Natl Ctr St Courts.

Description of the Western Isles of Scotland. Martin Martin. 440p. (C). 1981. 52.00 (*0-901824-01-1*, Pub. by Mercat Pr Bks UK) St Mut.

Description of the World, 2 vols., Set. Marco Polo. LC 74-5372. reprint ed. 225.00 (*0-404-11525-X*) AMS Pr.

Description of Tula Weapon Factory: In Regard to Historical & Technical Aspects. Losif Gamel. (C). 1988. 32.00 (*81-205-0072-5*, Pub. by Oxford IBH II) S Asia.

***Description of Ukraine.** Guillaume Le Vasseur & Sieur De Beauplan. Tr. by Andrew B. Pernal & Dennis F. Essar. LC 92-54347. (Harvard Series in Ukrainian Studies). (Illus.). 256p. (UKR.). 1990. write for info. (*0-916458-40-7*) Harvard Ukrainian.

***Description of Ukraine.** fac. ed. Guillaume Le Vasseur & Sieur De Beauplan. Tr. by Andrew B. Pernal & Dennis F. Essar. LC 92-54347. (Harvard Series in Ukrainian Studies). (Illus.). 112p. 1990. write for info. (*0-916458-39-3*) Harvard Ukrainian.

Description of Ukraine: Guillaume le Vasseur & Sieur de Beauplan. Guillaume Le Vasseur & Sieur De Beauplan. Tr. by Andrew B. Pernal & Dennis F. Essar. LC 92-54347. (Harvard Series in Ukrainian Studies). (Illus.). cxiv, 243p. (C). 1993. 75.00 (*0-916458-44-X*) Harvard Ukrainian.

Description of Various Leafcasters, 1956-1982: Translation of Selected Passages in Beschreibung verschiedener Anfaserungsgerate, 1983. Per M. Laursen. Ed. by Ellen R. McCrady. Tr. by Moya Tonnies. (Monograph to Abbey Newsletter: Suppl. 2). (Illus.). v, 23p. (Orig.). 1992. pap. 30.00 (*0-9622071-1-X*) Abbey Pubns.

Descriptionary. Marc McCutcheon. 356p. 1992. lib. bdg. 40.00 (*0-8160-2487-1*) Facts on File.

Descriptionary: A Thematic Dictionary. Marc McCutcheon. 496p. 1993. pap. 12.00 (*0-345-38256-0*, Ballantine Trade) Ballantine.

Descriptions. Don Ihde & Hugh J. Silverman. LC 84-26748. (Selected Studies in Phenomenology & Existential Philosophy: No. 11). 300p. 1985. 59.50 (*0-88706-075-7*); pap. 19.95 (*0-88706-076-5*) State U NY Pr.

Descriptions. Stephen Neale. 200p. 1989. 40.00 (*0-262-14045-4*) MIT Pr.

Descriptions. Stephen Neale. 304p. 1993. pap. 16.00 (*0-262-64031-7*, Bradford Bks) MIT Pr.

Descriptions see Imagines, Bks. 1 & 2

Descriptions de Dessins: Picture Descriptions in French. Carmen Waggoner. Ed. by Frederique Parr. (Illus.). 65p. (Orig.). (FRE.). (YA). (gr. 7 up). 1989. audio, pap. text ed. 32.00 (*0-939990-77-6*) Intl Linguistics.

Descriptions of Gem Materials. 3rd ed. Glenn Vargas & Martha Vargas. LC 85-50413. (Illus.). 192p. 1985. 15.00 (*0-917646-06-1*) Glenn Vargas.

Descriptions of New Indian Lepidoperous Insects from the Collection of Late Mr. W. S. Atkinson, M.A., F.L.S., Pts. 1-2. F. Moore. 1987. 750.00 (*0-685-21848-1*, Pub. by Intl Bk Distr II) St Mut.

Descriptions of New Indian Lepidoterous Insects from the Collection of Late Mr. W. S. Atkinson, Pts. 1-2. H. Hewitson. 1987. 375.00 (*81-7089-087-X*, Pub. by Intl Bk Distr II) St Mut.

Descriptions of New Indian Lepidoterous Insects from the Collection of Late Mr. W. S. Atkinson, Pts. 1-2. F. Moore. 1987. 375.00 (*81-7089-889-7*, Pub. by Intl Bk Distr II) St Mut.

Descriptions of New Indian Lepidoterous Insects from the Collection of Late Mr. W. S. Atkinson, Pts. 1-2. Ed. by F. Moore. (C). 1987. 600.00 (*0-685-61466-2*, Pub. by Intl Bk Distr II) St Mut.

Descriptions of New Indian Lepidoterous Insects from the Collection of Late Mr. W. S. Atkinson, Pts. 1 & 2. Ed. by F. Moore. 1987. 200.00 (*0-685-49626-0*, Pub. by Intl Bk Distr II) St Mut.

Descriptions of Seed Sources & Collections for Provenances of Pinus Caribaea. A. Greaves. 1978. 40.00 (*0-85074-035-5*) St Mut.

Descriptions of the Ancient Works in Ohio: Supplement to 1848 Ancient Monuments of the Mississippi Valley. Charles Whittlesey. (Archaeology, Ohio History, Prehistoric Indians Ser.). (Illus.). 40p. 1993. reprint ed. pap. 6.00 (*1-56651-082-1*) A W McGraw.

Descriptions of the Sheriffdoms of Lanark & Renfrew. William Hamilton. LC 75-168237. (Maitland Club, Glasgow. Publications: No. 12). reprint ed. 34.50 (*0-404-52943-7*) AMS Pr.

Descriptive Analyses of Piano Works. Edward Perry. 1977. lib. bdg. 59.95 (*0-8490-1708-4*) Gordon Pr.

Descriptive Analysis of Gascon. Reine C. Kelly. (Janua Linguarum, Series Practica: No. 138). 1973. pap. text ed. 61.55 (*90-279-2388-4*) Mouton.

Descriptive Analysis of Power. Jack H. Nagel. LC 74-14087. 214p. reprint ed. pap. 61.00 (*0-8357-8092-9*, 2033839) Bks Demand.

Descriptive Analysis of Standard Modern Greek. Peter Mackridge. 308p. 1987. pap. 29.95 (*0-19-815854-8*) OUP.

Descriptive & Bibliographic Catalog of the Circus & Related Arts Collection at Illinois State University. Robert Sokan. (Illus.). 219p. 1985. text ed. 45.00 (*0-916638-32-4*) Meyerbooks.

Descriptive & Historical Account of Hydraulic & Other Machines for Raising Water, Ancient & Modern. Thomas Ewbank. LC 72-5048. (Technology & Society Ser.). 598p. 1972. reprint ed. 36.95 (*0-405-04700-2*) Ayer.

Descriptive & Inferential Statistics: An Introduction. rev. ed. Herman Loether & Donald G. McTavish. 512p. (C). 1988. Instr's. manual avail. write for info. (*0-318-62200-9*, H11877) Allyn.

Descriptive & Inferential Statistics: An Introduction. 3rd rev. ed. Herman Loether & Donald G. McTavish. 512p. (C). 1988. text ed. 46.00 (*0-205-11186-6*, H11869) Allyn.

Descriptive & Inferential Statistics: An Introduction. 4th ed. Donald G. McTavish. LC 92-10348. 1992. text ed. write for info. (*0-205-14019-X*) Allyn.

Descriptive & Interpretive Studies of South American Platyrrhine Fossils: 1891-1952. R. A. Stirton et al. LC 78-72716. 41.50 (*0-404-18291-7*) AMS Pr.

Descriptive Appraisal of the Florida Public Guardianship Pilot Program Start-Up. W. Schmidt et al. 1983. write for info. (*0-318-58136-1*) FSU CSP.

Descriptive Bibliographic Catalog of the Music Printed by Hubert Waelrant & Jan de Laet. Robert L. Weaver. LC 94-11356. (Detroit Studies in Music Bibliography: No. 73). 1994. 40.00 (*0-08-999005-6*) Info Coord.

Descriptive Bibliography Catalog of the Music Printed by Hubert Waelrant & Jan de Laet. Robert L. Weaver. (Detroit Studies in Music Bibliography). 1994. 40.00 (*0-89990-058-5*) Info Coord.

Descriptive Bibliography of Civil War Manuscripts in Illinois. William L. Burton. LC 65-24627. 1966. 5.00 (*0-912226-09-9*) Ill St Hist Soc.

Descriptive Bibliography of Civil War Manuscripts in Illinois. William L. Burton. LC 65-24627. 410p. reprint ed. pap. 116.90 (*0-317-27797-9*, 2015290) Bks Demand.

Descriptive Bibliography of Lady Chatterley's Lover: With Essays Toward a Publishing History of the Novel. Jay A. Gertzman. LC 89-17181. (Bibliographies & Indexes in World Literature Ser.: No. 23). 328p. 1990. text ed. 59.95 (*0-313-26125-3*, GLD/, Greenwood Pr) Greenwood.

Descriptive Bibliography of One Thousand One Horse Books. Ed. by William E. Jones. 128p. 1972. pap. 4.95 (*0-912830-10-7*) Printed Horse.

Descriptive Bibliography of the Modern Library: 1917-1970. George M. Andes. LC 88-64071. (Illus.). 256p. 1989. 50.00 (*0-924097-01-9*) Boston Bk Annex.

Descriptive Catalog of Hemerocallis Clones, 1893-1948. Norton & Stuntz. 100p. 10.00 (*0-930653-02-5*) Intl Bulb Soc.

Descriptive Cataloging for AACR2 & USMARC: A How-to-Do-It Workbook for Librarians. Larry Millsap & Terry E. Ferl. (How-to-Do-It Ser.). 240p. 1991. 39.95 (*1-55570-098-5*) Neal-Schuman.

Descriptive Cataloging in a New Light: Polemical Chapters for Librarians. Herbert H. Hoffman. LC 76-380445. 171p. 1976. pap. 6.00 (*0-89537-000-X*) Headway Pubns.

Descriptive Cataloging of Library Materials. 5th ed. Shirley L. Hopkinson. LC 77-153880. 1977. pap. 10.00 (*0-913860-04-2*) Claremont House.

Descriptive Catalogue. William Blake. LC 90-40555. 84p. 1990. reprint ed. 35.00 (*1-85477-036-5*, Pub. by Woodstock Bks UK) Cassell.

Descriptive Catalogue of Impressions from Ancient Scottish Seals. Henry Laing. LC 75-171640. (Maitland Club, Glasgow. Publications: No. 68). reprint ed. 47.50 (*0-404-53081-8*) AMS Pr.

Descriptive Catalogue of Materials Relating to the History of Great Britain & Ireland to the End of the Reign of Henry VII, 3 vols. in 4, Set. Thomas D. Hardy. Incl. Vol. 1, Pts. 1 & 2. From the Roman Period to the Norman Invasion. 1972. (*0-8115-1042-5*); Vol. 2. From Ten Sixty-Six to Twelve Hundred. 1972. (*0-8115-1043-3*); Vol. 3. From Twelve Hundred to Thirteen Twenty-Seven. 1972. (*0-8115-1044-1*); (Rolls Ser.: No. 26). 1972. reprint ed. 180.00 (*0-685-09999-7*) Periodicals Srv.

Descriptive Catalogue of Seventeenth Century Religious Literature in the Kansas State University Library. William P. Williams. LC 67-63307. (Libraries Bibliography: No. 3). 1966. 1.50 (*0-686-20809-9*) KSU.

Descriptive Catalogue of the Bibliographies of Twentieth Century British Poets, Novelists & Dramatists. 2nd enl. rev. ed. Elgin W. Mellown. LC 79-193301. 414p. 1978. 22.50 (*0-87875-137-8*) Whitston Pub.

Descriptive Catalogue of the Collection of Tarantine Coins. O. E. Ravel & M. P. Vlastos. (Illus.). 1977. 70.00 (*0-916710-30-0*) Obol Intl.

Descriptive Catalogue of the Etched Works of Wenceslaus Hollar, 1607-1677. Richard Pennington. LC 81-51828. 452p. 1982. 300.00 (*0-521-22408-X*) Cambridge U Pr.

Descriptive Catalogue of the Indian Deep-Sea Fishes in the Indian Museum. A. Alcock. Ed. by P. K. Talwar. (Illus.). 228p. (C). 1994. text ed. 195.00 (*1-881570-44-4*) Intl Sci Pub.

Descriptive Catalogue of the Jorge Luis Borges Collection at the University of Virginia Library. C. Jared Loewenstein. 150p. 1993. text ed. 35.00 (*0-8139-1333-0*) U Pr of Va.

Descriptive Catalogue of the Letters of Charles & Mary Anne Lamb in the W. Hugh Peal Collection, University of Kentucky Libraries. Edwin W. Marrs, Jr. LC 84-50664. (University of Kentucky Libraries Occasional Papers). 48p. 1984. lib. bdg. 15.00 (*0-917519-02-7*) U of KY Libs.

Descriptive Catalogue of the Manuscripts in the Library of Corpus Christie College, Cambridge, 2 vols. Montague R. James. 1990. reprint ed. pap. 160.00 (*0-685-27121-8*) Periodicals Srv.

Descriptive Catalogue of the Manuscripts in the Library of Corpus Christie College, Cambridge, 2 vols., 1. Montague R. James. 1990. reprint ed. write for info. (*0-8115-3766-8*) Periodicals Srv.

Descriptive Catalogue of the Manuscripts in the Library of Corpus Christie College, Cambridge, 2 vols., 2. Montague R. James. 1990. reprint ed. write for info. (*0-8115-3767-6*) Periodicals Srv.

Descriptive Catalogue of the Manuscripts of the Works of John Gower. Derek Pearsall et al. (Literature Ser.). 300p. lib. bdg. 45.00 (*0-8240-9189-2*) Garland.

Descriptive Catalogue of the Works of the Camden Society. Ed. by John G. Nichols. (Camden Society, London. Publications, First Ser.: No. 80B). reprint ed. 25.00 (*0-404-50208-3*) AMS Pr.

Descriptive Checklist of Book Catalogues Separately Printed in America, 1693-1800. Robert B. Winans. 1981. 37.50 (*0-912296-47-X*, U Pr of Va) Am Antiquarian.

Descriptive, Contrastive & Applied Linguistics see Linguistics Across Historical & Geographical Boundaries in Honor of Jacek Fisiak on the Occasion of His Fiftieth Birthday

Descriptive Dictionary & Atlas of Sexology. Ed. by Robert T. Francoeur et al. LC 89-25860. 792p. 1991. text ed. 99.50 (*0-313-25943-7*, FUH/, Greenwood Pr) Greenwood.

Descriptive Directory of State Judicial Plans. 40p. 1983. Manuscript. 3.00 (*0-685-18275-4*, NCSC-053) Natl Ctr St Courts.

Descriptive Economics: An Introduction to Economic Theory & the U. K. Economy. 7th ed. C. Harbury. 288p. (C). 1986. text ed. 29.50 (*0-273-02483-3*) Trans-Atl Phila.

Descriptive English Grammar. 2nd ed. Susan E. Harman & H. House. 1950. text ed. write for info. (*0-13-199083-7*) P-H.

Descriptive Flora of Puerto Rico & Adjacent Islands: Spermatophyta, Vol. I. Henri A. Liogier. LC 84-22668. 352p. 1985. pap. 20.00 (*0-8477-2334-8*) U of PR Pr.

Descriptive Flora of Puerto Rico & Adjacent Islands, Vol. II: Leguminosae to Anacardiaceae. Henri A. Liogier. LC 84-25668. 481p. 1988. pap. 23.00 (*0-8477-2333-X*) U of PR Pr.

Descriptive Flora of the Maltese Islands Including the Ferns & Flowering Plants. John Borg. 846p. 1976. reprint ed. 109.50 (*3-87429-104-9*) Koeltz Sci Bks.

Descriptive Geometry. M. C. Hawk. (Orig.). (C). 1962. pap. text ed. 11.95 (*0-07-027290-5*) McGraw.

Descriptive Geometry. Gary Lamit. (Illus.). 464p. 1983. text ed. 79.00 (*0-13-199802-1*) P-H.

D

Descriptive Geometry. 8th ed. Eugene G. Pare et al. 1991. Workshop with Comp Graph, Ser. B. write for info. (0-318-68104-8); Workshop with Comp Graph, Ser. A. write for info. (0-318-68105-6) Macmillan.

Descriptive Geometry. 8th ed. Eugene G. Pare et al. 464p. (C). 1991. write for info. (0-02-391331-2) Macmillan.

Descriptive Geometry: Worksheets with Computer Graphics. 8th ed. Eugene G. Pare et al. 160p. (C). 1991. Series A. pap. write for info. (0-02-390951-X); Series B. pap. write for info. (0-02-391301-0) Macmillan.

Descriptive Geometry & Geometric Modeling. J. Alan Adams & Leon M. Billow. 476p. (C). 1988. text ed. 44.00 (0-03-009514-X) SCP.

Descriptive Grammar of Ecclesiastical Latin Based on Modern Structural Analysis. Richard J. O'Brien. LC 65-25149. (Georgetown University Latin Ser.). 283p. reprint ed. pap. 80.70 (0-8357-8566-1, 2034932) Bks Demand.

Descriptive Grammar of Fanti. William E. Welmers. (LD Ser.: No. 39). 1946. pap. 16.00 (0-527-00785-4) Periodicals Srv.

Descriptive Grammar of Jan Yperman's Cyrurgie. Colette M. Van Kerckvoorde. LC 92-40638. (Studies in Old Germanic Languages & Literatures: Vol. 4). 125p. (C). 1994. text ed. 35.95 (0-8204-2149-9) P Lang Pubs.

Descriptive Grammar of Nepali. Jayaraj Acharya. LC 91-10097. 391p. 1991. text ed. 30.00 (0-87840-282-9) Georgetown U Pr.

Descriptive Grammar of SAEI: Di Egyptian Colloquial Arabic. Abdelghany A. Khalafallah. (Janua Linguarum, Ser. Practica: No. 32). 1969. pap. text ed. 42.35 (90-279-0690-4) Mouton.

Descriptive Grammar of the Lubecker Bibel of 1494: German Language & Literature. Margaret S. Zelljadt. (European University Studies: Ser. 1, Vol. 216). 149p. 1979. pap. 22.80 (3-261-03020-8) P Lang Pubs.

Descriptive Inventories of Collections in the Social Welfare History Archives Center. Clarke A. Chambers. LC 73-102265. 846p. 1970. text ed. 85.00 (0-8371-3270-3, SWH/, Greenwood Pr) Greenwood.

Descriptive Inventories of Manuscripts Microfilmed for the Hill Monastic Manuscript Library, Austrian Libraries, Vol. 1. Ed. by Donald N. Yates. (Orig.). 1981. pap. 30.00 (0-940250-01-2) Hill Monastic.

Descriptive Inventories of Manuscripts Microfilmed for the Hill Monastic Manuscript Library, Austrian Libraries, Vol. II: Fiecht. Ed. by Peter Jeffery & Donald Yates. (Orig.). 1985. pap. 45.00 (0-940250-02-0) Hill Monastic.

Descriptive Inventories of Manuscripts Microfilmed for the Hill Monastic Manuscript Library, Austrian Libraries, Vol. III: Herzogenburg. Ed. by Hope Mayo. (Orig.). 1985. pap. 50.00 (0-940250-03-9) Hill Monastic.

Descriptive Inventories of Manuscripts Microfilmed for the Hill Monastic Manuscript Library, No. 1: Biblioteca Nacional de Lisboa, Fundo Alcobaca, Pt. 2. Ed. by Thomas Amos. 1989. 50.00 (0-940250-19-5) Hill Monastic.

Descriptive Inventories of Manuscripts Microfilmed for the Hill Monastic Manuscript Library, No. 1: Biblioteca Nacional de Lisboa, Fundo Alcobaca, Pt. 3. Ed. by Jonathan Black & Thomas Amos. 1990. 50.00 (0-940250-20-9) Hill Monastic.

Descriptive Inventories of Manuscripts Microfilmed for the Hill Monastic Manuscript Library, Portuguese Libraries, Vol. 1: Biblioteca Nacional de Lisboa, Fundo Alcobaca, Pt. 1. Ed. by Thomas L. Amos. (Orig.). 1988. 50.00 (0-940250-18-7) Hill Monastic.

Descriptive Inventory of the Texas Materials in the Rare Book Room of the Tarlton Law Library. 29p. 1989. 15.00 (0-935630-35-X) U of Tex Tarlton Law Lib.

Descriptive Key to the Grasses of Ohio Based on Vegetative Characters. Clara G. Weishaupt. Ed. by Veda M. Cafazzo. (Bulletin New Ser.: Vol. 7, No. 1). (Illus.). 100p. (Orig.). 1985. pap. text ed. 12.00 (0-86727-098-5) Ohio Bio Survey.

Descriptive List of Novels & Tales Dealing with American City Life. W. M. Griswold. 1976. lib. bdg. 59.95 (0-8490-1709-2) Gordon Pr.

Descriptive List of Treasure Maps & Charts in the Library of Congress: Treasure Maps & Charts. 2nd rev. ed. Donald A. Wise. LC 93-60996. 26p. 1993. pap. 10.00 (0-9638122-0-3) U Scandinavian.

***Descriptive Method.** Claude Royet-Journoud. Tr. by Keith Waldrop. 30p. (Orig.). 1995. pap. 7.00 (0-942996-23-2) Post Apollo Pr.

Descriptive Petrography of the Igneous Rocks. Albert Johannsen. LC 31-22687. reprint ed. Vol. 2: The Quartz-bearing Rocks. pap. 115.00 (0-317-26510-5, 2024049); reprint ed. Vol. 3: The Intermediate Rocks. pap. 93.80 (0-317-26511-3); reprint ed. Vol. 4: The Feldspathoid Rocks. The Periodites & Perknites. pap. 135.80 (0-317-26512-1) Bks Demand.

Descriptive Phonetics. 2nd rev. ed. Donald R. Calvert. LC 92-457. 1992. pap. text ed. 36.00 (0-86577-452-8) Thieme Med Pubs.

Descriptive Physical Oceanography: An Introduction. enl. ed. G. L. Pickard & W. J. Emery. (Illus.). 320p. 1990. pap. text ed. 26.00 (0-08-037952-4, Pergamon Pr) Elsevier.

Descriptive Physical Oceanography: An Introduction. 4th enl. ed. Ed. by G. L. Pickard & W. J. Emery. (International Series in Geophysics). (Illus.). 265p. 1982. text ed. 61.00 (0-08-026280-5, G145, G125, C145, Pergamon Pr); pap. text ed. 17.95 (0-08-026279-1, Pergamon Pr) Elsevier.

Descriptive Physical Oceanography: An Introduction. 5th enl. ed. G. L. Pickard & W. J. Emery. (Illus.). 320p. 1990. text ed. 65.00 (0-08-037953-2, Pergamon Pr) Elsevier.

***Descriptive Psychology.** Franz Brentano. Ed. & Tr. by Benito Mueller. LC 94-44167. (International Library of Philosophy). 1995. 55.00 (0-415-10811-X, C0403) Routledge.

Descriptive Regional Oceanography with Plates 1-19: Elementary Desc 4 Main Div of World Ocean Limits Forms, Etc. P. Tchernia & J. Swallow. Tr. by D. Densmore. LC 78-40287. (Pergamon Marine Ser.: Vol. 3). (Illus.). 256p. 1980. text ed. 114.00 (0-08-020925-4, Pub. by Pergamon Repr UK) Franklin.

Descriptive Set Theory. Y. N. Moschovakis. (Studies in Logic & the Foundations of Mathematics: Vol. 100). 638p. 1980. 128.25 (0-444-85305-7, North Holland) Elsevier.

Descriptive Set Theory. Y. N. Moschovakis. (Studies in Logic & the Foundations of Mathematics: No. 100). 638p. 1987. reprint ed. pap. 49.50 (0-444-70199-0, North Holland) Elsevier.

Descriptive Set Theory & the Structure of Sets of Uniqueness. Alexander S. Kechris & Alain Louveau. (London Mathematical Society Lecture Note Ser.: No. 128). 384p. 1987. pap. 54.95 (0-521-35811-6) Cambridge U Pr.

Descriptive Sketch of the Present State of Vermont. Ed. by John A. Graham. LC 86-51466. reprint ed. 19.95 (0-911853-09-X) Vermont Herit Pr.

Descriptive Sketches. William Wordsworth. Ed. by Eric Birdsall & Paul M. Zall. LC 82-14284. (Cornell Wordsworth Ser.). (Illus.). 316p. 1983. 61.50 (0-8014-1536-5) Cornell U Pr.

Descriptive Statistical Techniques for Librarians. Arthur W. Hafner. LC 89-144. 266p. 1990. pap. 15.00 (0-8389-0510-2) ALA.

Descriptive Statistics: A Contemporary Approach. Richard P. Runyon. LC 76-15467. (Statistics Ser.). (C). 1977. pap. text ed. write for info. (0-201-06652-1) Addison-Wesley.

Descriptive Study of the Network Television Western During the Seasons 1955-56 to 1962-63. Donald H. Kirkley, Jr. Ed. by Christopher H. Sterling. LC 78-21722. (Dissertations in Broadcasting Ser.). 1980. lib. bdg. 21.95 (0-405-11761-2) Ayer.

Descriptive Syntax & the English Verb. David Kilby. LC 84-45287. 250p. 1984. pap. 16.95 (0-7099-1553-5, Pub. by Croom Helm UK) Routledge Chapman & Hall.

Descriptive Syntax of Christopher Marlowe's Language. Ed. by Sadao Ando. 721p. 1976. 115.00 (0-86008-162-1, Pub. by U of Tokyo JA) Col U Pr.

Descriptive Syntax of the Old English Charters. Charles Carlton. LC 73-102955. (Janua Linguarum, Series Practica: No. 111). (Illus.). (Orig.). 1970. pap. text ed. 49.25 (90-279-0744-7) Mouton.

Descriptive Syntax of the Peterborough Chronicle from 1122 to 1154. David L. Shores. LC 70-111620. (Janua Linguarum, Ser. Practica: No. 103). (Illus.). (Orig.). 1971. pap. text ed. 92.35 (90-279-1613-6) Mouton.

Descriptive Technique of Panini: An Introduction. Vidya N. Misra. (Janua Linguarum, Series Practica: No. 18). 1966. pap. text ed. 58.50 (90-279-0637-8) Mouton.

Descriptive Theories of Bargaining: An Experimental Analysis of Two- & Three-Person Characteristic Function Bargaining. G. R. Uhlich. Ed. by Martin J. Beckmann & W. Krelle. (Lecture Notes in Economics & Mathematical Systems Ser.: Vol. 341). (Illus.). x, 165p. 1990. pap. 29.90 (0-387-52483-5) Spr-Verlag.

***Descriptive Translation Studies & Beyond.** Gideon Toury. (Benjamins Translation Library: Vol. 4). 300p. 1995. lib. bdg. 84.00x (1-55619-495-1); pap. 27.95x (1-55619-687-3) Benjamins North Am.

Descrittione Del Regno Di Scotia Di Petruccio Ubaldini. Petruccio Ubaldini. LC 71-177548. (Bannatyne Club, Edinburgh. Publications: No. 32). reprint ed. 18.50 (0-404-52738-8) AMS Pr.

Descrying the Ideal: The Philosophy of John William Miller. Stephen Tyman. LC 92-32269. 176p. (C). 1993. 19.95 (0-8093-1840-7) S Ill U Pr.

Descsriptions of New Indian Lepidoterous Insects from the Collection of Late Mr. W. S. Atkinson, Pts. 1-2. F. Moore. (C). 1987. text ed. 400.00 (0-685-52011-0, Pub. by Intl Bk Distr II) St Mut.

Descubra Su Propia Fe: Find Out Your Own Faith. Anna B. Mow. (SPA.). 4.95 (84-7228-590-1, 220258, Pub. by Edit Clie SP) TSELF.

Descubra una Nueva Vida: Discover a New Life. Salvador Iserte. (SPA.). 4.25 (84-7228-864-1, 220257, Pub. by Edit Clie SP) TSELF.

Descubramos Como Orar. Hope McDonald. Tr. by F. G. Coleman. 128p. (SPA.). 1987. reprint ed. pap. 3.95 (0-311-40040-X) Casa Bautista.

Descubre Aves. Scott Weidensaul. Tr. by University of Mexico City Staff. (Descubre - Spanish Ser.). (Illus.). 48p. (J). (gr. 3-8). 1993. lib. bdg. 16.95 (1-56674-047-9, HTS Bks) Forest Hse.

Descubre Dinosaurios. Joel E. Arem. Tr. by University of Mexico City Staff. (Descubre - Spanish Ser.). (Illus.). 48p. (J). (gr. 3-8). 1993. lib. bdg. 16.95 (1-56674-049-5, HTS Bks) Forest Hse.

Descubre Estrellas y Planetas. Toni Eugene. Tr. by University of Mexico City Staff. (Descubre - Spanish Ser.). (Illus.). 48p. (J). (gr. 3-8). 1993. lib. bdg. 16.95 (1-56674-052-5, HTS Bks) Forest Hse.

Descubre La Vida En el Oceano. Alice Jablonsky. Tr. by University of Mexico City Staff. (Descubre - Spanish Ser.). (Illus.). 48p. (J). (gr. 3-8). 1993. lib. bdg. 16.95 (1-56674-050-9, HTS Bks) Forest Hse.

Descubre Mariposas. Gary Dunn. Tr. by University of Mexico City Staff. (Descubre - Spanish Ser.). (Illus.). 48p. (J). (gr. 3-8). 1993. lib. bdg. 16.95 (1-56674-048-7, HTS Bks) Forest Hse.

Descubre Rocas y Minerales. Joel E. Arem. Tr. by University of Mexico City Staff. (Descubre - Spanish Ser.). (Illus.). 48p. (J). (gr. 3-8). 1993. lib. bdg. 16.95 (1-56674-051-7, HTS Bks) Forest Hse.

Descubre Tu Poder Interno. Eric Butterworth. LC 81-69933. Orig. Title: Discover the Power Within You. 336p. 1983. 7.95 (0-87159-026-3) Unity Bks.

Descubre Tus Dones Espirituales: Discover Your Spiritual Gifts. Rick Yohn. (SPA.). 5.50 (84-7228-778-5, 220260, Pub. by Edit Clie SP) TSELF.

Descubrelo Tu Mismo: Find Out for Yourself. Eugenia Price. (SPA.). 4.95 (84-7228-199-X, 220259, Pub. by Edit Clie SP) TSELF.

Descubridores De la Luz: Discoverers of Light. Freda Carver. (SPA.). 2.25 (84-399-3991-4, 220261, Pub. by Edit Clie SP) TSELF.

Descubriendo a Dios: Getting into God. Stuart Briscoe. (SPA.). 4.95 (84-7228-303-8, 220264, Pub. by Edit Clie SP) TSELF.

***Descubriendo Ecuador.** Ed. by Loup Langton & Pablo Corral. 238p. (SPA.). 60.00 (0-9644049-1-5) Descubriendo Ecu.

Descubriendo la Oracion (Discovering Prayer) A. Knowles. (SPA.). Date not set. 5.99 (0-8423-6321-1, 490203) Editorial Unilit.

Descubriendo la Oracion (Discovering Prayer) D. Needham. (SPA.). Date not set. 1.79 (1-56063-359-X, 498252) Editorial Unilit.

Descubriendo la Palabra De Dios (Discovering God's Word) J. G. Mitchell. (SPA.). Date not set. 1.79 (1-56063-361-1, 498224) Editorial Unilit.

Descubriendo-Memorizacion-De Escrituras (Discovering Scripture Memory) J. Braga. (SPA.). Date not set. 1.79 (1-56063-360-3, 498253) Editorial Unilit.

Descubrimiento de las Americas. Betsy Maestro & Giulio Maestro. Tr. by Juan G. Arturo. (Illus.). 48p. (J). (gr. 5-8). 1992. 13.95 (0-9625162-9-5) Lectorum Pubns.

***Descubrimiento de los Dinosaurios.** Alice Jablonsky. Tr. by DigiPro Staff. (Comes to Life Bks.). 16p. (SPA.). (J). (ps-2). 1994. write for info. (1-57234-012-6) YES Ent.

Descubrimientos: Discoveries. Eugenia Price. (SPA.). 4.25 (84-7228-337-2, 220267, Pub. by Edit Clie SP) TSELF.

Descubrir la Tierra (Discover the Earth) Francois Beautier. Tr. by Francisco-Javier Calzada. (Explorer Ser.). (Illus.). 96p. (SPA.). (J). (gr. 4 up). 1992. lib. bdg. 15.90 (1-56294-175-5) Millbrook Pr.

Descubrir y Crear. 3rd ed. Almeida. 1985. student ed, pap. 28.95 (0-8384-3753-2) Heinle & Heinle.

Desde la Esquina Donde la Luna Medita. Coral Zayas. LC 92-62624. (Illus.). 80p. (Orig.). (SPA.). 1993. pap. 8.00 (1-882573-00-5) Serena Bay.

Desde las Sombras. Elena Suarez. LC 83-60445. (Senda Narrativa Ser.). 95p. (Orig.). 1983. pap. 9.95 (0-918454-34-4) Senda Nueva.

Desde los Pobres de la Tierra see Religious Life & the Poor: Liberation Theology Perspectives

Desde Lutecia: Anacronismo y Modernidad en los Escritos Teatrales de Cesar Vallejo. Guido A. Podesta. 341p. (SPA.). 1995. pap. 18.00 (0-9640795-0-X) Latinoam Edit.

Desdemona: A Play about a Handkerchief. Paula Vogel. 1994. pap. 4.75 (0-8222-1391-5) Dramatists Play.

Desdemona: Twelve Going on Desperate. Beverly Keller. LC 86-10655. 160p. (J). (gr. 3-7). 1986. 15.00 (0-688-06076-5) Lothrop.

Desdemona: Twelve Going on Desperate. Beverly Keller. LC 87-45287. (Trophy Bk.). 160p. (J). (gr. 3-7). 1988. reprint ed. pap. 3.95 (0-06-440226-6, Trophy) HarpC Child Bks.

Desdemona Moves On. Beverly Keller. LC 92-7127. 176p. (J). (gr. 3-7). 1992. text ed. 13.95 (0-02-749751-8, Bradbury S&S) S&S Childrens.

***Desden Con el Desden.** 2nd ed. Agustin M. Cavanna. 268p. 1978. pap. 14.95 (0-7859-5183-0) Fr & Eur.

Desdichas de la Fortuna O Julianillo Valcarcel. Juan de Manara. Manuel Y. Machado. Ed. by Damaso Chicharro Chamorro. (Nueva Austral Ser.: Vol. 236). (SPA.). 1991. pap. text ed. 24.95x (84-239-7236-4) Elliots Bks.

Deseables Mas-Oro (More Precious-Gold) (SPA.). Date not set. 2.50 (0-8423-6311-4, 497301) Editorial Unilit.

Desegration in American Schools: Comparative Intervention Strategies. Brian L. Fife. LC 91-33163. 224p. 1992. text ed. 42.95 (0-275-94140-X, C4140, Praeger Pubs) Greenwood.

Desegregated Heart. Sarah P. Boyle. Ed. by Annette K. Baxter. LC 79-8777. (Signal Lives Ser.). 1980. reprint ed. lib. bdg. 32.95 (0-405-12826-6) Ayer.

Desegregated Housing & Interracial Neighborhoods: A Bibliographic Guide. Mark Beach. 91p. 1975. 1.00 (0-318-15821-3, N-5) Natl Neighbors.

Desegregating America's Colleges & Universities: Title VI Regulation of Higher Education. Ed. by John L. Williams, III. 256p. (C). 1987. text ed. 26.95 (0-8077-2870-5) Tchrs Coll.

Desegregating the Altar: The Josephites & the Struggle for Black Priests, 1871-1960. Stephen J. Ochs. LC 89-48219. (C). 1993. pap. 16.95 (0-8071-1859-1) La State U Pr.

Desegregation: Resistance & Readiness. Melvin M. Tumin. 1958. 47.50x (0-691-09313-X) Princeton U Pr.

***Desegregation: Resistance & Readiness.** Melvin M. Tumin. LC 58-13938. Date not set. reprint ed. pap. 82.10 (0-7837-9464-9, 2060206) Bks Demand.

Desegregation: The Illusion of Black Progress. Alvis V. Adair. LC 83-25914. 208p. 1984. pap. text ed. 22.50 (0-8191-3767-7) U Pr of Amer.

Desegregation & Hispanic Students: A Community Perspective. Tony Baez et al. LC 80-80311. 84p. (Orig.). 1980. pap. 5.25 (0-89763-023-8) Natl Clearinghse Bilingual Ed.

Desegregation & the Law: The Meaning of the School Segregation Cases. Albert P. Blaustein & Clarence C. Ferguson, Jr. (Illus.). xiv, 333p. 1985. reprint ed. lib. bdg. 32.50 (0-8377-0344-1) Rothman.

Desegregation from Brown to Alexander: An Exploration of Supreme Court Strategies. Stephen L. Wasby et al. LC 76-30792. 512p. 1977. 19.85 (0-8093-0805-3) S Ill U Pr.

Desegregation in Higher Education. Ed. by Samuel L. Myers, Sr. LC 88-39407. (Illus.). 98p. (Orig.). (C). 1989. pap. text ed. 13.50 (0-8191-7291-X, NAEOHE) U Pr of Amer.

Desegregation of Public Education. Ed. by Michal R. Belknap. LC 91-3621. (Civil Rights, White House & Justice Dept. Ser.: Vol. 7). 584p. 1991. 138.00 (0-8240-3375-2) Garland.

Desegregation of Public Transportation, Facilities, & Programs. Ed. by Michal R. Belknap. LC 91-3631. (Civil Rights, White House & Justice Dept. Ser.: Vol. 8). 248p. 1991. 77.00 (0-8240-3376-0) Garland.

Desegregation of the Mentally Ill. J. Hoenig & Marian Hamilton. (International Library of Sociology & Social Reconstruction). 1969. text ed. 24.95 (0-8464-0318-8) Beekman Pubs.

Desegregation Works: A Primer for Parents & Teachers. Lillian S. Calhoun. 1968. pap. 0.90 (0-912008-19-9) Equity & Excel.

Desemboque. Frank Graziano. 48p. (Orig.). 1979. pap. 5.00 (0-912449-01-2) Floating Island.

***Desenganos Amorosos.** Maria de Zayas y Sotomayor. Ed. by Agustin Gonzalez de Amezua. 463p. (SPA.). 1968. pap. 100.00 (0-614-00116-1) Elliots Bks.

***Desenganos Amorosos.** Maria de Zayas y Sotomayor. Ed. by Agustin Gonzalez de Amezua. 463p. (SPA.). 1968. pap. 100.00 (0-614-00221-4) Elliots Bks.

Desenmascarado. Rita Cabezas. 172p. (Orig.). 1988. pap. 3.99 (0-945792-04-2, 490239) Editorial Unilit.

Desenmascaramiento. Jan Van Rijckenborgh. (SPA.). 1987. pap. 6.00 (84-398-2798-9) Rosycross Pr.

Deseret Book History. Eleanor Knowles. LC 91-76472. vi, 170p. 1991. 14.95 (0-685-74749-2) Deseret Bk.

Deseret News-Church News Almanac 1989. Ed. by Dell Van Orden. 1988. 6.00 (0-318-32855-0) Deseret News.

Desert. Robert Burton. (Animal Homes Ser.). (Illus.). 24p. (J). (gr. k-4). 1991. lib. bdg. 10.40 (1-878137-17-4) Newington.

Desert. Ron Hirschi. (Discover My World Ser.: Bk. 3). (J). 1992. mass mkt. 4.99 (0-553-35497-3, Little Rooster) Bantam.

Desert. J. M. Le Clezio. (FRE.). 1985. pap. 13.95 (0-7859-0646-0, F113320) Fr & Eur.

Desert. J. M. Le Clezio. (Folio Ser.: No. 1670). (FRE.). pap. 10.95 (2-07-037670-2) Schoenhof.

Desert. Miranda MacQuitty. LC 93-21068. (Eyewitness Bks.). (J). 1994. 16.00 (0-679-86003-7); lib. bdg. 16.99 (0-679-96003-1) Knopf Bks Yng Read.

Desert. April P. Sayre. (Exploring Earth's Biomes Ser.). (Illus.). 64p. (J). (gr. 5-8). 1994. lib. bdg. 15.98 (0-8050-2825-0) TFC Bks NY.

Desert. George Sher. (Studies in Moral, Political, & Legal Philosophy). 256p. (C). 1989. text ed. 45.00 (0-691-07745-2); pap. text ed. 14.95 (0-691-02316-6) Princeton U Pr.

Desert. Pierre Loti. Tr. by Jay P. Minn. LC 93-10090. 164p. (ENG.). 1993. reprint ed. pap. 14.95 (0-87480-427-2) U of Utah Pr.

Desert: A Nature Panorama. Susan Deming. (Nature Panorama Ser.). (Illus.). 7p. (J). (ps-3). 1991. bds. 5.95 (0-8118-0291-4) Chronicle Bks.

***Desert: Hot & Dry but It's Home to Big Cats, Camels, Coyotes & More.** Joni P. Hunt. Ed. by Vicki Leon. LC 94-30870. (Close up: A Focus on Nature Ser.). (Illus.). 40p. (YA). (gr. 5 up). 1994. lib. bdg. 14.95 (0-382-24861-9); pap. 7.95 (0-382-24862-7) Silver Burdett Pr.

Desert a City: An Introduction to the Study of Egyptian & Palestinian Monasticism under the Christian Empire. Derwas J. Chitty. 222p. 1977. pap. 12.95 (0-913836-45-1) St Vladimirs.

Desert Airforce. Ian Black. (Osprey Colour Library). (Illus.). 128p. 1992. pap. 15.95 (1-85532-192-0, Pub. by Osprey Pubng Ltd UK) Motorbooks Intl.

Desert Airliners. Graham Robson. LC 93-49485. (Illus.). 112p. 1994. pap. 19.95 (0-87938-904-4) Motorbooks Intl.

Desert Alphabet Book. Jerry Pallotta. LC 93-42651. (Illus.). 32p. (Orig.). (J). (ps-4). 1994. 14.95 (0-88106-473-4); lib. bdg. 15.88 (0-88106-687-7); pap. 6.95 (0-88106-472-6) Charlesbridge Pub.

Desert & Mountain Plants of the Southwest. Dorothy V. Leake et al. LC 92-50716. (Illus.). 1993. pap. 18.95 (0-8061-2489-X) U of Okla Pr.

Desert & River in Nubia: Geomorphology & Prehistoric Environments at the Aswan Reservoir. Karl W. Butzer & Carl L. Hansen. LC 67-20761. (Illus.). 1968. 45.00 (0-299-04770-9) U of Wis Pr.

Desert & River in Nubia: Geomorphology & Prehistoric Environments at the Aswan Reservoir, Set. Karl W. Butzer & Carl L. Hansen. LC 67-20761. (Illus.). 1968. 20.00 (0-299-97001-9) U of Wis Pr.

Desert & the City. Frere Ivan. 126p. 1993. 29.00 (0-85439-447-8, Pub. by St Paul Pubns UK) St Mut.

Desert & the City: An Interpretation of the History of Christian Spirituality. Thomas M. Gannon & George W. Traub. 338p. (C). 1984. 10.35 (0-8294-0452-X) Loyola Univ Pr.

Desert & the Dream. Glyn Williams. xiii, 230p. 1975. 17.50 (0-7083-0579-2, Pub. by U of Wales UK) Bks Intl VA.

***Desert & the Market Place.** Ursula Fleming. 1995. pap. 12.95 (0-85244-289-0, Pub. by Gracewing UK) Morehouse Pub.

An Asterisk (*) at the beginning of an entry indicates that the title is appearing in BIP for the first time.

An Asterisk (*) at the beginning of an entry indicates that the title is appearing in BIP for the first time.

D

Desert Seasons. Illus. by Jan Mike & Samuel Mike. 32p. (J). (gr. k-8). 1995. 7.95 (*0-918080-49-5*, 20975) Treas Chest Bks.
Desert Shadows: A True Story of the Charles Manson Family in Death Valley. Bob Murphy. LC 93-93688. (Illus.). 144p. 1993. pap. 9.95 (*0-930704-29-0*) Sagebrush Pr.
Desert Shall Blossom: A Comprehensive Guide to Vegetable Gardening in the Mountain West. David E. Whiting. (Illus.). 112p. (Orig.). 1991. pap. 13.98 (*0-88290-418-3*) Horizon Utah.
Desert Shield. Frank Chadwick. 1991. pap. 10.00 (*1-55878-093-9*) Game Designers.
Desert Shield to Desert Storm: The Second Gulf War. Dilip Hiro. (Illus.). 592p. 1992. 59.95 (*0-415-90656-3*, A9502, Routledge NY); pap. 18.95 (*0-415-90657-1*, A9506, Routledge NY) Routledge.
Desert Sinner. Ralph McInerny. (WWL Mystery Ser.). 1994. mass mkt. 3.99 (*0-373-26158-6*, 1-26158-5) Harlequin Bks.
Desert Sinner. Ralph McInerny. (Father Dowling Mystery Ser.). 192p. 1992. 16.95 (*0-312-08177-4*) St Martin.
Desert Sinner. large type ed. Ralph McInerny. (Popular Ser.). 320p. 1993. reprint ed. pap. 17.95 (*1-56054-631-X*) Thorndike Pr.
Desert Skin: Photographs by Thomas Miller. Ed. by Edward Abbey. (Illus.). 101p. (Orig.). 1994. pap. 24.95 (*0-87480-460-4*) U of Utah Pr.
Desert Slaughter: The Imperialist War Against Iraq. Ed. by Martin McLaughlin. (Illus.). 508p. (Orig.). (C). 1991. pap. 18.95 (*0-929087-54-2*) Labor Pubns Inc.
Desert Slave. Miranda North. 1989. pap. 3.75 (*0-8217-2664-1*) Zebra.
Desert Smells Like Rain: A Naturalist in Papago Indian Country. Gary P. Nabhan. LC 81-81505. 192p. 1987. pap. 10.95 (*0-86547-050-2*, North Pt Pr) FS&G.
Desert Soil Fauna. John A. Wallwork. LC 81-12030. 304p. 1982. text ed. 65.00 (*0-275-90921-2*, C0921, Praeger Pubs) Greenwood.
Desert Soldiers. Julia Stein. 64p. (Orig.). 1992. pap. text ed. 6.95 (*1-879395-03-7*) CA Classics Bks.
Desert Solitaire. Edward Abbey. LC 87-36546. (Illus.). 255p. 1988. reprint ed. 35.00 (*0-8165-1057-1*) U of Ariz Pr.
Desert Solitaire: A Season in the Wilderness. Edward Abbey. (Ecological Main Event Ser.). 320p. 1985. mass mkt. 5.95 (*0-345-32649-0*) Ballantine.
Desert Solitaire: A Season in the Wilderness. Edward Abbey. 1990. pap. 9.95 (*0-671-69588-6*, Touchstone Bks) S&S Trade.
Desert Song. O'Banyon. 1994. pap. 9.99 (*0-06-108045-4*, PL) HarpC.
*__Desert Song.__ Constance Obanyon. 1994. pap. 5.99 (*0-06-108290-2*, Harp PBks) HarpC.
Desert Song. large type ed. Ann Boyle. (General Ser.). 352p. 1993. 21.95 (*0-7089-2836-6*) Ulverscroft.
Desert Stake-Out. large type ed. Harry Whittington. (Linford Western Library). 1990. pap. 12.95 (*0-7089-6947-X*, Trailtree Bookshop) Ulverscroft.
Desert Stake-Out. Harry Whittington. 160p. 1989. reprint ed. pap. 2.75 (*0-380-70730-6*) Avon.
Desert Star. Tom Willard. (Strike Fighters Ser.: No. 06). 1991. mass mkt. 3.95 (*0-06-100193-7*, Harp PBks) HarpC.
Desert Storm. Military History Magazine Staff. 176p. 1991. 34.95 (*0-943231-46-9*) Empire Pr.
Desert Storm. large type ed. Stella Whitelaw. (Linford Romance Library). 1990. pap. 12.95 (*0-7089-6834-1*, Trailtree Bookshop) Ulverscroft.
Desert Storm: The Gulf War & What We Learned. Michael J. Mazarr et al. LC 92-29687. 207p. (C). 1992. text ed. 37.00 (*0-8133-1598-0*) Westview.
Desert Storm: The War in the Persian Gulf. Time Magazine Editors. 1991. 19.95 (*0-316-85100-0*) Little.
Desert Storm - Desert Sand. Louise O. Neaderland. (Illus.). 1992. 12.00 (*0-942561-17-1*) Bone Hollow.
Desert Storm Air Power. Ray Bradbrook. (Desert Storm Ser.). (Illus.). 64p. pap. 11.95 (*1-85532-179-3*, 9541, Pub. by Osprey UK) Stackpole.
Desert Storm Air War. Robert F. Dorr. (Power Pro Ser.). (Illus.). 128p. 1991. pap. 9.98 (*0-87938-560-X*) Motorbooks Intl.
Desert Storm & the Mass Media. Bradley S. Greenberg & Walter Gantz. Ed. by Brenda Dervin. LC 92-35365. (Communication Series: Communication Alternatives). 464p. (C). 1993. text ed. 72.50 (*1-881303-34-9*); pap. text ed. 28.50 (*1-881303-35-7*) Hampton Pr NJ.
Desert Storm Ground War. Hans Halberstadt. (Illus.). 128p. 1991. pap. 9.98 (*0-87938-561-8*) Motorbooks Intl.
Desert Storm Journal: A Nurse's Story. Elizabeth Kassner. (Illus.). 96p. 1993. pap. 12.95 (*1-882063-19-8*) Cottage Pr MA.
Desert Storm Land Power. Tim Ripley. (Desert Storm Ser.). (Illus.). 64p. pap. 11.95 (*1-85532-177-7*, 9542, Pub. by Osprey UK) Stackpole.
Desert Storm Sea Power. Peter Gilchrist. (Desert Storm Ser.). (Illus.). 64p. pap. 11.95 (*1-85532-178-5*, 9540, Pub. by Osprey UK) Stackpole.
Desert Storm Sea War. Arnold Meisner. (Illus.). 128p. 1991. pap. 9.98 (*0-87938-562-6*) Motorbooks Intl.
Desert Survival Handbook. Charles A. Lehman. Ed. by Diane M. Fessler. (Illus.). 96p. 1993. pap. 5.00 (*0-935810-34-X*) Primer Pubs.
Desert Survival Manual. Michael Johansen. 104p. 1993. pap. 4.95 (*0-915030-00-4*) Tecolote Pr.
Desert Tiger: Captain James Paddy Graydon & the Civil War in the Far Southwest. Jerry D. Thompson. (Southwestern Studies: No. 97). (Illus.). 86p. (Orig.). 1992. pap. 12.50 (*0-87404-192-9*) Tex Western.
Desert Time. Diana Kappel-Smith. (Illus.). 262p. 1994. reprint ed. pap. 15.95 (*0-8165-1432-1*) U of Ariz Pr.
Desert Tortoise Council Symposium, 1976. Ed. by J. A. Amant. 15.00 (*0-318-23139-5*) Desert Tortoise Coun.
Desert Tortoise Council Symposium, 1977. Ed. by K. A. Hashagen. 15.00 (*0-318-23138-7*) Desert Tortoise Coun.
Desert Tortoise Council Symposium, 1978: Proceedings. 1978. 15.00 (*0-317-04933-X*) Desert Tortoise Coun.
Desert Tortoise Council Symposium, 1979: Proceedings. Ed. by K. A. Hashagen. 15.00 (*0-318-23137-9*) Desert Tortoise Coun.
Desert Tortoise Council Symposium, 1980: Proceedings. 1980. 15.00 (*0-317-04934-8*) Desert Tortoise Coun.
Desert Tortoise Council Symposium, 1980: Proceedings. Ed. by K. A. Hashagen. (Illus.). 179p. 1981. 15.00 (*0-318-13956-1*) Desert Tortoise Coun.
Desert Tortoise Council Symposium, 1981: Proceedings. 1981. 15.00 (*0-317-05501-1*) Desert Tortoise Coun.
Desert Tortoise Council Symposium, 1982: Proceedings. 1982. 15.00 (*0-317-05502-X*) Desert Tortoise Coun.
Desert Tortoise Council Symposium, 1983: Proceedings. 1983. 15.00 (*0-317-05503-8*) Desert Tortoise Coun.
Desert Tortoise Council Symposium, 1983: Proceedings. Mary Trather. 200p. 1986. 15.00 (*0-318-21751-1*) Desert Tortoise Coun.
Desert Tortoise Council Symposium, 1984: Proceedings. 1984. 15.00 (*0-317-04938-0*) Desert Tortoise Coun.
Desert Tortoise Council Symposium, 1984: Proceedings. Ed. by Mary Trotter. 1987. 15.00 (*0-318-23136-0*) Desert Tortoise Coun.
Desert Tortoise Council Symposium, 1985: Proceedings. 1985. 15.00 (*0-317-04939-9*) Desert Tortoise Coun.
Desert Tortoise Council Symposium, 1985: Proceedings. Ed. by Mary Trotter. 1989. 15.00 (*0-318-41055-9*) Desert Tortoise Coun.
Desert Tortoise Council Symposium, 1986: Proceedings. 1986. 15.00 (*0-317-04940-2*) Desert Tortoise Coun.
Desert Tortoise Council Symposium, 1987: Proceedings. 1993. write for info. (*0-317-04941-0*) Desert Tortoise Coun.
Desert Tortoise Council Symposium, 1988: Proceedings. 1993. write for info. (*0-317-04942-9*) Desert Tortoise Coun.
Desert Tortoise Council Symposium, 1989: Proceedings. 1993. write for info. (*0-317-04943-7*) Desert Tortoise Coun.
Desert Tortoise Council Symposium, 1990: Proceedings. 1993. write for info. (*0-317-04944-5*) Desert Tortoise Coun.
Desert Tortoise Council Symposium, 1991: Proceedings. 1993. write for info. (*0-317-04945-3*) Desert Tortoise Coun.
Desert Tortoise Council Symposium, 1992: Proceedings. 1992. 20.00 (*0-317-04946-1*) Desert Tortoise Coun.
Desert Tortoise Council Symposium,1981: Proceedings. Ed. by K. A. Hashagen. 214p. 1983. 45.00 (*0-318-16924-X*) Desert Tortoise Coun.
Desert Tracings: Six Classic Arabian Odes by 'Algama, Shanfara, Labid, 'Antara, Al-A'sha, & Dhu Al-Rumma. Tr. by Michael Sells. LC 88-28084. (Wesleyan Poetry in Translation Ser.). 87p. 1989. 12.95 (*0-8195-2157-4*, Wesleyan Univ Pr) U Pr of New Eng.
Desert Trackers: Men of the Border Patrol. Peter R. Odens. (Illus.). 70p. (Orig.). 1972. reprint ed. per., pap. 5.00 (*0-9609484-9-X*) P R Odens.
Desert Trail. Dane Coolidge. 1975. lib. bdg. 13.85 (*0-89966-059-2*) Buccaneer Bks.
Desert Trails. large type ed. John Blaze. (Linford Western Library). 288p. 1994. pap. 14.95 (*0-7089-7497-X*, Linford) Ulverscroft.
Desert Trails of Atacama. Isaiah Bowman. LC 76-111776. (BCL Ser. I). reprint ed. 20.00 (*0-404-00964-6*) AMS Pr.
Desert Treasures. Junior League of Phoenix Staff. (Illus.). 232p. 1992. 18.95 (*0-9613174-1-8*) Jr Leag Phoenix.
Desert Tree Finder: A Manual for Identifying Desert Trees of Ariz., Calif., N. Mex. May T. Watts & Tom Watts. 62p. 1974. pap. 2.50 (*0-912550-07-4*) Nature Study.
Desert Vendetta. Clarence Dawson. LC 93-41686. 260p. (Orig.). 1993. pap. 12.95 (*0-86534-205-9*) Sunstone Pr.
Desert Victory: The War for Kuwait. Norman Friedman. LC 92-21088. (Illus.). 435p. 1991. 35.00 (*1-55750-254-4*); pap. 21.95 (*1-55750-255-2*) Naval Inst Pr.
Desert Visions. Antonio J. Olivera. 1993. 10.95 (*0-533-10594-3*) Vantage.
Desert Voices. Byrd Baylor. LC 80-17061. (Illus.). 32p. (J). (ps-3). 1981. text ed. 14.95 (*0-684-16712-3*, C Scribner Sons Young) S&S Childrens.
Desert Voices. William Labarge. 1991. mass mkt. 4.95 (*0-06-100354-9*, Harp PBks) HarpC.
Desert Voices. Byrd Baylor. LC 92-24475. (Illus.). 32p. (J). (gr. 1-5). 1993. reprint ed. pap. 3.95 (*0-689-71691-5*, Aladdin Paperbacks) S&S Childrens.
Desert Voices. E. I. Edwards. LC 73-3752. (Illus.). 215p. 1973. reprint ed. text ed. 67.50 (*0-8371-6848-1*, EDDV, Greenwood Pr) Greenwood.
Desert Warfare. Wallace B. Black & Jean F. Blashfield. LC 91-27186. (World War II 50th Anniversary Ser.). (Illus.). 48p. (J). (gr. 5-6). 1992. text ed. 12.95 (*0-89686-561-4*, Crstwood Hse) Silver Burdett Pr.
Desert Warpaint. Peter R. March. (Osprey Colour Library). (Illus.). 128p. 1992. pap. 15.95 (*1-85532-193-9*, Pub. by Osprey Pubng Ltd UK) Motorbooks Intl.
*__Desert Warrior.__ Khaled bin Sultan & Patrick Seale. 1995. 35.00 (*0-06-017298-3*) HarpC.
*__Desert Water.__ Gary Parker. 312p. 1995. pap. 9.99 (*1-56476-450-8*, 6-3450, Victor Books) SP Pubns.
Desert Wife. Hilda Faunce. LC 80-22163. (Illus.). xiv, 305p. 1981. reprint ed. pap. 9.95 (*0-8032-6853-X*) U of Nebr Pr.
Desert Wild Flowers. rev. ed. Edmund C. Jaeger. LC 41-22485. (Illus.). xxx, 322p. 1941. 35.00 (*0-8047-0364-7*); pap. 12.95 (*0-8047-0365-5*) Stanford U Pr.
Desert Wildflowers. Mabel Crittenden. 288p. 1994. pap. 16.95 (*0-88839-282-6*) Hancock House.
Desert Wildlife. Edmund C. Jaeger. (Illus.). xii, 308p. 1961. 35.00 (*0-8047-0123-7*); pap. 12.95 (*0-8047-0124-5*) Stanford U Pr.
Desert Wildlife. Jinny Johnson. (Up-Close Ser.). (Illus.). 24p. (J). (gr. 4-7). 1993. 9.95 (*0-89577-536-0*) RD Assn.
Desert Wind. Duncan Long. 1991. mass mkt. 3.95 (*0-06-100139-2*, Harp PBks) HarpC.
Desert Wisdom. K. Douglas. Date not set. pap. 12.00 (*0-06-061997-X*, PL) HarpC.
Desert Wisdom. K. Douglas. 1995. 20.00 (*0-06-061996-1*, HarpT) HarpC.
Desert Wood: An Anthology of Nevada Poets. Ed. by Shaun T. Griffin. LC 91-3952. (Western Literature Ser.). 256p. 1991. 29.95 (*0-87417-175-X*); pap. 16.95 (*0-87417-181-4*) U of Nev Pr.
Desert Year. Carol Lerner. LC 90-44643. (Illus.). 48p. (J). 1991. 13.95 (*0-688-09382-5*); lib. bdg. 13.88 (*0-688-09383-3*) Morrow Jr Bks.
Desert Year. Joseph W. Krutch. LC 84-24127. 280p. 1985. reprint ed. pap. 13.95 (*0-8165-0923-9*) U of Ariz Pr.
Desert Years: Undreaming the American Dream. Cynthia Rich. LC 89-35667. 120p. (Orig.). 1989. pap. 7.95 (*0-933216-67-X*) Spinsters Ink.
Deserted: The Story of the Children Abandoned in Soviet Russia. Vladimir M. Zenzinov. Tr. by Agnes Platt. LC 74-10083. 216p. 1975. reprint ed. 21.45 (*0-88355-190-X*) Hyperion Conn.
Deserted by God? Sinclair B. Ferguson. LC 93-16299. 192p. 1993. 14.99 (*0-8010-3563-5*) Baker Bk.
Deserted Cities - Heart. Lewis Shiner. 1988. pap. 17.95 (*0-385-24637-4*, Spectra) Bantam.
Deserted Greenhouse. John Fandel. pap. 8.50 (*0-87957-004-0*) Roth Pub.
Deserted Library Mystery. Created by Gertrude C. Warner. (Boxcar Children Mysteries Ser.: No. 21). (Illus.). (J). (gr. 2-7). 1991. 10.95 (*0-8075-1561-2*); pap. 3.50 (*0-8075-1560-4*) A Whitman.
Deserted Medieval Villages. Maurice Beresford & John G. Hurst. (Illus.). 360p. (C). 1990. text ed. 48.00 (*0-86299-655-4*) A Sutton Pub.
Deserted Village: Diary of Rev. James Newton of Nuneham Courtenay, 1736-86. James Newton. Ed. by Gavin Hannah. (Illus.). 192p. (C). 1992. text ed. 30.00 (*0-7509-0205-1*) A Sutton Pub.
Deserter. Anton Fuchs. Tr. by Todd C. Hanlin. (Studies in Austrian Literature, Culture, & Thought. Translation Ser.). 270p. 1991. pap. 22.00 (*0-929497-19-8*) Ariadne CA.
Deserter. Robert Koch. 256p. (Orig.). 1990. pap. 8.95 (*0-8361-3519-9*) Herald Pr.
Deserter & Other Stories. Harold Frederic. (Collected Works of Harold Frederic). 1988. reprint ed. lib. bdg. 79.00 (*0-7812-1194-8*) Rprt Serv.
Deserter & Other Stories: A Book of Two Wars. Harold Frederic. LC 79-110190. (Short Story Index Reprint Ser.). 1977. 25.95 (*0-8369-3341-9*) Ayer.
Deserter & Other Stories see Collected Works of Harold Frederic
Deserter & Other Stories, a Book of Two Wars. Harold Frederic. LC 77-99245. (BCL Ser.: I). reprint ed. 29.50 (*0-404-02572-2*) AMS Pr.
Deserter-Immigrants of the American Revolution from Hessen-Hanau see Mercenaries from Hessen-Hanau Who Remained in Canada & the United States after the American Revolution
Deserter Troop. Jack Cummings. 192p. 1991. 18.95 (*0-8027-4121-5*) Walker & Co.
Deserter Troop. Jack Cummings. 256p. 1993. pap. 3.50 (*1-55817-715-9*, Pinnacle NY) Windsor NY.
*__Deserter Troop.__ braille ed. Jack Cummings. 297p. 1994. text ed. 23.76 (*1-56956-450-7*, BR9333) W A T Braille.
Deserter Troop. large type ed. Jack Cummings. 295p. 1992. reprint ed. lib. bdg. 17.95 (*1-56054-402-3*) Thorndike Pr.
Deserters & Disbanded Soldiers from British, German, & Loyalist Military Units in the South, 1782. Clifford N. Smith. (British-American Genealogical Research Monograph Ser.: No. 10). vi, 26p. (Orig.). 1991. pap. 15.00 (*0-915162-36-9*) Westland Pubns.
Deserteur. Jean Giono. (FRE.). 23.95 (*0-7859-0097-7*, M3496) Fr & Eur.
Deserteur et Autres Recit. Jean Giono. 278p. (FRE.). 1978. pap. 10.95 (*0-7859-2402-7*, 2070370127) Fr & Eur.
Deserteur et Autres Recits. Jean Giono. (Folio Ser.: No. 1012). (FRE.). pap. 8.95 (*2-07-037012-7*) Schoenhof.
Desertification: Associated Case Studies Prepared for the United Nations Conference on Desertification. Margaret R. Biswas & Asit K. Biswas. LC 80-40024. (Environmental Sciences & Applications Ser.: Vol. 12). (Illus.). 532p. 1980. 222.00 (*0-08-023581-6*, Pub. by Pergamon Repr UK) Franklin.
*__Desertification: Exploding the Myth.__ David S. G. Thomas & Nicholas J. Middleton. text ed. 44.95 (*0-470-23364-8*) Wiley.
*__Desertification: Exploding the Myth.__ David S.G. Thomas & Nicholas J. Middleton. 1994. text ed. 54.95 (*0-471-94815-2*) Wiley.
Desertification: Monitoring & Control. A. K. Tewari. 284p. (C). 1988. 135.00 (*81-85046-77-8*, Scientific) St Mut.
Desertification: Natural Background & Human Mismanagement. M. Mainguet. (Physical Environment Ser.: Vol. 9). (Illus.). xvi, 306p. 1991. 159.00 (*0-387-52519-X*) Spr-Verlag.
Desertification: Natural Background & Human Mismanagement. Monique Mainguet. LC 94-14998. 1994. 69.00 (*0-387-57746-7*) Spr-Verlag.
Desertification & Development: Dryland Ecology in Social Perspective. B. Spooner & H. S. Mann. 1983. text ed. 157.00 (*0-12-658050-2*) Acad Pr.
Desertification & Land Degradation in the European Mediterranean. F. Perez-Trejo. 69p. 1994. pap. 14.00 (*92-826-7059-7*, CG-NA-14850-ENC, Pub. by Europ Com) UNIPUB.
Desertification, Debt & Structural Adjustment in Sub-Saharan Africa. (Wilton Park Paper Ser.: No. 18). 25p. 1990. pap. 5.00 (*0-11-701229-7*, HM2297) UNIPUB.
Desertification in Europe. Ed. by R. Fantechi & N. S. Margaris. 1986. lib. bdg. 88.00 (*90-277-2230-7*) Kluwer Ac.
Desertification in the Sahelian & Sudanian Zones of West Africa. Jean Gorse & David Steeds. (Technical Paper Ser.: No. 61). 1987. 7.95 (*0-8213-0897-1*, BK0897) World Bank.
Desertification of Arid Lands. H. E. Dregne. LC 83-83969. (Advances in Desert & Arid Land Technology & Development Ser.: Vol. 3). (Illus.). 228p. 1983. text ed. 70.00 (*3-7186-0168-0*) Gordon & Breach.
Desertification of World & Their Control. T. S. Chouhan. (C). 1993. text ed. 225.00 (*81-7233-043-X*, Pub. by Scientific Pubs II) St Mut.
Desertified Grasslands: Their Biology & Management. Ed. by G. P. Chapman. (Linnean Society of London Symposium Ser.: No. 13). (Illus.). 376p. 1992. text ed. 99.50 (*0-12-168570-5*) Acad Pr.
Desertion During the Civil War. Ella Lonn. (History - United States Ser.). 251p. 1992. reprint ed. lib. bdg. 79.00 (*0-7812-6180-5*) Rprt Serv.
Desertion of Alabama Troops from the Confederate Army. Bessie Martin. LC 32-34110. (Columbia University. Studies in the Social Sciences: No. 378). reprint ed. 21.50 (*0-404-51378-6*) AMS Pr.
Deserts. (Discover Ser.). (Illus.). 48p. (J). 1993. 9.98 (*1-56173-424-1*) Pubns Intl Ltd.
Deserts. Sheri Amsel. LC 92-8789. (Habitats of the World Ser.). (Illus.). 32p. (YA). 1992. 19.97 (*0-8114-6300-1*) Raintree Steck-V.
Deserts. Chris Arvetis & Carole Palmer. LC 93-502. (Where Are We? Ser.). (Illus.). (J). 1993. 3.95 (*0-528-83574-2*) Rand McNally.
Deserts. Donna Bailey. LC 89-26120. (Facts About Ser.). (Illus.). 48p. (J). (gr. 2-6). 1990. lib. bdg. 21.36 (*0-8114-2511-8*) Raintree Steck-V.
Deserts. Norman S. Barrett. (Picture Library). (Illus.). (J). (ps-3). 1990. lib. bdg. 12.53 (*0-531-10832-5*) Watts.
Deserts. Keith Brandt. LC 84-8623. (Illus.). 32p. (J). (gr. 3-6). 1985. lib. bdg. 9.49 (*0-8167-0262-4*); pap. text ed. 2.95 (*0-8167-0263-2*) Troll Assocs.
Deserts. Jim Flegg. LC 92-46603. (Illus.). 160p. 1993. 29.95 (*0-8160-2902-4*) Facts on File.
Deserts. Michael George. (Images Ser.). (J). (gr. 5 up). 1992. lib. bdg. 16.95 (*0-88682-434-6*) Creative Ed.
Deserts. Michael George. 40p. (J). (gr. 4-7). 1993. 15.95 (*1-56846-054-6*) Creative Ed.
Deserts. Mel Higginson. LC 94-9403. (This Earth Is Ours Ser.). (J). 1994. write for info. (*0-86593-380-4*) Rourke Corp.
Deserts. Jill Hughes. (Finding Out about Ser.). (Illus.). 32p. (J). (gr. 4-6). 1991. 13.95 (*0-237-60175-3*, Pub. by Evans Bros Ltd UK) Trafalgar.
Deserts. Keith Lye. (Our World Ser.). (Illus.). 48p. (J). (gr. 5-8). 1987. lib. bdg. 12.95 (*0-382-09501-4*) Silver Burdett Pr.
Deserts. Tom Mariner. LC 89-17278. (Earth in Action Ser.). (Illus.). 32p. (J). (gr. 3-8). 1990. lib. bdg. 9.95 (*1-85435-192-3*) Marshall Cavendish.
Deserts. James McMahon. Ed. by Charles Elliott. LC 84-48674. (Audubon Society Nature Guides Ser.). (Illus.). 638p. 1985. pap. 19.00 (*0-394-73139-5*) Knopf.
*__Deserts.__ Neil Morris. (Wonders of Our World Ser.). (Illus.). 50p. (J). (gr. 1-4). 1995. lib. bdg. 17.95 (*0-86505-827-X*) Crabtree Pub Co.
*__Deserts.__ Neil Morris. (Wonders of Our World Ser.). (Illus.). 50p. (J). (gr. 1-4). 1995. pap. 6.95 (*0-86505-839-3*) Crabtree Pub Co.
Deserts. Joy Palmer. LC 92-12406. (First Starts Ser.). (Illus.). 32p. (J). (gr. 2-3). 1992. lib. bdg. 19.97 (*0-8114-3402-8*) Raintree Steck-V.
Deserts. Joy Palmer. (First Starts Ser.). (J). (ps-3). 1993. pap. 4.95 (*0-8114-4912-2*) Raintree Steck-V.
Deserts. Kate Petty. (Around & About Ser.). (Illus.). 32p. (J). (gr. 2-4). 1993. pap. 5.95 (*0-8120-1762-5*) Barron.
Deserts. Elsa Posell. LC 81-15548. (New True Bks.). (Illus.). 48p. (J). (gr. k-4). 1982. lib. bdg. 12.90 (*0-516-01613-X*); pap. 4.95 (*0-516-41613-8*) Childrens.
Deserts. Seymour Simon. LC 89-39738. (Illus.). 32p. (J). (gr. k up). 1990. 13.95 (*0-688-07415-4*); lib. bdg. 13.88 (*0-688-07416-2*) Morrow Jr Bks.
Deserts. Philip Steele. LC 90-20759. (Pocket Facts Ser.). (Illus.). 32p. (J). (gr. 5-6). 1991. text ed. 11.95 (*0-89686-588-6*, Crstwood Hse) Silver Burdett Pr.
Deserts. Richard Stephen. LC 89-20300. (Our Planet Ser.). (Illus.). 32p. (J). (gr. 4-6). 1990. lib. bdg. 11.59 (*0-8167-1969-1*); pap. text ed. 3.95 (*0-8167-1970-5*) Troll Assocs.
Deserts. L. Stone. (Ecozones Ser.). (Illus.). 48p. (J). (gr. 4-8). 1989. 11.95 (*0-685-67722-2*); lib. bdg. 15.94 (*0-86592-438-4*) Rourke Corp.
Deserts. Clint Twist. LC 91-22471. (Ecology Watch Ser.). (Illus.). 48p. (J). (gr. 4-6). 1991. text ed. 13.95 (*0-87518-490-1*, Dillon Silver Burdett) Silver Burdett Pr.
Deserts. Wilkes. (Explainers Ser.). (J). (gr. 4-6). 1980. lib. bdg. 11.96 (*0-88110-694-1*, Usborne); pap. 4.95 (*0-7460-0757-4*, Usborne) EDC.
Deserts. Lawrence Williams. LC 89-17340. (Last Frontiers Ser.). (Illus.). 48p. (J). (gr. 4-8). 1990. lib. bdg. 9.95 (*1-85435-169-9*) Marshall Cavendish.
Deserts. Jenny Wood. LC 91-15814. (Wonderworks of Nature Ser.). (Illus.). 32p. (J). (gr. 3-4). 1991. lib. bdg. 17.27 (*0-8368-0631-X*) Gareth Stevens Inc.

An Asterisk (*) at the beginning of an entry indicates that the title is appearing in BIP for the first time.

An Asterisk (*) at the beginning of an entry indicates that the title is appearing in BIP for the first time.

D

Design & Construction of Transportation Facilities: Research Problem Statements. (Transportation Research Circular Ser.: No. 340). 115p. 1988. 10.00 (*0-685-38562-0*) Transport Res Bd.
Design & Construction of Urban Stormwater Management Systems. (ASCE Manual & Report on Engineering Practice Ser.: No. 77). 700p. 1992. text ed. 60.00 (*0-87262-855-8*) Am Soc Civil Eng.
Design & Construction of Urban Stormwater Management Systems. Comp. by Urban Water Resources Research Council Staff. LC 92-36519. 724p. 1993. text ed. 60.00 (*1-881369-21-8*) Water Environ.
Design & Construction of Water Wells. National Water Well Association Staff. (Illus.). 256p. 1988. text ed. 54.95 (*0-442-26907-2*) Van Nos Reinhold.
Design & Construction of Wood Framed Buildings. Morton Newman. 1994. text ed. 49.00 (*0-07-046363-8*) McGraw.
Design & Construction Specification for Marine Loading Arms. OCIMF Staff. 1986. 310.00 (*0-317-61172-0*, Pub. by Witherby & Co UK) St Mut.
Design & Construction Specification for Marine Loading Arms. OCIMF Staff. (C). 1987. 315.00 (*0-685-36231-0*, Pub. by Witherby & Co UK) St Mut.
Design & Construction Specification for Marine Loading Arms. OCIMF Staff. 1993. 120.00 (*1-85609-071-X*, Pub. by Witherby & Co UK) St Mut.
Design & Construction Techniques for the Residential Builder. Frederick U. Hop. (Illus.). 480p. (C). 1988. text ed. 35.95 (*0-13-200064-4*) P-H.
Design & Control of Concrete Mixtures. 13th rev. ed. Portland Cement Association Staff. 212p. (Orig.). (C). 1992. reprint ed. pap. text ed. 33.00 (*0-89312-087-1*, EB001T) Portland Cement.
***Design & Corporate Success.** Clive Rassam. (Design Council - Strategies for Product Development Ser.: No. 3). 176p. 1995. 59.95 (*0-566-07534-2*, Pub. by Gower UK) Ashgate Pub Co.
Design & Creation of Jewelry. 3rd ed. Robert Von Neumann. LC 72-1500. 348p. 1982. pap. 19.95 (*0-8019-7067-9*) Chilton.
Design & Decision Support Systems in Architecture. Ed. by Harry Timmermans. LC 93-24413. (DIVS-Diverse Ser.). 264p. (C). 1993. lib. bdg. 90.00 (*0-7923-2444-7*) Kluwer Ac.
Design & Destiny: The Making of the Tucker Automobile. Philip S. Egan. LC 89-90666. (Illus.). 143p. (Orig.). 1989. pap. 12.95 (*0-924321-00-8*, 8-OM-0001) Auto Quarterly.
Design & Development of Expert Systems & Neural Networks. Larry Medsker & Jay Liebowitz. LC 93-3185. 273p. (C). 1994. text ed. write for info. (*0-02-380131-X*) Macmillan.
Design & Development of Knowledge-Based Systems. Giovanni Guida & Carlo Tasso. 360p. 1994. pap. text ed. 54.95 (*0-471-92808-9*) Wiley.
Design & Drawing: An Applied Approach. Richard L. Shadrin. LC 91-73901. (Illus.). 208p. 1992. 27.95 (*0-87192-243-6*) Davis Mass.
Design & Engineering of Production Systems. Farhad Azadivar. 630p. (C). 1984. text ed. 34.95 (*0-910554-43-9*) Engineering.
***Design & Enterprise.** James P. Cramer. 120p. 1994. 19.95 (*1-55835-131-0*) AIA Press.
Design & Evaluation of Computer - Human Interfaces: Issues for Librarians & Information Scientists: Proceedings of the 1988 Clinic on Library Applications of Data Processing. Ed. by Martin Siegel. 1991. text ed. 20.00 (*0-87845-079-3*) U of Ill Lib Info Sci.
Design & Evaluation of Public Library Buildings. Nolan A. Lushington & James M. Kusack. LC 91-8009. (Illus.). 250p. (C). 1991. lib. bdg. 39.50 (*0-208-02300-3*, Lib Prof Pubns) Shoe String.
Design & Evolution of C Plus Plus. Bjarne Stroustrup. 448p. (C). 1994. pap. text ed. 29.25 (*0-201-54330-3*) Addison-Wesley.
Design & Fabrication of Acousto-Optic Devices. Ed. by Goutzoulis et al. (Optical Engineering Ser.: Vol. 41). 512p. 1994. 165.00 (*0-8247-8930-X*) Dekker.
Design & Fabrication of Conventional & Unconventional Superconductors. E. W. Collings. LC 84-5923. (Illus.). 225p. 1984. 32.00 (*0-8155-0989-8*) Noyes.
Design & Figure Carving. Elmer J. Tangerman. (Illus.). 1940. pap. 4.95 (*0-486-21209-2*) Dover.
Design & Figure Carving. Elmer J. Tangerman. (Illus.). 13.25 (*0-8446-3049-7*) Peter Smith.
Design & Form: The Basic Course at the Bauhaus. 2nd rev. ed. Johannes Itten. 1975. pap. 19.95 (*0-442-24039-2*) Van Nos Reinhold.
Design & Implementation of a C-Band Single Antenna Polarimetric Active Radar Calibrator. James J. Ahne et al. (University of Michigan Report Ser.: No. 027587-1-T). 120p. reprint ed. pap. 34.20 (*0-7837-6291-7*, 2046006) Bks Demand.
Design & Implementation of a Flight Simulation System. Hassan B. Diab. (Illus.). 152p. (Orig.). (C). 1993. pap. text ed. 19.95 (*0-8156-6088-X*) Syracuse U Pr.
***Design & Implementation of a L-Band Single Antenna Polarimetric Active Radar Calibrator.** fac. ed. Kamal Sarabandi et al. (University of Michigan Report: No. 027587-2-T). 109p. 1994. pap. 31.10 (*0-7837-7691-8*, 2047447) Bks Demand.
***Design & Implementation of a Log-Structured File System.** Mendel Rosenblum. (International Series in Engineering & Computer Science). 144p. (C). 1994. lib. bdg. 76.00 (*0-7923-9541-7*) Kluwer Ac.
Design & Implementation of Administrative Controls: A Guide for Financial Executives. John P. Fertakis. LC 89-32885. 200p. 1989. text ed. 59.95 (*0-89930-454-0*, FDC, Quorum Bks) Greenwood.
Design & Implementation of Computer-Based Information Systems, No. 1. Ed. by N. Szperski & E. Grochla. (Information Systems Ser.). 383p. 1979. lib. bdg. 103.00 (*90-286-0519-3*) Kluwer Ac.
Design & Implementation of Concurrent Small Talk. Ed. by Yasuhiko Yokote. 172p. (C). 1990. text ed. 36.00 (*981-02-0112-5*) World Scientific Pub.
Design & Implementation of Intelligent Manufacturing Systems. Mohammed Jamshidi. 1995. text ed. 75.00 (*0-13-458217-9*) P-H.
***Design & Implementation of Intelligent Manufacturing Systems: From Expert Systems, Neural Networks, to Fuzzy Logic.** Ed. by Hamid R. Parsaei & Mo Jamshidi. LC 95-4068. (Environmental & Intelligent Manufacturing Systems Ser.). 1995. text ed. 75.00 (*0-13-192030-8*) P-H.
Design & Implementation of Optimization of Software, No. 28. Ed. by H. J. Greenberg. (NATO Advanced Study Institute, Applied Science Ser.). 566p. 1978. lib. bdg. 103.00 (*90-286-0728-5*) Kluwer Ac.
Design & Implementation of Programs in FORTRAN 77. Hans Lee & Paul Munsell. 448p. 1990. pap. text ed. 35.00 (*0-13-199993-1*) P-H.
Design & Implementation of Symbolic Computation Systems: International Symposium DISCO '90 Capri, Italy, April 10-12, 1990 Proceedings. Ed. by A. Miola et al. (Lecture Notes in Computer Science Ser.: Vol. 429). xii, 284p. 1990. pap. 32.70 (*0-387-52531-9*) Spr-Verlag.
Design & Implementation of Symbolic Computation Systems: International Symposium, DISCO '93, Bath, U. K. April 1992 Proceedings. Ed. by John Fitch. LC 93-34000. (Lecture Notes in Computer Science Ser.: Vol. 721). 1993. 39.00 (*0-387-57272-4*) Spr-Verlag.
Design & Implementation of Symbolic Computation Systems: International Symposium, DISCO '93, Gmunden, Austria, September 1993: Proceedings. Ed. by Alfonso Miola. LC 93-21040. (Lecture Notes in Computer Science Ser.: Vol. 722). 1993. 54.00 (*0-387-57235-X*) Spr-Verlag.
Design & Implementation of the 43BSD UNIX Operating System. John S. Quaterman et al. (Illus.). 448p. (C). 1989. text ed. 48.50 (*0-201-06196-1*) Addison-Wesley.
Design & Implementation of 4.3 BSD Unix Operation System Answer Book. Samuel J. Leffler et al. (Illus.). 64p. (C). 1991. pap. text ed. 10.75 (*0-201-54629-9*) Addison-Wesley.
Design & Inference in Finite Population Sampling. A. S. Hedayat & Bikas K. Sinha. (Probability & Mathematical Statistics: Applied Probability & Statistics Section Ser.). 400p. 1991. text ed. 74.95 (*0-471-88073-6*) Wiley.
Design & Innovation: Policy & Management. Ed. by Richard Langdon & Roy G. Rothwell. LC 85-26109. 220p. 1986. text ed. 29.95 (*0-312-19448-X*) St Martin.
***Design & Installation Pt. 1.** William Culross & Son Ltd. Staff. (C). 1991. 90.00x (*0-900323-86-8*, Pub. by W Culross & Son Ltd UK) St Mut.
Design & Installation of Comminution Circuits. Ed. by Andrew L. Mular & Gerald V. Jergensen. LC 82-71992. (Illus.). 1032p. reprint ed. pap. 180.00 (*0-8357-6642-X*, 2035309) Bks Demand.
Design & Installation of Concentration & Dewatering Circuits. Ed. by Andrew L. Mular & Mark A. Anderson. LC 85-63667. (Illus.). 852p. reprint ed. pap. 180.00 (*0-8357-6643-8*, 2035310) Bks Demand.
Design & Installation of on-Line Analyser System. EEMUA Staff. 1988. 125.00x (*0-85931-084-1*, Pub. by EEMUA UK) St Mut.
Design & Instrumentation of In-Situ Experiments in Underground Laboratories for Radioactive Waste Disposal: Proceedings of a Joint CEC-NEA Workshop, Brussels, 15-17 May 1984. B. Come et al. Ed. by P. Johnston & E. Muller. 500p. (C). 1984. text ed. 160.00 (*90-6191-594-5*, Pub. by A A Balkema NE) Ashgate Pub Co.
Design & Intent in African Literature. Ed. by David F. Dorsey et al. LC 82-50450. 137p. 1982. 22.00 (*0-89410-354-7*); pap. 14.00 (*0-89410-355-5*) Three Continents.
***Design & Interacting of the IBM PC, PS & Compatible.** Muhammad A. Mazidi & Janicer G. Mazidi. LC 94-29197. (Eighty X Eighty-Six IBM PC & Compatible Computers Ser.). 448p. 1994. text ed. 69.00 (*0-13-098567-8*) P-H.
Design & Layout of Foodservice Facilities. John C. Birchfield. (Illus.). 272p. (C). 1988. text ed. 44.95 (*0-442-21042-6*) Van Nos Reinhold.
Design & Light. Ed. by Wolfgang Hageney. (Illus.). 96p. (ENG, FRE, GER, ITA & SPA.). 1988. pap. 26.95 (*88-7070-063-1*) Belvedere USA.
Design & Maintenance of Accounting Manuals. 2nd ed. Harry L. Brown. (Institute of Management Accountants Professional Book Ser.). 1993. text ed. 90.00 (*0-471-59643-4*) Wiley.
***Design & Make Your Own Contemporary Sampler Quilt.** Katie Pasquini. LC 94-22078. (Needlework Ser.). (Illus.). 64p. 1994. pap. text ed. 5.95 (*0-486-28197-3*) Dover.
Design & Management for Energy Conservation. P. W. O'Callaghan. 1981. 150.00 (*0-08-027287-8*, Pub. by Pergamon Repr UK) Franklin.
Design & Management for Resource Recovery (Series), 3 vols. Ed. by P. Arne Vesilin. 95p. 1980. Vol. 2, High Technology - A Failure Analysis, 95p. 19.50 (*0-250-40311-0*); Vol. 3, Quantitative Decision-Making, 153p. 19.50 (*0-250-40313-7*) Technomic.
Design & Management of Poverty Reduction Programs & Projects in Anglophone Africa: Proceedings of a Seminar Sponsored Jointly by the Economic Development Institute of the World Bank & the Uganda Management Institute. Ed. by Michael Bamberger et al. LC 94-354. (EDI Seminar Ser.). 1994. write for info. (*0-8213-2767-4*) World Bank.
Design & Management of Sustainable Projects to Alleviate Poverty in South Asia: EDI Serminar Report Ser. Ed. by Michael Bamberger & Abdul Aziz. LC 93-8237. 350p. 1993. 19.95 (*0-8213-2472-1*, 12472) World Bank.
Design & Manufacture of Composite Structures. G. E. Eckold. 1994. text ed. 57.00 (*0-07-018961-7*) McGraw.
Design & Manufacture of Hypoid Gears. Boris A. Shtipelman. LC 78-8591. 410p. reprint ed. pap. 116.90 (*0-317-08002-4*, 2022245) Bks Demand.
Design & Marketing of New Products. 2nd ed. Glenn Urban & John R. Hauser. LC 93-7240. 640p. 1993. text ed. 70.00 (*0-13-201567-6*) P-H.
Design & Operating Guide for Aquaculture Seawater Systems. J. E. Huguenin. (Development in Aquaculture & Fisheries Science Ser.: No. 20). 264p. 1989. 74.50 (*0-444-87157-8*) Elsevier.
Design & Operation - Activated Sludge Processes Using Respirometry. Rozich. 1992. 69.95 (*0-87371-449-0*, TD756) Lewis Pubs.
Design & Operation Guidelines for Optimization of the High-Rate Filtration Process: Plant Survey Results. 328p. 1989. pap. 29.00 (*0-89867-478-6*, 90552) Am Water Wks Assn.
Design & Operation of Caving & Sublevel Stoping Mines. Ed. by Daniel R. Stewart. LC 81-68554. (Illus.). 880p. 1981. 15.00 (*0-89520-287-5*) SMM&E Inc.
Design & Operation of Farm Irrigation Systems. Ed. by M. E. Jensen. LC 81-65586. 829p. 1981. text ed. 51.00 (*0-916150-28-3*, MO181) Am Soc Ag Eng.
Design & Operation of Flexible Manufacturing Systems. Paul G. Ranky. xiv, 348p. 1984. 74.00 (*0-444-86819-4*, North Holland) Elsevier.
Design & Operation of Heat Exchangers: Proceedings of the EUROTHERM Seminar No. 18 Hamburg, February 27 - March 1, 1991. Ed. by W. Roetzel et al. (EUROTHERM Seminar Ser.: No. 18). (Illus.). 432p. 1992. 110.00 (*0-387-53771-6*) Spr-Verlag.
Design & Operation of Large Wastewater Treatment Plants: Proceedings of a Workshop Held in Vienna, Austria, 19-23 September. Ed. by W. Von Der Emde & H. B. Tench. (Illus.). 700p. 1985. pap. 145.00 (*0-08-031733-2*, Pergamon Pr) Elsevier.
Design & Operation of Pipeline Control Systems. Ed. by Louis Fletcher. 62p. 1984. 16.00 (*0-87262-419-6*) Am Soc Civil Eng.
Design & Operation of Sewage Treatment Plants in Coastal Tourist Areas: Proceedings of the IAWPRC Conference Held in Limassol, Cyprus, November 3-4, 1987. Ed. by M. Nicolaou & I. Hadjivassilis. (Water Science & Technology Ser.: No. 21). 158p. 1990. pap. 57.50 (*0-08-037374-7*, Pergamon Pr) Elsevier.
***Design & Operation of Small Wastewater Treatment Plants: Selected Proceedings of the Second International Conference on Design & Operation of Small Wastewater Treatment Plants, Held in Trondheim, Norway, 28-30 June 1993.** Second International Conference on Design & Operation of Small Wastewater Treatment Plants Staff. Ed. by H. Odegaard. (Water Science & Technology Ser.: Vol. 28). 396p. 1994. pap. 175.00 (*0-08-042493-7*, Pergamon Pr) Elsevier.
***Design & Operation of Smallholder Irrigation in South Asia.** D. E. Campbell. LC 94-29953. (Technical Paper, 256, Irrigation & Drainage Ser.: Vol. 256). 1994. write for info. (*0-8213-2995-2*) World Bank.
Design & Operational Effects of Geometrics. (Transportation Research Record Ser.: No. 1100). 57p. 1986. 8.80 (*0-309-04120-1*) Transport Res Bd.
Design & Origins in Astronomy. Ed. by George Mulfinger. (Creation Research Society Monograph Ser.: No. 2). (Illus.). 152p. (Orig.). 1984. pap. 8.95 (*0-940384-03-5*) Creation Research.
Design & Performance for Deep Foundations: Piles & Piers in Soil & Soft Rock: Proceedings of a Session Sponsored by the Committees on Deep Foundations & Rock Mechanics of the Geotechnical Engineering Division of the American Society of Civil Engineers in Conjunction with the ASCE Convention in Dallas, Texas, October 24-28, 1993. Ed. by Priscilla P. Nelson et al. LC 93-31658. (Geotechnical Special Publication Ser.: No. 36). 1993. write for info. (*0-87262-987-2*) Am Soc Civil Eng.
Design & Performance of Climate Control Systems. 88p. 1992. pap. 39.00 (*1-56091-233-2*, SP-916) Soc Auto Engineers.
Design & Performance of Earth Retaining Structures. Ed. by Philip C. Lambe & Lawrence A. Hansen. LC 90-771. 904p. 1990. pap. text ed. 70.00 (*0-87262-761-6*) Am Soc Civil Eng.
Design & Performance of Gas Turbine Power Plants. Ed. by William R. Hawthorne & W. T. Olson. LC 58-5027. (High Speed Aerodynamics & Jet Propulsion Ser.: No. 11). (Illus.). 577p. reprint ed. pap. 164.50 (*0-8357-8858-X*, 2052282) Bks Demand.
Design & Performance of Local Computer Networks. J. Shoch. 1981. 1.00 (*0-07-056984-3*) McGraw.
Design & Performance of Road Pavements. 2nd ed. David Croney. 1991. text ed. 72.00 (*0-07-707408-4*) McGraw.
Design & Performance of Underground Excavations. Ed. by E. T. Brown & J. A. Hudson. 518p. 1984. 126.00 (*0-7277-0211-4*, Pub. by T Telford UK) Am Soc Civil Eng.
Design & Planning of Engineering Systems. Dale D. Meredith et al. (Civil Engineering & Engineering Mechanics Ser.). (Illus.). 384p. 1973. Reference ed. 34.95 (*0-685-03823-8*) P-H.
Design & Planning of Engineering Systems. 2nd ed. Dale D. Meredith et al. (Illus.). 352p. (C). 1984. text ed. 76.00 (*0-13-200189-6*) P-H.
***Design & Planning of Research & Clinical Laboratory Facilities.** Leonard Mayer. LC 94-28955. 1995. text ed. 75.00 (*0-471-30623-1*) Wiley.
***Design & Practice Manual for Geotextiles.** Applications Engineering Group Staff. (Illus.). 217p. 1994. 49.95 (*1-887184-00-7*) Polyfelt Am.
Design & Primary Education. Design Council Staff. 64p. (C). 1987. pap. text ed. 25.00 (*0-85072-212-8*) St Mut.
***Design & Printing Buyer's Survival Guide.** Don Sparkman. LC 95-75299. 200p. 1995. pap. 18.95 (*1-880559-28-5*) Allworth Pr.
Design & Production of Corrugated Packaging & Displays. A. Howard Bessen. (Illus.). 256p. 1991. 84.95 (*0-9616302-4-8*) Jelmar Pub.
Design & Production of Media Presentations for Libraries. Patsy Cullen & John Kirby. 200p. 1985. text ed. 54.95 (*0-566-03548-0*) Ashgate Pub Co.
***Design & Production of Multimedia & Simulation-Based Learning Material.** Ed. by Ton De Jong & Luigi Sarti. LC 94-26572. (Diverse Ser.). 272p. (C). 1994. lib. bdg. 84.00 (*0-7923-3020-X*) Kluwer Ac.
Design & Protocol for Monitoring Indoor Air Quality. Ed. by N. L. Nagda & J. P. Harper. LC 88-37486. (Special Technical Publication Ser.: No. STP 1002). (Illus.). 310p. 1989. text ed. 53.00 (*0-8031-1176-2*) ASTM.
Design & Purpose: A Study in the Drama of Evolution. Henry T. Edge. (Study Ser.: No. 4). 1980. 2.00 (*0-913004-37-5*) Point Loma Pub.
Design & Realization of Bipolar Transistors. Peter Ashburn. LC 88-2438. (Design & Measurement in Electrical & Electronic Engineering Ser.). 198p. 1992. pap. text ed. 64.95 (*0-471-93570-0*) Wiley.
Design & Reform of Taxation Policy. Ed. by Gianluigi Galeotti. (Financial & Monetary Policy Issues Ser.). 224p. (C). 1992. lib. bdg. 116.00 (*0-7923-2016-6*) Kluwer Ac.
Design & Repair of Residential & Light Commercial Foundations. Robert W. Brown. (Illus.). 256p. 1990. text ed. 46.00 (*0-07-008192-1*) McGraw.
Design & Retrofit of Wastewater Treatment Plants for Biological Nutrient Removal. Ed. by Clifford W. Randall et al. LC 92-53521. (Water Quality Management Library: Vol. 5). 375p. 1992. text ed. 75.00 (*0-87762-922-6*) Technomic.
Design & Selection of Components for Enclosed Gear Drives. (AGMA Ser.: No. 6001-C88). (Illus.). 17p. 1988. pap. text ed. 60.00 (*1-55589-498-4*) AGMA.
Design & Sew It Yourself: A Workbook for Creative Clothing. rev. ed. Lois Ericson & Diane E. Frode. (Illus.). 120p. 1983. pap. 14.95 (*0-911985-00-X*) Erics Pr.
Design & Sizing of Active Solar Thermal Systems. T. Agami Reddy. (Illus.). 416p. 1987. 95.00 (*0-19-859016-4*) OUP.
Design & Synthesis. Ed. by Hiroyuki Yoshikawa. 1985. 179.50 (*0-444-87705-3*) Elsevier.
Design & Synthesis of Organic Molecules Based on Molecular Recognition. Ed. by G. V. Binst. (Illus.). 410p. 1986. 140.00 (*0-387-16123-6*) Spr-Verlag.
Design & Systems: General Applications of Methodology. Ed. by Arne Collen & Wojciech W. Gasparski. LC 93-6404. (Praxiology Ser.: Vol. 3). 1994. write for info. (*1-56000-140-2*) Transaction Pubs.
***Design & Systems: General Applications of Methodology.** Ed. by Arne Collen & Wojciech W. Gasparski. (Praxiology: International Annual of Practical Philosophy & Methodology Ser.: Vol. 3). 480p. (C). 1994. 49.95 (*1-56000-187-9*) Transaction Pubs.
Design & Targeted Reactions of Oligonucleotide Derivative. Dmitri G. Knorre et al. LC 93-19678. 1993. 169.95 (*0-8493-4856-0*, QP628) CRC Pr.
Design & Technology. John Aitken & George Mills. (C). 1989. 300.00 (*0-216-92625-4*, Pub. by Jordanhill College UK) St Mut.
Design & Technology. James R. Garratt. (Illus.). 319p. (C). 1992. pap. 23.50 (*0-521-36969-X*) Cambridge U Pr.
Design & Technology in the Primary School: Case Studies for Teachers. Hind Makiya & Margaret Rogers. LC 91-48095. 160p. 1992. 59.95 (*0-415-08089-4*, A7629) Routledge.
Design & Technology of Heat Pipes for Cooling & Heat Exchange. Calvin C. Silverstein. 550p. 1992. 99.50 (*0-89116-859-1*) Hemisp Pub.
Design & Technology of Integrated Circuits. Donard De Cogan. 230p. 1990. pap. text ed. 75.00 (*0-471-92237-4*) Wiley.
Design & Technology Through Home Economics. M. Jepson & P. Creighton. (C). 1990. 75.00 (*0-7487-0178-8*, Pub. by S Thornes Pubs UK) St Mut.
Design & Test Techniques for VLSI & WSI Circuits. Massara. 1990. 99.00 (*0-86341-165-7*, CM015) Inst Elect Eng.
Design & Testing of Roadside Safety Devices. (Transportation Research Record Ser.: No. 1233). 177p. 1989. 25.00 (*0-309-05005-7*) Transport Res Bd.
Design & the Handweaver. Mary M. Atwater. LC 61-4138. (Guild Monographs: No. 3). (Illus.). 26p. 1961. pap. 8.95 (*0-916658-03-1*) Shuttle Craft.
Design & the Public Good: Selected Writings of Serge Chermayeff, 1930 to 1980. Ed. by Serge Chermayeff & Richard A. Plunz. (Illus.). 336p. 1982. 40.00 (*0-262-16088-9*) MIT Pr.

D

An Asterisk (*) at the beginning of an entry indicates that the title is appearing in BIP for the first time.

D

An Asterisk (*) at the beginning of an entry indicates that the title is appearing in BIP for the first time.

1887

1995. reprint ed. pap. text ed. 17.95 (*1-885803-02-8*, 943) Paradise Res. A comprehensive study & analysis of the origins, principles & practices of the Oxford Group (also known as "A First Century Christian Fellowship") of which A.A. was an integral part in its formative years from 1933 to 1939. How the Oxford Group's Biblical principles contributed to & impacted upon A.A.'s Big Book, Twelve Steps, & early high success rate in the 1930s. Endorsed by Oxford Group authorities Garth Lean, James & Eleanor Forde Newton, Willard Hunter, James Houck, A.A. oldtimer Geraldine D., A.A. historian Ernest Kurtz, Ph.D., & Dr. Paul Wood, President, National Council on Alcoholism & Drug Dependence. Other Dick B. titles on A.A.'s spiritual roots: NEW LIGHT ON ALCOHOLISM: THE A.A. LEGACY FROM SAM SHOEMAKER; THE AKRON GENESIS OF ALCOHOLICS ANONYMOUS; DR. BOB'S LIBRARY; ANNE SMITH'S JOURNAL; THE BOOKS EARLY AA'S READ FOR SPIRITUAL GROWTH; & COURAGE TO CHANGE: THE CHRISTIAN ROOTS OF THE TWELVE STEP MOVEMENT (with Pittman). Titles now published only by Paradise Research Publications, Good Book Publishing Company, or Baker Book House. Reviewed in LIBRARY JOURNAL, BOOKSTORE JOURNAL, FOR A CHANGE, EPISCOPAL LIFE, THE LIVING CHURCH, RECOVERY NEWS, SOBER TIMES. Interviews in Cleveland Plain Dealer, Baltimore Sun, Akron Beacon Journal. Author a recovered alcoholic, retired attorney, & Bible student who has sponsored over sixty A.A.'s in recovery. ***Publisher Provided Annotation.***

Design for Maintainability. C. Parsloe. (C). 1992. 110.00x (*0-86022-308-6*, Pub. by Build Servs Info Assn UK) St Mut.

Design for Manufacturability: Getting It Right the First Time. Comp. by CAD-CIM Alert Editors. (Illus.). 400p. 1988. ring bd. 345.00 (*0-932007-15-5*) Mgmt Roundtable.

Design for Manufacturability: Optimizing Cost, Quality & Time-to-Market. David M. Anderson. LC 90-82921. (Illus.). 200p. 1990. text ed. 49.95 (*1-878072-11-0*) CIM Press.

***Design for Manufacturability: The 1995 National Design Engineering Show & Conference, March 13-17, 1995, Chicago, IL.** Ed. by J. R. Behun. (Design Engineering Ser.: Vol. 81). 128p. 1995. 80.00 (*0-7918-1299-5*, H00931) ASME.

Design for Manufacturability - Assembly. Richard K. Miller. 219p. 1990. pap. text ed. 955.00 (*0-89671-111-0*) SEAI Tech Pubns.

Design for Manufacturability - 1994. Ed. by J. Mason. LC 93-70158. (DE Ser.: Vol. 67). 132p. 1994. 32.50 (*0-7918-1269-3*, H00901) ASME.

***Design for Manufacturability of Ceramic Components: Proceedings of the Design for Manufacturability & Manufacture of Ceramic Components Symposium, Presented at the 96th Annual Meeting of the American Ceramic Society, Held in Indianapolis, IN, April 25-27, 1994.** Design for Manufacturability & Manufacture of Ceramic Components Symposium Staff. Ed. by Asish Ghosh et al. LC 95-10176. (Ceramic Transactions Ser.: Vol. 50). (Illus.). 272p. 1995. 83.00 (*0-944904-88-2*, 1EDG00A) Am Ceramic.

Design for Manufacturability 1993. Ed. by P. J. Guichelaar. LC 93-70158. 163p. 1993. pap. 45.00 (*0-7918-1136-0*, G00780) ASME.

Design for Manufacture: Reducing Life Cycle Costs While Improving Time to Market & Product Quality. Ed. by A. M. Agogino. (DE Ser.: Vol. 51). 72p. 1992. 30.00 (*0-7918-1110-7*, G00754) ASME.

Design for Manufacture: Strategy, Principles & Techniques. John Corbett. (C). 1991. pap. text ed. 45.25 (*0-201-41694-8*) Addison-Wesley.

Design for Manufacturing & Assembly in Apparel. Educational Foundation for the Fashion Industries Staff. Date not set. pap. write for info. (*0-13-042979-1*) P-H.

Design for Mountain Communities: A Landscape & Architectural Guide. Sherry Dorward. (Illus.). 448p. 1990. text ed. 54.95 (*0-442-22095-2*) Van Nos Reinhold.

Design for Movement. Lyn Oxenford. 1951. pap. 9.95 (*0-87830-561-0*, Theatre Arts Bks) Routledge Chapman & Hall.

Design for Murder. Carolyn G. Hart. 208p. (Orig.). 1988. 4.99 (*0-553-26562-8*) Bantam.

Design for Music Learning. Douglas Greer. LC 79-21117. 1980. pap. text ed. 17.95 (*0-8077-2573-0*) Tchrs Coll.

Design for Need. Ed. by J. Bicknell & L. McQuiston. 1977. 65.00 (*0-08-021500-9*, Pub. by Pergamon Repr UK) Franklin.

Design for News. Wallace W. Allen. LC 81-2022. (Illus.). 1981. spiral bd. 10.95 (*0-932272-04-5*) Minneapolis Tribune.

Design for Passenger Transport. Ed. by Frank Height. (Illus.). 1979. 63.00 (*0-08-023735-5*, Pub. by Pergamon Repr UK) Franklin.

Design for Political Science: Scope, Objectives, & Methods. Ed. by James C. Charlesworth. LC 74-117766. (Essay Index Reprint Ser.). 1977. 21.95 (*0-8369-1789-8*) Ayer.

Design for Preaching. H. Grady Davis. LC 58-5749. (Orig.). 1958. 18.00 (*0-8006-0806-2*, 1-806, Fortress Pr) Augsburg Fortress.

Design for Recyclability. M. E. Henstock. 172p. 1988. pap. text ed. 31.50 (*0-901462-46-2*, Pub. by Inst Materials UK) Ashgate Pub Co.

***Design for Safety.** David Thurston. 1994. pap. 18.95 (*0-07-064561-2*) TAB Bks.

***Design for Safety.** 2nd ed. David Thurston. 1994. text ed. 27.95 (*0-07-064560-4*) TAB Bks.

Design for Scholarship. Isaiah Bowman. LC 71-152159. (Essay Index Reprint Ser.). 1977. 18.95 (*0-8369-2181-X*) Ayer.

***Design for Society.** Nicel Whiteley. 192p. 1995. pap. 22.50 (*0-948462-65-5*, Reaktion Bks UK) U of Wash Pr.

Design for Strength & Production. C. Ruiz & F. Koenigsburger. 280p. 1970. text ed. 220.00 (*0-677-62050-0*) Gordon & Breach.

Design for Success: A Human-Centered Approach to Designing Successful Products & Systems. William B. Rouse. (Systems Engineering Ser.). 287p. 1991. text ed. 74.95 (*0-471-52483-2*) Wiley.

Design for Teaching & Training: A Self-Study Guide to Lesson Planning. Ford LeRoy. LC 77-87249. (Illus.). 1978. pap. 16.99 (*0-8054-3422-4*) Broadman.

Design for the Environment. Dorothy Mackenzie. LC 91-8409. (Illus.). 176p. 1991. 35.00 (*0-8478-1390-8*) Rizzoli Intl.

***Design for the Environment: Product Life Cycle Design Guidance Manual.** U.S. Environmental Protection Agency Staff. 181p. (Orig.). 1994. pap. text ed. 65.00 (*0-86587-384-4*) Gov Insts.

Design for the Real World: Human Ecology & Social Change. 2nd rev. ed. Victor Papanek. (Illus.). 405p. (C). 1992. reprint ed. pap. 17.00 (*0-89733-153-2*) Academy Chi Pubs.

Design for Thinking: A First Book in Semantics. rev. ed. Albert Upton. LC 61-14653. (Illus.). xii, 240p. (C). 1973. reprint ed. pap. text ed. 9.95 (*0-87015-207-6*) Pacific Bks.

Design for Total War: Arms & Economics in the Third Reich. Berenice A. Carroll. LC 68-15527. (Studies in European History: Vol. 17). 1968. text ed. 61.55 (*90-279-0299-2*) Mouton.

Design for Wholeness: Dealing with Anger, Learning to Forgive, Building Self-Esteem. Loughlan Sofield et al. LC 90-82098. 152p. (Orig.). 1990. pap. 6.95 (*0-87793-430-4*) Ave Maria.

Design for Work & Use: Case Studies in Ergonomics Practice, Vol. 2. Ed. by H. G. Maule & J. S. Weiner. LC 81-139177. 150p. 1981. 51.00 (*0-85066-208-7*) Taylor & Francis.

Design, Form, & Chaos. Paul Rand. (Illus.). 224p. (C). 1993. 45.00 (*0-300-05553-6*) Yale U Pr.

Design Formulas for Plastics Engineers. Natti S. Rao. 135p. (C). 1991. text ed. 27.95 (*1-56990-084-1*) Hanser-Gardner.

Design from Physical Principles: Papers from the 1992 Fall Symposium. Ed. by Brian Williams. (Technical Reports). (Illus.). 168p. (Orig.). (C). 1993. spiral bd. 25.00 (*0-929280-36-9*) Amer Artificial.

Design Fundamentals for Low Voltage Distribution & Control. Kussy & Warren. (Electrical Engineering & Electronics Ser.: Vol. 35). 416p. 1987. 150.00 (*0-8247-7515-5*) Dekker.

Design Futures: Key to International Management. James Woudhuysen. 148p. (C). 1993. pap. text ed. 130.00 (*0-85072-302-7*) St Mut.

Design Graphs for Concrete Shell Roofs. Charles B. Wilby. (Illus.). 148p. 1981. 48.75 (*0-85334-899-5*, Pub. by Elsevier Applied Sci UK) Elsevier.

Design Guide. HMSO Staff. 84p. 1991. pap. 55.00 (*0-11-321389-1*, HM9381) UNIPUB.

Design Guide, No. II. (Illus.). 394p. (Orig.). 1986. pap. 9.95 (*0-317-89907-4*) CA Design Pubns.

Design Guide for Cool Thermal Storage. Ed. by B. Parsons. (Illus.). 1993. pap. 72.00 (*1-883413-07-9*) Am Heat Ref & Air Eng.

***Design Guide for Frost-Protected Shallow Foundations.** Jay H. Crandell. (Illus.). 51p. (Orig.). (C). 1995. pap. text ed. 40.00x (*0-7881-1611-8*) Diane Pub.

***Design Guide for Involute Splines.** 64p. 1994. 59.00 (*1-56091-583-8*, M117) Soc Auto Engineers.

Design Guide for Secure Adult Correctional Facilities. LC 83-72162. (Illus.). 207p. 1983. 34.65 (*0-942974-47-6*, 340) Am Correctional.

***Design Guide for the Electrical Safety of Instrument Control Panels.** EEMUA Staff. 1994. 125.00 (*0-85931-080-9*, Pub. by EEMUA UK) St Mut.

***Design Guide for Thermally Activated Air Conditioning.** Gerald R. Guinn. (Illus.). 95p. (Orig.). (C). 1994. pap. text ed. 65.00x (*0-7881-1080-2*) Diane Pub.

Design Guide for Wildlife Protection & Conservation for Transportation Facilities. 1976. pap. 3.00 (*0-686-20957-5*, GWP-1) AASHTO.

Design Guide to the Uniform Building Code, 1991. 3rd ed. Alfred Goldberg. 552p. 1993. text ed. 89.95 (*0-471-30391-7*) Wiley.

Design Guide to the 1985 Uniform Building Code. Alfred Goldberg. (Illus.). (Orig.). (C). 1985. pap. 26.00 (*0-9614808-0-7*) GRDA Pubns.

Design Guide to the 1988 Uniform Building Code. Alfred Goldberg. LC 89-77097. (Illus.). (Orig.). 1988. pap. 43.50 (*0-9614808-4-X*) GRDA Pubns.

Design Guide to the 1988 Uniform Building Code, Supplement 1990. Alfred Goldberg. LC 89-77097. (Illus.). 64p. (Orig.). 1990. pap. 12.00 (*0-9614808-6-6*) GRDA Pubns.

Design Guide to the 1988 Uniform Building Code, 1989 Supplement. Alfred Goldberg. (Illus.). 64p. (Orig.). 1989. pap. 10.00 (*0-9614808-5-8*) GRDA Pubns.

Design Guide to the 1991 Uniform Building Code. Alfred Goldberg. LC 90-86363. (Illus.). 544p. (Orig.). 1991. 64.00 (*0-9614808-9-0*); pap. 55.00 (*0-685-47752-5*) GRDA Pubns.

***Design Guide to the 1991 Uniform Building Code: 1993 Supplement.** 3rd ed. Alfred Goldberg. Date not set. pap. text ed. write for info. (*0-471-30959-1*) Wiley.

***Design Guide to the 1994 Uniform Building Code.** Alfred Goldberg & John C. Canestro. 1994. text ed. 75.00 (*0-471-30957-5*) Wiley.

Design Guidelines for Desktop Publishing. Roberta Mantus. 128p. 1992. text ed. 16.95 (*0-8273-5075-9*) Delmar.

Design Guidelines for Desktop Publishing: Instructor's Guide. Roberta Mantus. 1992. 8.00 (*0-8273-5076-7*) Delmar.

Design Guidelines for Exhaust Hoods. L. J. Stewart. (C). 1985. 105.00 (*0-86022-142-3*, Pub. by Build Servs Info Assn UK) St Mut.

Design Guidelines for Surface Mount & Fine Pitch Technology. 2nd ed. Vern Solberg. 1995. text ed. 52.00 (*0-07-059577-1*) McGraw.

Design Guidelines for Surface Mount Technology. Vern Solberg. (Illus.). 208p. 1989. 52.00 (*0-8306-3199-2*, TAB/TPR) TAB Bks.

Design Guidelines for Surface Mount Technology. John E. Traister. 311p. 1990. text ed. 80.00 (*0-12-697400-4*) Acad Pr.

Design Guidelines Surface Mount Technology. Vern Solberg. 1989. text ed. 52.00 (*0-07-156692-9*) McGraw.

Design Guides for Radioactive Material Handling Facilities & Equipment. 1988. 35.00 (*0-89448-554-7*) Am Nuclear Soc.

Design Handbook for Model Railroads. Paul Mallery. (Illus.). 68p. 1990. pap. 8.95 (*0-911868-71-2*, C71) Carstens Pubns.

Design Handbook for Optical Fiber Systems. (User Manual & Handbook Ser.: Vol. II). 253p. 75.00 (*0-686-32956-2*) Info Gatekeepers.

Design Handbook in Accordance with the Strength Design Method of ACI 318-89, I. 544p. 1991. 133.95 (*0-317-32076-9*, SP-17(91)) ACI.

Design Handbook in Accordance with the Strength Design Method of ACI 318-89: Columns, Vol. 2. ACI Committee 340. 1990. ring bd. 118.50 (*0-685-85093-5*, SP-17A) ACI.

Design Handbook of Wastewater Systems, 4 vols., Set. Incl. Vol. 1. Wastewater Collection & Transportation. N. I. Likhachev et al. 150p. 1986. 100.00 (*0-89864-021-0*); Vol. 2. Methods of Wastewater Treatment. N. I. Likhachev et al. 500p. 1986. 185.00 (*0-89864-022-9*); Vol. 3. Municipal & Industrial Systems. N. I. Likhachev et al. 265p. 1986. 135.00 (*0-89864-023-7*); Vol. 4. Systems Integration & Ancillary Facilities. N. I. Likhachev et al. 150p. 1986. 100.00 (*0-89864-024-5*); (Illus.). 1986. 395.00 (*0-89864-025-3*) Allerton Pr.

Design Heritage of Noren: Traditional Japanese Storefront Art. Photos by Takashi Masuda. LC 88-80145. (Illus.). 200p. 1989. 55.00 (*0-87040-770-8*) Japan Pubns USA.

Design History: A Student's Handbook. Ed. by Hazel Conway. (Illus.). 224p. 1987. text ed. 49.95 (*0-04-709019-7*); pap. text ed. 16.95 (*0-04-709020-0*) Routledge Chapman & Hall.

***Design History: An Anthology.** Ed. by Dennis P. Doordan. (Illus.). 270p. (Orig.). 1995. pap. 15.95x (*0-262-54076-2*) MIT Pr.

Design History & the History of Design. John A. Walker. 243p. (C). 1989. text ed. 55.50 (*0-7453-0274-2*) Westview.

Design History & the History of Design. John A. Walker. 243p. (C). 1990. pap. text ed. 18.95 (*0-7453-0522-9*) Westview.

Design Human Engineering. Richard Bandler. Date not set. write for info. (*0-916990-30-3*) META Pubns.

Design Hydrology & Sedimentology for Small Catchments. C. T. Haan et al. (Illus.). 588p. 1994. text ed. 89.95 (*0-12-312340-2*) Acad Pr.

Design in Agricultural Engineering. Leslie L. Christianson & Roger P. Rohrbach. LC 86-71552. (Illus.). 312p. (C). 1986. 35.00 (*0-916150-80-1*, M1086) Am Soc Ag Eng.

Design in America: The Cranbrook Vision 1925-1950. LC 83-6343. (Illus.). 352p. 1984. 49.50 (*0-8109-0801-8*) Abrams.

Design in Chaucer's Troilus. Sanford B. Meech. LC 76-88981. 529p. 1969. reprint ed. text ed. 38.50 (*0-8371-2118-3*, MECT, Greenwood Pr) Greenwood.

Design in Depth. D. K. Holland. 256p. 1996. 49.99 (*1-56496-091-9*) Rockport Pubs.

Design in Familiar Places: What Makes Home Environments Look Good. Sidney Brower. LC 87-27889. 203p. 1988. text ed. 49.95 (*0-275-92686-9*, C2686, Praeger Pubs) Greenwood.

Design in Italy: Eighteen-Seventy to the Present. Penny Sparke. (Illus.). 240p. 1988. 55.00 (*0-89659-884-5*) Abbeville Pr.

Design in Liberal Learning. Maxwell H. Goldberg. LC 71-110645. (Jossey-Bass Higher Education Ser.). 208p. reprint ed. pap. 59.30 (*0-8357-9314-1*, 2013938) Bks Demand.

Design in Mind. Bryan Lawson. LC 93-50198. (Illus.). 160p. 1994. pap. 34.95 (*0-7506-1211-8*, Butterwrth Archit) Buttrwrth-Heinemann.

Design in Offshore Structures. 192p. 1983. 67.00 (*0-7277-0195-9*, Pub. by T Telford UK) Am Soc Civil Eng.

Design in Plastics. Doug Clemenshaw. Ed. by Blount & Co. Staff. (Design Sourcebook Ser.). 240p. 1989. 49.99x (*0-935603-11-5*, 30136) Rockport Pubs.

Design in Progress: What Happens Behind the Scenes. Ed. by Supon Design Group Staff. (Illus.). 160p. 1992. pap. 24.95 (*0-945814-05-4*, Nippan Pubns) Bks Nippan.

Design in Puritan American Literature. William J. Scheick. LC 91-35585. 176p. 1992. text ed. 25.00 (*0-8131-1775-5*) U Pr of Ky.

Design in Structural Steel. 3rd ed. John E. Lothers. LC 71-160254. (Civil Engineering & Engineering Mechanics Ser.). (Illus.). 1972. 38.95 (*0-685-03824-6*) P-H.

Design in Texas. Ed. by Jerry Herring. (Illus.). 272p. 1986. 35.00 (*0-917001-05-2*) Herring Pr.

Design in the Contemporary World: A Paper Prepared from the Proceedings of the Stanford Design Forum 1988. Jeffrey Meikle. 100p. (Orig.). 1989. write for info. (*0-318-65097-5*) Pentagram Design.

Design in the High Street. Michell. 1986. pap. 39.95 (*0-85139-159-1*, Butterwrth Archit) Buttrwrth-Heinemann.

Design in the Information Environment: How Computing Is Changing the Problems, Processes & Theories of Design. Ed. by Patrick F. Whitney & Cheryl Kent. 192p. (C). 1986. pap. text ed. 10.95 (*0-317-18603-5*, KnopfC) Knopf.

Design in the Information Environment: How Computing Is Changing the Problems, Processes & Theories of Design. Ed. by Patrick F. Whitney & Cheryl Kent. (Illus.). 183p. (C). 1985. text ed. 19.95 (*0-8093-1251-4*) S Ill U Pr.

Design in the Service of Beauty. Welleran Poltarnees. (Illus.). 48p. 1994. 18.95 (*0-9621131-8-2*) Blue Lantern Studio.

Design in the Theatre. George Sheringham & James Laver. LC 72-175893. (Illus.). 1972. reprint ed. 23.95 (*0-405-08965-1*) Ayer.

Design in Venezuelan Petroglyphs. Ruby De Valencia & Jeannine S. Volsky. Ed. by Pampero Foundation Staff. (Illus.). 409p. (ENG, FRE & SPA.). 1989. 75.00 (*0-685-45576-9*, Pub. by FUNDACOMUN VE) CDS Gallery.

Design Information Flow. L. J. Wild. (C). 1992. 110.00x (*0-86022-300-0*, Pub. by Build Servs Info Assn UK) St Mut.

Design, Innovation & Long Cycles in Economic Development. Ed. by Christopher Freeman. LC 85-26272. 200p. 1986. text ed. 32.50 (*0-312-19449-8*) St Martin.

***Design Innovations in Electric & Hybrid Electric Vehicles: 1995 International Congress & Exposition Meeting.** 1995. pap. 49.00 (*1-56091-639-7*, SP1089) Soc Auto Engineers.

Design Inquiry. Ed. by Bela Banathy. 150p. 1987. text ed. 15.95 (*0-318-32524-1*) Intersystems Pubns.

Design, Inspection & Operation of High Pressure Vessels & Piping Systems: Joint Conference of the Pressure Vessels & Piping, Materials, Nuclear Engineering, Solar Energy Divisions, 1981, Denver. Ed. by J. R. Sims. LC 81-65370. (PVP Ser.: No. 48). 169p. pap. 48.20 (*0-317-58257-7*, 2056395) Bks Demand.

Design Institute for Physical Property Data: Ten Years of Accomplishment. Ed. by Ted Selover, Jr. LC 90-779. (AIChE Symposium Ser.: Vol. 86, No. 275). 116p. 1990. pap. 50.00 (*0-8169-0487-1*) Am Inst Chem Eng.

Design Instructions. (EUITS Ser.: No. B-1). 78p. 1991. spiral bd. 69.50 (*0-87683-503-5*) GP Pub.

Design Integration for Minimal Energy & Cost. J. E. Halldane. 238p. 1989. 81.00 (*1-85166-292-8*) Elsevier.

Design Intervention. Wolfgang F. Preiser. 1991. text ed. 59.95 (*0-442-27333-9*) Van Nos Reinhold.

Design Issues in CSCW. Duska Rosenberg & Chris Hutchinson. LC 94-13514. (Computer Supported Cooperative Work Ser.). 1994. 59.00 (*0-387-19810-5*) Spr-Verlag.

***Design Issues in Optical Processing.** Ed. by John N. Lee. (Cambridge Studies in Modern Optics: 16). (Illus.). 265p. (C). 1995. 59.95 (*0-521-43048-8*) Cambridge U Pr.

Design Language for Computer-Assisted Instruction. R. E. Grubb. (Illus.). 155p. 1974. pap. text ed. 25.00 (*0-87567-103-9*) Entelek.

Design Liability in the Construction Industry. Ed. by D. L. Cornes. (C). 1988. 500.00 (*0-685-32834-1*, Pub. by Witherby & Co UK) St Mut.

***Design Library: Airbrush.** Date not set. 14.99 (*1-56496-159-1*) Rockport Pubs.

***Design Library: Brochure.** Date not set. 14.99 (*1-56496-160-5*) Rockport Pubs.

***Design Library: Logo & Letterhead.** Date not set. 14.99 (*1-56496-161-3*) Rockport Pubs.

***Design Library: Packaging.** Date not set. 14.99 (*1-56496-158-3*) Rockport Pubs.

***Design Library: Promotion.** Date not set. 14.99 (*1-56496-157-5*) Rockport Pubs.

Design Life of Buildings. 284p. 1985. 42.00 (*0-7277-0237-8*, Pub. by T Telford UK) Am Soc Civil Eng.

Design Load for Water Supply in Buildings. F. Kiya & S. Murakawa. Tr. by P. R. Kanade. (Illus.). 299p. (C). 1989. text ed. 85.00 (*90-6191-903-7*, Pub. by A A Balkema NE) Ashgate Pub Co.

Design Management. Peter Gorb. 1990. pap. 14.98 (*0-442-30363-7*) Van Nos Reinhold.

Design, Management, & Operation of Pavements. (Transportation Research Record Ser.: No. 1252). 49p. 1989. 9.00 (*0-309-04973-3*) Transport Res Bd.

1888

An Asterisk (*) at the beginning of an entry indicates that the title is appearing in BIP for the first time.

An Asterisk (*) at the beginning of an entry indicates that the title is appearing in BIP for the first time.

D

Design of Interactive Computer Displays: A Guide to the Select Literature. Ed. by Kate McGee & Catherine Matthews. LC 85-60627. 647p. 1985. pap. 84.50 (*0-916313-08-5*) Ergosyst Assocs.

Design of Interactive Computer Displays II: A Guide to Selected Periodicals. Ed. by Kate McGee et al. LC 85-28169. (Orig.). 1986. pap. 15.00 (*0-916313-10-7*) Ergosyst Assocs.

Design of Interpreters, Compilers, & Editors, for Augmented Transition Networks. Ed. by Leonard Bolc. (Symbolic Computation Ser.). (Illus.). 214p. 1985. 69.00 (*0-387-12789-5*) Spr-Verlag.

Design of Large Steam Turbine-Generator Foundations. Task Committee on Turbine Foundations of the Fossil Power Committee & the Nuclear Energy Committee of the Energy Division. 84p. 1987. 14.00 (*0-87262-597-4*) Am Soc Civil Eng.

Design of Latticed Steel Transmission Structures: An ASCE Standard, ASCE 10-90. 64p. 1992. pap. text ed. 39.00 (*0-87262-858-2*) Am Soc Civil Eng.

Design of Life. Renato Dulbecco. 466p. (C). 1990. reprint ed. 21.00 (*0-300-04477-1*) Yale U Pr.

Design of Liquid Retaining Concrete Structures. 2nd ed. Robert D. Anchor. LC 92-13614. 1993. text ed. 47.00 (*0-07-001763-8*) McGraw.

Design of Load-Bearing Wall Panels. (PCI Journal Reprints Ser.). 1974. pap. 10.00 (*0-937040-14-2*, JR-154) P-PCI.

Design of Low- & Medium-Rise Steel Buildings. Allison. 48p. 1991. 16.00 (*1-56424-028-2*, D805) Am Inst Steel Construct.

Design of Low-Cost Housing & Community Facilities, Vol. 2. (Basic Housing Case Studies). pap. 10.00 (*92-1-130012-6*, E.75.IV.2) UN.

Design of Low-Voltage Bipolar Operational Amplifiers. M. Jeroen Fonderie. LC 92-44955. (International Series in Engineering & Computer Science, VLSI, Computer Architecture, & Digital Screen Processing). 208p. (C). 1993. lib. bdg. 76.00 (*0-7923-9317-1*) Kluwer Ac.

***Design of Low-Voltage, Low Power Analog Integrated Devices & Their Application in Hearing Instruments.** W. A. Serdijn. 160p. (Orig.). 1994. pap. 52.50x (*90-6275-955-6*, Pub. by Delft U Pr NE) Coronet Bks.

Design of Machine & Structural Parts. Kurt M. Marshek. LC 87-6286. 222p. 1987. text ed. 79.95 (*0-471-84996-0*) Wiley.

Design of Machine Elements. 4th ed. Virgil M. Faires. 624p. (C). 1965. text ed. write for info. (*0-02-335950-1*) Macmillan.

Design of Machine Elements. 5th ed. Merhyle F. Spotts. (Illus.). 1978. 39.95 (*0-685-03825-4*) P-H.

Design of Machine Elements. 6th ed. Merhyle F. Spotts. (Illus.). 704p. (C). 1985. text ed. 77.00 (*0-13-200593-X*) P-H.

Design of Machinery: An Introduction to the Synthesis & Analysis of Mechanisms & Machines. Robert L. Norton. 1992. text ed. write for info. (*0-07-047799-X*) McGraw.

Design of Man-Computer Dialogues. James Martin. (Illus.). 496p. 1973. pap. text ed. 60.00 (*0-13-201251-0*) P-H.

Design of Marine & Offshore Structures: Proceedings of the Fourth International Conference on Computer Aided Design, Manufacture & Operation in the Marine & Offshore Industries (CADMO 92) Held in Madrid, Spain, October 27-29, 1992. Ed. by T. K. Murthy & J. A. Alaez. LC 92-82811. (CADMO Ser.). 828p. 1992. 324.00 (*1-56252-107-1*) Computational Mech MA.

Design of Marine Facilities. J. Gaythwaite. 1990. text ed. 85.00 (*0-442-22900-3*) Chapman & Hall.

Design of Marine Structures & Composite Materials. C. S. Smith. 39p. 1990. 144.00 (*1-85166-416-5*) Elsevier.

Design of Microprocessor-Based System. Nikitas Alexandridis. 528p. 1993. text ed. 75.00 (*0-13-588567-1*) P-H.

Design of Minor Irrigation & Canal Structures. C. Satyanarayana Murty. (C). 1991. pap. 16.00 (*81-224-0280-1*, Pub. by Wiley Eastern II) S Asia.

Design of Mission Operations Systems for Scientific Remote Sensing. Stephen D. Wall & Kenneth W. Ledbetter. (Illus.). 250p. 1991. 85.00 (*0-85066-860-3*, Pub. by Tay Francis Ltd UK) Taylor & Francis.

Design of Modern Concrete Highway Bridges. Conrad P. Heins & Richard A. Lawrie. LC 92-15561. 656p. (C). 1992. reprint ed. lib. bdg. 110.00 (*0-89464-760-1*) Krieger.

Design of Modern Control Systems. D. J. Bell et al. (Control Engineering Ser.: No. 20). 344p. 1982. pap. 99.00 (*0-906048-74-5*, CE020) Inst Elect Eng.

Design of Modern Steel Highway Bridges. Conrad P. Heins & D. A. Firmage. LC 78-9084. 475p. reprint ed. pap. 135.40 (*0-7837-2824-7*, 2057648) Bks Demand.

Design of Modern Turbine Combustors. A. M. Mellor. (Combustion Ser.). 557p. 1990. text ed. 237.00 (*0-12-490055-0*) Acad Pr.

Design of Multi-Storey Precast Concrete Structures. (FIP Commission on Prefabrication Ser.). 27p. 1986. 30.00 (*0-7277-0258-0*, Pub. by T Telford UK) Am Soc Civil Eng.

Design of Multiple Inheritance Hierarchies. Peter Eklund. 1994. 55.00 (*0-13-106089-9*) P-H.

Design of Multiple Inheritance Hierarchies. 3rd ed. Peter Eklund. 250p. 1994. pap. text ed. 36.00 (*0-13-104696-9*) P-H.

Design of Municipal Sludge Composting Facilities. 1978. 25.00 (*0-944989-14-4*, 040078) Hazardous Mat Control.

Design of Municipal Wastewater Treatment Plants. (ASCE Manual & Report on Engineering Practice Ser.: No. 76). 1600p. 1992. pap. text ed. 250.00 (*0-87262-834-5*) Am Soc Civil Eng.

Design of Municipal Wastewater Treatment Plants: MOP 8, 2 vols., I. (Illus.). 1592p. 1992. write for info. (*0-943244-84-6*) Water Environ.

Design of Municipal Wastewater Treatment Plants: MOP 8, 2 vols., II. (Illus.). 1592p. 1992. write for info. (*0-943244-85-4*) Water Environ.

Design of Municipal Wastewater Treatment Plants: MOP 8, 2 vols., Set. (Illus.). 1592p. 1992. 250.00 (*0-943244-83-8*) Water Environ.

Design of Networks for Monitoring Water Quality. Thomas Sanders et al. LC 83-61028. 336p. 1987. 38.00 (*0-918334-51-9*) WRP.

Design of New Materials. Ed. by D. L. Cocke & A. Clearfield. LC 87-3131. (Illus.). 378p. 1987. 79.50 (*0-306-42604-8*, Plenum Pr) Plenum.

***Design of Non-Impounding Mine Waste Dumps.** fac. ed. Society of Mining Engineers of AIME Staff. Ed. by M. K. McCarter. LC 85-71780. (Illus.). 222p. 1985. reprint ed. pap. 63.30 (*0-7837-7842-2*, 2047601) Bks Demand.

Design of Novel Chalcogen-Containing Organic Metals: Extensively Conjugated Electron Donors & Acceptors with Reduced On-site Coulomb Repulsion. F. Ogura & Y. Aso. (Sulfur Report Ser.). 1992. pap. text ed. 99.00 (*3-7186-5295-1*) Gordon & Breach.

Design of Nuclear Plants. A. N. Komarovskii. 496p. 1965. text ed. 152.50 (*0-7065-0488-7*, Pub. by Keter Pub IS) Coronet Bks.

Design of Office Information Systems. C. Ellis & N. Naffah. (Surveys in Computer Science Ser.). (Illus.). vii, 248p. 1987. 40.00 (*0-387-17810-4*) Spr-Verlag.

Design of Operating Systems for Small Computer Systems. Stephen H. Kaisler. 682p. (C). 1983. lib. bdg. 56.00 (*0-471-07774-7*) Krieger.

Design of Optical Systems Incorporating Low Power Lasers: Critical Review. Ed. by O'Shea. 221p. 1987. 48.00 (*0-89252-776-5*, 741) SPIE.

Design of OS-2. Harvey M. Deitel & M. S. Kogan. (Illus.). 448p. (C). 1992. text ed. 43.25 (*0-201-54889-5*) Addison-Wesley.

Design of OS 2. 2nd ed. M. S. Kogan. (C). 1995. text ed. 43.25 (*0-201-52886-X*) Addison-Wesley.

Design of Partially Prestressed Flexural Members. Prestressed Concrete Institute Staff. (PCI Journal Reprints Ser.). 20p. 1977. pap. 6.00 (*0-318-19854-1*, JR189) P-PCI.

Design of Partially Prestressed Flexural Members, Reader Comments. (PCI Journal Reprints Ser.). 14p. 1978. pap. 6.00 (*0-686-40107-7*, JR189A) P-PCI.

Design of Pile Foundations. (National Cooperative Highway Research Program Report Ser.: No. 042). 68p. 1977. 4.80 (*0-309-02544-3*) Transport Res Bd.

Design of Pile Foundations. U. S. Army Corps of Engineers. LC 92-43726. 112p. 1993. 24.00 (*0-87262-930-9*) Am Soc Civil Eng.

Design of Pilot-Plant Studies. 108p. 1982. pap. 17.50 (*0-89867-285-6*, 20164) Am Water Wks Assn.

Design of Plastic Moulds & Dies. L. Sors & I. Balazs. (Studies in Polymer Science: No. 3). 254p. 1989. 143.75 (*0-444-98902-1*) Elsevier.

Design of Pneumatic & Fluidic Control Systems. Edward L. Holbrook & Pah I. Chen. LC 84-61668. (Illus.). 431p. 1984. 35.00 (*0-9613851-0-3*) Pech Pub.

Design of Precast Prestressed Bridge Girders Made Continuous. (National Cooperative Highway Research Program Report Ser.: No. 322). 97p. 1989. 11.00 (*0-309-04619-X*) Transport Res Bd.

Design of Prestressed Concrete. R. I. Gilbert & Neil Mickleborough. (Illus.). 384p. (C). 1990. text ed. 115.00 (*0-04-445402-3*); pap. text ed. 29.95 (*0-04-445403-1*) Routledge Chapman & Hall.

Design of Prestressed Concrete. 2nd ed. Arthur H. Nilson. 592p. 1987. Net. text ed. write for info. (*0-471-83072-0*) Wiley.

Design of Prestressed Concrete Structures. 3rd ed. T. Y. Lin & Ned H. Burns. LC 80-20619. 646p. (C). 1981. Net. text ed. write for info. (*0-471-01898-8*) Wiley.

***Design of Process Equipment: Selected Topics.** 3rd ed. Kanti K. Mahajan. (Illus.). 1990. 68.00 (*0-615-00652-3*) Pressure.

Design of Prodrugs. Ed. by H. Bundgaard. 372p. 1986. 162.75 (*0-444-80675-X*) Elsevier.

Design of Rabelais's "Pantagruel" Edwin M. Duval. 240p. (C). 1991. text ed. 32.50x (*0-300-04803-3*) Yale U Pr.

***Design of Racing & High Performance Engines.** Joseph Harralson. (Progress in Technology Ser.). 200p. 1995. 59.00 (*1-56091-601-X*, PT53) Soc Auto Engineers.

Design of Real Time Applications. Maurice Blackman. LC 74-26960. (Illus.). 283p. reprint ed. pap. 80.70 (*0-8357-6302-1*, 2035575) Bks Demand.

Design of Regional Accounts: Papers Presented at the Conference on Regional Accounts, 1960. Conference on Regional Accounts Staff. Ed. by Werner Hochwald. LC 61-17653. 301p. reprint ed. pap. 85.80 (*0-7837-3125-6*, 2042862) Bks Demand.

Design of Reinforced & Prestressed Masonry. W. G. Curtin et al. 256p. 1988. 95.00 (*0-7277-1314-0*, Pub. by T Telford UK) Am Soc Civil Eng.

Design of Reinforced Concrete. 2nd ed. Jack C. McCormac. 624p. (C). 1989. text ed. 51.25 (*0-06-044345-6*); write for info. (*0-318-59890-6*) HarpCollege.

Design of Reinforced Concrete Elements. Patrick Morrell. (Illus.). 1977. pap. 26.95 (*0-8464-0320-X*) Beekman Pubs.

Design of Reinforced Concrete Structures. 2nd ed. Henry J. Cowan. 320p. 1988. boxed 52.00 (*0-13-201443-2*) P-H.

Design of Relational Databases. Kari-Jouko Raiha. (C). 1992. pap. text ed. 37.75 (*0-201-56523-4*) Addison-Wesley.

Design of Research & Analysis of Data in the Clinic: An Introductory Manual for Clinical Research. rev. ed. American Physical Therapy Association Staff. (Orig.). 1985. pap. 12.00 (*0-912452-58-7*) Am Phys Therapy Assn.

Design of Research & Analysis of Data in the Clinic: Introduction to Factorial Designs & Analysis of Variance. rev. ed. American Physical Therapy Association Staff. 1985. pap. 12.00 (*0-912452-59-5*) Am Phys Therapy Assn.

Design of Residential Areas: Basic Considerations, Principles & Methods. Thomas Adams. LC 73-2900. (Metropolitan America Ser.: Vol. 6). 334p. 1979. reprint ed. 31.95 (*0-405-05381-9*) Ayer.

Design of Rural Development: Lessons from Africa. Uma Lele. LC 75-10896. (World Bank Research Publication Ser.). (Illus.). 260p. 1975. pap. 11.95 (*0-8018-1769-2*) Johns Hopkins.

Design of Sedimentation Basins. (National Cooperative Highway Research Program Report Ser.: No. 070). 53p. 1980. 6.80 (*0-309-03027-7*) Transport Res Bd.

Design of Shearing Sheds & Sheep Yards. A. A. Barber & R. B. Freeman. (Illus.). 220p. 1986. 64.95 (*0-909605-35-1*, Pub. by Inkata Pr AT) Intl Spec Bk.

Design of Ships' Structures. HMSO Staff. 498p. 1993. 165.00 (*0-11-772717-2*, HM27172, Pub. by HMSO UK) UNIPUB.

Design of Slabs on Grade. 57p. 1992. 51.95 (*0-685-62951-1*) ACI.

Design of Small Canal Structure. USDI Staff. 435p. 1988. 300.00 (*0-685-18856-6*, Scientific) St Mut.

Design of Small Canal Structure. USDI Staff. (C). 1991. text ed. 200.00 (*0-7855-0106-1*, Pub. by Scientific Pubs II); text ed. 200.00 (*81-85046-48-4*, Pub. by Scientific Pubs II) St Mut.

Design of Small Canal Structures. 1992. lib. bdg. 350.95 (*0-8490-5550-4*) Gordon Pr.

Design of Small Dams. (Water Resources Technical Publication Ser.). 902p. 1987. 27.00 (*0-16-003373-X*, 024-003-00164-3) USGPO.

Design of Small Dams: A Guide to Safe Practices in the Design of Small Dams in Public Work Projects. 1992. lib. bdg. 489.95 (*0-8490-5553-9*) Gordon Pr.

***Design of Small Electrical Machines.** H.S. Hamdi. 1994. text ed. 67.95 (*0-471-95202-8*) Wiley.

Design of Smoke Management Systems. J. Klote & J. Milke. Ed. by M. Geshwiler. (Illus.). 225p. (C). 1992. text ed. 83.00 (*0-910110-88-3*) Am Heat Ref & Air Eng.

Design of Social Research. Russell L. Ackoff. LC 53-12546. 432p. reprint ed. pap. 123.20 (*0-685-15599-4*, 2026759) Bks Demand.

Design of Solid-State Power Supplies. 3rd ed. Eugene R. Hnatek. 1989. text ed. 74.95 (*0-442-20768-9*) Van Nos Reinhold.

Design of Spandrel Beams. 75p. 1988. 24.00 (*0-318-35233-8*, R&D5) P-PCI.

Design of Steel & Composite Beams with Web Openings, 1990. Darwin. 1990. 16.00 (*1-56424-031-2*, D802) Am Inst Steel Construct.

***Design of Steel Structures.** Elias G. Abu-Saba. LC 94-48546. 1995. write for info. (*0-412-98491-1*) Chapman & Hall.

Design of Steel Structures. 3rd ed. Edwin H. Gaylord. 1992. text ed. write for info. (*0-07-023054-4*) McGraw.

Design of Steel Transmission Pole Structures. Comp. by American Society of Civil Engineers Staff. 82p. 1978. pap. 6.00 (*0-87262-139-1*) Am Soc Civil Eng.

Design of Steel Transmission Pole Structures: ASCE Manual & Report on Engineering Practice, No. 72. 2nd ed. LC 90-422. 103p. 1990. pap. text ed. 18.00 (*0-87262-754-3*) Am Soc Civil Eng.

Design of Structural Concrete. 164p. 1983. 64.75 (*0-317-37036-7*, COMI-83); 33.25 (*0-317-37037-5*) ACI.

Design of Structural Elements: Concrete, Steelwork, Masonry, & Timber Design to British Standards & Eurocodes. C. Arya. LC 93-32219. 1993. write for info. (*0-419-17620-9*, E & FN Spon) Routledge Chapman & Hall.

Design of Structural Steelwork. Peter Knowles. (Illus.). 1977. 43.50 (*0-903384-16-7*) Trans-Atl Phila.

Design of Structures Against Fire. R. D. Anchor et al. (C). 1986. 300.00 (*0-685-32833-3*, Pub. by Witherby & Co UK) St Mut.

Design of Structures Against Fire: Proceedings of the International Conference of Design of Structure Against Fire, Aston University, Birmingham U. K., 15-16 April 1986. Ed. by Robert D. Anchor et al. 252p. 1986. 66.75 (*1-85166-012-7*) Elsevier.

Design of Structures & Foundations for Vibrating Machines. Suresh C. Arya et al. LC 78-56171. 190p. 1979. 39.00 (*0-87201-294-8*) Gulf Pub.

Design of Structures of Least Weight. H. Cox & R. Bisplinghoff. LC 65-14782. (International Series of Mono in Aeronautics & Astronautics: Vol. 8). 1965. 60.00 (*0-08-011165-3*, Pub. by Pergamon Repr UK) Franklin.

Design of Sunshading Devices. A. Monem Saleh. 116p. 1988. pap. text ed. 15.00 (*0-643-04892-8*, Pub. by CSIRO AT) Intl Spec Bk.

***Design of Supports in Mines.** Biron. 23p. 1987. text ed. 45.95 (*0-471-86726-8*) Krieger.

Design of Survivable Networks. Mechthild Stoer. LC 92-39266. (Lecture Notes in Mathematics Ser.: Vol. 1531). 1993. 35.00 (*0-387-56271-0*) Spr-Verlag.

Design of Synthetic Inhibitors of Thrombin. Ed. by G. Claeson et al. (Advances in Experimental Medicine & Biology Ser.: Vol. 340). 246p. 1994. 75.00 (*0-306-44593-X*, Plenum Pr) Plenum.

Design of Testable VSLI Circuits. Maly. 1994. write for info. (*0-8493-7281-X*) CRC Pr.

Design of Textiles for Industrial Applications. P. W. Harrison. 218p. 1977. 100.00 (*0-686-63759-3*) St Mut.

Design of the Appropriations Process in the House of Representatives, 1865-1921. Charles Stewart, III. (Political Economy of Institutions & Decisions Ser.: No. 5). (Illus.). 250p. (C). 1989. 54.95 (*0-521-35472-2*) Cambridge U Pr.

Design of the Electron Microscope Laboratory. Ed. by R. H. Alderson. (Practical Methods in Electron Microscopy Ser.: Vol. 4). 1975. pap. 18.00 (*0-444-10816-5*, North Holland) Elsevier.

Design of the Factory with a Future. J. T. Black. 256p. 1991. text ed. write for info. (*0-07-005551-3*); pap. text ed. write for info. (*0-07-005550-5*) McGraw.

Design of the Mach Operating System. Eric Sheinbrood et al. 480p. 1993. boxed 46.00 (*0-13-204595-8*) P-H.

***Design of the National Water-Quality Assessment Program: Occurrence & Distribution of Water-Quality Conditions.** Robert J. Gilliom et al. LC 95-12999. (Circulars Ser.: Vol. 1112). 1995. write for info. (*0-615-00693-0*) US Geol Survey.

Design of the OSF-1 Operating System. Open Software Foundation Staff. 1993. pap. text ed. 47.00 (*0-13-202813-1*) P-H.

Design of the UNIX Operating System. Maurice J. Bach. 512p. 1986. text ed. 69.00 (*0-13-201799-7*) P-H.

Design of Thermal Systems. 3rd ed. Wilbert F. Stoecker. (Illus.). 592p. 1989. text ed. write for info. (*0-07-061620-5*) McGraw.

Design of Tools for Deformation Processes. Ed. by T. A. Blazynski. 308p. 1986. 86.50 (*0-85334-389-6*, Pub. by Elsevier Applied Sci UK) Elsevier.

Design of Underground Hard-Coal Mines. J. Pazdziora. (Advances in Mining Science & Technology Ser.: Vol. 3). 1988. 89.75 (*0-444-98938-2*) Elsevier.

Design of Urban Runoff Quality Controls. Ed. by Larry A. Roesner et al. 502p. 1989. 43.00 (*0-87262-695-4*) Am Soc Civil Eng.

Design of Vibration Isolation Systems: S A E Committee G-5 Aerospace Shock & Vibration. Society of Automotive Engineers Staff. 1962. 59.00 (*0-08-009761-8*, Pub. by Pergamon Repr UK) Franklin.

Design of VSLI Systems: A Practical Introduction. Linda E. Brackenbury. (Computer Science Ser.). (Illus.). 164p. (C). 1987. text ed. 90.00 (*0-333-40821-7*); pap. text ed. 30.00 (*0-333-40822-5*) Scholium Intl.

Design of Warning Labels & Instructions. Alan Ryan. 1991. text ed. 59.95 (*0-442-31953-3*) Van Nos Reinhold.

Design of Wastewater & Stormwater Pumping Stations. Richard L. Anderton et al. LC 93-6136. (Manual of Practice Ser.: Vol. FD-4). 1993. 35.00 (*0-685-71446-2*) Water Environ.

Design of Wastewater & Stormwater Pumping Stations ('80) Manual of Practice, Facilities & Development-4, No. 4. Water Pollution Control Federation Staff. 152p. 1981. pap. 23.00 (*0-943244-20-X*, MOP FD-4) Water Environ.

Design of Water & Wastewater Services for Cold Climate Communities: Seminar in Edmonton in June 1980 of the 10th IAWPR Conference. Ed. by D. W. Smith & S. E. Hrudey. (Illus.). 190p. 1981. pap. 43.00 (*0-08-029079-5*, E140, Pergamon Pr) Elsevier.

Design of Water Intake Structures for Fish Protection. American Society of Civil Engineers Staff. LC 81-70988. (Illus.). 163p. reprint ed. pap. 49.90 (*0-685-23468-1*, 2056673) Bks Demand.

Design of Water Quality Monitors. R. Ward. 1990. text ed. 59.95 (*0-442-00156-8*) Van Nos Reinhold.

Design of Water-Retaining Structures. Ian Batty & Roger Westbrook. 202p. 1992. pap. text ed. 116.00 (*0-470-21846-0*) Halsted Pr.

Design of Welded Tubular Connections: Basis & Use of AWS Code Provisions. P. W. Marshall. (Developments in Civil Engineering Ser.: Vol. 37). 412p. 1991. 131.25 (*0-444-88201-4*) Elsevier.

Design of Well-Structured & Correct Programs. 4th ed. S. Alagic & Michael A. Arbib. (Texts & Monographs in Computer Science). (Illus.). x, 292p. 1991. reprint ed. text ed. 55.00 (*0-387-90299-6*) Spr-Verlag.

Design of William Morris' "The Earthly Paradise" Florence S. Boos. LC 89-12180. (Studies in British Literature: Vol. 6). 592p. 1991. lib. bdg. 119.95 (*0-88946-933-4*) E Mellen.

Design of Wood Structures. 3rd ed. Donald E. Breyer. 832p. 1993. text ed. 63.00 (*0-07-007678-2*) McGraw.

Design of Work & Development of Personnel in Advanced Manufacturing. Ed. by Gavriel Salvendy & Waldemar Karwowski. 575p. 1994. text ed. 84.95 (*0-471-59447-4*, Wiley-Interscience) Wiley.

Design of Worm & Spiral Gears. Earle Buckingham. LC 60-16525. 450p. 1981. 30.00 (*0-317-00957-5*) Buckingham Assoc.

Design Office Management Handbook. Ed. by Fred A. Stitt. 1990. pap. 22.50 (*0-931228-11-5*) Arts & Arch.

Design on File. (On File Ser.). 345p. ring bd. 155.00x (*0-87196-270-5*) Facts on File.

Design on the Land: The Development of Landscape Architecture. Norman T. Newton. LC 70-134955. (Illus.). 740p. 1971. 50.00 (*0-674-19870-0*) Belknap Pr.

***Design, Operation, & Closure of Municipal Solid Waste Landfills: Seminar Publication.** Gregory Richardson et al. (Illus.). 86p. (Orig.). (C). 1994. pap. text ed. 50.00x (*0-7881-1419-0*) Diane Pub.

Design-Operation Interactions at Large Waste Water Treatment Plants. S. H. Jenkins. 1978. pap. 55.00 (*0-08-020901-7*, Pergamon Pr) Elsevier.

Design Optimization. John S. Gero. (Notes & Reports in Mathematics in Science & Engineering Ser.). 1985. text ed. 81.00 (*0-12-280910-6*) Acad Pr.

Design Optimization. Eric Sandgren. (Mechanical Engineering Ser.). (Illus.). 384p. (C). 1995. text ed. 48.50 (*0-201-18544-X*) Addison-Wesley.

D

An Asterisk (*) at the beginning of an entry indicates that the title is appearing in BIP for the first time.

Design Optimization of Cyclic Oil Gas Processes for Peakload Gas Production. S. A. Weil et al. (Research Bulletin Ser.: No.37). iv, 70p. 1965. 5.00 (*0-685-43358-7*) Inst Gas Tech.

Design Paradigms: Case Histories of Error & Judgment in Engineering. Henry Petroski. LC 93-32560. (Illus.). 250p. (C). 1994. 42.95 (*0-521-46108-1*); pap. 17.95 (*0-521-46649-0*) Cambridge U Pr.

Design Pascal. Clancy. (C). 1995. text ed. write for info. (*0-7167-8264-2*) W H Freeman.

Design Patterns: Microarchitectures for Reusable Object-Oriented Software. Erich Gamma. 1995. 36.95 (*0-201-63361-2*) Addison-Wesley.

*__Design Patterns for Object-Oriented Software Development.__ Wolfgang Pree. (C). 1995. text ed. 39.75 (*0-201-42294-8*) Addison-Wesley.

Design, Performance, & Applications of Microwave Semiconductor Control Components. Kenneth E. Mortenson & Jose M. Borrego. LC 70-189394. (Modern Frontiers in Applied Science Ser.). (Illus.). 294p. reprint ed. pap. 83.80 (*0-8357-4176-1*, 2036954) Bks Demand.

*__Design Plan Oosterschelde Storm-Surge Barrier: Overall Design & Design Philosophy.__ (Illus.). 252p. (C). 1994. pap. 55.00 (*90-5410-107-5*, Pub. by A A Balkema NE) Ashgate Pub Co.

Design Planning for Freestanding Ambulatory Care Facilities. Bill Rostenberg. LC 86-17241. (Illus.). 142p. (Orig.). 1987. 40.00 (*0-939450-95-X*, 043181) AHPI.

Design Power. Ed. by Duane Hillmer. LC 83-90501. (Illus.). 48p. (Orig.). 1984. pap. text ed. 12.95 (*0-916065-00-6*) Hillmer Graph Co.

Design Practice of Open Drainage Channels in an Agricultural Land Drainage System: A World Wide Survey, 1984. 343p. 1984. 25.00 (*81-85068-09-7*) US Comm Irrigation.

Design Practices: Passenger Car Automatic Transmissions. 3rd ed. LC 93-50093. (Advances in Engineering Ser.: Vol. 18). 912p. 1994. 119.00 (*1-56091-506-4*) Soc Auto Engineers.

Design Practices for Covered Drains in an Agricultural Land Drainage System: A Worldwide Survey, 1987. 50.00 (*81-85068-14-3*) US Comm Irrigation.

Design Practices for Multiple-Seam Longwell Mines. Gregory J. Chekan & Jeffrey M. Listak. 1993. write for info. (*0-318-70187-1*) US Interior.

Design Presentation: Techniques for Marketing & Presentation of Project Proposals. 2nd ed. Ernest E. Burden. 1992. pap. text ed. 29.95 (*0-07-008938-8*) McGraw.

Design Presentation: Techniques for Marketing & Project Presentation. Ernest E. Burden. (Illus.). 256p. 1983. text ed. 60.00 (*0-07-008931-0*) McGraw.

Design Presentations for Architects. Michael Wahl. (Illus.). 136p. 1987. pap. 30.95 (*0-442-29150-7*) Van Nos Reinhold.

Design Primer: Geotextiles & Related Materials. 150p. 1991. 35.00 (*0-685-48639-7*) Indus Fabrics.

Design Principles & Problems. Paul Zelanski & Mary P. Fisher. (Illus.). 304p. (C). 1984. pap. text ed. 38.00 (*0-03-051166-6*) HB Coll Pubs.

Design Principles for Desktop Publishers. 2nd ed. Tom Lichty. 226p. 1994. pap. 19.95 (*0-534-23082-2*) Intl Thomson.

Design Principles of Metal Cutting Machine Tools. F. Koenigsberger. LC 63-12694. 1964. 140.00 (*0-08-010106-2*, Pub. by Pergamon Repr UK) Franklin.

Design Problem Solving: Knowledge Structures & Control Strategies. David Brown & B. Chandrasekaran. (Research Notes in Artificial Intelligence Ser.). (Illus.). 200p. (Orig.). 1989. pap. text ed. 29.95 (*0-934613-07-9*) Morgan Kaufmann.

Design Problem Solving: Knowledge Structures & Control Strategies. Ed. by David C. Brown & B. Chandrasekaran. 208p. (Orig.). (C). 1989. pap. text ed. 180.00 (*0-273-08766-5*, Pub. by Pitman Pubng UK) St Mut.

Design Procedure for Partially Prestressed Concrete Beams Based on Strength & Serviceability. (PCI Journal Reprints Ser.). 18p. 1985. pap. 7.00 (*0-318-19783-9*, JR266) P-PCI.

*__Design Process.__ H. Bradley Hammond. (Illus.). 245p. (C). 1994. pap. text ed. 21.00 (*1-57074-153-0*) Greyden Pr.

Design Process: A Primer for Architectural & Interior Design. Sam F. Miller. 240p. 1995. pap. 39.95 (*0-442-01394-9*) Van Nos Reinhold.

Design Process: Case Studies in Project Development. Ellen Shoshkes. (Illus.). 256p. 1989. 45.00 (*0-8230-1312-X*, Whitney Lib) Watsn-Guptill.

Design Process: Innovative Architecture in Portland, Seattle & Spokane. 1985. pap. 6.00 (*0-910524-13-0*) Eastern Wash.

Design Professional's Handbook of Business & Law. Ed. by Robert F. Cushman & James C. Dobbs. (Construction Law Library). 840p. 1991. text ed. 123.00 (*0-471-52284-8*) Wiley.

Design Professional's Handbook of Business & Law. Ed. by Robert F. Cushman & James C. Dobbs. 840p. 1992. pap. text ed. 65.00 (*0-471-55232-1*) Wiley.

*__Design Project Planning.__ W. T. Bond. LC 95-14235. 1995. write for info. (*0-13-349275-3*) P-H.

Design Proposals for Reinforced Concrete Corbels. (PCI Journal Reprints Ser.). 28p. 1985. pap. 7.00 (*0-318-19755-3*, JR173) P-PCI.

Design Proposals for Shear & Torsion. (PCI Journal Reprints Ser.). 72p. 1980. pap. 13.00 (*0-686-40133-6*, JR228) P-PCI.

Design Protection. Dan Johnson. 144p. 1987. 49.00 (*0-85072-165-2*) St Mut.

Design Protection. Dan Johnston. 200p. (C). 1989. text ed. 90.00 (*0-85072-248-9*) St Mut.

*__Design Protection: A Practical Guide to the Law on Plagiarism for Manufacturers & Designers.__ 4th ed. Dan Johnston. 330p. 1994. 67.95 (*0-566-07553-9*) Ashgate Pub Co.

Design Rationale: Concepts, Techniques, & Use. Ed. by Thomas P. Moran & John M. Carroll. (Computers, Cognition, & Work Ser.). 600p. 1994. text ed. 100.00 (*0-8058-1566-X*); pap. 50.00 (*0-8058-1567-8*) L Erlbaum Assocs.

Design Recommendations for Precast Concrete Structures. 8p. 1993. 9.50 (*0-685-72302-X*, 550R-93) ACI.

Design Recommendations for Room Air Distribution Systems. P. J. Jackman. 1990. 72.00 (*0-86022-252-7*, Pub. by Build Servs Info Assn UK) St Mut.

Design Representation Programming Interface: Electrical Connectivity, 4 vols., 1. Design Information Technical Committee Staff. 475p. 1993. pap. text ed. 150.00 (*1-882750-01-2*) CAD Framewk.

Design Representation Programming Interface: Electrical Connectivity, 4 vols., Set. Design Information Technical Committee Staff. 475p. 1993. pap. text ed. write for info. (*1-882750-00-4*) CAD Framewk.

Design Research Interactions. Ed. by Arvid Osterberg et al. (EDRA Proceedings Ser.). 600p. 1981. pap. text ed. 30.00 (*0-939922-03-7*) EDRA.

Design Resourcebook for Small Communities. Henry Sanoff. (Illus.). 51p. (C). 1988. pap. text ed. 6.95 (*0-317-93291-8*) H Sanoff.

*__Design Responsibilities.__ C. Parsloe. (C). 1994. 115.00x (*0-86022-371-X*, Pub. by Build Servs Info Assn UK) St Mut.

Design Review: Challenging Urban Aesthetic Control. Brenda C. Scheer & Wolfgang F. E. Preiser. LC 94-19274. 1994. 36.95 (*0-412-98351-6*); pap. 39.95 (*0-412-99161-6*) Chapman & Hall.

Design Rules for a CIM System. R. W. Yeomans et al. 454p. 1985. 57.50 (*0-444-87812-2*, North Holland) Elsevier.

Design, Sampling, Handling, & Applications of Infrared Microscopes. Ed. by Patricia B. Roush. LC 87-14345. (Special Technical Publication Ser.: No. 949). (Illus.). viii, 115p. 1987. 24.00 (*0-8031-0953-9*, 04-949000-39) ASTM.

Design Sensitivity: Statistical Power for Experimental Research. Mark W. Lipsey. (Illus.). 224p. (C). 1989. text ed. 49.95 (*0-8039-3062-3*); pap. text ed. 24.00 (*0-8039-3063-1*) Sage.

Design Sensitivity Analysis of Structural Systems. Edward J. Haug et al. (Mathematics in Science & Engineering Ser.). 1986. text ed. 106.00 (*0-12-332920-5*); pap. text ed. 63.00 (*0-12-332921-3*) Acad Pr.

Design since Nineteen Forty-Five. Peter Dormer. LC 92-80335. (World of Art Ser.). (Illus.). 216p. 1993. pap. 12.95 (*0-500-20261-3*) Thames Hudson.

Design since Nineteen Forty-Five. Kathryn B. Hiesinger & George H. Marcus. LC 83-17414. 251p. (Orig.). 1983. pap. 9.95 (*0-87633-056-1*) Phila Mus Art.

Design Skills in Human Resource Development, Set. J. William Pfeiffer & Arlette C. Ballew. LC 87-40536. (Training Technologies Set Ser.). 118p. (Orig.). 1988. pap. text ed. 139.00 (*0-88390-215-X*) Pfeiffer & Co.

Design Standards for School Art Facilities. 2nd ed. 32p. 1994. pap. 10.00 (*0-685-72170-1*) Natl Art Ed.

Design Statistics in Pharmacochemistry. Peter P. Mager. (Chemometrics Research Studies). 661p. 1991. text ed. 356.00 (*0-471-92953-0*) Wiley.

Design Study for a Macropermeability Test in an Argillaceous Formation. J. Brounders. (Nuclear Science & Technology Ser.). 63p. 1993. pap. 11.00 (*92-826-4738-2*, CD-NA-14478-EN-C, Pub. by Europ Com) UNIPUB.

Design Supplement to SSB-1-81. Prestressed Concrete Institute Staff. 80p. pap. 20.00 (*0-318-19822-3*, SSB-Z) P-PCI.

Design Synectics: Stimulating Creativity in Design. Nicholas Roukes. LC 88-70675. (Illus.). 224p. 1988. pap. 24.95 (*0-87192-198-7*) Davis Mass.

Design Tables for Beams on Elastic Foundations & Related Structural Problems. J. T. Iyengar et al. (Illus.). 140p. 1979. 66.75 (*0-85334-841-3*, Pub. by Elsevier Applied Sci UK) Elsevier.

Design Tables for Discrete Time Normalized Low-Pass Filters. Arild Lacroix & Karl-Heinz Witte. 295p. (C). 1986. pap. 19.00 (*0-89006-215-3*) Artech Hse.

Design Tables for Folded Plates. U. H. Varyani & K. N. Taneja. (Illus.). 355p. (C). 1982. 59.00 (*0-88065-224-1*, Pub. by Today & Tomorrows P & P II) Scholarly Pubns.

Design Talks! Ed. by Peter Gorb & Eric Schneider. 308p. (C). 1988. pap. 38.95x (*0-85072-218-7*, Pub. by Design Council Bks UK) Ashgate Pub Co.

Design Team Revolution: How to Cut Lead Times in Half & Double Your Productivity. Kenichi Sekin & Keisuke Arai. (Illus.). 328p. 1994. 85.00 (*1-56327-008-0*) Prod Press.

Design Techniques for Modern Lace. Veronica D. Sorenson. (Illus.). 152p. 1990. 39.95 (*0-7134-6021-0*, Pub. by Batsford UK) Trafalgar.

Design Techniques to Minimize Low-Temperature Asphalt Pavement Transverse Cracking. 76p. 1981. 15.00 (*0-318-17744-7*, RR-81-1) Asphalt Inst.

Design Technology: Children's Engineering. Susan Dunn & Larson. 230p. 1989. pap. 28.00 (*1-85000-590-7*, Falmer Pr) Taylor & Francis.

Design Technology Five Twelve. Pat Williams & David Jinks. (Illus.). 130p. 1985. pap. 27.50 (*1-85000-049-2*, Falmer Pr) Taylor & Francis.

Design Technology of Fusion Reactors. Ed. by M. Akiyama. 636p. (C). 1990. text ed. 109.00 (*9971-5-0727-7*) World Scientific Pub.

Design, Testing, & Optimization of Trading Systems. Robert Pardo. LC 92-372. (Traders Library). 176p. 1992. text ed. 34.95 (*0-471-55446-4*) Wiley.

Design, Testing & Reporting Performance Results of Automatic External Defibrillators. 18p. 1987. 49.00 (*0-685-65434-6*, TIR2-113) Assn Adv Med Instrn.

Design That Cares: Planning Health Facilities for Patients & Visitors. 2nd ed. Janet R. Carpman & Myron A. Grant. LC 93-24698. 327p. (Orig.). 1993. 49.95 (*1-55648-106-3*, 043182) AHPI.

Design Theory & Computer Science. Subrata Dasgupta. (Cambridge Tracts in Theoretical Computer Science Ser.: No. 15). 300p. (C). 1991. 69.95 (*0-521-39021-4*) Cambridge U Pr.

*__Design Theory & Methodology: Proceedings of the Sixth International Conference, Minneapolis, MN, 1994.__ 383p. 1994. pap. 65.00 (*0-7918-1282-0*) ASME.

Design Theory & Methodology - DTM'93. Ed. by T. K. Hight & L. A. Stauffer. (DE Ser.: Vol. 53). 268p. 1993. pap. 62.50 (*0-7918-1170-0*, G00814) ASME.

Design Theory Eighty-Eight. Ed. by S. L. Newsome et al. (Illus.). xi, 355p. 1989. 54.00 (*0-387-96976-4*) Spr-Verlag.

Design Theory for CAD: Proceedings of the IFIP WG 5.2 Working Conference, Tokyo, Japan, October 1-3, 1985. Ed. by Hiroyuki Yoshikawa & Ernest A. Warman. 460p. 1987. 95.00 (*0-444-70151-6*, North Holland) Elsevier.

Design Thinking. Peter G. Rowe. (Illus.). 242p. 1991. reprint ed. pap. 14.95x (*0-262-68067-X*) MIT Pr.

Design Through Discovery. 5th ed. Marjorie E. Bevlin. 368p. (C). 1989. pap. text ed. 38.00 (*0-03-026303-4*) HB Coll Pubs.

Design Through Discovery. 6th ed. Marjorie Bevlin. (C). 1993. pap. 39.25 (*0-03-076547-1*) HB Coll Pubs.

Design Through Discovery: Elements & Principles. Marjorie E. Bevlin. 190p. (C). 1985. pap. text ed. 27.50 (*0-03-071624-1*) HB Coll Pubs.

*__Design Through Discovery: The Elements & Principles.__ 2nd ed. Marjorie E. Bevlin. LC 93-77624. xv, 205p. 1995. pap. 29.50 (*0-15-500963-X*) HarBrace.

Design to Cost for Affordability. Jack V. Michaels & William P. Wood. 413p. 1989. text ed. 74.95 (*0-471-60900-5*) Wiley.

Design to Deceive. Jane M. Choate. 1993. 13.95 (*0-8034-9007-0*) Bouregy.

Design to Deceive. large type ed. Jane M. Choate. LC 93-42209. 1994. pap. 13.95 (*0-7862-0138-X*) Thorndike Pr.

Design to Reduce Technical Risk. AT&T Staff. 750p. 1993. text ed. 60.00i (*0-07-002561-4*) McGraw.

Design to Test. Jon Turino & H. Frank Binnedyk. (Illus.). 227p. 1982. text ed. 150.00 (*0-912253-01-0*) Logical Solns Tech.

Design to Test. 2nd ed. John L. Turino. 1990. text ed. 64.95 (*0-442-00170-3*) Van Nos Reinhold.

Design to Test. 2nd ed. Jon L. Turino. (Illus.). 380p. 1989. 195.00 (*0-912253-05-3*) Logical Solns Tech.

Design to Test Seminar-Workshop Notebook. Jon Turino. (Illus.). 350p. 1983. student ed. 225.00 (*0-912253-02-9*) Logical Solns Tech.

*__Design Tool Selection & Use.__ 1995. lib. bdg. 250.00 (*0-8490-6456-2*) Gordon Pr.

Design Tools for Energy Efficient Homes. 3rd ed. Ken Eklund & David Baylon. Ed. by Richard Beckerman & Annie Stewart. (Illus.). 126p. 1984. pap. 7.90 (*0-934478-25-2*) Ecotope.

Design Tools for The 90's: Fifteenth EUROMICRO Symp. on Microprocessing & Microprogramming (EUROMICRO 89), Cologne, FRG, 4-8 Sept., 1989. Ed. by L. Mezzalira & S. Winter. 852p. 1990. 141.00 (*0-444-88052-6*, North Holland) Elsevier.

Design Units on Tlingit Baskets. Erna Gunther. 20p. 1990. pap. text ed. 4.75 (*1-880475-01-4*) Friends of SJM.

Design Way: An Essay. Rene Loire. 456p. 1990. 14.95 (*0-9611614-5-0*) A Ghosh.

Design with Advanced Composite Materials. Ed. by Leslie N. Philips. (Illus.). 384p. (C). 1989. 59.95x (*0-85072-238-1*, Pub. by Design Council Bks UK) Ashgate Pub Co.

Design with Advanced Composite Materials. Ed. by L. N. Phillips. (Illus.). 360p. 1990. 77.00 (*0-387-51800-2*, 3659) Spr-Verlag.

Design with Climate: A Bioclimatic Approach to Architectural Regionalism. Victor Olgyay. (Illus.). 200p. 1992. pap. 29.95 (*0-442-01110-5*) Van Nos Reinhold.

Design with Energy: The Conservation & Use of Energy in Buildings. John Littler & Randall Thomas. (Cambridge Urban & Architectural Studies: 8). (Illus.). 320p. 1984. 89.95 (*0-521-24562-1*); pap. 47.95 (*0-521-28787-1*) Cambridge U Pr.

Design with Flowers. Herb Mitchell. 240p. 1991. 49.95 (*0-9627922-1-7*) CRB Pub.

Design with Illustrations. Steven Heller. (Illus.). 288p. 1990. text ed. 35.95 (*0-442-23277-2*) Van Nos Reinhold.

Design with Microcontrollers. John B. Peatman. 512p. 1988. text ed. write for info. (*0-07-049238-7*) McGraw.

Design with Microprocessors for Mechanical Engineeres. A. Kent Stiffler. 1992. text ed. write for info. (*0-07-061374-5*) McGraw.

Design with Nature. Ian L. McHarg. 208p. 1991. text ed. 69.95 (*0-471-55797-8*) Wiley.

*__Design with Nature.__ Ian L. McHarg. (Series in Sustainable Design). 1995. pap. text ed. 39.95 (*0-471-11460-X*) Wiley.

Design with Nature. Ian L. McHarg. LC 76-77344. 1971. pap. 15.95 (*0-385-05509-9*) Natural Hist.

Design with Non-Ductile Materials. W. E. Creyke et al. (Illus.). xix, 294p. 1982. 79.25 (*0-85334-149-4*, 1-359-82, Pub. by Elsevier Applied Sci UK) Elsevier.

Design with Operational Amplifiers & Analog Integrated Circuits. Sergio Franco. 656p. (C). 1988. text ed. write for info. (*0-07-021799-8*) McGraw.

Design with Reinforced Plastics: A Guide for Engineers & Designers. Ed. by Rayner M. Mayer. (Illus.). 212p. (C). 1993. pap. 42.95x (*0-85072-294-2*, Pub. by Design Council Bks UK) Ashgate Pub Co.

*__Design with the Land: Landscape Architecture of Michael Van Valkenburgh.__ Ed. by Brooke Hodges. LC 94-16259. (Illus.). 88p. (Orig.). 1994. pap. 24.95 (*1-56898-022-1*) Princeton Arch.

Design with Type. Carl Dair. LC 66-23932. 1982. pap. 19.95 (*0-8020-6519-8*) U of Toronto Pr.

Design with X. Dean Young. LC 87-27239. (Wesleyan New Poets Ser.). 64p. 1988. pap. 10.95 (*0-8195-1155-2*, Wesleyan Univ Pr) U Pr of New Eng.

Design Workbook. Sharon Mendola. 80p. (C). 1993. pap. text ed., spiral bd. 16.95 (*0-8403-8454-8*) Kendall-Hunt.

*__Design Workbook.__ Sharon Mendola. 80p. (C). 1995. spiral bd. 16.95 (*0-7872-0617-2*) Kendall-Hunt.

*__Design Your Future: Live Your Vision in the Ever-Changing Learning Society.__ Paul Siegel. LC 94-76685. 224p. (Orig.). 1995. pap. 17.95 (*0-9623769-6-5*) Lrng Soc Pubns.

Design Your Own Coat of Arms: An Introduction to Heraldry. Rosemary A. Chorzempa. 48p. (Orig.). 1987. pap. 2.95 (*0-486-24993-X*) Dover.

Design Your Own Life: From High School to Career. Alice Ruud. 1990. student ed 9.95 (*1-56117-000-3*) Telesis CA.

Design Your Own Model A Ford. William G. Narum. 1990. pap. 5.95 (*0-486-26516-1*) Dover.

Design Your Own Repeat Patterns: A Quick & Easy Approach. Ann V. Waterman. 48p. (Orig.). 1986. pap. 3.95 (*0-486-25132-2*) Dover.

Design Yourself! Kurt Hanks et al. Ed. by W. Philip Gerould. LC 91-22916. (Orig.). 1991. reprint ed. pap. 11.95 (*1-56052-046-9*) Crisp Pubns.

Designated Duty & Limited Engineer. (USCG Examination Questions & Answers Ser.: Bk. 1). 294p. (Orig.). 1990. pap. text ed. 39.95 (*0-932889-11-5*) Examco Inc.

Designated Duty & Limited Engineer. (USCG Examination Questions & Answers Ser.: Bk. 2). 253p. (Orig.). 1990. pap. text ed. 39.95 (*0-932889-12-3*) Examco Inc.

Designated Landmarks of the Niagara Frontier. Lawrence McIntyre. 1985. pap. 13.95 (*0-9620314-2-9*) Meyer Enter.

*__Designated Vocational Instructional: A Resource & Planning Guide.__ 2nd ed. Ann Kellogg. 287p. (C). 1995. pap. text ed. 30.00 (*1-57337-017-7*) WI Dept Pub Instruct.

Designation of Human Types. Tr. by B. C. Law. (C). 1922. 16.00 (*0-86013-009-6*, Pub. by Pali Text) Wisdom MA.

Designed by God: A Woman's Workshop on Wholeness. Kirkie Morrissey. (Woman's Workshop Ser.). 160p. (Orig.). 1985. pap. 7.99 (*0-310-45011-X*, 16246P) Zondervan.

Designed by God, So I Must Be Special. Bonnie Sose. 22p. (J). 1988. pap. 3.50 (*0-9615279-8-6*) Character Builders.

Designed by God So I Must Be Special. Bonnie Sose. (Illus.). 24p. (J). (ps-2). 1991. 10.95 (*0-9615279-6-X*); Afro-American version available. 10.95 (*0-9615279-4-3*) Character Builders.

Designed for Conquest: Biblical Models for Overcoming Life's Struggles. Roy L. Laurin. LC 90-36540. Orig. Title: Meet Yourself in the Bible. 189p. 1990. reprint ed. pap. 7.99 (*0-8254-3139-5*) Kregel.

*__Designed for Dependency: Moving from Emotional Isolation to Intimacy.__ Lori A. Varick. 192p. (Orig.). 1994. pap. 8.99 (*1-883002-04-4*) Emerald WA.

Designed for Dignity: What God Has Made It Possible For You to Be. Richard L. Pratt, Jr. 224p. 1993. 14.99 (*0-87552-380-3*) Presby & Reformed.

*__Designed for the Kill: The Jet Fighter - Development & Experience.__ Mike Spick. (Illus.). 178p. 1995. 33.95 (*1-85310-121-4*) Naval Inst Pr.

Designed Polymers by Carbocationic Macromolecular Engineering: Theory & Practice. Joseph P. Kennedy & Bela Ivan. 240p. (C). 1992. text ed. 94.50 (*1-56990-047-7*) Hanser-Gardner.

Designed Right! Alan Swann. (Illus.). 200p. 1990. 24.95 (*0-89134-332-6*, 30202) North Light Bks.

Designed to Annoy. Elizabeth Oldfield. (Presents Ser.). 1994. mass mkt. 2.99 (*0-373-11636-5*, 1-11636-7) Harlequin Bks.

Designed to Be Like Him: New Testament Insight for Becoming Christlike. J. Dwight Pentecost. 1994. pap. 10.99 (*0-929239-88-1*) Discovery Hse Pubs.

Designed to Cruise. Roger Marshall. (Illus.). 1990. 49.95 (*0-393-03333-3*) Norton.

Designed to Sell: Turn-of-the-Century American Posters in the Virginia Museum of Fine Arts. Frederick R. Brandt et al. Ed. by Monica S. Rumsey & Rosalie A. West. (Illus.). 111p. (Orig.). 1994. pap. 35.00 (*0-917046-38-2*) Va Mus Arts.

Designed to Work: People & Production Systems. Robert T. Lund et al. 224p. 1993. text ed. 56.00 (*0-13-203944-3*) P-H.

*__Designer Crimes: A Laura Di Palma Mystery.__ Lia Matera. LC 95-1701. 1995. 21.00 (*0-684-80312-7*) S&S Trade.

Designer Diets for the Healing Force Within: Healing Forces Within for Obesity & Disease. James F. Balch, Jr. Ed. by Phyllis Balch & Sharon Kean. (Illus.). 282p. 1987. pap. 19.95 (*0-942023-00-5*) P A B Bks.

Designer Drugs. Lawrence Clayton. Ed. by Ruth Rosen. (Drug Abuse Prevention Library). (YA). (gr. 7-12). 1993. 15.95 (*0-8239-1519-0*) Rosen Group.

Designer Drugs. Paula Goodman & Gabriel Koz. (Encyclopedia of Psychoactive Drugs Ser.: No. 2). (Illus.). 120p. 1988. lib. bdg. 19.95 (*1-55546-207-3*) Chelsea Hse.

D

Designer Drugs. Paul R. Robbins. LC 94-16314. (Drug Library). (Illus.). 112p. (YA). (gr. 6 up). 1995. lib. bdg. 17.95 (*0-89490-488-4*) Enslow Pubs.
Designer Duplex Home Plans. Piercy & Barclay Designers, Inc. Staff. (Illus.). 24p. 1985. 8.95 (*0-929939-08-5*) Piercy Barclay.
Designer Greeting Cards. 160p. 1994. 34.99 (*1-56496-081-1*) Rockport Pubs.
Designer Home Plans, Vol. 4. Piercy & Barclay Designers, Inc. Staff. (Illus.). 63p. 1982. 12.95 (*0-929939-02-6*) Piercy Barclay.
Designer Home Plans, Vol. 5. Piercy & Barclay Designers, Inc. Staff. (Illus.). 63p. 1985. 12.95 (*0-929939-03-4*) Piercy Barclay.
Designer Home Plans, Vol. 6. Piercy & Barclay Designers, Inc. Staff. (Illus.). 64p. 1990. pap. text ed. 12.95 (*0-929939-04-2*) Piercy Barclay.
Designer Interiors. Morris M. Charles. 160p. 1994. 29.95 (*0-86636-333-5*) Rizzoli Intl.
***Designer Interiors.** Charles M. Mount. 1994. 29.95 (*0-86636-346-7*) PBC Intl Inc.
Designer Kids. David Walsh. LC 90-83227. (Illus.). 134p. 1990. 10.95 (*0-925190-12-8*) Fairview Press.
***Designer Kitchens: A Who's Who in Kitchen Design.** Martin. 1995. 24.95 (*1-878667-05-X*) Amer Dist Serv.
***Designer Kitchens: A Who's Who in Kitchen Design.** Donald J. Martin. (Illus.). 176p. (C). 1995. pap. 15.00 (*1-886378-01-0*) Kasmar Pubns.
***Designer Kitchens: A Who's Who in Kitchen Design.** Ed. by Donald J. Martin. (Illus.). 176p. (C). 1995. 24.95 (*1-886378-00-2*) Kasmar Pubns.
Designer Knitting. Ed. by Hugh Ehrman. LC 86-13223. (Illus.). 95p. 1986. 17.50 (*0-938953-00-1*) Westminster Trading.
Designer Leisure Home Plans. Piercy & Barclay Designers, Inc. Staff. (Illus.). 1985. 8.95 (*0-929939-07-7*) Piercy Barclay.
Designer Music: A Study of Harmonization. Myra E. Boitos. Ed. by Adel Meisenheimer & Mark Zeeman. (Illus.). 17p. 1987. Multi-media print/cassette. 15.00 (*0-944582-01-X*) Song Crafters.
Designer Needlepoint. Ed. by Hugh Ehrman. LC 87-2158. (Illus.). 128p. 1987. 22.50 (*0-938953-01-X*) Westminster Trading.
Designer Notes for Microwave Antennas. Richard C. Johnson. (Artech House Antenna Library). 201p. 1991. text ed. 55.00 (*0-89006-521-7*) Artech Hse.
Designer Offices. Otto Riewolt. LC 94-17070. (Illus.). 240p. 1994. 60.00 (*0-86565-149-3*) Vendome.
***Designer Oil Crops: Breeding, Processing & Biotechnology.** Denis J. Murphy. 1994. 120.00 (*1-56081-827-1*) VCH Pubs.
Designer Photoshop. Robert Day. 1993. pap. 30.00 (*0-679-74394-4*) Random.
Designer Photoshop: From Monitor to Printed Page Covers Version X.0. 2nd ed. Rob Day. 1995. pap. 30.00 (*0-679-75326-5*) Random.
***Designer Politics: How Elections Are Won.** Margaret Scammell. LC 94-24883. 1994. write for info. (*0-312-12317-5*) St Martin.
Designer "Pot" Pourri. Joe Dickel. LC 91-67736. 152p. 1993. pap. 9.00 (*1-56002-140-3*, Univ Edtns) Aegina Pr.
Designer Primer. Tom Porter & Sue Goodman. (Illus.). 144p. 1988. pap. 14.95 (*0-684-18457-5*, Scribners) S&S Trade.
Designer QuarkXPress. Lauren Smith. 1994. Incl. diskette. disk, pap. 29.95 (*1-55828-379-X*) MIS Press.
***Designer Scam.** Colin McDowell. (Illus.). 232p. 1995. 29.95 (*0-09-177612-0*, Pub. by Hutchinson UK) Trafalgar.
Designer Source Listing, Vol. II. Maryanne Burgess. 109p. (Orig.). 1986. pap. 9.00 (*0-9616741-0-5*) Carikean Pub.
Designer Source Listing, Vol. III. Maryanne Burgess. 127p. (Orig.). (C). 1987. pap. 11.95 (*0-9616741-1-3*) Carikean Pub.
Designer Source Listing, Vol. III. Maryanne Burgess. 127p. (Orig.). (C). 1989. pap. 11.95 (*0-9616741-3-X*) Carikean Pub.
Designer Source Listing, Vol. IV. Maryanne Burgess. 180p. (Orig.). 1989. pap. 17.95 (*0-9616741-2-1*) Carikean Pub.
Designer Source Listing, Vol. 5. Maryanne Burgess. 186p. (Orig.). 1992. pap. 17.95 (*0-9616741-4-8*) Carikean Pub.
Designer Source Listing, 1993-94. Maryanne Burgess. 224p. (Orig.). 1993. pap. 17.95 (*0-9616741-5-6*) Carikean Pub.
Designer Sweatshirts. Mary Mulari. (Illus.). 44p. (Orig.). 1989. pap. 7.95 (*0-9613569-1-X*) Mary Prodns.
Designers Book of Home Plans, Vol. 2. Piercy & Barclay Designers, Inc. Staff. (Illus.). 48p. 1976. 12.95 (*0-929939-00-X*) Piercy Barclay.
Designers Book of Home Plans, Vol. 3. 2nd ed. Piercy & Barclay Designers, Inc. Staff. (Illus.). 1990. 12.95 (*0-929939-09-3*) Piercy Barclay.
Designers Book of Home Plans: Executive Homes. 4th ed. Piercy & Barclay Designers, Inc. Staff. (Illus.). 64p. 1991. 12.95 (*0-929939-12-3*) Piercy Barclay.
Designers Book of Home Plans: Narrow Lot Homes. 3rd ed. Piercy & Barclay Designers, Inc. Staff. (Illus.). 64p. 1991. 12.95 (*0-929939-11-5*) Piercy Barclay.
Designer's Collection Home Plans, No. DC01: Best-Selling Home Plans of 1989. (Illus.). 1990. pap. text ed. 6.95 (*0-945471-26-2*) HomeStyles Pub & Mkt.
Designer's Collection Home Plans, No. DC02: Creative Traditionals. (Illus.). 1990. pap. text ed. 6.95 (*0-945471-29-7*) HomeStyles Pub & Mkt.
Designer's Commonsense Business Book. Barbara Ganim. 192p. 1993. 29.95 (*0-8442-3376-5*, NTC Busn Bks) NTC Pub Grp.
***Designer's Commonsense Business Book.** rev. ed. Barbara Ganim. (Illus.). 224p. 1995. pap. 22.95 (*0-89134-618-X*) North Light Bks.
Designer's Dictionary Two. Bruce T. Barber. (Illus.). 407p. 1981. 10.00 (*0-911380-54-X*) ST Pubns.
Designer's Guide for Creative Women's Ministries. Dorothy Dahlman. LC 88-80894. (Enabling Ser.). (Illus.). 115p. (Orig.). 1988. pap. 7.99 (*0-935797-30-0*) Harvest IL.
Designer's Guide to Color, No. 5. Ikuyoshi Shibukawa & Yumi Takahashi. Tr. by Japan-Michi Interlingual Staff. 128p. 1991. 19.95 (*0-87701-871-5*); pap. 12.95 (*0-87701-878-2*) Chronicle Bks.
Designer's Guide to Color: Over One Thousand Color Combinations. James Stockton. LC 84-3203. (Designers Guide Ser.). (Illus.). (Orig.). 1984. 19.95 (*0-87701-331-4*); pap. 12.95 (*0-87701-317-9*) Chronicle Bks.
Designer's Guide to Color 2: Over One Thousand Additional Color Combinations, Vol. 2. James Stockton. LC 84-21482. (Designers Guide Ser.). (Illus.). 124p. 1984. 19.95 (*0-87701-340-3*); pap. 12.95 (*0-87701-345-4*) Chronicle Bks.
Designer's Guide to Color 3. Jeanne Allen. (Designers Guide Ser.: No. 3). (Illus.). 120p. (Orig.). 1986. 19.95 (*0-87701-415-9*); pap. 12.95 (*0-87701-408-6*) Chronicle Bks.
Designer's Guide to Color 4. Ikuyoshi Shibukawa & Yumi Takahashi. 136p. 1990. 19.95 (*0-87701-690-9*); pap. 12.95 (*0-87701-681-X*) Chronicle Bks.
Designer's Guide to Creating Charts & Diagrams. Nigel Holmes. (Illus.). 192p. 1991. pap. 22.50 (*0-8230-1338-3*, Watsn-Guptill) Watsn-Guptill.
Designer's Guide to Creating Corporate Identity Systems. Rose DeNeve. (Illus.). 144p. (Orig.). 1992. 27.95 (*0-89134-441-1*) North Light Bks.
Designer's Guide to Making Money with Your Desktop Computer. Jack Neff. (Illus.). 128p. 1992. pap. 19.95 (*0-89134-439-X*, 30423) North Light Bks.
Designer's Guide to PostScript Text Type. 2nd ed. Jean C. King. 1993. pap. 34.95 (*0-442-01454-6*) Van Nos Reinhold.
Designer's Guide to Print Production: A Step-by-Step Publishing Book. Ed. by Nancy Aldrich-Ruenzel. (Illus.). 160p. 1990. 29.95 (*0-8230-1314-6*, Watsn-Guptill) Watsn-Guptill.
***Designers Guide to SPICE & Spectre.** Kenneth S. Kundert. 400p. (C). 1995. 70.00 (*0-7923-9571-9*) Kluwer Ac.
Designer's Guide to Surfaces & Finishes. Penny Radford. (Illus.). 160p. 1991. pap. 22.50 (*0-8230-1311-1*, Whitney Lib) Watsn-Guptill.
Designer's Guide to Testable Logic Circuits. Colin Maunder. (Illus.). 208p. (C). 1992. pap. text ed. 35.50 (*0-201-56513-7*) Addison-Wesley.
Designer's Guide to Typography: A Step-by-Step Publishing Book. Ed. by Nancy Aldrich-Ruenzel. (Illus.). 160p. 1991. 32.50 (*0-8230-1308-1*, Watsn-Guptill) Watsn-Guptill.
***Designer's Guide to VHDL.** Peter Ashenden. 1995. 32.95 (*1-55860-270-4*) Morgan Kaufmann.
Designer's Guide to VHDL Synthesis. Douglas E. Ott & Thomas J. Wilderotter. LC 94-20003. 336p. (C). 1994. lib. bdg. 84.00 (*0-7923-9472-0*) Kluwer Ac.
Designer's Guide to Wind Loading of Building Structures. N. J. Cook. LC 85-16621. (Illus.). 352p. 1986. text ed. 95.00 (*0-408-00870-9*) Buttrwrth-Heinemann.
Designer's Guide to Wind Loading of Building Structures: Part Two: Static Structures. J. Cook. (Illus.). 586p. 1990. text ed. 200.00 (*0-408-00871-7*) Buttrwrth-Heinemann.
Designers' Handbook: Medical Electronics: The Handbook to Medical Electronics Engineering & Design. Intro. by Cheryl Doriot. (Illus.). 194p. (Orig.). (C). Date not set. pap. 35.00 (*0-9618649-7-4*) Canon Comns.
Designer's Handbook of Flat Sketching. Rizalito P. Guevarra. (Illus.). 88p. (C). 1992. 15.95 (*0-9633088-0-7*) Parungao Pub.
Designer's Handbook of Instrumentation & Control Circuits. Joseph J. Carr. 626p. 1991. text ed. 138.00 (*0-12-160640-6*) Acad Pr.
***Designers' Handbook to Eurocode 4 Pt. 1.1: Design of Composite Steel & Concrete Structures.** R. P. Johnson & D. Anderson. 194p. 1993. 96.00 (*0-7277-1690-5*) Am Soc Civil Eng.
Designers International Index, 3 vols., Set. Comp. by Leichester Polytechnic University Library Staff. 1700p. 1991. 640.00 (*0-86291-770-0*) U Pubns Amer.
Designer's Mix & Match Type. Ian Pape. 1992. 39.95 (*0-07-048758-8*) McGraw.
Designer's Mix & Match Type. Ian Pape. 224p. 1992. 39.95 (*0-8306-4269-2*, 4303, Design Pr) TAB Bks.
Designers on Mac. Diane Burns & Takenobu Igarashi. (Illus.). 224p. (C). 1993. pap. 49.95 (*3-927258-20-2*) Gingko Press.
Designing a Capitation Payment Plan for Medicare End Stage Renal Disease Services. Donna O. Farley et al. LC 94-1869. 1994. write for info. (*0-8330-1512-5*, MR-391-HCFA) Rand Corp.
Designing a Computer Support System for School: A Handbook for Administrators. Carleton K. Finch & David H. Dennen. (Computers in Education Ser.). 192p. 1986. text ed. 22.90 (*0-201-10564-0*) Addison-Wesley.
Designing a Data Entry & Verification System. Peter A. Tatian. LC 92-15309. (Methods & Applications for Using Microcomputers in Policy Research Ser.: Vol. 1). 1992. write for info. (*0-89629-324-6*) Intl Food Policy.
Designing a Decision Support System for Credit Management. (Credit Research Foundation Ser.). 22p. 1988. 40.00 (*0-939050-46-3*) Credit Res NYS.
Designing a Fair & Reasonable Basic Benefit Plan Using Clinical Guidelines. Ed. by David C. Hadorn & Deborah A. Lott. 1992. pap. write for info. (*0-9633681-0-9*) CA Public Emp Retire.
Designing a Garden: A Guide to Planning & Planting Through the Seasons. Allen Paterson. (Illus.). 160p. 1992. pap. 19.95 (*0-921820-45-3*, Pub. by Camden Hse CN) Firefly Bks Ltd.
Designing a House: An Architectural Design Profile. Charles Jencks & Terry Farrell. (Academy Architecture Bks.). (Illus.). 80p. 1987. pap. 21.95 (*0-312-19462-5*) St Martin.
Designing a Laboratory. Ed. by Joseph H. Barker et al. 210p. 1989. 40.00 (*0-87553-150-4*) Am Pub Health.
Designing a New Factory with Manufacturing Simulation & Planned Experimentation. Thomas S. Babin. LC 92-25878. (Six Sigma Research Institute Ser.). 1992. write for info. (*0-201-63419-8*) Addison-Wesley.
Designing a Photograph. Bill Smith. (Illus.). 144p. 1985. pap. 18.95 (*0-8174-3776-2*, Amphoto) Watsn-Guptill.
Designing a Place Called Home: Reordering the Surburbs. James W. Wentling. LC 94-19294. 290p. 1994. (*0-412-99191-8*) Chapman & Hall.
***Designing a Public School Choice Program That Can Pay for Itself.** Judy M. Cresanta. 12p. 1993. 7.00 (*1-886306-03-6*) Nevada Policy.
Designing a Scheme of Assessment. C. Ward. (C). 1980. 80.00 (*0-85950-428-X*, Pub. by S Thornes Pubs UK) St Mut.
Designing a System of Labor Market Statistics & Information. Robert S. Goldfarb & Arvil V. Adams. LC 93-5067. (Discussion Paper Ser.: Vol. 205). 64p. 1993. 6.95 (*0-8213-2514-0*, 21514) World Bank.
***Designing a 401(K) Plan: The Hands-on-Guide to Creating the Best Plan for Your Company.** William A. Schneider. 1994. 55.00 (*1-55738-830-X*) Probus Pub Co.
Designing Affordable Houses. 1986. lib. bdg. 250.00 (*0-8490-3534-1*) Gordon Pr.
Designing Against Vandalism. Design Council Staff. 108p. (C). 1979. pap. text ed. 40.00 (*0-85072-092-3*) St Mut.
***Designing Alternative Assessments for Interdisciplinary Curriculum.** Richard E. Maurer. LC 95-15017. 1996. write for info. (*0-205-17393-4*) Allyn.
Designing America: Creating Urban Identity. Joel B. Goldsteen & Cecil D. Elliott. LC 93-3265. 1994. pap. 39.95 (*0-442-01111-3*) Van Nos Reinhold.
Designing an Effective Compliance Program, 11 vols. Ed. by Dawes Murphy. (Corporate Compliance Ser.). 1993. 990.00 (*0-685-68839-9*) Clark Boardman Callaghan.
Designing an Effective Sales Compensation Program. John K. Moynahan. LC 79-54844. 222p. reprint ed. pap. 63.30 (*0-317-26019-7*, 2023891) Bks Demand.
***Designing & Achieving Competency: A Competency Based Approach.** R. Boam & P. Sparrow. 204p. (C). 1992. pap. 68.85x (*0-07-707572-2*, Pub. by IPM Hse UK) St Mut.
Designing & Building a Deck. L. Donald Meyers. (Illus.). 272p. 1988. text ed. 46.00 (*0-13-201816-0*) P-H.
***Designing & Building Applications for OS-2 Version 3.** David Reich. 1995. pap. text ed. 34.95 (*0-471-11586-X*) Wiley.
***Designing & Building Business Models Using Microsoft Excel.** Andrew J. Robson. LC 95-6597. 1995. pap. write for info. (*0-07-709058-6*) McGraw.
Designing & Building Children's Furniture, with 61 Projects. 2nd ed. Percy W. Blandford. (Furniture Woodshop Ser.). (Illus.). 192p. 1988. 21.95 (*0-8306-9264-9*, 3064); pap. 12.95 (*0-8306-9364-5*, 3064) TAB Bks.
Designing & Building Colonial & Early American Furniture-with 47 Projects. 2nd ed. Percy W. Blanford. (Furniture Woodshop Ser.). (Illus.). 192p. 1988. 21.95 (*0-8306-0914-8*, 3014H); pap. 12.95 (*0-8306-9314-9*, 3014P) TAB Bks.
Designing & Building Electronic Filters. Delton T. Horn. 248p. 1992. pap. 14.95 (*0-8306-3933-0*) TAB Bks.
Designing & Building Electronic Filters. deluxe ed. Delton T. Horn. 1992. text ed. 26.95 (*0-07-157828-5*) McGraw.
Designing & Building Electronic Filters: Deluxe Edition. Delton T. Horn. 320p. 1992. 26.95 (*0-8306-3920-9*, 1888) TAB Bks.
Designing & Building Outdoor Furniture With 57 Projects. 2nd ed. Percy W. Blandford. (Furniture Woodshop Ser.). (Illus.). 192p. 1988. 21.95 (*0-318-32689-2*, 3014H); pap. 12.95 (*0-318-32690-6*, 3014P) TAB Bks.
***Designing & Building Parallel Programs: Concepts & Tools for Parallel Software Engineering.** Ian Foster. LC 94-3661. (C). 1995. text ed. 48.50 (*0-201-57594-9*) Addison-Wesley.
Designing & Building Space-Saving Furniture, with 28 Projects. 2nd ed. Percy W. Blandford. (Furniture Woodshop Ser.). (Illus.). 192p. 1989. 21.95 (*0-8306-1274-2*, 3074); pap. 12.95 (*0-8306-9374-2*, 3074) TAB Bks.
Designing & Building the Sheet Metal Brake. David J. Gingery. LC 80-66142. (Build Your Own Metalworking Shop from Scrap Ser.). (Illus.). 52p. (Orig.). 1980. pap. 6.95 (*1-878087-06-1*) D J Gingery.
Designing & Building Your Own Frameset: An Illustrated Guide for the Amateur Bicycle Builder. 2nd rev. ed. Richard P. Talbot. (Illus.). 161p. 1984. 32.95 (*0-9602418-3-3*) R Talbot.
Designing & Building Your Professional Office. 2nd ed. Murray Schwartz. 352p. 1989. boxed 49.95 (*0-87489-477-8*) Med Economics.
***Designing & Coding Reusable C++** Martin D. Carroll & Margaret A. Ellis. 352p. (C). 1995. text ed. 33.95 (*0-201-51284-X*) Addison-Wesley.
Designing & Conducting Behavior Research. Clifford J. Drew. (C). 1985. pap. text ed. 35.95 (*0-205-14314-8*, H4314) Allyn.
Designing & Conducting Behavioral Research. Clifford J. Drew & M. L. Hardman. (General Psychology Ser.: No. 134). 311p. 1986. pap. write for info. (*0-08-033988-3*, Pergamon Pr) Elsevier.
Designing & Conducting Health Surveys: A Comprehensive Guide. Lu Ann Aday. LC 89-45590. (Health-Social & Behavioral Science Ser.). 428p. 1989. 39.95 (*1-55542-173-3*) Jossey-Bass.
Designing & Conducting Health Systems Research Projects. C. Varkevisser et al. (Health Systems Research Training Ser.: Vol. 2, Pts. 1 & 2). 582p. 1992. pap. 25.00 (*0-685-55376-0*, IDRC287.1.2, Pub. by IDRC CN) UNIPUB.
***Designing & Conducting Research: Inquiry in Education & Social Science.** rev. ed. Clifford J. Drew et al. 1995. 48.95 (*0-205-16699-7*); pap. 36.95 (*0-205-16698-9*) Allyn.
Designing & Conducting Survey Research: A Comprehensive Guide. Louis M. Rea & Richard A. Parker. LC 91-30033. (Public Administration Ser.). 280p. 1992. 32.95 (*1-55542-404-X*) Jossey-Bass.
Designing & Constructing Mobiles. Jack Wiley. (Illus.). 224p. (Orig.). 1985. 19.95 (*0-8306-0839-7*, 1839); pap. 12.60 (*0-8306-1839-2*, 1839P) TAB Bks.
Designing & Delivering Cost-Effective Training: And Measuring the Results. 2nd ed. Ed. by Ron Zemke & Philip Jones. 800p. 1989. 68.95 (*0-943210-04-6*) Lakewood Pubns.
***Designing & Delivering Successful Presentations: Communicating in Technical, Scientific, & Managerial Environments.** Peter J. Hager & H. J. Scheiber. (Illus.). (C). 1996. lib. bdg. write for info. (*0-89464-868-3*) Krieger.
Designing & Design Verification Tests for Fire Department Ground Ladders. National Fire Protection Association Staff. 1994. 20.25 (*0-317-63563-8*, 1931-94) Natl Fire Prot.
***Designing & Drawing for the Theatre.** Lynn Pecktal. LC 94-21038. 1994. 58.00 (*0-07-557232-X*) McGraw.
Designing & Evaluating Games & Simulations. Margaret Gredler. 240p. 1994. 24.95 (*0-88415-157-3*) Gulf Pub.
***Designing & Forming Custom Cartridges: For Rifles & Handguns.** Ken Howell. (Custom Cartridges Ser.). 608p. 1995. 59.95 (*0-9643623-0-9*) Inkhorn.
Designing & Gardening with the Plant Materials & Conditions of North Central Florida (New USDA Zone 9) A Companion Volume to Landscape Design & Gardening Procedures for the Not So Rich. Anne Magill. 118p. (Orig.). 1990. pap. 10.95 (*0-9627632-1-7*) Melrose Garden Pr.
Designing & Implementing a Career Information Center. Sandra T. Brown & Duane Brown. LC 90-32105. 60p. (Orig.). 1990. pap. 6.50 (*0-912048-73-5*) Garrett Pk.
Designing & Implementing Effective Workshops. Ed. by Thomas J. Sork. LC 83-82724. (New Directions for Adult & Continuing Education Ser.: No. ACE 22). 1984. 16.95 (*0-87589-992-7*) Jossey-Bass.
Designing & Implementing Ethernet Networks. Bill Hancock. LC 88-18617. 190p. 1988. pap. 39.95 (*0-89435-366-7*) Wiley.
Designing & Implementing Ethernet Networks. Bill Hancock. 1993. pap. text ed. 39.95 (*0-471-56565-2*, GD3667) Wiley.
Designing & Implementing On-Site Day Care: A Consultant's Perspective. (BNA Special Report Series on Work & Family: No. 36). 32p. 1990. 35.00 (*1-55871-195-3*, BSP199) BNA.
***Designing & Implementing Successful Diversity Programs.** Lawrence M. Baytos. LC 94-34051. 1994. 79.95 (*0-13-128034-1*) P-H.
Designing & Improving Courses & Curricula in Higher Education: A Systematic Approach. Robert M. Diamond. LC 88-28433. (Higher Education Ser.). 304p. 1989. 34.95x (*1-55542-129-6*) Jossey-Bass.
Designing & Maintaining Your Edible Landscape Naturally. Robert Kourik. Ed. by Mark Kane. LC 85-63207. (Illus.). 400p. (Orig.). 1986. pap. 25.00 (*0-9615848-0-7*) Metamorphic Pr.
Designing & Making Handwoven Rugs: Techniques for Creating European, Oriental & American Rugs & Household Fabrics. Osma G. Tod & Josephine C. Del Deo. LC 76-17665. 1976. reprint ed. pap. 7.95 (*0-486-23391-X*) Dover.
***Designing & Making Wooden Toys.** Terry Kelly. (Illus.). 200p. 1995. pap. 14.95 (*0-946819-43-2*) Sterling.
Designing & Managing Instructional Programs. (Instructor Training Ser.). (Illus.). 315p. 1983. teacher ed 75.00 (*0-87683-046-7*); pap. text ed. 59.50 (*0-87683-383-0*) GP Pub.
Designing & Managing Programs: An Effectiveness Based Approach. Peter M. Kettner et al. (Sourcebooks for the Human Services Ser.: Vol. 11). (Illus.). 216p. (C). 1990. text ed. 49.95 (*0-8039-3260-X*); pap. text ed. 24.00 (*0-8039-3261-8*) Sage.
Designing & Managing State Competitive Research Grant Programs: A Resource Guide. John J. Forrer. Ed. by Karen Glass. 172p. (Orig.). 1990. pap. text ed. 20.00 (*1-55877-111-5*) Natl Governor.
Designing & Managing Your Career. Ed. by Harry Levinson. 1989. text ed. 29.95 (*0-07-103249-5*) McGraw.
Designing & Painting for the Theatre. Lynn Pecktal. LC 74-31271. 416p. (C). 1975. text ed. 49.25 (*0-03-011901-4*) HB Coll Pubs.
Designing & Planning Bathrooms: A Guide to Innovative Organizing, Remodeling & Decorating Your Bathroom. Ed. by Kimberly Kerrigone. LC 91-71687. 96p. 1992. pap. 8.95 (*0-932944-99-X*) Creative Homeowner.
Designing & Planning Bedrooms: Lighting, Furnishing & Decorating Bedrooms for the Whole Family. Ed. by Kimberly Kerrigone. LC 91-71692. 96p. 1992. pap. 8.95 (*0-932944-94-9*) Creative Homeowner.
Designing & Planning Environmental Graphics. Gerry Rosentswieg & Wayne Hunt. (Illus.). 256p. 1995. 55.00 (*0-942604-35-0*) Madison Square.

An Asterisk (*) at the beginning of an entry indicates that the title is appearing in BIP for the first time.

An Asterisk (*) at the beginning of an entry indicates that the title is appearing in BIP for the first time.

***Designing Groupware for Real-Time Drawing.** Ed. by Saul Greenberg et al. LC 95-12573. 1995. pap. write for info. (*0-07-707899-3*) McGraw.

Designing Groupwork: Strategies for the Heterogen Classroom. 2nd ed. Elizabeth G. Cohen. LC 93-40799. 296p. (C). 1994. pap. text ed. 17.95 (*0-8077-3331-8*) Tchrs Coll.

Designing GUI Applications for Windows. John Levine. 1993. disk, pap. 39.95 (*1-55851-328-0*) M&T Bks.

Designing Health Communication Campaigns: What Works? Thomas E. Backer. 200p. (C). 1992. text ed. 42.00 (*0-8039-4331-8*); pap. text ed. 19.50 (*0-8039-4332-6*) Sage.

***Designing Health Messages: Public Health Practice & Communication Theory.** Edward Maibach & Roxanne L. Parrot. 250p. 1995. text ed. 42.00 (*0-8039-5397-6*); pap. text ed. 21.95 (*0-8039-5398-4*) Sage.

***Designing Healthy Cities.** Aicher. 1996. write for info. (*0-89464-927-2*) Krieger.

Designing Houses: An Illustrated Guide. Lester Walker & Jeff Milstein. LC 75-7684. (Illus.). 160p. 1979. 12.95 (*0-87951-096-X*) Overlook Pr.

Designing Human-Centered Technology. Ed. by Howard Rosenbrock. (Artificial Intelligence & Society Ser.). (Illus.). 225p. 1990. pap. 69.00 (*0-387-19567-X*, 3414) Spr-Verlag.

Designing Hypermedia for Learning. Ed. by David H. Jonassen & Heinz Mandl. (NATO ASI Series F: Computer & Systems Sciences, Special Programme AET: Vol. 67). xxv, 457p. 1990. 79.00 (*0-387-52958-6*) Spr-Verlag.

Designing in Batik & Tie Dye see Batik & Tie Dye Techniques

***Designing Individual & Group Learning.** IPM Staff. (Training Delivery Ser.: No. 4). (C). 1994. pap. 94.00x (*0-08-042160-1*, Pub. by IPM Hse UK) St Mut.

Designing Information: New Roles for Librarians. Ed. by Linda C. Smith & Prudence W. Dalrymple. 228p. reprint ed. pap. 65.00 (*0-7837-6451-0*, 2046450) Bks Demand.

Designing Information Systems. 1990. 79.95 (*0-7506-1038-7*) Buttrwrth-Heinemann.

***Designing Information Systems for Development Planning.** Shirin Madon. 171p. Date not set. 50.00 (*1-872474-11-X*, Pub. by Alfred Waller UK) Paul & Co Pubs.

Designing Information Systems Security. Richard Baskerville. LC 87-31959. (John Wiley Information Systems Ser.). 263p. reprint ed. pap. 75.00 (*0-7837-4512-5*, 2044291) Bks Demand.

***Designing Information Technology in the Postmodern Age: From Method to Metaphor.** Richard Coyne. LC 95-8253. (Leonardo Book Ser.). 1995. 35.00 (*0-262-03228-7*) MIT Pr.

Designing Instruction for Adult Learners. Gary J. Dean. LC 92-30576. 142p. (C). 1994. 19.50 (*0-89464-658-3*) Krieger.

Designing Instruction for Diverse Abilities & the Library Media Teacher's Role. M. Ellen Jay & Hilda L. Jay. LC 90-47945. (Illus.). 180p. 1990. lib. bdg. 34.00 (*0-208-02261-9*, Lib Prof Pubns); pap. text ed. 26.50 (*0-208-02262-7*, Lib Prof Pubns) Shoe String.

Designing Instruction for Library Users: A Practical Guide. Ed. by Svinicki & Schwartz. (Books in Library & Information Science Ser.: Vol. 50). 272p. 1988. 79.75 (*0-8247-7820-0*) Dekker.

Designing Instruction for the Adult Learner: Theory & Practice for Employee Training. Rita Richey. 224p. 1992. 69.00 (*0-7494-0477-9*, Pub. by Kogan Page Educ UK) Taylor & Francis.

Designing Instructional Strategies: The Prevention of Academic Problems. Edward J. Kameenui & Simmons. 512p. (C). 1990. pap. write for info. (*0-675-21004-6*, Merrill Pub Co) Macmillan.

Designing Instructional Systems: Decision-Making in Course Planning & Curriculum Design. A. J. Romiszowski. 418p. 1984. 34.95 (*0-89397-181-2*) Nichols Pub.

Designing Instructional Text. 3rd rev. ed. James Hartley. (Illus.). 176p. 1994. pap. 33.95 (*0-89397-399-8*) Nichols Pub.

Designing Instructional Visuals. Jerry M. Linker. (Bridges for Ideas Handbook Ser.). 1968. pap. text ed. 6.00 (*0-913648-01-9*) U Tex Austin Film Lib.

Designing Intelligence: A Framework for Smart Systems. Steven H. Kim. (Illus.). 288p. 1991. 39.95 (*0-19-506016-4*) OUP.

***Designing Intelligent Learning Environments: From Cognitive Analysis to Computer Implementation.** Miriam Reiner et al. (Cognition & Computing Ser.). 1995. write for info. (*1-56750-104-4*); pap. write for info. (*1-56750-127-3*) Ablex Pub.

Designing Intelligent Systems: An Introduction. Igor Aleksander. (Illus.). 166p. 1984. 22.95 (*0-89059-043-5*, 590435) Qual Resc.

Designing Interaction: Psychology at the Human-Computer Interface. Ed. by John M. Carroll. (Cambridge Series in Human-Computer Interaction: No. 4). (Illus.). 340p. (C). 1991. 69.95 (*0-521-40056-2*); pap. 29.95 (*0-521-40921-7*) Cambridge U Pr.

Designing Interactive Software. rev. ed. Greg P. Kearsley & Robin Halley. LC 85-28463. (Illus.). 154p. (Orig.). 1986. pap. 19.95 (*0-935749-25-X*) Park Row Pr.

Designing Interactive Strategy: From Value Chain to Value Constellation. Richard Normann & Rafael Ramirez. LC 94-7850. 1994. text ed. 48.95 (*0-471-95086-6*) Wiley.

Designing Interfaces for Technological Application: Ceramic-Ceramic, Ceramic-Metal Joining - Proceedings of the European Colloquium Organized by the Commission of the European Communities, Joint Research Center, Institute for Advanced Materials, Petten, the Netherlands, 20-21 April 1988. Ed. by S. D. Peteves. 312p. 1989. 70.25 (*1-85166-377-0*) Elsevier.

Designing Interiors. Rosemary Kilmer & W. Otie Kilmer. (Illus.). 640p. (C). 1992. pap. text ed. 42.75 (*0-03-032233-2*) HB Coll Pubs.

Designing International Software. David A. Schmitt. 350p. 1991. pap. text ed. 29.00 (*0-13-202870-0*) P-H.

Designing Interventions for Preschool Learning & Behavior Problems. David W. Barnett & Karen T. Carey. LC 91-38009. (Social & Behavioral Sciences Ser.). 491p. 1992. 42.95 (*1-55542-409-0*) Jossey-Bass.

Designing Interventions for the Helping Professions. Edwin J. Thomas. LC 84-3395. (Sourcebooks for Improving Human Services Ser.: No. 3). (Illus.). 303p. reprint ed. pap. 86.40 (*0-8357-4859-6*, 2037791) Bks Demand.

Designing Knitwear. Deborah Newton. Ed. by Christine Timmons. 272p. 1992. 39.95 (*0-942391-06-3*) Taunton.

***Designing Learning Programmes.** IPM Staff. (Training Design & Management Ser.: No. 3). (C). 1994. pap. 93.00x (*0-08-042166-0*, Pub. by IPM Hse UK) St Mut.

Designing Linear Control Systems with MATLAB. Katsuhiko Ogata. LC 93-34429. 1993. pap. text ed. 33.40 (*0-13-293226-1*) P-H.

***Designing Litigation Support Databases.** D. Kartson. Date not set. text ed. 105.00 (*0-471-08637-1*) Wiley.

Designing Machines & Dies for Polymer Processing with Computer Programs. Natti S. Rao. 208p. (C). 1981. text ed. 47.50 (*1-56990-083-3*) Hanser-Gardner.

Designing Machines & Dies for Polymer Processing with Computer Programs: Fortran & Basic. Natti S. Rao. (Illus.). 208p. 1981. 44.00 (*0-686-48155-0*, 1907) T-C Pubns CA.

Designing Magnetic Components for High Frequency DC-DC Converters. William T. McLyman. 435p. 1993. 80.00 (*1-883107-00-8*) KG Magnetics.

***Designing Major Policy Reform: Lessons from the Transport Sector.** Ian C. Heggie. (Discussion Paper Ser.: No. 115). 40p. 1991. 6.95 (*0-8213-1756-3*, 11756) World Bank.

***Designing Mal.** Howard Greer. (American Autobiography Ser.). 310p. 1995. reprint ed. lib. bdg. 89.00 (*0-7812-8540-2*) Rprt Serv.

Designing Men's & Boy's Garments. rev. ed. (Illus.). 140p. 1985. 20.00 (*0-318-18627-6*) Master Design.

Designing Messages for Development Communication: An Audience Participation-Based Approach. Bella Mody. 216p. (C). 1992. 49.95 (*0-8039-9105-3*); pap. 24.00 (*0-8039-9106-1*) Sage.

Designing Microprocessor-Based Digital Circuitry. S. J. Cahill. (Illus.). 192p. (C). 1985. pap. text ed. 16.95 (*0-685-09683-1*) P-H.

Designing Military Pay: Contributions & Implications of the Economics Literature. Beth J. Asch. LC 93-16003. 1993. write for info. (*0-8330-1391-2*, MR-161-FMP) Rand Corp.

***Designing Modernity: The Arts of Reform & Persuasion 1885-1945.** Ed. by Wendy Kaplan. LC 95-60480. (Illus.). 352p. 1995. 60.00 (*0-500-23706-9*) Thames Hudson.

***Designing Multimedia Systems.** Prabhat K. Andleigh. 1995. pap. text ed. 48.00 (*0-13-089095-2*) P-H.

Designing New Civilizations, Vol. 6, No. 12. Ed. by Leon Vickman. 60p. (Orig.). 1990. pap. 2.00 (*1-878814-00-1*) New Civilization.

Designing New Civilizations, Vol. 7, No. 1. Ed. by Leon Vickman. 55p. (Orig.). 1991. pap. 2.00 (*1-878814-01-X*) New Civilization.

***Designing New Traditions in Quilts.** Sharyn S. Craig. Ed. by Jack Braunstein & Jane Townswick. (Illus.). 96p. (Orig.). 1991. pap. 24.95 (*0-9622565-1-X*) Chariot Pub PA.

Designing Object-Oriented Software. Rebecca Brock. 1990. pap. text ed. 46.00 (*0-13-629825-7*) P-H.

Designing Object-Oriented User Interfaces. Dave Collins. (C). Date not set. text ed. 48.50 (*0-8053-1270-6*) Benjamin-Cummings.

***Designing Object-Oriented User Interfaces.** Dave Collins. LC 94-24586. (C). 1995. text ed. 48.50 (*0-8053-5350-X*) Benjamin-Cummings.

***Designing Object Systems: Object-Oriented Modeling with Syntropy.** Steve Cook & John Daniels. LC 94-30446. (Object-Oriented Ser.). 317p. 1994. text ed. 42.00 (*0-13-203860-9*) P-H.

***Designing Offsite Facilities by Use of Routing Diagrams.** fac. ed. Edward G. Musser. LC 83-5608. (Illus.). 78p. 1983. reprint ed. pap. 25.00 (*0-7837-8146-6*, 2047954) Bks Demand.

Designing Optimal Strategies for Mineral Exploration. J. G. De Geoffroy & T. K. Wignall. LC 85-19383. 380p. 1985. 85.00 (*0-306-41977-7*, Plenum Pr) Plenum.

Designing Organic Syntheses: A Programmed Introduction to the Synthon Approach. Stuart Warren. LC 77-15479. 285p. 1978. pap. text ed. 49.95 (*0-471-99612-2*, Wiley-Interscience) Wiley.

***Designing Organizations.** Daniel Robey. (C). 1981. 62.95 (*0-256-02513-4*) Irwin.

Designing Organizations. 3rd ed. Daniel Robey. 608p. (C). 1990. text ed. 60.95 (*0-256-06999-9*, 08-1397-03) Irwin.

Designing Organizations. 4th ed. David Robey & Carol A. Sales. LC 93-3727. 560p. (C). 1994. text ed. 65.95 (*0-256-11699-7*) Irwin.

Designing Organizations: A Decision-Making Perspective. Richard J. Butler. (Illus.). 240p. 1991. 69.95 (*0-415-05331-5*, A5490); pap. 19.95 (*0-415-05332-3*, A5494) Routledge.

Designing Organizations: A Macro Perspective. 3rd ed. Daniel Robey. (C). 1990. 46.50 (*0-685-38299-0*) Irwin.

***Designing Organizations: An Executive Briefing on Strategy, Structure, & Process.** Jay R. Galbraith. LC 94-47358. (Management Ser.). 144p. 1995. 25.95 (*0-7879-0091-5*) Jossey-Bass.

Designing Organizations for High Performance. David P. Hanna. (Organization Development Ser.). (Illus.). 144p. (C). 1988. pap. text ed. 26.95 (*0-201-12693-1*) Addison-Wesley.

Designing Organizations for Satisfaction & Efficiency. K. Legge & E. Mumford. 160p. 1978. text ed. 52.95 (*0-566-02102-1*) Ashgate Pub Co.

Designing OS-2 Applications. David E. Reich. 336p. 1993. pap. text ed. 34.95 (*0-471-58889-X*) Wiley.

***Designing Parks: An Examination of Contemporary Approaches to Design in Landscape Architecture.** Lodwijk Balijon. (Illus.). 322p. 1995. pap. 39.50 (*1-870673-15-8*, Pub. by Garden Art Pr UK) Antique Collect.

Designing Partial Dentures. D. M. Watt & A. R. MacGregor. (Illus.). 258p. 1984. 75.00 (*0-7236-0810-5*, Pub. by John Wright UK) Buttrwrth-Heinemann.

Designing Pascal Solutions, Vol. II. Michael Clancy. (C). 1995. text ed. 24.95 (*0-7167-8260-X*) W H Freeman.

Designing Pascal Solutions: A Case Study Approach. Michael J. Clancy & Marcia C. Linn. (Illus.). 448p. (C). 1995. pap. text ed. 24.95 (*0-7167-8258-8*) W H Freeman.

Designing Patterns: A Fresh Approach to Pattern Cutting. Hilary Campbell. (Illus.). 128p. (Orig.). 1980. pap. 33.50 (*0-85950-404-2*, Pub. by Stanley Thornes UK) Trans-Atl Phila.

***Designing Pension Security: The Central Pension Fund of the Operating Engineers.** Teresa Ghilarducci et al. LC 95-7960. 1995. text ed. write for info. (*0-89930-995-X*, Quorum Bks) Greenwood.

Designing Performance Appraisal Systems: Aligning Appraisals & Organizational Realities. Allan M. Mohrman, Jr. et al. LC 88-32894. (Management Ser.). 256p. 1989. 31.95x (*1-55542-149-0*) Jossey-Bass.

Designing Pictorial Symbols. Nigel Holmes & Rose DeNeve. (Illus.). 144p. 1990. pap. 19.95 (*0-8230-1330-8*, Watsn-Guptill) Watsn-Guptill.

Designing Plastic Parts for Assembly. Paul A. Tres. LC 94-1549. 1994. text ed. write for info. (*1-56990-168-6*) Hanser-Gardner.

***Designing Plastic Parts for Assembly.** 2nd rev. ed. Paul A. Tres. 272p. (C). 1995. pap. text ed. write for info. (*1-56990-199-6*) Hanser-Gardner.

Designing Pneumatic Control Circuits: Efficient Techniques for Practical Application. Bruce E. McCord. LC 82-2103. (Fluid Power & Control Ser.: No. 2). (Illus.). 176p. reprint ed. pap. 50.20 (*0-7837-0940-4*, 2041245) Bks Demand.

Designing Preschool Movement Programs. Stephen W. Sanders. LC 92-4595. (Illus.). 152p. 1992. pap. 16.00 (*0-87322-362-4*, BSAN0362) Human Kinetics.

Designing, Producing, Using Business Graphics: With the Personal Computer. Jay R. Alperson & Gordon McComb. 280p. 24.95 (*0-933186-17-7*) IBM Purchase.

Designing Productive Learning Environments. Frederick G. Knirk. LC 79-4031. (Illus.). 184p. 1979. 34.95 (*0-87778-137-0*) Educ Tech Pubns.

***Designing Products & Services That Customers Want.** Robert King. LC 95-12447. (Management Master Ser.: Vol. 13). (Illus.). 50p. 1995. 15.95 (*1-56327-092-7*) Prod Press.

***Designing Professional Development for Change: A Systemic Approach.** James Bellanca & Robin Fogarty. LC 95-75711. 64p. 1995. pap. 9.95 (*0-932935-94-X*) IRI-Skylght.

Designing Program Evaluations. Linda T. Bilheimer. Ed. by Karen Glass. (Strategies for Improving State Perinatal Programs Ser.). 70p. (Orig.). 1989. pap. text ed. 15.00 (*1-55877-060-7*) Natl Governor.

Designing, Purchasing, Processing: A Technical Update: Plastics for the Medical & Electronics Industries: Eighth Annual Pacific Technical Conference, February 19-21, 1985. Society of Plastics Engineers Staff. 255p. reprint ed. pap. 72.70 (*0-317-42294-4*, 2025800) Bks Demand.

Designing Qualitative Research. Catherine Marshall & Gretchen B. Rossman. 172p. (C). 1989. text ed. 39.95 (*0-8039-3157-3*); pap. text ed. 17.95 (*0-8039-3158-1*) Sage.

***Designing Qualitative Research.** 2nd ed. Catherine Marshall & Gretchen B. Rossman. 188p. 1994. 39.95 (*0-8039-5248-1*); pap. 17.95 (*0-8039-5249-X*) Sage.

Designing Quality & Balance into Your Life, Work & Play: A Self-Test Workbook That Shows You Where You Are Now & Guides You Where You'd Like To Be. Jack Riley. 128p. (Orig.). 1987. pap. 6.95 (*0-89997-077-X*) Wilderness Pr.

Designing Quality Databases with IDEFIX Information Models. Thomas A. Bruce. LC 91-18092. 584p. (C). 1992. text ed. 55.00 (*0-932633-18-8*) Dorset Hse Pub Co.

Designing Quilts: The Value of Value. Suzanne Hammond. Ed. by Ursula Reikes. (Illus.). 90p. (Orig.). 1994. pap. 19.95 (*1-56477-064-8*) That Patchwork.

Designing Regulatory Policy with Limited Information. David Besanko & David E. Sappington. LC 87-277. (Fundamentals of Pure & Applied Economics Ser.: Vol. 20). viii, 80p. (C). 1987. pap. text ed. 33.00 (*3-7186-0385-3*) Gordon & Breach.

Designing Resistance Training Programs. Steven J. Fleck & William J. Kraemer. LC 87-2850. (Illus.). 280p. 1987. text ed. 35.00x (*0-87322-113-3*, BFLE0113) Human Kinetics.

Designing Rooms For Children. Mary Gilliatt. 1991. pap. 18.95 (*0-316-31419-6*) Little.

Designing Safer Roads: Practices for Resurfacing, Restoration, & Rehabilitation. (Special Report Ser.: No. 214). 319p. 1987. 28.00 (*0-309-04453-7*) Transport Res Bd.

Designing School Health Curricula. Evelyn E. Ames et al. 256p. (C). 1992. pap. write for info. (*0-697-10158-4*) Brown & Benchmark.

Designing School Health Curruculam, Planning for Good Health. 2nd ed. Evelyn E. Ames et al. 256p. (C). 1995. pap. text ed. write for info. (*0-697-22363-9*) Brown & Benchmark.

Designing Screen Interfaces in C. James C. Pinson. 304p. 1991. pap. text ed. 38.60 (*0-13-201583-8*) P-H.

***Designing Skill-Based Pay: Satisfying the Yearning for Earning by Learning.** 2nd ed. Donald F. Barkman. (Illus.). 139p. 1994. 59.95 (*1-883655-01-3*) Busn Ctr.

***Designing Skill-Based Pay: Satisfying the Yearning for Earning by Learning.** 2nd ed. Donald F. Barkman. (South Africa Ser.). (Illus.). 139p. 1994. pap. write for info. (*1-883655-04-8*) Busn Ctr.

Designing Social Inquiry: Scientific Inference in Qualitative Research. Gary King et al. LC 93-39283. 1994. 55.00 (*0-691-03470-2*); pap. 19.95 (*0-691-03471-0*) Princeton U Pr.

Designing Spaces: Visualizing, Planning & Building. Education Development Staff. LC 94-35412. (Seeing & Thinking Mathematically in the Middle Grades Ser.). (Illus.). 200p. 1995. spiral bd. 35.00 (*0-435-08350-3*) Heinemann.

Designing Stair Pressurization Systems. Richard P. Thornberry. 1982. 4.65 (*0-686-37668-4*, TR 82-4) Society Fire Protect.

Designing State Machine Controllers Using Programmable Logic. Michael Treseler. 208p. 1991. text ed. 57.00 (*0-13-202938-3*) P-H.

Designing Stitched Textiles for the Church. Beryl Dean. (Illus.). 96p. 1993. 35.00 (*0-85532-752-9*, Pub. by Search Pr UK) A Schwartz & Co.

Designing Strategy: A How-to Book for Managers. George C. Sawyer. LC 85-17815. 267p. 1986. text ed. 29.95 (*0-471-81682-5*) Wiley.

Designing Structured Programs. David A. Higgins & David G. Scott. 256p. 1988. pap. text ed. 51.00 (*0-13-201468-8*) P-H.

Designing Successful Farmer-Managed Seed Systems. Sharanjit S. Bal & Johnson E. Douglas. (Discussion Paper Ser.). 28p. (Orig.). 1991. pap. 6.00 (*0-933595-62-X*) Winrock Intl.

***Designing Surveys: A Guide to Decisions & Procedures.** Ron Czaja & Johnny Blair. LC 94-48280. (Research Methods & Statistics Ser.). 1995. pap. write for info. (*0-8039-9056-1*) Pine Forge.

***Designing Surveys in Two & Three Dimensions.** Dale Stone. LC 94-27480. (Geophysical References Ser.: Vol. 5). 1994. 67.00 (*1-56080-073-9*) Soc Expl Geophys.

Designing Tasks for the Communicative Classroom. David Nunan. (Cambridge Language Teaching Library). (Illus.). 256p. (C). 1989. pap. 16.95 (*0-521-37915-6*) Cambridge U Pr.

***Designing TCP-IP Internetworks.** Geoff Bennett. (B & F - Computer Science Ser.). 400p. 1995. pap. 49.95 (*0-442-01880-0*) Van Nos Reinhold.

Designing Teaching Improvement Programs. Ed. by Jack Lindquist. LC 79-51475. 1978. reprint ed. pap. 12.95 (*0-937012-07-6*) Coun Indep Colleges.

***Designing Team-Based Organizations: New Forms for Knowledge Work.** Susan A. Mohrman et al. (Management Ser.). 400p. 1995. 29.95 (*0-7879-0080-X*) Jossey-Bass.

Designing Technical Reports. 2nd ed. J. C. Mathes. 528p. (C). 1991. pap. write for info. (*0-02-377095-3*) Macmillan.

Designing Tests for Evaluating Student Achievement. James S. Cangelosi. 230p. (C). 1990. pap. text ed. 27.50 (*0-8013-0263-3*, 75916) Longman.

Designing the City: A Guide for Advocates & Public Officials. Adele F. Bacow. LC 94-30144. (Illus.). 304p. (C). 1995. text ed. 45.00 (*1-55963-290-9*); pap. text ed. 27.50 (*1-55963-291-7*) Island Pr.

Designing the Cost-Effective Office: A Guide for Facilities Planners & Managers. Jack M. Fredrickson. LC 89-3791. (Illus.). 184p. 1989. text ed. 49.95 (*0-89930-258-0*, FDG/, Quorum Bks) Greenwood.

***Designing the Earth: The Human Impulse to Shape Nature.** David Bourdon. LC 95-10639. 1995. write for info. (*0-8109-3224-5*) Abrams.

Designing the Effective Message: Critical Thinking & Communications. Donald N. Wood. 160p. 1989. per. 25.95 (*0-8403-5517-3*) Kendall-Hunt.

Designing the Future. Robin Baker. LC 93-60202. (Illus.). 208p. 1993. 45.00 (*0-500-01578-3*) Thames Hudson.

Designing the Interior Landscape. Richard L. Austin. (Illus.). 160p. 1985. text ed. 44.95 (*0-442-20930-4*) Van Nos Reinhold.

Designing the Lateral Organization. Jay R. Galbraith. 1993. write for info. (*0-318-70112-X*) Addison-Wesley.

Designing the Molecular World: Chemistry at the Frontier. Philip Ball. LC 93-38151. 1994. 29.95 (*0-691-00058-1*) Princeton U Pr.

Designing the New City: A Systemic Approach. John E. Gibson. LC 76-44899. (Wiley Series on Systems Engineering & Analysis). 302p. 1977. reprint ed. pap. 86.10 (*0-7837-3444-1*, 2057768) Bks Demand.

Designing the Office of the Future: The Japanese Approach to Tomorrow's Workplace. Volker Hartkopf et al. 1993. text ed. 69.95 (*0-471-59569-1*) Wiley.

***Designing the Perfect Resume.** Pat Criscito. LC 95-5699. 1995. write for info. (*0-8120-9329-1*) Barron.

1894

An Asterisk (*) at the beginning of an entry indicates that the title is appearing in BIP for the first time.

An Asterisk (*) at the beginning of an entry indicates that the title is appearing in BIP for the first time.

1895

D

Desir et la Reflexion Dans la Philosophie De Spinoza. R. Misrahi. 382p. 1972. pap. text ed. 45.00 (0-677-50815-8) Gordon & Breach.

***Desirability of Currency Unification Theory & Some Evidence.** Bertholt Leeftink. (Tinbergen Institute Research Ser.: No. 92). 227p. 1995. pap. 26.50 (90-5170-328-7, Pub. by Thesis Pubs NE) IBD Ltd.

Desirable & Undesirable Characteristics of Offshore Yachts. Cruising Club of America Technical Committee et al. Ed. by John Rousmaniere. 1987. 29.95 (0-393-03311-2) Norton.

Desirable Physical Facilities for an Activity Program. Frank Long. LC 78-177007. (Columbia University. Teachers College. Contributions to Education Ser.: No. 593). reprint ed. 22.50 (0-404-55593-4) AMS Pr.

Desirable Residence. large type ed. Sheila A. Cole. (Dales General Fiction Ser.). 367p. 1993. pap. 16.95 (1-85389-426-5, Dales) Ulverscroft.

Desirable Residences & Other Stories. Sel. by Jack Adrian. 304p. 1991. 25.00 (0-19-212304-1) OUP.

Desirable Residences & Other Stories. E. F. Benson. 304p. 1992. pap. 9.95 (0-19-282977-7) OUP.

Desirable Women. (Chester's Books of Madrigals: Vol. 3). Date not set. pap. 7.50 (0-685-69019-9, Chester Music) Music Sales.

Desire. Jody Aliesan. 73p. 1989. pap. 7.00 (0-912887-11-7) Empty Bowl.

Desire. Phoebe Conn. 512p. 1993. mass mkt. 5.99 (0-8217-4086-5) Zebra.

Desire. Patricia Hagan. (Historical Ser.). 1992. mass mkt. 3.99 (0-373-28743-7, 1-28743-2) Harlequin Bks.

Desire. Amanda Quick. 1994. mass mkt. 5.99 (0-553-56153-7, Fanfare) Bantam.

Desire. Amanda Quick. 1994. 25.95 (1-56895-067-5) Wheeler Pub.

Desire: Its Role in Practical Reason & the Explanation of Action. G. F. Schueler. LC 94-18922. 1995. 52.50x (0-262-19355-8, Bradford Bks) MIT Pr.

Desire: Love Stories in Western Culture. Catherine Belsey. LC 94-14118. (Illus.). 280p. 1994. 49.95 (0-631-16813-3); pap. 21.95 (0-631-16814-1) Blackwell Pubs.

Desire: Selected Poems 1963-1987. David Bromige. LC 88-3409. 232p. (Orig.). 1988. 20.00 (0-87685-724-1) Black Sparrow.

Desire: Selected Poems 1963-1987, signed ed. deluxe ed. David Bromige. LC 88-3409. 232p. (Orig.). 1988. 30.00 (0-87685-725-X) Black Sparrow.

Desire: The Collective Unconscious. Telfer Stokes. 1989. 35.00 (0-932526-26-8) Nexus Pr.

***Desire: The Emotional Appetite for Success.** Melvin E. Murphy. Ed. by Carol Starks et al. LC 95-94334. (Illus.). 180p. (YA). 1995. 20.00 (0-9646799-0-6) M Murphy.

Desire & Anxiety: Circulations of Sexuality in Shakespearean Drama. Valerie Traub. LC 92-12275. (Gender, Culture, Difference Ser.). 224p. 1992. 55.00 (0-415-05526-1, A5159); pap. 14.95 (0-415-05527-X, A5163) Routledge.

Desire & Contradiction: Imperial Visions & Domestic Debates in Victorian Literature. D. Bivona. (Cultural Politics Ser.). 1991. text ed. 49.95 (0-7190-2953-8, Pub. by Manchester Univ Pr UK); text ed. 14.95 (0-7190-2954-6, Pub. by Manchester Univ Pr UK) St Martin.

Desire & Craving: A Cultural Theory of Alcoholism. Pertti Alasuutari. LC 91-22457. (SUNY Series in New Social Studies on Alcohol & Drugs). 226p. (C). 1992. 57.50 (0-7914-1097-8); pap. 18.95 (0-7914-1098-6) State U NY Pr.

Desire & Death in the Spanish Sentimental Romance. Patricia Grieve. Ed. by Thomas Lathrop et al. 147p. 1987. 14.50 (0-936388-22-6) Juan de la Cuesta.

***Desire & Deception.** Miranda Lee. (Presents Ser.). 1995. mass mkt. 3.25 (0-373-11760-4, 1-11760-5) Harlequin Bks.

Desire & Delight: A New Reading of Augustine's Confessions. Margaret R. Miles. 120p. 1992. 15.95 (0-8245-1163-8) Crossroad NY.

Desire & Destiny. Linda L. Miller. Ed. by Linda Marrow. 320p. (Orig.). 1990. mass mkt. 5.99 (0-671-70635-7) PB.

***Desire & Dissent: An Introduction to Luis Antonio de Villena.** Chris Perriam. Ed. by John E. Flower. (New Directions in European Writing Ser.). 160p. 1995. 39.95 (1-85973-057-4) Berg Pubs.

Desire & Domestic Fiction: A Political History of the Novel. Nancy Armstrong. LC 86-16482. 322p. 1987. 49.95 (0-19-504179-8) OUP.

Desire & Domestic Fiction: A Political History of the Novel. Nancy Armstrong. 322p. 1990. reprint ed. pap. 17.95 (0-19-506160-8) OUP.

***Desire & Imagination: Classic Essays in Sexuality.** Ed. by Regina Barreca. 256p. 1995. pap. 13.95 (0-452-01150-7, Mer) NAL-Dutton.

Desire & Its Discontents. Eugene Goodheart. 224p. 1991. text ed. 35.00 (0-231-07642-8) Col U Pr.

***Desire & It's Discontents.** Eugene Goodheart. 1994. pap. 16.00 (0-231-07643-6) Col U Pr.

Desire & Love in Henry James: A Study of the Late Novels. David McWhirter. (Illus.). (C). 1989. 64.95 (0-521-35328-9) Cambridge U Pr.

Desire & Pursuit of the Whole: A Romance of Modern Venice. Baron Corvo, pseud. (Quality Paperbacks Ser.). xvi, 300p. 1986. reprint ed. pap. 9.95 (0-306-80258-9) Da Capo.

Desire & Pursuit of the Whole: A Romance of Modern Venice. Frederick C. Rolfe. LC 77-10836. 299p. 1977. reprint ed. text ed. 35.00 (0-8371-9808-9, RODP, Greenwood Pr) Greenwood.

Desire & Pursuit of the Whole: A Romance of Modern Venice. Frederick W. Rolfe. LC 78-21374. (Gay Experience Ser.). reprint ed. 25.50 (0-404-61536-8) AMS Pr.

***Desire & Repression: The Dialectic of Self & Other in the Late Works of Henry James.** Donna Przybylowicz. LC 84-24068. 367p. 1986. pap. 104.60 (0-7837-8399-X, 2059210) Bks Demand.

Desire & Restraint in Shelley. F. Stovall. LC 70-95448. (Studies in Shelley: No. 25). 1969. reprint ed. lib. bdg. 49.95 (0-8383-1205-5) M S G Haskell Hse.

Desire & Restraint in Shelley. Floyd Stovall. 1971. reprint ed. 19.00 (0-403-01229-5) Scholarly.

Desire & Surrender. Katherine Sutcliffe. 400p. 1986. mass mkt. 4.99 (0-380-75067-8) Avon.

Desire & the Devil: Demonic Contracts in French & European Literature. Carlo Testa. LC 90-28412. (American University Studies: Romance Languages & Literature: Ser. II, Vol. 159). 208p. (C). 1991. text ed. 39.95 (0-8204-1439-5) P Lang Pubs.

***Desire & the Female Therapist: Engendered Gazes in Psychotherapy & Art Therapy.** Joy Schaverein. LC 94-48387. (Illus.). 240p. 1995. 69.95x (0-415-08700-7, C0036) Routledge.

***Desire & the Female Therapist: Engendered Gazes in Psychotherapy & Art Therapy.** Joy Schaverein. (Illus.). 240p. 1995. pap. 19.95 (0-415-08701-5, C0037) Routledge.

Desire & the Political Unconscious in American Literature: Eros & Ideology. Sam B. Girgus. LC 89-35600. 304p. 1990. text ed. 45.00 (0-312-03591-8); pap. 14.95 (0-312-03602-7) St Martin.

Desire & the Sign: Nineteenth-Century American Fiction. Fred G. See. LC 86-21088. 208p. 1987. text ed. 30.00 (0-8071-1313-1) La State U Pr.

Desire & Time: New Work from the Institute of American Indian Arts. Ed. by Penelope Gillen. (IAIA Anthology Ser.: No. 2). 64p. 1990. pap. 6.00 (1-881396-01-0) IOA Indian Arts.

Desire & Truth: Functions of Plot in Eighteenth-Century English Novels. Patricia M. Spacks. LC 89-27725. 248p. 1990. 32.00 (0-226-76845-7) U Ch Pr.

Desire & Truth: Functions of Plot in Eighteenth-Century English Novels. Patricia M. Spacks. x, 262p. 1994. pap. text ed. 14.95 (0-226-76847-3) U Ch Pr.

Desire (Arezo) Book of Poetry, Vol. I. Kazem Fathie. (Illus.). 752p. (Orig.). (ENG & PER.). 1990. 40.00 (0-9627148-0-1); pap. 35.00 (0-9627148-1-X) K Fathie.

***Desire Burn.** Ed. by Janet B. Gluckman. 272p. 1995. pap. 9.95 (0-7867-0259-1) Carroll & Graf.

***Desire by Numbers.** Klaus Kertess. LC 94-26819. (Illus.). 1994. 15.00 (0-9631095-3-7) Artspace Bks.

Desire, Death & Goodness: The Conflict of Ultimate Values in Theravada Buddhism. Grace G. Burford. LC 90-5969. (New Perspectives in Philosophical Scholarship Series: Texts & Issues: Vol. 1). 227p. (C). 1990. text ed. 38.95 (0-8204-1242-2) P Lang Pubs.

Desire for Control: Personality, Social & Clinical Perspectives. J. M. Burger. (Social - Clinical Psychology Ser.). (Illus.). 215p. 1992. 29.50 (0-306-44072-5, Plenum Pr) Plenum.

Desire for Origins: New Language, Old English, & Teaching the Tradition. Allaen J. Frantzen. LC 90-31077. 260p. (C). 1990. text ed. 40.00 (0-8135-1590-4); pap. text ed. 15.00 (0-8135-1591-2) Rutgers U Pr.

***Desire for the Land.** Richard Bear. (Illus.). 58p. (Orig.). 1995. pap. write for info. (0-9645574-0-1) Stony Run Pr.

Desire for White: New & Selected Poems. Allen Afterman. 97p. 1991. pap. 10.95 (1-878818-04-X) Sheep Meadow.

Desire in Belfast: Poems. Sean Haldane. 94p. 1993. pap. 13.95 (0-85640-496-9, Pub. by Blackstaff Pr IE) Dufour.

***Desire in Disguise.** Rebecca Brandewyne. (Orig.). 1994. reprint ed. lib. bdg. 22.00 (0-7278-4636-1) Severn Hse.

Desire in L. A. Martha C. Ronk. LC 89-34552. (Contemporary Poetry Ser.). 96p. 1990. 15.00 (0-8203-1175-8); pap. 7.95 (0-8203-1176-6) U of Ga Pr.

Desire in Language: A Semiotic Approach to Literature & Art. Julia Kristeva. Ed. by Leon S. Roudiez. Tr. by Alice A. Jardine & Thomas Gora. LC 80-10689. (European Perspectives Ser.). (Illus.). 336p. 1982. text ed. 42.00 (0-231-04806-8); pap. text ed. 17.50 (0-231-04807-6) Col U Pr.

***Desire in the Renaissance: Psychoanalysis & Literature.** Valeria Finucci. 1994. pap. 14.95 (0-691-00100-6) Princeton U Pr.

Desire in the Sun. Karen Robards. 400p. 1988. mass mkt. 5.99 (0-380-75554-8) Avon.

Desire My Love: (Sparhawk) Miranda Jarrett. (Historical Ser.). 1994. mass mkt. 3.99 (0-373-28847-6, 1-28847-1) Harlequin Bks.

Desire of Ages. Ellen G. White. 1940. reprint ed. 8.95 (0-8163-0029-1, 04259-8); reprint ed. 12.95 (0-8163-0032-1, 04257-2); reprint ed. pap. 9.50 (0-8163-0031-3, 04254-9) Pacific Pr Pub Assn.

***Desire of Ages: The Happiness Millions Desire Is Found in the Man Who Divided History.** E. G. White. (Bible Study Companion Set Ser.: Vol. 3). 544p. (Orig.). (C). 1993. pap. 7.95 (1-883012-52-X) Remnant Pubns.

***Desire of Divine Love: John McLeod Campbell's Doctrine of the Atonement.** Leanne Van Dyk. LC 94-30671. (Studies in Church History: Vol. 4). 200p. (C). 1995. text ed. 48.95 (0-8204-2647-4) P Lang Pubs.

Desire of My Eyes: The Life & Work of John Ruskin. Wolfgang Kemp. Tr. by Jan Van Heurck. (Illus.). 528p. 1992. pap. 17.00 (0-374-52348-7) FS&G.

Desire of the Righteous Granted. John Bunyan. 1974. pap. 5.99 (0-87377-018-8) GAM Pubns.

Desire on the Dunes. Nancy Bruff. 352p. 1984. pap. 3.50 (0-8439-2094-7) Dorchester Pub Co.

Desire One. Thaisa Frank. Ed. by Pat Dienstfrey. 52p. 1982. 4.75 (0-932716-15-6) Kelsey St Pr.

Desire Provoked. Tracy Daugherty. 1986. 15.95 (0-394-55334-9) Random.

Desire Seeking Expression: Mallarme's Prose pour des Esseintes. Marshall Olds. LC 82-82431. (French Forum Monographs: No. 42). 129p. (Orig.). 1983. pap. 10.95 (0-917058-41-0) French Forum.

Desire to Be God: Freedom & the Other in Sartre & Berdyaev. James M. McLachlan. LC 91-31770. (Studies in Phenomenological Theology: Vol. 1). 215p. (C). 1992. pap. text ed. 39.95 (0-8204-1711-4) P Lang Pubs.

Desire to Desire: The Woman's Film of the 1940s. Mary A. Doane. LC 85-45986. (Theories of Representation & Difference Ser.). (Illus.). 224p. 1987. 35.00 (0-253-31682-0); 12.95 (0-253-20433-X, MB-433) Ind U Pr.

Desire to Learn: Selected Writings. Eric Moon. LC 93-15146. (Illus.). 458p. 1993. 47.50 (0-8108-2686-0) Scarecrow.

Desire Unlimited: The Cinema of Pedro Almodovar. Paul J. Smith. LC 94-1436. 1994. 59.95 (0-86091-497-6, Pub. by Verso UK); pap. 17.95 (0-86091-662-6, Pub. by Verso UK) Routledge Chapman & Hall.

Desired. Thea Devine. 448p. 1994. mass mkt. 4.99 (0-8217-4585-9) Zebra.

***Desired.** Virginia Henley. 1995. pap. 5.99 (0-440-21703-2) Dell.

***Desired.** large type ed. Virginia Henley. LC 95-12547. 1995. write for info. (0-7838-1359-7) Hall.

Desired Track. James Gollin & Robert Allardyce. 200p. 1994. pap. 15.95 (1-883868-01-7) Am Vision Pub.

***Desiree.** Annemarie Selinko. LC 52-9706. 1994. reprint ed. lib. bdg. 27.95x (1-56849-548-X) Buccaneer Bks.

***Desiree's Baby.** Kate Chopin. (Kate Chopin Ser.). 1994. audio 16.95 (1-883049-13-X); audio, lib. bdg. 18.95 (1-883049-33-4) Commuters Lib.

***Desires & Deceptions.** Jasmine Cresswell. 1995. mass mkt. 4.99 (1-55166-036-9, 1-66036-4, Mira Bks) Harlequin Bks.

Desires & Disguises: Latin American Women Photographers. Amanda Hopkinson. 1993. pap. 19.99 (1-85242-280-7) Serpents Tail.

Desire's Blossom. Cassie Edwards. 496p. 1985. pap. 3.75 (0-8217-1536-4) Zebra.

Desire's Bride. Teresa Howard. 384p. 1992. mass mkt. 4.25 (0-8217-3973-5) Zebra.

Desire's Chains. Susan Sackett. 384p. 1991. mass mkt. 4.25 (0-8217-3428-8) Zebra.

Desire's Door. Lee McCarthy. (Roerich Poetry Prize Winner Ser.). 83p. 1991. pap. 10.95 (0-934257-85-X) Story Line.

Desire's Dream. Phyllis Herrmann. 384p. 1993. mass mkt. 4.25 (0-8217-4236-1) Zebra.

Desire's Embrace. Mary Martin. 448p. 1993. mass mkt. 4.50 (0-8217-4187-X) Zebra.

Desire's Endless Kiss. Millie Criswell. 1991. mass mkt. 4.25 (0-8217-3608-6) Zebra.

Desire's Experience Transformed: A Representative Anthology of Lope de Vega's Lyric Poetry. Tr. & Intro. by Carl W. Cobb. LC 91-60466. 305p. (ENG & SPA.). 1991. 40.00 (0-938972-18-9) Spanish Lit Pubns.

Desire's Flame. Carla Simpson. 1985. pap. 3.95 (0-8217-1587-9) Zebra.

Desire's Gamble. Rosalyn Alsobrook. 1989. mass mkt. 4.50 (0-8217-2812-1) Zebra.

Desire's Glory. Patricia Pellicane. 1992. mass mkt. 4.50 (0-8217-3989-1) Zebra.

Desires in Conflict. Joe Dallas. 1991. pap. 9.99 (0-89081-897-5) Harvest Hse.

***Desires of a Woman's Heart.** Beverly LaHaye. 272p. 1994. pap. 9.99 (0-8423-1372-9) Tyndale.

Desires of a Woman's Heart: Encouragement for Women When Traditional Values Are Challenged. Beverly LaHaye. LC 93-12911. 1993. 16.99 (0-8423-7945-2) Tyndale.

***Desires of Mothers to Please Others in Letters.** Bernadette Mayer. 350p. 1994. pap. 12.95 (0-9638433-1-1) Hard Pr MA.

Desires of the Human Heart: An Introduction to the Theology of Bernard Lonergan. Ed. by Vernon Gregson. 1988. pap. 12.95 (0-8091-3002-5) Paulist Pr.

Desires, Right & Wrong: The Ethics of Enough. Mortimer J. Adler. 384p. 1991. text ed. 22.95 (0-02-500281-3) Macmillan.

Desire's Slave. Linda Hilton. 1992. mass mkt. 4.25 (0-8217-3731-7) Zebra.

Desire's Song. Pamela Caldwell. 448p. 1994. mass mkt. 4.50 (0-8217-4624-3) Zebra.

Desire's Storm. Lindsay Randall. 512p. 1986. pap. 3.95 (0-8217-1920-3) Zebra.

***Desire's Treasure.** Linda Sandifer. 384p. 1995. mass mkt. 4.99 (0-8217-4899-8) Windsor NY.

***Desiring Flight.** Christianne Balk. LC 94-38209. 96p. (Orig.). 1995. pap. 12.95 (1-55753-062-9) Purdue U Pr.

Desiring God: Meditations of a Christian Hedonist. John Piper. LC 86-23818. 281p. 1987. pap. 10.99 (0-88070-221-4, Multnomah Bks) Questar Pubs.

Desiring Theology. Charles E. Winquist. 184p. 1994. pap. text ed. 12.95 (0-226-90213-7) U Ch Pr.

Desiring Theology. Charles E. Winquist. 184p. 1994. lib. bdg. 30.00 (0-226-90212-9) U Ch Pr.

***Desisions of the Executive Directors under Article IX of the Articles of Agreement on Questions of Interpretation of the Articles of Agreement: International Bank for Reconstruction & Development.** 28p. Date not set. write for info. (0-8213-1846-2, 11846) World Bank.

***Desisions of the Executive Directors under Article IX of the Articles of Agreement on Questions of Interpretation of the Articles of Agreement: International Bank for Reconstruction & Development.** 28p. (FRE.). Date not set. write for info. (0-8213-2002-5, 12002) World Bank.

***Desisions of the Executive Directors under Article IX of the Articles of Agreement on Questions of Interpretation of the Articles of Agreement: International Bank for Reconstruction & Development.** 28p. (SPA.). Date not set. write for info. (0-8213-2038-6, 12038) World Bank.

Desk & Derrick Standard Oil Abbreviator. 3rd ed. Desk & Derrick Club Staff. 330p. 1986. pap. 24.95 (0-87814-299-1, P4418) PennWell Bks.

Desk Book for Construction Superintendents. 2nd ed. King Royer. (Illus.). 1980. text ed. 27.50 (0-685-03826-2) P-H.

Desk Book for Setting Up A Closely Held Corporation. 2nd ed. Robert P. Hess. LC 85-18088. 549p. 1986. 69.95 (0-87624-114-3, Inst Busn Plan) P-H.

Desk-Book of Errors in English. Frank H. Vizetelly. 1995. reprint ed. 40.00 (1-55888-955-8) Omnigraphics Inc.

Desk Drawer Anthology. Ed. by Theodore Roosevelt. LC 72-99032. (Granger Index Reprint Ser.). 1977. 24.95 (0-8369-6107-2) Ayer.

***Desk in the Front of the Room & Other Tales Told Out of School.** Gerald D. Sullivan. LC 94-93918. (Illus.). 80p. (Orig.). 1995. pap. 9.95 (0-9644573-1-8) Shamrock Sky Bks.

Desk Ref. Thomas J. Glover. (Illus.). 492p. 1993. lib. bdg. 39.95 (0-9622359-1-1) Sequoia Pub Inc.

Desk Reference for Critical Care. Brenda K. Shelton & Jonelle E. Wright. (Nursing-Health Science Ser.). 1383p. (C). 1993. boxed 97.50 (0-86720-325-0) Jones & Bartlett.

Desk Reference for Neuroscience. 2nd ed. I. Lockard. (Illus.). 344p. 1991. pap. 43.00 (0-387-97715-5) Spr-Verlag.

Desk Reference for Organic Chemists. Michael B. East & David J. Ager. 1995. write for info. (0-89464-818-7) Krieger.

Desk Reference Guide: Cliff's Notes Hardbound Literary Libraries. 1990. pap. 3.95 (0-931013-88-7) Moonbeam Pubns.

Desk Reference on Significant U. S. Supreme Court Decisions Affecting Public School. Gwendolyn H. Gregory. 1992. pap. text ed. 25.00 (0-88364-135-6) Natl Sch Boards.

Desk Reference Set, 3 vols., Set. Signet Books Staff. 1989. Boxed set. boxed, pap. 16.48 (0-451-92249-2, Sig) NAL-Dutton.

Desk-Side Guide to the Rules of Bankruptcy. 56p. 1988. pap. 15.00 (0-685-18965-1, 549-0056-01) Amer Bar Assn.

Desk Stress. David Christopher. 16p. 1991. pap. 1.00 (1-880745-00-3) Global City.

Desk-Top Business Intelligence Sourcebook. Kent R. Frantzve. LC 91-72603. 192p. (Orig.). 1992. pap. 16.95 (1-880186-00-4) Hyde Pk Mktg.

Desk-Top Publishing: Writing & Publishing in the Computer Age. David R. Sullivan. LC 88-81363. 1989. teacher ed 3.56 (0-318-36902-8) HM.

Desk Top Risk Manager: An Employer's Guide to Reducing the Cost of Workers Compensation & Other Employee Benefits. William C. Neel. 220p. 1991. 145.00 (0-9628805-0-7) ECMS.

Desk Top Science. B. K. Hixson. 44p. 1989. pap. text ed. 16.99 (1-57156-008-4) Wild Goose UT.

Deskbook Encyclopedia of American Insurance Law. 7th ed. 84.25 (0-939675-35-8) Data Res MN.

Deskbook Encyclopedia of American School Law, 1994. 1994. pap. 93.25 (0-939675-38-2) Data Res MN.

Deskbook Encyclopedia of Employment Law. 2nd ed. LC 94-441. 1994. pap. 68.25 (0-939675-42-0) Data Res MN.

Deskbook Encyclopedia of Public Employment Law. 4th ed. 405p. 81.75 (0-939675-41-2) Data Res MN.

Deskbook of Art Law. 2nd ed. Leonard D. DuBoff & Sally H. Caplan. 1993. ring bd. 350.00 (0-379-20157-7) Oceana.

Deskbook of Building Construction: Charts, Tables, & Forms. Byron W. Maguire. (Illus.). 256p. (C). 1985. pap. text ed. 36.00 (0-13-202037-8) P-H.

Deskbook of Construction Contract Law: With Forms. H. Murray Hohns et al. LC 80-27862. 288p. 1981. text ed. 49.95 (0-13-202069-6, Busn) P-H.

Deskbook of Executive Excellence & Stress Management: Skills, Tactics, & Tips for Superior Job Performance. S. A. Swami. 170p. 1993. 14.95 (0-941553-02-7) Minibook Pub.

Desktop Basics with WorkPerfect 5.1. Margaret Brown. 260p. 1991. teacher ed 5.00 (1-56243-065-3, WDB/TM); spiral bd. 20.00 (1-56243-052-1, WDB); trans. 130.00 (1-56243-067-X, WD-13); trans. 200.00 (1-56243-068-8, WD-26); trans. 200.00 (1-56243-069-6, WD-12); disk 65.00 (1-56243-062-9, DD-77); disk 65.00 (1-56243-066-1, DD-85) DDC Pub.

Desktop Color Book. Verbum Magazine Editors. (Illus.). 64p. (Orig.). 1992. pap. 14.95 (1-882305-00-0) Verbum.

Desktop Color Book. 2nd ed. Michael Gosney & Linnea Dayton. (Illus.). 120p. 1995. pap. 19.95 (1-55828-365-X) Verbum.

Desktop Communications: IBM PC. PS-2, & Compatibles. David A. Honig et al. 404p. (Orig.). 1990. pap. text ed. 22.95 (0-471-60613-8) Wiley.

Desktop Computer Animation: A Guide to Low-Cost Computer Animation. Gregory MacNicol. (Illus.). 187p. 1992. 45.00 (0-240-80065-6, Focal) Buttrwrth-Heinemann.

An Asterisk (*) at the beginning of an entry indicates that the title is appearing in BIP for the first time.

D

An Asterisk (*) at the beginning of an entry indicates that the title is appearing in BIP for the first time.

Desmidioflorula Paulista I: Genero Arthordesmus Ehr. ex Ralfs Emend. Arch. C. E. Bicudo & M. T. Azevedo. (Bibliotheca Phycologica Ser.: No. 36). (Illus.). (POR.). 1978. text ed. 26.00 (*3-7682-1156-8*) Lubrecht & Cramer.

Desmidioflorula Paulista II: Genero Micrasterias C. Agardh ex Ralfs. C. Bicudo & L. Sormus. (Bibliotheca Phycologica Ser.: No. 57). (Illus.). 230p. (SPA.). 1982. pap. text ed. 52.00 (*3-7682-1225-4*) Lubrecht & Cramer.

Desmidioflorula Paulista III: Generos Bambu ina, Desmidium, Groenbladia, Nyalotheca, Onychonema, Phymatodos, Spondylosium, Teilingia. C. E. Bicudo & I. M. Samanez. (Bibliotheca Phycologica Ser.: No. 68). (Illus.). 138p. (POR.). 1984. pap. text ed. 32.50 (*3-7682-1388-9*) Lubrecht & Cramer.

***Desmidioflorula Paulista IV.** C. F. De M. Bicudo & A. A. De Castro. 95. (Illus.). 191p. (POR.). 1994. pap. 59.50 (*0-614-00209-5*) Lubrecht & Cramer.

Desmids from Papua New Guinea. Wim Vyverman. (Bibliotheca Phycologica Ser.: Vol. 87). 360p. 1991. pap. text ed. 115.20 (*3-443-60014-X*, Pub. by Cramer-Borntraeger GW) Lubrecht & Cramer.

Desmids of the English Lake District. Edna M. Lind & Alan J. Brook. 1980. 39.00 (*0-686-75592-8*) St Mut.

Desmond Hundred. Jane G. Austin. (Works of Jane (Goodin) Austin). 1989. reprint ed. lib. bdg. 79.00 (*0-7812-1829-2*) Rprt Serv.

Desmond Tutu. David Winner. LC 88-4883. (People Who Have Helped the World Ser.). (Illus.). 68p. (J). 1990. reprint ed. pap. 7.95 (*0-8192-1542-2*) Morehouse Pub.

Desmond Tutu: Bishop of Peace. Carol Greene. LC 86-9582. (Picture-Story Biographies Ser.). (Illus.). 32p. (J). (gr. 2-5). 1986. lib. bdg. 11.85 (*0-516-03634-3*); pap. 3.95 (*0-516-43634-1*) Childrens.

Desmond Tutu: Black Africa's Man of Destiny. Patrick Comerford. 1989. pap. 15.00 (*1-85390-005-2*, Pub. by Veritas IE) St Mut.

Desmond Tutu: Religious Leader Devoted to Freedom. David Wimer. LC 90-10044. (People Who Made a Difference Ser.). (Illus.). 64p. (J). (gr. 3-4). 1991. lib. bdg. 21.26 (*0-8368-0459-7*) Gareth Stevens Inc.

Desmond Tutu: The Courageous & Eloquent Archbishop Struggling Against Apartheid in South Africa. David Winner. Ed. by Rhoda Sherwood. LC 88-4883. (People Who Have Helped the World Ser.). (Illus.). 68p. (J). (gr. 5-6). 1989. lib. bdg. 21.26 (*1-55532-822-9*) Gareth Stevens Inc.

Desmond's Daughters. large type ed. Marjorie Warby. 336p. 1989. 17.95 (*0-7089-2001-2*) Ulverscroft.

Desmond's Guide to Perfect Entertaining. Desmond Atholl & Michael Cherkinian. (Illus.). 224p. 1993. 18.95 (*0-312-09921-5*, Pub. by Thomas Dunne Bks) St Martin.

Desmopressin in Bleeding Disorders. Ed. by G. Mariani et al. (NATO ASI Series A, Life Sciences: Vol. 242). (Illus.). 386p. (C). 1993. 105.00 (*0-306-44414-3*, Plenum Pr) Plenum.

Desobeissance. Alberto Moravia. (FRE.). 1973. pap. 10.95 (*0-7859-4022-7*) Fr & Eur.

Desolacion. G. Mistral. 230p. (SPA.). 1972. 10.50 (*0-8288-7130-2*, S8274) Fr & Eur.

Desolate City: Revolution in the Catholic Church. Anne R. Muggeridge. 1990. pap. 12.00 (*0-06-066046-5*) Harper SF.

Desolate South, Eighteen Sixty-Five to Eighteen Sixty-Six. John T. Trowbridge. LC 72-114899. (Select Bibliographies Reprint Ser.). 1977. 35.95 (*0-8369-5303-7*) Ayer.

Desolation Angels. Jack Kerouac. 1978. pap. 10.00 (*0-399-50385-4*, Perigee Bks) Berkley Pub.

***Desolation Angels.** Jack Kerouac. 432p. Date not set. pap. 12.00 (*1-57222-505-X*) Riverhead Bks.

***Desolation Angels.** Jack Kerouac. 1995. pap. 12.00 (*1-57322-505-3*) Riverhead Bks.

Desolation Island. Patrick O'Brian. 325p. 1991. pap. 10.95 (*0-393-30812-X*) Norton.

Desolation Island. Patrick O'Brian. 1994. 22.50 (*0-393-03705-3*) Norton.

Desolation of a City. Charles Phythian-Adams. LC 79-9967. (Past & Present Publications). (Illus.). 1980. 79.95 (*0-521-22604-X*) Cambridge U Pr.

***Desolation of Reality.** William R. Brashear. LC 94-40614. (American University Studies, Series V, Philosophy: Vol. 174). 1995. write for info. (*0-8204-2735-7*) P Lang Pubs.

Desolation River Guide: Green River Wilderness. Laura Evans & Buzz Belknap. LC 74-80877. (Illus.). 56p. 1974. 14.95 (*0-916370-06-2*); pap. 7.95 (*0-916370-05-4*) Westwater.

Desolation Wilderness: Fishing Guide. Mark Heskett. (Illus.). 72p. 1995. pap. 12.95 (*1-878175-62-9*) F Amato Pubns.

Desolation Wilderness & the South Lake Tahoe Basin. 2nd ed. Jeffrey P. Schaffer. LC 86-528029. (Illus.). 160p. 1985. pap. 13.95 (*0-89997-050-8*) Wilderness Pr.

***De'Sommi, Leone: The Three Sisters.** Tr. by Don Beecher & Massimo Ciavoletta. 132p. 1993. pap. 8.00 (*0-919473-81-4*, DH88P, Pub. by Dovehouse CN) MRTS.

***De'Sommi, Leone: The Three Sisters.** Tr. by Don Beecher & Massimo Ciavoletta. 132p. 1993. 20.00 (*0-919473-99-7*, DH88, Pub. by Dovehouse CN) MRTS.

***Desorden de Tu Nombre: The Disorder of Your Name.** Millas. 1995. pap. 12.50 (*0-679-76091-1*, Vin) Random.

Desorption Induced by Electron Transitions, DIET I. Ed. by N. H. Tolk et al. (Chemical Physics Ser.: Vol. 24). (Illus.). 269p. 1983. 63.00 (*0-387-12127-7*) Spr-Verlag.

Desorption Induced by Electron Transitions Diet V: Proceedings of the Fifth International Workshop, Taos, NM, March 31-April 4, 1992. Ed. by A. R. Burns et al. LC 93-7305. (Surface Sciences Ser.: Vol. 31). 1993. write for info. (*3-540-56473-X*) Spr-Verlag.

Desorption Induced by Electronic Transitions DIET Four: Proceedings of the Fourth International Workshop, Gloggnitz, Austria, October 2-4, 1989. Ed. by G. Betz & P. Varga. (Surface Sciences Ser.: Vol. 19). (Illus.). xvi, 392p. 1990. 75.00 (*0-387-52386-3*) Spr-Verlag.

Desorption Induced by Electronic Transitions, DIET V: Proceedings of the Fifth International Workshop, Taos, NM, March 31-April 4, 1992. Ed. by A. B. Burns et al. (Surface Sciences Ser.: Vol. 31). (Illus.). 360p. 1993. 119.00 (*0-387-56473-X*) Spr-Verlag.

DeSoto, Coronado, Cabrillo: Explorers of the Northern Mystery. David Lavender. LC 91-47633. (Handbook Ser.: No. 144). (Illus.). 112p. (Orig.). 1992. pap. 4.00 (*0-685-62342-4*, 024-005-01102-1) Natl Park Serv.

DeSoto Didn't Land at Tampa. Rolfe F. Schell. LC 66-17798. (Illus.). 1967. 10.95 (*0-87208-011-0*); pap. 8.95 (*0-87208-048-X*) Island Pr Pubs.

***DeSoto Parish History.** Illus. by Eugenia Manning. 1994. 50.00 (*0-9644415-0-0*) DeSoto Hist & Geneal.

Desouza in Stardust. large type ed. Freny Olbrich. (Mystery Ser.). 384p. 1983. 15.95 (*0-7089-0951-5*) Ulverscroft.

Desouza Pays the Price. large type ed. Freny Olbrich. (Mystery Ser.). 352p. 1982. 15.95 (*0-7089-0844-6*) Ulverscroft.

Despachos de los Consules Norteamericanos en Puerto Rico: 1818-1868, Tomo I. Ed. by Puerto Rico, Universidad. Facultad de Humanidades, Centro de Investigaciones Historicas Staff. LC 77-12721. 1395p. 1982. 25.00 (*0-8477-0845-4*) U of PR Pr.

Despair. Vladimir Nabokov. (International Ser.). 1989. pap. 11.00 (*0-679-72343-9*, Vin) Random.

Despair & Deliverance: Private Salvation in Contemporary Israel. Benjamin Beit-Hallahmi. LC 91-16392. (SUNY Series in Israeli Studies). (C). 1992. 59.50 (*0-7914-0999-6*); pap. 19.95 (*0-7914-1000-5*) State U NY Pr.

Despair & Personal Power in the Nuclear Age. Joanna R. Macy. 200p. 1983. lib. bdg. 39.95 (*0-86571-030-9*); pap. 16.95 (*0-86571-031-7*) New Soc Pubs.

Despair in Monterey Bay. David D. Connell & Jim Thurman. LC 93-183351. (Mathnet Casebks.: 2). (Illus.). (J). (gr. 3-7). 1993. pap. text ed. 3.95 (*0-7167-6502-0*, Sci Am Yng Rdrs) W H Freeman.

Despair in Monterey Bay. David D. Connell & Jim Thurman. LC 93-183351. (Mathnet Casebks.: 2). (Illus.). (J). (gr. 4-7). 1995. text ed. 10.95 (*0-7167-6505-5*, Sci Am Yng Rdrs) W H Freeman.

Despairing Developer: Diary of an Aid Worker in the Middle East. Timothy Morris. 224p. 1991. 49.95 (*1-85043-486-7*, Pub. by I B Tauris UK); text ed. 16.95 (*1-85043-350-X*, Pub. by I B Tauris UK) St Martin.

Desparados on the Loose see Adios, Bandido!

Despatches from Damascus: Gilbert Mackereth & British Policy in the Levant, 1933-1939. Ed. by Michael G. Fry & Itamar Rabinovich. 228p. (Orig.). 1986. pap. text ed. 11.95 (*0-8156-7052-4*, Pub. by Shiloah Ctr Mid East & African Studies IS) Syracuse U Pr.

Despatches of Michele Suriand & Marc'Antonio Barbaro, Venetian Ambassadors at the Court of France, 1560-1563. Ed. by Henry Layard. Bd. with Registers of the French Conformed Churches of St. Patrick & St. Mary, Dublin. (Huguenot Society of London Publications Ser.: Vol. 6 & 7). 1972. reprint ed. (*0-8115-1645-8*) Periodicals Srv.

Despenaperros. Jose M. Vaz de Soto. (Nueva Austral Ser.: Vol. 46). (SPA.). 1991. pap. text ed. 29.95x (*84-239-1846-7*) Elliots Bks.

Desperado. Rebecca Brandewyne. 304p. (Orig.). 1992. mass mkt. 5.99 (*0-446-35584-4*) Warner Bks.

Desperado. large type ed. Rebecca Brandewyne. LC 93-619. (Orig.). 1993. pap. 18.95 (*1-56054-721-9*) Thorndike Pr.

Desperado, No. 1. B. W. Lawton. 176p. (Orig.). 1993. pap. 3.99 (*0-515-11077-9*) Jove Pubns.

***Desperado & 35 Country Classics.** 128p. (Orig.). 1994. pap. 14.95 (*0-89724-243-2*) Warner Brothers.

Desperado Dream. Karen A. Bale. 1990. mass mkt. 4.50 (*0-8217-2983-7*) Zebra.

Desperado, No. 2: Edge of the Law. B. W. Lawton. 176p. (Orig.). 1993. pap. 3.99 (*0-515-11133-3*) Jove Pubns.

Desperado, No. 3: Hard Justice. B. W. Lawton. 1993. pap. 3.99 (*0-515-11213-5*) Jove Pubns.

Desperado Passion. Patricia Pellicane. 448p. 1991. mass mkt. 4.50 (*0-8217-3336-2*) Zebra.

Desperado Run. Patrick E. Andrews. 224p. 1987. pap. 2.50 (*0-8217-2077-5*) Zebra.

***Desperado (Timeless Love)** Patricia Rosemoor. 1995. mass mkt. 3.50 (*0-373-22346-3*) Harlequin Bks.

Desperadoes. Ron Hansen. 1990. pap. 8.95 (*0-393-30680-1*) Norton.

Desperadoes. Ben Thompson. 1977. pap. 1.25 (*0-8439-0514-X*) Dorchester Pub Co.

Desperadoes. large type ed. Ron Hansen. 470p. 1981. 15.95 (*0-7089-0644-3*) Ulverscroft.

Desperadoes, Throwing Smoke, Keyhole Lover. Keith Reddin. 1986. pap. 4.75 (*0-8222-0301-4*) Dramatists Play.

Desperados. Elaine Shannon. 1989. pap. 5.95 (*0-451-82207-2*, 043) NAL-Dutton.

Desperado's Caress. Carla Simpson. 1991. mass mkt. 4.50 (*0-8217-3506-3*) Zebra.

Desperado's Kiss. Joyce Myrus. 448p. 1991. mass mkt. 4.50 (*0-8217-3443-1*) Zebra.

***Desperate.** Kay David. (Intimate Moments Ser.). 1995. pap. 3.75 (*0-373-07624-X*, 1-07624-9) Silhouette.

***Desperate Call.** Laura Coburn. 352p. (Orig.). 1995. mass mkt. 4.99 (*0-451-18294-4*, Onyx) NAL-Dutton.

Desperate Character, Etc. Ivan S. Turgenev. Tr. by Constance Garnett. LC 74-132131. (Short Story Index Reprint Ser.). 1977. 18.95 (*0-8369-3688-4*) Ayer.

Desperate Characters: A Novella in Verse & Other Poems. Nicholas Christopher. 112p. 1989. pap. 12.50 (*0-14-012116-1*, Penguin Bks) Viking Penguin.

Desperate Choices. Sibylle Garrett. (Silhouette Intimate Moments Ser.). 1993. mass mkt. 3.39 (*0-373-07476-X*, 5-07476-0) Silhouette.

Desperate Circumstances, Dangerous Woman. Brenda M. Osbey. 103p. (Orig.). 1991. pap. 9.95 (*0-934257-57-4*) Story Line.

Desperate Deception. Maria Greene. 384p. (Orig.). 1988. pap. 3.95 (*0-380-75562-9*) Avon.

Desperate Dieters: A Book on Body Management & Self-Esteem. Kathy L. Shorter. 48p. Date not set. pap. text ed. 4.99 (*1-879686-01-5*) Wrd Faith Min.

Desperate Diplomacy: William H. Seward's Foreign Policy, 1861. Norman B. Ferris. LC 75-5509. 275p. reprint ed. 78.40 (*0-685-16019-X*, 2027558) Bks Demand.

Desperate Encounters: The Fifth Royal Gurkha Rifles (the Punjab Frontier Force) Robert Maxwell. 264p. (C). 1989. text ed. 65.00 (*0-946270-35-X*, Pub. by Pentland Pr UK) St Mut.

***Desperate Faction? The Jacobites of North-East England 1688-1745.** Leo Gooch. (Illus.). 229p. 1995. pap. 22.95 (*0-85958-636-7*) Paul & Co Pubs.

Desperate Faith: A Study of Bellow, Salinger, Mailer, Baldwin, & Updike. Howard M. Harper. LC 67-17034. 208p. reprint ed. pap. 59.30 (*0-8357-4410-8*, 2037230) Bks Demand.

Desperate for a Dog. Rose Impey. (Speedsters Ser.). (Illus.). 64p. (J). (gr. 2-5). 1991. pap. 3.99 (*0-14-034798-4*, Puffin) Puffin Bks.

***Desperate Gamble.** Janice Bennett. 320p. 1995. mass mkt. 3.99 (*0-8217-4815-7*) Windsor NY.

Desperate Gourmet. Lois Schenck. 160p. 1988. pap. 10.95 (*0-312-02191-7*) St Martin.

Desperate Hours. Joseph Hayes. 1976. 21.95 (*0-8488-0810-X*) Amereon Ltd.

Desperate Hours. Joseph Hayes. 389p. 1981. reprint ed. lib. bdg. 17.95 (*0-89968-230-8*, Lghtyr Pr) Buccaneer Bks.

Desperate Journey. Fred Rendrell & Tricia Watterson. (C). 1989. 550.00 (*1-85098-043-8*, Pub. by Jordanhill College UK) St Mut.

Desperate Journeys, Abandoned Souls: True Stories of Castaways & Other Survivors. Edward E. Leslie. LC 88-644. (Illus.). 448p. 1988. pap. 11.95 (*0-395-43608-7*) HM.

Desperate Justice. large type ed. Richard Speight. 1990. 21.95 (*0-7089-2179-5*) Ulverscroft.

Desperate Man. Wayne D. Overholser. 192p. 1992. pap. 3.50 (*0-8439-3175-2*) Dorchester Pub Co.

Desperate Measures. James Hannah. LC 87-26404. (Southwest Life & Letters Ser.). 208p. 1988. 17.95 (*0-87074-262-0*) SMU Press.

***Desperate Measures.** Fern Michaels. LC 94-27157. 1994. 22.00 (*0-345-38440-7*) Ballantine.

Desperate Measures. David Morrell. 416p. 1994. 22.95 (*0-446-51791-7*) Warner Bks.

***Desperate Measures.** David Morrell. 1995. mass mkt. 6.99 (*0-446-60239-6*, Warner Vision) Warner Bks.

Desperate Measures. large type ed. Sara Craven. 1992. reprint ed. lib. bdg. 18.95 (*0-263-13026-6*, Pub. by Mills & Boon UK) Thorndike Pr.

***Desperate Measures.** large type ed. Fern Michaels. LC 94-34299. 1995. write for info. (*0-7862-0337-4*) Thorndike Pr.

Desperate Night. large type ed. H. C. Davis. (Linford Mystery Library). 1990. pap. 12.95 (*0-7089-6851-1*, Trailtree Bookshop) Ulverscroft.

Desperate People. Farley Mowat. 240p. 1984. mass mkt. 5.99 (*0-7704-2323-X*) Bantam.

Desperate Pleasures. (Illus.). 140p. 1988. 23.95 (*0-945618-01-8*) Dorsoduro Pr.

Desperate Politics of Postmodernism. Henry S. Kariel. LC 88-14150. 200p. (Orig.). (C). 1989. lib. bdg. 30.00 (*0-87023-654-7*); pap. 13.95 (*0-87023-655-5*) U of Mass Pr.

Desperate Pursuit. Gloria D. Miklowitz. (J). (gr. 7 up). 1992. mass mkt. 3.99 (*0-553-29746-5*, Starfire) Bantam.

Desperate Remedy: An Edwina Crusoe Medical Mystery. Mary Kittredge. 208p. 1993. 18.95 (*0-312-09784-0*) St Martin.

Desperate Remedy: An Edwina Crusoe Mystery. large type ed. Mary Kittredge. LC 93-39981. 1994. pap. 17.95 (*0-7862-0109-6*) Thorndike Pr.

***Desperate Remedy Vol. 1.** Mary Kittredge. 1994. pap. 4.50 (*0-312-95330-5*) St Martin.

Desperate Search. Lee Rody. LC 88-63476. (American Adventure Ser.). 160p. (J). (gr. 2-6). 1989. pap. 5.99 (*1-55661-027-0*) Bethany Hse.

Desperate Spring: Lives of Algerian Women. Fettouma Tonati. 1990. pap. 9.95 (*0-7043-4053-4*, Pub. by Womens Pr UK) Interlink Pub.

Desperate Street. Roy B. McKeown. 68p. (Orig.). 1989. pap. 5.95 (*0-939497-19-0*) Promise Pub.

Desperate Viscount. Gayle Buck. 224p. (Orig.). 1993. pap. 3.99 (*0-451-17743-6*, Sig) NAL-Dutton.

Desperate Voyage. John Caldwell. 250p. 1991. pap. 14.95 (*0-924486-20-1*) Sheridan.

Desperate Witch. large type ed. Anthony Graham. (Mystery Ser.). 352p. 1992. 21.95 (*0-7089-2609-6*) Ulverscroft.

***Desperate Women Need to Talk to You.** Joan Frank. 154p. 1994. lib. bdg. 27.00 (*0-8095-5883-1*) Borgo Pr.

Desperately Seeking Crime Crushers. Wally Davis. (Illus.). 96p. (Orig.). 1986. pap. 4.95 (*0-938417-00-2*) Copouts Ink.

Desperately Seeking Julio. Maruja Torres. 181p. 1992. pap. 15.95 (*1-872180-79-5*, Pub. by Fourth Estate UK) Trafalgar.

Desperately Seeking Perfect Family. Fran Sciacca & Jill Sciacca. (Lifelines Ser.). (YA). 1987. pap. 3.95 (*0-89066-098-0*) World Wide Pubs.

Desperately Seeking Solutions: Macintosh Troubleshooting Guide to the Mac. Erica Kerwien. (Illus.). 256p. (Orig.). 1993. Incl. double density disk. disk, pap. 29.95 (*1-56830-009-3*) Hayden.

Desperately Seeking the Audience. Ien Ang. 192p. 1991. 55.00 (*0-415-05269-6*, A5064); pap. 15.95 (*0-415-05270-X*, A5068) Routledge.

Despertad America! Tomad Mi Corizon, Tomad Mi Mano: El Inspirador Relato de las Apariciones Marianas, Curaciones, y Fe en Conyers, Georgia. Anne M. Hancock. Tr. by Maria Siccardi. (Illus.). 200p. (Orig.). 1993. pap. 10.95 (*1-878901-89-3*) Hampton Roads Pub Co.

Despertamiento En Indonesia: Indonesia Revival: Focus on Timor. George W. Peters. (SPA.). 4.25 (*84-7228-171-X*, 220275, Pub. by Edit Clie SP) TSELF.

Despertar de la Gracia. Charles R. Swindoll. 192p. (Orig.). (SPA.). 1991. pap. 5.95 (*0-88113-018-4*) Edit Betania.

Despiertate, Iglesia!...La Victoria es Nuestra! (Brothers & Sisters, We Have a Problem) Nicky Cruz. 160p. (Orig.). (SPA.). 1988. 5.99 (*0-926557-07-6*, 490244) Editorial Unilit.

Despierte a la Vida: Wake up to Life. Salvador Iserte. (SPA.). 6.95 (*84-7228-937-0*, 223012, Pub. by Edit Clie SP) TSELF.

Despised & Rejected. A. T. Fitzroy, pseud. LC 75-12314. (Homosexuality Ser.). 1975. reprint ed. 19.95 (*0-405-07389-5*) Ayer.

Despiser of God? Doug Stringer. 16p. (Orig.). 1989. pap. write for info. (*0-944547-02-8*) Herit Hse Litho.

Despite a Generous Spirit: Denying Asylum in the United States. Silk James. Ed. by Virginia Hamilton. (Issue Brief Ser.). 1986. pap. 2.00 (*0-317-58042-6*) US Comm Refugees.

Despite It All. Chaim Lazar. Tr. by Goldie Wachsman. LC 84-50677. (Illus.). 208p. 1985. 13.95 (*0-88400-106-7*) Shengold.

Despite the Evidence. large type ed. Peter Alding. (Linford Mystery Library). 416p. 1992. pap. 14.95 (*0-7089-7301-9*, Trailtree Bookshop) Ulverscroft.

Despite the Plainness of the Day: Love Poems. David Ignatow. Ed. by Peter Oresick & Anthony Petrosky. 64p. (C). 1991. text ed. 20.00 (*0-9626023-0-2*); pap. 10.00 (*0-9626023-1-0*) Mill Hunk Bks.

Despite This Flesh: The Disabled in Stories & Poems. Ed. by Vassar Miller. 166p. 1985. 15.95 (*0-292-72449-7*); pap. 8.95 (*0-292-71550-1*) U of Tex Pr.

Despo Magoni: Recent Paintings. Alternative Museum Staff. LC 86-70055. (Illus.). 1986. pap. 4.00 (*0-932075-08-8*) Alternative Mus.

Desportes de Invierno. Charles M. Schulz. 64p. 1971. 4.95 (*0-686-56188-0*) Fr & Eur.

Despotic Rulers: Ash Shiah Wa Hakimun. rev. ed. Muhammad J. Mughniyyah. Ed. by S. M. Wasi & A. A. Aini. Tr. by M. Fazal Haq. 274p. reprint ed. pap. 8.00 (*0-941724-46-8*) Islamic Seminary.

Despotism & Differential Reproduction: A Darwinian View of History. Laura L. Betzig. LC 85-20010. (Foundations of Human Behavior Ser.). (Illus.). 182p. 1986. lib. bdg. 39.95 (*0-202-01171-2*) Aldine de Gruyter.

Despotism in America. Richard Hildreth. (Notable American Authors Ser.). 1992. reprint ed. lib. bdg. 75.00 (*0-7812-3125-6*) Rprt Serv.

Despotism in America: An Enquiry into the Nature, Results & Legal Basis of the Slaveholding System in the United States. Richard Hildreth. LC 69-16310. 1970. reprint ed. 39.50 (*0-678-00599-0*) Kelley.

Despotism in America: Or an Inquiry into the Nature & Results of the Slave-Holding System in the United States. Richard Hildreth. LC 77-81120. (Black Heritage Library Collection). 1977. 19.95 (*0-8369-8600-8*) Ayer.

Despotism of Freedom: Or, Tyranny & Cruelty of American Republican Slavemasters. David L. Child. LC 76-149865. (Black Heritage Library Collection). 1977. 15.95 (*0-8369-8747-0*) Ayer.

Despues De la Experiencia: Afterglow. Sherwood E. Wirt. (SPA.). 3.25 (*84-7228-049-7*, 220278, Pub. by Edit Clie SP) TSELF.

Despues De Un Ataque Cardiaco: Que Sigue? Julia A. Purcell et al. Ed. by Nancy R. Hull. Tr. by Olimpia De la Vega. LC 90-27143. (Illus.). 68p. (Orig.). 1991. pap. text ed. 4.90 (*0-939838-30-3*) Pritchett & Hull.

Despues del Silencio: Entrevistas al Padre Franciscano Fray Miguel Angel Loredo, O.F.M. por Nicolas Perez Diez-Arguelles. 2nd ed. Miguel A. Loredo. LC 89-84404. (Coleccion Cuba y Sus Jueces Ser.). (Illus.). 215p. (SPA.). 1989. reprint ed. pap. 15.00 (*0-89729-537-4*) Ediciones.

DESQview: Everything You Need to Know. Jonathan Kamin. (Illus.). 400p. (Orig.). 1992. pap. 22.95 (*1-55958-238-3*) Prima Pub.

Dessa Rose. Sherley A. Williams. 1987. mass mkt. 5.99 (*0-425-10337-4*) Berkley Pub.

Dessarollo Professional De Educadores De Alultos. Alexander N. Charters. 1977. 4.00 (*0-87060-077-X*, MSS 3) Syracuse U Cont Ed.

Dessert in Half the Time: Use Your Food Processor & Microwave to Make Great Desserts In Less Time Than It Takes to Buy a Pint of Ben & Jerry's. Linda W. Eckhardt & Diana C. Butts. LC 93-2734. (Illus.). 1993. 25.00 (*0-517-58721-1*, Crown) Crown Pub Group.

Dessert Lover's Cookbook: More Than 200 Spectacular Recipes with Step-by-Step Color Photographs. Marlene Sorosky. LC 84-43119. (Illus.). 256p. 1989. reprint ed. pap. 20.00 (*0-06-091658-3*, PL) HarpC.

Dessert Sampler. Jan Siegrist. (Illus.). 48p. (Orig.). 1992. pap. 3.95 (*0-933050-90-9*) New Eng Pr VT.

D

An Asterisk (*) at the beginning of an entry indicates that the title is appearing in BIP for the first time.

Dessert, the Grand Finale. Sedgewood Press Staff. 1993. 29.95 (0-696-02550-7) Meredith Bks.

***Desserts.** Sonia Allison. 1994. 9.95 (0-572-01660-3, Pub. by W Foulsham UK) Trans-Atl Phila.

Desserts. Miriam Canter. 160p. 1990. spiral bd. 5.50 (0-941016-56-0) Penfield.

Desserts. Barbara K. Morgan. 36p. (Orig.). 1989. pap. 2.75 (0-940844-33-8) Wellspring.

Desserts. Ed. by Amanda Murray. 100p. 1992. pap. 5.95 (1-882232-07-0) Kitchen Collect.

Desserts. Louise Stoltzfus. LC 94-14898. (Best of Favorite Recipes from Quilters Ser.). (Illus.). 64p. 1994. 7.95 (1-56148-116-5) Good Bks PA.

Desserts. Ed. by Carla Waldemar. (Land O Lakes Collector Ser.: Vol. 1). 1993. 14.95 (0-923944-49-4) Pub Partners.

Desserts. large type ed. pap. 5.50 (0-317-03506-1) Cath Guild Blind.

Desserts: From Amish & Mennonite Kitchens. Ed. by Phyllis P. Good & Rachel T. Pellman. (Pennsylvania Dutch Cookbooks Ser.). (Illus.). 32p. (Orig.). 1983. pap. 2.95 (0-934672-13-X) Good Bks PA.

Desserts: One Hundred & Fifty Delicious Ideas. 1994. 9.98 (0-681-45461-X) Longmeadow Pr.

Desserts - Les Desserts et Patisseries. Illus. by Nadine Wickenden. LC 94-14107. (Marie-Pierre Moine's French Kitchen Ser.). (ENG & FRE.). 1994. write for info. (0-671-89657-1) S&S Trade.

***Desserts around the World.** (Easy Menu Ethnic Cookbooks Ser.). (YA). (gr. 5 up). 1991. 14.95 (0-8225-9626-1, Lerner Publctns) Lerner Group.

Desserts Around the World. Photos by Robert L. Wolfe & Diane Wolfe. (Easy Menu Ethnic Cookbooks Ser.). (Illus.). 56p. (J). (gr. 5 up). 1991. lib. bdg. 14.95 (0-8225-0926-1, Lerner Publctns) Lerner Group.

Desserts for Diabetics. Mabel Cavaiani. 176p. (Orig.). 1992. pap. 13.00 (0-399-51734-0, Perigree Bks) Berkley Pub.

Desserts from Amish & Mennonite Kitchens. Phyllis P. Good. 1991. pap. 2.95 (1-56148-043-6) Good Bks PA.

Desserts from Your Bread Machine - Perfect Every Time: Cakes, Cookies, Pastries, Doughnuts... Lora Brody. 1994. 22.00 (0-688-13071-2) Morrow.

***Desserts (Frozen & Refrigerated) Market.** 100p. (Orig.). 1995. pap. 2,195.00 (0-7605-2208-1) Rector Pr.

***Desserts to Die For.** Marcel Desaulniers. LC 95-1152. (Illus.). 1995. 30.00 (0-684-81139-1) S&S Trade.

Desserts to Lower Your Fat Thermostat. Barbara W. Higa. 1989. pap. 9.95 (0-912547-06-5) Vitality Hse Int Inc.

Desserts with a Difference: Carrot Cake, Fennel Tart, & Other Surprising & Delicious Vegetable Desserts. Sally Stone & Martin Stone. LC 93-6566. 1993. pap. 18.00 (0-517-88072-5, C P Pubs) Crown Pub Group.

Destabilization & Subversion New Challenges. Ed. by Darbara Singh. (C). 1987. 9.00 (81-7050-058-3, Patriot) S Asia.

Destabilization of Nicaragua. Tom Barry. 39p. 1986. 5.95 (0-911213-09-0) Interhemisp Res Ctr.

Destabilizing Theory: Contemporary Feminist Debates. Ed. by Michele Barrett & Anne Phillips. LC 91-67234. 240p. (C). 1992. 39.50 (0-8047-2030-4); pap. 12.95 (0-8047-2031-2) Stanford U Pr.

***Destello el Dinosaurio: Dazzle the Dinosaur.** Marcus Pfister. LC 94-42452. (Illus.). 32p. (SPA.). (J). (gr. k-3). 1995. 16.95 (1-55858-387-4); lib. bdg. 16.88 (1-55858-388-2) North-South Bks NYC.

Desterradas del Paraiso Protagonistas en la Narrativa de Maria Luis Bombal. Intro. by Marjorie Agosin. LC 83-60448. (Senda de Estudios y Ensayos Ser.). 127p. (Orig.). 1983. pap. 12.95 (0-918454-32-8) Senda Nueva.

DeStijl. Paul Overy. LC 90-72120. (World of Art Ser.). (Illus.). 216p. (Orig.). 1991. pap. 12.95 (0-500-20240-0) Thames Hudson.

Destin Europeen de la Meuse see Conditions de Croissance des Economies Regionales en Etat de Suremploi: Le Cas de Liege

Destin International: La Compagnie de Saint-Gobain, 1830-1939. J. P. Daviet. 724p. (FRE.). 1988. pap. text ed. 77.00 (2-88124-220-0) Gordon & Breach.

Destinados a la Cruz: Destined for the Cross. Paul E. Billheimer. (SPA.). 3.25 (84-7228-786-6, 220276, Pub. by Edit Clie SP) TSELF.

Destinados a Vencer. Paul E. Billheimer. 96p. 1984. pap. 2.95 (0-88113-048-6) Edit Betania.

Destination. Sheldon Woodson. 1994. 7.95 (0-8062-4996-X) Carlton.

Destination: Antarctica. Robert Swan. (Illus.). 48p. (J). (gr. 2-7). 1989. pap. 5.95 (0-590-41286-8) Scholastic Inc.

Destination: Grand Canyon. Thomas E. Way. LC 90-3100. (Illus.). 112p. (Orig.). 1990. pap. 5.00 (0-914846-45-0) Golden West Pub.

Destination: North America. Dawne M. Flammger. 366p. 1993. pap. text ed. 31.95 (0-8273-5300-6) Delmar.

Destination: Phoenix - Hundreds of Things to Do in the Valley of the Sun. Dorothy Tegeler. (Illus.). 180p. (Orig.). 1990. pap. 9.95 (0-943169-20-8) Gem Guides Bk.

Destination: Showdown. Jake Davis. (Last Rangers Ser.: Bk. 3). 176p. (Orig.). 1993. pap. 3.99 (0-425-13705-8) Berkley Pub.

Destination--Discovery! Activities for Studying Columbus & Other Explorers. Frances L. Carroll. LC 94-7035. 212p. (Orig.). 1994. pap. 30.00 (0-8389-0634-6) ALA.

***Destination Acteens: Acteens Member Booklet.** Sammie Johnston. Ed. by Rebecca Nelson. 21p. (Orig.). (YA). (gr. 7-12). 1995. pap. text ed. 2.95 (1-56309-118-6) Womans Mission Union.

Destination Bethlehem: Seven Christmas Plays for Young People. Steve Trott. LC 93-19352. 64p. (Orig.). 1993. pap. 14.99 (0-8010-8906-9) Baker Bk.

***Destination Biafra.** Emecheta. (African Writers Ser.). 1994. pap. 10.95 (0-435-90992-4) Heinemann.

Destination College: A Guide to the College Admissions Process. Barbara G. Heyman. 96p. 1988. pap. 8.95 (0-446-38748-7) Warner Bks.

Destination Danger. large type ed. W. Colt MacDonald. 1979. 21.95 (0-7089-0389-4) Ulverscroft.

Destination Eternity: Az Janin Ta Janan. 2nd ed. Hazrat M. Angha. Ed. by Jim Swan. Tr. by Nahid Angha. (Sufism Ser.). Orig. Title: Az - Janin Ta-Janan. (Illus.). 185p. (Orig.). 1988. pap. 15.50 (0-918437-02-4) Intl Sufism.

Destination French. (BBC Phrase Books for Teenagers Ser.). 1995. 5.95 (0-8442-9236-2, Passport Bks) NTC Pub Grp.

***Destination Geography Vol. 1: Western Hemisphere.** Education Systems Staff. 296p. 1994. pap. text ed. 28.00 (1-879982-34-X) Educ Systs.

***Destination Geography Vol. 2: Eastern Hemisphere.** Education Systems Staff. 397p. 1994. pap. text ed. 28.00 (1-879982-35-8) Educ Systs.

***Destination Internet.** Paul Hoffman. 1995. pap. 14.99 (1-56884-469-7) IDG Bks.

Destination Japan: A Business Guide for the 1990s. 1993. lib. bdg. 274.95 (0-8490-9012-1) Gordon Pr.

Destination Japan: A Business Guide for the 90s. 67p. (Orig.). (C). 1994. pap. text ed. 30.00 (0-941375-84-6) Diane Pub.

Destination Marketing. Richard B. Gartrell. 336p. 1994. per. 49.95 (0-8403-8978-7) Kendall-Hunt.

Destination Moon. Herge. (Illus.). 62p. (J). 19.95 (0-8288-5027-5) Fr & Eur.

Destination Moon. Herge. (J). (gr. 3-8). ring bd. 19.95 (0-8288-5026-7) Fr & Eur.

Destination Moon. Herge. (Adventures of Tintin Ser.). 1976. mass mkt. 7.95 (0-316-35845-2, Joy St Bks) Little.

Destination: Moon. James Irwin. LC 89-3078. 48p. (gr. 3-7). 1989. 9.99 (0-88070-307-5, Gold & Honey) Questar Pubs.

***Destination Multimedia.** 1995. pap. 14.99 (1-56884-470-0) IDG Bks.

Destination Outer Space. Anna Alter. (Focus on Science Ser.). (J). (gr. 6 up). 1988. 4.95 (0-8120-3839-8) Barron.

Destination Retirement: Saturday Morning Planner. Craig Smith & Anita Jay. (Saturday Morning Planner). (Illus.). 120p. (Orig.). 1994. pap. text ed. 5.00 (0-9628583-1-5) Blue Sky Pub.

Destination Spanish. (BBC Phrase Books for Teenagers Ser.). 1995. 5.95 (0-8442-9237-0, Passport Bks) NTC Pub Grp.

Destination Tokyo: A Pictorial History of Doolittle's Tokyo Raid, April 18, 1942. rev. ed. Stan B. Cohen. LC 83-60014. (Illus.). 136p. 1992. pap. 12.95 (0-929521-52-8) Pictorial Hist.

Destination Unknown. Agatha Christie. 1992. mass mkt. 4.99 (0-06-100381-6, Harp PBks) HarpC.

Destination Unknown: A Tale of Survival. Rudolph Bachner. 200p. 1993. pap. 10.95 (0-8059-3446-4) Dorrance.

Destination: Void see Worlds Beyond Dune: The Best of Frank Herbert

***Destination Wa 92.** Alaska Northwest Books Staff. 1994. pap. 4.95 (0-88240-346-X) Alaska Northwest.

***Destination Zero: New & Selected Poems.** Sam Hamill. 184p. (Orig.). 1995. text ed. 25.00 (1-877727-55-5); pap. 15.00 (1-877727-53-9) White Pine.

***Destinations.** John W. Malenda. 180p. 1995. pap. 10.95 (1-886482-00-4) Guiding Lght.

Destinations. Jan Morris. 1982. pap. 9.95 (0-19-503069-9) OUP.

Destinations: A Canvass of American Literature since 1900. Gorham B. Munson. LC 70-131784. 1971. 7.00 (0-403-00671-6) Scholarly.

Destinations: A Canvass of American Literature since 1900. Gorham B. Munson. (BCL1-PS American Literature Ser.). 218p. 1992. reprint ed. lib. bdg. 79.00 (0-7812-6621-1) Rprt Serv.

Destinations: Essays from Rolling Stone. Jan Morris. (Illus.). 1980. 21.95 (0-19-502708-6) OUP.

Destinations: Grand Visions. Jerry Flack. (Journeys: an Individualized Reading, Writing, & Thinking Program Ser.). 112p. 1993. pap. text ed. 13.95 (0-944459-67-6) ECS Lrn Systs.

Destinations: How to Use All Kinds of Maps. Carlienne Frisch. LC 93-10577. (J). 1993. 13.95 (0-8239-1607-3) Rosen Group.

Destinations: North American & International Geography. Dennis L. Foster. 1990. 38.00 (0-02-680872-2) Macmillan.

Destinations: North American & International Geography. Dennis L. Foster. LC 93-23329. (Travel Professional Ser.). 1994. write for info. (0-02-801381-6); pap. write for info. (0-02-801383-2) Macmillan.

Destinations, Detours & Diversions: A Guide to Family Outings & Good Times. Betty Cothran. (Illus.). 75p. (Orig.). (YA). 1989. pap. 2.50 (0-9625229-0-2) Seaworthy Pubns.

Destinations of Southern California: The Guide to Exciting Restaurants, Attractions & Lodgings. 2nd rev. ed. David Vokac. (Illus.). 320p. 1995. pap. 9.95 (0-930743-05-9) West Press.

Destinations of the Southwest. David Vokac. (Illus.). 320p. (Orig.). 1988. pap. 8.95 (0-930743-03-2) West Press.

Destinations Past: Traveling Through History with John Lukacs. John Lukacs. LC 93-45629. 240p. 1994. 26.95 (0-8262-0956-4) U of Mo Pr.

Destined. Joanna Warren. (Belle Meade Ser.: No. 3). 432p. (Orig.). 1980. pap. 2.50 (0-89083-693-0) Zebra.

Destined for Dominion. rev. ed. A. L. Gill. 183p. 1993. pap. 7.95 (0-941975-12-6) Power Hse Pub.

Destined for Glory. large type ed. Margaret Clarkson. (Large Print Inspirational Ser.). 1987. pap. 9.95 (0-8027-2587-2) Walker & Co.

Destined for Greatness: Getting the Results You Desire from Yourself & Others. Robert L. Lawson. 160p. (Orig.). 1994. per., pap. text ed. 16.95 (0-8403-9339-3) Kendall-Hunt.

Destined for Greatness: Getting the Results You Desire from Yourself & Others. Robert L. Lawson. 160p. (Orig.). reprint ed. pap. text ed. 9.95 (0-935979-01-8) Prof Dynamics.

Destined for Hell. Luis Torez. LC 87-82615. 128p. 1985. pap. 5.95 (0-89221-133-4) New Leaf.

***Destined for Murder: Profiles of Six Serial Killers with Astrological Commentary.** Young et al. 224p. 1995. pap. text ed. 12.95 (1-56718-832-X) Llewellyn Pubns.

Destined for the Throne. Paul E. Billheimer. LC 83-15151. 140p. (Orig.). 1983. pap. 6.99 (0-87123-309-6) Bethany Hse.

Destined for the Throne. Paul E. Billheimer. (Orig.). 1990. pap. 5.95 (0-87508-040-5) Chr Lit.

Destined for You. large type ed. Kay Winchester. 336p. 1987. 16.95 (0-7089-1675-9) Ulverscroft.

Destined to be Wives: The Sisters of Beatrice Webb. Barbara Caine. 280p. 1987. 35.00 (0-19-820054-4) OUP.

***Destined to Love.** Suzanne Elizabeth. 1994. pap. 4.99 (0-06-108225-2, Harp PBks) HarpC.

Destined to Mature. Gerald Derstine. 144p. (Orig.). 1984. pap. 2.99 (0-88368-147-1) Whitaker Hse.

Destined to Meet. Jessica Steele. 1993. pap. 2.89 (0-373-03256-0, 1-03256-4) Harlequin Bks.

Destined to Overcome. Paul E. Billheimer. LC 82-4537. 123p. 1982. pap. 6.99 (0-87123-287-1) Bethany Hse.

Destined to Overcome. Paul E. Billheimer. 123p. 1993. pap. 5.95 (0-87508-044-8) Chr Lit.

Destined to Share the Throne. Ruth Billman. 1990. pap. 4.50 (0-87508-032-4) Chr Lit.

Destined to Win. Nicky Cruz. LC 91-60373. 208p. (Orig.). 1991. pap. 8.95 (0-89221-195-4) New Leaf.

Destinee Arbitraire. Robert Desnos. Ed. by J. Dumas. (FRE.). 1975. pap. 11.95 (0-7859-2779-4) Fr & Eur.

Destinee Arbitraire. Robert Desnos & Marie-Claire Dumas. (Poesie Ser.). 88p. (FRE.). 1975. 13.95 (2-07-032154-1) Schoenhof.

Destinees. Alfred De Vigny. Ed. by Saulnier. (Textes Litteraires Francais Ser.). (FRE.). pap. 7.95 (0-8288-9667-4, F75890) Fr & Eur.

Destinies. Karen H. Bouldin. Ed. by James B. Van Treese. 380p. 1994. pap. 9.95 (1-56901-165-6) NW Pub.

***Destinies.** Al C. Ward. 390p. Date not set. pap. 9.95 (0-614-04905-9) NW Pub.

Destinies of Darcy Dancer, Gentleman. J. P. Donleavy. 1990. pap. 9.95 (0-87113-289-3) Grove-Atltic.

Destinies of Individuals & of Nations. Rudolf Steiner. 258p. 1990. 24.95 (0-88010-206-3, 1177); pap. 16.95 (0-88010-205-5, 1176) Anthroposophic.

Destino. Rocco V. Traficante. 1993. 18.95 (0-533-10626-5) Vantage.

Destino Mas Alla De la Muerte: A Destiny Beyond Death. Bill Drost. (SPA.). 4.95 (84-7645-272-1, 223362, Pub. by Edit Clie SP) TSELF.

Destinos: An Introduction to Spanish. Bill Vanpatten. 1991. text ed. write for info. (0-07-002069-8) McGraw.

Destinos: An Introduction to Spanish, Level 1. Bill Van Patten et al. 1991. Wkbk. - study guide. student ed, pap. text ed. write for info. (0-07-002072-8) McGraw.

Destinos: An Introduction to Spanish, Level 2. Bill Van Patten et al. 1992. Wkbk. - study guide. student ed, pap. text ed. write for info. (0-07-002073-6) McGraw.

Destinos Homeviewer's Guide & Audiocassettes: An Introduction to Spanish. Bill V. Patten et al. 1993. Incl. audiocassettes. audio, pap. text ed. write for info. (0-07-911479-2) McGraw.

Destins. Francois Mauriac. 126p. (FRE.). 1928. pap. 9.95 (0-7859-1453-6, 2246144817) Fr & Eur.

Destins. Francois Mauriac. (Coll. Diamant). 1965. 11.95 (0-685-11133-4) Fr & Eur.

Destiny. Sally Beauman. 1988. mass mkt. 6.50 (0-553-27018-4) Bantam.

Destiny. Barbara Benedict. 416p. 1994. mass mkt. 4.50 (0-8217-4756-8) Zebra.

Destiny. David Edgar. 96p. 1978. pap. 8.95 (0-413-41070-6, A0074, Pub. by Methuen UK) Heinemann.

Destiny. Irma Myers. 404p. (Orig.). 1993. pap. 16.95 (1-880365-29-4) Prof Pr NC.

Destiny. Rose Toren. LC 91-60449. 174p. 1991. 16.95 (0-88400-151-2) Shengold.

Destiny. large type unabridged ed. Anne Hampson. (Nightingale Ser.). 228p. 1989. pap. 13.95 (0-8161-4674-8) G K Hall.

Destiny: A Flying Tigers Rendezvous with Fate. Erik Shilling. 328p. Date not set. lib. bdg. write for info. (1-882463-02-1) Ben-Wal Print.

Destiny: A Southeast Asia Saga 1928-1953. Laurence C. Bergquist. (Illus.). 336p. 1994. 24.95 (0-935553-06-1) Pacifica Pr.

Destiny: An Uncommon Journey. David W. Krueger & Jane Newfield. LC 90-70570. 61p. 1990. 9.95 (1-55523-350-3) Winston-Derek.

***Destiny: Gaia Matrix Oracle Numerology.** Rowena P. Kryder. Ed. by Linda Web. (Illus.). 112p. (Orig.). 1995. pap. 10.95 (0-9624716-8-2) Golden Point Prod.

Destiny & Control in Human Systems: Studies in the Interactive Connectedness of Time (Chronotopology) Charles Muses. 1984. lib. bdg. 68.00 (0-89838-156-8) Kluwer Ac.

Destiny & Desire. Nadine Crenshaw. 448p. 1992. mass mkt. 4.99 (1-55817-666-7, Pinnacle NY) Windsor NY.

Destiny & Desire. Lorinda Hagen. 1979. pap. 1.95 (0-8439-0639-1) Dorchester Pub Co.

Destiny & Disease in Mental Disorders. C. M. Campbell. 1977. lib. bdg. 59.95 (0-8490-1710-6) Gordon Pr.

Destiny & One Hundred Two Other Real-Life Mysteries. Paul Aurandt. 256p. 1984. mass mkt. 4.99 (0-553-26014-6) Bantam.

Destiny & Race: Selected Writings, 1840-1898. Alexander Crummell. Ed. by Wilson J. Moses. LC 91-44849. 320p. (C). 1992. lib. bdg. 35.00 (0-87023-788-8); pap. text ed. 16.95x (0-87023-789-6) U of Mass Pr.

Destiny at Cracker Creek. Dorothy Lindsay & Steele Lindsay. LC 84-61590. 192p. 1984. pap. 8.50 (0-88100-047-7) Natl Writ Pr.

***Destiny Awaits.** Elizabeth. 1995. mass mkt. 4.99 (0-06-108342-9, Harp PBks) HarpC.

Destiny Betrayed: JFK, Cuba, & the Garrison Case. James DiEugenio. 436p. 1992. 19.95 (1-879823-00-4) Sheridan Sq Pr.

Destiny by Choice. Thom Lemmons. 192p. (Orig.). 1989. pap. 7.99 (0-945564-13-9, Multnomah Bks) Questar Pubs.

Destiny by Choice: The Inaugural Addresses of the Governors of Texas. Ed. by Marvin E. De Boer. LC 91-15794. (Illus.). 496p. 1992. 45.00 (1-55728-232-3) U of Ark Pr.

***Destiny Calls - Pocahontas.** (Picture Window Ser.). 30p. (J). 1995. 9.98 (1-57082-241-7) Mouse Works.

Destiny Can Wait: The Polish Air Force in World War II. M. Lisiewicz et al. (Aviation Ser.). (Illus.). 401p. 1988. reprint ed. 29.95 (0-89839-113-X) Battery Pr.

Destiny Denied. abr. ed. Kirsten Snyder. 700p. 1995. pap. 14.95 (1-56901-500-7) NW Pub.

Destiny Forever. T. Curtis Watson. 1994. 15.95 (0-533-10964-7) Vantage.

***Destiny Going Sour.** Steven Levi. 1991. 5.00 (0-932593-19-4) Black Bear.

Destiny in Doubt. Barbara Rae. 1994. pap. 7.95 (1-56901-143-5) NW Pub.

Destiny Is Not a Matter of Chance: Essays in Reflection & Contemplation on the Destiny of Blacks. Emma S. Etuk. (American University Studies: History: Ser. IX, Vol. 52). 245p. (C). 1989. text ed. 28.50 (0-8204-1002-0) P Lang Pubs.

Destiny Makers. George Turner. 336p. 1993. mass mkt. 4.99 (0-380-71887-1, AvoNova) Avon.

Destiny Makers. George Turner. LC 92-2414. 1993. 20.00 (0-688-12187-X) Morrow.

Destiny Makers of Indian Industry: A Study of Scientists & Engineers. Vidula Jakatdar. 1990. 16.50 (0-86132-227-4, Pub. by Popular Prakashan II) S Asia.

Destiny Map, Pt. 1: The Relics of Power Trilogy. 64p. 12.00 (0-87431-309-0, 20551) West End Games.

***Destiny Mine.** Janelle Taylor. 352p. 1995. 18.95 (0-8217-4824-6) Zebra.

***Destiny Mine.** large type ed. Janelle Taylor. LC 95-6687. 448p. 1995. 23.95 (0-7838-1208-6, Large Print Bks) Hall.

Destiny Obscure: Autobiographies of Childhood, Education, & Family from the 1820s to the 1920s. John Burnett. LC 93-39254. (Modern British History Ser.). 388p. 1994. 79.95x (0-415-10400-9, B4094); pap. 22.95 (0-415-10401-7, B4098) Routledge.

Destiny of a Continent. Manuel Ugarte. Ed. by J. Fred Rippey. Tr. by Catherine A. Philips. LC 71-111476. reprint ed. 47.50 (0-404-06700-X) AMS Pr.

Destiny of a King. Georges Dumezil. Tr. by Alf Hiltebeitel. (Midway Reprint Ser.). 1973. lib. bdg. 15.00 (0-226-16975-8) U Ch Pr.

Destiny of a King. Georges Dumezil. Tr. by Alf Hiltebeitel. (Midway Reprint Ser.). 1988. pap. text ed. 11.95 (0-226-16976-6) U Ch Pr.

Destiny of America. Robert R. Leichtman & Carl Japikse. LC 83-70303. (From Heaven to Earth Ser.). 128p. 1984. 7.95 (0-89804-075-2); pap. 3.50 (0-89804-074-4) Ariel GA.

Destiny of America. Robert R. Leichtman. (From Heaven to Earth Ser.). 1996. pap. 11.95 (0-89804-086-8) Ariel GA.

Destiny of Angels. Richard McCulloch. (Illus.). 314p. 1986. 20.00 (0-9608928-1-8) Towncourt Ent.

Destiny of Capitalism in the Orient. N. Simoniya. 252p. (C). 1985. 50.00 (0-685-31542-8, Pub. by Collets UK) Pro-Am Music.

Destiny of Dreams. Michael Bowler. 200p. (Orig.). 1990. pap. 14.95 (1-85371-065-2, Pub. by Poolbeg Pr IE) Dufour.

Destiny of Isabelle Eberhardt. Cecily Mackworth. 228p. 1986. reprint ed. pap. 9.50 (0-88001-118-1) Ecco Pr.

Destiny of Man. Nikolai Berdiaev. Tr. by Natalie Duddington. LC 78-14100. 1993. reprint ed. 32.00 (0-88355-775-4) Hyperion Conn.

Destiny of Man Viewed in the Light of His Origin. John Fiske. (Notable American Authors Ser.). 1992. reprint ed. lib. bdg. 75.00 (0-7812-2845-X) Rprt Serv.

Destiny of Me. Larry Kramer. 160p. (Orig.). 1993. pap. 9.95 (0-452-27016-2, Plume) NAL-Dutton.

Destiny of Russian America, Seventeen Forty-One to Eighteen Sixty-Seven. Aleksandr I. Alekseev. Ed. by Richard A. Pierce. Tr. by Marina Ramsay. (Alaska History Ser.: No. 34). (Illus.). 1990. 35.00 (0-919642-13-6) Limestone Pr.

Destiny of the Mother Church. Bliss Knapp. (Twentieth-Century Biographers Ser.). (Illus.). 336p. 1992. 14.95 (0-87510-231-X) Christian Sci.

Destiny of the Nations. Alice A. Bailey. LC 89-195778. 1949. 16.00 (0-85330-002-X) Lucis.

***Destiny of the Nations.** Alice A. Bailey. LC 89-195778. 1971. pap. 8.00 (0-85330-102-6) Lucis.

Destiny of the Soul. rev. ed. Helen Roberts. Ed. by Franklin Loehr. LC 83-82485. Orig. Title: The Soul That Sinneth--It Shall Die. 1987. pap. 10.50 (0-915151-13-8) Religious Res Pr.

D

An Asterisk (*) at the beginning of an entry indicates that the title is appearing in BIP for the first time.

1899

Destiny of the Soul: Critical History of the Doctrine of a Future Life, 2 vols., Set. 10th ed. William R. Alger. LC 68-19263. 1968. reprint ed. text ed. 85.00 (0-8371-0003-8, ALDS) Greenwood.

Destiny of the Soul: Critical History of the Doctrine of a Future Life, 2 vols., Vol. 1. 10th ed. William R. Alger. LC 68-19263. 1968. reprint ed. text ed. 55.00 (0-313-21609-6, ALDA) Greenwood.

Destiny of the Soul: Critical History of the Doctrine of a Future Life, 2 vols., Vol. 2. 10th ed. William R. Alger. LC 68-19263. 1968. reprint ed. text ed. 55.00 (0-313-21610-X, ALDB) Greenwood.

Destiny of the Sword. David Duncan. (Seventh Sword Ser.: Bk. 3). 1988. mass mkt. 4.95 (0-345-35293-9, Del Rey) Ballantine.

Destiny of the World Between Socialism & Free Enterprise: The Worlds New Order. George Cattou. 135p. (Orig.). Date not set. pap. text ed. 7.00 (0-9637473-0-4) Euros Amer.

Destiny Our Choice. large type ed. John Attenborough. 496p. 1988. 23.95 (0-7089-8450-9, Trail West Pubs) Ulverscroft.

Destiny, the Web of... 7th ed. Max Heindel. Ed. by Rosicrucian Fellowship Staff. 1989. reprint ed. pap. text ed. 9.95 (0-911274-17-0) Rosicrucian.

Destiny to Mould: Selected Speeches by the Prime Minister of Guyana. Forbes Burnham. Ed. by C. A. Nascimento & R. Burrowes. LC 70-114298. 275p. 1970. 32.50 (0-8419-0042-6, Africana) Holmes & Meier.

Destiny's Bride: Brides of Montclair, No. 8. Jane Peart. 224p. 1991. pap. 8.99 (0-310-67021-7) Zondervan.

Destiny's Calendar. rev. ed. Gary Metras. 75p. 1988. reprint ed. pap. 7.00 (0-938566-39-3) Adastra Pr.

***Destiny's Child.** Bretton. 1995. mass mkt. 4.99 (1-55166-090-3, Mira Bks) Harlequin Bks.

***Destiny's Child.** Ann Major. (Western Lovers Ser.). 1995. mass mkt. 3.99 (0-373-88548-2, 1-88548-2) Harlequin Bks.

Destiny's Daughter. large type ed. Mary Williams. (Romance Ser.). 384p. 1992. 21.95 (0-7089-2635-5) Ulverscroft.

Destiny's Dawn. F. Rosanne Bittner. 384p. (Orig.). 1987. mass mkt. 3.95 (0-445-20468-0) Warner Bks.

Destiny's Desire. Victoria London. 464p. 1987. pap. 3.95 (0-8217-2089-9) Zebra.

Destiny's Downfall: A History of the Island of Guam. Robert F. Rogers. LC 94-25845. (Illus.). 416p. (C). 1995. text ed. 45.00x (0-8248-1616-1); pap. text ed. 24.95 (0-8248-1678-1) UH Pr.

Destiny's Dream. Joanna Jordan. 384p. (Orig.). 1990. pap. 3.95 (0-380-75790-7) Avon.

Destiny's Dream. Joan Smith. 368p. (Orig.). 1988. pap. 3.95 (0-8439-2628-7) Dorchester Pub Co.

Destiny's End. Timothy R. Sullivan. 320p. (Orig.). 1988. pap. 2.95 (0-380-75352-9) Avon.

Destiny's Journey. Doblin. 1994. pap. 24.95 (1-56924-990-3) Marlowe & Co.

Destiny's Lovers. Flora Speer. 1990. pap. 3.95 (0-8439-2985-5) Dorchester Pub Co.

***Destiny's Price: A Sourcebook of the Streets.** Contrib by Phil Brucato. (Black Dog Ser.). 1995. per., pap. 15.00 (1-56504-450-9, 4040) White Wolf.

Destiny's Promise. Laurel Pace. (Historical Ser.). 1993. mass mkt. 3.99 (0-373-28772-0, 1-28772-1) Harlequin Bks.

Destiny's Splendor. Kathleen Drymon. 1988. pap. 3.95 (0-8217-2527-0) Zebra.

Destiny's Temptress. Janelle Taylor. 544p. 1993. mass mkt. 4.99 (0-8217-3823-2) Zebra.

Destitutes & Development: A Study of the Bauri Community in Bokaro Region. Nirmal Sengupta. 1979. 11.00 (0-8364-0351-7) S Asia.

***Destroy All Monsters, 1975-1979: Geisha This Niagara.** 100p. Date not set. pap. 20.00 (1-881616-48-7) Dist Art Pubs.

Destroy Not the Dream. Sheila Lewis. (Rainbow Romances Ser.). 160p. 1993. 14.95 (0-7090-4914-5, Hale-Parkwest) Parkwest Pubns.

Destroy Not the Dream. large type ed. Sheila Lewis. (Romance Ser.). 288p. 1994. pap. 14.95 (0-7089-7544-5, Trailtree Bookshop) Ulverscroft.

Destroy, She Said. Marguerite Duras. Tr. by Barbara Bray. 144p. pap. 7.95 (0-8021-5154-X) Grove-Atltic.

Destroy the Kentucky. Bart Davis. Ed. by Paul McCarthy. 416p. (Orig.). 1992. mass mkt. 5.50 (0-671-69664-5) PB.

Destroyed Boston Buildings. (Picture Books Ser.). 32p. 1965. pap. 4.00 (0-934909-03-2) Mass Hist Soc.

Destroyer. Roy W. West. 288p. (Orig.). 1985. pap. 3.25 (0-8439-2218-4) Dorchester Pub Co.

Destroyer: Kill or Cure, No. 11. Warren Murphy & Richard Sapir. 1988. pap. 3.50 (1-55817-148-7, Pinnacle NY) Windsor NY.

Destroyer: Murder's Shield, No. 9. Warren Murphy & Richard Sapir. 1988. pap. 3.50 (1-55817-146-0, Pinnacle NY) Windsor NY.

Destroyer: Slave Safari, No. 12. Warren Murphy & Richard Sapir. 1988. pap. 3.50 (1-55817-149-5, Pinnacle NY) Windsor NY.

Destroyer: Summit Chase, No. 8. Warren Murphy & Richard Sapir. 1988. pap. 3.50 (1-55817-145-2, Pinnacle NY) Windsor NY.

Destroyer: Terror Squad, No. 10. Warren Murphy & Richard Sapir. 1988. pap. 3.50 (1-55817-147-9, Pinnacle NY) Windsor NY.

Destroyer: Union Bust, No. 7. Warren Murphy & Richard Sapir. pap. 3.50 (1-55817-144-4, Pinnacle NY) Windsor NY.

Destroyer & Preserver: Shelley's Poetic Skepticism. Lloyd R. Abbey. LC 79-9166. 183p. reprint ed. pap. 52.20 (0-7837-1815-2, 2042015) Bks Demand.

Destroyer Campbeltown. Al Ross. LC 90-60099. (Anatomy of the Ship Ser.). (Illus.). 128p. 1990. 36.95 (1-55750-725-2) Naval Inst Pr.

Destroyer Escort England. Al Ross. (Anatomy of the Ship Ser.). (Illus.). 96p. 1985. 36.95 (0-87021-140-4) Naval Inst Pr.

Destroyer Escort Sailor Association History Book. Destroyer Escort Sailors Association. LC 86-51635. 264p. 1987. 48.00 (0-938021-10-9) Turner Pub KY.

Destroyer Escort Sailors Association, Vol. II. 2nd ed. Turner Publishing Co., Staff. LC 86-51635. 551p. 1989. 48.00 (0-938021-49-4) Turner Pub KY.

Destroyer Escort Sailors Association--Trim but Deadly, Vol. III. Turner Publishing Co. Staff. LC 86-51635. (Illus.). 160p. 1992. 48.00 (1-56311-052-0) Turner Pub KY.

Destroyer Man. large type ed. John Alliston. 1991. 21.95 (0-7089-2421-2) Ulverscroft.

Destroyer, No. 29: The Final Death. Warren Murphy. 1990. pap. 3.50 (1-55817-319-6, Pinnacle NY) Windsor NY.

Destroyer, No. 32: Killer Chromosomes. Warren Murphy. 1990. pap. 3.50 (1-55817-355-2, Pinnacle NY) Windsor NY.

Destroyer, No. 33: Voodoo Die. Warren Murphy. 1990. pap. 3.50 (1-55817-370-6, Pinnacle NY) Windsor NY.

Destroyer No. 34: Chained Reaction. Warren Murphy. 1990. pap. 3.50 (1-55817-383-8, Pinnacle NY) Windsor NY.

Destroyer, No. 35: Last Call. Warren Murphy. 1990. pap. 3.50 (1-55817-395-1, Pinnacle NY) Windsor NY.

Destroyer, No. 36: Power Play. Warren Murphy. 1990. pap. 3.50 (1-55817-406-0, Pinnacle NY) Windsor NY.

Destroyer of the Iron Horse: General Joseph E. Johnston & Confederate Rail Transport, 1861-1865. Jeffrey N. Lash. LC 90-5372. (Illus.). 240p. 1991. 28.50x (0-87338-423-7) Kent St U Pr.

Destroyer, the Sullivans: Anatomy of the Ship. Al Ross. LC 87-63031. (Anatomy of the Ship Ser.). (Illus.). 120p. 1988. 36.95 (0-87021-617-1) Naval Inst Pr.

Destroyers. A. W. Miller. (Orig.). 1980. pap. 1.75 (0-8439-0738-X) Dorchester Pub Co.

Destroyers. Antony Preston. LC 77-82132. (Illus.). 1977. 14.95 (0-685-03827-0) P-H.

Destroyers. M. Walmer. (Sea Power Library). (Illus.). 48p. (J). (gr. 3-8). 1989. lib. bdg. 18.60 (0-86625-081-6) Rourke Corp.

Destroyers: The Underside of Human Nature. James K. Feibleman. (American University Studies Anthropology & Sociology: Ser. XI, Vol. 17). 187p. 1987. 26.00 (0-8204-0609-0) P Lang Pubs.

Destroyers & Frigates. Christopher Chant. (Illus.). 410p. 1994. text ed. 125.00 (0-08-040714-5, Pub. by Brasseys UK) Brasseys Inc.

Destroyers Escorts of the World War Two: Warship's Data Special. Thomas F. Walkowiak. LC 87-61286. 48p. (Orig.). 1987. pap. 7.95 (0-933126-88-3) Pictorial Hist.

Destroyers for Great Britain. Arnold Hague. LC 89-63588. (Illus.). 92p. 1990. 24.95 (0-87021-782-8) Naval Inst Pr.

Destroying Angel. Nancy Eimers. LC 90-50909. (Wesleyan New Poets Ser.). 64p. 1991. 22.50 (0-8195-2194-9, Wesleyan Univ Pr); pap. 10.95 (0-8195-1196-X, Wesleyan Univ Pr) U Pr of New Eng.

Destroying Angel. Richard Russo. 240p. 1992. pap. 4.50 (0-441-14273-7) Ace Bks.

Destroying Angel: Sex, Fitness, & Food in the Legacy of Degeneracy Theory, Graham Crackers, Kellogg's Corn Flakes, & American Health History. John Money. LC 84-43104. 213p. 1985. 27.95 (0-87975-277-7) Prometheus Bks.

Destroying Democracy: How Government Funds Partisan Politics. James T. Bennett & Thomas J. DiLorenzo. 561p. 1985. 7.00 (0-932790-53-4); pap. 3.00 (0-932790-54-2) Cato Inst.

Destroying Ethnic Identity: The Gypsies of Bulgaria. Helsinki Watch Staff. Ed. by Areyeh Neier. LC 91-73013. 60p. (Orig.). 1991. pap. 7.00 (1-56432-032-4) Hum Rts Watch.

***Destroying of Harry Blyne.** Peter M. Fotheringham. 1995. 18.95 (0-312-11775-2, Pub. by Thomas Dunne Bks) St Martin.

Destroying the Works of the Enemy. Phillip G. Goudeaux. 116p. 1992. text ed. 11.95 (1-56550-006-7); pap. text ed. 9.95 (1-56550-000-8) Vis Bks Intl.

***Destroying the Works of Witchcraft Through Prayer & Fasting.** Ruth Brown. 57p. 1994. pap. 4.95 (0-89228-110-3) Impact Christian.

Destruction. Harold L. McConnen. 128p. 1988. pap. write for info. (0-318-64421-5) Talking Leaf Pubs.

***Destruction & Reconstruction: Personal Experiences of the Civil War.** Richard Taylor. 288p. 1995. reprint ed. pap. 14.95 (0-306-80624-X) Da Capo.

Destruction & Reconstruction: Personal Experiences of the Late War. Richard Taylor. (Southern Classics Ser.). 274p. 1995. pap. 11.95 (1-879941-21-X) J S Sanders.

Destruction & Reconstruction: Personal Experiences of the Late War. Richard Taylor. LC 72-11349. (American South Ser.). 1973. reprint ed. 35.95 (0-405-05065-8) Ayer.

Destruction & Resistance. Chaim Lazar. LC 84-52354. (Illus.). 240p. 1985. pap. 15.95 (0-88400-113-X) Shengold.

Destruction at Noonday. Bill Robinson. 224p. 1992. 22.95 (0-924486-21-X) Sheridan.

Destruction by Demolition-Incendiaries & Sabotage. 1987. lib. bdg. 75.00 (0-8490-3951-7) Gordon Pr.

***Destruction Committee.** William J. Coughlin. 1994. lib. bdg. 24.95x (1-56849-408-4) Buccaneer Bks.

Destruction-Decouverte: Le Fonctionnement de la Rhetorique dans les Essais de Montaigne. Lawrence D. Kritzman. LC 80-66329. (French Forum Monographs: No. 21). 185p. (Orig.). 1980. pap. 12.95 (0-917058-20-8) French Forum.

Destruction in the English Civil Wars. Stephen Porter. 192p. 1994. 40.00 (0-7509-0516-6) A Sutton Pub.

Destruction of a Planet: Zionism Is Racism. Gyeorgos C. Hatonn & Anton. Tr. by Dharma. 221p. (Orig.). (C). 1991. pap. 10.00 (0-922356-60-2) Amer West Pubs.

Destruction of American Indian Families. Ed. by Steven Unger. LC 76-24533. 1977. pap. 4.25 (0-686-24119-3) Assn Am Indian.

Destruction of Ancient Rome. Rodolfo Lanciani. LC 67-23855. (Illus.). 1972. reprint ed. 20.95 (0-405-08726-8, Pub. by Blom Pubns UK) Ayer.

Destruction of Atlantis. Frank Joseph. (Illus.). 1987. 11.00 (0-318-22610-3) Atlantis Research.

Destruction of Atlantis: Ragnarok the Age of the Fire & Gravel. Ignatius Donnelly. LC 75-175055. (Illus.). 472p. 1989. reprint ed. pap. 16.50 (0-89345-220-3, Steinerbks) Garber Comm.

Destruction of Black Civilization. rev. ed. Chancellor Williams. 1987. 29.95 (0-88378-042-9); pap. 16.95 (0-88378-030-5) Third World.

Destruction of Brazilian Slavery, 1850-1888. 2nd ed. Robert E. Conrad. LC 92-11285. 254p. (C). 1993. pap. 19.50 (0-89464-750-4) Krieger.

Destruction of Convoy PQ-17. David Irving. 1989. mass mkt. 4.95 (0-312-91152-1) St Martin.

Destruction of Evidence. Jamie S. Gorelick et al. (Trial Practice Library). 516p. 1989. text ed. 135.00 (0-471-61138-7) Wiley.

Destruction of Evidence: 1992 Cumulative Supplement. Stephen Marzen et al. 280p. 1992. pap. 65.00 (0-471-57677-8) Wiley.

Destruction of Hazardous Chemicals in the Laboratory. George Lunn & Erci B. Sansone. 1990. text ed. 89.95 (0-471-51063-7) Wiley.

Destruction of Hazardous Chemicals in the Laboratory. 2nd ed. George Lunn & Eric B. Sansone. LC 93-35634. 1994. text ed. 79.95 (0-471-57399-X) Wiley.

Destruction of Nikolaevsk-on-Amur: An Episode in the Russian Civil War in the Far East, 1920. A. Ya. Gutman. Ed. by Richard A. Pierce. Tr. by Ella L. Wiswell. (Russia & Asia Ser.: No. 2). (Illus.). 395p. 1993. 28.00 (0-919642-35-7) Limestone Pr.

Destruction of Organic Matter. T. Gorsuch & R. Belcher. LC 71-109583. (International Series of Monographs on Analytical Chemistry: Vol. 39). 1970. 66.00 (0-08-015575-8, Pub. by Pergamon Repr UK) Franklin.

***Destruction of Our Children: Why Our Children Must Become Warriors.** Fay E. Butler. 130p. (Orig.). 1994. pap. 7.00 (1-883483-05-0) Ellis-Butler Minist.

Destruction of Pendleton: The West Virginia Flood of 1985. Rick Gillespie. (Illus.). 72p. (Orig.). 1986. pap. 9.95 (0-9616609-0-2) Pendleton Pubns.

Destruction of Pompeii & Other Stories. Vassily Aksyonov. (Contemporary Russian Prose Ser.). 183p. 1991. pap. 9.95 (0-679-73441-4, Vin) Random.

***Destruction of Reason.** Georg Lukacs. (C). 1952. text ed. 49.95 (0-85036-247-4, Pub. by Merlin Pr UK) Humanities.

Destruction of Slonim Jewry: The Story of the Jews During the Holocaust. Nachum Albert. Ed. & Tr. by Max Rosenfeld. LC 90-81303. (Illus.). 400p. 1990. pap. 13.95 (0-89604-137-9) Holocaust Pubns.

Destruction of Slonim Jewry: The Story of the Jews During the Holocaust. Nachum Alpert. Ed. & Tr. by Max Rosenfeld. LC 90-81303. (Illus.). 400p. 1990. 23.95 (0-89604-136-0) Holocaust Pubns.

***Destruction of Sodom, Gomorrah, & Jericho: Geological, Climatological, & Archaeological Background.** K. O. Emery & David Neev. (Illus.). 192p. 1995. text ed. 35.00 (0-19-509094-2) OUP.

Destruction of Success. Sam Lupi, II. 320p. 1994. 20.95 (0-8059-3551-7) Dorrance.

Destruction of the California Indians. Ed. by Robert F. Heizer. LC 92-37603. xxii, 321p. 1993. reprint ed. pap. 14.00 (0-8032-7262-6, Bison Books) U of Nebr Pr.

Destruction of the Christian Tradition. Rama P. Coomaraswamy. 287p. (Orig.). 1981. pap. 17.95 (0-900588-20-9) S Perennis.

***Destruction of the Environment: Racism & the Profit System.** David Perez. 26p. 1993. pap. 2.50 (0-614-02749-7) World View Forum.

Destruction of the European Jews, 3 vols. abr. rev. ed. Raul Hilberg. LC 84-18369. 1312p. 1985. pap. 16.95 (0-8419-0910-5) Holmes & Meier.

Destruction of the European Jews, 3 vols., Set. rev. ed. Raul Hilberg. LC 84-18369. 1312p. 1985. boxed 99.50 (0-8419-0832-X) Holmes & Meier.

Destruction of the Greek Empire & the Story of the Capture of Constantinople by the Turks. E. Pears. LC 68-25259. (World History Ser.: No. 48). (Illus.). 1969. reprint ed. lib. bdg. 75.00 (0-8383-0227-0) M S G Haskell Hse.

Destruction of the Jaguar: Poems from the Books of Chilam Balam. Tr. by Christopher Sawyer-Laucanno. (Orig.). 1987. pap. 5.95 (0-87286-210-0) City Lights.

***Destruction of the Natural Vegetation of North-Central Chile.** Conrad J. Bahre. LC 78-50836. (University of California Publications in Geography: No. 23). 138p. 1979. pap. 39.40 (0-7837-7470-2, 2049192) Bks Demand.

Destruction of Tilted Arc Documents. Ed. by Clara Weyergraf-Serra & Martha Buskirk. (Illus.). 406p. 1990. 37.50x (0-262-23155-7); pap. 17.95 (0-262-73089-8) MIT Pr.

Destruction of Yugoslavia. Branca Magas. LC 92-30825. 384p. 1993. 64.95 (0-86091-376-7, A3750, Pub. by Verso UK); pap. 19.95 (0-86091-593-X, A3754, Pub. by Verso UK) Routledge Chapman & Hall.

Destructiones Modorum Significandi. Ed. by Ludger Kaczmarek. LC 94-1372. (Bochumer Studien zur Philosophie Ser.: No. 9). xlix, 138p. (GER & LAT.). 1994. lib. bdg. 60.00 (90-6032-283-5) Benjamins North Am.

Destructive Achievers: Power & Ethics in the American Corporation. Charles M. Kelly. 1988. 19.95 (0-201-09039-2) Addison-Wesley.

Destructive & Useful Insects: Their Habits & Control. 5th ed. Robert L. Metcalf. LC 92-18374. 1992. text ed. 79.95 (0-07-041692-3) McGraw.

Destructive Behaviour in Developmental Disabilities: Diagnosis & Treatment. Ed. by Travis Thompson & David B. Gray. (Focus Editions Ser.: Vol. 170). 320p. (C). 1994. text ed. 49.95 (0-8039-5582-0); pap. text ed. 24.95 (0-8039-5583-9) Sage.

Destructive Element. Stephen Spender. 1970. 12.50 (0-87556-325-2) Saifer.

Destructive Impact of Karate Punches vs 9mm Ammunition Through Body Armor. Bernd W. Weiss et al. (KSI Report Ser.: No. 303). (Illus.). 10p. (Orig.). 1994. text ed. 2.00 (0-931373-03-4) Hiles & Hardin Pubs.

***Destructive Impulses: An Examination of an American Secret in Race Relations: White Violence.** A. J. Williams - Myers. 144p. (Orig.). (C). 1994. pap. text ed. 28.00 (0-8191-9663-0) U Pr of Amer.

***Destructive Impulses: An Examination of an American Secret in Race Relations: White Violence.** A. J. Williams-Myers. 144p. (Orig.). (C). 1994. lib. bdg. 46.50 (0-8191-9662-2) U Pr of Amer.

Destructive War: William Tecumseh Sherman, Stonewall Jackson, & the Americans. Charles Royster. LC 92-56370. 1992. pap. 15.00 (0-679-73878-9, Vin) Random.

Destructors. Graham Greene. (Creative Short Stories Ser.). (YA). (gr. 4-9). 1989. 13.95 (0-88682-348-X, 97213-098) Creative Ed.

Destry Rides Again. Max Brand. 208p. 1991. pap. 2.95 (0-671-73543-8) PB.

Destry Rides Again. Max Brand. 1990. reprint ed. lib. bdg. 19.95 (0-89968-485-8) Buccaneer Bks.

Desulfurization of Heavy Oils & Residua. Speight. (Chemical Industries Ser.: Vol. 4). 224p. 1981. 135.00 (0-8247-1506-3) Dekker.

Desulfurization of Iron & Steel & Sulfide Shape Control. William G. Wilson & Alex Mclean. LC 80-69613. 167p. reprint ed. pap. 47.60 (0-685-15244-8, 2027148) Bks Demand.

Desulphurisation: Technologies & Strategies for Reducing Sulphur Emissions. Ed. by W. S. Kyte. (Institution of Chemical Engineers Symposium Ser.: No. 123). 300p. 1991. 89.00 (1-56032-232-2) Hemisp Pub.

Desulphurization in Coal Combustion Systems. Ed. by W. S. Kyte et al. (European Federation of Chemical Engineering Ser.). 275p. 1989. 99.50 (0-89116-969-5) Hemisp Pub.

***Detached Retina: Aspects of SF & Fantasy.** Brian W. Aldiss. LC 95-133. 280p. 1995. 39.95 (0-8156-2681-9); pap. 16.95 (0-8156-0370-3) Syracuse U Pr.

Detaching with Love. Carolyn W. 19p. (Orig.). 1984. pap. 1.55 (0-89486-232-4, 1253B) Hazelden.

Detachment. Michel Serres. Tr. by James Genevieve & Raymond Federman. LC 89-35167. 115p. 1989. lib. bdg. 23.00 (0-8214-0935-2) Ohio U Pr.

Detachment: Seven Simple Steps. Judith M. Knowlton & Rebecca D. Chaitin. (Gifts of Growth Ser.). 56p. (Orig.). 1985. pap. 2.50 (0-934391-00-9) Quotidian.

Detachment & Concern: Essays in the Philosophy of Teaching & Teacher Education. Margret Buchmann et al. LC 93-1171. (Advances in Contemporary Educational Thought Ser.: No. 11). 312p. 1993. text ed. 42.00 (0-8077-3274-5); pap. 19.95 (0-8077-3273-7) Tchrs Coll.

Detachment & the Writing of History: Essays & Letters of Carl L. Becker. Carl L. Becker. Ed. by Phil L. Snyder. LC 70-152590. 240p. 1972. reprint ed. text ed. 55.00 (0-8371-6023-5, BEWH, Greenwood Pr) Greenwood.

Detail & Scale: A-7 Corsair II, Vol. 22. Bert Kinzey. (Illus.). 64p. 1986. pap. 10.95 (0-8306-8532-4, NO. 25032, TAB-Aero) TAB Bks.

Detail & Scale: Boeing 707 & AWACS, Vol. 23. Alwyn T. Lloyd. (Illus.). 64p. 1987. pap. 10.95 (0-8306-8533-2, NO. 25033, TAB-Aero) TAB Bks.

Detail & Scale: F4F Wildcat, Vol. 30. Bert Kinzey. (Illus.). 64p. 1988. pap. 10.95 (0-8306-8040-3, 25040P) TAB Bks.

Detail & Scale: USS Lexington, Vol. 29. Bert Kinzey. (Illus.). 64p. 1988. pap. 10.95 (0-8306-8039-X, 25039P) TAB Bks.

Detail & Scale, F-102 Delta Dagger, Vol. 35. Bert Kinzey. (Illus.). 72p. 1989. pap. 10.95 (0-8306-3046-5) TAB Bks.

Detail & Scale of the F-4C, F-4D, RF-4C. Bert Kinzey. (Detail & Scale Ser.: Vol. 42). 64p. 1992. pap. 10.95 (0-8306-3949-7, 25057) TAB Bks.

Detail & Scale, USS America, CVA-66, CV-66, Vol. 34. Bert Kinzey. (Illus.). 72p. 1989. pap. 10.95 (0-8306-0203-8) TAB Bks.

Detail & Scale, Vol. 26, F6F Hellcat. Bert Kinzey. (Illus.). 72p. 1988. pap. 8.95 (0-317-61094-5, 25036) TAB Bks.

Detail & Scale, Vol. 27: B-52 Stratofortress. Alwyn T. Lloyd. (Illus.). 72p. 1988. pap. 10.95 (0-8306-8037-3, 25037) TAB Bks.

Detail & Scale, Vol. 28, Av-8 Harrier, Part 1. Don Linn. (Illus.). 72p. 1987. pap. 10.95 (0-8306-8038-1, 25038) TAB Bks.

Detail & Scale, Vol. 31: F-8 Crusader. Bert Kinzey. (Illus.). 72p. 1988. pap. 10.95 (0-8306-8541-3, 25041) TAB Bks.

D

An Asterisk (*) at the beginning of an entry indicates that the title is appearing in BIP for the first time.

D

An Asterisk (*) at the beginning of an entry indicates that the title is appearing in BIP for the first time.

1901

Detectionary. Mill Roseman. Ed. by Otto Fenzler et al. LC 75-27326. (Illus.). 320p. 1977. pap. 12.95 (*0-87951-114-1*) Overlook Pr.

Detectionary. Mill Roseman. Ed. by Otto Fenzler et al. LC 75-27326. (Illus.). 320p. 1980. 22.95 (*0-87951-041-2*) Overlook Pr.

Detections of Dr. Sam: Johnson. Lillian De La Torre. LC 84-80238. (Johnson, Detector Ser.). 190p. 1984. reprint ed. pap. 4.95 (*0-930330-09-9*) Intl Polygonics.

Detective. 1985. 39.00 (*0-317-39064-3*, Pub. by P Norbury Pubns Ltd UK) St Mut.

Detective. Parnell Hall. LC 86-46386. 300p. 1987. 17.95 (*1-55611-026-X*) D I Fine.

Detective. Roderick Thorp. 29.95 (*0-8488-0375-2*) Amereon Ltd.

Detective & Mr. Dickens. William J. Palmer. 1992. reprint ed. mass mkt. 3.99 (*0-345-37471-1*) Ballantine.

Detective & Mystery Fiction: An International Bibliography of Secondary Sources. Ed. by Walter Albert. LC 89-140438. xii, 781p. 1984. 61.00x (*0-941028-02-X*, Brownstone Bks) Borgo Pr.

Detective & Mystery Fiction: International Bibliography of Secondary Sources. 2nd rev. ed. Walter Albert. (Brownstone Mystery Guides Ser.: No. 10). (Illus.). 1500p. Date not set. lib. bdg. write for info. (*0-941028-15-1*, Brownstone Bks) Borgo Pr.

Detective Dan & the Flying Frog Mystery. Timothy Roland. (Detective Dan Ser.). 48p. (J). (gr. 2-5). 1993. pap. 4.99 (*0-310-38121-5*) Zondervan.

Detective Dan & the Gooey Gumdrop Mystery. Timothy Roland. (Detective Dan Ser.). 48p. (J). (gr. 2-5). 1993. pap. 4.99 (*0-310-38111-8*) Zondervan.

Detective Dan & the Missing Marble Mystery. 2nd abr. rev. ed. Timothy Roland. (Detective Dan Ser.). 48p. (J). (gr. 2-5). 1993. pap. 4.99 (*0-310-38091-X*) Zondervan.

Detective Dan & the Puzzling Pizza Mystery. Timothy Roland. (Detective Dan Ser.). 48p. (J). (gr. 2-5). 1993. pap. 4.99 (*0-310-38101-0*) Zondervan.

Detective Dictionary: A Handbook for Aspiring Sleuths. Erich Ballinger. LC 93-11882. (Late-Night Library Ser.). (Illus.). 144p. (YA). (gr. 5 up). 1994. lib. bdg. 18.95 (*0-8225-0721-8*, Lerner Publctns) Lerner Group.

***Detective Dinosaur.** James Skofield. LC 94-42296. (I Can Read Bks.). (Illus.). (J). 1996. 14.00 (*0-06-024907-2*); lib. bdg. 13.89 (*0-06-024908-0*) HarpC.

Detective Duckworth to the Rescue. Annie Cobb. (Going Places Ser.). (Illus.). 32p. (J). (gr. k-3). 1991. 4.95 (*0-671-70398-6*); lib. bdg. 6.95 (*0-671-70394-3*) Silver Pr.

Detective Fiction: Crime & Compromise. Ed. by Dick Allen & David Chacko. 481p. (Orig.). (C). 1974. pap. text ed. 17.50 (*0-15-517408-8*) HB Coll Pubs.

Detective Fiction: The Collector's Guide. 2nd ed. John Cooper & Barry A. Pike. (Illus.). 230p. 1994. 59.95 (*0-85967-991-8*, Pub. by Scolar Pr UK) Ashgate Pub Co.

Detective Fiction from Latin America. Amelia S. Simpson. LC 88-46188. (Illus.). 224p. 1990. 35.00 (*0-8386-3377-3*) Fairleigh Dickinson.

Detective First Grade. Dan Mahoney. 384p. 1993. 21.95 (*0-312-09288-1*) St Martin.

***Detective First Grade Vol. 1: A Novel.** Dan Mahoney. 1994. pap. 5.99 (*0-312-95313-5*) St Martin.

Detective in Distress: Philip Marlowe's Domestic Dream. Gay Brewer. LC 90-35522. (Brownstone Mystery Guides Ser.: Vol. 5). 68p. (C). 1989. reprint ed. lib. bdg. 20.00x (*0-8095-6404-1*, Brownstone Bks); reprint ed. pap. 10.00x (*0-941028-08-9*, Brownstone Bks) Borgo Pr.

Detective in Film. William K. Everson. (Illus.). 256p. 1972. 9.95 (*0-8065-0298-3*, Citadel Pr); pap. 7.95 (*0-8065-0448-X*, Citadel Pr) Carol Pub Group.

Detective Investigator. Jack Rudman. (Career Examination Ser.: C-1247). 1994. pap. 34.95 (*0-8373-1247-7*) Nat Learn.

Detective Jardine: Crimes in Honolulu. John Jardine & Edward Rohrbough. Ed. by Bob Krauss. LC 84-8671. 230p. 1984. 14.95 (*0-8248-0962-9*) UH Pr.

Detective Mole & Halloween Mystery. Robert Quackenbush. (J). 1989. pap. 3.95 (*0-671-67830-2*, Litl Simon S&S) S&S Childrens.

Detective Mole & the Haunted Castle Mystery. Robert Quackenbush. LC 84-20141. (Illus.). 32p. (J). (gr. k-3). 1985. lib. bdg. 14.93 (*0-688-04641-X*) Lothrop.

Detective Novel of Manners: Hedonism, Morality, & the Life of Reason. Hanna Charney. LC 79-17634. 160p. 1981. 27.50 (*0-8386-3004-9*) Fairleigh Dickinson.

Detective Short Story: A Bibliography & Index. E. H. Mundell, Jr. & G. Jay Rausch. 1974. 15.00 (*0-318-22157-8*) KSU.

Detective Stars & the Case of the Super Soccer Team. Caroline A. Levine. LC 92-28600. (Illus.). 48p. (J). (gr. 1-4). 1994. 11.99 (*0-525-65134-9*, Cobblehill Bks) Dutton Child Bks.

Detective Stories from the Strand. Sel. by Jack Adrian. 368p. 1992. 22.95 (*0-19-212306-8*) OUP.

Detective Stories from the Strand. Intro. & Sel. by Jack Adrian. 400p. 1992. pap. 12.95 (*0-19-282998-X*) OUP.

Detective Tricks You Can Do. Judith Conaway. LC 85-28881. (Illus.). 48p. (J). (gr. 1-5). 1986. lib. bdg. 11.89 (*0-8167-0672-7*); pap. text ed. 3.50 (*0-8167-0673-5*) Troll Assocs.

Detective Zack & the Mystery at Thunder Mountain. Jerry D. Thomas. LC 93-41480. (Detective Zack Ser.: Vol. 4). (J). (gr. 4 up). 1994. pap. 5.95 (*0-8163-1212-5*) Pacific Pr Pub Assn.

Detective Zack & the Red Hat Mystery. Jerry D. Thomas. LC 93-4322. (Detective Zack Ser.: Vol. 3). (J). 1993. pap. 5.95 (*0-8163-1169-2*) Pacific Pr Pub Assn.

Detective Zack & the Secret of Noah's Flood: Starburst. Jerry D. Thomas. LC 92-5730. 128p. (J). 1992. pap. 5.95 (*0-8163-1107-2*) Pacific Pr Pub Assn.

Detective Zack & the Secrets in the Sand. Jerry D. Thomas. LC 92-29931. (J). 1993. pap. 5.95 (*0-8163-1129-3*) Pacific Pr Pub Assn.

***Detective Zacks Word Puzzle Safari.** Jerry Thomas. 1993. pap. 1.25 (*0-8163-1105-6*) Pacific Pr Pub Assn.

***Detectives.** Micheels. 1995. mass mkt. 5.50 (*0-312-95392-5*) St Martin.

Detectives: Their Toughest Cases in Their Own Words. Peter A. Micheels. (Illus.). 288p. 1994. 21.95 (*0-312-09785-9*) St Martin.

Detective's Handbook (B - U) A. Civardi et al. (Detective Guides Ser.). (Illus.). 192p. (J). (gr. 2-6). 1992. pap. 9.95 (*0-86020-278-X*) EDC.

Detectives in Togas. Henry Winterfeld. 249p. (J). (gr. 3-7). 1990. pap. 3.95 (*0-15-223415-2*, Odyssey) HarBrace.

Detective's Private Investigation Training Manual. William Patterson. (Illus.). 160p. 1979. pap. 14.95 (*0-87364-161-2*) Paladin Pr.

Detector Dogs: Hot on the Scent. Elizabeth Ring. LC 93-7275. (Good Dogs! Ser.). (Illus.). 32p. (J). (gr. 2-4). 1993. lib. bdg. 13.90 (*1-56294-289-1*) Millbrook Pr.

Detector Research & Development for the Superconducting Supercollider, Symposium on. T. Dombeck et al. 844p. 1991. text ed. 173.00 (*981-02-0445-0*) World Scientific Pub.

Detectors for Capillary Chromatography. Ed. by H. H. Hill & D. G. McMinn. (Chemical Analysis: a Series of Monographs on Analytical Chemistry & Its Applications). 464p. 1992. text ed. 110.00 (*0-471-50645-1*) Wiley.

Detectors for Particle Radiation. K. Kleinknecht. 206p. 1988. pap. 34.95 (*0-521-35852-3*) Cambridge U Pr.

Detectors in Heavy-Ion Reactions. Berlin, 1982: Proceedings. Ed. by W. Von Oertzen. (Lecture Notes in Physics Ser.: Vol. 178). 258p. 1983. pap. 29.00 (*0-387-12001-7*) Spr-Verlag.

Detente: Prospects for Democracy & Dictatorship. Aleksandr Solzhenitsyn. LC 79-66443. (Issues in Contemporary Civilization Ser.). 140p. reprint ed. pap. 39.90 (*0-317-20614-1*, 2024156) Bks Demand.

Detente: Prospects for Democracy & Dictatorship. Aleksandr Solzhenitsyn et al. LC 76-15233. (Issues in Contemporary Civilization Ser.). 1976. reprint ed. pap. text ed. 12.95x (*0-87855-629-X*) Transaction Pubs.

Detente After Brezhnev: The Domestic Roots of Soviet Foreign Policy. Alexander Yanov. Tr. by Robert Kessler. LC 77-620014. (Policy Papers in International Affairs Ser.: No. 2). x, 87p. 1977. pap. 4.95 (*0-87725-502-4*) U of Cal IAS.

Detente & Confrontation: American-Soviet Relations from Nixon to Reagan. Raymond L. Garthoff. LC 84-45855. 1147p. 1985. 49.95 (*0-8157-3044-6*); pap. 25.95 (*0-8157-3043-8*) Brookings.

Detente & Confrontation: American-Soviet Relations from Nixon to Reagan. rev. ed. Raymond L. Garthoff. 1000p. (C). 49.95 (*0-8157-3042-X*); pap. 24.95 (*0-8157-3041-1*) Brookings.

Detente & Defense: A Reader. Robert J. Pranger. LC 76-44607. (Foreign Affairs Study Ser.: No. 40). 456p. reprint ed. pap. 130.00 (*0-8357-4464-7*, 2037308) Bks Demand.

Detente & Peace in Europe. Ed. by Ruediger Juette. 148p. (C). 1982. text ed. 29.00 (*3-593-32219-6*) Irvington.

Detente & Socialist Democracy: A Discussion with Roy Medvedev. Ed. by Ken Coates. (European Socialist Thought Ser.: No. 6). 163p. (Orig.). 1975. pap. 24.00 (*0-85124-227-8*, Pub. by Spokesman Bks UK) Coronet Bks.

Detente & the Democratic Movement in the U. S. S. R. Frederick C. Barghoorn. LC 76-4425. 1976. 24.95 (*0-02-901850-1*) Free Pr.

Detente & the Nixon Doctrine. Robert S. Litwak. (International Studies). 240p. 1986. pap. 19.95 (*0-521-33834-4*) Cambridge U Pr.

Detente in Europe: The Soviet Union & the West since 1953. John Van Oudenaren. LC 90-25033. 510p. 1991. lib. bdg. 63.00 (*0-8223-1133-X*); pap. text ed. 31.95 (*0-8223-1141-0*) Duke.

Detente in Historical Perspective. 2nd ed. Ed. by George Schwab & H. Friedlander. 171p. (C). 1981. reprint ed. pap. text ed. 9.95 (*0-8290-0457-2*) Irvington.

Detente or Debacle. 108p. 1979. 3.95 (*0-318-13320-2*) Am Comm US Soviet.

Detention & Torture in South Africa: Psychological, Legal & Historical Studies. Don Foster & Dennis Davis. LC 86-33918. 240p. 1987. text ed. 39.95 (*0-312-00785-X*) St Martin.

Detention in Remand Homes: A Report of the Cambridge Department of Criminal Science on the Use of Sec. 54 of the Children & Young Persons Act, 1933. Cambridge Department of Criminal Science Staff. (Cambridge Studies in Criminology: Vol. 7). 1972. reprint ed. pap. 13.00 (*0-8115-0421-2*) Periodicals Srv.

Detention of Human Rights Workers & Lawyers from the West Bank & Gaza & Conditions of Detention at Ketziot. Virginia N. Sherry. Ed. by Michael Posner. 120p. (Orig.). 1989. pap. text ed. 10.00 (*0-934143-19-6*) Lawyers Comm Human.

Detergency: Theory & Test Methods, Pt. III. Cutler & Davis. (Surfactant Science Ser.: Vol. 5). 384p. 1981. 160.00 (*0-8247-6982-1*) Dekker.

Detergency: Theory & Test Methods, Part 1. Ed. by W. Gale Cutler & R. C. Davis. (Surfactant Science Ser.: No. 5). (Illus.). 463p. 1972. reprint ed. pap. 132.00 (*0-7837-3382-8*, 2043340) Bks Demand.

Detergency: Theory & Test Methods, Part 2. Ed. by Cutler & Davis. (Surfactant Science Ser.: Vol. 5). 296p. 1975. 170.00 (*0-8247-7260-1*) Dekker.

***Detergency Pt. 2: Theory & Test Methods.** fac. ed. Ed. by W. G. Cutler & R. C. Davis. LC 79-163921. (Surfactant Science Ser.: No. 5). (Illus.). 292p. 1972. pap. 83.30 (*0-7837-7306-4*, 2043340) Bks Demand.

Detergency Evaluation & Testing. Jay C. Harris. LC 53-10758. (Interscience Manuals Ser.: No.41). 220p. reprint ed. pap. 62.70 (*0-317-09365-7*, 2007392) Bks Demand.

Detergency, Pt. 4: Theory & Test Methods. Cutler & Kissa. (Surfactant Science Ser.: Vol. 20). 568p. 1987. 170.00 (*0-8247-7503-1*) Dekker.

Detergent Analysis: A Handbook for Cost-Effective Quality Control. Benjamin M. Milwidsky & Delia M. Gabriel. LC 81-19840. (Illus.). 303p. 1989. reprint ed. 65.00 (*0-9608752-3-9*) Micelle Pr.

Detergents & Textile Washing: Principles & Practice. Gunter Jakobi & Albrecht Lohr. LC 87-25299. (Illus.). 248p. 1988. lib. bdg. 90.00 (*0-89573-686-1*) VCH Pubs.

***Detering Democracy.** Noam Chomsky. Date not set. write for info. (*0-09-913501-9*) Random.

Deterioration & Race Education with Practical Application to the Condition of the People & Industry. Samuel Royce. LC 72-180587. (Medicine & Society in America Ser.). 596p. 1972. reprint ed. 39.95 (*0-405-03967-0*) Ayer.

Deterioration in the Quality of Foreign Bonds Issued in the United States, 1920-1930. Ilse Mintz. Ed. by Mira Wilkins. LC 78-3939. (International Finance Ser.). (Illus.). 1979. reprint ed. lib. bdg. 17.95 (*0-405-11240-8*) Ayer.

Deterioration in the Quality of Foreign Bonds Issued in the United States, 1920-1930. Ilse Mintz. (General Ser.: No. 52). 112p. 1951. reprint ed. 29.20 (*0-87014-051-5*) Natl Bur Econ Res.

Deterioration, Maintenance, & Repair of Structures. Sidney Johnson. 384p. 1981. reprint ed. 44.00 (*0-89874-095-9*) Krieger.

Deterioration of Book Stock: Causes & Remedies: Two Studies on the Permanence of Book Paper Conducted by W. J. Barrow. Ed. by Randolph W. Church. (Illus.). 70p. 1959. text ed. 5.00 (*0-685-62263-0*) VA State Lib.

Deterioration of Dams & Reservoirs: Examples & Their Analysis. Tr. by A. D. Penman. 368p. (C). 1984. text ed. 130.00 (*90-6191-546-5*, Pub. by A A Balkema NE) Ashgate Pub Co.

Deterioration of the Mexican Presidency: The Years of Luis Echeverria. Samuel Schmidt. Tr. by Dan A. Cothran. LC 91-17540. (PROFMEX Ser.). 222p. 1991. 37.50 (*0-8165-1235-3*) U of Ariz Pr.

Deterioration of the Public Sector Housing Stock. Diane Diacon. 280p. 1991. text ed. 68.95 (*1-85628-110-8*, Pub. by Avebury Pub UK) Ashgate Pub Co.

Deterioration of Water Quality in Distribution Systems. 176p. 1987. pap. 21.00 (*0-89867-396-8*, 90521) Am Water Wks Assn.

Determinants & Consequences of Trade Restrictions in the U. S. Economy. Victor A. Canto. LC 85-12211. 218p. 1985. text ed. 55.00 (*0-275-90050-9*, C0050, Praeger Pubs) Greenwood.

Determinants & Controls of Scientific Developments. Ed. by Karin D. Knorr et al. LC 75-16419. (Theory & Decision Library: No. 10). 460p. 1975. lib. bdg. 158.00 (*90-277-0600-X*) Kluwer Ac.

Determinants & Effects of Changes in the Stock of Money, 1875-1960. Phillip Cagan. (Business Cycles Ser.: No. 13). 408p. 1965. 106.10 (*0-87014-097-3*) Natl Bur Econ Res.

Determinants & Matrices. Alexander C. Aitken. LC 82-24168. (University Mathematical Texts Ser.). 144p. 1983. reprint ed. text ed. 49.75 (*0-313-23294-6*, AIDE, Greenwood Pr) Greenwood.

Determinants & Systemic Consequences of International Capital Flows, 1991. Morris Goldstein et al. LC 91-2289. (Occasional Paper Ser.: No. 77). vii, 94p. (Orig.). 1991. pap. 10.00 (*1-55775-205-2*) Intl Monetary.

Determinants & Their Applications in Mathematical Physics. Robert Vein & Paul Dale. 300p. 1995. text ed. 60.00 (*0-13-203019-5*) P-H.

Determinants of Change. Alice Golostein. 1985. text ed. 17.50 (*0-910430-02-0*, JSS3, Conf Jewsh Soc Studies) Col U Pr.

Determinants of Emigration from Mexico, Central America, & the Caribbean. Ed. by Sergio Diaz-Briquets & Sidney Weintraub. 356p. (C). 1991. pap. text ed. 62.00 (*0-8133-8142-8*) Westview.

Determinants of Executive Compensation: Corporate Ownership, Performance, Size, & Diversification. Ellen L. Pavlik & Ahmed R. Belkaoui. LC 90-26407. 176p. 1991. text ed. 59.95 (*0-89930-633-0*, PEZ/, Quorum Bks) Greenwood.

Determinants of Expenditures for Physicians' Services in the United States. Victor R. Fuchs & Marcia J. Kramer. (Occasional Papers: No. 117). 72p. 1973. reprint ed. 20.00 (*0-87014-247-X*) Natl Bur Econ Res.

Determinants of Fertility & Child Mortality in Cote d'Ivoire & Ghana. Kofi D. Benefo & T. Paul Schultz. LC 94-4997. (LSM Working Papers Ser.: No. 103). 102p. 1994. write for info. (*0-8213-2789-5*) World Bank.

Determinants of Fertility Decline: A Study of Rural Karnataka. N. Baskara Rao. 1986. 17.50 (*81-7003-060-9*, Pub. by S Asia Pubs II) S Asia.

Determinants of HMO Success. Peter D. Fox & LuAnn Heinen. LC 86-29553. 264p. (Orig.). 1987. pap. text ed. 28.00 (*0-910701-21-0*, 0866) Health Admin Pr.

Determinants of Hospital Costs: Outputs, Inputs, & Regulation in the 1980s. Jack Hadley & Stephen Zuckerman. LC 91-24292. (Report Ser.: No. 91-10). (Illus.). 236p. (Orig.). 1991. lib. bdg. 45.00 (*0-87766-551-6*); pap. text ed. 16.50 (*0-87766-552-4*) Urban Inst.

Determinants of Individual Productivity: A Study of Academic Researchers. Douglas Rebne. (Monograph & Research Ser.: No. 53). 155p. 1990. pap. 12.50 (*0-89215-162-5*) U Cal LA Indus Rel.

Determinants of Investment Behavior. Universities-National Bureau Staff. Ed. by Robert Ferber. (Conference Ser.: No. 18). 622p. 1967. reprint ed. 160.00 (*0-87014-309-3*) Natl Bur Econ Res.

Determinants of Low Wages for Women Workers. Mary H. Stevenson. LC 84-15032. (Landmark Dissertations in Women's Studies). 240p. 1984. text ed. 45.00 (*0-275-91278-7*, C1278, Praeger Pubs) Greenwood.

Determinants of Mandibular Form & Growth: Proceedings of a Sponsored Symposium Honoring Professor Robert E. Moyers. Symposium on Craniofacial Growth (2nd: 1975: University of Michigan) Staff. Ed. by James A. McNamara, Jr. LC 77-153464. (Craniofacial Growth Monograph Ser.: No. 4). (Illus.). 281p. reprint ed. pap. 80.10 (*0-685-24147-5*, 2033020) Bks Demand.

Determinants of Mortality Change & Differentials in Developing Countries. (Population Studies: No. 94). 170p. 1986. 19.50 (*92-1-151151-8*, E.85.XIII.4) UN.

Determinants of Neuronal Identity. Ed. by Marty Shankland & Eduardo R. Macagno. (Illus.). 528p. 1992. text ed. 69.00 (*0-12-638280-8*) Acad Pr.

Determinants of Political Participation: Women & Public Activity. Snehalata Panda. 1990. 20.00 (*0-685-34755-9*, Pub. by Ajanta II) S Asia.

Determinants of Public Policy: Cities, States, Nations. Virginia Gray & Thomas Dye. (C). 1979. pap. 12.00 (*0-918592-32-1*) Pol Studies.

Determinants of Reproductive Change in Bangladesh: Success in a Challenging Environment. John Cleland et al. LC 94-16613. (Regional & Sectoral Studies). 1994. write for info. (*0-8213-2849-2*) World Bank.

Determinants of Return in Real Estate Investment & the Role of Real Estate Management. George W. Gau. (Orig.). 1982. pap. text ed. 16.00 (*0-944298-28-1*, 869) Inst Real Estate.

Determinants of Self-Employment. G. De Wit. (Studies in Empirical Economics). (Illus.). xii, 193p. 1993. pap. 52.00 (*0-387-91451-X*) Spr-Verlag.

Determinants of Social Status in India. Ed. by S. C. Malik. xi, 192p. 1986. 22.00 (*81-208-0073-7*, Pub. by Motilal Banarsidass II) S Asia.

Determinants of Soil Loss Tolerance. Ed. by B. L. Schmidt et al. (ASA Special Publication Ser.). 153p. (C). 1982. pap. 8.50 (*0-89118-071-0*) Am Soc Agron.

Determinants of Substance Abuse: Biological, Psychological, & Environmental Factors. Ed. by Mark Galizio & Stephen A. Maisto. LC 85-3405. (Perspectives on Individual Differences Ser.). 454p. 1985. 70.00 (*0-306-41873-8*, Plenum Pr) Plenum.

Determinants of Total Family Charges for Health Care: United States, 1980 DHHS 91-20408. (Reports from the National Medical Care Utilization & Expenditure Survey, Analytical Report Ser. C: No. 8). 72p. 3.75 (*0-685-61595-2*, 017-022-01125-5) Natl Ctr Health Stats.

Determinants of Unauthorized Western Hemisphere Migration to the United States. Sidney Weintraub & Robert T. Green. (Special Project Report Ser.). 140p. 1989. 8.00 (*0-89940-867-2*) LBJ Sch Pub Aff.

Determinants of Value: An Annotated Bibliography. Robert C. Denne. (Bibliographic Ser.: No.1). 48p. 1976. pap. 11.00 (*0-88329-045-6*) IAAO.

Determinate Religion **see Lectures on the Philosophy of Religion**

Determinate Sentencing: The Promise & the Reality of Retributive Justice. Pamala L. Griset. LC 90-35293. (SUNY Series in Critical Issues in Criminal Justice). (Illus.). 237p. (C). 1991. 64.50 (*0-7914-0534-6*); pap. 21.95 (*0-7914-0535-4*) State U NY Pr.

Determination. Eleanor Ayer. (Values Library). (YA). (gr. 7-12). 1991. lib. bdg. 14.95 (*0-8239-1226-4*) Rosen Group.

Determination, Reading Level 2. Goley. (Learn the Value Ser.: Set II). (Illus.). 32p. (J). (gr. 1-4). 1989. 11.95 (*0-685-58779-7*); lib. bdg. 15.94 (*0-86592-389-2*) Rourke Corp.

Determination & Use of Stability Constants. 2nd ed. Arthur E. Martell & Ramumas J. Motekaitis. LC 91-45076. 200p. 1993. 45.00 (*1-56081-516-7*) VCH Pubs.

Determination, Courage, Destiny. Comp. by Esther Dykman-Gastwirth. LC 92-30855. 1992. write for info. (*0-9622584-2-3*) Oceanco Ltd.

Determination of Absorbed Dose in a Patient Irradiated by Beams of X or Gamma Rays in Radiotherapy Procedures, No. 24. International Commission on Radiation Units & Measurements. LC 76-22297. 1976. 30.00 (*0-913394-43-2*) Intl Comm Rad Meas.

Determination of Anions & Cations, Transitionmetals, Other Complex Ions, 1990. HMSO Staff. 126p. 1991. pap. 25.00 (*0-11-752331-3*, HM6331) UNIPUB.

***Determination of Aquifer Parameters Using Array & Regression Analysis.** Michael Kasenow & Paul Pare. 1994. spiral bd. 25.00 (*0-918334-86-1*) WRP.

Determination of Beta-Blockers in Biological Material. Ed. by V. Marko. (Techniques & Instrumentation in Analytical Chemistry Ser.: Vol. 4C). 334p. 1989. 148.75 (*0-444-87305-8*) Elsevier.

Determination of Carbon & Hydrogen & the Use of New Combustion Catalysts **see Methods in Microanalysis**

Determination of Carbon & Hydrogen in the Presence of Other Elements or Simultaneously with Them **see Methods in Microanalysis**

Determination of Carboxylic Functional Groups. R. D. Tiwari & J. P. Sharma. LC 73-104121. (C). 1970. 65.00 (*0-08-015516-2*, Pub. by Pergamon Repr UK) Franklin.

D

An Asterisk (*) at the beginning of an entry indicates that the title is appearing in BIP for the first time.

An Asterisk (*) at the beginning of an entry indicates that the title is appearing in BIP for the first time.

1903

D

Deterrence & Defense: Toward a Theory of National Security. Glenn H. Snyder. LC 75-18405. (Illus.). 294p. 1975. reprint ed. text ed. 48.50 (*0-8371-8333-2*, SNDD, Greenwood Pr) Greenwood.

Deterrence & Defense: Towards a Theory of National Security. Glenn H. Snyder. LC 61-12102. reprint ed. pap. 76.00 (*0-317-08306-6*, 200884) Bks Demand.

Deterrence & Defense in a Post-Nuclear World: Emerging Soviet & American Strategies. Gary L. Guertner. LC 89-36449. 240p. 1990. text ed. 39.95 (*0-312-03638-8*) St Martin.

Deterrence & Defense in Korea: The Role of U. S. Forces. Ralph N. Clough. LC 75-44466. (Studies in Defense Policy). 61p. 1976. pap. 7.95 (*0-8157-1481-5*) Brookings.

Deterrence & Juvenile Crime. A. L. Schneider. (Research in Criminology Ser.). (Illus.). x, 129p. 1989. 65.00 (*0-387-97057-6*, 3053) Spr-Verlag.

Deterrence & Strategic Culture: Chinese-American Confrontations, 1949-1958. Shu G. Zhang. LC 92-52777. (Cornell Studies in Security Affairs). 320p. 1993. 37.95 (*0-8014-2751-7*) Cornell U Pr.

Deterrence & the Revolution in Soviet Military Doctrine. Raymond L. Garthoff. 209p. 1990. 29.95 (*0-8157-3056-X*); pap. 11.95 (*0-8157-3055-1*) Brookings.

Deterrence, Arms Control, & Disarmament: Toward a Synthesis in National Security Policy. J. David Singer. LC 83-25950. (Illus.). 326p. (C). 1984. reprint ed. pap. text ed. 23.00 (*0-8191-3792-8*) U Pr of Amer.

Deterrence Before Hiroshima. George H. Quester. 214p. 1986. 32.95 (*0-88738-087-5*) Transaction Pubs.

Deterrence in American Foreign Policy: Theory & Practice. Alexander L. George et al. LC 74-7120. 666p. 1974. pap. text ed. 24.50 (*0-231-03838-0*) Col U Pr.

Deterrence in Decay: The Future of the U. S. Defense Industrial Base. John McCain et al. (CSIS Panel Report). 67p. 1989. 24.95 (*0-89206-139-1*) CSI Studies.

Deterrence in the Middle East: Where Theory & Practice Converge. Ed. by Aharon Klieman & Ariel Levite. LC 94-18405. (JCSS Study: No. 22). (C). 1994. pap. text ed. 34.50 (*0-8133-2220-0*) Westview.

Deterrence in the 1980s: Crisis & Dilemma. Ed. by R. B. Byers. LC 85-10755. 256p. 1985. text ed. 39.95 (*0-312-19593-1*) St Martin.

Deterrence Theory Revisited. Robert Jervis. (CISA Working Paper Ser.: No. 14). 72p. (Orig.). Date not set. pap. 10.00 (*0-86682-013-2*) Ctr Intl Relations.

Deterrent Diplomacy: Japan, Germany & the U. S. S. R., 1935-1940. Ed. by James Morley. LC 75-25524. (Japan's Road to the Pacific War Ser.). 380p. reprint ed. pap. 108.30 (*0-317-26658-6*, 2025109) Bks Demand.

Deterrents & Reinforcement: The Psychology of Insufficient Reward. Douglas H. Lawrence & Leon Festinger. vi, 180p. 1962. 27.50 (*0-8047-0117-2*) Stanford U Pr.

Deterrents to Participation: An Adult Education Dilemma. Craig L. Scanlan. (Eric Information Analysis Ser.). 62p. 1986. 7.00 (*0-318-22354-6*, IN308) Ctr Educ Trng Employ.

Deterring Criminals: Policy Making & the American Political Tradition. Jeffrey L. Sedgwick. 50p. 1980. pap. 12.50 (*0-8447-3385-7*) Am Enterprise.

Deterring Democracy. Noam Chomsky. 421p. 1992. pap. 15.00 (*0-374-52349-5*, Noonday) Hill & Wang.

Deterring Democracy. Noam Chomsky. 384p. 1991. 29.95 (*0-86091-318-X*, A5347, Pub. by Verso UK) Routledge Chapman & Hall.

Deterring Drug Abuse among Children & Adolescents: Prevention Research. 1993. lib. bdg. 255.99 (*0-8490-8501-2*) Gordon Pr.

Deterring Fraud: The Internal Auditor's Perspective. W. S. Albrecht et al. 169p. (C). 1984. text ed. 33.00 (*0-89413-117-6*) Inst Inter Aud.

Deth Makes Ya Horny. W. Gellis. 59p. 1987. pap. 10.00 (*0-917455-02-9*) Big Foot NY.

Dethroned Heiress. Eliza A. Dupuy. LC 76-76923. (American Fiction Reprint Ser.). 1977. 20.95 (*0-8369-7002-0*) Ayer.

Dethronement of Sabaoth: Studies in the Shen & Kabod Theologies. Tryggve Mettinger. (Coniectanea Biblica. Old Testament Ser.: No. 18). 158p. (Orig.). 1982. pap. 41.00x (*0-317-65792-5*) Coronet Bks.

Dethronement of the City Boss. John J. Hamilton. LC 79-37344. (Select Bibliographies Reprint Ser.). 1977. reprint ed. 21.95 (*0-8369-6691-0*) Ayer.

Detlev's Imitations. Hubert Fichte. Tr. by Martin Chalmers. 256p. (Orig.). 1992. pap. 14.99 (*1-85242-167-3*) Serpents Tail.

Detling Secret. large type ed. Julian Symons. 336p. 1983. 15.95 (*0-7089-1063-7*) Ulverscroft.

DeTomaso: The Man & the Machines. Wallace A. Wyss. LC 91-72450. (Illus.). 1991. write for info. (*0-9629682-0-X*) Adler Pub.

***Detonacion - Palabras en la Arena.** 2nd ed. Antonio B. Vallejo. 224p. 1987. pap. 8.95 (*0-7859-5203-9*) Fr & Eur.

Detonation of Condensed Explosives. Roger Cheret. LC 92-16118. 1992. write for info. (*0-387-53616-7*) Spr-Verlag.

Detonation of Condensed Explosives. Roger Cheret. Ed. by R. A. Graham. (High Pressure Shock Compression of Condensed Matter Ser.). (Illus.). 496p. 1992. 198.00 (*0-387-97898-4*) Spr-Verlag.

Detotalized Totalities: Synthesis & Disintegration in Naturalist, Existentialist, & Socialist Fiction. L. S. Dembo. 208p. (Orig.). (C). 1989. text ed. 37.50 (*0-299-12020-1*); pap. text ed. 15.75 (*0-299-12024-4*) U of Wis Pr.

Detour. Grace Kaiser. LC 90-3361. 192p. 1992. pap. 9.95 (*1-56148-062-2*) Good Bks PA.

Detour. Grace H. Kaiser. LC 90-3361. 192p. 1990. 15.95 (*0-934672-87-3*) Good Bks PA.

Detour. Helen Nielsen. LC 87-70476. 192p. 1988. reprint ed. pap. 4.95 (*0-88739-080-3*, Blk Lizard) Creat Arts Bk.

Detour: A Hollywood Story. Cheryl Crane & Cliff Jahr. 1989. mass mkt. 4.50 (*0-380-70580-X*) Avon.

Detour: Poems. Sandra Williams. pap. 7.00 (*0-932264-09-3*) Trask Hse Bks.

***Detour: Truth about Information Superhighway.** Michael Sullivan-Trainor. 1994. 22.99 (*1-56884-307-0*) IDG Bks.

Detour for Emmy. Marilyn Reynolds. (Illus.). 256p. (Orig.). 1993. 15.95 (*0-930934-75-X*); pap. 9.95 (*0-930934-76-8*) Morning Glory.

Detours: Biographies of Physically Disabled Achievers. Charles D. Abernathy. 36p. (Orig.). 1988. pap. 5.95 (*0-9620745-0-0*); pap. text ed. 3.95 (*0-9620745-1-9*) TEAM Savers.

Detour's Amsterdam: An Alternative Guide. Brian Hicks & Tom Hooper. Ed. by Augustus C. Caswell. (Orig.). 1994. pap. 13.95 (*0-9635983-7-6*) Detour Pubns.

Detour's London. Jon Nicholson & John Williams. Ed. by Augustus Caswell. LC 93-90988. (Detour Ser.). 304p. 1993. 13.95 (*0-9635983-1-7*) Detour Pubns.

Detour's Miami: An Alternative Guide. Joseph Downton. Ed. by Augustus C. Caswell. 304p. (Orig.). 1993. pap. 13.95 (*0-9635983-4-1*) Detour Pubns.

Detour's New York: An Alternative Guide. Joseph Downton & Eva Leonard. Ed. by Augustus C. Caswell. 304p. (Orig.). 1994. pap. 14.95 (*0-9635983-6-8*) Detour Pubns.

Detours of Desire: Readings in the French Baroque. Mitchell Greenberg. LC 83-19380. 175p. 1984. 36.50 (*0-8142-0359-0*) Ohio St U Pr.

Detour's Paris: The Alternative Guide. Brian Hicks & Tom Hooper. Ed. by Augustus C. Caswell. 240p. (Orig.). 1994. pap. 13.95 (*0-9635983-8-4*) Detour Pubns.

Detours (Passable but Unsafe) Philip S. Marden. LC 68-54360. (Essay Index Reprint Ser.). 1977. 19.95 (*0-8369-0677-2*) Ayer.

***Detour's San Francisco.** Robin Stevens. 1994. pap. 15.95 (*1-885526-00-8*) Detour Pubns.

Detour's Southern California: An Alternative Guide. Matthew Cibellis. Ed. by Augustus C. Caswell. 304p. (Orig.). 1994. pap. 14.95 (*0-9635983-9-2*) Detour Pubns.

Detour's Washington, D.C. Joseph Downton. Ed. by Augustus C. Caswell. 276p. 1993. pap. 13.95 (*0-9635983-3-3*) Detour Pubns.

Detox: Step One for the Alcoholic. Catherine Fellman. (American University Studies: Health Sciences Studies: Ser. XXIII, Vol. 1). 205p. (C). 1988. text ed. 33.80 (*0-8204-0698-8*) P Lang Pubs.

Detoxification & Natural Degradation of Chemical Warfare Agents. Ralf Trapp. (Chemical & Biologocal Warfare Agents Studies: No. 3). 104p. 1985. pap. 40.00 (*0-85066-309-1*) Taylor & Francis.

Detoxification Treatment Manual. 1986. lib. bdg. 75.00 (*0-8490-3510-4*) Gordon Pr.

Detoxify & Vitalize Your Life: Natural Remedies That Boost Your Immune Systeme; Detoxify from Chemical Pollutants, Radiation & X-Rays; Generate Optimal Vitality & Health. rev. ed. Steven R. Schechter. Ed. by Ruth Stockton. LC 90-70098. 294p. 1990. reprint ed. 17.95 (*0-685-33005-2*); reprint ed. pap. 9.95 (*1-878412-02-7*) Vitality CA.

DETPROB: Probability of Detection Calculation Software & User's Manual. William A. Skillman. (Artech House Radar Software Library). 50p. 1991. disk 100.00 (*0-89006-561-6*) Artech Hse.

***Detraditionalization: Critical Reflections on Authority & Identity at a Time of Uncertainty.** Ed. by Paul Heelas et al. 360p. (C). 1996. write for info. (*1-55786-554-X*) Blackwell Pubs.

***Detraditionalization: Critical Reflections on Authority & Identity at a Time of Uncertainty.** Ed. by Paul Heelas et al. 360p. (C). 1996. pap. write for info. (*1-55786-555-8*) Blackwell Pubs.

Detritus & Microbial Ecology in Aquaculture. Ed. by D. J. Moriarty & R. S. Pullin. (Conference Proceedings Ser.: No. 14). 1987. pap. 28.50 (*971-10-2229-X*, Pub. by ICLARM PH) Intl Spec Bk.

Detroit. Chanda K. Zimmerman. LC 88-35914. (Downtown America Bks.). (Illus.). 60p. (J). (gr. 3 up). 1989. text ed. 13.95 (*0-87518-409-X*, Dillon Silver Burdett) Silver Burdett Pr.

Detroit: City of Race & Class Violence. rev. ed. B. J. Widick. LC 88-33761. (Great Lakes Bks.). 292p. (C). 1989. reprint ed. pap. 15.95 (*0-8143-2104-6*) Wayne St U Pr.

Detroit: La Onda Latina en Poesia-Latin Sounds in Poetry, Vol. II. Casa de Unidad Staff. (Illus.). 72p. (Orig.). (ENG & SPA.). 1987. pap. 6.00 (*0-9615977-1-2*) Casa Unidad.

Detroit: Race & Uneven Development. Joe T. Darden et al. (Illus.). 336p. 1990. pap. 19.95 (*0-87722-776-4*) Temple U Pr.

Detroit: The Renaissance City. 2nd ed. Balthazar Korab. Ed. by Michael P. Spradlin & Carolyn M. Clark. (Illus.). 104p. reprint ed. 19.98 (*1-881892-00-X*) Spradlin & Assocs.

***Detroit: Visions of the Eagle.** Dale Fisher. Ed. by Mary Beth Fisher. LC 94-61438. (Illus.). 176p. 1994. 50.00 (*0-9615623-3-1*) Eyry Eagle Pub.

Detroit & the Problem of Order, 1830-1880: A Geography of Crime, Riot, & Policing. John C. Schneider. LC 79-16492. 187p. reprint ed. pap. 53.30 (*0-8357-2947-8*, 2039203) Bks Demand.

Detroit Architecture: AIA Guide. rev. ed. Ed. by Katharine M. Meyer & Martin P. McElroy. LC 80-132260. (Illus.). 272p. 1980. pap. 13.95 (*0-8143-1651-4*) Wayne St U Pr.

***D'Etroit Checkers: The Gem of French Draughts!** Karl W. Grube. 30p. 1995. pap. 15.00 (*0-614-03916-9*) Games By Grube.

Detroit Chefs Book. William Struns. Ed. by R. McMinn. 120p. (Orig.). 1989. pap. text ed. 6.95 (*0-935201-89-0*) Affordable Adven.

Detroit Collects Prints & Drawings. Detroit Institute Of Arts. LC 76-168631. 52p. 1972. 14.95x (*0-8143-1486-4*) Wayne St U Pr.

Detroit Deathwatch. Don Pendleton. (Executioner Ser.: No. 19). 1989. pap. 3.50 (*1-55817-218-1*, Pinnacle NY) Windsor NY.

Detroit, Fort Lernoult, & the American Revolution. Philip P. Mason. LC 64-18967. 34p. reprint ed. pap. 25.00 (*0-7837-3634-7*, 2043501) Bks Demand.

Detroit Goes to War: The American Auto Industry in World War II. V. Dennis Wrynn. LC 93-7693. 1993. 29.95 (*0-87938-773-4*) Motorbooks Intl.

Detroit Guide. Ed. by Martin Fischhoff. LC 82-74233. (Illus.). 486p. (Orig.). 1983. pap. 8.95 (*0-9600448-6-8*) Detroit Guide.

Detroit Images: Photographs of the Renaissance City. Ed. by John J. Bukowczyk et al. LC 88-27950. (Great Lakes Bks.). (Illus.). 278p. (C). 1989. 49.95 (*0-8143-1965-3*) Wayne St U Pr.

Detroit in Miniature. Ed Force & James Wieland. Date not set. write for info. (*0-910509-01-8*) J Wieland.

Detroit Insider: How to Buy Three & Four Year Old Cars at Four Hundred & Less - How to Buy a New Car at Lowest Possible Prices - Classic Cars for Fun & Profit. John V. Kamin. Incl. How to Buy Three-Four Year Old Cars at Four Hundred Dollars & Less. 1981. (*0-318-51903-8*); How to Buy a New Car at Lowest Possible Prices. 1981. (*0-318-51904-6*); Classic Cars for Fun & Profit. 1981. (*0-318-51905-4*); 38p. 1981. Set pap. 6.00 (*0-911353-09-7*) Forecaster Pub.

Detroit Institute of Arts: A Brief History. William Peck. (Illus.). 196p. 1991. pap. 19.95 (*0-89558-136-1*) Wayne St U Pr.

***Detroit Institute of Arts: A Visitor's Guide.** Ed. by Julia P. Henshaw. (Illus.). 336p. (C). 1995. 34.95 (*0-8143-2618-8*); pap. 19.95 (*0-8143-2619-6*) Wayne St U Pr.

***Detroit Jobbank.** 5th ed. Adams Inc. Staff. 1994. pap. 15.95 (*1-55850-451-6*) Adams Pubng.

Detroit Lakes Area Fishing Map Guide. James F. Billig & Thomas C. Billig. 1994. pap. 14.95 (*1-885010-07-9*) Sptsmans Connect.

Detroit Lions. Richard Rambeck. (NFL Today Ser.). 48p. (J). (gr. 4 up). 1991. lib. bdg. 14.95 (*0-88682-366-8*) Creative Ed.

Detroit Lives. Comp. by Robert H. Mast. LC 93-51007. (Conflicts in Urban & Regional Development Ser.). 288p. 1994. 49.95 (*1-56639-225-X*); pap. 19.95 (*1-56639-226-8*) Temple U Pr.

Detroit Longitudinal Study, 1967. Joel Aberbach & Jack Walker. 1974. write for info. (*0-89138-103-1*) ICPSR.

Detroit Memorial Park Cemetery: The Evolution of an African American Corporation. Roberta H. Wright. 1993. write for info. (*0-9629468-1-8*) Charro Bk.

Detroit, Monroe & Toledo Short Line Railway. Wilbur E. Hague & Kirk F. Hise. (Illus.). 80p. (Orig.). 1986. pap. 11.00 (*0-911940-43-X*) Cox.

Detroit Perspectives: Crossroads & Turning Points. Ed. by Wilma W. Henrickson. LC 90-37064. (Great Lakes Bks.). (Illus.). 594p. 1990. 35.00 (*0-8143-2013-9*); pap. 15.95 (*0-8143-2014-7*) Wayne St U Pr.

Detroit Pistons. rev. ed. Richard Rambeck. (NBA Today Ser.). (Illus.). 32p. (J). (gr. 4 up). 1993. lib. bdg. 14.95 (*0-88682-521-0*) Creative Ed.

Detroit Prototype of the NBER Urban Simulation Model. Gregory K. Ingram et al. (Urban & Regional Studies: No. 1). 252p. 1972. text ed. 66.30 (*0-87014-258-5*) Natl Bur Econ Res.

Detroit Publishing Company Collector's Guide. Ed. by James L. Lowe & Ben Papell. LC 75-4127. (Illus.). 288p. 1975. pap. 12.95 (*0-913782-07-6*) Deltiologists Am.

Detroit Publishing Company Handbook & Supplement. rev. ed. Burdick. 96p. 1986. reprint ed. pap. 4.95 (*0-686-40532-3*) Deltiologists Am.

Detroit Race Riot. Robert Shogan & Tom Craig. LC 76-1011. (FDR & the Era of the New Deal Ser.). 1976. reprint ed. lib. bdg. 27.50 (*0-306-70808-6*) Da Capo.

***Detroit Receiving Hospital Emergency Medicine Handbook.** 3rd ed. 1995. write for info. (*1-882663-01-2*) Plymouth MI.

Detroit Recorder's Court, Court Administrator-Clerk of Court Recruitment Project. National Center for State Courts Staff. 93p. 1978. 5.58 (*0-685-15230-8*, NCRO-002) Natl Ctr St Courts.

Detroit Red Wings. Vartan Kupelian. LC 93-47951. (NHL Today Ser.). 32p. (J). 1995. 14.95 (*0-88682-674-8*) Creative Ed.

Detroit Riot of Nineteen Sixty-Seven. Hubert G. Locke. LC 76-79479. (Illus.). 168p. reprint ed. pap. 47.90 (*0-7837-3816-1*, 2043636) Bks Demand.

Detroit River Connections: Historical & Biographical Sketches of the Eastern Great Lakes Border Region. Judy Jacobson. 208p. 1994. pap. 22.50 (*0-685-75125-2*, 9153) Clearfield Co.

Detroit Steel: The New Age of the Great American Performance Car. David Fetherston. (Color Library). (Illus.). 128p. 1994. pap. 15.95 (*1-85532-323-0*, Pub. by Osprey Pubng Ltd UK) Motorbooks Intl.

Detroit Style: Automotive Form 1925-1950. Ed. by Strother MacMinn. (Illus.). 120p. 1985. pap. 9.95 (*0-89558-113-2*) Det Inst Arts.

Detroit Tigers. Lieb. 1976. 20.95 (*0-8488-1578-5*) Amereon Ltd.

Detroit Tigers. Richard Rambeck. (Baseball: The Great American Game Ser.). 48p. (J). (gr. 4-10). 1991. lib. bdg. 14.95 (*0-88682-447-8*) Creative Ed.

Detroit Tigers: A Pictorial Celebration of the Greatest Players & Moments in Tigers' History. William M. Anderson. LC 91-3813. (Illus.). 1991. 39.95 (*0-912083-51-4*) Diamond Communications.

Detroit Tigers: A Pictorial Celebration of the Greatest Players & Moments in Tigers' History. William M. Anderson. LC 91-3813. (Illus.). 1992. 21.95 (*0-912083-55-7*) Diamond Communications.

Detroit Tigers: An Illustrated History. Gerald Astor & Joe Falls. (Illus.). 256p. 1989. 24.95 (*0-8027-1082-4*) Walker & Co.

Detroit to Fort Sackville, 1778-1779: The Journal of Normand MacLeod. Ed. by William A. Evans & Elizabeth S. Sklar. LC 77-13078. (Illus.). 181p. 1978. text ed. 24.95 (*0-8143-1589-5*) Wayne St U Pr.

Detroit Today. Dennis Cox. (Urban Portrait Color Ser.). 96p. 1991. 22.50 (*1-878005-29-4*) Northmont Pub.

Detroit, Toledo & Ironton R. R. Henry Ford's Railroad. Scott D. Trostel. Ed. by Russell J. Heine. (Ohio Railroad Heritage Ser.). (Illus.). 312p. 1988. 44.95 (*0-925436-02-X*) Cam-Tech Pub.

***Detroit Undercover.** Thomas J. Rundquist. 50p. (Orig.). 1995. pap. 7.95 (*1-884239-08-0*) Nova Media.

Detroit Yiddish Theater, 1920 to 1937. James Miller. LC 67-16851. 196p. reprint ed. pap. 55.90 (*0-7837-3796-3*, 2043616) Bks Demand.

Detruire, Dit-Elle. Marguerite Duras. (FRE.). 1969. pap. 14.95 (*0-7859-0042-X*, F99780) Fr & Eur.

***Detskii Eroticheskii Folklore - Children's Erotic Folklore.** Ed. & Pref. by Mikhail Armalinsky. 70p. (Orig.). (RUS.). 1995. pap. 6.00 (*0-916201-17-1*) M I P Co.

Dette De Coeur. James M. Cain. 245p. (FRE.). 1986. pap. 11.95 (*0-7859-2044-7*, 2070377636) Fr & Eur.

Dettes - A Catskill Legend: Their Story & Their Techniques. Eric Leiser. 264p. 1992. 35.00 (*0-9632705-0-8*) Willowkill Pr.

***Detwiler Directory of Medical Market Sources, 1995.** Ed. by Susan M. Detwiler. 1995. cd-rom 195.00x (*0-9644828-1-9*) S M Detwiler.

***Detwiler Directory of Medical Market Sources, 1995.** 4th ed. Ed. by Susan M. Detwiler. 512p. 1995. pap. 195.00x (*0-9644828-0-0*) S M Detwiler.

***Deucalion.** Brian Caswell. (YA). 1995. 12.95 (*0-7022-2865-6*, Pub. by Univ Queensland Pr AT) Intl Spec Bk.

Deuce. Robert O. Butler. 1994. 25.00 (*0-8050-3197-9*) H Holt & Co.

Deuce. Robert O. Butler. LC 93-6303. 1994. pap. 11.00 (*0-8050-3139-1*, Owl) H Holt & Co.

Deuces & Ladies Wild. large type ed. Richard S. Wheeler. LC 91-24917. 331p. (Orig.). 1992. reprint ed. lib. bdg. 16.95 (*1-56054-246-2*) Thorndike Pr.

Deus Destroyed: The Image of Christianity in Early Modern Japan. George Elison. LC 88-10944. (East Asian Monographs: No. 141). 564p. 1988. reprint ed. pap. 18.00 (*0-674-19962-6*) HUP.

Deus E Grande, Deus E Bom. Michael Griffith. 120p. (POR.). 1991. pap. 5.95 (*0-8297-1651-3*) Life Pubs Intl.

Deus Irae. Philip K. Dick & Roger Zelazny. LC 92-47045. 192p. 1993. pap. 8.00 (*0-02-031589-9*, Pub. by Gebrueder Borntraeger GW) Macmillan.

Deus Machine: A Novel. Pierre Ouellette. LC 93-18767. 1994. 22.50 (*0-679-42407-5*, Villard Bks) Random.

Deutero-Pauline Letters: Ephesians, Colossians, Second Thessalonians, First-Second Timothy, Titus. J. Paul Sampley et al. LC 93-31816. (Proclamation Commentaries Ser.). 1993. 10.00 (*0-8006-2802-0*) Augsburg Fortress.

Deuteromycete Studies: Collected Mycological Papers. R. T. Moore. (Bibliotheca Mycologica Ser.: Vol. 108). (Illus.). 180p. 1987. pap. text ed. 58.50 (*3-443-59009-8*) Lubrecht & Cramer.

Deuteronomic History. Terence E. Fretheim. Ed. by Lloyd R. Bailey & Victory P. Furnish. 160p. (Orig.). 1983. pap. 10.95 (*0-687-10497-1*, 82-20593) Abingdon.

Deuteronomio: El Evangelio del Amor (Comentario Biblico Portavoz) Samuel J. Schultz. Orig. Title: Deuteronomy (Everyman's Bible Commentary). 122p. (SPA.). 1979. pap. 5.99 (*0-8254-1658-2*) Kregel.

Deuteronomistic History. Martin Noth. 153p. (C). 1990. 12.50 (*0-905774-30-2*, Pub. by Sheffield Acad UK) CUP Services.

Deuteronomistische Pentateuchredaktion in Exodus 3-17. Werner Fuss. (Beiheft 126 zur Zeitschrift fuer die Alttestamentliche Wissenschaft Ser.). xii, 406p. (C). 1972. 123.10 (*3-11-003854-4*) De Gruyter.

Deuteronomy. A. D. Mayes. (New Century Bible Ser.). 352p. 1979. 15.95 (*0-551-00804-0*) Attic Pr.

Deuteronomy. A. D. Mayes. Ed. by Ronald E. Clements. (New Century Bible Commentary Ser.). 1981. pap. 19.99 (*0-8028-1882-X*) Eerdmans.

Deuteronomy. Eugene H. Merrill. LC 94-12543. (New American Commentary Ser.: Vol. 4). 480p. 1994. 27.99 (*0-8054-0104-0*, 4201-04) Broadman.

Deuteronomy. Patrick D. Miller. (Interpretation: a Bible Commentary for Preaching & Teaching Ser.). 276p. (Orig.). 1990. text ed. 22.00 (*0-8042-3105-2*) Westminster John Knox.

Deuteronomy. Samuel Schultz. (Everyman's Bible Commentary Ser.). 128p. (Orig.). (C). 1971. pap. 7.99 (*0-8024-2005-2*) Moody.

Deuteronomy. J. A. Thompson. Ed. by D. J. Wiseman. LC 74-14303. (Tyndale Old Testament Commentary Ser.). 320p. 1975. 17.99 (*0-87784-882-3*, 882); pap. 11.99 (*0-87784-255-8*, 255) InterVarsity.

Deuteronomy, Chapters 1-11. Moshe Weinfeld. 1991. 35.00 (*0-385-17593-0*) Doubleday.

Deuteronomy: A Commentary. Gerhard Von Rad. LC 66-23088. (Old Testament Library). 212p. 1966. 21.00 (*0-664-20734-0*, Westminster) Westminster John Knox.

Deuteronomy: A Favored Book of Jesus. Bernard N. Schneider. pap. 6.99 (*0-88469-051-2*) BMH Bks.

An Asterisk (*) at the beginning of an entry indicates that the title is appearing in BIP for the first time.

Deuteronomy: Critical & Exegetical Commentary. Samuel R. Driver. LC 02-25926. (International Critical Commentary Ser.). 556p. 1902. 39.95 (*0-567-05003-3*, Pub. by T & T Clark UK) Bks Intl VA.

Deuteronomy see Daily Study Bible - Old Testament

Deuteronomy see Concordant Version of the Old Testament

Deuteronomy & City Life: A Form Criticism of Texts with the Word City ('ir) in Deuteronomy 4: 41 -26: 19. Don C. Benjamin. LC 83-3609. (Illus.). 366p. (Orig.). (C). 1983. pap. text ed. 30.00 (*0-8191-3139-3*) U Pr of Amer.

Deuteronomy & the Death of Moses: A Theological Reading. Dennis T. Olson. LC 94-12729. 1994. pap. 14.00 (*0-8006-2639-7*, Fortress Pr) Augsburg Fortress.

Deuteronomy & the Deuteronomic School. Moshe Weinfeld. LC 91-41324. xviii, 467p. 1992. reprint ed. 27.50 (*0-931464-40-4*) Eisenbrauns.

Deuteronomy (Everyman's Bible Commentary) see Deuteronomio: El Evangelio del Amor (Comentario Biblico Portavoz)

Deuteronomy, with Excursus on Covenant & Law. Richard Clifford. LC 82-81222. (Old Testament Message Ser.: Vol. 4). 195p. 1982. pap. 12.95 (*0-8146-5239-5*) Liturgical Pr.

Deutsch: Erleben Wir Es! 2nd ed. Edda Weiss. Ed. by Joan Saslow. LC 80-16484. (Illus.). 344p. (GER.). (gr. 10). 1981. text ed. 29.00 (*0-07-069215-7*) McGraw.

Deutsch: Erleben Wir Es, Level 2. Edda Weiss. LC 72-8377. (Learning German the Modern Way Ser.). (Illus.). 418p. (gr. 10-12). 1973. text ed. 30.64 (*0-07-069081-2*) McGraw.

Deutsch: Intermediate German Lessons, 2 vols. Hugo Mueller. 350p. 1967. Bk. 1, pt. 2. 25.50 (*0-87559-207-4*); Bk. 3, 246p., 1973 German Lessons for Advanced Students. 22.50 (*0-87559-208-2*) Shalom.

Deutsch: Schritt Fur Schritt. Elke Godfrey. 576p. (C). 1986. text ed. 31.00 (*0-13-203380-1*) P-H.

***Deutsch: Schritt fur Schritt.** 2nd ed. Godfrey. (Illus.). 560p. 1994. text ed. write for info. (*0-13-203308-9*) P-H.

Deutsch: Schritt fur Schritt. 2nd ed. Elke Godfrey. (C). text ed. write for info. (*0-13-204017-4*) P-H.

Deutsch Aktiv, Level 1, Level 2. Incl. Lehrbuch Gerd Neuner et al. (Illus.). 160p. text ed. 15.95 (*3-468-49900-0*); Arbeitsbuch Gerd Neuner et al. 136p. 11.25 (*3-468-49901-9*); Lehrerhandbuch Gerd Neuner et al. 141p. 9.95 (*3-468-49902-7*); Glossary-English Gerd Neuner et al. 64p. 5.50 (*3-468-49930-2*); Glossary-French Gerd Neuner et al. 64p. 5.50 (*3-468-49931-0*); Austrian Supplement Gerd Neuner et al. 29p. 4.50 (*3-468-49905-1*); Companion Grammar Gerd Neuner et al. 96p. 10.00 (*3-468-49906-X*); Cassette 1A Gerd Neuner et al. 10.95 (*3-468-84450-6*); Cassette 1B Gerd Neuner et al. 10.95 (*3-468-84451-4*); Begleitheft zu Cassette 1B Gerd Neuner et al. 32p. 6.95 (*3-468-49903-5*); Cassette 1C Gerd Neuner et al. 10.95 (*3-468-84452-2*); Folien Gerd Neuner et al. Thirty transparencies. trans. 109.95 (*3-468-49904-3*); Tests Gerd Neuner et al. 33p. 51.95 (*3-468-49909-4*); write for info. (*0-318-56963-9*) Langenscheidt.

***Deutsch Aktiv, Level 2.** Incl. Cassette 2B Gerd Neuner et al. 10.95 (*3-468-84462-X*); Arbeitsbuch Gerd Neuner et al. 128p. 11.25 (*3-468-49911-6*); Lehrerhandbuch Gerd Neuner et al. 148p. 9.25 (*3-468-49912-4*); Glossary-English Gerd Neuner et al. 41p. 5.50 (*3-468-49940-X*); Glossary-French Gerd Neuner et al. 41p. 5.50 (*3-468-49941-8*); Companion Grammar Gerd Neuner et al. 96p. 9.95 (*3-468-49916-7*); Cassette 2A1 Gerd Neuner et al. 10.95 (*3-468-84460-3*); Cassette 2A2 Gerd Neuner et al. 10.95 (*3-468-84461-1*); Begleitheft zu Cassette 2B Gerd Neuner et al. 39p. 6.95 (*3-468-49913-2*); Folien Gerd Neuner et al. trans. 109.95 (*3-468-84463-8*); write for info. (*0-318-56962-0*) Langenscheidt.

Deutsch Aktiv, Level 3. Incl. Materialien fur die Mittelstuffe, Teil 1. Lehrbuch. Edelhoff et al. 96p. 15.95 (*3-468-49920-5*); Materialien fur die Mittelstuffe, Teil 2. Lehrbuch. Edelhoff et al. 112p. 15.95 (*3-468-49925-6*); Arbeitsbuch, Teile 1 & 2. Edelhoff et al. 136p. 13.95 (*3-468-49921-3*); Lehrerhandbuch, Teil 1. Edelhoff et al. 168p. 25.00 (*3-468-49922-1*); Cassette 3, Teil 1. Edelhoff et al. 10.95 (*3-468-84470-0*); Cassette 3, Teil 2. Edelhoff et al. 10.95 (*3-468-84471-9*); write for info. (*0-318-68064-5*) Langenscheidt.

Deutsch Aktiv Neu, Grundstufe 1 (Chapters 1-12) Incl. Lehrbuch. text ed. 20.95 (*3-468-49160-3*); Arbeitsbuch. 17.50 (*3-468-49161-1*); write for info. (*0-318-68074-2*) Langenscheidt.

Deutsch Aktiv Neu, Grundstufe 2 (Chapters 13-24) Incl. Lehrbuch. text ed. 20.95 (*3-468-49165-4*); Arbeitsbuch. 17.50 (*3-468-49166-2*); write for info. (*0-318-68075-0*) Langenscheidt.

Deutsch Aktiv Neu, Level 1A. Incl. Lehrbuch. Gerd Neuner et al. text ed. 13.95 (*3-468-49100-X*); Arbeitsbuch. Gerd Neuner et al. 11.25 (*3-468-49101-8*); Glossar-English. Neuner et al. 1987. 5.50 (*3-468-49103-4*); Glossar-French. Neuner et al. 1987. 5.50 (*3-468-49104-2*); Cassette 1A-1. Neuner et al. 1987. 10.95 (*3-468-84550-2*); Cassette 1A-2(a&b) Neuner et al. 1987. 24.95 (*3-468-84551-0*); Begleitheft zu Cassette 1A-2(a&b) Neuner et al. 1987. 5.25 (*3-468-49110-7*); Lehrerhandreichungen. Neuner et al. 1987. 23.95 (*3-468-49102-6*); Folien. Neuner et al. 42.50p. 1994. 109.95 (*3-468-84552-9*); 1987. write for info. (*0-318-68065-3*) Langenscheidt.

Deutsch Aktiv Neu, Level 1B. Incl. Lehrbuch. Gerd Neuner et al. text ed. 14.95 (*3-468-49120-4*); Arbeitsbuch. Neuner et al. 12.25 (*3-468-49121-2*); Glossar-English. Neuner et al. 6.50 (*3-468-49123-9*); Glossar-French. Neuner et al. 6.50 (*3-468-49124-7*); Cassette 1B-1. Neuner et al. 1988. 10.95 (*3-468-84555-3*); Cassette 1B-2(a&b) Neuner et al. 1988. 24.95 (*3-468-84556-1*); Begleitheft zu Cassette 1B-2(a&b) Neuner et al. 1988. 5.25 (*3-468-49130-1*); Lehrerhandreichungen. Neuner et al. 23.95 (*3-468-49122-0*); Folien. Neuner et al. 109.95 (*3-468-84557-X*); 1988p. 1988. write for info. (*0-318-68066-1*) Langenscheidt.

Deutsch Aktiv Neu, Level 1C. Incl. Lehrbuch. text ed. 15.95 (*3-468-49140-9*); Arbeitsbuch. 13.00 (*3-468-49141-7*); Glossar-English. 5.50 (*3-468-49143-3*); Glossar-French. 5.50 (*3-468-49144-1*); Cassette 1C. 10.95 (*3-468-84560-X*); Lehrerhandreichungen. 23.95 (*3-468-49142-5*); Folien. 109.95 (*3-468-84562-6*); 1989. write for info. (*0-318-68067-X*) Langenscheidt.

Deutsch Als Fremdsprache: Neubearbeitung. K. Braun et al. Incl. Pt. 1. Grundkurs. text ed. 19.95 (*3-12-554400-9*); (*0-318-55655-3*) Schoenhof.

Deutsch-Chinesische Beziehungen in Geschichte & Gegenwart. Ed. by Heng-yo Kuo & Leutner Mechthild. (Berliner China-Studien Ser.: Vol. 19). 445p. (GER.). 1990. pap. 36.00 (*3-597-10615-3*) K G Saur.

Deutsch-Chinesisches Standard Handworterbuch: Standard German-Chinese Dictionary. Commercial Press Staff. 1364p. (CHI & GER.). 1979. 49.95 (*0-8288-4753-3*, M9265) Fr & Eur.

***Deutsch-Deutsch: Ein Satirisches Woerterbuch.** Ernst Rohl. 103p. (GER.). 1991. 29.95 (*0-7859-8322-8*, 3359004957) Fr & Eur.

Deutsch-Ewe, Pt. II. Diedrich Westermann. (B. E. Ser.: No. 178). (GER.). 1906. 20.00 (*0-8115-3090-6*) Periodicals Srv.

Deutsch-Finnisches Schulworterbuch. A. Rosentahl et al. 673p. (FIN & GER.). 1976. 39.95 (*0-8288-5577-3*, M9637) Fr & Eur.

Deutsch Fuer Auslaender: Grundstufe. Hermann Kessler. Incl. Pt. 1. Leichter Anfang (Lehrbuch) pap. text ed. 16.95 (*0-685-47452-6*); Pt. 1a. Leichte Aufgaben (Arbeitsheft) pap. text ed. 9.95 (*0-685-47453-4*); Pt. 1b. Leichte Erzaelungen (Leseband) pap. text ed. 3.90 (*0-685-47455-0*); Pt. 1c. Sprachlaboruebungen. 3.90 (*0-685-47456-9*); Tonbaender fuer das Sprachlabor. audio 260.00 (*0-685-47457-7*); Tonband mit Lehrbuchtexten. audio 29.25 (*0-685-47458-5*); Set pap. write for info. (*0-318-55656-1*) Schoenhof.

Deutsch Fuer Auslaender: Mittelstufe. Incl. Pt. 2. Schneller Fortgang (Lehrbuch) Hermann Kessler. pap. text ed. 16.95 (*0-685-47459-3*); Pt. 2a. Kurze Uebungen (Arbeitsheft) Hermann Kessler. 9.95 (*0-685-47460-7*); Pt. 2b. Kurze Geschichten (Leseband) Hermann Kessler. pap. text ed. 3.90 (*0-685-47462-3*); Pt. 2c. Sprachlaboruebungen. 3.90 (*0-685-47463-1*); Tonbaender fuer das Sprachlabor. 260.00 (*0-685-47464-X*); Tonband mit Lehrbuchtexten. 29.25 (*0-685-47465-8*); Set pap. text ed. write for info. (*0-318-55657-X*) Schoenhof.

Deutsch Fuer Auslaender: Oberstufe. Hermann Kessler. Incl. Pt. 3. Deutschlandkunde (Lehrbuch) pap. text ed. 13.00 (*0-685-47466-6*); Pt. 3b. Moderne Dichtungen (Leseband) pap. text ed. 29.25 (*0-685-47467-4*); Pt. 3d. Dichter unserer Zeit. pap. text ed. 29.25 (*0-685-47469-0*); Set pap. write for info. (*0-318-55658-8*) Schoenhof.

***Deutsch Fur Alle.** 4th ed. Werner Haas et al. 1994. audio, text ed. write for info. (*0-471-11075-2*) Wiley.

Deutsch Fur Alle: Beginning College German - A Comprehensive Approach. 3rd ed. Werner Haas & Gustave B. Mathieu. 360p. 1987. Net. student ed write for info. (*0-471-83118-2*); teacher ed 30.00 (*0-471-85425-5*); Net. text ed. write for info. (*0-471-83115-8*) Wiley.

Deutsch Fur Alle: Beginning College German: A Comprehensive Approach. 4th ed. Werner Haas & Doris F. Merrifield. Ed. by Gustave B. Mathieu. 576p. (C). 1993. Net. text ed. write for info. (*0-471-57381-7*) Wiley.

Deutsch Fur Studenten Spicher Sprache-Aleman Para Estudiantes De Habla Espanola, Vol. 1. Hanne G. Reck. LC 78-18825. 193p. 1979. pap. text ed. 6.00 (*0-8477-3321-1*) U of PR Pr.

Deutsch Heute. 3rd ed. Jack R. Moeller & Helmut Liedloff. LC 83-81521. 480p. (GER.). 1984. audio 2.75 (*0-685-08252-0*) HM.

Deutsch Heute, 5 Vols. 5th ed. Jack R. Moeller et al. (C). 1992. text ed. 51.56 (*0-395-47299-7*) HM.

Deutsch Heute Nev Ausgabe. Sidwell & Capoore. write for info. (*0-318-69853-6*) Heinle & Heinle.

Deutsch Hier. Theo Scherling et al. 176p. (GER.). 1982. 14.95 (*3-468-49980-9*); trans. 109.95 (*3-468-84506-5*); audio 20.00 (*3-468-84505-7*); 15.95 (*3-468-49981-7*); 10.50 (*3-468-49989-2*) Langenscheidt.

***Deutsch Hier, Posters.** Theo Scherling et al. 1982. 43.95 (*3-468-84507-3*) Langenscheidt.

***Deutsch-Hindi Woerterbuch.** Krishna M. Sharma. 1216p. (GER & HIN.). 1978. 150.00 (*0-7859-8526-3*, 3873481014) Fr & Eur.

***Deutsch? Ja, Bitte.** Ed. by Editors of ELI Staff. (Illus.). 93p. (Orig.). (GER.). (J). (gr. 2-6). 1987. pap. 9.95 (*88-85148-04-2*, Pub. by Europ Lang Inst IT) Midwest European Pubns.

***Deutsch? Ja, Bitte, Band 2.** Ed. by Editors of ELI Staff. (Illus.). 98p. (Orig.). (GER.). (J). (gr. 2-6). 1990. pap. 9.95 (*88-85148-10-7*, Pub. by Europ Lang Inst IT) Midwest European Pubns.

***Deutsch? Ja, Bitte, Band 3.** Ed. by Editors of ELI Staff. (Illus.). 100p. (Orig.). (GER.). (J). (gr. 6-10). 1992. pap. 9.95 (*88-85148-43-3*, Pub. by Europ Lang Inst IT) Midwest European Pubns.

Deutsch Konkret, Level 1. Gerd Neuner & Peter Desmarets. Incl. Set. Textbook, 3 vols. 256p. 1983. 15.50 (*0-88729-754-4*); Lehrbuch. 96p. 1983. pap. text ed. 12.00 (*3-468-49850-0*); English Workbook. 128p. 1984. 9.95 (*3-468-96746-2*); Arbeitsbuch. 79p. 1983. 9.50 (*3-468-49851-9*); Glossar English. 17p. 1984. 4.95 (*3-468-49853-5*); Glossar French. 17p. 1984. 4.95 (*3-468-49854-3*); Teacher's Manual. 56p. 1984. 13.25 (*3-468-96747-0*); Lehrerhandreichungen. 112p. 1984. 11.95 (*3-468-49852-7*); Cassette 1A. 1984. 20.00 (*3-468-84430-3*); Cassette 1B. 1984. 29.95 (*3-468-84431-X*); Begleitheft zu Cassette 1B. 5.50 (*3-468-49859-4*); Folien, 30 transparencies. 1984. 109.95 (*3-468-84434-4*); Tests. 42.50 (*3-468-96743-8*); Resource Pkg. 49.95 (*3-468-49882-9*); write for info. (*0-318-68076-9*) Langenscheidt.

Deutsch Konkret, Level 2. Incl. Set. Textbook, 3 vols. 136p. 1984. 15.50 (*0-88729-755-2*); Set. Textbook, 2 vols. 168p. 1985. 12.95 (*0-88729-751-X*); Lehrbuch. 120p. 1984. pap. text ed. 12.00 (*3-468-49860-8*); English Workbook. 128p. 1986. 9.95 (*3-468-96748-9*); Arbeitsbuch. 96p. 1985. 9.50 (*3-468-49861-6*); Glossar English. 31p. 1985. 5.50 (*3-468-49863-2*); Glossar French. 32p. 1985. 5.50 (*3-468-49864-0*); Teacher's Manual. 80p. 1988. 13.25 (*3-468-96749-7*); Lehrerhandreichungen. 108p. 1987. 11.95 (*3-468-49862-4*); Cassette 2A. 1985. 20.00 (*3-468-84530-8*); Folien. 109.95 (*3-468-84534-0*); Tests. 42.50 (*3-468-49878-0*); Resource Pkg. 49.95 (*3-468-49883-7*); write for info. (*0-318-68077-7*) Langenscheidt.

Deutsch Konkret, Level 3. Incl. Set. Textbook, 3 vols. 120p. 1985. 15.50 (*0-88729-756-0*); Lehrbuch. Reiner Schmidt. 120p. 1985. text ed. 12.00 (*3-468-49870-5*); English Workbook. 128p. 1987. 12.00 (*3-468-96752-7*); Arbeitsbuch. 112p. 1986. 7.95 (*3-468-49871-3*); Glossar English. 24p. 1988. 5.50 (*3-468-49873-X*); Glossar French. 24p. 1988. 5.50 (*3-468-49874-8*); Lehrerhandreichungen. 96p. 1989. 14.95 (*3-468-49872-1*); Cassette 3A. 20.00 (*3-468-84540-5*); Folien. 109.95 (*3-468-84544-8*); Tests. 42.50 (*3-468-49879-9*); write for info. (*0-318-68091-2*) Langenscheidt.

***Deutsch-Kurdisch Woerterbuch.** Amirxan. 611p. (GER & KUR.). 1992. 150.00 (*0-7859-7243-9*, 3190063486) Fr & Eur.

Deutsch-Lateinisches Worter-Buch, 2 vols. in 1. Johann L. Frisch. (Documenta Linguistica, Reihe II Ser.). xviii, 1299p. 1977. reprint ed. write for info. (*3-487-06328-X*, Pub. by Georg Olms GW) Lubrecht & Cramer.

Deutsch Mit Emil. Ed. by Helga Tilton. (C). 1980. pap. text ed. 16.95 (*0-393-95111-1*) Norton.

Deutsch mit Erfolg, Level 1. Heinz Griesbach. 256p. (GER.). 1983. 20.00 (*3-468-49770-9*); 17.50 (*3-468-49771-7*); 5.25 (*3-468-49775-X*) Langenscheidt.

Deutsch mit Erfolg, No. 1A. Heinz Griesbach. 256p. (GER.). 1983. audio 20.00 (*3-468-84720-3*) Langenscheidt.

Deutsch mit Erfolg, No. 1B. Heinz Griesbach. 256p. (GER.). 1983. audio 20.00 (*3-468-84721-1*) Langenscheidt.

Deutsch mit Erfolg, No. 1C1-10. Heinz Griesbach. 256p. (GER.). 1983. audio 174.50 (*3-468-84722-X*) Langenscheidt.

Deutsch Mit Erfolg, Level 2. 240p. 20.95 (*3-468-49780-6*); 20.00 (*3-468-84741-6*) Langenscheidt.

Deutsch; Na Klar! An Introductory Course. Lida Baldwin & Michael Busges. 1991. pap. text ed. write for info. (*0-07-016844-X*) McGraw.

Deutsch Na Klar! An Introductory Course. Robert Di Donato et al. 1991. Instr's ed. teacher ed, text ed. write for info. (*0-07-557029-7*); Wkbk. pap. text ed. write for info. (*0-07-557027-0*) McGraw.

***Deutsch, Na Klar! An Introductory German Course.** 2nd ed. Robert Di Donato et al. LC 94-40903. 1994. student ed write for info. (*0-07-016969-1*); teacher ed write for info. (*0-07-016970-5*) McGraw.

Deutsch Naturlich! Gerhard Clausing & Lana Rings. (C). 1986. Tapescript; reel to reel recordings; cassettes & transparencies. write for info. (*0-318-62575-X*) HM.

Deutsch-Persisches Fachwoerterbuch Fuer Naturwissenschaft, Medezin und Landwirtschaft. B. Habibi. 240p. (GER & PER.). 1964. pap. 65.00 (*0-8288-6759-3*, M-7331, Pub. by Harrassowitz) Fr & Eur.

***Deutsch-Russiches, Russiches-Deutsch Woerterbuch.** A. W. Karelskij. 765p. (GER & RUS.). 1991. 39.95 (*0-7859-8546-8*, 3894510978) Fr & Eur.

***Deutsch-Russiches, Russiches-Deutsches Woerterbuch.** 2nd ed. Emilja Rimaschewskaja. 935p. (GER & RUS.). 1991. 69.95 (*0-7859-8547-6*, 3894511109) Fr & Eur.

***Deutsch-Russisches Woerterbuch, 2 vols.** 3rd ed. Bielfeldt. 2253p. (GER & RUS.). 1991. 295.00 (*0-7859-7441-5*, 3050017767) Fr & Eur.

***Deutsch-Russisches Woerterbuch fur Lernzwecke.** Evgenia Iwanowa. (GER & RUS.). 1992. 49.95 (*0-7859-8545-X*, 3894510803) Fr & Eur.

Deutsch-Russische Wirtschaftssprache. N. Grischen. 480p. (GER & RUS.). 1969. 75.00 (*0-8288-6571-X*, M-7332) Fr & Eur.

Deutsch-Russisches Meteorologisches Worterbuch: German - Russian Meteorological Dictionary. W. G. Martschenko. 392p. (GER & RUS.). 1973. 19.95 (*0-8288-6234-6*, M-9092) Fr & Eur.

Deutsch-Russisches Satzlexikon: German-Russian Syntax Lexicon, 2 vols., Set. K. A. Paffen. 1680p. (GER & RUS.). 1980. 110.00 (*0-8288-2310-3*, F19660) Fr & Eur.

Deutsch-Russisches Woerterbuch des Eisenbahn Wesens. 3rd ed. N. A. Fridman. 807p. (GER & RUS.). 1987. 95.00 (*0-8288-2371-5*, M1981) Fr & Eur.

Deutsch-Russisches Worterbuch der Forstund Holzwirtschaft: German-Russian Dictionary of Forestry of the Lumber Industry. E. A. Pawlow & O. I. Semjonowa. 477p. (GER & RUS.). 1978. 29.95 (*0-8288-4870-X*, M9058) Fr & Eur.

Deutsch-Russisches Worterbuch der Rechentechnik und Datenverarbeitung. deluxe ed. W. A. Scharow & A. L. Nowitschkowa. 400p. (GER & RUS.). 1976. 24.95 (*0-8288-5578-1*, M9057) Fr & Eur.

Deutsch-Russisches Worterbuch fur Eisenbahnwesen. A. P. Sulima-Samujillo et al. 536p. (GER & RUS.). 1960. pap. 24.95 (*0-8288-6834-4*, M-9069) Fr & Eur.

Deutsch-Russisches Worterbuch fur Eisenbahnwessen. D. A. Bunin et al. 531p. (GER & RUS.). 1957. 14.95 (*0-7859-0796-3*, M9060) Fr & Eur.

Deutsch-Russisches Worterbuch fur Ozeanographie. deluxe ed. N. N. Gorski et al. 240p. (GER & RUS.). 1957. 24.95 (*0-8288-6857-3*, M-9104) Fr & Eur.

Deutsch-Russisches Worterbuch fur Wasserbau. deluxe ed. L. B. Bernstein. 579p. (GER & RUS.). 1961. 39.95 (*0-8288-6814-X*, M9100) Fr & Eur.

***Deutsch-Schwabisch Eichborn Dialeky-Lexikon.** Reinhard Von Normann. (GER.). 1989. 19.95 (*0-7859-8505-0*, 3821812591) Fr & Eur.

Deutsch-Spanisches Glossarium Finanz und Wirtschaft: German - Spanish Glossary of Finance & Economics. Mario R. Lerche. 460p. (GER & SPA.). 1967. 75.00 (*0-8288-6671-6*, M8176) Fr & Eur.

Deutsch Syntax: Ansichten und Aussichten. Ed. by Ludger Hoffmann. (Institut fuer Deutsche Sprache - Jahrbuch, 1991 Ser.). vi, 613p. (GER.). (C). 1992. lib. bdg. 144.65 (*3-11-013706-2*) De Gruyter.

***Deutsch-Turkisches Woerterbuch.** Herbert Jansky. 502p. (GER & TUR.). 1961. 175.00 (*0-7859-8364-3*, 3447004924) Fr & Eur.

***Deutsch-Turkisches Woerterbuch.** 2nd ed. Karl Steuerwald. 669p. (GER & TUR.). 1987. 295.00 (*0-7859-8366-X*, 3447015845) Fr & Eur.

Deutsch-Turkisches Worterbuch Fur Technische Berufe. 2nd deluxe ed. Sadettin Bilginer. 448p. (GER & TUR.). 1966. 75.00 (*0-8288-6701-1*, M7348) Fr & Eur.

Deutsch Warum Nicht auf, Bk. 1: German Lessons for Beginners. Hannelore Driessle & Myrtle Rognebakke. 221p. 1972. 22.50 (*0-87559-206-6*) Shalom.

Deutsch X 3. Incl. Gespraechsbuch II "Meine Meinung" (Illus.). 1978. pap. text ed. 4.30 (*3-468-49656-7*); Glossar III, Einsprachig Deutsch. 1978. pap. text ed. 2.10 (*0-685-03165-9*); Lehrerheft III. 1978. pap. text ed. 2.10 (*0-685-03166-7*); Leseheft III, "Aktuell und interessant": Die wichtigsten Staedte in den deutsch sprachigen Laendern. (Illus.). 1978. pap. text ed. 3.75 (*0-685-03167-5*); Loesungsheft III. 1978. pap. text ed. 2.10 (*0-685-03168-3*); Sprachlabor-Cassetten II mit Sprechuebungen. 1978. audio (*0-685-60100-5*); Sprachlabor-Tonbaender II mit Sprechuebungen. 1978. audio (*0-685-60101-3*); Sprechuebungen II. 1978. pap. text ed. (*3-468-49646-X*); Text-Cassette II mit ausgewaehlten Lektionstexten. 1978. audio 10.90 (*0-685-03169-1*); Uebungsbuch III. 1978. pap. text ed. 3.20 (*0-685-03170-5*); 1978. write for info. (*0-318-54160-2*) M S Rosenberg.

Deutsch Zusammen: A Communicative Course in German. Frank E. Donahue & Johanna Watzinger. 624p. (C). 1990. text ed. write for info. (*0-13-204991-0*) P-H.

Deutsch Zusammen: A Communicative Course in German. Frank E. Donahue & Johanna Watzinger. 624p. (C). 1990. pap. text ed. write for info. (*0-13-205006-4*) P-H.

Deutsche Aussprache: Reine und gemaessigte Hochlautung mit Aussprachewoerterbuch. 19th rev. ed. Siebs. (C). 1984. 29.25 (*3-11-000325-2*) De Gruyter.

Deutsche Barockliteratur Von Opitz Bix Brockes. Victor M. Sammlung. iv, 96p. 1966. reprint ed. write for info. (*0-318-71863-4*, Pub. by Georg Olms GW) Lubrecht & Cramer.

Deutsche Bibliographie des Buddhismus. Hans L. Held. viii, 190p. 1973. reprint ed. write for info. (*3-487-04572-9*, Pub. by Georg Olms GW) Lubrecht & Cramer.

Deutsche Buchhandel und die Geistigen Stromungen der Letzten Hundert Jahre. Friedrich Schulze. 296p. 1990. reprint ed. write for info. (*3-487-09139-9*, Pub. by Georg Olms GW) Lubrecht & Cramer.

Deutsche Buchhandler, Deutsche Buchdrucker, 6 vols. in 1. Rudolf Schmidt. 1155p. 1979. reprint ed. write for info. (*3-487-06943-1*, Pub. by Georg Olms GW) Lubrecht & Cramer.

Deutsche Drama Des Mittelalters. Wolfgang Michael. (Grundriss der Germanischen Philologie Ser.: Vol. 20). 304p. (C). 1971. 119.25 (*3-11-003310-0*) De Gruyter.

***Deutsche Drucke des Barock 1600-1720: Abstract A, Vol. 8.** Ed. by Saur, K. G., Staff. 1989. write for info. (*3-598-32108-2*) K G Saur.

***Deutsche Drucke des Barock 1600-1720: Abstract A, Vol. 9.** Ed. by Saur, K. G., Staff. 1990. write for info. (*3-598-32109-0*) K G Saur.

***Deutsche Drucke des Barock 1600-1720: Abstract A, Vol. 10.** Ed. by Saur, K. G., Staff. 1994. write for info. (*3-598-32110-4*) K G Saur.

***Deutsche Drucke des Barock 1600-1720: Abstract A, Vol. 11.** Ed. by Saur, K. G., Staff. 1995. write for info. (*3-598-32111-2*) K G Saur.

***Deutsche Drucke des Barock 1600-1720: Abstract A, Vol. 12.** Ed. by Saur, K. G., Staff. 1995. write for info. (*3-598-32112-0*) K G Saur.

***Deutsche Drucke des Barock 1600-1720: Abstract A, Vol. 13.** Ed. by Saur, K. G., Staff. 1995. write for info. (*3-598-32113-9*) K G Saur.

***Deutsche Drucke des Barock 1600-1720: Abstract B, Vol. 12.** Ed. by Saur, K. G., Staff. 1990. write for info. (*3-598-32142-2*) K G Saur.

D

An Asterisk (*) at the beginning of an entry indicates that the title is appearing in BIP for the first time.

1905

***Deutsche Drucke des Barock 1600-1720: Abstract B, Vol. 19.** Ed. by Saur, K. G., Staff. 1992. write for info. (*3-598-32149-X*) K G Saur.

***Deutsche Drucke des Barock 1600-1720: Abstract B, Vol. 20.** Ed. by Saur, K. G., Staff. 1992. write for info. (*3-598-32150-3*) K G Saur.

***Deutsche Drucke des Barock 1600-1720: Abstract C, Vol. 4.** Ed. by Saur, K. G., Staff. 1988. write for info. (*3-598-32164-3*) K G Saur.

***Deutsche Drucke des Barock 1600-1720: Abstract C, Vol. 5.** Ed. by Saur, K. G., Staff. 1989. write for info. (*3-598-32165-1*) K G Saur.

***Deutsche Drucke des Barock 1600-1720: Abstract C, Vol. 6.** Ed. by Saur, K. G., Staff. 1989. write for info. (*3-598-32166-X*) K G Saur.

***Deutsche Drucke des Barock 1600-1720: Abstract C; Register zu den Banden.** Ed. by Saur, K. G., Staff. 1988. write for info. (*3-598-32800-1*) K G Saur.

***Deutsche Drucke des Barock 1600-1720: Abstract D, Vol. 1.** Ed. by Saur, K. G., Staff. 1993. write for info. (*3-598-32181-3*) K G Saur.

***Deutsche Drucke des Barock 1600-1720: Abstract D, Vol. 2.** Ed. by Saur, K. G., Staff. 1994. write for info. (*3-598-32182-1*) K G Saur.

Deutsche Drucke des Barock, 1600-1720: Katalog der Herzog August Bibliothek Wolfenbuttel, Abt B, Bd. 18. 334p. (GER.). 1992. lib. bdg. 225.00 (*3-598-32148-1*) K G Saur.

Deutsche Drucke des Barock, 1600-1720 - Katalog der Herzog August Bibliothek Wolfenbuttel: Deutsche Geschichte-Besonderes Abt. B, Band 13. ix, 280p. (GER.). 1990. lib. bdg. 230.00 (*3-598-32143-0*) K G Saur.

Deutsche Drucke des Barock 1600-1720 - Katalog der Herzog August Bibliothek Wolfgenbuttel: Deutsche geschichte-Allgemeines Abt. B, Band 11. ix, 272p. (GER.). 1990. lib. bdg. 230.00 (*3-598-32141-4*) K G Saur.

Deutsche Drucke des Barock 1600-1720 - Katalog der Herzog August Bibliothek Wolfgenbuttel: Historische Hilfswissenschaften - (A-N) ABT.B Band 9. ix, 265p. (GER.). 1990. lib. bdg. 230.00 (*3-598-32139-2*) K G Saur.

Deutsche Drucke des Barock 1600-1720 - Katalog der Herzog August Bibliothek Wolfgenbuttel: Neuere Geschichte (0-Z) - ABT - Band 10. v, 279p. (GER.). 1990. lib. bdg. 230.00 (*3-598-32140-6*) K G Saur.

Deutsche Drucke des Barock 1600-1720 in der Herzog August Bibliothek Wolfenbuttel Abteilung B: Mittlere Aufstellung Vol. 3: Theologica 1. Ed. by Martin Bircher. (Illus.). ix, 445p. 1986. lib. bdg. 160.00 (*3-598-32133-3*) K G Saur.

Deutsche Drucke des Barock 1600-1720 in der Herzog August Bibliothek Wolfenbuttel Abteilung B: Mittlere Aufstellung Vol. 5: Theologica 3. Ed. by Martin Bircher. (Illus.). ix, 491p. 1986. lib. bdg. 160.00 (*3-598-32135-X*) K G Saur.

Deutsche Drucke des Barock, 1600-1720, in der Herzog August Bibliothek Wolfenbuttel Abt. B Vol. 8: Biographische Schriften. ix, 321p. 1989. lib. bdg. write for info. (*3-598-32138-4*) K G Saur.

Deutsche Drucke des Barock, 1600-1720 in der Herzog August Bibliothek Wolfenbuttel, Abt. B-Vol. 7: Allgemeines, Buchwesen, Geographie, Wissenschaftskunde, Historische Hilfswissenschaften. (Illus.). ix, 272p. 1989. lib. bdg. write for info. (*3-598-32137-6*) K G Saur.

Deutsche Drucke des Barock 1600-1720 in der Herzog August Bibliothek Wolfenbuttel Abteilung B: Mittlere Aufstellung Vol. 4: Theologica 2. Ed. by Martin Bircher. (Illus.). ix, 572p. 1986. lib. bdg. 160.00 (*3-598-32134-1*) K G Saur.

Deutsche Drucke des Barock 1600-1720 in der Herzog August Bibliothek Wolfenbuttel Abtwilung B: Mittlere Aufstellung Vol. 6: Theologica 4. Ed. by Martin Bircher. (Illus.). 303p. 1986. lib. bdg. 160.00 (*3-598-32136-8*) K G Saur.

Deutsche Drucke des Barock 1600-1720 in der Herzog August Bibliothek Wolfenmittel, Abteilung A: Bibliotheca Augusta, 13 vols., Set. Ed. by Martin Bircher. write for info. (*3-598-32100-7*) K G Saur.

Deutsche Drucke des Barock 1600-1720 in der Herzog August Bibliothek Wolfenmittel, Abteilung A: Bibliotheca Augusta: Abstract A, 7 vols., Vol. 1. Ed. by Martin Bircher. 346p. 1977. 160.00 (*3-598-32101-5*) K G Saur.

Deutsche Drucke des Barock 1600-1720 in der Herzog August Bibliothek Wolfenmittel, Abteilung A: Bibliotheca Augusta: Abstract A, 7 vols., Vol. 2. Ed. by Martin Bircher. 1979. 160.00 (*3-598-32102-3*) K G Saur.

Deutsche Drucke des Barock 1600-1720 in der Herzog August Bibliothek Wolfenmittel, Abteilung A: Bibliotheca Augusta: Abstract A, 7 vols., Vol. 3. Ed. by Martin Bircher. 311p. 1980. 160.00 (*3-598-32103-1*) K G Saur.

Deutsche Drucke des Barock 1600-1720 in der Herzog August Bibliothek Wolfenmittel, Abteilung A: Bibliotheca Augusta: Abstract A, 7 vols., Vol. 4. Ed. by Martin Bircher. 348p. 1987. 160.00 (*3-598-32104-X*) K G Saur.

Deutsche Drucke des Barock 1600-1720 in der Herzog August Bibliothek Wolfenmittel, Abteilung A: Bibliotheca Augusta: Abstract A, 7 vols., Vol. 5. Ed. by Martin Bircher. 271p. 1980. 160.00 (*3-598-32105-8*) K G Saur.

Deutsche Drucke des Barock 1600-1720 in der Herzog August Bibliothek Wolfenmittel, Abteilung A: Bibliotheca Augusta: Abstract A, 7 vols., Vol. 6. Ed. by Martin Bircher. 271p. 1987. 160.00 (*3-598-32106-6*) K G Saur.

Deutsche Drucke des Barock 1600-1720 in der Herzog August Bibliothek Wolfenmittel, Abteilung A: Bibliotheca Augusta: Abstract A, 7 vols., Vol. 7. Ed. by Martin Bircher. 270p. 1987. 160.00 (*3-598-32107-4*) K G Saur.

Deutsche Drucke des Barock 1600-1720 in der Herzog August Bibliothek, Wolfenmittel, Abteilung B: Mittlere Aufstellung, 20 vols. Ed. by Martin Bircher. write for info. (*3-598-32130-9*) K G Saur.

Deutsche Drucke des Barock 1600-1720 in der Herzog August Bibliothek, Wolfenmittel, Abteilung B: Mittlere Aufstellung: Abstract B, 2 vols., Vol. 1. Ed. by Martin Bircher. 332p. 1987. Vol.1: Literatur 1: A-N, 1982, 332 pgs. 160.00 (*3-598-32131-7*) K G Saur.

Deutsche Drucke des Barock 1600-1720 in der Herzog August Bibliothek, Wolfenmittel, Abteilung B: Mittlere Aufstellung: Abstract B, 2 vols., Vol. 2. Ed. by Martin Bircher. 339p. 1982. Vol.2: Literatur 2: O-Z - Sprachwissenschaft, Kunst, 1982, 339 pgs. 160.00 (*3-598-32132-5*) K G Saur.

Deutsche Drucke des Barock 1600-1720 in der Herzog August Bibliothek, Wolfenmittel, Abteilung C: Helmstedter Bestande, 6 vols. Ed. by Martin Bircher. write for info. (*3-598-32160-0*) K G Saur.

Deutsche Drucke des Barock 1600-1720 in der Herzog August Bibliothek, Wolfenmittel, Abteilung C: Helmstedter Bestande: Abstract C, 3 vols., Vol. 1. Ed. by Martin Bircher. 1983. 160.00 (*3-598-32161-9*) K G Saur.

Deutsche Drucke des Barock 1600-1720 in der Herzog August Bibliothek, Wolfenmittel, Abteilung C: Helmstedter Bestande: Abstract C, 3 vols., Vol. 2. Ed. by Martin Bircher. viii, 369p. 1988. 160.00 (*3-598-32162-7*) K G Saur.

Deutsche Drucke des Barock 1600-1720 in der Herzog August Bibliothek, Wolfenmittel, Abteilung C: Helmstedter Bestande: Abstract C, 3 vols., Vol. 3. Ed. by Martin Bircher. vi, 365p. 1988. 160.00 (*3-598-32163-5*) K G Saur.

Deutsche Drucke des Barock, 1600-1720. Katalog der Herzog August Bibliothek Wolfenbuttel Abt. B: Naturwissenschaften: Abstract B, Vol. 17. 379p. (GER.). 1991. lib. bdg. 240.00 (*3-598-32147-3*) K G Saur.

Deutsche Drucke des Barock, 1600-1720. Katalog der Herzog August Bibliothek Wolfenbuttel, ABT. B, Bd. 14: Deutsche Geschichte (Braunschweig-Luneburg) viii, 297p. (GER.). 1990. lib. bdg. 225.00 (*3-598-32144-9*) K G Saur.

Deutsche Drucke des Barock, 1600-1720. Katalog der Herzog August Bibliothek Wolfenbuttel, ABT B, Bd. 15: Geschichte Einzelner Lander. 319p. (GER.). 1991. lib. bdg. 225.00 (*3-598-32145-7*) K G Saur.

Deutsche Drucke des Barock, 1600-1720. Katalog der Herzog August Bibliothek Wolfenbuttel, ABT.B, Bd. 16: Kulturgeschichte, Medizin, Naturwissenschaften. 294p. (GER.). 1991. lib. bdg. 225.00 (*3-598-32146-5*) K G Saur.

Deutsche Elemente in den Vereinigten Staaten von Nordamerika. Gustav P. Koener. (Crosscurrents, Writings of German Political Emigres in 19th Century America Ser.: Section II America & the Americans, Vol. 3). 468p. 1986. text ed. 68.00 (*0-8204-0045-9*) P Lang Pubs.

Deutsche Fachprosa des Mittelalters. Ausgewaehlte Texte. Wolfram Schmitt. (Kleine Texte fuer Vorlesungen und Uebungen Ser.: Vol. 190). 120p. (C). 1972. 24.60 (*3-11-003801-3*) De Gruyter.

Deutsche Fachsprache der Technik. Werner Reinhardt et al. (Studien Zu Sprache und Technik Ser.: Bd. 3). xi, 174p. (GER.). 1992. write for info. (*3-487-09608-0*, Pub. by Georg Olms GW) Lubrecht & Cramer.

Deutsche Filmwoche Anthology. Ed. by R. Gordon. 1976. lib. bdg. 200.00 (*0-8490-1711-4*) Gordon Pr.

Deutsche Fragen, Texte zur juengsten Vergangenheit. Ed. by Karl-Heinz Drochner & Erika Drochner-Kirchberg. 207p. pap. 17.50 (*3-468-49460-2*) Langenscheidt.

Deutsche Gegenwartssprache: Tendenzen und Perspektiven Institut fur Deutsche Sprache-Jahrbuch, 1989. Ed. by Gerhard Stickel. 420p. (C). 1990. lib. bdg. 101.55 (*3-11-012446-7*) De Gruyter.

Deutsche Grammatik. Helbig & Buscha. 1991. 26.95 (*3-324-00118-8*) Langenscheidt.

Deutsche Grammatik: Gotisch, Alt-, Mittel-, und Neuhochdeutsch, 3 vols. 3rd ed. Wilhelm Wilmanns. (C). 1967. reprint ed. 311.55 (*3-11-000315-5*) De Gruyter.

Deutsche Grammatik in Frage & Antwort. Gerhard Hofmann. 32.50 (*3-468-37110-1*) Langenscheidt.

Deutsche Inflation: Eine Zwischenbilanz. Ed. by Gerald D. Feldman et al. (Veroeffentlichungen der Historischen Kommission zu Berlin, Band 67, Beitraege zu Inflation und Wiederaufbau in Deutschland und Europa 1914-1924: Vol. 1). xxiii, 431p. (GER.). 1982. lib. bdg. 70.80 (*3-11-009679-X*) De Gruyter.

Deutsche Kolonialsprachen, 5 vols., Vols. 1-5. Ed. by Carl Meinhof et al. (B. E. Ser.: No. 177). 1972. 18.00 (*0-685-73993-7*) Periodicals Srv.

Deutsche Kolonialsprachen Vol. 1: Die Sprache der Herero in Deutsch-Sudwest-Afrika, 1937, 5 vols. Ed. by Carl Meinhof et al. (B. E. Ser.: No. 177). 1937. 18.00 (*0-8115-3087-6*) Periodicals Srv.

Deutsche Kolonialsprachen Vol. 3: Die Sprache der Haussa in Zentalafrika, 5 vols. Ed. by Carl Meinhof et al. (B. E. Ser.: No. 177). 1972. Vol. 3: Die Sprache der Haussa in Zentalafrika. 18.00 (*0-685-73994-5*) Periodicals Srv.

Deutsche Kolonialsprachen Vol. 5: Die Sprache der Jaund in Kamerun, 5 vols. Ed. by Carl Meinhof et al. (B. E. Ser.: No. 177). 1972. Vol. 5: Die Sprache der Jaunde in Kamerun. 18.00 (*0-685-73995-3*) Periodicals Srv.

Deutsche Kriegsernahrungs-Wirtschaft. August Skalweit. (Wirtschafts-Und Sozialgeschichte des Weltkrieges (Osterreichische Und Ungarische Serie)). (GER.). 1927. 100.00 (*0-317-27431-7*) Elliots Bks.

Deutsche Kultur in Epochen. Gerda Jordan. LC 92-10281. (American University Studies: German Languages & Literature: Ser. I, Vol. 99). 330p. (C). 1993. text ed. 44.95 (*0-8204-1804-8*) P Lang Pubs.

Deutsche Kulturfilme. Ed. by International Film Bureau, Inc. Staff. (European Studies-Germany). 32p. 1982. 3.00 (*0-8354-2547-9*) Intl Film.

Deutsche Lehrtexte Fur Auslander-Medizin. 1987. 10.50 (*3-324-00142-0*) Langenscheidt.

Deutsche Lied: Geistlich und Weltlich Bis Zum 18 Jahrhundert. Ed. by Martin Breslauer. No. 1. xv, 301p. 1966. reprint ed. write for info. (*0-318-71765-4*, Pub. by Georg Olms GW) Lubrecht & Cramer.

Deutsche Lied Des XV und XVI Jahrhunderts, 2 vols. in 1. Robert Eitner. LC 71-178529. reprint ed. 57.50 (*0-404-56542-5*) AMS Pr.

Deutsche Literarische Zeitschriften, 1945-1970: Ein Repertorium, 4 vols., Set. Ed. by Deutsches Literaturarchiv Marbach Am Neckar. 1304p. (GER.). 1992. lib. bdg. 500.00 (*3-598-22000-6*) K G Saur.

Deutsche Literartur Zeitschriften 1880-1945: Ein Repertorium, 5 vols., Set. Ed. by Deutschen Literaturarchiv Margach am Neckar Staff. 1623p. (GER.). 1988. lib. bdg. 500.00 (*3-598-10645-9*) K G Saur.

Deutsche Literaturgeschichte. Paul Hankamer. LC 72-120563. reprint ed. 42.50 (*0-404-03095-5*) AMS Pr.

***Deutsche Mittelalter in Seinen Dichtungen.** Albrecht Classen. 250p. (C). 1994. pap. text ed. 20.00 (*1-57074-231-6*) Greyden Pr.

Deutsche Mystik Im Elsab. Lothar Schreyer. Ed. by Brian Keith-Smith. LC 92-23070. (Lothar Schreyer Edition Ser.: No. 1). (Illus.). 284p. 1992. text ed. 89.95 (*0-7734-1338-3*) E Mellen.

Deutsche Namenkunde: Unsere Familiennamen nach ihrer Entstehung und Bedeutung. Max Gottschald. 1982. 161.55 (*3-11-008618-2*) De Gruyter.

Deutsche Namenkunde: Unsere Familiennamen nach ihrer Entstehung und Bedeutung. 4th ed. Max Gottschald. 1971. 67.70 (*3-11-006467-7*) De Gruyter.

Deutsche Oper: Grundzuege Ihres Werdens & Wesens. Ludwig Schiedermair. LC 80-2299. reprint ed. 38.50 (*0-404-18868-0*) AMS Pr.

Deutsche Peintre-Graveur, 5 vols., Set. Andreas Andresen & Rudolph Weigel. 1971. reprint ed. write for info. (*3-487-04004-2*, Pub. by Georg Olms GW) Lubrecht & Cramer.

Deutsche Phonetik Fur Auslander. 1991. 33.50 (*3-324-00145-5*) Langenscheidt.

Deutsche Professor der Gegenwart: The German Professor Today. Johannes Flach. Ed. by Walter P. Metzger. LC 76-55203. (Academic Profession Ser.). (GER.). 1977. reprint ed. lib. bdg. 21.95 (*0-405-10035-3*) Ayer.

Deutsche Rechtsalterthuemer: Nach der Ausgabe von A. Heusler & R. Huebner, 2 vols., Set. Jacob Grimm. Ed. by Ruth Schmidt-Wiegand. (J. & W. Grimm Werke Ser.: Vols. 17-18). (GER.). 1992. lib. bdg. 179.25 (*3-487-09597-1*, Pub. by Georg Olms GW) Lubrecht & Cramer.

Deutsche Rohstoffwirtschaft Im Weltkrieg Einschliesslich des Hindenburg-Programms. Otto Goebel. (Wirtschafts-Und Sozialgeschichte des Weltkrieges (Osterreichische Und Ungarische Serie)). (GER.). 1930. 100.00 (*0-317-27434-1*) Elliots Bks.

Deutsche Sagen: German Legends, 2 vols. in 1. Jacob Grimm & Wilhelm K. Grimm. Ed. by Richard M. Dorson. LC 77-70597. (International Folklore Ser.). (Illus.). 1977. reprint ed. lib. bdg. 41.95 (*0-405-10097-3*) Ayer.

Deutsche Schriften, 2 vols. in 1. Albrecht Von Eyb. xcv, 260p. 1984. write for info. (*3-615-00001-3*, Pub. by Georg Olms GW); Vol. I: Das Ehebuchlein. write for info. (*0-318-71252-0*, Pub. by Georg Olms GW); Vol. II: Die Dramenubertragungen. write for info. (*0-318-71253-9*, Pub. by Georg Olms GW) Lubrecht & Cramer.

Deutsche Schriften mit den Holzschnitten der Erstdrucke, 9 vols. Thomas Murner. Ed. by Franz Schultz. (C). 1969. reprint ed. 1,107.70 (*3-11-000276-0*) De Gruyter.

Deutsche Schrifttafeln des IX Bis XVI Jahrhunderts Aus Handschriften der Bayerischen Staatsbibliothek Munchen, 5 pts. in 1. Erich Petzet & Otto Glauning. 326p. 1975. reprint ed. write for info. (*3-487-05685-2*, Pub. by Georg Olms GW) Lubrecht & Cramer.

Deutsche Seitengewehre und Bajonette, 1740-1945. Klaus Lubbe. (Illus.). 279p. (GER.). 1991. pap. 32.00 (*3-926598-48-4*) Johnson Ref Bks.

Deutsche Sprach und Landeskunde. Incl. Joanna Ratyck. 1981. pap. text ed. 7.25 (*0-394-32649-0*); John E. Crean. 1981. pap. text ed. 7.25 (*0-394-32650-4*); 608p. (C). 1981. Set text ed. 20.00 (*0-394-32648-2*) Random.

Deutsche Sprach und Landeskunde. 2nd ed. John E. Crean, Jr. et al. (C). 1985. pap. text ed. 11.50 (*0-685-08395-0*) McGraw.

Deutsche Sprache Nach der Wende. K. Welke et al. (Germanistische Linguistik Ser.: Heft 110-111/92). xii, 180p. (GER.). 1992. write for info. (*3-487-09627-7*, Pub. by Georg Olms GW) Lubrecht & Cramer.

Deutsche Sprache und Landeskunde. 4th ed. John Crean et al. 1993. Workbook. student ed, pap. text ed. write for info. (*0-07-013514-2*) McGraw.

Deutsche Sprache und Landeskunde. 4th ed. John Crean et al. 1993. Laboratory Manual. student ed, pap. text ed. write for info. (*0-07-013515-0*) McGraw.

Deutsche Sprache und Landeskunde. 4th ed. John E. Crean, Jr. et al. LC 92-30218. (ENG & GER.). 1993. teacher ed write for info. (*0-07-013513-4*); text ed. write for info. (*0-07-013512-6*) McGraw.

Deutsche Sprachegeschichte: Vom Spatmittelalter Bis Zur Gegenwart Bd. 1: Einfuhrung - Grundbegriffe. Deutsch In der Fruhburgerlichen Zeit. Peter Von Polenz. (Sammlung Goschen Ser.: No. 2237). (Illus.). 380p. (GER.). (C). 1991. pap. 19.10 (*3-11-012458-0*) De Gruyter.

***Deutsche Sprachgeschichte Bd. II: Vom Spaetmittelalter Bis Zur Gegenwart.** Peter Von Polenz. (Jahrhundert Ser.: No. 17 und 18). 507p. (GER.). (C). 1994. lib. bdg. 66.15 (*3-11-014608-8*); pap. text ed. 43.10 (*3-11-013436-5*) De Gruyter.

Deutsche Sprachlehre Fuer Auslaender. Dora Schulz & Heinz Griesbach. Incl. Grundstufe in einem Band. 5.80 (*0-685-47471-2*); Grundstufe in einem Band. pap. text ed. 19.95 (*0-685-47472-0*); Grundstufe in einem Band. 3.95 (*0-685-47473-9*); Grundstufe in einem Band. (*0-685-47474-7*); Grundstufe in einem Band. 5.20 (*0-685-47475-5*); Grundstufe. Ausgabe in zwei Baenden. pap. text ed. 16.95 (*0-685-47476-3*); Grundstufe. Ausgabe in zwei Baenden. pap. text ed. 17.95 (*0-685-47477-1*); Mittelstufe; Moderner Deutscher Sprachgebrauch Ein Lehrgang Fuer Fortgeschrittene. pap. text ed. 29.95 (*0-685-47480-1*); Mittelstufe; Moderner Deutscher Sprachgebrauch Ein Lehrgang Fuer Fortgeschrittene. audio 31.20 (*0-685-47483-6*); Set pap. write for info. (*0-318-55659-6*) Schoenhof.

Deutsche Staatsfinanz-Wirtschaft im Kriege. Walther Lotz. (Wirtschafts-Und Sozialgeschichte des Weltkrieges (Osterreichische Und Ungarische Serie)). (GER.). 1927. 100.00 (*0-317-27438-4*) Elliots Bks.

Deutsche Staatsleban Vor der Revolution. Clemens T. Perthes. Ed. by J. P. Mayer. LC 78-67375. (European Political Thought Ser.). (GER.). 1979. lib. bdg. 28.95 (*0-405-11725-6*) Ayer.

Deutsche Syntax. 2nd ed. Hans-Juergen Heringer. (Sammlung Goeschen Ser.: Vol. 5246). (Illus.). (GER.). (C). 1972. 17.55 (*3-11-004015-8*) De Gruyter.

Deutsche Universitat im Schnittpunkt Amerikanischer & Sozialistischer Organisationsprinzipien. European Research Association Staff. (Transworld Identity Ser.: Vol. 1). 320p. 1982. 24.50 (*0-931922-01-1*) Eurolingua.

Deutsche Verbale Wendungen Fur Auslander. 1989. 13.00 (*3-324-00279-6*) Langenscheidt.

Deutsche Versepos im 18. Jahrhundert: Studien & Kommentierte Gattungsbibliographie. Dieter Martin. (Quellen und Forschungen zur Sprach und Kulturgeschichte der Germanischen Voelker Ser.: Bd 103). xi, 450p. (GER.). (C). 1993. lib. bdg. 161.55 (*3-11-013816-6*) De Gruyter.

Deutsche Volks- und Wanderlieder. Toni Hirtreiter. 144p. (GER.). 1981. pap. 7.25 (*3-581-66331-7*) Langenscheidt.

Deutsche Wanderer-Vagabunden-und Vagantenlyrik in den Jahren 1910 Bis 1933. Friedemann Spicker. (Quellen und Forschungen zur Sprach und Kulturgeschichte der Germanischen Voelker Ser.: NF). (C). 1976. text ed. 120.00 (*3-11-004936-8*) De Gruyter.

***Deutsche Wirtschaftssprache Fir Amerikaner.** 3rd ed. Doris F. Merrifield. 1994. disk, pap. text ed. write for info. (*0-471-10788-3*) Wiley.

Deutsche Wirtschaftssprache fur Amerikaner. 2nd ed. Doris F. Merrifield. 282p. 1989. Net. text ed. write for info. (*0-471-61374-6*); Net. audio write for info. (*0-471-50238-3*); audio 19.95 (*0-471-50237-5*) Wiley.

***Deutsche Wirtschaftssprache Fur Amerikaner.** 3rd ed. Doris F. Merrifield. 1994. text ed. write for info. (*0-471-30947-8*) Wiley.

Deutsche Wortbildung: Typen und Tendenzen der Gegenwartssprache. Maria Pumpel-Mader et al. Ed. by Institut fur Deutsche Sprache Staff. (Sprache der Gegenwart Ser.: No. 80). xx, 340p. (GER.). (C). 1992. lib. bdg. 127.15 (*3-11-012445-9*) De Gruyter.

Deutsche Worterbucher des 17 und 18 Jahrhunderts. Ed. by Helmut Henne. x, 168p. 1975. write for info. (*3-487-05469-8*, Pub. by Georg Olms GW) Lubrecht & Cramer.

Deutsche Wortfelder Fur Den Sprachunterricht. 1991. 17.50 (*3-324-00594-9*); 17.50 (*3-324-00596-5*); 14.95 (*3-324-00146-3*) Langenscheidt.

Deutsche Wortgeschichte, Vol. 1. 3rd ed. Ed. by Friedrich Maurer & Heinz Rupp. LC 73-88302. (Grundriss der Germanischen Philologie Ser.: Vol. 17, Pt. 1). 581p. (C). 1974. 157.70 (*3-11-003627-4*) De Gruyter.

Deutsche Wortgeschichte, Vol. 2. 3rd rev. ed. Ed. by Friedrich Maurer & Heinz Rupp. (Grundriss der Germanischen Philologie Ser.: Vol. 17, Pt. 2). vi, 698p. (GER.). (C). 1974. 169.25 (*3-11-003619-3*) De Gruyter.

Deutsche Wortgeschichte, Vol. 3. 3rd ed. Ed. by Friedrich Maurer & Heinz Rupp. (Grundriss der Germanischen Philologie Ser.: Vol. 17, Pt. 3). (C). 1978. 113.10 (*3-11-003620-7*) De Gruyter.

Deutsche Wortschatz nach Sachgruppen. 7th ed. Franz Dornseiff. (C). 1983. 84.65 (*3-11-000287-6*) De Gruyter.

Deutschen: Vergangenheit und Gegenwart. 3rd ed. Wulf Koepke. LC 84-22458. 491p. (C). 1985. pap. text ed. 24.00 (*0-03-000367-9*) HB Coll Pubs.

Deutschen: Vergangenheit und Gegenwart. 4th ed. Wulf Koepke. (Illus.). 450p. (C). 1993. pap. text ed. 26.75 (*0-03-074989-1*) HB Coll Pubs.

Deutschen: Vergangenheit Und Gegenwart. 4th ed. Wulf Koepke. 450p. (GER.). 1993. lib. bdg. write for info. (*0-318-70026-3*) HarBrace.

Deutschen Archivare 1500 to 1945,, Vol. 1 & 2. rev. ed. Wolfgang Leesch. 1005p. (GER.). 1992. lib. bdg. 58.00 (*3-598-10606-8*) K G Saur.

Deutschen Archivare 1500 to 1945, vol. 1: Verzeichnis nach ihren Wirkungsstatten. Wolfgang Leesch. 268p. (GER.). 1985. lib. bdg. 28.50 (*3-598-10530-4*) K G Saur.

D

An Asterisk (*) at the beginning of an entry indicates that the title is appearing in BIP for the first time.

An Asterisk (*) at the beginning of an entry indicates that the title is appearing in BIP for the first time.

***Developing a Comprehensive Faculty Evaluation System: A Handbook for College Faculty & Administrators on Designing & Operating a Comprehensive Faculty Evaluation System.** Raoul A. Arreola. 200p. (C). 1995. pap. text ed. 44.95 (*1-882982-03-7*) Anker Pub.

Developing a Computerized Personnel System: The Manager's & Buyer's Guide. David B. Windsor. 210p. (C). 1985. 570.00 (*0-85292-370-8*) St Mut.

Developing a Consulting Practice. Robert O. Metzger. (Survival Skills for Scholars Ser.: Vol. 3). (Illus.). 108p. (C). 1993. text ed. 27.50 (*0-8039-5046-2*); pap. text ed. 12.95 (*0-8039-5047-0*) Sage.

Developing a Consulting Services Control & Engagement Program. (MAS Practice Administration Aids Ser.). 1993. 14.00 (*0-317-37098-7*) Am Inst CPA.

Developing a Curriculum in Response to Change, Options: Expanding Educational Services for Adults. National Center for Research in Vocational Education Staff. 1987. 39.95 (*0-317-03874-5*, SP500E) Ctr Educ Trng Employ.

***Developing a Curriculum Leadership Role in Key Stage 1: A Handbook for Students & Newly Qualified Teachers.** Ed. by Mike Harrison. LC 95-7261. 224p. 1995. 75.00x (*0-7507-0422-5*, Falmer Pr); pap. 27.00x (*0-7507-0423-3*, Falmer Pr) Taylor & Francis.

***Developing a Curriculum Leadership Role in Key Stage 2: A Handbook for Students & Newly Qualified Teachers.** Ed. by Julie Davies. LC 95-7262. 208p. 1995. 75.00x (*0-7507-0424-1*, Falmer Pr); pap. 27.00x (*0-7507-0425-X*, Falmer Pr) Taylor & Francis.

***Developing a Disaster Guide for Farmworkers: A Guide for Service Providers.** Association of Farmworker Opportunity Programs Staff. 98p. 1994. pap. text ed. write for info. (*1-886567-02-6*) Assn Farmwrker.

***Developing a Divorce Recovery Ministry: A How-to Manual.** Bill Flanagan. Date not set. 19.95 (*0-7814-5039-X*, 87510) Cook.

Developing a Drama Group. Lamb's Players Staff. 1989. 19. 95 (*0-89066-185-5*) World Wide Pubs.

Developing a Financial Management Information System for Local Governments: The Key Systems. Rhett D. Harrell. LC 80-84383. (Illus.). 42p. 1980. pap. 8.00 (*0-686-84364-9*); pap. 7.00 (*0-686-84365-7*) Municipal.

Developing a Gender Policy in Secondary Schools. Jean Rudduck. LC 93-4049. 160p. 1994. 80.00 (*0-335-19153-3*, Open Univ Pr); pap. 24.00 (*0-335-19152-5*, Open Univ Pr) Taylor & Francis.

***Developing a Hazardous Materials Exercise Program: A Handbook for State & Local Officials.** 78p. (Orig.). (C). 1994. pap. text ed. 35.00x (*0-7881-1405-0*) Diane Pub.

***Developing a Healthy Lifestyle.** Janice L. Burggrabe & Kent C. Miller. (Healing Presence Ser.). 256p. (Orig.). 1994. pap. 34.95 (*0-89390-334-5*) Resource Pubns.

Developing a High School Chemistry Course Adapted to the Differentiated Needs of Boys & Girls. Margery Gillson. LC 75-176805. (Columbia University. Teachers College. Contributions to Education Ser.: No. 709). reprint ed. 37.50 (*0-404-55709-0*) AMS Pr.

Developing a Hospital Emergency Preparedness Program. rev. ed. Gregg C. Beatty. (Management & Compliance Ser.: Vol. 2). (Illus.). 110p. 1990. reprint ed. ring bd. 110.00 (*0-87258-451-8*, 055201) Am Hospital.

Developing a Lifelong Contract in the Sports Marketplace. Greg Cylkowski. 398p. 1994. pap. text ed. 23.70 (*0-685-66930-0*) Global Sports Prodns.

Developing a Lifelong Contract in the Sports Marketplace. 2nd rev. ed. Greg J. Cylkowski. (Illus.). 400p. (C). 1994. per., pap. text ed. 20.95 (*0-9636449-0-4*) Athletic Achieve.

Developing a Mariculture Business in Alaska: Information & Resources. R. RaLonde & B. Paust. (Aquaculture Note Ser.: No. 15). 40p. (Orig.). 1993. pap. 4.00 (*1-56612-020-9*) AK Sea Grant CP.

Developing a Mission Statement for the Middle Level School. NASSP Middle Level Council Staff. 40p. (Orig.). 1987. pap. text ed. 7.00 (*0-88210-204-4*) Natl Assn Principals.

***Developing a Multipurpose Canister System for Spent Nuclear Fuel.** Asiyih Davis & Cheryl Runyon. (State Legislative Report Ser.: Vol. 19, No. 4). 3p. 1994. 5.00 (*1-55516-095-6*, 7302-1904) Natl Conf State Legis.

Developing a National Consciousness: The Birth of Modern Turkey. 1978. 6.00 (*0-317-56410-2*) UM Ctr MENAS.

Developing a Partnership to Eliminate Alcohol & Other Drugs in Your Community. Sally S. Crawford. 82p. 1992. pap. text ed., spiral bd. 15.00 (*1-882802-01-2*) Healthy Life.

Developing a Personnel Manual. Lin Grensing. (Business Ser.). 152p. 1993. pap. 12.95 (*0-88908-282-0*) Self-Counsel Pr.

Developing a Police Anti-Corruption Capability. Mitchell Ware. (Criminal Justice Center Monographs). 1978. pap. text ed. 3.25x (*0-318-37492-7*) John Jay Pr.

Developing a Positive Self Concept, Pt. II. 1992. pap. 8.00 (*0-685-62438-2*, A261-08478) Home Econ Educ.

Developing a Practice in Ambulatory Surgery. Ed. by W. Beeson & H. Tobin. (American Academy of Facial Plastic & Reconstructive Surgery Monograph). (Illus.). 320p. 1993. pap. text ed. 79.00 (*0-86577-412-9*) Thieme Med Pubs.

***Developing a Profession of Librarianship in Australia: Travel Diaries & Other Papers.** John W. Metcalf. Ed. by W. Boyd Rayward. LC 94-32935. 1995. write for info. (*0-8108-2944-4*) Scarecrow.

Developing a Professional Sales Force: A Guide for Sales Trainers & Sales Managers. David A. Stumm. LC 86-8117. 234p. 1986. text ed. 55.00 (*0-89930-176-2*, SDV/, Quorum Bks) Greenwood.

Developing a Professional Vita or Resume. rev. ed. Carl McDaniels. LC 90-3029. (Illus.). 108p. 1990. pap. 10.95 (*0-912048-81-6*) Garrett Pk.

Developing a Programme for Delayed Motor Development in Children. David Stewart. 1990. 60.00 (*1-85000-526-5*, Falmer Pr); pap. 29.00 (*1-85000-527-3*, Falmer Pr) Taylor & Francis.

***Developing a Quality Curriculum.** Allan A. Glatthorn. LC 94-22689. 1994. write for info. (*0-87120-234-4*) Assn Supervision.

***Developing a Sports Career in the Sports Marketplace: The Sports Career Development Handbook.** Ed Kobak, Jr. (The Sports Career Development Handbook). (Illus.). 394p. (Orig.). (C). (gr. 11 up). 1995. per., pap. text ed. 21.95 (*0-9619181-9-5*) Global Sports Prodns.

Developing a Strategic Business Plan with Cases: An Entrepreneur's Advantage. 6th ed. Robert P. Crowner. 256p. (C). 1990. pap. text ed. 13.95 (*0-256-08636-2*, 31-1128-96) Irwin.

Developing a Strategy for a Multiagency Response to Clandestine Drug Laboratories. (Illus.). 133p. (Orig.). (C). 1994. pap. text ed. 40.00 (*0-7881-0581-7*) Diane Pub.

***Developing a Successful Physician - Hospital Organization.** Jennings Ryan & Kolb, Inc. Staff. Ed. by Peter F. Straley. LC 95-10043. 190p. 1995. pap. 57.50 (*1-55648-136-5*, 164100) AHPI.

Developing a Successful Tutoring Program. Patricia S. Koskinen & Robert M. Wilson. LC 81-18335. 1982. text ed. 16.95 (*0-8077-2673-7*) Tchrs Coll.

Developing a Successful Women's Track & Field Program. Dianna Lasco. LC 85-21790. 214p. 1986. text ed. 21.95 (*0-13-205261-X*, Busn) P-H.

Developing a Systems View of Education. Bela Banathy. (Systems Inquiry Ser.). 92p. (Orig.). 1980. pap. text ed. 10.95 (*0-914105-01-9*) Intersystems Pubns.

Developing a Teaching Style. Louisell & Descamps. (C). 1991. text ed. 46.50 (*0-06-044109-7*) HarpCollege.

Developing a Thinking Skills Program. Barry Beyer. 256p. (C). 1988. pap. text ed. 39.95 (*0-205-11133-5*, H11331, Longwood Div) Allyn.

Developing a Time Budget. D. L. Groves & S. L. Groves. 35p. (C). 1978. pap. text ed. 4.00 (*0-940414-00-7*) Appalach Assoc.

***Developing a Vibrant Parish Pastoral Council.** Arthur X. Deegan, II. LC 94-39971. 176p. (Orig.). 1995. pap. 11. 95 (*0-8091-3556-6*) Paulist Pr.

Developing a Vision: Strategic Planning & the Library Media Specialist. John D. Crowley. LC 94-2198. (Professional Guides in School Librarianship). 160p. 1994. text ed. 35.00 (*0-313-28835-6*, Greenwood Pr) Greenwood.

Developing a Vision for Ministry in the Twenty-First Century. Aubrey Malphurs. LC 91-42503. 192p. (Orig.). 1992. pap. 11.99 (*0-8010-6286-1*) Baker Bk.

Developing a Vital Congregation. Herb Miller. (Orig.). 1989. pap. write for info. (*0-937462-12-8*) Net Pr.

Developing a Winning Just-in-time Marketing Strategy: The Industrial Marketer's Guide. Charles O'Neal. 1990. text ed. 31.67 (*0-13-205303-9*) P-H.

Developing a Winning Marketing Plan. William A. Cohen. LC 86-32402. (Business Strategy Ser.). 324p. 1987. text ed. 39.95 (*0-471-84529-9*) Wiley.

Developing a Written Voice. Dona J. Hickey. LC 92-14928. 260p. (C). 1993. pap. text ed. 21.95 (*1-55934-049-5*) Mayfield Pub.

Developing a 21st Century Mind. Marsha Sinetar. 1991. 17. 50 (*0-679-40105-9*, Villard Bks) Random.

Developing Academic Programs: The Climate for Innovation. Daniel T. Seymour. LC 88-83590. (ASHE-ERIC Higher Education Report Ser.: No. 3). 128p. (Orig.). (C). 1988. pap. 15.00 (*0-913317-46-2*) GWU Schl E&HD.

Developing Academic Reading Skills. Laura D. Latulippe. (Illus.). 224p. (C). 1986. pap. text ed. 21.00 (*0-13-204157-X*) P-H.

Developing Achievement Motivation in Adolescents: Education for Human Growth. Alfred S. Alschuler. LC 72-84336. 330p. 1973. 34.95 (*0-87778-037-4*) Educ Tech Pubns.

Developing Active Readers: Ideas for Parents, Teachers, & Librarians. Ed. by Dianne L. Monson & DayAnn K. McClenathan. LC 79-9058. 112p. reprint ed. pap. 32.00 (*0-8357-4308-X*, 2037105) Bks Demand.

***Developing Adaptive Work Behaviors, Vol. 17.** Ed. by William H. Burke. (HDI Professional Series on Head Injury Rehabilitation). 45p. Date not set. pap. 8.00 (*1-882855-24-8*) HDI Pubs.

Developing, Administering, & Evaluating Adult Education. Knox, Alan B. & Associates. LC 80-7998. (Higher Education Ser.). 316p. 1980. 36.95 (*0-87589-467-4*) Jossey-Bass.

***Developing Administrative Excellence: Creating a Culture of Leadership.** Ed. by Sharon A. McDade & Phyllis H. Lewis. LC 85-644752. (New Directions for Higher Education Ser.: No. 87). 110p. (Orig.). 1994. pap. 16.95 (*0-7879-9986-5*) Jossey-Bass.

Developing Adult Day Care: An Approach to Maintaining Independence for Impaired Older Persons. Helen Padula. 192p. 1982. 15.00 (*0-910883-61-0*, 270) Natl Coun Aging.

Developing Africa: A Modernization Perspective. Ed. by Pradip K. Ghosh. LC 83-26672. (International Development Resource Bks.: No. 20). (Illus.). viii, 435p. 1984. text ed. 89.50 (*0-313-24156-2*, GAF/, Greenwood Pr) Greenwood.

Developing Agricultural Extension for Women Farmers. Katrine A. Saito & Daphne Spurling. (Discussion Paper Ser.: No. 156). 124p. 1992. pap. 7.95 (*0-8213-2078-5*, 12078) World Bank.

Developing Agriculture of the Middle East: Opportunities & Prospects. Ed. by K. S. McLackhlan. 74p. 1976. 43.00 (*0-86010-046-4*) G & T Inc.

***Developing Alert Listening Skills.** Jean G. DeGaetano. 84p. (J). 1995. pap. text ed. 24.00 (*1-886143-29-3*) Grt Ideas Tching.

Developing America's Northern Frontier. Ed. by Theodore Lane. LC 86-28233. (Illus.). 270p. (Orig.). 1987. pap. text ed. 25.00 (*0-8191-6082-2*, Inst Soc Econ Res) U Pr of Amer.

Developing an Adult Education Program Through Community Linkages. Harold Beder & Franceska Smith. 1977. 7.00 (*0-88379-009-2*) A A A C E.

Developing an Effective Major Gift Program: From Managing Staff to Soliciting Gifts. Roy Muir & Jerry May. 1993. pap. 37.00 (*0-89964-302-7*) Coun Adv & Supp Ed.

Developing an Effective Teacher Mentor Program. Melvin P. Heller & Nancy W. Sindelar. LC 91-60200. (Fastback Ser.: No. 319). (Orig.). 1991. pap. 1.25 (*0-87367-319-0*) Phi Delta Kappa.

***Developing An Effective Worship Ministry.** Tom Kraeuter. 120p. (Orig.). 1993. pap. 7.99 (*1-883002-05-2*) Emerald WA.

Developing an Employee Incentive Program. 30p. 1984. pap. 33.00 (*0-317-57891-X*, CS981) Natl Restaurant Assn.

Developing an Entrepreneurial Enterprise. John Durand. Ed. by Christopher A. Smith. (Illus.). 84p. (Orig.). (C). 1989. pap. 16.00 (*0-916671-90-9*) Material Dev.

Developing an Executive Frame of Mind. Janet Buell. Ed. by Audrey Cheney. LC 89-32049. (Illus.). 180p. (Orig.). 1989. pap. 20.95 (*0-929551-05-2*); audio 22.95 (*0-929551-06-0*) Ability Workshop Pr.

Developing an Individualized Behavior Management Plan. Kathleen A. Riley et al. 1994. 2.95 (*1-56456-087-2*, 285) W Gladden Found.

Developing an Interdisciplinary Science of Organizations. Karlene H. Roberts et al. LC 78-62568. (Jossey-Bass Social & Behavioral Science Ser.). 191p. reprint ed. pap. 54.50 (*0-8357-6889-9*, 2037941) Bks Demand.

Developing an Investment Philosophy. Philip A. Fisher. 115p. 1991. 14.95 (*0-931133-06-8*, Busn Class) Pac Pub Grp.

Developing an Occupational Drug Abuse Program: Considerations & Approaches. 1986. lib. bdg. 79.95 (*0-8490-3512-0*) Gordon Pr.

***Developing & Administering a Child Care Center.** 3rd ed. Dorothy J. Sciarra & Anne G. Dorsey. LC 94-30040. 528p. 1994. pap. text ed. 32.95 (*0-8273-5873-3*) Delmar.

Developing & Applying End of Arm Tooling. Ed. by P. McCormick. 264p. 1986. 42.00 (*0-87263-211-3*) SME.

Developing & Conducting Training for Foodservice Employees: A Guide for Trainers. Karen E. Drummond. LC 92-19567. 1992. student ed 10.25 (*0-685-60009-2*); student ed, audio 27.50 (*0-88091-102-6*) Am Dietetic Assn.

Developing & Directing Counselor Education Laboratories: Proceedings of an ACES National Conference Think Tank. Ed. by Jane E. Myers. LC 94-3946. 1994. 27.95 (*1-55620-137-0*) Am Coun Assn.

Developing & Distributing FoxPro 2.5 for Windows Application. Porus H. Havewala. LC 94-12422. 160p. 1994. disk 15.95 (*1-55622-428-1*) Wordware Pub.

Developing & Documenting the Curriculum. David G. Armstrong. 250p. 1988. text ed. 55.67 (*0-205-11852-6*, H1852-6) Allyn.

Developing & Enforcing a Code of Business Ethics. Gary Ward. LC 88-35685. (Illus.). 48p. (Orig.). 1989. pap. 5.00 (*0-87576-144-5*) Pilot Bks.

Developing & Evaluating Educational Research. Gary W. Moore. (C). 1987. text ed. 38.25 (*0-673-39172-8*) HarpCollege.

Developing & Implementing an Integrated Test Facility for Testing Computerized Systems. William E. Perry & Javier F. Kuong. 1979. 35.00 (*0-940706-09-1*, MAP-12) Management Advisory Pubns.

***Developing & Implementing Business Information Systems for Small Businesses.** Stanley X. Lewis, Jr. et al. 51p. 1990. pap. text ed. 19.50 (*0-933179-04-9*) Bus Account Pubns.

***Developing & Implementing Critical Pathways in Respiratory Care.** Deborah K. Wall et al. 91p. (Orig.). 1994. pap. text ed. write for info. (*0-916499-58-8*) Care Educ Grp.

Developing & Implementing Individualized Educational Programs. 3rd ed. Bonnie Strickland & Ann P. Turnbull. 480p. (C). 1990. pap. write for info. (*0-675-21142-5*, Merrill Pub Co) Macmillan.

Developing & Implementing Marketing Strategies. Volney Steffire. LC 85-12189. 269p. 1985. text ed. 57.95 (*0-275-92046-1*, C2046, Greenwood Pr) Greenwood.

Developing & Improving Irrigation & Drainage Systems: Selected Papers from World Bank Seminars. Ed. by Guy Le Moigne et al. LC 92-17888. (Technical Paper Ser.: No. 178). 177p. 1992. 10.95 (*0-8213-2165-X*, 12165) World Bank.

Developing & Increasing Intuitive Thinking. Sisk. 1991. pap. 10.00 (*0-89824-714-4*) Trillium Pr.

Developing & Institutionalizing a Self-Improvement Capability: Structures & Strategies of Secondary Schools. Herbert J. Klausmeier. LC 85-20194. 204p. (Orig.). (C). 1986. pap. text ed. 22.50 (*0-8191-4952-7*) U Pr of Amer.

Developing & Localizing International Software. Tom Madell et al. LC 93-41466. (Hewlett-Packard Professional Books Ser.). 224p. 1994. pap. text ed. 34.80 (*0-13-300674-3*) P-H Gen Ref & Trav.

Developing & Maintaining Video Collections in Libraries. James C. Scholtz. 175p. 1988. lib. bdg. 40.95 (*0-87436-497-3*, 2105-1) ABC-CLIO.

Developing & Managing a Nursing Home Volunteer Program. Vicki Parsons. (Orig.). (C). 1991. pap. text ed. 14.95 (*1-877735-32-9*, 179) M&H Pub Co TX.

Developing & Managing a Personal Injury Practice. (Litigation & Administrative Practice Course Handbook, 1983-84 Ser.). 183p. 1992. pap. 35.00 (*0-685-69411-9*) PLI.

Developing & Managing a Personal Injury Practice 1993. (Litigation & Administrative Practice Course Handbook, 1983-84 Ser.: Vol. 468). 148p. 1993. 35.00 (*0-685-69741-X*, H4-5165) PLI.

Developing & Managing an Effective Elder Law Practice. Cheryl C. Mitchell & F. H. Mitchell, Jr. 220p. 1991. pap. text ed. 50.00 (*1-879909-01-4*) Mitchell WA.

Developing & Managing Cardiac Rehabilitation Programs. Ed. by Linda K. Hall. (Illus.). 248p. 1993. text ed. 39.00 (*0-87322-358-6*, BHAL0358) Human Kinetics.

Developing & Managing Expert Systems. David S. Prerau. (Illus.). 384p. (C). 1990. text ed. 35.50 (*0-201-13659-7*) Addison-Wesley.

Developing & Managing Health-Fitness Facilities. Robert W. Patton et al. LC 88-13428. (Illus.). 376p. 1989. text ed. 42.00 (*0-87322-203-2*, BPAT0203) Human Kinetics.

Developing & Managing Open Organizations. Oscar G. Mink et al. LC 79-10195. 303p. 1991. pap. 19.95 (*0-318-21892-5*) Catapult Press.

Developing & Managing Open Organizations: A Model & Methods for Maximizing Organizational Potential. 2nd ed. Oscar G. Mink et al. Ed. by Karen I. Stelzner. (Illus.). 303p. (C). 1991. reprint ed. pap. 19.95 (*0-685-66131-8*) Catapult Press.

***Developing & Managing Your School Guidance Program.** 2nd ed. Norman C. Gysbers & Patricia Henderson. 501p. 1994. pap. 35.95 (*1-55620-119-2*) Am Coun Assn.

Developing & Operating a Records Retention Program Guideline. 86p. 1986. pap. 26.00 (*0-933887-18-3*, A4520) Assn Recs Mgrs & Admin.

Developing & Training Human Resources in Organization. 2nd ed. Wexley. (C). 1991. pap. text ed. 28.50 (*0-673-46160-2*) HarpCollege.

Developing & Using Decision Support Applications. Steven C. Ross et al. (Microcomputing Ser.). 266p. (C). 1988. pap. text ed. 28.50 (*0-314-30124-0*) West Pub.

Developing & Using Microcomputer Business Systems. Kathryn Huff. 224p. (C). 1987. pap. text ed. 27.25 (*0-314-34730-5*) West Pub.

Developing & Using Office Applications with AppleWorks: Versions 1.0 Through 2.0. M. S. Varnon. LC 86-24696. (Microcomputing Ser.). 366p. (Orig.). (C). 1987. pap. text ed. 31.00 (*0-314-34129-3*) West Pub.

Developing & Using Tests Effectively: A Guide for Faculty. Lucy C. Jacobs & Clinton I. Chase. LC 92-19335. (Higher & Adult Education Ser.). 256p. 1992. 29.95 (*1-55542-481-3*) Jossey-Bass.

Developing & Validating Multiple-Choice Test Items. Thomas M. Haladyna. 228p. 1994. text ed. 49.95 (*0-8058-1206-7*) L Erlbaum Assocs.

***Developing Applications with CA-Visual Objects.** Gary Stark et al. (Illus.). 880p. (Orig.). 1995. pap. 45.00 (*0-672-30566-6*) Sams.

***Developing Applications with Clarion for Windows.** Ross Santis & David Harms. (Illus.). (Orig.). 1995. pap. 45.00 (*0-672-30674-3*) Sams.

Developing Applications with Microsoft Office. Christine Solomon. 600p. 1994. disk 39.95 (*1-55615-665-0*) Microsoft.

***Developing Applications with Microsoft Office.** Christine Solomon. 1994. write for info. (*0-615-00252-8*) Microsoft.

***Developing Applications with Microsoft Office for Windows 95.** Christine Solomon. 1995. disk 39.95 (*1-55615-898-X*) Microsoft.

Developing Applications with Quattro Pro for Windows. John Walkenbach. 300p. 1993. pap. 29.95 (*1-883327-40-7*) TitleWave Pr.

Developing Areas: A Book of Readings & Research. Ed. by Vijayan K. Pillai & Lyle W. Shannon. 450p. 1994. 74.95 (*0-85496-741-9*) Berg Pubs.

Developing Areas: A Classed Bibliography of the Joint Bank-Fund Library, World Bank Group & International Monetary Fund, 3 vols, Set. Joint Bank-Fund Library (Washington, D. C.) Staff. Incl. Vol. 1. Latin America & the Caribbean. 1977. lib. bdg. 110.00 (*0-8161-0023-3*); Vol. 2. Africa & the Middle East. 1977. lib. bdg. 110.00 (*0-8161-0024-1*); Vol. 3. Asia & Oceania. 1977. lib. bdg. 110.00 (*0-8161-0025-X*); 1977. Set lib. bdg. 330.00 (*0-8161-0003-9*, Hall Library) G K Hall.

Developing Areas, Universities, & Public Policy. Ed. by Fred Lazin et al. 184p. (Orig.). 1986. pap. 12.00 (*0-918592-86-0*) Pol Studies.

Developing Arguments: Strategies for Reaching Audiences. Kathleen Bell. 737p. (C). 1990. pap. 22.95 (*0-534-12192-6*) Intl Thomson.

Developing Arts & Humanities Programming with the Elderly. Ronald J. Manheimer. LC 83-25864. (RASD Adult Services in Action Ser.: No. 2). 13p. 1984. pap. 2.00 (*0-8389-5656-4*) ALA.

Developing Assertiveness. Anni Townend. (Self-Development for Managers Ser.). 140p. 1991. pap. 12.95 (*0-415-04464-2*, A6229) Routledge.

Developing Assessment for the National Curriculum. Ed. by Caroline Gipps. (Bedford Way Ser.). 160p. 1992. pap. 32.50 (*0-7494-0837-5*, Pub. by Kogan Page Educ UK) Taylor & Francis.

Developing Attitudes Toward Learning. 2nd ed. Robert F. Mager. LC 83-60499. 1984. pap. 15.95 (*1-56103-337-5*) Lake Pub Co.

Developing Auto-Instructional Materials. A. J. Romiszowski. 460p. (Orig.). 1987. pap. 35.95 (*0-89397-269-X*) Nichols Pub.

Developing Basic Skills Programs in Secondary Schools. Ed. by Daisy G. Wallace. LC 81-70310. 141p. 1982. 5.00 (*0-87120-111-9*, 611-82264) Assn Supervision.

D

An Asterisk (*) at the beginning of an entry indicates that the title is appearing in BIP for the first time.

D

An Asterisk (*) at the beginning of an entry indicates that the title is appearing in BIP for the first time.

An Asterisk (*) at the beginning of an entry indicates that the title is appearing in BIP for the first time.

D

*__Developing Programs for Older Adults.__ A. U. Scannell. Date not set. pap. 8.75 (*1-56699-067-X*, OD45) Alban Inst.

Developing Programs for the Educationally Disadvantaged. Ed. by Harry Passow. LC 67-19026. reprint ed. pap. 95.00 (*0-317-41882-3*, 2026051) Bks Demand.

Developing Programs in Adult Education. Edgar J. Boone. (Illus.). 244p. (C). 1992. reprint ed. pap. text ed. 19.95 (*0-88133-689-0*) Waveland Pr.

Developing Proofreading Skill. Sue C. Camp. Ed. by Joseph Tinervia. LC 80-12596. (Illus.). 128p. (gr. 11-12). 1980. text ed. 6.96 (*0-07-009635-X*) McGraw.

Developing Proofreading Skill: With Editing Applications. 3rd ed. Sue C. Camp. LC 92-36771. 1993. 12.50 (*0-02-800897-9*) Glencoe.

Developing Psychic Abilities. Apryl J. Douglas. LC 87-50497. (Orig.). 1987. pap. 9.95 (*0-937533-07-6*) TEC Pubns.

Developing Public Library Collections Policies & Procedures: A How-to-Do-It Manual for Small & Medium Sized Public Libraries. Kay Cassell & Elizabeth Futas. (How-to-Do-It Ser.). 143p. 1991. pap. text ed. 39.95 (*1-55570-060-8*) Neal-Schuman.

*__Developing Quality Computer Systems.__ Anthony Coogan. 224p. Date not set. 29.95 (*1-85554-250-1*) Blackwell Pubs.

Developing Quality Schools. Ed. by Colin Bayne-Jardine & Peter Holly. 224p. 1994. 75.00 (*0-7507-0242-7*, Falmer Pr); pap. 26.00 (*0-7507-0243-5*, Falmer Pr) Taylor & Francis.

Developing Quality Systems & Educational Organisations. Ed. by Geoffrey D. Doherty. LC 93-47624. 224p. 1994. pap. 22.95 (*0-415-09829-7*, B4101) Routledge.

Developing Radiation Emergency Plans for Academic, Medical Or Industrial Facilities. LC 91-23659. (Report Ser.: No. 111). 129p. 1991. pap. text ed. 25.00 (*0-929600-20-7*) NCRP Pubns.

Developing Readers' Advisory Services: Concepts & Commitments. Ed. by Kathleen de la Pena McCook et al. LC 93-22853. 120p. 1993. pap. 29.95 (*1-55570-163-9*) Neal-Schuman.

Developing Readers & Writers in the Context Areas: K-12. 2nd ed. David Moore et al. LC 93-19974. 400p. (C). 1994. pap. text ed. 37.95 (*0-8013-0467-9*, 78297) Longman.

Developing Readers in the Middle Years. Elaine Millard. LC 93-29245. (English, Language & Education Ser.). 1994. 23.00 (*0-335-19071-5*, Open Univ Pr) Taylor & Francis.

*__Developing Reading Efficiency.__ (YA). (gr. 7-10). Date not set. 22.95 (*0-614-04294-1*) Develop Read Dist.

Developing Reading Efficiency. 4th ed. Lyle L. Miller. LC 79-55778. 1980. pap. text ed. write for info. (*0-8087-3958-1*) Burgess MN Intl.

Developing Reading Skills. Deanne K. Milan. 416p. (C). 1983. pap. text ed. write for info. (*0-394-32789-6*) Random.

Developing Reading Skills. 3rd ed. Deanne K. Milan. 496p. 1991. pap. text ed. write for info. (*0-07-041901-9*) McGraw.

Developing Reading Skills. 4th ed. Deanne Milan. LC 94-7827. 1994. pap. text ed. write for info. (*0-07-041914-0*) McGraw.

D

Developing Reading Skills: A Practical Guide to Reading Comprehension Exercises. Francoise Grellet. (New Directions in Language Teaching Ser.). 251p. 1981. pap. 16.95 (*0-521-28364-7*) Cambridge U Pr.

Developing Reading Skills: Advanced. 2nd ed. Linda Markstein & Louise Hirasawa. 232p. 1983. pap. 7.95 (*0-8384-2989-0*, Newbury); pap. 17.95 (*0-8384-2988-2*, Newbury) Heinle & Heinle.

Developing Reading Skills: Beginning. Linda Markstein. 160p. 1987. pap. 15.95 (*0-8384-2824-X*, Newbury) Heinle & Heinle.

Developing Reading Skills: Beginning. 2nd ed. Linda Markstein. LC 93-45815. 1994. pap. 17.95 (*0-8384-4987-5*) Heinle & Heinle.

Developing Reading Skills: Intermediate. Linda Markstein & Louise Hirasawa. 1981. pap. 15.95 (*0-8384-2826-6*, Newbury) Heinle & Heinle.

Developing Reading Skills: Intermediate. Linda Markstein & Louise Hirasawa. 1982. pap. 7.95 (*0-8384-3055-4*, Newbury) Heinle & Heinle.

Developing Reading Skills: Intermediate. 2nd ed. Linda Markstein & Louise Hirasawa. LC 93-46179. 1994. pap. 17.95 (*0-8384-5774-6*) Heinle & Heinle.

Developing Reading Versatility. 6th ed. W. R. Adams. 528p. (C). 1992. Answer key. pap. text ed. 2.00 (*0-03-096521-7*) HB Coll Pubs.

Developing Reading Versatility. 6th ed. W. R. Adams. 528p. 1993. text ed. write for info. (*0-03-079099-9*) HB Coll Pubs.

Developing Real-Time Embedded Software: In a Market Driven Company. Karen S. Ellison. 352p. 1994. pap. text ed. 44.95 (*0-471-59459-8*) Wiley.

Developing Recycling Markets & Industries. 41p. 1990. 10.00 (*1-55516-977-5*, 9334) Natl Conf State Legis.

Developing Reflective Judgment: Understanding & Promoting Intellectual Growth & Critical Thinking in Adolescents & Adults. Patricia M. King & Karen S. Kitchener. LC 93-43164. (Higher & Adult Education Series: Social & Behavioral Science Ser.). 351p. 1994. 34.95 (*1-55542-629-8*) Jossey-Bass.

Developing Relationships. David Bowker et al. (Patchwork Ser.: No. 4). (Illus.). 12p. 1993. pap. 18.00 (*1-873791-55-0*) Taylor & Francis.

Developing Relationships in Business Networks. Ed. by Hakan Hakansson & Ivan Snehota. LC 94-19938. 416p. 1995. 89.95x (*0-415-11570-1*, C0084) Routledge.

Developing Relationships Through Love. Don Clowers. 42p. (Orig.). 1986. student ed 4.95 (*0-914307-62-2*) R Tilton Ministries.

Developing Residential Practice: A Source Book of References & Resources for Staff Development. Ed. by Robin Douglas et al. (C). 1985. 59.00 (*0-685-40334-3*, Pub. by Natl Inst Soc Work) St Mut.

Developing Residential Practice: Five Role Play & Simulation Games for Staff in Residential Settings. Chris Payne & Robin Douglas. 1981. 50.00 (*0-317-05757-X*, Pub. by Natl Inst Soc Work) St Mut.

Developing Resiliency Through Children's Literature: A Guide for Teachers & Librarians, K-8. Nancy L. Cecil & Patricia L. Roberts. LC 91-51001. 224p. 1992. pap. 24.95 (*0-89950-707-7*) McFarland & Co.

Developing Resourceful Humans: Adult Education Within the Economic Context. Ed. by Lynn Burton. LC 91-45393. (International Perspectives on Adult & Continuing Education Ser.). 272p. 1992. 59.95 (*0-415-00121-8*, A5908) Routledge.

Developing Respite Services for the Elderly. Ed. by Rhonda J. Montgomery & Joyce Prothero. LC 85-40980. (Illus.). 82p. (Orig.). (C). 1986. 25.00 (*0-295-96386-7*); pap. 10.00 (*0-295-96347-6*) U of Wash Pr.

Developing Response to Fiction. Robert Protherough. 192p. 1983. pap. 27.00 (*0-335-10405-3*, Open Univ Pr) Taylor & Francis.

Developing Response to Poetry. Patrick Dias & Michael Hayhoe. (English, Language & Education Ser.). 128p. 1988. pap. 27.00 (*0-335-15833-1*, Open Univ Pr) Taylor & Francis.

Developing Responsive Human Services: New Perspectives about Residential Treatment Organizations. Ed. by Jack Thaw & Anthony J. Cuvo. 336p. (C). 1986. text ed. 69.95 (*0-89859-612-2*) L Erlbaum Assocs.

Developing Retirement Communities, 2 vols., Vol. 2. 2nd ed. Paul A. Gordon. LC 92-14056. (Real Estate Practice Library). 1264p. 1992. Set. text ed. 232.00 (*0-471-55583-5*) Wiley.

Developing Role of Short-Lived Radionuclides in Nuclear Medical Practice: Proceedings. DOE Technical Information Center Staff. Ed. by Peter Paras & J. W. Thiessen. LC 84-26718. (Symposium Ser.). 571p. 1985. pap. 22.95 (*0-87079-518-X*, CONF-820523); fiche 9.00 (*0-87079-519-8*, CONF-820523) DOE.

Developing Roots & Wings: A Trainer's Guide to Affirming Culture in Early Childhood Programs. Stacey York. LC 92-11974. 210p. (Orig.). 1992. pap. 24.95 (*0-934140-75-8*) Redleaf Pr.

Developing Rural India: Policies, Politics, & Progress. Walter C. Neale. LC 85-63424. (Perspectives on Asian & African Development Ser.: No. 3). 263p. 1990. 29.00 (*0-913215-15-5*) Riverdale Co.

Developing Safe, Effective & Reliable Medical Software. 46p. 1991. 65.00 (*0-910275-56-4*, MDS-113) Assn Adv Med Instrn.

Developing Safety Critical Systems with Ada. I. C. Pyle. 250p. 1991. pap. 39.00 (*0-13-204298-3*, 270406) P-H.

Developing Safety Skills with the Young Child. Diana E. Comer. LC 86-11438. 192p. (C). 1987. teacher ed 8.00 (*0-8273-2669-6*); pap. text ed. 19.95 (*0-8273-2668-8*) Delmar.

Developing Safety Training Programs. Joseph Saccaro. 192p. 1992. text ed. 44.95 (*0-442-01282-9*) Van Nos Reinhold.

Developing School. Ed. by Peter Holly & Geoff Southworth. 220p. 1989. 55.00 (*1-85000-484-6*, Falmer Pr); pap. 28.00 (*1-85000-485-4*, Falmer Pr) Taylor & Francis.

*__Developing School-Based Tobacco Use Prevention & Cessation Programs.__ Steve Sussman et al. 256p. 1994. 46.00 (*0-8039-4927-8*); pap. 22.95 (*0-8039-4928-6*) Sage.

Developing Science in the Primary Classroom. Wynne Harlen & Sheila Jelly. LC 89-26864. 72p. 1990. pap. text ed. 13.50 (*0-435-08305-8*, 08305) Heinemann.

Developing Second-Language Skills: Theory & Practice. 3rd ed. Kenneth Chastain. 438p. (C). 1988. pap. text ed. 16.00 (*0-15-517619-6*) HB Coll Pubs.

Developing Self-Awareness. 2nd ed. David A. Whetten & Cameron. (Developing Management Skills Modules Ser.). (C). 1993. 6.25 (*0-06-501795-1*) HarpCollege.

Developing Self-Concept for Exceptional Learners: A Handbook. rev. ed. John R. Moss & Louise Skelton. (C). 1977. pap. 7.00 (*0-937660-05-1*) PIP.

Developing Self-Control. Carol Foster. 136p. 1974. pap. text ed. 7.00 (*0-917472-02-0*) F Fournies.

*__Developing Self Control, Vol. 14.__ Ed. by William H. Burke. (HDI Professional Series on Head Injury Rehabilitation). 60p. Date not set. pap. 8.00 (*1-882855-21-3*) HDI Pubs.

Developing Self-Esteem. Matt Newman et al. LC 80-730732. (Illus.). 1980. pap. text ed. 165.00 (*0-89290-152-7*, A602-SATC) Soc for Visual.

Developing Self-Esteem. rev. ed. Connie Palladino. Ed. by W. Philip Gerould. LC 93-74716. (Illus.). 114p. (Orig.). 1994. pap. 9.95 (*1-56052-261-5*) Crisp Pubns.

Developing Self-Esteem for Students. Connie Palladino. Ed. by W. Philip Gerould. LC 93-74716. (Illus.). (Orig.). 1994. pap. 9.95 (*1-56052-289-5*) Crisp Pubns.

*__Developing Senior Faculty As Teacher.__ Ed. by Martin J. Finkelstein & Mark W. LaCelle-Peterson. LC 85-644763. (New Directions for Teaching & Learning Ser.: No. 55). 116p. (Orig.). 1993. pap. 16.95 (*1-55542-682-4*) Jossey-Bass.

Developing Sentence Sense. Martin M. McKoski & Lynne C. Hahn. (C). 1993. text ed. 14.75 (*0-673-46973-5*) HarpCollege.

Developing Sentence Skills. Barbara Hansen & Rebecca McDaniel. 384p. (C). 1990. pap. text ed. write for info. (*0-13-204520-6*) P-H.

Developing Services for the Elderly. 2nd ed. Ed. by Joyce Lishman. LC 85-40083. (Research Highlights in Social Work Ser.). 185p. 1985. text ed. 29.95 (*0-312-19715-2*) St Martin.

Developing Shelter Models for the Homeless: Three Program Design Options. Robert Mayer & Tillie Shuster. 107p. (Orig.). 1985. pap. 10.00 (*0-88156-028-6*) Comm Serv Soc NY.

Developing Shop Safety Skills. (Illus.). 84p. 1981. 10.00 (*0-89606-036-5*, 903); teacher ed 5.00 (*0-89606-157-4*, 903TG); student ed 3.50 (*0-89606-158-2*, 903SW) Am Assn Voc Materials.

Developing Skills for International Trade: A Practical Guide for Export Training. 2nd ed. Judee K. Benton. 230p. 1992. pap. text ed. write for info. (*1-884023-50-9*) Team Exports.

Developing Skills for International Trade: A Practical Guide for Export Training & Skills Workbook & Answer Book. 2nd ed. Judee K. Benton. 230p. 1992. pap. text ed. write for info. (*1-884023-52-5*) Team Exports.

Developing Skills for International Trade: Skills Workbook & Answer Book. 2nd ed. Judee K. Benton. 166p. 1992. pap. write for info. (*1-884023-51-7*) Team Exports.

Developing Skills in Algebra, Vol. I: A Lecture Worktext. 4th ed. J. Louis Nanney & John L. Cable. 264p. (C). 1987. pap. write for info. (*0-697-06768-8*) Wm C Brown Pubs.

Developing Skills in Geographical Education. R. Gerber & J. Lidstone. (C). 1988. 150.00 (*0-7016-2530-9*, Pub. by S Thornes Pubs UK) St Mut.

Developing Skills with Information Technology. Ed. by Lisanne Bainbridge & Antonio Ruiz-Quintanilla. 1989. text ed. 149.00 (*0-471-92396-6*) Wiley.

Developing Skills with People: Training for Person to Person Client Contact. Dainow. 201p. 1988. text ed. 47.50 (*0-471-91726-5*) Wiley.

*__Developing Social Skills, Vol. 9.__ Ed. by William H. Burke. (HDI Professional Series on Head Injury Rehabilitation). 60p. Date not set. pap. 8.00 (*1-882855-16-7*) HDI Pubs.

Developing Sociological Knowledge. 2nd ed. Bernard P. Cohen. 345p. (C). 1988. pap. text ed. 25.95 (*0-8304-1123-2*) Nelson-Hall.

Developing Sociological Knowledge: Theory & Method. B. Cohen. 1980. pap. 22.95 (*0-685-03828-9*) P-H.

Developing Software to Government Standards. William H. Roetzheim. 1990. text ed. 60.00 (*0-13-829755-X*) P-H.

Developing South Asia: A Modernization Perspective. Ed. by Pradip K. Ghosh. LC 83-26600. (International Development Resource Bks.: No. 18). xv, 582p. 1984. text ed. 105.00 (*0-313-24154-6*, GSA/, Greenwood Pr) Greenwood.

Developing Speaking Skill. Geraldine Chapey. 200p. 1989. pap. text ed. 9.95 (*0-07-010545-6*); audio 29.00 (*0-07-087528-6*); vhs 99.99 (*0-07-087088-8*) McGraw.

Developing Speaking Skills. James M. Jasper & Edith Morgan. (Illus.). 64p. (J). (gr. k-6). 1985. 8.95 (*0-86653-268-4*, GA 633) Good Apple.

Developing Spiritual Accuracy & Pinpointing. John Tetsola. Ed. by Perry M. Mallory. 125p. (Orig.). 1993. pap. 9.95 (*0-9634306-0-2*) End-Time Wave.

*__Developing Spiritual Growth in Junior High Students: A Step-by-Step Program to Guide Your Junior Highers into Spiritual Maturity.__ Ray Johnston. 144p. 1994. pap. 14.99 (*0-310-49041-3*) Zondervan.

*__Developing SQL Windows Applications.__ David Gugick. (Illus.). 550p. (Orig.). 1995. pap. 45.00 (*0-672-30511-9*) Sams.

Developing Staff Competencies for Supporting People with Developmental Disabilities: An Orientation Handbook. 2nd ed. James F. Gardner & Michael S. Chapman. LC 92-14330. 416p. (C). 1992. reprint ed. pap. text ed. 35.00 (*1-55766-107-3*, 1073) P H Brookes.

*__Developing Staff Skills.__ Ed. by Roger Neugebauer. (Best of Exchange Ser.). (Illus.). 48p. (Orig.). (C). 1990. pap. 10.00 (*0-942702-07-7*) Child Care.

*__Developing Strategic Thought: Rediscovering the Art of Direction-Giving.__ Ed. by Bob Garratt. (McGraw-Hill Developing Organizations Ser.). 1995. text ed. 29.95 (*0-07-707986-8*) McGraw.

Developing Structural Integrity in Bearing Wall Buildings. (PCI Journal Reprints Ser.). 33p. 1980. pap. 8.00 (*0-686-40151-4*, JR248) P-PCI.

Developing Structure of Temperament & Personality from Infancy to Adulthood. Ed. by Charles F. Halverson et al. 464p. 1994. text ed. 99.95 (*0-8058-1252-0*) L Erlbaum Assocs.

*__Developing Structure of Temperament & Personality from Infancy to Adulthood.__ Ed. by Charles F. Halverson et al. 464p. 1994. pap. 39.95 (*0-8058-1669-0*) L Erlbaum Assocs.

Developing Structured Systems: A Methodology Using Structured Techniques. Brian Dickinson. LC 80-54609. (Illus.). 360p. 1986. pap. 39.95 (*0-917072-23-5*, Yourdon) P-H.

Developing Student Autonomy in Learning. 2nd ed. Ed. by David Boud. 284p. 1988. 39.95 (*0-89397-291-6*) Nichols Pub.

*__Developing Student Capability Through Modular Courses.__ Ed. by Alan Jenkins et al. (Teaching & Learning in Higher Education Ser.). 192p. 1994. pap. 35.00x (*0-7484-1369-3*, Pub. by Kogan Page Educ UK) Taylor & Francis.

*__Developing Student Government Leadership.__ Ed. by Melvin C. Terrell & Michael J. Cuyjet. LC 85-644751. (New Directions for Student Services Ser.: No. 66). 108p. (Orig.). 1994. pap. 16.95 (*0-7879-9972-5*) Jossey-Bass.

Developing Student Leaders: How to Motivate, Select, Train & Empower Your Kids to Make a Difference. Ray Johnston. 160p. 1991. pap. 12.99 (*0-310-54331-2*) Zondervan.

Developing Study Skills in Secondary Schools. Ed. by Harold L. Herber. LC 65-5280. (Perspectives in Reading Ser.: No. 4). 175p. reprint ed. pap. 49.90 (*0-317-28181-X*, 2025446) Bks Demand.

Developing Style in Watercolour. Ray C. Smith. (Illus.). 128p. 1992. 24.95 (*0-7153-9956-X*, Pub. by D & C Pub UK) Sterling.

Developing Subjective Test Items. Susan S. Redfield & Lisa Kupetsky. (Illus.). 40p. (Orig.). 1987. pap. 16.50 (*0-87683-917-0*, A917-0) GP Pub.

Developing Substance: Mid-Range Theory in Nursing, Vol. 2. Ed. by Peggy L. Chinn. LC 94-7364. (Advances in Nursing Science Ser.). 286p. 1994. pap. 37.00 (*0-8342-0578-5*) Aspen Pub.

Developing Successful College Writing Programs. Edward M. White. LC 88-30416. (Higher & Adult Education Ser.). 256p. 1989. 32.95x (*1-55542-131-8*) Jossey-Bass.

*__Developing Successful Marketing Strategies.__ Allan Sutherlin. 1992. pap. 19.95 (*0-8442-3580-6*) NTC Pub Grp.

Developing Successful New Communities. Reid Ewing. LC 91-75046. 154p. 1991. 58.95 (*0-87420-719-3*) Urban Land.

Developing Successful New Products: A Guide to Product Planning. David Allen. (Financial Times Management Ser.). 320p. 1993. 114.00x (*0-273-60150-4*, Pub. by Pitman Pub Ltd UK) Trans-Atl Phila.

Developing Successful Worker Co-Operatives. Chris Cornforth et al. 256p. (C). 1988. text ed. 48.00 (*0-8039-8076-0*); pap. text ed. 17.95 (*0-8039-8077-9*) Sage.

Developing Superior Work Teams: Building Quality & the Competitive Edge. Dennis C. Kinlaw. 192p. 1990. text ed. 32.95 (*0-669-24983-1*) Free Pr.

*__Developing Superior Work Teams: Building Quality & the Competitive Edge.__ Dennis C. Kinlaw. 224p. 1995. 29.95 (*0-87425-257-1*) Human Res Dev Pr.

Developing Supervision of Teams in Field & Residential Social Work, 2 pts. Chris Payne & Tony Scott. (C). 1982. Pt. 1. 50.00 (*0-7855-0074-X*, Pub. by Natl Inst Soc Work); Pt. 2. 25.00 (*0-7855-0075-8*, Pub. by Natl Inst Soc Work) St Mut.

Developing Supervision of Teams in Field & Residential Social Work, Pt. 1. Chris Payne & Tony Scott. (C). 1982. 39.00 (*0-902789-24-4*, Pub. by Natl Inst Soc Work) St Mut.

Developing Supervision of Teams in Field & Residential Social Work, Pt. 1. Tony Scott & Chris Payne. 1982. 25.00 (*0-317-05758-8*, Pub. by Natl Inst Soc Work) St Mut.

Developing Supervision of Teams in Field & Residential Social Work, Pt. 2. Chris Payne & Tony Scott. (C). 1985. 29.00 (*0-685-28589-8*, Pub. by Natl Inst Soc Work); 25.00 (*0-902789-34-1*, Pub. by Natl Inst Soc Work) St Mut.

Developing Supervision of Teams in Field & Residential Social Work, pt.2. Chris Payne & Tony Scott. Ed. by National Institute for Social Work Staff. 1985. 12.50 (*0-317-40576-4*, Pub. by Natl Inst Soc Work) St Mut.

*__Developing Support Groups for Individuals with Early-Stage Alzheimer's Disease: Planning, Implementation, & Evaluation.__ Robyn Yale. LC 95-6672. 192p. 1995. pap. text ed. 27.00 (*1-878812-26-2*) Hlth Prof Pr.

*__Developing SYBASE Applications.__ Daniel Worden. (Illus.). 650p. (Orig.). 1995. pap. 39.99 (*0-672-30700-6*) Sams.

Developing Talent in Young People. Ed. by Benjamin S. Blood. 1985. pap. 9.95 (*0-345-31509-X*, Ballantine Trade) Ballantine.

*__Developing Teachers Developing Schools: Making INSET Effective for the School.__ Ed. by Howard Bradley et al. 208p. 1994. pap. 27.00x (*1-85346-321-3*, Pub. by D Fulton UK) Taylor & Francis.

Developing Teachers Professionally: Reflections for Initial & In-Service Trainers. Ed. by David Bridges & Trevor Kerry. LC 93-6981. 192p. 1993. 59.95 (*0-415-09295-7*, B0802); pap. write for info. (*0-415-09296-5*) Routledge.

Developing Teacher's Theories of Teaching: A Touchstone Approach. Bevis Yaxley. 240p. 1991. 65.00 (*1-85000-777-2*, Falmer Pr); pap. 30.00 (*1-85000-778-0*, Falmer Pr) Taylor & Francis.

Developing Teaching Competencies. James De Lee et al. LC 79-9910. 72p. 1979. pap. text ed. 9.95 (*0-88289-215-0*) Pelican.

Developing Teaching Skills in Physical Education. 3rd ed. Daryl Siedentop. LC 90-25194. 343p. (C). 1991. text ed. 39.95 (*0-87484-899-7*) Mayfield Pub.

Developing Technical Training: A Structured Approach for the Development of Classroom & Computer-Based Instructional Materials. Ruth C. Clark. (Illus.). 263p. (C). 1989. 37.95 (*0-201-14967-2*) Addison-Wesley.

Developing Technical Training: A Structured Approach for the Development of Classroom & Computer-Based Instructional Materials. Ruth C. Clark. LC 88-34964. (Training & Development Ser.). (Illus.). 272p. (C). 1994. reprint ed. pap. text ed. 31.95 (*0-9641045-0-4*) Buzzards Bay.

*__Developing Technology Managers in the Pacific Rim: Comparative Strategies.__ Ed. by Karen Minden & Poh-Kam Wong. LC 95-15666. (Illus.). 272p. 1995. 59.95 (*1-56324-618-X*, East Gate Bk); pap. 24.95 (*1-56324-619-8*, East Gate Bk) M E Sharpe.

Developing Test-Taking Skills. Maria Sosa. (Illus.). 1982. pap. text ed. 165.00 (*0-89290-183-7*, A191-SATC) Soc for Visual.

An Asterisk (*) at the beginning of an entry indicates that the title is appearing in BIP for the first time.

An Asterisk (*) at the beginning of an entry indicates that the title is appearing in BIP for the first time.

Development & Applications of a Decision Support System for Emergency Medical Services. David J. Eaton et al. (Working Paper Ser.: No. 46). 24p. 1988. pap. 5.00 (*0-685-24954-9*) LBJ Sch Pub Aff.

Development & Backwardness: Coexistence or Confrontation? S. Parameswara. (Sociological Publications in Honour of Dr. K. Ishwaran: No. 6). 1990. text ed. 30.00 (*81-85047-62-6*, Pub. by Reliance Pub Hse II) Apt Bks.

Development & Change: Essays in Honour of K. N. Raj. Ed. by Pranab Bardhan et al. (Illus.). 374p. 1994. 26.00 (*0-19-563122-6*) OUP.

Development & Change in Highland Yemen. Charles F. Swagman. LC 88-20603. (Illus.). 220p. reprint ed. pap. 62.70 (*0-7837-5981-9*, 2045785) Bks Demand.

Development & Change in India. R. T. Tewari & A. Joshi. (C). 1988. 62.00 (*81-7024-200-2*, Pub. by Ashish II) S Asia.

Development & Character of Gothic Architecture. Charles H. Moore. 1977. lib. bdg. 139.95 (*0-8490-1713-0*) Gordon Pr.

Development & Chemical Specificity Neurons: Proceedings of the International Symposium, Switzerland, Sept., 1978. Ed. by M. Cuenod et al. (Progress in Brain Research Ser.: Vol. 51). 1980. 134.00 (*0-444-80128-6*, North Holland) Elsevier.

Development & Chronology of Chaucer's Works. John S. Tatlock. (Chaucer Society Second Ser.: No. 37). 241p. reprint ed. pap. 9.95 (*0-935005-80-3*) Lincoln-Rembrandt.

Development & Clinical Uses of Haemophilus B Conjugate Vaccines. Ed. by Ronald W. Ellis & Dan M. Granoff. LC 94-302. (Infectious Disease & Therapy Ser.: Vol. 11). 520p. 1994. 175.00 (*0-8247-9186-X*) Dekker.

Development & Conservation of Ground-Water Resources & Water-Related Natural Disasters & Their Mitigation in Selected Least Developed Countries & Developing Island Countries in the ESCAP Region. (Water Resources Ser.: No. 66). 102p. 1990. 13.50 (*92-1-119552-7*, 89.II.F.18) UN.

Development & Control of Dust Explosions. Nagy & Verakis. (Occupational Safety & Health Ser.: Vol. 8). 296p. 1983. 110.00 (*0-8247-7004-8*) Dekker.

Development & Cultural Change: Cross-Cultural Perspectives. Ed. by Ilpyong J. Kim. 255p. (C). 1986. pap. 12.95 (*0-89226-041-6*, ICUS) Paragon Hse.

Development & Decline: The Evolution of Sociopolitical Organization. Ed. by Henri J. Claessen et al. LC 84-28258. 384p. (C). 1985. text ed. 65.00 (*0-89789-075-2*, Bergin & Garvey) Greenwood.

Development & Decline in Fukien Province in the 17th & 18th Centuries. Ed. by E. B. Vermeer. LC 90-43720. (Sinica Leidensia Ser.: Vol. 22). 488p. 1990. pap. 105.75 (*90-04-09171-8*) E J Brill.

Development & Democracy: Aid Policies in Latin America. 128p. (Orig.). 1992. pap. 30.00 (*92-64-13770-X*) OECD.

Development & Democracy in the Third World. Abbas Pourgerami. 210p. (C). 1991. pap. text ed. 33.50 (*0-8133-8005-7*) Westview.

Development & Democratization in the Third World: Myths, Hopes, & Realities. Ed. by Kenneth E. Bauzon. 250p. 1992. 54.50 (*0-8448-1722-8*, Crane Russak); pap. 24.50 (*0-8448-1723-6*, Crane Russak) Taylor & Francis.

Development & Design with Advanced Materials: Proceedings of the 2nd International Conference on Development & Design with Advanced Materials (ATMAM '89), Montreal, Quebec, Canada, 16-18 Aug., 1989. Ed. by G. C. Sih et al. 346p. 1990. 128.25 (*0-444-88706-7*, North Holland) Elsevier.

Development & Differentiation of Vertebrate Lymphocytes. J. Horton. (Developments in Immunology Ser.: Vol. 8). 1980. 70.25 (*0-444-80195-2*) Elsevier.

Development & Dilemmas in Science Education. Ed. by Peter Fensham. 225p. 1988. 70.00 (*1-85000-350-5*, Falmer Pr); pap. 32.50 (*1-85000-351-3*, Falmer Pr) Taylor & Francis.

Development & Disenchantment in Rural Tunisia: The Bourguiba Years. Mira Zussman. 212p. (C). 1992. pap. text ed. 41.50 (*0-8133-8238-6*) Westview.

Development & Dissemination of Model Systems for Hypertension Control in Organizational Settings. Andrea E. Foote & John C. Erfurt. 1974. 3.50 (*0-87736-322-6*) U of Mich Inst Labor.

Development & Distribution of Dejiao Associations in Malaysia & Singapore. Tan Chee-Beng. 100p. 1986. pap. 13.75 (*9971-988-14-3*, Pub. by Inst SE Asian Studies SI) Ashgate Pub Co.

Development & Diversity: Language Variation across Time & Space. Ed. by Jerold A. Edmondson et al. (Publications in Lingustics: No. 93). 688p. 1990. fiche 48.00 (*0-88312-908-6*) Summer Instit Ling.

Development & Effectiveness: Strategies for IS Organizational Transition. Vaughan Merlyn et al. LC 93-6045. (Ernst & Young Information Mangement Ser.). 300p. 1994. text ed. 45.00 (*0-471-58954-3*) Wiley.

Development & Environment: Proceedings. Conference on the Human Environment, Founex, Switzerland, June 4-12, 1971. Ed. by Maurice F. Strong. LC 72-75446. (Illus.). 225p. (Orig.). 1973. pap. text ed. 24.65 (*90-279-6990-6*) Mouton.

Development & Environment: Sustaining People & Nature. Intro. by Dharam Ghai. (Illus.). 268p. (C). 1994. pap. text ed. 17.95 (*0-631-19394-4*) Blackwell Pubs.

Development & Evaluation of a Rapid & Highly Sensitive Methodology for the Detection of Human Viruses in Water. 48p. 1989. pap. 12.50 (*0-89867-472-7*, 90546) Am Water Wks Assn.

Development & Evaluation of Job Performance Criteria: A Procedural Guide. Warren S. Blumenfeld. LC 76-18778. (Research Monograph: No. 64). 46p. 1976. spiral bd. 19.95 (*0-88406-096-9*) GA St U Busn Pr.

Development & Evaluation of Roadside Safety Features. LC 92-38101. (Transportation Research Record Ser.: No. 1367). 1993. 22.00 (*0-309-05408-7*) Transport Res Bd.

Development & Evolution. Ed. by B. C. Goodwin. LC 82-14728. (British Society for Developmental Biology Symposium Ser.: No. 6). 350p. 1983. 125.00 (*0-521-24949-X*) Cambridge U Pr.

Development & Evolution: Complexity & Change in Biology. Stanley N. Salthe. 400p. 1993. 52.50 (*0-262-19335-3*, Bradford Bks) MIT Pr.

Development & Evolution: Including Psychophysical Evolution, Evolution by Orthoplasy & the Theory of Genetic Modes. James M. Baldwin. LC 75-3022. (Philosophy in America Ser.). reprint ed. 42.50 (*0-404-59017-9*) AMS Pr.

Development & Evolution of Butterfly Wing Patterns. H. Frederik Nijhout. LC 90-24312. (Series in Comparative Evolutionary Biology). (Illus.). 336p. (C). 1991. 45.00 (*0-87474-921-2*); pap. text ed. 25.00 (*0-87474-917-4*) Smithsonian.

Development & Foreign Policy: Ghana's Experience, 1966-69. A. S. Shahid. iv, 190p. 1991. 18.00 (*81-85163-17-0*, Pub. by Kalinga Pubns) Nataraj Bks.

Development & Function of Roots. Ed. by John G. Torrey & D. Clarkson. 1975. text ed. 253.00 (*0-12-695750-9*) Acad Pr.

Development & Growth of the External Dimensions of the Human Body in the Fetal Period. Richard Scammon & Leroy A. Calkins. LC 29-23081. 391p. reprint ed. pap. 111.50 (*0-317-26311-0*, 2055910) Bks Demand.

Development & Growth of the Film Industry in Nigeria. Ed. by O. Nwuneli & A. Opubor. (Illus.). 114p. 1980. 19.95 (*0-89388-220-8*); pap. 11.95 (*0-685-59744-X*) Okpaku Communications.

Development & Handicap. Vicky A. Lewis. 256p. 1987. pap. text ed. 24.95 (*0-631-13633-9*) Blackwell Pubs.

Development & Impact of Right-Wing Politics in Britain, 1903-1932. Barbara S. Farr. Ed. by William H. McNeill & Peter Stansky. (Modern European History Ser.). 400p. 1987. lib. bdg. 15.00 (*0-8240-7806-3*) Garland.

Development & Implementation of an Accounting System for District Courts of Virginia. National Center for State Courts Staff. 18p. 1975. 1.08 (*0-685-15173-5*, MAB-042) Natl Ctr St Courts.

Development & Integration of Behaviour: Essays in Honor of Robert Hinde. Ed. by Patrick Bateson. (Illus.). 400p. (C). 1991. 110.00 (*0-521-40356-1*); pap. 34.95 (*0-521-40709-5*) Cambridge U Pr.

Development & Interrelationships of Oneota Culture in the Lower Missouri River Valley, Vol. 32. Dale R. Henning. Ed. by Robert T. Bray. (Missouri Archaeologist Ser.). (Illus.). 185p. (Orig.). 1970. pap. 3.00 (*0-943414-49-0*) MO Arch Soc.

Development & Laboratory Evaluation of the Haloform Potential Tests. 180p. 1989. pap. 21.00 (*0-89867-464-6*, 90547) Am Water Wks Assn.

Development & Learning: Conflict or Congruence? Lynn S. Liben. (Jean Piaget Symposium Ser.). 256p. 1987. 49.95 (*0-8058-0009-3*) L Erlbaum Assocs.

Development & Legal Services in Africa: Report of a Seminar on Development & Legal Services in Africa, Dakar-Senegal, April 1983, Organized by the Council for the Development of Economic & Social Research in Africa (CODESRIA) & the International Commission of Jurists (ICJ) Seminar on Development & Legal Services in Africa (1983: Dakar-Senegal). (CODESRIA Special Publications: No. 1). 193p. reprint ed. pap. 55.10 (*0-685-16102-1*, 2027735) Bks Demand.

Development & Maintenance of Prosocial Behavior: International Perspectives on Positive Morality. Ed. by Ervin Staub et al. LC 84-3355. (Critical Issues in Social Justice Ser.). 538p. 1984. 85.00 (*0-306-41299-3*, Plenum Pr) Plenum.

Development & Management Aspects of Irrigation & Drainage Systems. Ed. by Conrad G. Keyes, Jr. & Jim J. Ward. 496p. 1985. 48.00 (*0-87262-472-2*) Am Soc Civil Eng.

Development & Management of Agriculture. V. N. Asopa & P. N. Shingi. 413p. (C). 1987. 26.00 (*81-204-0221-9*, Pub. by Oxford IBH II) S Asia.

***Development & Management of Audiology Practices.** Ed. by Evelyn Cherow et al. 142p. 1994. pap. text ed. 25.00 (*0-614-06522-4*, 0111902) Am Speech Lang Hearing.

Development & Management of Counseling Programs & Guidance Services. Robert L. Gibson et al. 448p. (C). 1983. text ed. write for info. (*0-02-341770-6*) Macmillan.

Development & Management of University Research Groups. Robert V. Smith. (Illus.). 147p. (C). 1986. text ed. 17.50 (*0-292-71538-2*) U of Tex Pr.

***Development & Management of Visitor Attractions.** John Swarbrooke. (Illus.). 300p. 1995. pap. 32.95 (*0-7506-1979-1*, Focal) Buttrwrth-Heinemann.

Development & Meaning of Psychological Distance. Ed. by Rodney R. Cocking & K. Ann Renninger. 280p. 1992. text ed. 59.95 (*0-8058-0747-0*) L Erlbaum Assocs.

Development & Modes of Production in Marxian Economics (a Critical Evaluation) Alan Richards. (In the Fundamentals of Pure & Applied Economics Ser.: Volume 12). 160p. 1986. pap. text ed. 44.00 (*3-7186-0332-2*) Gordon & Breach.

***Development & Operation Manual for a Golf Practice Range Facility.** Jay K. Livingood. (Illus.). 300p. 1992. 195.00 (*0-9645721-0-9*) Livingood Consult.

Development & Physiology of Angiosperms. (Advances in Pollen Spore Research Ser.: Vol. III). 160p. 1978. 12.00 (*0-88065-167-9*, Messers Today & Tomorrow) Scholarly Pubns.

Development & Planning. Ignacy Sachs. Tr. by Peter Fawcett. (Illus.). 112p. 1987. 44.95 (*0-521-33454-3*) Cambridge U Pr.

Development & Planning Economy Environmental & Resource Issues. P. A. Stone. 256p. 1988. text ed. 59.50 (*0-419-13560-X*, E & FN Spon) Routledge Chapman & Hall.

Development & Plasticity of the Brain: An Introduction. Raymond D. Lund. (Illus.). 1978. pap. text ed. 19.95 (*0-19-502308-0*) OUP.

Development & Plasticity of the Mammalian Spinal Cord. Ed. by A. Gorio et al. 300p. 1986. 129.00 (*0-387-96366-9*) Spr-Verlag.

Development & Policy Concerning Children with Special Needs. Ed. by Marion Perlmutter. (Minnesota Symposia on Child Psychology Ser.: Vol. 16). 272p. (C). 1983. text ed. 49.95 (*0-89859-261-5*) L Erlbaum Assocs.

Development & Politics of Argentine Immigration Policy 1852-1914: To Govern Is to Populate. Donald S. Castro. LC 91-30100. 324p. 1991. lib. bdg. 99.95 (*0-7734-9980-6*) E Mellen.

Development & Present Status of Negro Education in East Texas. William R. Davis. LC 75-178798. (Columbia University. Teachers College. Contributions to Education Ser.: No. 626). reprint ed. 37.50 (*0-404-55626-4*) AMS Pr.

Development & Principles of International Humanitarian Law. Jean Pictet. 1985. pap. 16.95 (*0-318-18536-9*) Kluwer Ac.

Development & Procurement of Gliders in the Army Air Forces, 1941-1944. Paul M. Davis & Amy C. Fenwick. (USAF Historical Studies: No. 47). 208p. 1946. reprint ed. pap. 29.00 (*0-89126-148-6*) MA-AH Pub.

Development & Psychometric Characteristics of the Revised Illinois Test of Psycholinquistic Abilities. Samuel A. Kirk & John N. Paraskevopoulos. LC 69-19511. (Illus.). 243p. 1969. pap. 15.00 (*0-252-00007-2*) U of Ill Pr.

Development & Purpose: An Essay Towards a Philosophy of Evolution. Leonard T. Hobhouse. 1968. reprint ed. 59.00 (*0-403-00115-3*) Scholarly.

Development & Rearing of Zoae Larvae in Brachyura: Crustacea Decapoda. Ali Soltanpour-Gargari et al. LC 89-17306. (Crustaceana Supplements Ser.: No. 14). viii, 173p. (Orig.). 1989. pap. text ed. 34.50 (*90-04-08807-5*) E J Brill.

Development & Recognition of the Transformed Cell. Ed. by M. I. Greene & T. Hamaoka. LC 87-17175. (Illus.). 476p. 1987. 95.00 (*0-306-42636-6*, Plenum Pr) Plenum.

Development & Reform of Financial Systems in Central & Eastern Europe. Ed. by John P. Bonin & Istvan P. Szekely. 368p. 1995. 67.95 (*1-85898-024-0*, Pub. by E Elgar Pub UK) Ashgate Pub Co.

Development & Regeneration of Nervous System. Ed. by G. Toffano & G. Calderini. (Journal: Developmental Neuroscience: Vol. 5, No. 1). (Illus.). 116p. 1982. pap. 46.50 (*3-8055-3524-4*) S Karger.

Development & Regeneration of Skeletal Muscles. Ed. by B. Christ & R. Cihak. (Bibliotheca Anatomica Ser.: No. 29). (Illus.). viii, 224p. 1986. 143.25 (*3-8055-4227-5*) S Karger.

Development & Regeneration of the Nervous System. Ed. by S. Nona et al. (Eye & Brain: Biomedical & Clinical Aspects Ser.). (Illus.). 272p. 1992. 170.00 (*0-412-40280-7*, A9438) Chapman & Hall.

Development & Relationships. 2nd ed. Mollie S. Smart & Russell C. Smart. Incl. Vol. 3. 1978. 17.50 (*0-685-42251-8*); (Illus.). 1978. write for info. (*0-318-54208-0*) Macmillan.

Development & Scope of Higher Education in the United States. Richard Hofstadter & C. De Witt Hardy. LC 52-14741. 254p. 1952. text ed. 50.00 (*0-231-01956-4*) Col U Pr.

Development & Social Change in Rural Egypt. Richard H. Adams, Jr. LC 85-30251. (Contemporary Issues in the Middle East Ser.). (Illus.). 248p. 1986. text ed. 39.95x (*0-8156-2362-3*) Syracuse U Pr.

***Development & Social Change in the Chilean Countryside: From the Pre-Land Reform Period to the Democratic Transition.** Cristobal Kay & Patrico Silva. (CEDLA Latin America Studies (CLAS): No. 62). 344p. 1992. pap. 32.00 (*90-70280-63-9*, Pub. by Thesis Pubs NE) IBD Ltd.

Development & Social Change in the Pacific Islands. Alastair Couper. (Croom Helm Maritime Ser.). 176p. (C). 1989. lib. bdg. 55.00 (*0-415-00917-0*) Routledge.

Development & Social Justice: Micro-Action by Weaker Sections. Anil Bhatt. 220p. (C). 1989. text ed. 26.00 (*0-8039-9579-2*) Sage.

Development & Social Welfare: Indonesia's Experiences under the New Order. Ed. by Jan P. Dirkse et al. (Verhandelingen Ser.: No. 156). 306p. (Orig.). 1993. pap. 29.00 (*90-6718-056-4*, Pub. by KLTV Pr NE) Cellar.

Development & Structure of the Furniture Industry. J. L. Oliver. 1966. 97.00 (*0-08-011460-1*, Pub. by Pergamon Repr UK) Franklin.

Development & Structures of Creole Languages: Essays in Honor of Derek Bickerton. Ed. by Francis Byrne & Thom Huebner. LC 90-23249. (Creole Language Library: Vol. 9). x, 222p. 1991. 50.00x (*1-55619-162-6*) Benjamins North Am.

Development & Structures of the Body Image, 2 vols., Set. Seymour Fisher. 1986. text ed. 125.00 (*0-89859-700-5*) L Erlbaum Assocs.

Development & Structures of the Body Image, Vol. 1. Seymour Fisher. 344p. 1986. Vol. I, 344p. text ed. 69.95 (*0-89859-684-X*) L Erlbaum Assocs.

Development & Structures of the Body Image, Vol. 2. Seymour Fisher. 568p. 1986. Vol. II, 568p. text ed. 99.95 (*0-89859-699-8*) L Erlbaum Assocs.

Development & Sustaining of Self-Esteem in Childhood. Ed. by John E. Mack & Steven L. Ablon. LC 83-22726. xiv, 304p. 1984. 42.50x (*0-8236-1255-4*) Intl Univs Pr.

Development & Testing of a General Modelling Technique, No. EUR 12826. A. Behle et al. 117p. 1990. 12.00 (*92-826-1560-X*, CD-NA-12826-EN-C) UNIPUB.

Development & Testing of a Siesmic Pavement Analyzer. Soheil Nazarain et al. 165p. (Orig.). (C). 1993. pap. text ed. 15.00 (*0-309-05753-1*, SHRP-H-375) SHRP.

Development & the Arts: Critical Perspectives. Ed. by Margery B. Franklin & Bernard Kaplan. 280p. 1994. text ed. 59.95 (*0-8058-0487-0*) L Erlbaum Assocs.

Development & the Environment Crisis: Red or Green Alternatives. Michael Redclift. (Development & Underdevelopment Ser.). 176p. 1984. pap. 14.95 (*0-416-32140-2*, NO. 4020) Routledge Chapman & Hall.

Development & the Rule of Law: Prevention Verses Cure as a Human Rights Strategy. Philip Alston. 131p. reprint ed. pap. 37.40 (*0-8357-6645-4*, 2035312) Bks Demand.

Development & the State in Reforma Guatemala, 1871-1885. David McCreery. LC 81-22545. (Papers in International Studies: Latin America Ser.: No. 10). 128p. (Orig.). reprint ed. pap. 36.50 (*0-7837-6472-3*, 2046476) Bks Demand.

Development & Transfer of Industrial Technology. Ed. by O. C. C. Lin et al. LC 94-5799. (Advances in Industrial Engineering Ser.: Vol. 20). 292p. 1994. 200.00 (*0-444-81686-0*) Elsevier.

Development & Transfer of Pollution Prevention Technology. Ann Rappaport. LC 93-292. 224p. 1993. text ed. 55.00 (*0-89930-816-3*, Q816, Quorum Bks) Greenwood.

Development & Transformation: Themes & Variations in Indian Society. B. K. Nagla. (C). 1993. 36.00 (*81-7033-189-7*, Pub. by Rawat II) S Asia.

Development & Treatment of Childhood Aggression. Ed. by Debra Pepler & Kenneth H. Rubin. 488p. 1990. 95.00 (*0-8058-0370-X*) L Erlbaum Assocs.

Development & Underdevelopment: A Profile of the Third World. John Cole. 160p. 1987. pap. text ed. 9.95 (*0-416-92080-2*, 1205) Routledge Chapman & Hall.

Development & Underdevelopment: The History, Economics & Politics of North-South Relations. Hartmut Elsenhans. (Illus.). 176p. 1991. text ed. 22.50 (*0-8039-9679-9*) Sage.

Development & Underdevelopment: The Political Economy of Inequality. Ed. by Mitchell A. Seligson & John T. Passe-Smith. LC 93-9796. 456p. (Orig.). (C). 1993. pap. text ed. 22.00 (*1-55587-400-2*) Lynne Rienner.

Development & Underdevelopment in America: Contrasts of Economic Growth in North & Latin America in Historical Perspective. Ed. by Walther Bernecker & Hans W. Tobler. LC 93-11856. (Studies on North America: No. 8). iv, 335p. (C). 1993. lib. bdg. 129.25 (*3-11-013518-3*) De Gruyter.

Development & Underdevelopment in Historical Perspective. 2nd ed. Ed. by Gavin Kitching. (Development & Underdevelopment Ser.). 224p. 1989. pap. 14.95 (*0-415-03449-3*) Routledge.

Development & Use of the MMPI-2 Content Scales. Butcher et al. 200p. 1990. text ed. 24.95 (*0-8166-1817-8*) U of Minn Pr.

Development & Validation of Performance Prediction Models & Specifications for Asphalt Binders & Paving Mixes. Robert L. Lytton et al. 500p. (Orig.). (C). 1993. pap. text ed. 20.00 (*0-309-05617-9*, SHRP-A-357) SHRP.

***Development & Vulnerability in Close Relationships.** Ed. by Gil G. Noam & Kurt W. Fischer. (Jean Piaget Symposia Ser.). 270p. 1995. text ed. 45.00 (*0-8058-1369-1*) L Erlbaum Assocs.

Development & Water Pollution Control in Asia: Selected Proceedings of Asian Waterqual '91, the 3rd IAWPRC Regional Conference on Development & Water Pollution Control, 20-24 November, 1991, Shanghai, China. Ed. by R. Bhamidimarri et al. (Water Science & Technology Ser.: Vol. 28). (Illus.). 258p. 1994. pap. 97.00 (*0-08-042491-0*) Elsevier.

Development Anthropology. Riall Nolan. (C). 1996. text ed. 37.50 (*0-8133-0983-2*); pap. text ed. 19.95 (*0-8133-0984-0*) Westview.

Development As Action in Context. Ed. by Rainer K. Silbereisen et al. (Illus.). 335p. 1986. 119.00 (*0-387-13449-2*) Spr-Verlag.

Development As an Evolutionary Process, 1985, Vol. 198. Ed. by Rudolf A. Raff & Elizabeth C. Raff. 344p. 1987. text ed. 99.95 (*0-471-62922-7*) Wiley.

Development As Communication: A Perspective on India. Uma Narula & W. Barnett Pearce. LC 85-2088. 240p. 1986. text ed. 19.95 (*0-8093-1223-9*) S Ill U Pr.

Development as Social Transformation: Reflections on the Global Problematique. (United Nations University (UNU) Publications). 281p. 1989. 20.00 (*92-808-0483-9*, E.88.III.A.11) UN.

***Development Assistance, Export Promotion & Environmental Technology.** 1995. lib. bdg. 250.95 (*0-8490-7539-4*) Gordon Pr.

Development Assistance Manual: DAC Principles for Effective Aid. 152p. (Orig.). 1992. pap. 19.00 (*92-64-13779-3*) OECD.

Development at Crossroads: An African Experience. Ed. by Kwaku Osei-Hwedie & Muna Ndulo. LC 90-83110. (Illus.). 412p. (Orig.). 1990. pap. text ed. 24.95 (*1-55618-085-3*) Brunswick Pub.

Development Bank Business Market: What the MDBs Lend For, Why They Lend for It, & How Much They Lend, Including a Lending Scenario for the Year 2000. Nicholas H. Ludlow. LC 93-71061. (Illus.). 460p. 1993. 383.00 (*0-943781-03-5*) Develop Bank.

Development Banking in Mexico: The Case of the Nacional Financiera, S. A. Miguel D. Ramirez. LC 85-16700. 252p. 1985. text ed. 59.95 (*0-275-92032-1*, C2032, Praeger Pubs) Greenwood.

An Asterisk (*) at the beginning of an entry indicates that the title is appearing in BIP for the first time.

An Asterisk (*) at the beginning of an entry indicates that the title is appearing in BIP for the first time.

***Development Issues: Presentations to the 44th Meeting of the Development Committee, Washington, D. C.- September 21, 1992.** (Development Committee Report Ser.: No. 30). 128p. (SPA.). 1992. 7.95 (*0-8213-2274-5*, 12274) World Bank.

***Development Issues: Presentations to the 47th Meeting of the Development Committee, Washington, D. C.- September 27, 1993.** (Development Committee Report Ser.: No. 32). 152p. 1993. 9.95 (*0-8213-2710-0*, 12710) World Bank.

***Development Issues: Presentations to the 47th Meeting of the Development Committee, Washington, D. C.- September 27, 1993.** (Development Committee Report Ser.: No. 32). 152p. (FRE.). 1993. 9.95 (*0-8213-2711-9*, 12711) World Bank.

***Development Issues: Presentations to the 47th Meeting of the Development Committee, Washington, D. C.- September 27, 1993.** (Development Committee Report Ser.: No. 32). 152p. (SPA.). 1993. 9.95 (*0-8213-2712-7*, 12712) World Bank.

***Development Issues: Presentations to the 48th Meeting of the Development Committee, Washington, D.C., April 26, 1994.** 158p. 1994. lib. bdg. 9.95 (*0-8213-2870-0*) World Bank.

***Development Issues: Presentations to the 49th Meeting of the Development Committee, Madrid, Spain 1994.** World Bank Staff. 120p. 1994. 8.95 (*0-8213-3136-1*, 13136) World Bank.

Development Issues & Strategies in the New Europe. Ed. by Markku Tykkylainen. 220p. 1992. 68.95 (*1-85628-326-7*, Pub. by Avebury Pub UK) Ashgate Pub Co.

Development Issues in the Arab World. Allan M. Findlay. LC 93-5461. (Introductions to Development Ser.). Date not set. write for info. (*0-415-04200-3*) Routledge.

Development Issues: Presentations to the 46th Meeting of the Development Committee, Washington, D. C., May 1, 1993: Problemes De Developpement: Communicatins Faites a La 46e Reunion Du Comite Du Developpement, Washington, D. C. - Ler Mai 1993 - Cuestiones Relativas Al Desarollo: Exposiciones Presentadas En la XLVI Reunion Del Comite Para el Desarollo, Celebrada El la Ciudad De Washington, el 1 De Mayo De 1993. (Development Committee Report Ser.: No. 31). 236p. 1993. ENG. 13.95 (*0-8213-2499-3*, 12499); FRE. 13.95 (*0-8213-2500-0*, 12500); SPA. 13.95 (*0-8213-2501-9*, 12501) World Bank.

Development Land & Development Charge in Singapore. Leung Y. Kwong. 202p. 1987. 74.00 (*0-409-00537-1*) Butterworth Legal Pubs.

Development Land & Development Charge in Singapore. Leung. 1987. 74.00 (*0-409-99537-1*) Butterworth Legal Pubs.

***Development Macroeconomics.** Pierre-Richard Agenor & Peter J. Montiel. LC 95-2853. 1995. write for info. (*0-691-03413-3*) Princeton U Pr.

***Development Management in Africa: Toward Dynamism, Empowerment, & Entrepreneurship.** Sadig Rasheed. 283p. (C). 1994. pap. text ed. 49.95 (*0-8133-2147-6*) Westview.

Development, Marketing & Operation of Manufactured Home Communities. George Allen et al. 409p. (C). 1993. text ed. 73.00 (*0-471-59519-5*) Wiley.

Development, Methods, & Response Characteristics: National Mortality Followback Survey, 1986. LC 92-48960. (Vital & Health Statistics Ser.: No. 29). 1992. write for info. (*0-8406-0471-8*) Natl Ctr Health Stats.

Development Methods for Water Wells: Anthology. 94p. 1986. 6.25 (*1-56034-005-3*, K065) Natl Water Well.

Development Model for the Agricultural Sector of Portugal. Alvin C Egbert & Hyung M. Kim. LC 75-2662. (World Bank Occasional Paper Ser.: No. 20). (Illus.). 109p. 1975. pap. 6.95 (*0-8018-1793-5*) Johns Hopkins.

Development of a Classification of Travel-to-Work Areas. A. E. Green & D. W. Owen. (Progress in Planning Ser.: Vol. 34). (Illus.). 96p. 1990. pap. 45.00 (*0-08-040771-4*, Pergamon Pr) Elsevier.

Development of a CNC Spur Gear Generating System. Bernard J. Renggli & G. Wesley Blankenship. (Fall Technical Meeting Papers 88FTMS2). (Illus.). 19p. 1988. pap. text ed. 30.00 (*1-55589-522-0*) AGMA.

Development of a Copper-Bearing Age Hardenable Steel with High Strength Properties. Southern Research Institute Staff. 177p. 1969. 26.55 (*0-317-34507-9*, 107) Intl Copper.

Development of a Geochemical Mapping Method for the Prospecting of Deposits, Environmental Research & Regional Planning on the Basis of Multi-Element Investigations of Plant Ashes. Hansgeorg. Tr. by K. Allard. (Mineral Deposits on Monograph Ser.). (Illus.). 73p. 1981. text ed. 42.50 (*3-443-12019-9*, Pub. by Gebruder Borntraeger GW) Lubrecht & Cramer.

***Development of a Geographic Information System (GIS) Prototype Data Dictionary for Oil Spill Response Activities: Project Report.** 250p. (Orig.). (C). 1993. pap. text ed. 95.00x (*0-7881-0116-1*) Diane Pub.

Development of a Hydrogen Fueled Mass Transit Vehicle. 90p. 1981. 15.00 (*0-318-17350-6*, DG/81-327) Pub Tech Inc.

Development of a Kinetic Model Including Rate Constant Estimations on Iodine. A. Alonso et al. 88p. 1992. pap. 11.00 (*92-826-2858-2*, CD-NA-13790-EN-C, Pub. by Europ Com) UNIPUB.

Development of a Linguistic System in English Speaking American Children, Vol. 1. Inga Hanna & Joe E. Pierce. LC 77-91612. 1978. pap. 10.95 (*0-913244-13-9*) Hapi Pr.

Development of a Linguistic System in English Speaking American Children, Vol. 2. Joe E. Pierce. LC 77-91612. 125p. (Orig.). 1982. pap. 6.95 (*0-913244-56-2*) Hapi Pr.

Development of a Marxist Perspective in Africa. Nzongola Ntalaja. Ed. by Omenana Collective Staff. (Etudes et Analyses Marxistes en Afrique Ser.). 24p. (Orig.). (C). reprint ed. pap. 3.00 (*0-686-88663-1*) Omenana.

Development of a Modern Navy: French Naval Policy 1871-1904. Theodore Ropp. Ed. by Stephen S. Roberts. (Illus.). 439p. 1987. 36.95 (*0-87021-141-2*) Naval Inst Pr.

Development of a Modular Design Methodology to Facilitate Reuse. William D. Atwell. LC 92-25879. (Six Sigma Research Institute Ser.). 1992. write for info. (*0-201-63422-8*) Addison-Wesley.

Development of a Performance Assessment Process for Connecticut Trial Court Clerks' Offices. Lorraine Adams & Robert Lowe. 112p. 1989. 7.00 (*0-685-55346-9*, NERO254) Natl Ctr St Courts.

Development of a Phonological System in English Speaking American Children. Joe E. Pierce & Ingrid V. Hanna. (Illus.). 120p. 1972. pap. 6.95 (*0-913244-09-0*) Hapi Pr.

Development of a Planning Oriented Method for Estimating the Value of Development Easements on Agricultural Land. David E. Boyce et al. (Discussion Paper Ser.: No. 105). 1978. pap. 10.00 (*1-55869-024-7*) Regional Sci Res Inst.

Development of a Postmodern Self: A Computer-Assisted Comparative Analysis of Personal Documents. Michael Wood & Louis A. Zurcher. LC 87-23666. (Contributions in Sociology Ser.: No. 70). 192p. 1988. text ed. 45.00 (*0-313-25458-3*, WDV/, Greenwood Pr) Greenwood.

Development of a Professional Self: Teaching & Learning in Professional Helping Processes, Selected Writings, 1930-1968. Virginia P. Robinson. LC 77-78322. (Studies in Modern Society: Political & Social Issues: No. 12). 42.50 (*0-404-16015-8*) AMS Pr.

Development of a Regenerative Sulfur Dioxide Sorbent System. H. A. Akse & A. B. Hessink. 108p. 1991. pap. 11.00 (*92-826-3020-X*, CD-NA-13643-EN-C) UNIPUB.

Development of a Revolutionary Mentality: Papers Presented at the First Library of Congress Symposium on the American Revolution May 5 & 6, 1972. LC 72-11849. 157p. 1972. 1.50 (*0-8444-0045-9*) Lib Congress.

Development of a State School System: New Hampshire. Eugene A. Bishop. LC 78-176566. (Columbia University. Teachers College. Contributions to Education Ser.: No. 391). reprint ed. 37.50 (*0-404-55391-5*) AMS Pr.

Development of a Stress Reduction & Assistance Program for the Michigan Judiciary. Lorraine Adams & Nancy London. 71p. 1991. 4.50 (*0-685-50609-6*, NERO-252) Natl Ctr St Courts.

Development of a Variable Center Distance Gear Noise Test Facility. G. Wesley Blankenship. (Fall Technical Meeting Papers 88FTM13). (Illus.). 11p. 1988. pap. text ed. 30.00 (*1-55589-518-2*) AGMA.

Development of a Workshop Facility for the Quality Inspection of Gearboxes, No. EUR 13552-1. 194p. 1991. pap. 19.00 (*92-826-2826-4*, CD-NA-13552-EN-C) UNIPUB.

Development of a Workshop Facility for the Quality Inspection of Gearboxes, No. EUR 13552-2. 155p. 1991. pap. 16.00 (*92-826-2827-2*, CD-NB-13552-EN-C) UNIPUB.

Development of AAF Base Facilities in the United States, 1939-1945. Robert F. Futrell. (USAF Historical Studies: No. 69). 263p. 1951. pap. text ed. 31.95 (*0-89126-129-X*) MA-AH Pub.

Development of Ablaut in the Strong Verbs of the East Midland Dialects of Middle English. J. F. Rettger. (LD Ser.: No. 18). 1972. reprint ed. 16.00 (*0-527-00764-1*) Periodicals Srv.

Development of Achievement Motivation. Martin Maehr. (Advances in Motivation & Achievement Ser.: Vol. 3). 347p. 1984. 73.25 (*0-89232-289-6*) Jai Pr.

Development of Adaptive Intelligence: A Cross-Cultural Study. Carol F. Feldman et al. LC 73-22557. (Jossey-Bass Behavioral Science Ser.). 158p. reprint ed. pap. 45.10 (*0-8357-9315-X*, 2013920) Bks Demand.

Development of Admiralty Jurisdiction & Practice since 1800: An English Study with American Comparisons. F. L. Wiswall. LC 77-108113. 253p. reprint ed. pap. 72.20 (*0-685-43697-7*, 2027257) Bks Demand.

Development of Aeromedical Evacuation in the USAF, 1909-1960, Vol. 1. Robert F. Futrell. (USAF Historical Studies: No. 23). 446p. 1960. 43.00 (*0-89126-050-1*) MA-AH Pub.

Development of Aeromedical Evacuation in the USAF, 1909-1960, Vol. 2. Robert F. Futrell. (USAF Historical Studies: No. 23). 1960. reprint ed. pap. 39.95 (*0-89126-051-X*) MA-AH Pub.

Development of Aesthetic Experience. M. Ross. LC 82-3742. (Curriculum Issues in Arts Education Ser.: Vol. 3). 222p. 1982. 92.00 (*0-08-028908-8*, Pub. by Pergamon Repr UK) Franklin.

Development of African Drama. Michael Etherton. 368p. (Orig.). (C). 1983. 37.95 (*0-8419-0812-5*, Africana); pap. 17.50 (*0-8419-0813-3*, Africana) Holmes & Meier.

***Development of Aggression in Early Childhood.** Henri Parens. LC 94-41957. 426p. 1995. pap. 35.00 (*1-56821-441-3*) Aronson.

Development of Air Doctrine in the Army Air Arm, 1917-1941. Thomas H. Greer. (USAF Historical Studies: No. 89). 162p. 1955. pap. text ed. 30.00 (*0-89126-021-8*) MA-AH Pub.

Development of Air Doctrine in the Army Air Arm, 1917-1941. Thomas H. Greer. 154p. 1986. reprint ed. pap. write for info. (*0-318-60187-7*) Off Air Force.

Development of Aircraft Gun Turrets in the AAF, 1917-1944. Irving B. Holley, Jr. (USAF Historical Studies: No. 54). 279p. 1947. pap. text ed. 33.00 (*0-89126-139-7*) MA-AH Pub.

Development of Alfred Binet's Psychology see Serial Reactions Considered As Conditioned Reactions

Development of American Citizenship, 1608-1870. James H. Kettner. LC 78-954. 403p. reprint ed. pap. 114.90 (*0-7837-6863-X*, 2046692) Bks Demand.

Development of American Federalism. William H. Riker. (C). 1987. lib. bdg. 55.00 (*0-89838-225-4*) Kluwer Ac.

Development of American Gastroenterology. Joseph B. Kirsner. 480p. 1990. 69.00 (*0-88167-603-9*) Raven.

Development of American Karate: History & Skills. Ed. by Jerry Beasley. LC 83-62681. (Illus.). 96p. 1983. pap. 9.95 (*0-943736-02-1*) Ormsby.

Development of American Literary Criticism. Ed. by Floyd Stovall. 1955. pap. 13.95 (*0-685-01127-5*) NCUP.

Development of American Literary Criticism. Ed. by Floyd Stovall. LC 80-12269. ix, 262p. 1980. reprint ed. text ed. 59.75 (*0-313-22440-4*, STDE, Greenwood Pr) Greenwood.

Development of American Pharmacology: John J. Abel & the Shaping of a Discipline. John Parascandola. (Illus.). 224p. 1992. text ed. 33.50x (*0-8018-4416-9*) Johns Hopkins.

Development of American Physiology: Scientific Medicine in the Nineteenth Century. Bruce W. Fye. LC 86-46287. 288p. 1987. text ed. 44.50 (*0-8018-3459-7*) Johns Hopkins.

Development of American Prisons & Prison Customs, 1776-1845. Orlando F. Lewis. LC 93-39530. (Criminology, Law Enforcement, & Social Problems Ser.: No. 1). (Illus.). 1995. reprint ed. 25.00 (*0-87585-706-X*) Patterson Smith.

Development of American Public Policy: The Structure of Policy Restraint. David B. Robertson et al. (C). 1989. pap. text ed. 26.00 (*0-673-39881-1*) HarpCollege.

Development of American Romance: The Sacrifice of Relation. Michael D. Bell. LC 80-12241. xiv, 292p. (C). 1984. pap. text ed. 10.95 (*0-226-04213-8*) U Ch Pr.

Development of an African Working Class: Studies in Class Formation & Action. Ed. by Richard Sandbrook & Robin Cohen. 340p. reprint ed. pap. 96.90 (*0-318-34717-2*, 2031925) Bks Demand.

Development of an Application Level Communications Standard for Building Management Systems. 1989. 200.00 (*0-86022-304-3*, Pub. by Build Servs Info Assn UK) St Mut.

Development of an Artificial Intelligence System for Inventory Management. Mary K. Allen. 1987. 50.00 (*0-318-33303-1*) Coun Logistics Mgt.

Development of an Energy Action Plan: A Participatory Approach. 93p. 1982. 15.00 (*0-318-17330-1*, DG/82-305) Pub Tech Inc.

Development of an Environmental Bio-Industry: European Perceptions. Ann-Marie Prieels. 131p. 1993. pap. 17.00 (*92-826-4691-2*, SY-76-92-051-EN, Pub. by Europ Com) UNIPUB.

Development of Animal Production Systems. B. L. Nestel. (World Animal Science Ser.: Vol. 2A). 350p. 1984. 146.25 (*0-444-42050-9*, I-474-83) Elsevier.

Development of Anthropological Ideas. John J. Honigmann. LC 75-35107. (Dorsey Series in Anthropology). 446p. reprint ed. pap. 127.20 (*0-317-26336-6*, 2024231) Bks Demand.

Development of Anti-Icing Technology. Robert R. Blackcurn et al. 479p. (Orig.). (C). 1993. pap. text ed. 20.00 (*0-309-95761-3*, SHRP-H-385) SHRP.

Development of Applications for Copper-Plastic Combinations. U. S. Industrial Chemical Company Staff. 54p. 1964. 8.10 (*0-317-34508-7*, 40) Intl Copper.

***Development of Aquaculture: An Ecosystems Perspective.** E. W. Shell. (Agricultural Exp. Station Ser.). 265p. 1994. pap. 19.95 (*0-8173-0773-7*) U of Ala Pr.

Development of Arab-American Identity. Ed. by Ernest McCarus. 200p. 1994. text ed. 45.00 (*0-472-10439-X*) U of Mich Pr.

Development of Arabic Logic. Nicholas Rescher. LC 64-13361. 262p. reprint ed. pap. 74.70 (*0-317-08129-2*, 2015571) Bks Demand.

Development of Arabic Mathematics: Between Arithmetic & Algebra. Roshdi Rashed. Tr. by Angela Armstrong. LC 93-39784. (Boston Studies in the Philosophy of Science: Vol. 156). 1994. lib. bdg. 115.00 (*0-7923-2565-6*) Kluwer Ac.

***Development of Artistically Gifted Children: Selected Case Studies.** Ed. by Claire Golomb. 272p. 1995. text ed. 59.95 (*0-8058-1524-4*) L Erlbaum Assocs.

Development of Attachment & Affiliative Systems. Ed. by Robert N. Emde & Robert J. Harmon. LC 82-3818. (Topics in Developmental Psychobiology Ser.). 332p. 1982. 55.00 (*0-306-40849-X*, Plenum Pr) Plenum.

Development of Attention: Research & Theory. Ed. by J. T. Enns. (Advances in Psychology Ser.: No. 69). 570p. 1990. 131.00 (*0-444-88332-0*, North Holland) Elsevier.

Development of Ballistic Missiles in the United Air Force, 1945-1960. Jacob Neufeld. LC 89-71109. (Illus.). 425p. 1990. pap. 23.00 (*0-16-021154-9*, S/N 008-070-00641-3) USGPO.

Development of Banking in India: A Study of the Working of the State Financial Corporation. Sujit Sikidar. 1985. text ed. 28.50 (*0-685-14103-9*) Coronet Bks.

Development of Behavioral States & the Expression of Emotions in Early Infancy: New Proposals for Investigation. Peter H. Wolff. LC 86-16066. (Illus.). viii, 292p. (C). 1987. 32.50 (*0-226-90520-9*) U Ch Pr.

Development of Berkeley's Philosophy. Ed. by George Pitcher. (Philosophy of George Berkeley Ser.). 400p. 1988. lib. bdg. 35.00 (*0-8240-2436-2*) Garland.

Development of Biochemistry in Canada. Elrig G. Young. LC 75-44055. (Illus.). 145p. reprint ed. pap. 41.40 (*0-685-23512-2*, 2026480) Bks Demand.

***Development of Biological Systematics: Antoine-Laurent de Jussieu, Nature, & The Natural System.** Peter F. Stevens. LC 94-27231. 520p. 1994. 65.00 (*0-231-06440-3*) Col U Pr.

Development of Black Theater in America: From Shadows to Selves. Leslie C. Sanders. LC 87-13542. 280p. 1988. pap. 9.95 (*0-8071-1582-7*) La State U Pr.

Development of Botany in Selected Regions of North America Before 1900: An Original Anthology. Ed. by Keir B. Sterling. LC 77-81126. (Biologists & Their World Ser.). (Illus.). 1978. lib. bdg. 28.95 (*0-405-10722-6*) Ayer.

***Development of Brain & Behaviour in the Chicken.** L. J. Rogers. 280p. 1995. 77.50x (*0-85198-924-1*) CAB Intl.

Development of British Heathlands & their Soils. G. W. Dimbleby. 1962. 45.00 (*0-686-45495-2*) St Mut.

Development of British Monetary Orthodoxy 1797-1875. Frank W. Fetter. LC 76-30912. 1978. reprint ed. lib. bdg. 39.50 (*0-678-01386-1*) Kelley.

Development of Buddhism in England. Christmas Humphreys. LC 78-72442. reprint ed. 17.50 (*0-404-17308-X*) AMS Pr.

Development of Buddhist Ethics. G. S. Misra. 1984. text ed. 22.00 (*0-685-13698-1*) Coronet Bks.

Development of Buddhist Iconography in Eastern India. Mallar Ghosh. (Illus.). 1980. text ed. 44.00 (*0-685-13699-X*) Coronet Bks.

Development of Canadian Controls on Natural Gas Exports. G. C. Watkins. 20p. 1987. pap. 10.00 (*0-918714-13-3*) Intl Res Ctr Energy.

Development of Capitalism in Africa. John Sender & Sheila Smith. 250p. 1987. text ed. 59.95 (*0-416-37730-0*); pap. text ed. 16.95 (*0-416-37740-8*) Routledge Chapman & Hall.

Development of Capitalism in Northern Nigeria. Robert W. Shenton. LC 86-123444. 192p. reprint ed. pap. 54.80 (*0-7837-0417-8*, 2040740) Bks Demand.

Development of Capitalism in the Navajo Nation: A Political-Economic History. Lawrence D. Weiss. LC 83-17448. (Studies in Marxism: Vol. 15). 180p. 1984. 29.95 (*0-930656-37-7*); pap. 10.95 (*0-930656-38-5*) MEP Pubns.

Development of Capitalistic Enterprise in India. Daniel H. Buchanan. 489p. 1966. reprint ed. 35.00 (*0-7146-1998-1*, Pub. by F Cass Pubs UK) Intl Spec Bk.

Development of Certified Reference Materials for the National Reference System for the Clinical Laboratory, Vol. 4. National Committee for Clinical Laboratory Standards Staff. (Approved Guideline Ser.: Vol. 4). 1991. 40.00 (*1-56238-106-7*, NRSCL3-A) Natl Comm Clin Lab Stds.

***Development of Chemical Principles.** unabridged ed. Cooper H. Langford & Ralph A. Beebe. (Illus.). 384p. 1995. pap. text ed. 9.95 (*0-486-68359-1*) Dover.

Development of Chemotherapeutic Agents for Parasitic Diseases. Maurice Marois. 1976. 46.25 (*0-444-10996-X*, North Holland) Elsevier.

Development of Chess Style. Max Euwe. 1978. pap. 7.95 (*0-679-14045-X*) McKay.

Development of Children. 2nd ed. Michael Cole & Sheila R. Cole. LC 92-42001. (C). 1995. text ed. write for info. (*0-7167-2238-0*) W H Freeman.

Development of Chinese Agriculture, 1950-1959. Peter Schran. LC 69-17364. (Illinois Studies in the Social Sciences: No. 56). 254p. reprint ed. pap. 72.40 (*0-8357-6089-8*, 2034463) Bks Demand.

Development of Chinese Zen. Heinrich Dumoulin. 146p. 1990. reprint ed. pap. 15.00 (*957-9482-16-0*) Oriental Bk Store.

Development of Christian Doctrine: Some Historical Prolegomena. Jaroslav Pelikan. LC 69-14864. (St. Thomas More Lectures Ser.: No. 3). 162p. 1969. 25.00 (*0-300-01082-6*) Yale U Pr.

Development of Church Teaching on Prolonging Life. Kevin D. O'Rourke. 20p. 1988. pap. 3.00 (*0-87125-152-3*, 217) Cath Health.

Development of Circadian Rhythmicity & Photoperiodism in Mammals. Ed. by Steven M. Reppert. LC 89-23095. (Research in Perinatal Medicine Ser.: No. IX). (Illus.). 1989. 102.50 (*0-916859-42-8*) Perinatology.

Development of Civil Society in Communist Systems. Ed. by Robert F. Miller. 176p. 1992. pap. text ed. 19.95 (*1-86373-171-7*, Pub. by Allen Unwin AT) Paul & Co Pubs.

Development of Civilization: A Documentary History of Politics, Society & Thought, Vol. 2. Harry J. Carroll et al. LC 69-17828. 544p. reprint ed. pap. 155.10 (*0-7837-3010-1*, 2042930) Bks Demand.

Development of Class Structure in Eastern Europe: Poland & Her Southern Neighbors. Aleksander Gella. LC 87-37498. (Illus.). 326p. 1988. 74.50 (*0-88706-833-2*); pap. 24.95 (*0-88706-834-0*) State U NY Pr.

***Development of Coal Combustion Sensitivity Tests for Smoke Detectors.** John C. Edwards & Gerald S. Morrow. LC 94-47029. (Information Circular Ser., Bureau of Mines). 1995. write for info. (*0-615-00464-4*) US Interior.

Development of Coal Feed Systems for Pressurized Fluidized Bed Processes To, No. EUR 12820. British Coal Corporation Staff. 137p. 1990. pap. 13.50 (*92-826-1506-5*, CD-NA-12820-EN-C) UNIPUB.

Development of Cognition, Affect, & Social Relations Vol. 13: The Minnesota Symposium on Child Psychology. Ed. by W. Andrew Collins. LC 79-27560. (Minnesota Symposium on Child Psychology Ser.). (Illus.). 320p. 1980. text ed. 49.95 (*0-89859-023-X*) L Erlbaum Assocs.

***Development of Cognitive Anthropology.** Roy D'Andrade. (Illus.). 288p. (C). 1995. 54.95 (*0-521-45370-4*); pap. 16.95 (*0-521-45976-1*) Cambridge U Pr.

Development of Cognitive Processes. Ed. by Vernon Hamilton. 1977. text ed. 258.00 (*0-12-321750-4*) Acad Pr.

D

An Asterisk (*) at the beginning of an entry indicates that the title is appearing in BIP for the first time.

D

An Asterisk (*) at the beginning of an entry indicates that the title is appearing in BIP for the first time.

1917

Development of India's Resource Base: Patterns, Problems & Prospects. Ed. by V. Vidyanath. 524p. 1988. 38.00 (*81-212-0210-8*, Pub. by Gian Publng Hse II) S Asia.

Development of Industrial Societies. (Sociological Review Monographs: No. 8). 1972. reprint ed. pap. 15.00 (*0-8115-3314-X*) Periodicals Srv.

Development of Industrial Society in Ireland: The Third Joint Meeting of the Royal Irish Academy & the British Academy, Oxford, 1990. Ed. by John H. Goldthorpe & Christopher T. Whelan. (Proceedings of the British Academy: Vol. 79). (Illus.). 484p. 1994. reprint ed. pap. 23.00 (*0-19-726141-8*) OUP.

Development of Infants Born at Risk. Deborah L. Holmes & Joseph F. Pasternak. 272p. (C). 1984. text ed. 49.95 (*0-89859-283-6*) L Erlbaum Assocs.

Development of Infants of Drug Dependent Mothers. Anneloes Van Baar. 200p. 1991. 33.00 (*90-265-1189-2*, Pub. by Swets Pub Serv NE) Taylor & Francis.

Development of Infants with Disabilities & Their Families: Implications for Theory & Service Delivery. Jack P. Shonkoff et al. (Monographs of the Society for Research in Child Development: No. 232, Vol. 57, Nos. 6-7). 176p. (C). 1992. pap. text ed. 9.75 (*0-226-75351-4*) U Ch Pr.

Development of Informal Geometry. Robert Coleman. LC 78-176696. (Columbia University. Teachers College. Contributions to Education Ser.: No. 865). reprint ed. 37.50 (*0-404-55865-8*) AMS Pr.

Development of Information Systems: What Management Needs to Know. Donald F. Heany. LC 68-30891. (Illus.). 429p. reprint ed. pap. 122.30 (*0-317-10041-6*, 2012413) Bks Demand.

Development of Information Systems for Agriculture. 259p. 1993. pap. 15.00 (*92-833-2126-X*, APO126X, Pub. by Asian Prod Organ) UNIPUB.

Development of Integrated Sea Use Management. Hance D. Smith & Adalberto Vallega. 288p. 1991. 95.00 (*0-415-03816-2*, A5955) Routledge.

Development of Intelligence in Children. Alfred Binet & Thomas Simon. LC 73-2962. (Classics in Psychology Ser.). 1975. reprint ed. 25.95 (*0-405-05135-2*) Ayer.

Development of Intentional Action: Cognitive, Motivational, & Interactive Processes. Ed. by Merry Bullock. (Contributions to Human Development Ser.: Vol. 22). (Illus.). x, 84p. 1991. 59.25 (*3-8055-5411-7*) S Karger.

Development of International Humanitarian Law. Geza Herczegh. 240p. 1984. 48.00 (*0-569-08811-9*, Pub. by Collets UK) Pro-Am Music.

***Development of International Law by the European Court of Human Rights.** 2nd ed. J. G. Merrills. (Melland Schill Monographs in International Law). 272p. 1995. text ed. 24.95 (*0-7190-4560-6*, Pub. by Manchester Univ Pr UK) St Martin.

Development of International Law by the International Court. Hersch Lauterpacht. 427p. (C). 1982. 150.00 (*0-906496-30-6*, Pub. by Grotius Pubns UK) St Mut.

Development of International Markets. John Walmsley. (C). 1990. lib. bdg. 84.00 (*1-85333-279-8*, Pub. by Graham & Trotman UK) Kluwer Ac.

Development of Intersensory Perception: Comparative Perspectives. Ed. by David J. Lewkowicz & Robert Lickliter. 448p. 1994. text ed. 99.95 (*0-8058-1217-2*) L Erlbaum Assocs.

Development of IRI-90: Proceedings of a Workshop Held in Abingdon, UK, 7-9 August 1989. Ed. by Karl Rawer & W. R. Piggott. (Advances in Space Research Ser.: Vol. 10). 1991. pap. 105.00 (*0-08-040785-4*, Pergamon Pr) Elsevier.

D

Development of Iron Chelators for Clinical Use. Bergeron. 1994. 129.95 (*0-8493-8679-9*, RM666) CRC Pr.

Development of Islamic Library Collections in Western Europe & North America. Stephan Roman. 272p. 1990. text ed. 100.00 (*0-7201-2065-9*, Mansell Pub) Cassell.

Development of Islamic State & Society. M. M. Siddiqui. 1986. 22.50 (*0-935782-68-0*) Kazi Pubns.

Development of ISO-Footcandle Curves for Highway Lighting. Richard A. Zimmer. (Illus.). 105p. (Orig.). (C). 1994. pap. text ed. 45.00 (*0-7881-0306-7*) Diane Pub.

***Development of Jets & Turbines Aero Engines.** Bill Gunston. (Illus.). 224p. 1995. 39.95 (*1-85260-463-8*, Pub. by J H Haynes & Co UK) Motorbooks Intl.

Development of Job Design Theories & Techniques. David A. Buchanan. LC 79-83808. 180p. 1979. text ed. 55.00 (*0-275-90335-4*, C0335, Praeger Pubs) Greenwood.

Development of Judicial Control of the European Communities. Gerhard Bebr. 840p. 1981. lib. bdg. 321.00 (*90-247-2541-0*) Kluwer Ac.

Development of Kamakura Rule, 1180-1250: A History with Documents. Jeffrey P. Mass. LC 78-62271. xvi, 312p. 1979. 39.50 (*0-8047-1003-1*) Stanford U Pr.

Development of Labor Institutions in Thailand. Bevars D. Mabry. LC 79-113663. (Cornell University, Southeast Asia Program, Data Paper Ser.: No. 112). 164p. reprint ed. pap. 46.80 (*0-8357-6090-1*, 2034595) Bks Demand.

Development of Labour Law in Trinidad & Tobago. Roy D. Thomas. LC 89-61551. 160p. 1989. pap. 13.95 (*0-911565-06-X*) Calaloux Pubns.

Development of Language. 3rd ed. Jean Berko-Gleason. LC 92-28907. (Illus.). 493p. (C). 1993. text ed. write for info. (*0-02-344251-4*, Merrill Pub Co) Macmillan.

Development of Language & Language Researchers: Essay in Honor of Roger Brown. Ed. by Frank Kessel. 421p. 1987. text ed. 79.95 (*0-89859-906-7*); pap. text ed. 39.95 (*0-8058-0063-8*) L Erlbaum Assocs.

Development of Language & Literacy in Young Children. 3rd ed. Susanna Pflaum-Connor. 256p. (C). 1986. pap. write for info. (*0-675-20447-X*, Merrill Pub Co) Macmillan.

Development of Large Scale Structure in the Universe. Jeremiah P. Ostriker. (Lezione Fermiane Ser.). (Illus.). 120p. (C). 1992. pap. 22.95 (*0-521-42361-9*) Cambridge U Pr.

Development of Law in California. William J. Palmer & Paul P Selvin. 1983. write for info. (*0-318-58310-0*) West Pub.

Development of Law in Frontier California: Civil Law & Society, 1850-1890. Gordon M. Bakken. LC 84-25202. (Contributions in Legal Studies: No. 33). (Illus.). 162p. 1985. text ed. 45.00 (*0-313-24725-0*, BFC/, Greenwood Pr) Greenwood.

Development of Law on the Rocky Mountain Frontier: Civil Law & Society, 1850-1912. Gordon M. Bakken. LC 82-20984. (Contributions in Legal Studies: No. 27). ix, 200p. 1983. text ed. 49.95 (*0-313-23285-7*, BDL/, Greenwood Pr) Greenwood.

Development of Legitimating Ideas: Intellectuals & Politicians in Post-War Western Germany. Stephen D. Berger. LC 91-22959. (Harvard Studies in Sociology). 293p. 1991. 29.00 (*0-8240-8309-1*) Garland.

Development of Library Collections of Sound Recordings. F. Hoffmann. (Books in Library & Information Science: Vol. 28). 184p. 1979. 85.00 (*0-8247-6858-2*) Dekker.

Development of Library Services in India: Social Science Information. S. P. Agrawal. (C). 1989. 25.00 (*81-7022-233-8*, Pub. by Concept II) S Asia.

Development of Life Insurance Surrender Values in the United States. J. David Cummins. LC 73-87483. (S. S. Huebner Foundation Monographs: No. 2). 81p. (C). 1973. pap. 12.00 (*0-918930-02-2*) Huebner Foun Insur.

***Development of Literacy Through Social Interaction.** Ed. by Colette Daiute. LC 85-644581. (New Directions for Child Development Ser.: No. 61). 129p. (Orig.). 1993. pap. 17.95 (*1-55542-720-0*) Jossey-Bass.

Development of Livestock, Agriculture & Water Supplies in Botswana Before Independence: A Short History & Policy Analysis. Emery Roe. (Occasional Paper Ser.: No. 10). 56p. 1980. 6.45 (*0-86731-023-5*) Cornell CIS RDC.

Development of Local Energy Management Preparedness - Emergency Operations Project: A Unit Report from the Energy Task Force of the Urban Consortium. 65p. 1981. 10.00 (*0-318-17336-0*, DG/81-304) Pub Tech Inc.

***Development of Local Public Services, 1650-1860: Lessons from Middletown, Connecticut.** Hannah J. McKinney. LC 95-5269. (Contributions in Economics & Economic History Ser.: Vol. 166). 224p. 1995. text ed. 59.95 (*0-313-29590-5*, Greenwood Pr) Greenwood.

Development of Logic. William Kneale & Martha Kneale. (Illus.). 1985. pap. 35.00 (*0-19-824773-7*) OUP.

Development of Long-Span Bridge Building. Tom F. Peters. (Illus.). 188p. (Orig.). (ENG, FRE & GER.). 1980. pap. text ed. 19.95 (*0-686-78178-3*) Interbk Inc.

Development of Long Term Retention. Ed. by M. L. Howe et al. (Illus.). 272p. 1992. 76.00 (*0-387-97734-1*) Spr-Verlag.

Development of Mammalian Absorptive Processes. Ciba Foundation Staff. LC 79-20804. (Ciba Foundation Symposium: New Ser.: No. 70). 350p. reprint ed. pap. 99.80 (*0-317-29760-0*, 2022189) Bks Demand.

Development of Managerial Enterprise. Ed. by Kesaji Kobayashi & Hidemasa Morikawa. (International Conferences on Business History Ser.: No. 12). 320p. 1986. 49.50 (*0-86008-397-7*, Pub. by U of Tokyo JA) Col U Pr.

Development of Marginal Agricultural Land in Asia & the Pacific. APO Staff. 240p. 1993. pap. 15.00 (*92-833-2129-4*, APO1294, Pub. by Asian Prod Organ) UNIPUB.

Development of Market Agriculture in South Carolina, 1670-1785. David L. Coon. (Outstanding Studies in Early American History). 400p. 1989. reprint ed. 25.00 (*0-8240-6176-4*) Garland.

Development of Marketing in the Automobile Industry. Ed. by Akio Okochi & Koichi S. Shimokawa. (International Conferences on Business History Ser.: No. 7). 303p. 1981. 42.50 (*0-86008-288-1*, Pub. by U of Tokyo JA) Col U Pr.

Development of Markets for New Materials: A Study of Building New End-Product Markets for Aluminum, Fibrous Glass, & the Plastics. A. Raymond Corey. LC 56-9764. 279p. reprint ed. pap. 79.60 (*0-317-29992-1*, 2051840) Bks Demand.

Development of Marriage & Kinship. Charles S. Wake. Ed. by Rodney Needham. LC 66-20596. (Classics in Anthropology Ser.). 566p. reprint ed. pap. 161.40 (*0-685-15789-X*, 2026784) Bks Demand.

Development of Mathematics. unabridged ed. E. T. Bell. LC 92-24016. 637p. 1992. reprint ed. pap. 12.95 (*0-486-27239-7*) Dover.

Development of Mathematics in China & Japan. 2nd ed. Y. Mikami. LC 74-6716. 383p. 1974. text ed. 29.50 (*0-8284-0149-7*) Chelsea Pub.

Development of Mathematics in the Nineteenth Century. Felix Klein et al. (LIE Groups Ser.: No. 9). 1979. 80.00 (*0-915692-28-7*) Math Sci Pr.

***Development of Mathematics 1900-1950.** Jean-Paul P. Basel. LC 94-25339. (FRE.). 1994. 75.00 (*0-8176-2821-5*) Birkhauser.

Development of Mature Walking. David Sutherland et al. (Clinics in Developmental Medicine Ser.: Nos. 104/105). (Illus.). 227p. (C). 1991. 65.00 (*0-521-41221-8*, Pub. by Mc Keith Pr UK) Cambridge U Pr.

Development of Meaning see Study & Analysis of the Conditional Reflex

Development of Medical Bibliography. Estelle Brodman. 226p. 1981. reprint ed. 8.25 (*0-912176-00-8*) Med Lib Assn.

Development of Medical Techniques & Treatments: From Leeches to Heart Surgery. Martin Duke. LC 90-4666. 270p. 1991. 32.50 (*0-8236-1232-5*) Intl Univs Pr.

***Development of Medications for the Treatment of Opiate & Cocaine Addictions: Issues for the Government & Private Sector.** National Institute on Drug Abuse, National Research Council Committee. 272p. (Orig.). (C). 1995. pap. text ed. 37.00 (*0-309-05244-0*) Natl Acad Pr.

Development of Medicine as a Profession. Vern L. Bullough. LC 76-56850. 132p. 1966. 20.00 (*0-686-65683-0*) Watson Pub Intl.

Development of Melody in the Tone Poems of Richard Strauss: Motif, Figure & Theme. Denis Wilde. LC 90-6220. (Studies in the History & Interpretation of Music: Vol. 32). 436p. 1990. lib. bdg. 109.95 (*0-88946-487-1*) E Mellen.

Development of Memory in Children. 3rd ed. Robert Kail. (Illus.). 251p. (C). 1995. text ed. write for info. (*0-7167-2102-3*); pap. text ed. write for info. (*0-7167-2076-0*) W H Freeman.

Development of Metalinguistic Abilities in Children. David T. Hakes. (Language & Communication Ser.: Vol. 9). (Illus.). 119p. 1980. 31.00 (*0-387-10295-7*) Spr-Verlag.

Development of Methodism in the Old Southwest: 1783-1824. Walter B. Posey. LC 73-18408. (Perspectives in American History Ser.: No. 19). (Illus.). 151p. 1974. reprint ed. lib. bdg. 29.50 (*0-87991-339-8*) Porcupine Pr.

Development of Methodological Principles Documents for Analytes in the Clinical Laboratory: Tentative Guideline (1989) 1989. 40.00 (*1-56238-092-3*, NRSCL6-T) Natl Comm Clin Lab Stds.

Development of Methods for Dynamic Force Calibration, Pt. 1, No. EUR 12933. CEC Staff. 108p. 1990. pap. 12.00 (*92-826-1729-7*, CD-NA-12933-EN-C) UNIPUB.

Development of Methods for Dynamic Force Calibration, Pt. 2, No. EUR 12933/2. CEC Staff. 146p. 1990. pap. 15.50 (*92-826-1730-0*, CD-NB-12933-EN-C) UNIPUB.

***Development of Methods to Detect Sulfate-Reducing Bacteria: Agents of Microbiologically Influenced Corrosion, Pub. No. 37.** Ed. by D. H. Pope. (Illus.). 64p. 1990. 53.00 (*1-877914-19-3*) NACE Intl.

Development of Microbiology. Patrick Collard. LC 75-40987. 210p. reprint ed. pap. 59.90 (*0-317-07740-6*, 2022443) Bks Demand.

Development of Military Thought: The Nineteenth Century. Azar Gat. LC 92-11907. 310p. 1992. 69.00 (*0-19-820246-6*, Clarendon Pr) OUP.

***Development of Modern Behavioural Psychology.** John McLeish. 228p. (Orig.). (C). 1981. pap. text ed. 14.95x (*0-920490-20-4*) Temeron Bks.

Development of Modern Chemistry. Aaron J. Ihde. (Illus.). 851p. 1983. reprint ed. pap. 17.95 (*0-486-64235-6*) Dover.

Development of Modern Education in the Gulf. Sheikha Misnad. 386p. 1985. 40.00 (*0-685-14920-X*, Pub. by Ithaca UK) Evergreen Dist.

Development of Modern France 1870-1939, Vol. 2. rev. ed. D. W. Brogan. 16.50 (*0-8446-0515-8*) Peter Smith.

Development of Modern Italy. Cecil J. Sprigge. 1969. 40.00 (*0-86527-043-0*) Fertig.

Development of Modern Medicine: An Interpretation of the Social & Scientific Factors Involved. R. H. Shryock. LC 79-5401. 490p. 1980. reprint ed. pap. 13.95 (*0-299-07534-6*) U of Wis Pr.

Development of Modern Philosophy. Robert Adamson. Ed. by William R. Sorley. LC 76-165613. (Select Bibliographies Reprint Ser.). 1977. reprint ed. 25.95 (*0-8369-5920-5*) Ayer.

Development of Modern Turkey As Measured by Means of Its Press. Ahmed Emin. LC 72-76713. (Columbia University. Studies in the Social Sciences: No. 142). reprint ed. 29.50 (*0-404-51142-2*) AMS Pr.

Development of Moral Reasoning: Practical Approaches. Ed. by Donald B. Cochrane & Michael E. Manley-Casimir. LC 80-17141. 352p. 1980. text ed. 65.00 (*0-275-90464-4*, C0464, Praeger Pubs) Greenwood.

Development of Motor Abilities During the First Three Years. Nancy Bayley. (SRCD M: Vol. 1, No. 1). 1935. pap. 14.00 (*0-527-01486-9*) Periodicals Srv.

Development of Movement Control & Coordination. Ed. by J. Scott Kelso & Jane E. Clark. LC 81-14690. (Wiley Series in Developmental Psychology & Its Applications). 382p. reprint ed. pap. 108.90 (*0-8357-8859-8*, 2033617) Bks Demand.

Development of Multiplicative Reasoning in the Learning of Mathematics. Ed. by Guershon Harel & Jere Confrey. LC 93-19443. (SUNY Series, Reform in Mathematics Education). (Illus.). 407p. 1994. 74.50 (*0-7914-1763-8*); pap. 24.95 (*0-7914-1764-6*) State U NY Pr.

Development of Muslim Theology, Jurisprudence & Constitution Theory. D. B. MacDonald. 400p. 1985. 280.00 (*1-85077-066-2*, Darf Pubs Ltd) St Mut.

Development of National Administrative Organization in the United States. Lloyd M. Short. (Brookings Institution Reprint Ser.). reprint ed. lib. bdg. 34.00 (*0-697-00168-7*) Irvington.

Development of Natural History in Tudor England. F. D. Hoeniger & J. F. Hoeniger. LC 69-19336. (Folger Guides to the Age of Shakespeare Ser.). 1969. pap. 4.95 (*0-918016-29-0*) Folger Bks.

Development of Naturalist Legal Theory. H. McCoubrey. 224p. 1987. 59.95 (*0-7099-4669-4*, Pub. by Croom Helm UK) Routledge Chapman & Hall.

Development of Negro Religion. Ruby Johnston. (African Studies). reprint ed. 20.00 (*0-938818-69-4*) ECA Assoc.

Development of Neo-Confucian Thought, Vol. 1. Carsun Chang. 1957. pap. 16.95x (*0-8084-0105-X*) NCUP.

Development of Neuronal Connections. Ed. by L. M. Eisenman. (Journal: Brain, Behavior & Evolution: Vol. 31, No. 4, 1988). 76p. 1988. pap. 78.50 (*3-8055-4805-2*) S Karger.

Development of New NLO Crystals in the Borate Series. C. T. Chen. LC 92-41424. (Laser Science & Technology Ser.: Vol. 15). 1993. pap. text ed. 40.00 (*3-7186-5351-6*) Gordon & Breach.

Development of Newtonian Calculus in Britain, 1700-1810. Niccolo Guicciardini. (Illus.). 230p. (C). 1990. 74.95 (*0-521-36466-3*) Cambridge U Pr.

Development of Newtonian Optics in England. Henry J. Steffens. (Illus.). 1977. 20.00 (*0-88202-048-X*, Sci Hist) Watson Pub Intl.

Development of Nigerian Foreign Policy. Claude S. Phillips. LC 64-13703. (Northwestern University African Studies Ser.: No. 13). 166p. reprint ed. pap. 47.40 (*0-317-11319-4*, 2015305) Bks Demand.

Development of Nomadism in Ancient Northeast Africa. Karim Sadr. LC 91-14688. (Illus.). 160p. (C). 1991. text ed. 29.95x (*0-8122-3066-3*) U of Pa Pr.

Development of Nuclear Strategy. Bernard Brodie. (CISA Working Paper Ser.: No. 11). 30p. (Orig.). Date not set. pap. 10.00 (*0-86682-010-8*) Ctr Intl Relations.

Development of Numerical Competence: Animal and Human Models. Ed. by Sarah T. Boysen & E. John Capaldi. (Comparative Cognition & Neuroscience Ser.). 296p. 1992. text ed. 69.95 (*0-8058-0749-7*); pap. 29.95 (*0-8058-1231-8*) L Erlbaum Assocs.

***Development of Oldest-Old Mortality, 1950-1990: Evidence from 28 Developed Countries.** Vaino Kannisto. (Monographs on Population Aging: Vol. 1). (Illus.). 108p. 1994. 57.50x (*87-7838-015-4*, Pub. by Odense Universitets Forlag DK) Coronet Bks.

Development of Optical Fibers in Japan. H. Murata. xii, 156p. 1989. pap. text ed. 66.00 (*2-88124-372-X*) Gordon & Breach.

Development of Oral & Written Language in Social Contexts. Ed. by Anthony D. Pellegrini et al. LC 84-369. (Advances in Discourse Processes Ser.: Vol. 13). 288p. (Orig.). (C). 1984. text ed. 75.00 (*0-89391-171-2*); pap. text ed. 39.50 (*0-89391-172-0*) Ablex Pub.

Development of Oral Communication in the Classroom. Gerald M. Phillips et al. LC 71-77821. (C). 1970. text ed. write for info. (*0-672-60857-X*, Bobbs) Macmillan.

Development of Order in the Visual System. Ed. by S. R. Hilfer & J. B. Sheffield. (Cell & Developmental Biology of the Eye Ser.). (Illus.). xii, 249p. 1986. 104.00 (*0-387-96264-6*) Spr-Verlag.

Development of Orthographic Knowledge & the Foundations of Literacy: A Memorial Festschrift for Edmund H. Henderson. Ed. by Shane Templeton & Donald Bear. 384p. 1991. text ed. 79.95 (*0-8058-0825-6*) L Erlbaum Assocs.

Development of Ovule & Seed Coat Structure in Angiosperms. F. Bouman. (International Bioscience Monographs: No. 6). 80p. 1978. 7.50 (*0-88065-067-2*, Messers Today & Tomorrow) Scholarly Pubns.

Development of Palestine Exploration: Being the Ely Lectures for 1903. Frederick J. Bliss. Ed. by Moshe Davis. LC 77-70676. (America & the Holy Land Ser.). 1977. reprint ed. lib. bdg. 33.95 (*0-405-10228-3*) Ayer.

Development of Palestinian Resistance. Walter Lehn. (Information Papers: No. 14). 47p. (Orig.). (C). 1974. pap. 2.75 (*0-937694-30-4*) Assn Arab-Amer U Grads.

Development of Parliamentary Government in Serbia. Alex N. Dragnich. (East European Monographs: No. 44). 138p. 1978. text ed. 47.50 (*0-914710-37-0*) East Eur Quarterly.

Development of Pavement Structural Subsystems. (National Cooperative Highway Research Program Report Ser.: No. 291). 59p. 1987. 8.80 (*0-309-04414-6*) Transport Res Bd.

Development of Peirce's Philosophy. Murray G. Murphey. LC 61-13739. (Illus.). 440p. reprint ed. pap. 125.40 (*0-8357-9155-6*, 2006013) Bks Demand.

Development of Peirce's Philosophy. Murray G. Murphey. LC 93-2777. 448p. (C). 1993. reprint ed. lib. bdg. 38.95 (*0-87220-231-3*); reprint ed. pap. text ed. 19.95 (*0-87220-183-X*) Hackett Pub.

Development of Person-Context Relations. Ed. by Thomas A. Kindermann & Jaan Valsiner. 248p. 1995. text ed. 49.95 (*0-8058-1568-6*) L Erlbaum Assocs.

Development of Personal Construct Psychology. Robert A. Neimeyer. LC 84-17367. 186p. reprint ed. pap. 53.10 (*0-7837-6806-0*, 2046638) Bks Demand.

Development of Perturbative QCD. Guido Altarelli. 400p. 1994. text ed. 99.00 (*981-02-1702-1*); pap. text ed. 61.00 (*981-02-1703-X*) World Scientific Pub.

Development of Photography in Boston, Eighteen Forty to Eighteen Seventy-Five. Pamela Hoyle. LC 79-53041. (Illus.). 1979. pap. 7.50 (*0-934552-33-9*) Boston Athenaeum.

Development of Piston Aero Engines. Bill Gunston. (Illus.). 208p. 1993. 34.95 (*1-85260-385-2*, Pub. by J H Haynes & Co UK) Motorbooks Intl.

Development of Plasma Derivatives for Clinical Use: Proceedings of the American Red Cross Symposium, Washington, October 1971 - Journal: Vox Sanguinis, Vol. 23, Nos. 1 & 2. American National Red Cross Symposium Staff. Ed. by G. A. Jamieson. (Illus.). 1972. pap. 43.00 (*3-8055-1483-2*) S Karger.

***Development of Plastics.** Ed. by S. T. Mossman & P. J. Morris. 120p. 1994. 65.00 (*0-85186-575-5*, R6575) CRC Pr.

Development of Plastics Processing: Machinery & Methods. Joseph F. Chabot. (Society of Plastics Engineers Monographs). 208p. 1992. text ed. 79.95 (*0-471-54716-6*) Wiley.

1918

An Asterisk (*) at the beginning of an entry indicates that the title is appearing in BIP for the first time.

An Asterisk (*) at the beginning of an entry indicates that the title is appearing in BIP for the first time.

D

Development of the County-Unit School District in Utah: A Study in Adaptability. Edward A. Bateman. LC 75-176541. (Columbia University. Teachers College. Contributions to Education Ser.: No. 790). reprint ed. 37.50 (*0-404-55790-2*) AMS Pr.

Development of the Cranial Nerve Ganglia & Related Nuclei in the Rat. J. Altman & S. Bayer. (Advances in Anatomy, Embryology & Cell Biology Ser.: Vol. 74). (Illus.). 100p. 1982. pap. 38.00 (*0-387-11337-1*) Spr-Verlag.

Development of the Dentition. Frans P. Van der Linden. (Illus.). 216p. 1983. pap. text ed. 54.00 (*0-86715-103-X*) Quint Pub Co.

Development of the Detective Novel. Alma E. Murch. LC 69-10138. 272p. 1969. reprint ed. text ed. 35.00 (*0-8371-0581-1*, MUDN, Greenwood Pr) Greenwood.

Development of the Diencephalon of the Chinese Hamster: An Investigation of the Validity of the Criteria of Subdivision of the Brain. A. Keyser. (Journal: Acta Anatomica: Vol. 83, Suppl.). (Illus.). 1972. pap. 29.00 (*3-8055-1593-6*) S Karger.

Development of the Digestive System in the North American Opossum, Didelphis Virginiana. W. J. Krause & J. H. Cutts. (Advances in Anatomy, Embryology & Cell Biology Ser.: Vol. 125). (Illus.). vii, 151p. 1992. pap. 79.00 (*0-387-55149-2*) Spr-Verlag.

***Development of the Doctrine of the Holy Spirit in the Yoruba (African) Indigenous Christian Movement.** Caleb O. Oladipo. LC 94-35601. (American University Studies, Ser. VII: Vol. 185). 1994. write for info. (*0-8204-2708-X*) P Lang Pubs.

Development of the Drama. Brander Matthews. LC 79-39199. (Select Bibliographies Reprint Ser.). 1977. reprint ed. 23.95 (*0-8369-6801-8*) Ayer.

Development of the Dutch Welfare State: From Workers' Insurance to Universal Entitlement. Robert H. Cox. LC 93-6667. (Policy & Institutional Studies). 280p. (C). 1993. text ed. 59.95 (*0-8229-3760-3*) U of Pittsburgh Pr.

Development of the Ego: Implications for Personality Theory, Psychopathology, & the Psychotherapeutic Process. Stanley Greenspan. LC 89-2237. 390p. 1989. 50.00x (*0-8236-1230-9*) Intl Univs Pr.

Development of the English Law of Conspiracy. J. W. Bryan. LC 72-77737. (Law, Politics & History Ser.). 1970. reprint ed. lib. bdg. 25.00 (*0-306-71375-6*) Da Capo.

Development of the English Novel. Wilbur L. Cross. LC 78-90494. 329p. 1969. reprint ed. text ed. 59.75 (*0-8371-2204-X*, CREN, Greenwood Pr) Greenwood.

Development of the English Playhouse. Richard Leacroft. 368p. 1988. 49.95 (*0-413-60600-7*, A0075) Heinemann.

Development of the Equations of Electromagnetism in Material Continua. H. F. Tiersten. Ed. by Clifford A. Truesdell. (Tracts in Natural Philosophy Ser.: Vol. 36). 160p. 1990. 54.00 (*0-387-97241-2*) Spr-Verlag.

Development of the Federal Program of Flood Control on the Mississippi River. Arthur D. Frank. LC 68-58572. (Columbia University. Studies in the Social Sciences: No. 323). reprint ed. 21.00 (*0-404-51323-9*) AMS Pr.

Development of the Flour Milling Industry in the United States. Charles B. Kuhlman. LC 68-56240. (Library of Early American Business & Industry: No. 32). 1973. reprint ed. 39.50 (*0-678-00932-5*) Kelley.

Development of the Free Public High School in Illinois to 1860. Paul E. Belting. LC 71-89149. (American Education: Its Men, Institutions & Ideas, Ser. 1). 1977. reprint ed. 18.95 (*0-405-01386-8*) Ayer.

Development of the Frog. C. B. Powar & J. D. Sahasrabuddhe. 1992. 22.50 (*81-7040-447-9*, Pub. by Himalaya II) Apt Bks.

Development of the Genital System & the Male Pseudohermaphroditism. Jan E. Jirasek. Ed. by M. Michael Cohen, Jr. LC 72-128825. 150p. reprint ed. pap. 42.80 (*0-317-19868-8*, 2023106) Bks Demand.

Development of the German Air Force, Nineteen Nineteen to Nineteen Thirty-Nine. Richard Suchenwirth. LC 78-111597. (German Air Force in World War 2 Ser.). 1970. reprint ed. 21.95 (*0-405-00050-2*) Ayer.

Development of the German Air Force, 1919-1939. Richard Suchenwirth. Ed. by Harry Fletcher. (USAF Historical Studies: No. 160). 311p. 1968. reprint ed. pap. text ed. 33.95 (*0-89126-145-1*) MA-AH Pub.

Development of the Greek Economy, 1950-1991: An Historical, Empirical, & Econometric Analysis. George A. Jouganatos. LC 91-38211. (Contributions in Economics & Economic History Ser.: No. 132). 272p. 1992. text ed. 65.00 (*0-313-28344-3*, JGE, Greenwood Pr) Greenwood.

Development of the Greek Language. Wendy Moleas. (Studies in Modern Greek). 118p. (Orig.). (C). 1989. lib. bdg. 25.00 (*0-89241-485-5*); pap. text ed. 16.00 (*0-89241-486-3*) Caratzas.

Development of the Heavy Bomber, 1918-1944. Jean H. Dubuque & Robert F. Gleckner. (USAF Historical Studies: No. 6). 188p. 1951. pap. text ed. 25.00 (*0-89126-030-7*) MA-AH Pub.

Development of the Hill Areas. G. L. Dobhal. 1987. 27.00 (*0-8364-2242-2*, Pub. by Concept II) S Asia.

Development of the Idea of Detente: Coming to Terms. Michael Froman. LC 91-19066. 160p. 1992. text ed. 49.95 (*0-312-04777-0*) St Martin.

Development of the Idea of History in Antiquity. Gerald A. Press. LC 84-239837. (McGill-Queen's Studies in the History of Religion: No. 2). 191p. reprint ed. pap. 54.50 (*0-7837-1028-3*, 2041339) Bks Demand.

Development of the Inca State. Brian S. Bauer. (Illus.). 203p. 1992. text ed. 25.00 (*0-292-71563-3*) U of Tex Pr.

Development of the Indian National Congress, 1892-1909. rev. ed. Pansy C. Ghosh. 1985. 20.00 (*0-8364-1411-X*, KL Mukhopadhyay) S Asia.

Development of the Infant & Young Child: Normal & Abnormal. 9th ed. R. S. Illingworth. (Illus.). 364p. 1987. pap. 48.00 (*0-443-03840-6*) Churchill.

Development of the Italian Schools of Painting, 19 vols. Raimond Van Marle. LC 70-116366. (Illus.). 1970. reprint ed. 495.00 (*0-87817-048-0*) Hacker.

Development of the Labor Surplus Economy: Theory & Policy. John C. Fei & Gustav Ranis. LC 64-21024. (Publication of the Economic Growth Center, Yale University Ser.). (Illus.). 334p. reprint ed. pap. 95.20 (*0-8357-6091-X*, 2033766) Bks Demand.

Development of the Larval Pigment Patterns in Triturus Alpestrs & Ambystoma Mexicanum. H. H. Epperlein & J. Lofberg. (Advances in Anatomy, Embryology & Cell Biology Ser.: Vol. 118). (Illus.). 112p. 1990. pap. 70.60 (*0-685-32922-4*, 3510) Spr-Verlag.

Development of the Late Phoenician Scripts. J. Brian Peckham. LC 68-17629. (Semitic Ser.: No. 20). (Illus.). 245p. 1968. 15.00 (*0-674-20050-0*) HUP.

Development of the Law of Belligerent Occupation, 1863-1914. Doris A. Graber. LC 68-58584. (Columbia University. Studies in the Social Sciences: No. 543). reprint ed. 24.50 (*0-404-51543-6*) AMS Pr.

Development of the Logical Method in Ancient China. Shih Hu. 1973. lib. bdg. 79.95 (*0-87968-524-7*) Krishna Pr.

Development of the London Livery Companies: An Historical Essay & Select Bibliography. William F. Kahl. (Kress Library of Business & Economics Publication: No. 15). (Illus.). viii, 104p. 1960. pap. 9.95 (*0-678-09910-3*, Kress Lib Business) Kelley.

Development of the Long-Range Escort Fighter. Bernard Boylan. (USAF Historical Studies: No. 136). 321p. 1955. pap. text ed. 35.00 (*0-89126-141-9*) MA-AH Pub.

Development of the Mexican Tuna Industry, 1976-1986. Linda L. Hudgins. LC 87-505. (Research Report Ser.: No. 5). 54p. 1986. pap. text ed. 6.00 (*0-86638-091-4*, Eastwest Ctr Pr) UH Pr.

Development of the Mind: Psychoanalytic Papers on Clinical & Theoretical Problems. Jeanne Lampl-de Groot. LC 65-21749. 391p. 1965. text ed. 55.00 (*0-8236-1240-6*) Intl Univs Pr.

Development of the Modern Flute. Nancy Toff. LC 86-7116. (Illus.). 288p. 1986. reprint ed. 29.95 (*0-252-01358-1*) U of Ill Pr.

Development of the Modern Guitar. Ed. by Mark Grant. (Guitar Study Ser.: Vol. 2). (Illus.). 200p. (Orig.). 1992. pap. 12.95 (*0-933224-59-1*) Bold Strummer Ltd.

Development of the Modern Problems Course in the Senior High School. Manson V. Jennings. LC 70-176904. (Columbia University. Teachers College. Contributions to Education Ser.: No. 968). reprint ed. 37.50 (*0-404-55968-9*) AMS Pr.

Development of the Modern State: A Sociological Introduction. Gianfranco Poggi. LC 77-76148. xii, 175p. 1978. 24.50 (*0-8047-0959-9*); pap. 10.95 (*0-8047-1042-2*) Stanford U Pr.

Development of the Mongolian National Style Painting: Mongol Zurag. N. Tsultem. (Illus.). 222p. (C). 1986. text ed. 275.00 (*0-569-08992-1*, Pub. by Collets) St Mut.

Development of the Monist View of History. Georgi Plikhanou. 334p. 1972. reprint ed. 25.00 (*0-8464-1086-9*) Beekman Pubs.

Development of the National Home & Hospice Care Survey. Barbara J. Haupt. LC 94-12450. (Vital & Health Statistics, Series 1, Programs & Collection Procedures: No. 33). 1994. 11.00 (*0-8406-0492-0*) Natl Ctr Health Stats.

***Development of the National Home & Hospice Care Survey.** National Center for Health Statistics Staff. LC 94-1309. (Series Reports: Series 1, No. 33). 153p. Date not set. 11.00 (*0-614-02900-7*, 017-022-01265-1) Natl Ctr Health Stats.

Development of the Notion of Self: Understanding the Complexity of Human Interiority. William S. Schmidt. LC 93-20925. (Studies in the Psychology of Religion: Vol. 5). 416p. 1994. text ed. 109.95 (*0-7734-9341-7*) E Mellen.

Development of the Number Field Sieve. A. K. Lenstra & H. W. Lenstra, Jr. LC 93-5229. (Lecture Notes in Mathematics Ser.: Vol. 1554). 1994. 23.00 (*0-387-57013-6*) Spr-Verlag.

Development of the Office of Hazzan Through the Talmudic Period. Hyman I. Sky. LC 92-36311. 208p. 1992. 89.95 (*0-7734-9823-0*, Mellen Univ Pr) E Mellen.

Development of the Pacific Salmon-Canning Industry: A Grown Man's Game. Ed. by Diane Newell. (Illus.). 336p. (C). 1989. text ed. 49.95 (*0-7735-0717-5*, Pub. by McGill CN) U of Toronto Pr.

Development of the Peace Idea & Other Essays. Benjamin F. Trueblood. LC 70-137555. (Peace Movement in America Ser.). xxviii, 244p. 1972. reprint ed. lib. bdg. 30.95 (*0-89198-085-7*) Ozer.

Development of the Personality, Vol. 1. Liz Greene & Howard Sasportas. (Seminars in Psychological Astrology Ser.: Vol. 1). 333p. (Orig.). 1987. pap. 14.95 (*0-87728-673-6*) Weiser.

Development of the Principles & Plans on Which to Establish Self-Supporting Home Colonies. Robert Owen. LC 72-2941. reprint ed. 34.50 (*0-404-10707-9*) AMS Pr.

Development of the Private Sector in a Small Economy in Transition: The Case of Mongolia. Hongjoo Hahm. LC 93-41714. (Discussion Paper Ser.: No. 223). 52p. 1993. 6.95 (*0-8213-2721-6*, 12721) World Bank.

Development of the Pro-Choice Movement: Professional Organization & Grass-Roots Activism in the Abortion Conflict. Suzanne Staggenborg. 256p. 1991. 35.00 (*0-19-506596-4*) OUP.

Development of the Proto-Indo-European Laryngeals in Greek. R. S. Beekes. (Janua Linguarum, Ser. Practica: No. 42). 1969. pap. text ed. 89.25 (*90-279-0693-9*) Mouton.

Development of the Public Land Policy, 1783-1820, with Special Reference to Indiana. Charles J. Bayard. Ed. by Stuart Bruchey. LC 78-53556. (Development of Public Land Law in the U. S. Ser.). 1979. lib. bdg. 30.95 (*0-405-11364-1*) Ayer.

Development of the Puerto Rican Jibaro & His Present Attitude Towards Society. Jose C. Rosario. LC 74-14248. (Puerto Rican Experience Ser.). (Illus.). 124p. 1975. reprint ed. 11.95 (*0-405-06234-6*) Ayer.

Development of the Rat Spinal Cord: Immuno- & Enzyme Histochemical Approaches. Martin Oudega et al. LC 93-44601. 1994. write for info. (*3-540-57173-6*); 99.00 (*0-387-57173-6*) Spr-Verlag.

Development of the Red Pulp in the Spleen. V. Grouls & B. Helpap. (Advances in Anatomy, Embryology & Cell Biology Ser.: Vol. 75). (Illus.). 70p. 1982. pap. 34.00 (*0-387-11408-4*) Spr-Verlag.

Development of the Regional Policy of the European Communities. P. Tristan McGee. (C). 1982. 40.00 (*0-685-30279-2*, Pub. by Oxford Polytechnic UK) St Mut.

Development of the Resources of the Sea: India. J. N. Nanda. (C). 1988. 22.00 (*81-7022-220-6*, Pub. by Concept II) S Asia.

Development of the Role of the Security Council: Peace-Keeping & Peace-Building Workshop 1992 - Colloque 1992. Ed. by Rene-Jean Dupuy. (Recueil des Cours, Colloque Ser.). 516p. (C). 1993. lib. bdg. 158.00 (*0-7923-2318-1*) Kluwer Ac.

Development of the Roman Alphabet. Susan Westlake. (Illus.). 21p. (Orig.). 1992. spiral bd., pap. 1.80 (*0-939507-24-2*, B405) Amer Classical.

Development of the S. A. in Nurnberg, 1922-34. Eric G. Reiche. (Illus.). 352p. 1986. 49.95 (*0-521-30638-8*) Cambridge U Pr.

***Development of the Second Partner Review in Audit Engagements.** Michael S. Luehlfing. 20p. 1991. pap. text ed. 19.50 (*0-933179-05-7*) Bus Account Pubns.

Development of the Securities Market in Israel. Marshall Sarnat. 138p. 1966. lib. bdg. 30.00 (*0-685-14112-8*, Pub. by J C B Mohr GW) Coronet Bks.

Development of the Social Security Act. Edwin E. Witte. (Illus.). 238p. (C). 1962. pap. 4.00x (*0-299-02544-6*) U of Wis Pr.

Development of the Sonnet: An Introduction. Michael Spiller. LC 92-4868. 320p. 1992. 69.95 (*0-415-07744-3*, A9657); pap. 16.95 (*0-415-08741-4*, A9661) Routledge.

Development of the Soviet Budgetary System. Robert W. Davies. LC 78-23596. 373p. 1979. reprint ed. text ed. 69.50 (*0-313-21191-4*, DADS, Greenwood Pr) Greenwood.

Development of the Tachi in Japan. Hawley. 1990. pap. 4.95 (*0-910704-02-3*) Hawley.

Development of the Teaching of Agriculture in Mississippi with Special Emphasis on Agriculture As a Part of School Curricula. Ronald J. Slay. LC 78-177780. (Columbia University. Teachers College. Contributions to Education Ser.: No. 310). reprint ed. 37.50 (*0-404-55310-9*) AMS Pr.

Development of the Television Network Oligopoly. Stewart L. Long. Ed. by Christopher H. Sterling. LC 78-21725. (Dissertations in Broadcasting Ser.). (Illus.). 1980. lib. bdg. 17.95 (*0-405-11764-7*) Ayer.

Development of the Top Forty Radio Format. David T. MacFarland. Ed. by Christopher H. Sterling. LC 78-21726. (Dissertations in Broadcasting Ser.). (Illus.). 1980. lib. bdg. 48.95 (*0-405-11765-5*) Ayer.

Development of the U. S. Urban System: Concepts, Structures, Regional Shifts, Vol. II. Edgar S. Dunn, Jr. LC 81-47619. 266p. 1983. 75.00 (*0-8018-2638-1*) Resources Future.

Development of the U. S. Urban System, Vol. 1: Concepts, Structures, Regional Shifts. Edgar S. Dunn. LC 79-2180. (Illus.). 227p. reprint ed. pap. 64.70 (*0-7837-6144-9*, 2043726) Bks Demand.

Development of the Vascular System. Ed. by R. N. Feinberg et al. (Issues in Biomedicine Ser.: Vol. 14). (Illus.). viii, 192p. 1991. 176.00 (*3-8055-5285-8*) S Karger.

Development of the Vertebrate Retina. Ed. by B. L. Finlay & D. R. Sengelub. (Perspectives in Vision Research Ser.). (Illus.). 308p. 1989. 79.50 (*0-306-43060-6*, Plenum Pr) Plenum.

Development of the Vertebrate Skull. Gavin R. De Beer. LC 85-1081. (Illus.). xxiv, 730p. 1985. reprint ed. lib. bdg. 55.00 (*0-226-13958-1*); reprint ed. pap. text ed. 22.50 (*0-226-13960-3*) U Ch Pr.

Development of the Visual System. Ed. by Dominic M. Lam & Carla J. Shatz. (Bradford - Proceedings of the Retina Foundation Symposium Ser.: Vol. 3). (Illus.). 256p. 1991. 70.00 (*0-262-12154-9*, Bradford Bks) MIT Pr.

***Development of the Welfare State in the Western World.** Thomas Katsaros. LC 95-3033. 414p. (C). 1995. lib. bdg. 56.00 (*0-8191-9871-4*); pap. text ed. 42.50 (*0-8191-9872-2*) U Pr of Amer.

Development of the Worcester Police Department. Leahy. pap. 6.00 (*0-914206-13-3*) Clark U Pr.

Development of Therapeutic Skills. Mary Jo Bulbrook. 1980. text ed. 14.95 (*0-316-11472-3*, Little Med Div) Little.

Development of Thought. G. S. Halford. (Illus.). 464p. (C). 1982. text ed. 89.95 (*0-89859-177-5*) L Erlbaum Assocs.

Development of Transportation in Modern England. 2nd ed. W. T. Jackman. 820p. 1962. 42.50 (*0-7146-1326-6*, Pub. by F Cass Pubs UK) Intl Spec Bk.

Development of Tropical Lands: Policy Issues in Latin America. Michael Nelson. LC 72-12363. (Resources for the Future Ser.). 323p. 1973. 27.00 (*0-8018-1488-X*) Johns Hopkins.

Development of Tropical Lands: Policy Issues in Latin America. Michael Nelson. LC 72-12363. (Illus.). 326p. reprint ed. pap. 93.00 (*0-685-20405-7*, 2030212) Bks Demand.

Development of Tubewell Irrigation in India. Ed. by R. K. Dhawan. 256p. 1982. 29.95 (*0-318-36788-2*) Asia Bk Corp.

Development of Underdevelopment in China: A Symposium. Ed. by Philip C. Huang. LC 80-51203. 138p. reprint ed. pap. 39.40 (*0-317-41947-1*, 2026135) Bks Demand.

Development of University Libraries in India after Independence. O. P. Gupta. (C). 1992. 25.00 (*81-7022-409-8*, Pub. by Concept II) S Asia.

Development of Urban Low-Income Neighbourhoods in the Third World. Ed. by E. Bruno et al. 408p. 1986. pap. text ed. 50.00 (*3-923578-05-9*) Cassell.

Development of Urban Systems in Africa. Ed. by Robert A. Obudho & Salah S. El-Shakhs. LC 78-19766. 432p. 1979. text ed. 65.00 (*0-275-90404-0*, C0404, Praeger Pubs) Greenwood.

***Development of Vegetable Oils in Human Nutrition.** Ed. by R. Przbylski & B. McDonald. 1995. write for info. (*0-935315-66-7*) AOCS Pr.

Development of Wage Theory in Britain in the 19th Century. David R. Grossman. 225p. (Orig.). (C). 1988. pap. write for info. (*0-9621435-0-2*) Political Econ Pr.

Development of "Walden" A Genetic Text. Ronald Clapper. LC 80-2503. 1981. 75.00 (*0-404-19051-0*) AMS Pr.

Development of Weak Interaction Theory. Ed. by P. K. Kabir. (International Science Review Ser.). (Illus.). 312p. 1963. text ed. 169.00 (*0-677-00320-X*) Gordon & Breach.

Development of Weldable, Hot Workable High Strength Copper-Bearing Structural Steels. University of Ghent Staff. 83p. 1975. 12.45 (*0-317-34513-3*, 151) Intl Copper.

Development of Welfare States in Europe & America. Ed. by Peter Flora & Arnold J. Heidenheimer. LC 79-65227. 420p. 1981. pap. 21.95 (*0-87855-920-5*) Transaction Pubs.

Development of Western Music: A History, 1. 2nd ed. K. Marie Stolba. 752p. 1994. write for info. (*0-697-12549-1*) Brown & Benchmark.

Development of Western Music: A History, 2. 2nd ed. K. Marie Stolba. 752p. 1994. write for info. (*0-697-12550-5*) Brown & Benchmark.

Development of Western Music: A History, Set. 2nd ed. K. Marie Stolba. 752p. 1994. boxed write for info. (*0-697-12547-5*) Brown & Benchmark.

Development of Western Music: A History, Brief Version. 2nd ed. K. Marie Stolba. 576p. (C). 1994. pap. text ed. write for info. (*0-697-12693-5*) Brown & Benchmark.

Development of Wireless to 1920. George Sheirs. LC 75-23900. (Historical Studies in Telecommunications). (Illus.). 1977. 56.95 (*0-405-07759-9*) Ayer.

Development of Women's Entrepreneurship in India. Shanta K. Chandra. (C). 1991. 14.00 (*81-7099-302-4*, Pub. by Mittal II) S Asia.

Development of Word Meaning. Ed. by S. A. Kuczaj, II & M. D. Barrett. (Cognitive Development Ser.). (Illus.). 390p. 1985. 115.00 (*0-387-96152-6*) Spr-Verlag.

Development of Word Order Patterns in Old English. Marian C. Bean. LC 82-22722. (Illus.). 150p. (C). 1983. text ed. 42.00 (*0-389-20356-4*, 07216) B&N Imports.

Development of World Dominion. C. H. Douglas. 1972. 59.95 (*0-8490-0021-1*) Gordon Pr.

Development of World Dominion. C. H. Douglas. 157p. 1986. pap. 6.00 (*0-317-53300-2*) Noontide.

***Development of World Economy, 1975-1991.** Ed. by Alain Geledan. (Social Science Monograph). 288p. 1994. 40.00 (*0-88033-969-1*) East Eur Quarterly.

Development of Written Estonian. George Kurman. LC 67-65322. (Uralic & Altaic Ser.: Vol. 90). 120p. 1968. pap. text ed. 9.00 (*0-87750-036-3*) Res Inst Inner Asian Studies.

Development of X-Ray Analysis. rev. unabridged ed. Lawrence Bragg. Ed. by D. C. Phillips & H. Lipson. LC 92-39217. (Illus.). 270p. 1993. reprint ed. pap. text ed. 8.95 (*0-486-67316-2*) Dover.

***Development Officer in Higher Education: Toward an Understanding of the Role.** Michael J. Worth & James W. Asp, 2nd. Ed. & Frwd. by Jonathan D. Fife. (ASHE-ERIC Higher Education Report: No. 4, 1994). 100p. (C). Date not set. pap. 18.00 (*1-878380-60-5*) GWU Schl E&HD.

Development Options in Europe. Ed. by Bjorn Hettne. (Gothenburg University Department of Peace Research Studies). 100p. (Orig.). 1988. pap. 31.00x (*91-87380-03-X*) Coronet Bks.

Development or Destruction: The Conversion of Tropical Forest to Pasture in Latin America. Ed. by Henry A. Pearson et al. 405p. (C). 1992. pap. text ed. 60.50 (*0-8133-7824-9*) Westview.

Development or Deterioration? Work in Rural Asia. Ed. by Bruce Koppel et al. LC 93-40819. 328p. 1994. lib. bdg. 45.00 (*1-55587-471-1*) Lynne Rienner.

Development Perspectives. Ed. by K. S. Ramachandran. 1991. text ed. 25.00 (*0-7069-5332-0*, Pub. by Vikas II) S Asia.

Development Perspectives: Problems, Strategies & Policies. V. V. Bhatt. (Illus.). 352p. 1980. text ed. 138.00 (*0-08-025774-7*, Pub. by Pergamon Repr UK) Franklin.

Development Perspectives for the 1990s. Ed. by Renee Prendergast & H. W. Singer. LC 91-24054. 350p. 1991. text ed. 69.95 (*0-312-06803-4*) St Martin.

D

An Asterisk (*) at the beginning of an entry indicates that the title is appearing in BIP for the first time.

Development Planning: Origin & Growth. Ratnakar Gedam. 250p. 1991. 100.00 (*81-7158-229-X*, Pub. by Scientific Pubs II) St Mut.

Development Planning: The Indian Experience. Sukhamoy Chakravarty. 148p. 1987. 45.00 (*0-19-828555-8*) OUP.

Development Planning: The Indian Experience. Sukhamoy Chakravarty. 156p. 1993. reprint ed. pap. 4.95 (*0-19-562346-0*) OUP.

Development Planning & Aboriginal Rights: The Case of Northern Canada. A. L. Swiderski. (Progress in Planning Ser.: No. 37). 82p. 1992. pap. 66.00 (*0-08-041848-1*, Pergamon Pr) Elsevier.

Development Planning & Local Economic Growth: A Study of Process & Policy in Bracknell New Town. Ivan Turok. (Progress in Planning Ser.: Vol. 31). 96p. 1989. pap. 30.00 (*0-08-037365-8*, Pub. by Aberdeen U Pr) Macmillan.

Development Planning & Policy Design: A System Dynamics Approach. Khalid Saeed. LC 94-8824. 288p. 1994. 59.95 (*1-85628-672-X*, Pub. by Avebury Pub UK) Ashgate Pub Co.

Development Planning & Population Policy in Puerto Rico: From Historical Evolution Towards a Plan for Population Stabilization. Ken C. Earnhardt. LC 77-11187. (Planning Ser.: No. S-5). 1982. 6.00 (*0-8477-2441-7*) U of PR Pr.

***Development Planning for School Improvement.** David Hargreaves & David Hopkins. (School Development Ser.). (Illus.). 1995. 65.00 (*0-304-33101-5*); pap. 19.95 (*0-304-33103-1*) Cassell.

***Development Planning Guide.** Dennis E. Coates. 48p. 1994. pap. text ed. 18.00 (*1-886713-01-4*) Perform Support Systs.

Development Planning in an African Economy: The Experience of Nigeria, Vol. I: 1950-1980. Satish C. Mehta. 1990. 36.00 (*81-85163-14-6*, Pub. by Kalinga) S Asia.

Development Planning in an African Economy, Vol. 1: 1950-1980: The Experience of Nigeria. Satish C. Mehta. (Illus.). vii, 244p. 1990. 22.00 (*0-685-63300-4*, Pub. by Kalinga Pubns) Nataraj Bks.

Development Planning in an African Economy, 1950-1980, Vol. 1: The Experience of Nigeria. Satish C. Mehta. (Illus.). vii, 244p. 1990. 22.00 (*0-685-62647-4*, Pub. by Kalinga Pubns) Nataraj Bks.

Development Planning in Bangladesh: A Study in Political Economy. Nurul Islam. LC 77-77354. 1977. text ed. 29.95 (*0-312-19694-6*) St Martin.

Development Planning in India. Mary Parmar. 1993. 30.00 (*0-685-65106-1*, Pub. by Reliance Pub Hse II) Apt Bks.

Development Planning in Mixed Economies. (United Nations University (UNU) Publications). 359p. 1989. 25.00 (*92-808-0637-8*, E.88.III.A.6) UN.

Development Policy. B. Krishnarao. 1992. text ed. 25.00 (*81-207-0943-8*, Pub. by Sterling Pubs II) Apt Bks.

Development Policy. Ed. by Soumitra Sharma. LC 92-6772. 262p. 1993. text ed. 69.95 (*0-312-08096-4*) St Martin.

Development Policy & Economic Theory. Ed. by Kaushik Basu & Pulin Nayak. (Illus.). 336p. (C). 1993. 24.95 (*0-19-562764-4*) OUP.

Development Policy & Planning: A Third World Perspective. Ed. by Pradip K. Ghosh. LC 83-26492. (International Development Resource Bks.: No. 8). (Illus.). xvii, 626p. 1984. text ed. 105.00 (*0-313-24144-9*, GDP/, Greenwood Pr) Greenwood.

Development Policy & Planning: An Introduction to Models & Techniques. Anis Chowdhury & Colin Kirkpatrick. LC 93-7404. 1994. 45.00 (*0-415-09888-2*); pap. 14.95 (*0-415-09889-0*) Routledge.

Development Policy & Public Action. Ed. by Marc Wuyts et al. (Illus.). 320p. 1993. 55.00 (*0-19-877336-6*); pap. 17.95 (*0-19-877337-4*) OUP.

Development Policy in East Asia: Economic Growth & Poverty Alleviation. Romeo M. Bautista. 62p. 1992. pap. 10.00 (*981-3016-25-6*, Pub. by Inst SE Asian Studies SI) Ashgate Pub Co.

***Development Policy in the Cold War Era.** Brigitte H. Schultz. (C). 1995. pap. text ed. 31.25 (*3-8258-2148-X*) Westview.

Development Policy of a Communist Government: West Bengal Since 1977. Ross Mallick. LC 92-20010. (Cambridge South Asian Studies: No. 54). (Illus.). 240p. (C). 1994. 59.95 (*0-521-43292-8*) Cambridge U Pr.

Development Policy Two: The Pakistan Experience. Ed. by Walter P. Falcon & Gustav F. Papanek. LC 70-160113. (Center for International Affairs Ser.). (Illus.). 283p. 1971. 29.95 (*0-674-20270-8*) HUP.

Development Policymaking in Mexico: The Sistema Alimentario Mexicano (SAM) Michael R. Redclift. (Research Report Ser.: No. 24). 26p. (Orig.). (C). 1981. pap. 5.00 (*0-935391-23-1*, RR-24) UCSD Ctr US-Mex.

Development Politics: Private Development & the Public Interest. Robert Hollister & Tunney Lee. Ed. by Michael Barker. LC 79-67386. (Studies in State Development Policy: Vol. 8). 93p. 1979. pap. 11.95 (*0-934842-07-8*) CSPA.

Development, Politics & Social Theory: Essays in Honour of S P Varma, the Doyen of Political Scientists in India. Ed. by Iqbal Narain. 400p. 1989. text ed. 40.00 (*81-207-0850-4*, Pub. by Sterling Pubs II) Apt Bks.

Development Problems in Latin America: An Analysis. (With a Foreword by Carlos Quintana) United Nations, Economic Commission for Latin America. LC 71-111930. (Special Publication of the Institute of Latin American Studies, University of Texas at Austin). 366p. reprint ed. pap. 104.40 (*0-685-16459-4*, 2027321) Bks Demand.

Development Problems of an Open-Access Resource: The Fisheries of Peninsular Malaysia. Ooi Jin Bee. 61p. 1990. pap. text ed. 10.00 (*981-3035-46-3*, Pub. by Inst SE Asian Studies SI) Ashgate Pub Co.

Development Process: A Spatial Perspective. Akin L. Mabogunje. LC 80-19939. 357p. 1980. 36.50 (*0-8419-0659-9*) Holmes & Meier.

Development Process in Small Island States. Ed. by Douglas G. Lockart et al. LC 92-26122. (Illus.). 224p. 1993. 59.95 (*0-415-06984-X*, B0204) Routledge.

Development Program Planning, a Process Approach. David H. Spaeth. LC 91-76993. (International Museum of Cultures Publications: No. 24). x, 164p. (Orig.). 1991. pap. 12.50 (*0-88312-178-6*); fiche 12.00 (*0-88312-907-8*) Summer Instit Ling.

Development Programmes in Agriculture & the Weaker Sections. N. Desinga Raj. 217p. 1987. 26.00 (*81-85076-16-2*, Pub. by Chugh Pubns II) S Asia.

Development Projects As Policy Experiments: An Adaptive Approach to Development Administration. Dennis A. Rondinelli. LC 83-8117. (Development & Underdevelopment Ser.). 180p. 1983. pap. 10.95 (*0-416-73640-8*, NO. 3914) Routledge Chapman & Hall.

Development Projects As Policy Experiments: An Adaptive Approach to Development Administration. 2nd ed. Dennis A. Rondinelli. LC 92-17773. (Development & Underdevelopment Ser.). (Illus.). 192p. 1993. 59.95 (*0-415-06622-0*, A9845, Routledge NY); pap. 16.95 (*0-415-06623-9*, A9849, Routledge NY) Routledge.

Development Projects Observed. Albert O. Hirschman. LC 67-27683. 211p. reprint ed. pap. 60.20 (*0-685-15234-0*, 2027141) Bks Demand.

***Development Projects Observed: With a New Preface by the Author.** Albert O. Hirschman. 197p. (C). 1995. 19.95x (*0-8157-3652-5*) Brookings.

Development Psychology of Music. David J. Hargreaves. LC 86-13660. 270p. 1987. pap. 21.95 (*0-521-31415-1*) Cambridge U Pr.

Development Puzzle: Some Insights from Africa. Ed. by Kwaku Osei-Hwedie & Muna Ndulo. LC 90-83111. (Illus.). 520p. (Orig.). (C). 1990. pap. text ed. 24.95 (*1-55618-084-5*) Brunswick Pub.

Development, Regeneration, & Plasticity of the Autonomic Nervous System. Ed. by I. A. Hendry & C. E. Hill. LC 92-49663. (Autonomic Nervous System Ser.: Vol. 3). 1993. text ed. 148.00 (*3-7186-5136-X*) Gordon & Breach.

***Development Regulation & Housing Affordability.** Ira S. Lowry. 180p. 1992. pap. text ed. 42.95 (*0-87420-729-0*) Urban Land.

***Development Report Card for the States, 1995: Economic Benchmarks for State & Corporate Decisionmakers.** 202p. (Orig.). 1995. 70.00 (*1-883187-05-2*) Corp Ent Dev.

Development Report Card, 1994: Economic Benchmarks for State & Corporate Decisionmakers. 8th ed. 210p. 1994. spiral bd. 70.00 (*1-883187-01-X*) Corp Ent Dev.

Development Research: The Environmental Challenge. Ed. by James T. Winpenny. 228p. (C). 1992. pap. text ed. 19.50 (*0-8133-1604-9*) Westview.

Development Review & Outlook, 1984-85. Urban Land Institute Staff. LC 83-647869. 511p. reprint ed. pap. 145.70 (*0-8357-8094-5*, 2033943) Bks Demand.

Development, Sale & Purchase of Manufactured Home Landlease Communities. George Allen. Ed. by Nora Freese. (Monograph Ser.: No. 2). 30p. 1993. 25.00 (*1-878350-02-1*) PMN Pub.

Development Science & Art of Minerals Surveying: Proceedings of the 6th International Congress of the International Society for Mine Surveying, Harrogate, 9-13 Sept. 1985, 2 vols., Set. 1098p. (C). 1985. text ed. 305.00 (*90-6191-615-1*, Pub. by A A Balkema NE) Ashgate Pub Co.

Development Self. Ed. by Robert J. Leahy. (Developmental Psychology Ser.). 1985. text ed. 59.00 (*0-12-439870-7*) Acad Pr.

Development, Sociology & Anthropology: An Annotated Bibliography of World Bank Publications & Documents in Sociology & Anthropology. Michael M. Cernea & April L. Adams. LC 94-1864. (Technical Paper Ser.: No. 241). 1994. write for info. (*0-8213-2781-X*) World Bank.

Development States in East Asia. Ed. by Gorden White. 200p. 1988. text ed. 49.95 (*0-312-01341-8*) St Martin.

Development Strategies: A New Synthesis. Ed. by John P. Lewis. (U. S. Third World Policy Perspectives Ser.). 128p. 1985. 32.95 (*0-88738-044-1*); pap. 17.95 (*0-87855-991-4*) Transaction Pubs.

Development Strategies & Policies in Latin America: A Historical Perspective. Corbo. 30p. 1992. pap. 5.00 (*1-55815-181-8*) ICS Pr.

***Development Strategies & Policy Implementation: The Case of Korea.** Il Sakong. (Occasional Papers: No. 60). 1995. write for info. (*1-55815-432-9*) ICS Pr.

Development Strategies as Ideologies: Puerto Rico's Export-Led Industrialization Experience. Emilio Pantojas-Garcia. LC 90-33397. 208p. 1990. lib. bdg. 37.00 (*1-55587-198-4*) Lynne Rienner.

Development Strategies As Ideology. Emilio Pantojas-Garcia. LC 90-33397. 205p. 1990. 18.50 (*0-8477-0175-1*) U of PR Pr.

Development Strategies in Africa: Current Economic, Socio-Political, & Institutional Trends & Issues. Aguibou Y. Yansane. (Contributions in Afro-American & African Studies). 1995. 55.00 (*0-313-28994-8*, Greenwood Pr) Greenwood.

Development Strategies in Rural Colombia: The Case of Caqueta. Robin R. Marsh. LC 82-620032. (Latin American Studies: Vol. 55). 1983. text ed. 22.95 (*0-87903-055-0*) UCLA Lat Am Ctr.

Development Strategies in Semi-Industrial Economies. Bela A. Balassa. LC 81-15558. (World Bank Research Publication Ser.). 408p. reprint ed. pap. 116.30 (*0-7837-5379-9*, 2045143) Bks Demand.

Development Strategy & the Economy of Sierra Leone. John Weeks. LC 91-39069. 130p. 1992. text ed. 65.00 (*0-312-07212-0*) St Martin.

***Development Studies: A Reader.** Corbridge. Date not set. pap. text ed. 31.95 (*0-470-23528-4*) Wiley.

Development Studies: Critique & Renewal. Raymond Apthorpe & Andras Krahl. viii, 264p. 1986. pap. 53.75 (*90-04-07714-6*) E J Brill.

Development Studies & Colonial Policy. Ed. by B. Ingham & C. Simmons. (Illus.). 296p. 1988. text ed. 35.00 (*0-7146-3231-7*, Pub. by F Cass Pubs UK) Intl Spec Bk.

Development Studies Revisited: Twenty-Five Years of the Journal of Development Studies. Ed. by Charles L. Cooper & Eur Fitzgerald. 548p. 1989. text ed. 65.00 (*0-7146-3376-3*, Pub. by F Cass Pubs UK) Intl Spec Bk.

Development Study of Factors Related to Children's Clothing Preferences. Lucille A. Hunt. (SRCD M: Vol. 24, No. 1). 1959. 14.00 (*0-527-01577-6*) Periodicals Srv.

Development Teaching Style in Adult Eductaion. Joe E. Heimlich & Emmalou Norland. LC 94-8094. (Higher & Adult Education Ser.). 376p. 1994. 29.95 (*0-7879-0013-3*) Jossey-Bass.

Development, Technology & Flexibility: Brazil Faces the Industrial Divide. Joao C. Ferraz et al. LC 91-38284. (Illus.). 240p. 1992. 75.00 (*0-415-07089-9*, A7406) Routledge.

Development, Technology, Education & Culture. Biman Sen. (C). 1991. 25.00 (*81-202-0293-7*, Pub. by Ajanta II) S Asia.

Development Theory: Critiques & Explorations. A. H. Somjee. LC 90-8552. 180p. 1991. text ed. 55.00 (*0-312-04886-6*) St Martin.

Development Theory & the Three Worlds. Bjorn Hettne. (Longman Development Studies). 1990. pap. text ed. 41.95 (*0-470-21519-4*) Halsted Pr.

***Development Theory & the Three Worlds: Towards an International Political Economy of Development.** 2nd ed. Bjorn Hettne. LC 95-1462. (Development Studies). 1995. pap. text ed. 34.95 (*0-470-23498-9*) Wiley.

Development Through Dialogue & Training: A Conceptual Framework. Paul Kevenhorster. 94p. 1988. pap. 23.00 (*3-7890-1590-3*, Pub. by Nomos Verlags GW) Intl Bk Import.

Development Through Drama. Brian Way. LC 90-4597. (C). 1967. pap. 15.00 (*0-391-00296-1*) Humanities.

Development Through Dualism? Land Tenure, Policy, & Poverty in Malawi. David E. Sahn & Jehan Arulpragasm. (Working Paper Ser.). (C). 1991. pap. text ed. 7.00 (*1-56401-109-7*) Cornell Food.

Development Through Health. Henry D. Molumphy. (Illus.). 16p. 1985. 1.00 (*0-918397-01-4*) Foster Parents.

Development Through Integration: Lessons from East Africa. Parbati K. Sircar. (Illus.). xv, 193p. 1990. 18.00 (*0-685-62646-6*, Pub. by Kalinga Pubns) Nataraj Bks.

Development Through Integration: Lessons from East Africa. Parbati K. Sircar. 1990. 27.50 (*81-85163-15-4*, Pub. by Kalinga) S Asia.

Development Through Life: A Handbook for Clinicians. M. Rutter & D. Hay. (Illus.). 720p. 1994. 125.00 (*0-632-03693-1*, Pub. by Blckwell Sci Pubns UK) Blackwell Sci.

Development Through Life: A Psychosocial Approach. 5th ed. Newman. LC 90-25467. 708p. (C). 1991. text ed. 49.95 (*0-534-15396-8*) Brooks-Cole.

***Development Through Life: A Psychosocial Approach.** 6th ed. Barbara M. Newman & Philip R. Newman. 763p. 1995. text ed. 49.95 (*0-534-23334-1*) Brooks-Cole.

Development Through Non-Governmental Organizations in Nepal. D. Chand. (C). 1991. 108.00 (*0-7855-0176-2*); text ed. 75.00 (*0-7855-0134-7*) St Mut.

Development Through Self-Reliance in the SADDC Region. Ed. by Achola & Msimuko. 170p. 1987. pap. text ed. 10.95 (*0-943852-26-9*) Prof World Peace.

Development Today: A Fund Raising guide for Nonprofit Organizations. 5th ed. Jeffrey Lant. 282p. 1993. pap. 24.95 (*0-940374-25-0*) JLA Pubns.

Development under Siege, Constraints & Opportunities in a Changing Global Economy: The CDP Report 1987. 21p. 1987. pap. 3.00 (*92-1-104212-7*, E.87.II.A.18) UN.

***Development, Use, & Performance of Exterior Insulation & Finish Systems, STP 1187.** Ed. by Mark F. Williams & Richard G. Lampo. LC 93-3637. (Special Technical Publication Ser.: Vol. 1187). (Illus.). 400p. 1995. text ed. 73.00 (*0-8031-2019-2*, 04-011870) ASTM.

Development Versus Stagnation: Technological Continuity & Agricultural Progress in Pre-modern China. Gang Deng. LC 92-19427. (Contributions in Economics & Economic History Ser.: No. 141). 288p. 1993. text ed. 57.95 (*0-313-28646-9*, DDV, Greenwood Pr) Greenwood.

Development with Trade: LDCs & the International Economy. Ed. by Anne O. Krueger. LC 88-28460. (Sequoia Seminar Publication). 250p. (C). 1988. 29.95 (*1-55815-042-0*); pap. 12.95 (*1-55815-041-2*) ICS Pr.

Development Without Destruction: Evolving Environment, Perceptions. Mostafa K. Tolba. 208p. 1982. text ed. 85.00 (*0-907567-22-3*, Tycooly Pub); pap. text ed. 45.00 (*0-907567-23-1*, Tycooly Pub) Weidner & Sons.

Developmental - Adapted Physical Education: Making Ability Count. 3rd ed. Carl B. Eichstaedt & Leonard H. Kalakian. LC 92-37930. 672p. (C). 1993. text ed. write for info. (*0-02-331701-9*) Macmillan.

Developmental Academic Advising. Roger B. Winston et al. LC 84-48001. (Joint Publication in the Jossey-Bass Higher Education Series & the Jossey-Bass Social & Behavioral Science Ser.). 603p. reprint ed. pap. 171.90 (*0-7837-6530-4*, 2045642) Bks Demand.

***Developmental & Acquired Dyslexia: Neuropsychological & Neurolinguistic Perspectives.** Ed. by Che K. Leong. (Neuropsychology & Cognition Ser.). 300p. (C). 1995. lib. bdg. 112.00 (*0-7923-3166-4*) Kluwer Ac.

Developmental & Neonatal Hematology. Ed. by James A. Stockman, III & Carl Pochedly. (Pediatric Hematology-Oncology Ser.). (Illus.). 352p. 1988. text ed. 99.50 (*0-88167-330-7*) Raven.

Developmental & Perceptual Assessment of Learning-Disabled Children: Theoretical Concepts & Diagnostic Testing. Sidney Groffman & Harold A. Solan. Ed. by Sally M. Corngold. (Illus.). 216p. (C). 1994. lib. bdg. 18.00 (*0-943599-73-3*) OEPF.

Developmental Approach to Adult Psychopathology. Edward Zigler & Marion Glick. LC 85-31447. (Wiley Series on Personality Processes). 357p. reprint ed. pap. 101.80 (*0-7837-2797-6*, 2057676) Bks Demand.

Developmental Approach to Algebraic Concepts. Mauro Cassano et al. 416p. 1993. per. 39.50 (*0-8403-8701-6*) Kendall-Hunt.

Developmental Approach to Problems of Acting Out. rev. ed. Ed. by Eveoleen N. Rexford. LC 77-17666. 223p. 1978. text ed. 32.50x (*0-8236-1221-X*) Intl Univs Pr.

***Developmental Approach to Urban Transport Planning: An Indonesian Illustration.** Harry Dimitiriou. 215p. (C). 1995. boxed, pap. text ed. 59.95 (*1-85972-004-8*, Pub. by Avebury Pub UK) Ashgate Pub Co.

Developmental Apraxia of Speech: Theory & Clinical Practice. Penelope K. Hall et al. LC 92-42727. (C). 1993. text ed. 34.00 (*0-89079-582-7*, 6596) PRO-ED.

Developmental Art Therapy. Geraldine H. Williams & Mary M. Wood. LC 77-8121. (Illus.). 198p. 1977. pap. 29.00 (*0-936104-60-0*, 1115) PRO-ED.

Developmental Aspects of Craniofacial Dysmorphology. Ed. by Michael Melnick & Ronald Jorgenson. LC 79-2487. (Alan R. Liss Ser.: Vol. 15, No. 8). 1979. 19.00 (*0-685-42252-6*) March of Dimes.

Developmental Aspects of Health Compliance Behavior. Ed. by Norman Krasnegor et al. 368p. 1992. text ed. 79.95 (*0-8058-1112-5*) L Erlbaum Assocs.

Developmental Aspects of Temporomandibular Joint Disorders. Ed. by D. S. Carlson et al. (Craniofacial Growth Ser.: Vol. 16). (Illus.). 298p. 1985. 49.00 (*0-929921-12-7*) UM CHGD.

Developmental Assessment & Intervention with Children & Adolescents. Ann Vernon. LC 93-13261. 168p. 1993. 27.95 (*1-55620-122-2*) Am Coun Assn.

Developmental Assessment in Clinical. Johnson. (C). 1992. text ed. 55.95 (*0-205-14381-4*, H4381) Allyn.

Developmental Behavior Genetics: Neural, Biometrical, & Evolutionary Approaches. Ed. by Martin E. Hahn et al. (Illus.). 352p. 1990. 59.00 (*0-19-505446-6*) OUP.

Developmental-Behavioral Disorders: Selected Topics, Vol. 1. Ed. by M. I. Gottlieb & J. E. Williams. (Critical Issues in Developmental & Behavioral Pediatrics Ser.). (Illus.). 392p. 1988. 75.00 (*0-306-42753-2*, Plenum Med Bk) Plenum.

Developmental-Behavioral Disorders: Selected Topics, Vol. 2. Ed. by M. I. Gottleib & J. E. Williams. (Critical Issues in Developmental & Behavioral Pediatrics Ser.). (Illus.). 310p. 1989. 65.00 (*0-306-43124-6*, Plenum Med Bk) Plenum.

Developmental-Behavioral Disorders: Selected Topics, Vol. 3. Ed. by M. I. Gottlieb & J. E. Williams. (Illus.). 330p. 1991. 75.00 (*0-306-43748-1*, Plenum Pr) Plenum.

Developmental Behavioral Neuroscience: The Minnesota Symposia on Child Psychology, Vol. 24. Ed. by M. R. Gunnar & C. Nelson. (Minnesota Symposium on Child Psychology Ser.). 248p. (C). 1991. text ed. 49.95 (*0-8058-0977-5*) L Erlbaum Assocs.

Developmental Biology. Nigel Holder & Virginia Walbot. 1987. text ed. write for info. (*0-07-554564-0*) McGraw.

Developmental Biology. Paul Kugrens. 308p. (C). 1994. pap. text ed., spiral bd. 24.95 (*0-8403-9156-0*) Kendall-Hunt.

Developmental Biology. Mark Taylor. 176p. 1991. spiral bd. 25.95 (*0-8403-7007-5*) Kendall-Hunt.

Developmental Biology. 3rd ed. Leon W. Browder et al. 754p. (C). 1991. pap. text ed. 57.25 (*0-03-013514-1*) SCP.

Developmental Biology. 4th rev. ed. Scott F. Gilbert. LC 93-42036. (Illus.). 900p. (C). 1994. text ed. 59.95 (*0-87893-249-6*) Sinauer Assocs.

Developmental Biology: A Guide for Experimental Study. Mary S. Tyler. LC 94-2607. (Illus.). 110p. (Orig.). (C). 1994. pap. text ed. 19.95 (*0-87893-846-X*) Sinauer Assocs.

Developmental Biology: A Comprehensive Synthesis, Vol. 1: Oogenesis. Ed. by Leon W. Browder. LC 85-3406. 644p. 1985. 110.00 (*0-306-41866-5*, Plenum Pr) Plenum.

Developmental Biology: A Comprehensive Synthesis, Vol. 2: The Cellular Basis of Morphogenesis. Ed. by Leon W. Browder. LC 85-3406. 668p. 1986. 110.00 (*0-306-42164-X*, Plenum Pr) Plenum.

Developmental Biology: A Comprehensive Synthesis, Vol. 3: The Cell Surface in Development & Cancer. Ed. by Malcolm S. Steinberg. LC 85-3406. 380p. 1986. 85.00 (*0-306-42165-8*, Plenum Pr) Plenum.

Developmental Biology: A Comprehensive Synthesis, Vol. 4: Manipulation of Mammalian Development. Ed. by Ralph B. Gwatkin. LC 85-3406. 402p. 1986. 85.00 (*0-306-42166-6*, Plenum Pr) Plenum.

Developmental Biology: A Comprehensive Synthesis, Vol. 5: The Molecular Biology of Cell Determination & Cell Differentiation. Ed. by Leon W. Browder. LC 85-3406. (Illus.). 460p. 1988. 89.50 (*0-306-42735-4*, Plenum Pr) Plenum.

Developmental Biology: A Comprehensive Synthesis, Vol. 6: Genomic Adaptability in Somatic Cell Specialization. Ed. by M. A. DiBerardino & L. D. Etkin. LC 85-3406. (Illus.). 256p. 1989. 75.00 (*0-306-43177-7*, Plenum Pr) Plenum.

D

An Asterisk (*) at the beginning of an entry indicates that the title is appearing in BIP for the first time.

Developmental Biology: A Comprehensive Synthesis, Vol. 7: Conceptual History of Modern Embryology. Ed. by S. F. Gilbert. (Illus.). 276p. 1991. 75.00 (*0-306-43842-9*, Plenum Pr) Plenum.

Developmental Biology & Cancer. Ed. by Gisele M. Hodges & Charles Rowlatt. LC 93-9560. 528p. 1993. 179.95 (*0-8493-8869-4*, RC268) CRC Pr.

Developmental Biology of Ascidians. Noriyuki Satoh. (Developmental & Cell Biology Ser.: No. 29). (Illus.). 300p. (C). 1994. 64.95 (*0-521-35221-5*) Cambridge U Pr.

Developmental Biology of Fern Gametophytes. V. Raghaven. (Illus.). 250p. (C). 1989. 89.95 (*0-521-33022-X*) Cambridge U Pr.

Developmental Biology of Prokaryotes. Ed. by J. H. Parish. LC 79-10275. (Studies in Microbiology: Vol. 1). 1979. 85.00 (*0-520-04016-3*) U CA Pr.

Developmental Biology of the Axolotl. Ed. by John Armstrong & George M. Malacinski. (Illus.). 336p. 1989. 65.00 (*0-19-505073-8*) OUP.

Developmental Breakdown & Psychoanalytic Treatment in Adolescence. Moses Laufer & M. Egle Laufer. LC 88-38741. 224p. (C). 1989. text ed. 32.00 (*0-300-04437-2*) Yale U Pr.

Developmental Cardiology: Morphogenesis & Function. Edward B. Clark & Atsuyoshi Takao. (Illus.). 732p. 1990. 135.00 (*0-87993-382-8*) Futura Pub.

Developmental Challenge Course. W. G. Alston. (Illus.). 110p. 1985. pap. 14.95 (*0-932392-23-7*) Mouvement Pubns.

Developmental Challenge in Malaysia. Siew N. Chee. LC 69-104443. (Papers in International Studies: Southeast Asia Ser.: No. 3). 26p. reprint ed. pap. 25.00 (*0-317-09525-0*, 2004377) Bks Demand.

Developmental Changes in Myocardial Inotropic Responsiveness. Michael Artman. (Medical Intelligence Unit Ser.). 118p. 1994. 89.95 (*1-57059-127-X*, LN9127) R G Landes.

Developmental Concordance & Discordance During Puberty & Early Adolescence. D. M. Mort. (SRCD Ser.: Vol. 18, No. 1). 1953. 12.00 (*0-527-01557-1*) Periodicals Srv.

Developmental Continuity Across Preschool & Primary Grades. Nita H. Barbour & Carol Seefeldt. LC 93-599. 1993. write for info. (*0-87173-128-2*) ACEI.

Developmental Craniofacial Biology. Harold C. Slavkin. LC 79-850. (Illus.). 479p. reprint ed. pap. 136.60 (*0-8357-7659-X*, 2056986) Bks Demand.

Developmental Defects of the Axial Skeleton in Paleopathology. Ethne Barnes. (Illus.). 368p. 1994. 39.95 (*0-685-66949-1*) Univ Pr Colo.

Developmental Defects of the Axial Skeleton in Paleopathology. Ethne Barnes. LC 93-48329. 360p. 1994. 39.95 (*0-87081-316-1*) Univ Pr Colo.

Developmental Delay & Mental Retardation. Steven Coker. (Neurologic Illness: Diagnosis & Treatment Ser.). (Illus.). 200p. 1989. 50.00 (*0-89335-310-8*) PMA Pub Corp.

Developmental Deviations & Personality. D. R. Alexsandrowicz. 128p. 1989. pap. text ed. 38.00 (*2-88124-298-7*) Gordon & Breach.

Developmental Diagnosis in Treatment of Handicapped Individuals. Shoji Nishimura. (Illus.). 240p. 1988. 27.50 (*0-87562-097-3*) Spec Child.

Developmental Dimension of Domestic Groups in India: An Anthropological Analysis of Domestic Groups Demography & Economy of a Tribe in Central India. Ratish Srivastava. 141p. 1979. 14.00 (*1-55528-027-7*, Pub. by Today & Tomorrows P & P II) Scholarly Pubns.

Developmental Disabilities: A Handbook for Best Practices. Phillip J. McLaughlin & Paul Wehman. 328p. 1992. 45.00 (*1-56372-023-X*) PRO-ED.

***Developmental Disabilities: A Handbook for Best Practices.** Ed. by Phillip J. McLaughlin & Paul Wehman. 1995. write for info. (*0-89079-657-2*) PRO-ED.

***Developmental Disabilities: A Handbook for Interdisciplinary Practice.** Bruce Thyer & Nancy Kropf. 256p. 1995. pap. text ed. 29.95 (*1-57129-003-6*) Brookline Bks.

Developmental Disabilities: A Handbook for Occupational Therapists. Ed. by Jerry A. Johnson & David A. Ethridge. LC 89-20012. (Occupational Therapy in Health Care Ser.: Vol. 6, Nos. 2 & 3). (Illus.). 249p. 1989. text ed. 39.95 (*0-86656-959-6*) Haworth Pr.

Developmental Disabilities: Delivery of Medical Care for Children & Adults. I. Leslie Rubin & Allen C. Crocker. LC 87-2840. 526p. reprint ed. pap. 150.00 (*0-7837-2743-7*, 2043123) Bks Demand.

Developmental Disabilities: Management Through Diet & Medication. Eric Denhoff & Steven A. Feldman. LC 81-15138. (Pediatric Habilitation Ser.: No. 2). (Illus.). 277p. reprint ed. pap. 79.00 (*0-7837-0913-7*, 2041218) Bks Demand.

Developmental Disabilities: No Longer a Private Tragedy. Ed. by Lynn Wikler & Maryanne Keenan. LC 83-17405. (Readings in Social Work Ser.). 235p. (C). 1983. pap. text ed. 18.95 (*0-87101-117-4*) Natl Assn Soc Wkrs.

***Developmental Disabilities: No Longer a Private Tragedy.** fac. ed. Ed. by Lynn Wikler & Maryanne P. Keenan. LC 83-17405. (Readings in Social Work Ser.). 245p. 1994. pap. 69.90 (*0-7837-7704-3*, 2047462) Bks Demand.

Developmental Disabilities: Psychologic & Social Implications. Ed. by Daniel Bergsma. LC 76-44446. (Alan R. Liss, Inc. Ser.: Vol. 12, No. 4). 1976. 25.00 (*0-686-18080-1*) March of Dimes.

Developmental Disabilities: Psychosocial Aspects. George S. Baroff. LC 90-43702. (Illus.). 259p. (C). 1991. pap. text ed. 27.00 (*0-89079-412-X*, 1590) PRO-ED.

Developmental Disabilities: Theory, Assessment & Intervention. Ed. by Michael Lewis & Lawrence Taft. 288p. 1982. text ed. 35.00 (*0-88331-134-8*) Luce.

Developmental Disabilities & Sacramental Access. Edward Foley. 168p. (Orig.). 1994. pap. text ed. 11.95 (*0-8146-2280-1*) Liturgical Pr.

***Developmental Disabilities in Infancy & Childhood, 2 Vols., Set.** Capute & Accardo. 1360p. 1995. boxed 195.00 (*0-614-06526-7*, CAP) P H Brookes.

***Developmental Disabilities in Infancy & Childhood Vol. I: Neurodevelopmental Diagnosis & Treatment.** 2nd ed. Arnold J. Capute & Pasquale J. Accardo. LC 94-34249. 736p. 1995. boxed 115.00 (*1-55766-178-2*) P H Brookes.

***Developmental Disabilities in Infancy & Childhood Vol. II: The Spectrum of Developmental Disabilities.** 2nd ed. Arnold J. Capute & Pasquale J. Accardo. LC 94-34249. 624p. 1995. boxed 100.00 (*1-55766-194-4*) P H Brookes.

Developmental Disabilities Program Aide. Jack Rudman. (Career Examination Ser.: C-864). 1994. pap. 23.95 (*0-8373-0864-X*) Nat Learn.

Developmental Disabilities Program Specialist. (Career Examination Ser.: C-3368). 1994. pap. 27.95 (*0-8373-3368-7*) Nat Learn.

Developmental Disorders: The Transitional Space in Mental Breakdown & Creative Integration. Peter L. Giovacchini. LC 86-10877. 385p. 1986. 45.00 (*0-87668-919-5*) Aronson.

Developmental Disorders of Language. Betty B. Brown & Margaret Edwards. (Illus.). 234p. (Orig.). (C). 1991. pap. text ed. 34.95 (*1-879105-06-3*, A011) Singular Publishing.

***Developmental Dyslexia: Studies in Disorders of Communication.** 3rd ed. Michael Thomson. 320p. 1989. 62.25 (*0-614-00862-X*, 0071) Singular Publishing.

Developmental Dyslexia & Learning Disorders: Child Health & Development, Vol. 5. Ed. by D. Bakker et al. (Illus.). vi, 166p. 1987. 56.00 (*3-8055-4585-1*) S Karger.

Developmental Dyspraxia & Adult-Onset Apraxia: A Lecture Prepared for Sensory Integration International. A. Jean Ayres. LC 88-151167. 85p. (Orig.). 1985. pap. 15.00 (*1-882068-00-9*) Sensory Integration.

Developmental Education in the 1990's: 92 of the Questions Frequently Asked by Teachers & Parents, with Answers That Will Clarify the Issues & Help Children Now. Jim Grant. 136p. (Orig.). 1991. pap. 10.95 (*0-935493-42-5*) Modern Learn Pr.

Developmental Effects of Irradiation on the Brain of the Embryo & Fetus. Ed. by International Commission of Radiological Protection. (International Commission of Radiological Protection Ser.: No. 49). (Illus.). 50p. 1987. pap. 35.00 (*0-08-035203-0*, Pergamon Pr) Elsevier.

Developmental Examination of Infants & Preschool Children. Dorothy F. Egan. (Clinics in Developmental Medicine Ser.: No. 112). (Illus.). 84p. (C). 1991. 37.95 (*0-521-41197-1*, Pub. by Mc Keith Pr UK) Cambridge U Pr.

Developmental Experiences: Treatment of Developmental Disorders in Children. David S. Levin. LC 84-24318. 352p. 1985. 40.00 (*0-87668-760-5*) Aronson.

Developmental Follow-Up: Concepts, Domains, & Methods. Ed. by Sarah L. Friedman & H. Carl Haywood. (Illus.). 406p. 1994. boxed 75.00 (*0-12-267855-9*) Acad Pr.

***Developmental Follow-Up: Concepts, Domains, & Methods.** Ed. by Sarah L. Friedman & H. Carl Haywood. (Illus.). 406p. 1995. pap. 45.00 (*0-12-267856-7*) Acad Pr.

***Developmental-Functionalist Approach to Child Language.** Nancy Budwig. 264p. 1995. text ed. 30.00 (*0-8058-0520-6*) L Erlbaum Assocs.

Developmental Genetics of Vertebrates. B. V. Konyukhov. 1990. 32.00 (*81-7087-051-8*, Pub. by Oxford IBH II) S Asia.

Developmental Group Care of Children & Youth: Concepts & Practice. Henry W. Maier et al. LC 87-7421. (Child & Youth Services Ser.: Vol. 9, No. 2). 233p. 1987. text ed. 49.95 (*0-86656-655-4*) Haworth Pr.

Developmental Guidance & Counseling: A Practical Approach. 2nd ed. Robert D. Myrick. LC 93-70231. 390p. (C). 1993. pap. text ed. 29.95 (*0-932796-53-2*) Ed Media Corp.

Developmental Gymnastics, Pt. I: Building Physical Skills for Children. Garland O'Quinn. LC 77-91498. (Illus.). 125p. 1978. 18.00 (*0-292-71514-5*) U of Tex Pr.

Developmental Immunology. Edwin L. Cooper & Eric Nisbet-Brown. (Illus.). 496p. 1993. 95.00 (*0-19-504353-7*) OUP.

Developmental Impact of Rural Infrastructure in Bangladesh. Raisuddin Ahjmed & Mahabub Hossain. 150p. 1990. 10.00 (*0-89629-086-7*) Intl Food Policy.

Developmental Instability: Its Origins & Evolutionary Implications: Proceedings of the International Conference, Tempe, Arizona, U. S. A., 14-15 June 1993. Ed. by Theresa A. Markow. LC 94-1934. (Contemporary Issues in Genetics & Evolution Ser.: Vol. 2). 436p. (C). 1994. lib. bdg. 199.00 (*0-7923-2678-4*) Kluwer Ac.

Developmental Issues in Discourse. Ed. by Jonathan Fine & Roy O. Freedle. LC 82-22831. (Advances in Discourse Processes Ser.: Vol. 10). 328p. 1983. text ed. 75.00 (*0-89391-160-7*); pap. text ed. 39.50 (*0-89391-161-5*) Ablex Pub.

Developmental Issues in Small Island Economies. David L. McKee & Clement A. Tisdell. LC 90-31967. 208p. 1990. text ed. 55.00 (*0-275-93393-8*, C3393, Praeger Pubs) Greenwood.

Developmental Language Curriculum. Cheney et al. 1988. 50.00 (*0-295-96654-8*) U of Wash Pr.

Developmental, Learning, & Emotional Problems, Health of Our Nation's Children, United States, 1988: PHS 91-1250. No. 190. write for info. (*0-318-69619-3*) Natl Ctr Health Stats.

Developmental Logic of Social Systems. Henry Teune & Zdravko Mlinar. LC 77-26099. (Sage Library of Social Research: Vol. 60). 176p. reprint ed. pap. 50.20 (*0-317-07992-1*, 2021963) Bks Demand.

Developmental Management: Learning to Manage with Vision. Ronnie Lessem. (Illus.). 220p. 1990. text ed. 32.95 (*0-631-16844-3*) Blackwell Pubs.

Developmental Math. Arnold R. Steffensen & L. Murphy Johnson. (C). 1990. pap. text ed. 63.00 (*0-673-46230-7*) HarpCollege.

Developmental Mathematics. 2nd ed. Mervin L. Keedy & Marvin L. Bittinger. 832p. (C). 1988. pap. text ed. 47.50 (*0-201-14354-2*) Addison-Wesley.

Developmental Mathematics. 2nd ed. David Novak. 947p. (C). 1988. pap. text ed. 28.00 (*0-669-17092-5*); Student guide to margin exercises. student ed 8.50 (*0-669-17096-8*); Instr.'s guide. teacher ed 2.00 (*0-669-17093-3*); Answer key. 2.00 (*0-669-17094-1*); Topics in basic Mathematics. write for info. (*0-669-27651-0*) Heath.

Developmental Mathematics. 3rd ed. C. L. Johnston et al. 616p. (C). 1991. pap. 48.95 (*0-534-14208-7*) PWS Pubs.

Developmental Mathematics. 3rd ed. Mervin L. Keedy et al. (Illus.). 977p. (C). 1993. text ed. 44.95 (*0-201-53770-2*) Addison-Wesley.

***Developmental Mathematics.** 4th ed. Marvin L. Bittinger et al. 1024p. (C). 1996. pap. text ed. write for info. (*0-201-62978-X*) Addison-Wesley.

***Developmental Mathematics.** 4th ed. C. L. Johnston et al. LC 94-22941. 688p. 1995. pap. 47.95 (*0-534-94500-7*) PWS Pubs.

Developmental Mathematics. 4th ed. Martha M. Wood et al. 688p. (C). 1990. text ed. 49.95 (*0-534-92123-X*) PWS Pubs.

***Developmental Mathematics.** 5th ed. Martha M. Wood & Peggy Capell. LC 94-24712. 1995. pap. 45.95 (*0-534-93654-7*) PWS Pubs.

Developmental Mathematics: Graphing Calculator Investigations. Dennis C. Ebersole. LC 92-35403. (C). 1992. 10.50 (*0-06-501439-1*) HarpCollege.

Developmental Mathematics: TASP Version. 2nd ed. Mervin L. Keedy & Marvin L. Bittinger. (Illus.). 944p. (C). 1989. text ed. 48.50 (*0-201-50355-7*) Addison-Wesley.

Developmental Mathematics: TASP Version. 3rd ed. Mervin L. Keedy et al. LC 92-24311. 977p. (C). 1993. pap. text ed. 47.50 (*0-201-52591-7*) Addison-Wesley.

Developmental Mathematics-Arithmetic & Algebra. Mervin L. Keedy & Marvin L. Bittinger. (Illus.). 608p. 1984. teacher ed write for info. (*0-201-14809-9*); write for info. (*0-201-14833-1*); pap. write for info. (*0-201-14808-0*) Addison-Wesley.

Developmental Mathematics I: A Workbook. Theresa Noel & Andre Joseph. 1984. 10.00 (*0-936264-14-4*) Andres & Co.

Developmental Mathematics II: A Workbook. Theresa Noel & Andre Joseph. 1984. 10.00 (*0-936264-15-2*) Andres & Co.

***Developmental Mechanisms of Heart Disease.** Edward B. Clark et al. LC 94-23123. (Illus.). 768p. 1995. 159.00 (*0-87993-160-4*) Futura Pub.

Developmental Metrics. Fred Justus. (Math Ser.). 24p. (gr. 2-4). 1978. student ed 5.00 (*0-8209-0105-9*, A-15) ESP.

Developmental Migration: A Processual Analysis of Inter State Rural-Rural Migration. B. R. Raju. (C). 1989. 22.50 (*81-7022-205-2*, Pub. by Concept II) S Asia.

Developmental Models of Thinking. Ed. by Rainer H. Kluwe & Hans Spada. LC 79-6780. (Developmental Psychology Ser.). 1980. text ed. 54.00 (*0-12-416450-1*) Acad Pr.

Developmental Modulation of Neuronal Cell Surface Determinants see Cleavage Lines of the Skin

Developmental Motor Activities for All Children from Theory to Practice. Harold A. Lerch & Christine Stopka. 199p. (C). 1992. pap. text ed. write for info. (*0-697-14479-8*) Brown & Benchmark.

Developmental Motor Speech Disorders. Michael A. Crary. LC 93-3711. (Illus.). 297p. (Orig.). (C). 1993. pap. text ed. 42.50x (*1-879105-92-6*) Singular Publishing.

Developmental Movement Exercises for Children. David L. Gallahue. 397p. (C). 1982. pap. write for info. (*0-02-340330-6*) Macmillan.

Developmental Nephrology. Wallace W. McCrory. LC 72-75399. (Commonwealth Fund Publications). (Illus.). 230p. 1972. 29.95 (*0-674-20275-9*) HUP.

Developmental Network Approach to Therapeutic Foster Care. Paul Fine. 1994. 18.95 (*0-87868-509-X*) Child Welfare.

Developmental Neurobiology. Philippe Evrard & Alexandre Minkowski. (Nestle Nutrition Workshop Ser.: Vol. 12). 334p. 1989. 61.00 (*0-88167-544-X*) Raven.

Developmental Neurobiology. 3rd ed. M. Jacobson. (Illus.). 920p. 1991. 89.50 (*0-306-43797-X*, Plenum Pr) Plenum.

Developmental Neurobiology of Breathing. Ed. by Gabriel G. Haddad & Jay P. Farber. (Lung Biology in Health & Disease Ser.: Vol. 53). 800p. 1991. 210.00 (*0-8247-8459-6*) Dekker.

Developmental Neurobiology of the Autonomic Nervous System. Ed. by Phyllis Gootman. LC 86-3077. (Contemporary Neuroscience Ser.). (Illus.). 440p. 1986. 79.50 (*0-89603-080-6*) Humana.

Developmental Neurochemistry. Ed. by Richard C. Wiggins et al. (Illus.). 326p. 1985. text ed. 40.00 (*0-292-71548-X*) U of Tex Pr.

Developmental Neurocognition - Speech & Face Processing in the First Year of Life: Proceedings of the NATO Advanced Research Workshop. Ed. by Benedicte De Boysson Bardies et al. LC 93-9598. (NATO Advanced Study Institutes Series D, Behavioural & Social Sciences: No. 69). 516p. (C). 1993. Acid-free paper. lib. bdg. 189.00 (*0-7923-2188-X*) Kluwer Ac.

Developmental Neurology. Hans C. Lou. (Illus.). 305p. 1982. text ed. 75.50 (*0-89004-700-6*) Raven.

Developmental Neuropathology. 2nd ed. R. L. Friede. (Illus.). 625p. 1990. 150.00 (*0-387-19280-8*) Spr-Verlag.

Developmental Neuropathology of Schizophrenia. Ed. by Sarnoff A. Mednick et al. (NATO ASI Series A, Life Sciences: Vol. 217). (Illus.). 210p. 1992. 79.50 (*0-306-44081-4*, Plenum Pr) Plenum.

Developmental Neuropsychiatry. Ed. by Michael Rutter. LC 83-1633. 632p. 1983. lib. bdg. 65.00 (*0-89862-621-8*) Guilford Pr.

***Developmental Neuropsychiatry Vol. 1: Fundamentals.** James C. Harris. (Illus.). 256p. 1995. 45.00 (*0-19-506824-6*) OUP.

***Developmental Neuropsychiatry Vol. 2: Assessment, Diagnosis, & Treatment of Developmental Disorders.** James C. Harris. (Illus.). 544p. 1995. 75.00 (*0-19-509849-8*) OUP.

Developmental Neuropsychobiology. Ed. by William T. Greenough & Janice M. Juraska. (Behavioral Biology Ser.). 1986. text ed. 112.00 (*0-12-300270-2*); pap. text ed. 59.00 (*0-12-300271-0*) Acad Pr.

Developmental Neuropsychology. 2nd ed. Otfried Spreen et al. (Illus.). 608p. 1995. 65.00 (*0-19-506736-3*); pap. 39.95 (*0-19-506737-1*) OUP.

Developmental Neuroscience-Physiological, Pharmacological & Clinical Aspects: Proceedings of the International Meeting of the International Society for Developmental Neuroscience, 5th, Held in Chieti, Italy, 24-28 June, 1984. Ed. by F. Caciagli et al. (Giovanni Lorenzini Foundation Symposia Ser.: Vol. 20). 404p. 1985. 144.75 (*0-444-80640-7*) Elsevier.

Developmental Neurotoxicity of Lead. Christopher Winder. 1984. lib. bdg. 108.50 (*0-85200-776-0*) Kluwer Ac.

Developmental Neurotoxicology. Gaylia J. Harry. 1994. 89.95 (*0-8493-4427-1*, RC347) CRC Pr.

Developmental Nutrition. Lucille S. Hurley. (Illus.). 1979. text ed. 25.95 (*0-685-03829-7*) P-H.

Developmental Nutrition. Kretchmer. 1994. write for info. (*0-8493-8887-2*, CRC Reprint) Franklin.

Developmental Optometry: The Optometric Appraisal of Vision Development & Visual Performance. 2nd ed. G. N. Getman. Ed. by Sally M. Corngold. LC 87-82198. (Introduction to Behavioral Optometry Ser.). (Illus.). 117p. 1992. reprint ed. pap. 18.00 (*0-943599-23-7*) OEPF.

Developmental Order: Its Origin & Regulation. Ed. by Stephen Subtelny & Paul B. Green. 1982. text ed. 179.95 (*0-471-56256-4*) Wiley.

Developmental Orthography. Philip Luelsdorff. LC 91-7333. xii, 258p. 1991. 89.00x (*90-272-2065-4*) Benjamins North Am.

Developmental Pathogenesis & Treatment of Borderline & Narcissistic Personalities. Donald B. Rinsley. LC 89-17506. 192p. 1989. 27.50 (*0-87668-828-8*) Aronson.

Developmental Pathology of the Embryo & Fetus. James E. Dimmick & Dagmar K. Kalousek. (Illus.). 896p. 1992. text ed. 165.00 (*0-397-51040-3*) Lippincott.

Developmental Patterning of the Vertebrate Limb. Ed. by J. R. Hinchliffe et al. (NATO ASI Series A, Life Sciences: Vol. 205). (Illus.). 446p. 1991. 125.00 (*0-306-43927-1*, Plenum Pr) Plenum.

***Developmental Person Through Childhood & Adolescence.** 4th ed. Kathleen S. Berger. 1995. text ed. 54.95x (*1-57259-002-5*); student ed, pap. 12.95x (*1-57259-009-2*) Worth.

Developmental Perspectives on Craniofacial Problems. Rebecca A. Eder. LC 93-31776. 1995. 98.00 (*0-387-94168-1*) Spr-Verlag.

Developmental Perspectives on Depression. Ed. by Dante Cicchetti & Sheree L. Toth. LC 92-18117. (Rochester Symposium on Developmental Psychopathology Ser.: Vol. 4). 384p. (C). 1992. text ed. 69.50 (*1-878822-16-0*) Univ Rochester Pr.

Developmental Perspectives on Motivation. Ed. by Janis E. Jacobs. LC 53-11655. (Nebraska Symposium on Motivation Ser.: Vol. 40). xiii, 299p. 1993. 35.00 (*0-8032-2575-X*); pap. 19.95 (*0-8032-7576-5*) U of Nebr Pr.

Developmental Perspectives on Teaching & Learning Thinking Skills. Deanna Kuhn. (Contributions to Human Development Ser.: Vol. 21). (Illus.). x, 140p. 1990. 23.75 (*3-8055-5205-X*) S Karger.

Developmental Physical Education for Today's Elementary School Children. David L. Gallahue. (Illus.). 759p. (C). 1987. text ed. write for info. (*0-02-340380-2*) Macmillan.

Developmental Physical Education for Today's School Children. 2nd ed. David L. Gallahue. 640p. (C). 1993. boxed write for info. (*0-697-14208-6*) Brown & Benchmark.

Developmental Physiology: A Tribute to the Influence of Alfred Jost - Journal: Biology of the Neonate, Vol. 55, No. 6, 1989. Ed. by J. Girard. (Illus.). 80p. 1989. pap. 46.50 (*3-8055-5041-3*) S Karger.

Developmental Pragmatics. Ed. by Elinor Ochs. LC 78-20047. 1979. text ed. 59.00 (*0-12-524550-5*) Acad Pr.

Developmental Problems in Infancy & the Preschool Years. Ed. by Barbara K. Keogh. (Advances in Special Education Ser.: Vol. 5). 1986. 73.25 (*0-89232-313-2*) Jai Pr.

Developmental Problems of Drug-Exposed Infants. Ed. by Louis M. Rossetti. (Illus.). 77p. (Orig.). (C). 1992. pap. text ed. 21.50x (*1-56593-064-9*, 0370) Singular Publishing.

Developmental Processes: Heinz Werner's Selected Writings, 2 vols. Ed. by Sybil S. Barten & Margery B. Franklin. LC 77-92187. 562p. (Orig.). 1978. Vol. 1: General Theory & Perceptual Experience. text ed. 50.00 (*0-8236-1250-3*); Vol. 2: Cognition, Language & Symbolization. text ed. 50.00 (*0-8236-1251-1*) Intl Univs Pr.

D

An Asterisk (*) at the beginning of an entry indicates that the title is appearing in BIP for the first time.

An Asterisk (*) at the beginning of an entry indicates that the title is appearing in BIP for the first time.

D

Developments in Antitrust Health Care Law. 208p. 1989. pap. 50.00 (*0-685-47175-6*, 503-0080) Amer Bar Assn.

Developments in Applied Spectroscopy: Proceedings of the Mid-America Symposium on Spectroscopy, 13th Annual Symposium, Chicago, Illinois, April 30-May 3, 1962, Vol. 2. Society for Applied Spectroscopy Staff. Ed. by J. R. Ferraro & J. S. Ziomek. LC 61-17720. 448p. reprint ed. pap. 127.70 (*0-317-28823-7*, 2020721) Bks Demand.

Developments in Applied Spectroscopy: Proceedings of the Sixteenth Annual Mid-America Spectroscopy Symposium Held in Chicago, IL, June 14-17, 1965, Vol. 5. Mid-America Spectroscopy Symposium (16th: 1965, Chicago). Ed. by L. R. Pearson & E. L. Grove. LC 61-17720. 516p. reprint ed. pap. 147.10 (*0-685-15709-1*, 2026293) Bks Demand.

Developments in Applied Spectroscopy, Vol. 3: Proceedings of the Mid-America Symposium on Spectroscopy, 13th Annual Symposium, Chicago, Illinois May 20-23, 1963. Society for Applied Spectroscopy Staff. Ed. by J. E. Forrette & E. Lanterman. LC 61-17720. (Illus.). 423p. reprint ed. pap. 120.60 (*0-317-07933-6*, 2020722) Bks Demand.

Developments in Applied Spectroscopy, Vol. 4: Proceedings of the Mid-America Symposium on Spectroscopy, 13th Annual Symposium, Chicago, Illinois, June 2-5, 1964. Society for Applied Spectroscopy Staff. Ed. by Elwin N. Davis. LC 61-17720. (Illus.). 558p. reprint ed. pap. 159.10 (*0-317-07928-X*, 2020723) Bks Demand.

Developments in Applied Spectroscopy, Vol. 6: Proceedings of the Mid-America Symposium on Spectroscopy, 13th Annual Symposium, Chicago, Illinois, May 15-18, 1967. Society for Applied Spectroscopy Staff et al. Ed. by William K. Baer & Alfred J. Perkins. LC 61-17720. (Illus.). 413p. reprint ed. pap. 117.80 (*0-317-07921-2*, 2020724) Bks Demand.

Developments in Applied Spectroscopy: Vol. 7-A: Proceedings of the Mid-America Symposium on Spectroscopy, 13th Annual Symposium, Chicago, Illinois, May 13-17, 1968. Society for Applied Spectroscopy Staff. Ed. by E. L. Grove & Alfred J. Perkins. LC 61-17720. (Illus.). 351p. reprint ed. pap. 100.10 (*0-317-07908-5*, 2020726) Bks Demand.

Developments in Applied Spectroscopy Vol. 8: Proceedings of the Mid-America Symposium on Spectroscopy, 13th Annual Symposium, Chicago, Illinois, May 12-15, 1969. Society for Applied Spectroscopy Staff. Ed. by E. L. Grove. LC 61-17720. (Illus.). 335p. reprint ed. pap. 95.50 (*0-317-07916-6*, 2020725) Bks Demand.

Developments in Arid Zone Ecology & Environmental Quality, Vol. 1. Ed. by Hillel I. Shuval. xiv, 418p. write for info. (*0-86689-005-X*) Balaban Intl Sci Serv.

Developments in Asia: Economic, Political & Cultural Aspects. Ed. by Christine Effenberg. (Illus.). 545p. (Orig.). 1987. pap. 62.50 (*3-515-05049-3*) Coronet Bks.

Developments in Astrometry & Their Impact on Astrophysics & Geodynamics: Proceedings of the 156th Symposium of the International Astronomical Union Held in Shanghai, China, September 15-19, 1992. Ed. by Ivan I. Mueller & Barbara Kolaczek. LC 93-16750. 1993. lib. bdg. 129.00 (*0-7923-2237-1*) Kluwer Ac.

Developments in Australian Politics. Ed. by Judith Brett et al. 464p. 1994. 64.95 (*0-7329-2010-8*, Pub. by Macmill Educ AT); pap. 32.95 (*0-7329-2009-4*, Pub. by Macmill Educ AT) Paul & Co Pubs.

D

Developments in Aviation Products Liability. Ian Awford. (C). 1985. 550.00 (*0-685-32832-5*, Pub. by Witherby & Co UK) St Mut.

Developments in Biodegradation of Hydrocarbons, Vol. 1. Ed. by R. J. Watkinson. (Illus.). 232p. 1978. 74.00 (*0-85334-751-4*, Pub. by Elsevier Applied Sci UK) Elsevier.

Developments in Block Copolymers, No. 2. Ed. by I. R. Goodman. 316p. 1985. 90.00 (*0-85334-372-1*, Pub. by Elsevier Applied Sci UK) Elsevier.

Developments in Block Copolymers, Vol. 1. Ed. by I. R. Goodman. (Illus.). xiv, 358p. 1982. 117.00 (*0-85334-145-1*, I-360-82, Pub. by Elsevier Applied Sci UK) Elsevier.

Developments in Boundary Element Methods, Vol. 1. Ed. by P. K. Banerjee & R. B. Butterfid. 292p. 1979. 110.00 (*0-85334-845-6*, Pub. by Elsevier Applied Sci UK) Elsevier.

Developments in Boundary Element Methods, Vol. 2. Ed. by P. K. Banerjee & R. P. Shaw. (Illus.). 288p. 1982. 110.00 (*0-85334-112-5*, Pub. by Elsevier Applied Sci UK) Elsevier.

Developments in Boundary Element Methods, Vol. 3. P. K. Banerjee & S. Mukherjee. 328p. 1984. 97.25 (*0-85334-253-9*, I-167-84, Pub. by Elsevier Applied Sci UK) Elsevier.

Developments in Boundary Element Methods, Vol. 4. Ed. by P. K. Banerjee & J. O. Watson. 360p. 1986. 95.50 (*0-85334-376-4*, Pub. by Elsevier Applied Sci UK) Elsevier.

Developments in Breakwaters. (Conference Proceedings Ser.). 330p. 1986. 58.00 (*0-7277-0266-1*, Pub. by T Telford UK) Am Soc Civil Eng.

Developments in British Politics 2. rev. ed. Ed. by Henry Drucker et al. 430p. 1988. pap. 14.95 (*0-312-02341-3*) St Martin.

Developments in British Politics 4. Ed. by Patrick Dunleavy et al. LC 93-10892. 1993. text ed. 45.00 (*0-312-10087-6*); pap. 16.95 (*0-312-10088-4*) St Martin.

Developments in Building Maintenance, Vol. 1. Ed. by E. J. Gibson. (Illus.). xi, 260p. 1979. 63.00 (*0-85334-801-4*, Pub. by Elsevier Applied Sci UK) Elsevier.

Developments in Cancer Chemotherapy, Vol. I. Ed. by R. I. Glazer. 296p. 1984. 180.00 (*0-8493-5778-0*, RC271, CRC Reprint) Franklin.

Developments in Cancer Chemotherapy, Vol. II. Ed. by Robert I. Glazer. 224p. 1988. 122.00 (*0-8493-5770-5*, RC271, CRC Reprint) Franklin.

Developments in Carbohydrate Chemistry. Ed. by Richard J. Alexander & Henry F. Zobel. LC 92-71691. (Illus.). 386p. 1992. 79.00x (*0-913250-76-7*) Am Assn Cereal Chem.

Developments in Ceramic & Metal-Matrix Composites. Ed. by K. Upadhya & J. J. Moore. (Illus.). 450p. 1992. 128.00 (*0-87339-145-4*, 432) Minerals Metals.

Developments in Characteristic Function Theory. E. Lukacs. (Charles Griffin Book Ser.). 190p. 1987. reprint ed. 35.00 (*0-19-520577-4*) OUP.

Developments in Chemical Engineering: A Festschrift for P. V. Danckwerts. Ed. by J. Bridgwater. (Illus.). 190p. 1983. pap. 39.00 (*0-08-030251-3*, Pergamon Pr) Elsevier.

Developments in Chromatography, 2 vols. Ed. by C. E. Knapman. (Illus.). 1980. Vol. 1 1978. 38.00 (*0-85334-748-4*, Pub. by Elsevier Applied Sci UK) Elsevier.

Developments in Civil & Construction Engineering Computing. Civil Comp Editors. 1990. pap. 165.00 (*0-948749-17-2*, Pub. by Civil-Comp UK) St Mut.

Developments in Clinical & Experimental Neuropsychology. Ed. by J. R. Crawford & D. M. Parker. (Illus.). 346p. 1989. 85.00 (*0-306-43244-7*, Plenum Pr) Plenum.

Developments in Close Range Photogrammetry, Vol. 1. Ed. by K. B. Atkinson. (Illus.). 220p. 1982. 74.00 (*0-85334-882-0*, Pub. by Elsevier Applied Sci UK) Elsevier.

Developments in Coastal & Estuarine Pollution: Proceedings of an IAWPRC Conference Held in Fukuoka, Japan, 18-21 October, 1987. W. R. Parker. LC 82-645900. (Water Science & Technology Ser.: No. 20). (Illus.). 300p. 1988. pap. 155.00 (*0-08-036885-9*, Pergamon Pr) Elsevier.

Developments in Cognitive Psychotherapy. Ed. by Windy Dryden & Peter Trower. 288p. (C). 1988. text ed. 47.50 (*0-8039-8134-1*) Sage.

Developments in Composite Material, Vol. 1. Ed. by G. S. Holister. (Illus.). 245p. 1977. 68.50 (*0-85334-740-9*, Pub. by Elsevier Applied Sci UK) Elsevier.

Developments in Composite Materials. Ed. by G. S. Holister. (Applied Science Developments Ser.). (Illus.). 234p. 1977. 55.00 (*0-686-48243-3*, 0703) T-C Pubns CA.

Developments in Composite Materials, Vol. 2. Ed. by G. S. Holister. (Developments Ser.). (Illus.). 207p. 1981. 74.00 (*0-85334-966-5*, Pub. by Elsevier Applied Sci UK) Elsevier.

Developments in Computational Engineering Mechanics. Civil Comp Editors. 1993. pap. 150.00 (*0-948749-21-0*, Pub. by Civil-Comp UK) St Mut.

Developments in Concrete Technology, Vol. 1. Ed. by F. D. Lydon. (Illus.). 325p. 1979. 79.25 (*0-85334-855-3*, Pub. by Elsevier Applied Sci UK) Elsevier.

Developments in Concurrency & Communication. C. A. Hoare. (University of Texas at Austin Year of Programming Ser.). (Illus.). 400p. (C). 1990. text ed. 31.25 (*0-201-17232-1*) Addison-Wesley.

Developments in Crime & Crime Control Research: German Studies on Victims, Offenders, & the Public. Ed. by K. Sessar et al. (Research in Criminology Ser.). 200p. 1990. 48.00 (*0-387-97081-9*) Spr-Verlag.

Developments in Crystalline Polymers, Vol. 1. Ed. by D. C. Bassett. 279p. 1982. 97.25 (*0-85334-116-8*, Pub. by Elsevier Applied Sci UK) Elsevier.

Developments in Crystalline Polymers, Vol. 2. Ed. by D. C. Bassett. 350p. 1988. 99.00 (*1-85166-133-6*) Elsevier.

Developments in Dairy Chemistry, Vol. 2. Ed. by P. F. Fox. (Illus.). 436p. 1984. 120.75 (*0-85334-224-5*, Pub. by Elsevier Applied Sci UK) Elsevier.

Developments in Dairy Chemistry - Four: Functional Milk Proteins. Ed. by P. F. Fox. 390p. 1990. 99.00 (*1-85166-368-1*) Elsevier.

Developments in Dairy Chemistry, Vol 1: Proteins. Ed. by P. F. Fox. (Illus.). x, 409p. 1982. 120.75 (*0-85334-142-7*, I-361-82, Pub. by Elsevier Applied Sci UK) Elsevier.

Developments in Dairy Chemistry 3: Lactose & Minor Constituents. Ed. by P. F. Fox. 416p. 1985. 108.00 (*0-85334-370-5*, Pub. by Elsevier Applied Sci UK) Elsevier.

Developments in Debt Conversion Programs & Conversion Activities. Woonki Sung & Rosaria Troia. LC 92-10095. (Technical Paper Ser.: No. 170). 55p. 1992. 6.95 (*0-8213-2103-X*, 12103) World Bank.

***Developments in Dementia & Functional Disorders in the Elderly.** Ed. by Raymond Levy & Robert Howard. LC 94-47442. 232p. 1995. 75.00 (*1-871816-27-0*, Pub. by Wrightson Biomed UK) Taylor & Francis.

Developments in Design & Operation of Large Wastewater Treatment Plants: Proceedings of an IAWPRC Workshop Held in Budapest, Hungary, 14-18 September 1987. Paul Benedek et al. LC 82-645900. (Water Science & Technology Ser.). (Illus.). 318p. 1988. pap. 120.00 (*0-08-036882-4*, Pergamon Pr) Elsevier.

Developments in Design Methodology. Ed. by Nigel Cross. LC 84-7433. 367p. reprint ed. pap. 104.60 (*0-8357-2799-8*, 2039926) Bks Demand.

Developments in Diesel Particulate Control Systems. 1989. 19.00 (*0-89883-432-5*, SP775) Soc Auto Engineers.

Developments in Distribution Switchgear. (IEE Conference Publications). 1986. 46.00 (*0-85296-328-9*, IC261) Inst Elect Eng.

Developments in Diving Technology, Vol. 1. Society for Underwater Technology Staff. (Advances in Underwater Technology & Offshore Engineering Ser.). (Illus.). 160p. 1985. lib. bdg. 84.00 (*0-86010-625-X*) G & T Inc.

Developments in Drugs Used in Anesthesia. Ed. by J. Spierdijk et al. 1982. lib. bdg. 80.00 (*90-6021-492-7*) Kluwer Ac.

Developments in Dynamic & Activity-Based Approaches to Travel Analysis. Ed. by Peter Jones. (Illus.). 479p. 1990. text ed. 69.95 (*0-566-07023-5*, Pub. by Avebury Pub UK) Ashgate Pub Co.

Developments in Dynamic Soil-Structure Interaction: Proceedings of the NATO Advanced Study Institute, Kemer, Antalya, Turkey, July 8-16, 1992. Ed. by Polat Gulkan. (NATO Advanced Science Institutes Series C: Mathematical & Physical Sciences). 456p. (C). 1993. lib. bdg. 196.00 (*0-7923-2144-8*) Kluwer Ac.

Developments in East European Politics. Stephen White et al. LC 93-5037. 318p. 1993. lib. bdg. 45.00 (*0-8223-1429-0*); pap. text ed. 19.95 (*0-8223-1435-5*) Duke.

Developments in Econometric Analyses of Productivity. Ali Dogramaci. (Studies in Productivity Analysis). 1982. lib. bdg. 49.50 (*0-89838-101-0*) Kluwer Ac.

Developments in Educational Testing, 2 vols. Ed. by K. Ingenkamp. 450p. 1969. Vol. 1, 450p. text ed. 149.00 (*0-677-61700-3*) Gordon & Breach.

Developments in Educational Testing, 2 vols., Vol. 2. Ed. by K. Ingenkamp. 504p. 1969. text ed. 149.00 (*0-677-61710-0*); Set. text ed. 251.00 (*0-677-61720-8*) Gordon & Breach.

Developments in Electoral Geography. Ed. by R. J. Johnston et al. 288p. 1990. 67.50 (*0-415-04133-3*, A4100) Routledge.

Developments in Electronics for Offshore Fields, Vol. 1. Ed. by C. Bedwell. (Illus.). 230p. 1978. 63.00 (*0-85334-753-0*, Pub. by Elsevier Applied Sci UK) Elsevier.

***Developments in Electrorheological Flows & Measurement Uncertainty: 1994 International Mechanical Engineering Congress & Exposition, Chicago, Illinois - November 6-11, 1994.** D. A. Siginer. LC 94-79147. (FED,AMD Ser.: Vol. 205, Vol. 190). 196p. 1994. 74.00 (*0-7918-1438-6*, G00933) ASME.

Developments in Engineering Mechanics: Proceedings of the Technical Sessions on Developments in Engineering Mechanics Held at the Canadian Society for Civil Engineering Centennial Conference, Montreal, Quebec, Canada, May 18-22, 1987. Ed. by A. P. Selvadurai. (Studies in Applied Mechanics: Vol. 16). 468p. 1987. 125.75 (*0-444-42896-8*) Elsevier.

Developments in Environmental Control & Public Health, Vol. 1. Ed. by A. Porteous. (Illus.). 311p. 1979. 83.00 (*0-85334-834-0*, Pub. by Elsevier Applied Sci UK) Elsevier.

Developments in Environmental Control & Public Health, Vol. 2. Ed. by A. Porteous. (Illus.). 311p. 1981. 83.00 (*0-85334-941-X*, Pub. by Elsevier Applied Sci UK) Elsevier.

Developments in Expert Systems. Coombs. 1984. text ed. 43.00 (*0-12-187580-6*) Acad Pr.

Developments in Family Therapy: Theories & Applications Since 1948. Ed. by Sue Walrond-Skinner. 248p. (Orig.). 1981. pap. 18.95 (*0-7100-0812-0*, RKP) Routledge.

Developments in Fertility Control: Proceedings of the WHO Scientific Group, Geneva, 1968. WHO Staff. (Technical Report Ser.: No. 424). 1969. pap. 2.00 (*92-4-120424-9*) World Health.

Developments in Filtration. Shirley Institute Staff. (C). 1984. 135.00 (*0-685-54101-0*, Pub. by British Textile Tech UK) St Mut.

Developments in Fire Protection of Offshore Platforms, Vol. 1. Ed. by R. G. Gowar. (Illus.). 232p. 1978. 74.00 (*0-85334-792-1*, Pub. by Elsevier Applied Sci UK) Elsevier.

Developments in Flow Measurement, Vol. 1. Ed. by R. W. Scott. (Illus.). 333p. 1982. 102.75 (*0-85334-976-2*, Pub. by Elsevier Applied Sci UK) Elsevier.

Developments in Food Analysis, Vols. 1 & 2. Ed. by R. D. King. 1980. Vol. 2, 1980. 79.25 (*0-85334-921-5*, Pub. by Elsevier Applied Sci UK) Elsevier.

Developments in Food Analysis Techniques, Vol. 3. R. D. King. (Illus.). 228p. 1984. 66.75 (*0-85334-262-8*, I-123-84, Pub. by Elsevier Applied Sci UK) Elsevier.

Developments in Food Carbohydrates, Vol. 1. Ed. by Gordon G. Birch & Robert S. Shallenberger. 189p. 1977. 66.75 (*0-85334-733-6*, Pub. by Elsevier Applied Sci UK) Elsevier.

Developments in Food Carbohydrates, Vol. 2. Ed. by C. K. Lee. (Illus.). 219p. 1980. 117.00 (*0-85334-857-X*, Pub. by Elsevier Applied Sci UK) Elsevier.

Developments in Food Carbohydrates, Vol. 3. Ed. by C. K. Lee. (Illus.). xii, 216p. 1982. 84.75 (*0-85334-996-7*, Pub. by Elsevier Applied Sci UK) Elsevier.

Developments in Food Colours, Vol. 1. Ed. by J. Walford. (Illus.). 259p. 1980. 66.75 (*0-85334-881-2*, Pub. by Elsevier Applied Sci UK) Elsevier.

Developments in Food Colours, Vol. 2. Ed. by J. Walford. 264p. 1984. 74.00 (*0-85334-244-X*, I-519-83, Pub. by Elsevier Applied Sci UK) Elsevier.

***Developments in Food Engineering: Sixth International Congress on Engineering & Food, Chiba, Japan, 1993.** Ed. by Toshimasa Yano et al. 1085p. 1994. 249.95 (*0-7514-0224-9*, Pub. by Blackie Acad & Prof UK) Routledge Chapman & Hall.

Developments in Food Flavours. Ed. by Gordon G. Birch & M. G. Lindley. 282p. 1987. 88.25 (*1-85166-037-2*, Pub. by Elsevier Applied Sci UK) Elsevier.

Developments in Food Microbiology, No. 2. Ed. by R. K. Robinson. 200p. 1986. 66.75 (*0-85334-432-9*, Pub. by Elsevier Applied Sci UK) Elsevier.

Developments in Food Microbiology, Vol. 4. Ed. by R. K. Robinson. 250p. 1988. 84.75 (*1-85166-169-7*) Elsevier.

Developments in Food Packaging, Vol. 1. Ed. by S. J. Palling. (Illus.). 192p. 1980. 66.75 (*0-85334-917-7*, Pub. by Elsevier Applied Sci UK) Elsevier.

Developments in Food Perservation, No. 3. Ed. by S. N. Thorne. 300p. 1986. 83.00 (*0-85334-384-5*, Pub. by Elsevier Applied Sci UK) Elsevier.

Developments in Food Preservation, No. 5. Ed. by S. N. Thorne. 332p. 1989. 97.25 (*1-85166-259-6*) Elsevier.

Developments in Food Preservation, Vol. 1. Ed. by S. N. Thorne. (Illus.). 271p. 1981. 93.75 (*0-85334-979-7*, Pub. by Elsevier Applied Sci UK) Elsevier.

Developments in Food Preservation, Vol. 2. Ed. by S. N. Thorne. 192p. 1983. 63.00 (*0-85334-212-1*, Pub. by Elsevier Applied Sci UK) Elsevier.

Developments in Food Preservation, Vol. 4. Ed. by S. N. Thorne. 280p. 1987. 83.00 (*1-85166-030-5*, Pub. by Elsevier Applied Sci UK) Elsevier.

Developments in Food Preservatives, Vol. 1. Ed. by R. H. Tilbury. 168p. 1980. 54.00 (*0-85334-918-5*, Pub. by Elsevier Applied Sci UK) Elsevier.

Developments in Food Proteins, No. 6. Ed. by B. J. Hudson. 338p. 1988. 101.00 (*1-85166-199-9*) Elsevier.

Developments in Food Proteins, Vol. 1. Ed. by B. J. Hudson. (Illus.). 339p. 1982. 97.25 (*0-85334-987-8*, Pub. by Elsevier Applied Sci UK) Elsevier.

Developments in Food Proteins, Vol. 2. Ed. by B. J. Hudson. (Illus.). 328p. 1983. 97.25 (*0-85334-176-1*, Pub. by Elsevier Applied Sci UK) Elsevier.

Developments in Food Proteins, Vol. 3. Ed. by B. J. Hudson. (Illus.). 288p. 1984. 79.25 (*0-85334-271-7*, I-260-84, Pub. by Elsevier Applied Sci UK) Elsevier.

Developments in Food Proteins, Vol. 5. Ed. by B. J. Hudson. 344p. 1987. 101.00 (*1-85166-082-8*, Pub. by Elsevier Applied Sci UK) Elsevier.

Developments in Food Proteins, Vol. 7. Ed. by B. J. Hudson. 278p. 1991. 130.00 (*1-85166-535-8*) Elsevier.

Developments in Food Proteins-4. B. J. Hudson. 360p. 1986. 101.00 (*0-85334-412-4*) Elsevier.

Developments in Four-Dimensional Geodesy. F. K. Brunner & C. Rizos. (Lecture Notes in Earth Sciences Ser.: Vol. 29). (Illus.). x, 264p. 1990. pap. 41.00 (*0-387-52332-4*) Spr-Verlag.

Developments in Fracture Mechanics, Vols. 1 & 2. Ed. by G. G. Chell. 1981. Vol. 1, 1979. 84.75 (*0-85334-858-8*, Pub. by Elsevier Applied Sci UK); Vol. 2, 1981. 88.25 (*0-85334-973-8*, Pub. by Elsevier Applied Sci UK) Elsevier.

Developments in Fracture Mechanics Test Methods Standardization - STP 632. Ed. by W. F. Brown & J. G. Kaufman. 290p. 1977. 24.75 (*0-8031-0321-2*, 04-632000-30) ASTM.

Developments in French Politics. Ed. by Peter A. Hall et al. LC 90-8199. 304p. 1990. text ed. 49.95 (*0-312-04751-7*); pap. 16.95 (*0-312-04752-5*) St Martin.

Developments in Geophysical Exploration Methods, Vol. 1. Ed. by A. A. Fitch. (Illus.). 310p. 1979. 84.75 (*0-85334-835-9*, Pub. by Elsevier Applied Sci UK) Elsevier.

Developments in Geophysical Exploration Methods, Vol. 2. Ed. by A. A. Fitch. (Illus.). 235p. 1981. 66.75 (*0-85334-930-4*, Pub. by Elsevier Applied Sci UK) Elsevier.

Developments in Geophysical Exploration Methods, Vol. 3. Ed. by A. A. Fitch. (Illus.). 320p. 1982. 88.25 (*0-85334-126-5*, Pub. by Elsevier Applied Sci UK) Elsevier.

Developments in Geophysical Exploration Methods, Vol. 4. Ed. by A. A. Fitch. (Illus.). 200p. 1983. 63.00 (*0-85334-174-5*, I-454-82, Pub. by Elsevier Applied Sci UK) Elsevier.

Developments in Geophysical Exploration Methods, Vol. 5. Ed. by A. A. Fitch. 262p. 1983. 88.25 (*0-85334-216-4*, Pub. by Elsevier Applied Sci UK) Elsevier.

Developments in Geophysical Exploration Methods, Vol. 6. Ed. by A. A. Fitch. (Illus.). 280p. 1985. 63.00 (*0-85334-344-6*, Pub. by Elsevier Applied Sci UK) Elsevier.

Developments in Geoscience, 1989. Ed. by Chinese Academy of Sciences Staff et al. (Illus.). 1990. pap. 38.00 (*7-03-001376-X*, Pub. by Science Pr CH) Intl Spec Bk.

Developments in Geotechnical Aspects of Embankments, Excavations & Buried Structures: Proceedings of the Symposium Held in 1988 & 1990 in Bangkok on Underground Excavations in Soils & Rocks. Ed. by A. S. Balasubramaniam et al. (Illus.). 608p. (C). 1991. text ed. 140.00 (*90-5410-019-2*, Pub. by A A Balkema NE) Ashgate Pub Co.

***Developments in Geotechnical Engineering from Harvard to New Delhi 1936-1994: Proceedings Symposium on Developments in Geotechnical Engineering, Bangkok, Thailand 12-16 January 1994.** Symposium on Developments in Geotechnical Engineering Staff. Ed. by A. S. Balasubramniam. (Illus.). 593p. 1994. 130.00 (*90-5410-522-4*) Balkema RSA.

Developments in German Politics. Ed. by Gordon Smith et al. LC 92-12051. 368p. 1992. text ed. 55.00 (*0-8223-1260-3*); pap. text ed. 21.95 (*0-8223-1266-2*) Duke.

Developments in GRP Technology, Vol. 1. Ed. by B. Harris. (Illus.). 268p. 1983. 84.75 (*0-85334-204-0*, Pub. by Elsevier Applied Sci UK) Elsevier.

Developments in Heat Exchanger Technology, Vol. 1. Ed. by D. Chisholm. (Illus.). 294p. 1980. 97.25 (*0-85334-913-4*, Pub. by Elsevier Applied Sci UK) Elsevier.

Developments in Highway Pavement Engineering, Vol. 1. Ed. by P. S. Pell. (Illus.). 285p. 1978. 83.00 (*0-85334-781-6*, Pub. by Elsevier Applied Sci UK) Elsevier.

Developments in Highway Pavement Engineering, Vol. 2. Ed. by P. S. Pell. (Illus.). 196p. 1978. 66.75 (*0-85334-804-9*, Pub. by Elsevier Applied Sci UK) Elsevier.

An Asterisk (*) at the beginning of an entry indicates that the title is appearing in BIP for the first time.

An Asterisk (*) at the beginning of an entry indicates that the title is appearing in BIP for the first time.

Developments in Reinforced Plastics, Vol. 1. Ed. by G. Pritchard. (Illus.). 283p. 1980. 93.75 (*0-85334-919-3*, Pub. by Elsevier Applied Sci UK) Elsevier.

Developments in Reinforced Plastics, Vol. 2. Ed. by G. Pritchard. (Illus.). 196p. 1982. 61.25 (*0-85334-125-7*, Pub. by Elsevier Applied Sci UK) Elsevier.

Developments in Reinforced Plastics, Vol. 3. Ed. by G. Pritchard. (Illus.). 202p. 1984. 63.00 (*0-85334-266-0*, I-169-84, Pub. by Elsevier Applied Sci UK) Elsevier.

Developments in Reinforced Plastics, Vol. 4. Ed. by G. Pritchard. (Illus.). 272p. 1985. 88.25 (*0-85334-305-5*, Pub. by Elsevier Applied Sci UK) Elsevier.

Developments in Reinforced Plastics, No. 5. Ed. by G. Pritchard. 284p. 1986. 84.75 (*0-85334-400-0*, Pub. by Elsevier Applied Sci UK) Elsevier.

Developments in River Basin Management: Proceedings of an IAWPRC Conference Held in Sao Paulo, Brazil, 13-15 August, 1986. Ed. by N. L. Nucci et al. LC 82-645900. (Water Science & Technology Ser.: Vol. 19). (Illus.). 280p. 1988. pap. 77.00 (*0-08-035593-5*, Pergamon Pr) Elsevier.

Developments in Rubber & Rubber Composites, Vol. 1. Ed. by C. W. Evans. (Illus.). 184p. 1980. 54.00 (*0-85334-892-8*, Pub. by Elsevier Applied Sci UK) Elsevier.

Developments in Rubber & Rubber Composites, Vol. 2. Ed. by C. W. Evans. (Illus.). 183p. 1983. 63.00 (*0-85334-173-7*, I-460-82, Pub. by Elsevier Applied Sci UK) Elsevier.

Developments in Rubber Technology, Vol. 3. Ed. by A. Whelan & K. S. Lee. (Illus.). 240p. 1982. 86.50 (*0-85334-135-4*, Pub. by Elsevier Applied Sci UK) Elsevier.

Developments in Rubber Technology, Vol. 4. A. Whelan & K. S. Lee. 1987. 95.50 (*1-85166-083-6*, Pub. by Elsevier Applied Sci UK) Elsevier.

Developments in Rubber Technology, Vols. 1 & 2. Ed. by A. Whelan & K. S. Lee. 1981. Vol. 1, 1979. 79.25 (*0-85334-862-6*, Pub. by Elsevier Applied Sci UK); Vol. 2, 1981. 74.00 (*0-85334-949-5*, Pub. by Elsevier Applied Sci UK) Elsevier.

Developments in Russian & Post-Soviet Politics. 3rd ed. Ed. by Stephen White et al. LC 94-10629. 384p. 1994. lib. bdg. 58.00 (*0-8223-1507-6*); pap. text ed. 21.95 (*0-8223-1518-1*) Duke.

Developments in School & Public Assessment. Ed. by Brian Low & Graeme Withers. (C). 1992. 65.00 (*0-86431-070-6*, Pub. by Aust Coun Educ Res AT) St Mut.

Developments in School Mathematics Education Around the World, Vol. 1. Izaak Wirszup & Robert Streit. 725p. (J). (gr. k-12). 1987. pap. 22.00 (*0-87353-249-X*) NCTM.

Developments in School Mathematics Education Around the World, Vol. 3. University of Chicago School Mathematics Project Staff. Ed. by Izaak Wirszup & Robert Streit. (Illus.). 501p. (Orig.). 1993. pap. 22.00 (*0-87353-356-9*) NCTM.

Developments in School Mathematics Education Around the World, Vol. 2: Applications-Oriented Curricula & Technology-Supported Learning for All Students. Ed. by Izaak Wirszup & Robert Streit. (Illus.). 475p. (Orig.). 1990. pap. 22.00 (*0-87353-302-X*) NCTM.

Developments in Sedimentary Provenance Studies. Ed. by A. C. Morton et al. (Geological Society Special Publications: No. 57). (Illus.). 376p. 1991. 130.00 (*0-903317-56-7*, Pub. by Geol Soc Pub Hse UK) AAPG.

Developments in Semantics. Alex Orenstein & Raphael Stern. LC 83-83299. (Language, Logic & Linguistics Ser.). 402p. (C). 1984. 65.00 (*0-930586-34-4*); pap. text ed. 29.00 (*0-930586-13-1*) Haven Pubns.

Developments in Sewerage, Vol. 1. Ed. by R. E. Bartlett. (Illus.). 180p. 1979. 54.00 (*0-85334-831-6*, Pub. by Elsevier Applied Sci UK) Elsevier.

Developments in Social Skills Training. Ed. by Sue Spence & Geoff Shepherd. 1983. text ed. 88.00 (*0-12-656620-8*) Acad Pr.

Developments in Soft Drink Technology, Vol. 3. Ed. by W. H. Houghton. 256p. 1984. 66.75 (*0-85334-278-4*, I-319-84, Pub. by Elsevier Applied Sci UK) Elsevier.

Developments in Soil Mechanics. 566p. 1983. 82.00 (*0-7277-0180-0*, Pub. by T Telford UK) Am Soc Civil Eng.

Developments in Soil Mechanics, Vol. 1. Ed. by C. R. Scott. (Illus.). 441p. 1978. 120.75 (*0-85334-771-9*, Pub. by Elsevier Applied Sci UK) Elsevier.

Developments in Soil Mechanics & Foundation Engineering, Vol. 1. Ed. by P. K. Banerjee & R. Butterfield. (Illus.). 266p. 1984. 84.75 (*0-85334-222-9*, Pub. by Elsevier Applied Sci UK) Elsevier.

Developments in Soviet & Post-Soviet Politics. 2nd ed. Ed. by Stephen White et al. LC 92-12050. 348p. 1992. text ed. 58.00 (*0-8223-1259-X*); pap. text ed. 21.95 (*0-8223-1267-0*) Duke.

Developments in Soviet Coking Technology. Mark Loba. Ed. by Janna Gross. (Institute of Minerals Fuels IGA Ser.). 159p. (Orig.). 1986. pap. text ed. 75.00 (*1-55831-028-2*) Delphic Associates.

Developments in Soviet Metal Rolling. Konstantiu Radtchenko. Ed. by Jonathan Gallant. Tr. by Elizabeth Squires. (Illus.). 125p. (Orig.). 1989. pap. text ed. 75.00 (*1-55831-094-0*) Delphic Associates.

Developments in Soviet Politics. Ed. by Stephen White et al. 327p. (C). 1990. lib. bdg. 55.50 (*0-8223-1084-8*); pap. text ed. 21.95 (*0-8223-1089-9*) Duke.

Developments in Space Law: Issues & Policies. Stephen Gorove. (Utrecht Studies in Air & Space Law). 428p. (C). 1991. lib. bdg. 125.50 (*0-7923-1444-1*) Kluwer Ac.

Developments in Stamens of Viola Odorata. H. Olsen-Gisel. (Dissertationes Botanicae Ser.: Vol. 70). (Illus.). 192p. 1983. pap. text ed. 48.00 (*3-7682-1362-5*) Lubrecht & Cramer.

Developments in Stress Analysis, Vol. 1. Ed. by G. S. Holister. (Illus.). 197p. 1979. 63.00 (*0-85334-812-X*, Pub. by Elsevier Applied Sci UK) Elsevier.

Developments in Stress Analysis for Pressurized Components, Vol. 1. Ed. by R. W. Nichols. (Illus.). 210p. 1977. 79.25 (*0-85334-724-7*, Pub. by Elsevier Applied Sci UK) Elsevier.

Developments in Sweeteners, Vol. 1. Ed. by C. A. Hough et al. (Illus.). 192p. 1979. 66.75 (*0-85334-820-0*, Pub. by Elsevier Applied Sci UK) Elsevier.

Developments in Sweeteners, Vol. 2. Ed. by T. H. Grenby et al. (Illus.). 264p. 1983. 84.75 (*0-85334-202-4*, I-206-83, Pub. by Elsevier Applied Sci UK) Elsevier.

Developments in Sweetners. T. H. Grenby. 1987. 84.75 (*1-85166-104-2*) Elsevier.

Developments in Tender Offers for Corporate Control, 1973-76. Edward R. Aranow et al. LC 77-4235. 411p. 1977. text ed. 103.00 (*0-231-04170-5*) Col U Pr.

Developments in the Air Cargo Industry. ICHCA Staff. (C). 1988. 190.00 (*0-685-54105-3*, Pub. by ICHCA UK) St Mut.

Developments in the Air Cargo Industry. D. W. Peak. 98p. (C). 1981. 190.00 (*0-906297-17-6*, Pub. by ICHCA UK) St Mut.

***Developments in the Analysis of Lipids.** Ed. by John H. Tyman & Michael H. Gordon. 216p. 1994. 89.95 (*0-85186-971-8*, R6971, Pub. by Royal Soc Chem UK) CRC Pr.

Developments in the Annealing of Sheet Steels. Ed. by R. Pradhan & I. Gupta. (Illus.). 510p. 1992. 115.00 (*0-87339-181-0*, 440) Minerals Metals.

Developments in the Assessment & Treatment of Addictive Behaviors. Ted D. Nirenberg & Stephen Maisto. Ed. by Glenn R. Caddy. LC 87-11446. (Developments in Clinical Psychology Ser.: Vol. 5). 400p. 1987. text ed. 59.50 (*0-89391-170-4*) Ablex Pub.

Developments in the Centrifuge Separation Project: AEC Technical Information Center. AEC Technical Information Center Staff et al. (National Nuclear Energy Ser.: Div. X, Vol. 1). 269p. 1951. 36.50 (*0-87079-179-6*, TID-5230); mic. film 10.00 (*0-87079-180-X*, TID-5230) DOE.

Developments in the Clothing Industry. D. L. Munden & C. M. Dorkin. 56p. 1973. 95.00 (*0-686-63760-7*) St Mut.

Developments in the Clothing Industry, Vol. 5, No. 1. D. L. Munden & C. M. Dorkin. (C). 1973. pap. text ed. 85.00 (*0-685-46407-5*, Pub. by Textile Institue UK) St Mut.

Developments in the Drawing of Metals. 644p. (Orig.). 1983. pap. text ed. 52.50 (*0-904357-56-2*, Pub. by Inst Materials UK) Ashgate Pub Co.

***Developments in the Education of Adults in Europe.** Ed. by Peter Jarvis & Franz Poggeler. LC 94-31774. (Studies in Pedagogy, Andragogy & Gerontology: Vol. 21). 1994. write for info. (*3-631-47458-X*) P Lang Pubs.

Developments in the European Community, January - June 1992. HMSO Staff. (Command Paper Ser.: No. 2065). 91p. 1992. pap. 20.00 (*0-10-120652-6*, HM06526, Pub. by HMSO UK) UNIPUB.

Developments in the European Community July-December 1881. HMSO Staff. (Command Paper Ser.: No. 1857). 96p. 1992. pap. 25.00 (*0-10-118572-3*, HM85723, Pub. by HMSO UK) UNIPUB.

Developments in the Fiber Optic Sensors Market, 2 vols., Set. Corporate Strategic Intelligence Inc. Staff. (Illus.). 200p. (Orig.). 1988. pap. 1,495.00 (*0-918435-54-4*) Info Gatekeepers.

Developments in the Field of Drug Abuse: Proceedings. National Association for the Prevention of Addiction to Narcotics. Ed. by Edward Senay. 1130p. 1975. 69.95 (*0-87073-388-5*) Transaction Pubs.

Developments in the Finishing of Cotton & Man-Made Fiber Fabrics. D. H. Wyles. 81p. 1973. 70.00 (*0-686-63761-5*) St Mut.

Developments in the Finishing of Cotton & Man-Made Fibre Fabrics, Vol. 5, No. 4. D. H. Wyles. 81p. (C). 1973. pap. text ed. 70.00 (*0-685-36090-3*, Pub. by Textile Institue UK) St Mut.

Developments in the Law of Treaties. Shabtai Rosenne. (Cambridge Studies in International & Comparative Law). 566p. (C). 1989. 94.95 (*0-521-33318-0*) Cambridge U Pr.

Developments In the Management of Chemotherapy-Induced Nausea & Vomiting: A Workshop Held At Lake Tahoe Nevada, April 11, 1987. David Basedow. (Illus.). 24p. (Orig.). 1987. write for info. (*0-944036-00-7*) Medicine Grp USA.

Developments in the Market for Self-Assembly Furniture 1986. 1986. 175.00 (*0-317-43747-X*) St Mut.

Developments in the Methodology of Social Science. Werner Leinfellner & E. Koehler. LC 74-83003. (Theory & Decision Library: No. 6). 400p. 1974. lib. bdg. 140.00 (*90-277-0493-7*); pap. text ed. 90.00 (*90-277-0539-9*) Kluwer Ac.

Developments in the Organic Chemistry of Sulfur: Proceedings of the XIII International Symposium on the Organic Chemistry of Sulfur, August 7-12, 1988, Odense, Denmark. Ed. by C. Th. Pedersen & J. Becher. 394p. 1989. text ed. 70.00 (*0-677-22140-1*) Gordon & Breach.

Developments in the Power Industry: Heat Exchanger Technologies & Materials Improvements. J. R. Maurer. LC 93-73003. (PWR Ser.: Vol. 23). 124p. 1993. 35.00 (*0-7918-0998-6*, H00830) ASME.

Developments in the Rorschach Technique, 3 vols. Bruno Klopfer et al. Incl. Vol. 1. Technique & Theory. 726p. (C). 1954. text ed. 45.25 (*0-15-517626-9*); Vol. 2. Fields of Application. 828p. (C). 1956. text ed. 45.25 (*0-15-517627-7*); Vol. 3. Aspects of Personality Structure. 446p. (C). 1970. text ed. 45.25 (*0-15-517628-5*); (C). 1970. Set text ed. write for info. (*0-318-52966-1*) HB Coll Pubs.

Developments in the Science & Practice of Toxicology: Proceedings of the Third International Congress of Toxicology, San Diego, CA, August 28 - September 3, 1983. Ed. by A. W. Hayes et al. (Developments in Toxicology & Environmental Science Ser.: Vol. 11). 614p. 1984. 202.75 (*0-444-80547-8*) Elsevier.

Developments in the Science & Technology of Composite Materials: Proceedings of the Third European Conference Held in Bordeaux, France, 20-23 March 1989. Ed. by A. R. Bunsell et al. 836p. 1990. 234.00 (*1-85166-359-2*) Elsevier.

Developments in the Science & Technology of Composite Materials - ECCM 4: Proceedings of the Fourth European Conference, Held in Stuttgart, Germany, 25-28 Sept. 1990, Organized by EACM. Ed. by J. Fuller et al. 1100p. 1991. 330.00 (*1-85166-562-5*) Elsevier.

Developments in the Study of Criminal Behaviour, 2 vols., 1. Ed. by Philip Feldman. LC 81-21946. reprint ed. pap. 64.50 (*0-8357-4612-7*, 2037545) Bks Demand.

Developments in the Study of Criminal Behaviour, 2 vols., 2. Ed. by Philip Feldman. LC 81-21946. 264p. reprint ed. pap. 75.30 (*0-8357-4613-5*) Bks Demand.

Developments in the Terminology of Physics & Technology. Kerstin Klasson. 202p. (Orig.). 1977. pap. text ed. 28.75x (*91-22-00124-7*, Pub. by Almqv & Wiksell SW) Coronet Bks.

Developments in the Theory of Fundamental Interactions. Ed. by L. Turko & A. Pekalski. (Studies in High Energy Physics: Vol. 3). 598p. (C). 1981. 160.00 (*3-7186-0104-4*) Gordon & Breach.

Developments in the Use of Compensation Orders in Magistrates' Courts Oct 88. D. Corkery Moxon & C. Hedderman. (Home Office Research Study Ser.: No. 126). 58p. 1992. pap. 14.00 (*0-11-341042-5*, HM10425, Pub. by HMSO UK) UNIPUB.

Developments in Theoretical & Applied Mechanics, Vol. XIV. Ed. by R. M. Hackett et al. (Illus.). 576p. 1988. 50.00 (*0-685-56670-6*) U MS Schl Eng.

Developments in Theoretical & Applied Mechanics, Vol. XIV. Ed. by S. Y. Wang et al. (Illus.). 576p. 1988. 50.00 (*0-937099-01-5*) U MS Schl Eng.

Developments in Theoretical & Applied Mechanics, Vol. 17: Proceedings of SECTAM Seventeen. Ed. by Ing-Chang Jong & Fred A. Akl. 600p. (C). 1994. 80.00 (*0-9640094-0-4*) U Ark LA Tech.

Developments in Theoretical Physics. Ed. by S. M. Roy et al. 1989. 32.00 (*81-204-0470-X*, Pub. by Oxford IBH II) S Asia.

Developments in Thin-Walled Structures, Vol. 1. Ed. by J. Rhodes & A. C. Walker. (Illus.). 290p. 1982. 93.75 (*0-85334-123-0*, Pub. by Elsevier Applied Sci UK) Elsevier.

Developments in Thin-Walled Structures, Vol. 2. Ed. by J. Rhodes & A. C. Walker. (Illus.). 244p. 1984. 79.25 (*0-85334-247-4*, I-520-83, Pub. by Elsevier Applied Sci UK) Elsevier.

Developments in Thin-Walled Structures, Vol. 3. Ed. by J. Rhodes & A. C. Walker. 290p. 1987. 88.25 (*1-85166-076-3*, Pub. by Elsevier Applied Sci UK) Elsevier.

Developments in Tidal Energy. 334p. 1990. text ed. 105.00 (*0-7277-1571-2*) Am Soc Civil Eng.

Developments in Time Series Analysis: In Honor of Maurice B. Priestley. T. Subba Rao. LC 93-3344. 1993. write for info. (*0-412-49260-1*) Chapman & Hall.

***Developments in Training in Social Services.** Dhanwant K. Rai. 1994. pap. 21.00 (*0-902789-91-0*, Pub. by Natl Inst Soc Work) St Mut.

Developments in U. S. Strategic Nuclear Policy under the Carter Administration. Desmond Ball. (CISA Working Paper Ser.: No. 21). 23p. (Orig.). Date not set. pap. 10.00 (*0-86682-020-5*) Ctr Intl Relations.

Developments in Water Treatment, 1. Ed. by W. M. Lewis. (Illus.). 1980. 66.75 (*0-85334-902-9*, Pub. by Elsevier Applied Sci UK) Elsevier.

Developments in Water Treatment, 2. Ed. by W. M. Lewis. (Illus.). 1980. 66.75 (*0-85334-903-7*, Pub. by Elsevier Applied Sci UK) Elsevier.

Developments in West German Politics. Ed. by Gordon Smith et al. LC 89-23392. 360p. (Orig.). (C). 1989. lib. bdg. 58.00 (*0-8223-1025-2*); pap. text ed. 21.95 (*0-8223-1043-0*) Duke.

Developments of Cancer Chemotherapy. Ed. by K. Lapis. (Journal: Oncology: Vol. 37, Suppl. 1). (Illus.). iv, 120p. 1980. pap. 26.50 (*3-8055-1588-X*) S Karger.

Developments of Control Theory for Economic Analysis. Ed. by C. Carraro & D. Sartore. (C). 1987. lib. bdg. 107.00 (*90-247-3345-6*) Kluwer Ac.

Developments of New Volatile Inhalation Anaesthetics. Ed. by A. B. Dobkin. (Monographs in Anaesthesiology: Vol. 6). 1979. 102.75 (*0-444-80064-6*, Excerpta Medica) Elsevier.

Developments of Thin Gauge Materials, EUR 13304. A. Jenkins. 132p. 1991. pap. 17.00 (*92-826-2394-7*, CD-NA-13304-EN-C) UNIPUB.

Developments Underground (No-Dig 89) Ed. by John E. James. 322p. 1989. pap. text ed. 63.00 (*0-7277-1567-4*, Pub. by T Telford UK) Am Soc Civil Eng.

Developments Using Occam: Proceedings of the 8th Occam User Group Technical Meeting, Sheffield, U. K. March 27-29, 1988. Ed. by J. Kerridge. (Transputer & Occam Engineering Ser.). 214p. 1988. 50.00 (*90-5199-002-2*, Pub. by IOS Pr NE) IOS Press.

Developments with Natural Rubber. Ed. by J. A. Brydson. (Illus.). 148p. 1967. 38.00 (*0-85334-062-5*, Pub. by Elsevier Applied Sci UK) Elsevier.

***Developpement des Cooperatives et Autres Organizations - The Development of Cooperatives & Other Rural Organizations: La Role de la Banque Mondiale - The Role of the World Bank.** Pekka Hussi et al. (Document Technique de la Banque Mondiale Ser.). 146p. 1994. 7.95 (*0-8213-2848-4*, 12848) World Bank.

Developpement des Systemes Indigenes d'Exploitation Agricole Integres au Sahel. Mike Speirs & Ole Olsen. (Technical Paper Ser.: No. 179F). 92p. 1993. 7.95 (*0-8213-2532-9*) World Bank.

Developpement et Environment: Fait et Perspectives dans les Pays Industrialises et en Voie de Developpement. Albert Sasson. LC 74-78190. 423p. (FRE.). 1975. pap. text ed. 63.10 (*90-279-7596-5*) Mouton.

Developpment de la Physique Cartesienne 1646-1712 (the Development of Cartesian Physics) Paul Mouy. Ed. by I. Bernard Cohen. LC 80-2138. (Development of Science Ser.). 1981. reprint ed. lib. bdg. 33.95 (*0-405-13893-8*) Ayer.

***Develpment of the Artificial Disc: SB Charite.** Karin Buttner-Janz. Tr. by Rocky Mountain Translators Staff. 200p. 1993. text ed. write for info. (*0-9635430-0-8*) Hundley & Assocs.

Devendorf Family. O. W. Bell. (Illus.). 111p. 1994. reprint ed. lib. bdg. 29.50 (*0-8328-4207-9*); reprint ed. pap. 19.50 (*0-8328-4208-7*) Higginson Bk Co.

***Devendorf Family.** O. W. Bell. (Illus.). 111p. 1994. reprint ed. lib. bdg. 29.50 (*0-8328-4525-6*); reprint ed. pap. 19.50 (*0-8328-4526-4*) Higginson Bk Co.

***Devenir et la Conscience Cosmique Chez Saint-Exupery.** Pierre Nguyen-Van-Huy. LC 94-38773. 188p. (FRE.). 1995. text ed. 79.95 (*0-7734-2912-3*) E Mellen.

Devenish: Historical & Genealogical Records of the Devenish Families of England & Ireland. Robert J. Devenish & Charles H. McLaughlin. (Illus.). 409p. 1993. reprint ed. lib. bdg. 72.50 (*0-8328-3100-X*); reprint ed. pap. 62.50 (*0-8328-3101-8*) Higginson Bk Co.

Devereaux File. Ross H. Spencer. 1990. 18.95 (*1-55611-212-2*) D I Fine.

De'veri Precetti Della Pittura Libri Tre. Giovanni B. Armenini. 232p. 1971. reprint ed. write for info. (*0-318-71578-3*, Pub. by Georg Olms GW) Lubrecht & Cramer.

***Devetsil Czech Avant-Garde Art: Architecture & Design of the 1920s & 30s.** Frwd. by D. Elliott & H. Rees. 115p. 1990. pap. 45.00 (*0-905836-70-7*, Pub. by Museum Modern Art UK) St Mut.

Devi. Suzanne Ironbiter. 125p. (Orig.). 1987. pap. 8.95 (*0-938999-02-8*) Yuganta Pr.

Devi Mahatmya: The Crystalization of the Goddess Tradition. Thomas B. Coburn. (C). 1989. reprint ed. 26.00 (*81-208-0557-7*, Pub. by Motilal Banarsidass II) S Asia.

Devi-Mahatmyam (the Chandi) Tr. by Swami Jagadiswarananda. Bilingual ed. pap. 3.95 (*0-87481-426-X*) Vedanta Pr.

Deviance. Ed. by Richard F. Tomasson. (Comparative Social Research Ser.: Vol. 8). 352p. 1985. 73.25 (*0-89232-520-8*) Jai Pr.

Deviance: An Introduction. Visano. 1993. pap. write for info. (*0-409-80939-X*, Pub. by Buttrwrth Can Acad CN) Buttrwrth-Heinemann.

Deviance: Anthropological Perspectives. Ed. by Morris Freilich et al. LC 91-2037. 264p. 1991. text ed. 49.95 (*0-89789-205-4*, H205, Bergin & Garvey); pap. text ed. 16.95 (*0-89789-204-6*, G204, Bergin & Garvey) Greenwood.

Deviance: Being, Behaving, & Branding. David A. Ward et al. LC 93-19695. 1993. text ed. write for info. (*0-205-13752-0*) Allyn.

Deviance: The Interactionist Perspective. 5th ed. Earl Rubington & Martin A. Weinberg. 580p. (C). 1987. pap. write for info. (*0-02-404390-7*) Macmillan.

Deviance & Conformity. Stuart Palmer. 1969. 21.95 (*0-317-18409-1*) NCUP.

Deviance & Control: Theory, Research & Social Policy. Craig B. Little. LC 88-64161. 419p. 1989. pap. 30.00 (*0-87581-341-0*) Peacock Pubs.

Deviance & Control: Theory, Research, & Social Policy. 3rd ed. Craig B. Little. 420p. 1995. pap. text ed. write for info. (*0-87581-395-X*) Peacock Pubs.

Deviance & Decency: The Ethics of Research with Human Subjects. Ed. by Carl B. Klockars & Finbarr W. O'Connor. LC 79-18034. (Sage Annual Reviews of Studies in Deviance: No. 3). 284p. reprint ed. pap. 81.00 (*0-8357-8441-X*, 2034705) Bks Demand.

Deviance & Medicalization: From Badness to Sickness. enl. ed. Peter Conrad & Joseph W. Schneider. LC 92-13441. 352p. (C). 1992. reprint ed. 49.95 (*0-87722-998-8*); reprint ed. pap. 22.95 (*0-87722-999-6*) Temple U Pr.

Deviance & Mental Illness. Ed. by Walter R. Gove. LC 82-3386. (Sage Annual Reviews of Studies in Deviance: No. 6). 303p. reprint ed. pap. 86.40 (*0-8357-4799-9*, 2037736) Bks Demand.

Deviance & Moral Boundaries: Witchcraft, the Occult, Science Fiction, Deviant Sciences & Scientists. Nachman Ben-Yehuda. LC 85-1167. x, 260p. (C). 1987. pap. text ed. 12.95 (*0-226-04336-3*) U Ch Pr.

Deviance & Psychopathology: The Sociology & Psychology of Outsiders. Robert Endleman. LC 88-13949. 308p. (C). 1990. lib. bdg. 34.50 (*0-89464-344-4*) Krieger.

***Deviance & Psychopathology: The Sociology & Psychology of Outsiders.** Robert Endleman. 308p. 1995. pap. 19.50 (*0-89464-958-2*) Krieger.

Deviance & Social Control. S. J. Pfohl. 416p. 1985. text ed. write for info. (*0-07-049757-5*) McGraw.

D

An Asterisk (*) at the beginning of an entry indicates that the title is appearing in BIP for the first time.

An Asterisk (*) at the beginning of an entry indicates that the title is appearing in BIP for the first time.

1927

Devil Rock. Scott Westerfield. LC 85-90287. (Illus.). 217p. 1986. 14.95 (0-9615537-0-7) Westerfield.

Devil Sang in Tune. Andonis Fostieris. Tr. by Kimon Friar. (Contemporary Poets Ser.: No. 3). (Illus.). 64p. (Orig.). 1983. pap. 3.95 (0-916982-28-9, RL228) CCR Pubns.

Devil Sits among the Congregation. H. Chalk. 88p. (C). 1989. 60.00 (0-7223-2221-6, Pub. by A H S Ltd UK) St Mut.

*__Devil Soldier: The American Soldier of Fortune Who Became a God in China.__ Caleb Carr. 1995. 15.00 (0-679-76128-4) Random.

Devil Soldier: The Story of Frederick Townsend Ward, the Most Honored & Controversial American in Chinese History. Caleb Carr. 1991. 25.00 (0-679-41114-3) Random.

Devil Stick Book. Todd Strong. LC 90-34819. (Illus.). 107p. (Orig.). 1990. pap. 9.95 (0-917643-07-0) B Dube.

Devil Stories: Modern Man in Search of a Resort. Alan Rosenus. LC 78-64543. (Illus.). 1979. 18.95 (0-913522-07-4); pap. 10.95 (0-913522-08-2) Urion Pr CA.

Devil Stories: Modern Man in Search of a Resort. limited ed. Alan Rosenus. LC 78-64543. (Illus.). 1979. 40.00 (0-913522-09-0) Urion Pr CA.

Devil Storm. Theresa Nelson. LC 87-5493. 224p. (J). (gr. 5-7). 1987. 15.95 (0-531-05711-9); lib. bdg. 15.99 (0-531-08311-X) Orchard Bks Watts.

Devil Strike. David Robbins. (Blade Ser.: No. 8). 192p. (Orig.). 1990. pap. 2.95 (0-8439-2964-2) Dorchester Pub Co.

Devil Take a Crooked House. Tomas O'Leary. LC 88-1214. 1990. 15.95 (0-89924-063-1); pap. 8.00 (0-89924-055-0) Lynx Hse.

Devil Take Her: A Study of the Rebellious Lover in English Poetry. L. B. Salomon. 1972. 59.95 (0-8490-0024-6) Gordon Pr.

Devil Take the Youngest. Winkie Pratney. LC 85-90017. 271p. (Orig.). 1985. pap. 8.99 (0-910311-29-3) Huntington Hse.

Devil Take You, Sweetest. large type ed. Mary Romney. 336p. 1987. 16.95 (0-7089-1669-4) Ulverscroft.

Devil Tales. Virginia F. Boyle. LC 70-38643. (Black Heritage Library Collection). (Illus.). 1977. reprint ed. 23.95 (0-8369-9001-3) Ayer.

Devil Theory of War: An Inquiry into the Nature of History & the Possibility of Keeping Out of War. Charles A. Beard. LC 68-54771. (Illus.). 124p. 1969. reprint ed. text ed. 35.00 (0-8371-0300-2, BEDT, Greenwood Pr) Greenwood.

Devil Thumbs a Ride & Other Unforgettable Films. Barry Gifford. LC 87-34638. 160p. 1988. pap. 7.95 (0-8021-3078-X) Grove-Atltic.

Devil to Pay. Glen Chase. (Cherry Delight Ser.). 1977. pap. 1.50 (0-8439-0473-9) Dorchester Pub Co.

Devil to Pay. Mark Daniel. LC 92-11547. 1993. 19.95 (0-316-17265-0) Little.

*__Devil to Pay.__ Mark Daniel. 256p. 1995. mass mkt. 4.99 (0-380-72328-X) Avon.

Devil to Pay. Robin Moore. 415p. 1991. 19.95 (1-879915-02-2) Affil Writers America.

Devil to Pay. Cole Riley. 217p. (Orig.). 1994. pap. 3.95 (0-87067-742-X) Holloway.

*__Devil to Pay.__ large type ed. Mark Daniel. LC 95-13707. 391p. 1995. 19.95 (0-7838-1351-1, Large Print Bks) Hall.

Devil-Tree of el Dorado: A Novel. Frank Atkins. Ed. by R. Reginald & Douglas Melville. LC 77-84196. (Lost Race & Adult Fantasy Ser.). (Illus.). 1978. reprint ed. lib. bdg. 36.95 (0-405-10955-5) Ayer.

Devil Undone: The Life & Poetry of Benjamin Church, 1734-1778. Jeffrey B. Walker & Benjamin Church. 1981. 27.95 (0-405-14111-4) Ayer.

Devil Visits Confidence. C. Marcus Parr. (Petites Major Ser.). 40p. 1993. pap. 4.00 (1-884754-00-7) Potpourri Pubns.

Devil Was Handsome. large type ed. Maurice Procter. (Mystery Ser.). 1979. 15.95 (0-7089-0259-6) Ulverscroft.

Devil Water. Anya Seton. 30.95 (0-8488-0318-3) Amereon Ltd.

Devil Water. large type ed. Anya Seton. 1977. 16.95 (0-85456-554-X) Ulverscroft.

Devil We Knew: Americans & the Cold War. H. W. Brands, Jr. LC 92-29030. 256p. 1993. 27.50 (0-19-507499-8) OUP.

Devil We Knew: Americans & the Cold War. H. W. Brands. 254p. 1994. reprint ed. pap. 10.95 (0-19-509377-1) OUP.

Devil Wears Wings. rev. ed. Harry Whittington. LC 86-71964. 160p. 1987. reprint ed. pap. 3.95 (0-88739-036-6, Blk Lizard) Creat Arts Bk.

*__Devil Wire.__ Cameron Judd. 1995. 3.99 (0-553-57171-0) Bantam.

Devil Wire. Cameron Judd. 272p. 1986. pap. 2.50 (0-8217-1937-8) Zebra.

Devil Wire. large type ed. Wayne C. Lee. LC 92-41945. 1993. 19.95 (0-7927-1552-7, Curley Lrg Print) Chivers N Amer.

Devil with James Bond. Ann Boyd. LC 73-15312. 123p. 1975. reprint ed. text ed. 38.50 (0-8371-7182-2, BOJB, Greenwood Pr) Greenwood.

Devil with the Three Golden Hairs. Jacob Grimm & Wilhelm K. Grimm. LC 82-12735. (Illus.). 40p. (J). (gr. k-3). 1983. lib. bdg. 10.99 (0-394-95560-9) Knopf Bks Yng Read.

Devil Won't Let Me In. Alice Olds-Ellingson. 64p. (Orig.). 1990. pap. 6.95 (0-916397-11-4) Manic D Pr.

Devil Worship. Isya Joseph. 222p. 1972. spiral bd. 7.70 (0-7873-0483-2) Mokelumne.

Devil You Say. Elisa DeCarlo. 192p. (Orig.). 1993. mass mkt. 4.50 (0-380-76993-X, AvoNova) Avon.

Devilbirds: The Story of the United States Marine Corps Aviation in World War II. John M. De Chant. LC 79-16257. reprint ed. 23.95 (0-89201-050-9) Zenger Pub.

Devilish but True: The Doctor Looks at Spiritualism. Harold Dearden. (Illus.). 288p. 1975. reprint ed. 22.00 (0-8464-0324-2) Beekman Pubs.

Devilish Earl. Rachelle Edwards. (Orig.). 1994. mass mkt. 3.99 (0-449-22321-3) Fawcett.

Devilishness. Rius. (Diabluras: Un Libro de Todos Los Diablos Ser.). 70p. 1987. pap. 9.00 (0-910309-50-7, 5438) Am Atheist.

DeVilliers - the Acquisition of English. Ed. by DeVilliers. (Crosslinguistic Study of Language Acquisition Ser.). 136p. 1986. pap. 14.95 (0-89859-840-0) L Erlbaum Assocs.

Devils. Isaac Asimov et al. (Isaac Asimov's Magical Worlds of Fantasy Ser.: No. 8). 1987. pap. 3.50 (0-451-14867-3, Sig) NAL-Dutton.

Devils. Fyodor Dostoyevsky. Ed. & Tr. by Michael R. Katz. (World's Classics Ser.). 672p. (Orig.). 1992. pap. 7.95 (0-19-281850-3) OUP.

Devils. Fyodor Dostoyevsky. Tr. by David Magarshack. (Classics Ser.). (Orig.). 1954. mass mkt. 8.95 (0-14-044035-6, Penguin Classics) Viking Penguin.

Devils. J. C. Wall. 1972. 59.95 (0-8490-0025-4) Gordon Pr.

*__Devil's Adjutant: Jochen Peiper, Panzer Leader.__ Michael Reynolds. (Illus.). 320p. 1995. 27.50 (1-885119-15-1) Sarpedon.

Devils Advocate. 1989. pap. 4.50 (0-8216-5070-X) Carol Pub Group.

Devil's Advocate. Morris L. West. 1959. 17.95 (0-688-01453-4) Morrow.

Devil's Advocate. large type ed. Morris West. 1974. 12.00 (0-85456-274-5) Ulverscroft.

Devil's Advocate. Taylor Caldwell. 1976. reprint ed. lib. bdg. 24.95 (0-88411-163-6, Aeonian Pr) Amereon Ltd.

Devil's Advocates: Decadence in Modern Literature. Thomas R. Whissen. LC 89-2108. (Contributions to the Study of World Literature Ser.: No. 33). 158p. 1989. text ed. 45.00 (0-313-26483-X, WDS, Greenwood Pr) Greenwood.

Devil's Advocates: The Unnatural History of Lawyers. Jonathan Roth & Andrew Roth. (Illus.). 192p. (Orig.). 1989. pap. 12.95 (0-87337-101-1) Nolo Pr.

Devil's Alphabet. Kurt E. Koch. LC 76-160692. 158p. 1972. pap. 6.99 (0-8254-3004-6) Kregel.

Devil's Alternative. Frederick Forsyth. 416p. 1982. mass mkt. 6.99 (0-553-26490-7) Bantam.

Devil's Alternative. large type ed. Frederick Forsyth. 1980. 12.00 (0-7089-0529-3) Ulverscroft.

Devils & Angels: Textual Editing & Literary Theory. Ed. by Philip Cohen. (C). 1991. text ed. 29.50 (0-8139-1315-2) U Pr of Va.

Devils & Demons. Ed. by Marvin Kaye. (Dorset Classic Reprints Ser.). 600p. 1991. 19.95 (0-88029-662-3) Marboro Bks.

Devils & Evil Spirits of Babylonia, 2 vols., Set. R. C. Thompson. 1972. 200.00 (0-8490-0026-2) Gordon Pr.

Devils & Evil Spirits of Babylonia, 2 vols., Set. Reginald C. Thompson. LC 73-18855. (Luzac's Semitic Text & Translation Ser.: Nos. 14-15). (Illus.). reprint ed. 47.50 (0-404-11353-2) AMS Pr.

Devil's Angel. Marlene Suson. 384p. (Orig.). 1994. mass mkt. 4.50 (0-380-77613-8) Avon.

Devil's Anvil: The Assault on Peleliu. James H. Hallas. LC 93-13532. 297p. 1994. text ed. 27.50 (0-275-94646-0, Praeger Pubs) Greenwood.

Devils Are among Us: The War for Namibia. D. Herbstein & J. Evenson. LC 89-48796. (Illus.). 208p. (C). 1989. text ed. 49.95 (0-86232-896-9, Pub. by Zed Books UK); pap. 15.00 (0-86232-897-7, Pub. by Zed Books UK) Humanities.

Devil's Arithmetic. Jane Yolen. 160p. (J). 1988. pap. 15.99 (0-670-81027-4) Viking Child Bks.

Devil's Arithmetic. Jane Yolen. (YA). 1990. pap. 3.99 (0-14-034535-3, Puffin) Puffin Bks.

Devil's Arithmetic: A Study Guide. Michael Golden. Ed. by J. Friedland & R. Kessler. (Novel Ties Ser.). 29p. (J). (gr. 4-7). 1992. pap. text ed. 15.95 (0-88122-697-1) Lrn Links.

Devil's Auction. Robert Weinberg. (Weird Tales Library). (Illus.). 155p. 1988. 18.95 (0-913896-25-X) Owlswick Pr.

Devil's Auction. Robert Weinberg. 320p. 1990. reprint ed. pap. 3.95 (0-8439-2997-9) Dorchester Pub Co.

Devil's Backbone. Terry C. Johnston. 1991. mass mkt. 4.99 (0-312-92574-3) St Martin.

Devil's Backbone: The Story of the Natchez Trace. Jonathan Daniels. LC 84-3222. 270p. 1985. reprint ed. pap. 4.25 (0-88289-438-2) Pelican.

Devil's Band. Robert McCaig. (Orig.). 1986. pap. 2.25 (0-8217-1903-3) Zebra.

*__Devil's Bargain.__ Karen Harbaugh. (Regency Romance Ser.). 224p. (Orig.). 1995. mass mkt. 3.99 (0-451-18318-5, Sig) NAL-Dutton.

Devil's Bargain. Marlene Suson. 224p. (Orig.). 1992. mass mkt. 3.99 (0-380-76470-9) Avon.

Devil's Bestseller. William Mitchum. (Illus.). 151p. 1983. 9.95 (0-9612120-0-4); pap. 3.50 (0-9612120-1-2) Para-Bk-Pr.

Devil's Bodyguard. Jim Phillips. LC 83-61388. (Illus.). 350p. 1986. 19.95 (0-932572-12-X) Phillips Pubns.

Devil's Bondman. Sylvia Thorpe. 1980. pap. 1.75 (0-449-50034-9, Coventry) Fawcett.

Devil's Bounty. large type ed. Larry J. Martin. LC 92-18699. 342p. 1992. reprint ed. lib. bdg. 16.95 (1-56054-480-5) Thorndike Pr.

Devil's Bouquet. Florence Morrison. 70p. 1974. 5.75 (0-87881-018-8) Mojave Bks.

Devil's Bridge. Cynthia DeFelice. 96p. (J). (gr. 5 up). 1994. pap. 3.50 (0-380-72117-1) Avon.

Devil's Bridge. Cynthia DeFelice. LC 92-7497. 96p. (J). (gr. 5 up). 1992. text ed. 13.95 (0-02-726465-3, Mac Bks Young Read) S&S Childrens.

Devil's Butcher Shop: The New Mexico Prison Uprising. Roger Morris. LC 88-4005. 277p. 1988. reprint ed. pap. 16.95 (0-8263-1062-1) U of NM Pr.

Devil's Butte. large type ed. Ray Hogan. LC 93-7857. 1993. 16.95 (1-56054-574-7) Thorndike Pr.

Devils Canyon. large type ed. Hank Mitchum. LC 92-18451. (General Ser.). 312p. 1992. pap. 14.95 (0-8161-5595-X) G K Hall.

Devil's Canyon Double Cross. large type ed. Clifford Blair. 251p. 1992. reprint ed. lib. bdg. 14.95 (1-56054-572-0) Thorndike Pr.

Devil's Captain. Philip Shea. 320p. 1992. mass mkt. 3.99 (1-55817-624-1, Pinnacle NY) Windsor NY.

Devil's Cat. William W. Johnstone. (Horror Ser.). 384p. 1987. pap. 3.95 (0-8217-2091-0) Zebra.

Devil's Charter. Barnabe Barnes. LC 71-133638. (Tudor Facsimile Texts. Old English Plays Ser.: No. 121). reprint ed. 49.50 (0-404-53421-X) AMS Pr.

Devil's Church & Other Stories. Joaquim M. Machado de Assis. Tr. by Jack Schmitt & Lorie Ishimatsu. LC 76-53828. (Texas Pan American Ser.). (Illus.). 166p. (C). 1977. pap. 9.95 (0-292-71542-0) U of Tex Pr.

*__Devil's Claw Root: And Other Natural Remedies for Arthritis.__ rev. ed. Rachel Carston. LC 94-910296. 112p. 1994. pap. 9.95 (0-920470-36-X) Alive Bks.

Devil's Cocktail. Alexander Wilson. 360p. 1977. reprint ed. lib. bdg. 15.75 (0-89966-258-7) Buccaneer Bks.

Devils Coin. Mark Manley. 1990. pap. 3.95 (0-8217-3094-0) Zebra.

Devil's Coup. Jimmy Tait. (Illus.). 158p. 1991. 22.95 (0-575-04620-1, Pub. by V Gollancz UK) Trafalgar.

Devil's Cradle. Kate Stewart. 320p. 1992. mass mkt. 4.50 (0-8217-3802-X) Zebra.

Devil's Creek. Levinson. (Pecos Kid Ser.: No. 5). 1994. mass mkt. 3.50 (0-06-100656-4, Harp PBks) HarpC.

Devil's Cub. Georgette Heyer. 341p. 1984. lib. bdg. 21.95 (0-89966-497-0) Buccaneer Bks.

Devil's Cub. Georgette Heyer. (Signet Regency Romance Ser.). 256p. 1992. pap. 4.99 (0-451-17211-6) NAL-Dutton.

Devil's Cub. Georgette Heyer. 232p. 1993. 19.95 (1-56723-049-0) Yestermorrow.

Devil's Cuspidor. Beatrice LaForce. 1981. pap. 1.75 (0-686-37157-7) Eldridge Pub.

*__Devil's Darling.__ Casey Claybourne. 208p. (Orig.). 1994. pap. 4.50 (0-515-11492-8) Jove Pubns.

Devil's Darling. large type ed. Violet Winspear. (Linford Romance Library). 314p. 1984. pap. 11.95 (0-7089-6042-1, Trailtree Bookshop) Ulverscroft.

Devil's Daughter. Catherine Coulter. 1985. pap. 4.99 (0-451-15863-6, Onyx) NAL-Dutton.

Devil's Deception. Suzannah Davis. 400p. 1990. pap. 3.95 (0-380-75673-0) Avon.

Devil's Delight. DeLoras Scott. 384p. (Orig.). 1992. mass mkt. 4.50 (0-380-76343-5) Avon.

Devil's Delilah. Loretta Chase. 288p. 1990. pap. 3.95 (0-449-21894-5, Crest) Fawcett.

Devil's Delilah. Loretta Chase. 228p. 1989. 19.95 (0-8027-1058-1) Walker & Co.

Devil's Delilah. large type ed. Loretta Chase. LC 90-10731. 401p. 1990. lib. bdg. 18.95 (0-89621-970-4) Thorndike Pr.

Devil's Den, at Gettysburg: Forty-Fourth Alabama Regiment (Confederate), Its Action, Roster, & Family Connections. Charles E. Boyd. 1987. text ed. 26.95 (0-87121-445-8); pap. 19.95 (0-685-10283-1) Banner Pr AL.

Devil's Desire. Laurie McBain. 1976. mass mkt. 5.50 (0-380-00295-7) Avon.

Devil's Device: Robert Whitehead & the History of the Torpedo. rev. ed. Edwyn Gray. LC 90-48675. (Illus.). 320p. 1991. 32.95 (0-87021-245-1) Naval Inst Pr.

*__Devil's Dictionaries: The Best of the Devil's Dictionary & the American Heretic's Dictionary.__ expanded ed. Ambrose Bierce & Chaz Bufe. 1995. pap. 9.95 (1-884365-06-X) See Sharp Pr.

Devil's Dictionary. Ambrose Bierce. 376p. reprint ed. lib. bdg. 21.95 (0-89190-186-8) Amereon Ltd.

Devil's Dictionary. Ambrose Bierce. 1990. reprint ed. lib. bdg. 22.95 (0-89968-478-5) Buccaneer Bks.

Devil's Dictionary. Ambrose Bierce. LC 92-46179. (Thrift Editions Ser.). 144p. 1993. reprint ed. pap. 1.00 (0-486-27542-6) Dover.

Devil's Dictionary. Ambrose G. Bierce. (Principle Works of Ambrose Gwinett Bierce). 1989. reprint ed. lib. bdg. 79.00 (0-7812-1966-3) Rprt Serv.

Devil's Dictionary & Other Works. Ambrose Bierce & Gahan Wilson. (Classics Illustrated Ser.). (Illus.). 52p. (YA). Date not set. pap. 4.95 (1-57209-018-9) Classics Int Ent.

Devil's Dinero. large type ed. Marshall Grover. (Linford Western Library). 272p. 1988. pap. 11.95 (0-7089-6489-3, Trailtree Bookshop) Ulverscroft.

Devil's Disaster. Stephen McNamee. LC 87-5576. 287p. 1987. 17.75 (0-930950-07-0); pap. 10.75 (0-930950-09-7) Nopoly Pr.

Devil's Disciple. George Bernard Shaw. Ed. by Robert F. Whitman. LC 79-56706. (Bernard Shaw Early Texts: Play Manuscripts in Facsimile). 1981. lib. bdg. 20.00 (0-8240-4581-5) Garland.

Devil's Disciple. George Bernard Shaw. LC 90-53571. 1991. pap. 6.00 (0-88734-229-9) Players Pr.

Devil's Disciple. George Bernard Shaw. 14.95 (0-8488-1161-5) Amereon Ltd.

Devil's Disciple. Doyle Trent. 256p. 1993. pap. 3.50 (0-8217-4403-8) Zebra.

Devil's Disciples. Jeff Godwin. (Illus.). 352p. (Orig.). 1986. pap. 11.50 (0-937958-23-9) Chick Pubns.

Devil's Disciple's Dictionary & Monodialogues. Morton Leeds. (Illus.). 136p. (Orig.). 1988. pap. text ed. 4.95 (0-317-91132-5) Lone Oak Pr.

Devil's Ditties: Being Stories of the Kentucky Mountain People, Told by Jean Thomas, with the Songs They Sing. Jean Thomas. (Illus.). 1976. reprint ed. 46.00 (1-55888-956-6) Omnigraphics Inc.

Devil's Dominion: Magic & Religion in Early New England. Richard Godbeer. 272p. (C). 1992. 32.95 (0-521-40329-4) Cambridge U Pr.

Devil's Dominion: Magic & Religion in Early New England. Richard Godbeer. 272p. (C). 1994. pap. 14.95 (0-521-46670-9) Cambridge U Pr.

Devil's Donkey. Bill Brittain. LC 80-7907. (Illus.). 128p. (J). (gr. 3-7). 1981. lib. bdg. 14.89 (0-06-020683-7) HarpC Child Bks.

Devil's Donkey. Bill Brittain. LC 80-7907. (Trophy Bk.). (Illus.). 128p. (J). (gr. 3-7). 1982. pap. 3.95 (0-06-440129-4, Trophy) HarpC Child Bks.

Devil's Door. Sharan Newman. 384p. 1994. 21.95 (0-312-85420-X) Forge NYC.

*__Devil's Door.__ Sharan Newman. 416p. 1995. mass mkt. 4.99 (0-8125-2295-8) Forge NYC.

Devil's Doorstep see also Cougar of Canyon Caballo

Devil's Dozen. Tr. by Brenda Walker & Belin Tonchev. LC 90-71089. 1991. pap. 21.00 (0-948259-84-1) Dufour.

Devil's Dozen. large type ed. Marshall Grover. (Linford Western Library). 256p. 1986. pap. 11.95 (0-7089-6218-1, Linford) Ulverscroft.

Devil's Dozen: Thirteen Bulgarian Women Poets. Ed. by Brenda Walker & Belin Tonchev. Tr. by Belin Tonchev. (Illus.). 174p. (Orig.). 1992. pap. 21.00 (0-685-60746-1, Pub. by Forest Bks UK) Dufour.

Devil's Drainpipe: A Nuclear Waste Comedy. Keith Kirts. 288p. (Orig.). 1993. pap. 10.95 (1-882639-01-4) Synapse Cent.

Devil's Dream. Lee Smith. 320p. 1993. pap. 10.00 (0-345-38291-9, Ballantine Trade) Ballantine.

Devil's Dream. large type ed. Lee Smith. LC 92-30448. 533p. 1993. reprint ed. lib. bdg. 20.95 (1-56054-563-1) Thorndike Pr.

Devils, Drugs & Doctors. Howard Haggard. (Illus.). 1980. reprint ed. 30.00 (0-89182-023-X) Charles River Bks.

Devil's Due. large type ed. Maurice Procter. 1972. 12.00 (0-85456-133-1) Ulverscroft.

Devil's Due: A Letter to the Editor of "The Examiner" see Jonas Fisher: A Poem in Brown & White

Devil's Embrace. Catherine Coulter. 1985. pap. 4.99 (0-451-14198-9, Onyx) NAL-Dutton.

Devil's Empire. C. C. Cribb. LC 77-70211. pap. 2.95 (0-932046-02-9) Manhattan Ltd NC.

Devil's End. D. A. Fowler. Ed. by John Scognamiglio. 320p. (Orig.). 1992. mass mkt. 4.99 (0-671-72659-5) PB.

*__Devil's Eye.__ H. L. Richardson. LC 95-15550. 1995. write for info. (0-8499-3855-4) Word Pub.

Devil's Fingerprints. Anton Van Casteren. 1994. 16.95 (0-8062-4953-6) Carlton.

Devil's Food. Janice Weber. 1996. write for info. (0-446-51772-0) Warner Bks.

Devil's Ford. Robert Kammen. 192p. 1987. pap. 2.50 (0-8217-2102-X) Zebra.

Devil's Game. Poul Anderson. 1985. mass mkt. 4.99 (0-671-55995-8) Baen Bks.

Devils Gate. Elizabeth Ergas. 1991. mass mkt. 4.50 (1-55817-498-2, Pinnacle NY) Windsor NY.

Devil's Gauntlet. Os Guinness. LC 89-31325. (Viewpoint Pamphlet Ser.). 32p. 1989. pap. 2.99 (0-8308-1108-7, 1108) InterVarsity.

Devils, Ghosts, & Witches: Occult Folklore of the Upper Ohio Valley. George Swetnam. Ed. by Helene Smith. LC 88-90519. (Anthology Ser.). (Illus.). 120p. (Orig.). 1988. pap. 14.95 (0-945437-03-X) MacDonald-Sward.

*__Devil's Gonna Get Him.__ Valerie W. Wesley. 1995. 19.95 (0-399-14027-1) Putnam Pub Group.

Devil's Guns. Clay Dawson. (Long Rider Ser.: No. 26). 1993. pap. 3.99 (1-55773-954-4) Diamond.

Devil's Hand. Jack McKinney. 1988. mass mkt. 4.95 (0-345-35300-5, Del Rey) Ballantine.

Devil's Heart. William W. Johnstone. 1983. pap. 2.95 (0-8217-1156-3) Zebra.

Devil's Heart. William W. Johnstone. 1987. pap. 3.95 (0-8217-2110-0) Zebra.

Devil's Heart. Carmen Carter. Ed. by Kevin Ryan. (Star Trek: The Next Generation Ser.). 320p. 1994. reprint ed. mass mkt. 5.99 (0-671-79426-4, Pocket Star Bks) PB.

*__Devil's Heaven.__ Thomas Adcock. Ed. by Jane Chelius. 336p. 1995. 20.00 (0-671-89778-0) PB.

Devil's Highway. Harold B. Wright. 39.95 (1-56723-106-3) Yestermorrow.

Devil's Hole. large type ed. Patricia Ainsworth. 352p. 1987. 16.95 (0-7089-1566-3) Ulverscroft.

*__Devils Hole: A Novel.__ Bill Branon. 1995. 23.00 (0-06-017760-8) HarpC.

Devils in Amber: The Baltics. Phillip Bonosky. Ed. by Dieterich Steffan. LC 91-45096. 305p. (Orig.). 1992. pap. 9.95 (0-7178-0699-5) Intl Pubs Co.

Devil's Island: Colony of the Damned. Alexander Miles. (Illus.). 224p. 1988. pap. 9.95 (0-89815-275-5) Ten Speed Pr.

Devil's Jug, the Crying Tree & Me. Ken W. Kite. (Illus.). 343p. 1992. pap. 14.95 (0-9634418-0-9) Moonshine WA.

Devil's Juggler. Murray Smith. Ed. by Bill Grose. 672p. 1994. reprint ed. mass mkt. 5.99 (0-671-78468-4, Pocket Star Bks) PB.

Devil's Kiss. William W. Johnstone. (Orig.). 1981. pap. 3.95 (0-8217-2109-7) Zebra.

Devil's Kiss. large type ed. Sally Blake. (Magna Historical Fiction Ser.). 372p. 1992. 21.95 (0-7505-0396-3) Ulverscroft.

An Asterisk (*) at the beginning of an entry indicates that the title is appearing in BIP for the first time.

An Asterisk (*) at the beginning of an entry indicates that the title is appearing in BIP for the first time.

D

Devotional Theology: Meditations on Christian Existence. Egil Grislis. LC 87-50523. 175p. (Orig.). 1987. 24.95 (0-317-89500-1); pap. text ed. 14.95 (1-55605-007-0) Wyndhall Pr.

Devotional Warm-ups for Church Choirs. Kenneth W. Osbeck. LC 85-17222. 96p. 1985. pap. 4.99 (0-8254-3421-1); pap. 54.00 (0-8254-3423-8) Kregel.

Devotionals for Teachers. Nelle Vander Ark. 80p. 1975. 8.99 (0-8010-9263-9) Baker Bk.

Devotions. Harry Hewitt. Ed. by Elizabeth Hewitt. 56p. (Orig.). 1990. pap. 8.00 (0-9627244-0-8, MPI) Penn Sounds.

Devotions & Prayers in Honor of St. Joseph. Jerome F. Coniker. (Living Meditation & Prayerbook). (Illus.). 34p. (Orig.). 1978. pap. text ed. 2.50 (0-932406-04-1) AFC.

Devotions Day by Day. Ed. by Phyllis A. Frantz. 192p. 1988. pap. 10.00 (0-8170-1128-5) Judson.

Devotions for a Deeper Life. Oswald Chambers. Ed. by Glenn D. Black. 320p. 1986. 12.99 (0-310-38710-8, 17070) Zondervan.

Devotions for a New Mother. Mildred Tengbom. LC 83-14928. 127p. 1983. reprint ed. pap. 6.99 (0-87123-294-4) Bethany Hse.

Devotions for Any Occasion. Jerry Hayner. 1987. pap. 4.50 (0-687-10513-7) Abingdon.

Devotions for Church School Teachers. Richard Andersen. LC 76-2158. 64p. 1976. pap. 2.95 (0-570-03722-0, 12-2624) Concordia.

Devotions for Dieters. pap. 5.95 (1-55748-029-X) Barbour & Co.

Devotions for Divorcing. William E. Thompson. LC 85-42827. 96p. 1984. pap. 8.99 (0-8042-2525-7, John Knox) Westminster John Knox.

Devotions for Early Teens, 1. Ruth I. Johnson. (J). (gr. 7-12). 1974. pap. 4.50 (0-8024-2181-4) Moody.

Devotions for Gardeners. Jean Shaw. LC 93-39073. 1994. pap. 12.99 (0-310-37510-X) Zondervan.

Devotions for Graduates. Hester Monsma. 25p. (Orig.). 1984. pap. 2.49 (0-8010-2939-2) Baker Bk.

***Devotions for Kindred Spirits.** Roy B. Zock. LC 95-13296. 392p. 1983. pap. 10.99 (0-8254-4065-3) Kregel.

Devotions for Later Years. Wallace Fridy. 1991. pap. 6.25 (0-687-10516-1) Abingdon.

***Devotions for Little Boys & Girls: Jesus & His Friends.** Joan C. Webb. LC 94-67874. (Illus.). 112p. (Orig.). (J). 1995. pap. 6.99 (0-7847-0295-0, 12-02755) Standard Pub.

Devotions for Little Boys & Girls: New Testament. Joan C. Webb. (Illus.). 112p. (J). (ps-00). 1992. pap. 5.99 (0-87403-682-8, 12-02822) Standard Pub.

Devotions for Little Boys & Girls: Old Testament. Joan C. Webb. (Illus.). 112p. (Orig.). (J). (ps-00). 1992. pap. 5.99 (0-87403-681-X, 12-02821) Standard Pub.

***Devotions for Little Boys & Girls: What Is God Like?** Joan C. Webb. LC 94-67875. (Illus.). 112p. (Orig.). (J). 1995. pap. 6.99 (0-7847-0294-2, 12-02754) Standard Pub.

Devotions for Living with Loss. Mary C. Miller. 1991. 7.95 (0-910452-72-5) Covenant.

Devotions for Mothers. Hester Monsma. 30p. 1984. pap. 1.99 (0-8010-2942-2) Baker Bk.

***Devotions for New Moms.** Ruth Conrad. 1996. 9.99 (0-87788-172-3) Shaw Pubs.

Devotions for New Mothers. Bonnie Taylor. 128p. 1987. 12.00 (0-8170-1081-5); pap. 10.00 (0-8170-1115-3) Judson.

Devotions for New Parents. Alfred M. Buls. (Orig.). 1972. pap. 1.95 (0-570-03675-5, 74-1010) Concordia.

Devotions for the Alcoholic Christian. Carl Nelson. Ed. by Michael Sherer. (Orig.). 1988. pap. 5.00 (1-55673-033-0, 8817) CSS OH.

Devotions for the Blended Family. Margaret Smith-Broersma. LC 94-17861. 160p. 1994. pap. 10.99 (0-8254-2150-0) Kregel.

Devotions for the Children's Hour. 2nd ed. Kenneth Taylor. (J). (gr. 1-8). 1987. pap. 7.99 (0-8024-2226-8) Moody.

Devotions for the Children's Hour see Meditaciones para Ninos

Devotions for the Holy Souls. Reginald Cap. 1989. pap. 22.00 (0-86217-299-3, Pub. by Veritas IE) St Mut.

Devotions for Women in the Workplace. Miriam Neff. 1991. pap. 7.99 (0-8024-1727-2) Moody.

***Devotions for Young Readers.** Janet Bair. (Illus.). 224p. (J). 1995. pap. 9.99 (0-7847-0331-0, 12-02756) Standard Pub.

Devotions for Youth Groups on the Go. Cindy Hansen & Dan Hansen. 96p. 1992. pap. 11.99 (1-55945-075-4) Group Pub.

Devotions from Famous Hymn Stories. Lindsay Terry. (Good Morning Lord Ser.). 1974. pap. 4.99 (0-8010-8882-8) Baker Bk.

***Devotions to Strengthen Your Walk with God.** Busha. (Proverbs for Busy Women Ser.: Vol. 1). 1995. pap. text ed. (0-8054-5386-5) Broadman.

Devotions to the Saints. Anna Riva. 112p. 1982. pap. 4.50 (0-943832-08-X) Intl Imports.

Devotions upon Emergent Occasions. John Donne. Ed. by Anthony Raspa. LC 76-361973. 248p. reprint ed. pap. 70.70 (0-317-26281-5, 2024263) Bks Demand.

Devour the Snow. Abe Polsky. 1979. pap. 4.75 (0-8222-0304-9) Dramatists Play.

Devouring. Douglas D. Hawk. 368p. (Orig.). 1994. mass mkt., pap. text ed. 4.50 (0-8439-3642-8) Dorchester Pub Co.

Devouring Fungus, Tales of the Computer Age. Karla Jennings. 1990. pap. 10.95 (0-393-30732-8) Norton.

Devouring Whirlwind: Terror & Transcendence in the Cinema of Cruelty. Will H. Rockett. LC 88-10254. (Contributions to the Study of Popular Culture Ser.: No. 21). 221p. 1988. text ed. 49.95 (0-313-25998-4, RCY/, Greenwood Pr) Greenwood.

Devout Humanism As a Style. Cecilian Streebing. LC 70-128930. (Catholic University Romance Literature Ser.: No. 50). reprint ed. 37.50 (0-404-50350-0) AMS Pr.

Devoutly I Adore Thee: The Hymns & Prayers of St. Thomas Aquinas. St. Thomas Aquinas. Ed. by Robert Anderson & Johann Moser. Tr. by Johann Moser. LC 93-37487. 122p. 1993. 13.95 (0-918477-19-0) Sophia Inst Pr.

Devs of Cincvad: A Lineage & State in Maharashtra. Laurence W. Preston. 300p. 1989. 64.95 (0-521-34633-9) Cambridge U Pr.

Dew Drop Dead. James Howe. 128p. (YA). 1991. pap. 3.99 (0-380-71301-2, Camelot) Avon.

Dew Drop Dead: A Sebastian Barth Mystery. James Howe. LC 89-34697. (Sebastian Barth Mysteries Ser.). 160p. (J). (gr. 3-7). 1990. text ed. 14.00 (0-689-31425-6, Atheneum Bks Young) S&S Childrens.

Dew of Hermon. Janis Fedor. LC 88-72110. 320p. (Orig.). 1989. pap. 5.95 (0-918897-04-1) Devonshire Pub.

DeWain Valentine. Peter Plagens. 24p. 1975. 7.00 (0-686-99813-8) Mus Contemp Art.

Dewar Manuscripts. 397p. 1982. 75.00 (0-85335-004-3, Pub. by Stuart Titles Ltd UK); pap. 20.00 (0-685-06806-4, Pub. by Stuart Titles Ltd UK) St Mut.

Dewatering: Avoiding Its Unwanted Side Effects. J. Patrick Powers. (C). 1986. 115.00 (0-685-54221-1, Scientific) St Mut.

Dewatering: Avoiding Its Unwanted Side Effects. American Society of Civil Engineers Staff. Ed. by J. Patrick Powers. LC 85-70483. (Illus.). 84p. reprint ed. pap. 25.00 (0-8357-8676-5, 2056833) Bks Demand.

Dewatering-Avoiding Its Unwanted Side Effects. Ed. by J. Patrick Powers. (C). 1987. reprint ed. text ed. 100.00 (0-685-22082-6, Scientific) St Mut.

Dewatering Municipal Wastewater Sludges. Orris E. Albertson et al. LC 90-23202. (Pollution Technology Review Ser.: No. 202). (Illus.). 189p. 1991. 45.00 (0-8155-1266-X) Noyes.

Dewatring-Avoiding Its Unwanted Side Effects. Ed. by J. P. Powers. (C). 1987. text ed. 55.00 (0-685-61675-4, Pub. by Scientific Pubs II) St Mut.

Dewdney, the Magic Machine: More Computer Recreations from Scientific American. A. K. Dewdney. LC 90-31250. 320p. 1995. text ed. write for info. (0-7167-2125-2); pap. text ed. write for info. (0-7167-2144-9) W H Freeman.

Dewdrops of Wisdom. Foundation of I, Inc. Staff. (Illus.). 62p. (Orig.). 1984. reprint ed. pap. text ed. 7.50 (1-878791-05-2) Found Of I.

Dewdrops on a Lotus Leaf. Norma N. Bordeaux. (Illus.). 28p. 1974. pap. 2.95 (0-89564-076-7) IBS Intl.

Dewdrops on a Lotus Leaf: Zen Poems of Ryokan. Ryokan. Ed. & Tr. by John Stevens. LC 93-20221. (Centaur Editions Ser.). (Illus.). 172p. (Orig.). 1993. pap. 11.00 (0-87773-884-X) Shambhala Pubns.

Deweese & Saunders Otolaryngology Head & Neck. Schuller & Schleining. 550p. 1993. 62.00 (0-8016-6842-5) Mosby Yr Bk.

Dewey. Jim E. Tiles. 256p. 1989. 39.50 (0-415-00908-1) Routledge.

Dewey. Jim E. Tiles. 284p. 1991. pap. 16.95 (0-415-05310-2, A5236) Routledge.

Dewey: An International Perspective. 173p. 1991. 55.00 (3-598-11060-X) K G Saur.

Dewey & His Critics. John Dewey. Ed. by Sidney Morgenbesser. LC 77-94488. 752p. (C). 1977. lib. bdg. 37.50 (0-931206-00-6); pap. text ed. 19.50 (0-931206-01-4) Hackett Pub.

***Dewey Bartlett Legacy.** Bob Burke. Ed. by Kenny A. Franks & Gini M. Campbell. (Oklahoma Statesmen Ser.). (Illus.). 215p. 1995. 20.00 (1-885596-01-4) OK Heritage.

Dewey Decimal Classification. Marie-Jose Shaw. (Sound Filmstrip Kits Ser.). (gr. 4-8). 1981. teacher ed 34.00 (0-8209-0447-3, FCW-24) ESP.

Dewey Decimal Classification: A Practical Guide. Lois M. Chan et al. LC 93-23733. 211p. 1994. pap. 40.00 (0-910608-49-0) Forest Pr.

Dewey Decimal Classification: A Study Manual. 20th ed. John P. Comaromi. 303p. 1991. lib. bdg. 45.00 (0-87287-870-8) Libs Unl.

Dewey Decimal Classification: History & Current Status. John P. Comaromi & M. P. Satija. 300p. 1988. pap. text ed. 25.00 (0-938719-30-0, Envoy Pr); pap. text ed. 10.95 (0-938719-35-1, Envoy Pr) Apt Bks.

Dewey Decimal Classification: 200 Religion Class. LC 89-27221. 191p. 1989. reprint ed. pap. 15.00 (0-910608-43-1) Forest Pr.

Dewey Decimal Classification: 200 Schedules Expanded for Use. rev. ed. Mary C. Bauer. iii, 113p. (Orig.). 1988. pap. 25.00 (0-87507-042-6) Cath Lib Assn.

Dewey Decimal Classification & Relative Index, 3 vols. 18th ed. Incl. Vol. 1. Introduction & Tables. LC 78-140002. 20.00 (0-910608-10-5); Vol. 2. Schedules. LC 78-140002. 20.00 (0-685-01661-7); Vol. 3. Index. LC 78-140002. 20.00 (0-910608-11-3); LC 78-140002. (Illus.). 2692p. 1971. Set. 60.00 (0-685-26876-4) Forest Pr.

Dewey Decimal Classification & Relative Index, 4 vols., Set. 20th ed. Melvil Dewey. LC 88-24629. 1989. 275.00 (0-910608-37-7) Forest Pr.

Dewey Decimal Classification for British Schools: Introduction. 4th ed. Ed. by Mary L. South. 179p. 1986. 40.00 (0-910608-35-0) Forest Pr.

Dewey Experiment in China: Educational Reform & Political Power in the Early Republic. Barry Keenan. (East Asian Monographs: No. 81). 350p. 1977. 22.50 (0-674-20277-5) HUP.

Dewey on Education: Selections, with an Introduction & Notes. Ed. by Martin Dworkin. LC 59-15893. (Classics in Education Ser.). (Illus.). 1959. pap. text ed. 7.00 (0-8077-1263-9) Tchrs Coll.

Dewey, Russell, Whitehead: Philosophers as Educators. Brian Hendley. LC 85-2148. 200p. (Orig.). (C). 1985. pap. text ed. 14.95 (0-8093-1243-3) S Ill U Pr.

Dewey y la Crisis de la Education en los Estados Unidos. Jose Sanchez-Boudy. LC 89-85122. (Coleccion Polymita Ser.). 177p. (Orig.). (SPA.). 1990. pap. 12.00 (0-89729-547-1) Ediciones.

Dewey's Amusing Rubber Antics. Ralph G. Dewey. 16p. 1989. pap. 3.50 (1-880215-09-8) Deweys GNB.

Dewey's Balloon & Clown Notebook. Ralph G. Dewey. 52p. 1981. pap. 5.50 (1-880215-00-4) Deweys GNB.

Dewey's Basic Balloon Sculpturing Course. Ralph G. Dewey. 12p. 1978. pap. 3.50 (1-880215-10-1) Deweys GNB.

Dewey's Bubble Buddies. Ralph G. Dewey. 48p. 1978. pap. 4.50 (1-880215-07-1) Deweys GNB.

Dewey's Celebrity Balloons. Ralph G. Davey. 36p. 1994. pap. text ed. 6.00 (1-880215-22-5) Deweys GNB.

Dewey's Clown Gags & Giggles. Ralph G. Dewey. 32p. 1990. pap. 5.00 (1-880215-13-6) Deweys GNB.

Dewey's Easy Gospel Chalk Talks. Ralph G. Dewey. 48p. 1983. pap. 4.50 (1-880215-02-0) Deweys GNB.

***Dewey's Ethical Thought.** Jennifer Welchman. 256p. 1995. 35.00x (0-8014-2729-0) Cornell U Pr.

Dewey's Extra Easy Balloons. Ralph G. Dewey. 32p. 1987. pap. 4.00 (1-880215-15-2) Deweys GNB.

Dewey's Gospel Balloon Routines, No. 1. Ralph G. Dewey. 14p. 1977. pap. 3.50 (1-880215-04-7) Deweys GNB.

Dewey's Gospel Balloon Routines, No. 2. Ralph G. Dewey. 32p. 1985. pap. 4.00 (1-880215-05-5) Deweys GNB.

Dewey's Gospel Balloon Routines, No. 3. Ralph G. Dewey. 28p. 1988. pap. 4.00 (1-880215-06-3) Deweys GNB.

Dewey's Gospel Cartoon Chalk Talks. Ralph G. Dewey. 36p. 1979. pap. 4.00 (1-880215-01-2) Deweys GNB.

Dewey's Gospel Cartoon Fun. Ralph G. Dewey. 32p. 1989. pap. 4.00 (1-880215-03-9) Deweys GNB.

Dewey's Gospel Clown Skits, No. 1. Ralph G. Dewey. 30p. 1986. pap. 4.00 (1-880215-18-7) Deweys GNB.

Dewey's Gospel Clown Skits, No. 2. Ralph G. Dewey. 32p. 1992. pap. 4.00 (1-880215-21-7) Deweys GNB.

Dewey's Gospel Juggling Skits. Ralph G. Dewey. 16p. 1990. pap. 3.50 (1-880215-12-8) Deweys GNB.

Dewey's Gospel Paper Tricks. Ralph G. Dewey. 28p. 1991. pap. 4.00 (1-880215-14-4) Deweys GNB.

***Dewey's Klown Komedy.** Ralph G. Dewey. 36p. 1994. pap. text ed. 6.00 (1-880215-23-3) Deweys GNB.

Dewey's Mammoth Multiple Balloons. Ralph G. Dewey. 28p. 1985. pap. 4.00 (1-880215-08-X) Deweys GNB.

Dewey's Metaphysics. Raymond D. Boisvert. LC 88-80074. xii, 227p. 1988. 35.00 (0-8232-1196-7) Fordham.

Dewey's New Balloon Animals. Ralph G. Dewey. 46p. 1976. pap. 5.00 (1-880215-11-X) Deweys GNB.

Dewey's New Logic: A Reply to Russell. Tom Burke. LC 94-1618. 1994. 32.00 (0-226-08069-2) U Ch Pr.

Dewey's Rubber Rascals. Ralph G. Dewey. 44p. 1984. pap. 5.00 (1-880215-16-0) Deweys GNB.

Dewey's Supressed Psychology. Scudder Klyce. LC 75-3215. reprint ed. 42.00 (0-404-59211-2) AMS Pr.

Dewey's Zany Balloons. Ralph G. Dewey. 44p. 1991. pap. 4.00 (1-880215-17-9) Deweys GNB.

Dewhurst's Paediatric & Adolescent Gynaecology. John Dewhurst & D. K. Edmonds. (Illus.). 148p. 1989. text ed. 150.00 (0-407-01520-5) Buttrwrth-Heinemann.

Dewhurst's Textbook of Obstetrics & Gynaecology for Postgraduates. C. R. Whitfield. 550p. 1994. write for info. (0-632-02547-6) Blackwell Sci.

Dewi. William Constandse. 168p. 1983. pap. 6.95 (0-317-01757-8) Utama Pubns Inc.

DEX-UCS Service Supplier Directory. 1990. 15.00 (0-318-50037-X) Uniform Code.

Dexter Gordon: A Musical Biography. Stan Britt. (Quality Paperbacks Ser.). (Illus.). 192p. 1989. pap. 11.95 (0-306-80361-5) Da Capo.

***Dexterity & Its Development.** N. A. Bernstein. Ed. by Mark L. Latash & Michael Turvey. (Resources for Ecological Psychology Ser.). 500p. 1995. text ed. 75.00 (0-8058-1646-1) L Erlbaum Assocs.

Dextrous Robot Hands. Ed. by S. T. Venkataraman & T. Iberall. (Illus.). viii, 345p. 1989. 59.00 (0-387-97190-4, 3671) Spr-Verlag.

Dextrous Robotic Hands. Richard K. Miller & Terri C. Walker. LC 88-80903. (Survey on Technology & Markets Ser.: No. 19). 50p. 1989. pap. text ed. 200.00 (1-55865-018-0) Future Tech Surveys.

Deyo (Deyoe) Family. Kenneth E. Hasbrouck & Ruth P. Heidgerd. 547p. 1980. 53.00 (0-318-14366-6) Huguenot Hist.

Dezbah & the Dancing Tumbleweeds. Margaret K. Garaway. (Illus.). 175p. (Orig.). (J). (gr. 3-5). 1990. pap. 7.95 (0-918080-50-9) Treas Chest Bks.

***Dezbah & the Dancing Tumbleweeds.** 2nd ed. Margaret K. Garaway. (Illus.). 82p. (Orig.). (J). (gr. 4-8). 1994. pap. 7.95 (0-9638851-2-X) Old Hogan Pubng.

DFaster DBetter. R. David Dornbusch. 100p. 1984. ring bd. 35.00 (0-930627-12-1) Paradigm Comm.

***DFT: An Owner's Manual for the Discrete Fourier Transform.** William L. Briggs & Van E. Henson. LC 95-3232. 1995. pap. 37.50 (0-89871-342-0) Soc Indus-Appl Math.

DFT-FFT & Convolution Algorithms & Implementation. C. S. Burrus & Thomas W. Parks. LC 84-18808. (Topics in Digital Signal Processing Ser.). 232p. 1985. pap. text ed. 64.95 (0-471-81932-8) Wiley.

DG: Memoirs of a British Broadcaster. Alasdair Milne. (Illus.). 236p. 1989. 29.95 (0-340-42772-8, Pub. by H & S UK) Trafalgar.

***dGeneral Index to the Documents Relating to the Colonial History of the State of New Jersey: First Series, in Ten Volumes.** Frederick W. Ricord. 198p. 1994. 22.50 (0-614-03824-3, 4895) Genealog Pub.

DH 88: The Story of the DeHaviland Racing Comet. David Ogilvy. LC 84-73107. (Illus.). 174p. 1985. 19.95 (0-911139-02-8) Flying Bks.

Dhahr Mirzbaneh Tombs: Three Intermediate Bronze Age Cemeteries in Jordan. Paul W. Lapp. (American Schools of Oriental Research Publications of the Jerusalem School Archaeology: Vol. 4). x, 117p. 1966. pap. text ed. 12.50 (0-317-04129-0) Am Schls Oriental.

Dhahran's American Consulate: The History of the United States Consulate General Dhahran, Saudi Arabia. Kay H. Campbell. (Illus.). 82p. (Orig.). 1991. pap. 12.95 (0-9615945-3-5) Chiefton Pub.

Dhaka Summit an SAARC. Pramod K. Mishra. (C). 1986. 9.50 (81-7074-000-2, Pub. by KP Bagchi IA) S Asia.

Dhammapada. ix, 139p. 1955. 3.00 (0-317-00026-8) Cunningham Pr.

Dhammapada. (Life Companion Library). 116p. (Orig.). 1983. pap. 3.95 (0-89744-016-1) Auromere.

Dhammapada. Nikunja V. Banerjee. (C). 1989. 19.50 (0-685-37834-9, Pub. by Munshiram Manoharial II) S Asia.

Dhammapada. Gautama Buddha. Tr. by Irving Babbitt. LC 64-23655. 1965. pap. 7.95 (0-8112-0004-3, NDP188) New Directions.

Dhammapada. Gautama Buddha. Tr. by K. Sri Dhammananda. (Illus.). 669p. (C). 1988. text ed. 39.95 (983-99523-0-7, Buddhist Missionary Society) Wisdom MA.

Dhammapada. Buddha Sakyamuni. Ed. & Tr. by Dharma Publishing Staff. Tr. by Gedun Choephel. (Tibetan Translation Ser.: Vol. 12). (Illus.). 381p. (Orig.). 1985. pap. 17.95 (0-913546-98-4) Dharma Pub.

Dhammapada. Tr. by John R. Carter & Mahinda Palihawadana. 544p. 1987. 65.00 (0-19-504162-3) OUP.

Dhammapada. Tr. by Eknath Easwaran. 75.00 (0-939489-10-4) Engdahl Typo.

Dhammapada. Intro. by Eknath Easwaran & Stephen Ruppenthal. LC 85-29869. 1986. 18.00 (0-915132-38-9); pap. 9.95 (0-915132-37-0) Nilgiri Pr.

Dhammapada. Tr. by Juan Mascaro. (Classics Ser.). 1973. mass mkt. 7.95 (0-14-044284-7, Penguin Classics) Viking Penguin.

Dhammapada. 3rd ed. Bhuddha. 24p. 1973. pap. 3.50 (0-942401-03-4) Am Vegan Soc.

Dhammapada: Anonymous Translation with Explanatory Notes & a Short Essay on Buddha's Thought. ix, 139p. 1955. 4.00 (0-938998-16-1) Theosophy.

Dhammapada: Sayings of Buddha. Tr. by Thomas Cleary. LC 94-16628. 1995. pap. 6.95 (0-553-37376-5) Bantam.

***Dhammapada: The Path of Truth.** Buddha. Tr. by Ananda Maitreya & Rose Kramer. 110p. (Orig.). 1995. pap. 7.00 (0-938077-87-2) Parallax Pr.

Dhammapada: The Sayings of the Buddha. Thomas Byrom. LC 93-535. (Pocket Classics Ser.). 144p. 1993. pap. 6.00 (0-87773-966-8) Shambhala Pubns.

Dhammapada: The Way of the Buddha, 12 vols. Osho. Ed. by Swami Krishna Prabhu. Incl. 1991. Vol. I, 253p. (3-89338-091-4); 1991. Vol. II, 258p. (3-89338-092-2); 1991. Vol. III, 258p. (3-89338-093-0); 1991. Vol. IV, 265p. (3-89338-094-9); 1991. Vol. V, 264p. (3-89338-095-7); 1991. Vol. VI, 281p. (3-89338-096-5); 1991. Vol. VII, 229p. (3-89338-097-3); 1991. Vol. VIII, 310p. (3-89338-098-1); 1991. Vol. IX, 232p. (3-89338-099-X); 1991. Vol. X, 313p. (3-318-68806-9); 1991. Vol. XI, 239p. (3-89338-101-5); 1991. Vol. XII, 247p. (3-89338-102-3); (Buddha Ser.). 3149p. 1991. Set boxed 166.00 (0-685-50849-8, Pub. by Rebel Hse GW) Osho Chidvilas.

Dhammapada, Wisdom of the Buddha. Tr. by Harischandra Kaviratna. LC 80-52031. 211p. 1980. 14.00 (0-911500-39-1); pap. 9.00 (0-911500-40-5) Theos U Pr.

Dhamnapada Sanskrit Text. N. V. Banerjee. (C). 1989. 21.50 (0-685-30708-5, Pub. by Munshiram Manoharial II) S Asia.

Dharani Sutra. Tr. by Buddhist Text Translation Society Staff. 328p. 1976. pap. 300.00 (0-917512-13-8) Buddhist Text.

Dharma. Annie Besant. 1986. 4.50 (0-8356-7116-X) Theos Pub Hse.

Dharma. Roberto Valero. LC 85-70432. (Coleccion Espejo de Paciencia Ser.). (Illus.). 70p. (Orig.). (SPA.). 1985. pap. 8.95 (0-89729-371-1) Ediciones.

Dharma: That Benefits All Beings Impartially Like the Light of the Sun & Moon. Kalu Rinpoche. LC 86-5941. 222p. 1986. 49.50 (0-88706-156-7); pap. 16.95 (0-88706-157-5) State U NY Pr.

***Dharma & Development: Religion As Resource in the Sarvodaya Self-Help Movement.** fac. rev. ed. Joanna Macy. LC 85-236. (Illus.). 119p. 1994. pap. 34.00 (0-7837-7573-3, 2047326) Bks Demand.

Dharma Bums. Jack Kerouac. 1976. 20.95 (0-8488-1399-5) Amereon Ltd.

Dharma Bums. Jack Kerouac. 192p. 1976. lib. bdg. 21.95 (0-89966-135-1) Buccaneer Bks.

Dharma Bums. Jack Kerouac. 1959. pap. 3.95 (0-451-15275-1, Sig) NAL-Dutton.

Dharma Bums. Jack Kerouac. 256p. 1971. pap. 10.95 (0-14-004252-0, Penguin Bks) Viking Penguin.

Dharma Family Treasures: Sharing Mindfulness with Children. Ed. by Sandy Eastoak. LC 93-24517. 280p. 1994. pap. 14.95 (1-55643-172-4) North Atlantic.

Dharma Flower Sutra: Belief & Understanding, Vol. V. Tr. by Buddhist Text Translation Society. (Illus.). 200p. (Orig.). (C). 1980. pap. 8.00 (0-917512-64-2) Buddhist Text.

Dharma Flower Sutra: Devadatta, Vol. X. Tr. by Buddhist Text Translation Society Staff. 150p. (Orig.). 1982. pap. 7.50 (0-917512-34-0) Buddhist Text.

Dharma Flower Sutra: Expedient Methods, Vol. III. Tr. by Buddhist Text Translation Society. (Illus.). 183p. (Orig.). 1979. pap. 8.00 (0-917512-26-X) Buddhist Text.

D

An Asterisk (*) at the beginning of an entry indicates that the title is appearing in BIP for the first time.

Dharma Flower Sutra: Introduction, Vol. II. Tr. by Buddhist Text Translation Society. (Illus.). 324p. (Orig.). (CHI.). 1978. pap. 9.00 (*0-917512-22-7*) Buddhist Text.

Dharma Flower Sutra: Masters of the Dharma, Vol. IX. Tr. by Buddhist Text Translation Society. (Illus.). 270p. (Orig.). (C). 1981. pap. 8.50 (*0-917512-85-5*) Buddhist Text.

Dharma Flower Sutra: Medicinal Herbs, Vol. VI. Tr. by Buddhist Text Translation Society. (Illus.). 161p. (Orig.). (C). 1980. pap. 8.00 (*0-917512-65-0*) Buddhist Text.

Dharma Flower Sutra; Vol. I: Introduction. Comment by Tripitaka Master Hua & Buddhist Text Translation Society. (Illus.). 85p. (Orig.). 1977. pap. 5.00 (*0-917512-16-2*) Buddhist Text.

Dharma Flower Sutra, Vol. IV: A Parable. Tr. by Buddhist Text Translation Society. (Illus.). 371p. (Orig.). (C). 1979. pap. 9.00 (*0-917512-62-6*) Buddhist Text.

Dharma Flower Sutra, Vol. VII: Parable of the Transformation City. Tr. by Buddhist Text Translation Society. (Illus.). 250p. (Orig.). 1980. pap. 8.50 (*0-917512-67-7*) Buddhist Text.

Dharma Flower Sutra, Vol. VIII: Five Hundred Disciples Receive Predictions. Tr. by Buddhist Text Translation Society. (Illus.). 160p. (Orig.). 1980. pap. 8.00 (*0-917512-71-5*) Buddhist Text.

Dharma Flower Sutra, Vol. VIII: Five Hundred Disciples Receive Predictions, Set. Tr. by Buddhist Text Translation Society. (Illus.). 160p. (Orig.). 1980. 79.50 (*0-685-57673-6*) Buddhist Text.

Dharma for All. 264p. 1987. pap. 2.95 (*0-87481-539-8*, Pub. by Ramakrishna Math II) Vedanta Pr.

Dharma Gaia: A Harvest of Essays in Buddhism & Ecology. Ed. by Allan Hunt-Badiner. LC 90-34216. (Illus.). 268p. (Orig.). 1990. per., pap. 15.00 (*0-938077-30-9*) Parallax Pr.

Dharma Lion: A Biography of Allen Ginsberg. Michael Schumacher. (Illus.). 752p. 1992. 35.00 (*0-312-08179-0*) St Martin.

Dharma Lion: A Biography of Allen Ginsberg. Michael Schumacher. 784p. 1994. pap. 18.95 (*0-312-11263-7*) St Martin.

***Dharma: or The Religion of Enlightenment: An Exposition of Buddhism.** Paul Carus. 134p. 1995. pap. 11.00 (*0-89540-325-0*) Sun Pub.

Dharma; or, the Religious Enlightenment; an Exposition of Buddhism. 5th enl. rev. ed. Paul Carus. LC 78-72393. reprint ed. 24.00 (*0-404-17253-9*) AMS Pr.

Dharma Paths. Khenpo Karthar. Ed. by Laura M. Roth. 270p. (Orig.). 1993. pap. 14.95 (*1-55939-002-6*) Snow Lion Pubns.

Dharma Realm Buddhist University Catalog 1983. (Illus.). 246p. (Orig.). pap. 10.00 (*0-88139-000-3*) Buddhist Text.

Dharma-Samgraha, an Ancient Collection of Buddhist Technical Terms. Kenju Kasawara. Ed. by F. Max Muller & H. Wenzel. LC 78-72425. reprint ed. 17.50 (*0-404-17286-5*) AMS Pr.

***Dharma Talks by a Living Buddha.** Sheng-Yen Lu. Tr. by Janny Chow. LC 94-36517. 1994. pap. 10.00 (*1-881493-05-9*) Purple Lotus Soc.

Dharma's Daughters: Contemporary Indian Women & Hindu Culture. Sara S. Mitter. LC 90-19387. (Illus.). 250p. (C). 1991. text ed. 40.00 (*0-8135-1677-3*); pap. 12.95 (*0-8135-1678-1*) Rutgers U Pr.

***Dharmic Challenge: Putting Sathya Sai Baba's Teachings into Practice.** Ed. & Comp. by Judy Warner. 190p. (Orig.). 1995. pap. 12.00 (*0-9629835-6-X*) Leela Pr.

Dhatu Katha Pakarana & Its Commentary. Ed. by Edmund R. Gooneratne. LC 78-72426. reprint ed. 21.50 (*0-404-17287-3*) AMS Pr.

Dhaulagiri - und Annapurna-Himalaya, Pts. 1-2: Ein Beitrag Zur Geomorphologie Extremer Hochgebirge, Atlas & Text. M. Kuhle. (Annals of Gemorphology Supplement Ser.: Vol. 41). (Illus.). 229p. (GER.). 1982. pap. text ed. 135.80 (*3-443-21041-4*, Pub. by Gebrueder Borntraeger GW) Lubrecht & Cramer.

***DHEA: Unlocking the Secrets to the Fountain of Youth. James Jamieson & Beth Ley. 176p. (Orig.). 1995. pap. 14.95 (*0-9642703-3-1*) B L Pubns.**
THE HOTTEST ANTI-AGING NEWS AROUND THE WORLD IS ON DHEA! DHEA, produced by the adrenal glands, is the precursor hormone to estrogen, progesterone, testosterone & all of the other corticosteroids in the body. Levels of this amazing pro-hormone are highest when we are in the prime of life, age 18-25, after which production gradually begins to slow down. Supplemental DHEA has therapeutic potential for numerous medical conditions. Studies show that an increase in blood levels of DHEA is associated with a 36% reduction in mortality from any cause. Studies also show that we can actually prevent disease if we can maintain high levels of DHEA! AND WE CAN! Safely & naturally through supplementation from an extract from a food grown in Mexico, wild yams! James Jamieson, Pharmacologist, & nutrition writer Beth Ley, tell you how you may benefit from DHEA, & how it may even save your life! Find out why stress is your worst enemy against healthy DHEA levels & against degenerate diseases associated with aging! Find out how to end PMS, symptoms of menopause, osteoporosis, heart disease, sexual problems, diabetes, high cholesterol, obesity, cancer, Alzheimer's, memory deficits, autoimmune diseases, immune disorders, chronic fatigue, & the list goes on, & on.
Publisher Provided Annotation.

***DHHS Infant Care.** 1993. pap. 4.00 (*0-614-06324-8*) Claitors.

***DHHS Social Security Handbook.** 1993. pap. 20.00 (*0-87511-630-2*) Claitors.

Dhimals Miraculour Migrants of Himalyan Anthropological Study of a Nepalese Ethnic Group. R. R. Regmi. (C). 1991. text ed. 75.00 (*0-7855-0133-9*, Pub. by Ratna Pustak Bhandar) St Mut.

Dhimmi: Jews & Christians under Islam. Bat Ye'or. Tr. by David Maisel et al. LC 84-47749. (Illus.). 444p. 1985. 39.50 (*0-8386-3233-5*) Fairleigh Dickinson.

***Dhodia: Industrialisation & Change in a Primitive Community.** Amitabha Sarkar. (C). 1994. 20.00 (*81-212-0442-9*, Pub. by Gian Publng Hse II) S Asia.

Dhow Chasing in Zanzibar Waters & on the Eastern Coast of Africa. G. L. Sulivan. (Illus.). 453p. 1968. reprint ed. 35.50 (*0-7146-1855-1*, BHA-01855, Pub. by F Cass Pubs UK) Intl Spec Bk.

Dhvanyaloka of Anandavardhana with the Locana of Abhinavagupta. Anandavardhana & Abhinavagupta. Tr. by Daniel H. Ingalls et al. LC 88-8806. (Oriental Ser.: No. 49). 873p. 1990. 50.00 (*0-674-20278-3*) HUP.

Dhyana. M. P. Pandit. 60p. 1990. reprint ed. pap. 1.95 (*0-941524-03-5*) Lotus Light.

Di & Dock on the Mountain Top. S. Diane Sholley. Ed. by Sandra Sholley. LC 93-72604. (Mountain Top Ser.). (Orig.). 1993. pap. 19.95 (*0-9638204-0-0*) Aaronwood.

Di & I. Peter Lefcourt. LC 93-38837. 1994. 20.00 (*0-679-42583-7*) Random.

***Di & I: A Novel.** Peter Lefcourt. 1995. pap. 12.00 (*0-06-097668-3*, PL) HarpC.

Di-Dos of a Farm Boy in the Roaring Twenties. Howard W. Werry. LC 83-51839. (Illus.). 200p. 1984. 7.95 (*0-916405-00-1*) Wilmot Pub Co.

Di Fiore's Atlas of Histology with Functional Correlations. 7th ed. Victor Eroschenko. (Illus.). 350p. 1992. spiral bd. 35.95 (*0-8121-1560-0*) Williams & Wilkins.

***Di Fiore's Atlas of Histology with Functional Correlations.** 8th ed. Victor P. Eroschenko. LC 94-47275. 1995. write for info. (*0-683-02818-9*) Williams & Wilkins.

***Di Serambi: On the Verandah: A Bilingual Anthology of Modern Indonesian Poetry.** Ed. by Iem Brown & Joan Davis. (Illus.). 180p. (C). 1995. 49.95 (*0-521-47202-4*) Cambridge U Pr.

***Di Serambi: On the Verandah: A Bilingual Anthology of Modern Indonesian Poetry.** Ed. by Iem Brown & Joan Davis. (Illus.). 180p. (C). 1995. pap. 12.95 (*0-521-47714-X*) Cambridge U Pr.

Di-(2-Ethylhexyl) Phthalate. (BUA Report Ser.: Vol. 4). 75p. 1993. pap. 48.00 (*1-56081-234-6*) VCH Pubs.

Dia de Bodas. Pablo A. Deiros. 174p. (Orig.). (SPA.). 1987. pap. text ed. 5.95 (*0-89922-237-4*) Edit Caribe.

Dia de Fiesta por la Manana & El Dia de Fiesta por la Tarde. Juan De Zabaleta. reprint ed. write for info. (*0-318-71631-3*, Pub. by Georg Olms GW) Lubrecht & Cramer.

Dia de Futbol. Lynn Salem & Josie Stewart. Tr. by Mariana Robles. (Illus.). 8p. (J). (gr. 1). 1994. pap. 3.50 (*1-880612-27-5*) Seedling Pubns.

Dia de las Madres. 32p. 1990. reprint ed. pap. 1.50 (*0-311-07301-8*) Casa Bautista.

Dia de los Muertos: Day of the Dead. Alternative Museum Staff. LC 88-83426. (Illus.). 1988. pap. 10.00 (*0-932075-23-1*) Alternative Mus.

Dia de los Muertos, No. 3: Homelessness. Alternative Museum Staff. LC 90-55614. (Orig.). 1990. pap. 10.00 (*0-932075-32-0*) Alternative Mus.

***Dia de Miranda para Bailar.** Jackie Schaefer. (J). 1994. 14.95 (*0-02-781112-3*, Aladdin Paperbacks) S&S Childrens.

Dia de Nieve. Ezra J. Keats. (Illus.). 32p. (SPA.). (J). (ps-1). 1991. pap. 4.99 (*0-14-054363-5*, Puffin) Puffin Bks.

Dia de Nieve. Ezra J. Keats. (SPA.). (J). (ps). 1991. 12.95 (*0-670-83747-4*) Viking Child Bks.

***Dia De Nieve.** Ezra J. Keats. (Illus.). (J). (gr. k-3). 1991. audio, pap. 14.95 (*0-87499-245-1*); audio, pap. 22.95 (*0-87499-246-X*) Live Oak Media.

***Dia De Nieve, 4 bks., Set.** Ezra J. Keats. (Illus.). (J). (gr. k-3). 1991. audio, pap. 31.95 (*0-87499-247-8*) Live Oak Media.

Dia Del Bien, Dia Del Mal (Good Day, Bad Day) A. H. Mottesi. (SPA.). Date not set. 1.79 (*0-685-74927-4*, 498506) Editorial Unilit.

***Dia Feliz - Happy Day.** Ruth Krauss. LC 94-37256. (Illus.). 30p. (SPA.). (J). (ps-3). 1995. 14.95 (*0-06-025450-5*) HarpC Child Bks.

Dia Lluvioso. (J). (ps-3). 1993. pap. 2.25 (*0-307-50064-0*, Golden Pr) Western Pub.

Dia-Logo Therapy: Psychonarration & the Pardes. Mordechai Rotenberg. LC 90-44250. 192p. 1991. text ed. 55.00 (*0-275-92943-4*, C2943, Praeger Pubs) Greenwood.

***Dia Menospensado: Historia de los Presidiarios en Puerto Rico 1793-1993.** Fernando Pico. 198p. 1994. pap. text ed. 9.95 (*0-929157-27-3*) Ediciones Huracan.

Dia por Dia. Anthony Atwell, Jr. LC 85-2691. 96p. (Orig.). 1985. pap. 16.95 (*0-86534-058-7*) Sunstone Pr.

Dia-Tras-Dia Con Billy Graham. Comp. by Joan W. Brown. Orig. Title: Day by Day with Billy Graham. 192p. 1987. reprint ed. 6.50 (*0-311-40039-6*, Edit Mundo) Casa Bautista.

Diabelli Variations: Sixteen Contemporaries of Beethoven on a Waltz Tune. Ed. by William S. Newman. 31p. reprint ed. pap. 25.00 (*0-317-09716-4*, 2004337) Bks Demand.

Diabelli Variations: Variations on a Theme by Fifty Composers & Virtuosos. Anton Diabelli et al. pap. 25.00 (*0-912028-09-2*) Music Treasure.

Diabetes. Paul Almonte & Theresa Desmond. LC 90-45745. (Facts About Ser.). (Illus.). 48p. (J). (gr. 5-6). 1991. text ed. 12.95 (*0-89686-604-1*, Crstwood Hse) Silver Burdett Pr.

Diabetes. James W. Anderson. 224p. 1987. mass mkt. 5.99 (*0-446-34399-4*) Warner Bks.

***Diabetes.** Maria Barnwell & Patsy R. Smith. (Outline Ser.). 300p. (Orig.). (C). 1994. pap. text ed. 16.95 (*1-56930-031-3*) Skidmore Roth Pub.

***Diabetes.** Ed. by Richard M. Cowett. LC 95-810. (Nestle Nutrition Workshop Ser.: Vol. 35). 1995. write for info. (*0-7817-0324-7*) Raven.

Diabetes. Barbara Goodheart. LC 90-31328. (Venture Bks.). (Illus.). 128p. (YA). (gr. 9-12). 1990. lib. bdg. 14.28 (*0-531-10882-1*) Watts.

Diabetes. Elaine Landau. (Understanding Illness Ser.). (Illus.). 64p. (J). (gr. 5-8). 1994. lib. bdg. 15.98 (*0-8050-2988-5*) TFC Bks NY.

Diabetes. Marjorie Little. (Medical Disorders & Their Treatment Ser.). (Illus.). 112p. (YA). (gr. 6-12). 1991. 18.95 (*0-7910-0061-3*) Chelsea Hse.

***Diabetes.** Carol M. Semple. LC 94-26501. (Healthwatch Ser.). (J). 1995. 13.95 (*0-89686-860-5*, Crstwood Hse) Silver Burdett Pr.

Diabetes. Alvin Silverstein et al. LC 93-41199. (Diseases & People Ser.). (Illus.). 128p. (YA). (gr. 6 up). 1994. lib. bdg. 17.95 (*0-89490-464-7*) Enslow Pubs.

Diabetes. Steven Tiger. LC 86-23498. (Understanding Disease Ser.). (Illus.). 72p. (J). (gr. 4-8). 1987. lib. bdg. 13.98 (*0-671-63273-6*, Julian Messner) Silver Burdett Pr.

Diabetes. Wm Brady et al. 40p. 1965. reprint ed. spiral bd. 5.50 (*0-7873-1016-6*) Mokelumne.

Diabetes: A Guide to Living Well. Gary Arsham & Ernest Lowe. LC 88-31040. 396p. (Orig.). 1992. pap. 10.95 (*0-937721-51-4*) Chronimed.

Diabetes: Caring for Your Emotions As Well As Your Health. Jerry Edelwich & Archie Brodsky. LC 86-10868. 256p. 1986. 17.95 (*0-201-10609-4*); pap. 13.46 (*0-201-10608-6*) Addison-Wesley.

Diabetes: Clinical Management. Ed. by Robert Tattersall & Edwin Gale. (Illus.). 382p. 1990. text ed. 59.95 (*0-443-02273-9*) Churchill.

Diabetes: Clinical Science in Practice. Ed. by R. D. Leslie & David C. Robbins. (Illus.). 550p. (C). 1995. 150.00 (*0-521-45029-2*) Cambridge U Pr.

Diabetes: Current Research & Future Directions in Management & Cure. Pasquale Covelli & Melvin Wiedman. LC 88-42643. (Illus.). 159p. (Orig.). 1988. pap. 16.95x (*0-89950-361-6*) McFarland & Co.

Diabetes: Instructor's Guide. Mary D. Litchford & Laura Yordy. (C). 1991. 5.00 (*1-880989-25-5*); 3.5 hd 99.00 (*1-880989-11-5*); 3.5 hd 99.00 (*1-880989-09-3*); 5.25 hd 99.00 (*1-880989-10-7*); 5.25 hd 99.00 (*1-880989-08-5*); 5.00 (*1-880989-24-7*) Case Sftware.

Diabetes: Its Causes & Treatment. Andrew Gold. 11p. 1993. reprint ed. spiral bd. 3.30 (*0-7873-0351-8*) Mokelumne.

Diabetes: Questions You Have - Answers You Need. Paula Brisco. 1993. pap. 9.95 (*1-882606-02-7*) Peoples Med Soc.

***Diabetes: Reducing Your Risk.** Gerald Bernstein. (If It Runs in Your Family Ser.). 1994. 4.99 (*0-553-56906-6*) Bantam.

Diabetes: The Facts That Let You Regain Control of Your Life. Charles Kilo et al. LC 87-6136. 208p. 1987. pap. text ed. 12.95 (*0-471-85801-3*) Wiley.

Diabetes: Your Complete Exercise Guide. Neil F. Gordon. LC 92-39741. (Illus.). 152p. 1993. pap. 40.00x (*0-87322-427-2*, PGOR0427) Human Kinetics.

***Diabetes: 1995 Vital Statistics.** American Diabetes Association Staff. 64p. 1995. pap. 17.50 (*0-945448-43-0*, PMDVS95) Am Diabetes.

Diabetes A to Z. American Diabetes Association Staff. 128p. 1988. 9.95 (*0-945448-03-1*) Am Diabetes.

Diabetes & Artherosclerosis: Molecular Basis & Clinical Aspects. Ed. by Boris Draznin & Robert H. Eckel. 448p. 1993. 79.00 (*0-412-04431-5*) Chapman & Hall.

Diabetes & Atherosclerosis. Ed. by Robert W. Stout. (Developments in Cardiovascular Medicine Ser.). (C). 1992. lib. bdg. 151.50 (*0-7923-1310-0*) Kluwer Ac.

Diabetes & Atherosclerosis: Molecular Basis & Clinical Aspects. Ed. by Boris Draznin & Robert H. Eckel. LC 92-48854. 1993. write for info. (*0-444-01665-1*) Elsevier.

Diabetes & Brief Illness. Marion J. Franz & Judy O. Joynes. 1987. pap. 2.00 (*0-937721-04-2*) Chronimed.

Diabetes & Doing Your Best. Nick Walters. (Illus.). 112p. (Orig.). 1990. 7.95 (*0-911071-01-6*) Olde Maryland.

Diabetes & Exercise. R. C. Cantu. (Illus.). write for info. (*0-318-62009-X*) Mouvement Pubns.

Diabetes & Exercise: Guidelines for Safe & Enjoyable Activity. Marion J. Franz. Ed. by Michael P. Moore. (Illus.). 20p. 1988. 2.50 (*0-937721-05-0*) Chronimed.

Diabetes & Heart Disease. R. J. Jarrett. (Metabolic Aspects of Cardiovascular Disease Ser.: Vol. 2). 1984. 87.25 (*0-444-80536-2*, I-270-84) Elsevier.

Diabetes & Hemostasis. J. Van de Loo. (Journal: Haemostasis: Vol. 17, No. 1). (Illus.). vi, 90p. 1987. pap. 69.00 (*3-8055-4448-0*) S Karger.

Diabetes & Hypoglycemia. Michael T. Murray. LC 93-36307. (Getting Well Naturally Ser.). 1994. pap. 9.95 (*1-55958-426-2*) Prima Pub.

Diabetes & Impotence: A Concern for Couples. Priscilla Hollander. (Illus.). 6p. 1985. pap. 2.00 (*0-937721-09-3*) Chronimed.

Diabetes & Its Management. Ed. by P. J. Watkins et al. (Illus.). 288p. 1990. pap. 49.95 (*0-632-02692-8*) Blackwell Sci.

Diabetes & Its Ocular Complications. William E. Benson et al. (Illus.). 256p. 1988. text ed. 90.95 (*0-03-014263-6*) Saunders.

Diabetes & Pregnancy. Chahul & Hawkins. 1989. 85.00 (*0-7236-1331-1*, Pub. by John Wright UK) Buttrwrth-Heinemann.

Diabetes & Pregnancy: Teratology, Toxicity & Treatment. Ed. by Lois Jovanovic et al. LC 85-31705. 451p. 1986. text ed. 95.00 (*0-275-92092-5*, C2092, Praeger Pubs) Greenwood.

Diabetes & Pregnancy: What to Expect. American Diabetes Association. (Illus.). 70p. 1989. 9.95 (*0-945448-05-8*, CPREDP) Am Diabetes.

Diabetes & Primary Eye Care. A. Ariffin et al. (Modern Optometry Ser.). (Illus.). 224p. 1992. 65.00 (*0-632-03142-5*) Blackwell Sci.

Diabetes & Protein Glycosylation. M. P. Cohen. (Illus.). 170p. 1986. 61.00 (*0-387-96297-2*) Spr-Verlag.

Diabetes & the Heart. Ed. by Kenneth G. Taylor. LC 92-18892. (Oxford Medical Publications). 1992. pap. 25.00 (*0-19-263026-1*) OUP.

Diabetes & the Kidney. Ed. by A. Heidland. (Contributions to Nephrology Ser.: Vol. 73). (Illus.). 232p. 1989. 135.25 (*3-8055-4968-7*) S Karger.

Diabetes & Vascular Disease. Morris D. Kerstein. (Illus.). 328p. 1989. text ed. 55.00 (*0-397-50985-5*) Lippincott.

Diabetes Annual, No. 5. Ed. by K. G. Alberti & L. P. Krall. 700p. 1990. 275.00 (*0-444-81207-5*) Elsevier.

Diabetes Annual, Vol. 6. K. G. Alberti & L. P. Krall. 1991. 215.50 (*0-444-89251-6*) Elsevier.

***Diabetes Annual, Vol. 8.** Ed. by S. M. Marshall & P. H. Home. 504p. 1994. text ed. 214.50 (*0-444-81788-3*) Elsevier.

Diabetes Annual 7. Ed. by S. M. Marshall et al. 384p. 1993. 185.75 (*0-444-89694-5*) Elsevier.

Diabetes As a Disease of Civilization: The Impact of Culture Change on Indigenous Peoples. Ed. by Jennie R. Joe & Robert S. Young. LC 93-10649. (New Babylon Studies in the Social Sciences: No. 50). (Illus.). vi, 527p. (C). 1993. lib. bdg. 206.15 (*3-11-013474-8*) Mouton.

Diabetes: Beating the Odds: The Doctor's Guide to Reducing Your Risk. Elliot J. Rayfield & Cheryl Solimini. LC 92-14725. (Illus.). 198p. 1992. pap. 8.61 (*0-201-57784-4*) Addison-Wesley.

Diabetes Carbohydrate & Calorie Counter. Annette B. Natow & Jo-Ann Heslin. Ed. by Sally Peters. 288p. (Orig.). 1991. mass mkt. 5.99 (*0-671-69565-7*) PB.

Diabetes Care. Dornan. 200p. 1988. pap. 32.95 (*0-433-00005-8*) Buttrwrth-Heinemann.

Diabetes Care Made Easy: A Simple Step-by-Step Guide for Controlling Your Diabetes. Allison Nemaneic et al. LC 92-11193. (J). 1992. 9.95 (*1-56561-013-X*) Chronimed.

***Diabetes Care Made Easy, for Kids: A Simple Step by Step Guide for Controlling Your Diabetes.** Allison Nemaniec. 1993. pap. 9.95 (*1-56561-014-8*) Chronimed.

Diabetes Complicating Pregnancy: The Joslin Clinic Method. Ed. by John W. Hare. 173p. 1989. text ed. 72.95 (*0-471-50808-X*) Wiley.

***Diabetes Complicating Pregnancy: The Joslin Clinic Method.** 2nd ed. Ed. by Brown & Hare. Date not set. text ed. 69.95 (*0-471-11031-0*) Wiley.

Diabetes Control & the Kosher Diet. Ada P. Kahn. LC 84-51535. 180p. 1985. pap. 9.95 (*0-930121-00-7*) Wordscope Inc.

***Diabetes Dictionary.** (Illus.). 101p. (Orig.). (C). 1994. pap. text ed. 20.00x (*0-7881-1023-3*) Diane Pub.

Diabetes Education. Ed. by Arun K. Baksi et al. LC 83-25976. (Wiley-Medical Publication Ser.). 149p. reprint ed. pap. 42.50 (*0-8357-8631-5*, 2035055) Bks Demand.

Diabetes Education Course. Competence Assurance Systems Staff. (Illus.). 1986. pap. text ed. 75.00 (*0-89147-064-6*) CAS.

***Diabetes Education Goals.** LC 95-10032. (Practical Approaches in Diabetes Care Ser.). 1995. write for info. (*0-945448-49-X*) Am Diabetes.

Diabetes from the Inside Out: A Resource Manual. large type ed. Char Gast. (Illus.). 215p. 1992. Incl. Aid to Meal Planning in back cover. 19.95 (*0-9632453-0-9*); Aid to Meal Planning, OTA or EURO bdg. write for info. (*0-9632453-1-7*) Diabetes Educ.

Diabetes Guide. K. Johansen & S. Dagogo-Jack. (Illus.). xv, 121p. 1992. pap. 18.00 (*0-387-54429-1*) Spr-Verlag.

Diabetes in America: Diabetes Data Complied 1984. Illus. by Richard F. Hamman. 678p. (Orig.). pap. 23.00 (*0-16-002633-4*, S/N 017-045-00102-1) USGPO.

Diabetes in Childhood & Adolescence. Ed. by D. W. Kaplan. (Journal: Pediatrician: Vol. 12, No. 4, 1983-85). (Illus.). iv, 72p. 1986. pap. 38.50 (*3-8055-4400-6*) S Karger.

Diabetes in Elderly People. Ed. by Colin M. Kesson & Paul V. Knight. 200p. 1990. pap. 22.95 (*0-412-32870-4*, A4450) Chapman & Hall.

***Diabetes in Hispanic Americans: Current Research & Education Programs.** (Illus.). 107p. (Orig.). (C). 1994. pap. text ed. 50.00x (*0-7881-1084-5*) Diane Pub.

Diabetes in Juveniles: Proceedings of the 2nd Beilinson, Symposium on the Various Faces in Juveniles, Jerusalem, Israel. 2nd ed. International Beilinson Symposium Staff. Ed. by Zvi Laron. (Illus.). 1977. 59.25 (*3-8055-2698-9*) S Karger.

D

An Asterisk (*) at the beginning of an entry indicates that the title is appearing in BIP for the first time.

*Diabetes in Old Age. Ed. by Paul Finucane & Alan Sinclair. LC 94-39718. 1995. text ed. 64.95 (0-471-95344-X) Wiley.
Diabetes in Practice. Ed. by H. Connor & A. J. Boulton. 1989. text ed. 65.95 (0-471-92087-8) Wiley.
Diabetes in the Family. Dorothy Born. LC 81-18024. (Illus.). 1982. pap. 9.95 (0-13-208463-5) P-H.
*Diabetes in the United States: A Strategy for Prevention. 61p. (Orig.). (C). 1993. pap. text ed. 45.00x (0-7881-0112-9) Diane Pub.
Diabetes Insipidus in Man. Ed. by P. Czernichow & A. D. Robinson. (Frontiers of Hormone Research Ser.: Vol. 13). (Illus.). x, 326p. 1985. 132.00 (3-8055-3921-5) S Karger.

***Diabetes Is Not a Piece of Cake: Prescribed for Family, Friends & Co-workers of Folks with Diabetes. Janet Meirelles. LC 94-75824. (Illus.). 1994. pap. 15.95 (1-884929-75-3) Lincoln Pubng.**
THIS YEAR MORE THAN 650,000 PEOPLE WILL BE DIAGNOSED WITH DIABETES. DIABETES IS NOT A PIECE OF CAKE...(1-884929-75-3), $15.95, is the FIRST BOOK anyone newly diagnosed with diabetes should buy or receive! It's the ONLY book for friends, family, co-workers & supervisors. 288 great pages. DIABETES... has the latest information, plus over 300 diabetics told this nurse-author their true stories: Kira's paramedics; The $200.00 sandwich; When Jo cuddles--give her sugar; The hostage in Lebanon with diabetes. What you need to know about diabetes--whether you have it or not, including a chapter "Do I have it, will I get it?" 24 pages of great recipes. Recommended by physicians & diabetics: "My husband read it & finally understood." "Thanks for the recipe for fat-free, sugar-free cheesecake." "The glossary & index are great helps." (Ask us for details). Available to the trade through IPG, Pacific Pipeline & Ingram Books. For additional information from the Publisher call (800) BOOKS-4-U. Due to requests from readers, the 128 page DIABETES IS NOT A PIECE OF CAKE COOKBOOK (1-884929-82-6), $11.75, has just been completed.
Publisher Provided Annotation.

*Diabetes is Not a Piece of Cake Cookbook. Janet Meirelles. 128p. (Orig.). 1995. pap. 11.75 (1-884929-82-6) Lincoln Pubng.
Diabetes, Liver & Digestive Diseases. Wrynn Smith. (Profile of Health & Disease in America Ser.). (Illus.). 176p. 1988. 40.00 (0-8160-1459-0) Facts on File.
Diabetes Management. International Diabetes Center Staff. 56p. 1991. student ed, pap. 2.95 (0-937721-90-5) Chronimed.
Diabetes Management in the Nineteen Eighties: The Role of Home Blood Glucose Monitoring & New Insulin Delivery Systems. Charles M. Peterson. LC 82-80561. 344p. 1982. text ed. 75.00 (0-275-91377-5, C1377, Praeger Pubs) Greenwood.
Diabetes Markets. (Market Research Reports: No.381). 143p. 1993. 795.00 (0-317-05461-9) Theta Corp.
Diabetes Mellitus. (Technical Report Ser.: No. 727). 113p. 1985. pap. 5.40 (92-4-120727-2) World Health.
Diabetes Mellitus. Ed. by K. Oberdisse. (Handbuch der Inneren Medigin Ser.: Vol. 7/2). 1977. 327.00 (0-387-07741-3) Spr-Verlag.
Diabetes Mellitus, Vol. 5. Ed. by Harold Rifkin & Philip Raskin. (Illus.). 391p. 1980. text ed. 22.95 (0-87619-747-0) P-H.
*Diabetes Mellitus: A Practical Handbook. 6th rev. ed. Suellyn K. Milcovich & Barbara Dunn-Long. LC 94-23731. 1995. pap. 12.95 (0-923521-31-3) Bull Pub.
Diabetes Mellitus: A Source Guide. 1991. lib. bdg. 250.00 (0-8490-4893-1) Gordon Pr.
Diabetes Mellitus: Aspects of the Worldwide Epidemiology of Diabetes Mellitus & its Long-Term Complications. J. M. Ekoe. 272p. 1989. 92.50 (0-444-81003-X) Elsevier.
Diabetes Mellitus: Diagnosis & Treatment. 2nd ed. Mayer B. Davidson. LC 85-20167. (Wiley Medical Publication). (Illus.). 603p. reprint ed. pap. 171.90 (0-8357-3063-8, 2039319) Bks Demand.
Diabetes Mellitus: Diagnosis & Treatment. 3rd ed. Mayer B. Davidson. (Illus.). 435p. 1991. pap. text ed. 42.00 (0-443-08718-0) Churchill.
Diabetes Mellitus: Etiopathogenesis & Metabolic Aspects. Ed. by F. Belfiore et al. (Frontiers in Diabetes Ser.: Vol. 4). (Illus.). x, 282p. 1984. 169.75 (3-8055-3771-9) S Karger.
Diabetes Mellitus: Management & Complications. Ed. by Jerrold M. Olefsky & Robert S. Sherwin. (Contemporary Issues in Endocrinology & Metabolism Ser.: Vol. 1). (Illus.). 399p. 1985. text ed. 50.00 (0-443-08379-7) Churchill.
*Diabetes Mellitus: Management & Complications. fac. ed. Ed. by Jerrold M. Olefsky & Robert S. Sherwin. LC 84-29258. (Contemporary Issues in Endocrinology & Metabolism Ser.). (Illus.). 413p. 1985. reprint ed. pap. 117.80 (0-7837-7899-6, 2047655) Bks Demand.
Diabetes Mellitus: Pathophysiology & Therapy. Ed. by W. Creutzfeldt & Pierre J. Lefebvre. (Illus.). xxvi, 358p. 1989. pap. 104.00 (0-387-50506-7) Spr-Verlag.
Diabetes Mellitus in Children & Adolescents. Luther B. Travis et al. (Major Problems in Clinical Pediatrics Ser.). (Illus.). 360p. 1987. text ed. 60.50 (0-7216-8899-3) Saunders.
Diabetes Mellitus in East Asia: Proceedings of the 1st China-Japan Symposium on Diabetes Mellitus, Beijing, China, 5-6 May, 1987. Ed. by Goro Mimura et al. (International Congress Ser.: No. 771). 406p. 1988. 118.00 (0-444-80992-9, Excerpta Medica) Elsevier.
*Diabetes Mellitus in Pregnancy. 2nd ed. Ed. by E. Albert Reece & Donald R. Coustan. LC 95-12415. 1995. write for info. (0-443-08979-5) Churchill.
Diabetes Mellitus in Pregnancy: Principles & Practice. Ed. by Albert Reece & Donald R. Coustan. (Illus.). 652p. 1988. text ed. 98.00 (0-443-08470-X) Churchill.
Diabetes Mellitus in the Elderly: A Practical Guide. Ed. by Steven R. Gambert et al. 288p. 1990. 80.50 (0-88167-624-1) Raven.
Diabetes Mellitus...From Theory to Therapy: Proceedings of the Ninth Annual Arnold O. Beckman Conference in Clinical Chemistry. Ed. by Michael W. Steffes. (Special Issue of Clinical Chemistry Ser.: Vol. 32, No. 10(B)). 106p. 1986. pap. 10.00 (0-915274-38-8) Am Assn Clinical Chem.
*Diabetes, Natural Way. Catherine Steven. 1995. pap. 5.95 (1-85230-705-6) Element MA.
Diabetes Nineteen Eighty-Eight: Proceedings of the Thirteenth Congress of the International Diabetes Federation, Sydney, 20-25 Nov., 1988. Ed. by R. G. Larkins et al. (International Congress Ser.: No. 800). 1246p. 1989. 205.25 (0-444-81086-2) Elsevier.
Diabetes Nineteen Eighty-Five. Ed. by M. Serrano-Rios & Pierre J. Lefebvre. (International Congress Ser.: No. 700). 1154p. 1986. 249.75 (0-444-80812-4) Elsevier.
Diabetes Nursing Care. Sandra Winter. LC 94-60361. (Illus.). 224p. (Orig.). (C). 1993. pap. 49.95 (1-878025-56-2) Western Schls.
Diabetes, Obesity & Hyperlipidemias, No. II. Ed. by Gaetano Crepaldi et al. 1983. text ed. 109.00 (0-12-195480-3) Acad Pr.
Diabetes, Obesity & Hyperlipidemias: Proceedings of the European Symposium on Metabolism, 5th, Padova, 15-17 May, 1989. Ed. by G. Crepaldi et al. (International Congress Ser.: Vol. 4, No. 872). 472p. 1990. 138.50 (0-444-81151-6, Excerpta Medica) Elsevier.
Diabetes, Obesity & Hyperlipidemias, V: The Plurimetabolic Syndrom; Proceedings of the European Symposium on Metabolism, Padova, 24-26 May, 1993. Ed. by G. Crepaldi et al. LC 93-38467. (International Congress Ser.: No. 1039). 1993. 193.75 (0-444-81639-9, Excerpta Medica) Elsevier.
Diabetes Prevention & Care in the Villages of Alaska. Cynthia Schraer et al. (Illus.). 228p. (Orig.). (C). 1993. pap. text ed. 45.00 (1-56806-489-6) Diane Pub.
Diabetes Product Markets: Product Penetration Increases with Patient Awareness. Market Intelligence Staff. 300p. 1992. 1,995.00 (1-56753-404-X) Frost & Sullivan.
Diabetes Record Book. International Diabetes Center Staff. 56p. 1991. student ed. pap. 2.95 (0-937721-91-3) Chronimed.
*Diabetes-Related Programs for Black Americans: A Resource Guide. (Illus.). 107p. (Orig.). (C). 1994. pap. text ed. 45.00x (0-7881-1027-6) Diane Pub.
Diabetes Secondary to Pancreatopathy: Proceedings of the Post EASD International Symposium on Diabetes Secondary to Pancreatopathy, Padova, Italy, 21-22 Sept. 1987. Ed. by A. K. Tiengo & K. G. Alberti. (International Congress Ser.: No. 764). 292p. 1988. 92.50 (0-444-80990-2, Excerpta Medica) Elsevier.
Diabetes Self-Care Method: The Breakthrough Program of Self-Management That Will Help You Lead a Better, Freer, More Normal Life. rev. ed. Charles M. Peterson & Lois Jovanovic-Peterson. (Illus.). 160p. 1990. reprint ed. pap. 12.95 (0-929923-29-4) Lowell Hse.
*Diabetes Sourcebook. Diana W. Guthrie & Richard A. Guthrie. 256p. 1995. pap. 15.00 (1-56565-261-4) Lowell Hse.
Diabetes Sourcebook, Vol. 3. Ed. by Peter Dresser. (Health Reference Ser.). 1994. lib. bdg. 80.00 (1-55888-751-2) Omnigraphics Inc.
Diabetes Sourcebook: Today's Methods & Ways to Give Yourself the Best Care. Diana W. Guthrie & Richard A. Guthrie. (Illus.). 260p. 1990. 21.95 (0-929923-30-8) Lowell Hse.
Diabetes Sourcebook: Today's Methods & Ways to Give Yourself the Best Care. Diana W. Guthrie & Richard A. Guthrie. 256p. 1992. pap. 12.95 (0-929923-79-0) Lowell Hse.
*Diabetes Sports & Exercise Book: How to Play Your Way to Better Health. Claudia Graham et al. LC 94-42097. 208p. 1995. 25.00 (1-56565-206-1) Lowell Hse.
Diabetes Support Groups for Young Adults: A Facilitator's Manual. Rose Shalom & Janice J. Ryan. 66p. 1989. pap. 19.95 (0-945448-06-6, PEDSGYA) Am Diabetes.
Diabetes Type II & What to Do. Virginia Valentine et al. LC 92-37694. 180p. 1993. 21.95 (1-56565-034-4, Anodyne) Lowell Hse.
Diabetes Type II & What to Do. Virginia Valentine. 184p. 1994. pap. 12.95 (1-56565-149-9) Lowell Hse.
Diabetes Type Two: Living a Long, Healthy Life Through Blood-Sugar Normalization. Richard K. Bernstein. (Illus.). 352p. 1990. 21.95 (0-13-208679-4) P-H.
Diabetes und Graviditaet. Ed. by A. Reist et al. (Fortschritte der Geburtshilfe & Gynaekologie Ser.: Vol. 54). (Illus.). 1975. pap. 15.25 (3-8055-2144-8) S Karger.
Diabetes, Visual Impairment, & Group Support: A Guidebook. Judith Caditz. LC 89-90678. (Illus.). 77p. 1989. pap. text ed. 12.95 (0-9622368-1-0) Ctr Partially.
Diabetes, Visual Impairment & Group Support: A Guidebook. large type ed. Judith Caditz. LC 89-90678. (Illus.). 114p. 1989. pap. text ed. 12.95 (0-9622368-0-2) Ctr Partially.
Diabetes Without Fear. Joseph I. Goodman & W. Watts Biggers. 1979. mass mkt. 4.99 (0-380-43562-4) Avon.
Diabetes Youth Curriculum: A Toolbox for Educators: Resource & Activities Guide - "The Toolbox", Bk. 2. Patricia M. Moynihan. Ed. by Patricia B. Raab. LC 88-7112. (Illus.). 260p. (Orig.). 1988. ring bd. 55.00 (0-937721-50-6) Chronimed.
Diabetes Youth Curriculum: A Toolbox for Educators, Bk. 1: The Curriculum. P. Moynihan et al. LC 88-7111. (Illus.). 136p. (Orig.). 1988. pap. text ed. 95.00 (0-937721-49-2) Chronimed.
Diabetes 101: A Pure & Simple Guide for People Who Use Insulin. 2nd rev. ed. Richard Dolinar & Betty P. Brackenridge. 1993. pap. 9.95 (1-56561-024-5) Chronimed.
Diabetic Always: Insulin No More - or Any Other Darn Pills. Julian Goldstein. 111p. (Orig.). 1994. pap. 11.95 (1-884295-03-7) Ananta Prnting.
Diabetic Angiopathy in Children. Ed. by B. Weber. (Pediatric & Adolescent Endocrinology Ser.: Vol. 9). (Illus.). xvi, 380p. 1981. 158.50 (3-8055-1574-X) S Karger.
Diabetic Cakes, Pies & Other Scrumptuous Desserts. Mary J. Finsand. LC 87-26749. 160p. 1988. pap. 9.95 (0-8069-6672-6) Sterling.
Diabetic Candy, Cookie & Dessert Cookbook. Mary J. Finsand. LC 81-85024. (Illus.). 160p. 1982. pap. 9.95 (0-8069-7586-5) Sterling.
Diabetic Chocolate Cookbook. Mary J. Finsand. LC 84-8454. 160p. 1985. pap. 9.95 (0-8069-7900-3) Sterling.
Diabetic Complications: Early Diagnosis & Treatment. Ed. by Domenico Andreani et al. LC 87-18967. (Wiley-Medical Publication Ser.). (Illus.). 330p. reprint ed. pap. 94.10 (0-8357-8629-3, 2035053) Bks Demand.
Diabetic Cook Book. Better Homes & Gardens Staff. 112p. 1992. 12.95 (0-696-01988-4) Meredith Bks.
Diabetic Cookbook. (Illus.). 96p. 1994. 7.98 (0-7853-0177-1, 2022700) Pubns Intl Ltd.
Diabetic Cookies. Mary J. Finsand. LC 93-43893. 160p. 1994. pap. 9.95 (0-8069-0506-9) Sterling.
*Diabetic Cooking from Around the World. Vilma L. Chantiles. LC 94-25252. 1995. 9.99 (0-517-12284-7) Random Hse Value.
Diabetic Cooking from Around the World. braille ed. Vilma L. Chantiles. 659p. 1992. vinyl bd. 52.72 (1-56956-221-0, BR8070) W A T Braille.
Diabetic Delights. Carol LaForge & Linda Morse. LC 93-70972. 184p. 1993. spiral bd. 16.95 (0-9637774-0-8) Diabetic Delghts.
Diabetic Diet Exchange Lists. Margaret B. Salmon. (Illus.). 1980. pap. 1.50 (0-918662-02-8) Techkits.
Diabetic Diet Exchange Lists for Low Sodium Diets. Margaret B. Salmon. (Illus.). 1980. pap. 1.50 (0-918662-06-0) Techkits.
Diabetic Doctor Looks at Diabetes: His & Yours. Peter A. Lodewick. (Illus.). 204p. 1984. pap. 7.95 (0-910117-00-4) RMI.
*Diabetic Foot. John E. McDermott. 1995. 30.00 (0-89203-119-0) Amer Acad Ortho Surg.
Diabetic Foot. 5th ed. Marvin E. Levin et al. LC 92-49437. 635p. 1992. 89.00 (0-8016-6878-6) Mosby Yr Bk.
Diabetic Foot Care. American Diabetes Association Staff. 12p. 1990. pap. 5.75 (0-945448-13-9, PMFOOT) Am Diabetes.
*Diabetic Gourmet. Francine Prince. 320p. 1994. write for info. (0-9631701-3-9) R A Rapaport.
Diabetic Heart. Makoto Nagano & Naranjan S. Dhalla. 560p. 1991. 115.00 (0-88167-743-4) Raven.
Diabetic Macro- & Microangiopathy. Julian Mincu. LC 73-82434. (C). 1975. 150.00 (3-11-004533-8) De Gruyter.
Diabetic Man: A Guide to Health & Success in All Areas of Your Life. Peter A. Lodewick et al. 336p. 1992. pap. 15.00 (0-929923-78-2) Lowell Hse.
Diabetic Microangiopathy. Ed. by H. Abe & M. Hoshi. (Frontiers in Diabetes Ser.: Vol. 3). (Illus.). xii, 500p. 1983. 221.00 (3-8055-3787-5) S Karger.
Diabetic Microwave Cookbook. Mary J. Finsand. LC 89-19693. 160p. 1989. pap. 9.95 (0-8069-6960-1) Sterling.
Diabetic Neuropathy. Peter J. Dyck et al. (Illus.). 336p. 1987. text ed. 94.50 (0-7216-2125-2) Saunders.
Diabetic Neuropathy. Ed. by J. D. Ward & Y. Goto. 1990. text ed. 215.00 (0-471-92486-5) Wiley.
Diabetic Pancreas. 2nd ed. Ed. by Bruno W. Volk & Edward R. Arquilla. LC 84-26413. 652p. 1985. 115.00 (0-306-41781-2, Plenum Med Bk) Plenum.
Diabetic Pregnancy. J. M. Brudenell et al. (Current Reviews in Obstetrics & Gynaecology Ser.). (Illus.). 147p. 1989. pap. text ed. 44.95 (0-443-02792-7) Churchill.
Diabetic Retinopathy: Practical Management. R. Joseph Olk & Carol M. Lee. LC 92-48876. 1993. 89.50 (0-397-51167-1) Lippincott.
Diabetic Sweet Tooth Cookbook. Mary J. Finsand. LC 92-31090. 160p. 1993. pap. 9.95 (0-8069-8530-5) Sterling.
Diabetic Woman: All Your Questions Answered. Lois Jovanovic et al. 272p. 1988. pap. 11.95 (0-87477-410-1) J P Tarcher.
Diabetic's Book: All Your Questions Answered. large type ed. J. Biermann & B. Toohey. 1993. 21.95 (1-56895-022-5) Wheeler Pub.
Diabetic's Book: All Your Questions Answered. 3rd rev. ed. June Bierman & Barbara Toohey. 256p. 1994. pap. 12.95 (0-87477-773-9, J P T-Putnam) Putnam Pub Group.
Diabetic's Book: All Your Questions Answered. 3rd rev. ed. June Biermann & Barbara Toohey. 256p. 1994. pap. 12.95 (0-685-74797-2) J P Tarcher.
Diabetic's Brand Name Food Exchange Handbook. rev. ed. Ed. by Clara M. Schneider. LC 88-43387. 192p. 1991. pap. 14.95 (0-89471-596-8) Running Pr.
Diabetics' Cookbook. Roberta Longstaff & Jim Mann. write for info. (0-318-59667-9) S&S Trade.
Diabetics' Get Fit Book. Jacki Winter & Barbara Boucher. write for info. (0-318-59668-7) S&S Trade.
Diabetic's Guide to Health & Fitness. Kris E. Berg. LC 86-2916. (Illus.). 272p. 1986. pap. 16.95 (0-88011-347-2, PBER0347) Human Kinetics.
Diabetic's Handbook. 2nd ed. Anthony M. Sindoni. LC 59-12119. (Illus.). 301p. reprint ed. pap. 85.80 (0-317-07877-1, 2012577) Bks Demand.
Diabetic's Innovative Cookbook: A Positive Approach to Living with Diabetes. Josepher Juliano & Diane Young. LC 93-41241. 1994. 25.00 (0-8050-2518-9) H Holt & Co.
*Diabetic's Innovative Cookbook: A Positive Approach to Living with Diabetes, with 145 Heart-Healthy Recipes. Joseph Juliano & Dianne Young. 432p. 1995. pap. 14.95 (0-8050-3785-3, Owl) H Holt & Co.
Diabetic's Jet Ejectors: Diabetic Gun for Personal Insulin Injection. C. Chicka & Anthony Chimpa. LC 88-92324. (Illus.). 78p. (Orig.). 1989. pap. 9.95 (0-922958-03-3) H W Parker.
Diabetic's Total Health Book. 3rd rev. ed. June Biermann & Barbara Toohey. 272p. 1992. pap. 11.95 (0-87477-689-9) J P Tarcher.
Diable Amoureux. Jacques Cazotte. (FRE.). 1981. pap. 10.95 (0-7859-1934-1, 2070372723) Fr & Eur.
Diable au Corps. Raymond Radiguet. (Coll. Diamant). 118p. (FRE.). 1991. pap. 6.95 (0-7859-1492-7, 2277229695) Fr & Eur.
Diable au Corps. Raymond Radiguet. (Folio Ser.: No. 1391). 192p. (FRE.). 1955. pap. 8.95 (2-07-037391-6) Schoenhof.
Diable, Dieu et Autres Contes de Menterie. Pierre Gripari. (FRE.). 1980. pap. 11.95 (0-7859-2433-7, 2070371905) Fr & Eur.
Diable et le Bon Dieu. Jean-Paul Sartre. (FRE.). 1976. pap. 10.95 (0-8288-3745-7, F125311) Fr & Eur.
Diable et le Bon Dieu with Putain Respectueuse. Jean-Paul Sartre. (Folio Ser.: No. 869). pap. 8.95 (2-07-036869-6) Schoenhof.
Diable Vert. Muriel Cerf. 288p. (FRE.). 1981. pap. 10.95 (0-7859-1943-0, 2070373355) Fr & Eur.
*Diablerie: Britain. (Vampire). Date not set. 10.00 (1-56504-074-0) White Wolf.
Diables Amoureux. Guillaume Apollinaire. 384p. (FRE.). 1981. pap. 12.95 (0-7859-3465-0, 2070354458) Fr & Eur.
*Diablesse & the Baby. Richardo Keens-Douglas. (Illus.). 24p. (J). (gr. k up). 1994. lib. bdg. 15.95 (1-55037-993-3, Pub. by Annick CN); pap. 5.95 (1-55037-992-5, Pub. by Annick CN) Firefly Bks Ltd.
*Diablesse et le Bebe (La Diablesse & the Baby) Richardo Keens-Douglas. (Illus.). 24p. (J). (ps-2). 1994. lib. bdg. 15.95 (1-55037-995-X, Pub. by Annick CN); pap. 6.95 (1-55037-994-1, Pub. by Annick CN) Firefly Bks Ltd.
Diablo at Daybreak. Dale Colter. 1991. mass mkt. 3.50 (0-06-100140-6, PL) HarpC.
Diablo Grant. Reasoner. 240p. (Orig.). 1995. mass mkt. 4.99 (0-671-87142-0) PB.
Diablo Mundo - Poesia - Estudiante de Salamanca. Esproneda. 316p. (SPA.). 1987. 9.95 (0-8288-7126-4, S7877) Fr & Eur.
Diabole bei Lysias. Walter Voegelin. Ed. by Gregory Vlastos. LC 78-14599. (Morals & Law in Ancient Greece Ser.). (GER & GRE.). 1979. reprint ed. lib. bdg. 17.95 (0-405-11579-2) Ayer.
Diaboliad & Other Stories. Mikhail Bulgakov. 1993. pap. 13.00 (0-679-74892-X, Vin) Random.
Diabolical Baron. Mary J. Putney. 224p. 1993. lib. bdg. 20.00 (0-7278-4528-4) Severn Hse.
*Diabolical Designs: Paintings, Interiors, & Exhibitions of James McNeill Whistler. Deanna M. Bendix. LC 94-24957. 1995. write for info. (1-56098-415-5) Smithsonian.
Diabolical Game to Win Man's Soul: A Rhetorical & Structural Approach to Mankind. Dorothy R. Castle. LC 89-13662. (American University Studies: English Language & Literature: Ser. IV, Vol. 70). 215p. (C). 1990. text ed. 41.50 (0-8204-1237-6) P Lang Pubs.
Diabolical Principle & the Dithyrambic Spectator. Wyndham Lewis. LC 78-176495. (English Literature Ser.: No. 33). 1971. reprint ed. lib. bdg. 75.00 (0-8383-1362-0) M S G Haskell Hse.
Diaboliques. Jules Barbey d'Aurevilly. (FRE.). 1987. pap. 11.95 (0-7859-1736-5, 2070363422) Fr & Eur.
Diaboliques. Boileau-Narcejac. (Celle Qui N'etait Plus Ser.). (FRE.). 1973. pap. 10.95 (0-7859-1731-4, 2070363260) Fr & Eur.
Diaboliques. Pierre Boileau & Thomas Narcejac. (Folio Ser.: No. 326). 185p. (FRE.). 1952. pap. 8.95 (2-07-036326-0) Schoenhof.
Diaboliques. Barbey D'Aurevilly. (Dedalus Modern European Fiction Classics Ser.). 384p. 1987. pap. 11.95 (0-946626-13-8, Pub. by Dedalus Bks UK) Hippocrene Bks.
Diabolist. Mary A. Drew. (Orig.). 1978. pap. 0.95 (0-380-00235-3, 21451) Avon.
Diabolo Book. Todd Strong. LC 93-43737. 1994. write for info. (0-917643-10-0) B Dube.
Diabolo Book. Jack Wiley. (Illus.). 29p. (gr. 6 up). 1988. pap. 6.95 (0-913999-23-7) Solipaz Pub Co.

D

An Asterisk (*) at the beginning of an entry indicates that the title is appearing in BIP for the first time.

An Asterisk (*) at the beginning of an entry indicates that the title is appearing in BIP for the first time.

D

Diagnosis & Treatment of Acute Radiation Injury: Proceedings. International Atomic Energy Agency Staff & World Health Organization Staff. (Illus.). 425p. (ENG, FRE & RUS.). 1961. 10.80 (*92-4-156024-X*) World Health.

Diagnosis & Treatment of Alcoholism. 2nd ed. Gary G. Forrest. 362p. 1978. spiral bd., pap. 38.95x (*0-398-03780-9*) C C Thomas.

Diagnosis & Treatment of Alcoholism. 2nd ed. Ed. by Gary G. Forrest. LC 94-72312. 364p. 1994. pap. 35.00 (*1-56821-330-1*) Aronson.

Diagnosis & Treatment of Anxiety Disorders. Robert O. Pasnau. LC 84-447. 272p. 1984. text ed. 31.00 (*0-88048-022-X*, 48-022-X) Am Psychiatric.

Diagnosis & Treatment of Anxiety Disorders: A Physician's Handbook. 2nd ed. Ed. by Thomas J. McGlynn & Harry L. Metcalf. 118p. Date not set. spiral bd. 28.50 (*0-88048-523-X*) Am Psychiatric.

Diagnosis & Treatment of Brain Ischemia: CT Brain Blood Flow, Brain Hemodynamics, & Carotid & Vertebral Artery Surgery. Ed. by Andrew L. Carney & Evelyn M. Anderson. (Advances in Neurology Ser.: Vol. 30). (Illus.). 424p. 1981. 126.00 (*0-89004-529-1*) Raven.

Diagnosis & Treatment of Carcinoma of the Cervix in Developing Areas: Proceedings of the Meeting of the International Working Party & International Conference on Diagnosis & Treatment of Carcinoma of the Cervix in Developing Areas, Pattaya & Bangkok, Thailand, January 28 - February 2, 1985. International Working Party for Treatment of Cancer of Cervix in Developing Areas, Meeting (8th: 1985: Ban Phattaya, Thailand) Staff. Ed. by R. F. Mould & Kawee Tungsubutra. LC 86-133595. 378p. 1985. reprint ed. pap. 107.80 (*0-7837-4507-9*, 2044284) Bks Demand.

Diagnosis & Treatment of Cardiac Arrhythmias: Proceedings of the International Symposium on Diagnosis & Treatment of Cardiac Arrhythmias, Barcelona, Spain, Oct 5-8, 1977. International Symposium on Diagnosis & Treatment of Cardiac Arrhythmias Staff. Ed. by A. J. De Luna. (Illus.). 1980. 414.00 (*0-08-024426-2*, Pub. by Pergamon Repr UK) Franklin.

Diagnosis & Treatment of Cardiac Arrhythmias Following Open Heart Surgery: Emphasis on the Use of Atrial & Ventricular Epicardial Wire Electrodes. Albert L. Waldo & William A. Maclean. LC 80-65680. (Illus.). 280p. 1983. 32.50 (*0-87993-132-9*) Futura Pub.

Diagnosis & Treatment of Carotid Artery Disease. 2nd rev. ed. Intro. by William H. Baker. (Illus.). 264p. 1985. 34. 50 (*0-87993-224-4*) Futura Pub.

***Diagnosis & Treatment of Chronic Depression.** James H. Kocsis & Daniel N. Klein. 1995. lib. bdg. 27.50 (*0-89862-849-0*, C2849) Guilford Pr.

Diagnosis & Treatment of Chronic Pain. 2nd ed. Nelson H. Hendler et al. 1989. 29.95 (*0-88416-615-5*, Yr Bk Med Pubs) Mosby Yr Bk.

***Diagnosis & Treatment of Common Pain of Vertebral Origin: A New Approach.** Robert Maigne. Ed. & Tr. by Walter L. Nieves. LC 94-29321. Orig. Title: Diagnostic et Traitement des Douleurs Commones d'Origine Rachidienne. 1995. write for info. (*0-683-05376-0*) Williams & Wilkins.

Diagnosis & Treatment of Depression in Late Life: Results of the NIH Consensus Development Conference. Ed. by Lon S. Schneider et al. LC 93-4216. 416p. 1993. text ed. 46.50 (*0-88048-556-6*) Am Psychiatric.

***Diagnosis & Treatment of Dermatology, 2 vols., Set.** 2nd ed. Richard Ashton & Barbara Leppard. 1995. pap. 69. 95 (*1-85775-093-4*); pap. 69.95 (*0-614-07389-8*, Radcliffe Med Pr) Scovill Paterson.

Diagnosis & Treatment of Diseases in Ayurveda, Pt. 3. Dash Kashyap. (C). 1984. 59.00 (*0-8364-2483-2*, Pub. by Concept II) S Asia.

Diagnosis & Treatment of Diseases in Ayurveda, Pt. 4. Vaidya B. Dash & Lalitesh Kashyap. 1987. 58.00 (*81-7022-024-6*, Pub. by Concept II) S Asia.

Diagnosis & Treatment of Diseases in Ayurveda, Pt. V. Bhagwan Dash. 1991. 74.00 (*81-7022-348-2*, Pub. by Concept II) S Asia.

Diagnosis & Treatment of Diseases in Ayurveda, Vols. 1-3. Bhagwan Dass. (C). 1988. 190.00 (*0-317-92343-9*, Scientific) St Mut.

Diagnosis & Treatment of Dissociative Disorders. Ed. by Jon G. Allen & William H. Smith. LC 94-27324. 136p. 1995. pap. 20.00 (*1-56821-275-5*) Aronson.

Diagnosis & Treatment of Drug & Alcohol Abuse. Ed. by Sidney Cohen & James F. Callahan. LC 85-24833. 305p. 1986. text ed. 69.95 (*0-86656-479-9*) Haworth Pr.

***Diagnosis & Treatment of Early Melanoma.** 1995. lib. bdg. 250.99 (*0-8490-6727-8*) Gordon Pr.

Diagnosis & Treatment of Erectile Disturbances: A Guide for Clinicians. Ed. by R. Taylor Segraves & Harry W. Schoenberg. LC 85-3714. 266p. 1985. 49.50 (*0-306-41871-1*, Plenum Med Bk) Plenum.

Diagnosis & Treatment of Extrauterine Pregnancies. Nicholas Kadar. 256p. 1990. 86.50 (*0-88167-672-1*) Raven.

Diagnosis & Treatment of Functional Infertility. B. Lunenfeld et al. 1993. 65.00 (*3-89412-129-7*) Blackwell Sci.

Diagnosis & Treatment of Global Aphasia. Michael Collins. (Illus.). 194p. (Orig.). (C). 1991. reprint ed. pap. text ed. 45.00x (*1-879105-23-3*, A013) Singular Publishing.

Diagnosis & Treatment of Infantile Autism. Ed. by C. Gillberg. LC 89-71050. (Illus.). 460p. 1989. 95.00 (*0-306-43481-4*, Plenum Pr) Plenum.

Diagnosis & Treatment of Lead Poisoning. Ed. by J. J. Chisolm, Jr. et al. 213p. 1976. text ed. 39.50 (*0-8422-7262-3*) Irvington.

Diagnosis & Treatment of Low Back Pain. Neil Kahanovitz. 160p. 1991. 76.50 (*0-88167-775-2*) Raven.

Diagnosis & Treatment of Mental Illness: An Introduction. Jonathan P. Beard et al. LC 88-5507. (Illus.). 217p. 1989. 34.95 (*0-8143-1920-3*); pap. 17.95 (*0-8143-1921-1*) Wayne St U Pr.

Diagnosis & Treatment of Minimal Brain Dysfunction in Children: A Clinical Approach. Ed. by Ruth Ochroch. LC 80-15858. 303p. 1981. 45.95 (*0-87705-503-3*) Human Sci Pr.

Diagnosis & Treatment of Multiple Personality Disorder. Frank W. Putnam. LC 88-11217. (Guilford Foundations of Modern Psychiatry Ser.). 351p. 1989. lib. bdg. 38.95 (*0-89862-177-1*) Guilford Pr.

Diagnosis & Treatment of Muscle Pain. Ed. by Kraus. (Illus.). 116p. 1988. pap. text ed. 42.00 (*0-86715-166-8*, 1668) Quint Pub Co.

Diagnosis & Treatment of Odontogenic Infections: A Self-Instructional Guide, Bk. 9. Thomas H. Hohl et al. Ed. by James R. Hooley & Robert J. Whitacre. (Illus.). 288p. 1983. pap. 44.50 (*0-89939-090-0*) Stoma Pr.

Diagnosis & Treatment of Old Age Dementias. Ed. by T. A. Ban & H. Peter Lehmann. (Modern Problems of Pharmacopsychiatry Ser.: Vol. 23). (Illus.). viii, 112p. 1989. 57.75 (*3-8055-4844-3*) S Karger.

Diagnosis & Treatment of Phonological Disorders. Camarata. 375p. 1994. 41.95 (*0-8016-6448-9*) Mosby Yr Bk.

Diagnosis & Treatment of Prevalent Diseases of North American Indian Populations. Melvin Lee et al. (American Indian Health Ser.: Vol. 1). 302p. 1974. text ed. 27.50 (*0-8422-7215-1*) Irvington.

Diagnosis & Treatment of Prevalent Diseases of North American Indian Populations. Max J. Miller et al. (American Indian Health Ser.: Vol. 2). 250p. 1974. text ed. 24.50 (*0-8422-7216-X*) Irvington.

Diagnosis & Treatment of Pulmonary Hypertension. Ed. by E. Kenneth Weir et al. (Illus.). 416p. 1992. 69.00 (*0-87993-516-2*) Futura Pub.

Diagnosis & Treatment of Shock: Diagnosis & Treatment. 2nd ed. Max H. Weil et al. LC 92-48454. (Illus.). 468p. 1994. 95.00 (*0-683-08897-1*) Williams & Wilkins.

Diagnosis & Treatment of Temporomandibular Joint & Myofascial Pain Dysfunctions. Errol Lader. Tr. by Calvin Hogue. LC 83-50819. (Illus.). 150p. 1983. pap. text ed. 75.00 (*0-9610782-4-3*) Vadare.

Diagnosis & Treatment of the Personality Disorders. Martin Kantor. Ed. by Gregory Hacke. 323p. 1992. text ed. 35.00 (*0-912791-89-6*) Ishiyaku Euro.

***Diagnosis & Treatment of the Young Male Victim of Sexual Abuse.** William Breer. (Illus.). 236p. 1992. pap. 28.95 (*0-398-06029-0*) C C Thomas.

Diagnosis & Treatment of the Young Male Victim of Sexual Abuse. William Breer. (Illus.). 236p. (C). 1992. text ed. 45.95x (*0-398-05816-4*) C C Thomas.

Diagnosis & Treatment of Upper Gastrointestinal Tumors. Ed. by M. Friedman et al. (International Congress Ser.: No. 542). 538p. 1981. 137.50 (*0-444-90189-2*, Excerpta Medica) Elsevier.

***Diagnosis & Treatment of Voice Disorders.** Rubin et al. 1995. write for info. (*0-89640-276-2*) Igaku-Shoin.

Diagnosis & Treatment Planning in Counseling. Linda Seligman. LC 85-19728. (Illus.). 353p. (C). 1986. pap. 23.95 (*0-89885-262-5*) Human Sci Pr.

Diagnosis & Treatment Planning in Dentofacial Orthopedics. Frans P. Van der Linden. 1987. pap. text ed. 68.00 (*1-85097-005-X*) Quint Pub Co.

Diagnosis & Treatment Product for Immune Diseases, No. C-141. Business Communications Co., Inc. Staff. 162p. 1991. 2,750.00 (*0-89336-832-6*) BCC.

Diagnosis & Treatment Selection for Anxiety Disorders. Samuel Knapp & Leon VandeCreek. Ed. by Harold H. Smith, Jr. LC 88-43469. (Practitioner's Resource Ser.). 94p. 1989. pap. 13.95 (*0-943158-30-3*, DTSBP) Pro Resource.

Diagnosis & Troubleshooting of Automotive Electrical, Electronic & Computer Science. James D. Halderman. 352p. 1991. pap. text ed. 51.00 (*0-13-208729-4*) P-H.

Diagnosis, Assessment & Management. Ed. by Abdul-Majeed Salmasi & A. N. Nicolaides. (Developments in Cardiovascular Medicine Ser.). (C). 1991. lib. bdg. 164. 50 (*0-7923-1188-4*) Kluwer Ac.

Diagnosis Cancer: Your Guide Through the First Few Months. Wendy S. Harpham. (Illus.). 176p. 1992. 22.95 (*0-393-03187-X*); pap. 10.95 (*0-393-30892-8*) Norton.

Diagnosis, Dimensions, & the DSM IV Special Issues Journal of Abnormal Psychology: The Science of Classification, Vol. 100, No. 3. Ed. by David H. Barlow. 150p. 1991. text ed. 20.00 (*1-55798-135-3*) Am Psychol.

***Diagnosis for Disaster: The Devastating Truth About False Memory Syndrome & Its Impact on Accusers & Families.** Claudette Wassil-Grimm. 320p. 1995. 22.95 (*0-87951-572-4*) Overlook Pr.

Diagnosis for Organizational Change: Methods & Models. Ann Howard et al. (Professional Practice Ser.). 288p. 1994. lib. bdg. 35.00 (*0-89862-480-0*) Guilford Pr.

Diagnosis from the Spine. B. H. Jones. 255p. 1974. spiral bd. 16.50 (*0-7873-0478-6*) Mokelumne.

Diagnosis from the Spine: A Practical Method of Diagnosis & Non-Medical Treatment, Combining Manual Therapy, Hydrotherapy & Psychotherapy. B. H. Jones. 1991. lib. bdg. 75.00 (*0-8490-4188-0*) Gordon Pr.

Diagnosis in Andrology. Ed. by J. Bain & E. S. Hafez. (Clinics in Andrology Ser.: No. 4). (Illus.). 255p. 1980. lib. bdg. 129.50 (*90-247-2365-5*) Kluwer Ac.

Diagnosis in Orthopaedics. Leon Gillis. LC 70-361941. (Illus.). 320p. reprint ed. pap. 91.20 (*0-317-41708-8*, 2025721) Bks Demand.

Diagnosis in Speech-Language Pathology. Ed. by Bruce J. Tomblin et al. 320p. 1994. 39.95 (*1-56593-147-5*, 0506) Singular Publishing.

Diagnosis Is Cancer: A Psychological & Legal Resource Handbook for Cancer Patients, Their Families & Helping Professionals. Edward J. Larschan & Richard J. Larschan. 144p. 1986. pap. 9.95 (*0-915950-77-4*) Bull Pub.

Diagnosis of Acute Abdominal Disease. John M. Beal & John G. Raffensperger. LC 79-811. 177p. reprint ed. pap. 50.50 (*0-317-07819-4*, 2055415) Bks Demand.

Diagnosis of Acute Abdominal Pain, No. 2E. F. T. DeDombal. (Illus.). 274p. 1990. text ed. 39.95 (*0-443-03487-7*) Churchill.

Diagnosis of Alcohol Abuse. Ed. by Ronald R. Watson. 288p. 1989. 119.00 (*0-8493-6381-0*, RC565) CRC Pr.

Diagnosis of Bone & Joint Disorders, 6 vols., Set. 3rd ed. Donald Resnick. LC 93-48321. (Illus.). 1994. text ed. 695.00 (*0-7216-5066-X*) Saunders.

Diagnosis of Chest Pain. Albert J. Miller. (Illus.). 240p. 1988. text ed. 72.00 (*0-88167-400-1*) Raven.

Diagnosis of Child Sexual Abuse: Guidance for Doctors. 1988. pap. 11.00 (*0-11-321155-4*, HM3856, Pub. by HMSO UK) UNIPUB.

Diagnosis of Cholecystoses. J. H. Ruijs. 1977. pap. text ed. 62.00 (*90-247-1932-1*) Kluwer Ac.

Diagnosis of Colorectal & Ovarian Carcinoma: Application of Immunoscintigraphic Technology. Ed. by Maguire & Van Nostrand. (Targeted Diagnosis & Therapy Ser.: Vol. 6). 268p. 1992. 110.00 (*0-8247-8646-7*) Dekker.

***Diagnosis of Deep Vein Thrombosis & Pulmonary Embolism.** Ed. by G. Agnelli & H. R. Bueller. (Journal: Vol. 25, No. 1-2, 1995). (Illus.). 88p. 1994. pap. 89.00 (*3-8055-6116-4*) S Karger.

Diagnosis of Defective Colour Vision. Jennifer Birch. LC 92-48986. (Oxford Medical Publications). (Illus.). 204p. 1993. write for info. (*0-19-261870-9*) OUP.

Diagnosis of Defective Colour Vision. Jennifer Birch. LC 92-48986. (Oxford Medical Publications). (Illus.). 204p. 1993. 33.00 (*0-19-262388-5*) OUP.

Diagnosis of Depression. J. P. Feighner & W. F. Boyer. (Perspectives in Psychiatry Ser.). 202p. 1991. text ed. 85.00 (*0-471-92891-7*, Wiley-Liss) Wiley.

Diagnosis of Depressive Disorders: Medical Analysis Index with Research Bibliography. Eva L. Johansson. LC 85-47874. 1987. 44.50 (*0-88164-420-X*); pap. 39.50 (*0-88164-421-8*) ABBE Pubs Assn.

Diagnosis of Disease by Observation of the Eye, Pt. II, Vol. I. Peter J. Thiel. 100p. 1993. reprint ed. spiral bd. 8.25 (*0-7873-0862-5*) Mokelumne.

Diagnosis of Diseases of the Chest, Vol. I. 3rd ed. Robert G. Fraser et al. (Illus.). 706p. 1988. text ed. 99.00 (*0-7216-3870-8*) Saunders.

Diagnosis of Diseases of the Chest, Vol. II. 3rd ed. Robert G. Fraser et al. 900p. 1989. text ed. 105.00 (*0-7216-3871-6*) Saunders.

Diagnosis of Diseases of the Chest, Vol. IV. 3rd ed. Robert G. Fraser & J. A. Pare. LC 76-20932. (Illus.). 1990. text ed. 105.00 (*0-7216-3873-2*) Saunders.

Diagnosis of Endometrial Biopsies & Curetting: A Practical Approach. Michael T. Mazur & Robert J. Kurman. LC 94-10428. 1994. 79.00 (*0-387-94230-0*) Spr-Verlag.

Diagnosis of Endometrial Biopsies & Curetting: A Practical Approach. Michael T. Mazur & Robert J. Kurman. LC 94-10428. 1994. 158.00 (*3-540-94230-0*) Spr-Verlag.

Diagnosis of Energy Systems in Developing Countries, EUR 13068. J. Girod. 268p. 1992. pap. 30.00 (*92-826-2048-4*, CD-NA-13068-EN-C, Pub. by Europ Com) UNIPUB.

Diagnosis of Heart Disease. N. O. Fowler. (Illus.). 416p. 1991. 87.00 (*0-387-97428-8*) Spr-Verlag.

Diagnosis of Herbicide Damage to Crops. D. J. Eagle & D. J. Caverly. (Illus.). 1981. 52.50 (*0-8206-0294-9*) Chem Pub.

Diagnosis of Human Viruses by Polymerase Chain Reaction Technology. Ed. by Y. Becker & G. Darai. LC 92-49412. (Frontiers of Virology Ser.: Vol. 1). (Illus.). 340p. 1992. 125.00 (*0-387-55461-0*) Spr-Verlag.

***Diagnosis of Ill-Health in Amenity Trees.** R. G. Strouts & T. G. Winter. (Research for Amenity Trees Ser.: No. 2). 400p. 1994. pap. 60.00 (*0-11-752919-2*, HM29192) UNIPUB.

Diagnosis of Mental Disorders: Medical Subject Analysis with Research Bibliography. Gabriella M. Meir. LC 84-45651. 150p. 1985. 37.50 (*0-88164-228-2*); pap. 29.50 (*0-88164-229-0*) ABBE Pubs Assn.

Diagnosis of Metabolic Bone Disease. Paull Grech et al. (Illus.). 384p. 1986. text ed. 98.95 (*0-7216-2151-1*) Saunders.

Diagnosis of Mineral Disorders in Plants. Ed. by J. B. Robinson. 1984. Vol. 1, Principles. 66.50 (*0-8206-0311-2*); Vol. 2, Vegetables. 82.50 (*0-8206-0312-0*) Chem Pub.

Diagnosis of Mineral Disorders in Plants: Vegetables, Vol. II. Ed. by J. B. Robinson. 100p. 1982. 110.00 (*0-11-240804-4*, Pub. by HMSO UK) UNIPUB.

Diagnosis of Mycotoxicoses. Ed. by J. L. Richard & J. R. Thurston. (Current Topics in Veterinary Medicine & Animal Science Ser.). 1986. lib. bdg. 216.00 (*0-89838-751-5*) Kluwer Ac.

Diagnosis of Non-Palpable Breast Lesions: Ultrasonographical Controlled Fine Needle Aspiration. Jacqueline Mouriquand et al. LC 93-13055. (Illus.). x, 72p. 1993. 69.00 (*3-8055-5747-7*) S Karger.

Diagnosis of Our Time: Wartime Essays of a Sociologist. Karl Mannheim. LC 86-22787. (International Library of Sociology & Social Reconstruction). 190p. 1987. reprint ed. text ed. 52.50 (*0-313-25165-7*, MDIA) Greenwood.

Diagnosis of Plant Diseases: A Field & Laboratory Manual Emphasizing the Most Practical Methods for Rapid Identification. Rubert B. Streets. LC 68-13545. (Illus.). 258p. reprint ed. pap. 73.60 (*0-7837-1912-4*, 2042116) Bks Demand.

Diagnosis of Plant Virus Diseases. Matthews. 1993. 99.50 (*0-8493-4284-8*, SB736) CRC Pr.

Diagnosis of Salivary Gland Disorders. Ed. by K. Graamans & H. P. Van Den Akker. (C). 1991. lib. bdg. 84.00 (*0-7923-1384-4*) Kluwer Ac.

Diagnosis of Speech & Language Disorders. 2nd ed. James E. Nation & Dorothy M. Aram. (Illus.). (C). 1991. reprint ed. pap. text ed. 45.00x (*1-879105-05-5*, A055) Singular Publishing.

Diagnosis of Stupor & Coma. 3rd ed. Fred Plum & Jerome Posner. LC 80-10300. (Contemporary Neurology Ser.: No. 19). (Illus.). 377p. 1982. pap. text ed. 31.00 (*0-8036-6993-3*) Davis Co.

Diagnosis of the Temporomandibular Joint. Richard W. Katzberg & Per-Lennart Westesson. (Illus.). 416p. 1993. text ed. 132.50 (*0-7216-2368-9*) Saunders.

Diagnosis Related Groups. Ed. by Peter Allen. 200p. 1984. pap. 995.00 (*0-931634-38-5*) FIND-SVP.

Diagnosis Related Groups in Europe: Uses & Perspectives. M. Casas & M. Wiley. LC 93-33225. 1993. 54.00 (*0-387-57168-X*) Spr-Verlag.

Diagnostic Analysis of the Casebooks of Ticehurst House Asylum, 1845-1890. Trevor H. Turner. (Psychological Medicine Monograph Supplements Ser.: No. 21). (Illus.). 50p. (C). 1993. pap. 23.95 (*0-521-42986-2*) Cambridge U Pr.

Diagnostic & Interventional Catherization in Cogenital Heart Disease. James E. Lock et al. 208p. (C). 1987. lib. bdg. 93.00 (*0-89838-831-7*) Kluwer Ac.

Diagnostic & Interventional Radiology: A Clinical Manual. Gaylord et al. 336p. 1989. pap. text ed. 34.50 (*0-7216-2333-6*) Saunders.

Diagnostic & Laboratory Testing in Psychiatry. Ed. by Mark S. Gold & A. L. Pottash. LC 85-24465. (Critical Issues in Psychiatry Ser.). 300p. 1986. 49.50 (*0-306-42054-6*, Plenum Med Bk) Plenum.

Diagnostic & Operative Arthroscopy of the Knee-Joint. 2nd enl. rev. ed. W. Glinz. LC 88-9378. (Illus.). 170p. (C). 1990. text ed. 120.00 (*0-920887-34-1*) Hogrefe & Huber Pubs.

Diagnostic & Operative Arthroscopy of the Temporomandibular Joint. McCain. (Illus.). 300p. 1993. 129.00 (*0-8016-6074-2*) Mosby Yr Bk.

Diagnostic & Operative Gynecologic Laparoscopy. Gobel & Taylor. 360p. 1995. 125.00 (*0-8016-7823-4*) Mosby Yr Bk.

Diagnostic & Operative Hysteroscopy a Test & Atlas... Baggish. 326p. 1988. 175.00 (*0-8151-0460-X*, Yr Bk Med Pubs) Mosby Yr Bk.

Diagnostic & Remedial Mathematics in Special Education. Gerard Giordano. LC 93-21630. (Illus.). 320p. (C). 1993. spiral bd. 59.95x (*0-398-05882-2*) C C Thomas.

Diagnostic & Remedial Reading for Classroom Teaching. 6th ed. Wilson & Cleland. 480p. (C). 1989. write for info. (*0-675-20640-5*, Merrill Pub Co) Macmillan.

Diagnostic & Statistical Manual of Mental Disorders. 3rd ed. American Psychiatric Association Staff. LC 79-55868. 506p. reprint ed. pap. 144.30 (*0-8357-3037-9*, 2039285) Bks Demand.

Diagnostic & Statistical Manual of Mental Disorders: DSM-IV. American Psychiatric Association Staff. LC 94-6304. 1994. pap. text ed. 42.95 (*0-89042-062-9*, 2062) Am Psychiatric.

Diagnostic & Statistical Manual of Mental Disorders: DSM-IV. 4th ed. American Psychiatric Association Staff. LC 94-6304. 1994. boxed 54.95 (*0-89042-061-0*) Am Psychiatric.

***Diagnostic & Structured Interviewing: A Handbook for Psychologists.** Ricard Rogers. LC 94-42415. 411p. 1995. 59.00 (*0-911907-20-3*) Psych Assess.

Diagnostic & Surgical Arthroscopy in the Horse. 2nd ed. C. Wayne McIlwraith. LC 89-2463. (Illus.). 227p. 1990. text ed. 98.50 (*0-8121-1186-9*) Williams & Wilkins.

Diagnostic & Surgical Arthroscopy of the Shoulder. Johnson. (Illus.). 556p. 1992. 179.00 (*0-8016-2400-2*) Mosby Yr Bk.

Diagnostic & Surgical Arthroscopy of the Temporomandibular Joint. Sanders. 208p. 1989. text ed. 147.00 (*0-7216-2453-7*) Saunders.

Diagnostic & Therapeutic Assessments in Alzheimer's Disease. Ed. by C. G. Gottfries et al. 248p. 1991. 85.00 (*1-871816-12-2*, Pub. by Wrighston Biomed UK) Taylor & Francis.

Diagnostic & Therapeutic Cardiac Catheterization. 2nd ed. Ed. by Pepine, Carl J., & Associates Staff et al. LC 93-14866. 710p. 1994. 95.00 (*0-683-06845-8*) Williams & Wilkins.

Diagnostic & Therapeutic Cardiovascular Interventions, Vol. 1425. George S. Abela. 1991. 62.00 (*0-8194-0515-9*) SPIE.

Diagnostic & Therapeutic Cardiovascular Interventions II. Ed. by George S. Abela. 1992. 62.00 (*0-8194-0788-7*, 1642) SPIE.

Diagnostic & Therapeutic ERCP: Technical Aspects & Atlas. Neuhaus Von Bernard & Bernard Hogemann. Tr. by Konrad H. Soergel & Michael J. Schmalz. (Illus.). 328p. 1992. 170.00 (*0-683-06433-9*) Williams & Wilkins.

Diagnostic & Therapeutic Problems in Connective Tissue Diseases. R. A. Asherson et al. (C). 1988. lib. bdg. 83. 00 (*0-7462-0051-X*) Kluwer Ac.

Diagnostic & Therapeutic Problems in Pediatruc Epileptology: Proceedings of the 1st International Symposium, Parma, Italy, 8-9 June, 1987. Ed. by C. Faienza & G. L. Prati. (International Congress Ser.: No. 781). 200p. 1988. 92.50 (*0-444-80986-4*, Excerpta Medica) Elsevier.

Diagnostic Angiography: Monographs in Clinical Radiology. Saadoon Kadir. (Illus.). 734p. 1986. text ed. 132.50 (*0-7216-1055-2*) Saunders.

An Asterisk (*) at the beginning of an entry indicates that the title is appearing in BIP for the first time.

Diagnostic Approach to Organizational Behavior. 3rd ed. Judith R. Gordon. 800p. 1991. text ed. 51.00 (*0-205-12090-3*, H20902) Allyn.

Diagnostic Approach to Organizational Behavior. 4th ed. Judith R. Gordon. LC 92-16368. 1992. text ed. write for info. (*0-205-14520-5*) Allyn.

Diagnostic Assays for Colon Cancer. Abulkalam Shamsuddin. (Illus.). 168p. 1991. 87.00 (*0-8493-6540-6*, RC280, CRC Reprint) Franklin.

Diagnostic Atlas of the Heart. Ed. by J. Willis Hurst & Joseph S. Alpert. 576p. 1994. 160.00 (*0-7817-0058-2*); sl. write for info. (*0-7817-0059-0*) Raven.

Diagnostic Audiology. Ed. by John T. Jacobson & Jerry L. Northern. 333p. (C). 1991. write for info. (*0-318-68766-6*) Allyn.

***Diagnostic Bacteriology Protocols.** Ed. by Jenny Howard & David Whitcombe. LC 95-15032. (Methods in Molecular Biology Ser.: Vol. 46). (Illus.). 296p. 1995. spiral bd. 69.50 (*0-89603-297-3*) Humana.

Diagnostic Biosensor Polymers: Developed from a Symposium Sponsored by the Division of Industrial & Engineering Chemistry, at the 205th National Meeting of the American Chemical Society, Denver, Colorado, March 28-April 2, 1993. Ed. by Arthur M. Usmani & Naim Akmal. LC 94-895. (ACS Symposium Ser.: Vol. 556). 1994. 89.95 (*0-8412-2908-2*) Am Chemical.

Diagnostic Breast Pathology: A Text & Colour Atlas. Ali Ahmed. (Illus.). 151p. 1992. text ed. 129.95 (*0-443-03185-1*) Churchill.

Diagnostic Bronchoscopy: A Teaching Manual. 6th ed. Peter Stradling. (Illus.). 184p. 1991. text ed. 133.95 (*0-443-04293-4*) Churchill.

***Diagnostic Classification of Mental Health & Developmental Disorders of Infancy & Early Childhood.** Zero to Three Nat. Ctr. Clinical Infant Programs Staff. 150p. (Orig.). 1994. pap. 25.00 (*0-943657-32-6*) Zero To Three.

Diagnostic Clinical Dermatology. J. A. Hunter et al. Ed. by J. A. Savin & M. V. Dahl. 1990. 42.95 (*0-632-01955-7*) Blackwell Sci.

Diagnostic Clinical Microbiology: A Benchtop Perspective. Sandra Fessia et al. (Illus.). 224p. 1988. pap. text ed. 29.50 (*0-7216-2326-3*) Saunders.

Diagnostic Clinical Neuropsychology. rev. ed. Erin D. Bigler. (Illus.). 288p. 1988. text ed. 47.50 (*0-292-71537-4*) U of Tex Pr.

Diagnostic Constants of Minerals. Feklichev. 1992. 151.95 (*0-8493-7540-1*, QE369) CRC Pr.

Diagnostic Criteria for Functional Psychoses. 2nd ed. P. Berner et al. 288p. (C). 1992. 90.00 (*0-521-42315-5*) Cambridge U Pr.

Diagnostic Cytology of the Dog & Cat. Ed. by R. L. Cowell & R. D. Tyler. LC 88-83423. (Illus.). 264p. 1989. 74.95 (*0-939674-25-4*) Am Vet Pubns.

Diagnostic Cytology of the Urinary Tract. N. D. Holmqvist. Ed. by G. L. Wied. (Monographs in Clinical Cytology: Vol. 6). (Illus.). 1977. 37.75 (*3-8055-2685-7*) S Karger.

***Diagnostic Cytology of the Urinary Tract: With Histopathologic & Clinical Correlations.** Leopold G. Koss. LC 95-15499. 1995. write for info. (*0-615-00782-1*) Lippincott.

***Diagnostic Cytopathology.** Paul Richman. 1994. vdisk 400.00 (*1-56815-031-8*) Image Premast.

Diagnostic Cytopathology: A Text & Colour Atlas. Chandra Grubb. (Illus.). 214p. 1988. text ed. 85.00 (*0-443-03050-2*) Churchill.

Diagnostic Cytopathology of the Uterine Cervix. 2nd ed. S. F. Patten. (Monographs in Clinical Cytology: Vol. 3). (Illus.). 1977. 78.50 (*3-8055-2194-4*) S Karger.

Diagnostic Decisions in Neurology. Klaus Poeck. LC 85-18801. 145p. 1985. 39.00 (*0-387-15779-4*) Spr-Verlag.

Diagnostic Dermatopathology. Richard A. Jacoby & William Halmi. 1992. pap. text ed. 90.00 (*0-07-032243-0*) McGraw.

Diagnostic Devices Manual & Directory: Immunology & Microbiology, 2 vols., Set. R. W. Stevens. 1728p. 1986. Vol. 1, 1728p. 190.00 (*0-8247-7426-4*); Vol. 2. 190.00 (*0-8247-7459-0*) Dekker.

Diagnostic Dysmorphology: An Approach to the Patient with Multiple Congenital Anomalies. J. M. Aase. (Illus.). 290p. 1990. 52.50 (*0-306-43444-X*, Plenum Pr) Plenum.

Diagnostic Electrocardiographic Devices. 39p. 1991. 53.00 (*0-685-65435-4*, EC11-113) Assn Adv Med Instrn.

Diagnostic Electron Microscopy, Vols. 1-3. Ed. by Benjamin F. Trump & Raymond T. Jones. LC 77-12817. (Wiley-Medical Publication Ser.). (Illus.). 360p. reprint ed. Vol. 1, 360p. pap. 102.60 (*0-7837-3064-0*, 2042742); reprint ed. Vol. 2, 415p. pap. 118.30 (*0-7837-3065-9*, 2042742); reprint ed. Vol. 3, 550p. pap. 156.80 (*0-7837-3066-7*, 2042742) Bks Demand.

Diagnostic Electron Microscopy: A Text-Atlas. Richard Dickersin. LC 87-30997. (Illus.). 640p. 1988. 105.50 (*0-89640-137-5*) Igaku-Shoin.

***Diagnostic Electron Microscopy in Practical Dermatology.** J. Daroczy & I. Racz. 213p. (C). 1987. 150.00x (*963-05-4152-1*) St Mut.

Diagnostic Electron Microscopy of Tumors. 2nd ed. F. N. Ghadially. LC 79-42839. 1985. text ed. 185.00 (*0-407-00299-5*) Buttrwrth-Heinemann.

Diagnostic Electronics & Imaging Equipment Markets: A Detailed Database on a 13 Billion Dollar Market. Market Intelligence Staff. 370p. 1992. 995.00 (*1-56753-086-9*) Frost & Sullivan.

Diagnostic Enzymology. David Hawcroft. LC 86-28305. (Analytical Chemistry by Open Learning Ser.). 280p. 1987. pap. text ed. 64.95 (*0-471-91399-5*) Wiley.

Diagnostic Enzymology. Ed. by Eugene L. Coodley. LC 78-85839. 336p. reprint ed. pap. 95.80 (*0-317-07924-7*, 2055417) Bks Demand.

Diagnostic Errors in Medicine: International Survey with Medical Research Subject Index & Bibliography. Elizabethe W. Hamilton. LC 83-70083. 148p. 1983. 37.50 (*0-941864-46-4*); pap. 29.50 (*0-941864-47-2*) ABBE Pubs Assn.

Diagnostic et Traitement des Douleurs Commones d'Origine Rachidienne see Diagnosis & Treatment of Common Pain of Vertebral Origin: A New Approach

Diagnostic Evaluation of the Knee. M. Strobel & H. W. Stedtfeld. (Illus.). xviii, 356p. 1990. 149.00 (*0-387-50710-8*) Spr-Verlag.

Diagnostic Foraminiferal Assemblages of Shallow-Water Modern Environments: South Florida & the Bahamas, No. VI. P. R. Rose & B. Lidz. (Sedimenta Ser.: Vol. VI). 55p. 1977. 9.00 (*0-932981-05-4*) Univ Miami CSL.

Diagnostic Function Tests in Chemical Pathology. P. T. Lascelles & D. Donaldson. 224p. 1990. lib. bdg. 65.00 (*0-7462-0108-7*) Kluwer Ac.

Diagnostic Function Tests in Chemical Pathology. P. T. Lascelles & D. Donaldson. (C). 1990. lib. bdg. 55.00 (*0-685-32873-2*); pap. text ed. 43.50 (*0-7462-0107-9*) Kluwer Ac.

Diagnostic Gastro Pathology. Richman. 1993. 250.00 (*0-685-65405-2*) Mosby Yr Bk.

Diagnostic Hematology. Bernadette F. Rodak. LC 94-11097. (Illus.). 608p. 1995. text ed. 57.00 (*0-7216-4727-8*) Saunders.

Diagnostic Hematology Clinical & Technical Principles. Powers. (Illus.). 576p. 1989. text ed. 41.95 (*0-8016-4042-3*) Mosby Yr Bk.

Diagnostic Histopathology of Neuroendocrine Tumours. Ed. by Julia M. Polak. LC 92-49111. 500p. 1993. 150.00 (*0-443-04480-5*) Churchill.

Diagnostic Histopathology of the Breast. David L. Page & Thomas J. Anderson. (Illus.). 362p. 1987. text ed. 149.95 (*0-443-02240-2*) Churchill.

***Diagnostic Histopathology of Tumors.** Ed. by Christopher D. Fletcher. LC 94-24321. 1995. write for info. (*0-443-04295-0*) Churchill.

***Diagnostic History & Physical Exam in Medicine for Newton.** Paul D. Chan. (Current Clinical Strategies Ser.). 275p. (C). 1995. disk 34.95 (*1-57443-003-3*) Educ Res Lab.

Diagnostic Imaging: An Algorithmic Approach. 2nd ed. Ronald L. Eisenberg. LC 65-9491. 1987. text ed. 95.00 (*0-397-58300-1*, Lippincott Medical) Lippincott.

***Diagnostic Imaging: Instruments & Agents.** 1995. 26.50 (*0-614-03484-1*, C189) BCC.

Diagnostic Imaging & Radiology Product Comparison System, 1994, 3 vols., Set. Ed. by Garry Hayner. 1994. 695.00 (*0-941417-06-9*) ECRI.

Diagnostic Imaging Asia, No. 2. William H. Straub. 1989. 10.95 (*0-316-81889-5*) Little.

***Diagnostic Imaging Centers Directory.** 105p. (Orig.). 1995. pap. 795.00 (*0-7605-2295-2*) Rector Pr.

Diagnostic Imaging Equipment. (Market Research Reports: No. 325). 166p. 1993. 325.00 (*0-317-05472-4*) Theta Corp.

Diagnostic Imaging in Infertility. Alan C. Winfield & Anne C. Wentz. (Illus.). 336p. 1992. 85.00 (*0-683-09149-2*) Williams & Wilkins.

Diagnostic Imaging in Infertility & Reproductive Endocrinology. Ed. by Richard Jaffe et al. (Illus.). 500p. 1994. 110.00 (*0-397-51351-8*) Lippincott.

Diagnostic Imagining in Ophthalmology. Ed. by C. Gonzalez et al. (Illus.). 576p. 1985. 248.00 (*0-387-96140-2*) Spr-Verlag.

Diagnostic Imaging Medicine. Richard Reba et al. 1983. lib. bdg. 186.50 (*90-247-2798-7*) Kluwer Ac.

Diagnostic Imaging Methods in Hepatology. Ed. by H. Lutz & L. Demling. 1984. lib. bdg. 148.00 (*0-85200-807-4*) Kluwer Ac.

Diagnostic Imaging of Infants & Children, 3 vols., Set. John R. Sty et al. LC 91-18267. 1200p. 1991. 262.50 (*0-8342-0165-8*) Raven.

Diagnostic Imaging of the Acute Abdomen. D. Beyer & U. Modder. (Illus.). 470p. 1988. 150.00 (*0-387-17520-2*) Spr-Verlag.

Diagnostic Imaging of the Ear. 2nd ed. P. D. Phelps & G. A. Lloyd. (Illus.). 234p. 1990. 226.00 (*0-387-19570-X*) Spr-Verlag.

Diagnostic Imaging of the Jaws. Robert P. Langlais et al. (Illus.). 715p. (C). 1994. pap. text ed. 62.95 (*0-683-04849-X*) Williams & Wilkins.

Diagnostic Imaging of the Liver, Biliary Tract, & Pancreas. S. Sakuma et al. (Illus.). 300p. 1987. 91.00 (*0-387-16667-X*) Spr-Verlag.

Diagnostic Imaging of the Lower Genitourinary Tract. Matthew D. Rifkin. (Illus.). 352p. 1985. text ed. 108.50 (*0-88167-045-6*) Raven.

Diagnostic Imaging of the Lung. Putman. (Lung Biology in Health & Disease Ser.: Vol. 46). 752p. 1990. 225.00 (*0-8247-8318-2*) Dekker.

Diagnostic Imaging of the Premature Infant. Ed. by Rodrigo Dominguez. (Illus.). 288p. 1992. text ed. 94.95 (*0-443-08740-7*) Churchill.

Diagnostic Imaging of the Shoulder. Leeane L. Seeger. (Illus.). 208p. 1992. 90.00 (*0-683-07637-X*) Williams & Wilkins.

***Diagnostic Imaging Survey, 2 vols., Set.** 500p. (Orig.). 1995. pap. 2,295.00 (*0-7605-2294-4*) Rector Pr.

Diagnostic Immunocytochemistry & Electron Microscopy. Hossein Yazdi & Irving Dardick. LC 91-20908. (Guides to Clinical Aspiration Biopsy Ser.). (Illus.). 344p. 1992. text ed. 97.00 (*0-89640-214-2*) Igaku-Shoin.

Diagnostic Immunology. David F. Keren & Jeffrey S. Warren. (Illus.). 384p. 1992. 85.00 (*0-683-04596-2*) Williams & Wilkins.

Diagnostic Immunology Laboratory Manual. Ronald J. Harbeck & Patricia C. Giclas. 346p. 1991. 61.00 (*0-88167-811-2*) Raven.

Diagnostic Immunology-Serology, Fascicle I. 140p. 15.00 (*0-317-33952-4*, LM5) Coll Am Pathol.

Diagnostic Immunopathology. 2nd ed. Ed. by Robert B. Colvin et al. LC 93-41659. 848p. 1995. 235.00 (*0-7817-0020-5*) Raven.

***Diagnostic Immunopathology: Laboratory Practice & Clinical Application.** Heddy Zola et al. (Illus.). 326p. (C). 1992. write for info. (*0-521-43331-2*) Cambridge U Pr.

Diagnostic Interviewing. Ed. by Michel Hersen & Samuel M. Turner. LC 85-19298. 376p. 1985. 52.50 (*0-306-42050-3*, Plenum Pr) Plenum.

Diagnostic Interviewing. 2nd ed. Ed. by M. Hersen & S. M. Turner. (Illus.). 365p. (C). 1994. write for info. (*0-306-44755-X*, Plenum Pr) Plenum.

Diagnostic Interviewing for Consultants & Auditors. John G. Quay. 104p. (Orig.). 1986. pap. 18.75 (*0-9616062-0-7*) Quay Assocs.

Diagnostic Issuses in Anorexia Nervosa & Bulimia Nervosa. Ed. by David M. Garner & Paul E. Garfinkel. LC 87-35534. (Brunner-Mazel Eating Disorders Monograph Ser.: No. 2). 240p. 1988. 27.95 (*0-87630-502-8*) Brunner-Mazel.

Diagnostic Laryngology: Adults & Children. Benjamin. (Illus.). 192p. 1989. text ed. 129.00 (*0-7216-2838-9*) Saunders.

Diagnostic Liver Pathology. Christopher S. Foster. (C). 1994. disk 300.00 (*1-56815-010-5*) Image Premast.

Diagnostic Manual: Essentials for the Diagnosis of Chemical Dependency, Vol. II. Robert M. McAuliffe & Mary B. McAuliffe. LC 75-13360. 1975. 6.95 (*0-317-00369-0*) Am Chem Dep Soc.

Diagnostic Math Test for M. A. P. S. Charles T. Gatje & John F. Gatje. Tr. by Rafael Marcos. (Orig.). 1977. pap. text ed. 35.00 (*0-937534-06-4*) G&G Pubs.

Diagnostic Math Test for M. A. P. S. Charles T. Gatje & John F. Gatje. Tr. by Rafael Marcos. (Orig.). 1981. pap. 35.00 (*0-937534-08-0*) G&G Pubs.

***Diagnostic Mathematical Tasks: Grades 1-8.** rev. ed. H. E. Schleiger. (VCP Ser.). 268p. (C). 1993. 105.00x (*0-909184-41-0*, Pub. by Deakin Univ AT) St Mut.

Diagnostic Measurements in LSI & VLSI Integrated Circuits Production. A. Jakubowski et al. (Series in Elect & Comp Engineering: Vol. 7). 372p. (C). 1991. text ed. 74.00 (*981-02-0282-2*, E-B1142) World Scientific Pub.

Diagnostic Medical Parasitology. Lynn S. Garcia & David A. Bruckner. 595p. 1988. 55.75 (*0-444-01280-X*) Elsevier.

Diagnostic Medical Parasitology. 2nd ed. Lynne S. Garcia & David A. Bruckner. LC 92-48336. 700p. 1993. text ed. 75.00 (*1-55581-046-2*) Am Soc Microbio.

Diagnostic Medical Sonography, Vol. I: Obstetrics & Gynecology. Mimi C. Berman et al. (Illus.). 662p. 1990. text ed. 95.00 (*0-397-50952-9*) Lippincott.

Diagnostic Medical Sonography, Vol. II: Echocardiography. Marveen Craig et al. (Illus.). 461p. 1991. text ed. 95.00 (*0-397-50953-7*) Lippincott.

Diagnostic Medical Sonography, Vol. III: Abdomen. Diane M. Kawamura et al. (Illus.). 656p. 1992. text ed. 100.00 (*0-397-50951-0*) Lippincott.

Diagnostic Medical Ultrasound Examination Review. 2nd ed. B. Peters & G. P. Kocheril. (Allied Health Ser.). 300p. 1988. pap. 37.00 (*0-444-01334-2*) Elsevier.

Diagnostic Methods in Clinical Thyroidology. Ed. by Joel I. Hamburger. (Illus.). 250p. 1989. 85.00 (*0-387-96923-3*) Spr-Verlag.

Diagnostic Methods in Critical Care: Automated Data Collection & Interpretation. Ed. by William C. Shoemaker & Edward Abraham. LC 86-19746. (Basic & Clinical Cardiology Ser.: No. 9). (Illus.). 518p. reprint ed. pap. 147.70 (*0-7837-4317-3*, 2044003) Bks Demand.

***Diagnostic Microbiology & Cytology of the Eye.** Kathleen A. Byrne et al. LC 94-28598. 176p. 1995. pap. 59.95 (*0-7506-9607-9*) Buttrwrth-Heinemann.

Diagnostic Molecular Biology. Theodore E. Mifflin et al. 1992. text ed. 47.50 (*0-07-041933-7*) McGraw.

Diagnostic Molecular Microbiology: Principles & Applications. Ed. by David H. Persing et al. LC 92-38523. 700p. 1993. spiral bd. 65.00 (*1-55581-056-X*) Am Soc Microbio.

Diagnostic Molecular Pathology: A Practical Approach, Vol. II. Ed. by C. S. Herrington & James O. McGee. (Practical Approach Ser.). (Illus.). 240p. 1992. 70.00 (*0-19-963239-1*, IRL Pr); pap. 39.00 (*0-19-963238-3*, IRL Pr) OUP.

Diagnostic Molecular Pathology, Vol. 1: A Practical Approach: Phenotyping & Genotyping of Intact Cells. Ed. by C. S. Herrington & O. D. McGee. (Practical Approach Ser.). (Illus.). 296p. 1993. 70.00 (*0-19-963237-5*, IRL Pr); pap. 39.00 (*0-19-963236-7*, IRL Pr) OUP.

Diagnostic Molecular Pathology, Vols. I & II: A Practical Approach. Ed. by C. S. Herrington & James O. McGee. (Practical Approach Ser.). (Illus.). 536p. 1993. 123.00 (*0-19-963241-3*, IRL Pr); pap. 70.00 (*0-19-963240-5*, IRL Pr) OUP.

Diagnostic Monitoring of Skill & Knowledge Acquisition. Ed. by N. Frederickson et al. 528p. (C). 1990. text ed. 99.95 (*0-89859-992-X*) L Erlbaum Assocs.

Diagnostic Neuropathology. M. Esiri & D. Oppenheimer. 1989. 175.00 (*0-632-01951-4*) Blackwell Sci.

Diagnostic Neuroradiology - a Text - Atlas. Anne G. Osborn. 800p. 1993. 185.00 (*0-8016-7486-7*) Mosby Yr Bk.

Diagnostic Nuclear Medicine, 2 vols. 2nd ed. Alexander Gottschalk et al. (Illus.). 1288p. 1988. 260.00 (*0-683-03670-X*) Williams & Wilkins.

***Diagnostic Nuclear Medicine.** 3rd ed. Ed. by Martin P. Sandler. LC 94-32470. 1995. write for info. (*0-683-07503-9*) Williams & Wilkins.

Diagnostic Obstetrical Ultrasound. John P. McGahan & Manuel Porto. (Illus.). 640p. 1994. 99.00 (*0-397-51320-8*) Lippincott.

Diagnostic Parasitology for Veterinary Technicians. Ed. by J. Colville. LC 90-85892. (Illus.). 250p. 1991. 24.50 (*0-939674-32-7*) Am Vet Pubns.

Diagnostic Pathology of Infectious Diseases. Gail Woods. (Illus.). 705p. 1993. text ed. 97.50 (*0-8121-1604-6*) Williams & Wilkins.

Diagnostic Pathology of Liver & Biliary Tract. 2nd ed. Ruebner. 1991. 145.00 (*1-56032-060-5*) Hemisp Pub.

Diagnostic Pathology of Parasitic Infections with Clinical Correlations. Yezid Gutierrez. LC 89-12270. (Illus.). 532p. 1990. text ed. 89.00 (*0-8121-1237-7*) Williams & Wilkins.

Diagnostic Pathology of the Intestinal Mucosa. W. O. Dobbins. (Illus.). x, 217p. 1989. 131.00 (*0-387-97059-2*, 3051) Spr-Verlag.

Diagnostic Patient Studies in Surgery. Bernard Sigel. LC 85-23999. 461p. reprint ed. pap. 131.40 (*0-7837-2747-X*, 2043127) Bks Demand.

Diagnostic Pediatric Imaging. C. M. Hall & S. Lingam. (Illus.). 416p. 1986. 64.00 (*0-387-16202-X*) Spr-Verlag.

Diagnostic Picture Test in Pediatric Dentistry. Rock. 1988. 19.95 (*0-8151-7381-4*, Yr Bk Med Pubs) Mosby Yr Bk.

Diagnostic Picture Tests in Cardiology. Patterson. 1990. 14.95 (*0-8151-6623-0*, Yr Bk Med Pubs) Mosby Yr Bk.

Diagnostic Picture Tests in Clinical Medicine, 4 vols., Set. Chesell. (LAT.). 1991. 49.00 (*0-8151-1658-6*) Mosby Yr Bk.

Diagnostic Picture Tests in Clinical Neurology. Malcolm Parson. (Illus.). 128p. 1987. pap. text ed. 14.95 (*0-8151-6616-8*, Yr Bk Med Pubs) Mosby Yr Bk.

Diagnostic Picture Tests in Clinical Surgery. William Walker. LC 92-8485. 128p. 1992. 14.95 (*0-8151-9087-5*) Mosby Yr Bk.

Diagnostic Picture Tests in Dentistry. Lamey. 1989. 14.95 (*0-7234-0982-X*, Wolfe Pub) Mosby Yr Bk.

Diagnostic Picture Tests in Dermatology. Levene. (SPA.). 1991. 26.15 (*0-7234-1670-2*, Wolfe Pub) Mosby Yr Bk.

Diagnostic Picture Tests in Dermatology. Ed. by G. M. Levene. (Illus.). 128p. 1986. 14.95 (*0-8151-5407-0*, DTD-1, Yr Bk Med Pubs) Mosby Yr Bk.

Diagnostic Picture Tests in Endocrinology. Reginald Hall. 128p. 1991. 14.95 (*0-8151-4076-2*) Mosby Yr Bk.

Diagnostic Picture Tests in ENT. Bull. 1991. 14.95 (*0-8151-1310-2*, Yr Bk Med Pubs) Mosby Yr Bk.

Diagnostic Picture Tests in Gastroenterology. Sarner. 1991. write for info. (*0-8151-7516-7*, Yr Bk Med Pubs) Mosby Yr Bk.

Diagnostic Picture Tests in General Medicine. Zatouroff. 1988. 14.95 (*0-8151-9884-1*, Yr Bk Med Pubs) Mosby Yr Bk.

Diagnostic Picture Tests in General Surgery. Walker. 1988. 14.95 (*0-8151-9147-2*, Yr Bk Med Pubs) Mosby Yr Bk.

Diagnostic Picture Tests in Geriatric Medicine. Kamal. 1989. 14.95 (*0-8151-4981-6*, Yr Bk Med Pubs) Mosby Yr Bk.

Diagnostic Picture Tests in Hematology. Bellingham. 128p. 1993. pap. 14.95 (*0-8151-5224-8*, Yr Bk Med Pubs) Mosby Yr Bk.

Diagnostic Picture Tests in Infectious Diseases. Ronald T. Emond. (Illus.). 128p. 1987. 14.95 (*0-8151-3111-9*, Yr Bk Med Pubs) Mosby Yr Bk.

Diagnostic Picture Tests in Injury in Sport. Williams. 1988. 14.95 (*0-8151-9349-1*, Yr Bk Med Pubs) Mosby Yr Bk.

Diagnostic Picture Tests in Obstetrics & Gynecology. Victor R. Tindall. (Illus.). 128p. 1987. pap. text ed. 14.95 (*0-8151-8813-7*, Yr Bk Med Pubs) Mosby Yr Bk.

Diagnostic Picture Tests in Ophthalmology. Ed. by C. Montague Ruben. (Illus.). 128p. 1987. 14.95 (*0-8151-7447-0*, POP-1, Yr Bk Med Pubs) Mosby Yr Bk.

Diagnostic Picture Tests in Oral Medicine. Ed. by W. R. Tyldesley. (Illus.). 128p. 1986. 14.95 (*0-8151-8910-9*, DTM-1, Yr Bk Med Pubs) Mosby Yr Bk.

Diagnostic Picture Tests in Orthopedics. Kessel. 1988. 14.95 (*0-8151-5049-0*, Yr Bk Med Pubs) Mosby Yr Bk.

Diagnostic Picture Tests in Pediatric Dentistry. Rock. 1988. 14.95 (*0-7234-0984-6*, Wolfe Pub) Mosby Yr Bk.

Diagnostic Picture Tests in Pediatrics. 2nd ed. Milner. 160p. 1991. pap. 14.95 (*0-8016-6292-3*) Mosby Yr Bk.

Diagnostic Picture Tests in Respiratory Medicine. Peter R. Studdy. (Illus.). 128p. 1990. 14.95 (*0-8151-8246-5*, Yr Bk Med Pubs) Mosby Yr Bk.

Diagnostic Picture Tests in Rheumatology. Ed. by Verna Wright. (Illus.). 128p. 1987. 14.95 (*0-8151-9358-0*, PIT-1, Yr Bk Med Pubs) Mosby Yr Bk.

Diagnostic Picture Tests in Urology. George. 128p. 1991. pap. 14.95 (*0-8016-6289-3*) Mosby Yr Bk.

Diagnostic Prescriptive Reading Instruction: A Guide for Classroom Teachers. 4th ed. Martha D. Collins & Earl H. Cheek. 512p. (C). 1993. boxed write for info. (*0-697-12575-0*) Brown & Benchmark.

Diagnostic Problems in Clinical Ophthalmology. Ed. by Curtis Margo et al. LC 92-49132. (Illus.). 896p. 1993. text ed. 89.50 (*0-7216-3659-4*) Saunders.

Diagnostic Procedure Handbook. J. A. Golish. 564p. 1992. 34.95 (*0-683-03619-X*) Williams & Wilkins.

Diagnostic Procedures for Bacterial Infections. 7th ed. Ed. by Berttina B. Wentworth. LC 87-19306. 886p. 1988. 80.00 (*0-87553-149-0*) Am Pub Health.

Diagnostic Procedures for Mycotic & Parasitic Infections. 7th ed. Ed. by Berttina B. Wentworth. 650p. 1988. 75.00 (*0-87553-156-3*) Am Pub Health.

Diagnostic Procedures for Viral, Rickettsial, & Chlamydial Infections. 6th ed. Ed. by Nathalie J. Schmidt & Richard W. Emmons. 1244p. 1989. 85.00 (*0-87553-155-5*) Am Pub Health.

D

An Asterisk (*) at the beginning of an entry indicates that the title is appearing in BIP for the first time.

Diagnostic Procedures in Cardiology: A Clinician's Guide. Ed. by James V. Warren & Richard P. Lewis. LC 84-25725. (Illus.). 508p. reprint ed. pap. 144.80 (*0-8357-6312-9*, 2035585) Bks Demand.

Diagnostic Procedures in Veterinary Bacteriology & Mycology. 5th ed. Ed. by Gary R. Carter & John R. Cole, Jr. 620p. 1990. text ed. 39.95 (*0-12-161775-0*) Acad Pr.

Diagnostic Psychological Testing. David Rapaport et al. LC 68-16993. 562p. 1968. text ed. 65.00 (*0-8236-1260-0*) Intl Univs Pr.

Diagnostic Pulmonary Cytology. 2nd ed. Geno Saccomanno. LC 85-7477. 1986. text ed. 100.00 (*0-89189-189-7*, 16-3-007-00) Am Soc Clinical.

Diagnostic Radiography: A Concise Practical Manual. 4th ed. Glenda J. Bryan. LC 87-8072. (Illus.). 500p. 1987. pap. text ed. 46.00 (*0-443-02992-X*) Churchill.

Diagnostic Radiology, 3 vols., Set. 2nd ed. Ed. by Ronald G. Grainger & David J. Allison. (Illus.). 2760p. 1991. text ed. 485.00 (*0-443-04112-1*) Churchill.

Diagnostic Radiology see Encyclopedia of Urology

Diagnostic Radiology in Emergency Medicine. Rosen et al. (Illus.). 704p. 1991. 120.00 (*0-8016-6267-2*) Mosby Yr Bk.

Diagnostic Radiology in Emergency Medicine. Rosen et al. (SPA.). 1993. 109.65 (*84-8086-047-2*) Mosby Yr Bk.

Diagnostic Radiology of the Brain: CT, DSA, NMR. 2nd ed. Ruth G. Ramsey. (Advanced Exercises in Diagnostic Radiology Ser.: Vol. 9). (Illus.). 320p. 1984. pap. text ed. 55.95 (*0-7216-1177-X*) Saunders.

Diagnostic Radiology of the Dog & Cat. 2nd ed. J. Kevin Kealy. (Illus.). 528p. 1987. text ed. 72.50 (*0-7216-1853-7*) Saunders.

Diagnostic Radiology of the Horse, Pt. 2: Diseases of the Hind Limb. Dik & Gunsser. (Illus.). 148p. 1989. text ed. 142.00 (*0-7216-2959-8*) Saunders.

Diagnostic Radiology of the Horse, Pt. 3: Diseases of the Head, Neck & Throat. Dik & Gunsser. (Illus.). 172p. 1990. text ed. 152.00 (*0-7216-3448-6*) Saunders.

Diagnostic Reading Inventory for Primary & Intermediate Grades. Janet M. Scott & Sheila C. McCleary. 151p. (C). 1993. spiral bd. 28.98 (*0-9636225-0-1*) Scott & McCleary Pub.

Diagnostic Reasoning & Treatment Decision Making. Doris L. Carnevali. 1993. text ed. 29.95 (*0-397-54921-0*) Lippincott.

Diagnostic Recognition of Genetic Disease. William L. Nyhan & Nadia A. Sakati. LC 86-21132. 766p. reprint ed. pap. 180.00 (*0-7837-2735-6*, 2043115) Bks Demand.

Diagnostic Respiratory Cytopathology. William W. Johnston. LC 79-84478. (Illus.). 328p. 1979. 62.00 (*0-89352-047-0*, MA047, Yr Bk Med Pubs) Mosby Yr Bk.

Diagnostic Seminars in Pathology, Vol. 1. Ekkehard Grundmann. 318p. (Orig.). 1990. pap. 65.00 (*0-89574-324-8*) G F Verlag.

Diagnostic Sonography: Principles & Clinical Applications. 2nd ed. Arthur Fleischer & Donna Kepple. LC 94-1695. (Illus.). 608p. 1995. text ed. 160.00 (*0-7216-3764-7*) Saunders.

Diagnostic Spelling Potential Test (DSPT) John Arena. 18.00 (*0-87879-305-4*) Acad Therapy.

Diagnostic Strategies for Common Medical Problems. Ed. by Robert J. Panzer et al. 550p. 1991. pap. 38.00 (*0-943126-20-7*, DIS91) Amer Coll Phys.

Diagnostic Study of the Subject Matter of High School Chemistry. Samuel R. Powers. LC 79-177164. (Columbia University. Teachers College. Contributions to Education Ser.: No. 149). reprint ed. 37.50 (*0-404-55149-1*) AMS Pr.

Diagnostic Surgical Pathology, Set. 2nd ed. Ed. by Stephen S. Sternberg et al. LC 93-20274. (Illus.). 2480p. 1994. 335.00 (*0-7817-0043-4*) Raven.

***Diagnostic Techniques for Semiconductor Materials & Devices.** D. K. Schroder et al. 400p. 1994. 58.00 (*1-56677-092-0*, PV 94-33) Electrochem Soc.

Diagnostic Techniques for Semiconductor Materials & Devices, Vol. 92-2: Proceedings. Ed. by J. Benton et al. LC 92-70113. 250p. 1992. 36.00 (*1-56677-001-7*) Electrochem Soc.

Diagnostic Techniques for Semiconductor Materials Processing, Vol. 324: Materials Research Society Symposium Proceedings. Ed. by O. J. Glembocki et al. 1994. text ed. 71.00 (*1-55899-223-5*) Materials Res.

Diagnostic Techniques in Medical Parasitology. S. Fleck & A. H. Moody. (Illus.). 135p. 1988. pap. 34.95 (*0-7236-0776-1*, Pub. by John Wright UK) Buttrwrth-Heinemann.

Diagnostic Techniques in Pulmonary Disease, Part 2. Sackner. (Lung Biology in Health & Disease Ser.: Vol. 16). 424p. 1981. 140.00 (*0-8247-1182-3*) Dekker.

Diagnostic Techniques in Pulmonary Disease, Pt. 1. Sackner. (Lung Biology in Health & Disease Ser.: Vol. 16). 560p. 1980. 155.00 (*0-8247-1059-2*) Dekker.

Diagnostic Techniques in Renal Disease. Robert G. Narins. (Contemporary Issues in Nephrology Ser.). (Illus.). 384p. 1992. text ed. 85.00 (*0-443-08806-3*) Churchill.

Diagnostic Techniques in Urology. O'Reilly et al. (Illus.). 640p. 1990. text ed. 210.00 (*0-7216-3116-9*) Saunders.

Diagnostic Test Implications. Springhouse Publishing Company. (Clinical Skillbuilders Ser.). 1992. 24.95 (*0-87434-380-1*) Springhouse Pub.

Diagnostic Test of Aptitude for Clerical Office Work Based on an Analysis of Clerical Operations. Allen M. Ruggles. LC 74-177215. (Columbia University. Teachers College. Contributions to Education Ser.: No. 148). reprint ed. 37.50 (*0-404-55148-3*) AMS Pr.

Diagnostic Testing & Nursing Implications: A Case Study Approach. Pagana. (Illus.). 528p. 1990. pap. 25.95 (*0-8016-5841-1*) Mosby Yr Bk.

Diagnostic Testing & Nursing Implications: A Case Study Approach. 4th ed. Kathleen D. Pagana & Timothy J. Pagana. LC 93-5961. 540p. 1993. pap. 24.95 (*0-8016-6779-8*) Mosby Yr Bk.

Diagnostic Testing Handbook for Clinical Decision Making. Goldenberg. 320p. 1989. 22.95 (*0-8151-0487-1*, Yr Bk Med Pubs) Mosby Yr Bk.

Diagnostic Testing of Deaf Children. A. Van Uden. viii, 216p. 1983. 35.50 (*90-265-0436-5*, Pub. by Swets Pub Serv NE) Taylor & Francis.

Diagnostic Tests. Ed. by Susan Williams & Barbara McVan. LC 85-12540. (Clinical Pocket Manual Ser.). 187p. 1985. pap. 15.95 (*0-87434-002-0*) Springhouse Pub.

Diagnostic Tests: Medical Subject Analysis with Research Bibliography. John C. Bartone. LC 84-45646. 150p. 1987. 44.50 (*0-88164-238-X*); pap. 39.50 (*0-88164-239-8*) ABBE Pubs Assn.

Diagnostic Tests & Nursing Implications. V. F. Valasek. 704p. 1983. 1.00 (*0-07-066805-1*) McGraw.

Diagnostic Tests Handbook. Ed. by Regina D. Ford. 703p. 1987. 23.95 (*0-87434-138-8*) Springhouse Pub.

Diagnostic Tests in Endocrinology & Diabetes. Ed. by Pierre M. Bouloux & Lesley H. Rees. LC 93-20474. (Diagnostic Test Ser.: Vol. 4). 1993. write for info. (*0-412-35200-1*) Chapman & Hall.

Diagnostic Tests in Neurology. Paul M. Matthews & Douglas R. Arnold. (Illus.). 372p. 1990. pap. text ed. 44.95 (*0-443-08621-4*) Churchill.

***Diagnostic Tools in Atmospheric Physics.** G. Fiocco et al. LC 94-73353. 1995. 130.00 (*90-5199-202-5*) IOS Press.

Diagnostic Transmission Electron Microscopy of Tumors: With Clinicopathological, Immunohistochemical, & Cytogenic Correlations. Robert A. Erlandson. LC 93-1632. 880p. 1994. 195.00 (*0-7817-0042-6*) Raven.

Diagnostic Trouble Controls Code Manual 1980-86. 960p. 1992. pap. 50.00 (*0-8019-8283-9*) Chilton.

Diagnostic Trouble Controls Code Manual 1987-89. 928p. 1992. pap. 50.00 (*0-8019-8284-7*) Chilton.

Diagnostic Trouble Controls Code Manual 1990-91. 1152p. 1992. pap. 50.00 (*0-8019-8285-5*) Chilton.

Diagnostic Ultrasonics: Principles & Use of Instruments. 3rd ed. W. N. McDicken. (Illus.). 367p. 1991. text ed. 85.00 (*0-443-04132-6*) Churchill.

Diagnostic Ultrasonography Test & Syllabus. Thomas L. Lawson et al. LC 94-16701. (Professional Self-Evaluation Program Ser.: Vol. 38). (Illus.). 940p. 1994. 200.00 (*1-55903-038-0*) Am Coll Radiology.

Diagnostic Ultrasound. Carol M. Rumack. 1504p. 1991. 235.00 (*0-8016-9040-4*) Mosby Yr Bk.

Diagnostic Ultrasound: Physics, Biology & Instrumentation. Bushong & Archer. (Illus.). 192p. 1991. 35.95 (*0-8016-0394-3*) Mosby Yr Bk.

Diagnostic Ultrasound: Principles, Instruments & Exercises. 4th ed. Frederick W. Kremkau. LC 92-48829. (Illus.). 368p. 1993. text ed. 42.00 (*0-7216-4308-6*) Saunders.

Diagnostic Ultrasound: Proceedings of the First International Conference, University of Pittsburgh, 1965. Ed. by Charles C. Grossman. LC 65-27810. 532p. reprint ed. pap. 151.70 (*0-317-27899-1*, 2055788) Bks Demand.

Diagnostic Ultrasound: Text & Cases. 2nd ed. Dennis A. Sarti. 1200p. 1987. 159.00 (*0-8151-7537-X*, Yr Bk Med Pubs) Mosby Yr Bk.

Diagnostic Ultrasound Applied to Ob-Gyn. Rudy E. Sabbagha. 1993. 125.00 (*0-397-51241-4*) Lippincott.

Diagnostic Ultrasound Applied to Obstetrics & Gynecology. 2nd ed. Rudy E. Sabbagha et al. LC 65-8634. (Illus.). 608p. 1987. text ed. 95.00 (*0-397-50699-6*, Lippincott Medical) Lippincott.

Diagnostic Ultrasound in Clinical Obstetrics & Gynecology. Ed. by Horace E. Thompson & Richard L. Bernstine. LC 78-562. (Wiley Medical Publication). (Illus.). 204p. reprint ed. pap. 58.20 (*0-7837-3477-8*, 2057809) Bks Demand.

Diagnostic Ultrasound in Gastroenterology: Instrumentation, Clinical Problems & Atlas. L. Bolondi et al. 544p. 1984. text ed. 64.00 (*1-57235-054-7*) Piccin NY.

Diagnostic Ultrasound in Gastrointestinal Disease. Ed. by Kenneth J. Taylor. LC 78-21895. (Clinics in Diagnostic Ultrasound Ser.: No. 1). 188p. reprint ed. pap. 53.60 (*0-7837-3150-7*, 2042835) Bks Demand.

Diagnostic Ultrasound in Obstetrics. Ed. by John C. Hobbins. LC 79-15350. (Clinics in Diagnostic Ultrasound Ser.: No. 3). (Illus.). 202p. reprint ed. pap. 57.60 (*0-7837-2558-2*, 2042717) Bks Demand.

Diagnostic Ultrasound in the Dog & Cat. F. Barr. 1990. pap. 75.00 (*0-632-02845-9*) Blackwell Sci.

Diagnostic Ultrasound of the Lower Abdomen. A. Tranta et al. 198p. 1985. text ed. 40.00 (*1-57235-024-5*) Piccin NY.

Diagnostic Ultrasound Test & Syllabus, Vol. 23. Michael L. Manco-Johnson et al. (Professional Self-Evaluation & Continuing Education Program Ser.). (Illus.). 700p. 1988. 150.00 (*1-55903-023-2*) Am Coll Radiology.

Diagnostic Ultrastructural Pathology I: Text Atlas Case Studies. Dvorak. 1992. 99.95 (*0-8493-4404-2*, RB643) CRC Pr.

***Diagnostic Ultrastructural Pathology II: A Text-Atlas of Case Studies Emphasizing Respiratory & Nervous Systems.** Ed. by Ann M. Dvorak & Rita A. Monahan-Earley. LC 94-47018. 416p. 1995. 495.00 (*0-8493-4490-5*, 4490) CRC Pr.

***Diagnostic Ultrastructural Pathology III: A Text-Atlas of Case Studies Emphasizing Endocrine & Hematopoietic Systems.** Ann M. Dvorak & Rita A. Monahan-Earley. LC 94-47673. 432p. 1995. 275.00 (*0-8493-9474-0*, 9474) CRC Pr.

Diagnostic Ultrastructure of Non-Neoplastic Diseases. Ed. by John M. Papadimitriou et al. (Illus.). 728p. 1992. text ed. 375.00 (*0-443-03464-8*) Churchill.

Diagnostic Use of Rorschach with Children. Jesse Francis-Williams. 1969. 73.00 (*0-08-013057-7*, Pub. by Pergamon Repr UK) Franklin.

Diagnostic Veterinary Clinical Pathology. Cowell & Tyler. 500p. pap. 45.00 (*0-8016-1173-3*) Mosby Yr Bk.

Diagnostico de Enfermeria. 2nd ed. Mija Kim. 1990. pap. text ed. 29.95 (*0-07-104011-0*) McGraw.

Diagnostics. 2nd ed. Ed. by Matthew Cahill & Minnie B. Rose. LC 85-12626. (Nurse's Reference Library). (Illus.). 1108p. 1986. 29.95 (*0-916730-89-1*) Springhouse Pub.

Diagnostics. 2nd ed. Ed. by Helen Hamilton & Minnie B. Rose. 1108p. (C). pap. 24.95 (*0-87434-007-1*) Springhouse Pub.

Diagnostics According to F. X. Mayr: Criteria of Good, Marginal & Ill Health. Erich Rauch. Tr. by David M. Fogg. (Illus.). 129p. (Orig.). 1993. pap. text ed. 25.00 (*2-8043-4004-X*, Pub. by Edits Haug Intl) Medicina Bio.

Diagnostics & Applications of Thin Films: Proceedings of the International Summer School, May 1991, Czechoslovakia. Ed. by L. Eckertova & T. Ruzicka. (Illus.). 328p. 1992. 144.00 (*0-7503-0165-1*) IOP Pub.

Diagnostics & Vaccines for Parasitic Diseases. Ed. by M. Tiru & W. Hennessen. (Developments in Biological Standardization Ser.: Vol. 62). viii, 162p. 1986. pap. 56.00 (*3-8055-4266-6*) S Karger.

Diagnostics in the Year 2000. Ed. by Prithipal Singh et al. LC 92-49894. 1993. text ed. 79.95 (*0-442-00972-0*) Chapman & Hall.

Diagnostics of Adrenal Cortex Diseases: An Integrated Approach, 2 vols. Luigi Troncone. 1986. Vol. I, 240 pgs., Vol. II, 272 pgs. 188.00 (*0-8493-6359-4*, RC659) CRC Pr.

Diagnostics of Adrenal Cortex Diseases, Vol. 1: Integrated Approach. L. Troncone. LC 85-25522. 1986. 107.00 (*0-8493-6360-8*) CRC Pr.

Diagnostics of Adrenal Cortex Diseases, Vol. 2: Integrated Approach. L. Troncone. LC 85-25522. 1986. 152.00 (*0-8493-6361-6*, CRC Reprint) Franklin.

Diagnostik des Hodentumors und Seiner Metastasen. Ed. by L. Weissbach & Roswitha Bussar-Maatz. (Beitraege zur Onkologie, Contributions to Oncology Ser.: Vol. 28). (Illus.). x, 194p. 1987. 53.75 (*3-8055-4614-9*) S Karger.

Diagnostik und Therapie der Erektilen Dysfunktion mit Vasoaktiven Substanzen. Ed. by U. Wetterauer & C. G. Stief. (Illus.). viii, 156p. (C). 1990. lib. bdg. 75.40 (*3-11-012183-2*) De Gruyter.

Diagnostik und Therapie des Prostatakarzinoms. Ed. by H. Goettinger. (Beitraege zur Urologie Ser.: Vol. 1). 1979. pap. 26.50 (*3-8055-0294-X*) S Karger.

Diagonal Line. August J. Nigro. LC 83-50945. 192p. 1984. 32.50 (*0-941664-02-3*) Susquehanna U Pr.

Diagonalization & Self-Reference. Raymond Smullyan. (Logic Guides Ser.). 288p. 1994. 75.00 (*0-19-853450-7*) OUP.

Diagonals: Active Graphic Design. 80p. 1991. pap. 18.95 (*88-7070-160-3*) Belvedere USA.

Diagonsis for Man: Technology, the New Diseases, & Our Present Dilemma. John A. Green, III. 16p. 1985. 3.00 (*0-89756-016-7*) Two Rivers.

Diagram & List of Goshen Presbyterian Church Pews, 1796. Orange County Genealogical Society Staff. 1986. pap. text ed. 0.50 (*0-937135-02-X*) Orange County Genealog.

Diagram Cohomology & Isovariant Homotopy Theory. Giora Dula & Reinhard Schultz. LC 94-14405. (Memoirs of the American Mathematical Society Ser.: No. 527). 1994. write for info. (*0-8218-2589-5*) Am Math.

Diagram Geometrics. A. Pasini. (Mathematical Monographs). 350p. 1994. 95.00 (*0-19-853497-3*) OUP.

Diagram Graphics. P. I. E. Books Editors. (Illus.). 224p. 1993. 79.95 (*4-938586-34-7*) Bks Nippan.

Diagram of Synoptic Relationships. Allan Barr. 1938. 33.95 (*0-567-02021-5*, Pub. by T & T Clark UK) Bks Intl VA.

Diagram Techniques in Group Theory. Geoffrey E. Stedman. (Illus.). 250p. (C). 1990. 110.00 (*0-521-32787-3*) Cambridge U Pr.

***Diagrammatic Reasoning: Cognitive & Computational Perspectives.** N. Hari Narayanan. Ed. by Janice Glasgow et al. LC 95-14683. (AAAI Press Ser.). 500p. (C). 1995. pap. 39.95x (*0-262-57112-9*) MIT Pr.

Diagrammatica: The Path to Feynman Diagrams. Martinus Veltman. (Cambridge Lecture Notes in Physics Ser.: No. 4). (Illus.). 200p. (C). 1994. pap. 29.95 (*0-521-45692-4*) Cambridge U Pr.

Diagrammatical Analysis. Lee L. Kantenwein. 98p. pap. 8.99 (*0-88469-150-0*) BMH Bks.

Diagramming Techniques for Analysts & Programmers. James Martin & Carma L. McClure. (Illus.). 416p. (C). 1984. text ed. 96.00 (*0-13-208794-4*) P-H.

Diagramming the Greek New Testament. Richard P. Belcher. 62p. 1993. reprint ed. pap. write for info. (*1-883265-06-1*) Richbarry Pr.

Diagrams for Faceting, Vol. I. Glenn Vargas & Martha Vargas. LC 75-21404. (Illus.). 190p. 1975. 25.00 (*0-917646-02-9*) Glenn Vargas.

Diagrams for Faceting, Vol. II. Glenn Vargas & Martha Vargas. LC 75-21404. (Illus.). 176p. (C). 1983. 25.00 (*0-917646-05-3*) Glenn Vargas.

Diagrams for Faceting, Vol. III. Glenn Vargas & Martha Vargas. LC 75-21404. (Illus.). 176p. 1987. 25.00 (*0-917646-07-X*) Glenn Vargas.

Diagrams for Living: The Bible Unveiled. Emmet Fox. LC 91-58895. 1993. reprint ed. pap. 10.00 (*0-06-250335-9*) Harper SF.

Diagraphics II. JCA Books Staff. (Illus.). 328p. 1994. 75.00 (*4-931154-21-2*, Pub. by Japan Creat Assn JA) Bks Nippan.

Diakka, & Their Earthly Victims. Andrew J. Davis. 102p. 1971. reprint ed. spiral bd. 5.50 (*0-7873-0259-7*) Mokelumne.

Diakonate. Dale Rumble. 240p. (Orig.). 1990. pap. 7.99 (*1-56043-020-6*) Destiny Image.

Diakonia: Re-interpreting the Ancient Sources. John N. Collins. 384p. 1990. 55.00 (*0-19-506067-9*) OUP.

Diakonia: Studies in Honor of Robert T. Meyer. Ed. by Thomas Halton & Joseph P. Williman. LC 85-21254. 346p. 1986. 24.95 (*0-8132-0596-4*) Cath U Pr.

***Diakonia: Studies in Honor of Robert T. Meyer.** Ed. by Thomas P. Halton & Joseph P. Williman. LC 85-21254. (Illus.). reprint ed. pap. 103.20 (*0-7837-9191-7*, 2049892) Bks Demand.

***Diakonia in the Classical Reformed Tradition & Today.** fac. ed. Elsie A. McKee. LC 89-39372. 151p. (Orig.). 1989. reprint ed. pap. 43.10 (*0-7837-7963-1*, 2047719) Bks Demand.

Dial: A Monthly Magazine for Literature, Philosophy & Religion, Vol. 1, Nos. 1-12. Ed. by Moncure D. Conway. reprint ed. lib. bdg. 76.50 (*0-404-19515-6*) AMS Pr.

Dial: Arts & Letters in the 1920s. Ed. by Gaye L. Brown. LC 80-54667. (Illus.). 160p. (Orig.). 1983. pap. 14.95 (*0-87023-407-2*) U of Mass Pr.

Dial a Christian Message. Olive Martin. Ed. by Jean Oglethorpe. (C). 1989. pap. 30.00 (*1-85072-022-3*, Pub. by W Sessions UK) St Mut.

Dial-a-Croc. Mike Dumbleton. LC 90-25385. (Illus.). 32p. (J). (ps-2). 1991. 14.95 (*0-531-05945-6*); 14.99 (*0-531-08545-7*) Orchard Bks Watts.

***Dial-a-Croc.** Mike Dumbleton. LC 90-25385. (Illus.). 32p. (J). (ps-2). 1995. pap. text ed. 5.95 (*0-531-07059-X*) Orchard Bks Watts.

Dial-a-Dinosaur: Instant Guide to Dinosaurs. Kidsbooks, Inc. Staff. (Illus.). 16p. (Orig.). (J). (gr. 1-4). 1988. pap. 4.95 (*0-8431-2289-7*) Price Stern.

Dial-A-Fax: Fax Phone Box. 1991. 85.00 (*0-945622-01-5*) Dial-A-Fax.

Dial-a-Fax Directory: The Fax Phone Book. Dial-a-Fax Directories Corp. Staff. LC 87-656600. (Illus.). 1500p. 1991. reprint ed. pap. 94.00 (*0-945622-00-7*) Dial-A-Fax.

Dial-a-Porn: Verbal Intercourse or Mass Corruption? Laura Lee. (Orig.). 1993. pap. 16.95 (*0-9634724-0-2*) Bench Pr CA.

Dial-an-Atheist: Greatest Hits from Ohio. Frank R. Zindler. LC 90-46497. 432p. (Orig.). 1991. pap. 15.00 (*0-910309-67-1*, 5566) Am Atheist.

Dial B for Birder: Private Files of a Real Life Bird Detective. Lola Oberman. Ed. by Greg Liinder. 200p. (Orig.). 1992. pap. 12.95 (*1-55971-186-8*) NorthWord.

Dial D for Destiny. Ann Logan. (Superromance Ser.). 1994. mass mkt. 3.50 (*0-373-70585-9*, 1-70585-4) Harlequin Bks.

Dial Detective. Maria-Kay Simms. (Illus.). 112p. (Orig.). 1989. pap. 12.95 (*0-935127-09-7*) ACS Pubns.

Dial Eight Hundred for Health. Comp. by People's Medical Society Staff. LC 92-45044. 1993. pap. 5.95 (*0-9627334-9-0*) Peoples Med Soc.

Dial-It 976 & 900 Report. 130p. 1991. 45.00 (*0-317-04254-8*) NARUC.

***Dial "L" for Loveless.** Alison Tyler. (Orig.). Date not set. mass mkt., pap. 5.95 (*1-56333-386-4*) Masquerade.

Dial M for Murder. Frederick Knott. 1954. pap. 4.75 (*0-8222-0305-7*) Dramatists Play.

***Dial Nine One-One: Peaceful Christians & Urban Violence.** fac. ed. Dave Jackson. LC 81-2541. 152p. 1994. pap. 43.40 (*0-7837-7324-2*, 2047253) Bks Demand.

Dial Nine to Get Out! Commentaries on Business Life...As Heard on Public Radio's "Marketplace" David Graulich. LC 94-3958. 100p. (Orig.). 1994. pap. 9.95 (*1-881052-50-8*) Berrett-Koehler.

Dial 800 for Health. People's Medical Society Staff. LC 93-27097. 1994. 4.99 (*0-517-10025-8*, Pub. by Wings Bks) Random Hse Value.

Dialect & Accent in Industrial West Yorkshire. K. M. Petyt. LC 85-20136. (Varieties of English Around the World General Ser.: 6). viii, 401p. 1985. pap. 87.00x (*90-272-4864-8*) Benjamins North Am.

Dialect & Education: Some European Perspectives. Ed. by Jenny Cheshire et al. 270p. 1989. 99.00 (*1-85359-036-3*, Pub. by Multilingual Matters UK); pap. 39.95 (*1-85359-035-5*, Pub. by Multilingual Matters UK) Taylor & Francis.

Dialect & Language Variation. Harold E. Allen & Michael D. Linn. 1986. pap. text ed. 49.00 (*0-12-051130-4*) Acad Pr.

Dialect & Provenance of the Middle English Poem "The Owl & the Nightingale". A Linguistic Study. B. Sundby. (Lund Studies in English: Vol. 18). 1972. reprint ed. pap. 25.00 (*0-8115-0561-8*) Periodicals Srv.

Dialect & Standard in Highly Industrialized Societies. Ed. by Ulrich Ammon. (International Journal of the Sociology of Language Ser.: No. 21). 1979. text ed. 60.00 (*90-279-7858-1*) Mouton.

Dialect Ballads. Charles F. Adams. LC 78-166640. (Illus.). 1971. reprint ed. 19.00 (*0-403-01415-8*) Scholarly.

Dialect Boundaries & the Question of Franco-Provencal. George Jochnowitz. (Janua Linguarum, Series Practica: No. 147). 1973. pap. text ed. 63.10 (*90-279-2480-5*) Mouton.

Dialect in Use: Sociolinguistic Variation in Cardiff English. Nikolas Coupland. xii, 176p. 1987. 35.00 (*0-7083-0958-5*, Pub. by U of Wales UK) Bks Intl VA.

Dialect Intelligibility Testing. Eugene Casad. (Publications in Linguistics & Related Fields: No. 38). 201p. 1974. pap. 8.00 (*0-88312-040-2*); fiche 12.00 (*0-88312-440-8*) Summer Instit Ling.

An Asterisk (*) at the beginning of an entry indicates that the title is appearing in BIP for the first time.

D

An Asterisk (*) at the beginning of an entry indicates that the title is appearing in BIP for the first time.

Dialogical Apologetics: A Person-Centered Approach to Christian Defense. David K. Clark. LC 92-31661. 208p. (Orig.). 1993. pap. text ed. 12.99 (*0-8010-2573-7*) Baker Bk.

Dialogical Imperative: A Christian Reflection on Interfaith Encounter. David Lochhead. LC 88-1570. (Faith Meets Faith Ser.). 120p. 1988. 39.95 (*0-88344-612-X*); pap. 16.95 (*0-88344-611-1*) Orbis Bks.

Dialogical Philosophy from Kierkegaard to Buber. Shmuel H. Bergman. Tr. by Arnold A. Gerstein. LC 90-38138. (SUNY Series in Jewish Philosophy). 257p. (C). 1991. 64.50 (*0-7914-0623-7*); pap. 21.95 (*0-7914-0624-5*) State U NY Pr.

Dialogical Self: Meaning As Movement. Hubert J. Hermans & Harry J. Kempen. (Illus.). 195p. 1993. text ed. 54.95 (*0-12-342320-1*) Acad Pr.

Dialogical Theatre: Dramatizations of the Conquest of Mexico & the Question of the Other. Max Harris. LC 92-19478. 1993. text ed. 45.00 (*0-312-08562-1*) St Martin.

Dialogicall Discourses of Spirits & Devils, Declaring Their Proper Essence. John Deacon & John Walker. LC 76-57377. (English Experience Ser.: No. 795). 1977. reprint ed. lib. bdg. 55.00 (*90-221-0795-7*) Walter J Johnson.

Dialogics of Critique: M. M. Bakhtin & the Theory of Ideology. Michael Gardiner. LC 91-37484. 240p. 1992. 49.95 (*0-415-06064-8*, A7339); pap. 15.95 (*0-415-07975-6*, A7343) Routledge.

Dialogics of Dissent in the English Novel. Cates Baldridge. LC 93-41021. 219p. (C). 1994. 39.95x (*0-87451-666-8*) U Pr of New Eng.

Dialogics of the Oppressed. Peter Hitchcock. 320p. (C). 1992. text ed. 49.95 (*0-8166-2106-3*); pap. text ed. 19.95 (*0-8166-2107-1*) U of Minn Pr.

Dialogism: Bakhtin & His World. Michael Holquist. (New Accents Ser.). 272p. 1990. 55.00 (*0-415-01179-5*, A4347); pap. 13.95 (*0-415-01180-9*) Routledge.

Dialogo. Primo Levi & Tullio Regge. Tr. by Raymond Rosenthal. 112p. (C). 1989. pap. text ed. 15.95 (*0-691-08545-5*) Princeton U Pr.

***Dialogo - Dialogue - Comhra.** Lucy Lippard et al. (Illus.). 272p. Date not set. pap. 29.95 (*0-9646426-1-1*) Dist Art Pubs.

Dialogo Dos Montes: Spanish Text, English Verse Translation. Reheul Jessurun. Ed. by Philip Polack. (Serie B: Textos, XIX). (Illus.). 153p. (Orig.). (C). 1975. pap. 36.00 (*0-900411-95-3*, Pub. by Tamesis Bks Ltd UK) Boydell & Brewer.

***Dialogo Sobre la Mision.** Stott. 1987. pap. text ed. (*0-8028-0905-7*) Eerdmans.

Dialogos, No. 128. Juan Luis Vives. 153p. (SPA.). 1959. write for info. (*0-8288-8580-X*) Fr & Eur.

Dialogos Bilingues para Todos, Bk. I. John Staulo. 280p. (Orig.). (ENG & SPA.). (C). 1992. pap. text ed. 39.50 (*0-8191-8592-2*) U Pr of Amer.

Dialogos Evangelisticos (Dialogues That Witness) Para Alcanzar a Mas Jovenes para Cristo (Reaching Youth for Christ) Lloyd Mann & Wilma Mann. 96p. (SPA.). 1991. pap. 3.50 (*0-311-12334-1*) Casa Bautista.

Dialogos (Gorgias - Fedon - el Banquete) Platon. Tr. by Luis Roig de Lluis. (Nueva Austral Ser.: Vol. 22). (SPA.). 1991. pap. text ed. 24.95x (*84-239-1822-X*) Elliots Bks.

***Dialogos Y Cuadernos: Introduccion A La Literatura Hispanica.** Peter Ashworth & Harold Moon. 288p. (C). 1994. per., pap. text ed. 34.95 (*0-8403-9599-X*) Kendall-Hunt.

Dialogs: Reading & Writing in the Disciplines. Jeffrey Carroll. (Illus.). 544p. (C). 1992. pap. write for info. (*0-02-319590-8*) Macmillan.

Dialogue. Mark Dunster. 15p. (Orig.). 1985. pap. 4.00 (*0-89642-120-1*) Linden Pubs.

Dialogue. Lewis Turco. (Elements of Fiction Writing Ser.). 128p. 1989. 13.95 (*0-89879-349-1*) Writers Digest.

Dialogue: An-Interdisciplinary Approach. Ed. by Marcelo Dascal. LC 84-24202. (Pragmatics & Beyond Companion Ser.: No. 1). xiv, 473p. 1985. 130.00x (*0-915027-47-X*) Benjamins North Am.

Dialogue: Australian Studies in Art History. Ian Burn. (Illus.). 208p. (Orig.). 1992. pap. text ed. 19.95 (*1-86373-086-9*, Pub. by Allen Unwin AT) Paul & Co Pubs.

Dialogue - An Exhibition of Original Paintings by Dan Kedar. 40p. (Orig.). 1989. pap. text ed. 15.00 (*0-940429-06-3*) M B Glass Assocs.

Dialogue - 89 - The Conservation of Bronze Sculpture in the Outdoor Environment: A Dialogue among Conservators, Curators, Environmental Scientists, & Corrosion Engineers. Intro. by T. Drayman-Weisser. (Illus.). 398p. 1992. pap. text ed. 69.00 (*1-877914-38-X*) NACE Intl.

Dialogue about Catholic Sexual Teaching. Ed. by Charles E. Curran & Richard A. McCormick. LC 93-4370. (Readings in Moral Theology Ser.: No. 8). 624p. 1993. pap. 22.95 (*0-8091-3414-4*) Paulist Pr.

Dialogue & Armed Conflict: Negotiating the Civil War in El Salvador. Riordan Roett & Frank Smyth. (FPI Case Studies: No. 12). 56p. (Orig.). (C). 1989. lib. bdg. 26.75 (*0-941700-36-4*); pap. text ed. 10.00 (*0-941700-37-2*) JH FPI SAIS.

Dialogue & Critical Discourse: Language, Culture, Critical Theory. Ed. by Michael S. Macovski. LC 92-28231. 224p. 1995. 45.00 (*0-19-507063-1*); pap. 21.00 (*0-19-508124-2*) OUP.

Dialogue & Deconstruction: The Gadamer-Derrida Encounter. Ed. by Diane P. Michelfelder & Richard E. Palmer. LC 88-24792. (SUNY Series in Contemporary Continental Philosophy). 352p. 1989. 59.50 (*0-7914-0008-5*); pap. 19.95 (*0-7914-0009-3*) State U NY Pr.

Dialogue & Dialectic: Eight Hermeneutical Studies on Plato. Hans-Georg Gadamer. LC 79-18887. 1983. 13.00 (*0-300-02983-7*) Yale U Pr.

Dialogue & Difference: English for the 1990s. Ed. by Peter Brooker & Peter Humm. 256p. 1989. 49.95 (*0-415-01643-6*, A3622); pap. 13.95 (*0-415-01644-4*, A3626) Routledge.

Dialogue & Disagreement: Franz Rosenzweig's Relevance to Contemporary Jewish-Christian Understanding. Ronald H. Miller. LC 89-35492. 234p. (Orig.). (C). 1990. lib. bdg. 57.00 (*0-8191-7539-0*) U Pr of Amer.

Dialogue & Discovery: A Study in Socratic Method. Kenneth Seeskin. LC 86-14514. (SUNY Series in Philosophy). 179p. (C). 1987. 59.50 (*0-88706-337-3*); pap. 19.95 (*0-88706-336-5*) State U NY Pr.

Dialogue & History: Constructing South India, 1795-1895. Eugene F. Irschick. LC 93-10238. 1994. 45.00 (*0-520-08404-7*); pap. 18.00 (*0-520-08405-5*) U CA Pr.

***Dialogue & Instruction.** M. Reiner. Ed. by R. J. Beun & M. Baker. (NATO ASI Ser.: Vol. 142). 368p. 1995. 90.00 (*3-540-58834-5*) Spr-Verlag.

***Dialogue & Instruction: Modelling Interaction in Intelligent Tutoring Systems.** Ed. by Robbert-Jan Beun et al. LC 95-6511. (NATO ASI Ser.: Series F, Computer & Systems Sciences: Vol. 142). 1995. write for info. (*0-387-58834-5*) Spr-Verlag.

Dialogue & Literature: Apostrophe, Auditors, & the Collapse of Romantic Discourse. Michael Macovski. 250p. 1994. 38.00 (*0-19-506965-X*) OUP.

Dialogue & Syncretism: An Interdisciplinary Approach. Ed. by J. D. Gort et al. (Currents of Encounter Ser.). 240p. (Orig.). (C). 1989. pap. 20.99 (*0-8028-0501-9*) Eerdmans.

Dialogue & Technology: Art & Knowledge. Ed. by Bo Goranzon & M. Florin. (Artificial Intelligence & Society Ser.). xviii, 197p. 1991. pap. 51.00 (*0-387-19574-2*) Spr-Verlag.

Dialogue & the Human Image: Beyond Humanistic Psychology. Maurice Friedman. 300p. (C). 1992. text ed. 38.95 (*0-8039-4368-7*); pap. text ed. 17.95 (*0-8039-4369-5*) Sage.

Dialogue and the Interpretation of Illness: Conversations in a Cameroon Village. Robert Pool. LC 93-4290. (Explorations in Anthropology Ser.). 250p. 1994. 49.95 (*0-85496-873-3*); pap. 19.95 (*1-85973-016-7*) Berg Pubs.

Dialogue at the Margins: Whorf, Bakhtin, & Linguistic Relativity. Emily A. Schultz. LC 90-50097. (New Directions in Anthropological Writing Ser.). 198p. (Orig.). (C). 1991. text ed. 37.50 (*0-299-12700-1*); pap. text ed. 16.95 (*0-299-12704-4*) U of Wis Pr.

Dialogue Between Bergson, Aristotle, & Philologos. 3rd enl. ed. Constantine Cavarnos. LC 88-80318. 80p. 1988. pap. 6.50 (*0-914744-79-8*) Inst Byzantine.

Dialogue Between Philosophy & Religion: The Perspective of Karl Jaspers. Bernard F. O'Connor. LC 87-34685. 228p. (Orig.). (C). 1988. pap. text ed. 22.00 (*0-8191-6863-7*) U Pr of Amer.

Dialogue Between Some Young Men & Sundry Ancient Men. William Bradford. (Works of William Bradford). 1989. reprint ed. lib. bdg. 79.00 (*0-7812-2035-1*) Rprt Serv.

Dialogue Between the Tax Administration & the Taxpayer up to the Filing of the Tax Return. (Cahiers de Droit Fiscal International Ser.: Vol. LXVa). 444p. 1980. pap. 80.00 (*90-200-0603-7*) Kluwer Law Tax Pubs.

Dialogue Between the Tax Administration & the Taxpayer up to the Filing of the Tax Return, Vol. LXVa. 444p. pap. 37.00 (*0-686-41004-1*) Kluwer Ac.

Dialogue Concerning Heresies: Complete Works of St. Thomas More, Set, Vol. 6, Pts. 1 & 2. Ed. by Thomas More et al. LC 63-7949. (Illus.). 910p. (C). 1981. Set. text ed. 95.00 (*0-300-02211-5*) Yale U Pr.

Dialogue Concerning Natural Religion. David Hume. 1972. pap. 5.95 (*0-317-30530-1*) Free Pr.

Dialogue Concerning the Slavery of the Africans. Samuel Hopkins. Bd. with Selling of Joseph. LC 75-82201. LC 75-82201. (Anti-Slavery Crusade in America Ser.). 82p. 1975. reprint ed. 13.95 (*0-405-00640-3*) Ayer.

Dialogue Concerning the Two Chief World Systems, Ptolemaic & Copernican. 2nd rev. ed. Galileo Galilei. Tr. by Stillman Drake. 1967. pap. 17.00 (*0-520-00450-7*) U CA Pr.

Dialogue Dans la Marecage. Marguerite Yourcenar. 47p. (FRE.). 1988. 19.95 (*0-7859-0467-0*, 2070711986) Fr & Eur.

Dialogue de Betes. Colette. (Folio Ser.: No. 701). 160p. (FRE.). 1974. 6.95 (*2-07-036701-0*) Schoenhof.

Dialogue des Carmelites. Georges Bernanos. (Coll. Le Livre de Vie). (FRE.). pap. 10.95 (*0-8288-9079-X*, F87641) Fr & Eur.

Dialogue, Dialectic, & Conversation: A Social Perspective on the Function of Writing. Gregory Clark. LC 89-6214. 120p. (C). 1989. pap. text ed. 12.95 (*0-8093-1579-3*) S Ill U Pr.

Dialogue-Discourse-Research. Eleanor Antin et al. LC 79-54783. (Orig.). 1979. pap. 17.50 (*0-89951-033-7*) Santa Barb Mus Art.

Dialogue: From Birth to One Year: Understanding & Communicating with Your Baby. Helen Whitehouse. (Illus.). 142p. 1986. 15.95 (*0-9617341-0-8*) Helen Whitehouse.

Dialogue Games. Lauri Carlson. 1982. lib. bdg. 107.50 (*90-277-1455-X*) Kluwer Ac.

***Dialogue in a Major Key: Women Scholars Speak.** Ed. & Prol. by Mary H. Maguire. LC 95-3985. 200p. (Orig.). 1995. pap. 20.00 (*0-8141-0881-4*) NCTE.

Dialogue in American Drama. Ruby Cohn. LC 76-154898. 348p. reprint ed. pap. 99.20 (*0-8357-9202-1*, 2017613) Bks Demand.

Dialogue in Children. T. Slama-Cazacu. 1977. 60.80 (*90-279-7754-2*) Mouton.

Dialogue in Early Modern France (1547-1630) Art & Argument. Prol. by Colette H. Winn. LC 92-35530. 304p. 1993. 57.95 (*0-8132-0777-0*) Cath U Pr.

Dialogue in Teaching: Theory & Practice. Nicholas C. Burbules. LC 92-44879. (Advances in Contemporary Educational Thought Ser.: Vol. 10). 208p. (C). 1993. text ed. 43.00 (*0-8077-3242-7*); pap. text ed. 21.95 (*0-8077-3241-9*) Tchrs Coll.

Dialogue in Williamsburg: The Turning Point for South Africa? Michael K. Briand. LC 89-28989. 1989. pap. 10.95 (*1-55815-068-4*) ICS Pr.

Dialogue Is Not a Chaste Event: Comments by Paulo Freire on Issues in Participatory Research. Comp. by Paul Jurmo. (Issues & Concepts Ser.). 35p. (C). pap. 3.00 (*0-932288-78-2*) Ctr Intl Ed U of MA.

Dialogue Journal Communication. Jana Staton et al. Ed. by Marcia Farr. LC 87-27885. (Writing Research Ser.: Vol. 10). 352p. 1988. text ed. 49.50 (*0-89391-338-3*); pap. text ed. 27.50 (*0-89391-431-2*) Ablex Pub.

Dialogue Journal Writing with Nonnative English Speakers: A Handbook for Teachers. Joy K. Peyton & Leslie Reed. LC 89-51727. 1990. pap. 9.95 (*0-939791-37-4*) Tchrs Eng Spkrs.

Dialogue Journal Writing with Nonnative English Speakers: An Instructional Packet for Teachers & Workshop Leaders. Joy K. Peyton & Jana Staton. 152p. 1992. pap. 19.95 (*0-939791-39-0*) Tchrs Eng Spkrs.

Dialogue Journals: Writing as Conversation. Kathy E. Danielson. LC 88-660076. (Fastback Ser.: No. 266). 50p. (Orig.). 1988. pap. 1.25 (*0-87367-266-6*) Phi Delta Kappa.

Dialogue Journals in the Multilingual Classroom: Building Language Fluency & Writing Skills Through Written Interaction. Joy K. Peyton & Jana Staton. Ed. by Marcia Farr. LC 92-10058. (Writing Research Ser.). 320p. (C). 1992. text ed. 49.95 (*0-89391-660-9*); pap. text ed. 24.95 (*0-89391-661-7*) Ablex Pub.

Dialogue of Comfort Against Tribulation. Thomas More. (Complete Works of St. Thomas More: No. 12). 1976. 90.00 (*0-300-01609-3*) Yale U Pr.

Dialogue of Hope: Talking Our Way Through Cancer. Charles Downes & Peggy Downes. LC 93-84083. (Illus.). 136p. 1993. pap. 10.00 (*0-931104-37-8*) Sunflower Ink.

Dialogue of Justice: Toward a Self-Reflective Society. James S. Fishkin. 240p. (C). 1993. text ed. 30.00 (*0-300-05112-3*) Yale U Pr.

Dialogue of Mercury & Charon. Alfonso de Valdes. Tr. & Intro. by Joseph V. Ricapito. LC 84-48489. 224p. 1986. 25.00 (*0-253-31700-2*) Ind U Pr.

Dialogue of Reason: An Analysis of Analytical Philosophy. L. Jonathan Cohen. 256p. 1989. pap. 24.95 (*0-19-824865-2*) OUP.

Dialogue of Religions. Ninian Smart. LC 79-8730. (Library of Philosophy & Theology). 142p. 1981. reprint ed. text ed. 45.00 (*0-313-22187-1*, SMDR, Greenwood Pr) Greenwood.

Dialogue of Salomon & Saturn. Salomon & Saturn. LC 78-178552. (Medieval Studies). reprint ed. 30.00 (*0-404-56667-7*) AMS Pr.

Dialogue of St. Catherine of Siena. St. Catherine of Siena. Tr. & Intro. by Algar Thorold. 1976. reprint ed. pap. 9.00 (*0-89555-037-7*) TAN Bks Pubs.

Dialogue of the Deaf: The India-Pakistan Divide. D. D. Khanna & Kishore Kumar. 224p. (C). 1992. text ed. 25.00 (*81-220-0274-9*, Pub. by Konark Pubs Pvt Ltd II) Advent Bks Div.

Dialogue of the Immortality of the Soul. Plato. LC 73-161797. (Augustan Translators Ser.). reprint ed. 49.50 (*0-404-54134-8*) AMS Pr.

***Dialogue of Touch: Developmental Play Therapy. Viola A. Brody. 373p. (C). 1993. pap. text ed. 20.00 (0-9646232-0-X) Devel Play Trng Assocs.**

A casebook for professionals, parents, teachers, students illustrating how a child & the therapist create a relationship through touch. How to relate to an attachment-problem child. "This is a book as practical as a mother's lap & as tender as a father's belief in you."--S. Simon, University of Massachusetts. "The professions & the world needs to hear what you say in this book."-- C.A. Pinkard, University of South Florida. CONTENTS: Introduction: The History & Method of Developmental Play Therapy; Touching the Self: The Developmental Play Dialogue; The Structure of Developmental Play Therapy; Touching Autism: Developmental Play with Jason; Touching Psychosis: Developmental Play Therapy with Kenny; The Developmental Play Group Program: The One-to-One Child-Adult Play; Circle Time; Training; The Supervisory Model; Appendix: Developmental Play Games. To order write to: Viola A. Brody, 519 Plaza Seville Ct., #38, Treasure Island, FL 33706. 813-323-6113. $20 Libraries & Bookstores 20% discount. ***Publisher Provided Annotation.***

Dialogue of Violence: Filmmaking in World War II's Pacific Theater. Ed. by Abe Mark Nornes & Fukushima Yukio. LC 92-40162. (Studies in Film & Video). 1994. pap. text ed. 18.00 (*3-7186-0562-7*) Gordon & Breach.

Dialogue of Voices: Feminist Theory & Bakhtin. Ed. by Karen Hohne & Helen Wussow. LC 93-8711. 1994. text ed. 44.95 (*0-8166-2295-7*); pap. text ed. 17.95 (*0-8166-2296-5*) U of Minn Pr.

Dialogue on Awakening: Communion with a Loving Brother. Carpenter. 288p. (Orig.). 1992. pap. 12.95 (*0-9633051-0-7*) Carpenters Hl.

Dialogue on Comparable Worth. Michael E. Gold. LC 83-8508. 120p. (Orig.). 1983. 16.00 (*0-87546-098-4*); pap. 7.95 (*0-87546-099-2*) ILR Pr.

Dialogue on Debt: Alternative Analyses & Solutions. George A. Potter. 160p. (Orig.). (C). 1988. pap. text ed. 7.95 (*0-934255-06-7*) Center Concern.

Dialogue on Dialects. Walt Wolfram & Donna Christian. (Dialects & Educational Equity Ser.: No. 1). 20p. (C). 1979. pap. 3.33 (*0-13-209818-0*, P-H) Ctr Appl Ling.

Dialogue on Diversity: A New Agenda for Women. Ed. by Barbarba Peters & Victoria Samuels. 88p. 1978. pap. 1.95 (*0-87495-003-1*) Am Jewish Comm.

Dialogue on Education. Ed. by Robert Theobald. LC 67-21396. (Dialogue Ser.: No. 3). 1967. pap. 3.40 (*0-672-60910-X*, DS3, Bobbs) Macmillan.

Dialogue on G. E. Moore's Ethical Philosophy: Together with an Account of Three Talks with Moore on Diverse Philosophical Questions. Constantine Cavarnos. LC 79-65479. 68p. 1979. 7.95 (*0-914744-43-7*); pap. 5.00 (*0-914744-44-5*) Inst Byzantine.

Dialogue on Personal Identity & Immortality. John R. Perry. LC 78-52943. 60p. (C). 1978. lib. bdg. 21.50 (*0-915144-91-3*); pap. text ed. 3.95 (*0-915144-53-0*) Hackett Pub.

Dialogue on Poetry & Literary Aphorisms. Friedrich Schlegel. Tr. by Ernst Behler & Roman Struc. LC 67-27115. 1968. 28.50 (*0-271-73136-2*) Pa St U Pr.

Dialogue on Technology. Ed. by Robert Theobald. (Dialogue Ser.: No. 2). (Orig.). 1967. pap. 3.20 (*0-672-60909-6*, DS2, Bobbs) Macmillan.

Dialogue on the Control of Human Behavior. Carl Rogers & B. F. Skinner. Ed. by Gerald Gladstein. 30p. 1976. audio 49.50 (*0-88432-028-6*, S29244) Audio-Forum.

Dialogue on the Government of Florence. Francesco Guicciardini. Ed. by Alison Brown. (Cambridge Texts in the History of Political Thought Ser.). 256p. (C). 1994. 59.95 (*0-521-38450-8*); pap. 18.95 (*0-521-45623-1*) Cambridge U Pr.

Dialogue on the Path of Initiation: An Introduction to the Life & Thought of Karlfried Graf Durckheim. Alphonse Goettmann. Tr. by Theodore Nottingham & Rebecca Nottingham. LC 91-77024. (Illus.). 168p. 1992. pap. 12.95 (*0-936385-26-X*) J Friedlander.

Dialogue on the Soul. Aelred Of Rievaulx. (Cistercian Fathers Ser.: No. 22). Orig. Title: De Anima. 1981. 10.95 (*0-87907-222-9*) Cistercian Pubns.

Dialogue on Wealth & Welfare: An Alternative View of World Capital Formation, a Report to the Club of Rome. Orio Giarini. LC 80-412680. (Pergamon International Library Science Technology Engineering & Social Studies). (Illus.). 368p. 1980. 167.00 (*0-08-026088-8*, Pub. by Pergamon Repr UK) Franklin.

Dialogue on Women. Ed. by Robert Theobald. LC 67-26798. (Dialogue Ser.: No. 4). (Orig.). 1967. pap. 2.65 (*0-672-60911-8*, DS4, Bobbs) Macmillan.

Dialogue Partly on Political Liberty. Tibor R. Machan & John O. Nelson. 82p. (Orig.). (C). 1989. pap. text ed. 13.50 (*0-8191-7736-9*) U Pr of Amer.

Dialogue Rejoined: Theology & Ministry in the United States Hispanic Reality. Robert Schreiter & Ana M. Pineda. 160p. (Orig.). 1995. 10.95 (*0-8146-2206-2*) Liturgical Pr.

Dialogue upon the Gardens of the Right Honourable the Lord Viscount Cobham, at Stow. William Gilpin. (Augustan Reprints Ser.: No. 176 (1976)). reprint ed. 12.00 (*0-404-70176-0*) AMS Pr.

Dialogue with a Difference. Ed. by Tony Bayfield & Marcus Braybrooke. 192p. (Orig.). 1992. pap. 18.00 (*0-334-01980-X*, SCM Pr) TPI PA.

Dialogue with a Dolphin: A Journey in Self-Awareness. ViAnn Oden. Ed. by Paul M. Hartloff & Tanya Reid. (Illus.). (Orig.). 1991. pap. 10.95 (*0-944474-28-4*) Anvipa Pr.

Dialogue with Albert Ellis: Against Dogma. Wendy Dryden. (Therapeutically Speaking Ser.). 160p. 1991. 80.00 (*0-335-09286-1*, Open Univ Pr); pap. 32.00 (*0-335-09285-3*, Open Univ Pr) Taylor & Francis.

Dialogue with Arnold Lazarus: "It Depends" Wendy Dryden. (Therapeutically Speaking Ser.). 160p. 1991. 80.00 (*0-335-09280-2*, Open Univ Pr); pap. 32.00 (*0-335-09279-9*, Open Univ Pr) Taylor & Francis.

Dialogue with B. F. Skinner. Richard I. Evans. LC 81-15377. 156p. 1981. text ed. 45.00 (*0-275-90612-4*, C0612, Praeger Pubs) Greenwood.

Dialogue with C. G. Jung. Richard I. Evans. LC 81-15371. 256p. 1981. text ed. 55.00 (*0-275-90616-7*, C0616, Praeger Pubs) Greenwood.

Dialogue with Carl Rogers. Richard I. Evans. LC 81-15373. 286p. 1981. text ed. 49.95 (*0-275-90618-3*, C0618, Praeger Pubs) Greenwood.

Dialogue with Christ. Torkom Saraydarian. LC 77-86722. 1979. pap. 4.00 (*0-911794-42-5*) Aqua Educ.

Dialogue with Death: A Journey Through Consciousness. 2nd ed. Eknath Easwaran. LC 92-38898. 240p. 1992. text ed. 22.00 (*0-915132-73-7*); pap. 13.95 (*0-915132-72-9*) Nilgiri Pr.

Dialogue with Death: Shri Aurobindo's Savitri: A Mystical Approach. Ed. by Rohit Mehta. (C). 1983. reprint ed. 17.50 (*0-8364-2507-3*, Pub. by Motilal Banarsidass II) S Asia.

D

An Asterisk (*) at the beginning of an entry indicates that the title is appearing in BIP for the first time.

Dialogue with Deviance: The Hasidic Ethic & the Theory of Social Contraction. Mordechai Rotenberg. LC 93-6901. 283p. (C). 1993. reprint ed. pap. 18.95 (0-8191-8975-8) U Pr of Amer.

Dialogue with Erich Fromm. Richard I. Evans. LC 81-15376. 160p. 1981. text ed. 45.00 (0-275-90614-0, C0614, Praeger Pubs) Greenwood.

***Dialogue with Erik Erikson.** Richard I. Evans. 190p. 1995. pap. 22.50 (1-56821-561-4) Aronson.

Dialogue with Friends. Patricia Gilmore. Incl. Letters from Friends. 1988. (0-318-63125-3); 1988. Set pap. 6.95 (0-9618242-1-2) Horizon Soc Pubns.

Dialogue with God. Mark Vikler. LC 86-70744. 260p. 1986. pap. 7.95 (0-88270-620-9) Bridge Pub.

Dialogue with Hassidic Tales: Hallowing the Everyday. Maurice Friedman. (Insight Book Ser.). 163p. 1989. 29.95 (0-89885-407-5) Human Sci Pr.

Dialogue with Heidegger on Values: Ethics for Times of Crisis. Ernest Joos. LC 91-38671. (American University Studies: Philosophy: Ser. V, Vol. 127). 198p. (C). 1992. text ed. 37.95 (0-8204-1649-5) P Lang Pubs.

Dialogue with Jean Piaget. Richard I. Evans. LC 81-15374. 254p. 1981. text ed. 55.00 (0-275-90619-1, C0619, Praeger Pubs) Greenwood.

Dialogue with Jehovah's Witnesses, 2 vols., I. Duane Magnani. 1983. 13.95 (1-883858-08-9) Witness CA.

Dialogue with Jehovah's Witnesses, 2 vols., II. Duane Magnani. 1983. 13.95 (1-883858-09-7) Witness CA.

Dialogue with Jehovah's Witnesses, 2 vols., Set. Duane Magnani. 1983. 22.95 (1-883858-07-0) Witness CA.

Dialogue with John Norcross: Toward Integration. Wendy Dryden. (Therapeutically Speaking Ser.). 160p. 1991. 80.00 (0-335-09441-4, Open Univ Pr); pap. 32.00 (0-335-09440-6, Open Univ Pr) Taylor & Francis.

***Dialogue with Masks.** Mary Melfi. 80p. 1995. lib. bdg. 25.00 (0-8095-4537-3) Borgo Pr.

Dialogue with Nature: Nine Contemporary Sculptors. Linda L. Johnson. LC 92-30181. (Illus.). 32p. 1992. pap. 10.00 (0-943044-18-9) Phillips Coll.

***Dialogue with Photography.** Paul Hill & Thomas Cooper. 352p. 1995. pap. 17.95 (0-948797-66-5) Dist Art Pubs.

Dialogue with R. D. Laing. Richard I. Evans. LC 81-15372. 250p. 1981. text ed. 55.00 (0-275-90617-5, C0617, Praeger Pubs) Greenwood.

Dialogue with Sammy: A Psychoanalytic Contribution to the Understanding of Child Psychosis. Joyce McDougall & Serge Lebovici. 296p. 1989. pap. 20.00 (1-85343-109-5) Col U Pr.

Dialogue with Street Fighters. Alfred Fleishman. LC 81-80600. 140p. 1981. pap. text ed. 8.00 (0-918970-29-6) Intl Gen Semantics.

Dialogue with the Dogcatcher. Janet McCann. 50p. (Orig.). 1987. 10.95 (0-941720-52-7); pap. 3.95 (0-941720-53-5) Slough Pr TX.

Dialogue with the Masters. C. Richards. Ed. by G. Arledge. 54p. (Orig.). 1994. pap. text ed. 4.00 (0-9625067-1-0) Helpers Pr.

Dialogue with the Other: Martin Buber & the Quaker Experience. Janet E. Schroeder. LC 73-92486. 32p. (Orig.). 1973. pap. 3.00 (0-87574-192-4) Pendle Hill.

Dialogue with the Other: The Interreligious Dialogue. David Tracy. 272p. (Orig.). 1991. pap. 14.99 (0-8028-0562-0) Eerdmans.

Dialogues. Stanley Berne. LC 62-7479. (Illus.). 108p. 1962. pap. 100.00 (0-913844-15-2) Am Canadian.

Dialogues. Gilles Deleuze & Claire Parnet. Tr. by Hugh Tomlinson & Barbara Habberjam. (European Perspectives Ser.). 200p. 1989. text ed. 40.50 (0-231-06600-7); pap. text ed. 16.00 (0-231-06601-5) Col U Pr.

Dialogues. Louise O. Neaderland. (Illus.). 13p. (Orig.). 1990. 12.00 (0-942561-15-5) Bone Hollow.

Dialogues. Lucius Annaeus Seneca. Ed. by Leighton D. Reynolds. (Oxford Classical Texts Ser.). 1977. text ed. 29.95 (0-19-814659-0) OUP.

Dialogues. Abbey Strauss. LC 91-67746. 208p. 1993. pap. 11.95 (1-56002-147-0, Univ Edtns) Aegina Pr.

Dialogues. Paul Valery. (Bollingen Ser.). 1989. pap. 9.95 (0-691-01878-2) Princeton U Pr.

***Dialogues.** Gregory. Tr. by Odo J. Zimmerman. (Fathers of the Church Ser.: Vol. 39). 303p. Date not set. reprint ed. pap. 86.40 (0-7837-9144-5, 2049944) Bks Demand.

Dialogues. Igor Stravinsky & Robert Craft. LC 82-50247. (Illus.). 152p. reprint ed. pap. 43.40 (0-7837-4848-5, 2044495) Bks Demand.

Dialogues, 1. Lucian. (Loeb Classical Library: No. 14, 54, 130, 162, 302, 430-432). 486p. 1913. text ed. 18.95 (0-674-99015-3) HUP.

Dialogues, 2. Lucian. (Loeb Classical Library: No. 14, 54, 130, 162, 302, 430-432). 530p. 1915. text ed. 18.95 (0-674-99060-9) HUP.

Dialogues, 3. Lucian. (Loeb Classical Library: No. 14, 54, 130, 162, 302, 430-432). 498p. 1921. text ed. 18.95 (0-674-99144-3) HUP.

Dialogues, 4. Lucian. (Loeb Classical Library: No. 14, 54, 130, 162, 302, 430-432). 430p. 1925. text ed. 18.95 (0-674-99179-6) HUP.

Dialogues, 5. Lucian. (Loeb Classical Library: No. 14, 54, 130, 162, 302, 430-432). 548p. 1936. text ed. 18.95 (0-674-99333-0) HUP.

Dialogues, 6. Lucian. (Loeb Classical Library: No. 14, 54, 130, 162, 302, 430-432). 280p. 1959. text ed. 18.95 (0-674-99474-4) HUP.

Dialogues, 7. Lucian. (Loeb Classical Library: No. 14, 54, 130, 162, 302, 430-432). 488p. 1961. text ed. 18.95 (0-674-99475-2) HUP.

Dialogues, 8. Lucian. (Loeb Classical Library: No. 14, 54, 130, 162, 302, 430-432). 544p. 1967. text ed. 18.95 (0-674-99476-0) HUP.

Dialogues, 2 vols., I. Plato. Tr. by Benjamin E. Jowett. 1937. 25.00 (0-394-42004-7) Random.

Dialogues: The Dying & the Living. Austin H. Kutscher & Lillian G. Kutscher. 1979. 20.95 (0-405-12511-9) Ayer.

Dialogues - Dialogi: Literary & Cultural Exchanges Between (Ex) Soviet & American Women. Susan H. Aiken et al. LC 93-8650. (Illus.). 440p. 1994. lib. bdg. 35.00 (0-8223-1375-8); pap. text ed. 19.95 (0-8223-1390-1) Duke.

Dialogues about Adoption: Conversations Between Parents & Their Children. Linda Bothun. LC 94-69688. 216p. (Orig.). 1994. pap. 12.95 (0-9619559-1-0) Swan Pubns.

Dialogues & Debates in Social Psychology. Ed. by Jeannette Murphy et al. 368p. 1985. pap. 19.95 (0-86377-020-7) L Erlbaum Assocs.

Dialogues & Dramas. Ed. by Lewis B. Monroe. LC 78-38602. (Granger Index Reprint Ser.). 1977. reprint ed. 19.95 (0-8369-6334-2) Ayer.

Dialogues & Ideologues. Thomas Molnar. 1977. reprint ed. 4.95 (0-8199-0679-4, Frncscn Herld) Franciscan Pr.

Dialogues & Monologues. Humbert Wolfe. LC 74-121515. (Essay Index Reprint Ser.). 1977. 20.95 (0-8369-1818-5) Ayer.

Dialogues Concerning Natural Religion. David Hume. Ed. by Richard H. Popkin. LC 79-25349. (HPC Classics Ser.). 132p. (C). 1980. lib. bdg. 22.50 (0-915144-46-8); pap. text ed. 4.50 (0-915144-45-X) Hackett Pub.

Dialogues Concerning Natural Religion. David Hume. Ed. by Henry D. Aiken. (Library of Classics: No. 5). 128p. 1970. pap. 11.95 (0-02-846180-0) Hafner.

Dialogues Concerning Natural Religion. David Hume. (Great Books in Philosophy). 114p. 1989. pap. text ed. 5.95x (0-87975-527-X) Prometheus Bks.

Dialogues Concerning Natural Religion. David Hume. (Classics Ser.). 160p. 1990. pap. 7.95 (0-14-044536-6, Penguin Classics) Viking Penguin.

Dialogues Concerning Natural Religion: Hume. Norman K. Smith. 264p. (C). 1947. pap. write for info. (0-02-412930-5) Macmillan.

Dialogues Concerning Natural Religion & the Natural History of Religion. David Hume. Ed. & Intro. by J. C. Gaskin. LC 93-18246. (World's Classics Ser.). 1994. 7.95 (0-19-282932-7) OUP.

Dialogues Concerning the Foundations of Ethics. K. Richard Garrett. 200p. (C). 1990. text ed. 59.00 (0-8476-7639-0); pap. text ed. 14.95 (0-8476-7640-4) Rowman.

Dialogues Concerning Two New Sciences. Galileo Galilei. (Illus.). 300p. 1914. pap. text ed. 7.95 (0-486-60099-8) Dover.

Dialogues Concerning Two New Sciences. Galileo Galilei. (Great Minds Ser.). 294p. 1991. pap. 9.95 (0-87975-707-8) Prometheus Bks.

Dialogues Concerning Two New Sciences. Galileo Galilei. Tr. by Henry Crew & Alfonso De Salvio. (University Studies Ser.). 316p. reprint ed. pap. 90.10 (0-8357-9453-9, 2015284) Bks Demand.

Dialogues de Betes. Sidonie-Gabrielle Colette. (FRE.). 1975. pap. 10.95 (0-7859-1811-6, 2070367010) Fr & Eur.

Dialogues for Diversity: Community & Ethnicity on Campus. LC 93-31063. 184p. 1994. pap. 16.50 (0-89774-867-0) Oryx Pr.

Dialogues for Practice in Idiomatic Italian. Giuliana Katz. 160p. 1988. teacher ed 1.00 (0-8020-6680-1); pap. text ed. 14.95 (0-8020-6670-4) U of Toronto Pr.

Dialogues from Delphi. Jacob Loewenberg. LC 77-121485. (Essay Index Reprint Ser.). 1977. 21.95 (0-8369-1886-X) Ayer.

Dialogues in a Cave. Charlotte M. Stein. 239p. (Orig.). 1975. pap. 3.49 (0-916634-01-9) Double M Pr.

Dialogues in a Monastery. Constantine Tsatsos. xii, 182p. 1988. 15.95 (0-917653-14-9); pap. 10.95 (0-318-35071-8) Hellenic Coll Pr.

Dialogues in Academia I: Introduction to a New Faith for Mankind. Kathryn E. Ruggles. LC 91-66271. 247p. (Orig.). 1991. pap. 12.00 (0-9623596-1-0) Natl Spir Assy HI.

Dialogues in American Politics. Donald Roy. 160p. 1993. spiral bd. 26.95 (0-8403-8661-3) Kendall-Hunt.

Dialogues in French & English. William Caxton. Ed. by H. Bradley. (EETS, ES Ser.: No. 79). 1972. reprint ed. pap. 25.00 (0-527-00281-X) Periodicals Srv.

Dialogues in Judaism: Jewish Dilemmas Defined, Debated, & Explored. William Berkowitz. LC 91-8732. 552p. 1991. 39.95 (0-87668-654-4) Aronson.

Dialogues in Metapsychiatry. Thomas Hora. LC 77-8268. 238p. 20.00 (0-913105-16-3) PAGL Pr.

***Dialogues in Neurological Surgery.** Ed. by Mark N. Hadley. 1995. 65.00 (0-942219-76-7) Quality Med Pub.

Dialogues in Paradise. Can Xue. Tr. by Ronald Janssen & Jian Zhang. 173p. (Orig.). 1989. pap. 9.95 (0-8101-0831-3) Northwestern U Pr.

Dialogues in Perception. Bela Julesz. 730p. 1994. 49.95x (0-262-10052-5, Bradford Bks) MIT Pr.

Dialogues in Phenomenologie. Ihde & Zaner. (Selected Studies in Phenomenology & Existential Philosophy: No. 5). 1975. pap. text ed. 74.50 (90-247-1665-9) Kluwer Ac.

Dialogues in Swing: Intimate Conversations with the Stars of the Big Band Era. Fred Hall. Ed. by Eugene D. Wheeler. LC 89-9273. 240p. (Orig.). 1989. pap. 9.95 (0-934793-19-0) Pathfinder CA.

Dialogues in Swing: Intimate Conversations with the Stars of the Big Band Era. Fred Hall. 240p. (Orig.). 1991. reprint ed. lib. bdg. 33.00x (0-8095-5907-2) Borgo Pr.

Dialogues in the English & Malaiane Languages. Gothard Arthus. Tr. by A. Spalding. LC 74-80160. (English Experience Ser.: No. 640). 1974. reprint ed. 20.00 (90-221-0640-3) Walter J Johnson.

Dialogues of Alfred North Whitehead. Alfred N. Whitehead. LC 76-49903. (Illus.). 396p. 1977. reprint ed. text ed. 72.50 (0-8371-9341-9, WHDI, Greenwood Pr) Greenwood.

Dialogues of Athing & Other Poems. Harold Holden. 112p. 1993. 16.00 (0-9641178-0-0) Inland Bks.

Dialogues of Fundamental Equations of Science & Philosophy. A. Pfeiffer & J. Mendelssohn. LC 66-30633. 1967. 60.00 (0-08-012231-0, Pub. by Pergamon Repr UK) Franklin.

Dialogues of G. de Purucker, 3 vols., Set. G. De Purucker. Ed. by Arthur L. Conger. LC 79-65630. 1420p. 1948. 35.00 (0-911500-59-6) Theos U Pr.

Dialogues of Gurdjieff: An Allegorical Adventure. enl. rev. ed. Jan, pseud. 318p. 1981. 20.00 (0-936380-02-0) Chan Shal Imi.

Dialogues of Lewis & Clark: A Narrative Poem. Robert E. Lee. LC 78-67631. (Illus.). 87p. reprint ed. pap. 25.00 (0-8357-5504-5, 2035119) Bks Demand.

Dialogues of Plato. Plato. 400p. 1986. 5.95 (0-553-21371-7, Bantam Classics) Bantam.

Dialogues of Plato. Plato. Ed. by Justin E. Kaplan. Tr. by Benjamin E. Jowett. 400p. (C). 1984. mass mkt. 5.99 (0-671-52524-7, WSP) PB.

Dialogues of Plato, Vol. 1. R. E. Allen. LC 84-17349. 384p. (Orig.). (C). 1989. pap. 17.00 (0-300-04488-7) Yale U Pr.

Dialogues of Plato: Euthyphro; Apology; Crito; Meno; Gorgias; Menexenus, Vol. I. Tr. by R. E. Allen. LC 84-17349. 384p. 1985. text ed. 47.00 (0-300-03226-9) Yale U Pr.

Dialogues of Plato Vol. II: The Symposium, Translated with Commentary. Reginald E. Allen. 184p. 1991. text ed. 30.00x (0-300-04874-2) Yale U Pr.

Dialogues of Plato, Vol. II: The Symposium. Tr. & Comment by R. E. Allen. 189p. (C). 1993. pap. 12.00 (0-300-05699-0) Yale U Pr.

Dialogues of the Buddha, 3 vols., 1. Tr. by T. W. Davids & C. A. Davids. (C). 1977. 32.50 (0-86013-033-9, Pub. by Pali Text) Wisdom MA.

Dialogues of the Buddha, 3 vols., 2. Tr. by T. W. Davids & C. A. Davids. (C). 1977. 32.50 (0-86013-034-7, Pub. by Pali Text) Wisdom MA.

Dialogues of the Buddha, 3 vols., 3. Tr. by T. W. Davids & C. A. Davids. (C). 1977. 30.00 (0-86013-035-5, Pub. by Pali Text) Wisdom MA.

Dialogues of the Buddha, 3 vols., Set. Tr. by T. W. Davids & C. A. Davids. (C). 1977. 91.00 (0-86013-258-7, Pub. by Pali Text) Wisdom MA.

Dialogues of the Courtesans see Maillol Nudes: Thirty-Five Lithographs by Aristide Maillol

Dialogues of the Soul & Mortal Self in Time. Jane Roberts. 1979. pap. 4.95 (0-685-03831-9) P-H.

Dialogues of the Word: The Bible As Literature According to Bakhtin. Walter L. Reed. LC 92-36420. 248p. (C). 1993. 39.95 (0-19-507997-3) OUP.

Dialogues on A Course in Miracles. Tara Singh. LC 86-82912. (Orig.). 1987. 19.95 (1-55531-130-X); pap. 14.95 (1-55531-131-8) Life Action Pr.

Dialogues on Art. Edouard Roditi. LC 79-91612. 250p. 1980. pap. 11.95 (0-915520-21-4) R-E CA.

***Dialogues on Course.** Tara Singh. Date not set. pap. write for info. (0-345-38402-4) Ballantine.

Dialogues on Development: For the Development Approach to Education. 110p. (Orig.). 1986. pap. 8.95 (0-935493-03-4, RRB 306) Programs Educ.

Dialogues on Developmental Curriculum: K-1. Ed. by James K. Uphoff. 257p. (Orig.). 1987. pap. text ed. 11.95 (0-935493-10-7, RRB 334) Programs Educ.

Dialogues on Moral Education. John Wilson & Barbara Cowell. LC 83-4433. 170p. (Orig.). 1983. pap. 12.95 (0-89135-035-7) Religious Educ.

Dialogues on the Arcana of Love & Venus. Luisa S. Toletana. Tr. by Donald A. McKenzie. 174p. 1974. 10.00 (0-87291-069-5) Coronado Pr.

Dialogues on the Philosophy of Marxism: Proceedings of the Society for the Philosophical Study of Dialectical Materialism. John Somerville & Howard L. Parsons. LC 77-149963. (Contributions in Philosophy Ser.: No. 6). 420p. 1974. text ed. 75.00 (0-8371-6062-6, PAD/) Greenwood.

Dialogues on the Psychology of Language & Thought: Conversations with Noam Chomsky, Charles Osgood, Jean Piaget, Ulric Neisser, & Marcel Kinsbourne. Ed. by Robert W. Rieber. LC 82-42850. (Cognition & Language Ser.). 174p. 1983. 42.50 (0-306-41185-7, Plenum Pr) Plenum.

Dialogues on the Supersensual Life. Jacob Boehme. Tr. by William Law. 144p. 1992. pap. 17.95 (1-56459-216-2) Kessinger Pub.

Dialogues on the Teaching of Literature. Bertrand Evans & James J. Lynch. 14.95 (0-8084-0397-4); pap. 10.95 (0-8084-0398-2) NCUP.

Dialogues on Time, Being & Awareness. Elias H. Chacalos. LC 75-25220. 1976. 18.95 (0-917262-01-8) Potomac Pr Cir.

Dialogues on Verbal Behavior. Ed. by Linda J. Hayes & Philip N. Chase. (International Institute on Verbal Relations Ser.). 349p. 1991. text ed. 54.95 (1-878978-06-3); pap. text ed. 34.95 (1-878978-00-4) Context Pr.

Dialogues Philosophiques. Francois-Marie de Voltaire. 538p. 1966. 49.95 (0-8288-7420-4) Fr & Eur.

Dialogues sur le Commandement. Andre Maurois. (FRE.). 1924. pap. 13.95 (0-7859-5316-7) Fr & Eur.

Dialogues with a Modern Mystic. Mark Matousek & Andrew Harvey. (Illus.). 200p. (Orig.). 1994. pap. 12.00 (0-8356-0704-6, Quest) Theos Pub Hse.

Dialogues with Children. Gareth B. Matthews. 136p. 1984. 17.95 (0-674-20282-1) HUP.

Dialogues with Children. Gareth B. Matthews. 136p. 1992. pap. 10.95 (0-674-20284-8) HUP.

Dialogues with Contemporary Continental Thinkers: Richard Kearney in Dialogue with Paul Ricoeur, Emmanuel Levinas, Herbert Marcuse, Stanislas Breton & Jacques Derrida. Richard Kearney. LC 84-17162. 160p. 1988. text ed. 15.95 (0-7190-1729-7, Pub. by Manchester Univ Pr UK) St Martin.

Dialogues with Convention: Essays in Renaissance Poetry. R. D. Bedford. LC 89-20269. 204p. 1990. 34.50 (0-472-10171-4) U of Mich Pr.

Dialogues with Death. Willie M. Boyd. 1993. 8.95 (0-8062-4510-7) Carlton.

Dialogues with God. Frances J. Roberts. 1968. 9.50 (0-932814-07-7); pap. 6.50 (0-932814-08-5) Kings Farspan.

Dialogues with God: Sonnet Psalms on the Significance of Being Human. Benito F. Reyes. LC 78-244706. 139p. 1969. reprint ed. pap. 10.00 (0-939375-37-0) World Univ Amer.

Dialogues with Kohelet: The Book of Ecclesiastes, Translation & Commentary. Tr. & Comment by T. A. Perry. LC 92-16256. 256p. (C). 1993. 25.00 (0-271-00882-2) Pa St U Pr.

Dialogues with Leuco. Cesare Pavese. Tr. by William Arrowsmith. LC 89-83807. 201p. 1989. 17.95 (0-941419-38-X, Eridanos Library) Marsilio Pubs.

Dialogues with Marcel Duchamp. Pierre Cabanne. (Quality Paperbacks Ser.). (Illus.). 152p. 1987. reprint ed. pap. 9.95 (0-306-80303-8) Da Capo.

Dialogues with Northwest Writers: Interviews with Nine Writers, Including Tom Robbins, Mary Barnard & Richard Hugo. Ed. by John Witte. LC 82-19063. (Illus.). 280p. (Orig.). 1982. pap. 8.00 (0-918402-06-9) NW Review Bks.

Dialogues with Scientists & Sages. Renee Weber. 1988. pap. 12.95 (0-14-019087-2, Penguin Bks) Viking Penguin.

Dialogues with the Dead: The Discussion of Mortality among the Sora of Eastern India. Piers Vitebsky. (Cambridge Studies in Social & Cultural Anthropology: No. 88). (Illus.). 288p. (C). 1993. 59.95 (0-521-38447-8) Cambridge U Pr.

Dialogues with the Devil. Taylor Caldwell. 20.95 (0-89190-279-1, Am Repr) Amereon Ltd.

Dialogues with the Devil. Taylor Caldwell. 1987. pap. 3.50 (0-449-21508-3) Fawcett.

Dialogus de Oratoribus. Tacitus. Ed. by Charles E. Bennett. (College Classical Ser.). 1983. 25.00 (0-89241-380-8); pap. 12.50 (0-89241-226-7) Caratzas.

Dialogus Inter Militem et Clericum: Richard FitzRalph's Sermon. J. Trevisa. (EETS, OS Ser.: No. 167). 1972. reprint ed. 40.00 (0-527-00164-3) Periodicals Srv.

***Dialysis.** James Fowlds & Linda Skidmore-Roth. (Outline Ser.). 300p. (Orig.). (C). Date not set. pap. text ed. 16.95 (1-56930-030-5) Skidmore Roth Pub.

Dialysis & the Treatment of Renal Insufficiency. John C. Van Stone. 386p. 1983. text ed. 88.00 (0-8089-1566-5, 794699, Grune) Saunders.

Dialysis & Transplantation: Diagnostics & Techniques. Karl M. Koch & Philip H. Halloran. Ed. by Norman M. Kaplan & M. Donald Blaufox. (Current Opinion in Nephrology & Hypertension Ser.). (Illus.). 1026p. (Orig.). 1993. pap. text ed. 49.95 (1-85922-006-1) Current Science.

***Dialysis & Transplantation: Diagnostics & Techniques.** Karl M. Koch & Phillip F. Halloran. Ed. by Norman M. Kaplan & M. Donald Blaufox. (Current Opinion in Nephrology & Hypertension Ser.). (Illus.). 664p. (Orig.). 1994. pap. text ed. 49.95 (1-85922-617-5) Current Science.

Dialysis Instant Instructor. Fowlds. spiral bd. write for info. (1-56930-020-8) Skidmore Roth Pub.

***Dialysis Membranes: Structure & Predictions.** Ed. by V. Bonomini. (Contributions to Nephrology Ser.: Vol. 113). (Illus.). viii, 140p. 1995. 117.75 (3-8055-6061-3) S Karger.

***Dialysis Nurse's Survival Guide.** James Fowlds & Linda Skidmore-Roth. (Nurse's Survival Guide Ser.). 300p. (Orig.). (C). 1995. pap. text ed. 24.95 (1-56930-019-4) Skidmore Roth Pub.

***Dialysis-Related Amyloidosis.** Ed. by K. Maeda & T. Shinzato. (Contributions to Nephrology Ser.: Vol. 112). (Illus.). viii, 192p. 1994. 152.00 (3-8055-6046-X) S Karger.

Dialysis Therapy. 2nd ed. Ed. by Allen R. Nissenson & Richard N. Fine. 417p. (Orig.). 1992. pap. text ed. 53.00 (1-56053-058-8) Hanley & Belfus.

Dialysis Therapy in the 1990s. Ed. by H. Tanaka. (Contributions to Nephrology Ser.: Vol. 82). (Illus.). 116p. 1991. 87.25 (3-8055-5188-6) S Karger.

Dialysis, Transplantation & Nephrology: Proceedings, Vol. 12. European Dialysis & Transplant Association Staff. Ed. by J. F. Moorhead. (Illus.). 1976. text ed. 65.00 (0-8464-0327-7) Beekman Pubs.

Dialysis, Transplantation & Nephrology: Proceedings of the European Dialysis & Transplant Association, Tel Aviv, 1974, Vol. 11. European Dialysis & Transplant Association Staff. Ed. by John Moorhead. (Illus.). 600p. 1975. 65.00 (0-8464-0326-9) Beekman Pubs.

Dialysis, Transplantation, Nephrology: Proceedings European Dialysis & Transplant Assoc. Volume 13. Ed. by Brian Robinson. (Illus.). 1977. 65.00 (0-8464-0328-5) Beekman Pubs.

Dialysis, Transplantation, Nephrology: Proceedings, European Dialysis & Transplant Association. Brian Robinson. (Illus.). 1978. 65.00 (0-8464-0329-3) Beekman Pubs.

D

An Asterisk (*) at the beginning of an entry indicates that the title is appearing in BIP for the first time.

Dialysis, Transplantation, Nephrology: Proceedings, European Dialysis & Transplant Association, Vol. 15. Ed. by Brian Robinson. (Illus.). 662p. 1979. 65.00 (*0-8464-1087-7*) Beekman Pubs.

Dialysis, Transplantation, Nephrology: Proceedings, European Dialysis & Transplant Association, Vol. 16. Ed. by J. H. Robinson et al. (Illus.). 785p. 1979. 65.00 (*0-8464-1067-2*) Beekman Pubs.

Diamante Gedenkzuilen en Leerzaeme Voorbeelden: Een Bespreking van Johan van Gools "Nieuwe Schouburg" Lyckle De Vries. (Illus.). 280p. (DUT.). 1991. 55.00 (*90-6980-032-2*, Pub. by Egbert Forsten NE) Benjamins North Am.

Diamat As Philosophy of Nature. F. Spratt. 1980. lib. bdg. 59.95 (*0-8490-3082-X*) Gordon Pr.

Diamond. Gordon Davies. (Illus.). 267p. 1984. 69.00 (*0-85274-512-5*) IOP Pub.

Diamond. Mark Dunster. 17p. (Orig.). 1994. pap. 4.00 (*0-89642-238-0*) Linden Pubs.

Diamond. R. V. Huddlestone. (Butterworth Gem Ser.). (Illus.). 208p. 1989. text ed. 29.95 (*0-7506-1054-9*) Buttrwrth-Heinemann.

Diamond. Bobby Owens. LC 93-90791. 217p. 1993. 34.00 (*1-884308-01-5*); pap. text ed. 10.95 (*1-884308-02-3*) Enlisted Ldrship.

Diamond. Sharon Sala. 1994. mass mkt. 4.50 (*0-06-108196-5*, Harp PBks) HarpC.

Diamond: Baseball Writings of Mark Harris. Mark Harris. LC 93-74482. 256p. 1994. 21.95 (*1-55611-398-6*) D I Fine.

***Diamond: Baseball Writings of Mark Harris.** Mark Harris. 300p. 1995. pap. 12.95 (*1-55611-431-1*) D I Fine.

***Diamond: Electronic Properties & Applications.** Ed. by Lawrence S. Pan. (International Series in Engineering & Computer Science, Natural Language Processing & Machine Translation). 488p. (C). 1994. lib. bdg. 145.00 (*0-7923-9524-7*) Kluwer Ac.

***Diamond Age: Or, Young Lady's Illustrated Primer.** Neal Stephenson. LC 94-30486. 1995. pap. 22.95 (*0-553-09609-5*) Bantam.

Diamond & Diamond-Like Films & Coatings. Ed. by R. E. Clausing et al. (NATO ASI Series B, Physics: Vol. 266). (Illus.). 890p. 1991. 175.00 (*0-306-44004-0*, Plenum Pr) Plenum.

Diamond & Jewelry Trade Directory. Ed. by Peter Glenn et al. 1987. 20.00 (*0-87314-077-X*); pap. 3.00 (*0-87314-076-1*) Peter Glenn.

Diamond Anthology of Prose & Poetry: Seventy-Fifth Year. Writers' League of Washington Staff. Ed. by Marijane Ricketts et al. (Illus.). 112p. (YA). (gr. 8-12). 1992. pap. write for info. (*0-9618223-2-5*) M G Ricketts.

Diamond Before You Die. large type ed. Chris Wiltz. 1990. 21.95 (*0-7089-2194-9*) Ulverscroft.

Diamond Bessie & the Shepherds. Ed. & Intro. by Wilson M. Hudson. (Annual Pubns. Ser., No. 36). (Illus.). 170p. 1972. 15.00 (*0-88426-011-9*) Encino Pr.

Diamond Bird. Y. Weinberg. (Diamond Twin Adventure Ser.). 1991. 10.95 (*0-89906-410-8*); 7.95 (*0-89906-411-6*) Mesorah Pubns.

Diamond Buckow. A. J. Arnold. (Novel of the West Ser.). 1993. 16.95 (*0-87131-731-1*) M Evans.

Diamond Buying Guide. 1989. write for info. (*0-318-66973-0*) Briarcliff Pr.

***Diamond Cat.** Marian Babson. 224p. 1995. 20.95 (*0-312-13049-X*, Pub. by Thomas Dunne Bks) St Martin.

Diamond Champs. Matt Christopher. (J). (gr. 4-7). 1990. mass mkt. 3.95 (*0-316-14006-6*) Little.

Diamond Classics: Essays on One Hundred of the Best Baseball Books Ever Published. Mike Shannon. LC 89-42571. 471p. 1989. lib. bdg. 32.50x (*0-89950-320-9*) McFarland & Co.

Diamond Curse. Fred Kamil. 1993. 16.95 (*0-533-10168-9*) Vantage.

Diamond Cut Diamond. large type ed. Donnelly. 1991. pap. 15.95 (*0-7927-0406-1*, AS039, Atlantic Lrg Print) Chivers N Amer.

Diamond Cuts Diamond. large type ed. Mary Street. (Linford Romance Library). 1986. pap. 7.95 (*0-7089-6315-3*, Linford) Ulverscroft.

Diamond Days: An Oral History of the University of Texas at El Paso. Ed. by Charles H. Martin & Rebecca M. Craver. 226p. 1991. pap. 10.00 (*0-87404-245-3*) Tex Western.

Diamond Deceit. Carolyn Keene. Ed. by Anne Greenberg. (Nancy Drew Files Ser.: No. 83). 160p. (Orig.). (J). 1993. mass mkt. 3.99 (*0-671-73087-8*, Archway) PB.

Diamond Dies. 15.00 (*0-318-03180-9*, 7510) Wire Assn Intl.

Diamond Dust. Ed. by Jonathan Berry. (Illus.). vii, 121p. (Orig.). 1991. pap. 9.95 (*1-879479-00-1*) ICE WA.

Diamond Films: A Survey on Technology & Markets, No. 14. Richard K. Miller & Terri C. Walker. LC 88-80492. 34p. 1989. pap. text ed. 200.00 (*1-55865-013-X*) Future Tech Surveys.

Diamond Films & Coatings: Developments, Properties, & Applications. Ed. by Robert F. Davis. LC 92-35011. (Illus.). 415p. 1993. 78.00 (*0-8155-1323-2*) Noyes.

Diamond Fire. Gina Robins. 496p. 1986. pap. 3.95 (*0-8217-1943-2*) Zebra.

Diamond Greats: Profiles & Interviews with Sixty-Five of Baseball's History Makers. Rich Westcott. (Illus.). 400p. 1988. lib. bdg. 22.50 (*0-88736-220-6*) Mecklermedia.

Diamond Growth & Films. Ed. by Universities' Carbon Films & Materials Group Staff. 276p. 1990. 108.00 (*1-85166-811-X*) Elsevier.

Diamond Hard. Andrew MacAllan. 672p. 1992. pap. 11.95 (*0-7472-3513-9*, Pub. by Headline UK) Trafalgar.

Diamond Head: A Miss Danforth Mystery. Marian J. Jackson. LC 92-16867. 167p. 1992. 18.95 (*0-8027-1247-9*) Walker & Co.

Diamond Heart, Bk. Two: The Freedom to Be. A. H. Almaas. 212p. (Orig.). 1989. pap. 12.00 (*0-936713-04-6*) Diamond Bks CA.

Diamond Heart, Bk. 1: Elements of the Real in Man. A. H. Almaas. LC 86-71832. 280p. (Orig.). 1987. pap. 10.00 (*0-936713-01-1*) Diamond Bks CA.

Diamond Hindi-English Dictionary. Ed. by Giriraj S. Agarwal & Baljit Singh. 420p. (Orig.). 1993. pap. 5.95 (*1-881338-38-X*) Nataraj Bks.

Diamond Hitch Days. J. N. Hessel. LC 91-8056. (Illus.). 1991. pap. 14.95 (*0-87004-344-7*) Caxton.

Diamond Hunters. Wilbur Smith. 224p. 1990. mass mkt. 4.95 (*0-449-21614-4*, Crest) Fawcett.

Diamond Hunters. large type ed. Wilbur Smith. 1992. pap. 14.95 (*0-7927-0668-4*, Paragon Lrg Print) Chivers N Amer.

***Diamond in Disguise.** Elizabeth Hewitt. 384p. 1995. 4.99 (*0-451-40564-1*, Topaz) NAL-Dutton.

Diamond in the Buff. Susan Dunlap. 1991. mass mkt. 4.99 (*0-440-20788-6*) Dell.

Diamond in the Darkness. Veni Raj. (Illus.). 32p. 1984. pap. 4.50 (*0-85398-161-2*) G Ronald Pub.

Diamond in the Rough. Millie Criswell. 1994. mass mkt. 4.99 (*0-06-108093-4*, Harp PBks) HarpC.

Diamond in the Rough. Suzanne Simmons. 384p. 1994. 4.99 (*0-451-40384-3*, Topaz) NAL-Dutton.

Diamond in the Rough: An Illustrated History of Arizona. Marshall Trimble. 250p. 1988. 35.00 (*0-89865-585-4*) Donning Co.

***Diamond in the Rough: The Secret to Finding Your Own Value & Making Your Own Success.** Barry J. Farber. 256p. (Orig.). 1995. pap. 12.00 (*0-425-14733-9*, Berkley Trade) Berkley Pub.

Diamond in the Window. Jane Langton. (J). (gr. 5 up). 17.50 (*0-8446-6414-6*) Peter Smith.

Diamond in the Window. Jane Langton. LC 62-7312. (Trophy Bk.). (Illus.). 256p. (J). (gr. 5 up). 1973. reprint ed. pap. 3.95 (*0-06-440042-5*, Trophy) HarpC Child Bks.

Diamond Jenness Collections from Bering Strait. David A. Morrison. (Canadian Museum of Civilization Mercury Ser.). (Illus.). 171p. 1992. pap. 19.95 (*0-660-12922-1*) U Ch Pr.

Diamond Lane. Karen Karbo. 316p. 1993. pap. 13.95 (*0-87951-486-8*) Overlook Pr.

Diamond Lens & Other Stories. Fitz-James O'Brien. LC 70-109502. (Illus.). reprint ed. 26.50 (*0-404-00613-2*) AMS Pr.

Diamond Lens & Other Stories. Fitz-James O'Brien. LC 76-131791. (Illus.). 1971. reprint ed. 29.00 (*0-403-00678-3*) Scholarly.

Diamond Man. Paul Preuss. (Arthur C. Clarke's Venus Prime Ser.: Vol. 5). 1990. pap. 3.95 (*0-380-75349-9*) Avon.

***Diamond Mask.** Julian May. (Galactic Milieu Ser.: Bk. 2). 1995. mass mkt., pap. 5.99 (*0-345-36248-9*, Del Rey) Ballantine.

Diamond Mask: A Novel. Julian May. LC 93-37802. (Galactic Milieu Trilogy Ser.: Vol. 2). 1994. 22.00 (*0-679-43310-4*) Knopf.

***Diamond Materials: Fourth International Symposium.** K. V. Ravi et al. 1995. 72.00 (*1-56677-098-X*, PV 95-4) Electrochem Soc.

***Diamond Nebula: A Novel.** Jeremy Reed. 200p. 1995. 28.00 (*0-7206-0891-0*, Pub. by P Owen Ltd UK) Dufour.

Diamond on Ice. Lacey Dancer. 224p. (Orig.). 1991. pap. 2.75 (*1-878702-34-3*, Kismet) Meteor Pub.

Diamond Optics, Vol. 969. Ed. by A. Feldman & S. Holly. 1988. 45.00 (*0-8194-0004-1*) SPIE.

Diamond Optics Four. 1992. 53.00 (*0-8194-0662-7*, 1534) SPIE.

Diamond Optics II. Ed. by Albert Feldman & Sandor Holly. 244p. 1990. 53.00 (*0-8194-0182-X*, VOL. 1146) SPIE.

Diamond Optics Three, Vol. 1325. A. Feldman & S. Holly. 1990. 62.00 (*0-8194-0386-5*) SPIE.

Diamond Park Dinosaur. Gibbs Davis. (Never Sink Nine Ser.: No. 9). (J). 1994. pap. 3.25 (*0-553-48131-2*, Skylark) Bantam.

Diamond Rainbow: Euphoria (Transcension) Superlove. LC 94-92006. (Illus.). 244p. 1994. Comb bdg. ring bd., spiral bd. 44.00 (*0-9602334-4-X*) Superlove.

Diamond Rainbow: Superlove. 2nd ed. Date not set. write for info. (*0-9602334-5-8*) Superlove.

Diamond Ring: Business, Politics, & Precious Stones in South Africa, 1867-1945. Colin W. Newbury. (Illus.). 448p. 1990. 89.00 (*0-19-821775-0*) OUP.

Diamond Ring Buying Guide: How to Spot Value & Avoid Ripoffs. 4th ed. Renee Newman. LC 93-9741. (Illus.). 151p. (C). 1993. pap. 12.95 (*0-929975-20-0*) Intl Jewelry Pubns.

Diamond Ring River Valley: The Story of Saragail & Her Battle Against the Forces of Solitude. James Belcher. 87p. 1988. per., pap. 5.00 (*0-318-41277-2*) Pudding Hse Pubns.

Diamond Rock: A Tale of the Paoli Massacre. Clifton Lisle. 1993. reprint ed. lib. bdg. 89.00 (*0-7812-5483-3*) Rprt Serv.

Diamond Series: Introduction to Bridge Play of the Hand. Aubrey Grant. 1994. pap. 9.95 (*0-943855-11-X*) Amer Contrct Brdg Lge.

Diamond Setting: The Professional Approach. Robert R. Wooding. LC 84-70977. (Illus.). 181p. 1984. text ed. 29.95 (*0-9613545-1-8*) Dry Ridge.

Diamond, Silicon Carbide & Nitrite Wide-Bandgap Semiconductors: Materials Research Society Symposium Proceedings, Vol. 339. Ed. by C. H. Carter, Jr. et al. 1994. text ed. 48.00 (*1-55899-239-1*) Materials Res.

Diamond, Silicon Carbide & Related Wide Bandgap Semiconductors: Materials Research Society Symposium Proceedings, Vol. 162. Ed. by J. T. Glass et al. 1990. text ed. 41.00 (*1-55899-050-X*) Materials Res.

Diamond Smugglers. Ian Fleming. 15.95 (*0-88411-873-8*, Aeonian Pr) Amereon Ltd.

***Diamond Solitaire.** 1993. pap. 5.13 (*1-56054-804-5*) Thorndike Pr.

Diamond Solitaire. Peter Lovesey. 352p. 1993. 18.95 (*0-89296-535-5*) Mysterious Pr.

Diamond Solitaire. Peter Lovesey. 336p. 1994. mass mkt. 5.50 (*0-446-40347-4*, Mysterious Paperbk) Warner Bks.

Diamond Solitaire. large type ed. Peter Lovesey. LC 93-35504. 1993. 20.95 (*0-7862-0076-6*) Thorndike Pr.

Diamond State Trolleys: Electric Railways of Delaware. Harold E. Cox. (Illus.). 88p. (Orig.). 1991. pap. 14.00 (*0-911940-49-9*) Cox.

***Diamond Street: The Story of the Little Town with the Big Red Light District.** Bruce E. Hall. (Illus.). 222p. (Orig.). 1994. pap. 13.95 (*1-883789-01-X*) Blk Dome Pr.

Diamond Sutra. Kevin O'Neil. 1978. pap. 5.00 (*0-86627-004-3*) Crises Res Pr.

Diamond Sutra & the Sutra of Hui-Neng. Tr. by A. F. Price & Wong Mou-Lam. 1974. pap. 9.95 (*0-394-73019-4*) Shambhala Pubns.

Diamond Sutra & the Sutra of Hui Neng. Tr. by A. F. Price & Wong Mou-Lam. LC 78-237407. 192p. 1974. reprint ed. pap. 14.00 (*0-87773-005-9*) Shambhala Pubns.

Diamond That Cuts Through Illusion: Commentaries on the Prajnaparamita Diamond Sutra. Thich Nhat Hanh. LC 92-13502. 115p. 1992. pap. 9.00 (*0-938077-51-1*) Parallax Pr.

Diamond Throne. David Eddings. (Elenium Ser.: Bk. 1). 448p. 1990. mass mkt. 5.99 (*0-345-36769-3*, Del Rey) Ballantine.

Diamond Tiger. Maxwell. 1994. pap. 2.99 (*0-06-108260-0*, PL) HarpC Child Bks.

Diamond Tiger. Anne Maxwell. (Orig.). 1992. mass mkt. 4.99 (*0-06-104079-7*, Harp PBks); mass mkt. 4.99 (*0-06-104181-5*, Harp PBks) HarpC.

Diamond Tree: Jewish Tales from Around the World. Howard Schwartz & Barbara Rush. LC 90-32420. (Illus.). 120p. (J). (gr. 2-5). 1991. lib. bdg. 16.89 (*0-06-025243-X*) HarpC Child Bks.

Diamond Tree: Jewish Tales from Around the World. Howard Schwartz & Barbara Rush. LC 90-32420. (Illus.). 120p. (J). (gr. 2-5). 1991. 17.00 (*0-06-025239-1*) HarpC Child Bks.

Diamond Truths. Gro Warling. 96p. 1993. pap. 6.95 (*1-879244-81-0*) Windom Bks.

***Diamond War.** Zilpha K. Snyder. (Castle Court Kids Ser.: No. 1). (J). (gr. 2-6). 1995. mass mkt. 3.50 (*0-440-40985-3*) Dell.

Diamond Web. Alan Watts. Ed. by Mark Watts. LC 87-71203. 160p. (Orig.). 1987. pap. 8.95 (*0-89708-152-8*) And Bks.

Diamond Willow. Kathleen Eagle. (Silhouette Intimate Moments Ser.). 1993. mass mkt. 3.39 (*0-373-07480-8*, 5-07480-2) Silhouette.

Diamond Years. H. W. Darst. 368p. 1988. 12.00 (*0-89114-170-7*) Baptist Pub Hse.

Diamond Years. Allen E. Roberts. (History of Babcock Lodge Ser.: No. 322). (Illus.). 316p. 1987. 12.50 (*0-935633-04-9*) Anchor Comm.

Diamondfield Jack: A Study in Frontier Justice. David Grover. LC 85-40940. (Illus.). 208p. (Orig.). 1986. pap. 8.95 (*0-8061-1979-9*) U of Okla Pr.

Diamonds. Elizabeth Anderson. 400p. (Orig.). 1991. pap. 4.50 (*0-8439-3060-8*) Dorchester Pub Co.

Diamonds. Dale Herd. (Orig.). 1975. pap. 2.50 (*0-914726-14-5*) Mudra.

Diamonds. Fred Ward. Ed. by Charlotte Ward. (Fred Ward Gem Book Ser.). (Illus.). 64p. 1993. pap. 14.95 (*0-9633723-2-7*) Gem Bk Pubs.

Diamonds. 2nd ed. Eric Burton. LC 78-66362. (Illus.). 566p. 1979. 60.00 (*0-8019-6789-9*) Chilton.

Diamonds: Fascinating Facts. Renee Newman. (Gemstones Ser.). (Illus.). 16p. (C). 1990. 3.95 (*0-929975-01-4*) Intl Jewelry Pubns.

Diamonds: From Birth to Eternity. Arthur N. Wilson. Ed. by Michael Ross & Dianne Eash. 1982. 29.95 (*0-87311-010-2*) Gemological.

***Diamonds: The Evolution of the Ballpark from Elysian Fields to Camden Yards.** Michael Gershman. 1995. pap. 19.95 (*0-395-73524-6*) HM.

Diamonds & Coral: Anglo-Dutch Jews & Eighteenth-Century Trade. Gedalia Yogev. LC 78-301. 360p. 1978. 39.50 (*0-8419-0369-7*) Holmes & Meier.

Diamonds & Defaults: Studies in Pure & Applied Intensional Logic. Ed. by Maarten De Rijke. LC 93-17749. (Synthese Library: Vol. 229). 400p. (C). 1993. lib. bdg. 116.00 (*0-7923-2342-4*) Kluwer Ac.

Diamonds & Dreams. Rebeca Paisley. 432p. (Orig.). 1991. mass mkt. 4.50 (*0-380-76564-0*) Avon.

Diamonds & Gold in South Africa. Theodore Reunert. LC 72-3916. (Black Heritage Library Collection). 1977. reprint ed. 32.95 (*0-8369-9106-0*) Ayer.

Diamonds & Precious Stones. Harry Emmanuel. 1977. 79.95 (*0-8490-1716-5*) Gordon Pr.

Diamonds & Rust: A Bibliography & Discography on Joan Baez. Joan Swanekamp. LC 79-91336. (Illus.). 88p. 1980. 28.50 (*0-87650-113-7*) Popular Culture.

Diamonds & Toads: A Classic Fairy Tale. Ellen Schecter. LC 93-14096. (Bank Street Ready-to-Read Ser.). (Illus.). (J). 1994. pap. 10.95 (*0-553-09046-1*); mass mkt. 3.99 (*0-553-37339-0*) Bantam.

Diamonds Are a Dyke's Best Friend: Reflections, Reminiscences, & Reports from the Field on the Lesbian National Pastime. Yvonne Zipter. LC 88-30897. 224p. (Orig.). 1988. lib. bdg. 20.95 (*0-932379-48-6*); pap. 9.95 (*0-932379-47-8*) Firebrand Bks.

Diamonds Are a Girl's Best Friend: Women Writers on Baseball. Ed. by Elinor Nanen. 295p. 1995. pap. 12.95 (*0-571-19853-8*) Faber & Faber.

Diamonds are a Girl's Best Friend: Women Writers on Baseball. Ed. by Elinor Nauen. 276p. 1994. 22.95 (*0-571-19819-8*) Faber & Faber.

***Diamonds Are Dancing: A History of Conesus Lake.** H. T. Anderson. 57p. 1993. 25.00 (*1-884849-06-7*) R&R Bks.

Diamonds Are Forever. (BookCard Ser.). 1993. pap. 4.95 (*0-8118-0305-8*) Chronicle Bks.

Diamonds Are Forever. Ian Fleming. 1976. 19.95 (*0-8488-1005-8*) Amereon Ltd.

Diamonds Are Forever. Ian Fleming. pap. 2.95 (*0-685-11139-3*) Fr & Eur.

***Diamonds Are Forever.** Ian Fleming. (James Bond Ser.). 1995. reprint ed. 6.98 (*1-56731-050-8*, MJF Bks) Fine Comms.

Diamonds Are Forever: Artists & Writers on Baseball. Ed. by Peter H. Gordon. LC 87-14585. (Illus.). 168p. 1987. pap. 19.95 (*0-87701-468-X*) Chronicle Bks.

Diamonds Are Forever: The Business of Baseball. Ed. by Paul M. Sommers. 208p. (C). 1992. 19.95 (*0-8157-8042-7*) Brookings.

Diamonds Are Not Forever. William Jackson. 72p. 1994. pap. 9.95 (*0-9641792-5-3*) Analyn Pubng.

Diamonds Can Cut Glass & Unrepeatable Miracle. LC 88-22564. 286p. 1988. 17.75 (*0-930950-28-3*); pap. 10.75 (*0-930950-29-1*) Nopoly Pr.

Diamond's Compass: A Novel. P. H. Liotta. LC 92-33371. 1993. 18.95 (*0-945575-74-2*) Algonquin Bks.

Diamonds for Dusty Roads. Joy Haney. 1992. pap. write for info. (*1-880969-07-6*) Schl Prophet.

Diamonds in a Frozen Cavern: Nine L. A. Pierce College Students Speak Out on AIDS. 20p. 1992. 3.00 (*1-881168-21-2*) Red Danceflr.

Diamonds in Daniel. W. G. Heslop. 1975. pap. 3.99 (*0-88019-018-3*) Schmul Pub Co.

Diamonds in the Desert. Cookbook Committee Staff. LC 87-90525. (Illus.). 350p. 1989. reprint ed. 13.95 (*0-9618029-0-1*) Ozona Womans.

Diamonds in the Dust. Joni E. Tada. 368p. 1993. Printed caseside. pap. 14.99 (*0-310-37950-4*) Zondervan.

Diamonds in the Dust: Discover & Develop Your Child's Gifts. Jackie Mallis. 448p. (Orig.). 1982. pap. 14.95 (*0-86617-020-0*) Multi Media TX.

Diamonds in the Dust: Discover & Develop Your Child's Gifts. 2nd ed. Jackie Mallis. 448p. (Orig.). 1992. pap. 19.95 (*0-86617-056-1*) Multi Media TX.

Diamonds in the Rough. Jim Bowman & Joel Zoss. LC 89-8131. 480p. 1989. text ed. 29.95 (*0-02-633590-5*) Macmillan.

Diamonds in the Rough. Charles E. Cravey. 64p. (Orig.). 1986. pap. 4.00 (*0-938645-00-5*) In His Steps.

Diamonds in the Rough. Steven A. Seager. 64p. (Orig.). 1993. pap. 7.95 (*1-56167-123-1*) Am Literary Pr.

Diamond's Japan Business Directory, 1993. 27th ed. 1500p. 1993. 400.00 (*4-924360-01-5*) Diamond Head.

***Diamonds of Dixie: Travels Through the Southern Minor Leagues.** Ernest J. Green. 1995. write for info. (*1-56833-043-X*) Madison Bks UPA.

Diamonds of the Night. rev. ed. Arnost Lustig. 287p. 1986. reprint ed. pap. 15.95 (*0-8101-0706-6*) Northwestern U Pr.

***Diamonds of the North: A Concise History of Baseball in Canada.** William A. Humber. (Illus.). 224p. 1995. pap. 15.95 (*0-19-541039-4*) OUP.

Diamonds or Rubies? Lynn G. Colson. (Illus.). 150p. 1995. pap. write for info. (*0-318-72816-8*) Peace Pub Co.

Diamonds Past. abr. ed. Bob Altman. 340p. 1995. pap. 9.95 (*1-56901-496-5*) NW Pub.

Diamonds Wrought by Man. B. V. Derjaguin & D. V. Fedoseev. 142p. (C). 1985. 40.00 (*0-685-36909-9*, Pub. by Collets) St Mut.

Dian Fossey. Jack Roberts. LC 94-6841. (Importance of Ser.). (Illus.). 128p. (J). (gr. 5-9). 1995. 16.95 (*1-56006-068-9*) Lucent Bks.

Diana. Jorge De Montemayor. Tr. by Roseanna Mueller. LC 88-1730. (Spanish Studies: Vol 1). 250p. 1989. lib. bdg. 89.95 (*0-88946-735-8*) E Mellen.

Diana. Bill Deemer. (Orig.). 1966. pap. 1.00 (*0-940556-01-4*) Coyote.

Diana: A Modern Metaphysical Fairy Tale. Nancy L. MacCauley. Ed. by Carrie Teasdale. LC 85-73902. 320p. (Orig.). 1986. pap. 9.95 (*0-251-93702-X*) Another Way.

Diana: A Princess & Her Troubled Marriage. Nicholas Davies. (Illus.). 320p. 1992. 21.95 (*1-55972-115-4*, Birch Ln Pr) Carol Pub Group.

***Diana: A Strange Autobiography.** Diana Frederics. LC 75-12315. (The Cutting Edge: Lesbian Life & Literature Ser.). 280p. 1995. 35.00 (*0-8147-2632-1*); pap. 15.95 (*0-8147-2635-6*) NYU Pr.

Diana: A Strange Autobiography. Diana Frederics. LC 75-12315. (Homosexuality Ser.). 1975. reprint ed. 19.95 (*0-405-07359-3*) Ayer.

Diana: An Intermediate Language for Ada. Ed. by G. Goos et al. 201p. 1987. pap. 28.00 (*0-387-12695-3*) Spr-Verlag.

***Diana: Her New Life.** Andrew Morton. 1994. 23.00 (*0-684-80009-8*) S&S Trade.

***Diana: Her New Life.** large type ed. Andrew Morton. LC 95-2572. 1995. write for info. (*0-7862-0425-7*) Thorndike Pr.

Diana: Her True Story. Andrew Morton. Ed. by Julie Rubenstein & Sally Peters. 288p. 1992. mass mkt. 5.99 (*0-671-79878-2*) PB.

An Asterisk (*) at the beginning of an entry indicates that the title is appearing in BIP for the first time.

Diana: Her True Story. large type ed. Andrew Morton. 304p. 1993. reprint ed. lib. bdg. 21.95 (*1-56054-608-5*); reprint ed. pap. 13.95 (*1-56054-889-4*) Thorndike Pr.

Diana: Twentieth-Century Princess. Patricia R. Giff. (Women of Our Time Ser.). (Illus.). 64p. (J). (gr. 3-5). 1992. pap. 3.99 (*0-14-034707-0*, Puffin) Puffin Bks.

Diana & Persis. Louisa May Alcott. Ed. by Sarah Elbert. LC 77-11663. (Individual Publications). (Illus.). 1978. lib. bdg. 18.95 (*0-405-10521-5*) Ayer.

Diana & Prince Charles Fashion Paper Dolls in Full Color. Tom Tierney. (J). 1985. pap. 3.95 (*0-486-24961-1*) Dover.

Diana at Her Bath & the Women of Rome. Pierre Klossowski. Tr. by Stephen Sartarelli & Sophie Hawkes. LC 89-83810. (Illus.). 139p. 1990. 17.95 (*0-941419-42-8*, Eridanos Library) Marsilio Pubs.

Diana Cooper. large type ed. Phillip Ziegler. 598p. 1982. 23.95 (*0-7089-8059-7*, Trail West Pubs) Ulverscroft.

Diana Does It. George Middleton. 1961. pap. 4.75 (*0-8222-0306-5*) Dramatists Play.

Diana Guest: Stonecarver. Diana Guest et al. LC 92-21487. (Illus.). 144p. 1992. 60.00 (*0-944439-16-0*) Clark City Pr.

Diana in Private: The Princess Nobody Knows. large type ed. Colin Campbell. LC 92-30414. (General Ser.). 471p. 1993. 21.95 (*0-8161-5608-5*) G K Hall.

Diana in Private: The Princess Nobody Knows. Colin Campbell. 1992. reprint ed. mass mkt. 5.99 (*0-312-95051-9*) St Martin.

Diana of Montemayor as Social & Religious Teaching. Bruno M. Damiani. LC 83-3608. (Studies in Romance Languages: No. 28). 124p. reprint ed. pap. 35.40 (*0-7837-5811-1*, 2045478) Bks Demand.

Diana of the Crossways. George Meredith. reprint ed. lib. bdg. 79.00 (*0-7812-0098-9*) Rprt Serv.

Diana of the Crossways. George Meredith. LC 70-145177. 1971. reprint ed. 89.00 (*0-403-01105-1*) Scholarly.

Diana, Princess of Wales. Carol Greene. LC 85-12751. (Picture-Story Biographies Ser.). (Illus.). 32p. (J). (gr. 2-4). 1985. pap. 3.95 (*0-516-43538-8*) Childrens.

*__Diana Ross: Entertainer.__ Ed. by Nathan I. Huggins. (Black Americans of Achievement). (Illus.). 144p. (YA). (gr. 5 up). 1995. 18.95 (*0-7910-1882-2*) Chelsea Hse.

Diana Stair. Floyd Dell. LC 74-26100. reprint ed. 49.50 (*0-404-58419-5*) AMS Pr.

*__Diana, the Goddess Who Hunts Alone.__ Carlos Fuentes. Tr. by Alfred MacAdam. LC 95-10846. 224p. 1995. 21.00 (*0-374-13903-2*) FS&G.

Diana's Gift: An Inspirational Journey of Breast Cancer Awareness. Barbara Berghole & Eva Shaw. 200p. 1992. pap. 8.95 (*0-685-59741-5*) L Cooper Fnd.

Diana's Hunt: Caccia Di Diana: Boccaccio's First Fiction. Ed. by Anthony K. Cassell & Victoria Kirkham. Tr. by Victoria Kirkham. LC 90-45815. (Middle Ages Ser.). (Illus.). 288p. (C). 1991. text ed. 34.95x (*0-8122-8219-1*) U of Pa Pr.

Diana's Step-by-Step Family Scrapbook. Suzanne Weyn. (J). (gr. 4-7). 1993. pap. 4.95 (*0-590-47199-6*) Scholastic Inc.

*__Diana's Watercolor Jacket.__ Diana Leone. (Illus.). 32p. 1995. pap. text ed. 14.95 (*0-942786-37-8*) Leone Pubns.

Diane Arbus. Patricia Bosworth. 464p. 1985. pap. 10.95 (*0-380-69927-3*) Avon.

Diane Arbus. Patricia Bosworth. 400p. 1995. pap. 14.00 (*0-393-31207-0*) Norton.

Diane Arbus: An Aperture Monograph. (Illus.). 184p. 40.00 (*0-912334-40-1*); pap. 29.95 (*0-912334-41-X*) Aperture.

Diane Arbus: Magazine Work Essay. Ed. by Thomas W. Southall. LC 84-70444. (Illus.). 176p. 1986. pap. 29.95 (*0-89381-233-1*) Aperture.

Diane Burko. Contrib by John Perreault et al. LC 87-63191. (Illus.). 48p. (Orig.). 1990. reprint ed. pap. 15.00 (*0-9623799-6-4*) Locks Gallery.

Diane de Poitiers. Philippe Erlanger. 384p. (FRE.). 1974. pap. 10.95 (*0-7859-2338-1*, 2070365522) Fr & Eur.

Diane Goode Book of American Folk Tales & Songs. Illus. by Diane Goode. LC 89-1097. 64p. (J). (ps-5). 1989. 15.95 (*0-525-44458-0*, DCB) Dutton Child Bks.

Diane Goode's American Christmas. Diane Goode. LC 89-25605. (Illus.). 80p. (J). (ps up). 1990. 14.95 (*0-525-44620-6*, DCB) Dutton Child Bks.

Diane Goode's Book of Scary Stories & Songs. Comp. by Diane Goode. LC 93-32610. (Illus.). 64p. (J). (ps up). 1994. 15.99 (*0-525-45175-7*, DCB) Dutton Child Bks.

Diane Goode's Book of Silly Stories & Songs. Diane Goode. LC 91-38192. (Illus.). 64p. (J). (ps-6). 1992. 15.00 (*0-525-44967-1*, DCB) Dutton Child Bks.

Diane Goode's Christmas Magic: Poems & Carols. Illus. by Diane Goode. LC 92-6366. (Pictureback Ser.). 32p. (Orig.). (J). (ps-3). 1992. pap. 2.25 (*0-679-82427-8*) Random Bks Yng Read.

Diane Seed's Mediterranean Dishes. Diane Seed. LC 93-27855. (Illus.). 1993. pap. 15.95 (*0-89815-579-7*) Ten Speed Pr.

Dianetica. L. Ron Hubbard. 1995. pap. 5.99 (*0-88404-304-5*) Bridge Pubns Inc.

Dianetics. rev. ed. L. Ron Hubbard. 1989. pap. 4.95 (*0-685-76384-6*) Church of Scient Info.

Dianetics: Evolution of a Science. L. Ron Hubbard. 20.00 (*0-686-30777-1*) Church Scient NY.

Dianetics: The Evolution of a Science. L. Ron Hubbard. 252p. 1983. 22.00 (*0-88404-141-7*) Bridge Pubns Inc.

Dianetics: The Modern Science of Mental Health. L. Ron Hubbard. 675p. 1995. mass mkt. 6.99 (*0-88404-632-X*) Bridge Pubns Inc.

Dianetics: The Modern Science of Mental Health. L. Ron Hubbard. 25.00 (*0-686-30776-3*) Church Scient NY.

Dianetics: The Modern Science of Mental Health. rev. ed. L. Ron Hubbard. 1986. 22.00 (*0-88404-258-8*) Bridge Pubns Inc.

Dianetics & Scientology Technical Dictionary. L. Ron Hubbard. 1975. 62.50 (*0-88404-037-2*) Bridge Pubns Inc.

Dianetics & Scientology Technical Dictionary. L. Ron Hubbard. 50.00 (*0-686-30803-4*) Church Scient NY.

Dianetics Fifty-Five. L. Ron Hubbard. 20.00 (*0-686-13920-8*) Church Scient NY.

*__Dianetics Lectures & Demonstrations: Four Lectures.__ L. Ron Hubbard. Date not set. 24.99 (*0-88404-784-9*) Bridge Pubns Inc.

Dianetics, the Original Thesis. L. Ron Hubbard. 20.00 (*0-686-13917-8*) Church Scient NY.

Dianetics Today. L. Ron Hubbard. 76.00 (*0-686-30802-6*) Church Scient NY.

Dianetics 55. L. Ron Hubbard. 246p. 1989. 28.00 (*0-88404-417-3*) Bridge Pubns Inc.

Dianion Chemistry. Thompson. 1994. write for info. (*0-8493-7868-0*) CRC Pr.

Dianne Feinstein: Never Let Them See You Cry. Jerry Roberts. 224p. 1994. 20.00 (*0-06-258508-8*) HarpC West.

*__Diaper Market.__ 150p. (Orig.). 1995. pap. 2,195.00 (*0-7605-2043-7*) Rector Pr.

Diapering & Infant Skin Care: Journal, Pediatrician, Supplement 1, 1987, Vol. 14. Ed. by A. L. Norins. (Illus.). iv, 52p. 1987. pap. 17.75 (*3-8055-4615-7*) S Karger.

Diapering Baby: Simply, Healthfully, Economically, & Ecologically. Anna Hanson. LC 90-85752. (Illus.). 80p. (C). 1991. pap. 9.95 (*0-9628302-3-2*) FamilyWorks Pr.

Diapers, Deadlines & Decisions: Careers & Children. Edward E. Pullman & Durlynn C. Anema. 168p. 1988. spiral bd. 21.95 (*0-8403-4725-1*) Kendall-Hunt.

Diapers Doo-Doo & Diddlypoop - Baby's First Year. I. Alterman. 96p. 1993. 5.95 (*0-88032-435-X*) Ivory Tower Pub.

Diaphragm Shear Connections Between Flanges of Prestressed Concrete T Beams. (PCI Journal Reprints Ser.). 12p. 1985. pap. 6.00 (*0-318-19742-1*, JR94) P-PCI.

Diaporthales in North America with Emphasis on Gnomonia & Its Segregates. M. E. Barr. (Mycologia Memoirs Ser.: No. 7). (Illus.). 1977. lib. bdg. 55.50 (*3-7682-1189-4*) Lubrecht & Cramer.

Diapseniaceae to Myoporaceae see Flora Europaea

Diapsid Reptile from the Pennsylvanian of Kansas. Robert R. Reisz. (Special Publication Ser.: No. 7). 74p. (Orig.). 1981. pap. 5.00 (*0-89338-011-3*) U of KS Mus Nat Hist.

Diaria De Bello Carolino (Diary of the Caroline War 1496) Alessandro Benedetti. Ed. by Dorothy M. Schullian. LC 66-21028. (Renaissance Text Ser.: No. 1). x, 276p. 1967. 8.50 (*0-9602696-0-6*) Renaiss Society Am.

Diaries & Correspondence of the Earl of Malmesbury, 4 Vols, 1. 2nd ed. James H. Malmesbury. LC 73-121023. reprint ed. write for info. (*0-404-04171-X*) AMS Pr.

Diaries & Correspondence of the Earl of Malmesbury, 4 Vols, 2. 2nd ed. James H. Malmesbury. LC 73-121023. reprint ed. write for info. (*0-404-04172-8*) AMS Pr.

Diaries & Correspondence of the Earl of Malmesbury, 4 Vols, 3. 2nd ed. James H. Malmesbury. LC 73-121023. reprint ed. write for info. (*0-404-04173-6*) AMS Pr.

Diaries & Correspondence of the Earl of Malmesbury, 4 Vols, 4. 2nd ed. James H. Malmesbury. LC 73-121023. reprint ed. write for info. (*0-404-04174-4*) AMS Pr.

Diaries & Correspondence of the Earl of Malmesbury, 4 Vols, Set. 2nd ed. James H. Malmesbury. LC 73-121023. reprint ed. 265.00 (*0-404-04170-1*) AMS Pr.

Diaries & Journals of Literary Women from Fanny Burney to Virginia Woolf. Judy Simons. LC 89-52172. 228p. 1990. text ed. 28.95x (*0-87745-291-1*) U of Iowa Pr.

Diaries & Letters of American Women: An Annotated Bibliography. Joyce D. Goodfriend. LC 87-17908. 187p. 1987. text ed. 35.00 (*0-8161-8778-9*, Hall Reference) Macmillan.

Diaries & Memoirs of a Sailor. W. J. Moore. 80p. (C). 1989. pap. 30.00 (*0-7223-1728-X*, Pub. by A H S Ltd UK) St Mut.

Diaries & Writing of Ann Morrison Reed, 1849-1921. Ed. by John E. Reller. 1978. 7.95 (*0-910312-48-6*) Calif Hist.

Diaries, Eighteen Seventy-One to Eighteen Eighty-Two, of Samuel P. Avery, Art Dealer. Samuel P. Avery. Ed. by Madeleine Fidell-Beaufort et al. 1979. 72.95 (*0-405-11517-2*) Ayer.

Diaries, Letters, & Recollections: The War Between the States. 133p. 1955. pap. write for info. (*0-318-64324-3*) Winchester-Frederick Cty Hist Soc.

Diaries of a Hessian Chaplain & the Chaplain's Assistant. Tr. & Intro. by Bruce Burgoyne. 50p. (Orig.). (C). 1990. pap. 4.00 (*0-939016-17-6*) Johannes Schwalm Hist.

Diaries of Absalom Watkin: A Manchester Man, 1787-1861. Absalom Watkin. Ed. by Magdalen Goffin. LC 93-33706. 1993. 34.00 (*0-7509-0417-8*) A Sutton Pub.

Diaries of Adam & Eve. Mark Twain. 91p. 1971. 7.50 (*0-87291-012-1*) Coronado Pr.

*__Diaries of Adam & Eve.__ Mark Twain. 1991. pap. 5.00 (*0-681-86201-7*) Longmeadow Pr.

*__Diaries of Assadollah Alam Vol. I: 1347-1348.__ Assadollah Alam. Ed. by Ali-Naqhi Alikhani. 414p. (PER.). 1992. 25.00x (*0-936347-57-0*) Iran Bks.

*__Diaries of Assadollah Alam Vol. II: 1349-1351.__ Assadollah Alam. Ed. by Alinaghi Alikhani. 424p. (PER.). 1993. 25.00x (*0-936347-58-9*) Iran Bks.

Diaries of Charles Ora Card: The Canadian Years, 1886-1903. Ed. by Donald G. Godfrey & Brigham Y. Card. (Illus.). 720p. 1993. 45.00 (*0-87480-410-8*) U of Utah Pr.

Diaries of Charlotte Perkins Gilman, 2 vols., Set, Vol. 1: 1879-1887; Vol. 2: 1890-1935. Ed. by Denise D. Knight. LC 94-4988. 1096p. (C). 1994. text ed. 89.50 (*0-8139-1524-4*) U Pr of Va.

Diaries of Court Ladies of Old Japan. Tr. by Annie S. Omori & Doi Kochi. LC 72-111775. reprint ed. 29.50 (*0-404-04819-6*) AMS Pr.

*__Diaries of Dawn Powell 1920-1967.__ Dawn Powell. Ed. & Intro. by Tim Page. 475p. 1995. 30.00 (*1-883642-08-6*) Steerforth Pr.

Diaries of Donald MacDonald. Donald MacDonald. LC 72-77060. 233p. 1973. reprint ed. lib. bdg. 29.50 (*0-678-00914-7*) Kelley.

Diaries of Edward Lee Hicks: Bishop of Lincoln 1910-1919. Ed. by Graham Neville. (Publications of the Lincoln Record Society: Vol. 82). 256p. 1993. 35.00 (*0-901503-55-X*) Boydell & Brewer.

Diaries of Franz Kafka, Vol. 1: 1910-1913. Franz Kafka. Ed. by Max Brod. Tr. by Joseph Kresh. LC 48-6432. (Illus.). 1988. write for info. (*0-8052-3054-8*); pap. 15.00 (*0-8052-0906-9*) Schocken.

Diaries of Franz Kafka, Vol. 2: 1914-1923. Franz Kafka. Ed. by Max Brod. Tr. by Martin Greenberg. LC 48-6432. (Illus.). 1987. 10.50 (*0-8052-3055-6*); pap. 8.95 (*0-8052-0425-3*) Schocken.

Diaries of George Bird, Victorian Wheelwright, 1862-83. J. Little. (C). 1980. text ed. 35.00 (*0-685-22180-6*, Pub. by Univ Nottingham UK) St Mut.

Diaries of George Washington. George Washington. Ed. by Donald Jackson & Dorothy Twohig. Incl. Vol. V, July 1786-December 1789. 1979. 37.50 (*0-8139-0801-9*); (Papers of George Washington). 559p. write for info. (*0-318-56215-4*) U Pr of Va.

Diaries of George Washington: January 1790 to December 1799, Vol. 6. George Washington. Ed. by Donald Jackson. 1980. 37.50 (*0-8139-0807-8*) U Pr of Va.

Diaries of George Washington: Volume 4, 1784 - June 1786. George Washington. Ed. by Donald Jackson & Dorothy Twohig. LC 75-41365. (Papers of George Washington). (Illus.). 405p. 1978. 37.50 (*0-8139-0722-5*) U Pr of Va.

Diaries of George Washington: 1771-75, 1780-81. George Washington. Ed. by Donald Jackson & Dorothy Twohig. Incl. Vol. II: 1766-70. 1976. 37.50 (*0-8139-0688-1*); Vol. III: 1771-1775, 1780-1781. 1978. 37.50 (*0-8139-0721-7*); write for info. (*0-318-56216-2*) U Pr of Va.

Diaries of George Washington, Vol. 1: 1748-65. George Washington. Ed. by Donald Jackson & Dorothy Twohig. LC 75-41365. (Illus.). 431p. reprint ed. pap. 122.90 (*0-7837-3538-3*, 2043361) Bks Demand.

Diaries of Hannah Cullwick, Victorian Maidservant. Hannah Cullwick. Ed. by Liz Stanley. LC 84-11638. (Illus.). 385p. 1984. pap. 14.00 (*0-8135-1071-6*) Rutgers U Pr.

Diaries of Hans Christian Andersen. Hans Christian Andersen et al. Ed. by Patricia Conroy & Sven H. Rossel. (Illus.). 512p. 1990. 45.00 (*0-295-96845-1*) U of Wash Pr.

Diaries of Henry Hill of Slackfields Farm, 1872-96. J. Heath. (C). 1988. text ed. 35.00 (*0-685-22179-2*, Pub. by Univ Nottingham UK) St Mut.

Diaries of Jane Somers. Doris Lessing. 1984. pap. 12.00 (*0-394-72955-2*, Vin) Random.

Diaries of John M. Miller of Westwood - Cincinnati Ohio: Excerpts from 1869-1870 & 1881-1894. Susan R. Alexander. LC 92-93448. (Illus.). 634p. 1993. 49.95 (*0-9633141-0-6*) S R Alexander.

Diaries of Lady Anne Clifford. Ed. by D. J. Clifford. (Illus.). 320p. 1992. pap. 24.00 (*0-7509-0163-2*) A Sutton Pub.

Diaries of Margaret Scholl Hood, 1851-1861. Margaret S. Hood. LC 91-68231. (Illus.). 480p. 1992. 25.00 (*0-929539-91-5*) Picton Pr.

Diaries of Mario M. Cuomo: The Campaign for Governor. Mario M. Cuomo. LC 83-43200. (Illus.). 484p. 1984. 19.95 (*0-394-53695-9*) Random.

Diaries of Paul Klee, 1898-1918. Paul Klee. Ed. & Intro. by Felix Klee. 434p. 1964. pap. 15.00 (*0-520-00653-4*) U CA Pr.

Diaries of Peter Pears, 1939-1979. Ed. & Anno. by Philip Reed. (Aldeburgh Studies in Music: No. 2). 160p. (C). 1995. text ed. 45.00 (*0-85115-364-X*) Boydell & Brewer.

Diaries of Tchaikovsky. Petr I. Tchaikovsky. Tr. by Wladimir Lakond. LC 79-138104. (Illus.). 365p. 1973. reprint ed. text ed. 45.50 (*0-8371-5680-7*, CHDI, Greenwood Pr) Greenwood.

Diaries of the Popish Plot. Ed. by Douglas Greene. LC 77-938. 1977. 50.00 (*0-8201-1288-7*) Schol Facsimiles.

Diaries of Theodor Herzl. Theodor Herzl. Ed. by Lowenthal. 16.50 (*0-8446-2247-8*) Peter Smith.

Diaries of Walter Murray Gibson, 1886-1887. Jacob Adler & Gwynn W. Barrett. LC 75-188977. (Illus.). 200p. 1973. 14.00 (*0-8248-0211-X*) UH Pr.

Diaries of Willard Motley. Ed. by Jerome Klinkowitz. 180p. 1979. 19.95 (*0-8138-0140-0*) Iowa St U Pr.

Diaries of William Charles Macready, 2 vols., 1. William C. Macready. Ed. by William C. Toynbee. LC 78-84519. 1972. 24.95 (*0-405-08773-X*, Pub. by Blom Pubns UK) Ayer.

Diaries of William Charles Macready, 2 vols., 2. William C. Macready. Ed. by William C. Toynbee. LC 78-84519. 1972. 24.95 (*0-405-08774-8*, Pub. by Blom Pubns UK) Ayer.

Diaries of William Charles Macready, 2 vols., Set. William C. Macready. Ed. by William C. Toynbee. LC 78-84519. 1972. 48.95 (*0-405-08772-1*, Pub. by Blom Pubns UK) Ayer.

Diaries, Prayers & Annals. Samuel Johnson. Ed. by E. L. McAdam, Jr. et al. (Works of Samuel Johnson Ser.: Vol. 1). 1958. 65.00 (*0-300-00733-7*) Yale U Pr.

Diaries to an English Professor: Pain & Growth in the Classroom. Jeffrey Berman. LC 94-10564. 304p. (C). 1995. lib. bdg. 45.00 (*0-87023-927-9*); pap. 17.95 (*0-87023-928-7*) U of Mass Pr.

Diaries Written from 1492 to 1844 see American Diaries: An Annotated Bibliography of Published American Diaries & Journals to 1980

Diaries Written from 1845 to 1980 see American Diaries: An Annotated Bibliography of Published American Diaries & Journals to 1980

Diario De Hostos 1986-1869: Obras Completas. Eugenio M. De Hostos. LC 87-25566. 290p. (SPA.). 1990. 12.95 (*0-8477-3607-5*); pap. 8.50 (*0-8477-3608-3*) U of PR Pr.

Diario de Oracions Privada. John Baillie. 1979. pap. 5.00 (*0-8358-0412-7*) Upper Room Bks.

*__Diario de Pedro - Pedro's Journal.__ Pam Conrad. (J). (gr. 4-7). 1994. pap. 2.95 (*0-590-47402-2*) Scholastic Inc.

Diario de un Caracol. Mercedes Ares. LC 86-83092. (Coleccion Espejo de Paciencia Ser.). 28p. (Orig.). 1987. pap. 6.00 (*0-89729-422-X*) Ediciones.

Diario de un Cubanito. Ralph Rewes. LC 87-82650. (Coleccion Caniqui Ser.). 180p. (Orig.). (SPA.). 1988. pap. 9.95 (*0-89729-464-5*) Ediciones.

Diario de un Viajero Desesperado. Charles R. Swindoll. 208p. (Orig.). (SPA.). 1989. pap. 4.95 (*0-88113-046-X*) Edit Betania.

Diario de Zenobia Camprubi Tomo I. Graciela P. De Nemes. 376p. 1991. 16.60 (*0-8477-3652-0*) U of PR Pr.

Diario Di Sidney Sonnino. Incl. Vol. Primo. 1866-1912. Ed. by Benjamin F. Brown. xiv, 536p. 1974. (*0-7006-0116-3*); Vol. Secondo. 1914-1916. Ed. by Pietro Pastorelli. xii, 374p. 1974. (*0-7006-0117-1*); Vol. Terzo. 1916-1922. Ed. by Pietro Pastorelli. 1974. (*0-7006-0118-X*); (Opera Omnia di - The Complete Works of Sidney Sonnino Ser.). (ITA.). 1974. Set. 35.00 (*0-686-92521-1*) U Pr of KS.

Diario of Christopher Columbus' First Voyage to America 1492-1493. Christopher Columbus. Ed. by James E. Kelley, Jr. LC 87-40551. (American Exploration & Travel Ser.: Vol. 70). (Illus.). 424p. 1989. 65.00x (*0-8061-2101-7*) U of Okla Pr.

Diario of Christopher Columbus's First Voyage to America, 1492-1493. Christopher Columbus. Tr. by Oliver Dunn & James E. Kelley, Jr. LC 87-40551. (American Exploration & Travel Ser.: Vol. 70). (Illus.). 504p. 1991. pap. 24.95 (*0-8061-2384-2*) U of Okla Pr.

Diariusz Podrozny of Pylyp Orlyk: (1720-1726) Intro. by Orest Subtelny & Omelijan Pritsak. LC 88-84116. (Library of Early Ukrainian Literature: Vol. 5). xiiv, 794p. (C). 1988. text ed. 35.00 (*0-916458-25-3*) Harvard Ukrainian.

Diariusz Podrozny of Pylyp Orlyk: (1727-1730) Intro. by Omeljan Pritsak & Orest Subtelny. LC 88-84116. (Library of Early Ukrainian Literature: Vol. 6). xxviii, 868p. (C). 1989. text ed. 35.00 (*0-916458-26-1*) Harvard Ukrainian.

*__Diariusz Podrozny of Pylyp Orlyk: (1731-1733)__ Intro. by Omeljan Pritsak & Orest Subtelny. (Library of Early Ukrainian Literature: Vol. 7). (C). Date not set. text ed. write for info. (*0-916458-34-2*) Harvard Ukrainian.

Diarrhea. Michael Gracey. 1991. 98.95 (*0-8493-8819-8*, RC862) CRC Pr.

Diarrhea & Constipation. (Incontinence Ser.). 1991. lib. bdg. 250.00 (*0-87700-963-5*) Revisionist Pr.

Diarrhea & Malnutrition: Interactions, Mechanisms, & Interventions. Ed. by Lincoln C. Chen & Nevin S. Scrimshaw. LC 82-18894. 334p. 1983. 85.00 (*0-306-41046-X*, Plenum Pr) Plenum.

Diarrhea & Malnutrition in Childhood. J. A. Walker-Smith & A. S. McNeish. 264p. 1986. pap. text ed. 65.00 (*0-407-00401-7*) Buttrwrth-Heinemann.

Diarrheal Diseases. Ed. by M. Field. 528p. 1991. 82.00 (*0-8385-1684-X*, A1684-8) Appleton & Lange.

Diarrhoea & PHC. Ed. by Ivan Wolffers. (Orig.). 1992. pap. text ed. 16.00 (*90-5383-042-1*, Pub. by VU Univ Pr NE) Paul & Co Pubs.

Diary. Stacie Johnson. (Young Adults Ser.). 1994. pap. 3.50 (*0-553-56563-X*) Bantam.

Diary. John Lamont. LC 78-171649. (Maitland Club, Glasgow. Publications: No. 7). reprint ed. 22.00 (*0-404-52933-X*) AMS Pr.

Diary. James Melville. LC 70-172723. (Bannatyne Club, Edinburgh. Publications: No. 34). reprint ed. 32.50 (*0-404-52740-X*) AMS Pr.

Diary, Set. Witold Gombrowicz. Ed. by Jan Kott. Tr. by Lillian Vallee. 1994. pap. 19.95 (*0-8101-1151-9*) Northwestern U Pr.

Diary, 2 Vols, Set. Gino C. Speranza. Ed. by Florence C. Speranza. LC 71-176000. reprint ed. 28.50 (*0-404-06194-X*) AMS Pr.

Diary, Vol. 1. Witold Gombrowicz. Ed. by Jan Kott. Tr. by Lillian Vallee. 232p. 1988. pap. 12.95 (*0-8101-0715-5*) Northwestern U Pr.

Diary, Vol. 2. Witold Gombrowicz. Ed. by Jan Kott. Tr. by Lillian Vallee. 239p. 1989. pap. 12.95 (*0-8101-0717-1*) Northwestern U Pr.

Diary, Vol. 3. Witold Gombrowicz. Ed. by Jan Kott. Tr. by Lillian Vallee. 220p. 1993. 29.95 (*0-8101-0718-X*); pap. 12.95 (*0-8101-0719-8*) Northwestern U Pr.

Diary, Vols. 1 & 2. Benjamin R. Haydon. Ed. by Willard B. Pope. Incl. Vol. 1. 1808-1815. LC 60-5394. (Illus.). 495p. 1960. (*0-318-53047-3*); Vol. 2. 1816-1824. LC 60-5394. (Illus.). 553p. 1960. (*0-318-53048-1*); LC 60-5394. 1960. Set. 60.00 (*0-674-20349-6*) HUP.

Diary: From November 10, 1824 to April 20, 1825. William Owen. (American Biography Ser.). 134p. 1991. reprint ed. lib. bdg. 59.00 (*0-7812-8304-3*) Rprt Serv.

Diary after Death. rev. ed. Franklin Loehr. LC 83-82486. 148p. 1992. reprint ed. pap. 7.50 (*0-915151-04-9*) Religious Res Pr.

Diary & Autobiography of John Adams, 4 Vols, Set. John Adams. Ed. by L. H. Butterfield et al. LC 60-5387. (Adams Papers Ser.: No. 1, Diaries). (Illus.). 1813p. 1961. 170.00 (*0-674-20300-3*) HUP.

Diary & Correspondence of Salmon P. Chase. Salmon P. Chase. LC 74-75301. (Law, Politics & History Ser.). 1971. reprint ed. lib. bdg. 59.50 (*0-306-71264-4*) Da Capo.

D

An Asterisk (*) at the beginning of an entry indicates that the title is appearing in BIP for the first time. 1941

Diary & Correspondence of Salmon P. Chase. Salmon P. Chase. (American Biography Ser.). 527p. 1991. reprint ed. lib. bdg. 99.00 (*0-7812-8066-4*) Rprt Serv.
Diary & Journal of Richard Clough Anderson, Jr., 1814-1826. Richard C. Anderson. Ed. by Alfred Tischendorf & E. Taylor Parks. LC 64-19178. 374p. reprint ed. pap. 106.60 (*0-317-55480-8*, 2052208) Bks Demand.
Diary & Letters: With an Account of His Administration. Thomas Hutchinson. (Notable American Authors Ser.). 1992. reprint ed. lib. bdg. 75.00 (*0-7812-3302-X*) Rprt Serv.
Diary & Letters of Gouverneur Morris, 2 Vols. Gouverneur Morris. Ed. by Anne C. Morris. LC 70-98691. (American Public Figures Ser.). 1970. reprint ed. lib. bdg. 130.00 (*0-306-71835-9*) Da Capo.
Diary & Letters of His Excellency Thomas Hutchinson, 2 vols., Set. Thomas Hutchinson. LC 74-170056. reprint ed. 165.00 (*0-404-03464-0*) AMS Pr.
Diary & Letters of His Excellency Thomas Hutchinson: Captain-General & Governor-in-Chief of His Late Magesty's Province of Massachusetts Bay in North America; Compiled by Peter O. Hutchinson, 2 vols., Set. Thomas Hutchinson. (American Biography Ser.). 1991. reprint ed. lib. bdg. 148.00 (*0-7812-8206-3*) Rprt Serv.
Diary & Letters of Kaethe Kollwitz. Kaethe Kollwitz. Tr. by Richard Winston & Clara Winston. (Illus.). 260p. 1988. pap. 15.95 (*0-8101-0761-9*) Northwestern U Pr.
Diary & Life, of William Bryd II of Virginia, 1674-1744. Kenneth A. Lockridge. 1991. pap. 10.95 (*0-393-95682-2*) Norton.
Diary, & Life, of William Byrd II of Virginia, 1674-1744. Kenneth A. Lockridge. LC 86-40425. (Institute of Early American History & Culture Ser.). xiv, 202p. 1987. 27.50 (*0-8078-1736-8*) U of NC Pr.
Diary & Sundry Observations of Thomas Alva Edison. Thomas A. Edison. Ed. by Dagobert D. Runes. LC 68-28588. (Illus.). 181p. 1968. reprint ed. text ed. 49.75 (*0-8371-0067-4*, EDTE, Greenwood Pr) Greenwood.
Diary Fiction: Writing As Action. H. Porter Abbott. LC 84-7111. 240p. 1984. 31.50 (*0-8014-1713-9*) Cornell U Pr.
***Diary for 1861.** Alexander Means. (American Autobiography Ser.). 46p. 1995. reprint ed. lib. bdg. 69.00 (*0-7812-8588-7*) Rprt Serv.
Diary from a Journey to the Middle of the World. John Brandi. 1979. per. 8.00 (*0-685-99725-1*) Figures.
Diary from a Journey to the Middle of the World. deluxe ed. John Brandi. 1979. per. 10.00 (*0-935724-57-5*) Figures.
Diary from Age Two see Speech Development of a Bilingual Child
Diary from Baja California. John Brandi. (Illus.). 1978. 4.00 (*0-87922-103-8*) Christophers Bks.
Diary from Dixie. Mary B. Chesnut. Ed. by Ben A. Williams. 600p. 1980. pap. text ed. 16.95 (*0-674-20291-0*) HUP.
Diary from Dixie. Mary B. Chesnut. Ed. by Isabella Martin & Myrta L. Avary. (Illus.). 28.25 (*0-8446-1109-3*) Peter Smith.
Diary from Dixie. Mary B. Chesnut. (History - United States Ser.). 423p. 1992. reprint ed. lib. bdg. 99.00 (*0-7812-6183-X*) Rprt Serv.
Diary from the Years of Occupation, 1939-44. Zygmunt Klukowski. Ed. by Andrew Klukowski & Helen K. May. Tr. by George Klukowski. LC 92-11032. (Illus.). 408p. (C). 1993. 44.95 (*0-252-01960-1*) U of Ill Pr.
Diary in the Sand. Maurice L. Smith. 116p. 1992. pap. 17.95 (*0-9632593-0-X*) Lelands.
Diary in the Strict Sense of the Term. Bronislaw Malinowski. 360p. 1989. 45.00 (*0-8047-1706-0*); pap. 16.95 (*0-8047-1707-9*) Stanford U Pr.
Diary into the Unknown. Eugene E. Whitworth & Ruth E. Whitworth. Ed. by Daniel W. Fry. 170p. 1988. 5.00 (*0-317-90588-0*) Grt Western Univ.
Diary Kept by T. E. Lawrence: While Traveling in Arabia During 1911. T. E. Lawrence. 86p. 1993. 45.00 (*1-873938-24-1*, Pub. by Ithaca UK) Paul & Co Pubs.
Diary of a Baby. Daniel N. Stern. LC 90-80241. 176p. 1992. pap. 11.00 (*0-465-01640-5*) Basic.
Diary of a Bomb Aimer. C. Muirhead. 160p. (C). 1991. 65.00 (*0-946771-75-8*, Pub. by Spellmount UK) St Mut.
Diary of a Bomb Aimer (WW2) Spellmount Ltd. Publishers Staff. (C). 1986. 90.00 (*0-685-60222-2*, Pub. by Spellmount UK) St Mut.
Diary of a Canny Man 1818-1828: Adam Mackie, Farmer, Merchant & Innkeeper in Fyvie. William Mackie. (Aberdeen University Press Bks.). (Illus.). 96p. 1991. pap. 13.90 (*0-08-041213-0*, Pub. by Aberdeen U Pr) Macmillan.
***Diary of a Cat: True Confessions & Lifelong Observations of a Well-Adjusted House Cat.** Leigh W. Rutledge. 128p. 1995. 11.95 (*0-525-94003-0*, Dutton) NAL-Dutton.
Diary of a Cattle Drive. William E. Jackson. Ed. by J. Orin Oliphant. 38p. 1984. pap. 4.95 (*0-87770-298-5*) Ye Galleon.
Diary of a Chambermaid. Octave Mirbeau. (Dedalus European Fiction Classics Ser.). 356p. 1992. pap. 14.95 (*0-7818-0008-0*, Pub. by Dedalus Bks UK) Hippocrene Bks.
Diary of a Chambermaid. Octave Mirbeau. 1992. pap. 14.95 (*0-946626-82-0*, Pub. by Dedalus Bks UK) Hippocrene Bks.
Diary of a City Priest. John McNamee. LC 93-11924. 270p. (Orig.). 1993. pap. 14.95 (*1-55612-662-X*) Sheed & Ward MO.
Diary of a Civil Servant. Cyro DosAnjos. Tr. by Arthur Brakel. LC 86-46325. (Illus.). 184p. 1988. 29.50 (*0-8386-3315-3*) Fairleigh Dickinson.
Diary of a Coastwatcher in the Solomons. Snowy Rhoades. 1982. pap. 5.00 (*0-685-09256-9*) Adm Nimitz Foun.
Diary of a Colonial Wife: An African Experience. Joan Sharwood-Smith. (Illus.). 160p. 1992. text ed. 39.50 (*1-85043-524-3*, Pub. by I B Tauris UK) St Martin.
Diary of a Common Soldier in the American Revolution, 1775-1783: An Annotated Edition of the Military Journal of Jeremiah Greenman. Ed. by Robert C. Bray & Paul E. Bushnell. LC 77-18528. (Illus.). 333p. 1978. pap. 12.50 (*0-87580-528-0*) N Ill U Pr.
Diary of a Communist Undergraduate. Nikolai Ognyov, pseud. Tr. by Alexander Werth. LC 72-90304. (Soviet Literature in English Translation Ser.). 288p. 1973. reprint ed. 21.50 (*0-88355-015-6*) Hyperion Conn.
Diary of a Congressman. G. W. Whitehurst. Ed. by Robert Friedman. LC 83-16523. 272p. 1983. pap. 7.95 (*0-89865-335-5*); 15.95 (*0-89865-353-3*) Donning Co.
Diary of a Congressman: ABSCAM & Beyond, Vol. 2. G. William Whitehurst. Ed. by Robert Friedman. LC 83-16523. 327p. 1985. 16.95 (*0-89865-376-2*); pap. 8.95 (*0-89865-375-4*) Donning Co.
Diary of a Cotswold Parson: Rev. F. E. Witts. Ed. by David Verey. (Illus.). 192p. 1993. pap. text ed. 14.00 (*0-685-63405-1*) A Sutton Pub.
Diary of a Country Priest. Georges Bernanos. 304p. 1984. pap. 8.95 (*0-88184-013-0*) Carroll & Graf.
Diary of a County Executive. James P. Coughlin. 160p. 1991. 15.95 (*0-938627-14-7*) New Past Pr.
Diary of a Daly Debutante. Dora Knowlton. LC 72-79946. 1972. 18.95 (*0-405-08713-6*, Pub. by Blom Pubns UK) Ayer.
Diary of a Deaf Mute. David Chagall. 1971. pap. 3.50 (*0-916538-01-X*) Millenium Hse.
***Diary of a Designing Woman.** Jeri Holmes. 1995. 17.95 (*0-8062-5196-4*) Carlton.
Diary of a Disaster: British Aid to Greece, 1940-1941. Robin Higham. LC 86-9177. 296p. 1986. 32.00 (*0-8131-1564-7*) U Pr of Ky.
Diary of a District Officer. John Morley. (Illus.). 200p. 1992. text ed. 39.50 (*1-85043-526-X*, Pub. by I B Tauris UK) St Martin.
Diary of a Dog. Olivia Long. (Pets & Their People Ser.). (Illus.). 32p. (J). (ps-4). Date not set. 9.95 (*1-880042-06-1*, SL12456) Shelf-Life Bks.
***Diary of a Dream: A History of the National Archives Independence Movement, 1980-1985.** Robert M. Warner. LC 94-37951. 241p. 1995. 32.50 (*0-8108-2956-8*) Scarecrow.
Diary of a Drug Fiend. Aleister Crowley. 1973. lib. bdg. 250.00 (*0-87968-110-1*) Krishna Pr.
Diary of a Drug Fiend. Aleister Crowley. LC 79-142495. 384p. 1970. pap. 11.95 (*0-87728-146-7*) Weiser.
Diary of a Drug Fiend. Aleister Crowley. 384p. 1989. reprint ed. lib. bdg. 26.95 (*0-89966-593-4*) Buccaneer Bks.
Diary of a Dude-Wrangler. Maxwell S. Burt. (BCL1 - United States Local History Ser.). 331p. 1991. reprint ed. lib. bdg. 89.00 (*0-7812-6327-1*) Rprt Serv.
***Diary of a Duffer.** George Blake. LC 94-44889. (Illus.). (Orig.). 1995. pap. 12.95 (*1-57028-020-7*) Masters Pr IN.
Diary of a Fat Housewife: A True Story of Humor, Heartbreak & Hope. Rosemary Green. 352p. 1995. 21.95 (*0-446-51789-5*) Warner Bks.
Diary of a Film see Beauty & the Beast: Diary of a Film
Diary of a First Class Jerk. Debbie Mitchell. LC 87-50267. 96p. (YA). (gr. 6-8). 1987. 8.95 (*1-55523-079-2*) Winston-Derek.
Diary of a Forty-Niner. Alfred Jackson. 193p. 1995. reprint ed. pap. 12.95 (*0-9627987-3-8*) Turtle Point Pr.
Diary of a Frantic Kid Sister. Hila Colman. (J). (gr. 4-6). 1985. pap. 2.95 (*0-671-61926-8*, Archway) PB.
Diary of a Frontier Bishop: The Journals of Theophile Meerschaert. Ed. by James D. White. LC 94-66879. xx, 638p. (Orig.). (C). 1994. pap. 29.50 (*0-9641702-0-5*) Sarto Pr.
Diary of a Girl in Changi 1941-45. Sheila Bruhn. (Illus.). 144p. (Orig.). 1994. pap. 14.95 (*0-86417-619-8*, Pub. by Kangaroo Pr AT) Seven Hills Bk.
Diary of a Human Shield. Glenda Lockwood. (Illus.). 230p. 1992. pap. 17.95 (*0-7475-1090-3*, Pub. by Bloomsbury Pub Ltd UK) Trafalgar.
***Diary of a Humiliated Man.** Felix De Azua. Tr. by Julie Jones. (Verba Mundi Ser.). 337p. 1995. 21.95 (*1-56792-032-2*) Godine.
Diary of a Japanese Innkeeper's Daughter. Kazuko Smith. Ed. by Robert J. Smith. Tr. by Miwa Kai. LC 83-150220. (Cornell East Asia Ser.: No. 36). 200p. (Orig.). 1984. pap. 9.00 (*0-939657-36-8*) Cornell East Asia Pgm.
Diary of a Journey Across Arabia, 1819. George F. Sadleir. (Arabia Past & Present Ser.: Vol. 5). (Illus.). 1977. 26.95 (*0-902675-59-1*) Oleander Pr.
Diary of a Journey Across Tibet. Hamilton Bower. 310p. (C). 1976. reprint ed. 125.00 (*0-89771-101-7*, Pub. by Ratna Pustak Bhandar) St Mut.
Diary of a Journey from the Mississippi to the Coasts of the Pacific: With a United States Government Expedition, 2 vols., Set. Baldwin Mollhausen. (American Biography Ser.). 1991. reprint ed. lib. bdg. 148.00 (*0-7812-8287-X*) Rprt Serv.
***Diary of a Kriegie.** Edward Beattie. (American Autobiography Ser.). 312p. 1995. reprint ed. lib. bdg. 89.00 (*0-7812-8453-8*) Rprt Serv.
***Diary of a Lost Boy.** Harry Kondoleon. LC 95-1679. 1995. pap. 14.95 (*1-57322-504-5*) Riverhead Bks.
Diary of a Loving Heart. June M. Bacher. LC 83-82322. (Pioneer Romance Ser.). 176p. 1984. mass mkt., pap. 3.99 (*1-56507-049-6*) Harvest Hse.
Diary of a Loving Heart. large type ed. June M. Bacher. LC 87-34061. 1988. pap. 8.95 (*0-8027-2623-2*) Walker & Co.
Diary of a Mad Old Man. Junichiro Tanizaki. LC 90-50614. 192p. 1991. pap. 10.00 (*0-679-73024-9*, Vin) Random.
Diary of a Madman. Nikolai V. Gogol. Tr. by Ronald Wilks. (Classics Ser.). 1973. mass mkt. 6.95 (*0-14-044273-1*, Penguin Classics) Viking Penguin.
Diary of a Madman. rev. ed. William-Alan Landes & Marilyn Standish. LC 90-52545. 1985. pap. 5.00 (*0-88734-109-8*) Players Pr.
Diary of a Madman & Other Stories. Nicolai Gogol. 1976. 14.95 (*0-8488-0505-4*) Amereon Ltd.
Diary of a Madman & Other Stories. Lu Xun. Tr. by William A. Lyell. LC 90-36785. (Illus.). 432p. 1990. text ed. 40.00 (*0-8248-1278-6*); pap. 18.95 (*0-8248-1317-0*) UH Pr.
Diary of a Madman & Other Stories. Andrew R. MacAndrew. Tr. by Andrew MacAndrew. 1961. pap. 4.95 (*0-451-52403-9*, CE1824, Sig Classics) NAL-Dutton.
Diary of a Napoleonic Foot Soldier. Jakob Walter. (Illus.). 128p. 1993. pap. 10.00 (*0-14-016559-2*, Penguin Bks) Viking Penguin.
***Diary of a Nobody.** George Grossmith & Weedon Grossmith. (Oxford Popular Fiction Ser.). (Illus.). 224p. 1995. pap. 7.95 (*0-19-282404-X*) OUP.
***Diary of a Nobody.** George Grossmith & Weedon Grossmith. (Illus.). 288p. 1993. pap. 8.95 (*0-460-87227-3*, Everyman's Classic Lib) C E Tuttle.
Diary of a Nobody. large type ed. George Grossmith & Weedon Grossmith. (Mainstream Ser.). (Illus.). 296p. 1987. lib. bdg. 16.95 (*1-85089-040-4*, Pub. by ISIS UK) Transaction Pubs.
Diary of a Nobody. George Grossmith & Weedon Grossmith. (Illus.). 192p. 1991. reprint ed. 30.00 (*0-86299-927-8*) A Sutton Pub.
Diary of a Non-Deflector: Selected Poems. Jim Dine. (Illus.). 80p. (Orig.). 1987. pap. text ed. 10.00 (*0-910457-13-1*) Arion Pr.
Diary of A. O. Barnabooth. Valery Larbaud. Tr. by Gilbert Cannan. LC 90-46619. (Recovered Classics Ser.). 336p. 1990. reprint ed. 18.00 (*0-929701-14-3*); reprint ed. pap. 10.00 (*0-929701-15-1*) McPherson & Co.
Diary of a Parish Clerk. Steen S. Blicher. 50p. 1991. pap. 5.95 (*1-880755-01-7*) Mermaid Pr.
Diary of a Pigeon Watcher. Schverin. 1994. pap. 8.95 (*1-56924-948-2*) Marlowe & Co.
Diary of a Pilgrimage. Jerome K. Jerome. (Jerome K. Jerome Ser.). (Illus.). 176p. (YA). (gr. 6-9). 1990. pap. 8.00 (*0-86299-010-6*) A Sutton Pub.
***Diary of a Rapist.** Evan S. Connell. LC 94-43665. 1995. write for info. (*0-88001-408-3*) Ecco Pr.
Diary of a Reluctant Recruit. Dick Bernal. 182p. 1988. pap. 6.95 (*0-88144-127-9*) Christian Pub.
Diary of a Russian Censor: Aleksandr Nikitenko. Ed. & Tr. by Helen S. Jacobson. LC 74-78977. 424p. 1975. 37.50 (*0-87023-152-9*) U of Mass Pr.
Diary of a Russian Priest. 2nd ed. Alexander Elchaninov. Ed. by Kallistos T. Ware. LC 82-16795. (Illus.). 225p. (Orig.). 1982. reprint ed. pap. 10.95 (*0-88141-000-4*) St Vladimirs.
Diary of a Russian Schoolteacher. F. Vigdorova. Tr. by Rose Prokofieva. LC 73-7078. 256p. 1973. reprint ed. text ed. 38.50 (*0-8371-6909-7*, VIRS, Greenwood Pr) Greenwood.
Diary of a School-Marm. Geraldine Squires. 1985. 50.00 (*0-7223-1885-5*, Pub. by A H S Ltd UK) St Mut.
Diary of a Sea Captain's Wife: Tales of Santa Cruz Island. Margaret H. Eaton & Vera E. Amey. Ed. by Janice Timbrook. (Illus.). 272p. 1980. 16.50 (*0-87461-032-X*); pap. 9.50 (*0-87461-033-8*) McNally & Loftin.
Diary of a Shirtwaist Striker. Theresa S. Malkiel. (Literature of American Labor Ser.). 224p. 1990. pap. 12.95 (*0-87546-168-9*) ILR Pr.
Diary of a Single Woman. Marianna Sommerfeld. 240p. (Orig.). 1991. pap. write for info. (*0-9629863-0-5*) Beach Grass.
Diary of a Sit-in. 2nd ed. Merrill Proudfoot. (Blacks in the New World Ser.). (Illus.). 272p. 1990. 11.95 (*0-252-06062-8*) U of Ill Pr.
Diary of a Somebody: Based on the Orton Diaries. John Lahr. LC 88-37726. 79p. (Orig.). 1989. pap. 7.95 (*0-87910-124-5*) Limelight Edns.
Diary of a Southern Queen: An HIV Plus Vision Quest. J. Michael Clark. LC 90-44705. 108p. (Orig.). 1990. pap. 8.00 (*0-930383-17-6*) Monument Pr.
***Diary of a Southern Refugee During the War.** Judith W. McGuire. 368p. 1995. pap. 12.00 (*0-8032-8223-0*, Bison Books) U of Nebr Pr.
Diary of a Southern Refugee, During the War. Judith W. McGuire. LC 72-2614. (American Women Ser.: Images & Realities). 364p. 1974. reprint ed. 32.95 (*0-405-04468-2*) Ayer.
Diary of a Sportscaster. Ken Coleman & Dan Valenti. LC 82-82096. 176p. (Orig.). 1982. pap. 6.95 (*0-943514-03-7*) Literations.
Diary of a Square Peg. Maralene Wesner. 98p. 1987. pap. 4.95 (*0-936715-07-3*) Diversity Okla.
***Diary of a Strike.** 2nd ed. Bernard Karsh. LC 81-10403. 195p. 1982. reprint ed. pap. 55.60 (*0-7837-8074-5*, 2047827) Bks Demand.
Diary of a Superfluous Man. Ivan S. Turgenev. Tr. by David Patterson. 80p. 1986. pap. 4.95 (*0-393-30306-3*) Norton.
Diary of a Superfluous Man, & Other Stories. Ivan S. Turgenev. Tr. by Isabel F. Hapgood. LC 72-150488. (Short Story Index Reprint Ser.). 1977. reprint ed. 19.95 (*0-8369-3829-1*) Ayer.
***Diary of a Survivor: 19 Years in Castro's Prisons.** Ana Rodriguez & Glenn Garvin. 336p. 1995. 22.95 (*0-312-13050-3*) St Martin.
***Diary of a Trademark.** Ian Stephens. 1995. pap. 12.00 (*0-919754-51-1*) InBook.
Diary of a Trolley Road. Michael C. DeVito. (Illus.). 1975. 10.00 (*0-910506-16-7*) De Vito.
***Diary of a Vampire.** Gary Bowen. (Orig.). 1995. pap. text ed. 6.95 (*1-56333-331-7*) Masquerade.
Diary of a Victorian Miss on Holiday. Ed. by Helen Kelsall & Keith Kelsall. 156p. 1992. 39.95 (*1-874718-00-8*, Pub. by Hallamshire Pr UK) St Mut.
***Diary of a Visiting Mother Vol. III: One Family's Journey Through Our Courts, Vol. III.** Louise Wallace. LC 94-69179. (Visiting Mother Ser.). 200p. 1995. pap. 12.00 (*1-885800-02-9*) PineTree Pr.
Diary of a Westward Voyage. Rabindranath Tagore. Tr. by Indu Dutt. LC 74-27392. 137p. 1975. reprint ed. text ed. 38.50 (*0-8371-7904-1*, TAWV, Greenwood Pr) Greenwood.
Diary of a Whacked-out Bitch or How to Change the Universe Starting with Yourself. Judith A. Heinz. Ed. by DonnaLee Dox. LC 92-90828. (Illus.). 195p. (Orig.). 1992. pap. 9.95 (*0-9636245-0-4*) Wind Bag Bks.
Diary of a Witness: Diary of a Witness to the War in Africa. Pedro Alarcon. Tr. by Bern Keating. (C). 1988. 39.95 (*0-940561-10-7*) White Rose Pr.
Diary of a Woman Doctor. Marilyn Gilman. 1981. pap. 2.75 (*0-89083-718-X*) Zebra.
Diary of a Working Man: Bill Williams, Forest of Dean, 1872-1873. Ed. by Bess Anstis & Ralph Anstis. LC 94-1791. 1994. write for info. (*0-7509-0584-0*) A Sutton Pub.

Diary of a Writer: An Andrew Neill Case. Jonathan Gage. 368p. 1994. 18.95 (*0-9639608-1-4*); pap. 6.50 (*0-9639608-0-6*) Higher Ground Pub. Today Andrew Neill inherited over forty million dollars. Only, to wish he hadn't... On February 12, Jake Neill, famous best-selling novelist, died from a heart attack. At least, that's what everyone was told. Jake wrote about unresolved mysteries from all over the world. He would look into a particular case, find the answer & write a book about it. His last book, DIARY OF A WRITER, tells the story of a man that, searching for the truth behind the death of his wife, unveils a plot of deceit of international scale, fiercely kept in secret for decades. There is only one problem with DIARY OF A WRITER, it wasn't supposed to get published. It threatened too many powerful people, & they would do anything to stop the book from seeing the light. Only, they left out a slight detail... You see, Jake Neill had the tricky habit of secretly sending a copy of his books to his brother Andrew, before anybody else knew about them. DIARY OF A WRITER is a fast paced mystery novel full of thrill & action. If you like Tom Clancy, John Grisham & Stephen King, DIARY OF A WRITER is a must in your library. Order from: Higher Ground Publishing, P.O. Box 4317, Westlake Village, CA 91359-1317; 818-889-9452, FAX 818-889-9682. ***Publisher Provided Annotation.***

Diary of a Young Girl. Anne Frank. 1994. 13.50 (*0-679-60124-4*) Knopf.
Diary of a Young Girl. Anne Frank. 1993. mass mkt. 4.99 (*0-553-29698-1*) Bantam.
Diary of a Young Girl. Anne Frank. 1989. mass mkt. 5.50 (*0-671-69009-4*) PB.
Diary of a Young Girl. Anne Frank. LC 58-11474. 285p. 1978. 13.50 (*0-394-60451-2*, Modern Lib) Random.
***Diary of a Young Girl, the Definitive Education.** Anne Frank. 1995. 25.00 (*0-385-47378-8*) Doubleday.
Diary of a Young Man Growing Old: A Baby Boomer's Thoughts at Middle Age. Robert D. Fry. 122p. (Orig.). 1993. pap. 7.95 (*1-883234-01-8*) Little Burro.
Diary of a Young Soul Rebel. Isaac Julien & Colin MacCabe. (Illus.). 208p. 1991. 45.00 (*0-253-33117-X*, Pub. by British Film Inst UK); pap. 18.95 (*0-85170-310-0*, Pub. by British Film Inst UK) Ind U Pr.
Diary of a Yuppie. Louis Auchincloss. 1987. pap. 3.95 (*0-312-90761-3*) St Martin.
Diary of a Yuppie. Louis Auchincloss. 1987. pap. 3.95 (*0-317-62209-9*) St Martin.
***Diary of Adam & Eve.** Mark Twain. 1972. 3.00 (*0-87129-452-4*, D15) Dramatic Pub.
Diary of Alice James. Alice James. (American Biography Ser.). 241p. 1991. reprint ed. lib. bdg. 69.00 (*0-7812-8211-X*) Rprt Serv.
Diary of an Ad Man. James W. Young. 1990. pap. 11.95 (*0-8442-3245-9*, NTC Busn Bks) NTC Pub Grp.
Diary of an Affair. Jeannie Sakol. 224p. 1989. 17.95 (*1-55611-136-3*) D I Fine.
Diary of an Affair. Jeannie Sakol. 1990. pap. 3.95 (*1-55817-397-8*, Pinnacle NY) Windsor NY.
Diary of an Alchemist. Douglas Baker. (C). 1987. 80.00 (*0-317-90362-4*, Pub. by Claregate Coll UK) St Mut.
Diary of an Angel. rev. ed. Alizarin Lake. 192p. (Orig.). 1991. mass mkt. 4.95 (*1-878320-71-8*) Masquerade.

An Asterisk (*) at the beginning of an entry indicates that the title is appearing in BIP for the first time.

An Asterisk (*) at the beginning of an entry indicates that the title is appearing in BIP for the first time.

***Diary of James Horne Morrison, (1894-1895) A Scots Missionary in Canada.** Ed. by Boyd S. Schlenther. LC 94-20998. 1994. write for info. (0-7734-9024-8) E Mellen.

Diary of Jesus H. Christ. Ed. by J. P. Sculley. 110p. 1988. pap. 6.95 (0-941913-01-5) Ventura Arts.

Diary of John Manningham. John Manningham. Ed. by John Bruce. LC 17-1264. (Camden Society, London. Publications, First Ser.: No. 99). reprint ed. 49.50 (0-404-50199-0) AMS Pr.

Diary of John Manningham of the Middle Temple, 1602-1603: Newly Edited in Complete & Unexpurgated Form from the Original Manuscript in the British Museum. John Manningham. LC 74-22553. 485p. reprint ed. pap. 138.30 (0-8357-6520-2, 2035891) Bks Demand.

Diary of John Quincy Adams: Nov. 1779-Dec. 1788, Set, Vols. 1 & 2. John Q. Adams. Ed. by David G. Allen et al. LC 81-6197. (Adams Papers Ser.). (Illus.). 1017p. (C). 1982. Set. 95.00 (0-674-20420-4) HUP.

Diary of John Rous, Incumbent of Santon Downham, Suffolk, from 1625 to 1642. John Rous. Ed. by Mary A. Green. (Camden Society, London. Publications, First Ser.: No. 66). reprint ed. 35.00 (0-404-50166-4) AMS Pr.

Diary of Joseph Farington, 2 vols., Set. Joseph Farington. Ed. by Kathryn Cave. LC 78-7056. (Studies in British Art). 1984. text ed. 125.00 (0-300-03183-1) Yale U Pr.

Diary of Joseph Farington, 2 vols., Set. Joseph Farington. Ed. by Kathryn Cave. LC 78-7056. (Studies in British Art). 1985. text ed. 125.00 (0-300-03270-6) Yale U Pr.

Diary of Joseph Farington, Set, Vols. 11 & 12. Joseph Farington. Ed. by Kathryn Cave. LC 78-7056. (Studies in British Art). 1000p. 1983. Set. text ed. 125.00 (0-300-03124-6) Yale U Pr.

Diary of Joseph Farington, Vol. XIII. Joseph Farington. Ed. by Kathryn Cave. 320p. 1984. write for info. (0-318-57887-5) Yale U Pr.

Diary of Joseph Farington, Vol. XIV. Joseph Farington. Ed. by Kathryn Cave. 384p. 1984. write for info. (0-318-57888-3) Yale U Pr.

Diary of Joseph Farington, Vol. XV. Joseph Farington. Ed. by Kathryn Cave. 320p. 1985. write for info. (0-318-57889-1) Yale U Pr.

Diary of Joseph Farington, Vol. XVI. Joseph Farington. Ed. by Kathryn Cave. 328p. 1985. write for info. (0-318-57890-5) Yale U Pr.

Diary of Joseph Farington: January 1808 Through December 1810, Set, Vols. 9 & 10. Joseph Farington. Ed. by Kathryn Cave. LC 78-7056. (Studies in British Art). 1000p. 1982. Set. text ed. 125.00 (0-300-02859-8) Yale U Pr.

Diary of Joseph Farington, R. A. Volumes 7 & 8: January 1805 Through December 1807, Set. Joseph Farington. LC 78-7056. (Published for the Paul Mellon Center for Studies in British Art Ser.). 360p. (C). 1982. text ed. 125.00 (0-300-02768-0) Yale U Pr.

Diary of Joshua Hempstead of New London, Conn., 1711-1758. Joshua Hempstead. (Illus.). 750p. 1985. 45.00 (0-9607744-1-6) New London County.

Diary of Joshua Hempstead, 1711-1758, with an Account of a Journey Made from New London to Maryland. Joshua Hempstead. 750p. reprint ed. lib. bdg. 120.00 (0-8328-0934-9); reprint ed. pap. 112.50 (0-8328-0935-7) Higginson Bk Co.

Diary of Josiah Atkins. Josiah Atkins. 1976. 17.95 (0-405-10472-3, 12625) Ayer.

Diary of Juliet Thompson. Juliet Thompson. 396p. 1983. pap. 13.95 (0-933770-27-8) Kalimat.

Diary of Kenneth Macrae. Ed. by Iain H. Murray. (Illus.). 535p. 1980. 29.95 (0-85151-297-6) Banner of Truth.

Diary of Kido Takayoshi, Vol. 1. Sydney Brown. 1983. 74.50 (0-86008-328-4) Col U Pr.

Diary of Kido Takayoshi, Vol. 3. Ed. by Sidney D. Brown & Akiko Hirota. 380p. 1986. 99.50 (0-86008-386-1, Pub. by U of Tokyo JA) Col U Pr.

Diary of Kido Takayoshi, Vol. 2: 1871-1874. Kido Takayoshi. Ed. by Sidney D. Brown & Akiko Hirota. 540p. 1985. 74.50 (0-86008-350-0, Pub. by U of Tokyo JA) Col U Pr.

Diary of Latoya Hunter. Latoya Hunter. LC 92-8384. (J). 1992. 16.00 (0-517-58511-1, Crown) Crown Pub Group.

Diary of Latoya Hunter: My First Year in Junior High. Latoya Hunter. LC 93-13106. (YA). 1993. pap. 8.00 (0-679-74606-4, Vin) Random.

Diary of Lieutenant Anthony Allaire of Fergusons Corps. Anthony Allaire. LC 67-29025. (Eyewitness Accounts of the American Revolution Ser., No. 1). 1976. reprint ed. 16.95 (0-405-01102-4) Ayer.

Diary of Lost Boy. Harry Kondoleon. LC 93-24257. 1994. 20.00 (0-679-43067-9) Knopf.

Diary of Madam Egout Pour Sweet. Rina Hands. 88p. (Orig.). 1991. 11.95 (0-89756-017-5) Two Rivers.

Diary of Madox Brown. Ford B. Madox. Ed. by Virginia Surtees. LC 81-51344. (Paul Mellon Centre for Studies in British Art). (Illus.). 320p. (C). 1981. 42.50 (0-300-02743-5) Yale U Pr.

Diary of Marquis Kido, Nineteen Thirty-One to Nineteen Forty-Five: Selected Translations Into English. Marquis K. Koichi. LC 83-21646. 500p. 1984. text ed. 75.00 (0-313-27055-4, U7055, Greenwood Pr) Greenwood.

Diary of Martha Ballard, 1785-1812. Tr. by Robert R. McCausland & Cynthia M. McCausland. LC 92-67980. 992p. 1992. 59.95 (0-929539-62-1) Picton Pr.

Diary of Master William Silence. Dodgson H. Madden. (BCL1-PR English Literature Ser.). 386p. 1992. reprint ed. lib. bdg. 89.00 (0-7812-7309-9) Rprt Serv.

Diary of Master William Silence: A Study of Shakespeare & Elizabethan Sport. Dodgson H. Madden. LC 71-95440. (Studies in Shakespeare: No. 24). 1970. reprint ed. lib. bdg. 61.95 (0-8383-0993-3) M S G Haskell Hse.

Diary of Master William Silence: A Study of Shakespeare & of Elizabethan Sport. Dodgson H. Madden. LC 78-89018. 386p. 1970. reprint ed. text ed. 65.00 (0-8371-2322-4, MAMS, Greenwood Pr) Greenwood.

***Diary of Matthew Patten of Bedford, NH, 1754-1788.** (Illus.). 640p. 1993. 49.50 (0-89725-111-3) Picton Pr.

Diary of Michael Wigglesworth, 1653 to 1657: The Conscience of a Puritan. Michael Wigglesworth. Ed. by Edmund Morgan. 11.25 (0-8446-0808-4) Peter Smith.

Diary of Military Government in Germany, 1945. Ed. by B. N. Reckitt. 78p. (C). 1989. 35.00 (0-7223-2301-8, Pub. by A H S Ltd UK) St Mut.

Diary of Miss Emma Holmes, 1861-1866. Ed. by John F. Marszalek. (Library of Southern Civilization). (Illus.). 528p. 1994. reprint ed. pap. 16.95 (0-8071-1940-7) La State U Pr.

***Diary of My Gerbil Colony.** Eva Fischer-Dixon. 120p. 1995. pap. 7.95 (0-7610-0046-1) NW Pub.

Diary of Northwest Trout Flies. Dan Homel. (Illus.). 96p. 1991. pap. 7.95 (1-879522-00-4) Forrest Pk.

Diary of One of Garibaldi's Thousand. Giuseppe C. Abba. Tr. by E. R. Vincent. LC 80-24181. (Oxford Library of Italian Classics). (Illus.). xxi, 166p. 1981. reprint ed. text ed. 52.50 (0-313-22446-3, ABDO, Greenwood Pr) Greenwood.

Diary of Patrick Breen - One of the Donner Party. Patrick Breen. Ed. by Frederick J. Teggart. (Illus.). 16p. 1978. reprint ed. pap. 3.95 (0-89646-048-7) Vistabooks.

Diary of Peaches Browning: The World, Close at Hand & Far Away, as Seen by an Intelligent Labrador. Thomas C. Thomsen. Ed. by Eleanor Mann. 148p. (Orig.). 1992. pap. 7.95 (0-945288-02-6) Cross River Pr.

Diary of Philip Hone 1828-1851, 2 Vols. in 1. Ed. by Allan Nevins. LC 77-112559. (Rise of Urban America Ser.). (Illus.). 1970. reprint ed. 57.95 (0-405-02468-1) Ayer.

Diary of Philip Leget Edwards, the Great Cattle Drive from California to Oregon in 1839. Philip L. Edwards. 62p. 1989. 14.95 (0-87770-465-1) Ye Galleon.

Diary of Pierre Laval. Pierre Laval. LC 72-6725. reprint ed. 22.50 (0-404-10644-7) AMS Pr.

Diary of Private Prayer. Donald M. Baillie. 136p. 1949. text ed. 14.00 (0-684-30997-1, Scribners) S&S Trade.

Diary of Private Prayer. John Baillie. 144p. 1979. pap. 7.00 (0-684-16323-3, Scribners) S&S Trade.

Diary of Private Prayer. large type ed. John Baillie. (Large Print Inspirational Ser.). 144p. 1986. pap. 8.95 (0-8027-2519-8) Walker & Co.

Diary of Public Transactions & Other Occurrences, Chiefly in Scotland. John Nicoll. LC 71-173084. (Bannatyne Club, Edinburgh. Publications: No. 52). reprint ed. 37.50 (0-404-52762-0) AMS Pr.

Diary of Ralph Macfarlane, 1616-1683. Ralph Josselin. Ed. by Alan Macfarlane. (Records of Social & Economic History, New Series British Academy: No. III). (Illus.). 754p. 1991. pap. 59.00 (0-19-726103-5) OUP.

Diary of Readings. John Baillie. 400p. 1986. pap. 4.95 (0-02-048360-0, Pub. by Gebrueder Borntraeger GW) Macmillan.

Diary of Rev. William Bentley: 1784-1819, Vols. 2 & 4. William Bentley. 18.00 (0-8446-1071-2) Peter Smith.

Diary of Rexford G. Tugwell: The New Deal, 1932-1935. Ed. by Michael V. Namorato. LC 92-1166. (Contributions in Economics & Economic History Ser.: No. 136). 544p. 1992. text ed. 65.00 (0-313-28017-7, NDY/, Greenwood Pr) Greenwood.

Diary of Richard L. Burtsell, Priest of New York the Early Years, 1865-1868. Richard L. Burtsell & Nelson J. Callahan. 1978. 41.95 (0-405-10813-3) Ayer.

Diary of Ruth Anna Hatch, Woods Hole, 1881. Ed. by M. L. Smith. (Illus.). (YA). 1992. text ed. write for info. (0-9611374-3-6) Woods Hole Hist.

Diary of Samuel Pepys. Samuel Pepys. Ed. by O. F. Morshead. (Illus.). 1960. 25.75 (0-8446-2727-5) Peter Smith.

Diary of Samuel Pepys, 9 vols. Samuel Pepys. Ed. by Robert Latham & William Matthews. Incl. Vol. 1. 1660. 1970. 42.00 (0-520-01575-4); Vol. 2. 1661. 1970. 42.00 (0-520-01576-2); Vol. 3. 1662. 1970. 42.00 (0-520-01577-0); Vol. 4. 1663. 1971. 42.00 (0-520-01857-5); Vol. 5. 1664. 1971. 42.00 (0-520-01858-3); Vol. 6. 1665. 1972. 42.00 (0-520-01859-1); Vol. 7. 1666. 1972. 42.00 (0-520-02094-4); Vol. 8. 1667. 1974. 42.00 (0-520-02095-2); Vol. 9. 1668-1669. 1976. 42.00 (0-520-02096-0); Vol. 10. Companion. 1983. 42.00 (0-520-02097-9); Vol. 11. Index. 1983. 42.00 (0-520-02098-7); write for info. (0-318-56007-0) U CA Pr.

Diary of Samuel Pepys, 10 Vols, Set. Samuel Pepys. Ed. by Henry B. Wheatley. Tr. by Mynors Bright. LC 68-57227. reprint ed. lib. bdg. 825.00 (0-404-05030-1) AMS Pr.

Diary of Samuel Sewall, 1674-1729, 2 vols. Ed. by Halsey M. Thomas. (Illus.). 1254p. 1973. 30.00 (0-374-13952-0) FS&G.

Diary of Samuel Sewall, 1674-1729, 3 Vols, 1. Samuel Sewall. LC 77-141102. (Research Library of Colonial Americana). (Illus.). 1972. reprint ed. 48.95 (0-405-03312-5) Ayer.

Diary of Samuel Sewall, 1674-1729, 3 Vols, 2. Samuel Sewall. LC 77-141102. (Research Library of Colonial Americana). (Illus.). 1972. reprint ed. 48.95 (0-405-03313-3) Ayer.

Diary of Samuel Sewall, 1674-1729, 3 Vols, 3. Samuel Sewall. LC 77-141102. (Research Library of Colonial Americana). (Illus.). 1972. reprint ed. 48.95 (0-405-03314-1) Ayer.

Diary of Samuel Sewall, 1674-1729, 3 Vols, Set. Samuel Sewall. LC 77-141102. (Research Library of Colonial Americana). (Illus.). 1972. reprint ed. 145.95 (0-405-03311-7) Ayer.

Diary of Samuel Sewall, 1674-1729, 2 vols., Set. Samuel Sewall. (American Biography Ser.). 1991. reprint ed. lib. bdg. 148.00 (0-7812-8350-7) Rprt Serv.

Diary of Sigmund Freud: Vienna & London, 1929-1939. Sigmund Freud. (Illus.). 256p. 1992. text ed. 50.00 (0-684-19329-9, Scribners) S&S Trade.

Diary of Signs & Wonders. Maria Woodworth-Etter. 584p. (Orig.). 1981. pap. 14.95 (0-89274-184-8) Harrison Hse.

Diary of Simeon Perkins, 1766-1780, Vol. 29. Simeon Perkins. Ed. by Harold A. Innes. LC 69-14503. 298p. 1969. reprint ed. text ed. 55.00 (0-8371-5067-1, PEDI, Greenwood Pr) Greenwood.

Diary of Simeon Perkins, 1780-1789, Vol. 36. Simeon Perkins. Ed. by D. C. Harvey. LC 69-14503. 531p. 1969. reprint ed. text ed. 75.00 (0-8371-5068-X, PEDJ, Greenwood Pr) Greenwood.

Diary of Sir Edward Hamilton: 1885-1906. Ed. by Dudley W. Bahlman. 475p. 1994. 39.95 (0-85958-612-X, Pub. by Hull Univ Pr UK) Paul & Co Pubs.

Diary of Soren Kierkegaard. Soren Kierkegaard. Ed. by Peter P. Rohde. 1971. reprint ed. pap. 5.95 (0-8065-0251-7, Citadel Pr) Carol Pub Group.

Diary of the Alarcon Expedition into Texas 1718-1719. Fray F. Celiz. Ed. by Fritz L. Hoffman. LC 67-24717. (Quivira Society Publications, Vol. 5). 1967. reprint ed. 19.95 (0-405-00075-8) Ayer.

Diary of the American Revolution: From Newspapers & Original Documents, 2 vols., 1. Ed. by Frank Moore & Peter Decker. LC 72-76563. (Eyewitness Accounts of the American Revolution Ser., No. 1). (Illus.). 1969. reprint ed. 23.95 (0-405-01166-0) Ayer.

Diary of the American Revolution: From Newspapers & Original Documents, 2 vols., 2. Ed. by Frank Moore & Peter Decker. LC 72-76563. (Eyewitness Accounts of the American Revolution Ser., No. 1). (Illus.). 1969. reprint ed. 23.95 (0-405-01167-9) Ayer.

Diary of the American Revolution: From Newspapers & Original Documents, 2 vols., Set. Ed. by Frank Moore & Peter Decker. LC 72-76563. (Eyewitness Accounts of the American Revolution Ser., No. 1). (Illus.). 1969. reprint ed. 46.95 (0-405-01165-2) Ayer.

Diary of the Cavaliere Bernini's Visit to France. Paul F. De Chantelou. Ed. by Anthony Blunt. Tr. by Margery Corbett. LC 85-42680. (Illus.). 376p. 1985. text ed. 69.50x (0-691-04028-1) Princeton U Pr.

***Diary of the Cavaliere Bernini's Visit to France.** Ed. by Anthony Blunt. LC 85-42680. reprint ed. pap. 117.50 (0-7837-9314-6, 2060054) Bks Demand.

***Diary of the Century: Tales from America's Greatest Diarist.** Edward R. Ellis & Pete Hamill. Ed. by Philip Turner. (Illus.). 592p. 1995. 25.00 (1-56836-080-0) Kodansha.

Diary of the Civil War. John C. Spence. 350p. 1991. text ed. write for info. (0-9621673-1-2) C B Arnette.

Diary of the French Revolution, 2 vols. Gouverneur Morris. Ed. by Beatrix C. Davenport. LC 70-110859. (Illus.). 1972. reprint ed. text ed. 75.00 (0-8371-4528-7, MOFR) Greenwood.

Diary of the French Revolution, 2 vols, 1. Gouverneur Morris. Ed. by Beatrix C. Davenport. LC 70-110859. (Illus.). 1972. reprint ed. text ed. 45.00 (0-8371-4529-5, MOFS) Greenwood.

Diary of the French Revolution, 2 vols., Set. Gouverneur Morris. Ed. by Beatrix C. Davenport. LC 71-157348. (Select Bibliographies Reprint Ser.). 1977. reprint ed. 72.95 (0-8369-5809-8) Ayer.

Diary of the French Revolution, 2 vols, Vol. 2. Gouverneur Morris. Ed. by Beatrix C. Davenport. LC 70-110859. (Illus.). 1972. reprint ed. text ed. 45.00 (0-8371-4530-9, MOFT) Greenwood.

Diary of the Lord's Place. Joe Ranieri. 128p. (Orig.). 1992. pap. 7.95 (0-9631517-5-4) Jeremiah Pr.

Diary of the Marches of the Royal Army During the Great Civil War. Richard Symonds. Ed. by Charles E. Long. (Camden Society, London. Publications, First Ser.: No. 74). reprint ed. 72.00 (0-404-50174-5) AMS Pr.

Diary of the Proceedings in the Parliament & Privy Council of Scotland. Ed. by David H. Crossrig. LC 72-1026. (Bannatyne Club, Edinburgh. Publications: No. 27). reprint ed. 10.00 (0-404-52733-7) AMS Pr.

Diary of the Public Correspondence of Sir Thomas Hope. Thomas Hope. LC 74-170048. (Bannatyne Club, Edinburgh. Publications: No. 76). reprint ed. 27.50 (0-404-52797-3) AMS Pr.

Diary of the Sinai Campaign. Moshe Dayan. (Quality Paperbacks Ser.). (Illus.). 236p. 1991. reprint ed. pap. 12.95 (0-306-80451-4) Da Capo.

Diary of the Sinai Campaign. Moshe Dayan. LC 78-27859. (Illus.). 236p. 1979. reprint ed. text ed. 35.00 (0-313-20928-6, DADO, Greenwood Pr) Greenwood.

***Diary of the Trail.** Paul Lamb. iii, 239p. (Orig.). 1995. pap. text ed. 10.00 (0-9639719-1-3) Lambs Fold Ranch.

Diary of the "Y" Miriam S. Baruch. 120p. 1978. write for info. (0-8187-0049-1) Harlo Press.

Diary of Time Remembered Back Along, up Bremridge. Dorinda Jeynes. 233p. (C). 1988. 59.00 (1-85200-022-8, Pub. by United Writers Pubns UK) St Mut.

Diary of Unborn Child - Inner Dialogues: A Baby Speaks from His Mother's Womb. Manuel D. Coudris. Ed. by Rene Coudris. Tr. by Pat Campbell. (Illus.). 192p. (Orig.). 1995. pap. 11.95 (0-946551-80-4, Pub. by Gateway Bks UK) Atrium Pubs.

Diary of Valery Bryusov (1893-1905). With Reminiscences by V. F. Khodasevich & Marina Tsvetaeva. Valery Bryusov. Ed. by Joan D. Grossman. LC 78-66013. (Documentary Studies in Modern Russian Poetry: No. 1). 200p. 1980. 38.00 (0-520-03858-4) U CA Pr.

Diary of Vaslav Nijinsky. Ed. by Romola Nijinsky. (Illus.). 1968. pap. 11.95 (0-520-00945-2) U CA Pr.

Diary of Virginia Woolf, Vol. 5: 1936-1941. Virginia Woolf. Ed. by Anne O. Bell. 416p. 1985. pap. 10.95 (0-15-626040-9, Harvest Bks) HarBrace.

Diary of Virginia Woolf: Vol. 1, 1915-1919. Ed. by Anne O. Bell. LC 78-23882. 356p. 1979. pap. 12.95 (0-15-626036-0, Harvest Bks) HarBrace.

Diary of Virginia Woolf: Vol. 2, 1920-1924. Ed. by Anne O. Bell. LC 78-23882. 371p. 1980. pap. 10.95 (0-15-626037-9, Harvest Bks) HarBrace.

Diary of Virginia Woolf: Vol. 3, 1925-1930. Ed. by Anne O. Bell. LC 77-73111. 400p. 1981. pap. 11.95 (0-15-626038-7, Harvest Bks) HarBrace.

Diary of Virginia Woolf: Vol. 4, 1931-1935. Ed. by Anne O. Bell. 402p. 1983. reprint ed. pap. 10.95 (0-15-626039-5, Harvest Bks) HarBrace.

Diary of Walter Yonge. Walter Yonge. Ed. by George Roberts. (Camden Society, London. Publications, First Ser.: No. 41). reprint ed. 37.50 (0-404-50141-9) AMS Pr.

Diary of William Dunlap, 3 Vols. in 1. William Dunlap. LC 78-84204. 1972. 63.95 (0-405-08474-9, Pub. by Blom Pubns UK) Ayer.

Diary of William Dunlap, 1766-1839: The Memoirs of a Dramatist, Theatrical Manager, Painter, Critic, Novelist, & Historian. William Dunlap. (American Biography Ser.). 502p. 1991. reprint ed. lib. bdg. 99.00 (0-7812-8116-4) Rprt Serv.

Diary of William Harvey. Jean Hamburger. Tr. by Barbara Wright. LC 91-46771. 224p. (C). 1992. 35.00 (0-8135-1825-3); pap. 14.95 (0-8135-1826-1) Rutgers U Pr.

Diary of William J. Schierholt in World War One. William J. Schierholt. 17p. 1978. pap. 15.00 (0-89126-061-7) MA-AH Pub.

Diary of William Owen from Nov. 10, 1824 to April 20, 1825. William Owen. Ed. by Joel W. Hiatt. LC 72-77057. 1973. reprint ed. lib. bdg. 27.50 (0-678-00918-X) Kelley.

Diary of William Pynchon of Salem. William Pynchon. Ed. by Fitch E. Oliver. LC 75-31131. reprint ed. 52.50 (0-404-13608-7) AMS Pr.

Diary on Information Theory. Alfred Renji. 192p. (C). 1984. 67.50x (963-05-3876-8, Pub. by Akad Kiado HU) St Mut.

Diary, Reminiscences, & Correspondence, 3 vols., Set. Henry C. Robinson. (BCL1-PR English Literature Ser.). 1992. reprint ed. lib. bdg. 225.00 (0-7812-7622-5) Rprt Serv.

Diary, Reminiscences, & Correspondence of Henry Crabb Robinson, 2 Vols. Henry C. Robinson. Ed. by Thomas Sadler. reprint ed. write for info. (0-318-50557-6) AMS Pr.

Diary, Reminiscences, & Correspondence of Henry Crabb Robinson, 2 Vols, 1. Henry C. Robinson. Ed. by Thomas Sadler. LC 28-15241. reprint ed. write for info. (0-404-05366-1) AMS Pr.

Diary, Reminiscences, & Correspondence of Henry Crabb Robinson, 2 Vols, 2. Henry C. Robinson. Ed. by Thomas Sadler. LC 28-15241. reprint ed. write for info. (0-404-05367-X) AMS Pr.

Diary, Reminiscences, & Correspondence of Henry Crabb Robinson, 2 Vols, Set. Henry C. Robinson. Ed. by Thomas Sadler. LC 28-15241. reprint ed. 115.00 (0-404-05365-3) AMS Pr.

Diary Sixty-Four to Sixty-Five. Chiara Lubich. 184p. 1987. 6.95 (0-911782-55-9) New City.

Diary, 1851. John M. Mackenzie. (C). 1992. text ed. 75.00 (0-86152-872-7, Pub. by Acair Ltd UK) St Mut.

Dias Acratas: Sin Ley ni Dios. Alberto Guigou. LC 80-53561. (Senda Narrativa Ser.). 276p. (Orig.). (SPA.). 1981. pap. 10.95 (0-918454-24-7) Senda Nueva.

Dias Contados. Juan A. Corretjer. (Illus.). 51p. (SPA.). 1985. pap. 3.50 (0-685-24435-0) Editorial El Coqui.

Dias Cubanos de Hernan Cortes y Su Lucha Por un Ideal. Angel Aparicio-Laurencio. 40p. (Orig.). (SPA.). 1988. pap. 5.00 (84-86662-09-5) Ediciones.

Dias de Circo. Alma F. Ada. (Cuentos con Alma Ser.). (Illus.). 24p. (SPA.). (J). (gr. 3-9). 1993. 16.95 (1-56492-127-1) Laredo.

Dias Sin Gloria. Jose R. Estrada. 64p. (SPA.). 1982. reprint ed. pap. 3.05 (0-311-08213-0, Edit Mundo) Casa Bautista.

Dias Terrenales. Jose Revueltas. Ed. by Evodio Escalante. (Coleccion Archivos). 386p. (SPA.). (C). 1991. 34.95 (84-00-07113-1) U of Pittsburgh Pr.

Dias y Dias de Poesia: Complete Program. Alma F. Ada. (Orig.). (SPA.). (ps-6). 1992. pap. 370.00 (1-56334-258-8) Hampton-Brown.

Dias y Dias de Poesia: Complete Program - Small Books, 36 bks. Alma F. Ada. (Illus.). (Orig.). (SPA.). (J). (ps-6). 1992. pap. 580.00 (1-56334-259-6) Hampton-Brown.

***Diaspora.** Jake Berry. (Illus.). (YA). (gr. 7 up). 1989. audio 3.00 (0-929611-07-1) Plutonium Pr.

Diaspora Jews & Judaism: Essays in Honor of & in Dialogue with A. Thomas Kraabel. J. Andrew Overman & Robert MacLennan. (USF Studies in the History of Judaism). 388p. (C). 1992. 74.95 (1-55540-696-3, 240041) Scholars Pr GA.

***Diasporas: Poems 1973-1977.** Seymour Mayne. 128p. 1995. lib. bdg. 27.00 (0-8095-4538-1) Borgo Pr.

Diasporas in Antiquity. Ed. by Shaye J. Cohen & Ernest S. Frerichs. LC 93-37125. (Brown Judaic Studies: No. 288). 130p. 1993. 39.95 (1-55540-918-0, 140288) Scholars Pr GA.

Diastematomyelia. F. B. Maroun. LC 75-17393. (Illus.). 144p. 1976. 10.60 (0-87527-143-X) Green.

Diastolic Relaxation of the Heart: The Biology of Diastole in Health & Disease. 2nd ed. Ed. by William Grossman & Beverly H. Lorell. LC 93-35878. 368p. (C). 1994. lib. bdg. 125.00 (0-7923-2611-3) Kluwer Ac.

D

An Asterisk (*) at the beginning of an entry indicates that the title is appearing in BIP for the first time.

Dia...Tal Vez un Viernes: Una Novela No Muy Seria, Pero Eso Si, Romantica. Carlos Deupi. LC 92-70486. (Coleccion Caniqui Ser.). 243p. (Orig.). (SPA.). 1992. pap. 19.00 (*0-89729-638-9*) Ediciones.

Diathesis in the Semitic Languages: A Comparative Morphological Study. Jan Retso. LC 89-39786. (Studies in Semitic Languages & Linguistics: Vol. XIV). xvii, 254p. 1989. text ed. 55.00 (*90-04-08818-0*) E J Brill.

Diatom Flora in Springs in Jutland Denmark. N. Foged. (Illus.). 344p. 1984. lib. bdg. 70.00 (*3-7682-1378-1*) Lubrecht & Cramer.

Diatom Flora of Blue Lake Warm Soring, Utah, U. S. A. A Contribution to the Freshwater Diatom Flora of the Hawaiian Islands. Kaczmarska & S. R. Rushforth. (Bibliotheca Diatomologica Ser.: No. 2). (Illus.). 280p. 1983. text ed. 65.00 (*3-7682-1363-3*) Lubrecht & Cramer.

Diatom Flora of the Provo River, Utah (U. S. A.) L. L. Lawson & S. R. Rushforth. 1975. 30.00 (*3-7682-0955-5*) Lubrecht & Cramer.

Diatom Flora of the Swan River Esturary Western Australia. Jacob John. (Bibliotheca Phycologica Ser.: No. 64). (Illus.). 360p. 1983. lib. bdg. 60.00 (*3-7682-1360-9*) Lubrecht & Cramer.

Diatom Stratigraphy & Human Settlement in Minnesota. John P. Bradbury. LC 75-21066. (Geological Society of America, Special Paper Ser.: No. 171). 79p. reprint ed. pap. 25.00 (*0-317-29090-8*, 2023739) Bks Demand.

Diatom Studies of the Headwaters of Henrys Fork of the Snake River, Island Park, Idaho, U. S. A. R. L. Clark & S. R. Rushforth. (Bibliotheca Phycologica Ser.: No. 33). 1977. pap. text ed. 30.00 (*3-7682-1149-5*) Lubrecht & Cramer.

Diatom Types of Heinrich Heiden in Heiden & Kolbe 1928. Reimer Simonsen. (Bibliotheca Diatomologica Ser.: Vol. 24). (Illus.). 100p. 1992. pap. text ed. 85.00 (*3-443-57015-1*, Pub. by Cramer-Borntraeger GW) Lubrecht & Cramer.

Diatomaceae III: Festschrift Niels Foged on the Occasion of his 75th Birthday. Ed. by H. Hakansson & J. Gerloff. (Nova Hedwigia Beiheft Ser.: 73.). (Illus.). 386p. (Orig.). (ENG & GER.). 1982. lib. bdg. 98.00 (*3-7682-5473-9*) Lubrecht & Cramer.

***Diatomeen, Bacillariophyceae in Ehrenbergs Material von Cayenne, Guyana Gallica, 1843.** Irwin Reichardt & Horst Lange-Bertalot. (Iconographia Diatomologica, Annotated Diatom Micrographs, Taxonomy Ser.). (Illus.). x, 92p. 1994. 56.00 (*3-87429-371-8*) Koeltz Sci Bks.

Diatomeen der Altmuehl. E. Reichardt. (Bibliotheca Diatomologica Ser.: Vol. 6). (Illus.). 170p. 1985. lib. bdg. 39.00 (*3-7682-1411-7*) Lubrecht & Cramer.

Diatomeen von Schweden und Finnland, 5 pts. A. Cleve-Euler. (Kungl. Sv. Vetenskapsak Handl Ser.). (Illus.). 1968. pap. 350.00 (*3-7682-0550-9*) Lubrecht & Cramer.

Diatomeenflora van Nederland, 10 fasc. in one vol. A. Van Der Werff & H. Huls. 581p. 1976. reprint ed. ring bd. 245.00 (*3-87429-113-8*) Koeltz Sci Bks.

Diatomeenschalen im Elektronenmikroskopischen Bild. Incl. Part 6. J. G. Helmcke & W. Krieger. 1966. (*3-7682-0174-0*); Part 7. Marine Diatoms. J. G. Helmcke & W. Krieger. Ed. by H. Okumo. 1969. (*3-7682-0175-9*); (Illus.). 90.00 (*0-685-03112-8*) Lubrecht & Cramer.

Diatomees des Alpes et du Jura et de la Region Suisse et Francaise des environs de Geneve. J. Brun. (Illus.). 1965. 22.00 (*90-6123-028-4*) Lubrecht & Cramer.

Diatomees Marines de France et des Districts Maritimes Voisins. H Peragallo & M. Peragallo. (Illus.). 552p. (FRE.). 1984. reprint ed. lib. bdg. 329.50 (*3-87429-219-3*) Koeltz Sci Bks.

Diatomic Interaction Potential Theory, 2 vols. Jerry Goodisman. Incl. Vol. 1. Fundamentals. 1973. 73.50 (*0-12-290201-7*); Vol. 2. Applications. 1973. 78.00 (*0-12-290202-5*); (Physical Chemistry Ser.). write for info. (*0-318-50257-7*) Acad Pr.

Diatoms. John J. Dodd. LC 86-17696. (Illustrated Flora of Illinois Ser.). (Illus.). 491p. 1987. text ed. 40.00 (*0-8093-1154-2*) S Ill U Pr.

Diatoms. F. E. Round et al. (Illus.). (C). 1990. 285.00 (*0-521-36318-7*) Cambridge U Pr.

Diatoms & Lake Acidity. Ed. by J. P. Smol et al. (Developments in Hydrobiology Ser.). 1986. lib. bdg. 193.50 (*90-6193-536-9*) Kluwer Ac.

***Diatoms from British Columbia (Canada) Lakes & Their Relationship to Salinity, Nutrients & Other Limnological Variables.** B. F. Cumming et al. (Bibliotheca Diatomologica Ser.: Vol. 31). (Illus.). 207p. 1995. pap. 136.00x (*3-443-57022-4*, Pub. by Cramer-Borntraeger GW) Lubrecht & Cramer.

Diatoms from Papua New Guinea. Wim Vyverman. (Bibliotheca Diatomologica Ser.: Vol. 22). (Illus.). 434p. 1991. pap. text ed. 165.00 (*3-443-57013-5*, Pub. by Cramer-Borntraeger GW) Lubrecht & Cramer.

Diatoms from Viti Levu, Fiji Islands. Niels Foged. (Bibliotheca Diatomologica Ser.: Vol. 14). (Illus.). 194p. 1987. pap. 63.00 (*3-443-57005-4*) Lubrecht & Cramer.

Diatoms in Alaska. Niels Foged. (Bibliotheca Phycologica Ser.: No. 53). (Illus.). 318p. 1981. text ed. 56.00 (*3-7682-1303-X*) Lubrecht & Cramer.

Diatoms in Bornholm, Denmark. Niels Foged. (Bibliotheca Phycologica Ser.: No. 59). (Illus.). 104p. 1982. 32.50 (*3-7682-1328-5*) Lubrecht & Cramer.

Diatoms in Eastern Australia. Niels Foged. (Bibliotheca Phycologica Ser.: No. 41). (Illus.). 1979. 39.00 (*3-7682-1203-3*) Lubrecht & Cramer.

Diatoms in Gambia & in the Volo Bay, Greece. Niels Foged. (Bibliotheca Diatomologica Monograph: No. 12). (Illus.). 222p. 1986. 70.00 (*3-443-57002-X*) Lubrecht & Cramer.

Diatoms in New Zealand, the North Island. Niels Foged. (Bibliotheca Phycologica Ser.: No. 47). (Illus.). 1979. pap. text ed. 42.00 (*3-7682-1253-X*) Lubrecht & Cramer.

Diatoms in Oland, Sweden. Niels Foged. (Bibliotheca Phycologica Ser.: No. 49). (Illus.). 194p. 1980. pap. 35.00 (*3-7682-1269-6*) Lubrecht & Cramer.

Diatoms in Samos, a Greek Island in the Aegean: Diatoms in Kos & Kalymnos, Two Greek Islands. Niels Foged. (Bibliotheca Diatomologica Ser.: No. 10). (Illus.). 226p. 1985. lib. bdg. 52.00 (*3-7682-1443-5*) Lubrecht & Cramer.

Diatoms in the Thames Estuary, England: Ecology, Palaeoecology, & Salinity Transfer Function. S. Juggins. (Bibliotheca Diatomologica Ser.: Vol. 25). (Illus.). 216p. 1992. pap. text ed. 63.00 (*3-443-57016-X*, Pub. by Cramer-Borntraeger GW) Lubrecht & Cramer.

Diatoms of North America. 2nd ed. William C. Vinyard. (Illus.). 120p. (C). 1979. pap. 9.95 (*0-916422-15-1*) Mad River.

Diatoms of Recent Bottom Sediments of Utah Lake, Utah, U. S. A. Judith A. Grimes & S. R. Rushforth. (Bibliotheca Phycologica Ser.: No. 55). (Illus.). 180p. 1982. text ed. 39.00 (*3-7682-1310-2*) Lubrecht & Cramer.

Diatoms of Southwestern U. S. A. Diatoms of Lower Lake Powell & Vicinity, Vol. 1. D. B. Czarnecki & D. W. Blinn. (Bibliotheca Phycologica Ser.: No. 28). 1977. pap. text ed. 24.00 (*3-7682-1102-9*) Lubrecht & Cramer.

Diatoms of Southwestern U. S. A. Diatoms of the Colorado River in Grand Canyon National Park and Vicinity, Vol. 2. D. B. Czarnecki & D. W. Blinn. (Illus.). 1978. pap. text ed. 30.00 (*3-7682-1182-7*) Lubrecht & Cramer.

Diatoms of the Sundays & Great Fish Rivers in the Eastern Cape Province of South Africa. R. E. M. Archibald. (Bibliotheca Diatomologica Ser.: Vol.1). 432p. 1983. text ed. 72.00 (*3-7682-1365-X*) Lubrecht & Cramer.

Diatoms of the Tittabawassee River, Michigan. E. D. Wujek & R. F. Rupp. (Bibliotheca Phycologica Ser.: No. 50). (Illus.). 160p. 1981. pap. text ed. 26.00 (*3-7682-1271-8*) Lubrecht & Cramer.

Diatoms of the U. S. S. R. Fossil & Recent, Vol. 1. S. I. Gleser et al. (Illus.). 403p. 1979. reprint ed. lib. bdg. 194.00 (*3-87429-168-5*) Koeltz Sci Bks.

Diatoms of the United States (Exclusive of Alaska & Hawaii), Set. Ruth Patrick & Charles W. Reimer. LC 65-29113. (Monograph: No. 13-1). (Illus.). 688p. 1966. 50.00 (*0-910006-19-9*) Acad Nat Sci Phila.

Diatoms of the United States (Exclusive of Alaska & Hawaii), Vol. 1. Ruth Patrick & Charles W. Reimer. LC 65-29113. (Monograph: No. 13-1). (Illus.). 688p. 1966. lib. bdg. 30.00 (*0-910006-20-2*) Acad Nat Sci Phila.

Diatoms of the United States (Exclusive of Alaska & Hawaii), Vol. 2, Pt. 1. Ruth Patrick & Charles W. Reimer. (Monograph: No. 13-2). (Illus.). 213p. 1975. lib. bdg. 20.00 (*0-910006-21-0*) Acad Nat Sci Phila.

Diatoms to Dinosaurs: The Size & Scale of Living Things. Christopher McGowan. (Illus.). 272p. 1994. 24.95 (*1-55963-304-2*) Island Pr.

Diatribe to Dr. Steele. Charles Gullans. 18p. 1982. 15.00 (*0-936576-09-X*) Symposium Pr.

Diavolessa (Galuppi) see Italian Opera Librettos, Vol. IV, 1640-1770

***Diazo Chemistry I: Aromatic & Heteroaromatic Compounds.** Heinrich Zollinger. 453p. 1994. 115.00 (*1-56081-878-6*) VCH Pubs.

Diazo Compounds: Properties & Synthesis. Manfred Regitz & Gerhard Maas. 1987. text ed. 196.00 (*0-12-585840-X*) Acad Pr.

Diazonaphthoquinone-Based Resists. Ralph Dammel. LC 92-25724. (Tutorial Texts in Optical Engineering Ser.: Vol. TT 11). 1992. 42.00 (*0-8194-1019-5*) SPIE.

Dibble & Dabble. Dave Saunders & Julie Saunders. LC 88-24127. (Illus.). 32p. (J). (ps-1). 1990. text ed. 14.95 (*0-02-781071-2*, Bradbury S&S) S&S Childrens.

Dibble & the Great Blob: A Parable for Children Over & Under 21. Jim Ballard. LC 75-25393. (Mandala Series in Education). 1975. pap. 3.50 (*0-916250-06-7*) Irvington.

Dibdin's Ghost. Eugene Field. (Notable American Authors Ser.). (J). 1992. reprint ed. lib. bdg. 75.00 (*0-7812-2649-X*) Rprt Serv.

Dibenzanthracenes & Environmental Carcinogenesis. Walter Karcher. (Monographs on Cancer Research). 256p. (C). 1992. 125.00 (*0-521-30382-6*) Cambridge U Pr.

Dibjua ... Luego, Escribe. Joy Evans & Jo E. Moore. Tr. by Liz Wolfe & Dora Ficklin. (Illus.). 32p. (SPA.). (J). (gr. k-3). 1990. pap. text ed. 4.95 (*1-55799-181-2*) Evan-Moor Corp.

Diblos Notebook. James Merrill. LC 94-9180. 160p. 1994. reprint ed. pap. 9.95 (*1-56478-064-3*) Dalkey Arch.

Dibre Shir(Poems) Literaria Judaica No. 41. Meir H. Letteris. reprint ed. 49.50 (*0-404-13862-4*) AMS Pr.

Dibs in Search of Self. Virginia M. Axline. 1986. mass mkt. 5.99 (*0-345-33925-8*) Ballantine.

Dibujos Que Hablan Al Corazon: Drawings That Speak to the Heart. Felipe Saint. (SPA.). 4.95 (*84-7645-395-7*, 223519, Pub. by Edit Clie SP) TSELF.

Dic. Popular De la Biblia (Popular Bible Dictionary) Juan Rojas. (Illus.). (SPA.). 1992. 8.99 (*1-56063-191-0*, 497693); pap. 5.99 (*0-685-74928-2*, 497692) Editorial Unilit.

Dicc. Dificultades Y: Encyclopedia of Bible Difficulties. Haley-Escuain. (SPA.). 23.95 (*84-7645-323-X*, 223309, Pub. by Edit Clie SP) TSELF.

Dicc. Etimologico Sinonimos: Etymological Dictionary. Samuel Vila. (SPA.). 23.95 (*84-7645-158-X*, 223212, Pub. by Edit Clie SP) TSELF.

Dicc. Expositivo N. T. - Tomo: Exp. Dict. of N. T. - Words, 4 vols., 1. W. Vine. (SPA.). 23.95 (*0-317-06112-7*, 222317, Pub. by Edit Clie SP) TSELF.

Dicc. Expositivo N. T. - Tomo: Exp. Dict. of N. T. - Words, 4 vols., II. W. Vine. (SPA.). 23.95 (*84-7645-045-1*, 222318, Pub. by Edit Clie SP) TSELF.

Dicc. Expositivo N. T. - Tomo: Exp. Dict. of N. T. - Words, 4 vols., III. W. Vine. (SPA.). 23.95 (*84-7645-118-0*, 222319, Pub. by Edit Clie SP) TSELF.

Dicc. Expositivo N. T. - Tomo: Exp. Dict. of N. T. - Words, 4 vols., IV. W. Vine. (SPA.). 23.95 (*84-7645-201-2*, 223241, Pub. by Edit Clie SP) TSELF.

Dicc. Figuras De Diccion Usadas En: Dictionary of Figures of Speech. E. W. Bullinger. (SPA.). 23.95 (*84-7645-065-6*, 223146, Pub. by Edit Clie SP) TSELF.

Diccionario del Cine: Dictionary of the Cinema, 2 vols., Set. Georges Sadoul. 800p. (SPA.). 1977. pap. 29.95 (*0-8288-5303-7*, S50057) Fr & Eur.

Diccionario Nuevos Directores Franceses. Augusto Martinez Torres. 176p. (SPA.). 1976. pap. 9.95 (*0-8288-5579-X*, S50075) Fr & Eur.

Dictionaire Basque Pour Tous: Francais-Basque. Michel Nihelena Ormazebel. 660p. 1975. pap. 6.95 (*0-7859-6033-3*, 8440082304) Fr & Eur.

Diccionari Actual II: Iustrat de la Llengua Catalana. Miguel Arimany Coma. 431p. 1983. 14.95 (*0-8288-1754-5*, S40318) Fr & Eur.

Diccionari Alemany-Catala. 2nd ed. Lluis B. Porcioles. 716p. (CAT & GER.). 1990. 41.95 (*0-7859-6336-7*, 8485194187) Fr & Eur.

Diccionari Alemany-Catala, Catala-Alemany. 2nd ed. Roser Guardia Bassols. 544p. 1986. 36.95 (*0-7859-6215-8*, 8473061713) Fr & Eur.

Diccionari Barcanova de la Llengua. Barcanova. 816p. (CAT.). 1991. 55.00 (*0-7859-6231-X*, 8475332250) Fr & Eur.

Diccionari Barcanova de la Llengua Basic. Barcanova. 592p. (CAT.). 1991. 24.95 (*0-7859-6232-8*, 8475334210) Fr & Eur.

Diccionari Barcanova d'Historia de Catalunya. Barcanova. 320p. (CAT.). 1990. 35.00 (*0-7859-6234-4*, 8475334571) Fr & Eur.

Diccionari Basic Catala-Castella, Castella-Catala. 9th ed. Miquel Arimany Coma. 390p. (CAT & SPA.). 1975. pap. 9.95 (*0-8288-5797-0*, S50359) Fr & Eur.

Diccionari Castella-Valencia, Valencia-Castella. Rosendo C. Lisboa. 1100p. 1989. 19.95 (*0-7859-6400-2*, 8486488036) Fr & Eur.

Diccionari Catala-Alemany. Enc Catalana Staff. 1060p. 1991. 59.95 (*0-7859-6298-0*, 8477392595) Fr & Eur.

Diccionari Catala-Alemany, Alemany-Catala. Andrea Rienitz. 288p. 1990. pap. 11.95 (*0-7859-6036-8*, 8440461976) Fr & Eur.

Diccionari Catala-Angles. 3rd ed. Salvador O. Llinas. 1088p. 1991. 59.95 (*0-7859-6498-3*) Fr & Eur.

Diccionari Catala-Angles i Angles-Catala. Mariana Soler. 288p. 1990. pap. 11.95 (*0-7859-6038-4*, 8440461992) Fr & Eur.

Diccionari Catala-Castella i Castella-Catala. De Vecchi. 968p. (CAT & SPA.). 1988. 69.95 (*0-7859-5901-7*, 8431501820) Fr & Eur.

Diccionari Catala de Falses Etimologies. Josep M. Massip. 224p. (SPA.). 1984. pap. 19.95 (*0-7859-5879-7*, 8429722114) Fr & Eur.

Diccionari Catala de Sinonims: Catalan Dictionary of Synonyms. Albert Jane. 606p. (CAT.). 1972. 24.95 (*0-8288-6352-0*, S-50214) Fr & Eur.

Diccionari Catala E G B Vox. Antoni Homs. 400p. 1985. 19.95 (*0-7859-6165-8*, 8471533359) Fr & Eur.

Diccionari Catala-Frances. Enc Catalana Staff. 544p. 1990. 41.95 (*0-7859-6337-5*, 8485194497) Fr & Eur.

Diccionari Catala-Frances i Frances-Catala. Renee Mathieu. 288p. 1990. pap. 11.95 (*0-7859-6037-6*, 8440461984) Fr & Eur.

Diccionari Catala-Hongares. Enc Catalana Staff. 675p. 1990. pap. 51.95 (*0-7859-6295-6*, 8477390622) Fr & Eur.

Diccionari Catala-Italia, Italia-Catala. Ronaldo Delguerra. 288p. 1990. pap. 11.95 (*0-7859-6471-1*) Fr & Eur.

Diccionari Catala-Portugues. Manuel D. Seabra Ferreira & Manuel Vimala Devi. 1008p. 1989. 59.95 (*0-7859-6296-4*, 8477390827) Fr & Eur.

Diccionari Catala Valencia Balear, 10 vols. Anthony M. Alcover et al. 1985. 1,495.00 (*0-8288-2080-5*, S31549) Fr & Eur.

Diccionari Catala Valencia Balear. 7th ed. Antoni M. Sureda. 888p. (SPA & VAL.). 1985. pap. 135.00 (*0-7859-5840-1*, 8427303874) Fr & Eur.

Diccionari Catala Valencia Balear, Vol. 1. 6th ed. Antoni M. Sureda. 1080p. (SPA & VAL.). 1985. 135.00 (*0-7859-5839-8*, 8427303866) Fr & Eur.

Diccionari Catala Valencia Balear, Vol. 2. 6th ed. Antoni M. Sureda. 1008p. (SPA & VAL.). 1985. 135.00 (*0-7859-5841-X*) Fr & Eur.

Diccionari Catala Valencia Balear, Vol. 3. 6th ed. Antoni M. Sureda. 1004p. (SPA & VAL.). 1985. pap. 135.00 (*0-7859-6455-X*, 842730210X) Fr & Eur.

Diccionari Catala Valencia Balear, Vol. 4. 6th ed. Antoni M. Sureda. 992p. (SPA.). 1985. pap. 135.00 (*0-7859-5834-7*, 8427302118) Fr & Eur.

Diccionari Catala Valencia Balear, Vol. 5. 6th ed. Antoni M. Sureda. 998p. (SPA & VAL.). 1985. 135.00 (*0-7859-5838-X*, 8427302266) Fr & Eur.

Diccionari Catala Valencia Balear, Vol. 6. 6th ed. Antoni M. Sureda. 1006p. (SPA & VAL.). 1985. pap. 135.00 (*0-7859-5836-3*, 8427302231) Fr & Eur.

Diccionari Catala Valencia Balear, Vol. 7. 6th ed. Antoni M. Sureda. 950p. (SPA & VAL.). 1985. pap. 135.00 (*0-7859-6456-8*, 842730224X) Fr & Eur.

Diccionari Catala Valencia Balear, Vol. 8. Quintin A. Vaquero. (SPA.). 1987. pap. write for info. (*0-7859-5683-2*, 840064313) Fr & Eur.

Diccionari Catala Valencia Balear, Vol. 9. Quintin A. Vaquero. (SPA.). 1972. pap. write for info. (*0-7859-5680-8*, 8400038851) Fr & Eur.

Diccionari Catala Valencia Balear, Vol. 10. 6th ed. Antoni M. Sureda. 888p. (SPA & VAL.). 1985. pap. 135.00 (*0-7859-5835-5*, 8427302126); pap. 135.00 (*0-7859-5837-1*, 8427302258) Fr & Eur.

Diccionari, Catalan. Susaeta Staff. 88p. (CAT & SPA.). 1983. pap. 10.95 (*0-7859-5892-4*, 8430513388) Fr & Eur.

Diccionari de la Ciencia i la Tecnologia Nuclears. Antoni L. Orriols. 316p. (SPA.). 1979. pap. 29.95 (*0-7859-5876-2*, 8429714766) Fr & Eur.

Diccionari de la Llengua Catalana. 2nd ed. J. Carreras et al. 1677p. (CAT.). 1983. 37.50 (*0-8288-2083-X*, S40777) Fr & Eur.

Diccionari de la Musica. 2nd ed. Roland de Cande. 224p. (SPA.). 1985. pap. 10.95 (*0-7859-5875-4*, 8429705783) Fr & Eur.

Diccionari de l'Empress Electrica. Jordi Garcia Soler. 159p. 1990. 39.95 (*0-7859-6209-3*, 8472794474) Fr & Eur.

Diccionari de l'Esport Catala-Castella, Castella-Catala. Enric Baneres. 408p. (CAT & SPA.). 1989. 41.95 (*0-7859-6494-0*, 847739072X) Fr & Eur.

Diccionari de Locutions i Frases Fetes. 5th ed. Joana R. Juanola. 426p. (SPA.). 1991. 69.95 (*0-7859-5878-9*, 8429721878) Fr & Eur.

Diccionari de Noms de Persona. 2nd ed. Santiago A. Gubern. 584p. (CAT & SPA.). 1978. 10.95 (*0-8288-4871-8*, S31551) Fr & Eur.

Diccionari de Noms de Persona. 6th ed. Jose-Maria A. Olivart. 368p. (CAT.). 1991. 39.95 (*0-7859-5877-0*, 8429715738) Fr & Eur.

Diccionari De Quimica. Miguel P. Cardona. 110p. 1984. pap. 11.95 (*0-7859-6473-8*) Fr & Eur.

Diccionari de Robotica. 2nd ed. Carles Riba. 92p. 1991. 35.00 (*0-7859-6251-4*, 8476531443) Fr & Eur.

Diccionari De Sinonims. 5th ed. Manuel F. Lluelles. 1234p. (CAT.). 1986. 59.95 (*0-7859-5117-2*) Fr & Eur.

Diccionari de Sinonims i Antonims. 13th ed. Santiago P. Estrany. 864p. (SPA.). 1991. pap. 42.95 (*0-7859-5895-9*, 8430781412) Fr & Eur.

Diccionari de Tintin. Toni Costa Lopez. 80p. (SPA.). 1987. pap. 19.95 (*0-7859-5830-4*, 8426122744) Fr & Eur.

Diccionari d'Economia. Tribo Sansalvado. 116p. 1987. pap. 12.95 (*0-7859-6474-6*) Fr & Eur.

Diccionari del Nacionalisme. Imma Tubella. 120p. 1978. 25.95 (*0-7859-6222-0*, 8474100348) Fr & Eur.

Diccionari d'Electronica. Luis Marquet. 208p. (CAT.). 1977. pap. 9.95 (*0-8288-5304-5*, S50184) Fr & Eur.

Diccionari dels Sants de Cada Dia. Philippe Rouillard. 442p. (SPA.). 1965. pap. 12.95 (*0-7859-5852-5*, 8428100616) Fr & Eur.

Diccionari d'Homonims i Paronims. Joana Raspall Juanola. 256p. 1988. 19.95 (*0-7859-6233-6*, 8475334334) Fr & Eur.

***Diccionari d'Informatica.** 2nd ed. Camera Offical de Comercio Staff. 1982. 12.95 (*0-7859-5039-7*) Fr & Eur.

Diccionari Enciclopedic de Medicina. Enc Catalana Staff. 1730p. 1990. 195.00 (*0-7859-6297-2*, 8477390932) Fr & Eur.

Diccionari Escolar Catala Arimany, 3 vols. in 1. 7th ed. Miguel Arimany Coma. 1418p. (CAT.). 1983. 59.95 (*0-8288-2081-3*, S50049) Fr & Eur.

Diccionari Escolar Catala-Castella, Castella-Catala. 4th ed. Nina M. Marques. 500p. (SPA.). 1991. pap. 27.95 (*0-7859-5842-8*, 8427304609) Fr & Eur.

Diccionari Escolar Catala-Frances i Frances-Catala. Renee Mathieu. 208p. 1988. pap. 19.95 (*0-7859-6197-6*, 8472111598) Fr & Eur.

Diccionari Escolar Catala-Ingles i Ingles-Catala. Mariana Soler. 208p. 1988. pap. 19.95 (*0-7859-6198-4*, 8472111601) Fr & Eur.

Diccionari Escolar Valencia, 3 vols. in 1. Miguel Arimany Coma. 310p. (CAT.). 1980. pap. 12.95 (*0-8288-2082-1*, S50050) Fr & Eur.

Diccionari Etimologic i Complementari de la Llengua Catalana, Vol. 1. 6th ed. Joan Corominas i Vigneaux. 900p. 1991. 150.00 (*0-7859-6201-8*, 8472561747) Fr & Eur.

Diccionari Etimologic i Complementari de la Llengua Catalana, Vol. 2. 5th ed. Joan Corominas i Vigneaux. 1120p. 1990. 150.00 (*0-7859-6202-6*, 8472561917) Fr & Eur.

Diccionari Etimologic i Complementari de la Llengua Catalana, Vol. 3. 3rd ed. Joan Corominas i Vigneaux. 1054p. 1985. 150.00 (*0-7859-6203-4*, 8472562042) Fr & Eur.

Diccionari Etimologic i Complementari de la Llengua Catalana, Vol. 4. 4th ed. Joan Corominas i Vigneaux. 964p. 1991. 150.00 (*0-7859-6204-2*, 8472562190) Fr & Eur.

Diccionari Etimologic i Complementari de la Llengua Catalana, Vol. 5. 3rd ed. Joan Corominas i Vigneaux. 996p. 1990. 150.00 (*0-7859-6205-0*, 8472562484) Fr & Eur.

Diccionari Etimologic i Complementari De la Llengua Catalana, Vol. 6. 3rd ed. Joan C. Vigneauz. 977p. 1990. 150.00 (*0-7859-6488-6*) Fr & Eur.

Diccionari Etimologic i Complementari de la Llengua Catalana, Vol. 7. 3rd ed. Joan Corominas i Vigneaux. 1007p. 1991. 150.00 (*0-7859-6206-9*, 8472562972) Fr & Eur.

Diccionari Etimologic i Complementari de la Llengua Catalana, Vol. 8. 2nd ed. Joan Corominas i Vigneaux. 1000p. 1988. 150.00 (*0-7859-6207-7*, 8472563154) Fr & Eur.

Diccionari Frances-Catala. Enc Catalana Staff. 1095p. 1988. 41.95 (*0-7859-6040-6*, 8440464754) Fr & Eur.

An Asterisk (*) at the beginning of an entry indicates that the title is appearing in BIP for the first time.

1945

Diccionari Herladic. Armand De Fluvia i Escorsa. 142p. 1987. pap. 12.95 (0-7859-6396-0, 8486387302) Fr & Eur.

Diccionari Illustrat Catala-Castella i Castella-Catala. Pere E. Busqueta. 740p. (CAT & SPA.). 1989. 31.95 (0-7859-5889-4, 8430310967) Fr & Eur.

Diccionari Italia-Catala, Catala-Italia. 2nd ed. Jordi Fornas Prat. 616p. 1985. 34.95 (0-7859-6217-4, 8473061837) Fr & Eur.

Diccionari Japones-Catala, Catala-Japones. 2nd ed. Albert Toras Graell. 540p. 1985. 51.95 (0-7859-6338-3, 8485194500) Fr & Eur.

Diccionari Juridic Catala. Col Legi d'Advocats Staff. 480p. 1986. 55.00 (0-7859-6340-5, 8485194799) Fr & Eur.

Diccionari Lujan De Gastronomie Catalana. 2nd ed. Nestor Lujan. 192p. 1990. pap. 34.95 (0-7859-6401-0, 8486491347) Fr & Eur.

Diccionari Manual Castella-Catala. 2nd ed. Miguel Arimany Coma. 413p. (CAT.). 1975. 24.95 (0-8288-5798-9, S50358) Fr & Eur.

Diccionari Manual Castella-Catala, Catala-Castella. 4th ed. Vox Staff. 712p. 1991. 35.00 (0-7859-4941-0) Fr & Eur.

Diccionari Manual Catala-Castella. 2nd ed. Miguel Arimany Coma. 535p. (CAT.). 1975. 35.00 (0-8288-5799-7, S50357) Fr & Eur.

Diccionari Manual Catala-Castella i Castella-Catala. 9th ed. Miguel Arimany Coma. 956p. (CAT.). 1976. 39.95 (0-8288-5803-9, S50360) Fr & Eur.

Diccionari Manual de la Llengua Catalana. Joseph M. Montserrat. 1401p. (CAT.). 1975. 65.00 (0-8288-5800-4, S31550) Fr & Eur.

Diccionari Manual de Sinonims Amb I Exemples. 4th ed. Vox Staff. 320p. (SPA.). 1982. 24.95 (0-8288-2086-4, S50217) Fr & Eur.

Diccionari Manuel Vox Llengua Catalana de Sinonims i Antonims. Vox Staff. 335p. 1991. 22.95 (0-7859-6163-1, 8471533251) Fr & Eur.

***Diccionari Pera Ociosos.** 3rd ed. Joan Fuster Ortells. 1991. pap. 11.95 (0-7859-5040-0) Fr & Eur.

Diccionari Politic. Gustau B. Barba. 144p. 1990. pap. 13.95 (0-7859-6393-6, 8486175119) Fr & Eur.

Diccionari Politic de Catalunya. Victor Lluelles Cardona. 344p. (CAT.). 1977. pap. 24.95 (0-8288-5306-1, S50183) Fr & Eur.

Diccionari Portugues-Catala. Manuel D. Seabra Ferreira. 896p. 1985. pap. 51.95 (0-7859-6339-1, 8485194624) Fr & Eur.

Diccionari Portugues-Catala, Catala-Portugues. Clara Prat Turu. 512p. 1982. 31.95 (0-7859-6216-6, 8473061829) Fr & Eur.

Diccionari Practic de Sinonims Catalans: Mots i Frases: Practical Catalan Dictionary of Snyonyms, Words & Phrases. 2nd ed. Joana De Cahue. 640p. (CAT.). 1979. write for info. (0-7859-5112-1) Fr & Eur.

Diccionari Pratic de Comerc Exterior Catala-Angles, Angles-Catala. Joan Ferrer Santalo. 192p. 1988. pap. 16.95 (0-7859-6045-7, 8450079608) Fr & Eur.

Diccionari Terminologic de l'Administracio Municipal. Jordi B. Cortal. 100p. (CAT.). 1980. pap. 6.95 (0-7859-6043-0, 8450036704) Fr & Eur.

Diccionari Usual de Sinonims Catalans: Mots i Frases. Joana Raspall de Cauhe et al. 572p. (CAT.). 1975. 29.95 (0-8288-5801-2, S50048) Fr & Eur.

Diccionari Vox Angles-Catala, Catala-Angles. Vox Staff. 688p. 1991. 39.95 (0-7859-6166-6, 8471533367) Fr & Eur.

Diccionario: Atlas De Mineralogia. 2nd ed. Vincenzo De Michele. 216p. (SPA.). 1978. 17.50 (0-8288-5164-6, S50260) Fr & Eur.

Diccionario Abrente De Terminos Economico-Financieros. Abrente. 208p. (SPA.). 1989. pap. 21.95 (0-7859-6420-7, 8487402003) Fr & Eur.

Diccionario Abrente de Terminos Economico-Financieros. 9th ed. Hermann J. Abs et al. 880p. (GER.). 1973. 275.00 (0-7859-6900-4, 3411012595) Fr & Eur.

Diccionario Abreviado Espanol-Chino: Spanish-Chinese Dictionary. deluxe ed. Commercial Press Staff. 1244p. (CHI & SPA.). 1979. 39.95 (0-8288-4754-1, S33189) Fr & Eur.

Diccionario Abreviado Frances-Espanol, Espanol-Frances. Vox Staff. 784p. 1989. 17.95 (0-7859-6159-3, 8471532190) Fr & Eur.

Diccionario Abreviado Vox de la Lengua Espanol. 16th ed. Manuel Gili Goya. 536p. 1991. 14.95 (0-7859-6156-9, 8471532018) Fr & Eur.

Diccionario Abreviado Vox Ingles-Espanol, Espanol-Ingles. Vox Staff. 832p. 1991. 19.95 (0-7859-6160-7, 8471532204) Fr & Eur.

Diccionario Abreviado Vox Latino-Espanol, Espanol-Latino. Vox Staff. 316p. 1991. 16.95 (0-7859-6161-5, 8471532212) Fr & Eur.

Diccionario Actual de la Lengua Espano Vox. Manuel A. Ezquerra. 1696p. (SPA.). 1991. 95.00 (0-7859-6152-6, 8471531747) Fr & Eur.

Diccionario Actual de la Lengua Espanol Vox. Juan J. Alzugaray. 126p. 1979. write for info. (0-7859-5027-3) Fr & Eur.

***Diccionario Akateko-Espanol.** Jose J. Tomas & Domingo A. Tomas. Ed. by Fernando Penalosa. 350p. (Orig.). (SPA.). 1995. pap. 19.95 (1-886502-07-2, Ediciones Yax Te) Yax Te Press.

Diccionario Alcoyano De Musica y Musicos. Ernesto V. Calatayud. 460p. 1988. pap. 59.95 (0-7859-6368-5, 8485878094) Fr & Eur.

Diccionario Aleman-Espanol, Espanol-Aleman, 2 vols. Emilio M. Amador. (GER & SPA.). 1991. 87.50 (0-685-68144-0) Fr & Eur.

Diccionario Aleman-Espanol, Espanol-Aleman. Muller. 900p. (GER & SPA.). 24.25 (0-7859-0883-8, S-50384) Fr & Eur.

Diccionario Aleman-Espanol, Espanol-Aleman, 2 vols., Set. Emilo M. Amador. 2096p. (SPA.). 1991. 150.00 (0-7859-5891-6, 8430311130) Fr & Eur.

Diccionario Aleman-Espanol, Espanol-Aleman, 2 vols., Vol. 1. Emilio M. Amador. 1056p. (GER & SPA.). 1991. 75.00 (0-7859-3352-2, 8430311149) Fr & Eur.

Diccionario Aleman-Espanol, Espanol-Aleman, 2 vols., Vol. 2. Emilio M. Amador. 1040p. (GER & SPA.). 1991. 75.00 (0-7859-3353-0, 8430311157) Fr & Eur.

Diccionario Amaia De la Lengua Vasca. Jaime Kerexeta-Gallostegui. 1100p. 1990. 350.00 (0-7859-6418-5, 8487279279) Fr & Eur.

Diccionario Anadaluz, 4 vols. Antonio M. Molera. 2000p. (SPA.). 1980. 175.00 (0-7859-3708-0, 8430027696) Fr & Eur.

Diccionario Anadaluz, Vol. 1. Antonio M. Molera. 500p. 1980. 45.00 (0-7859-6460-6) Fr & Eur.

Diccionario Andaluz, Vol. 2. Antonio M. Molera. 500p. (SPA.). 1980. 45.00 (0-7859-5880-0, 8430027718) Fr & Eur.

Diccionario Andaluz, Vol. 3. Antonio M. Molera. 500p. (SPA.). 1980. 45.00 (0-7859-5881-9, 8430027726) Fr & Eur.

Diccionario Andaluz, Vol. 4. Antonio M. Molera. 500p. (SPA.). 1980. 45.00 (0-7859-5882-7, 8430027734) Fr & Eur.

Diccionario Arabe-Espanol. Federico Corriente. 880p. (ARA & SPA.). 1991. 125.00 (0-7859-5828-2, 8425417635) Fr & Eur.

Diccionario Arabe-Espanol, Espanol-Arabe. M. Kaplanian. 1252p. (ARA & SPA.). 95.00 (0-7859-0439-5, S50424) Fr & Eur.

Diccionario Atlas de Anatomia Humana. 2nd ed. Nicola Piscitelli. (Illus.). 256p. (SPA.). 1980. pap. write for info. (0-7859-5106-7) Fr & Eur.

Diccionario Atomico. Victorin Charles. 296p. (SPA.). 49.95 (0-7859-0719-X, S-33057) Fr & Eur.

Diccionario Austral de la Lengua Espanol. Austral Staff. 350p. 1991. pap. 12.95 (0-7859-5748-0) Fr & Eur.

Diccionario Austral De la Lengua Espanola. 2nd ed. (Nueva Austral Ser.: No. 83). 502p. (SPA.). 1994. pap. text ed. 19.95x (84-239-1883-1) Elliots Bks.

***Diccionario Auxiliar del Traductor Espanol-Ingles.** 2nd ed. Jose Merino-Bustamante. 240p. 1991. pap. 39.95 (0-7859-5041-9) Fr & Eur.

Diccionario Basic del IBM-PC. Eddie Adamis. 224p. (SPA.). 1985. pap. 55.00 (0-8288-1364-7, S60234) Fr & Eur.

Diccionario Basico Anaya de la Lengua. Anaya Staff. 736p. (SPA.). 1991. 24.95 (0-7859-5734-0, 8420721956) Fr & Eur.

Diccionario Basico da Lingua Galega. 5th ed. Instituto da Lingua Galega. 288p. (SPA.). 1987. pap. write for info. (0-7859-4952-6) Fr & Eur.

Diccionario Basico de la Lengua Espanola. 5th ed. Aquilino Sanchez Perz. 1976p. 1992. pap. 35.00 (0-7859-6144-5, 8471433508) Fr & Eur.

Diccionario Basico de Matematicas. 5th ed. Mariano Diaz Velasquez. 224p. (SPA.). 1990. pap. 22.95 (0-7859-5733-2, 8420714348) Fr & Eur.

Diccionario Basico Del Ordenador. 2nd ed. Rolf Lohberg. 48p. 1987. pap. 8.95 (0-7859-6449-5) Fr & Eur.

Diccionario Basico Escolar de la Lengua Espanola. 2nd ed. Juan Capdevila Font. 398p. (SPA.). 1975. pap. 4.75 (0-8288-5802-0, S50255) Fr & Eur.

Diccionario Basico Espasa, 5 vols., Set. Espasa Staff. (ENG, FRE, GER, ITA & SPA.). 1981. 1,295.00 (0-8288-2009-0, S19891) Fr & Eur.

Diccionario Basico Frances-Espanol, Espanol-Frances. Vox Staff. 928p. 1991. 24.95 (0-7859-6154-2, 8471531887) Fr & Eur.

Diccionario Basico Illustrado Espanol - English - Catalan, 6 vols., Set. Credsa Staff. 1242p. (CAT, ENG & SPA.). 1990. 595.00 (0-7859-3359-X, 8470592797) Fr & Eur.

Diccionario Basico Illustrado Espanol - Ingles - Gallego, 4 vols. Mediterreneo Staff. 1200p. (ENG & SPA.). 1982. 395.00 (0-7859-3445-6) Fr & Eur.

Diccionario Basico Illustrado Espanol-Ingles-Euskera, 4 vols., Set. Mediterreneo Staff. 1200p. (BAS, ENG & SPA.). 1982. 395.00 (0-7859-3370-0, M29970) Fr & Eur.

Diccionario Basico Ilustrado Espanol-Euskera, 6 vols., Set. Credsa Staff. 1220p. 1988. 450.00 (0-7859-6479-7) Fr & Eur.

Diccionario Basico Ilustrado Espanol-Euskera, 6 vols., Set. Credsa Staff. 1989. 395.00 (0-7859-6100-3, 8470563335) Fr & Eur.

Diccionario Basico Ilustrado Espanol-Euskera, Vol. 1. Credsa Staff. 200p. 1988. 75.00 (0-7859-6094-5, 8470562878) Fr & Eur.

Diccionario Basico Ilustrado Espanol-Euskera, Vol. 1. Credsa Staff. 200p. 1989. 75.00 (0-7859-6101-1, 8470563343) Fr & Eur.

Diccionario Basico Ilustrado Espanol-Euskera, Vol. 2. Credsa Staff. 212p. 1988. 75.00 (0-7859-6095-3, 8470562886) Fr & Eur.

Diccionario Basico Ilustrado Espanol-Euskera, Vol. 3. Credsa Staff. 196p. 1988. 75.00 (0-7859-6096-1, 8470562894) Fr & Eur.

Diccionario Basico Ilustrado Espanol-Euskera, Vol. 3. Credsa Staff. (Illus.). 196p. 1989. 75.00 (0-7859-6480-0) Fr & Eur.

Diccionario Basico Ilustrado Espanol-Euskera, Vol. 4. Credsa Staff. 212p. 1989. 75.00 (0-7859-6103-8, 8470563378) Fr & Eur.

Diccionario Basico Ilustrado Espanol-Euskera, Vol. 5. Credsa Staff. 196p. 1988. 75.00 (0-7859-6098-8, 8470562916) Fr & Eur.

Diccionario Basico Ilustrado Espanol-Euskera, Vol. 5. Credsa Staff. 196p. 1989. 75.00 (0-7859-6104-6, 8470563386) Fr & Eur.

Diccionario Basico Ilustrado Espanol-Euskera, Vol. 6. Credsa Staff. 204p. 1988. 75.00 (0-7859-6099-6, 8470562924) Fr & Eur.

Diccionario Basico Ilustrado Espanol-Euskera, Vol. 6. Credsa Staff. 228p. 1989. 75.00 (0-7859-6105-4, 8470563394) Fr & Eur.

Diccionario Basico Ilustrado Espanol-Ingles-Catalan, 6 vols., Set. Credsa Staff. 1990. 595.00 (0-7859-6087-2, 8470562797) Fr & Eur.

Diccionario Basico Ilustrado Espanol-Ingles-Catalan, Vol. 1. Credsa Staff. 200p. 1990. 105.00 (0-7859-6088-0, 8470562800) Fr & Eur.

Diccionario Basico Ilustrado Espanol-Ingles-Catalan, Vol. 2. Credsa Staff. 212p. 1990. 105.00 (0-7859-6089-9, 8470562819) Fr & Eur.

Diccionario Basico Ilustrado Espanol-Ingles-Catalan, Vol. 3. Credsa Staff. 196p. 1990. 105.00 (0-7859-6090-2, 8470562827) Fr & Eur.

Diccionario Basico Ilustrado Espanol-Ingles-Catalan, Vol. 4. Credsa Staff. 212p. 1990. 105.00 (0-7859-6091-0, 8470562835) Fr & Eur.

Diccionario Basico Ilustrado Espanol-Ingles-Catalan, Vol. 5. Credsa Staff. 196p. 1990. 105.00 (0-7859-6092-9, 8470562843) Fr & Eur.

Diccionario Basico Ilustrado Espanol-Ingles-Catalan, Vol. 6. Credsa Staff. 204p. 1990. 105.00 (0-7859-6093-7, 8470562851) Fr & Eur.

Diccionario Basico Ingles-Espanol, Espanol-Ingles. Vox Staff. 672p. 1991. 24.95 (0-7859-6146-1, 8471531550) Fr & Eur.

Diccionario Basico Ladino - Espanol. Pascal Pascual Recuero. 182p. (LAD & SPA.). 1977. pap. 29.95 (0-7859-3362-X, 8472130886) Fr & Eur.

Diccionario Basico Latino-Espanol, Espanol-Latino. Vox Staff. 880p. 1991. 29.95 (0-7859-6162-3, 8471532239) Fr & Eur.

Diccionario Basico Norteamericano: Diccionario Fundamental Para el Estudio Del Ingles. 240p. (ENG & SPA.). 1991. pap. 7.95 (0-8442-7970-6, Passport Bks) NTC Pub Grp.

Diccionario Biblico Arqueologico. Ed. by Charles F. Pfeiffer. Tr. by Roberto Gama. 768p. (SPA.). 1982. 30.95 (0-311-03667-8) Casa Bautista.

Diccionario Biblico Compendiado. Louis Monloubou. 300p. 1991. pap. 39.95 (0-7859-6086-4, 8470502689) Fr & Eur.

Diccionario Biblico Manual. 3rd ed. Heinz Obermayer. 352p. (SPA.). 1987. pap. 14.95 (0-7859-4887-2) Fr & Eur.

Diccionario Biblico Universal. A. R. Buckland. Orig. Title: Buckland Bible Dictionary. (Illus.). 456p. 1981. 15.95 (0-8297-0836-7) Life Pubs Intl.

Diccionario Bibliografico De Liegos Sueltos Poeticos, Siglo XVI. Antonio Rodriguez Monino. 740p. (SPA.). 1970. 53.95 (0-8288-6494-2, S-7006) Fr & Eur.

Diccionario Bilingue de Economia y Empresa: Bilingual Spanish-English, English-Spanish Economics, 10 vols., Set. Jose M. Lozano Irueste. 1991. pap. write for info. (0-7859-5991-2, 8436806441) Fr & Eur.

Diccionario Bilingue de Economia y Empresa (English-Spanish, Spanish-English) Bilingual Spanish-English, English-Spanish Economics & Business Dictionary. Jose M. L. Irueste. 816p. (ENG & SPA.). 1991. 150.00 (0-8288-2395-2, S35000) Fr & Eur.

Diccionario Bilingue de Economia y Empresa, Vol. 1: Bilingual Spanish-English, English-Spanish Economics. Jose M. Lozano Irueste. 128p. 1991. pap. write for info. (0-7859-5981-5, 8436806344) Fr & Eur.

Diccionario Bilingue de Economia y Empresa, Vol. 10: Bilingual Spanish-English, English-Spanish Economics. Jose M. Lozano Irueste. 128p. 1991. pap. write for info. (0-7859-5990-4, 8436806433) Fr & Eur.

Diccionario Bilingue de Economia y Empresa, Vol. 2: Bilingual Spanish-English, English-Spanish Economics. Jose M. Lozano Irueste. 128p. 1991. pap. write for info. (0-7859-5982-3, 8436806352) Fr & Eur.

Diccionario Bilingue de Economia y Empresa, Vol. 3: Bilingual Spanish-English, English-Spanish Economics. Jose M. Lozano Irueste. 128p. 1991. pap. write for info. (0-7859-5983-1, 8436806360) Fr & Eur.

Diccionario Bilingue de Economia y Empresa, Vol. 5: Bilingual Spanish-English, English-Spanish Economics. Jose M. Lozano Irueste. 128p. 1991. pap. write for info. (0-7859-5985-8, 8436806387) Fr & Eur.

Diccionario Bilingue de Economia y Empresa, Vol. 6: Bilingual Spanish-English, English-Spanish Economics. Jose M. Lozano Irueste. 128p. 1991. pap. write for info. (0-7859-5986-6, 8436806395) Fr & Eur.

Diccionario Bilingue de Economia y Empresa, Vol. 7: Bilingual Spanish-English, English-Spanish Economics. Jose M. Lozano Irueste. 128p. 1991. pap. write for info. (0-7859-5987-4, 8436806409) Fr & Eur.

Diccionario Bilingue de Economia y Empresa, Vol. 8: Bilingual Spanish-English, English-Spanish Economics. Jose M. Lozano Irueste. 128p. 1991. pap. write for info. (0-7859-5988-2, 8436806417) Fr & Eur.

Diccionario Bilingue de Economia y Empresa, Vol. 9: Bilingual Spanish-English, English-Spanish Economics. Jose M. Lozano Irueste. 128p. 1991. pap. write for info. (0-7859-5989-0, 8436806425) Fr & Eur.

Diccionario Bilingue De Psicologia. Adela Alcantud. LC 78-50649. (Senda Lexicografica Ser.). (SPA.). 1978. pap. 7.95 (0-918454-05-0) Senda Nueva.

Diccionario Bilingue Ingles-Espano, Espanol, Ingles. Espasa Calpe Staff. 1300p. 1990. 125.00 (0-7859-5749-9) Fr & Eur.

Diccionario Biografico. A. Gavalda. 651p. (SPA.). 1962. 59.95 (0-8288-6804-2, S-37664) Fr & Eur.

Diccionario Biografico de la Musica. 2nd ed. Juan Ricart Matas. 1144p. (SPA.). 1986. 150.00 (0-7859-5124-5) Fr & Eur.

Diccionario Biografico Historico Dominicano. R. Martinez. (SPA.). write for info. (0-318-56669-9) Fr & Eur.

Diccionario Biografico y Bibliografico de Escritores y Artistas del Siglo, 2 vols., Set. Antonio E. De Molins. (Illus.). lii, 1475p. 1972. reprint ed. write for info. (3-487-04220-7, Pub. by Georg Olms GW) Lubrecht & Cramer.

Diccionario Bolsillo Cuyas Ingles-Espanol, Espanol-Ingles. Arthur S. Butterfield. 464p. 1985. pap. 14.95 (0-7859-6248-4, 8476400268) Fr & Eur.

Diccionario Bolsillo Cuyas Italiano-Espanol, Spagnuelo-Italiano. 4th ed. Fernando Ayala. 639p. (ITA & SPA.). 1958. 24.95 (0-7859-6192-5, 8471830604) Fr & Eur.

Diccionario Bompiano de Autores Literarios, Vol. 2. Planeta Staff. 616p. 1987. 29.95 (0-7859-6005-8, 8439506457) Fr & Eur.

Diccionario Bompiano de Autores Literarios, Vol. 3. Planeta Staff. 632p. 1988. 29.95 (0-7859-6006-6, 8439506465) Fr & Eur.

Diccionario Bompiano de Autores Literarios, Vol. 4. Planeta Staff. 632p. 1988. 29.95 (0-7859-6007-4, 8439506473) Fr & Eur.

Diccionario Bompiano de Autores Literarios, Vol. 5. Planeta Staff. 640p. 1988. 29.95 (0-7859-6008-2, 8439506481) Fr & Eur.

Diccionario Botanico Canario. Gunther Kunkel. 280p. 1986. 59.95 (0-7859-6345-6, 8485438469) Fr & Eur.

Diccionario Brasileiro Contemporaneo. F. Fernandes. (POR.). write for info. (0-318-56671-0) Fr & Eur.

Diccionario Cambridge Ilustrado de Informatica. Arthur Godman. (Illus.). 272p. 1987. 39.95 (0-7859-5811-8) Fr & Eur.

Diccionario Castella-Catala, Catala-Castella Vox Compacte. Cox Staff. 608p. 1989. 14.95 (0-7859-6484-3) Fr & Eur.

Diccionario Castellano - Vasco. Placido Mugica Berrondo. 1032p. (BAQ & SPA.). 1987. 95.00 (0-7859-3346-8) Fr & Eur.

Diccionario Castellano-Hebreo-Castellano. 4th ed. Yeshayahu Austridan. 400p. (HEB & SPA.). 1988. pap. 29.95 (0-8288-0463-X, S37819) Fr & Eur.

Diccionario Castellano Ilustrado. Porrua Staff. (Illus.). (SPA.). pap. 17.95 (0-7859-0429-8, S31405) Fr & Eur.

Diccionario Castellano-Vasco. 4th ed. Placido Mugika. 1027p. 95.00 (0-8288-6235-4, S-50441) Fr & Eur.

Diccionario Castellano-Vasco. 4th ed. P. Roman de Bera. 524p. (BAQ & SPA.). 1975. 39.95 (0-8288-5804-7, S50440) Fr & Eur.

Diccionario Catala-Castella y Castellano-Catalan. 2nd ed. Assumpta Falgueras. 608p. 1989. pap. 16.95 (0-7859-5767-7) Fr & Eur.

***Diccionario Catala-Frances, Frances-Catala: Catalan-French, French-Catalan Dictionary, 2 vols.** Carles Castellanos Llorenc & Rafael Castellanos Llorenc. 1090p. 1983. write for info. (0-7859-5032-X) Fr & Eur.

Diccionario Catalan-Castellano, Castellano-Catalan, 12 vols. Santiago A. Gubern. 768p. (CAT & SPA.). 1990. pap. write for info. (0-7859-3372-7, 8487584136) Fr & Eur.

Diccionario Catalan-Castellano, Castellano-Catalan, 12 vols., Set. Santiago A. Gubern. 64p. (CAT & SPA.). 1990. pap. write for info. (0-7859-6434-7, 8487584128) Fr & Eur.

Diccionario Catalan-Castellano, Castellano-Catalan, Vol. 1. Santiago A. Gubern. 64p. 1990. pap. write for info. (0-318-72435-9, 8487584012); pap. write for info. (0-7859-6426-6, 8487584020) Fr & Eur.

Diccionario Catalan-Castellano, Castellano-Catalan, Vol. 2. Santiago A. Gubern. 64p. (CAT & SPA.). 1990. pap. write for info. (0-7859-6428-2, 8487584047) Fr & Eur.

Diccionario Catalan-Castellano, Castellano-Catalan, Vol. 5. Santiago A. Gubern. 64p. (CAT & SPA.). 1990. pap. write for info. (0-7859-6431-2, 8487584071) Fr & Eur.

Diccionario Catalan-Castellano, Castellano-Catalan, Vol. 6. Santiago A. Gubern. 64p. (CAT & SPA.). 1990. pap. 32.95 (0-7859-6506-8, 848758408X) Fr & Eur.

Diccionario Catalan-Castellano, Castellano-Catalan, Vol. 7. Santiago A. Gubern. 64p. (CAT & SPA.). 1990. pap. write for info. (0-7859-6432-0, 8487584098) Fr & Eur.

Diccionario Catalan-Castellano, Castellano-Catalan, Vol. 8. Santiago A. Gubern. 64p. (CAT & SPA.). 1990. pap. 10.95 (0-7859-6425-8, 8486726441) Fr & Eur.

Diccionario Catalan-Castellano, Castellano-Catalan, Vol. 9. Santiago A. Gubern. 64p. (CAT & SPA.). 1990. pap. 65.00 (0-7859-6507-6, 848758411X) Fr & Eur.

Diccionario Catalan-Castellano, Castellano-Catalan, Vol. 10. Santiago A. Gubern. 64p. (CAT & SPA.). 1990. pap. write for info. (0-7859-6429-0, 8487584055); pap. write for info. (0-7859-6433-9, 8487584101) Fr & Eur.

Diccionario Catalan-Castellano, Castellano-Catalan, Vol. 11. Santiago A. Gubern. 64p. (CAT & SPA.). 1990. pap. write for info. (0-7859-6427-4, 8487584039) Fr & Eur.

Diccionario Catalan-Castellano, Castellano-Catalan, Vol. 12. Santiago A. Gubern. 64p. (CAT & SPA.). 1990. pap. write for info. (0-7859-6430-4, 8487584063) Fr & Eur.

Diccionario Catalan-Castellano, Castellano-Catalan: Large Castilian & Catalan Dictionary, Vol. 3. 9th ed. Santiago A. Gubern. 1182p. (CAT.). 1978. 75.00 (0-8288-4878-5, S50294) Fr & Eur.

Diccionario Catalan-Castellano, Castellano-Catalan: Small Castilian-Catalan, Catalan-Castilian Dictionary, Vol. 4. 2nd ed. Santiago A. Gubern. 340p. (CAT.). 1977. pap. 19.95 (0-8288-5309-6, S50289) Fr & Eur.

Diccionario Cavinena-Castellano Castellano-Cavinena con Bosquejo de la Gramatica Cavinena. Elizabeth L. Camp & Millicent R. Liccardi. xvi, 363p. (Orig.). (MIS & SPA.). 1989. fiche 28.00 (0-88312-723-7) Summer Instit Ling.

Diccionario Ceramico Cientifico-Pratico. Claudio Guillem Monzonis. 320p. 1987. pap. write for info. (0-7859-6032-5, 8439887450) Fr & Eur.

Diccionario Cheli. 2nd ed. Francisco Umbral. 262p. 1983. pap. 14.95 (0-7859-5803-7) Fr & Eur.

An Asterisk (*) at the beginning of an entry indicates that the title is appearing in BIP for the first time.

An Asterisk (*) at the beginning of an entry indicates that the title is appearing in BIP for the first time.

D

Diccionario de Filosofia. Miguel A. Quintanilla Fisac. 300p. 1991. pap. 39.95 (*0-7859-6145-3*, 8471517094) Fr & Eur.

Diccionario de Filosofia. 9th ed. Walter Breugger. 684p. (SPA.). 1978. pap. 39.95 (*84-254-0146-1*, S50197) Fr & Eur.

Diccionario de Filosofia, 1. Jose Ferrater-Mora. 1991. 105.00 (*0-7859-5744-8*) Fr & Eur.

Diccionario de Filosofia, 3. Jose Ferrater-Mora. 1991. 105.00 (*0-7859-5745-6*) Fr & Eur.

Diccionario de Filosofia, 4. Jose Ferrater-Mora. 1991. 1, 105.00 (*0-7859-5746-4*) Fr & Eur.

Diccionario De Filosofia, Vol. 2. Jose F. Mora. 960p. 1991. 105.00 (*0-7859-6448-7*) Fr & Eur.

Diccionario de Filosofia: Dictionary of Philosophy. Armand Cuvillier. 228p. (SPA.). 1961. 22.50 (*0-8288-6815-8*, S-33052) Fr & Eur.

***Diccionario de Filosofia Abreviado: Abbreviated Dictionary of Philosophy.** 4th ed. Jose Ferrater Mora. 416p. 1991. 25.95 (*0-7859-5042-7*) Fr & Eur.

Diccionario de Filosofia de Bolsillo, Vol. 1 A-H. 6th ed. Jose Ferrater Mora. 384p. (SPA.). 1991. pap. 16.95 (*0-7859-5722-7*, 8420619442) Fr & Eur.

Diccionario de Filosofia de Bolsillo, Vol. 2 I-Z. 6th ed. Jose Ferrater Mora. 416p. (SPA.). 1991. pap. 16.95 (*0-7859-5723-5*, 8420619450) Fr & Eur.

Diccionario de Filosofia Gran Vox. Vox Staff. 834p. 1991. write for info. (*0-7859-6172-0*, 8471533480) Fr & Eur.

Diccionario de Fisica. Area Staff. 676p. (SPA.). 1990. pap. write for info. (*0-7859-6435-5*, 8487606016) Fr & Eur.

Diccionario de Fisica. Eduardo A. Malisani. 320p. (SPA.). 1987. pap. 55.00 (*0-7859-6402-9*, 8486592402) Fr & Eur.

Diccionario de Fisica. Jose A. Peris. 464p. (SPA.). 1987. pap. 110.00 (*0-7859-3337-9*, 8420515299) Fr & Eur.

Diccionario de Fotografia. Hugo Schoettle. 357p. 1982. pap. 32.95 (*0-7859-6085-6*, 8470314793) Fr & Eur.

Diccionario de Gastronomia. 3rd ed. Carlos Delgado Gonzalez. 240p. (SPA.). 1991. pap. 12.95 (*0-7859-5716-2*, 8420600997) Fr & Eur.

Diccionario de Gentilicios y Toponimos: Dictionary of Place Names & Proper Names. Daniel Santano & Daniel Leon. (SPA.). 1981. 45.00 (*0-8288-2061-9*, S14225) Fr & Eur.

Diccionario de Gentilicos y Toponimos: Dictionary of Place Names & Proper Names. Domingo Caparros. (SPA.). 1981. 49.95 (*0-8288-2031-7*, F107510) Fr & Eur.

Diccionario de Geografia. Akal Staff. 624p. 1991. 125.00 (*0-7859-6237-9*, 8476006810) Fr & Eur.

Diccionario de Geografia. O. S. Akhmanova & E. Wilson. 1055p. 1988. 22.95 (*0-8288-7391-7*, M2909) Fr & Eur.

Diccionario de Geografia: Dictionary of Geography. W. C. Moore. 158p. (SPA.). 1972. 19.95 (*0-8288-6354-7*, S-50246) Fr & Eur.

Diccionario de Geografia Fisica. John B. Whittow. 568p. (SPA.). 1988. 125.00 (*0-7859-5728-6*, 8420652318) Fr & Eur.

Diccionario de Geologia. Alain Foucault. 324p. (SPA.). 1985. 85.00 (*0-7859-3355-7*, 8431103795) Fr & Eur.

Diccionario de Gobierno y Legislacion. Josep de Ayala. 5040p. (SPA.). 1988. write for info. (*0-7859-3363-8*, 8472324494) Fr & Eur.

Diccionario De Grafologia y Terminos Psicologicos Afines. 4th ed. Augusto V. Andreo. 532p. 1991. pap. 49.95 (*0-7859-6454-1*) Fr & Eur.

Diccionario de Hacienda Publica. Enriaue Langa Mora. 448p. 1990. pap. 45.00 (*0-7859-5975-0*, 8436802489) Fr & Eur.

Diccionario de Hebreo Biblico - A Dictionary of Biblical Hebrew. Moises Chavez. 864p. (SPA.). 1992. 35.50 (*0-311-42094-X*) Casa Bautista.

***Diccionario de Historia de Espana.** German Bleiberg. 1986. write for info. (*0-7859-5033-8*) Fr & Eur.

Diccionario de Historia de Espana, Vol. 1. 3rd ed. German Bleiberg. 1368p. (SPA.). 1986. 105.00 (*0-7859-5724-3*, 8420652059) Fr & Eur.

Diccionario de Historia de Espana, Vol. 2. German Bleiberg. 1192p. (SPA.). 1986. 105.00 (*0-7859-5725-1*, 8420652067) Fr & Eur.

Diccionario de Historia Ecclesiastica de Espana, 4 vols. Quintin Aldea Vaquero. 3200p. (SPA.). 1972. 195.00 (*0-7859-3335-2*, 8400038835) Fr & Eur.

Diccionario de Historia Eclesiastica de Espana, 4 vols., Vol. 1 Suppl. Quintin Aldea Vaquero. (SPA.). 1987. pap. write for info. (*0-318-72224-0*, 8400064313) Fr & Eur.

Diccionario de Historia Eclesiastica de Espana, Vol. 2. Quintin A. Vaquero. (SPA.). 1972. pap. write for info. (*0-7859-5681-6*, 8400038878) Fr & Eur.

Diccionario de Historia Eclesiastica de Espana, Vol. 3. 2nd ed. Vicente A. Merlo. 128p. 1990. pap. 15.95 (*0-7859-5157-1*) Fr & Eur.

Diccionario de Historia Eclesiastica de Espana, Vol. 4. 4th ed. Vicente A. Merlo. 224p. 1990. pap. 14.95 (*0-7859-5158-X*, S19856) Fr & Eur.

Diccionario de Historia Eclesiastica de Espana, Vol. 1: Supplement. Quintin A. Vaquero. (SPA.). 1972. pap. write for info. (*0-7859-6552-1*, 840003886X) Fr & Eur.

Diccionario de Homofonos Castellaros. Hipolito F. Aschiero. 120p. (SPA.). 1975. 22.50 (*0-8288-5809-8*, S33053) Fr & Eur.

***Diccionario de Hosteleria.** Gallego. 488p. (SPA.). 1993. pap. 39.95 (*0-7859-7491-1*, 8428320152) Fr & Eur.

Diccionario de Iconografia. Federico Revilla. 408p. 1990. pap. 32.95 (*0-7859-6001-5*, 8437609291) Fr & Eur.

Diccionario de Immunologia. Francisco L. Corbian. 256p. 1991. pap. 25.95 (*0-7859-6502-5*) Fr & Eur.

Diccionario de Immunologia. W. J. Herbert & P. C. Wilkinson. 256p. (SPA.). 1974. 45.00 (*0-7859-0648-7*, S50055) Fr & Eur.

Diccionario de Incorrecciones, Particularidades, Curiosidades del Lenguaje. 5th ed. Andres S. Chavarria & A. Cuartas. 520p. (SPA.). 1992. pap. 29.95 (*0-7859-3687-4*, S12185) Fr & Eur.

Diccionario de Informatica. Anthony Chandor. 480p. (SPA.). 1989. pap. 125.00 (*0-7859-5730-8*, 8420652350) Fr & Eur.

Diccionario de Informatica. Michel Ginguay. 272p. (SPA.). 1985. pap. 75.00 (*0-8288-6356-3*, S-50130) Fr & Eur.

Diccionario de Informatica Gran Vox. Vox Staff. 352p. 1990. write for info. (*0-7859-6168-2*, 8471533405) Fr & Eur.

Diccionario de Informatica Ingles-Espanol. Olivetti Staff. 272p. (ENG & SPA.). 1989. pap. 39.95 (*0-685-53860-5*, S50364) Fr & Eur.

Diccionario de Informatica y Electronica, 16 vols. Ingelek Staff. 2048p. (SPA.). 1987. 450.00 (*0-7859-3368-9*, 8477080496) Fr & Eur.

***Diccionario de Informes Financieros: Ingles-Espanol, Espanol-Ingles.** Peter Donaghy & Coopers & Lybrand. 365p. (ENG & SPA.). 1993. 75.00 (*0-7859-7480-6*, 8423407551) Fr & Eur.

Diccionario de Ingeneria Industrial: Espanol - Ingles Mecanica. Etsi Ind Madrid Staff. 384p. (ENG & SPA.). 1991. 39.95 (*0-7859-3366-2*, 8474840678) Fr & Eur.

Diccionario de Ingeneria Industrial: Espanol - Ingles Organizacion. Etsi Ind Madrid Staff. 260p. (ENG & SPA.). 1990. 39.95 (*0-7859-3365-4*, 8474840643) Fr & Eur.

Diccionario de Ingeneria Industrial, Espanol - Ingles Construccion. Etsi Ind Madrid Staff. 256p. (ENG & SPA.). 1991. 39.95 (*0-685-68775-9*) Fr & Eur.

Diccionario De Ingenieria Ambiental y Ciencias Afines see Dictionary of Environmental Engineering & Related Sciences

Diccionario de Insurgentes. Jose Maria Miquel I Verges. (SPA.). 29.95 (*0-7859-0934-6*, S-12335) Fr & Eur.

Diccionario de Interjecciones Espanol-Ingles-Espanol. Francisca Arana de Love. (ENG & SPA.). 1985. 19.95 (*0-8288-2324-3*, S10647) Fr & Eur.

Diccionario de la Astronomica y Astronautica. Pedro Mateu Sancho. 350p. (SPA.). 1962. 49.95 (*0-8288-6806-9*, S-12334) Fr & Eur.

Diccionario de la Biblia. 9th ed. Herbert Haag. 1080p. (SPA.). 1987. 125.00 (*0-7859-3344-1*, 8425400775) Fr & Eur.

Diccionario de la Civilizacion Griega: Dictionary of the Greek Civilization. Pierre Devambez. 482p. (SPA.). 1972. 53.95 (*0-8288-6357-1*, S-50367) Fr & Eur.

Diccionario de la Cocina Clasica Americana y Europea. Gran Encyclopedia Vasca Staff. 1154p. (SPA.). 1981. 395.00 (*0-7859-3341-7*, 8424807286) Fr & Eur.

Diccionario de la Cocina Clasica Americana y Europea, 1. Gran Enc. Vasca Staff. 1981. 85.00 (*0-7859-5781-2*) Fr & Eur.

Diccionario de la Cocina Clasica Americana y Europea, 2. Gran Enc. Vasca Staff. 1981. 85.00 (*0-7859-5782-0*) Fr & Eur.

Diccionario de la Cocina Clasica Americana y Europea, 3. Gran Enc. Vasca Staff. 1981. 85.00 (*0-7859-5783-9*) Fr & Eur.

Diccionario de la Cocina Clasica Americana y Europea, 4. Gran Enc. Vasca Staff. 1981. 85.00 (*0-7859-5784-7*) Fr & Eur.

Diccionario de la Cocina Clasica Americana y Europea, Vol. 5. Gran Enc Vasca Staff. 230p. 1981. 85.00 (*0-7859-5973-4*, 8434807332) Fr & Eur.

Diccionario de la Cocina Clasica Mejicana y Europea, 1. Gran Enc. Vasca Staff. 1981. 85.00 (*0-7859-5777-4*) Fr & Eur.

Diccionario de la Cocina Clasica Mejicana y Europea, 2. Gran Enc. Vasca Staff. 1981. 85.00 (*0-7859-5778-2*) Fr & Eur.

Diccionario de la Cocina Clasica Mejicana y Europea, 3. Gran Enc. Vasca Staff. 1981. 85.00 (*0-7859-5779-0*) Fr & Eur.

Diccionario de la Cocina Clasica Mejicana y Europea, 5. Gran Enc. Vasca Staff. 1981. 85.00 (*0-7859-5780-4*) Fr & Eur.

Diccionario de la Cocina Clasica Mejicana y Europea, 5 vols., Set. deluxe ed. Gran Encyclopedia Vasca Staff. 1154p. (SPA.). 1981. 395.00 (*0-7859-3340-9*, 8424807227) Fr & Eur.

Diccionario De la Cocina Clasica Mejicana y Europea, Vol. 4. Gran Enc Vasca Staff. 230p. 1981. 85.00 (*0-7859-6451-7*) Fr & Eur.

Diccionario de la Communicacion, 2 vols., Set. Ignacio H. De la Mota Oreja. 744p. (ENG & SPA.). 1988. 110.00 (*0-7859-3686-6*, 8428316074) Fr & Eur.

Diccionario de la Communicacion, Vol. 2. Ignacio H. Mota Oreja. 368p. (SPA.). 1988. 59.95 (*0-7859-5856-8*, 8428316090) Fr & Eur.

Diccionario De la Construccio. Itec Staff. 320p. 1986. pap. 85.00 (*0-7859-6390-1*, 8485954327) Fr & Eur.

Diccionario de la Construccion: Construction Dictionary. Equipo Reactor de Ceac Staff. 650p. (SPA.). 1978. pap. 49.95 (*0-8288-4886-6*, S50225) Fr & Eur.

Diccionario de la Construccion y Obras Publicas Ingles-Espanol, 2 vols., Set. Jose Benito Bacho. 268p. (ENG & SPA.). 1975. 95.00 (*0-8288-5811-X*, S50117) Fr & Eur.

Diccionario de la Construccion y Obras Publicas, Tomo 2: Span. Jose Benito Bacho. 110p. (SPA.). 1975. 49.95 (*0-8288-5812-8*, S50119) Fr & Eur.

Diccionario de la Construcion y de Obras Publicas, Tomo I: Ingles. Jose Benito Bacho. 168p. (SPA.). 1975. 49.95 (*0-8288-5813-6*, S50118) Fr & Eur.

Diccionario de la Contruccion. CEAC Staff. 622p. (SPA.). 1991. pap. 59.95 (*0-7859-5906-8*, 8432926086) Fr & Eur.

Diccionario de la Decoracion: Dictionary of Decoration. Equipo Reactor de Ceac Staff. 792p. (ENG, FRE, GER, ITA & SPA.). 1973. 95.00 (*0-8288-6238-9*, S-12256) Fr & Eur.

Diccionario de la Edicion y la Artes Graficas. John Dreyfus. 724p. 1990. 105.00 (*0-7859-5980-7*, 8436805127) Fr & Eur.

Diccionario de la Electronica. 3rd ed. Jean F. Arnaud. 368p. (SPA.). 1976. pap. 9.95 (*0-8288-5592-7*, S14211) Fr & Eur.

Diccionario de la Exportacion. Martin A. Pedraz. 928p. (SPA.). 1986. 150.00 (*0-7859-6212-3*, 8472991709) Fr & Eur.

Diccionario de la Felicidad. 2nd ed. Jorge S. Pros. 1046p. (SPA.). 1988. pap. 75.00 (*0-7859-4897-X*) Fr & Eur.

Diccionario de la Gestion Financiera. P. Conso. (SPA.). 1991. write for info. (*0-7859-3705-6*, 8428318514) Fr & Eur.

Diccionario de la Historia. Miguel V. Santos. 171p. 1991. pap. 35.00 (*0-7859-6250-6*, 8476520573) Fr & Eur.

Diccionario de la Industrias; Industrial Dictionary. Conseil International de la Language Francaise Staff. write for info. (*0-8288-7667-3*) Fr & Eur.

Diccionario de la Informacion, Comunicacio y Periodismo. 6th ed. Jose M. De Sousa. 584p. (SPA.). 1992. pap. 65.00 (*0-7859-3707-2*, 8428318840) Fr & Eur.

Diccionario de la Jerga del Estudiante Universitario Puertorriqueno del Sistema Publico. Josefina Claudio de la Torre. LC 87-25559. 1989. 12.95 (*0-8477-2010-1*) U of PR Pr.

Diccionario de la Lengua. Anaya Staff. 1080p. (SPA.). 1991. 59.95 (*0-7859-5736-7*, 8420741485) Fr & Eur.

Diccionario de la Lengua Castellana. Academia Espanola Staff. (SPA.). 1989. 450.00 (*0-7859-3369-7*, 8478483985) Fr & Eur.

Diccionario de la Lengua Castellana, Vol. 1. Academia Espanola Staff. (SPA.). 1989. pap. 75.00 (*0-7859-6321-9*, 8478482059) Fr & Eur.

Diccionario de la Lengua Castellana, Vol. 2. Academia Espanola Staff. (SPA.). 1989. pap. 75.00 (*0-7859-6322-7*, 8478482067) Fr & Eur.

Diccionario de la Lengua Castellana, Vol. 3. Academia Espanola Staff. (SPA.). 1989. pap. 75.00 (*0-7859-6323-5*, 8478482075) Fr & Eur.

Diccionario de la Lengua Castellana, Vol. 4. Academia Espanola Staff. (SPA.). 1989. pap. 75.00 (*0-7859-6324-3*, 8478482083) Fr & Eur.

Diccionario de la Lengua Castellana, Vol. 5. Academia Espanola Staff. (SPA.). 1989. pap. 75.00 (*0-7859-6325-1*, 8478482091) Fr & Eur.

Diccionario de la Lengua Castellana, Vol. 6. Acervo. 190p. (SPA.). 1982. 14.95 (*0-8288-2022-8*, S40787) Fr & Eur.

Diccionario de la Lengua Espanol, 2 vols., Set. 19th ed. Real Academia de la Lengua Espanol Staff. 1456p. (SPA.). 1986. 295.00 (*0-8288-4402-X*, S12257) Fr & Eur.

Diccionario de la Lengua Espanola. 228p. (SPA.). 4.95 (*0-7859-0706-8*, S-25231); lib. bdg. 295.00 (*0-8288-2735-4*) Fr & Eur.

***Diccionario de la Lengua Espanola.** 3rd ed. Ed. by Espasa Staff. (Espasa de Bolsillo Ser.). 916p. (SPA.). 1994. 29.95x (*84-239-5993-7*) Elliots Bks.

Diccionario de la Lengua Espanola, 2 Vols. 20th ed. Real Academia Espanola Staff. (SPA.). 1984. 220.00 (*84-239-4774-2*) Colton Bk.

Diccionario de la Lengua Espanola. 21th ed. Ed. by Real Academia Espanola Staff. 1548p. (SPA.). 1992. 289.50x (*84-239-4399-2*) Elliots Bks.

***Diccionario de la Lengua Espanola, 2 vols., Set.** 21th ed. Ed. by Real Academia Espanola Staff. 2192p. (SPA.). 1994. pap. text ed. 89.50x (*84-239-9200-4*) Elliots Bks.

Diccionario de la Lengua Espanola: Dictionary of the Spanish Language, 2 vols., Set. Nauta Staff. 704p. (SPA.). 1978. 195.00 (*0-8288-4887-4*, S50030) Fr & Eur.

Diccionario de la Lengua Espanola Cantabrica. Cantabrica Staff. 1736p. (SPA.). 1985. 295.00 (*0-7859-3338-7*, 8422104687) Fr & Eur.

Diccionario de la Lengua Mechada. Ignacio Guasp. (SPA.). 24.95 (*0-7859-0715-7*, S-5248) Fr & Eur.

Diccionario de la Limpieza. Djenane Chappat. 234p. (SPA.). 1970. pap. 6.95 (*0-8288-6496-9*, S-12249) Fr & Eur.

Diccionario De la Literatura, 2 vols., Set. 3rd ed. Federico C. Sainz de Robles Corr. 1232p. 1982. 115.00 (*0-7859-6437-1*, 8703279922) Fr & Eur.

Diccionario de la Literatura, Vol. 1. 3rd ed. Sainz De Robles & Federico Carlos Corriente Cordoba. 576p. (SPA.). 1982. 65.00 (*0-7859-5708-1*, 8403270747) Fr & Eur.

Diccionario de la Literatura, Vol. 2. Alianza Staff. Tr. by Adell. 864p. (SPA.). 1982. 95.00 (*0-8288-1575-5*, S29973) Fr & Eur.

Diccionario De la Literatura Gran Vox. Vox Staff. 436p. 1990. 125.00 (*0-7859-6485-1*) Fr & Eur.

Diccionario de la Literatura Mundial. 2nd ed. Joseph T. Shipley. 564p. (SPA.). 1974. 44.95 (*0-8288-5981-7*, S12359) Fr & Eur.

Diccionario De la Literatura Tres Autores Extranjeros. 3rd ed. Federico C. Sainz de Robles Corr. 1232p. 1967. write for info. (*0-7859-6445-2*) Fr & Eur.

Diccionario de la Literatura Universal: Universal Dictionary of Literature. Juan Capdevila Font. 536p. (SPA.). 1977. 22.50 (*0-8288-5315-0*, S50261) Fr & Eur.

Diccionario de la Literature Clasica. M. C. Howatson. 832p. (SPA.). 1991. pap. 175.00 (*0-7859-5732-4*, 8420652393) Fr & Eur.

Diccionario De la Mitologia Clasica, Vol. 2, I-Z. 8th ed. Constantino F. Martinez. 304p. 1991. pap. 14.95 (*0-7859-6447-9*) Fr & Eur.

Diccionario de la Mitologia Clasica: Dictionary of Classical Mythology, 2 vols. Constantino Falcon Martinez. 633p. (SPA.). 1980. pap. 35.00 (*0-8288-2194-1*, S32723) Fr & Eur.

Diccionario de la Mitologia Classica, Vol. 1 A-H. 8th ed. Constantino Falcon Martinez. 368p. 1991. pap. 14.95 (*0-7859-5721-9*, 8420617911) Fr & Eur.

Diccionario de la Mitologia Mundial: Dictionary of World Mythology. Edaf Staff. 387p. (SPA.). 1984. pap. write for info. (*0-7859-5115-6*) Fr & Eur.

Diccionario de la Musica. 8th ed. Manuel Valls Gorina. 264p. (SPA.). 1991. pap. 13.95 (*0-7859-5719-7*, 8420613347) Fr & Eur.

Diccionario de la Musica, Vol. I. Marc Honegger. Tr. by T. Marco. 632p. (SPA.). 1987. lib. bdg. 49.95 (*0-7859-5014-1*, 842395398X) Fr & Eur.

Diccionario de la Musica, Vol. II. Marc Honegger. 624p. (SPA.). 1987. lib. bdg. 49.95 (*0-7859-5015-X*, 8423953998) Fr & Eur.

Diccionario de la Musica: Historico y Tecnico. 4th ed. Michel Brenet. 566p. (SPA.). 1981. write for info. (*0-7859-5084-2*) Fr & Eur.

Diccionario de la Musica: Los Hombres y Sus Obras, 2 vols., Set. Marc Honegger. Tr. by Tomas Marco. 1257p. (SPA.). 1989. 375.00 (*84-239-5397-1*) Elliots Bks.

Diccionario de la Naturaleza. Ramos. 976p. (SPA.). 1987. lib. bdg. 49.95 (*0-7859-5016-8*, 8423969495) Fr & Eur.

Diccionario de la Naturaleza: Hombre, Ecologio, Paisaje. Ed. by Angel Ramos. (Illus.). 1032p. (SPA.). 1989. 239.50 (*84-239-6949-5*) Elliots Bks.

Diccionario de la Psicologia. 4th ed. Norberth Sillamy. 344p. (SPA.). 1974. 14.95 (*0-8288-5982-5*, S12360) Fr & Eur.

Diccionario de la Real Academia Expanola. 2nd ed. Real Academia Espanola Staff. 980p. 1991. 275.00 (*0-7859-6048-1*, 8460076059) Fr & Eur.

Diccionario de la Revolucion Francesa. Francois Furet. 920p. (SPA.). 1989. 150.00 (*0-7859-5729-4*, 8420652334) Fr & Eur.

Diccionario de la Santa Biblia. W. W. Rand. (Illus.). 768p. (SPA.). 1969. reprint ed. pap. 16.25 (*0-89922-003-7*) Edit Caribe.

Diccionario de la Tecnicas de Grupo. Anne A. Schutzenberger. 260p. (SPA.). 1974. pap. 19.95 (*0-8288-5983-3*, S50365) Fr & Eur.

Diccionario de la Vida Sexual. Juan Capdevila Font. 200p. (SPA.). 1976. 14.95 (*0-8288-5594-3*, S50262) Fr & Eur.

Diccionario de l'Art I Els Oficis de la Construccion. 5th ed. Miguel F. Llompart. 440p. (CAT.). 1988. pap. 69.95 (*0-7859-5107-5*) Fr & Eur.

Diccionario de las Americas. A. Plaza. 1216p. (SPA.). 1991. 125.00 (*0-7859-5684-0*, 8401601657) Fr & Eur.

Diccionario de las Ciencias. Lionel Salem. 528p. 1991. 85.00 (*0-7859-5972-6*, 8434552868) Fr & Eur.

Diccionario de las Ciencias de la Vida. McGraw Hill Staff. 940p. 1990. 125.00 (*0-7859-6236-0*, 8476006195) Fr & Eur.

Diccionario de las Lenguas Espanola y Alemana, Vol. 1. 10th ed. Rudolph Slaby. 1348p. 1991. 150.00 (*0-7859-5817-7*) Fr & Eur.

Diccionario de las Lenguas Espanola y Alemana: Dictionary of the German & Spanish Languages, 2 vols., Set. 8th ed. Rudolf Slaby. 2472p. (GER & SPA.). 1991. 295.00 (*0-8288-5316-9*, S50380) Fr & Eur.

Diccionario de las Religiones. Konig. 816p. (SPA.). 1977. 49.95 (*0-8288-5317-7*, S50201) Fr & Eur.

Diccionario de las Religiones. Pedro Rodriguez Santidrian. 472p. (SPA.). 1989. pap. 18.95 (*0-7859-5718-9*, 8420603732) Fr & Eur.

Diccionario de Linguistica. Anaya Staff. 328p. (SPA.). 1986. 55.00 (*0-7859-6230-1*, 8475253660) Fr & Eur.

Diccionario de Linguistica. Ermano Ancilli. 732p. (SPA.). 1982. 105.00 (*0-7859-5822-3*, 8425412641) Fr & Eur.

Diccionario De Linguistica. Mounin. (SPA.). 32.95 (*0-7859-0895-1*, S-50062) Fr & Eur.

Diccionario de Linguistica: Dictionary of Linguistics. Jean Dubois. (SPA.). 1979. pap. 62.50 (*0-8288-4758-4*, S-50086) Fr & Eur.

***Diccionario de Linguistica de la Escuela Espanola.** F. Abad. 284p. (SPA.). 1993. pap. 59.50 (*84-249-1042-7*) Elliots Bks.

Diccionario de los Alimentos. Cedel Staff. 1988. 65.00 (*0-7859-5974-2*, 8435203387) Fr & Eur.

Diccionario de los Asesinos. Rene Reouven. 386p. (SPA.). 1976. pap. 24.95 (*0-8288-5595-1*, S50083) Fr & Eur.

Diccionario de los Medios de Comunicacion: Tecnica, Semiologia, Linguistica. Jean-Baptiste Fages. 288p. (SPA.). 1978. pap. 29.95 (*0-8288-4889-0*, S50121) Fr & Eur.

Diccionario de los Papas. Juan Dacio. (SPA.). 59.95 (*0-7859-0863-3*, S50110) Fr & Eur.

Diccionario de los Reyes de Espana. Alfonso Espinet. 434p. 1989. pap. 59.95 (*0-7859-6249-2*, 8476520379) Fr & Eur.

Diccionario de los Santos de Cada Dia. 2nd ed. Dom P. Rouillard. 336p. (SPA.). 1989. pap. write for info. (*0-7859-5125-3*) Fr & Eur.

Diccionario de los Simbolos. 3rd ed. Jean Chevalier. 1108p. (SPA.). 1991. 175.00 (*0-7859-5826-6*, 8425415144) Fr & Eur.

Diccionario de los Sintomas: Los Testa de Su Salud. A. Saponaro. 333p. (SPA.). 1973. 29.95 (*0-7859-0809-9*, S-13713) Fr & Eur.

Diccionario de Management: Management Dictionary. H. Johannsen et al. 244p. (SPA.). 1972. 35.00 (*0-8288-6358-X*, S-31465) Fr & Eur.

Diccionario de Marina. 2nd ed. Jose L. Pando y Villaroya. 252p. 1985. pap. 39.95 (*0-7859-6031-7*, 8439847068) Fr & Eur.

D

An Asterisk (*) at the beginning of an entry indicates that the title is appearing in BIP for the first time.

Diccionario de Marketing. 3rd ed. Bernardo R. Asenjo et al. 168p. (SPA.). 1990. pap. 35.00 (*0-7859-4919-4*) Fr & Eur.

Diccionario de Matematica Gran Vox. Vox Staff. 400p. 1990. 150.00 (*0-7859-6169-0*, 8471533421) Fr & Eur.

Diccionario de Matematica Moderna. Dario Maravall Casesnoves. 332p. (SPA.). 1975. pap. 19.95 (*0-8288-5814-4*, S50009) Fr & Eur.

Diccionario de Matematicas. Juan Capdevila Font. 160p. (SPA.). 1976. 14.95 (*0-8288-5596-X*, S50263) Fr & Eur.

Diccionario de Materiales y Procesos de Ingenieria. H. R. Clauser. 820p. (SPA.). 1970. 125.00 (*0-8288-6497-7*, S-50067) Fr & Eur.

***Diccionario de Maximas Pensamientos y Sentacias.** 9th ed. Jorge S. Pros. 744p. 1989. write for info. (*0-7859-5026-5*) Fr & Eur.

Diccionario de Medicina. Ed. by E. Dabout. (SPA.). 24.95 (*0-7859-0587-1*, S-37586) Fr & Eur.

Diccionario de Medicina. Andre Duranteau. 396p. 1987. 39.95 (*0-7859-5809-6*) Fr & Eur.

Diccionario de Medicina de Urgencia: Dictionary of Emergency Medicine. 2nd ed. Cedel Staff. 208p. (SPA.). 1977. 9.95 (*0-8288-5318-5*, S13672) Fr & Eur.

Diccionario de Medicina Gran Vox. Vox Staff. 382p. 1990. 150.00 (*0-7859-6170-4*, 8471533448) Fr & Eur.

Diccionario de Medicos Puertorriquenos Que Se Man Distinguico Fuera de la Medicina. Soto Arana. 22.50 (*0-8288-8094-8*, S5070) Fr & Eur.

Diccionario de Medicos Puertorriquenos Que Se Man Distinguico Fuera de la Medicina. Arana Soto. (SPA.). 17.50 (*0-8288-9020-X*, S5070) Fr & Eur.

Diccionario de Mejicanismos. Francisco J. Santamaria. (SPA.). 95.00 (*0-7859-0711-4*, S-12355) Fr & Eur.

Diccionario de Metologia Estadistica: Dictionary of Statistical Methodology. Gonzalo Gonsalvo Mainar. 184p. (SPA.). 1978. pap. 24.95 (*0-8288-4890-4*, S50010) Fr & Eur.

Diccionario de Metrica Espanola. 2nd ed. Dominguez Caparros. (SPA.). 1992. write for info. (*0-7859-3681-5*, 8428313660) Fr & Eur.

Diccionario de Mitologia. Henri Aubert. 238p. (SPA.). 1961. 19.95 (*0-8288-6816-6*, S33055) Fr & Eur.

Diccionario de Mitologia Universal. Arthur Cotterell. 288p. (SPA.). 1988. pap. 24.95 (*0-7859-5926-2*, 8434410826) Fr & Eur.

Diccionario de Mitologia Universal, 2 vols. Jean-Francois M. Niel. 1266p. 1991. pap. 95.00 (*0-7859-6254-9*, 8476723571) Fr & Eur.

Diccionario De Mitologia Universal, Vol. 1. Jean-Francois M. Niel. 1266p. 1991. pap. 95.00 (*0-7859-6489-4*) Fr & Eur.

Diccionario de Mitologia Universal, Vol. 2. Jean-Francois M. Niel. 1266p. 1991. pap. 95.00 (*0-7859-6255-7*, 8476723598) Fr & Eur.

Diccionario de Modismos Inglese y Norteamericanos. 2nd ed. Alfonso Torrents dels Prats. 304p. (ENG & SPA.). 1979. 49.95 (*0-8288-4760-6*, S12364) Fr & Eur.

Diccionario De Modismos Ingleses y Norte Americanos: English & North American Dictionary of Idioms for Spanish Speaking People. 4th ed. A. Torrents del Prats. 472p. 1985. 34.00 (*84-261-0838-5*) IBD Ltd.

Diccionario de Modismos y Lenguaje Coloquial: Espanol - Aleman. Renner. (GER & SPA.). 1991. write for info. (*0-7859-3704-8*, 8428318506) Fr & Eur.

Diccionario de Moral Cristiana: Dictionary of Christian Morals. 2nd ed. Karl Hoermann. 704p. (SPA.). 1978. pap. 59.95 (*0-7859-0871-4*, S50192) Fr & Eur.

***Diccionario de Moral Cristiana: Dictionary of Christian Morals.** 3rd ed. Karl Hoermann. (SPA.). 1985. 59.95 (*0-7859-5043-5*) Fr & Eur.

***Diccionario de Motivos de la Literatura Universal.** Elisabeth Frenzel. 412p. (SPA.). 1993. 100.00 (*84-249-0057-X*) Elliots Bks.

***Diccionario de Mujeres Celebres.** Ed. by Espasa Staff. (Espasa de Bolsillo Ser.). (Illus.). 496p. (SPA.). 1994. 34.95x (*84-239-9211-X*) Elliots Bks.

Diccionario de Musica Sevilla 1818. Angel Medina. 107p. 1991. write for info. (*0-7859-6225-5*, 8474682924) Fr & Eur.

Diccionario de Optometria. Michel Millodot. 304p. 1990. write for info. (*0-7859-6039-2*, 8440464142) Fr & Eur.

Diccionario de Ortografia Tecnica. Jose M. De Sousa. 424p. (SPA.). 1987. write for info. (*0-7859-4955-0*) Fr & Eur.

Diccionario de Palabras y Frases Extranjeros. 2nd ed. Arturo del Hoyo. 424p. 1990. 22.95 (*0-7859-5710-3*, 8403870558) Fr & Eur.

Diccionario de Pedagogia. Paul Foulquie. 464p. (SPA.). 1976. 95.00 (*0-8288-5597-8*, S50016) Fr & Eur.

Diccionario de Pedagogia Labor, 2 vols., Set. 3rd ed. Victor Garcia Hoz. 444p. (SPA.). 1974. 75.00 (*0-8288-5984-1*, S12488) Fr & Eur.

Diccionario de Pedogogia. Paul Foulquie. 464p. (SPA.). 1976. pap. 79.95 (*0-8288-5598-6*, S50015) Fr & Eur.

Diccionario de Philosofia Contemporanea. 3rd ed. Miguel A. Fisac. 492p. (SPA.). 1985. pap. write for info. (*0-7859-5085-0*) Fr & Eur.

Diccionario de Pintores. Carlos M. Pasamontes. (SPA.). 1987. pap. 250.00 (*0-7859-5910-6*, 8433310216) Fr & Eur.

Diccionario de Pliegos Sueltos Poeticos: Poetry Manuscripts, 16th Century. Antonio Rodriguez-Monino. 735p. (SPA.). 1970. 49.95 (*0-8288-8564-8*) Fr & Eur.

Diccionario de Politica. Rafael Garzaro. 426p. 1987. pap. 34.95 (*0-7859-6347-2*, 8485664299) Fr & Eur.

Diccionario de Politica, Vol. 1, A-J. Norberto Bobbio & N. Matteucci. 896p. (SPA.). 1982. 105.00 (*0-7859-5903-3*, 8432304301) Fr & Eur.

Diccionario de Politica, Vol. 2, K-Z. Norberto Bobbio & N. Matteucci. 884p. (SPA.). 1983. 105.00 (*0-7859-5904-1*, 8432304611) Fr & Eur.

Diccionario De Proceso De Datos. Europe Company Corporation Staff. 184p. 1987. pap. 41.95 (*0-7859-6367-7*, 8485838491) Fr & Eur.

Diccionario de Psicoanalisis Clasico. Friedrich W. Doucet. 232p. (SPA.). 1974. pap. 24.95 (*0-8288-5985-X*, S50069) Fr & Eur.

Diccionario de Psicologia. C. Genovard Rossello. 284p. (SPA.). 1980. 53.95 (*0-8288-2216-6*, S37535) Fr & Eur.

Diccionario de Psicologia Evolutiva y da le Educacion. Rom Harre. 320p. 1990. 65.00 (*0-7859-6229-8*, 8475096077) Fr & Eur.

Diccionario de Psicologia Para Educadores. PPU Staff. 374p. 1989. pap. 39.95 (*0-7859-6252-2*, 8476653476) Fr & Eur.

Diccionario de Psicologia Sexual. 2nd ed. Georges Bastin. 412p. (SPA.). 1978. pap. 39.95 (*0-7859-5086-9*, S13099) Fr & Eur.

Diccionario de Psicopedagogia y Psiqiatria del Nino: French - Spanish. 5th ed. Robert Lafon. 1056p. (FRE & SPA.). 1993. lib. bdg. write for info. (*0-7859-3677-7*, 8428107556) Fr & Eur.

Diccionario de Psiquiatria. Raymond Battegay. 680p. (SPA.). 1989. 150.00 (*0-7859-5827-4*, 8425415802) Fr & Eur.

Diccionario de Psiquiatria. James A. Brussel & George L. Cantzlaar. 306p. (SPA.). pap. 49.50 (*0-7859-0781-5*, S50209) Fr & Eur.

Diccionario de Psiquiatria, Vol. 1. 3rd ed. Antoine Porot. 650p. (SPA.). 1977. 59.95 (*0-7859-5924-6*, 8433566695) Fr & Eur.

Diccionario de Psiquiatria, Vol. 2. 3rd ed. Antoine Porot. 650p. (SPA.). 1977. 59.95 (*0-7859-5925-4*, 8433566709) Fr & Eur.

Diccionario de Psiquiatria: Dictionary of Psychiatry, 2 vols., Set. 3rd ed. Antoine Porot. 650p. (SPA.). 1977. 125.00 (*0-8288-5320-7*, S50071) Fr & Eur.

Diccionario de Publicidad y Marketing. Eduardo Parra Murga. 238p. 1990. 75.00 (*0-7859-6348-0*, 8485783069) Fr & Eur.

Diccionario de Qheshwa-Espanol, Espanol-Qheshwa. 3rd ed. Jesus Lara. 430p. (MIS & SPA.). 1990. pap. write for info. (*0-7859-4889-9*) Fr & Eur.

Diccionario de Quimica. Iciaro Lazaro. 130p. 1988. 32.95 (*0-7859-6030-9*, 8439712693) Fr & Eur.

Diccionario de Quimica, 11 vols. D. W. Sharp. 584p. (SPA.). 1988. pap. 150.00 (*0-7859-5715-4*, 8420517372) Fr & Eur.

Diccionario de Quimica Gran Vox. Vox Staff. 400p. 1991. write for info. (*0-7859-6171-2*, 8471533472) Fr & Eur.

Diccionario de Radio. 104p. (SPA.). 1979. 19.95 (*84-201-0368-3*) Fr & Eur.

Diccionario De Radio y Television. J. Cebrian Herrero. 382p. 1981. pap. 32.95 (*0-7859-6446-0*) Fr & Eur.

Diccionario de Refranes. Juana Barella Campos & Ana G. Barella Campos. 534p. (SPA.). 1975. pap. 54.95 (*0-8288-5815-2*, S50116) Fr & Eur.

***Diccionario de Refranes.** J. G. Campos & A. Barella. 432p. (SPA.). 1993. pap. 49.50x (*84-239-5984-8*) Elliots Bks.

Diccionario de Regionalismos de la Provincia de la Rioja. Julian Caceres Freire. (SPA.). 75.00 (*0-7859-0705-X*, S33066) Fr & Eur.

Diccionario de Religiones Comparadas, 2 vols., Set. Samuel G. Brandon. 1553p. (SPA.). 1975. 125.00 (*0-8288-5816-0*, S50104) Fr & Eur.

Diccionario de Religiones Comparadas, Vol. 1. S. G. Brandon. 750p. 1975. 55.00 (*0-7859-6106-2*, 8470571893) Fr & Eur.

Diccionario de Religiones Comparadas, Vol. 2. S. G. Brandon. 726p. 1975. 55.00 (*0-7859-6107-0*, 8470571907) Fr & Eur.

Diccionario de Retorica, Critica y Terminologia Literaria. 3rd ed. Angelo Marchese. 448p. (SPA.). 1991. pap. 45.00 (*0-7859-5927-0*, 8434483866) Fr & Eur.

Diccionario de Ro de Qheshwa-Espanol, Espanol-Qheshwa. Jesus Lara. (SPA.). 39.95 (*0-686-56703-X*) Fr & Eur.

Diccionario de Seguros. H. L. Mueller-Lutz. 282p. (ENG, FRE, GER & SPA.). 1977. pap. 15.75 (*0-7859-0901-X*, S-50035) Fr & Eur.

Diccionario de Seudonimos Literarios Espanoles, Con Algunas Iniciales. P. P. Rogers & F. A. Lapuente. 610p. (SPA.). 1977. 75.00 (*0-8288-5322-3*, S50152); pap. 49.95 (*0-8288-5325-8*, S31444) Fr & Eur.

Diccionario de Seudonimos Literarios Espanoles, Con Algunas Iniciales. P. P. Rogers & F. A. Lapuente. 610p. (SPA.). 1993. 69.50x (*84-249-1352-3*) Elliots Bks.

Diccionario De Seudonimos y Escritores Iberoamericanos. Gerardo Saenz. LC 90-86230. (Coleccion Diccionarios Ser.). 405p. (Orig.). (SPA.). 1992. pap. 39.00 (*0-89729-597-8*) Ediciones.

Diccionario de Sigles de Organismos Nacionales e Internacionales. Javier Gomez de Cadiz. 64p. (SPA.). 1976. pap. 9.95 (*0-8288-5601-X*, S50584) Fr & Eur.

Diccionario de Simbolos. 8th ed. Juan E. Cirlot. 476p. (SPA.). 1991. pap. 34.95 (*0-7859-5921-1*, 8433535048) Fr & Eur.

Diccionario de Sinonimos, Antonimos e Ideas Afines: Dictionary of Synonyms, Antonyms & Related Ideas. Andres Santamaria. 429p. (SPA.). 1981. 9.95 (*0-8288-2060-0*, S12277) Fr & Eur.

***Diccionario de Sinonimos, Antonimos y Paronimos.** 4th ed. Michel Doezis. 528p. 1990. pap. 13.95 (*0-7859-5034-6*) Fr & Eur.

Diccionario de Sinonimos Con Antonimos y Paronimos. 2nd rev. ed. Ed. by Frank Calderon. 432p. (Orig.). (SPA.). 1992. pap. 5.00 (*1-56259-021-9*) Editorial Amer.

Diccionario de Sinonimos e Ideas Afines y de la Rima (Dictionary of Synonyms, Related Ideas & Rhyming) 4th ed. J. Horta Massanes. 363p. (SPA.). 1991. pap. 17.95 (*0-7859-3738-2*, S50243) Fr & Eur.

Diccionario de Sinonimos Easa con Antonimos y Paranimos. Ed. by Frank Calderon. LC 87-402057. (Orig.). (SPA.). 1986. pap. 5.00 (*0-944499-03-1*) Editorial Amer.

Diccionario de Sinonimos Espanoles. Porrua Staff. (SPA.). 9.95 (*0-7859-0422-0*, S12253) Fr & Eur.

Diccionario de Sinonimos Valle. F. Gordo. 252p. (SPA.). 1980. 9.95 (*0-8288-2010-4*, S29130) Fr & Eur.

***Diccionario de Sinonimos y Antonimos.** Ed. by Espasa Staff. 1226p. (SPA.). 1994. 149.50x (*84-239-2170-0*) Elliots Bks.

***Diccionario de Sinonimos y Antonimos.** Ed. by Espasa Staff. (Espasa de Bolsillo Ser.). 808p. (SPA.). 1993. 34.95x (*84-239-9204-7*) Elliots Bks.

Diccionario de Sintomas. Joan Gomez. 625p. (SPA.). 1976. 69.95 (*0-8288-5602-8*, S31421) Fr & Eur.

Diccionario de Sociologia. Nicolas Abercrombie. 288p. (SPA.). 1986. pap. 26.95 (*0-7859-6000-7*, 8473606357) Fr & Eur.

Diccionario de Sociologia. 2nd ed. Mitchell G. Duncan. 240p. 1986. 24.95 (*0-7859-5799-5*) Fr & Eur.

Diccionario de Sociologia: Dictionary of Sociology. 2nd ed. Helmut Schoeck. 392p. (SPA.). 1977. pap. 20.95 (*0-8288-5326-6*, S50188) Fr & Eur.

Diccionario de Sociologia - Dictionary of Sociology. 4th ed. Helmut Schoeck. 392p. (SPA.). 1985. pap. 49.95 (*0-7859-5060-5*) Fr & Eur.

Diccionario de Sus Suenos. Indira Shankar. 208p. (Orig.). (SPA.). 1985. pap. 4.95 (*0-939193-00-0*) Edit Concepts.

Diccionario de Teminos Literarios. Akal Staff. 600p. (SPA.). 1990. 125.00 (*0-7859-6235-2*, M2815) Fr & Eur.

Diccionario de Teologia. Ed. by Everett Harrison. Tr. by Guillermo Serrano & Humberto R. Casanova. 558p. 1993. reprint ed. 22.50 (*0-939125-33-1*) Evangelical Lit.

Diccionario de Teologia: Dictionary of Theology. 6th ed. Louis Bouyer. 672p. (SPA.). 1990. write for info. (*0-7859-5061-3*) Fr & Eur.

Diccionario de Teologia Biblica. 2nd ed. Johannes B. Bauer. 582p. (SPA.). 1985. 69.95 (*0-7859-5087-7*, S50203) Fr & Eur.

Diccionario de Teologia Contemporanea. Bernard Ramm. Tr. by Roger V. Valle. 143p. 1984. reprint ed. pap. 4.50 (*0-311-09064-8*) Casa Bautista.

Diccionario de Terminologia Forestal Dictionary of Forest Terminology. 2nd ed. James R. Anderson & Steven Walker. 92p. reprint ed. pap. text ed. write for info. (*0-9619526-0-1*) J R Anderson.

***Diccionario de Terminologia Linguistica Actual.** Werner Abraham. 512p. (SPA.). 1993. 79.50 (*84-249-0080-4*) Elliots Bks.

Diccionario de Terminologia Linguistica Actual: Dictionary of Modern Linguistic Terminology. Werner Abraham. 511p. (SPA.). 1981. 85.00 (*0-8288-2027-9*, S60080) Fr & Eur.

Diccionario de Terminologia Militar Espanol-Frances, 2 vols., Set. Pierre Peyrous. 1989. pap. 49.95 (*0-7859-6317-0*, 8478230394) Fr & Eur.

Diccionario de Terminologia Militar Espanol-Frances, Vol. 1. 2nd ed. Pierre Peyrous. 658p. 1991. pap. 29.95 (*0-7859-6318-9*, 8478230408) Fr & Eur.

Diccionario de Terminologia Militar Espanol-Frances, Vol. 2. 2nd ed. Pierre Peyrous. 631p. 1991. pap. 29.95 (*0-7859-6319-7*, 8478230416) Fr & Eur.

Diccionario de Terminologia Militar Frances-Espanol. Pierre Peyrous. 368p. 1976. pap. 49.95 (*0-7859-6044-9*, 8450075289) Fr & Eur.

Diccionario de Terminos Aerauticos. Ruben D. Rosario. (ENG & SPA.). 125.00 (*0-685-42438-3*, S-37343) Fr & Eur.

Diccionario de Terminos Artisticos y Arqueologicos. Estela Ocampo. 240p. 1988. pap. 24.95 (*0-7859-6247-6*, 8476390769) Fr & Eur.

Diccionario de Terminos Cientificos, Vol. 1. McGraw Hill Staff. 336p. 1987. 39.95 (*0-7859-6013-9*, 8439506651) Fr & Eur.

Diccionario de Terminos Cientificos, Vol. 2. McGraw Hill Staff. 312p. 1988. 39.95 (*0-7859-6470-3*) Fr & Eur.

Diccionario de Terminos Cientificos, Vol. 3. McGraw Hill Staff. 312p. 1988. 39.95 (*0-7859-6014-7*, 8439506678) Fr & Eur.

Diccionario de Terminos Cientificos, Vol. 4. McGraw Hill Staff. 320p. 1988. 39.95 (*0-7859-6015-5*, 8439506686) Fr & Eur.

Diccionario de Terminos Cientificos, Vol. 5. McGraw Hill Staff. 320p. 1988. 39.95 (*0-7859-6016-3*, 8439506694) Fr & Eur.

Diccionario de Terminos Cientificos, Vol. 6. McGraw Hill Staff. 320p. 1988. 39.95 (*0-7859-6017-1*, 8439506708) Fr & Eur.

Diccionario de Terminos Comerciales. P. Gaballi Prat. 634p. (ENG & SPA.). 1963. 69.95 (*0-8288-6784-4*, S-31618) Fr & Eur.

Diccionario de Terminos Contables: Dictionary of Accounting Terms. Joaquin Blanes Prieto. 430p. (ENG & SPA.). 1991. pap. 49.95 (*0-8288-6359-8*, S28549) Fr & Eur.

Diccionario De Terminos De Arte. Luis Monreal y Tejada & R. G. Haggar. 426p. 1992. pap. 28.00 (*84-261-2701-0*) IBD Ltd.

Diccionario de Terminos de Proceso de Datos: Con Vocabulario Espanol-Ingles, Ingles-Espanol. 2nd ed. Angel Salto Dolla. 446p. (ENG & SPA.). 1979. 20.95 (*0-7859-0880-3*, S-50371) Fr & Eur.

Diccionario de Terminos Equivicos Ingles - Espanol, Ingles - Espanol. Miguel Cuenca. 224p. (ENG & SPA.). 1989. pap. 39.95 (*0-7859-5713-8*, 8420515485) Fr & Eur.

Diccionario de Terminos Filologicos. 3rd ed. Fernando Lazarro-Carreter. 444p. 1990. pap. 29.95 (*0-7859-5787-1*) Fr & Eur.

Diccionario de Terminos Geograficos: Dictionary of Geographical Terms. F. J. Monkhouse. 560p. (SPA.). 1978. 150.00 (*0-8288-4894-7*, S50017) Fr & Eur.

Diccionario de Terminos Historicos y Alfines. Istmo Staff. 329p. 1990. pap. 18.95 (*0-7859-6110-0*, 8470901303) Fr & Eur.

Diccionario De Terminos Juridicos. 2nd ed. Ignacio R. Garcia. 700p. (SPA.). 1985. 32.50 (*0-88063-500-2*, Equity Pub NH) Michie Butterworth.

Diccionario de Terminos Juridicos. 2nd ed. Ignacio Rivera. 1987. write for info. (*0-318-62483-4*) Equity Pubng NH.

Diccionario de Terminos Juridicos en Cuatro Idiomas. Edgard Le Docte. 760p. 1987. 295.00 (*0-7859-6220-4*, 8473984692) Fr & Eur.

Diccionario de Terminos Literarios. Alain. 384p. (FRE.). 1990. pap. 11.95 (*0-7859-1673-3*, F80950) Fr & Eur.

Diccionario De Terminos Literarios y Artisticos. Editorial America, S. A. Staff. Ed. by Maria E. Del Real. (Illus.). 392p. (Orig.). (SPA.). 1990. pap. write for info. (*0-944499-68-6*) Editorial Amer.

Diccionario de Terminos Marxistos. Mascitelli. 416p. (SPA.). 1979. pap. 19.95 (*0-8288-4766-5*, S50073) Fr & Eur.

Diccionario de Terminos Medicos Ingles-Espanol, Espanol-Ingles. 7th ed. 872p. 1991. 150.00 (*0-7859-4904-6*) Fr & Eur.

Diccionario de Terminos Mineralogicos y Cristalograficos. Carlos Marino & Rogelio Diaz-Guerrero. 608p. (SPA.). 1991. 75.00 (*0-7859-5731-6*, 8420652377) Fr & Eur.

Diccionario de Terminos Panamenos. Arnoldo Higuero. 97p. (Orig.). (SPA.). 1993. pap. text ed. 15.00 (*0-9605082-5-2*) Allied Ent.

Diccionario de Terminos Religiosos. Aquillino De Pedro Hernandez. 312p. (SPA.). 1990. pap. 26.95 (*0-7859-5858-4*, 8428513775) Fr & Eur.

Diccionario de Tipografia y del Libro. 2nd ed. Jose Martinez de Sousa. (SPA.). 1981. write for info. (*0-7859-3680-7*, 8428311323) Fr & Eur.

Diccionario de Traumatologia Jims. Jims Staff. 288p. 1991. pap. 59.95 (*0-7859-6111-9*, 88470923463) Fr & Eur.

Diccionario de Unidadaes y Tablas de Conversion. 3rd ed. Vasco Costa & Osvald Frances. 168p. (SPA.). 1977. pap. 17.95 (*0-8288-5328-2*, S50579) Fr & Eur.

Diccionario de Unidades Cientificas. 4th ed. H. G. Jerrard. 216p. 1980. pap. 29.95 (*0-8288-1161-X*, S50215) Fr & Eur.

Diccionario de Uso del Espagnol, 2 vols., Set. M. Moliner. 1991. 170.00 (*84-249-1344-2*) IBD Ltd.

Diccionario de Uso del Espagnol, Vol. 1. M. Moliner. 1446p. 1991. write for info. (*0-318-72431-6*) IBD Ltd.

Diccionario de Uso del Espagnol, Vol. 2. M. Moliner. 1585p. 1991. write for info. (*0-318-72432-4*) IBD Ltd.

Diccionario de Uso del Espanol, 2 vols. 4th ed. Maria Moliner. 3088p. 1993. 239.50 (*0-685-75413-8*) Elliots Bks.

Diccionario de Uso del Espanol, 1. Maria Moliner. 1991. write for info. (*0-7859-5791-X*) Fr & Eur.

Diccionario de Uso del Espanol, 2. Maria Moliner. 1991. 150.00 (*0-7859-5792-8*) Fr & Eur.

Diccionario de Uso del Espanol, Set. Maria Moliner. 1991. 295.00 (*0-7859-5790-1*) Fr & Eur.

Diccionario de Verbos e Regimes. Fernandes. 606p. (POR.). 49.95 (*0-7859-0589-8*, M-9212) Fr & Eur.

Diccionario de Verbos Ingleses con Particula. Enrique Lavin Camacho. 240p. (ENG & SPA.). 1989. pap. 32.95 (*0-7859-5714-6*, 8420516724) Fr & Eur.

Diccionario de Vinos Espanoles. Jose Perez & Ramon Alsina. 238p. (SPA.). 1991. reprint ed. 19.95 (*0-7859-5894-0*, 8430781358) Fr & Eur.

Diccionario de Vitaminas. Leonard Mervyn. 240p. (CAT.). 1985. pap. write for info. (*0-7859-4920-8*) Fr & Eur.

Diccionario de Voces Indigenas de Puerto Rico. Luis Hernandez Aquino. (SPA.). 18.95 (*0-7859-0714-9*, S-27651) Fr & Eur.

Diccionario de Voces Natulares. Vicente Garcia de Diego. 724p. (SPA.). 1986. 32.50 (*0-8288-2046-5*, S11993) Fr & Eur.

Diccionario de Zoologia. 3rd ed. Umberto Parenti. 244p. (SPA.). 1982. 29.95 (*0-8288-2390-1*, S50257) Fr & Eur.

Diccionario del Amor. Aline de Nanxe. 122p. (SPA.). 1969. pap. 9.95 (*0-8288-6572-8*, S-50136) Fr & Eur.

Diccionario del Arte Actual: Dictionary of Modern Art. Thomas Karin. 224p. (SPA.). 1978. pap. 19.95 (*0-8288-4895-5*, S50064) Fr & Eur.

Diccionario del Automovil: Dictionary of the Automobile. Ed. by Equipo Reactor de Ceac Staff. 916p. (SPA.). 1978. 69.95 (*0-8288-4896-3*, S14232) Fr & Eur.

Diccionario del Automovil: Dictionary of the Automobile. 4th ed. Roger Guerber. 237p. (ENG, FRE, GER & SPA.). 1972. pap. 24.95 (*0-8288-6360-1*, S-14249) Fr & Eur.

Diccionario del Basic. Hart. (SPA.). 1985. write for info. (*0-7859-3682-3*, 8428313784) Fr & Eur.

Diccionario del Budo: Artes Marciales. Raymond Thomas. 128p. (JPN, KOR & SPA.). 1978. pap. 19.95 (*0-8288-4897-1*, S50092) Fr & Eur.

***Diccionario del Cine Espanol.** A. M. Torres. (Espasa de Bolsillo Ser.). (Illus.). 504p. (SPA.). 1994. 34.95x (*84-239-9203-9*) Elliots Bks.

Diccionario del Cine Espanol, 1896-1968: Dictionary of the Spanish Cinema, 1896-1968. 359p. (SPA.). 1970. pap. 19.95 (*0-8288-6498-5*, S-50008) Fr & Eur.

Diccionario del Cine Negro. 3rd ed. Javier Coma. 264p. (SPA.). 1991. 125.00 (*0-7859-5685-9*, 8401604893) Fr & Eur.

Diccionario del Cristianismo. 2nd ed. Olivier De La Brosse. 1104p. (SPA.). 1987. write for info. (*0-7859-5088-5*) Fr & Eur.

D

An Asterisk (*) at the beginning of an entry indicates that the title is appearing in BIP for the first time.

Diccionario Del Diablo: The Devil's Alphabet. Kurt Koch. (SPA.). 4.95 (*84-7228-033-0*, 220281, Pub. by Edit Clie SP) TSELF.

Diccionario del Espanol Chicano. Roberto A. Galvan & Richard V. Teschner. 152p. 1991. pap. text ed. 9.95 (*0-8325-9634-5*, Passport Bks) NTC Pub Grp.

Diccionario del Espanol Chicano. 2nd ed. (BBC Phrase Bks.). 1994. pap. 12.95 (*0-8442-7967-6*, Passport Bks) NTC Pub Grp.

Diccionario del Espanol Chicano. 2nd ed. (BBC Phrase Bks.). 1994. 17.95 (*0-8442-7966-8*, Passport Bks) NTC Pub Grp.

Diccionario del Espanol Equivoco: Spanish Dictionary of Ambiguities. M. Crido de Val. 122p. (SPA.). 1981. pap. 12.95 (*0-8288-2041-4*, S38322) Fr & Eur.

Diccionario del Espanol Moderno: Dictionary of Modern Spanish. 5th ed. Martin Alonso. 1100p. (SPA.). 1978. 125.00 (*0-8288-4898-X*, S12229) Fr & Eur.

Diccionario del Hogar Catolico. Hogar Staff. 1180p. (SPA.). 1962. 25.95 (*0-8288-6807-7*, S-12259) Fr & Eur.

Diccionario del Hombre Contemporaneo. Bertrand Russell. (SPA.). pap. 17.50 (*0-686-56655-6*) Fr & Eur.

Diccionario del Lenguaje Filosofico. Paul Foulquie. 1100p. (SPA.). 1966. 85.00 (*0-8288-6704-6*, S-50065) Fr & Eur.

***Diccionario del Marketing.** Gonzalez. 273p. (SPA.). 1992. pap. 35.00 (*0-7859-7496-2*, 8428319898) Fr & Eur.

Diccionario del Nuevo Testamento: Dictionary of the New Testament. Xavier Leon-Dufour. 480p. (SPA.). 1977. 29.95 (*0-8288-5329-0*, S50103) Fr & Eur.

Diccionario del Pendulo de Foucault. Luigi Bauco. 320p. (SPA.). 1989. pap. 39.95 (*0-7859-6314-6*, 8478170081) Fr & Eur.

Diccionario del Plastico. J. A. Wordingham & P. Reboul. 208p. (SPA.). 24.95 (*0-7859-0720-3*, S-33051) Fr & Eur.

Diccionario del Psicoanalisis. 3rd deluxe ed. Jean Laplanche & Jean-Bertrand Pontalis. Ed. by Fernando Cervantes Gimeno. 558p. (SPA.). 1977. 65.50 (*0-7859-0894-3*, S-31445) Fr & Eur.

Diccionario del Teatro: Dramaturgia, Estetica, Semiologia. 2nd ed. Patrice Pavis. 605p. 1991. pap. 69.95 (*0-7859-6227-1*, 8475092373) Fr & Eur.

Diccionario del Verbo Castellano: Dictionary of Castilian Verbs. Santiago Lazzati. 438p. (SPA.). 1977. pap. 24.95 (*0-8288-5332-0*, S12049) Fr & Eur.

Diccionario Diplomatico. Santiago Martinez. 252p. 1986. pap. 29.95 (*0-7859-6199-2*, 8472324095) Fr & Eur.

Diccionario Disney. Walt Disney. 112p. (SPA.). 1973. pap. 9.95 (*0-8288-6241-9*, S-24118) Fr & Eur.

Diccionario Durvan de la Lengua Espanola. Durvan Staff. 1312p. (SPA.). 1977. 69.95 (*0-8288-5333-9*, S11956) Fr & Eur.

Diccionario EASA Ingles-Espanol Espanol-Ingles. 2nd rev. ed. Ed. by Maria E. Alvarez del Real. (Illus.). 808p. (Orig.). (ENG & SPA.). (YA). 1992. pap. 5.95 (*1-56259-017-0*) Editorial Amer.

Diccionario Economia General y Empresa, 4 vols., Set. Manuel A. Quintillan. 112p. (SPA.). 1991. pap. write for info. (*0-7859-5993-9*, 8436806522) Fr & Eur.

Diccionario Economia General y Empresa, Vol. 1. Manuel A. Quintillan. 112p. (SPA.). 1991. pap. write for info. (*0-7859-5994-7*, 8436806530) Fr & Eur.

Diccionario Economia General y Empresa, Vol. 2. Manuel A. Quintillan. 112p. (SPA.). 1991. pap. write for info. (*0-7859-5995-5*, 8436806549) Fr & Eur.

Diccionario Economia General y Empresa, Vol. 3. Manuel A. Quintillan. 112p. (SPA.). 1991. pap. write for info. (*0-7859-5996-3*, M2818) Fr & Eur.

Diccionario Economia General y Empresa, Vol. 4. 5th ed. Karl-Heinz Ahlheim. 768p. 1992. 65.00 (*0-8288-7721-1*, M7346) Fr & Eur.

Diccionario Economia General y Empressa, 4 vols., Set. Manuel A. Quintillan. 448p. (SPA.). 1991. pap. write for info. (*0-7859-5992-0*, 8436806514) Fr & Eur.

Diccionario Economico de la Empresa: Dictionary of the Economics of Free Enterprise. Andres S. Suarez. 384p. (SPA.). 1977. 29.95 (*0-8288-5334-7*, S50181) Fr & Eur.

Diccionario Empresarial. 3rd ed. Marcelino E. De Juan. 560p. 1990. 85.00 (*0-7859-5344-2*, 8485378865) Fr & Eur.

Diccionario Empresarial Stanford, 5 vols., Set. Argos Vergara Staff. 384p. (SPA.). 1987. pap. 95.00 (*0-7859-6274-3*, 8477090203) Fr & Eur.

Diccionario en Color de Arbustos: Shrub Dictionary in Color. S. Millar Gault. 210p. (SPA.). 1978. write for info. (*0-7859-5062-1*) Fr & Eur.

Diccionario Enciclopedia Larousse: Larousse Encyclopedia Dictionary (Spanish Edition), 12 vols., Set. Larousse Staff. (SPA.). 995.00 (*0-8288-8245-2*) Fr & Eur.

Diccionario Enciclopedia Salvat Universal, 20 vols., Set. Salvat Staff. 10080p. (SPA.). 1969. 3,500.00 (*0-8288-6574-4*, S-12270) Fr & Eur.

Diccionario Enciclopedia Universal, 13 vols., Set. Credsa Staff. 5036p. (ENG, FRE, GER, ITA & SPA.). 650.00 (*0-7859-0423-9*, S12271) Fr & Eur.

Diccionario Enciclopedias Labor: Encyclopedia Dictionary of Labor, 9 vols. 7th ed. Ed. by Javier Lasso de La Vega & Jose M. Rubert Candau. 6500p. (ENG, FRE, GER, POR & SPA.). 1978. 495.00 (*0-8288-5127-1*, S12269) Fr & Eur.

Diccionario Enciclopedica Informatica. P. L. Monit. 275p. 1989. 39.95 (*0-7859-6257-3*, 8476761166) Fr & Eur.

Diccionario Enciclopedica Labor, 10 vols., Set. Labor Staff. 3758p. (SPA.). 1990. 1,795.00 (*0-7859-5911-4*, 8433503901) Fr & Eur.

Diccionario Enciclopedica Labor, Vol. 1. Labor Staff. 374p. 1990. 195.00 (*0-7859-6462-2*) Fr & Eur.

Diccionario Enciclopedica Labor, Vol. 2. Labor Staff. 374p. (SPA.). 1990. 195.00 (*0-7859-5912-2*, 8433503928) Fr & Eur.

Diccionario Enciclopedica Labor, Vol. 3. Labor Staff. 374p. (SPA.). 1990. 195.00 (*0-7859-5913-0*, 8433503936) Fr & Eur.

Diccionario Enciclopedica Labor, Vol. 4. Labor Staff. 374p. (SPA.). 1990. 195.00 (*0-7859-5914-9*, 8433503944) Fr & Eur.

Diccionario Enciclopedica Labor, Vol. 5. Labor Staff. 374p. (SPA.). 1990. 195.00 (*0-7859-5915-7*, 8433503952) Fr & Eur.

Diccionario Enciclopedica Labor, Vol. 6. Labor Staff. 374p. (SPA.). 1990. 195.00 (*0-7859-5916-5*, 8433503960) Fr & Eur.

Diccionario Enciclopedica Labor, Vol. 7. Labor Staff. 374p. (SPA.). 1990. 195.00 (*0-7859-5917-3*, 8433503979) Fr & Eur.

Diccionario Enciclopedica Labor, Vol. 8. Labor Staff. 374p. (SPA.). 1990. 195.00 (*0-7859-5918-1*, 8433503987) Fr & Eur.

Diccionario Enciclopedica Labor, Vol. 9. Labor Staff. 374p. (SPA.). 1990. 195.00 (*0-7859-5919-X*, 8433503995) Fr & Eur.

Diccionario Enciclopedica Labor, Vol. 10. Labor Staff. (SPA.). 1990. 195.00 (*0-7859-5920-3*, 8433504002) Fr & Eur.

Diccionario Enciclopedica Vasco, Vol. 1: A-Amuzti. 4th ed. Bernardo Estornes Lasa. 654p. 1978. 195.00 (*0-7859-6058-9*, 8470250892) Fr & Eur.

Diccionario Enciclopedica Vasco, Vol. 10: Echau-Enti. Bernardo Estornes Lasa. 616p. 1979. 195.00 (*0-7859-6067-8*, 8470251910) Fr & Eur.

Diccionario Enciclopedica Vasco, Vol. 11: Ento-Esubi. Bernardo E. Lasa. 624p. 1980. 195.00 (*0-7859-6475-4*) Fr & Eur.

Diccionario Enciclopedica Vasco, Vol. 12: Esuin-Facen. Bernardo Estornes Lasa. 608p. 1981. 195.00 (*0-7859-6068-6*, 8470252046) Fr & Eur.

Diccionario Enciclopedica Vasco, Vol. 13: Facer-Fortes. Bernardo Estornes Lasa. 592p. 1982. 195.00 (*0-7859-6069-4*, 8470252070) Fr & Eur.

Diccionario Enciclopedica Vasco, Vol. 14: Fortif-Gallet. Bernardo E. Lasa. 592p. 1982. 195.00 (*0-7859-6070-8*, 8470252143) Fr & Eur.

Diccionario Enciclopedica Vasco, Vol. 15: Galleta-Geog. 2nd ed. Bernardo Estornes Lasa. 592p. 1988. 195.00 (*0-7859-6071-6*, 8470252151) Fr & Eur.

Diccionario Enciclopedica Vasco, Vol. 16: Geol-Gruzeta. Bernardo E. Lasa. 592p. 1984. 195.00 (*0-7859-6477-0*) Fr & Eur.

Diccionario Enciclopedica Vasco, Vol. 17: Gu-Hablista. Bernardo Estornes Lasa. 600p. 1985. 195.00 (*0-7859-6072-4*, 8470252194) Fr & Eur.

Diccionario Enciclopedica Vasco, Vol. 18: Hace-Hurania. Bernardo Estornes Lasa. 592p. 1985. 195.00 (*0-7859-6073-2*, 8470252208) Fr & Eur.

Diccionario Enciclopedica Vasco, Vol. 2: An-Artazu. 4th ed. Bernardo Estornes Lasa. 656p. 1986. 195.00 (*0-7859-6060-0*, 8470250973) Fr & Eur.

Diccionario Enciclopedica Vasco, Vol. 20: Inta-Ituriz. Bernardo Estornes Lasa. 584p. 1986. 195.00 (*0-7859-6074-0*, 8470252224) Fr & Eur.

Diccionario Enciclopedica Vasco, Vol. 22: Kobau-Landap. Bernardo Estornes Lasa. 584p. 1987. 195.00 (*0-7859-6076-7*, 8470252240) Fr & Eur.

Diccionario Enciclopedica Vasco, Vol. 23: Landara-Lecu. Bernardo Estornes Lasa. 584p. 1987. 195.00 (*0-7859-6077-5*, 8470252259) Fr & Eur.

Diccionario Enciclopedica Vasco, Vol. 24: Lecumbe-Liba. Bernardo Estornes Lasa. 574p. 1988. 195.00 (*0-7859-6078-3*, 8470252275) Fr & Eur.

Diccionario Enciclopedica Vasco, Vol. 25: Libano-Llavo. 2nd ed. Bernardo Estornes Lasa. 592p. 1988. 195.00 (*0-7859-6079-1*, 8470252305) Fr & Eur.

Diccionario Enciclopedica Vasco, Vol. 26: Lle-Marruza. Bernardo Estornes Lasa. 576p. 1989. 195.00 (*0-7859-6080-5*, 8470252313) Fr & Eur.

Diccionario Enciclopedica Vasco, Vol. 27: Mars-Mendix. Bernardo E. Lasa. 576p. 1989. 195.00 (*0-7859-6478-9*) Fr & Eur.

Diccionario Enciclopedica Vasco, Vol. 28: Mendiz-Mome. Bernardo Estornes Lasa. 576p. 1990. 195.00 (*0-7859-6081-3*, 8470252356) Fr & Eur.

Diccionario Enciclopedica Vasco, Vol. 29: Momio-Mulat. Bernardo Estornes Lasa. 574p. 1990. 195.00 (*0-7859-6082-1*, 8470252364) Fr & Eur.

Diccionario Enciclopedica Vasco, Vol. 3: Art-Balzategui. 3rd ed. Bernardo Estornes Lasa. 624p. 1977. 195.00 (*0-7859-6059-7*, 8470250957) Fr & Eur.

Diccionario Enciclopedica Vasco, Vol. 31: Nage-Navarra. Bernardo Estornes Lasa. 576p. 1991. 225.00 (*0-7859-6084-8*, 8470252380) Fr & Eur.

Diccionario Enciclopedica Vasco, Vol. 4: Balzola-Bi. 3rd ed. Bernardo Estornes Lasa. 624p. 1977. 195.00 (*0-7859-6063-5*, 8470251481) Fr & Eur.

Diccionario Enciclopedica Vasco, Vol. 5: Bi-Caballe. 3rd ed. Bernardo Estornes Lasa. 638p. 1978. 195.00 (*0-7859-6064-3*, 8470251651) Fr & Eur.

Diccionario Enciclopedica Vasco, Vol. 6: Caballo-Cer. 3rd ed. Bernardo Estornes Lasa. 622p. 1978. 195.00 (*0-7859-6065-1*, 8470251740) Fr & Eur.

Diccionario Enciclopedica Vasco, Vol. 8: Corral-Decla. 2nd ed. Bernardo Estornes Lasa. 624p. 1977. 195.00 (*0-7859-6061-9*, 8470251252) Fr & Eur.

Diccionario Enciclopedica Vasco, Vol. 9: Decli-Echats. Bernardo Estornes Lasa. 612p. 1978. 195.00 (*0-7859-6062-7*, 8470251430) Fr & Eur.

Diccionario Enciclopedico, 6 vols. A. Plaza. 3796p. (SPA.). 1991. 895.00 (*0-7859-5686-7*, 8401607256) Fr & Eur.

Diccionario Enciclopedico, 15 vols., Set. (J). (gr. 7 up). 199. 00 (*0-8347-5189-5*) Ency Brit Ed.

Diccionario Enciclopedico: El Ateneo. 3rd ed. Juan C. Y Equipo Merlo. (SPA.). 995.00 (*0-7859-0709-2*, S-33045) Fr & Eur.

Diccionario Enciclopedico: Gran Omeba, 12 vols., Set. Porrua Staff. (SPA.). 450.00 (*0-7859-0430-1*, S33046) Fr & Eur.

Diccionario Enciclopedico Abreviado. Espasa Staff. (SPA.). lib. bdg. 1,295.00 (*0-8288-2726-5*) Fr & Eur.

Diccionario Enciclopedico Areas, 10 vols., Set. Nauta Staff. 4140p. (SPA.). 1990. 1,495.00 (*0-7859-5843-6*, 8427813597) Fr & Eur.

Diccionario Enciclopedico Areas, Vol. 2. Nauta Staff. 424p. (SPA.). 1990. 150.00 (*0-7859-5844-4*, 8427813619) Fr & Eur.

Diccionario Enciclopedico Areas, Vol. 3. Nauta Staff. 404p. (SPA.). 1990. 150.00 (*0-7859-5845-2*, 8427813627) Fr & Eur.

Diccionario Enciclopedico Areas, Vol. 4. Nauta Staff. 424p. (SPA.). 1990. 150.00 (*0-7859-5846-0*, 8427813635) Fr & Eur.

Diccionario Enciclopedico Areas, Vol. 5. Nauta Staff. 416p. (SPA.). 1990. 150.00 (*0-7859-5847-9*, 8427813643) Fr & Eur.

Diccionario Enciclopedico Areas, Vol. 6. Nauta Staff. 416p. (SPA.). 1990. 150.00 (*0-7859-5848-7*, 8427813651) Fr & Eur.

Diccionario Enciclopedico Areas, Vol. 7. Nauta Staff. 416p. 1990. 150.00 (*0-7859-6457-6*) Fr & Eur.

Diccionario Enciclopedico Areas, Vol. 8. Nauta Staff. 408p. (SPA.). 1990. 150.00 (*0-7859-5849-5*, 8427813678) Fr & Eur.

Diccionario Enciclopedico Areas, Vol. 9. Nauta Staff. 408p. (SPA.). 1990. 150.00 (*0-7859-5850-9*, 8427813686) Fr & Eur.

Diccionario Enciclopedico Areas, Vol. 10. Nauta Staff. 404p. (SPA.). 1990. 150.00 (*0-7859-5851-7*, 8427813694) Fr & Eur.

Diccionario Enciclopedico Argos-Vergara, 10 vols. Argos Vergara Staff. 4440p. (SPA.). 1984. 59.95 (*0-7859-6486-X*, 847178565X) Fr & Eur.

Diccionario Enciclopedico Argos-Vergara, 12 vols., 444p. ea. Argos Vergara Staff. (SPA.). 1984. 59.95 (*0-7859-6191-7*, 8471785730) Fr & Eur.

Diccionario Enciclopedico Argos-Vergara, Vol. 1. Argos Vergara Staff. 444p. (SPA.). 1984. 59.95 (*0-7859-6184-4*, 8471785668) Fr & Eur.

Diccionario Enciclopedico Argos-Vergara, Vol. 2. Argos Vergara Staff. 444p. (SPA.). 1984. 59.95 (*0-7859-6186-0*, 8471785684) Fr & Eur.

Diccionario Enciclopedico Argos-Vergara, Vol. 3. Argos Vergara Staff. 444p. (SPA.). 1984. 59.95 (*0-7859-6187-9*, 8471785692) Fr & Eur.

Diccionario Enciclopedico Argos-Vergara, Vol. 4. Argos Vergara Staff. 444p. (SPA.). 1984. 59.95 (*0-7859-6188-7*, 8471785706) Fr & Eur.

Diccionario Enciclopedico Argos-Vergara, Vol. 5. Argos Vergara Staff. 444p. (SPA.). 1984. 59.95 (*0-7859-6189-5*, 8471785714) Fr & Eur.

Diccionario Enciclopedico Argos-Vergara, Vol. 6. Argos Vergara Staff. 444p. (SPA.). 1984. 59.95 (*0-7859-6190-9*, 8471785722) Fr & Eur.

Diccionario Enciclopedico Argos-Vergara, Vol. 7. Argos Vergara Staff. 3860p. (SPA.). 1990. 1,495.00 (*0-7859-6281-6*, 8477090815) Fr & Eur.

Diccionario Enciclopedico Argos-Vergara, Vol. 8. Argos Vergara Staff. 304p. (SPA.). 1990. 125.00 (*0-7859-6282-4*, 8477090823) Fr & Eur.

Diccionario Enciclopedico Argos-Vergara, Vol. 9. Argos Vergara Staff. 324p. (SPA.). 1990. 125.00 (*0-7859-6290-5*, 8477090912) Fr & Eur.

Diccionario Enciclopedico Argos-Vergara, Vol. 10. Argos Vergara Staff. 444p. (SPA.). 1984. 59.95 (*0-7859-6185-2*, 8471785676) Fr & Eur.

Diccionario Enciclopedico de Anatomia de Peces: Ingles-Espanol. A. Rojo. (ENG & SPA.). write for info. (*0-318-56672-9*, S-36994) Fr & Eur.

Diccionario Enciclopedico de Anatomia de Peces, Ingles-Espanol. Alfonso L. Rojo. 564p. 1988. write for info. (*0-7859-6226-3*) Fr & Eur.

Diccionario Enciclopedico De Astronomia. C. Lamberti. 284p. 1989. 39.95 (*0-7859-6406-1*, 8486761131) Fr & Eur.

Diccionario Enciclopedico De Contabilidad. Piero Mella. 1989. 39.95 (*0-7859-6504-1*) Fr & Eur.

Diccionario Enciclopedico de Educacion Especial, 4 vols., Set. Santillana Staff. 2152p. (SPA.). 1991. 795.00 (*0-7859-5860-6*, 8429423257) Fr & Eur.

Diccionario Enciclopedico de Educacion Especial, Vol. 1. Santillana Staff. 520p. (SPA.). 1991. 200.00 (*0-7859-5861-4*, 8429423265) Fr & Eur.

Diccionario Enciclopedico de Educacion Especial, Vol. 2. Santillana Staff. 488p. (SPA.). 1991. 200.00 (*0-7859-5862-2*, 8429423273) Fr & Eur.

Diccionario Enciclopedico de Educacion Especial, Vol. 3. Santillana Staff. 504p. (SPA.). 1991. 200.00 (*0-7859-5863-0*, 8429423281) Fr & Eur.

Diccionario Enciclopedico De Educacion Especial, Vol. 4. Santillana Staff. 640p. 1991. 200.00 (*0-7859-6458-4*) Fr & Eur.

Diccionario Enciclopedico De Geologia. R. Carimati. 271p. 1989. 39.95 (*0-7859-6408-8*, 8486761174) Fr & Eur.

Diccionario Enciclopedico de la Vida Sexual, 5 vols., Set. Jesus Noguer More. 792p. (SPA.). 1974. 250.00 (*0-8288-5987-6*, S50029) Fr & Eur.

Diccionario Enciclopedico de lla Mitologia. 2nd ed. Juan C. Fernandez. 512p. (SPA.). 1989. pap. 49.95 (*0-7859-5900-9*, 8431501685) Fr & Eur.

Diccionario Enciclopedico de Medicina "Jims" 4th ed. L. Braier. (ENG, FRE, GER, ITA, LAT & SPA.). 1980. 125.00 (*0-8288-0580-6*, S33099) Fr & Eur.

Diccionario Enciclopedico de Metalurgia. Oliver Bader & Michel Theret. 960p. (ENG, FRE & SPA.). 1975. 75.00 (*0-8288-5817-9*, S50132) Fr & Eur.

Diccionario Enciclopedico de Teologia Moral: Encyclopedic Dictionary of Theological Morality. Leandro Rossi & Ambrogio Valsecchi. 1488p. (SPA.). 1978. pap. 35.00 (*0-8288-5458-0*, S50078) Fr & Eur.

Diccionario Enciclopedico de Teologia Moral: Encyclopedic Dictionary of Theological Morality. 3rd ed. Leandro Rossi & Ambrogio Valsecchi. 1488p. (SPA.). 1978. 53.95 (*0-8288-5129-8*, S50077) Fr & Eur.

Diccionario Enciclopedico de Teologia Moral: Suplemento: Encyclopedic Dictionary of Theological Morality, Supplement. Leandro Rossi & Ambrogio Valsecchi. 256p. (SPA.). 1978. 49.95 (*0-8288-5130-1*, S50079) Fr & Eur.

Diccionario Enciclopedico del Arte, 8 vols., Set. Grupo Libro 88 Staff. 1992. 1,500.00 (*0-7859-6334-0*, 8479062215) Fr & Eur.

Diccionario Enciclopedico del Arte, Vol. 2. Grupo Libro 88 Staff. 256p. 1992. 195.00 (*0-7859-6327-8*, 8479062142) Fr & Eur.

Diccionario Enciclopedico del Arte, Vol. 3. Grupo Libro 88 Staff. 272p. 1992. 195.00 (*0-7859-6328-6*, 8479062150) Fr & Eur.

Diccionario Enciclopedico del Arte, Vol. 4. Grupo Libro 88 Staff. 288p. 1992. 195.00 (*0-7859-6329-4*, 8479062169) Fr & Eur.

Diccionario Enciclopedico del Arte, Vol. 5. Grupo Libro 88 Staff. 272p. 1992. 195.00 (*0-7859-6330-8*, 8479062177) Fr & Eur.

Diccionario Enciclopedico del Arte, Vol. 6. Grupo Libro 88 Staff. 272p. 1992. 195.00 (*0-7859-6332-4*, 8479062185) Fr & Eur.

Diccionario Enciclopedico del Arte, Vol. 7. Grupo Libro 88 Staff. 304p. 1992. 195.00 (*0-7859-6331-6*, 8479062183) Fr & Eur.

Diccionario Enciclopedico del Arte, Vol. 8. Grupo Libro 88 Staff. 304p. 1992. 195.00 (*0-7859-6333-2*, 8479062207) Fr & Eur.

Diccionario Enciclopedico des Sidervsgia. Jeronimo Vasquez Lopez. 376p. (SPA.). 1975. pap. 97.50 (*0-8288-5818-7*, S50004) Fr & Eur.

Diccionario Enciclopedico Durvan: Durvan Encyclopedic Dictionary, 12 vols., Set. Durvan Staff. 5632p. (SPA.). 1978. 995.00 (*0-8288-5131-X*, S12265) Fr & Eur.

Diccionario Enciclopedico Edaf, 18 vols., Set. 5th ed. EDAF Staff. 8752p. (SPA.). 1974. 995.00 (*0-8288-5988-4*, S30680) Fr & Eur.

Diccionario Enciclopedico Electronica. A. Marini. 376p. 1989. 39.95 (*0-7859-6503-3*) Fr & Eur.

Diccionario Enciclopedico Escolar Basico. 808p. (SPA.). 1974. pap. 60.00 (*0-8288-5989-2*, S50044) Fr & Eur.

Diccionario Enciclopedico Espasa, 24 vols., Set. Espasa Staff. (SPA.). 1980. 2,495.00 (*0-8288-4687-1*, S37369) Fr & Eur.

Diccionario Enciclopedico Espasa 1. (Illus.). 1800p. (SPA.). 1993. 179.50x (*84-239-5913-9*) Elliots Bks.

Diccionario Enciclopedico Espasa 1 A-Z. Espasa Staff. (SPA.). lib. bdg. 150.00 (*0-8288-2725-7*, S15561) Fr & Eur.

Diccionario Enciclopedico Estudiantil. Editorial America, S. A. Staff. Ed. by Maria E. Del Real. 386p. (Orig.). (SPA.). 1990. pap. write for info. (*0-944499-54-6*) Editorial Amer.

***Diccionario Enciclopedico Exito, 8 vols.** Oceano Staff. 4044p. 1990. write for info. (*0-7859-5044-3*) Fr & Eur.

Diccionario Enciclopedico Exito, Vol. 1. Oceano Staff. 456p. 1990. 250.00 (*0-7859-6311-1*, 8477644683) Fr & Eur.

Diccionario Enciclopedico Exito, Vol. 2. Oceano Staff. 435p. 1991. 250.00 (*0-7859-6299-9*, 8477640467) Fr & Eur.

Diccionario Enciclopedico Exito, Vol. 3. Oceano Staff. 458p. 1991. 250.00 (*0-7859-6300-6*, 8477640475) Fr & Eur.

Diccionario Enciclopedico Exito, Vol. 4. Oceano Staff. 468p. 1991. 250.00 (*0-7859-6301-4*, 8477640483) Fr & Eur.

Diccionario Enciclopedico Exito, Vol. 5. Oceano Staff. 480p. 1991. 250.00 (*0-7859-6302-2*, 8477640491) Fr & Eur.

Diccionario Enciclopedico Exito, Vol. 6. Oceano Staff. 736p. 1990. 250.00 (*0-7859-6496-7*) Fr & Eur.

Diccionario Enciclopedico Exito, Vol. 8. Oceano Staff. 508p. 1990. 250.00 (*0-7859-6313-8*, 8477644756) Fr & Eur.

Diccionario Enciclopedico Grijalbo, 3 vols. Grijalbo Staff. 2344p. 1990. 350.00 (*0-7859-5808-8*) Fr & Eur.

Diccionario Enciclopedico Grijalbo, 6 Vols. Grijalbo Staff. 2368p. 1991. 595.00 (*0-7859-5806-1*) Fr & Eur.

Diccionario Enciclopedico Illustrado, Vol. 10: Tripolitan. Argos Vergara Staff. (Illus.). 384p. (SPA.). 1987. pap. 95.00 (*0-7859-6492-4*, 847709022X) Fr & Eur.

Diccionario Enciclopedico Illustrado, Vol. 2: Bayaceto-Co. Argos Vergara Staff. 384p. (SPA.). 1987. pap. 95.00 (*0-7859-6276-X*, 8477090238) Fr & Eur.

Diccionario Enciclopedico Illustrado, Vol. 3: Comicios-Es. Argos Vergara Staff. 384p. (SPA.). 1987. pap. 95.00 (*0-7859-6277-8*, 8477090246) Fr & Eur.

Diccionario Enciclopedico Illustrado, Vol. 4: Espana-Grand Bretagne. Argos Vergara Staff. 384p. (SPA.). 1987. pap. 95.00 (*0-7859-6278-6*, 8477090254) Fr & Eur.

Diccionario Enciclopedico Illustrado, Vol. 5: Gran Bretan. Argos Vergara Staff. 384p. (SPA.). 1987. pap. 95.00 (*0-7859-6279-4*, 8477090262) Fr & Eur.

Diccionario Enciclopedico Illustrado, Vol. 6: Lanzarot-M. Argos Vergara. (Illus.). 384p. (SPA.). 1987. pap. 95.00 (*0-7859-6439-8*, 8777090270) Fr & Eur.

D

An Asterisk (*) at the beginning of an entry indicates that the title is appearing in BIP for the first time.

Diccionario Enciclopedico Illustrado, Vol. 7: Munataner-P. Argos Staff. (SPA.). 1984. 695.00 (*0-8288-2011-2*, S50444) Fr & Eur.

Diccionario Enciclopedico Illustrado, Vol. 8: Piramo-S.A. Argos Vergara Staff. 4552p. (SPA.). 1984. 595.00 (*0-7859-6182-8*, 8471785633) Fr & Eur.

Diccionario Enciclopedico Illustrado, Vol. 9: Salt-Tripo. Argos Vergara Staff. 448p. (SPA.). 1984. 59.95 (*0-7859-6183-6*, 8471785641) Fr & Eur.

Diccionario Enciclopedico Ilustrado, 3 vols., Set. Porrua Staff. (Illus.). (SPA.). 125.00 (*0-7859-0431-X*, S33077) Fr & Eur.

Diccionario Enciclopedico Ilustrado Argos Vergara, 12 vols. Argos Vergara Staff. (SPA.). 1990. 125.00 (*0-7859-6291-3*, 8477090920) Fr & Eur.

Diccionario Enciclopedico Ilustrado Argos Vergara, Vol. 10. Argos Vergara Staff. 324p. 1990. 125.00 (*0-685-70608-7*, 8477090912) Fr & Eur.

Diccionario Enciclopedico Ilustrado Argos Vergara, Vol. 1: Avellaneda. Argos Vergara Staff. 296p. (SPA.). 1990. 125.00 (*0-7859-6292-1*, 8477090939) Fr & Eur.

Diccionario Enciclopedico Ilustrado Argos Vergara, Vol. 10: Redova-Sobreperico. Argos Vergara Staff. 324p. (SPA.). 1990. 125.00 (*0-7859-6283-2*, 8477090831) Fr & Eur.

Diccionario Enciclopedico Ilustrado Argos Vergara, Vol. 11: Sobrequilla-Uzcudun. Argos Vergara Staff. (Illus.). 340p. (SPA.). 1990. 125.00 (*0-7859-6493-2*, 847709084X) Fr & Eur.

Diccionario Enciclopedico Ilustrado Argos Vergara, Vol. 12: V-Zworikin. Argos Vergara Staff. 328p. (SPA.). 1990. 125.00 (*0-7859-6284-0*, 8477090858) Fr & Eur.

Diccionario Enciclopedico Ilustrado Argos Vergara, Vol. 2: Avellaneda-Carol I. Argos Vergara Staff. 328p. (SPA.). 1990. 125.00 (*0-7859-6285-9*, 8477090866) Fr & Eur.

Diccionario Enciclopedico Ilustrado Argos Vergara, Vol. 3: Carol II-Desideratum. Argos Vergara Staff. 332p. (SPA.). 1990. 125.00 (*0-7859-6286-7*, 8477090874) Fr & Eur.

Diccionario Enciclopedico Ilustrado Argos Vergara, Vol. 4: Desierto-Faceta. Argos Vergara Staff. 324p. (SPA.). 1990. 125.00 (*0-7859-6287-5*, 8477090882) Fr & Eur.

Diccionario Enciclopedico Ilustrado Argos Vergara, Vol. 5: Facial-Hannibal. Argos Vergara Staff. 320p. (SPA.). 1990. 125.00 (*0-7859-6288-3*, 8477090890) Fr & Eur.

Diccionario Enciclopedico Ilustrado Argos Vergara, Vol. 6: Hannon-Lazaro. Argos Vergara Staff. 320p. (SPA.). 1990. 125.00 (*0-7859-6289-1*, 8477090904) Fr & Eur.

Diccionario Enciclopedico Ilustrado Argos Vergara, Vol. 7: Lazaro-Carreter. 2nd ed. Miguel A. Coma. 1046p. (CAT.). 1987. 29.95 (*0-7859-6196-8*, 8472111571) Fr & Eur.

Diccionario Enciclopedico Ilustrado Argos Vergara, Vol. 8: Monoclamidea-Parpado. 12th ed. Miguel A. Coma. 304p. (CAT.). 1983. pap. 10.95 (*0-7859-6195-X*, S50050) Fr & Eur.

Diccionario Enciclopedico Ilustrado Argos Vergara, Vol. 9: Parpallo-Redoute. 2nd ed. Miguel A. Coma. 310p. (CAT.). 1987. pap. 15.95 (*0-7859-6487-8*, 847211158X) Fr & Eur.

Diccionario Enciclopedico Ilustrado de Medicina. 26th ed. Emalsa Staff. 1760p. 1987. 225.00 (*0-7859-6242-5*, 8476054122) Fr & Eur.

Diccionario Enciclopedico Ilustrado de Medicina, 3 vols., Set. Emalsa Staff. 1985. 595.00 (*0-7859-6241-7*, 8476052235) Fr & Eur.

Diccionario Enciclopedico Ilustrado de Medicina, Vol. 1. Emalsa Staff. 650p. 1985. 225.00 (*0-7859-6238-7*, 8476052200) Fr & Eur.

Diccionario Enciclopedico Ilustrado de Medicina, Vol. 2. Emalsa Staff. 650p. 1985. 225.00 (*0-7859-6239-5*, 8476052219) Fr & Eur.

Diccionario Enciclopedico Ilustrado de Medicina, Vol. 3. Emalsa Staff. 650p. 1985. 225.00 (*0-7859-6240-9*, 8476052227) Fr & Eur.

Diccionario Enciclopedico Ilustrado Deca90, 12 vols., Set. Durvan Staff. 1991. 1,295.00 (*0-7859-6258-1*, 8476772211) Fr & Eur.

Diccionario Enciclopedico Ilustrado Deca90, Vol. 1. Durvan Staff. (Illus.). 524p. 1991. 125.00 (*0-7859-6490-8*) Fr & Eur.

Diccionario Enciclopedico Ilustrado Deca90, Vol. 3. Durvan Staff. 520p. 1991. 125.00 (*0-7859-6260-3*, 8476772246) Fr & Eur.

Diccionario Enciclopedico Ilustrado Deca90, Vol. 4. Durvan Staff. 524p. 1991. 125.00 (*0-7859-6261-1*, 8476772254) Fr & Eur.

Diccionario Enciclopedico Ilustrado Deca90, Vol. 6. Durvan Staff. 520p. 1991. 125.00 (*0-7859-6263-8*, 8476772270) Fr & Eur.

Diccionario Enciclopedico Ilustrado Deca90, Vol. 7. Durvan Staff. 520p. 1991. 125.00 (*0-7859-6264-6*, 8476772289) Fr & Eur.

Diccionario Enciclopedico Ilustrado Deca90, Vol. 8. Durvan Staff. 516p. 1991. 125.00 (*0-7859-6265-4*, 8476772297) Fr & Eur.

Diccionario Enciclopedico Ilustrado Deca90, Vol. 9. Durvan Staff. 520p. 1991. 125.00 (*0-7859-6266-2*, 8476772300) Fr & Eur.

Diccionario Enciclopedico Ilustrado Deca90, Vol. 10. Durvan Staff. 520p. 1991. 125.00 (*0-7859-6267-0*, 8476772319) Fr & Eur.

Diccionario Enciclopedico Ilustrado Deca90, Vol. 11. Durvan Staff. 550p. 1991. 125.00 (*0-7859-6268-9*, 8476772327) Fr & Eur.

Diccionario Enciclopedico Ilustrado Deca90, Vol. 12. Durvan Staff. 512p. 1991. 125.00 (*0-7859-6269-7*, 8476772335) Fr & Eur.

Diccionario Enciclopedico Ilustrado Sopena: Sopena Encyclopedic Illustrated Dictionary, 5 vols., Set. Sopena Staff. 4920p. (SPA.). 1977. 450.00 (*0-8288-5336-3*, S50528) Fr & Eur.

***Diccionario Enciclopedico Larousse: Larousse Encyclopedia Dictionary: Spanish Edition, 12 vols.** Larousse Staff. 1992. write for info. (*0-7859-5231-4*) Fr & Eur.

Diccionario Enciclopedico Oceano, 5 vols., Set. Oceano Staff. 1990. 695.00 (*0-7859-6303-0*, 8477640998) Fr & Eur.

Diccionario Enciclopedico Oceano, Vol. 1. Oceano Staff. 424p. 1990. 150.00 (*0-7859-6304-9*, 8477641005) Fr & Eur.

Diccionario Enciclopedico Oceano, Vol. 2. Oceano Staff. 424p. 1990. 150.00 (*0-7859-6305-7*, 8477641013) Fr & Eur.

Diccionario Enciclopedico Oceano, Vol. 3. Oceano Staff. 424p. 1990. 150.00 (*0-7859-6495-9*); 150.00 (*0-7859-6306-5*, 8477641021) Fr & Eur.

Diccionario Enciclopedico Oceano, Vol. 5. Oceano Staff. 364p. 1990. 150.00 (*0-7859-6307-3*, 8477641048) Fr & Eur.

Diccionario Enciclopedico Quimica. deluxe ed. Miguel A. Del Arco Torres. 736p. (SPA.). 1984. 150.00 (*0-7859-6051-1*, 8470162586) Fr & Eur.

Diccionario Enciclopedico Salvat Alfa, 10 vols., Set. Salvat Staff. 3500p. (SPA.). 1972. 495.00 (*0-8288-6361-X*, S-50518) Fr & Eur.

Diccionario Enciclopedico Santillana, 10 vols., Set. Santillana Staff. 3504p. (SPA.). 1991. 1,295.00 (*0-7859-5864-9*, 8429432507) Fr & Eur.

Diccionario Enciclopedico Santillana, Vol. 1. Santillana Staff. 352p. (SPA.). 1991. 135.00 (*0-7859-5865-7*, 8429432515) Fr & Eur.

Diccionario Enciclopedico Santillana, Vol. 2. Santillana Staff. 340p. (SPA.). 1991. 135.00 (*0-7859-5866-5*, 8429432523) Fr & Eur.

Diccionario Enciclopedico Santillana, Vol. 3. Santillana Staff. 356p. (SPA.). 1991. 135.00 (*0-7859-5867-3*, 8429432531) Fr & Eur.

Diccionario Enciclopedico Santillana, Vol. 4. Santillana Staff. 372p. 1991. 135.00 (*0-7859-6459-2*) Fr & Eur.

Diccionario Enciclopedico Santillana, Vol. 5. Santillana Staff. 340p. (SPA.). 1991. 135.00 (*0-7859-5868-1*, 8429432558) Fr & Eur.

Diccionario Enciclopedico Santillana, Vol. 7. Santillana Staff. 372p. (SPA.). 1991. 135.00 (*0-7859-5870-3*, 8429432574) Fr & Eur.

Diccionario Enciclopedico Santillana, Vol. 8. Santillana Staff. 372p. (SPA.). 1991. 135.00 (*0-7859-5871-1*, 8429432582) Fr & Eur.

Diccionario Enciclopedico Santillana, Vol. 10. Santillana Staff. 320p. (SPA.). 1991. 135.00 (*0-7859-5873-8*, 8429432604) Fr & Eur.

Diccionario Enciclopedico Slavat, 26 vols., Set. Salvat Staff. 3744p. 1992. 995.00 (*0-7859-6436-3*, 8488063415) Fr & Eur.

Diccionario Enciclopedico Tecnico: Materiales Siderurgicos. F. Rapatz & F. Roll. 260p. (SPA.). 1968. 49.95 (*0-8288-6624-4*, S-33724) Fr & Eur.

Diccionario Enciclopedico Tecnico Magnitudes y Unidades Fisicas. Alfred Sacklowski. (Diccionario Enciclopedico Tecnico Ser.). 224p. (SPA.). 1973. write for info. (*0-7859-5089-3*) Fr & Eur.

Diccionario Enciclopedico Tecnico Mecansimos Engranajes y Acoplamientos. Schalitz Jehlicka. 289p. (SPA.). 1969. 39.95 (*0-8288-6575-2*, S-33735) Fr & Eur.

Diccionario Enciclopedico Teide, 4 vols., Set. deluxe ed. Teide Staff. 2478p. (SPA.). 1977. 150.00 (*0-8288-5337-1*, S50447) Fr & Eur.

Diccionario Enciclopediica Vasco, Vol. 21: Ituriz-Koba. Bernardo Estornes Lasa. 592p. 1986. 195.00 (*0-7859-6075-9*, 8470252232) Fr & Eur.

Diccionario Escolar. 2nd ed. Ed. by Maria E. Alvarez del Real. LC 83-80787. (Illus.). 228p. (SPA.). (J). (gr. 2). 1986. pap. 3.75 (*0-944499-13-9*) Editorial Amer.

***Diccionario Escolar: Espanol-Ingles - English-Spanish.** Ed. by Espasa-Harrap's Staff. (Espasa de Bolsillo Ser.). 656p. 1994. 34.95x (*84-239-9208-X*) Elliots Bks.

Diccionario Escolar Centroamericano. Francisco Morales Santos. 600p. 1988. pap. write for info. (*0-7859-6335-9*, 8483772310) Fr & Eur.

Diccionario Escolar de Sinonimos y Antonimos: Students Dictionary of Synonyms & Antonyms. 2nd ed. Vox Staff. 370p. (SPA.). 1980. 29.95 (*0-8288-2067-8*, S39159) Fr & Eur.

Diccionario Escolar Etimologico: Student's Etymological Dictionary. 4th ed. Victor Garcia Hoz. 752p. (SPA.). 1991. pap. 34.95 (*0-7859-5063-X*) Fr & Eur.

Diccionario Escolar Hispanoamericano. 4th ed. Vasco Ame. 600p. (SPA.). 1975. pap. 5.95 (*0-8288-5819-5*, S27088) Fr & Eur.

Diccionario Escolar Sopena Color de la Lengua Espanola. Sopena Staff. 928p. (SPA.). 1976. pap. 55.00 (*0-8288-5607-9*, S50144) Fr & Eur.

Diccionario Esencial Diafora Espanol-Ingles-Espanol: Essential Diafore Spanish-English-Spanish Dictionary. B. Dutton et al. 425p. (ENG & SPA.). 1981. 19.95 (*0-8288-2326-X*, S40509) Fr & Eur.

Diccionario Esencial Frances-Espanol, Espanol-Frances. Jean-Paul Vidal. 598p. 1981. pap. 12.95 (*0-7859-6341-3*, 8485205901) Fr & Eur.

Diccionario Esencial Santillana. Santillana Staff. 1376p. (SPA.). 1991. 39.95 (*0-7859-5874-6*, 8429434151) Fr & Eur.

Diccionario Esloveno-Espanol. Ed. by Anton Grad. 747p. (SLO & SPA.). 1979. 49.95 (*0-8288-4767-3*, S37817) Fr & Eur.

Diccionario Espanol - Frances - Arabe. Ola A. Soliman. 1991. 40.00 (*0-86685-465-7*) Intl Bk Ctr.

Diccionario Espanol-Aleman, Aleman-Espanol Militar. Carlos Ruiz Jodar. 375p. (GER & SPA.). 1975. pap. 24.95 (*0-8288-5820-9*, S50101) Fr & Eur.

Diccionario Espanol-Arabe: Spanish - Arabic Dictionary. 2nd ed. Federico C. Cordoba. 862p. (ARA & SPA.). 1986. pap. 36.95 (*0-7859-5118-0*) Fr & Eur.

***Diccionario Espanol de la Lengua China.** Fernando Mateos et al. 1381p. (SPA.). 1990. 339.50x (*84-239-4771-8*) Elliots Bks.

Diccionario Espanol de la Lengua China: Spanish Dictionary of the Chinese Language. 2nd ed. Miguel Otegui et al. 1381p. (CHI & SPA.). 1979. 350.00 (*0-8288-5339-8*, S31804) Fr & Eur.

Diccionario Espanol Etimologico: Spanish Etymological Dictionary. Felix Diez Mateo. 396p. (SPA.). 1972. 16.95 (*0-8288-6362-8*, S-12291) Fr & Eur.

Diccionario Espanol-Frances, Espagnol-Francais. Miguel Gimenez Sales. 736p. (FRE & SPA.). 1975. pap. 8.75 (*0-8288-5821-7*, S50394) Fr & Eur.

Diccionario Espanol-Ingles - Ingles-Espanol Universidad de Miami: English-Spanish - Spanish-English Dictionary University of Miami. rev. ed. Ed. by Gerald G. Curtis. 584p. (ENG & SPA.). 1993. pap. 4.50 (*1-56259-028-6*) Editorial Amer.

Diccionario Espanol-Ingles English-Spanish Dictionary. 2nd ed. Edwin B. Williams. 1549p. (ENG & SPA.). 1989. text ed. 19.95 (*0-07-070421-X*) McGraw.

Diccionario Espanol-Ingles, Ingles-Espanol. 800p. (ENG & SPA.). 1979. pap. 6.95 (*84-346-0310-1*) Fr & Eur.

Diccionario Espanol-Ingles, Ingles-Espanol. Lib. Sanchez Staff. 1704p. 1991. 55.00 (*0-7859-6246-8*, 8476300980) Fr & Eur.

Diccionario Espanol-Ingles, Ingles-Espanol, 2 vols., Set. Oceano Staff. 1989. 195.00 (*0-7859-6308-1*, 8477644454) Fr & Eur.

Diccionario Espanol-Ingles, Ingles-Espanol, Vol. 2. Oceano Staff. 484p. 1989. 105.00 (*0-7859-6310-3*, 8477644470) Fr & Eur.

Diccionario Espanol-Ruso: Spanish - Russian Dictionary. 944p. (RUS & SPA.). 1961. 39.95 (*0-8288-6817-4*, S-31679) Fr & Eur.

Diccionario Espanol-Ruso de le Prospeccion y Refinacion del Petroleo. A. Pinkevich & B. Amelin. Ed. by A. F. Dobriansky. 424p. (RUS & SPA.). 1966. 39.95 (*0-8288-6705-4*, S-37368) Fr & Eur.

Diccionario Espanol-Ruso, Ruso-Espanol. 2nd ed. K. Marzishevskaya et al. 512p. (RUS & SPA.). 1992. pap. 29.95 (*0-7859-1087-5*, 5200021677) Fr & Eur.

Diccionario Espanol-Vasco, Vol. 1. Bernardo Estornes Lasa. 224p. 1965. pap. 19.95 (*0-7859-6057-0*, 8470250256) Fr & Eur.

Diccionario Espanol-Vasco, Vol. 2. Bernardo Estornes Lasa. 186p. 1965. pap. 19.95 (*0-7859-6056-2*, 8470250248) Fr & Eur.

Diccionario Espanol-Vasco, Vol. 3. Bernardo E. Lasa. 170p. 1965. pap. 19.95 (*0-7859-6476-2*) Fr & Eur.

Diccionario Espanol-Vasco, Vol. 4. Bernardo Estornes Lasa. 178p. 1965. pap. 19.95 (*0-7859-6055-4*, 8470250221) Fr & Eur.

Diccionario Espanol-Vasco, Vol. 5. Bernardo Estornes Lasa. 1965. pap. 19.95 (*0-7859-6054-6*, 8470250213) Fr & Eur.

Diccionario Espiritualidad, 3 vols., Set. Ermano Ancilli. 728p. (SPA.). 1983. 105.00 (*0-7859-5823-1*, 8425413370) Fr & Eur.

Diccionario Espiritualidad, Vol. 1. Ermano Ancilli. 652p. (SPA.). 1983. 105.00 (*0-7859-5824-X*, 8425413656) Fr & Eur.

Diccionario Espiritualidad, Vol. 2. 2nd ed. 524p. 1983. write for info. (*0-7859-5012-5*) Fr & Eur.

Diccionario Espiritualidad, Vol. 3. 3rd ed. A. Anderson. 277p. (ENG & GER.). 1989. lib. bdg. 95.00 (*0-8288-3878-X*, F107850) Fr & Eur.

Diccionario Estudiantil. 3rd ed. 326p. (SPA.). 1972. pap. 6.95 (*84-7165-051-7*) Fr & Eur.

Diccionario Etimologico. Alfredo San Jose Requejo. 128p. 1989. pap. 10.95 (*0-7859-6294-8*, 8477290407) Fr & Eur.

Diccionario Etimologico Abreviado. 2nd ed. Fernando Coripio Perez. 320p. (SPA.). 1976. pap. 9.95 (*0-8288-5608-7*, S50161) Fr & Eur.

Diccionario Everest Cumbre Frances. Everest Staff. 656p. 1990. pap. 14.95 (*0-7859-5764-2*) Fr & Eur.

Diccionario Everest Cuspide Frances-Espanol y Espanol Frances. Everest Staff. 990p. 1988. pap. 16.95 (*0-7859-5765-0*) Fr & Eur.

Diccionario Everest Italiano. Everest Staff. 896p. 1991. pap. 12.95 (*0-7859-5768-5*) Fr & Eur.

Diccionario Everest Vertice Ingles. Everest Staff. 700p. 1990. pap. 10.95 (*0-7859-5762-6*) Fr & Eur.

Diccionario Familiar de Medicina Natural: Colloquial Dictionary of Natural Medicine. Emmerick-Armand Maury & C. Rudder. 441p. (SPA.). 1981. 19.95 (*0-8288-1867-3*, S37815) Fr & Eur.

Diccionario Familiar Larousse, 2 vols. 128p. (SPA.). 1991. 95.00 (*0-7859-5705-7*, 8401614066) Fr & Eur.

Diccionario Familiar Larousse, Vol. 1: Espanol - Ingles. Plaza Janes Staff. 66p. (ENG & SPA.). 1991. pap. 39.95 (*0-7859-5706-5*, 8401614074) Fr & Eur.

Diccionario Familiar Larousse, Vol. 2: Ingles - Espanol. Plaza Janes Staff. 62p. (ENG & SPA.). 1991. pap. 39.95 (*0-7859-5707-3*, 8401614082) Fr & Eur.

Diccionario Filosofico. Voltaire. 264p. 1988. pap. 32.95 (*0-7859-6409-6*, 8486955017) Fr & Eur.

Diccionario Filosofico. Francois-Marie de Voltaire. 378p. (SPA.). 1976. pap. 15.75 (*0-7859-0906-0*, S-50148) Fr & Eur.

Diccionario Filosofico. 3rd ed. 520p. 1987. pap. 14.95 (*0-7859-4895-3*) Fr & Eur.

Diccionario Filosofico, 2 vols., Set. Francois-Marie de Voltaire. 616p. (SPA.). 1978. 17.50 (*0-7859-0905-2*, S-50012) Fr & Eur.

Diccionario Frances-Espanol de la Construccion y Obras Publicas. Herbert Bucksch & Arturo Galan e Hildalgo. 564p. (FRE & SPA.). 1975. 56.95 (*0-8288-5822-5*, S50133) Fr & Eur.

Diccionario Frances-Espanol, Espanol-Frances Collins Pocket. 7th ed. Carlos Giordano. 512p. 1990. 24.95 (*0-7859-5802-9*) Fr & Eur.

Diccionario Frances-Espanol, Espanol-Frances Gran Vox. Vox Staff. 376p. 1990. write for info. (*0-7859-6167-4*, 8471533383) Fr & Eur.

Diccionario Frances-Espanol, Espanol-Frances Vox Compacto. Vox Staff. 608p. 1988. pap. 14.95 (*0-7859-6157-7*, 8471532050) Fr & Eur.

Diccionario Fraseologico Comercial. Dusan Zavada et al. 435p. (GER & POR.). 1978. 27.50 (*0-686-92497-5*, M-9026) Fr & Eur.

Diccionario Galego-Castelan, Castelan-Galego. Xose Feixo Cid. 1330p. 1988. pap. 29.95 (*0-7859-6273-5*, 8476800088) Fr & Eur.

Diccionario Galego-Castelan e Vocabulario Castelan-Galego. 4th ed. Xose L. Franco Grande. 970p. (SPA.). 1978. 34.95 (*0-8288-5135-2*, S50436) Fr & Eur.

Diccionario Gallego-Castellano, Castelan-Galego. Xuntanza Staff. 350p. 1988. pap. 11.95 (*0-7859-6404-5*, 8486614279) Fr & Eur.

Diccionario General de Acustica y Electro Acustica. Henri Piraux. 374p. (SPA.). 1967. 29.95 (*0-8288-6672-4*, S-50237) Fr & Eur.

Diccionario General De Bibliografia Espanola, 7 vols., Set. Dionisio Hidalgo. xxvi, 3530p. 1973. reprint ed. write for info. (*3-487-04678-4*, Pub. by Georg Olms GW) Lubrecht & Cramer.

Diccionario General de Ciencias Humanas: General Dictionary of the Human Sciences. Georges Thines & Agnes Lempereur. 976p. (SPA.). 1978. 125.00 (*0-8288-5136-0*, S50146) Fr & Eur.

Diccionario General de Habilidades. Juan M. Gonzalez-Cremona. 336p. 1991. 19.95 (*0-7859-5747-2*) Fr & Eur.

Diccionario General de Turismo. G. Novo. (SPA.). 19.50 (*0-7859-0917-6*, S-28710) Fr & Eur.

Diccionario General Espanol-Ingles, 2 vols., Set. Ramon Garcia-Pelayo. 998p. 1989. 125.00 (*0-7859-6415-0*, 8487227155) Fr & Eur.

Diccionario General Espanol-Ingles, Vol. 1. Ramon Garcia-Pelayo. 480p. 1989. 75.00 (*0-7859-6416-9*, 8487227163) Fr & Eur.

Diccionario General Espanol-Ingles, Vol. 2. Ramon Garcia-Pelayo. 518p. 1989. 75.00 (*0-7859-6417-7*, 8487227171) Fr & Eur.

Diccionario General Illustrado de la Lengua Espanol. deluxe ed. Manuel A. Ezquerra. 1230p. (SPA.). 1991. 175.00 (*0-7859-4894-5*, S12377) Fr & Eur.

Diccionario General y Tecnico: Hiztegi Orokor-Teknikoa, 2 vols., Set. Luis M. Urdangarin. 618p. 1983. 95.00 (*0-7859-5064-8*) Fr & Eur.

Diccionario Geografico Universal. 2nd ed. Ed. by Maria E. Alvarez del Real. LC 81-71535. (Illus.). 836p. (SPA.). 1986. pap. 6.00 (*0-944499-00-7*) Editorial Amer.

Diccionario Geografico Universal. 3rd rev. ed. Ed. by Maria E. Alvarez del Real. (Illus.). 876p. (SPA.). 1992. pap. 5.95 (*1-56259-020-0*) Editorial Amer.

Diccionario Gramatical y de Dudas del Idioma. Sopena Staff. 1500p. (SPA.). 75.00 (*0-7859-0424-7*, S12275) Fr & Eur.

Diccionario Griego-Espanol. deluxe ed. Sopena Staff. 1544p. (GRE & SPA.). 125.00 (*0-7859-0440-9*, S50425) Fr & Eur.

Diccionario Griego-Espanol. 2nd ed. Miguel Balaguer. 940p. (GRE & SPA.). 1977. 29.95 (*0-8288-5342-8*, S50344) Fr & Eur.

Diccionario Griego-Espanol. 2nd ed. Francisco Rodriguez Adrados. 320p. (GRE & SPA.). 1989. pap. 85.00 (*0-7859-5682-4*, 8400046528) Fr & Eur.

Diccionario-Guia de Redaccion. 5th ed. J. Vinoly. 188p. (SPA.). 1983. write for info. (*0-7859-5096-6*) Fr & Eur.

Diccionario Heraldico. 2nd ed. Vincente De Cadenas Vicent. 340p. (SPA.). 1989. pap. write for info. (*0-7859-5090-7*) Fr & Eur.

Diccionario Historia de La. Caribe Editorial Staff. (SPA.). Date not set. 22.99 (*0-89922-300-1*) Edit Caribe.

***Diccionario Historico de la Lengua Espanola: Fascicles 1-10, Bound Together.** Real Academia Espanola Staff. (SPA.). 1991. 650.00 (*84-600-3782-7*) Elliots Bks.

Diccionario Historico de la Lengua Espanola (Faciculos) Real Academia Espanola Staff. 156p. 1984. pap. 29.95 (*0-7859-6046-5*, 8460037835) Fr & Eur.

Diccionario Historico Geografico Ilustrado del Pais Vasco, Vol. 3. Prol. by Jose M. De Retena. 384p. 1975. 75.00 (*0-7859-4896-1*) Fr & Eur.

Diccionario Humano. 2nd ed. Mercedes Iribarren Reta. 552p. (SPA.). 1975. pap. 19.95 (*0-8288-5823-3*, S50088) Fr & Eur.

Diccionario Humoristico. V. Claraso. 297p. (SPA.). 1966. 35.00 (*0-8288-6706-2*, S-37662) Fr & Eur.

Diccionario Humoristico. 3rd ed. Jorge S. Pros. 552p. (SPA.). 1982. pap. write for info. (*0-7859-4898-8*) Fr & Eur.

Diccionario Ideologico de la Lengua Castellana. 2nd ed. Julio C. Sanchez. 1446p. (SPA.). 1992. write for info. (*0-7859-4948-8*) Fr & Eur.

Diccionario Ideologico Feminista. Victoria Sau Sanchez. 280p. 1981. pap. 12.95 (*0-7859-6223-9*, 8474260728) Fr & Eur.

Diccionario Illustrado de Terminos Taurinos. 3rd ed. Luis Nieto-Manjon. 438p. 1991. pap. 65.00 (*0-7859-5751-0*) Fr & Eur.

Diccionario Ilustrado Aleman-Espanol y Espanol-Aleman. Sopena Staff. 520p. (SPA.). 1990. 32.95 (*0-7859-5888-6*, 8430310940) Fr & Eur.

D

An Asterisk (*) at the beginning of an entry indicates that the title is appearing in BIP for the first time. 1951

Diccionario Ilustrado Danae de la Lengua Espanola. deluxe ed. Danae Staff. (Illus.). (SPA.). write for info. (*0-7859-0434-4*, S50207) Fr & Eur.

Diccionario Ilustrado de Artes Marciales. Louis Frederic. 368p. 1989. pap. 79.95 (*0-7859-6342-1*, 8485269640) Fr & Eur.

Diccionario Ilustrado de Astronomia y Astronautica. Ian Didpath. (Illus.). 264p. 1987. 19.95 (*0-7859-5770-7*) Fr & Eur.

Diccionario Ilustrado de Efemerides, 2 vols. Vincente Vega. 1901p. (SPA.). 1968. pap. 38.95 (*0-685-01697-8*, S-50279) Fr & Eur.

Diccionario Ilustrado de Efemerides, 2 vols., Set. deluxe ed. Vincente Vega. 1901p. (SPA.). 1968. 47.95 (*0-7859-0870-6*, S-12366) Fr & Eur.

Diccionario Ilustrado de Electronica. Humberto Ramirez Villareal. 192p. (SPA.). 24.95 (*0-7859-0708-4*, S-25248) Fr & Eur.

Diccionario Ilustrado de la Arquitectura Contemporanea. 4th ed. Gerd Hatje. Ed. by Gerd Sabater. 360p. (SPA.). 1982. pap. 39.95 (*0-7859-5103-2*) Fr & Eur.

Diccionario Ilustrado de la Biblia. Gerhard Bellinger. (Illus.). 664p. 1991. 85.00 (*0-7859-5772-3*) Fr & Eur.

Diccionario Ilustrado de la Biblia. Ed. by Wilton M. Nelson. (Illus.). 735p. (SPA.). 1974. 20.95 (*0-89922-033-9*); pap. 17.95 (*0-89922-099-1*) Edit Caribe.

Diccionario Ilustrado de la Lengua Espanola. Aristos. 640p. (SPA.). 24.95 (*0-7859-0881-1*, S12234) Fr & Eur.

Diccionario Ilustrado de la Lengua Espanola. Carlos Arniches. 67p. (SPA.). 1964. 5.95 (*0-8288-7100-0*, S8718) Fr & Eur.

Diccionario Ilustrado de la Lengua Espanola. Atilano Rances. 480p. (SPA.). 1983. pap. 14.95 (*0-7859-5108-3*) Fr & Eur.

Diccionario Ilustrado de Rarezas, Inverosimilitudes y Curiosidades. 4th deluxe ed. Vicente Vega. 622p. (SPA.). 1971. 24.75 (*0-7859-0867-6*, S-12368) Fr & Eur.

Diccionario Ilustrado de Terminologia Textil Aleman-Espanol, Espanol-Aleman. Carlos Scheengluth. 700p. (GER & SPA.). 1975. 66.00 (*0-8288-5825-X*, S50056) Fr & Eur.

Diccionario Ilustrado de Trucos. deluxe ed. J. L. Chardans & Vicente Vega. 700p. (SPA.). 1970. 24.75 (*84-252-0206-X*) Fr & Eur.

Diccionario Ilustrado en Color de Plantas de Interior. Roy Hay et al. 231p. (SPA.). 1976. 75.00 (*0-8288-5611-7*, S50277) Fr & Eur.

Diccionario Ilustrado en Color de Plantas de Jardin con Plantas de Interior y de Invernadero. R. Har & Patrick M. Synge. 364p. (SPA.). 1977. 95.00 (*0-8288-5343-6*, S12330) Fr & Eur.

Diccionario Ilustrado Italiano-Espanol, Espanol-Italiano. Sopena Staff. 640p. (ITA & SPA.). 1990. 32.95 (*0-7859-5890-8*, 8430310975) Fr & Eur.

Diccionario Ilustrado Vox Ingles-Espanol, 6 vols., Set. Vox Staff. 1991. 695.00 (*0-7859-6174-7*, 8471536528) Fr & Eur.

Diccionario Ilustrado Vox Ingles-Espanol, Vol. 1. Vox Staff. 204p. 1991. 125.00 (*0-7859-6175-5*, 8471536536) Fr & Eur.

Diccionario Ilustrado Vox Ingles-Espanol, Vol. 2. Vox Staff. 200p. 1991. 125.00 (*0-7859-6176-3*, 8471536544) Fr & Eur.

D

Diccionario Ilustrado Vox Ingles-Espanol, Vol. 3. Vox Staff. 200p. 1991. 125.00 (*0-7859-6177-1*, 8471536552) Fr & Eur.

Diccionario Ilustrado Vox Ingles-Espanol, Vol. 5. Vox Staff. 200p. 1991. 125.00 (*0-7859-6179-8*, 8471536579) Fr & Eur.

Diccionario Ilustrado Vox Ingles-Espanol, Vol. 6. Vox Staff. 192p. 1991. 125.00 (*0-7859-6180-1*, 8471536587) Fr & Eur.

Diccionario Infantil Fher. Angel J. Gomez de Segura Beaumont. 24p. (SPA.). 1978. pap. 9.95 (*0-7859-0864-1*, S50076) Fr & Eur.

Diccionario Infantil Ilustrado. 190p. (SPA.). (J). 1975. 20.50 (*0-7859-0876-5*, S50006); pap. 17.95 (*0-8288-5827-6*, S50007) Fr & Eur.

Diccionario Ingenieria Industrial: Espanol - Ingles Tecnicas. Etsi Ind Madrid Staff. 184p. (ENG & SPA.). 1990. 39.95 (*0-7859-3364-6*, 8474840635) Fr & Eur.

Diccionario Ingles. American Heritage Dictionary Editors. 1982. 9.95 (*0-395-31254-X*); pap. 9.95 (*0-395-31255-8*) HM.

Diccionario Ingles-Espanol, Espanol-Ingles. Robertson. 894p. (ENG & SPA.). 12.25 (*84-303-0107-0*, S-50396); pap. 49.95 (*84-303-0108-9*, S-50397) Fr & Eur.

Diccionario Ingles-Espanol, Espanol-Ingles. 3rd ed. Francisco Bruguera Grane. 680p. (ENG & SPA.). 1979. pap. 6.95 (*0-8288-4770-3*, S50345) Fr & Eur.

Diccionario Ingles-Espanol, Espanol-Ingles de Terminoligia Teatral. Rafael Portillo-Garcia. 232p. 1986. pap. 29.95 (*0-7859-5773-1*) Fr & Eur.

Diccionario Ingles-Espanol y Espanol-Ingles: English-Spanish, Spanish-English, 2 vols., Set. 6th ed. EDAF Staff. 3000p. (ENG & SPA.). 1977. 175.00 (*0-8288-5344-4*, S12391) Fr & Eur.

Diccionario Internacional de Derecho de Autor. Pau M. Sala. 486p. 1988. pap. 69.95 (*0-7859-6403-7*, 8486592518) Fr & Eur.

Diccionario Internacional de Senales Maritimes, 3 vols. Associcio Internacional de Senales Maritimes Staff. (SPA.). 1990. pap. write for info. (*0-7859-6224-7*, 8474336449) Fr & Eur.

***Diccionario Inverso de la Lengua Espanola.** I. Bosque & M. Perez Fernandez. 716p. (SPA.). 1993. 125.00 (*84-249-1080-X*) Elliots Bks.

Diccionario Italiano-Espanol y Espanol-Italiano, 2 vols., Set. Emilio M. Amador. 1984p. (ITA & SPA.). 1988. 150.00 (*0-7859-5884-3*, 8430310762) Fr & Eur.

Diccionario Italiano-Espanol y Espanol-Italiano, Vol. 1. Emilio M. Amador. 1040p. (ITA & SPA.). 1988. pap. 75.00 (*0-7859-5885-1*, 8430310770) Fr & Eur.

Diccionario Iter Aleman-Espanol, Espanol-Aleman: Iter German-Spanish, Spanish-German Dictionary. Iter. 512p. (GER & SPA.). 1977. 9.95 (*0-8288-5346-0*, S50377) Fr & Eur.

Diccionario Juridico. Espana Calpe Staff. 1216p. 1991. 125.00 (*0-7859-5753-7*) Fr & Eur.

Diccionario Juridico. 4th ed. Julia I. Lope. 320p. (SPA.). 1990. pap. 45.00 (*0-7859-5899-1*, 8431500549) Fr & Eur.

Diccionario Juridico del Leasing. Garcia Sole Fernando. 160p. 1991. pap. 34.95 (*0-7859-6221-2*, 8473988442) Fr & Eur.

Diccionario Juridico Espasa. F. T. Moro. 1010p. (SPA.). 1991. 119.50x (*84-239-5988-0*) IBD Ltd.

Diccionario Juridico Frances-Espanol-Frances. Olivier Merlin-Walch & Amoros Rica. 800p. (FRE & SPA.). 1986. 175.00 (*0-8288-0407-9*, S 36030) Fr & Eur.

Diccionario-Juridico Segun la Jurisprudencia Del Tribunal Supremo De Puerto Rico: Palabras, Frases y Doctrinas, 2 vols., Set. Mariano Morales-Lebron. 925p. (SPA.). Date not set. 195.00 (*0-685-73078-6*) U Cinn Law.

***Diccionario-Juridico Segun la Jurisprudencia del Tribunal Supremo de Puerto Rico: Palabras, Frases y Doctrinas, 2 vols., Set.** Mariano Morales-Lebron. 925p. (SPA.). Date not set. 195.00 (*0-9626291-1-1*) U Cinn Law.

Diccionario Kapeluse de la Lengua Espanola. 1552p. (SPA.). 1979. 59.95 (*0-8288-4771-1*, S33044) Fr & Eur.

Diccionario Karten Ilustrado. 1680p. (SPA.). 1977. pap. 125.00 (*0-8288-5348-7*, S33047) Fr & Eur.

Diccionario Konkani-Portuguez. M. S. Dalgado. 602p. 1983. write for info. (*0-8288-1774-X*, F24950) Fr & Eur.

Diccionario Laboral. Ramon Bayod Serrat. 546p. (SPA.). 1969. pap. 14.95 (*0-8288-6576-0*, S50139) Fr & Eur.

Diccionario Larousse de Historia Univeral, Vol. 1. Planeta Staff. 680p. 1988. 29.95 (*0-7859-6019-8*, 8439507690) Fr & Eur.

Diccionario Larousse de Historia Univeral, Vol. 2. Planeta Staff. 760p. 1988. 29.95 (*0-7859-6003-1*, 8439407704) Fr & Eur.

Diccionario Larousse de Historia Univeral, Vol. 3. Planeta Staff. 776p. 1988. 29.95 (*0-7859-6020-1*, 8439507712) Fr & Eur.

Diccionario Larousse de Historia Univeral, Vol 5. Planeta Staff. 832p. 1988. 29.95 (*0-7859-6022-8*, 8439509731) Fr & Eur.

Diccionario Larousse de la Pintura, 6 vols. Planeta Staff. 1988. write for info. (*0-7859-6023-6*, 8439509766) Fr & Eur.

Diccionario Larousse de la Pintura, Vol. 1. Planeta Staff. 368p. 1989. 16.95 (*0-7859-6024-4*, 8439509774) Fr & Eur.

Diccionario Larousse de la Pintura, Vol. 2. Planeta Staff. 376p. 1989. 16.95 (*0-7859-6025-2*, 8439509782) Fr & Eur.

Diccionario Larousse de la Pintura, Vol. 3. Planeta Staff. 360p. 1989. 16.95 (*0-7859-6026-0*, 8439509790) Fr & Eur.

Diccionario Larousse de la Pintura, Vol. 4. Planeta Staff. 368p. 1989. 16.95 (*0-7859-6027-9*, 8439509804) Fr & Eur.

Diccionario Larousse de la Pintura, Vol. 5. Planeta Staff. 328p. 1989. 16.95 (*0-7859-6028-7*, 8439509812) Fr & Eur.

Diccionario Larousse de la Pintura, Vol. 6. Planeta Staff. 344p. 1989. 16.95 (*0-7859-6029-5*, 8439509820) Fr & Eur.

Diccionario Larousse del Espanol Moderno. Ramon Garcia-Palayo Gross & Gross. 640p. (SPA.). 1983. pap. 4.95 (*0-451-12352-2*, Sig) NAL-Dutton.

Diccionario Latino-Espanol, Espanol-Latino, 3 vols., Set. deluxe ed. Blanquez. 2703p. (LAT & SPA.). 395.00 (*0-7859-0885-4*, S50419) Fr & Eur.

Diccionario Lengua Espanola Forja. 24th ed. Jose Garcia Mercadal. 488p. (SPA.). 1977. 9.95 (*0-8288-5349-5*, S50034) Fr & Eur.

Diccionario Lexicon, Aleman-Espanol, Espanol-Aleman: German-Spanish, Spanish-German Dictionary Lexicon. Hans Muller. 384p. (GER & SPA.). 1977. pap. 14.95 (*0-8288-5350-9*, S31392) Fr & Eur.

Diccionario Lexicon Esperanto-Espanol, Espanol-Esperanto. Sopena Staff. 400p. (ESP & SPA.). pap. 14.95 (*84-303-0147-X*, S50402) Fr & Eur.

Diccionario Lexicon Esperanto-Espanol, Espanol-Esperanto. deluxe ed. Sopena Staff. 400p. (ESP & SPA.). 14.95 (*0-7859-0435-2*, S50403) Fr & Eur.

Diccionario Lexicon Finlandes-Espanol, Espanol-Finlandes. Sopena Staff. 400p. (FIN & SPA.). pap. 14.95 (*84-303-0149-6*, S-50404) Fr & Eur.

Diccionario Lexicon Finlandes-Espanol, Espanol-Finlandes. deluxe ed. Sopena Staff. 400p. (FIN & SPA.). 14.95 (*0-7859-0954-0*, S-50405) Fr & Eur.

Diccionario Lexicon Frances-Espanol, Espanol-Frances. deluxe ed. E. Gimeno. 384p. (FRE & SPA.). 1975. 15.95 (*0-8288-5828-4*, S31393) Fr & Eur.

Diccionario Lexicon Holandes-Espanol y Espanol-Holandes. Sopena Staff. 384p. (DUT & SPA.). 1974. pap. 14.95 (*0-7859-0436-0*, S50408) Fr & Eur.

Diccionario Lexicon Holandes-Espanol y Espanol-Holandes. deluxe ed. Sopena Staff. 384p. (DUT & SPA.). 1974. pap. 14.95 (*0-8288-5994-9*, S50409) Fr & Eur.

Diccionario Lexicon Ingles-Espanol, Espanol-Ingles. D. Macarulla. 384p. (ENG & SPA.). 1974. pap. 13.95 (*0-8288-5996-5*, S31391) Fr & Eur.

Diccionario Lexicon Italiano-Espanol, Espanol-Italiano. Sopena Staff. 400p. (ITA & SPA.). pap. 7.95 (*0-7859-0428-X*, S31394) Fr & Eur.

Diccionario Lexicon Noruego-Espanol, Espanol-Noruego. Sopena Staff. 400p. (NOR & SPA.). 14.95 (*0-7859-0438-7*, S50418); pap. 14.95 (*84-303-0164-X*, S-50417) Fr & Eur.

Diccionario Lexicon Portugues-Espanol, Espanol-Portugues. Sopena Staff. 400p. (POR & SPA.). 14.95 (*0-7859-0441-7*, S50429); pap. 14.95 (*84-303-0143-7*, S-50430) Fr & Eur.

Diccionario Lexicon Sueco-Espanol, Espanol-Sueco. Sopena Staff. 400p. (SPA.). 1975. 14.95 (*0-7859-0437-9*, S50416); pap. 14.95 (*84-303-0145-3*, S50415) Fr & Eur.

Diccionario Literario de Obras y Personajes de Todos los Tiempos y Paises, 2 vols., Set. Gonzalez Porto-Bompiani. 1538p. (SPA.). 1979. 150.00 (*0-8288-4772-X*, S50244) Fr & Eur.

Diccionario Literario de Obras y Personajes de Todos los Tiempos y Paises, 12 vols., Set. 2nd ed. Ed. by Martin De Riquer. 11000p. (SPA.). 1972. 1,995.00 (*0-8288-6364-4*, S-12328) Fr & Eur.

Diccionario Literario Obras Personajes Bompiani, 12 vols., Set. Bompiani. 1987. 2,795.00 (*0-7859-6369-3*, 8485950356) Fr & Eur.

Diccionario Literario Obras Personajes Bompiani, Vol. 1. Bompiani. 585p. 1987. 195.00 (*0-7859-6370-7*, 8485950364) Fr & Eur.

Diccionario Literario Obras Personajes Bompiani, Vol. 2. Bompiani. 920p. 1987. 195.00 (*0-7859-6371-5*, 8485950372) Fr & Eur.

Diccionario Literario Obras Personajes Bompiani, Vol. 3. Bompiani. 944p. 1987. 195.00 (*0-7859-6372-3*, 8485950380) Fr & Eur.

Diccionario Literario Obras Personajes Bompiani, Vol. 4. Bompiani. 976p. 1987. 195.00 (*0-7859-6373-1*, 8485950399) Fr & Eur.

Diccionario Literario Obras Personajes Bompiani, Vol. 6. Bompiani. 920p. 1987. 195.00 (*0-7859-6375-8*, 8485950410) Fr & Eur.

Diccionario Literario Obras Personajes Bompiani, Vol. 7. Bompiani. 960p. 1987. 195.00 (*0-7859-6376-6*, 8485950429) Fr & Eur.

Diccionario Literario Obras Personajes Bompiani, Vol. 8. Bompiani. 790p. 1987. 195.00 (*0-7859-6377-4*, 8485950437) Fr & Eur.

Diccionario Literario Obras Personajes Bompiani, Vol. 9. Bompiani. 888p. 1987. 195.00 (*0-7859-6378-2*, 8485950445) Fr & Eur.

Diccionario Literario Obras Personajes Bompiani, Vol. 10. Bompiani. 840p. 1987. 195.00 (*0-7859-6379-0*, 8485950453) Fr & Eur.

Diccionario Literario Obras Personajes Bompiani, Vol. 11. Bompiani. 1987. 195.00 (*0-7859-6380-4*, 8485950461) Fr & Eur.

Diccionario Literario Obras Personajes Bompiani, Vol. 12. Bompiani. 648p. 1987. 195.00 (*0-7859-6501-7*) Fr & Eur.

Diccionario Literario Obras Personajes Bompiani, Appendix 1. Bompiani. 776p. 1987. 195.00 (*0-7859-6381-2*, 8485950488) Fr & Eur.

Diccionario Literario Obras Personajes Bompiani, Appendix 2. Bompiani. 792p. 1987. 195.00 (*0-7859-6382-0*, 8485950496) Fr & Eur.

Diccionario Literario Obras Personajes Bompiani, Appendix 3. Bompiani. 550p. 1989. 195.00 (*0-7859-6389-8*, 8485950607) Fr & Eur.

Diccionario Literario Universal. Jose A. Perez Rioja. 994p. (SPA.). 1977. 89.95 (*0-8288-5351-7*, S31441) Fr & Eur.

***Diccionario Magico Infantil.** Eulalia Goma. 52p. 1989. 19.95 (*0-7859-5045-1*) Fr & Eur.

Diccionario Magico Infantil en Seis Lenguas. 2nd ed. Eulalia Goma. 96p. (CAT, ENG, FRE & SPA.). (J). 1978. 29.95 (*0-8288-5140-9*, S50028) Fr & Eur.

Diccionario Manual. 4th ed. Real Academia Espano. 1668p. 1989. 195.00 (*0-7859-5752-9*) Fr & Eur.

Diccionario Manual Aleman-Espanol, Espanol-Aleman: German & Spanish. Felix Diez Mateo. 952p. (GER & SPA.). 1978. pap. 14.95 (*0-8288-5142-5*, S50383) Fr & Eur.

Diccionario Manual Aleman-Espanol, Spanisch-Deutsch. 17th ed. E. M. Amador. 936p. (GER & SPA.). 1977. 14.95 (*0-8288-5352-5*, S50382) Fr & Eur.

Diccionario Manual Amador Aleman-Espanol, Espanol-Aleman. 9th ed. Jean Amery et al. 839p. (GER.). 1977. 275.00 (*0-7859-6911-X*, 3411012714) Fr & Eur.

Diccionario Manual Amador Aleman-Espanol,Espanol-Aleman. E. M. Amador. 1400p. (GER & SPA.). 1988. 89.95 (*0-7859-0882-X*, S50385) Fr & Eur.

Diccionario Manual Amador Frances-Espanol y Espanol-Frances. Leopoldo Gimeno Font. 1248p. (FRE & SPA.). 1991. 89.95 (*0-8288-5829-2*, S50401) Fr & Eur.

Diccionario Manual Amador Ingles-Espanol, Espanol-Ingles. E. M. Amador. 944p. (ENG & SPA.). 35.00 (*0-7859-0953-2*, S-50395) Fr & Eur.

Diccionario Manual Auxiliar Basico. 2nd ed. Plaza Janes Staff. 432p. (SPA.). 1991. write for info. (*0-7859-5091-5*) Fr & Eur.

Diccionario Manual de la Lengua Espanola. rev. ed. Editorial Vosgos Staff. (Coleccion Diccionarios Ser.). (Illus.). 623p. (SPA.). 1988. 9.95 (*0-318-42006-6*) Ediciones.

Diccionario Manual de Sinonimos, Antonimos e Ideas Afines. 512p. (SPA.). pap. 9.95 (*84-303-0066-X*, S-12277) Fr & Eur.

Diccionario Manual e Ilustrado de la Lengua Espanola. 4th ed. Ed. by Real Acadeimia Espanola Staff. (Illus.). 1666p. (SPA.). 1989. 275.00x (*84-239-5978-3*) Elliots Bks.

Diccionario Manual e Ilustrado de la Lengua Espanola, 1. Real Academia Espano Staff. 1983. 45.00 (*0-7859-5754-5*) Fr & Eur.

Diccionario Manual e Ilustrado de la Lengua Espanola, 2. Real Academia Espano Staff. 1983. 45.00 (*0-7859-5755-3*) Fr & Eur.

Diccionario Manual e Ilustrado de la Lengua Espanola, 3. Real Academia Espano Staff. 1983. 45.00 (*0-7859-5756-1*) Fr & Eur.

Diccionario Manual e Ilustrado de la Lengua Espanola, 5. Real Academia Espano Staff. 1983. 45.00 (*0-7859-5758-8*) Fr & Eur.

Diccionario Manual e Ilustrado de la Lengua Espanola, 6. Real Academia Espano Staff. 1983. 45.00 (*0-7859-5759-6*) Fr & Eur.

Diccionario Manual Frances-Espanol, Espagnol-Francais: French & Spanish. 36th ed. Arturo Cuyas Armengol. 830p. (FRE & SPA.). 1977. 14.95 (*0-8288-5353-3*, S50390) Fr & Eur.

Diccionario Manual Frances-Espanol, Espanol-Frances: French - Spanish, Spanish - French. Felix Diez Mateo & Frida Hochleitner. 992p. (FRE & SPA.). 1971. 27.95 (*0-8288-6439-X*, S-50389) Fr & Eur.

Diccionario Manual Frances-Espanol-Frances. Vox Staff. 953p. (FRE & SPA.). 1980. 39.95 (*0-8288-2336-7*, S12418) Fr & Eur.

Diccionario Manual Herder Frances-Espanol, Espanol-Frances. 3rd ed. Gunther Haensch. 644p. (FRE & SPA.). 1989. write for info. (*0-7859-5092-3*) Fr & Eur.

Diccionario Manual Illustrado de Arquitectura con los Terminos Mas Comunes: Illustrated Dictionary of Architecture. D. Ware. (Illus.). 224p. (SPA.). 1981. pap. 29.95 (*0-8288-1197-0*, S50275) Fr & Eur.

Diccionario Manual Ingles-Espanol, Espanol-Ingles. 3rd ed. Felix Diez Mateo & Frida Hochleitner. 1008p. (ENG & SPA.). 1985. pap. write for info. (*0-7859-5116-4*) Fr & Eur.

Diccionario Manual Ingles-Espanol, Spanish-English. 35th ed. Arturo Cuyas Armengol. 768p. (ENG & SPA.). 1978. pap. 9.95 (*0-8288-5144-1*, S12389) Fr & Eur.

Diccionario Manual Italiano-Espanol, Spagnuolo-Italiano: Spanish & Italian. 16th ed. Jose Ortiz De Burgos. 960p. (ITA & SPA.). 1977. 14.95 (*0-8288-5354-1*, S50432) Fr & Eur.

Diccionario Manual Vox Barcanova de la Llengua Catalana. Vox Staff. 1478p. 1991. write for info. (*0-7859-6151-8*, 8471531704) Fr & Eur.

Diccionario Manual Vox Frances-Espanol, Espanol-Frances. Vox Staff. 232p. 1991. 39.95 (*0-7859-6173-9*, 8471533944) Fr & Eur.

Diccionario Manual Vox Griago-Espanol. Vox Staff. 724p. 1991. 45.00 (*0-7859-6155-0*, 8471531925) Fr & Eur.

Diccionario Manual Vox Ilustrado de la Lengua Espanola. Vox Staff. 1312p. 1991. 24.95 (*0-7859-6153-4*, 8471531755) Fr & Eur.

Diccionario Manuel e Ilustrado de la Lengua Espanol, 5 vols., Set. 4th ed. Real Academia de la Lengua Espanol Staff. 1666p. (SPA.). 1989. 195.00 (*0-8288-2736-2*, S38002) Fr & Eur.

Diccionario Marin de al Lengua Espanola, Vol. 2. Marin Staff. 1668p. (SPA.). 1982. 250.00 (*0-8288-2017-1*, S2556) Fr & Eur.

Diccionario Marino Espanol-Ingles, Ingles-Espanol Para Uso. Juan J. Martinez de Espinoza. 802p. 1989. 35.00 (*0-7859-6218-2*, 8473410483) Fr & Eur.

Diccionario Maritimo. Fausto Arocena. 215p. (SPA.). 1963. pap. 19.95 (*0-7859-6053-8*, 8470250159) Fr & Eur.

Diccionario Maritimo. 4th ed. Julian Arnich. 472p. (SPA.). 1991. 55.00 (*0-7859-5829-0*, S12232) Fr & Eur.

Diccionario Maritimo: Ingles - Espanol, Espanol - Ingoles. Rodriquez-Barrientos. (ENG & SPA.). 1987. write for info. (*0-7859-3684-X*, 8428315140) Fr & Eur.

Diccionario Maritimo Ilustrado Vasco-Castellano, Castellano-Vasco. Ignacio de Garmendia y Berasategui. (SPA.). 59.95 (*0-7859-0866-8*, S-50054) Fr & Eur.

Diccionario McGraw-Hill de Biologia. Ed. by Sybil P. Parker. 1992. text ed. 32.95 (*0-07-104155-9*) McGraw.

Diccionario McGraw-Hill de Computacion. Ed. by Sybil P. Parker. 1992. text ed. 32.95 (*0-07-104152-4*) McGraw.

Diccionario McGraw-Hill de Fisica. Ed. by Sybil P. Parker. 1992. text ed. 32.95 (*0-07-104157-5*) McGraw.

Diccionario McGraw-Hill de Ingenieria Electrica y Electronica. Ed. by Sybil P. Parker. 1992. text ed. 32.95 (*0-07-104153-2*) McGraw.

Diccionario McGraw-Hill de Ingenieria Mecanica. Ed. by Sybil P. Parker. 1992. text ed. 32.95 (*0-07-104154-0*) McGraw.

Diccionario McGraw-Hill de Quimica. Ed. by Sybil P. Parker. 1992. text ed. 32.95 (*0-07-104156-7*) McGraw.

Diccionario Medico. Salvat Staff. 738p. 1990. pap. 45.00 (*0-7859-5930-0*, 8434524775) Fr & Eur.

Diccionario Medico. 7th ed. Luigi Segatore & Gianangelo Poli. 1200p. (SPA.). 1982. write for info. (*0-7859-5104-0*) Fr & Eur.

Diccionario Medico: De Bosillo. 2nd deluxe ed. Prol. by Jose M. Mascaro Y Porcar. 632p. (SPA.). 1974. 39.95 (*0-8288-5997-3*, S13673) Fr & Eur.

Diccionario Medico: Medical Dictionary. F. Beer-Poitevin. 352p. (SPA.). 1979. 95.00 (*0-8288-4776-2*, S3751) Fr & Eur.

Diccionario Medico de Bolsillo. Salvat Staff. 640p. (SPA.). 1989. pap. 36.95 (*0-7859-5928-9*, 8434517892) Fr & Eur.

Diccionario Medico Dorland (Bolsillo) Dorland. 900p. 1988. pap. 45.00 (*0-7859-6243-3*, 8476152825) Fr & Eur.

Diccionario Medico Illustrado. 27th ed. Dorland. (Illus.). 1991. text ed. 55.00 (*0-07-104004-8*) McGraw.

Diccionario Medico Labor para la Familia. H. Mommsen. (SPA.). 1979. write for info. (*0-8288-4775-4*, S50063) Fr & Eur.

Diccionario Medico Labor para la Familia. 6th ed. H. Mommsen. 880p. (SPA.). 1982. 150.00 (*0-7859-5093-1*) Fr & Eur.

An Asterisk (*) at the beginning of an entry indicates that the title is appearing in BIP for the first time.

Diccionario Medico Practico Para el Hogar. Editorial America, S. A. Staff. Ed. by Maria E. Del Real. (Illus.). 384p. (SPA.). 1988. pap. 4.75 (*0-944499-32-5*) Editorial Amer.

Diccionario Medico Teide. Teide Staff. 660p. (SPA.). 1988. 39.95 (*0-7859-5893-2*, 8430780165) Fr & Eur.

Diccionario Medieval Espanol, 2 vols. Martin A. Pedraz. 784p. (SPA.). 1986. 150.00 (*0-7859-6213-1*, 8472991717) Fr & Eur.

Diccionario Medieval Espanol, Vol. 1. Damaso Alonso. 176p. 1991. pap. 12.95 (*0-7859-5143-1*) Fr & Eur.

Diccionario Medieval Espanol, Vol. 2. 3rd ed. Damaso Alonso. 216p. 1991. pap. 12.95 (*0-7859-5144-X*) Fr & Eur.

Diccionario Militar, 2 vols., Set. Jose Almirante. 700p. (SPA.). 1988. pap. 55.00 (*0-7859-6497-5*, 847823005X); pap. 105.00 (*0-7859-6315-4*, 8478230033) Fr & Eur.

Diccionario Militar, Vol. 1. Jose Almirante. 600p. (SPA.). 1988. pap. 55.00 (*0-7859-6316-2*, 8478230041) Fr & Eur.

Diccionario Militar, Vol. 1. Abel A. Hernandez. 1728p. (SPA.). 1986. 250.00 (*0-7859-6126-7*, 8471305151) Fr & Eur.

Diccionario Militar, Vol. 2. Martin A. Pedraz. 1712p. (SPA.). 1986. 295.00 (*0-7859-6211-5*, 8472991695) Fr & Eur.

Diccionario Militar Espanol-Ruso, Ruso-Espanol. deluxe ed. 632p. (ENG, RUS & SPA.). 1965. 39.95 (*0-8288-6737-2*, S-31871) Fr & Eur.

Diccionario Militar Estrategico & Politico. Fernando De Bordeje Morencos. 199p. (SPA.). 1981. pap. 24.95 (*0-8288-1913-0*, S60466) Fr & Eur.

***Diccionario Mini: Espanol-Ingles - English-Spanish.** Ed. by Espasa-Harrap's Staff. (Espasa de Bolsillo Ser.). 640p. 1994. 24.95x (*84-239-5996-1*) Elliots Bks.

Diccionario Mini Sopena Ingles-Espanol. Sopena Staff. 320p. (ENG & SPA.). 1975. pap. 5.95 (*0-8288-5831-4*, S50398) Fr & Eur.

Diccionario Mitilogico. Francisco C. Yarza. 304p. 1991. pap. 14.95 (*0-7859-6491-6*) Fr & Eur.

Diccionario Mitologia Griega & Romana. Dorothea Coenen. 256p. 1984. 16.95 (*0-7859-5739-1*) Fr & Eur.

Diccionario Mitologico. A. Gavalda. 900p. (SPA.). 49.95 (*0-7859-0806-4*, S-37663) Fr & Eur.

Diccionario Mitologico. C. Gaytan. (SPA.). 14.95 (*0-7859-0702-5*, S-25775) Fr & Eur.

Diccionario Moderno. 9th ed. Ed. by Maria E. Alvarez del Real. LC 83-80788. (Illus.). 640p. (ENG & SPA.). 1983. pap. text ed. 4.50 (*0-944499-05-8*) Editorial Amer.

Diccionario Moderno. 10th rev. ed. Ed. by Maria E. Alvarez del Real. 640p. (SPA.). (C). Date not set. pap. 4.50 (*0-944499-99-6*) Editorial Amer.

Diccionario Moderno de Sinonimos y Contrarios. 2nd ed. Jose M. Erro. 256p. (SPA.). 1989. pap. 16.95 (*0-7859-5898-3*, 8431500352) Fr & Eur.

Diccionario Moderno Espanol-Ingles. Ramon Garcia-Palayo Gross. 984p. 1989. 65.00 (*0-7859-6412-6*, 8487227082) Fr & Eur.

Diccionario Moderno Herder Aleman-Espanol, Espanol-Aleman: Herder Modern German-Spanish, Spanish-German Dictionary. 2nd ed. Gunther Haensch. 684p. (GER & SPA.). 1982. write for info. (*0-7859-5066-4*) Fr & Eur.

Diccionario Moderno Larousse Espanol-Ingles, English-Spanish. Ramon Garcia-Pelayo. 1992p. (ENG & SPA.). 1976. 39.95 (*0-8288-5616-8*, F48340) Fr & Eur.

Diccionario Monografico de Bellas Artes. deluxe ed. Vox Staff. (SPA.). 1979. 19.95 (*0-8288-4777-0*, S36147) Fr & Eur.

Diccionario Monografico de Medicina y Salud: Monographic Dictionary of Medicine & Health. deluxe ed. Ed. by Vox Staff. (SPA.). 1979. 24.95 (*0-8288-4778-9*, S36145) Fr & Eur.

Diccionario Monografico del Reino Animal: Monographic Dictionary of the Animal Kingdom. Vox Staff. 286p. 1980. 29.95 (*0-8288-2391-X*, S32725) Fr & Eur.

Diccionario Monografico Vox de Tecnologia: Vox Monographic Dictionary of Technology. Vox Staff. 320p. (SPA.). 1980. 249.95 (*0-8288-2146-1*, S36145) Fr & Eur.

Diccionario Monografico Vox del Reino Vegetal: Vox Monographic Dictionary of the Plant Kingdom. Vox Staff. 288p. (SPA.). 1980. 29.95 (*0-8288-1247-0*, S2553) Fr & Eur.

Diccionario Multilingue CD-ROM. Anaya Staff. 36p. (SPA.). 1988. 1,895.00 (*0-7859-5735-9*, 8420729876) Fr & Eur.

Diccionario Multiple. 4th ed. Onieva. (SPA.). 1987. write for info. (*0-7859-3678-5*, 8428304009) Fr & Eur.

Diccionario Nautico: Nautical Dictionary. deluxe ed. Jose M. Martinez Hidalgo Teran. 540p. (ENG, FRE & SPA.). 1977. 125.00 (*0-8288-5356-8*, S50095) Fr & Eur.

Diccionario Naval: Ingles-Espanol, Espanol-Ingles. 4th ed. Luis L. Leal. 232p. (ENG & SPA.). 1987. pap. 39.95 (*0-7859-3679-3*, S38405) Fr & Eur.

Diccionario Onomastico y Heraldico Vasco, Vol. 5. Jaime Querexeta Gallostequi. 288p. (SPA.). 1974. 79.95 (*0-8288-5998-1*, S50375) Fr & Eur.

Diccionario Oriente, 4 vols., Set. Porrua Staff. (SPA.). 350.00 (*0-7859-0432-8*, S33078) Fr & Eur.

Diccionario Ortografico Iter. Iter. 640p. (SPA.). 1978. pap. 18.95 (*0-8288-5146-8*, S50142) Fr & Eur.

***Diccionario Ortografico Iter.** Iter. 528p. 1984. pap. write for info. (*0-7859-5046-X*) Fr & Eur.

Diccionario Ortografico Mikron. 51th ed. Plans y de Gabriel Sanz de Bremond, Fructuoso Staff. 640p. (SPA.). 1978. 9.95 (*0-8288-5147-6*, S50033) Fr & Eur.

Diccionario para Crucigramas. Ed. by Maria E. Alvarez del Real. 384p. (Orig.). (SPA.). 1986. pap. 4.00 (*0-944499-15-5*) Editorial Amer.

Diccionario Para Crucigramas. 3rd rev. ed. Editorial America, S. A. Staff. Ed. by Maria E. Del Real. (Illus.). 384p. (SPA.). 1990. pap. write for info. (*0-944499-74-0*) Editorial Amer.

Diccionario para Ingenieros y Tecnicos Frances-Espanol-Frances. Luis Carcamo. 1106p. (FRE & SPA.). 195.00 (*0-8288-0671-3*, S2560) Fr & Eur.

Diccionario para Obras Publica, Edificacion y Maquinaria en Obra. Bucksch. 1116p. (GER & SPA.). 1976. 150.00 (*0-8288-5617-6*, S50187) Fr & Eur.

***Diccionario Plus: Espanol-Ingles - English-Spanish.** Ed. by Espasa-Harrap's Staff. (Espasa de Bolsillo Ser.). 840p. 1994. 34.95x (*84-239-5997-X*) Elliots Bks.

***Diccionario Pocket: Espanol-Frances - Frances-Espanol.** Ed. by Espasa-Harrap's Staff. 606p. (SPA.). 1994. 34.95x (*84-239-5998-8*) Elliots Bks.

***Diccionario Pocket: Espanol-Ingles - English-Spanish.** Espasa-Harrap's Staff. (Espasa de Bolsillo Ser.). 640p. 1994. 29.95x (*84-239-5995-3*) Elliots Bks.

Diccionario Politico. 6th ed. Eduardo Haro Tecglen. 288p. (SPA.). 1977. pap. 9.95 (*0-8288-5357-6*, S50024) Fr & Eur.

Diccionario Politico para Occidente. Antonio Marquez Bessa. 288p. (SPA.). 1978. pap. 14.95 (*0-8288-5149-2*, S50003) Fr & Eur.

Diccionario por Fechas de Historia Universal. 3rd ed. Christfried Coler. 480p. (SPA.). 1985. write for info. (*0-7859-5067-2*) Fr & Eur.

Diccionario Porrua de la Lengua Espanola. Antonio Raluy Poudevila. Ed. by Francisco Monterde. (SPA.). pap. 10.95 (*0-686-56694-7*, S-12281) Fr & Eur.

Diccionario Porrua de la Lengua Espanola Para Escuelas Primarias. Antonio Raluy Poudevila. Ed. by Francisco Monterde. 461p. (SPA.). pap. 8.95 (*0-7859-0712-2*, S-12282) Fr & Eur.

Diccionario Portugues-Espanol, Espanol-Portugues, 2 vols., Set. David Ortega Cavero. 1856p. (POR & SPA.). 1975. 175.00 (*0-8288-5832-2*, S12405) Fr & Eur.

Diccionario Practico: Asesor de la Propiedad & Copropiedad Inmobiliaria. Jose M. Plans Sanz De Bremond. 392p. (SPA.). 1975. pap. 24.95 (*0-7859-0649-5*, S50138) Fr & Eur.

Diccionario Practico de la Lengua Espanola del Nuevo Mundo: Practical Dictionary of the Spanish. Passport Books Staff. 1993. 9.95 (*0-8442-7968-4*, Passport Bks) NTC Pub Grp.

Diccionario Practico de Psicopatologia. Yves Poinso. 324p. (SPA.). 1976. 29.95 (*0-8288-5618-4*, S50194); pap. 29.95 (*0-8288-5619-2*, S50186) Fr & Eur.

Diccionario Practico Easa de la Lengua Espanola. 5th ed. Ed. by Maria E. Alvarez del Real. LC 81-72102. (Illus.). 800p. (ENG & SPA.). 1986. pap. 5.00 (*0-944499-04-X*) Editorial Amer.

Diccionario Pratico Espanol-Ingles. Ramon Garcia-Palayo Gross. 640p. 1989. pap. 18.95 (*0-7859-6414-2*, 8487227120) Fr & Eur.

Diccionario Pratico Frances-Espanol. Ramon Garcia-Palayo Gross. 640p. 1989. pap. 16.95 (*0-7859-6413-4*, 8487227112) Fr & Eur.

Diccionario Pratico Russo-Portugues. deluxe ed. N. Voinova & S. Starets. 643p. (POR & RUS.). 1964. 14.95 (*0-8288-6760-7*, M-9098) Fr & Eur.

Diccionario Pschyrembel de Ginecologia y Obstetricia. (Illus.). xii, 295p. (SPA.). 1988. lib. bdg. 52.35x (*0-89925-534-5*) De Gruyter.

Diccionario Punto Frances. Everest Staff. 592p. 1990. pap. 8.95 (*0-7859-5763-4*) Fr & Eur.

Diccionario Punto Ingles-Epsanol, Espanol-Ingles. Everest Staff. 448p. 1991. pap. 8.95 (*0-7859-5761-8*) Fr & Eur.

Diccionario Rapanui-Espanol, Redactado en la Isla de Pascua. Sebastian Englert. LC 75-35191. (SPA.). reprint ed. 20.00 (*0-404-14219-2*) AMS Pr.

Diccionario Razonado de Sinonimos y Contrarios. 2nd ed. Jose M. Erro. 752p. (SPA.). 1991. write for info. (*0-7859-5068-0*) Fr & Eur.

Diccionario Religioso Para los Hombres De Hoy. Josep Vilaro et al. 260p. (SPA.). 1976. pap. 12.95 (*0-8288-5620-6*, S50025) Fr & Eur.

Diccionario Retana de Autoridades de la Lengua Vasca, 2. Manuel De Sota Aburto. 1976. 105.00 (*0-7859-5775-8*) Fr & Eur.

Diccionario Retana de Autoridades de la Lengua Vasca, 3. Manuel De Sota Aburto. 1976. 105.00 (*0-7859-5776-6*) Fr & Eur.

Diccionario Retana de Autoridades de la Lengua Vasca, 4 vols., Set. deluxe ed. Manuel de Sota Aburto. (BAQ & SPA.). 1976. 395.00 (*0-8288-5621-4*, S50053) Fr & Eur.

Diccionario Retana De Autoridades De la Lengua Vasca, Vol. 4. Manuel De Sota Aburto. 512p. 1977. 105.00 (*0-7859-6450-9*) Fr & Eur.

Diccionario Rioduero: Arte, Vol. 1. Ursula Boeing-Haeusgen. 312p. (SPA.). 1978. pap. 14.95 (*0-8288-5153-0*, S50170) Fr & Eur.

Diccionario Rioduero: Biologia. 3rd ed. Rainer Bergfeld. 244p. (SPA.). 1982. pap. write for info. (*0-7859-5070-2*) Fr & Eur.

Diccionario Rioduero: Fisica. 2nd ed. Rolf Sauermost. 256p. (SPA.). 1979. write for info. (*0-7859-5094-X*) Fr & Eur.

Diccionario Rioduero: Fisica del Espacio: Astro-Physics. Udo Becker. 264p. (SPA.). 1978. pap. 14.95 (*0-8288-5152-2*, S50163) Fr & Eur.

Diccionario Rioduero: Geografia. 2nd ed. Margit Klein & Johannes Klein. (SPA.). 1977. 35.00 (*0-8288-5363-0*, S50173) Fr & Eur.

Diccionario Rioduero: Geologia y Mineralogia. 2nd deluxe ed. Catolica Editorial Staff. (SPA.). 1978. 35.00 (*0-8288-5151-4*, S50168) Fr & Eur.

Diccionario Rioduero: Literatura, Vol. 1. Peter Mueller. 304p. (SPA.). 1977. 14.95 (*0-8288-5360-6*, S50164) Fr & Eur.

Diccionario Rioduero: Paises de la Tierra. Johannes Klein. 296p. (SPA.). 1978. 35.00 (*0-8288-5154-9*, S50165) Fr & Eur.

Diccionario Rioduero: Quimica. 3rd ed. Peter Ottokar. 272p. (SPA.). 1982. write for info. (*0-7859-5071-0*) Fr & Eur.

Diccionario Rioduero: Zoologia. Catolica Editorial Staff. 432p. (SPA.). 1979. 35.00 (*0-8288-4780-0*, S50171) Fr & Eur.

Diccionario Rioduero, Arte, Vol. 2. Ursula Boeing-Haeusgen. 352p. (SPA.). 1980. pap. 14.95 (*0-7859-5737-5*, 8422009331) Fr & Eur.

Diccionario Rioduero Literatura, Vol. 2. Udo Mueller. 352p. (SPA.). 1978. 14.95 (*0-7859-5750-2*, 8422008602) Fr & Eur.

Diccionario Rioduero Matematica. 2nd ed. Jurgen Reck. 224p. (SPA.). 1982. write for info. (*0-7859-5069-9*) Fr & Eur.

Diccionario Rioduero Pedagogia. Bjorn Kaluza. 240p. 1980. 12.95 (*0-7859-5738-3*) Fr & Eur.

Diccionario Ruso-Espanol. Lorenzo Martinez Calvo. 2000p. (RUS & SPA.). 75.00 (*0-7859-0884-6*, S-50410) Fr & Eur.

Diccionario Ruso-Espanol: Russian-Spanish Dictionary. deluxe ed. J. Nogueira & G. Turover. 956p. (RUS & SPA.). 1979. 39.95 (*0-8288-4781-9*, S33593) Fr & Eur.

Diccionario Sinonimos-Antonimos, Ideas Afines, Paronimos. Sopena Staff. 640p. (SPA.). 1990. 31.95 (*0-7859-5887-8*, 8430310932) Fr & Eur.

Diccionario Sinonimos y Antonimos. 11th ed. 638p. (SPA.). 1993. 20.00 (*84-241-1501-5*) IBD Ltd.

Diccionario Sopena De Literatura, 3 vols., Set. Parnaso. 1820p. (SPA.). 150.00 (*0-7859-0886-2*, S-50140) Fr & Eur.

Diccionario Susaeta. Susaeta Staff. 96p. (SPA.). 1982. pap. 9.95 (*0-8288-1514-3*, S25795) Fr & Eur.

Diccionario Tacana-Castellano Castellano-Tacana. Aida B. De Ottaviano & Juan Ottaviano. viii, 233p. (Orig.). (SPA.). 1989. fiche 16.00 (*0-88312-722-9*) Summer Instit Ling.

Diccionario Tecnico de la Construccion, Edificacion y Obras Publicas Frances-Espanol y Espanol-Frances. M. Machado. 576p. (FRE & SPA.). 1969. 59.95 (*0-8288-6577-9*, S-50242) Fr & Eur.

Diccionario Tecnico de la Industria del Petroleo y Derivados: Technical Dictionary of Petroleum & Petroleum Products Industry. A. Mendez. 588p. (ENG, FRE & SPA.). 1980. 95.00 (*0-8288-0715-9*, S37582) Fr & Eur.

Diccionario Tecnico de la Plasticos Aleman-Espanol: Technical Dictionary of Plastics, German - Spanish. Annemarie Wittfoht & M. A. Achon. 544p. (GER & SPA.). 1970. 125.00 (*0-8288-6501-9*, S-50005) Fr & Eur.

Diccionario Tecnico de Terminologia Comercial Cantable y Bancaria. Jaime Garza Bores. (SPA.). 19.95 (*0-7859-0707-6*, S-25235) Fr & Eur.

Diccionario Tecnico del Agua: Technical Dictionary of Water. Jose Catalan Lafuente. 301p. (SPA.). 1977. pap. 39.95 (*0-8288-5365-7*, S50098) Fr & Eur.

Diccionario Tecnico Espanol-Aleman-Espanol. 6th ed. Herman Mink. 1560p. 1989. 195.00 (*0-8288-2143-7*, S50189) Fr & Eur.

Diccionario Tecnico Espanol-Frances. Hermann Mink. 1356p. (FRE & SPA.). 1988. 195.00 (*0-7859-5825-8*, 8425414814) Fr & Eur.

Diccionario Tecnico Espanol-Frances: Spanish-French Technical Dictionary. deluxe ed. Guy Malgorn. (FRE & SPA.). 1979. write for info. (*0-8288-4782-7*, S50241) Fr & Eur.

Diccionario Tecnico Espanol-Ingles. 5th ed. Guy Malgorn. 576p. (ENG & SPA.). 1990. pap. write for info. (*0-7859-4906-2*) Fr & Eur.

Diccionario Tecnico Frances-Espanol: French - Spanish Technical Dictionary. L. Malcolm. 544p. (FRE & SPA.). 1973. 39.95 (*0-8288-6242-7*, S-31563) Fr & Eur.

***Diccionario Tecnico Frances-Espanol (French-Spanish Technical Dictionary)** 3rd ed. Hermann Mink. 1152p. (FRE & SPA.). 1989. write for info. (*0-7859-5028-1*) Fr & Eur.

Diccionario Tecnico Hostelero. Fernando Molina Aranda. 245p. (SPA.). 1972. pap. 19.95 (*0-8288-6365-2*, S-50021) Fr & Eur.

Diccionario Tecnico Ilustrado de Edificacion y Obras Publicas: Technical Dictionary of Construction & Public Works. Maurice Barbier et al. 177p. (SPA.). 1981. pap. 29.95 (*0-8288-1327-2*, S50273) Fr & Eur.

Diccionario Tecnico Informatica y Electronica. 2nd ed. Juan L. Garcia. 640p. 1987. 19.95 (*0-7859-6395-2*, 8486367034) Fr & Eur.

Diccionario Tecnico Ingles-Espanol. 7th ed. Guy Malgorn. 632p. (ENG & SPA.). 1991. pap. 34.95 (*0-7859-3715-3*, 842830923X) Fr & Eur.

***Diccionario Tecnico Ingles-Portuguese de Maquinas e Ferramentas.** J. A. Martins. 229p. (ENG & POR.). 1983. 35.00 (*0-7859-7152-1*) Fr & Eur.

Diccionario Tecnico Militar. A. de Urquia Gomez. 372p. (ENG & SPA.). 1980. pap. 39.95 (*0-8288-1912-2*, S50129) Fr & Eur.

Diccionario Tecnico, Tomo 1: Aleman-Espanol. 8th ed. Herman Mink. 1908p. (GER & SPA.). 1991. 225.00 (*0-8288-5157-3*, S50190) Fr & Eur.

Diccionario Tecnico Vol. 2 Espanol-Aleman. 7th ed. Hermann Mink. 1560p. 1991. 195.00 (*0-7859-5819-3*) Fr & Eur.

Diccionario Tecnologico: Maquinaria y Equipos Agricoles. Cemagref Staff. 1295p. 1990. pap. 325.00 (*0-7859-6124-0*, 8471142805) Fr & Eur.

Diccionario Tecnologico de Salud Publica Veterinaria. Laureano Saez Moreno. 166p. 1990. pap. 21.95 (*0-7859-6219-0*, 8473600975) Fr & Eur.

Diccionario Tecnologico del Plasticos. 160p. (SPA.). 1978. 49.95 (*0-8288-5159-X*, S50059) Fr & Eur.

Diccionario Tecnologico Ingles-Espanol. 3rd ed. Francisco Franco Ibeas. 600p. (ENG & SPA.). 1989. pap. write for info. (*0-7859-4905-4*) Fr & Eur.

Diccionario Tematico de Agricultura y Ciencias Afines. Maria J. Gozalo. 618p. 1990. pap. 105.00 (*0-7859-6125-9*, 8471143127) Fr & Eur.

Diccionario Tematico de Antropologia. Angel Aguirre. 694p. (SPA.). 1989. pap. 59.95 (*0-7859-6253-0*, S60822) Fr & Eur.

Diccionario Tematico de Antropologia. Manuel A. Quintillan. 316p. (SPA.). 1985. 49.95 (*0-8288-1285-3*, S60822) Fr & Eur.

Diccionario Tematico de Sinomimos y Antonimos. Everest Staff. 640p. 1991. pap. 19.95 (*0-7859-5769-3*) Fr & Eur.

Diccionario Tematico Ingles-Espanol, Espanol-Ingles. 2nd ed. Jose M. Bustamante. 448p. (ENG & SPA.). 1990. pap. 35.00 (*0-7859-3698-X*, S31559) Fr & Eur.

Diccionario Teologico del Antiguo Testamento: Theological Dictionary of the Old Testament, 4 vols., Set. G. Johannes Botterweck. 1116p. (SPA.). 1978. 450.00 (*0-8288-5161-1*, S50106) Fr & Eur.

Diccionario Teologico Manual del Antiguo Testamento, Vol. 1. Ernst Jenni. 642p. 1978. 85.00 (*0-7859-6108-9*, 8470572415) Fr & Eur.

Diccionario Teologico Manual del Antiguo Testamento, Vol. 2. Ernst Jenni. 734p. 1985. 85.00 (*0-7859-6109-7*, 8470573713) Fr & Eur.

Diccionario Teologico Manual del Antiguo Testamento: Theological Dictionary of the Old Testament, 2 vols. Ernst Jenni. 1397p. (SPA.). 1985. 150.00 (*0-7859-5047-8*) Fr & Eur.

Diccionario Teorico y Practico del Juicio de Amparo. Eduardo Pallares. 321p. (SPA.). 24.95 (*0-7859-0717-3*, S-21916) Fr & Eur.

Diccionario Terminologia Politica. Thierrey Maulmier. 340p. (SPA.). 1977. pap. 19.95 (*0-8288-5366-5*, S50250) Fr & Eur.

Diccionario Terminologico de Ciencias Medicas. Cientificas y Tecnic Staff. 1424p. 1991. 150.00 (*0-7859-6042-2*, 8445800701) Fr & Eur.

Diccionario Terminologico de Ciencias Medicas: Terminological Dictionary of the Medical Sciences. 13th ed. Salvat Staff. 1088p. (SPA.). 1978. 250.00 (*0-7859-5048-6*) Fr & Eur.

Diccionario Terminologico De Economia, Comercio y Derecho, 2 vols., Set. Emilio G. Castro. 1768p. 1990. 595.00 (*0-7859-6423-1*, 8487532020) Fr & Eur.

Diccionario Terminologico De Economia, Comercio y Derecho, Vol. 1. Emilio G. Castro. 1768p. 1990. 395.00 (*0-7859-6421-5*, 8487532004) Fr & Eur.

Diccionario Terminologico De Economia, Comercio y Derecho, Vol. 2. Emilio G. Castro. 900p. 1990. 300.00 (*0-7859-6422-3*) Fr & Eur.

Diccionario Terminologico De Medios De Communicacion: Ingles-Espanol. Florencio Prieto. 400p. 1991. pap. 55.00 (*0-7859-6392-8*, 8486168627) Fr & Eur.

Diccionario Terminologico de Minas, Canteras y Mineralurgia. Laureano Fueyo Cuesta. 272p. (SPA.). 1973. 24.95 (*0-8288-6243-5*, S-50112) Fr & Eur.

Diccionario Terminologico de Quimica. 2nd ed. Jose R. Matutano. 786p. (ENG, GER & SPA.). 1982. pap. 105.00 (*0-7859-5095-8*) Fr & Eur.

Diccionario Turistico de Cataluna, Baleares y Andora. deluxe ed. J. Munso. 693p. (SPA.). 1975. 125.00 (*0-8288-5835-7*, S32722) Fr & Eur.

Diccionario Tzotzil de San Andres con variaciones dialectales. Agustin R. Sanchez. (Vocabularios Indigenas Ser.: No. 22). (Illus.). 481p. (Orig.). 1978. fiche 20.00x (*0-88312-372-X*) Summer Instit Ling.

Diccionario UNESCO de Ciencias Sociales, Vol. 1. Planeta Staff. 624p. 1987. 29.95 (*0-7859-6009-0*, 8439506619) Fr & Eur.

Diccionario UNESCO de Ciencias Sociales, Vol. 2. Planeta Staff. 592p. 1988. 29.95 (*0-7859-6010-4*, 8439506627) Fr & Eur.

Diccionario UNESCO de Ciencias Sociales, Vol. 3. Planeta Staff. 616p. 1988. 29.95 (*0-7859-6011-2*, 8439506635) Fr & Eur.

Diccionario UNESCO de Ciencias Sociales, Vol. 4. Planeta Staff. 568p. 1988. 29.95 (*0-7859-6012-0*, 8439506643) Fr & Eur.

Diccionario Universal del Arte y de los Artistas: Pintores: Universal Dictionary of Art & Artists: Painters, 3 vols., Set. 934p. (SPA.). 1970. 89.85 (*0-8288-6502-7*, S-50287) Fr & Eur.

Diccionario Universal del Arte y de los Artistas: Arquitectos: Universal Dictionary of Art & Artists: Architects. 323p. (SPA.). 1970. 29.95 (*0-8288-6503-5*, S-50282) Fr & Eur.

Diccionario Universal del Arte y de los Artistas: Arte Occidental y del Proximo Oriente, I: Universal Dictionary of Art & Artists; Western & Near Eastern Art. 300p. (SPA.). 1969. 29.95 (*0-8288-6581-7*, S-50285) Fr & Eur.

Diccionario Universal del Arte y de los Artistas: Arte Occidental y del Proximo Oriente, II: Universal Dictionary of Art & Artists; Western & Near Eastern Art. 300p. (SPA.). 1969. 29.95 (*0-8288-6580-9*, S-50284) Fr & Eur.

Diccionario Universal del Arte y de los Artistas: Arte Oriental, Precolombino y de los Pueblos Primitivos: Universal Dictionary of Art; Oriental, Pre-Columbian & the Art of Primitive Peoples. 315p. (SPA.). 1969. 29.95 (*0-8288-6578-7*, S-50286) Fr & Eur.

Diccionario Universal del Arte y de los Artistas: Escultores: Universal Dictionary of Art & Artists: Sculptors. 301p. (SPA.). 1970. 29.95 (*0-8288-6507-8*, S-50281) Fr & Eur.

D

An Asterisk (*) at the beginning of an entry indicates that the title is appearing in BIP for the first time.

1953

Diccionario Universal del Arte y de los Artistas: Estilos y Tendencias En el Arte Occidental: Universal Dictionary of Art & Artists, Styles & Tendencies in Western Art. 320p. (SPA.). 1969. 29.95 (*0-8288-6579-5*, S-50283) Fr & Eur.

Diccionario Universal del Arte y los Artistas: Universal Dictionary of Art & Artists, 9 vols., Set. Juan-Eduardo C. Cirlot. 2794p. (SPA.). 1969. 229.50 (*0-8288-6582-5*) Fr & Eur.

Diccionario Universal Herder Aleman-Espanol, Espanol-Aleman: Universal Herder German-Spanish, Spanish-German Dictionary. 4th deluxe ed. Herder Staff. 388p. (GER & SPA.). 1977. 7.95 (*0-8288-5367-3*, S50378) Fr & Eur.

Diccionario Universal Herder de la Lengua Espanola. Herder Staff. 460p. (SPA.). 1975. pap. 7.95 (*0-8288-5836-5*, S50195) Fr & Eur.

Diccionario Universal Herder Frances-Espanol, Espanol-Frances: Universal Herder French-Spanish, Spanish-French Dictionary. 5th deluxe ed. Herder Staff. 368p. (FRE & SPA.). 1977. 7.95 (*0-8288-5368-1*, S12394) Fr & Eur.

Diccionario Universal Herder Holandes-Espanol y Holandes-Espanol. Herder Staff. 264p. 1990. pap. 10.95 (*0-7859-5820-7*) Fr & Eur.

Diccionario Universal Herder Ingles-Espanol y Espanol-Ingles. Herder Staff. 340p. 1990. pap. 10.95 (*0-7859-5821-5*) Fr & Eur.

Diccionario Universal Herder Italiano-Espanol, Espanol-Italiano. Herder Staff. 368p. 1990. pap. 10.95 (*0-7859-5818-5*) Fr & Eur.

Diccionario Vasco-Castellano. 6th ed. Isaak Lopez Mendizabal. 452p. 1976. 49.95 (*0-8288-5624-9*, S50439) Fr & Eur.

Diccionario Vasco-Castellano: Basque-Spanish Dictionary, 2 vols., Set. P. Mukjika. (BAQ & SPA.). 1991. 195.00 (*0-8288-7253-8*, 8427112696) Fr & Eur.

Diccionario Vasco-Castellano, Castellano-Vasco: Basque-Spanish, Spanish-Basque Dictionary. 2nd ed. J. L. Arriaga. (BAQ & SPA.). 1991. 24.95 (*0-8288-7254-6*, 8427113943) Fr & Eur.

Diccionario Vasco-Castellano, Castellano-Vasco de Voces Comunes a Dos o Mas Dialectos del Euskera. Aberlaitz & P. Buenaventura De Oreyegui. (SPA.). 14.95 (*0-7859-0865-X*, S3099) Fr & Eur.

Diccionario Vasco-Espanol-Frances, 2 vols., Set. deluxe ed. Resurreccion M. Azkue. (FRE & SPA.). 195.00 (*0-7859-0952-4*, S12384) Fr & Eur.

Diccionario Visual Altea del Cuerpo Humano. Equipo Dorling Staff. 64p. 1992. pap. 45.00 (*0-7859-5997-1*, 8437245184) Fr & Eur.

Diccionario Vox Esencial Castella-Catala, Catala-Castella. Vox Staff. 608p. 1991. pap. 19.95 (*0-7859-6149-6*, 8471531682) Fr & Eur.

Diccionario Vox Esencial Frances-Espanol, Espanol-Frances. Vox Staff. 608p. 1991. pap. 19.95 (*0-7859-6148-8*, 8471531674) Fr & Eur.

Diccionario Vox Harrap's Manual Ingles-Espanol, Espanol-Ingles. Vox Staff. 1448p. 1991. 19.95 (*0-7859-6483-5*) Fr & Eur.

Diccionario Zen. E. Wood. 190p. (SPA.). 1980. pap. 24.95 (*0-8288-2202-6*, S32724) Fr & Eur.

Diccionarios del Saber Moderno: La Politica en Su Entorno Historico Actual. J. Ontza. 671p. (SPA.). 1980. 45.00 (*0-8288-2269-7*, S35606) Fr & Eur.

Diccionarios del Saber Moderno: La Pedagogia: Dictionaries of Modern Knowledge; Pedagogy. 2nd ed. H. Cormary et al. 580p. (SPA.). 1980. 59.95 (*0-8288-1398-1*, S35605) Fr & Eur.

Diccionarios Rioduero: Sociologia. W. Strobl. 278p. (SPA.). 1980. 17.95 (*0-8288-2368-5*, S 35929) Fr & Eur.

Dice & Dots: A Book of Mathematical Games. Michael Sentlowitz & Margaret Trivisone. 1988. pap. 12.50 (*0-201-06982-2*) Addison-Wesley.

Dice Games New & Old. William E. Tredd. (Games & Pastimes Ser.: Vol. 3). (Illus.). 64p. 1981. 9.95 (*0-906672-00-7*); pap. 4.95 (*0-906672-01-5*) Oleander Pr.

Dice Playing God: Reflections on Life in a Post-Modern Age. Werner Krieglstein. 264p. (Orig.). (C). 1991. lib. bdg. 48.00 (*0-8191-8091-2*); pap. text ed. 28.50 (*0-8191-8092-0*) U Pr of Amer.

Dicey's Song. Cynthia Voigt. 1987. pap. 3.95 (*0-449-70276-6*, Juniper) Fawcett.

Dicey's Song. Cynthia Voigt. LC 82-3882. 204p. (YA). (gr. 6 up). 1982. text ed. 15.95 (*0-689-30944-9*, Atheneum Bks Young) S&S Childrens.

Dicey's Song: A Literature Unit. Mari L. Robbins. (Literature Units Ser.). (Illus.). 48p. (Orig.). 1993. student ed, pap. 6.95 (*1-55734-422-1*) Tchr Create Mat.

Dicey's Song: A Study Guide. Suzann Morin. (Novel-Ties Ser.). (gr. 6-10). 1987. student ed, teacher ed 15.95 (*0-88122-112-0*) Lrn Links.

Dicha De Ganar Ninos Para Cris. Frank Coleman. 204p. (SPA.). 1990. 6.95 (*0-8297-1220-8*) Life Pubs Intl.

Dicha De Ser Mujer (Joy of Being a Woman) Ingrid Trobisch. (SPA.). 1990. reprint ed. 3.25 (*0-8423-6345-9*, 490245) Editorial Unilit.

Dicha Merecida: A Happiness Deserved. Quero De Tossini. (SPA.). 5.50 (*84-7228-605-3*, 220924, Pub. by Edit Clie SP) TSELF.

Dichapetalaceae & Rhabdodendraceae. Ghillean T. Prance. LC 73-180015. (Flora Neotropica Monograph Ser.: No. 10-11). (Illus.). 106p. (Orig.). 1972. pap. 13.95 (*0-89327-293-0*) NY Botanical.

Dicho y Hecho. Laila M. Dawson & Albert C. Dawson. LC 88-20784. 480p. 1989. Net. text ed. write for info. (*0-471-63136-1*); Net. audio write for info. (*0-471-50247-2*) Wiley.

***Dicho y Hecho.** 4th ed. Laila M. Dawson & lbert C. Dawson. 1994. audio, text ed. write for info. (*0-471-07675-9*) Wiley.

Dicho y Hecho: Beginning Spanish. 4th ed. Laila M. Dawson & Albert C. Dawson. 576p. (C). 1993. Net. text ed. write for info. (*0-471-57385-X*) Wiley.

***Dicho y Hecho: Beginning Spanish.** 4th ed. Laila M. Dawson & Albert C. Dawson. 1994. text ed. 0.01 (*0-471-07655-4*) Wiley.

***Dicho y Hecho: Text & Cassette Set.** 4th ed. Laila M. Dawson & Albert C. Dawson. 1993. audio, text ed. write for info. (*0-471-03227-1*) Wiley.

Dichos: Sayings & Proverbs from the Spanish. rev. ed. Charles Aranda. LC 77-78611. (Illus.). 32p. (ENG & SPA.). 1983. pap. 4.95 (*0-913270-47-4*) Sunstone Pr.

Dichos, Retranes y Opiniones. Juan Amaro & Cindy Elder. Ed. & Illus. by John Culpepper. 40p. (Orig.). (ENG & SPA.). (C). 1989. pap. write for info. (*0-9624186-1-7*) Warm Days Retirement.

Dichotomy Project No. 18: Installation - Performance. Margot De Wit et al. (Illus.). 24p. (Orig.). 1989. write for info. (*0-318-65109-2*) M de Wit.

Dichroic Dyes for Liquid Crystal Displays. Aleksandr V. Ivashchenko. 1994. 225.00 (*0-8493-4886-2*, TK7872) CRC Pr.

Dichten & Denken der Dschagganeger. Bruno Gutmann. (B. E. Ser.: No. 121). (GER.). 1909. 21.00 (*0-8115-3049-3*) Periodicals Srv.

Dichter see Augustus der Dichter

Dichter, Denker und Erzahler: A German Reader. Peter Heller & Edith Ehrlich. 429p. (C). 1989. reprint ed. pap. text ed. 22.95 (*0-88133-432-4*) Waveland Pr.

Dichter-Helden in der DDR-Literatur der Siebziger Jahre. Wolfgang Mueller. (DDR-Studien - East German Studies: Vol. 5). 220p. (C). 1989. text ed. 40.95 (*0-8204-0897-2*) P Lang Pubs.

Dichterliebe. rev. ed. Robert Schumann. Ed. by Arthur Komar. (Critical Scores Ser.). (Illus.). 136p. (C). 1971. pap. text ed. 8.95 (*0-393-09904-0*) Norton.

Dichtkunst. Aristoteles. (Documenta Semiotica Serie 2). xx, 421p. (GER.). 1973. reprint ed. write for info. (*3-487-04767-5*, Pub. by Georg Olms GW) Lubrecht & Cramer.

Dichtkunst Virgils. 3rd rev. ed. Viktor Poeschl. (C). 1977. 46.15 (*3-11-006885-0*) De Gruyter.

Dichtung der Afrikaner. Carl Meinhof. (B. E. Ser.: No. 43). (GER.). 1911. 22.00 (*0-8115-2994-0*) Periodicals Srv.

Dichtungen. Johann Fischart. LC 78-168026. reprint ed. 22.00 (*0-404-02387-8*) AMS Pr.

Dicing for Pearls. Jeremy Reed. 38p. (Orig.). 1990. 25.00 (*1-870612-85-X*, Pub. by Enitha Pr UK); pap. 10.95 (*1-870612-80-9*, Pub. by Enitha Pr UK) Dufour.

Dicionario Alamao - Portugues - German - Portuguese Dictionary. Porto Editora Staff. 1991. 75.00 (*0-8288-8543-5*) Fr & Eur.

Dicionario Basico Ladino - Espanol: Basic Ladino - Spanish Dictionary. Pascal Recuero. 153p. (LAD & SPA.). 1977. pap. 29.95 (*0-8288-9419-1*, S36126) Fr & Eur.

Dicionario Cambridge de Fisica. Teresa Rickards. 256p. 1988. 39.95 (*0-7859-5812-6*) Fr & Eur.

Dicionario da Lingua Portuguesa. F. Fernandes. (POR.). write for info. (*0-318-56670-2*) Fr & Eur.

Dicionario Da Lingua Portuguesa. Porto Editora Staff. 591p. 1992. 29.95 (*0-8288-8529-X*) Fr & Eur.

Dicionario de Administracao de Recursos Humanos con Termos: Ingles-Portugues, Portugues-Ingles: English-Portuguese, Portuguese-English Dictionary of Human Resources Administration. F. Toledo & B. Milioni. 156p. (ENG & POR.). 1979. pap. 24.95 (*0-8288-4783-5*, M9356) Fr & Eur.

Dicionario de Bolso Portugues-Russo. I. Chalaguina. 343p. (POR & RUS.). 1976. 9.95 (*0-8288-5626-5*, M9103) Fr & Eur.

Dicionario de Bolso Russo-Portuguese. C. Nunes. 376p. (POR & RUS.). 1976. 9.95 (*0-8288-5627-3*, M9062) Fr & Eur.

Dicionario De Espanhol Portugues - Spanish - Portuguese Dictionary. Julio Martinez Almoyna. 1068p. (POR & SPA.). 1990. 75.00 (*0-8288-8541-9*) Fr & Eur.

Dicionario de Expressoes Idiomaticas; Locucoes Mas Usuais da Lingua Portuguesa. M. Pugliese. 309p. (POR.). 1981. pap. 14.95 (*0-8288-1996-3*, M14432) Fr & Eur.

Dicionario De Frances Portuges - French - Portuguese Dictionary. Olivio Da Costa Carvalho. 798p. 1991. 65.00 (*0-8288-8539-7*) Fr & Eur.

Dicionario de Ingles - Portugues, Portugues - Ingles. 13th ed. L. Vallandro. (ENG & POR.). 1989. write for info. (*85-250-0622-X*, M903) Fr & Eur.

Dicionario De Portugues Espanhol: Portuguese - Spanish Dictionary. Julio Martinez Almoyna. 1332p. (POR & SPA.). 1990. 75.00 (*0-8288-8540-0*) Fr & Eur.

Dicionario De Portugues Frances - Portuguese - French Dictionary. Olivio Da Costa Carvalho. 853p. 1991. 65.00 (*0-8288-8537-0*) Fr & Eur.

Dicionario De Sinonimos. Tertulia Edipica. 1125p. (POR.). 1990. 85.00 (*0-8288-8535-4*) Fr & Eur.

Dicionario de Sinonimos: Dictionary of Synonyms. 3rd ed. A. Nascentes. 485p. (POR.). 1981. 22.50 (*0-8288-1995-5*, M14429) Fr & Eur.

Dicionario de Sinonimos e Antonimos da Lingua Portuguesa: Dictionary of Synonyms & Antonyms of the Portuguese Language. 3rd ed. F. Fernandes & C. P. Luft. 870p. (POR.). 1980. 75.00 (*0-8288-1994-7*, M9321) Fr & Eur.

Dicionario de Termos Tecnicos Ingles-Portugues. 5th ed. Luiz M. Antas. (ENG & POR.). 1980. pap. 110.00 (*0-685-65229-7*, F11375) Fr & Eur.

Dicionario de Termos Tecnicos Ingles-Portugues: English-Portuguese Dictionary of Technical Terms, 2 vols., Set. 11th ed. E. Furstenau. 1157p. (ENG & POR.). 1980. 195.00 (*0-8288-0652-7*, M9211) Fr & Eur.

Dicionario de Termos Tecnicos Portugues-Ingles. 3rd ed. Luiz M. Antas. 335p. (ENG & POR.). 1991. pap. 75.00 (*0-7859-0346-1*, F60022) Fr & Eur.

Dicionario Dos Verbos Portugueses. E. Silva & A. Tavares. 848p. (POR.). 1992. 75.00 (*0-8288-8538-9*) Fr & Eur.

Dicionario Espanhol - Portugues, Portugues - Espanhol - Portuguese - Spanish, Span ish - Portuguese Dictionary. Porto Editora Staff. 1195p. 1990. 49.95 (*0-8288-8533-8*) Fr & Eur.

Dicionario Etimologico Nova Fronteira da Lingua Portuguesa: Etymological Dictionary of the Portuguese Language. A. Correia Da Cunha. 839p. 1982. 45.00 (*0-8288-1992-0*, M14426) Fr & Eur.

Dicionario Ingles - Portugues - English - Portuguese Dictionary. Porto Editora Staff. 1991. 75.00 (*0-8288-8542-7*) Fr & Eur.

Dicionario Ingles-Portugues: English-Portuguese Dictionary. L. Vallandro. 1174p. (ENG & POR.). 1979. 39.95 (*0-8288-4784-3*, M903) Fr & Eur.

Dicionario Ingles-Portugues, Portugues-Ingles: English-Portuguese, Portuguese-English Dictionary. L. Vallandro. 981p. (ENG & POR.). 1980. 95.00 (*0-8288-4688-X*, M9213) Fr & Eur.

Dicionario Italiano - Portugues - Italian - Portuguese Dictionary. Porto Editora Staff. 1991. 75.00 (*0-8288-8547-8*) Fr & Eur.

Dicionario Latim - Portugues - Latin - Portuguese Dictionary. Porto Editora Staff. 1991. 75.00 (*0-8288-8545-1*) Fr & Eur.

Dicionario Portugues - Alemao - Portuguese - German Dictionary. Porto Editora Staff. 1991. 75.00 (*0-8288-8544-3*) Fr & Eur.

Dicionario Portugues - Espanhol - Portuguese - Spanish Dictionary. Porto Editora Staff. 594p. 1989. 29.95 (*0-8288-8531-1*) Fr & Eur.

Dicionario Portugues - Frances - Portuguese French Dictionary. Porto Editora Staff. 652p. 1991. 29.95 (*0-8288-8530-3*) Fr & Eur.

Dicionario Portugues - Italiano - Portuguese - Italian Dictionary. Porto Editora Staff. 1991. 75.00 (*0-8288-8548-6*) Fr & Eur.

Dicionario Portugues - Latim - Portuguese - Latin Dictionary. Porto Editora Staff. 1991. 75.00 (*0-8288-8546-X*) Fr & Eur.

Dicionario Portugues-Ingles: Portuguese-English Dictionary. H. Aliandro. 311p. (ENG & POR.). 1980. pap. 12.95 (*0-8288-0490-7*, M9216) Fr & Eur.

Dicionario Romeno - Portugues - Romanian - Portuguese Dictionary. Porto Editora Staff. 1991. 75.00 (*0-8288-8549-4*) Fr & Eur.

Dicionario Sobre Comercio Esterior Portugues - Ingles - Portugues. 3rd ed. (ENG & POR.). 1990. pap. 95.00 (*0-7859-0908-7*, F91250) Fr & Eur.

Dicionario Tecnico Contabil - Portugues-Ingles, Ingles-Portugues: Portuguese-English, English-Portuguese Techncal Accounting Dictionary. M. Altman. 126p. (ENG & POR.). 0199. pap. 35.00 (*0-8288-4017-2*, M9355) Fr & Eur.

Dicionario Tecnico de Electronica Ingles - Portugues. Isaac Ledermann. (ENG & POR.). 1986. pap. 39.95 (*0-8288-3966-2*, F92230) Fr & Eur.

Dick & Jane As Victims: Sex Stereotyping in Children's Readers. 2nd ed. LC 74-77374. 1975. pap. 3.00 (*0-9600724-1-1*) Women on Words.

Dick & the Devil. Robert Dichiara. 1990. mass mkt. 4.95 (*0-8125-1698-2*) Tor Bks.

Dick Bong, Ace of Aces. George C. Kenney. reprint ed. 17.95 (*0-89201-094-0*) Zenger Pub.

Dick Bruna's Picture Wordbook. Dick Bruna. (Illus.). 64p. (J). 1991. 5.99 (*0-517-05662-3*) Random Hse Value.

Dick Cepek Off-Road Handbook. Ed. by Tom Madigan. (Illus.). 224p. 1984. pap. 9.95 (*0-933506-11-2*) Darwin Pubns.

Dick Clark's American Bandstand Gold Vol. 1: 1955-1965. Ed. by Milton Okun. pap. 16.95 (*0-89524-713-5*) Cherry Lane.

Dick Clark's American Bandstand Gold Vol. 2: 1965-1975. Ed. by Milton Okun. 142p. (Orig.). (YA). 1994. pap. 16.95 (*0-89524-815-8*, 02502123) Cherry Lane.

***Dick Connor Remembered: Writing on Sports & Life.** Mary K. Connor. LC 94-37940. (Illus.). 288p. 1995. 22.95 (*1-55591-216-8*) Fulcrum Pub.

Dick Cossitt Memorial Exhibition. Mario Amaya. (Illus.). 13p. 1978. pap. 3.00 (*0-940744-21-X*) Chrysler Museum.

Dick Deterred: A Play in Two Acts. David Edgar. LC 74-7789. 112p. reprint ed. pap. 32.00 (*0-7837-6989-X*, 2046801) Bks Demand.

Dick Francis. J. Madison Davis. (English Authors Ser.). 200p. (C). 1989. text ed. 21.95 (*0-8057-6970-6*, TEAS 464, Twayne) Macmillan.

Dick Francis: Four Complete Novels. Dick Francis. 720p. 1988. 8.99 (*0-517-38806-5*) Random Hse Value.

Dick Francis Treasury of Great Racing Stories. John Welcome & Dick Francis. 1992. mass mkt. 5.99 (*0-449-22049-4*, Crest) Fawcett.

Dick Francis Treasury of Great Racing Stories. large type ed. Ed. by Dick Francis & John Welcome. (Anthologies Ser.). 454p. 1991. text ed. 22.95 (*0-8161-5171-7*) G K Hall.

Dick Gregory's Natural Diet for Folks Who Eat: Cookin' with Mother Nature. Dick Gregory. Ed. by James R. McGraw & Alvenia M. Fulton. 192p. 1974. reprint ed. mass mkt. 6.50 (*0-06-080315-0*, P315, PL) HarpC.

Dick Hodgson's Complete Guide to Catalog Marketing. Dick Hodgson. 420p. 1991. ring bd. 91.50 (*0-85013-176-6*) Dartnell Corp.

Dick Hyman's Professional Chord Changes & Substitutions for One Hundred Tunes Every Musician Should Know. Dick Hyman. 1986. 15.95 (*0-943748-14-3*) Ekay Music.

Dick Powell Story. Tony Thomas. (Illus.). 160p. (Orig.). 1992. pap. 19.95 (*1-880756-02-1*) Riverwood Pr.

Dick Ritger Academy: Coaches-Instructors' Manual. Dick Ritger. (Illus.). 68p. (C). 1987. write for info. (*0-318-63408-2*) R Ritger.

Dick Rutan & Jeana Yeager: Flying Non-Stop Around the World. Laurie Rozakis. Ed. by Bruce Glassman. LC 94-20399. (Partners Ser.). (Illus.). 48p. (J). (gr. 2-5). 1994. lib. bdg. 12.95 (*1-56711-087-8*) Blackbirch.

Dick Sands, the Boy Captain. Jules Verne. (Illus.). 1976. reprint ed. lib. bdg. 29.95 (*0-88411-904-1*, Aeonian Pr) Amereon Ltd.

Dick Smith's Monster Make-Up Book. Dick Smith. Ed. by Robert V. Michelucci. LC 84-62835. (Illus.). 104p. 1985. pap. 9.95 (*0-911137-02-5*) Imagine.

Dick Stedler's Sports Corner. Richard Stedler. Ed. by Daniel Locche & Brenda Alesii. (Illus.). 100p. (Orig.). 1994. 6.95 (*1-877697-02-8*) Brendan Ventures.

Dick Tracy. (Piano-Vocal-Guitar Ser.). (Illus.). 64p. 1990. pap. 12.95 (*0-7935-0287-X*, 00490516) H Leonard.

Dick Tracy: America's Most Famous Detective. Chester Gould. Ed. by Bill Crouch, Jr. (Illus.). 192p. 1987. pap. 14.95 (*0-8065-1059-5*, Citadel Pr) Carol Pub Group.

Dick Tracy: The Secret Files. Martin H. Greenberg. 1990. mass mkt. 4.95 (*0-8125-1010-0*) Tor Bks.

Dick Tracy: The Thirties, Tommy Guns & Hard Times. Chester Gould. Ed. by Herb Galewitz. LC 78-56876. (Illus.). 1980. 15.00 (*0-87754-071-3*); pap. 9.95 (*0-87754-123-X*) Chelsea Hse.

Dick Tracy: Tracy's Wartime Memories. Max Collins. (U. S. Classics Ser.). (Illus.). 64p. 1986. pap. 5.95 (*0-912277-32-7*) K Pierce Inc.

Dick Tracy & American Culture: Morality & Mythology, Text & Context. Garyn G. Roberts. LC 92-56687. (Illus.). 350p. 1993. lib. bdg. 45.00 (*0-89950-880-4*) McFarland & Co.

Dick Tracy & Nightmare Machine. Max A. Collins. 1991. pap. 3.50 (*0-8125-1344-4*) Tor Bks.

Dick Tracy Casebook. Comp. by Max A. Collins & Dick Locher. (Illus.). 224p. (Orig.). 1990. pap. 15.96 (*0-685-33413-9*) St Martin.

Dick Tracy's Fiendish Foes: A Sixtieth Anniversary Celebration. limited ed. Ed. by Dick Locher. (Illus.). 288p. (Orig.). 1991. 50.00 (*0-312-06337-7*) St Martin.

Dick Van Dyke Show. Ginny Wiessman & Coyne S. Sande. (Illus.). 160p. 1983. pap. 9.95 (*0-312-19977-5*) St Martin.

Dick Van Dyke Show Book. rev. ed. Ginny Weissman & Coyne S. Sanders. LC 92-44034. 1993. pap. 12.95 (*0-312-08766-7*) St Martin.

Dick Whittington. (Illus.). (ARA.). (J). (gr. 4-12). 1987. 3.95 (*0-86685-196-8*) Intl Bk Ctr.

Dick Whittington. Illus. by Kathleen Garry-McCord. LC 80-28171. 32p. (J). (gr. k-4). 1981. lib. bdg. 9.79 (*0-89375-482-X*); pap. text ed. 2.50 (*0-89375-483-8*) Troll Assocs.

Dick Whittington. Told by Catherine Storr. LC 85-16904. (Legends & Folktales Ser.). (Illus.). 32p. (J). (gr. 2-5). 1985. lib. bdg. 19.97 (*0-8172-2507-2*) Raintree Steck-V.

Dick Whittington: Fact & Fable. John Attwood. 112p. (C). 1988. 35.00 (*0-7212-0739-1*, Pub. by Regency Press) St Mut.

Dick Whittington & His Amazing Cat. Pat Hume. (Orig.). (J). (gr. k up). 1980. 5.00 (*0-87602-230-1*) Anchorage.

Dick Whittington & His Cat. Marcia Brown. LC 50-9157. (Illus.). 32p. (J). (gr. k-3). 1988. reprint ed. text ed. 14.95 (*0-684-18998-4*, C Scribner Sons Young) S&S Childrens.

Dick Whittington & His Cat: A Musical Play Based on an English Folk Tale. Jeff Church. (Illus.). 56p. (Orig.). (J). (ps-7). 1990. pap. 4.00 (*0-88680-340-3*); 10.00 (*0-88680-341-1*) I E Clark.

Dickens. (Little Brown Notebook Ser.). (Illus.). 256p. 6.95 (*1-897954-24-7*) Sterling.

Dickens. Christopher Martin. (Life & Works Ser. II). (Illus.). 112p. (YA). (gr. 7 up). 1990. lib. bdg. 19.94 (*0-86593-016-3*); lib. bdg. 14.95 (*0-685-36352-X*) Rourke Corp.

Dickens. Bernard Darwin. LC 73-8958. (Studies in Dickens: No. 52). 1973. reprint ed. lib. bdg. 45.95 (*0-8383-1710-3*) M S G Haskell Hse.

Dickens. O. Sitwell. LC 72-6293. (Studies in Dickens: No. 52). (C). 1972. reprint ed. lib. bdg. 75.00 (*0-8383-1623-9*) M S G Haskell Hse.

Dickens. Adolphus W. Ward. Ed. by John Morley. (English Men of Letters Ser.). reprint ed. lib. bdg. 27.50 (*0-404-51738-2*) AMS Pr.

Dickens: "Bleak House" Graham Storey. (Landmarks of World Literature Ser.). 128p. 1986. 29.95 (*0-521-32817-9*); pap. 10.95 (*0-521-31691-X*) Cambridge U Pr.

Dickens: A Biography. Fred Kaplan. 656p. 1990. pap. 12.95 (*0-380-70896-5*) Avon.

Dickens: A Biography. Fred Kaplan. LC 88-12859. (Illus.). 544p. 1988. 24.95 (*0-688-04341-0*) Morrow.

Dickens Advertiser: A Collection of the Advertisements in the Original Parts of Novels by Charles Dickens. Bernard A. Darwin. LC 72-152553. (Studies in Dickens: No. 52). 1971. reprint ed. lib. bdg. 39.95 (*0-8383-1234-9*) M S G Haskell Hse.

Dickens Aesthetic. Richard Lettis. LC 87-45808. (Studies in the Nineteenth Century: No. 6). 1989. 37.50 (*0-404-61486-8*) AMS Pr.

Dickens' All Year Round: An Index. Ann Oppenlander. LC 82-50403. 752p. 1985. 55.00 (*0-87875-252-8*) Whitston Pub.

Dickens & Charity. Norris Pope, Jr. LC 78-3867. 303p. 1978. text ed. 42.00 (*0-231-04478-X*) Col U Pr.

***Dickens & Crime.** 3rd ed. Philip Collins. LC 94-25477. 1994. write for info. (*0-312-12327-2*) St Martin.

Dickens & Daughter. Gladys Storey. LC 79-164657. (English Literature Ser.: No. 33). 1971. reprint ed. lib. bdg. 59.95 (*0-8383-1321-3*) M S G Haskell Hse.

An Asterisk (*) at the beginning of an entry indicates that the title is appearing in BIP for the first time.

An Asterisk (*) at the beginning of an entry indicates that the title is appearing in BIP for the first time.

1955

Dictatorship on Trial. Ed. by Otto Forst-Battaglia. LC 72-99635. (Essay Index Reprint Ser.). 1977. 30.95 (*0-8369-1607-7*) Ayer.

Dictatorship over Needs. Ferenc Feher et al. LC 83-3180. 320p. 1983. text ed. 39.95 (*0-312-20022-6*) St Martin.

Dictatorship, Workers, & the City: Labour in Greater Barcelona since 1939. Sebastian Balfour. (Illus.). 304p. 1989. 69.00 (*0-19-822740-X*) OUP.

Dictatorships & Ultimate Decrees in the Early Roman Republic. Arthur Kaplan. 1975. lib. bdg. 250.00 (*0-87700-245-2*) Revisionist Pr.

Dictee. Theresa H. Cha. (Illus.). 192p. 1994. reprint ed. pap. 12.95 (*0-943219-12-4*) Third Woman.

Diction: Italian, Latin, French, German . . . the Sounds & 81 Exercises for Singing Them. John Moriarty. LC 74-17158. 1975. pap. 15.00 (*0-911318-09-7*) E C Schirmer.

Diction for Singers: A Concise Reference for English, Italian, Latin, German, French, & Spanish Pronunciation. Joan Wall et al. 29.95 (*1-877761-51-6*) Pst Inc.

Dictionaire de Termes Officiels. Delegation Generale. 334p. 1993. 69.95 (*0-7859-5610-7*, 2110734299) Fr & Eur.

Dictionaire des Expressions et Locutions Figurees. (FRE.). 1979. Not Set by Publisher (*0-318-51978-X*) Fr & Eur.

Dictionaire des Horlogers Francais: Dictionary of French Watch & Clock Making. Tardy. 350p. (FRE.). 1979. pap. 225.00 (*0-7859-5072-9*) Fr & Eur.

Dictionaire des Litteratures, 4 vols. Philippe Van Tieghem. 4392p. (FRE.). 1984. 150.00 (*0-8288-6627-9*, 213038742X) Fr & Eur.

Dictionaire des Synonymes: Dictionary of Synonyms. Henri Benac. 1026p. (FRE.). 1981. 49.95 (*0-8288-1928-9*, M4558) Fr & Eur.

Dictionaire des Termes Odontostomatologiques. 3rd ed. Louis Verchere. 200p. (FRE.). 1992. 65.00 (*0-8288-9475-2*, M15415) Fr & Eur.

Dictionaire Detaille des Noms de Vetements Chez Les Arabes. R. Dozy. (ARA & FRE.). 1985. 25.00 (*0-86685-404-5*) Intl Bk Ctr.

Dictionaire Francais-Anglais, Anglais-Francaisde Medecine Physique de Reedaptaticn Ponctionelles. Herman L. Kamenetz & Georgette Kamenetz. 192p. (ENG & FRE.). 1972. 39.95 (*0-8288-6366-0*, M-6325) Fr & Eur.

Dictionaire Francais-Anglais d'electro-technique et d'electronique. Henri Piraux. (FRE.). 75.00 (*0-685-36687-1*) Fr & Eur.

Dictionaire Francais-Arabe. Louis Saisse. (ARA & FRE.). 1980. pap. 12.00 (*0-86685-112-7*) Intl Bk Ctr.

Dictionaire Technique Francais-Espagnol. 2nd ed. Guy Malgorn. 544p. (FRE & SPA.). 1974. 69.95 (*0-8288-6000-9*, M6387) Fr & Eur.

Dictionanaire Francais-Breton. Hemon Roparz. 42p. (BRE & FRE.). 1984. pap. 14.95 (*0-7859-4890-2*) Fr & Eur.

Dictionar de Constructii de Masini Rus-Roman: Russian-Rumanian Dictionary of Construction. Ludmila Farcas. (RUM & RUS.). 1981. write for info. (*0-8288-1330-2*, M15843) Fr & Eur.

Dictionar de Mecanica. Artexim. (RUM.). 1980. write for info. (*0-8288-2161-5*, M15837) Fr & Eur.

Dictionar Tehnic Poliglot. Editura Tehnica. 1233p. (C). 1967. text ed. 124.50 (*0-8290-0987-6*) Irvington.

Dictionarie Critique et Documentaire der Peintres, Sculpteurs, Dessinateurs et Graveurs. Emmanuel Benezit. (FRE.). 1976. 495.00 (*0-8150-0844-9*) Wittenborn.

Dictionaries: The Art & Craft of Lexicography. Sidney I. Landau. 384p. (C). 1989. pap. 18.95 (*0-521-36725-5*) Cambridge U Pr.

Dictionaries & the Authoritarian Tradition: A Study in English Usage & Lexicography. Ronald A. Wells. 1973. pap. text ed. 334.65 (*90-279-2428-7*) Mouton.

Dictionaries, Encyclopedias, & Other Word-Related Books, 2 vols. 4th ed. Ed. by Annie M. Brewer. 1333p. 1987. 520.00 (*0-8103-0440-6*) Gale.

Dictionaries for Adults & Children. Rashelle Karp & Frances Corcoran. Ed. by Sandy Whiteley. (Illus.). 46p. (Orig.). 1991. pap. 4.95 (*0-8389-7556-9*) ALA.

Dictionaries of English: Prospects for the Record of Our Language. Ed. by Richard W. Bailey. 192p. (C). 1987. text ed. 32.50 (*0-472-10087-4*) U of Mich Pr.

Dictionaries of John de Garlande. Tr. by Barbara B. Rubin. 98p. (C). 1981. 10.00 (*0-87291-155-1*) Coronado Pr.

***Dictionaries of Psychology.** Ed. by Ian Stuart-Hamilton. 800p. 1995. 126.00 (*1-85302-342-6*, Pub. by J Kingsley Pubs UK) Taylor & Francis.

Dictionario Da Lingua Portuguesa. 6th ed. J. Almeida Costa. 1811p. 1992. 95.00 (*0-8288-8536-2*) Fr & Eur.

Dictionario Frances - Portugues. Porto Editora Staff. 543p. 1992. 29.95 (*0-8288-8534-6*) Fr & Eur.

Dictionario Frances - Portugues, Portugues - Frances. Porto Editora Staff. 1195p. 1992. 49.95 (*0-8288-8532-X*) Fr & Eur.

Dictionariolum Puerorum Tribus Linguis: Lat., Ang. & Gall. Conscriptum. Robert Estienne. LC 72-194. (English Experience Ser.: No. 351). 616p. (ENG, FRE & LAT.). 1971. reprint ed. 95.00 (*90-221-0351-X*) Walter J Johnson.

Dictionarium Latinogermanicum. Petrus Dasypodius. (Documenta Linguistica, Reihe I: Worterbucher Des Vol. 15 & 16. Jahrhunderts Ser.). x, 982p. (GER.). 1974. reprint ed. write for info. (*3-487-05325-X*, Pub. by Georg Olms GW) Lubrecht & Cramer.

Dictionarium Latinogermanicum. Joannes Serranus. (Documenta Linguistica, Reihe I: Worterbucher Des Vol. 15 & 16. Jahrhunderts Ser.). ix, 416p. (GER.). 1974. reprint ed. write for info. (*3-487-05266-0*, Pub. by Georg Olms GW) Lubrecht & Cramer.

Dictionarium Museologium. 2nd ed. 774p. 1986. 135.00 (*3-598-07530-8*) K G Saur.

Dictionarium Musica, Being a Complete Dictionary, or, Treasury of Music. John Hoyle. (Monuments of Music & Music Literature in Facsimile: Series II, Vol. 83). 1976. reprint ed. lib. bdg. 40.00 (*0-8450-2283-0*) Broude.

Dictionarium, Seu Repertorium Morale Petri Berchorii Ordinis Divi Benedicti. Pierre Bersuire. civ, 1683p. reprint ed. write for info. (*0-318-72000-0*, Pub. by Georg Olms GW) Lubrecht & Cramer.

Dictionarium Teutonicolatinum. Cornelius Kiliaan. (Documenta Linguistica, Reihe I: Worterbucher Des Vol. 15 & 16. Jahrhunderts Ser.). xii, 239p. (GER.). 1975. reprint ed. write for info. (*3-487-05227-X*, Pub. by Georg Olms GW) Lubrecht & Cramer.

Dictionarium Theopharasti Paracelsi. Gerardus Dorneus. 94p. 1981. reprint ed. write for info. (*3-487-07066-9*, Pub. by Georg Olms GW) Lubrecht & Cramer.

Dictionary. Brooke M. Beebe & Ruth Y. Rosenblatt. LC 77-730283. (Illus.). (J). (gr. 3-5). 1977. pap. text ed. 165.00 (*0-89290-121-7*, A151-SATC) Soc for Visual.

Dictionary. Jessie C. Holton & Barbara A. Whitwell. (Angling for Words Ser.). 352p. pap. 15.00 (*0-87879-517-0*) Acad Therapy.

Dictionary. Dale McMasters. (Language Arts Ser.). 24p. (gr. 6 up). 1980. student ed 5.00 (*0-8209-0308-6*, D-1) ESP.

Dictionary. Betty Root. LC 91-26178. (Picture Pockets Ser.). (Illus.). 96p. (J). (gr. 1-5). 1992. pap. 13.00 (*0-671-76002-5*, S&S Bks Young Read); pap. 8.00 (*0-671-76003-3*, S&S Bks Young Read) S&S Childrens.

Dictionary. Marie-Jose Shaw. (Sound Filmstrip Kits Ser.). (gr. 3-6). 1981. teacher ed 34.00 (*0-8209-0441-4*, FCW-18) ESP.

Dictionary: Chontal to Spanish-English, Spanish to Chontal. Paul R. Turner & Shirley Turner. LC 78-164366. (Illus.). 384p. reprint ed. pap. 109.50 (*0-8357-8588-2*, 2034960) Bks Demand.

Dictionary - Lexicon of Industrial Measurement. P. Profos. 417p. (GER.). 1986. spiral bd. 95.00 (*0-8288-7941-9*) Fr & Eur.

Dictionary - Outline of Basic Statistics. John E. Freund & Frank J. Williams. (Illus.). 208p. reprint ed. pap. 5.95 (*0-486-66796-0*) Dover.

Dictionary According to Mommy. Joyce Armor. LC 88-3644. 104p. 1989. pap. 5.00 (*0-88166-162-7*) Meadowbrook.

Dictionary Amharic - English English - Amharic. A. Zekaria. 1991. lib. bdg. 59.95 (*0-8288-2622-6*) Fr & Eur.

Dictionary & Auction Catalogues of the Library of the American Numismatic Society: First Supplement 1962-67. American Numismatic Society, New York Staff. 1970. lib. bdg. 120.00 (*0-8161-0788-2*, Hall Library) G K Hall.

Dictionary & Auction Catalogues of the Library of the American Numismatic Society: Second Supplement. American Numismatic Society, New York Staff. 1973. lib. bdg. 120.00 (*0-8161-1058-1*, Hall Library) G K Hall.

Dictionary & Auction Catalogues of the Library of the American Numismatic Society: Third Supplement. 1978. lib. bdg. 225.50 (*0-8161-0247-3*, Hall Library) G K Hall.

Dictionary & Auction Catalogues of the Library of the American Numismatic Society, New York. American Numismatic Society New York Staff. 1970. Dictionary catalog, 7 vols. lib. bdg. 765.00 (*0-8161-0630-4*, Hall Library); Auction catalog, 1 vol. lib. bdg. 110.00 (*0-8161-0102-7*, Hall Library) G K Hall.

Dictionary & Auction Catalogues of the Library of the American Numismatic Society, New York, Set. American Numismatic Society New York Staff. 1970. lib. bdg. 655.00 (*0-8161-1489-7*, Hall Library) G K Hall.

Dictionary & Glossary of Koran. John Penrice. 167p. 1978. 29.95 (*0-318-37174-X*) Asia Bk Corp.

Dictionary & Glossary of the Holy Quran. rev. ed. John Penrice. 24.95 (*0-934905-09-6*) Kazi Pubns.

Dictionary & Glossary of the Koran. John Penrice. (ARA & ENG.). 1968. 20.00 (*0-86685-088-0*) Intl Bk Ctr.

Dictionary & Glossary of the Koran. John Penrice. 166p. (ARA & ENG.). 1987. 49.95 (*0-8288-1201-2*, M9962) Fr & Eur.

Dictionary & Glossary of the Koran. John Penrice. 180p. (C). 1985. text ed. 39.95 (*0-7007-0001-3*, Pub. by Curzon Pr UK) Humanities.

Dictionary & Glossary of the Koran. John Penrioe. 172p. (Orig.). (C). text ed. 27.50 (*81-85006-16-4*, Pub. by Sterling Pubs II) Apt Bks.

Dictionary & Glossary of the Koran. John Penrice. 1990. reprint ed. 10.00 (*81-85395-89-6*, Pub. by Low Price II) S Asia.

Dictionary & Glossary of the Koran, with Copious Grammatical References & Explanations. John Penrice. LC 70-90039. (ARA.). 1969. reprint ed. 25.00 (*0-8196-0252-3*) Biblo.

Dictionary & Glossary of the Koran, with Copious Grammatical References & Explanations of the Text. J. Penrice. 176p. 1978. text ed. 26.00 (*0-685-14040-7*) Coronet Bks.

Dictionary & Glossary of the Koran with Grammatical References & Explanations. John Penrice. 1980. lib. bdg. 55.00 (*0-8490-3123-0*) Gordon Pr.

Dictionary Arabic-Chinese. Commercial Press Staff. 1505p. (ARA & CHI.). 1978. 75.00 (*0-8288-5165-4*, M9288) Fr & Eur.

Dictionary Catalog & Shelf List of the Spencer Collection of Illustrated Books & Manuscripts & Fine Bindings, 2 vols., Set. New York Public Library, Research Libraries Staff. 1970. lib. bdg. 220.00 (*0-8161-0862-5*, Hall Library) G K Hall.

Dictionary Catalog of American Books Pertaining to the 17th Through 19th Centuries, 20 vols., Set. LC 76-103820. 1970. text ed. 3,750.00 (*0-8371-3265-7*, AAS, Greenwood Pr) Greenwood.

Dictionary Catalog of Jewish Collection, 14 Vols, Set. New York Public Library, Research Libraries Staff. 1970. lib. bdg. 1,365.00 (*0-8161-0409-3*, Hall Library) G K Hall.

Dictionary Catalog of Materials on New York City. New York Public Library, Research Libraries Staff. 1977. lib. bdg. 330.00 (*0-8161-0079-9*, Hall Library) G K Hall.

Dictionary Catalog of Printed Books, 38 Vols, No. 1. suppl. ed. Mitchell Library, Sydney, Australia Staff. 1970. lib. bdg. 155.00 (*0-8161-0848-X*, Hall Library) G K Hall.

Dictionary Catalog of Printed Books, 38 Vols, Set. Mitchell Library, Sydney, Australia Staff. 1970. lib. bdg. 4,110.00 (*0-8161-0790-4*, Hall Library) G K Hall.

Dictionary Catalog of the Albert A. & Henry W. Berg Collection of English & American Literature, First Supplement. New York Public Library, Research Libraries Staff. 1975. lib. bdg. 120.00 (*0-8161-0014-4*, Hall Library) G K Hall.

Dictionary Catalog of the American Indian Collection. Huntington Free Library, Reading Room Staff. 1977. lib. bdg. 435.00 (*0-8161-0065-9*, Hall Library) G K Hall.

Dictionary Catalog of the Applied Life Studies Library, First Supplement, 2 vols., Set. (C). 1982. lib. bdg. 270.00 (*0-8161-0390-9*, Hall Library) G K Hall.

Dictionary Catalog of the Applied Life Studies Library, University of Illinois at Urbana-Champaign, 4 vols. 1976. lib. bdg. 410.00 (*0-8161-0047-0*, Hall Library) G K Hall.

Dictionary Catalog of the Art & Architecture Division, Supplement 1974. New York Public Library, Research Libraries Staff. 1976. lib. bdg. 95.00 (*0-8161-0061-6*, Hall Library) G K Hall.

Dictionary Catalog of the Art & Architecture Division, The Research Libraries of The New York Public Library, 30 vols., Set. New York Public Library, Research Libraries Staff. 1975. lib. bdg. 3,380.00 (*0-8161-1157-X*, Hall Library) G K Hall.

Dictionary Catalog of the Arthur B. Spingarn Collection of Negro Authors, 2 vols. Howard University Library, Washington, D.C. 1970. lib. bdg. 220.00 (*0-8161-0872-2*, Hall Library) G K Hall.

Dictionary Catalog of the Children's Collection in the General Library, 5 vols., Set. 1974. 200.00 (*0-89073-020-2*) Boston Public Lib.

Dictionary Catalog of the Dance Collection, Performing Arts Research Center, 10 vols., Set. New York Public Library, Research Libraries Staff. 1974. lib. bdg. 940.00 (*0-8161-1124-3*, Hall Library) G K Hall.

Dictionary Catalog of the Department Library, 37 Vols, Set. Ed. by U. S. Department of the Interior, Washington, D. C. Staff. 1970. lib. bdg. 4,000.00 (*0-8161-0715-7*, Hall Library) G K Hall.

Dictionary Catalog of the Department Library, Fourth Suppl, 8 vols, Set. Ed. by U. S. Department of the Interior, Washington, D. C. Staff. 1975. lib. bdg. 910.00 (*0-8161-0016-0*, Hall Library) G K Hall.

Dictionary Catalog of the Edward E. Ayer Collection of Americana & American Indians, 16 Vols, Set. Newberry Library, Chicago Staff. 1970. lib. bdg. 1,280.00 (*0-8161-0586-3*, Hall Library) G K Hall.

Dictionary Catalog of the Edward E. Ayer Collection of Americana & American Indians, First Supplement, 3 vol., Set. Newberry Library, Chicago Staff. 1970. lib. bdg. 365.00 (*0-8161-0810-2*, Hall Library) G K Hall.

Dictionary Catalog of the G. Robert Vincent Library. Michigan State University, East Lansing Staff. 1974. lib. bdg. 85.00 (*0-8161-1149-9*, Hall Library) G K Hall.

Dictionary Catalog of the General Library, Boston Public Library, 61 vols. 1976. 36.50 (*0-89073-002-4*) Boston Public Lib.

Dictionary Catalog of the George Foster Peabody Collection of Negro Literature & History, 2 vols., Set. Fritz J. Malval. 1972. text ed. 315.00 (*0-8371-6065-0*, HIL/, Greenwood Pr) Greenwood.

Dictionary Catalog of the Giannini Foundation of Agricultural Economics Library, 12 vols. Ed. by University of California, Berkeley Staff. 1971. lib. bdg. 1,305.00 (*0-8161-0908-7*, Hall Library) G K Hall.

Dictionary Catalog of the Henry W. & Albert A. Berg Collection of English & American Literature, 5 Vols, Set. New York Public Library, Research Libraries Staff. 1970. lib. bdg. 535.00 (*0-8161-0870-6*, Hall Library) G K Hall.

Dictionary Catalog of the History of the Americas Collection, 28 Vols, Set. New York Public Library, Research Libraries Staff. 1970. lib. bdg. 2,520.00 (*0-8161-0540-5*, Hall Library) G K Hall.

Dictionary Catalog of the History of the Americas Collection, First Supplement, 9 vols., Set. New York Public Library, Research Libraries Staff. 1974. lib. bdg. 1,085.00 (*0-8161-0771-8*, Hall Library) G K Hall.

Dictionary Catalog of the J. Lloyd Eaton Collection of Science Fiction & Fantasy Literature, 3 vols., Set. 1982. lib. bdg. 330.00 (*0-8161-0379-8*, Hall Library) G K Hall.

Dictionary Catalog of the Jesse E. Moorland Collection of Negro Life & History, 9 vols., Set. Howard University Library, Washington, D.C. 1970. lib. bdg. 980.00 (*0-8161-0871-4*, Hall Library) G K Hall.

Dictionary Catalog of the Jesse E. Moorland Collection of Negro Life & History, First Supplement, 3 vols. Howard University Library, Washington, D.C. 1976. lib. bdg. 400.00 (*0-8161-0944-3*, Hall Library) G K Hall.

Dictionary Catalog of the Jewish Collection, First Supplement, 8 vols., Set. New York Public Library, Research Libraries Staff. 5424p. 1975. lib. bdg. 960.00 (*0-8161-0773-4*, Hall Library) G K Hall.

Dictionary Catalog of the Library of the Bernice P. Bishop Museum, 9 vols. Bishop, Bernice P., Museum Editors. 1970. Supp. 1. lib. bdg. 130.00 (*0-8161-0722-X*, Hall Library); Supp. 2. lib. bdg. 120.00 (*0-8161-0834-X*, Hall Library) G K Hall.

Dictionary Catalog of the Library of the Bernice P. Bishop Museum, 9 vols., Set. Bishop, Bernice P., Museum Editors. 1970. lib. bdg. 980.00 (*0-8161-0679-7*, Hall Library) G K Hall.

Dictionary Catalog of the Library of the Center for Applied Linguistics, Washington, D. C., 4 vols., Set. Center for Applied Linguistics Staff. 1974. lib. bdg. 410.00 (*0-8161-1114-6*, Hall Library) G K Hall.

Dictionary Catalog of the Library of the Freer Gallery of Art, 6 Vols, Set. Smithsonian Institution, Washington, D. C. Staff. 1970. lib. bdg. 610.00 (*0-8161-0799-8*, Hall Library) G K Hall.

Dictionary Catalog of the Library of the Mariners Museum, 9 Vols, Set. Mariners Museum Library - Newport News - Virginia Staff. 1970. lib. bdg. 980.00 (*0-8161-0674-6*, Hall Library) G K Hall.

Dictionary Catalog of the Library of the Massachusetts Horticultural Society, 3 Vols, Set. Massachusetts Horticultural Society, Boston Staff. 1970. lib. bdg. 285.00 (*0-8161-0648-7*, Hall Library) G K Hall.

Dictionary Catalog of the Library of the Massachusetts Horticultural Society, First Supplement. Massachusetts Horticultural Society, Boston Staff. 1972. lib. bdg. 120.00 (*0-8161-1038-7*, Hall Library) G K Hall.

Dictionary Catalog of the Library of the Pontifical Institute of Medieval Studies: First Supplement. Pontifical Institute of Medieval Studies, Toronto Staff. 1979. lib. bdg. 145.00 (*0-8161-1061-1*, Hall Library) G K Hall.

Dictionary Catalog of the Local History & Genealogy Division, 20 vols., Set. New York Public Library, Research Libraries Staff. 1974. lib. bdg. 1,760.00 (*0-8161-0784-X*, Hall Library) G K Hall.

Dictionary Catalog of the M. C. Migel Memorial Library, 2 vols., Set. American Foundation for the Blind (New York) Staff. 1970. lib. bdg. 170.00 (*0-8161-0705-X*, Hall Library) G K Hall.

Dictionary Catalog of the Manuscript Division, 2 Vols, Set. New York Public Library, Research Libraries Staff. 1970. lib. bdg. 170.00 (*0-8161-0750-5*, Hall Library) G K Hall.

Dictionary Catalog of the Map Division, 10 vols., Set. New York Public Library, Research Libraries Staff. 1971. lib. bdg. 1,090.00 (*0-8161-0783-1*, Hall Library) G K Hall.

Dictionary Catalog of the Music Collection. 2nd ed. New York Public Library, Research Libraries Staff. 1983. lib. bdg. 6,865.00 (*0-8161-0374-7*, Hall Library) G K Hall.

Dictionary Catalog of the Music Collection, 33 Vols, Set. New York Public Library, Research Libraries Staff. 1974. lib. bdg. 2,750.00 (*0-8161-0709-2*, Hall Library) G K Hall.

Dictionary Catalog of the Music Collection, Boston Public Library, 20 vols. Boston Public Library Staff. 15617p. 1976. First suppl., 4 vols. lib. bdg. 485.00 (*0-8161-1014-X*, Hall Library) G K Hall.

Dictionary Catalog of the Music Collection, Boston Public Library, 20 vols., Set. Boston Public Library Staff. 15617p. 1976. lib. bdg. 2,175.00 (*0-8161-0956-7*, Hall Library) G K Hall.

Dictionary Catalog of the Music Collection, Supplement II, 10 vols., Set. New York Public Library, Research Libraries Staff. 1978. lib. bdg. 1,490.00 (*0-8161-0760-2*, Hall Library) G K Hall.

Dictionary Catalog of the Music Collection, Supplement 1974. New York Public Library, Research Libraries Staff. 1976. lib. bdg. 95.00 (*0-8161-0059-4*, Hall Library) G K Hall.

Dictionary Catalog of the Negro Collection of the Fisk University Library, 6 vols., Set. Fisk University Library Editors, Nashville. 1974. lib. bdg. 560.00 (*0-8161-1055-7*, Hall Library) G K Hall.

Dictionary Catalog of the Oriental Collection, 16 Vols, Set. New York Public Library, Research Libraries Staff. 1970. lib. bdg. 1,320.00 (*0-8161-0410-7*, Hall Library) G K Hall.

Dictionary Catalog of the Oriental Collection: First Supplement, 8 vols., Set. New York Public Library, Research Libraries Staff. 1976. lib. bdg. 1,100.00 (*0-8161-0775-0*, Hall Library) G K Hall.

Dictionary Catalog of the P. K. Yonge Library of Florida History, the University of Florida, Gainesville. 1977. lib. bdg. 435.00 (*0-8161-0019-5*, Hall Library) G K Hall.

Dictionary Catalog of the Pacific Northwest Collection of the University of Washington Libraries, 6 vols., Set. University of Washington at Seattle Staff. 1972. lib. bdg. 730.00 (*0-8161-0985-0*, Hall Library) G K Hall.

Dictionary Catalog of the Princeton University Plasma Physics Laboratory Library, 4 vols, Set. Princeton University Staff. 1970. lib. bdg. 435.00 (*0-8161-0881-1*, Hall Library) G K Hall.

Dictionary Catalog of the Princeton University Plasma Physics Laboratory Library, First Supplement. Princeton University Staff. 1973. lib. bdg. 175.00 (*0-8161-1032-8*, Hall Library) G K Hall.

Dictionary Catalog of the Prints Division, 5 vols., Set. New York Public Library, Research Libraries Staff. 1975. lib. bdg. 545.00 (*0-8161-1148-0*, Hall Library) G K Hall.

Dictionary Catalog of the Rare Book Division, 21 vols, Set. New York Public Library, Research Libraries Staff. 1971. lib. bdg. 2,280.00 (*0-8161-0782-3*, Hall Library) G K Hall.

Dictionary Catalog of the Rare Book Division: First Supplement. New York Public Library, Research Libraries Staff. 1973. lib. bdg. 125.00 (*0-8161-1089-1*, Hall Library) G K Hall.

Dictionary Catalog of the Rodgers & Hammerstein Archives of Recorded Sound, 15 vols., Set. 1981. lib. bdg. 1,690.00 (*0-8161-0359-3*, Hall Library) G K Hall.

An Asterisk (*) at the beginning of an entry indicates that the title is appearing in BIP for the first time.

Dictionary Catalog of the Schomburg Collection of Negro Literature & History, 9 vols. New York Public Library, Research Libraries Staff. LC 66-1573. 1973. Supp. 1, 2 vols. lib. bdg. 130.00 (*0-8161-0735-1*, Hall Library); Supp. 2, 4 vols. lib. bdg. 485.00 (*0-8161-0820-X*, Hall Library) G K Hall.

Dictionary Catalog of the Schomburg Collection of Negro Literature & History, 9 vols., Set. New York Public Library, Research Libraries Staff. LC 66-1573. 1973. lib. bdg. 915.00 (*0-8161-0632-0*, Hall Library) G K Hall.

Dictionary Catalog of the Schomburg Collection of Negro Literature & History, Supplement 1974. New York Public Library Staff. 1976. lib. bdg. 120.00 (*0-8161-0062-4*, Hall Library) G K Hall.

Dictionary Catalog of the Slavonic Collection, 44 vols., Set. 2nd rev. ed. New York Public Library, Research Libraries Staff. 1974. lib. bdg. 4,355.00 (*0-8161-0777-7*, Hall Library) G K Hall.

Dictionary Catalog of the Stefansson Collection on the Polar Regions, 8 Vols, Set. Dartmouth College Library, Hanover, N. H. Staff. 1970. lib. bdg. 790.00 (*0-8161-0676-2*, Hall Library) G K Hall.

Dictionary Catalog of the United States Department of Housing & Urban Development Library & Information Division, 19 vols., Set. Ed. by U. S. Department of Housing & Urban Development, Washington, D. C. Staff. 1972. lib. bdg. 2,070.00 (*0-8161-1007-7*, Hall Library) G K Hall.

Dictionary Catalog of the United States Department of Housing & Urban Development Library & Information Division, First Supplement, 2 vols., Set. Ed. by U. S. Department of Housing & Urban Development, Washington, D. C. Staff. 1974. lib. bdg. 240.00 (*0-8161-1135-9*, Hall Library) G K Hall.

Dictionary Catalog of the United States Department of Housing & Urban Development, Library & Information Division, Second Supplement, 2 vols, Set. U. S. Department of Housing & Urban Development, Washington, D. C. Staff. 1975. lib. bdg. 240.00 (*0-8161-0012-8*, Hall Library) G K Hall.

Dictionary Catalog of the Vivian G. Harsh Collection of Afro-American History & Literature: Chicago Public Library, 4 vols., Set. 1978. lib. bdg. 405.00 (*0-8161-0252-X*, Hall Library) G K Hall.

Dictionary Catalog of the Water Resources Center Archives, 5 vols. Ed. by University of California, Berkeley Staff. 1972. lib. bdg. 545.00 (*0-8161-0884-6*, Hall Library); Supp. 1, 1971. lib. bdg. 125.00 (*0-8161-0895-1*, Hall Library); Supp. 2, 1972. lib. bdg. 125.00 (*0-8161-0983-4*, Hall Library) G K Hall.

Dictionary Catalog of the Water Resources Center Archives: Sixth Supplement, 2 vols., Set. Ed. by University of California, Berkeley Staff. 1978. lib. bdg. 285.00 (*0-8161-0244-9*, Hall Library) G K Hall.

Dictionary Catalog of the Water Resources Center Archives, Fourth Supplement. Ed. by University of California, Berkeley Staff. 942p. 1975. lib. bdg. 125.00 (*0-8161-0002-0*, Hall Library) G K Hall.

Dictionary Catalog of the Whitney M. Young, Jr., Memorial Library of Social Work. Columbia University, School of Social Work Staff. 1980. lib. bdg. 1,465.00 (*0-8161-0307-0*, Hall Library) G K Hall.

Dictionary Catalog of William Andrews Clark Memorial Library, 15 vols, Set. Clark, William Andrews, Memorial Library, Los Angeles Staff. 1974. lib. bdg. 1, 545.00 (*0-8161-1049-2*, Hall Library) G K Hall.

Dictionary Catalog on Deafness & the Deaf, 2 vols., Set. Gallaudet College Library Editors, Washington, D. C. 1970. lib. bdg. 190.00 (*0-8161-0877-3*, Hall Library) G K Hall.

Dictionary Catalogue. Emanuel Molho. LC 80-67876. 250p. 1988. 14.95 (*0-8288-0150-9*) Fr & Eur.

Dictionary-Catalogue of Operas & Operettas, 2 vols. John Towers. LC 67-25996. (Music Reprint Ser.). 1967. reprint ed. lib. bdg. 95.00 (*0-306-70962-7*) Da Capo.

Dictionary Catalogue of the Blacker - Wood Library of Zoology & Ornithology, 9 vols., Set. McGill University, Blacker - Wood Library of Zoology & Ornithology Staff. 6300p. 1970. lib. bdg. 930.00 (*0-8161-0719-X*, Hall Library) G K Hall.

Dictionary Catalogue of the Byzantine Collection of the Dumbarton Oaks Research Library, 12 vols, Set. Harvard University Dumbarton Oaks Research Library Staff. 1975. lib. bdg. 1,530.00 (*0-8161-1150-2*, Hall Library) G K Hall.

Dictionary Catalogue of the Columbia University Law Library, 28 Vols, Set. Columbia University Law Library Staff. 1970. lib. bdg. 3,145.00 (*0-8161-0800-5*, Hall Library) G K Hall.

Dictionary Catalogue of the Columbia University Law Library, First Supplement, 7 vols., Set. Columbia University Law Library Staff. 1978. lib. bdg. 1,035.00 (*0-8161-0802-1*, Hall Library) G K Hall.

Dictionary Catalogue of the Harris Collection of American Poetry & Plays, Brown University, 13 vols., Set. Brown University Staff. 1975. lib. bdg. 1,860.00 (*0-8161-0974-5*, Hall Library) G K Hall.

Dictionary Catalogue of the History of Printing from the John M. Wing Foundation, 6 Vols, Set. Newberry Library, Chicago Staff. 1970. lib. bdg. 655.00 (*0-8161-0587-1*, Hall Library) G K Hall.

Dictionary Catalogue of the History of Printing from the John M. Wing Foundation, First Supplement, 3 vols., Set. Newberry Library, Chicago Staff. 1970. lib. bdg. 365.00 (*0-8161-0809-9*, Hall Library) G K Hall.

Dictionary Catalogue of the History of Printing from the John M. Wing Foundation, Second Supplement. John M. Wing Foundation, Newberry Library Staff. 1981. lib. bdg. 500.00 (*0-8161-0326-7*, Hall Library) G K Hall.

Dictionary Catalogue of the Library of Sports in the Racquet & Tennis Club with Special Collections on Tennis, Lawn Tennis, & Early American Sports, 2 vols, Set. Racquet & Tennis Club, New York Staff. 1971. lib. bdg. 220.00 (*0-8161-0916-8*, Hall Library) G K Hall.

Dictionary Catalogue of the Library of the Pontifical Institute of Medieval Studies, 5 vols., Set. Pontifical Institute of Medieval Studies, Ontario Staff. 1973. lib. bdg. 555.00 (*0-8161-0970-2*, Hall Library) G K Hall.

Dictionary Catalogue of the Library of the Provincial Archives of British Columbia, 8 vols., Set. Provincial Archives Staff & Victoria, British Columbia. 1971. lib. bdg. 870.00 (*0-8161-0912-5*, Hall Library) G K Hall.

Dictionary Catalogue of the Library of the School of Library Service, 7 Vols, Set. Columbia University Editors. 1970. lib. bdg. 765.00 (*0-8161-0634-7*, Hall Library) G K Hall.

Dictionary Catalogue of the Library of the School of Library Service, First Supplement, 4 vols, Set. Columbia University Editors. 1976. lib. bdg. 530.00 (*0-8161-1166-9*, Hall Library) G K Hall.

Dictionary Catalogue of the London School of Hygiene & Tropical Medicine, 7 Vols, Set. University of London Staff. 1970. lib. bdg. 675.00 (*0-8161-0703-3*, Hall Library) G K Hall.

Dictionary Catalogue of the Teachers College Library, 36 vols., Set. Columbia University Editors. 1979. lib. bdg. 4,290.00 (*0-8161-0855-2*, Hall Library) G K Hall.

Dictionary Catalogue of the Teachers College Library, First Supplement, 5 vols., Set. Columbia University Editors. 1971. lib. bdg. 605.00 (*0-8161-0958-3*, Hall Library) G K Hall.

Dictionary Catalogue of the Teachers College Library, Second Supplement, 2 vols, Set. Columbia University Editors. 1973. lib. bdg. 300.00 (*0-8161-1039-5*, Hall Library) G K Hall.

Dictionary Catalogue of the Yale Forestry Library, 12 Vols, Set. Yale University - Henry S. Graves Memorial Library Staff. 1970. lib. bdg. 1,305.00 (*0-8161-0631-2*, Hall Library) G K Hall.

Dictionary Clinical Medicine. Stephan Dressler. 841p. (ENG & GER.). 1990. lib. bdg. 115.00 (*0-89573-993-3*) VCH Pubs.

Dictionary Clinical Medicine English, German. S. Dressler. 400p. (ENG & GER.). 1990. lib. bdg. 195.00 (*0-8288-3408-3*, 3527154639) Fr & Eur.

***Dictionary d'Architecture & Des Arts.** Afif Bahnassi. 200p. (ARA & FRE.). 1994. 35.00 (*0-86685-647-1*) Intl Bk Ctr.

Dictionary des Terms Economiques et Commerciaux (French-English-Arabic) Mustapha Henni. 1982. 30.00 (*0-86685-111-9*) Intl Bk Ctr.

Dictionary Dig. Linda Schwartz. (Study Skills Ser.). 48p. (J). (gr. 4-6). 1980. 5.95 (*0-88160-033-4*, LW 218) Learning Wks.

Dictionary Doughnut Shop. Elayne Weimann & Rita Friedman. (Fables from the Letter People Ser.). (Illus.). 30p. (J). (ps-1). 1989. lib. bdg. 12.95 (*0-89796-003-3*) New Dimens Educ.

Dictionary English - Thai. S. Charubhun. 691p. (ENG & THA.). 1991. reprint ed. lib. bdg. 59.95 (*0-8288-2623-4*, F55520) Fr & Eur.

Dictionary English & Sanskrit. Monier Williams. (C). 1992. reprint ed. text ed. 48.00 (*81-208-0454-6*, Pub. by Motilal Banarsidass II) S Asia.

Dictionary for Automotive Engineering. 3rd enl. ed. Jean De Coster. 628p. (ENG, FRE & GER.). 1990. lib. bdg. 100.00 (*3-598-10881-8*) K G Saur.

Dictionary for Banks & Stock Exchanges: Woerterbuch Fuer das Banwesen und Borsenwesen. 3rd ed. Hans N. Zahn. 440p. (ENG & GER.). 1991. 69.96 (*0-8288-0321-8*, M15098) Fr & Eur.

Dictionary for Brain Tumor Patients. 1993. write for info. (*0-944093-27-2*) Am Brain Tumor.

***Dictionary for Business & Finance.** 3rd ed. John V. Terry. LC 94-25151. 1995. write for info. (*1-55728-344-3*) U of Ark Pr.

Dictionary for Dreamers. Tom Chetwynd. 1993. pap. 10.00 (*1-85538-295-4*, Pub. by Aquarian Pr UK) Thorsons SF.

Dictionary for Dreamers. Tom Chetwynd. LC 73-163190. 255p. reprint ed. pap. 72.70 (*0-317-10393-8*, 2012170) Bks Demand.

Dictionary for Engineers & Technicians: Dictionnaire pour Ingenieurs et Techniciens: Francais-Espagnol-Francais. 4th ed. Luis Carcamo. 1988. write for info. (*0-8288-2103-8*, F12480) Fr & Eur.

Dictionary for Foreign Trade & International Co-Operation. D. Van Hoof. 1072p. (DUT, ENG, FRE & GER.). 1991. 150.00 (*90-6215-275-9*, Pub. by Maklu Uitgevers BE) W W Gaunt.

Dictionary for Lupus Patients. Ed. by Linda K. Rohner. 60p. 1993. pap. text ed. 9.95 (*0-9638245-0-3*) Mtn Gem Pubng.

Dictionary for Marine Technology, 2 vols., 1. Ed. by Robert Dluhy. (ENG & GER.). 1982. 235.00 (*3-87870-188-8*) Adlers Foreign Bks.

Dictionary for Marine Technology, 2 vols., 2. Ed. by Robert Dluhy. (ENG & GER.). 1982. 235.00 (*3-87870-189-6*) Adlers Foreign Bks.

Dictionary for Marine Technology, Vol. 1: German - English. 5th ed. Robert Dluhy. 776p. (ENG & GER.). 1987. 275.00 (*0-8288-0417-6*, M15459) Fr & Eur.

Dictionary for Marine Technology, Vol. 2: English - German. 5th ed. Robert Dluhy. 776p. (ENG & GER.). 1987. 295.00 (*0-8288-0418-4*, M15460) Fr & Eur.

***Dictionary for Patents in Five Languages.** Gy. L. Szedy. 1088p. 1987. 75.00x (*963-05-4436-9*, Pub. by Akad Kiado HU) St Mut.

Dictionary for Physicians. 2nd ed. F. Lejeune & Werner E. Bunjes. 459p. (ENG & GER.). 1968. 175.00 (*0-7859-0829-3*, M-7106) Fr & Eur.

Dictionary for Plant Engineering English-Japanese. T. Kotani. 664p. (ENG & JPN.). 1989. 225.00 (*0-8288-7218-X*, 4871982203) Fr & Eur.

Dictionary for Plant Engineering Japanese-English. T. Kotani. 730p. 1989. 225.00 (*0-8288-7217-1*, 4871982221) Fr & Eur.

Dictionary for Priests & Educators: Diccionario para Padres y Educadores. Hans H. Groothoff. 348p. (SPA.). 1978. pap. 24.95 (*0-8288-5148-4*, S50026) Fr & Eur.

Dictionary for Psychotherapists: Dynamic Concepts in Psychotherapy. Richard D. Chessick. LC 92-23967. 424p. 1993. 50.00 (*0-87668-338-3*) Aronson.

Dictionary for Spontaneous Descriptions. Douglas Moore & Harris Winitz. 120p. (Orig.). 1985. pap. text ed. 15.00 (*0-939990-43-1*) Intl Linguistics.

Dictionary for the Electrician with Formulas. Tom Henry. (Illus.). (Orig.). (C). 1988. pap. text ed. 18.00 (*0-945495-09-9*) T Henrys CECB.

Dictionary for the Idle. Joan Fuster. Tr. by Dominic Keown. 141p. (C). 1991. 7.95 (*1-85075-712-7*, Pub. by Sheffield Acad UK) CUP Services.

Dictionary for the Mental Health Professional: Psychiatrists, Psychologists. Dorothy H. Mills. 250p. 1993. 24.95 (*0-8288-1871-1*, S50021) Fr & Eur.

Dictionary for the Petroleum Industry. Illus. by T. Rey Calderon. 324p. 1991. pap. 35.00 (*0-88698-152-2*, 1. 40010) PETEX.

Dictionary for Tourists: English-Polish-English. J. Jaslan & J. Stanislawski. 712p. (ENG & POL.). 1981. 14.95 (*0-8288-1631-X*, M9819) Fr & Eur.

Dictionary for Veterinary Science & Biosciences. Roy Mack. 324p. (ENG & GER.). 1987. pap. 85.00 (*0-8288-2385-5*, M4375) Fr & Eur.

Dictionary for 12 Step Programs. Robert Barnhart. (Publications for Recovery). 68p. 1994. pap. 4.95 (*1-884780-04-0*) Phoenix Pubng.

***Dictionary Geological Engineering: Worterbuch GoeTechnik.** Herbert Bucksch. LC 95-14636. (ENG & GER.). 1995. write for info. (*0-387-58164-2*) Spr-Verlag.

***Dictionary Grammatical Analysis Holy Qur'an.** Mohammed Qubayya. 830p. (ARA.). 1995. 65.00 (*0-86685-645-5*) Intl Bk Ctr.

Dictionary-Handbook of Nuclear Medicine & Clincal Imaging. Iturralde. 1995. write for info. (*0-8493-4218-X*) CRC Pr.

Dictionary-Handbook of Nuclear Medicine & Clinical Imaging. Ed. by Mario P. Iturralde. 520p. 1990. 104.95 (*0-8493-3233-8*, RC78) CRC Pr.

Dictionary-Handbook to Hymns for the Living Church. George H Shorney, Jr. LC 77-75916. 1978. 19.95 (*0-916642-09-7*) Hope Pub.

Dictionary Hebrew Verbs. Moses Debahy. (ARA & HEB.). 1974. 19.95 (*0-86685-123-2*) Intl Bk Ctr.

Dictionary in Assamese & English. M. Bronson. (ASM & ENG.). 1987. 59.95 (*0-8288-1595-X*, F136031) Fr & Eur.

Dictionary Industrial Chemistry: English-Chinese. Commercial Press Staff. 81p. (CHI & ENG.). 1977. pap. 19.95 (*0-8288-5373-8*, M9585) Fr & Eur.

Dictionary Korean-Chinese. Commercial Press Staff. 1274p. (CHI & KOR.). 1978. 49.95 (*0-8288-5166-2*, M9289) Fr & Eur.

Dictionary-Lexicon of Micro-Computers: Dictionnaire-Lexique Micro-Informatique. Helene Chuquet. 264p. (FRE.). 1985. pap. 55.00 (*0-8288-1352-3*, M535) Fr & Eur.

Dictionary Marine Technique: English - French, French - English. Dobenik. lib. bdg. 195.00 (*0-8288-2490-8*, F34890) Fr & Eur.

Dictionary Ocean: Eng - Fr, Ger - Fr, Span - Fr. Raoul Piboubes. 761p. (ENG, FRE, GER & SPA.). 1989. write for info. (*0-7859-4578-4*) Fr & Eur.

Dictionary of Abbreviations & Symbols. E. F. Allen. 22.50 (*0-87559-167-1*) Shalom.

Dictionary of Abbreviations in Information Science. 406p. 1976. 55.00 (*0-686-44776-X*, Pub. by Collets UK) St Mut.

Dictionary of Abbreviations in Medical Science. R. Heister. 287p. (ENG & GER.). 1989. lib. bdg. 85.00 (*0-8288-3587-X*, F122440) Fr & Eur.

Dictionary of Abbreviations in Medical Sciences. R. Heister. 280p. 1989. 43.00 (*0-387-50487-7*) Spr-Verlag.

Dictionary of Abbreviations of the Russian Language. D. I. Alekseev. 486p. (ENG & RUS.). 1983. write for info. (*0-8288-0752-3*, M15485) Fr & Eur.

Dictionary of Accepted Ideas. Gustave Flaubert. 1976. 14. 95 (*0-8488-0485-6*) Amereon Ltd.

Dictionary of Accepted Ideas. rev. ed. Gustave Flaubert. Tr. by Jaques Barzun. LC 68-15880. 1954. pap. 6.95 (*0-8112-0054-X*, NDP230) New Directions.

Dictionary of Accounting. Peter Collin. 260p. 1992. pap. 16. 95 (*0-948549-27-0*, Pub. by Peter Collin UK) IBD Ltd.

***Dictionary of Accounting.** Comp. by Market House Books Staff. (Oxford Paperback Reference Ser.). 350p. 1995. pap. 12.95 (*0-19-280029-9*) OUP.

Dictionary of Accounting. David L. Scott & George Fiebelkorn. LC 84-27619. 150p. (C). 1985. 38.00 (*0-8476-1647-9*); pap. 14.00 (*0-8226-0384-5*) Rowman.

Dictionary of Accounting. 2nd ed. Ralph Estes. 160p. 1985. reprint ed. pap. 10.95 (*0-262-55011-3*) MIT Pr.

Dictionary of Accounting & Finance. Raymond Brockington. 320p. (Orig.). 1993. pap. 33.50 (*0-273-60112-1*, Pub. by Pitman Pub Ltd UK) Trans-Atl Phila.

***Dictionary of Accounting & Financial Management.** Louis Menard. 994p. 1994. write for info. (*0-7859-8752-5*) Fr & Eur.

***Dictionary of Accounting & of Financial Management.** Louis Menard. (ENG & FRE.). 1994. 156.60 (*0-7859-8886-6*) Fr & Eur.

Dictionary of Accounting & Related Disciplines: Dictionnaire de la Comptabilite et des Disciplines Connexes. 2nd ed. F. Sylvain. 662p. (ENG & FRE.). 1982. 125.00 (*0-8288-0807-4*, F363) Fr & Eur.

Dictionary of Accounting Terms. Joel Siegel & Jae Shim. (Financial Guides Ser.). 448p. 1987. pap. 10.95 (*0-8120-3766-9*) Barron.

***Dictionary of Accounting Terms.** 2nd ed. Joel G. Siegel & Jae K. Shim. LC 94-21214. 1995. write for info. (*0-8120-1918-0*) Barron.

Dictionary of Acoustics: English-German, German-English. H. Weissing. 260p. (ENG & GER.). 1992. 125.00 (*0-8288-5167-0*) Fr & Eur.

Dictionary of Actors. Edwin Nungezer. LC 75-173803. reprint ed. 27.50 (*0-404-04806-4*) AMS Pr.

Dictionary of Actors & of Other Persons Associated with the Public Representation of Plays in England Before 1642. Edwin Nungezer. LC 68-57633. 437p. 1969. reprint ed. text ed. 65.00 (*0-8371-0593-5*, NUDI, Greenwood Pr) Greenwood.

Dictionary of Actuarial & Life Insurance Terms: English-French-Italian-Spanish-German. Witherby's & Co. Ltd. Staff. (C). 1983. 300.00 (*0-685-32831-7*, Pub. by Witherby & Co UK) St Mut.

Dictionary of Acupuncture Terms, Concepts & Points. Ralph A. Dale. 1993. 39.00 (*1-877589-11-X*) Dialectic Pubns.

Dictionary of Administration & Management: Twenty Thousand New Terms & Concepts Used in Business & Public Sector Organizations, Agencies, Institutions & Systems. Systems Research Institute Staff. 1340p. 1986. 49.95 (*0-912352-08-6*) Systems Res.

Dictionary of Administrative & Legislative Terms English - Hindi. J. L. Gupta. (ENG & HIN.). 1992. reprint ed. 49.95 (*0-8288-8447-1*) Fr & Eur.

Dictionary of Admirals of the U. S. Navy, Vol. I: 1862-1900. William B. Cogar. (Illus.). 256p. 1989. 45.00 (*0-87021-431-4*) Naval Inst Pr.

Dictionary of Admirals of the U. S. Navy, Vol. II: 1901-1918, Vol. 2. William B. Cogar. LC 89-3339. (Illus.). 416p. 1991. 55.00 (*0-87021-195-1*) Naval Inst Pr.

Dictionary of Advanced Manufacturing Technology. V. Daniel Hunt. 1987. 55.50 (*0-444-01208-7*) Elsevier.

Dictionary of Advertising. Frank Jefkins. 192p. (Orig.). 1989. pap. 27.50 (*0-273-03136-8*, Pub. by Pitman Pub Ltd UK) Trans-Atl Phila.

Dictionary of Advertising. Sweetman R. Smith. 272p. 1991. 27.50 (*0-87005-714-6*) Fairchild.

Dictionary of Advertising. Ed. by Laurence Urdang. LC 76-45506. 212p. (Orig.). 1986. pap. text ed. 15.95 (*0-8442-3040-5*, Crain Bks) NTC Pub Grp.

Dictionary of Advertising & Marketing: Woerterbuch der Werbung und des Marketing. Clemens M. Gruber. 312p. (ENG & GER.). 1982. 59.95 (*0-8288-0094-4*, M6942) Fr & Eur.

Dictionary of Advertising Terms: French - English. Michael Barnard. 160p. (ENG & FRE.). 1992. 95.00 (*0-7859-0503-0*, 2852068184) Fr & Eur.

Dictionary of Aerodynamics. Commercial Press Staff. 250p. (CHI & ENG.). 1974. pap. 49.95 (*0-8288-6001-7*, M9595) Fr & Eur.

Dictionary of Aeronautical Terms. 2nd ed. Comp. by Dale Crane. (Mechanic Ser.). (Illus.). 661p. 1991. pap. 16.95 (*1-56027-071-3*, ASA-DAT-2) Av Suppl & Acad.

Dictionary of Aeronautics: Dictionar de Astronautica. D. Andrescu. (RUM.). 1983. write for info. (*0-8288-1172-5*, M15850) Fr & Eur.

Dictionary of Aeronautics Engineering: Diccionario Tecnico Aeronautico. Iberia Airlines Staff. 787p. (ENG & SPA.). 1983. 150.00 (*0-8288-0017-0*, S37343) Fr & Eur.

Dictionary of Aerospace Engineering. Michail G. Kotik. 900p. (ENG, GER & RUS.). 1986. 225.75 (*0-444-99506-4*) Elsevier.

Dictionary of Aerospace Teledetection: Dictionnaire de Teledetection Aero-Spatiale. S. Paul. 256p. (ENG & FRE.). 1982. 225.00 (*0-8288-0012-X*, M14360) Fr & Eur.

Dictionary of African Historical Biography. enl. ed. Mark R. Lipschultz & R. Kent Rasmussen. 1986. pap. 16.00 (*0-520-06611-1*) U CA Pr.

Dictionary of African Historical Biography. 2nd enl. ed. Mark R. Lipschultz & R. Kent Rasmussen. 1986. 55.00 (*0-520-05179-3*) U CA Pr.

Dictionary of Africanisms: Contributions of Sub-Saharan Africa to the English Language. Gerard M. Dalgish. LC 82-9366. xviii, 203p. 1982. text ed. 59.95 (*0-313-23585-6*, DDA/, Greenwood Pr) Greenwood.

Dictionary of Afro-American Slavery. Ed. by Randall M. Miller & John D. Smith. LC 87-37543. 882p. 1988. text ed. 95.00 (*0-313-23814-6*, SMS/, Greenwood Pr) Greenwood.

Dictionary of Afro-Latin American Civilization. Benjamin Nunez. LC 79-7731. (Illus.). xxxv, 525p. 1980. text ed. 69.50 (*0-313-21138-8*, NAL/, Greenwood Pr) Greenwood.

Dictionary of Agri-Business: Dictionnaire Permanent Entreprise Agricole. Legis Administration Staff. 1722p. (FRE.). 1983. 195.00 (*0-8288-1173-3*, M15326) Fr & Eur.

Dictionary of Agricultural & Food Engineering. Arthur W. Farrall & James A. Basselman. LC 78-71856. 450p. 1979. 26.60 (*0-8134-2023-7*, 2023); text ed. 19.95 (*0-685-02538-1*) Interstate.

***Dictionary of Agricultural Equipment & Machinery: French, English, German, Spanish, Italian & Portuguese.** J. Baudel. 1400p. (ENG, FRE & GER.). 1989. 150.00 (*0-7859-7458-X*, 2856080340) Fr & Eur.

Dictionary of Agriculture. Chhatwal Gurdeep. 318p. 1988. 80.00 (*81-7041-039-8*, Pub. by Scientific Pubs II) St Mut.

D

An Asterisk (*) at the beginning of an entry indicates that the title is appearing in BIP for the first time.

1957

Dictionary of Agriculture. A. Stephans. 260p. 1990. pap. text ed. 16.95 (*0-948549-13-0*, Pub. by Peter Collin UK) IBD Ltd.

***Dictionary of Agriculture: From Abaca to Zoonosis.** Kathryn L. Lipton. LC 94-25260. 375p. 1995. lib. bdg. 70.00 (*1-55587-523-8*) Lynne Rienner.

Dictionary of Agriculture: In German, English, French, Spanish, Italian, & Russian. 5th rev. ed. G. Haensch & G. Haberkamp De Anton. 1350p. 1987. 259.00 (*0-444-99512-9*) Elsevier.

Dictionary of Agriculture, Forestry, Horticulture. P. Muhle et al. 732p. (ENG & GER.). 1990. 141.00 (*0-444-98782-7*) Elsevier.

Dictionary of Agrometeorology: English-Serbian, Serbian-English. Otorepec Silva. 211p. (ENG & SER.). 1990. 95.00 (*0-8288-8224-X*) Fr & Eur.

Dictionary of Agronomy, 4 pts., Set. L. L. Somani. (C). 1989. 170.00 (*81-7099-114-5*, Pub. by Mittal II) S Asia.

Dictionary of AIDS-Related Terminology. Jeffrey T. Huber. 172p. 1993. 39.95 (*1-55570-117-5*) Neal-Schuman.

Dictionary of Alaskan English. Ed. by Russell Tabbert. 302p. (Orig.). 1991. pap. 47.50 (*0-938737-23-6*) Denali Press.

Dictionary of Albanian Literature. Robert Elsie. LC 85-31693. 178p. 1986. text ed. 49.95 (*0-313-25186-X*, EDA/, Greenwood Pr) Greenwood.

Dictionary of Alchemy: From Maria Prophetissa to Isaac Newton. Mark Haeffner. (Illus.). 1992. pap. 22.95 (*1-85538-085-4*, Pub. by Aquarian Pr UK) Thorsons SF.

Dictionary of Alcohol Use & Abuse: Slang, Terms & Terminology. Comp. by Ernest L. Abel. LC 85-22521. xvi, 189p. 1985. text ed. 69.50 (*0-313-24631-9*, ABA/, Greenwood Pr) Greenwood.

Dictionary of Alkaloids, 2 vols., Set. Ed. by T. W. Southon & John B. Buckingham. 1850p. 1989. text ed. 295.00 (*0-412-24910-3*) Chapman & Hall.

Dictionary of All Religious Denominations: Jewish, Heathen, Mahometan, Christian, Ancient, & Modern. Hannah Adams. LC 92-15133. (American Academy of Religion, Classics in Religious Studies). 396p. 1992. 39.95 (*1-55540-727-7*, 010508); pap. 24.95 (*1-55540-728-5*) Scholars Pr GA.

Dictionary of All Scriptures & Myths. G. A. Gaskell. 1993. 11.99 (*0-517-34663-X*) Random Hse Value.

Dictionary of Alternative Defense. Bjorn Moller. LC 92-27347. 540p. 1995. lib. bdg. 79.95 (*1-55587-386-3*) Lynne Rienner.

***Dictionary of American & European Educationists.** Peter Gordon & Richard Aldrich. 1995. text ed. write for info. (*0-7130-0193-3*, Pub. by Woburn Pr); text ed. write for info. (*0-7130-4022-X*, Pub. by Woburn Pr) Intl Spec Bk.

Dictionary of American Art. Matthew Baigell. LC 78-24824. 390p. 1980. pap. text ed. 17.00 (*0-06-430078-1*, IN 78, Icon Edns) HarpC.

Dictionary of American Authors. Oscar F. Adams. 1972. 75.00 (*0-8490-0031-9*) Gordon Pr.

Dictionary of American Biography, 17 vols., Set. Ed. by American Council of Learned Societies. LC 44-41895. 1981. text ed. 1,399.00 (*0-684-17323-9*, Scribners) S&S Trade.

Dictionary of American Biography, Supplement 7. Ed. by American Council of Learned Societies Staff. 1981. lib. bdg. 85.00 (*0-684-16794-8*, Scribners) S&S Trade.

Dictionary of American Biography: Biographical Index Guide. Ed. by American Council of Learned Societies Staff. (Orig.). 1981. pap. 13.45 (*0-684-17152-X*, Scribners) S&S Trade.

***Dictionary of American Biography: Supplement Nin, 1974-1975.** Ed. by Kenneth T. Jackson et al. 952p. 1995. 95.00 (*0-684-15054-9*, Scribners) S&S Trade.

***Dictionary of American Biography: Supplement Ten, 1976-1980.** Ed. by Kenneth T. Jackson et al. 928p. 1995. 95.00 (*0-684-19399-X*, Scribners) S&S Trade.

Dictionary of American Biography: Supplement 8. 776p. 1988. text ed. 95.00 (*0-684-18618-7*, Scribners) S&S Trade.

Dictionary of American Biography Containing Nearly Ten Thousand Notices. Francis S. Drake. (Notable American Authors Ser.). 1992. reprint ed. lib. bdg. 75.00 (*0-7812-2688-0*) Rprt Serv.

Dictionary of American Biography Including Men of the Time. Francis S. Drake. 1974. reprint ed. 98.00 (*1-55888-957-4*) Omnigraphics Inc.

Dictionary of American Bird Names. rev. ed. Ernest Choate. LC 84-28975. 226p. 1985. pap. 10.95 (*0-87645-117-2*) Harvard Common Pr.

Dictionary of American Book Collectors. Donald C. Dickinson. LC 85-5580. 399p. 1986. text ed. 69.50 (*0-313-22544-3*, DBC/, Greenwood Pr) Greenwood.

Dictionary of American Children's Fiction, 1859-1959: Books of Recognized Merit. Althea K. Helbig & Agnes R. Perkins. LC 84-19278. xv, 666p. 1985. text ed. 69.50 (*0-313-22590-7*, HEC/, Greenwood Pr) Greenwood.

Dictionary of American Children's Fiction, 1960-1984: Recent Books of Recognized Merit. Althea K. Helbig & Agnes R. Perkins. LC 85-24778. 930p. 1986. text ed. 75.00 (*0-313-25233-5*, HAB/, Greenwood Pr) Greenwood.

Dictionary of American Children's Fiction 1985-1989: Books of Recognized Merit. Althea K. Helbig & Agnes R. Perkins. LC 92-19613. 320p. 1993. text ed. 55.00 (*0-313-27719-2*, HDO, Greenwood Pr) Greenwood.

Dictionary of American Clock & Watch Makers. Kenneth A. Sposato. 200p. 1983. 30.00 (*0-9612832-0-3*) K A Sposato.

Dictionary of American Communal & Utopian History. Robert S. Fogarty. LC 79-7476. 320p. 1980. text ed. 69.50 (*0-313-21347-X*, FDA/, Greenwood Pr) Greenwood.

Dictionary of American Conservatism: A Complete Guide to People, Issues, Organizations & Events. Louis Filler. 1988. reprint ed. pap. 12.95 (*0-8065-1087-0*, Citadel Pr) Carol Pub Group.

Dictionary of American Diplomatic History. 2nd rev. ed. John E. Findling. LC 88-7701. 707p. 1989. text ed. 59.95 (*0-313-26024-9*, FDT, Greenwood Pr) Greenwood.

Dictionary of American Food & Drink. John F. Mariani. 1994. pap. 19.95 (*0-688-10139-9*) Morrow.

Dictionary of American Foreign Affairs. Stephen Flanders & Carl Flanders. 833p. 1993. text ed. 90.00 (*0-02-897146-9*) Macmillan.

Dictionary of American Hand Tools: A Pictorial Synopsis. Alvin Sellens. LC 89-70210. (Illus.). 1990. 49.00 (*0-9612068-4-5*) Sellens.

Dictionary of American History. Michael Martin & Leonard Gelber. 728p. 1990. 19.95 (*0-88029-431-0*) Dorset Pr.

Dictionary of American History. enl. rev. ed. Michael Martin & Leonard Gelber. (Quality Paperback Ser.: No. 124). 742p. 1981. reprint ed. pap. 16.95 (*0-8226-0124-9*) Littlefield.

Dictionary of American Idioms. 2nd rev. ed. Adam Makkai et al. 480p. 1987. pap. 11.95 (*0-8120-3899-1*) Barron.

***Dictionary of American Idioms.** 3rd ed. Adam Makkai. 1995. pap. 12.95 (*0-8120-1248-8*) Barron.

***Dictionary of American Idioms: English-Arabic.** Said Salah. 420p. 1993. 16.00 (*1-887584-06-4*) Intl Prom Art.

Dictionary of American Immigration History. Ed. by Francesco Cordasco. LC 89-37041. 810p. 1990. 97.50 (*0-8108-2241-5*) Scarecrow.

Dictionary of American Legal Usage. David Mellinkoff. 708p. 1993. reprint ed. text ed. 39.95 (*0-314-00068-2*) West Pub.

Dictionary of American Legal Usage. David Mellinkoff. 703p. (C). 1993. reprint ed. pap. text ed. 24.00 (*0-314-01060-2*) West Pub.

Dictionary of American Literary Characters. Benjamin Franklin. 560p. 1989. 60.00 (*0-8160-1917-7*) Facts on File.

Dictionary of American Medical Biography, 2 vols., 1. Ed. by Martin Kaufman, III et al. LC 82-21110. 600p. 1984. text ed. 100.00 (*0-313-24333-6*, KDA/01) Greenwood.

Dictionary of American Medical Biography, 2 vols., Set. Ed. by Martin Kaufman, III et al. LC 82-21110. 600p. 1984. text ed. 195.00 (*0-313-21378-X*, KDA/) Greenwood.

Dictionary of American Medical Biography, 2 vols., Vol. 2. Ed. by Martin Kaufman, III et al. LC 82-21110. 600p. 1984. text ed. 100.00 (*0-313-24334-4*, KDA/02) Greenwood.

Dictionary of American Military Biography, 3 vols., 1. Ed. by Roger J. Spiller et al. LC 83-12574. xv, 1368p. 1984. text ed. 105.00 (*0-313-24161-9*, SAM/01) Greenwood.

Dictionary of American Military Biography, 3 vols., Set. Ed. by Roger J. Spiller et al. LC 83-12574. xv, 1368p. 1984. text ed. 250.00 (*0-313-21433-6*, SAM/) Greenwood.

Dictionary of American Military Biography, 3 vols., Vol. 2. Ed. by Roger J. Spiller et al. LC 83-12574. xv, 1368p. 1984. text ed. 105.00 (*0-313-24162-7*, SAM/02) Greenwood.

Dictionary of American Military Biography, 3 vols., Vol. 3. Ed. by Roger J. Spiller et al. LC 83-12574. xv, 1368p. 1984. text ed. 105.00 (*0-313-24399-9*, SAM/03) Greenwood.

***Dictionary of American Naval Aviation Squadrons, Vol. 1.** Roy A. Grossnick. LC 94-35647. 1994. write for info. (*0-945274-29-7*) Naval Hist Ctr.

Dictionary of American Naval Fighting Ships, 8 vols., Set. 1992. lib. bdg. 3,555.95 (*0-8490-8857-7*) Gordon Pr.

Dictionary of American Negro Biography. Ed. by Rayford W. Logan & Michael R. Winston. LC 81-9629. 1983. 65.00 (*0-393-01513-0*) Norton.

Dictionary of American Nursing Biography. Ed. by Martin Kaufman et al. LC 87-25454. 480p. 1988. text ed. 59.95 (*0-313-24520-7*, KAU/, Greenwood Pr) Greenwood.

Dictionary of American Painters, Sculptors & Engravers. rev. ed. Mantle Fielding. Ed. by Genevieve Doran. 480p. 1975. reprint ed. 17.50 (*0-913274-03-8*) Modern Bks.

Dictionary of American Painters, Sculptors & Engravers. Mantle Fielding. 433p. 1993. reprint ed. lib. bdg. 99.00 (*0-7812-5270-9*) Rprt Serv.

Dictionary of American Painters, Sculptors & Engravers: Enlarged. Mantle Fielding. 1974. 25.00 (*0-685-47043-1*) Assoc Bk.

Dictionary of American Penology: An Introductory Guide. Vergil L. Williams. LC 77-94751. 530p. 1979. text ed. 105.00 (*0-313-20327-X*, WAP/, Greenwood Pr) Greenwood.

Dictionary of American Pop - Rock. Shaw. 1985. 19.95 (*0-02-872350-3*) Macmillan.

Dictionary of American Portraits. Hayward Cirker & Blanche Cirker. Ed. by Dover Staff. 1967. 80.00 (*0-486-21823-6*) Dover.

Dictionary of American Proverbs. Ed. by Wolfgang Mieder et al. 736p. 1991. 55.00 (*0-19-505399-0*) OUP.

Dictionary of American Regional English, Vol. 1 A-C. Ed. by Frederic G. Cassidy. (Illus.). 1056p. 1985. text ed. 73.50 (*0-674-20511-1*) Belknap Pr.

Dictionary of American Regional English: D-H, Vol. 2. Ed. by Frederic G. Cassidy & Joan H. Hall. 1175p. (C). 1991. text ed. 70.00 (*0-674-20512-X*) Belknap Pr.

Dictionary of American Religious Biography. 2nd enl. rev. ed. Henry W. Bowden. LC 92-35524. 720p. (Orig.). 1993. text ed. 75.00 (*0-313-27825-3*, BDO, Greenwood Pr) Greenwood.

Dictionary of American Sculptors: Eighteenth Century to the Present. Ed. by Glenn B. Opitz. (Illus.). 656p. 85.00 (*0-938290-03-7*) Apollo.

Dictionary of American Sign Language on Linguistic Principles. William C. Stokoe. LC 65-28740. 1965. 17.95 (*0-932130-00-3*) Linstok Pr.

Dictionary of American Sign Language on Linguistic Principles. 2nd rev. ed. W. C. Stokoe. LC 65-28740. 1976. pap. 14.95 (*0-932130-01-1*) Linstok Pr.

Dictionary of American Social Change. Louis Filler. LC 82-10036. 266p. (Orig.). 1982. 23.50 (*0-89874-242-0*); pap. 14.50 (*0-89874-564-0*) Krieger.

Dictionary of American Social Reform. Louis Filler. LC 74-90505. 854p. 1969. reprint ed. text ed. 95.00 (*0-8371-2137-X*, FIAS, Greenwood Pr) Greenwood.

Dictionary of American Spelling. David Downing. LC 91-60024. 336p. 1992. text ed. 9.95 (*0-8442-5476-2*, Natl Textbk) NTC Pub Grp.

Dictionary of American Temperance Biography: From Temperance Reform to Alcohol Research, the 1600s to the 1980s. Mark E. Lender. LC 83-12589. xv, 572p. 1984. text ed. 105.00 (*0-313-22335-1*, LAT/, Greenwood Pr) Greenwood.

Dictionary of Americanism: A Glossary of Words & Phrases, Usually Regarded As Peculiar to the United States. John R. Bartlett. 1976. reprint ed. 79.00 (*0-403-06365-5*, Regency) Scholarly.

Dictionary of Americanisms. John R. Bartlett. 440p. 1991. 7.99 (*0-517-69686-X*) Random Hse Value.

Dictionary of Americanisms: A Glossary of Words & Phrases, Usually Regarded As Peculiar. John R. Bartlett. 1988. reprint ed. lib. bdg. 69.00 (*0-7812-0500-X*) Rprt Serv.

Dictionary of Americanisms: Diccionario de Americanismos. Marcos A. Morinigo. 400p. (SPA.). 1985. 75.00 (*0-8288-1205-5*, S12121) Fr & Eur.

Dictionary of Americanisms for Czech Speakers. J. Peprnik. 620p. (C). 1985. 65.00 (*0-685-37237-5*, Pub. by Collets); 60.00 (*0-89771-908-5*, Pub. by Collets) St Mut.

Dictionary of Analytical Chemistry in English, German, French, Polish & Russian. G. Maludzinska. 392p. (ENG, FRE, GER, POL & RUS.). 1990. 225.00 (*0-8288-9226-1*) Fr & Eur.

Dictionary of Analytical Chemistry. Raj Kumar & Satish Anand. 1990. 33.50 (*81-7041-271-4*, Pub. by Anmol II) S Asia.

Dictionary of Analytical Chemistry: English, German, French, Polish & Russian. Ed. by G. Maludzinska. 400p. (ENG, FRE, GER, POL & RUS.). 1991. 143.00 (*0-444-98729-0*) Elsevier.

Dictionary of Analytical Reagents. Ed. by Z. Marczenko et al. 2000p. 1993. 975.00 (*0-412-35150-1*, A9622) Chapman & Hall.

***Dictionary of Anatomical Eponyms.** Regis Olry. LC 94-23697. 1994. write for info. (*1-56081-407-1*) VCH Pubs.

***Dictionary of Ancient Egypt.** Margaret Bunson. (Illus.). 320p. 1995. pap. 14.95 (*0-19-509989-3*) OUP.

Dictionary of Ancient History. Ed. by Graham Speake. (Illus.). 768p. 1994. 59.95 (*0-631-18069-9*) Blackwell Pubs.

Dictionary of Ancient Near Eastern Architecture. Gwendolyn Leick. 272p. 1988. text ed. 52.50 (*0-415-00240-0*) Routledge.

Dictionary of Ancient Near Eastern Mythology. Gwendolyn Leick. (Illus.). 240p. 1991. 55.00 (*0-415-00762-3*, A5254) Routledge.

Dictionary of Ancient Roman Coins. John M. Jones. (Illus.). 329p. 1990. 65.00 (*1-85264-026-X*, Pub. by Seaby UK) Trafalgar.

Dictionary of Angels. Gustav Davidson. 1994. pap. 19.95 (*0-02-907052-X*) Free Pr.

Dictionary of Anglo-Belgian Law. L. E. Anspach & A. M. Coutanche. 181p. 1988. reprint ed. lib. bdg. 27.50 (*0-8377-1905-4*) Rothman.

Dictionary of Animal Health Terminology: In English, French, Spanish, German, & Latin. Ed. by Roy Mack. LC 92-9212. 1992. write for info. (*0-444-88085-2*) Elsevier.

Dictionary of Animal Health Terminology in English, French, Spanish, German & Latin. Office International des Epizooties Staff. Ed. by Roy Mack. 426p. (ENG, FRE, GER, LAT & SPA.). 1992. 250.00 (*0-8288-9215-6*) Fr & Eur.

Dictionary of Animal Names in Five Languages. Ed. by V. E. Sokolov. (ENG, FRE, GER, LAT & RUS.). 1989. 75.00 (*0-8288-3961-1*, M6748) Fr & Eur.

Dictionary of Animal Names in Five Languages: Mammals, Vol. 1. V. E. Sokolov. 352p. (ENG, FRE, GER, LAT & RUS.). 1984. 79.00 (*0-317-42879-9*, Pub. by Collets UK) St Mut.

Dictionary of Animal Production: English, French, Spanish, German & Latin. European Association for Animal Production Staff. 684p. 1985. 166.75 (*0-444-45472-1*) Elsevier.

Dictionary of Animal Production Terminology. 2nd rev. ed. European Association for Animal Production Staff. 683p. (ENG, FRE, GER, LAT & SPA.). 1993. 395.00 (*0-8288-0035-9*, F138140) Fr & Eur.

Dictionary of Animal Production Terminology: In English, French, Spanish, German, & Latin. 2nd enl. rev. ed. Ed. by Sophie Straszewska & Louis Ollivier. LC 93-3149. (EAAP Publication Ser.: No. 60). (ENG, FRE, GER, LAT & SPA.). 1993. write for info. (*0-444-88072-0*) Elsevier.

Dictionary of Animal Words & Phrases. enl. rev. ed. Darryl Lyman. LC 94-10106. Orig. Title: The Animal Things We Say. 1994. 19.95 (*0-8246-0378-8*) Jonathan David.

Dictionary of Animals: Dictionnaire des Animaux. Pierre Rousselet-Blanc. 250p. (FRE.). 1981. 19.95 (*0-8288-4443-7*, M9771) Fr & Eur.

Dictionary of Anonymous Literature, 7 Vols., Set. Samuel Halkett & John Laing. LC 72-171232. (Reference Ser.: No. 44). 1971. reprint ed. lib. bdg. 490.00 (*0-8383-1245-4*) M S G Haskell Hse.

Dictionary of Anthropology. S. N. Madan. 328p. 1989. 80.00 (*81-7041-163-7*, Pub. by Scientific Pubs II) St Mut.

Dictionary of Anthropology. Ed. by Charlotte Seymour-Smith. (Social Sciences Ser.). 450p. (C). 1987. text ed. 45.00 (*0-8161-8817-3*, Hall Reference) Macmillan.

Dictionary of Anthropology. Charles Winick. LC 77-88976. 578p. 1970. reprint ed. text ed. 55.50 (*0-8371-2094-2*, WIDA, Greenwood Pr) Greenwood.

Dictionary of Antibiotic-Producing Organisms. John S. Glasby. 300p. 1992. boxed write for info. (*0-13-210584-5*) P-H.

Dictionary of Antibiotics & Related Substances. Ed. by B. W. Bycroft. 964p. 1987. text ed. 675.00 (*0-412-25450-6*) Chapman & Hall.

Dictionary of Antonyms of the Russian Language. M. R. Livov. 381p. (RUS.). 1984. 19.95 (*0-8288-2005-8*, M15178) Fr & Eur.

Dictionary of Antonyms of the Russian Language. M. R. L'vov. 400p. (C). 1978. 35.00 (*0-317-92414-1*, Pub. by Collets UK) Pro-Am Music.

Dictionary of Aphrodisiacs. Harry E. Wedeck. LC 91-15843. 160p. 1992. pap. 9.95 (*0-87131-675-7*) M Evans.

Dictionary of Applied Linguistics: Arabic. Khuli. 1986. 35.00 (*0-685-51719-5*) Intl Bk Ctr.

Dictionary of Applied Physics, Vols. 2,3,4,5. Ed. by Richard Glazebrook. 24.00 (*0-8446-1199-9*) Peter Smith.

Dictionary of Aquatic Sports. C. Doberman. 875p. (ENG & GER.). 1987. 150.00 (*0-8288-7701-7*, F26730) Fr & Eur.

Dictionary of Arab Names: Arabic-Arabic, 2 vols., Set. Sultan Qaboos University Staff. 1991. 75.00 (*0-86685-503-3*) Intl Bk Ctr.

Dictionary of Arabic & Islamic Proverbs. Paul Lunde & Justin Wintle. 200p. 1984. 19.95 (*0-7102-0179-6*, RKP) Routledge.

Dictionary of Arabic Grammar Terminology: Al-Khalil. George Abdul-Massih. 1990. 35.00 (*0-86685-464-9*) Intl Bk Ctr.

Dictionary of Arabic Homonyms: Arabic - Arabic. Abdullhalim M. Qunbos. 1987. 22.00 (*0-86685-437-1*) Intl Bk Ctr.

Dictionary of Arabic-Persian Quotes. Claud Field. (ARA, ENG & PER.). 1974. 20.00 (*0-86685-168-2*) Intl Bk Ctr.

Dictionary of Arabic Proverbs. Kilani-Ashour. 1991. 24.95 (*0-86685-499-1*) Intl Bk Ctr.

Dictionary of Arabic Topography & Place Names. Nigel Groom. 373p. (ARA & ENG.). 1983. 95.00 (*0-8288-1458-9*, F22060) Fr & Eur.

***Dictionary of Archaeological & Artistic Terms English-French-Arabic.** Ghietas Azeez. 1994. 25.00 (*0-86685-611-0*) Intl Bk Ctr.

Dictionary of Archaic & Provincial Words, Obsolete Phrases, Proverbs, & Ancient Customs, from the Fourteenth Century, 2 Vols, Set. 3rd ed. James O. Halliwell-Phillipps. LC 76-168221. reprint ed. 82.00 (*0-404-03055-6*) AMS Pr.

Dictionary of Archaic & Provincial Words, Obsolete Phrases, Proverbs & Ancient Customs, from the Fourteenth Century, 2 vols., Set. James O. Halliwell-Phillipps. 1968. reprint ed. 95.00 (*1-55888-958-2*) Omnigraphics Inc.

Dictionary of Archeo-Zoology. K. Murthy & P. K. Murthy. (C). 1990. 28.00 (*81-202-0287-2*, Pub. by Ajanta II) S Asia.

Dictionary of Archeology: Dizionario d'Archeologia. Warwick Bray & David Trump. 336p. (ITA.). 1980. 29.95 (*0-8288-1199-7*, F72520) Fr & Eur.

Dictionary of Architectural & Building Technology. Henry J. Cowan & P. R. Smith. (Illus.). x, 287p. 1986. 36.00 (*0-85334-402-7*) Elsevier.

Dictionary of Architecture. Henry H. Saylor. LC 52-8260. 240p. 1994. pap. text ed. 24.95 (*0-471-75601-6*) Wiley.

Dictionary of Architecture, 3 vols., Set. Robert Meikleham. 1980. lib. bdg. 500.00 (*0-8490-3122-2*) Gordon Pr.

Dictionary of Architecture: Bildworterbuch der Architektur. 2nd ed. Hans Koepf. 459p. (GER.). 1985. 59.95 (*0-8288-1194-6*, M15144) Fr & Eur.

***Dictionary of Architecture & Arts: Arabic-English & English-Arabic with an English-French Glossary.** Afif Bahnassi. (ARA & FRE.). 1995. 35.00 (*0-86685-656-0*) Intl Bk Ctr.

Dictionary of Architecture & Building, 3 vols. R. Sturgis. 1972. 300.00 (*0-8490-0032-7*) Gordon Pr.

Dictionary of Architecture & Building: English-German. U. Gelbrich. 500p. 1990. 128.25 (*0-444-98864-5*) Elsevier.

Dictionary of Architecture & Building, Biographical & Descriptive, 3 vols., Set. Russell Sturgis. (Illus.). 1995. reprint ed. 90.00 (*1-55888-959-0*) Omnigraphics Inc.

Dictionary of Architecture & Construction. Cyril M. Harris. 553p. 1987. 85.00 (*0-8288-1192-X*, M7786) Fr & Eur.

Dictionary of Architecture & Construction. 2nd ed. J. R. Forbes. 432p. (ENG & FRE.). 1990. 175.00 (*0-8288-0196-7*, F 12491) Fr & Eur.

Dictionary of Architecture & Construction. 2nd ed. Cyril M. Harris. 768p. 1993. text ed. 59.50 (*0-07-026888-6*) McGraw.

Dictionary of Architecture, Building Construction & Materials, Vol. 1. 2nd ed. Herbert Bucksch. 942p. (ENG & GER.). 1980. 295.00 (*0-8288-0199-1*, M7131) Fr & Eur.

Dictionary of Architecture, Building Construction & Materials, Vol. 2. 2nd ed. Herbert Bucksch. 1137p. (ENG & GER.). 1983. 295.00 (*0-8288-0198-3*, M7130) Fr & Eur.

Dictionary of Architecture Building Trades. 6th ed. A. Zboinski & L. Tyszynski. LC 62-22062. (ENG, GER, POL & RUS.). 1963. 204.00 (*0-08-010260-3*, Pub. by Pergamon Repr UK) Franklin.

Dictionary of Archival Technology: English, French with Dutch, German, Italian, Russian, Spanish Equivalents. P. Walne. 212p. (ENG & FRE.). 1989. lib. bdg. 115.00 (*0-8288-3397-4*, F94792) Fr & Eur.

D

1958

An Asterisk (*) at the beginning of an entry indicates that the title is appearing in BIP for the first time.

Dictionary of Archival Terminology, Vol. 2. F. B. Evans et al. 226p. (DUT, ENG, FRE, GER, ITA & RUS.). 1984. 59.95 (*0-8288-0188-6*, M14492) Fr & Eur.

Dictionary of Archival Terminology: English & French with Equivalents in Dutch, German, Italian, Russian & Spanish. 2nd rev. ed. Ed. by Peter Walne. (ICA Handbook Ser.: Vol. 7). 212p. 1988. lib. bdg. 43.00 (*3-598-20279-2*) K G Saur.

***Dictionary of Art, Set, 34 vols.** Ed. by Jane Turner. 1996. 8,000.00 (*1-884446-00-0*) Dictionary Art.

Dictionary of Art: Bildwoerterbuch der Kunst. 3rd ed. Heinrich Luetzeler. 448p. (GER.). 1980. pap. 45.00 (*0-8288-1422-8*, M7310) Fr & Eur.

Dictionary of Art & Archaeology Terms with Elements of Numismatics: Diccionario de Terminos de Arte y Arqueologia, y Elementos de Numismatica. 5th ed. Guillermo Fatas Cabeza & G. M. Borras. 280p. (SPA.). 1991. pap. 18.95 (*0-7859-4931-3*) Fr & Eur.

Dictionary of Art & Artists. rev. ed. Peter Murray & Linda Murray. (Reference Ser.). 1984. pap. 8.95 (*0-14-051133-4*, Penguin Bks) Viking Penguin.

Dictionary of Art Quotations. Ian Crofton. 224p. 1989. text ed. 19.95 (*0-02-870621-8*) Schirmer Bks.

***Dictionary of Art Terms English-French--French-English.** Claude Ferment. (ENG & FRE.). 1994. 150.00 (*0-7859-8889-0*) Fr & Eur.

Dictionary of Artificial Intelligence. Dennis Mercadal. 1990. pap. 39.95 (*0-442-00451-6*) Van Nos Reinhold.

Dictionary of Asian American History. Ed. by Hyung-Chan Kim. LC 85-30188. 642p. 1986. text ed. 85.00 (*0-313-23760-3*, KDH/, Greenwood Pr) Greenwood.

Dictionary of Asian Philosophies. St. Elmo Naumann, Jr. 1978. pap. 5.95 (*0-8065-0617-2*, Citadel Pr) Carol Pub Group.

Dictionary of Assyrian Botany. Reginald C. Thompson. LC 78-72767. (Ancient Mesopotamian Texts & Studies). reprint ed. 45.00 (*0-404-18221-6*) AMS Pr.

Dictionary of Assyrian Chemistry & Geology. Reginald C. Thompson. LC 78-72768. (Ancient Mesopotamian Texts & Studies). reprint ed. 24.50 (*0-404-18222-4*) AMS Pr.

***Dictionary of Astrology.** H. E. Wedeck. (Illus.). 288p. 1995. reprint ed. pap. 8.95 (*0-8065-1712-3*, Citadel Pr) Carol Pub Group.

Dictionary of Astronautics Vol. 1: Terms & Definitions. 3rd ed. Centre National d'Etudes Spatiales Staff. 332p. (ENG, GER, RUS & SPA.). 1992. 125.00 (*0-7859-4705-1*, F71240) Fr & Eur.

Dictionary of Astronomical Names. Adrian Room. 1988. 27.50 (*0-415-01298-8*) Routledge.

Dictionary of Astronomy. Commercial Press Staff. 103p. (CHI & ENG.). 1974. pap. 24.95 (*0-8288-6002-5*, M9574) Fr & Eur.

Dictionary of Atheism. M. P. Novikov. 559p. (RUS.). 1983. 39.95 (*0-8288-2316-2*, M15213) Fr & Eur.

Dictionary of Audiovisual Communication. Ahuadero F. Francisco. 190p. (ENG & SPA.). 1991. 49.95 (*0-8288-6057-2*, 8428318794) Fr & Eur.

Dictionary of Australian Artists, Painters, Sketchers, Photographers & Engravers to 1870. Ed. by Joan P. Kerr. (Illus.). 912p. 1993. 225.00 (*0-19-553290-2*) OUP.

Dictionary of Authors, Works & Personalities of Greek Literature: Diccionario de Autores, Obras y Personajes de la Literatura Griega. Vicente Lopez Soto. 316p. (SPA.). 1984. pap. 12.50 (*0-8288-1577-1*, S60272) Fr & Eur.

Dictionary of Automatic Data Processing. Habil E. Burger. 480p. (ENG, FRE, GER, RUS & SLO.). 1980. 80.00 (*0-569-08521-7*, Pub. by Collets UK) St Mut.

Dictionary of Automatical Technique. Ed. by Jiri Sykora. 1023p. (ENG, FRE, GER, POL, RUS, SLV & SPA.). 1975. 150.00 (*0-8288-5837-3*, M9892) Fr & Eur.

Dictionary of Automation Techniques. Jiri Sykora. 1024p. 1975. 95.00 (*0-569-08528-4*, Pub. by Collets UK) St Mut.

***Dictionary of Automobile Engineering.** (Illus.). 250p. 1995. pap. 20.00 (*0-948549-66-1*) IBD Ltd.

Dictionary of Automotive Emission Control. Peter A. Schmitt. 182p. (ENG & GER.). 1986. 85.00 (*0-8288-0044-8*, F20010) Fr & Eur.

Dictionary of Automotive Engineering. Don Goodsell. 182p. 1989. 48.00 (*0-89883-766-9*, R101) Soc Auto Engineers.

Dictionary of Aviation. Ed. by R. J. Hall & R. D. Campbell. LC 90-63665. 352p. 1991. lib. bdg. 45.00 (*1-55862-106-7*) St James Pr.

Dictionary of Bahamian English. John A. Holm & Alison W. Shilling. LC 82-83045. 270p. (C). 1982. 42.00 (*0-936368-03-9*) Lexik Hse.

Dictionary of Ballet Terms. Leo Kersley & Janet Sinclair. LC 78-27421. (Paperback Ser.). 1979. reprint ed. pap. 8.95 (*0-306-80094-2*) Da Capo.

Dictionary of Banking. 254p. 1989. 14.95 (*1-55520-100-8*) Probus Pub Co.

Dictionary of Banking. G. Klein. 289p. (Orig.). 1992. pap. 27.50 (*0-273-03788-9*, Pub. by Pitman Pub Ltd UK) Trans-Atl Phila.

Dictionary of Banking. Jerry M. Rosenberg. (Business Dictionaries Ser.). 384p. 1992. text ed. 49.95 (*0-471-57435-X*); pap. text ed. 14.95 (*0-471-57436-8*) Wiley.

***Dictionary of Banking.** 2nd ed. Gerald Klein. 320p. 1995. pap. 44.50 (*0-273-61424-X*) Trans-Atl Phila.

Dictionary of Banking. 3rd ed. F. E. Perry. 378p. 1988. pap. 27.50 (*0-273-02961-4*, Pub. by MacDonald & Evans UK) Trans-Atl Phila.

***Dictionary of Banking: Over 4,000 Terms Defined & Explained.** Charles J. Woelfel. 1994. 24.95 (*1-55738-728-1*) Probus Pub Co.

Dictionary of Banking & Finance. P. H. Collin. 260p. 1991. pap. text ed. 16.95 (*0-948549-12-2*, Pub. by Peter Collin UK) IBD Ltd.

Dictionary of Banking & Finance. Lewis E. Davids. (Quality Paperbacks Ser.: No. 336). 229p. 1980. reprint ed. pap. 9.95 (*0-8226-0336-5*) Rowman.

Dictionary of Banking & Stock Exchange in Six Languages. Iu A. Bobylev. 286p. (C). 1992. text ed. 75.00 (*0-569-17111-3*, Pub. by Collets) St Mut.

Dictionary of Banking Terms. 2nd ed. Thomas P. Fitch. Ed. by Irwin Kellner et al. LC 92-32712. 1993. pap. 11.95 (*0-8120-1530-4*) Barron.

Dictionary of Baptists in America. Ed. by Bill J. Leonard. LC 94-31573. 298p. (Orig.). 1994. pap. 16.99 (*0-8308-1447-7*, 1447) InterVarsity.

Dictionary of Basic Historical Terms: Diccionario de Terminos Basicos para la Historia. A. Santabarbara. 626p. (SPA.). 1983. pap. 55.00 (*0-8288-1498-8*, S21336) Fr & Eur.

Dictionary of Basic Joseki, 3 vols. Nine-Dan Ishida Yoshio. 1977. write for info. (*0-318-64432-0*) Ishi Pr Intl.

Dictionary of Basic Joseki, 3 vols., 1. Nine-Dan Ishida Yoshio. 1977. 29.95 (*4-87187-021-9*, G21) Ishi Pr Intl.

Dictionary of Basic Joseki, 3 vols., 2. Nine-Dan Ishida Yoshio. 1977. 29.95 (*4-87187-022-7*, G22) Ishi Pr Intl.

Dictionary of Basic Joseki, 3 vols., 3. Nine-Dan Ishida Yoshio. 1977. 29.95 (*4-87187-023-5*, G23) Ishi Pr Intl.

Dictionary of Basic Linguistic Terminology: Woerterbuch der Linguistiche Grundbegriffe. 4th ed. Winfried Ulrich. 217p. (GER.). 1987. 49.95 (*0-8288-1982-3*, M6914) Fr & Eur.

Dictionary of Basque Names: Diccionario de Apellidos Vascos. 6th ed. Nicolas N. Iraola. 304p. (BAQ & SPA.). 1989. pap. 26.95 (*0-7859-4934-8*) Fr & Eur.

Dictionary of Battles. T. B. Harbottle. 1972. 69.95 (*0-8490-0033-5*) Gordon Pr.

Dictionary of Battles: The World's Key Battles from 405 B.C. to Today. Ed. by David Chandler. (Illus.). 255p. 1991. 14.99 (*0-517-05475-2*) Random Hse Value.

Dictionary of Beer & Brewing. Comp. by Carl Forgel. 186p. 1988. pap. 19.95 (*0-937381-10-1*) Brewers Pubns.

Dictionary of Behavior Therapy. Alan S. Bellack. (C). 1985. 59.95 (*0-205-14280-X*, H4280) Allyn.

Dictionary of Behavior Therapy. Alan S. Bellack. (C). 1992. pap. text ed. 32.95 (*0-205-14279-6*, H4279) Allyn.

Dictionary of Behavioral Science. 2nd ed. Ed. by Benjamin B. Wolman. 720p. 1989. text ed. 39.95 (*0-12-762455-4*) Acad Pr.

Dictionary of Beverages: Dictionnaire des Alcools. Jacques Salle & Bernard Salle. 320p. (FRE.). 1986. pap. 19.95 (*0-8288-1178-4*, F114710) Fr & Eur.

Dictionary of Bhagavad Gita. R. J. Venkateswaran. 224p. 1990. text ed. 27.95 (*81-207-1151-3*, Pub. by Sterling Pubs II) Apt Bks.

Dictionary of Bharata Natya. Krishna Rao. (Illus.). 100p. 1980. text ed. 15.95 (*0-86131-155-8*, Pub. by Orient Longman Ltd II) Apt Bks.

Dictionary of Bharatnatyam. K. U. Rao. (Illus.). 92p. 1980. 16.95 (*0-318-36307-0*) Asia Bk Corp.

Dictionary of Bias-Free Usage: A Guide to Nondiscriminatory Language. Rosalie Maggio. 304p. 1991. pap. 25.00 (*0-89774-653-8*) Oryx Pr.

Dictionary of Bible. John Mackenzie. 976p. 1967. pap. 15.95 (*0-02-087720-X*) Macmillan.

Dictionary of Bible & Religion. Ed. by William H. Gentz. (Illus.). 1152p. 1986. 18.95 (*0-687-10757-1*) Abingdon.

Dictionary of Bible Imagery. Ed. by Alice S. Sechrist. LC 79-63409. 384p. 1972. 5.00 (*0-87785-118-2*) Swedenborg.

Dictionary of Bible Places. (Ichthus Ser.). 1990. pap. 3.95 (*0-687-18302-2*) Abingdon.

***Dictionary of Bible Symbols.** Grace Publications Staff. 1992. 8.99 (*0-85234-527-5*, Pub. by Evangel Pr UK) Presby & Reformed.

Dictionary of Biblical Hebrew & Aramean. P. Reymond. 1104p. (FRE & HEB.). 1991. 125.00 (*0-8288-6920-0*, 2204044636) Fr & Eur.

Dictionary of Biblical Interpretation. Ed. by R. J. Coggins & J. L. Houlden. LC 89-28178. 850p. 1990. 49.95 (*0-334-00294-X*) TPI PA.

Dictionary of Biblical Judaism, 2 vols., 1. Ed. by Jacob Neusner. 1994. lib. bdg. 62.50 (*0-685-71134-X*) Macmillan.

Dictionary of Biblical Judaism, 2 vols., 2. Ed. by Jacob Neusner. 1994. lib. bdg. 62.50 (*0-02-897289-9*) Macmillan.

Dictionary of Biblical Judaism, 2 vols., Set. Ed. by Jacob Neusner. 1994. text ed. 125.00 (*0-685-59239-1*) Macmillan.

Dictionary of Biblical Terms & Symbols: Woerterbuch Biblischer Bilder und Symbole. 4th ed. Manfred Lurker. 505p. (GER.). 1990. 75.00 (*0-8288-2308-1*, M7046) Fr & Eur.

***Dictionary of Biblical Theology.** 2nd ed. Ed. by Xavier Leon-Dufour. Tr. by P. Joseph Cahill & E. M. Stewart. 744p. (FRE.). 1995. pap. 29.95 (*0-932085-09-1*) Word Among Us.

Dictionary of Biblical Theology: Dizionario di Teologia Biblica. Xavier Leon-Dufour & G. Viola. 1424p. (ITA.). 1980. 110.00 (*0-8288-2314-6*, M7691) Fr & Eur.

Dictionary of Biblical Tradition in English Literature. Ed. by David L. Jeffrey. 1992. 79.99 (*0-8028-3634-8*) Eerdmans.

Dictionary of Bibliographic Abbreviations Found in the Scholarship of Classical Studies & Related Disciplines. Comp. by Jean S. Wellington. LC 82-21068. xv, 393p. 1983. text ed. 79.50 (*0-313-23523-6*, WLC/, Greenwood Pr) Greenwood.

Dictionary of Bibliometrics. Virgil Diodato. LC 93-3952. (Illus.). 1994. lib. bdg. 29.95 (*1-56024-852-1*) Haworth Pr.

Dictionary of Biochemistry. Satish Anand & Raj Kumar. 1990. 33.50 (*81-7041-272-2*, Pub. by Anmol II) S Asia.

Dictionary of Biochemistry & Molecular Biology. 2nd ed. Jochanan Stenesh. 1989. text ed. 110.00 (*0-471-84089-0*) Wiley.

Dictionary of Biographical Quotations: The Most Complete Dictionary of Who Said What about Whom. Ed. by Richard Kenin & Justin Wintle. (Reprints Ser.). 860p. 1989. reprint ed. 29.95 (*0-88029-344-6*) Dorset Pr.

Dictionary of Biography. Herbert S. Robinson et al. (Quality Paperback Ser.: No. 281). 530p. 1975. reprint ed. pap. 7.25 (*0-8226-0281-4*) Littlefield.

Dictionary of Biography: Past & Present, Containing the Chief Events in the Lives of Eminent Persons of All Ages & Nations. Benjamin Vincent. 1974. reprint ed. 78.00 (*1-55888-960-4*) Omnigraphics Inc.

Dictionary of Biology. C. Stockley. (Illustrated Dictionaries Ser.). (Illus.). 128p. (J). (gr. 6 up). 1987. lib. bdg. 16.96 (*0-88110-229-6*); pap. 10.95 (*0-86020-819-2*) EDC.

Dictionary of Biology. 2nd enl. rev. ed. G. Haensch & G. Haberkamp De Anton. 680p. (ENG, FRE, GER & SPA.). 1981. 169.25 (*0-444-41968-3*) Elsevier.

Dictionary of Biology. 6th ed. M. Abercrombie et al. (Reference Ser.). (Orig.). 1951. pap. 8.95 (*0-14-051003-6*, Penguin Bks) Viking Penguin.

Dictionary of Biology: Diccionario de Biologia. Faustino Cordon. 389p. 1985. 49.95 (*0-8288-0784-1*, S16351) Fr & Eur.

Dictionary of Biology: Diccionario de Biologia. 2nd ed. T. Lender. 208p. (SPA.). 1985. write for info. (*0-7859-4915-1*) Fr & Eur.

Dictionary of Biology & Ecology: Woerterbuecher der Biologie: Oekologie. 2nd ed. W. Tischler. (GER.). 1983. 59.95 (*0-8288-1222-5*, M15335) Fr & Eur.

Dictionary of Biomedical Acronyms & Abbreviations. 2nd ed. Ed. by Jacques Dupayrat. 162p. 1990. pap. text ed. 59.95 (*0-471-92649-3*) Wiley.

Dictionary of Biotechnology. Rolf Schmid & Saburo Fukui. 1324p. (ENG, GER & JPN.). 1986. 450.00 (*0-8288-0786-8*, 787) Fr & Eur.

Dictionary of Biotechnology. 2nd ed. James Coombs. 376p. 1992. pap. 90.00 (*1-56159-074-6*, Stockton Pr) Groves Dictionaries.

Dictionary of Biotechnology: English - German. W. Babel et al. 116p. (ENG & GER.). 1989. 150.00 (*0-8288-9308-X*, M1721) Fr & Eur.

Dictionary of Biotechnology: English-German. W. Babel et al. 116p. 1988. 64.00 (*0-444-98900-5*) Elsevier.

Dictionary of Biotechnology in English-Japanese-German. R. D. Schmid & Saburo Fukui. 1350p. 1986. 295.00 (*0-387-15566-X*) Spr-Verlag.

Dictionary of Biotechnology, Japanese-English-Japanese. Inter Group Staff. 441p. (ENG & JPN.). 1987. 125.00 (*0-8288-0782-5*, F34188) Fr & Eur.

Dictionary of Birds. Ed. by Bruce Campbell & Elizabeth Lack. LC 84-72101. (Illus.). 700p. 1985. 75.00 (*0-931130-12-3*) Harrell Bks.

Dictionary of Blue & White Printed Pottery, Vol. 2. A. W. Coysh & R. K. Henrywood. (Illus.). 240p. 1989. 49.50 (*1-85149-093-0*) Antique Collect.

Dictionary of Blue & White Printed Pottery 1780-1880. A. W. Coysh & R. K. Henrywood. (Illus.). 420p. 1982. 79.50 (*0-907462-06-5*) Antique Collect.

Dictionary of Body Chemistry. Richard B. Fisher. 208p. 1983. pap. 8.00 (*0-586-08382-0*, Pub. by Granada UK) Academy Chi Pubs.

Dictionary of Books Relating to America, 29 Vols. in 2, Set. Joseph Sabin. LC 66-31865. 1966. reprint ed. 325.00 (*0-8108-0033-0*) Scarecrow.

Dictionary of Botany, Vol. 2: General Terms. P. Macura. 744p. (ENG, FRE, GER & RUS.). 1982. 169.25 (*0-444-41977-2*) Elsevier.

Dictionary of Bowing Terms for Stringed Instruments. 3rd ed. Barbara G. Jackson et al. 1987. 11.00 (*0-89917-498-1*) Am String Tchrs.

Dictionary of Brazilian Literature. Ed. by Irwin Stern. LC 87-17744. 452p. 1988. text ed. 79.50 (*0-313-24932-6*, SDB/, Greenwood Pr) Greenwood.

Dictionary of British & American Women Writers, 1660-1800. Ed. by Janet Todd. LC 84-2123. (Illus.). 368p. 1985. pap. text ed. 27.25 (*0-8476-7556-4*) Rowman.

Dictionary of British & Irish Botanists & Horticulturalists: (Including Plant Collectors, Flower Painters, & Garden Designers) rev. ed. Ed. by Ray Desmond & Christine Ellwood. 900p. 1993. 250.00 (*0-85066-843-3*, Pub. by Tay Francis Ltd UK) Taylor & Francis.

Dictionary of British Art, Vol. I: Sixteenth & Seventeenth Century British Painters. Ellis Waterhouse. (Illus.). 308p. 1988. 89.50 (*1-85149-036-1*) Antique Collect.

Dictionary of British Art, Vol. 2: British Eighteenth Century Painters. Ellis Waterhouse. (Illus.). 443p. 1981. 89.50 (*0-902028-93-6*) Antique Collect.

Dictionary of British Art, Vol. 4: Victorian Painters. 2nd ed. Christopher Wood. (Illus.). 764p. 1978. 99.50 (*0-902028-72-3*) Antique Collect.

Dictionary of British Art, Vol. 5: British Artists 1880-1940. Antique Collector's Club Staff. 567p. 1976. 89.50 (*0-902028-36-7*) Antique Collect.

Dictionary of British Art, Vol. 6: Twentieth Century Painters & Sculptors. Spalding & Collins. (Illus.). 484p. 1991. 99.50 (*1-85149-106-6*) Antique Collect.

Dictionary of British Cartoonists & Caricaturists. Mark Bryant & Simon Heneage. LC 93-21363. 252p. 1994. 54.95 (*0-85967-976-4*, Pub. by Scolar Pr UK) Ashgate Pub Co.

Dictionary of British Children's Fiction, Vol. 1. Althea K. Helbig. LC 88-17788. 887p. 1989. text ed. 150.00 (*0-313-27239-5*, Greenwood Pr) Greenwood.

Dictionary of British Children's Fiction, Vol. 2. Althea K. Helbig. LC 88-17788. 782p. 1989. text ed. 150.00 (*0-313-27240-9*, Greenwood Pr) Greenwood.

Dictionary of British Children's Fiction: Books of Recognized Merit. Althea K. Helbig & Agnes R. Perkins. LC 88-17788. 1652p. 1989. text ed. 150.00 (*0-313-22591-5*, HBC/, Greenwood Pr) Greenwood.

***Dictionary of British Educationists.** Richard Aldrich & Peter Gordon. (Illus.). 276p. 1989. text ed. 35.00 (*0-7130-0177-1*, Pub. by Woburn Pr); pap. text ed. 19.50 (*0-7130-4011-4*, Pub. by Woburn Pr) Intl Spec Bk.

Dictionary of British Equestrian Artists. Sally Mitchell. (Illus.). 518p. 1985. 89.50 (*0-907462-42-1*) Antique Collect.

Dictionary of British Folk-Tales in the English Language, 2 vols. Katherine M. Briggs. 1168p. 1991. reprint ed. Pt. A: Folk Narratives, 1168p. pap. 45.00 (*0-415-06694-8*, A6235); reprint ed. Pt. B: Folk Legends, 1408p. pap. 45.00 (*0-415-06695-6*, A6239) Routledge.

Dictionary of British Folk-Tales in the English Language, 2 vols., Set. Katherine M. Briggs. 2576p. 1991. reprint ed. pap. 80.00 (*0-415-06696-4*, A6231) Routledge.

Dictionary of British Institutions: A Student's Guide. John Oakland. LC 92-38180. (Illus.). 176p. 1993. 57.50 (*0-415-07109-7*, B0108); pap. write for info. (*0-415-07110-0*) Routledge.

Dictionary of British Literary Characters. 1993. 60.00 (*0-8160-2179-1*) Facts on File.

Dictionary of British Literary Characters. John R. Greenfield. 1994. 65.00 (*0-8160-2180-5*) Facts on File.

Dictionary of British Literary Characters, 2 vols., Set. John Greenfield. 560p. 1991. 95.00 (*0-8160-2178-3*) Facts on File.

Dictionary of British Studio Potters. Pat Carter. (Illus.). 192p. 1990. text ed. 39.95 (*0-85967-800-8*, Pub. by Scolar Pr UK) Ashgate Pub Co.

Dictionary of British Watercolour Artists up to 1920: Vol. 1, The Text. 2nd ed. M. L. Mallalieu. 304p. 1986. 79.50 (*1-85149-025-6*) Antique Collect.

Dictionary of British Watercolour Artists Up to 1920: Vol. 2, The Plates. H. L. Mallalieu. (Illus.). 284p. 1979. 69.50 (*0-902028-63-4*) Antique Collect.

Dictionary of British Watercolour Artists up to 1920: Vol. 3. H. L. Mallalieu. (Illus.). 288p. 1991. 69.50 (*1-85149-111-2*) Antique Collect.

***Dictionary of Buddhist Literature & Literary Personalities.** K. Krishna Murthy. (C). 1994. 34.00x (*81-85067-88-0*, Pub. by Sundeep II) S Asia.

Dictionary of Buddhist Terms & Terminologies. K. Krishna Murthy. 1991. 37.00 (*81-85067-67-8*, Pub. by Sundeep II) S Asia.

Dictionary of Building. Randall McMullan. 256p. 1991. 59.50 (*0-87683-601-5*) GP Pub.

Dictionary of Building & Civil Engineering: Dictionnaire Multilingue de Construction et de Genie Civil. S. N. Korchomkin. 600p. (DUT, ENG, FRE, GER & RUS.). 1986. 250.00 (*0-8288-0222-X*, F 1924) Fr & Eur.

Dictionary of Building Construction. Cyril M. Harris. 1992. pap. 14.95 (*0-07-026895-9*) McGraw.

Dictionary of Building Construction. G. Sebestyen. 286p. (ENG, FRE, GER, HUN & RUS.). 1983. 39.95 (*0-8288-1336-1*, M 6212) Fr & Eur.

Dictionary of Building Engineering. S. N. Korchomkin. 1985. 105.00 (*90-201-1863-3*, Pub. by Kluwer NE) IBD Ltd.

***Dictionary of Business: French-English-German.** 3rd ed. Academie de Sciences Staff. (ENG, FRE & GER.). 1994. 250.00 (*0-7859-8885-8*) Fr & Eur.

Dictionary of Business & Credit Terms. Ben Berman. Ed. by James J. Andover. LC 82-14231. 208p. 1983. 16.95 (*0-934914-45-1*) NACM.

Dictionary of Business & Economics. rev. ed. Christine Ammer & Dean S. Ammer. 508p. (C). 1984. 40.00 (*0-02-900790-9*) Free Pr.

Dictionary of Business & Economics: Revised & Expanded Edition. enl. rev. ed. Christine Ammer & Dean S. Ammer. 517p. 1986. pap. 27.95 (*0-02-901480-8*) Free Pr.

Dictionary of Business & Finance. Hans Schnellman. 120p. (ENG & GER.). 1987. 95.00 (*0-8288-0104-5*, M4943) Fr & Eur.

Dictionary of Business & Finance: Worterbuch Handel und Finanzen. Hans Schnellman. 120p. (GER.). 1987. 95.00 (*0-8288-0819-8*) Fr & Eur.

***Dictionary of Business & Finance Terms.** George E. Oldham. 1993. pap. 9.95 (*1-882912-01-2*) Sunrise TN.

Dictionary of Business & Management. 2nd ed. Jerry M. Rosenberg. 684p. 1985. 49.95 (*0-8288-4408-9*, M7802) Fr & Eur.

Dictionary of Business & Management. 3rd ed. Jerry M. Rosenberg. (Business Dictionaries Ser.). 384p. 1992. text ed. 45.00 (*0-471-57812-6*); pap. text ed. 14.95 (*0-471-54536-8*) Wiley.

Dictionary of Business Biography: A Biographical Dictionary of Business Leaders Active in Britain in the Period, 1860-1980, 5. Ed. by David Jeremy. (Illus.). 1986. text ed. 200.00 (*0-406-27345-6*) Buttrwrth-Heinemann.

***Dictionary of Business, Law, & Finance.** Robert Herbst. (ENG, FRE & GER.). 1995. 140.00 (*0-930267-32-X*) Bergh Pub.

Dictionary of Business Quotations. Ed. by Robert Parker. 240p. 1990. 30.00 (*0-685-35584-5*) S&S Trade.

Dictionary of Business Quotations. Julia Vitullo-Martin & J. Robert Moskin. 352p. 1993. 30.00 (*0-19-507836-5*) OUP.

Dictionary of Business Terms. Ed. by Jack P. Friedman et al. 500p. 1987. pap. 10.95 (*0-8120-3775-8*) Barron.

Dictionary of Business Terms. 2nd ed. Jack Friedman et al. 700p. (C). 1994. pap. 11.95 (*0-8120-1833-8*) Barron.

Dictionary of Cable Engineering: English-German-French. C. Richling & I. Drewitz. 610p. (ENG, FRE & GER.). 1976. pap. 60.00 (*3-87097-072-3*) IBD Ltd.

An Asterisk (*) at the beginning of an entry indicates that the title is appearing in BIP for the first time.

Dictionary of Canadian Abbreviations. Terese Dobroslavic. 400p. (C). 1993. text ed. 70.00 (*1-55022-196-5*, Pub. by ECW Press CN) Genl Dist Srvs.

Dictionary of Canadian Biography, Vols. I-XII. Incl. Vol. I. 1000-1700. Ed. by G. W. Brown & Marcel Trudel. LC 66-31909. xxiii, 755p. 1966. 75.00 (*0-8020-3142-0*); Vol. II. 1701-1740. Ed. by David Hayne & Andre Vachon. LC 66-31909. xli, 759p. 1969. 75.00 (*0-8020-3240-0*); Vol. II. 1701-1740. Ed. by David Hayne & Andre Vachon. LC 66-31909. xli, 759p. 1969. 150.00 (*0-8020-3249-4*); Vol. III. 1741-1770. Ed. by Marc La Terreur. LC 66-31909. 1974. 75.00 (*0-8020-3314-8*); Vol. III. 1741-1770. Ed. by Marc La Terreur. LC 66-31909. 1974. 150.00 (*0-8020-3315-6*); Vol. IV. 1771-1800. Ed. by Frances Halpenny. LC 66-31909. 1979. 75.00 (*0-8020-3351-2*); Vol. IV. 1771-1800. Ed. by Frances Halpenny. LC 66-31909. 1979. 150.00 (*0-8020-3352-0*); Vol. IX. 1861-1870. Ed. by Jean Hamelin. LC 66-31909. 1976. 75.00 (*0-8020-3319-9*); Vol. IX. 1861-1870. Ed. by Jean Hamelin. LC 66-31909. 1976. 150.00 (*0-8020-3320-2*); Vol. X. 1871-1880. Ed. by Marc La Terreur. LC 66-31909. 1972. 75.00 (*0-8020-3287-7*); Vol. X. 1871-1880. Ed. by Marc La Terreur. LC 66-31909. 1972. 150.00 (*0-8020-3288-5*); Vol. XI. 1881-1890. Ed. by Francess G. Halpenny. LC 66-31909. 1100p. 1982. 75.00 (*0-8020-3367-9*); Vol. XI. 1881-1890. Ed. by Francess G. Halpenny. LC 66-31909. 1100p. 1982. 150.00 (*0-8020-3368-7*); LC 66-31909. write for info.*0-318-56149-2*) U of Toronto Pr.

Dictionary of Canadian Biography: Index to Volumes I to IV (1000-1800) Ed. by Francess G. Halpenny & Jean Hamelin. 192p. 1981. 45.00 (*0-8020-3326-1*); 100.00 (*0-8020-3388-1*) U of Toronto Pr.

Dictionary of Canadian Biography: Index to Volumes I to XII. Ed. by Francess G. Halpenny & Jean Hamelin. 608p. 1991. 85.00 (*0-8020-3464-0*); 150.00 (*0-8020-3465-9*) U of Toronto Pr.

Dictionary of Canadian Biography: 1801-1820, Vol. V. Ed. by Francess G. Halpenny. 1069p. 1983. 75.00 (*0-8020-3398-9*) U of Toronto Pr.

Dictionary of Canadian Biography - Dictionnaire Biographique du Canada, Vol. XIII: 1901-1910. Ed. by Ramsay Cook. 1300p. 1994. 85.00 (*0-8020-3998-7*) U of Toronto Pr.

Dictionary of Canadian Biography, Vol. Eight: 1851-1860. Ed. by Francess G. Halpenny & Jean Hamelin. 1029p. 1985. 80.00 (*0-8020-3422-5*); 150.00 (*0-8020-3423-3*) U of Toronto Pr.

Dictionary of Canadian Biography, Vol. Twelve: 1891-1900. Ed. by Francess G. Halpenny & Jean Hamelin. 1200p. 1990. 80.00 (*0-8020-3460-8*); 150.00 (*0-8020-3461-6*) U of Toronto Pr.

Dictionary of Canadian Biography, Vol. VI: 1821-35. Ed. by Francess G. Halpenny. 75.00 (*0-8020-3436-5*) U of Toronto Pr.

Dictionary of Canadian Biography, Vol. VI: 1821-35, Laurentian Edition. Ed. by Francess G. Halpenny. 1986. Laurentian ed., 1986. 150.00 (*0-8020-3437-3*) U of Toronto Pr.

Dictionary of Canadian Biography, Vol. VII: 1836-1850. Ed. by Francess G. Halpenny. 1117p. 1988. 75.00 (*0-8020-3452-7*); 150.00 (*0-8020-3453-5*) U of Toronto Pr.

Dictionary of Canadian Quotations. Ed. by John Colombo. 671p. Date not set. 29.95 (*0-7737-2515-6*, Pub. by Stoddart Pubng CN) Genl Dist Srvs.

Dictionary of Card Games. David Parlett. (Oxford Paperback Reference). (Illus.). 400p. 1992. pap. 12.95 (*0-19-869173-4*) OUP.

Dictionary of Cardiac Pacing, Electrophysiology & Arrhythmias. David L. Hayes et al. LC 93-83653. (Illus.). 171p. 1993. text ed. 65.00 (*1-881645-01-0*) Peritus.

Dictionary of Cardiology: Dictionnaire de Cardiologie. Paul E. Valere. 352p. (FRE.). 1986. 95.00 (*0-8288-1829-0*, F28480) Fr & Eur.

Dictionary of Catch Phrases: American & British, from the Sixteenth Century to the Present Day. rev. ed. Eric Partridge. Ed. by Paul Beale. LC 85-40997. 408p. 1992. 24.95 (*0-8128-3101-2*, Scrbrough Hse); pap. 12.95 (*0-8128-8536-8*, Scrbrough Hse) Madison Bks UPA.

Dictionary of Catholic Devotions. Michael Walsh. LC 91-55417. 320p. 1994. 22.00 (*0-06-069271-5*) Harper SF.

Dictionary of Cebuano Visayan, Vols. 1 & 2. John U. Wolff. LC 73-158699. (Cornell University, Southeast Asia Program, Data Paper Ser.: No. 87). 560p. reprint ed. Vol. 1, 560p. pap. 159.60 (*0-8357-3675-X*, 2036400); reprint ed. Vol. 2, 645p. pap. 180.00 (*0-8357-3676-8*, 2036400) Bks Demand.

***Dictionary of Celebrated Phrases: Diccionario de Frases Celabres.** 6th ed. Jorge S. Pros. 1000p. 1988. 69.95 (*0-7859-5025-7*) Fr & Eur.

***Dictionary of Cell Biology.** 2nd ed. Ed. by J. M. Lackie & J. A. T. Dow. (Illus.). 380p. 1995. text ed. 45.00 (*0-12-432562-9*) Acad Pr.

***Dictionary of Cell Biology.** 2nd ed. Ed. by J. M. Lackie & J. A. T. Dow. (Illus.). 380p. 1995. pap. text ed. write for info. (*0-12-432563-7*) Acad Pr.

Dictionary of Celtic Myth & Legend. Miranda Green. LC 91-65265. (Illus.). 240p. 1992. 35.00 (*0-500-01516-3*) Thames Hudson.

Dictionary of Celtic Mythology. Peter B. Ellis. 232p. 1992. lib. bdg. 55.00 (*0-87436-609-7*) ABC-CLIO.

Dictionary of Celtic Mythology. Peter B. Ellis. LC 93-30262. 240p. 1994. pap. 9.95 (*0-19-508961-8*) OUP.

Dictionary of Cement Manufacture & Technology: Zement-Woerterbuch. 2nd ed. Carel Von Amerongen. 328p. (ENG & GER.). 1986. 175.00 (*0-8288-0879-1*, M 7127) Fr & Eur.

Dictionary of Ceramic Science & Engineering. 2nd ed. I. J. McColm. 1994. 75.00 (*0-306-44542-5*, Plenum Pr) Plenum.

***Dictionary of Ceramics.** 3rd ed. A. E. Dodd. 240p. 1994. 90.00 (*0-901716-56-1*) Ashgate Pub Co.

Dictionary of Ceramics & Earths: English-German, German-English: Worterbuch Keramik und Erden: Englisch-Deutsch, Deutsch-Englisch. Berd Pfannkuche & Johanna Baur. LC 93-12989. (ENG & GER.). 1993. 96.00 (*1-56081-207-9*) VCH Pubs.

Dictionary of Cereal Processing & Cereal Chemistry. R. Schneeweiss. 520p. (ENG, FRE, GER, LAT & RUS.). 1982. 174.50 (*0-444-42049-5*, I-274-82) Elsevier.

Dictionary of Characters & Proper Names in the Works of Shakespeare. Francis G. Stokes. 1977. lib. bdg. 134.95 (*0-8490-1718-1*) Gordon Pr.

Dictionary of Characters & Proper Names in the Works of Shakespeare. Francis G. Stokes. 1981. reprint ed. lib. bdg. 69.00 (*0-00-003880-6*) Scholarly.

Dictionary of Chemical Engineering: English, German, Spanish, French. Aksel L. Lydersen & Ingrid Dahlo. LC 92-12716. 250p. (ENG, FRE, GER & SPA.). 1992. pap. text ed. 79.95 (*0-471-93392-9*) Wiley.

Dictionary of Chemical Engineering & Laboratory Equipment. enl. ed. Hans Schnellman. 312p. (ENG & GER.). 1987. 175.00 (*0-8288-0170-3*, F93771) Fr & Eur.

Dictionary of Chemical Names & Synonyms. Philip H. Howard & Michael W. Neal. 1800p. 1991. 149.95 (*0-87371-396-6*, TP9) Lewis Pubs.

Dictionary of Chemical Terminology. Dobromila Kryt. 600p. (ENG, FRE, GER, POL & RUS.). 1980. 118.00 (*0-444-99788-1*) Elsevier.

Dictionary of Chemical Terms. McGraw-Hill Editors. LC 85-11696. 464p. 1986. pap. text ed. 27.95 (*0-07-045417-5*) McGraw.

Dictionary of Chemistry. J. Wertheim & C. Oxlade. (Illustrated Dictionaries Ser.). (Illus.). 128p. (J). (gr. 6 up). 1987. lib. bdg. 16.96 (*0-88110-230-X*); pap. 10.95 (*0-86020-821-4*) EDC.

Dictionary of Chemistry, Vol. 1. Richard R. Ernst. (ENG & GER.). 1961. 95.00 (*0-8288-6818-2*, M7037) Fr & Eur.

Dictionary of Chemistry, Vol. 2. Richard R. Ernst. (ENG & GER.). 1963. 85.00 (*0-8288-6785-2*, M7036) Fr & Eur.

Dictionary of Chemistry & Chemical Engineering. 2nd ed. Helmut Gross. 636p. (ENG & GER.). 1983. 175.00 (*0-8288-0167-3*, M15545) Fr & Eur.

Dictionary of Chemistry & Chemical Engineering, 2 vols., Set. 2nd ed. Incl. Vol. 1. German-English. 849p. 1979. 260.00 (*0-89573-010-3*); Vol. 2. English-German. 781p. 1987. 260.00 (*0-89573-025-1*); (ENG & GER.). 1979. write for info. (*0-685-05245-1*) VCH Pubs.

Dictionary of Chemistry & Chemical Engineering, 2 vols., Vol. 1. 2nd ed. Incl. Vol. 1. German-English. 849p. 1979. 260.00 (*0-89573-010-3*); Vol. 2. English-German. 781p. 1987. 260.00 (*0-89573-025-1*); (ENG & GER.). 1979. write for info. (*0-685-05246-X*) VCH Pubs.

Dictionary of Chemistry & Chemical Engineering, Vol. 1. 3rd ed. Louis De Vries & H. Kolb. 851p. (ENG & GER.). 1983. 350.00 (*0-8288-0165-7*, M7126) Fr & Eur.

Dictionary of Chemistry & Chemical Engineering, Vol. 2. Louis De Vries. (ENG & GER.). 1972. pap. 350.00 (*0-8288-6367-9*, M-7125) Fr & Eur.

Dictionary of Chemistry & Chemical Technology. 3rd ed. Helmut Gross. 720p. (ENG & GER.). 1984. 175.00 (*0-8288-0168-1*, M15545) Fr & Eur.

Dictionary of Chemistry & Chemical Technology: English-German. H. W. Gross et al. 768p. 1989. 154.00 (*0-444-98863-7*) Elsevier.

Dictionary of Chemistry & Chemical Technology: Japanese, English, Chinese. C. Huimin & B. Wenchu. 1720p. 1989. 205.25 (*0-444-87371-6*) Elsevier.

Dictionary of Chemistry & Chemical Technology in Japanese, English & Chinese. C. Huimin & B. Wenchu. 1716p. (CHI, ENG & JPN.). 1989. 350.00 (*0-8288-9224-5*) Fr & Eur.

Dictionary of Chemistry English - French. Raymond Cornubert. (ENG & FRE.). 1977. 85.00 (*0-8288-9465-5*) Fr & Eur.

Dictionary of Chess. N. P. Zelepukhin. 206p. (RUS.). 1982. 14.95 (*0-8288-2350-2*, M 15539) Fr & Eur.

Dictionary of Child Psychiatry & Psychology: Diccionario de Psicologia y Psiquiatria Infantil. Alberto L. Merani. 176p. (ENG, GER, ITA & SPA.). 1983. 28.50 (*0-8288-2221-2*, S39839) Fr & Eur.

Dictionary of Childhood Health: Diccionario de la Salud Infantil. J. Ratel. 480p. (SPA.). 1983. pap. 19.95 (*0-8288-1875-4*, S60549) Fr & Eur.

Dictionary of Children's Fiction from Australia, Canada, India, New Zealand & Selected African Countries. Althea K. Helbig & Agnes R. Perkins. LC 91-35234. (Books of Recognized Merit). 608p. 1992. text ed. 85.00 (*0-313-26126-1*, HCD/, Greenwood Pr) Greenwood.

Dictionary of China's Rural Economy. K. Broadbent. 406p. (CHI & ENG.). 1978. 125.00 (*0-8288-5169-7*, M9712) Fr & Eur.

Dictionary of Chinese Buddhist Terms. Ed. by William E. Soothill & Lewis Hodous. (C). 1987. reprint ed. 44.00 (*81-208-0319-1*, Pub. by Motilal Banarsidass II) S Asia.

***Dictionary of Chinese Buddhist Terms: With Sanskrit & English Equivalents & a Sanskrit-Pali Index.** William E. Soothill & Lewis Hodous. 550p. (C). 1995. reprint ed. text ed. 189.00 (*0-7007-0355-1*, Pub. by Curzon Pr UK) Humanities.

Dictionary of Chinese Characters' Information. Science Press Staff. 1346p. (CHI.). 1988. 95.00 (*0-8288-7326-7*, 7030008626) Fr & Eur.

Dictionary of Chinese Classifiers. 160p. 1989. pap. 5.95 (*0-89346-312-4*) Heian Intl.

Dictionary of Chinese History. Michael Dillon. 240p. 1979. 35.00 (*0-7146-3107-8*, Pub. by F Cass Pubs UK) Intl Spec Bk.

Dictionary of Chinese Law & Government: Chinese-English. Philip R. Bilancia. LC 73-80618. 832p. 1981. 85.00 (*0-8047-0864-9*) Stanford U Pr.

Dictionary of Chinese Symbols: Dictionnaire des Symboles Chinois. Wolfram Eberhard. 368p. (CHI & FRE.). 1984. pap. 45.00 (*0-8288-1608-5*, F85350) Fr & Eur.

Dictionary of Chinese Symbols: Hidden Symbols in Chinese Life & Thought. Wolfram Eberhard. 384p. 1988. pap. 16.95 (*0-415-00228-1*) Routledge.

Dictionary of Christian Art. Diane Apostolos-Cappadona. (Illus.). 380p. (C). 1994. 39.50 (*0-8264-0779-X*) Continuum.

***Dictionary of Christian Biography.** Ed. by Henry Wace & William Piercy. 1040p. 1994. 29.95 (*1-56563-057-2*) Hendrickson MA.

Dictionary of Christian Biography, Literature, Sects & Doctrines: Being a Continuation of the Dictionary of the Bible, 4 Vols, Set. Ed. by William Smith & Henry Wace. LC 12-3122. 1968. reprint ed. 495.00 (*0-527-84200-1*) Periodicals Srv.

Dictionary of Christian Biography, Literature, Sects & Doctrines: Being a Continuation of the "Dictionary of the Bible", 4 vols., Set. Ed. by William Smith & Henry Wace. LC 12-3122. reprint ed. 495.00 (*0-404-06140-0*) AMS Pr.

Dictionary of Christian Lore & Legend. J. C. Metford. LC 82-50815. (Illus.). 272p. 1991. pap. 14.95 (*0-500-27373-1*) Thames Hudson.

Dictionary of Christianity in America: A Comprehensive Resource on the Religious Impulse That Shaped a Continent. Harry S. Stout et al. Ed. by Daniel G. Reid et al. LC 89-29953. 1306p. 1990. 44.99 (*0-8308-1776-X*, 1776) InterVarsity.

Dictionary of Church Music. George W. Stubbins. 128p. 1993. reprint ed. lib. bdg. 69.00 (*0-7812-9679-X*) Rprt Serv.

Dictionary of Civil Engineering. V. N. Vazirani. (C). 1992. text ed. 20.00 (*81-204-0740-7*, Pub. by Oxford IBH II) S Asia.

Dictionary of Civil Engineering: Dictionnairre du Batiment, French & German. Hans Schnellman. 120p. (FRE & GER.). 1987. 95.00 (*0-8288-0881-3*, M15025) Fr & Eur.

Dictionary of Civil Engineering: Woerterbuch fuer Bautechnik und Baumaschinen. 5th rev. ed. Herbert Bucksch. 875p. (FRE & GER.). 1982. pap. 195.00 (*0-8288-4425-9*, M15075) Fr & Eur.

Dictionary of Civil Engineering: Woerterbuch Fuer Bautechnik und Baumaschinen. 8th rev. ed. Herbert Bucksch. (ENG & GER.). 1982. 225.00 (*0-8288-0202-5*, M7121) Fr & Eur.

Dictionary of Civil Engineering & Construction Machinery & Equipment, Vol. 1. 5th ed. Herbert Bucksch. 420p. (ENG & FRE.). 1976. 125.00 (*0-8288-5629-X*, M4647) Fr & Eur.

Dictionary of Civil Engineering & Construction Machinery & Equipment, Vol. 2. 5th ed. Herbert Bucksch. 548p. (ENG & FRE.). 1976. 150.00 (*0-8288-5630-3*, M6050) Fr & Eur.

Dictionary of Civil Engineering, German & English. enl. ed. Hans Schnellman. 312p. (ENG & GER.). 1987. 195.00 (*0-8288-0210-6*, F25840) Fr & Eur.

Dictionary of Civil Engineering, Spanish & English. Hans Schnellman. 120p. (ENG & SPA.). 1987. pap. 95.00 (*0-8288-0889-9*, F21020) Fr & Eur.

Dictionary of Civil Engineering, Vol. 2: Woerterbuch Fuer Bautechnik und Baumaschinen. 8th rev. ed. Herbert Bucksch. 1219p. (ENG & GER.). 1982. 225.00 (*0-8288-0203-3*, M7122) Fr & Eur.

Dictionary of Classical Ballet in Labanotation. Alan Miles. 108p. (Orig.). 1995. pap. 15.00 (*0-932582-17-6*) Dance Notation.

Dictionary of Classical, Biblical, & Literary Allusions. Abraham H. Lass. 1988. mass mkt. 5.99 (*0-449-14565-4*) Fawcett.

Dictionary of Classical Mythology. Zimmerman. (YA). (gr. 9 up). 1983. mass mkt. 5.99 (*0-553-25776-5*) Bantam.

Dictionary of Classical Mythology: Symbols, Attributes, & Associations. Robert E. Bell. LC 81-19141. 390p. 1980. lib. bdg. 60.00 (*0-87436-305-5*) ABC-CLIO.

***Dictionary of Classical Mythology & Religion.** 1995. pap. 14.99 (*0-517-12311-8*) Random.

Dictionary of Cliches. James Rogers. 1986. mass mkt. 5.99 (*0-345-33814-6*) Ballantine.

Dictionary of Cliches. 5th ed. Eric Partridge. 1978. reprint ed. pap. 13.95 (*0-7100-0049-9*, RKP) Routledge.

Dictionary of Cliches. James Rogers. 320p. 1992. reprint ed. pap. 8.99 (*0-517-06020-5*, Pub. by Wings Bks) Random.

Dictionary of Clinical Medicine. Stephan Dressler. 878p. (ENG & GER.). 1991. lib. bdg. 115.00 (*0-89573-992-5*) VCH Pubs.

Dictionary of Clinical Pharmacology for Doctors & Pharmacists: Woerterbuch der Klinischen Pharmakologie Fuer Mediziner und Pharmazeuten. R. K. Liedtke. 245p. 1980. 49.95 (*0-8288-1838-X*, M15389) Fr & Eur.

Dictionary of Clinical Tests. O. Potparic & J. Gibson. (Illus.). 250p. 1992. 48.00 (*1-85070-416-3*) Prthnon Pub.

***Dictionary of Clothes from Lisan al-Arab.** Ahmed Matloub. 142p. (ARA.). 1995. 18.95 (*0-86685-652-8*) Intl Bk Ctr.

***Dictionary of Coal Chemistry & Petrochemistry.** W. Leipnitz. (ENG, FRE, GER & RUS.). 1992. 158.00 (*0-7859-8833-5*) Fr & Eur.

Dictionary of Coal Chemistry & Petrochemistry: English-German-French-Russian. rev. ed. Walter Leipnitz. 340p. (ENG, FRE, GER & RUS.). 1992. 158.00 (*3-86117-039-6*, Pub. by A Hatier GW) IBD Ltd.

Dictionary of Coal Science & Technology. Comp. by Roy D. Meritt. LC 86-31143. (Illus.). 384p. 1987. 48.00 (*0-8155-1124-8*) Noyes.

***Dictionary of Code Symbols for Cables & Insulated Cord According to UDE, CENELEC & IEC: German-English.** 4th ed. Ewald Retzlaff. 152p. (ENG & GER.). 1993. 49.95 (*0-7859-8693-6*, 380071860x) Fr & Eur.

***Dictionary of Cognitive Psychology.** Ed. by Ian Stuart-Hamilton. 250p. 1995. 49.95 (*1-85302-202-0*, Pub. by J Kingsley Pubs UK) Taylor & Francis.

Dictionary of Collective Nouns. 3rd ed. 1905. 88.00 (*0-8103-5530-2*) Gale.

Dictionary of Colloid & Surface Science. Becher. 216p. 1990. 99.75 (*0-8247-8326-3*) Dekker.

Dictionary of Colonial American Printers' Ornaments & Illustrations. Elizabeth C. Reilly. LC 75-5023. (Illus.). xxxvi, 514p. 1975. 60.00 (*0-912296-06-2*, U Pr of Va) Am Antiquarian.

Dictionary of Colorful Phrases. Gibson Carothers & James Lacey. (Illus.). 96p. 1994. pap. 6.95 (*0-8069-4639-3*) Sterling.

Dictionary of Combinations Equivalent to a Word. Ed. by R. Rogozhnikova. 144p. (C). 1983. 75.00 (*0-685-46807-0*, Pub. by Collets) St Mut.

Dictionary of Commerce. Abrol Gupta. 392p. 1991. 80.00 (*81-7041-120-3*, Pub. by Scientific Pubs II) St Mut.

Dictionary of Commercial & Business Law: Diccionario de Derecho Comercial y de la Empresa. Saul A. Argeri. 398p. (SPA.). 1982. pap. 42.50 (*0-8288-1527-5*, S40508) Fr & Eur.

Dictionary of Commercial & Economic English: Dictionnaire de L'Anglais Economique et Commercial. 2nd ed. Michel Marcheteau. 620p. (ENG & FRE.). 1990. pap. 24.95 (*0-8288-0075-8*, M513) Fr & Eur.

Dictionary of Commercial, Financial & Legal Terms in Two Languages. R. Herbst. (ENG & GER.). Vol. A, Eng. to Ger. 157.75 (*3-85942-003-8*); Vol. B, Ger. to Eng. 157.75 (*3-85942-004-6*) Adlers Foreign Bks.

***Dictionary of Commercial Law: English, German & French.** Udo Becker. 1000p. (ENG, FRE & GER.). 1980. 150.00 (*0-7859-7459-8*, 285608012X) Fr & Eur.

Dictionary of Commercial Terms & Abbreviations. Alan E. Branch. 458p. (C). 1984. pap. 150.00 (*0-900886-90-0*, Pub. by Witherby & Co UK) St Mut.

Dictionary of Commerical Law. 2nd ed. U. Becker. 1000p. (ENG, FRE & GER.). 1980. 142.50 (*2-85608-012-X*) IBD Ltd.

Dictionary of Common Fallacies, 2 vols., Set. Philip Ward. 616p. 1989. 59.95 (*0-87975-511-3*) Prometheus Bks.

Dictionary of Common Mistakes in Modern Written Arabic: Arabic-Arabic. Muhammad Adnani. 1984. 30.00 (*0-86685-104-6*) Intl Bk Ctr.

Dictionary of Common Words. V. D. Arakin et al. 567p. (ENG & RUS.). 1981. 17.95 (*0-8288-1226-8*, F60770) Fr & Eur.

Dictionary of Communication & Media Studies. rev. ed. Ed. by James Watson & Anne Hill. 224p. 1989. 49.00 (*0-7131-6586-3*, Pub. by E Arnold UK); pap. 16.95 (*0-7131-6585-5*, Pub. by E Arnold UK) Routledge Chapman & Hall.

Dictionary of Communication & Media Studies. 3rd ed. Jim Watson & Anne Hill. 224p. 1993. pap. 17.95 (*0-340-57425-9*, B0093, Pub. by E Arnold UK) Routledge Chapman & Hall.

***Dictionary of Communication Design.** Petra Wilhelm. LC 94-46575. (ENG & GER.). 1994. 29.95 (*0-387-57779-3*) Spr-Verlag.

***Dictionary of Communication Disorders.** 2nd ed. Morris. 244p. 1992. pap. 37.75 (*1-56593-371-0*, 0319) Singular Publishing.

***Dictionary of Communications Technology: Terms, Definitions & Abbreviations.** Held. Date not set. text ed. 69.95 (*0-471-95542-6*) Wiley.

***Dictionary of Communications Technology: Terms, Definitions, & Abbreviations.** 2nd ed. Gilbert Held. LC 94-33840. 1994. pap. text ed. 49.95 (*0-471-95126-9*) Wiley.

Dictionary of Company Law. 2nd ed. A. H. Hudson. 1991. U.K. pap. 30.00 (*0-406-68164-3*) Butterworth Legal Pubs.

***Dictionary of Comparative Proverbs, English-Arabic-French-Latin.** Kamal Khalaili. 236p. (ARA & FRE.). 1994. 19.95 (*0-86685-651-X*) Intl Bk Ctr.

Dictionary of Comparative Religions. Samuel G. Brandon. LC 76-11390. 712p. 1978. text ed. 60.00 (*0-684-15561-3*, Scribners) S&S Trade.

Dictionary of Composers. Ed. by Charles Osborne. LC 78-58291. (Illus.). 380p. 1981. pap. 17.95 (*0-8008-2195-5*) Taplinger.

Dictionary of Composers & Their Music. Eric Gilder. 1993. 12.99 (*0-517-09295-6*) Random Hse Value.

Dictionary of Composite Materials Technology. Stuart Lee. LC 89-50813. 171p. 1989. 49.00 (*0-87762-600-6*) Technomic.

Dictionary of Computer & Data Processing Terms: English with Arabic Glossary. Haddad. 1988. 19.95 (*0-86685-434-7*) Intl Bk Ctr.

Dictionary of Computer & Video Terms. William MacNair. (Illus.). 87p. (Orig.). 1987. lib. bdg. 49.95 (*0-941303-35-7*); pap. 14.50 (*0-941303-05-5*) Comput & Arts Pubns.

***Dictionary of Computer Graphics Technology & Applications.** 2nd ed. Roy Latham. LC 94-36569. 1995. 19.00 (*0-387-94405-2*) Spr-Verlag.

Dictionary of Computer Programming & Data Processing. 386p. 1976. 90.00 (*0-686-44722-0*, Pub. by Collets UK) St Mut.

***Dictionary of Computer Science French-English, English-French.** Afnor Staff. 374p. (ENG & FRE.). 1989. pap. 95.00 (*0-7859-7740-6*, 2124869116) Fr & Eur.

Dictionary of Computer Science in English-Arabic. Boutros-Sbeih. 1989. 24.95 (*0-86685-504-1*) Intl Bk Ctr.

An Asterisk (*) at the beginning of an entry indicates that the title is appearing in BIP for the first time.

D

An Asterisk (*) at the beginning of an entry indicates that the title is appearing in BIP for the first time.

1961

Dictionary of Econometrics. Adrian C. Darnell. 512p. 1994. 112.95 (*1-85278-389-3*, Pub. by E Elgar Pub UK) Ashgate Pub Co.

Dictionary of Economic & Commercial Portuguese: Dictionnaire du Portugais Economique et Commercial. (FRE & POR.). 1988. 65.00 (*0-8288-0826-0*, M512) Fr & Eur.

Dictionary of Economic Plants. 2nd enl. rev. ed. J. C. Uphof. 1968. 49.00 (*3-7682-0001-9*) Lubrecht & Cramer.

Dictionary of Economic, Political & Legal Science. M. E. Benissad. 258p. (ARA, ENG & FRE.). 1983. pap. 49.95 (*0-7859-4862-7*) Fr & Eur.

Dictionary of Economic Products of India, 6 vols., Set. G. A. Watt. (C). 1988. text ed. 600.00 (*0-685-22086-9*, Scientific) St Mut.

Dictionary of Economic Products of Malaya, Vols. 1-2 Rep. A. Burkil. (C). 1986. 600.00 (*0-317-92347-1*, Scientific) St Mut.

Dictionary of Economic Quotations. 2nd ed. Comp. by Simon James. 256p. (C). 1984. pap. 14.00 (*0-8226-0390-X*) Littlefield.

Dictionary of Economic Spanish: Dictionnaire de l'Espagnol Economique. Bordas Staff. (FRE & SPA.). 1985. 65.00 (*0-8288-0828-7*, F49990) Fr & Eur.

Dictionary of Economic Terms. S. Bubic. 1048p. (CRO, ENG & SER.). 1975. 95.00 (*0-8288-5838-1*, M9699) Fr & Eur.

Dictionary of Economic Terms. rev. ed. J. R. Winton. 80p. 1987. 18.50 (*0-87559-173-6*) Shalom.

Dictionary of Economics, 2 vols. R. V. Eichborn. Incl. Vol. 1. English & German. 1982. 215.00 (*3-921392-06-3*); Vol. 2. German & English. 1982. 215.00 (*3-921392-07-1*); (ENG & GER.). 1982. 336.00 (*0-685-41956-8*) Adlers Foreign Bks.

Dictionary of Economics. A. I. Goranin. 316p. (RUS.). 1983. 24.95 (*0-8288-1283-7*, M 15094) Fr & Eur.

Dictionary of Economics. Frank Livesey. 320p. (Orig.). 1993. pap. 33.50 (*0-273-60034-6*, Pub. by Pitman Pub Ltd UK) Trans-Atl Phila.

Dictionary of Economics. P. N. Roy. (C). 1989. 45.00 (*0-89771-426-1*, Current Dist) St Mut.

Dictionary of Economics. Ed. by Donald Rutherford. (Illus.). 448p. 1991. 85.00 (*0-415-06566-6*, A6024) Routledge.

Dictionary of Economics. Randall S. Schuler. 580p. (ENG & GER.). 1990. pap. 95.00 (*0-685-62925-2*, 3817111029) Fr & Eur.

***Dictionary of Economics.** Jae K. Shim. (Business Dictionary Ser.). 1995. text ed. 39.95 (*0-471-01317-X*) Wiley.

***Dictionary of Economics.** Jae K. Shim & Joel G Siegel. (Business Dictionary Ser.). 1995. pap. text ed. 16.95 (*0-471-01314-5*) Wiley.

Dictionary of Economics: Ekonomiordbok. N. F. Edstrom et al. (ENG & SWE.). 1987. 125.00 (*0-8288-0136-3*, F39010) Fr & Eur.

Dictionary of Economics: Oekonomisches Woerterbuch. F. Munniksma. 764p. (ENG & GER.). 1980. 95.00 (*0-8288-0099-5*, M 15199) Fr & Eur.

Dictionary of Economics: Woerterbuch der Wirtschaft. 10th ed. Horst C. Recktenwald. 706p. (GER.). 1987. 59. 95 (*0-8288-1279-9*, M6941) Fr & Eur.

***Dictionary of Economics & Business.** Vladimir Kovalev. (ITA & RUS.). Date not set. 150.00 (*0-7859-8873-4*) Fr & Eur.

***Dictionary of Economics & Business & of Modern Language.** Fernando Picchi. (ENG & ITA.). Date not set. 100.00 (*0-7859-8874-2*) Fr & Eur.

Dictionary of Economics & Commerce. Zacharia Nasr. 320p. (ARA, ENG & FRE.). 1980. write for info. (*0-8288-0151-7*, M15757) Fr & Eur.

Dictionary of Economics & Finance: Diccionario Economico y Financiero. 3rd ed. Yves Bernard et al. 1341p. (SPA.). 1981. 150.00 (*0-8288-1287-X*, S33136) Fr & Eur.

Dictionary of Economics, Business, & Finance (English & Arabic with Arabic Glossary) Nabih Ghattas. 1985. 35. 00 (*0-86685-271-9*) Intl Bk Ctr.

Dictionary of Economics, 1990. Randall S. Schuler. 580p. (ENG & GER.). 1990. 150.00 (*0-8288-3892-5*) Fr & Eur.

Dictionary of Education. Derek Rowntree. 362p. (C). 1982. text ed. 45.00 (*0-389-20263-0*, 07081) B&N Imports.

Dictionary of Education. John Dewey. Ed. by Ralph B. Winn. LC 72-139129. 150p. 1972. reprint ed. text ed. 45.00 (*0-8371-5745-5*, DEDE, Greenwood Pr) Greenwood.

***Dictionary of Education Terms.** Ed. by David Blake & Vincent Hanley. 150p. 1995. boxed 51.95 (*1-85742-256-2*, Pub. by Arena UK); pap. write for info. (*1-85742-253-8*, Pub. by Arena UK) Ashgate Pub Co.

Dictionary of Educational Evaluation & Research: Dictionnaire de l'Evaluation et de la Recherche en Education. Gilbert De Landsheere. 352p. (FRE.). 1979. 99.50 (*0-8288-4793-2*, M6108) Fr & Eur.

***Dictionary of Educational Opportunities.** Donald Rosen et al. LC 94-24738. 166p. 1994. pap. 18.00 (*0-911907-19-X*) Psych Assess.

Dictionary of Effects & Phenomena in Physics. Joachim Schubert. 140p. 1987. lib. bdg. 35.00 (*0-89573-487-7*) VCH Pubs.

Dictionary of Egyptian Arabic. Martin Hinds. 981p. (ARA & ENG.). 1987. 125.00 (*0-8288-0434-6*, F24540) Fr & Eur.

Dictionary of Egyptian Arabic: (Arabic-English) Hinds & Badawi. 1987. 65.00 (*0-86685-421-5*) Intl Bk Ctr.

Dictionary of Egyptian Gods & Goddesses. George Hart. (Illus.). 227p. (Orig.). 1986. pap. text ed. 13.95 (*0-7102-0167-2*, RKP) Routledge.

Dictionary of Egyptian Gods & Goddesses. George Hart. 1986. pap. 14.95 (*0-415-05909-7*) Routledge.

Dictionary of Eighteenth Century Russian Language, Vol. 3. S. Barkhudarov. 296p. (C). 1987. 90.00 (*0-685-46814-3*, Pub. by Collets) St Mut.

Dictionary of Eighteenth Century Russian Language, Vol. 5. S. Barkhudarov. 256p. (C). 1989. 90.00 (*0-685-37144-1*, Pub. by Collets) St Mut.

Dictionary of Eighteenth Century Russian Language, Vol. 4. Ed. by S. Barkhudarov. 256p. (C). 1988. 90.00 (*0-685-37145-X*, Pub. by Collets) St Mut.

Dictionary of Eighteenth Century World History. Jeremy Black. Ed. by Roy Porter. 832p. 1994. 59.95 (*0-631-18068-0*) Blackwell Pubs.

Dictionary of Electrical & Electronics Engineering. 5th ed. Hans Schwenkhagen. 868p. (ENG & GER.). 1992. 295. 00 (*0-8288-4013-X*, M6928) Fr & Eur.

Dictionary of Electrical Civil Engineering. U. B. Chopra. 1989. 33.50 (*81-7041-140-8*, Pub. by Anmol II) S Asia.

Dictionary of Electrical Engineering. K. L. Raina. 1989. 33. 50 (*81-7041-162-9*, Pub. by Anmol II) S Asia.

***Dictionary of Electrical Engineering: English, German, French, Dutch & Russian.** Kluwer Staff. 479p. (DUT, FRE & GER.). 1987. 135.00 (*0-7859-7703-1*, 2040164715) Fr & Eur.

Dictionary of Electrical Engineering: English, German, French, Dutch, Russian. Ed. by Y. N. Luginsky et al. (C). 1987. lib. bdg. 124.50 (*90-201-1910-9*) Kluwer Ac.

Dictionary of Electrical Engineering: Erosarmu Elektrotechnika. L. Gador. 583p. (ENG, FRE, GER, HUN & RUS.). 1985. 49.95 (*0-8288-0310-2*, M7882) Fr & Eur.

Dictionary of Electrical Engineering & Electronics: English-German. Peter-Klaus Budig. 1985. 187.25 (*0-444-99595-1*, I-422-84) Elsevier.

Dictionary of Electrical Engineering & Electronics: German-English. Ed. by Peter-Klaus Budig. 690p. 1985. 219.00 (*0-444-99594-3*) Elsevier.

Dictionary of Electrical Engineering & Electronics, Vol. 1: English - German. 5th ed. Peter-Klaus Budig. 800p. (ENG & GER.). 1992. 250.00 (*0-8288-0288-2*, M7394) Fr & Eur.

Dictionary of Electrical Engineering & Electronics, Vol. 2: German - English. 5th ed. Peter-Klaus Budig. 704p. (ENG & GER.). 1992. 250.00 (*0-685-63364-0*, F45830) Fr & Eur.

Dictionary of Electrical Engineering & Electronics, Vol. 2: German-English. 4th ed. Peter-Klaus Budig. 700p. (ENG & GER.). 1985. 250.00 (*0-8288-0287-4*, F45830) Fr & Eur.

Dictionary of Electrical Engineering, Electronics & Related Applications: Dictionnaire de l'Electrotechnique, l'Electronique & Applications Connexes. Henri Piraux. 272p. (FRE & GER.). 1983. 75.00 (*0-8288-0923-2*, M6455) Fr & Eur.

Dictionary of Electrical Science & Technology. A. Colella. 759p. (ENG & ITA.). 1988. 195.00 (*0-8288-4038-5*, F135870) Fr & Eur.

Dictionary of Electrical Terms: Japanese-Arabic-English. 425p. (ARA, ENG & JPN.). 1982. 125.00 (*0-8288-0308-0*, F55998) Fr & Eur.

Dictionary of Electromechanics: Diccionario Tecnico de Electromecanica. Luis Weis Ballesteros. 298p. (ENG & SPA.). 1980. pap. 19.95 (*0-8288-0303-X*, S 60504) Fr & Eur.

Dictionary of Electronic & Computer Music Technology. Richard Dobson. 232p. 1992. 45.00 (*0-19-311344-9*) OUP.

Dictionary of Electronic Packaging, Microelectronic, & Interconnection Term. Martin B. Miller. 186p. 1990. 39.95 (*0-9625930-0-1*) Technology Seminars.

Dictionary of Electronics. E. C. Young. (Reference Ser.). 1979. pap. 7.95 (*0-14-051074-5*, Penguin Bks) Viking Penguin.

Dictionary of Electronics. 2nd ed. S. W. Amos. (Illus.). 324p. 1987. 49.95 (*0-408-02750-9*) Buttrwrth-Heinemann.

Dictionary of Electronics, Vol. 1. Alfred Oppermann. 1987p. (ENG & GER.). 195.00 (*0-8288-0294-7*, M 15118) Fr & Eur.

Dictionary of Electronics: English, German, French, Dutch, Russian. Ed. by R. G. Mirimanov et al. 1985. lib. bdg. 105.50 (*90-201-1788-2*) Kluwer Ac.

Dictionary of Electronics & Computer Science. McGraw-Hill Editors. 582p. 1985. text ed. 49.50 (*0-07-045416-7*) McGraw.

***Dictionary of Electronics & Electrical Engineering.** Pierre Renyi & Dominique Amrouni. (Illus.). 1130p. 1986. text ed. 143.00 (*0-921137-01-X*) Technip.

Dictionary of Electronics & Electrical Engineering: English-Japanese-German-Russian. 3rd ed. Ed. by Seiichi Ishibashi. LC 87-42812. 1804p. 1987. 250.00 (*0-306-42749-4*, Plenum Pr) Plenum.

Dictionary of Electronics & Hydro-Vacuum Technology, 2 vols. (ENG, FRE, GER & RUS.). 1983. 75.00 (*0-8288-0306-4*, M15593) Fr & Eur.

Dictionary of Electronics & Information Processing: Enzyklopadisches Worterbuch der Elektrotechnik und Elektronik, 2 vols., Set. Peter Wennrich. 770p. (ENG & GER.). 1990. lib. bdg. 170.00 (*3-598-10885-0*) K G Saur.

Dictionary of Electronics & Waveguides. Hans Schnellman. 120p. (GER & SPA.). 1990. pap. 95.00 (*0-8288-0935-6*, M 1610) Fr & Eur.

Dictionary of Electronics & Waveguides, Computers & Data Processing. enl. ed. Hans Schnellman. 240p. (ENG & GER.). 1987. 150.00 (*0-8288-0295-5*, M930) Fr & Eur.

Dictionary of Electronics, Communications & Electrical Engineering, 2 vols., 1. H. Wernicke. 1300p. 52.50 (*0-685-05199-4*) Adlers Foreign Bks.

Dictionary of Electronics, Communications & Electrical Engineering, 2 vols., 2. H. Wernicke. 1300p. 52.50 (*0-685-05200-1*) Adlers Foreign Bks.

***Dictionary of Electronics, Computing & Telecommunications, Vol. 1 German-English.** Vittorio Ferretti. 636p. (ENG & GER.). 1992. 225.00 (*0-7859-6962-4*) Fr & Eur.

***Dictionary of Electronics, Computing & Telecommunications, Vol. 2 English-German.** Vittorio Ferretti. 669p. (ENG & GER.). 1992. 225.00 (*0-7859-6963-2*) Fr & Eur.

Dictionary of Electronics, Computing, & Telecommunications, English-German: Worterbuch der Elektronik, Datentechnik und Telekommunikation, Englisch-Deutsch. Vittorio Ferretti. LC 92-17916. 1992. 99.00 (*0-387-54202-7*) Spr-Verlag.

Dictionary of Electronics Engineering. Commercial Press Staff. 785p. (CHI & ENG.). 1976. 49.95 (*0-8288-5632-X*, M956) Fr & Eur.

Dictionary of Electronics, German & English. enl. ed. Hans Schnellman. 1987. 135.00 (*0-8288-0296-3*, M1199) Fr & Eur.

Dictionary of Electronics, Telecommunications & Vacuum Technology, 2 vols., Set. E. Redl & E. Oldal. 1269p. (ENG, FRE, GER, HUN & RUS.). 1983. 75.00 (*0-8288-0315-3*, M6649) Fr & Eur.

Dictionary of Electronics, Vol. 2. Alfred Oppermann. 800p. (ENG & GER.). 1987. 225.00 (*0-8288-0293-9*, M8702) Fr & Eur.

Dictionary of Eleventh & Seventeenth Century Russian Language, Vol. 13. Ed. by D. Shmelev. 320p. (C). 1987. 90.00 (*0-685-46816-X*, Pub. by Collets) St Mut.

Dictionary of Eleventh & Seventeenth Century Russian Language, Vol. 14. Ed. by L. Astakhina. 312p. (C). 1988. 90.00 (*0-685-54120-7*, Pub. by Collets) St Mut.

Dictionary of Emergency Homeopathy (Dictionnaire Homeopathique d'Urgence) 13th ed. Louis Pommier. 765p. (FRE.). 1985. 75.00 (*0-7859-4836-8*, M6461) Fr & Eur.

Dictionary of Eminent Librarians. Robert B. Downs. LC 90-84054. 256p. 1990. 24.50 (*0-9623333-5-2*) High Plns WY.

Dictionary of Employment Law. Norman Selwyn. 1985. 44. 00 (*0-406-20790-9*, U.K.) Butterworth Legal Pubs.

***Dictionary of Endocrinology & Related Biomedical Sciences.** Constance R. Martin. (Illus.). 800p. 1995. 59. 95 (*0-19-506033-4*) OUP.

Dictionary of Energy. Hall & Hinman. (Energy, Power & Environment Ser.: Vol. 18). 280p. 1983. 89.75 (*0-8247-1793-7*) Dekker.

Dictionary of Energy. 2nd ed. Ed. by Malcolm Slesser. 320p. 1988. 59.95 (*0-89397-320-3*) Nichols Pub.

Dictionary of Energy Science: Nuclear & Non-Nuclear Energy. Karl-Heinz Mannhardt. 166p. (ENG & GER.). 1981. 110.00 (*0-8288-0700-0*, M 15045); 75.00 (*0-8288-2292-1*, M15046); 110.00 (*0-8288-2293-X*, M 15047) Fr & Eur.

Dictionary of Engineering. McGraw-Hill Editors. Ed. by Sybil P. Parker. 659p. 1985. text ed. 49.50 (*0-07-045412-4*) McGraw.

Dictionary of Engineering Acronyms & Abbreviations. Uwe Herb & Harald Keller. 315p. 1989. 75.00 (*1-55570-028-4*) Neal-Schuman.

Dictionary of Engineering Acronyms & Abbreviations. 2nd ed. Uwe Erb & Harald Keller. LC 93-11570. 878p. 1994. 125.00 (*1-55570-129-9*) Neal-Schuman.

Dictionary of Engineering & Technology: English-German, Vol. II. 5th ed. Richard R. Ernst. 1985. 125.00 (*0-19-520485-9*) OUP.

Dictionary of Engineering & Technology, Vol. 1: German-English. 5th ed. Richard R. Ernst. (Illus.). 1268p. 1989. 125.00 (*0-19-520820-X*) OUP.

Dictionary of English & Sindhi. George Stack. 238p. (ENG & SNH.). 1986. 39.95 (*0-8288-8484-6*) Fr & Eur.

Dictionary of English-Arabic Commercial International Trade & Shipping Terms. Alan E. Branch & Juma A. Hakmeh. 257p. (C). 1988. 210.00 (*0-948691-61-1*, Pub. by Witherby & Co UK) St Mut.

Dictionary of English-Arabic-French Management Terms. Coveney-Moore. 1990. 11.95 (*0-86685-505-X*) Intl Bk Ctr.

Dictionary of English, Bengali & Manipuri. Star Publications Staff. 1992. reprint ed. 95.00 (*0-8288-8485-4*) Fr & Eur.

Dictionary of English Collocations: Based on the Brown Corpus, 3 vols. set. Goran Kjellmer. 2304p. 1994. 295. 00 (*0-19-823903-3*) OUP.

Dictionary of English Furniture, 3 vols., Set. Ralph Edwards. (Illus.). 1986. boxed, pap. 175.00 (*1-85149-037-X*) Antique Collect.

Dictionary of English Furniture, Vol. I. Ralph Edwards. (Illus.). 362p. 1986. write for info. (*0-318-61588-6*) Antique Collect.

Dictionary of English Furniture, Vol. II. Ralph Edwards. (Illus.). 396p. 1986. write for info. (*0-318-61589-4*) Antique Collect.

Dictionary of English Furniture, Vol. III. Ralph Edwards. (Illus.). 388p. 1986. write for info. (*0-318-61590-8*) Antique Collect.

Dictionary of English Idioms. Libr. du Liban Staff. (ARA & ENG.). 1989. 29.95 (*0-86685-512-2*) Intl Bk Ctr.

Dictionary of English Law. William J. Byrne. 1991. reprint ed. lib. bdg. 97.50 (*0-8377-1952-6*) Rothman.

Dictionary of English Literature. William D. Adams. 1972. 75.00 (*0-8490-0035-1*) Gordon Pr.

Dictionary of English Literature: Being a Comprehensive Guide to English Authors & Their Works. 2nd ed. W. Davenport Adams. LC 89-26524. 708p. 1992. reprint ed. lib. bdg. 65.00 (*1-55888-898-5*) Omnigraphics Inc.

Dictionary of English Normative Grammar 1700-1800. Bertil Sundby et al. LC 91-43663. (Studies in the History of the Language Sciences: No. 63). x, 486p. 1991. 106.00x (*1-55619-358-0*) Benjamins North Am.

Dictionary of English Personal Names. Ed. by A. Rybakin. 222p. (C). 1989. 40.00 (*0-685-46806-2*, Pub. by Collets) St Mut.

Dictionary of English Phrases with Illustrative Sentences. Kwong Ki Chaou. (Illus.). 1995. reprint ed. 60.00 (*1-55888-961-2*) Omnigraphics Inc.

Dictionary of English Place Names. A. D. Mills. LC 92-43070. (C). 1993. pap. 6.99 (*0-19-283131-3*) OUP.

Dictionary of English Place Names. Ed. by David Mills. 424p. 1992. 27.50 (*0-19-869156-4*) OUP.

Dictionary of English Proverbs in Modern Use. M. Bukovskaia. 232p. (C). 1985. 45.00 (*0-685-33704-9*, Pub. by Collets) St Mut.

Dictionary of English Proverbs in Modern Use. Ed. by M. Bukovskaia. 232p. (C). 1985. 40.00 (*0-685-46805-4*, Pub. by Collets) St Mut.

***Dictionary of English Surnames.** 3rd ed. P. H. Reaney & R. M. Wilson. 584p. 1995. pap. 15.95 (*0-19-863146-4*) OUP.

Dictionary of English Surnames. 3rd ed. P. H. Reaney & R. M. Wilson. 640p. 1991. 75.00 (*0-685-49859-X*, A5791) Routledge.

Dictionary of English Synonyms & Synonymous Parallel Expressions. rev. ed. Ed. by Richard Soule & G. Howson. 488p. 42.50 (*0-87559-043-8*); 47.50 (*0-87559-044-6*) Shalom.

Dictionary of English Weights & Measures: From Anglo-Saxon Times to the Nineteenth Century. Ronald E. Zupko. LC 68-14038. reprint ed. pap. 60.00 (*0-317-08979-X*, 2015376) Bks Demand.

Dictionary of Entomology. A. W. Leftwich. LC 75-27143. 368p. pap. 104.90 (*0-318-34739-3*, 2031996) Bks Demand.

***Dictionary of Environment: French - English with English-French Index.** Comuvir. 351p. (ENG & FRE.). 1992. 105.00 (*0-7859-7479-2*, 2853192431) Fr & Eur.

Dictionary of Environment & Development: People, Places, Ideas, & Organizations. Andy Crump. LC 92-36484. (Illus.). 272p. (C). 1993. 40.00x (*0-262-03207-4*); pap. 16.95x (*0-262-53117-8*) MIT Pr.

Dictionary of Environment, Health & Safety. U. S. Department of Energy, Office of Environment, Safety, & Health Staff. 1992. 79.95 (*0-87371-876-3*, TD169) Lewis Pubs.

Dictionary of Environmental Engineering & Related Sciences. Jose T. Villate. LC 78-67002. (Coleccion Diccionarios Ser.). Orig. Title: Diccionario De Ingenieria Ambiental y Ciencias Afines. 445p. (ENG & SPA.). 1979. 25.00 (*0-89729-209-X*) Ediciones.

***Dictionary of Environmental Protection: French-German, German-French.** Dieter Lukhaup. 500p. (FRE & GER.). 1993. 250.00 (*0-7859-8418-6*, 3527282432) Fr & Eur.

Dictionary of Environmental Protection Technology. Egon Seidel. 528p. (ENG, FRE, GER & RUS.). 1987. 225.00 (*0-8288-0947-X*, M6035) Fr & Eur.

Dictionary of Environmental Protection Technology: English-German-French-Russian-Bulgarian. rev. ed. Egon Seidel. 664p. (BUL, ENG, FRE, GER & RUS.). 1991. 110.00 (*3-86117-002-7*, Pub. by A Hatier GW) IBD Ltd.

Dictionary of Environmental Protection Technology: In English, German, French, Russian. Egon Seidel. 527p. 1988. 148.75 (*0-444-98971-4*) Elsevier.

Dictionary of Environmental Quotations. Barbara K. Rodes & Rice Odell. 288p. 1992. 35.00 (*0-13-210576-4*) S&S Trade.

Dictionary of Environmental Science & Technology. Andrew Porteous. (Illus.). 416p. 1991. 75.00 (*0-335-09231-4*); pap. 33.00 (*0-335-09230-6*) Wiley.

Dictionary of Environmental Science & Technology. rev. ed. Andrew Porteous. 439p. 1992. pap. text ed. 37.95 (*0-471-93544-1*) Wiley.

Dictionary of Epidemiology. 2nd ed. Ed. by John M. Last. (Handbooks Sponsored by the IEA & WHO Ser.). (Illus.). 160p. 1988. pap. 14.95 (*0-19-505481-4*) OUP.

***Dictionary of Epidemiology.** 3rd ed. John M. Last. (Illus.). 208p. 1995. 35.00 (*0-19-509667-3*) OUP.

***Dictionary of Epidemiology.** 3rd ed. John M. Last. (Illus.). 208p. 1995. pap. 16.95 (*0-19-509668-1*) OUP.

Dictionary of Epilepsy: Part I - Definitions. H. Gastaut. 1973. 8.00 (*92-4-154027-3*) World Health.

Dictionary of Epithets & Terms of Address. Leslie Dunkling. 352p. 1990. 27.95 (*0-415-00761-5*, A4699) Routledge.

Dictionary of Eponymic Names of Diseases & Syndromes. E. P. Mezhenina. 182p. 1982. 19.95 (*0-8288-1858-4*, M15443) Fr & Eur.

Dictionary of Eponyms. 2nd ed. Cyril L. Beeching. (Oxford Paperback Reference Ser.). 272p. 1988. pap. 9.95 (*0-19-282156-3*) OUP.

Dictionary of Esoteric Words. Ann Cattell. (Orig.). 1967. pap. 1.75 (*0-8065-0175-8*, C205, Citadel Pr) Carol Pub Group.

Dictionary of Essential English. Marion McGuire. (Illus.). 464p. 1987. teacher ed 12.99 (*0-86601-625-2*); student ed 4.99 (*0-86601-626-0*); text ed. 18.49 (*0-86601-624-4*) Media Materials.

Dictionary of Essential Quotations. Comp. by Kevin Goldstein-Jackson. LC 83-2815. 188p. (C). 1983. text ed. 26.50x (*0-389-20393-9*, N7271); pap. 14.00 (*0-8226-0389-6*) Littlefield.

***Dictionary of Ethics, Society & Theology.** Andrew Linzey & Paul A. Clarke. 600p. 1995. 99.95 (*0-415-06212-8*, B0385) Routledge.

Dictionary of Ethology. Klaus Immelmann & Colin Beer. LC 88-21360. (Illus.). 352p. 1989. 46.50 (*0-674-20506-5*) HUP.

Dictionary of Ethology. Klaus Immelmann & Colin Beer. (Illus.). 352p. 1992. 19.95 (*0-674-20507-3*) HUP.

***Dictionary of Euphemisms.** Hugh Rawson. Date not set. 14.00 (*0-517-88297-3*) Random.

1962

An Asterisk (*) at the beginning of an entry indicates that the title is appearing in BIP for the first time.

***Dictionary of European Community Terms Swedish-English-German-French.** Rosman Jahja. 224p. 1994. 27.00 (*91-7150-537-7*) IBD Ltd.

Dictionary of European Proverbs. Emanuel Strauss. 3000p. 1994. 520.00 (*0-415-09624-3*, B0401) Routledge.

Dictionary of Even More Diseased English. Kenneth Hudson. 160p. 1983. pap. 7.95 (*0-89733-079-X*) Academy Chi Pubs.

Dictionary of Evolutionary Fish Osteology. Alfonso L. Rojo. (Illus.). 280p. 1991. 49.95 (*0-8493-4214-7*, QL639) CRC Pr.

Dictionary of Explosives. Arthur Marshall. (Explosives Ser.). 1989. lib. bdg. 250.00 (*0-8490-3967-3*) Gordon Pr.

Dictionary of Eye Terminology. 2nd ed. Barbara Cassin & Sheila Solomon. Ed. by Melvin L. Rubin. (Illus.). 285p. (Orig.). 1990. pap. text ed. 17.95 (*0-937404-33-0*) Triad Pub FL.

***Dictionary of False Friends: German-English.** Barnickel. 215p. (ENG & GER.). 1992. 49.95 (*0-7859-7247-1*, 3861170000) Fr & Eur.

Dictionary of Family Psychology & Family Therapy: A Dictionary of Concepts & Terms. 2nd ed. S. Richard Sauber et al. LC 93-1588. (Illus.). 468p. (C). 1993. text ed. 65.00 (*0-8039-5332-1*); pap. text ed. 29.95 (*0-8039-5333-X*) Sage.

Dictionary of Family Therapy. Jacques Miermont. Ed. by Hugh Jenkins. Tr. by Chris Turner. (Illus.). 600p. (C). 1994. text ed. 95.00 (*0-631-17048-0*) Blackwell Pubs.

Dictionary of Fantastic Art. Jorg Krichbaum & Rein Zondergeld. (Pocket Art Ser.). (Illus.). 1985. pap. 6.95 (*0-8120-2110-X*) Barron.

Dictionary of Feminist Theory. Maggie Humm. 304p. 1990. pap. text ed. 20.00 (*0-8142-0507-0*) Ohio St U Pr.

***Dictionary of Feminist Theory.** 2nd ed. Maggie Humm. 354p. 1995. pap. text ed. 20.00 (*0-8142-0667-0*) Ohio St U Pr.

***Dictionary of Feminist Theory.** 2nd ed. Maggie Humm. LC 94-48253. 354p. 1995. text ed. 59.50 (*0-8142-0666-2*) Ohio St U Pr.

Dictionary of Fictional Characters. Martin Seymour-Smith. (Orig.). 1992. reprint ed. pap. 18.95 (*0-87116-166-4*) Writer.

Dictionary of Film Producers (Dictionnaire des Cinfastes) 4th enl. rev. ed. George Sadoul. 347p. (FRE.). 1990. pap. 19.95 (*0-7859-4706-X*, F79852) Fr & Eur.

***Dictionary of Film Quotations.** Melinda Corey & George Ochoa. LC 94-44227. 1995. pap. 24.00 (*0-517-88067-9*) Random.

***Dictionary of Film Terms: The Aesthetic Companion to Film Analysis.** rev. ed. Frank Beaver. (Twayne's Filmmakers Ser.). (Illus.). 324p. 1994. text ed. 29.95x (*0-8057-9333-X*, Twayne); pap. 15.95 (*0-8057-9334-8*, Twayne) Macmillan.

Dictionary of Films. Georges Sadoul. Tr. by Peter Morris. LC 78-136028. 1972. pap. 16.00 (*0-520-02152-5*) U CA Pr.

Dictionary of Finance. LC 92-42735. (Oxford Reference Ser.). (C). 1993. pap. 11.95 (*0-19-285279-5*) OUP.

Dictionary of Finance. Etan A. Auneyon. 486p. 1988. text ed. 65.00 (*0-02-916420-6*) Macmillan.

Dictionary of Finance & Investment Terms. 3rd ed. John Downes & Jordan E. Goodman. 500p. (Orig.). 1991. pap. 10.95 (*0-8120-4631-5*) Barron.

Dictionary of Financial Management: Dictionnaire de la Gestion Financiere. 3rd ed. Pierre Conso et al. 496p. (ENG & FRE.). 1984. 125.00 (*0-8288-0316-1*, M7776) Fr & Eur.

Dictionary of Financial Risk Management. Swiss Bank Corporation Staff & Gary L. Gastineau. 225p. 1993. 45.00 (*1-55738-443-6*) Probus Pub Co.

Dictionary of Firing & Heating Technology, Vol. 1: Oil-Firing. Manfred Katz. 191p. (ENG, FRE & GER.). 1981. 125.00 (*0-8288-0965-8*, M 8252) Fr & Eur.

Dictionary of First Names. Patrick Hanks & Flavia Hodges. 400p. 1990. 35.00 (*0-19-211651-7*) OUP.

Dictionary of First Names. Alfred J. Kolatch. 544p. 1990. pap. 11.00 (*0-399-51633-6*, Perigree Bks) Berkley Pub.

Dictionary of Fishes. Rube Allyn. LC 52-334. (Orig.). 1952. pap. 7.95 (*0-8200-0101-5*) Great Outdoors.

Dictionary of Fishing Terms: Japanese-English, English-Japanese. 443p. (ENG & JPN.). 1980. 95.00 (*0-8288-4689-8*, M9344) Fr & Eur.

Dictionary of Flexible Manufacturing Systems & Robotics. B. Voskoboynikov. 392p. (DUT, ENG, FRE, GER & RUS.). 1991. pap. 150.00 (*0-8288-7234-1*, 902012269X) Fr & Eur.

Dictionary of Flexible Manufacturing Systems & Robotics. B. S. Voskoboynikov. 392p. (DUT, ENG, FRE, GER & RUS.). 1991. 105.00 (*90-201-2269-X*, Pub. by Kluwer NE) IBD Ltd.

Dictionary of Flowering Plants & Ferns. Ed. by J. C. Willis. 1245p. (C). 1982. text ed. 500.00 (*81-7089-003-9*, Pub. by Intl Bk Distr II) St Mut.

Dictionary of Flowering Plants & Ferns. rev. ed. J. C. Willis. 1245p. (C). 1982. reprint ed. 360.00 (*0-685-21844-9*, Pub. by Intl Bk Distr II) St Mut.

Dictionary of Fly-Fishing. C. B. McCully. LC 92-32413. (Oxford Paperback Reference Ser.). (Illus.). 288p. (C). 1993. pap. 11.95 (*0-19-283126-7*) OUP.

Dictionary of Folklore: English-Arabic. Abdul H. Younis. 1983. 35.00 (*0-86685-307-3*) Intl Bk Ctr.

Dictionary of Food & Agriculture. Vladimir Beck. 278p. (ENG, FRE, GER, HUN & RUS.). 1980. 75.00 (*0-8288-0033-2*, M15600) Fr & Eur.

Dictionary of Food Hygiene. R. Bowman & E. D. Emmett. 244p. (Orig.). 1992. pap. 29.50 (*0-7487-1405-7*, Pub. by Stanley Thornes UK) Trans-Atl Phila.

Dictionary of Food Ingredients. 2nd ed. Igoe. 1989. text ed. 39.95 (*0-442-31927-4*) Chapman & Hall.

***Dictionary of Food Ingredients.** 3rd ed. Robert S. Igoe & Y. H. Hui. LC 95-4648. 1995. write for info. (*0-412-07281-5*); pap. write for info. (*0-412-07291-2*) Chapman & Hall.

Dictionary of Food Microbiology. Hanns K. Frank. LC 92-62872. 290p. 1993. text ed. 75.00 (*1-56676-010-0*) Technomic.

***Dictionary of Food Mircobiology.** Hanns K. Frank. 290p. 1992. 98.00 (*3-86022-035-7*) IBD Ltd.

Dictionary of Food, Nutrition & Cookery. Erich Luck. 392p. (ENG & GER.). 1983. 175.00 (*0-8288-0842-2*, M15385) Fr & Eur.

Dictionary of Foods. Gaylord Hauser & Ragnar Berg. 156p. 1971. pap. 2.25 (*0-87904-008-4*) Lust.

Dictionary of Forces' Slang: 1939-1945. Ed. by Eric Partridge et al. LC 75-117899. (Select Bibliographies Reprint Ser.). 1977. reprint ed. 21.95 (*0-8369-5352-5*) Ayer.

Dictionary of Foreign Expressions & Words. A. M. Babkin & V. V. Shendetsov. 654p. (C). 1987. 105.00 (*0-317-92481-8*, Pub. by Collets UK) Pro-Am Music.

Dictionary of Foreign Musical Terms & Handbook of Orchestral Instruments. Tom S. Wotton. 1988. reprint ed. lib. bdg. 59.00 (*0-7812-0090-3*) Rprt Serv.

Dictionary of Foreign Musical Terms & Handbook of Orchestral Instruments. Tom S. Wotton. LC 79-166268. 226p. 1907. reprint ed. 29.00 (*0-403-01389-5*) Scholarly.

Dictionary of Foreign Phrases & Abbreviations. 3rd ed. Tr. by Kevin Guinagh. LC 82-8486. 288p. 1982. 44.00 (*0-8242-0675-4*) Wilson.

Dictionary of Foreign Quotations. Robert L. Collison & Mary Collison. LC 81-124080. 415p. reprint ed. pap. 118.30 (*0-317-20687-7*, 2025151) Bks Demand.

Dictionary of Foreign Trade: Dicionario del Comercio Exterior. D. Valentin Budic. 328p. (ENG & SPA.). 1983. pap. 39.95 (*0-8288-0134-7*, S50552) Fr & Eur.

Dictionary of Foreign Words & Phrases. Ed. by L. E. Smith. 1992. lib. bdg. 255.75 (*0-8490-5566-0*) Gordon Pr.

Dictionary of Foreign Words & Phrases. Maxim Newmark. LC 70-88915. 245p. 1969. reprint ed. text ed. 35.00 (*0-8371-2103-5*, NEFW, Greenwood Pr) Greenwood.

Dictionary of Foreign Words & Phrases in Current English. A. J. Bliss. 400p. 1983. pap. 14.95 (*0-7100-9521-X*, RKP) Routledge.

Dictionary of Foreign Words & Phrases in Current English. Alan Bliss. 400p. 1983. pap. 14.95 (*0-415-05905-4*, 9521X) Routledge.

Dictionary of Forest Fires. S. S. Sagwal. (C). 1991. 10.00 (*81-7024-410-2*, Pub. by Ashish II) S Asia.

Dictionary of Forest Mensuration & Management. S. S. Sagwal. (C). 1992. 110.00 (*81-7136-032-7*, Pub. by Periodical Expert India) St Mut.

Dictionary of Forestry. S. S. Negi. (C). 1988. 62.50 (*81-7136-010-6*, Pub. by Periodical Expert India) St Mut.

Dictionary of Forestry. J. Weck. 513p. (ENG, FRE, GER, RUS & SPA.). 1966. 146.25 (*0-444-40626-3*) Elsevier.

Dictionary of Forestry - Chinese & English. Commercial Press Staff. 274p. (CHI & ENG.). 1977. pap. 19.95 (*0-8288-5375-4*, M9594) Fr & Eur.

Dictionary of Forestry in German, English, French, Spanish & Russian. Johannes V. Weck. 608p. (ENG, FRE, GER, RUS & SPA.). 1986. reprint ed. 250.00 (*0-8288-6736-4*, M-7826) Fr & Eur.

Dictionary of Freemasonary. Robert Macoy. 704p. 1989. 9.99 (*0-517-69213-9*) Random Hse Value.

***Dictionary of French & International Acronyms.** 3rd ed. J. Carton. 380p. (FRE.). 1987. pap. 55.00 (*0-7859-7475-X*, 2856080251) Fr & Eur.

Dictionary of French Furniture Makers of the 18th Century - Dictionnaire Des Ebenistes et Des Menuisiers. Pierre Kjellberg. (Illus.). 896p. (FRE.). 1989. 250.00 (*1-55660-194-8*) A Wofsy Fine Arts.

Dictionary of French Furniture Makers of the 19th Century - Dictionnaire Des Ebenistes et Des Menuisiers. Denise Ledoux-Lebard. (Illus.). 736p. 250.00 (*1-55660-195-6*) A Wofsy Fine Arts.

Dictionary of French Language Literature: Dictionnaire des Litteratures de Langue Francaise, Vol. 1: A-C. Jean-Pierre De Beaumarchais et al. 766p. (FRE.). 1994. 185.00 (*0-8288-1562-3*, M6181) Fr & Eur.

Dictionary of French Literature. Ed. by Sidney D. Braun. LC 70-138576. (Illus.). 362p. (C). 1971. reprint ed. text ed. 35.00 (*0-8371-5775-7*, BRDF, Greenwood Pr) Greenwood.

Dictionary of French Place Names in the U. S. A. Rene Coulet du Gard. 450p. (C). 1986. 39.00 (*0-939586-06-1*) Edns des Deux Mondes.

Dictionary of French Pronunciation: Dictionnaire de la Prononciation Francaise. Leon Warnant. 990p. (FRE.). 1987. 150.00 (*0-8288-1954-8*, M6602) Fr & Eur.

Dictionary of Fundamental Theology. Ed. by Rene Latourelle & Rino Fisichella. LC 93-42818. 1280p. 1994. 75.00 (*0-8245-1395-9*) Crossroad NY.

***Dictionary of Fundamental Theology.** Rene Latourelle & Rino Fisichella. 1264p. 1992. lib. bdg. 200.00 (*0-85439-395-1*, Pub. by St Paul Pubns UK) St Mut.

Dictionary of Furniture. Charles Boyce. 1988. pap. 19.95 (*0-8050-0752-0*, Owl) H Holt & Co.

Dictionary of Futures & Options: Over One Thousand International Terms Defined & Explained. Alan Webber. 1994. 35.00 (*1-55738-595-5*) Probus Pub Co.

Dictionary of Futurology & Social Sciences: Dictionnaire de Futurologie et des Sciences Sociales. Yvan Venev. 118p. (ENG, FRE & RUS.). 1987. pap. 95.00 (*0-8288-2370-7*, F137300) Fr & Eur.

Dictionary of Gambling & Gaming. Thomas L. Clark. LC 87-82866. xxi, 263p. 1988. 48.00 (*0-936368-06-3*) Lexik Hse.

Dictionary of Gaming, Modelling & Simulation. G. Ian Gibbs. LC 78-59784. 174p. reprint ed. pap. 49.60 (*0-317-11019-5*, 2021906) Bks Demand.

Dictionary of Gardening - Supplement. Ed. by Patrick M. Synge. 1969. 74.00 (*0-19-869116-5*) OUP.

Dictionary of Garment Terminology. Gerhard Rebmann. 450p. (ENG, FRE & GER.). 1984. 295.00 (*0-8288-0747-7*, M6966) Fr & Eur.

Dictionary of Gas Turbine Installation. 170p. (CHI & ENG.). 1973. pap. 24.95 (*0-8288-6245-1*, M-9566) Fr & Eur.

Dictionary of Gastronomy - Hotel Industry - Tourism, Vol. 1: German - English - French. J. P. Duboux. 608p. (ENG, FRE & GER.). 1990. 98.50 (*3-907950-01-1*) IBD Ltd.

Dictionary of Gastronomy - Hotel Industry - Tourism, Vol. 2: English - French - German. J. P. Duboux. 608p. (ENG, FRE & GER.). 1990. 98.50 (*3-907950-02-X*) IBD Ltd.

Dictionary of Gemmology. 2nd ed. Peter G. Read. (Illus.). 256p. 1988. text ed. 59.95 (*0-408-02925-0*) Buttrwrth-Heinemann.

***Dictionary of Gemmology.** 2nd ed. Peter G. Read. (Illus.). 272p. 1994. pap. 29.95 (*0-7506-1675-X*) Buttrwrth-Heinemann.

Dictionary of Gems & Gemology. 6th ed. Robert M. Shipley. 1974. 7.50 (*0-87311-007-2*) Gemological.

Dictionary of Genealogy. 3rd ed. Terrick V. Fitzhugh. (Illus.). 320p. 1992. 39.95 (*0-7136-3348-4*, Pub. by A&C Black UK) Talman.

Dictionary of General Psychology: Basic Terminology & Key Concepts. rev. ed. Charles A. Heidenreich. (C). 1970. pap. text ed. 7.95 (*0-8403-0171-5*) Heidenreich.

***Dictionary of Generic Names of Seed Plants.** Tatiana Wielgorskaya. Ed. by Armen Tahktajan. 472p. 1994. 80.00 (*0-231-07892-7*) Col U Pr.

Dictionary of Genetics. 4th ed. Robert C. King & William D. Stansfield. (Illus.). 416p. (C). 1990. pap. text ed. 19.95 (*0-19-506371-6*) OUP.

Dictionary of Geodesics, Photogrammetrics-Teledicition & Cartography: Dictionar de Geodezie, Fotogrammetrie-Teledetectie si Cartografie. Mihail Albota. 548p. 1980. write for info. (*0-8288-0361-7*, M15715) Fr & Eur.

Dictionary of Geographical Literacy: The Complete Geography Reference. Kieran O'Mahony. Ed. by Bernadette O'Mahony. (Illus.). 380p. (Orig.). (C). 1993. pap. 19.95 (*0-944638-08-2*) EduCare Pr.

Dictionary of Geography. rev. ed. W. G. Moore. (Reference Ser.). (Orig.). 1950. pap. 7.95 (*0-14-051002-8*, Penguin Bks) Viking Penguin.

Dictionary of Geography & Language: Diccionario de Geografia y Lenguaje. Justo Corchon. 230p. (SPA.). 1983. pap. write for info. (*0-7859-4932-1*) Fr & Eur.

Dictionary of Geography & Natural Environment, Monkhouse & Small: English with English - Arabic Glossary. Ahmed S. Khatib. 1983. 20.00 (*0-86685-078-3*) Intl Bk Ctr.

Dictionary of Geological Terms. 3rd rev. ed. American Geological Institute Staff. LC 82-45315. (Illus.). 576p. 1984. pap. 12.95 (*0-385-18101-9*, Anchor NY) Doubleday.

Dictionary of Geology. Whitten & Brooks. (Reference Ser.). 1973. pap. 12.95 (*0-14-051049-4*, Penguin Bks) Viking Penguin.

Dictionary of Geology (Dictionnaire de Geologie) 3rd ed. Alain Foucault. 352p. (FRE.). 1988. pap. write for info. (*0-7859-4639-X*) Fr & Eur.

Dictionary of Geology, Oil & Gas: Slovar po Geologii Nefti i Gaza. K. A. Chernikov. 700p. (RUS.). (C). 1988. text ed. 325.00 (*0-934393-54-0*) Rector Pr.

Dictionary of Geopolitics. Ed. by John O'Loughlin. LC 93-25072. 304p. 1993. text ed. 69.50 (*0-313-26313-2*, ODG/, Greenwood Pr) Greenwood.

Dictionary of Georgia Biography, 2 vols., Set. Ed. by Kenneth Coleman & Charles S. Gurr. LC 82-17341. 1144p. 1983. 75.00 (*0-8203-0662-2*) U of Ga Pr.

Dictionary of Geosciences, 2 vols. A. Watznauer. (ENG & GER.). 1982. English-German. 77.00 (*0-444-99702-4*); German-English. 77.00 (*0-444-99701-6*) Elsevier.

Dictionary of Geosciences, Band 1: Waterbush Der Geowissenscrackers. 3rd ed. Adolf Watznauer. 388p. (ENG & GER.). 1987. 95.00 (*0-8288-0356-0*, M 6917) Fr & Eur.

Dictionary of Geosciences, Band 2 Vol. 1: Woerterbuch Geowissenschaftern. 3rd ed. Adolf Watznauer. 400p. (ENG & GER.). 1988. 150.00 (*0-8288-0357-9*, M 6916) Fr & Eur.

Dictionary of Geosciences, English - German. 3rd ed. Adolf Watznauer. 400p. (ENG & GER.). 1988. 95.00 (*0-8288-4047-4*, M6917) Fr & Eur.

Dictionary of Geotechnical Engineering. R. A. Leme. 159p. (ENG & POR.). 1980. pap. 39.95 (*0-8288-0958-5*, M6073) Fr & Eur.

Dictionary of German & English Legal & Economic Terminology: Woerterbuch der Rechtssprache und Wirtschaftssprache, Vol. 1. 4th ed. Alfred Romain. 854p. (ENG & GER.). 1989. 225.00 (*0-8288-0393-5*, M 7101) Fr & Eur.

Dictionary of German & English Legal & Economic Terminology: Woerterbuch der Rechtssprache und Wirtschaftssprache, Vol. 2. 2nd ed. Alfred Romain. 882p. (ENG & GER.). 1985. 225.00 (*0-8288-0394-3*, M7100) Fr & Eur.

Dictionary of German Economic Terms: Dictionnaire de l'Allemand Economique. Jurgen Boelcke. (FRE & GER.). 1988. 65.00 (*0-8288-0810-4*, M590) Fr & Eur.

Dictionary of German Folklore: Woerterbuch der Deutschen Volkskunde. 3rd ed. Richard Beitl. 1005p. (GER.). 1981. 59.95 (*0-8288-1186-5*, M7112) Fr & Eur.

Dictionary of German Military Terms, Abbreviations & Map Symbols. W. Victor Madeja. 146p. 1992. 18.00 (*0-941052-75-3*) Valor Pub.

Dictionary of German Synonyms. 3rd ed. R. B. Farrell. LC 75-36175. (GER.). 1977. pap. 29.95 (*0-521-29068-6*) Cambridge U Pr.

Dictionary of Gerontology. Diana K. Harris. LC 87-25142. 208p. 1988. text ed. 49.95 (*0-313-25287-4*, HGE/, Greenwood Pr) Greenwood.

Dictionary of Gifted, Talented, & Creative Education Terms. Ed. by Mary M. Frasier et al. 135p. 1984. pap. 15.00 (*0-89824-021-2*) Trillium Pr.

Dictionary of Glass-Making. Leon M. Dubrul. 268p. (CZE, ENG & RUS.). 1985. 60.00 (*0-317-59482-6*, Pub. by Collets UK) Pro-Am Music.

Dictionary of Glass Making. International Commission on Glass Staff. 402p. (ENG, FRE & GER.). 1983. 146.25 (*0-444-42048-7*) Elsevier.

Dictionary of Glass-Making. International Commission on Glass Staff. 402p. (ENG, FRE & GER.). 1983. pap. write for info. (*0-8288-1304-3*, M 8392) Fr & Eur.

Dictionary of Glass-making: Diccionairio Del Vidrio - Dicionario Do Vidro. Ed. by UNESCO, European Community Staff. LC 92-26660. 1992. write for info. (*0-444-89622-8*) Elsevier.

Dictionary of Glass Making in English, French & German. International Commission on Glass Staff. 402p. (ENG, FRE & GER.). 1983. 295.00 (*0-8288-9280-6*) Fr & Eur.

Dictionary of Glass Making in English, Spanish & Portuguese. International Commission on Glass Staff. 358p. (ENG, POR & SPA.). 1992. 295.00 (*0-8288-9281-4*) Fr & Eur.

Dictionary of Global Climate Change. Comp. by W. John Maunder. LC 92-19059. 256p. 1992. 45.00 (*0-412-03901-X*, A9802, Chap & Hall NY) Chapman & Hall.

***Dictionary of Global Climate Change.** 2nd ed. John W. Maunder. LC 92-19059. 257p. 1995. pap. 24.95 (*0-412-99581-6*) Chapman & Hall.

Dictionary of Global Culture. Ed. by Henry Louis Gates, Jr. & Kwame A. Appiah. LC 93-43132. 1995. 35.00 (*0-394-58581-X*) Knopf.

Dictionary of Gods & Goddesses, Devils & Demons. Manfred Lurker. 460p. 1987. 45.00 (*0-415-03943-6*, 08774, RKP); pap. 15.95 (*0-415-03944-4*, 11066, RKP) Routledge.

Dictionary of Gods & Goddesses, Devils & Demons. Manfred Lurker. LC 86-21911. 451p. (C). 1987. 45.00 (*0-7102-0877-4*, RKP); pap. 15.95 (*0-7102-1106-6*, RKP) Routledge.

Dictionary of Good French: Dictionnaire du Bon Francais. J. Girodet. 896p. (FRE.). 1981. lib. bdg. 65.00 (*0-8288-4445-3*, M9362) Fr & Eur.

Dictionary of Government & Politics. P. H. Collin. 225p. 1988. pap. text ed. 16.95 (*0-948549-05-X*, Pub. by Peter Collin UK) IBD Ltd.

Dictionary of Grammatical Terms in Linguistics. Robert L. Trask. LC 92-24806. 320p. 1993. 59.95 (*0-415-08627-2*, B0412, Routledge NY); pap. 17.95 (*0-415-08628-0*, B0416, Routledge NY) Routledge.

Dictionary of Graphic Arts Terms: A Communication Tool for People Who Buy Type & Printing. Patricia Mintz. 328p. 1981. text ed. 32.95 (*0-442-26711-8*) Van Nos Reinhold.

Dictionary of Graphic Images. Comp. by Philip Thompson & Peter Davenport. 258p. 1981. 30.00 (*0-312-20108-7*) St Martin.

Dictionary of Graphology: The A-Z of Your Personality. Gloria Hargreaves & Peggy Wilson. 1983. 28.00 (*0-685-11947-5*) Dufour.

***Dictionary of Great Books.** Wigoder. Date not set. 50.00 (*0-13-051567-1*) P-H.

Dictionary of Greek & Roman Biography & Mythology, 3 Vols, Set. Ed. by William Smith. LC 11-24983. reprint ed. 565.00 (*0-404-06130-3*) AMS Pr.

Dictionary of Greek & Roman Geography, 2 Vols, Set. Ed. by William Smith. LC 74-14843. reprint ed. write for info. (*0-404-06134-6*) AMS Pr.

Dictionary of Greek & Roman Mythology: Diccionario de Mitologia Griega y Romana. 5th ed. Pierre Grimal. 634p. (SPA.). 1991. pap. 69.95 (*0-7859-4964-X*) Fr & Eur.

Dictionary of Greek & Roman Mythology: Dictionnaire de la Mythologie Grecque et Romaine. 12th ed. Pierre Grimal. 608574p. (FRE.). 1994. 150.00 (*0-8288-2190-9*, M6299) Fr & Eur.

Dictionary of Greek Coin Inscriptions. Severin Icard. (ENG & GRE.). 1979. reprint ed. 30.00 (*0-916710-42-4*); reprint ed. pap. 20.00 (*0-916710-43-2*) Obol Intl.

Dictionary of Greek Coin Inscriptions. Severin Icard. (ENG & GRE.). 1979. reprint ed. lib. bdg. 45.00 (*0-915262-31-2*) S J Durst.

Dictionary of Greek Literature. James H. Mantinband. (Quality Paperback Ser.: No. 145). 409p. 1966. reprint ed. pap. 12.95 (*0-8226-0145-1*) Littlefield.

Dictionary of Guatamalan Popular Expressions: Diccionario de al Espresion Popular Guatemalteca. Daniel Armas. 438p. (SPA.). 1982. 45.00 (*0-8288-2029-5*, S15747) Fr & Eur.

Dictionary of Guitarists: A Biographical-Bibliographical-Historical-Critical Dictionary of Guitars (Related Instruments), Guitarists (Teachers-Composers-Performers-Luthiers-Amateurs), Guitar-Makers (Luthiers), Dances & Songs - Terminology. Intro. by Matanya Ophee. LC 86-80463. 488p. (SPA.). 1988. reprint ed. 135.00 (*0-936186-18-6*); reprint ed. pap. 95.00 (*0-685-17660-6*) Edit Orphee.

Dictionary of Gynecology: Dictionnaire de Gynecologie. Henri Rozenbaum. 312p. (FRE.). 1981. 85.00 (*0-8288-1826-6*) Fr & Eur.

D

An Asterisk (*) at the beginning of an entry indicates that the title is appearing in BIP for the first time.

Dictionary of Haiku. Jane Reichhold. 320p. (Orig.). 1991. pap. 12.95 (*0-944676-87-1*) AHA Bks.

Dictionary of Haitian Creole Verbs with Phrases & Idioms. Emmanuel W. Vedrine. (Illus.). 244p. (Orig.). 1993. pap. 16.00 (*0-938534-04-1*) Soup Nuts Pr.

***Dictionary of Hawaiian Legal Land-Terms.** Comp. by Paul H. Lucas. LC 95-12500. 1995. write for info. (*0-8248-1636-6*) UH Pr.

Dictionary of Health Physics & Nuclear Sciences Terms. Rex J. Borders. Ed. by K. Paul Steinmeyer. 440p. 1991. 95.00 (*0-9630191-0-4*) RSA Pubns.

Dictionary of Helminthology & Plant Nematology. Ed. by G. I. Pozniak. 108p. (ENG & RUS.). 1979. 35.00 (*0-8288-4786-X*) Fr & Eur.

***Dictionary of Heraldry.** Joseph Foster. (Illus.). 224p. 1995. 22.98 (*0-8317-2155-3*) Smithmark.

Dictionary of Heraldry: Feudal Coats of Arms & Pedigrees. Joseph Forster. (Illus.). 256p. 1989. 24.99 (*0-517-68638-4*) Random Hse Value.

Dictionary of Herbs, Spices, Seasonings, & Natural Flavorings. Carole J. Skelly. LC 93-28205. (Reference Library of Social Science: Vol. 918). 504p. 1994. 75.00 (*0-8153-1465-5*, SS918) Garland.

Dictionary of Herpetology. Peters. 1985. 16.95 (*0-02-850230-2*) Macmillan.

Dictionary of High-Energy Physics. R. Sube. 164p. (C). 1987. 395.00 (*0-685-54131-2*, Pub. by Collets) St Mut.

Dictionary of High Energy Physics. R. Sube. 164p. (C). 1987. text ed. 405.00 (*0-7855-0111-8*, Pub. by Collets) St Mut.

Dictionary of High Energy Physics: In English, German, French & Russian. Rolf Sube. 176p. 1987. 105.25 (*0-444-98983-8*) Elsevier.

Dictionary of High Polymer Macromolecule. 54p. (CHI & ENG.). 1974. pap. 19.95 (*0-686-92619-6*) Fr & Eur.

Dictionary of Hindu Architecture. P. K. Acharya. 1981. text ed. 58.50 (*0-685-13704-X*) Coronet Bks.

Dictionary of Historic Documents. George C. Kohn. 1991. 40.00 (*0-8160-1978-9*) Facts on File.

Dictionary of Historic Nicknames: A Treasury of More Than 7,500 Famous & Infamous Nicknames from World History. Carl Sifakis. LC 82-15430. 584p. reprint ed. pap. 166.50 (*0-7837-1574-9*, 2041866) Bks Demand.

Dictionary of Historical Allusions. Thomas B. Harbottle. LC 89-29253. 306p. 1990. reprint ed. lib. bdg. 40.00 (*1-55888-899-3*) Omnigraphics Inc.

Dictionary of Historical Terms. Chris Cook. Date not set. 22.95 (*0-8488-0794-4*) Yestermorrow.

Dictionary of Historical Terms. 2nd ed. Chris Cook. LC 89-14934. 352p. (C). 1990. 34.95 (*0-87226-331-2*) P Bedrick Bks.

Dictionary of Historical Terms. 2nd ed. Ed. by Chris Cook. LC 89-14934. 352p. 1991. pap. 14.95 (*0-87226-241-3*) P Bedrick Bks.

Dictionary of History. Satish Ganjoo. 1990. 33.50 (*81-7041-237-4*, Pub. by Anmol II) S Asia.

Dictionary of Holland Occupational Codes (DHOC) 2nd ed. Gary D. Gottfredson & John L. Holland. LC 89-8390. 634p. 1989. pap. 35.00 (*0-911907-03-3*) Psych Assess.

***Dictionary of Homeopathic Medical Terminology.** 3rd ed. Jay Yasgur. 250p. (C). 1994. pap. text ed. 14.95 (*1-886149-00-3*) Van Hoy Pubs.

Dictionary of Homonyms. Ellyson. 1976. 18.95 (*0-88411-136-9*) Amereon Ltd.

Dictionary of Homonyms: New Word Patterns. Louise Ellyson. 166p. 1979. lib. bdg. 15.95 (*0-685-00359-0*, Aeonian Pr) Amereon Ltd.

Dictionary of Homonyms of the Russian Language. Ed. by O. Akhmanova. 448p. (C). 1986. 59.00 (*0-685-46804-6*, Pub. by Collets) St Mut.

Dictionary of Homonyms of the Russian Language. 3rd ed. O. S. Achmanova. 448p. (RUS.). 1986. 49.95 (*0-8288-2000-7*, M1254) Fr & Eur.

Dictionary of Horse & Rider: Dictionnaire du Cheval et du Chevalier. C. Cassart & R. Moirant. 288p. (FRE.). 1979. 69.95 (*0-8288-4795-9*, M6064) Fr & Eur.

Dictionary of Horse-Drawn Vehicles. D. J. Smith. 190p. 1990. pap. 32.00 (*0-85131-468-6*, Pub. by J A Allen & Co UK) St Mut.

Dictionary of Hotels, Tourism & Catering Management. 256p. 1994. pap. 16.95 (*0-948549-40-8*) IBD Ltd.

Dictionary of Human Factors: Ergonomics. Stramler. 1992. 59.95 (*0-8493-4236-8*, TA66) CRC Pr.

Dictionary of Human Geography. R. J. Johnston et al. 1981. 45.00 (*0-317-30514-X*) Free Pr.

Dictionary of Human Geography. 3rd ed. Ed. by R. J. Johnston et al. LC 92-44285. 576p. 1993. 89.95 (*0-631-18141-5*); pap. 22.95 (*0-631-18142-3*) Blackwell Pubs.

Dictionary of Human Oncology: A Concise Guide to Tumors. J. Gibson & O. Potparic. LC 93-35740. 1993. 55.00 (*1-85070-472-4*) Prthnon Pub.

Dictionary of Humorous Quotes. Evan Esar. 1976. 21.95 (*0-8488-0998-X*) Amereon Ltd.

Dictionary of Hungarian Slang. Alex Sandri-White. (HUN.). 8.95 (*0-685-22762-6*) Aurea.

Dictionary of Hunting Terms: Woerterbuch der Weidmannsprache. Franz Kehrein & Joseph Kehrein. 338p. (GER.). 1985. 110.00 (*0-8288-2347-2*, M6943) Fr & Eur.

Dictionary of Hydraulic Machinery. A. T. Troskolanski. 736p. (ENG, FRE, GER, ITA, RUS & SPA.). 1986. 197.50 (*0-444-99728-8*) Elsevier.

Dictionary of Hydraulics & Pneumatics. Gunter Neubert. 226p. 1980. 60.00 (*0-569-08523-3*, Pub. by Collets UK) St Mut.

Dictionary of Hydraulics & Pneumatics: English-German-Russian-Spanish & French. G. Neubert. 226p. (ENG, FRE, GER, RUS & SPA.). 1973. 95.00 (*0-7859-0814-5*, M-8178) Fr & Eur.

Dictionary of Hymnology: Origin & History of Christian Hymns, 4 vols., Set. Ed. by J. Julian. 1977. lib. bdg. 1,200.00 (*0-8490-1719-X*) Gordon Pr.

Dictionary of Hypnotism. Anita Evangelista. LC 90-36941. 288p. 1991. text ed. 49.95 (*0-313-25967-4*, EVH/, Greenwood Pr) Greenwood.

Dictionary of Ideas: Closeness. Harry A. Wilmer. (Illus.). 75p. (Orig.). (C). 1989. pap. text ed. write for info. (*0-318-65243-9*) IH Salado.

Dictionary of Idiomatic French Expressions. B. Lafleur. 670p. (FRE.). 1991. 65.00 (*0-685-62923-6*, 2801109479) Fr & Eur.

Dictionary of Idiomatic French Expressions. 2nd ed. B. Lafleur. 670p. (FRE.). 1991. lib. bdg. 65.00 (*0-8288-3314-1*, 2801109479) Fr & Eur.

Dictionary of Idioms: And Their Origins. Linda Flavell & Roger Flavell. 288p. 1994. pap. 12.95 (*1-85626-129-8*) Trafalgar.

Dictionary of Imaginary Places. Alberto Manguel & Gianni Guadalupi. (Illus.). 1987. pap. 18.95 (*0-15-626054-9*, Harvest Bks) HarBrace.

Dictionary of Imaginery Places. Manguel. 1980. 24.95 (*0-02-579310-1*) Macmillan.

Dictionary of Immunology. W. J. Herbert & P. C. Wilkinson. 282p. (ENG & GER.). 1980. 29.95 (*0-8288-0570-9*, M6595) Fr & Eur.

Dictionary of Immunology. Ed. by Frederick S. Rosen et al. 233p. 1990. pap. 28.00 (*0-444-01478-0*) Elsevier.

Dictionary of Immunology. Ed. by Frederick S. Rosen et al. 200p. 1988. 60.00 (*0-935859-58-6*, Stockton Pr) Groves Dictionaries.

***Dictionary of Immunology.** 4th ed. Ed. by W. John Herbert et al. (Illus.). 256p. 1995. text ed. 45.00 (*0-12-752025-2*) Acad Pr.

Dictionary of Indian Biography. C. E. Buckland. LC 68-26350. (Reference Ser.: No. 44). 1969. reprint ed. lib. bdg. 85.00 (*0-8383-0277-7*) M S G Haskell Hse.

Dictionary of Indian History. Sachchidananda Bhattacharya. LC 77-1105. 963p. 1977. reprint ed. text ed. 58.50 (*0-8371-9515-2*, BHDI, Greenwood Pr) Greenwood.

Dictionary of Indian Tribes of the Americas, 4 vols., Set. 2nd ed. 2000p. 1981. lib. bdg. 285.00 (*0-937862-25-8*) Am Indian Pubs.

Dictionary of Indian Tribes of the Americas, 3 vols., Set. 2nd ed. LC 93-8019. 1993. 375.00 (*0-937862-28-2*) Am Indian Pubs.

Dictionary of Indians of North America, 3 vols., Set. Ed. by Harry Waldman. 1978. 145.00 (*0-403-01799-8*) Scholarly.

***Dictionary of Indo-Persian Literature.** Nabi Hadi. (C). 1995. 64.00x (*81-7017-311-6*, Pub. by Abhinav II) S Asia.

Dictionary of Indology, Vol. 4. Ashim K. Roy & N. N. Gidwani. 335p. 1986. 24.00 (*0-317-53540-4*, Pub. by Oxford IBH II) S Asia.

Dictionary of Indology, Vol. 3: L-R. Ashim Roy & N. N. Gidwani. 1986. 24.00 (*81-204-0036-4*, Pub. oy Oxford IBH II) S Asia.

Dictionary of Indonesian Islam. Howard M. Federspiel. (Monographs in International Studies, Southeast Asia Ser.: No. 94). 320p. (Orig.). (C). 1994. pap. text ed. 25.00 (*0-89680-182-9*) Ohio U Pr.

Dictionary of Industrial Chemistry. 164p. (CHI & ENG.). 1979. pap. 19.95 (*0-686-92529-7*) Fr & Eur.

Dictionary of Industrial Digital Computer Terminology. Purdue Workshop on Standardization of Industrial-Computer Languages, Glossary Committee. LC 72-81778. 96p. reprint ed. pap. 27.40 (*0-317-08566-2*, 2051117) Bks Demand.

Dictionary of Industrial Engineering: Woerterbuch der Industriallen Technik. 4th ed. Richard R. Ernst. 1092p. (ENG & GER.). 1980. 250.00 (*0-8288-0624-1*, M7001) Fr & Eur.

Dictionary of Industrial Engineering: Woerterbuch der Industriellen Technik, Vol. 2. 5th ed. Richard R. Ernst. 1422p. (ENG & GER.). 1985. 250.00 (*0-8288-0623-3*, M7000) Fr & Eur.

Dictionary of Industrial Furnaces & Refractories. H. Y. El-Desouki & A. A. Kasim. 300p. (ARA, ENG, FRE & GER.). 1981. 24.95 (*0-8288-0711-6*, M15463) Fr & Eur.

Dictionary of Industrial Property Legal & Related Terms. Francis J. Kase. 232p. (ENG, FRE, GER & SPA.). 1980. 150.00 (*0-8288-0411-7*, M15566) Fr & Eur.

Dictionary of Industrial Property, Legal & Related Terms: English, Spanish, French & German. Ed. by Francis J. Kase. 232p. (ENG, FRE, GER & SPA.). 1980. lib. bdg. 107.50 (*90-286-0619-X*) Kluwer Ac.

Dictionary of Industrial Security. Stewart Kidd. LC 87-4672. 1987. 45.00 (*0-7102-0794-8*, RKP) Routledge.

Dictionary of Industrial Technology: In English, German, & Portuguese. Comp. by H. E. Philippsborn. LC 94-1644. (ENG, GER & POR.). 1994. write for info. (*0-444-89945-6*) Elsevier.

***Dictionary of Infections & Infectious Diseases.** O. Potparic & J. Gibson. 140p. (C). 1995. 35.00 (*1-85070-607-7*) Prthnon Pub.

Dictionary of Informal Brazilian Portuguese: With English Index. Bobby J. Chamberlain & Ronald M. Harmon. LC 84-13735. 720p. (C). 1984. text ed. 29.95 (*0-87840-091-5*) Georgetown U Pr.

Dictionary of Information. 2nd ed. 120p. (ENG, POL & RUS.). 1981. 14.95 (*0-8288-0264-5*, M15560) Fr & Eur.

Dictionary of Information Processing. Finnish Data Processing Association Staff. 233p. (ENG, FIN, FRE, GER, RUS & SWE.). 1985. 125.00 (*0-8288-0907-0*, M15082) Fr & Eur.

Dictionary of Information Science. Frank George. 1987. write for info. (*0-670-80140-2*) Viking Penguin.

Dictionary of Information Science: In English, German, French, & Russian. Comp. by Erich Burger. 903p. 1989. 202.75 (*0-444-98904-8*) Elsevier.

Dictionary of Information Science & Technology. Carolyn Watters. (Illus.). 300p. 1992. text ed. 24.95 (*0-12-738510-X*) Acad Pr.

Dictionary of Information Security Standards Concepts & Terms. 2nd ed. Dennis Longley et al. 632p. 1993. 130.00 (*1-56159-069-X*, Stockton Pr) Groves Dictionaries.

Dictionary of Information Technology. S. M. Collin. 232p. 1987. pap. text ed. 16.95 (*0-948549-03-3*, Pub. by Peter Collin UK) IBD Ltd.

Dictionary of Information Technology. 2nd ed. Dennis Longley & Michael Shain. (Illus.). 382p. 1986. 29.95 (*0-19-520519-7*) OUP.

Dictionary of Information Technology & Computer Science. 2nd ed. Tony Gunton. 343p. 1994. 39.95 (*1-85554-327-3*) Blackwell Pubs.

Dictionary of Initials. Betsy M. Parks. 1981. 12.95 (*0-8065-0750-0*, Citadel Pr) Carol Pub Group.

***Dictionary of Initials of Scientific, Technical & Commercial Organization.** 2nd ed. J. Murith. 471p. 1993. write for info. (*0-7859-8800-9*) Fr & Eur.

Dictionary of Initials of Scientific, Technical & Commercial Organizations. 2nd ed. J. Murith. 471p. 1993. 180.00 (*2-85206-384-0*) IBD Ltd.

Dictionary of Inorganic Compounds. Ed. by Jane E. Macintyre. (C). 1992. text ed. 3,995.00 (*0-412-30120-2*, A6962) Chapman & Hall.

Dictionary of Insurance. 7th rev. ed. Lewis E. Davids. LC 89-36094. 516p. 1990. pap. text ed. 17.95 (*0-8226-3000-1*) Littlefield.

Dictionary of Insurance Law. E. R. Ivamy. (C). 1981. 120.00 (*0-685-32830-9*, Pub. by Witherby & Co UK) St Mut.

Dictionary of Insurance Terms. Tayseer H. Treky. 395p. (ARA & ENG.). (C). 1985. 340.00 (*0-900886-96-X*, Pub. by Witherby & Co UK) St Mut.

Dictionary of Insurance Terms. 2nd ed. Harvey W. Rubin. 416p. 1991. pap. 9.95 (*0-8120-4632-3*) Barron.

***Dictionary of Insurance Terms.** 3rd ed. Harvey W. Rubin. LC 95-6527. 1995. write for info. (*0-8120-3379-5*) Barron.

Dictionary of Interior Design. Martin Pegler. (Illus.). 260p. (C). 1983. 28.50 (*0-87005-447-3*) Fairchild.

Dictionary of International & Comparative Law. James R. Fox. 495p. 1992. lib. bdg. 65.00 (*0-379-20430-4*) Oceana.

Dictionary of International Biography, 1993-94. 22th ed. 800p. 1993. 199.00 (*0-948875-90-9*, Pub. by Melrose UK) Taylor & Francis.

***Dictionary of International Biography 1994-1995.** 23th ed. 800p. 1994. 199.00x (*0-948875-41-0*, Pub. by Melrose UK) Taylor & Francis.

Dictionary of International Economics: German, Russian, English, French, Spanish. Ed. by S. Kohls. 620p. (ENG, FRE, GER, RUS & SPA.). 1976. lib. bdg. 70.00 (*90-286-0505-3*) Kluwer Ac.

Dictionary of International Finance. 2nd ed. Julian Walmsley. 222p. 1986. text ed. 69.95 (*0-471-83654-0*) Wiley.

Dictionary of International Law. B. M. Klimenko. 244p. (RUS.). 1982. 29.95 (*0-8288-1526-7*, M15490) Fr & Eur.

Dictionary of International Law. B. M. Klimenko. 295p. (C). 1986. 55.00 (*0-685-31520-7*, Pub. by Collets UK) Pro-Am Music.

Dictionary of International Medical Abbreviations. M. A. Touati. 474p. 1994. 60.00 (*2-85608-058-8*, Pub. by La Maison Du Dict FR) IBD Ltd.

***Dictionary of International Medical Abbreviations.** M. A. Touati. 474p. 1994. write for info. (*0-7859-8755-X*) Fr & Eur.

Dictionary of International Public Law, Vol. 1. S. Simonelli. 197p. (ENG & ITA.). 1981. pap. 39.95 (*0-8288-0398-6*, M15424) Fr & Eur.

Dictionary of International Public Law, Vol. 2. S. Simonelli. 184p. (ENG & ITA.). 1983. pap. 39.95 (*0-8288-0399-4*, M 9476) Fr & Eur.

***Dictionary of International Relations: Diccionario de Relaciones Internacionales.** J. P. Plano & Roy Olton. 465p. (SPA.). 1980. pap. 14.95 (*0-8288-2270-0*) Fr & Eur.

Dictionary of International Relations & Conference Terminology. Hassan Abdallah. 654p. (ARA & ENG.). 1982. 85.00 (*0-8288-2248-4*, F53990) Fr & Eur.

Dictionary of International Slurs. A. A. Roback. LC 76-5696. (Maledicta Press Publications Ser.: Vol. 5). (C). 1979. reprint ed. pap. 15.00 (*0-916500-05-5*) Maledicta.

Dictionary of International Trade. Jerry M. Rosenberg. (Business Dictionaries Ser.). 336p. 1993. text ed. 45.00 (*0-471-59732-5*); pap. text ed. 14.95 (*0-471-59731-7*) Wiley.

Dictionary of International Trade: 4,071 International Trade, Economic, Banking, Legal & Shipping Terms. 280p. Date not set. 16.50 (*0-9631864-8-5*) Wrld Trade Pr.

Dictionary of International Trade Fairs, 3 vols., Set. T. Martius. 1267p. 1980. 125.00 (*0-569-05140-1*, Pub. by Collets UK) St Mut.

Dictionary of Investing. Jerry M. Rosenberg. (Business Dictionaries Ser.). 384p. 1992. text ed. 49.95 (*0-471-57433-3*); pap. text ed. 14.95 (*0-471-57434-1*) Wiley.

Dictionary of Iraqi-Arabic. Ed. by Wayne Beene. 523p. (ARA & ENG.). (C). 1991. reprint ed. pap. text ed. 22.95 (*0-87840-281-0*) Georgetown U Pr.

Dictionary of Iraqi Arabic. Ed. by Karl Stowasser & Ronald G. Wolfe. (Richard Slade Harrell Arabic Ser.). 218p. (ARA & ENG.). 1991. reprint ed. pap. text ed. 15.95 (*0-87840-280-2*) Georgetown U Pr.

Dictionary of Irish Archaeology. Laurence Flanagan. 300p. (C). 1992. text ed. 77.50 (*0-389-20972-4*) B&N Imports.

Dictionary of Irish Literature. Ed. by Robert T. Hogan. LC 78-20021. 815p. 1979. text ed. 65.00 (*0-313-20718-6*, HDI/, Greenwood Pr) Greenwood.

Dictionary of Irish Mythology. Peter B. Ellis. 240p. 1989. lib. bdg. 50.00 (*0-87436-553-8*) ABC-CLIO.

Dictionary of Irish Mythology. Peter B. Ellis. 240p. 1992. pap. 10.95 (*0-19-282871-1*) OUP.

Dictionary of Irish Place Names. 2nd ed. Adrian Room. 144p. 1994. reprint ed. pap. 12.95 (*0-86281-460-X*, Pub. by Appletree Pr IE) Irish Bks Media.

Dictionary of Irish Quotations. Sean Sheehan. 160p. 1993. pap. 11.95 (*1-85635-052-5*, Pub. by Mercier Pr IE) Dufour.

Dictionary of Irrigation & Drainage. 2nd ed. 1012p. (ENG, FRE, GER & SPA.). 1983. 75.00 (*0-8288-0959-3*, F39710) Fr & Eur.

Dictionary of Islam. T. P. Hughes. 49.00 (*0-935782-70-2*) Kazi Pubns.

Dictionary of Islam. Thomas P. Hughes. 1976. reprint ed. 37.50 (*0-8364-0395-9*) S Asia.

Dictionary of Islam, 2 vols., Set. Thomas P. Hughes. 1980. lib. bdg. 199.95 (*0-8490-3121-4*) Gordon Pr.

Dictionary of Islam: A Cyclopedia of the Muhammadan Religion. Thomas P. Hughes. (Reprints in History Ser.). (Illus.). 750p. reprint ed. lib. bdg. 35.00 (*0-697-00053-2*) Irvington.

Dictionary of Islamic Architecture. Andrew Petersen. (Illus.). 352p. 1995. 75.00 (*0-415-06084-2*, B0381) Routledge.

Dictionary of Italian-American Poets. Ferdinando P. Alfonsi. (American University Studies: Romance Languages & Literature: Ser. II, Vol. 112). 174p. (C). 1989. text ed. 30.95 (*0-8204-0916-2*) P Lang Pubs.

Dictionary of Italian Literature. Peter E. Bondanella. Ed. by Julia C. Bondanella. LC 78-4022. 621p. 1979. text ed. 59.95 (*0-313-20421-7*, BDI/, Greenwood Pr) Greenwood.

Dictionary of Jamaican English. 2nd ed. Ed. by Frederic G. Casidy & R. B. Le Page. LC 78-17799. 1980. 150.00 (*0-521-22165-X*) Cambridge U Pr.

Dictionary of Japanese Affiliated Companies in the U. S. A. & Canada. 1992. lib. bdg. 300.00 (*0-8490-5354-4*) Gordon Pr.

Dictionary of Japanese & English Idiomatic Equivalents. Charles Corwin et al. LC 68-11818. 302p. 1980. 28.00 (*0-87011-111-6*) Kodansha.

Dictionary of Japanese & English Idiomatic Equivalents. Ed. by Charles Corwin et al. 302p. 1994. pap. 19.00 (*4-7700-1843-6*) Kodansha.

Dictionary of Japanese Buddhist Terms. Hisao Inagaki. LC 88-82776. 550p. (C). 1989. 34.50 (*0-89346-311-6*) Heian Intl.

Dictionary of Japanese Culture. Setsuko Kojima & Gene A. Crane. 1990. pap. text ed. 20.00 (*9971-68-144-7*, Pub. by Chopmen Singapore SI) Advent Bks Div.

Dictionary of Japanese Culture. Setsuko Kojima & Gene A. Crane. 413p. 1990. reprint ed. 19.95 (*0-89346-336-1*) Heian Intl.

Dictionary of Japanese Culture, Japanese-English. M. Yamaguchi. 408p. (ENG & JPN.). 1987. 95.00 (*0-8288-2365-0*, F55760) Fr & Eur.

Dictionary of Japanese Financial Terms. Dominic Williams. 240p. 1995. pap. 19.95 (*1-873410-12-3*, Pub. by Japan Library) Humanities.

Dictionary of Japanese Financial Terms. Dominic Williams. 240p. (C). 1995. text ed. 70.00 (*1-873410-11-5*, Pub. by Japan Library) Humanities.

Dictionary of Jargon. Jonathon Green. LC 87-4960. 832p. 1988. lib. bdg. 57.50 (*0-7100-9919-3*, RKP) Routledge.

Dictionary of Jesus & the Gospels: A Compendium of Contemporary Biblical Scholarship. Ed. by Joel B. Green et al. LC 91-32382. 1000p. 1992. 37.99 (*0-8308-1777-8*, 1777) InterVarsity.

Dictionary of Jewish Biography. Geoffrey Wigoder. 576p. 1991. 55.00 (*0-13-210105-X*) S&S Trade.

Dictionary of Jewish Surnames from the Russian Empire. Alexander Eider. (Illus.). 784p. 1993. 75.00 (*0-9626373-3-5*) Avotaynu.

Dictionary of Journalism: Diccionario del Periodismo. 5th ed. Antonio Lopez de Zuazo Algar. 256p. (SPA.). 1990. pap. 35.00 (*0-7859-4921-6*) Fr & Eur.

Dictionary of Judaism. Dagobert D. Runes. 236p. 1981. 8.95 (*0-8065-0787-X*, Citadel Pr) Carol Pub Group.

Dictionary of Judaism & Christianity. Daniel Cohn-Sherbok. LC 91-22076. 224p. (Orig.). (C). 1991. pap. 15.95 (*1-56338-030-7*) TPI PA.

Dictionary of Kashmiri Proverbs & Sayings. James H. Knowles. 1972. 59.95 (*0-8490-0036-X*) Gordon Pr.

Dictionary of Kathakali. K. P. Menon. (Illus.). 80p. 1981. text ed. 15.95 (*0-86131-046-2*, Pub. by Orient Longman Ltd II) Apt Bks.

Dictionary of Kathakali. K. P. Menon. (Illus.). 80p. 1979. 14.95 (*0-318-36308-9*) Asia Bk Corp.

Dictionary of Key Words in Psychology. Frank J. Bruno. 274p. 1988. pap. 14.95 (*0-7102-1394-8*, A3116, RKP) Routledge.

Dictionary of Khotan Saka. Harold W. Bailey. LC 77-80825. 1979. 285.00 (*0-521-21737-7*) Cambridge U Pr.

Dictionary of Kleinian Thought. R. D. Hinshelwood. 520p. 1991. 50.00 (*0-87668-556-4*) Aronson.

Dictionary of Kleinian Thought. enl. rev. ed. R. D. Hinshelwood. 490p. 1989. 49.50 (*0-946960-82-8*) Col U Pr.

Dictionary of Kleinian Thought. rev. ed. R. D. Hinshelwood. 482p. 1991. pap. 37.00 (*0-946960-83-6*) NYU Pr.

Dictionary of Labour Biography, 9 vols., 1. Ed. by Joyce M. Bellamy & John Saville. LC 78-185417. 1987. lib. bdg. 55.00 (*0-678-07008-3*) Kelley.

An Asterisk (*) at the beginning of an entry indicates that the title is appearing in BIP for the first time.

Dictionary of Labour Biography, 9 vols., 2. Ed. by Joyce M. Bellamy & John Saville. LC 78-185417. 1987. lib. bdg. 55.00 (*0-678-07018-0*) Kelley.

Dictionary of Labour Biography, 9 vols., 3. Ed. by Joyce M. Bellamy & John Saville. LC 78-185417. 1987. lib. bdg. 55.00 (*0-333-14415-5*) Kelley.

Dictionary of Labour Biography, 9 vols., 4. Ed. by Joyce M. Bellamy & John Saville. LC 78-185417. 1987. lib. bdg. 55.00 (*0-333-19704-6*) Kelley.

Dictionary of Labour Biography, 9 vols., 5. Ed. by Joyce M. Bellamy & John Saville. LC 78-185417. 1987. lib. bdg. 55.00 (*0-333-22015-3*) Kelley.

Dictionary of Labour Biography, 9 vols., 6. Ed. by Joyce M. Bellamy & John Saville. LC 78-185417. 1987. lib. bdg. 55.00 (*0-333-24095-2*) Kelley.

Dictionary of Labour Biography, 9 vols., 7. Ed. by Joyce M. Bellamy & John Saville. LC 78-185417. 1987. lib. bdg. 55.00 (*0-333-33181-8*) Kelley.

Dictionary of Labour Biography, 9 vols., 8. Ed. by Joyce M. Bellamy & John Saville. LC 78-185417. 1987. lib. bdg. 55.00 (*0-333-38782-1*) Kelley.

Dictionary of Labour Biography, 9 vols., 9. Ed. by Joyce M. Bellamy & John Saville. LC 78-185417. 1987. lib. bdg. 85.00 (*0-333-38783-X*) Kelley.

Dictionary of Lace. Pat Earnshaw. (Illus.). 240p. 1988. pap. 25.00 (*0-85263-700-4*, Pub. by Shire Pubns UK) Lubrecht & Cramer.

Dictionary of Lacquer Technology. H. Clausen. 562p. (ENG, FRE & GER.). 1980. 125.00 (*0-8288-1303-5*, M8339) Fr & Eur.

Dictionary of Lahu. James A. Matisoff. (Publications in Linguistics: Vol. III). 1989. 115.00 (*0-520-09711-4*) U CA Pr.

Dictionary of Landscape. George A. Goulty. 320p. 1991. text ed. 59.95 (*1-85628-214-7*, Pub. by Avebury Pub UK) Ashgate Pub Co.

Dictionary of Language Games, Puzzles & Amusements. Harry E. Eiss. LC 85-27280. 295p. 1986. text ed. 42.95 (*0-313-24467-7*, EID/, Greenwood Pr) Greenwood.

Dictionary of Late Egyptian, Vol. 1 of 4 Vols. Ed. by Leonard H. Lesko. (EGY.). 1982. lib. bdg. 35.00 (*0-930548-03-5*); pap. text ed. 20.00 (*0-930548-04-3*) B C Scribe.

Dictionary of Late Egyptian, Vol. 2. v, 214p. 1984. lib. bdg. 35.00 (*0-930548-05-1*); pap. 25.00 (*0-930548-06-X*) B C Scribe.

Dictionary of Late Egyptian, Vol. 3. v, 173p. 1987. lib. bdg. 35.00 (*0-930548-07-8*); pap. 20.00 (*0-930548-08-6*) B C Scribe.

Dictionary of Late Egyptian, Vol. 4. viii, 170p. 1989. lib. bdg. 40.00 (*0-930548-10-8*); pap. 25.00 (*0-930548-11-6*) B C Scribe.

Dictionary of Late Egyptian Vol. 5: The Index. iii, 109p. 1990. pap. 15.00 (*0-930548-12-4*) B C Scribe.

Dictionary of Latin American Racial & Ethnic Terminology: Spanish American Terms - Brazilian Portuguese Terms, Pts. 1 & 2. Thomas M. Stephens. 400p. 1990. lib. bdg. 53.95 (*0-8130-0965-0*) U Press Fla.

Dictionary of Latin & Greek Theological Terms. Richard A. Muller. LC 85-70795. 1985. 27.99 (*0-8010-6185-7*) Baker Bk.

Dictionary of Latin Literature. James H. Mantinband. (Quality Paperback Ser.: No. 152). 303p. 1964. reprint ed. pap. 9.95 (*0-8226-0152-4*) Littlefield.

Dictionary of Latin Phrases & Expressions: Diccionario de Expresiones y Frases Latinas. V. J. Herrero. 253p. (LAT & SPA.). 1980. 39.95 (*0-8288-1031-1*, S32727) Fr & Eur.

Dictionary of Latin Phrases & Quotations. Richard Branyon. 160p. 1994. pap. 11.95 (*0-7818-0260-1*) Hippocrene Bks.

Dictionary of Latin Standard Quotations. N. T. Babicev. 958p. (LAT & RUS.). 1982. 45.00 (*0-8288-2286-7*, M15185) Fr & Eur.

Dictionary of Law. 2nd ed. P. H. Collin. Orig. Title: English Law Dictionary. 328p. 1992. pap. 16.95 (*0-948549-33-5*, Pub. by Peter Collin UK) IBD Ltd.

Dictionary of Law. 3rd ed. L. B. Curzon. 448p. 1988. pap. 32.50 (*0-273-02962-2*, Pub. by Pitman Pub Ltd UK) Trans-Atl Phila.

Dictionary of Law. 3rd ed. Ed. by Elizabeth A. Martin. LC 93-36843. (Paperback Reference Ser.). 448p. (C). 1994. 29.95 (*0-19-211700-9*); pap. 13.95 (*0-19-280000-0*) OUP.

Dictionary of Law & Economics: Woerterbuch der Rechtssprache & Wirtschaftssprache, Vol. 1. 4th ed. Michel Doucet. 624p. (FRE & GER.). 1987. 150.00 (*0-8288-0976-3*, M15089) Fr & Eur.

Dictionary of Law, Containing Definitions of Terms & Phrases of American & English Jurisprudence, Ancient & Modern: Including the Principal Terms of International, Constitutional & Commercial Law; with a Collection of Legal Maxims & Numerous Select Titles from the Civil Law & Other Foreign Systems. Henry C. Black. LC 91-62383. x, 1253p. 1991. reprint ed. lib. bdg. 95.00 (*0-9630106-0-3*) Lawbk Exchange.

Dictionary of Legal & Commercial Terms: Woerterbuch der Rechtssprache & Wirtschaftssprache. Liu-Shing-I. 410p. (CHI & GER.). 1984. 250.00 (*0-8288-0974-7*, M15021) Fr & Eur.

Dictionary of Legal, Commercial, & Political Terms, Vol. 2. 3rd rev. ed. Clara-Erika Dietl et al. 821p. (ENG & GER.). 1988. 375.00 (*0-8288-3877-1*, M 15095) Fr & Eur.

Dictionary of Legal, Commercial, & Political Terms, Vol. 1: English - German. 5th ed. Clara-Erika Dietl. 937p. (ENG & GER.). 1990. 350.00 (*0-8288-3876-3*, F132140) Fr & Eur.

***Dictionary of Legal, Political & Commercial Terms Vol. 2: German-English.** 4th ed. C. Dietl. 849p. (ENG & GER.). 1992. 375.00 (*0-7859-7545-4*, 3406366546) Fr & Eur.

Dictionary of Legal Quotations. Simon R. James & Chantal Stebbings. LC 87-12255. 250p. 1987. text ed. 14.95 (*0-02-916002-2*) Macmillan.

Dictionary of Legal Quotations. J. W. Norton-Kyshe. 1972. 300.00 (*0-8490-0037-8*) Gordon Pr.

Dictionary of Legal Quotations. James W. Norton-Kyshe. xxi, 344p. 1984. reprint ed. 47.50 (*0-89941-375-7*, 303500) W S Hein.

Dictionary of Legal Terms. Garcia I. Rivera. 704p. (ENG & SPA.). 1985. 75.00 (*0-8288-7956-7*, F36820) Fr & Eur.

Dictionary of Legal Terms: A Simplified Guide to the Language of Law. 2nd ed. Stephen H. Gifis. LC 93-22322. 520p. 1993. pap. 8.95 (*0-8120-1411-1*) Barron.

Dictionary of Legal Terms - Spanish-English - English-Spanish: Diccionario de Terminos Juridicos - Espanol-Ingles - Ingles-Espanol. Julio Romanach, Jr. 216p. 1992. pap. text ed. 34.50 (*0-9633610-0-7*) Lawrence LA.

Dictionary of Legal Terms & Citations. H. Sturgess & A. Hewitt. 1976. 300.00 (*0-87968-408-9*) Gordon Pr.

Dictionary of Legal Terms (Diccionario de Terminos Lagales) Spanish-English, English-Spanish. Louis A. Robb. (ENG & SPA.). 1976. pap. 15.00 (*968-18-0384-1*) Intl Lang.

***Dictionary of Legal Words & Phrases, Vol. 1.** C. J. Claassen. Date not set. boxed 114.00 (*0-409-01890-2*, SA) Butterworth Legal Pubs.

***Dictionary of Legal Words & Phrases, Vol. 2.** C. J. Claassen. Date not set. boxed 114.00 (*0-409-01891-0*, SA) Butterworth Legal Pubs.

***Dictionary of Legal Words & Phrases, Vol. 3.** C. J. Claassen. Date not set. boxed 114.00 (*0-409-01892-9*, SA) Butterworth Legal Pubs.

***Dictionary of Legal Words & Phrases, Vol. 4.** C. J. Claassen. Date not set. boxed 114.00 (*0-409-01893-7*, SA) Butterworth Legal Pubs.

Dictionary of Lexical Difficulties Encountered in Literary Texts. Ed. by V. Makarov & N. Matveeva. 368p. (C). 1989. 60.00 (*0-685-54119-3*, Pub. by Collets) St Mut.

Dictionary of Librarianship: English-German - German-English. Ed. by Eberhard Sauppe. 428p. 1988. lib. bdg. 90.00 (*3-598-10618-1*) K G Saur.

Dictionary of Library & Educational Technology. 3rd enl. ed. Kenyon C. Rosenberg. 196p. 1989. lib. bdg. 32.50 (*0-87287-623-3*) Libs Unl.

***Dictionary of Library & Information Management.** 200p. 1995. pap. 20.00 (*0-948549-68-8*) IBD Ltd.

Dictionary of Library & Information Science: English - German, German - English Worterbuch Bibliotheks & Informationswissenschaft. Saledah Von Keitz & W. Von Keitz. LC 92-16849. 527p. (ENG & GER.). 1992. 65.00 (*1-56081-199-4*) VCH Pubs.

Dictionary of Library & Information Science (English & German) 2nd ed. S. Keitz. 527p. (ENG & GER.). 1992. lib. bdg. 150.00 (*0-8288-3392-3*, F107243) Fr & Eur.

Dictionary of Library & Information Sciences. Li Heng. 400p. (CHI & ENG.). 1984. 150.00 (*0-8288-0179-7*, M15588) Fr & Eur.

Dictionary of Library Science. R. N. Chopra. 1990. 33.50 (*81-7041-291-9*, Pub. by Anmol II) S Asia.

Dictionary of Library Science Information & Documentation. rev. ed. W. E. Clason & S. Salem. 708p. (ARA, DUT, ENG, FRE, GER, ITA & SPA.). 1977. 187.25 (*0-444-41475-4*) Elsevier.

Dictionary of Lighting Engineering: English, German, French, & Russian. R. Zimmermann. 430p. 1990. 141.00 (*0-444-98850-5*) Elsevier.

Dictionary of Lille Patois: Dictionnaire du Patois de Lille. Pierre Legrand. 174p. (FRE.). 1990. pap. write for info. (*0-7859-4858-9*) Fr & Eur.

Dictionary of Linguistics: Diccionario de Linguistica. 2nd ed. Theodor Lewandowski. 464p. (SPA.). 1986. pap. 59.95 (*0-7859-4953-4*) Fr & Eur.

Dictionary of Linguistics: Diccionario de Linguistica. 3rd ed. Jean Dubois et al. 712p. (SPA.). 1986. write for info. (*0-7859-4951-8*) Fr & Eur.

Dictionary of Linguistics & Phonetics. 3rd ed. David Crystal. (Language Library). (Illus.). 432p. 1991. pap. text ed. 19.95 (*0-631-17871-6*) Blackwell Pubs.

Dictionary of Literary & Linguistic Terms: Arabic-Arabic. Magdi Wahba. 1974. 35.00 (*0-86685-131-3*) Intl Bk Ctr.

Dictionary of Literary Biography, 96 vols. write for info. (*0-318-59849-3*) Gale.

Dictionary of Literary Biography, Vol. 2. Mary Bruccoli. (Documentary Ser.: Vol. 2). (Illus.). 480p. 1982. 128.00 (*0-8103-1114-3*) Gale.

Dictionary of Literary Biography, Vol. 5. (Documentary Ser.: Vol. 5). (Illus.). 450p. 1987. 128.00 (*0-8103-2639-6*) Gale.

Dictionary of Literary Biography, Vol. 6. (Documentary Ser.). 450p. 1988. 128.00 (*0-8103-2781-3*) Gale.

Dictionary of Literary Biography, Vol. 135. Mary Bruccoli et al. 1993. 128.00 (*0-8103-5394-6*, 007470) Gale.

Dictionary of Literary Biography, Vol. 136. Mary LaymaBruccoli et al. 1994. 128.00 (*0-8103-5395-4*, 007471) Gale.

Dictionary of Literary Biography, Vol. 137. Mary Bruccoli et al. 1994. 128.00 (*0-8103-5396-2*, 007472) Gale.

Dictionary of Literary Biography, Vol. 138. Mary Bruccoli et al. 1994. 128.00 (*0-8103-5397-0*, 007473) Gale.

Dictionary of Literary Biography, Vol. 139. Mary Bruccoli et al. 1994. 128.00 (*0-8103-5398-9*, 007474) Gale.

Dictionary of Literary Biography, Vol. 141. Mary Bruccoli et al. 1994. 128.00 (*0-8103-5555-8*, 007476) Gale.

Dictionary of Literary Biography, Vol. 142. Mary Bruccoli et al. 1994. 128.00 (*0-8103-5556-6*, 007477) Gale.

Dictionary of Literary Biography, Vol. 143. Mary Bruccoli et al. 1994. 128.00 (*0-8103-5557-4*, 007478) Gale.

Dictionary of Literary Biography, Vol. 144. Mary Bruccoli et al. 1994. 128.00 (*0-8103-5558-2*, 007479) Gale.

Dictionary of Literary Biography, Vol. 145. Mary Bruccoli et al. 1994. 128.00 (*0-8103-5559-0*, 007480) Gale.

Dictionary of Literary Biography: Modern American Poets: James Dickey, Robert Frost, & Marianne Moore, Vol. 7. Ed. by Mary Bruccoli et al. (Documentary Ser.: Vol. 7). (Illus.). 1989. 128.00 (*0-8103-2782-1*) Gale.

***Dictionary of Literary Biography: Twentieth-Century Spanish Poets, Vol. 134.** Ed. by Jerry P. Winfield. 366p. 1993. 120.00 (*0-8103-5393-8*) Gale.

Dictionary of Literary Biography - Concise British, 8 Vols., Vol. 1. 1991. 500.00 (*0-8103-7980-5*) Gale.

Dictionary of Literary Biography Documentary: An Illustrated Chronicle, Vol. 1. Ed. by Margaret A. Van Antwerp. (Dictionary of Literary Biography Ser.). (Illus.). 440p. 1982. 128.00 (*0-8103-1112-7*) Gale.

Dictionary of Literary Biography Documentary Series, Vol. 4. Ed. by Perry J. Ashley. 456p. 1983. 128.00 (*0-8103-1113-5*) Gale.

Dictionary of Literary Biography Documentary Series, Vol. 8. 1991. 128.00 (*0-8103-7579-6*) Gale.

Dictionary of Literary Biography Documentary Series, Vol. 11. 1993. 128.00 (*0-8103-5542-6*) Gale.

Dictionary of Literary Biography Documentary Series: An Illustrated Chronicle, Vol. 3. Ed. by Mary Bruccoli. 416p. 1983. 128.00 (*0-8103-1115-1*) Gale.

Dictionary of Literary Biography, No. 85: Austrian Writers after 1914, Vol. 85. Mary Bruccoli. 1989. 128.00 (*0-8103-4563-3*) Gale.

Dictionary of Literary Biography, No. 86: American Short-Story Writers, 1910-1945, First Series, Vol. 86. Mary Bruccoli. 1989. 128.00 (*0-8103-4564-1*) Gale.

Dictionary of Literary Biography, Vol. 80: Restoration Dramatists & 18th Century Dramatists, First Series, Vol. 80. Mary Bruccoli. 1989. 128.00 (*0-8103-4558-7*) Gale.

Dictionary of Literary Biography, Vol. 81: Austrian Fiction Writers, 1875-1913, Vol. 81. Mary Bruccoli. 1989. 128.00 (*0-8103-4559-5*) Gale.

Dictionary of Literary Biography, Vol. 82: Chicano Writers, First Series, Vol. 82. Mary Bruccoli. Ed. by Carl R. Shirley. 350p. 1989. 128.00 (*0-8103-4560-9*) Gale.

Dictionary of Literary Biography, Vol. 83: French Novelists since 1960, Vol. 83. Mary Bruccoli. 1989. 128.00 (*0-8103-4561-7*) Gale.

Dictionary of Literary Biography, Vol. 84: Restoration & 18th Century Dramatists, Vol. 84. Mary Bruccoli. (Second Ser.). 350p. 1989. 128.00 (*0-8103-4562-5*) Gale.

Dictionary of Literary Biography, Vol. 87: British Mystery & Thriller Writers since 1940, First Series, Vol. 87. Braccdi. 1989. 128.00 (*0-8103-4565-X*) Gale.

Dictionary of Literary Biography, Vol. 88: Canadian Writers, 1920-1959, Second Series, Vol. 88. Ed. by Mary Bruccoli. (Second Ser.). 1989. 128.00 (*0-8103-4566-8*) Gale.

Dictionary of Literary Biography, Vol. 89: Restoration & 18th Century Dramatists, Vol. 89. Ed. by Mary Bruccoli et al. (Third Ser.). 1989. 128.00 (*0-8103-4567-6*) Gale.

Dictionary of Literary Biography, Vol. 90: German Writers in the Age of Goethe, 1789-1832, Vol. 90. Ed. by Mary Bruccoli et al. 1989. 128.00 (*0-8103-4568-4*) Gale.

Dictionary of Literary Biography, Vol. 91: American Magazine Journalists, 1900-1960, Vol. 91. Ed. by Sam G. Riley. LC 89-48356. (First Ser.). (Illus.). 416p. 1990. text ed. 128.00 (*0-8103-4571-4*, 006559) Gale.

Dictionary of Literary Biography, Vol. 92: Canadian Writers, 1890-1920, Vol. 92. Ed. by W. H. New. LC 89-48355. (Illus.). 487p. 1990. text ed. 128.00 (*0-8103-4572-2*) Gale.

Dictionary of Literary Biography, Vol. 93: British Romantic Poets, 1789-1832, Vol. 93. Ed. by John R. Greenfield. LC 90-2888. (First Ser.). (Illus.). 437p. 1990. text ed. 128.00 (*0-8103-4573-0*) Gale.

Dictionary of Literary Biography, Vol. 94: German Writers in the Age of Goethe: Sturm und Drang to Classicism, Vol. 94. Ed. by James Hardin & Christoph E. Schweitzer. LC 90-3382. (Illus.). 427p. 1990. text ed. 128.00 (*0-8103-4574-9*) Gale.

Dictionary of Literary Biography, Vol. 95: Eighteenth-Century British Poets, Vol. 95. Ed. by John Sitter. LC 90-3500. (First Ser.). (Illus.). 446p. 1990. 128.00 (*0-8103-4575-7*) Gale.

Dictionary of Literary Biography, Vol. 96: British Romantic Poets, 1789-1832, Vol. 96. Ed. by John R. Greenfield. (Second Ser.). (Illus.). 1990. text ed. 128.00 (*0-8103-4576-5*) Gale.

Dictionary of Literary Biography, Vol. 97: German Writers from the Enlightenment to Sturm und Drang, 1720-1764, Vol. 97. Ed. by James Hardin & Christoph E. Schweitzer. (Illus.). 1990. text ed. 128.00 (*0-8103-4577-3*) Gale.

Dictionary of Literary Biography, Vol. 98: Modern British Essayists, Vol. 98. (Illus.). 1990. text ed. 128.00 (*0-8103-4578-1*) Gale.

Dictionary of Literary Biography Yearbook, 1980. Ed. by Karen L. Rood et al. LC 81-4188. 344p. 1981. 128.00 (*0-8103-1600-5*) Gale.

Dictionary of Literary Biography Yearbook, 1982. Ed. by Richard Ziegfeld. (Illus.). 432p. 1983. 128.00 (*0-8103-1626-9*) Gale.

Dictionary of Literary Biography Yearbook, 1984. Ed. by Jean W. Ross. 380p. 1985. 128.00 (*0-8103-1628-5*) Gale.

Dictionary of Literary Biography Yearbook, 1985. 350p. 1986. 128.00 (*0-8103-1629-3*) Gale.

Dictionary of Literary Biography Yearbook, 1986. 460p. 1987. 128.00 (*0-8103-2094-0*) Gale.

Dictionary of Literary Biography Yearbook, 1987. Dictionary of Literary Biography Editors Staff. (Illus.). 1988. 128.00 (*0-8103-1835-0*) Gale.

Dictionary of Literary Biography Yearbook, 1988. Mary Bruccoli. 1989. 128.00 (*0-8103-1836-9*) Gale.

Dictionary of Literary Biography Yearbook, 1992. 1993. 128.00 (*0-8103-5543-4*) Gale.

Dictionary of Literary Biography 124, Vol. 124. 1993. 128.00 (*0-8103-5383-0*) Gale.

Dictionary of Literary Biography 125, Vol. 125. 1993. 128.00 (*0-8103-5384-9*) Gale.

Dictionary of Literary Biography 127, Vol. 127. 1993. 128.00 (*0-8103-5386-5*) Gale.

Dictionary of Literary Biography 128: 20th Century Italian Poets, Vol. 128. Siegfried Mews & James Hardin. (Second Ser.). 1993. 128.00 (*0-8103-5387-3*) Gale.

Dictionary of Literary Biography 129, Vol. 129. 1993. 128.00 (*0-8103-5388-1*) Gale.

Dictionary of Literary Biography 130, Vol. 130. 1993. 128.00 (*0-8103-5389-X*) Gale.

Dictionary of Literary Biography 131, Vol. 131. 1993. 128.00 (*0-8103-5390-3*) Gale.

Dictionary of Literary Biography 132, Vol. 132. 1993. 128.00 (*0-8103-5391-1*) Gale.

Dictionary of Literary Biography 134. 1993. 120.00 (*0-8103-5993-6*) Gale.

Dictionary of Literary, Dramatic, & Cinematic Terms. 2nd ed. Sylvan Barnet et al. (C). 1987. pap. text ed. 9.50 (*0-673-39194-9*) HarpCollege.

***Dictionary of Literary Pseudonyms in the English Language.** T. J. Carty. 500p. 1995. lib. bdg. 75.00 (*1-884964-13-3*) Fitzroy Dearborn.

Dictionary of Literary Quotations. Meic Stephens. 240p. 1989. 25.00 (*0-415-04129-5*, A3895) Routledge.

Dictionary of Literary-Rhetorical Conventions of the English Renaissance. Marjorie Donker & George M. Muldrow. LC 81-4266. xvi, 268p. 1982. text ed. 55.00 (*0-313-23000-5*, DER/, Greenwood Pr) Greenwood.

Dictionary of Literary Terms. J. A. Cuddon. 1982. pap. 9.95 (*0-14-051112-1*, Penguin Bks) Viking Penguin.

Dictionary of Literary Terms. Gagan Raj. 1990. 33.50 (*81-7041-284-6*, Pub. by Anmol II) S Asia.

Dictionary of Literary Terms see Concise Dictionary of Literary Terms

Dictionary of Literary Terms & Literary Theory. 3rd ed. J. A. Cuddon. 1076p. 1991. 56.95 (*0-631-17214-9*) Blackwell Pubs.

Dictionary of Literary Terms (English-French-Arabic) Magdi Wahba. 1974. 39.95 (*0-86685-117-8*) Intl Bk Ctr.

Dictionary of Literary Themes & Motifs, 2 vols. Ed. by Jean-Charles Seigneuret. LC 87-12004. 1530p. 1988. text ed. 250.00 (*0-313-22943-0*, SLT/, Greenwood Pr) Greenwood.

Dictionary of Literature in the English Language, 2 vols. Robin Myers. LC 68-18529. 1978. From Chaucer to 1970. 842.00 (*0-08-023684-7*, Pub. by Pergamon Repr UK) Franklin.

Dictionary of Literature in the English Language, 2 vols, 1. Robin Myers. LC 68-18529. 1978. 400.00 (*0-08-012079-2*, Pub. by Pergamon Repr UK) Franklin.

Dictionary of Literature in the English Language, 2 vols, 2. Robin Myers. LC 68-18529. 1978. 224.00 (*0-08-016142-1*, Pub. by Pergamon Repr UK) Franklin.

Dictionary of Literature in the English Language, 2 vols, Set. Robin Myers. LC 68-18529. 1978. 623.00 (*0-08-016143-X*, Pub. by Pergamon Repr UK) Franklin.

Dictionary of Literature in the English Language, Vol. 3: From 1940-1970. Robin Myers. 1978. 265.00 (*0-08-018050-7*, Pergamon Pr) Elsevier.

Dictionary of Liturgical Terms. Philip Pfatteicher. LC 91-22075. 160p. (Orig.). (C). 1991. 15.95 (*1-56338-026-9*) TPI PA.

***Dictionary of Liturgical Terms.** Philip Pfatteicher. LC 91-22075. 160p. (Orig.). (C). 1991. pap. 11.00 (*1-56338-125-7*) TPI PA.

Dictionary of Loanwords Usage: Katakana-English. Prem Motwani. 258p. (ENG & JPN.). 1991. 125.00 (*0-8288-7340-2*) Fr & Eur.

Dictionary of Logic As Applied in the Study of Language: Concepts - Methods - Theories. Ed. by Witold Marciszewski. 464p. 1981. lib. bdg. 145.50 (*90-247-2123-7*) Kluwer Ac.

Dictionary of Love. Comp. by Gil Friedman. LC 89-90140. 192p. (Orig.). 1990. pap. 9.95 (*0-913038-02-4*) Yara Pr.

Dictionary of Macedonian: Recnick Na Makedonskiot Jazik. 1706p. (SLV.). 1986. 49.95 (*0-8288-2077-5*, F80010) Fr & Eur.

Dictionary of Management. K. R. Balan. 1993. 25.00 (*81-207-1503-9*, Pub. by Sterling Pubs II) Apt Bks.

Dictionary of Management. R. Chopra. 192p. 1990. 80.00 (*81-7041-134-3*, Pub. by Scientific Pubs II) St Mut.

Dictionary of Manufacturing Terms. Ed. by R. Veilleux. 133p. 1987. 21.00 (*0-87263-279-2*) SME.

Dictionary of Marine Artists. Dorothy E. Brewington. (Illus.). xix, 450p. 1982. 45.00 (*0-913372-24-2*) Mystic Seaport.

Dictionary of Marine Engineering Terms. M. Masuda. 318p. (ENG & JPN.). 1980. 125.00 (*0-8288-0420-6*, M9339) Fr & Eur.

Dictionary of Marine Insurance Terms. R. H. Brown. 395p. 1975. 150.00 (*0-900886-11-0*, Pub. by Witherby & Co UK) St Mut.

Dictionary of Marine Insurance Terms & Clauses. 5th ed. Robert H. Brown. 656p. (C). 1989. 250.00 (*0-948691-43-3*, Pub. by Witherby & Co UK) St Mut.

Dictionary of Marine Technology. D. A. Taylor. (Illus.). 244p. 1989. text ed. 110.00 (*0-408-02195-0*) Buttrwrth-Heinemann.

Dictionary of Maritime Terms: Mercantile & Naval Shipping. Ed. by John Siemss et al. 838p. (GER.). 1984. 80.00 (*3-9800987-0-2*) IR Pubns.

Dictionary of Marketing. A. Ivanovic. 207p. 1989. pap. text ed. 16.95 (*0-948549-08-4*, Pub. by Peter Collin UK) IBD Ltd.

D

An Asterisk (*) at the beginning of an entry indicates that the title is appearing in BIP for the first time.

***Dictionary of Marketing.** Wolfgang J. Koschnick. 950p. 1995. 102.95 (*0-566-07612-8*, Pub. by Gower UK) Ashgate Pub Co.

Dictionary of Marketing. Rona Ostrow & Sweetman R. Smith. (Illus.). 250p. 1987. text ed. 26.50 (*0-87005-573-9*) Fairchild.

***Dictionary of Marketing & Advertising.** Jerry M. Rosenberg. LC 94-25576. 1995. text ed. 39.95 (*0-471-02503-8*); pap. text ed. 17.95 (*0-471-02502-X*) Wiley.

Dictionary of Marketing & Advertising. 2nd ed. Michael J. Baker. (Illus.). 1990. 57.50 (*0-89397-372-6*) Nichols Pub.

Dictionary of Marketing Research. Ed. & Contrib by J. J. Van Minden. 301p. 1987. 38.00 (*0-912289-57-0*) St James Pr.

Dictionary of Marketing Terms. Ed. by Peter D. Bennett. LC 88-24116. 220p. 1989. text ed. 35.00 (*0-87757-194-5*) Am Mktg.

Dictionary of Marketing Terms. Betsy-Ann Toffler & Jane Imber. LC 93-23235. 1994. pap. 11.95 (*0-8120-1783-8*) Barron.

Dictionary of Marketing Terms. 4th ed. Irving J. Shapiro. LC 80-25669. 280p. 1981. 12.95 (*0-8226-0363-2*) Rowman.

Dictionary of Marks: An Antique Collector's Guide. Margaret M. Taylor. 1989. 7.99 (*0-517-68476-4*) Random Hse Value.

Dictionary of Marks: Pottery & Porcelain. Ralph M. Kovel & Terry H. Kovel. 288p. 1953. 14.95 (*0-517-00141-1*, Crown) Crown Pub Group.

Dictionary of Marks N - E: Ceramics, Metalwork, Furniture, Tapestry. Margaret McDonald-Taylor. (Illus.). 336p. 1993. pap. 22.95 (*0-7126-5303-1*, Pub. by Barrie & Jenkins) Trafalgar.

Dictionary of Marxist Thought. Ed. by Thomas B. Bottomore. 544p. 1983. 50.00 (*0-674-20525-1*) HUP.

Dictionary of Marxist Thought. Ed. by Thomas B. Bottomore. 544p. 1985. pap. text ed. 15.95 (*0-674-20526-X*) HUP.

Dictionary of Marxist Thought. 2nd ed. Tom Bottomore. Ed. by Lawrence Harris et al. 672p. 1992. 69.95 (*0-631-16481-2*); pap. 27.95 (*0-631-18082-6*) Blackwell Pubs.

Dictionary of Materia Medica & Therapeutics. C. Henri Leonard & Thomas Christy. 1980. lib. bdg. 75.00 (*0-8490-3120-6*) Gordon Pr.

Dictionary of Material Testing, Vol. 2. Werner Goedecke. 486p. (ENG, FRE & GER.). 1980. 150.00 (*0-8288-0218-1*, M9029) Fr & Eur.

Dictionary of Material Testing, Vol. 3. Werner Goedecke. 458p. (ENG, FRE & GER.). 1980. 150.00 (*0-8288-0219-X*, M9028) Fr & Eur.

Dictionary of Materials & Manufacturing. Ed. by Vernon John. (Illus.). 400p. 1990. 59.95 (*0-89397-371-8*) Nichols Pub.

***Dictionary of Materials Engineering & Technology.** Claus G. Goetzel & Lilo K. Goetzel. 753p. (ENG & GER.). (C). 1995. text ed. write for info. (*1-56990-148-1*) Hanser-Gardner.

Dictionary of Mathematical Games, Puzzles, & Amusements. Harry E. Eiss. LC 87-280. 292p. 1988. text ed. 49.95 (*0-313-24714-5*, EDM/, Greenwood Pr) Greenwood.

D

Dictionary of Mathematics. 252p. (CHI & ENG.). 1974. pap. 49.95 (*0-686-92280-8*) Fr & Eur.

Dictionary of Mathematics. Japan Ministry of Education Staff & Jordan. 300p. (ENG & JPN.). 1980. 49.95 (*0-8288-1893-2*, M9346) Fr & Eur.

Dictionary of Mathematics. R. Sube & G. Eisenreich. 1458p. (C). 1985. text ed. 645.00 (*0-7855-0112-6*, Pub. by Collets) St Mut.

Dictionary of Mathematics. 3rd ed. Francois Le Lionnais. 848p. (ENG & FRE.). 1992. 150.00 (*0-7859-4704-3*, F70764) Fr & Eur.

Dictionary of Mathematics, 2 vols., Set. Gunther Eisenreich & Rolf Sube. 1460p. (ENG, FRE, GER & RUS.). 1982. 218.00 (*0-444-99706-7*) Elsevier.

Dictionary of Mathematics: Dictionnaire de Mathematiques. L. Chambadal. 312p. 1982. 69.95 (*0-8288-1896-7*, M6625) Fr & Eur.

Dictionary of Mathematics, English-German-French-Russian. Ed. by Collet's Holdings, Ltd. Staff. 1985. 455.00 (*0-317-46608-9*, Pub. by Collets UK) Pro-Am Music.

Dictionary of Mathematics Terms. Douglas Downing. (C). 1987. pap. 10.95 (*0-8120-2641-1*) Barron.

***Dictionary of Mathematics Terms.** 2nd ed. Douglas Downing. LC 95-12039. (Professional Guides Ser.). 1995. write for info. (*0-8120-3097-4*) Barron.

Dictionary of Mauritian Creole. P. Baker et al. 365p. (CRP & FRE.). 1987. 59.95 (*0-8288-7296-1*, 2858029733) Fr & Eur.

Dictionary of Measurement Technology for Computers. Commercial Press Staff. 161p. (CHI & ENG.). 1977. pap. 39.95 (*0-8288-5376-2*, M9565) Fr & Eur.

Dictionary of Mechanical Engineering. S. B. Chopra. 1989. 33.50 (*81-7041-169-6*, Pub. by Anmol II) S Asia.

Dictionary of Mechanical Engineering. Commercial Press Staff. 608p. (CHI & ENG.). 1974. pap. text ed. 65.00 (*0-8288-6005-X*, M9586) Fr & Eur.

Dictionary of Mechanical Engineering. 3rd ed. G. H. Nayler. (Illus.). 400p. 1985. text ed. 84.95 (*0-408-01505-5*) Buttrwrth-Heinemann.

Dictionary of Mechanics, Strength of Materials & Materials in Two Volumes. R. Walther. (ENG & GER.). 1965. 146.00 (*0-08-010859-8*, Pub. by Pergamon Repr UK) Franklin.

Dictionary of Mechanisms. deluxe ed. Herbert Bucksch. (ENG & GER.). 1976. 195.00 (*0-8288-5633-8*, M7111) Fr & Eur.

Dictionary of Medical Acronyms & Abbreviations. 2nd ed. Stanley Jablonski. 300p. 1992. pap. 18.00 (*1-56053-052-9*) Hanley & Belfus.

Dictionary of Medical & Health Terminology: English-Hebrew, Hebrew-English. Ed. by Ellen Feingold et al. 450p. 1991. 50.00 (*0-13-210253-6*) S&S Trade.

Dictionary of Medical & Surgical Syndromes. J. Gibson & O. Potparic. (Illus.). 200p. (C). 1992. 48.00 (*1-85070-338-8*) Prthnon Pub.

Dictionary of Medical Eponyms. B. G. Firkin & J. A. Whitworth. (Illus.). 590p. 1987. 48.00 (*1-85070-138-5*) Prthnon Pub.

***Dictionary of Medical Eponyms.** 2nd ed. B. G. Firkin & J. A. Whitworth. (Illus.). 590p. (C). 1995. text ed. 59.00 (*1-85070-477-5*) Prthnon Pub.

Dictionary of Medical Equipment. Malcom Brown et al. 336p. 1987. 65.00 (*0-317-56144-8*, 1148) Chapman & Hall.

Dictionary of Medical Folklore. Carol A. Rinzler. 1980. pap. 2.75 (*0-345-28791-6*) Ballantine.

Dictionary of Medical Siglas: Dictionnaire des Sigles Medicaux. J. P. Poinsotte. 146p. (FRE.). 1982. pap. text ed. 24.95 (*0-8288-4420-8*, M9772) Fr & Eur.

Dictionary of Medical Syndromes. 3rd ed. Magalini. (Illus.). 900p. 1990. text ed. 99.00 (*0-397-50882-4*) Lippincott.

Dictionary of Medical Terms: English-Spanish, Spanish-English. 6th ed. Ruiz Torres. 880p. 1989. 79.00 (*0-87201-195-X*) Gulf Pub.

Dictionary of Medical Terms for the Nonmedical Person. 3rd ed. Mikel A. Rothenberg & Charles F. Chapman. LC 93-31122. 628p. 1994. pap. 9.95 (*0-8120-1852-4*) Barron.

Dictionary of Medical Terms in Galen. Richard J. Durling. LC 92-39986. (Studies in Ancient Medicine: No. 5). xiii, 344p. (ENG & GRE.). 1993. 114.50 (*90-04-09754-6*) E J Brill.

Dictionary of Medicine. Klaus P. Eschenbach. 606p. (ENG & GER.). 1983. 49.95 (*0-8288-0568-7*, M6454) Fr & Eur.

Dictionary of Medicine. Jurgen Nohring. 1984. 166.75 (*0-444-99641-9*, I-050-84) Elsevier.

Dictionary of Medicine: German-English. Jurgen Nohring. 850p. 1987. 202.75 (*0-444-98982-X*) Elsevier.

Dictionary of Medicine: Russian - French. G. Bejenar. (FRE & RUS.). lib. bdg. 75.00 (*0-8288-2615-3*, F12776) Fr & Eur.

Dictionary of Medicine, German & English. Jurgen Nohring. 848p. (ENG & GER.). 1987. 195.00 (*0-8288-0572-5*, M1735) Fr & Eur.

Dictionary of Medieval Knighthood & Chivalry: Concepts & Terms. Bradford B. Broughton. LC 84-29036. (Illus.). 614p. 1986. text ed. 79.50 (*0-313-24552-5*, BKD/, Greenwood Pr) Greenwood.

Dictionary of Medieval Knighthood & Chivalry: People, Places, & Events. Bradford B. Broughton. LC 87-18163. (Illus.). 800p. 1988. text ed. 55.00 (*0-313-25347-1*, BPN/, Greenwood Pr) Greenwood.

Dictionary of Medieval Latin from British Sources, Fascicule 4; F-G-H. Ed. by D. R. Howlett. 320p. 1990. pap. 98.00 (*0-19-726082-9*) OUP.

Dictionary of Medieval Romance & Romance Writers. Lewis Spence. 1972. 200.00 (*0-8490-0039-4*) Gordon Pr.

Dictionary of Mental Handicap. May P. Lindsey. 304p. 1989. 55.00 (*0-415-02810-8*) Routledge.

Dictionary of Mental Health. Richard B. Fisher. (Illus.). 268p. 1983. pap. 8.00 (*0-586-08339-1*, Pub. by Granada UK) Academy Chi Pubs.

Dictionary of Mercantile Law: Diccionario de Derecho Mercantil. 3rd ed. Jose M. Codera-Martin. 344p. (SPA.). 1987. write for info. (*0-7859-4937-2*) Fr & Eur.

Dictionary of Mesa Grande Diegueno. Ted Couro & Christina Hutcheson. 1973. pap. 7.50 (*0-939046-14-8*) Malki Mus Pr.

Dictionary of Mesa Grande Diegueno: 'Lipay Aa-English - English - 'Lipay Aa. Ted Couro & Christina Hutcheson. Tr. by Leanne Hinton. 118p. (C). 1993. reprint ed. lib. bdg. 23.00x (*0-8095-6208-1*) Borgo Pr.

Dictionary of Metal-Cutting Machine Tools. deluxe ed. Henry G. Freeman. 561p. (ENG & GER.). 1965. 125.00 (*0-8288-6738-0*, M-7110) Fr & Eur.

Dictionary of Metallurgy. Ed. by A. Dollinger. 767p. (ENG, FRE, GER, POL, RUS & SLV.). 1974. 150.00 (*0-8288-6006-8*, M9893) Fr & Eur.

Dictionary of Metallurgy. J. L. Taylor. 619p. (ENG & POR.). 1981. pap. 95.00 (*0-8288-1918-1*, M8957) Fr & Eur.

Dictionary of Metallurgy: Dictionnaire de Metalurgie. Maria L. Breba. (FRE.). 1984. write for info. (*0-8288-1923-8*, M15832) Fr & Eur.

Dictionary of Metallurgy & Foundry Technology: English - German. Karl Stolzel. 418p. (ENG & GER.). 1984. 250.00 (*0-8288-9289-X*, S60220) Fr & Eur.

Dictionary of Metallurgy & Foundry Technology: English-German. Karl Stolzel. 1984. 141.00 (*0-444-99612-5*, I-423-84) Elsevier.

Dictionary of Metallurgy & Foundry Technology: German-English. Karl Stolzel. 450p. 1987. 133.50 (*0-444-99514-5*) Elsevier.

Dictionary of Meteorology. Commercial Press Staff. 207p. (CHI & ENG.). 1974. pap. 39.95 (*0-8288-6007-6*, M9567) Fr & Eur.

Dictionary of Mexican American History. Ed. by Matt S. Meier & Feliciano Rivera. LC 80-24750. (Illus.). 472p. 1981. text ed. 49.95 (*0-313-21203-1*, NMD/, Greenwood Pr) Greenwood.

Dictionary of Mexican American Proverbs. Comp. by Mark Glazer. LC 87-23721. 376p. 1987. text ed. 65.00 (*0-313-25385-4*, GMP/, Greenwood Pr) Greenwood.

Dictionary of Mexican Literature. Ed. by Eladio Cortes. LC 91-10529. 816p. 1992. text ed. 85.00 (*0-313-26271-3*, CMX/, Greenwood Pr) Greenwood.

Dictionary of Michelangelo's Watermarks. Jane Roberts. 49p. (Orig.). 1988. pap. 5.95 (*0-685-60732-1*) Natl Gallery Art.

Dictionary of Micro-Electronics. A. M. Prochorov. (DUT, ENG, FRE, GER & RUS.). 150.00 (*0-8288-9438-8*) Fr & Eur.

Dictionary of Microbial Taxonomic Usage. S. T. Cowan. 1968. 15.00 (*0-934454-28-0*) Lubrecht & Cramer.

Dictionary of Microbiology & Molecular Biology. 2nd ed. Paul Singleton & Diana Sainsbury. LC 87-19047. 1019p. 1993. text ed. 189.95 (*0-471-91114-3*) Wiley.

***Dictionary of Microbiology & Molecular Biology.** 2nd ed. Paul Singleton & Diana Sainsbury. 1993. pap. text ed. 59.95 (*0-471-94052-6*) Wiley.

Dictionary of Microelectronics: English-German & German-English. Ed. by Werner Bindmann. 480p. 1985. 154.00 (*0-444-99619-2*, I-187-84) Elsevier.

Dictionary of Microelectronics: English, Russian, German, French, Dutch. A. M. Prokhorov. 544p. (DUT, ENG, FRE, GER & RUS.). 1991. 95.00 (*0-7859-1084-0*, 5200006376) Fr & Eur.

Dictionary of Microprocessor Systems. Ed. by D. Muller. 312p. (ENG, FRE, GER & RUS.). 1984. 100.00 (*0-444-99645-1*, I-401-83) Elsevier.

Dictionary of Microprocessor Systems. 2nd rev. ed. D. Muller. 448p. (ENG, FRE, GER & RUS.). 1990. 154.00 (*0-685-47417-8*) Elsevier.

Dictionary of Microprocessor Systems. 4th ed. Dieter Muller. 448p. (ENG, FRE, GER & RUS.). 1990. 175.00 (*0-8288-0270-X*, M 13124) Fr & Eur.

Dictionary of Microprocessor Systems: English-German-French-Russian. rev. ed. Dieter Muller. 448p. (ENG, FRE, GER & RUS.). 1990. 75.00 (*3-86117-013-2*, Pub. by A Hatier GW) IBD Ltd.

Dictionary of Military Abbreviations. Norman Polmar et al. LC 93-34566. 307p. 1994. 24.95 (*1-55750-680-9*) Naval Inst Pr.

Dictionary of Military & Associated Terms. 1991. lib. bdg. 250.00 (*0-8490-4946-6*) Gordon Pr.

Dictionary of Military & Naval Quotations. Comp. by Robert D. Heinl, Jr. LC 66-22342. 1966. 25.95 (*0-87021-149-8*) Naval Inst Pr.

Dictionary of Military & Technological Abbreviations & Acronyms. Bernhard Pretz. 450p. 1983. 45.00 (*0-7100-9274-1*, RKP) Routledge.

Dictionary of Military, Defense Contractor & Troop Slang Acronyms. Philip C. Gutzman. 392p. 1990. lib. bdg. 125.00 (*0-87436-589-9*) ABC-CLIO.

Dictionary of Military History. rev. ed. Ed. by Andre Corvisier. Tr. by Chris Turner. LC 92-46136. (Illus.). 944p. 1994. 64.95 (*0-631-16848-6*) Blackwell Pubs.

Dictionary of Military Law: Chinese-English, English-Chinese. Joseph D. Lowe. LC 83-83213. (Illus.). xiv, 775p. 1994. 130.00 (*0-9605506-6-6*) Lowe Pub.

Dictionary of Military Law, Chinese & English. Joseph D. Lowe. 750p. (CHI & ENG.). 1987. 175.00 (*0-8288-0973-9*, M8721) Fr & Eur.

Dictionary of Military Terms. Trevor N. Dupuy et al. LC 85-26592. 233p. 1986. 42.00 (*0-8242-0717-3*) Wilson.

Dictionary of Military Terms. A. Plekhov. 336p. (C). 1988. 125.00 (*0-685-37189-1*, Pub. by Collets) St Mut.

Dictionary of Military Terms. rev. ed. Joint Chiefs of Staff. 428p. 1991. 44.95 (*1-85367-085-5*, 5491) Stackpole.

***Dictionary of Military Terms.** 3rd ed. Comp. by U. S. Joint Chiefs of Staff. LC 95-13988. 512p. 1995. 44.95 (*1-85367-217-3*, Pub. by Greenhill Bks UK) Stackpole.

Dictionary of Military Terms & Military Intelligence Phrases: Chinese-English & English-Chinese. limited ed. Joseph D. Lowe. LC 88-91316. (Illus.). 725p. (CHI & ENG.). 1994. 130.00 (*0-930325-11-7*) Lowe Pub.

Dictionary of Milling Technology. J. Bure et al. 136p. (ENG, GER, ITA & SPA.). 1980. pap. 24.95 (*0-8288-0032-4*, F10139) Fr & Eur.

Dictionary of Mind & Spirit. Comp. by Donald A. Watson. 416p. (Orig.). 1992. pap. 12.50 (*0-380-71792-1*) Avon.

Dictionary of Ming Biography, 1364-1644, 2 vols, Set. Ed. by L. Carrington Goodrich & Chaoying Fang. LC 75-26938. (Illus.). 1976. 191.00 (*0-685-62034-4*) Col U Pr.

Dictionary of Ming Biography, 1364-1644, Vol. 1. Ed. by L. Carrington Goodrich & Chaoying Fang. LC 75-26938. (Illus.). 1054p. 1976. write for info. (*0-231-03801-1*) Col U Pr.

Dictionary of Ming Biography, 1364-1644, Vol. 2. Ed. by L. Carrington Goodrich & Chaoying Fang. LC 75-26938. (Illus.). 634p. 1976. write for info. (*0-231-03833-X*) Col U Pr.

Dictionary of Mining & Processing. Helmut Schmidt. 692p. 1980. 99.00 (*0-317-59287-4*, Pub. by Collets UK) Pro-Am Music.

Dictionary of Mining Technology & Manufacturing. Helmut Schmidt. 691p. (ENG & GER.). 1981. 125.00 (*0-8288-0596-2*, M14275) Fr & Eur.

Dictionary of Mining Terminology. 3rd ed. Baron. 478p. (RUS.). 1981. 15.95 (*0-8288-1919-X*, M8853) Fr & Eur.

Dictionary of Mining, Vol. 1: English-German. H. Georgen. 520p. (ENG & GER.). 1981. 75.00 (*0-8288-0589-X*, M9049) Fr & Eur.

Dictionary of Mining, Vol. 2: German-English. H. Georgen. 530p. (ENG & GER.). 1981. 59.95 (*0-8288-0590-3*, M14220) Fr & Eur.

Dictionary of Minor Planet Names. Lutz D. Schmadel. LC 92-10894. ix, 687p. 1992. 59.00 (*0-387-54384-8*) Spr-Verlag.

Dictionary of Minor Planet Names. 2nd enl. rev. ed. Lutz D. Schmadel. LC 93-21310. 1993. 69.00 (*0-387-57260-0*) Spr-Verlag.

Dictionary of Minton. Paul Atterbury & Maureen Batkin. (Illus.). 368p. 1990. 69.50 (*1-85149-073-6*) Antique Collect.

Dictionary of Miracles. Ebenezer Brewer. 1972. 75.00 (*0-8490-0040-8*) Gordon Pr.

Dictionary of Miracles: Imitative, Realistic, & Dogmatic. rev. ed. E. Cobham Brewer. LC 89-28194. 582p. 1992. reprint ed. lib. bdg. 55.00 (*1-55888-900-0*) Omnigraphics Inc.

Dictionary of Misconduct Connected with Work Concepts & a Glossary of Terms Used in Labor Relations see Dictionary of the Principles of Misconduct in the Workplace & a Glossary of Labor Terms

Dictionary of Misinformation. Tom Burnam. 1985. pap. 2.95 (*0-345-32134-0*) Ballantine.

Dictionary of Misinformation. Tom Burnam. 1993. pap. 12.00 (*0-06-272050-3*) HarpC.

Dictionary of Modern Business. Louis Robb. (ENG & SPA.). 1960. 35.00 (*0-910136-00-9*) Anderson Kramer.

Dictionary of Modern Colloquial French. Rene J. Herail & Edwin A. Lovatt. 352p. 1984. pap. 13.95 (*0-7102-1099-X*, 1099X, RKP) Routledge.

Dictionary of Modern Colloquial French. Rene J. Herail & Edwin A. Lovatt. 1985. 32.50 (*0-7100-9704-2*, RKP) Routledge.

Dictionary of Modern Colloquial French. Rene J. Herail. 1987. pap. 15.95 (*0-415-05893-7*) Routledge.

Dictionary of Modern Critical Terms. Ed. by Roger Fowler. 288p. 1987. 35.00 (*0-7102-1021-3*, 10213, RKP); pap. 12.95 (*0-7102-1022-1*, 10211, RKP) Routledge.

Dictionary of Modern Critical Terms: Hermeneutics as Method, Philosophy, & Critique. Ed. by Roger Fowler. 1987. pap. 14.95 (*0-415-05884-8*) Routledge.

Dictionary of Modern English Usage. 2nd ed. Henry W. Fowler. (C). 1983. reprint ed. pap. 10.95 (*0-19-281389-7*) OUP.

Dictionary of Modern English Usage. 2nd rev. ed. Henry W. Fowler. 750p. 1987. 24.95 (*0-19-869115-7*) OUP.

Dictionary of Modern French Literature: From the Age of Reason Though Realism. Sandra W. Dolbow. LC 85-15492. 375p. 1986. text ed. 65.00 (*0-313-23784-0*, Greenwood Pr) Greenwood.

Dictionary of Modern Herbalism: The Complete Guide to Herbs & Herbal Therapy. Simon Mills. 208p. 1985. pap. 10.95 (*0-89281-238-9*) Inner Tradit.

Dictionary of Modern Italian History. Ed. by Frank J. Coppa. LC 84-6704. xxvi, 496p. 1985. text ed. 105.00 (*0-313-22983-X*, CMI/, Greenwood Pr) Greenwood.

Dictionary of Modern Lebanese Proverbs. Anis Freyha. (ARA & ENG.). 1974. 25.00 (*0-86685-086-4*) Intl Bk Ctr.

Dictionary of Modern Legal Usage. 2nd ed. Bryan A. Garner. 896p. 1995. 45.00 (*0-19-507769-5*) OUP.

Dictionary of Modern Legal Usage. Bryan A. Garner. 616p. 1990. reprint ed. pap. 17.95 (*0-19-506578-6*) OUP.

Dictionary of Modern Linguistic Terms: English-Arabic, Arabic-English. Muhammad Bakalla. 1975. 30.00 (*0-86685-304-9*) Intl Bk Ctr.

Dictionary of Modern Medicine: A Sourcebook of Current Medical Expressions, Jargon & Technical Terms. J. C. Segen. (Illus.). 900p. (C). 1992. 75.00 (*1-85070-321-3*) Prthnon Pub.

Dictionary of Modern Military Technology. Frank Barnaby. 400p. 1991. 54.50 (*0-685-38705-4*, Pub. by I B Tauris UK) St Martin.

Dictionary of Modern Music & Musicians. 543p. 1993. reprint ed. lib. bdg. 99.00 (*0-7812-9708-7*) Rprt Serv.

Dictionary of Modern Music & Musicians. Ed. by A. Eaglefield-Hull. LC 78-139192. (Music Ser.). 1971. reprint ed. lib. bdg. 65.00 (*0-306-70086-7*) Da Capo.

Dictionary of Modern Music & Musicians. Ed. by Arthur E. Hull. LC 72-1619. reprint ed. 47.50 (*0-404-08315-3*) AMS Pr.

Dictionary of Modern Music & Musicians. Ed. by Arthur E. Hull. LC 77-166238. 543p. 1924. reprint ed. 69.00 (*0-403-01365-8*) Scholarly.

Dictionary of Modern Politics. 400p. 1993. 80.00 (*0-946653-75-5*, 101894, Pub. by Europa UK) Gale.

Dictionary of Modern Politics & Political Sociology. B. P. Singh. 1987. 32.00 (*81-7099-032-7*, Pub. by Mittal II) S Asia.

Dictionary of Modern Technology: English-German, 2 vols., Vol. 1. 2nd ed. Alfred Oppermann. 1935p. (ENG & GER.). 1990. 375.00 (*0-8288-0631-4*, M6982) Fr & Eur.

***Dictionary of Modern Technology: English-German, 2 vols., Vol. 2.** Alfred Oppermann. 2044p. (GER.). 1987. 375.00 (*0-8288-0632-2*) Fr & Eur.

Dictionary of Modern Theological German. 2nd ed. Helmut W. Ziefle. LC 92-47081. 384p. (Orig.). 1992. reprint ed. pap. 14.99 (*0-8010-9931-5*); reprint ed. audio 7.95 (*0-8010-9932-3*) Baker Bk.

Dictionary of Modern Theological German. 2nd ed. Helmut W. Ziefle. LC 92-11697. 384p. (Orig.). 1992. pap. text ed. 19.99 (*0-8010-9935-8*) Baker Bk.

Dictionary of Modern Welsh: Y Geiriadur Cyfoes. H. Meurig Evans. 624p. (C). 1992. 59.00 (*0-7154-0725-2*, Pub. by C Davies Pubs) St Mut.

Dictionary of Modern Words (Dictionnaire des Mots Contemporains) P. Gilbert. 739p. (FRE.). 1989. 69.95 (*0-7859-4819-8*, M6128) Fr & Eur.

Dictionary of Modern Written Arabic. 4th ed. Hans Wehr. (ARA & ENG.). 1979. 170.00x (*0-86685-422-3*) Intl Bk Ctr.

Dictionary of Modern Written Arabic. 5th ed. Hans Wehr. 1452p. (ARA & ENG.). 1985. 295.00 (*0-8288-0995-X*, M9964) Fr & Eur.

Dictionary of Modern Written Arabic. Hans Wehr. Tr. by J. Milton Cowan. xvii, 1301p. (ARA & ENG.). 1993. reprint ed. 175.00 (*0-87950-002-6*) Spoken Lang Serv.

1966

An Asterisk (*) at the beginning of an entry indicates that the title is appearing in BIP for the first time.

An Asterisk (*) at the beginning of an entry indicates that the title is appearing in BIP for the first time.

D

Dictionary of Optics & Optical Engineering: German-English, English-German. 2nd ed. Werner Bindmann. 688p. (ENG & GER.). 1992. 195.00 (*0-8288-7380-1*, M7402) Fr & Eur.

Dictionary of Optoelectronics: English-Serbocroat & Serbocroat-English. S. Tankosic. 314p. (C). 1988. 100.00 (*0-685-36919-6*, Pub. by Collets) St Mut.

Dictionary of Optometry. 3rd ed. Michel Millodot. 208p. 1993. pap. 30.00 (*0-7506-0847-1*) Buttrwrth-Heinemann.

Dictionary of Oregon History. 2nd ed. Ed. by Howard M. Corning. LC 89-61196. 281p. 1989. 35.00 (*0-8323-0449-2*) Binford Mort.

Dictionary of Organic Compounds: First Supplement. Ed. by John B. Buckingham et al. 1983. 450.00 (*0-412-17010-8*, NO. 6798) Chapman & Hall.

Dictionary of Organic Compounds: Tenth Supplement. Ed. by John B. Buckingham. 720p. 1993. 832.50 (*0-412-17100-7*, A9625) Chapman & Hall.

Dictionary of Organic Compounds: The Eighth Supplement. 5th ed. Ed. by John B. Buckingham. 704p. 1990. 599.00 (*0-412-17080-9*, A5185) Chapman & Hall.

Dictionary of Organic Compounds: The Fifth Supplement. 5th ed. Ed. by John B. Buckingham. 1300p. 1987. text ed. 799.00 (*0-412-17050-7*) Chapman & Hall.

Dictionary of Organic Compounds: The Seventh Supplement. Ed. by John B. Buckingham. 740p. 1990. 499.00 (*0-412-17070-1*, A3817) Chapman & Hall.

Dictionary of Organic Compounds: Third Supplement. 5th ed. Ed. by John B. Buckingham. 800p. 1985. 450.00 (*0-412-17030-2*, 9553) Chapman & Hall.

Dictionary of Organometallic Compounds, 3 vols., Set. Ed. by John B. Buckingham et al. 3000p. 1984. 1,100.00 (*0-412-24710-0*, NO. 9075) Chapman & Hall.

Dictionary of Organometallic Compounds: Fifth Supplement. Ed. by Jane E. Macintyre. 1125p. 1990. 895.00 (*0-412-28180-5*, A3821) Chapman & Hall.

Dictionary of Organometallic Compounds: First Supplement. Ed. by John B. Buckingham et al. 400p. 1985. 350.00 (*0-412-26320-3*, NO. 9076) Chapman & Hall.

Dictionary of Organometallic Compounds: Fourth Supplement. Ed. by Jane E. Macintyre. (Illus.). 600p. 1988. 695.00 (*0-412-28170-8*, A1997) Chapman & Hall.

Dictionary of Organometallic Compounds: Second Supplement. 636p. 1986. 350.00 (*0-412-26330-0*, 9980) Chapman & Hall.

Dictionary of Organometallic Compounds: Structure Index for Supplements 1-5. Ed. by Jane E. Macintyre. 208p. 1990. 275.00 (*0-412-35680-5*, A4395) Chapman & Hall.

Dictionary of Organometallic Compounds: Third Supplement. Ed. by Jane E. Macintyre. 600p. 1988. text ed. 450.00 (*0-412-26340-8*) Chapman & Hall.

Dictionary of Organophosphorus Compounds. Ed. by R. S. Edmundson. 1342p. 1987. text ed. 725.00 (*0-412-25790-4*) Chapman & Hall.

***Dictionary of Oriental Philosophy.** Ed. by Ruth Reyna. 419p. 1993. 57.50x (*81-215-0118-0*, Pub. by M Manoharial II) Coronet Bks.

Dictionary of Oriental Quotations. Claud Field. 1972. 75.00 (*0-8490-0043-2*) Gordon Pr.

Dictionary of Painters, Sculptors & Graphic Artists, 10 vols., Set. rev. ed. E. Benezit. (Illus.). (FRE.). 1976. 550.00 (*2-7000-0149-4*) Edns Publisol.

Dictionary of Pali Proper Names, 2 vols. Malalasekera. (PLI.). 1983. 250.00 (*0-8288-1721-9*, F 27380) Fr & Eur.

D

Dictionary of Pali Proper Names, 2 vols. G. P. Malasekera. (C). 1938. 72.50 (*0-86013-269-2*, Pub. by Pali Text) Wisdom MA.

Dictionary of Palmistry. J. S. Bright. 237p. 1984. 9.95 (*0-318-36394-1*) Asia Bk Corp.

Dictionary of Papago Usage: Vol. I, B-K. Madeleine Mathiot. (Language Science Ser.: No. 8-1). 504p. 1974. pap. text ed. 82.35 (*90-279-2677-8*) Mouton.

Dictionary of Paper. 4th ed. 489p. 1980. 20.00 (*951-9309-61-6*, 1501APID) TAPPI.

Dictionary of Parapsychology: Diccionario de Parapsicolgia, 2 vols. W. Bonin. (SPA.). 1983. pap. 25.95 (*0-8288-2201-8*, S15803) Fr & Eur.

Dictionary of Parapsychology: Diccionario de Parapsicologia. Julio Roca Muntanola. 272p. (SPA.). 1979. 29.95 (*0-8288-4761-4*, S50093) Fr & Eur.

Dictionary of Parisian Music Publishers (1700-1950) Cecil Hopkinson. LC 79-9521. (Music Reprint Ser.). 1979. reprint ed. 27.50 (*0-306-79577-9*) Da Capo.

Dictionary of Pastoral Care. Alastair V. Campbell. 320p. 1987. 24.50 (*0-8245-0834-3*) Crossroad NY.

Dictionary of Pastoral Care & Counseling. Ed. by Rodney J. Hunter. 1376p. 1990. 59.95 (*0-687-10761-X*) Abingdon.

Dictionary of Patent Practice: Woerterbuch der Patentpraxis. 4th ed. J. R. Uexkull & H. J. Reich. 175p. (ENG & GER.). 1994. 135.00 (*0-8288-0395-1*, M7107) Fr & Eur.

Dictionary of Patent Terminology: Woerterbuch der Patentfachssprache. 5th ed. E. Berthold Klaften & F. C. Allison. 520p. (ENG & GER.). 1986. 195.00 (*0-8288-0391-9*, M 6974) Fr & Eur.

Dictionary of Pathogenic Agents of Cultivated Plants. I. Fiala & F. Fevre. 136p. (ENG, FRE & LAT.). 1992. 125.00 (*0-8288-7188-4*, 2738003354) Fr & Eur.

Dictionary of Paul & His Letters: A Compendium of Contemporary Biblical Scholarship. Ed. by Gerald F. Hawthorne et al. LC 93-36044. 1038p. (Orig.). 1993. 37.99 (*0-8308-1778-6*, 1778) InterVarsity.

Dictionary of Pedagogy: Woerterbuch der Paedagogik. 12th ed. Wilhelm Hehlmann. 586p. (GER.). 1982. pap. 45.00 (*0-8288-1392-2*, M6976) Fr & Eur.

Dictionary of Pediatric Dermatology: Dictionnaire de Dermatologie Pediatrique. J. L. Bonafe. 1985. 110.00 (*0-8288-1790-1*, M15583) Fr & Eur.

Dictionary of Pentecostal & Charismatic Movements. Stanley M. Burgess & Gary B. McGee. Ed. by Patrick H. Alexander. 960p. 1988. 34.99 (*0-310-44100-5*) Zondervan.

Dictionary of Persian Loan Words in the Arabic Language. Al-Sayyid Addi-Shir. (ARA & PER.). 1980. 25.00 (*0-86685-128-3*) Intl Bk Ctr.

Dictionary of Personal Finance. Ed. by Joel G. Siegel et al. 416p. 1992. text ed. 75.00 (*0-02-897393-3*) Macmillan.

Dictionary of Personal Finance. Joel G. Siegel et al. 391p. 1993. pap. 20.00 (*0-02-897394-1*) Macmillan.

***Dictionary of Personnal & Educational Terms: English-German, German-English.** Rory O'Flanagan. 263p. (ENG & GER.). 1991. 95.00 (*0-7859-7111-4*) Fr & Eur.

Dictionary of Personnel & Human Resources Management. Roger Bennett. 288p. (Orig.). 1992. pap. 42.50 (*0-273-03877-X*, Pub. by Pitman Pub Ltd UK) Trans-Atl Phila.

Dictionary of Personnel Management. A. Ivanovic. 193p. 1988. pap. text ed. 16.95 (*0-948549-06-8*, Pub. by Peter Collin UK) IBD Ltd.

Dictionary of Pesticide (Chinese-English-Russian-Japanese) Science Press Staff. 1019p. (CHI, ENG, JPN & RUS.). 1984. 75.00 (*0-8288-6993-6*) Fr & Eur.

Dictionary of Petroleum Exploration, Drilling, & Production. Norman J. Hyne. 631p. 1991. 89.95 (*0-87814-352-1*, P4474) PennWell Bks.

Dictionary of Petroleum Technology: English-French - French-English. Magdeleine Moureau. 1991. lib. bdg. 325.00 (*0-8288-3189-0*) Fr & Eur.

Dictionary of Petrology. S. I. Tomkeieff. LC 81-19836. 680p. 1983. text ed. 299.95 (*0-471-10159-1*) Wiley.

Dictionary of Pharmaceutical Medicine. Gerhard Nahle. LC 94-11648. 1994. 25.00 (*0-387-82557-6*) Spr-Verlag.

Dictionary of Philosophical Quotations. Ed. by A. J. Ayer & J. O'Grady. 544p. (C). 1993. text ed. 49.95x (*0-631-17015-4*) Blackwell Pubs.

Dictionary of Philosophical Quotations. Ed. by A. J. Ayer & J. O'Grady. 544p. (C). 1994. pap. text ed. 21.95 (*0-631-19478-9*) Blackwell Pubs.

Dictionary of Philosophy. Ed. by Ivan Frolov. LC 83-244. 464p. 1985. 8.95 (*0-7178-0604-9*) Intl Pubs Co.

Dictionary of Philosophy. A. R. Lacey. 266p. 1990. pap. 15.95 (*0-415-05872-4*, A4927) Routledge.

***Dictionary of Philosophy.** Ed. & Intro. by Thomas Mautner. 640p. Date not set. text ed. write for info. (*0-631-18459-7*) Blackwell Pubs.

Dictionary of Philosophy. K. Srinivas. vi, 199p. (C). 1993. 25.00 (*81-7024-518-4*, Pub. by Ashish Pub Hse II) Nataraj Bks.

Dictionary of Philosophy. enl. rev. ed. Ed. by Dagobert D. Runes. LC 81-80240. 360p. (C). 1984. pap. 14.95 (*0-8226-0392-6*) Littlefield.

Dictionary of Philosophy. 2nd ed. Antony G. Flew. 388p. 1984. pap. 14.95 (*0-312-20923-1*) St Martin.

Dictionary of Philosophy. 21th ed. Walter Brugger. 592p. (ENG & GER.). 1992. 75.00 (*0-8288-2277-8*, M7587) Fr & Eur.

Dictionary of Philosophy: Dictionnaire des Philosophes, 2 vols., Set. D. Huisman. 2768p. (FRE.). 1984. 450.00 (*0-8288-2273-5*, F70760) Fr & Eur.

Dictionary of Philosophy: Philosophisches Woerterbuch. 22th ed. Heirich Schmidt. 817p. (GER.). 1991. 59.95 (*0-8288-2280-8*, M15205) Fr & Eur.

Dictionary of Philosophy & Psychology. James M. Baldwin et al. 1977. lib. bdg. 395.00 (*0-8490-1721-1*) Gordon Pr.

Dictionary of Philosophy & Psychology. Incl. Vol. 3, Pt. 1. Bibliography of Philosophy, Psychology and Cognate Subjects. Pt. 1. 24.00 (*0-8446-1049-6*); Vol. 3, Pt. 2. Bibliography of Philosophy, Psychology and Cognate Subjects. Pt. 2. (*0-8446-1050-X*); write for info. (*0-318-55250-7*) Peter Smith.

***Dictionary of Philosophy & Religion.** 2nd ed. Reese. (C). Date not set. text ed. write for info. (*0-391-03864-8*); pap. write for info. (*0-391-03865-6*) Humanities.

Dictionary of Philosophy & Religion: Eastern & Western Thought. William L. Reese. LC 78-12561. 644p. (C). 1980. pap. 25.00 (*0-391-00941-9*) Humanities.

***Dictionary of Phonetics & Phonology.** R. L. Trask. LC 95-16583. 1995. pap. write for info. (*0-415-11261-3*) Routledge.

***Dictionary of Phonetics & Phonology.** Robert L. Trask. LC 95-16583. 1995. write for info. (*0-415-11260-5*) Routledge.

Dictionary of Photography: Technique - Art - Design: Diccionario de la Fotografia: Tecnica - Arte - Diseno. H. Shottle. 358p. (SPA.). 1982. pap. 21.75 (*0-8288-2094-5*, S40500) Fr & Eur.

Dictionary of Phraseological Synonyms of the Russian Language. V. P. Zhukov & M. I. Sidorenko. 442p. (C). 1987. 75.00 (*0-317-92479-6*, Pub. by Collets) St Mut.

Dictionary of Physical Chemistry. Satish Anand & Raj Kumar. 1990. 23.50 (*81-7041-238-2*, Pub. by Anmol II) S Asia.

Dictionary of Physical Metallurgy. R. K. Freiwillig et al. 192p. (ENG, FRE, GER, RUS & SPA.). 1987. 113.00 (*0-444-99527-7*) Elsevier.

Dictionary of Physical Metallurgy. E. F. Tyrkiel. 402p. (ENG, FRE, GER, POL & RUS.). 1978. 133.50 (*0-444-99810-1*) Elsevier.

Dictionary of Physical Metallurgy. E. F. Tyrkiel. 402p. (ENG, FRE, GER, POL & RUS.). 1977. 250.00 (*0-8288-9293-8*, M7855) Fr & Eur.

Dictionary of Physics. Commercial Press Staff. 1689p. (CHI & ENG.). 1978. 19.95 (*0-8288-5170-0*, M9287) Fr & Eur.

Dictionary of Physics. L. Hoffman. 107p. (ENG, FRE & RUS.). 1982. 19.95 (*0-8288-2243-3*, M1989) Fr & Eur.

Dictionary of Physics, 2 vols. Science Press Staff. 2720p. 1988. lib. bdg. 125.00 (*0-7859-3661-0*, 7030008324) Fr & Eur.

Dictionary of Physics. C. Stockley. (Illustrated Dictionaries Ser.). (Illus.). 128p. (J). (gr. 6 up). 1988. lib. bdg. 16.96 (*0-88110-308-X*); pap. 10.95 (*0-86020-987-3*) EDC.

Dictionary of Physics: Dictionnaire de Physique. Elie Devy. 904p. (FRE.). 1988. 195.00 (*0-8288-2234-4*, F65440) Fr & Eur.

***Dictionary of Physics: English-German.** Sube Ralf & Guenther Eisenreich. 1008p. (ENG & GER.). 1987. 225.00 (*0-7859-7072-X*) Fr & Eur.

***Dictionary of Physics: English-German-French-Russian.** 2nd ed. Sube Ralf & Guenther Eisenreich. 2896p. (ENG, FRE & GER.). 1984. 750.00 (*0-7859-7069-X*) Fr & Eur.

Dictionary of Physics: Russian, English, German, & French. V. J. Rydnik et al. 392p. 1989. 128.25 (*0-444-70490-6*) Elsevier.

Dictionary of Physics, English-German-French-Russian. Collet's Holdings, Ltd. Staff. 1986. 700.00 (*0-317-52906-4*, Pub. by Collets UK) Pro-Am Music.

Dictionary of Physics in Russian, German, English & French. V. J. Rydnik et al. 392p. (ENG, FRE, GER & RUS.). 1989. 250.00 (*0-8288-9318-7*) Fr & Eur.

Dictionary of Pictorial Subjects from Classical Literature: A Guide to Their Identification in Works of Art. Percy Preston. LC 83-4470. (Illus.). 336p. 1983. 39.95 (*0-684-17913-X*, Scribners) S&S Trade.

Dictionary of Picture Postcards in Britain 1894-1939. A. W. Coysh. (Illus.). 312p. 1986. pap. 59.50 (*1-85149-015-9*) Antique Collect.

Dictionary of Plant Names. Allen J. Coombes. 207p. 1985. lib. bdg. 10.95 (*0-600-35770-8*) Lubrecht & Cramer.

***Dictionary of Plant Names: Botanical Names & Their Common Name Equivalents.** rev. ed. Allen J. Coombes. 208p. 1994. 10.95 (*0-88192-294-3*) Timber.

Dictionary of Plant Names: Handwoerterbuch der Pflanzennamen. 13th ed. Robert Zander. 769p. (GER.). 1984. 95.00 (*0-8288-1244-6*, M7735) Fr & Eur.

Dictionary of Plant Names & Botany: Botanisches Woerterbuch: Pflanzennamen und Botanische Fachworter. 11th ed. Rudolf Schubert & Gunther Wagner. 645500p. (GER.). 1993. 55.00 (*0-8288-1243-8*, M15345) Fr & Eur.

Dictionary of Plant Pathology. Ed. by Paul Holliday. 448p. (C). 1989. 69.95 (*0-521-33117-X*) Cambridge U Pr.

Dictionary of Plant Pathology. Ed. by Paul Holliday. 392p. (C). 1992. pap. 24.95 (*0-521-42475-5*) Cambridge U Pr.

Dictionary of Plant Virology: In English, Russian, German, French & Spanish. V. Bojnansky & A. Fargasova. 500p. 1991. 141.00 (*0-444-98740-1*) Elsevier.

Dictionary of Plant Virology in English, Russian, German, French & Spanish. V. Bojnansky & A. Fargasova. 472p. (ENG, FRE, GER, RUS & SPA.). 1991. 250.00 (*0-8288-9202-4*) Fr & Eur.

Dictionary of Plastics. J. A. Wordingham & P. Reboul. (Quality Paperback Ser.: No. 174). 1967. reprint ed. pap. 10.50 (*0-8226-0174-5*) Littlefield.

Dictionary of Plastics Engineering. Hans Schnellman. 120p. (ENG & ITA.). 1986. pap. 95.00 (*0-8288-0729-9*, M 6973) Fr & Eur.

Dictionary of Plastics Technology. A. M. Abd-El-Wahed. Ed. by H. Y. El-Desouki. (ARA, ENG, FRE & GER.). 1980. 75.00 (*0-8288-0731-0*, M9754) Fr & Eur.

Dictionary of Plastics Technology. R. J. Heath & A. W. Birley. 256p. 1992. 59.95 (*0-412-02961-8*, A5309, Blackie & Son-Chapman NY) Chapman & Hall.

Dictionary of Plastics Technology. H. D. Junge. 315p. 1987. lib. bdg. 150.00 (*0-89573-525-3*) VCH Pubs.

Dictionary of Plastics Technology. Gisbert Kaliske. 384p. (ENG, FRE, GER & RUS.). 1983. 100.00 (*0-444-99687-7*, 1-479-82) Elsevier.

Dictionary of Plastics Technology. Gisbert Kaliske. 408p. (ENG, FRE, GER & RUS.). 1983. 175.00 (*0-8288-0732-9*, M14273) Fr & Eur.

***Dictionary of Plays of Shadow Theatre.** Mounir Khayyal. 232p. (ARA.). 1995. 35.00 (*0-86685-648-X*) Intl Bk Ctr.

Dictionary of Polish Literature. E. J. Czerwinski. LC 93-49540. 504p. 1994. text ed. 85.00 (*0-313-26222-5*, Greenwood Pr) Greenwood.

Dictionary of Polish Obscenities (Polish-English) 3rd ed. Stanislaw Kielbasa. 93p. (POL.). (C). 1994. pap. 6.95 (*0-933884-93-1*, Scythian Bks) Berkeley Slavic.

Dictionary of Political Parties & Organizations in Russia. Vladimir Pribylovskii. Ed. by Dauphine Sloan & Sarah Helmstadter. (Significant Issues Ser.). 1992. pap. text ed. 21.00 (*0-89206-180-4*) CSI Studies.

Dictionary of Political Phrases & Allusions. Hugh Montgomery. 1972. 75.00 (*0-8490-0044-0*) Gordon Pr.

Dictionary of Political Psychology: Handwoerterbuch der Politischen Psychologie. E. Lippert. 380p. (GER.). 1983. 65.00 (*0-8288-2256-5*, M15264) Fr & Eur.

Dictionary of Political Science: Diccionario de Ciencia Politica. Axel Gorlitz. 628p. (SPA.). 1980. pap. 95.00 (*0-8288-2268-9*, S50058) Fr & Eur.

Dictionary of Political Terminology. Comp. by M. B. Khopkar. 1970. pap. 2.75 (*0-88253-149-2*) Ind-US Inc.

Dictionary of Political Terms: Chinese-English, English-Chinese. Joseph D. Lowe. LC 80-85163. (Illus.). 1250p. (CHI & ENG.). 1994. 160.00 (*0-9605506-0-7*) Lowe Pub.

Dictionary of Political Thought. Roger Scruton. 512p. 1984. pap. 12.95 (*0-8090-1524-2*) Hill & Wang.

Dictionary of Politics: Diccionario de Politica, 2 vols. Norberto Bobbio & N. Matteucci. 1751p. (SPA.). 1983. 225.00 (*0-8288-2266-2*, S40514) Fr & Eur.

Dictionary of Politics: Sachwoerterbuch der Politik. 2nd ed. Reinhart Beck. 1111p. (GER.). 1986. 75.00 (*0-8288-2255-7*, M8026) Fr & Eur.

Dictionary of Politics: Selected American & Foreign Political & Legal Terms. 7th ed. Walter J. Raymond. LC 92-14215. (Illus.). 762p. 1992. 60.00 (*1-55618-008-X*) Brunswick Pub.

Dictionary of Polling: The Language of Contemporary Opinion Research. Michael L. Young. LC 91-24198. 288p. 1992. text ed. 59.95 (*0-313-27598-X*, YDP, Greenwood Pr) Greenwood.

Dictionary of Polygraphy: Fachworterbuch Polygrafie. Wolfgang Miller. 1020p. (ENG, FRE, GER & RUS.). 1981. 175.00 (*0-8288-2228-X*, M11292) Fr & Eur.

Dictionary of Polynesian Mythology. Robert D. Craig. LC 89-7479. 472p. 1989. text ed. 59.95 (*0-313-25890-2*, Greenwood Pr) Greenwood.

Dictionary of Popular Music. Peter Gammond & Cl Gammond. 1988. reprint ed. lib. bdg. 59.00 (*0-7812-0388-0*) Rprt Serv.

Dictionary of Popular Music. Peter Gammond & Peter Clayton. LC 73-166229. 274p. 1961. reprint ed. 59.00 (*0-403-01563-4*) Scholarly.

***Dictionary of Portuguese-African Civilization Vol. 1: From Discovery to Independence, 2 vols.** Benjamin Nunez. 1060p. 1995. 220.00 (*1-873836-70-8*, Pub. by H Zell Pubs UK) Bowker-Saur.

***Dictionary of Portuguese-African Civilization Vol. 2: Biographies: From Ancient Kings to Presidents.** Benjamin Nunez. 500p. 1995. 90.00 (*1-873836-65-1*) K G Saur.

Dictionary of Post-Classical Yemeni Arabic, Vol. I. Moshe Piamenta. LC 90-2137. xxiv, 274p. (ARA & ENG.). 1990. 94.50 (*90-04-09261-7*) E J Brill.

Dictionary of Post-Classical Yemeni Arabic, Vol. 2. Moshe Piamenta. LC 90-2137. 267p. (ARA & ENG.). 1991. 94.50 (*90-04-09293-5*) E J Brill.

Dictionary of Power Engineering: German-English with Definitions & English Index. Bharat Heavy Electricals Ltd. Staff. LC 93-16449. 326p. (ENG & GER.). 1993. 156.25 (*0-444-89984-7*) Elsevier.

Dictionary of Power Engineering & Automation, Vol. 1. Heinrich Bezner. 537p. (ENG & GER.). 1987. 125.00 (*0-8288-0621-7*, M15791) Fr & Eur.

Dictionary of Power Engineering & Automation, Vol. 2. Heinrich Bezner. 545p. (ENG & GER.). 1987. 125.00 (*0-8288-0622-5*, M15792) Fr & Eur.

Dictionary of Power Plant Engineering: Conventional Steam Power Plants, Pt. I. F. Stattmann. 252p. (FRE & GER.). 1971. 95.00 (*0-8288-6441-1*, M-7103) Fr & Eur.

Dictionary of Power Plant Engineering: Nuclear Power Plants, Pt. II. F. Stattmann. 316p. (FRE & GER.). 1973. 69.95 (*0-7859-0843-9*, M-7102) Fr & Eur.

Dictionary of Practical Law. Charles F. Hemphill, Jr. & Phyllis D. Hemphill. 1979. text ed. 12.95 (*0-13-210567-5*, Spectrum Bks) P-H.

Dictionary of Practical Materia Medica, 3 vols. 2585p. (C). 1980. text ed. 224.95 (*0-8464-1004-4*) Beekman Pubs.

Dictionary of Prehistoric Indian Artifacts of the American Southwest. Franklin Barnett. LC 73-82865. (Illus.). 148p. 1973. reprint ed. pap. 12.95 (*0-87358-120-2*) Northland AZ.

Dictionary of Prince Edward Island English. T. K. Pratt. 224p. (C). 1988. 30.00 (*0-8020-5781-0*) U of Toronto Pr.

Dictionary of Principal Medications: Dictionnaire des Medicaments Principaux. Lagier Lechat. 528p. 1982. 110.00 (*0-8288-1815-0*, M15386) Fr & Eur.

Dictionary of Printed Circuit Technology. G. Bohss. (ENG & GER.). 1986. 79.50 (*0-444-99555-2*) Elsevier.

Dictionary of Printing & Publishing. P. H. Collin. 1989. pap. text ed. 16.95 (*0-948549-09-2*, Pub. by Peter Collin UK) IBD Ltd.

Dictionary of Problem Words & Expressions. rev. ed. Harry Shaw. 320p. 1987. text ed. 18.95 (*0-07-056517-1*) McGraw.

Dictionary of Problem Words & Expressions. Harry Shaw. 1985. reprint ed. mass mkt. 5.99 (*0-671-54558-2*, WSP) PB.

Dictionary of Process Technology: English, German, French, & Russian. K. Hartman et al. 460p. 1990. 128.25 (*0-444-98888-2*) Elsevier.

Dictionary of Production Engineering: Electroerosive & Electrochemical Removal, Vol. 9. G. Pahlitzsch. 170p. (ENG, FRE & GER.). 1984. 75.00 (*0-8288-0606-3*, M 4000) Fr & Eur.

Dictionary of Professional Management: Fifty Thousand New Terms & Concepts Used in Private, Public & Third Sector Organizations. Systems Research Institute Staff. 1500p. (C). 1994. 59.95 (*0-912352-09-4*) Systems Res.

Dictionary of Project Management: Francais-Anglais. 2nd ed. Association Francaise des Ingenieurs Staff. 218p. (ENG & FRE.). 1992. pap. 95.00 (*0-7859-0974-5*, 2124843214) Fr & Eur.

Dictionary of Pronunciation. 4th ed. Samuel Noory. LC 81-66273. 512p. 1982. 19.95 (*0-8453-4722-5*, Cornwall Bks) Assoc Univ Prs.

Dictionary of Pronunciation of Artists' Names, with Their Schools & Dates for American Readers & Students. Gustave E. Kaltenbach. LC 88-64108. viii, 74p. 1989. reprint ed. 38.00 (*1-55888-804-7*) Omnigraphics Inc.

***Dictionary of Prophetic Traditions in Sahih Al-Bukharti Vol. 1.** M. Abul-Foutouh. 555p. 1993. 45.00 (*0-86685-609-9*) Intl Bk Ctr.

Dictionary of Proto-Circassian Roots. A. H. Kuipers. ii, 93p. 1975. pap. 22.00 (*0-685-53315-8*) Benjamins North Am.

Dictionary of Protopharmacology: Therapeutic Practices 1700-1850. J. Worth Estes. (Illus.). 220p. 1990. 39.95 (*0-88135-068-0*, Sci Hist) Watson Pub Intl.

Dictionary of Proverbs: And Their Origins. Linda Flavell & Roger Flavell. 272p. 1994. 24.95 (*1-85626-068-2*); text ed. 12.95 (*1-85626-141-7*) Trafalgar.

***Dictionary of Proverbs from Folk Literature.** Mounir Khayyal. 334p. (ARA.). Date not set. 25.00 (*0-86685-649-8*) Intl Bk Ctr.

An Asterisk (*) at the beginning of an entry indicates that the title is appearing in BIP for the first time.

An Asterisk (*) at the beginning of an entry indicates that the title is appearing in BIP for the first time.

1969

D

Dictionary of SDI. Harry Waldman. LC 87-12477. (Illus.). 192p. 1988. 40.00 (*0-8420-2281-3*); pap. 19.95 (*0-8420-2295-3*) Scholarly Res Inc.

Dictionary of Sea Painters. 3rd ed. E. H. Archibald. (Illus.). 576p. 1989. 89.50 (*1-85149-047-7*) Antique Collect.

Dictionary of Sea Terms. 3rd ed. A. Ansted. (Illus.). 360p. 1985. 35.00 (*0-85174-481-8*, Pub. by Brown Son & Ferguson UK) Sheridan.

Dictionary of Seashore Life. Cricket Harris. (Orig.). 1961. pap. 3.95 (*0-8200-0205-4*) Great Outdoors.

Dictionary of Sects, Heresies, Ecclesiastical Parties, & Schools of Religious Thought. Ed. by John H. Blunt. LC 89-29543. 647p. 1990. reprint ed. lib. bdg. 75.00 (*1-55888-903-5*) Omnigraphics Inc.

Dictionary of Seed Plants' Names: Latin - Chinese - English. Science Press Staff. 1036p. (CHI, ENG & LAT.). 1989. lib. bdg. 95.00 (*0-7859-3664-5*, 7030013905) Fr & Eur.

Dictionary of Seismic Prospecting: English-French - French-English. Chambre Syndical Du Petrole et Du Gaz Staff. lib. bdg. 195.00 (*0-8288-9088-9*, F1790) Fr & Eur.

Dictionary of Seismic Prospecting, English & French. Chambre Syndical Du Petrole et Du Gaz Staff. 328p. (ENG & FRE.). 1987. 175.00 (*0-8288-2289-1*, F1790) Fr & Eur.

Dictionary of Selected Synonyms in the Principal Indo-European Languages. Carl D. Buck. 416p. 1988. pap. text ed. 29.95 (*0-226-07937-6*) U Ch Pr.

Dictionary of Semiconductor Physics & Electronics: English German - German English. Werner Bindmann. LC 65-23853. 1965. 252.00 (*0-08-011592-6*, Pub. by Pergamon Repr UK) Franklin.

Dictionary of Sexual Language & Imagery in Shakespearean & Stuart Literature, 3 vols., Set. Gordon Williams. 1500p. (C). 1994. text ed. 599.00 (*0-685-74476-0*, Pub. by Athlone Pr UK) Humanities.

Dictionary of Sexual Slang: Words, Phrases, & Idioms from AC - DC to Zig-Zag. Alan Richter. LC 92-6316. 272p. 1993. text ed. 29.95 (*0-471-54057-9*) Wiley.

*Dictionary of Shakespeare's Sexual Pluns & Their Significance. Frankie Rubinstein. LC 95-5836. 1995. write for info. (*0-312-12677-8*) St Martin.

Dictionary of Shipbuilding, Shipping & Fisheries. V. Dipl-Ling & Erhard Bensch. 784p. 1980. vinyl bd. 150.00 (*0-686-30016-5*, Pub. by Collets UK) St Mut.

Dictionary of Shipping: International Trade Terms & Abbreviations. Alan E. Branch. 279p. 1982. 80.00 (*0-900886-70-6*, Pub. by Witherby & Co UK) St Mut.

Dictionary of Shipping: International Trade Terms & Abbreviations. Alan E. Branch. 587p. (C). 1986. pap. 145.00 (*0-948691-20-4*, Pub. by Witherby & Co UK) St Mut.

Dictionary of Shipping Terms. 591p. (ENG & JPN.). 1977. 175.00 (*0-8288-5378-9*, M9333) Fr & Eur.

Dictionary of Shipping Terms. Peter Brodie. 192p. (ENG & FRE.). 1989. pap. 50.00 (*1-85044-245-2*) Lloyds London Pr.

Dictionary of Shipping Terms. Peter Brodie. Tr. by John S. Vlassopulos. 174p. (ENG & GRE.). 1989. pap. 60.00 (*1-85044-173-1*) Lloyds London Pr.

Dictionary of Shipping Terms. 2nd ed. Peter Brodie. 1993. pap. 35.00 (*1-85044-069-7*) Lloyds London Pr.

Dictionary of Shipping Terms Italian-English. Peter Brodie & Enrico Vincenzini. 171p. (ENG & ITA.). 1988. pap. 50.00 (*1-85044-174-X*) Lloyds London Pr.

Dictionary of Shipping Terms Spanish-English. Peter Brodie & Marc Possemiers. 205p. (ENG & SPA.). 1988. pap. 50.00 (*1-85044-153-7*) Lloyds London Pr.

Dictionary of Signatures & Monograms of American Artists. Peter H. Falk. LC 88-92695. (Illus.). 556p. 1989. lib. bdg. 115.00 (*0-932087-04-3*) Sound View Pr.

Dictionary of Silviculture. S. S. Sagwal. 129p. 1992. 98.00 (*81-7089-162-0*, Pub. by Intl Bk Distr II) St Mut.

Dictionary of Similes. 2nd enl. rev. ed. Frank J. Wilstach. LC 89-63017. 578p. 1990. reprint ed. lib. bdg. 45.00 (*1-55888-847-0*) Omnigraphics Inc.

Dictionary of Slang & Unconventional English. Eric Partridge. 1980. 45.00 (*0-02-594970-5*) Macmillan.

Dictionary of Slang & Unconventional English. 8th ed. Eric Partridge. 1408p. 1985. text ed. 75.00 (*0-02-594980-2*) Macmillan.

Dictionary of Slavic Word Families. Louis J. Herman. LC 74-13341. (Illus.). 679p. reprint ed. pap. 180.00 (*0-317-10092-0*, 2012116) Bks Demand.

Dictionary of Soccer. rev. ed. Rick Braithwaite. LC 89-9796. (Illus.). 72p. 1989. pap. 5.95 (*0-940893-02-9*) Cool Change Pub.

Dictionary of Social Sciences: English-French-Arabic. Zaki Badawi. 1981. 30.00 (*0-86685-115-1*) Intl Bk Ctr.

Dictionary of Social Welfare. Noel Timms & Rita Timms. 228p. 1982. 25.00 (*0-7100-9084-6*, RKP) Routledge.

Dictionary of Social Work - Philippine Setting: Philippine Setting. Leonora Serafica-De Guzman. v, 100p. (Orig.). (C). 1988. pap. 9.75 (*971-10-0361-9*, Pub. by New Day Pub PH) Cellar.

Dictionary of Socialism. Angelo S. Rappoport. 1976. lib. bdg. 44.00 (*0-8490-1723-8*) Gordon Pr.

Dictionary of Sociology: Soziologisches Woerterbuch. 11th ed. Helmut Schoeck. 400p. (GER.). 1982. pap. 24.95 (*0-8288-2363-4*, M7622) Fr & Eur.

Dictionary of Sociology & Related Sciences. Henry P. Fairchild. LC 76-110377. 342p. 1970. reprint ed. text ed. 38.50 (*0-8371-4581-3*, FADS, Greenwood Pr) Greenwood.

Dictionary of Sodium, Fats, & Cholesterol. 2nd ed. Barbara Kraus. 384p. 1990. pap. 13.00 (*0-399-51572-0*, Perigree Bks) Berkley Pub.

Dictionary of Soil Science. 2nd enl. rev. ed. Jean Lozet & Clement Mathieu. 358p. (FRE.). (C). 1991. text ed. 95.00 (*90-5410-201-2*, Pub. by A A Balkema NE) Ashgate Pub Co.

Dictionary of Solar Energy: Diccionario de Energia Solar. Jose Aguilar Peris et al. 226p. (SPA.). 1982. pap. 39.95 (*0-8288-2294-8*, S21887) Fr & Eur.

Dictionary of Solid State Physics & Electronics Technology: English-German, German-English. W. Bindmann. (Technical Dictionary Ser.). 1973. 31.50 (*0-685-27547-7*) Adlers Foreign Bks.

Dictionary of South African English. Jean Branford & William Branford. 444p. 1992. 45.00 (*0-19-570595-5*) OUP.

Dictionary of South African English. 4th ed. Jean Bradford. 361p. (AFR & ENG.). 1991. 39.95 (*0-7859-4864-3*, M9418) Fr & Eur.

Dictionary of South Carolina Biography, Vol. 1. Ed. by Richard N. Cote & Patricia H. Williams. (Illus.). 404p. 1985. 30.00 (*0-89308-275-9*) Southern Hist Pr.

Dictionary of Space English. Adam Makkai. viii, 72p. (Orig.). 1973. pap. 10.00 (*0-933104-23-5*) Jupiter Pr.

Dictionary of Space Management: French-English-German-Spanish. H. J. Calsat et al. 703p. (ENG, FRE, GER & SPA.). 1993. 225.00 (*2-85319-245-8*) IBD Ltd.

*Dictionary of Space Management: French-English-German-Spanish. H. J. Calsat. 703p. (ENG, FRE, GER & SPA.). 1993. write for info. (*0-7859-8766-5*) Fr & Eur.

Dictionary of Space Technology. Mark Williamson. (Illus.). 416p. 1990. 50.00 (*0-85274-339-4*) IOP Pub.

Dictionary of Spanish Literature. Maxim Newmark. LC 72-141263. 314p. 1972. reprint ed. text ed. 35.00 (*0-8371-5859-1*, NESL, Greenwood Pr) Greenwood.

Dictionary of Spanish Place Names, Vol. V. Rene C. Du Gard. 210p. 1986. 39.00 (*0-939586-05-3*) Edns des Deux Mondes.

Dictionary of Spanish Place Names of the Northwest Coast of America: California, Vol. I. Rene Coulet du Gard. 190p. (ENG & SPA.). (C). 1982. 24.00 (*0-939586-01-0*) Edns des Deux Mondes.

Dictionary of Spanish Place Names of the Northwest Coast of America: Oregon, Washington State, British Columbia, Alaska, Vol. II. Rene Coulet du Gard. 190p. (ENG & SPA.). (C). 1983. 24.00 (*0-939586-02-9*) Edns des Deux Mondes.

Dictionary of Spanish Place Names, Vol. III: New Mexico. Rene Coulet du Gard. 380p. 1983. 39.00 (*0-939586-03-7*) Edns des Deux Mondes.

Dictionary of Spanish Place Names, Vol. IV: Texas, Arizona. 140p. 1983. 28.00 (*0-939586-04-5*) Edns des Deux Mondes.

Dictionary of Spatiologie: Terms & Definitions. 3rd ed. Consei International de la Langue Francaise Staff. 352p. (ENG, GER, RUS & SPA.). 1992. 150.00 (*0-7859-1010-7*, 2853192393) Fr & Eur.

Dictionary of Special Education & Rehabilitation. 3rd ed. Glenn A. Vergason. LC 89-84596. 207p. 1990. pap. text ed. 19.95 (*0-89108-212-5*) Love Pub Co.

Dictionary of Speech Therapy. David W. Morris. 200p. 1988. pap. 27.00 (*0-85066-444-6*) Singular Publishing.

Dictionary of Spice Technology. Commercial Press Staff. 172p. (CHI & ENG.). 1978. pap. 19.95 (*0-8288-5171-9*, M9568) Fr & Eur.

Dictionary of Spoken American English (Dictionnaire de l'Americain Parle) Adrienne. 735p. (ENG & FRE.). 1990. pap. 69.95 (*0-7859-4867-8*, M971) Fr & Eur.

Dictionary of Spoken German: Deutsches Bildwoerterbuch der Sprache Brockhaus. 8th ed. Brockhaus. 972p. (GER.). 1981. 59.95 (*0-8288-1971-8*, M9299) Fr & Eur.

Dictionary of Spoken Nepali: Nepali-English, English-Nepali, with Phrases & Grammar Reference Notes. Earl R. Mosburg. viii, 111p. (Orig.). (ENG & NEP.). 1991. pap. 14.95 (*0-9629545-2-7*) E R Mosburg.

Dictionary of Spoken Palestinian Arabic: Dictionnaire de l'Arabe Parle Palestinien. 2nd ed. Yoharan Elihai. 416p. (ARA & FRE.). 1984. pap. 59.95 (*0-8288-1589-5*, F29510) Fr & Eur.

Dictionary of Spoken Russian: Russian-English: English-Russian. U. S. War Department Staff. (ENG & RUS.). 1959. pap. 10.95 (*0-486-20496-0*) Dover.

Dictionary of Spoken Spanish: Spanish-English, English-Spanish. U. S. War Department Staff. (ENG & SPA.). pap. 7.95 (*0-486-20495-2*) Dover.

Dictionary of Spoken Spanish Words, Phrases, Sentences. U. S. Armed Forces Staff. LC 30-900. (ENG & SPA.). 1960. pap. 12.95 (*0-385-00976-3*) Doubleday.

Dictionary of Sport Science. E. Beyer. 770p. (ENG, FRE & GER.). 1987. spiral bd. 75.00 (*0-8288-7615-0*) Fr & Eur.

Dictionary of Sporting Artists. Mary A. Wingfield. 356p. 1992. 89.50 (*1-85149-140-6*) Antique Collect.

Dictionary of Sports Idioms. Robert S. Palmatier & Harold L. Ray. 228p. 1993. pap. 14.95 (*0-8442-9123-4*, Natl Textbk) NTC Pub Grp.

Dictionary of Sports Quotations. Comp. by Barry Liddle. 1987. 24.95 (*0-7102-0785-9*, RKP) Routledge.

Dictionary of Sri Aurobindo's Yoga. Sri Aurobindo. Ed. by M. P. Pandit. LC 92-74994. 320p. 1992. pap. 11.95 (*0-941524-74-4*) Lotus Light.

Dictionary of St. Lucian Creole, 2 pts. Ed. by Lawarence D. Carrington. LC 92-10018. (Trends in Linguistics, Documentation Ser.: Vol. 7). xi, 626p. (C). 1992. lib. bdg. 229.25 (*3-11-012625-7*) Mouton.

Dictionary of Standard Abbreviations of the French Language. J. C. Faudouas. 256p. 1990. pap. 32.50 (*2-85608-038-3*) IBD Ltd.

Dictionary of Standard C. Rex Jaeschke. LC 91-26931. 165p. (Orig.). 1991. pap. 12.00 (*1-878956-07-8*) CBM Bks.

Dictionary of Statistical, Scientific & Technical Terms. H. Sahai & J. Berrios. 143p. (ENG & SPA.). 1981. 35.00 (*0-8288-2352-9*, S 36265) Fr & Eur.

Dictionary of Statistical Terms. 5th ed. Ed. by F. H. Marriott. 1990. pap. text ed. 76.95 (*0-470-21349-3*) Halsted Pr.

Dictionary of Statistics. Banday & Shah. 342p. 1989. 80.00 (*81-7041-228-5*, Pub. by Scientific Pubs II) St Mut.

Dictionary of Statistics. Michael G. Mulhall. 1972. 300.00 (*0-8490-0046-7*) Gordon Pr.

Dictionary of Statistics. 2nd enl. rev. ed. M. Korolev. 623p. (C). 1989. 125.00 (*0-685-46845-3*, Pub. by Collets) St Mut.

Dictionary of Statistics & Methodology: A Non-Technical Guide for the Social Sciences. W. Paul Vogt. (Illus.). 256p. (C). 1993. text ed. 46.00 (*0-8039-5276-7*); pap. text ed. 21.95 (*0-8039-5277-5*) Sage.

Dictionary of Steam Generator Engineering. 2nd ed. A. Bachmair. 768p. (ENG, FRE, GER & SPA.). 1983. 115.00 (*0-8288-4023-7*, M9010) Fr & Eur.

Dictionary of Steam Generator Engineering in Four Languages. 2nd ed. 768p. (ENG, FRE, GER & SPA.). 1983. pap. 193.00 (*3-8027-2504-2*) IBD Ltd.

Dictionary of Steroids, 2 vols., Set. Ed. by D. N. Kirk et al. 1824p. 1991. 1,350.00 (*0-412-27060-9*, A5565) Chapman & Hall.

Dictionary of Stock Market Terms in Four Languages. B. L. Thole & Theodor Gilissen. (DUT, ENG, FRE & GER.). 22.50 (*0-87559-068-3*) Shalom.

Dictionary of Street Alcohol & Drug Terms. 4th ed. Peter Johnson et al. 200p. (Orig.). (C). 1993. pap. 27.95 (*0-941375-48-X*) Diane Pub.

Dictionary of Stress Marks for Radio & Television Employees. F. L. Agreenko & M. V. Zarva. 808p. (C). 1984. 75.00 (*0-317-92477-X*, Pub. by Collets UK) Pro-Am Music.

Dictionary of Structural Engineering. Cyril M. Harris. 1992. pap. 14.95 (*0-07-026893-2*) McGraw.

Dictionary of Stylistics. Katie Wales. (Studies in Language & Linguistics). (Orig.). (C). 1989. pap. text ed. 40.95 (*0-582-03139-7*, 79406) Longman.

Dictionary of Subjects & Symbols in Art. rev. ed. James A. Hall. LC 74-6578. (Icon Editions Ser.). (Illus.). 1979. pap. 15.00 (*0-06-430100-1*, IN-100, Icon Edns) HarpC.

*Dictionary of Substances & Their Effects Vol. 5: I to M. Mervyn Richardson. 1000p. 1994. 325.00 (*0-85186-371-X*, R6371) CRC Pr.

Dictionary of Superstitions. Ed. by Iona Opie & Moira Tatem. 510p. 1989. 39.95 (*0-19-211597-9*) OUP.

Dictionary of Superstitions. Ed. by Iona Opie & Moira Tatem. 512p. 1992. pap. 14.95 (*0-19-282916-5*) OUP.

Dictionary of Surface Active Agents, Cosmetics & Toiletries. G. Carriere. 198p. 1978. 79.50 (*0-444-99809-8*) Elsevier.

Dictionary of Surface Active Agents, Cosmetics & Toiletries. G. Carriere. 198p. (DUT, ENG, FRE, GER, ITA, POL & SPA.). 1978. 175.00 (*0-8288-9220-2*, M15544) Fr & Eur.

Dictionary of Surface Water Hydrology. M. F. Roche. 288p. (ENG, FRE, GER & SPA.). 1986. pap. 65.00 (*2-225-80739-6*, Masson) IBD Ltd.

Dictionary of Surfactants. K. Siekamnn. 160p. (ENG & GER.). 1987. pap. 95.00 (*0-8288-7991-5*) Fr & Eur.

Dictionary of Surnames. Patrick Hanks & Flavia Hodges. (Illus.). 880p. 1989. 85.00 (*0-19-211592-8*) OUP.

Dictionary of Symbolism: Cultural Icons & the Meanings Behind Them. Hans Biedermann. Tr. by James Hulbert. (Illus.). 592p. 1992. lib. bdg. 45.00 (*0-8160-2593-2*) Facts on File.

Dictionary of Symbolism: Cultural Icons & the Meanings Behind Them. Han Biedermann. Tr. by James Hulbert. LC 93-30616. (Illus.). 480p. 1994. reprint ed. pap. 19.95 (*0-452-01118-3*, Mer) NAL-Dutton.

Dictionary of Symbols. Ed. by Alain Cheerbrant. Tr. by John Buchanan-Brown. (Illus.). 1216p. 1994. 39.95 (*0-631-19265-4*) Blackwell Pubs.

Dictionary of Symbols. Tom Chetwynd. 1994. pap. 11.00 (*1-85538-296-2*, Pub. by Aquarian Pr UK) Thorsons SF.

Dictionary of Symbols. Juan-Eduardo C. Cirlot. Tr. by J. Sage. 476p. 1983. pap. write for info. (*0-415-03649-6*, A2298:XUSA) Routledge.

Dictionary of Symbols. Carl G. Liungman. 608p. 1995. pap. 18.00 (*0-393-31236-4*) Norton.

Dictionary of Symbols: Dictionnaire des Symboles. 2nd ed. J. Chevalier & A. Gheerbrant. 1060p. 1982. pap. 45.00 (*0-8288-0751-5*, M6068) Fr & Eur.

Dictionary of Symbols: Western Ideograms. Carl G. Liungman. 596p. 1991. lib. bdg. 65.00 (*0-87436-610-0*) ABC-CLIO.

*Dictionary of Symbols & Imagery. 1985. 126.50 (*0-7204-8021-3*) Elsevier.

Dictionary of Symbols & Imagery. 2nd rev. ed. A. De Vries. 516p. 1976. 89.50 (*0-444-10607-3*, North Holland) Elsevier.

Dictionary of Symbols & Myths: Diccionario de Simbolos y Mitos. 3rd ed. Jose A. Rioja. 436p. (SPA.). 1988. pap. 29.95 (*0-7859-4965-8*) Fr & Eur.

Dictionary of Symptoms. rev. ed. Joan Gomez. LC 82-42525. (Illus.). 383p. 1983. pap. 8.95 (*0-8128-6230-9*, Scrbrough Hse) Madison Bks UPA.

Dictionary of Synonyms: Dictionnaire des Synonymes. H. B. Du Chazaud. 520p. (FRE.). 1983. 69.95 (*0-8288-1933-5*, M5227) Fr & Eur.

Dictionary of Synonyms: Synonymordboken. A. Stromberg. 534p. (SWE.). 1986. 125.00 (*0-8288-2074-0*, F64174) Fr & Eur.

Dictionary of Synonyms: Synonyymisanasto. 10th ed. Y. Kivimies. 180p. (FIN.). 1986. 59.95 (*0-8288-2075-9*, M1697) Fr & Eur.

Dictionary of Synonyms, Analogies & Antonyms: Dictionnaire des Synonymes, Analogies et Antonymes. R. Boussinot. 1031p. (FRE.). 1981. 59.95 (*0-8288-1930-0*, M4559) Fr & Eur.

Dictionary of Synonyms & Antonyms. Joseph Devlin. 384p. 1984. mass mkt. 4.99 (*0-446-31310-6*) Warner Bks.

Dictionary of Synonyms & Antonyms. V. J. Smith. 42.50 (*0-87559-045-4*); 47.50 (*0-87559-046-2*) Shalom.

Dictionary of Synonyms & Antonyms: Diccionario de Sinonimos y Antonimos. 3rd ed. Mariano O. Manzano. 368p. (SPA.). 1990. write for info. (*0-7859-4956-9*) Fr & Eur.

Dictionary of Synonyms & Antonyms: Dizionario dei Sinonimi e dei Contrari. D. Cinti. 587p. (ITA.). 1983. 49.95 (*0-8288-1987-4*, M14419) Fr & Eur.

Dictionary of Synonyms & Antonyms: Woerterbuch der Synonyme und Antonyme. E. Bulitta & H. Bulitta. 795p. (GER.). 1983. 85.00 (*0-8288-1972-6*, F50310) Fr & Eur.

Dictionary of Synonyms & Antonyms see Reference Collection Boxed Set

Dictionary of Synonyms of the Russian Language. 5th ed. Z. E. Aleksandrova. 400p. (RUS.). 1986. 49.95 (*0-8288-2001-5*, M1973) Fr & Eur.

Dictionary of Synonyms, Related & Contrary Ideas: Diccionario de Sinonimos, Ideas Afines y Contrarios. 14th ed. Santiago P. Estrany & J. Ruiz Calonja. 528p. (SPA.). 1991. pap. write for info. (*0-7859-4957-7*) Fr & Eur.

Dictionary of Syrian Arabic: English-Arabic. Ed. by Karl Stowasser & Moukhtar Ani. (Richard Slade Harrell Arabic Ser.). 202p. (ARA & ENG.). 1964. pap. 14.95 (*0-87840-010-9*) Georgetown U Pr.

Dictionary of Syrian Arabic: English-Arabic. Karl Stowasser & Moukhtar Ani. (Georgetown University, Washington, D.C., Institute of Languages & Linguistics. Richard Slade Harrell-Arabic Ser.: No. 5). 287p. reprint ed. pap. 81.80 (*0-685-15251-0*, 2056163) Bks Demand.

Dictionary of Systems Analysis & Operation Research. G. Szepesi. 154p. (ENG, FRE, GER, HUN & RUS.). 1980. 24.95 (*0-8288-0908-9*, M 15553) Fr & Eur.

Dictionary of Tamil Proverbs. H. Jensen. (C). 1988. 76.00 (*0-8364-2345-3*) S Asia.

Dictionary of Tax Terms. D. Larry Crumbley et al. LC 93-23218. 1994. pap. 9.95 (*0-8120-1780-3*) Barron.

*Dictionary of Technical Abbreviations: English - Arabic. Said Salah. 220p. 1993. 12.00 (*1-887584-05-6*) Intl Prom Art.

Dictionary of Technical Acoustics. L. Reichardt. (FRE, GER, HUN, POL, RUS, SLO & SPA.). 1978. 20.50 (*0-685-92166-2*) Adlers Foreign Bks.

Dictionary of Technical Information. 144p. (ENG, GER, HUN & RUS.). 1980. 25.00 (*0-8288-1331-0*, M15041) Fr & Eur.

Dictionary of Technical Information. 182p. 1980. 40.00 (*0-569-08388-5*, Pub. by Collets) St Mut.

Dictionary of Technical Information. S. Kaliszky. 143p. (ENG, GER, HUN & RUS.). 1980. 49.95 (*0-8288-1334-5*, M8652) Fr & Eur.

Dictionary of Technical Information: Agriculture & Feeding, 2 vols. V. Beck. 891p. (C). 1980. 250.00 (*0-569-08636-1*, Pub. by Collets) St Mut.

Dictionary of Technical Information: Agriculture & Feeding, 2 vols., Set. V. Beck. 891p. (C). 1980. 150.00 (*0-89771-914-X*, Pub. by Collets) St Mut.

Dictionary of Technical Information: Construction Mechanics. Z. Viktor & S. Gyula. 456p. (C). 1986. 120.00 (*0-89771-915-8*, Pub. by Collets) St Mut.

Dictionary of Technical Information: Construction Mechanics. Ed. by Z. Viktor & S. Gyula. 456p. (C). 1986. 110.00 (*0-685-58758-4*, Pub. by Collets) St Mut.

Dictionary of Technical Information: Meteorology. C. Rudolf & S. Dezsone. 596p. (C). 1986. 100.00 (*0-685-58757-6*, Pub. by Collets); 120.00 (*0-89771-916-6*, Pub. by Collets) St Mut.

Dictionary of Technical Information: Power Electronics. G. Laszlo. 584p. (C). 1985. 125.00 (*0-685-60802-6*, Pub. by Collets) St Mut.

Dictionary of Technical Information: Power Electronics. Ed. by G. Laszlo. 584p. (C). 1985. 125.00 (*0-685-49865-4*, Pub. by Collets) St Mut.

Dictionary of Technical Information: Power Electronics, Vols. 54-55. Ed. by Collet's Holdings Staff. 584p. 1985. 110.00 (*0-317-42861-6*, Pub. by Collets UK) St Mut.

Dictionary of Technical Information Building & Construction. Gyula Sebestyen. 286p. (ENG, FRE, GER, HUN & RUS.). 1983. 50.00 (*0-317-59484-2*, Pub. by Collets UK) Pro-Am Music.

Dictionary of Technical Medical Terms: Diccionario de los Terminos Tecnicos de Medicina. 20th ed. M. Garnier & Valery Delamare. 1114p. (SPA.). 1981. 39.95 (*0-8288-1866-5*, S60551) Fr & Eur.

Dictionary of Technical Medical Terms: Dictionnaire des Termes Techniques de Medecine. 21th ed. Valery Delamare & M. Garnier. 880p. 1984. 95.00 (*0-8288-1806-1*) Fr & Eur.

Dictionary of Technical Terms. Henry G. Greeman. 703p. (ENG & GER.). 1983. 175.00 (*0-8288-0627-6*, M14483) Fr & Eur.

Dictionary of Technical Terms, 2 vols., Set. Julius O. Kettridge. (ENG & FRE.). 1980. 150.00 (*0-685-11207-1*) Fr & Eur.

Dictionary of Technical Terms & Phrases, Vol. 2. Julius O. Kettrdige. 667p. (ENG & FRE.). 1980. 150.00 (*0-8288-0617-9*, F137172) Fr & Eur.

Dictionary of Technology: English-German. Ed. by R. Walther. 1200p. 1985. 187.25 (*0-444-99591-9*) Elsevier.

Dictionary of Telecommunication: German-English-French. 397p. (ENG, FRE & GER.). 1992. 190.00 (*3-7785-2080-6*) IBD Ltd.

An Asterisk (*) at the beginning of an entry indicates that the title is appearing in BIP for the first time.

Dictionary of Telecommunications. John Graham. LC 82-15675. 199p. reprint ed. pap. 56.80 (*0-8357-8775-3*, 2031558) Bks Demand.

Dictionary of Telecommunications: Dicionario de Telecommunicacoes. J. V. Neto. 689p. (ENG & POR.). 1981. 75.00 (*0-8288-0184-3*, F45000) Fr & Eur.

Dictionary of Telecommunications: Dictionnaire des Telecommunications: Anglais-Francais. Johanne De Luca. 408p. (ENG & FRE.). 1988. pap. 125.00 (*0-8288-0180-0*, M972) Fr & Eur.

Dictionary of Telecommunications: English-Chinese. Commercial Press Staff. 721p. (CHI & ENG.). 1961. pap. 29.95 (*0-8288-6819-0*, M-9589) Fr & Eur.

Dictionary of Teleliteracy: A Personal Guide to Television from 1948 to the Present. David Bianculli. (Illus.). 288p. 1995. 22.95 (*0-8264-0577-0*) Continuum.

Dictionary of Telugu & English: Explaining English Idioms & Phrases in Telugu, 2 vols. Charles P. Brown. (ENG & TEL.). 1977. reprint ed. 214.95 (*0-518-19008-0*) Ayer.

Dictionary of Ten Forty Deductions. Bender's Editorial Staff. 1980. Annual. write for info. (*0-8205-1306-7*) Bender.

Dictionary of Terms. Ed. by Jac L. Williams. 544p. 1991. reprint ed. pap. 15.00 (*0-7083-0977-1*, Pub. by U of Wales UK) Bks Intl VA.

Dictionary of Terms & Techniques in Archaeology. Sara Champion. LC 80-66774. 144p. reprint ed. pap. 41.10 (*0-317-20683-4*, 2025147) Bks Demand.

Dictionary of Terms in Art. Frederick W. Fairholt. 1972. 59.95 (*0-8490-0047-5*) Gordon Pr.

Dictionary of Terms in Federal Acquisition Regulation (FAR) W. Noel Keyes. 174p. 1985. pap. 45.00 (*0-379-20786-9*) Oceana.

Dictionary of Terms in Music. 4th ed. Ed. by Horst Leuchtmann. 411p. (ENG & GER.). 1992. pap. 55.00 (*3-598-10913-X*) K G Saur.

Dictionary of Terms of Declension & Structure in Universal Arabic Grammar: English - Arabic & Arabic - English. Antoine El-Dahdah. 1988. 30.00 (*0-86685-435-5*) Intl Bk Ctr.

Dictionary of Terms Used in the Safety Profession. 3rd ed. Contrib by Stanley A. Abercrombie. 72p. 1988. pap. 25.00 (*0-939874-79-2*) ASSE.

Dictionary of Terpenoids. Ed. by J. D. Connolly & R. A. Hill. 1800p. (C). 1992. text ed. 1,595.00 (*0-412-25770-X*, A6858) Chapman & Hall.

Dictionary of the African Left: Parties, Movements & Groups. 2nd ed. Donald I. Ray. 290p. 1989. text ed. 59.95 (*1-85521-014-2*, Pub. by Dartmth Pub UK) Ashgate Pub Co.

Dictionary of the Alabama Language. Cora Sylestine et al. LC 92-30925. 765p. (C). 1993. text ed. 35.00 (*0-292-73077-2*) U of Tex Pr.

Dictionary of the American Indian. John Stoutenburgh, Jr. 1990. 9.99 (*0-517-69416-6*) Random Hse Value.

Dictionary of the American West. Win Blevins. (Illus.). 304p. 1992. lib. bdg. 35.00 (*0-8160-2031-0*) Facts on File.

Dictionary of the American West. Winfred Blevins. 1993. pap. 17.95 (*0-8160-2858-3*) Facts on File.

Dictionary of the Arts. LC 94-16276. 1994. 29.95 (*0-8160-3205-X*) Facts on File.

***Dictionary of the Atakapa Language Accompanied by Text Material.** Ed. by Albert Gatschet & John Swanton. (Bureau of American Ethnology Bulletins Ser.). 181p. 1995. lib. bdg. 79.00 (*0-7812-4108-1*) Rprt Serv.

Dictionary of the Automobile Industry, English & German. Hans Schnellman. 120p. (ENG & GER.). 1987. 95.00 (*0-8288-0045-6*, F132160) Fr & Eur.

Dictionary of the Avant-Gardes. Richard Kostelanetz. LC 93-17793. (Illus.). 400p. 1993. pap. 20.00 (*1-55652-202-9*) A cappella Bks.

Dictionary of the Bach Flower Remedies. 18th ed. T. W. Jones. 48p. pap. 5.95 (*0-8464-4192-6*) Beekman Pubs.

Dictionary of the Bengali Language, 2 Vols. W. Carey. 2160p. (BEN & ENG.). 1981. 195.00 (*0-8288-1120-2*, M14468) Fr & Eur.

Dictionary of the Bengali Language, 2 Vols. William Carey. 2160p. 1986. reprint ed. 140.00 (*0-685-14467-4*, Pub. by Manohar II) S Asia.

Dictionary of the Bible. (J). (gr. 2 up). 1994. pap. 5.95 (*0-685-74709-3*) Running Pr.

Dictionary of the Bible. Ed. by James Hastings. 1088p. 1978. text ed. 75.00 (*0-684-15556-7*, Scribners) S&S Trade.

Dictionary of the Bible. James Hastings. 1008p. 1989. 24.95 (*0-943575-22-2*) Hendrickson MA.

Dictionary of the Bible, 5 vols., Set. James Hastings. (Illus.). 4656p. 1988. reprint ed. 149.50 (*0-943575-07-9*) Hendrickson MA.

Dictionary of the Bible & Its Religions: Judaism, Christianity & Islam: Dictionnaire de la Bible & des Religions du Livre: Judaisme, Christianisme, Islam. BREPOLS Staff. 456p. (FRE.). 1985. 175.00 (*0-8288-1202-0*, M7938) Fr & Eur.

***Dictionary of the Biloxi & Ofo Languages.** Dorsey & Swanton. (Bureau of American Ethnology Bulletins Ser.). 340p. 1995. lib. bdg. 99.00 (*0-7812-4047-6*) Rprt Serv.

Dictionary of the Biochemistry of Food & Nutrition: Dictionnaire de Biochimie Alimentaire et de Nutruition. Jean Adrian et al. 320p. (FRE.). 1981. 125.00 (*0-8288-4440-2*, M9626) Fr & Eur.

Dictionary of the Black Theatre: Broadway, Off-Broadway, & Selected Harlem Theatre. Allen Woll. LC 82-21090. (Illus.). xvi, 359p. 1983. text ed. 49.95 (*0-313-22561-3*, WDB/, Greenwood Pr) Greenwood.

***Dictionary of the Body.** Dorling Kindersley Staff. (J). (gr. 4-7). 1995. 19.95 (*0-7894-0011-1*) Dorling Kindersley.

Dictionary of the Catalan Language: Diccionari Manual de la Llengua Catalana. 9th ed. Pompeu F. Poch. 1360p. (CAT.). 1991. 49.95 (*0-7859-4960-7*) Fr & Eur.

Dictionary of the Characters & Proper Names in the Works of Shakespeare. Francis G. Stokes. 1988. reprint ed. lib. bdg. 69.00 (*0-7812-0001-6*) Rprt Serv.

Dictionary of the Characters & Proper Names in the Works of Shakespeare. Francis G. Stokes. reprint ed. 49.00 (*0-403-04029-9*) Somerset Pub.

Dictionary of the Characters & Scenes in the Novels, Romances & Short Stories of H. G. Wells. G. Connes. LC 73-174698. (Reference Ser.: No. 44). 1971. reprint ed. lib. bdg. 63.95 (*0-8383-1353-1*) M S G Haskell Hse.

Dictionary of the Characters & Scenes in the Stories & Poems of Rudyard Kipling, 1886-1911. W. Arthur Young. (BCL1-PR English Literature Ser.). 231p. 1992. reprint ed. lib. bdg. 79.00 (*0-7812-7583-0*) Rprt Serv.

Dictionary of the Characters in the Waverly Novels of Sir Walter Scott. M. F. Husband. 1977. lib. bdg. 59.95 (*0-8490-1724-6*) Gordon Pr.

Dictionary of the Chinese Particles: With a Prolegomenon in Which the Problems of the Particles Are Considered & They Are Classified by Their Grammatical Functions. W. A. Dobson. LC 73-91242. 917p. reprint ed. pap. 180.00 (*0-317-55678-9*, 2029329) Bks Demand.

Dictionary of the Chinook Jargon, or Trade Languages of Oregon. George Gibbs. LC 76-168142. (Library of American Linguistics: No. 12). (CHN.). reprint ed. 42.75 (*0-404-50992-4*) AMS Pr.

***Dictionary of the Choctaw Language.** Cyrus Byington. (Bureau of American Ethnology Bulletins Ser.). 611p. 1995. lib. bdg. 149.00 (*0-7812-4046-8*) Rprt Serv.

Dictionary of the Choctaw Language. Cyrus Byington. Ed. by Henry S. Halbert. xii, 611p. 1990. reprint ed. lib. bdg. 59.00 (*1-878592-07-6*); reprint ed. pap. 39.00 (*1-878592-06-8*) Native Amer Bk Pubs.

Dictionary of the Cinema: Dictionnaire du Cinema, 2 vols., Set. Jean Tulard. (FRE.). 1984. 65.00 (*0-8288-2093-7*, F15225) Fr & Eur.

Dictionary of the Difficulties of the Russian Language. 3rd ed. D. E. Rozental. 704p. (RUS.). 1984. 35.00 (*0-8288-2006-6*, M15156) Fr & Eur.

***Dictionary of the Earth.** John Farndon & Neil Ardley. LC 94-35497. (Illus.). 192p. (J). (gr. 4-7). 1995. 19.95 (*0-7894-0049-9*) Dorling Kindersley.

Dictionary of the Ecumenical Movement. Ed. by Geoffrey Wainwright et al. (Illus.). 1104p. 1991. 59.99 (*0-8028-2428-5*) Eerdmans.

Dictionary of the English Language, 2 vols. Samuel Johnson. 2328p. 1990. boxed 350.00 (*0-582-07380-4*, 78935) Longman.

Dictionary of the English Language, 2 Vols. Samuel Johnson. LC 74-181906. reprint ed. write for info. (*0-404-09840-1*) AMS Pr.

Dictionary of the English Language. Samuel Johnson. LC 79-14941. (Illus.). 2320p. 1980. reprint ed. 150.00 (*0-405-12414-7*) Ayer.

Dictionary of the English Language, 2 vols., Set. Samuel Johnson. 1978. 240.00 (*0-86685-125-9*) Intl Bk Ctr.

Dictionary of the English Language: In Which the Words Are Deduced from Their Originals & Illustrated in Their Different Significations by Examples from the Best Writers, 2 vols., Set. Samuel Johnson. 1968. reprint ed. 617.75 (*3-487-01935-3*) Adlers Foreign Bks.

Dictionary of the Environment. 2nd ed. Michael Allaby. 608p. 1984. 85.00 (*0-8288-1399-X*, M8686) Fr & Eur.

Dictionary of the Environment. 3rd ed. Michael Allaby. 304p. 1991. pap. 20.00 (*0-8147-0597-9*) NYU Pr.

Dictionary of the Environment. 3rd ed. Michael Allaby. 304p. 1989. 80.00 (*0-8147-0591-X*) NYU Pr.

Dictionary of the Environment: Diccionario del Medio Ambiente. Michael Allaby. 421p. (SPA.). 1984. pap. 35.50 (*0-8288-1403-1*, S40721) Fr & Eur.

Dictionary of the French & English Tongues. Randle Cotgrave. (Anglistica & Americana Ser.: No. 77). 1970. reprint ed. 167.70 (*0-685-66455-4*, 05103206, Pub. by Georg Olms GW) Lubrecht & Cramer.

Dictionary of the French & English Tongues. Randle Cotgrave. No. 77. 10p. 1970. reprint ed. write for info. (*0-318-71449-3*, Pub. by Georg Olms GW) Lubrecht & Cramer.

Dictionary of the French Chanson(song) Dictionnaire de la Chanson Francaise. Sevran Pascal. 384p. (FRE.). 1986. 32.50 (*0-8288-2173-9*, M2355) Fr & Eur.

Dictionary of the French Cinema: Dictionnaire du Cinema Francais. Jean-Loup Passek. 867p. 1987. 28.95 (*0-8288-2602-1*, F11830) Fr & Eur.

Dictionary of the Fungi. 7th ed. Ainsworth & Bisby. 445p. 1983. 125.00 (*0-8288-5172-7*, M9711) Fr & Eur.

Dictionary of the Gas Industry. 2nd ed. International Gas Union Staff. 794p. (ENG, FRE, GER & RUS.). 1982. 195.00 (*0-8288-0713-2*, M 15522) Fr & Eur.

Dictionary of the Gas Industry. 2nd ed. International Gas Union Staff. 800p. (ARA, ENG, ITA, POR & SPA.). 1985. 350.00 (*0-8288-0712-4*, M 15564) Fr & Eur.

Dictionary of the Gathic Language of the Zend Avesta. Lawrence H. Mills. LC 74-21253. (GAE.). reprint ed. 72.50 (*0-404-12804-1*) AMS Pr.

Dictionary of the Graphic Arts Industry. Ed. by W. Muller. 1020p. (ENG, FRE, GER, HUN, POL, RUS, SLO & SPA.). 1981. 156.50 (*0-444-99745-8*) Elsevier.

Dictionary of the Graphic Arts Industry. W. Muller. 1020p. (ENG, FRE, GER, HUN, POL, RUS, SLO & SPA.). 1981. 295.00 (*0-8288-9284-9*) Fr & Eur.

***Dictionary of the High Court Rules.** C. A. McVeigh. 216p. 1989. pap. 63.00 (*0-409-78793-0*, NZ) Butterworth Legal Pubs.

Dictionary of the History of France. V. Pierre-Michel. 464p. (FRE.). 1991. 49.95 (*0-8288-6924-3*, 2203156031) Fr & Eur.

Dictionary of the History of Science. Ed. by William F. Bynum et al. LC 81-47116. 528p. 1985. 75.00 (*0-691-08287-1*); pap. 19.95x (*0-691-02384-0*) Princeton U Pr.

Dictionary of the History of the American Brewing & Distilling Industries. William L. Downard. LC 79-6826. (Illus.). xxv, 268p. 1980. text ed. 69.50 (*0-313-21330-5*, DOD/, Greenwood Pr) Greenwood.

Dictionary of the Huazalinguillo Dialect of Nahuatl with Grammatical Sketch & Readings. Geoffrey Kimball. 131p. 1980. pap. 3.00 (*0-317-43425-X*) Tulane Lat Am Lib.

Dictionary of the Information Age. Lewis B. Sckolnick. (Illus.). 300p. (Orig.). (C). 1994. pap. 175.00 (*1-57205-230-9*) Rector Pr.

Dictionary of the Italian & Croatian Languages: Dizionario della Lingua Italiana e Croata, Vol. 1. G. Androvic. (CRO & ITA.). 1980. 24.95 (*0-8288-1055-9*, F42510) Fr & Eur.

Dictionary of the Italian & Croatian Languages: Dizionario della Lingue Italiana e Croata, Vol. 2. G. Androvic. (CRO & ITA.). 1980. 27.95 (*0-8288-1638-7*, F42710) Fr & Eur.

***Dictionary of the Jewish-Christian Dialogue.** rev. ed. Ed. by Leon Klinicki & Geoffrey Wigoder. LC 95-15509. 1995. write for info. (*0-8091-3582-5*) Paulist Pr.

Dictionary of the Jewish-Christian Dialogue. Ed. by Leon Klenicki & Geoffrey Wigoder. LC 83-62021. (Studies in Judaism & Christianity). 222p. (Orig.). reprint ed. pap. 63.30 (*0-8357-2702-5*, 2039814) Bks Demand.

Dictionary of the Kanuri Language. N. Cytter & J. Hutchison. (PALL Ser.: No. 13). 200p. 1990. pap. 75.40 (*90-6765-412-4*) Mouton.

***Dictionary of the Kashmiri Language.** George A. Grierson. (C). 1993. 48.00x (*81-85557-87-X*, Pub. by Low Price II) S Asia.

Dictionary of the Kentish Dialect & Provicialisms in Use in the County of Kent. W. D. Parish & W. F. Shaw. (English Dialect Society Publications Ser.: No. 54). 1972. reprint ed. pap. 20.00 (*0-8115-0476-X*) Periodicals Srv.

Dictionary of the Khazars: Female Edition. Milorad Pavic. Tr. by Christina Pribicevic-Zoric. 1989. pap. 13.00 (*0-679-72754-X*, Vin) Random.

Dictionary of the Khazars: Male Edition. Milorad Pavic. Tr. by Christina Pribicevic-Zoric. 1989. pap. 13.00 (*0-679-72461-3*, Vin) Random.

Dictionary of the Language of Bugotu, Santa Isabel Island, Solomon Islands. Walter G. Ivens. LC 75-35125. reprint ed. 32.50 (*0-404-14141-2*) AMS Pr.

Dictionary of the Language of Rennell & Bellona: Part One: Rennellese & Bellonese to English. Samuel H. Elbert. 364p. 1975. 35.00 (*0-8248-0490-2*) UH Pr.

Dictionary of the Languages of Spain: Diccionario de las Lenguas de Espana. Enrique Fontanillo Merino. (SPA.). 1985. 59.95 (*0-8288-2045-7*, F90180) Fr & Eur.

Dictionary of the Latvian Language A-Z. R. Balina et al. 883p. (C). 1987. 150.00 (*0-685-37165-4*, Pub. by Collets) St Mut.

Dictionary of the Lepcha Language. G. B. Mainwaring & A. Grunwedel. (C). 1979. 130.00 (*0-89771-111-4*, Pub. by Ratna Pustak Bhandar) St Mut.

Dictionary of the Lepcha Language. C. B. Mainwarsng & A. Grunwedel. 1979. 80.00 (*0-7855-0267-X*, Pub. by Ratna Pustak Bhandar) St Mut.

Dictionary of the Lepcha Language. M. Mainwarsng & G. Grunwedel. 1979. 80.00 (*0-7855-0310-2*, Pub. by Ratna Pustak Bhandar) St Mut.

Dictionary of the Literature of the Iberian Peninsula, 2 vols., Set. Ed. by German Bleiberg et al. LC 90-2755. 1840p. 1993. text ed. 195.00 (*0-313-21302-X*, BLD/, Greenwood Pr) Greenwood.

Dictionary of the Literature of the Iberian Peninsula, Vol. 1, A-L. Ed. by German Bleiberg et al. LC 90-2755. 1840p. 1993. text ed. 195.00 (*0-313-28731-7*, Greenwood Pr) Greenwood.

Dictionary of the Literature of the Iberian Peninsula, Vol. 2. Ed. by German Bleiberg et al. LC 90-2755. 1840p. 1993. text ed. 195.00 (*0-313-28732-5*, Greenwood Pr) Greenwood.

Dictionary of the Liturgy. Jovian Lang. 1989. 9.95 (*0-89942-273-X*) Catholic Bk Pub.

Dictionary of the Machine & Auto Industry, English & German. exp. ed. Hans Schnellman. 312p. (ENG & GER.). 1987. 135.00 (*0-8288-0046-4*, M1206) Fr & Eur.

Dictionary of the Martial Arts. Louis Frederic. Ed. & Tr. by Paul Crompton. LC 91-61445. (Illus.). 304p. (Orig.). 1991. 29.95 (*0-8048-1753-7*); pap. 19.95 (*0-8048-1750-2*) C E Tuttle.

Dictionary of the Middle Ages, 13 vols., Set. Ed. by Joseph R. Strayer. 1989. text ed. 990.00 (*0-684-19073-7*, Scribners) S&S Trade.

Dictionary of the Middle Ages, Vol. 1. Ed. by Joseph R. Strayer. LC 82-5904. 1982. text ed. 89.00 (*0-684-16760-3*, Scribners) S&S Trade.

Dictionary of the Middle Ages, Vol. 2. Ed. by Joseph R. Strayer. LC 82-5904. 1983. text ed. 89.00 (*0-684-17022-1*, Scribners) S&S Trade.

Dictionary of the Middle Ages, Vol. 3. Ed. by Joseph R. Strayer. LC 82-5904. 1984. text ed. 89.00 (*0-684-17023-X*, Scribners) S&S Trade.

Dictionary of the Middle Ages, Vol. 4. Ed. by Joseph R. Strayer. LC 82-5904. 1984. text ed. 89.00 (*0-684-17024-8*, Scribners) S&S Trade.

Dictionary of the Middle Ages, Vol. 5. Ed. by Joseph R. Strayer. LC 82-5904. 1985. text ed. 89.00 (*0-684-18161-4*, Scribners) S&S Trade.

Dictionary of the Middle Ages, Vol. 6. Joseph R. Strayer. LC 82-5904. 1985. text ed. 89.00 (*0-684-18168-1*, Scribners) S&S Trade.

Dictionary of the Middle Ages, Vol. 7. Ed. by Joseph R. Strayer. LC 82-5904. 1986. text ed. 89.00 (*0-684-18169-X*, Scribners) S&S Trade.

Dictionary of the Middle Ages, Vol. 8. Ed. by Joseph R. Strayer. LC 82-5904. 1987. text ed. 89.00 (*0-684-18274-2*, Scribners) S&S Trade.

Dictionary of the Middle Ages, Vol. 9. Ed. by Collet's Holdings, Ltd. Staff. LC 82-5904. 1987. text ed. 89.00 (*0-684-18275-0*, Scribners) S&S Trade.

Dictionary of the Military. Beijing Military Science Staff. 1030p. (ARA, CHI, ENG, FRE, GER, RUS & SPA.). 1989. 75.00 (*0-8288-9445-0*) Fr & Eur.

Dictionary of the Modern Politics of South-East Asia. Ed. by Michael Leifer. (Dictionaries of Contemporary Politics Ser.). (Illus.). 384p. 1995. 75.00 (*0-415-04219-4*, A9989) Routledge.

***Dictionary of the Modern United States Military: Over 15,000 Weapons, Agencies, Acronyms, Slang, Installations, Medical Terms & Other Lexical Units of Warfare.** S. F. Tomajczyk. 816p. 1995. lib. bdg. 125.00 (*0-7864-0127-3*) McFarland & Co.

Dictionary of the Names of Animals: Amphibians & Reptiles. V. Sokolov. 556p. (C). 1988. 125.00 (*0-89771-917-4*, Pub. by Collets) St Mut.

Dictionary of the Names of Animals: Amphibians & Reptiles. Ed. by V. Sokolov. 556p. (C). 1988. 90.00 (*0-685-46869-0*, Pub. by Collets) St Mut.

Dictionary of the Names of Animals: Fishes. V. Sokolov. 734p. (C). 1989. 135.00 (*0-89771-918-2*, Pub. by Collets) St Mut.

Dictionary of the Names of Animals: Fishes. Ed. by V. Sokolov. 734p. (C). 1992. 95.00 (*0-685-46868-2*, Pub. by Collets) St Mut.

Dictionary of the Names of Marine Fishes. A. Kotliar. 288p. (C). 1984. 65.00 (*0-569-08971-9*, Pub. by Collets); 125.00 (*0-89771-919-0*, Pub. by Collets) St Mut.

Dictionary of the Names of Marine Fishes in Six Languages. A. N. Kotliar. 288p. (ENG, FRE, GER, LAT, RUS & SPA.). 1986. 50.00 (*0-317-59481-8*, Pub. by Collets UK) Pro-Am Music.

Dictionary of the Napoleonic Wars. David G. Chandler. LC 93-805. 1993. 70.00 (*0-13-177288-0*) S&S Trade.

***Dictionary of the North-West Semitic Inscriptions Vol. 1, Set.** Jacob Hoftijzer & K. Jongeling. LC 94-39945. 9940. 314.50 (*90-04-09817-8*) E J Brill.

***Dictionary of the North-West Semitic Inscriptions Vol. 2, Set.** Jacob Hoftijzer & K. Jongeling. LC 94-39945. 1995. 314.50 (*90-04-09820-8*) E J Brill.

Dictionary of the Noted Names in Fiction: Including Also Familiar Pseudonyms, Surnames Bestowed on Eminent Men, & Analagous Popular Appellations Often Referred to in Literature & Conversation. William A. Wheeler. LC 89-26590. 440p. 1990. reprint ed. lib. bdg. 40.00 (*1-55888-902-7*) Omnigraphics Inc.

Dictionary of the Occult. Ed. by Julian Franklyn. 1995. reprint ed. 40.00 (*1-55888-963-9*) Omnigraphics Inc.

Dictionary of the Occult Sciences. L. Stebbing. 1973. lib. bdg. 250.00 (*0-87968-449-6*) Krishna Pr.

Dictionary of the Ojibway Language. 3rd ed. Frederic Baraga. LC 92-28915. 736p. 1992. reprint ed. pap. 24.95 (*0-87351-281-2*, Borealis Book) Minn Hist.

Dictionary of the Old West, 1850-1900. Peter Watts. LC 94-18340. 1994. reprint ed. pap. 9.99 (*0-517-11913-7*, Pub. by Wings Bks) Random.

Dictionary of the Older Scottish Tongue, Pts. XXVII-XXXI. Ed. by A. J. Aitken & James A. Stevenson. (Dictionary of the Older Scottish Tongue Ser.: Vol. 5). 620p. 1994. 225.00 (*0-08-028490-6*, Pergamon Pr) Elsevier.

Dictionary of the Older Scottish Tongue: From the Twelfth Century to the End of the Seventeenth, 6 vols. Ed. by A. J. Aitken & James A. Stevenson. LC 38-21689. 1988. 1,050.00 (*0-08-030675-6*, Pub. by Aberdeen U Pr) Macmillan.

Dictionary of the Older Scottish Tongue: From the Twelfth Century to the End of the Seventeenth. Ed. by A. J. Aitken & James A. Stevenson. LC 38-21689. (Dictionary of the Older Scottish Tongue Ser.: No. 38). 120p. 1994. pap. 52.00 (*0-08-030677-2*, Pub. by Aberdeen U Pr) Macmillan.

Dictionary of the Older Scottish Tongue: From the Twelfth Century to the End of the Seventeenth, No. 37. A. J. Aitken & James A. Stevenson. LC 38-21689. 120p. 1994. pap. 52.00 (*0-08-030676-4*, Pub. by Aberdeen U Pr) Macmillan.

Dictionary of the Older Scottish Tongue: From the Twelfth Century to the End of the Seventeenth, Pt. 33. Ed. by A. J. Aitken & James A. Stevenson. 120p. 1994. pap. 52.00 (*0-08-030394-3*, Pub. by Aberdeen U Pr) Macmillan.

Dictionary of the Older Scottish Tongue: From the Twelfth Century to the End of the Seventeenth, Pt. 34. Ed. by A. J. Aitken & James A. Stevenson. (DOST Ser.). 120p. 1994. pap. 52.00 (*0-08-030395-1*, Pub. by Aberdeen U Pr) Macmillan.

Dictionary of the Older Scottish Tongue: From the Twelfth Century to the End of the Seventeenth, Pt. 35. Ed. by A. J. Aitken & James A. Stevenson. (Dictionary of the Older Scottish Tongue Ser.). 120p. 1994. pap. 52.00 (*0-08-030396-X*, Pub. by Aberdeen U Pr) Macmillan.

Dictionary of the Older Scottish Tongue: From the Twelfth Century to the End of the Seventeenth, Pt. 36. A. J. Aitken & James A. Stevenson. LC 38-21689. 120p. 1994. pap. 52.00 (*0-08-030673-X*, Pub. by Aberdeen U Pr) Macmillan.

Dictionary of the Older Scottish Tongue: From the Twelfth Century to the End of the Seventeenth, Pt. 40. Ed. by A. J. Aitken & James A. Stevenson. (Dictionary of the Older Scottish Tongue Ser.). 120p. 1994. pap. 52.00 (*0-08-030679-9*, Pergamon Pr) Elsevier.

D

An Asterisk (*) at the beginning of an entry indicates that the title is appearing in BIP for the first time.

1971

Dictionary of the Older Scottish Tongue, Part 42: Ru-Sanct: From the Twelfth Century to the End of the Seventeenth. Ed. by A. J. Aitken et al. (Dictionary of the Older Scottish Tongue Ser.). 120p. 1994. pap. 52.00 (*0-08-030683-7*, Pub. by Aberdeen U Pr) Macmillan.

Dictionary of the Older Scottish Tongue, Pt. 32: From the Twelfth Century to the End of the Seventeenth. Ed. by A. J. Aitken & James A. Stevenson. 120p. 1994. pap. 52.00 (*0-08-030393-5*, Pergamon Pr) Elsevier.

Dictionary of the Older Scottish Tongue, Pt. 39: From the Twelfth Century to the End of the Seventeenth. A. J. Aitken & James A. Stevenson. LC 38-21689. 120p. 1994. pap. 52.00 (*0-08-030678-0*, Pergamon Pr) Elsevier.

Dictionary of the Older Scottish Tongue, Pt. 41: From the Twelfth Century to the End of the Seventeenth. A. J. Aitken & James A. Stevenson. 120p. 1994. pap. 52.00 (*0-08-030680-2*, Pub. by Aberdeen U Pr) Macmillan.

Dictionary of the Older Scottish Tongue, Vol. 7 (37-41) From the Twelfth Century to the End of the Seventeenth. Ed. by A. J. Aitken & James A. Stevenson. LC 38-21689. 600p. 1994. 225.00 (*0-08-030681-0*, Pub. by Aberdeen U Pr) Macmillan.

Dictionary of the Older Scottish Tongue, Vols. 1-7: From the Twelfth Century to the End of the Seventeenth. A. J. Aitken et al. (Dictionary of the Older Scottish Tongue Ser.: No. 7). 4200p. 1990. 1,900.00 (*0-08-030682-9*, Pub. by Aberdeen U Pr) Macmillan.

***Dictionary of the Osage Language.** Francis La Flesche. (Bureau of American Ethnology Bulletins Ser.). 406p. 1995. lib. bdg. 109.00 (*0-7812-4109-X*) Rprt Serv.

Dictionary of the Osage Language. Francis La Flesche. reprint ed. 69.00 (*0-403-03580-5*) Scholarly.

Dictionary of the Osage Language. Francis La Flesche. LC 90-43115. 412p. 1990. reprint ed. lib. bdg. 59.00 (*1-878592-20-3*); reprint ed. pap. 39.00 (*1-878592-19-X*) Native Amer Bk Pubs.

Dictionary of the Persian & English Languages. Fazl-I-Ali. 668p. (ENG & PER.). 1987. 75.00 (*0-8288-1122-9*, M14112) Fr & Eur.

Dictionary of the Persian Arabic: Arabic-English. John Richardson. (ARA, ENG & PER.). 1986. 150.00 (*0-8288-0546-6*, M 6600) Fr & Eur.

Dictionary of the Pharmach: Woerterbuch der Pharmazie, Vol. 1: Biologie, Chemie, Technolgie. H. Auterhoff. 532p. (GER.). 1981. 95.00 (*0-8288-1835-5*, M15388) Fr & Eur.

Dictionary of the Photographic & a Comprehensive & Systematic Catalogue of Photographic Apparatus Material: Manufactured, Imported & Sold by E. Anthony, 2 vols. in 1. Henry H. Snelling & E. Anthony. Ed. by Peter C. Bunnell & Robert A. Sobieszek. LC 76-23059. (Sources of Modern Photography Ser.). (Illus.). 1979. reprint ed. lib. bdg. 27.95 (*0-405-09623-2*) Ayer.

Dictionary of the Physical Sciences: Terms, Formulas, Data. Cesare Emiliani. (Illus.). 384p. 1987. 19.95 (*0-19-503651-4*) OUP.

Dictionary of the Principles of Misconduct in the Workplace & a Glossary of Labor Terms. 3rd ed. Clarence C. Terry. LC 83-91491. Orig. Title: Dictionary of Misconduct Connected with Work Concepts & a Glossary of Terms Used in Labor Relations. 176p. (C). 1984. pap. 17.95 (*0-9625419-0-7*) DeAcklen-Terry Pub Co.

Dictionary of the Print Trade in Ireland, 1550-1775. Robert Munter. LC 88-80279. 351p. reprint ed. pap. 100.10 (*0-7837-5615-1*, 2045522) Bks Demand.

Dictionary of the Printing Industry, English & German. Hans Schnellman. 120p. (ENG & GER.). 1987. 95.00 (*0-8288-0690-X*, F127160) Fr & Eur.

Dictionary of the Puk'hto, Pus'hto, or Language of the Afghans; with Remarks on the Originality of the Language & Its Affinity to the Semitic & Other Oriental Tongues. H. G. Raverty. 1987. reprint ed. 52.00 (*81-206-0286-2*, Pub. by Asian Educ Servs II) S Asia.

Dictionary of the Pulp & Paper Industry: In Five Languages, English, German, French, Spanish, & Russian. Comp. by Milos Svaton. LC 92-30831. 1992. write for info. (*0-444-98789-4*) Elsevier.

Dictionary of the Pushto Language: Pushto - English Dictionary. H. G. Raverty. 1140p. 1987. 79.95 (*0-8288-8477-3*) Fr & Eur.

Dictionary of the Quebec Cinema: Dictionnaire de la Cinema Quebecois. Houle. (FRE.). 1979. 59.95 (*0-8288-4796-7*, M6132) Fr & Eur.

Dictionary of the Rheumatic Diseases: Health Status Measurement, Vol. III. American College of Rheumatology, Glossary Committee. 80p. (C). 1988. pap. text ed. write for info. (*0-911059-03-2*) Cntct Assocs Intl.

***Dictionary of the Roman Empire.** Matthew Bunson. (Illus.). 512p. 1995. pap. 17.95 (*0-19-510233-9*) OUP.

Dictionary of the Rules of Substantive Nouns & Adjectives: Dicionario de Regimes de Substantivos y Adjetivos. F. Ferdandes. 684p. (SPA.). 1982. 29.95 (*0-8288-1993-9*, M14509) Fr & Eur.

Dictionary of the Russian Academy, 7 vols., Set. Ed. by M. Oesterby. (RUS.). 1981. reprint ed. 1,100.00 (*0-915346-76-1*) A Wofsy Fine Arts.

Dictionary of the Russian Language. S. I. Ozhegov. 798p. (C). 1988. 135.00 (*0-569-07728-1*, Pub. by Collets) St Mut.

Dictionary of the Russian Language: 1981-84, 4 vols. 2976p. (RUS.). 1984. 350.00 (*0-8288-1999-8*, F53020) Fr & Eur.

Dictionary of the Russian Revolution. Ed. by George Jackson & Robert Devlin. LC 88-17771. 722p. 1989. text ed. 95.00 (*0-313-21131-0*, DRU/, Greenwood Pr) Greenwood.

Dictionary of the Sciences of Education: Diccionario De las Ciencias De la Educacion, 2 vols., Set. Santillana Staff. 1528p. (SPA.). 1985. write for info. (*0-7859-4927-5*) Fr & Eur.

Dictionary of the Second World War. Elizabeth A. Wheal et al. LC 90-312. (Illus.). 640p. 1990. 39.95 (*0-87226-337-1*) P Bedrick Bks.

Dictionary of the Secrets of Ibiza: Diccionario de Secretos de Ibiza. M. Planells. 345p. (SPA.). 1982. pap. 16.95 (*0-8288-1463-5*, S39884) Fr & Eur.

***Dictionary of the Sport & Exercise Sciences.** Patty Freedson et al. Ed. by Mark H. Anshel. LC 90-45252. 176p. (Orig.). 1991. pap. text ed. 19.00 (*0-87322-379-9*, BANS0379) Human Kinetics.

Dictionary of the Sussex Dialect & Collection of Provincialisms in Use in the County of Sussex. W. D. Parrish. (English Dialect Society Publications Ser.: No. 6). 1972. reprint ed. pap. 16.00 (*0-8115-0440-9*) Periodicals Srv.

Dictionary of the Swahili Language. Ed. by Ludwig Krapf. LC 72-77205. (Illus.). 433p. (ENG & SWA.). 1971. reprint ed. text ed. 37.50 (*0-8371-1276-1*, KRS/, Negro U Pr) Greenwood.

***Dictionary of the Synthesizer & Computer Music: French-English, English-French.** Olivier Gilkain. 255p. (ENG & FRE.). 1992. pap. 17.95 (*0-7859-7900-X*, 2501017153) Fr & Eur.

Dictionary of the Tarot. Bill Butler. LC 74-9230. (Illus.). 1987. pap. 14.00 (*0-8052-0559-4*) Schocken.

Dictionary of the Theatre: Dictionnaire du Theatre Termes et Concepts de l'Analyse Theatrale. Patricia Pavis. 477p. (ENG, FRE, GER & SPA.). 1987. 150.00 (*0-8288-2188-7*, M15589) Fr & Eur.

Dictionary of the Theatre: Woerterbuch der Darstellenden Kuenste. G. Fischborn. 256p. (GER & RUS.). 1984. 39.95 (*0-8288-1418-X*, M15139) Fr & Eur.

Dictionary of the Undersea World: Enciclopedia Del Mundo Submarino. 2nd ed. Miguel Arimany Coma. 711p. (SPA.). 1981. 75.00 (*0-8288-1582-8*, S23069) Fr & Eur.

Dictionary of the Vietnam War. Ed. by James S. Olson. LC 87-12023. 593p. 1988. text ed. 75.00 (*0-313-24943-1*, OVW/, Greenwood Pr) Greenwood.

Dictionary of the Welsh Language - Geiriadur Prifysgol Cymru, Vol. 1, Pts. I-XXI: A - Ffysur. Ed. by Gareth A. Bevan. xx, 1366p. 90.00 (*0-7083-0504-0*, Pub. by U of Wales UK) Bks Intl VA.

Dictionary of the Welsh Language - Geiriadur Prifysgol Cymru, Vol. 2, Pts. XXII-XXXVI: G - Llys. Ed. by Gareth A. Bevan. xxi, 925p. 70.00 (*0-7083-0981-X*, Pub. by U of Wales UK) Bks Intl VA.

Dictionary of Theatre Anthropology: The Secret Art of the Performer. Eugenio Barba & Nicola Savarese. Tr. by Richard Fowler. (Illus.). 272p. 1991. pap. 29.95 (*0-415-05308-0*, A6232) Routledge.

Dictionary of Theoretical Concepts in Biology. Keith E. Roe & Richard G. Frederick. LC 80-19889. 380p. 1981. 32.50 (*0-8108-1353-X*) Scarecrow.

Dictionary of Theoretical Linguistics: English-Arabic with Arabic-English Glossary. Muhammad A. Al-Khuli. 1983. 35.00 (*0-86685-306-5*) Intl Bk Ctr.

Dictionary of Theories. Ed. by Jennifer Bothamley. 1993. 80.00 (*1-873477-05-8*, 101460, Gale Res Intl) Gale.

Dictionary of Tibetan & English Language. A. D. Koros. (ENG & TIB.). 1987. 95.00 (*0-8288-1143-1*, M15747) Fr & Eur.

Dictionary of Tools in Woodworking Almanac. Raphael Salaman. 1986. 60.00 (*0-02-606760-9*) Macmillan.

Dictionary of Toxicology. Ed. by Ernest Hodgson et al. 470p. 1988. text ed. 99.95 (*0-442-31842-1*) Van Nos Reinhold.

Dictionary of Toys in America, Vol. II. Ed. by Ida Long & Earnest Long. (Illus.). 72p. 1987. reprint ed. pap. 15.00 (*0-9604406-4-X*) Longs Americana.

Dictionary of Toys Sold in America, Vol. I. Ernest A. Long & Earnest A. Long. (Illus.). 83p. (Orig.). 1987. reprint ed. pap. 15.00 (*0-9604406-3-1*) Longs Americana.

Dictionary of Trade Name Origins. Adrian Room. 1990. 39.95 (*0-7102-0174-5*, RKP) Routledge.

Dictionary of Trade Name Origins. rev. ed. Adrian Room. 1991. 39.95 (*0-8442-3190-8*, Natl Textbk) NTC Pub Grp.

Dictionary of Traditional South-East Asian Theatre. Ghulam-Sarwar Yousof. (Illus.). 370p. 1994. pap. 32.00 (*967-65-3032-8*) OUP.

Dictionary of Translated Names & Titles. Adrian Room. 336p. 1986. 57.50 (*0-7100-9953-3*, RKP) Routledge.

***Dictionary of Transport & Combatant Vessels, Steam & Sail Employed by the Union Army, 1861-1868.** Charles D. Gibson & E. Kay Gibson. (Army's Navy Ser.). (Illus.). 450p. (C). 1995. lib. bdg. write for info. (*0-9608996-4-2*) Ensign Pr.

Dictionary of Travel, Tourism & Hospitality. S. Medlik. 240p. 1993. pap. 21.95 (*0-7506-0953-2*) Buttrwrth-Heinemann.

Dictionary of Trees. Fred Walden. LC 63-2400. (Orig.). 1963. pap. 3.95 (*0-8200-0401-4*) Great Outdoors.

Dictionary of Trees & Shrubs of Europe: A Dictionary in Eight Languages. Ed. by S. Z. Priszter. 300p. 1983. 59.00 (*963-05-2946-7*, Pub. by Akade Kiado HU) IBD Ltd.

Dictionary of Twentieth Century British Book Illustrators. Alan Horne. (Illus.). 400p. 1994. 79.50 (*1-85149-108-2*) Antique Collect.

Dictionary of Twentieth-Century British Business Leaders. Ed. by David Jeremy & Geoffrey Tweedale. 263p. 1994. lib. bdg. 60.00 (*0-86291-594-5*) Bowker-Saur.

Dictionary of Twentieth-Century Cuban Literature. Ed. by Julio A. Martinez. LC 88-35805. 537p. 1990. text ed. 75.00 (*0-313-25185-1*, MZC/, Greenwood Pr) Greenwood.

Dictionary of Twentieth Century Design. John Pile. (Illus.). 320p. 1990. 35.00 (*0-8160-1811-1*) Facts on File.

Dictionary of Twentieth Century Design. John Pile. LC 93-39780. (Illus.). 320p. 1994. reprint ed. pap. 18.95 (*0-306-80569-3*) Da Capo.

Dictionary of Twentieth-Century History: 1914-1990. Peter Teed. 520p. 1992. 30.00 (*0-19-211676-2*) OUP.

Dictionary of Twentieth-Century History: 1914-1990. Peter Teed. 528p. 1992. pap. 9.95 (*0-19-285207-8*) OUP.

Dictionary of Twentieth Century Italian Violin Makers & Import Dealers Scrapbook. 2nd ed. Marlin Brinser. 1978. pap. 22.50 (*0-9602298-1-7*) Timberwood.

Dictionary of Twentieth-Century World Biography. Ed. by Asa Briggs. 624p. 1992. 30.00 (*0-19-211679-7*) OUP.

Dictionary of Twentieth-Century World Biography. Ed. by Asa Briggs. 624p. 1993. reprint ed. pap. 12.95 (*0-19-283124-0*) OUP.

Dictionary of Twentieth-Century World Culture: Post-World War II America, Vol. 1. 352p. 1994. 60.00 (*0-8103-8481-7*, 008570) Gale.

Dictionary of Twentieth-Century World Politics. Jay M. Shafritz et al. (Illus.). 784p. 1993. 60.00 (*0-8050-1976-6*) H Holt & Co.

Dictionary of U. S. Government Statistical Terms. Ed. by Alfred N. Garwood & Louise L. Hornor. 261p. 1991. lib. bdg. 50.00 (*0-931845-25-4*); pap. 45.00 (*0-931845-24-6*) Info Pubns.

Dictionary of United States Economic History. James S. Olson. LC 91-32193. 680p. 1992. text ed. 85.00 (*0-313-26532-1*, OEH/, Greenwood Pr) Greenwood.

Dictionary of Universal Arabic Grammar, in Charts & Tables. Antoine Dahdah. (Illus.). (ARA.). 1982. 35.00 (*0-86685-292-1*) Intl Bk Ctr.

Dictionary of Universal Biography of All Ages & of All Peoples. Albert M. Hyamson. 679p. 1994. reprint ed. lib. bdg. 65.00 (*0-7808-0010-9*) Omnigraphics Inc.

Dictionary of Urdu, Classical Hindi & English. John T. Platts. (ENG, HIN & URD.). 1987. 95.00 (*0-8288-1745-6*, F29960) Fr & Eur.

Dictionary of Urdu Classical Hindi & English. 2nd ed. John T. Platts. (C). 1988. 52.00 (*0-8364-2410-7*) S Asia.

Dictionary of Useful & Everyday Plants & Their Common Names. F. N. Howes. LC 73-91701. 300p. 1974. 59.95 (*0-521-08520-9*) Cambridge U Pr.

Dictionary of Ventilation & Health. Wolfgang Lindeke. 186p. 1980. 65.00 (*0-569-08522-5*, Pub. by Collets UK) St Mut.

Dictionary of Vertebrate Zoology: Russian-English, English-Russian. George J. Jacobs. LC 78-16321. 1978. pap. text ed. 8.50 (*0-87474-551-9*, JADVP) Smithsonian.

Dictionary of Veterinary & Zoological Terms: Dictionnaire des Termes Veterinaires et Zootech-Niques. 3rd ed. Martial Villemin. 470p. 1984. 95.00 (*0-8288-2384-7*, M4674) Fr & Eur.

Dictionary of Veterinary Medicine. Gotthard Ilchmann. 450p. (ENG, FRE, GER & RUS.). 1993. 180.00 (*3-86117-037-X*, Pub. by A Hatier GW) IBD Ltd.

Dictionary of Victorian Wood Engravers. Rodney K. Engen. 304p. 1985. text ed. 97.50 (*0-85964-139-2*, Pub. by Scolar Pr UK) Ashgate Pub Co.

Dictionary of Video: English - Spanish. Tomas P. Benito. 96p. (ENG & SPA.). 1992. pap. 14.95 (*0-7859-3683-1*, M3151) Fr & Eur.

Dictionary of Visual Science. 4th ed. David Cline et al. LC 88-20235. (Illus.). 848p. 1989. text ed. 55.00 (*0-8019-7862-9*) Chilton.

Dictionary of Vitamins: Dictionnaire des Vitamines. Daniel Nani. 1986. 24.95 (*0-8288-1820-7*, M2330) Fr & Eur.

Dictionary of Vocal Terminology: An Analysis. Cornelius L. Reid. LC 81-86074. xxi, 478p. 1983. 39.95 (*0-915282-07-0*) J Patelson Mus.

Dictionary of War Quotations. Justin Wintle. 1989. text ed. 35.00 (*0-02-935411-0*) Free Pr.

Dictionary of Wars. George C. Kohn. LC 87-6863. 600p. 1987. pap. 16.95 (*0-385-24207-7*, Anchor NY) Doubleday.

Dictionary of Wars. George C. Kohn. 592p. 1986. 40.00 (*0-8160-1005-6*) Facts on File.

Dictionary of Water: Dictionnaire de l'Eau. Colf. 545p. (ENG & FRE.). 1981. pap. 59.95 (*0-8288-1484-8*, F38100) Fr & Eur.

Dictionary of Water & Sewage Engineering. 2nd rev. ed. Fritz Meinck & K. Mohle. 738p. (ENG, FRE, GER & ITA.). 1977. 197.50 (*0-444-99811-X*) Elsevier.

Dictionary of Water & Wastewater Treatment Trademarks & Brand Names. Tom M. Pankratz. 160p. 1991. 49.95 (*0-87371-673-6*, HD0971) Lewis Pubs.

Dictionary of Water Chemistry. Friedrich Von Ammon. 203p. 1985. pap. 80.00 (*0-89573-434-6*) VCH Pubs.

Dictionary of Wedgwood. Robin Reilly & George Savage. (Illus.). 414p. 1980. 79.50 (*0-902028-85-5*) Antique Collect.

Dictionary of Weeds of Eastern Europe: Their Common Names & Importance in Latin, Albanian, Bulgarian, Czech, German, English, Greek, Hungarian, Polish, Romanian, Russian, Serbo-Croat, & Slovak. G. Williams & K. Hunyadi. 480p. 1988. 151.50 (*0-444-98969-2*) Elsevier.

Dictionary of Weeds of Eastern Europe: Their Names & Importance. G. H. Williams & K. Hunyadi. (ALB, BUL, CZE, ENG, GER, HUN, POL, RUM, RUS, SER & SLO.). 1987. 295.00 (*0-8288-7197-3*, F45230) Fr & Eur.

***Dictionary of Weeds of Eastern Europe Their Common Names & Importance.** G. H. Williams & K. Hunyardi. 479p. 1987. 54.00x (*963-05-4392-3*, Pub. by Akad Kiado HU) St Mut.

Dictionary of Weights & Measures for the British Isles: The Middle Ages Through the Twentieth Century. Ronald E. Zupko. LC 68-14038. (Memoirs Ser.: Vol. 168). 512p. 1985. 30.00 (*0-87169-168-X*, M168-ZUR) Am Philos.

Dictionary of Welding. A. Kleiber. 396p. (ENG & GER.). 1970. 35.00 (*0-8417-1026-0*) Adlers Foreign Bks.

Dictionary of Welding Technology: Woerterbuch der Schweisstechnik. Achim Kleiber. 572p. (ENG & GER.). 1985. 110.00 (*0-8288-0593-8*, M6959) Fr & Eur.

Dictionary of Welding Technology: Woerterbuch der Schweisstechnik. Achim Kleiber. 576p. (ENG & GER.). 1986. 125.00 (*0-8288-0594-6*, M 15603) Fr & Eur.

Dictionary of Wellerisms. Ed. by Wolfgang Mieder & Stewart A. Kingsbury. 208p. 1994. 24.95 (*0-19-508318-0*) OUP.

Dictionary of Western Church Music. David Poultney. LC 91-12325. (Illus.). 272p. 1991. 45.00 (*0-8389-0569-2*) ALA.

Dictionary of Winds. L. Z. Prokh. 312p. (RUS.). 1983. 19.95 (*0-8288-1402-3*, M15586) Fr & Eur.

Dictionary of Wines 1991. 4th ed. Gerard Debuigne. 400p. (FRE.). 1991. 35.00 (*0-8288-6958-8*, F118400) Fr & Eur.

Dictionary of Women Artists: An International Dictionary of Women Artists Born Before 1900. Chris Petteys. LC 84-22511. 872p. 1985. lib. bdg. 75.00 (*0-8161-8456-9*, Hall Reference) Macmillan.

Dictionary of Wood & Woodworking Practice, Vol. 1: Holz-Woerterbuch. 2nd ed. Herbert Bucksch. 461p. (ENG & GER.). 1986. 150.00 (*0-8288-0330-7*, M7465) Fr & Eur.

Dictionary of Wood & Woodworking Practice, Vol. 2: Holz-Woerterbuch. Herbert Bucksch. 536p. (ENG & GER.). 1986. 175.00 (*0-8288-0329-3*, M7466) Fr & Eur.

Dictionary of Wood Construction & Woodworking. Cyril M. Harris. 1992. pap. 14.95 (*0-07-026894-0*) McGraw.

Dictionary of Wood Science & Technology: English-German - German-English. Peter Muhle. 466p. 1992. 183.00 (*3-87097-157-6*, Pub. by O Brandstetter Verlag GW) IBD Ltd.

Dictionary of Woodworking Tools. rev. ed. Raphael Salaman & Philip Walker. LC 89-40478. (Illus.). 545p. 1990. pap. 31.95 (*0-942391-51-9*) Taunton.

Dictionary of Worcester Porcelain, Vol. 1: 1751-1851. John Sandon. (Illus.). 384p. 1993. 89.50 (*1-85149-156-2*) Antique Collect.

Dictionary of Word Origins. 2nd ed. Joseph T. Shipley. LC 69-14079. 430p. 1970. reprint ed. text ed. 52.50 (*0-8371-1966-9*, SHWO, Greenwood Pr) Greenwood.

Dictionary of Word Origins. John Ayto. 592p. (C). 1993. reprint ed. pap. 16.95 (*1-55970-214-1*) Arcade Pub Inc.

Dictionary of Word Origins. Joseph T. Shipley. (Quality Paperback Ser.: No. 121). 442p. 1979. reprint ed. pap. 17.00 (*0-8226-0121-4*) Littlefield.

Dictionary of Word Roots & Combining Forms. Donald J. Borror. LC 60-15564. 134p. (C). 1960. pap. text ed. 9.95 (*0-87484-053-8*) Mayfield Pub.

Dictionary of Words about Alcohol. 2nd ed. M. Keller et al. LC 81-620046. 1982. 19.50 (*0-911290-12-5*) Rutgers Ctr Alcohol.

Dictionary of Words & Phrases Used in Ancient & Modern Law. Arthur English. 979p. 1987. reprint ed. lib. bdg. 85.00 (*0-8377-2104-0*) Rothman.

Dictionary of Works of Vocal Art, Vol. 2, G-O. M. Honegger & Abbe F. Prevost. 1991. lib. bdg. 185.00 (*0-7859-3949-0*) Fr & Eur.

Dictionary of Works of Vocal Art, Vol. 1: A-F. 255p. 1990. pap. 49.95 (*0-7859-4579-2*) Fr & Eur.

***Dictionary of World Myth.** Ed. by Peter Bently. LC 94-44700. 1995. write for info. (*0-8160-3300-5*); pap. write for info. (*0-8160-3325-0*) Facts on File.

Dictionary of World Mythology. Arthur Cotterell. (Oxford Paperback Reference Ser.). (Illus.). 320p. 1990. pap. 11.95 (*0-19-217747-8*) OUP.

Dictionary of World Place-Names Derived from English Names. Adrian Room. (Illus.). 272p. 1989. 35.00 (*0-415-02811-6*) Routledge.

Dictionary of World Politics. Ed. by Graham Evans & Jeffrey Newnham. 460p. 1991. 55.00 (*0-13-210527-6*) S&S Trade.

Dictionary of Yiddish Slang & Idioms. Fred Kogos. 168p. (YID.). 1995. pap. 7.95 (*0-8065-0347-5*, Citadel Pr) Carol Pub Group.

Dictionary of Yugoslavian Political-Economics Systems Terminology: Rjecnik Terminologije Jugoslavenskog Politicko-Ekonomoskog Sistema. Vlasta Andrlic. 144p. (ENG & SER.). 1985. pap. 24.95 (*0-8288-2264-6*, F107450) Fr & Eur.

Dictionary of Zoology: English-Chinese. Commercial Press Staff. 52p. (CHI & ENG.). 1975. pap. 39.95 (*0-8288-5840-3*, M9571) Fr & Eur.

Dictionary of Zoology: Zoologisches Woerterbuch. 5th ed. Erwin Hentschel & Guenter Wagner. 576p. (GER.). 1993. 55.00 (*0-8288-2386-3*, M15302) Fr & Eur.

Dictionary of 20th Century World Culture, Vol. 2. Ed. by Catharine S. Brosman. 1995. 60.00 (*0-8103-8482-5*) Gale.

Dictionary of 20th Century World Culture, Vol. 3. 1995. 60.00 (*0-8103-8483-3*) Gale.

Dictionary of 20th Century World Culture, Vol. 4. 1995. 60.00 (*0-8103-8484-1*) Gale.

Dictionary of 20th Century World Culture: French Culture, 1900-1975, Vol. 5. Ed. by Catharine S. Brosman. (Dictionary of 20th Century Culture Ser.: No. 2). 449p. 1996. 60.00 (*0-8103-8485-X*) Gale.

Dictionary Reference Guide for Respiratory Therapy. J. Owen Krasowski. LC 77-77500. 124p. reprint ed. pap. 35.40 (*0-8357-7596-8*, 2056916) Bks Demand.

D

An Asterisk (*) at the beginning of an entry indicates that the title is appearing in BIP for the first time.

Dictionary Roman Coins. Stevenson. 1982. reprint ed. lib. bdg. 75.00 (*0-686-45266-6*, Pub. by Seaby UK) S J Durst.

Dictionary Skills. Sylvia J. Foust. (Illus.). 48p. (J). (gr. 2-6). 1986. student ed 6.95 (*1-55734-339-X*) Tchr Create Mat.

Dictionary Skills. Barbara Gregorich. (Horizons II Ser.). (Illus.). 24p. (J). (gr. 3-4). 1980. student ed 3.50 (*0-89403-605-X*) EDC.

Dictionary Slovene-Serbocroatian-Slovene. Janko Jurancic. 566p. (CRO, SER & SLV.). 1978. 19.95 (*0-8288-5173-5*, M9703) Fr & Eur.

Dictionary Source Book. Ed. by Charles M. Stacy. 10p. (Orig.). 1984. pap. 9.75 (*0-916409-01-5*) Specialized Intl Biblio.

Dictionary Techniques of Graphics Industry: English - French, French - English. J. C. Faudouas. 1991. lib. bdg. 150.00 (*0-8288-2489-4*, F36010) Fr & Eur.

Dictionary to Plays & Novels of Shaw. C. L. Broad & V. M. Broad. 1973. 250.00 (*0-87968-016-4*) Gordon Pr.

Dictionary to Plays & Novels of Shaw. C. Lewis Broad & V. M. Broad. LC 75-92947. (Studies in Irish Literature: No. 16). 1969. reprint ed. lib. bdg. 75.00 (*0-8383-0961-5*) M S G Haskell Hse.

Dictionary to the Novels of James Fenimore Cooper. Mitchell E. Summerlin. 380p. (C). 30.00 (*0-317-59619-5*) Penkevill.

Dictionary to the Plays & Novels of Bernard Shaw: With Bibliography of His Works. C. L. Broad & Broad Broad. 1988. reprint ed. lib. bdg. 49.00 (*0-7812-0555-7*) Rprt Serv.

Dictionary to the Plays & Novels of Bernard Shaw: With Bibliography of His Works & of the Literature Concerning Him with the Record of the Principle Shawian Play Production. C. Lewis Broad & Violet M. Broad. LC 76-131645. (Illus.). 1972. reprint ed. 39.00 (*0-403-00532-9*) Scholarly.

***Dictionary Worcester Vol. 2: 1852-1952.** Sandon. 1995. pap. text ed. write for info. (*1-85149-157-0*) Antique Collect.

Dictionnaire a l'Usage des Plaisanciers. 160p. (ENG & FRE.). 1969. pap. 24.95 (*0-8288-6583-3*, M-6569) Fr & Eur.

***Dictionnaire Abkhaz.** Catherine Paris & Niaz Batouka. 1992. write for info. (*0-7859-8185-3*, 2-87723-044-9) Fr & Eur.

***Dictionnaire Abrege De Peinture et D'Architecture.** Francois-Marie De Marsy. 1972. write for info. (*0-7859-8043-1*, 2-8266-0228-4) Fr & Eur.

***Dictionnaire Abrege des Imprimateurs/Editeurs Francais du 16 Siecle.** Jean Muller. 150p. (FRE.). 1970. pap. 125.00 (*0-7859-8525-5*, 3873200309) Fr & Eur.

***Dictionnaire Abrege des Imprimeurs/Editeurs Francais Du.** 16th ed. Jean Muller. 1970. write for info. (*0-7859-8670-7*, 3873200309) Fr & Eur.

***Dictionnaire Abrege des Termes de Medecine.** Jacques Delamare. 1990. write for info. (*0-7859-7822-4*, 2-224-01940-8) Fr & Eur.

***Dictionnaire Abrege du Surrealisme.** Andre Breton & Paul Eluard. 1991. write for info. (*0-7859-7942-5*, 2-7143-0421-4) Fr & Eur.

Dictionnaire Abrege du Surrealisme. Annie C. Dobbs. (FRE.). pap. 39.95 (*0-7859-0756-4*, M-6165) Fr & Eur.

Dictionnaire Abrege Grec-Francais: Greek - French Dictionary. Anatole Bailly. 1012p. (FRE & GRE.). 1969. pap. 65.00 (*0-8288-6584-1*, M6019) Fr & Eur.

Dictionnaire Abrege Latin-Francais. Felix Gaffiot. 1720p. (FRE & LAT.). 1970. pap. 39.95 (*0-8288-6505-1*, M-6258) Fr & Eur.

Dictionnaire Actuel de l'Education. 2nd ed. Renald Legendre. 679p. (ENG & FRE.). 1993. 79.95 (*0-8288-1387-6*, M 520) Fr & Eur.

***Dictionnaire Affectif des Plantes.** Bernard Vial. 1990. write for info. (*0-7859-8230-2*, 2-905030-71-2) Fr & Eur.

***Dictionnaire Agricole.** 5th rev. ed. Gunther Haensch & Gisela Haberkamp de Anton. 1987. write for info. (*0-7859-8104-7*, 2-85608-022-7) Fr & Eur.

Dictionnaire Agro-Alimentaire (Dictionary Food Science) Anglais-Francais, Francais-Anglais. Jean Adrian. 346p. (ENG & FRE.). 1990. pap. 150.00 (*0-8288-2612-9*, F136010) Fr & Eur.

***Dictionnaire Allemand-Francais et Francais-Allemand.** Karl Rotteck & G. Kister. 1978. write for info. (*0-7859-8004-0*, 2-7370-0085-8) Fr & Eur.

***Dictionnaire Allemand-Francais et Francais-Allemand.** P. Siegfried Villain. 1979. write for info. (*0-7859-8005-9*, 2-7370-0107-2) Fr & Eur.

Dictionnaire Allemand-Francais et Francais-Allemand: German - French & French - German Dictionary. Denis Eckel & Hofer Manfred. 1324p. (FRE & GER.). 1970. 49.95 (*0-8288-6506-X*, M-6184) Fr & Eur.

Dictionnaire Allemand-Francais, Francais-Allemand. Ed. by Rotteck. 980p. (FRE & GER.). 1970. pap. 10.95 (*0-7859-0753-X*, M-6115) Fr & Eur.

Dictionnaire Analogique de la Publicite et des Medias. Remi-Pierre Heude. 396p. 1993. pap. 79.95 (*0-7859-5615-8*, 2212036280) Fr & Eur.

Dictionnaire Analogique et de Synonymes pour la Resolution des Problemes des Mots Croises: Dictionary of Analogies & Synonyms for Resolving the Problems of Crossword Puzzles. 6th ed. Maurice Denis-Papin. (FRE.). 1989. reprint ed. pap. 29.95 (*0-7859-5119-9*) Fr & Eur.

***Dictionnaire Analphabetique.** Bruno Masure. 202p. (FRE.). 1990. pap. 29.95 (*0-7859-8102-0*, 2855655986) Fr & Eur.

***Dictionnaire Anglais Elementaire.** Peter H. Collin. 1991. write for info. (*0-7859-8585-9*, 0-245-50152-5) Fr & Eur.

***Dictionnaire Anglais, Francais, Espagnol, Allemand, Russe, A.** Science Militaire Staff. 1989. 95.00 (*0-7859-8705-3*, 7800210804) Fr & Eur.

***Dictionnaire Anglais-Francais et Francais-Anglais.** Eugene Kuentz. 1976. write for info. (*0-7859-7768-6*, 2211410251) Fr & Eur.

***Dictionnaire Anglais-Francais et Francais-Anglais.** Jean Vincent. 1979. write for info. (*0-7859-8007-5*, 2-7370-0172-2) Fr & Eur.

Dictionnaire Anglais-Francais et Francais-Anglais des Termes et Locutions Maritimes. 2nd ed. Henri Paasch. 320p. (ENG & FRE.). 1974. pap. 23.50 (*0-7859-0749-1*, M-6437) Fr & Eur.

***Dictionnaire Arabe-Francais.** Alfred L. De Premare. 1993. write for info. (*0-7859-8018-0*, 2-7384-1859-7) Fr & Eur.

***Dictionnaire Arabe-Francais.** Daniel Reig. 1991. write for info. (*0-7859-8607-3*, 203451209X) Fr & Eur.

Dictionnaire Arabe-Francais. Ben Sedira & Charles Belkacem. 628p. (ARA & FRE.). 1980. pap. 24.95 (*0-8288-0439-7*, M 9305) Fr & Eur.

Dictionnaire Arabe-Francais-Anglais, 1: Arabic - French - Arabic Dictionary, 4 vols., Set. Regis Blachere & Moustafa Chouemi. (ARA, ENG & FRE.). 1967. 750.00 (*0-8288-6674-0*, M6034) Fr & Eur.

Dictionnaire Arabe-Francais-Arabe. Jean-Jacques Schmidt. 320p. (ARA & FRE.). 1991. 39.95 (*0-8288-1591-7*, F330) Fr & Eur.

Dictionnaire Arabe Moderne Larousse (Larousse Dictionary of Modern Arabic) Philosophie, Musique, Science, Vol. 1: A-Co. R. Georr. 360p. (ARA & FRE.). 1973. 29.95 (*0-7859-4841-4*) Fr & Eur.

***Dictionnaire Archaeologique de la France, 2 vols.** Atlas Staff. (FRE.). 1990. 295.00 (*0-7859-7981-6*, 2731205008) Fr & Eur.

Dictionnaire Archeologique de la Bible: Archeological Dictionary of the Bible. Ed. by Abraham Negev. 350p. (FRE.). 1970. 75.00 (*0-8288-6510-8*, M-6117) Fr & Eur.

***Dictionnaire Archeologique, Historique et Touristique des Ch.** Charles Floquet. 1991. write for info. (*0-7859-8656-1*, 285554050X) Fr & Eur.

Dictionnaire Astrologique. Henry J. Gouchou. 670p. (FRE.). 1975. 95.00 (*0-8288-5842-X*, M6284) Fr & Eur.

Dictionnaire Atlas D'Anatomie, 3 vols., Set. Pierre Kamina. 1984. lib. bdg. 395.00 (*0-8288-2620-X*, 2224009321) Fr & Eur.

***Dictionnaire Atlas d'Anatomie A-F.** Pierre Kamina & Annie Zwobada-Kamina. 1983. write for info. (*0-7859-7817-8*, 2-224-00930-5) Fr & Eur.

Dictionnaire Banda-Francais. Ch. Tisserant. 611p. (FRE.). 1931. 59.95 (*0-8288-6886-7*, M-6585) Fr & Eur.

Dictionnaire Beethoven. Barry Cooper. 600p. (FRE.). 1991. 195.00 (*0-8288-9447-7*) Fr & Eur.

***Dictionnaire Berrichon Avec Citations Litteraires.** Jean Tissier. 1987. write for info. (*0-7859-7992-1*, 2-7348-0734-3) Fr & Eur.

***Dictionnaire Bibliographique des Auteurs Juifs, de Leurs Ouv.** M. Kayserling. 1968. write for info. (*0-614-00416-0*, 9060040856) Fr & Eur.

Dictionnaire Biblique. Joseph Dheilly. 1284p. (FRE.). 1964. 29.95 (*0-8288-6761-5*, M-6114) Fr & Eur.

***Dictionnaire Biblique Abrege.** Louis Monloubou. 1989. 59.95 (*0-7859-7959-X*, 2-7189-0399-6) Fr & Eur.

***Dictionnaire Bilingue.** Paul Pauliat. 1976. write for info. (*0-7859-7652-3*, 2034017366) Fr & Eur.

***Dictionnaire Bilingue: French-German, German-French.** Jean Clediere & Daniel Rocher. 560p. (FRE & GER.). 1984. pap. 14.95 (*0-7859-7847-X*, 2253002801) Fr & Eur.

***Dictionnaire Bilingue: French-Italian, Italian-French.** Giuseppe Padovani. 536p. (FRE & ITA.). 1987. pap. 14.95 (*0-7859-7846-1*, 2253002798) Fr & Eur.

Dictionnaire Bilingue de l'Edition: French-English, English-French. Philippe Schuwer. 447p. (ENG & FRE.). 1993. pap. 95.00 (*0-7859-4837-6*, M6508) Fr & Eur.

***Dictionnaire Biographique.** 1986. write for info. (*0-7859-7988-3*, 2-7342-0105-4) Fr & Eur.

***Dictionnaire Biographique de Touraine.** Michel Laurencin. 1990. write for info. (*0-7859-8654-5*, 285443210X) Fr & Eur.

Dictionnaire Biographique des Auteurs de Tous les Temps et de Tous les Pays, 2 tomes, Set. 109.50 (*0-685-35955-7*) Fr & Eur.

Dictionnaire Biographique des Comediens Francais du 17e Siecle. 3rd ed. Georges Mongredien & Jean Robert. 330p. (FRE.). 1981. 75.00 (*0-7859-4842-2*) Fr & Eur.

***Dictionnaire Biographique des Createurs de la Region de Joli.** Rejean Olivier. 1975. write for info. (*0-7859-8255-8*, 2-920249-28-2) Fr & Eur.

Dictionnaire Biographique des Personnages Fictifs de la Comedie Humaine: Dictionnaire des Personnages Fictifs Anonymes. Fernand Lotte. 96p. (FRE.). 1952. 18.95 (*0-7859-5129-6*) Fr & Eur.

***Dictionnaire Biographique du Canada.** Presses de l'Universite Laval Staff. 1982. write for info. (*0-7859-8456-9*, 2-7637-6950-0) Fr & Eur.

Dictionnaire Biographique du Canada, Vol. 1: 1000-1700. Laval Staff. 800p. (FRE.). 1966. 95.00 (*0-8288-9452-3*) Fr & Eur.

Dictionnaire Biographique du Canada, Vol. 10: 1871-1880. Laval Staff. 926p. (FRE.). 1972. 95.00 (*0-8288-9460-4*, 2763766382) Fr & Eur.

Dictionnaire Biographique du Canada, Vol. 11: 1881-1890. Laval Staff. 1212p. (FRE.). 1982. 95.00 (*0-8288-9461-2*) Fr & Eur.

Dictionnaire Biographique du Canada, Vol. 2: 1701-1740. Laval Staff. 834p. (FRE.). 1969. 95.00 (*0-8288-9453-1*) Fr & Eur.

Dictionnaire Biographique du Canada, Vol. 3: 1741-1770. Laval Staff. 888p. (FRE.). 1974. 95.00 (*0-8288-9454-X*) Fr & Eur.

Dictionnaire Biographique du Canada, Vol. 4: 1771-1800. Laval Staff. 1044p. (FRE.). 1980. 95.00 (*0-8288-9455-8*) Fr & Eur.

Dictionnaire Biographique du Canada, Vol. 5: 1801-1820. Laval Staff. 1168p. (FRE.). 1983. 95.00 (*0-8288-9456-6*) Fr & Eur.

Dictionnaire Biographique du Canada, Vol. 6: 1821-1835. Laval Staff. 1243p. (FRE.). 1987. 95.00 (*0-8288-9457-4*, 2763770983) Fr & Eur.

Dictionnaire Biographique du Canada, Vol. 8: 1851-1860. Laval Staff. 1243p. (FRE.). 1985. 95.00 (*0-8288-9458-2*, 276377069X) Fr & Eur.

Dictionnaire Biographique du Canada, Vol. 9: 1861-1870. Laval Staff. 1060p. (FRE.). 1977. 95.00 (*0-8288-9459-0*) Fr & Eur.

***Dictionnaire Biographique du Canada 1701-1740.** Presses de l'Universite Laval Staff. 1969. write for info. (*0-7859-8028-8*, 2-7637-0007-1) Fr & Eur.

***Dictionnaire Biographique du Canada 1741-1770.** Presses de l'Universite Laval Staff. 1974. write for info. (*0-7859-8031-8*, 2-7637-6736-2) Fr & Eur.

***Dictionnaire Biographique du Canada 1771-1800.** Presses de l'Universite Laval Staff. 1980. write for info. (*0-7859-8033-4*, 2-7637-6900-4) Fr & Eur.

***Dictionnaire Biographique du Canada 1821-1835.** Presses de l'Universite Laval Staff. 1987. write for info. (*0-7859-8034-2*, 2-7637-7099-1) Fr & Eur.

***Dictionnaire Biographique du Canada 1861-1870.** Presses de l'Universite Laval Staff. 1977. write for info. (*0-7859-8032-6*, 2-7637-6812-1); write for info. (*0-7859-8592-1*, 0774668113) Fr & Eur.

***Dictionnaire Biographique du Canada 1871-1880.** Presses de l'Universite Laval Staff. 1972. write for info. (*0-7859-8029-6*, 2-7637-0010-1) Fr & Eur.

Dictionnaire Biographique du Mouvement Ouvrier Francais, 8 vols., Set. Jean Maitron. (FRE.). 295.00 (*0-7859-0939-7*, M-6384) Fr & Eur.

Dictionnaire Biographique du Movement Ouvrier Francais: De la Revolution Francaise a la Fondation de la Premiere Internationale (1789-1864, 3 tomes. Jean Maitron. Incl. Tome I. De A a C. 16.95 (*0-685-36060-1*); Tome II. De D a L. 19.95 (*0-685-36061-X*); Tome III. De M a Z. 19.95 (*0-685-36062-8*); write for info. (*0-318-51979-8*) Fr & Eur.

Dictionnaire Biographique International Des Ecrivains. Emile Carnoy. 946p. 1987. reprint ed. write for info. (*3-487-06703-X*, Pub. by Georg Olms GW) Lubrecht & Cramer.

Dictionnaire Birman-Francais. Denise Bernot. 324p. (FRE.). 1993. pap. 65.00 (*0-7859-5665-4*, 2877230465) Fr & Eur.

***Dictionnaire Bobo-Francais.** Pierre Le Bris & Andre Prost. 1981. write for info. (*0-7859-8653-7*, 285297102X) Fr & Eur.

Dictionnaire Bobo-Francais. P. Lebris. 416p. (FRE.). 1981. 69.95 (*0-8288-1599-2*, F37450) Fr & Eur.

Dictionnaire Bordas. Maurice Davau. 49.95 (*0-8288-9324-1*, M6102) Fr & Eur.

***Dictionnaire Bordas.** Robert Jarnier. 1974. write for info. (*0-7859-8612-X*, 204011338X) Fr & Eur.

***Dictionnaire Bordas de Litterature Francaise.** Henri Lemaitre. 1994. write for info. (*0-7859-8614-6*, 204019682X) Fr & Eur.

Dictionnaire Bordas des Rimes. Pierre DesFeuilles. 365p. (FRE.). 1993. 39.95 (*0-7859-0964-8*, 2040195130) Fr & Eur.

***Dictionnaire Bordas le Cadet.** Didier. 1990. write for info. (*0-7859-7706-6*, 2040183604) Fr & Eur.

***Dictionnaire Breton-Francais, Francais-Breton.** Garnier Staff. 816p. 1986. pap. 125.00 (*0-7859-5036-2*) Fr & Eur.

***Dictionnaire Breton-Gallois.** Rita Williams. 1984. write for info. (*0-7859-8159-4*, 2-86863-001-4) Fr & Eur.

Dictionnaire Bulgare-Francais: Bulgarian - French Dictionary. L. Stephanova. 978p. (BUL & FRE.). 1973. 95.00 (*0-7859-0812-9*, M-9834) Fr & Eur.

Dictionnaire Canadien-Francais. Sylva Clapin. 394p. (FRE.). 1974. 49.95 (*0-8288-6009-2*, M6587) Fr & Eur.

***Dictionnaire Cegos.** Christiane Morvan. 1986. write for info. (*0-7859-8642-1*, 271240307X) Fr & Eur.

***Dictionnaire Chinois-Francais.** 1990. write for info. (*0-7859-8237-X*, 2-906658-62-6) Fr & Eur.

***Dictionnaire Chinois-Francais.** Weng Zhongfu. 1988. write for info. (*0-7859-8236-1*, 2-906658-21-9) Fr & Eur.

Dictionnaire Chinois-Francais: Chinese-French Dictionary. Commercial Press Staff. 673p. (CHI & FRE.). 1979. 39.95 (*0-8288-2283-2*, M9268) Fr & Eur.

***Dictionnaire Chinois-Francais de Termes et Expressions Moder.** Chen Rongsheng. 1989. 75.00 (*0-7859-8706-1*, 7800280144) Fr & Eur.

***Dictionnaire Chinois-Francais des Termes Medicaux Usuels.** L'Hygiene Populaire Staff. 1990. write for info. (*0-7859-8702-9*, 7117006668) Fr & Eur.

Dictionnaire Classique: Francais-Neerlandais, Neerlandais-Francais. 22th ed. Ludovic Grootaers. 1018p. (DUT & FRE.). 1990. 125.00 (*0-8288-6585-X*, M-6300) Fr & Eur.

Dictionnaire Classique Anglais-Francais et Francais-Anglais. Charles Petit & William Savage. 686p. (ENG & FRE.). 1967. pap. 59.95 (*0-8288-6675-9*, M-6444) Fr & Eur.

***Dictionnaire Classique Francais-Breton Vol. 2: C-Debla.** Rene Le Gleau. 352p. (BRE & FRE.). 1984. pap. 45.00 (*0-7859-7999-9*, 2736800087) Fr & Eur.

***Dictionnaire Classique Francais-Breton Vol. 3: Deblo-Embeg.** Rene Le Gleau. 352p. (BRE & FRE.). 1986. pap. 45.00 (*0-7859-8000-8*, 2736800141) Fr & Eur.

***Dictionnaire Classique Francais-Breton Vol. 6.** Rene Le Gleau. 384p. (BRE & FRE.). 1987. pap. 55.00 (*0-7859-8001-6*, 2736800184) Fr & Eur.

***Dictionnaire Classique Francais-Breton Vol. 6.** Rene Le Gleau. 384p. (BRE & FRE.). 1988. pap. 45.00 (*0-7859-8002-4*, 2736800206) Fr & Eur.

***Dictionnaire Classique Francais-Breton Vol. 6.** Rene Le Gleau. 348p. (BRE & FRE.). 1989. pap. 45.00 (*0-7859-8003-2*, 2736800265) Fr & Eur.

***Dictionnaire Clinique des Therapies Familiales Systemiques.** Jean-Claude Benoit et al. 1988. write for info. (*0-7859-7935-2*, 2-7101-0694-9) Fr & Eur.

***Dictionnaire Collins Francais-Allemand, Allemand-Francais.** Veronika Schnorr. 1990. write for info. (*0-7859-7892-5*, 2-501-01444-8) Fr & Eur.

***Dictionnaire Collins Francais-Anglais, Anglais-Francais.** Pierre-Henri Cousin. 1990. write for info. (*0-7859-7893-3*, 2-501-01445-6) Fr & Eur.

***Dictionnaire Collins Francais-Italien, Italien-Francais.** Ettore Zelioli et al. 1990. write for info. (*0-7859-7894-1*, 2-501-01447-2) Fr & Eur.

***Dictionnaire Collins Super Gem Francais-Italien, Italien-Francais.** Paola Banfichi Ferrari & Adriana Secondo. 216p. (FRE & ITA.). 1985. 23.95 (*0-7859-7605-1*, 2010116631) Fr & Eur.

Dictionnaire Commente de l'Oeuvre de General de Gaulle. 880p. (FRE.). 1975. 39.95 (*0-8288-5843-8*, M6589) Fr & Eur.

***Dictionnaire Commercial.** Academie des Sciences Commerciales Staff. 1987. write for info. (*0-7859-7934-4*, 2-7101-0646-9) Fr & Eur.

Dictionnaire Commercial: Francais-Italien, Italien-Francais. Mario Mormile. (FRE & ITA.). 1978. lib. bdg. 125.00 (*0-7859-3907-5*) Fr & Eur.

Dictionnaire Commerciale: Commercial Dictionary. Alf. 297p. (FRE.). 1979. pap. 59.95 (*0-8288-4791-6*, M9307) Fr & Eur.

Dictionnaire Complet des Mots Croises. 400p. (FRE.). 1981. 24.95 (*0-686-56804-4*, F-136830) Fr & Eur.

***Dictionnaire Comptable et Financier: French-German, German-French.** Jurgen Boelcke et al. 196p. (FRE & GER.). 1993. pap. 75.00 (*0-7859-7940-9*, 2712704045) Fr & Eur.

***Dictionnaire Conseil des Medicaments Vendus Sans Ordonnance.** Jean-Paul Giroud & Charles Hagege. 1987. write for info. (*0-7859-7877-1*, 2-268-00440-6) Fr & Eur.

Dictionnaire Constitutionnel. Olivier Duhamel & Yves Meny. 1120p. (FRE.). 1992. 275.00 (*0-7859-0976-1*, 2130442560) Fr & Eur.

***Dictionnaire Contextuel de la Corrosion.** Robert Serre. (FRE.). 1984. write for info. (*0-7859-8597-2*, 0969095031) Fr & Eur.

***Dictionnaire Correctif du Francais au Canada.** Gaston Dulong. 1968. write for info. (*0-7859-8030-X*, 2-7637-6363-4) Fr & Eur.

Dictionnaire Corse-Francais, Pierre d'Evisa. 2nd ed. Mathieu Ceccaldi. 464p. (COR & FRE.). 1988. pap. 115.00 (*0-7859-4811-2*, M6066) Fr & Eur.

Dictionnaire Creole-Francais. Hector Poullet. 480p. (CRE & FRE.). 1991. pap. write for info. (*0-7859-0505-7*, 2868770061) Fr & Eur.

***Dictionnaire Creole Francais.** Hector Poullet et al. 1991. write for info. (*0-7859-8164-0*, 2-86877-006-1) Fr & Eur.

Dictionnaire Critique de la Communication, 2 vols. Lucien Sfez. 1808p. 1993. 695.00 (*0-7859-5611-5*, 2130439381) Fr & Eur.

Dictionnaire Critique de la Revolution Francaise. Francois Furet & Mona Ozouf. 1128p. (FRE.). 1988. 195.00 (*0-8288-9463-9*) Fr & Eur.

***Dictionnaire Critique De la Revolution Francaise, 4 vols.** Francois Furet. (FRE.). 1992. pap. 79.95 (*0-7859-7720-1*, 2080812637) Fr & Eur.

Dictionnaire Critique des Drogues: Critical Dictionary of Drugs. Ronald Verbeke. 160p. (FRE.). 1978. 59.95 (*0-8288-5175-1*, M6548) Fr & Eur.

Dictionnaire Critique et Documentaire des Peintres, Sculpteurs, Dessinateurs, et Graveurs de Tous les Temps et de Tous les Pays, 10 tomes, Set. Benezit. (FRE.). 1976. 895.00 (*0-8288-5635-4*, F1850) Fr & Eur.

***Dictionnaire Culturel de la Bible.** CERF Staff. 302p. (FRE.). 1990. 45.00 (*0-7859-7763-5*, 2204040282) Fr & Eur.

***Dictionnaire Culturel de la Mythologie Greco-Romaine.** Rene Martin. 1992. write for info. (*0-7859-7721-X*, 2091800740) Fr & Eur.

***Dictionnaire Culturel du Christianisme.** Nicole Lemaitre et al. 332p. 1994. 59.95 (*0-7859-7723-6*, 2091800813) Fr & Eur.

Dictionnaire d'Agriculture CILF. Salvador A. Sanroma. 64p. (CAT.). 1977. pap. 12.95 (*0-7859-6210-7*, S50060) Fr & Eur.

***Dictionnaire d'Amboise Pays de Savoie, 23 vols.** Valery D'Amboise. (FRE.). 1988. pap. 2,750.00 (*0-7859-8222-1*, 2903795134) Fr & Eur.

***Dictionnaire d'Amenagement d'Espace: French-English-German-Spanish.** H. J. Calsat. 703p. (FRE, GER & SPA.). 1993. 225.00 (*0-7859-7474-1*, 2853192458) Fr & Eur.

Dictionnaire D'Archeologie Chretienne et De Liturgie, 28 vols. Letouzey & Ane. (FRE.). 1903. write for info. (*0-7859-0497-2*, 2706301562) Fr & Eur.

Dictionnaire d'Archeologie Chretienne et de Liturgie, 28 vols., Set. Dom H. Leclercq & Henri Marron. (FRE.). 1903. 2,995.00 (*0-8288-6892-1*, M-6342) Fr & Eur.

***Dictionnaire D'Argot.** 2nd ed. Evariste Nouguier. 167p. (FRE.). 1993. pap. 32.95 (*0-7859-8197-7*, 2877710173) Fr & Eur.

Dictionnaire d'Argot et des Principales Locutions Populaires: Histoire de l'Ar. Andre La Rue & Clement Casciani. 190p. (FRE.). 1986. pap. 14.95 (*0-8288-1939-4*, F136760) Fr & Eur.

Dictionnaire de Ballet Moderne. (FRE.). 43.25 (*0-685-35976-X*) Fr & Eur.

Dictionnaire de Banque et Bourse. Yves Crozet. 336p. 1993. pap. 32.95 (*0-7859-5612-3*, 2200213077) Fr & Eur.

D

Dictionnaire de Base Francais-Provencal. Institut d'Estudis Occitan Staff. 431p. (FRE & PRO.). 1992. pap. 75.00 (0-7859-1020-4, 2909774007) Fr & Eur.

Dictionnaire de Bayle et la Lute Philosophique au 18e Siecle. Pierre Retat. 556p. (FRE.). 1972. pap. 45.00 (0-7859-0731-9, FA-410) Fr & Eur.

Dictionnaire de Biographie Francaise, Fasc. 1018 & 31-60. Floriane Prevot & Jean-Claude Roman-D'Amat. 230.00 (0-685-35951-4) Fr & Eur.

Dictionnaire de Biographie Francaise: French Biographical Dictionary, 16 vols., Set. Michel Prevost & Jean-Claude Roman-D'Amat. 8040p. (FRE.). 1972. 2,495.00 (0-8288-6370-9, M-6466) Fr & Eur.

***Dictionnaire de Biologie.** 2nd ed. Theodore Lender. 448p. (FRE.). 1992. 275.00 (0-7859-7747-3, 2130447031) Fr & Eur.

Dictionnaire de Botanique. Bernard Boulard. (FRE.). 1988. lib. bdg. 49.95 (0-8288-2598-X) Fr & Eur.

***Dictionnaire de Cardiologie.** Masson Staff. 352p. (FRE.). 1986. 135.00 (0-7859-7827-5, 2225802521) Fr & Eur.

Dictionnaire de Chimie Allemand-Francais: German-French Chemistry Dictionary. 3rd ed. Raymond Cornubert. 240p. (FRE & GER.). 1977. pap. 65.00 (0-8288-5381-9, M6088) Fr & Eur.

***Dictionnaire de Citations Chretiennes.** Philippe Engelhard. 224p. (FRE.). 1987. pap. 29.95 (0-7859-7762-7, 2204027162) Fr & Eur.

***Dictionnaire de Critique Litteraire.** Garde-Tamine. 320p. (FRE.). 1993. pap. 32.95 (0-7859-7758-9, 2200213778) Fr & Eur.

***Dictionnaire de Culture Biblique.** Maurice Carrez. 356p. (FRE.). 1993. 79.95 (0-7859-7795-3, 2220034208) Fr & Eur.

Dictionnaire de Danse. Jacques Baril. 288p. (FRE.). 1964. pap. 24.95 (0-8288-6762-3, M6590) Fr & Eur.

***Dictionnaire de Danse.** Charles Compan. 420p. (FRE.). 1979. pap. 135.00 (0-7859-8048-2, 2826606778) Fr & Eur.

Dictionnaire de Demographie. Roland Pressat. 304p. (FRE.). 1979. 75.00 (0-8288-9468-X, F70763) Fr & Eur.

Dictionnaire de Dermatologie. Francois Daniel. 760p. (FRE.). 1990. lib. bdg. 225.00 (0-8288-2593-9) Fr & Eur.

Dictionnaire de Diagnostic Clinique et Topographique. Alain Blacque-Belair & Bernard M. de Fossey. 1250p. (FRE.). 1969. 75.00 (0-8288-6586-8, M6037) Fr & Eur.

Dictionnaire de Didactique des Langues. Ed. by R. Galisson & D. Coste. 612p. (FRE.). 1976. 39.95 (0-8288-5638-9, M6591) Fr & Eur.

Dictionnaire de Dietique. G. Moioli. 364p. (FRE.). 1993. pap. 59.95 (0-7859-5640-9, 2732817066) Fr & Eur.

Dictionnaire de Domotique. Witold Zaniewicki. 552p. (FRE.). 1990. 295.00 (0-8288-9469-8) Fr & Eur.

Dictionnaire de Droit Canonique, 7 vols., Set. R. Naz. (FRE.). 1965. 1,195.00 (0-8288-6739-9, M-6423) Fr & Eur.

Dictionnaire de Droit Social Francais-Allemand. F. Frankl. 258p. (FRE & GER.). 1970. write for info. (3-19-006279-X) Fr & Eur.

Dictionnaire de Franglais. Grund Editorial Staff. 175p. (FRE.). 1980. pap. 24.95 (0-8288-4690-1, M8980) Fr & Eur.

Dictionnaire de Frequence des Mots du Francais Parle au Quebec. Pierre Martel et al. LC 91-5120. (American University Studies: Linguistics: Ser. XIII, Vol. 26). 768p. (Orig.). (C). 1992. pap. text ed. 110.95 (0-8204-1740-8) P Lang Pubs.

***Dictionnaire de Genetique.** Philippe L'Heritier. 272p. (FRE.). 1979. pap. 69.95 (0-7859-7824-0, 2225526575) Fr & Eur.

Dictionnaire de Genetique with English - French Index. Jean-Charles Sournia. 351p. (ENG & FRE.). 1991. pap. 125.00 (0-8288-9470-1) Fr & Eur.

Dictionnaire de Geographie Ancienne et Moderne. 2nd ed. Pierre Deschamps. 804p. (FRE.). 1990. 225.00 (0-7859-5127-X) Fr & Eur.

Dictionnaire De Geographie Ancienne et Moderne A l'Usage Du Libraire et De l'Amateur Des Livres. Pierre Deschamps. 796p. 1965. reprint ed. write for info. (0-318-71337-3, Pub. by Georg Olms GW) Lubrecht & Cramer.

Dictionnaire De Geographie Ancienne et Moderne a l'Usage Du Libraire et De l'Amateur Des Livres. Pierre C. Deschamps. 796p. (GER.). 1965. reprint ed. write for info. (0-318-70585-0, Pub. by Georg Olms GW) Lubrecht & Cramer.

Dictionnaire de Geographie Ancienne et Moderne a l'Usage Due Libraire et de l'Amateur des Livres. Pierre C. Deschamps. 796p. 1965. reprint ed. write for info. (0-318-71764-6, Pub. by Georg Olms GW) Lubrecht & Cramer.

Dictionnaire de Geographie Historique de la Gaule et de la France: Historical Dictionary of the Geography of Gaul & France. Joseph Moreau. 426p. (FRE.). 1972. pap. 99.50 (0-8288-6371-7, M-6593) Fr & Eur.

***Dictionnaire de Geopolitique.** Yves Lacoste. 1679p. (FRE.). 1993. 185.00 (0-7859-8616-2, 208035101x) Fr & Eur.

***Dictionnaire de Graphologie et des Termes Psychologiques Correspondants.** Augusto Vels. 659p. (FRE.). 1993. pap. 95.00 (0-7859-7987-5, 2733904221) Fr & Eur.

Dictionnaire De Gynecologie et D'Obstetrique: Termes Usuels S'Hier et D'Aujourd'Hui. Alain Mavel. 592p. (FRE.). 1990. pap. write for info. (0-7859-0499-9, 2718404957) Fr & Eur.

Dictionnaire De G026327255 Ancienne et Moderne a l'Usage Du Libraire et De l'Amateur Des Livres. Pierre C. Deschamps. 796p. 1965. reprint ed. write for info. (0-318-70735-7, Pub. by Georg Olms GW) Lubrecht & Cramer.

***Dictionnaire de la Bande Dessinee.** Henri Filippini. 732p. (FRE.). 1989. 195.00 (0-7859-7707-4, 2040184554) Fr & Eur.

Dictionnaire de la Beaute Feminine. Floriane Prevot. 268p. (FRE.). 1972. pap. 10.95 (0-7859-1444-7, 2203221011) Fr & Eur.

***Dictionnaire de la Betise et des Erreurs de Jugement.** Guy Bechtel. 820p. (FRE.). 1991. pap. 55.00 (0-7859-7808-9, 2221067479) Fr & Eur.

***Dictionnaire de la Bible.** Andre-Marie Gerard. 1478p. (FRE.). 1990. pap. 65.00 (0-7859-7806-2, 2221057600) Fr & Eur.

***Dictionnaire de la Bible Hebraique.** 3rd ed. Rabbin Marchand-Ennery. 304p. (FRE & HEB.). 1986. pap. 19.95 (0-7859-8086-5, 2853320456) Fr & Eur.

***Dictionnaire de la Chanson Francaise.** Pascal Sevran. 384p. (FRE.). 1988. pap. 31.95 (0-7859-8156-X, 2868043372) Fr & Eur.

Dictionnaire de la Chimie et de Ses Applications: Dictionary of Chemistry & Its Applications. 3rd ed. C. Duval. 1100p. (FRE.). 1977. 450.00 (0-8288-5383-5, M6183) Fr & Eur.

***Dictionnaire de la Chimie et du Genie Chimique: French-English-German.** Joachim C. Hitzke. (ENG, FRE & GER.). 1989. pap. 95.00 (0-7859-8257-4, 2950151841) Fr & Eur.

Dictionnaire de la Civilisation. Guy Rachet. 256p. (FRE.). 1992. 59.95 (0-8288-7354-2) Fr & Eur.

Dictionnaire de la Civilisation Egytienne: Dictionary of the Egyptian Civilization. Georges Posener. 326p. (FRE.). 1988. 79.95 (0-8288-6512-4, M-6462) Fr & Eur.

***Dictionnaire de la Civilisation Grecque.** Claude Mosse. 512p. (FRE.). 1992. 125.00 (0-7859-8173-X, 2870274416) Fr & Eur.

Dictionnaire de la Civilisation Grecque. Guy Rachet. 272p. (FRE.). 1992. 59.95 (0-8288-7353-4) Fr & Eur.

***Dictionnaire de la Civilisation Indienne.** Louis Frederic. 1276p. (FRE.). 1987. pap. 55.00 (0-7859-7797-X, 2221012585) Fr & Eur.

***Dictionnaire de la Civilisation Phenicienne et Punique.** Edouard Lipinski. 501p. (FRE.). 1993. 285.00 (0-7859-7902-6, 2503500331) Fr & Eur.

***Dictionnaire de la Civilisation Romaine.** Jean-Charles Fredouille. 256p. (FRE.). 1992. pap. 28.95 (0-7859-7682-5, 2037200749) Fr & Eur.

Dictionnaire de la Commune, Vol. 1. Bernard Noel. (FRE.). 1978. pap. 9.95 (0-8288-5177-8, M6428) Fr & Eur.

***Dictionnaire de la Communication.** Jean-Paul Truxillo. 480p. (FRE.). 1991. 125.00 (0-7859-7760-0, 2200420188) Fr & Eur.

***Dictionnaire de la Comptabilite.** 4th ed. Erik De La Villguerin. 1431p. (FRE.). 1993. pap. 165.00 (0-7859-8143-8, 2865212181) Fr & Eur.

***Dictionnaire de la Coree.** Louis Frederic. 456p. (FRE.). 1988. pap. 65.00 (0-7859-8152-7, 2866450434) Fr & Eur.

Dictionnaire de la Cuisine de Nord-Pas-de-Calais. Bonneton Staff. 160p. (FRE.). 1993. 39.95 (0-7859-5661-1, 2862531413) Fr & Eur.

***Dictionnaire de la Cuisine de Normandie.** Anne Prevel. 160p. (FRE.). 1993. 39.95 (0-7859-8120-9, 2862531480) Fr & Eur.

***Dictionnaire de la Cuisine des Ardennes Recettes Francaises et Belges.** Monique Esquerre-Anciaux. 155p. (FRE.). 1992. 39.95 (0-7859-8117-9, 2862531308) Fr & Eur.

***Dictionnaire de la Cuisine Lorraine.** Jean-Marie Cuny. 159p. (FRE.). 1992. 39.95 (0-7859-8119-5, 2862531367) Fr & Eur.

Dictionnaire de la Culture Physique. Marcel Rouet. 304p. (FRE.). 1975. 39.95 (0-8288-5846-2, M6494) Fr & Eur.

Dictionnaire De la Danse Historique, Theorique, Pratique et Bibliographique. G. Desrat. vi, 484p. 1977. reprint ed. write for info. (3-487-06327-1, Pub. by Georg Olms GW) Lubrecht & Cramer.

***Dictionnaire de la Foi Catholique.** Guy-Marie Oury. 267p. (FRE.). 1986. 59.95 (0-7859-8088-1, 2854431162) Fr & Eur.

Dictionnaire de la Foi Chretienne (Dictionary of the Christian Faith), 2 vols. Ed. by Antonin M. Henry & Olivier De LaBrosse. 420p. (FRE.). 1989. pap. 79.95 (0-7859-4843-0) Fr & Eur.

Dictionnaire de la Franc-Maconnerie, 2 vols., Set. 3rd ed. Daniel Ligou. 1344p. (FRE.). 1991. 175.00 (0-7859-4767-1, M267) Fr & Eur.

Dictionnaire de la Franc-Maconnerie et des Francs-Macons. Allec Mellor. 324p. (FRE.). 1989. reprint ed. pap. 49.95 (0-7859-4834-1) Fr & Eur.

***Dictionnaire de la France Medievale.** Jean Favier. 1016p. (FRE.). 1993. 295.00 (0-7859-7777-5, 2213031398) Fr & Eur.

Dictionnaire de la Geographie. 5th ed. Pierre George. 520p. 1993. lib. bdg. 145.00 (0-8288-2607-2, M6267) Fr & Eur.

***Dictionnaire de la Lande Francaise.** Charles Daney. 347p. (FRE.). 1992. 115.00 (0-7859-8124-1, 2862661635) Fr & Eur.

Dictionnaire de la Langue des Iles Marquises. Ildefonse Dordillon. 598p. (FRE.). 1932. 49.95 (0-8288-6885-9, M-6597) Fr & Eur.

Dictionnaire de la Langue Francaise. Paul-Emile Littre. 6809p. (FRE.). 1983. lib. bdg. 1,150.00 (0-7859-4626-8) Fr & Eur.

***Dictionnaire de la Langue Philosophique.** Paul Foulquie. 512p. (FRE.). 1991. pap. 26.95 (0-7859-7745-7, 2130437893) Fr & Eur.

Dictionnaire de la Langue Philosophique. 6th ed. P. Foulquie & R. St. Jean. 800p. (FRE.). 1992. 125.00 (0-7859-4635-7, F18420) Fr & Eur.

Dictionnaire de la Langue Quebecoise: Dictionary of Quebecoise. L. Bergeron. 574p. (FRE.). 1980. pap. 125.00 (0-8288-1092-3, M9360) Fr & Eur.

***Dictionnaire de la Langue Romano-Castraise et des Contrees Limitrophes.** J. P. Couzinte. 563p. (FRE.). 1976. 125.00 (0-7859-7990-5, 2734803003) Fr & Eur.

***Dictionnaire de la Langue Verte: Arcaismes, Locutions Etrangeres, Patois.** fac. ed. Hector France. 504p. (FRE.). 1990. pap. 155.00 (0-7859-8196-9, 2877710157) Fr & Eur.

***Dictionnaire de la Linguistique.** Georges Mounin. 346p. (FRE.). 1974. 105.00 (0-7859-7741-4, 2130331335) Fr & Eur.

***Dictionnaire de la Linguistique.** Georges Mounin. 384p. (FRE.). 1993. pap. 31.95 (0-7859-8625-1, 213044881x) Fr & Eur.

Dictionnaire de la Litterature Francaise et Francophone, 3 vols. Jacques Demougin. 1987. A-E. write for info. (0-8288-2617-X); E-N. write for info. (0-8288-2618-8); N-Z. write for info. (0-8288-2619-6) Fr & Eur.

Dictionnaire de la Litterature Francaise et Francophone, 3 vols., Set. Jacques Demougin. 1987. lib. bdg. 89.95 (0-7859-5550-X) Fr & Eur.

Dictionnaire de la Litterature Francaise et Francophone, Vol. 1. Jacques Demougin. 504p. 1987. pap. 26.95 (0-7859-5602-6, 2037200218) Fr & Eur.

Dictionnaire de la Litterature Francaise et Francophone, Vol. 2. Jacques Demougin. 506p. 1987. pap. 26.95 (0-7859-5603-4, 2037200226) Fr & Eur.

Dictionnaire de la Litterature Francaise et Francophone, Vol. 3. Jacques Demougin. 527p. 1987. pap. 26.95 (0-7859-5604-2, 2037200234) Fr & Eur.

***Dictionnaire de la Medecine Larousse.** Larousse Staff. (FRE.). 1990. pap. 16.95 (0-7859-7850-X, 2253037842) Fr & Eur.

Dictionnaire de la Montagne. Jacques Gautrat. 256p. (FRE.). 1970. pap. 14.95 (0-8288-6513-2, M-6598) Fr & Eur.

***Dictionnaire de la Morale Catholique.** Jean-Louis Brugues. 473p. (FRE.). 1991. 105.00 (0-7859-8093-8, 2854432193) Fr & Eur.

***Dictionnaire de la Musique.** Gerard Pernon. 448p. (FRE.). 1992. 75.00 (0-7859-8013-X, 2737311853) Fr & Eur.

***Dictionnaire de la Musique.** 3rd fac. ed. Sebastien De Brossard. 400p. (FRE.). 1992. pap. 225.00 (0-7859-8049-0, 2826608851) Fr & Eur.

Dictionnaire de la Musique: Les Hommes et Leurs Oeuvres,, Vol. 2, L-Z. M. Honegger. 1986. lib. bdg. 195.00 (0-7859-3948-2) Fr & Eur.

Dictionnaire de la Musique: Science de la Musique, 2 vols., Set. M. Honegger. 1216p. (FRE.). 1976. 325.00 (0-8288-5640-0, M6599) Fr & Eur.

***Dictionnaire de la Musique en France aux XVIIe et XVIIIe Siecles.** Marcelle Benoit. (FRE.). 1992. 235.00 (0-7859-7775-9, 2213028249) Fr & Eur.

***Dictionnaire de la Mystique.** Peter Dinzelbacher. 786p. (FRE.). 1993. 135.00 (0-7859-7908-5, 2503503179) Fr & Eur.

***Dictionnaire de la Mythologie.** Odile Gandon. 537p. (FRE.). 1992. pap. 16.95 (0-7859-8600-6, 201019201x) Fr & Eur.

Dictionnaire de la Mythologie Grecque et Romaine. Pierre Grimal. 1990. lib. bdg. 135.00 (0-8288-2616-1) Fr & Eur.

***Dictionnaire de la Mythologie Grecque et Romaine.** Dorothea von Coenen. 412p. (FRE.). 1992. 79.95 (0-7859-7905-0, 2503502474) Fr & Eur.

Dictionnaire de la Navigation: Dictionary of Navigation. Gianni Cazzaroli. 392p. (FRE.). 1973. 39.95 (0-7859-0730-0, M-4650) Fr & Eur.

***Dictionnaire de la Negritude.** Mongo Beti. 246p. (FRE.). 1989. pap. 55.00 (0-7859-8015-6, 2738404944) Fr & Eur.

Dictionnaire de la Noblesse, 10 vols., Set. Francais Aubert de la Chenaye-Desbois. 9800p. (FRE.). 1978. 1,695.00 (0-8288-5178-6, M6015) Fr & Eur.

Dictionnaire de la Noblesse Francais, 2 vols., Set. Etienne De Sereville & F. de Saint-Simon. 1246p. (FRE.). 1990. 350.00 (0-7859-5105-9) Fr & Eur.

***Dictionnaire de la Nouvelle Dietetique.** Albert-Francois Creff. 607p. (FRE.). 1984. 69.95 (0-7859-8631-6, 222104276x) Fr & Eur.

***Dictionnaire de la Peche et de l'Eau.** Bernard Breton. 374p. (FRE.). 1988. 32.95 (0-7859-8646-4, 273730170x) Fr & Eur.

***Dictionnaire de la Peinture Allemande et d'Europe Centrale.** Larousse Staff. 414p. (FRE.). 1990. pap. 79.95 (0-7859-7693-0, 2037400179) Fr & Eur.

Dictionnaire de la Peinture Francaise. Larousse Staff. 520p. (FRE.). 1989. pap. 89.95 (0-8288-2596-3, 203740011X) Fr & Eur.

Dictionnaire de la Peinture Italienne. Larousse Staff. 528p. (FRE.). 1989. pap. 79.95 (0-7859-5540-2, 2037400136) Fr & Eur.

Dictionnaire de la Peinture Surrealiste: Dictionary of Surrealist Painting. Sarane Alexandrian. 58p. (FRE.). 1973. 59.95 (0-7859-0406-9, M6601) Fr & Eur.

***Dictionnaire de la Pensee Politique.** J. Bremond. 854p. (FRE.). 1989. pap. 45.00 (0-7859-7785-6, 2218020076) Fr & Eur.

Dictionnaire de la Plaisance. Centre Nautique de G. 140p. 1993. pap. 36.95 (0-7859-5574-7, 2020197170) Fr & Eur.

Dictionnaire de la Plongee Sous-Marine; Dictionary of Skin-diving. Jean-Pierre Didier. 262p. (ENG, FRE, GER, ITA & SPA.). 1985. pap. 110.00 (0-8288-2351-0, F71220) Fr & Eur.

Dictionnaire de la Prehistoire. Andre L. Gourhan. 1232p. (FRE.). 1988. lib. bdg. 195.00 (0-8288-2597-1, 2130414591) Fr & Eur.

Dictionnaire de la Presse et des Medias: French-Arabic, Arabic-French Dictionary of the Press & Media. Conseil International de la Language Francaise Staff. (ARA & FRE.). pap. write for info. (0-8288-7675-4) Fr & Eur.

***Dictionnaire de la Priere.** Guy-Marie Oury. 236p. (FRE.). 1990. 75.00 (0-7859-8091-1, 2854432169) Fr & Eur.

Dictionnaire de la Prononciation: Pronounciation Dictionary. A. Lerond. 589p. (FRE.). 1980. 45.00 (0-8288-1943-2, M9124) Fr & Eur.

Dictionnaire de la Prononciation Francaise dans Son Usage Reel: Dictionary of French Pronunciation in Its Real Application. Andre Martinet & Henriette Walter. 932p. (FRE.). 1973. 125.00 (0-7859-0729-7, M-4739) Fr & Eur.

Dictionnaire De la Prospection Sismique: French - English, English - French. Chambre Syndical Du Petrole et Du Gaz Naturel Staff. 328p. 1987. pap. write for info. (0-7859-0498-0, 2710805278) Fr & Eur.

***Dictionnaire De la Qualite: French-English.** Michel Perigord. 351p. (FRE.). 1993. pap. 105.00 (0-7859-7739-2, 2124678116) Fr & Eur.

***Dictionnaire de la Reforme.** Edouard Belladur. 297p. (FRE.). 1992. pap. 49.95 (0-7859-7776-7, 2213030189) Fr & Eur.

***Dictionnaire de la Relieure-Dorure Manuelle: With English-French Lexicon.** Jean-Claude Faudouas. 115p. (ENG & FRE.). 1991. 75.00 (0-7859-7770-8, 2212008074) Fr & Eur.

Dictionnaire De la Robinette et De la Tuyauterie Industrielles: Office De la Langue Francaise Quebec. Monique Heroux. 302p. (ENG & FRE.). 1992. pap. 29.95 (0-7859-0496-4, 2551149835) Fr & Eur.

***Dictionnaire de la Robinetterie et de la Tuyauterie Industrielles: English-French.** Monique Heroux. 302p. (FRE.). 1992. pap. 75.00 (0-7859-7772-4, 2212008112) Fr & Eur.

***Dictionnaire de la Sagesse Orientale Bouddhisme, Hindouisme, Taoisme, Zen.** Laffont Staff. 780p. (FRE.). 1989. pap. 45.00 (0-7859-7805-4, 2221056116) Fr & Eur.

Dictionnaire de la Science Economique. 3rd ed. Alain Cotta. 448p. (FRE.). pap. 39.95 (0-7859-0740-8, M-6092) Fr & Eur.

Dictionnaire de la Sexualite. Georges Valensin. 392p. (FRE.). 1967. 10.95 (0-686-56826-5, M-6604) Fr & Eur.

Dictionnaire de la Theologie Fondamentale. Rene Latourelle. (FRE.). 1993. pap. 195.00 (0-7859-3020-5) Fr & Eur.

***Dictionnaire de la Turquie.** Helene Willemart. 316p. (FRE.). 1989. pap. 59.95 (0-7859-8153-5, 2866450493) Fr & Eur.

***Dictionnaire de la Vie - Dictionary of Life: Rijecnik Zivota: French-English-Serbocroate.** Students of Sarajevo Staff. 111p. (ENG, FRE & SER.). 1993. pap. 32.95 (0-7859-8666-9, 295067061x) Fr & Eur.

Dictionnaire de la Vie Affective et Sexuelle. Jean Cohen et al. 272p. (FRE.). 1974. 29.95 (0-8288-6016-5, M6605) Fr & Eur.

***Dictionnaire de la Vie Politique et Sociale.** Dominique Chagnollaud. 251p. (FRE.). 1993. pap. 24.95 (0-7859-7778-3, 2218003155) Fr & Eur.

***Dictionnaire de la Violence et du Crime.** Roger Dufour-Gompers. 458p. (FRE.). 1992. pap. 115.00 (0-7859-8148-9, 2865862178) Fr & Eur.

Dictionnaire de la Virilite: Dictionary of Virility. P. Vincent. 370p. (FRE.). 1973. 19.95 (0-7859-0768-8, M-6553) Fr & Eur.

Dictionnaire de la Voile: Dictionary of Flight. Ed. by Michel Barberousse. 256p. (FRE.). 1970. pap. 19.95 (0-8288-6514-0, M6606) Fr & Eur.

***Dictionnaire de l'Academia Francaise Vol. 1: A-Barattage.** 9th ed. Academie Francaise Staff. 116p. (FRE.). 1986. pap. 21.95 (0-7859-7732-5, 2110808926) Fr & Eur.

***Dictionnaire de l'Academie Francaise: A-Enz.** Academie Francaise Staff. 834p. (FRE.). 1992. 195.00 (0-7859-7736-8, 2110812494) Fr & Eur.

***Dictionnaire de l'Academie Francaise Vol. 3.** 9th ed. Academie Francaise Staff. (FRE.). 1987. pap. 21.95 (0-7859-7733-3, 2110809205) Fr & Eur.

***Dictionnaire de l'Academie Francaise Vol. 3.** 9th ed. Academie Francaise Staff. (FRE.). 1988. pap. 24.95 (0-7859-7734-1, 2110809531) Fr & Eur.

***Dictionnaire de l'Academie Francaise Vol. 4.** 9th ed. Academie Francaise Staff. (FRE.). 1989. pap. 24.95 (0-7859-7735-X, 2110810521) Fr & Eur.

***Dictionnaire de l'Academie Francaise Vol. 5: Deux-Encyclique.** 9th ed. Academie Francaise Staff. 582p. (FRE.). 1990. pap. 28.95 (0-7859-8620-0, 211081117x) Fr & Eur.

***Dictionnaire de l'Alimentation.** John Yudkin. 520p. (FRE.). 1988. pap. 29.95 (0-7859-8633-2, 222105475x) Fr & Eur.

***Dictionnaire de l'Allemand dD'Aujourd'hui: German-French, French-German.** Philippe Magere. 743p. (FRE & GER.). 1987. pap. 19.95 (0-7859-8009-1, 2737002699) Fr & Eur.

***Dictionnaire de l'Allemand des Affaires.** Guillaume De La Roque. 475p. (FRE & GER.). 1989. pap. 16.95 (0-7859-7854-2, 2253045799) Fr & Eur.

Dictionnaire de l'Allemand Economique et Commercial. Jurgen Boelcke et al. 482p. (FRE & GER.). 1982. pap. write for info. (0-7859-4737-X) Fr & Eur.

Dictionnaire de L'Amerique Francaise. Charles Dufresne. 1988. lib. bdg. 69.95 (0-8288-2594-7) Fr & Eur.

***Dictionnaire de l'Amerique Francaise.** Charles Dufresne. 396p. (FRE.). 1988. pap. 49.95 (0-7859-8021-0, 2760302164) Fr & Eur.

Dictionnaire de l'Ancien Francais. Algirdas J. Greimas. 630p. (FRE.). 1992. 75.00 (0-8288-1937-8, F133970) Fr & Eur.

D

An Asterisk (*) at the beginning of an entry indicates that the title is appearing in BIP for the first time.

Dictionnaire de l'Anglais Contemporain. F. Dubois-Charlier. 863p. (ENG & FRE.). 1980. 22.50 (*0-8288-0776-0*, M14141) Fr & Eur.

***Dictionnaire de l'Anglais des Affaires.** Guillaume De La Roque. 446p. (ENG & FRE.). 1988. pap. 16.95 (*0-7859-7853-4*, 2253045780) Fr & Eur.

Dictionnaire de l'Anglais Economique et Commercial: Dictionary of Commercial & Economic English. J-P. Berman et al. 412p. (ENG & FRE.). 1980. pap. 22.95 (*0-8288-1254-3*, M4800) Fr & Eur.

***Dictionnaire de l'Archaeologie.** Guy Rachet. 1060p. (FRE.). 1982. pap. 49.95 (*0-7859-7814-3*, 2221503228) Fr & Eur.

Dictionnaire de l'Argot Moderne: Dictionary of Modern Slang. 11th ed. Georges Sandry. 456p. (FRE.). 1980. 24.95 (*0-8288-1952-1*, F136790) Fr & Eur.

***Dictionnaire de l'Argot Parisien.** Eitenne-Loredan Larchey. 252p. (FRE.). 1985. pap. 32.95 (*0-7859-8233-7*, 2905291036) Fr & Eur.

***Dictionnaire de l'Art Moderne Contemporain.** Gerard Durozoi. 700p. (FRE.). 1992. 225.00 (*0-7859-8056-3*, 2850252662) Fr & Eur.

Dictionnaire De l'Astrologie: Dictionary of Astrology. Michele Curcio. (FRE.). 1980. pap. 19.95 (*0-8288-1189-X*, M6607) Fr & Eur.

Dictionnaire de l'Audio-Visuel: Francais-Anglais, Anglais-Francais. Guitta Pessis-Pasternak. 384p. (ENG & FRE.). 1976. pap. 39.95 (*0-8288-5639-7*, M6442) Fr & Eur.

***Dictionnaire de l'Automobile: French-English-American.** ETAI Staff. 141p. (FRE.). 1986. 65.00 (*0-7859-7974-3*, 2726880266) Fr & Eur.

***Dictionnaire de L'EAO: With English-French Index.** Don Didier. 248p. (FRE.). 1988. pap. 34.95 (*0-7859-7930-1*, 2708005847) Fr & Eur.

***Dictionnaire de L'Economie.** 4th ed. Jean-Francois Phelizon. 352p. (FRE.). 1985. pap. 39.95 (*0-7859-7952-2*, 2717810382) Fr & Eur.

Dictionnaire de l'Economie du Droit et du Commerce, Vol. 2: Francais - Allemand. Miguel De Toro y Gisbert. 546p. 1987. pap. text ed. 12.95 (*0-7859-4870-8*) Fr & Eur.

Dictionnaire de l'Enfantement. Max Ploquin. 264p. (FRE.). 1974. pap. 39.95 (*0-8288-6012-2*, M6459) Fr & Eur.

***Dictionnaire de l'Entreprise.** Pol Guyomarc'h. 190p. (FRE.). 1993. pap. 24.95 (*0-7859-7788-0*, 2218037661) Fr & Eur.

Dictionnaire de l'Environnement. Georges Thines & Agnes Lempereur. 1034p. (FRE.). 1984. pap. write for info. (*0-7859-4839-2*) Fr & Eur.

Dictionnaire de l'Esoterisme. Pierre Riffard. 396p. 1993. pap. 36.95 (*0-7859-5620-4*, 2228886548) Fr & Eur.

***Dictionnaire de l'Espagnol des Affaires.** Guillaume De La Roque. 447p. (FRE & SPA.). 1988. pap. 16.95 (*0-7859-7855-0*, 2253045802) Fr & Eur.

Dictionnaire de l'Espagnol Economique et Commercial. J. Chapron & Gerboin. (FRE & SPA.). 1988. 65.00 (*0-8288-0830-9*, M511) Fr & Eur.

***Dictionnaire de L'Esprit: Two Thousand Citations de Rabelias a Coluche.** Raymond Castans. 344p. (FRE.). 1991. pap. 39.95 (*0-7859-8179-9*, 2877061167) Fr & Eur.

***Dictionnaire de l'Estampe en France 1830-1950.** Janine Bailly-Herzberg. 384p. (FRE.). 1985. 195.00 (*0-7859-7717-1*, 2080120131) Fr & Eur.

Dictionnaire de l'Ethnologie et de Anthropologie. P. Bonte. (FRE.). 1991. lib. bdg. 195.00 (*0-8288-3830-5*, F112720) Fr & Eur.

***Dictionnaire de l'Ethnologie et de l'Anthropologie.** 2nd ed. Michel Izard. 768p. (FRE.). 1992. 195.00 (*0-7859-8624-3*, 213044539x) Fr & Eur.

***Dictionnaire de L'Ethologie.** Klaus Immelmann. 293p. (FRE.). 1990. pap. 85.00 (*0-7859-8172-1*, 2870093888) Fr & Eur.

Dictionnaire de l'Extreme-Gauche: De 1945 a Nos Jours: Dictionary of the Extreme Left from 1945 to Present. Roland Biard. 384p. (FRE.). 1978. pap. 39.95 (*0-8288-5176-X*, M6033) Fr & Eur.

***Dictionnaire de l'Humour et du Libertinage.** Maurice Maloux. 360p. (FRE.). 1983. 34.95 (*0-7859-7835-6*, 2226017674) Fr & Eur.

Dictionnaire de l'Informatique Tcheque-Francais-Tcheque: Czech-French, French-Czech Computers Dictionary. K. Janos & J. Laitl. 351p. (CZE & FRE.). 1980. 95.00 (*0-8288-0906-2*, M14278) Fr & Eur.

Dictionnaire de l'Insolite et du Fantastique. Jean-Louis Bernard. 356p. (FRE.). 1974. 24.95 (*0-8288-6013-0*, M6608) Fr & Eur.

***Dictionnaire de l'Intelligence Artificielle.** Philippe Genthon. 156p. (FRE.). 1989. 85.00 (*0-7859-8150-0*, 2866011740) Fr & Eur.

***Dictionnaire de Liturgie.** Robert Le Gall. 279p. (FRE.). 1987. pap. 38.95 (*0-7859-8089-X*, 2854431359) Fr & Eur.

Dictionnaire de Locutions, Francais-Anglais. Marguerite-Marie Dubois. 392p. (ENG & FRE.). 1973. 59.95 (*0-685-57711-2*, M-6173) Fr & Eur.

Dictionnaire de l'Opera. Harold D. Rosenthal & John Warrack. 420p. (FRE.). 1974. pap. 59.95 (*0-8288-6014-9*, M416) Fr & Eur.

***Dictionnaire de L'OSI: French-English.** Afnor Staff. 176p. (ENG & FRE.). 1992. pap. 65.00 (*0-7859-8621-9*, 212481611x) Fr & Eur.

***Dictionnaire de l'Outillage et de la Machine Outil: French-English, English-French.** Jean-Pierre Michaux. (ENG & FRE.). 1976. pap. 22.95 (*0-7859-7928-X*, 2708004441) Fr & Eur.

Dictionnaire de l'Urbanisme et de l'Amenagement. Pierre Merlin & Francoise Choay. 744p. (FRE.). 1988. 195.00 (*0-8288-2359-6*, M 414) Fr & Eur.

Dictionnaire de Management et Controle du Gestion. B. Dervaux. 233p. (ENG & FRE.). 1986. 75.00 (*0-8288-7696-7*) Fr & Eur.

Dictionnaire de Marine, Francais et Anglais: Marine Dictionary, French & English. Robert Gruss. 368p. (ENG & FRE.). 1978. 49.95 (*0-8288-5179-4*, M6302) Fr & Eur.

Dictionnaire de Matiere Medicale Homeopathique. Andre O. Julian. 496p. (FRE.). 1981. 150.00 (*0-8288-1811-8*) Fr & Eur.

***Dictionnaire de Maximes et Locutions Latines Utilissees en Droit Quebecois.** Albert Mayrand. 235p. (FRE & LAT.). 1972. 39.95 (*0-7859-8020-2*, 2760107787) Fr & Eur.

***Dictionnaire de Medecine du Sport.** Philippe Most. 274p. (FRE.). 1987. pap. 95.00 (*0-7859-7828-3*, 2225810176) Fr & Eur.

Dictionnaire de Medecine Flammarion. 5th ed. Serge Kernbaum. 1024p. (FRE.). 1994. 95.00 (*0-8288-2613-7*, M6123) Fr & Eur.

Dictionnaire de Medecine Physique de Reeducation et Readaptation Fonctionelles. Herman L. Kamenetz & Georgette Kamenetz. 208p. (FRE.). 1972. 19.95 (*0-686-56986-5*, M-6324) Fr & Eur.

***Dictionnaire de Medicine Chinoise Traditionelle.** Jean-Francois Borsarello. 248p. (FRE.). 1984. 225.00 (*0-7859-7826-7*, 2225800855) Fr & Eur.

Dictionnaire de Meteorologie Populaire. rev. ed. Jean-Philippe Chassany. 410p. (FRE.). 1989. pap. 185.00 (*0-7859-4812-0*) Fr & Eur.

***Dictionnaire de Musique.** J. J. De Meude-Monpas. 256p. (FRE.). 1982. pap. 95.00 (*0-7859-8047-4*, 2826606662) Fr & Eur.

Dictionnaire de Musique dans Lequel on Simplifie les Expressions et les Definitions Mathematiques et Physiques Qui Ont Rapport a Cet Art. Jean J. De Meude-Monpas. LC 76-43927. (Music & Theatre in France in the 17th & 18th Centuries Ser.). (FRE.). reprint ed. 26.00 (*0-404-60175-8*) AMS Pr.

***Dictionnaire de Mythes Litteraires.** Pierre Brunel. 1436p. (FRE.). 1988. 275.00 (*0-7859-7878-X*, 2268007146) Fr & Eur.

***Dictionnaire de Mythologie Celte Dieux et Heros.** 2nd ed. Jean-Paul Persigout. 319p. (FRE.). 1990. pap. 55.00 (*0-7859-7879-8*, 2268009688) Fr & Eur.

***Dictionnaire de Mythologie Celtique.** Jean-Paul Persigout. (FRE.). 1985. pap. 32.95 (*0-7859-7876-3*, 2268003507) Fr & Eur.

Dictionnaire de Napoleon. Jean Tulard. 1769p. (FRE.). 1987. 295.00 (*0-8288-1490-2*, F69650) Fr & Eur.

***Dictionnaire de Parasitologie.** Patrice Bouree. 126p. (FRE.). 1989. pap. 29.95 (*0-7859-7979-4*, 2729889248) Fr & Eur.

***Dictionnaire de Pathologies Professionelles et Medecine du Travail.** Frejaville Hachet. 1004p. (FRE.). 1988. 195.00 (*0-7859-7819-4*, 2224017243) Fr & Eur.

Dictionnaire de Pharmacologie Dentaire: Dictionary of Dental Pharmacology. Roger Viellefosse. 228p. (FRE.). 1970. 49.95 (*0-8288-6516-7*, M-6550) Fr & Eur.

***Dictionnaire de Philosophie.** Jacqueline Russ. 383p. (FRE.). 1991. pap. 45.00 (*0-7859-7709-0*, 2040193014) Fr & Eur.

***Dictionnaire De Philosophie.** 2nd ed. Gerard Durozoi. 367p. (FRE.). 1990. 45.00 (*0-7859-7724-4*, 2091801135) Fr & Eur.

Dictionnaire de Physique. Gabriel Laitier. 276p. (FRE.). 1968. pap. 55.00 (*0-8288-6632-5*, M-6328) Fr & Eur.

***Dictionnaire de Physique.** Elie Levy. 890p. (FRE.). 1988. 250.00 (*0-7859-8622-7*, 213039311x) Fr & Eur.

***Dictionnaire de Poche Anglais: English-French, French-English.** Denis Girard. 698p. (ENG & FRE.). 1994. pap. 19.95 (*0-7859-7861-5*, 2253065153) Fr & Eur.

***Dictionnaire de Poche Espagnol: Spanish-English, English-Spanish.** Lydia Behar-Velay. 660p. (FRE & SPA.). 1994. pap. 19.95 (*0-7859-7860-7*, 2253064483) Fr & Eur.

Dictionnaire de Poche Francais-Chinois. Commercial Press Staff. 558p. (CHI & FRE.). 1975. pap. 14.95 (*0-8288-5849-7*, M9579) Fr & Eur.

Dictionnaire de Poetique. Michele Aquien. 344p. (FRE.). 1993. pap. 22.95 (*0-7859-5627-1*, 2253063622) Fr & Eur.

Dictionnaire De Poetique et De Rhetorique. 4th ed. Henri Morier. 1320p. (FRE.). 1989. 350.00 (*0-7859-0469-7*, 2130400973) Fr & Eur.

Dictionnaire de Politique: Coll. le Present en Question: Dictionary of Politics. 350p. (FRE.). 1979. 39.95 (*0-8288-4794-0*, M6124) Fr & Eur.

***Dictionnaire de Politique Internationale.** Charles Zorgbibe. 736p. (FRE.). 1988. pap. 85.00 (*0-7859-8623-5*, 213041897x) Fr & Eur.

Dictionnaire de Proverbes & Dictons. Jean Robert. 45.00 (*0-317-45633-4*) Fr & Eur.

***Dictionnaire de Psychologie.** Roland Doron. 776p. (FRE.). 1991. pap. 175.00 (*0-7859-7744-9*, 2130435513) Fr & Eur.

Dictionnaire de Psychologie en Trois Langues (Dictionary of Psychology in Three Languages) French-German-English, Vol. 2. Hubert C. Duijker. 356p. 1977. ring bd. 165.00 (*0-7859-4782-5*, M4660) Fr & Eur.

Dictionnaire de Psychologie en 3 Langues, 3 vols. Hubert C. Duijker & Maria Van Sijswijk. 416p. (ENG, FRE & GER.). 1977. ring bd. 165.00 (*0-7859-0938-9*, M-4661) Fr & Eur.

***Dictionnaire de Rhetorique.** Georges Molinie. 352p. (FRE.). 1992. pap. 22.95 (*0-7859-8635-9*, 225306257x) Fr & Eur.

***Dictionnaire de Sciences Biologiques du College a L'Universite.** Jean-Louis Morere. 320p. (FRE.). 1991. pap. 69.95 (*0-7859-7978-6*, 2729841261) Fr & Eur.

Dictionnaire De Sigillographie Pratique. Louis-Alphonse Chassant & P. J. Delbarre. vi, 264p. reprint ed. write for info. (*3-487-07942-9*, Pub. by Georg Olms GW) Lubrecht & Cramer.

***Dictionnaire de Sigles Domaines Economique et Sociaux.** Danielle Candel. 740p. (FRE.). 1992. 155.00 (*0-7859-8105-5*, 2856080456) Fr & Eur.

Dictionnaire de Sigles Nationaux et Internationaux: Dictionary of National & International Siglas. Michel Dubois. 479p. (FRE.). 1977. pap. 125.00 (*0-8288-5384-3*, M6609) Fr & Eur.

***Dictionnaire de Sociologie.** Gilles Ferreol. 300p. (FRE.). 1991. pap. 32.95 (*0-7859-7759-7*, 2200330790) Fr & Eur.

Dictionnaire de Sociologie: Dictionary of Sociology. Joseph Sumpf & Michel Hugues. 256p. (FRE.). 1973. pap. 24.95 (*0-7859-0767-X*, M-6527) Fr & Eur.

Dictionnaire de Sociologie: Sociology - Dictionary. Emilio Willems. 314p. (FRE.). 1970. pap. 29.95 (*0-8288-6517-5*, M-6573) Fr & Eur.

Dictionnaire de Spiritualite. Andre Derville. 1993. pap. 325.00 (*0-7859-5633-6*, 2701012783) Fr & Eur.

Dictionnaire de Spiritualite: Dictionary of Spirituality, 12 vols., Set. Andre Rayez. (FRE.). 1970. 4,995.00 (*0-8288-6518-3*, M-6565) Fr & Eur.

***Dictionnaire de Sylviculture: French, German, English, Spanish, Italian.** Alberto Bruttini. 384p. (FRE, GER & SPA.). 1930. pap. 95.00 (*0-7859-7963-8*, 2720501670) Fr & Eur.

***Dictionnaire de Synonymes pour Mots Croises, Par Nombre de Lettres.** Paul Martin. 110p. (FRE.). 1986. pap. 12.95 (*0-7859-8081-4*, 2853191737) Fr & Eur.

Dictionnaire de Theologie. Peter Eicher. 1988. lib. bdg. 275.00 (*0-8288-2592-0*, 2204027707) Fr & Eur.

Dictionnaire de Theologie Catholique, Tables Generales: De Raison a Stolz: Dictionary of Catholic Theology, 3 vols., Set. Bernard Loth & Albert Michel. (FRE.). 1970. 995.00 (*0-8288-6519-1*, M-6379) Fr & Eur.

***Dictionnaire de Votre Argent.** Nathalie Cadart. (FRE.). 1989. pap. 45.00 (*0-614-00411-X*, 2501012496) Fr & Eur.

***Dictionnaire D'Economie.** Jean-Pierre Paulet. 265p. (FRE.). 1992. pap. 49.95 (*0-7859-7771-6*, 2212008082) Fr & Eur.

Dictionnaire d'Economie et de Sciences Sociales. Jean-Yves Capul. 475p. 1993. pap. 29.95 (*0-7859-5616-6*, 2218059363) Fr & Eur.

***Dictionnaire d'Economie et de Sciences Sociales.** Claude-Daniele Echaudemaison. 447p. (FRE.). 1993. pap. 28.95 (*0-7859-7725-2*, 2091803162) Fr & Eur.

***Dictionnaire d'Economie, Finance, Banque et Comptabilite: French-English-Italian.** Michel Valente. 1516p. (ENG, FRE & ITA.). 1993. 295.00 (*0-7859-7844-5*, 2247016359) Fr & Eur.

***Dictionnaire d'Emile Zola: Dictionnaire des Rougon-Macquart.** Colette Becker. 720p. (FRE.). 1993. pap. 49.95 (*0-7859-7813-5*, 2221076125) Fr & Eur.

***Dictionnaire D'Epidemiologie.** Jammal. 171p. (FRE.). 1988. pap. 65.00 (*0-7859-7820-8*, 2224018029) Fr & Eur.

Dictionnaire D'Epidemiologie. Annette Leclerc et al. 143p. (FRE.). 1990. write for info. (*0-7859-0506-5*, 2876710382) Fr & Eur.

Dictionnaire des Abreviations Courantes de la Langue Francaise. J. C. Faudouas. 256p. (FRE.). 1992. 75.00 (*0-7859-5658-1*, 2856080383) Fr & Eur.

Dictionnaire Des Abreviations Latines et Francaises. Louis-Alphonse Chassant. xlviii, 172p. 1989. reprint ed. write for info. (*3-487-05406-X*, Pub. by Georg Olms GW) Lubrecht & Cramer.

Dictionnaire des Abreviations Latines et Francaises Usitees Dans les Inscriptions Lapidaires et Metalliques, le Manuscrits et les Chartes Du Moyen Age. Louis A. Chassant. xlviii, 172p. 1970. reprint ed. write for info. (*0-318-72005-1*, Pub. by Georg Olms GW) Lubrecht & Cramer.

Dictionnaire des Affaires Francais-Anglais, Anglais-Francais. Delmas-Harrap. 508p. (ENG & FRE.). 1981. 75.00 (*0-8288-9544-9*, M9452) Fr & Eur.

Dictionnaire des Aliments pour les Animaux. Marcello Picconi. 620p. (FRE.). 1965. 65.00 (*0-8288-6741-0*, M-6452) Fr & Eur.

Dictionnaire des Americanismes. 8th ed. Etienne Deak & Simone Deak. 823p. (FRE.). 1987. pap. 69.95 (*0-7859-4818-X*, M6103) Fr & Eur.

***Dictionnaire des Anciennes Familles de Touraine.** Luc Boisnard. 464p. (FRE.). 1992. 250.00 (*0-7859-8101-2*, 2855540542) Fr & Eur.

Dictionnaire des Anecdotes Historiques. Armand Isnard. 371p. 1993. pap. 49.95 (*0-7859-5647-6*, 2840690160) Fr & Eur.

Dictionnaire des Anglicismes (Dictionary of Anglicisms) G. Rey-Debove. 1150p. (FRE.). 1990. 75.00 (*0-7859-4769-8*, M3259) Fr & Eur.

Dictionnaire des Animaux. Richard Scarry. 96p. (FRE.). (J). (gr. 3-8). 1992. 39.95 (*0-7859-1543-5*, 2719203341) Fr & Eur.

Dictionnaire des Anthropologistes. Paul-Emile Duroux. 336p. (FRE.). 1974. pap. 59.95 (*0-8288-6018-1*, M6182) Fr & Eur.

***Dictionnaire des Antiquites Romaines et Gracques.** Anthony Rich. 740p. (FRE.). 1987. pap. 79.95 (*0-7859-8067-9*, 2851994255) Fr & Eur.

***Dictionnaire des Arbres et Arbustes des Jardins.** Andre Belot. 399p. (FRE.). 1989. 95.00 (*0-7859-8240-X*, 2908041006) Fr & Eur.

***Dictionnaire des Architectes de l'Antiquite a nos Jours.** Bernard Oudin. 568p. (FRE.). 1983. pap. 34.95 (*0-7859-7796-1*, 2221010906) Fr & Eur.

Dictionnaire des Argots Francais. Esnault. (FRE.). 22.65 (*0-7859-0626-6*, F136740) Fr & Eur.

***Dictionnaire des Articles Medico-Chirurgicaux, Articles de Pansements.** ETIM Staff. 1200p. (FRE.). 1988. 295.00 (*0-7859-8231-0*, 2905201045) Fr & Eur.

***Dictionnaire des Artistes et Ouvriers d'Art de Bourgogne Vol. 1: A-K.** Sylvain Laveissiere. 290p. (FRE.). 1980. pap. 145.00 (*0-7859-8066-0*, 2851890069) Fr & Eur.

***Dictionnaire des Arts de Peinture et Gravure, 5 vols.** fac. ed. Claude-Henri Watelet. (FRE.). 1972. 895.00 (*0-7859-8044-X*, 2826602764) Fr & Eur.

***Dictionnaire des Arts Martiaux.** Louis Frederic. 384p. (FRE.). 1988. 65.00 (*0-7859-8151-9*, 2866450396) Fr & Eur.

***Dictionnaire des Arts Metiers et Professions.** Alfred Franklin. 856p. (FRE.). 1987. 49.95 (*0-7859-7125-4*, M9135) Fr & Eur.

Dictionnaire des Assassins. rev. ed. Rene Reouven. 429p. (FRE.). 1986. 85.00 (*0-7859-4844-9*) Fr & Eur.

***Dictionnaire des Associations et des Mutuelles.** 2nd ed. Marie-Therese Gravier. 216p. (FRE.). 1988. pap. 59.95 (*0-7859-8146-2*, 2865440303) Fr & Eur.

Dictionnaire des Assurances Sociales. Jean-Charles Sournia. 112p. (FRE.). 1973. 75.00 (*0-8288-6259-1*, M-6522) Fr & Eur.

Dictionnaire Des Athees Anciens et Modernes. Pierre S. Marechal. 438p. reprint ed. write for info. (*0-318-71376-4*, Pub. by Georg Olms GW) Lubrecht & Cramer.

Dictionnaire des Auteurs, 4 vols., Set. Robert Laffont. 1980. lib. bdg. 150.00 (*0-8288-2614-5*, F12570) Fr & Eur.

Dictionnaire des Auteurs de Langue Francaise. Yves-Alain Favre. 1980. lib. bdg. 45.00 (*0-8288-2591-2*, 2705002944) Fr & Eur.

***Dictionnaire des Auteurs de Langue Francaise en Amerique du Nord.** Reginald Hamel. 1364p. (FRE.). 1992. pap. 125.00 (*0-7859-8027-X*, 2762114756) Fr & Eur.

Dictionnaire des Auteurs de Tous les Temps et de Tous les Pays, 2 tomes, Set. 109.50 (*0-685-36080-6*) Fr & Eur.

***Dictionnaire des Auteurs du Radio-Feuilleton Quebecois.** Renee Legris. 200p. (FRE.). 1981. pap. 29.95 (*0-7859-8026-1*, 2762110904) Fr & Eur.

***Dictionnaire des Auteurs et des Themes de la Philosophie.** Sylvain Auroux. 526p. (FRE.). 1991. pap. 36.95 (*0-7859-7607-8*, 2010159705) Fr & Eur.

***Dictionnaire des Auteurs Grecs et Latins de l'Antiquite et du Moyen Age.** Wolfgang Buchwald. 897p. (FRE.). 1992. 135.00 (*0-7859-7901-8*, 2503500161) Fr & Eur.

***Dictionnaire des Auteurs Maghrebins Se Langue Francaise.** Jean Dejeux. 400p. (FRE.). 1984. pap. 59.95 (*0-7859-8144-6*, 2865370852) Fr & Eur.

Dictionnaire des Auteurs, Vol. 4: Qa-Zw. Robert Laffont. 759p. (FRE.). 1980. pap. 45.00 (*0-7859-4429-X*, 2221501756) Fr & Eur.

Dictionnaire des Autorites. Georges Vajda. 226p. (FRE.). 1963. pap. 35.00 (*0-8288-6786-0*, M-6611) Fr & Eur.

Dictionnaire des Belgicismes. Joseph Hanse. (FRE.). 1991. lib. bdg. 95.00 (*0-8288-9749-2*, 2801109649) Fr & Eur.

Dictionnaire des Belgicismes, 2 vols., Set. Francois Massion. 946p. (FRE.). 1987. write for info. (*0-8288-9464-7*) Fr & Eur.

Dictionnaire des Biographies, 2 vols., Set. Pierre Grimal. (FRE.). 1958. 395.00 (*0-8288-7400-X*, F12930) Fr & Eur.

Dictionnaire des Biographies, 2 Tomes, Set. Grinial. 67.90 (*0-685-35950-6*) Fr & Eur.

***Dictionnaire des Biographies Vol. 1: L'Antiquite.** Jean-Maurice Biziere. 272p. (FRE.). 1992. pap. 34.95 (*0-7859-7753-8*, 2200211074) Fr & Eur.

***Dictionnaire des Biographies Vol. 2: Le Moyen Age.** Jean-Maurice Biziere. 309p. (FRE.). 1993. pap. 39.95 (*0-7859-7757-0*, 2200213719) Fr & Eur.

***Dictionnaire des Biographies Vol. 3: La France Moderne.** Jean-Maurice Biziere. 272p. (FRE.). 1993. pap. 36.95 (*0-7859-7754-6*, 2200211082) Fr & Eur.

***Dictionnaire des Biographies Vol. 5: XIXe Siecle.** Jean-Maurice Biziere. 256p. (FRE.). 1994. pap. 36.95 (*0-7859-7755-4*, 2200211090) Fr & Eur.

***Dictionnaire des Biographies Vol. 6: Twentieth Century.** Jean-Maurice Biziere. 272p. (FRE.). 1992. pap. 39.95 (*0-7859-7756-2*, 2200212313) Fr & Eur.

***Dictionnaire des Bruits.** Jean-Claude Trait. 449p. (FRE.). 1990. pap. 12.95 (*0-7859-8024-5*, 2761908414) Fr & Eur.

***Dictionnaire des Calories.** Christopher Arden. 192p. (FRE.). 1990. pap. 12.95 (*0-7859-7983-2*, 2732841307) Fr & Eur.

Dictionnaire des Changements de Noms 1803-1956. Jerome. 238p. (FRE.). 1964. pap. 23.95 (*0-8288-6764-X*, M-6613) Fr & Eur.

Dictionnaire des Changements de Noms 1957-1962. Jerome. 104p. (FRE.). 1964. pap. 23.95 (*0-8288-6765-8*, M-6614) Fr & Eur.

Dictionnaire des Chansons de la Revolution. G. Marty. 1988. lib. bdg. 89.95 (*0-8288-2590-4*, 2235018009) Fr & Eur.

***Dictionnaire des Chanteurs de l'Opera de Paris du 17e Siecle a Nos Jours.** Jean Gourret. 320p. (FRE.). 1987. 79.95 (*0-7859-7975-1*, 2727301642) Fr & Eur.

***Dictionnaire des Chanteurs Francophones de 1900 a nos Jours.** Alain-Pierre Noyer. 210p. (FRE.). 1989. pap. 59.95 (*0-7859-8082-2*, 2853192091) Fr & Eur.

***Dictionnaire Des Charades.** Nelly Charbonneaux. (FRE.). 1994. pap. 14.95 (*0-614-00408-X*) Fr & Eur.

***Dictionnaire des Charades.** Nelly Charbonneaux. 1994p. 1994. pap. 14.95 (*0-7859-7629-9*) Fr & Eur.

Dictionnaire des Chateaux de France: Bourgogne-Nivernais: Dictionary of the Chateaux of France: Bourgogne-Nivernais. Francoise Vignier. 300p. (FRE.). 1980. 135.00 (*0-8288-1193-8*, M6615) Fr & Eur.

An Asterisk (*) at the beginning of an entry indicates that the title is appearing in BIP for the first time. 1975

Dictionnaire des Cineastes. 4th enl. rev. ed. George Sadoul. 357p. (FRE.). 1990. pap. 19.95 (*0-7859-4707-8*, F79854) Fr & Eur.

***Dictionnaire Des Citations.** Olivier Millet. 409p. (FRE.). 1992. pap. 16.95 (*0-7859-7859-3*, 2253061409) Fr & Eur.

***Dictionnaire Des Citations Chretiennes.** Jean Dorcase. 610p. (FRE.). 1990. 115.00 (*0-7859-7837-2*, 2227362189) Fr & Eur.

***Dictionnaire des Citations de l'Histoire de France.** Michele Ressi. 800p. (FRE.). 1992. pap. 155.00 (*0-7859-7880-1*, 2268010171) Fr & Eur.

Dictionnaire des Citations du Monde Entier. Jean Robert. 45.00 (*0-317-45621-0*) Fr & Eur.

***Dictionnaire des Citations Francaises et Etrangeres.** Florence Montreynuad. 544p. (FRE.). 1985. 69.95 (*0-7859-7727-9*, 2092910612) Fr & Eur.

***Dictionnaire des Combinaisons Alimentaires.** A. Tentori. 232p. (FRE.). 1991. pap. 55.00 (*0-7859-7982-4*, 2732807680) Fr & Eur.

***Dictionnaire des Communes.** Lavauzelle Staff. 1787p. (FRE.). 1984. 125.00 (*0-7859-7915-8*, 2702500757) Fr & Eur.

***Dictionnaire des Communes Vol. 1: Departement de la Meuse.** fac. ed. H. Lemoine. (FRE.). 1991. pap. 185.00 (*0-7859-8250-7*, 2909112047) Fr & Eur.

***Dictionnaire des Communes Vol. 2: Departement du Loiret.** fac. ed. Patron. 586p. (FRE.). 1991. pap. 115.00 (*0-7859-8248-5*, 2909112012); pap. 125.00 (*0-7859-8249-3*, 2909112020) Fr & Eur.

Dictionnaire des Communes (de France) (FRE.). 20.95 (*0-685-36659-6*) Fr & Eur.

***Dictionnaire des Communes Savoyardes.** Philippe Paillard. 450p. (FRE.). 1981. 150.00 (*0-7859-7949-2*, 2717102299) Fr & Eur.

***Dictionnaire des Communes, Vaucluse.** Robert Bailly. 476p. (FRE.). 1986. 95.00 (*0-7859-8211-6*, 2903044279) Fr & Eur.

***Dictionnaire des Composants Electroniques.** Dunod Staff. 256p. (FRE.). 1994. pap. 75.00 (*0-7859-7730-9*, 2100012932) Fr & Eur.

***Dictionnaire des Compositeurs de Musique en Bretagne.** Vefa de Bellaing. 280p. (FRE.). 1992. pap. 75.00 (*0-7859-8243-4*, 2908261111) Fr & Eur.

Dictionnaire des Constantes Biologiques et Physiques: Dictionary of Biological & Physical Constants. 5th ed. Alain Blacque-Belair. 2200p. (FRE.). 1980. 175.00 (*0-8288-1219-5*, M15349) Fr & Eur.

***Dictionnaire des Constituants 1789-91, 2 vols.** Edna H. Lemay. (FRE.). 1991. 395.00 (*0-7859-8019-9*, 2740000030) Fr & Eur.

***Dictionnaire des Correspondents de Teilhard de Chardin.** Gerard-Henry Baudard. 200p. (FRE.). 1974. pap. 18.95 (*0-7859-8204-3*, 2900588030) Fr & Eur.

***Dictionnaire des Decouvertes.** Roger Caratini. 486p. (FRE.). 1990. 115.00 (*0-7859-8136-5*, 2863913522) Fr & Eur.

***Dictionnaire Des Devises Heraldiques: Avec Supplement.** Louis-Alphonse Chassant. 1624p. (FRE.). Date not set. 165.00 (*0-7859-8402-X*, 3487071827) Fr & Eur.

Dictionnaire Des Devises Historiques et Heraldiques - Supplement Au Dictionnaire Des Devises Historiques et Heraldiques, 3 vols. in 1. Louis-Alphonse Chassant & Henri Tausin. xlviii, 1624p. 1980. reprint ed. write for info. (*3-487-07180-0*, Pub. by Georg Olms GW) Lubrecht & Cramer.

***Dictionnaire des Difficultes: French-English, English-French.** Lilian Hecart-Evans. 195p. (FRE.). 1991. pap. 13.95 (*0-7859-7984-0*, 2732841471) Fr & Eur.

Dictionnaire des Difficultes de la Langue Francaise. Larousse Staff. 435p. (FRE.). 1992. 55.00 (*0-7859-0962-1*, 2033409023) Fr & Eur.

***Dictionnaire des Difficultes de la Langue Francaise au Canada.** 2nd ed. Gerard Dagenias. 538p. (FRE.). 1984. 39.95 (*0-7859-8023-7*, 2761810376) Fr & Eur.

Dictionnaire des Difficultes du Francais. Jean Robert. 45.00 (*0-317-45622-9*) Fr & Eur.

***Dictionnaire des Dinosaures.** Rupert Matthews. 48p. (FRE.). 1990. 22.95 (*0-7859-7960-3*, 2719215236) Fr & Eur.

***Dictionnaire des Diplomates de Napolean Histoire et Dictionnaire du Corps Diplomatique Consulaire et Imperial.** Jacques Henri-Robert. 368p. (FRE.). 1990. 125.00 (*0-7859-8068-7*, 2851995340) Fr & Eur.

***Dictionnaire des Disques et des Compacts Guide Critique de la Musique Classique Enregistree.** 4th ed. Jean-Michel Damian. 1367p. (FRE.). 1991. pap. 59.95 (*0-7859-7807-0*, 2221066820) Fr & Eur.

***Dictionnaire des Domaines de L'Unesco: Education, Science Sociales, Culture et Commmunication: English, French, Russian, Bulgarian.** Yvan Venev. 230p. (BUL, FRE & RUS.). 1984. pap. 95.00 (*0-7859-7950-6*, 2717807772) Fr & Eur.

Dictionnaire des Dynasties Bourgecises et du Monde des Affaires. Ed. by Henry Coston. 599p. (FRE.). 1975. 75.00 (*0-8288-5850-0*, M6617) Fr & Eur.

Dictionnaire des Echecs. 2nd ed. Francois Le Lionnais & E. Maget. (FRE.). 1984. 115.00 (*0-8288-2341-3*, F60500) Fr & Eur.

Dictionnaire des Ecrivains Francais: Dictionary of French Writers. Jean Malignon. 576p. (FRE.). 1971. 39.95 (*0-8288-6445-4*, M-6388) Fr & Eur.

***Dictionnaire des Ecrivains Francais pour la Jeunesse 1914-1991.** Nic Diament. 783p. (FRE.). 1993. 325.00 (*0-7859-7767-8*, 2211071252) Fr & Eur.

***Dictionnaire des Editeurs de Musique Francais Vol. 1: Origines a 1820.** Anik Devries. 770p. (FRE.). 1979. 495.00 (*0-7859-8045-8*, 2826604600) Fr & Eur.

***Dictionnaire des Editeurs de Musique Francais Vol. 2: 1820-1914.** Anik Devries. 512p. (FRE.). 1988. 550.00 (*0-7859-8046-6*, 2826604619) Fr & Eur.

***Dictionnaire des Editeurs d'Estampes a Paris Sous l'Ancien Regime.** Maxime Preaud. 334p. (FRE.). 1987. pap. 145.00 (*0-7859-8214-0*, 2903181608) Fr & Eur.

Dictionnaire des Eglises de France, 5 tomes. Incl. Tome I. Histoire Generale des Eglises de France. 91.95 (*0-685-73261-4*); Tome II. Region Centre et Sud-Est. 91.95 (*0-685-73262-2*); Tome III. Region Sud-Ouest. 91.95 (*0-685-73263-0*); Tome IV. Region ouest de Paris, Paris et ses environs, Bretagne, Normandie. 91.95 (*0-685-73264-9*); Tome V. Nord, Est, Belgique, Luxembourg, Suisse. 91.95 (*0-685-73265-7*); write for info. (*0-318-51980-1*) Fr & Eur.

***Dictionnaire des Engins de Peche.** Jean-Paul George. 278p. (FRE.). 1991. pap. 79.95 (*0-7859-8012-1*, 2737308380) Fr & Eur.

***Dictionnaire des Eponymes Medicaux: French-English.** Henri Van Hoof. 405p. (ENG & FRE.). 1993. pap. 105.00 (*0-7859-8187-X*, 2877230716) Fr & Eur.

***Dictionnaire Des Examens Biologiques et Investigations Paracliniques.** 3rd ed. Herve Durand. 488p. (FRE.). 1991. pap. 110.00 (*0-7859-7917-4*, 2704006687) Fr & Eur.

***Dictionnaire des Expressions.** Bruno Lafleur. 672p. (FRE.). 1984. 59.95 (*0-7859-7698-1*, 2040152679) Fr & Eur.

Dictionnaire des Expressions & Locutions Figurees. Jean Robert. 45.00 (*0-317-45624-5*) Fr & Eur.

***Dictionnaire des Expressions Imagees.** Robert Galisson. 144p. (FRE.). 1984. 26.95 (*0-7859-7752-X*, 2190332729) Fr & Eur.

***Dictionnaire des Expressions Juridiques.** Henri Roland. 440p. (FRE.). 1983. pap. 36.95 (*0-7859-8116-0*, 2859341102) Fr & Eur.

***Dictionnaire des Expressions Paillardes et Libertines de la Litterature Francaise.** Jean-Marc Richard. 271p. (FRE.). 1993. pap. 49.95 (*0-7859-8053-9*, 2850183806) Fr & Eur.

***Dictionnaire des Facteurs d'Instruments de Musique en Wallonie et a Bruxelles du 9e Siecle a Nos Jours.** Malou Haine. 770p. (FRE.). 1986. 250.00 (*0-7859-8171-3*, 2870092504) Fr & Eur.

Dictionnaire des Faux-Amis Francais - Anglais. Jacques Van Roey. 794p. (ENG & FRE.). 1991. pap. 65.00 (*0-7859-4577-6*) Fr & Eur.

Dictionnaire des Femmes. (FRE.). 8.95 (*0-686-56844-3*) Fr & Eur.

***Dictionnaire des Femmes Celebres.** Lucienne Mazenod. 940p. (FRE.). 1992. pap. 59.95 (*0-7859-7803-8*, 2221052927) Fr & Eur.

Dictionnaire des Figures et des Personnages. C. Aziza et al. 464p. (FRE.). 1981. 39.95 (*0-8288-1218-7*, M14213) Fr & Eur.

Dictionnaire des Forets. 5th ed. Georges Plaisance. (FRE.). 1975. pap. 49.95 (*0-8288-5851-9*, M6457) Fr & Eur.

Dictionnaire des Frequences, Vocabulaire Litteraire des 19 et 20 Siecles, 4 vols. Ed. by Centre de Recherche Pour un Tresor de la Langue Francaise Staff. 2284p. (FRE.). 1976. pap. 110.00 (*0-8288-5641-9*, M6620) Fr & Eur.

Dictionnaire des Fromages: Cheese Dictionary. Robert H. Courtine. 250p. (FRE.). 1972. pap. 17.95 (*0-8288-6374-1*, F83160) Fr & Eur.

***Dictionnaire des Grandes Oeuvres de la Litterature Francaise.** Robert Staff. 720p. (FRE.). 1992. 85.00 (*0-7859-8060-1*, 2850361968) Fr & Eur.

***Dictionnaire des Grands Economistes.** Janine Bremond. 192p. (FRE.). 1992. pap. 32.95 (*0-7859-8251-5*, 2909420027) Fr & Eur.

Dictionnaire des Grands Evenements de l'Histoire: Dictionary of the Great Events of History. Georges Masquet. 315p. (FRE.). 1973. pap. 15.95 (*0-8288-6260-5*, M-174) Fr & Eur.

***Dictionnaire Des Grands Nome de la Seconde Guerre Mondiale.** John Keegan. 224p. (FRE.). 1982. 75.00 (*0-7859-7863-1*, 2258030013) Fr & Eur.

***Dictionnaire des Grands Noms de la Chose Imprimee.** Jean-Claude Faudouas. 190p. (FRE.). 1991. pap. 39.95 (*0-7859-7969-7*, 2725613922) Fr & Eur.

***Dictionnaire des Gros Maux de L'Entreprise.** Jissey Helbe. 109p. (FRE.). 1990. 49.95 (*0-7859-7966-2*, 2723412857) Fr & Eur.

Dictionnaire des Groupes Industriels & Financiers en France. 360p. (FRE.). 1978. 17.95 (*0-686-57102-9*) Fr & Eur.

Dictionnaire des Heresies Meridionales. Rene Nelli. 384p. (FRE.). 18.50 (*0-8288-9194-X*) Fr & Eur.

***Dictionnaire des Histoires Droles Super Erotiques.** Claude Laborde. (FRE.). 1993. pap. 45.00 (*0-7859-8051-2*, 2840690543) Fr & Eur.

Dictionnaire des Hommes de Theatre Francais Contemporains. 152p. (FRE.). pap. 39.95 (*0-7859-0724-6*, F-17640) Fr & Eur.

Dictionnaire des Homonymes de la Langue Francaise. Jean Camion. 683p. (FRE.). 1986. lib. bdg. 135.00 (*0-8288-2588-2*, 2906444006) Fr & Eur.

***Dictionnaire des Huiles Vegetales.** Paul Mensier. 771p. (FRE.). 1957. pap. 165.00 (*0-7859-7964-6*, 2720504211) Fr & Eur.

Dictionnaire des Idees dans l'Oeuvre d'Andre Malraux. Ileana Juilland. 325p. (FRE.). 1968. 45.00 (*0-8288-6633-3*, F-11080) Fr & Eur.

Dictionnaire des Idees dans l'Oeuvre de Marcel Proust. Pauline Newman Gordon. (FRE.). 1968. 59.95 (*0-8288-6634-1*, M-6624) Fr & Eur.

Dictionnaire des Idees dans l'Oeuvre de Simone de Beauvoir. Christian van den Berghe. (Collection Dictionnaires des Idees, Litterature Francaise: No. 1). (FRE.). 1966. 21.50 (*0-686-20917-6*) Mouton.

Dictionnaire des Idees dans l'Oeuvre de Simone de Beauvoir. Christian L. Van den Berghe. 290p. (FRE.). 1966. 39.95 (*0-8288-6708-9*, F85920) Fr & Eur.

Dictionnaire des Idees par le Mots. Jean Robert. 45.00 (*0-317-45630-X*) Fr & Eur.

***Dictionnaire des Identites Culturelles de la Francophonie.** Psul Wijnands. 447p. (FRE.). 1993. 150.00 (*0-7859-8084-9*, 2853192490) Fr & Eur.

***Dictionnaire Des Illustrateurs: 1890-1945, No. 2.** Marcus Osterwalder. 1384p. (FRE.). 1989. text ed. 325.00 (*0-7859-8038-5*, 2825800392) Fr & Eur.

***Dictionnaire des Illustrateurs Vol. 1: 1800-1914.** Marcus Osterwalder. 1223p. (FRE.). 1989. 325.00 (*0-7859-8037-7*, 2825800309) Fr & Eur.

***Dictionnaire des Industries: German-French, French-German.** Christian Schmitt. 1183p. (FRE & GER.). 1993. 595.00 (*0-7859-8083-0*, 2853192474) Fr & Eur.

Dictionnaire des Industries Alimentaires. Jean-Michel Clement. 361p. (FRE.). 1978. 85.00 (*0-8288-5184-0*, M6071) Fr & Eur.

***Dictionnaire des Inquisateurs.** Galilee Staff. 464p. (FRE.). 1981. pap. 75.00 (*0-7859-7958-1*, 2718602007) Fr & Eur.

***Dictionnaire des Jeux de Lettres.** Larousse Staff. 1088p. (FRE.). 1994. pap. 32.95 (*0-7859-7689-2*, 2037300913) Fr & Eur.

Dictionnaire des Journalistes, 1600-1789. Jean Sgard & Michel Gilot. 1210p. (FRE.). 1991. 595.00 (*0-7859-4838-4*) Fr & Eur.

Dictionnaire des Journaux. G. N. Henderson & D. J. Coffey. 272p. (FRE.). 1986. 110.00 (*0-7859-4825-2*) Fr & Eur.

***Dictionnaire des Lettres Francaises Vol. 1: Moyen Age.** Georges Grente. 1568p. (FRE.). 1992. pap. 75.00 (*0-7859-7857-7*, 2253056626) Fr & Eur.

Dictionnaire des Lettres Francaises (le Moyen Age) Georges F. Grente. 768p. (FRE.). 1972. 79.95 (*0-8288-6375-X*, M-6577) Fr & Eur.

Dictionnaire des Lettres Francaises, 18e Siecle (A-K), 2 vols. Georges F. Grente. 672p. (FRE.). 1960. 175.00 (*0-8288-6836-0*, M-6578) Fr & Eur.

Dictionnaire des Lettres Francaises, 18e Siecle (L-Z), 2 vols. Georges F. Grente. 568p. (FRE.). 1973. 85.00 (*0-8288-6261-3*, M-6580) Fr & Eur.

Dictionnaire des Lettres Francaises, 19e Siecle: A-K. Georges F. Grente. 549p. (FRE.). 1971. 85.00 (*0-685-57712-0*, M-6296) Fr & Eur.

Dictionnaire des Lettres Francaises, 19e Siecle: L-Z. Georges F. Grente. 568p. (FRE.). 1973. 85.00 (*0-8288-6262-1*, M-6297) Fr & Eur.

Dictionnaire des Lieux qui Racontent l'Histoire. Gilles Henri. 280p. 1993. pap. 55.00 (*0-7859-5621-2*, 2235021166) Fr & Eur.

Dictionnaire des Litteratures, 3 vols., Set. Philippe Van Tieghem. 1968. 150.00 (*0-685-61099-3*) Fr & Eur.

Dictionnaire des Litteratures, Vol. 1: A-F. Philippe Van Tieghem. 1461p. 1968. write for info. (*0-8288-7449-2*) Fr & Eur.

Dictionnaire des Litteratures, Vol. 2: G-N. Philippe Van Tieghem. 1440p. 1968. write for info. (*0-8288-7450-6*) Fr & Eur.

Dictionnaire des Litteratures, Vol. 3: O-Z. Philippe Van Tieghem. 1440p. 1968. write for info. (*0-8288-7451-4*) Fr & Eur.

Dictionnaire des Litteratures de Langue Francaise, Vol. 2, E-L. Jean-Pierre De Beaumarchais. 774p. (FRE.). 1994. lib. bdg. 185.00 (*0-7859-3950-4*, 2040163522) Fr & Eur.

Dictionnaire des Litteratures de Langue Francaise, Vol. 3, M-R. Jean-Pierre De Beaumarchais. 764p. (FRE.). 1984. lib. bdg. 185.00 (*0-7859-3951-2*) Fr & Eur.

***Dictionnaire des Litteratures de Langue Francaise, Vol. 4 S-Z.** Jean P. Beaumarchais. 665p. (FRE.). 1994. 185.00 (*0-7859-3952-0*) Fr & Eur.

Dictionnaire des Litteratures de Langue Francaise, Vol. 4, S-Z. Jean-Pierre De Beaumarchais. (FRE.). 1984. lib. bdg. 185.00 (*0-685-68102-5*) Fr & Eur.

***Dictionnaire des Litteratures Francaise et Etrangeres.** Jacques Demougin. 1861p. (FRE.). 1992. pap. 250.00 (*0-7859-7667-1*, 2035083044) Fr & Eur.

***Dictionnaire des Litteratures Suisses.** Pierre-Olivier Walzer. 500p. (FRE.). 1991. pap. 55.00 (*0-7859-8198-5*, 2881080774) Fr & Eur.

***Dictionnaire des Locutions en Moyen Francais.** Giuseppe Di Stefano. 930p. (FRE.). 1992. 375.00 (*0-7859-8595-6*, 0919089550) Fr & Eur.

***Dictionnaire des Locutions Idiomatiques Francaises.** Bruno Lafleur. 669p. (FRE.). 1980. pap. 105.00 (*0-7859-8292-2*, 3261048042) Fr & Eur.

***Dictionnaire des Locutions Populaires du Bon Pays de Rennes en Bretagne.** H. Coulabin. 392p. (FRE.). 1978. 85.00 (*0-7859-7989-1*, 2734802961) Fr & Eur.

***Dictionnaire des Malades: Choix des Examens Complementaires.** Herve Durand. 316p. (FRE.). 1989. pap. 79.95 (*0-7859-7916-6*, 2704005982) Fr & Eur.

***Dictionnaire des Matechaux de France du Moyen Age a nos Jours.** Genevieve Maze-Sencier. 452p. (FRE.). 1988. 115.00 (*0-7859-8637-5*, 226200546x) Fr & Eur.

***Dictionnaire des Mathematiques.** 4th ed. Alain Bouvier. 968p. (FRE.). 1993. 235.00 (*0-7859-7750-3*, 2130454917) Fr & Eur.

Dictionnaire des Matieres Plastiques. Annemarie Wittfoht. 325p. (ENG & FRE.). 1976. pap. 52.50 (*0-7859-0728-9*, M-6574) Fr & Eur.

Dictionnaire des Media. Jean-Baptiste Fages & Christian Pagano. 364p. (FRE.). 1971. pap. 39.95 (*0-8288-6447-0*, M-6626) Fr & Eur.

***Dictionnaire des Medicaments.** Vittorio Fattorusso. 1000p. (FRE.). 1992. 79.95 (*0-7859-7832-1*, 2225826935) Fr & Eur.

***Dictionnaire des Medicaments.** Jean Thuillier. 940p. (FRE.). 1990. pap. 55.00 (*0-7859-7809-7*, 2221067916) Fr & Eur.

Dictionnaire des Medicaments: Dictionary of Medications. Maurice Neuman. 432p. (FRE.). 1971. pap. 35.00 (*0-8288-6446-2*, M-6424) Fr & Eur.

***Dictionnaire des Medicaments Conseil.** 5th ed. Jean-Marie Hardre. 513p. (FRE.). 1992. pap. 85.00 (*0-7859-8074-1*, 2852704366) Fr & Eur.

***Dictionnaire des Medicaments Veterinaires et des Parapharmacies Animales.** 6th ed. Etienne Meisonnier. 1328p. (FRE.). 1992. pap. 110.00 (*0-7859-8659-6*, 286326091x) Fr & Eur.

***Dictionnaire des Meubles et Objets D'Art: 8,000 Prix En Ventes Publiques.** Enrique Mayer. 720p. (FRE.). 1993. 450.00 (*0-7859-7836-4*, 2226059601) Fr & Eur.

***Dictionnaire des Mille Oeuvres Cles de la Philosophy.** Denis Huisman. 573p. (FRE.). 1994. 59.95 (*0-7859-7722-8*, 2091800759) Fr & Eur.

Dictionnaire des Miniaturistes du Moyen Age de la Renaissance. 2nd ed. E. Aeschlimann. Ed. by P. D'Ancona. 1972. 140.00 (*0-8115-0032-2*) Periodicals Srv.

***Dictionnaire des Ministres de 1789 a 1989.** Benoit Yvert. 1264p. (FRE.). 1990. 150.00 (*0-7859-7867-4*, 2262007101) Fr & Eur.

***Dictionnaire des Monogrammes, Chiffres, Lettres Initiales, Logoriphes, Rebus, etc. Sous Leguels le Plus Celebres Peintres, Graveurs et Dessinateurs ont Dessine Leurs Noms.** Jean-Frederic Christ. 484p. (FRE.). 1972. 275.00 (*0-7859-8648-0*, 282660161x) Fr & Eur.

***Dictionnaire des Monuments de Paris.** Jean Colson. 920p. (FRE.). 1992. 450.00 (*0-7859-8213-2*, 2903118663) Fr & Eur.

***Dictionnaire des Mots Croises.** rev. ed. Larousse Staff. 904p. (FRE.). 1991. pap. 32.95 (*0-7859-7690-6*, 2037302150) Fr & Eur.

Dictionnaire des Mots d'Esprit. Jean Delacour. 352p. (FRE.). 1976. pap. 16.95 (*0-8288-5644-3*, M6627) Fr & Eur.

***Dictionnaire des Mots Historiques de Cesar a Churchill.** Francois Bluche. 401p. (FRE.). 1992. pap. 45.00 (*0-7859-8180-2*, 2877061493) Fr & Eur.

***Dictionnaire des Mots qui n'Existent Pas.** Jean-Loup Chiflet. 168p. (FRE.). 1992. pap. 36.95 (*0-7859-7864-X*, 2258035724) Fr & Eur.

Dictionnaire des Mots Qui Ont une Histoire. Gilles Henry. 250p. (FRE.). 1989. pap. 49.95 (*0-8288-2601-3*, 2235016782) Fr & Eur.

***Dictionnaire des Mots Suisses de la Langue Francaise.** Alain Nicollier. 171p. (FRE.). 1990. pap. 49.95 (*0-7859-8200-0*, 2881150055) Fr & Eur.

Dictionnaire des Musiciens. Roland de Cande. 288p. (FRE.). 1974. pap. 29.95 (*0-8288-6020-3*, F17742) Fr & Eur.

***Dictionnaire des Mythes.** Nadia Julien. 607p. (FRE.). 1992. pap. 19.95 (*0-7859-7899-2*, 2501016939) Fr & Eur.

Dictionnaire des Neologismes Officiels. Commisariat General de la Language Francaise Staff. 238p. (ENG & FRE.). 1988. pap. 49.95 (*0-8288-7664-9*) Fr & Eur.

Dictionnaire des Noms d'Agents Pathogenes: French & English Dictionary of Pathogenic Agents. Conseil International de la Language Francaise Staff. (ENG & FRE.). write for info. (*0-8288-7671-1*) Fr & Eur.

***Dictionnaire des Noms de Communes, Treves et Paroisses du Finistere.** Bernard Tanguy. 280p. (FRE.). 1990. 135.00 (*0-7859-8221-3*, 2903708258) Fr & Eur.

***Dictionnaire des Noms de Rues.** Bernard Stephane. 744p. (FRE.). 1988. 45.00 (*0-7859-8657-X*, 285620211x) Fr & Eur.

***Dictionnaire des Noms Propres de la Bible.** Olivier Odelain. 536p. (FRE.). 1978. 115.00 (*0-7859-7761-9*, 2204011630) Fr & Eur.

Dictionnaire des Noms Propres de la Bible: Dictionary of Biblical Proper Names. 536p. (FRE.). 1978. 89.95 (*0-8288-5186-7*, M6628) Fr & Eur.

***Dictionnaire des Noms Propres de l'Academie de Nimes.** Christian Lacour. 155p. (FRE.). 1990. pap. 105.00 (*0-7859-8168-3*, 2869712324) Fr & Eur.

Dictionnaire des Nouvelles Technologies, English-French Vol. 2. 3rd rev. ed. Renee Fisher. 575p. (ENG & FRE.). 1991. pap. 125.00 (*0-8288-0613-6*, F25760) Fr & Eur.

Dictionnaire des Oeuvres Algeriennes en Langue Francais. Christiane Achour. 383p. (FRE.). 1990. pap. 95.00 (*0-8288-7583-9*, 2738409490) Fr & Eur.

Dictionnaire des Oeuvres de la Litterature Russe: Dictionary of the Works of Russian Literature. Jacques Sancan. 246p. (FRE.). 1973. pap. 19.95 (*0-8288-6263-X*) Fr & Eur.

Dictionnaire des Oeuvres de Tous les Tempes et de Tous les Pays. Ed. by Robert Laffont. 1980. pap. 45.00 (*0-7859-4426-5*) Fr & Eur.

Dictionnaire des Oeuvres de Tous les Temps et de Tous les Pays. Bompiani Laffont. 1981. lib. bdg. 275.00 (*0-8288-2600-5*) Fr & Eur.

Dictionnaire des Oeuvres de Tous les Temps et de Tous les Pays (Dictionary of the Works of All Times & Places) Litterature. Robert Laffont. 882p. (FRE.). pap. 45.00 (*0-7859-4622-5*) Fr & Eur.

***Dictionnaire des Oeuvres de Tous les Temps et de Tous les Pays Litterature, Philosophie, Musique, Sciences, 7 vols.** Robert Laffont & Valentino Bompiano. (FRE.). 1980. 265.00 (*0-7859-8630-8*, 222101183x) Fr & Eur.

Dictionnaire des Oeuvres et des Themes de la Litterature Allemande: Dictionary of Works & Themes in German Literature. Jean Chassard & Gonthier Weil. (FRE.). 1973. pap. 19.95 (*0-8288-6264-8*, M-6631) Fr & Eur.

Dictionnaire des Oeuvres et des Themes de la Litterature Americane. Alfred Fontenilles & Pierre Marambaud. 282p. (FRE.). 1976. pap. 24.95 (*0-8288-5645-1*, M6632) Fr & Eur.

1976 An Asterisk (*) at the beginning of an entry indicates that the title is appearing in BIP for the first time.

Dictionnaire des Oeuvres Politiques: Dictionary of Political Works. 2nd ed. Francois Chatelet et al. 1168p. (FRE.). 1989. 175.00 (*0-8288-7648-7*) Fr & Eur.

***Dictionnaire des Officiers de l'Armee Royale Qui Ont Combattu Aux Etats-Unis Pedant la Guerre D'Independence.** Gilbert Bodinier. 498p. (FRE.). 1982. pap. 55.00 (*0-7859-8133-0*, 2863230158) Fr & Eur.

Dictionnaire des Operas, 2 vols., Set. Felix Clement & Pierre Larousse. LC 69-15617. (Music Reprint Ser.). (FRE.). 1969. reprint ed. 135.00 (*0-306-71197-4*) Da Capo.

***Dictionnaire des OSBL: Associations, Congregations, Fondations, Mutuelles, Syndicats.** Marie-Therese Gravier. 232p. (FRE.). 1993. pap. 79.95 (*0-7859-8147-0*, 2865440524) Fr & Eur.

Dictionnaire des Ouvrages Anonymes. 3rd ed. Antoine-Alexandre Barbier. 1646p. (FRE.). 1964. lib. bdg. 995.00 (*0-8288-2493-2*, F12410) Fr & Eur.

Dictionnaire des Ouvrages Anonymes, 4 vols., Set. Antoine-Alexandre Barbier. xlv, 2533p. 1986. reprint ed. write for info. (*3-487-00550-6*, Pub. by Georg Olms GW) Lubrecht & Cramer.

Dictionnaire des Papes. Hans Kuhner. (FRE.). pap. 14.95 (*0-7859-0732-7*, M-6634) Fr & Eur.

Dictionnaire des Parlementaires Francais Comprenant Tous les Membres des Assemblees Francaises et Tous les Ministres Francais depuis le Ler Mai 1789 Jusqu'au Ler Mai 1889, 5 vols. Adolphe Robert & Gaston Cougny. xvi, 3189p. reprint ed. write for info. (*0-318-71403-5*, Pub. by Georg Olms GW) Lubrecht & Cramer.

Dictionnaire des Parlers Arabes de Syrie, Liban et Palestine. Claude Denizeau. 581p. (ARA & FRE.). 1961. pap. 105.00 (*0-7859-4893-7*) Fr & Eur.

Dictionnaire des Partis Communistes et des Mouvements Revolutionnaires: Dictionary of Communist Parties & Revolutionary Movements. Francois Fejto. 236p. (FRE.). 1971. pap. 19.95 (*0-8288-6449-7*, M-6635) Fr & Eur.

***Dictionnaire des Patronymes Basques: Euskal Deiruren Hiztegia, Vol. 1.** Philippe Oyhamburu. 788p. (BAQ & FRE.). 1991. 75.00 (*0-7859-8242-6*, 2908132028) Fr & Eur.

***Dictionnaire des Peintres Corses et de la Corse 1800-1850.** Giansily. 127p. (FRE.). 1993. pap. 45.00 (*0-614-00415-2*, 286523102X) Fr & Eur.

***Dictionnaire des Peintres et Sculpteurs de Provence-Alpes-Cote d'Azur.** Andre Alauzen. 522p. (FRE.). 1986. 165.00 (*0-7859-8128-4*, 2862761311) Fr & Eur.

Dictionnaire des Peintres et Sculpteurs Provencaux. Jean Pierre Camard & Anne Marie Belfort. 444p. (FRE.). 1974. pap. 19.95 (*0-8288-6021-1*, M6636) Fr & Eur.

Dictionnaire des Peintres, Sculpteurs, Dessinateurs et Graveurs: Nouvelle Edition, 10 vols., Set. E. Benezit. 7400p. (FRE.). 1976. reprint ed. lib. bdg. 550.00 (*2-7000-0157-5*, Pub. by Lib Grund FR) Dealers Choice.

Dictionnaire des Personnages. 3rd ed. Robert Laffont & Valentino Bompiani. 776p. (FRE.). 1984. pap. 49.95 (*0-7859-5120-2*) Fr & Eur.

***Dictionnaire des Personnages de la Revolution.** Roger Caratini. 575p. (FRE.). 1988. 79.95 (*0-7859-7943-3*, 2714422322) Fr & Eur.

Dictionnaire des Personnages de Tous les Temps & de Tous les Pays. (FRE.). 81.50 (*0-685-36081-4*) Fr & Eur.

***Dictionnaire des Personnages du Cinema.** Gilles Horvilleur. 624p. (FRE.). 1988. 195.00 (*0-7859-7702-3*, 2040163999) Fr & Eur.

Dictionnaire des Personnages Litteraires et Dramatiques de Tous les Tempes et de Tous les Pays. Bompiani Laffont. (FRE.). 83.95 (*0-8288-9900-2*, F12885) Fr & Eur.

***Dictionnaire des Personnages Vian.** Gilbert Pestereau. 426p. (FRE.). 1993. pap. 28.95 (*0-7859-7874-7*, 2267012006) Fr & Eur.

***Dictionnaire des Philosophes, 2 vols.** 2nd ed. Denis Huisman. 3104p. (FRE.). 1993. 750.00 (*0-7859-7751-1*, 2130455247) Fr & Eur.

***Dictionnaire des Philosophes Antiques Vol. 1: Abam(m)on a Axiothea.** Richard Goulet. 854p. (FRE.). 1989. pap. 175.00 (*0-7859-7815-1*, 2222040426) Fr & Eur.

Dictionnaire des Photographes. rev. ed. Naggar. 567p. (FRE.). 1982. write for info. (*0-8288-7909-5*, 8185243077) Fr & Eur.

Dictionnaire des Pierrettes et des Parfums Magiques. E. N. Santini de Riols. 256p. (FRE.). 1981. pap. write for info. (*0-8288-4444-5*, M9770) Fr & Eur.

***Dictionnaire des Poetes.** Jacque Charpentreau. 432p. (FRE.). 1983. 34.95 (*0-7859-7716-3*, 2070510190) Fr & Eur.

Dictionnaire des Poetes et de la Poesie. J. Charpentreau & G. Jean. (Folio - Junior Ser.). 427p. (FRE.). (J). (gr. 5-10). 1983. 27.95 (*2-07-051019-0*) Schoenhof.

Dictionnaire des Poincons Officiels Francais et Etrangers, Anciens et Modernes de Leur Creation (14e Siecle) a Nos Jours. Beuque. (FRE.). 1976. lib. bdg. 250.00 (*0-8288-2603-X*, F64050) Fr & Eur.

Dictionnaire Des Precieuses, 2 vols. in 1. Antoine B. Somaize. lxiv, 704p. 1972. reprint ed. write for info. (*3-487-04417-X*, Pub. by Georg Olms GW) Lubrecht & Cramer.

***Dictionnaire des Presages et des Superstitions.** Philippa Waring. 271p. (FRE.). 1990. pap. 45.00 (*0-7859-7882-8*, 2268013383) Fr & Eur.

***Dictionnaire des Proverbes Africains.** Mwamba Cabakulu. 302p. (FRE.). 1992. pap. 59.95 (*0-7859-8017-2*, 2738416853) Fr & Eur.

***Dictionnaire des Proverbes et des Dictions de France.** Jean-Yves Dournon. 347p. (FRE.). 1988. pap. 16.95 (*0-7859-7856-9*, 2253046795) Fr & Eur.

***Dictionnaire des Proverbes, Sentences, et Maximes.** Maurice Maloux. (FRE.). 1994. pap. 32.40 (*0-7859-8887-4*) Fr & Eur.

Dictionnaire des Proverbs, Sentences, et Maximes: Larousse Dictionary of Proverbs, Sayings & Maxims. 2nd ed. Maurice Maloux. 628p. (FRE.). 1990. pap. write for info. (*0-7859-4738-8*) Fr & Eur.

Dictionnaire Des Pseudonymes. Georges D'Heylli, pseud. iii, 559p. 1977. reprint ed. write for info. (*3-487-06339-5*, Pub. by Georg Olms GW) Lubrecht & Cramer.

Dictionnaire des Racines Semitiques, 2 vols. David C. Cohen. 76p. (FRE.). 1976. pap. 79.95 (*0-8288-5646-X*, M6640, Mouton) Fr & Eur.

***Dictionnaire des Regicides 1793.** Jacques-Philippe Giboury. 441p. (FRE.). 1989. 75.00 (*0-7859-8638-3*, 226200594x) Fr & Eur.

***Dictionnaire des Reines.** Chriatian Bouyer. 260p. (FRE.). 1992. 85.00 (*0-7859-7868-2*, 2262007896) Fr & Eur.

***Dictionnaire des Relieurs Francais Ayant Exerce de 1800 a Nos Jours.** Julien Flety. 225p. (FRE.). 1988. pap. 59.95 (*0-7859-8228-0*, 2904918078) Fr & Eur.

***Dictionnaire des Religions.** Mircea Eliade. 364p. (FRE.). 1990. 75.00 (*0-7859-7865-8*, 2259020305) Fr & Eur.

***Dictionnaire des Religions.** Mircea Eliade. (FRE.). 1992. pap. 22.95 (*0-7859-7873-9*, 2266050125) Fr & Eur.

***Dictionnaire des Religions.** Marguerite-Marie Thiollier. 300p. (FRE.). 1990. pap. 75.00 (*0-7859-8137-3*, 2864690624) Fr & Eur.

Dictionnaire des Religions. 2nd ed. Paul Poupard. 1856p. (FRE.). 1985. 225.00 (*0-8288-9471-X*) Fr & Eur.

***Dictionnaire des Religions, 2 vols.** 3rd ed. Paul Poupard. 2248p. (FRE.). 1993. 495.00 (*0-7859-7749-X*, 2130451128) Fr & Eur.

***Dictionnaire des Reves.** Luc Uyttenhove. 286p. (FRE.). 1987. pap. 13.95 (*0-7859-7885-2*, 2501009142) Fr & Eur.

***Dictionnaire des Reves de A a Z: Le Guide Complet pour l'Analyse et l'Interpretation des Reves.** Hanns Kurth. 416p. (FRE.). 1982. pap. 38.95 (*0-7859-7875-5*, 2268001946) Fr & Eur.

***Dictionnaire des Rimes Orales et Ecrites.** Leon Warnant. 576p. (FRE.). 1992. pap. 29.95 (*0-7859-7677-9*, 2037102186) Fr & Eur.

***Dictionnaire des Science de l'Environnement Terminologie.** Sylvain Parent. 748p. (ENG & FRE.). 1991. 95.00 (*0-7859-7911-5*, 2700211065) Fr & Eur.

***Dictionnaire des Sciences Economiques et Sociales.** Henri Bourachot. 192p. (FRE.). 1992. pap. 24.95 (*0-7859-7710-4*, 2040193030) Fr & Eur.

Dictionnaire des Sciences et Techniques Nucleaires. 3rd ed. Commissariat a l'Energie Atomique. 492p. (FRE.). 1975. 125.00 (*0-7859-0650-9*, M6081) Fr & Eur.

***Dictionnaire Des Sciences Historiques.** Andre Burguiere. 704p. (FRE.). 1986. pap. 125.00 (*0-7859-7742-2*, 2130393616) Fr & Eur.

***Dictionnaire des Sciences Occultes.** Frederic Boutet. 412p. (FRE.). 1993. pap. 45.00 (*0-7859-8109-8*, 2857043899) Fr & Eur.

Dictionnaire des Sciences Occultes de l'Esoterisme et des Arts Divinitoires. Olivier Beigbeder. 436p. (FRE.). 1989. 95.00 (*0-7859-4806-6*) Fr & Eur.

Dictionnaire des Scours d'Urgence en Cas de Catastophe. S. W. Gunn. 217p. (ENG & FRE.). 1984. 39.95 (*0-8288-1798-7*, M14130) Fr & Eur.

Dictionnaire des Sculpteurs de l'Ecole Francaise, 8 Vols. 1972. 720.00 (*0-8115-0036-5*) Periodicals Srv.

Dictionnaire des Sculpteurs Francais du Moyen Age. Michele Beaulieu. 312p. (FRE.). 1992. 225.00 (*0-8288-9472-8*) Fr & Eur.

Dictionnaire des Services Publics Relevant de l'Etat: Dictionary of Public Services Related to Government. J. LeBrun. 1020p. (FRE.). 1978. 175.00 (*0-8288-5187-5*, M6341) Fr & Eur.

***Dictionnaire des Sigles Informatique.** Virga. 224p. (FRE.). 1992. pap. 15.95 (*0-7859-7897-6*, 2501015878) Fr & Eur.

***Dictionnaire des Sigles Scientifiques, Techniques et Economiques.** 2nd ed. Jean Murith. 470p. (FRE.). 1987. 250.00 (*0-7859-8071-7*, 2852063840) Fr & Eur.

***Dictionnaire des Signes et des Symptomes en Homeopathie et des Remedes Correspondent.** Yves Le Penven. 412p. (FRE.). 1986. 95.00 (*0-7859-7818-6*, 2224011733) Fr & Eur.

Dictionnaire des Societes Secretes en Occident. Pierre Mariel. (FRE.). 1971. pap. 29.95 (*0-8288-6450-0*, M-6642) Fr & Eur.

Dictionnaire des Songes, dans Dicitonnaire des Sciences Occultes. 416p. (FRE.). 1976. pap. 39.95 (*0-8288-5647-8*, M6643) Fr & Eur.

***Dictionnaire des Sports Aeriens Ultralegers: French-English, English-French.** Raphael Dalla-Costa. 88p. (ENG & FRE.). 1988. pap. 18.95 (*0-7859-8087-3*, 2854281829) Fr & Eur.

Dictionnaire des Structures de Vocabulaire Savant. 4th rev. ed. H. Cottez. 515p. (FRE.). 1988. 75.00 (*0-7859-4865-1*, M9516) Fr & Eur.

Dictionnaire des Structures du Vocabulaire Savant. Jean Robert. 45.00 (*0-317-45634-2*) Fr & Eur.

***Dictionnaire des Substances Chimiques Reglementees.** Afnor Staff. 812p. (FRE.). 1987. pap. 395.00 (*0-7859-7738-4*, 2124201115) Fr & Eur.

***Dictionnaire des Superstitions.** Annie Holmes. 167p. (FRE.). 1994. pap. 12.95 (*0-7859-7986-7*, 2732842036) Fr & Eur.

Dictionnaire des Superstitions et des Croyances. Pierre Canavaggio. 353p. 1993. pap. 85.00 (*0-7859-5652-2*, 2850765546) Fr & Eur.

***Dictionnaire des Symboles.** Marianne Oesterreicher-Mollwo. 312p. (FRE.). 1992. pap. 59.95 (*0-7859-7903-4*, 2503502458) Fr & Eur.

Dictionnaire des Synonymes. R. DeNoter & P. Vuillermoz. 284p. (FRE.). 1969. 19.95 (*0-8288-6590-6*, M-6113) Fr & Eur.

Dictionnaire des Synonymes. Jean Robert. 45.00 (*0-317-45635-0*) Fr & Eur.

***Dictionnaire des Synonymes: Repertoire des Mots Francais Usuels Ayant un Sens Sembable, Analogue ou Approche.** 140th ed. Raphael Noter. 283p. (FRE.). 1992. pap. 28.95 (*0-7859-7746-5*, 2130442404) Fr & Eur.

Dictionnaire des Synonymes et des Antonymes. Hector Dupuis & Romain Legare. 608p. (FRE.). 1975. 39.95 (*0-8288-5860-8*, M6180) Fr & Eur.

Dictionnaire des Synonymes et des Equivalences. Jean Lecointe. 354p. 1993. pap. 19.95 (*0-7859-5625-5*, 2253061417) Fr & Eur.

Dictionnaire des Techniques Aeronautiques et Spatiales--Trilingue. 2nd ed. 1152p. 1984. 275.00 (*0-7859-5606-9*, 2040101241) Fr & Eur.

Dictionnaire des Techniques Aeronautiques et Spatiales--Trilingue: Francais, Anglais, Allemand: 24,000 Entrees dans Chaque Langue. 1200p. (ENG, FRE & GER.). 1978. 175.00 (*2-04-010124-1*) Fr & Eur.

***Dictionnaire des Techniques et Technologies Modernes Vol. 2: French-English.** J. R. Forbes. 582p. (ENG & FRE.). 1993. 225.00 (*0-7859-8652-9*, 285206880X) Fr & Eur.

Dictionnaire des Techniques et Technologies Modernes, Anglais. 2nd ed. J. R. Forbes. 594p. (ENG & FRE.). 1993. 225.00 (*0-8288-9473-6*, F135020) Fr & Eur.

***Dictionnaire des Telecommunications.** Antoine Odier. 352p. (FRE.). 1992. pap. 17.95 (*0-7859-7898-4*, 2501016742) Fr & Eur.

Dictionnaire des Termes d'Anatomie, d'Embryologie et d'Histologie. Ernst Lovasy. 624p. (FRE.). 1954. 65.00 (*0-8288-6871-9*, M-6380) Fr & Eur.

***Dictionnaire des Termes de la Sociologie.** Adriaan Hermans. 94p. (FRE.). 1991. pap. 14.95 (*0-7859-7895-X*, 2501015401) Fr & Eur.

***Dictionnaire des Termes de l'Art: English-French, French-English.** Claude Ferment. 544p. (ENG & FRE.). 1994. pap. 150.00 (*0-7859-8107-1*, 2856080596) Fr & Eur.

***Dictionnaire des Termes de Medecine.** 23th ed. Marcle Garnier. 1068p. (FRE.). 1992. 105.00 (*0-7859-7823-2*, 2224021259) Fr & Eur.

Dictionnaire Des Termes D'Imprimerie De Reliure et De Papeterie: French - English. Michael Barnard. 232p. (ENG & FRE.). 1992. 125.00 (*0-7859-0502-2*, 2852067994) Fr & Eur.

***Dictionnaire des Termes Economiques.** Mathilde Menard. 94p. (FRE.). 1990. pap. 15.95 (*0-7859-7890-9*, 2501014154) Fr & Eur.

***Dictionnaire des Termes Juridiques.** Christian Rudelle. 221p. (FRE.). 1992. pap. 45.00 (*0-7859-8202-7*, 2883990662) Fr & Eur.

***Dictionnaire des Termes Juridiques et Commerciaux.** Annie Mouthier. 227p. (FRE.). 1991. pap. 39.95 (*0-7859-8645-6*, 273280102x) Fr & Eur.

Dictionnaire des Termes Medicaux Francais - Neerlandais & Neerlandais - Francais. R. Vanden Driessche. 1884p. (DUT & FRE.). 1989. 395.00 (*0-8288-9474-4*, 2870170408) Fr & Eur.

***Dictionnaire des Termes Officiels de la Langue Francaise: January 1994 Edition.** Journal Officiel Staff. 461p. (FRE.). 1994. pap. 75.00 (*0-7859-8619-7*, 211073499X) Fr & Eur.

***Dictionnaire des Termes Scientifiques.** Jean-Noel Von Der Weid. 96p. (FRE.). 1990. pap. 12.95 (*0-7859-7891-7*, 2501014162) Fr & Eur.

Dictionnaire des Termes Techniques d'Entomologies Elementaire. Eugene Seguy. 465p. (FRE.). 1967. 175.00 (*0-8288-6679-1*, M-6512) Fr & Eur.

***Dictionnaire des Termes Techniques, l'Atelier du Peintre.** Larousse Staff. 408p. (FRE.). 1990. pap. 79.95 (*0-7859-7696-5*, 2037400667) Fr & Eur.

Dictionnaire Des Termes Typographiques et De Design: French - English. Michael Barnard. 192p. (ENG & FRE.). 1992. 95.00 (*0-7859-0504-9*, 2852068192) Fr & Eur.

***Dictionnaire des Termes Veterinaires et Animlaiers: French-English, English-French.** Roy Mack. 576p. (ENG & FRE.). 1991. 195.00 (*0-7859-8134-9*, 2863260863) Fr & Eur.

Dictionnaire des Terms Normalises de Sciences et Techniques. Association National Staff & Serge Paul. 409p. (FRE.). 1993. pap. 55.00 (*0-7859-5609-3*, 2110729139) Fr & Eur.

Dictionnaire des Theatres Parisiens au Xixe Siecle. Nicole Wild. 1989. lib. bdg. 125.00 (*0-8288-2586-6*) Fr & Eur.

***Dictionnaire des Theories et Mecanismes Economiques.** Janine Bremond. (FRE.). 1984. pap. 32.95 (*0-7859-7791-0*, 2218071290) Fr & Eur.

***Dictionnaire des Traducteurs et de la Litterature Traduite en Ancien et Moyen Francais 842-1600.** Paul Chavy. 1545p. (FRE.). 1988. 495.00 (*0-7859-7712-0*, 2051008590) Fr & Eur.

***Dictionnaire des Unites et Valeurs Approximatives.** Pierre Dauchin. 180p. (FRE.). 1992. pap. 49.95 (*0-7859-7945-X*, 2714428754) Fr & Eur.

Dictionnaire des Urgences Medicales de l'Adulte (Dictionary of Adult Emergency Medicine) 2nd ed. Arnaud Cenac et al. 416p. (FRE.). 1989. ring bd. 85.00 (*0-7859-4621-7*, F126640) Fr & Eur.

***Dictionnaire des Vins et Alcools.** Myriam Huet. 432p. (FRE.). 1990. pap. 34.95 (*0-7859-8212-4*, 2903118566) Fr & Eur.

***Dictionnaire des Vitamines.** Daniel Nani. 155p. (FRE.). 1993. pap. 12.95 (*0-7859-7985-9*, 2732841870) Fr & Eur.

Dictionnaire Des Vocabulaires Techniques Du De Architectura De Vitruve. Vitruvius. Ed. by Louis Callebat. Bd. CXXIII. 750p. Date not set. write for info. (*0-318-71244-X*, Pub. by Georg Olms GW) Lubrecht & Cramer.

Dictionnaire des 10,000 Dirigeants Politiques Francais. Pierre-Marie Dioudonnat & Sabine Bragadir. 756p. (FRE.). 1978. 95.00 (*0-8288-5181-6*, M6164) Fr & Eur.

***Dictionnaire d'Etymologie Daco-Romane, 2 vols., Set.** fac. ed. Alexandre de Cihac. 1188p. (FRE.). 1978. 695.00 (*0-7859-8457-7*, 3764802049) Fr & Eur.

Dictionnaire d'Etymologie Sumerienne et Grammaire Comparee. Colman G. Gostony. 204p. (FRE.). 1975. pap. 95.00 (*0-7859-0776-9*, M6283) Fr & Eur.

Dictionnaire d'Histoire de France: Dictionary of the History of France. Alain Decaux et al. (FRE.). 1981. 225.00 (*0-8288-1487-2*, M14212) Fr & Eur.

Dictionnaire d'Histoire de l'Art. Jean-Pierre Neraudau. 544p. (FRE.). 1985. 125.00 (*0-8288-1417-1*, F26160) Fr & Eur.

***Dictionnaire d'Histoire de l'Eglise.** Guy Bedouelle. 333p. (FRE.). 1994. 79.95 (*0-7859-8095-4*, 2854432517) Fr & Eur.

***Dictionnaire d'Histoire du XXe Siecle.** Anne Carol. 499p. (FRE.). 1993. pap. 24.95 (*0-7859-7792-9*, 2218071924) Fr & Eur.

Dictionnaire d'Histoire et du Geographie Ecclesiastiques, 16 vols., Set. Roger Aubert & Van Cauwenberg. (FRE.). pap. 2,795.00 (*0-7859-0389-5*, M6014) Fr & Eur.

***Dictionnaire d'Homeopathie Pediatrique a l'Usage des Familles et des Medecins de Famille.** Herman Leduc. 494p. (FRE.). 1990. pap. 79.95 (*0-7859-7910-7*, 2700211057) Fr & Eur.

Dictionnaire d'Informatique. George A. Nania. 1000p. (ENG, FRE, ITA, POR & SPA.). 1983. 150.00 (*0-8288-0272-6*, M 14464) Fr & Eur.

Dictionnaire d'Informatique: English - French, French - English. Jacques Hildebert. 926p. (ENG & FRE.). 1993. pap. 39.95 (*0-7859-0998-2*, 2266053736) Fr & Eur.

Dictionnaire D'Informatique: English-French with French-English Dictonary. Lavoisier & Hermann. 680p. (FRE.). 1991. 175.00 (*0-7859-0501-4*, 2852067587) Fr & Eur.

Dictionnaire d'Informatique Francais-Anglias. 6th rev. ed. Michel Ginguay. 232p. 1993. pap. 85.00 (*0-7859-5618-2*, 225840350) Fr & Eur.

Dictionnaire d'Intelligence Artificielle, Anglais-Francais. Noel Lazure. 216p. 1993. pap. 115.00 (*0-7859-5617-4*, 2225840288) Fr & Eur.

***Dictionnaire d'ORL (Oto-Rhino-Laryngologie) dOrthophonie et de Chirurgie Maxillo-Faciale: French with English Translations.** Yves Guerrier. 351p. (ENG & FRE.). 1993. pap. 225.00 (*0-7859-7957-3*, 2718406399) Fr & Eur.

***Dictionnaire d'Orthographe et des Difficultes du Francais.** Jean-Yves Dournon. (FRE.). 1987. pap. 18.95 (*0-7859-7849-6*, 2253028851) Fr & Eur.

Dictionnaire d'Oto-Rhino-Laryngologie, 5 vols. Augustin Larrauri. (ENG, FRE, GER, ITA & SPA.). 1971. 95.00 (*0-8288-6442-X*, M-6338) Fr & Eur.

Dictionnaire du Bearnais et du Gascon Modernes. Simin Palay. 1072p. (FRE.). 1991. 95.00 (*0-8288-6022-X*, M6645) Fr & Eur.

Dictionnaire du Blues. Jean-Claude Arnaudon. 296p. (FRE.). 1978. 59.95 (*0-8288-5191-3*, M6646) Fr & Eur.

***Dictionnaire du Breton Parle a Douarnenez Vol. 3: Geriadur Brehoneg Douarnenez, Ar Sevel-Bagou, Lien, Gwerniou.** Per Denez. 136p. (BRE & FRE.). 1984. pap. 19.95 (*0-7859-8158-6*, 2868630006) Fr & Eur.

***Dictionnaire du Breton Parle a Douarnenez Vol. 4: Geriadur Brehoneg Douarnenez, Ar Beskerezh, No. 4.** Per Denez. 152p. (BRE & FRE.). 1985. pap. 24.95 (*0-7859-8161-6*, 2868630103) Fr & Eur.

Dictionnaire du Bricolage et du Depannage Menager. Francis Genette. 450p. (FRE.). 1972. pap. 49.95 (*0-8288-6378-4*, M-6265) Fr & Eur.

Dictionnaire du Bridge. G. Versini. 420p. (FRE.). 1968. 95.00 (*0-8288-6636-8*, M-6549) Fr & Eur.

Dictionnaire du Chien. Pierre Rousselet-Blanc & Josette Rousselet-Blanc. 267p. (FRE.). 1976. 49.95 (*0-8288-5648-6*, M6647) Fr & Eur.

***Dictionnaire du Christianisme.** Jean Mathieu-Rosay. 316p. (FRE.). 1990. pap. 17.95 (*0-7859-7888-7*, 2501012887) Fr & Eur.

***Dictionnaire du Christianisme Ancien.** Joeseph F. Kelly. 277p. (FRE.). 1994. 79.95 (*0-7859-7907-7*, 2503503020) Fr & Eur.

Dictionnaire du Cinema. Jean-Loup Passek. 867p. (FRE.). 1986. 150.00 (*0-8288-2090-2*, F11830) Fr & Eur.

***Dictionnaire du Cinema Vol. 1: Realisateurs.** 2nd ed. Jean Tulard. 1128p. (FRE.). 1984. pap. 45.00 (*0-7859-7799-6*, 2221045424) Fr & Eur.

***Dictionnaire du Cinema Vol. 2: Les Actuers.** Laffont Staff. 1128p. (FRE.). 1984. pap. 55.00 (*0-7859-7811-9*, 2221071638) Fr & Eur.

***Dictionnaire du Cinema Africain Vol. 1.** Association des Trois Mondes, Paris Staff. 398p. (FRE.). 1991. pap. 65.00 (*0-7859-8145-4*, 2865372979) Fr & Eur.

Dictionnaire du Cinema Americain (A-K) Michel Ciment. (FRE.). 1988. lib. bdg. 35.00 (*0-8288-2498-3*) Fr & Eur.

Dictionnaire du Cinema Americain (K-Z) Michel Ciment. (FRE.). 1988. lib. bdg. 35.00 (*0-8288-2499-1*) Fr & Eur.

***Dictionnaire du Comportement Animal.** David McFarland. 1013p. (FRE.). 1990. pap. 55.00 (*0-7859-7802-X*, 2221052811) Fr & Eur.

Dictionnaire du Costume. Michel Leloir. 400p. (FRE.). 1992. 295.00 (*0-8288-9477-9*) Fr & Eur.

Dictionnaire du Diabetique. Philippe Renou. 320p. (FRE.). 1991. 79.95 (*0-8288-9478-7*) Fr & Eur.

***Dictionnaire du Diable.** Roland Villeneuve. 428p. (FRE.). 1989. 145.00 (*0-7859-8131-4*, 2863111841) Fr & Eur.

Dictionnaire du Droit des Societes a Responsabilite Limitee, 8 vols. Joly Legal Dictionaries Staff. (FRE.). 1984. 350.00 (*0-8288-1518-6*, M6134) Fr & Eur.

D

An Asterisk (*) at the beginning of an entry indicates that the title is appearing in BIP for the first time.

1977

*Dictionnaire du Droit des Societes a Responsabilite Limitee, 9 vols. Joly Legal Dictionaries Staff. (FRE.). 1990. 1,095.00 (0-7859-8655-3, 285522019x) Fr & Eur.

Dictionnaire du Droit des Societes Anonymes, 12 vols., Set. GLN-Joly Staff. (FRE.). 1990. 1,495.00 (0-7859-4899-6) Fr & Eur.

Dictionnaire du Francais. Marie Gatard. 1989. lib. bdg. 45.00 (0-8288-2497-5, 2010152166) Fr & Eur.

Dictionnaire Du Francais. Hagege, C & Hachette Staff. 1768p. (FRE.). 1987. pap. write for info. (0-7859-0446-8, 2010123077) Fr & Eur.

Dictionnaire du Francais. 2nd ed. Hachette Staff. 1807p. (FRE.). 1992. 59.95 (0-7859-0961-3, 2010188772) Fr & Eur.

Dictionnaire du Francais Argotique et Populaire: Dictionary of Slang & Popular French. Francois Caradec. 255p. (FRE.). 1977. pap. 17.95 (0-8288-5385-1, M4968) Fr & Eur.

Dictionnaire du Francais Classique. Jean Dubois & Rene Lagane. 511p. (FRE.). 1992. pap. 85.00 (0-8288-6451-9, F-133960) Fr & Eur.

Dictionnaire du Francais Contemporain Manual et Travaux Pratiques. Larousse Staff. 29.95 (0-317-45626-1) Fr & Eur.

Dictionnaire du Francais d'Algerie. Jeanne Duclos. 159p. (FRE.). 1992. 49.95 (0-7859-1012-3, 2862531227) Fr & Eur.

*Dictionnaire du Francais Fondamental en Image pour les Ruraux. Guy-Jose Bretones. 274p. (FRE.). 1982. pap. 45.00 (0-7859-8111-X, 2858022275) Fr & Eur.

Dictionnaire du Francais Langue Etrangere. J. Dubois. 910p. 1988. 55.00 (0-7859-4786-8) Fr & Eur.

Dictionnaire du Francais-Langue Etrangere. 2nd ed. Jean Dubois. (FRE.). 1986. lib. bdg. 39.95 (0-7859-3943-1) Fr & Eur.

Dictionnaire du Francais Parle. Charles Bernet. (FRE.). 1989. lib. bdg. 69.95 (0-8288-2496-7) Fr & Eur.

*Dictionnaire du Francais Parle. rev. ed. Pierre Rezau. 382p. (FRE.). 1991. pap. 17.95 (0-7859-7627-2, 2020128683) Fr & Eur.

Dictionnaire du Francais Regional de Beaujolais. Anne-Marie Vurpas & Claude Michel. 191p. (FRE.). 1992. 59.95 (0-7859-1013-1, 2862531340) Fr & Eur.

Dictionnaire du Francais Regional de Berry-Bourbonnais. Pierrette Debuisson. 160p. (FRE.). 1993. 39.95 (0-7859-5660-3, 2862531405) Fr & Eur.

Dictionnaire du Francais Regional de Bourgogne. Gerard Taverdet. 159p. (FRE.). 1991. 50.00 (0-8288-9543-0) Fr & Eur.

*Dictionnaire du Francais Regional de Champagne. Michel Tamine. 160p. (FRE.). 1993. 39.95 (0-7859-8122-5, 2862531510) Fr & Eur.

Dictionnaire du Francais Regional de Lorraine. Jean Lanher & Alain Litaize. 160p. (FRE.). 1990. 125.00 (0-8288-9479-5) Fr & Eur.

*Dictionnaire du Francais Regional de Normandie. Rene Lepelley. 157p. (FRE.). 1993. 39.95 (0-7859-8121-7, 2862531502) Fr & Eur.

Dictionnaire du Francais Regional de Pilat. Jean-Baptiste Martin. 280p. (FRE.). 1989. 59.95 (0-8288-9486-8) Fr & Eur.

Dictionnaire du Francais Regional de Poitou-Charentes et de Vendee. Pierre Rezeau. 159p. (FRE.). 1990. 50.00 (0-8288-9480-9, 2862530972) Fr & Eur.

Dictionnaire du Francais Regional de Provence. Philippe Blanchet. 157p. (FRE.). 1991. 50.00 (0-8288-9481-7) Fr & Eur.

*Dictionnaire du Francais Regional de Savoie. Anita Gagny. 159p. (FRE.). 1993. 39.95 (0-7859-8123-3, 2862531529) Fr & Eur.

*Dictionnaire du Francais Regional des Ardennes. Michel Tamine. 157p. (FRE.). 1992. 39.95 (0-7859-8118-7, 2862531359) Fr & Eur.

Dictionnaire du Francais Regional des Pays Aquitaines. Jacques Boisgontier. 157p. (FRE.). 1991. 50.00 (0-8288-9482-5) Fr & Eur.

Dictionnaire du Francais Regional du Languedoc. Christian Camps. 160p. (FRE.). 1991. 50.00 (0-8288-9483-3) Fr & Eur.

Dictionnaire du Francais Regional du Midi Toulousain et Pyreneen. Jacques Boisgontier. 157p. (FRE.). 1992. 50.00 (0-8288-9484-1) Fr & Eur.

Dictionnaire du Francais Regional du Nord-Pas-de-Calais. Fernand Carton & Denise Poulet. 125p. (FRE.). 1991. 50.00 (0-8288-9485-X) Fr & Eur.

Dictionnaire du Francais Regional du Roussillon. Christian Camps. 93p. (FRE.). 1991. 50.00 (0-8288-9487-6) Fr & Eur.

Dictionnaire du Francais Vivant: Dictionary of Living French. Maurice Davau et al. 1360p. (FRE.). 1972. pap. 49.95 (0-8288-6379-2, M-6102) Fr & Eur.

Dictionnaire du Francias Regional du Velay. Claudine Frechet. 159p. (FRE.). 1993. 39.95 (0-7859-5663-8, 2862531472) Fr & Eur.

*Dictionnaire du Jazz. Philippe Carles. 1160p. (FRE.). 1988. pap. 55.00 (0-7859-7798-8, 2221045165) Fr & Eur.

Dictionnaire du Jazz. rev. ed. Hughes Panassie & M. Gautier. 384p. (FRE.). 1987. pap. 49.95 (0-8288-2170-4, M6648) Fr & Eur.

*Dictionnaire du Jazz a Bruxelles et en Wallonie. Conseil de la Musique, Belgique Staff. 327p. (FRE.). 1991. pap. 95.00 (0-7859-8662-6, 287009468x) Fr & Eur.

Dictionnaire du Marche Commun. GLN-Joly Staff. 5000p. (FRE.). 1990. 1,495.00 (0-8288-9488-4) Fr & Eur.

Dictionnaire du Marche Commun: Dictionary of the Common Market, 4 vols., Set. Joly Legal Dictionaries Staff. (FRE.). 1978. 350.00 (0-8288-5192-1, M6135) Fr & Eur.

Dictionnaire du Marche de l'Art: Dictionary of the Art market. Didier Romand & Gerald Schurr. 416p. (FRE.). 1978. pap. 95.00 (0-8288-5193-X, M6490) Fr & Eur.

*Dictionnaire du Marketing et des Affaires. Remi Van Dick. 201p. (FRE.). 1991. pap. 95.00 (0-7859-8626-X, 221200804x) Fr & Eur.

Dictionnaire du Monde Religieux dans la France Contemporaine, Vol. 1: Les Jesuites. Jean-Marie Mayeur & Yves-Marie Hilaire. Ed. by Paul Duclos. 272p. (FRE.). 1985. 125.00 (0-8288-9489-2) Fr & Eur.

Dictionnaire du Monde Religieux dans la France Contemporaine, Vol. 2: L'Alsace. Jean-Marie Mayeur & Yves-Marie Hilaire. Ed. by Bernard Vogler. 483p. (FRE.). 1987. 125.00 (0-8288-9490-6) Fr & Eur.

*Dictionnaire du Monde Religieux dans la France Contemporaine, Vol. 3: La Bretagne. Jean-Marie Mayeur & Yves-Marie Hilaire. Ed. by Michel Lagree. 428p. (FRE.). 1985. pap. write for info. (0-7859-5243-8) Fr & Eur.

Dictionnaire du Monde Religieux dans la France Contemporaine, Vol. 4: Lille-Flandres. Jean-Marie Mayeur & Yves-Marie Hilaire. Ed. by Andre Caudron. 504p. (FRE.). 1990. 125.00 (0-8288-9492-2) Fr & Eur.

*Dictionnaire du Parfait Cynique. Roland Jaccard. 159p. (FRE.). 1991. pap. 12.95 (0-7859-7858-5, 2253057142) Fr & Eur.

*Dictionnaire du Parler Bourbonnais. Frantz Brunet. 258p. (FRE.). 1993. 75.00 (0-7859-8245-0, 2908592177) Fr & Eur.

*Dictionnaire du Patois de Lille. fac. ed. Pierre Legrand. 180p. (FRE.). 1987. pap. 79.95 (0-7859-8229-9, 2904951288) Fr & Eur.

*Dictionnaire du Pere Noel. Gregoire Solotareff. (FRE.). 1991. 55.00 (0-7859-8615-4, 207056598x) Fr & Eur.

Dictionnaire du Ski. Jacques Gautrat. 256p. (FRE.). 1969. pap. 19.95 (0-8288-6591-4, M-6651) Fr & Eur.

Dictionnaire du Strabisme: Phisiologie et Clinique. Phillippe Lanthony. 202p. (FRE.). 1983. 79.95 (0-8288-1813-4, M15412) Fr & Eur.

Dictionnaire du Style et des Usages Administratifs. Marcel Spreutels. 484p. (FRE.). 24.95 (0-7859-0766-1, M-6523) Fr & Eur.

Dictionnaire du Symbolisme Animal. Jean-Paul Clebert. 455p. (FRE.). 1974. pap. 35.00 (0-8288-6023-8, M581) Fr & Eur.

Dictionnaire du Theatre Francais Contemporain: Dictionary of French Contemporary Theatre. Alfred Simon. 250p. (FRE.). 1970. pap. 14.95 (0-8288-6522-1, M-675) Fr & Eur.

Dictionnaire du Transport Aerien. Pascal Cambournac. 136p. (FRE.). 1993. pap. 65.00 (0-7859-5669-7, 2908537087) Fr & Eur.

Dictionnaire du Vin: Dictionary of Wine. Yves Renouil & Yves de Traversay. (FRE.). 1962. 95.00 (0-8288-6809-3, M-6482) Fr & Eur.

Dictionnaire du Vocabulaire Essentiel: Dictionary of Essential Vocabulary. 6th ed. Georges Matore. 360p. (FRE.). 1980. pap. 23.95 (0-8288-1945-9, M6652) Fr & Eur.

*Dictionnaire Economique. Douglas Greenwald. 1987. write for info. (0-7859-7953-0, 2-7178-1288-1) Fr & Eur.

Dictionnaire Economique de l'Anglais et du Francais: Systeme Banquaire. Banque de France Staff. 232p. (ENG & FRE.). 1992. pap. 125.00 (0-7859-1005-0, 2717822798) Fr & Eur.

*Dictionnaire Economique de l'Anglais et du Francais Vol. 2: Credit, Taux D'Interet. Banque de France Staff. (ENG & FRE.). 1992. pap. 105.00 (0-7859-7956-5, 2717823581) Fr & Eur.

*Dictionnaire Economique et Juridique. 3rd rev. ed. Jean Baleyte et al. 1992. write for info. (0-7859-7883-6, 2-275-00643-5) Fr & Eur.

Dictionnaire Economique et Social: Social & Economic Dictionary. Thomas H. Suarvet. 526p. (FRE.). 1973. 49.95 (0-8288-6265-6, M-6526) Fr & Eur.

Dictionnaire Economoqie et Juridique: Francais-Anglais, Anglais-Francais. 3rd ed. Jean Baleyte et al. 725p. (ENG & FRE.). 1992. pap. 150.00 (0-8288-0381-1, M8442) Fr & Eur.

*Dictionnaire Electronique. Sylvie Segre. 1991. write for info. (0-7859-7931-X, 2-7080-0646-0) Fr & Eur.

*Dictionnaire Elementaire Breton-Francais. Iwan Kadored. 1984. write for info. (0-7859-8160-8, 2-86863-002-2) Fr & Eur.

*Dictionnaire Elementaire Creole Haitien-Francais. Ed. by Alain Bentolila. 1976. write for info. (0-7859-7787-2, 2218036002) Fr & Eur.

Dictionnaire Elementaire Creole Haitien-Francais. Pierre Nougayrol et al. Ed. by Alain Bentolila. 511p. (FRE.). 1976. 69.95 (0-8288-5649-4, M6430) Fr & Eur.

Dictionnaire Elementaire Francais-Creole. Pierre Pinalie. 237p. (FRE.). 1992. 59.95 (0-8288-9493-0) Fr & Eur.

Dictionnaire en Couleurs des Animaux. Maurice Burton. 400p. (FRE.). 1974. 75.00 (0-8288-6024-6, M6653) Fr & Eur.

*Dictionnaire Encyclopedique Alpha. Alpha Staff. 1983. write for info. (0-7859-8050-4, 2-8270-0295-7) Fr & Eur.

Dictionnaire Encyclopedique d'Agrometeorology: French, English & Spanish Dictionary of Agrometeorology. Conseil International de la Language Francaise Staff. (ENG, FRE & SPA.). write for info. (0-8288-7672-X) Fr & Eur.

*Dictionnaire Encyclopedique de la Bible. Centre Informatique et Bible (Maredsous, Belgique) Staff. 1987. write for info. (0-7859-7909-3, 2-503-59002-0) Fr & Eur.

*Dictionnaire Encyclopedique de la Liturgie A-L. Domenico Sartore & Achille M. Triacca. Ed. by Henri Delhougne. 1992. 250.00 (0-7859-7906-9, 2-503-50248-2) Fr & Eur.

Dictionnaire Encyclopedique de la Pedagogie Moderne. Fernand Hotyat & D. Delepine. (FRE.). 1974. 49.95 (0-8288-6025-4, M6319) Fr & Eur.

*Dictionnaire Encyclopedique de l'Ecologie et des Sciences De. Francois Ramade. 1993. write for info. (0-7859-8052-0, 2-84074-037-0) Fr & Eur.

*Dictionnaire Encyclopedique de Theorie et de Sociologie du D. 2nd ed. Andre-Jean Arnaud et al. 1993. write for info. (0-7859-8640-5, 227500601X) Fr & Eur.

*Dictionnaire Encyclopedique des Aliments. Solange Monette. 1991. write for info. (0-7859-8203-5, 2-89037-475-0) Fr & Eur.

Dictionnaire Encyclopedique des Citations. Jean Dissere. 395p. (FRE.). 1970. 19.95 (0-7859-0733-5, M-6654) Fr & Eur.

Dictionnaire Encyclopedique des Finances Publiques. Loic Philip. 1647p. (FRE.). 1991. 225.00 (0-8288-9494-9) Fr & Eur.

Dictionnaire Encyclopedique des Sports, des Sportifs et des Performances. Bernard LeRoy. 864p. (FRE.). 1973. 135.00 (0-8288-6266-4, M-6353) Fr & Eur.

Dictionnaire Encyclopedique d'Histoire: Encyclopedic Dictionary of History, 8 vols., Set. Michel Mourre. 5480p. (FRE.). 1978. 595.00 (0-8288-5194-8, M6420) Fr & Eur.

Dictionnaire Encyclopedique d'Histoire et Geographie Agraires: French, English, German, Italian & Spanish Dictionary of Agrarian Geography & History. 2nd ed. Fenelon, Paul & Conseil International de la Language Francaise Staff. 801p. (ENG, FRE, GER, ITA & SPA.). 1991. pap. 285.00 (0-8288-6169-2, 2853192105) Fr & Eur.

Dictionnaire Encyclopedique du Christianisme Ancien. CERF Staff. 1200p. (FRE.). 1990. 795.00 (0-8288-9495-7) Fr & Eur.

*Dictionnaire Encyclopedique du Christianisme Ancien Vol. 2: J-Z. Angelo Di Berardino. Ed. by Francois Vial. 1990. write for info. (0-7859-7764-3, 2204041823) Fr & Eur.

*Dictionnaire Encyclopedique du Judaisme. Ed. by Geoffrey Wigoder & Sylvie A. Goldberg. 1800p. 1993. 395.00 (0-7859-7765-1, 2204045411) Fr & Eur.

Dictionnaire Encyclopedique du Theatre. Michel Corvin. 940p. (FRE.). 1991. 195.00 (0-8288-9496-5) Fr & Eur.

*Dictionnaire Encyclopedique Economique et Social. 2nd ed. Claude Alquier. 1990. write for info. (0-7859-7955-7, 2-7178-1834-0) Fr & Eur.

*Dictionnaire Encyclopedique Juniors. Hachette Staff. Date not set. write for info. (0-7859-7604-3, 2010114280) Fr & Eur.

Dictionnaire Encyclopedique Larousse L1. Larousse Staff. (FRE.). 1979. 250.00 (0-7859-0127-2, M7733) Fr & Eur.

Dictionnaire Encyclopedique Lidis, 3 vols., Set. Lidis Staff. 1104p. (FRE.). 1977. 350.00 (0-8288-5386-X, M6138) Fr & Eur.

*Dictionnaire Encyclopedique Medical. Maurice Rapin. 1986. write for info. (0-7859-8636-7, 225710482x) Fr & Eur.

*Dictionnaire Encyclopedique Suisse. Alain Nicollier. 1988. write for info. (0-7859-8199-3, 2-88115-001-2) Fr & Eur.

Dictionnaire Encylopedique d'Agrometeorologie. S. De Parceveaux. 328p. (ENG, FRE & SPA.). 1990. lib. bdg. 75.00 (0-685-48306-1, M6119) Fr & Eur.

Dictionnaire Encylopedique Quillet, 10 vols., Set. Quillet Staff. (FRE.). 1977. 1,295.00 (0-8288-5387-8, M6139) Fr & Eur.

*Dictionnaire Erotique. Alfred Delvau. 288p. (FRE.). 1990. 95.00 (0-7859-7946-8, 2714443370) Fr & Eur.

Dictionnaire Erotique. Pierre Guiraud. 648p. (FRE.). 1978. pap. 39.95 (0-8288-5195-6, M6306) Fr & Eur.

*Dictionnaire Erotique. Pierre Guiraud. 1993. write for info. (0-7859-7839-9, 2-228-88693-9) Fr & Eur.

Dictionnaire Espagnol-Francais et Francais-Espagnol. Serge Denis et al. 904p. (FRE & SPA.). 1976. 85.00 (0-8288-5650-8, S33062) Fr & Eur.

*Dictionnaire Espagnol-Francais et Francais-Espagnol. Robert Larrieu. 1978. write for info. (0-7859-8006-7, 2-7370-0109-9) Fr & Eur.

Dictionnaire Espagnol-Francais et Francais-Espagnol: French - Spanish, Spanish - French. Ed. by Vicente Salva & Robert Larrieu. 1580p. (FRE & SPA.). 1951. 55.00 (0-7859-0775-0, F-140811) Fr & Eur.

Dictionnaire Essentiel d'Ecologie. Jean Touffet. 112p. (FRE.). 1982. 19.95 (0-8288-1400-7, M15270) Fr & Eur.

Dictionnaire et Armorial des Noms de Famille de France. Claude-Pierre Blanche. 312p. (FRE.). 1974. pap. 75.00 (0-8288-6026-2, M6038) Fr & Eur.

*Dictionnaire et Ideologie. Domenico D'Oria. 1989. 95.00 (0-7859-8709-6, 8875142858) Fr & Eur.

Dictionnaire et Origine des Instruments de Musique. Pierre-Andre Sable. 96p. (FRE.). 1980. 14.95 (0-8288-2172-0, M15204) Fr & Eur.

*Dictionnaire Etim-Freisz 1990. 7th ed. ETIM Staff. 1990. write for info. (0-7859-8232-9, 2-905201-06-1) Fr & Eur.

Dictionnaire Etymologique. Jean Robert. 45.00 (0-317-45625-3) Fr & Eur.

*Dictionnaire Etymologique de la Flore Francaise. Jean-Patrick Ferrari. 1984. write for info. (0-7859-7965-4, 2-7205-0518-8) Fr & Eur.

Dictionnaire Etymologique de la Langue Francaise. 10th ed. Oscar Bloch & Walter Von Wartburg. 720p. (FRE.). 1994. 135.00 (0-8288-5855-1, FC1016) Fr & Eur.

Dictionnaire Etymologique de la Langue Latine: Etymological Dictionary of the Latin Language. 4th ed. A. Ernout & A. Meillet. 946p. (FRE & LAT.). 1980. 225.00 (0-8288-1022-2, M6697) Fr & Eur.

*Dictionnaire Etymologique de la Langue Wallone, 3 vols. fac. ed. Charles-Marie Grandgagnage. 1275p. 1969. pap. write for info. (0-7859-5213-6) Fr & Eur.

*Dictionnaire Etymologique des Noms de Communes de Normandie. Rene Lepelley. 1993. write for info. (0-7859-8096-2, 2-85480-455-4) Fr & Eur.

Dictionnaire Etymologique des Noms de Famille. Marie-Therese Moriet. 1120p. (FRE.). 1991. 150.00 (0-8288-9497-3) Fr & Eur.

Dictionnaire Etymologique des Noms de Famille et Prenoms de France. Albert Dauzat. 626p. (FRE.). 1985. write for info. (0-8288-9498-1) Fr & Eur.

*Dictionnaire Etymologique des Noms de Famille Gascons. Michel Grosclaude. 1992. 95.00 (0-7859-8261-2, 2-9507255-0-3) Fr & Eur.

Dictionnaire Etymologique des Noms de Pays et de Peuples: Eymological Dictionary of People's & Place Names. Serge Losique. 243p. (FRE.). 1971. pap. 35.00 (0-8288-6453-5, F-135990) Fr & Eur.

Dictionnaire Etymologique des Noms de Rivieres et de Montagnes en France. Albert Dauzat et al. (FRE.). 1982. pap. 95.00 (0-7859-4817-1, M6101) Fr & Eur.

Dictionnaire Etymologique des Noms des Lieux en France. 2nd ed. Albert Dauzat. 786p. (FRE.). 1979. 85.00 (0-8288-9499-X, EM74) Fr & Eur.

*Dictionnaire Etymologique des Noms d'Hommes et de Dieux. Andre Cherpillod. 1988. write for info. (0-7859-7830-5, 2-225-81556-9) Fr & Eur.

*Dictionnaire Etymologique et Historique du Francais. rev. ed. Jean M. DuBois & Henri Mitterand. 1993. write for info. (0-7859-7680-9, 2037102283) Fr & Eur.

*Dictionnaire etymologique Marabout. Jean Mathieu-Rosay. 544p. (FRE.). 1985. pap. 17.95 (0-7859-8641-3, 250100664x) Fr & Eur.

*Dictionnaire Europa. Larousse Staff. 1959. write for info. (0-7859-7649-3, 2034010329) Fr & Eur.

Dictionnaire Europeen des Medicaments et Leurs Equivalents. 2nd ed. Christian Gariot. 1699p. (FRE.). 1991. 295.00 (0-8288-9522-8) Fr & Eur.

*Dictionnaire Europeen des Mots Usuels. Monique Goursau & Henri Goursau. 1989. 69.95 (0-7859-8223-X, 2-904105-02-6) Fr & Eur.

Dictionnaire Explicatif et Combinatoire du Francais Contemporain (DECFC), Vol. 1: Recherches Lexico-Semantiques. Ed. by Igor Mel'cuk. 172p. (FRE.). 1984. 44.00x (2-7606-0658-9, Pub. by Les Presses CN) Benjamins North Am.

Dictionnaire Explicatif et Combinatoire du Francais Contemporain (DECFC), Vol. 2: Recherches Lexico-Semantiques. Ed. by Igor Mel'cuk. 344p. (FRE.). 1988. 89.00x (2-7606-0804-2, Pub. by Les Presses CN) Benjamins North Am.

Dictionnaire Explicatif et Combinatoire du Francais Contemporain (DECFC), Vol. 3: Recherches Lexico-Semantiques. Ed. by Igor Mel'cuk. 325p. (FRE.). 1992. 65.00x (2-7606-1559-6, Pub. by Les Presses CN) Benjamins North Am.

*Dictionnaire Extraordinaire des Mots Ordinaires. Rene Drouin. 1991. write for info. (0-7859-7944-1, 2-7144-2567-4) Fr & Eur.

Dictionnaire Familial des Medecines Naturelles. Emmerick-Armand Maury & Chantal De Rudder. (FRE.). 1982. 105.00 (0-8288-9523-6, M6832) Fr & Eur.

*Dictionnaire Familial D'Homeopathie. Emmerick-Armand Maury. 1982. write for info. (0-7859-7938-7, 2-7113-0026-9) Fr & Eur.

*Dictionnaire Familial D'Homeopathie. Emmerick-Armand Maury. 1991. write for info. (0-7859-7896-8, 2-501-01546-0) Fr & Eur.

*Dictionnaire Feminin-Masculin des Professions, des Titres Et. Geneve (Canton) Bureau de l'Egalite des Droits Entre Homme et Femme. 1991. write for info. (0-7859-8201-9, 2-88340-012-1) Fr & Eur.

*Dictionnaire Fiduciaire Financier. 2nd ed. Erik De La Villeguerin. 1991. write for info. (0-7859-8140-3, 2-86521-156-8) Fr & Eur.

*Dictionnaire Fiscal 1992. 1992. 95.00 (0-7859-8142-X, 2-86521-192-4) Fr & Eur.

*Dictionnaire Fondamental du Francais Litteraire. Philippe Forest & Gerard Conio. 1993. write for info. (0-7859-8132-2, 2-86311-244-9) Fr & Eur.

Dictionnaire Forestier Multilingue. Andre Metro. 434p. (FRE.). 1976. 125.00 (0-8288-5651-6, M6409) Fr & Eur.

Dictionnaire Foucher de Stenographie. G. Brousse. 346p. (FRE.). 1980. pap. 24.95 (0-8288-4692-8, M6699) Fr & Eur.

*Dictionnaire Foulfoulde-Francais. Dominique Noye. 1989. 150.00 (0-7859-7925-5, 2-7053-0484-3) Fr & Eur.

Dictionnaire Francais - Arabe Detaille: Al-Kamel al-Wasit. Youssef M. Reda. 1990. 45.00 (0-86685-463-0) Intl Bk Ctr.

Dictionnaire Francais - Chinois de l'Electronique. Industrie Electronique Staff. 1484p. (CHI & FRE.). 1987. 95.00 (0-8288-9524-4) Fr & Eur.

Dictionnaire Francais - Chinois de Mecanique et d'Electricite. Yongguang Zheng et al. 1910p. (CHI & FRE.). 1989. 250.00 (0-8288-9525-2) Fr & Eur.

Dictionnaire Francais - Chinois des Travaux de Construction. Science Press Staff. 1914p. (CHI & FRE.). 1986. 95.00 (0-8288-9527-9) Fr & Eur.

Dictionnaire Francais - Chinois du Chemin de Fer. Chemins de fer China Staff. 1140p. (CHI & FRE.). 1991. 95.00 (0-8288-9528-7) Fr & Eur.

Dictionnaire Francais - Chinois en Automatique. Connaissance Staff. 630p. (CHI & FRE.). 1990. 50.00 (0-8288-9529-5) Fr & Eur.

*Dictionnaire Francais-Allemand, Allemand-Francais. Jean Clediere & Daniel Rocher. 1987. write for info. (0-7859-7654-X, 2034020537) Fr & Eur.

*Dictionnaire Francais-Allemand, Allemand-Francais. Hatier. Date not set. write for info. (0-7859-7779-1, 2218005018) Fr & Eur.

An Asterisk (*) at the beginning of an entry indicates that the title is appearing in BIP for the first time.

***Dictionnaire Francais-Allemand, Allemand-Francais.** Wolfgang Loffler & Kristin Waeterloos. 1993. write for info. (*0-7859-7616-7*, 2010206576); write for info. (*0-7859-7619-1*) Fr & Eur.

Dictionnaire Francais-Allemand des Locutions. F. Dubois & P. Werny. (FRE & GER.). 1976. 39.95 (*0-8288-5652-4*, M6172) Fr & Eur.

***Dictionnaire Francais-Allemand, Deutsch-Franzosich.** Jean Clediere et al. Date not set. write for info. (*0-7859-7650-7*, 2034016114) Fr & Eur.

Dictionnaire Francais-Allemand, Deutsch-Franzosisch. A. Pinloche. 805p. (FRE & GER.). pap. 6.50 (*0-7859-0817-X*, M-9043) Fr & Eur.

***Dictionnaire Francais-Anglais.** 1993. write for info. (*0-7859-7997-2*, 2-7367-0902-0) Fr & Eur.

***Dictionnaire Francais-Anglais, Anglais-Francais.** Pierre-Henry Cousin. (ENG & FRE.). 1988. write for info. (*0-7859-7602-7*, 2010095804) Fr & Eur.

***Dictionnaire Francais-Anglais, Anglais-Francais.** Hatier. Date not set. write for info. (*0-7859-7780-5*, 2218005026) Fr & Eur.

***Dictionnaire Francais-Anglais, Anglais-Francais.** Michael Janes et al. 1993. write for info. (*0-7859-7614-0*, 2010206517) Fr & Eur.

***Dictionnaire Francais-Anglais, Anglais-Francais.** Michael Janes et al. 1993. write for info. (*0-7859-8601-4*, 201020655x) Fr & Eur.

Dictionnaire Francais-Anglais, Anglais-Francais des Termes et Locutions de la Marine Marchande. (ENG & FRE.). 25.00 (*0-7859-0754-8*, M-6140) Fr & Eur.

Dictionnaire Francais-Anglais-Chinois de l'Electronique. Science & Technologie Staff. 238p. (CHI, ENG & FRE.). 1993. 45.00 (*0-7859-5678-6*, 7502314806) Fr & Eur.

Dictionnaire Francais-Anglais de l'Economie. David Lambert. 264p. (ENG & FRE.). 1975. pap. 49.95 (*0-8288-5857-8*, M63299) Fr & Eur.

Dictionnaire Francais-Anglais et Anglais-Francais: French - English, English - French Dictionary. Denis Girard. 1464p. (ENG & FRE.). 1972. 49.95 (*0-8288-6382-2*, M-6274) Fr & Eur.

Dictionnaire Francais-Anglais et Anglais-Francais des Termes Medicaux et Biologiques. 2nd ed. Pierre Lepine. 896p. (ENG & FRE.). 1974. 175.00 (*0-8288-6027-0*, M4665) Fr & Eur.

Dictionnaire Francais-Anglais et Anglais-Francais des Termes Techniques de Medecine. Delamare. (ENG & FRE.). 95.00 (*0-685-36680-4*) Fr & Eur.

Dictionnaire Francais-Arabe. Abdel-Nour. 1985. 39.95 (*0-86685-415-0*) Intl Bk Ctr.

Dictionnaire Francais-Arabe: French-Arabic Dictionary. Louis Saisse & C. Iskandar. 425p. (ARA & FRE.). 1980. pap. 14.95 (*0-8288-1590-9*, M994) Fr & Eur.

Dictionnaire Francais-Arabe: French-Arabic Dictionary. Ben Sedira & Charles Belkacem. 820p. (ARA & FRE.). 1980. pap. 39.95 (*0-8288-0440-0*, M9306) Fr & Eur.

Dictionnaire Francais-Arabe de la Presse et des Medias: French & Arabic Dictionary of the Press & Media. Conseil International de la Language Francaise Staff. (ARA & FRE.). write for info. (*0-8288-7673-8*) Fr & Eur.

***Dictionnaire Francais Azed.** Hatier. Date not set. write for info. (*0-7859-7789-9*, 2218049856) Fr & Eur.

***Dictionnaire Francais-Breton des Expressions Figurees.** 1993. write for info. (*0-7859-8155-1*, 2-86775-122-5) Fr & Eur.

Dictionnaire Francais-Breton Vannetais. Herrieu. 200p. (BRE & FRE.). 1982. 19.95 (*0-8288-1116-4*, F 34900) Fr & Eur.

***Dictionnaire Francais Chinois.** 1988. write for info. (*0-7859-8577-8*, 7-5327-0505-6) Fr & Eur.

***Dictionnaire Francais-Chinois.** 1985. write for info. (*0-7859-8583-2*, 9-6207-0017-1) Fr & Eur.

Dictionnaire Francais-Chinois. Commercial Press Staff. 1498p. (CHI & FRE.). 1979. 24.95 (*0-8288-4797-5*) Fr & Eur.

***Dictionnaire Francais-Chinois de la Science et de la Technologie des Aliments.** 1992. 95.00 (*0-7859-8575-1*, 7-5019-1313-7) Fr & Eur.

Dictionnaire Francais-Chinois de l'Aeronautique et de l'Espace. Editions de l'Industrie Aeronautique Staff. 2017p. (CHI & FRE.). 1991. 125.00 (*0-7859-1037-9*, 7800463672) Fr & Eur.

Dictionnaire Francais Chinois de Metallurgie. Industrie Metallurgie Staff. 1005p. (CHI & FRE.). 1983. 50.00 (*0-8288-9526-0*) Fr & Eur.

***Dictionnaire Francais-Chinois des Expressions Francaises Cou.** 1988. write for info. (*0-7859-8576-X*, 7-5327-0339-8) Fr & Eur.

Dictionnaire Francais-Corse. Jean Albertini. 349p. (FRE.). 1974. pap. 49.95 (*0-8288-6028-9*, M6001) Fr & Eur.

Dictionnaire Francais-Creole. Jules Faine. 480p. 1975. pap. 95.00 (*0-8288-5858-6*, M4608) Fr & Eur.

Dictionnaire Francais-Cri (Dialecte Quebecois) Philippe Vaillancourt. 460p. 1992. pap. 125.00 (*0-7859-5646-8*, 2760507084) Fr & Eur.

***Dictionnaire Francais de l'Informatique et des Sciences.** Ivan Venev. 1984. write for info. (*0-7859-7951-4*, 2-7178-0792-6) Fr & Eur.

Dictionnaire Francais de Medicine et de Biologie, Vol. 3. A. Mauila et al. 1200p. (FRE.). 1972. 195.00 (*0-7859-0746-7*, M-6394) Fr & Eur.

Dictionnaire Francais de Medicine et de Biologie, Vol. 4. A. Manuila et al. 580p. (FRE.). 1975. 1,195.00 (*0-8288-5856-X*, M15420) Fr & Eur.

Dictionnaire Francais de Medicine et de Biologie, Vol. 4: Annexes. A. Manuila et al. 580p. (FRE.). 1975. 325.00 (*0-7859-4432-X*, 2225287767) Fr & Eur.

***Dictionnaire Francais-Espagnol, Espagnol-Francais.** Hachette Staff. (FRE & SPA.). 1993. write for info. (*0-7859-7615-9*, 2010206525) Fr & Eur.

***Dictionnaire Francais-Espagnol, Espagnol-Francais.** Hatier. Date not set. write for info. (*0-7859-7781-3*, 2218005034) Fr & Eur.

***Dictionnaire Francais-Espagnol, Espagnol-Francais.** A. Gonzalez Hermoso & M. Sanchez Alfaro. 1993. write for info. (*0-7859-7618-3*, 2010206568) Fr & Eur.

***Dictionnaire Francais-Espagnol, Espagnol-Francais.** Miguel De Toro y Gisbert. 1987. write for info. (*0-7859-7653-1*, 2034020510) Fr & Eur.

Dictionnaire Francais-Ewe. Kofi J. Adzomada. 245p. (FRE.). 1992. 75.00 (*0-7859-1019-0*, 2906718327) Fr & Eur.

Dictionnaire Francais-Francais des Mots Rare et Precieux. (FRE.). pap. 8.95 (*0-7859-4313-7*) Fr & Eur.

Dictionnaire Francais-Hebreu. rev. ed. Marc M. Cohn. 760p. (FRE & HEB.). 1988. 79.95 (*0-7859-4813-9*) Fr & Eur.

***Dictionnaire Francais-Indonesien.** Farida Soemargono. 1994. write for info. (*0-7859-8208-6*, 2-901795-57-9) Fr & Eur.

***Dictionnaire Francais-Italien, Italien-Francais.** Enea Balmas. 1993. write for info. (*0-7859-7617-5*, 2010206541) Fr & Eur.

***Dictionnaire Francais-Italien, Italien-Francais.** Bordas. 1990. write for info. (*0-7859-7708-2*, 2040192441) Fr & Eur.

***Dictionnaire Francais-Italien, Italien-Francais.** Bordas. 1990. write for info. (*0-7859-8613-8*, 204019228X) Fr & Eur.

***Dictionnaire Francais-Italien, Italien-Francais.** Hatier. Date not set. write for info. (*0-7859-7784-8*, 2218019817) Fr & Eur.

Dictionnaire Francais-Kurde. Halkawt Hakim. 247p. 1993. pap. 59.95 (*0-7859-5624-7*, 2252029005) Fr & Eur.

Dictionnaire Francais-Langue d'Oc. Piat. 1000p. (FRE.). 75.00 (*0-7859-0723-8*, M-6451) Fr & Eur.

***Dictionnaire Francais-Latin.** Jean E. Decahors. 1957. write for info. (*0-7859-7782-1*, 2218005301) Fr & Eur.

Dictionnaire Francais-Latin. Georges Edon. (FRE & LAT.). 85.00 (*0-7859-0763-7*, M-6703) Fr & Eur.

***Dictionnaire Francais-Latin.** Henri Goelzer. 1977. write for info. (*0-7859-7918-2*, 2-7050-0091-7) Fr & Eur.

***Dictionnaire Francais-Latin.** Ed. by Henri Goelzer. 1966. write for info. (*0-7859-8618-9*, 208070124X) Fr & Eur.

***Dictionnaire Francais-Latin.** Louis Quicherat. 1967. write for info. (*0-7859-7600-0*, 2010041844) Fr & Eur.

***Dictionnaire Francais-Luxembourgeois.** Henri Rinnen. 1170p. (FRE.). 1988. 95.00 (*0-7859-8664-2*, 287963007x) Fr & Eur.

Dictionnaire Francais-Malgache. R. P. Malzac. 861p. (FRE.). 1953. pap. 59.95 (*0-8288-6876-X*, M-6390) Fr & Eur.

Dictionnaire Francais-Neerlandais. C. Herckenrath & A. Dory. 509p. (DUT & FRE.). 1980. 49.95 (*0-8288-0452-4*, M9743) Fr & Eur.

***Dictionnaire Francais-Polonais.** 5th ed. Bernard Hamel. 1987. write for info. (*0-7859-8209-4*, 2-902957-00-9) Fr & Eur.

***Dictionnaire Francais-Pyreneen, Pyreneen-Francais.** Nicole Lacour et al. 1991. write for info. (*0-7859-8170-5*, 2-86971-317-7) Fr & Eur.

***Dictionnaire Francais-Russe.** V. G. Gak & J. Triomphe. 1991. write for info. (*0-7859-8098-9*, 2-85536-010-2) Fr & Eur.

***Dictionnaire Francais-Russe et Russe-Francais de la Langue D.** Robert Giraud. 1991. write for info. (*0-7859-7962-X*, 2-7204-0216-8) Fr & Eur.

Dictionnaire Francais-Serbocroate. 632p. (CRO, FRE & SER.). pap. 29.95 (*0-686-57109-6*, M-6142) Fr & Eur.

Dictionnaire Francais-Serbocroate-Francais. Branislav Grujic. 631p. (FRE & SER.). 1982. 29.95 (*0-8288-1045-1*, M 6142) Fr & Eur.

Dictionnaire Francais-Tahitien et Tahitien-Francais: Tahitian - French - Tahitian Dictionary. Mai-Aru & J. Anisson du Perron. 380p. (FRE.). 1973. 39.95 (*0-8288-6267-2*, M-6383) Fr & Eur.

Dictionnaire Francais-Tamoul; French-Tamil Dictionary. Mousset & Hector Dupuis. 1253p. (FRE & TAM.). 1990. 150.00 (*0-8288-1108-3*, M223) Fr & Eur.

***Dictionnaire Francais-Thailandais.** 1991. write for info. (*0-7859-8584-0*, 974-210-483-2) Fr & Eur.

Dictionnaire Francais-Tibetain (Tibet Oriental) A. Giraudeau & Francis Gore. 310p. (FRE & TIB.). 1956. 125.00 (*0-8288-6861-1*, M-6275) Fr & Eur.

***Dictionnaire Francais-Turc.** Cybele Berk & Michel Bozdemir. 1991. write for info. (*0-7859-8207-8*, 2-901795-42-0) Fr & Eur.

***Dictionnaire Francais-Vietnamien.** Comite des Sciences Sociales de la Republique Socialiste du Viet-Nam Staff. 1988. write for info. (*0-7859-8712-6*, 9290280344) Fr & Eur.

Dictionnaire Francasi-Malgache. Narivelo Rajaonarimanana. 192p. (FRE.). 1993. pap. 39.95 (*0-7859-5666-2*, 2901795544) Fr & Eur.

***Dictionnaire Francias-Chinois de l'Aeronautique & de l'Espa.** L'Industrie Aeronautique Staff. 1991. write for info. (*0-7859-8707-X*, 7800463672) Fr & Eur.

Dictionnaire Franco-Arabe de la Langue Parlee en Algerie: French-Arabic Dictionary of Spoken Algerian Arabic. Charles Ben Sedira Belkacem. 756p. (ARA & FRE.). 1980. 75.00 (*0-8288-1587-9*, F5080) Fr & Eur.

Dictionnaire Francois, 2 vols. in 1. Pierre Richelet. 1128p. 1973. reprint ed. write for info. (*3-487-04587-7*, Pub. by Georg Olms GW) Lubrecht & Cramer.

***Dictionnaire Futunien-Francais.** Claire Moyse-Faurie. 1993. write for info. (*0-7859-8186-1*, 2-87723-070-8) Fr & Eur.

***Dictionnaire Garzanti Bordas.** Bordas. 1988. write for info. (*0-7859-7705-8*, 2040182330) Fr & Eur.

Dictionnaire Garzanti Francais-Italien, Italien-Francais. Garzanti. 2046p. (FRE & ITA.). 150.00 (*0-686-57110-X*, M-6143) Fr & Eur.

Dictionnaire Genealogique des Familles Canadiennes, 1. Cyprien Tanguay. LC 73-101091. reprint ed. 20.00 (*0-404-06341-1*) AMS Pr.

Dictionnaire Genealogique des Familles Canadiennes, Set. Cyprien Tanguay. LC 73-101091. reprint ed. lib. bdg. 225.00 (*0-404-06340-3*) AMS Pr.

Dictionnaire Genealogique des Familles Canadiennes, Vols. 2-7. Cyprien Tanguay. LC 73-101091. reprint ed. 34.50 (*0-685-73118-9*) AMS Pr.

***Dictionnaire Genealogique des Familles de l'Inde Francais.** Lucien-Jean Bord & Michel Gaudart de Soulages. 1984. write for info. (*0-7859-8256-6*, 2-9500353-0-2) Fr & Eur.

Dictionnaire General de la Francophonie. J. J. Luthi. 390p. (FRE.). 1986. 95.00 (*0-8288-1944-0*, F59710) Fr & Eur.

Dictionnaire General de la Langue Francaise du Commencement du 17e Siecle Jusqu'a Nos Jours: General Dictionary of the French Language from the Beginning of the 17th Century to the Present, 2 vols., Set. Adophe Hatzfeld & Arsene Darmesteter. 1468p. (FRE.). 1964. 150.00 (*0-8288-6766-6*, F-134240) Fr & Eur.

Dictionnaire General de la Technique Industrielle: Francais - Allemand. 3rd ed. Alain Paris. 1110p. 1990. pap. 49.95 (*0-7859-4740-X*) Fr & Eur.

Dictionnaire General de Surrealisme et de ses Environs. Adam Biro & Rene Passeron. 468p. (FRE.). 1982. 150.00 (*0-8288-9530-9*) Fr & Eur.

***Dictionnaire General Francais-Allemand, Allemand-Francais.** Pierre Grappin. Ed. by Ralf Brockmeier. 1994. write for info. (*0-7859-7662-0*, 2034513355) Fr & Eur.

***Dictionnaire General Francais-Italien, Italien-Francais.** Claude Margueron & Gianfranco Eolena. 1994. write for info. (*0-7859-7661-2*, 2034513347) Fr & Eur.

***Dictionnaire General pour la Maitrise de la Langue Francaise.** Larousse Staff. 1993. write for info. (*0-7859-7641-8*, 2033203026) Fr & Eur.

Dictionnaire Geographique De l'Ancienne Egypte. Heinrich K. Brugsch. 1420p. 1974. reprint ed. write for info. (*3-487-05312-8*, Pub. by Georg Olms GW) Lubrecht & Cramer.

***Dictionnaire Geographique, Historique et Biographique D'Indr.** J. Carre De Busserole. 1988. write for info. (*0-7859-8100-4*, 2-85554-031-3) Fr & Eur.

Dictionnaire Geographique, Historique et Politque des Guales et de la France, 6 vols., Set, Paris 1762-1770. Jean J. Expilly. (FRE.). 1972. Set, Paris, 1762-1770. 750.00 (*0-318-23477-7*) Periodicals Srv.

Dictionnaire Geologique: Francais-Russe: French - Russian Dictionary of Geology. deluxe ed. V. Dybovskaia & I. Kirillova. 406p. (FRE & RUS.). 1958. 19.95 (*0-8288-6847-6*, M-9099) Fr & Eur.

Dictionnaire Grec-Francais. C. Georgin. (FRE & GRE.). 1992. reprint ed. pap. 39.95 (*0-7859-4823-6*) Fr & Eur.

Dictionnaire Grec-Francais: Greek - French Dictionary. Anatole Bailly. 2230p. (FRE & GRE.). 1967. pap. 125.00 (*0-8288-6680-5*, M6020) Fr & Eur.

Dictionnaire Grec-Francais: Greek - French Dictionary. Victor Magnien & M. Lacroix. 2168p. (FRE & GRE.). 1969. 79.95 (*0-8288-6592-2*, M-6382) Fr & Eur.

Dictionnaire Grec-Francais: Greek - French Dictionary. Emile Pessoneaux. 896p. (FRE & GRE.). 1953. 59.95 (*0-8288-6877-8*, M-6443) Fr & Eur.

Dictionnaire Grec-Francais du Nouveau Testament. 3rd ed. Maurice Carrez & Francois Morel. 270p. (FRE & GRE.). 1985. pap. write for info. (*0-7859-4810-4*) Fr & Eur.

Dictionnaire Hachette de la Langue Francais. Hachette Staff. 75.00 (*0-317-45629-6*) Fr & Eur.

Dictionnaire Hachette de la Langue Francaise: Hachette Dictionary of the French Language. Setton. 1183p. (FRE.). 1980. 59.95 (*0-8288-1953-X*, M9373) Fr & Eur.

Dictionnaire Hachette du Francais. 2nd ed. Ed. by Marie Gatard. 1824p. (ENG & FRE.). (C). 1993. pap. 32.50 (*2-01-018877-2*) OUP.

***Dictionnaire Hachette Encyclopedique Illustre.** Hatchette Staff. 2065p. (FRE.). 1994. 85.00 (*0-7859-7613-2*, 2010202554) Fr & Eur.

***Dictionnaire Hachette Juniors.** Ed. by Paul Bonnevie & Philippe Amiel. Date not set. write for info. (*0-7859-7606-X*, 2010143981) Fr & Eur.

***Dictionnaire Hachette Juniors Encyclopedie, Noms Propres.** Paul Bonnevie. 1990. write for info. (*0-7859-7609-4*, 2010164636) Fr & Eur.

***Dictionnaire Hachette Juniors Langue Francaise.** Paul Bonnevie. 1990. write for info. (*0-7859-7608-6*) Fr & Eur.

***Dictionnaire Hassaniyya-Francais: Dialecte Arabe de Mauritanie, Dal-Ra, Vol. 4.** Catherine Taine-Cheikh. 265p. (FRE.). 1991. pap. 95.00 (*0-7859-7922-0*, 2705303715) Fr & Eur.

***Dictionnaire Hassaniyya-Francais: Dialecte Arabe de Mauritanie, Ha-Xa, Vol. 3.** Catherine Taine-Cheikh. 230p. (FRE.). 1989. pap. 55.00 (*0-7859-7921-2*, 2705303707) Fr & Eur.

***Dictionnaire Hassaniyya-Francais: Dialecte Arabe de Mauritanie, Introduction Hamza-Ba, Vol. 1.** Catherine Taine-Cheikh. 186p. (FRE.). 1989. pap. 95.00 (*0-7859-7919-0*, 2705303685) Fr & Eur.

***Dictionnaire Hassaniyya-Francais: Dialecte Arabe de Mauritanie, Sin-Sad, Vol. 6.** Catherine Taine-Cheikh. 204p. (FRE.). 1991. pap. 55.00 (*0-7859-7924-7*, 2705303731) Fr & Eur.

***Dictionnaire Hassaniyya-Francais: Dialecte Arabe de Mauritanie, Ta-Zim, Vol. 2.** Catherine Taine-Cheikh. 176p. (FRE.). 1989. pap. 55.00 (*0-7859-7920-4*, 2705303693) Fr & Eur.

***Dictionnaire Hassaniyya-Francais: Dialecte Arabe de Mauritanie, Za-Sin, Vol. 5.** Catherine Taine-Cheikh. 197p. (FRE.). 1991. pap. 55.00 (*0-7859-7923-9*, 2705303723) Fr & Eur.

***Dictionnaire Hebreu-Francais.** N. P. Sander & Isaac-Leon Trenel. (FRE & HEB.). 1982. pap. write for info. (*0-7859-8579-4*, 90-04-01949-9) Fr & Eur.

***Dictionnaire Hindi-Francais.** Federica Boschetti. 1991. write for info. (*0-7859-8260-4*, 2-9506068-0-6) Fr & Eur.

***Dictionnaire Historique de la Papaute.** Philippe Levillain. 1776p. Date not set. 375.00 (*0-7859-8720-7*) Fr & Eur.

***Dictionnaire Historique de la Revolution Francaise.** Albert Soboul. Ed. by Jean-Rene Suratteau & Francois Gendron. 1989. write for info. (*0-7859-7743-0*, 2130425224) Fr & Eur.

Dictionnaire Historique de la Terminologie Optique des Grecs. Charles Mugler. 460p. (FRE.). 1964. pap. 150.00 (*0-8288-6767-4*, M-6421) Fr & Eur.

***Dictionnaire Historique de la Terminologie Optique des Grecs.** Charles Mugler. 460p. (FRE.). 1964. pap. 165.00 (*0-7859-7845-3*, 2252001674) Fr & Eur.

***Dictionnaire Historique de la Ville de Paris et de Ses Envir.** Hurtaut & Magny. 1977. write for info. (*0-7859-8040-7*, 2-8266-0115-6) Fr & Eur.

Dictionnaire Historique de l'Ancien Langage Francois Ou Glossaire de la Langue Francoise, 10 vols., Set. Jean B. La Curne De Sainte Palaye. lxxxvi, 4775p. 1972. reprint ed. write for info. (*3-487-04251-7*, Pub. by Georg Olms GW) Lubrecht & Cramer.

***Dictionnaire Historique des Fascismes et du Nazisme.** Serge Berstein & Pierre Milza. 1992. 175.00 (*0-7859-8174-8*, 2-87027-463-7) Fr & Eur.

***Dictionnaire Historique des Fiefs, Chatellenies et Paroisses.** Guillaume-Michel Chabrol. 1973. write for info. (*0-7859-8054-7*, 2-85023-006-5) Fr & Eur.

***Dictionnaire Historique des Francs-Macons.** Jean-Andre Faucher. 1988. write for info. (*0-7859-7866-6*, 2-262-00463-3) Fr & Eur.

Dictionnaire Historique des Musiciens, Artistes et Amateurs, Morts ou Vivant, 2 vols., Set. A. E. Choron & F. J. Fayolle. 965p. 1910. lib. bdg. 193.70 (*0-685-13867-4*, 05103285, Pub. by Georg Olms GW) Lubrecht & Cramer.

Dictionnaire Historique Des Musiciens, Artistes et Amateurs, Morts Ou Vivants, 2 vols., Set. Alexandre E. Choron & Francois J. Fayolle. xcii, 905p. 1971. reprint ed. write for info. (*0-318-71330-6*, Pub. by Georg Olms GW) Lubrecht & Cramer.

Dictionnaire Historique des Musiciens, Artistes et Amateurs, Morts Ou Vivants, 2 vols., Set. Alexandre E. Choron & Francois J. Fayolle. 1971. reprint ed. write for info. (*0-318-71894-4*, Pub. by Georg Olms GW) Lubrecht & Cramer.

Dictionnaire Historique des Rues de Marseilles. Adrien Bles. 442p. (FRE.). 1989. 250.00 (*0-8288-9531-7*) Fr & Eur.

Dictionnaire Historique des Rues de Paris. Jacques Hillairet. (FRE.). 1987. 395.00 (*0-8288-9532-5*) Fr & Eur.

Dictionnaire Historique des Rues de Paris: Supplement. Jacques Hillairet. 150p. (FRE.). 1975. 59.95 (*0-8288-9533-3*) Fr & Eur.

Dictionnaire Historique du Breton: Geriadur Istorel ar Brezhoneg. Roparz. (FRE.). 1975. reprint ed. 695.00 (*0-8288-9534-1*) Fr & Eur.

Dictionnaire Historique et Biographique de la Revolution et de l'Empire: 1789-1815, 2 vols. J. F. Robinet et al. 1899. 220.00 (*0-318-23476-9*) Periodicals Srv.

Dictionnaire Historique et Heraldique De la Noblesse Francaise, 2 vols., Set. Philippe D. Mailhol. vii, 1452p. reprint ed. write for info. (*0-318-71375-6*, Pub. by Georg Olms GW) Lubrecht & Cramer.

***Dictionnaire Historique et Pittoresque du Theatre et des Art.** Arthur Pougin. 1985. write for info. (*0-7859-7980-8*, 2-7307-0280-6) Fr & Eur.

***Dictionnaire Historique Geographique et Statistique de L'Ind.** Hubert. 1985. write for info. (*0-7859-7932-8*, 2-7084-0125-4) Fr & Eur.

Dictionnaire Historique, Georgraphique et Biographique de Maine et Loire, 3 vols., Set. C. Port. 896p. (FRE.). 1978. 595.00 (*0-8288-5197-2*, M6463) Fr & Eur.

***Dictionnaire Historique, Litteraire et Statistique des Depar.** Jean-Louis Grillet. 1973. write for info. (*0-7859-7991-3*, 2-7348-0411-5) Fr & Eur.

***Dictionnaire Historique, Thematique et Technique des Littera.** Ed. by Jacques Demougin. 1986. write for info. (*0-7859-7666-3*, 2035083028) Fr & Eur.

***Dictionnaire Historique, Thematique et Technique des Littera A-K.** Ed. by Jacques Demougin. 1985. write for info. (*0-7859-8608-1*, 203508301X) Fr & Eur.

***Dictionnaire Homeopathique.** Louis Pommier. 1986. write for info. (*0-7859-7851-8*, 2-253-03815-6) Fr & Eur.

***Dictionnaire Humoristique de A a Z.** Tristan Bernard. Ed. by Pierre Drachline. 1993. write for info. (*0-7859-8125-X*, 2-86274-287-2) Fr & Eur.

***Dictionnaire Iaai.** Francoise Ozanne-Rivierre. 1984. write for info. (*0-7859-8078-4*, 2-85297-126-7) Fr & Eur.

***Dictionnaire Iconologique.** Honore Lacombe de Prezel. 1972. write for info. (*0-7859-8042-3*, 2-8266-0209-8) Fr & Eur.

Dictionnaire Illustre: Dictionnaire Illustre: Francais-Russe. A. Kolesnikova & L. Lulchak. (Illus.). 856p. (FRE & RUS.). 1977. 29.95 (*0-7859-0811-0*, M9070) Fr & Eur.

Dictionnaire Illustre de L'Histoire de France. Alain Decaux. 1989. lib. bdg. 85.00 (*0-8288-2495-9*) Fr & Eur.

Dictionnaire Illustre de Rhumathologie. A. K. Bhalla & P. L. Williams. 352p. (FRE.). 1990. 150.00 (*0-8288-9535-X*) Fr & Eur.

***Dictionnaire Illustre des Antiquites et de la Brocante.** Jean Bedel. 1988. write for info. (*0-7859-7668-X*, 2035091063) Fr & Eur.

D

An Asterisk (*) at the beginning of an entry indicates that the title is appearing in BIP for the first time.

***Dictionnaire Illustre des Explorateurs et Grands Voyageurs Francais du XIX Siecle Vol. 1: Afrique.** Numa Broc. 346p. (FRE.). 1988. 150.00 (*0-7859-7994-8*, 2735501582) Fr & Eur.

***Dictionnaire Illustre des Explorateurs et Grands Voyageurs Francais du XIX Siecle Vol. 2: Asie.** Numa Broc. 452p. (FRE.). 1992. 175.00 (*0-7859-7995-6*, 2735502333) Fr & Eur.

Dictionnaire Illustre Multilingue de la Ceramique du Proche-Orient Ancien. Marguerite Yon. 312p. (FRE.). 1982. 125.00 (*0-8288-9537-6*) Fr & Eur.

Dictionnaire Illustre Multilingue de l'Architecture du Proche-Orient Ancien. Olivier Aurenche. 391p. (FRE.). 1977. 150.00 (*0-8288-9536-8*) Fr & Eur.

Dictionnaire Illustre Multilinque de l'Architecture du Proche-Orient Ancien: Multilingual Illustrated Dictionary of the Architecture of the Ancient Near-East. Olivier Aurenche. 392p. (FRE.). 1978. 125.00 (*0-8288-5199-9*, M6017) Fr & Eur.

Dictionnaire Illustre Technique Automobile en 6 Langues. Czeslaw Blok et al. 680p. (DUT, ENG, FRE, GER, ITA & RUS.). 1981. 195.00 (*0-8288-0050-2*, M9475) Fr & Eur.

***Dictionnaire Ilustre de Mythologie Basque.** Ed. by Jose M. De Barandiaran & Michel Duvert. 1993. write for info. (*0-7859-8708-8*, 8479173297) Fr & Eur.

***Dictionnaire Inattendu des Citations.** Alain Dag'Naud & Olivier Dazat. 1992. 95.00 (*0-7859-7612-4*, 2010177363) Fr & Eur.

***Dictionnaire Inespere de Fifty-Five Termes Visites par Jacques Lacan.** Oreste Saint-Drome. 1994. write for info. (*0-7859-7630-2*, 2020213508) Fr & Eur.

Dictionnaire Informatique, Vol. 2: French-English. 3rd rev. ed. R. Fisher. (ENG & FRE.). 1991. 110.00 (*0-685-48812-8*, M14514) Fr & Eur.

Dictionnaire Initiatique. rev. ed. Herre Masson. 430p. (FRE.). 1984. 55.00 (*0-7859-4833-3*) Fr & Eur.

***Dictionnaire Initiatique de L'Orant.** Roland Nadaus. 1993. write for info. (*0-7859-8190-X*, 2-87744-154-7) Fr & Eur.

Dictionnaire International d'Abbreviations Scientifiques et Techniques. Azzaretti. 300p. (FRE.). 1978. lib. bdg. 95.00 (*0-7859-3905-9*, 2856080030) Fr & Eur.

***Dictionnaire International des Abreviations Medicales.** Maurice A. Touati. 1994. write for info. (*0-7859-8106-3*, 2-85608-058-8) Fr & Eur.

***Dictionnaire International des Mots Usuels.** Monique Goursau & Henri Goursau. 1989. 69.95 (*0-7859-8224-8*, 2-904105-03-4) Fr & Eur.

***Dictionnaire International des Termes Litteraires.** Francke. 1980. write for info. (*0-7859-8667-7*, 331701475X) Fr & Eur.

***Dictionnaire International du Commerce et de l'Economie.** Ed. by F. Munniksma. 1990. write for info. (*0-7859-8704-5*, 7505200259) Fr & Eur.

Dictionnaire International du Commerce et de L'Economie: French, English, Esperanto, German, Spanish, Italian, Portuguese, Swedish, Japanese, Chinese. F. Munniksma. 1990. 75.00 (*0-685-48811-X*, M15696) Fr & Eur.

***Dictionnaire International du Cyclisme 1993.** Claude Sudres. 1993. write for info. (*0-7859-8252-3*, 2-910048-01-2) Fr & Eur.

Dictionnaire Inverse de l'Ancien Francais. Ralph De Gorog. LC 81-18874. (Medieval & Renaissance Texts & Studies: Vol. 4). 272p. 1982. 32.00 (*0-86698-010-5*) MRTS.

***Dictionnaire Inverse de l'Ancien Francais.** Douglas C. Walker. 832p. (FRE.). 1982. 45.00 (*0-7859-8022-9*, 2760348105) Fr & Eur.

***Dictionnaire Inverse et Analyse Statistique de la Langue Esp.** Silvia Faitelson-Weiser. 1988. write for info. (*0-7859-8035-0*, 2-7637-7137-8) Fr & Eur.

***Dictionnaire Italien D'Aujourd'Hui.** Pierre Noaro et al. 1993. write for info. (*0-7859-7872-0*, 2-266-02936-3) Fr & Eur.

***Dictionnaire Italien-Francais et Francais-Italien.** Herselin. 1978. write for info. (*0-7859-8008-3*, 2-7370-0173-0) Fr & Eur.

Dictionnaire Italien-Francais et Francais-Italien: Italian - French, French - Italian Dictionary. Pierre Rouede & Denise Rouede. 1256p. (FRE & ITA.). 1970. 55.00 (*0-8288-6526-4*, M-6493) Fr & Eur.

***Dictionnaire Italien-Francais, Francais-Italien.** Ed. by Jacqueline Bloncourt-Herselin. 1969. write for info. (*0-7859-8617-0*, 208070009X) Fr & Eur.

Dictionnaire Jersais-Francais, 2 tomes, Set. Le Maistre. (FRE.). 150.00 (*0-685-57713-9*, F136580) Fr & Eur.

***Dictionnaire Joly Bourse et Produits Financiers.** Laurent Faugerolas. 1990. write for info. (*0-7859-8097-0*, 2-85522-030-0) Fr & Eur.

***Dictionnaire Joly Concurence.** Xavier de Roux & Dominique Voillemot. 1988. write for info. (*0-7859-8238-8*, 2-907512-00-5) Fr & Eur.

***Dictionnaire Joly, Pratique des Contrats Internationaux.** 2nd ed. GLN-Joly Staff. 1990. write for info. (*0-7859-8239-6*, 2-907512-01-3) Fr & Eur.

***Dictionnaire Judiciare des Communes 1992.** Sofiac. 900p. (FRE.). 1992. pap. 295.00 (*0-7859-8065-2*, 2851301047) Fr & Eur.

Dictionnaire Juridique. Lemeunier. (FRE.). 1988. pap. 75.00 (*0-7859-3914-8*) Fr & Eur.

Dictionnaire Juridique. Mario Matteucci. (FRE & ITA.). 1963. write for info. (*0-7859-4892-9*) Fr & Eur.

***Dictionnaire Juridique des Communautes Europeennes.** Ami Barav & Christian Philip. 1993. write for info. (*0-7859-7748-1*, 2130449123) Fr & Eur.

Dictionnaire Juridique, Diccionario Juridico: French - Spanish, Spanish - French. 3rd ed. Olivier Merlin-Walch & Narciso Amoros Rica. 933p. (FRE & SPA.). 1993. 195.00 (*0-7859-1078-6*, S36030) Fr & Eur.

***Dictionnaire Juridique et Economique: French-English, English-French.** Michel Doucet. 769p. (ENG & FRE.). 1979. 150.00 (*0-7859-8103-9*, 2856080111) Fr & Eur.

Dictionnaire Juridique et Economique: Russian - French, French - Russian. Doucet Long. 1984. lib. bdg. 175.00 (*0-8288-2492-4*) Fr & Eur.

Dictionnaire Juridique et Economique Doucet: Legal & Economic Dictionary, Vol. 1. 3rd ed. Michel Doucet. 625p. (ENG & FRE.). 1980. 150.00 (*0-8288-0382-X*, M6147) Fr & Eur.

Dictionnaire Juridique Italien-Francais-Italien. 2nd ed. G. Tortora. 808p. (FRE & ITA.). 1991. 195.00 (*0-7859-3723-4*) Fr & Eur.

***Dictionnaire Juridique Multilingue: English-French-Spanish-Dutch.** L. D. Egbert. 573p. (DUT, FRE & SPA.). 1978. pap. write for info. (*0-7859-8580-8*, 9028602674) Fr & Eur.

***Dictionnaire Juridique Sport.** Francois Alaphilippe & Jean-Pierre Karaquillo. 1990. write for info. (*0-7859-7843-7*, 2-247-01093-8) Fr & Eur.

***Dictionnaire Kazakh-Francais.** Dominique Indjoudjian & Larissa Kydyrbayeva. (FRE & KAZ.). 1983. pap. write for info. (*0-7859-7948-4*, 2-7169-0182-1) Fr & Eur.

Dictionnaire Laitier: Francais, Allemand, Anglais. Jacques Casalis. (ENG, FRE & GER.). 1963. 85.00 (*0-8288-6787-9*, M-6063) Fr & Eur.

Dictionnaire Laotien-Francais: Laotian - French Dictionary, 2 vols., Set. Marc Reinhorn. 2000p. (FRE & LAO.). 1970. 175.00 (*0-8288-6527-2*, M-6481) Fr & Eur.

***Dictionnaire Larousse Bilingue de Poche.** Larousse Staff. Date not set. write for info. (*0-7859-8605-7*, 203401104X) Fr & Eur.

Dictionnaire Latin-Francais. Felix Gaffiot. 628p. (FRE & LAT.). 1989. pap. 18.95 (*0-7859-4822-8*) Fr & Eur.

***Dictionnaire Latin-Francais.** Felix Gaffiot. 1967. write for info. (*0-7859-8598-0*, 201000535x) Fr & Eur.

***Dictionnaire Latin-Francais.** A. Gariel. 1959. write for info. (*0-7859-8628-6*, 221800531X) Fr & Eur.

***Dictionnaire Latin-Francais.** Ed. by Henri Goelzer. 1966. write for info. (*0-7859-7718-X*, 2080701231) Fr & Eur.

Dictionnaire Latin-Francais. Charles Lebaigue. 1382p. (FRE & LAT.). 59.95 (*0-7859-0744-0*, M-6340) Fr & Eur.

Dictionnaire Latin-Francais: Latin - French Dictionary. Henri Bornecque & Fernand Cauet. 560p. (FRE & LAT.). 1953. 75.00 (*0-8288-6878-6*, M6044) Fr & Eur.

Dictionnaire Liturgique, Historique et Theorique de Plainchant et de Musique d'Eglise. M. J. D'Ortigue. LC 79-155353. (Music Ser.). (FRE.). 1971. reprint ed. lib. bdg. 110.00 (*0-306-70165-0*) Da Capo.

***Dictionnaire Maconnique.** Jëan-Andre Faucher. 1981. write for info. (*0-7859-8138-1*, 2-86477-035-0) Fr & Eur.

***Dictionnaire Maloine de l'Infirmiere et Aide-Memoire des Pri.** B. F. Cape & P. Dobson. 1979. write for info. (*0-7859-7816-X*, 2224005210) Fr & Eur.

***Dictionnaire Manuel de Gerontologie Sociale.** Nicolas Zay. 1982. write for info. (*0-7859-8647-2*, 276376925X) Fr & Eur.

Dictionnaire-Manuel du Negociant en Vins et Spiriteaux et du Maitre de Chai: Manual-Dictionary for Wine & Spirits Merchants. Edouard Feret. 633p. 1981. 95.00 (*0-8288-0758-2*, M14200) Fr & Eur.

Dictionnaire Marabout des Mots Croises. Leon Noel & Marynel Leon. 508p. 1993. Vol. 2, I-Z. pap. 17.95 (*0-7859-5632-8*, 2501018850) Fr & Eur.

***Dictionnaire Marabout des Trucs.** Laura Fronty. 1985. write for info. (*0-7859-7884-4*, 2-501-00646-1) Fr & Eur.

***Dictionnaire Marial.** Robert Pannet et al. 1991. write for info. (*0-7859-8092-X*, 2-85443-217-7) Fr & Eur.

***Dictionnaire Marketing.** Yves Le Golvan. 1988. write for info. (*0-7859-7704-X*, 2040169962) Fr & Eur.

***Dictionnaire Medical.** Georges Bellicha & Pierre Bellicha. 480p. (FRE.). 1987. pap. 79.95 (*0-7859-7701-5*, 2040163506) Fr & Eur.

***Dictionnaire Medical.** 5th ed. Ludmila Manuila. 504p. (FRE.). 1991. pap. 39.95 (*0-7859-7833-X*, 2225827958) Fr & Eur.

Dictionnaire Medical; Allemand - Francais, Francais - Allemand. Dieter W. Unseld. 550p. (FRE & GER.). 1992. lib. bdg. 150.00 (*0-7859-3644-0*, 2856080502) Fr & Eur.

Dictionnaire Medical Chinois-Francois. 1599p. (CHI & FRE.). 1993. 140.00 (*0-7859-5675-1*, 7117011556) Fr & Eur.

Dictionnaire Medical de l'Infirmiere. 4th rev. ed. J. Quevauvilliers & L. Perlemuter. 1344p. (FRE.). 1992. 130.00 (*0-7859-4749-3*, M1900) Fr & Eur.

***Dictionnaire Medical de Poche.** Ludmila Manuila et al. 1994. write for info. (*0-7859-7862-3*, 2-253-08521-9) Fr & Eur.

Dictionnaire Medical Illustre De Semiologie Patronymique. Maloine Staff. (FRE.). 1979. 49.95 (*0-8288-4798-3*, M6149) Fr & Eur.

***Dictionnaire Mes 10,000 Mots.** Marcel Didier. Date not set. write for info. (*0-7859-7700-7*, 2040161538) Fr & Eur.

Dictionnaire Meteorologique: Francais-Russe: French-Russian Dictionary of Meteorology. deluxe ed. P. V. Silvestrov. 191p. (FRE & RUS.). 1978. 29.95 (*0-7859-0810-2*, M9122) Fr & Eur.

***Dictionnaire Methodique de l'Architecture Grecque et Romaine: With French, German, English, Italian & Greek Vocabulary.** Ecole Francaise De Rome Staff. 307p. (FRE.). 1985. 135.00 (*0-7859-7976-X*, 2728301050) Fr & Eur.

Dictionnaire Minier Russe-Francais. (FRE & RUS.). 1973. pap. 25.00 (*0-8288-6268-0*, M-6150) Fr & Eur.

Dictionnaire Misogyne. Agnes Michaux. 1993. pap. 45.00 (*0-7859-5635-2*, 2709612585) Fr & Eur.

Dictionnaire Moderne Larousse Saturne Francais-Anglais, Anglais-Francais. Larousse Staff. 49.95 (*0-317-45631-8*) Fr & Eur.

Dictionnaire Moderne Larousse Saturne Francais-Anglais, Anglais-Francaise. Larousse Staff. (ENG & FRE.). write for info. (*0-8288-7839-0*) Fr & Eur.

Dictionnaire Moderne: Slovene & Francais: Modern Slovene-French Dictionary. Anton Grad. 745p. (FRE & SLV.). 1978. 49.95 (*0-8288-5461-0*, M9705) Fr & Eur.

***Dictionnaire Mondial des Chanteurs.** Christian Dureau. 1989. 59.95 (*0-7859-8149-7*, 2-86594-048-9) Fr & Eur.

***Dictionnaire Mondial des Mouvements Litteraires et Artistique.** Odette Virmaux & Alain Virmaux. 1992. 135.00 (*0-7859-7881-X*, 2-268-01268-9) Fr & Eur.

Dictionnaire Mongol-Francais. Jacques LeGrand & Tsegmidijn Suk-Hbaatar. 288p. (FRE & MON.). 1992. 49.95 (*0-7859-1018-2*, 2901795498) Fr & Eur.

Dictionnaire Mongol-Russe-Francais, 3 vols., Set. J. E. Kowalewski. (FRE, MON & RUS.). 1993. reprint ed. 150.00 (*957-638-149-5*) Oriental Bk Store.

Dictionnaire Montagnais-Francais. Lynn Drapeau. 904p. (FRE.). 1991. 125.00 (*0-7859-1009-3*, 2760506614) Fr & Eur.

***Dictionnaire Mozabite-Francais.** Jean Delheure. 1984. write for info. (*0-7859-8080-6*, 2-85297-166-6) Fr & Eur.

Dictionnaire Mytho-Hermetique. Antione-Joseph Pernety. 548p. (FRE.). 1980. pap. 150.00 (*0-8288-2191-7*, M6441) Fr & Eur.

Dictionnaire Napoleon. Jean Tulard. 1989. lib. bdg. 295.00 (*0-8288-2491-6*, F69650) Fr & Eur.

***Dictionnaire National des Communes de France.** 21th ed. 1984. write for info. (*0-7859-7913-1*, 2-7013-0560-8) Fr & Eur.

Dictionnaire National des Communes de France. 40th ed. Michel Albin Staff. 1342p. (FRE.). 1992. 150.00 (*0-8288-6917-0*, 2226057242) Fr & Eur.

Dictionnaire National des Communes de France: National Dictionary of French Communes. 20th ed. Dominique de Fleurian. Ed. by Jacques Simond & Jacques Frenay. 1150p. (FRE.). 1977. 79.95 (*0-8288-5391-6*, M6254) Fr & Eur.

Dictionnaire Naval Francais - Chinois. Defense Nationale Staff. 994p. (CHI & FRE.). 1985. 95.00 (*0-8288-9538-4*) Fr & Eur.

***Dictionnaire Normand-Francais.** Jean-Paul Bourdon et al. 1993. write for info. (*0-7859-8085-7*, 2-85319-250-4) Fr & Eur.

***Dictionnaire Nostradamus.** Michel Dufresne. 1989. 89.95 (*0-7859-8254-X*, 2-920176-54-4) Fr & Eur.

***Dictionnaire Officiel des Mots de Tete.** Alain Baudot et al. 1984. write for info. (*0-7859-8596-4*, 0919762719) Fr & Eur.

***Dictionnaire Ou Traite De la Police Generale Des Villes, Bou.** Edme De La Poix de Fremenville. 1989. 95.00 (*0-7859-8167-5*, 2-86971-149-2) Fr & Eur.

***Dictionnaire Oxford.** Michael Janes. 1987. write for info. (*0-7859-7719-8*, 2080704850) Fr & Eur.

Dictionnaire Paici-Francais, Suivi d'un Lexique Francais-Paici. Rivierre. 372p. (FRE.). 1984. 39.95 (*0-8288-1628-X*, F37540) Fr & Eur.

Dictionnaire Persan-Francais. Gilbert Lazard. LC 90-40583. xvii, 482p. (FRE & PER.). 1990. 114.50 (*90-04-08549-1*) E J Brill.

Dictionnaire Petrolier des Techniques de Diagraphique, Forage et Production. Sonia Ketchian. 376p. (ENG, FRE, GER & RUS.). 1965. 250.00 (*0-8288-6742-9*, M-6326) Fr & Eur.

Dictionnaire Philosophique. Francois-Marie De Voltaire. Ed. by Raymond Naves. (Illus.). 384p. (FRE.). 1964. pap. 11.95 (*0-7859-1419-6*, 2080700286) Fr & Eur.

***Dictionnaire Philosophique.** Voltaire. 702p. (FRE.). 1987. pap. 49.95 (*0-7859-8010-5*, 2737002877) Fr & Eur.

Dictionnaire Philosophique. Francois-Marie de Voltaire. Ed. by Rene Pomeau. 384p. 1964. 4.50 (*0-686-55745-X*) Fr & Eur.

***Dictionnaire Philosophique de Citations.** Leon-Louis Grateloup. 1991. write for info. (*0-7859-7610-8*, 2010165802) Fr & Eur.

***Dictionnaire Phonologique et Orthographique du Francais Fond.** Jean-Louis Bouttaz. 1979. write for info. (*0-7859-7941-7*, 2-7135-0277-2) Fr & Eur.

***Dictionnaire Picard des Parlers et Traditions du Beauvaisis.** Francois Beauvy. 1990. write for info. (*0-7859-8110-1*, 2-85706-020-3) Fr & Eur.

***Dictionnaire Pittoresque et Historique ou Description D'Arch.** Hebert. 1972. write for info. (*0-7859-8041-5*, 2-8266-0195-4) Fr & Eur.

Dictionnaire Plus. Sel. by Reader's Digest Staff. 703p. (FRE.). 1992. 110.00 (*0-7859-1004-2*, 2709803704) Fr & Eur.

Dictionnaire Politique, Economique et Diplomatique Chinois - Francais. Traductions de Chine Staff. 1371p. (CHI & FRE.). 1990. 95.00 (*0-8288-9539-2*) Fr & Eur.

***Dictionnaire Politique, Economique et Diplomatique Chinois-F.** Traductions de Chine Staff. 1990. write for info. (*0-7859-8703-7*, 7500100906) Fr & Eur.

Dictionnaire Politique et Diplomatique. Pierre Sandahl & Louise de Bea. 194p. (FRE.). 1976. pap. 24.95 (*0-8288-5653-2*, M6503) Fr & Eur.

***Dictionnaire Politique Portatif en Cinq Mots.** Jean-Pierre Faye. 1982. write for info. (*0-7859-7715-5*, 2070354741) Fr & Eur.

***Dictionnaire Polonais-Francais.** 5th ed. Bernard Hamel. 1987. write for info. (*0-7859-8210-8*, 2-902957-01-7) Fr & Eur.

***Dictionnaire Polyglotte des Termes d'Art et d'Archeologie.** Louis Reau. 1977. write for info. (*0-7859-8668-5*, 3535015502) Fr & Eur.

Dictionnaire Polyglotte des Termes d'Art et d'Archeologie. Louis Reau. 961p. (FRE.). 1977. reprint ed. 595.00 (*0-8288-9540-6*, M6612) Fr & Eur.

Dictionnaire Polytechnique Russe: French & Russian Polytechnical Dictionary. I. Ichlinski. 608p. (FRE & RUS.). 1980. 65.00 (*0-8288-2132-1*, M15070) Fr & Eur.

***Dictionnaire Portatif de Peinture, Sculpture et Gravure.** Antoine-Joseph Pernety. 1972. write for info. (*0-7859-8649-9*, 282660242X) Fr & Eur.

Dictionnaire Portugais. Rouse & Ersillo Cardoso. 1820p. (SPA.). (J). (gr. 9-12). 1963. 49.95 (*0-685-57714-7*, M-6495) Fr & Eur.

Dictionnaire pour l'Architecture, le Batiment et les Materiaux de Construction, 2 vols., Band I. Bucksch. 820p. (FRE & GER.). 1977. 350.00 (*0-8288-5392-4*, M7095) Fr & Eur.

Dictionnaire pour l'Architecture, le Batiment et les Materiaux de Construction, 2 vols., Band II. Bucksch. 688p. (FRE & GER.). 1979. 350.00 (*0-8288-4725-8*, M7096) Fr & Eur.

Dictionnaire pour les Travaux Publics et l'Equipement des Chartiers de Construction, 2 vols., Band I. deluxe ed. Bucksch. 875p. (FRE & GER.). 1976. 195.00 (*3-7625-0379-6*) Fr & Eur.

Dictionnaire pour les Travaux Publics et l'Equipement des Chartiers de Construction: Dictionary of Public Works & Construction Equipment, 2 vols., Band II. deluxe ed. Bucksch. 911p. (FRE & GER.). 1978. 195.00 (*0-8288-5200-6*, M7098) Fr & Eur.

***Dictionnaire pour les Travaux Publics, le Batiment et l'Equipement des Chantiers en Construction Vol. 2: French-English.** Hector Bucksch. 550p. (ENG & FRE.). 1985. 165.00 (*0-7859-7774-0*, 2212010869) Fr & Eur.

***Dictionnaire pour les Travaux Publics, le Batiment et l'Equipement des Chantiers en Construction Vol. 3: German-French.** 3rd ed. Hector Bucksch. 878p. (FRE & GER.). 1972. 350.00 (*0-7859-8627-8*, 221201080x) Fr & Eur.

***Dictionnaire pour les Travaux Publics, le Batiment et l'Equipement des Chantiers en Construction Vol. 4: French-German.** 4th ed. Hector Bucksch. 912p. (FRE & GER.). 1978. pap. 350.00 (*0-7859-7773-2*, 2212010818) Fr & Eur.

***Dictionnaire pour Rever, S'Amuser et Chanter.** Odile Arlaud. 1991. write for info. (*0-7859-7673-6*, 2036515150) Fr & Eur.

Dictionnaire Practique des Homonymes: Practical Dictionary of Homonyms. J. Bertrand. 224p. (FRE.). 1980. 29.95 (*0-8288-1929-7*, M12401) Fr & Eur.

***Dictionnaire Pratique.** 2nd ed. Ed. by M. Puy-Costa. 1966. write for info. (*0-7859-8602-2*, 203220620X); write for info. (*2-03-220620-X*) Fr & Eur.

***Dictionnaire Pratique D'Astrologie.** Catherine Aubier & Patrick Ravignant. 1989. 69.95 (*0-7859-8154-3*, 2-86676-476-5) Fr & Eur.

***Dictionnaire pratique de bacteriologie clinique.** Jean - Loup Avril. 1988. write for info. (*0-7859-8644-8*, 272988842x) Fr & Eur.

Dictionnaire Pratique de Droit Medicale. J. Pouletti. 424p. (FRE.). 1982. 110.00 (*0-8288-4421-6*, M9773) Fr & Eur.

***Dictionnaire Pratique de Graphologie.** Ed. by Pierre Faideau. 1991. write for info. (*0-7859-7870-4*, 2-263-01714-3) Fr & Eur.

***Dictionnaire Pratique de la Chimie.** J. F. Le Marechal & L. Soulie. 158p. (FRE.). 1984. pap. 16.95 (*0-7859-7790-2*, 2218056070) Fr & Eur.

***Dictionnaire Pratique de l'Acupuncture et de L'Acupressure.** Pierre Crepon. 1980. write for info. (*0-7859-7968-9*, 2-7256-1308-6) Fr & Eur.

Dictionnaire Pratique de l'Acupuncture et l'Acupressure: Practical Dictionary of Acupuncture & Acupressure. Pierre Crepon. 192p. 1980. 39.95 (*0-8288-1797-9*, M8979) Fr & Eur.

***Dictionnaire Pratique de L'Alimentation.** Andre Levy & Jacqueline Duffour. 1987. write for info. (*0-7859-7914-X*, 2-7021-1649-3) Fr & Eur.

***Dictionnaire Pratique de l'Edition en 20 Langues.** 3rd ed. Imre Mora. 1984. write for info. (*0-7859-8669-3*, 3598104499) Fr & Eur.

Dictionnaire Pratique de Pharmacologie: Clinique. Yvan Touitou & Leon Perlemuter. 1204p. (FRE.). 1976. 250.00 (*0-8288-5655-9*, M6536) Fr & Eur.

***Dictionnaire Pratique de Sexualite.** Yves Moigno. 1991. write for info. (*0-7859-7889-5*, 2-501-01407-3) Fr & Eur.

***Dictionnaire Pratique de Therapeutique Canine et Feline.** 3rd rev. ed. Robert Moraillon et al. 1992. 195.00 (*0-7859-7831-3*, 2-225-82579-3) Fr & Eur.

Dictionnaire Pratique de Therapeutique Pediatrique: Practical Dictionary of Pediatric Therapeutics. Robert Steinschneider. 824p. (FRE.). 1980. 125.00 (*0-8288-1828-2*, F58400) Fr & Eur.

***Dictionnaire Pratique des Collectivites Territoriales.** Andre Lefebvre. 1988. write for info. (*0-7859-8176-4*, 2-87603-010-1) Fr & Eur.

***Dictionnaire Pratique des Mathematiques Vol. 1: Analyse.** Pierre Lambert. 284p. (FRE.). 1989. pap. 22.95 (*0-7859-7793-7*, 2218079429) Fr & Eur.

***Dictionnaire Pratique des Mathematiques Vol. 2: Algebre.** Pierre Lambert. 285p. (FRE.). 1990. pap. 22.95 (*0-7859-7786-4*, 2218025760) Fr & Eur.

***Dictionnaire Pratique des Medicaments.** Larousse Staff. (FRE.). 1989. write for info. (*0-7859-8609-X*, 203510128X) Fr & Eur.

***Dictionnaire Pratique des Soins et du Soutien a Domicile.** Gil Roucoules & Leon Perlemuter. 1990. write for info. (*0-7859-7829-1*, 2-225-81308-6) Fr & Eur.

Dictionnaire Pratique du Creole de Guadeloupe. Henry Tourneux & Maurice Barbotin. 488p. (CRP & FRE.). 1990. lib. bdg. 150.00 (*2-86537-248-0*) Fr & Eur.

Dictionnaire Pratique Francais-Polonais. K. Kupisz & B. Kielski. 1036p. (FRE & POL.). 1976. 39.95 (*0-8288-5656-7*, M9327) Fr & Eur.

An Asterisk (*) at the beginning of an entry indicates that the title is appearing in BIP for the first time.

Dictionnaire Pratique Mercure: Francais-Espagnol, Espagnol-Francais. 2nd ed. M. Pay-Costa. 1024p. (FRE & SPA.). 1966. 24.95 (*0-7859-0762-9*, M-6471) Fr & Eur.

***Dictionnaire Promenade.** Jean Hamburger. 1989. write for info. (*0-7859-7625-6*, 2020107686) Fr & Eur.

Dictionnaire Quadrilingue de la Presse et des Medias: French, Portuguese, Italian & Spanish Dictionary of the Press & Media. Conseil International de la Language Francaise Staff. (FRE, ITA, POR & SPA.). write for info. (*0-8288-7674-6*) Fr & Eur.

***Dictionnaire Quartet-Systems du Macintosh.** Joelle Piard & Christian Piard. 1990. write for info. (*0-7859-8247-7*, 2-908796-00-7) Fr & Eur.

Dictionnaire Quillet de la Langue Francais, 4 vols., Set. Quillet Staff. 2132p. (FRE.). 495.00 (*0-7859-0390-9*, M6153) Fr & Eur.

***Dictionnaire Raisonne des Mots Croises.** Jacqueline Charron. 1977. write for info. (*0-7859-8593-X*, 0775905410) Fr & Eur.

Dictionnaire Raisonne des Superstitions et des Croyances Populaires: Superstitions & Popular Belief. Pierre Canavaggio. 247p. (FRE.). 1977. pap. 39.95 (*0-8288-5393-2*, M6059) Fr & Eur.

Dictionnaire Raisonne du Mobilier Francais de l'Epoque Carlovingienne a la Renaissance, 6 Vols. 2nd ed. Eugene E. Viollet-Le-Duc. (Illus.). (FRE.). reprint ed. write for info. (*0-318-50558-4*) AMS Pr.

Dictionnaire Raisonne du Mobilier Francais de l'Epoque Carlovingienne a la Renaissance, 6 Vols, 1. 2nd ed. Eugene E. Viollet-Le-Duc. LC 76-153606. (Illus.). (FRE.). reprint ed. 57.00 (*0-404-09751-0*) AMS Pr.

Dictionnaire Raisonne du Mobilier Francais de l'Epoque Carlovingienne a la Renaissance, 6 Vols, 2. 2nd ed. Eugene E. Viollet-Le-Duc. LC 76-153606. (Illus.). (FRE.). reprint ed. 57.00 (*0-404-09752-9*) AMS Pr.

Dictionnaire Raisonne du Mobilier Francais de l'Epoque Carlovingienne a la Renaissance, 6 Vols, 3. 2nd ed. Eugene E. Viollet-Le-Duc. LC 76-153606. (Illus.). (FRE.). reprint ed. 57.00 (*0-404-09753-7*) AMS Pr.

Dictionnaire Raisonne du Mobilier Francais de l'Epoque Carlovingienne a la Renaissance, 6 Vols, 4. 2nd ed. Eugene E. Viollet-Le-Duc. LC 76-153606. (Illus.). (FRE.). reprint ed. 57.00 (*0-404-09754-5*) AMS Pr.

Dictionnaire Raisonne du Mobilier Francais de l'Epoque Carlovingienne a la Renaissance, 6 Vols, 5. 2nd ed. Eugene E. Viollet-Le-Duc. LC 76-153606. (Illus.). (FRE.). reprint ed. 57.00 (*0-404-09755-3*) AMS Pr.

Dictionnaire Raisonne du Mobilier Francais de l'Epoque Carlovingienne a la Renaissance, 6 Vols, 6. 2nd ed. Eugene E. Viollet-Le-Duc. LC 76-153606. (Illus.). (FRE.). reprint ed. 57.00 (*0-404-09756-1*) AMS Pr.

Dictionnaire Raisonne du Mobilier Francais de l'Epoque Carlovingienne a la Renaissance, 6 Vols, Set. 2nd ed. Eugene E. Viollet-Le-Duc. LC 76-153606. (Illus.). (FRE.). reprint ed. lib. bdg. 345.00 (*0-404-09750-2*) AMS Pr.

***Dictionnaire Raisonne et Illustre du Th/atre A L'Italienne.** Alain Roy. 1992. 65.00 (*0-7859-8166-7*, 2-86943-357-3) Fr & Eur.

Dictionnaire Reunionnais-Francais. Daniel Baggioni. 376p. (FRE & PAT.). 1990. 75.00 (*0-8288-9462-0*) Fr & Eur.

Dictionnaire Rimbaud. Claude Jeancolas. 400p. (FRE.). 1991. 95.00 (*0-8288-6956-1*, 2715809018) Fr & Eur.

***Dictionnaire Russe-Francais des Termes en Usage Dans l'Eglise Russe.** 2nd ed. Martine Roty. 160p. (FRE & RUS.). 1983. pap. 24.95 (*0-7859-7961-1*, 2720401935) Fr & Eur.

Dictionnaire Russe-Francais du Batiment: Russian-French Dictionary of Construction. V. V. Voronine. Ed. by A. I. Denissov. 462p. (FRE & RUS.). 1978. 24.95 (*0-8288-5201-4*, M9064) Fr & Eur.

***Dictionnaire Sachs No. 2.** Larousse Staff. Date not set. write for info. (*0-7859-7634-5*, 2030281034) Fr & Eur.

***Dictionnaire Sachs-Villate No. 1.** Larousse Staff. Date not set. write for info. (*0-7859-7633-7*, 2030281034) Fr & Eur.

***Dictionnaire Sachs-Villate Francais-Allemand, Allemand-Francais.** Larousse Staff. (FRE & GER.). Date not set. 450.00 (*0-7859-7632-9*) Fr & Eur.

Dictionnaire Samoa-Francais-Anglais et Francais-Samoa-Anglais. Louis Violette. LC 75-35215. (ENG & FRE.). reprint ed. 44.50 (*0-404-14238-9*) AMS Pr.

***Dictionnaire San-Antonio.** Serge Le Doran. 638p. (FRE.). 1993. text ed. 65.00 (*0-7859-7871-2*, 2265049646) Fr & Eur.

***Dictionnaire Sango.** Luc Bouquiaux et al. 1978. write for info. (*0-7859-8076-8*, 2-85297-016-3) Fr & Eur.

Dictionnaire Sanskrit-Francais. N. Stchoupak. 897p. (FRE & SAN.). 1987. reprint ed. pap. 250.00 (*0-7859-4913-5*) Fr & Eur.

***Dictionnaire Selectif des arbres, des Plantes et des Fleurs.** Jean-Pierre Michaux. 1979. write for info. (*0-7859-7929-8*, 2-7080-0463-8) Fr & Eur.

***Dictionnaire Selectif et Commente des Difficultes de la Vers.** Jean Rey. 1973. write for info. (*0-7859-7927-1*, 2-7080-0066-7) Fr & Eur.

***Dictionnaire Social 1992.** Revue Fiduciaire Staff. 1992. 85.00 (*0-7859-8141-1*, 2-86521-191-6) Fr & Eur.

***Dictionnaire Superflu.** Pierre Desproges. 1985. write for info. (*0-7859-7624-8*, 2020086581) Fr & Eur.

***Dictionnaire Symbolique des Animaux.** Pierre Miquel. 1991. write for info. (*0-7859-8660-X*, 286377106X) Fr & Eur.

***Dictionnaire Symbolique et Pratique de la Franc-Maconnerie.** Jean Ferre. 1994. write for info. (*0-7859-8063-6*, 2-85076-611-9) Fr & Eur.

Dictionnaire Synonymique. Anthony Guerronnan. Ed. by Peter C. Bunnell & Robert A. Sobieszek. LC 76-23055. (Sources of Modern Photography Ser.). (FRE.). 1979. reprint ed. lib. bdg. 15.95 (*0-405-09620-8*) Ayer.

***Dictionnaire Tauromachique.** Paul Casanova. 190p. (FRE.). 1982. pap. 75.00 (*0-7859-8126-8*, 2862760439) Fr & Eur.

Dictionnaire Technique Anglais-Francais. Guy Malgorn. 495p. (ENG & FRE.). 1976. 89.95 (*0-8288-5657-5*, M6385) Fr & Eur.

Dictionnaire Technique Arabe-Francais. Jean-Jacques Schmidt. (FRE.). 1986. lib. bdg. 150.00 (*0-7859-3912-1*) Fr & Eur.

***Dictionnaire Technique de la Bourse et des Marches.** Jeanne France De Villeneuve. 352p. (FRE.). 1994. 195. 00 (*0-7859-8259-0*, 2950495036) Fr & Eur.

***Dictionnaire Technique de la Peinture Vol. 1: A-B.** Andre Beguin. 230p. (FRE.). 1978. pap. 59.95 (*0-7859-8215-9*, 2903319073) Fr & Eur.

***Dictionnaire Technique de la Peinture Vol. 2: C-E.** Andre Beguin. 202p. (FRE.). 1979. pap. 59.95 (*0-7859-8665-0*, 290331909x) Fr & Eur.

***Dictionnaire Technique de la Peinture Vol. 3: F-H.** Andre Beguin. 204p. (FRE.). 1980. pap. 59.95 (*0-7859-8216-7*, 2903319111) Fr & Eur.

***Dictionnaire Technique de la Peinture Vol. 4: I-M.** Andre Beguin. 202p. (FRE.). 1981. pap. 59.95 (*0-7859-8217-5*, 2903319146) Fr & Eur.

***Dictionnaire Technique de la Peinture Vol. 5: N-P.** Andre Beguin. 230p. (FRE.). 1982. pap. 59.95 (*0-7859-8218-3*, 2903319162) Fr & Eur.

***Dictionnaire Technique de la Peinture Vol. 6: Q-Z.** Andre Beguin. 270p. (FRE.). 1984. pap. 59.95 (*0-7859-8219-1*, 2903319189) Fr & Eur.

Dictionnaire Technique de l'Automobile. George Zlatovski. 184p. (ENG, FRE & GER.). 1973. pap. 39.95 (*0-8288-6269-9*, M-6575) Fr & Eur.

Dictionnaire Technique de l'Eau. Grund Staff. (FRE.). pap. 29.95 (*0-7859-0391-7*, M6156) Fr & Eur.

Dictionnaire Technique des Peintures et des Travaux de Peinturage: Technical Dictionary of Painting & the Painting Industry. Association Francaise De Normalisation Staff. 156p. (FRE.). 1980. 95.00 (*0-8288-1415-5*, M14358) Fr & Eur.

Dictionnaire Technique des Termes Utilises dans l'Industrie du Petrole, Anglais-Francais, Francais-Anglais: English-French, French-English Dictionary of the Petroleum Industry. Magdeleine Moureau & Janine Rouge. 914p. (ENG & FRE.). 1977. 325.00 (*0-8288-5394-0*, M6419) Fr & Eur.

Dictionnaire Technique du Bois en 4 Langues. 640p. (ENG, FRE, GER & RUS.). 37.50 (*0-686-57116-9*) Fr & Eur.

***Dictionnaire Technique du Papier et des Encres.** Jean-Claude Faudouas. 117p. (FRE.). 1991. pap. 75.00 (*0-7859-7769-4*, 2212008066) Fr & Eur.

Dictionnaire Technique et Administratif de la Navigation Interieure. Henri Berna. 393p. (FRE.). 1977. 125.00 (*0-8288-5395-9*, M6030) Fr & Eur.

Dictionnaire Technique et Critique du Dessin. Andre Beguin. (FRE.). 1978. 150.00 (*0-8288-5202-2*, M6027) Fr & Eur.

***Dictionnaire Technique et Scientifique Vol. 1: English-French.** Henri Goursau. 940p. (ENG & FRE.). 1994. 125.00 (*0-7859-8225-6*, 2904105042) Fr & Eur.

Dictionnaire Technique Francais-Anglais (French-English Technical Dictionary) G. Malgorn. 475p. 1972. 105.00 (*0-7859-4831-7*) Fr & Eur.

Dictionnaire Technique Illustre des Outils Coupants pour l'Usinage des Metaux. Toni Heiler. 474p. (ENG, FRE, GER, ITA & SPA.). 1965. 115.00 (*0-8288-6743-7*, M-6313) Fr & Eur.

Dictionnaire Technique Russe-Francais de la Preparation. 129p. (FRE & RUS.). 1973. pap. 29.95 (*0-7859-0727-0*, M-6160) Fr & Eur.

Dictionnaire Technique Universal Kluwer, Francais-Neerlandais: Kluwer's Universal French-Dutch Technical Dictionary. G. Schuurmans-Stekhoven. 636p. (DUT & FRE.). 1978. 150.00 (*0-8288-5203-0*, M6506) Fr & Eur.

Dictionnaire Technique Universal Kluwer, Neerlandais-Francais: Kluwer's Universal Dutch-French Technical Dictionary. G. Schuurmans-Stekhoven. 656p. (DUT & FRE.). 1978. 150.00 (*0-8288-5204-9*, M6507) Fr & Eur.

Dictionnaire Technologique Vol. 2: Supplement in Portuguese. Michel Feutry et al. 400p. (ENG, FRE, GER & SPA.). 1976. 95.00 (*0-7859-5657-3*, 2856080014) Fr & Eur.

Dictionnaire Technologique, (Ebenisterie-Menuiserie-Scierie-Technologie) Vol. 6. Moirand. 356p. (FRE.). 1986. pap. 150.00 (*0-7859-3910-5*, 2856080219) Fr & Eur.

Dictionnaire Technologique, Vol. 1 Mecanique, Metallurgie, Hydraulique et Industrie Annexes: English, French, German. Michel Feutry et al. 736p. (ENG, FRE & GER.). 1976. 125.00 (*0-7859-3904-0*, 2856080006) Fr & Eur.

Dictionnaire Technologique, Vol. 1P. Michel Feutry et al. 380p. (ENG, FRE, GER & POR.). 1981. pap. 75.00 (*0-7859-3908-3*) Fr & Eur.

***Dictionnaire Thematique des Heros de Bandes Dessinees Vol. 1: Histoire, Western.** Henri Filippini. 448p. (FRE.). 1992. 175.00 (*0-7859-7967-0*, 2723414795) Fr & Eur.

Dictionnaire Thematique des Langues de la Region Hienghene Nouvelle Caledonie. Andre-Georges Haudricourt. 285p. 1982. pap. 59.95 (*0-8288-1629-8*, F123790) Fr & Eur.

Dictionnaire Thematique Francais-Argot. H. Leveque. (FRE.). 1991. 49.95 (*0-685-48813-6*, F83770) Fr & Eur.

Dictionnaire Thematique Japonais-Francais. You-Feng Staff. 853p. (FRE & JPN.). 1993. 69.95 (*0-7859-5667-0*, 2906658839) Fr & Eur.

Dictionnaire Theologique Portatif. Pons-Augustin Alletz. viii, 679p. reprint ed. write for info. (*0-318-71995-9*, Pub. by Georg Olms GW) Lubrecht & Cramer.

Dictionnaire Topographique de la France. Henri Stein. 738p. (FRE.). 1954. pap. 49.95 (*0-8288-6872-7*, M-6525) Fr & Eur.

***Dictionnaire Topographique du Department du Calvados Comprenant les Noms de Lieu Anciens et Modernes.** Celestin Hippeau. 386p. (FRE.). 1981. pap. 79.95 (*0-7859-8073-3*, 2852261294) Fr & Eur.

Dictionnaire Trilingue de Definitions Technologiques de Peche: Trilingual Dictionary of Technological Definitions of Fishing. 85p. (FRE.). 1980. pap. 14.95 (*0-8288-1427-9*, F22500) Fr & Eur.

Dictionnaire Universal de l'Art et des Artistes, 3 tomes, Set. (FRE.). 341.25 (*0-685-36013-X*) Fr & Eur.

Dictionnaire Universel, Contenant Generalement Tous les Mots Francois, 4 vols., Set. Antoine Furetiere. 4400p. 1972. reprint ed. write for info. (*3-487-04466-8*, Pub. by Georg Olms GW) Lubrecht & Cramer.

***Dictionnaire Usuel de l'Environnement et de l'Ecologie Vol. 1.** Jean Ternisian. (FRE.). 1981. 24.95 (*0-7859-8069-5*, 2852052210) Fr & Eur.

***Dictionnaire Usuel de l'Environnement et de l'Ecologie Vol. 2.** Jean Ternisien. 1982. write for info. (*0-7859-8070-9*, 2-85205-222-9) Fr & Eur.

Dictionnaire Usuel de Psychologie. N. Sillamy. 784p. (FRE.). 1991. 130.00 (*0-7859-4747-7*, M15538) Fr & Eur.

Dictionnaire Usuel Illustre. Flammarion Staff. 1944p. (FRE.). 1983. 49.95 (*0-8288-1927-0*, F134430) Fr & Eur.

Dictionnaire Usuel Illustre Flammarion. Flammarion Staff. 45.95 (*0-8288-8439-0*) Fr & Eur.

Dictionnaire Vidal (French Physicians Desk Reference) 68th ed. Vidal. 2296p. (FRE.). 1994. 295.00 (*0-8288-9541-4*) Fr & Eur.

***Dictionnaire Vivant du Batiment et des Travaux Publics.** Pierre Dusserre Telmon. 181p. (FRE.). 1988. pap. 59.95 (*0-7859-8258-2*, 2950329802) Fr & Eur.

Dictionnaire Wolof-Francais. A. Fall et al. 336p. (FRE.). 1990. lib. bdg. 150.00 (*2-86537-233-2*) Fr & Eur.

***Dictionnaire Xaracuu-Francais (Nouvelle-Caledonie)** Claire Moyse-Faurie & Marie-Adele Joredie. 1986. write for info. (*0-7859-8235-3*, 2-906341-00-2) Fr & Eur.

Dictionnaire Yiddish - Francais. Noe Gruss & Samuel Kerner. 371p. (FRE & YID.). 1982. 125.00 (*0-8288-9542-2*) Fr & Eur.

***Dictionnairede Mathematiques.** Christian Lixi. 239p. (FRE.). 1988. 42.95 (*0-7859-7726-0*, 2091889512) Fr & Eur.

Dictionnaires de Genetique: Genetics Dictionary with English-French Index. CILF Staff. 352p. (ENG & FRE.). 1991. pap. 125.00 (*0-8288-6166-8*, F116440) Fr & Eur.

Dictionnaires des Maladies. Jean P. Barbier & Francois C. Hugues. 528p. (FRE.). 1973. 59.95 (*0-7859-0725-4*, M6022) Fr & Eur.

Dictionnaires des Mots Tordus. Pef. (Folio - Cadet Bleu Ser.: No. 192). 79p. (FRE.). (J). (gr. 1-5). 1989. pap. 10. 95 (*2-07-031192-9*) Schoenhof.

***Dictionnaires des Oeuvres Litteraires du Quebec Vol. 1: Origines a 1900.** rev. ed. Maurice Lemire. 998p. (FRE.). 1980. 250.00 (*0-7859-5221-7*) Fr & Eur.

Dictionnaires des Proverbes et Dictons de France. Jean-Yves Dournon. 75.00 (*0-8288-7714-9*) Fr & Eur.

***Dictionnaires des Reves.** Yves Marguerite. 385p. (FRE.). 1990. pap. 38.95 (*0-7859-8639-1*, 226801004x) Fr & Eur.

Dictionnaires des Sigles Anglais Utilises en Electronique et en Informatique. Jean-Louis Le Brizault. 240p. (FRE.). 1990. pap. 125.00 (*0-8288-2587-4*, 2852065835) Fr & Eur.

Dictionnaires Electroniques et Analyse Automatique de Textes. Max Silberztein. 248p. 1993. pap. 85.00 (*0-7859-5619-0*, 2225841578) Fr & Eur.

Dictionnaires Oeuvres Contemporains: Dictionary of Contemporary Works. Bompiani Laffont. (FRE.). 1977. 225.00 (*0-8288-5462-9*, M6129) Fr & Eur.

Dictyostelids. Kenneth B. Raper & Ann W. Rahn. LC 83-43089. (Illus.). 448p. 1984. 95.00 (*0-691-08345-2*) Princeton U Pr.

Dicynodonts: A Study in Palaeobiology. Gillian King. 200p. 1990. 75.00 (*0-412-33080-6*, A3815) Chapman & Hall.

***Did Big Brother Give You Permission to Go Wee-Wee?** Thomas F. Metzger. (Illus.). 144p. (Orig.). 1994. pap. 12.95 (*0-931892-98-8*) B Dolphin Pub.

Did Big Brother Give You Permission to Go Wee Wee? rev. ed. Thomas F. Metzger. Ed. by Rainell M. Metzger. (Illus.). 144p. 1994. pap. 12.95 (*0-9641789-0-7*) Metzger Ent.

Did Britain Make It? Ed. by Penny Sparke. 160p. 1986. 65.00 (*0-85072-168-7*) St Mut.

Did British Capitalism Breed Inequality? Jeffrey G. Williamson. (Illus.). 272p. 1985. text ed. 60.00 (*0-04-942186-7*) Routledge Chapman & Hall.

Did Charles Darwin Become a Christian? Wilbert H. Rusch, Sr. & John W. Klotz. 44p. (Orig.). 1988. pap. text ed. 3.95 (*0-940384-05-1*) Creation Research.

Did Christ Die for All? George E. Failing. 1980. 1.25 (*0-937296-02-3*, 222-B) Presence Inc.

Did Christ Die Only for the Elect? Charles R. Smith. 1979. pap. 1.50 (*0-88469-025-3*) BMH Bks.

Did Christ Make Love? Chandler Brossard. LC 72-89690. 1973. 6.95 (*0-672-51730-2*, Bobbs) Macmillan.

Did Christ Rule Out Women Priests, 1977. J. N. Wijnaards. 96p. (C). 1988. pap. 3.50 (*0-85597-204-1*, Pub. by McCrimmon Pub) Attic Pr.

Did Darwin Get It Right? Essays on Games, Sex & Evolution. John M. Smith. 264p. 1992. pap. 15.95 (*0-412-03821-8*, A9764, Chapman & Hall) Chapman & Hall.

Did-Done, Ran-Run, & Saw-Seen. Marie-Jose Shaw. (English Sound Filmstrip Kits Ser.). (gr. 3). 1980. teacher ed 34.00 (*0-8209-0471-6*, FCW3E-18) ESP.

***Did Elvis Sing in Your Hometown?** Lee Cotten. (Illus.). 250p. 1995. 26.95 (*0-9646588-0-I*); pap. 14.95 (*0-9646588-1-X*) High Sierra Bks.

Did God Make Them Black? Isaac O. Olaleye. LC 88-51961. 262p. 1990. 14.95 (*1-55523-223-X*) Winston-Derek.

Did God Use Evolution to "Create"? A Critique of Biological Evolution, Geological Evolution, & Astronomical Evolution. Christopher Chui. 350p. (Orig.). 1993. pap. 12.95 (*0-9640005-0-4*) Logos Pubs.

Did Gustav Mahler Ski? Judy Gahagan. LC 90-21601. 128p. 1991. 18.95 (*0-8112-1162-2*); pap. 9.95 (*0-8112-1163-0*, NDP711) New Directions.

***Did I Do Something Wrong? A Supportive Guide for Parents & Loved Ones of People in Therapy.** Heidi H. Spencer. LC 94-66758. 288p. 1995. pap. 13.95 (*0-88282-128-8*) New Horizon NJ.

Did I Ever Tell You About How Our Family Got Started? Building Togetherness & Values by Sharing Stories about Your Family. Deborah S. Lewis & Gregg Lewis. (Family Share Together Ser.). 112p. 1994. pap. 7.99 (*0-310-42111-X*) Zondervan.

Did I Ever Tell You about the Time When You Were Little? Building Togetherness & Values by Sharing Stories about Your Family. Deborah S. Lewis & Gregg Lewis. (Family Share Together Ser.). 112p. 1994. pap. 7.99 (*0-310-41071-1*) Zondervan.

Did I Ever Tell You about When Mom & Dad Were Young? Building Togetherness & Values by Sharing Stories about Your Family. Deborah S. Lewis & Gregg Lewis. (Family Share Together Ser.). 112p. 1994. pap. 7.99 (*0-310-42101-2*) Zondervan.

Did I Ever Tell You about When Your Grandparents Were Children? Building Togetherness & Values by Sharing Stories about Your Family. Deborah S. Lewis & Gregg Lewis. (Family Share Together Ser.). 112p. 1994. pap. 7.99 (*0-310-42121-7*) Zondervan.

Did I Ever Tell You How Lucky You Are? Dr. Seuss. (Illus.). (J). (ps-4). 1973. 11.00 (*0-394-82719-8*); lib. bdg. 11.99 (*0-394-92719-2*) Random Bks Yng Read.

Did I Ever Tell You How Lucky You Are? Dr. Seuss. (Dr. Seuss Book & Cassette Classics Ser.). (Illus.). 64p. (J). (ps up). 1993. audio 13.00 (*0-679-84993-9*) Random Bks Yng Read.

Did I Hear a Buck Snort? Max Short. (Illus.). 112p. (Orig.). 1994. pap. 7.95 (*0-9640061-0-3*) Buckmoth Pr.

Did I Win? A Farewell to George Sheehan. Joe Henderson. 208p. 1995. 19.95 (*1-56796-066-9*) WRS Group.

***Did I Win? A Farewell to George Sheehan.** Joe Henderson. 208p. 1995. pap. 12.95 (*1-56796-106-1*) WRS Group.

Did It Matter That I Ever Was? Maria Van Doren. 30p. (Orig.). 1993. pap. 10.00 (*0-9629364-1-3*) Bourdon Pub.

Did Jesus Die Spiritually? Exposing the J. D. S. Heresy. Hobart E. Freeman. 73p. (Orig.). 1983. pap. 2.95 (*1-878725-10-6*) Faith Min & Pubns.

Did Jesus Die Twice? Ed. by Gene Tolliver. LC 85-63545. 100p. (Orig.). 1986. pap. 3.75 (*0-937357-00-6*) Substance Faith.

Did Jesus Exist? G. A. Wells. 250p. pap. 19.95 (*0-87975-395-1*) Prometheus Bks.

Did Jesus Know He Was God? Francois Dreyfus. 1988. 5.95 (*0-8199-0899-1*, Frncscn Herld) Franciscan Pr.

Did Jesus Know What He Was Talking About? Ralph H. Peterson. 112p. 1982. 6.95 (*0-8187-0045-9*) Am Developing.

Did Jesus Live One Hundred B. C.? G. R. Mead. 440p. 1992. pap. 29.95 (*1-56459-130-1*) Kessinger Pub.

Did Jesus Live One Hundred B.C.? G. R. Mead. 440p. 1993. spiral bd. 16.50 (*0-7873-0603-7*) Mokelumne.

Did Jesus Live One Hundred Years B. C. An Inquiry into the Talmud Jesus Stories, the Toldoth, Jeschu, a Study of Christian Origins. G. R. Mead. 1991. lib. bdg. 79.95 (*0-8490-4304-2*) Gordon Pr.

Did Jesus Teach Capitalism? Spiros Zodhiates. LC 82-71267. (Illus.). 1982. pap. 5.99 (*0-89957-548-X*) AMG Pubs.

Did Molly Pitcher Say That? Glackens. 1989. 18.95 (*0-86316-097-2*); pap. 12.95 (*0-86316-094-8*) Writers & Readers.

Did Monetary Forces Cause the Great Depression? Peter Temin. (Illus.). 201p. (C). 1975. pap. text ed. 9.95 (*0-393-09209-7*) Norton.

Did My First Mother Love Me? A Story for an Adopted Child. Kathryn M. Miiller. (Illus.). 48p. (Orig.). (J). (ps-3). 1994. 12.95 (*0-930934-85-7*) Morning Glory.

Did My First Mother Love Me? A Story for an Adopted Child. Kathryn M. Miller. (Illus.). 48p. (Orig.). (J). (ps-3). 1994. pap. 5.95 (*0-930934-84-9*) Morning Glory.

Did My Mama Like to Dance? And Other Stories about Mothers & Daughters. Ed. by Geeta Kothari. 192p. 1994. pap. 10.00 (*0-380-77101-2*) Avon.

Did Pocahontas Save Captain John Smith? J. A. Lemay. LC 92-791. (Illus.). 144p. 1992. 22.50 (*0-8203-1461-7*) U of Ga Pr.

Did Politics Influence Jesus? Gordon Lindsay. 1979. per. 3.95 (*0-89985-113-4*) Christ for the Nations.

Did Shakespeare Write "Titus Andronicus"? John M. Robertson. LC 77-39875. reprint ed. 31.50 (*0-404-05361-0*) AMS Pr.

Did She Have Time to Say, "Lord Have Mercy on My Soul"? Hermine S. Hamilton. 1994. 12.95 (*0-533-10784-9*) Vantage.

Did She Leave Me Any Money? Alyce P. Cornyn-Selby. 198p. 1991. pap. text ed. 11.95 (*0-941383-11-3*) Beynch Pr.

D

An Asterisk (*) at the beginning of an entry indicates that the title is appearing in BIP for the first time.

1981

Did the Children Cry? Hitler's War Against Jewish & Polish Children, 1939-1945. Richard C. Lukas. (Illus.). 320p. 1994. 22.50 (0-7818-0242-3) Hippocrene Bks.

Did the Eagle Get You, Dr. Moss? A Memoir of Ephraim Summers. Charles F. Wiley. LC 90-38033. (Illus.). 225p. 1990. 20.00 (0-940473-17-8); pap. 11.95 (0-940473-18-6) Wm Caxton.

Did the Greeks Believe in Their Myths? An Essay on the Constitutive Imagination. Paul Veyne. Tr. by Paula Wissing. xii, 162p. 1988. pap. text ed. 11.95 (0-226-85434-5) U Ch Pr.

Did the Phoenicians Discover America? Thomas C. Johnston. reprint ed. 4.95 (0-686-05042-8) St Thomas.

Did the Proto-Indo-European Priesthood Commit Treason in the Period of P.I.E. Unity? When & Where? An Attempt to Locate the Time & Place of the Proto-Indo-European Homeland. 2nd rev. ed. Frederick W. Ballantine & James L. Oswald. (Illus.). 273p. (C). reprint ed. 12.75 (0-685-45712-5) G J Ludwig.

Did the Sun Shine Before You Were Born? A Sex Education Primer. Sol Gordon & Judith Gordon. (J). (ps-3). 1982. pap. 7.95 (0-934978-03-4) Ed-U Pr.

Did the Sun Shine Before You Were Born: A Sex Education Primer. Sol Gordon & Judith Cohen. LC 74-82733. (J). (ps-2). 1974. 12.00 (0-89388-179-1) Okpaku Communications.

Did the Sun Shine Before Your Were Born? Sol Gordon & Judith Gordon. (Young Readers Ser.). (Illus.). 48p. (Orig.). (J). (gr. k-5). 1992. pap. 8.95 (0-87975-723-X) Prometheus Bks.

***DID 3: Architecture & Design World Review.** S. A. Rotovision. 264p. 1994. 45.00 (0-8230-6321-6) Watsn-Guptill.

***Did Triceratops Have Polka Dots? First Questions & Answers about Dinosaurs.** Editors of Time Life Inc. Ed. by Allan Fallow. LC 95-18649. (Time-Life Library of First Questions & Answers). (Illus.). 48p. (J). 1995. write for info. (0-7835-0903-0) Time-Life.

DID Two: The International Directory of Architecture & Design. Rotovision S. A. Staff. (Illus.). 224p. 1992. 65.00 (0-8230-6207-4, Watsn-Guptill) Watsn-Guptill.

Did W. D. Custead Fly First? The Story of W. D. Custead of Elm Mott - Waco, Texas - Airship Builder Before the Wrights Flew. Nick Pocock. LC 74-83996. (Illus.). 1974. pap. 17.95 (0-915376-00-8); mic. film 20.00 (0-915376-01-6) Spec Aviation.

Did Ya See the Masked Man? Sean M. Rice. LC 91-51083. (Orig.). 1985. pap. 5.00 (0-88734-304-X) Players Pr.

Did You Carry the Flag Today, Charley? Rebecca Caudill. LC 66-11422. (Illus.). 96p. (J). (gr. 2-4). 1966. 15.95 (0-8050-1201-X, Bks Young Read) H Holt & Co.

Did You Carry the Flag Today, Charley? Rebecca Caudill. LC 66-11422. (Illus.). 96p. (J). (gr. 2-4). 1971. 3.95 (0-03-086620-0, Bks Young Read) H Holt & Co.

Did You Carry the Flag Today, Charley? Rebecca Caudill. (J). (gr. k-6). 1988. reprint ed. pap. 3.25 (0-440-40092-9) Dell.

Did You Ever Meet a Texas Hero? Marj Gurasich. LC 91-19544. (Illus.). (J). (gr. 3-5). 1992. 12.95 (0-89015-819-3) Sunbelt Media.

Did You Ever Sing a Mooley Cow? see Everybody Sings!

Did You Ever Talk to God Above? Francis Roth. (Illus.). 1974. 6.99 (3-901170-23-5) CEF Press.

Did You Hear Something? Michael Teitelbaum. (Slightly Spooky Stories Ser.). (Illus.). (J). 1992. 2.98 (0-685-60663-5) Kidsbks.

Did You Hear the One About ... Soupy Sales. 1987. 4.95 (0-685-46250-1, Collier S&S) S&S Trade.

***Did You Hear Wind Sing Your Name?** Sandra Orie. (Illus.). 32p. (J). 1995. 14.95 (0-8027-8350-3); lib. bdg. 15.85 (0-8027-8351-1) Walker & Co.

Did You Know? Deborah Pease. Ed. by Constance Hunting. 58p. 1993. pap. 8.95 (0-913006-52-1) Puckerbrush.

Did You Know? Fascinating Facts & Fallacies about Business. D. Keith Denton & Charles Boyd. LC 93-47947. 1994. write for info. (0-13-032194-X) P-H.

Did You Know? New Insights into a World that is Full of Astonishing Facts & Astonishing Stories. Reader's Digest Editors. (Illus.). 384p. 1993. 32.95 (0-276-42014-4, Random) RD Assn.

***Did You Know That?** (Spin-a-Quiz Bks.). (Illus.). 16p. (J). (gr. k-2). 1994. pap. 5.95 (1-56144-431-6, Honey Bear Bks) Modern Pub NYC.

***Did You Know That...? Surprising but True Facts about History, Science, Art, Technology.** Marko Perko. 304p. (Orig.). 1994. pap. text ed. 5.50 (0-425-14343-0) Berkley Pub.

***Did You Know That ... of & about Jesus' Life as Recorded in the Holy Scriptures?** (Walk with Jesus Ser.). 12p. 1987. pap. 5.00 (1-57277-206-9) Truth Center.

Did You Know That? Baja Shells from the Northern Sea of Cortez. Wesley M. Farmer. (Illus.). 24p. 1992. 4.25 (0-937772-05-4) W M Farmer.

***Did You Know This Was in the Bible.** Bruce Carroll. (Illus.). 244p. (Orig.). 1995. pap. 18.00x (0-614-07030-9, Red River Pr) Archival Servs.

Did You Lose the Car Again? Paula K. Feder. (Speedsters Ser.). (Illus.). 64p. (J). (gr. 2-5). 1991. pap. 3.99 (0-14-034800-X, Puffin) Puffin Bks.

Did You Really Fall into a Vat of Anchovies? And Other Activities for Language Arts. Ed. by Cheri Armstrong. 96p. 1993. 18.95 (1-877673-18-8, VAT) Cottonwood Pr.

Did You Receive the Spirit? rev. ed. Simon Tugwell. 144p. 1982. pap. 6.95 (0-87243-108-8) Templegate.

Did You Say Ghosts? Richard Michelson. LC 92-30134. (Illus.). 32p. (J). (ps up). 1993. text ed. 14.95 (0-02-766915-7, Mac Bks Young Read) S&S Childrens.

Did You See My Ad? Larry Semon. LC 88-6990. 128p. 1988. pap. 12.95 (0-931790-78-6) Brick Hse Pub.

Did Your Eyes Deceive You? Expert Psychological Testimony on the Unreliability of Eyewitness Identification. F. Woocher. (Monograph Ser.: No. CR-41). 1978. 4.00 (1-55524-042-9) Ctr Respon Psych.

Did Your Granny Have a Hammer? A History of the Irish Women's Suffrage Movement. Rosemary C. Ohlens et al. (Illus.). (C). 1989. pap. 7.95 (0-946211-14-0, Pub. by Attic IE) InBook.

Did Your Jeweler Tell You? An Insider's Guide to Facts You Need to Know about Your Jewelry & Its Care. Dawn King. LC 90-91535. (Orig.). 1990. pap. 5.95 (1-878672-00-2) King Enterprises.

Didache: The Teaching of the Twelve Apostles. Ed. by Philotheos Bryennios. (GRE.). 1989. Original Greek text. pap. text ed. 2.50 (0-89981-204-X) Eastern Orthodox.

Didache: The Teaching of the Twelve Apostles. Tr. by Roswell Hitchcock. 1989. English translation. pap. text ed. 1.50 (0-89981-205-8) Eastern Orthodox.

***Didache: The Teaching of the Twelve Apostles.** large type ed. Tr. by Francis Brown & Roswell Hitchcock. 1994. pap. 3.00 (0-89981-304-6) Eastern Orthodox.

***Didache in Context.** Ed. by Clayton N. Jefford. 480p. 1994. 97.25 (90-04-10045-8) E J Brill.

Didache, the Epistle of Barnabas, the Epistle & Martyrdom of St. Polycarp, the Fragments of Papias, the Epistle of Diognetus. Ed. by W. J. Burghardt et al. LC 78-62453. (Ancient Christian Writers Ser.: No. 6). 241p. 1948. 16.95 (0-8091-0247-1) Paulist Pr.

Didactic Muse. Willard Spiegelman. (Studies in Contemporary American Poetry). 264p. (C). 1990. text ed. 47.50 (0-691-06799-6); pap. text ed. 13.95 (0-691-01460-4) Princeton U Pr.

Didactic Strategies in Physical Education. Linus J. Dowell. (Illus.). 232p. (Orig.). 1980. pap. text ed. 11.95x (0-89641-047-1) American Pr.

Didactic Structure & Content of el Libro de Calila e Digna. Margaret Parker. LC 76-51194. (Coleccion de Estudios Hispanicos - Hispanic Studies Collection). 1978. pap. 10.00 (0-89729-188-3) Ediciones.

Didactic Verses by Henry Pfaff: Poetry of Labor Struggles, Life & Capital. 62p. 1983. 2.00 (0-685-08826-X) Indus Workers World.

Didactic Verses of an Old-Time Wobbly. Henry J. Pfaff. 62p. 1983. pap. 3.95 (0-88286-106-9) C H Kerr.

Didactical Phenomenology of Mathematical Structure. Hans Freudenthal. 1986. pap. text ed. 58.00 (90-277-2261-7) Kluwer Ac.

Didactics: Social, Literary, & Political, 2 vols. Robert Walsh. LC 72-1290. (Essay Index Reprint Ser.). 1977. reprint ed. 44.95 (0-8369-2873-3) Ayer.

Didactics: Social, Literary, & Political, 2 vols, 1. Robert Walsh. LC 72-1290. (Essay Index Reprint Ser.). 1979. reprint ed. 23.95 (0-8369-9982-7) Ayer.

Didactics: Social, Literary, & Political, 2 vols, 2. Robert Walsh. LC 72-1290. (Essay Index Reprint Ser.). 1977. reprint ed. 23.95 (0-8369-9983-5) Ayer.

Didactics for the Undergraduate Student. Fraser. 1991. pap. 34.95 (0-409-10193-1) Buttrwrth-Heinemann.

Didactics of Mathematics as a Scientific Discipline. Ed. by Rolf Biehler et al. LC 93-39782. (Mathematics Education Library: Vol. 13). 1993. lib. bdg. 150.00 (0-7923-2613-X) Kluwer Ac.

Didactologie et Phonetique Appropriative. Jacques Roy. (American University Studies: Linguistics: Ser. XIII, Vol. 8). 202p. (C). 1989. text ed. 33.00 (0-8204-0754-2) P Lang Pubs.

Didaktik und Methodik Deutsch als Fremdsprache. Dieter Strauss. 157p. pap. 24.50 (3-468-49432-7) Langenscheidt.

Didascalicon of Hugh of St. Victor. Jerome Taylor. (Records of Western Civilization Ser.). 254p. 1991. text ed. 58.00 (0-231-02444-4); pap. text ed. 12.50 (0-231-09630-5) Col U Pr.

Diddie, Dumps & Tot. Louise-Clarke Pyrnelle. (Illus.). 117p. (J). (gr. 4-8). 1963. 14.95 (0-911116-17-6) Pelican.

Diddle Diddle Red Hot Fiddle. Patricia Powell. (Illus.). 32p. (J). (gr. 1-8). 1990. pap. text ed. 6.95 (0-944512-01-1) Radiant LA.

Diddledee Dog, the Dirt Digger. Harry B. Kircher. LC 68-57271. (Illus.). 20p. 1968. pap. 1.00 (0-8134-1061-4, 1061) Interstate.

***Diddy Waw Diddy: Passage of an American Son.** Billy Porterfield. (Southwest Life & Letters Ser.). (Illus.). 448p. 1995. pap. 12.95 (0-87074-382-1) SMU Press.

Diddy Waw Diddy: The Passage of an American Son. Billy Porterfield. LC 93-25301. (Illus.). 416p. 1994. 23.00 (0-06-016999-0, HarpT) HarpC.

Diderot. Otis Fellows. (World Authors Ser.: No. 425). 232p. 1989. text ed. 26.95 (0-8057-8225-7, TWAS 425, Twayne) Macmillan.

Diderot: Thresholds of Representation. James Creech. LC 85-25881. 213p. 1986. 42.50 (0-8142-0393-0) Ohio St U Pr.

Diderot & Descartes: A Study of Scientific Naturalism in the Enlightment. Aram Vartanian. LC 52-8781. (History of Ideas Ser.: No. 6). reprint ed. pap. 85.80 (0-317-09015-1, 2000885) Bks Demand.

Diderot & Rousseau's Contributions to Aesthetics. Servanne Woodward. LC 90-22971. (New Studies in Aesthetics: Vol. 8). 335p. (C). 1991. text ed. 53.00 (0-8204-1477-8) P Lang Pubs.

Diderot & the Family. William F. Edmiston. (Stanford French & Italian Studies: Vol. 39). 192p. 1985. pap. 46.50 (0-915838-51-6) Anma Libri.

Diderot & the Jews. Leon Schwartz. LC 78-73304. 208p. 1981. 32.50 (0-8386-2377-8) Fairleigh Dickinson.

Diderot, Denis. T. Dlugach. 237p. (C). 1988. 45.00 (0-685-31618-1, Pub. by Collets UK) Pro-Am Music.

Diderot: Digression & Dispersion: A Bicentennial Tribute. Ed. by Jack Undank & Herbert Josephs. LC 84-81852. (French Forum Monographs: No. 58). 282p. (Orig.). 1984. pap. 17.95 (0-917058-58-5) French Forum.

Diderot et l'Amour. Alice M. Laborde. (Stanford French & Italian Studies: No. 17). vi, 114p. 1979. pap. 46.50 (0-915838-22-2) Anma Libri.

Diderot et Mme. de Puisieux. Alice M. Laborde. (Stanford French & Italian Studies: Vol. 36). 1985. pap. 46.50 (0-915838-54-0) Anma Libri.

Diderot, Interpreter of Nature: Selected Writings. Denis Diderot. Ed. & Tr. by Jonathon Kemp. Tr. by Jean Stewart. LC 78-65607. 1990. reprint ed. 35.00 (0-88355-841-6) Hyperion Conn.

***Diderot on Art, Vol. 1.** Tr. by John Goodman. LC 95-10638. (Illus.). 1995. write for info. (0-300-06248-6) Yale U Pr.

***Diderot on Art, Vol. 1.** Tr. by John Goodman. LC 95-10638. (Illus.). 1995. pap. write for info. (0-300-06251-6) Yale U Pr.

***Diderot on Art, Vol. 2.** Tr. by John Goodman. LC 95-10638. (Illus.). 1995. write for info. (0-300-06249-4) Yale U Pr.

***Diderot on Art, Vol. 2.** Tr. by John Goodman. LC 95-10638. (Illus.). 1995. pap. write for info. (0-300-06252-4) Yale U Pr.

Diderot Pictorial Encyclopedia of Trades & Industry, 2 Vols., 1. Denis Diderot. Ed. by Charles C. Gillispie. 1959. 29.95 (0-486-22284-5) Dover.

Diderot Pictorial Encyclopedia of Trades & Industry, 2 Vols., 2. Denis Diderot. Ed. by Charles C. Gillispie. 1959. 29.95 (0-486-22285-3) Dover.

Diderot Pictorial Encyclopedia of Trades & Industry: Manufacturing & the Technical Arts in Plates Selected from "L'Encyclopedie, ou Dictionnaire Raisonne des Sciences, des Arts et des Metiers", 2 vols., 1. Intro. & Notes by Charles C. Gillispie. LC 92-31820. (Pictorial Archive Ser.). (Illus.). 936p. 1993. reprint ed. pap. 17.95 (0-486-27428-4) Dover.

Diderot Pictorial Encyclopedia of Trades & Industry: Manufacturing & the Technical Arts in Plates Selected from "L'Encyclopedie, ou Dictionnaire Raisonne des Sciences, des Arts et des Metiers", 2 vols., 2. Intro. & Notes by Charles C. Gillispie. LC 92-31820. (Pictorial Archive Ser.). (Illus.). 936p. 1993. reprint ed. pap. 17.95 (0-486-27429-2) Dover.

Diderot's Cat: Selected Poems. Michael Kruger. Tr. by Richard Dove. LC 93-38504. 1994. 14.95 (0-8076-1343-6) Braziller.

Diderot's Chaotic Order: Approach to Synthesis. Lester G. Crocker. LC 73-16756. 188p. 1974. 39.50 (0-691-07199-3) Princeton U Pr.

Diderot's Dream. Wilda Anderson. LC 89-43478. 272p. 1990. text ed. 39.50x (0-8018-3976-9) Johns Hopkins.

Diderot's Early Philosophical Works. Denis Diderot. Ed. by Margaret Jourdain. LC 70-147967. reprint ed. 34.50 (0-404-08219-X) AMS Pr.

Diderot's Imagery: A Study of a Literary Personality. Eric M. Steel. LC 68-1793. (Studies in French Literature: No. 45). 1969. reprint ed. lib. bdg. 75.00 (0-8383-0628-4) M S G Haskell Hse.

Diderot's Vie de Seneque: A Swan Song Revised. Douglas A. Bonneville. LC 66-63483. (University of Florida Humanities Monographs: No. 19). 59p. reprint ed. pap. 25.00 (0-7837-5016-1, 2044683) Bks Demand.

Diderot's Writings on the Theatre. Denis Diderot. Ed. by F. C. Green. LC 76-43916. (Music & Theatre in France in the 17th & 18th Centuries Ser.). reprint ed. 57.50 (0-404-60157-X) AMS Pr.

***Didgeridoo: Ritual Origins & Playing Techniques.** Dirk Schellberg. (Illus.). 158p. 1994. pap. 12.95 (90-74597-13-0) Weiser.

Didier Leschenet. Jane Bernstein. LC 90-752744. (Sixteenth Century Chanson Ser.: Vol. 18). 312p. 1990. 86.00 (0-8240-3117-2) Garland.

***Didja' Ever Make Butter? And Other Hilarious Childhood Survival Tales.** Gary M. Corbett. 217p. Date not set. 19.95 (1-886882-00-2) Polo Springs.

Didman. John Speicher. LC 77-123987. 1971. 25.00 (0-89366-108-2) Ultramarine Pub.

Didn't It Rain? Will It Be Fire? Solutions for Global Air Warming. James M. DeVone, Sr. & Susu Akhenaton. LC 89-92762. (Illus.). 50p. (C). 1989. pap. text ed. 9.95 (0-9625092-1-3) Schl Univ Studies.

Didn't You Kill My Mother in Law: The Story of Alternative Comedy in Britain from the Comedy Store to Saturday Live. Roger Wilmut & Peter Rosengard. (Methuen Humor Ser.). (Illus.). 285p. (Orig.). (C). 1989. pap. 15.95 (0-413-17390-9, A0420, Pub. by Methuen UK) Heinemann.

Didn't You Read My Book? Richard Eby. 172p. 1992. 7.99 (1-56043-448-1, Treasure Hse) Destiny Image.

Dido. Mark Dunster. 14p. (Orig.). 1994. pap. 4.00 (0-89642-237-2) Linden Pubs.

Dido. Christopher Marlowe & Thomas Nash. LC 70-133703. (Tudor Facsimile Texts. Old English Plays Ser.: No. 72). reprint ed. 49.50 (0-404-53372-8) AMS Pr.

Dido & Aeneas, an Opera. Henry Purcell. Ed. by Curtis Price. (Critical Scores Ser.). 1986. 27.50 (0-393-02407-5) Norton.

Dido & Aeneas, an Opera. Henry Purcell. Ed. by Curtis Price. (Critical Scores Ser.). (C). 1986. pap. text ed. 9.95 (0-393-95528-1) Norton.

Dido en la Literatura Espanola: Su Retrato y Defensa. Maria R. De Malkiel. (Serie A: Monagrafias, XXXVII). 166p. (Orig.). (SPA.). (C). 1974. pap. 36.00 (0-900411-85-6, Pub. by Tamesis Bks Ltd UK) Boydell & Brewer.

Didon. Niccolo Piccinni. Ed. by Gustave Lefevre. (Chefs-d'oeuvre classiques de l'opera francaise Ser.: Vol. 28). (Illus.). 334p. (FRE.). 1970. reprint ed. pap. 35.00 (0-8450-1128-6) Broude.

Didone Abbandonata (Vinci) see Italian Opera Librettos, Vol. IV, 1640-1770

Didyaeverhavaday? A Cookbook. Pamela Weis. 482p. (Orig.). 1988. pap. 18.88 (0-9621841-0-1) Raspberry Patch Pr.

Didyma: Apollo's Oracle, Cult, & Companions. Joseph Fontenrose. 1988. 50.00 (0-520-05845-3) U CA Pr.

Didymus. Tom W. Decker. LC 95-68666. (Illus.). 280p. (Orig.). 1995. pap. 9.95 (1-887097-13-9) Dayssprng Pr. Two Thousand years ago a man named Thomas witnessed a series of miracles performed by an obscure rabbi but couldn't accept what he saw. Anticipating disclosing him as a charlatan, he temporarily joined the rabbi & his small group as they went about their vague mission. Instead he became involved in a series of events that today would shake humanity to the core. This is a realistic journey through the days of the Gospels as told in fiction by the man Jesus called DIDYMUS (Thomas). Whether a Christian or not, you'll find this book a believable tale of a small motley group of men & Thomas, the Apostle; a traveler & educator who enjoyed life, was drawn to Jesus through curiosity, could not fully accept all the things he witnessed, & doubted almost all of it to the end. A human, heartwarming tale of love, fear, awe & a triumph that didn't come easy. The plot follows the Bible's four Gospels plus the first part of Acts. It required substantial research to sort out the events in logical order, so any reader interested in Scripture will find this book a handy reference since it contains ample footnotes. To order: The Dayspring Press, P.O. Box 40214, Mobile, AL 36604.** ***Publisher Provided Annotation.

Didymus the Blind & the Text of the Gospels. Bart D. Ehrman. LC 86-24845. (Society of Biblical Literature New Testament in the Greek Fathers Ser.). 292p. 1987. 24.95 (1-55540-083-3, 06-30-01); pap. 17.95 (1-55540-084-1) Scholars Pr GA.

Die All, Die Merrily. Leo Bruce. (Carolus Deene Mystery Ser.). 192p. 1987. pap. 5.95 (0-89733-253-9) Academy Chi Pubs.

***Die Asiatische Hydra: Die Cholera von 1830-31 in Berlin und den Preussischen Provinzen Posen, Preussen und Schlesien.** Barbara Dettke. (Veroeffentlichungen der Historischen Kommision Zu Berlin Ser.: Bd. 89). xiii, 383p. (GER.). (C). 1995. lib. bdg. 152.30 (3-11-014493-X) De Gruyter.

Die-Cast Metals, Light Metals & Alloys Including Electrical Conductors (114 Standards) see ASTM Annual Book of Standards, 1986

Die Casting of Copper Alloys. Case Western Reserve University Staff. 115p. 1973. 17.25 (0-317-34514-1, 189) Intl Copper.

Die Design Fundamentals. 2nd ed. J. R. Paquin & R. E. Crowley. LC 86-19132. (Illus.). 256p. 1987. 26.95 (0-8311-1172-0) Indus Pr.

Die Design Handbook. 3rd ed. Intro. by David A. Smith. LC 89-63763. (Illus.). 928p. 1990. 120.00 (0-87263-375-6) SME.

Die Dreaming: An Owen Keane Mystery. Terence Faherty. 272p. 1994. 20.95 (0-312-11045-6, Pub. by Thomas Dunne Bks) St Martin.

Die Erkenntnis des Uebersinnlichen in unserer Zeit und deren Bedeutung fuer see Supersensible Knowledge

Die for Big Betsy. large type ed. Bill Knox. (Linford Mystery Library). 1990. pap. 12.95 (0-7089-6844-9, Traitree Bookshop) Ulverscroft.

Die for Love. Elizabeth Peters. 288p. 1992. mass mkt. 4.50 (0-8125-2470-5) Tor Bks.

Die for Love. Elizabeth Peters. 288p. 1993. reprint ed. lib. bdg. 20.00 (0-7278-4491-1) Severn Hse.

Die for Me. Carol Gorman. 144p. (Orig.). (J). (gr. 7-12). 1992. pap. 3.50 (0-380-76686-8, Flare) Avon.

***Die Grundzahlworter der Uralischen Sprachen.** L. Honti. 355p. (GER.). 1994. 48.00 (963-05-6458-0, Pub. by A K HU) Intl Spec Bk.

***Die Hard III.** Chiel. 1995. mass mkt. 4.99 (0-312-95676-2) St Martin.

Die Krise des Modernen Islams see Crisis of Modern Islam: A Preindustrial Culture in the Scientific-Technological Age

Die Laughing. Vincent Courtney. (Nightmare Club Ser.: No. 10). 224p. 1994. pap. 3.50 (0-8217-4511-5) Zebra.

Die Laughing. S. S. Rafferty. 200p. pap. 4.95 (0-930330-16-1) Intl Polygonics.

Die Laughing. large type ed. Richard Lockridge. LC 91-40154. 303p. 1992. lib. bdg. 19.95 (1-56054-240-3) Thorndike Pr.

Die Like a Dog. large type ed. Brett Halliday. (Linford Mystery Library). 336p. 1993. pap. 14.95 (0-7089-7267-5, Traitree Bookshop) Ulverscroft.

D

An Asterisk (*) at the beginning of an entry indicates that the title is appearing in BIP for the first time.

An Asterisk (*) at the beginning of an entry indicates that the title is appearing in BIP for the first time.

1983

Diesel Fuels for the Nineties: Composition & Additives to Meet Emissions & Performance Needs. (International Fuels & Lubricants Meeting & Exposition, 1993 Ser.). pap. 45.00 (*1-56091-433-5*, SP-994) Soc Auto Engineers.

Diesel Fundamentals: Principles & Service. Frank J. Thiessen & Davis N. Dales. (C). 1986. teacher ed write for info. (*0-8359-1287-6*, Reston) P-H.

Diesel Fundamentals: Principles & Service. 2nd ed. Frank J. Thiessen & Davis N. Dales. (C). 1986. text ed. 76.00 (*0-8359-1286-8*, Reston) P-H.

Diesel Generator Handbook. L. L. Mahon. (Illus.). 416p. 1992. 195.00 (*0-7506-1147-2*) Buttrwrth-Heinemann.

Diesel Locomotive Rosters: United States, Canada & Mexico. 3rd ed. Charles W. McDonald. Ed. by George Drury. (Illus.). 240p. (Orig.). 1992. pap. 16.95 (*0-89024-112-0*) Kalmbach.

Diesel Locomotives in Preservation, Vol. 2: Former BR LMSR Loco's. Peter Nicholson. 28p. (C). 1987. pap. 30.00 (*0-317-90465-5*, Pub. by Picton UK) St Mut.

Diesel Mechanics. Zdenko Geda. LC 81-730632. 1981. student ed 5.00 (*0-8064-0193-1*, 472); audio 359.00 (*0-8064-0194-X*) Bergwall.

Diesel Mechanics. 2nd ed. Erich J. Schulz. 496p. 1983. text ed. 39.95 (*0-07-055639-3*) McGraw.

Diesel Mechanics. 3rd ed. Erich J. Schultz & Ben L. Evridge. 1989. pap. text ed. write for info. (*0-07-055891-4*) McGraw.

Diesel Mechanics. 3rd ed. Erich J. Schulz & Ben L. Evridge. (Illus.). 480p. 1988. pap. text ed. 39.95 (*0-07-055836-1*) McGraw.

Diesel Mechanics an Introduction. Little. 1982. 35.95 (*0-534-01054-7*) Delmar.

Diesel Mechanics II: Engine Assembly. Zdenko Gega. 1983. student ed 7.00 (*0-8064-0195-8*, 473); audio 279.00 (*0-8064-0196-6*) Bergwall.

Diesel Mechanics III. Zdenko Gega. LC 83-730096. 1983. student ed 7.00 (*0-8064-0197-4*, 474); audio 279.00 (*0-8064-0198-2*) Bergwall.

Diesel Particulate Control Trap, & Filtration Systems. 312p. 1992. pap. 79.00 (*1-56091-213-8*, SP-896) Soc Auto Engineers.

Diesel Particulate Emissions: Measurement Techniques, Fuel Effects & Control Technology. Ed. by John H. Johnson et al. 658p. 1992. 79.00 (*1-56091-304-5*, PT-42) Soc Auto Engineers.

Diesel Plant Operations Handbook. Clive T. Jones. 608p. 1991. text ed. 69.50 (*0-07-032814-5*) McGraw.

Diesel Preventive Maintenance. Ed. by Kelly Gorham. (Automotive Ser.). 28p. (YA). (gr. 10 up). 1993. student ed 7.00 (*0-8064-0013-7*, A37); audio 439.00 (*0-8064-0012-9*) Bergwall.

Diesel Problem in New York City. E. Goldstein & M. Paly. 1985. 5.00 (*0-318-20474-6*) Natl Resources Defense Coun.

***Diesel's Devious Deed.** Thomas. 1994. 3.99 (*0-517-13549-3*) Random Hse Value.

Diesel's Devious Deed & Other Thomas the Tank Engine Stories. W. Awdry. LC 91-21133. (Thomas the Tank Engine Picturebacks Ser.). (Illus.). 32p. (Orig.). (J). (ps-3). 1992. pap. 2.25 (*0-679-81976-2*) Random Bks Yng Read.

Diesel's Devious Deed & Other Thomas the Tank Engine Stories. W. Awdry. Ed. by Ringo Starr. (Thomas the Tank Engine & Friends Ser.). (Illus.). 32p. (Orig.). (J). (ps-3). 1992. audio, pap. 6.95 (*0-679-83474-5*) Random Bks Yng Read.

Diesel's Engine, Vol. 1: From Conception to 1918. C. Lyle Cummins, Jr. Ed. by Jeanne Cummins. LC 93-74475. (Illus.). xiv, 746p. 1993. 55.00 (*0-917308-03-4*) Carnot Pr.

Diesels of the Espee: Alco PA's. Ed. by R. M. Cortani. LC 75-38238. (Illus.). 1975. 25.00 (*0-89685-034-X*) Chatham Pub CA.

Diesels of the Sunrise Trail. John J. Scala. LC 83-91415. (Railroad Ser.). (Illus.). 152p. 1985. 31.95 (*0-9612814-0-5*) Weekend Chief.

Diet: A Key to Health. R. Swinburne Clymer. 1966. 4.95 (*0-686-05800-3*) Philos Pub.

Diet: And Health. Brian Ward. LC 90-31200. (Health Guides Ser.). (Illus.). 32p. (YA). 1991. lib. bdg. 13.23 (*0-531-14095-4*) Watts.

Diet - in Life, Food, Old Age & Research: Index of New Information with Authors & Subjects. Melba J. Milligan. 180p. 1993. 49.50 (*1-55914-842-X*); pap. 39.50 (*1-55914-843-8*) ABBE Pubs Assn.

Diet - Investigations, Research & Results: Index of New Information with Authors & Subjects. Melba J. Milligan. 180p. 1993. 49.50 (*1-55914-844-6*); pap. 39.50 (*1-55914-845-4*) ABBE Pubs Assn.

***Diet Aids Market.** 150p. (Orig.). 1995. pap. 2,195.00 (*0-7605-2262-6*) Rector Pr.

Diet Alternative. Diane Hampton. Orig. Title: Scriptural Eating Patterns. 144p. (Orig.). 1984. pap. 4.99 (*0-88368-148-X*) Whitaker Hse.

***Diet & Breast Cancer.** American Institute for Cancer Research Staff. (Advances in Experimental Medicine & Biology Ser.: Vol. 364). (Illus.). 182p. (C). 1994. 69.50 (*0-306-44895-5*, Plenum Pr) Plenum.

Diet & Cancer. William A. Creasey. LC 84-21845. 231p. reprint ed. pap. 65.90 (*0-7837-2696-1*, 2043074) Bks Demand.

Diet & Cancer: Markers, Prevention & Treatment. Ed. by M. M. Jacobs. (Advances in Experimental Medicine & Biology Ser.: Vol. 354). (Illus.). 249p. (C). 1994. 79.50 (*0-306-44723-1*, Plenum Pr) Plenum.

***Diet & Cancer: Molecular Mechanisms of Interactions.** Ed. by American Institute for Cancer Research Staff. (Advances in Experimental Medicine & Biology Ser.: Vol. 375). 220p. (Orig.). 1995. 79.50 (*0-306-45067-4*) Plenum.

Diet & Diet Reform. M. K. Gandhi. Ed. by B. Kumarappa. 185p. (Orig.). 1983. pap. 12.50 (*0-934676-61-5*) Greenlf Bks.

***Diet & Disease.** 3rd ed. E. Cheraskin et al. (Illus.). 384p. (Orig.). 1995. pap. 14.95 (*0-87983-666-0*) Keats.

Diet & Domestic Life in Society. Ed. by Anne Sharman et al. 288p. 1990. 34.95 (*0-87722-751-9*) Temple U Pr.

Diet & Drug Interactions. Daphne A. Roe. (Illus.). 288p. 1989. text ed. 52.95 (*0-442-20487-6*) Van Nos Reinhold.

Diet & Exercise. (Looking Good Ser.). (Illus.). (J). (gr. 5 up). 1987. 11.95 (*0-685-73926-0*); lib. bdg. 15.94 (*0-86625-280-0*) Rourke Corp.

Diet & Exercise Diary. Bonnie R. Wegener. 80p. 1988. pap. text ed. 2.95 (*0-318-23797-0*) Think Thin Think Shapely Pubns.

Diet & Exercise Guide. rev. ed. Family Circle Food Staff & Mary Milo. LC 73-11787. (Family Circle Bks.). (Illus.). 160p. 1977. 12.95 (*0-405-09844-8*) Ayer.

Diet & Exercise Made Easy. Sylvan R. Lewis. (Illus.). 128p. (Orig.). 1980. pap. 2.00 (*0-936320-00-1*) Compact Books.

Diet & Health: Implications for Reducing Chronic Disease Risk. National Research Council Staff. 768p. 1989. 54.95 (*0-309-03994-0*) Natl Acad Pr.

***Diet & Health Benefits of HCA.** Dallas Clouatre. 1994. pap. 3.50 (*0-87983-656-3*) Keats.

Diet & Health in Europe - the Evidence. Ed. by G. B. Brubacher. (Journal: Annals of Nutrition & Metabolism: Vol. 35, Suppl. 1, 1991). (Illus.). iv, 120p. 1991. pap. 35.25 (*3-8055-5400-1*) S Karger.

Diet & Health of Isolated Populations. G. R. Wadsworth. 232p. 1984. 168.00 (*0-8493-6101-X*, RC623, CRC Reprint) Franklin.

Diet & Human Carcinogenesis. Ed. by J. V. Joosens et al. (International Congress Ser.: No. 685). 360p. 1986. 106.25 (*0-444-80761-6*, Excerpta Medica) Elsevier.

Diet & Nutrition. R. Ballentine. LC 78-110274. 634p. (C). 1978. pap. 15.95 (*0-89389-048-0*) Himalayan Pubs.

Diet & Nutrition. Ed. by Charles B. Clayman. LC 90-8382. (American Medical Association Home Medical Library). (Illus.). 144p. 1991. 16.98 (*0-89577-358-9*) RD Assn.

Diet & Nutrition Activities. Patricia R. Toner. LC 93-4965. (Just for the Health of It Ser.: Unit 2). 1993. pap. 18.95 (*0-87628-265-6*) Ctr Appl Res.

Diet & Obesity. Ed. by G. A. Bray et al. (Illus.). xiv, 248p. 1989. 128.00 (*3-8055-4980-6*) S Karger.

Diet & Physical Efficiency: Influence of Frequency of Meals Upon Physical Efficiency & Industrial Productivity. Howard W. Haggard & Leon A. Greenberg. Ed. by Leon Stein. LC 77-70500. (Work Ser.). (Illus.). 1977. lib. bdg. 23.95 (*0-405-10171-6*) Ayer.

Diet & Prevention of Coronary Heart Disease & Cancer: Proceedings of the Fourth International Berzelius Symposium. Ed. by Bo Hallgren et al. 232p. 1986. text ed. 91.50 (*0-88167-219-X*) Raven.

Diet & the Aetiology of Cancer. Ed. by A. B. Miller. (ESO Monographs). (Illus.). 84p. 1989. 62.00 (*0-387-50681-0*) Spr-Verlag.

Diet Bible. Maureen Salaman. 1994. 17.50 (*0-913087-03-3*) Statford CA.

Diet Center Program: Lose Weight & Keep It off Forever. rev. ed. Sybil Ferguson. 1990. pap. 10.95 (*0-316-27902-1*) Little.

Diet Center Program: Lose Weight Fast & Keep It Off Forever. Sybil Ferguson. 424p. 1983. 16.95 (*0-316-27901-3*) Little.

Diet, Crime & Delinquency. 4th ed. Alexander G. Schauss. LC 80-80927. 108p. 1988. pap. 6.95 (*0-939764-00-8*) Life Sci Pr.

Diet, Demography, & Disease: Changing Perspectives of Anemia. Ed. by Patricia Stuart-Macadam & Susan Kent. LC 92-11086. (Foundations of Human Behavior Ser.). 294p. 1992. lib. bdg. 61.95 (*0-202-01189-5*) Aldine de Gruyter.

Diet, Diabetes & Atherosclerosis. Ed. by Guido Pozza et al. 296p. 1984. text ed. 86.00 (*0-88167-017-0*) Raven.

Diet Diary: The Culinary Companion for a New You! Andrew Ludy. (Illus.). 193p. (Orig.). 1984. pap. 4.95 (*0-943912-01-6*) Landing Pr.

***D.I.E.T. (Did I Eat That?) The Finding of Myself, the Losing of 135 Pounds.** Judy M. Cowart. 150p. 1995. pap. 12.95 (*0-9644073-0-2*) CC Production.

Diet Evaluation: A Guide to Planning a Healthy Diet. Ed. by G. Richard Jansen et al. 279p. 1990. spiral bd. 59.95 (*0-12-380215-6*) Acad Pr.

Diet, Exercise, & Coronary Heart Disease. Larry W. Gibbons & William J. Wilkinson. 25p. 1989. ring bd. 39.00 (*0-88091-050-X*) Am Dietetic Assn.

Diet Foods. Business Communications Co., Inc. Staff. (Illus.). 195p. 1986. pap. 1,450.00 (*0-89336-487-8*, GA-058) BCC.

Diet for a Gentle World: Eating with Conscience. Leslie R. Inglis. LC 92-511. 160p. 1993. pap. 7.95 (*0-89529-581-4*) Avery Pub.

Diet for a Happy Heart. Jeanne Jones. LC 88-72345. 1989. 17.95 (*0-89721-189-8*, One Hund One Prods) Cole Group.

Diet for a New America: How Your Food Choices Affect Your Health, Happiness & the Future of Life on Earth. John Robbins & Joanna R. Macy. LC 87-61157. (Illus.). 432p. 1987. pap. 13.95 (*0-913299-54-5*) Stillpoint.

Diet for a Poisoned Planet: How to Choose Safe Foods for You & Your Family. David Steinman. 400p. 1992. pap. 12.50 (*0-345-37465-7*, Ballantine Trade) Ballantine.

Diet for a Small Planet. 20th ed. Frances M. Lappe. 528p. 1991. pap. 14.00 (*0-345-37366-9*, Ballantine Trade) Ballantine.

Diet for a Small Planet: 10th Anniversary Edition. Frances M. Lappe. 1986. mass mkt. 6.99 (*0-345-32120-0*, Ballantine Trade) Ballantine.

Diet for a Strong Heart. Michio Kushi. (Illus.). 566p. 1986. pap. 14.95 (*0-312-00120-7*) St Martin.

Diet for All Seasons. Elson Haas. 224p. (Orig.). 1994. pap. 12.95 (*0-89087-732-7*) Celestial Arts.

Diet for Healthy Living. Raj K. Anand & Nirmal Anand. 65p. (Orig.). 1985. pap. 3.95 (*0-318-04445-5*) Raj Anand.

Diet for Natural Beauty. Aveline Kushi. 1991. 23.00 (*0-87040-789-9*) Japan Pubns USA.

Diet for One Hundred Healthy Happy Years: Health Secrets from the Caucasus. Morvyth McQueen-Williams & Barbara Apisson. Ed. by Norman Ober. LC 76-30710. 1977. 9.95 (*0-685-03832-7*) P-H.

Diet in Pregnancy: A Randomized Controlled Trail of Nutritional Supplements. Ed. by David Rush et al. LC 79-3846. (Alan R. Liss Ser.: Vol. 16, No. 3). 1980. 31.00 (*0-685-03286-8*) March of Dimes.

Diet Is a Dirty Word: The I-Can-Relate-to-That Weight-Loss Book. Ann M. Collins. LC 93-84485. (Illus.). 128p. (Orig.). 1993. pap. 9.95 (*0-9636558-0-9*) Persnl Power.

Diet Is a Four Letter Word. Suzie Heyman. LC 89-51575. 256p. (Orig.). 1990. pap. 12.95 (*0-9624680-0-2*) Starlight FL.

Diet Is a Four Letter Word: Mary Wright's Success with the Duke Diet & Fitness Program. Mary Wright. Ed. by Pamela Westland. (Illus.). 187p. 1988. 14.95 (*0-7198-0024-2*) M A Enter.

Diet Jokes. Bill Stott. Ed. by Helen Exley & Samantha Armstrong. (Joke Bks.). (Illus.). 60p. 1992. 6.99 (*1-85015-321-3*) Exley Giftbooks.

Diet, Lifestyle, & Mortality in China: A Study of the Characteristics of 65 Chinese Counties. Junshi Chen et al. Ed. by T. Colin Campbell et al. LC 89-38882. (Illus.). 920p. 1990. 175.00 (*0-8014-2453-4*) Cornell U Pr.

Diet Manual. Newark Beth Israel Medical Center, Dietary Department Staff. LC 80-82889. 92p. (Orig.). 1980. pap. 10.00 (*0-937714-00-3*) Newark Beth.

Diet Manual: A Compilation of Food Allowances Prescribed in Normal & Abnormal States of Health for the Use of Physicians, Paramedical Personnel & Trainees. 1991. lib. bdg. 79.95 (*0-8490-5053-7*) Gordon Pr.

Diet, Nutrition, & Cancer. National Research Council. 496p. 1982. pap. 29.95 (*0-309-03280-6*) Natl Acad Pr.

Diet, Nutrition, & Cancer: A Critical Evaluation. Ed. by Bandaru S. Reddy & Leonard A. Cohen. 184p. 1986. Vol. I, 184p. 144.00 (*0-8493-6332-2*, RC268); Vol. II, 208p. 106.00 (*0-8493-6333-0*) Franklin.

Diet, Nutrition, & Cancer: Directions for Research. National Research Council U. S. Staff. LC 83-61699. 86p. reprint ed. pap. 25.00 (*0-7837-2039-4*, 2042305) Bks Demand.

Diet, Nutrition & Cancer: Proceedings of the 16th International Symposium of the Princess Takamatsu Cancer Research Fund, Japan, 1985. Ed. by Y. Hayaishi et al. 344p. 1986. lib. bdg. 144.00 (*90-6764-085-9*, Pub. by VSP NE) Coronet Bks.

Diet, Nutrition & Dental Research. Ed. by M. E. Curzon & J. M. Ten Cate. (Journal: Caries Research: Vol. 24, Suppl. 1, 1990). (Illus.). iv, 80p. 1990. pap. 33.75 (*3-8055-5305-6*) S Karger.

Diet, Nutrition, & Health. K. K. Carroll. 368p. (C). 1990. text ed. 55.00 (*0-7735-0733-7*, Pub. by McGill CN); pap. text ed. 27.95 (*0-7735-0741-8*, Pub. by McGill CN) U of Toronto Pr.

Diet, Nutrition & Immunity. Kabbash. 1994. write for info. (*0-8493-6744-1*) CRC Pr.

Diet, Nutrition & the Prevention of Chronic Disease: Report of a WHO Study Group Technical Report No. 797. 203p. 1990. pap. 23.40 (*92-4-120797-3*) World Health.

Diet or Die see Greatest Diet in the World

Diet Pill, a Pretty Rock & a Live Snake for the Teacher. Helen M. Reed. 100p. 1991. 8.95 (*0-9630217-0-2*) H M Reed.

Diet Reference Manual. Massachusetts General Hospital Department of Dietetics Staff. Ed. by Ruth D. Palombo & Mary Carey. 240p. 1984. spiral bd. 17.50 (*0-316-54947-9*) Little.

Diet-Related Diseases: The Modern Epidemic. 2nd ed. Ed. by Stephen Seely et al. 1985. text ed. 54.95 (*0-87055-503-0*) AVI.

Diet Right! The Consumer's Guide to Diet & Weight Loss Programs. Matthew Quincy. 128p. (Orig.). 1991. reprint ed. lib. bdg. 23.00x (*0-8095-5855-6*) Borgo Pr.

Diet Selection: An Interdisciplinary Approach to Foraging Behaviour. Ed. by R. N. Hughes. LC 92-27323. 1993. 54.95 (*0-632-03559-5*) Blackwell Sci.

***Diet Therapy.** Sue R. Williams. LC 94-21373. 1994. write for info. (*0-8016-9128-1*) Mosby Yr Bk.

Diet Therapy: Self Instruction Modules. Stanfield. (Health Science Ser.). 350p. (C). 1995. pap. 32.50 (*0-86720-337-4*) Jones & Bartlett.

Diet Therapy for the Dietary Manager. DMA Staff. 416p. 1992. per. 47.50 (*0-8403-7856-4*) Kendall-Hunt.

***Diet Therapy in Traditional Chinese Medicine.** Ed. by Liu Chi-Lin. LC 94-44954. 1995. write for info. (*0-443-04967-X*) Churchill.

Diet to Die For. Joan Hess. (Claire Mallory Mystery Ser.). 1992. reprint ed. mass mkt. 4.50 (*0-345-36654-9*) Ballantine.

Diet to Lose & Win. enl. rev. ed. Merilyn Cummings. 52p. 1987. 24.95 (*0-9617195-1-6*); teacher ed 30.00 (*0-9617195-2-4*); audio 19.95 (*0-9617195-9-1*) Abrahamson Pub.

Diet to Lose & Win. 3rd enl. rev. ed. Merilyn Cummings. 52p. 1987. pap. 19.95 (*0-9617195-8-3*) Abrahamson Pub.

***Diet Workshop's Recipes for Healthy Living.** Lois L. Lindauer & Sally Sampson. LC 94-26401. 1995. 25.00 (*0-385-47251-X*) Doubleday.

Dieta Definitiva. Frank Calderon. 128p. (Orig.). (SPA.). 1986. pap. 2.95 (*0-939193-06-X*) Edit Concepts.

Dieta Definitiva. Ed. by Creative Publishing Concepts Staff. (Orig.). (SPA.). 1990. pap. write for info. (*0-944499-80-5*) Editorial Amer.

Dieta Diabetica Para Buena Salud: (Diabetic Diet Exchange Lists) Margaret B. Salmon. (Illus.). (SPA.). 1979. pap. 1.50 (*0-918662-05-2*) Techkits.

Dietary & Environmental Lead: Human Health Effects. Ed. by Kathryn R. Mahaffey. (Topics in Environmental Health Ser.: Vol. 7). 472p. 1985. 189.75 (*0-444-80609-1*) Elsevier.

Dietary Excesses & Health Disease Implications. John J. Anderson. (Illus.). 1984. pap. 18.95 (*0-938938-13-4*) Health Sci Comm.

Dietary Factors & Birth Defects. Ed. by Raghubir P. Sharma. LC 93-12186. 380p. (Orig.). 1993. pap. text ed. 28.50 (*0-934394-08-3*) AAASPD.

Dietary Fat Requirements in Health & Development. Ed. by Joyce Beare-Rogers. 216p. (C). 1988. 65.00 (*0-685-47962-5*) AOCS Pr.

Dietary Fats: Determinants of Preference, Selection, & Consumption. Ed. by D. J. Mela. LC 92-5798. 1992. write for info. (*1-85166-865-9*) Elsevier.

Dietary Fats & Health. Ed. by E. G. Perkins & Willard Visek. 978p. 1983. 40.00 (*0-935315-07-1*) AOCS Pr.

Dietary Fats & Thrombosis: Proceedings of the Inserm Symposium at Lyon, 1973. Inserm-International Symposium Staff. Ed. by S. Renaud & A. Nordoy. (Journal: Haemostasis: Vol. 2, Nos. 1-4). (Illus.). 200p. 1974. 67.25 (*3-8055-1712-2*) S Karger.

Dietary Fats, Prostanoids & Arterial Thrombosis. G. Hornstra. 1982. lib. bdg. 103.00 (*90-247-2667-0*) Kluwer Ac.

Dietary Fiber. (Landmark Ser.). 1979. 22.50 (*0-8422-4126-4*) Irvington.

Dietary Fiber. Shirley S. Lorenzani. (Good Health Guide Ser.). 32p. (Orig.). 1988. pap. 1.95 (*0-87983-479-X*) Keats.

Dietary Fiber: Basic & Clinical Aspects. Ed. by George V. Vahouny & David Kritchevsky. LC 85-19159. 586p. 1986. 125.00 (*0-306-42028-7*, Plenum Pr) Plenum.

Dietary Fiber: Chemistry, Physiology, & Health Effects. Ed. by David Kritchevsky et al. LC 90-6710. (Illus.). 586p. 1990. 125.00 (*0-306-43310-9*, Plenum Insight) Plenum.

Dietary Fiber: Subject Survey & Research Index with Bibliography. Vincent A. Spedding. LC 87-47661. 150p. 1987. 39.50 (*0-88164-676-8*); pap. 34.50 (*0-88164-677-6*) ABBE Pubs Assn.

Dietary Fiber, Calories & Cancer: Index of Modern Authors & Subjects with Guide for Rapid Research. Joseph M. Bahr. LC 90-56290. 160p. 1991. 44.50 (*1-55914-380-0*); pap. 39.50 (*1-55914-381-9*) ABBE Pubs Assn.

Dietary Fiber, Calories & Cancer: Index of Modern Authors & Subjects with Guide for Rapid Research. Joseph M. Bahr. LC 92-36369. 1992. 44.50 (*1-55914-958-2*); pap. 39.50 (*1-55914-959-0*) ABBE Pubs Assn.

Dietary Fiber in Health & Disease. Ed. by David Kritchevsky & Charles Bonfield. LC 94-62014. (Illus.). 486p. 1995. 119.00x (*0-9624407-6-0*) Eagan Pr.

Dietary Fiber in Health & Disease. Ed. by George V. Vahouny & David Kritchevsky. LC 82-7549. (GWUMC Department of Biochemistry Annual Spring Symposia Ser.). 344p. 1982. 85.00 (*0-306-40926-7*, Plenum Pr) Plenum.

Dietary Fiber Research. Z. Madar & S. H. Odes. (Progress in Biochemical Pharmacology Ser.: Vol. 24). (Illus.). viii, 148p. 1990. 107.25 (*3-8055-5043-X*) S Karger.

Dietary Fiber Weight Control. Brumback. 1989. 21.95 (*0-8151-0749-8*, Yr Bk Med Pubs) Mosby Yr Bk.

Dietary Fibre. Ed. by Gordon G. Birch & K. J. Parker. (Illus.). 304p. 1983. 88.25 (*0-85334-178-8*, Pub. by Elsevier Applied Sci UK) Elsevier.

***Dietary Fibre.** Ed. by M. I. Gurr & N. G. Asp. 23p. 1994. pap. 12.50 (*0-944398-24-3*) ILSI.

Dietary Fibre - A Component of Food: Nutritional Function in Health & Disease. Ed. by T. F. Scheizer et al. (ILSI Human Nutrition Reviews Ser.). (Illus.). xx, 354p. 1992. 159.00 (*0-387-19718-4*) Spr-Verlag.

Dietary Fibre, Fibre-Depleted Foods & Disease. Ed. by H. C. Trowell et al. 1985. text ed. 134.00 (*0-12-701160-9*) Acad Pr.

Dietary Guidelines & Your Diet. 1994. lib. bdg. 250.00 (*0-8490-5760-4*) Gordon Pr.

Dietary Influences on Cancer: Traditional & Modern. Ed. by R. Schoental. 272p. 1982. 135.00 (*0-8493-5647-4*, RC262, CRC Reprint) Franklin.

Dietary Intake of Food Additives in the U. K. Initial Surveillance. (Food Surveillance Paper Ser.: No. 37). 67p. 1993. pap. 15.00 (*0-11-242951-3*, HM29513, Pub. by HMSO UK) UNIPUB.

***Dietary Intake of Vitamins, Minerals, & Fiber of Persons Ages 2 Months & over in the United States: Third National Health & Nutrition Examination Survey, Phase 1, 1988-91.** National Center for Health Statistics Staff. (Advance Data Ser.: No. 258). 28p. Date not set. write for info. (*0-614-02945-7*) Natl Ctr Health Stats.

Dietary Iron: Birth to Two Years. L. J. Filer, Jr. 202p. 1989. 47.50 (*0-88167-571-7*, 2051) Raven.

Dietary Journal. Celestine L. Simmons. 140p. 1994. pap. 12.95 (*0-9641756-0-6*) Townsend Ent.

Dietary Lipids & Insulin Action: Second International Smolenice Insulin Symposium. Ed. by I. Klimes et al. LC 93-11065. (Annals Ser.). 1993. write for info. (*0-89766-797-2*); pap. write for info. (*0-89766-798-0*) NY Acad Sci.

***Dietary Lipids & Postnatal Development.** fac. ed. Ed. by Claudio Galli et al. LC 73-79580. (Illus.). 286p. Date not set. pap. 81.60 (*0-7837-7157-6*, 2047140) Bks Demand.

D

An Asterisk (*) at the beginning of an entry indicates that the title is appearing in BIP for the first time.

An Asterisk (*) at the beginning of an entry indicates that the title is appearing in BIP for the first time.

1985

D

Differences in Nursing Care: Area 1. Jack Rudman. (ACT Proficiency Examination Program Ser.: PEP-43). 1994. pap. 23.95 (0-8373-5543-5) Nat Learn.

Differences in Nursing Care: Area 1. Jack Rudman. (Regents External Degree Ser.: REDP-21). 1994. pap. 23.95 (0-8373-5621-0) Nat Learn.

Differences in Nursing Care: Area 2. Jack Rudman. (ACT Proficiency Examination Program Ser.: PEP-44). 1994. pap. 23.95 (0-8373-5544-3) Nat Learn.

Differences in Nursing Care: Area 2. Jack Rudman. (Regents External Degree Ser.: REDP-22). 1994. pap. 23.95 (0-8373-5622-9) Nat Learn.

Differences in Nursing Care: Area 3. Jack Rudman. (ACT Proficiency Examination Program Ser.: PEP-45). 1994. pap. 23.95 (0-8373-5545-1) Nat Learn.

Differences in Nursing Care: Area 3. Jack Rudman. (Regents External Degree Ser.: REDP-23). 1994. pap. 23.95 (0-8373-5623-7) Nat Learn.

Differences in Tax Treatment: Between a Domestic Subsidiary & a Domestic Branch of a Non-Resident Company. Ed. by John I. Forry. 175p. 1983. 40.00 (0-686-41017-3) Kluwer Ac.

Differences in Tax Treatment Between Local & Foreign Investors & Effects of International Treaties. (Cahiers de Droit Fiscal International Ser.: Vol. LXIIIb). 512p. 1978. pap. 100.00 (90-200-0519-7) Kluwer Law Tax Pubs.

Differences in Tax Treatment Between Local & Foreign Investors & Effects of International Treaties, Vol. LXIIIb. 512p. pap. 37.00 (0-686-41000-9) Kluwer Ac.

Differences in the Activities of Teachers in Rural One-Teacher Schools & of Grade Teachers in Cities. Verne McGuffey. LC 79-177026. (Columbia University. Teachers College. Contributions to Education Ser.: No. 346). reprint ed. 22.50 (0-404-55346-X) AMS Pr.

Differences in the Way Men & Women Perceive Love. Earnie Larsen. 19p. 1986. 1.00 (0-936098-50-3) Intl Marriage.

Differences of the Churches of the Separation Containing a Description of the Leitourgie & Ministerie of the Visible Church. John Smyth. LC 73-6161. (English Experience Ser.: No. 624). 32p. 1973. reprint ed. 5.00 (90-221-0624-1) Walter J Johnson.

Differences That Make a Difference: Examining Assumptions in Gender Research. Ed. by Lynn H. Turner & Helen M. Sterk. LC 94-16453. 248p. 1994. text ed. 55.00 (0-89789-387-5, Bergin & Garvey) Greenwood.

Differences That Work: Organizational Excellence. Mary C. Gentile. 1994. text ed. 29.95 (0-07-103581-8) McGraw.

Differences That Work: Organizational Excellence Through Diversity. Intro. by Mary C. Gentile. LC 93-37088. 320p. 1994. 29.95 (0-87584-499-5) Harvard Busn.

Differend: Phrases in Dispute. Jean-Francois Lyotard. Tr. by Georges Van Den Abbeele. LC 88-4780. (Theory & History of Literature Ser.: Vol. 46). 224p. (Orig.). 1989. text ed. 39.95 (0-8166-1610-8); pap. 14.95 (0-8166-1611-6) U of Minn Pr.

Different Accent. Michael Henderson. 144p. 1985. pap. 3.95 (0-901269-90-5) Grosvenor USA.

Different & Alike. 3rd ed. Nancy P. McConnell. Ed. by Donna Cliff. LC 93-70957. (Illus.). 40p. (J). (gr. 1-6). 1993. pap. 7.20 (0-944943-32-2, CODE 22164-6) Current Inc.

Different & Wonderful: Raising Black Children in a Race-Conscious Society. Darlene P. Hopson & Derek S. Hopson. 272p. 1992. pap. 10.00 (0-671-75518-8, Fireside) S&S Trade.

***Different Angle: Fly Fishing Stories by Women.** Ed. by Holly Morris. LC 94-39386. 288p. (Orig.). 1995. 22.95 (1-878067-63-X) Seal Pr Feminist.

Different Arrangements. Sharon Chmielarz. LC 82-61650. (Minnesota Voices Project Ser.: No. 10). (Illus.). 103p. 1982. pap. 3.00 (0-89823-042-X) New Rivers Pr.

Different but Equal. David D. Weisher. 1994. 21.95 (0-533-10519-6) Vantage.

Different by Design. John MacArthur. 192p. (Orig.). 1994. pap. 9.99 (1-56476-247-5, Victor Books) SP Pubns.

Different by Design: The Context & Character of Three Magnet Schools. Mary H. Metz. 288p. 1986. 29.95 (0-7102-0071-4, RKP) Routledge.

Different by Design: The Context & Character of Three Magnet Schools. Mary H. Metz. 288p. 1992. pap. 16.95 (0-415-90521-4, A6804) Routledge.

Different Call: Women's Ministries in the Episcopal Church. Mary S. Donovan. LC 86-18032. 216p. (Orig.). 1986. 19.95 (0-8192-1396-9) Morehouse Pub.

Different Children, Different Needs. Charles F. Boyd. 9.99 (0-88070-685-6) Questar Pubs.

Different Choices-A Game of Jewish Survival see Kadima Kesher Series

***Different Christianity: Early Christian Esotericism & Modern Thought.** Robin Amis. 384p. 1995. text ed. 59.50x (0-7914-2571-1); pap. text ed. 19.95x (0-7914-2572-X) State U NY Pr.

Different Colored Dreams. Christine B. J. Fulwylie. (Illus.). 93p. (Orig.). 1994. pap. 7.50 (1-885742-02-9) Boaz-Fulwylic.

Different Cookbook: Designed for Beginning Cooks, with over 1800 Selected & Tested Recipes. Robert H. Stone. LC 84-90143. (Illus.). 400p. 1986. 19.95 (0-9609192-2-8) R H Stone.

Different Cultures Same School: Ethnic Minority Children in Europe. Ed. by Lotty Eldering & Jo Kloprogge. 220p. 1989. 25.00 (90-265-0989-8, Pub. by Swets Pub Serv NE) Taylor & Francis.

Different Dances. Shel Silverstein. 19.95 (0-8488-1168-2) Amereon Ltd.

Different Daughters: A Book by Mothers of Lesbians. Ed. by Louise Rafkin. LC 86-72846. 160p. (Orig.). (C). 1987. 21.95 (0-939416-12-3); pap. 9.95 (0-939416-13-1) Cleis Pr.

Different Doorway: Adventures of a Caesarean Born. Jane B. English. LC 85-80840. (Illus.). 143p. 1985. pap. 7.95 (0-934747-39-3) Earth Heart.

Different Dragons. Jean Little. (Illus.). 144p. (J). (gr. 3-7). 1989. pap. 3.95 (0-14-031998-0, Puffin) Puffin Bks.

Different Drum: Community Making & Peace. M. Scott Peck. 336p. 1988. pap. 12.00 (0-671-66833-1, Touchstone Bks) S&S Trade.

Different Drum, Community Making & Peace. M. Scott Peck. 1987. 14.95 (0-671-64633-8) S&S Trade.

Different Drummer. William M. Kelley. 1990. mass mkt. 9.95 (0-385-41390-4) Doubleday.

Different Drummer. large type ed. Clive Egleton. 512p. 1987. 16.95 (0-7089-1585-X) Ulverscroft.

Different Drummer: Homosexuality in America. Elaine Landau. (YA). (gr. 7 up). 1986. lib. bdg. write for info. (0-671-54997-9, Julian Messner) Silver Burdett Pr.

Different Drummer: The Story of E. J. Banfield, the Beachcomber of Dunk Island. Michael Noonan. LC 86-16027. (Illus.). 237p. 1987. pap. 14.95 (0-7022-2027-2, Pub. by Univ Queensland Pr AT) Intl Spec Bk.

Different Drummers. Bill Mintz. (Illus.). 96p. 1975. pap. 11.95 (0-8256-2660-9, AM38035) Music Sales.

Different Drummers: A Study of Cultural Alternatives in Fiction. Meredith Cary. LC 84-1346. 300p. 1984. 27.50 (0-8108-1689-X) Scarecrow.

Different Drummers: Jazz in Nazi Germany. Michael H. Kater. 304p. 1992. 30.00 (0-19-505009-6) OUP.

Different Elements of a General Science of Culture. C. Blok et al. 116p. 1990. text ed. 35.00 (1-85628-065-9, Pub. by Avebury Pub UK) Ashgate Pub Co.

Different Existence: Principles of Phenomenological Psychopathology. Jan H. Van Den Berg. LC 72-182104. 152p. 1972. pap. text ed. 14.50x (0-8207-0244-7) Duquesne.

Different Faces of Motherhood. Ed. by B. Birns & D. Hay. LC 88-16878. (Perspectives in Developmental Psychology Ser.). (Illus.). 312p. 1988. 45.00 (0-306-42887-3, Plenum Pr) Plenum.

Different Flesh. Harry Turtledove. 304p. 1994. reprint ed. mass mkt. 4.99 (0-671-87622-8) Baen Bks.

Different Fleshes: A Novel-Poem. Albert Goldbarth. 1979. text ed. 4.95 (0-934888-00-0) Hobart & Wm Smith.

Different Frontier: Alaska Criminal Justice, 1935-1965. K. S. Kynell. 384p. (Orig.). (C). 1991. lib. bdg. 49.00 (0-8191-8052-1) U Pr of Amer.

Different Gospel: A Historical & Biblical Analysis of the Modern Faith Movement. Dan R. McConnell. 208p. 1988. pap. 7.95 (0-913573-78-7) Hendrickson MA.

***Different Gospel: Biblical & Historical Insights into the Word of Faith Movement.** rev. ed. Dan R. McConnell. 224p. 1995. pap. 12.95 (1-56563-132-3) Hendrickson MA.

Different Gospels: The Meaning of Apostasy, Vol. 10. Ed. by Richard J. Neuhaus. (Encounter Ser.). 1989. pap. 9.99 (0-8028-0210-9) Eerdmans.

Different Hunger. A. Sivanandan. (C). 1982. pap. text ed. 17.50 (0-86104-371-5) Westview.

Different Images: Portraits of Remembered People. Hildegarde Flanner. LC 86-32809. 112p. (Orig.). 1987. pap. 10.00 (0-936784-28-8) J Daniel.

***Different Is Not Bad, Different Is the World: A Book about Disabilities.** Sally L. Smith. (Illus.). 36p. (J). (gr. 2-6). 1994. pap. text ed. 9.00 (1-57035-030-2, 64BOOK) Sopris.

Different Kind of Classroom: Teaching with Dimensions of Learning. Pref. by Robert J. Marzano & Stephanie P. Marshall. LC 92-9069. 191p. (Orig.). 1992. pap. 15.95 (0-87120-192-5, 611-92107) Assn Supervision.

Different Kind of Diplomacy: A Source Book for International Health Volunteers. Ed. by Jack C. Fisher & Debra Armstrong. (Illus.). 200p. (Orig.). (C). 1987. pap. 10.95 (0-9618734-0-X) PSRF Pub.

Different Kind of Healing: Doctors Speak Candidly about Their Successes with Alternative Medicine. Oscar Janiger & Philip Goldberg. LC 92-37215. 256p. 1993. 21.95 (0-87477-728-3, J P T-Putnam) Putnam Pub Group.

Different Kind of Healing: Why Mainstream Doctors Are Embracing Alternative Medicine. Oscar Janiger & Philip Goldberg. 224p. 1994. pap. 12.95 (0-87477-787-9, J P T-Putnam) Putnam Pub Group.

Different Kind of Husband. Paul E. Hopkins. LC 92-17738. 144p. (Orig.). 1992. pap. 12.99 (0-8272-0619-4) Chalice Pr.

Different Kind of Listening. K. Chernin. 1994. 22.00 (0-06-017118-9, HarpT) HarpC.

Different Kind of Man. Barbara Andrews. (Candlelight Supreme Ser.: No. 119). 1986. pap. write for info. (0-440-12039-X) P-H.

***Different Kind of Person & "Room for Doubt"** Veronica Boyle. 1995. 17.95 (0-533-11366-0) Vantage.

Different Kind of Season. Lisa Binkowski. LC 93-93800. 104p. (Orig.). 1994. pap. 9.00 (1-56002-328-7, Univ Edtns) Aegina Pr.

Different Kind of State: Popular Power & Democratic Administration. Ed. by Gregory Albo et al. 256p. (C). 1993. pap. 24.95 (0-19-540907-8) OUP.

Different Kind of Victory. James R. Leutze. LC 81-4005. (Illus.). 362p. 1981. 34.95 (0-87021-056-4) Naval Inst Pr.

Different Kinds of Love. Leland Bardwell. 121p. (C). 1987. pap. 7.95 (0-946211-34-5, Pub. by Attic IE) InBook.

Different Kinds of Prayer. Perry A. Gaspard. 60p. 1984. pap. text ed. 3.50 (0-931867-08-8) Abundant Life Pubns.

Different Language: Gertrude Stein's Experimental Writing. Marianne DeKoven. LC 82-70558. (Illus.). 208p. 1983. 25.00 (0-299-09210-0) U of Wis Pr.

***Different Light.** Stewart. 1995. mass mkt. 5.99 (0-671-86855-1) PB.

Different Like Me: A Book for Teens Who Worry about Their Parents' Use of Alcohol - Drugs. Evelyn Leite & Pamela Espeland. (Illus.). 120p. (Orig.). 1987. pap. text ed. 8.95 (0-935908-34-X, P097) Johnsn Inst.

Different Losses - Different Issues, Vol. 2: What to Expect & How to Help. Johnette Hartnett. LC 93-90775. (Good Mourning Ser.). 64p. 1993. pap. 6.95 (1-883171-94-6) Good Mourning.

Different Loving: An Exploration of the World of Sexual Dominance & Submission. Gloria G. Brame et al. LC 92-37144. 1993. 25.00 (0-679-40873-8, Villard Bks) Random.

***Different Minds, Different Voices.** Virginia Aronson. (Illus.). 192p. (Orig.). 1995. pap. 24.99 (1-56790-148-4) Cool Hand Comms.

Different Mirror: A History of Multicultural America. Ronald Takaki. 1994. pap. 13.95 (0-316-83111-5) Little.

Different Mirror: The Making of Multicultural America. Ronald T. Takaki. 1993. 27.95 (0-316-83112-3) Little.

Different Moon. Ara Watson. 1983. pap. 4.75 (0-8222-0309-X) Dramatists Play.

Different Mothers: Sons & Daughters of Lesbians Talk about Their Lives. Ed. by Louise Rafkin. 160p. (Orig.). 1990. 24.95 (0-939416-40-9); pap. 9.95 (0-939416-41-7) Cleis Pr.

Different Paths: Poems by Lauren Mittermann. Lauren Mittermann. 52p. 1994. pap. 6.95 (0-9638558-0-8) Maple Grove.

Different Paths of Inupiat Men & Women in the Wage Economy. Judith Kleinfeld. 1981. 2.00 (0-685-52897-9) Univ AK Ctr CCS.

Different People: Pictures of Some Japanese. Donald Richie. LC 87-81681. 198p. 1988. pap. 16.95 (0-87011-820-X) Kodansha.

Different People see Geisha, Gangster, Neighbor, Nun: Scenes from Japanese Lives

Different Person. James Merrill. LC 94-7687. 288p. 1994. pap. 14.00 (0-06-251079-7) Harper SF.

Different Person: A Memoir. James Merrill. LC 92-37974. 1993. 12.50 (0-679-42317-6) Knopf.

Different Perspectives on Wavelets. Ed. by Ingrid Daubechies. LC 93-33264. (Proceedings of Symposia in Applied Mathematics Ser.: No. 47). 205p. 1993. 45.00 (0-8218-5503-4) Am Math.

Different Places, Different Voices: Gender & Develpment in Africa, Asia, & Latin America. Ed. by Janet H. Momsen & Vivian Kinnaird. LC 92-18427. (International Studies of Women & Places). (Illus.). 352p. 1993. 55.00 (0-415-07538-6, A9887, Routledge NY); pap. 16.95 (0-415-07563-7, A9891, Routledge NY) Routledge.

Different Point of View: Sara Jeannette Duncan. Misao Dean. 208p. (C). 1991. text ed. 39.95 (0-7735-0792-2, Pub. by McGill CN) U of Toronto Pr.

Different Rainbows. Judith Daniels. (Voices Romance Ser.: No. 2). 224p. 1994. pap. 3.50 (0-8217-4580-8) Zebra.

Different Reality: Studies on the Work of Elena Garro. Ed. by Anita K. Stoll. LC 88-43228. 208p. 1990. 38.50 (0-8387-5166-0) Bucknell U Pr.

Different Season. David Klass. LC 87-19969. 208p. (YA). (gr. 7 up). 1988. 15.99 (0-525-67237-0, Lodestar Bks) Dutton Child Bks.

Different Seasons. Stephen King. LC 82-70145. 468p. 1982. pap. 29.95 (0-670-27266-3) Viking Penguin.

Different Seasons. Stephen King. 512p. 1983. reprint ed. pap. 6.99 (0-451-16753-8, Sig) NAL-Dutton.

Different Sexual Worlds: Contemporary Case Studies of Sexuality. Dick Skeen. 208p. 1991. text ed. 27.95 (0-669-27277-9); pap. 13.95 (0-669-27278-7) Free Pr.

Different Shades of Courage: A Coloring & Activities Book of African American Achievement, Vol. 1. Eric Brown. Ed. by Jen Sheen. (Illus.). 53p. (Orig.). (J). (gr. 4 up). 1993. pap. 9.95 (0-9636468-0-X) Little Tike.

Different Sin. Rochelle Schwab. 192p. 1993. pap. 9.95 (1-879603-08-X) Los Hombres.

Different Sort of Time: The Life of Jerrold R. Zacharias Scientist, Engineer, Educator. Jack S. Goldstein. (Illus.). 408p. 1992. 35.00x (0-262-07138-X) MIT Pr.

***Different Spokes.** Violet M. Franck. 300p. 1995. pap. 8.95 (1-56901-845-6) NW Pub.

Different Story: A Black History of Fredericksburg, Stafford & Spotsylvania, Virginia. Ruth C. Fitzgerald. LC 79-67534. (Illus.). 336p. 1980. 21.95 (0-9604564-2-2) Fitzg Unicorn.

Different Strokes. Andros, Phil, & Co. Staff. 140p. 1993. reprint ed. pap. 7.95 (1-55583-222-9) Alyson Pubns.

Different Strokes for Different Folks: Access & Barriers to Adult Education & Training. Ivan Charner & Bryna S. Fraser. 118p. 1986. 10.00 (0-86510-054-3) Natl Inst Work.

Different Systems of Penal Codes in Europe: Also, a Report on the Administrative Changes in France since the Revolution of 1848. H. S. Sanford. 404p. 1988. reprint ed. lib. bdg. 47.50 (0-8377-1152-5) Rothman.

***Different Transition Path: Ownership, Performance, & Influence of Chinese Rural Industrial Enterprises.** rev. ed. Chenggang Xu. LC 94-46983. (Garland Studies on Industrial Productivity). (Illus.). 184p. 1995. 46.00 (0-8153-1629-1) Garland.

Different Tune. Barbara Gregorich. Ed. by Joan Hoffman. (Start to Read! Ser.). (Illus.). 16p. (Orig.). (J). (gr. k-2). 1991. pap. 2.25 (0-88743-028-7, 06028) Sch Zone Pub Co.

Different Tune. Bruce Witty. Ed. by Joan Hoffman. (Read & Think Ser.). (Illus.). 32p. (J). (gr. k-2). 1987. student ed 1.99 (0-88743-103-8, 02603) Sch Zone Pub Co.

***Different Tune.** Bruce Witty. (Start to Read Ser.). (Illus.). 32p. (J). (gr. k-2). 1992. 3.95 (0-88743-422-3) Sch Zone Pub Co.

Different Types of Stories & Poems. Tabitha Grubbs & Tiffany McQueen. (Illus.). 52p. (J). (gr. k-3). 1983. lib. bdg. 25.00 (1-56611-000-9); pap. 15.00 (1-56611-349-0) Jonas.

Different Valor, the Story of General Joseph E. Johnston, C.S.A. Gilbert E. Govan & James W. Livingood. LC 73-9372. (Illus.). 470p. 1973. reprint ed. text ed. 35.00 (0-8371-7012-5, GOVD, Greenwood Pr) Greenwood.

Different View. Clark Johnson & Dale Withers. LC 85-73311. 80p. 1986. 9.00 (0-86690-313-5, J2354-014) Am Fed Astrologers.

Different Views for Christian Thinking. Robert V. Moser. 72p. 1988. 6.95 (0-9621065-0-X) R V Moser.

Different Voices: A Social, Cultural, & Historical Framework for Change in the American Art Museum. Carol Becker et al. (Illus.). 150p. (Orig.). 1992. pap. text ed. write for info. (1-880974-00-2) AAMD.

Different Voices: Women & the Holocaust. Ed. by Carol Rittner & John K. Roth. LC 92-28233. (Illus.). 384p. 1993. 25.95 (1-55778-503-1, Athena); pap. 18.95 (1-55778-504-X, Athena) Paragon Hse.

Different Voices - Shared Vision: Male & Female in the Trinitarian Community. Marie Meyer et al. 96p. (Orig.). (C). Date not set. pap. text ed. 4.00 (0-9633142-1-1) Am Luth Pub Bur.

Different Voices, Different Truths: The 1827 Murder at Cherry Hill (A Social History Teaching Unit) Rebecca Watrous et al. (Illus.). 280p. (Orig.). 1990. pap. 25.00 (0-943366-08-9) Hist Cherry Hill.

Different War: Vietnam in Art. Lucy R. Lippard. LC 89-70103. (Illus.). 120p. (Orig.). 1990. pap. 18.95 (0-941104-43-5) Real Comet.

Different Waterfronts: A Wooden Boat Reader. Peter H. Spectre. (Illus.). 256p. 1991. reprint ed. pap. 14.95 (0-88448-079-8) Tilbury Hse.

Different Way. Kathryn Makris. 192p. (J). 1989. pap. 2.95 (0-380-75728-1, Flare) Avon.

Different Way of Seeing. Richard L. Shenk. LC 88-92748. (Illus.). 60p. 1989. 40.00 (0-685-25261-2) Sheyna Pubns.

Different Woman. large type ed. Jan Webster. 1991. 21.95 (0-7089-2437-9) Ulverscroft.

Different Woman: A Novel. Janine Boissard. Tr. by Mary Feeney. 224p. 1989. 17.95 (0-316-10104-4) Little.

Different Women, Different Work: Gender & Industrialisation in Indonesia. Ed. by Mies Grijns et al. 243p. 1994. 55.95 (1-85628-636-3, Pub. by Avebury Pub UK) Ashgate Pub Co.

Different World. Zulfikar Ghose. LC 84-42674. 318p. 1986. 22.50 (0-87951-982-7); pap. 10.95 (0-87951-207-5) Overlook Pr.

Different World. large type ed. Joan Mellows. 1989. 17.95 (0-7089-2077-2) Ulverscroft.

Different World for Women: The Life of Millicent Garrett Fawcett. David Rubinstein. 320p. 1991. lib. bdg. 42.50 (0-8142-0564-X) Ohio St U Pr.

Different Worlds: A Sociological Study of Taste, Choice & Success in Art. Ed. by Liah Greenfeld. (ASA Rose Monograph Ser.). (Illus.). 224p. (C). 1989. 49.95 (0-521-36064-1) Cambridge U Pr.

Different Worlds: Interracial & Cross-Cultural Dating. Janet Bode. LC 88-30380. 1989. lib. bdg. 14.21 (0-531-10663-2) Watts.

Differentes Vues de Quelques Restes...de l'Ancienne Ville de Pesto. Giovanni B. Piranesi. (Illus.). 25p. 1973. 95.00 (1-55660-198-0) A Wofsy Fine Arts.

Differentiable Manifolds. G. De Rham. Tr. by F. R. Smith. (Grundlehren der Mathematischen Wissenschaften Ser.: Vol. 266). (Illus.). 180p. 1984. 74.00 (0-387-13463-8) Spr-Verlag.

Differentiable Manifolds. Yozo Matsushima. Tr. by E. T. Kobayashi. LC 71-182215. (Pure & Applied Mathematics Ser.: No. 9). 315p. reprint ed. pap. 89.80 (0-8357-6094-4, 2034547) Bks Demand.

Differentiable Manifolds: A First Course. Laurence Conlon. LC 92-31098. xiii, 395p. 1994. 49.50 (0-8176-3626-9) Birkhauser.

Differentiable Manifolds & Quadratic Forms. F. Hirzebruch et al. LC 70-176304. (Lecture Notes in Pure & Applied Mathematics Ser.: Vol. 4). 126p. reprint ed. pap. 36.00 (0-8357-9080-0, 2017692) Bks Demand.

Differentiable Operators & Nonlinear Equations. Victor Khatskevich & David Shoiykhet. Tr. by Mircea Martin. LC 93-40439. (Operator Theory, Advances & Applications Ser.: Vol. 66). 296p. 1993. 117.00 (0-8176-2929-7) Birkhauser.

Differential Algebra & Algebraic Groups. E. R. Kolchin. (Pure & Applied Mathematics Ser.: Vol. 55). 1973. text ed. 136.00 (0-12-417650-X) Acad Pr.

Differential Algebraic Equations & Their Numerical Treatment. Ed. by Collet's Holdings, Ltd. Staff. 1986. 42.00 (0-317-46611-9, Pub. by Collets UK) Pro-Am Music.

Differential Algebraic Groups. E. R. Kolchin. (Pure & Applied Mathematics Ser.). 1985. text ed. 101.00 (0-12-417640-2) Acad Pr.

Differential Algebraic Groups of Finite Dimension. A. Buium. (Lecture Notes in Mathematics Ser.: Vol. 1506). xv, 145p. 1992. pap. 29.00 (0-387-55181-6) Spr-Verlag.

Differential Algebras in Topology. David Anick. LC 93-12604. (Research Notes in Mathematics Ser.). 304p. (C). 1993. text ed. 54.95 (1-56881-001-6) AK Peters.

Differential Analysis in Infinite Dimensional Spaces. Sundaresan & Swaminathan. LC 86-3510. (Contemporary Mathematics Ser.: Vol. 54). 122p. 1986. pap. text ed. 25.00 (0-8218-5059-8, CONM-54) Am Math.

An Asterisk (*) at the beginning of an entry indicates that the title is appearing in BIP for the first time.

D

An Asterisk (*) at the beginning of an entry indicates that the title is appearing in BIP for the first time.

Differential Equations with Derive. David C. Arney. 284p. (Orig.). (C). 1993. pap. text ed. 22.95 (*0-9623629-3-X*) MathWare.

Differential Equations with Discontinuous Righthand Sides. A. F. Filippov. (C). 1988. lib. bdg. 142.00 (*90-277-2699-X*) Kluwer Ac.

Differential Equations with Linear Algebra. Zbigniew H. Nitecki & Martin M. Guterman. 640p. (C). 1986. text ed. 55.00 (*0-03-002719-5*) SCP.

Differential Equations with Maple V. Martha L. Abell & James P. Braselton. 640p. 1994. pap. 44.95 (*0-12-041548-8*, AP Prof) Acad Pr.

Differential Equations with Mathematica. Martha L. Abell & James P. Braselton. 631p. 1993. pap. 44.95 (*0-12-041539-9*, AP Prof) Acad Pr.

***Differential Equations with Mathematica.** Kevin R. Coombes. 218p. 1995. pap. 20.95 (*0-471-10874-X*) Wiley.

Differential Forecasts of Achievement & Their Use in Educational Counseling. Ralph R. Wolf. Bd. with Time-Sampling Studies of Child Behavior. R. E. Arrington.; Factor Analysis of Texts Designed to Measure Persistence. G. R. Thornton.; Principles of Conditioning in Human Goal Behavior. A. J. Mitrano.; Vol. 3. Studies in the Psychology of Art. Ed. by Norman C. Meier. (Psychology Monographs General & Applied: Vol. 51). 1972. reprint ed. Set pap. 35.00 (*0-8115-1450-1*) Periodicals Srv.

***Differential Forms & Applications.** Manfredo P. Do Carmo. LC 94-21965. (Universitext Ser.). Orig. Title: Formas Differencias e Aplicacoes. 1994. 29.50 (*0-387-57618-5*) Spr-Verlag.

Differential Forms & Connections. R. W. Darling. LC 93-46634. (Illus.). 280p. (C). 1994. 49.95 (*0-521-46259-2*); pap. 19.95 (*0-521-46800-0*) Cambridge U Pr.

Differential Forms in Algebraic Topology. R. Bott & L. W. Tu. (Graduate Texts in Mathematics Ser.: Vol. 82). (Illus.). 288p. 1995. 49.50 (*0-387-90613-4*) Spr-Verlag.

Differential Forms in Mathematical Physics. rev. ed. C. Von Westenholz. (Studies in Mathematics & Its Applications: Vol. 3). 564p. 1981. 128.25 (*0-444-85435-5*, North Holland); pap. 59.00 (*0-444-85437-1*, North Holland) Elsevier.

Differential Forms Orthogonal to Holomorphic Functions or Forms, & Their Properties. Sh. A. Dautov & L. A. Aizenberg. LC 83-2696. (Translations of Mathematical Monographs: Vol. 56). 165p. 1983. 52.00 (*0-8218-4508-X*, MMONO-56) Am Math.

Differential Forms With Application. Harley Flanders. 1990. pap. 6.95 (*0-486-66169-5*) Dover.

Differential Function Fields & Moduli of Algebraic Varieties. A. Buium. (Lecture Notes in Mathematics Ser.: Vol. 1226). ix, 146p. 1987. pap. 25.00 (*0-387-17194-0*) Spr-Verlag.

Differential Galois Theory. J. F. Pommaret. LC 81-6298. (Mathematics & Its Applications Ser.: Vol. 15). 775p. 1983. text ed. 432.00 (*0-677-05670-2*) Gordon & Breach.

Differential Games. Avner Friedman. LC 73-15872. (CBMS Regional Conference Series in Mathematics: No. 18). 66p. 1982. reprint ed. pap. 24.00 (*0-8218-1668-3*, CBMS-18) Am Math.

Differential Games. Avner Friedman. LC 75-155119. (Pure & Applied Mathematics Ser.: No. 25). 361p. reprint ed. pap. 102.90 (*0-7837-3519-7*, 2057853) Bks Demand.

Differential Games: Theory & Applications. American Society of Mechanical Engineers. LC 74-128583. 147p. reprint ed. pap. 41.90 (*0-317-08724-X*, 2013312) Bks Demand.

Differential Games: Theory & Methods for Solving Game Problems with Singular Surfaces. Joseph Lewin. LC 93-33448. 1993. 49.00 (*0-387-19841-5*) Spr-Verlag.

Differential Games - Developments in Modelling & Computation: Proceedings of the 4th International Symposium on Differential Games & Applications August 9-10, 1990, Helsinki, Finland. Ed. by R. P. Hamalainen et al. (Lecture Notes in Control & Information Sciences Ser.: Vol. 156). (Illus.). xiii, 292p. 1991. pap. 51.00 (*0-387-53787-2*) Spr-Verlag.

Differential Games & Applications. Ed. by Tamer S. Basar & P. Bernard. (Lecture Notes in Control & Information Sciences Ser.: Vol. 119). (Illus.). 201p. 1989. pap. 38.00 (*0-387-50758-2*) Spr-Verlag.

Differential Games & Applications: Proceedings of a Workshop, Enschede, Netherlands, March 16-25,1977. Ed. by P. Hagedorn et al. (Lecture Notes in Control & Information Sciences Ser.: Vol. 3). 1977. pap. text ed. 19.00 (*0-387-08407-X*) Spr-Verlag.

Differential Games & Control Theory: Proceedings of a National Science Foundation-Conference Board of the Mathematical Sciences Regional Research Conference, Held at University of Rhode Island, Kingston, Rhode Island, June 4-8, 1973: the Invited Lectures & Contributed Papers. Regional Research Conference on Differential Games & Control Theory Staff. LC 74-21593. (Lecture Notes in Pure & Applied Mathematics Ser.: No. 10). 422p. reprint ed. pap. 120.30 (*0-7837-4774-8*, 2044529) Bks Demand.

Differential Games & Control Theory III: Proceedings of the Third Kingston Conference, Pt. A. Liu & Roxin. (Lecture Notes in Pure & Applied Mathematics Ser.: Vol. 44). 256p. 1979. 115.00 (*0-8247-6845-0*) Dekker.

Differential Games & Control Theory Two: Proceedings of the Second Kingston Conference Held at University of Rhode Island, Kingston, Rhode Island, June 7 to 10, 1976. Kingston Conference on Differential Games & Control Theory Staff. Ed. by Emilio D. Roxin et al. LC 77-4689. (Lecture Notes in Pure & Applied Mathematics Ser.: No. 30). (Illus.). 503p. reprint ed. pap. 143.40 (*0-7837-3381-X*, 2043339) Bks Demand.

Differential Games of Pursuit. L. Petrosian. LC 93-24420. (Series on Optimization: Vol. 2). 560p. 1993. text ed. 104.00 (*981-02-0979-7*) World Scientific Pub.

Differential Geometric Control Theory. Ed. by Roger Brockett et al. (Progress in Mathematics Ser.: Vol. 27). 340p. 1982. 46.50 (*0-8176-3091-0*) Birkhauser.

Differential Geometric Methods in Mathematical Physics. Ed. by H. D. Doebner & J. D. Hennig. (Lecture Notes in Mathematics Ser.: Vol. 1139). vi, 337p. 1985. pap. 46.20 (*0-387-15666-6*) Spr-Verlag.

Differential Geometric Methods in Mathematical Physics. P. L. Garcia & A. Perez Rendon. (Lecture Notes in Mathematics Ser.: Vol. 1251). vii, 300p. 1987. pap. 43.60 (*0-387-17816-3*) Spr-Verlag.

Differential Geometric Methods in Theoretical Physics: Proceedings of the XIII International Conference, Shumen, Bulgaria, August 1984. Ed. by H. D. Doebner & T. D. Palev. 380p. 1986. pap. 52.00 (*9971-5-0071-X*) World Scientific Pub.

Differential Geometric Methods in Theoretical Physics: Proceedings of the 19th International Conference Held at Rapallo, Italy, 19-24 June 1990. Ed. by Claudio Bartocci et al. (Lecture Notes in Physics Ser.: Vol. 375). xx, 401p. 1991. 50.00 (*0-387-53763-5*) Spr-Verlag.

Differential Geometric Methods in Theoretical Physics: Proceedings of the 21st International Conference. C. N. Yang et al. 624p. 1993. text ed. 137.00 (*981-02-1210-0*) World Scientific Pub.

Differential Geometric Methods in Theoretical Physics: Twentieth International Conference, 2 vols., Set. Ed. by S. Catto & A. Rocha. 1300p. 1992. text ed. 239.00 (*981-02-0993-2*) World Scientific Pub.

Differential Geometry. R. Goreaux. (C). 1989. 30.00 (*0-89771-391-5*, Current Dist) St Mut.

Differential Geometry. Heinrich Guggenheimer. pap. text ed. 7.95 (*0-486-63433-7*) Dover.

Differential Geometry. Ed. by V. L. Hansen. (Lecture Notes in Mathematics Ser.: Vol. 1263). xi, 288p. 1987. pap. 29.30 (*0-387-18012-5*) Spr-Verlag.

Differential Geometry. Erwin Kreyszig. 1991. pap. 8.95 (*0-486-66721-9*) Dover.

Differential Geometry. Martin Lipschutz. (Schaum's Outline Ser.). 1969. pap. text ed. 12.95 (*0-07-037985-8*) McGraw.

Differential Geometry. Ed. by A. M. Naveira. (Lecture Notes in Mathematics Ser.: Vol. 1045). viii, 194p. 1984. pap. 27.00 (*0-387-12882-4*) Spr-Verlag.

Differential Geometry. Okubo. (Pure & Applied Mathematics Ser.: Vol. 112). 816p. 1987. 199.00 (*0-8247-7700-X*) Dekker.

Differential Geometry. Ed. by G. Soos & J. Szenthe. (Colloquia Mathematica Societatis Janos Bolyai Ser.: Vol. 31). 830p. 1983. 187.25 (*0-444-86197-1*, North Holland) Elsevier.

Differential Geometry. J. J. Stoker. 1989. pap. text ed. 49.95 (*0-471-50403-3*) Wiley.

Differential Geometry, 2 pts. Pure Mathematics Symposium Staff. Ed. by S. S. Chern & R. Osserman. LC 75-6593. (Proceedings of Symposia in Pure Mathematics Ser., Humboldt State University, Arcata, CA, July 29-August 16, 1974: Vol. 27). 451p. 1982. reprint ed. Pt. 1, 451 p. pap. 66.00 (*0-8218-0247-X*, PSPUM-27.1); reprint ed. Pt. 2, 443 p. pap. 73.00 (*0-8218-0248-8*, PSPUM-27.2) Am Math.

Differential Geometry. Pure Mathematics Symposium Staff. Ed. by C. B. Allendoerfer. LC 50-1183. (Proceedings of Symposia in Pure Mathematics Ser., Humboldt State University, Arcata, CA, July 29-August 16, 1974: Vol. 3). 200p. 1983. reprint ed. 36.00 (*0-8218-1403-6*, PSPUM-3) Am Math.

Differential Geometry, 3 vols., Set. Ed. by Robert E. Greene & S. T. Yau. (Proceedings of Symposia in Pure Mathematics Ser., Humboldt State University, Arcata, CA, July 29-August 16, 1974: Vol. 54). 2000p. 1993. 259.00 (*0-8218-1493-1*, PSPUM/54C) Am Math.

Differential Geometry, 2 pts., Set. Pure Mathematics Symposium Staff. Ed. by S. S. Chern & R. Osserman. LC 75-6593. (Proceedings of Symposia in Pure Mathematics Ser., Humboldt State University, Arcata, CA, July 29-August 16, 1974: Vol. 27). 894p. 1982. reprint ed. pap. 113.00 (*0-8218-1427-3*, PSPUM-27) Am Math.

Differential Geometry: Geometry in Mathematical Physics & Related Topics. Ed. by Robert Greene & S. T. Yau. LC 92-32831. (Proceedings of Symposia in Pure Mathematics Ser., Humboldt State University, Arcata, CA, July 29-August 16, 1974: Vol. 54, Pt. 2). 655p. 1993. 96.00 (*0-8218-1495-8*) Am Math.

Differential Geometry: Partial Differential Equations on Manifolds. Ed. by Robert Greene & S. T. Yau. LC 92-32827. (Proceedings of Symposia in Pure Mathematics Ser., Humboldt State University, Arcata, CA, July 29-August 16, 1974: Vol. 54, Pt. 1). 560p. 1993. 89.00 (*0-8218-1494-X*) Am Math.

Differential Geometry: Proceedings of the Symposium in Honor of Professor Buchin Su's 90th Birthday. C. H. Gu et al. 348p. 1993. text ed. 81.00 (*981-02-1096-5*) World Scientific Pub.

Differential Geometry: Proceedings, Special Year, Maryland 1981-1982. Ed. by Robert Brooks et al. (Progress in Mathematics Ser.: Vol. 32). 263p. 1983. 36.50 (*0-8176-3134-8*) Birkhauser.

Differential Geometry: The Interface Between Pure & Applied Mathematics. Luksic et al. LC 87-30648. (CONM Ser.: Vol. 68). 273p. 1991. pap. text ed. 37.00 (*0-8218-5075-X*, CONM-68) Am Math.

Differential Geometry - Pensicola, 1989. Ed. by F. J. Carreras et al. (Lecture Notes in Mathematics Ser.: Vol. 1410). vi, 308p. 1989. pap. 41.60 (*0-387-51885-1*, 3761) Spr-Verlag.

Differential Geometry & Calculus of Variations. 3rd ed. N. V. Efimov et al. (Translations Ser.: No. 1 Vol. 6). 504p. 1990. 42.00 (*0-8218-1606-3*, TRANS 1-6) Am Math.

Differential Geometry & Complex Analysis. Ed. by Isaac Chavel & H. M. Farkas. (Illus.). 225p. 1984. 85.00 (*0-387-13543-X*) Spr-Verlag.

Differential Geometry & Differential Equations. Ed. by C. H. Gu et al. (Lecture Notes in Mathematics Ser.: Vol. 1255). xii, 243p. 1987. pap. 39.30 (*0-387-17849-X*) Spr-Verlag.

Differential Geometry & Differential Equations: Proceedings of the 1980 Conference in Beijing, The People's Republic of China, 3 vols., Set. S. S. Chen. 1780p. 1982. text ed. 882.00 (*0-677-31120-6*) Gordon & Breach.

Differential Geometry & Gauge Fields. H. Rund. 1994. text ed. 68.00 (*981-02-1230-5*) World Scientific Pub.

Differential Geometry & Its Applications. Ed. by D. Krupka & A. Svec. (C). 1987. lib. bdg. 154.50 (*90-277-2487-3*) Kluwer Ac.

Differential Geometry & Mathematical Physics. Ed. by John Beem & Krishan L. Duggal. LC 94-20799. 1994. write for info. (*0-8218-5172-1*) Am Math.

Differential Geometry & Relativity. Ed. by M. Cahen & M. Flato. (Mathematical Physics & Applied Mathematics Ser: No. 3). 1976. lib. bdg. 94.00 (*90-277-0745-6*) Kluwer Ac.

Differential Geometry & Statistics. Michael Murray & John Rice. LC 93-12009. (Monographs on Statistics & Applied Probability: Vol. 48). 1993. write for info. (*0-412-39860-5*) Chapman & Hall.

Differential Geometry & Topology. R. Caddeo & F. Tricerri. 300p. 1993. text ed. 105.00 (*981-02-1401-4*) World Scientific Pub.

Differential Geometry & Topology. A. T. Fomenko. Tr. by D. A. Leites. LC 87-2444. (Contemporary Soviet Mathematics Ser.). (Illus.). 338p. 1987. 89.50 (*0-306-10995-6*, Consultants) Plenum.

Differential Geometry & Topology. Z. Hou et al. (Lecture Notes in Mathematics Ser.: Vol. 1369). vi, 366p. 1989. pap. 47.90 (*0-387-51037-0*) Spr-Verlag.

Differential Geometry & Topology. Jacob T. Schwartz. 180p. 1968. text ed. 129.00 (*0-677-01510-0*) Gordon & Breach.

Differential Geometry, Calculus of Variations & Their Applications: Calculus of Variations & Their Applications. Rassias. (Lecture Notes in Pure & Applied Mathematics Ser.: Vol. 100). 544p. 1985. 140.00 (*0-8247-7267-9*) Dekker.

Differential Geometry, Gauge Theories, & Gravity. M. Gockeler & T. Schucker. (Cambridge Monographs on Mathematical Physics). 200p. 1987. 74.95 (*0-521-32960-4*) Cambridge U Pr.

Differential Geometry, Gauge Theories & Gravity. M. Gockeler & T. Schucker. (Cambridge Monographs on Mathematical Physics). 248p. (C). 1989. pap. 29.95 (*0-521-37821-4*) Cambridge U Pr.

Differential Geometry, Global Analysis, & Topology. Ed. by A. Nicas & W. F. Shadwick. LC 92-5152. (Conference Proceedings, Canadian Mathematical Society Ser.: Vol. 12). 185p. 1992. 50.00 (*0-8218-6017-8*, CMSAMS/12C) Am Math.

Differential Geometry, Group Representations & Quantization. Ed. by J. D. Hennig et al. (Lecture Notes in Physics Ser.: Vol. 379). 280p. 1991. 39.00 (*0-387-53941-7*) Spr-Verlag.

Differential Geometry in Statistical Inference. S. Amari et al. LC 87-82603. (IMS Lecture Notes - Monograph Ser.: Vol. 10). iv, 232p. 1987. pap. 25.00 (*0-940600-12-9*) Inst Math.

Differential Geometry in the Large. 2nd ed. H. C. Hopf. (Lecture Notes in Mathematics Ser.: Vol. 1000). vii, 184p. 1989. pap. 31.30 (*0-387-51497-X*, 3377) Spr-Verlag.

Differential Geometry in the Large: Seminar Lectures New York University 1946 & Stanford University 1956. H. Hoff. (Lecture Notes in Mathematics Ser.: Vol. 1000). 184p. 1983. pap. 14.60 (*0-387-12004-1*) Spr-Verlag.

Differential Geometry, Lie Groups & Symmetric Spaces. Sigurdur Helgason. (Pure & Applied Mathematics Ser.). (C). 1978. text ed. 44.95 (*0-12-338460-5*) Acad Pr.

Differential Geometry-Manifolds, Curves & Surfaces. M. Berger & B. Gostiaux. (Graduate Tests in Mathematics Ser.: Vol. 115). 480p. 1987. 54.00 (*0-387-96626-9*) Spr-Verlag.

Differential Geometry of Complex Vector Bundles. Shoshichi Kobayashi. (Publications of the Mathematical Society of Japan: No. 15). 310p. 1987. text ed. 65.00 (*0-691-08467-X*) Princeton U Pr.

Differential Geometry of Curves & Surfaces. Manfredo P. Do Carmo. (C). 1976. text ed. 71.00 (*0-13-212589-7*) P-H.

Differential Geometry of Folitations: The Fundamental Integrability Problem, Set. B. L. Reinhart. (Ergebnisse der Mathematik Ser.: Folge 2, Vol. 99). 195p. 1983. 69.00 (*0-387-12269-9*) Spr-Verlag.

Differential Geometry of Submanifolds. K. Kenmotsu. (Lecture Notes in Mathematics Ser.: Vol. 1090). vi, 132p. 1984. pap. 28.10 (*0-387-13873-0*) Spr-Verlag.

Differential Geometry on Complex & Almost Complex Space. K. Yano & I. N. Sneddon. LC 63-10097. (International Series of Monographs on Pure & Applied Mathematics: Vol. 49). 1964. 140.00 (*0-08-010259-X*, Pub. by Pergamon Repr UK) Franklin.

Differential Geometry, Pensacola 1985. Ed. by A. M. Naveira et al. (Lecture Notes in Mathematics Ser.: Vol. 1209). 306p. 1986. pap. 39.30 (*0-387-16801-X*) Spr-Verlag.

Differential Inclusions: Set-Valued Maps & Viability Theory. Jean P. Aubin & A. Cellina. LC 84-1327. (Grundlehren der Mathematischen Wissenschaften Ser.: Vol. 264). (Illus.). 350p. 1984. 98.00 (*0-387-13105-1*) Spr-Verlag.

Differential Inclusions in Nonsmooth Mechanical Problems: Shocks & Dry Friction. Manuel D. Monteiro Marques. LC 93-17931. (Progress in Nonlinear Differential Equations & Their Applications Ser.: Vol. 9). 179p. 1993. 69.00 (*0-8176-2900-9*) Birkhauser.

Differential Invariants of Generalized Spaces. 2nd ed. Tracey Y. Thomas. LC 91-75374. x, 241p. (C). 1991. lib. bdg. 27.50 (*0-8284-0336-8*, 336) Chelsea Pub.

Differential Item Functioning. Ed. by Paul Holland & Howard Wainer. 456p. 1992. text ed. 89.95 (*0-8058-0972-4*) L Erlbaum Assocs.

Differential Management & Motivation: An Advanced Understanding of Human Development & Motivation. rev. ed. James S. Payne. 197p. 1994. pap. text ed. 14.95 (*1-57171-000-0*) Lincoln-Rembrandt.

Differential Manifold & Theoretical Physics. W. D. Curtis & F. R. Miller. 416p. 1986. pap. text ed. 65.00 (*0-12-200231-8*) Acad Pr.

Differential Manifolds. Antoni A. Kosinski. (Illus.). 248p. 1992. text ed. 59.95 (*0-12-421850-4*) Acad Pr.

Differential Manifolds. 2nd ed. Serge A. Lang. (Illus.). ix, 230p. 1988. pap. 29.80 (*0-387-96113-5*) Spr-Verlag.

***Differential Models of Hysteresis.** Augusto Visintin. LC 94-47313. (Applied Mathematical Sciences Ser.: Vol. 111). 1994. write for info. (*0-387-54793-2*) Spr-Verlag.

Differential Mortality: Methodological Issues & Biosocial Factors. Ed. by Lado Ruzicka et al. (International Studies in Demography). (Illus.). 272p. 1989. 65.00 (*0-19-828651-1*) OUP.

Differential Mortality: Methodological Issues & Biosocial Factors. Ed. by Lado Ruzicka et al. (International Studies in Demography). (Illus.). 272p. 1995. reprint ed. pap. 17.95 (*0-19-828882-4*) OUP.

Differential Mortality in the United States: A Study in Socio-Economic Epidemiology. Evelyn M. Kitagawa & Philip M. Hauser. LC 72-93951. (Vital & Health Statistics Monographs, American Public Health Association). 288p. 1973. 29.00 (*0-674-20561-8*) HUP.

Differential Operations of Infinite Order with Real Arguments & Their Applications. Tran Duc Van & Dinh Nho Hao. 248p. 1994. text ed. 45.00 (*981-02-1611-4*) World Scientific Pub.

Differential Operators & Highest Weight Representations. Davidson et al. LC 91-27804. (MEMO Ser.: No. 94/455). 102p. 1991. 20.00 (*0-8218-2509-7*, MEMO 94/455) Am Math.

Differential Patterns in Higher Plants. Ed. by Krystyna M. Urbanska. 272p. 1987. text ed. 70.00 (*0-12-709425-3*) Acad Pr.

Differential Police Response Strategies. Michael T. Farmer et al. LC 81-80183. (Illus.). 193p. (Orig.). (C). 1981. pap. text ed. 7.00 (*1-878734-04-0*) Police Exec Res.

Differential Psychology. Henry L. Minton & Frank W. Schneider. (Illus.). 514p. (C). 1985. reprint ed. text ed. 32.95x (*0-88133-152-X*) Waveland Pr.

Differential Psychopharmacology on Anxiolytics & Sedatives. Ed. by J. R. Boissier et al. (Modern Problems of Pharmacopsychiatry Ser.: Vol. 14). (Illus.). 1977. 43.25 (*3-8055-2777-2*) S Karger.

***Differential Release & Impact of Antibiotic-Induced Endotoxin.** Ed. by Eugen Faist. LC 94-47586. 1995. write for info. (*0-7817-0321-2*) Raven.

Differential Rotation & Stellar Convection - Sun & Solar Type Stars. G. Rudiger. (Fluid Mechanics of Astrophysics & Geophysics Ser.). 1989. text ed. 206.00 (*2-88124-066-6*) Gordon & Breach.

Differential Scanning Calorimetry of Polymers: Physics, Chemistry, Analysis, Technology. V. A. Bershtein & V. M. Egorov. Ed. & Tr. by T. J. Kemp. LC 93-27823. (Ellis Horwood Series in Polymer Science & Technology). 1994. text ed. write for info. (*0-13-218215-7*, Tavistock-E Horwood) Routledge Chapman & Hall.

***Differential Selling.** James S. Payne et al. 124p. (Orig.). 1994. pap. 14.95x (*1-57171-001-9*) Lincoln-Rembrandt.

Differential Systems & Isometric Embeddings. Phillip A. Griffiths & Gary R. Jensen. 200p. 1987. text ed. 49.50 (*0-691-08429-7*); pap. text ed. 24.95 (*0-691-08430-0*) Princeton U Pr.

Differential Therapeutics in Psychiatry: The Art & Science of Treatment Selection. Allen Frances et al. LC 84-5883. 440p. 1984. 47.95 (*0-87630-360-2*) Brunner-Mazel.

Differential Therapy of Depression: Possibilities & Limitations. Ed. by H. Hippius & N. Matussek. (Advances in Pharmacotherapy Ser.: Vol. 2). (Illus.). x, 238p. 1986. 149.00 (*3-8055-4049-3*) S Karger.

Differential Thermal Analysis: Application & Results in Mineralogy. W. Smykatz-Kloss. LC 74-17490. (Minerals & Rocks Ser.: Vol. 11). (Illus.). xiv, 185p. 1974. 34.00 (*0-387-06906-2*) Spr-Verlag.

Differential Topology. Victor Guillemin & Alan Pollack. (Mathematics Ser.). (Illus.). 324p. 1974. text ed. 63.00 (*0-13-212605-2*) P-H.

Differential Topology. Ed. by U. Koschorke. (Lecture Notes in Mathematics Ser.: Vol. 1350). vi, 269p. 1988. pap. 39.30 (*0-387-50369-2*) Spr-Verlag.

Differential Topology. J. Margalef-Roig & E. Outerelo Dominguez. LC 92-10918. (North-Holland Mathematics Studies: Vol. 173). 1992. write for info. (*0-444-88434-3*, North Holland) Elsevier.

***Differential Topology.** 5th ed. M. W. Hirsch. (Graduate Texts in Mathematics Ser.: Vol. 33). x, 222p. 1976. reprint ed. 39.00 (*0-387-90148-5*) Spr-Verlag.

D

An Asterisk (*) at the beginning of an entry indicates that the title is appearing in BIP for the first time.

An Asterisk (*) at the beginning of an entry indicates that the title is appearing in BIP for the first time.

D

Diffractive & Miniaturized Optics: Proceedings of a Conference Held 12-13 July 1993, San Diego, California. Ed. by Sing H. Lee. LC 93-47390. (Critical Reviews of Optical Science & Technology Ser.: Vol. CR49). 1993. 91.00 (*0-8194-1292-9*); 76.00 (*0-8194-1291-0*) SPIE.

Diffractive Optics. LC 94-65361. (Nineteen Ninety-Four Technical Digest Ser.: Vol. 11). 250p. (Orig.). 1994. pap. 75.00 (*1-55752-349-5*); pap. text ed. 48.00 (*1-55752-348-7*) Optical Soc.

Diffractive Optics: Design, Fabrication, & Applications. LC 92-80615. (Technical Digest Series, 1992: Vol. 9). 200p. (Orig.). 1992. Postconference. pap. 75.00 (*1-55752-234-0*); Conference. pap. 48.00 (*1-55752-233-2*) Optical Soc.

Diffractive Processes in Nuclear Physics. W. E. Frahn. (Oxford Studies in Nuclear Physics). (Illus.). 1985. 45.00 (*0-19-851512-X*) OUP.

Diffractometry Tutorial. (American Crystallographic Association Lecture Notes Ser.: No. 4). 1978. pap. 15.00 (*0-686-47204-7*) Polycrystal Bk Serv.

Diffuse Coatings on Iron & Steel. N. S. Gorbunov. 174p. 1960. text ed. 46.00 (*0-7065-0094-6*, Pub. by Keter Pub IS) Coronet Bks.

Diffuse Diseases of the Lung: A Team Approach. Thurlbeck et al. (Illus.). 256p. (C). 1991. 82.00 (*1-55664-197-4*) Mosby Yr Bk.

Diffuse Matter in Galaxies. Ed. by Jean Audouze et al. 1983. lib. bdg. 84.00 (*90-277-1626-9*) Kluwer Ac.

Diffuse Matter in the Solar System: Comet Halley & Other Studies: Proceeding of the Royal Society Held on May 21 & 22, 1986. Ed. by G. Turner & C. T. Pillinger. (Illus.). 199p. 1987. text ed. 105.00 (*0-85403-325-4*, Pub. by Royal Soc Chem UK) Scholium Intl.

Diffuse Pollution. Ed. by H. Olem. (Water Science & Technology Ser.: Vol. 28). 722p. 1993. pap. 335.00 (*0-08-042345-0*) Elsevier.

***Diffusing Geography: Essays for Peter Haggett.** Ed. by Andrew Cliff et al. (IBG Special Publications). (Illus.). 384p. (C). 1995. text ed. 74.95 (*0-631-19534-3*) Blackwell Pubs.

Diffusing Marketing Theory & Research: The Contributions of Bauer, Green, Kotler & Levitt. Ed. by A. Andreasen & D. Gardner. LC 78-10544. (Proceedings Ser.). 1979. 15.00 (*0-87757-116-3*) Am Mktg.

Diffusing Marketing Theory & Research: The Contributions of Bauer, Green, Kotler, & Levitt. Ed. by Alan R. Andreasen & David M. Gardner. LC 78-10544. (American Marketing Association, Proceedings Ser.). 154p. reprint ed. pap. 43.90 (*0-8357-6873-2*, 2035571) Bks Demand.

Diffusing the Power. Michael Meacher. (C). 1992. pap. text ed. 23.00 (*0-7453-0693-4*) Westview.

Diffusing the Power. Michael Meacher. (C). 1992. text ed. 55.50 (*0-7453-0692-6*, Pub. by Pluto Pr UK) Westview.

Diffusion: Mass Transfer in Fluid Systems. E. L. Cussler. (Illus.). 537p. 1985. pap. 37.95 (*0-521-29846-6*) Cambridge U Pr.

Diffusion: Papers Presented at a Seminar of the American Society for Metals, October 14 & 15, 1972. American Society for Metals Staff. LC 73-88315. 383p. reprint ed. pap. 109.20 (*0-685-10839-2*, 2019479) Bks Demand.

Diffusion Analysis & Applications. Ed. by R. W. Heckel et al. LC 89-61029. (Illus.). 450p. 1989. 10.00 (*0-87339-080-6*, 328) Minerals Metals.

Diffusion Analysis & Applications: Proceedings of a Symposium on Diffusion Analysis & Applications - Jointly Sponsored by the Minerals, Metals & Materials Society & the Atomic Transport Activities Committee of ASM, Held During the TMS Fall Meeting, September 25-29, 1988, Chicago, Illinois. Metallurgical Society of AIME Staff. Ed. by A. D. Romig, Jr. & M. A. Dayananda. LC 89-61029. 373p. reprint ed. pap. 106.40 (*0-7837-5640-2*, 2052492) Bks Demand.

Diffusion & Belief in a Collective Delusion: The Seattle Windshield Pitting Epidemic. Nahum Z. Medalia & Otto N. Larsen. (Reprint Series in Social Sciences). (C). 1993. reprint ed. pap. text ed. 1.90 (*0-8290-2718-1*, S-602) Irvington.

Diffusion & Convection in Porous Catalysts. Ed. by Ian A. Webster. LC 88-34405. (AIChE Symposium Ser.: Vol. 84, No. 266). 96p. 1988. pap. 38.00 (*0-8169-0458-8*, S 266) Am Inst Chem Eng.

Diffusion & Interfaces: Microscopic Concepts. Ed. by M. Grunze et al. (Surface Sciences Ser.: Vol. 12). (Illus.). 215p. 1988. 66.00 (*0-387-19212-3*) Spr-Verlag.

Diffusion & Membrane Technology. Sidney B. Tuwiner. LC 62-20783. (ACS Monograph: No. 156). 1962. 39.95 (*0-8412-0284-2*) Am Chemical.

***Diffusion & Perfusion Magnetic Resonance Imaging.** Ed. by Denis Le Bihan. LC 94-24643. 408p. 1995. 149.00 (*0-7817-0244-5*) Raven.

***Diffusion & Reactions: From Basics to Applications.** Jerzy Jedlinski. (Solid State Phenomena Ser.: Vol. 41). (Illus.). 320p. (C). 1995. text ed. 94.00 (*3-908450-08-X*, Pub. by Trans Tech SZ) LPS Dist Ctr.

***Diffusion & Structure of Metals.** S. Z. Bokshtein. Tr. by S. C. Dhamija. (Illus.). 178p. 1985. text ed. 55.00 (*81-205-0004-0*, Pub. by Oxonion Pr Pvt Ltd) Science Pubs.

***Diffusion & Transport of Pollutants in Atmospheric Mesoscale Flow Fields.** Ed. by Albert Gyr & Frans S. Rys. LC 94-39300. (ERCOFTAC Ser.: Vol. 1). 1995. write for info. (*0-7923-3260-1*) Kluwer Ac.

Diffusion & Use of Geographic Information Technologies: Proceedings of the NATO Advanced Research Workshop on Modeling the Diffusion & Use of Geographic Information Technologies, Sounion, Greece, April 8-11, 1992. Ed. by Ian Masser & Harlan J. Onsrud. LC 93-9597. (NATO Advanced Study Institutes Series D, Behavioural & Social Sciences: No. 70). 364p. (C). 1993. Alk. paper. lib. bdg. 136.00 (*0-7923-2190-1*) Kluwer Ac.

Diffusion Approximations & Bounds for Queues. Fridrikh I. Karpelevich & A. Y. Kreinin. LC 94-12418. (Translations of Mathematical Monographs: Vol. 137). 1994. write for info. (*0-8218-4597-7*) Am Math.

Diffusion, Atomic Ordering, & Mass Transport: Selected Problems in Geochemistry. Ed. by J. Ganguly & S. Saxena. (Advances in Physical Geochemistry Ser.: Vol. 8). (Illus.). 632p. 1990. 181.00 (*0-387-97287-0*) Spr-Verlag.

Diffusion Bonding, No. 2. D. J. Stephenson. 1991. 110.00 (*1-85166-591-9*) Elsevier.

Diffusion Bonding of Materials. N. F. Kazakov. 450p. 1985. 134.00 (*0-08-032550-5*, Pub. by PPL UK) Franklin.

Diffusion Bonding, Vol. 2: Proceedings of the International Conference on Diffusion Bonding, 2nd, Held at Cranfield Institute of Technology, U. K., 28-29 March, 1990. Ed. by D. J. Stephenson. 328p. 1991. 110.00 (*0-685-40618-0*) Elsevier.

Diffusion Chamber Culture: Hemopoiesis, Cloning of Tumors, Cytogenetic & Carinogenic Assays. E. P. Cronkite & A. L. Carstens. (Illus.). 270p. 1980. pap. 61.00 (*0-387-10064-4*) Spr-Verlag.

Diffusion Chromizing of Alloys. G. N. Dubinin. Tr. by K. M. Pai. (Illus.). 526p. (RUS.). (C). 1987. 38.00 (*81-205-0069-5*, Pub. by Oxford IBH II) S Asia.

Diffusion-Controlled Stress Relaxation of Swollen Rubber-Like Networks. D. E. Knibbe. 60p. 1968. pap. text ed. 69.00 (*0-677-61185-4*) Gordon & Breach.

Diffusion Equations. Seizo Ito. LC 92-24069. (Translations of Mathematical Monographs: Vol. 114). 225p. 1992. 93.00 (*0-8218-4570-5*) Am Math.

***Diffusion in Amorphous Materials: Proceedings of the International Symposium Sponsored by Atomic Transport Activity Committee of American Society of Materials, Pittsburgh, PA, 1994.** LC 94-78685. 241p. 1995. 70.00 (*0-87339-243-4*) Minerals Metals.

Diffusion in & Through Polymers: Principles & Applications. Wolf R. Vieth. 322p. (C). 1991. text ed. 62.50 (*1-56990-106-6*) Hanser-Gardner.

Diffusion in High Technology Materials. Ed. by M. A. Dayananda et al. 400p. 1988. text ed. 88.00 (*0-87849-561-4*, Pub. by Trans Tech GW) LPS Dist Ctr.

Diffusion in Materials. Ed. by A. L. Laskar et al. (C). 1990. lib. bdg. 215.00 (*0-7923-0653-8*) Kluwer Ac.

Diffusion in Materials: DIMAT 92. Ed. by M. Koiwa et al. (Defect & Diffusion Forum Ser.: Vol. 95-98). (Illus.). 1288p. (C). 1993. text ed. 295.00 (*0-87849-662-9*, Pub. by Trans Tech SZ) LPS Dist Ctr.

Diffusion in Metals & Alloys. V. Z. Bugakov. 136p. 1971. text ed. 44.00 (*0-7065-1071-2*, Pub. by Keter Pub IS) Coronet Bks.

Diffusion in Metals & Alloys: DIMETA 88. Ed. by F. J. Kedves & D. L. Beke. 1550p. 1989. text ed. 170.00 (*3-908044-03-0*, Pub. by Trans Tech GW) LPS Dist Ctr.

Diffusion in Metals & Alloys: Proceedings of an International Conference Held at Tihany, Hungary. Ed. by F. J. Kedves & D. L. Beke. (Diffusion & Defect Monograph Ser.: Vol. 7). 685p. (C). 1983. text ed. 170.00 (*0-87849-527-4*, Pub. by Trans Tech GW) LPS Dist Ctr.

Diffusion in Ordered Alloys & Intermetallic Compounds. Ed. by B. Fultz et al. (Illus.). 234p. 1993. 44.00 (*0-87339-204-3*) Minerals Metals.

Diffusion in Reactor Materials. G. B. Fedorov & E. A. Smirnov. (Diffusion & Defect Monograph Ser.: Vol. 8). 182p. 1984. 42.00 (*0-87849-531-2*, Pub. by Trans Tech GW) LPS Dist Ctr.

Diffusion in Solids. Ed. by A. L. Laskar et al. (Material Science Forum Ser.: Vol. 1). 290p. (C). 1984. pap. text ed. 78.00 (*0-87849-533-9*, Pub. by Trans Tech GW) LPS Dist Ctr.

Diffusion in Solids. Paul Shewmon. LC 89-61758. (Illus.). 246p. (C). 1989. 45.00 (*0-87339-105-5*) Minerals Metals.

Diffusion in Solids. Paul G. Shewmon. 203p. 33.00 (*0-930745-12-4*) Williams Bk Co.

Diffusion in Solids: Unsolved Problems. Ed. by Graeme Murch. 294p. 1992. text ed. 72.00 (*0-87849-631-9*, Pub. by Trans Tech GW) LPS Dist Ctr.

Diffusion in Solids & High Temperature Oxidations of Metals. Ed. by J. Nowotny. 446p. 1992. text ed. 146.00 (*0-87849-626-2*, Pub. by Trans Tech GW) LPS Dist Ctr.

Diffusion in Solids II. Ed. by Graeme E. Murch & Arthur S. Nowick. (Materials Science & Technology Ser.). 1984. text ed. 140.00 (*0-12-522662-4*) Acad Pr.

Diffusion in Zeolites: And Other Microporous Solids. Douglas M. Ruthven & Jorg Karger. 640p. 1992. text ed. 175.00 (*0-471-50907-8*) Wiley.

Diffusion Kinetics for Atoms in Crystals. John R. Manning. LC 68-20921. 274p. reprint ed. pap. 78.10 (*0-317-09190-5*, 2005790) Bks Demand.

***Diffusion, Markov Processes & Martingales.** 2nd ed. L. C.G. Rogers & D. Williams. (Probability & Mathematic Ser.: 1). 1995. text ed. 79.95 (*0-471-95061-0*) Wiley.

Diffusion of Advanced Telecommunications in Developing Countries. OECD Staff. 111p. (Orig.). 1991. pap. 19.00 (*92-64-13578-2*) OECD.

Diffusion of an American Montessori Education. Judith W. Meyer. LC 74-80719. (Research Papers Ser.: No. 160). 97p. 1975. pap. 12.00 (*0-89065-067-5*) U Chicago Comm Geo.

Diffusion of an Innovation in an Urban System: The Spread of Planned Regional Shopping Centers in the United States, 1949-1968. Yehoshua S. Cohen. LC 72-76011. (Research Papers Ser.: No. 140). 136p. 1972. pap. 12.00 (*0-89065-047-0*) U Chicago Comm Geo.

Diffusion of Classical Art in Antiquity. John Boardman. LC 94-16269. (A. W. Mellon Lectures in the Fine Arts Ser.: Vol. XXXV, 42). 1995. 49.50 (*0-691-03680-2*) Princeton U Pr.

Diffusion of Contaminants in the Ocean. R. V. Ozmidov. (C). 1990. lib. bdg. 164.00 (*0-7923-0611-2*) Kluwer Ac.

Diffusion of Distances: Dialogues Between Chinese & Western Poetics. Wai-Lim Yip. LC 92-15325. (C). 1993. 30.00 (*0-520-07736-9*) U CA Pr.

Diffusion of Electrolytes in Polymers. G. E. Zaikov et al. (New Concepts in Polymer Science Ser.). 325p. 1988. lib. bdg. 202.00 (*90-6764-077-8*, Pub. by VSP NE) Coronet Bks.

Diffusion of Electronic Data Interchange. H. K. Pfeiffer. (Contributions to Management Science Ser.). (Illus.). xiv, 257p. 1992. pap. 69.00 (*0-387-91428-5*) Spr-Verlag.

***Diffusion of Gases.** H. A. Neidig & J. N. Spencer. (Modular Laboratory Program in Chemistry Ser.). 7p. (C). 1990. pap. text ed. 1.25x (*0-87540-385-9*) Chem Educ Res.

***Diffusion of Gases & Graham's Law.** Grover W. Everett, Jr. Ed. by H. A. Neidig. (Modular Laboratory Program in Chemistry Ser.). 7p. (C). 1992. pap. text ed. 1.25x (*0-87540-412-X*) Chem Educ Res.

Diffusion of Influenza: Patterns & Paradigms. Gerald F. Pyle. LC 86-1780. (Illus.). 240p. (C). 1986. 60.50 (*0-8476-7429-0*, R7429) Rowman.

***Diffusion of Information Technology: Experience of Industrial Countries & Lessons for Developing Countries.** Nagy Hanna et al. LC 95-7495. (Discussion Papers: Vol. 281). 1995. write for info. (*0-8213-3216-3*) World Bank.

Diffusion of Innovations. 3rd ed. Everett M. Rogers. (Illus.). 512p. 1982. text ed. 29.95 (*0-02-926650-5*) Free Pr.

***Diffusion of Innovations.** 4th ed. Everett M. Rogers. LC 94-24947. 1995. pap. 29.95 (*0-02-926671-8*) Free Pr.

Diffusion of Innovations: A Select Bibliography. Ed. by William H. Kennedy. LC 89-7489. (Bibliographies & Indexes in Sociology Ser.: No. 17). 264p. 1989. text ed. 69.50 (*0-313-26698-0*, Greenwood Pr) Greenwood.

Diffusion of Innovations in English Language Teaching: The ELEC Effort in Japan, 1956-1968. Lynn E. Henrichsen. LC 89-11906. (Contributions to the Study of Education Ser.: No. 33). (Illus.). 252p. 1989. text ed. 49.95 (*0-313-26617-4*, HDU/, Greenwood Pr) Greenwood.

Diffusion of Innovations in the Public Sector: Proceedings of a Conference. Ed. by Glen H. Cope. (Institute & Seminar Proceedings Sr.). 1992. write for info. (*0-89940-101-5*) LBJ Sch Pub Aff.

Diffusion of Medical Innovations: An Applied Network Analysis. Mary L. Fennel & Richard B. Warnecke. LC 88-2475. (Environment Development, & Public Policy: Public Policy & Social Services Ser.). (Illus.). 300p. 1988. 45.00 (*0-306-42752-4*, Plenum Pr) Plenum.

Diffusion of New Industrial Processes: An International Study. Ed. by Lars Nabseth & G. F. Ray. LC 73-88309. (National Institute of Economic & Social Research Occasional Papers: No. 29). 346p. reprint ed. pap. 98.70 (*0-317-27314-0*, 2024504) Bks Demand.

Diffusion of New Process Technologies in Hungary. Ray Oakley et al. LC 92-28351. 1993. 59.00 (*0-86187-062-X*, Pub. by Pinter Pubs UK) St Martin.

Diffusion of Process Innovations. Stephen Davies. LC 78-15143. 207p. reprint ed. pap. 59.00 (*0-317-28007-4*, 2025580) Bks Demand.

Diffusion of Science. Jesse Lee Bennett. LC 74-26250. (History, Philosophy & Sociology of Science Ser.). 1975. reprint ed. 19.95 (*0-405-06580-9*) Ayer.

Diffusion of Technological Change in the Pennsylvania Pig Iron Industry: 1850-1870. William D. Walsh. LC 75-2601. (Dissertations in American Economic History Ser.). (Illus.). 1975. 30.95 (*0-405-07222-8*) Ayer.

Diffusion of Technologies & Social Behavior. Ed. by N. Nakicenovic & A. Grubler. (Illus.). xxvi, 605p. 1991. 149.00 (*0-387-53846-1*) Spr-Verlag.

Diffusion of the Reformation in Southwestern Germany, 1518-1534. Manfred Hannemann. LC 75-14120. (Research Papers Ser.: No. 167). (Illus.). 1975. pap. 12.00 (*0-89065-074-8*) U Chicago Comm Geo.

Diffusion of War: A Study of Opportunity & Willingness. Randolph M. Siverson & Harvey Starr. (Illus.). 200p. 1991. text ed. 32.50 (*0-472-10247-8*) U of Mich Pr.

Diffusion Phenomena in Thin Films & Microelectronic Materials. Ed. by Devendra Gupta & Paul S. Ho. LC 88-22634. (Illus.). 588p. 1989. 86.00 (*0-8155-1167-1*) Noyes.

Diffusion Process in Solid Phase Welding of Materials. V. M. Faichenko. (C). 1984. 34.00 (*0-8364-2118-3*, Pub. by Oxford IBH II) S Asia.

Diffusion Processes, 2 vols. Ed. by J. N. Sherwood et al. 444p. 1971. Vol. 2, 444p. 198.00 (*0-677-14830-5*); Vol. 1, xiv, 400p. text ed. 222.00 (*0-677-14820-8*) Gordon & Breach.

Diffusion Processes, 2 vols., Vol. 2. Ed. by J. N. Sherwood et al. 1971. Set. text ed. 432.00 (*0-677-14260-9*) Gordon & Breach.

***Diffusion Processes Vol. 438: Experiment, Theory, Simulations: Proceedings of the Fifth Max Born Symposium, Held at Kudowa, Poland, 1-4 June 1994.** Ed. by Andrzej Pekalski. LC 94-39108. (Lecture Notes in Physics Ser.). 1994. write for info. (*3-540-58653-9*) Spr-Verlag.

Diffusion Processes & Location. Lawrence Brown. (Bibliography Ser.: No. 4). 177p. 1968. 20.00 (*1-55869-026-3*) Regional Sci Res Inst.

Diffusion Processes & Partial Differential Equations. Kazuaki Taira. (Mathematics in Science & Engineering Ser.). 452p. 1988. text ed. 112.00 (*0-12-682220-4*) Acad Pr.

Diffusion Processes & Related Problems in Analysis. Mark A. Pinsky. 600p. 1991. 58.50 (*0-8176-3516-5*) Birkhauser.

Diffusion Processes & Related Problems in Analysis, Vol. II: Stochastic Flows. Ed. by Mark A. Pinsky & V. Wihstutz. (Progress in Probability Ser.: Vol. 27). ix, 346p. 1991. 68.50 (*0-8176-3543-2*) Birkhauser.

Diffusion Processes & Related Topics in Biology. L. M. Ricciardi. LC 77-7464. (Lecture Notes in Biomathematics Ser.: Vol. 14). 1977. pap. 27.00 (*0-387-08146-1*) Spr-Verlag.

Diffusion Processes & Their Sample Paths. K. Ito & H. P. McKean, Jr. (Grundlehren der Mathematischen Wissenschaften Ser.: Vol. 125). 1965. 45.00 (*0-387-03302-5*) Spr-Verlag.

Diffusion Processes During Drying of Solids. K. N. Shukla. 168p. 1990. text ed. 48.00 (*981-02-0278-4*) World Scientific Pub.

Diffusion Processes in Iron Alloys. M. A. Krishtal. 238p. 1970. text ed. 61.00 (*0-7065-1017-8*, Pub. by Keter Pub IS) Coronet Bks.

Diffusion Processes in Metals. Ed. by V. N. Svechnikov. 158p. 1970. text ed. 44.00 (*0-7065-1016-X*, Pub. by Keter Pub IS) Coronet Bks.

Diffusion Processes in Nuclear Materials. Ed. by R. P. Agarwala. LC 92-26715. x, 440p. 1992. write for info. (*0-444-89146-3*, North Holland) Elsevier.

***Diffusion Processes in Ordered Alloys.** L. N. Larikov et al. Tr. by S. P. Pednekar. (Illus.). 184p. (C). 1981. text ed. 64.00 (*0-614-01343-7*, Pub. by Oxonion Pr Pvt Ltd) Science Pubs.

***Diffusion Processes in Solid-Phase Welding of Materials.** V. M. Fel'chenko et al. Tr. by S. C. Dhamija. (Illus.). 208p. (C). 1984. text ed. 65.00 (*0-614-01345-3*, Pub. by Oxonion Pr Pvt Ltd) Science Pubs.

Diffusion Rate Data & Mass Transport Phenomena for Cooper Systems. National Bureau of Standards Staff. (INCRA Monograph). 322p. 1977. 20.00 (*0-317-42799-7*) Intl Copper.

Diffusion Research in Rural Sociology: The Record & Prospects for the Future. Frederick C. Fliegel. LC 92-19426. (Contributions in Sociology Ser.: No. 103). 152p. 1992. text ed. 47.95 (*0-313-26447-3*, FDF, Greenwood Pr) Greenwood.

Diffusion, Transfer, & Implementation of Information Technology: Proceedings of the IFIP TC8 Working Conference on Diffusion, Transfer, & Implementation of Information Technology, Pittsburgh, PA, U.S.A., 11-13 October 1993. Ed. by Linda Levine. LC 94-4643. (IFIP Transactions A: Computer Science & Technology Ser.: Vol. A-45). 1994. write for info. (*0-444-81856-1*, North Holland) Elsevier.

Diffusional Creep of Materials. B. Burton. 1977. 36.00 (*0-87849-506-1*, Pub. by Trans Tech GW) LPS Dist Ctr.

Diffusional Mass Transfer. A. H. Skelland. LC 84-14403. 528p. (C). 1985. reprint ed. lib. bdg. 69.50 (*0-89874-792-9*) Krieger.

Diffusionless Phase Transitions & Related Structures in Oxides. C. Boulesteix. 348p. 1992. text ed. 96.00 (*0-87849-629-7*, Pub. by Trans Tech GW) LPS Dist Ctr.

***Diffusionless Phase Transitions in Oxides: And Some Reconstructive & Martensitic Phase Transitions.** Ed C. Boulesteix. (Key Engineering Materials Ser.: Vol. 101-102). (Illus.). 442p. (C). 1995. text ed. 172.00 (*0-87849-691-2*, Pub. by Trans Tech SZ) LPS Dist Ctr.

Diffusions, Markov Processes, & Martingales, Vol. 1: Foundations. David Williams. LC 78-16634. 251p. reprint ed. pap. 71.60 (*0-685-20651-3*, 2030437) Bks Demand.

***Diffusive Scattering of X-Rays & Neutrons by Fluctuation: Inhomogeneities in Imperfect Crystals.** Mikhail A. Krivoglaz. LC 94-3791. 1994. write for info. (*3-540-57627-4*) Spr-Verlag.

Dig. Alan D. Foster. (Orig.). 1996. write for info. (*0-446-51853-0*, Aspect) Warner Bks.

Dig: An Archaeological Reconstruction of a West Coast Village. George F. MacDonald & Richard I. Inglis. (Canadian Prehistory Ser.). (Illus.). x, 90p. 1985. pap. text ed. 8.50 (*0-317-18868-2*, 56528-9, Pub. by Natl Mus Sci Tech CN) U Ch Pr.

Dig: Poems by Lynn Emanuel. Lynn Emanuel. 64p. (Orig.). 1992. pap. 10.95 (*0-252-06251-5*) U of Ill Pr.

Dig a Narrow Grave see This Land Turns Evil Slowly

Dig & Hotel Fiesta, Vol. 2. Lynn Emanuel. LC 94-7703. 144p. 1994. pap. 13.95 (*0-252-06420-8*) U of Ill Pr.

Dig Dig. Leslie Wood. (Cat on the Mat Ser.). (Illus.). 16p. (J). (ps up). 1988. pap. 3.50 (*0-19-272185-2*) OUP.

Dig, Drill, Dump, Fill. Tana Hoban. LC 75-11987. (Illus.). 32p. (J). (ps-3). 1975. 13.88 (*0-688-84016-7*) Greenwillow.

Dig, Drill, Dump, Fill. Tana Hoban. LC 75-11987. (Illus.). 32p. (J). (ps up). 1992. pap. 3.95 (*0-688-11703-1*, Mulberry) Morrow.

Dig Here. Thomas Penfield. (Illus.). 240p. (Orig.). 1987. reprint ed. pap. 10.00 (*0-918080-38-X*) Treas Chest Bks.

***Dig Hole, Soft Mole.** Carolyn Lesser. LC 95-11697. (Illus.). (J). 1996. write for info. (*0-15-223491-8*) HarBrace.

Dig in Time. Peni R. Griffin. LC 92-18958. 160p. (J). (gr. 3-7). 1992. pap. 3.99 (*0-14-036001-8*) Puffin Bks.

Dig in Time. Peni R. Griffin. LC 90-47388. 192p. (J). (gr. 4-7). 1991. text ed. 14.95 (*0-689-50525-6*, McElderry) S&S Childrens.

An Asterisk (*) at the beginning of an entry indicates that the title is appearing in BIP for the first time.

Dig Me Up. Suzanne Chance. 176p. (Orig.). (YA). 1992. pap. 3.50 (*0-380-76917-4*, Flare) Avon.

Dig My Grave Deep. Peter Rabe. LC 87-72697. 144p. 1988. reprint ed. pap. 4.95 (*0-88739-092-7*, Blk Lizard) Creat Arts Bk.

Dig That Hole! John Light. LC 91-39036. (Light Reading Ser.). (J). (gr. 5 up). 1991. 3.95 (*0-85953-503-7*) Childs Play.

Dig the Spurs Deep. Peter Field. (Powder Valley Western Ser.). 176p. 1988. pap. 2.75 (*0-380-70421-8*) Avon.

Dig This! How Archaeologists Uncover Our Past. Michael Avi-Yonah. LC 92-28305. (Buried Worlds Ser.). (YA). (gr. 6 up). 1993. 22.95 (*0-8225-3200-X*, Lerner Publctns) Lerner Group.

Dig We Must! - into the Coal Operator's Profits! 1970. pap. 0.25 (*0-87898-055-5*) New Outlook.

Dig Your Own Gold. Ellen G. Genta. 1976. 4.95 (*0-89036-062-6*) Hawkes Pub Inc.

Digalo en Espanol: Review Grammar for Communication. Marta De La Portilla. (Illus.). (C). 1988. pap. text ed. write for info. (*0-13-211178-0*) P-H.

Digalo en Ingles, (Say It in English for Spanish-Speaking People) Leon J. Cohen & A. C. Rogers. (Orig.). pap. 3.50 (*0-486-20802-8*) Dover.

Digase la Verdad. William Backus & Marie Chaplan. 1983. 4.95 (*0-88113-049-4*) Edit Betania.

Digby. Joseph Dougherty. 1986. pap. 4.75 (*0-8222-0308-1*) Dramatists Play.

***Digby.** Barbara S. Hazan. LC 95-1689. (I Can Read Bks.). (J). 1996. 14.95 (*0-06-026253-2*) HarpC Child Bks.

Digby. large type ed. Pamela Hill. 1990. 21.95 (*0-7089-2331-3*) Ulverscroft.

Digby. David Walker. reprint ed. lib. bdg. 21.95 (*0-88411-866-5*, Aeonian Pr) Amereon Ltd.

Digby & Kate. Barbara Baker. LC 87-24455. (Easy Reader Ser.). (Illus.). 48p. (J). (ps-2). 1988. 9.95 (*0-525-44370-3*, 0966-290, DCB) Dutton Child Bks.

Digby & Kate. Barbara Baker. LC 93-6555. (Easy-to-Read Ser.: Level 2). (Illus.). (J). (gr. k-3). 1993. pap. 3.25 (*0-14-036547-8*, Puffin) Puffin Bks.

Digby & Kate Again. Barbara Baker. LC 88-25677. (Easy Reader Ser.). (Illus.). 48p. (J). (ps-2). 1989. 9.95 (*0-525-44477-7*, DCB) Dutton Child Bks.

Digby & Kate Again. Barbara Baker & Martha Winborn. (Easy-to-Read Ser.: Level 2 (Red)). (Illus.). (J). (gr. k-3). 1994. pap. 3.25 (*0-14-036665-2*) Puffin Bks.

Digby Plays. Ed. by F. J. Furnivall. (EETS ES Ser.: Vol. 70). 1972. 15.00 (*0-685-09932-6*) Periodicals Srv.

Digby Plays: The Digby Mysteries, from the Mss. by . . . Ed. by F. J. Furnivall. (New Shakespeare Society, London, Ser. 7: No. 1). 1972. reprint ed. pap. 15.00 (*0-8115-0247-3*) Periodicals Srv.

Digenes Akrites: New Approaches to Byzantine Heroic Poetry. Roderick Beaton & David Ricks. (Center for Hellenic Studies: Vol. 2). 1993. 59.95 (*0-86078-395-2*, Pub. by Variorum UK) Ashgate Pub Co.

Digenis Akritas. Tr. by Denison B. Hull. LC 79-141384. 148p. 1986. pap. text ed. 14.95 (*0-8214-0833-X*) Ohio U Pr.

Digest: Annotated British, Commonwealth & European Cases, 75 vols., Set. Ed. by Butterworth Staff. 1942. boxed 5,000.00 (*0-406-02500-2*) Michie Butterworth.

Digest & Index of the Minutes of General Synod, 1958-1977. Mildred Schuppert. 1979. pap. 10.99 (*0-8028-1774-2*) Eerdmans.

Digest, Cases & Materials, Land Acquisition & Compensation Cases. B. Banerjee. (C). 1990. 110.00 (*0-89771-302-8*) St Mut.

Digest, Cases & Materials, on Civil Procedure Code, 1970-1989. Chandra B. Upadhyay. (C). 1990. 190.00 (*0-89771-238-2*) St Mut.

Digest, Cases & Materials on Limitation Act. A. K. Banerji. (C). 1990. 125.00 (*0-89771-251-X*) St Mut.

Digest File. Ed. by W. A. Johnson. 60p. (Orig.). pap. 12.95 (*0-914981-06-4*) Res Pubns AZ.

Digest for the Successful Terrarium. Richard Bartlett. (Illus.). 80p. 6.95 (*3-89356-035-1*, 16040) Tetra Pr.

Digest, No. IX, 2: Lex Aquilia. Ed. & Tr. by C. H. Monro. LC 93-79700. 106p. 1994. reprint ed. 30.00 (*1-56169-058-9*) W W Gaunt.

Digest of Agricultural Census Statistics: United Kingdom 1992. 134p. 1993. pap. 35.00 (*0-11-242958-0*, HM29580, Pub. by HMSO UK) UNIPUB.

Digest of All India Control of Rent & Eviction Cases, 1970-1976. P. R. Verma. 136p. 1977. pap. 55.00 (*0-317-57753-0*) St Mut.

Digest of American Indian Law: Cases & Chronology. H. Barry Holt & Gary Forrester. x, 138p. 1990. 35.00 (*0-8377-0684-X*) Rothman.

Digest of Australian Constitutional Cases. 3rd ed. P. H. Lane. xxi, 487p. 1988. 102.00 (*0-455-20812-3*, Pub. by Law Bk Co); pap. 63.00 (*0-455-20813-1*, Pub. by Law Bk Co) W W Gaunt.

Digest of Australian Constitutional Cases. 4th ed. P. H. Lane. 483p. 1992. 110.00 (*0-455-21145-0*, Pub. by Law Bk Co); pap. 68.00 (*0-455-21146-9*, Pub. by Law Bk Co) W W Gaunt.

***Digest of Building Contract Awards.** 26th ed. Marshall & Swift Staff. (Illus.). 450p. 1995. pap. 52.95 (*1-56842-269-5*) Marshall & Swift.

Digest of Building Contract Awards: The Hard Facts - Comparables on Actual Project Listings. Pascal Lothoir. 383p. 1993. write for info. (*1-56842-003-X*) Marshall & Swift.

Digest of Business Law. 3rd ed. Willis W. Hagen et al. 1991. pap. text ed. 32.75 (*0-314-93184-8*) West Pub.

Digest of Bylaws & Buy-Sell Agreements. 162p. 1976. 27.50 (*0-933948-04-2*, 13-0000-902) Med Group Mgmt.

Digest of Commercial Laws of the World, 11 bdrs. National Association of Credit Management Staff. LC 65-22163. 1966. Approx. 4 releases per yr. write for info. (*0-318-54751-1*) Oceana.

Digest of Commercial Laws of the World, 11 bdrs. National Association of Credit Management Staff & Lester Nelson. LC 65-22163. 1966. ring bd. 1,100.00 (*0-379-01000-3*) Oceana.

Digest of Commercial Laws of the World: Forms of Commercial Agreements, 2 vols., Set. National Association of Credit Management Staff. 1984. ring bd. 200.00 (*0-379-01045-3*) Oceana.

Digest of Commercial Laws of the World: State Variations of Commercial Law, 2 vols. National Association of Credit Management Staff & Lester Nelson. 1985. ring bd. 200.00 (*0-379-01031-3*); Approx. 4 releases per yr. write for info. (*0-318-64270-0*) Oceana.

Digest of Date for the Construction Industry, January 1994. 86p. 1994. pap. 19.00 (*0-11-752801-3*, HM28013, Pub. by HMSO UK) UNIPUB.

Digest of Decisions of the Rental Housing Commission: Real Estate, Housing & Land Use Section. 25.00 (*0-317-62691-4*) DC Bar.

***Digest of Education Statistics.** 1994. pap. 33.00 (*0-16-045251-1*) Claitors.

Digest of Education Statistics, 2 vols., Set. 1994. lib. bdg. 595.00 (*0-8490-5774-4*) Gordon Pr.

***Digest of Educational Statistics (1993)** (Illus.). 459p. (Orig.). (C). 1994. pap. text ed. 75.00x (*0-7881-1154-X*) Diane Pub.

***Digest of Educational Statistics 1994.** Ed. by National Center for Education Statistics Staff. 536p. 1994. pap. 33.00 (*0-89059-032-X*) Bernan Pr.

Digest of English Grammar, Synthetical & Analytical. L. T. Covell. LC 89-24052. 1989. reprint ed. 50.00 (*0-8201-1441-3*) Schol Facsimiles.

Digest of Environmental Protection & Water Statistics. 66p. 1988. pap. 20.00 (*0-11-752082-9*, HM3143, Pub. by HMSO UK) UNIPUB.

***Digest of Environmental Protection & Water Statistics 1994.** HMSO Staff. No. 16. 179p. 1994. pap. 35.00 (*0-11-752939-7*, HM29397, Pub. by HMSO UK) UNIPUB.

Digest of Health Service Finance. Dan Tosey. (C). 1987. pap. 40.00 (*0-685-28610-X*) St Mut.

Digest of Intellectual Property Laws of the World, 3 vols. National Association of Credit Management Staff. Ed. by Lester Nelson. LC 65-22163. 1990. Approx. 4 releases per yr. write for info. (*0-318-68974-X*) Oceana.

Digest of Intellectual Property Laws of the World, 3 vols., Set. National Association of Credit Management Staff & Lester Nelson. LC 65-22163. 1990. ring bd. 495.00 (*0-379-01015-1*) Oceana.

Digest of International Law, 8 Vols, Set. John B. Moore. LC 77-101908. reprint ed. 1,045.00 (*0-404-04420-4*) AMS Pr.

Digest of International Law: Washington, D.C., 1940-1944, 8 vols. Green H. Hackworth. LC 73-5440. reprint ed. write for info. (*0-404-11140-8*) AMS Pr.

Digest of Investigations in the Teaching of Science in the Elementary & Secondary Schools. Francis D. Curtis. LC 74-153694. 369p. reprint ed. pap. 105.20 (*0-685-12281-6*, 2026000) Bks Demand.

Digest of Justinian, 4 vols., Set. Ed. by Alan Watson et al. LC 84-17236. 1985. text ed. 439.95 (*0-8122-7945-X*) U of Pa Pr.

Digest of Laws of Texas. Oliver C. Hartley. LC 74-19607. reprint ed. 87.50 (*0-404-12323-6*) AMS Pr.

Digest of Legal Activities of International Organizations & Other Institutions. 10th ed. International Institute for the Unification of Private Law Staff. Ed. by Paula Howarth. LC 74-19327. 1990. ring bd. 150.00 (*0-379-00525-5*) Oceana.

***Digest of Mining Claim Laws.** 4th ed. 224p. 1990. pap. 19.50 (*0-614-06616-6*, DMC4) Rocky Mtn Mineral Law Found.

Digest of Motor Accident Claims & Compensation. B. L. Bansal. (C). 1989. 250.00 (*0-685-36525-5*) St Mut.

Digest of Muhammadan Law, 2 vol. set. Neil Baillie. 420p. 1980. 65.00 (*1-56744-234-X*) Kazi Pubns.

Digest of Muhammadan Law, 2 vols., Set. N. Baillie. 65.50 (*0-935782-72-9*) Kazi Pubns.

Digest of Muhammadan Law, Vol. 2. Neil Baillie. 420p. 1980. write for info. (*1-56744-260-9*) Kazi Pubns.

Digest of Official Actions. Incl. 1959-1968. pap. 11.50 (*0-89970-031-4*, OP-21); 1969-1978. pap. 22.50 (*0-89970-091-8*, OP-317); 1979-1980. 144p. 1984. pap. 6.00 (*0-89970-155-8*, OP 161); 1981-1982. 122p. 1984. pap. 6.00 (*0-89970-167-1*, OP 231); write for info. (*0-318-50517-7*, OP021) AMA.

Digest of Papers: COMPCON Spring '94, 39th International Computer Conference. 500p. 1994. pap. text ed. 80.00 (*0-8186-5380-9*, 5380) IEEE Comp Soc.

Digest of Roman Law: Theft, Rapine, Damage & Insult. Justinian. Tr. by C. F. Kolbert. (Classics Ser.). 1979. mass mkt. 9.95 (*0-14-044343-6*, Penguin Classics) Viking Penguin.

Digest of Selected California Laws Related to Certificated Personnel. 112p. 1990. pap. text ed. 15.00 (*0-943397-12-X*) Assn Calif Sch Admin.

Digest of Selected California Laws Related to Certified Personnel, 1994. Raj Prasad. 100p. 1994. pap. text ed. 25.00 (*0-943397-25-1*, 115) Assn Calif Sch Admin.

Digest of Selected California Laws Related to Classified Personnel, 1990. 79p. 1990. pap. text ed. 15.00 (*0-943397-13-8*) Assn Calif Sch Admin.

Digest of State Accountancy Laws & State Board Regulations, 1987-88. American Institute of Certified Public Accountants Staff. 113p. pap. 32.30 (*0-8357-6903-8*, 2037961) Bks Demand.

***Digest of State Accountancy Laws & State Board Regulations, 1992.** American Institute of Certified Public Accountants Staff. LC 78-643269. 154p. 1992. pap. 180.00 (*0-7837-8536-4*, 2049349) Bks Demand.

Digest of State Accounting Laws & State Board Regulations. American Institute of Certified Public Accountants Staff. 144p. 1992. pap. text ed. 26.00 (*0-87051-086-X*) Am Inst CPA.

Digest of State Land Sales Regulations. Ed. by Stuart M. Bloch & William B. Ingersoll. 200p. 150.00 (*0-318-19273-X*) Land Dev Inst.

Digest of State Lotteries. John T. Lang. (Illus.). 96p. (Orig.). 1983. pap. write for info. (*0-913397-00-8*) Hilltop Publishing.

***Digest of Statistics on Social Protection in Europe - General Neediness, Vol. 8.** Eurostat Staff. 208p. 1994. pap. 11.00 (*92-826-8414-8*, CA84-94-662ENC, Pub. by Europ Com) UNIPUB.

Digest of Statistics on Social Protection in Europe, Vol. 2: Invalidity Disability. Eurostat Staff. 208p. 1992. pap. 25.00 (*92-826-3720-4*, CA-82-91-002-EN-C, Pub. by Europ Com) UNIPUB.

Digest of Statistics on Social Protection in Europe, Vol. 4: Family. Eurostat Staff. 208p. 1993. pap. 25.00 (*92-826-3722-0*, CA-82-91-004-EN-C, Pub. by Europ Com) UNIPUB.

Digest of Summer School Programs for College & High School Students. 1991. 27.50 (*0-685-39169-8*) Graduate Group.

Digest of the Criminal Law: Crimes & Punishments. James F. Stephen. lxxvi, 424p. 1991. reprint ed. lib. bdg. 42.50 (*0-8377-2648-4*) Rothman.

Digest of the Decisions of the International Court of Justice, 1976-1985. R. Bernhardt et al. (Fontes Iuris Gentium Ser.: Vol. 7). 768p. 1990. 259.00 (*0-387-51726-X*, 3606) Spr-Verlag.

Digest of the Divine Law. Howard B. Rand. 1943. 8.00 (*0-685-08802-2*) Destiny.

***Digest of the Early Connecticut Probate Records, 3 Vols., Set.** Charles W. Manwaring. 2224p. 1995. reprint ed. 150.00 (*0-8063-1472-9*) Genealog Pub.

Digest of the English Law of Trusts. Keeton & Sheridan. 1987. U.K. text ed. 66.00 (*0-903486-50-4*, U.K.) Butterworth Legal Pubs.

Digest of the Law of Evidence. James F. Stephen. xiv, 226p. 1991. reprint ed. lib. bdg. 32.50 (*0-8377-2647-6*) Rothman.

Digest of the Law of Evidence in Civil & Criminal Cases & a Treatise on Bills of Exchange, & Promissory Notes. Zephaniah Swift. LC 70-37990. (American Law Ser.: The Formative Years). 412p. 1972. reprint ed. 26.95 (*0-405-04035-0*) Ayer.

Digest of the Law of Partnership. Frederick Pollock. xxxvi, 135p. 1988. reprint ed. lib. bdg. 25.00 (*0-8377-2514-3*) Rothman.

Digest of the Law of Trade-Marks & Unfair Trade. Norman F. Hesseltine. xlviii, 390p. 1991. reprint ed. lib. bdg. 42.50 (*0-8377-2245-4*) Rothman.

Digest of the Laws & Decisions Relating to the Appointment, Salary & Compensation of the Officials of the United States Courts, with the Instructions of the Attorney-General to United States District Attorneys, Clerks & Marshals. Ed. by Robert M. Cousar. 300p. 1991. reprint ed. lib. bdg. 37.50 (*0-8377-2018-4*) Rothman.

Digest of the Leos Summer Topical Meetings, 1994. IEEE (Lasers & Electro-Optics Society) Staff. LC 93-80387. 320p. 1994. pap. write for info. (*0-7803-1752-1*, 94TH0606-4); fiche write for info. (*0-7803-1753-X*) Inst Electrical.

Digest of the Public Record of Communism in the United States. Fund for the Republic, Inc. Staff. Ed. by Gerald Grob. LC 76-46078. (Anti-Movements in America Ser.). 1977. lib. bdg. 63.95 (*0-405-09951-7*) Ayer.

Digest of United Kingdom Energy Statistics: 1992. 111p. 1992. pap. 40.00 (*0-11-414158-4*, HM41584) UNIPUB.

Digest of United Kingdom Energy Statistics, 1993. 189p. 1993. pap. 35.00 (*0-11-515328-4*, HM53284, Pub. by HMSO UK) UNIPUB.

Digest of United States Practice in International Law: Cumulative Index, 1973-1980. Marian L. Leich. 371p. 1989. boxed 17.00 (*0-16-021551-X*, S/N 044-000-02282-6) USGPO.

Digest of United States Practice in International Law, 1979. Marian L. Nash. (State Department Publications: No. 9374). 1955p. 1983. 22.00 (*0-16-004393-X*, S/N 044-000-01937-0) USGPO.

Digest of Wills Cases, 1900-1988. A. S. Arora. (C). 1988. 140.00 (*0-685-36458-5*) St Mut.

Digest Shakespeareanae. Ed. by James A. Morgan. LC 75-172743. (Shakespeare Society of New York. Publications: No. 4, Pts. 1 & 7). reprint ed. 37.50 (*0-404-04419-0*) AMS Pr.

Digesta, Vol. I. Justinianus Augustus. Ed. by Paulus Kreuger & Theodorus Mommsen. 960p. 1962. write for info. (*3-296-13801-3*, Pub. by Georg Olms GW) Lubrecht & Cramer.

Digesta, Vol. II. Justinianus Augustus. Ed. by Paulus Kreuger & Theodorus Mommsen. iv, 1044p. 1963. write for info. (*3-296-13802-1*, Pub. by Georg Olms GW) Lubrecht & Cramer.

Digestibility & Amino Acid Availability in Cereals & Oilseeds. Ed. by John W. Finley & Daniel T. Hopkins. LC 85-72941. 304p. 1985. 89.00 (*0-913250-40-6*) Am Assn Cereal Chem.

Digesting the Child Within: And Other Cartoons to Live By. John Callahan. (Illus.). 104p. 1991. pap. 8.00 (*0-688-09488-0*, Quill) Morrow.

Digestion: The Digestive System. Jenny Bryan. LC 92-35052. (Body Talk Ser.). (Illus.). 48p. (J). (gr. 5 up). 1993. text ed. 13.95 (*0-87518-564-9*, Dillon Silver Burdett) Silver Burdett Pr.

Digestion & Dyspepsia. R. T. Trall. 160p. 1975. spiral bd. 9.35 (*0-7873-0892-7*) Mokelumne.

Digestion & the Structure & Function of the Gut. D. F. Magee & A. F. Dalley. (Continuing Education Ser.: Vol. 8). (Illus.). viii, 360p. 1986. 118.50 (*3-8055-4204-6*) S Karger.

Digestion, Assimilation, Elimination & You. Ed Bashaw. 35p. 1987. pap. 2.95 (*0-913923-43-5*) Woodland UT.

Digestive Cancer. A. Canonico et al. (Advances in Medical Oncology Ser.: Vol. 9). 1979. 174.00 (*0-08-024392-4*, Pub. by Pergamon Repr UK) Franklin.

Digestive Disease Pathology, Vol. I. Watanabe. 1988. text ed. 88.00 (*0-07-105328-X*) McGraw.

Digestive Diseases. Albert Mendeloff & James P. Dunn. LC 71-158432. (Vital & Health Statistics Monographs, American Public Health Association). (Illus.). 190p. 1971. 26.50 (*0-674-20580-4*) HUP.

Digestive Diseases in Dogs & Cats. Simpson. 287p. 1991. pap. 65.00 (*0-632-02931-5*) Blackwell Sci.

Digestive Disorders. Joyce Sorenson & Nancy Murray. (Menus for Better Health Ser.). 36p. (Orig.). 1983. pap. 1.95 (*0-911638-08-3*) Witkower.

Digestive Enzymes. Jeffrey Bland. Ed. by Richard A. Passwater & Earl Mindell. (Good Health Guide Ser.). 1983. pap. 2.50 (*0-87983-331-9*) Keats.

Digestive System. Regina Avraham. (Healthy Body Ser.). (Illus.). 104p. (YA). (gr. 6-12). 1989. 18.95 (*0-7910-0015-X*) Chelsea Hse.

Digestive System. Glenn F. Bastian. LC 94-1897. 139p. (C). 1994. pap. 5.25 (*0-06-501710-2*) HarpCollege.

Digestive System. Merce Parramon. (Invisible World Ser.). (Illus.). 32p. (J). (gr. 4 up). 1994. lib. bdg. 14.95 (*0-7910-2126-2*, Am Art Analog) Chelsea Hse.

Digestive System. Alvin Silverstein et al. (Human Body Systems Ser.). (Illus.). 96p. (J). (gr. 5-8). 1994. lib. bdg. 16.98 (*0-8050-2832-3*) TFC Bks NY.

Digestive System see Anatomy & Physiology: A Programmed Approach

Digestive System in Mammals: Food, Form, & Function. Ed. by David J. Chivers & Peter Langer. LC 93-32561. (Illus.). 400p. (C). 1994. 84.95 (*0-521-44016-5*) Cambridge U Pr.

Digestive System: Liver, Biliary Tract & Pancreas see C I B A Collection of Medical Illustrations

Digestive System: Lower Digestive Tract see C I B A Collection of Medical Illustrations

Digestive System: Upper Digestive Tract see C I B A Collection of Medical Illustrations

***Digestive Tract Surgery: A Text & Atlas.** Ed. by Richard H. Bell, Jr. et al. LC 95-981. 1995. write for info. (*0-397-51344-5*) Lippincott.

Digestive Tract Tumors. Ed. by Kiyoshi Inokuchi et al. LC 86-42515. (GANN Monographs on Cancer Research: No. 31). 288p. 1986. 85.00 (*0-306-42297-2*, Plenum Pr) Plenum.

Digesto de Puerto Rico: 1974-1994. suppl. ed. 1994. 90.00 (*0-685-74141-9*) Butterworth Legal Pubs.

Digesto de Puerto Rico: 1974-1994, 23 vols., Set. (SPA.). 1974. boxed 700.00 (*0-88063-501-0*) Michie Butterworth.

Digger Phelps & Notre Dame Basketball. Richard Phelps & Pat Scanlon. LC 81-43. (Illus.). 216p. 1981. 9.95 (*0-685-03834-3*) P-H.

Digger Smoked Out. Warren Murphy. 256p. 1994. 4.95 (*0-7867-0177-3*) Carroll & Graf.

***Diggers.** Patricia Armentrout & David Armentrout. LC 95-3978. (Heavy Equipment Ser.). (J). 1995. write for info. (*1-55916-134-5*) Rourke Bk Co.

Diggers. C. Young. (Machine Board Bks.). (Illus.). 12p. (J). (ps). 1993. bds. 4.50 (*0-7460-1096-6*) EDC.

Diggers. large type ed. Margaret W. Brown. LC 94-7995. (Illus.). 32p. (J). (ps-1). 1995. 14.95 (*0-7868-0006-2*); lib. bdg. 14.89 (*0-7868-2001-2*) Hyprn Child.

Diggers. Paul Stickland. LC 93-12533. (Illus.). 14p. (J). (ps). 1993. reprint ed. 3.50 (*0-525-67453-5*, Lodestar Bks) Dutton Child Bks.

Diggers: Makers of the Australian Military Tradition. Chris D. Coulthard-Clark. (Illus.). 367p. 1993. 44.95 (*0-522-84470-7*) Intl Spec Bk.

Diggers & Cranes. C. Young. (Young Machines Ser.). (Illus.). 32p. (J). (ps-2). 1991. lib. bdg. 13.96 (*0-88110-552-X*, Usborne); pap. 5.95 (*0-7460-0625-X*, Usborne) EDC.

Diggers & Dump Trucks. LC 91-16119. (Eye Openers Ser.). (Illus.). 24p. (J). (gr. 1-6). 1991. pap. 7.95 (*0-689-71516-1*, Aladdin Paperbacks) S&S Childrens.

Diggers & Dumpers. (Snapshop Big Picture Paperbacks Ser.). (Illus.). 32p. (J). (ps-3). 1994. 4.95 (*1-56458-731-2*) Dorling Kindersley.

Digging Deeper: Investigations into Rocks, Shocks, Quakes, & Other Earthy Matters. Sandra Markle. LC 86-27412. (Illus.). 128p. (J). (gr. 4-9). 1987. 15.00 (*0-688-05986-4*) Lothrop.

Digging Deeper: Issues in the Miners' Strike. Ed. by Huw Beynon. 252p. 1985. pap. text ed. 13.95 (*0-86091-820-3*, Pub. by Verso UK) Routledge Chapman & Hall.

Digging Diamonds Daily, 1. C. C. Cribb. LC 77-70215. 12.95 (*0-932046-07-X*) Manhattan Ltd NC.

Digging Diamonds Daily, 2. C. C. Cribb. LC 77-70215. 12.95 (*0-932046-08-8*) Manhattan Ltd NC.

Digging Diamonds Daily, Set. C. C. Cribb. LC 77-70215. write for info. (*0-932046-09-6*) Manhattan Ltd NC.

Digging Dinosaurs. John R. Horner & James Gorman. LC 88-40226. 208p. 1988. 17.95 (*0-89480-220-8*, 1604) Workman Pub.

D

An Asterisk (*) at the beginning of an entry indicates that the title is appearing in BIP for the first time.

Digging Dinosaurs: The Search That Unraveled the Mystery of Baby Dinosaurs. John R. Horner & James Gorman. LC 89-46099. (Illus.). 224p. 1990. reprint ed. pap. 13.00 (*0-06-097314-5*, PL) HarpC.

Digging Down to China. Lesley Frost. (Illus.). 64p. (J). (gr. 1-4). 1968. 9.95 (*0-8159-5306-2*) Devin.

Digging for Buried Treasure. Marilyn Lashbrook. (Illus.). 12p. (J). (gr. k-6). 1984. pap. text ed. 4.25 (*1-55976-141-5*) CEF Press.

Digging for Carter's Grove. Ivor Noel Hume. LC 73-88326. (Archaeological Ser.: No. 8). (Illus.). 61p. (Orig.). 1974. pap. 5.95 (*0-87935-016-4*) Colonial Williamsburg.

Digging for Dinosaurs. Melvin Berger. (Ranger Rick Science Spectacular Ser.). 16p. (J). (gr. 2-4). 1994. pap. text ed. 14.95 (*1-56784-205-4*) Newbridge Comms.

***Digging for Fire & New Morning.** Hughes. 112p. 1994. pap. 11.95 (*0-413-68250-1*, Pub. by Methuen UK) Heinemann.

Digging for Gold. Horatio Alger, Jr. (Works of Horatio Alger Jr.). 1989. reprint ed. lib. bdg. 79.00 (*0-7812-3562-6*) Rprt Serv.

Digging for Gold: Papers on Archaeology for Profit. William K. Macdonald. (Technical Reports: No. 5). 1976. pap. 2.00 (*0-932206-14-X*) U Mich Mus Anthro.

Digging for Gold in Your Own Back Yard: The Complete Homeowners Guide to Lowering Your Real Estate Taxes. Gary Whalen. LC 90-91764. 266p. (Orig.). 1990. pap. 19.95 (*0-9626829-0-X*) REI Pr.

Digging for Gold in Your Own Backyard: The Complete Homeowners Guide to Lowering Your Real Estate Taxes. Gary Whalen. 1992. pap. 19.95 (*0-9626829-1-8*) REI Pr.

Digging for Gold Without a Shovel: Letters of Daniel Wadsworth Coit from Mexico & California. limited ed. Daniel W. Coit. Ed. by George P. Hammond. (Illus.). 1967. 35.00 (*0-912094-11-7*) Old West.

Digging for Indians: Poems. Gary Gildner. LC 77-158183. (Pitt Poetry Series, Pitt Paperback: No. 68). 78p. reprint ed. pap. 25.00 (*0-7837-7052-9*, 2046864) Bks Demand.

Digging for Irish Roots: How to Search for Your Ancestors. Don Cahalan. (Illus.). 220p. 1989. 17.95 (*0-915474-10-7*) Decalogue Bks.

Digging for Shark Teeth. Rick Lott. 1984. pap. 5.00 (*0-938078-19-4*) Anhinga Pr.

Digging In. Robin Bradford. 28p. (Orig.). 1989. pap. 4.00 (*0-945926-04-9*) Paradigm RI.

Digging in Camp Counselor's Handbook, 12 Bks. Jerry Glashagel et al. 40p. 1976. pap. 20.00x (*0-88035-022-9*, 492, YMCA USA) Human Kinetics.

Digging in Camp Director's Handbook. Jerry Glashagel et al. 56p. 1976. pap. 8.50 (*0-88035-025-3*, 491, YMCA USA) Human Kinetics.

Digging into Custer's Last Stand. Sandy Barnard. (Illus.). 72p. (Orig.). 1986. pap. 10.00 (*0-9618087-0-5*) AST Pr.

Digging into Dinosaurs. National Wildlife Federation Staff. (J). (gr. k-8). 1991. pap. 7.95 (*0-945051-33-6*, 75002) Natl Wildlife.

Digging into Language. Carla Heymsfeld. (J). (gr. 5-8). 1987. pap. 9.99 (*0-8224-1916-5*) Fearon Teach Aids.

Digging into Literature. Maureen E. Hay & Margy Kuntz. (J). (gr. 5-8). 1987. pap. 7.99 (*0-8224-1917-3*) Fearon Teach Aids.

Digging into Logic. Sandra Eads & Beverly Post. (J). (gr. 5-12). 1987. pap. 7.99 (*0-8224-4458-5*) Fearon Teach Aids.

Digging into Popular Culture. Ed. by Ray B. Browne & Pat Browne. (Illus.). 186p. (C). 1991. lib. bdg. 34.95 (*0-87972-521-4*); pap. text ed. 17.95 (*0-87972-522-2*) Bowling Green Univ.

Digging into the Past. Deborah Lattimore. (BrainBooster Ser.). (Illus.). 32p. (J). (gr. 3 up). 1986. 5.95 (*0-88679-460-9*) Educ Insights.

Digging into the Past: Twenty-Five Years of Archaeology in Denmark. Ed. by Steen Hvass & Birger Storgaard. (Illus.). 312p. 1993. 87.50 (*87-7288-568-8*, Pub. by Aarhus Univ Pr DK) Coronet Bks.

Digging of Soils by Earthmovers with Powered Parts. V. K. Rudnev. Tr. by M. Sivaramakrishnan. 144p. (C). 1985. text ed. 90.00 (*90-6191-450-7*, Pub. by A A Balkema NE) Ashgate Pub Co.

Digging the Gold: A Story of California. Horatio Alger. 1976. reprint ed. lib. bdg. 23.95 (*0-88411-816-9*, Aeonian Pr) Amereon Ltd.

Digging Through Archaeology. F. Richard Olenchak. (Triad Prototype Ser.). 36p. 1989. pap. 8.95 (*0-936386-49-5*) Creative Learning.

***Digging Through Darkness: Chronicles of an Archaeologist.** Carmel Schrire. LC 94-30778. (Illus.). 304p. (C). 1995. 29.95 (*0-8139-1558-9*) U Pr of Va.

Digging to Australia. Lesley Glaister. 192p. 1993. text ed. 19.00 (*0-689-12162-8*, Atheneum S&S) S&S Trade.

Digging to Australia. large type ed. Lesley Glaister. LC 93-11695. 1993. 17.95 (*0-7862-0031-6*) Thorndike Pr.

Digging to China: Down & out in the Middle Kingdom. J. D. Brown. LC 91-7805. 230p. 1991. 18.95 (*0-939149-51-6*) Soho Press.

Digging to China: Down & Out in the Middle Kingdom. J. D. Brown. LC 91-7805. 230p. 1993. pap. 10.00 (*0-939149-88-5*) Soho Press.

Digging to the Past: Excavations in Ancient Lands. W. John Hackwell. LC 86-13115. (Illus.). 64p. (J). (gr. 3-7). 1986. text ed. 14.95 (*0-684-18692-6*, C Scribner Sons Young) S&S Childrens.

Digging up Bones. 3rd rev. ed. D. R. Brothwell. LC 80-66914. (Illus.). 196p. 1981. pap. 29.95 (*0-8014-9875-9*) Cornell U Pr.

Digging Up Butch & Sundance. Anne Meadows. (Illus.). 416p. 1994. 24.95 (*0-312-10968-7*, Pub. by Thomas Dunne Bks) St Martin.

Digging up Dinosaurs. Aliki. (Let's-Read-&-Find-Out Bk. & Cassette). 32p. (J). (ps-2). 1991. pap. 7.95 (*1-55994-302-5*, Caedmon) HarperAudio.

Digging up Dinosaurs. rev. ed. Aliki. LC 85-42979. (Trophy Let's-Read-&-Find-Out Bk.). (Illus.). 32p. (J). (gr. k-3). 1988. pap. 4.95 (*0-06-445078-3*, Trophy) HarpC Child Bks.

Digging up Dinosaurs. rev. ed. Aliki. LC 87-29949. (Let's-Read-&-Find-Out Science Bk.). (Illus.). 32p. (J). (ps-3). 1988. 15.00i (*0-690-04714-2*) HarpC Child Bks.

Digging up Dinosaurs. rev. ed. Aliki. LC 87-29949. (Let's-Read-&-Find-Out Science Bk.). (Illus.). 32p. (J). (ps-3). 1988. lib. bdg. 14.89 (*0-690-04716-9*, Crowell Jr Bks) HarpC Child Bks.

Digging up Old Moans & Groans. Leona Ferstler. Ed. by Beverly Thorp. 80p. 1989. pap. 7.00 (*1-877628-04-2*) Ironwood Pr.

***Digging up the Bones.** Teresa N. Roberts. 70p. (Orig.). 1994. pap. 7.00 (*0-944920-12-8*) Bellowing Ark Pr.

Digging up the Bones... Pharmacology, Microbiology, Pathology & Biochemistry, 4 vols., Set B. Nikos M. Linardakis. 400p. (Orig.). (C). 1994. Vol. 1, Pharmacology. pap. text ed. 16.00 (*1-884084-00-1*); Vol. 2, Microbiology. pap. text ed. 16.00 (*1-884084-01-X*); Vol. 3, Pathology. pap. text ed. 16.00 (*1-884084-02-8*); Vol.4, Biochemistry. pap. text ed. write for info. (*1-884084-04-4*) Michaelis Med.

Digging up the Bones... Pharmacology, Microbiology, Pathology & Biochemistry, 4 vols., Set B, Set. Nikos M. Linardakis. 400p. (Orig.). (C). 1994. pap. text ed. 64.00 (*1-884084-10-9*) Michaelis Med.

***Digging up the Bones... Vol. 5: Behavioral Science.** Nikos M. Linardakis. (Illus.). 80p. (C). 1995. pap. text ed. 16.00 (*1-884084-11-7*) Michaelis Med.

***Digging up the Bones... Vol. 6: Psychiatry.** Alexander Z. Golbin & Nikos M. Linardakis. (Illus.). 100p. (C). Date not set. pap. text ed. 16.00 (*1-884084-12-5*) Michaelis Med.

Digging up the Mountains: Selected Stories. Neil Bissoondath. 247p. 1986. pap. 4.95 (*0-7715-9246-9*, Pub. by Stoddart Pubng CN) Genl Dist Srvs.

***Digging up the Past.** Randall K. Meyer. (Illus.). 595p. (Orig.). 1994. write for info. (*0-9641984-0-1*) NAP AL.

Digging up the Past. 2nd ed. Charles L. Woolley. LC 77-13325. (Illus.). 125p. 1978. reprint ed. text ed. 35.00 (*0-8371-9853-4*, WODU, Greenwood Pr) Greenwood.

Digging up the Past: The Story of an Archaeological Adventure. Carollyn James. (Illus.). 64p. (J). (gr. 5-8). 1990. lib. bdg. 12.60 (*0-531-10878-3*) Watts.

Digging up Tyrannosaurus Rex. Jack Horner & Don Lessem. LC 92-2204. (Face to Face with Science Ser.). (Illus.). 36p. (J). (gr. 2-6). 1992. 15.00 (*0-517-58783-1*); lib. bdg. 15.99 (*0-517-58784-X*) Crown Bks Yng Read.

***Digging up Tyrannosaurus Rex.** John R. Horner & Don Lessen. 36p. (J). (gr. 2-6). 1995. pap. 6.99 (*0-517-88336-8*) Crown Bks Yng Read.

Diggingest Dog. Al Perkins. LC 67-21920. (Illus.). 72p. (J). (gr. k-3). 1967. 7.99 (*0-394-80047-8*) Beginner.

Diggingest Dog. Al Perkins. LC 67-21920. (Illus.). 72p. (J). (gr. k-3). 1967. lib. bdg. 9.99 (*0-394-90047-2*) Beginner.

Diggings & Doings in Park City. Rae C. Ringholtz. 1977. reprint ed. 7.95 (*0-914740-16-4*) Western Epics.

Diggs-Caminetti Case 1913-1917: For Any Other Immoral Purpose, Set. Robert L. Anderson. LC 90-6004. (Studies in Twentieth Century American History: Vol. 1). 468p. 1990. lib. bdg. 109.95 (*0-88946-320-4*) E Mellen.

Diggstown. Leonard Wise. 1992. mass mkt. 4.99 (*0-312-95089-6*) St Martin.

Diggy Armadillo Goes to Fort Worth Stock Show & Rodeo, Bk. 2: Further Adventures: "Finding Rosita" Ann Pugh et al. LC 93-73103. (Illus.). 54p. (J). (gr. 3-6). 1993. 7.95 (*1-879465-02-7*) Diggy & Assocs.

***Digit-Serial Computation.** Richard Hartley & Keshab K. Parhi. LC 95-6885. (The Kluwer International Ser. in Engineering & Computer Science). 320p. (C). 1995. lib. bdg. 99.50 (*0-7923-9573-5*) Kluwer Ac.

Digital & Analog Communication Systems. 4th ed. Leon W. Couch, II. (Illus.). 832p. (C). 1993. text ed. write for info. (*0-02-325281-2*) Macmillan.

Digital & Analogue Interfacing for Computers. 1990. 87.95 (*0-632-02862-9*) Buttrwrth-Heinemann.

***Digital & Kalman Filtering: An Introduction to Discrete-Time Filtering & Optimum Linear Estimation.** 2nd ed. S. M. Bozic. LC 94-36554. 1994. pap. write for info. (*0-470-23401-6*) Halsted Pr.

Digital & Microprocessor Electronics for Scientific Application. Dennis Barnaal. (Illus.). 384p. (C). 1989. reprint ed. pap. text ed. 21.95 (*0-88133-421-9*) Waveland Pr.

Digital & Microprocessor Engineering. 2nd ed. S. J. Cahill & I. McCrum. LC 93-6499. (Ellis Horwood Series in Electrical & Electronic Engineering). 576p. 1993. write for info. (*0-13-217928-8*, Tavistock-E Horwood); pap. 45.00 (*0-13-213398-9*, Tavistock-E Horwood) Routledge Chapman & Hall.

Digital & Microprocessor Fundamentals: Theory & Applications. William Kleitz. 560p. 1990. text ed. 52.00 (*0-13-209891-1*) P-H.

Digital & Microprogram Electronics: Theory Application Troubleshooting. Byron W. Putman. (Illus.). 416p. (C). 1986. text ed. 52.00 (*0-13-214354-2*) P-H.

Digital at Work: Snapshots from the First Thirty-Five Years. Ed. by Jamie P. Pearson. (History Ser.). (Illus.). 212p. (Orig.). 1992. pap. 19.95 (*1-55558-092-0*, EY-J826E-DP, Digital DEC) Buttrwrth-Heinemann.

Digital at Work: Snapshots of the First Thirty-Five Years. Jamie Pearson. 225p. 1992. pap. 19.95 (*0-13-213489-6*) P-H.

Digital Audio & Compact Disc Technology. 2nd ed. Luc Baert et al. 256p. 1992. pap. 37.95 (*0-7506-0614-2*) Buttrwrth-Heinemann.

***Digital Audio & Compact Disc Technology.** 3rd ed. Luc Baert et al. LC 94-36853. 320p. 1995. pap. 37.95 (*0-240-51397-5*, Focal) Buttrwrth-Heinemann.

Digital Audio Broadcasting: Status Report & Outlook. National Association of Broadcasters Staff. 69p. (Orig.). 1990. pap. 45.00 (*0-89324-098-2*) Natl Assn Broadcasters.

Digital Audio Broadcasting: 1991 Market & Policy Developments. Marcia De Sonne. 100p. 1991. 60.00 (*0-89324-094-X*) Natl Assn Broadcasters.

Digital Audio Engineering: An Anthology. Ed. by John Strawn et al. LC 85-18. (Computer Music & Digital Audio Ser.: Vol. 3). (Illus.). 144p. 1985. 29.95 (*0-86576-087-X*) A-R Eds.

Digital Audio Operations. Francis Rumsey. 256p. 1991. 47.95 (*0-240-51311-8*, Focal) Buttrwrth-Heinemann.

***Digital Audio Signal Processing.** Ed. by John Strawn. (Computer Music & Digital Audio Ser.: Vol. 1). (Illus.). xiv, 283p. (C). 1993. pap. 21.95 (*0-89579-279-6*) A-R Eds.

Digital Avionics Systems. Gary R. Spitzer. 288p. 1987. text ed. 39.95 (*0-13-211517-4*, Busn) P-H.

Digital Avionics Systems: Principles & Practice. 2nd ed. Gary R. Spitzer. 1992. text ed. 50.00 (*0-07-060333-2*) McGraw.

Digital BiCMOS Integrated Circuit Design. S. H. Embabi et al. LC 92-29636. (International Series in Engineering & Computer Science, VLSI, Computer Architecture, & Digital Screen Processing). (C). 1992. lib. bdg. 109.00 (*0-7923-9276-0*) Kluwer Ac.

Digital Biosignal Processing. Ed. by R. Weitkunat. (Techniques in the Behavioral & Neural Sciences Ser.: No. 5). 400p. 1991. 274.50 (*0-444-81140-0*); pap. 80.00 (*0-685-48728-8*) Elsevier.

Digital Board Testing. Test Engineering Institute Staff. (Illus.). 400p. 1981. 450.00 (*0-912253-03-7*) Logical Solns Tech.

Digital Broadband Networks & Services. Lindberg. 1994. text ed. 50.00 (*0-07-037936-X*) McGraw.

Digital Bus Handbook. Joseph Giacomo. 1990. text ed. 68.50 (*0-07-016923-3*) McGraw.

Digital Calculations of Engine Cycles. SAE Staff. LC 64-21831. 1964. 56.00 (*0-08-011104-1*, Pub. by Pergamon Repr UK) Franklin.

***Digital Cameras: The New Era of Color Photography.** John Larish. 1995. 27.95 (*0-941845-14-1*) Micro Pub Pr.

Digital Cardiac Imaging. Ed. by Andrew J. Buda & Edward J. Delp. 1985. lib. bdg. 137.50 (*0-89838-697-7*) Kluwer Ac.

Digital Cartography. Robert G. Cromley. (Illus.). 336p. 1991. text ed. 70.00 (*0-13-710930-X*, 530801) P-H.

Digital Cellular Radio. George Calhoun. (Telecommunications Applications Library). 450p. 1988. text ed. 69.00 (*0-89006-266-8*) Artech Hse.

Digital Cellular Systems. William C. Lee. (Series in Telecommunications). 1994. text ed. write for info. (*0-471-52430-1*) Wiley.

Digital Cellular Telecommunications Systems. Douglas A. Kerr. 1996. text ed. 50.00 (*0-07-034232-6*) McGraw.

***Digital Circuit Design for Computer Science Students: An Introductory Textbook.** N. Wirth. 200p. 1995. 34.50 (*3-540-58577-X*) Spr-Verlag.

Digital Circuit Fundamentals I. Buck Engineering Staff. Ed. by Buck Engineering Tech. Writers. (F. A. C. E. T. Ser.: Vol. 15). (Illus.). 216p. 1990. ring bd. 12.00 (*0-86657-036-5*) Buck Eng Co.

Digital Circuit Fundamentals II. Buck Engineering Staff. Ed. by Buck Engineering Tech. Writers. (F. A. C. E. T. Ser.: Vol. 16). (Illus.). 216p. 1990. ring bd. 12.00 (*0-86657-038-1*) Buck Eng Co.

Digital Circuit Fundamentals, No. I: Instructor's Guide. Buck Engineering Staff. Ed. by Buck Engineering Tech Writers. (F. A. C. E. T. Ser.: Vol. 15). (Illus.). 80p. 1991. pap. text ed. 11.00 (*0-86657-037-3*) Buck Eng Co.

Digital Circuit Logic & Design Through Experimentation. Darrell D. Rose. (Illus.). 256p. (C). 1982. pap. text ed. 12.50 (*0-911908-13-7*) Tech Ed Pr.

Digital Circuit Testing: A Guide to DFT, & Other Techniques. Francis C. Wang. (Illus.). 233p. 1991. text ed. 79.00 (*0-12-734580-9*) Acad Pr.

Digital Circuits. Kenneth Muchow et al. (Illus.). 480p. (C). 1987. 16.95 (*0-685-17183-3*) P-H.

Digital Circuits. J. R. Nowicki & L. J. Adam. (Illus.). 320p. 1991. pap. 27.95 (*0-7131-3641-3*, A6451, Pub. by E Arnold UK) Routledge Chapman & Hall.

Digital Circuits. William J. Streib. (Illus.). 408p. 1990. text ed. 37.28 (*0-87006-713-3*) Goodheart.

Digital Circuits: A Preparation for Microprocessors. Charles W. McKay. LC 77-13058. (Illus.). 1978. 32.95 (*0-685-03835-1*) P-H.

Digital Circuits: Engineers Tutor Series, 3 vols. Amalou Abdelilah. (Illus.). (Orig.). pap. write for info. (*0-318-64993-4*); Vol. 1, 03/1989, 154p. pap. 12.95 (*0-938862-67-7*); Vol. 2, 04/1989, 118p. pap. 12.95 (*0-929704-04-5*) Weber Systems.

Digital Circuits & Microprocessors. Herbert Taub. (Electrical Engineering Ser.). (Illus.). 608p. 1982. text ed. write for info. (*0-07-062945-5*) McGraw.

Digital Circuits & Systems. Richard L. Castellucis. 356p. 1981. teacher ed write for info. (*0-8359-1298-1*, Reston) P-H.

Digital Circuits & Systems. Douglas V. Hall. 560p. (C). 1989. text ed. 38.95 (*0-07-025537-7*) McGraw.

Digital Circuits Engineers Tut. Amalou Abdelilah. 1989. pap. 12.95 (*0-929704-06-1*) Weber Systems.

Digital Circuits with Microprocessor Applications. Paul M. Chirlian. 432p. (C). 1981. text ed. 49.95 (*0-916460-32-0*, Matrix Pubs Inc) Weber Systems.

Digital Codes & Numbering Systems. Leo Rizzo. (Series 870). (Orig.). 1983. student ed, pap. 6.00 (*0-8064-0355-1*, 870); audio 159.00 (*0-8064-0356-X*) Bergwall.

Digital Communication. Edward A. Lee & David G. Messerschmitt. 736p. (C). 1988. lib. bdg. 82.50 (*0-89838-274-2*) Kluwer Ac.

Digital Communication. 2nd ed. Edward A. Lee. LC 93-26197. 912p. (C). 1993. lib. bdg. 120.00 (*0-7923-9391-0*) Kluwer Ac.

***Digital Communication: Overview Summary.** Dave Adamy. (Overview Summaries Ser.). 32p. 1995. pap. 4.95 (*1-885897-08-1*) Lynx Pubng.

Digital Communication: Solutions Manual. 2nd ed. Edward A. Lee. 112p. (C). 1993. pap. text ed. 20.00 (*0-7923-9405-4*) Kluwer Ac.

Digital Communication & Signal Processing. Lapp. Date not set. text ed. write for info. (*0-318-72278-X*) Van Nos Reinhold.

Digital Communication & Signal Processing. T. Lapp. 1988. text ed. write for info. (*0-442-26042-5*) Van Nos Reinhold.

Digital Communication Techniques: Signal Design & Detection, Vol. 1. Marvin K. Simon et al. LC 93-9053. 912p. 1994. text ed. 76.00 (*0-13-200610-3*) P-H.

Digital Communications. Ed. by E. Biglieri & G. Prati. 363p. 1986. 87.25 (*0-444-87911-0*, North Holland) Elsevier.

Digital Communications. Simon Haykin. LC 87-28573. 597p. 1988. Net. text ed. write for info. (*0-471-62947-2*) Wiley.

Digital Communications. 2nd ed. John G. Proakis. (Electrical Engineering Ser.). 928p. (C). 1989. text ed. write for info. (*0-07-050937-9*) McGraw.

***Digital Communications.** 3rd ed. John G. Proakis. LC 94-41620. (Electrical & Computer Engineering Ser.). 1995. text ed. write for info. (*0-07-051726-6*) McGraw.

Digital Communications: Microwave Applications. Kamilo Feher. 1981. text ed. 66.00 (*0-13-214080-2*) P-H.

Digital Communications by Satellite: Modulaton, Multiple Access & Coding. Vijay K. Bhargava et al. LC 91-4052. 592p. 1991. reprint ed. text ed. 84.50 (*0-89464-629-X*) Krieger.

Digital Communications with Space Applications. S. Golomb et al. (Illus.). 228p. 1981. 21.95 (*0-932146-05-8*) Peninsula CA.

***Digital Compression in Video & Audio.** John Watkinson. (Illus.). 256p. 1995. pap. 47.95 (*0-240-51394-0*, Focal) Buttrwrth-Heinemann.

***Digital Compression of Still Images & Video.** Roger Clarke. (Signal Processing & Its Applications Ser.). (Illus.). 480p. 1995. text ed. 65.00 (*0-12-175720-X*) Acad Pr.

Digital Computer. K. Parton. LC 64-14147. 1964. 62.00 (*0-08-012250-7*, Pub. by Pergamon Repr UK) Franklin.

Digital Computer Applications to Process Control: Proceedings of the IFAC-FIP Conference, 6th, Dusseldorf, Brd, Oct., 1980. IFAC-IFIP Conference Staff. Ed. by R. Isermann & H. Kaltenecker. LC 80-41343. (IFAC Proceedings Ser.). 550p. 1981. 245.00 (*0-08-026749-1*, Pub. by Pergamon Repr UK) Franklin.

Digital Computer Basics. 1986. lib. bdg. 79.95 (*0-8490-3758-1*) Gordon Pr.

Digital Computer Basics. (Illus.). 302p. reprint ed. per., pap. 8.50 (*0-16-002068-9*, S/N 008-047-002) USGPO.

Digital Computer Circuits & Concepts. 3rd ed. Bill R. Deem et al. (Illus.). 1980. teacher ed write for info. (*0-8359-1300-7*, Reston) P-H.

Digital Computer Control Systems. G. S. Virk. 240p. (C). 1991. text ed. 40.00 (*0-07-067512-0*) McGraw.

Digital Computer Design Principles with Introduction to Microprocessors. N. L. Sarda. 286p. 1989. 35.00 (*81-209-0018-9*, Pub. by Pitambar Pub II) St Mut.

Digital Computer Electronics: An Introduction to Microcomputers. 2nd ed. Albert P. Malvino. LC 83-8952. (Illus.). 384p. 1983. text ed. 39.95 (*0-07-039901-8*); text ed. write for info. (*0-07-040023-7*) McGraw.

Digital Computer Fundamentals. 6th ed. Thomas C. Bartee. 1985. text ed. write for info. (*0-07-003899-6*) McGraw.

Digital Computer Operator. Jack Rudman. (Career Examination Ser.: C-197). 1994. pap. 23.95 (*0-8373-0197-1*) Nat Learn.

Digital Computer Programmer. Jack Rudman. (Career Examination Ser.: C-198). 1994. pap. 27.95 (*0-8373-0198-X*) Nat Learn.

Digital Computer Specialist. Jack Rudman. (Career Examination Ser.: C-199). 1994. pap. 27.95 (*0-8373-0199-8*) Nat Learn.

Digital Computer Systems Analyst. Jack Rudman. (Career Examination Ser.: C-200). 1994. pap. 27.95 (*0-8373-0200-5*) Nat Learn.

Digital Computer Systems Operator. Jack Rudman. (Career Examination Ser.: C-1249). 1994. pap. 223.95 (*0-8373-1249-3*) Nat Learn.

Digital Computer Systems Programmer. Jack Rudman. (Career Examination Ser.: C-1250). 1994. pap. 27.95 (*0-8373-1250-7*) Nat Learn.

Digital Computer Systems Specialist. Jack Rudman. (Career Examination Ser.: C-1251). 1994. pap. 27.95 (*0-8373-1251-5*) Nat Learn.

Digital Computer Systems Technician. Jack Rudman. (Career Examination Ser.: C-1252). 1994. pap. 29.95 (*0-8373-1252-3*) Nat Learn.

Digital Computers Made Simple. Saul Heller. LC 77-101399. 1978. pap. 2.50 (*0-912146-12-5*, 18-01) Ameco.

Digital Concepts & Applications. Amin R. Ismail & Victor M. Rooney. 965p. (C). 1990. text ed. 56.00 (*0-03-026628-9*); Test bank. write for info. (*0-03-047177-X*) SCP.

An Asterisk (*) at the beginning of an entry indicates that the title is appearing in BIP for the first time.

An Asterisk (*) at the beginning of an entry indicates that the title is appearing in BIP for the first time.

***Digital Imaging & Sound Technology: Telecommunications in the 21st Century.** Stanley Baron. 1995. pap. 42.95 (*0-442-02106-2*) Van Nos Reinhold.

Digital Imaging for Mini-Labs. Roger W. Burdette & Carolyn A. Thieme-Busch. 200p. 1993. pap. 55.00 (*0-9637554-0-4*) Burdette Assocs.

Digital Imaging for Visual Artists. Sally Weiner. 1994. pap. text ed. 49.95 (*0-07-025067-7*) McGraw.

Digital Imaging in Diagnostic Radiology. Ed. by John D. Newell & Charles A. Kelsey. (Illus.). 163p. 1990. text ed. 64.00 (*0-443-08634-6*) Churchill.

***Digital Imaging in Diagnostic Radiology.** fac. ed. Ed. by John D. Newell, Jr. & Charles A. Kelsey. LC 90-2231. (Illus.). 173p. 1990. reprint ed. pap. 49.40 (*0-7837-7876-7*, 2047633) Bks Demand.

Digital Imaging in Health Care. 174p. 1987. 48.00 (*92-1-116380-3*, E.86.II.E.29) UN.

Digital Integrated Circuit Testing from a Quality Perspective. Eugene R. Hnatek. LC 93-13739. 1993. text ed. 54.95 (*0-442-00643-8*) Van Nos Reinhold.

Digital Integrated Circuits. Joseph E. Kasper & Steven A. Feller. 197p. 1982. pap. 12.95 (*0-685-06128-0*) P-H.

Digital Integrated Electronics. Herbert Taub & Donald L. Schilling. (E & EE). (Illus.). (C). 1977. text ed. write for info. (*0-07-062921-8*) McGraw.

Digital Interface Handbook. Francis Rumsey & John Watkinson. LC 93-16385. (Illus.). 224p. 1993. pap. 35.00 (*0-240-51333-9*) Buttrwrth-Heinemann.

***Digital Interface Handbook.** 2nd ed. Francis Rumsey & John Watkinson. (Illus.). 288p. 1995. pap. 47.95 (*0-240-51396-7*, Focal) Buttrwrth-Heinemann.

***Digital Jam Trax-Blues.** 1994. 14.95 (*0-614-01265-1*, AM92218) Omnibus NY.

***Digital Jam Trax-Chicago Blues.** 1994. 14.95 (*0-8256-1425-2*, AM92222) Omnibus NY.

***Digital Jam Trax-Jazz.** 1994. 14.95 (*0-8256-1426-0*, AM92223) Omnibus NY.

***Digital Jam Trax-Modern Blues.** 1994. 14.95 (*0-8256-1423-6*, AM92220) Omnibus NY.

***Digital Jam Trax-More Blues.** 1994. 14.95 (*0-8256-1422-8*, AM92219) Omnibus NY.

***Digital Jam Trax-Rock.** 1994. 14.95 (*0-8256-1424-4*, AM92221) Omnibus NY.

Digital Logic: Analysis, Application & Design. Susan A. Garrod & Robert J. Borns. 970p. (C). 1991. text ed. 57.25 (*0-03-023099-3*) SCP.

Digital Logic: Analysis, Application & Design. Susan A. Garrod & Robert J. Borns. 970p. (C). 1991. Instr.'s manual with transparency masters, test items, & lab results. teacher ed, pap. text ed. 11.00 (*0-03-023102-7*) SCP.

Digital Logic: Analysis, Application & Design. Susan A. Garrod & Robert J. Borns. 970p. (C). 1991. Laboratory manual. student ed, pap. text ed. 25.50 (*0-03-023193-0*) SCP.

Digital Logic Analysis & Design. Ed. by George W. Zobrist. (Computer Engineering & Computer Science Ser.). 208p. (C). 1995. 55.00 (*0-89391-782-6*) Ablex Pub.

Digital Logic & Computer Design. M. Morris Mano. 1979. text ed. 48.00 (*0-13-214510-3*) P-H.

Digital Logic & State Machine Design. 2nd ed. David J. Comer. 514p. (C). 1990. text ed. 63.00 (*0-03-031038-5*); Solutions manual. write for info. (*0-03-031039-3*) SCP.

***Digital Logic Circuit Analysis & Design.** 2nd ed. Victor P. Nelson. LC 94-35122. 1995. text ed. 69.00 (*0-13-463894-8*) P-H.

D

Digital Logic Design. 2nd ed. Brian Holdsworth. 448p. 1987. pap. text ed. 49.95 (*0-408-01566-7*) Buttrwrth-Heinemann.

Digital Logic Design. 3rd ed. B. Holdsworth. LC 94-705. 1994. 15.95 (*0-7506-1615-6*) Buttrwrth-Heinemann.

Digital Logic Design: Tutorials & Laboratory Exercises. John Passafiume & Michael Douglas. 128p. 1984. Net. text ed. write for info. (*0-471-60345-7*) Wiley.

Digital Logic Fundamentals. Buck Engineering Staff. Ed. by Buck Engineering Tech. Writers. (F. A. C. E. T. Ser.: Vol. 14). (Illus.). 242p. 1989. ring bd. 13.00 (*0-86657-034-9*) Buck Eng Co.

Digital Logic Fundamentals. Buck Engineering Staff. Ed. by Buck Engineering Tech. Writers. (F. A. C. E. T. Ser.: Vol. 14). (Illus.). 92p. 1990. teacher ed, pap. text ed. 11.00 (*0-86657-035-7*) Buck Eng Co.

Digital Logic Testing & Simulation. Alexander Miczo. 480p. (C). 1985. Net. text ed. write for info. (*0-471-60365-1*); 10.00 (*0-471-60422-4*) Wiley.

Digital Logic Tutor I: An Introduction to Combinational Logic. Gerard N. Foster. 80p. (C). 1994. pap. write for info. (*0-02-338735-1*) Macmillan.

Digital Magnetic Recording. 2nd ed. Al Hoagland & James E. Monson. 1991. text ed. 79.95 (*0-471-40144-7*) Wiley.

Digital Magnetic Recording. Albert S. Hoagland. LC 82-23203. 164p. (C). 1983. reprint ed. lib. bdg. 16.50 (*0-89874-591-8*) Krieger.

***Digital Mammography: Proceedings of the 2nd International Workshop on Digital Mammography, York, England, 10-12 July 1994.** Ed. by Alastair G. Gale. LC 94-32879. (International Congress Ser.: Vol. 1069). 1994. write for info. (*0-444-81916-9*) Elsevier.

Digital Mantras: The Language of Abstract & Virtual Worlds. Steven R. Holtzman. (Illus.). 460p. 1994. 32.50x (*0-262-08228-4*) MIT Pr.

Digital Mathematics, Infinity & Revival. Jack Ott. (Illus.). 130p. (Orig.). 1988. pap. 7.95 (*0-9621493-0-6*) J Appleseed Pr.

***Digital MBA.** Dan Burnstein. 1995. cd-rom, pap. text ed. 39.95 (*0-07-882099-5*) McGraw.

***Digital Medial Tools.** Wallace. 1995. pap. text ed. 39.95 (*0-12-732855-6*, AP Prof) Acad Pr.

Digital Methods for Signal Analysis. Kenneth G. Beauchamp & C. K. Yuen. (Illus.). 1979. text ed. 65.00 (*0-04-621027-X*) Routledge Chapman & Hall.

Digital Microelectronics. Haldun Haznedar. (C). 1991. text ed. 64.50 (*0-8053-2821-1*) Benjamin-Cummings.

Digital Microwave Receivers. James B. Tsui. (Microwave Library). 288p. 1989. text ed. 78.00 (*0-89006-339-7*) Artech Hse.

Digital Microwave Transmission. I. Frigyes et al. (Studies in Electrical & Electronic Engineering: Vol. 38). 1990. 151.50 (*0-444-98858-0*) Elsevier.

***Digital Modulation & Coding.** Stephen G. Wilson. LC 95-13968. 1995. text ed. 74.00 (*0-13-210071-1*) P-H.

Digital MOS Integrated Circuits. Ed. by Mohamed Elmasry. LC 81-6522. 504p. 1981. 59.95 (*0-87942-151-7*, PC01503) Inst Electrical.

Digital MOS Integrated Circuits: Design for Applications. Niantsu Wang. 426p. 1989. text ed. 87.00 (*0-13-213109-9*) P-H.

Digital MOS Integrated Circuits, No. II: With Applications to Processors & Memory Design. Ed. by M. I. Elmasry. LC 91-40913. (Illus.). 472p. (C). 1992. text ed. 69.95 (*0-87942-275-0*, PC0269-1) Inst Electrical.

***Digital Moving Pictures: Coding & Transmission on ATM Networks.** Jean-Pierre Leduc. LC 94-27698. 1994. 168.50 (*0-444-81786-7*) Elsevier.

***Digital Multimedia Cross-Industry Guide.** Ed. by Philip V. Dodds. 350p. 1995. pap. 49.95 (*0-240-80205-5*, Focal) Buttrwrth-Heinemann.

Digital Networking & T-Carrier Multiplexing. Gilbert Held. 1990. text ed. 54.95 (*0-471-92800-3*) Wiley.

Digital Neural Networks. Sun-Yuang Kung. 400p. 1993. text ed. 65.00 (*0-13-612326-0*) P-H.

Digital Neurocomputing: From Theory to Implementation. Sun-Yuang Kung. 400p. 1991. text ed. 50.00 (*0-685-50516-2*) P-H.

Digital Nonlinear Editing: New Approaches to Editing Film & Video. Thomas A. Ohanian. LC 92-32378. (Illus.). 304p. 1993. 49.95 (*0-240-80175-X*, Focal) Buttrwrth-Heinemann.

Digital Novice. Jim Grubbs. LC 86-90696. (Illus.). 128p. (Orig.). 1987. pap. 9.95 (*0-931387-21-3*) QSKY Pub.

Digital Optical Cellular Image Processor. K. S. Huang. (Series in Computer Science: Vol. 24). 284p. (C). 1990. text ed. 36.00 (*981-02-0337-3*) World Scientific Pub.

Digital Optical Computing. Ed. by Arrathoon. 243p. 1987. 50.00 (*0-89252-787-0*, 752) SPIE.

Digital Optical Computing. Ed. by Ravindra A. Athale. (Critical Reviews of Optical Science & Technology Ser.: Vol. CR 35). 322p. 1990. 73.00 (*0-8194-0274-5*); pap. 58.00 (*0-8194-0255-9*) SPIE.

Digital Optical Computing II. Ed. by R. Arrathoon. 1990. 77.00 (*0-8194-0256-7*, VOL. 1215) SPIE.

Digital Oscilloscope Handbook. Charles G. Masi. (Test & Measurement Ser.). 250p. 1995. 29.95 (*0-7506-9434-3*) Buttrwrth-Heinemann.

Digital Pattern Recognition. 2nd ed. Ed. by K. S. Fu. (Communications & Cybernetics Ser.: Vol. 10). (Illus.). 234p. 1980. pap. 50.00 (*0-387-10207-8*) Spr-Verlag.

Digital Phase Modulation. John B. Anderson et al. (Applications of Communications Theory Ser.). 516p. 1986. 110.00 (*0-306-42195-X*, Plenum Pr) Plenum.

Digital Photo Illustration. J. Gardiner. (Design & Graphic Design Ser.). 1994. text ed. 39.95 (*0-442-01167-9*) Van Nos Reinhold.

Digital Photography. Mikkel Aaland. 1992. pap. 20.00 (*0-679-74260-3*, Random Ref) Random.

Digital Photography: Pictures of Tomorrow. John Larish. 1994. pap. 27.95 (*0-941845-08-7*) Micro Pub Pr.

Digital Piano Complete Method: A Composite of 4 Instruction Books. (Digital Piano Ser.). 1989. pap. 19.95 (*0-88188-847-8*, HL 00242900) H Leonard.

Digital Picture Processing. L. P. Yaroslavsky. (Information Sciences Ser.: Vol. 9). (Illus.). 290p. 1985. 79.00 (*0-387-11934-5*) Spr-Verlag.

Digital Picture Processing, 1. 2nd ed. Azriel Rosenfeld & Avinash C. Kak. LC 81-17611. (Computer Science & Applied Mathematics Ser.). 1982. text ed. 72.00 (*0-12-597301-2*) Acad Pr.

Digital Picture Processing, 2. 2nd ed. Azriel Rosenfeld & Avinash C. Kak. LC 81-17611. (Computer Science & Applied Mathematics Ser.). 1982. text ed. 72.00 (*0-12-597302-0*) Acad Pr.

Digital Pictures: Representation & Compression. A. N. Netravali & B. G. Haskell. LC 87-32722. (Applications of Communications Theory Ser.). 602p. 1988. 105.00 (*0-306-42791-5*, Plenum Pr) Plenum.

***Digital Pictures: Representation, Compression & Standards.** 2nd ed. Arun N. Netravali & Barry G. Haskell. LC 94-42988. (Applications of Communications Theory Ser.). 686p. 1995. 95.00 (*0-306-44917-X*, Plenum Pr) Plenum.

Digital Prepress Book, Vol. 1. Diane Burns. (Illus.). 270p. 1993. 115.00 (*4-87246-287-4*) Bks Nippan.

***Digital Preservation Consortium: Mission & Goals Statement.** Donald Waters & Anne Kenney. 8p. 1994. pap. 10.00 (*1-887334-31-9*) Comm Preserv & Access.

Digital Principles & Applications. Donald P. Leach & Albert P. Malvino. LC 93-29589. 1993. write for info. (*0-02-801821-4*) Glencoe.

Digital Principles & Applications. 3rd ed. Albert P. Malvino & Donald P. Leach. LC 80-19631. (Illus.). 496p. (C). 1981. text ed. 43.95 (*0-07-039875-5*) McGraw.

Digital Principles & Applications. 4th ed. Albert P. Malvino & Donald P. Leach. 544p. 1985. text ed. 42.95 (*0-07-039883-6*) McGraw.

Digital Private Branch Exchanges (PBXs) Edwin R. Coover. LC 88-82227. 384p. 1988. pap. 5.95 (*0-8186-0829-3*, 829) IEEE Comp Soc.

Digital Processing of Analog Signals. Thomas V. Young. (Illus.). 400p. (C). 1985. text ed. 34.95 (*0-685-09147-3*) P-H.

Digital Processing of Geophysical Data: A Review. Roy O. Lindseth. (Course Notes Ser.: No. 1). 282p. 1982. reprint ed. pap. 46.00 (*0-931830-50-8*, 456) Soc Expl Geophys.

Digital Processing of Random Signals. Boaz Porat. 1993. text ed. 74.00 (*0-13-063751-3*) P-H.

Digital Processing of Signals: Theory & Practice. 2nd ed. Maurice Bellanger. 1989. pap. text ed. 79.95 (*0-471-92101-7*) Wiley.

Digital Processing of Signals in Communications, No. 340. (IEE Conference Publications). 1991. pap. text ed. 98.00 (*0-85296-522-2*) Inst Elect Eng.

Digital Processing of Speech Signals. Lawrence R. Rabiner & Ronald W. Schafer. (Signal Processing Ser.). 1978. text ed. 81.00 (*0-13-213603-1*) P-H.

***Digital Productions on the Mbone & the Internet.** Kumar. 300p. 1995. 35.00 (*1-56205-451-1*) New Riders Pub.

***Digital Productions on the Mbone & the Internet.** New Riders Development Group Staff. (Illus.). 300p. (Orig.). 1995. pap. 32.00 (*1-56205-397-3*) New Riders Pub.

***Digital Projects for Musicians.** Contrib by Craig Anderson. 1994. 24.95 (*0-8256-1384-1*, AM91244) Music Sales.

Digital Protection: Protective Relaying from Electromechanical to Microprocessor. L. P. Singh. LC 94-21799. 1995. text ed. 29.95 (*0-470-23436-9*) Wiley.

***Digital Protection for Power Systems.** A. T. Johns & S. K. Salman. (IEEE Power Ser.: No. 15). xii, 204p. 1995. boxed 85.00 (*0-86341-195-9*) Inst Elect Eng.

Digital Radiography. William R. Brody. (Illus.). 240p. 1984. text ed. 80.00 (*0-89004-242-X*) Raven.

Digital Radiography: Selected Topics. Ed. by James G. Kereiakes et al. LC 86-3259. 208p. 1986. 59.50 (*0-306-42188-7*, Plenum Pr) Plenum.

Digital Satellite Communications. 2nd ed. Tri T. Ha. 172p. 1990. student ed 19.95 (*0-685-46983-2*) McGraw.

Digital Satellite Communications Systems & Technologies: Military & Civil Applications. Ed. by Nejat Ince. LC 92-23872. (International Series in Engineering & Computer Science, VLSI, Computer Architecture, & Digital Screen Processing). 624p. (C). 1992. lib. bdg. 144.00 (*0-7923-9254-X*) Kluwer Ac.

Digital Seismology & Fine Modeling of the Lithosphere. Ed. by R. Cassinis et al. (Ettore Majorana International Science Series, Life Sciences: Vol. 42). (Illus.). 432p. 1989. 105.00 (*0-306-43211-0*, Plenum Pr) Plenum.

Digital Signal Compression. Henrique S. Malvar. 1994. 55.00 (*0-13-605882-5*) P-H.

Digital Signal Computers & Processors. Ed. by Andres C. Salazar. LC 77-82295. 352p. 1977. 39.95 (*0-87942-099-5*, PC00968) Inst Electrical.

Digital Signal Processing. Ed. by Vito Cappellini & A. G. Constantinides. 1980. text ed. 139.00 (*0-12-159080-1*) Acad Pr.

Digital Signal Processing. Inmos Limited Staff. 200p. 1989. pap. text ed. 29.80 (*0-13-212804-7*) P-H.

Digital Signal Processing. Murat Kunt. 500p. 1986. text ed. 29.00 (*0-89006-187-4*) Artech Hse.

Digital Signal Processing. Wataru Mayeda. 352p. 1992. text ed. 74.00 (*0-13-211301-5*) P-H.

Digital Signal Processing. Alan V. Oppenheim & Ronald W. Schafer. LC 74-17280. (Illus.). 608p. 1975. text ed. 76.00 (*0-13-214635-5*) P-H.

Digital Signal Processing. Ed. by Lawrence R. Rabiner & Charles N. Rader. LC 72-90358. (Illus.). 528p. 1972. pap. 39.95 (*0-87942-018-9*, PP00182) Inst Electrical.

Digital Signal Processing. Richard A. Roberts & Clifford T. Mullis. (Electrical Engineering Ser.). (Illus.). 650p. (C). 1987. text ed. 67.95 (*0-201-16350-0*) Addison-Wesley.

Digital Signal Processing. 2nd ed. Andrew Sekey. (Illus.). 1987. 498.00 (*0-87942-465-6*, HL0408-5) Inst Electrical.

Digital Signal Processing. 2nd ed. William D. Stanley & James Dougherty. (C). 1984. text ed. 58.00 (*0-8359-1321-X*, Reston); write for info. (*0-318-58075-6*, Reston) P-H.

Digital Signal Processing. Abraham Peled & Bede Liu. LC 85-7984. 320p. 1985. reprint ed. lib. bdg. 34.50 (*0-89874-864-X*) Krieger.

Digital Signal Processing: A Laboratory Approach Using PC-DSP. 2nd ed. Oktay Alkin. LC 93-34430. 1994. pap. text ed. 38.80 (*0-13-328139-6*) P-H.

Digital Signal Processing: A Practical Approach. Emmanuel Ifeachor & Barrie W. Jervis. LC 93-15001. (Electronic Systems Engineering Ser.). (C). 1993. text ed. 66.75 (*0-201-54413-X*) Addison-Wesley.

Digital Signal Processing: A System Design Approach. David J. DeFatta et al. 661p. 1988. Net. text ed. write for info. (*0-471-83788-1*) Wiley.

Digital Signal Processing: Applications to Communications & Algebraic Coding Theories. Salvatore D. Morgera & Hari Krishna. 233p. 1989. text ed. 66.00 (*0-12-506995-2*) Acad Pr.

Digital Signal Processing: Efficient Convolution & Fourier Transform Techniques. Myers. 320p. 1990. boxed 45.00 (*0-13-211814-9*) P-H.

Digital Signal Processing: Principles, Devices & Applications. Jones. 1990. 99.00 (*0-86341-210-6*, CE042) Inst Elect Eng.

Digital Signal Processing: Theory, Applications & Hardware. Richard A. Haddad & Thomas W. Parsons. (Illus.). 624p. (C). 1995. text ed. write for info. (*0-7167-8206-5*) W H Freeman.

Digital Signal Processing: A Laboratory Approach Using PC-DSP. 2nd ed. Oktay Alkin. 1994. pap. text ed. 21.75 (*0-13-102203-2*) P-H.

Digital Signal Processing & Time Series Analysis. Enders A. Robinson & Manuel T. Silvia. 1978. 49.95 (*0-8162-7264-6*) Holden-Day.

***Digital Signal Processing Application Using the ADSP2100 Family Vol. 2.** Analog Devices Staff. 688p. 1994. pap. text ed. 33.60 (*0-13-178567-2*) P-H.

Digital Signal Processing Applications with the TMS320 Family, Vol. 1. Texas Instruments Engineering Staff. 724p. 1986. 38.95 (*0-685-62500-1*, SPRA012A) Tex Instr Inc.

Digital Signal Processing Applications with the TMS320 Family, Vol. 2. Texas Instruments Engineering Staff. 650p. 1990. 38.95 (*0-685-62501-X*, SPRA016) Tex Instr Inc.

Digital Signal Processing Applications with the TMS320 Family, Vol. II. Texas Instruments, Inc. Staff & Panos Papamichalis. 640p. 1990. boxed, text ed. 69.00 (*0-13-212952-3*) P-H.

Digital Signal Processing Applications with the TMS320 Family, Vol. 3. Texas Instruments Engineering Staff. 650p. 1990. 38.95 (*0-685-62502-8*, SPRA017) Tex Instr Inc.

Digital Signal Processing Applications with the TMS320 Family, Vol. III. Texas Instruments, Inc. Staff & Panos Papamichalis. 576p. 1990. text ed. 77.00 (*0-13-212960-4*) P-H.

Digital Signal Processing Design. Ed. by Andrew Bateman & Warren Yates. 400p. (C). 1988. pap. text ed. 225.00 (*0-273-02787-5*, Pub. by Pitman Pubng UK) St Mut.

Digital Signal Processing 'Eighty-Seven: Proceedings of the International Conference, Florence, Italy, 7-10 September. Ed. by Vito Cappellini & A. G. Constantinides. 1002p. 1988. 184.75 (*0-444-70297-0*, North Holland) Elsevier.

Digital Signal Processing in Communication Systems. Marvin E. Frerking. LC 93-25299. 1994. text ed. 69.95 (*0-442-01616-6*) Van Nos Reinhold.

Digital Signal Processing Laboratory Using the ADSP-2101 Microcomputer. Analog Devices, Inc. Staff et al. 1991. text ed. 45.00 (*0-13-218181-9*, 330601) P-H.

Digital Signal Processing Sysltems Using Fsm. Zhang & Dooley. 1994. text ed. write for info. (*0-07-707788-1*) McGraw.

Digital Signal Processing Systems - Finite State Machine Realization. LC 93-12483. 1993. 69.95 (*0-8493-7759-5*, QA) CRC Pr.

***Digital Signal Processing Technology: Proceedings of a Conference Held 17-18 April, 1995, Orlando, Florida.** Ed. by Panos Papamichalis & Robert Kerwin. LC 95-131. (Critical Reviews of Optical Science & Technology Ser.: Vol. 57). 1995. write for info. (*0-8194-1847-1*) SPIE.

Digital Signal Processing Using the Motorola Digital Signal Processor Family. Robert J. Simpson. LC 93-41383. 464p. 1994. pap. text ed. 55.00 (*0-13-490632-2*) P-H.

Digital Signal Processing with C & the TMS320C30. Ralph Chassaing. LC 92-10635. (Topics in Digital Signal Processing Ser.). 1992. text ed. 110.00 (*0-471-55780-3*); pap. text ed. 54.95 (*0-471-57777-4*) Wiley.

Digital Signal Processing with the TMS320C25. Ralph Chassaing & Darrell Horning. LC 08-934031. (Topics in Digital Signal Processing Ser.). 1990. text ed. 74.95 (*0-471-51066-1*) Wiley.

Digital Signal Processing-84: Proceedings of the International Conference Held in Florence, Italy, 5-8 September 1984. Ed. by Vito Cappellini & A. G. Constantinides. 886p. 1985. 161.75 (*0-444-87583-2*, North Holland) Elsevier.

Digital Signal Processing '91: Proceedings of the International Conference, Florence, Italy, 4-6 Sept., 1991. Ed. by Vito Cappellini & A. G. Constantinides. 784p. 1991. 169.00 (*0-444-88890-X*) Elsevier.

Digital Signal Processor, DSP, Markets: Cost Barriers Broken, Hypergrowth Expected Within 18 months. Market Intelligence Staff. 265p. (Orig.). 1992. 1,695.00 (*1-56753-073-7*) Frost & Sullivan.

Digital Signal Transmission. Chris Bissell & David Chapman. (Illus.). 275p. (C). 1992. 84.95 (*0-521-41537-3*); pap. 37.95 (*0-521-42557-3*) Cambridge U Pr.

Digital Simulation in Electrochemistry. 2nd rev. ed. D. Britz. (Illus.). 235p. 1988. pap. 46.00 (*0-387-18979-3*) Spr-Verlag.

Digital Simulation of Dynamic Systems: A Control Theory Approach. Tom T. Hartley et al. LC 94-2660. 416p. 1994. text ed. 61.00 (*0-13-219957-2*) P-H.

***Digital Sourcebook: The Digital Sourcebook.** American Showcase Staff. (New Media Showcase Ser.: No. 4). 220p. 1994. pap. 29.95 (*0-8230-6364-X*) Watsn-Guptill.

Digital Special Analysis with Applications in C & Matlab. Lawrence S. Marple, Jr. 1993. text ed. write for info. (*0-13-015140-8*) P-H.

Digital Spectral Analysis with Applications. Lawrence S. Marple, Jr. (Illus.). 480p. 1987. text ed. 79.00 (*0-13-214149-3*) P-H.

Digital Speech for Low Bit Rate Communication Systems. A. Kondoz. LC 94-4942. (Series in Communication & Distributed Systems). 1995. text ed. 89.95 (*0-471-95064-5*) Wiley.

Digital Style Guide. Susan I. Schultz et al. LC 92-36320. (Software Development Ser.). (Illus.). 349p. (Orig.). 1992. pap. text ed. 24.95 (*1-55558-104-8*, EYJ883EDP, Digital DEC) Buttrwrth-Heinemann.

Digital Subtraction Angiography. Arina Van Breda & Barry T. Katzen. 240p. 1986. 52.00 (*0-316-10774-3*, Little Med Div) Little.

Digital Subtraction Arteriography: An Application of Computerized Fluoroscopy. Charles Mistretta. LC 81-14721. (Illus.). 175p. reprint ed. pap. 49.90 (*0-8357-7623-9*, 2056946) Bks Demand.

Digital Subtraction Imaging in Infants & Children. Ed. by Eric N. Faerber. (Illus.). 208p. 1989. 42.00 (*0-87993-340-2*) Futura Pub.

Digital Switching Control Architectures. Giuseppe Fantauzzi. (Artech House Telecom Engineering Library). 180p. 1990. text ed. 66.00 (*0-89006-452-0*) Artech Hse.

1994

An Asterisk (*) at the beginning of an entry indicates that the title is appearing in BIP for the first time.

D

An Asterisk (*) at the beginning of an entry indicates that the title is appearing in BIP for the first time.

1995

Dilemma of Mexico's Development: The Roles of the Private & Public Sectors. Raymond Vernon. LC 63-17214. 248p. reprint ed. pap. 70.70 (*0-7837-1531-5*, 2041808) Bks Demand.

Dilemma of Modernity: Philosophy, Culture, & Anti-Culture. Lawrence E. Cahoone. LC 86-30195. (SUNY Series in Philosophy). 325p. 1987. 59.50 (*0-88706-549-X*); pap. 19.95 (*0-88706-550-3*) State U NY Pr.

Dilemma of Narcissus. Louis Lavelle. Tr. by William T. Gairdner. 230p. 1993. reprint ed. 22.95 (*0-943914-61-2*); reprint ed. pap. 15.95 (*0-943914-62-0*) Larson Pubns.

Dilemma of Our Times: An Historical Essay. Harold J. Laski. LC 68-14930. 1968. reprint ed. 37.50 (*0-678-05062-7*) Kelley.

***Dilemma of Priestless Sundays.** James Dallen. LC 94-31579. 154p. (Orig.). 1994. pap. 9.95 (*1-56854-042-6*, DP SUN) Liturgy Tr Pubns.

Dilemma of Qualitative Method: Herbert Blumer & the Chicago Tradition. Martyn Hammersley. 270p. 1990. pap. 17.95 (*0-415-01772-6*, A4823) Routledge.

Dilemma of Siting a High-Level Nuclear Waste Repository. Douglas Easterling & Howard Kunreuther. LC 93-45901. 296p. (C). 1995. lib. bdg. 99.95 (*0-7923-9439-9*) Kluwer Ac.

Dilemma of Style: Architectural Ideas from the Picturesque to the Postmodern. Mordaunt J. Crook. LC 87-10821. (Illus.). 340p. 1987. 45.00 (*0-226-12119-4*) U Ch Pr.

Dilemma of Swedish Energy Policy: Implications for International Policymakers. Ragnar Lofstedt. LC 93-24407. (Studies in Green Research). 233p. 1993. 59.95 (*1-85628-217-1*, Pub. by Avebury Pub UK) Ashgate Pub Co.

Dilemma of the Alcoholic Marriage. Al-Anon Family Group Headquarters, Inc. Staff. LC 70-182133. 100p. 1971. 6.00 (*0-910034-18-4*) Al-Anon.

***Dilemma of the Fetus: Fetal Research, Medical Progress, & Moral Politics.** Steven Maynard-Moody. 1995. 23.95 (*0-312-11785-X*) St Martin.

***Dilemma of the Italian-Americans.** Richard Gambino. (Essay Ser.: No. 26). 388p. 1995. 18.00 (*1-55071-037-0*) Guernica Editions.

***Dilemma of the Modern in Japanese Fiction.** Dennis C. Washburn. LC 94-31373. 1995. 30.00 (*0-300-05997-3*) Yale U Pr.

Dilemma of Third World Defense Industries: Supplier Control or Recipient Autonomy, Vol. 3. Ed. by Kwang-il Baek et al. (Monographs of the Center for International Studies, Inha University). (Illus.). 278p. (C). 1989. text ed. 64.50 (*0-8133-0582-9*) Westview.

Dilemma of Toxic Substance Regulation: How Overregulation Causes Underregulation. John Mendeloff. (Regulation of Economic Activity Ser.: No. 17). 450p. 1988. 42.00 (*0-262-13230-3*) MIT Pr.

Dilemma of Wilderness. Corry McDonald. LC 86-5839. 120p. (Orig.). 1987. pap. 10.95 (*0-86534-088-9*) Sunstone Pr.

Dilemmas. 224p. 1982. pap. 3.95 (*0-911605-00-2*) Avalon Hill.

***Dilemmas.** Graham Bennett. Date not set. 22.00 (*0-614-06171-7*, Pub. by Erthscan Pubns UK) Island Pr.

Dilemmas. Gilbert Ryle. (C). 1954. pap. 16.95 (*0-521-09115-2*) Cambridge U Pr.

Dilemmas: A Christian Approach to Moral Decision Making. Richard Higginson. LC 88-29755. 238p. 1989. pap. 11.99 (*0-664-25068-8*) Westminster John Knox.

Dilemmas: Stories & Studies in Sentiment. Ernest C. Dowson. LC 71-157774. (Short Story Index Reprint Ser.). 1977. reprint ed. 16.95 (*0-8369-3886-0*) Ayer.

Dilemmas & Contradictions in Social Theory. G. LLewellyn Watson. 206p. (Orig.). 1987. lib. bdg. 47.50 (*0-8191-6638-3*); pap. 21.00 (*0-8191-6639-1*) U Pr of Amer.

Dilemmas & Difficulties in the Management of Psychiatric Patients. Ed. by Keith E. Hawton & Philip Cowen. (Illus.). 272p. 1990. 75.00 (*0-19-261883-0*); pap. 38.95 (*0-19-261944-6*) OUP.

Dilemmas & Directions in Corrections. Ed. by Peter J. Benekos & Alida V. Merlo. LC 92-81967. (ACJS-Anderson Monograph Ser.). 195p. (C). 1992. pap. text ed. write for info. (*0-87084-235-8*) Anderson Pub Co.

Dilemmas in Clincal Cardiology. Ed. by Melvin D. Cheitlin. LC 70-6558. (Cardiovascular Clinics Ser.: Vol. 21, No. 1). (Illus.). 315p. (C). 1990. text ed. 75.00 (*0-8036-1712-7*) Davis Co.

***Dilemmas in Educational Change.** Ed. by Ted Riecken & Deborah Court. 106p. (Orig.). (C). 1993. pap. text ed. 17.95x (*1-55059-053-7*) Temeron Bks.

Dilemmas in Health Care. rev. ed. Ed. by Basiro Davey & Jennie Popay. LC 92-44760. (Health & Disease Ser.: Bk. 7). 1993. pap. 27.50 (*0-335-19119-3*, Open Univ Pr) Taylor & Francis.

Dilemmas in Human Service Management. Raymond S. Mayers et al. LC 93-50540. (Social Work Ser.: Vol. 23). 184p. (C). 1994. text ed. 31.95 (*0-8261-7740-9*) Springer Pub.

Dilemmas in Modern Jewish Thought: The Dialectics of Revelation & History. Michael L. Morgan. LC 92-7724. 224p. 1992. 35.00 (*0-253-33878-6*) Ind U Pr.

Dilemmas in Regional Policy. Ed. by Antoni Kuklinski & J. G. Lamboy. (Regional Planning Ser.: No. 12). xiv, 457p. 1983. 142.35 (*90-279-3279-4*) Mouton.

Dilemmas in School Finance. Ed. by J. Alan Thomas & Robert K. Wimpelberg. LC 77-17669. 1978. pap. 6.00 (*0-931080-05-3*) U Chicago Midwest Admin.

Dilemmas in the Study of Information: Exploring the Boundaries of Information Science. S. D. Neill. LC 91-24835. (Contributions in Librarianship & Information Science Ser.: No. 70). 208p. 1992. text ed. 49.95 (*0-313-27734-6*, NDN, Greenwood Pr) Greenwood.

Dilemmas of a Reconciler. Richard K. Ullmann. (C). 1963. pap. 3.00 (*0-87574-131-2*) Pendle Hill.

Dilemmas of Activism: Class, Community, & the Politics of Local Mobilization. Ed. by Joseph M. Kling & Prudence S. Posner. 384p. 1990. 39.95 (*0-87722-696-2*) Temple U Pr.

Dilemmas of an Upright Man: Max Planck As Spokesman for German Science. John L. Heilbron. 250p. 1986. 38.00 (*0-520-05710-4*); pap. 13.00 (*0-520-06171-3*) U CA Pr.

Dilemmas of Appeasement: British Deterrence & Defense, 1934-1937. Gaines Post, Jr. LC 92-27606. (Cornell Studies in Security Affairs). 384p. 1993. 48.50 (*0-8014-2748-7*) Cornell U Pr.

Dilemmas of Black Politics: Issues of Leadership & Strategy. Ed. by Georgia A. Persons. LC 92-19599. (C). 1992. text ed. 24.00 (*0-06-500509-0*) HarpCollege.

***Dilemmas of Brief Psychotherapy.** James P. Gustafson. (Illus.). 240p. 1995. 39.50 (*0-306-44975-7*) Plenum.

Dilemmas of Change in British Politics. Ed. by Donley T. Studlar & Jerold L. Waltman. LC 83-14782. 250p. 1984. 29.50 (*0-87805-195-3*) U Pr of Miss.

Dilemmas of Choice. Ed. by Kent A. Price. LC 86-195396. 270p. reprint ed. pap. 77.00 (*0-7837-0116-0*, 2040393) Bks Demand.

Dilemmas of Contemporary Religion. David Martin. LC 78-17704. 1978. text ed. 29.95 (*0-312-21055-8*) St Martin.

Dilemmas of Corrections: Contemporary Readings. 2nd ed. Kenneth C. Haas & Geoffrey P. Alpert. (Illus.). 554p. (Orig.). (C). 1991. pap. text ed. 21.95 (*0-88133-535-5*) Waveland Pr.

***Dilemmas of Corrections: Contemporary Readings.** 3rd rev. ed. Ed. by Kenneth C. Haas & Geoffrey P. Alpert. (Illus.). 622p. (C). 1995. pap. text ed. 24.95x (*0-88133-826-5*) Waveland Pr.

Dilemmas of Democracy: Tocqueville & Modernization. Seymour Drescher. LC 68-12725. 316p. reprint ed. pap. 90.10 (*0-317-26641-1*, 2025437) Bks Demand.

Dilemmas of Development: Reflections on the Counter-Revolution in Development Economics. 2nd ed. John Toye. LC 92-47385. 224p. 1993. text ed. 49.95 (*0-631-18547-X*); pap. text ed. 21.95 (*0-631-18548-8*) Blackwell Pubs.

Dilemmas of Development Assistance: The What, Why & Who of Foreign Aid. Sarah J. Tisch & Michael B. Wallace. LC 93-27343. (Dilemmas in World Politics Ser.). 174p. (C). 1994. text ed. 52.50 (*0-8133-8408-7*); pap. text ed. 14.95 (*0-8133-8409-5*) Westview.

Dilemmas of Discourse: Controversies about the Sociological Interpretation of Language. Anthony J. Wootton. LC 75-35651. (Controversies in Sociology Ser.: No. 4). 122p. 1981. 19.75 (*0-8419-0247-X*) Holmes & Meier.

Dilemmas of Dying: The Ethics of Terminal Care. Ian Thompson. 227p. 1979. 24.00 (*0-85224-367-7*, Pub. by Edinburgh U Pr UK) Col U Pr.

Dilemmas of Enlightenment: Studies in the Rhetoric & Logic of Ideology. Oscar Kenshur. LC 92-36297. (New Historicism Ser.: No. 26). 1993. 45.00 (*0-520-08155-2*) U CA Pr.

***Dilemmas of Freedom.** E. Ancsel. 104p. (C). 1978. 27.00x (*963-05-1694-2*, Pub. by Akad Kiado HU) St Mut.

Dilemmas of Freedom. Eva Ancsel. 104p. 1978. 33.75 (*0-317-53751-2*, Pub. by Collets) St Mut.

Dilemmas of Independence: Ukraine after Totalitarianism. Alexander J. Motyl. LC 93-16966. 200p. 1993. pap. 17.95 (*0-87609-131-1*) Coun Foreign.

Dilemmas of Indian Polity. S. N. Singh. 140p. (C). 1985. 90.00 (*81-85009-13-9*, Pub. by Print Hse II) St Mut.

Dilemmas of Individualism: Status, Liberty, & American Constitutional Law. Michael J. Phillips. LC 82-15580. (Contributions in American Studies: No. 67). x, 226p. 1983. text ed. 55.00 (*0-313-23690-9*, PSF/, Greenwood Pr) Greenwood.

Dilemmas of Internationalism: French Syndicalism & the International Labour Movement, 1900-1914. Susan Milner. LC 90-374. 268p. 1991. 65.00 (*0-85496-617-X*) Berg Pubs.

Dilemmas of Law in the Welfare State. Ed. by Gunther Teubner. (European University Institute, Series A (Law): No. 3). viii, 341p. 1985. 115.40 (*3-11-010495-4*) De Gruyter.

Dilemmas of Law in the Welfare States. Ed. by Gunther Teubner. (European University Institute, Series A (Law): No. 3). 341p. (C). 1988. pap. text ed. 27.95 (*3-11-011491-7*) De Gruyter.

Dilemmas of Leadership: Decision Making & Ethics in the Community College. George B. Vaughan et al. LC 92-8187. (Higher & Adult Education Ser.). 248p. 1992. 29.95 (*1-55542-468-6*) Jossey-Bass.

Dilemmas of Life & Death: Hindu Ethics in a North American Context. S. Cromwell Crawford. LC 93-50087. 233p. (C). 1994. text ed. 57.50 (*0-7914-2165-1*); pap. text ed. 17.95 (*0-7914-2166-X*) State U NY Pr.

Dilemmas of Planning Practice: Values, Skills & Ethics. Patsy Healey & Huw Thomas. 270p. 1991. text ed. 68.95 (*1-85628-173-6*, Pub. by Avebury Pub UK) Ashgate Pub Co.

Dilemmas of Pluralist Democracy: Autonomy vs. Control. Robert A. Dahl. LC 81-16111. (Studies in Political Science: No. 31). 1983. pap. 14.00x (*0-300-03076-2*) Yale U Pr.

Dilemmas of Political Development. 4th ed. Monte Palmer. LC 88-60934. 403p. 1989. pap. 29.00 (*0-87581-331-3*) Peacock Pubs.

Dilemmas of Presidential Leadership: From Washington Through Lincoln. Richard Ellis & Aaron Wildavsky. 245p. (C). 1991. 21.95 (*1-56000-553-X*) Transaction Pubs.

Dilemmas of Presidential Leadership: From Washington Through Lincoln. Aaron Wildavsky & Richard Ellis. 546p. 1989. 39.95 (*0-88738-221-5*); pap. 19.95 (*0-685-50121-3*) Transaction Pubs.

Dilemmas of Reform in China: Political Conflict & Economic Debate. Joseph Fewsmith. LC 93-34487. (Socialism & Social Movements Ser.). 304p. (C). 1994. text ed. 55.00 (*1-56324-327-X*, East Gate Bk); pap. text ed. 21.95 (*1-56324-328-8*, East Gate Bk) M E Sharpe.

Dilemmas of Schooling. Ann Berlak & Harold Berlak. 1989. pap. 15.95 (*0-416-74140-1*, 3566) Routledge Chapman & Hall.

Dilemmas of Social Democracy: The Spanish Socialist Workers Party in the 1980s. Donald Share. LC 88-25102. (Contributions in Political Science Ser.: No. 230). 181p. 1989. text ed. 47.95 (*0-313-26074-5*, SRI/, Greenwood Pr) Greenwood.

Dilemmas of Social Reform: Poverty & Community Action in the U. S. 2nd ed. Peter Marris & Martin Rein. LC 81-16361. (C). 1982. pap. text ed. 7.95 (*0-226-50657-6*) U Ch Pr.

Dilemmas of the American Self. John P. Hewitt. 304p. 1989. 34.95 (*0-87722-656-3*) Temple U Pr.

Dilemmas of the American Self. John P. Hewitt. 304p. 1991. pap. 19.95 (*0-87722-837-X*) Temple U Pr.

Dilemmas of the Dollar: The Economics & Politics of United States International Monetary Policy. rev. ed. C. Fred Bergsten. 608p. 1995. pap. text ed. 35.00 (*0-87332-600-8*) M E Sharpe.

Dilemmas of U. S. Health Care. Eli Ginzberg. 180p. 1994. text ed. 22.95 (*0-02-911715-1*) Free Pr.

Dilemmas of Welfare Policy: Why Work Strategies Haven't Worked. Mildred Rein. LC 82-3726. 190p. 1982. text ed. 49.95 (*0-275-90883-6*, C0883, Praeger Pubs) Greenwood.

Dilemmas of World Politics: International Issues in a Changing World. Ed. by John Baylis & N. J. Rengger. 456p. 1992. 68.00 (*0-19-827351-7*); pap. 19.95 (*0-19-827350-9*) OUP.

Dilemme de l'Etre et du Neant Chez Saint Augustin: Des Premiers Dialogues aux "Confessions" Emilie Z. Brunn. (Bochumer Studien zur Philosophie Ser.: Band 4). iv, 102p. (FRE.). 1984. 22.00 (*90-6032-234-7*, Pub. by B R Gruener NE) Benjamins North Am.

Dilemmes du Roman. Ed. by Catherine Lafarge. LC 89-84497. (Stanford French & Italian Studies: Vol. 65). 364p. (FRE.). 1990. pap. 46.50 (*0-915838-80-X*) Anma Libri.

Diligence in Love. Daisy Newman. 252p. 1992. pap. 11.95 (*0-944350-22-4*) Friends United.

Diligence Produces Results. Billy J. Daugherty. (Orig.). 1991. pap. 0.50 (*1-56267-035-2*) Victory Ctr OK.

Diligence Temples under Cons. Coyle. 1986. pap. 2.95 (*0-87123-408-4*) Bethany Hse.

Dillard's, the First Fifty Years. Leon J. Rosenberg. LC 87-25499. 162p. (Orig.). 1988. 15.95 (*1-55728-021-5*) U of Ark Pr.

Dilligas. Mike Stone. 350p. 1994. 27.95 (*1-883897-02-5*); pap. 14.95 (*1-883897-03-3*) River Rock CA.

Dillinger. Jack Higgins. Ed. by Julie Rubenstein. 208p. 1991. mass mkt. 4.95 (*0-671-67619-9*) PB.

Dillinger: A Short & Violent Life. Robert Cromie & Joseph Pinkston. 266p. reprint ed. lib. bdg. 14.95 (*0-685-35129-7*); reprint ed. pap. text ed. 10.95 (*0-924772-06-9*) CH Bookworks.

Dillinger: The Untold Story. G. Russell Girardin & William J. Helmer. LC 93-35737. 1994. 27.50 (*0-253-32556-0*) Ind U Pr.

***Dillinger Days.** John Toland. (Illus.). 397p. 1995. reprint ed. pap. 14.95 (*0-306-80626-6*) Da Capo.

Dillinger Dossier. Jay R. Nash. LC 83-72087. (Illus.). 312p. 1983. pap. 19.95 (*0-913204-16-1*) December Pr.

Dillinger Poems, Bk. One. Todd Moore. 1978. pap. 2.00 (*0-930600-01-0*) Uzzano Pr.

Dillon after Dark. Leandra Logan. (Temptation Ser.: No. 362). 1991. mass mkt. 2.99 (*0-373-25462-8*) Harlequin Bks.

Dillon Press Book of the Earth. Tom Mariner & Anyon Ellis. LC 94-16855. (J). (gr. 3 up). 1994. text ed. 16.95 (*0-87518-640-8*, Mac Bks Young Read) S&S Childrens.

Dillon Press Children's Atlas. Contrib by Malcolm Porter. LC 93-15593. (Illus.). 96p. (J). (gr. 5 up). 1993. text ed. 16.95 (*0-87518-606-8*, Dillon Silver Burdett) Silver Burdett Pr.

Dillon's Promise. large type ed. Cinda Richards. LC 93-1348. 1993. 19.95 (*0-7927-1630-2*, Curley Lrg Print); pap. 17.95 (*0-7927-1629-9*, Curley Lrg Print) Chivers N Amer.

***Dillon's Reckoning.** Dee Holmes. (Intimate Moments Ser.). 1995. pap. 3.75 (*0-373-07628-2*, 1-07628-0) Silhouette.

Dillsboro. Dillard Noggle & Carolyn Jeffries. LC 86-82646. 187p. (Orig.). 1986. pap. 10.00 (*0-931889-05-7*) Epistemology Pubs.

Dilly Dilly Piccalilli: Poems for the Very Young. Myra C. Livingston. (Illus.). 80p. (J). (gr. 1 up). 1989. text ed. 13.95 (*0-689-50466-7*, McElderry) S&S Childrens.

Dilly the Dinosaur. Tony Bradman. (Illus.). 64p. (J). (gr. 2-5). 1988. pap. 3.95 (*0-14-032337-6*, Puffin) Puffin Bks.

***Dilmun Temple at Saar: Bahrain & Its Archaeological Inheritance.** Harriet Crawford et al. LC 95-15529. 1995. write for info. (*0-7103-0487-0*, Pub. by Kegan Paul Intl UK) Routledge Chapman & Hall.

Dilophosaurus. Oliver. (Dinosaur Library: Set III). (Illus.). 24p. (J). 1984. lib. bdg. 14.00 (*0-86592-215-2*) Rourke Enter.

Dilthey: Philosopher of the Human Studies. Dilthey. Ed. by Rudolf Makkreel. LC 92-25042. 469p. (C). 1993. pap. text ed. 18.95 (*0-691-02097-3*) Princeton U Pr.

Dilthey & Phenomenology. Ed. by Rudolf A. Makkreel & John Scanlon. LC 87-8102. (Current Continental Research Ser.: No. 006). 182p. (Orig.). (C). 1987. lib. bdg. 46.00 (*0-8191-6305-8*, Ctr Adv Res) U Pr of Amer.

Dilthey & the Narrative of History. Jacob Owensby. 208p. 1994. 29.95 (*0-8014-3011-9*) Cornell U Pr.

Dilthey Today: A Critical Appraisal of the Contemporary Relevance of His Work. H. P. Rickman. LC 87-31779. (Contributions in Philosophy Ser.: No. 35). 224p. 1988. text ed. 49.95 (*0-313-25933-X*, RDT/, Greenwood Pr) Greenwood.

Diltheys Erlebnisbegriff: Entstehung, Glanzzeit und Verkuemmerung eines literaturhistorischen Begriffs. Karol Sauerland. 182p. (C). 1972. 74.60 (*3-11-003599-5*) De Gruyter.

Dilue Rose: The Girl Who Saw Texas Independence. Jan Seale. (Texas History Biography Ser.). (Illus.). 30p. (J). (gr. k-3). 1986. pap. 2.95 (*0-936927-21-6*) Knowing Pr.

Diluted Magnetic Semiconductors. Ed. by J. K. Furdyna et al. (Semiconductors & Semimetals Ser.: Vol. 25). 470p. 1988. text ed. 140.00 (*0-12-752125-9*) Acad Pr.

Diluted Magnetic Semiconductors. Ed. by M. Jain. 600p. (C). 1991. text ed. 118.00 (*981-02-0176-1*) World Scientific Pub.

Diluted Magnetic (Semimagnetic) Semiconductors. Ed. by R. L. Aggarwal et al. (MRS Symposium Proceedings Ser.: Vol. 89). 1987. text ed. 37.00 (*0-931837-54-5*) Materials Res.

Diluvio Del Genesis: The Genesis Flood. John Whitcomb. (SPA.). 20.95 (*84-7228-717-3*, 220285, Pub. by Edit Clie SP) TSELF.

***Dilvish the Damned.** Zelazny. 1982. mass mkt. 4.99 (*0-345-33417-5*, Del Rey) Ballantine.

Dilvish the Damned. Roger Zelazny. 1985. mass mkt. 4.99 (*0-345-90175-4*, Del Rey) Ballantine.

Dilworth Theorems: Selected Papers of R. P. Dilworth. K. Bogart et al. (Contemporary Mathematicians Ser.). 450p. 1990. 68.50 (*0-8176-3434-7*) Birkhauser.

Dilys. Grossman. 1982. 12.98 (*0-02-545840-X*) Macmillan.

***Dilys Powell Film Reader.** Dilys Powell. Ed. by Christopher Cook. (Film Reader Ser.). 468p. 1995. 39.95 (*1-55783-206-4*) Applause Theatre Bk Pubs.

Dilys Powell Film Reader. Dilys Powell. Ed. by Christopher Cook. LC 92-12538. 480p. 1993. pap. 17.95 (*0-19-283082-1*) OUP.

Dim-Mak: Death-Point Striking. Erle Montaigue. (Illus.). 240p. 1993. pap. 25.00 (*0-87364-718-1*) Paladin Pr.

***Dim Roads & Dark Nights.** Ruby P. Tartt. Ed. by Alan Brown. 200p. (Orig.). 1993. 21.95 (*0-942979-10-9*); pap. 12.95 (*0-942979-11-7*) Livingston U Pr.

Dim Sum. Rhoda Yee. LC 77-89297. (Illus.). 1977. pap. 5.95 (*0-394-73463-7*, Random) Taylor & Ng.

Dim Sum: Fast & Festive Chinese Cooking. Ruth Law. Ed. by Nancy Crossman. LC 82-45410. (Illus.). 256p. 1985. reprint ed. pap. 9.95 (*0-9614250-9-1*) Whats Cooking.

Dim Sum: How About Some? A Guide to New York's Liveliest Chinese Dining & How to Make a Day of It. Wanda Chin & Michael P. Danowski. LC 90-62423. (Illus.). (Orig.). 1991. pap. 8.95 (*0-9627444-0-9*) NY Niche Pr.

Dim Tales. John Knoepfle. 145p. 1989. pap. 7.00 (*0-935153-12-8*) Stormline Pr.

DIMACO, Dictionnaire des Mathematiques au College. rev. ed. Michel Bouty. 447p. (FRE.). 1991. 29.95 (*0-7859-4846-5*) Fr & Eur.

***DiMaggio: An Illustrated Life.** Dick Johnson & Glenn Stout. (Illus.). 256p. 1995. 29.95 (*0-8027-1311-4*) Walker & Co.

***DiMaggio, the Last American Knight.** Joseph Durso. LC 94-40795. 288p. 1995. 22.95 (*0-316-19730-0*) Little.

Dimanche de la Vie. Raymond Queneau. (FRE.). 1973. pap. 10.95 (*0-8288-3768-6*, M3945) Fr & Eur.

Dimanche de la Vie. Raymond Queneau. (Folio Ser.: No. 442). (FRE.). pap. 8.95 (*2-07-036442-9*) Schoenhof.

Dimanches d'Aout. Patrick Modiano. (FRE.). 1989. pap. 10.95 (*0-7859-2918-5*) Fr & Eur.

Dimanches d'Aout. Patrick Modiano. (Folio Ser.: No. 2042). (FRE.). 1989. pap. 8.95 (*2-07-038130-7*) Schoenhof.

Dimanches d'un Bourgeois de Paris. Guy De Maupassant. 93p. (FRE.). 1988. pap. 19.95 (*0-7859-4763-9*) Fr & Eur.

Dime. Richard Deutch. 1970. pap. 2.50 (*0-685-57777-5*) New Rivers Pr.

Dime Capitan: Raflexiones Sobre la Masculinidad. Rafael L. Ramirez. LC 93-74310. 133p. (Orig.). 1993. pap. 7.95 (*0-929157-18-4*) Ediciones Huracan.

Dime Como Funciona (How Things Work) Steve Parker. (Illus.). 164p. (SPA.). (J). (gr. 4 up). 1992. lib. bdg. 19.90 (*1-56294-179-8*) Millbrook Pr.

Dime, Constanza. Michael L. Noricks. 142p. 1984. pap. 6.50 (*0-88334-180-8*) Longman.

Dime Detectives. Ron Goulart. LC 88-40074. (Illus.). 272p. 1988. 17.95 (*0-89296-191-0*) Mysterious Pr.

Dime for Every Minute of Your Time, That It Takes to Finish a Rhyme: And Other Funraising Poems. Alpha Pyramis. 10p. 1985. pap. 21.95 (*0-913597-75-9*) Prosperity & Profits.

Dime Novel Detective. Ed. by Gary Hoppenstand. LC 82-61847. 254p. 1982. 19.95 (*0-87972-213-4*); pap. 14.95 (*0-87972-214-2*) Bowling Green Univ.

Dime Novel Roundup: Annotated Index 1931-1981. Michael L. Cook. LC 82-73847. 1983. 13.95 (*0-87972-227-4*); pap. 7.95 (*0-87972-228-2*) Bowling Green Univ.

Dime Novel Western. Daryl Jones. LC 78-61073. 1978. 10.95 (*0-87972-098-0*); pap. 5.95 (*0-87972-097-2*) Bowling Green Univ.

Dime Novels. Frank O'Brien. (Illus.). 99p. reprint ed. pap. 25.00 (*0-87556-183-7*) Saifer.

D

An Asterisk (*) at the beginning of an entry indicates that the title is appearing in BIP for the first time.

Dimensions of Loss & Death Education

Curriculum & Resource Guide. 3rd ed. Patricia H. Zalaznik. 474p. 1992. 89.95 (0-931152-12-7) Abundant Res.

The most comprehensive curriculum in death education in America today is now in its third edition. DIMENSIONS OF LOSS & DEATH EDUCATION CURRICULUM & RESOURCE GUIDE, a 474-page loose-leaf bound resource & accompanying teaching aids now include research & investigations done as recently as 1992. HIV/AIDS, CHRONIC & LIFE-THREATENING CONDITIONS & CELEBRATION OF LIFE are new units; a greatly expanded unit on SOCIAL ISSUES balances the edition. Each of the 21 units has its own bibliography & is indexed. This curriculum includes over 3,700 references, print & non-print. The book begins with an extensive TEACHER PREPARATION section. Units are: APPRAISAL OF INITIAL & PERSONAL FEELINGS ABOUT DYING & DEATH; LANGUAGE, DEFINITIONS & THEORIES OF DYING & DEATH; LOSS EXPERIENCES FOLLOWED BY GRIEVING; CULTURAL & HISTORICAL WAYS; RELIGIOUS, SPIRITUAL & PHILOSOPHICAL VIEWS; CHRONIC & LIFE-THREATENING ILLNESSES; HIV/AIDS; PROCESSES OF DYING & DEATH; GRIEF; RESPONSES TO GRIEF OF ANOTHER; FUNERALS & THE FUNERAL PROCESS;

D

An Asterisk (*) at the beginning of an entry indicates that the title is appearing in BIP for the first time.

1997

DENIAL & AVOIDANCE; SUICIDE; SOCIAL ISSUES; THE "SOCIALLY INVISIBLE;" ECONOMIC & LEGAL FACTORS; LIVING PREVENTIVELY; SUMMARY; & CELEBRATION OF LIFE. Also included are an extensive bibliography & an appendix including Patient Self-determination Act, Donor Document, etc. The curriculum is designed for professional education, adult & secondary education. Accompanying items are STUDENT ACTIVITY WORKBOOK (ISBN 0-931152-13-5), $9.95 (Quantity discounts available) & ANSWER KEY, (ISBN 0-931152-14-3), $8.95. Contact: Abundant Resources, Inc., Suite 240, 15655 40th Ave. No., Minneapolis, MN 55446; Phone: 612-557-0272; FAX: 612-557-6334. ***Publisher Provided Annotation.***

Dimensions of Meaning. Ed. by S. I. Hayakawa & William Dresser. LC 68-24164. (Composition & Rhetoric Ser.). (Orig.). (C). 1970. pap. write for info. (*0-672-60902-9*, CR16, Bobbs) Macmillan.

Dimensions of Moral Education. Robert E. Carter. 254p. 1984. pap. 15.95 (*0-8020-6540-6*) U of Toronto Pr.

Dimensions of Morning Sky. Clarence Maloney. 1964. pap. 10.00 (*0-685-62611-3*) Atlantis Edns.

Dimensions of Musical Thinking. Intro. by Eunice Boardman. (Illus.). 128p. (Orig.). (C). 1989. pap. 10.00 (*0-940796-62-7*, 1081) Music Ed Natl.

Dimensions of National Integration: The Experiences & Lessons of Indian History. Nisith R. Ray. (C). 1993. 40.00 (*81-85094-62-4*, Pub. by Punthi Pus II) S Asia.

Dimensions of New Contraceptives, Norplant & Women: A Publication from the Kaiser Forums Sponsored by the Henry J. Kaiser Family Foundation. Ed. by Sarah E. Samuels & Mark D. Smith. 123p. (Orig.). 1992. pap. text ed. 5.00 (*0-944525-11-3*) H J Kaiser.

Dimensions of Non-Alignment. Lazar Mojsov. 282p. 1981. 65.00 (*0-317-53806-3*, Pub. by Collets UK) Pro-Am Music.

Dimensions of Non-Commerical Foodservice Management. A. McCool. 392p. 1994. text ed. 44.95 (*0-442-01358-2*) Van Nos Reinhold.

Dimensions of Nursing Administration. Ed. by Beverly Henry et al. (Illus.). 750p. 1988. pap. 43.95 (*0-86542-051-3*) Mosby Yr Bk.

Dimensions of Orthodox Judaism. Ed. by Rueven P. Bulka. LC 83-260. 471p. 1983. 35.00 (*0-87068-894-4*) Ktav.

Dimensions of Pakistan Movement. Muhammad Munawwar. 367p. 1987. 39.95 (*1-56744-261-7*) Kazi Pubns.

***Dimensions of Parking.** 2nd ed. Urban Land Institute Staff. LC 83-50079. (Illus.). 160p. 1983. reprint ed. pap. 45.60 (*0-7837-8918-1*, 2049630) Bks Demand.

***Dimensions of Parking.** 3rd ed. NPA Staff & ULI Staff. 335p. 1993. pap. text ed. 34.95 (*0-87420-744-4*, D85) Urban Land.

Dimensions of Parking. Urban Land Institute Staff. LC 79-64130. 128p. reprint ed. pap. 36.50 (*0-317-20855-1*, 2023882) Bks Demand.

Dimensions of Peace & Nonviolence: The Gandhian Perspective. Anima Bose. 176p. 1987. 17.50 (*81-212-0076-8*, Pub. by Gian Publng Hse II) S Asia.

Dimensions of Personality: Essays in Honour of H. J. Eysenck. Ed. by R. Lynn. (Illus.). 490p. 1981. 162.00 (*0-08-024294-4*, Pub. by Pergamon Repr UK) Franklin.

Dimensions of Political Communication West Bengal: Nineteen Seventies. Srabani Raichaudhuri. 1986. 17.50 (*0-317-47415-4*, Pub. by KP Bagchi IA) S Asia.

Dimensions of Professional Nursing. 6th ed. Lucie Y. Kelly. (Illus.). 760p. 1991. text ed. 39.50 (*0-08-040303-4*, Pub. by PPI UK) McGraw.

***Dimensions of Professional Nursing.** 7th ed. Lucie Y. Kelly & Lucille A. Joel. LC 94-36655. 768p. 1995. pap. text ed. 33.50 (*0-07-105477-4*) Hlth Prof Div.

Dimensions of Project Management: Fundamentals, Techniques, Organization, Applications. Ed. by H. Reschke & H. Schelle. (Illus.). xvii, 336p. 1990. pap. 77.00 (*0-387-53157-2*) Spr-Verlag.

Dimensions of Psychoanalysis. Ed. by Joseph Sandler. 280p. 1990. 35.00 (*0-8236-1293-7*) Intl Univs Pr.

Dimensions of Psychotherapy: An Experimental & Clinical Approach. Donald R. Stieper & Daniel N. Wiener. LC 65-22494. 1965. 39.50 (*0-89197-622-1*) Irvington.

Dimensions of Radionics: Techniques of Instrumented Distant Healing. 2nd ed. David V. Tansley & Malcolm Rae. (Illus.). 208p. 1992. reprint ed. pap. 16.95 (*0-914732-29-3*) Bro Life Inc.

Dimensions of Reading Difficulties. A. T. Ravenette. 1968. 53.00 (*0-08-012956-0*, Pub. by Pergamon Repr UK) Franklin.

***Dimensions of Register Variation: A Cross-Linguistic Comparison.** Douglas Biber. 512p. (C). 1995. 59.95 (*0-521-47331-4*) Cambridge U Pr.

Dimensions of Renunciation in Advaita Vedanta. Kapil N. Tiwari. 1977. 11.00 (*0-8364-0109-3*) S Asia.

Dimensions of Ring Theory. Constantin Nastasescu & Freddy Van Oystaeyen. 1987. lib. bdg. 124.50 (*90-277-2461-X*) Kluwer Ac.

Dimensions of Rural Transportation. Ed. by D. Panduranga Rao. (C). 1989. 78.50 (*81-210-0235-4*, Pub. by Inter-India Pubns) S Asia.

Dimensions of Scheduled Caste Development in India. Ed. by R. S. Tripathi & P. D. Tiwari. (C). 1991. text ed. 27.50 (*81-85024-99-5*, Pub. by Uppal Pub Hse II) S Asia.

Dimensions of Self Experience: Progress in Self Psychology, Vol. 5. Ed. by Arnold Goldberg. (Progress in Self Psychology Ser.). 320p. 1989. text ed. 36.00 (*0-88163-086-1*) Analytic Pr.

Dimensions of Social Change. M. N. Srinivas. 518p. 1977. 15.95 (*0-318-36966-4*) Asia Bk Corp.

Dimensions of Social Life: Essays in Honor of David G. Mandelbaum. Ed. by Paul Hockings. (New Babylon Studies in the Social Sciences: No. 48). (Illus.). xiv, 712p. (C). 1987. lib. bdg. 226.95 (*0-89925-292-3*) Mouton.

Dimensions of Social Welfare Policy. 2nd ed. Neil Gilbert & Harry Specht. LC 85-20488. (Illus.). 256p. 1985. text ed. write for info. (*0-13-214404-2*, Busn) P-H.

Dimensions of Social Welfare Policy. 3rd ed. Neil Gilbert et al. 256p. (C). 1992. text ed. write for info. (*0-13-218108-8*) P-H.

Dimensions of Socio-Political Change in Mysore, 1918-1940. S. Chandrasekhar. 1985. 32.00 (*0-8364-1471-3*, Pub. by Ashish II) S Asia.

Dimensions of Sociolinguistics in South Asia. Ed. by Edward Dimock. (C). 1992. 42.00 (*81-204-0573-0*, Pub. by Oxford IBH II) S Asia.

Dimensions of Spaces of Siegel Cusp Forms of Degree Two & Three. Minking Eie. LC 84-10956. (Memoirs of the American Mathematical Society Ser.: Vol. 304). 184p. 1984. 17.00 (*0-8218-2305-1*, MEMO/50/304C) Am Math.

Dimensions of Spiritual Education. Norman Dowsett & Sita R. Jayaswal. (Integral Education Ser.: No.4). (Illus.). 91p. 1975. pap. 2.50 (*0-89071-216-6*) Aurobindo Assn.

Dimensions of Spirituality in the Black Experience. Robert E. Dungy. 64p. (Orig.). 1991. 4.95 (*0-8358-0634-0*); teacher ed, pap. 6.95 (*0-8358-0635-9*) Upper Room Bks.

Dimensions of Sport Sociology. Ed. by March L. Krotee. 256p. 1979. text ed. 14.95 (*0-685-03025-3*, Scribners) S&S Trade.

Dimensions of State Mental Health Policy. Ed. by Christopher G. Hudson & Arthur J. Cox. LC 90-7595. 320p. 1990. text ed. 55.00 (*0-275-93252-4*, C3252, Praeger Pubs) Greenwood.

Dimensions of Strategy: Some Indian Perspectives. Ed. by Jayantanuja Bandhopadhyaya. 1989. 21.50 (*81-85195-25-0*, Pub. by Minerva II) S Asia.

Dimensions of Substitute Child Care: A Comparative Study of Foster & Residential Care Practice. M. J. Colton. 301p. 1988. text ed. 59.95 (*0-566-05612-7*, Pub. by Avebury Pub UK) Ashgate Pub Co.

Dimensions of the Americas: Art & Social Change in Latin America & the United States. Shifra M. Goldman. LC 94-7458. 1994. lib. bdg. 80.00 (*0-226-30123-0*); pap. text ed. 29.95 (*0-226-30124-9*) U Ch Pr.

Dimensions of the Cancer Problem. Fikri M. Meleka. xii, 144p. 1983. pap. 39.25 (*3-8055-3622-4*) S Karger.

***Dimensions of the Hermeneutic Circle.** Ronald Bontekoe. 256p. (C). 1996. text ed. 49.95 (*0-391-03933-4*) Humanities.

Dimensions of the Holocaust. 2nd ed. Elie Wiesel et al. 90p. 1990. pap. 9.95 (*0-8101-0908-5*) Northwestern U Pr.

Dimensions of the Holocaust: A Series of Lectures Presented at Northwestern University & Coordinated by the Department of History. 64p. 3.50 (*0-88464-091-4*) ADL.

Dimensions of the Hospitality Industry: A College Introduction. Paul R. Dittmer & Gerald G. Griffin. LC 92-17463. 1993. text ed. 39.95 (*0-442-00770-1*) Van Nos Reinhold.

Dimensions of the Modern Presidency. Edward Kearny. LC 80-68461. (Orig.). 1981. pap. text ed. write for info. (*0-88273-268-4*) Forum Pr IL.

Dimensions of the Sign in Art. Albert Cook. LC 88-5564. (Illus.). 276p. 1989. text ed. 40.00 (*0-87451-448-7*) U Pr of New Eng.

Dimensions of the Word. 6.84 (*0-8215-9805-8*) Sadlier.

Dimensions of Thinking: A Framework for Curriculum & Instruction. Robert J. Marzeno et al. LC 87-72733. 162p. (Orig.). (C). 1988. pap. 10.00 (*0-87120-148-8*, 611-87040) Assn Supervision.

***Dimensions of Thinking & Cognitive Instruction: Implications for Educational Reform.** Ed. by Beau F. Jones & Laura Idol. 536p. 1989. 99.95 (*0-8058-0346-7*) L Erlbaum Assocs.

Dimensions of Thinking & Cognitive Instruction: Implications for Educational Reform, 2 vols., Set. Ed. by Beau F. Jones & Laura Idol. 1989. text ed. 149.95 (*0-8058-0365-3*) L Erlbaum Assocs.

Dimensions of Thought: Current Explorations in Time, Space & Knowledge, 2 vols., 1. Tarthang Tulku. Ed. by Ralph Moon & Steve Randall. 1980. 21.95 (*0-913546-77-1*) Dharma Pub.

Dimensions of Thought: Current Explorations in Time, Space & Knowledge, 2 vols., 1. Tarthang Tulku. Ed. by Steve Randall. 1981. pap. 12.95 (*0-913546-79-8*) Dharma Pub.

Dimensions of Thought: Current Explorations in Time, Space & Knowledge, 2 vols., 2. Tarthang Tulku. Ed. by Ralph Moon & Steve Randall. 1980. 21.95 (*0-913546-78-X*) Dharma Pub.

Dimensions of Thought: Current Explorations in Time, Space & Knowledge, 2 vols., II. Tarthang Tulku. Ed. by Steve Randall. 1981. pap. 12.95 (*0-913546-80-1*) Dharma Pub.

Dimensions of Time & Life. Ed. by J. T. Fraser & Marlene P. Soulsby. (Study of Time Ser.: Vol. VIII). 278p. 1995. text ed. 37.50 (*0-8236-1295-3*) Intl Univs Pr.

Dimensions of Tolerance: What Americans Believe about Civil Liberties. Herbert McClosky & Alida Brill. LC 82-72959. 525p. 1983. 45.00 (*0-87154-591-8*) Russell Sage.

Dimensions of Tolerance: What Americans Believe about Civil Liberties. Herbert McClosky & Alida Brill. 512p. (C). 1986. pap. 17.95 (*0-87154-592-6*) Russell Sage.

Dimensions of Tourism. Joseph Fridgen. Ed. by Ann Halm. LC 90-49122. (Illus.). 316p. 1991. text ed. 62.95 (*0-86612-049-1*) Educ Inst Am Hotel.

Dimensions of Tribal Movements in India. M. C. Paul. (C). 1989. 18.00 (*81-210-0219-2*, Pub. by Inter-India Pubns) S Asia.

Dimensions of Wasteland Development. Hridai R. Yadav. (C). 1989. 56.00 (*81-7022-264-8*, Pub. by Concept II) S Asia.

Dimensions of Work. Richard H. Hall. LC 85-11925. 351p. reprint ed. pap. 100.10 (*0-7837-1125-5*, 2041655) Bks Demand.

Dimensions of Writing. Ann Kinmont. (Studies in Primary Education). 128p. (Orig.). 1990. pap. 24.95 (*0-8464-4330-9*) Beekman Pubs.

Dimensions World Politics. Hastedt. (C). 1990. text ed. 52.00 (*0-06-042674-8*) HarpCollege.

Dimethyl Sulfate. (Environmental Health Criteria Ser.: No. 48). 55p. 1985. pap. 4.80 (*92-4-154188-1*) World Health.

***Dimethyl Sulfoxide (DMSO) Index of New Information with Authors & Subjects.** rev. ed. Science & Life Consultants Association Staff. LC 94-34920. 139p. 1994. 44.50 (*0-7883-0400-3*); pap. 39.50 (*0-7883-0401-1*) ABBE Pubs Assn.

Dimethyl Sulfoxide, Vol. 1: Basic Concepts of DMSO. Ed. by Stanley W. Jacob et al. LC 70-134700. 495p. reprint ed. pap. 141.10 (*0-7837-0643-X*, 2040984) Bks Demand.

Dimethylsulphide: Oceans, Atmosphere & Climate: Proceedings of the International Symposium Held in Belgirate, Italy, 13-15 October 1992. Ed. by Giambattista Restelli. LC 93-30136. 412p. (C). 1993. lib. bdg. 136.00 (*0-7923-2490-0*) Kluwer Ac.

Dimetrodon. Oliver. (Dinosaur Library: Set II). (Illus.). 24p. (J). 1984. lib. bdg. 14.00 (*0-86592-210-1*) Rourke Enter.

Dimetrodon: The Sail-Backed Dinosaur. Elizabeth Sandell. Ed. by Marjorie Oelerich & Harlan S. Hansen. LC 88-39802. (Dinosaur Discovery Era Ser.). (Illus.). 32p. (J). (gr. k-5). 1989. lib. bdg. 12.95 (*0-944280-15-3*); pap. text ed. 5.95 (*0-944280-21-8*) Bancroft-Sage.

Diminished Anti-Poverty Impact of Economic Growth, the Shift to Services, & the Feminization of Poverty. Emily Northrop. LC 93-36057. 192p. 1993. 43.00 (*0-8153-1674-7*) Garland.

Diminished by Death. Ross. (Black Dagger Crime Ser.). 16.50 (*0-86220-824-6*, BD023, Black Dagger) Chivers N Amer.

***Diminished Capacity.** Sherwood Kivaly. 256p. (Orig.). 1995. pap. 10.00 (*0-425-14951-X*, Berkley Trade) Berkley Pub.

Diminished Mind: A Study of Planned Mediocrity in Our Public Schools. Mortimer B. Smith. LC 71-95136. 150p. 1970. reprint ed. text ed. 49.75 (*0-8371-2583-9*, SMDM, Greenwood Pr) Greenwood.

Diminished Mind: One Family Extraordinary Battle with Alzheimer's. Jean Tyler & Harry Anifantakis. 1990. text ed. 16.95 (*0-07-157187-6*) McGraw.

Diminished Mind: One Family's Extraordinary Battle with Alzheimer's. Jean Tyler. 1990. 16.95 (*0-8306-3465-7*) TAB Bks.

Diminished Mind: One Family's Extraordinary Battle with Alzheimer's: The Jean Tyler Story. large type ed. Harry Anifantakis. LC 92-31108. (General Ser.). 420p. 1993. lib. bdg. 20.95 (*0-8161-5602-6*) G K Hall.

Diminished Responsibility. large type ed. Geoffrey Toye. (Mystery Ser.). 608p. 1992. 21.95 (*0-7089-2704-1*) Ulverscroft.

Diminishing Fictions: Essays on the Modern American Novel & Its Critics. Bruce Bawer. LC 87-83084. 336p. 1988. 22.00 (*1-55597-109-1*) Graywolf.

Diminishing Returns in Agriculture. F. Lester Patton. LC 68-57575. (Columbia University. Studies in the Social Sciences: No. 284). reprint ed. 20.00 (*0-404-51284-4*) AMS Pr.

Diminutive, Augmentative & Pejorative Suffixes in Modern Spanish. A. Gooch. (C). 1970. pap. text ed. 3.50 (*0-685-03999-4*, Pergamon Pr) Elsevier.

Diminutive Dramas. 4th ed. Maurice Baring. LC 77-70343. (One-Act Plays in Reprint Ser.). 1977. reprint ed. 18.50 (*0-8486-2012-7*) Roth Pub Inc.

Dimitri Shostakovich: A Catalogue, Bibliography, & Discography. 2nd ed. David Hulme. (Illus.). 400p. 1991. 105.00 (*0-19-816204-9*) OUP.

Dimitri Shostakovich, the Man & His Work: Music Book Index. Ivan I. Martynov. 197p. 1993. reprint ed. lib. bdg. 69.00 (*0-7812-9620-X*) Rprt Serv.

Dimitri Tiomkin: A Portrait. Christopher Palmer. (Illus.). 144p. 1985. 22.00 (*0-9509439-0-8*, Pub. by Scolar Pr UK) Ashgate Pub Co.

Dimitrov of Bulgaria. Charles Moser. LC 79-90385. 360p. 1979. 14.95 (*0-89803-011-0*) Green Hill.

Dimity Convictions: The American Woman in the Nineteenth Century. Barbara Welter. LC 76-8305. 230p. 1976. 16.95 (*0-8214-0352-4*); pap. 12.95 (*0-8214-0358-3*) Ohio U Pr.

Dimona: The Third Temple? The Story Behind the Vanunu Revelation. Mark Gaffney. (Illus.). 300p. (Orig.). (C). 1989. pap. 12.50 (*0-915597-77-2*) Amana Bks.

Dimorphandra (Caesalpiniaceae) M. F. Da Silva. LC 86-647083. (Flora Neotropica Monograph Ser.: No. 44). (Illus.). 128p. 1986. 44.75 (*0-89327-310-4*) NY Botanical.

Dimorphic Fungi in Biology & Medicine. Ed. by H. Vanden Bossche et al. 105.00 (*0-306-44493-3*, Plenum Pr) Plenum.

Dimorphodon. Oliver. (Dinosaur Library: Set III). (Illus.). 24p. (J). 1986. lib. bdg. 14.00 (*0-86592-217-9*) Rourke Enter.

Dimpled Lunatics: The Mad, Mad World of Babyhood. Suzanne Slesin et al. LC 92-8966. 48p. 1993. 14.00 (*0-517-58932-X*, C P Pubs) Crown Pub Group.

Dimyarian Pelecypods of the Mississippi Marshall Sandstone of Michigan see Palaeontographica Americana: No. 2

Dinah for President. Claudia Mills. LC 91-34839. 128p. (J). (gr. 3-7). 1992. text ed. 13.95 (*0-02-766999-8*, Mac Bks Young Read) S&S Childrens.

Dinah for President. Claudia Mills. LC 93-44668. 128p. (J). (gr. 3-7). 1994. pap. 3.95 (*0-689-71854-3*, Aladdin Paperbacks) S&S Childrens.

***Dinah Forever.** Claudia Mills. LC 94-42136. 114p. (J). 1995. 14.00 (*0-374-31788-7*) FS&G.

Dinah in Love. Claudia Mills. LC 93-19256. 144p. (J). (gr. 3-7). 1993. text ed. 13.95 (*0-02-766998-X*, Mac Bks Young Read) S&S Childrens.

Dinah's Mad, Bad Wishes. Barbara M. Joosse. LC 88-884. (Illus.). 32p. (J). (gr. k-3). 1989. lib. bdg. 13.89 (*0-06-023099-1*) HarpC Child Bks.

Dinah's Pain & Other Poems of the Black Life Experience. Big Mama. LC 88-90222. 101p. (Orig.). (C). 1988. pap. 8.95 (*0-9620373-0-3*) Cultral Alliance Foundation.

Dinah's Rebellion: A Biblical Parable for Our Time. Ita Sheres. 176p. 1990. 17.95 (*0-8245-1014-3*) Crossroad NY.

Dinamation's Dinosaur's Alive! Dinamation International Corp. Staff. LC 92-82913. (Illus.). 32p. (J). (ps-2). 1993. pap. 3.95 (*0-590-47082-5*, Cartwheel) Scholastic Inc.

Dinamica de Adiestrar Discipulos. Gary W. Kuhne. 160p. 1980. 3.95 (*0-88113-040-0*) Edit Betania.

Dinamica De Evangelismo: Dynamics of Personal Follow-Up. Gary W. Kuhne. (SPA.). 6.95 (*84-7228-344-5*, 220284, Pub. by Edit Clie SP) TSELF.

Dinamicas de la Escuela Dominical. Ed. by Wilfredo Calderon. 108p. (SPA.). 1973. pap. 4.95 (*0-87148-255-X*) Pathway Pr.

Dinarbas. Ellis C. Knight. Ed. by Ann Messenger. (Early Women Writers 1650-1800 Ser.: No. 2). 160p. 1993. 16.95 (*0-937191-49-3*) Colleagues Pr Inc.

Dinars & Dirhams: Coins of the Islamic Lands: The Early Period. Michael Bates & Elizabeth Savage. (Nasser D. Khalili Collection of Islamic Art: Vol. XIX). (Illus.). 304p. (C). 1995. 245.00 (*0-19-727617-2*) OUP.

Dina's Book. Herbjorg Wassmo. Tr. by Nadia Christensen. 448p. 1994. 22.95 (*1-55970-243-5*) Arcade Pub Inc.

Dindon. Georges Feydeau. (FRE.). 1989. pap. 10.95 (*0-7859-3148-1*, 2253048771) Fr & Eur.

Dine: Orgin Myths of the Navaho Indians. Aileen O'Brien. 1988. reprint ed. lib. bdg. 75.00 (*0-7812-0065-2*) Rprt Serv.

***Dine: Origin Myths of the Navaho Indians.** Aileen O'Bryan. (Bureau of American Ethnology Bulletins Ser.). 187p. 1995. lib. bdg. 79.00 (*0-7812-4163-4*) Rprt Serv.

Dine Bahane: The Navajo Creation Story. Paul G. Zolbrod. LC 84-6920. 442p. 1987. reprint ed. pap. 16.95 (*0-8263-1043-5*) U of NM Pr.

Dine Orange County: The Orange County Register Guide to Great Eating. Kinney Littlefield & Kitty Morgan. (Register Bookshelf Ser.). (Illus.). 128p. (Orig.). 1994. pap. text ed. 1.37 (*0-9635868-9-0*) OC Register.

Dine Out & Lose Weight. Michel Montignac. 1991. pap. 19.95 (*2-906236-17-9*, Pub. by Editions Artulen) Montignac USA.

Dine, the Navajo. Ed. by Susan L. Shaffer. (Native Peoples of the Southwest Ser.: Level 6). (Illus.). (J). (gr. 6). 1987. teacher ed 197.95 (*0-934351-26-0*); student ed 4.95 (*0-934351-31-7*); sl. 294.43 (*0-934351-15-5*) Heard Mus.

Dinefwr Castle. Rob Gittins. (C). 1983. pap. 15.00x (*0-86383-032-3*, Pub. by Gomer Pr UK) St Mut.

Diner De Babette. Karen Blixen. 253p. (FRE.). 1989. pap. 11.95 (*0-7859-2107-9*, 2070380955) Fr & Eur.

Diner en Ville. Claude Mauriac. (FRE.). 1985. pap. 13.95 (*0-7859-4229-7*) Fr & Eur.

Diner Guys. Chip Silverman. Ed. by Stewart Richardson. 416p. 1989. 18.95 (*1-55972-009-3*, Birch Ln Pr) Carol Pub Group.

***Diner on the Wall.** Tom Soybel. 60p. (J). (ps up). 1995. pap. 8.95 (*1-883650-23-2*) Windswept Hse.

Dinero: Money. Andrew Murray. (SPA.). 2.95 (*84-7228-824-2*, 220286, Pub. by Edit Clie SP) TSELF.

Dinero para la Universidad: Una Guia para Padres: Companero para Cash for College. Cynthia R. Mckee. 1994. pap. 9.00 (*0-688-13611-7*) Hearst Bks.

Dinero, Sexo y Poder. Richard J. Foster. Tr. by Juan S. Araujo. 208p. (SPA.). (C). 1989. pap. 4.95 (*0-88113-057-5*) Edit Betania.

***Diners.** rev. ed. John Baeder. LC 94-21218. 1995. write for info. (*0-8109-2611-3*) Abrams.

Diner's Dictionary: Food & Drink from A to Z. John Ayto. LC 93-11306. 400p. (C). 1994. 25.00 (*0-19-866193-2*) OUP.

Diner's Guide to Japan: Wining & Dining the Japanese Way. Boye De Mente. LC 89-51720. (Illus.). 154p. (Orig.). 1990. pap. 5.95 (*0-8048-1641-7*) C E Tuttle.

Dinetah: An Early History of the Navajo People. Lawrence D. Sundberg. Ed. by James C. Smith, Jr. LC 94-32959. (Illus.). 128p. (Orig.). (J). (gr. 5-12). 1995. pap. 10.95 (*0-86534-221-0*) Sunstone Pr.

Dinetah: Navajo History, Vol. II. Robert A. Roessel. 180p. 1983. 24.00 (*0-936008-09-1*) Rough Rock Pr.

Dinetah Tapes. Dale Freeman. 160p. 1993. pap. 7.95 (*1-880365-85-5*) Prof Pr NC.

Ding: The Life of Jay Norwood Darling. David L. Lendt. LC 89-7432. (Iowa Heritage Collection). (Illus.). 216p. 1989. reprint ed. pap. 10.95 (*0-8138-0406-X*) Iowa St U Pr.

1998

An Asterisk (*) at the beginning of an entry indicates that the title is appearing in BIP for the first time.

D

An Asterisk (*) at the beginning of an entry indicates that the title is appearing in BIP for the first time.

1999

Dinner with Doctor Rocksteady. Frank Russell. 64p. (Orig.). 1987. pap. 9.95 (*0-938507-11-7*) Ion Books.

Dinners & Nightmares. 3rd ed. Diane Di Prima. 1994. pap. 12.95 (*0-86719-395-6*) Last Gasp.

***Dinners for Two.** O'Connor. 1994. 24.95 (*1-883914-07-8*) Menus & Music.

Dinner's in the Freezer! More Mary & Less Martha. 3rd ed. Jill Bond. (Illus.). 256p. 1993. Wkbk. student ed 18.00 (*0-9645396-0-8*) Great Chr Bks.

***Dinner's Ready: Fifty-Two Weekly Schemes that Transform One Meal into Five.** Andrew Schloss & Ken Bookman. LC 94-26834. (Illus.). 1995. write for info. (*0-688-12720-7*) Morrow.

Dinner's Ready: Turning Cooking into Child's Play. Shelley M. Hess & Bruce Gleason. (Illus.). 50p. (Orig.). 1991. pap. text ed. 9.99 (*0-9624448-4-7*) S Hess Facemaker.

Dinner's Ready, Mom. Helen Gustafson. LC 86-11802. 96p. (Orig.). (J). (gr. k-3). 1986. pap. 8.95 (*0-89087-470-0*) Celestial Arts.

Dinnertime. Claire Henley. (Animal Board Bks.). (Illus.). 14p. (J). (ps). 1994. bds. 3.95 (*0-448-40826-0*, G&D) Putnam Pub Group.

Dinnertime. Jan Pienkowski. (Pienkowski Minipops Ser.). (Illus.). 10p. (J). (ps up). 1991. 4.95 (*0-8431-2963-8*); pap. 9.95 (*0-8431-0961-0*) Price Stern.

***Dinnertime.** Winton. 1995. 2.99 (*0-517-12100-X*) Random Hse Value.

Dinnertime for Animals see Books for Young Explorers

Dinny & the Witches. William Gibson. 1961. pap. 4.75 (*0-8222-0311-1*) Dramatists Play.

***Dino: Grosse PC Lexikon der Dinosaurier 1 CD-ROM (12 CM)** Sybex Staff. (CD-ROM (12 CM)). (GER.). 1994. cd-rom 55.00 (*0-7859-8500-X*, 3815597633) Fr & Eur.

Dino: Living High in the Dirty Business of Dreams. Nick Tosches. 1993. mass mkt. 5.99 (*0-440-21412-2*) Dell.

Dino & Yo - Dino & Me: Bilingual Puzzles - Rompecabezas Bilingues. Ed. by Ariel Kochane. Tr. & Illus. by Mercedes D'Adderio. (Ser. 1). 16p. 1990. student ed 2.50 (*0-9626264-0-6*) El Dado Milagroso.

Dino Campana: Orphic Songs. Tr. by I. L. Salomon. 1968. 7.95 (*0-8079-0036-2*); pap. 3.95 (*0-8079-0037-0*) October.

Dino Compagni's Chronicle of Florence. Daniel E. Bornstein. LC 85-29512. (Middle Ages Ser.). (Illus.). 140p. (Orig.). (C). 1986. pap. text ed. 17.95 (*0-8122-1221-5*) U of Pa Pr.

Dino Den. YES Entertainment Corp. Staff. (Pop-Up Storybook). 2p. (J). (ps-2). 1993. write for info. (*1-883366-03-8*) YES Ent.

Dino Dots. Dougal Dixon. LC 88-28583. 96p. (J). 1988. pap. 4.95 (*0-88166-122-8*) Meadowbrook.

Dino Dots. Dougal Dixon. 1989. 4.95 (*0-671-67084-0*) S&S Trade.

Dino Dreams ABCs: Learning the ABCs. (J). (ps). 1994. 6.95 (*1-57036-016-2*, Bedrock Press) Turner Pub GA.

Dino Expert. Julie Brillhart. LC 92-43474. (J). 1993. write for info. (*0-8075-1597-3*) A Whitman.

Dino, Godzilla, & the Pigs: My Life on Our Missouri Hog Farm. Mary E. Fricke. LC 93-17898. 185p. 1993. 20.00 (*0-939149-96-6*) Soho Press.

Dino Hug. Connie E. Kelly. 15p. (J). (ps-3). 1994. pap. text ed. 3.95 (*0-9641814-0-1*) C E Kelly.

***Dino-Might.** Rick Walton. (Illus.). 64p. (Orig.). (J). 1995. pap. 3.99 (*1-885628-08-0*) Buckaroo Bks.

D

Dino-Mite Dinosaur Jokes. Jeff Rovin. Ed. by Ruth Ashby. (Illus.). 96p. (J). 1994. pap. 2.99 (*0-671-88258-9*, Minstrel Bks) PB.

Dino Mites Declare War! FamilyVision Press Staff. LC 93-71624. (Dino Mites Ser.). (Illus.). 80p. (J). 1993. pap. 8.95 (*1-56969-100-2*) FamilyVision.

Dino Petriali, No. 23. Ed. by Kyoichi Tsuzuki. (Art Random Ser.). (Illus.). 48p. 1990. 32.95 (*4-7636-8540-6*) Bks Nippan.

***Dino Quiz Book.** Schlein. 1995. pap. (*0-590-48121-5*) Scholastic Inc.

Dino, the Ding Bat Cat. Jean Richardson. LC 92-17736. (Illus.). 48p. (J). (gr. 1-3). 1992. 12.95 (*0-89015-869-X*) Sunbelt Media.

Dino, the Star Keeper. Marek Mann. Ed. by Jill Max. Tr. by Mangold Verlag. LC 91-21304. (Magic Mountain Fables Ser.). (Illus.). 24p. (J). (gr. k-3). 1991. lib. bdg. 14.60 (*1-56074-028-0*) Garrett Ed Corp.

***Dino-Trekking: The Ultimate Family Guide to Fun with Dinosaurs.** Kelly M. Halls. LC 95-7877. 1995. write for info. (*0-471-11498-7*) Wiley.

Dino Valentino. Randy M. Taylor. (Illus.). 33p. (J). (gr. k-5). 1988. write for info. (*0-937745-05-7*) Traditions Pr.

Dinoflagellate Cysts from the Nordic Seas. Amy L. Dale & Barry Dale. Ed. by Susumu Honjo. (Ocean Biocoenosis Ser.: No. 5). (Illus.). 20p. (Orig.). 1992. pap. text ed. 10.00 (*1-880224-04-6*) Woods Hole Ocean.

Dinoflagellates. David L. Spector. 1984. text ed. 158.00 (*0-12-656520-1*) Acad Pr.

Dinoflagellates of the Coastal Waters of the Western Pacific. A. Bohm. (BMB Ser.). 1936. pap. 15.00 (*0-527-02243-8*) Periodicals Srv.

***Dino's Ski Adventure.** Meg Hilly-Anderson. 32p. (J). 1995. write for info. (*0-9632484-2-7*) Tempest Bk.

Dinosaur. (Jumbo Fun Coloring & Activity Bks.). (Illus.). 288p. (J). 1991. pap. 2.99 (*0-517-67870-5*) Random Hse Value.

Dinosaur. (Ultimate Sticker Ser.). (J). (ps-3). 1993. pap. 6.95 (*1-56458-247-7*) Dorling Kindersley.

Dinosaur. Dougal Dixon. (DK Action Packs Ser.). (Illus.). (J). (gr. 3-7). 1994. 19.95 (*1-56458-683-9*) Dorling Kindersley.

Dinosaur. David Norman & Angela Miller. LC 88-27167. (Eyewitness Bks.). (Illus.). 64p. (J). (gr. 5 up). 1989. 16.00 (*0-394-82253-6*); lib. bdg. 16.99 (*0-394-92253-0*) Knopf Bks Yng Read.

Dinosaur. David Norman. (Illus.). 192p. 1991. 25.00 (*0-13-218140-1*) P-H Gen Ref & Trav.

Dinosaur. David Norman. 1993. pap. 15.00 (*0-671-87472-1*) P-H Gen Ref & Trav.

Dinosaur. 2nd ed. Carl E. Baugh & Clifford A. Wilson. (Illus.). 184p. 1991. reprint ed. pap. 12.95 (*0-939497-01-8*) Promise Pub.

Dinosaur: The Story Behind the Scenery. rev. ed. Allen Hagood & Linda West. LC 90-60037. (Illus.). 48p. 1990. pap. 6.95 (*0-88714-041-6*) KC Pubns.

Dinosaur ABC's Activity Book. rev. ed. Ed. by Richard B. Bliss. (Illus.). 32p. (J). (gr. k-3). 1986. pap. 3.95 (*0-89051-113-6*) Master Bks.

Dinosaur Action Set. Malcolm Whyte. (Action Sets Ser.). (Illus.). 24p. (Orig.). (J). (gr. 1 up). 1986. pap. 5.95 (*0-8431-1758-3*, Troubador) Price Stern.

Dinosaur Activity Book. (Illus.). 64p. (Orig.). (J). (gr. 2-5). 1993. pap. 2.95 (*1-56144-300-X*, Honey Bear Bks) Modern Pub NYC.

Dinosaur Activity Fun Box. (Illus.). (J). (gr. k-3). 1993. 25.41 (*1-56144-306-9*, Honey Bear Bks) Modern Pub NYC.

***Dinosaur Adventure.** Date not set. pap. 35.00 (*1-56997-090-4*) Knowldge Adv.

Dinosaur Almanac. Q. L. Pearce. (Illus.). 96p. (J). (gr. 1 up). 1994. pap. 4.95 (*1-56565-175-8*) Lowell Hse Juvenile.

Dinosaur Alphabet Book. Jerry Pallotta. (Jerry Pallotta's Alphabet Bks.). (Illus.). 32p. (Orig.). (J). (ps-4). 1990. 14.95 (*0-88106-467-X*); lib. bdg. 15.88 (*0-88106-683-4*); pap. 6.95 (*0-88106-466-1*) Charlesbridge Pub.

Dinosaur Alphabet Book. Patricia Whitehead. LC 84-8839. (ABC Adventures Ser.). (Illus.). 32p. (J). (gr. k-2). 1985. lib. bdg. 11.59 (*0-8167-0363-9*); pap. text ed. 2.95 (*0-8167-0364-7*) Troll Assocs.

Dinosaur & Other Prehistoric Animal Factfinder. Michael Benton. LC 92-53119. (Illus.). 256p. (Orig.). (J). (gr. 4-8). 1992. pap. 12.95 (*1-85697-802-8*, Kingfisher LKC) LKC.

***Dinosaur Ate My Homework.** Ray Nelson et al. (Illus.). 48p. (J). (gr. k-6). 1994. 14.95 (*1-56977-400-5*) Flying Rhino.

Dinosaur Babies. Maida Silverman. LC 88-4690. (Illus.). (J). 1990. pap. 4.95 (*0-671-69438-3*, Litl Simon S&S) S&S Childrens.

Dinosaur Babies, Set, Bk. 1 of 2. Ed. by Jane H. Buxton. (Pop-Up Set Ser.). (Illus.). (J). (ps-3). 1991. Set. 21.95 (*0-87044-841-2*) Natl Geog.

Dinosaur Babies: A Step One Book. Lucille R. Penner. LC 90-36045. (Step into Reading Bks.). (Illus.). 32p. (Orig.). (J). (ps-1). 1991. pap. 3.50 (*0-679-81207-5*) Random Bks Yng Read.

Dinosaur Babies: A Step One Book. Lucille R. Penner. LC 90-36045. (Step into Reading Bks.). (Illus.). 32p. (Orig.). (J). (ps-1). 1991. lib. bdg. 7.99 (*0-679-91207-X*) Random Bks Yng Read.

Dinosaur Beach. Liza Donnelly. (Illus.). 32p. (Orig.). (J). (ps-3). 1991. pap. 2.50 (*0-685-43744-2*) Scholastic Inc.

Dinosaur Bob: And His Adventures with the Family Lazardo. William Joyce. LC 87-30796. (Illus.). 32p. (J). (ps-3). 1988. 15.00 (*0-06-023047-9*); lib. bdg. 14.89 (*0-06-023048-7*) HarpC Child Bks.

Dinosaur Bob & His Adventures with the Family Lazardo. William Joyce. LC 87-30796. (Illus.). 48p. (J). (ps-3). 1994. pap. 4.95 (*0-06-443247-5*, Trophy) HarpC Child Bks.

***Dinosaur Bob & His Adventures with the Family Lazardo.** limited ed. William Joyce. LC 94-19100. (Laura Geringer Book Ser.). (Illus.). 48p. (J). (ps-3). 1995. 150.00 (*0-06-025429-7*) HarpC Child Bks.

Dinosaur Bob & His Adventures with the Family Lazaro. Joyce. (J). 1995. lib. bdg. 14.89 (*0-06-021075-3*) HarpC.

Dinosaur Bob & His Adventures with the Family Lazaro. William Joyce. (J). (ps-3). 1995. 15.00 (*0-06-021074-5*, HarpT) HarpC.

***Dinosaur Bob Doll.** William Joyce. (Illus.). (J). (ps-3). 1995. 15.95 (*0-694-00696-3*, Festival) HarpC Child Bks.

Dinosaur Bob Gift Edition. Joyce. (J). Date not set. 40.00 (*0-06-023851-8*, HarpT) HarpC.

Dinosaur Bones. Aliki. LC 85-48246. (Let's-Read-&-Find-Out Science Bk.). (Illus.). 32p. (J). (ps-3). 1988. lib. bdg. 14.89 (*0-690-04550-6*, Crowell Jr Bks) HarpC Child Bks.

Dinosaur Bones. Aliki. (Trophy Let's-Read-&-Find-Out Bk.). (Illus.). 32p. (J). (gr. k-4). 1990. pap. 4.95 (*0-06-445077-5*, Trophy) HarpC Child Bks.

Dinosaur Bones! C. E. Thompson. (Illus.). 32p. (J). (ps-3). 1992. 6.95 (*0-448-41087-7*, G&D) Putnam Pub Group.

Dinosaur Book. G. Zanini. (Fascinating World of Dinosaurs Ser.). (Illus.). 32p. (J). (gr. k-6). 1985. 5.98 (*0-517-42525-4*) Random Hse Value.

Dinosaur Brains: Dealing with All Those Impossible People at Work. Albert J. Bernstein & Sydney C. Rozen. 1993. mass mkt. 4.95 (*0-345-36713-8*) Ballantine.

Dinosaur Brains: Dealing with All Those Impossible People at Work. Albert J. Bernstein & Sydney C. Rozen. 1989. text ed. 27.95 (*0-471-61808-X*) Wiley.

Dinosaur Carton Craft. Hideharu Naito. (Illus.). 68p. (Orig.). 1992. pap. 10.95 (*0-87040-911-5*) Japan Pubns USA.

Dinosaur Chase. Carolyn B. Otto. LC 90-2021. (Illus.). 32p. (J). (ps-1). 1991. lib. bdg. 14.89 (*0-06-021614-X*) HarpC Child Bks.

Dinosaur Color & Pattern Book. Jerome C. Brown. (J). (gr. k-3). 1989. pap. 9.99 (*0-8224-2322-7*) Fearon Teach Aids.

Dinosaur Coloring Book. V. Nichols. (Illus.). 32p. (Orig.). (J). (gr. k-6). 1993. pap. 2.95 (*1-879424-50-9*) Nickel Pr.

Dinosaur Coloring Book. Anthony Rao. (Illus.). (J). (gr. k-3). 1980. pap. 2.50 (*0-486-24022-3*) Dover.

Dinosaur Coloring Book. Malcolm White. (Color & Story Bks.). (Illus.). 32p. (Orig.). (J). (gr. 1-6). 1982. pap. 4.95 (*0-8431-1708-7*, Troubador) Price Stern.

***Dinosaur Cookbook.** Michael L. Ellis, 3rd. (Illus.). (Orig.). 1993. pap. text ed. 3.50 (*0-929178-22-X*) Valley Forge Pub.

Dinosaur Cousins? Bernard Most. LC 86-18485. (Illus.). 40p. (J). (ps-3). 1987. 13.95 (*0-15-223497-7*, HB Juv Bks) HarBrace.

Dinosaur Cousins? Bernard Most. 32p. (J). (ps-3). 1990. pap. 4.95 (*0-15-223498-5*, Voyager Bks) HarBrace.

Dinosaur Cowboys Puppet Theatre. Judy Lichtenstein. (J). (ps-3). 1994. 10.95 (*1-55550-882-0*) Universe.

Dinosaur Creatures & More. (Dinosaur Flip-Ups Ser.). (Illus.). 5p. (J). (gr. k-3). 1993. bds. 3.50 (*1-56144-355-7*, Honey Bear Bks) Modern Pub NYC.

Dinosaur Cut & Color Activity Book. 1988. pap. 3.99 (*0-517-66281-7*) Random Hse Value.

Dinosaur Cut & Use Stencils. Ellen Sandbeck. 64p. 1989. pap. 4.95 (*0-486-25923-4*) Dover.

Dinosaur Dances. Jane Yolen. (Illus.). 40p. (J). 1990. 14.95 (*0-399-21629-4*, Putnam) Putnam Pub Group.

Dinosaur Data Book. Diagram Group Staff. 320p. (Orig.). 1990. pap. 12.95 (*0-380-75896-2*) Avon.

Dinosaur Day. Liza Donnelly. 32p. (J). (ps-3). 1987. pap. 2.50 (*0-590-41800-9*) Scholastic Inc.

***Dinosaur Days.** Marilynn Barr. (Illus.). 48p. 1993. teacher ed, pap. 5.95 (*0-87827-956-3*, MM 1977) Evan-Moor Corp.

Dinosaur Days. Marilynn G. Barr. (Illus.). 48p. (J). (ps-1). 1993. pap. 5.95 (*1-878279-56-4*) Monday Morning Bks.

Dinosaur Days. David Lloyd. Incl. Silly Games. 1985. 3.95 (*0-394-87380-7*); Breakfast. 1985. 3.95 (*0-394-87378-5*); Terrible Thing. 1985. 3.95 (*0-394-87381-5*); (Illus.). 32p. (J). (ps-1). 1985. write for info. (*0-318-59173-1*) Random Bks Yng Read.

Dinosaur Days. Linda Manning. LC 93-28443. (Illus.). 32p. (J). (ps-2). 1993. lib. bdg. 12.95 (*0-8167-3315-5*); pap. 3.95 (*0-8167-3316-3*) BrdgeWater.

Dinosaur Days. Joyce Milton. LC 84-17861. (Step into Reading Bks.). (Illus.). 48p. (J). (gr. k-3). 1985. lib. bdg. 7.99 (*0-394-97023-3*); pap. 3.99 (*0-394-87023-9*) Random Bks Yng Read.

Dinosaur Days. Joyce Milton. (Step into Reading Book & Cassette Library). 48p. (J). (gr. k-3). 1988. audio, pap. 6.99 (*0-394-89774-9*) Random Bks Yng Read.

Dinosaur Days in Texas. Tom Allen et al. LC 88-37237. (Illus.). 64p. (J). (gr. 3 up). 1989. lib. bdg. 15.95 (*0-937460-30-3*); pap. 11.95 (*0-937460-92-3*) Hendrick-Long.

Dinosaur Debut. rev. ed. Aunt Eeebs. (Illus.). 24p. (J). (ps-2). 1991. reprint ed. pap. write for info. (*1-878908-00-6*) Rivercrest Indus.

Dinosaur Detective. Beverly Armstrong. (Skill Builder Ser.). (Illus.). 32p. (J). (gr. k-3). 1979. 3.95 (*0-88160-075-X*, LW 808) Learning Wks.

Dinosaur Diary: My Triassic Homeland. Lynett Gillette. (Illus.). 32p. (J). (gr. 4). 1988. pap. 2.95 (*0-945695-00-4*) Petrified Forest Mus Assn.

Dinosaur Dictionary. D. F. Glut. (Fascinating World of Dinosaurs Ser.). (Illus.). (J). (gr. 2-6). 1985. pap. 5.98 (*0-517-45589-7*) Random Hse Value.

Dinosaur Dictionary. Donald F. Glut. (YA). (gr. 9 up). 1972. 12.50 (*0-8065-0283-5*, Citadel Pr) Carol Pub Group.

Dinosaur Dictionary. Donald F. Glut. (Illus.). 218p. 1976. reprint ed. pap. 6.95 (*0-8065-0519-2*, Citadel Pr) Carol Pub Group.

Dinosaur Dig. Kathryn Lasky. LC 89-13212. (Illus.). 64p. (J). (gr. 3 up). 1990. 13.95 (*0-688-08574-1*); lib. bdg. 13.88 (*0-688-08575-X*) Morrow Jr Bks.

Dinosaur Digs: A Guide to Museums, Sites & Opportunities to Learn about Dinosaurs in U. S. & Canada. Richard Will & Margery Read. LC 92-73118. (Illus.). 150p. (Orig.). 1992. pap. 18.95 (*1-56626-004-3*) Country Rds.

Dinosaur Dilemma: Fact or Fantasy. Dennis G. Lindsay. (Creation Science Ser.: Vol. 7). 1990. per. 6.95 (*0-89985-279-3*) Christ for the Nations.

Dinosaur Dioramas to Cut & Assemble. Matthew Kalmenoff. (J). 1983. pap. 4.95 (*0-486-24541-1*) Dover.

Dinosaur Discoveries: How to Create Your Own Prehistoric World. Robin West. (Craft Bks.). (Illus.). 72p. (J). (gr. k-5). 1989. lib. bdg. 19.95 (*0-87614-351-6*, Carolrhoda) Lerner Group.

Dinosaur Discovery. Carrel Muller & Ethel M. Jacques. (Illus.). 32p. (J). (gr. 4-6). 1987. student ed 5.00 (*0-915785-02-1*) Bonjour Books.

Dinosaur Discovery Era, 12 vols., Set. 199.00 (*0-944280-24-2*) Ency Brit Ed.

Dinosaur Dot-To-Dot Activity Book. Jill Osborne. 32p. (J). 1989. pap. 1.25 (*0-89375-837-X*) Troll Assocs.

Dinosaur Dots. Monica Russo. (Illus.). 96p. (J). 1991. pap. 4.95 (*0-8069-7388-9*) Sterling.

Dinosaur Dream. Dennis Nolan. LC 89-78208. (Illus.). 32p. (J). (ps-2). 1990. text ed. 14.95 (*0-02-768145-9*, Mac Bks Young Read) S&S Childrens.

Dinosaur Dream. Dennis Nolan. LC 93-48409. (Illus.). 32p. (J). (gr. k-3). 1994. pap. 4.95 (*0-689-71832-2*, Aladdin Paperbacks) S&S Childrens.

Dinosaur Dreams. Allan Ahlberg. LC 90-2943. (Illus.). 24p. (J). (ps up). 1991. 12.95 (*0-688-09955-6*); lib. bdg. 12.88 (*0-688-09956-4*) Greenwillow.

Dinosaur Dreams. Kerry Westell. (Annick Press Ser.: Series 8). (Illus.). 24p. (Orig.). (J). (ps-2). 1989. pap. 0.99 (*1-55037-049-9*, Pub. by Annick CN) Firefly Bks Ltd.

Dinosaur Dreams. Allan Ahlberg. Ed. by Amy Cohn. LC 90-2943. (Funnybones Ser.). (Illus.). 32p. (J). (gr. k up). 1994. reprint ed. pap. 4.95 (*0-688-13641-9*, Mulberry) Morrow.

Dinosaur Dress Up. Allen Sirois. LC 91-10583. (Illus.). 32p. (J). (ps-3). 1992. 15.00 (*0-688-10459-2*, Tambourine Bks); lib. bdg. 14.93 (*0-688-10460-6*, Tambourine Bks) Morrow.

Dinosaur Drove. Ed. by Workbench Magazine Staff. (Workbench Plans Ser.). (Illus.). 15p. Date not set. 12.95 (*0-86675-067-3*) KC Pub.

Dinosaur Dynasty, 5 titles. Dougal Dixon. 160p. (J). (gr. k-4). 1994. lib. bdg. 99.65 (*1-884756-00-X*) Davidson Titles.

Dinosaur Egg Mystery. M. Christine Butler. (J). (ps-3). 1992. 11.95 (*0-8120-6297-3*); pap. 5.95 (*0-8120-1379-4*) Barron.

Dinosaur Eggs. Francis Mosley. (Illus.). 32p. (J). (ps-2). 1992. pap. 5.95 (*0-8120-4959-4*) Barron.

Dinosaur Eggs & Babies. Ed. by Kenneth Carpenter et al. (Illus.). 448p. (C). 1994. 79.95 (*0-521-44342-3*) Cambridge U Pr.

Dinosaur Encyclopedia. Michael J. Benton. Ed. by Wendy Barish. (Illus.). 192p. (J). (gr. 3-7). 1984. pap. 7.95 (*0-671-51046-0*, S&S Bks Young Read) S&S Childrens.

Dinosaur Faces. Pierre-Marie Valat. (Illus.). 16p. (J). (ps up). 1990. 14.95 (*0-525-44631-1*, DCB) Dutton Child Bks.

Dinosaur Family Tree. Kunihiko Hisa & Sylvia A. Johnson. (Discovering Dinosaurs Ser.). (Illus.). 64p. (J). (gr. 4 up). 1990. lib. bdg. 17.50 (*0-8225-2203-9*, Lerner Publctns) Lerner Group.

Dinosaur Fantastic. Ed. by Mike Resnick & Martin H. Greenberg. 320p. (Orig.). 1993. mass mkt. 4.99 (*0-88677-566-3*) DAW Bks.

Dinosaur for a Day. Jim Murphy. (Illus.). (J). 1992. 15.95 (*0-590-42866-7*, Scholastic Hardcover) Scholastic Inc.

Dinosaur for Gerald. Helena C. Pittman. (Gerald Bks.). (Illus.). 32p. (J). (ps-3). 1990. lib. bdg. 18.95 (*0-87614-431-8*, Carolrhoda) Lerner Group.

Dinosaur Fossils. Alvin Granowsky. LC 91-23407. (World of Dinosaurs Ser.). (Illus.). 32p. (J). (gr. 1-4). 1992. lib. bdg. 19.97 (*0-8114-3253-X*); pap. 3.95 (*0-8114-6228-5*) Raintree Steck-V.

Dinosaur Fright. Colin Threadgall. LC 91-40049. (Illus.). 32p. (J). (ps up). 1993. 15.00 (*0-688-11733-3*, Tambourine Bks); lib. bdg. 14.93 (*0-688-11734-1*, Tambourine Bks) Morrow.

Dinosaur Fun File. Clive Hopwood. (Illus.). (J). (gr. 3-6). 1992. pap. 4.95 (*1-56680-508-2*) Mad Hatter Pub.

Dinosaur Funbook. William Johnson. (Illus.). 40p. (J). (gr. 1 up). 1982. pap. 3.50 (*0-8431-1704-4*, Troubador) Price Stern.

Dinosaur Funny Bones. Jean B. Polhamus. Ed. by Cherie Rayburn. (Illus.). 27p. (J). (gr. k-6). 1994. pap. text ed. 14.25 (*0-944943-53-5*, 23846-0) Current Inc.

Dinosaur Funny Bones. Jean B. Polhamus & M. Funai. (J). 1980. 4.95 (*0-13-214536-7*) P-H.

Dinosaur Garden. Liza Donnelly. (Illus.). 32p. (J). (ps-3). 1991. pap. 2.50 (*0-590-43172-2*) Scholastic Inc.

Dinosaur Giants & More. (Dinosaur Flip-Ups Ser.). (Illus.). 5p. (J). (gr. k-3). 1993. bds. 3.50 (*1-56144-356-5*, Honey Bear Bks) Modern Pub NYC.

Dinosaur Heresies. Robert T. Bakker. 480p. 1995. pap. 12.95 (*0-8217-2859-8*) Zebra.

Dinosaur Heresies: New Theories Unlocking the Mystery of the Dinosaurs & Their Extinction. Robert T. Bakker. Ed. by Maria D. Guarnaschelli. LC 86-12643. (Illus.). 448p. 1986. 24.95 (*0-688-04287-2*) Morrow.

***Dinosaur Hill.** Diana Loski & Linda Sniffen. (Illus.). (Orig.). (J). (gr. 3-8). 1995. pap. 3.75 (*1-885101-16-3*) Writers Pr Srv.

***Dinosaur Hunt.** (J). (gr. k-3). 1995. 15.95 (*0-399-22777-6*, Grosset-Putnam) Putnam Pub Group.

Dinosaur Hunt! Rolf E. Johnson & Carol A. Piggins. LC 91-50336. (True Adventure Ser.). (Illus.). 32p. (J). (gr. 2-8). 1993. lib. bdg. 15.93 (*0-8368-0740-5*); lib. bdg. 17.27 (*0-685-61502-2*) Gareth Stevens Inc.

Dinosaur Hunt Activity Book. Jeffrey Nelson. (Orig.). (J). 1994. pap. 2.99 (*0-8125-9439-8*) Tor Bks.

Dinosaur Hunters. Kate McMullan. LC 88-30742. (Step into Reading Bks.). (Illus.). 48p. (Orig.). (J). (gr. 2-4). 1989. 3.50 (*0-394-81150-X*); lib. bdg. 7.99 (*0-394-91150-4*) Random Bks Yng Read.

Dinosaur Hunters: Eccentric Amateurs & Obsessed Professionals. David Spalding. LC 93-15319. 1993. 24.95 (*1-55958-338-X*) Prima Pub.

***Dinosaur Hunters: Eccentric Amateurs & Obsessed Professionals.** David A. Spalding. 1994. pap. 14.95 (*1-55958-590-0*) Prima Pub.

Dinosaur Hunter's Kit. (Discovery Kit Ser.). (Illus.). 64p. (Orig.). (J). (gr. 2 up). 1990. pap. 17.95 (*0-89471-804-5*) Running Pr.

Dinosaur in Trouble. Sharon Gordon. (Illus.). 32p. (J). (gr. k-2). 1980. lib. bdg. 7.89 (*0-89375-374-2*); pap. 1.95 (*0-89375-274-6*) Troll Assocs.

Dinosaur Invasion. Malcolm Hulke. (Dr. Who Ser.: No. 3). 1989. pap. 3.50 (*1-55817-190-8*, Pinnacle NY) Windsor NY.

Dinosaur Is the Biggest Animal That Ever Lived & Other Wrong Ideas You Thought Were True. Seymour Simon. LC 83-48960. (Illus.). 64p. (J). (gr. 2-5). 1984. lib. bdg. 14.89 (*0-397-32076-0*, Lipp Jr Bks) HarpC Child Bks.

Dinosaur Is the Biggest Animal That Ever Lived, & Other Wrong Ideas You Thought Were True. Seymour Simon. LC 83-48960. (Trophy Nonfiction Bk.). (Illus.). 64p. (J). (gr. 2-5). 1986. reprint ed. pap. 5.95 (*0-06-446053-3*, Trophy) HarpC Child Bks.

Dinosaur Island. Max Haynes. LC 90-48148. (Illus.). 32p. (J). (ps up). 1991. 13.95 (*0-688-10329-4*); lib. bdg. 13.88 (*0-688-10330-8*) Lothrop.

Dinosaur Island. Edward Packard. (Choose Your Own Adventure Ser.: No. 138). (J). (gr. 4-7). 1993. pap. 3.50 (*0-553-56007-7*) Bantam.

***Dinosaur Island.** large type ed. Edward Packard. LC 94-24103. (ChooseYour own Adventure Ser.: No. 138). (Illus.). 128p. (J). 1995. lib. bdg. 15.93 (*0-8368-1306-5*) Gareth Stevens Inc.

An Asterisk (*) at the beginning of an entry indicates that the title is appearing in BIP for the first time.

Dinosaur Jokes. Judy Bixenman. (Funny Side up Ser.). (Illus.). 32p. (J). (gr. 1-4). 1991. 19.93 (*0-89565-728-7*) Childs World.

Dinosaur Jokes & Riddles Book. Jeffrey Nelson. (Illus.). 24p. (J). (gr. 3 up). 1988. pap. 1.95 (*1-56288-341-0*) Checkerboard.

Dinosaur Journal: Making Sense of a Young Son's Death. Curtis Mortimer. (Illus.). 150p. 1995. pap. 12.95 (*0-940895-19-6*) Cornerstone IL.

Dinosaur Lady. Anne M. Duquette. (Romance Ser.). 1994. mass mkt. 2.99 (*0-373-03328-1*, 1-03328-1) Harlequin Bks.

Dinosaur Learning Fun. Imogene Forte. (Illus.). 48p. (J). (ps-3). 1987. pap. 2.95 (*0-86530-145-X*, IP 100-6) Incentive Pubns.

Dinosaur Library, 4 bks., Set I. Sheehan. (Illus.). 96p. (J). 1981. Set. lib. bdg. write for info. (*0-86592-110-5*) Rourke Enter.

Dinosaur Library, 13 bks., Set II. Oliver & Wilson. (Illus.). 312p. (J). 1984. Set. lib. bdg. write for info. (*0-86592-200-4*) Rourke Enter.

Dinosaur Library, 6 bks., Set III. Oliver. (Illus.). 144p. (J). 1986. Set. lib. bdg. write for info. (*0-86592-214-4*) Rourke Enter.

Dinosaur Library, 6 bks., Set IV. White & Swann. (Illus.). 144p. (J). 1989. Set. lib. bdg. write for info. (*0-86592-516-X*) Rourke Enter.

Dinosaur Library, 6 bks., Set V. White & Swann. (Illus.). 144p. (J). 1984. Set. lib. bdg. write for info. (*0-86592-523-2*) Rourke Enter.

Dinosaur Life Activity Book. Donald Silver & Patricia Wynne. 32p. (J). (gr. 1-3). 1988. pap. 2.50 (*0-486-25809-2*) Dover.

Dinosaur Mad Libs. Leonard Stern & Roger Price. (Mad Libs Ser.). 48p. (Orig.). (J). (gr. 1 up). 1993. bds. 2.95 (*0-8431-3528-X*) Price Stern.

Dinosaur Man: Tales of Madness & Enchantment from the Back Ward. Susan Baur. LC 90-55948. (Illus.). 224p. 1992. reprint ed. pap. 10.00 (*0-06-098104-0*, PL) HarpC.

Dinosaur Masks & Puppets. Ronald Mah. (J). (gr. 2 up). pap. 4.50 (*0-8431-1952-7*, Troubador) Price Stern.

Dinosaur Mazes. Rich Latta. 48p. (J). (gr. 2 up). 1990. bds. 2.95 (*0-8431-2822-4*) Price Stern.

Dinosaur Mazes: Educational Activity-Coloring Book. Peter M. Spizzirri. Ed. by Linda Spizzirri. (Illus.). 32p. (J). (gr. k-5). 1984. pap. 1.00 (*0-86545-057-9*) Spizzirri.

Dinosaur Mobiles. Anne Wild. (Illus.). 32p. (Orig.). (J). (gr. 2 up). 1990. pap. 5.95 (*0-906212-18-9*, Pub. by Tarquin UK) Parkwest Pubns.

Dinosaur Monsters & More. (Dinosaur Flip-Ups Ser.). (Illus.). 5p. (J). (gr. k-3). 1993. bds. 3.50 (*1-56144-357-3*, Honey Bear Bks) Modern Pub NYC.

Dinosaur Mountain. Caroline Arnold. (J). (gr. 4-7). 1993. pap. 6.95 (*0-395-66503-5*, Clarion Bks) HM.

Dinosaur Mountain. Caroline Arnold. 1990. 15.95 (*0-89919-693-4*) Ticknor & Fields.

***Dinosaur Musical.** Willie Reale & Robert Reale. 1995. 25.00 (*0-8222-1446-6*) Dramatists Play.

Dinosaur Mysteries. Mary O'Neill. LC 89-4789. (Illus.). 32p. (J). (gr. 3-7). 1989. lib. bdg. 12.89 (*0-8167-1635-8*); pap. text ed. 3.95 (*0-8167-1636-6*) Troll Assocs.

Dinosaur Mystery. Gertrude C. Warner. (Boxcar Children Mysteries Ser.: No. 44). (Illus.). 192p. (J). (gr. 2-7). 1995. lib. bdg. 10.95 (*0-8075-1603-1*); pap. 3.50 (*0-8075-1604-X*) A Whitman.

Dinosaur Named after Me. Bernard Most. Ed. by Diane D'Andrade. (Illus.). 32p. (J). (ps-3). 1991. 12.95 (*0-15-223494-2*) HarBrace.

***Dinosaur Named after Me.** Bernard Most. LC 90-36272. (J). (ps-2). 1995. pap. 5.00 (*0-15-223493-4*, Voyager Bks) HarBrace.

***Dinosaur National Monument.** David Petersen. LC 94-35655. (New True Bks.). 48p. (J). (gr. k-4). 1995. lib. bdg. 12.90 (*0-516-01074-3*) Childrens.

Dinosaur National Monument, UT & CO. rev. ed. Ed. by Trails Illustrated Staff. (Illus.). 1993. Folded topographical map. 8.99 (*0-925873-20-9*) Trails Illustrated.

Dinosaur Nexus. Lee Grimes. 224p. (Orig.). 1994. mass mkt. 4.99 (*0-380-77319-8*, AvoNova) Avon.

Dinosaur Paper Chains. Stewart Walton & Sally Walton. (Illus.). 32p. (J). (gr. 3 up). 1994. pap. 6.95 (*0-688-13413-0*, Tupelo Bks) Morrow.

***Dinosaur Park Vol. 1.** Hayford Peirce. 1994. pap. 4.99 (*0-8125-5040-4*) Tor Bks.

Dinosaur Planet. Anne McCaffrey. 1984. mass mkt. 5.99 (*0-345-31995-8*, Del Rey) Ballantine.

Dinosaur Planet Survivors. Anne McCaffrey. 304p. 1984. mass mkt. 4.95 (*0-345-27246-3*, Del Rey) Ballantine.

Dinosaur Plays. C. D. Arnold. LC 83-8446. (Gay Play Script Ser.). (Illus.). 73p. 1984. pap. 5.95 (*0-935672-09-5*) JH Pr.

Dinosaur Plots & Other Intrigues in Natural History. Leonard Krishtalka. 1990. pap. 8.95 (*0-380-70998-8*) Avon.

Dinosaur Pop-Up ABC. Arlene Maguire. (J). 1995. 14.95 (*0-671-89076-X*, Litl Simon S&S) S&S Childrens.

Dinosaur Poster Book. David Norman. 1988. pap. 2.00 (*0-517-65263-3*) Random Hse Value.

Dinosaur Princess & Other Prehistoric Riddles. David A. Adler. LC 87-25121. (Illus.). 64p. (J). (gr. 1-4). 1988. lib. bdg. 12.95 (*0-8234-0686-5*) Holiday.

***Dinosaur Provincial Park: Land of Vanished Dinosaurs.** Gord Reid. (Illus.). 64p. 1995. lib. bdg. 33.00 (*0-8095-4832-1*) Borgo Pr.

Dinosaur Punch out Stencils. A. G. Smith. (J). 1989. pap. 3.50 (*0-486-25305-8*) Dover.

Dinosaur Puzzles & Mazes. (Illus.). 64p. (Orig.). (J). (gr. 2-5). 1993. pap. 2.95 (*1-56144-301-8*, Honey Bear Bks) Modern Pub NYC.

Dinosaur Question & Answer Book: Everything Kids Want to Know about Dinosaurs, Fossils, And... Owl Magazine Staff. (J). (gr. 4-7). 1992. 16.95 (*0-316-67736-1*, Joy St Bks) Little.

***Dinosaur Questions.** Bernard Most. LC 94-42630. (J). 1995. write for info. (*0-15-292885-5*) HarBrace.

***Dinosaur Relatives.** Janet Riehecky. (Dinosaur Bks.). (Illus.). 32p. (ENG & SPA.). (J). (ps-2). 1990. lib. bdg. 21.36 (*1-56766-125-4*) Childs World.

Dinosaur Relatives. Janet Riehecky. (Dinosaur Bks.). (Illus.). 32p. (ENG & SPA.). (J). (ps-2). 1990. lib. bdg. 21.36 (*0-89565-626-4*) Childs World.

Dinosaur Riddles. Joseph Heck. Ed. by Wendy Barish. (Illus.). 128p. (J). (gr. 3-7). 1982. reprint ed. 9.29 (*0-685-05613-9*, Litl Simon S&S) S&S Childrens.

Dinosaur River Guide: Flaming Gorge, Dinosaur National Monument. Laura Evans & Buzz Belknap. LC 73-79803. (Illus.). 64p. 1973. 14.95 (*0-916370-04-6*); pap. 6.95 (*0-916370-03-8*) Westwater.

Dinosaur Roar! Paul Stickland & Henrietta Stickland. LC 93-43959. (Illus.). 32p. (J). (ps-1). 1994. 9.99 (*0-525-45276-1*, DCB) Dutton Child Bks.

Dinosaur Safari Guide: Tracking North America's Prehistoric Past. Vincenzo Costa. LC 93-21362. 1994. pap. 14.95 (*0-89658-231-0*) Voyageur Pr.

Dinosaur Scrapbook. Donald F. Glut. 1980. 19.95 (*0-8065-0671-7*, Citadel Pr) Carol Pub Group.

Dinosaur Scrapbook. Donald F. Glut. 320p. 1982. pap. 9.95 (*0-8065-0816-7*, Citadel Pr) Carol Pub Group.

Dinosaur Shaman: Nine Tales from the Xenozoic Age. Mark Schultz. Ed. by Dave Schreiner. LC 90-21624. (Xenozoic Tales Ser.). (Illus.). 128p. 1990. 29.95 (*0-87816-117-1*); pap. 14.95 (*0-87816-118-X*) Kitchen Sink.

***Dinosaur Skeletons & Other Prehistoric Animals.** Jinny Johnson. LC 94-35362. (Illus.). 48p. (J). 1995. 16.95 (*0-89577-678-2*, Readers Digest Kids) RD Assn.

***Dinosaur Snaps.** (J). Date not set. write for info. (*0-7894-0104-5*) Dorling Kindersley.

Dinosaur Stamps of the World. Stuart Baldwin & Beverly Halstead. (Illus.). 128p. (C). 1989. pap. 79.00 (*0-9508063-4-X*, Pub. by S A Baldwin UK) St Mut.

Dinosaur Stencil Book. (J). 1991. 7.99 (*0-517-05410-8*) Random Hse Value.

Dinosaur Sticker Atlas. C. Bloch. (Illus.). 32p. (J). (gr. k-6). 1993. reprint ed. pap. 3.95 (*1-879424-19-3*) Nickel Pr.

Dinosaur Sticker Book. Anna Pomaska. (Illus.). (J). (gr. k-3). 1989. pap. 1.00 (*0-486-25907-2*) Dover.

Dinosaur Sticker Paper Doll. Nina Barbaresi. (Illus.). (J). (gr. k-3). 1991. pap. 1.00 (*0-486-26224-3*) Dover.

Dinosaur Story. Joanna Cole. LC 74-5931. (Illus.). 32p. (J). (gr. k-3). 1974. lib. bdg. 13.93 (*0-688-31826-6*) Morrow Jr Bks.

Dinosaur Systematics: Approaches & Perspectives. Ed. by Kenneth Carpenter & Philip J. Currie. (Illus.). 375p. (C). 1990. 64.95 (*0-521-36672-0*) Cambridge U Pr.

Dinosaur Systematics: Approaches & Perspectives. Ed. by Kenneth Carpenter & Philip J. Currie. (Illus.). 334p. (C). 1992. pap. 32.95 (*0-521-43810-1*) Cambridge U Pr.

Dinosaur That Followed Me Home. Bruce Coville. (Camp Haunted Hills Ser.). 160p. (Orig.). (J). (gr. 3-6). 1990. pap. 3.50 (*0-671-64750-4*, Minstrel Bks) PB.

Dinosaur Time. Peggy Parish & Arnold Lobel. (I Can Read Bk. & Cassette). 32p. (J). (ps-2). 1990. pap. 6.95 (*1-55994-262-2*, Caedmon) HarperAudio.

Dinosaur Time. Peggy Parish. LC 73-14331. (Early I Can Read Bk.). (Illus.). 32p. (J). (gr. k-3). 1974. 14.95 (*0-06-024653-7*); lib. bdg. 14.89 (*0-06-024654-5*) HarpC Child Bks.

Dinosaur Time. Peggy Parish. LC 73-14331. (Trophy Early I Can Read Bk.). (Illus.). 32p. (J). (ps-2). 1983. pap. 3.50 (*0-06-444037-0*, Trophy) HarpC Child Bks.

Dinosaur Titans & More. (Dinosaur Flip-Ups Ser.). (Illus.). 5p. (J). (gr. k-3). 1993. bds. 3.50 (*1-56144-358-1*, Honey Bear Bks) Modern Pub NYC.

Dinosaur Tracks. Tony Thulborn. (Illus.). 384p. 1990. 69.95 (*0-412-32890-9*, A4398) Chapman & Hall.

Dinosaur Tracks & Murder. John Dellinger. 160p. 1994. pap. 7.95 (*1-56901-307-1*) NW Pub.

***Dinosaur Tracks & Other Fossil Footprints of the Western United States.** Martin Lockley & Adrian Hunt. 1995. 29.50 (*0-231-07926-5*) Col U Pr.

Dinosaur Tracks & Traces. Ed. by David D. Gillette & Martin Lockley. (Illus.). 450p. (C). 1989. 64.95 (*0-521-36354-3*) Cambridge U Pr.

Dinosaur Tracks & Traces. Ed. by David D. Gillette & Martin Lockley. (Illus.). 461p. (C). 1991. pap. 37.95 (*0-521-40788-5*) Cambridge U Pr.

Dinosaur Tree. Douglas Henderson. LC 93-34204. (Illus.). 32p. (J). (gr. 1-5). 1994. text ed. 15.95 (*0-02-743547-4*, Bradbury S&S) S&S Childrens.

Dinosaur Triangle: Land of the 'Terrible Lizards' James Keener. (Illus.). (Orig.). 1989. pap. 4.50 (*0-929290-01-1*) Grand Rivr CO.

Dinosaur Trivia for Kids: I'm Saury! Carole Marsh. (Quantum Leap Ser.). (Illus.). (Orig.). (J). (gr. 2 up). 1994. lib. bdg. 24.95 (*1-55609-162-1*); pap. 14.95 (*0-935326-54-5*) Gallopade Pub Group.

Dinosaur Valentine. Liza Donnelly. (Illus.). 32p. (J). (ps-2). 1994. pap. 2.50 (*0-590-46415-9*, Cartwheel) Scholastic Inc.

Dinosaur Valley. Mitsuhiro Kurokawa. LC 92-10788. (Illus.). 48p. (J). (gr. 1-5). 1992. 14.95 (*0-8118-0257-4*) Chronicle Bks.

***Dinosaur Who Lived in My Backyard.** B. G. Hennessy. (Illus.). (J). (gr. k-3). 1991. audio 22.95 (*0-87499-199-4*); audio, pap. 14.95 (*0-87499-198-6*) Live Oak Media.

Dinosaur Who Lived in My Backyard. B. G. Hennessy. (Illus.). 32p. (J). (ps-3). 1990. pap. 4.99 (*0-14-050736-1*, Puffin) Puffin Bks.

Dinosaur Who Lived in My Backyard. B. G. Hennessy. LC 87-19867. (Illus.). 32p. (J). (ps-1). 1988. pap. 13.99 (*0-670-81685-X*) Viking Child Bks.

***Dinosaur Who Lived in My Backyard, 4 bks., Set.** B. G. Hennessy. (Illus.). (J). (gr. k-3). 1991. audio, pap. 29.95 (*0-87499-200-1*) Live Oak Media.

Dinosaur with an Attitude. Hanna Johansen. Tr. by Elisabetta Maccari. LC 94-60000. (Illus.). 143p. (Orig.). (J). (gr. 4-7). 1994. 12.95 (*1-57143-018-0*, Wetlands Pr) RDR Bks.

***Dinosaur with an Attitude.** Hanna Johansen. Tr. by Elisabetta Maccari. LC 94-60000. (Illus.). 143p. (Orig.). (J). (gr. 4-7). 1995. pap. 7.95 (*1-57143-022-9*, Wetlands Pr) RDR Bks.

Dinosaur World see Rand McNally Fact Books

Dinosaure. Illus. by J. Prunier & H. Galeron. (Gallimard - Mes Premieres Decouvertes Ser.: No. 30). (FRE.). (J). (ps-1). 1991. 17.95 (*2-07-056642-0*) Schoenhof.

Dinosaure Follow-the Dots Coloring Bk. Patricia Wynne. (Little Activity Bks.). (J). 1994. pap. 1.00 (*0-486-27991-X*) Dover.

Dinosauria. Ed. by David B. Weishampel. 733p. 1990. 95.00 (*0-520-06726-6*) U CA Pr.

Dinosauria. David B. Weishampel et al. 1992. pap. 40.00 (*0-520-06727-4*) U CA Pr.

Dinosaurian Faunas of China. Z. M. Dong. 200p. 1992. 133.00 (*0-387-52084-8*) Spr-Verlag.

Dinosauring: A Channels to Children Activity Guide. Roberta Simmons et al. (Illus.). 75p. 1989. spiral bd., pap. 12.95 (*0-9616396-1-X*) Channels Children.

Dinosaurios: Dinosaurs. Mary Clark. Tr. by Lada Kratky. (Spanish New True Bks.). (Illus.). 48p. (SPA.). (J). (gr. k-4). 1984. lib. bdg. 13.28 (*0-516-31612-5*); pap. 5.50 (*0-516-51612-4*) Childrens.

Dinosaurios Gigantes. (SPA.). (J). 1989. pap. 19.95 (*0-590-73764-3*) Scholastic Inc.

Dinosaurios Gigantes (Giant Dinosaurs) Erna Rowe. Tr. by Argentina Palacios. (Illus.). 32p. (J). (ps-2). pap. 4.95 (*0-590-40647-7*) Scholastic Inc.

***Dinosaurios y Otros Animales Prehistoricos-Dinosaurs & Other Prehistoric Animals Factfinder: Y Otros Animales Prehistoricos (Dinosaurs & Other Prehistoric Animals Factfinder)** Michael Benton. (Illus.). 256p. (SPA.). (J). (gr. 4-8). 1995. pap. 12.95 (*1-85697-542-8*, Kingfisher LKC) LKC.

Dinosaurium. Barbara A. Brenner. LC 91-6335. (Bank Street Museum Bks.: No. 1). (J). (ps-3). 1993. mass mkt. 9.50 (*0-553-35427-2*) Bantam.

Dinosauro en Peligro. Sharon Gordon. (Illus.). 32p. (SPA.). (J). (gr. k-2). 1981. lib. bdg. 7.89 (*0-89375-554-0*); pap. 1.95 (*0-685-42386-7*) Troll Assocs.

***Dinosaurs.** (Learners Ser.). 48p. (J). Date not set. 3.50 (*0-7214-1701-9*) Ladybird Bks.

***Dinosaurs.** (J). 1995. pap. text ed. 4.95 (*0-307-08050-1*, Golden Pr) Western Pub.

***Dinosaurs.** (Press Out Bks.). 16p. (J). 1995. 5.95 (*0-7894-0130-4*, 5-70589) Dorling Kindersley.

***Dinosaurs.** Brenda Apsley. (Illus.). 24p. (J). (ps-2). 1995. pap. 1.95 (*1-56293-573-9*) McClanahan Bk.

Dinosaurs. B. Armstrong. (Science Ser.). 32p. (J). (gr. 1-7). 1988. 3.95 (*0-88160-160-8*, LW 265) Learning Wks.

Dinosaurs. Illus. by Dorothea Barlowe et al. LC 77-70862. (Pop-Up Bks.: No. 33). (J). (ps-3). 1977. 10.00 (*0-394-83538-7*) Random Bks Yng Read.

Dinosaurs. Michael Benton. LC 94-9362. (First Facts Ser.). (Illus.). 128p. (J). (gr. k-4). 1994. pap. 5.95 (*1-85697-524-X*, Kingfisher LKC) LKC.

Dinosaurs. Michael J. Benton. LC 93-19072. (Picturepedia Ser.). (Illus.). (J). 1993. 12.95 (*1-56458-382-1*) Dorling Kindersley.

Dinosaurs. Michael J. Benton. LC 90-30837. (Picture Pockets Ser.). (Illus.). 96p. (J). (gr. 1-5). 1992. pap. 13.00 (*0-671-75998-1*, S&S Bks Young Read); pap. 8.00 (*0-671-75999-X*, S&S Bks Young Read) S&S Childrens.

Dinosaurs. Melvin Berger. (Stranger Than Fiction Ser.). 128p. (J). 1990. pap. 2.95 (*0-380-76052-5*, Camelot) Avon.

Dinosaurs. Mary L. Clark. LC 81-7750. (New True Bks.). (Illus.). 48p. (J). (gr. k-4). 1981. lib. bdg. 13.50 (*0-516-01612-1*); pap. 5.50 (*0-516-41612-X*) Childrens.

Dinosaurs. Neil Clark & William Lindsay. LC 93-48880. (DK Pocket Ser.). (Illus.). 160p. (YA). (gr. 7 up). 1995. pap. 5.95 (*1-56458-662-6*) Dorling Kindersley.

***Dinosaurs.** Neil Clark. (Look Inside Ser.). (Illus.). 16p. (J). (gr. 2-5). 1995. 9.95 (*0-89577-689-8*, J Morris NY) RD Assn.

Dinosaurs. Claude Delafosse & James Prunier. (First Discovery Bks.). (Illus.). (J). (gr. 4 up). 1993. 11.95 (*0-590-46358-6*) Scholastic Inc.

***Dinosaurs.** Gloria Evangelista. LC 93-87110. (Step Ahead Beginning Readers Ser.). (Illus.). 24p. (Orig.). (J). (ps up). 1994. pap. 7.99 (*0-679-86194-7*) Random Bks Yng Read.

Dinosaurs. Gloria Evangelistar. Date not set. write for info. (*0-318-72413-8*) Random.

Dinosaurs. Eugene S. Gaffney. (Golden Guide Ser.). (J). (gr. 3 up). 1990. pap. write for info. (*0-307-24076-2*) Western Pub.

Dinosaurs. Gail Gibbons. LC 87-364. (Illus.). 32p. (J). (ps-3). 1987. lib. bdg. 15.95 (*0-8234-0657-1*); pap. 5.95 (*0-8234-0708-X*) Holiday.

Dinosaurs. Judith E. Greenberg & Helen H. Carey. (Science Adventures Ser.). (Illus.). 32p. (J). (gr. 2-4). 1990. lib. bdg. 10.95 (*0-8172-3751-8*) Raintree Steck-V.

Dinosaurs. David Hately. (J). 1987. Series S808-13. boxed 3.95 (*0-7214-9543-5*) Ladybird Bks.

Dinosaurs. Lee B. Hopkins. (Illus.). 47p. (J). (ps-3). 1987. 12.95 (*0-15-223495-0*) HarBrace.

Dinosaurs. Lee B. Hopkins. (J). 1990. pap. 4.95 (*0-15-223496-9*, Voyager Bks) HarBrace.

***Dinosaurs.** Richard Krueger. LC 94-46552. (Prehistoric North America Ser.). (Illus.). (J). 1995. write for info. (*1-56294-548-3*) Millbrook Pr.

***Dinosaurs.** Little Golden Books Staff. (J). Date not set. 1.39 (*0-307-08571-6*, Golden Pr) Western Pub.

Dinosaurs. John Man. 1988. 4.98 (*0-671-06145-3*) S&S Trade.

Dinosaurs. Edward Mast & Lenore Bensinger. (Orig.). (J). 1994. 5.00 (*0-87602-327-8*) Anchorage.

Dinosaurs. Sue Mayes. (Young Nature Ser.). (Illus.). 32p. (J). (gr. k-1). 1993. lib. bdg. 13.96 (*0-88110-641-0*, Usborne); pap. 5.95 (*0-7460-1020-6*, Usborne) EDC.

Dinosaurs. McCord. (Picture History Ser.). (Illus.). (J). (gr. 4-6). 1977. lib. bdg. 13.96 (*0-88110-680-1*, Usborne); pap. 6.95 (*0-7460-1469-4*, Usborne) EDC.

***Dinosaurs.** Lisa Miles. (Hotshots Ser.). (Illus.). 32p. (J). (gr. 1 up). 1995. pap. 2.95 (*0-7460-2277-8*, Usborne) EDC.

***Dinosaurs.** Ed. by Angela Milner. LC 95-12938. (Discoveries Ser.). (Illus.). 64p. (J). (gr. 4-7). 1995. write for info. (*0-7835-4765-X*) Time-Life.

Dinosaurs. Ting Morris & Neil Morris. LC 92-32915. (Sticky Fingers Ser.). (J). 1993. lib. bdg. 12.95 (*0-531-14258-2*) Watts.

Dinosaurs. Don Nardo. LC 93-4314. (Exploring the Unknown Ser.). (J). (gr. 5 up). 1994. 17.95 (*1-56510-154-5*) Lucent Bks.

Dinosaurs. Judy Nayer. (At Your Fingertips Ser.). (Illus.). 12p. (J). (ps-2). 1993. bds. 6.95 (*1-56293-336-1*) McClanahan Bk.

***Dinosaurs.** Kate Needham. LC 95-14023. (Time Trekkers Visit the...Ser.). (Illus.). (J). 1995. lib. bdg. write for info. (*1-56294-942-X*, Copper Beech Bks) Millbrook Pr.

Dinosaurs. Illus. by Gena Neilson. (J). (ps-1). 1986. spiral bd. 9.95 (*0-937763-00-4*) Lauri Inc.

Dinosaurs. D. Norman. (Spotter's Guides Ser.). (Illus.). 64p. (YA). (gr. 10 up). 1993. pap. 4.95 (*0-86020-458-8*) EDC.

Dinosaurs. David Norman. (Fact Finders Ser.). (Illus.). 64p. 1989. 7.99 (*0-517-67728-8*) Random Hse Value.

Dinosaurs. Mary Packard. (Illus.). 48p. (J). (ps-3). 1981. pap. 9.95 (*0-671-43040-8*, S&S Bks Young Read) S&S Childrens.

Dinosaurs. Steve Pollock. (Illus.). 48p. (J). (gr. 7-9). 1992. 13.95 (*0-563-34753-8*, BBC-Parkwest); pap. 7.50 (*0-563-34607-8*, BBC-Parkwest) Parkwest Pubns.

Dinosaurs. Jim Rothaus. (Zoobooks Ser.). 24p. (J). (gr. 3). 1988. lib. bdg. 14.95 (*0-88682-223-8*) Creative Ed.

Dinosaurs. Running Press Staff. LC 93-83583. (Unfolding World Ser.). (Illus.). (J). (gr. 4-7). 1993. 5.95 (*1-56138-319-8*) Running Pr.

Dinosaurs. Karen Shuey. (Illus.). 48p. (J). (gr. k-4). 1987. student ed 6.95 (*1-55734-218-0*) Tchr Create Mat.

Dinosaurs. Kathie B. Smith. (Sticker Bks.). (J). 1987. pap. 2.95 (*0-671-63238-8*, Litl Simon S&S) S&S Childrens.

***Dinosaurs.** Scott Steedman. LC 95-76. (Worldwise Ser.). (Illus.). (J). 1995. lib. bdg. 14.98 (*0-531-14377-5*) Watts.

***Dinosaurs.** Scott Steedman. (Worldwise Ser.). (Illus.). 48p. (J). (gr. 3-5). 1995. pap. text ed. 7.00 (*0-531-15283-9*) Watts.

Dinosaurs. Wendy Stein. LC 93-15919. (Great Mysteries Ser.). (YA). 1994. 16.95 (*1-56510-096-4*) Greenhaven.

Dinosaurs. John B. Wexo. (Prehistoric Zoobks.). 24p. (J). (gr. 3 up). 1991. lib. bdg. 14.95 (*0-88682-393-5*) Creative Ed.

Dinosaurs. Wildlife Education, Ltd. Staff. (Illus.). 20p. (Orig.). (J). (gr. k-12). 1985. pap. 2.75 (*0-937934-34-8*) Wildlife Educ.

Dinosaurs! Ed. by World Book, Inc. Staff. LC 65-25105. (Childcraft - The How & Why Library: The 1987 Childcraft Annual). (Illus.). 304p. (J). (gr. 3-7). 1987. lib. bdg. write for info. (*0-7166-0687-9*) World Bk.

Dinosaurs. Peter Zallinger. LC 76-24178. (Pictureback Ser.). (Illus.). (J). (ps-1). 1977. pap. 2.50 (*0-394-83485-2*) Random Bks Yng Read.

Dinosaurs. 2nd ed. John Ostrom. Ed. by J. J. Head. LC 84-71139. (Carolina Biology Readers Ser.: No. 98). (Illus.). 32p. (J). (gr. 10 up). 1984. pap. 3.00 (*0-89278-201-3*, 45-9698) Carolina Biological.

Dinosaurs: A Celebration, No. 1. 48p. 1992. 4.95 (*0-87135-904-9*) Marvel Entmnt.

Dinosaurs: A Celebration, No. 2. 48p. 1992. 4.95 (*0-87135-905-7*) Marvel Entmnt.

Dinosaurs: A Celebration, No. 3. 48p. 1992. 4.95 (*0-87135-924-3*) Marvel Entmnt.

Dinosaurs: A Celebration, No. 4. 48p. 1992. 4.95 (*0-87135-925-1*) Marvel Entmnt.

Dinosaurs: A Closer Look. Dougal Dixon. (Dinosaur Dynasty Ser.). 32p. (J). (gr. k-4). 1994. lib. bdg. 19.93 (*1-884756-04-2*) Davidson Titles.

***Dinosaurs: A Closer Look.** Dougal Dixon. 32p. (J). (gr. 3 up). 1995. write for info. (*1-56397-533-5*, Wordsong) Boyds Mills Pr.

Dinosaurs: A Closer Look. Highlights for Children Staff. (Dino Ser.). (Illus.). 32p. (J). (gr. 3-10). 1992. pap. 3.50 (*0-87534-316-3*) Highlights.

Dinosaurs! A Drawing Book. Michael Emberley. (Reading Rainbow Ser.). (Illus.). 48p. (J). (gr. 3 up). 1985. mass mkt. 6.95 (*0-316-23631-4*) Little.

Dinosaurs: A New Discovery. J. Stewart. (Illus.). 32p. (J). (gr. 1-6). 1989. 10.95 (*0-88625-234-2*) Durkin Hayes Pub.

Dinosaurs: A New Discovery. Chris Walker. (J). (gr. 4-7). 1989. pap. 5.95 (*0-88625-235-0*) Durkin Hayes Pub.

***Dinosaurs! A Sport-the-Difference Puzzle Book.** Steve Parker. LC 94-34687. (Illus.). (J). 1995. 12.00 (*0-679-86715-5*) Random Bks Yng Read.

Dinosaurs: A Thematic Unit. Diann Culver. (Thematic Units Ser.). (Illus.). 80p. (J). (gr. 3-5). 1993. student ed 8.95 (*1-55734-238-5*) Tchr Create Mat.

An Asterisk (*) at the beginning of an entry indicates that the title is appearing in BIP for the first time.

Dinosaurs: All Shapes & Sizes. Dougal Dixon. (Dinosaur Dynasty Ser.). 32p. (J). (gr. k-4). 1994. lib. bdg. 19.93 (*1-884756-03-4*) Davidson Titles.

***Dinosaurs: All Shapes & Sizes.** Dougal Dixon. 32p. (J). (gr. 3 up). 1995. write for info. (*1-56397-535-1*, Wordsong) Boyds Mills Pr.

Dinosaurs: All Shapes & Sizes. Highlights for Children Staff. (Dino Ser.). (Illus.). 32p. (J). (gr. 3-10). 1992. pap. 3.50 (*0-87534-315-5*) Highlights.

Dinosaurs: An A to Z Guide. Michael Benton. 1988. 7.99 (*0-517-66877-7*) Random Hse Value.

Dinosaurs: An Educational Coloring Book. Spizzirri Publishing Co. Staff. Ed. by Linda Spizzirri. (Illus.). 32p. (J). (gr. 1-8). 1981. pap. 1.75 (*0-86545-019-6*) Spizzirri.

Dinosaurs: An Integrated Unit. Kathy Rogers. (Primary Thematic Units Ser.). (Illus.). 96p. (Orig.). 1993. pap. 12.95 (*0-944459-79-X*) ECS Lrn Systs.

Dinosaurs: Back in Time. Jane B. Moncure. LC 89-38469. (Discovery World Ser.). (Illus.). 32p. (J). (ps-2). 1990. lib. bdg. 21.36 (*0-89565-550-0*) Childs World.

Dinosaurs: Facts Fun, & Fantastic Crafts. Imogene Forte. LC 86-82932. (Tabletop Learning Ser.). (Illus.). 80p. (J). (gr. k-6). 1987. pap. text ed. 3.95 (*0-86530-149-2*, IP 944) Incentive Pubns.

Dinosaurs: Find the Difference. (J). 1992. pap. 4.99 (*0-517-06725-0*) Random Hse Value.

Dinosaurs: Giants of the Earth. Dougal Dixon. (Dinosaur Dynasty Ser.). 32p. (J). (gr. k-4). 1994. lib. bdg. 19.93 (*1-884756-01-8*) Davidson Titles.

***Dinosaurs: Giants of the Earth.** Dougal Dixon. 32p. (J). (gr. 3 up). 1995. write for info. (*1-56397-534-3*, Wordsong) Boyds Mills Pr.

Dinosaurs: Giants of the Earth. Highlights for Children Staff. (Dino Ser.). (Illus.). 32p. (J). (gr. 3-10). 1992. pap. 3.50 (*0-87534-313-9*) Highlights.

Dinosaurs: Pop-Up. (J). (ps-3). 1993. pap. 4.95 (*0-8167-2925-5*) Troll Assocs.

***Dinosaurs! Strange & Wonderful.** Laurence Pringle. (Illus.). 32p. (J). (ps-2). 1995. 14.95 (*1-878093-16-9*) Boyds Mills Pr.

Dinosaurs: Superdoodles. LC 92-74102. (J). (gr. 3 up). 1993. pap. 4.95 (*0-88160-223-X*, LW301) Learning Wks.

Dinosaurs: Superfacts. (J). 1992. 4.99 (*0-517-07325-0*) Random Hse Value.

Dinosaurs: The Bible, Barney & Beyond. Phil Phillips. 200p. 1995. pap. 9.95 (*0-914984-59-4*) Starburst.

Dinosaurs: The Encyclopedia. Donald F. Glut. (Illus.). 1040p. 1995. lib. bdg. 145.00 (*0-89950-917-7*) McFarland & Co.

***Dinosaurs: The Fastest, the Fiercest, the Most Amazing.** Elizabeth MacLeod. (Illus.). 32p. (J). (gr. 1-4). 1995. 11.99 (*0-670-86026-3*) Viking Child Bks.

Dinosaurs: The Fossil Hunters. Dougal Dixon. (Dinosaur Dynasty Ser.). 32p. (J). (gr. k-4). 1994. lib. bdg. 19.93 (*1-884756-05-0*) Davidson Titles.

***Dinosaurs: THe Fossil Hunters.** Dougal Dixon. 32p. (J). (gr. 3 up). 1995. write for info. (*1-56397-532-7*, Wordsong) Boyds Mills Pr.

Dinosaurs: the Fossil Hunters. Highlights for Children Staff. (Dino Ser.). (Illus.). 32p. (J). (gr. 3-10). 1992. pap. 3.50 (*0-87534-317-1*) Highlights.

Dinosaurs: The Real Monsters. Dougal Dixon. (Dinosaur Dynasty Ser.). 32p. (J). (gr. k-4). 1994. lib. bdg. 19.93 (*1-884756-02-6*) Davidson Titles.

***Dinosaurs: The Real Monsters.** Dougal Dixon. 32p. (J). (gr. 3 up). 1995. write for info. (*1-56397-536-X*, Wordsong) Boyds Mills Pr.

Dinosaurs: The Real Monsters. Highlights for Children Staff. (Dino Ser.). (Illus.). 32p. (J). (gr. 3-10). 1992. pap. 3.50 (*0-87534-314-7*) Highlights.

Dinosaurs: The Textbook. Spencer G. Lucas. 320p. (C). 1993. pap. write for info. (*0-697-14429-1*) Wm C Brown Pubs.

Dinosaurs: Those Terrible Lizards. Duane T. Gish. LC 77-89152. (Illus.). 1977. 10.95 (*0-89051-039-3*) Master Bks.

Dinosaurs: Unearthing the Secrets of Ancient Beasts. Don Nardo. (Encyclopedia of Discovery & Invention Ser.). (Illus.). (J). (gr. 5-8). 1994. 17.95 (*1-56006-253-3*) Lucent Bks.

Dinosaurs see Books for Young Explorers

Dinosaurs -- Concepts, Histology & Stratigraphy, Vol. 18. A. S. William. (Halstead Memorial Ser.: Vol. 18, Pt. 3). 1993. pap. text ed. 208.00 (*2-88124-907-8*) Gordon & Breach.

Dinosaurs - A Journey Through Time: A Children's Activity Book. Dennis Schatz. 48p. (J). (ps-6). 1987. pap. 9.95 (*0-935051-01-5*) Pacific Sci Ctr.

Dinosaurs - Prehistoric Animals. (J). (gr. k-2). 1991. pap. 1.29 (*0-87449-189-4*) Modern Pub NYC.

Dinosaurs Activity Book. (Illus.). (J). (ps-6). pap. 2.95 (*0-565-01078-6*, Pub. by Natural Hist Mus UK) Parkwest Pubns.

Dinosaur's Adventure in Alphabet Town. D. Cook. LC 91-20544. (Read Around Alphabet Town Ser.). (Illus.). 32p. (J). (ps-2). 1992. lib. bdg. 12.23 (*0-516-05404-X*) Childrens.

Dinosaurs Alive! Shelly Ritthaler. 96p. (Orig.). (J). (gr. 2 up). 1994. pap. 3.50 (*0-380-77323-6*, Camelot Young) Avon.

Dinosaurs Alive & Well! A Guide to Good Health. Laurene K. Brown & Marc T. Brown. (J). (ps-3). 1990. 15.95 (*0-316-10998-3*, Joy St Bks) Little.

Dinosaurs Alive & Well! A Guide to Good Health. Laurie K. Brown. (J). (ps-3). 1992. mass mkt. 5.95 (*0-316-11009-4*, Joy St Bks) Little.

Dinosaurs All Around: An Artist's View of the Prehistoric World. Caroline Arnold. LC 92-5726. (Illus.). 48p. (J). (gr. 3-6). 1993. 14.95 (*0-395-62363-4*, Clarion Bks) HM.

Dinosaur's Alphabet. Richard Fortey. (J). (gr. 4-8). 1990. 14.95 (*0-8120-6202-7*) Barron.

Dinosaurs & Birds. Giuseppe Minelli. (History of Life on Earth Ser.). (Illus.). 64p. (YA). 1988. 15.95 (*0-8160-1559-7*) Facts on File.

Dinosaurs & Cousin Armadillo. Gra Delle Duncan. 1990. pap. 3.95 (*0-89015-744-8*) Sunbelt Media.

Dinosaurs & How They Lived. Steve Parker. LC 91-60143. (See & Explore Library). (Illus.). 64p. (J). (gr. 3 up). 1991. 11.95 (*1-879431-13-0*); lib. bdg. 12.99 (*1-879431-28-9*) Dorling Kindersley.

Dinosaurs & Love. Marie Lobue. LC 92-91075. 64p. 1994. pap. 7.00 (*1-56002-247-7*, Univ Edtns) Aegina Pr.

***Dinosaurs & Man: A Fantasy Natural History of the Future.** Graham Coleman. LC 95-2455. (Illus.). (J). 1995. write for info. (*0-8120-9413-1*) Barron.

Dinosaurs & Other Extinct Animals. Gabriel Beaufay. (Focus on Science Ser.). (Illus.). 80p. (J). (gr. 7 up). 1987. pap. 4.95 (*0-8120-3836-3*) Barron.

Dinosaurs & Other First Animals. Dean Morris. LC 87-16670. (Read about Animals Ser.). (Illus.). 48p. (J). (gr. 2-6). 1987. lib. bdg. 10.95 (*0-8172-3206-0*) Raintree Steck-V.

***Dinosaurs & Other Prehistoric Animals.** Maria Flugel. LC 95-12377. (Animals at a Glance Ser.). (Illus.). (J). 1995. write for info. (*0-8368-1354-5*) Gareth Stevens Inc.

Dinosaurs & Other Prehistoric Animals. Jo E. Moore. (Illus.). 48p. 1992. pap. 9.95 (*1-55799-213-4*) Evan-Moor Corp.

Dinosaurs & Other Prehistoric Animals. Robin Wright. LC 90-38028. (Illus.). 96p. (J). (gr. 3-6). 1991. lib. bdg. 14.89 (*0-8167-2232-3*); pap. text ed. 6.95 (*0-8167-2233-1*) Troll Assocs.

***Dinosaurs & Other Prehistoric Creatures.** Kathryn Senior. LC 94-30821. (The X-Ray Picture Bks.). (Illus.). 48p. (J). (gr. 5-8). 1995. lib. bdg. 14.95 (*0-531-14352-X*) Watts.

***Dinosaurs & Other Prehistoric Creatures.** Kathryn Senior. LC 94-30821. (Illus.). 48p. (J). (ps-3). 1995. pap. 8.95 (*0-531-15732-6*) Orchard Bks Watts.

Dinosaurs & Other Prehistorics. William R. Johnson. Ed. by Pauline D. Johnson. (BLIP Production Reference Board Bks.). (Illus.). 48p. (J). (gr. 3-6). 1986. pap. 4.95 (*0-936917-02-4*, B606) Blip Prods.

Dinosaurs & Prehistoric Animals. Kay Quinn. (Sixty Things I Can Draw Ser.). (Illus.). 64p. (J). (gr. 2-10). 1990. 4.99 (*0-517-03566-9*) Random Hse Value.

Dinosaurs & Prehistoric Animals Coloring Book. E. Vernel Wagner. (Illus.). 64p. (J). (gr. 3-5). 1988. pap. 3.00 (*0-941875-05-9*) Wolverine Gallery.

Dinosaurs & Prehistoric Creatures. (Dinosaur Bind-Ups Ser.). (Illus.). 240p. (J). (gr. k-2). 1989. 19.95 (*0-87449-513-X*) Modern Pub NYC.

Dinosaurs & Prehistoric Creatures. (Illus.). 24p. (J). (gr. 2-5). 1993. pap. 2.50 (*1-56144-290-9*, Honey Bear Bks) Modern Pub NYC.

Dinosaurs & Prehistoric Creatures. Michael Teitelbaum. LC 93-50056. (Facts about Dinosaurs Ser.). (J). 1994. write for info. (*0-86593-355-3*) Rourke Corp.

Dinosaurs & Prehistoric Life: A Look at the Animals & Plants of Prehistory. LC 93-85520. (Gem Ser.). (Illus.). 240p. (J). 1994. pap. 5.95 (*1-56138-381-3*) Running Pr.

Dinosaurs & the Bible. David W. Unfred. LC 90-80887. (Illus.). 47p. (J). (gr. 3-8). 1990. 12.99 (*0-910311-70-6*) Huntington Hse.

Dinosaurs & Their Relatives in Action. Tanner O. Gay. (Early Reader Pop-Ups Ser.). (Illus.). 16p. (J). (ps-3). 1990. pap. 7.95 (*0-689-71434-3*, Aladdin Paperbacks) S&S Childrens.

Dinosaurs & Their Young. Russell Freedman. LC 83-6160. (Illus.). 32p. (J). (gr. 1-4). 1983. lib. bdg. 13.95 (*0-8234-0496-X*) Holiday.

Dinosaurs Are Different. Aliki. LC 84-45332. (Let's-Read-&-Find-Out Science Bk.). (Illus.). 32p. (J). (ps-3). 1985. 15.00 (*0-690-04456-9*, Crowell Jr Bks); lib. bdg. 14.89 (*0-690-04458-5*, Crowell Jr Bks) HarpC Child Bks.

Dinosaurs Are Different. Aliki. LC 84-45332. (Trophy Let's-Read-&-Find-Out Book & Cassette Set). (Illus.). 32p. (J). (ps-3). 1986. pap. 4.95 (*0-06-445056-2*, Dealer Bank) HarpC Child Bks.

Dinosaurs Are 568. Jean Rogers. LC 88-5501. (Illus.). 96p. (J). (gr. 3 up). 1988. 10.95 (*0-688-07931-8*) Greenwillow.

Dinosaurs Aren't Forever. Jessica Hatchigan. 112p. (Orig.). (J). 1991. pap. 2.95 (*0-380-76137-8*, Camelot) Avon.

Dinosaurs at the Supermarket. Lindsay Camp. LC 92-16936. (Illus.). 32p. (J). (gr. 3-8). 1993. 13.99 (*0-670-84802-6*) Viking Child Bks.

Dinosaurs Before Dark. Mary P. Osborne. LC 91-51106. (First Stepping Stone Bks.). (Illus.). 80p. (Orig.). (J). (gr. 1-4). 1992. pap. 2.99 (*0-679-82411-1*) Random Bks Yng Read.

Dinosaurs Before Dark. Mary P. Osborne. LC 91-51106. (First Stepping Stone Bks.). (Illus.). 80p. (Orig.). (J). (gr. 1-4). 1992. lib. bdg. 9.99 (*0-679-92411-6*) Random Bks Yng Read.

Dinosaurs, Beware! A Safety Guide. Marc T. Brown & Stephen Krensky. LC 82-15207. (Illus.). 32p. (J). (ps-3). 1982. 15.95 (*0-316-11228-3*, Pub. by H K Lewis UK) Little.

Dinosaurs, Beware! A Safety Guide. Marc T. Brown & Stephen Krensky. LC 82-15207. (Illus.). 32p. (J). (ps-3). 1984. mass mkt. 6.95 (*0-316-11219-4*, Joy St Bks) Little.

Dinosaurs Big & Small. (J). (gr. k-2). 1991. pap. 1.29 (*0-87449-186-X*) Modern Pub NYC.

Dinosaurs Big & Small. (Illus.). 24p. (J). (gr. 2-5). 1993. pap. 2.50 (*1-56144-292-5*, Honey Bear Bks) Modern Pub NYC.

Dinosaurs, Big & Small. Michael Teitelbaum. LC 93-50058. (Facts about Dinosaurs Ser.). (J). 1994. write for info. (*0-86593-352-9*) Rourke Corp.

***Dinosaur's Busy Day.** Liane Onish. (Doll Book Ser.). (Illus.). 8p. (J). (ps-2). 1995. bds. 4.95 (*1-56293-802-9*) McClanahan Bk.

Dinosaurs by Design. Duane T. Gish. (Illus.). 88p. 1992. 14.95 (*0-89051-165-9*) Master Bks.

Dinosaurs Came to Town. Dom Mansell. (J). (ps-3). 1991. 13.95 (*0-316-54584-8*) Little.

***Dinosaurs Can Fly: Creating the High Performance International Petroleum Company.** John Elting Treat. LC 94-23727. 1994. write for info. (*0-87814-429-3*) PennWell Bks.

Dinosaurs' Christmas. Liza Donnelly. 32p. (J). 1991. 12.95 (*0-590-44797-1*, Scholastic Hardcover) Scholastic Inc.

***Dinosaurs' Christmas.** Liza Donnelly. (J). (ps-3). 1994. pap. 2.50 (*0-590-44798-X*) Scholastic Inc.

Dinosaurs-Coloring Book. (J). 1985. pap. 1.95 (*0-88388-084-9*) Bellerophon Bks.

Dinosaurs Colouring Book. (Illus.). (J). (ps-6). pap. 2.95 (*0-565-00825-0*, Pub. by Natural Hist Mus UK) Parkwest Pubns.

Dinosaurs Cut-Out Model. I. Ashman. (Cut Out Models Ser.). (Illus.). 32p. (J). (gr. 4-8). 1994. pap. 9.95 (*0-7460-1320-5*, Usborne) EDC.

***Dinosaurs Depart.** Bob Barner. LC 95-10630. (Start Smart Math Bks.: Vol. 5). (J). 1996. pap. write for info. (*0-553-37584-9*) Bantam.

***Dinosaurs, Diamonds & Things from Outer Space: The Great Extinction.** David B. Carlisle. LC 94-32694. 1995. pap. 17.95 (*0-8047-2494-6*) Stanford U Pr.

***Dinosaurs, Diamonds, & Things from Outer Space: The Great Extinction.** David B. Carlisle. LC 94-32694. 1995. 45.00 (*0-8047-2392-3*) Stanford U Pr.

Dinosaurs, Dinosaurs. Byron Barton. LC 88-22938. (Illus.). 40p. (J). (ps-1). 1989. lib. bdg. 14.89 (*0-690-04768-1*) HarpC Child Bks.

Dinosaurs, Dinosaurs. Byron Barton. LC 88-22938. (Illus.). 40p. (J). (ps-1). 1989. 10.95 (*0-694-00269-0*, Crowell Jr Bks) HarpC Child Bks.

Dinosaurs, Dinosaurs. Byron Barton. LC 88-22938. (Big Bk.). (Illus.). 40p. (J). (ps-1). 1991. 19.95 (*0-06-020410-9*) HarpC Child Bks.

Dinosaurs, Dinosaurs. Byron Barton. LC 88-22938. (Trophy Picture Bk.). (Illus.). 40p. (J). (ps-1). 1993. pap. 4.95 (*0-06-443298-X*, Trophy) HarpC Child Bks.

Dinosaurs, Dinosaurs Board Book. Byron Barton. (Illus.). 32p. (J). (ps). 1994. 6.95 (*0-694-00625-4*, Festival) HarpC Child Bks.

Dinosaurs Divorce: A Guide for Changing Families. Laurene K. Brown & Marc T. Brown. (Illus.). 32p. (J). (ps-3). 1986. 15.95 (*0-316-11248-8*) Little.

Dinosaurs Divorce: A Guide for Changing Families. Laurene K. Brown & Marc T. Brown. (Illus.). 32p. (J). (ps-3). 1988. mass mkt. 6.95 (*0-316-10996-7*) Little.

Dinosaurs Don't Do Drugs: Say NO to Drugs with C, D, & E. Sydney Skochko & Stephen Skochko. LC 92-85568. (Illus.). 47p. (J). (ps-3). 1992. 13.95 (*1-880125-26-9*) Newmark CA.

Dinosaurs Down Under: And Other Fossils from Australia. Caroline Arnold. (Illus.). 48p. (J). (gr. 3-7). 1990. 15.95 (*0-89919-814-7*, Clarion Bks) HM.

Dinosaurs down Under: And Other Fossils from Australia. Caroline Arnold. (J). (gr. 4-7). 1994. pap. 6.95 (*0-395-69119-2*, Clarion Bks) HM.

Dinosaurs, Dragonflies & Diamonds: All About Natural History Museums. Gail Gibbons. LC 88-38831. (Illus.). 32p. (J). (gr. k-3). 1988. text ed. 13.95 (*0-02-737240-5*, Four Winds Pr) S&S Childrens.

Dinosaurs, Dunes, & Drifting Continents: The Geohistory of the Connecticut Valley. 2nd ed. Richard D. Little. (Illus.). 107p. 1986. pap. 8.50 (*0-9616520-0-4*) Val Geol Pubns.

Dinosaur's Egg. 2nd ed. Edmund Candler. LC 92-63034. 312p. Date not set. pap. 12.95 (*0-9627987-5-4*) Turtle Point Pr.

Dinosaurs Existed? Mike Benton. LC 94-16252. (How Do We Know? Ser.). (J). 1995. lib. bdg. write for info. (*0-8114-3878-3*) Raintree Steck-V.

Dinosaurs for Christmas. Scott Thomas. (J). 1993. 8.75 (*0-8062-4764-9*) Carlton.

Dinosaurs for Dessert: Book & Cookie Cutter Set. Stephanie St. Pierre. (Illus.). 16p. (J). (gr. k-3). 1991. pap. 3.95 (*0-590-68985-1*) Scholastic Inc.

Dinosaurs for Hire, Vol. 1: Guns 'N Lizards. Tom Mason. (Illus.). 88p. 1989. pap. 5.95 (*0-944735-21-5*) Malibu Graphics.

Dinosaurs for Hire, Vol. 2: Dinosaurs Rule! Tom Mason. (Illus.). 78p. 1990. pap. 5.95 (*0-944735-31-2*) Malibu Graphics.

Dinosaurs for Lunch. Shelly Ritthaler. 80p. (Orig.). (J). (gr. 2). 1993. pap. 3.50 (*0-380-76796-1*, Camelot Young) Avon.

Dinosaurs from A to Z. Keith McConnell. (NaturEncyclopedia Library). (Illus.). 40p. (Orig.). (J). (gr. 2 up). 1988. pap. 5.95 (*0-88045-095-9*) Stemmer Hse.

Dinosaurs Galore. Cecilia R. Telles. (Illus.). 32p. (J). (ps-2). 1993. pap. 3.50 (*0-87406-652-2*) Willowisp Pr.

***Dinosaurs Grow Again.** Union Baptist Day Care Preschoolers. (Wee Write Bks.: No. 10). (Illus.). 31p. (J). (ps-2). 1994. 32.95 (*1-884987-35-4*); lib. bdg. 17.95 (*1-884987-33-8*); pap. 7.95 (*1-884987-34-6*) WeWrite.

***Dinosaurs Grow Again.** Union Baptist Day Care Staff. (Wee Write Bks.: No. 10). (Illus.). 25p. (J). (ps-3). 1994. lib. bdg. 17.95 (*1-994987-33-2*) WeWrite.

Dinosaurs' Halloween. Liza Donnelly. (J). (ps-3). 1988. pap. 2.50 (*0-590-41006-7*) Scholastic Inc.

Dinosaurs I Have Known. Barry L. Polisar. (Illus.). 48p. (Orig.). (J). (gr. 2-6). 1988. 9.95 (*0-938663-00-3*); pap. 7.95 (*0-938663-05-4*) Rainbow Morn.

Dinosaurs in God's World Long Ago. Henrietta D. Gambill. Ed. by Shirley Beegle. (Happy Day Bks.). (Illus.). 24p. (J). (ps-3). 1994. reprint ed. pap. 1.89 (*0-7847-0253-5*) Standard Pub.

Dinosaurs in the Attic: An Excursion into the American Museum of Natural History. Douglas J. Preston. (Illus.). 256p. 1993. pap. 13.95 (*0-312-10456-1*) St Martin.

Dinosaurs in the Garden: A Naturalist's Guide to Backyard Biology & Evolution. R. Gary Raham. (Illus.). 280p. 1988. 22.95 (*0-937548-10-3*) Plexus Pub.

Dinosaurs in the Morning: Forty-One Pieces on Jazz. Whitney Balliett. LC 78-93. 224p. 1978. text ed. 42.50 (*0-313-20283-4*, BADI, Greenwood Pr) Greenwood.

Dinosaurs in Your Backyard. William Mannetti. LC 81-7998. (Illus.). 160p. (J). (gr. 4-7). 1982. text ed. 13.95 (*0-689-30906-6*, Atheneum Bks Young) S&S Childrens.

Dinosaurs' Last Days. Alvin Granowsky. LC 91-23408. (World of Dinosaurs Ser.). (Illus.). 32p. (J). (gr. 1-4). 1992. lib. bdg. 19.97 (*0-8114-3250-5*); pap. 3.95 (*0-8114-6225-0*) Raintree Steck-V.

***Dinosaurs Next Door.** H. Castor. (Reading for Beginners Ser.). (Illus.). 24p. (J). (gr. k-3). 1995. lib. bdg. 11.96 (*0-88110-744-1*, Usborne); pap. 4.95 (*0-7460-1531-3*, Usborne) EDC.

Dinosaurs of Africa. Louis L. Jacobs. LC 92-15080. 1993. 24.50 (*0-685-57388-5*, Villard Bks) Random.

Dinosaurs of All Sizes. Alvin Granowsky. LC 91-22343. (World of Dinosaurs Ser.). (Illus.). 32p. (J). (gr. 1-4). 1992. lib. bdg. 19.97 (*0-8114-3251-3*); pap. 3.95 (*0-8114-6229-3*) Raintree Steck-V.

Dinosaurs of Jurassic Park: An All Aboard Reading Book. Michael Crichton. (J). (ps-3). 1993. pap. 3.50 (*0-448-40178-9*, Platt & Munk Pubs) Putnam Pub Group.

Dinosaurs of North America. Helen R. Sattler. LC 80-27411. (Illus.). 160p. (J). (gr. 2 up). 1981. 18.00 (*0-688-51952-0*) Lothrop.

Dinosaurs of Prey: An Educational Coloring Book. Spizzirri Publishing Co. Staff. Ed. by Linda Spizzirri. (Illus.). 32p. (J). (gr. k-5). 1985. pap. 1.75 (*0-86545-063-3*) Spizzirri.

Dinosaurs of the Land, Sea & Air. (Dinosaur Bind-Ups Ser.). (Illus.). 240p. (J). (gr. k-2). 1989. 19.95 (*0-87449-512-1*) Modern Pub NYC.

Dinosaurs of the Land, Sea & Air. (Illus.). 24p. (J). (gr. 2-5). 1993. pap. 2.50 (*1-56144-289-5*, Honey Bear Bks) Modern Pub NYC.

Dinosaurs of the Land, Sea, & Air. Michael Teitelbaum. LC 93-49614. (Facts about Dinosaurs Ser.). (J). 1994. write for info. (*0-86593-353-7*) Rourke Corp.

Dinosaurs of the Prehistoric Era. (Illus.). 24p. (Orig.). (J). (gr. 2-5). 1993. pap. 2.50 (*1-56144-291-7*, Honey Bear Bks) Modern Pub NYC.

Dinosaurs of the Prehistoric Era. Michael Teitelbaum. LC 93-50057. (Facts about Dinosaurs Ser.). (J). 1994. write for info. (*0-86593-354-5*) Rourke Corp.

Dinosaurs on Parade. Adapt. by Francine Hughes. (We're Back! Books & Cassette Tapes Ser.). (Illus.). (J). (ps-3). 1993. pap. 2.50 (*0-448-40446-X*, G&D); audio, pap. 5.95 (*0-448-40448-6*, G&D) Putnam Pub Group.

Dinosaurs Past & Present, Vol. 1. Ed. by Sylvia J. Czerkas & Everett C. Olson. LC 87-60944. (Illus.). 180p. (Orig.). 1987. pap. 29.95 (*0-938644-24-6*) Nat Hist Mus.

Dinosaurs Past & Present, Vol. I. Ed. by Sylvia J. Czerkas & Everett C. Olson. LC 87-60944. (Illus.). 180p. (Orig.). 1987. pap. 29.95 (*0-295-96707-2*) U of Wash Pr.

Dinosaurs Past & Present, Vol. 2. Ed. by Sylvia J. Czerkas & Everett C. Olson. LC 87-60944. (Illus.). 164p. (Orig.). 1988. pap. 29.95 (*0-938644-23-8*) Nat Hist Mus.

Dinosaurs Past & Present, Vol. II. Ed. by Sylvia J. Czerkas & Everett C. Olson. (Illus.). 164p. (Orig.). 1988. pap. 29.95 (*0-295-96708-0*) U of Wash Pr.

Dinosaurs-Pop Up. (J). 1989. 9.95 (*0-8167-0901-7*) Troll Assocs.

Dinosaurs Postcard Book. Running Press Staff. (Postcard Book Ser.). (Illus.). 64p. (Orig.). (J). 1987. pap. 7.95 (*0-89471-553-4*) Running Pr.

Dinosaurs Rediscovered: New Discoveries That Are Revolutionizing Our Understanding of Dinosaurs. Don Lessem. (Illus.). 320p. 1992. 25.00 (*0-671-73491-1*) S&S Trade.

Dinosaurs Rediscovered: New Findings Which Are Revolutionizing Dinosaur Science. Don Lessem. (Illus.). 368p. 1993. pap. 12.00 (*0-671-79715-8*, Touchstone Bks) S&S Trade.

Dinosaurs, Spitfires, & Sea Dragons. Christopher McGowan. LC 90-41552. (Illus.). 384p. 1991. text ed. 29.95 (*0-674-20769-6*, MCGDIN) HUP.

Dinosaurs, Spitfires, & Seadragons. Christopher McGowan. (Illus.). 384p. (Orig.). 1992. pap. text ed. 14.95 (*0-674-20770-X*) HUP.

Dinosaurs Sticker Book. 1988. pap. 5.99 (*0-517-64547-5*) Random Hse Value.

Dinosaurs to the Rescue: A Guide to Protecting Our Planet. Laurene K. Brown & Marc T. Brown. (Illus.). (J). (ps-3). 1992. 14.95 (*0-316-11087-6*, Joy St Bks) Little.

Dinosaurs to the Rescue: A Guide to Protecting Our Planet. Marc Brown. (J). (ps-3). 1994. 5.95 (*0-316-11397-2*) Little.

Dinosaurs Travel, Vol. 1. Laurie K. Brown. (J). (ps-3). 1991. mass mkt. 5.95 (*0-316-11253-4*) Little.

Dinosaurs Travel: A Guide for Families on the Go. Laurene K. Brown & Marc T. Brown. (Illus.). 32p. (J). (ps-3). 1988. 13.95 (*0-316-11076-0*) Little.

Dinosaurs Trivia Fun Book. Elvira Gamiello. (Illus.). 32p. (Orig.). (J). 1989. pap. 1.50 (*0-942025-09-1*) Kidsbks.

Dinosaurs!, Vol. 1: A Drawing Book. Michael Emberley. (J). 1980. 14.95 (*0-316-23417-6*) Little.

An Asterisk (*) at the beginning of an entry indicates that the title is appearing in BIP for the first time.

An Asterisk (*) at the beginning of an entry indicates that the title is appearing in BIP for the first time.

D

Diplomacy: The Dialogue Between States. Adam Watson. 240p. 1992. pap. 18.95 (*0-415-06559-3*, A9852) Routledge.

Diplomacy: The Role of the Wife, a Symposium. Ed. by Martin F. Herz. 90p. (C). 1985. reprint ed. pap. text ed. 12.00 (*0-8191-5066-5*, Inst Study Diplomacy) U Pr of Amer.

***Diplomacy: Theory & Practice.** G. R. Berridge. LC 95-6414. 1995. write for info. (*0-13-433889-8*) P-H.

***Diplomacy, Administration & Policy: The Ideas & Careers of Frederick E. Nolting, Jr., Frederick C. Mosher, & Paul T. David.** Ed. by Kenneth W. Thompson. 248p. (Orig.). (C). 1995. pap. text ed. 24.50 (*0-8191-9883-8*) U Pr of Amer.

Diplomacy & Dogmatism: Bernardino de Mendoza & the French Catholic League. DeLamar Jensen. LC 63-20769. (Illus.). 334p. 1964. 32.00 (*0-674-20800-5*) HUP.

Diplomacy & Revolution: The Franco-American Alliance of 1778. Ed. by Ronald Hoffman & Peter J. Albert. LC 80-13931. (U. S. Capitol Historical Society, Perspectives on the American Revolution Ser.). 200p. 1981. 25.00 (*0-8139-0864-7*) U Pr of Va.

Diplomacy & Strategy of Survival: British Policy & Franco's Spain, 1940-1941. Denis Smyth. 352p. 1986. 69.95 (*0-521-22819-0*) Cambridge U Pr.

Diplomacy & the American Democracy. David D. Newsom. LC 87-45438. 240p. 1988. 25.00 (*0-253-31816-5*); pap. 9.95 (*0-253-20470-4*, MB-470) Ind U Pr.

Diplomacy at the U. N. Ed. by Geoff R. Berridge & A. Jennings. LC 84-11733. 256p. 1985. text ed. 39.95 (*0-312-21117-1*) St Martin.

Diplomacy During the Persian Gulf War. Allan E. Goodman. (Pew Case Studies in International Affairs). 50p. (C). 1992. pap. text ed. 2.50 (*1-56927-349-9*) Geo U Inst Dplmcy.

Diplomacy for the Future. Ed. by George C. McGhee. LC 87-3455. 116p. (Orig.). 1987. pap. text ed. 13.00 (*0-934742-41-3*) Geo U Inst Dplmcy.

Diplomacy for the Future. Ed. by George C. McGhee. LC 87-3455. 118p. (Orig.). 1987. lib. bdg. 35.50 (*0-8191-6487-9*, Inst Study Diplomacy); pap. text ed. 13.00 (*0-8191-6488-7*, Inst Study Diplomacy) U Pr of Amer.

Diplomacy for Victory: FDR & Unconditional Surrender. Raymond G. O'Connor. LC 70-155986. (Essays in American History Ser.). (Illus.). (C). 1971. pap. text ed. 7.95 (*0-393-09765-X*) Norton.

Diplomacy, Force, & Leadership: Essays in Honor of Alexder L. George. Timothy J. McKeown. Ed. by Dan Caldwell. LC 93-19811. 322p. 1993. text ed. 65.00 (*0-8133-1745-2*) Westview.

Diplomacy in a Democracy. Henry M. Wriston. LC 74-7541. 115p. 1974. reprint ed. text ed. 49.75 (*0-8371-7580-1*, WRDD, Greenwood Pr) Greenwood.

Diplomacy in Early Islam. A. Iqbal. 22.50 (*0-935782-74-5*) Kazi Pubns.

Diplomacy in Iron. Louis L. Snyder. LC 84-17175. 248p. (C). 1985. lib. bdg. 28.50 (*0-89874-794-5*) Krieger.

Diplomacy in Peace & War. T. N. Kaul. 251p. 1979. 16.95 (*0-7069-0749-3*) Asia Bk Corp.

***Diplomacy in the Former Soviet Republics.** James P. Nichol. LC 95-3353. 256p. 1995. text ed. 55.00 (*0-275-95192-8*, Praeger Pubs) Greenwood.

Diplomacy in the Near & Middle East, 1535-1956, 2 vols., Set. J. C. Hurewitz. 750p. (C). 1987. text ed. 600.00 (*1-85207-077-3*, Pub. by Archive Res Ltd UK) St Mut.

Diplomacy of a New Age: Major Issues in U. S. Policy Since 1945. Dexter Perkins. LC 67-13034. 190p. reprint ed. pap. 54.20 (*0-8357-9203-X*, 2017635) Bks Demand.

Diplomacy of a Tiny State. 2nd ed. K. C. Lee. 364p. 1993. pap. text ed. 29.00 (*981-02-1219-4*) World Scientific Pub.

Diplomacy of Aggression. Issraeljian & Kutakov. 450p. 1975. 25.00 (*0-8464-1252-7*) Beekman Pubs.

Diplomacy of Asymmetry: Korean-American Relations to 1910. Jongsuk Chay. LC 89-20502. 272p. 1990. text ed. 32.00 (*0-8248-1236-0*) UH Pr.

Diplomacy of Biological Disarmament: Vicissitudes of a Treaty in Force 1975-1985. Nicholas A. Sims. LC 86-11875. 1988. text ed. 55.00 (*0-312-21119-8*) St Martin.

Diplomacy of Fear: Canada & the Cold War, 1941-1948. Dennis Smith. 300p. 1988. pap. 18.95 (*0-8020-6684-4*) U of Toronto Pr.

Diplomacy of Fear: Canada & the Cold War, 1941-1948. Denis Smith. LC 88-198113. 299p. reprint ed. pap. 85.30 (*0-8357-3784-5*, 2036514) Bks Demand.

Diplomacy of German Unification. Stephen F. Szabo. LC 92-17119. 1992. text ed. 35.00 (*0-312-08057-3*) St Martin.

***Diplomacy of German Unification Vol. 1.** Stephen F. Szabo. 1994. text ed. 17.95 (*0-312-12160-1*) St Martin.

Diplomacy of Hope: Canada & Disarmament, 1945-1988. Albert Legault & Michel Fortmann. 632p. 1992. 75.00 (*0-7735-0920-8*, Pub. by McGill CN); pap. 29.95 (*0-7735-0955-0*, Pub. by McGill CN) U of Toronto Pr.

Diplomacy of Ideas: U. S. Foreign Policy & Cultural Relations, 1938-1950. F. A. Ninkovich. 256p. 1981. 49.95 (*0-521-23241-4*) Cambridge U Pr.

Diplomacy of Illusion: The British Government & Germany, 1937-1939. Keith Middlemas. (Modern Revivals in History Ser.). 510p. 1992. 62.50 (*0-7512-0009-3*, Pub. by Gregg Revivals UK) Ashgate Pub Co.

Diplomacy of Imperial Retreat: Britain's South China Policy, 1924-1931. Edmund S. Fung. (East Asian Historical Monographs). 300p. 1991. 53.00 (*0-19-585284-2*) OUP.

Diplomacy of Isolation: South African Foreign Policy Making. Deon Geldenhuys. LC 83-40515. 295p. 1984. text ed. 39.95 (*0-312-21132-5*) St Martin.

Diplomacy of Modernization: Colombian-American Relations 1920-1940. Stephen J. Randall. LC 77-4480. 251p. reprint ed. pap. 71.60 (*0-685-43698-5*, 2026440) Bks Demand.

Diplomacy of Power: Soviet Armed Forces as a Political Instrument. Stephen S. Kaplan. LC 80-25006. 733p. 1981. pap. 19.95 (*0-8157-4823-X*) Brookings.

Diplomacy of Pragmatism: Britain & the Formation of NATO, 1942-1949. John Baylis. LC 92-5602. (American Diplomatic History Ser.: No. 5). 208p. 1993. 35.00 (*0-87338-471-7*) Kent St U Pr.

Diplomacy of Surprise: Hitler, Nixon, Sadat. Michael I. Handel. (Harvard Studies in International Affairs: No. 44). 382p. 1984. reprint ed. lib. bdg. 52.00 (*0-8191-4054-6*); reprint ed. pap. text ed. 28.00 (*0-8191-4055-4*) U Pr of Amer.

Diplomacy of the American Revolution. Samuel F. Bemis. LC 83-12977. xii, 293p. 1983. reprint ed. text ed. 45.50 (*0-313-24173-2*, BEDI, Greenwood Pr) Greenwood.

Diplomacy of the Crucial Decade: American Foreign Relations During the 1960s. Ed. by Diane B. Kunz. LC 93-37995. 372p. (C). 1994. 50.00 (*0-231-08176-6*); pap. 16.50 (*0-231-08177-4*) Col U Pr.

Diplomacy of the Mexican Empire, 1863-1867. Arnold Blumberg. LC 85-23965. 334p. (C). 1987. reprint ed. pap. 19.95 (*0-89874-931-X*) Krieger.

Diplomacy of the New Republic, 1776-1815. Reginald Horsman. Ed. by John H. Franklin & A. S. Eisenstadt. LC 84-236910. (American History Ser.). 164p. (C). 1985. pap. text ed. write for info. (*0-88295-829-1*) Harlan Davidson.

Diplomacy of the Oppressed: New Directions in International Feminism. Ed. by Georgina Ashworth. 256p. (C). 1995. text ed. 55.00 (*1-85649-143-9*, Pub. by Zed Books UK); pap. 22.50 (*1-85649-144-7*, Pub. by Zed Books UK) Humanities.

Diplomacy of the Russo-Japanese War. John A. White. LC 63-23417. 429p. reprint ed. pap. 122.30 (*0-317-08455-0*, 2000697) Bks Demand.

Diplomacy of the Sino-French War (1883-85) Global Complications of an Undeclared War. Lewis M. Chere. LC 87-72449. (West & the Wider World Ser.). xii, 350p. 1988. 35.85x (*0-940121-06-9*) Cross Cultural Pubns.

Diplomacy of Zhou Enlai. Ronald C. Keith. LC 89-30667. (Illus.). 304p. 1989. text ed. 49.95 (*0-312-03100-9*) St Martin.

Diplomacy: The Role of the Wife: A Symposium. Ed. by Martin F. Herz. LC 81-917. 88p. (Orig.). 1981. pap. 7.00 (*0-934742-10-3*) Geo U Inst Dplmcy.

Diplomacy under a Foreign Flag: When Nations Break Relations. Ed. by David D. Newsom. LC 89-19983. 144p. (Orig.). 1990. pap. text ed. 9.95 (*0-934742-46-4*) Geo U Inst Dplmcy.

Diplomacy under a Foreign Flag: When Nations Break Relations. Ed. by David D. Newsom. LC 89-19983. 144p. (Orig.). 1990. text ed. 39.95 (*0-312-04051-2*) St Martin.

Diplomacy, War & Parliamentary Democracy: Further Lessons from the Falklands or, Advice from Academe. Robert A. Burns. 62p. (Orig.). 1985. pap. text ed. 14.00 (*0-8191-4610-2*) U Pr of Amer.

Diplomacy, War & Technology Since 1830. Maurice Pearton. LC 84-7272. (Studies in Government & Public Policy). 288p. 1984. pap. 9.95 (*0-7006-0254-2*) U Pr of KS.

Diplomas & Thatch Houses: Asserting Tradition in a Changing Micronesia. Juliana Flinn. 220p. (C). 1992. text ed. 34.50 (*0-472-10306-7*) U of Mich Pr.

Diplomas or Degrees: Fast, Legal, Inexpensive. 5th rev. ed. Richard M. Zink. (Illus.). 64p. 1994. pap. 14.95x (*0-939469-40-5*) Zinks Career Guide.

Diplomat. Charles W. Thayer. LC 74-6780. 299p. 1975. reprint ed. text ed. 79.50 (*0-8371-7570-4*, THDI, Greenwood Pr) Greenwood.

Diplomat Among Warriors. Robert D. Murphy. LC 75-42364. (Illus.). 470p. 1976. reprint ed. text ed. 65.00 (*0-8371-7693-X*, MUDW, Greenwood Pr) Greenwood.

Diplomat in Berlin, 1933-1939: Papers & Memoirs of Jozef Lipski, Ambassador of Poland. Jozef Lipski. Ed. by Waclaw Jedrzejewicz. LC 67-25871. 727p. reprint ed. pap. 180.00 (*0-317-09473-4*, 2006109) Bks Demand.

Diplomat in Carpet Slippers: Abraham Lincoln Deals with Foreign Affairs. Jay Monaghan. LC 79-39200. (Select Bibliographies Reprint Ser.). 1977. reprint ed. 34.95 (*0-8369-6802-6*) Ayer.

Diplomat in Chief. LC 85-16741. 528p. 1985. text ed. 59.95 (*0-275-92040-2*, Greenwood Pr) Greenwood.

Diplomat in Exile: Francis Pulszky's Political Activities in England, 1849-1860. Thomas Kabdebo. (Monographs: No. 56). 208p. 1979. text ed. 47.50 (*0-914710-47-8*) East Eur Quarterly.

Diplomat in Japan. Ernest M. Satow. reprint ed. 47.50 (*0-404-05561-3*) AMS Pr.

Diplomat in Khaki: Major General Frank Ross McCoy & American Foreign Policy, 1898-1949. A. J. Bacevich. LC 89-5749. (Modern War Studies). (Illus.). xii, 276p. 1989. 29.95 (*0-7006-0401-4*) U Pr of KS.

Diplomat Looks Back. Lewis Einstein. Ed. by Lawrence E. Gelfand. LC 67-24497. 305p. reprint ed. pap. 87.00 (*0-8357-8704-4*, 2033715) Bks Demand.

Diplomat of the Americas: A Biography of William I. Buchanan, 1852-1909. Harold F. Peterson. LC 76-22652. 458p. 1977. 59.50 (*0-87395-346-0*) State U NY Pr.

Diplomatarium of the Crusader Kingdom of Valencia: The Registered Charters of Its Conqueror, Jaume I, 1257-1276. Volume I: Society & Documentation in Crusader Valencia. Robert I. Burns. LC 84-17828. (Illus.). 288p. 1985. text ed. 55.00x (*0-691-05435-5*) Princeton U Pr.

Diplomatarium of the Crusader Kingdom of Valencia: The Registered Charters of Its Conqueror Jaume I, 1257-1276, Vol. II: The Foundations of Crusader Valencia: Revolt & Recovery. Robert I. Burns. 474p. 1990. text ed. 75.00 (*0-691-05474-6*) Princeton U Pr.

Diplomate Directory, 1989-1990. ABECSW Staff. Ed. by John A. Chambers. 1989. write for info. (*0-318-65923-9*) ABECSW.

Diplomatic Chronicles of the Middle East: A Biography of Ambassador Raymond A. Hare. Ed. by Paul J. Hare. 160p. (C). 1993. lib. bdg. 39.50 (*0-8191-8935-9*) U Pr of Amer.

Diplomatic Code of the United States of America (As American Diplomatic Code, 1834) Jonathan Elliot. (Notable American Authors Ser.). 1992. reprint ed. lib. bdg. 75.00 (*0-7812-2799-2*) Rprt Serv.

Diplomatic Death. large type ed. Charles Forsyte. 336p. 1988. 15.95 (*0-7089-1864-6*) Ulverscroft.

Diplomatic Dispute: U. S. Conflict with Iran, Japan & Mexico. Ed. by Robert L. Paarlberg et al. (Harvard Studies in International Affairs: No. 39). 174p. 1984. reprint ed. pap. text ed. 24.00 (*0-8191-4063-5*) U Pr of Amer.

Diplomatic History of America: Its First Chapter, 1452-1493-1494. Henry Harrisse. (Reprints in History Ser.). reprint ed. lib. bdg. 34.00 (*0-697-00007-9*); reprint ed. pap. 8.95 (*0-89197-731-7*) Irvington.

Diplomatic History of British Honduras, 1638 to 1901. Robert A. Humphreys. LC 81-4635. (Illus.). ix, 196p. 1981. reprint ed. text ed. 35.00 (*0-313-22995-3*, HUDH, Greenwood Pr) Greenwood.

Diplomatic History of Bulgaria, 1870-1886. Arthur M. Hyde. LC 72-136537. (University of Illinois Studies in the Social Sciences: Vol. 16, No. 3). 172p. 1972. reprint ed. text ed. 49.75 (*0-8371-5458-8*, HYHB, Greenwood Pr) Greenwood.

Diplomatic History of Ireland, 1948-49: The Republic, the Commonwealth & NATO. Ian McCabe. 212p. 1992. text ed. 39.50 (*0-7165-2461-9*, Pub. by Irish Acad Pr IE) Intl Spec Bk.

Diplomatic History of Modern Iraq. Abid A. Al-Marayati. 1961. 9.95 (*0-8315-0108-1*) Speller.

Diplomatic History of the American People. 10th ed. Thomas A. Bailey. (Illus.). 1980. text ed. 60.00 (*0-13-214726-2*) P-H.

Diplomatic History of the American Revolution. Jonathan R. Dull. LC 85-5306. (Illus.). 224p. 1987. pap. 15.00x (*0-300-03886-0*) Yale U Pr.

Diplomatic History of the Southern Confederacy. James M. Callahan. (History - United States Ser.). 304p. 1992. reprint ed. lib. bdg. 89.00 (*0-7812-6182-1*) Rprt Serv.

Diplomatic History, 1713-1933. Charles A. Petrie. LC 83-45834. reprint ed. 35.00 (*0-404-20199-7*) AMS Pr.

Diplomatic Ideas & Practices of Asian States. Ed. by Ashok Kapur. LC 90-2065. (International Studies in Sociology & Social Anthropology: No. 53). 133p. 1990. pap. 28.75 (*90-04-09289-7*) E J Brill.

Diplomatic Immunity. Grant V. McClanahan. 290p. 1989. pap. 15.95 (*0-312-02832-6*) St Martin.

Diplomatic Immunity: Principles, Practices, Problems. 1989. write for info. (*0-318-66025-3*) St Martin.

Diplomatic Laws in Contemporary International Relations. A. Chaturvedi. 200p. 1986. 24.95 (*0-318-37233-9*) Asia Bk Corp.

***Diplomatic List: The Official Directory of Foreign Diplomats & Their Staff in the U. S.** (Illus.). 76p. (Orig.). (C). 1995. pap. text ed. 45.00x (*0-7881-1612-6*) Diane Pub.

Diplomatic Lover. Elsie Lee. 256p. 1987. pap. 2.95 (*0-8217-2234-4*) Zebra.

***Diplomatic Moves.** Sally James. (Illus.). 192p. 1995. text ed. 39.50 (*1-85043-924-9*) St Martin.

Diplomatic Negotiations of American Naval Officers 1778-1883. Charles O. Paullin. 11.75 (*0-8446-1342-8*) Peter Smith.

Diplomatic Passport: More Undiplomatic Diaries. Charles Ritchie. 200p. 1986. pap. 4.95 (*0-7715-9258-2*, Pub. by Stoddart Pubng CN) Genl Dist Srvs.

Diplomatic Pleasures. pap. 4.50 (*0-8216-5092-0*, Univ Books) Carol Pub Group.

***Diplomatic Pouch.** Genevieve Chartier. (Illus.). 184p. 1995. pap. 11.95 (*0-9634891-3-5*) La Presse des Mich.

Diplomatic Protection of Americans in Mexico. F. S. Dunn. (MLA MS). 1972. reprint ed. 37.00 (*0-527-25750-8*) Periodicals Srv.

***Diplomatic Pursuits.** Joseph Von Westphalen. Tr. by Melanie Richter-Bernburg. LC 94-42791. 300p. (Orig.). 1995. pap. 14.95 (*0-945774-28-1*, PT2685.E825I413) Catbird Pr.

Diplomatic Ramifications of Unrestricted Submarine Warfare, 1939-1941. Janet M. Manson. LC 90-34130. (Contributions in Military Studies: No. 104). 326p. 1990. text ed. 55.00 (*0-313-26894-0*, MGC, Greenwood Pr) Greenwood.

Diplomatic Record, 1989-1990. Ed. by David D. Newsom. (Illus.). 250p. 1990. text ed. 73.00 (*0-8133-1142-X*) Westview.

Diplomatic Record, 1989-1990. Ed. by David D. Newsom. (Diplomatic Record Ser.). (Illus.). 256p. (Orig.). 1991. pap. text ed. 12.50 (*0-934742-65-0*) Geo U Inst Dplmcy.

Diplomatic Record, 1990-1991. Ed. by David D. Newsom. (Diplomatic Record Ser.). (Illus.). 337p. 1992. pap. text ed. 12.50 (*0-934742-66-9*) Geo U Inst Dplmcy.

Diplomatic Record, 1990-1991. Ed. by David D. Newsom. (Illus.). 331p. 1992. text ed. 61.00 (*0-8133-1386-4*) Westview.

Diplomatic Record, 1991-1992. Ed. by Hans Binnendijk & Mary E. Locke. 319p. (C). 1992. pap. text ed. 21.50 (*0-8133-1688-X*) Westview.

Diplomatic Record, 1991-1992. Ed. by Hans Binnendijk & Mary E. Locke. 319p. (C). 1993. text ed. 61.00 (*0-8133-1687-1*) Westview.

Diplomatic Record 1992-1993. Ed. by Allan E. Goodman. 288p. 1994. text ed. 65.00 (*0-8133-2067-4*) Westview.

Diplomatic Records: A Select Catalog of National Archives Microfilm Publications. LC 86-679. 245p. 1986. pap. 2.00 (*0-911333-10-X*, 200029) National Archives & Recs.

Diplomatic Relations. Ray Fleming. LC 81-82660. 59p. (YA). (gr. 9-12). 1982. per., pap. 4.00 (*0-916418-34-0*) Lotus.

Diplomatic Relations. Nanos Valoritis. 68p. 1972. 6.00 (*0-915572-07-9*) Panjandrum.

Diplomatic Relations Between the United States & Brazil. L. F. Hill. 1976. lib. bdg. 59.95 (*0-8490-1725-4*) Gordon Pr.

Diplomatic Relations Between the United States & Brazil. Lawrence F. Hill. LC 76-169489. reprint ed. 45.00 (*0-404-03268-0*) AMS Pr.

Diplomatic Relations Between the United States & Brazil. Lawrence F. Hill. LC 32-18335. 1969. reprint ed. 26.00 (*0-527-40650-3*) Periodicals Srv.

Diplomatic Relations Between the United States & Brazil. Lawrence F. Hill. LC 72-145088. 1971. reprint ed. 13.00 (*0-403-01027-6*) Scholarly.

Diplomatic Relations Between the United States & the Kingdom of the Two Sicilies, 2 vols., Set. Ed. by Howard R. Marraro. 1951. 45.00 (*0-913298-56-5*) S F Vanni.

Diplomatic Sailor. John Parkinson. 1981. 23.00 (*0-7223-1360-8*, Pub. by A H S Ltd UK) St Mut.

Diplomatic Secrets. 1993. pap. 4.50 (*0-8216-5095-5*, Univ Books) Carol Pub Group.

Diplomatic Service List, 1993. HMSO Staff. 357p. 1992. pap. 40.00 (*0-11-591744-6*, HM17446, Pub. by HMSO UK) UNIPUB.

Diplomatic Significance of Ionian Neutrality, 1821-31. W. D. Wrigley. (American University Studies: History: Ser. IX, Vol. 41). 340p. 1988. 41.95 (*0-8204-0696-1*) P Lang Pubs.

Diplomatic Studies in Latin & Greek Documents from the Carolingian Age. Luitpold Wallach. (Illus.). 352p. 1977. 56.50 (*0-8014-1019-3*) Cornell U Pr.

Diplomatic Witness. Paul Hasluck. 316p. 1980. 29.95 (*0-522-84186-4*) Intl Spec Bk.

Diplomatic Wives. Louise Page. (Methuen Modern Plays Ser.). 90p. (Orig.). 1989. pap. 9.95 (*0-413-61430-1*, Pub. by Methuen UK) Heinemann.

Diplomatische und Politische Geschichte Kroatiens. rev. ed. Ivo Omrcanin. 416p. 1990. 25.00 (*1-878716-03-4*) Ivor Pr.

Diplomatist. large type ed. William Haggard. 1993. 39.95 (*0-7066-1024-5*, Pub. by Remploy Pr CN) St Mut.

Diplomats & Terrorists: What Works, What Doesn't - A Symposium. Ed. & Intro. by Martin F. Herz. LC 82-6078. 80p. (Orig.). 1982. pap. 7.00 (*0-934742-17-0*) Geo U Inst Dplmcy.

Diplomats & Terrorists: What Works, What Doesn't, a Symposium. Ed. by Martin F. Herz. 80p. (C). 1985. reprint ed. pap. text ed. 12.50 (*0-8191-5068-1*, Inst Study Diplomacy) U Pr of Amer.

Diplomats & Terrorists II: Overseas Security - Our People Are the Key. Harold G. Bean. LC 87-3138. (Illus.). 96p. (Orig.). 1987. pap. 7.00 (*0-934742-42-1*) Geo U Inst Dplmcy.

Diplomats at Work: Three Renaissance Studies. Joycelyne G. Russell. (Illus.). 160p. (C). 1992. text ed. 55.00 (*0-7509-0032-6*) A Sutton Pub.

Diplomat's Handbook of International Law & Practice. 2nd ed. B. Sen. 1979. lib. bdg. 117.00 (*90-247-2142-3*) Kluwer Ac.

Diplomat's Handbook of International Law & Practice. 3rd rev. ed. B. Sen. (C). 1988. lib. bdg. 162.00 (*90-247-3647-1*) Kluwer Ac.

***Diplomats in Buckskins: A History of Indian Delegations in Washington City.** Herman J. Viola. LC 95-5146. 1995. pap. write for info. (*0-9630731-9-2*) Rivilo Bks.

Diplomat's Wife in Mexico. Edith L. O'Shaughnessy. LC 73-111727. (American Imperialism: Viewpoints of United States Foreign Policy, 1898-1941 Ser.). 1970. reprint ed. 34.95 (*0-405-02042-2*) Ayer.

Diplomat's Wife in Mexico. Edith L. O'Shaughnessy. (American Biography Ser.). 355p. 1991. reprint ed. lib. bdg. 79.00 (*0-7812-8303-5*) Rprt Serv.

Diplomats, 1919-1939. Gordon A. Craig. (C). 1994. pap. 24.95 (*0-691-03660-8*) Princeton U Pr.

Diplomats, 1939-1979. Gordon A. Craig. (C). 1994. 35.00 (*0-691-03613-6*) Princeton U Pr.

Diplomatska i Politicka Povijest Hrvatske, 4 vols., Set. Ivo Omrcanin. 298p. (CRO.). 1992. pap. 25.00 (*1-878716-06-9*) Ivor Pr.

Diplomatska i Politicka Povijest Hrvatske, Vol. 1. Ivo Omrcanin. 272p. (CRO.). 1991. pap. 20.00 (*0-614-03039-0*) Ivor Pr.

Diplomatska i Politicka Povijest Hrvatske, Vol. 2. Ivo Omrcanin. 303p. (CRO.). 1991. pap. 20.00 (*0-685-59169-7*) Ivor Pr.

Diplomatska i Politicka Povijest Hrvatske, Vol. 3. 309p. (CRO.). 1992. pap. 20.00 (*0-685-60640-6*) Ivor Pr.

Diplomatska i Politicka Povijest Hrvatske, Vol. 4. 300p. (CRO.). 1992. pap. 20.00 (*0-685-60641-4*) Ivor Pr.

Diplomazia Pontificia. Paolo Brezzi. 449p. reprint ed. write for info. (*0-318-71583-X*, Pub. by Georg Olms GW) Lubrecht & Cramer.

Dipole Moments & Birefringence of Polymers. Enrique Saiz & Evaristo Riande. 360p. 1991. text ed. 94.00 (*0-13-218199-1*) P-H.

An Asterisk (*) at the beginning of an entry indicates that the title is appearing in BIP for the first time.

Dipole Radiation Presence of a Conducting Half Space. A. Banos & A. Cullen. LC 65-14781. (International Series of Monographs in Electromagnetic Waves: Vol. 9). 1966. 110.00 (0-08-011171-8, Pub. by Pergamon Repr UK) Franklin.

Dipper. Stephanie J. Tyler et al. 1989. pap. 25.00 (0-85263-955-4, Pub. by Shire UK) St Mut.

*Dippers. Stephanie Tyler & Stephen Ormerod. (Illus.). 225p. 1995. text ed. 29.95 (0-85661-093-3) Acad Pr.

Dippy Diplodocus: Story & Gameboard. Carnegie Museum of Natural History, Division of Education Staff. (Illus.). 16p. (Orig.). (J). (ps-2). 1988. pap. 4.95 (0-911239-23-5) Carnegie Mus.

Dippy Diplodocus: Story Only. Carnegie Museum of Natural History, Division of Education Staff. (Illus.). 16p. (Orig.). (J). (ps-2). 1988. pap. 1.50 (0-911239-40-5) Carnegie Mus.

*Dips. Susan Puckett. (Illus.). 96p. 1995. 14.95 (1-56352-241-1) Longstreet Pr Inc.

Dip's Country Cooking. Mildred Council. (Illus.). 250p. (Orig.). 1992. pap. 16.95 (0-944337-06-6) New View Pubns.

Dips 'n' Doodles. Symons & Alvin Westcott. LC 74-108726. (Illus.). 48p. (J). (gr. 3-5). 1970. lib. bdg. 10.95 (0-87783-011-8) Oddo.

Dips 'n' Doodles. deluxe ed. Symons & Alvin Westcott. LC 74-108726. (Illus.). 48p. (J). (gr. 3-5). 1970. pap. 3.94 (0-87783-090-8) Oddo.

Dipsea: The Greatest Race. Barry Spitz. LC 93-85457. 240p. (Orig.). 1993. 27.95 (0-9620715-4-4); pap. 18.95 (0-9620715-5-2) Potrero Meadow Pub.

Diptera: Brachycera, Vol. II. E. Brunetti. (Fauna of British India Ser.). (Illus.). x, 410p. 1977. reprint ed. 30.00 (0-88065-071-0, Messers Today & Tomorrow) Scholarly Pubns.

*Diptera: Brachycera II-Cyclorrhapha I. E. Zimmerman & E. Hardy. (Insects of Hawaii Ser.: Vol. 11). (Illus.). 486p. 1964. 15.00 (0-614-05659-4) Entomol Soc.

*Diptera: Cyclorrhapha II. E. Zimmerman & E. Hardy. (Insects of Hawaii Ser.: Vol. 12). (Illus.). 824p. 1965. 15.00 (0-614-05660-8) Entomol Soc.

*Diptera: Cyclorrhapha III. E. Zimmerman & E. Hardy. (Insects of Hawaii Ser.: Vol. 13). (Illus.). 451p. 1980. 15.00 (0-614-05661-6) Entomol Soc.

*Diptera: Cyclorrhapha IV. E. Zimmerman & E. Hardy. (Insects of Hawaii Ser.: Vol. 14). (Illus.). 491p. 1981. 15.00 (0-614-05662-4) Entomol Soc.

Diptera: Diptera, Family Culicidae, Tribe Anophelini, Vol. 4. S. Christophers. (Fauna of British India Ser.). (Illus.). vi, 372p. 1977. reprint ed. 30.00 (0-88065-042-7, Messers Today & Tomorrow) Scholarly Pubns.

Diptera: Family Calcidae, Tribe Megarhinini & Cuiicini, Vol. 5. P. J. Barraud. (Fauna of British India Ser.). (Illus.). xxviii, 484p. 1977. reprint ed. 30.00 (0-685-04534-X, Messers Today & Tomorrow) Scholarly Pubns.

Diptera: Family Calliphoridae, Vol. 6. R. S. White et al. (Fauna of British India Ser.). (Illus.). xiv, 294p. 1977. reprint ed. 30.00 (0-88065-210-1, Messers Today & Tomorrow) Scholarly Pubns.

Diptera: Family Culicidae, Tribe Anophelini, Vol. 4. S. Christophers. (Fauna of British India Ser.). 1977. reprint ed. 30.00 (0-88065-043-5, Pub. by Today & Tomorrows P & P II) Scholarly Pubns.

*Diptera: Nematocera-Brachyccera I. E. Zimmerman & E. Hardy. (Insects of Hawaii Ser.: Vol. 10). (Illus.). 380p. 1960. 15.00 (0-614-05658-6) Entomol Soc.

Diptera: Nematocera (Excluding Chironomidae & Culcidae), Vol. 1. E. Brunetti. (Fauna of British India Ser.). (Illus.). xxviii, 610p. 1977. reprint ed. 30.00 (0-685-04535-8, Messers Today & Tomorrow) Scholarly Pubns.

Diptera: Pipunculidae, Syrphidae, Conopidae, Ostridae, Vol. III. E. Brunetti. (Fauna of British India Ser.). (Illus.). xii, 436p. 1977. reprint ed. 30.00 (0-88065-072-9, Messers Today & Tomorrow) Scholarly Pubns.

Diptera Types in the National Collection of Insects, Pt. 2: Brachycera. Bruce E. Cooper & Jeffrey M. Cumming. 112p. (Orig.). 1993. pap. 32.45 (0-660-57979-0, Pub. by Canada Commun Grp CN) Accents Pubns.

Diptico Cubano: La Mueca de la Paloma Negra Desertores del Paraiso. Jorge Ronet & Lazaro G. Carriles. (Biblioteca Cubana Contemporanea Ser.). 126p. (Orig.). (SPA.). 1988. pap. 12.00 (84-359-0539-X, Pub. by Editorial Playor SP) Ediciones.

Diptych Rome-London. Ezra Pound. (Bibelot Ser.). 64p. 1994. pap. 5.00 (0-8112-1268-8, NDP783) New Directions.

Dipyrone: Recent Investigations on Its Mode of Action, Pharmacokinetics, & Clinical Use, Berlin, October 24, 1991. Ed. by Kay Brune. LC 92-49454. vii, 45p. 1992. write for info. (3-7643-2804-5, Pub. by Birkhauser Vlg SZ); 18.00 (0-8176-2804-5, Pub. by Birkhauser Vlg SZ) Birkhauser.

Diquarks II. Isi Anselmino & E. Predazzi. 304p. 1994. text ed. 86.00 (981-02-1676-9) World Scientific Pub.

DIR Guide to Japanese Economic Statistics. Mikihiro Matsuoka & Brian Rose. 304p. 1994. 37.50 (0-19-828861-1) OUP.

Dir of Religious Organizations In The U. S. 3rd ed. J. Gordon Melton. 1992. 125.00 (0-685-48433-5) Gale.

Dirac: A Scientific Biography. Helge S. Kragh. (Illus.). 400p. (C). 1990. 54.95 (0-521-38089-8) Cambridge U Pr.

Dirac Equation. Bernd Thaller. LC 92-12288. (Texts & Monographs in Physics). 376p. 1993. 89.00 (3-540-54883-1); 89.00 (0-387-54883-1) Spr-Verlag.

Dirac Kets, Gamow Vectors & Gel'fand Triplets. Arno Bohm & M. Gadella. (Lecture Notes in Physics Ser.: Vol. 348). (Illus.). vii, 119p. 1989. 31.00 (0-387-51916-5, 3730) Spr-Verlag.

Dirac Structures & Integrability of Nonlinear Equations. Irene Dorfman. (Nonlinear Science, Theory & Applications Ser.). 176p. 1993. text ed. 84.95 (0-471-93893-9) Wiley.

Diradicals. Ed. by Weston T. Borden. LC 82-8604. (Illus.). 357p. reprint ed. pap. 101.80 (0-685-23822-9, 2056603) Bks Demand.

Dirae Im Romischen Epos. Wolfgang Hubner. Bd. 21. x, 231p. (GER.). 1969. write for info. (0-318-70625-3, Pub. by Georg Olms GW) Lubrecht & Cramer.

Dirae Im Romischen Epos. Wolfgang Hubner. Bd. XXI. 134p. 1970. write for info. (0-318-71150-8, Pub. by Georg Olms GW) Lubrecht & Cramer.

Dire Coasts. John C. Holmes. 36p. (Orig.). 1988. pap. 10.00 (0-931659-02-7) Limberlost Pr.

*Dire Happenings at Scratch Ankle. Celestine Sibley. 1994. pap. 4.50 (0-06-109050-6, Harp PBks) HarpC.

Dire Happenings at Scratch Ankle: A Kate Mulcay Mystery. Celestine Sibley. LC 92-56203. 224p. 1993. 19.00 (0-06-017703-9, HarpT) HarpC.

Dire la Parodie: Colloque de Cerisy. Ed. by Clive Thomson & Alain Pages. (American University Studies: Romance Languages & Literature: Ser. II, Vol. 91). 397p. (C). 1989. text ed. 58.95 (0-8204-0751-8) P Lang Pubs.

Dire Mastery: Discipleship from Freud to Lacan. Francois Roustang. Tr. by Ned Lukacher. LC 86-20572. 178p. 1986. pap. text ed. 13.00 (0-88048-259-1, 48-259-1) Am Psychiatric.

Dire Mastery: Discipleship from Freud to Lacan. Francois Roustang. Tr. by Ned Lukacher. LC 82-6552. 160p. 1982. text ed. 30.00x (0-8018-2675-6) Johns Hopkins.

Dire Straits. Gordon Matthews. (Orig.). 1987. pap. 2.95 (0-345-33885-5) Ballantine.

Dire Straits: Making Movies. 1980. 7.95 (0-89898-051-8) Almo Pubns.

*Dire Wolf: And Other Fearful & Fanciful Works by Sculptor George Roberts. George Roberts. Ed. by Robert Jacobson. LC 95-7063. 152p. (Orig.). 1995. pap. 25.00 (0-89301-182-7) U of Idaho Pr.

Direccion de Personal. Ferdinand F. Fournies. 1991. pap. text ed. 12.95 (0-07-104048-X) McGraw.

Direcorty of Library & Information Professionals. 3rd ed. 1904. 380.00 (0-8103-7910-4) Gale.

Direct Access to Physical Therapy Services: An Educational Module. 250p. 1991. ring bd., sl. 130.00 (0-685-65751-5, E-22) Am Phys Therapy Assn.

Direct Acting Steam Pump Standard for Nomenclature, Definitions, Application & Operation, No. 8.1-8.5. (Hydraulic Institute Ser.: No. 8.1-8.5). 1994. 39.00 (1-880952-13-0, S117) Hydraulic Inst.

Direct Action & Desegregation, 1960-1962: Toward a Theory of the Rationalization of Protest. James H. Laue. LC 89-9867. (Martin Luther King, Jr., & the Civil Rights Movement Ser.: Vol. 15). 440p. 1989. 90.00 (0-926019-09-0) Carlson Pub.

Direct Action & Sabotage! Three Classic IWW Pamphlets. Intro. by Salvatore Salerno. (Illus.). 120p. (Orig.). 1991. reprint ed. lib. bdg. 22.95 (0-88286-186-7); reprint ed. pap. 12.00 (0-88286-185-9) C H Kerr.

Direct & Allosteric Control of Glutamate Receptors. Ed. by Michael G. Palfreyman et al. LC 94-7075. (Series on Pharmacology & Toxicology). 1994. 129.95 (0-8493-8307-2, 8307) CRC Pr.

Direct & Alternating Current Circuits. Bernard Grob. 624p. 1985. text ed. 42.95 (0-07-024959-8) McGraw.

Direct & Alternating Current Circuits. 2nd ed. Bernard Grob. 1990. text ed. write for info. (0-07-025128-2) McGraw.

Direct & Alternating Current Machinery. 2nd ed. Jack Rosenblatt & M. Harold Friedman. 568p. (C). 1984. write for info. (0-675-20160-8, Merrill Pub Co) Macmillan.

*Direct & Indirect Costs of Diabetes in the United States in 1992. American Diabetes Association Staff. 32p. 1993. pap. 16.95 (0-945448-32-5, PMD1C92) Am Diabetes.

Direct & Indirect Objects. Marie-Jose Shaw. (English Sound Filmstrip Kits Ser.). (gr. 5). 1980. teacher ed 34.00 (0-8209-0505-4, FCW5E-12) ESP.

Direct & Indirect Speech. Ed. by Florian Coulmas. (Trends in Linguistics, Studies & Monographs: No. 31). (Illus.). x, 370p. 1986. text ed. 130.80 (0-89925-176-5) Mouton.

Direct & Inverse Imbedding Theorems. L. D. Kudrjavcev. Tr. by S. Smith. LC 73-22139. (Translations of Mathematical Monographs: Vol. 42). 206p. 1974. 66.00 (0-8218-1592-X, MMONO-42) Am Math.

Direct & Inverse Methods in Radar Polarimetry, 2 vols., Set. Ed. by Wolfgang M. Boerner. (C). 1992. lib. bdg. 434.50 (0-7923-1498-0) Kluwer Ac.

Direct & Inverse Problems: Potentials in Quantum Scattering. B. N. Zakhariev & A. A. Suzko. (Illus.). 240p. 1990. pap. 32.00 (0-387-52484-3) Spr-Verlag.

Direct & Inverse Scattering on the Line. Beals et al. LC 88-14487. (SURV Ser.: No. 28). 209p. 1988. text ed. 66.00 (0-8218-1530-X, SURV-28) Am Math.

*Direct & Large-Eddy Simulation One: Selected Papers from the First ERCOFTAC Workshop on Direct & Large-Eddy Simulation. Ed. by Peter R. Voke et al. LC 94-32855. (Fluid Mechanics & Its Applications Ser.: 26). 448p. (C). 1994. lib. bdg. 183.00 (0-7923-3106-0) Kluwer Ac.

Direct Approach to Counterpoint in Sixteenth Century Style: Music Book Index. Gustave F. Soderlund. 133p. 1993. reprint ed. lib. bdg. 69.00 (0-7812-9664-1) Rprt Serv.

Direct Awareness of the Self: A Translation of the Aparoksanubhuti by Sankara with Historical Introduction & Commentary. Sankara. LC 94-18054. (Studies in Asian Thought & Religion: Vol. 17). 170p. 1994. text ed. 79.95 (0-7734-9077-9) E Mellen.

Direct Broadcast by Satellite: Issues of Regulations, Barriers to Communication. Jon T. Powell. LC 85-6342. xviii, 300p. 1985. text ed. 65.00 (0-89930-067-7, PDP/, Quorum Bks) Greenwood.

Direct Connections: Making Your Personal Computer Communicate. Arielle Emmett & David Gabel. 1986. 21.95 (0-317-01183-9, Plume) NAL-Dutton.

Direct Contact Heat Transfer. Ed. by Frank Kreith & Robert F. Boehm. 402p. 1988. 121.00 (0-89116-635-1) Hemisp Pub.

*Direct Contracting Manual. Date not set. 350.00 (0-937925-94-2, DCM) Capitol Publns.

Direct Conversion of Nuclear Radiation Energy. George H. Miley. LC 70-155742. (ANS Monographs). 532p. 1970. 40.00 (0-89448-004-9, 300003) Am Nuclear Soc.

Direct Costing. William E. Arnstein & Frank Gilabert. LC 79-54827. 288p. reprint ed. pap. 82.10 (0-317-10203-6, 2022615) Bks Demand.

Direct Creativity. Robert P. Crawford. LC 64-8437. 1979. reprint ed. 11.00 (0-87034-009-3) Fraser Pub Co.

Direct Current Circuit Analysis Through Experimentation. 5th ed. Kenneth Fiske & James H. Harter. 256p. 1987. pap. 12.50 (0-911908-17-X) Tech Ed Pr.

Direct Current Fundamentals. Orla E. Loper & Edgar Tedson. LC 94-10135. 1995. 34.95 (0-8273-6572-1) Delmar.

*Direct Current Fundamentals. Orla E. Loper & Edgar Tedson. 1995. pap. write for info. (0-8273-6573-X) Delmar.

Direct Current Fundamentals. 3rd ed. Orla E. Loper & Edgar Tedsen. 386p. 1986. teacher ed 12.00 (0-8273-2236-4); text ed. 34.95 (0-8273-2235-6) Delmar.

Direct Current Fundamentals. 4th ed. Orla E. Loper & Edgar Tedsen. 516p. 1991. 34.95 (0-8273-4146-6); teacher ed 12.00 (0-8273-4148-2); pap. 29.95 (0-8273-4147-4) Delmar.

Direct-Current Hysteresigraphs - STP 526. 62p. 1973. pap. 6.00 (0-8031-0118-X, 04 526000 06) ASTM.

Direct-Current Magnetic Measurements for Soft Magnetic Materials - STP 371-S1. 72p. 1970. pap. 6.25 (0-8031-0736-6, 04-371001-06) ASTM.

Direct Current Motors & Generators: Repairing, Rewinding & Redesigning, 3 vols., Set. Samuel Heller. LC 82-72814. (Illus.). 1660p. (Orig.). 1982. pap. 188.00 (0-911740-09-0) Datarule.

Direct Current Traction Motor. D. A. Lightband. 436p. 1970. 35.00 (0-8464-1461-9) Beekman Pubs.

Direct Decision Therapy. Harold Greenwald. LC 73-75565. 1973. text ed. 14.50 (0-912736-15-1) EDITS Pubs.

Direct Democracy: The Politics of Initiative, Referendum, & Recall. Thomas E. Cronin. LC 88-14859. (Twentieth Century Fund Study). (Illus.). 289p. 1989. 29.50 (0-674-21025-5) HUP.

Direct Democracy: The Politics of Initiative, Referendum, & Recall. Thomas E. Cronin. (Twentieth Century Fund Study). 304p. 1990. pap. 16.95 (0-674-21026-3) HUP.

Direct Democracy & International Politics: Deciding International Issues Through Referendums. John T. Rourke et al. LC 92-8773. 202p. 1992. lib. bdg. 37.00 (1-55587-263-8) Lynne Rienner.

Direct Democracy in South Dakota: The People Conducting Their Own Business. C. Kenneth Meyer et al. 1979. 10.00 (1-55614-033-9) U of SD Gov Res Bur.

*Direct Digital Control: A Guide to Distributed Building Automation. John J. McGowan. LC 94-32120. 1994. write for info. (0-88173-166-8) Fairmont Pr.

Direct Digital Control for Building HVAC Systems. Michael J. Coffin. (Illus.). 272p. 1992. text ed. 49.95 (0-442-23797-9) Chapman & Hall.

Direct Digital Control of Building Systems: Theory & Practice. H. Michael Newman. (Series of Practical Construction Guides). 264p. 1994. text ed. 54.95 (0-471-51696-1) Wiley.

*Direct Digital Control Systems. J. B. Knowles. (Industrial Control, Computers & Communications Ser.). 413p. 1994. text ed. 69.95 (0-471-95147-1) Wiley.

Direct Digital Controls for Hvac Systems. Thomas B. Hartman. 1993. text ed. 38.00 (0-07-026977-7) McGraw.

Direct Disposal of Spent Nuclear Fuel. W. Bechthold et al. (C). 1987. lib. bdg. 89.00 (1-85333-079-5) Kluwer Ac.

Direct Drilling & Reduced Cultivations. H. Allen. (Illus.). 219p. 27.95 (0-85236-113-0, Pub. by Farming Pr UK) Diamond Farm Bk.

Direct-Drive Robot: Theory & Practice. Haruhiko Asada & Kamal Youcef-Toumi. (Illus.). 300p. 1987. 40.00 (0-262-01088-7) MIT Pr.

Direct Elections to the European Parliament, 1984. Ed. by Juliet Lodge. LC 85-10791. 309p. 1986. text ed. 32.50 (0-312-21213-5) St Martin.

Direct Electric Utility Competition: The Natural Monopoly Myth. Walter J. Primeaux. LC 85-20487. 316p. 1985. text ed. 59.95 (0-275-90032-0, C0032, Praeger Pubs) Greenwood.

Direct Examination. Scott Baldwin. (Art of Advocacy Ser.). 1981. Looseleaf updates available. write for info. (0-8205-1036-X) Bender.

Direct Foreign Investment: Costs & Benefits. Richard D. Robinson. LC 87-17750. 244p. 1987. text ed. 65.00 (0-275-92717-2, C2717, Praeger Pubs) Greenwood.

Direct Foreign Investment in the United States. Harvey A. Poniachek. 272p. 1986. text ed. 45.00 (0-669-11076-0) Free Pr.

Direct Foreign Investment in Turkish Manufacturing: An Analysis of the Conflicting Objectives & Frustrated Expectations of a Host Country. Asim Erdilek. 317p. 1982. lib. bdg. 78.50 (3-16-344464-4, Pub. by J C B Mohr GW) Coronet Bks.

Direct Foreign Investment in Yugoslavia: A Microeconomic Model. T. Misha Sarkovic. LC 86-8890. 224p. 1986. text ed. 55.00 (0-275-92159-X, C2159, Praeger Pubs) Greenwood.

Direct French Conversation, 2 Bks, Bk. 2. Henriette D. Betourne et al. (Orig.). (FRE.). (gr. 9 up). 1966. pap. text ed. 3.25 (0-88345-041-0, 17471) Prentice ESL.

Direct Healing. Paul Ellsworth. 173p. 1973. spiral bd. 6.60 (0-7873-0307-0) Mokelumne.

*Direct Hit: How to Make Direct Marketing Work in the Real World. Merlin Stone. (Pitman Marketing Ser.). 320p. 1995. pap. 19.95 (0-273-61689-7, Pub. by Pitman Pub UK) Natl Bk Netwk.

*Direct Hit: Real-World Insights & Common Sense Advice from a Direct Marketing Pro. Dave Majure. 1994. 22.95 (1-55738-821-0) Probus Pub Co.

Direct Instruction. Siegfried Engelmann. Ed. by Danny G. Langdon. LC 79-24814. (Instructional Design Library). 128p. 1980. 23.95 (0-87778-142-7) Educ Tech Pubns.

Direct Instruction: Handicapped Children in Nepal. Joshi Narayan. 53p. 1983. pap. 9.00 (0-318-03448-4) Am-Nepal Ed.

Direct Instruction Mathematics. 2nd ed. Jerry Silbert et al. 528p. (C). 1990. pap. write for info. (0-675-21208-1, Merrill Pub Co) Macmillan.

Direct Instruction Reading. 2nd ed. Douglas Carnine et al. 480p. (C). 1990. write for info. (0-675-21014-3, Merrill Pub Co) Macmillan.

Direct Integral Theory. Nielsen. (Lecture Notes in Pure & Applied Mathematics Ser.: Vol. 61). 184p. 1980. 99.75 (0-8247-6971-6) Dekker.

Direct Interactions & Nuclear Reaction Mechanisms. E. Clementel & C. Villi. 1238p. 1963. text ed. 591.00 (0-677-10070-1) Gordon & Breach.

Direct Investment & European Integration: Competition among Firms & Governments. Stephen Thomsen & Stephen Woolcock. LC 93-2176. 1993. 14.95 (0-87609-150-8) Coun Foreign.

Direct Investment & Joint Ventures in China: A Handbook for Corporate Negotiations. James E. Shapiro et al. LC 91-15. 342p. 1991. text ed. 59.95 (0-89930-646-2, BDJ, Quorum Bks) Greenwood.

Direct Investment Tax Initiatives of the European Community. Ed. by Fred C. De Hosson. 160p. 1990. pap. 48.00 (90-6544-521-8) Kluwer Law Tax Pubs.

Direct Investments in the European Community, 1984-1988. 204p. 1991. pap. 25.00 (92-826-2725-X, CA-59-90-548-EN-C) UNIPUB.

Direct Laplace Transforms, Vol. 4. A. P. Prudnikov et al. (Integrals & Ser.). 1992. text ed. 190.00 (2-88124-837-3) Gordon & Breach.

Direct Legislation: Voting on Ballot Propositions in the United States. David B. Magleby. LC 83-22265. 284p. reprint ed. pap. 81.00 (0-7837-4275-4, 2043967) Bks Demand.

Direct Lending see Installment Credit Series

Direct-Line Distances: International Edition. Gary L. Fitzpatrick & Marilyn J. Modlin. LC 85-27748. (Illus.). 320p. 1985. 42.50 (0-8108-1872-8) Scarecrow.

Direct-Line Distances: United States Edition. Gary L. Fitzpatrick & Marilyn J. Modlin. LC 85-27684. (Illus.). 320p. 1986. 42.50 (0-8108-1871-X) Scarecrow.

Direct-Line Distances: United States Edition, Set. Gary L. Fitzpatrick & Marilyn J. Modlin. LC 85-27684. (Illus.). 320p. 1986. 72.50 (0-8108-2024-2) Scarecrow.

Direct Logic. Stephen N. Thomas. LC 88-90263. 190p. (C). 1990. pap. text ed. 14.95 (0-9618359-0-7) Worthington.

Direct Mail & Mail Order Handbook. 3rd ed. Richard S. Hodgson. 1555p. 1980. 49.95 (0-85013-116-2) Dartnell Corp.

Direct Mail Copy That Sells. Herschell G. Lewis. (Illus.). 1986. 12.95 (0-13-214750-5, Busn) P-H.

Direct Mail, Fall-Winter 1991. 1991. write for info. (0-8306-2517-8); write for info. (0-8306-3982-9); write for info. (0-8306-3983-7) TAB Bks.

Direct Mail for Book Publishers. 3rd ed. Dan Poynter. (Book Publishing Consultation with Dan Poynter Ser.). (Illus.). 55p. 1990. student ed 19.95 (0-915516-59-4) Para Pub.

Direct Mail Fund Raising. Public Management Institute Staff. LC 80-80195. 400p. 1980. ring bd. 49.00 (0-916664-26-0) Datarex Corp.

Direct Mail Fund Raising: Letters That Work. R. L. Torre & M. A. Bendixen. LC 88-14862. (Nonprofit Management & Finance Ser.). (Illus.). 326p. 1988. 45.00 (0-306-42535-1, Plenum Pr) Plenum.

Direct Mail Graphics. Pie Books Staff. (Illus.). 224p. 1994. 79.95 (4-938586-60-6, Pub. by PIE Bks JA) Bks Nippan.

Direct Mail Magic. Charles Mallory. Ed. by Elaine Brett. LC 90-83478. (Fifty-Minute Ser.). (Illus.). 73p. (Orig.). 1991. pap. 9.95 (1-56052-075-2) Crisp Pubns.

Direct Mail Marketing Design. 160p. 1994. 34.99 (1-56496-080-3) Rockport Pubs.

Direct Mail Profits. Bob Bly. 1987. pap. 53.95 (0-87280-153-5, 3355, Asher-Gallant) Caddylak Systs.

Direct Mail, Spring-Summer 1991. 1991. write for info. (0-8306-0877-X) TAB Bks.

Direct Mail Testing for Fund Raisers. Joseph P. Kachorek. LC 91-60005. 185p. 1991. 40.00 (0-944496-23-7) Precept Pr.

Direct Marketer's Workbook. Herman R. Holtz. LC 86-13340. 348p. 1986. text ed. 55.00 (0-471-83066-6) Wiley.

Direct Marketing. 2nd ed. Herbert Katzenstein & William S. Sachs. (Illus.). 528p. (C). 1992. text ed. write for info. (0-02-362425-6) Macmillan.

Direct Marketing: Strategy, Planning, Execution. 3rd ed. Edward L. Nash. 1994. text ed. 44.95 (0-07-046032-9) McGraw.

D

An Asterisk (*) at the beginning of an entry indicates that the title is appearing in BIP for the first time.

Direct Marketing & the Law: What Managers Need to Know. Arthur Winston. 320p. 1993. text ed. 70.00 (*0-471-51993-6*) Wiley.

Direct Marketing Challenge: How to Use Powerful Direct Marketing Tools to Build Your Organization. Christopher J. Ryan. LC 89-50224. 191p. 1989. pap. write for info. (*0-9636236-0-5*) IdeaWorks MD.

Direct Marketing Checklists. John Stockwell & Henry Shaw. LC 93-6694. 256p. 1994. 19.95 (*0-8442-3224-6*, NTC Busn Bks) NTC Pub Grp.

Direct Marketing Coupon Designs: 300 Creative, Copyright Free Camera-Ready Professional Layouts. Clip Away. 1990. pap. 19.95 (*0-8306-3482-7*) TAB Bks.

Direct Marketing, Direct Selling, & the Mature Consumer: A Research Study. James R. Lumpkin et al. LC 88-18519. 240p. 1989. text ed. 55.00 (*0-89930-298-X*, LDT/, Quorum Bks) Greenwood.

Direct Marketing Handbook. 2nd ed. Edward L. Nash. 832p. 1992. text ed. 69.50 (*0-07-046027-2*) McGraw.

Direct Marketing Lessons You Shouldn't Have to Learn the Hard Way. Barry D. Silverstein. 52p. 1989. pap. 9.95 (*0-9623323-0-5*) Directech Inc.

Direct Marketing Management. Mary L. Roberts & Paul Berger. 440p. 1989. text ed. 65.00 (*0-13-214784-X*) P-H.

***Direct Marketing Market Place: The Networking Source of the Direct Marketing Industry.** Ed. by National Register Press Editing Staff. LC 79-649244. 1323p. 1995. pap. 189.00 (*0-87217-329-1*) Natl Register.

Direct Marketing Market Place - 1987. Ed. by Edward L. Stern. LC 79-649244. 664p. 1987. pap. 85.00 (*0-934464-09-X*) Hilary Hse Pubs.

Direct Marketing Market Place, 1994: The Directory of the Direct Marketing Industry. National Register Publishing Staff. LC 79-649244. 1179p. 1994. 179.99 (*0-87217-328-3*) Natl Register.

Direct Marketing Mergers, Acquisitions & Strategic Activities Yearbook. Michael Petsky. Ed. by Melissa D. Jones. 1995. pap. 345.00 (*0-9632267-1-1*) Vos Gruppo & Capell.

***Direct Marketing Rules of Thumb: Thousand Practical & Profitable Ideas to Help You Improve...** Nat G. Bodian. 1995. text ed. 59.95 (*0-07-006340-0*) McGraw.

Direct Marketing Strategies & Tactics. Herschell G. Lewis. (Illus.). 360p. 1992. 49.95 (*0-85013-220-7*) Dartnell Corp.

Direct Marketing Success: What Works & Why. Freeman F. Gosden, Jr. 225p. 1989. pap. text ed. 16.95 (*0-471-51328-8*) Wiley.

Direct Marketing Success Stories. Bob Stone. Ed. by Anne Knudsen. LC 94-17227. 1995. 29.95 (*0-8442-3665-9*, NTC Busn Bks) NTC Pub Grp.

***Direct Marketing Through Broadcast Media.** Alvin Eicoff. Ed. by Anne Knudsen. 1995. 29.95 (*0-8442-3518-0*, NTC Busn Bks) NTC Pub Grp.

Direct Marketing User's Guide. Barry D. Silverstein. 1991. pap. 9.95 (*0-9623323-1-3*) Directech Inc.

Direct Mass Spectrometry of Body Metabolites: Quantitative Methodology & Clinical Applications. John M. Mee. (Illus.). ix, 135p. 1984. pap. 15.00 (*0-318-04438-2*) Brandon-Lane-Pr.

Direct Methods for Sparse Matrices. I. S. Duff et al. (Monographs on Numerical Analysis). (Illus.). 360p. 1989. pap. 29.95 (*0-19-853421-3*) OUP.

Direct Methods in Crystallography. Carmelo Giacovazzo. 1980. text ed. 184.00 (*0-12-282450-4*) Acad Pr.

Direct Methods in Crystallography: Proceedings of the 1976 Intercongress Symposium. Ed. by H. A. Hauptman. 297p. 1978. pap. text ed. 13.50 (*0-9602470-0-9*) Polycrystal Bk Serv.

Direct Methods in the Calculus of Variations. B. Dacorogna. (Applied Mathematical Sciences Ser.: Vol. 79). (Illus.). ix, 308p. 1989. 59.00 (*0-387-50491-5*) Spr-Verlag.

Direct Methods of Qualitative Spectral Analysis of Singular Differential Operators. I. M. Glazman. 244p. 1965. text ed. 63.50 (*0-7065-0562-X*, Pub. by Keter Pub IS) Coronet Bks.

Direct Methods of Solving Crystal Structures. Ed. by H. Schenk. (NATO ASI Series B, Physics: Vol. 274). (Illus.). 428p. 1991. 115.00 (*0-306-44040-7*, Plenum Med Bk) Plenum.

Direct-Mind Experience. Richard Rose. (Illus.). 316p. (Orig.). 1985. 14.00 (*1-878683-08-X*); pap. 10.00 (*1-878683-01-2*) TAT Found.

Direct Model Reference Adaptive Control: Theory & Applications. Howard Kaufman et al. LC 93-29789. (Communications & Control Engineering Ser.). 1993. 69.00 (*0-387-94155-X*) Spr-Verlag.

Direct Nuclear Reaction Theories. Norman Austern. LC 78-100327. (Interscience Monographs & Texts in Physics & Astronomy: Vol. 25). 400p. reprint ed. pap. 114.00 (*0-317-08487-9*, 2006343) Bks Demand.

Direct Nuclear Reactions: Monograph. Norman R. Glendenning. LC 82-24365. 392p. 1983. text ed. 136.00 (*0-12-286320-8*) Acad Pr.

Direct Objects. Marie-Jose Shaw. (English Sound Filmstrip Kits Ser.). (gr. 4). 1979. teacher ed 34.00 (*0-8209-0483-X*, FCW4E-10) ESP.

Direct Observation of Imperfections in Crystals: Proceedings. Ed. by J. B. Newkirk & J. H. Wernick. LC 61-16633. 629p. reprint ed. pap. 179.30 (*0-317-08753-3*, 2000684) Bks Demand.

Direct Option. Richard Bartlett. 1992. pap. 11.95 (*0-13-218090-1*) P-H.

Direct Option. Richard C. Bartlett. LC 93-19819. 304p. 1994. 19.95 (*0-89096-583-8*); pap. 9.95 (*0-89096-584-6*) Tex A&M Univ Pr.

Direct Participation Programs Limited Representative: Principles & Practices, Questions & Answers. 10th ed. LC 91-18709. (Passtrak Ser.: No. 22). 240p. 1991. 95.00 (*0-7931-0149-2*, 3622-0110) Dearborn Trade.

Direct Path to Enlightenment see Great Path of Awakening

***Direct Practice Research in Human Service Agencies.** Betty J. Blythe et al. LC 94-24325. 1995. 49.50 (*0-231-07366-6*); pap. 22.50 (*0-231-07367-4*) Col U Pr.

Direct Psychotherapy: Twenty-Eight American Originals, Set. Ed. by Ratibor-Ray M. Jurjevich. LC 75-163841. 915p. 1972. 25.00 (*0-87024-218-0*) U of Miami Pr.

Direct Purchase of Natural Gas by End-Users. 2nd ed. Ed. by Government Institutes, Inc. Staff. 192p. (Orig.). 1988. pap. 89.00 (*0-86587-492-1*) Gov Insts.

Direct-Reading Colorimetric Indicator Tubes Manual. 2nd ed. Ed. by Barbara Dawson. (Illus.). 65p. (C). 1993. pap. 28.00 (*0-932627-53-6*, 175-SI-93) Am Indus Hygiene.

Direct Realism. Moltke S. Gram. 1983. lib. bdg. 80.00 (*90-247-2870-3*) Kluwer Ac.

***Direct Reduced Iron: Technology & Economics of Production & Use.** fac. ed. Iron & Steel Society of AIME Staff. Ed. by Robert L. Stephenson. LC 80-82727. (Illus.). 255p. 1994. pap. 72.70 (*0-7837-7322-6*, 2047250) Bks Demand.

Direct Reference: A Philosophical Essay on Meaning. Francois Recanati. LC 92-29857. 350p. 1993. 49.95 (*0-631-18154-7*) Blackwell Pubs.

Direct Response Marketing: An Entrepreneurial Approach. William A. Cohen. LC 83-19825. (Illus.). 510p. reprint ed. pap. 145.40 (*0-7837-3504-9*, 2057837) Bks Demand.

Direct Response Television: The Authoritative Guide. Frank Brady & John A. Vasquez. LC 94-17786. 1995. 47.95 (*0-8442-3548-2*, NTC Busn Bks) NTC Pub Grp.

Direct Sales: Be Better Than Good - Be Great! Joyce M. Ross. LC 91-7387. (Illus.). 208p. 1991. 17.95 (*0-88289-782-9*) Pelican.

Direct Sales, Commission Sales, Etc. Word Mapping Encyclopaedia. Data Notes Research Staff. LC 83-90738. (Bibliography Ser.). 60p. 1984. pap. 21.95 (*0-911569-61-8*) Prosperity & Profits.

Direct Seeded Rice. Singh & Bhattacharya. (C). 1989. 15.00 (*81-204-0446-7*) S Asia.

Direct Selling Channels. Intro. by Bert Rosenbloom. LC 92-40395. (Journal of Marketing Channels: Vol. 2, No. 2). (Illus.). 124p. 1993. lib. bdg. 29.95 (*1-56024-445-3*); pap. text ed. 14.95 (*1-56024-446-1*) Haworth Pr.

Direct Selling Revolution: Understanding the Growth of the Amway Corporation. Dominique Xardel. 196p. 1994. 39.95 (*0-631-19229-8*) Blackwell Pubs.

Direct Sequence Spread Spectrum Techniques. J. E. Hershey. (Illus.). 151p. (C). 1984. lib. bdg. 42.30 (*0-89412-097-2*); pap. 32.80 (*0-89412-071-9*) Aegean Park Pr.

Direct Social Work Practice: Theory & Skills. 4th ed. Dean H. Hepworth & Jo A. Larsen. (C). 1993. text ed. 50.95 (*0-534-19956-9*) Brooks-Cole.

Direct Spirit Writing (Psychography) A Treatise on One of the Objective Forms: Psychic or Spiritual Phenomena. W. Stainton Moses. 152p. 1972. reprint ed. spiral bd. 6.60 (*0-7873-0627-4*) Mokelumne.

***Direct Sticking Measurements in Muon Catalyzed Fusion.** H. De Hahn. 116p. (Orig.). 1994. pap. 47.50x (*90-6275-993-9*, Pub. by Delft U Pr NE) Coronet Bks.

Direct Stock: New York Gold Staff. (Illus.). 142p. 1993. pap. 19.95 (*0-685-66916-5*) Watsn-Guptill.

Direct Stock 3. New York Gold Staff. (Illus.). 142p. 1994. pap. 24.95 (*0-8230-6316-X*, Watsn-Guptill) Watsn-Guptill.

***Direct Stock 4.** 1995. pap. text ed. (*0-8230-6060-8*) Watsn-Guptill.

Direct Stone Sculpture. Milt Liebson. LC 90-64436. (Illus.). 160p. 1991. text ed. 29.95 (*0-88740-305-0*) Schiffer.

Direct Taxes Annual Digest. S. K. Kackar. (C). 1989. 100.00 (*0-685-44800-2*) St Mut.

Direct Taxes Circulars, 1983-1990. B. Bhargava & B. Bhandari. (C). 1990. 150.00 (*0-89771-277-3*) St Mut.

Direct Taxes Digest, 1984-1990. B. Bhargava & B. Bhandari. (C). 1990. 275.00 (*0-89771-279-X*) St Mut.

Direct Taxes Digest, 1988-1990. B. Bhargava & B. Bhandari. (C). 1990. 135.00 (*0-89771-278-1*) St Mut.

Direct Taxes Law & Practice. S. Singhania. (C). 1990. 65.00 (*0-89771-260-9*) St Mut.

Direct Taxes Ready Referencer. Shiavax Mistry. (C). 1990. 125.00 (*0-89771-261-7*) St Mut.

Direct Temperature Measurements of Deposits, Mount St. Helens, Washington, 1980-1981. Norman G. Banks & Richard P. Hoblitt. Vol. 1387. write for info. (*0-318-70233-9*) US Geol Survey.

Direct Theory: Experimental Film - Video As Major Genre. Edward S. Small. LC 94-44885. (Illus.). 144p. (C). 1994. pap. 13.95 (*0-8093-1920-9*) S Ill U Pr.

***Direct Theory: Experimental Film - Video As Major Genre.** Edward S. Small. LC 94-44885. (Illus.). 144p. (C). 1994. 19.95 (*0-8093-1919-5*) S Ill U Pr.

Direct Use of Online Bibliographic Information Systems by Untrained End Users: A Review of Research. Michael Eisenberg. 40p. 1983. 3.00 (*0-937597-05-8*, IR-64) ERIC Clear.

Direct Use of the Sun's Energy. Farrington Daniels. LC 64-20913. (Trends in Science Ser.: No. 5). (Illus.). 402p. reprint ed. pap. 114.60 (*0-7837-5309-8*, 2080332) Bks Demand.

Direct Utilization of Geothermal Energy: A Layman's Guide. (Special Report Ser.: No. 8). 97p. 1979. 6.00 (*0-934412-08-1*) Geothermal.

Direct Way: A Programmed Study of the English Sentence. George L. Dickson. 108p. (Orig.). 1979. pap. text ed. 7.95x (*0-89641-023-4*) American Pr.

Direct Your Subconscious & Drive to Succeed. Paul Harris. 128p. 1995. pap. 9.95 (*0-572-01573-9*, Pub. by Foulsham UK) Atrium Pubs.

Directed by Dorothy Arzner. Judith Mayne. LC 93-51496. 1995. 29.95 (*0-253-33716-X*); pap. 15.95 (*0-253-20896-3*) Ind U Pr.

Directed by Jack Arnold. Dana M. Reemes. LC 87-46382. (Illus.). 255p. 1988. lib. bdg. 32.50x (*0-89950-331-4*) McFarland & Co.

Directed Drug Delivery. Ed. by Ronald T. Borchardt et al. LC 85-2291. (Experimental Biology & Medicine Ser.). (Illus.). 384p. 1985. 89.50 (*0-89603-089-X*) Humana.

Directed-Energy Weapons: A Juridical Analysis. Edward A. Fessler. LC 79-65950. 204p. 1980. text ed. 55.00 (*0-275-90479-2*, C0479, Praeger Pubs) Greenwood.

Directed Models of Polymers, Interfaces & Clusters: Scaling & Finite-Size Properties. V. Privman & N. M. Svrakic. (Lecture Notes in Physics Ser.: Vol. 338). vi, 120p. 1989. 31.00 (*0-387-51429-5*, 3454) Spr-Verlag.

Directed Mutagenesis: A Practical Approach. Ed. by M. J. McPherson. (Practical Approach Ser.). (Illus.). 282p. 1991. pap. 44.00 (*0-19-963140-9*, IRL Pr) OUP.

Directed Reading Maturity. Stauffer. 1990. reprint ed. pap. 19.99 (*0-89824-233-9*) Trillium Pr.

Directed Sonar Sensing for Mobile Robot Navigation. John J. Leonard. (International Series in Engineering & Computer Science, VLSI, Computer Architecture, & Digital Screen Processing). 208p. (C). 1992. lib. bdg. 75.50 (*0-7923-9242-6*) Kluwer Ac.

Directeur de l'Opera. Jean Anouilh. 1972. pap. 8.95 (*0-8288-9014-5*, M5849) Fr & Eur.

Directeur de l'Opera see Rendez-Vous de Senlis Suivi de Leocadia

Directing: Film Techniques & Aesthetics. Michael Rabiger. (Illus.). 412p. 1989. pap. 36.95 (*0-240-80011-7*, Focal) Buttrwrth-Heinemann.

Directing: The Television Commercial. Ben Gradus. (Illus.). 236p. 1981. text ed. 29.95 (*0-240-51751-2*, Focal); pap. 27.95 (*0-240-51749-0*, Focal) Buttrwrth-Heinemann.

***Directing a Play.** rev. ed. Michael McCaffery. (Theater Manuals Ser.). (Illus.). 128p. 1995. reprint ed. pap. 14.95 (*0-7148-2513-1*, Pub. by Phaidon Press UK) Chronicle Bks.

Directing a Play, Vol. 1. Michael McCaffery. Ed. by David Mayer. (Theatre Manuals Ser.). 1991. pap. 8.95 (*0-02-871342-7*) Schirmer Bks.

***Directing Actors: Creating Memorable Performances for Film & Television.** Judith Weston. 1995. pap. 24.95 (*0-941188-24-8*) M Wiese Prodns.

Directing Beckett. Lois Oppenheim. LC 94-13121. (Illus.). 469p. 1994. 42.50 (*0-472-10535-3*) U of Mich Pr.

Directing Christian Education: The Changing Role of the Christian Education Specialist. Michael S. Lawson & Robert J. Choun, Jr. 1992. pap. 17.99 (*0-8024-1702-7*) Moody.

Directing Corporate Video. Ray DiZazzo. 288p. 1993. 26.95 (*0-240-80164-4*) Buttrwrth-Heinemann.

Directing Drama. John Miles-Brown. LC 87-60978. (Illus.). 172p. 1980. pap. 18.95 (*0-7206-0688-8*, Pub. by P Owen Ltd UK) Dufour.

Directing Ecological Succession. James O. Luken. 192p. 1990. 77.50 (*0-412-34450-5*, A5005) Chapman & Hall.

***Directing for the Stage: A Workshop Guide of Creative Exercises & Projects.** Terry J. Converse. Ed. by Theodore O. Zapel. (Illus.). (Orig.). (C). 1995. pap. text ed. 14.95 (*1-56608-014-2*, B169) Meriwether Pub.

***Directing General Education Outcomes.** Ed. by Neal A. Raisman. LC 85-644753. (New Directions for Community Colleges Ser.: No. 81). 107p. (Orig.). 1993. pap. 16.95 (*1-55542-686-7*) Jossey-Bass.

Directing in the Theatre. Hugh Morrison. LC 73-83996. 1974. pap. 10.95 (*0-87830-587-4*, Theatre Arts Bks) Routledge Chapman & Hall.

Directing in the Theatre: A Casebook. 2nd ed. J. Robert Wills. LC 93-29274. 224p. 1993. 29.50 (*0-8108-2735-2*) Scarecrow.

Directing of S & L Associations. 31th ed. 1985. 50.00 (*0-911304-05-3*) T K Sanderson.

Directing Plays: A Working Professional's Method. Stuart Vaughan. LC 92-16875. 320p. (C). 1993. text ed. 53.95 (*0-8013-0623-X*, 78562) Longman.

Directing Poiesis. Naum Panovski. LC 92-43331. (American University Studies: Fine Arts: Ser. XX, Vol. 18). 235p. (C). 1994. text ed. 49.95 (*0-8204-2074-3*) P Lang Pubs.

Directing Postmodern Theater: Shaping Signification in Performance. Jon Whitmore. LC 94-1272. (Illus.). 236p. 1994. text ed. 39.50 (*0-472-09557-9*); pap. text ed. 16.95 (*0-472-06557-2*) U of Mich Pr.

Directing Puppet Theater Step-by-Step. Carol Fijan & Frank Ballard. LC 88-35659. (Illus.). 96p. (C). 1990. pap. 15.00 (*0-89390-126-1*) Resource Pubns.

Directing Strategy: The Keys to High Performance. Lloyd S. Baird & Alan L. Frohman. 128p. 1992. text ed. 33.33 (*0-13-220302-2*) P-H.

Directing Television & Film. 2nd ed. Alan A. Armer. 386p. (C). 1990. text ed. 32.95 (*0-534-11616-7*) Intl Thomson.

Directing the Action: Acting & Directing in Contemporary Theatre. Charles Marowitz. (Acting Ser.). 1991. pap. 12.95 (*1-55783-072-X*) Applause Theatre Bk Pubs.

Directing the Children's Choir: A Comprehensive Resource. Shirley W. McRae. (Illus.). 232p. 1991. text ed. 26.00 (*0-02-871785-6*) Schirmer Bks.

Directing the Documentary. 2nd ed. Ed. by Michael Rabiger. 382p. 1992. pap. 39.95 (*0-240-80126-1*, Focal) Buttrwrth-Heinemann.

Directing the Film: Film Directors on Their Art. Eric Sherman. 360p. 1988. reprint ed. pap. 14.95 (*0-918226-15-5*) Acrobat.

Directing Video. Tom Kennedy. (Illus.). 204p. 1988. 39.95 (*0-86729-172-9*); student ed 27.95 (*0-86729-186-9*) Knowledge Indus.

Directing Your Directing Career: A Resource Book & Agent Guide for Directors. 290p. 1995. pap. 15.95 (*1-878355-01-5*) Sweden Pr.

***Directing Your Own Mutual Fund Investments: The Investors Series Educational Kit.** (Illus.). 48p. 1994. pap. 15.00 (*1-887283-01-3*) Mut Fund Educ All.

Direction: The Confrontation Between Nature & Mystery. limited ed. Mary C. Snotherly. Ed. by Mary B. Campbell. (Persephone Press Poetry Book Publication Award Ser.: No. 3). (Illus.). 24p. (Orig.). 1994. pap. 8.00 (*1-979009-14-7*) S P-Persephone Pr.

Direction: The Essential Dimension. Charles W. Williams. 1960. 8.95 (*0-8315-0003-4*) Speller.

***Direction: Where Do We Go from Here?** Kentrell D. Ellis. LC 94-92286. (Lifestyles Ser.). 97p. (Orig.). 1994. pap. text ed. 6.95 (*0-9632738-2-5*) K D Ellis Pubns.

Direction Finding from Arterials to Destinations. (National Cooperative Highway Research Program Report Ser.). 50p. 1980. 6.40 (*0-309-03031-5*) Transport Res Bd.

***Direction Finding Techniques: Overview Summary.** Dave Adamy. (Overview Summaries Ser.). 32p. 1994. pap. 4.95 (*1-885897-05-7*) Lynx Pubng.

Direction for Search of Records. Thomas Powell. LC 74-80208. (English Experience Ser.: No. 685). 1974. reprint ed. 9.50 (*90-221-0685-3*) Walter J Johnson.

Direction for the English Traveller. Jacob Van Langeren. LC 72-211. (English Experience Ser.: No. 197). 1969. reprint ed. 8.00 (*90-221-0197-5*) Walter J Johnson.

Direction for the Health of Magistrates & Students. Gulielmus Gratarolus. Tr. by Thomas Newton. LC 72-38192. (English Experience Ser.: No. 462). 172p. 1972. reprint ed. 30.00 (*90-221-0462-1*) Walter J Johnson.

Direction for Travailers for the Behoofe of the Young Earle of Bedford, Being Now Ready to Travell. Justus Lipsius. LC 77-7414. (English Experience Ser.: No. 878). 1977. reprint ed. lib. bdg. 15.00 (*90-221-0878-3*) Walter J Johnson.

***Direction of Church Growth: Ambassadors Magazine Collection.** Ed. by Edwin Su et al. (Ambassadors Magazine Collection: No. 6). 144p. (Orig.). (CHI.). 1994. pap. 5.50 (*1-882324-10-2*) Ambssdrs Christ.

Direction of Computer Use in Teaching Mathematics & Science. Ed. by William L. Blubaugh. 106p. (Orig.). 1993. pap. 20.00 (*1-880094-07-X*) Assn Advan Comput Educ.

Direction of Time. Hans Reichenbach. Ed. by Maria Reichenbach. 350p. 1991. pap. 16.00 (*0-520-07414-9*) U CA Pr.

Direction of Trade Policy. Ed. by Charles Pearson & James Riedel. 256p. (C). 1990. text ed. 54.95 (*1-55786-080-7*) Blackwell Pubs.

Direction of Trade Statistics Yearbook, 1992. International Monetary Fund Staff. 426p. 1992. 25.00 (*1-55775-239-7*) Intl Monetary.

***Directional Astrology: And Complete Sets of Tables.** Sepharial. 192p. 1995. pap. 17.00 (*0-89540-320-X*, Sun Bks) Sun Pub.

Directional Drilling. T. A. Inglis. (C). 1988. lib. bdg. 90.50 (*0-86010-716-7*, Pub. by Graham & Trotman UK) Kluwer Ac.

Directional Drilling & Deviation Control Technology. French Oil & Gas Industry Association Technical Committee. 160p. (FRE.). 1989. 125.00 (*0-8288-7373-9*, 2710805669) Fr & Eur.

Directional Drilling & Deviation Control Technology. French Oil & Gas Industry Association Technical Committee. (French Oil & Gas Industry Association Publications Ser.). (Illus.). 290p. (C). 1990. 129.00 (*2-7108-0566-9*, Pub. by Edits Technip FR) St Mut.

Directional Hearing. Ed. by William A. Yost & G. Gourevitch. (Illus.). 305p. 1987. 98.00 (*0-387-96493-2*) Spr-Verlag.

Directional Ocean Wave Spectra. Ed. by Robert C. Beal. LC 91-16779. (Studies in Earth & Space Sciences). (Illus.). 240p. 1991. text ed. 65.00 (*0-8018-4261-1*) Johns Hopkins.

Directional Properties of Materials. Ed. by H. J. Bunge. (Illus.). 265p. 1988. pap. text ed. 60.00 (*3-88355-136-8*, Pub. by DGM Metallurgy Info GW) IR Pubns.

Directional Solidification of Steel Castings. R. Wlodawer & L. Hewitt. LC 64-20641. 1966. 100.00 (*0-08-010536-X*, Pub. by Pergamon Repr UK) Franklin.

Directional Wave Spectra Applications. Ed. by Robert L. Wiegel. LC 82-70873. 501p. 1982. pap. 40.00 (*0-87262-303-3*) Am Soc Civil Eng.

Directionary to Financial Freedom. 3rd ed. Albert R. Steward, III. Ed. by Frank Walford. 320p. 1992. pap. text ed. 29.95 (*1-881180-14-X*) S Three.

Directions: A Collection of Poems. Thomas M. Hartman. Ed. & Intro. by Judy Gilley. 80p. 1986. pap. 5.95 (*0-9616013-1-0*) Midwest Media.

DIRECTIONS: Directory of Health & Human Care Service Agencies in San Diego County. United Way of San Diego County Resource Center Staff. 1991. 35.00 (*0-9629793-0-9*) United Way SD.

Directions: From the Word of God. David Rinden. 62p. 1992. pap. 3.95 (*0-943167-15-9*) Faith & Fellowship Pr.

Directions: Las Vegas. 340p. 1992. pap. 21.95 (*0-9635072-0-6*) Directions.

Directions: Quality Assurance Manual for Physician Office Laboratories. Robyn Lee. (C). 1991. 121.00 (*0-933948-39-5*, 2891) Ctr Res Ambulatory.

Directions & Directing. H. S. Green. 88p. 3.00 (*0-86690-111-6*, G1155-014) Am Fed Astrologers.

Directions & Implications of Advanced Computing, Vol. 1. Ed. by Jonathan Jacky & Douglas Schuler. LC 89-7019. 240p. (C). 1990. text ed. 39.50 (*0-89391-558-0*) Ablex Pub.

Directions & Implications of Advanced Computing, Vol. 2. Ed. by Nancy Leveson & Douglas Schuler. (Directions & Implications of Advanced Computing Ser.). 288p. (C). 1993. text ed. 59.95 (*0-89391-619-6*) Ablex Pub.

An Asterisk (*) at the beginning of an entry indicates that the title is appearing in BIP for the first time.

An Asterisk (*) at the beginning of an entry indicates that the title is appearing in BIP for the first time.

2007

D

Directors' & Officers' Liability, 1992: A Satellite Program. (Commercial Law & Practice Course Handbook Ser.). 1992. pap., vhs 195.00 (*0-685-70148-4*) PLI.

Directors' & Officers' Liability 1993: A Satellite Program. (Commercial Law & Practice Course Handbook Ser.: Vol. 657). 600p. 1993. 70.00 (*0-685-69712-6*, A4-4425) PLI.

Directors & Their Films: A Comprehensive Reference, 1895-1990. Brooks Bushnell. LC 92-56633. 1045p. 1993. lib. bdg. 125.00 (*0-89950-766-2*) McFarland & Co.

Directors & Their Functions. John C. Baker. LC 73-1990. (Big Business; Economic Power in a Free Society Ser.). 1973. reprint ed. 12.95 (*0-405-05074-7*) Ayer.

Directors' Fiduciary Duties: The Continuing Problem of Effective Enforcement. A. J. Boyle. (Forum Internationale Ser.: No. 10). 1988. 24.00 (*90-6544-379-7*) Kluwer Law Tax Pubs.

Director's Guide. Colin McArthur & Ian Barnard. (Waterlow Practitioner's Library). 144p. 1990. pap. 26. 00 (*0-08-040121-X*, Pergamon Pr) Elsevier.

Director's Guide to Place Me with Your Son: Ignatian Spirituality in Everyday Life. James W. Skehan. 80p. 1994. pap. 5.95 (*0-87840-569-0*) Georgetown U Pr.

Directors Handbook. 1977. text ed. 62.50 (*0-07-084487-9*) McGraw.

Directors in Rehearsal: A Hidden World. Susan Cole. 1992. 49.95 (*0-87830-018-X*, Theatre Arts Bks); pap. 15.95 (*0-685-59368-1*, Theatre Arts Bks) Routledge Chapman & Hall.

Directors in Rehearsal: A Hidden World. Susan Cole. 1992. pap. 15.95 (*0-87830-019-8*, Theatre Arts Bks) Routledge Chapman & Hall.

Director's Invitational, September 16-November 6, 1988. Frwd. by Wendell L. Ott. (Illus.). 14p. (Orig.). 1988. pap. 2.00 (*0-924335-06-8*) Tacoma Art Mus.

*__Director's Management Bookshelf.__ Dora C. Fowler. 12p. 1992. text ed. 1.00 (*1-57323-019-7*) Woodhaven Pbg.

Directors Manual. (Crayola Creativity Ser.). (Illus.). 80p. 1988. 50.00 (*0-86696-212-3*) Binney & Smith.

Director's Manual: Discovering: A Junior High Religion Program. Michael Carotta. Ed. by Thomas Zanzig. (Discovering Program Ser.). 134p. (Orig.). 1989. teacher ed, ring bd. 56.00 (*0-88489-212-3*) St Marys.

Director's Method for Film & Television. Ron Richards. 256p. 1992. pap. 34.95 (*0-240-80119-9*, Focal) Buttrwrth-Heinemann.

Directors of Development: Influences on the Development of Children's Thinking. Ed. by Lynn Okagaki & Robert J. Sternberg. 304p. 1991. text ed. 59.95 (*0-8058-0627-X*); pap. 29.95 (*0-8058-0628-8*) L Erlbaum Assocs.

Directors on Directing: A Sourcebook of the Modern Theatre. Toby Cole & Helen K. Chinoy. 479p. (C). 1963. pap. text ed. write for info. (*0-02-323300-1*) Macmillan.

*__Director's Ready Reference.__ CUNA Staff. 160p. 1995. pap. text ed., spiral bd. 18.02 (*0-7872-0499-4*) Kendall-Hunt.

Director's Taste & Achievement. A. Everett Austin, Jr. (Illus.). 92p. 1958. pap. 2.50 (*0-317-13586-4*) Wadsworth Atheneum.

Directors Version. (Crayola Creativity Ser.). (Illus.). 80p. 1988. 150.00 (*0-86696-216-6*) Binney & Smith.

Director's Vision: Play Direction from Analysis to Production. Louis E. Catron. 358p. (C). 1989. text ed. 42.95 (*0-87484-760-5*) Mayfield Pub.

Director's Voice. Contrib by Arthur Bartow. LC 88-4937. 360p. 1988. pap. 14.95 (*0-930452-74-7*) Theatre Comm.

*__Directort of Corporate Meeting Planners 1995.__ 1500p. 1995. 345.00 (*0-87228-071-3*) Salesmans.

Directory - American Society of Journalists & Authors, 1988. (Annual Directory Ser.). 80p. 1987. pap. 50.00 (*0-9612200-5-8*) Am Soc Jrnl & Auth.

Directory - American Society of Journalists & Authors, 1989. (Annual Directory Ser.). 86p. 1988. pap. 50.00 (*0-9612200-6-6*) Am Soc Jrnl & Auth.

*__Directory - French Research Development Databases: An Overview.__ OECD Staff. 126p. (Orig.). 1994. pap. 20. 00x (*92-64-04262-8*) OECD.

Directory & Gazetteer of Leeds & Clothing Districts of Yorkshire. William White. LC 71-83368. 1969. reprint ed. 57.50 (*0-678-05503-3*) Kelley.

Directory & Guide to Catalogues: Everything from A to Z by Mail. 1992. lib. bdg. 79.75 (*0-8490-5343-9*) Gordon Pr.

Directory & Statistics of Colorado Coal Mines with Distribution & Electric Generation Map, 1989. Edwin A. Kuhn. (Resource Ser.: No. 29). 49p. (Orig.). 1990. pap. 8.00 (*1-884216-34-X*) Colo Geol Survey.

Directory for Exceptional Children. 13th ed. Ed. by Porter Sargent Staff. LC 54-4975. (Special Education Ser.). (Illus.). 1312p. 1994. 60.00 (*0-87558-131-5*) Porter Sargent.

Directory for Performance Improvement. Dennis J. Kravetz. LC 89-8011. 432p. 1989. pap. 34.95 (*0-927764-00-8*) D J Kravetz & Assocs.

Directory for Small-Scale Agriculture. 109p. (Orig.). (C). 1993. pap. text ed. 30.00 (*1-56806-344-X*) Diane Pub.

Directory for Successful Publishing in Legal Periodicals. Ed. by Alphonso D. Joyner. LC 86-62889. 694p. (Orig.). 1987. pap. 44.99 (*0-940579-00-6*) Qucoda Pub.

Directory for Sunday Celebrations in the Absence of a Priest. Congregation for Divine Worship Staff. Tr. by Int'l Committee on English in the Liturgy Staff. 20p. (Orig.). 1988. pap. 3.50 (*1-55586-251-9*) US Catholic.

Directory for Traveling Friends, 1990-91. 7th rev. ed. Ed. by Carolyn Terrell. (Illus.). 170p. 1990. pap. 15.00 (*0-9620912-1-9*) Friends Genl Conf.

Directory of AAAS Fellows, 1985. Ed. by AAAS Office of Communications Staff. 237p. 1985. pap. 11.95 (*0-87168-282-6*, 85-20S) AAAS.

Directory of Academic Institutions & Organizations: Drug, Alcohol & Employee Assistance Program Educational Resources. 1990. lib. bdg. 250.00 (*0-87700-895-7*) Revisionist Pr.

Directory of Academic Institutions & Organizations with Drug, Alcohol & Employee Assistance Program Educational Resources. 1991. lib. bdg. 88.95 (*0-8490-4370-0*) Gordon Pr.

Directory of Accessible Van Rentals. Helen Hecker. 1994. pap. 9.95 (*0-685-60646-5*) Twin Peaks Pr.

*__Directory of Accessible Van Rentals.__ Helen Hecker. 1995. pap. 9.95 (*0-933261-09-8*) Twin Peaks Pr.

Directory of Accredited Institutions with Programs in Biocommunications. 79p. 1986. 8.50 (*0-318-20442-8*) Health Sci Comm.

*__Directory of Adaptive Technologies to Aid Library Patrons & Staff with Disabilities.__ Dennis A. Norlin et al. LC 94-36089. 1994. write for info. (*0-8389-7754-5*) ALA.

Directory of Advertising & Marketing Services, 1993-1994. 160p. 1993. 75.00 (*0-917168-15-1*) Executive Comm.

Directory of Advertising & Marketing Services, 1994-1995. 1994. 75.00 (*0-917168-16-X*) Executive Comm.

*__Directory of African American Religious Bodies.__ 1995. 49. 95 (*0-614-06547-X*, PADR) Howard U Pr.

*__Directory of African American Religious Bodies.__ 1995. pap. 29.95 (*0-614-06548-8*, PADRP) Howard U Pr.

Directory of African American Religious Bodies. Payne. 1990. pap. 29.95 (*0-88258-065-5*) Howard U Pr.

*__Directory of African American Religious Bodies: A Comependium by the Howard University School of Divinity.__ 2nd ed. Ed. by Wardell J. Payne. LC 95-10152. 1995. write for info. (*0-88258-184-8*); pap. write for info. (*0-88258-185-6*) Howard U Pr.

Directory of African American Writers & Poets, 1992. Abimbola Adama. 1992. pap. text ed. 10.00 (*0-9629532-1-0*) Black Angels.

Directory of African & Afro-American Studies in the United States. 7th ed. Ed. by John A. Distefano. 275p. 1988. 20.00 (*0-918456-61-4*, Crossroads) African Studies Assn.

Directory of African Experts, Vol I, No. 1. 120p. 1984. 14. 00 (*92-1-025004-4*, 84.II.K.1) UN.

Directory of African Experts, 1984: Supplement II, Vol. 1. 96p. 1986. 14.50 (*92-1-025049-4*, E/F.84.II.K.2) UN.

Directory of African Experts, 1984: Supplement III, Vol. I. 106p. 1986. 14.50 (*92-1-025050-8*, E/F.84.II.K.3) UN.

Directory of African Experts, 1984: Supplement IV, Vol. I. 118p. 1986. 15.50 (*92-1-025051-6*, E/F.84.II.K.4) UN.

Directory of African Film-Makers & Films. Comp. by Keith Shiri. LC 92-22105. 1992. write for info. (*0-948911-60-3*, Greenwood Pr); text ed. 79.50 (*0-313-28756-2*, GR8756, Greenwood Pr) Greenwood.

Directory of Agencies & Organizations Serving Deaf-Blind Individuals. 1987. 15.00 (*0-317-99715-7*) H Keller Natl Ctr.

Directory of Agencies Collecting Statistical Data from College & University Libraries. Ed. by Lynn LaBrake. 46p. 1986. 15.00 (*0-8389-7033-8*) Library Admin.

Directory of Agricultural & Forestry Equipment Manufacturers in Western Europe. 1986. 210.00 (*0-686-75441-7*) St Mut.

Directory of Agriculture & Horticulture Organizations. 1991. lib. bdg. 79.95 (*0-8490-5177-0*) Gordon Pr.

Directory of American & Canadian Publishers of Materials on East European Subjects. Zbigniew Kantorosinski. 72p. (Orig.). (C). 1993. pap. text ed. 30.00 (*1-56806-319-9*) Diane Pub.

Directory of American Book Workers. Comp. by Renee Roff. LC 80-52837. 1981. 19.95 (*0-935164-05-7*) Prairie Bk Ctr.

Directory of American Bridge-Building Companies 1840-1900. Victor C. Darnell. LC 84-51536. 110p. 1984. pap. text ed. 8.00 (*0-685-51546-X*, SIA4) Am Soc Civil Eng.

Directory of American Disc Record Brands & Manufacturers, 1891-1943. Allan Sutton. LC 93-44460. 304p. 1994. text ed. 65.00 (*0-313-29200-0*, Greenwood Pr) Greenwood.

Directory of American Film Scholars: Who's Who in American Film Scholarship. Ed. by Gordon Press Staff. 1977. 75.00 (*0-87968-226-4*) Gordon Pr.

Directory of American Firms Operating in Foreign Countries, 3 vols. 12th ed. World Trade Academy Press, Inc. Staff. 1991. 195.00 (*0-8360-0033-1*) World Trade.

Directory of American Firms Operating in Foreign Countries, 3 vols., Set. 13th ed. 1700p. 1994. 200.00 (*0-8360-0038-2*) World Trade.

Directory of American Libraries with Genealogy or Local History Collections. Ed. by P. William Filby. LC 87-37109. 330p. 1988. 75.00 (*0-8420-2286-4*) Scholarly Res Inc.

Directory of American Philosophers, 1994-95. 17th ed. Ed. by Archie Bahm. 480p. 1994. 109.00 (*0-912632-95-X*) Philos Document.

Directory of American Poetry Books. Poets House Staff. LC 93-17778. 96p. (Orig.). 1993. pap. 8.95 (*1-55921-099-0*, Asphodel Pr) Moyer Bell.

Directory of American Poetry Books. 2nd ed. Poets House Staff. LC 93-17778. 160p. (Orig.). 1994. pap. 9.95 (*1-55921-122-9*, Asphodel Pr) Moyer Bell.

Directory of American Poets & Fiction Writers. 288p. 1991. pap. 21.95 (*0-913734-23-3*) Poets & Writers.

Directory of American Poets & Fiction Writers, 1989-90. rev. ed. 288p. 1989. pap. 19.95 (*0-913734-20-9*) Poets & Writers.

Directory of American Poets & Fiction Writers, 1993-94. 7th ed. 320p. 1992. pap. 23.95 (*0-913734-26-8*) Poets & Writers.

Directory of American Poets & Fiction Writers, 1995-1996 Edition. 300p. (Orig.). 1995. pap. 25.95 (*0-913734-47-0*) Poets & Writers.

*__Directory of American Research & Technology 1996.__ Ed. by Bowker, R. R., Staff. 820p. 1995. 339.95 (*0-8352-3675-7*) Bowker.

Directory of American Research & Technology 1994. 28th ed. Ed. by Bowker, R. R., Staff. 820p. 1993. 315.00 (*0-8352-3395-2*) Bowker.

Directory of American Research & Technology 1995. 29th ed. Ed. by Bowker, R. R., Staff. 820p. 1994. 339.95 (*0-8352-3524-6*) Bowker.

Directory of American Savings & Loan Associations: The Complete Directory. 31th ed. T. K. Sanderson. 500p. 1985. 50.00 (*0-911304-02-9*) T K Sanderson.

Directory of American Savings & Loan Associations 1985. 32th ed. 500p. 1986. 50.00 (*0-911304-06-1*) T K Sanderson.

Directory of American Savings & Loan Associations, 1989. 34th ed. 500p. 1989. 55.00 (*0-911304-09-6*) T K Sanderson.

Directory of American Scholars, 4 vols., Set. 8th ed. Ed. by Jacques Cattell Press Staff. Incl. Vol. 1. History. 90.00 (*0-8352-1478-8*); Vol. II. English, Speech, Drama. 1982. 90.00 (*0-8352-1479-6*); Vol. III. Foreign Language, Linguistics, & Philology. 1982. 90.00 (*0-8352-1481-8*); Vol. IV. Philosophy, Religion & Law. 1982. 90.00 (*0-8352-1482-6*); 3152p. 1982. 325.00 (*0-8352-1476-1*) Bowker.

Directory of American Youth Organizations 1994-1995: A Guide to 500 Clubs, Groups, Troops, Teams, Societies, Lodges, & More for Young People. 5th rev. ed. Judith B. Erickson. 200p. (YA). (gr. k-12). 1994. pap. 18.95 (*0-915793-63-6*) Free Spirit Pub.

Directory of Ancestral Heads of New England Families: 1620-1700. Frank R. Holmes. LC 64-19755. 274p. 1989. reprint ed. 20.00 (*0-8063-0182-1*) Genealog Pub.

Directory of Appliances, Equipment, Construction Materials, & Components Evaluated in Accordance with International Publications 1994. (C). 1994. pap. text ed. 6.00 (*1-55989-542-X*) Underwrtrs Labs.

Directory of Applications Software of the United Nations System. 1990. 15.00 (*92-1-100350-4*, GV.90.0.2) UN.

Directory of Aquaculture in the Northeast. Nica Bell. 56p. (Orig.). 1991. pap. 5.00 (*1-56172-003-8*) MIT Sea Grant.

Directory of Arab Businesses & Services. 1992. lib. bdg. 445.95 (*0-8490-5594-6*) Gordon Pr.

*__Directory of Art & Design Faculties in Colleges & Universities, U. S. & Canada, 1994-95 Edition.__ 3rd ed. Intro. by Robby Gunstream. 525p. (Orig.). 1994. pap. 55.00 (*1-881913-01-5*) CMS Pubns.

Directory of Art & Music Colleges. 3rd ed. Ed. by Roberta Carr. 350p. (YA). (gr. 8-12). 1994. pap. 16.95 (*1-880468-09-3*) Col Connect.

Directory of Art Bronze Foundries. Michael S. Edge. 95p. 1990. pap. 14.95 (*1-879257-01-7*) Artesia Pr.

Directory of Art Libraries & Visual Resource Collections in North America. Judith A. Hoffberg & Stanley W. Hess. LC 78-61628. 298p. 1978. text ed. 49.95 (*0-918212-05-7*) Neal-Schuman.

Directory of Associate Members: Suppliers of Retail Services & Products. 15.00 (*0-87102-101-3*, 80-1014) Natl Ret Merch.

Directory of Association Meeting Planners & Conference-Convention Directors, 1994. Ed. by Edgar Adcock et al. 1053p. (Orig.). 1993. pap. 227.00 (*0-87228-044-6*) Salesmans.

***Directory of Association Meeting Planners & Conference/Convention Directors 1995. exp. ed. Ed. by Edgar Adcock et al. 1056p. 1995. pap. 237.00 (*0-87228-067-5*) Salesmans.**
Updated & expanded with over 2,500 new meeting planners & more than 500 new associations, this time-saving guide lists more than 8,700 national associations that hold more than 29,000 conventions, seminars & meetings. Listings identify over 14,000 meeting planner alphabetically by city & state & also include: * association name, with acronym * complete address & telephone & fax numbers * name of executive director & meeting planner * number of conventions, & smaller meetings & seminars * past & future convention locations * months held * number of days meetings/conventions are held * approximate number of attendees * booking schedules * type of facility used * professional speaker usage * exhibit space required. Also included: an Acronym Index to quickly find out the official name of an association, & a SPECIAL SECTION LISTING MAJOR ASSOCIATION MANAGEMENT COMPANIES, their meeting planners, & the associations they represent. *Publisher Provided Annotation.*

Directory of Associations in Louisiana. Dolores B. Owen. 303p. 1991. spiral bd. 22.50 (*0-9630719-0-4*) Owen Hse.

Directory of Associations of Women Lawyers. 20p. 1993. pap. 15.00 (*0-685-29660-1*, 492-0008) Amer Bar Assn.

Directory of Athletic Scholarships see **Athletic Scholarships: Thousands of Grants & Over 200 Million Dollars for College-Bound Athletes**

Directory of Atomic, Molecular, & Optical Scientists. National Research Council (U. S.), Committee on Atomic & Molecular Science Staff. LC 86-62825. 191p. reprint ed. pap. 54.50 (*0-8357-6812-0*, 2035495) Bks Demand.

Directory of Audio-Visual Sources: History of Science, Medicine & Technology. Bruce Eastwood. 160p. 1979. 20.00 (*0-88202-185-0*) Watson Pub Intl.

Directory of Australian Directories. 2nd rev. ed. Ed. by Ralph Reid. 256p. 1991. pap. 55.00 (*0-909532-80-X*) D W Thorpe.

*__Directory of Authors of New Medical & Scientific Reviews of Alcoholism with Subject Index.__ Science & Life Consultants Assn. Staff. 160p. 1995. 37.50 (*0-7883-0558-1*) ABBE Pubs Assn.

*__Directory of Authors of New Medical & Scientific Reviews of Alcoholism with Subject Index.__ Science & Life Consultants Assn. Staff. 160p. 1995. pap. 34.50 (*0-7883-0559-X*) ABBE Pubs Assn.

*__Directory of Authors of New Medical & Scientific Reviews of Ambulatory Surgery with Subject Index.__ Science & Life Consultants Assn. Staff. 160p. 1995. 37.50 (*0-7883-0526-3*) ABBE Pubs Assn.

*__Directory of Authors of New Medical & Scientific Reviews of Ambulatory Surgery with Subject Index.__ Science & Life Consultants Assn. Staff. 160p. 1995. pap. 34.50 (*0-7883-0527-1*) ABBE Pubs Assn.

*__Directory of Authors of New Medical & Scientific Reviews of Anti-Cancer Agents with Subject Index.__ 160p. 1995. 37.50 (*0-7883-0530-1*) ABBE Pubs Assn.

*__Directory of Authors of New Medical & Scientific Reviews of Anti-Cancer Agents with Subject Index.__ 160p. 1995. pap. 34.50 (*0-7883-0531-X*) ABBE Pubs Assn.

*__Directory of Authors of New Medical & Scientific Reviews of Antibiotics with Subject Index.__ Science & Life Consultants Assn. Staff. 160p. 1995. 37.50 (*0-7883-0562-X*) ABBE Pubs Assn.

*__Directory of Authors of New Medical & Scientific Reviews of Antibiotics with Subject Index.__ Science & Life Consultants Assn. Staff. 160p. 1995. pap. 34.50 (*0-7883-0563-8*) ABBE Pubs Assn.

*__Directory of Authors of New Medical & Scientific Reviews of Antigens of Neoplasms with Subject Index.__ Science & Life Consultants Assn. Staff. 160p. 1995. 37.50 (*0-7883-0552-2*) ABBE Pubs Assn.

*__Directory of Authors of New Medical & Scientific Reviews of Antigens of Neoplasms with Subject Index.__ Science & Life Consultants Assn. Staff. 160p. 1995. pap. 34.50 (*0-7883-0553-0*) ABBE Pubs Assn.

*__Directory of Authors of New Medical & Scientific Reviews of Biopsy & Related Factors with Subject Index.__ Science & Life Consultants Assn. Staff. 160p. 1995. 37. 50 (*0-7883-0554-9*) ABBE Pubs Assn.

*__Directory of Authors of New Medical & Scientific Reviews of Biopsy & Related Factors with Subject Index.__ Science & Life Consultants Assn. Staff. 160p. 1995. pap. 34.50 (*0-7883-0555-7*) ABBE Pubs Assn.

*__Directory of Authors of New Medical & Scientific Reviews of Carcinogens with Subject Index.__ Science & Life Consultants Assn. Staff. 160p. 1995. 44.50 (*0-7883-0544-1*) ABBE Pubs Assn.

*__Directory of Authors of New Medical & Scientific Reviews of Carcinogens with Subject Index.__ Science & Life Consultants Assn. Staff. 160p. 1995. pap. 39.50 (*0-7883-0545-X*) ABBE Pubs Assn.

*__Directory of Authors of New Medical & Scientific Reviews of Cell Membranes with Subject Index.__ Science & Life Consultants Assn. Staff. 160p. 1995. 37.50 (*0-7883-0504-2*) ABBE Pubs Assn.

*__Directory of Authors of New Medical & Scientific Reviews of Cell Membranes with Subject Index.__ Science & Life Consultants Assn. Staff. 160p. 1995. pap. 34.50 (*0-7883-0505-0*) ABBE Pubs Assn.

*__Directory of Authors of New Medical & Scientific Reviews of Cervix Neoplasms with Subject Index.__ Science & Life Consultants Assn. Staff. 160p. 1995. 37.50 (*0-7883-0514-X*) ABBE Pubs Assn.

*__Directory of Authors of New Medical & Scientific Reviews of Cervix Neoplasms with Subject Index.__ Science & Life Consultants Assn. Staff. 160p. 1995. pap. 34.50 (*0-7883-0515-8*) ABBE Pubs Assn.

*__Directory of Authors of New Medical & Scientific Reviews of Coenzymes with Subject Index.__ Science & Life Consultants Assn. Staff. 160p. 1995. 37.50 (*0-7883-0522-0*) ABBE Pubs Assn.

*__Directory of Authors of New Medical & Scientific Reviews of Coenzymes with Subject Index.__ Science & Life Consultants Assn. Staff. 160p. 1995. pap. 34.50 (*0-7883-0523-9*) ABBE Pubs Assn.

*__Directory of Authors of New Medical & Scientific Reviews of Contraception with Subject Index.__ Science & Life Consultants Assn. Staff. 160p. 1995. 37.50 (*0-7883-0506-9*) ABBE Pubs Assn.

*__Directory of Authors of New Medical & Scientific Reviews of Contraception with Subject Index.__ Science & Life Consultants Assn. Staff. 160p. 1995. pap. 34.50 (*0-7883-0507-7*) ABBE Pubs Assn.

*__Directory of Authors of New Medical & Scientific Reviews of Cystic Fibrosis with Subject Index.__ Science & Life Consultants Assn. Staff. 160p. 1995. 37.50 (*0-7883-0532-8*) ABBE Pubs Assn.

*__Directory of Authors of New Medical & Scientific Reviews of Cystic Fibrosis with Subject Index.__ Science & Life Consultants Assn. Staff. 160p. 1995. pap. 34.50 (*0-7883-0533-6*) ABBE Pubs Assn.

*__Directory of Authors of New Medical & Scientific Reviews of Diabetes Mellitus with Subject Index.__ Science & Life Consultants Assn. Staff. 160p. 1995. 37.50 (*0-7883-0548-4*) ABBE Pubs Assn.

D

An Asterisk (*) at the beginning of an entry indicates that the title is appearing in BIP for the first time.

*Directory of Authors of New Medical & Scientific Reviews of Diabetes Mellitus with Subject Index. Science & Life Consultants Assn. Staff. 160p. 1995. pap. 34.50 (0-7883-0549-2) ABBE Pubs Assn.

*Directory of Authors of New Medical & Scientific Reviews of Diets with Subject Index. Science & Life Consultants Assn. Staff. 160p. 1995. 37.50 (0-7883-0536-0) ABBE Pubs Assn.

*Directory of Authors of New Medical & Scientific Reviews of Diets with Subject Index. Science & Life Consultants Assn. Staff. 160p. 1995. pap. 34.50 (0-7883-0537-9) ABBE Pubs Assn.

*Directory of Authors of New Medical & Scientific Reviews of Domestic Animals with Subject Index. Science & Life Consultants Assn. Staff. 160p. 1995. 37.50 (0-7883-0560-3) ABBE Pubs Assn.

*Directory of Authors of New Medical & Scientific Reviews of Domestic Animals with Subject Index. Science & Life Consultants Assn. Staff. 160p. 1995. pap. 34.50 (0-7883-0561-1) ABBE Pubs Assn.

*Directory of Authors of New Medical & Scientific Reviews of Ecology with Subject Index. Science & Life Consultants Assn. Staff. 160p. 1995. 37.50 (0-7883-0538-7) ABBE Pubs Assn.

*Directory of Authors of New Medical & Scientific Reviews of Ecology with Subject Index. Science & Life Consultants Assn. Staff. 160p. 1995. pap. 34.50 (0-7883-0539-5) ABBE Pubs Assn.

*Directory of Authors of New Medical & Scientific Reviews of Homeostasis with Subject Index. Science & Life Consultants Assn. Staff. 160p. 1995. 37.50 (0-7883-0510-7) ABBE Pubs Assn.

*Directory of Authors of New Medical & Scientific Reviews of Homeostasis with Subject Index. Science & Life Consultants Assn. Staff. 160p. 1995. pap. 34.50 (0-7883-0511-5) ABBE Pubs Assn.

*Directory of Authors of New Medical & Scientific Reviews of Immunoglobulins with Subject Index. 160p. 1995. 37.50 (0-7883-0512-3) ABBE Pubs Assn.

*Directory of Authors of New Medical & Scientific Reviews of Immunoglobulins with Subject Index. 160p. 1995. pap. 34.50 (0-7883-0513-1) ABBE Pubs Assn.

*Directory of Authors of New Medical & Scientific Reviews of Immunotherapy with Subject Index. Science & Life Consultants Assn. Staff. 160p. 1995. 37.50 (0-7883-0534-4) ABBE Pubs Assn.

*Directory of Authors of New Medical & Scientific Reviews of Immunotherapy with Subject Index. Science & Life Consultants Assn. Staff. 160p. 1995. pap. 34.50 (0-7883-0535-2) ABBE Pubs Assn.

*Directory of Authors of New Medical & Scientific Reviews of Intelligence with Subject Index. Science & Life Consultants Assn. Staff. 160p. 1995. 37.50 (0-7883-0516-6) ABBE Pubs Assn.

*Directory of Authors of New Medical & Scientific Reviews of Intelligence with Subject Index. Science & Life Consultants Assn. Staff. 160p. 1995. pap. 34.50 (0-7883-0517-4) ABBE Pubs Assn.

*Directory of Authors of New Medical & Scientific Reviews of Leukocytes with Subject Index. Science & Life Consultants Assn. Staff. 160p. 1995. 37.50 (0-7883-0518-2) ABBE Pubs Assn.

*Directory of Authors of New Medical & Scientific Reviews of Leukocytes with Subject Index. Science & Life Consultants Assn. Staff. 160p. 1995. pap. 34.50 (0-7883-0519-0) ABBE Pubs Assn.

*Directory of Authors of New Medical & Scientific Reviews of Malaria with Subject Index. Science & Life Consultants Assn. Staff. 160p. 1995. 37.50 (0-7883-0520-4) ABBE Pubs Assn.

*Directory of Authors of New Medical & Scientific Reviews of Malaria with Subject Index. Science & Life Consultants Assn. Staff. 160p. 1995. pap. 34.50 (0-7883-0521-2) ABBE Pubs Assn.

*Directory of Authors of New Medical & Scientific Reviews of Mental Disorders with Subject Index. Science & Life Consultants Assn. Staff. 160p. 1995. 37.50 (0-7883-0524-7) ABBE Pubs Assn.

*Directory of Authors of New Medical & Scientific Reviews of Mental Disorders with Subject Index. Science & Life Consultants Assn. Staff. 160p. 1995. pap. 34.50 (0-7883-0525-5) ABBE Pubs Assn.

*Directory of Authors of New Medical & Scientific Reviews of Mineral Oil (Liquid Petrolatum) with Subject Index. Science & Life Consultants Assn. Staff. 160p. 1995. 37.50 (0-7883-0550-6) ABBE Pubs Assn.

*Directory of Authors of New Medical & Scientific Reviews of Mineral Oil (Liquid Petrolatum) with Subject Index. Science & Life Consultants Assn. Staff. 160p. 1995. pap. 34.50 (0-7883-0551-4) ABBE Pubs Assn.

*Directory of Authors of New Medical & Scientific Reviews of Neurotransmitter Receptors with Subject Index. Science & Life Consultants Assn. Staff. 160p. 1995. 37.50 (0-7883-0556-5) ABBE Pubs Assn.

*Directory of Authors of New Medical & Scientific Reviews of Neurotransmitter Receptors with Subject Index. Science & Life Consultants Assn. Staff. 160p. 1995. pap. 34.50 (0-7883-0557-3) ABBE Pubs Assn.

*Directory of Authors of New Medical & Scientific Reviews of Phagocytes & Phagocytosis with Subject Index. Science & Life Consultants Assn. Staff. 160p. 1995. 37.50 (0-7883-0508-5) ABBE Pubs Assn.

*Directory of Authors of New Medical & Scientific Reviews of Phagocytes & Phagocytosis with Subject Index. Science & Life Consultants Assn. Staff. 160p. 1995. pap. 34.50 (0-7883-0509-3) ABBE Pubs Assn.

*Directory of Authors of New Medical & Scientific Reviews of Phylogeny with Subject Index. Science & Life Consultants Assn. Staff. 160p. 1995. 37.50 (0-7883-0542-5) ABBE Pubs Assn.

*Directory of Authors of New Medical & Scientific Reviews of Phylogeny with Subject Index. Science & Life Consultants Assn. Staff. 160p. 1995. pap. 34.50 (0-7883-0543-3) ABBE Pubs Assn.

*Directory of Authors of New Medical & Scientific Reviews of Post-Operative Complications with Subject Index. Science & Life Consultants Assn. Staff. 160p. 1995. 37.50 (0-7883-0528-X) ABBE Pubs Assn.

*Directory of Authors of New Medical & Scientific Reviews of Post-Operative Complications with Subject Index. Science & Life Consultants Assn. Staff. 160p. 1995. pap. 34.50 (0-7883-0529-8) ABBE Pubs Assn.

*Directory of Authors of New Medical & Scientific Reviews of Rheumatic Diseases with Subject Inde. Science & Life Consultants Assn. Staff. 160p. 1995. 37.50 (0-7883-0566-2) ABBE Pubs Assn.

*Directory of Authors of New Medical & Scientific Reviews of Rheumatic Diseases with Subject Inde. Science & Life Consultants Assn. Staff. 160p. 1995. pap. 34.50 (0-7883-0567-0) ABBE Pubs Assn.

*Directory of Authors of New Medical & Scientific Reviews of Sudden Cardiac Deaths with Subject Index. Science & Life Consultants Assn. Staff. 160p. 1995. 37.50 (0-7883-0546-8) ABBE Pubs Assn.

*Directory of Authors of New Medical & Scientific Reviews of Sudden Cardiac Deaths with Subject Index. Science & Life Consultants Assn. Staff. 160p. 1995. pap. 34.50 (0-7883-0547-6) ABBE Pubs Assn.

*Directory of Authors of New Medical & Scientific Reviews of Tumor Necrosis Factors with Index. Science & Life Consultants Assn. Staff. 160p. 1995. 37.50 (0-7883-0564-6) ABBE Pubs Assn.

*Directory of Authors of New Medical & Scientific Reviews of Tumor Necrosis Factors with Index. Science & Life Consultants Assn. Staff. 160p. 1995. pap. 34.50 (0-7883-0565-4) ABBE Pubs Assn.

*Directory of Authors of New Medical & Scientific Reviews of Xenobiotics with Subject Index. Science & Life Consultants Assn. Staff. 160p. 1995. 37.50 (0-7883-0540-9) ABBE Pubs Assn.

*Directory of Authors of New Medical & Scientific Reviews of Xenobiotics with Subject Index. Science & Life Consultants Assn. Staff. 160p. 1995. pap. 34.50 (0-7883-0541-7) ABBE Pubs Assn.

Directory of Autocephalous Bishops of the Churches of the Apostolic Succession. 6th ed. Karl Pruter. LC 92-24123. (Autocephalous Orthodox Churches Ser.: No. 1). 96p. 1993. lib. bdg. 23.00 (0-912134-12-7, 26217486) Borgo Pr.

*Directory of Autocephalous Bishops of the Churches of the Apostolic Succession. 7th expanded rev. ed. Karl Pruter. LC 95-5114. (Autocephalous Orthodox Churches Ser.: No. 1). 1995. pap. write for info. (0-912134-25-9) Borgo Pr.

*Directory of Autocephalous Bishops of the Churches of the Apostolic Succession. 7th expanded rev. ed. Karl Pruter. LC 95-5114. (Autocephalous Orthodox Churches Ser.: Vol. 1). 1995. lib. bdg. write for info. (0-912134-24-0) Borgo Pr.

*Directory of Automated Criminal Justice Information Systems 1993 Vol. I: Law Enforcement. 848p. (Orig.). (C). 1994. pap. text ed. 75.00 (0-7881-1477-8) Diane Pub.

*Directory of Automated Criminal Justice Information Systems 1993 Vol. II: Corrections, Courts, Probation-Parole, Prosecution. 633p. (Orig.). (C). 1994. pap. text ed. 75.00 (0-7881-1478-6) Diane Pub.

Directory of Automated Library Systems. 2nd ed. John Corbin. 315p. 1989. pap. text ed. 55.00 (1-55570-050-0) Neal-Schuman.

Directory of Automotive Aftermarket Suppliers, 1993-94. Ed. by Michael Jarvis. 696p. 1992. pap. 225.00 (0-86730-571-1, CSG Info Servs) Lebhar Friedman.

Directory of Back Issue Treasure Magazine Buyers, Sellers, & Traders. John H. Reed. 41p. (Orig.). 1987. pap. 6.95 (0-940519-02-X) Res Discover Pubns.

Directory of Ballroom Dancing & Who's Who in the Ballroom Dancing World. L. Gordon & H. Gordon. (Ballroom Dance Ser.). 1985. lib. bdg. 79.95 (0-8490-3243-1) Gordon Pr.

*Directory of Bankruptcy Attorneys, 1995. 2372p. 1994. 225.00 (0-13-169245-3) Aspen Law.

Directory of Banks of the Former Soviet Republics, 1993-94, Vol. 1, No. 1. Ed. by East West Information Communication Staff. 400p. (C). 1994. lib. bdg. 420.00 (1-85333-926-1, Pub. by Graham & Trotman UK) Kluwer Ac.

Directory of Banks of the Former Soviet Republics 1993-94, Vol. 1, No. 2. Ed. by East West Information Communication (EWIC) Staff. 400p. 1994. lib. bdg. 420.00 (1-85333-931-8, Pub. by Graham & Trotman UK) Kluwer Ac.

Directory of Barter Directories. Comp. by Frieda Carrol. LC 83-90673. 100p. 1983. pap. 19.95 (0-911617-55-8, Barter Pub) Prosperity & Profits.

Directory of Bay Area Associations. Lorri Fien. (Illus.). 248p. (Orig.). 1990. pap. 24.95 (0-9623232-4-1) Bay Area Resource.

Directory of Bay Area Associations: Bay Area Contacts at Your Fingertips. rev. ed. Ed. by Lorri Fien. (Illus.). 240p. (Orig.). 1995. disk write for info. (0-9623232-9-2) Bay Area Resource.

Directory of Bay Area Associations: Bay Area Contacts at Your Fingertips. 2nd rev. ed. Ed. by Lorri Fien. (Illus.). 256p. (Orig.). 1995. pap. 79.95 (0-9623232-8-4) Bay Area Resource.

Directory of Bay Area Libraries, 1990. Ed. by Katharine Scarborough. 406p. 1990. 74.04 (0-318-50078-7) BAL & Info Sys.

Directory of Biomedical & Health Care Grants 1995. 9th ed. 664p. 1994. pap. 84.50 (0-89774-910-3) Oryx Pr.

*Directory of Biomedical & Health Care Grants 1996. 10th ed. Oryx Press Staff. Ed. by Millie Hannum & Janet Woolum. 664p. 1995. pap. 84.50 (0-89774-878-6, 2277) Oryx Pr.

Directory of Biomedical & Life Science Online Databases. Cuadra Staff & Elsevier Science Publishing Staff. 1987. 29.95 (0-444-01196-X) Elsevier.

Directory of Biotechnology Centers, 1993. 6th ed. North Carolina Biotechnology Center Staff. Ed. by Janet E. Hafer. 65p. 1993. pap. 40.00 (0-945597-19-3) NC Biotech Ctr.

Directory of Biotechnology Companies: U. S. Companies, Eastern Region I. Ed. by M. J. Sullivan et al. 60p. (C). 1991. pap. 18.50 (1-880343-03-7) A Gee.

Directory of Biotechnology Companies: U. S. Companies, Eastern Region II. Ed. by M. J. Sullivan et al. 60p. (C). 1991. pap. 18.50 (1-880343-04-5) A Gee.

Directory of Biotechnology Companies: U. S. Companies, Western Region I. Ed. by M. J. Sullivan et al. 60p. (C). 1991. pap. 18.50 (1-880343-00-2) A Gee.

Directory of Biotechnology Companies: U. S. Companies, Western Region I. 2nd ed. Ed. by M. J. Mullivan et al. 95p. 1992. pap. 23.95 (1-880343-06-1) A Gee.

Directory of Biotechnology Companies: U. S. Companies, Western Region II. Ed. by M. J. Sullivan et al. 60p. (C). 1991. pap. 18.50 (1-880343-01-0) A Gee.

Directory of Biotechnology Companies in the U. S. Ed. by M. J. Sullivan et al. 240p. (C). 1991. pap. 65.00 (1-880343-05-3) A Gee.

Directory of Biotechnology Recruiters. Ed. by M. J. Sullivan et al. 50p. (C). 1991. pap. 24.95 (1-880343-02-9) A Gee.

Directory of Black Historians, Ph.D's & Others, 1975-1976: Essays, Commentaries & Publications, Nos. 870-872. Ed. by Gossie H. Hudson. 1975. 12.50 (0-686-20367-4) CPL Biblios.

Directory of Black Nursing Faculty: Baccalaureate & Higher Degree Programs. Sallie T. Allen. LC 88-146305. 169p. (C). 1988. pap. 50.00 (0-923950-00-1) Tucker IL.

Directory of Blacks in the Performing Arts. 2nd ed. Edward Mapp. LC 89-30477. 612p. 1990. 57.50 (0-8108-2222-9) Scarecrow.

Directory of Bodies Concerned with Urban & Regional Research. 443p. 1990. 60.00 (92-1-116488-5) UN.

Directory of Book Printers. Marie Kiefer. LC 92-80438. 1993. pap. 9.95 (0-912411-39-2) Open Horizons.

Directory of Booksellers & Distributors for Independent Publishers. 750p. (Orig.). 1987. pap. 14.95 (0-936111-05-4) Persun & Berlin.

Directory of British Architects, 1834-1900. Ed. by Alison Felstead et al. (Illus.). 1072p. 1993. 300.00 (0-7201-2158-2, Mansell Pub) Cassell.

Directory of British Associations. 12th ed. 1994. 4,500.00 (0-8103-9917-2, 073003) Gale.

*Directory of British Associations & Associations in Ireland. 12th ed. 610p. 1994. 250.00 (0-900246-63-4) CBD Res.

Directory of British Geological Museums. Ed. by J. R. Nudds. (Geological Society Misc. Paper Ser.: No. 18). (Illus.). vii, 142p. 1994. 25.00 (1-897799-08-X, Pub. by Geol Soc Pub Hse UK) AAPG.

Directory of British Importers, 1990. 6th ed. Trade Research Publications Staff. 1983. 650.00 (0-685-51078-6, Pub. by Trade Rsch Pubns UK) St Mut.

Directory of British Official Publications: A Guide to Sources. 2nd ed. Stephen Richard. LC 84-12559. 468p. 1984. 120.00 (0-7201-1706-2, Mansell Pub) Cassell.

Directory of British Peerages from the Earliest Times to the Present Day. Francis L. Leeson. LC 85-70013. 174p. 1986. pap. 12.50 (0-8063-1121-5) Genealog Pub.

*Directory of British Political Organizations. 2nd ed. Paul Mercer. 450p. 1995. pap. 150.00 (1-56159-146-7, Stockton Pr) Groves Dictionaries.

Directory of Broodmare Buyers. Ed. by Jan Meerdink. 200p. 1992. ring bd. 125.00 (0-685-55024-9) R Meerdink Co Ltd.

Directory of Broodmare Buyers, 1990. Research Staff of the Russell Meerdink Company. Ed. by Jan Meerdink. 225p. 1990. ring bd. 125.00 (0-929346-07-6) R Meerdink Co Ltd.

Directory of Broodmare Buyers, 1989. 217p. 125.00 (0-929346-03-3) R Meerdink Co Ltd.

Directory of Building & Equipment Grants. Richard M. Eckstein. 200p. (Orig.). 1988. pap. 34.50 (0-945078-01-3) Rsch Grant Guides.

Directory of Building & Equipment Grants. 2nd ed. Contrib by Richard M. Eckstein. 216p. (Orig.). 1992. pap. 49.50 (0-945078-04-8) Rsch Grant Guides.

*Directory of Building & Equipment Grants. 3rd ed. Ed. by Richard M. Eckstein. 236p. 1994. pap. 57.50 (0-945078-08-0) Rsch Grant Guides.

Directory of Building Services Technical Software. J. Wix. (C). 1984. 175.00 (0-86022-191-1, Pub. by Build Servs Info Assn UK) St Mut.

Directory of Buried Or Sunken Treasures & Lost Mines of the United States. Thomas Penfield. (True Treasure Ser.). (Illus.). 134p. (Orig.). 1979. reprint ed. pap. text ed. 8.95 (0-941620-06-9) Carson Ent.

Directory of Business & Financial Information Services. 9th ed. Charles J. Popovich & M. Rita Costello. 471p. 1994. 75.00 (0-87111-420-8) SLA.

Directory of Business Archives in the United States & Canada. 96p. 1990. pap. 12.00 (0-931828-74-0) Soc Am Archivists.

*Directory of Business Information. Lawrence Rasie. 1995. text ed. 85.00 (0-471-59816-X) Wiley.

Directory of Business Information Resources: Associations, Newsletters, Magazines & Trade Shows. Ed. by Leslie Mackenzie. 1992. 135.00 (0-939300-11-7); pap. 120.00 (0-939300-15-X) Grey Hse Pub.

Directory of Business Information Resources, 1994. Ed. by Leslie Mackenzie. 887p. 1994. pap. 145.00 (0-939300-26-5) Grey Hse Pub.

Directory of Business Periodical Special Issues: The Definitive Guide to Indexed Business, Science, & Technology Periodicals. Trip Wyckoff. 250p. 1994. 49.95 (1-878753-60-6) Ref Press.

Directory of Business to Business Catalogs. Ed. by Leslie Mackenzie. 600p. 1992. pap. text ed. 110.00 (0-939300-16-8) Grey Hse Pub.

Directory of Buyers. 2nd ed. Frances Hulme. 1981. pap. 9.95 (0-936588-01-2) Buyer's Directory.

Directory of Buyout Financing Sources. Ed. by Yong Lim. 520p. Date not set. 225.00 (0-914470-68-X) SDC Pubng.

*Directory of Buyout Financing Sources. Ed. by Yong Lim & Ted Weissberg. 579p. 1994. 225.00 (0-914470-72-8) Venture Econ Inc.

Directory of Camps for Blind & Visually Impaired Children, Youths, & Adults. Comp. by Irene Ludwig. 34p. 1989. 15.95 (0-89128-159-2) Am Foun Blind.

Directory of Campus-Business Linkages. Ed. by Dorothy C. Fenwick. (Ace-Macmillan Series on Higher Education). 192p. 1983. write for info. (0-686-46066-9) Macmillan.

Directory of Canadian Private Residential Schools. Higgins Thomson. 461p. Date not set. write for info. (0-318-72336-0, Pub. by Stoddart Pubng CN) Genl Dist Srvs.

Directory of Canadian Residential Schools. Higgins Thomson. 461p. 1986. pap. 19.95 (0-458-80090-2, Pub. by Stoddart Pubng CN) Genl Dist Srvs.

Directory of Canadian Trademaarks. Thomson & Thomson Staff. (Nineteen Ninety-Four Edition Ser.). 1579p. 1993. pap. 210.00 (1-57123-012-2) Thomson & Thomson.

*Directory of Canadian Trademarks. Thomson & Thomson Staff. Ed. by Lisa M. DePasquale. 1600p. 1995. pap. 225.00 (1-57123-024-6) Thomson & Thomson.

Directory of Capillary Electrophoresis. Ed. by D. Coleman. (TrAC Supplement Ser.: No. 1). 156p. 1994. pap. 70.00 (0-444-81798-0) Elsevier.

Directory of Career Resources for Minorities. 89.50 (0-916270-16-5) Ready Ref Pr.

Directory of Career Resources for Women. 89.50 (0-916270-07-6) Ready Ref Pr.

Directory of Career Training & Development Programs, 2 vols. First Edition. 47.50 (0-916270-08-4); Suppl. 47.50 (0-916270-26-2) Ready Ref Pr.

Directory of Career Training & Development Programs, 2 vols., Set. 95.00 (0-916270-27-0) Ready Ref Pr.

Directory of Caribbean-American Restaurants, Cuisines & Fast Food Outlets. Trevor Fraser. 75p. 1992. pap. 2.99 (0-9632225-0-3) Vidcapt.

Directory of Caribbean-American Restaurants, Cuisines & Fast Food Outlets. 2nd ed. Trevor Fraser. 72p. 1993. pap. 2.99 (0-9632225-1-1) Vidcapt.

Directory of Caribbean Scholars. Ed. by Roland I. Perusse. 1978. lib. bdg. 300.00 (0-8490-1394-1) Gordon Pr.

Directory of Caribbeanists. Comp. by Sylvia Potter. 82p. (Orig.). 1989. pap. 8.00 (0-317-93928-9) Editorial Academica.

Directory of Catalog Houses. 7.00 (0-931113-44-X) Success Publ.

Directory of Catalogers in the Special Libraries Association. Dorothy McGarry. LC 89-111094. (Illus.). 96p. reprint ed. pap. 27.40 (0-7837-1182-4, 2041711) Bks Demand.

Directory of Catholic Boarding Schools. National Catholic Educational Association Staff. 1991. 5.30 (1-55833-072-0); pap. 4.00 (0-685-48506-4) Natl Cath Educ.

Directory of Catholic Charities, 1989: Agencies & Institutions. 110p. 1989. 15.00 (0-318-41152-0) Catholic Charities.

Directory of Catholic Special Educational Programs & Facilities, 1989. Ed. by Suzanne E. Hall & Geri M. Garvey. 100p. (Orig.). 1989. pap. 11.00 (1-55833-012-7) Natl Cath Educ.

Directory of Central America Classroom Resources, K-12. 2nd rev. ed. Ed. by Mary A. Swenson & Kay Dunne. 172p. 1990. pap. 12.95 (0-9617743-3-9) Res Ctr Amer.

Directory of Certification Examination Review Courses 1994-1995. 1994. 18.75 (1-55810-079-2, AC-08) Am Nurses Pub.

Directory of Certification Programs in North America. Philip C. Wright. 456p. 1994. pap. 24.95 (0-8020-7776-5) U of Toronto Pr.

Directory of Certified Clinical Specialists in Physical Therapy. 150p. 17.00 (0-685-65746-9, CERT-1) Am Phys Therapy Assn.

Directory of Certified Eight(a) Contractors, 1993: Headquartered in Alabama, Georgia, Kentucky, Mississippi, North Carolina, Tennessee, & Virginia. Tennessee Valley Authority Staff. 750p. 1993. pap. 90.00 (0-9636853-0-9) TCRD.

*Directory of Certified Surgical Technologists & Certified First Assistants, 1995. LCC-ST Staff. Ed. by Nadine A. Davis. 1995. pap. text ed. write for info. (0-9622332-5-0) Liaison Coun.

Directory of Chain Restaurant Operators, 1993. Ed. by Jim Tierney. 960p. 1993. pap. 279.00 (0-86730-585-1, CSG Info Servs) Lebhar Friedman.

Directory of Chemistry Software, 1992. Ed. by Wendy A. Warr et al. 204p. 1992. pap. 34.95 (0-9518236-0-4) Am Chemical.

D

An Asterisk (*) at the beginning of an entry indicates that the title is appearing in BIP for the first time. 2009

Directory of Child Day Care Centers, 4 vols. Ed. by Oryx Press Staff. Incl. Vol. 1. Northeast. 440p. 1986. (*0-89774-256-7*); Vol. 2. North Central. 464p. 1986. (*0-89774-328-8*); Vol. 3. West. 528p. 1986. (*0-89774-329-6*); South. 440p. 1986. pap. 62.50 (*0-89774-330-X*); Set. Set pap. 250.00 (*0-685-12389-8*); Incl. Vol. 1. (*0-89774-256-7*); Vol. 2. (*0-89774-328-8*); Vol. 3. (*0-89774-329-6*); pap. 62.50 (*0-89774-330-X*); Set pap. 26.95 (*0-318-60458-2*); Incl. Vol. 1. (*0-89774-256-7*); Vol. 2. (*0-89774-328-8*); Vol. 3. (*0-89774-329-6*); pap. 62.50 (*0-89774-330-X*); Set pap. 26.95 (*0-318-60459-0*); Incl. Vol. 1. (*0-89774-256-7*); Vol. 2. (*0-89774-328-8*); Vol. 3. (*0-89774-329-6*); pap. 62.50 (*0-89774-330-X*); Set pap. 26.95 (*0-318-60460-4*); Incl. Vol. 1. (*0-89774-256-7*); Vol. 2. (*0-89774-328-8*); Vol. 3. (*0-89774-329-6*); pap. 62.50 (*0-89774-330-X*); Set pap. 26.95 (*0-318-60461-2*) Oryx Pr.

Directory of Child Protective Programs & Services in the Southeastern United States. Ed. by Clara L. Johnson. 326p. 1979. 10.00 (*0-318-16352-7*, B19) Regional Inst Social Welfare.

Directory of Children's Theatres in the United States. Comp. by Gayle Cornelison. 164p. (C). 1983. reprint ed. pap. text ed. 27.00 (*0-8191-3526-7*) U Pr of Amer.

Directory of Chinese Agricultural & Related Organizations. Ed. by Qiaogaio Zhang. 350p. 1994. 85.00x (*0-85198-789-3*) CAB Intl.

Directory of Chinese-American Librarians. 2nd ed. Chung-Tze Li. 45p. 1986. pap. 6.00 (*0-937256-04-8*) Chinese Cult Serv.

Directory of Chinese Foreign Trade, 1986. China Council for the Promotion of International Trade. 295p. 1987. 95.00 (*0-85121-050-3*, Pub. by Longman Grp UK) Gale.

Directory of Chinese Government Organs. Ed. by Jin Mingyuan. Tr. by Chang Yanrui. 944p. (CHI.). 1991. 108.00 (*962-7167-13-4*, Pub. by New China News UK) Cypress Co.

Directory of Chinese Learned Organizations. Ed. by Y. L. Wang & R. Y. Wu. 900p. 1991. 159.00 (*0-387-53013-4*) Spr-Verlag.

Directory of Chinese Libraries. Ed. by Wu Renyong et al. (World Books Reference Guide: No. 3). 500p. (CHI & ENG.). 1982. 84.00 (*0-8103-4354-1*) Gale.

Directory of City Policy Officials. 111p. 1985. 25.00 (*0-317-36858-3*, 2002); 10.00 (*0-317-36859-1*) Natl League Cities.

Directory of Civic & Professional Organizations: Central Florida Edition. George Fencl. 65p. (Orig.). 1992. 14.95 (*0-942827-13-9*) Edge Pub.

Directory of Clothing Research. M. S. Davies et al. 136p. 1968. 60.00 (*0-686-63762-3*) St Mut.

Directory of Clothing Research. M. S. Davies & A. Dewings. 136p. (C). 1968. pap. text ed. 110.00 (*0-685-46406-7*, Pub. by Textile Institue UK) St Mut.

Directory of College Alumni Groups: Networking - Local & International Business Sales, Grants & Information for Students. Edward Rosenwasser. Ed. by Barbara Komer. 304p. (Orig.). 1993. pap. 19.95 (*0-932495-06-0*) Student Coll.

Directory of College & University Foodservice, 1992-93. Ed. by Ron Boch. 462p. 1992. pap. 249.00 (*0-86730-562-2*) Lebhar Friedman.

Directory of College Stores. Barry T. Klein. 300p. 1996. pap. 75.00 (*0-915344-26-2*) Todd Pubns.

Directory of College Stores. 262p. 1995. 35.00 (*0-685-00662-X*) B Klein Pubns.

***Directory of Colleges & Universities Offering GIS Courses.** John M. Morgan, 4th & Genevieve R. Bennett. 70p. 1990. pap. 25.00 (*0-614-06095-8*, L333) Am Congrs Survey.

Directory of Colleges & Universities with Accredited Social Work Degree Programs. 1994. pap. 10.00 (*0-685-74777-8*) Coun Soc Wk Ed.

***Directory of Colorado Manufacturers.** Ed. by Ginny S. Hayden et al. LC 48-45467. 560p. 1995. pap. text ed. 80.00 (*0-89478-066-2*) U CO Busn Res Div.

Directory of Colorado Manufacturers, 1992. Ed. by Ginny S. Hayden. 433p. 1992. pap. text ed. 75.00 (*0-89478-024-7*) U CO Busn Res Div.

Directory of Communications Professionals, 1995. 194p. 1995. 30.00 (*0-317-04701-9*) NARUC.

Directory of Community College Graduate-Level Courses on Two-Year Institutions. Barry Lumsden & G. Bryan Stewart. 1992. pap. 10.00 (*0-87117-246-1*) Am Assn Comm Coll.

Directory of Community, Junior, & Technical College with Home Economics & Related Program. Beth L. Brusius. 133p. reprint ed. pap. 38.00 (*0-7837-1919-1*, 2042123) Bks Demand.

Directory of Community Legislation in Force As at 1 December 1993, 2 vols. 1064p. 1993. pap. 135.00 (*92-77-59927-8*, Pub. by Europ Com) UNIPUB.

Directory of Community Legislation in Force As of June 1992, 2 vols., Set. 19th ed. European Communities Staff. 1064p. 1992. pap. 125.00 (*92-77-41891-5*, FX-89-92-000-EN-C, Pub. by Europ Com) UNIPUB.

Directory of Community Legislation in Force, June 1993, 2 vols. 21th ed. European Communities Staff. 1064p. 1993. pap. 140.00 (*92-77-54034-6*, JX-19-93-000-EN-C) UNIPUB.

Directory of Community Services: Directorio de Servicios para la Comunidad (in the Bronx, Manhattan & Staten Island) (ENG & SPA.). 1993. 40.00 (*0-87104-722-5*, Branch Libraries) NY Pub Lib.

***Directory of Community Services: First Call for Help.** United Way of Minneapolis Area Staff. 700p. 1995. pap. 16.50 (*1-887418-00-8*) United Way MN.

Directory of Community Social Work in Scotland: An Initial Appraisal. Ed. by David Crosbie et al. (C). 1989. 40.00 (*0-685-40341-6*, Pub. by Natl Inst Soc Work) St Mut.

Directory of Community Social Work Initiatives: England. Lynette Domoney. (C). 1989. 40.00 (*0-685-40342-4*, Pub. by Natl Inst Soc Work) St Mut.

Directory of Community Social Work Initiatives: Scotland. Comp. by Wendy Beecher. (C). 1987. 45.00 (*0-685-28601-0*, Pub. by Natl Inst Soc Work) St Mut.

Directory of Community Substance Abuse Programs in Virginia. 56p. (Orig.). (C). 1993. pap. text ed. 25.00 (*0-7881-0045-9*) Diane Pub.

Directory of Companies Involved in the Conventional & Hazardous Waste Business. Business Communications Company, Inc. Staff. 175.00 (*0-685-62471-4*) BCC.

Directory of Companies Offering Dividend Reinvestment Plans. 5th ed. Ed. by Sumie Kinoshita. 140p. 1988. 24.95 (*0-933183-03-8*) Evergreen Ent.

Directory of Companies Offering Dividend Reinvestment Plans. 6th ed. Ed. by Sumie Kinoshita. 140p. 1989. 24.95 (*0-933183-04-6*) Evergreen Ent.

Directory of Companies Offering Dividend Reinvestment Plans. 7th ed. Sumie Kinoshita. 140p. 1990. pap. 28.95 (*0-933183-06-2*) Evergreen Ent.

Directory of Companies Offering Dividend Reinvestment Plans. 8th ed. Sumie Kinoshita. 144p. 1991. 28.95 (*0-933183-08-9*) Evergreen Ent.

Directory of Companies Offering Dividend Reinvestment Plans. 10th ed. Ed. by Sumie Kinoshita. 142p. 1993. 28.95 (*0-933183-12-7*) Evergreen Ent.

Directory of Companies Offering Dividend Reinvestment Plans. 11th ed. Ed. by Sumie Kinoshita. 160p. 1994. 28.95 (*0-933183-15-1*) Evergreen Ent.

***Directory of Companies Offering Dividend Reinvestment Plans. 12th ed. Ed. by Sumie Kinoshita. 170p. (Orig.). 1995. 29.95x (*0-933183-17-8*) Evergreen Ent.**
Dividend reinvestment plans (DRPs) offer owners of common stocks a CONVENIENT & systematic way to invest their dividends & the opportunity to purchase additional shares with cash payments. Over 64 percent of S&P companies offer DRPs. The FIRST! Evergreen has published the DIRECTORY since 1982. The directory's editor, S. Kinoshita, is considered "THE" authority in the dividend reinvestment plans. She has been referred to as the "doyenne" (WORKING WOMAN), the "first lady" (OREGONIAN), & the "guru" (INVESTOR RELATIONS INSTITUTE) of dividend reinvestment. Personal finance writers love DRPs because they are a true BARGAIN for individual investors. DRPs are a proven, SAFE method for investing in quality companies. It's for the long-term, patient investor. In a DRP, the stockholder does not receive dividend checks. The dividends are used to purchase more stock, no matter how small the dividend, usually without paying brokerage commissions. In addition, the investor may send in additional money to purchase more shares, all without going to a broker. The directory lists over 800 companies that have DRPs, with addresses, telephone numbers & plan features. This encourages the prospective shareholder to call & investigate the company before investing. Evergreen Enterprises, Box 763, Laurel, MD 20725, 301-549-3939. ***Publisher Provided Annotation.***

***Directory of Companies Required to File Annual Reports with the Securities & Exchange Commission.** 1993. pap. 33.00 (*0-16-043094-1*) Claitors.

Directory of Computer & High Technology Grants. Ed. by Richard M. Eckstein. 200p. (Orig.). 1991. pap. text ed. 44.50 (*0-945078-03-X*) Rsch Grant Guides.

Directory of Computer & High Technology Grants. 2nd ed. Ed. by Richard M. Eckstein. 232p. (Orig.). 1994. pap. 56.50 (*0-945078-07-2*) Rsch Grant Guides.

Directory of Computer Education & Research, 2 vols., Set. Ed. by T. C. Hsiao. Incl. Vol. 1. Senior Colleges. LC 72-91675. 1973. (*0-318-55706-1*); Vol. 2. Junior Colleges. LC 72-91675. 1973. (*0-318-55707-X*); LC 72-91675. (U. S. Edition Ser.). 1800p. 1973. 150.00 (*0-912291-00-1*) Sci & Tech Pr.

Directory of Computer Education & Research: (International Edition), 2 vols. Ed. by T. C. Hsiao. LC 75-16507. 1800p. 1978. 150.00 (*0-912291-02-8*) Sci & Tech Pr.

Directory of Computer Education & Research: (U. S. Edition) Ed. by T. C. Hsiao. LC 81-51816. 1100p. 1985. 120.00 (*0-912291-06-0*) Sci & Tech Pr.

Directory of Computer Programs for Assessment of Radioactive Waste Disposal, 2 vols., Vol. 2. J. Ashton et al. (EUR Ser.: No. 11201). 1993. pap. 75.00 (*92-826-5179-7*, CD-NB-14201-EN-C, Pub. by Europ Com) UNIPUB.

Directory of Computers & Software Retailers, 1993. Ed. by Kim Reinhardt. 814p. pap. 275.00 (*0-685-65049-9*, CSG Info Servs) Lebhar Friedman.

Directory of Connecticut & Rhode Island High Technology Companies. 2nd ed. Mass Tech Times, Inc. Staff. Ed. by Anne S. Lillie. 200p. 1991. pap. 125.00 (*0-927452-03-0*) Mass Tech Times.

Directory of Connecticut Libraries & Media Centers: 1992. Ed. by Andrew Ippolito. 350p. 1995. per. 79.95 (*0-935912-53-3*) LDA Pubs.

Directory of Connecticut Manufacturers, 1993-1994. George D. Hall Co. Staff. 1993. pap. write for info. (*1-56803-003-7*) G D Hall Co.

Directory of Construction Industry Consultants, 1992. Wiley Law Publications Editorial Staff. (Construction Law Library: No. 1815). 464p. 1992. pap. text ed. 125.00 (*0-471-56947-X*) Wiley.

Directory of Consultants & Management Training Programs Intended for Local Non-Profit Groups, 1985. Marvin L. Peebles. 100p. 1985. ring bd. 20.00 (*0-939020-27-0*) MLP Ent.

Directory of Consumer Electronics, 1993. Ed. by Kim Reinhardt. 136p. pap. 125.00 (*0-685-65050-2*, CSG Info Servs) Lebhar Friedman.

Directory of Contemporary American Musical Instrument Makers. Susan C. Farrell. LC 80-24924. (Illus.). 232p. 1981. text ed. 27.50 (*0-8262-0322-1*) U of Mo Pr.

***Directory of Controlled Release Technologies, Products & Organizations.** Intro. by David Williams. 1995. disk 305.00 (*1-85617-239-2*) Elsevier.

Directory of Convenience Stores, 1993. rev. ed. Ed. by Adrienne Toth et al. 1993. pap. 220.00 (*0-911790-60-8*) Trade Dimensns.

Directory of Convenience Stores, 1994. rev. ed. Ed. by Adrienne Toth et al. 1994. pap. 220.00 (*0-911790-18-7*) Trade Dimensns.

Directory of Corporate Affiliations, 6 vols., Set. 1994. 950.00 (*0-87217-046-2*) Natl Register.

***Directory of Corporate Affiliations: Who Owns Whom, 5 vols.** Ed. by National Register Press Editing Staff. Incl. Directory of Corporate Affiliations: Master Index Volume I. LC 67-22770. 1812p. 1995. pap. (*0-87217-160-4*); Directory of Corporate Affiliations: Master Index Volume II. LC 67-22770. 2150p. 1995. pap. (*0-87217-161-2*); Directory of Corporate Affiliations: U. S. Public Companies. LC 67-22770. 2372p. 1995. pap. (*0-87217-163-9*); Directory of Corporate Affiliations: U. S. Private Companies. LC 67-22770. 1476p. 1995. pap. (*0-87217-164-7*); Directory of Corporate Affiliations: International Public & Private Companies. LC 67-22770. 1922p. 1995. pap. (*0-87217-162-0*); LC 67-22770. 950.00 (*0-87217-165-5*) Natl Register.

Directory of Corporate Affiliations - International, 1994. National Register Publishing Staff. LC 67-22770. 1784p. 1994. 685.00 (*0-87217-182-5*) Natl Register.

Directory of Corporate Affiliations - U.S. Private, 1994. National Register Publishing Staff. LC 87-659005. 1900p. 1994. 685.00 (*0-87217-202-3*) Natl Register.

Directory of Corporate Affiliations - U.S. Public, 1994, 2 vols., Set. National Register Publishing Staff. LC 67-22770. 2900p. 1994. 795.00 (*0-87217-154-X*) Natl Register.

***Directory of Corporate Affiliations Library, 5 Vols. Ed. by National Register Publishing Staff. 1995. 950.00 (*0-87217-157-4*) Natl Register.**
The new 1995 edition of the DIRECTORY OF CORPORATE AFFILIATIONS LIBRARY, the definitive source of who owns whom, is now available exclusively as a completely updated, comprehensive 5-volume series. Only the most influential public & private companies in the U.S. & overseas are included - those with at least $10 million in revenue. Everything you & your patrons need to know about corporate linkage is at your fingertips. At-a-glance "family tree" listings make it easy to determine exactly who owns whom, & provide you with valuable insights into corporate hierarchy & the responsibilities of parent companies, subsidiaries, affiliates & divisions. For 1995, over 117,000 of the world's leading companies with 286,000 key executives have been selected for inclusion. Over 5,000 companies are all-new to this edition. The set features a 2-volume master Index, offering quick access to individual entries by company name, brand name, S.I.C. code, personnel, & geographic location. The three other volumes feature the latest information about new mergers, acquisitions, management changes, & more. Five volumes of essential business information at one low price! Your cost for the DIRECTORY OF CORPORATE AFFILIATIONS LIBRARY is only $950.00. You get the Directory of Corporate Affiliations/ U.S. Public, Directory of Corporate Affiliations/U.S. Private, & Directory of Corporate Affiliations/International, plus the 2- volume Master Index. ***Publisher Provided Annotation.***

***Directory of Corporate & Foundation Givers, 1995: A National Listing of the 8,000 Major Funding Sources for Nonprofits, 2 vols.** 4th ed. Ed. by Katherine Jankowski. 4023p. 1994. pap. 225.00 (*0-930807-76-6*) Taft Group.

Directory of Corporate & Foundation Givers 1996, 2 vol., 1. Katherine Jankowski. 1995. write for info. (*1-56995-009-1*) Taft Group.

Directory of Corporate & Foundation Givers 1996, 2 vol., 2. Katherine Jankowski. 1995. write for info. (*1-56995-010-5*) Taft Group.

Directory of Corporate & Foundation Givers 1996, 2 Vols., Vol. 1. Katherine Jankowski. 1995. Set. 230.00 (*1-56995-008-3*) Taft Group.

Directory of Corporate & Foundation Givers 1997, 2 vol., 1. Katherine Jankowski. 1996. write for info. (*1-56995-012-1*) Taft Group.

Directory of Corporate & Foundation Givers 1997, 2 vol., 2. Katherine Jankowski. 1996. write for info. (*1-56995-013-X*) Taft Group.

Directory of Corporate & Foundation Givers 1997, 2 vol., Set. Katherine Jankowski. 1996. 210.00 (*1-56995-011-3*) Taft Group.

Directory of Corporate Art Collections. 4th ed. Ed. by Shirley R. Howarth. 310p. 1986. pap. 69.95 (*0-943488-03-6*) Intl Art Alliance.

Directory of Corporate Art Collections. 5th ed. Ed. by Shirley R. Howarth. 500p. 1988. pap. 89.95 (*0-317-60390-6*) Intl Art Alliance.

***Directory of Corporate Counsel, 1994-95, 2 vols., Set.** 15th ed. Prentice-Hall Editorial Staff. 2850p. 1994. 375.00 (*0-13-165664-3*) Aspen Law.

Directory of Corporate Environmental Professionals. Lyle Hoyt. 372p. 1993. pap. 150.00 (*0-9634631-0-1*) Wortham Pub.

Directory of Corporate Name Changes. Howard R. Jarrell. LC 93-34327. 355p. 1993. 69.50 (*0-8108-2761-1*) Scarecrow.

Directory of Cosmetic & Toiletry Ingredients. 2nd ed. Ed. by Susan Rich. 365p. 1982. pap. 985.00 (*0-686-84482-3*) Kline.

Directory of Credentials in Counseling & Psychotherapy. Daniel R. Martin & J. Richard Cookerly. (Reference Bks.). 270p. 1989. text ed. 35.00 (*0-8161-9062-3*, Hall Reference) Macmillan.

Directory of Criminal Justice Information Sources. 57p. (Orig.). (C). 1993. pap. text ed. 35.00 (*1-56806-858-1*) Diane Pub.

***Directory of Criminal Justice Information Sources.** 9th ed. 65p. (Orig.). (C). 1994. pap. text ed. 40.00x (*0-7881-1340-2*) Diane Pub.

Directory of Crocodilian Farming Operation. 2nd ed. Ed. by R. A. Luxmoore. 352p. 1992. 30.00 (*2-8317-0078-7*, Pub. by IUCN SZ) Island Pr.

Directory of Current Research on Sheep & Goats. Ed. by J. W. King. 271p. (Orig.). 1988. pap. text ed. 27.50 (*0-85198-611-0*) CAB Intl.

Directory of Curriculum Materials Centers, 1990. Ed. by Carol Wright et al. 240p. 1991. 39.54 (*0-8389-7439-2*); 32.94 (*0-685-58904-8*) Assn Coll & Res Libs.

***Directory of Dance Faculties in Colleges & Universities, U. S. & Canada, 1994-95 Edition.** 3rd ed. Intro. by Robby Gunstream. 140p. (Orig.). 1994. pap. 55.00 (*1-881913-02-3*) CMS Pubns.

Directory of Defense Electronic Products & Services. 200p. 60.00 (*0-318-14039-X*); 30.00 (*0-318-14040-3*) Elec Ind Assn.

Directory of Department Stores, 1993. 672p. pap. 239.00 (*0-86730-577-0*) Lebhar Friedman.

Directory of Designers, 1993. Design Council Staff. 224p. (C). 1993. text ed. 175.00 (*0-85072-295-0*) St Mut.

Directory of Development Finance Institutions. 94p. 1987. 11.00 (*92-1-006005-9*, EFS.86.11.B.4) UN.

Directory of Development Research & Training Institutes in Africa. OECD Staff. 248p. (Orig.). 1992. pap. 40.00 (*92-64-03539-7*) OECD.

Directory of Development Research & Training Institutes in Europe. OECD Staff. 237p. (Orig.). (ENG & FRE.). 1991. pap. 40.00 (*92-64-03505-2*) OECD.

Directory of Directories on the Internet. Gregory B. Newby. (Supplement to Small Computers in Libraries Ser.: No. 33). 175p. 1993. pap. text ed. 29.50 (*0-88736-768-2*) Mecklermedia.

Directory of Directories 1988: Publishers Volume. Ed. by Cecilia A. Marlow. (Directory of Directories Ser.). 608p. 1987. 155.00 (*0-8103-2509-8*) Gale.

Directory of Directors in the City of New York & Tri-State Area. 738p. 1986. 160.00 (*0-936612-07-X*) DODC.

Directory of Directors in the City of New York & Tri-State Area. 750p. 1988. 175.00 (*0-936612-09-6*) DODC.

Directory of Directors in the City of New York & Tri-State Area. 770p. 1989. 185.00 (*0-936612-10-X*) DODC.

Directory of Directors in the City of New York & Tri-State Area. 770p. 1990. 190.00 (*0-936612-11-8*) DODC.

Directory of Directors in the City of New York & Tri-State Area. 682p. 1991. 195.00 (*0-936612-12-6*) DODC.

Directory of Directors in the City of New York & Tri-State Area. 675p. 1992. 199.00 (*0-936612-13-4*) DODC.

Directory of Directors in the City of New York & Tri-State Area. 675p. 1993. 210.00 (*0-936612-14-2*) DODC.

Directory of Directors in the City of New York & Tri-State Area. 700p. 1994. 215.00 (*0-936612-15-0*) DODC.

***Directory of Directors in the City of New York & Tri-State Area.** 675p. 1995. 220.00x (*0-936612-16-9*) DODC.

D

2010

An Asterisk (*) at the beginning of an entry indicates that the title is appearing in BIP for the first time.

Directory of Directors in the City of New York & Tri-State Area. A. M. Dahl. 750p. 1984. 145.00 (*0-936612-05-3*) DODC.

Directory of Directors in the City of New York & Tri-State Area. A. M. Dahl. 727p. 1985. 150.00 (*0-936612-06-1*) DODC.

Directory of Directors in the City of New York & Tri-State Area. A. M. Dahl. 750p. 1987. 170.00 (*0-936612-08-8*) DODC.

Directory of Discount Department Stores, 1993. Ed. by Janice Backer. 718p. 245.00 (*0-86730-583-5*, CSG Info Servs) Lebhar Friedman.

Directory of Dissertations in Accounting. J. David Spiceland. LC 86-40096. (Reference Books in Accounting Ser.). 250p. (C). 1986. 39.95 (*0-910129-39-8*) Wiener Pubs Inc.

Directory of Distinguished Americans. 4th ed. J. M. Evans. LC 81-71699. 500p. 1988. 62.50 (*0-934544-46-8*) Am Biog Inst.

Directory of Distinguished Americans. 5th ed. Ed. by J. M. Evans. LC 81-71699. 500p. 1989. 62.50 (*0-318-40137-1*) Am Biog Inst.

Directory of Doctoral Programs in Theatre Studies in the U. S. A. & Canada. Ed. by Simon Williams & Thomas Postlewait. 110p. 1992. pap. 8.95 (*0-9631991-0-2*) Am Soc Theatre Res.

*__Directory of Doctoral Programs in Theatre Studies in the U. S. A. & Canada.__ 2nd ed. Ed. by Thomas Postlewait & Peter A. Davis. 1995. write for info. (*0-614-04176-7*) Am Soc Theatre Res.

Directory of Doctoral Research on Puerto Ricans in the United States of America. Luis A. Cardona. LC 89-83369. 136p. (Orig.). 1990. pap. text ed. 33.95 (*0-914199-07-2*) Carreta Pr.

Directory of Doctoral Study in Rehabilitation. 2nd ed. Ed. by Dennis R. Maki & Norman L. Berven. 62p. 1992. 10.00 (*1-55620-116-8*, 72253) Am Coun Assn.

Directory of Drug Store & HBC Chains, 1993. Ed. by Patrice Petti. pap. 260.00 (*0-86730-576-2*) Lebhar Friedman.

Directory of East European Businesses, Vol. 1: Manufacturing. 216p. 1992. pap. 74.95 (*1-85252-116-3*, Pub. by Mercury Books UK) Ref Press.

Directory of Eastern European Film-Makers & Films 1945-1991. Grzegorz Balski. LC 91-22023. 540p. 1992. text ed. 85.00 (*0-313-28278-1*, BOG, Greenwood Pr) Greenwood.

Directory of Eastern Orthodox Parishes in Present Day Poland. Jonathan D. Shea & Constance M. Ochnio. (Illus.). 30p. 1991. pap. text ed. write for info. (*0-945440-04-9*) Pol Geneal CT.

Directory of EC Industry Information Sources. James Hogan. 354p. 1992. 95.00 (*1-56159-050-9*, Stockton Pr) Groves Dictionaries.

Directory of Economic Development Programs at State Colleges & Universities. 182p. 1989. 22.50 (*0-317-05051-6*) Natl Coun Econ Dev.

Directory of Economic Development Programs at State Colleges & Universities. AASCU Staff. LC 88-16975. 188p. (C). 1989. lib. bdg. 52.25 (*0-88044-095-3*); pap. text ed. 31.50 (*0-88044-094-5*) AASCU Press.

Directory of Edinburgh in 1752. James Gilhooley. 128p. 1989. 30.00 (*0-85224-595-5*, Pub. by Edinburgh U Pr UK) Col U Pr.

Directory of Educational Contests for Students K-12. Kim Long. 300p. 1991. lib. bdg. 40.00 (*0-87436-586-4*) ABC-CLIO.

Directory of Educational Institutions Offering Courses in Nondestructive Testing. American Society for Nondestructive Testing (ASNT) Staff. 7p. (Orig.). 1991. pap. 4.50 (*0-931403-84-7*, 114) Am Soc Nondestructive.

Directory of Educational Software in Nursing. C. Bolwell. 1991. 79.95 (*0-88737-521-9*, 41-2405) Natl League Nurse.

Directory of Educational Statistics: A Guide to Sources. Malcolm C. Hamilton. LC 74-14673. 1974. 19.50 (*0-87650-054-8*) Pierian.

Directory of Eighteen Fifteen: Pittsburgh, PA. & Vicinity. 29p. 1985. reprint ed. pap. 6.00 (*0-933227-11-6*) Closson Pr.

Directory of Electronic Mail Addresses. 4th ed. Donnalyn Frey & Rick Adams. Ed. by Tim O'Reilly. (Nutshell Handbook Ser.). 662p. 1994. pap. 9.95 (*1-56592-046-5*) OReilly & Assocs.

Directory of Employee Leasing Firms: With a Guide to the Industry. T. Joe Willey. (International Standard Serial Ser.: No. 1056/6112). (Illus.). 199p. (Orig.). (C). 1991. pap. 37.50 (*0-944308-12-0*) Aegis Consulting.

Directory of Employers Associations, Trade Unions, Joint Organizations: September 1993. 106p. 1993. pap. 25.00 (*0-11-361332-6*, HM13326, Pub. by HMSO UK) UNIPUB.

*__Directory of Employers Associations, Trade Unions Joint Organizations Etc. March 1994.__ HMSO Staff. 106p. 1994. pap. 25.00 (*0-11-361334-2*, HM13342, Pub. by HMSO UK) UNIPUB.

Directory of Employers Associations, Trade Unions Joint Organizations, etc., September 1990 Edition. Her Majesty's Stationery Office Staff. 106p. 1990. pap. 22.00 (*0-11-361317-2*, HM713X) UNIPUB.

Directory of Energy Data Collection Forms. (Illus.). 72p. (Orig.). (C). 1994. pap. text ed. 45.00 (*0-7881-0496-9*) Diane Pub.

Directory of Energy Information Administration Models 1993. rev. ed. 96p. (C). 1993. pap. text ed. 60.00 (*1-56806-594-9*) Diane Pub.

*__Directory of Energy Information Administration Models 1994.__ 91p. (Orig.). (C). 1994. pap. text ed. 60.00x (*0-7881-1317-8*) Diane Pub.

Directory of Energy Professionals, 1995. 319p. 1995. 40.00 (*0-317-04702-7*) NARUC.

Directory of Engineering & Engineering Technology Undergraduate Programs, 1993. American Society for Engineering Education Staff. (Illus.). 1993. pap. 49.95 (*0-87823-143-9*) Am Soc Eng Ed.

Directory of Engineering & Engineering Technology Undergraduate Programs, 1994. American Society for Engineering Education Staff. (Illus.). 1994. pap. 49.95 (*0-87823-147-1*) Am Soc Eng Ed.

Directory of Engineering Document Sources. 4th ed. Global Engineering Documents Staff. Ed. by Vasantha Nathan. 274p. 1989. pap. 125.00 (*0-912702-45-1*) Global Eng Doc.

Directory of Engineering Graduate Studies & Research, 1993. American Society for Engineering Education Staff. (Illus.). (C). 1993. pap. 69.95 (*0-87823-146-3*) Am Soc Eng Ed.

Directory of Engineering Societies & Related Organizations. 13th ed. Gordon Davis. 400p. (Orig.). 1989. pap. 150.00 (*0-87615-005-9*) AAES.

Directory of Entertainment & Sports Attorneys 1995. 1994. 195.00 (*0-13-104611-X*) Aspen Law.

Directory of Environment Statistics. 311p. 30.00 (*92-1-161196-2*) UN.

Directory of Environmental Asset Data Bases & Valuation Studies. David Yardas et al. 128p. reprint ed. pap. 36.50 (*0-7837-3039-X*, 2042887) Bks Demand.

*__Directory of Environmental Attorneys, 1995.__ Prentice-Hall Editorial Staff. 1756p. 1994. 195.00 (*0-13-169269-0*) Aspen Law.

Directory of Environmental Consultants: 1994-95. Patricia J. Scharlin. 250p. 1994. 67.00 (*0-9631675-3-7*) Environ Grp.

Directory of Environmental Information Sources. 4th ed. Ed. by Thomas F. Sullivan. 322p. 1992. pap. text ed. 74.00 (*0-86587-326-7*) Gov Insts.

Directory of Environmental Investing. Michael Silverstein. 150p. (Orig.). 1991. pap. 75.00 (*0-941375-15-3*) Diane Pub.

Directory of EPA - State Contacts by Specialty. 73p. (Orig.). (C). 1992. pap. text ed. 39.95 (*1-56806-051-3*) Diane Pub.

Directory of Essential Oils. 2nd ed. Wanda Sellar. 192p. pap. 26.95 (*0-8464-4191-8*) Beekman Pubs.

*__Directory of Ethnic Minority Professionals in Psychology.__ 3rd ed. Comp. by APA, Ethnic Minority Affairs Office Staff. 349p. 1994. 20.00 (*1-55798-253-8*) Am Psychol.

Directory of Ethnic Professionals in LIS. Comp. by George C. Grant. 335p. 1991. 52.95 (*0-9625423-3-4*) Four-G Pubs.

Directory of Euromarket Borrowers. Ed. by Euromoney Staff. 1985. 160.00 (*0-686-79167-3*, Pub. by Euromoney UK) St Mut.

Directory of European Anthropologists in North America. Comp. by Carol Rogers et al. 1987. 6.00 (*0-913167-20-7*) Am Anthro Assn.

Directory of European Banking & Financial Associations. Ed. by Philip Molyneux. 238p. 1990. lib. bdg. 65.00 (*1-55862-077-X*) St James Pr.

Directory of European Business. Ed. by World of Information Staff. 392p. 1992. 195.00 (*0-86291-617-8*) Bowker-Saur. "The User's Guide is very informative & useful. Recommended for any library with a strong international business collection."--CHOICE. "An excellent feature is the business information section." -- BUSINESS INFORMATION ALERT. "...an invaluable resource that will help anyone who wants to understand the business environment & the importance of Europe in today's world...no other international directory< is as comprehensive in scope as this compilation."--RRB BOOKLIST. The most comprehensive guide of its kind, the Directory gives you instant access to 4,000 business & government organizations & 12,000 names in the 33 countries of both East & West Europe. Users will find: Complete coverage of Europe's 4,000 leading business & government organizations selected by size. Top personnel, full contact information, sales, head count, ownership, & main activities. Tables ranking each sector in each country. An operating environment section for each country, with details of the political system, economic climate, business culture, banking & legal systems, currency, tax structure, trade regulations, investment incentives, accountancy practice, & sources of finance. *Publisher Provided Annotation.*

Directory of European Environmental Organizations. 2nd ed. Mireille Deziron & Leigh M. Bailey. LC 93-2028. 224p. 1993. 59.95 (*0-631-19114-3*) Blackwell Pubs.

Directory of European Growth Markets. (Illus.). 92p. (Orig.). (C). 1991. pap. text ed. 40.00 (*0-941375-31-5*) Diane Pub.

Directory of European Industrial & Trade Associations, Pt. 1. 5th ed. Anderson. 1991. 275.00 (*0-900246-55-3*, 001574) Gale.

Directory of European Industrial & Trade Associations, 6 Vols., Vol. 1. 5th ed. Anderson. 1994. 795.00 (*0-8103-9736-6*) Gale.

Directory of European Industries & Trade Associations. 6th ed. (Directory of European Associations Ser.: Pt. 1). 1995. 275.00 (*0-685-59079-8*, 001576) Gale.

*__Directory of European Institutions.__ 2nd ed. Gerhard Hitzler. Date not set. pap. text ed. write for info. (*0-406-02286-0*, UK) Butterworth Legal Pubs.

Directory of European Institutions. 2nd ed. Gerhard Hitzler. 1991. pap. 126.00 (*0-406-04511-9*, U.K.) Butterworth Legal Pubs.

Directory of European Learned Assocs, 1995, Vol. 2. Anderson. 1994. write for info. (*0-8103-9737-4*, 001575, Pub. by CBD Res Ltd UK) Gale.

Directory of European Porcelain. Ludwig Danckert. (Illus.). 684p. 1990. 70.00 (*0-7198-0003-X*, Pub. by NAG Press UK) Antique Collect.

Directory of European Professional & Learned Societies: CDB Research National Learned, Scientific, & Technical Societies, Vol. 2. 4th ed. Anderson. 1989. 180.00 (*0-900246-51-0*, 001573) Gale.

Directory of European Regional Standards - Related Organizations. Natl. Inst. of Standards & Technology (NIST) Staff & Maureen Breitenberg. 184p. 1991. pap. 27.00 (*0-912702-58-3*) Global Eng Doc.

Directory of European Regional Standards-Related Organizations. Ed. by Maureen Breitenberg. 188p. (Orig.). (C). 1994. pap. text ed. 50.00 (*0-7881-0730-5*) Diane Pub.

Directory of European Research & Development, 2 vols. 3000p. 1995. 400.00 (*1-85739-092-X*) Bowker-Saur. From product development & innovation to applied & basic research, the DIRECTORY OF EUROPEAN RESEARCH & DEVELOPMENT encompasses all forms of research & every type of facility: academic, commercial, public, private, or joint venture. The main criterion for inclusion is that the project be of at least one year's duration. In all, some 20,000 facilities & 10,000 key personnel from 39 countries in eastern & western Europe, are profiled, including elusive labs tucked away in corporations... universities...& independent facilities. Entries are categorized by type of facility--Business Enterprises, Government, Private Non-Profit, Higher Education & Consultancies-& arranged alphabetically by name. Each entry includes the full name of the organization (in English & the original language), full contact details, main organizational activities, date founded, research expenditure, source of funding, parent organization, affiliation, publications & a listing of full-time research staff, including project managers. A convenient index of 630 subjects helps easily locate any research facility. *Publisher Provided Annotation.*

Directory of European Trade Fairs: A Key to the World for Exporters. 153p. (Orig.). (C). 1992. pap. text ed. 49.95 (*0-941375-52-8*) Diane Pub.

Directory of Executive Compensation Consultants. Ed. by James H. Kennedy. (Orig.). 1993. student ed, pap. 47.50 (*0-916654-81-8*) Kennedy Pubns.

*__Directory of Executive Recruiters: Corporate Edition, 1995-96.__ Ed. by James H. Kennedy. 800p. 1995. text ed. 99.00 (*0-916654-95-8*) Kennedy Pubns.

Directory of Executive Recruiters, 1994. 23th ed. Ed. by James H. Kennedy. 890p. (Orig.). 1994. pap. 39.95 (*0-916654-84-2*) Kennedy Pubns.

***Directory of Executive Recruiters, 1995. 24th ed. Ed. by James H. Kennedy. 960p. (Orig.). 1995. pap. 39.95 (*0-916654-92-3*) Kennedy Pubns. The definitive guide to working with "headhunters" (who never charge the job-seeker), published annually since '71. Profiles 2,890 firms. Heavily indexed by geography, management specialty & industry. Also identifies over 6,700 principals in these firms. Individuals in a job-change mode make their availability known to these recruiters & are called for interviews if their qualifications match current assignments - a small chance statistically, but a worthwhile element of the complete job-search process - Even those not ready to switch jobs get into the recruiter data banks so they'll be called in the future. Mentioned in the Kiplinger Washington Letter, Marilyn Moats Kennedy's Career Strategies, National Business Employment Weekly, Sylvia Porter's Personal Finance Magazine, Forbes, Knock 'Em Dead, What Color Is Your Parachute? Updated annually.** *Publisher Provided Annotation.*

---

*__Directory of Executive Temporary Placement Firms.__ Ed. by James H. Kennedy. 40p. (Orig.). 1994. pap. text ed. 19.00 (*0-916654-96-6*) Kennedy Pubns.

*__Directory of Experiential Therapy & Adventure-Based Counseling Programs.__ Jackie Gerstein. 1992. 15.00 (*0-614-05767-1*) Assn Exper Ed.

Directory of Expert System Research & Development in the Construction & Building Services Industries. G. Hamilton et al. (C). 1990. 340.00 (*0-685-33894-0*, Pub. by Build Servs Info Assn UK) St Mut.

Directory of Experts, Authorities & Spokespersons: An Encyclopedia of Sources. 6th ed. Ed. by Mitchell P. Davis & Marnie E. Wiss. (Illus.). 480p. 1989. pap. 37.25 (*0-934333-07-6*) Broadcast Inter.

Directory of Experts, Authorities & Spokespersons: The Talk Show Guest Directory. 4th ed. Ed. by Mitchell P. Davis. (Illus.). 304p. (Orig.). 1987. pap. 25.00 (*0-934333-04-1*) Broadcast Inter.

Directory of Experts, Authorities & Spokespersons Fifth Annual '88-'89 Ed. Talk Show Guest Directory. Ed. by Mitchell P. Davis. (Illus.). 488p. 1988. pap. 37.25 (*0-934333-05-X*) Broadcast Inter.

Directory of Export Buyers in the UK. 4th ed. Trade Research Publications Staff. (C). 1983. 315.00 (*0-317-89783-7*, Pub. by Trade Rsch Pubns UK) St Mut.

Directory of Facilities & Services for the Learning Disabled, 1995-96. 176p. 1995. 4.00 (*0-685-48386-X*) Acad Therapy.

Directory of Family Associations, 1993-94. Elizabeth P. Bentley. 344p. 1993. pap. 29.95 (*0-8063-1383-8*, 426) Genealog Pub.

Directory of Family 'One-Name' Periodicals. J. Konrad. 50p. 1994. 10.00 (*0-685-20964-4*, Heritge Hse) Ye Olde Genealogie Shoppe.

Directory of Family One-Name Periodicals. rev. ed. Ed. by J. Konrad. 60p. 1993. pap. 8.00 (*1-878311-15-8*, Heritge Hse) Ye Olde Genealogie Shoppe.

Directory of Family One-Name Periodicals. rev. ed. Ed. by J. Konrad. 60p. 1994. pap. 10.00 (*1-878311-08-5*, Heritge Hse) Ye Olde Genealogie Shoppe.

Directory of Federal Aid for Education. 1982. 47.50 (*0-916270-31-9*) Ready Ref Pr.

Directory of Federal Aid for Health & Allied Fields. 1982. 47.50 (*0-916270-35-1*) Ready Ref Pr.

Directory of Federal Aid for the Aging. 1982. 47.50 (*0-916270-39-4*) Ready Ref Pr.

Directory of Federal Aid for the Handicapped. 1982. 47.50 (*0-916270-30-0*) Ready Ref Pr.

Directory of Federal Aid for Veterans. 1982. 47.50 (*0-916270-33-5*) Ready Ref Pr.

Directory of Federal Aid for Women & Minorities. 1982. 47.50 (*0-916270-32-7*) Ready Ref Pr.

Directory of Federal & State Nutrition Monitoring Activities. 1994. lib. bdg. 261.95 (*0-8490-5634-9*) Gordon Pr.

*__Directory of Federal Anti-Drug Grants.__ 1994. lib. bdg. 250.75 (*0-8490-6427-9*) Gordon Pr.

Directory of Federal CD-ROM Titles: What Is Available & How Are They Priced. (Illus.). 52p. (Orig.). (C). 1994. pap. text ed. 40.00 (*0-7881-0480-2*) Diane Pub.

Directory of Federal Historical Programs & Activities. 88p. (Orig.). 1990. pap. 10.00 (*0-685-48052-6*) Am Hist Assn.

Directory of Federal Historical Programs & Activities. (Orig.). 1994. 10.00 (*0-685-73046-8*) Am Hist Assn.

*__Directory of Federal Jobs & Employers.__ Ronald L. Krannich & Caryl R. Krannich. 250p. (Orig.). 1995. pap. 21.95 (*1-57023-033-1*) Impact VA.

Directory of Federal Laboratory & Technology Resources: A Guide to Services, Facilities & Expertise. 230p. (Orig.). (C). 1994. pap. text ed. 125.00 (*0-7881-0191-9*) Diane Pub.

Directory of Federal Laboratory & Technology Resources: A Guide to Services, Facilities, & Expertise. 5th ed. Intro. & Pref. by Edward J. Lehmann. 1993. pap. 65.00 (*0-934213-40-2*, PB93-100097) Natl Tech Info.

Directory of Federal Libraries. 2nd ed. William R. Evinger. LC 86-42744. 384p. 1993. 97.50 (*0-89774-674-0*) Oryx Pr.

Directory of Feeds & Feed Ingredients. 2nd ed. Charles Macgregor. 85p. (C). Date not set. pap. text ed. 7.00 (*0-932147-20-8*, Hoards Dairyman) Hoard & Sons Co.

Directory of Feeds & Feed Ingredients. 2nd ed. Charles A. Macgregor. LC 89-85192. 64p. (C). 1989. pap. text ed. 6.00 (*0-932147-07-0*) Hoard & Sons Co.

Directory of Fellows with By-Laws, Councils Commissions, Committees & Task Forces, 1987-88. 400p. 1994. 55.00 (*0-317-64275-8*) Am Coll Obstetric.

Directory of Financial Aid for American Undergraduates Interested in Overseas Study & Travel. Joseph Lurie. 1981. pap. 9.00 (*0-88461-007-1*) Adelphi Univ.

Directory of Financial Aids for Minorities, 1993-1995. 5th ed. Gail A. Schlachter & R. David Weber. (Financial Aid for Special Needs Groups Ser.). 660p. (C). 1993. lib. bdg. 47.50 (*0-918276-21-7*) Ref Serv Pr.

Directory of Financial Aids for Minorities, 1993-95. 600p. 55.00 (*0-685-55408-2*) B Klein Pubns.

Directory of Financial Aids for Women, 1993-1995. Gail A. Schlachter & R. David Weber. 506p. (C). 1993. lib. bdg. 45.00 (*0-918276-20-9*) Ref Serv Pr.

D

Directory of Financial Aids for Women, 1993-95. 5th ed. 450p. 50.00 (*0-685-55409-0*) B Klein Pubns.

Directory of Financial Services for State & Local Government. 210p. 1982. pap. 15.00 (*0-686-84359-2*); pap. 9.00 (*0-686-84360-6*) Municipal.

Directory of Florida Industries, 1988. Florida Chamber of Commerce. 1988. 49.95 (*0-685-19234-2*) Trend Bk Div.

Directory of Florida Industry, 1994. 1994. 85.00 (*1-55600-484-2*) Harris Pub.

Directory of Florida Markets, 1992. 112p. 1991. pap. 15.95 (*0-942980-17-4*) CNW.

Directory of Food & Nutrition Information for Professionals & Consumers. 2nd ed. Ed. by Robyn C. Frank & Holly B. Irving. 344p. 1992. pap. 55.00 (*0-89774-689-9*) Oryx Pr.

Directory of Foodservice Distribution, 1992. Ed. by Gael Murphy. 852p. 1992. pap. 249.00 (*0-86730-564-9*, CSG Info Servs) Lebhar Friedman.

Directory of Foreign Banks & Other Foreign-Owned Financial Institutions in the United States. IBPC Staff. (International Banking Ser.). 1992. pap. 95.00 (*0-88115-102-5*) I B P C Inc.

Directory of Foreign Firms Operating in the United States, 3 pts., Set. 7th rev. ed. 696p. 1992. 145.00 (*0-8360-0037-4*) World Trade.

Directory of Foreign Investors of the U.S. 1992. Nancy Garman. 1993. 215.00 (*0-8103-8043-9*) Gale.

Directory of Foreign Investors of U. S. 1994. 3rd ed. Nancy Garman. 1996. 205.00 (*0-8103-8044-7*) Gale.

Directory of Foreign Language Service Organizations, No. 3. Sophia A. Behrens. (Language in Education Ser.). 148p. 1987. pap. text ed. 11.00 (*0-13-214859-5*) P-H.

Directory of Foreign Law Collections in Selected Law Libraries. Ed. by Ellen G. Schaffer & Thomas R. Bruce. LC 91-11812. (American Association of Law Libraries Publications Ser.: No. 41). xii, 273p. 1991. 37.50 (*0-8377-0141-4*) Rothman.

Directory of Foreign Manufacturers in the United States. 5th enl. ed. Ed. by Jeffrey S. Arpan & David A. Ricks. 419p. 1993. 195.00 (*0-88406-255-4*) GA St U Busn Pr.

Directory of Foreign Trade Organizations in Eastern Europe: Bulgaria, Czechoslovakia, East Germany, Hungary, Poland, Romania & U. S. S. R. Vance T. Petrunoff. LC 88-84163. 300p. (Orig.). 1989. pap. 85.00 (*0-926476-00-9*) Intl Trade Pr.

Directory of Foreign Trade Organizations in Eastern Europe: Bulgaria, Czechoslovakia, East Germany, Hungary, Poland, Romania & U. S. S. R. 2nd ed. Intro. by Vance T. Petrunoff. LC 89-85034. 325p. (Orig.). 1989. pap. 125.00 (*0-926476-01-7*) Intl Trade Pr.

Directory of Foreign Trade Organizations in Eastern Europe: Bulgaria, Czechoslovakia, East Germany, Hungary, Poland, Romania & U. S. S. R. 3rd ed. Intro. by Vance T. Petrunoff. LC 90-80534. 370p. (Orig.). 1990. pap. 125.00 (*0-926476-02-5*) Intl Trade Pr.

Directory of Forestry & Natural Resources Computer Software. rev. ed. Ed. by David Gilluly. (Illus.). 250p. 1989. text ed. 100.00 (*0-317-91085-X*) Forest Res Syst.

*__Directory of Foundation & Corporate Members of the European Foundation Centre.__ 1993. pap. text ed. 88.00 (*2-9600051-2-0*) Foundation Ctr.

Directory of Foundations of the Greater Washington Area, 1984. Community Foundation of Greater Washington Staff. 125p. 1984. 10.00 (*0-318-03830-7*) Comm Foun DC.

D

Directory of Franchise Opportunities: A Handbook for Assisting Entrepreneur - Franchise Investors with the Sources for Public - Private Aid. LaVerne Ludden. 300p. (Orig.). 1994. pap. 14.95 (*1-57112-062-9*, PA2054, Park Avenue) JIST Works.

*__Directory of Franchising Organizations.__ Pilot Books Staff & Samuel Small. LC 62-39831. 80p. 1995. 5.95 (*0-87576-190-9*) Pilot Bks.

Directory of Free Programs, Performing Talent & Attractions. Robert D. Shelley & Eileen E. Shelley. 1983. 75.00 (*0-914623-00-1*) Pageant Pub Co.

Directory of Freight Forwarders & Custom House Brokers. 106p. 1995. 35.00 (*0-685-56478-9*) B Klein Pubns.

Directory of Freight Forwarders & Custom House Brokers. 4th ed. Ed. by Tyler G. Hicks. 108p. 1990. pap. 17.50 (*0-934311-85-4*) Intl Wealth.

Directory of Freight Forwarders & Custom House Brokers. 5th ed. Ed. by Tyler G. Hicks. 108p. 1992. pap. 17.50 (*1-56150-036-4*) Intl Wealth.

Directory of Freight Forwarders & Custom House Brokers. 6th ed. Ed. by Tyler G. Hicks. 108p. 1993. pap. 17.50 (*1-56150-086-0*) Intl Wealth.

Directory of Freight Forwarders & Custom House Brokers. 7th ed. Ed. by Tyler G. Hicks. 108p. 1994. pap. 17.50 (*1-56150-133-6*) Intl Wealth.

Directory of Fund Raising & Nonprofit Management Consultants. Ed. by Janice McLean. 390p. 1992. pap. 50.00 (*0-930807-25-1*, 600313) Fund Raising.

*__Directory of Funding Sources for Community Development.__ Ed. by Oryx Press Staff. 416p. 1995. pap. 47.50 (*0-89774-947-2*) Oryx Pr.

Directory of Genealogical & Historical Societies in the U. S. & Canada, 1994. Ed. by Dina C. Carson. 500p. 1994. lib. bdg. 85.00 (*1-879579-01-4*); pap. 45.00 (*1-879579-04-9*) Iron Gate Pub.

Directory of Genealogical & Historical Society Libraries, Archives & Collections in the U. S. & Canada, 1994. Ed. by Dina C. Carson. 300p. 1994. lib. bdg. 85.00 (*1-879579-00-6*); pap. 45.00 (*1-879579-03-0*) Iron Gate Pub.

Directory of Genealogical & Historical Society Publications in the U. S. & Canada, 1994. Ed. by Dina C. Carson. 500p. 1994. lib. bdg. 85.00 (*1-879579-02-2*); pap. 45.00 (*1-879579-05-7*) Iron Gate Pub.

Directory of General & International Business Journals. P. R. Chandy & Sharon Garrison. 293p. (Orig.). 1993. pap. 24.95 (*0-87563-435-4*) Stipes.

Directory of General Merchandise - Variety & Specialty Stores, 1993. Ed. by Janice Backer. 1390p. pap. 245.00 (*0-86730-584-3*, CSG Info Servs) Lebhar Friedman.

Directory of Georgia Markets, 1992. 50p. 1991. pap. 9.95 (*0-942980-19-0*) CNW.

Directory of Geoscience Departments. 30th rev. ed. Nicholas H. Claudy. 408p. (Orig.). 1991. pap. 22.00 (*0-922152-12-8*) Am Geol.

Directory of Geoscience Departments. 31th rev. ed. Ed. by Nicholas H. Claudy. 464p. (Orig.). 1992. pap. 26.00 (*0-922152-15-2*) Am Geol.

Directory of Geoscience Departments. 32th ed. Ed. by Nicholas H. Claudy. 480p. (Orig.). 1993. pap. 26.00 (*0-922152-19-5*) Am Geol.

Directory of Geoscience Departments. 33th rev. ed. Ed. by Nicholas H. Claudy. (Orig.). 1994. pap. write for info. (*0-922152-22-5*) Am Geol.

Directory of Geoscience Libraries, U. S. & Canada. 3rd ed. Ed. by Liz Frebold et al. LC 88-173640. 107p. reprint ed. pap. 30.50 (*0-7837-2488-8*, 2042653) Bks Demand.

*__Directory of Geoscience Libraries, U. S. & Canada.__ 4th ed. Ed. by C. J. Manson. 1992. 35.00 (*0-934485-20-8*) Geosci Info.

Directory of Gold & Silversmiths, Jewellers & Allied Traders 1838-1914, 2 vols. John Culme. (Illus.). 550p. 1988. Vol. I, 550 pgs. write for info. (*0-318-62838-4*); Vol. II, 392 pgs. write for info. (*0-318-62839-2*) Antique Collect.

Directory of Gold & Silversmiths, Jewellers & Allied Traders 1838-1914, 2 vols., Set. John Culme. (Illus.). 1988. 350.00 (*0-907462-46-4*) Antique Collect.

Directory of Government Document Collections & Librarians. 5th ed. Ed. by Barbara Kile. 658p. 1987. 37.50 (*0-88692-124-4*) Cong Info.

Directory of Government Documents Collections in Nassau & Suffolk Counties, New York. 3rd ed. Long Island Library Resources Council Committee on Government Information Staff. 1992. pap. 16.50 (*0-938435-33-7*) LI Lib Resources.

Directory of Government Production Primecontractors: Annual. 424p. 1988. pap. 15.00 (*0-318-35155-2*) Gov Data Pubns.

Directory of Governmental Officials in South Dakota, 1967. 5.00 (*1-55614-034-7*) U of SD Gov Res Bur.

*__Directory of Governors of the American States, Commonwealths, & Territories, January 1994.__ Ed. by Alicia C. Aebersold. (Illus.). 68p. (Orig.). 1994. pap. text ed. 8.95 (*1-55877-177-8*) Natl Governor.

*__Directory of Governors of the American States, Commonwealths, & Territories, January 1995.__ Ed. by Alicia C. Aebersold. (Illus.). 68p. (Orig.). 1995. pap. text ed. 9.95 (*1-55877-229-4*) Natl Governor.

Directory of Governors of the American States, Commonwealths, & Territories 1988. Ed. by Gerry R. Feinstein & Mark Miller. 1988. 8.95 (*1-55877-001-1*) Natl Governor.

Directory of Governors of the American States, Commonwealths, & Territories, 1989. National Governors' Association Staff. 68p. (Orig.). 1989. pap. text ed. 8.95 (*1-55877-034-8*) Natl Governor.

Directory of Governors of the American States, Commonwealths, & Territories, 1990. National Governors' Association Staff. Ed. by Mark Miller. 76p. (Orig.). 1990. pap. text ed. 8.95 (*1-55877-073-9*) Natl Governor.

Directory of Governors of the American States, Commonwealths & Territories 1991. Ed. by Mark Miller. (Illus.). 76p. (Orig.). 1991. pap. text ed. 8.95 (*1-55877-083-6*) Natl Governor.

Directory of Governors of the American States, Commonwealths & Territories 1992. Ed. by Mark Miller. (Illus.). 76p. (Orig.). 1992. pap. text ed. 8.95 (*1-55877-142-5*) Natl Governor.

*__Directory of Governors of the American States, Commonwealths, & Territories-1993.__ Ed. by Alicia C. Aebersold. (Illus.). 68p. (Orig.). 1993. pap. text ed. 8.95 (*1-55877-201-4*) Natl Governor.

Directory of Graduate Law Degree Programs. 3rd ed. Ed. by Richard L. Hermann et al. LC 90-656316. 112p. 1992. 16.95 (*0-929728-18-1*) Federal Reports Inc.

Directory of Graduate Law Degree Programs, 1990-1991. Ed. by Linda P. Sutherland & Richard L. Hermann. 130p. 1990. pap. 16.95 (*0-929728-08-4*) Federal Reports Inc.

Directory of Graduate Medical Education Program, 1991-1992. 1991. 40.00 (*0-89970-435-2*, OP416791) AMA.

Directory of Graduate Medical Education Programs. American Medical Association Staff. 1992. 45.00 (*0-89970-463-8*, OP416792) AMA.

Directory of Graduate Programs. 13th ed. 1991. Vol. B: Engineering & Business. pap. 17.00 (*0-446-39380-0*); Vol. C: Social Sciences & Education. pap. 17.00 (*0-446-39382-7*); Vol. D: Arts, Humanities & Other Fields. pap. 17.00 (*0-446-39384-3*) Warner Bks.

Directory of Graduate Programs. 13th ed. 1991. Vol. A: Natural Sciences. pap. 17.00 (*0-446-39378-9*) Warner Bks.

Directory of Graduate Programs. 14th ed. 1993. Vol. A Natural Sciences. pap. 18.00 (*0-446-39554-4*); Vol. B Engineering & Business. pap. 18.00 (*0-446-39549-8*); Vol. C Social Sciences & Education. pap. 18.00 (*0-446-39552-8*) Warner Bks.

Directory of Graduate Programs: 1986 & 1987, 4 vols., A. 10th ed. (Illus.). 1200p. (C). 1985. pap. 14.95 (*0-88685-027-4*) Educ Testing Serv.

Directory of Graduate Programs: 1986 & 1987, 4 vols., B. 10th ed. (Illus.). 1200p. (C). 1985. pap. 14.95 (*0-88685-028-2*) Educ Testing Serv.

Directory of Graduate Programs: 1986 & 1987, 4 vols., C. 10th ed. (Illus.). 1200p. (C). 1985. pap. 14.95 (*0-88685-029-0*) Educ Testing Serv.

Directory of Graduate Programs: 1986 & 1987, 4 vols., D. 10th ed. (Illus.). 1200p. (C). 1985. pap. 14.95 (*0-88685-030-4*) Educ Testing Serv.

Directory of Graduate Programs: 1986 & 1987, 4 vols., Set. 10th ed. (Illus.). 1200p. (C). 1985. pap. 59.80 (*0-88685-031-2*) Educ Testing Serv.

*__Directory of Graduate Programs Vol. A: Natural Sciences.__ 15th ed. 1995. pap. 20.00 (*0-446-39591-9*) Warner Bks.

*__Directory of Graduate Programs Vol. B: Engineering & Business.__ 15th ed. 1995. pap. 20.00 (*0-446-39593-5*) Warner Bks.

*__Directory of Graduate Programs Vol. C: Social Sciences & Education.__ 15th ed. 1995. pap. 20.00 (*0-446-39595-1*) Warner Bks.

*__Directory of Graduate Programs Vol. D: Arts, Humanities & Other Fields.__ 15th ed. 1995. pap. 20.00 (*0-446-39597-8*) Warner Bks.

Directory of Graduate Programs, Vol. D: Arts, Humanities, & Other Fields. 14th ed. Educational Testing Service Staff. 1993. pap. 18.00 (*0-446-39553-6*) Warner Bks.

Directory of Graduate Programs, 1988-89, 4 vols. Educational Testing Service Staff. 1987. Vol. A: Agriculture, Biological Sciences, Psychology, Health Sciences & Home Economics. pap. 14.95 (*0-446-38654-5*); Vol. B: Arts & Humanities. pap. 14.95 (*0-446-38656-1*); Vol. C: Physical Sciences, Mathematics & Engineering. pap. 14.95 (*0-446-38658-8*); Vol. D: Social Sciences & Education. pap. 14.95 (*0-446-38660-X*) Warner Bks.

Directory of Grant Support & Technical Assistance for Native American Initiatives. 800p. 1993. pap. 50.00 (*1-884324-00-2*) NMSU Ctr Econ.

*__Directory of Grant Support & Technical Assistance for Native American Initiatives 1994-1995.__ 4th ed. 450p. 1994. pap. text ed. 50.00 (*1-884324-01-0*) NMSU Ctr Econ.

Directory of Grants for Organizations Serving People with Disabilities. 8th ed. Ed. by Richard M. Eckstein. 228p. 1993. pap. 49.50 (*0-945078-06-4*) Rsch Grant Guides.

Directory of Grants in the Humanities 1994-95. 8th ed. Oryx Press Staff. 712p. 1994. pap. 84.50 (*0-89774-908-1*) Oryx Pr.

*__Directory of Grants in the Humanities 1995-96.__ 9th ed. Oryx Press Staff. Ed. by Millie Hannum & Janet Woolum. 720p. 1995. pap. 84.50 (*0-89774-911-1*, 2333) Oryx Pr.

*__Directory of Great Lakes Education Material.__ 3rd fac. ed. Great Lakes Science Advisory Board Staff. LC 88-174981. 78p. 1989. pap. 25.00 (*0-7837-8622-0*, 2075233) Bks Demand.

Directory of Greeting Card Sales Representatives in the United States, 1988-89. Ed. by Patti Brickman & Victoria O'Malley. 200p. (Orig.). 1988. pap. 25.00 (*0-938369-04-0*) Greeting Card Assn.

Directory of Greeting Card Sales Representatives, 1991-1992. rev. ed. Ed. by Paula A. Richmond. 200p. 1991. pap. 50.00 (*0-938369-11-3*) Greeting Card Assn.

Directory of Hard Facing & Wear Research Topics. 1978. 20.00 (*0-318-18635-7*) Welding Res Coun.

Directory of Hardlines Distributors, 1993-94. Ed. by Michael Jarvis. 550p. 1992. pap. 199.00 (*0-86730-588-6*, CSG Info Servs) Lebhar Friedman.

Directory of Health Care Professionals. 2400p. 1995. pap. 299.00 (*1-880678-37-3*) HCIA.

Directory of Health, Education & Research Journals. Lee Pratt. LC 83-49214. 144p. 1984. 29.50 (*0-8386-3213-0*) Fairleigh Dickinson.

*__Directory of Healthcare Group Purchasing Organizations.__ 460p. 1994. 315.00 (*1-56363-107-5*) Med Econ Data.

Directory of Healthcare Group Purchasing Organizations, 1994. Heidi M. Garrett. 1994. write for info. (*1-56363-062-1*) Med Econ Data.

Directory of High-Discount Merchandise & Product Sources for Distributors & Mail-Order Wealth Builders. 4th ed. S. David Hicks. 100p. 1990. pap. 17.50 (*0-934311-66-8*) Intl Wealth.

Directory of High-Discount Merchandise & Product Sources for Distributors & Mail-Order Wealth Builders. 5th ed. S. David Hicks. 100p. 1992. pap. 17.50 (*1-56150-017-8*) Intl Wealth.

Directory of High-Discount Merchandise & Product Sources for Distributors & Mail-Order Wealth Builders. 6th ed. S. David Hicks. 100p. 1993. pap. 17.50 (*1-56150-067-4*) Intl Wealth.

Directory of High-Discount Merchandise & Product Sources for Distributors & Mail-Order Wealth Builders. 7th ed. S. David Hicks. 100p. 1994. pap. 17.50 (*1-56150-115-8*) Intl Wealth.

Directory of High Discount Merchandise Sources. 116p. 1995. 35.00 (*0-685-56479-7*) B Klein Pubns.

Directory of High Volume Independent Drug Stores, 1993-94. Ed. by Patricc Petti. 1296p. 1992. pap. 285.00 (*0-86730-580-0*, CSG Info Servs) Lebhar Friedman.

Directory of High Volume Independent Restaurants, 1992-93. Ed. by Ron Boch. 1128p. 1992. pap. 270.00 (*0-86730-565-7*, CSG Info Servs) Lebhar Friedman.

*__Directory of Higher Education Institutions in the EFTA States: Austria, Finland, Ireland, Liechtenstein, Norway, Sweden, Switzerland.__ Comp. by ERASMUS, Human Resources, Education, Training & Youth Task Force Staff. 228p. 1994. pap. 36.00x (*0-7494-0489-2*, Pub. by Kogan Page Educ UK) Taylor & Francis.

Directory of Higher Education Institutions in the European Community. 2nd ed. European Communities Staff. 567p. 1992. pap. 55.00 (*92-826-2750-0*, CE-70-91-944-2A-C, Pub. by Europ Com) UNIPUB.

Directory of Higher Education Programs in Ground Water Science. 165p. 1987. 9.50 (*1-56034-006-1*, K401) Natl Water Well.

Directory of Historic American Theatres. Ed. by John Frick & Carlton Ward. LC 87-10709. 415p. 1987. text ed. 75.00 (*0-313-24868-0*, WDH/, Greenwood Pr) Greenwood.

Directory of History Departments & Organizations in the United States & Canada, 1993-94. 19th ed. Ed. by Roxanne M. Spencer. 800p. (Orig.). 1993. pap. 60.00 (*0-685-54257-2*) Am Hist Assn.

Directory of Holistic Medicine & Alternate Health Care Services in the U. S. Ed. by Shirley Linde & Donald J. Carrow. LC 85-13193. 264p. 1986. pap. 6.95 (*0-932090-18-4*) Mosby Yr Bk.

Directory of Holistic Practitioners for the Greater Boston Area. Ed. by David I. Weiss et al. LC 87-90042. 106p. (Orig.). 1987. pap. 6.00 (*0-9618049-0-4*) D I Weiss.

Directory of Holocaust Institutions. 1989. lib. bdg. 250.00 (*0-87700-881-7*) Revisionist Pr.

Directory of Home Center Operators & Hardware Chains, 1992. Ed. by Michael Jarvis. 1440p. 1992. pap. 239.00 (*0-86730-566-5*, CSG Info Servs) Lebhar Friedman.

Directory of Home Furnishings Retailers, 1993. Ed. by Pam Selman. 1024p. pap. 280.00 (*0-86730-582-7*, CSG Info Servs) Lebhar Friedman.

Directory of Homebuilt Ultra Light Aircraft. Hal Adkins. (Illus.). 106p. (Orig.). 1982. pap. 10.00 (*0-910907-00-5*) Haljan Pubns.

Directory of Homosexual Organizations & Publications: 1985-1986. 7th ed. Ed. by Ursula E. Copely. 100p. (Orig.). pap. 6.00 (*0-686-26160-7*) Homosexual Info.

*__Directory of Hospital Personnel.__ 2340p. 1994. 325.00 (*1-56363-103-2*) Med Econ Data.

Directory of Hospital Personnel, 1987. Ed. by William J. Feinberg. 1100p. (Orig.). 1986. pap. text ed. 259.00 (*0-938184-18-0*) Whole World.

Directory of Hospital Personnel, 1994. Heidi M. Garrett. 1994. write for info. (*1-56363-063-X*) Med Econ Data.

Directory of Human Resource Services, 1983-84. Human Resource Communication Group Staff. LC 82-80673. 128p. (Orig.). 1982. pap. 17.95 (*0-9609088-1-1*) Human Res Comm.

Directory of Humor Magazines & Humor Organizations in America (& Canada) 3rd ed. Ed. by Glenn C. Ellenbogen. LC 91-68398. (Illus.). 288p. (Orig.). 1992. 34.95 (*0-9606190-5-4*) Wry-Bred Pr.

Directory of Hydrogen Energy Products & Services, 1980-1981. IAHO Staff. 32p. 1981. pap. 12.00 (*0-08-027326-2*, Pergamon Pr) Elsevier.

Directory of Illustration, No. 9. Ed. by Glen R. Serbin. 256p. 1992. 39.95 (*0-9628858-1-9*, 30505) Serbin Commns.

*__Directory of Importers in Latin America.__ Comp. by Carlos Singer. 260p. 1994. pap. 195.00 (*0-9642542-0-4*) Americas Resch.

*__Directory of Importers in Latin America, 1994.__ 260p. 1994. pap. 195.00x (*0-8002-4321-8*) Intl Pubns Serv.

Directory of In-House Training Providers. American Bar Association, Young Lawyers Division Staff. 30p. 1988. pap. 5.00 (*0-685-21542-3*, 549-0070) Amer Bar Assn.

Directory of Incentives for Business Investment & Development in the United States: A State-by-State Guideline. 3rd ed. National Association of State Development Agencies Staff. LC 86-157140. (Illus.). 790p. (C). 1991. lib. bdg. 163.00 (*0-87766-515-X*); pap. text ed. 75.00 (*0-87766-501-X*) Urban Inst.

Directory of Indexing & Abstracting Courses & Seminars. LC 92-46651. 1993. 15.00 (*0-936547-17-0*) Am Soc Index.

Directory of Indian Film-Makers & Films. Comp. by Sanjit Narwekar. LC 93-44642. 576p. 1994. text ed. 85.00 (*0-313-29284-1*, Greenwood Pr) Greenwood.

Directory of Indian Publishers & Distributors. Ed. by Indian Bibliographic Centre Staff. 117p. 1987. text ed. 8.00 (*0-318-21412-1*, Pub. by Ind Biblio Ctr II) Univ Bks Ltd.

Directory of Indiana Children's Authors & Illustrators. 2nd rev. ed. Ed. by Katharyn E. Puckett & Sara Laughlin. 48p. 1991. pap. 6.95 (*0-9624180-1-3*) Stone Hills Area Lib Servs.

*__Directory of Indiana Donors, 3 vols., Set.__ Indiana Donors Alliance Staff. Date not set. pap. 15.00 (*1-886445-00-1*) Indiana Donors.

*__Directory of Indiana Donors, 1992-1993.__ Indiana Donors Alliance Staff. 242p. (Orig.). 1992. pap. 20.00 (*1-886445-03-6*) Indiana Donors.

*__Directory of Indiana Foundations, Set.__ Indiana Donors Alliance Staff. Date not set. pap. 35.00 (*1-886445-04-4*) Indiana Donors.

*__Directory of Indiana Foundations, 1995-1996.__ Indiana Donors Alliance Staff. Ed. by Susan R. Overs. 400p. (Orig.). 1994. pap. 35.00 (*1-886445-05-2*) Indiana Donors.

Directory of Industrial Designers 1991-92. 75.00 (*0-318-23072-0*) Indus Design.

Directory of Industrial Heat Processing & Combustion Equipment, 1984. Industrial Heating Equipment Association Staff. Ed. by Richard K. Miller. 150p. 1984. pap. text ed. 25.00 (*0-915586-80-0*) Fairmont Pr.

Directory of Information Resources for the Handicapped. 47.50 (*0-916270-28-9*) Ready Ref Pr.

Directory of Information Resources in Housing & Urban Development. 3rd ed. (Illus.). 205p. (C). 1994. pap. text ed. 60.00 (*0-7881-0287-7*) Diane Pub.

*__Directory of Information Sources on Scientific Research Related to the Preservation of Sound Recordings, Still & Moving Images, & Magnetic Tape.__ Margaret Child. 16p. 1993. pap. 10.00 (*1-887334-27-0*) Comm Preserv & Access.

An Asterisk (*) at the beginning of an entry indicates that the title is appearing in BIP for the first time.

Directory of Innovations in High School. Glorida Frazier & Robert Sickles. 408p. 1993. 39.95 (*1-883001-00-5*) Eye On Educ.

Directory of Institutions & Individuals Active in Environmentally-Sound & Appropriate Technologies. United Nations Environment Programme Staff. 1979. 64.00 (*0-08-025658-9*, Pub. by Pergamon Repr UK) Franklin.

Directory of Instructional Programs (K-8) Language Arts. 192p. (Orig.). 1990. teacher ed, pap. 15.95 (*0-9621503-2-0*) Brown Pub Network.

Directory of Instructional Programs (K-8) Mathematics. 240p. (Orig.). 1990. teacher ed, pap. 15.95 (*0-9621503-4-7*) Brown Pub Network.

Directory of Instructional Programs (K-8) Reading. 440p. (Orig.). 1990. teacher ed, pap. 24.95 (*0-9621503-1-2*) Brown Pub Network.

Directory of Instructional Programs (K-8) Science-Health. 184p. (Orig.). 1990. teacher ed, pap. 11.95 (*0-9621503-6-3*) Brown Pub Network.

Directory of Instructional Programs (K-8) Social Studies. 176p. (Orig.). 1990. teacher ed, pap. 11.95 (*0-9621503-5-5*) Brown Pub Network.

Directory of Instructional Programs (K-8) Spelling-Handwriting. 152p. (Orig.). 1990. teacher ed, pap. 15. 95 (*0-9621503-3-9*) Brown Pub Network.

Directory of Instructional Programs (K-8) Whole Language-Literature. 216p. (Orig.). 1990. teacher ed, pap. 11.95 (*0-9621503-7-1*) Brown Pub Network.

***Directory of Intellectual Property Attorneys, 1995.** 1684p. 1994. 195.00 (*0-13-169368-9*) Aspen Law.

Directory of Intentional Communities: A Guide to Cooperative Living. rev. ed. Ed. by Fellowship for Intentional Community Staff. (Illus.). 328p. 1991. pap. 16.00 (*0-9602714-1-4*) Fllwshp Intent.

Directory of Intentional Communities: A Guide to Cooperative Living. rev. ed. Ed. by Fellowship for Intentional Community Staff. (Illus.). 328p. 1992. pap. 16.00 (*0-9602714-2-2*) Fllwshp Intent.

Directory of Intentional Communities, 1990-91: A Guide to Cooperative Living. Ed. by Fellowship for Intentional Community Staff. (Illus.). 312p. (Orig.). 1990. pap. 12.00 (*0-9602714-0-6*) Fllwshp Intent.

Directory of International & National Medical Societies. Ed. by Zeitak. 350p. 1982. pap. 115.00 (*0-08-027991-0*, Pergamon Pr) Elsevier.

Directory of International & Regional Organizations Conducting Standards Activities. Ed. by Maureen Breitenberg. 436p. 1989. 44.00 (*0-912702-66-4*) Global Eng Doc.

Directory of International & Regional Organizations Conducting Standards-Related Activities. Ed. by Maureen Breitenberg. 436p. (Orig.). (C). 1993. pap. text ed. 50.00 (*1-56806-481-0*) Diane Pub.

Directory of International Business, 2 vols., Set. Jack A. Gottschalk. 1994. lib. bdg. 115.00 (*0-89356-822-8*) Salem Pr.

***Directory of International Careers 1994-1995.** rev. ed. Francis M. Jeffries. 600p. 1995. pap. 75.00 (*1-878974-22-X*) Jeffries & Assocs.

Directory of International Compatible Environmental Data. Carter & Diamondston. 1990. 79.00 (*1-56032-059-1*) Hemisp Pub.

Directory of International Grants & Fellowships in the Health Sciences. 100p. (Orig.). (C). 1994. pap. text ed. 50.00 (*0-7881-0343-1*) Diane Pub.

Directory of International Migration Study Centers, Research Program, & Library Resources. Ed. by Diane Zimmerman et al. LC 86-28418. (Bibliographies & Documentation Ser.). 299p. 1987. 35.00 (*0-685-19189-3*) Ctr Migration.

Directory of International Periodicals & Newsletters on the Built Environment. 2nd ed. Frances Gretes. 464p. 1992. text ed. 84.95 (*0-442-00792-2*) Van Nos Reinhold.

***Directory of International Resources for Indiana.** Comp. by William R. Adams & Veronica Fanning. LC 94-41027. (Illus.). 128p. 1994. pap. 14.95 (*0-253-20921-8*) Ind U Pr.

Directory of Internships, Work Experience Programs & On-the-Job Training Opportunities. 2nd ed. 89.50 (*0-916270-48-3*) Ready Ref Pr.

Directory of Interscholastic Moot Court Competitions, 1989. George Washington University Moot Court Board. 40p. (C). 1989. 12.00 (*0-9623329-0-9*) GWU MCB.

Directory of Irish Archives. 2nd ed. Ed. by Seamus Helferty & Raymond Refausse. 160p. 1993. text ed. 35. 00 (*0-7165-2507-0*, Pub. by Irish Acad Pr IE); pap. text ed. 19.50 (*0-7165-2508-9*, Pub. by Irish Acad Pr IE) Intl Spec Bk.

Directory of Islamic Banking & Financial Institutions. John R. Presley. 384p. 1988. lib. bdg. 120.00 (*0-7099-1347-8*) Routledge Chapman & Hall.

Directory of Italian American Associations in the Tri-State Area: Connecticut, Eastern New Jersey & New York. Comp. by Ezio Marchetto. 200p. 1989. 14.95 (*0-934733-44-9*) Ctr Migration.

***Directory of Japan Specialists & Japanese Studies Institutions in the United States & Canada: Japanese Studies in the United States, Vol. 1.** Japan Foundation Staff & Kokusai K. Kikin. LC 94-39856. (Japanese Studies: Vol. 24). 1994. write for info. (*0-924304-22-7*) Assn Asian Studies.

Directory of Japanese-Affiliated Companies in Asia, 1994-95. 357p. 1994. pap. 165.00 (*4-8224-0644-X*, Pub. by JETRO JA) Taylor & Francis.

Directory of Japanese Affiliated Companies in the E.C. 1991-92. 310p. 1992. pap. 150.00 (*4-8224-0550-8*, Pub. by Japan External Trade JA) Taylor & Francis.

***Directory of Japanese Affiliated Companies in the USA & Canada 1995-96.** 760p. 1995. 260.00x (*4-8224-0689-X*, Pub. by JETRO JA) Taylor & Francis.

Directory of Japanese-Affiliated Companies in U. S. A. & Canada, 1993-94. 677p. 1993. pap. 190.00 (*4-8224-0604-0*, Pub. by JETRO JA) Taylor & Francis.

Directory of Japanese Giving. Corporate Philanthropy Report Editors. 318p. 1991. pap. 190.00 (*1-881065-02-2*) Corp Philan.

Directory of Japanese Technical Reports 1989-1990. rev. ed. Intro. by Janet Geffner. (Japanese Directories Ser.). 550p. 1990. pap. 35.00 (*0-934213-29-1*, PB90-163098) Natl Tech Info.

Directory of Jewish Archival Institutions. Philip P. Mason. LC 75-15504. 77p. reprint ed. pap. 25.00 (*0-7837-3652-5*, 2043523) Bks Demand.

Directory of Jobs & Careers Abroad. 8th ed. Alex Lipinski. 352p. 1993. pap. 16.95 (*1-85458-025-6*, Pub. by Vacation-Work UK) Petersons Guides.

***Directory of Juvenile & Adult Correctional Departments, Institutions, Agencies & Paroling Authorities, 1995.** 740p. 1995. pap. 75.00 (*1-56991-024-3*) Am Correctional.

Directory of Key Executives: Non-Ferrous Wire Edition. Richard J. Callahan. Ed. by Eugene S. Reed & Amy G. Staniszewski. 425p. (Orig.). 1989. pap. 60.00 (*0-929833-00-7*) Hungerford & Holland.

Directory of Key Executives, Ferrous Wire Edition. Richard J. Callahan. Ed. by Eugene S. Reed & Amy G. Staniszewski. 400p. (Orig.). 1989. pap. 60.00 (*0-929833-01-5*) Hungerford & Holland.

Directory of Labour Organizations in Canada, 1992-93. Bureau of Labour Information Staff. 276p. (Orig.). 1992. pap. 32.45 (*0-660-57415-2*, Pub. by Canada Commun Grp CN) Accents Pubns.

Directory of Language Training & Services for Business: A Guide to Resources in Further & Higher Education. Colin Mellors et al. 500p. 1993. 74.50 (*0-415-09998-6*, B2530) Routledge.

Directory of Latin American Philosophers. Ed. by Jorge J. Gracia. (Council on International Studies & Programs Special Studies: No. 156). 122p. 1988. pap. text ed. 15. 00 (*0-317-92544-X*, 156) SUNYB Coun Intl Studies.

Directory of Law-Related CD-ROMS, 1993. Ed. by Arlene L. Eis. 100p. 1992. pap. text ed. 44.00 (*0-939486-26-1*) Infosources.

Directory of Law School Alternative Dispute Resolution Courses & Programs. 162p. 1989. pap. 20.00 (*0-89707-535-8*, 474-0039) Amer Bar Assn.

Directory of Law School Joint Degree Programs. 2nd ed. Ed. by Richard L. Hermann et al. 220p. 1991. 25.00 (*0-929728-14-9*) Federal Reports Inc.

Directory of Law School Joint Degree Programs, 1989-1990 Edition. Ed. by Richard Hermann et al. 241p. 1989. pap. 25.00 (*0-929728-02-5*) Federal Reports Inc.

Directory of Law School Transfer Policies: 3rd. 1992. 27. 50 (*0-685-53121-X*) Graduate Group.

Directory of Lawyer Disciplinary Agencies & Clients' Security Funds. Center for Professional Responsibility Staff. 25p. 1990. pap. 12.95 (*0-685-60842-5*, 561-0117-01) Amer Bar Assn.

Directory of Lawyer Referral Services. 31p. pap. 7.00 (*0-685-60843-3*, 409-0020-01) Amer Bar Assn.

Directory of Leading Chain Stores in the United States, 1993. 1992. pap. 279.00 (*0-86730-581-9*, CSG Info Servs) Lebhar Friedman.

Directory of Legal Employers, 1991. 1472p. 1991. pap. 120.00 (*0-318-02081-5*) NALP.

Directory of Legal Employers, 1992. 1450p. (Orig.). 1992. pap. 120.00 (*1-55733-001-8*) NALP.

Directory of Legal Employers, 1994. 1450p. (Orig.). 1994. pap. 120.00 (*1-55733-005-0*) NALP.

Directory of Legislative Leaders, 1993. NCSL Staff. 112p. 1993. pap. text ed. 15.00 (*1-55516-742-X*, 7135) Natl Conf State Legis.

***Directory of Legislative Leaders 1995.** NCSL Legislative Management Staff & Monica Root. 137p. 1994. 15.00 (*1-55516-744-6*, 7141) Natl Conf State Legis.

Directory of Libraries. 4th ed. 44p. 1992. 6.95 (*0-8213-2066-1*, 12066) World Bank.

Directory of Libraries: January 1993. 5th ed. 44p. 1992. 6.95 (*0-8213-2333-4*, 12333) World Bank.

***Directory of Libraries: The World Bank Depository Library Program.** 56p. 1994. 6.95 (*0-8213-2794-1*, 12794) World Bank.

***Directory of Libraries: The World Bank Depository Library Program 1995.** 60p. 1995. 6.95 (*0-8213-3210-4*, 13210) World Bank.

Directory of Library & Information Organization in the United Kingdom. Peter Dale. 192p. 1993. pap. 60.00 (*1-85604-092-5*, LAP0925, Pub. by Lib Assn Pub UK) UNIPUB.

Directory of Library & Information Profs. 2nd ed. 1991. 380.00 (*0-8103-7713-6*) Gale.

Directory of Library & Information Retrieved Software for Microcomputers. Ed. by Alison Gunson. 1990. text ed. 38.95 (*0-566-03628-2*, Pub. by Gower UK) Ashgate Pub Co.

Directory of Library Automation Software, Systems & Services. Ed. by Pamela Cibbarelli. 350p. 1992. pap. 79. 00 (*0-938734-65-2*) Learned Info.

***Directory of Library Automation Software, Systems & Services.** Ed. by Pamela R. Cibbarelli. 374p. 1994. pap. 79.00 (*0-938734-82-2*) Learned Info.

Directory of Library Networks & Cooperative Library Organizations. 1986. lib. bdg. 79.95 (*0-8490-3782-4*) Gordon Pr.

Directory of Library Systems in New York State. New York State Library Staff & New York State Division of Library Development Staff. 191p. 1992. 8.00 (*0-317-05248-9*) NYS Library.

Directory of Literary Magazines. Council of Literary Magazines & Presses Staff. 224p. 1991. pap. text ed. 9.95 (*1-55921-050-8*) Moyer Bell.

Directory of Literary Magazines & Presses, 1994-1995. Council of Literary Magazines & Presses Staff. 274p. 1994. pap. 11.95 (*1-55921-112-1*) Moyer Bell.

Directory of Literary Magazines 1992-1993: Council of Literary Magazines & Presses. 160p. 1992. pap. 9.95 (*1-55921-065-6*) Moyer Bell.

Directory of Literary Magazines 1994-1995. 1994. pap. 11. 95 (*1-55921-118-0*) Moyer Bell.

***Directory of Literary Magazines 1994-1995.** Council of Literary Magazines & Presses Staff. 350p. 1995. pap. 11. 95 (*1-55921-134-2*) Moyer Bell.

Directory of Litigation Attorneys, 1995-96, 2 vols. 5080p. 1993. 450.00 (*0-13-503302-0*) Aspen Law.

Directory of Living Aids for the Handicapped. 1984. 47.50 (*0-916270-41-6*) Ready Ref Pr.

Directory of London Stationers & Book Artisans, 1300-1500. C. Paul Christianson. LC 89-15064. 1989. 65.00 (*0-914930-11-7*) Biblio Soc Am.

***Directory of Louisiana Manufacturers, 1994.** 1994. 55.00 (*0-614-00286-9*) Harris Pub.

Directory of Low Cost Vacations with a Difference. J. Crawford. LC 85-29717. 68p. 1992. pap. 5.95 (*0-87576-161-5*) Pilot Bks.

Directory of Low Temperature Research in Europe. P. McDonald. (Illus.). 408p. 1992. 102.00 (*0-7503-0176-7*) IOP Pub.

Directory of Mail Drop Addresses & Zip Codes. 5th ed. Larry Schwartz & Pearl Sax. 250p. 1993. 605.50 (*0-914801-07-4*) Nat Assn Credit.

Directory of Mail Order Catalogs, No. 7. Ed. by Richard Gottlieb. 556p. 1992. pap. 135.00 (*0-939300-18-4*) Grey Hse Pub.

Directory of Mail Order Catalogs, No. 7. Ed. by Richard Gottlieb. 538p. 1994. pap. 145.00 (*0-939300-51-6*) Grey Hse Pub.

Directory of Mail Order Catalogues. 1992. lib. bdg. 255.95 (*0-8490-5518-0*) Gordon Pr.

Directory of Mailing List Companies. Ed. by B. Klein. 175p. 1995. pap. 45.00 (*0-915344-44-0*) Todd Pubns.

Directory of Mailing List Companies. 11th ed. Ed. by Barry T. Klein. 150p. 1991. 55.00 (*0-915344-18-1*) B Klein Pubns.

Directory of Maine, New Hampshire & Vermont High Technology Companies. rev. ed. Mass Tech Times, Inc. Staff. Ed. by Anne S. Lillie. 140p. 1989. pap. 125.00 (*0-927452-01-4*) Mass Tech Times.

Directory of Maine, New Hampshire & Vermont High Technology Companies. 2nd ed. Mass Tech Times, Inc. Staff. 1992. pap. write for info. (*0-927452-04-9*) Mass Tech Times.

***Directory of Major Companies in South East Asia.** 500p. 1995. 550.00 (*0-86338-555-9*, Pub. by Euromonitor Pubns UK) Gale.

Directory of Major Mailers & What They Mail, 1992: The Most Powerful Database on Direct Marketing Ever Created! 1992. 395.00 (*0-925133-21-3*) North Am Pub Co.

***Directory of Major Malls.** 14th ed. Ed. & Pref. by Tama J. Shor. (Illus.). 1138p. 1993. pap. 365.00 (*0-932599-11-7*) JOMURPA Pub.

***Directory of Major Malls.** 15th ed. Ed. & Pref. by Tama J. Shor. (Illus.). 1216p. 1994. pap. 385.00 (*0-932599-12-5*) JOMURPA Pub.

***Directory of Major Malls.** 16th ed. Ed. & Pref. by Tama J. Shor. (Illus.). 1256p. 1995. pap. 399.00 (*0-932599-13-3*) JOMURPA Pub.

Directory of Major Malls, 1985. 6th ed. Ed. by Tama J. Shor. (Illus.). 728p. 1985. pap. 200.00 (*0-932599-00-1*) JOMURPA Pub.

Directory of Major Malls, 1986. 7th ed. Ed. by Murray Shor. (Illus.). 812p. 1986. pap. 225.00 (*0-932599-01-X*) JOMURPA Pub.

Directory of Major Malls, 1987. 8th ed. Ed. by Murray Shor & Tama J. Shor. (Illus.). 856p. 1987. pap. 250.00 (*0-932599-02-8*) JOMURPA Pub.

Directory of Major Malls 1988. 9th ed. Ed. by Tama J. Shor. (Illus.). 776p. 1988. pap. 275.00 (*0-932599-03-6*) JOMURPA Pub.

Directory of Major Malls 1989. 10th ed. Ed. by Tama J. Shor. (Illus.). 836p. 1989. pap. 300.00 (*0-932599-04-4*) JOMURPA Pub.

Directory of Major Malls 1990. 11th ed. Ed. by Tama J. Shor. (Illus.). 834p. 1990. pap. 315.00 (*0-932599-06-0*) JOMURPA Pub.

Directory of Major Malls 1991. 12th ed. Ed. by Tama J. Shor. (Illus.). 990p. 1991. pap. 325.00 (*0-932599-07-9*) JOMURPA Pub.

Directory of Major Malls, 1992. 13th ed. Ed. by Murray Shor & Tama J. Shor. (Illus.). 1056p. 1992. pap. 349.00 (*0-932599-10-9*) JOMURPA Pub.

***Directory of Management Consultants, 1995-96.** 7th ed. Ed. by James H. Kennedy. 800p. 1994. text ed. 99.95 (*0-916654-94-X*) Kennedy Pubns.

Directory of Management Resources for Community Based Organizations. 6th ed. Marvin L. Peebles. 125p. 1987. ring bd. 20.00 (*0-939020-06-8*) MLP Ent.

Directory of M&A Intermediaries. Ed. by Yong Lim. 564p. Date not set. 225.00 (*0-914470-69-8*) SDC Pubng.

***Directory of M&A Intermediaries.** Ed. by Yong Lim & Ted Weissberg. 597p. 1994. 225.00 (*0-914470-73-6*) Venture Econ Inc.

Directory of Manufacturers & Wholesale Distributors. 1987. lib. bdg. 79.95 (*0-8490-3896-0*) Gordon Pr.

Directory of Manufacturers of Vacuum Plant, Components & Associated Equipment in the U. K., 1982. Ed. by J. S. Colligon. 56p. 1982. pap. 14.50 (*0-08-029323-9*, C145, A145, Pergamon Pr) Elsevier.

Directory of Marine Monitoring Programs in Massachusetts. Agnes Ayuso & Judith Pederson. Date not set. 6.00 (*1-56172-009-7*) MIT Sea Grant.

Directory of Maritime Periodicals. Ed. by Donna G. Fricke. 300p. (C). 1989. 35.95 (*0-9619447-1-4*) Maine Maritime Pr.

Directory of Mass Merchandisers, 1994. rev. ed. Ed. by Adrienne Toth et al. (Illus.). 1993. pap. 199.00 (*0-911790-15-2*, Progress Grocer) Trade Dimensns.

Directory of Massachusetts Foundations. 2nd ed. Ed. by John P. Huber. LC 76-15808. 1976. pap. 15.00 (*0-915884-12-7*) Eastern CT St Univ Fdn.

Directory of Massachusetts High Technology Companies. rev. ed. Mass Tech Times, Inc. Staff. Ed. by Anne S. Lillie. 324p. 1989. pap. write for info. (*0-927452-00-6*) Mass Tech Times.

Directory of Massachusetts High Technology Companies. 2nd ed. Mass Tech Times, Inc. Staff. Ed. by Anne S. Lillie. 365p. 1990. pap. write for info. (*0-927452-02-2*) Mass Tech Times.

Directory of Massachusetts Manufacturers, 1993-1994. George D. Hall Co. Staff. 1993. pap. write for info. (*1-56803-002-9*) G D Hall Co.

Directory of Massachusetts Photographers, 1840-1900. Chris Steele & Ronald Polito. LC 92-62230. (Illus.). 1993. 89.50 (*0-929539-76-1*) Picton Pr.

Directory of MasterCard & VISA Credit Card Sources. Ed. by Louis Gorchof. 400p. 1996. 75.00 (*0-915344-53-X*) Todd Pubns.

Directory of Master's Programs in Foreign Languages, Foreign Literatures, & Linguistics. Ed. by Modern Language Association Staff. LC 87-11254. ix, 173p. (Orig.). 1987. pap. 15.00 (*0-87352-169-2*, D312P) Modern Lang.

***Directory of Medical & Dental Schools Worldwide.** 6th ed. Ed. by U. S. Directory Service Staff. 312p. 1995. 59. 95 (*0-87228-063-2*) K G Saur.

Directory of Medical & Dental Schools Worldwide. 6th rev. ed. Ed. by Edgar Adcock et al. 280p. 1994. text ed. 59.95 (*0-916524-48-5*) US Direct Serv.

Directory of Medical Health & Health Care Libraries in U. K. & Ireland. 8th ed. D. J. Wright. 295p. 1992. pap. 50. 00 (*1-85604-066-6*, LAP0666, Pub. by Lib Assn Pub UK) UNIPUB.

Directory of Medical Health & Health Care Libraries in UK & Ireland. 9th ed. D. J. Wright. 300p. 1994. pap. 50.00 (*1-85604-120-4*, LAP1204, Pub. by Lib Assn Pub UK) UNIPUB.

***Directory of Medical Management Software.** Gary Knox. 91p. 1993. pap. 39.95 (*1-887212-02-7*) AQC Resource.

***Directory of Medical Management Software.** rev. ed. Gary Knox. 91p. 1995. pap. 39.95 (*1-887212-03-5*) AQC Resource.

Directory of Medical Rehabilitation Programs. 275p. 1993. disk 699.00 (*0-685-69246-9*) HCIA.

Directory of Medical Rehabilitation Programs. 275p. 1995. 195.00 (*1-880678-06-3*) HCIA.

Directory of Medical Schools Worldwide. 5th rev. ed. Ed. by Stanley Alperin. 1992. 44.95 (*0-916524-41-8*) US Direct Serv.

Directory of Medical Specialists from Kerala India. A. Enas Enas. 140p. (Orig.). 1986. pap. 25.00 (*0-9616232-0-9*) EA Enas.

Directory of Medical Specialists, 1991-1992, 3 vols., Set. 25th rev. ed. 6314p. 1991. 295.00 (*0-8379-0527-3*) Marquis.

***Directory of Member Agencies.** Family Service America Staff. 104p. 1995. pap. 250.00 (*0-87304-278-6*) Families Intl.

Directory of Members of ASJA. 1990. write for info. (*0-9612200-7-4*) Am Soc Jrnl & Auth.

***Directory of Members of Savings & Community Bankers of America.** Thomson Financial Publishing, Inc., Staff. 1994. pap. 95.00 (*1-56310-070-3*) Amer Bank Bond Buyer.

Directory of Members of the Savings & Community Bankers Association of America, 1993. Thomson Financial Publishing Inc. Staff. 1993. pap. 90.00 (*1-56310-049-5*) Amer Bank Bond Buyer.

Directory of Members, 1994-96. 448p. 1994. pap. 55.00 (*1-878147-12-9*) Am Political.

Directory of Men's & Boys' Wear Specialty Stores, 1993. 800p. pap. 180.00 (*0-86730-568-1*, CSG Info Servs) Lebhar Friedman.

Directory of Mental Health Libraries & Information Centers: Compiled Under the Auspices of the Association of Mental Health Librarians with the Support of the Mental Health Librarians Section, Medical Library Association. Ed. by Barbara A. Epstein & Ellen G. Detlefsen. LC 84-21582. 311p. reprint ed. pap. 88.70 (*0-8357-7809-6*, 2036181) Bks Demand.

Directory of Mergers & Acquisitions Firms & Professionals. Ed. by Kathryn Wolden. 308p. (Orig.). 1992. 150.00 (*0-8027-4896-1*) Walker & Co.

Directory of Michigan Municipal Officials. Michigan Municipal League Staff. 1994. 35.00 (*0-318-19475-9*) MI Municipal.

Directory of Microcomputer Retailers on Diskette. 1987. 995.00 (*0-317-64352-5*) Chromatic Comm.

Directory of Microcomputer Software for Cost Engineering. Calin Popescu & Abdelwahab Hamiani. LC 85-12847. 199p. reprint ed. pap. 56.80 (*0-7837-3365-8*, 2043323) Bks Demand.

Directory of Microcomputer Software for Libraries. Robert A. Walton & Nancy Taylor. LC 86-42725. 584p. 1986. pap. 37.00 (*0-89774-342-3*) Oryx Pr.

Directory of Microcomputer Software for Mechanical Engineering Design. Ed. by Colette O'Connell et al. LC 85-1540. 431p. reprint ed. pap. 122.90 (*0-7837-4320-3*, 2044006) Bks Demand.

D

An Asterisk (*) at the beginning of an entry indicates that the title is appearing in BIP for the first time. 2013

Directory of Microcomputer Software for School Business Administration. California Department of Education Staff. 136p. 1990. pap. 8.50 (*0-8011-0833-0*) Calif Education.

Directory of Mine Supply Houses, Distributors & Sales Agents. 300p. 1993. pap. 57.00 (*0-929531-21-3*) MacLn Hunter Pub.

Directory of Mineral-Related Organizations. 1994. lib. bdg. 250.00 (*0-8490-8417-2*) Gordon Pr.

Directory of Minority & Women-Owned Architectural & Engineering Firms. 116p. 1986. 10.00 (*0-686-48338-3*) Am Consul Eng.

***Directory of Minority Health Data Resources of the Public Health Service.** 1995. lib. bdg. 250.00 (*0-8490-6525-9*) Gordon Pr.

***Directory of Minority Health Data Resources of the Public Health Service.** 1995. lib. bdg. 253.99 (*0-8490-7570-X*) Gordon Pr.

Directory of MIT Sea Grant College Program Publications, 1971-1990. Comp. by Hilary Thornton. 70p. (Orig.). 1990. pap. text ed. (*1-56172-002-X*) MIT Sea Grant.

Directory of MIT Sea Grant College Program Publications: 1971-1991. (Orig.). 1991. pap. text ed. write for info. (*1-56172-004-6*) MIT Sea Grant.

Directory of Mixed-Use Developers. Urban Land Institute Staff. LC 83-145296. 49p. reprint ed. pap. 25.00 (*0-317-30050-4*, 2025041) Bks Demand.

Directory of Money Sources for Small Business. 1992. lib. bdg. 195.95 (*0-8490-5348-X*) Gordon Pr.

Directory of Mosquito Control Agencies in the United States & Canada, 1981. 2nd ed. Ed. by Gilbert L. Challet & Justine Keller. 39p. 1981. 20.00 (*0-9606210-3-2*) Am Mosquito.

Directory of Motor Component Manufacturers in Western Europe. 1986. 190.00 (*0-686-75442-5*) St Mut.

Directory of Multimedia Equipment Software & Services. 3rd ed. 525p. 1994. 52.00 (*0-939718-15-4*) Internatl Comms.

Directory of Multinationals, 2 Vols., Set. 4th ed. John Stopford. 1511p. 1992. 595.00 (*1-56159-053-3*, Stockton Pr) Groves Dictionaries.

***Directory of Music Faculties in Colleges & Universities, U. S. & Canada, 1994-95 Edition.** 16th ed. Intro. by Robby Gunstream. 869p. (Orig.). 1994. pap. 55.00 (*1-881913-04-X*) CMS Pubns.

Directory of Mutual Funds 1991. Investment Company Institute Staff. Ed. by Arlene Zuckerberg. (Illus.). 207p. 1991. pap. 5.00 (*1-878731-01-7*) Invest Co Inst.

Directory of Mutual Funds 1992. Investment Company Institute Staff. 231p. 1992. pap. 5.00 (*1-878731-04-1*) Invest Co Inst.

***Directory of National Helplines: A Guide to Toll-Free Public Service Numbers, 1995.** Pierian. 1995. pap. 7.00 (*0-87650-340-7*) Pierian.

Directory of National Information Sources on Disabilities. 5th ed. 105p. (Orig.). (C). 1994. pap. text ed. 34.95 (*0-7881-0715-1*) Diane Pub.

Directory of National Information Sources on Handicapping Conditions & Related Services. 1984. lib. bdg. 250.00 (*0-87700-551-6*) Revisionist Pr.

Directory of National Women's Organizations. Ed. by Paulette Tulloch. 686p. 1992. pap. text ed. 40.00 (*1-880547-08-2*) Nat Coun Res Wom.

Directory of National Women's Organizations. Paulette Tulloch. 1993. pap. 40.00 (*1-880547-10-4*) Nat Coun Res Wom.

Directory of Natural Science Centers 1984. Ed. by Mildred DeScherer. (Illus.). 1985. spiral bd., pap. 15.00 (*0-317-20046-1*) Natural Sci Youth.

***Directory of NCTM Individual Members, 1994.** NCTM Staff. 1012p. (Orig.). 1994. pap. 40.00 (*0-87353-382-8*) NCTM.

Directory of Neotropical Protected Areas. International Union for Conservation of Nature & Natural Resources (IUCN) Staff & Commission on National Parks & Protected Areas (CNPPA). (Illus.). 436p. 1982. 90.00 (*0-907567-63-0*, Tycooly Pub); pap. 60.00 (*0-907567-62-2*, Tycooly Pub) Weidner & Sons.

***Directory of New & Emerging Foundations.** 1994. pap. text ed. 95.00 (*0-87954-553-4*) Foundation Ctr.

Directory of New England Manufacturers, 1993-1994. George D. Hall Co. Staff. 1993. pap. write for info. (*1-56803-004-5*) G D Hall Co.

Directory of New Mexico Manufacturers. 1992. pap. 50.00 (*1-884324-25-8*) NMSU Ctr Econ.

Directory of Newsletters Related to Health, Medicine, Nutrition, & Sports. Ed. by Greg Landry & Nancy Landry. 48p. (Orig.). 1988. write for info. (*0-929363-00-0*) FIT Pub.

Directory of No-Credit-Check Lenders & Other Sources. James P. Severin. (Illus.). (Orig.). 1987. pap. 15.00 (*0-942853-00-8*) North Am Finan Grp.

Directory of Non-Governmental Environment & Development Organisations in OECD Member Countries. OECD Staff. 410p. (Orig.). 1992. pap. 68.00 (*92-64-03536-2*) OECD.

Directory of Non Traditional Training & Employment Programs Serving Women. 157p. (Orig.). (C). 1993. pap. text ed. 45.00 (*1-56806-937-5*) Diane Pub.

Directory of Nonfuel-Mineral Producers in Pennsylvania. 4th ed. Samuel W. Berkheiser, Jr. et al. (Information Circular Ser.: No. 54). (Illus.). 170p. 1985. pap. 6.00 (*0-8182-0070-7*) Commonweal PA.

Directory of North American Fisheries & Aquatic Scientists. 2nd ed. Ed. by Beth D. McAleer. LC 86-72933. 1987. pap. 13.00 (*0-913235-40-7*) Am Fisheries Soc.

Directory of Nursing Homes. 1620p. 1993. disk 2,500.00 (*0-685-69247-7*) HCIA.

Directory of Nursing Homes. 1620p. 1995. 249.00 (*1-880678-09-8*) HCIA.

***Directory of Object Technology.** Gaumer. 1995. pap. text ed. 69.00 (*0-13-352692-5*) P-H.

***Directory of Object Technology.** Dale J. Gaumer. LC 95-23. 360p. (Orig.). 1995. pap. 69.00 (*1-884842-08-9*) SIGS Bks.

***Directory of Occupational Health & Safety Software: Version 8.0.** 7th ed. Kent W. Peterson & Linda F. David. 462p. 1995. pap. 75.00 (*1-885190-02-6*) Comput in Occupat.

Directory of Office Supplies & Equipment. 7.00 (*0-931113-43-1*) Success Publ.

Directory of Officials & Organizations in China: A Quarter Century Guide. Malcolm Lamb. LC 94-12103. (Contemporary China Papers - Australian National University Ser.). 1392p. 1994. text ed. 160.00 (*1-56324-427-6*) M E Sharpe.

Directory of Officials & Staff, 1993. American Medical Association Staff. 164p. 1993. Spiral bdg. spiral bd. 40.00 (*0-89970-529-4*) AMA.

Directory of Oklahoma: State Almanac. 43th ed. Oklahoma Department of Libraries Staff. Ed. by Marilyn Vesely & Patricia Lester. (Illus.). 792p. 1991. pap. 12.00 (*1-880438-00-3*) OK Dept Lib.

Directory of Oklahoma see Oklahoma Almanac

Directory of Oklahoma Foundations. 2nd rev. ed. Thomas E. Broce & Daniel P. Junkin. LC 82-6984. 304p. 1982. 29.95 (*0-8061-1827-X*) U of Okla Pr.

Directory of On-Going Research in Cancer Epidemiology 1981. Calum S. Muir & G. Wagner. (IARC Scientific Publications: No. 38). 696p. 1986. pap. 26.95 (*0-19-723038-5*) OUP.

Directory of On-Going Research in Cancer Epidemiology 1982. Calum S. Muir & G. Wagner. (IARC Scientific Publications: No. 46). 722p. 1986. pap. 32.00 (*0-19-723046-6*) OUP.

Directory of On-Going Research in Cancer Epidemiology, 1983. G. Wagner. Ed. by Calum S. Muir. (IARC Scientific Publications: No. 50). 740p. 1986. pap. 32.00 (*0-19-723050-4*) OUP.

Directory of On-Going Research in Cancer Epidemiology, 1984. Ed. by Calum S. Muir & G. Wagner. (IARC Scientific Publications: No. 62). 748p. 1985. pap. 26.50 (*0-19-723062-8*) OUP.

Directory of On-Going Research in Cancer Epidemiology, 1988. Ed. by Michel P. Coleman & J. Wahrendorf. (IARC Scientific Publications: No. 93). 690p. 1988. pap. 60.00 (*92-832-1193-6*) OUP.

Directory of On-Going Research in Cancer Epidemiology, 1989-90. Ed. by Michel P. Coleman & J. Wahrendorf. (IARC Scientific Publications: No. 101). 864p. 1990. pap. 79.00 (*92-832-2101-X*) OUP.

Directory of On-Going Research in Cancer Epidemiology 1991. Ed. by Michel P. Coleman & J. Wahrendorf. (IARC Scientific Publications: No. 110). 792p. 1991. pap. 90.00 (*92-832-2110-9*) OUP.

Directory of On-Going Research in Cancer Epidemiology, 1992. Ed. by Michel P. Coleman et al. (IARC Scientific Publications: No. 117). 700p. 1992. pap. 98.00 (*92-832-2117-6*) OUP.

Directory of On-Going Research in Cancer Epidemiology, 1994. R. Sankaranarayanan et al. (IARC Scientific Publications: Vol. 130). 800p. 1994. pap. 95.00 (*92-832-2130-3*) OUP.

Directory of Online Databases. 95.00 (*0-685-17450-6*) Elsevier.

Directory of Online Healthcare Databases. 4th ed. Ed. by Karen Peterkin & Donald V. Black. 62p. 1989. spiral bd. 26.00 (*0-931712-09-2*) Alpine Guild.

Directory of Online Healthcare Databases. 5th rev. ed. Karen Peterkin & Donald V. Black. 80p. 1990. spiral bd. 35.00 (*0-931712-10-6*) Alpine Guild.

Directory of Operating Grants. Intro. by Richard M. Eckstein. 150p. (Orig.). 1992. pap. 42.50 (*0-945078-05-6*) Rsch Grant Guides.

Directory of Operating Small Business Investment Companies. 80p. (Orig.). (C). 1994. pap. text ed. 14.95 (*1-56806-220-6*) Diane Pub.

Directory of Oral History Collections. Allen Smith. 152p. 1988. 55.00 (*0-89774-322-9*) Oryx Pr.

Directory of Organizations & Institutions Advocating Coexistence Between Arabs & Jews in Israel. 1992. lib. bdg. 288.95 (*0-8490-5601-2*) Gordon Pr.

Directory of Orthodox Parishes & Institutions, 1994. Ed. by Philip Tamoush. 1994. 8.95 (*0-87903-816-0*) Oakwood Pubns.

***Directory of Outplacement Firms, 1995-96.** 8th ed. Ed. by James H. Kennedy. 500p. (Orig.). 1994. pap. text ed. 74.95 (*0-916654-93-1*) Kennedy Pubns.

Directory of Outreach Services in Public Libraries. American Library Association Staff. 640p. reprint ed. pap. 180.00 (*0-317-26558-X*, 2023944) Bks Demand.

Directory of Overseas Employers: Getting a Job Overseas. 1992. lib. bdg. 92.00 (*0-8490-5469-9*) Gordon Pr.

***Directory of Overseas Summer Jobs, 95.** 26th ed. Petersons Staff. 192p. 1995. pap. 14.95 (*1-85458-123-6*, Pub. by Vacation-Work UK) Petersons Guides.

Directory of Paleontologists of the World. 5th ed. Rex A. Doescher. 447p. (Orig.). 1989. pap. 25.00 (*0-9622577-0-2*) Intl Palaeontological.

Directory of Pan-European Organisations. Ed. by Euromonitor Staff. 450p. 1992. lib. bdg. 335.00 (*0-86338-405-6*, Pub. by Euromonitor Pubns UK) Gale.

Directory of Patent Attorneys & Agents. LC 80-23400. 328p. 1980. pap. 24.00 (*0-08-026343-7*, Pergamon Pr) Elsevier.

Directory of Pathology Training Program, 1987-88. 19th ed. Ed. by Judy Graves. (Illus.). 518p. 1986. pap. 50.00 (*0-317-56241-X*) Intersoc Comm Path Info.

Directory of Pathology Training Programs in the United States & Canada, 1990-91: Anatomic, Clinical, Specialized. 22th rev. ed. Ed. by Intersociety Committee on Pathology Information Staff & Eileen Lavine. (Illus.). 608p. 1989. pap. 55.00 (*0-318-42745-1*) Intersoc Comm Path Info.

Directory of Pathology Training Programs, 1985-1986. 17th ed. Ed. by Judy Graves. (Illus.). 500p. (Orig.). 1984. pap. 45.00 (*0-317-04534-2*) Intersoc Comm Path Info.

Directory of Pathology Training Programs, 1986-87. 18th ed. Ed. by Judy Graves. (Illus.). 505p. 1985. pap. 45.00 (*0-937888-02-8*) Intersoc Comm Path Info.

Directory of Pathology Training Programs, 1988-89. 20th ed. Ed. by Eileen Lavine. (Illus.). 518p. 1987. pap. 50.00 (*0-937888-04-4*) Intersoc Comm Path Info.

Directory of Pathology Training Programs, 1989-90. 21th rev. ed. Ed. by Eileen Lavine. (Illus.). 550p. (Orig.). 1988. pap. 55.00 (*0-937888-05-2*) Intersoc Comm Path Info.

Directory of Pathology Training Programs, 1991-1992. 23th rev. ed. Ed. by Intersociety Committee on Pathology Information Staff & Eileen Lavine. 604p. (Orig.). 1990. pap. 55.00 (*0-937888-07-9*) Intersoc Comm Path Info.

***Directory of Pennsylvania Foundations.** 5th ed. Ed. by S. Damon Kletzien. 464p. 1995. pap. 68.50 (*0-9616806-2-8*) Triadvocates Pr.

Directory of Periodicals Online: Indexed, Abstracted & Full-Text, Vol. 1. 2nd ed. Ed. by Catherine Chung. 350p. (Orig.). 1986. text ed. 125.00 (*0-932929-09-5*) Fed Doc Retrieval.

Directory of Periodicals Online: Indexed, Abstracted, & Full Text, News, Law & Business. Ed. by Maria S. Sims. 1987. pap. 75.00 (*0-932929-11-7*) Fed Doc Retrieval.

Directory of Periodicals Online: Indexed, Abstracted, & Full Text, News, Law & Business. 4th ed. Ed. by Maria S. Sims. 1988. pap. 75.00 (*0-932929-13-3*) Fed Doc Retrieval.

Directory of Periodicals Online: Indexed, Abstracted, & Full Text, Science & Technology. Ed. by Maria S. Sims. 1988. pap. 125.00 (*0-932929-02-8*) Fed Doc Retrieval.

Directory of Periodicals Online: Indexed, Absracted, & Full Text, Vol. 1: News, Law & Business. Ed. by Catherine Chung. 524p. 1985. pap. 90.00 (*0-932929-00-1*) Fed Doc Retrieval.

Directory of Periodicals Online: Indexed, Abstracted, & Full Text, Vol. 2: Medicine & Social Science. Ed. by Maria S. Sims. pap. write for info. (*0-932929-01-X*) Fed Doc Retrieval.

Directory of Periodicals Published in India 1986-1987. Susheel Kaur. (C). 1988. 400.00 (*0-685-36506-9*) St Mut.

Directory of Personal Image Consultants: 1992-93 Edition. 9th ed. Ed. by Jacqueline Thompson. (Illus.). 224p. (Orig.). 1992. pap. 40.00 (*0-933406-09-6*) Image Industry.

Directory of Personal Image Consultants, 1988-1989. Ed. by Jacqueline Thompson & Image Industry Publications. 180p. 1988. pap. 35.00 (*0-317-61811-3*) Image Industry.

Directory of Personal Image Consultants, 1990-91. rev. ed. 288p. 1990. pap. 35.00 (*0-933406-08-8*) Image Industry.

Directory of Physical Therapy Education Programs. 500p. 1993. 34.95 (*0-912452-79-X*, E-24) Am Phys Therapy Assn.

Directory of Physicians in the U. S. American Medical Association Staff. 1992. 545.00 (*0-89970-523-5*, OP390892) AMA.

Directory of Physics & Astronomy Staff Members, 1984-85. Ed. by Dion Shea. 412p. 1984. pap. 30.00 (*0-88318-458-3*) Am Inst Physics.

Directory of Physics & Astronomy Staff, 1990-1991. American Institute of Physics Staff. 402p. 1990. 60.00 (*0-88318-809-0*) Am Inst Physics.

Directory of Planning & Development Consultants. RICS Staff. 80p. (C). 1989. text ed. 85.00 (*0-85406-424-9*, Pub. by Surveyors Pubns) St Mut.

Directory of Plants Containing Secondary Metabolites. John S. Glasby. 100p. 1991. 220.00 (*0-85066-423-3*) Taylor & Francis.

***Directory of Poetry Publishers.** 10th ed. Ed. by Len Fulton. 364p. 1994. pap. 18.95 (*0-916685-44-6*) Dustbooks.

***Directory of Poetry Publishers.** 11th rev. ed. Ed. by Len Fulton. 400p. 1995. pap. 19.95 (*0-916685-54-3*) Dustbooks.

Directory of Poetry Publishers: 1993-94. 9th rev. ed. Ed. by Len Fulton. 400p. 1993. pap. 17.95 (*0-916685-38-1*) Dustbooks.

Directory of Polish Roman Catholic Parishes in the Territory of the former Austrian Partition. Jonathan D. Shea & Constance M. Ochnio. LC 91-61438. 119p. 1991. 14.00 (*0-945440-07-3*) Pol Geneal CT.

Directory of Polish Roman Catholic Parishes in the Territory of the Former Russian Partition. Jonathan D. Shea & Constance M. Ochnio. LC 89-63283. (Illus.). 265p. 1991. pap. 20.00 (*0-945440-03-0*) Pol Geneal CT.

Directory of Political Newsletters (1994 Edition) A Guide to Sources of Insider's Information about Government & Politics. rev. ed. Ed. by Lynn Hellebust. 150p. 1994. spiral bd. 45.00 (*1-879929-09-0*) Govt Res Serv.

Directory of Popular Culture Collections. Ed. by Christopher D. Geist et al. 248p. 1989. 50.00 (*0-89774-351-2*) Oryx Pr.

Directory of Portable Databases. 288p. 1989. 49.95 (*0-444-01522-1*) Elsevier.

Directory of Portable Databases, Vol. 2, No. 1. 471p. 1990. 49.95 (*0-444-01555-8*) Elsevier.

Directory of Portable Databases, Vol. 2, No. 2. Cuadra-Elsevier Staff. 642p. 1990. 59.95 (*0-444-01596-5*) Elsevier.

Directory of Postsecondary Institutions, 1989- 1990, Vol. 1: 4 Year & 2 Year. Susan G. Broyles. 571p. 1990. per., pap. 28.00 (*0-16-026774-9*, S/N 065-000-004) USGPO.

Directory of Power Plants in Asia & Australia. Utility Data Institute, Inc. Staff. Ed. by Chris Bergesen. 500p. (Orig.). (C). 1994. pap. 395.00 (*1-56760-011-5*, UDI2051-94) Utility Data Inst.

Directory of Power Plants in Canada. 2nd ed. Utility Data Institute Staff. 200p. 1992. pap. 225.00 (*1-56760-009-3*) Utility Data Inst.

Directory of Power Plants in Latin America & the Caribbean. Utility Data Institute Staff. Ed. by Chris Bergesen. 300p. 1993. pap. 395.00 (*1-56760-012-3*) Utility Data Inst.

Directory of Power Plants in the European Community. 4th ed. Utility Data Institute Staff. 425p. 1992. pap. 395.00 (*1-56760-008-5*) Utility Data Inst.

Directory of Practice: Examples in Residential Care for Elderly People. Ed. by Lynette Domoney & Ruth Halves. (C). 1989. 50.00 (*0-7855-0085-5*, Pub. by Natl Inst Soc Work) St Mut.

Directory of Practice Examples in Residential Care for Elderly People. Lynette Domoney & Ruth Halves. (C). 1989. 75.00 (*0-902789-62-7*, Pub. by Natl Inst Soc Work); 40.00 (*0-685-40332-7*, Pub. by Natl Inst Soc Work) St Mut.

Directory of Practice Parameters, Guidelines & Technology Assessments. 45.00 (*0-89970-539-1*, OP270293) AMA.

Directory of Primes: Annual. 160p. 1988. pap. 15.00 (*0-318-35156-0*) Gov Data Pubns.

Directory of Print Media Advertising Resources. R. L. Ehler. LC 90-63643. (Print Media Advertising Ser.: Bk. 2). 85p. (Orig.). 1992. pap. text ed. 44.95 (*1-879299-12-7*) Richler.

***Directory of Printers 1994-95.** E. Marie Kiefer & John Kremer. 392p. 1995. pap. write for info. (*0-912411-43-0*) Open Horizons.

Directory of Prison & Jail Addresses & Zip Codes. 5th ed. Larry Schwartz & Pearl Sax. 250p. 1993. 505.50 (*0-914801-01-5*) Nat Assn Credit.

***Directory of Professional Genealogists 1995.** (Illus.). 150p. 1995. pap. text ed. 15.00 (*0-614-05487-7*) Assn Prof Genealogists.

***Directory of Professional Preparation Programs in TESOL in the United States, 1995-1997.** Ed. by Helen Kornblum. 243p. 1995. pap. write for info. (*0-614-06964-5*) Tchrs Eng Spkrs.

Directory of Professional Workers in State Agricultural Experiment Stations & Other Cooperating Institutions. 1994. lib. bdg. 259.95 (*0-8490-9033-4*) Gordon Pr.

***Directory of Professionals.** AIA Staff. 160p. 1994. per., pap. text ed. 16.00 (*0-7872-0332-7*) Kendall-Hunt.

Directory of Programs for Gifted Children. 1991. 27.50 (*0-685-39170-1*) Graduate Group.

***Directory of Psychiatric Residency Training Programs.** 6th rev. ed. American Psychiatric Association, Dept. of Education Staff. 1995. pap. write for info. (*0-89042-706-2*, 2706) Am Psychiatric.

Directory of Psychiatry Residency Training Programs. 3rd ed. Ed. by Carolyn B. Robinowitz et al. 647p. reprint ed. pap. 180.00 (*0-8357-3038-7*, 2039287) Bks Demand.

Directory of Psychiatry Residency Training Programs: 0-89042-705-4. 5th ed. APA Office of Education Staff. 624p. 1990. pap. text ed. 19.95 (*0-685-72956-7*) Am Psychiatric.

***Directory of Psychics: How to Find, Evaluate, & Communicate with Professional Psychics & Mediums.** Hans Holzer. (Illus.). 256p. 1995. pap. 12.95 (*0-8092-3561-7*) Contemp Bks.

Directory of Psychological Tests in the Sport & Exercise Sciences. Ed. by Andrew C. Ostrow. LC 90-84378. (Illus.). 291p. (C). 1990. text ed. 36.00 (*0-9627926-0-8*) Fit Info Tech.

***Directory of Psychology Internships: Programs Offering Behavioral Training.** 100p. 1990. pap. 20.00 (*0-614-04145-7*) Assn Advance Behav Therapy.

Directory of Public Companies: Stockbrokers Bible. Gary Mair. 400p. 1993. 49.95 (*1-884821-00-6*) Wall St Finan.

Directory of Public Elementary & Secondary Education Agencies, 2 vols., Set. 1994. lib. bdg. 450.00 (*0-8490-5739-6*) Gordon Pr.

Directory of Public Officials, 1991-92. rev. ed. East-West Gateway Coordinating Council Staff. (Illus.). (C). 1991. pap. 14.95 (*0-9627998-1-5*) East-West Gateway.

Directory of Public Utility Commission Libraries. 1991. 7.00 (*0-317-02701-8*) NARUC.

Directory of Public Vocational Technical Schools & Institutes in the U. S. A. Ed. by Marliss Johnston. 400p. 1992. lib. bdg. 65.00 (*0-933474-50-4*) Media Mktg Group.

Directory of Public Vocational Technical Schools & Institutes in the U. S. A. 1994-1995. 7th rev. ed. Ed. by Marliss Johnston. 450p. 1994. lib. bdg. 65.00 (*0-933474-51-2*) Media Mktg Group.

Directory of Publications Resources: Selected Books, Periodicals, Software, Courses Organizations, Contests. rev. ed. Ed. by Linda Jorgensen. (Illus.). 120p. 1993. pap. 14.00 (*0-935012-15-X*) Edit Experts.

Directory of Publishing Opportunities for Teachers of Writing. Ed. by William F. Woods. LC 79-54036. 52p. 1979. pap. 3.50 (*0-930388-04-6*) Comm Collaborators.

Directory of Puerto Rican Scholars. Ed. by Raoul Gordon. 1976. lib. bdg. 75.00 (*0-8490-0048-3*) Gordon Pr.

Directory of Pump, Valve & Compressor Manufacturers in Western Europe. Ed. by European Directories Staff. 1986. 200.00 (*0-686-78876-1*) St Mut.

Directory of Purchasing Professionals, Vol. 1. 680p. 1994. 130.00 (*1-873477-50-3*, M89334-101467) Gale.

D

An Asterisk (*) at the beginning of an entry indicates that the title is appearing in BIP for the first time.

***Directory of Real Estate Development & Related Education Programs.** 3rd ed. Urban Land Institute Staff. LC 91-65046. 121p. 1991. reprint ed. pap. 34.50 (*0-7837-8917-3*, 2049628) Bks Demand.

***Directory of Real Estate Development & Related Education Programs.** 4th ed. Urban Land Institute Staff. LC 92-64327. 140p. 1992. reprint ed. pap. 39.90 (*0-7837-9007-4*, 2049629) Bks Demand.

***Directory of Real Estate Development & Related Education Programs.** 5th ed. ULI Staff. 140p. 1994. pap. text ed. 15.95 (*0-87420-759-2*) Urban Land.

Directory of Real Estate Development & Related Education Programs. Urban Land Institute Staff. LC 89-50094. 87p. reprint ed. pap. 25.00 (*0-8357-3189-8*, 2039459); reprint ed. pap. 33.10 (*0-7837-1002-X*, 2041312) Bks Demand.

Directory of Record & CD Retailers: 1990-1991 Edition. Keith Whelan. 368p. (Orig.). 1990. pap. 14.95 (*0-9627592-0-1*) Power Commn Gp.

Directory of Recreational Marine Product Dealers, 1993-94. Ed. by Janice Backer. 1092p. pap. 345.00 (*0-685-65051-0*, CSG Info Servs) Lebhar Friedman.

Directory of Recycable Wastes, Bk. 2. Ed. by Billy Mason. (Orig.). (C). 1981. pap. 11.95 (*0-942140-00-1*) Kelso.

Directory of Recyclable Wastes. Billy Mason. (Illus.). 1976. pap. text ed. 11.95 (*0-942140-01-X*) Kelso.

Directory of References & Resources for Direct Marketing of Training Programs. 2nd ed. Ed. by Susan F. Cottam & Don M. Schrello. 60p. (Orig.). 1985. pap. 14.95 (*0-935823-04-2*) Schrello Market.

Directory of Registered Environmental Organizations. 75p. (Orig.). (C). 1993. pap. text ed. 30.00 (*1-56806-530-2*) Diane Pub.

Directory of Registered Investment Advisors with the Securities & Exchange Commission, 1995. 1995. 345.00 (*0-685-73085-9*) Money Mkt.

Directory of Regulatory Compliance Products & Services. 1992. 79.95 (*0-8493-4630-4*) CRC Pr.

Directory of Religious & Parareligious Bodies & Organizations in the United States. Ed. by James V. Geisendorfer. 440p. 1990. lib. bdg. 109.95 (*0-88946-644-0*) E Mellen.

Directory of Religious Organizations in the U. S. 3rd ed. Melton. 1992. 130.00 (*0-8103-9890-7*, 072216) Gale.

Directory of Repositories of Family History in New Hampshire. Scott E. Green. 61p. 1993. pap. 10.95 (*0-685-69923-4*, 9125) Clearfield Co.

Directory of Research & Development: Activities in the U. K. in Land Survey & Related Fields. RICS Staff. 100p. (C). 1987. text ed. 65.00 (*0-85406-356-0*, Pub. by Surveyors Pubns) St Mut.

Directory of Research & Training Institutes in Latin America. OECD Staff. 154p. (Orig.). 1993. pap. 27.00 (*92-64-03705-5*) OECD.

Directory of Research Grants 1995. 1224p. 1995. pap. 135.00 (*0-89774-909-X*) Oryx Pr.

***Directory of Research Grants 1996, 2276.** Ed. by Millie Hannum & Janet Woolum. 1995. pap. 135.00 (*0-89774-877-8*) Oryx Pr.

Directory of Research Partners, EUR 14993. 420p. 1993. pap. 95.00 (*92-826-6245-4*, CD-NA-14993-EN-C, Pub. by Europ Com) UNIPUB.

Directory of Research Workers in Agriculture & Allied Sciences. Ed. by R. Vernon. 500p. 1989. text ed. 161.50 (*0-85198-623-4*) CAB Intl.

Directory of Residential Centers for Adults with Mental Illnesses. Oryx Press Staff. 328p. 1990. pap. 68.50 (*0-89774-563-9*) Oryx Pr.

Directory of Residential Centers for Adults with Developmental Disabilities. 408p. 1989. pap. 78.50 (*0-89774-533-7*) Oryx Pr.

Directory of Resources for Aging, Gerontology & Retirement. 2nd ed. Ed. by Michael R. Gabriel. 250p. 1986. lib. bdg. 75.00 (*0-933474-41-5*) Media Mktg Group.

Directory of Resources for Australian Studies in North America. Nan B. Albinski. 211p. 1992. 15.00 (*0-7326-0435-4*, Pub. by Natl Ctr Austln AT) Austlia-NZ Studies.

Directory of Resources for Educational Planning & Management. Ed. by Lyle O. Wright. 386p. 1975. ring bd. 49.95 (*0-916236-01-3*) Western Educ Serv.

Directory of Resources for Technology in Education, 1984. 242p. (Orig.). 1984. 19.95 (*0-914409-02-6*); pap. 12.95 (*0-685-08178-8*) Far West Lab.

***Directory of Resources to Assist Receivers of Insolvent Insurance Companies.** annuals 50p. (C). 1994. 25.00 (*0-89382-306-6*) Nat Assn Insu Comm.

Directory of Retirement Facilities. 1250p. 1994. disk 2,500.00 (*0-685-69244-2*) HCIA.

Directory of Retirement Facilities. 1250p. 1995. 249.00 (*1-880678-40-3*) HCIA.

Directory of Russian MP's. 284p. 1992. 260.00 (*0-582-09647-2*, 101872, Pub. by Longman Grp UK) Gale.

***Directory of Russian Scientists & Engineers.** Ed. by Yuri Khol'kin et al. LC 95-75936. 289p. (Orig.). 1995. pap. text ed. 20.00 (*0-9645120-3-3*) K-M Consult.

Directory of Safety Related Computer Resources. 2nd ed. Roger Brauer. 264p. 1993. pap. 64.95 (*0-939874-91-1*, 4343) ASSE.

***Directory of Safety Related Computer Resources, 1994.** Roger L. Brauer. LC 94-28647. 1994. 24.95 (*1-885581-01-7*) ASSE.

Directory of Scholarly Journals in English Language & Literature. L. L. Lee & Ellwood Johnson. 250p. 1990. 25.00 (*0-87875-401-6*) Whitston Pub.

Directory of Scientific Instrument Makers 1550-1851. Gloria Clifton. (Illus.). 272p. 1994. 95.00 (*0-302-00634-6*, Pub. by P Wilson Pubs) Sothebys Pubns.

Directory of Scots Banished to the American Plantations, 1650-1775. David Dobson. 239p. 1990. reprint ed. 15.00 (*0-685-60510-8*, 1485) Clearfield Co.

Directory of Scottish Settlers in North America, 1625-1825, Vol. I. David Dobson. LC 83-82470. 267p. 1988. 20.00 (*0-8063-1054-5*) Genealog Pub.

Directory of Scottish Settlers in North America, 1625-1825, Vol. II. David Dobson. LC 83-82470. 126p. 1986. 15.00 (*0-8063-1074-X*) Genealog Pub.

Directory of Scottish Settlers in North America, 1625-1825, Vol. III. David Dobson. LC 83-82470. 194p. 1984. 17.50 (*0-8063-1087-1*) Genealog Pub.

Directory of Scottish Settlers in North America, 1625-1825, Vol. IV. David Dobson. LC 83-82470. 161p. 1985. 17.50 (*0-8063-1105-3*) Genealog Pub.

Directory of Scottish Settlers in North America, 1625-1825, Vol. V. David Dobson. LC 83-82470. 312p. 1985. 20.00 (*0-8063-1124-X*) Genealog Pub.

***Directory of Scottish Settlers in North America, 1625-1825, Vol. VI.** David Dobson. 126p. 1994. 15.00 (*0-614-03809-X*, 1482) Genealog Pub.

Directory of Selected Automated Information Systems in New York State Government. Robert A. Carter. 99p. 1984. 5.00 (*0-318-22979-X*) NYS Library.

***Directory of Selected Chinese Universities & Colleges Open to Foreign Students.** Ed. by Xiong Binsan. 445p. 1993. 150.00 (*7-04-004372-6*, Pub. by Deakin Univ AT) St Mut.

Directory of Selected Collections of United Nations System Publications. 126p. 1990. 25.00 (*92-1-100351-2*, GV.90.0.4) UN.

Directory of Selected National Testing Programs. Educational Testing Service Staff. 288p. 1987. pap. 38.50 (*0-89774-386-5*) Oryx Pr.

Directory of Selected Research & Policy Centers Working on Women's Issues. 5th ed. Comp. by Mary A. Jorgensen. 48p. 1989. 10.50 (*0-87111-364-3*) SLA.

***Directory of Selected U. S. Cogeneration, Small Power & Industrial Power Plants, 2 vols., Set.** 11th ed. Ed. by Chris Bergesen & Fred Yost. (Illus.). 1994. pap. text ed. 395.00 (*1-56760-059-X*, UDI-2018-94) Utility Data Inst.

***Directory of Selected U. S. Cogeneration, Small Power & Industrial Power Plants, Vol. 1.** 11th ed. Ed. by Chris Bergesen & Fred Yost. (Illus.). 300p. 1994. pap. text ed. write for info. (*0-614-03047-1*) Utility Data Inst.

***Directory of Selected U. S. Cogeneration, Small Power & Industrial Power Plants, Vol. 2.** 11th ed. Ed. by Chris Bergesen & Fred Yost. (Illus.). 420p. 1994. pap. text ed. write for info. (*0-614-03048-X*) Utility Data Inst.

Directory of Self Help & Mutual Aid Groups. 7th ed. 250p. 1992. pap. 45.00 (*1-881605-00-0*) Self Help Ctr.

Directory of Services for Handicapping Conditions (1988) rev. ed. Information Protection & Advocacy Center for Handicapped Individuals, Inc. Staff. LC 88-26606. 251p. 1988. pap. 10.00 (*0-929813-00-6*) IPACHI.

Directory of Services for Persons with Disabilities 1993. 2nd ed. Information Protection & Advocacy Center for Handicapped Individuals, Inc. Staff. 300p. 1992. 25.00 (*0-929813-04-9*) IPACHI.

Directory of Sheffield. LC 69-18826. (Architecture & Decorative Art Ser.). 1969. reprint ed. 25.00 (*0-306-71251-2*) Da Capo.

Directory of Shopping Centers in the United States, 4 vols. LC 58-2082. 1988. 145.00 (*0-317-54925-1*) Natl Res Bur.

Directory of Shopping Centers in the United States, 4 vols., Set. LC 58-2082. 1988. 300.00 (*0-912610-19-0*); 300.00 (*0-912610-44-1*) Natl Res Bur.

Directory of Short-Run Book Printers. 1987. lib. bdg. 79.95 (*0-8490-3915-0*) Gordon Pr.

Directory of Simulation Software, 1991. Ed. by Elliot Estrine. 44p. 1991. 20.00 (*1-56555-006-4*, DSS-91) Soc Computer Sim.

Directory of Simulation Software, 1993. Ed. by Rodriguez. 56p. 1992. pap. 30.00 (*1-56555-015-3*, DSS-93) Soc Computer Sim.

Directory of Single Unit Supermarket Operators, 1992-93. Ed. by Jim Tierney. 728p. pap. 219.00 (*0-86730-552-5*, CSG Info Servs) Lebhar Friedman.

Directory of Small Magazine - Press Editors & Publishers. 23th ed. Ed. by Len Fulton. 300p. 1992. pap. 21.95 (*0-916685-33-0*) Dustbooks.

***Directory of Small Magazine - Press Editors & Publishers.** 26th rev. ed. Ed. by Len Fulton. 300p. 1995. pap. text ed. 23.95 (*0-916685-52-7*) Dustbooks.

Directory of Small Magazine Press Editors & Publishers, 1993-94. 24th rev. ed. Ed. by Len Fulton. 300p. 1993. pap. 22.95 (*0-916685-39-X*) Dustbooks.

Directory of Small-Scale Agriculture. 1991. lib. bdg. 79.95 (*0-8490-4954-7*) Gordon Pr.

Directory of Small-Scale Agriculture: Persons, Activities & Projects Information for Users. 1991. lib. bdg. 79.95 (*0-8490-4346-8*) Gordon Pr.

Directory of Social Change: Community. Michael Norton. 1988. 40.00 (*0-7045-0285-2*) St Mut.

Directory of Social Change: Education & Play. Michael Norton. 1988. 40.00 (*0-7045-0291-7*) St Mut.

Directory of Social Change: Women. Ellen Friedman. 1988. 40.00 (*0-7045-0335-2*) St Mut.

Directory of Social Research Organisations in the United Kingdom. Wendy Sykes et al. 320p. 1993. pap. text ed. 70.00 (*0-7201-2165-5*, Mansell Pub) Cassell.

Directory of Social Science Information Courses. UNESCO. 192p. 1988. 74.95 (*0-85496-240-9*) Berg Pubs.

Directory of Social Science Information Courses, 1988. (World Social Science Information Directories Ser.: No. 6). 167p. 1988. pap. 25.00 (*92-3-002525-9*, U1649) UNIPUB.

Directory of Software for Retailers. 65.00 (*0-87102-076-9*, 30-3069) Natl Ret Merch.

Directory of Software for Retailers 2. 400p. 1987. pap. 65.00 (*0-87102-125-0*, 30-5071) Natl Ret Merch.

Directory of Soviet Research Organization. National Foreign Assessment Center Staff. LC 79-121624. 300p. reprint ed. pap. 85.50 (*0-8357-2914-1*, 2039153) Bks Demand.

Directory of Spanish & Portuguese Film-Makers & Films. Ed. by Rafael De Espana. LC 94-17610. 264p. 1994. text ed. 69.50 (*0-313-29459-3*, Greenwood Pr) Greenwood.

Directory of Spare Capacity. 1981. 110.00 (*0-317-43698-8*) St Mut.

Directory of Special Collections in Western Europe. Ed. by Alison Gallico. 250p. 1993. lib. bdg. 75.00 (*0-86291-616-X*) Bowker-Saur.

Directory of Special Libraries, 2 vols., Vol. 1. 17th ed. Kirby. 1993. 435.00 (*0-8103-8017-X*) Gale.

Directory of Special Libraries, 2 vols., Vol. 1. 18th ed. Kirby. 1994. 435.00 (*0-8103-8524-4*) Gale.

Directory of Special Libraries, Vol. 1, Pt. 1 A-N. 17th ed. Kirby. 1993. write for info. (*0-8103-8018-8*) Gale.

Directory of Special Libraries, Vol. 1, Pt. 1 A-N. 18th ed. Kirby. 1994. write for info. (*0-8103-8525-2*) Gale.

Directory of Special Libraries, Vol. 1, Pt. 2 C-Z. 17th ed. Kirby. 1993. write for info. (*0-8103-8019-6*) Gale.

Directory of Special Libraries, Vol. 1, Pt. 2 O-Z. 18th ed. Kirby. 1994. write for info. (*0-8103-8526-0*) Gale.

Directory of Special Libraries, Vol. 2. 18th ed. Kirby. 1994. 380.00 (*0-8103-8527-9*) Gale.

Directory of Special Programs for Minority Group Members: Career Information Services, Employment Skills Banks, Financial Aid Sources. 5th ed. Ed. by Willis L. Johnson. LC 73-93533. (Illus.). 320p. (Orig.). 1990. pap. 30.00 (*0-912048-89-1*) Garrett Pk.

Directory of Specialized American Bookdealers. 3rd ed. Ed. by American Book Collector Magazine Staff. 520p. 1987. 47.50 (*0-89679-013-4*) Moretus Pr.

Directory of Specialized American Bookdealers, 1981-1982. Ed. by American Book Collector Magazine Staff. 1981. 19.95 (*0-89679-005-3*) Moretus Pr.

Directory of Specialized American Bookdealers, 1984-1985. 2nd ed. Comp. by American Book Collector Magazine Staff. xiv, 344p. 1984. lib. bdg. 35.00 (*0-89679-012-6*) Moretus Pr.

Directory of Stained Glass: Books & Patterns Thru 1988. 2nd ed. Melanie Mayo. Ed. by Stained Glass Images Inc. Staff. 208p. 1989. text ed. write for info. (*0-936459-10-7*) Stained Glass.

Directory of Stained Glass Books & Patterns: 1989 Through 1991. 3rd ed. Melanie M. Collins. Ed. by Stained Glass Images Inc. Staff. 116p. Date not set. spiral bd. 19.95 (*0-936459-17-4*) Stained Glass.

***Directory of Stained Glass Books & Patterns, 1992-94.** 4th ed. Melanie M. Collins. Ed. by Stained Glass Images Staff. 110p. (YA). Date not set. 21.95 (*0-936459-31-X*) Stained Glass.

Directory of State Court Clerks & County Courthouses, 1993. 1992. pap. 65.00 (*0-942008-61-8*) Want Pub.

Directory of State Hazardous Waste Officials. Inter-Face Staff. 204p. (Orig.). 1986. pap. 35.00 (*0-318-20050-3*) Interface Assocs.

Directory of State Industrial & Economic Departments, Commerce Departments & Purchasing Agencies. 30p. 1995. 30.00 (*0-317-55623-1*) B Klein Pubns.

***Directory of State Licensing Requirements for Psychologists.** John H. Gagnon. write for info. (*0-471-63615-0*) Wiley.

Directory of States' Biotechnology Centers, 1988. rev. ed. North Carolina Biotechnology Center Staff. 30p. 1988. pap. 10.00 (*0-945597-01-0*) NC Biotech Ctr.

Directory of Statewide Rural & Agricultural Leadership Programs. Ed. by Daryl K. Heasley. 50p. 1987. reprint ed. ring bd. 25.00 (*0-9609010-3-5*) NE Regional Ctr.

Directory of Statistical Microcomputer Software. Wayne A. Woodward et al. LC 85-207901. 472p. reprint ed. pap. 134.60 (*0-8357-6095-2*, 2034578) Bks Demand.

Directory of Statistical Microcomputer Software: 1987-88 Edition. Ed. by Woodward et al. 728p. 1988. 99.75 (*0-8247-7846-4*) Dekker.

Directory of Steel Foundries, 1993-94. 1995. 70.00 (*0-685-28243-0*) Steel Founders.

***Directory of Summer Jobs in Britain 1995.** 26th ed. Emily Hatchwell. 232p. 1995. pap. 15.95 (*1-85458-126-0*, Pub. by Vacation-Work UK) Petersons Guides.

Directory of Summer Music Programs, 1995. Sandy Caviezel. 105p. 1995. pap. 17.95 (*1-885383-02-9*) Music Resources.

Directory of Summer Music Programs, 1996. Sandy Caviezel. 135p. 1996. pap. 16.95 (*1-885383-03-7*) Music Resources. THE DIRECTORY OF SUMMER MUSIC PROGRAMS 1996 is a needed reference for all libraries, high school & college music departments, career counseling offices, music teachers, educational consultants, parents, & music enthusiasts of all ages. THE DIRECTORY is an annual comprehensive compilation of over 750 programs, classes & workshops offered by over 400 national & international organizations. THE DIRECTORY contains over 130 pages (no ads), 8 1/2 by 11, with title, ISBN & press imprinted on a durable comb binding. Program descriptions include information on: major focus, application deadlines, selection process, age & ability levels, faculty, dates of program, living accommodations, all fees for tuition, room & board, program & contact location, availability of private lessons, performance opportunities, & special events. Readers can easily match interests & abilities to programs, classes, & workshops in: classical, rock, pop, folk, jazz, new music, opera, chorus, musical theater, band, orchestra, chamber ensembles, history, theory, conducting, music technology, music education, & recording. Purchase of THE DIRECTORY includes THE NOVEMBER UPDATE OF SUMMER MUSIC PROGRAMS - a 6 page newsletter listing programs with early deadlines in December, January, & February. THE DIRECTORY is published early February. All orders received before January 15, 1996 receive both the 1995 & the 1996 NOVEMBER UPDATE.** ***Publisher Provided Annotation.

Directory of Summer School Programs at Home & Abroad for High School & College Students. Graduate Group Staff. 960p. (Orig.). 1991. pap. 20.00 (*0-685-41474-4*) Graduate Group.

Directory of Supermarket, Grocery & Convenience Store Chains, 1993. Ed. by Ron Bock. 1032p. 1992. pap. 285.00 (*0-86730-575-4*, CSG Info Servs) Lebhar Friedman.

Directory of Surveys in Developing Countries: Data on Families & Households, 1975-1992. Cynthia B. Lloyd & Catherine M. Marquette. LC 92-62578. 1992. pap. 25.00 (*0-87834-074-2*) Population Coun.

Directory of Talent & Model 1992. Chip Brill. 1992. 25.00 (*0-87314-136-9*) Peter Glenn.

***Directory of Tax-Exempt Funds of Health Service Organizations.** 1994. 335.00 (*0-614-04766-8*) Money Mkt.

Directory of Teaching Innovations in Psychology. James B. Maas & Douglas A. Kleiber. 610p. reprint ed. pap. 173.90 (*0-7837-0485-2*, 2040809) Bks Demand.

Directory of Technical & Scientific Directories. Ed. by A. P. Harvey. 280p. 1988. 95.00 (*0-582-00602-3*, Oryx Pr) Longman.

Directory of Technical Co-operation in Statistics. 64p. 1990. 9.00 (*92-1-161318-3*, 90.XVII.10) UN.

Directory of Technical Magazines & Directories. Richard K. Miller. 1982. text ed. 45.00 (*0-915586-33-9*) Fairmont Pr.

Directory of Technical Placement Resources 1988: Southern California Edition. Ed. by Regina Silver. 208p. (Orig.). 1988. pap. text ed. 24.00 (*0-929252-00-4*) Silver Crown.

Directory of Testing Laboratories, Commercial-Institutional. American Society for Testing & Materials Staff. LC 82-71209. (ASTM Special Technical Publication Ser.: No. 333E). 194p. reprint ed. pap. 55.30 (*0-8357-6822-8*, 2035504) Bks Demand.

Directory of Testing Laboratories, 1988. American Society for Testing & Materials Staff. 266p. reprint ed. pap. 75.90 (*0-8357-6821-X*, 2035503) Bks Demand.

Directory of Testing Laboratories, 1991 Edition. American Society for Testing & Materials Staff. LC 88-659052. 374p. reprint ed. pap. 106.60 (*0-7837-4796-9*, 2044837) Bks Demand.

***Directory of Texas Manufacturers, 2 vols., Set.** 1300p. 1995. 130.00 (*0-87755-337-8*) Bureau Busn UT.

Directory of Texas Manufacturers, 2 vols., Set. LC 34-27861. 1300p. (Orig.). 1994. pap. 130.00 (*0-87755-336-X*) Bureau Busn UT.

Directory of Texas Wholesalers, 1992. rev. ed. LC 90-656102. 679p. (Orig.). 1992. pap. 70.00 (*0-87755-328-9*) Bureau Busn UT.

Directory of the American Psychological Society, 1991. Intro. by Sharon Hantman. 494p. 1994. pap. 25.00 (*0-685-35617-5*) Amer Psy Soc.

Directory of the APA, 1993. Ed. by John A. Lazo. 1952p. 1993. 70.00 (*1-55798-210-4*) Am Psychol.

Directory of the Black Caucus of the American Library Association. 10.00 (*0-686-14255-1*) Black Caucus Am Lib.

Directory of the Canning, Freezing, Preserving Industries, 1990-91. 13th ed. Edward E. Judge & Sons, Inc. Staff. Ed. by Daniel P. Judge. 704p. 1990. pap. 125.00 (*1-880821-00-1*) E E Judge & Sons.

Directory of the Canning, Freezing, Preserving Industries, 1992-93. deluxe ed. Edward E. Judge & Sons, Inc. Staff. Ed. by Daniel P. Judge. 1360p. 1990. lib. bdg. 225.00 (*1-880821-01-X*) E E Judge & Sons.

Directory of the Canning, Freezing, Preserving Industries, 1992-93. 2nd ed. Edward E. Judge & Sons, Inc. Ed. by Daniel P. Judge. 1376p. 1992. lib. bdg. 235.00 (*1-880821-04-4*) E E Judge & Sons.

Directory of the Canning, Freezing, Preserving Industries, 1992-93. 14th ed. Edward E. Judge & Sons, Inc. Ed. by Daniel P. Judge. 720p. 1992. pap. 135.00 (*1-880821-03-6*) E E Judge & Sons.

Directory of the Cornell Southeast Asia Program, 1951-1976. Cornell University, Southeast Asia Program. LC 76-379099. (Cornell University, Southeast Asia Program, Data Paper Ser.: No. 103). 88p. reprint ed. pap. 25.10 (*0-317-55768-8*, 2029290) Bks Demand.

D

An Asterisk (*) at the beginning of an entry indicates that the title is appearing in BIP for the first time.

2015

***Directory of the European Commission: December 1993.** European Communities Staff. 151p. 1994. pap. 10.00 (*92-826-7377-4*, CB82-94-278ENC, Pub. by Europ Com) UNIPUB.

***Directory of the European Commission June 1994.** European Communities Staff. 151p. 1994. pap. 10.00 (*92-826-8491-1*, CB84-94-829ENC, Pub. by Europ Com) UNIPUB.

Directory of the Marian Clerics under the Title of the Immaculate Conception of the Most Blessed Virgin Mary. 124p. 1991. pap. write for info. (*0-933820-08-9*) Marian Fathers.

Directory of the Medical Library Association, 1989-90. Medical Library Association Staff. 151p. 1989. pap. 43.75 (*0-912176-27-X*) Med Lib Assn.

Directory of the Medical Library Association, 1990-91. Medical Library Association Staff. 168p. 1990. pap. 43.75 (*0-912176-31-8*) Med Lib Assn.

Directory of the Medical Library Association, 1991-92. Medical Library Association Staff. 175p. 1991. pap. 95.00 (*0-912176-32-6*) Med Lib Assn.

Directory of the Medical Library Association, 1993-94. Medical Library Association Staff. 200p. 1993. pap. 150.00 (*0-912176-35-0*) Med Lib Assn.

***Directory of the Medical Library Association 1993-94.** Medical Library Association Staff. (ISSN: 0543-2772). 196p. 1993. pap. 150.00 (*0-614-01349-6*) Med Lib Assn.

***Directory of the Medical Library Association, 1994-95.** 221p. 1994. pap. 150.00 (*0-912176-36-9*) Med Lib Assn.

***Directory of the Medical Library Association 1994-95.** Medical Library Association Staff. (ISSN: 0543-2772 (Annual)). 221p. 1994. pap. 150.00 (*0-614-01350-X*) Med Lib Assn.

Directory of the Membership, 1994. 100p. 1994. pap. text ed. write for info. (*1-882549-03-1*) Natl Asn Col Aux.

Directory of the Networks. 1973. 2.00 (*0-686-09552-9*) Network Project.

Directory of the Province of Ontario, 1857. Thomas B. Wilson & Emily S. Wilson. 712p. 1987. lib. bdg. 35.00 (*0-912606-30-4*) Hunterdon Hse.

Directory of the World Landslide Inventory. Ed. by William M. Brown, III et al. (Illus.). 163p. (Orig.). 1993. pap. text ed. 60.00 (*1-56806-402-0*) Diane Pub.

***Directory of Theatre Faculties in Colleges & Universities, U. S. & Canada, 1994-95 Edition.** 3rd ed. Intro. by Robby Gunstream. 321p. (Orig.). 1994. pap. 55.00 (*1-881913-03-1*) CMS Pubns.

Directory of Theatre Programs. 3rd ed. Ed. by Robert Wills. 112p. 1987. pap. 9.00 (*0-318-40106-1*) ACA VA.

Directory of Theatre Training Programs. 4th ed. Ed. by Jill Charles. 204p. 1993. pap. 22.95 (*0-933919-25-5*) Theatre Directories.

***Directory of Theatre Training Programs.** 5th ed. Ed. by Jill Charles. 220p. 1995. pap. 24.95 (*0-933919-31-X*) Theatre Directories.

Directory of Theme & Amusement Parks. rev. ed. Ray Carlson & Eleanor Popelka. LC 87-29206. 64p. 1991. pap. 5.95 (*0-87576-138-0*) Pilot Bks.

Directory of Toxic & Related Test Labs. Dominguez. 1991. 58.00 (*0-89116-904-0*) Hemisp Pub.

Directory of Trade Unions in the European Economic Community. Ed. by Micheal Williams. 124p. 1900. 23.00 (*0-86010-118-5*) G & T Inc.

***Directory of Traditional Latin Masses, 1994-1995.** Ed. by M. E. Morrison. 80p. (Orig.). 1994. pap. 10.00 (*1-883511-05-4*) Veritas Pr CA.

Directory of Traditional Music. Ed. by D. Christensen. 100p. 1995. 10.00 (*0-317-01462-5*) Intl Coun Trad.

Directory of Translators & Translating Agencies in the United Kingdom. 2nd ed. Ed. by Philip Morris & Geoff Weston. 352p. 1990. lib. bdg. 65.00 (*0-86291-277-6*) Bowker-Saur.

Directory of Transportation Professionals, 1995. 180p. 1995. 23.00 (*0-317-04703-5*) NARUC.

Directory of Travel Agencies for the Disabled. Helen Hecker. 80p. 1995. pap. 19.95 (*0-933261-04-7*) Twin Peaks Pr.

Directory of Travel Agencies for the Disabled. 3rd ed. Helen Hecker. 1995. audio 19.95 (*0-685-53174-0*); digital audio 19.95 (*0-685-53173-2*) Twin Peaks Pr.

Directory of Treasure Hunting, Prospecting & Related Organizations. John H. Reed. LC 86-63262. 191p. 1987. pap. 12.95 (*0-940519-00-3*) Res Discover Pubns.

Directory of Twenty-Five Hundred Active Real Estate Lenders. 4th ed. Ed. by Tyler G. Hicks. 200p. 1990. pap. 25.00 (*0-934311-75-7*) Intl Wealth.

Directory of Twenty-Five Hundred Active Real Estate Lenders. 5th ed. Ed. by Tyler G. Hicks. 200p. 1992. pap. 25.00 (*1-56150-026-7*) Intl Wealth.

Directory of Twenty-Five Hundred Active Real Estate Lenders. 7th ed. Tyler G. Hicks. 200p. 1994. pap. 25.00 (*1-56150-124-7*) Intl Wealth.

Directory of Two Thousand Five Hundred Active Real Estate Lenders. 6th ed. Tyler G. Hicks. 200p. 1993. pap. 25.00 (*1-56150-076-3*) Intl Wealth.

Directory of Two-Year-Old Buyers. Ed. by Jan Meerdink. 1992. ring bd. 125.00 (*0-685-55023-0*) R Meerdink Co Ltd.

Directory of Two Year Old Buyers, 1989. 253p. ring bd. 125.00 (*0-929346-04-1*) R Meerdink Co Ltd.

Directory of Two Year Old Buyers, 1990. Ed. by Jan Meerdink. 255p. (Orig.). 1990. ring bd. 125.00 (*0-929346-08-4*) R Meerdink Co Ltd.

Directory of U. K. & Irish Republic Geoscience Departments. 52p. (C). 1993. pap. text ed. 6.60 (*0-903317-95-8*, Pub. by Geol Soc Pub Hse UK) AAPG.

Directory of U. S. & Canadian Marketing Surveys & Services: Supplements Through 1983. 4th ed. Ed. by Marian Deitsch. 1981. ring bd. 145.00 (*0-917148-75-4*) Kline.

Directory of U. S. Army Forts, Camps, & Airfields (1789 to 1945) Tom Kneitel. (Illus.). 144p. (Orig.). 1992. pap. 15.95 (*0-939780-16-X*) CRB Res.

***Directory of U. S. Colleges & Universities Offering a Curriculum in Long Term Care Administration & State Board Licensure Requirements for Nursing Home Administrators.** Ed. by Jerome A. Miller & James E. Allen. 284p. (Orig.). (C). 1994. pap. 29.00 (*0-9635064-1-2*) Nat Asn Bds Exam.

Directory of U. S. Credit Bureau. Larry Schwartz & Pearl Sax. 99p. 89.95 (*0-914801-19-8*) Nat Assn Credit.

Directory of U. S. Government Datafiles. 1992. lib. bdg. 475.95 (*0-8490-5582-2*) Gordon Pr.

Directory of U. S. Government Datafiles for Mainframes & Microcomputers. (Orig.). 1993. pap. 65.00 (*0-934213-39-9*, PB93-111557) Natl Tech Info.

***Directory of U. S. Government Datafiles for Mainframes & Microcomputers.** 400p. 1995. pap. text ed. 65.00 (*0-934213-43-7*) Natl Tech Info.

Directory of U. S. Government Inventions. 1480p. 1991. pap. 225.00 (*1-56868-010-4*) Gov Data Pubns.

Directory of U. S. Government Inventions. (Illus.). 1480p. (Orig.). (C). 1994. pap. 395.00 (*0-7881-0430-6*) Diane Pub.

Directory of U. S. Government Software for Mainframes & Microcomputers. (Orig.). 1993. pap. text ed. 65.00 (*0-934213-37-2*, PB93-111565) Natl Tech Info.

***Directory of U. S. Government Software for Mainframes & Microcomputers.** 300p. (Orig.). 1995. pap. text ed. 65.00 (*0-934213-44-5*) Natl Tech Info.

***Directory of U. S. Government Software for Mainframes & Microcomputers: 1994 Edition.** 250p. (Orig.). (C). 1994. pap. text ed. 95.00x (*0-7881-1184-1*) Diane Pub.

***Directory of U. S. Labor Organizations, 1994-95 Edition.** Courtney D. Gifford. 124p. 1994. pap. 45.00 (*0-87179-850-6*) BNA.

***Directory of U. S. Marine Oceans CD-ROM's.** Ed. by Lynda S. Kuntz et al. (Illus.). 102p. (Orig.). (C). 1994. pap. text ed. 45.00x (*0-7881-1305-4*) Diane Pub.

Directory of U. S. Nursing Homes & Nursing Home Chains, 1994. Heidi M. Garrett. 1994. write for info. (*1-56363-071-0*) Med Econ Data.

Directory of U. S. Resources on the Rule of Law for the Independent States of the Former Soviet Union. Intro. by Samuel W. Lewis. LC 92-33149. (Orig.). 1992. pap. 14.95 (*1-878379-16-X*) US Inst Peace.

***Directory of U. S. Trademarks: All Class, 1995 Edition, Vols. VIII, IX & X.** Thomson & Thomson Staff. Ed. by Lisa M. DePasquale. 4382p. 1995. pap. 315.00 (*1-57123-022-X*) Thomson & Thomson.

***Directory of U. S. Trademarks: Class-by-Class, All Class & Updates, 1995 Edition.** 2nd ed. Thomson & Thomson Staff. Ed. by Lisa M. DePasquale. 16810p. 1995. pap. 1,190.00 (*1-57123-014-9*) Thomson & Thomson.

Directory of U. S. Trademarks: Class-by-Class & All Class & Updates, 10 vols. Thomson & Thomson Staff. (Nineteen Ninety-Four Edition Ser.). 15896p. 1994. pap. 1,145.00 (*1-57123-002-5*) Thomson & Thomson.

***Directory of U. S. Trademarks: Class-by-Class, 1995 Edition, Vol. I.** Thomson & Thomson Staff. Ed. by Lisa M. DePasquale. 1341p. 1995. pap. 225.00 (*1-57123-015-7*) Thomson & Thomson.

***Directory of U. S. Trademarks: Class-by-Class, 1995 Edition, Vol. II.** Thomson & Thomson Staff. Ed. by Lisa M. DePasquale. 1472p. 1995. pap. 225.00 (*1-57123-016-5*) Thomson & Thomson.

***Directory of U. S. Trademarks: Class-by-Class, 1995 Edition, Vol. III.** Thomson & Thomson Staff. Ed. by Lisa M. DePasquale. 1340p. 1995. pap. 225.00 (*1-57123-017-3*) Thomson & Thomson.

***Directory of U. S. Trademarks: Class-by-Class, 1995 Edition, Vol. IV.** Thomson & Thomson Staff. Ed. by Lisa M. DePasquale. 1318p. 1995. pap. 225.00 (*1-57123-018-1*) Thomson & Thomson.

***Directory of U. S. Trademarks: Class-by-Class, 1995 Edition, Vol. V.** Thomson & Thomson Staff. Ed. by Lisa M. DePasquale. 1061p. 1995. pap. 225.00 (*1-57123-019-X*) Thomson & Thomson.

***Directory of U. S. Trademarks: Class-by-Class, 1995 Edition, Vol. VI.** Thomson & Thomson Staff. Ed. by Lisa M. DePasquale. 1142p. 1995. pap. 225.00 (*1-57123-020-3*) Thomson & Thomson.

***Directory of U. S. Trademarks: Class-by-Class, 1995 Edition, Vol. VII.** Thomson & Thomson Staff. Ed. by Lisa M. DePasquale. 1554p. 1995. pap. 225.00 (*1-57123-021-1*) Thomson & Thomson.

Directory of U. S. Trademarks: First Update, Second Update, Third Update. Thomson & Thomson Staff. (Nineteen Ninety-Four Edition Ser.). 2419p. 1994. pap. 430.00 (*1-57123-011-4*) Thomson & Thomson.

***Directory of U. S. Trademarks: First Update, Second Update, Third Update, 1995 Edition.** Thomson & Thomson Staff. Ed. by Lisa M. DePasquale. 3200p. 1995. pap. 445.00 (*1-57123-023-8*) Thomson & Thomson.

Directory of U. S. Trademarks, Vol. I: Class-by-Class. Thomson & Thomson Staff. (Nineteen Ninety-Four Edition Ser.). 1452p. 1994. pap. 215.00 (*1-57123-003-3*) Thomson & Thomson.

Directory of U. S. Trademarks, Vol. II: Class-by-Class. Thomson & Thomson Staff. (Nineteen Ninety-Four Edition Ser.). 1467p. 1994. pap. 215.00 (*1-57123-004-1*) Thomson & Thomson.

Directory of U. S. Trademarks, Vol. III: Class-by-Class. Thomson & Thomson Staff. (Nineteen Ninety-Four Edition Ser.). 1422p. 1994. pap. 215.00 (*1-57123-005-X*) Thomson & Thomson.

Directory of U. S. Trademarks, Vol. IV: Class-by-Class. Thomson & Thomson Staff. (Nineteen Ninety-Four Edition Ser.). 1356p. 1994. pap. 215.00 (*1-57123-006-8*) Thomson & Thomson.

Directory of U. S. Trademarks, Vol. V: Class-by-Class. Thomson & Thomson Staff. (Nineteen Ninety-Four Edition Ser.). 1110p. 1994. pap. 215.00 (*1-57123-007-6*) Thomson & Thomson.

Directory of U. S. Trademarks, Vol. VI: Class-by-Class. Thomson & Thomson Staff. (Nineteen Ninety-Four Edition Ser.). 1076p. 1994. pap. 215.00 (*0-685-71185-4*) Thomson & Thomson.

Directory of U. S. Trademarks, Vol. VII: Class-by-Class. Thomson & Thomson Staff. (Nineteen Ninety-Four Edition Ser.). 1442p. 1994. pap. 215.00 (*1-57123-008-4*) Thomson & Thomson.

Directory of U. S. Trademarks, Vols. VIII, IX & X: All Class. Thomson & Thomson Staff. (Nineteen Ninety-Four Edition Ser.). 4121p. 1994. pap. 305.00 (*1-57123-010-6*) Thomson & Thomson.

Directory of UK Space Capabilities 1991. 270p. 1991. pap. 95.00 (*0-11-515268-7*, HM2768) UNIPUB.

***Directory of Undergraduate Internships in the Humanities.** fac. ed. Modern Language Association of America Staff. LC 84-25486. 154p. 1984. reprint ed. pap. 43.90 (*0-7837-8037-0*, 2047793) Bks Demand.

Directory of Undergraduate Political Science Faculty, 1993-1995. 4th ed. American Political Science Association Staff. 160p. (C). 1993. pap. text ed. 35.00 (*1-878147-10-2*) Am Political.

Directory of Unique Museums. Ed. by Bill Truesdell. LC 85-42726. 176p. 1985. pap. 29.95 (*0-89774-197-8*) Oryx Pr.

Directory of United Nations Databases & Information Services. 4th ed. 484p. 1990. 40.00 (*92-1-100349-0*, GV.90.0.1) UN.

Directory of United Nations Serial Publications, 1988. 500p. 1988. 30.00 (*92-1-100337-7*, EGV.87.0.3) UN.

Directory of Unpublished Experimental Mental Measures, Vol. 1: Through 1970, Vol. 1. Ed. by Bert A. Goldman & John Saunders. LC 73-17342. 223p. (C). 1974. 49.95 (*0-87705-130-5*) Human Sci Pr.

Directory of Unpublished Experimental Mental Measures, Vol. 2: 1971-1972. Ed. by Bert A. Goldman. LC 73-17342. 518p. 1978. 49.95 (*0-87705-300-6*) Human Sci Pr.

Directory of Unpublished Experimental Mental Measures, Vol. 4: 1974-1980. Ed. by Bert A. Goldman & Larry Osborne. 288p. 1985. 49.95 (*0-89885-100-9*) Human Sci Pr.

Directory of Unpublished Experimental Mental Measures, 1973: 1973-74, Vol. 3. Ed. by Bert A. Goldman & John C. Busch. LC 73-17342. 448p. 1982. 49.95 (*0-89885-095-9*) Human Sci Pr.

Directory of Unusual Majors. rev. ed. Ed. by Roberta Carr. 100p. 1991. pap. text ed. 25.00 (*1-880468-01-8*) Col Connect.

Directory of U.S. Government Data Files for Mainframes & Microcomputers. 147p. (Orig.). (C). 1993. pap. text ed. 125.00 (*1-56806-399-7*) Diane Pub.

Directory of U.S. Military Bases Worldwide. 2nd ed. Ed. by William R. Evinger. LC 94-38709. 416p. 1994. 125.00 (*0-89774-822-0*) Oryx Pr.

Directory of Value Added Resellers, 1993. Ed. by Kim Reinhardt. 884p. pap. 275.00 (*0-685-65052-9*, CSG Info Servs) Lebhar Friedman.

Directory of Vendors of Latin American Library Materials. 4th rev. ed. Howard L. Karno & Beverly Joy-Karno. (Bibliography & Reference Ser.: No. 32). vii, 42p. (Orig.). 1993. pap. 19.50 (*0-917617-35-5*) SALALM.

Directory of Victim Assistance Programs & Resources, 1994 Edition. NOVA Staff. 320p. (C). 1994. pap. text ed., spiral bd. 30.00 (*0-8403-9460-8*) Kendall-Hunt.

Directory of Video, Computer & Audio-Visual Products. 40th ed. 650p. 1995. 72.00 (*0-939718-14-6*) Internatl Comms.

Directory of Washington Lobbyists, Lawyers & Interest Groups: Summer 1993. Ed. by Edward Zuckerman. 500p. Date not set. pap. 90.00 (*0-939676-10-9*) Amward Pubns.

***Directory of Washington Lobbyists, Lawyers & Interest Groups: Winter 1995.** Ed. by Edward Zuckerman. 416p. 1995. 97.50 (*0-939676-12-5*) Amward Pubns.

Directory of Waste Utilization Technologies in Europe & the United States. Brenda Platt et al. LC 88-28436. 225p. 1989. pap. text ed. 25.00 (*0-917582-41-1*) Inst Local Self Re.

Directory of Water-Sewer & Related Industries Professionals, 1995. 155p. 1995. 27.00 (*0-317-04704-3*) NARUC.

Directory of Wedding Services & Planner for Spartanburg County, 1989-1990. Sandra Sheldon & Martin Sheldon. (Illus.). 50p. (Orig.). 1989. pap. text ed. 3.75 (*0-9623130-0-9*) Info Servs SC.

Directory of Wetlands of International Importance. Ramsar Convention Bureau Staff. 796p. 1990. 50.00 (*2-8317-0014-0*, Pub. by IUCN SZ) Island Pr.

Directory of Wholesale Grocers, 1993. Ed. by Gael Murphy. 672p. 1992. pap. 260.00 (*0-86730-578-9*, CSG Info Servs) Lebhar Friedman.

Directory of Wholesale Printing & Office Supplies Sources. 1987. lib. bdg. 69.95 (*0-8490-3866-9*) Gordon Pr.

Directory of Wholesale Printing & Office Supply Sources. Joe Soukup. 1991. pap. 10.00 (*0-915665-22-0*) Premier Publishers.

Directory of Wisconsin Owned & Managed Mutual Funds. 1988. pap. 5.00 (*0-318-23654-0*) UWIM CCA.

Directory of Women Business Owners: Megamarketplace East-West, 1987. 264p. (Orig.). 1987. pap. 12.00 (*0-16-000184-6*, S/N 003-000-00651-4) USGPO.

Directory of Women in African Studies. Comp. by African Studies Association, Women's Caucus Staff. 1984. pap. 8.00 (*0-918456-53-3*) African Studies Assn.

Directory of Women's & Childrens Wear Specialty Stores, 1993. Ed. by Jennifer Nemetz. 1100p. 1992. pap. 180.00 (*0-86730-569-X*, CSG Info Servs) Lebhar Friedman.

Directory of Women's Health Care Centers: In Cooperation with the National Association of Women's Health Professionals. Oryx Press Staff. 160p. 1989. pap. 45.00 (*0-89774-525-6*) Oryx Pr.

Directory of Women's Media. Ed. by Paulette Tulloch. 272p. 1992. pap. text ed. 30.00 (*1-880547-07-4*) Nat Coun Res Wom.

Directory of Women's Studies Programs & Library Resources. Ed. by Beth Stafford. 176p. 1990. pap. 55.00 (*0-89774-507-8*) Oryx Pr.

Directory of Wooden Boat Builders. WoodenBoat Magazine Staff. 1987. pap. text ed. 9.50 (*0-07-157317-8*) McGraw.

***Directory of Wooden Boat Builders & Designers.** 1994. 14.95 (*0-937822-30-2*) WoodenBoat Pubns.

***Directory of Worker's Compensation.** Date not set. 149.00 (*1-56925-027-8*, WCDI) Capitol Publns.

***Directory of Workers' Compensation Managed Care Organizations, 1995.** Ed. by Kathleen Gutman. 304p. 1994. pap. 149.00 (*1-884561-00-4*) Capitol Publns.

Directory of Workers' Education Institutions & Programmes in Developing Countries. 2nd ed. 244p. (ENG & FRE.). 1982. 22.00 (*92-2-003347-X*) Intl Labour Office.

Directory of Works in Progress: Research on Women. Ed. by Debra Schultz. 464p. 1992. pap. text ed. 30.00 (*1-880547-09-0*) Nat Coun Res Wom.

Directory of World Futures & Options Markets. M. J. Robertson. 656p. 1990. boxed 125.00 (*0-13-217951-2*) P-H.

Directory of World Sports Cars: Group C & IMSA Cars from 1982. Mike Cotton. (Illus.). 81p. 1988. pap. 21.95 (*0-946627-38-X*, Pub. by Aston Pubns UK) Motorbooks Intl.

Directory of World Stock Exchanges. Economist Publications Staff. LC 88-2353. 400p. 1988. text ed. 95.00 (*0-8018-3717-0*) Johns Hopkins.

Directory of Yearling Buyers, 1989. 288p. ring bd. 125.00 (*0-929346-02-5*) R Meerdink Co Ltd.

Directory of Yearling Buyers, 1990. Research Staff of the Russell Meerdink Company. Ed. by Jan Meerdink. 290p. 1990. ring bd. 125.00 (*0-929346-06-8*) R Meerdink Co Ltd.

Directory of Yearling Buyers, 1992. Ed. by Jan Meerdink. 200p. 1992. ring bd. 125.00 (*0-929346-16-5*) R Meerdink Co Ltd.

Directory on European Training Institutions in the Fields of Bilateral & Multilateral Diplomacy, Public Administration & Management, Economic & Social Development. 496p. (ENG & FRE.). 1987. pap. 30.00 (*92-1-057006-5*, EF87.III.K.DS/7) UN.

Directory on Mixed Marriages. Veritas Publications Staff. 1989. pap. 22.00 (*0-86217-111-3*, Pub. by Veritas IE) St Mut.

DIRECTORY Personal Phone Directory Reference Guide. Mohammed Alsaeed. (Illus.). 80p. (Orig.). Date not set. pap. 10.00 (*1-877628-03-4*) Ironwood Winona.

Directory Portable Databases 1990 Oct. 1990. write for info. (*0-318-68469-1*) Gale.

Directory Portable Databases 1992-93, 2 Vols., Vol. 1. Young & Kathleen Y. Marcaccio. 1994. 135.00 (*0-8103-8442-6*) Gale.

Directory Portable Databases 1993 Jan. Young & Kathleen Y. Marcaccio. 1992. write for info. (*0-8103-8440-X*) Gale.

Directory Portable Databases 1994 Apr. Young & Kathleen Y. Marcaccio. 1993. write for info. (*0-8103-8443-4*) Gale.

Directory Portable Databases 1994-95, 2 Vols., Vol. 1. Young & Kathleen Y. Marcaccio. 1995. 140.00 (*0-8103-8448-5*) Gale.

Directory Portable Databases 1995 Apr, Vol. 1. Young & Kathleen Y. Marcaccio. 1994. write for info. (*0-8103-8445-0*) Gale.

Directory to Free Stock Photography 2. LC 80-640589. 88p. 1986. pap. 14.50 (*0-939209-00-4*) Art Dir.

Directory to Industrial Design. Charles H. Burnette. 256p. 1992. pap. 49.95 (*0-442-00969-0*) Van Nos Reinhold.

***Directory to Limited Edition Collectible Stores.** Ed. by Diane C. Jones. 292p. 1993. pap. 14.95 (*0-930785-14-2*) Collectors Info.

Directory to Medical Product Manufacturing Consultants, 1993: The First Step to Finding a Consultant. 72p. (Orig.). 1993. pap. 15.00 (*0-9618649-8-2*) Canon Comns.

Directory to Secondary Market Retailers: Buying & Selling Limited Edition Artwork. Diane C. Jones. 212p. 1992. pap. 11.95 (*0-930785-10-X*) Collectors Info.

***Directory to Secondary Market Retailers: Your Complete Guide to Buying & Selling Limited Edition.** 2nd ed. 166p. 1994. pap. 11.95 (*0-930785-17-7*) Collectors Info.

Directory to the Bicentennial Inventory of American Painting Executed Before 1914. Smithsonian Institution, National Collection of Fine Arts Staff. 1976. 15.95 (*0-405-09545-7*, 19380) Ayer.

***Directory World Yellow Pages Industry Source Book: 1994-1995 Edition.** SIMBA Information, Inc., Staff. 593p. 1994. write for info. (*0-88709-060-5*) Simba Info Inc.

Directory, 1991-92: Japanese-Affiliated Companies in U. S. A. & Canada. 677p. 1991. pap. 150.00 (*4-8224-0314-9*, Pub. by Japan External Trade JA) Taylor & Francis.

***Dirge for a Dorset Druid.** Margot Arnold. 240p. 1995. pap. 6.00 (*0-88150-334-7*, Foul Play) Countryman.

Dirge for a Dorset Druid: A Penny Spring & Sir Toby Glendower Mystery. Margot Arnold. (Penny Spring & Sir Toby Glendower Mystery Ser.). 240p. 1993. 20.00 (*0-88150-266-9*, Foul Play) Countryman.

An Asterisk (*) at the beginning of an entry indicates that the title is appearing in BIP for the first time.

D

An Asterisk (*) at the beginning of an entry indicates that the title is appearing in BIP for the first time.

2017

Disability Benefits: Delivery of Disability Living Allowance & Disability Working. HMSO Staff. 74p. 1993. pap. 30.00 (*0-10-020313-2*, HM03132, Pub. by HMSO UK) UNIPUB.

Disability Benefits: Factors Determining Applications & Awards. Ed. by Han Emanuel et al. (Contemporary Studies in Economic & Financial Analysis: Vol. 59). 1987. 73.25 (*0-89232-824-X*) Jai Pr.

Disability Business: Political Economy of Rehabilitation in America. Gary L. Albrecht. (Library of Social Research: Vol. 190). 320p. (C). 1992. text ed. 49.95 (*0-8039-3630-3*); pap. text ed. 24.00 (*0-8039-3631-1*) Sage.

Disability, Civil Rights, & Public Policy: The Politics of Implementation. Stephen L. Percy. LC 89-30317. 328p. (C). 1990. pap. 21.95 (*0-8173-0668-4*) U of Ala Pr.

Disability Determination: The Administrative Process & the Role of Medical Personnel. Frank S. Bloch. LC 91-33483. (Studies in Social Welfare Policies & Programs: No. 13). 248p. 1992. text ed. 49.95 (*0-313-27638-2*, BNP/, Greenwood Pr) Greenwood.

***Disability, Discrimination, & Equal Opportunities: A Comparative Study of the Employment Rights of Disabled Persons.** Brian Doyle. LC 94-34931. (Studies in Labor & Social Law). 320p. 1995. 85.00 (*0-7201-2242-2*, Mansell Pub); pap. 30.00 (*0-7201-2244-9*, Mansell Pub) Cassell.

Disability Discrimination in Employment. John J. Coleman. LC 91-22911. 1991. ring bd. 125.00 (*0-87632-818-4*) Clark Boardman Callaghan.

Disability Discrimination in Employment Law. Robert L. Burgdorf, Jr. & Chai R. Feldblum. 1995. text ed. 195.00 (*0-87179-744-5*, 0744) BNA.

Disability Drama in Television & Film. Lauri E. Klobas. LC 88-42520. 496p. 1988. lib. bdg. 55.00 (*0-89950-309-8*) McFarland & Co.

***Disability Etiquette in the Workplace.** Patricia Morrissey. 38p. 1991. 20.00 (*0-916559-35-1*, 2032-TM-4045) EPF.

Disability Etiquette in the Workplace: Special Legi-Slate Edition. Patricia A. Morrisey. 64p. 1993. pap. text ed. write for info. (*1-880955-02-4*) Legi-Slate.

Disability Evaluation in Biomedicine: Subject Analysis & Research Index with Bibliography. Roy R. Zimmerman. LC 83-48720. 159p. 1984. 37.50 (*0-88164-080-8*); pap. 29.50 (*0-88164-081-6*) ABBE Pubs Assn.

Disability Evaluation of the Musculoskeletal System. Charles H. Epps, Jr. 1993. text ed. write for info. (*0-397-50922-7*) Lippincott.

Disability Handbook. Alan Balsam & Albert P. Zabin. LC 90-49913. (Illus.). 1100p. 1990. text ed. 95.00 (*0-07-172213-0*) Shepards-McGraw.

Disability Handbook. HMSO Staff. 311p. 1992. pap. 30.00 (*0-11-761907-8*, HM6170, Pub. by HMSO UK) UNIPUB.

Disability Helper's Guide to Mastering Resistance & Motivating Change. Gene L. Dent. (Practical Management Ser.). (C). 1991. pap. write for info. (*1-878403-04-4*) Martin-Dennison Pr.

Disability in America: Toward a National Agenda for Prevention. Institute of Medicine Staff. 376p. 1991. 29.95 (*0-309-04378-6*) Natl Acad Pr.

Disability in the United States: A Comprehensive Review of the State of the Knowledge. Ed. by Susan Thompson-Hoffman & Inez Storck. 280p. 1991. 38.95 (*0-8261-6770-5*) Springer Pub.

Disability Income: The Sale, the Product, the Market. Jeff Sadler. LC 91-61719. 304p. (Orig.). 1991. pap. 31.95 (*0-87218-487-0*) Natl Underwriter.

Disability Income Insurance. Ed. by Thomas O'Hare & Sherry Schlossnagle. 41p. (Orig.). 1993. pap. text ed. write for info. (*1-879143-23-2*) Health Ins Assn Am.

Disability Income Insurance: The Unique Risks. 2nd ed. Charles E. Soule. 300p. 1988. text ed. 50.00 (*1-55623-182-2*) Irwin Prof Pubng.

Disability Income Insurance: The Unique Risks. 3rd ed. Charles E. Soule. 300p. 1993. text ed. 50.00 (*1-55623-958-0*) Irwin Prof Pubng.

Disability Issues in Public Policy. Ed. by Sara Watson & David Pfeiffer. (Orig.). 1993. pap. 12.00 (*0-944285-35-X*) Pol Studies.

Disability Law Compliance Manual. Gary S. Marx & Gary G. Goldberger. 1991. text ed. 135.00 (*0-685-69658-8*, DLCM) Warren Gorham & Lamont.

Disability Law Compliance Report. Gary Marx. 130.00 (*0-685-69659-6*, ADAR) Warren Gorham & Lamont.

Disability Law in the United States: A Legislative History of the Americans with Disabilities Act of 1990, Public Law 101-336, 6 vols. Bernard D. Reams et al. LC 92-28987. (Federal Disabilities Laws Ser.). 3470p. 1992. 550.00 (*0-89941-797-3*, 307400) W S Hein.

Disability, Liberation & Development. Peter Coleridge. 160p. (C). 1993. text ed. 80.00 (*0-85598-194-6*, Pub. by Oxfam Pubns UK); pap. text ed. 28.00 (*0-85598-195-4*, Pub. by Oxfam Pubns UK) St Mut.

Disability Management: A Complete System to Reduce Costs, Increase Productivity, Meet Employee Needs, & Ensure Legal Compliance. Sheila H. Akabas et al. 288p. 1992. 59.95 (*0-8144-5027-X*) AMACOM.

***Disability Medical Handbook.** 400p. (C). 1994. 395.00 (*0-7605-0655-8*) Rector Pr.

***Disability Oppression.** Maurianne Adams. 86p. (C). 1994. 15.00 (*0-7872-0035-2*) Kendall-Hunt.

Disability Policies & Government Programs. Ed. by Edward D. Berkowitz et al. 206p. 1979. 33.95 (*0-03-051431-2*, Praeger Pubs) Greenwood.

Disability Policy. Ed. by William Johnson. 240p. (Orig.). 1987. pap. 12.00 (*0-918592-94-1*) Pol Studies.

***Disability Politics & Practice.** Ed. by Sara Watson & David Pfeiffer. 192p. (Orig.). 1994. pap. 12.00 (*0-944285-37-6*) Pol Studies.

Disability Practice Manual, 3 vols., Set. 1988. pap. 55.00 (*0-933945-01-9*) Legal Coun Elderly.

Disability Practice Manual, 1992: SSI & Social Security, 3 vols., Set. 600p. 1993. pap. 75.00 (*0-933945-08-6*) Legal Coun Elderly.

Disability Prevention: The Global Challenge. Ed. by John Wilson. (Illus.). 1984. 19.95 (*0-19-261375-8*) OUP.

Disability, Sexuality, & Abuse: An Annotated Bibliography. Sobsey. 208p. 1991. pap. 27.00 (*1-55766-068-9*, 0689) P H Brookes.

Disability Statistics Compendium. 356p. 1990. 49.00 (*92-1-161324-8*, 90.XVII.17) UN.

Disability, Stigma, & Recovery: The Patient As Anthropologist. Jimmie R. Rankin. (Literature of a Patient Response Ser.). 75p. 1994. pap. 14.95 (*1-883938-13-9*) Dry Bones Pr.

Disability Studies: A Reader. Stuart Carruthers & Jim Sandu. 220p. 1994. pap. 34.00 (*1-85302-189-X*, Pub. by J Kingsley Pubs UK) Taylor & Francis.

Disability, Theatre & Education. Richard Tomlinson. LC 83-49406. (Human Horizon Ser.). (Illus.). 186p. (Orig.). 1982. pap. 17.95 (*0-253-31779-7*) Brookline Bks.

Disability Under the Social Security Act: An Outline & Analysis of Caselaw. 1986. 25.00 (*0-685-30193-1*, 40, 685) NCLS Inc.

Disability, Work & Social Policy: Models for Social Welfare. Aliki Coudroglou & Dennis L. Poole. (Social Work Ser.: Vol. 2). 160p. 1984. 20.95 (*0-8261-4520-5*) Springer Pub.

Disability Workbook for Social Security Applicants: Managing Your Application for Disability Insurance Benefits. 2nd ed. Douglas M. Smith. Ed. by Barbara W. Smith. (Illus.). 180p. 1993. 18.95 (*1-878140-01-9*) Phys Dis Servs.

Disabled & Their Parents: A Counseling Challenge. Leo F. Buscaglia. LC 75-13822. 382p. 1983. 14.95 (*0-943432-13-8*) SLACK Inc.

Disabled & Their Parents: A Counseling Challenge. rev. ed. Leo F. Buscaglia. LC 83-50284. 398p. 1989. pap. 22.95 (*0-8050-1079-3*, Owl) H Holt & Co.

***Disabled & Their Parents: A Counseling Challenge.** 3rd rev. ed. Leo Buscaglia. 420p. 1994. pap. 22.95 (*1-55642-257-1*) SLACK Inc.

Disabled Child in the Library see Disabilities, Children, & Libraries: Mainstreaming Services in Public Libraries & School Media Centers

Disabled Children: Services, Transport & Education. Howard Meltzer et al. 162p. 1989. pap. 35.00 (*0-11-691266-9*, HM2669) UNIPUB.

Disabled, Female, & Proud! Stories of Ten Women with Disabilities. Harilyn Rousso et al. LC 93-26049. (Illus.). 1993. pap. text ed. 12.95 (*0-89789-358-1*, Bergin & Garvey) Greenwood.

Disabled God: Toward a Liberation Theology of Disability. Nancy L. Eiesland. LC 94-8887. 160p. (Orig.). 1994. pap. 13.95 (*0-687-10801-2*) Abingdon.

Disabled in the Soviet Union: Past & Present, Theory & Practice. Ed. by William O. McCagg & Lewis Siegelbaum. LC 89-40206. (Series in Russian & East European Studies). 310p. 1989. 49.95 (*0-8229-3622-4*) U of Pittsburgh Pr.

Disabled Learner. Ed. by Paul Satz & J. L. Ross. (Modern Approaches to the Diagnosis & Instruction of Multi-Handicapped Children Ser.: Vol. 8). xvi, 298p. 1973. 38.75 (*90-237-4107-2*, Pub. by Swets Pub Serv NE) Taylor & Francis.

Disabled Man & His Vocational Adjustment: A Study of the Types of Jobs Held by 4,404 Orthopedic Cases in Relation to the Specific Disability. Roy N. Anderson. Ed. by William R. Phillips & Janet Rosenberg. LC 79-6893. (Physically Handicapped in Society Ser.). 1980. reprint ed. lib. bdg. 17.95 (*0-405-13104-6*) Ayer.

Disabled People. Pam Adams. (Who Cares Ser.). (J). (gr. 4 up). 1990. 7.95 (*0-85953-361-1*); pap. 3.95 (*0-85953-351-4*) Childs Play.

Disabled People As Second Class Citizens. Myron G. Eisenberg et al. (Series on Rehabilitation: Vol. 2). (Illus.). 320p. 1982. 31.95 (*0-8261-3220-0*) Springer Pub.

Disabled Persons: Their Education & Rehabilitation. Oscar M. Sullivan & Kenneth O. Snortum. Ed. by William R. Phillips & Janet Rosenberg. LC 79-6925. (Physically Handicapped in Society Ser.). 1980. reprint ed. lib. bdg. 61.95 (*0-405-13132-1*) Ayer.

Disabled Persons - Statistical Data, Vol. 2: B, DK, E, IRL, I, UK. Eurostat Staff. 200p. 1992. pap. 35.00 (*92-826-4966-0*, CA-75-92-437-EN-C, Pub. by Europ Com) UNIPUB.

Disabled Persons & Earthquake Hazards. Kathleen J. Tierney et al. (Program on Environment & Behavior Monograph Ser.: No. 46). 165p. (Orig.). (C). 1988. pap. 10.00 (*0-685-28120-5*) Natural Hazards.

Disabled Persons & the Law. Bruce D. Sales et al. LC 82-9089. (Law, Society, & Policy Ser.: Vol. 1). 902p. 1982. 125.00 (*0-306-41094-X*, Plenum Pr) Plenum.

Disabled Person's Job Search Organizer: PLUS...Things You Need to Know about ADA Title I & Now You're Not Afraid to Ask!! Valentino W. Nardo & Anthony J. Landry. LC 92-3975. 94p. 1992. pap. 7.95 (*0-9632679-1-4*) LanNar Pub.

Disabled Physician: Problem - Solving Strategies for the Medical Staff. Daniel A. Lang. LC 89-6673. 148p. (Orig.). 1989. 37.50 (*1-55648-033-4*, 145103) AHPI.

Disabled Policy: America's Programs for the Handicapped. Edward D. Berkowitz. (C). 1989. pap. 19.95 (*0-521-38930-5*) Cambridge U Pr.

Disabled Reader: Education of the Dyslexic Child. Ed. by John Money. LC 66-20713. 441p. reprint ed. pap. 125.70 (*0-8357-9266-8*, 2011900) Bks Demand.

Disabled Readers: Insight, Assessment, Instruction. Ed. by Diane J. Sawyer. LC 79-17153. 137p. (Orig.). reprint ed. pap. 39.10 (*0-8357-8599-8*, 2034976) Bks Demand.

Disabled Soldier. Douglas C. McMurtrie. Ed. by William R. Phillips & Janet Rosenberg. LC 79-6921. (Physically Handicapped in Society Ser.). (Illus.). 1980. reprint ed. lib. bdg. 25.95 (*0-405-13140-2*) Ayer.

Disabled State. Deborah A. Stone. (Health, Society, & Policy Ser.). 295p. 1986. pap. 17.95 (*0-87722-362-9*) Temple U Pr.

Disabled Tankers: Report of Studies on Drift & Towage. OCIMF Staff. 1981. 450.00 (*0-900886-63-3*, Pub. by Witherby & Co UK) St Mut.

Disabled, the Media, & the Information Age. Ed. by Jack A. Nelson. LC 93-7700. (Contributions to the Study of Mass Media & Communications Ser.: No. 42). 264p. 1994. text ed. 55.00 (*0-313-28472-5*, NDM/, Greenwood Pr) Greenwood.

Disabled Veterans Programs: U. S. Eligibility & Benefit Types Compared with Five Other Countries. (Illus.). 96p. (Orig.). (C). 1994. pap. text ed. 50.00 (*0-7881-0561-2*) Diane Pub.

Disabled Village Children: A Guide for Health Workers, Rehabilitation Workers & Families. David Werner. LC 86-81738. (Illus.). 672p. (Orig.). 1987. pap. 15.00 (*0-942364-06-6*) Hesperian Found.

Disabled We Stand. Allan T. Sutherland. LC 83-49408. 159p. 1988. pap. 17.95 (*0-253-21255-3*) Brookline Bks.

Disabled Youth: From School to Work. OECD Staff. 70p. (Orig.). 1991. pap. 16.00 (*92-64-13448-4*) OECD.

***Disabled Youth & Employment.** OECD Staff. 135p. (Orig.). 1994. pap. 13.00x (*92-64-14152-9*) OECD.

Disablement in the Community. Donald L. Patrick & Hedle Peach. (Illus.). 248p. 1989. pap. 39.95 (*0-19-261434-7*) OUP.

Disabling Barriers - Enabling Environments. John Swain et al. 320p. (C). 1993. text ed. 65.00 (*0-8039-8824-9*); pap. text ed. 22.95 (*0-8039-8825-7*) Sage.

***Disabling Laws, Enabling Acts: Disability Rights in Britain & America.** Caroline Gooding & Ziauddin Sardar. (Law & Social Theory Ser.). (C). 1994. pap. text ed. 16.95 (*0-7453-0771-X*, Pub. by Pluto Pr UK) Westview.

***Disabling Laws, Enabling Acts: Disability Rights in Britain & America.** Caroline Gooding. LC 94-26208. (Law & Social Theory Ser.). (C). 1994. text ed. 68.00 (*0-7453-0770-1*, Pub. by Pluto Pr UK) Westview.

Disabling Policies? A Comparative Approach to Education, Policy & Disability. Gillian Fulcher. 300p. 1989. 70.00 (*1-85000-315-7*, Falmer Pr); pap. 38.00 (*1-85000-316-5*, Falmer Pr) Taylor & Francis.

Disabling Professions. Ivan Illich et al. (Ideas in Progress Ser.). 128p. 1987. reprint ed. pap. 9.95 (*0-7145-2510-3*) M Boyars Pubs.

Disadvantage & Education. Jo Mortimore & Tessa Blackstone. (SSRC-DHSS Studies in Deprivation & Disadvantage: No. 4). 216p. 1982. text ed. 28.95 (*0-435-82608-5*) Ashgate Pub Co.

Disadvantaged Gifted see Reaching for the Stars: A Minicourse for Education of Gifted Students

Disadvantaged Post-Adolescents: Approaches to Education & Rehabilitation. Reuvan Kohen-Raz. (Special Aspects of Education Ser.: Vol. 1). 233p. 1983. text ed. 72.00 (*0-677-06010-6*) Gordon & Breach.

Disadvantages of Inequality: A Study of Social Deprivation. Richard Berthoud. (Illus.). 1976. text ed. 25.00 (*0-8464-0338-2*) Beekman Pubs.

Disaffected Patriots: London Supporters of Revolutionary America. John Sainsbury. 364p. 1986. 44.95 (*0-7735-0556-3*, Pub. by McGill CN) U of Toronto Pr.

Disaffection & Diversity: Overcoming Barriers for Adult Learners. Ed. by Judith Calder. LC 92-27883. 224p. 1992. 95.00 (*0-7507-0117-X*, Falmer Pr); pap. 34.00 (*0-7507-0118-8*, Falmer Pr) Taylor & Francis.

Disaffection from School. Ken Reid. 230p. 1988. pap. text ed. 15.95 (*0-423-51550-0*) Routledge Chapman & Hall.

Disaffection from Schooling: An Early Years Perspectives. Ed. by Gill Barrett. 250p. 1989. 60.00 (*1-85000-440-4*, Falmer Pr); pap. 30.00 (*1-85000-441-2*, Falmer Pr) Taylor & Francis.

Disaggregation: Problems in Manufacturing & Service Organizations. Ed. by Larry P. Ritzman et al. 1979. lib. bdg. 96.00 (*0-89838-003-0*) Kluwer Ac.

Disaggregation in Economic Modelling. T. S. Barker & M. H. Pesaran. 320p. 1989. 39.95 (*0-415-00918-9*, A4140) Routledge.

Disagreeable Woman. Horatio Alger. 1976. lib. bdg. 14.95 (*0-88411-809-6*, Aeonian Pr) Amereon Ltd.

Disagreeable Woman: A Social Mystery. Horatio Alger, Jr. 190p. 1978. reprint ed. 24.00 (*0-686-35752-3*) G K Westgard.

Disagreeing with the IRS: Tax Guide 503. Holmes F. Crouch. Ed. by Irma J. Crouch. LC 92-73886. (Five Hundred: Audits & Appeals Ser.). (Illus.). 224p. 1992. pap. text ed. 16.95 (*0-944817-16-5*) Allyear Tax.

Disappearance. James Cohen. 1991. mass mkt. 4.50 (*1-55817-488-5*, Pinnacle NY) Windsor NY.

Disappearance. Rosa Guy. 256p. (J). (gr. 7 up). 1992. pap. 3.50 (*0-440-92064-7*, LFL) Dell.

Disappearance. Yury Trifonov. Tr. by David Lowe. 1991. 23.95 (*0-87501-089-X*) Ardis Pubs.

Disappearance. Colin Wilcox. 17.95 (*0-89190-580-4*, Am Repr) Amereon Ltd.

Disappearance. Philip Wylie. 1993. reprint ed. lib. bdg. 18.95 (*0-89968-415-7*, Lghtyr Pr) Buccaneer Bks.

Disappearance at Harmony Festivel. Eileen Charbonneau. (You-Solve-It Mysteries Ser.: No. 5). 224p. 1994. mass mkt. 3.50 (*0-8217-4674-X*) Zebra.

Disappearance of Childhood. Neil Postman. LC 94-16385. 1994. write for info. (*0-679-75166-1*) Vintage NY.

Disappearance of Gargoyles. Mary Makofske. 64p. (Orig.). 1988. pap. 5.95 (*0-939395-10-X*) Thorntree Pr.

Disappearance of General Jason. Percival C. Wren. 1976. lib. bdg. 18.50 (*0-89968-139-5*, Lghtyr Pr) Buccaneer Bks.

Disappearance of General Jason. Percival C. Wren. 17.95 (*0-8488-1516-5*) Amereon Ltd.

Disappearance of General Jason. Percival C. Wren. 438p. 1973. reprint ed. 15.00 (*0-85468-473-5*) Ultramarine Pub.

***Disappearance of God: A Reverent Investigation of Three Divine Mysteries.** Richard E. Friedman. LC 95-11393. 1995. 24.95 (*0-316-29434-9*) Little.

Disappearance of Introspection. William Lyons. 216p. 1988. 25.00 (*0-262-12115-8*, Bradford Bks); pap. 10.95 (*0-262-62062-6*, Bradford Bks) MIT Pr.

Disappearance of John Longworthy. Maurice F. Egan. 1978. 26.95 (*0-405-10818-4*) Ayer.

Disappearance of Representative Government: A California Solution. Robert T. Monagan. (Illus.). 184p. (Orig.). 1990. pap. 10.95 (*0-933994-10-9*) Comstock Bon.

Disappearance of the American Voter. rev. ed. LC 90-85323. 128p. 1990. pap. 5.00 (*0-89707-608-7*, 357-0011) Amer Bar Assn.

Disappearance of the Butterfly. Takashi Tsujii. Ed. by Thomas Fitzsimmons. Tr. by Robert Brady & Akemi Wegmuller. LC 94-9980. (Asian Poetry in Translation: Japan Ser.: No. 16). 96p. (C). 1994. 24.95 (*0-942668-43-X*); pap. 12.95 (*0-942668-44-8*) Katydid Bks.

Disappearance of the Dowry: Women, Families, & Social Change in Sao Paulo, Brazil, 1600-1900. Muriel Nazzari. 272p. 1991. 37.50 (*0-8047-1928-4*) Stanford U Pr.

Disappearance of the Small Landowner. A. H. Johnson. 1977. lib. bdg. 59.95 (*0-8490-1727-0*) Gordon Pr.

Disappearance of the Small Landowner. Arthur H. Johnson. (Illus.). 176p. 1979. reprint ed. lib. bdg. 29.50 (*0-678-08077-1*) Kelley.

Disappearance of Time: An Essay on the Philosophy of Kurt Godel. Palle Yourgrau. (Illus.). 200p. (C). 1991. 47.95 (*0-521-41012-6*) Cambridge U Pr.

Disappearances. (Illus.). 13p. 1989. pap. 5.00 (*0-9624615-3-9*) Nahan Contemporary.

Disappearances. Paul Auster. 96p. 1989. pap. 12.95 (*0-87951-341-1*) Overlook Pr.

Disappearances. Carol Fuchs. (Unexplained Ser.). 48p. (J). (gr. 3-4). 1991. lib. bdg. 11.95 (*1-56065-041-9*) Capstone Pr.

Disappearances. Howard Mosher. LC 77-22083. 272p. 1984. pap. 12.95 (*0-87923-524-1*) Godine.

Disappearances: A Workbook. Ed. by Becky B. Martos. 168p. (Orig.). 1981. pap. 4.95 (*0-939994-00-3*) Amnesty Intl USA.

Disappearances: Selected Poems. Paul Auster. 96p. 1988. 16.95 (*0-87951-328-4*) Overlook Pr.

***Disappearances & Political Killings: A Manual for Action.** Amnesty International, Dutch Section Staff. (Human Rights Crisis of the 1990s Ser.). 300p. (Orig.). 1994. pap. 16.95 (*0-939994-91-7*) Amnesty Intl USA.

Disappearing ABC Game Book. Hazel S. Gamec. (Illus.). 12p. (J). write for info. (*0-938042-02-5*) Printek.

Disappearing Act. Judy Blundell. (Ghostwriter Ser.). (J). 1994. pap. 3.50 (*0-553-37308-0*) Bantam.

Disappearing Acts. Terry McMillan. Ed. by Jane Rosenman. 384p. 1993. pap. 6.99 (*0-671-87200-1*, Pocket Star Bks) PB.

Disappearing Acts. Terry McMillan. LC 88-40412. 272p. 1989. 23.95 (*0-670-82461-5*) Viking Penguin.

Disappearing Acts. large type ed. Terry McMillan. LC 93-30217. 1993. 24.95 (*1-56895-033-0*) Wheeler Pub.

Disappearing American Voter. Ruy Teixeira. 242p. (C). 1992. 31.95 (*0-8157-8302-7*); pap. 14.95 (*0-8157-8303-5*) Brookings.

Disappearing Bike Shop. Elvira Woodruff. LC 91-29863. 176p. (J). (gr. 3-7). 1992. 13.95 (*0-8234-0933-3*) Holiday.

Disappearing Bike Shop. Elvira Woodruff. (J). (gr. 4-7). 1994. pap. 3.50 (*0-440-40938-1*) Dell.

Disappearing Border: Mexico-United States Relations to the 1990s. Clint E. Smith. (Portable Stanford Book Ser.). (Illus.). 208p. (Orig.). 1992. pap. 12.95 (*0-916318-50-8*) Stanford Alumni Assn.

Disappearing Bridegroom. large type ed. Margaret Erskine. 1991. 21.95 (*0-7089-2408-5*) Ulverscroft.

Disappearing Daily. Oswald G. Villard. LC 69-18939. (Essay Index Reprint Ser.). 1977. 21.95 (*0-8369-0056-1*) Ayer.

Disappearing Dwarf. James P. Blaylock. 288p. (Orig.). 1985. pap. 2.95 (*0-345-33089-7*, Del Rey) Ballantine.

Disappearing Faces: Florida's Animals in Danger. rev. ed. Carol A. Wallin. (Illus.). 64p. (Orig.). (J). (gr. 2 up). 1993. pap. 7.95 (*0-9639432-0-0*) Cardinal FL.

Disappearing Friend Mystery. Created by Gertrude C. Warner. (Boxcar Children Mysteries Ser.: No. 30). 192p. (J). (gr. 2-7). 1992. 10.95 (*0-8075-1627-9*); pap. 3.50 (*0-8075-1628-7*) A Whitman.

Disappearing Granny. Sheila Lavelle. (Banana Bks.). (Illus.). 42p. (J). (gr. 2-4). 1989. 3.95 (*0-8120-6134-9*) Barron.

Disappearing Grasslands. Kevin Cook. LC 93-1193. (Environment Alert! Ser.). (J). 1993. 17.27 (*0-8368-0483-X*) Gareth Stevens Inc.

Disappearing in Mississippi Latitudes, Vol. 2: A Mississippi Trilogy, Vol. 2. Louis D. Brodsky. 121p. 1994. 18.95 (*1-877770-80-9*); pap. 12.50 (*1-877770-81-7*) Time Being Bks.

Disappearing Jewel of Madagascar. Sigmund Brouwer. 132p. 1990. pap. text ed. 4.99 (*0-89693-014-9*) SP Pubns.

***Disappearing Jewel of Madagascar.** Sigmund Brouwer. 132p. (YA). (gr. 8-12). 1990. pap. text ed. 4.99 (*1-56476-373-0*, 6-3373, Victor Books) SP Pubns.

An Asterisk (*) at the beginning of an entry indicates that the title is appearing in BIP for the first time.

An Asterisk (*) at the beginning of an entry indicates that the title is appearing in BIP for the first time.

D

2019

Disaster Survival Planning: A Practical Guide for Businesses: Everything You Need to Know to Develop, Implement, & Test Your Own Recovery Plans. Judy K. Bell. (Illus.). 216p. (Orig.). 1991. 19.95 (0-9630580-0-2) Disaster Survival.

Disaster Teacher's Resource Guide. Irene Welch. Ed. by Liz Parker. (Take Ten Bks.). 35p. (Orig.). 1993. pap. text ed. 14.95 (1-56254-076-9) Saddleback Pubns.

Disaster Technology: An Annotated Bibliography. D. Manning. 300p. 1976. 125.00 (0-08-019984-4, Pub. by Pergamon Repr UK) Franklin.

Disaster Trail. Al Cody. 1993. 14.95 (0-7451-4581-7, Gunsmoke) Chivers N Amer.

Disaster Zone - U.S.A. Jack J. Morris. LC 90-85799. 192p. (Orig.). 1991. pap. text ed. write for info. (0-9628670-0-4) Avanti Pub Hse.

Disaster...& After. Ruth M. Everest. 1992. 8.95 (0-533-09417-8) Vantage.

Disasters! 2nd ed. Dan Dramer. (Critical Reading Ser.). 158p. (Orig.). (J). (gr. 6-8). 1995. pap. 9.00 (0-89061-766-X, 768) Jamestown Pubs.

Disasters: From the Pages of the New York Times. Ed. by Arleen Keylin & Gene Brown. (Illus.). 1976. 18.95 (0-405-06681-3) Ayer.

Disasters: Medical Organization. Ed. by Jan De Boer & Thomas W. Baillie. (Illus.). 112p. 1980. 50.00 (0-08-025491-8, Pub. by Pergamon Repr UK) Franklin.

***Disasters: Mental Health Interventions.** John D. Weaver. LC 95-3891. (Crisis Management Ser.). 220p. (Orig.). 1995. pap. 22.95 (1-56887-011-6, DMHBP, Prof Resc Pr) Pro Resource.

Disasters: Planning for a Caring Response. HMSO Staff. 120p. 1991. pap. 35.00 (0-11-321370-0, HM7006) UNIPUB.

Disasters: Violence of Nature & Threats by Man. Charles H. Ebert. 384p. 1993. per. 28.95 (0-8403-7608-1) Kendall-Hunt.

Disasters & Disaster Planning: Medical Analysis Index with Research Bibliography. American Health Research Institute Staff. LC 85-47857. 150p. 1987. 39.50 (0-88164-390-4); pap. 34.50 (0-88164-391-2) ABBE Pubs Assn.

Disasters & Mental Health: Contemporary Perspectives & Innovation in Services to Disaster Victims. National Institute of Mental Health Staff. Ed. by Barbara J. Sowder & Mary Lystad. LC 86-20616. (Illus.). 412p. 1986. reprint ed. pap. text ed. 18.50 (0-88048-261-3, 48-261-3) Am Psychiatric.

***Disasters & the Environment: Economic & Policy Issues.** Ed. by Caroline Guarnizo & Mohan Munasinghe. LC 95-5659. 1995. write for info. (0-8213-3212-0) World Bank.

Disasters & the Mass Media: Proceedings of the Committee on Disasters & the Mass Media Workshop, February 1979. National Research Council, Committee on Disasters & the Mass Media Staff. LC 79-27615. (Illus.). 315p. reprint ed. pap. 89.80 (0-8357-4270-9, 2037066) Bks Demand.

Disasters & the Small Dwelling. Ed. by I. Davis. 220p. 1981. 100.00 (0-08-024753-9, Pub. by Pergamon Repr UK) Franklin.

Disasters & the Small Dwelling: Perspectives for the U. N. IDNDR. Ed. by Yasemin Aysan & Ian Davis. (Illus.). 256p. (Orig.). (C). 1992. 60.00 (1-873936-07-9, Pub. by J & J Sci Pubs UK) Bks Intl VA.

***Disasters at Sea.** Milton H. Watson. (Illus.). 216p. 1995. 29.95 (1-85260-505-7, Pub. by J H Haynes & Co UK) Motorbooks Intl.

Disasters at Sea: Titanic to Exxon Valdez. 2nd ed. Richard A. Cahill. (Illus.). 290p. 1991. reprint ed. 29.95 (0-9630018-9-2) Nautical TX.

Disasters at Sea: Titantic to Exxon Valdez. Richard A. Cahill. 288p. 1992. pap. 19.95 (0-9630018-8-4) Nautical TX.

Disasters, Collective Behavior, & Social Organization. Ed. by Russell R. Dynes & Kathleen J. Tierney. LC 93-46766. (C). 1994. write for info. (0-87413-498-6) U Delaware Pr.

Disasters, Development & Environment. Ann Varley. 224p. 1994. text ed. 54.95 (0-470-22017-1) Halsted Pr.

Disasters, Development, & Environment. Ed. by Anne Varley. LC 94-2540. 1995. text ed. 54.95 (0-471-94993-0) Wiley.

Disasters: Hospital Planning. P. E. Savage. 1979. 67.00 (0-08-024914-0, Pub. by Pergamon Repr UK) Franklin.

Disasters of War. Leighton Rollins & Daniel Corrigan. LC 80-69430. (Illus.). 48p. 1981. pap. 4.00 (0-932274-15-3) Cadmus Eds.

Disasters of War. deluxe limited ed. Leighton Rollins & Daniel Corrigan. LC 80-69430. (Illus.). 48p. 1981. 15.00 (0-932274-16-1) Cadmus Eds.

Disasters of War. Francisco Goya. (Illus.). (gr. 7-12). 1968. reprint ed. pap. 6.95 (0-486-21872-4) Dover.

Disasters, Planning, & Development: Managing Natural Hazards to Reduce Loss. 25.00 (0-8270-3007-X) OAS.

Disasters That Shook the World. Cathie Cush. LC 93-10299. (Twenty Events Ser.). (Illus.). 48p. (J). (gr. 5-7). 1993. lib. bdg. 22.80 (0-8114-4929-7) Raintree Steck-V.

***Disastrous Encounters.** large type ed. Kerry Allyne. (Magna Large Print Ser.). 1994. 18.95 (0-7505-0669-5, Pub. by Magna Print Bks) Ulverscroft.

Disastrous Love Affair of Moon & Mars. Alfred De Grazia. (Quantavolution Ser.). 278p. (Orig.). 1984. pap. 17.00 (0-940268-09-4) Metron Pubns.

Disastrous Twilight: A Personal Record of the Partition of India. 2nd ed. S. Shahid Hamid. (Illus.). 364p. 1993. 47.50 (0-85052-396-6, Pub. by L Cooper Bks UK) Trans-Atl Phila.

Disbursement Handbook. 64p. (ENG, FRE, POR & SPA.). 1986. English. 7.95 (0-8213-0746-0); French. 7.95 (0-8213-0748-7); Portuguese. 7.95 (0-8213-1348-7) World Bank.

***Disbursement Handbook.** 114p. (SPA.). 1993. 7.95 (0-8213-2315-6, 12315) World Bank.

Disbursement Handbook - Manuel de Decaissement. 114p. (FRE.). 1993. 7.95 (0-8213-2481-0, 12471) World Bank.

Disbursement Handbook - Manual de Desembolsos. 114p. (POR.). 1993. 7.95 (0-8213-2471-3, 12471) World Bank.

Disc of Clear Water. Charlotte Mandel. LC 80-25317. (Illus.). 66p. (Orig.). 1981. pap. 5.00 (0-938158-00-7) Saturday Pr.

Disc Set. 2nd ed. Haydock. 1989. 125.00 (0-316-35186-5) Little.

Discard Your Disability Doldrums. Kelly J. Bauer. 64p. 1994. pap. 7.95 (0-8059-3547-9) Dorrance.

Discarded Image: An Introduction to Medieval & Renaissance Literature. C. S. Lewis. (Canto Bk.). 240p. (C). 1994. pap. 9.95 (0-521-47735-2) Cambridge U Pr.

Discarded Legacy: Politics & Poetics in the Life of Frances E. W. Harper, 1825-1911. Melba J. Boyd. LC 93-36922. (African American Life Ser.). (Illus.). 254p. (C). 1994. pap. text ed. 12.95 (0-8143-2489-4) Wayne St U Pr.

Discarding Images: Reflections on Music & Culture in Medieval France. Christopher Page. (Illus.). 256p. 1993. 42.00 (0-19-816346-0) OUP.

Discarding the Asylum: From Child Rescue to the Welfare State in English-Canada (1800-1950) Patricia T. Rooke & R. L. Schnell. LC 83-10569. (Illus.). 510p. (Orig.). (C). 1983. pap. text ed. 36.00 (0-8191-3305-1) U Pr of Amer.

Discarding the Throwaway Society. John E. Young. 70p. (Orig.). 1991. pap. 5.00 (1-878071-02-5) Worldwatch Inst.

***Discerner of Hearts: And Other Stories.** Olive Senior. (Orig.). 1995. pap. 13.95 (0-7710-8053-0, Pub. by McClelland & Stewart CN) Firefly Bks Ltd.

Discerning Art: Concepts & Issues. Ed. by George W. Hardiman & Theodore Zernich. 650p. (C). 1989. text ed. 27.80 (0-87563-327-7) Stipes.

Discerning Christian: How the Believer Detects Truth from Error in the Midst of Today's Religious Confusion. K. Neill Foster. 104p. (Orig.). (C). 1990. pap. 9.95 (0-87509-312-4, Pub. by Horizon Books CN) Chr Pubns.

Discerning God's Will. Ben C. Johnson. 168p. (Orig.). 1990. pap. 12.99 (0-664-25146-3) Westminster John Knox.

Discerning God's Will: Ignatius of Loyola's Teaching on Christian Decision-Making. Jules Toner. LC 91-75156. (Original Studies Composed in English Series III: No. 8). x, 344p. 1991. 37.95 (0-912422-82-3); pap. 24.95 (0-912422-83-1) Inst Jesuit.

Discerning Heart. Jos. V. Pieters. LC 91-34761. (Warbler Cottage Romances Ser.). 192p. 1992. pap. 7.99 (0-8007-5435-2) Revell.

Discerning Heart: Discovering a Personal God. Maureen Conroy. LC 93-12508. 272p. (Orig.). (C). 1993. pap. 13.95 (0-8294-0752-9, Campion Bks) Loyola Univ Pr.

Discerning Spirit: A Theology of Revelation. Timothy J. Gorringe. LC 90-38709. 160p. (Orig.). (C). 1990. pap. 12.95 (0-334-02462-5) TPI PA.

Discerning the Body. R. L. Black. 98p. (Orig.). 1984. pap. 3.95 (0-934942-42-0, 1264) White Wing Pub.

Discerning the Mystery: An Essay on the Nature of Theology. Andrew Louth. 168p. 1990. reprint ed. pap. 19.95 (0-19-826196-9) OUP.

Discerning the Spirit of Life in Making Decisions about Death. Robert R. Gillogly. 58p. (Orig.). 1992. pap. 3.75 (0-9634870-0-0) Asterisk Pubns.

Discerning the Subject. Paul Smith. LC 87-35926. (Theory & History of Literature Ser.: Vol. 55). 220p. 1988. pap. text ed. 15.95x (0-8166-1639-6) U of Minn Pr.

Discerning Traveler's Guide to Romantic Hideaways of the East Coast. David Glickstein & Linda Glickstein. LC 93-475. (Illus.). 224p. (Orig.). 1993. pap. 14.95 (0-312-09272-5) St Martin.

Discerning Traveler's Guide to the Middle Atlantic States. David Glickstein. 1991. pap. 17.95 (0-312-05857-8) St Martin.

Discerning Vocations to Marriage, Celibacy, & Singlehood. Maria T. Coombs & Francis K. Nemeck. LC 94-6148. 224p. 1994. 12.95 (0-8146-5505-X) Liturgical Pr.

***Discerning Your Call: An Introduction to Catechist Formation.** 74p. (Orig.). 1985. pap. text ed. 7.00 (1-887158-02-2) Educ Services.

Discerning Your Spiritual Gifts. Lloyd Edwards. LC 88-25728. 150p. (Orig.). 1988. pap. 9.95 (0-936384-65-4) Cowley Pubns.

Discernment: Seeking God in Every Situation. Chris Aridas. 120p. (Orig.). 1981. pap. 6.95 (0-914544-37-3) Living Flame Pr.

Discernment: The Art of Choosing Well. Pierre Wolff. LC 92-7922. 160p. (Orig.). 1993. pap. 9.95 (0-89243-485-6, Triumph Books) Liguori Pubns.

Discernment E politica see **Spiritual Discernment & Politics: Guidelines for Religious Communities**

Discharge & Velocity Measurements: Proceedings of a Short Course, Zurich, 26-27 August 1987. Ed. by Andreas Muller. 280p. (C). 1988. text ed. 95.00 (90-6191-782-4, Pub. by A A Balkema NE) Ashgate Pub Co.

Discharge Characteristics. D. S. Miller. (Hydraulic Structures Design Manual Ser.: Vol. 8). (Illus.). 270p. (C). 1994. 110.00 (90-5410-180-6, Pub. by A A Balkema NE) Ashgate Pub Co.

Discharge for Cause: Arbitral Enforcement under the Collective Bargaining Agreement. Douglas H. Thompson. LC 89-16065. 176p. 1989. text ed. 49.95 (0-275-92623-0, C2623, Praeger Pubs) Greenwood.

Discharge Lamps. C. Meyer & H. Nienhuis. Tr. by E. F. Van Rees Vellinga. (Philips Technical Library). (Illus.). 312p. 1989. text ed. 120.00 (90-201-2147-2) Scholium Intl.

Discharge of Sewage from Sea Outfalls. A. L. Gameson. 1975. 194.00 (0-08-018302-6, Pub. by Pergamon Repr UK) Franklin.

Discharge Planning: A Manual for Psychiatric Nurses. Babich & Brown. 193p. 1991. 20.00 (1-55642-201-6) SLACK Inc.

Discharge Planning: A Practitioner's Guide to Policies, Procedures & Protocols, Guideline Manual. Jackie Birmingham. 1992. 90.00 (1-879575-25-6) Acad Med Sys.

Discharge Planning: Assuring the Continuity of Care. O'Hare & Terry. 196p. 1987. 65.00 (0-87189-895-0, 89895) Aspen Pub.

Discharge Planning for Health Care Facilities. Faith J. Crittenden. LC 81-12894. 224p. 1982. pap. text ed. 29.95 (0-89303-210-7) P-H.

Discharge Planning for Home Health Care: A Multidisciplinary Approach. Barbara S. Gingerich & Deborah A. Ondeck. 258p. 1994. ring bd. 87.00 (0-8342-0572-6, 20572) Aspen Pub.

Discharge Planning Handbook. Judith W. Rorden. (Illus.). 384p. 1990. pap. text ed. 32.95 (0-7216-2845-1) Saunders.

Discharges from Nursing Homes: 1985 National Nursing Home Survey (PHS 90-1764) Edward S. Sekscenski. (Series 13: No. 103). 87p. text ed. 4.75 (0-685-28485-9, PB90-218744) Natl Ctr Health Stats.

Discharging to Atmosphere from Laboratory-Scale Processes. D. Hughes. (Handbook Ser.: No. 4). (C). 1989. 96.00 (0-948237-03-1, Pub. by H&H Sci Cnslts UK) St Mut.

Disciple. Juan C. Ortiz. LC 74-29650. 144p. 1975. pap. 7.99 (0-88419-145-1, Creation Hse) Strang Comms Co.

Disciple. Paul Bourget. xvii, 341p. 1976. reprint ed. 45.00 (0-86527-238-7) Fertig.

Disciple - Pastor: Enabling & Equipping the Church for Discipleship. E. Lynn Brown. LC 93-78819. (Reader Resource Ser.). 100p. (Orig.). 1993. pap. text ed. 6.00 (1-883667-01-1) Christian Meth.

Disciple & Other Poems. deluxe ed. George MacDonald. 1989. 27.50 (0-940652-87-0) Sunrise Bks.

Disciple & the Master: St. Bonaventure's Sermons on St. Francis of Assisi. Eric Doyle. 220p. 1983. 6.95 (0-8199-0842-8, Frncscn Herld) Franciscan Pr.

Disciple-Maker Workbook. Albert L. Kurz. Date not set. pap. 12.99 (0-8024-2217-9) Moody.

Disciple-Making Church. Bill Hull. LC 90-35377. 256p. 1990. 14.99 (0-8007-1641-8) Revell.

Disciple-Making Pastor. Bill Hull. LC 88-18321. 1988. 14.99 (0-8007-1608-6) Revell.

Disciple of a Master: (How to Hit a Baseball to Your Potential) Stephen J. Ferroli. (Illus.). 136p. (Orig.). (J). (gr. 9-12). 1986. pap. 9.95 (0-939905-00-0) Line Drive.

Disciple Story: Every Christian's Journey. Gregory M. Corrigan. LC 89-84737. 144p. (Orig.). 1989. pap. 5.95 (0-87793-408-8) Ave Maria.

Discipled to Christ. Stephen Kaung. Ed. by Herbert L. Fader. 88p. 1976. pap. 3.50 (0-935008-17-9) Christian Fellow Pubs.

Discipled to Christ. Stephen Kaung. Tr. by Lily Hsu. (CHI.). 1984. pap. write for info. (0-941598-13-6) Living Spring Pubns.

Disciplemakers' Handbook: Helping People Grow in Christ. Ed. by Alice Fryling. LC 89-36648. 224p. (Orig.). 1989. pap. 9.99 (0-8308-1266-0, 1266) InterVarsity.

Disciplemaking: Self-Study Course in Understanding & Applying Jesus' Command to "Make Disciples" Ed. by Robert E. Coleman et al. (Illus.). 231p. (Orig.). 1994. pap. 39.95 (1-879089-12-2); 9.95 (1-879089-13-0) B Graham Ctr.

Discipler's Manual: Thirty-Four Studies for Christian Life & Service. F. E. Marsh. LC 79-2550. 344p. 1991. pap. 10.99 (0-8254-3238-3) Kregel.

Disciples. Charles Marowitz. 71p. 1987. pap. 4.75 (0-8222-0313-8) Dramatists Play.

Disciples: A Novel. Joseph J. Andrew. 464p. 1993. 20.00 (0-671-79599-6) S&S Trade.

Disciples & American Culture: A Bibliography of Works by Disciples of Christ Members, 1866-1984. Leslie R. Galbraith & Heather F. Day. (American Theological Library Association Monograph: No. 26). 393p. 1990. 45.00 (0-8108-2361-6) Scarecrow.

***Disciples & Democracy: Religious Conservatives & the Future of American Politics.** Ed. by Michael Cromartie. 152p. (Orig.). 1994. pap. 12.99 (0-8028-0847-6) Eerdmans.

Disciples & Discipleship: Studies in the Gospel According to Mark. Ernest Best. 256p. 1986. 37.95 (0-567-09369-7, Pub. by T & T Clark UK) Bks Intl VA.

Disciples & Leaders: The Origins of Christian Ministry in the New Testament. John F. O'Grady. 1991. pap. 9.95 (0-8091-3269-9) Paulist Pr.

Disciples Are Made, Not Born. Walter A. Henrichsen. 156p. 1988. pap. 8.99 (0-89693-442-X) SP Pubns.

Disciples at the Crossroads: Perspectives on Worship & Church Leadership. Eleanor Bernstein. 168p. (Orig.). 1993. pap. text ed. 10.95 (0-8146-2146-5) Liturgical Pr.

Disciple's Christology: Appraisals of Kraus's Jesus Christ Our Lord. Ed. by Richard A. Kauffman. (Occasional Papers: No. 13). 112p. (Orig.). 1989. pap. text ed. 7.00 (0-936273-15-1) Inst Mennonite.

Disciples Family Album. Ed. by Peter M. Morgan. 96p. (Orig.). 1990. pap. 7.99 (0-8272-0617-8) Chalice Pr.

Disciples of Destruction: The Religious Origins of War & Terrorism. Charles W. Sutherland. LC 86-42915. 451p. 1986. 30.95 (0-87975-349-8) Prometheus Bks.

Disciples of Jesus. J. C. Wenger. LC 77-86343. (Mennonite Faith Ser.: No. 5). 72p. 1977. pap. 2.95 (0-8361-1836-7) Herald Pr.

Disciples of Jesus, Beginner-Primary Teacher. Carol E. Miller. 1984. pap. 2.25 (0-915374-47-1) Rapids Christian.

Disciples of Jesus Junior-Junior High Teacher. 1984. pap. 2.25 (0-915374-48-X) Rapids Christian.

Disciples of Light: Photographs in the Brewster Album. Graham Smith. LC 89-24563. (Illus.). 200p. 1990. 49.95 (0-89236-158-1) J P Getty Trust.

Disciples of the Buddha. Ed. by Zenno Ishigami. 208p. (Orig.). 1990. pap. 6.50 (4-333-01423-9, Pub. by Kosei Pub Co JA) C E Tuttle.

Disciples of the Wise. Joseph Zeitlin. LC 71-121517. (Essay Index Reprint Ser.). 1977. 21.95 (0-8369-1859-2) Ayer.

***Disciples Redeemed: A Dramatic Commemoration of the Last Supper.** Raymond I. Keffer. 28p. (Orig.). 1995. pap. 4.50 (0-7880-0373-9) CSS OH.

Disciple's Study Bible. Ed. by James Draper et al. 1988. 36.99 (1-55819-014-7) Holman Bible Pub.

Disciple's Study Bible. deluxe ed. Ed. by James Draper et al. 1988. 59.99 (1-55819-162-3); 69.99 (1-55819-025-2) Holman Bible Pub.

***Disciple's Wedding: Planning a Wedding That Gives Glory to God.** Nancy Orr & Kay McKean. 80p. 1994. pap. 6.99 (1-884553-21-4) Discipleshp.

***Discipleship.** J. Heinrich Arnold. Ed. by Hutterian Brethren Staff. 300p. 1994. pap. 12.50 (0-87486-066-0) Plough.

Discipleship: Creation, Covenant, Community. Marshal Gilmore et al. LC 94-76824. (Reader Resource Ser.). 125p. (Orig.). 1994. pap. text ed. 6.00 (1-883667-10-0) Christian Meth.

Discipleship: Giving God Your Best. Greg Laurie. LC 92-20897. 1993. pap. 3.99 (1-56507-039-9) Harvest Hse.

Discipleship: Growing up As a Christian. G. Campbell Morgan. LC 91-15196. 121p. 1991. reprint ed. pap. 7.99 (0-8254-3259-6) Kregel.

***Discipleship: Learning to Walk with Jesus.** Debbie Bentley. (Basic Christian Doctrine Ser.: No. 2). 11p. (Orig.). (YA). 1995. pap. 1.00 (1-885090-01-3) Cosecha Latina.

Discipleship: The Best Writing from the Most Experienced Disciple Makers. rev. ed. Ed. by Billie Hanks, Jr. & William A. Shell. 192p. 1993. pap. 9.99 (0-310-51001-5) Zondervan.

Discipleship: The Growing Christian's Lifestyle. Jim & Martha Reapsome. (Fisherman Bible Studyguide Ser.). 64p. 1984. 4.99 (0-87788-175-8) Shaw Pubs.

***Discipleship: The Growing Christian's Lifestyle.** James Reapsome & Martha Reapsome. Tr. by Yi-Hsin Ting. 57p. (CHI.). 1990. pap. 3.50 (1-56582-009-6) Christ Renew Min.

Discipleship & Family Ties in Mark & Matthew. Stephen C. Barton. LC 93-46383. (Society for New Testament Studies Monographs: No. 80). 281p. (C). 1995. 59.95 (0-521-46530-3) Cambridge U Pr.

Discipleship for All Believers: Christian Ethics & the Kingdom of God. Philip LeMasters. 160p. (Orig.). 1992. pap. 14.95 (0-8361-3579-2) Herald Pr.

Discipleship for Ordinary People. Stuart Briscoe. 208p. 1995. pap. 8.99 (0-87788-176-6) Shaw Pubs.

Discipleship: Growing with Jesus: A Gospel Guide to Fullness of Life. Malcolm Cornwell. 116p. (Orig.). 1989. pap. 6.95 (0-914544-70-5) Living Flame Pr.

***Discipleship II.** 238p. 1995. ring bd. 20.00 (0-9643021-6-0) Reality Living.

Discipleship in Principle & in Practice. Marshall Gilmore. LC 93-78180. (Reader Resource Ser.). 120p. 1993. pap. text ed. 6.00 (1-883667-00-3) Christian Meth.

***Discipleship in the Ancient World & Matthew's Gospel.** 2nd ed. Michael J. Wilkins. 288p. 1995. pap. 19.99 (0-8010-2007-7) Baker Bk.

Discipleship in the New Age, Vol. 1. Alice A. Bailey. LC 44-28587. 1944. 32.00 (0-85330-003-8) Lucis.

Discipleship in the New Age, Vol. 1. Alice A. Bailey. LC 44-28587. 1972. pap. 20.00 (0-85330-103-4) Lucis.

Discipleship in the New Age, Vol. 2. Alice A. Bailey. LC 44-28587. 1955. 32.00 (0-85330-004-6) Lucis.

Discipleship in the New Age, Vol. 2. Alice A. Bailey. LC 44-28587. 1972. pap. 20.00 (0-85330-104-2) Lucis.

Discipleship of Equals: A Critical Feminist Ekklesia-logy of Liberation. Elisabeth S. Fiorenza. LC 92-31264. 384p. (Orig.). 1993. pap. 19.95 (0-8245-1244-8) Crossroad NY.

Discipleship of the Mind: Learning to Love God in the Ways We Think. James W. Sire. LC 89-48575. 250p. (Orig.). 1990. pap. 11.99 (0-87784-985-4, 985) InterVarsity.

***Discipleship Or Pilgrimage? The Educator's Quest for Philosophy.** Tony W. Johnson. LC 94-28018. (SUNY Series, the Philosophy of Education). 1995. pap. text ed. 16.95x (0-7914-2504-5) State U NY Pr.

***Discipleship Or Pilgrimage? The Educator's Quest for Philosophy.** Tony W. Johnson. LC 94-28018. (SUNY Series, the Philosophy of Education). 222p. (C). 1995. text ed. 49.50x (0-7914-2503-7) State U NY Pr.

Discipleship Principles for Effective Church Administration. William H. Graves. LC 93-81267. 100p. (Orig.). 1993. pap. text ed. 6.00 (1-883667-08-9) Christian Meth.

Discipleship Therapy: Healthy Christians, Healthy Churches. Albert H. Epp. 277p. (Orig.). 1993. pap. text ed. 12.95 (0-9638185-7-0) Stairway Disciple.

Disciplina Clericalis of Petrus Alfonsi. Petrus Alfonsi. Ed. by Eberhard Hermes. Tr. by P. R. Quarrie. LC 73-94434. (Islamic World Ser.). 250p. 1977. 45.00 (0-520-02704-3) U CA Pr.

Disciplina De Cuatro a Doce (Discipline from Four to Twelve) J. Dobson. (SPA.). Date not set. 1.79 (0-685-74929-0, 497412) Editorial Unilit.

An Asterisk (*) at the beginning of an entry indicates that the title is appearing in BIP for the first time.

An Asterisk (*) at the beginning of an entry indicates that the title is appearing in BIP for the first time.

Disciplining One Another. Anne Ortlund. 185p. 1983. pap. write for info. (0-8499-2960-1) Word Inc.

Disciplining the Devil's Country. Carole Borges. LC 87-72607. 72p. (Orig.). 1988. 15.95 (0-914086-76-6); pap. 9.95 (0-914086-77-4) Alicejamesbooks.

***Disciplining the Soul, Vol. 1.** Winter. 1995. 49.95 (0-946621-42-X); pap. 23.95 (0-946621-43-8) Atrium Pubs.

Disciplining Your Preschooler & Feeling Good about It. rev. ed. Mitch Golant & Susan K. Golant. 208p. 1993. pap. 11.95 (1-56565-052-2) Lowell Hse.

Discipulado Cristiano: The Christian Disciple. G. Campbell Morgan. (SPA.). 3.25 (84-7228-826-9, 220312, Pub. by Edit Clie SP) TSELF.

Discipulado Para Todos. Stuart Briscoe. 240p. (SPA.). 1990. pap. 4.95 (0-8297-0956-8) Life Pubs Intl.

Discipulo. Juan C. Ortiz. 192p. 1978. 3.95 (0-88113-065-6) Edit Betania.

Discipulo Se Hace, No Nace: Disciples Are Made, Not Born. Walter Henrichsen. (SPA.). 4.95 (84-7228-046-2, 220313, Pub. by Edit Clie SP) TSELF.

Disclaimers in Estate Planning: A Guide to Their Effective Use. 325p. 1990. pap. 59.95 (0-89707-542-0, 543-0306) Amer Bar Assn.

Disclosing Tilt: Law, Belief & Criticism. David S. Caudill. 188p. 1993. pap. 23.50 (90-6256-752-5, Pub. by VU Univ Pr NE) Paul & Co Pubs.

***Disclosure.** Michael Crichton. 1994. pap. 6.99 (0-345-39175-6) Ballantine.

***Disclosure.** Michael Crichton. 1994. mass mkt. 6.99 (0-345-39105-5) Ballantine.

Disclosure. large type ed. Michael Crichton. 1994. pap. 23.00 (0-679-75143-2) Random.

Disclosure: A Novel. Michael Crichton. 1994. 24.00 (0-679-41945-4) Random.

Disclosure Checklists & Illustrative Financial Statements for Banks: January, 1989. American Institute for Certified Public Accountants Staff. Ed. by J. Byrne Kelly. LC 89-648499. (Financial Accounting & Reporting Practice Aid Ser.). 85p. reprint ed. pap. 25.00 (0-8357-4107-9, 2036873) Bks Demand.

Disclosure Checklists & Illustrative Financial Statements for Corporations. American Institute of Certified Public Accountants Staff. Ed. by Michael A. Tursi. LC 89-29254. (Financial Accounting & Reporting Practice Aid Ser.). 110p. reprint ed. pap. 31.40 (0-7837-1058-5, 2041538) Bks Demand.

Disclosure Checklists & Illustrative Financial Statements for Corporations: Winter 1988. American Institute of Certified Public Accountants Staff. Ed. by Michael A. Tursi. LC 89-29254. (Financial Accounting & Reporting Practice Aid Ser.). 118p. reprint ed. pap. 33.70 (0-8357-4108-7, 2036874) Bks Demand.

Disclosure Checklists & Illustrative Financial Statements for Credit Unions: Winter 1988. American Institute of Certified Public Accountants Staff. Ed. by J. Byrne Kelly. LC 89-29255. (Financial Accounting & Reporting Practice Aid Ser.). 54p. reprint ed. pap. 25.00 (0-8357-4106-0, 2036872) Bks Demand.

Disclosure Checklists & Illustrative Financial Statements for Nonprofit Organizations: January, 1989. American Institute of Certified Public Accountants Staff. Ed. by Michael A. Miceli. LC 89-648512. 95p. reprint ed. pap. 27.10 (0-8357-4109-5, 2036875) Bks Demand.

Disclosure Checklists & Illustrative Financial Statements for Savings & Loan Associations: January, 1989. American Institute of Certified Public Accountants Staff. Ed. by J. Byrne Kelly. LC 89-648456. (Financial Accounting & Reporting Practice Aid Ser.). 83p. reprint ed. pap. 25.00 (0-8357-4105-2, 2036871) Bks Demand.

Disclosure Checklists & Illustrative Financial Statements for State & Local Governmental Units: Winter 1988. American Institute of Certified Public Accountants Staff. Ed. by Susan Cornwall. LC 89-29257. (Financial Accounting & Reporting Practice Aid Ser.). 132p. reprint ed. pap. 37.70 (0-8357-4110-9, 2036877) Bks Demand.

D

Disclosure Criteria & Segment Reporting: Proceedings of a Conference Sponsored by the Accounting Research Center & the Public Policy Research Center of the College of Business, University of Florida. Ed. by Russell M. Barefield & Gary L. Holstrum. LC 79-21130. (University of Florida Accounting Ser.: No. 10). 167p. reprint ed. pap. 47.60 (0-7837-4957-0, 2044623) Bks Demand.

Disclosure in Company Accounts. R. K. Agarwal. (C). 1989. 140.00 (0-685-36547-6) St Mut.

Disclosure in Insurance: the Changing Scene & Judicial Review in England. B. Rudden & J. M. Yeats. (Lectures on the Common Law Ser.: Vol. 3). 60p. 1991. pap. 28.00 (90-6544-540-4) Kluwer Law Tax Pubs.

Disclosure of Corporate Social Performance: Survey, Evaluation, & Prospects. Harold L. Johnson. LC 78-10594. (Praeger Special Studies). 140p. 1979. text ed. 45.00 (0-275-90371-0, C0371, Praeger Pubs) Greenwood.

***Disclosure Processes in Children & Adolescents.** Ed. by Ken J. Rotenberg. (Cambridge Studies in Social & Emotional Development). (Illus.). 240p. (C). 1995. 44.95 (0-521-47098-6) Cambridge U Pr.

Disclosures. Katherine Goodman. (New York University Ottendorfer Ser.: Vol. 24). 241p. (C). 1986. text ed. 34.95 (0-8204-0398-9) P Lang Pubs.

Disco. Chelsea Farraday. 1978. pap. 1.95 (0-8439-0599-9) Dorchester Pub Co.

Disco Candy & Other Stories. L. C. Phillips. LC 78-72027. 210p. 1979. 16.95 (0-912282-07-X) Pulse-Finger.

Disco Dance Steps. J. Villari & K. Villari. (Ballroom Dance Ser.). 1986. lib. bdg. 79.95 (0-8490-3387-X) Gordon Pr.

Disco Dance Steps. J. Villari & K. Villari. (Ballroom Dance Ser.). 1985. lib. bdg. 76.00 (0-87700-722-5) Revisionist Pr.

Disco Dancing. G. Lloyd. (Ballroom Dance Ser.). 1986. lib. bdg. 69.95 (0-8490-3294-6) Gordon Pr.

Disco Dancing. G. Lloyd. (Ballroom Dance Ser.). 1985. lib. bdg. 79.00 (0-87700-821-3) Revisionist Pr.

Disco-File: The Discographical Catalog of American Race, Rhythm & Blues, Rock & Roll & Soul. 3rd ed. Fernando L. Gonzalez. Date not set. 80.00 (0-9601090-2-1) F L Gonzalez.

Disco Hustle. C. Lovisone. (Ballroom Dance Ser.). 1986. lib. bdg. 79.95 (0-8490-3316-0) Gordon Pr.

Disco Hustle. C. Lovisone. (Ballroom Dance Ser.). 1985. lib. bdg. 74.00 (0-87700-819-1) Revisionist Pr.

Disco in Spain. large type ed. Monica Ware. (Linford Romance Library). 256p. 1989. pap. 11.95 (0-7089-6695-0, Linford) Ulverscroft.

Disco Nixon. Marilyn Werden & David Arenson. 1995. pap. 10.00 (0-671-89816-7, Fireside) S&S Trade.

Disco-Rock. (Ballroom Dance Ser.). 1985. lib. bdg. 69.50 (0-87700-725-X) Revisionist Pr.

Disco Rock, Bk. 1. Kolar & Ramal. (Keyboard Beginning Ser.). 1990. 5.95 (0-685-31452-9, T720) Hansen Ed Mus.

Disco to Tango & Back: Skippy Blair on Contemporary Social Dance. Skippy Blair. 1978. pap. 22.50 (0-932980-01-5) Golden St Dance Teach Assn.

***Disco to Tango & Back: Skippy Blair on Contemporary Social Dance.** rev. ed. Skippy Blair. (Illus.). 196p. 1992. audio, ring bd. 40.00 (0-932980-06-6) Golden St Dance Teach Assn.

***Discografia de la Musica Cubana I, 1898-1925.** Cristobal D. Ayala. (Illus.). 365p. (Orig.). (SPA.). 1994. pap. 29.95 (0-89729-721-0) Ediciones.

Discographies of Commercial Recordings of the Cleveland Orchestra (1924-1977) and the Cincinnati Symphony Orchestra (1917-1977) Comp. by Betty Meyers & Frederick P. Fellers. LC 78-3122. 211p. 1978. text ed. 42.95 (0-313-20375-X, MDI/) Greenwood.

Discography of Hindustani & Karnatic Music. Michael S. Kinnear. LC 85-5584. (Discographies Ser.: No. 17). xix, 594p. 1985. text ed. 79.50 (0-313-24479-0, KDI/, Greenwood Pr) Greenwood.

Discography of Historical Records on Cylinders & 78s. Comp. by Brian Rust. LC 78-60530. 327p. 1979. text ed. 69.50 (0-313-20561-2, RRC/, Greenwood Pr) Greenwood.

Discography of Solo Song: Supplement Nineteen Seventy-Five to Nineteen Eighty-Two. Dorothy Stahl. LC 84-19794. (Detroit Studies in Music Bibliography: No. 52). 236p. 1984. 25.00 (0-89990-023-2) Info Coord.

Discography of Treble Voice Recordings. Comp. by James Laster. LC 84-22179. 157p. 1984. 20.00 (0-8108-1760-8) Scarecrow.

***Disconcerted Europe: The Search for a New Security Architecture.** Alexander Moens & Christopher Anstis. LC 94-21959. (C). 1994. text ed. 56.95 (0-8133-2324-X) Westview.

Disconnected. P. Kimball. LC 72-6349. 317p. 1972. text ed. 44.00 (0-231-03696-5) Col U Pr.

Disconnected: Public Opinion & Politics in Alabama. Patrick R. Cotter et al. LC 94-6169. 1994. pap. 14.95 (0-9630700-8-8) Vision AL.

Disconnecting Bell: The Impact of the AT&T Divestiture. Ed. by Harry M. Shooshan, III. (Illus.). 176p. 1984. 44.00 (0-08-030173-8, Pergamon Pr); pap. 20.00 (0-08-030172-X, Pergamon Pr) Elsevier.

Disconnection. Claude Ollier. Tr. by Dominic Di Bernardi. LC 89-35215. 130p. 1989. 19.95 (0-916583-47-3) Dalkey Arch.

Disconnection: How to Interface Computers and Video. Gerald A. Souter. (Professional Librarian Ser.). (Illus.). 208p. 1988. 45.00 (0-86729-218-0, Hall Reference); student ed, pap. 27.95 (0-86729-219-9, Hall Reference) Macmillan.

***Disconsolate Empires: French, British & Elgian Military Involvement in Post - Colonial Sub - Saharan Africa.** Alain Rouvez et al. 468p. (C). 1994. lib. bdg. 52.50 (0-8191-9643-6) U Pr of Amer.

Discontented Discourses: Feminism, Textual Intervention, Psychoanalysis. Ed. by Marleen S. Barr & Richard Feldstein. LC 88-11943. 264p. 1989. 29.95 (0-252-01562-2); pap. 12.50 (0-252-06023-7) U of Ill Pr.

Discontents. Dennis Cooper. 1991. pap. 12.95 (0-927200-10-4) Amethyst NY.

***Discontinuation of Hospice Care: Ethical Issues.** National Hospice Organization, Ethics Committee. 15p. 1993. 15.75 (0-931207-22-3) Natl Hospice.

Discontinued. Julian F. Thompson. 304p. (YA). (gr. 7 up). 1985. 12.95 (0-590-33321-6) Scholastic Inc.

Discontinued. Julian F. Thompson. 304p. (YA). (gr. 7 up). 1986. pap. 3.50 (0-590-42464-5) Scholastic Inc.

Discontinuidad y Ruptura en Guillermo Cabrera Infante. Isabel Alvarez-Borland. LC 82-84325. 144p. 1983. pap. text ed. 10.00 (0-935318-09-7) Edins Hispamerica.

Discontinuities in Wave Guides. Julian Schwinger & D. Saxon. 178p. 1968. text ed. 130.00 (0-677-01840-1); pap. text ed. 66.00 (0-677-01845-2) Gordon & Breach.

Discontinuity Analysis for Rock Engineering. Stephen D. Priest. LC 92-27172. 1992. write for info. (0-412-47600-2) Chapman & Hall.

Discontinuous - Fiber - Reinforced Composites. L. M. Bagaasen. 22p. 1991. reprint ed. 27.00 (0-938648-28-4) T-C Pubns CA.

Discontinuous Automatic Control. Irmgard Fluegge-Lotz. LC 52-13156. (Illus.). 176p. reprint ed. pap. 50.20 (0-317-10759-3, 2000032) Bks Demand.

***Discontinuous Change: Leading Organizational Transformation.** David A. Nadler et al. LC 94-30752. (Management Ser.). 388p. 1994. 28.95 (0-7879-0042-7) Jossey-Bass.

Discontinuous Discourses in Modern Russian Literature. Ed. by Catriona Kelly et al. LC 88-18157. 256p. 1989. text ed. 35.00 (0-312-01996-3) St Martin.

Discontinuous Groups & Automorphic Functions. Joseph Lehner. LC 63-11987. (Mathematical Surveys Ser.: Vol. 8). 425p. 1990. reprint ed. pap. 49.00 (0-8218-1508-3, SURV-8) Am Math.

Discontinuous Groups & Reimann Surfaces. Ed. by Leon Greenberg. LC 73-16783. (Annals of Mathematics Studies: No. 79). 450p. 1974. text ed. 65.00 (0-691-08138-7) Princeton U Pr.

Discontinuous Solidification of an Aluminum-Copper Alloy. Queen's University at Kingston Staff. 81p. 1965. 12.15 (0-317-34515-X, 66) Intl Copper.

Discopaedia of the Violin, 1889-1971. James L. Creighton. LC 79-185708. 1003p. reprint ed. pap. 180.00 (0-685-15889-6, 2056116) Bks Demand.

Discord & Collaboration: Essays on International Politics. Arnold Wolfers. 303p. 1962. pap. 14.95x (0-8018-0691-7) Johns Hopkins.

***Discord & Collaboration in a New Europe: Essays in Honor of Arnold Wolfers.** Ed. by Douglas T. Stuart & Stephen F. Szabo. LC 94-13205. 1994. 19.95 (0-941700-88-7) JH FPI SAIS.

Discord in the Pacific: Challenges to the Japanese-American Alliance. Ed. by Henry Rosovsky. LC 72-93017. 1972. pap. 3.00 (0-910416-16-8) Am Assembly.

Discordant Harmonies: A New Ecology for the Twenty-First Century. Daniel B. Botkin. (Illus.). 256p. 1990. 22.95 (0-19-505491-1) OUP.

Discordant Harmonies: A New Ecology for the Twenty-First Century. Daniel B. Botkin. 256p. 1992. pap. 11.95 (0-19-507469-6) OUP.

***Discordant Voices: The Non-Russian Soviet Literature 1952-1973.** George S. Luckyj. 160p. 1995. lib. bdg. 27.00 (0-8095-4935-2) Borgo Pr.

***Discorde Chez l'Ennemi.** Charles De Gaulle. 283p. 1971. 34.95 (0-7859-5242-X) Fr & Eur.

Discords Mingled: Essays on Music. Carl Engel. LC 67-28752. (Essay Index Reprint Ser.). 1977. 18.95 (0-8369-0417-6) Ayer.

Discorsi Politici: 1902-1923. Enrico Corradini. LC 76-180395. (ITA.). reprint ed. 55.00 (0-404-56116-0) AMS Pr.

Discorso Sopra la Mascherata Della Genealogia Delg'Iddei, Repr. Of 1565 Ed. Baccio Baldini. Bd. with Discorso Sopra Li Dei De'Gentili. LC 75-27852. LC 75-27852. (Renaissance & the Gods Ser.: Vol. 10). (Illus.). 1976. Set lib. bdg. 88.00 (0-8240-2059-6) Garland.

Discorso Sopra Li Dei De'Gentili see Discorso Sopra la Mascherata Della Genealogia Delg'Iddei

Discotheque at the Y: Nine Short Dances. (Ballroom Dance Ser.). 1986. lib. bdg. 79.95 (0-8490-3427-2) Gordon Pr.

Discotheque at the Y: Nine Short Dances. (Ballroom Dance Ser.). 1985. lib. bdg. 68.00 (0-87700-837-X) Revisionist Pr.

Discotheque Dancing. D. Lavelle. (Ballroom Dance Ser.). 1986. lib. bdg. 69.95 (0-8490-3257-1) Gordon Pr.

Discotheque Dancing. D. Lavelle. (Ballroom Dance Ser.). 1985. lib. bdg. 72.00 (0-87700-849-3) Revisionist Pr.

Discount & Equivalent Interest Tables No. 948. Ed. by Financial Publishing Co. Staff. 244p. 1981. 40.00 (0-87600-448-6) Finan Pub.

Discount & Equivalent Interest Yield Tables: Fifteen Percent to Twenty Percent. Financial Publishing Co. Staff. 244p. 1979. pap. 40.00 (0-87600-348-X) Finan Pub.

Discount & Equivalent Interest Yield Tables: Ten Percent to Fifteen Percent. Financial Publishing Co. Staff. 244p. 1973. pap. 40.00 (0-87600-248-3) Finan Pub.

Discount & Equivalent Interest Yield Tables: Twenty-five Percent to Thirty Percent. Financial Publishing Co. Staff. 244p. 1981. pap. 35.00 (0-87600-548-2) Finan Pub.

Discount Brokerage Survey: Stocks. Ed. by Mark Coler. 1994. pap. write for info. (1-877638-25-0) Mercer Inc.

Discount Buyers of America: The Catalog. Discount Buyers of America Staff. 172p. (Orig.). 1992. pap. text ed. 29.95 (0-934180-01-6) Money Business.

Discount Guide for Travelers over 55. 3rd rev. ed. Walter Weintz & Caroline Weintz. 320p. 1985. pap. 7.95 (0-525-48169-9, Dutton) NAL-Dutton.

Discount Terms Impact on Cash Inflows. 11p. 1979. 40.00 (0-939050-19-6) Credit Res NYS.

***Discount Travel U. S. A.** J. P. Drew. 200p. 1994. pap. write for info. (0-9640397-1-0) J P Drew.

Discounted Cash Flow, a Method of Investment Appraisal. Learning Systems Ltd. Staff. 1967. 45.00 (0-08-014026-2, Pub. by Pergamon Repr UK) Franklin.

Discounting for Time & Risk in Energy Policy. Robert C. Lind et al. 468p. 1982. 42.50 (0-8018-2709-4) Resources Future.

Discounting Human Lives: Uranium & Global Equity. Benjamin Goldman. (Studies in Green Research). 309p. 1994. 68.95 (1-85628-981-8, Pub. by Avebury Pub UK) Ashgate Pub Co.

Discounting in Financial Accounting & Reporting: Issues in the Literature. Raj Aggarwal & Charles Gibson. 141p. (Orig.). 1989. pap. 6.00 (0-910586-72-1, 077-89) Finan Exec.

Discounting Practices in the Computer Industry: A Monitoring Service for Optimizing the Acquisition of DP Equipment. Ed. by Rebecca Stedman. 166p. 1991. ring bd. 16,400.00 (0-945052-03-0) Computer Econ.

Discourager of Hesitancy see Lady or the Tiger

Discours. Honore Mirabeau. (FRE.). 1973. pap. 10.95 (0-7859-4005-7) Fr & Eur.

Discours: Derniers Vers. Pierre De Ronsard. Ed. by Y. Bellenger. (FRE.). 1979. pap. 10.95 (0-7859-2973-8) Fr & Eur.

Discours a Madame de la Sabliere sur l'Ame des Animaux. Jean De La Fontaine. 107p. (FRE.). 1950. 9.95 (0-8288-9929-0, F37970) Fr & Eur.

Discours Aspectualise. Ed. by Jaques Fontanille. (Nouveaux Actes Semiotiques Ser.: No. 1). 234p. pap. 44.00 (90-272-2267-3) Benjamins North Am.

Discours aux Nuages. Georges Duhamel. 276p. (FRE.). 1947. pap. 18.95 (0-7859-5415-5) Fr & Eur.

Discours de la Methode. Rene Descartes. (Illus.). (FRE.). 1965. pap. 10.95 (0-8288-9574-0, 2253012181) Fr & Eur.

Discours De la Methode. Rene Descartes. Ed. by F. De Buzon. 341p. (FRE.). 1991. pap. 11.95 (0-7859-1674-1, 2070326136) Fr & Eur.

Discours de la Methode: Avec: Extraits de la Dioptrique, des Meteores, du Mond, de Homme, de Lettres et de la Vie de Descartes par Baillet. Rene Descartes. 254p. (FRE.). 1966. 9.95 (0-7859-1169-3, 2080701096) Fr & Eur.

Discours de la Methode (Discourse on the Method) A Bilingual Edition with an Interpretive Essay. Rene Descartes. Tr. by George Heffernan. LC 93-42435. (ENG & FRE.). (C). 1994. text ed. 26.95 (0-268-00870-1); pap. text ed. 7.95 (0-268-00871-X) U of Notre Dame Pr.

Discours de la Methode et Essais see Oeuvres

Discours de la Servitude Volontaire ou le Contr'un. Michel E. De Montaigne & Etienne De la Boetie. 90p. (FRE.). 1947. 13.95 (0-8288-9628-3, 2080703943) Fr & Eur.

Discours de Reception a l'Academie Francaise. Henry De Montherlant. 88p. (FRE.). 1963. pap. 10.95 (0-7859-1290-8, 2070245942) Fr & Eur.

Discours de Reception a l'Academie Francaise. Francois Mauriac. (FRE.). 1934. pap. 10.95 (0-7859-5305-1) Fr & Eur.

Discours De Reception a l'Academie Francaise et Response a Jean D'Ormesson. Marguerite Yourcenar. 88p. (FRE.). 1981. 24.95 (0-7859-0452-2, 2070243656) Fr & Eur.

Discours de Reception et Reponse du Professeur Delay. Eugene Ionesco. (FRE.). pap. 11.95 (0-8288-9824-3, F105915) Fr & Eur.

Discours de Suede. Albert Camus. 1958. pap. 27.95 (0-7859-0595-2, F90560) Fr & Eur.

Discours des Miseres de Ce Temps. Pierre D. Ronsard & Jean Baillou. 290p. (FRE.). 1949. pap. 18.95 (0-7859-1460-9, 2251360913) Fr & Eur.

Discours d'Oxford. Jean Cocteau. 64p. (FRE.). 1956. 10.95 (0-8288-9122-2, F96490) Fr & Eur.

Discours du Docteur O'Grady. Andre Maurois. (FRE.). 1968. pap. 26.95 (0-7859-5549-6) Fr & Eur.

Discours et Messages, 5 tomes. Charles De Gaulle. Incl. Tome I. Pendant la Guerre (Juin 1940-Janv. 1946) 31.95 (0-685-73268-1); Tome II. Dans l'Attente (Fev. 46-Avr. 58) 39.95 (0-685-73269-X); Tome III. Vers le Renouveau (Mai 58-Juill. 62) 39.95 (0-685-73270-3); Tome IV. Pour l'Effort (Aout 62-Dec. 65) 39.95 (0-685-73271-1); Tome V. Vers le Terme (Jano. 66-Avril 69) 39.95 (0-685-73272-X); write for info. (0-318-51981-X) Fr & Eur.

***Discours et Messages Tome I: Pendant la Guerre (Juin 1940-Janv. 1946)** Charles De Gaulle. 750p. (FRE.). 1970. write for info. (0-7859-5245-4) Fr & Eur.

***Discours et Messages Tome II: Dans l'Attente Feb. '46-Apr. '58.** Charles De Gaulle. 750p. 1970. write for info. (0-7859-5244-6) Fr & Eur.

***Discours et Messages Tome III: Vers le Renouveau (Mai '58-Juill. '62)** Charles De Gaulle. 480p. (FRE.). 1970. 39.95 (0-7859-5246-2) Fr & Eur.

***Discours et Messages Tome V: Vers le Terme (Jano. '66-Apr. '69)** Charles De Gaulle. 750p. 1970. 39.95 (0-7859-5247-0) Fr & Eur.

Discours et Messages, Tome IV: Pour l'Effort (Aout 62-Dec. 65) Charles De Gaulle. 486p. (FRE.). 1970. 39.95 (0-7859-1217-7, F101753) Fr & Eur.

Discours et Nouveaux discours ou Docteur O'Grady see Silences du Colonel Bramble

Discours et Pouvoir. Ed. by Ross Chambers. LC 81-50963. (Michigan Romance Studies: Vol. 2). 262p. (Orig.). 1982. pap. 8.00 (0-939730-01-4) Mich Romance.

Discours Feminins dans la Litterature Postmoderne au Quebec. Ed. by Raija Koski et al. LC 93-27050. 420p. (FRE.). 1993. pap. 39.95 (0-7734-1968-3) E Mellen.

Discours Parlementaires de M. Thiers, 16 Vols, Set. Adolphe Thiers. LC 74-176147. reprint ed. 275.00 (0-404-07520-7) AMS Pr.

Discours Particulier D'Escosse. Jacques Makgill & Jean Bellenden. Ed. by Thomas Thomson. LC 72-172710. (Bannatyne Club, Edinburgh. Publications: No. 5). reprint ed. 17.50 (0-404-52706-X) AMS Pr.

Discours Preliminaire (Plan of the French Encyclopedia) Jean D'Alembert. 1972. 59.95 (0-8490-0049-1) Gordon Pr.

"Discours Siciliens" d'Aelius Aristede. rev. ed. Laurent Pernot. Ed. by W. R. Connor. LC 80-2662. (Monographs in Classical Studies). 1981. lib. bdg. 43.95 (0-405-14047-9) Ayer.

Discours sous la Coupole. Marcel Pagnol. 76p. (FRE.). 1961. pap. 10.95 (0-7859-5389-2) Fr & Eur.

Discours sur L'Ambasade. Aeschines. Ed. by W. R. Connor. LC 78-18585. (Greek Texts & Commentaries Ser.). (FRE & GRE.). 1979. reprint ed. lib. bdg. 19.95 (0-405-11427-3) Ayer.

Discours sur le Colonialisme. Aime Cesaire. pap. 13.95 (0-8288-9083-8, 2708705318) Fr & Eur.

Discours sur les Sciences et les Arts. Jean-Jacques Rousseau. Ed. by G. R. Havens. (MLA Ser.: No. 15). 1946. 26.00 (0-527-77300-X) Periodicals Srv.

2022

An Asterisk (*) at the beginning of an entry indicates that the title is appearing in BIP for the first time.

An Asterisk (*) at the beginning of an entry indicates that the title is appearing in BIP for the first time.

Discourse of Trade, from England unto the East-Indies. Thomas Mun. LC 68-30534. (Reprints of Economic Classics Ser.). 58p. 1971. reprint ed. 17.50 (0-678-00873-6) Kelley

Discourse of Trade Unto the East Indies. Thomas Mun. LC 72-6257. (English Experience Ser.: No. 85). 58p. 1969. reprint ed. 11.50 (90-221-0085-5) Walter J Johnson.

Discourse on Colonialism. Aime Cesaire. Tr. by Joan Pinkham. LC 72-178714. 96p. 1972. 10.00 (0-686-86362-3, CL-2059); pap. 8.00 (0-85345-226-1) Monthly Rev.

Discourse on Disenchantment: Reflections on Politics & Technology. Gilbert G. Germain. LC 92-284. (SUNY Series in Political Theory: Contemporary Issues). 187p. (C). 1993. 57.50 (0-7914-1319-5); pap. 18.95 (0-7914-1320-9) State U NY Pr.

Discourse on Elements. Tr. by Ven U. Narada. (C). 1962. 24.00 (0-86013-025-8, Pub. by Pali Text) Wisdom MA.

Discourse on Free Will. Desiderius Erasmus & Martin Luther. Tr. by Ernst F. Winter. LC 60-53363. (Milestones of Thought Ser.). 150p. 1985. pap. text ed. 10.95 (0-8044-6140-6, F Ungar Bks) Continuum.

Discourse on Hip: Selected Writings of Milton Klonsky. Ed. & Frwd. by Ted Solotaroff. LC 90-11979. 337p. 1990. 24.95 (0-8143-1972-6) Wayne St U Pr.

Discourse on Inequality. Jean-Jacques Rousseau. Tr. by Maurice W. Cranston. (Classics Ser.). 208p. 1985. mass mkt. 8.95 (0-14-044439-4, Penguin Classics) Viking Penguin.

Discourse on Metaphysics see Rationalists: Five Basic Works on Rationalism

Discourse on Metaphysics & Other Essays. G. W. Leibniz. Ed. by Daniel Garber. Tr. by Roger Ariew & Daniel Garber. (HPC Classics Ser.). 96p. (C). 1991. lib. bdg. 24.50 (0-87220-133-3); pap. text ed. 4.95 (0-87220-132-5) Hackett Pub.

Discourse on Metaphysics & the Monadology. Gottfried W. Leibniz. (Great Books in Philosophy). 123p. 1992. pap. 6.95 (0-87975-775-2) Prometheus Bks.

Discourse on Method: Descartes. Laurence J. Lafleur. 72p. (C). 1956. pap. write for info. (0-02-367160-2) Macmillan.

Discourse on Method & Meditations. Rene Descartes. Tr. by Laurence J. Lafleur. LC 60-13395. 1960. pap. write for info. (0-672-60278-4, LLA 89) Macmillan.

Discourse on Method & Meditations on First Philosophy. 3rd ed. Rene Descartes. Tr. by Donald Cress. LC 93-18772. (HPC Classics Ser.). 128p. (C). 1993. lib. bdg. 21.50 (0-87220-173-2); pap. text ed. 4.95 (0-87220-172-4) Hackett Pub.

Discourse on Method & Other Writings. Rene Descartes. Tr. by Arthur N. Wollaston. (Classics Ser.). (Orig.). 1968. mass mkt. 5.95 (0-14-044206-5, Penguin Classics) Viking Penguin.

Discourse on Method & the Meditations. Rene Descartes. Tr. by John Veitch. (Great Books in Philosophy). 123p. 1989. pap. text ed. 6.95x (0-87975-526-1) Prometheus Bks.

Discourse on Novelty & Creation. Carl Hausman. LC 83-17986. (SUNY Series in Philosophy). 159p. 1985. 59.50 (0-87395-864-0); pap. 19.95 (0-87395-865-9) State U NY Pr.

Discourse on Policy-Making: American Foreign Policy. Ed. by Kenneth W. Thompson. LC 87-10446. (Exxon Education Foundation Series on Rhetoric & Political Discourse: Vol. 10). 142p. (Orig.). (C). 1987. lib. bdg. 39.00 (0-8191-6338-4, Pub. by White Miller Center) U Pr of Amer.

Discourse on Political Economy & the Social Contract. Jean-Jacques Rousseau. Tr. & Intro. by Christopher Betts. LC 93-48985. (World's Classics Ser.). 240p. 1994. pap. 5.95 (0-19-282750-2) OUP.

Discourse on Popular Culture: Class, Gender, & History in Cultural Analysis, 1730 to the Present. Morag Shiach. LC 88-63329. 238p. 1989. 35.00 (0-8047-1720-6) Stanford U Pr.

Discourse on Statesmanship: The Design & Transformation of the American Polity. Paul Eidelberg. LC 74-8913. 480p. reprint ed. pap. 136.80 (0-317-41909-9, 2025917) Bks Demand.

Discourse on Terrorism Vol. 6: Political Violence & the Subcommittee on Security & Terrorism, 1981-1986. Michael Gold-Biss. LC 93-50228. (Major Concepts in Politics & Political Theory). 194p. (Orig.). (C). 1994. pap. text ed. 29.95 (0-8204-2421-8) P Lang Pubs.

Discourse on the All-Embracing Net of Views: The Brahmajala Sutta & Its Commentaries. Gautama Buddha. Tr. by Bhikkhu Bodhi. 360p. (Orig.). (C). 1989. pap. 13.95 (955-24-0052-X, Pub. by Buddhist Pubns Soc CE) Wisdom MA.

Discourse on the Character of George Washington. Timothy Dwight. (Notable American Authors Ser.). 1992. reprint ed. lib. bdg. 75.00 (0-7812-2742-9) Rprt Serv.

Discourse on the Fruits of Recluseship: The Samannaphala Sutta & Its Commentaries. Tr. by Bhikkhu Bodhi. 190p. (Orig.). (C). 1989. pap. 10.00 (955-24-0045-7, Pub. by Buddhist Pubns Soc CE) Wisdom MA.

Discourse on the Genuineness & Authenticity of the New Testament. Timothy Dwight. (Notable American Authors Ser.). 1992. reprint ed. lib. bdg. 75.00 (0-7812-2739-9) Rprt Serv.

Discourse on the Life & Character of Gov. Tazewell. 2nd ed. Hugh B. Grigsby. LC 91-70142. (Illus.). 116p. 1991. reprint ed. pap. 13.00 (1-878515-60-8) W S Dawson.

Discourse on the Life & Genius of James Fenimore Cooper. William C. Bryant. (Works of William Cullen Bryant). 1989. reprint ed. lib. bdg. 79.00 (0-7812-2138-2) Rprt Serv.

Discourse on the Life, Character & Genius of Washington Irving. William C. Bryant. (Works of William Cullen Bryant). 1989. reprint ed. lib. bdg. 79.00 (0-7812-2139-0) Rprt Serv.

Discourse on the Life Character & Work of Guilian Crommelin Verplanck. William C. Bryant. (Works of William Cullen Bryant). 1989. reprint ed. lib. bdg. 79.00 (0-7812-2142-0) Rprt Serv.

Discourse on the Love of Our Country. Richard Price. 104p. 1992. reprint ed. 40.00 (1-85477-108-6, Pub. by Woodstock Bks UK) Cassell.

Discourse on the Origin of Inequality. Jean-Jacques Rousseau. Tr. by Donald A. Cress. LC 92-20421. 112p. (C). 1992. lib. bdg. 27.50 (0-87220-151-1); pap. text ed. 3.95 (0-87220-150-3) Hackett Pub.

Discourse on the Origin of Inequality. Jean-Jacques Rousseau. Ed. by Patrick Coleman. Tr. by Franklin Philip. (World's Classics Ser.). 176p. 1994. pap. 6.95 (0-19-282947-5) OUP.

Discourse on the Origins of Inequality (Second Discourse), Polemics, & Political Economy. Jean-Jacques Rousseau. Ed. by Roger D. Masters & Christopher Kelly. Tr. by Judith R. Bush et al. LC 92-53866. (Collected Writings of Rousseau: Vol. 3). (Illus.). 242p. 1993. 40.00 (0-87451-603-X) U Pr of New Eng.

Discourse on the Plague. 9th enl. rev. ed. Richard Mead. LC 75-23742. reprint ed. 45.00 (0-404-13297-9) AMS Pr.

Discourse on the Real Nature of Self. Sankaracarya. Tr. by Deb K. Das. (Writers Workshop Redbird Ser.). 1977. lib. bdg. 8.00 (0-89253-617-9) Ind-US Inc.

Discourse on the Sciences & Arts (First Discourse) & Polemics. Jean J. Rousseau. Ed. by Roger D. Masters & Christopher Kelly. Tr. by Christopher Kelly et al. LC 91-50820. (Collected Writings of Rousseau: Vol. 2). (Illus.). 259p. 1992. 40.00 (0-87451-580-7) U Pr of New Eng.

Discourse on the Transfiguration. St. Gregory the Sinaite. Tr. by David Balfour. LC 85-13299. 170p. 1985. reprint ed. lib. bdg. 29.00x (0-89370-862-3) Borgo Pr.

Discourse on Thinking. Martin Heidegger. Tr. by J. M. Anderson & E. Hans Freund. (C). 1969. pap. text ed. 11.00 (0-06-131459-5, TB 1459, Torch) HarpC.

Discourse on Thinking. Martin Heidegger. Tr. by John M. Anderson & E. Hans Freund. 93p. 1991. reprint ed. lib. bdg. 27.00x (0-8095-9088-3) Borgo Pr.

Discourse Particles. Descriptive & Theoretical Investigations on the Logical, Syntactic & Pragmatic Properties of Discourse Particles in German. Ed. by Werner Abraham. LC 90-28425. (Pragmatics & Beyond New Ser.: Vol. 12). viii, 338p. 1991. 89.00x (1-55619-278-9) Benjamins North Am.

***Discourse Particles in Latin: A Study of Nam, Enim, Autem, Vero, & At.** Caroline Kroon. (Amsterdam Studies in Classical Philology: No. 4). xiv, 402p. 1995. lib. bdg. 83.00x (90-5063-447-8, Pub. by Gieben NE) Benjamins North Am.

Discourse Perspectives on Syntax. Ed. by Flora Klein-Andreu. 1983. text ed. 51.00 (0-12-413720-2) Acad Pr.

Discourse, Power & Justice: Towards a New Sociology of Improvement. Brian Longhurst & Michael Adler. LC 93-46106. (International Library of Sociology). 304p. 1993. 79.95x (0-415-04237-2, B3563) Routledge.

Discourse-Pragmatic Approaches to the Verb: The Evidence from Romance. Ed. by Suzanne Fleischman. (Romance Linguistics Ser.). 240p. 1991. 95.00 (0-415-05720-5, A5634) Routledge.

Discourse Pragmatics & Semantic Categorization: The Case of Negation & Tense-Aspect with Special Reference to Swahili. Ellen Contini-Morava. (Discourse Perspectives on Grammar Ser.: No. 1). xii, 205p. (C). 1989. lib. bdg. 79.25 (0-89925-436-5) Mouton.

Discourse Preached in the Center Church. Leonard Bacon. LC 78-168507. (Black Heritage Library Collection). 1977. reprint ed. 14.95 (0-8369-8861-2) Ayer.

Discourse Processing: An Edited Selection of Papers Presented at the International Symposium, Fribourg, Switzerland. Ed. by A. Flammer & Walter Kintsch. (Advances in Psychology Ser.: Vol. 8). 614p. 1982. 100.00 (0-444-86515-2, North Holland) Elsevier.

Discourse Production: A Computer Model of Some Aspects of a Speaker. Anthony Davey. 168p. 1979. 24.00 (0-85224-339-1, Pub. by Edinburgh U Pr UK) Col U Pr.

Discourse Production & Comprehension. Ed. by Roy O. Freedle. (Advances in Discourse Processes Ser.: Vol. 1). (Illus.). 346p. 1977. text ed. 75.00 (0-89391-001-5); pap. text ed. 39.50 (0-89391-128-3) Ablex Pub.

Discourse Production Model for "Twenty Questions" Michael Fortescue. (Pragmatics & Beyond Ser.: Vol. 1, No. 2). x, 137p. 1980. pap. 29.00x (90-272-2505-2) Benjamins North Am.

Discourse Strategies. John J. Gumperz. LC 81-20627. (Studies in Interactional Sociolinguistics: No. 1). 200p. 1982. pap. 19.95 (0-521-28896-7) Cambridge U Pr.

Discourse Structure & Anaphora: Written & Conversational English. Barbara A. Fox. (Cambridge Studies in Linguistics: No. 48). (Illus.). 181p. (C). 1993. pap. 18.95 (0-521-43990-6) Cambridge U Pr.

Discourse Studies: An Introductory Textbook. Jan Renkema. LC 93-1453. ix, 224p. 1993. 53.00x (1-55619-492-7); pap. 22.95 (1-55619-493-5) Benjamins North Am.

Discourse Studies in Honor of James L. Kinneavy. Ed. by Rosalind J. Gabin. 245p. Date not set. 45.00 (0-916379-57-4) Scripta.

Discourse Studies in Meso American Languages, 2 vols., 1. Ed. by Robert E. Longacre & Linda K. Jones. (Publications in Linguistics: No. 58). 1979. fiche 16.00x (0-88312-578-1) Summer Instit Ling.

Discourse Studies in Meso American Languages, 2 vols., 2. Ed. by Robert E. Longacre & Linda K. Jones. (Publications in Linguistics: No. 58). 1979. fiche 12.00x (0-88312-480-7) Summer Instit Ling.

Discourse Studies in Meso American Languages, 2 vols., Set. Ed. by Robert E. Longacre & Linda K. Jones. (Publications in Linguistics: No. 58). 1979. fiche 28.00x (0-88312-478-5) Summer Instit Ling.

Discourse, Tendered to the High Court of Parliament. LC 74-28870. (English Experience Ser.: No. 749). 1975. reprint ed. 3.50 (90-221-0749-3) Walter J Johnson.

Discourse Upon the Institution of Medical Schools in America. John Morgan. LC 74-26276. (History, Philosophy & Sociology of Science Ser.). 1975. reprint ed. 16.95 (0-405-06604-X) Ayer.

Discourse upon Usury. Thomas Wilson. 392p. 1962. 35.00 (0-7146-1260-X, Pub. by F Cass Pubs UK) Intl Spec Bk.

Discourse Written by a Learned Frier see Philosophical Discourse Concerning Speech

Discourse...Being Introductory to His Course of Lectures on Elocution & the English Language. Thomas Sheridan. (Augustan Reprints Ser.: No. 137 (1969)). reprint ed. 12.00 (0-404-70136-1) AMS Pr.

Discourses. Thomas H. Gallaudet. 1972. 59.95 (0-8490-0050-5) Gordon Pr.

Discourses. Niccolo Machiavelli. Ed. by Bernard Crick. (Classics Ser.). 1984. mass mkt. 8.95 (0-14-044428-9, Penguin Classics) Viking Penguin.

Discourses. Joshua Reynolds. 432p. 1992. 10.95 (0-14-043278-7, Penguin Classics) Viking Penguin.

***Discourses.** 7th ed. Meher Baba. Ed. by Eruch Jessawala et al. LC 94-36972. (Illus.). 450p. 1995. reprint ed. 25.00 (1-880619-08-3); reprint ed. pap. 15.00 (1-880619-09-1) Sheriar Found.

Discourses, 5 vols., 1. Dio Chrysostom. (Loeb Classical Library: No. 257, 339, 358, 376, 385). 586p. 1932. 18.95 (0-674-99283-0) HUP.

Discourses, 2 Vols, 1. Epictetus. (Loeb Classical Library: No. 131, 218). 482p. 1925. 18.95 (0-674-99145-1) HUP.

Discourses, 5 vols., 2. Dio Chrysostom. (Loeb Classical Library: No. 257, 339, 358, 376, 385). 448p. 1939. 18.95 (0-674-99374-8) HUP.

Discourses, 2 Vols, 2. Epictetus. (Loeb Classical Library: No. 131, 218). 566p. 1928. 18.95 (0-674-99240-7) HUP.

Discourses, 5 vols., 3. Dio Chrysostom. (Loeb Classical Library: No. 257, 339, 358, 376, 385). 490p. 1940. 18.95 (0-674-99395-0) HUP.

Discourses, 5 vols., 4. Dio Chrysostom. (Loeb Classical Library: No. 257, 339, 358, 376, 385). 478p. 1946. 18.95 (0-674-99414-0) HUP.

Discourses, 5 vols., 5. Dio Chrysostom. (Loeb Classical Library: No. 257, 339, 358, 376, 385). 510p. 1951. 18.95 (0-674-99424-8) HUP.

Discourses: Conversations in Postmodern Art & Culture. Ed. by Russell Ferguson et al. (Illus.). 488p. 1989. 29.95 (0-262-06125-2) New Mus Contemp Art.

Discourses: Conversations in Postmodern Art & Culture. Ed. by Russell Ferguson et al. (Illus.). 480p. 1992. reprint ed. pap. 19.95x (0-262-56063-1) MIT Pr.

DisCourses: More Readings for Thinkers on Airplanes. Michael Phillips. Ed. by Tom Speer. LC 89-92418. (Illus.). 142p. (Orig.). 1990. pap. 10.00 (0-931425-19-0) Clear Glass.

Discourses see Prince & Other Discourses

Discourses Against Judaizing Christians. John Chrysostom. Tr. by Paul W. Harkins. LC 77-8466. (Fathers of the Church Ser.: Vol. 68). 286p. 1979. 39.95 (0-8132-0068-7) Cath U Pr.

Discourses & Essays. Francis B. Bickerstaffe-Drew. LC 78-107683. (Essay Index Reprint Ser.). 1977. reprint ed. 20.95 (0-8369-1489-9) Ayer.

Discourses & Mathematical Illustrations Pertaining to the Extinction Shift Principle under the Electrodynamics of Galilean Transformations. Edward H. Dowdye, Jr. 1992. 29.95 (0-9634471-2-2); pap. 19.95 (0-9634471-3-0) E H Dowdye.

Discourses & Sayings of Our Lord. John Brown. 528p. 1990. 74.95 (0-85151-581-9) Banner of Truth.

Discourses Concerning Government. Algernon Sidney. Ed. by J. P. Mayer. LC 78-67387. (European Political Thought Ser.). 1980. reprint ed. lib. bdg. 37.95 (0-405-11739-6) Ayer.

Discourses Concerning Government. Algernon Sidney. Ed. by Thomas G. West. LC 89-37095. (Liberty Classics Ser.). xlv, 600p. (C). 1990. reprint ed. 27.50 (0-86597-088-2); reprint ed. pap. 10.00 (0-86597-089-0) Liberty Fund.

Discourses from the Spirit World. R. P. Wilson. 197p. 1973. spiral bd. 7.15 (0-7873-0976-1) Mokelumne.

Discourses in America. Matthew Arnold. reprint ed. lib. bdg. 59.00 (0-7812-0319-8) Rprt Serv.

Discourses in America. Matthew Arnold. LC 76-131610. 1970. reprint ed. 25.00 (0-403-00497-7) Scholarly.

***Discourses in Dialect: 10 New Black Poets.** Christal Archibald et al. 111p. (Orig.). 1992. pap. 6.95 (1-886986-00-2) Blackface Bks.

Discourses in Mathematics. Judith Mousley & Genee Marks. 112p. (C). 1991. pap. 60.00x (0-7300-1291-3, ECT403, Pub. by Deakin Univ AT) St Mut.

Discourses in Reading & Linguistics. Ed. by Virginia Teller. (Annals Ser.: Vol. 433). 225p. 1984. lib. bdg. 52.00 (0-89766-260-1); pap. 52.00 (0-89766-261-X) NY Acad Sci.

Discourses of Algernon Sidney, Vol. 24, No. 45. Scott A. Nelson. LC 91-58939. 176p. 1993. 33.50 (0-8386-3438-9) Fairleigh Dickinson.

Discourses of Authority in Medieval & Renaissance Literature. Ed. by Kevin Brownlee & Walter Stephens. LC 88-40346. 309p. 1989. text ed. 40.00 (0-87451-471-1) U Pr of New Eng.

Discourses of Brigham Young. Ed. by John A. Widtsoe. xiv, 497p. 1954. 18.95 (0-87747-066-9) Deseret Bk.

Discourses of Desire: Gender, Genre, & Epistolary Fictions. Linda S. Kauffman. LC 85-48196. (Illus.). 336p. (C). 1986. 39.95 (0-8014-1853-4); pap. 15.95 (0-8014-9510-5) Cornell U Pr.

***Discourses of Development: State, Market & Polity in the Analysis of Complex Change.** Peter W. Preston. 256p. 1994. pap. 63.95 (1-85972-026-9, Pub. by Ashgate UK) Ashgate Pub Co.

Discourses of Difference: An Analysis of Women's Travel Writing & Colonialism. Sara Mills. 208p. 1992. 55.00 (0-415-04629-7, A6766) Routledge.

Discourses of Difference: An Analysis of Women's Travel Writing & Colonialism. Sara Mills. (Illus.). 208p. 1993. pap. 16.95 (0-415-09664-2, B2566) Routledge.

***Discourses of Epictetus.** Epictetus. Ed. by Christopher Gill & Robin Hard. 422p. (Orig.). 1995. pap. 8.50 (0-460-87312-1, Everyman's Classic Lib) C E Tuttle.

Discourses of Ethnicity: Culture & Protest in Jharkhand. Susana DeValle. (Illus.). 276p. (C). 1992. text ed. 32.50 (0-8039-9416-8) Sage.

Discourses of Extremity: Radical Ethics & Post-Marxist Extravagance. Norman Geras. 200p. 1990. 45.00 (0-86091-266-3, A3747); pap. 15.95 (0-86091-980-3, A3751) Routledge Chapman & Hall.

Discourses of Global Politics: A Critical (Re) Introduction to International Relations. Jim George. LC 93-32719. (Critical Perspectives on World Politics Ser.). 266p. (C). 1994. lib. bdg. 45.00 (1-55587-444-4); pap. text ed. 18.95 (1-55587-446-0) Lynne Rienner.

Discourses of Gotama Buddha: Middle Collection. David W. Evans. 34.95 (1-85756-025-6, Pub. by Janus Pub UK) Intl Spec Bk.

Discourses of Machiavelli, 2 vols., Set. Ed. & Tr. by Leslie J. Walker. 1000p. (C). 1991. text ed. 210.00 (0-415-05995-X, A5089) Routledge.

Discourses of Martyrdom in English Literature, 1563-1694. John R. Knott, Jr. (Illus.). 297p. (C). 1993. 64.95 (0-521-43365-7) Cambridge U Pr.

***Discourses of Power: From Hobbes to Foucault.** Barry Hindess. 192p. (C). 1996. write for info. (0-631-19092-9); pap. write for info. (0-631-19093-7) Blackwell Pubs.

Discourses of Rumi. Tr. by Arthur J. Arberry. 288p. (C). 1993. pap. 19.95 (0-7007-0274-1, Pub. by Curzon Pr UK) Humanities.

Discourses of Science. Marcello Pera. Tr. by Clarissa Botsford. LC 94-14169. 1994. 29.95 (0-226-65617-9) U Ch Pr.

Discourses of Sexuality: From AIDS to Aristotle. Ed. by Domna C. Stanton. (Illus.). 300p. (C). 1992. text ed. 42.50 (0-472-09513-7); pap. 14.95 (0-472-06513-0) U of Mich Pr.

***Discourses of the Lord Jesus Christ in the Gospels.** (Walk with Jesus Ser.). 280p. 1988. pap. 40.00 (1-57277-230-1) Truth Center.

Discourses of the Prophet Joseph Smith. Alma P. Burton. LC 77-23977. viii, 280p. 1965. 19.95 (0-87747-067-7) Deseret Bk.

***Discourses of the Vanishing: Modernity, Phantasm, Japan.** Marilyn Ivy. 1995. lib. bdg. 45.95 (0-226-38832-8); pap. text ed. 17.95 (0-226-38833-6) U Ch Pr.

Discourses of Wilford Woodruff. G. Homer Durham. 9.95 (0-88494-000-4) Bookcraft Inc.

Discourses on Society: The Shaping of the Social Science Disciplines. Ed. by Peter Wagner. (C). 1990. lib. bdg. 144.00 (0-7923-1001-2) Kluwer Ac.

Discourses on the Christian Spirit & Life: With an Introduction. 2nd ed. Cyrus A. Bartol. LC 72-4951. (Romantic Tradition in American Literature Ser.). 418p. 1972. reprint ed. 33.95 (0-405-04622-7) Ayer.

***Discourses on the First Book of Herodotus.** James A. Arieti. LC 95-14368. 240p. (C). 1995. text ed. 59.50 (0-8226-3038-9); pap. text ed. 22.95 (0-8226-3039-7) Littlefield.

Discourses on the Gita. M. K. Gandhi. 73p. (Orig.). 1983. pap. 2.00 (0-934676-55-0) Greenlf Bks.

Discourses on the Meaning of History. William Kluback. (American University Studies: Philosophy: Ser. V, Vol. 23). 254p. 1988. 39.00 (0-8204-0387-3) P Lang Pubs.

Discourses on the Miracles of Our Savior. Thomas Woolston. Ed. by Rene Wellek. LC 75-11268. (British Philosophers & Theologians of the 17th & 18th Centuries Ser.: Vol. 67). 565p. 1979. lib. bdg. 15.00 (0-8240-1778-1) Garland.

Discourses on the Sober Life: How to Live One Hundred Years. L. Cornaro. (Longevity Ser.). 1991. lib. bdg. 79.95 (0-8490-4189-9) Gordon Pr.

Discourses on the Sober Life: How to Live 100 Years. Luigi Cornaro. 72p. 1993. spiral bd. 4.40 (0-7873-0223-6) Mokelumne.

Discourses on Various Important Subjects. Jonathan Edwards. (Notable American Authors Ser.). 1992. reprint ed. lib. bdg. 75.00 (0-7812-2764-X) Rprt Serv.

Discourses on War. William E. Channing. 1972. 59.95 (0-8490-0051-3) Gordon Pr.

Discourses on War. William E. Channing. LC 71-137531. (Peace Movement in America Ser.). lxi, 229p. 1972. reprint ed. lib. bdg. 29.95 (0-89198-059-8) Ozer.

Discourses That Pretend to Inform or Instruct. Roger Elliott. (C). 1989. 35.00 (0-907839-32-0, Pub. by Brynmill Pr Ltd UK) St Mut.

Discourses to the Aged. Job Orton. Ed. by Leon Stein. LC 79-8697. (Growing Old Ser.). 1980. reprint ed. lib. bdg. 33.95 (0-405-12795-2) Ayer.

Discourses upon Seneca the Tragedian. William Cornwallis. LC 52-10576. 1978. reprint ed. 50.00 (0-8201-1220-8) Schol Facsimiles.

D

An Asterisk (*) at the beginning of an entry indicates that the title is appearing in BIP for the first time.

Discoursing Sweet Music: Brass Bands & Community Life in Turn-of-the Century Pennsylvania. Kenneth Kreitner. LC 89-4766. (Music in American Life Ser.). (Illus.). 224p. 1990. 22.50 (*0-252-01661-0*) U of Ill Pr.

Discover. Katherine Grier. 1990. pap. 8.61 (*0-201-52322-1*) Addison-Wesley.

***Discover Level K: Skills for Life.** Merita Thompson & Johanna Strange. 7p. (J). (gr. k). 1991. text ed. 7.55 (*0-942277-56-2*) Am Guidance.

Discover a New World of Healing: Answers for Successful Living in These Times. Robin Llast. (Illus.). 234p. (Orig.). 1992. pap. text ed. 12.95 (*0-929240-52-9*) Essential Med Info Syst Inc.

Discover a Richer Life. Ernest Holmes. Ed. by Willis H. Kinnear. 96p. 1961. pap. 5.95 (*0-911336-27-3*) Sci of Mind.

Discover Aerodynamics with Paper Airplanes. Norman Schmidt. (Illus.). 48p. (Orig.). (YA). (gr. 7-12). 1991. pap. 14.95 (*0-920541-43-7*) Peguis Pubs Ltd.

Discover African Wildlife: Activity Book. Laura C. Beattie. (Discover Ser.). (Illus.). 24p. (Orig.). (J). (gr. 3-7). 1993. student ed, pap. 2.95 (*0-911239-38-3*) Carnegie Mus.

Discover Alaska: An Introduction to America's Last Frontier. Ed. by Alaska Northwest Staff. (Illus.). 64p. (Orig.). 1992. pap. 8.95 (*0-88240-412-1*) Alaska Northwest.

Discover America. Ed. by Carol B. Lutyk. (Illus.). 336p. (YA). 1989. 26.95 (*0-87044-804-8*); 36.95 (*0-87044-805-6*); lib. bdg. 39.95 (*0-87044-806-4*) Natl Geog.

Discover! America's Great River Road: A Guide to the Heritage, Natural History, & Recreational Resources of the Upper Mississippi River Valley. Pat Middleton. LC 88-82228. (Illus.). 224p. (Orig.). (J). (gr. 4-12). 1990. pap. 11.95 (*0-9620823-0-9*) Heritage WI.

Discover! America's Great River Road, Vol. 1 (WI, IA, MN, IL) A Guide to the Heritage, Natural History, & Recreational Resources of the Upper Mississippi River Valley. Pat Middleton. (Illus.). 224p. (Orig.). 1991. pap. 11.95 (*0-9620823-3-3*) Heritage WI.

Discover! America's Great River Road, Vol. 2 (IL, IA, MO) A Guide to the Heritage, Natural History, & Recreational Resources of the Middle Mississippi. (Illus.). 256p. (Orig.). 1992. pap. 11.95 (*0-9620823-1-7*) Heritage WI.

Discover Ancient Egypt: Activity Book. Tracy Harrast & Louise Craft. (Discover Ser.). (Illus.). 24p. (J). (gr. 3-7). 1990. student ed, pap. 2.95 (*0-911239-28-6*) Carnegie Mus.

Discover & Introductory Psychology. Peterson. (C). 1991. text ed. 61.50 (*0-673-52189-3*) HarpCollege.

Discover & Psychology. 3rd ed. Henry L. Roediger, III. (C). 1991. text ed. 44.50 (*0-673-52188-5*) HarpCollege.

***Discover Animal Life.** Contrib by Lynne H. Baptista & Mark Rosenthal. (Discover Ser.). (Illus.). 48p. (J). (gr. 3-6). Date not set. lib. bdg. 14.95 (*1-56674-106-8*, HTS Bks) Forest Hse.

Discover Animals. Loveland Comm. Staff. (J). 1992. 4.49 (*1-55513-910-8*, Chariot Bks) Chariot Family.

***Discover Another Nashville: An Updated Essential Guide for Natives & Newcomers with Hundreds of Interesting, Unusual & Alternative Listings.** rev. ed. Noa Ben-Amotz. Date not set. pap. write for info. (*0-9637105-1-6*) Common Ground.

Discover Another Nashville: With over 700 Listings. Noa Ben-Amotz. 1994. pap. 6.95 (*0-9637105-0-8*) Common Ground.

Discover Arizona! Rick Harris. LC 90-23407. (Illus.). 112p. (Orig.). 1991. pap. 6.95 (*0-914846-52-3*) Golden West Pub.

Discover Arizona's Night Sky. Frank Zullo. 56p. 1991. pap. 7.95 (*0-916179-30-3*) Ariz Hwy.

Discover Art - Kindergarten. Cynthia Colbert & Martha Taunton. (J). (gr. k). 1990. pap. text ed. 199.50 (*0-87192-219-3*) Davis Mass.

Discover Birds. Todd A. Culver. (Discover Ser.). (Illus.). 48p. (J). (gr. 3-6). 1992. lib. bdg. 14.95 (*1-878363-66-2*, HTS Bks) Forest Hse.

Discover Bones: Explore the Science of Skeletons. Lesley Grant. 1992. pap. 8.61 (*0-201-63237-3*) Addison-Wesley.

Discover Bookkeeping & Accounts. David Spurling. 256p. (Orig.). 1988. pap. 27.50 (*0-273-02870-7*, Pub. by Pitman Pub Ltd UK) Trans-Atl Phila.

Discover Brittany. Berlitz Staff. 336p. 1994. pap. 17.95 (*2-8315-0660-3*) Berlitz.

Discover Business & Commerce. D. Spurling & G. Whitehead. 256p. (Orig.). (C). 1986. pap. text ed. 26.50 (*0-273-02036-6*) Trans-Atl Phila.

Discover Butterflies. Betty L. Faber. (Discover Ser.). (Illus.). 48p. (J). (gr. 3-6). 1992. lib. bdg. 14.95 (*1-878363-67-0*, HTS Bks) Forest Hse.

Discover Colorado: Cripple Creek & Victor Tours. Annette L. Student. (Illus.). 71p. (Orig.). 1989. spiral bd. 6.95 (*1-877695-03-3*) Student Pubns.

Discover Colorado: Historic Denver Tours, 2 vols., Set. Annette L. Student. (Illus.). (Orig.). 1990. spiral bd., pap. 17.95 (*1-877695-10-6*) Student Pubns.

Discover Colorado: Leadville Tours. Annette L. Student. (Illus.). 70p. (Orig.). 1989. spiral bd. 6.95 (*1-877695-07-6*) Student Pubns.

***Discover Colors.** Marie-Agnes Gaudrat & Thierry Courtin. LC 94-39683. (J). 1995. write for info. (*0-8120-6497-6*) Barron.

Discover Colors. Loveland Comm. Staff. (J). 1992. 4.49 (*1-55513-916-7*, Chariot Bks) Chariot Family.

Discover Computers. Donald D. Spencer. LC 88-6044. 240p. (J). (gr. 6-9). 1988. teacher ed 19.95 (*0-89218-123-0*, NO. 3084); student ed 6.95 (*0-89218-122-2*, NO. 3085); pap. 14.95 (*0-89218-121-4*, NO. 3083) Camelot Pub.

Discover Creative Living. William W. Moore. 64p. (Orig.). 1988. pap. 2.95 (*0-945563-00-0*) Penumbra Pub.

***Discover Dallas: A Child's Guide, 1995-96.** rev. ed. Elaine Velvin. (Illus.). 68p. (J). (gr. 2-7). 1995. pap. 5.95 (*1-885777-09-4*) Hendrick-Long.

Discover Denver: A Pennywise Survival Handbook. rev. ed. Kay Kane & Louise Gold. (Illus.). 1983. 7.95 (*0-9604430-1-0*) Gold-Kane Ent.

Discover Deserts. Howard E. Lawler. (Discover Ser.). (Illus.). 48p. (J). (gr. 3-6). 1992. lib. bdg. 14.95 (*1-56674-029-0*, HTS Bks) Forest Hse.

Discover Devils Tower National Monument. Bobbi Salts. 32p. (J). (gr. 3-5). 1992. 2.50 (*1-881667-00-6*) Devils Tower NHA.

Discover Dinosaurs. Peter Dodson. (Discover Ser.). (Illus.). 48p. (J). (gr. 3-6). 1992. lib. bdg. 14.95 (*1-878363-68-9*, HTS Bks) Forest Hse.

***Discover Dinosaurs.** Jessica Esslinger. 20p. (J). Date not set. pap. text ed. 2.95 (*1-879373-77-7*) R Rinehart.

Discover Dinosaurs. Alice Jablonsky. (Comes to Life Bks.). 16p. (J). (ps-2). 1994. write for info. (*1-883366-36-4*) YES Ent.

Discover Dinosaurs: A Royal Ontario Museum Book. Christopher McGowan. (Illus.). (J). (gr. 3-7). 1993. pap. 10.95 (*1-55074-048-2*) Addison-Wesley.

Discover Dinosaurs: Activity Book. Jessica Esslinger. (Discover Ser.). (Illus.). 20p. (J). (gr. 1-6). 1988. student ed, pap. 2.95 (*0-911239-26-X*) Carnegie Mus.

Discover Dinosaurs: Become a Dinosaur Detective. Christopher McGowan. LC 92-42627. (Illus.). 96p. (J). (gr. 4-7). 1993. pap. 9.57 (*0-201-62267-X*) Addison-Wesley.

***Discover Dinosaurs Activity Book: A Comprehensive Teacher's Guide for Elementary & Middle Schools.** Carnegie Museum of Natural History Staff & Patte Kelley. (Illus.). 40p. (Orig.). 1995. pap. text ed. 6.95 (*0-911239-47-2*) Carnegie Mus.

***Discover DXing! An Introduction to AM, FM, & TV DXing.** John Zondlo. (Illus.). 52p. 1993. pap. 4.95 (*1-882123-44-1*) Universal Radio Rsch.

Discover Europe. Berlitz Staff. 480p. 1994. pap. 21.95 (*2-8315-0673-5*) Berlitz.

Discover Families. Loveland Comm. Staff. (J). 1992. 4.49 (*1-55513-911-6*, Chariot Bks) Chariot Family.

Discover Florida. Robert Tolf. 10.00 (*0-8103-2125-4*) Trend Bk Div.

Discover French Words in Your English Vocabulary. Emilio M. Binzoni. 256p. (Orig.). (C). 1987. pap. 6.95 (*0-9620465-0-7*) Dialogue AZ.

Discover George Mason: Home, State, & Country: A Sampler of Lesson Plans, Activities, & Resources for Teachers of Students in Grades 3 Through 6. rev. ed. Denise McHugh. (Illus.). vi, 101p. 1993. pap. 9.50 (*1-884085-02-4*) Bd Regents.

Discover Girls in Action. Ethel McIndoo. 22p. (Orig.). (SPA.). (J). (gr. 4-6). 1988. pap. text ed. 1.50 (*0-936625-74-0*); pap. text ed. 1.50 (*0-936625-41-4*) Womans Mission Union.

Discover Grand Teton National Park. Bobbi Salts. Ed. by NPS Staff. (Illus.). 32p. (J). 1992. pap. 3.95 (*0-931895-22-7*) Grand Teton NHA.

Discover Graphology: A Straightforward & Practical Guide to Handwriting Analysis. Margaret Gullan-Whur. LC 92-44046. (Illus.). 176p. 1993. pap. 9.95 (*0-8069-0356-2*) Sterling.

Discover Historic California. rev. ed. George Roberts & Jan Roberts. Ed. by April G. Ping & Robin Nordhues. LC 94-76113. (Illus.). 560p. 1994. pap. 12.95 (*0-935182-74-8*) Gem Guides Bk.

***Discover Houston Downtown.** Sandra S. Lord. (Discover Houston Ser.). (Illus.). 32p. (Orig.). 1994. pap. 5.00 (*0-9638792-1-9*) CitiWalks Pr.

Discover Illinois. James Piety. (Illus.). 144p. (C). 1990. student ed 11.80 (*0-87563-291-2*) Stipes.

Discover Indian Reservations U.S.A. A Visitor's Welcome Guide. Ed. by Veronica E. Tiller. 402p. (Orig.). 1992. pap. 19.95 (*0-9632580-0-1*) Council Pubns.

Discover Intensive Phonics for Yourself. rev. ed. Charlotte F. Lockhart. LC 83-71502. 452p. (J). 1983. teacher ed 49.95 (*0-9605654-1-8*) Char-L.

Discover Intensive Phonics for Yourself. 4th rev. ed. Charlotte F. Lockhart. LC 88-91180. 420p. reprint ed. teacher ed, audio 70.00 (*0-9605654-6-9*) Char-L.

Discover Intensive Phonics for Yourself: Teachers Edition. rev. ed. LC 85-71828. 458p. 1985. ring bd. 61.00 (*0-9605654-2-6*) Char-L.

Discover Ireland. Berlitz Staff. 336p. 1994. pap. 18.95 (*2-8315-0683-2*) Berlitz.

Discover It! Mary Laycock & Manuel Dominques. 32p. (Orig.). (J). (gr. 5-10). 1986. pap. 7.50 (*0-918932-87-4*) Activity Resources.

Discover It Yourself: Where Did You Get Those Eyes? Kay Cooper. 80p. (J). 1993. pap. 3.50 (*0-380-71304-7*, Camelot) Avon.

Discover It Yourself: Where in the World Are You? Kay Cooper. (Illus.). 96p. (J). 1993. reprint ed. pap. 3.50 (*0-380-71299-7*, Camelot) Avon.

Discover It Yourself: Who Put the Canon in the Courthouse Square? Kay Cooper. 96p. (J). 1993. pap. 3.50 (*0-380-71298-9*, Camelot) Avon.

Discover Japan Vol. 1: Words, Customs & Concepts. Japan Culture Institute Staff. LC 82-48294. (Discover Japan Ser.). (Illus.). 216p. 1988. pap. 9.00 (*0-87011-835-8*) Kodansha.

Discover Japan Vol. 2: Customs & Concepts. Japan Culture Institute Staff. LC 82-48294. (Discover Japan Ser.). (Illus.). 216p. 1988. pap. 10.00 (*0-87011-836-6*) Kodansha.

Discover Jesus: Guaranteed Security in an Uncertain World. Mark Finley & David B. Smith. LC 92-46451. 1993. 4.95 (*0-8163-1149-8*) Pacific Pr Pub Assn.

***Discover Life Through the Ages: A Carnegie Activity Book.** Laura C. Beattie. (Discover Ser.). (Illus.). 28p. (Orig.). (J). (gr. 3-8). 1995. student ed, pap. 3.95 (*1-57098-030-6*) R Rinehart.

***Discover Light & Sound.** Illus. by Peg Gerrity & Lorie Robare. (Discover Ser.). 48p. (J). (gr. 3-6). Date not set. lib. bdg. 14.95 (*1-56674-107-6*, HTS Bks) Forest Hse.

Discover Loire Valley. Berlitz Staff. 352p. 1994. pap. 17.95 (*2-8315-0662-X*) Berlitz.

Discover Marin State Parks: Angel Island, Mt. Tamalpais, China Camp, Tomales Bay, Olompali. rev. ed. Tacy Dunham. (Marin Trail Guide Ser.). (Illus.). 56p. 1989. reprint ed. pap. 6.95 (*0-685-27206-0*) Cttnwd Pr.

Discover Meditation: A Practical Introduction to the Art of Meditation. Simon Court. LC 93-43008. (Illus.). 112p. 1994. pap. 9.95 (*0-8069-0640-5*) Sterling.

Discover Michigan. David B. McConnell. LC 81-6722. (Illus.). 144p. (J). (gr. 4). 1989. teacher ed 7.45 (*0-910726-33-7*); text ed. 19.95x (*0-910726-07-8*) Hillsdale Educ.

***Discover Native America: Arizona Colorado New Mexico & Utah.** Tish Minear & Janet Limon. (Illus.). 300p. (Orig.). 1995. pap. 16.95 (*0-7818-0327-6*) Hippocrene Bks.

***Discover Nature at Sundown: Things to Know & Things to Do.** Elizabeth P. Lawlor. (Illus.). 224p. (J). 1995. pap. 14.95 (*0-8117-2527-8*) Stackpole.

Discover Nature at the Seashore: Things to Know & Things to Do. Elizabeth P. Lawlor. LC 91-17260. (Discover Nature Ser.). (Illus.). 224p. (J). 1992. pap. 12.95 (*0-8117-3079-4*) Stackpole.

Discover Nature Close to Home: Things to Know & Things to Do. Elizabeth P. Lawlor. (Discover Nature Ser.). (Illus.). 224p. (Orig.). (YA). (gr. 8 up). 1993. pap. 14.95 (*0-8117-3077-8*) Stackpole.

***Discover Nature in the Garden: Things to Know & Things to Do.** Jim Conrad. (Illus.). 224p. 1996. pap. 14.95 (*0-8117-2442-5*) Stackpole.

Discover New England. Berlitz Editors. (Discover Ser.). 352p. 1994. pap. 18.95 (*2-8315-1321-9*) Berlitz.

Discover Normandy. Berlitz Staff. 336p. 1994. pap. 17.95 (*2-8315-0663-8*) Berlitz.

Discover Numerology: Understanding & Using the Power of Numbers. Julia Line. LC 93-24780. (Illus.). 224p. 1993. pap. 9.95 (*0-8069-0464-X*) Sterling.

Discover Ocean Life. Alice Jablonsky. (Discover Ser.). (Illus.). 48p. (J). (gr. 3-6). 1992. lib. bdg. 14.95 (*1-878363-69-7*, HTS Bks) Forest Hse.

Discover Oklahoma Cookin' Oklahoma Four-H Staff. LC 93-72517. 1993. write for info. (*0-87197-388-X*) Favorite Recipes.

Discover Oregon Wineries, 1909-1990. rev. ed. Nancy H. Daniel. (Illus.). 45p. 1989. 1.00 (*0-942367-03-0*) Oreg Winegrowers Assn.

Discover Oregon Wineries 1987-1988. rev. ed. Nancy H. Daniel. (Illus.). 38p. 1987. 1.00 (*0-942367-00-6*) Oreg Winegrowers Assn.

Discover Oregon Wineries 1988-1989. rev. ed. Ed. by Nancy H. Daniel. (Illus.). 45p. 1988. 1.00 (*0-942367-02-2*) Oreg Winegrowers Assn.

Discover Portugal. Berlitz Editors. (Discover Ser.). 336p. 1995. pap. 18.95 (*2-8315-0684-0*) Berlitz.

Discover Powerful Secrets of Retailing Never Revealed: An Invaluable Guide for the Beginning or Experienced Retailer. Wendy Carter. (Illus.). 128p. (Orig.). 1989. pap. text ed. 14.95 (*0-926658-00-X*) Wencar.

***Discover Psalms: Hope When We're Hurting.** Carol V. Rudie. (Discover Your Bible Ser.). 1995. teacher ed write for info. (*1-56212-092-1*) CRC Pubns.

Discover Pyrenees. Berlitz Staff. 336p. 1994. pap. 17.95 (*2-8315-0664-6*) Berlitz.

Discover Rain Forests. Richard Block. (Discover Ser.). (Illus.). 48p. (J). (gr. 3-6). 1992. lib. bdg. 14.95 (*1-56674-030-4*, HTS Bks) Forest Hse.

Discover Reincarnation see Discover Your Past Lives: A Practical Course

***Discover Rivers: A Discovery Book.** Dick Ruehrwein & Julie North. (Illus.). 32p. (Orig.). (J). (gr. 5-7). 1995. pap. 3.75 (*0-915992-73-6*) Eastern Acorn.

Discover Rocks & Minerals. W. R. Shedenhelm. (Discover Ser.). (Illus.). 48p. (J). (gr. 3-6). 1992. lib. bdg. 14.95 (*1-878363-70-0*, HTS Bks) Forest Hse.

Discover Rocks & Minerals: Activity Book. Laura C. Beattie. (Discover Ser.). (Illus.). 24p. (J). (gr. 3-8). 1991. student ed, pap. 2.95 (*0-911239-36-7*) Carnegie Mus.

Discover Romanian: An Introduction to the Language & Culture. Rodica Botoman. (Illus.). 425p. (C). 1995. pap. text ed. 47.50 (*0-8142-0536-4*) Ohio St U Pr.

Discover Runes: Understanding & Using the Power of Runes. Tony Willis. LC 92-44470. (Illus.). 176p. 1993. pap. 9.95 (*0-8069-0354-6*) Sterling.

Discover San Diego. 15th rev. ed. Leander Peik & Rosalie Peik. (Illus.). 136p. 1988. pap. 2.50 (*0-9620402-0-7*) Peiks Enter.

Discover San Diego. 16th ed. Leander Peik. 1991. pap. 3.50 (*0-9620402-5-8*) Peiks Enter.

***Discover Seashores: A Discovery Book.** Barbara Moses. (Illus.). 32p. (J). (gr. 5-7). 1995. pap. 3.75 (*0-915992-72-8*) Eastern Acorn.

Discover Seattle with Kids: Where to Go & What to See in the Puget Sound Area. 5th ed. Rosanne Cohn. (Illus.). 224p. 1987. reprint ed. pap. 8.95 (*0-9691246-4-3*) J&SAI.

***Discover Shapes.** Francoise Audry-Iljic & Thierry Courtin. LC 94-37327. (J). 1995. write for info. (*0-8120-6499-2*) Barron.

Discover Sizes & Shapes. Loveland Comm. Staff. (J). 1992. 4.49 (*1-55513-909-4*, Chariot Bks) Chariot Family.

***Discover: Skills for Life Level 1: Student Edition Big Book.** Merita L. Thompson & Johanna Strange. (Illus.). 64p. 1991. text ed. 76.95 (*0-942277-43-0*) Am Guidance.

Discover: Skills for Life, Level K: Pupil Edition. Merita L. Thompson & Johanna Strange. (Illus.). 48p. (J). (gr. k). 1991. text ed. 11.95 (*0-7854-0153-9*, 15001) Am Guidance.

Discover: Skills for Life, Level K: Spanish Home Worksheets. Merita L. Thompson & Johanna Strange. (Illus.). 7p. (SPA.). (J). (gr. k). 1991. text ed. 8.95 (*0-7854-0204-7*, 15305) Am Guidance.

Discover: Skills for Life, Level K: Student Edition Big Book. Merita L. Thompson & Johanna Strange. (Illus.). 48p. (J). (gr. k). 1991. text ed. 87.95 (*0-7854-0174-1*, 15004) Am Guidance.

Discover: Skills for Life, Level K: Teacher's Edition. Merita L. Thompson & Johanna Strange. 80p. 1991. text ed. 33.95 (*0-7854-0154-7*, 15002) Am Guidance.

Discover: Skills for Life, Level K: Total Teacher Support System. Merita L. Thompson & Johanna Strange. (Illus.). 168p. 1991. text ed. 97.95 (*0-7854-0155-5*, 15003) Am Guidance.

Discover: Skills for Life, Level 1: Pupil Book. Merita L. Thompson & Johanna Strange. (Illus.). 48p. (J). (gr. 1). 1991. text ed. 11.95 (*0-7854-0156-3*, 15011) Am Guidance.

Discover: Skills for Life, Level 1: Spanish Home Worksheets. Merita L. Thompson & Johanna Strange. (Illus.). 7p. (SPA.). (J). (gr. 1). 1991. text ed. 8.95 (*0-7854-0106-7*, 15315) Am Guidance.

Discover: Skills for Life, Level 1: Student Edition Big Book. Merita L. Thompson & Johanna Strange. (Illus.). 64p. (J). (gr. 1). 1991. text ed. 87.95 (*0-7854-0194-6*, 15014) Am Guidance.

Discover: Skills for Life, Level 1: Teacher's Edition. Merita L. Thompson & Johanna Strange. (Illus.). 96p. 1991. text ed. 33.95 (*0-7854-0157-1*, 15012) Am Guidance.

Discover: Skills for Life, Level 1: Total Teacher Support System. Merita L. Thompson & Johanna Strange. (Illus.). 168p. 1991. text ed. 97.95 (*0-7854-0158-X*, 15013) Am Guidance.

Discover: Skills for Life, Level 2: Spanish Home Worksheet. Merita L. Thompson & Johanna Strange. (Illus.). 7p. (SPA.). (J). (gr. 2). 1991. text ed. 8.95 (*0-7854-0107-5*, 15325) Am Guidance.

Discover: Skills for Life, Level 2: Student Book. Merita L. Thompson & Johanna Strange. (Illus.). 64p. (J). (gr. 2). 1991. text ed. 11.95 (*0-7854-0159-8*, 15021) Am Guidance.

Discover: Skills for Life, Level 2: Teacher's Edition. Merita L. Thompson & Johanna Strange. (Illus.). 112p. 1991. text ed. 33.95 (*0-7854-0160-1*, 15022) Am Guidance.

Discover: Skills for Life, Level 2: Total Teacher Support System. Merita L. Thompson & Johanna Strange. (Illus.). 1991. text ed. 97.95 (*0-7854-0161-X*, 15023) Am Guidance.

Discover: Skills for Life, Level 3: Spanish Home Worksheet. Merita L. Thompson & Johanna Strange. (Illus.). 7p. (SPA.). (J). (gr. 3). 1991. text ed. 8.95 (*0-7854-0108-3*, 15335) Am Guidance.

Discover: Skills for Life, Level 3: Student Book. Merita L. Thompson & Johanna Strange. (Illus.). 80p. (J). (gr. 3). 1991. text ed. 12.95 (*0-7854-0162-8*, 15031) Am Guidance.

Discover: Skills for Life, Level 3: Teacher's Edition. Merita L. Thompson & Johanna Strange. (Illus.). 112p. 1991. text ed. 36.95 (*0-7854-0163-6*, 15032) Am Guidance.

Discover: Skills for Life, Level 3: Total Teacher Support System. Merita L. Thompson & Johanna Strange. (Illus.). 186p. 1991. text ed. 99.95 (*0-7854-0164-4*, 15033) Am Guidance.

Discover: Skills for Life, Level 4: Spanish Home Worksheets. Merita L. Thompson & Johanna Strange. (Illus.). 7p. (SPA.). (J). (gr. 4). 1991. text ed. 8.95 (*0-7854-0109-1*, 15345) Am Guidance.

Discover: Skills for Life, Level 4: Student Book. Merita L. Thompson & Johanna Strange. (Illus.). 80p. (J). (gr. 4). 1991. text ed. 12.95 (*0-7854-0165-2*, 15041) Am Guidance.

Discover: Skills for Life, Level 4: Teacher's Edition. Merita L. Thompson & Johanna Strange. (Illus.). 116p. 1991. text ed. 36.95 (*0-7854-0166-0*, 15042) Am Guidance.

Discover: Skills for Life, Level 4: Total Teacher Support. Merita L. Thompson & Johanna Strange. (Illus.). 216p. 1991. text ed. 99.95 (*0-942277-19-8*, 15043) Am Guidance.

Discover: Skills for Life, Level 5: Spanish Home Worksheets. Merita L. Thompson & Johanna Strange. (Illus.). 7p. (SPA.). (J). (gr. 5). 1991. text ed. 8.95 (*0-7854-0110-5*, 15355) Am Guidance.

Discover: Skills for Life, Level 5: Student Book. Merita L. Thompson & Johanna Strange. (Illus.). 128p. (J). (gr. 5). 1991. text ed. 13.95 (*0-7854-0168-7*, 15051) Am Guidance.

Discover: Skills for Life, Level 5: Teacher's Edition. Merita L. Thompson & Johanna Strange. (Illus.). 168p. 1991. text ed. 36.95 (*0-7854-0169-5*, 15052) Am Guidance.

Discover: Skills for Life, Level 5: Total Teacher Support System. Merita L. Thompson & Johanna Strange. (Illus.). 216p. 1991. text ed. 99.95 (*0-7854-0170-9*, 15053) Am Guidance.

Discover: Skills for Life, Level 6: Spanish Home Worksheets. Merita L. Thompson & Johanna Strange. (Illus.). 7p. (SPA.). (J). (gr. 6). 1991. text ed. 8.95 (*0-7854-0111-3*, 15365) Am Guidance.

Discover: Skills for Life, Level 6: Student Book. Merita L. Thompson & Johanna Strange. (Illus.). 144p. (J). (gr. 6). 1991. text ed. 14.95 (*0-7854-0095-8*, 15061) Am Guidance.

Discover: Skills for Life, Level 6: Total Teacher Support System. Merita L. Thompson & Johanna Strange. (Illus.). 224p. 1991. text ed. 99.95 (*0-7854-0096-6*, 15063) Am Guidance.

D

An Asterisk (*) at the beginning of an entry indicates that the title is appearing in BIP for the first time.

2025

Discover: Skills for Life, Level 7: Student Book. Merita L. Thompson & Johanna Strange. (Illus.). 240p. (J). (gr. 7). 1991. text ed. 18.95 (*0-7854-0097-4*, 15071) Am Guidance.

Discover: Skills for Life, Level 7: Teacher's Edition. Merita L. Thompson & Johanna Strange. (Illus.). 256p. 1991. text ed. 41.95 (*0-7854-0098-2*, 15072) Am Guidance.

Discover: Skills for Life, Level 7: Total Teacher Support System. Educational Assessment Publishing Company Staff. (Illus.). 396p. 1991. text ed. 220.95 (*0-7854-0099-0*, 15073) Am Guidance.

Discover: Skills for Life, Level 8: Student Book. Educational Assessment Publishing Company Staff. (Illus.). 240p. (J). (gr. 8). 1991. text ed. 18.95 (*0-7854-0150-4*, 15081) Am Guidance.

Discover: Skills for Life, Level 8: Teacher's Edition. Educational Assessment Publishing Company Staff. (Illus.). 256p. 1991. text ed. 41.95 (*0-7854-0151-2*, 15082) Am Guidance.

Discover: Skills for Life, Level 8: Total Teacher Support System. Educational Assessment Publishing Company Staff. (Illus.). 396p. 1991. text ed. 220.95 (*0-7854-0152-0*, 15083) Am Guidance.

Discover Sociology. Ray Power et al. 300p. (Orig.). (C). 1986. pap. text ed. 26.50 (*0-273-02282-2*) Trans-Atl Phila.

Discover Southeast Alaska with Pack & Paddle. 2nd ed. Margaret H. Piggott. LC 90-36104. (Illus.). 240p. 1990. pap. 12.95 (*0-89886-242-6*) Mountaineers.

Discover Southern Ontario. Annette Snowdon. (Illus.). 518p. 1985. 14.95 (*0-7725-1526-3*, Pub. by Stoddart Pubng CN) Genl Dist Srvs.

Discover Stars & Planets. Toni Eugene. (Discover Ser.). (Illus.). 48p. (J). (gr. 3-6). 1992. lib. bdg. 14.95 (*1-878363-71-9*, HTS Bks) Forest Hse.

Discover the Apocrypha. JoLinda Lewis & Danny Lewis. 25p. 1972. 3.95 (*0-932807-02-X*) Overmountain Pr.

Discover the Best Jobs for You! One Hundred & One Tools & Strategies for Career Success. 2nd ed. Ron Krannich. 1993. 24.95 (*0-942710-82-7*); pap. 11.95 (*0-942710-79-7*) Impact VA.

Discover the Career Within You. 3rd ed. Clarke G. Carney & Cinda F. Wells. 312p. (C). 1990. pap. 21.95 (*0-534-14952-9*) Brooks-Cole.

***Discover the Career Within You.** 4th rev. ed. Clarke G. Carney & Cinda F. Wells. LC 94-21844. 304p. 1995. pap. 20.95 (*0-534-25638-4*) Brooks-Cole.

***Discover the CSU: A Subjective Guide to the California State University.** Pat Dever & Margy Arthur. LC 94-79125. 208p. (Orig.). 1994. pap. 10.00 (*0-9643053-0-5*) Coll Campus.

Discover the Fun of Cake Decorating. Ed. by Eugene T. Sullivan & Marilynn C. Sullivan. LC 79-11150. 1979. 12.99 (*0-912696-15-X*) Wilton.

Discover the Good Life in Rural America: The City Slicker's Guide to Buying Country Real Estate Without Losing Your Shirt. Bob Bone. Ed. & Frwd. by Marilyn Ross. 1994. pap. 19.95 (*0-918880-36-X*) Comm Creat.

Discover the Harmonica. R. Yoder. 1990. 2.95 (*0-685-32193-2*, P072) Hansen Ed Mus.

***Discover the Hidden New Jersey.** Russell Roberts. (Illus.). 300p. (C). 1995. pap. 18.95 (*0-8135-2252-8*) Rutgers U Pr.

Discover the Kazoo. C. Anderson. (Miscellaneous Ser.). 1990. 1.95 (*0-685-32015-4*, G281) Hansen Ed Mus.

***Discover the Limitless Power of Positive Decision Making Technology.** Afrikan Culture Institute Staff. LC 91-72700. (Afrikan Motivational Ser.). 200p. 1995. write for info. (*1-56454-038-3*) Cont Afrikan.

***Discover the Limitless Power of Positive Goal Achievement Technology.** Afrikadzata Deku (Afrikan Culture Institute) Staff. LC 91-72698. (Afrikan Motivational Ser.). 300p. 1995. write for info. (*1-56454-036-7*) Cont Afrikan.

***Discover the Limitless Power of Positive Planning Technology.** Afrikan Culture Institute Staff. LC 91-72702. 80p. 1995. write for info. (*1-56454-040-5*) Cont Afrikan.

***Discover the Limitless Power of Positive Self-Knowledge Technology.** Afrikadzata Deku (Afrikan Culture Institute) Staff. LC 91-72697. (Afrikan Motivational Ser.). 300p. 1995. write for info. (*1-56454-035-9*) Cont Afrikan.

***Discover the Limitless Power of Positive Team-Building Technology.** Afrikan Culture Institute Staff. LC 91-72701. (Afrikan Motivational Ser.). 100p. 1995. write for info. (*1-56454-039-1*) Cont Afrikan.

***Discover the Olympic Spirit Inside of You.** Kim D. Fellwock. 140p. (Orig.). 1995. pap. write for info. (*1-57502-027-0*) Morris Pub.

Discover the Oregon Trail. Bobbi Salts. (Illus.). 32p. (Orig.). (J). (gr. 4-6). 1992. pap. 3.95 (*0-931056-06-3*) Jefferson Natl.

Discover the Power Within You: A Guide to the Unexplored Depths Within. Eric Butterworth. LC 91-58166. 256p. 1992. reprint ed. pap. 12.00 (*0-06-250115-1*) Harper SF.

Discover the Power Within You *see* **Descubre Tu Poder Interno**

Discover the Right Job for You: A Guide to Creating Job & Career Success. Ronald L. Krannich & Caryl R. Krannich. 167p. (Orig.). 1991. 22.95 (*0-942710-32-0*); pap. 11.95 (*0-942710-33-9*) Impact VA.

Discover the Rockies: 1992-1993 Travel & Recreation Guide. Colorado Publishing Company Staff. 320p. 1992. pap. text ed. 14.95 (*0-9632304-0-9*) CO Pub Co.

Discover the Stars: Star Watching Using the Naked Eye, Binoculars, or a Telescope. Richard Berry. (Illus.). 96p. 1987. pap. 12.95 (*0-517-56529-3*, Harmony) Crown Pub Group.

Discover the Wines You Don't Know. 1988. 2.00 (*0-685-44004-4*, 111) Am Bartenders.

Discover the World: Helping Children Develop Respect for Themselves, Others & the Earth. Ed. by Susan Hopkins & Jeff Winters. 160p. (Orig.). 1990. lib. bdg. 39.95 (*0-86571-191-7*); pap. 14.95 (*0-86571-192-5*) New Soc Pubs.

Discover the World of Trucking. John H. Ware. 160p. 1993. pap. 12.95 (*1-880365-31-6*) Prof Pr NC.

Discover Truth & Be Free. Dwight O. Nichols. 68p. (Orig.). 1994. pap. 4.95 (*0-9624064-1-4*) New Era Trng.

Discover Turkey: Year-Round Recipes for Parts & Leftovers. Leah Christian. 24p. (Orig.). 1988. pap. 4.00 (*0-685-25279-5*) Family Rm Pr.

Discover Tuscany. Berlitz Editors. (Discover Ser.). 352p. 1995. pap. 18.95 (*2-8315-0685-9*) Berlitz.

Discover Volcanoes & Earthquakes. Bruce A. Bolt. (Discover Ser.). (Illus.). 48p. (J). (gr. 3-6). 1992. lib. bdg. 14.95 (*1-56674-031-2*, HTS Bks) Forest Hse.

Discover Weather. Robert W. Grumbine. (Discover Ser.). (Illus.). 48p. (J). (gr. 3-6). 1992. lib. bdg. 14.95 (*1-56674-032-0*, HTS Bks) Forest Hse.

***Discover Western Australia.** Jocelyn Burt. Date not set. 29.95 (*1-875560-21-1*, Pub. by Univ of West Aust Pr AT) Intl Spec Bk.

Discover Westward Expansion. Bobbi Salts. (Illus.). 32p. (Orig.). (J). (gr. 4-6). 1992. pap. text ed. 3.95 (*0-931056-03-9*) Jefferson Natl.

Discover What You're Best At. rev. ed. Barry Gale. 1990. pap. 12.00 (*0-671-69589-4*) S&S Trade.

Discover Windows 3.1 Multimedia. Roger Jennings. 1992. pap. 39.95 (*1-56529-060-7*) Que.

Discover Your Best Possible Future: A Step-by-Step Guide to Choosing a College, a Major, a Career. Diane Eble & Richard Hagstrom. 160p. 1993. 8.99 (*0-310-54491-2*) Zondervan.

Discover Your Best Self. Robert N. James. LC 78-57043. 1979. 7.95 (*0-686-24751-5*) Discoveries.

Discover Your Business Potential: A Comprehensive Self-Evaluation. Teresa Patty. 96p. 1992. student ed write for info. (*0-9633989-0-3*) New Start Cnslting.

Discover Your Chess Strength. Raymond Keene. 128p. 1992. pap. 19.95 (*0-8050-2432-8*, Pub. by Batsford Chess UK) H Holt & Co.

Discover Your Children's Gifts: A Parents Handbook to Recognize & Develop Your Children's God-Given Gifts. Don Fortune & Katie Fortune. LC 89-32990. 224p. 1989. pap. 11.99 (*0-8007-9151-7*) Chosen Bks.

Discover Your God-Given Gifts. Don Fortune & Katie Fortune. LC 87-20543. 276p. (Orig.). 1987. pap. 11.99 (*0-8007-9108-8*) Chosen Bks.

Discover Your Inner Spirit. Ruth Fishel. (Meditative Moments Ser.). (Illus.). 72p. (Orig.). 1993. pap. 1.95 (*1-55874-255-7*, 2557) Health Comm.

Discover Your Own Literacy. Donald Graves. LC 89-36848. (Reading-Writing Teacher's Companion Ser.). 137p. (Orig.). 1989. pap. text ed. 13.00 (*0-435-08487-9*) Heinemann.

Discover Your Past Lives. Brad Steiger & Francie Steiger. Ed. by Julie Lockhart. LC 87-62094. 288p. 1987. reprint ed. pap. 15.95 (*0-914918-76-1*, Whitford Pr) Schiffer.

Discover Your Past Lives: A Practical Course. J. H. Brennan. LC 93-44450. Orig. Title: Discover Reincarnation. 160p. 1994. reprint ed. pap. 9.95 (*0-8069-0642-1*) Sterling.

***Discover Your Perfect Soul Mate.** Judith Powell. 1995. audio, pap. text ed. 12.95 (*1-56087-078-8*) Top Mtn Pub.

Discover Your Roots: A New, Easy Guide for Tracing Your Family Tree. Marilyn M. Heimberg. LC 77-77291. (Illus.). 1977. pap. 3.95 (*0-918880-00-9*) Comm Creat.

Discover Your Spiritual Gift & Use It. Rick Yohn. 1982. pap. 7.99 (*0-8423-0626-9*) Tyndale.

***Discover Your Spiritual Type: A Guide to Individual & Congregational Growth.** Corinne Ware. 1994. 14.95 (*1-56699-149-8*, AL159) Alban Inst.

Discover Your Talent & Find Fulfillment: A Guide to Using Your Skills to Get What You Need & Want Out of Life. Roscoe Barnes, III. 80p. 1994. pap. 6.95 (*0-9626420-0-2*) McKinley & Henson.

***Discover Your True Self-Esteem.** David J. Gilbert. 1995. pap. 7.95 (*0-533-10237-5*) Vantage.

Discover Yourself. rev. ed. Paul Brunton. LC 83-60832. 320p. 1983. reprint ed. pap. 14.95 (*0-87728-592-6*) Weiser.

Discover Yourself at a Greater Columbus Bed & Breakfast. Jennifer Bosveld. 70p. (Orig.). 1994. pap. 8.95 (*0-685-53842-7*) Pudding Hse Pubns.

Discover Zion: Five Language Guide. Victor L. Jackson. LC 77-73070. (Illus.). 88p. (ENG, FRE, GER, JPN & SPA.). 1978. 4.95 (*0-915630-05-2*) Zion.

Discovered! Clay Coleman. (Escape from Lost Island Ser.: No. 4). (YA). (gr. 9-12). 1991. pap. 2.95 (*0-06-106044-5*, PL) HarpC.

Discovered: Sodom & Gomorrah. Jim Pinkoski. (Illus.). 24p. (Orig.). 1992. 2.95 (*0-945383-40-1*) Teach Servs.

Discovered: True! The Genesis Story of Creation. Jim Pinkoski. (Illus.). 32p. (Orig.). 1992. 2.95 (*0-945383-39-8*) Teach Servs.

Discovered Country: Tourism & Survival in the American West. Ed. by Scott Norris. LC 94-66179. (Illus.). 248p. (Orig.). 1994. pap. 17.95 (*0-9637623-0-3*) Stone Ladder.

Discovered Lands, Invented Pasts: Transforming Visions of the American West. Jules D. Prown et al. LC 92-53537. 217p. (C). 1992. pap. 30.00 (*0-89467-061-1*) Yale Art Gallery.

Discovered Lands, Invented Pasts: Transforming Visions of the American West. Jules D. Prown et al. (Illus.). 256p. (C). 1992. pap. text ed. 40.00 (*0-300-05722-9*) Yale U Pr.

Discovered Lands, Invented Pasts: Transforming Visions of the American West. Jules D. Prown et al. (Illus.). 232p. 1994. pap. 25.00 (*0-300-05731-8*) Yale U Pr.

***Discovered Light.** Craig T. Putnam. 56p. 1995. pap. 7.00 (*0-8059-3694-7*) Dorrance.

***Discoverers.** Date not set. pap. 22.00 (*1-56997-095-5*) Knowldge Adv.

Discoverers. Daniel J. Boorstin. 1983. 40.00 (*0-394-40229-4*) Random.

Discoverers. Daniel J. Boorstin. 1993. pap. 16.00 (*0-394-25633-6*, Vin) Random.

Discoverers. Paul King. 1994. mass mkt. 5.99 (*0-553-29831-3*) Bantam.

Discoverers: A History of Man's Search to Know His World & Himself. Daniel J. Boorstin. 768p. 1985. pap. 16.00 (*0-394-72625-1*, Vin) Random.

Discoverers: An Illustrated History of Man's Search to Know His World & Himself, 2 vols. Daniel J. Boorstin. (Illus.). 1024p. 1991. boxed 75.00 (*0-8109-3207-5*) Abrams.

Discoverers, Explorers, Settlers: The Diligent Writers of Early America. Wayne Franklin. LC 79-4390. (Illus.). xiv, 252p. 1989. pap. text ed. 14.95 (*0-226-26072-0*) U Ch Pr.

Discoverers for Medicine. William H. Woglom. LC 78-156733. (Essay Index Reprint Ser.). 1977. reprint ed. 18.95 (*0-8369-2432-0*) Ayer.

Discoverers of America. Harold Faber. LC 91-17001. (Illus.). 304p. (YA). (gr. 9 up). 1992. text ed. 17.95 (*0-684-19217-9*, C Scribner Sons Young) S&S Childrens.

Discoverers of the Lost World: An Account of Some of Those Who Brought Back to Life South American Mammals Long Buried in the Abyss of Time. George G. Simpson. LC 84-2243. (Illus.). 224p. 1984. 17.00 (*0-300-03188-2*) Yale U Pr.

Discoverie & Historie of the Gold Mynes in Scotland. Stephen Atkinson. LC 77-38492. (Bannatyne Club, Edinburgh. Publications: No. 14). reprint ed. 24.50 (*0-404-52714-0*) AMS Pr.

Discoverie of the Large, Rich & Bewtiful Empire of Guiana, Performed in the Yeare 1595, by Sir W. Ralegh. Walter Raleigh. LC 68-27482. (English Experience Ser.: No. 3). 112p. 1968. reprint ed. 11.50 (*90-221-0003-0*) Walter J Johnson.

Discoverie of Witchcraft. Reginald Scot. (J). 1989. pap. 7.95 (*0-486-26030-5*) Dover.

Discoveries. Koshi. 1992. pap. 19.95 (*0-8384-2386-8*) Heinle & Heinle.

Discoveries: African Art from the Smiley Collection. Ed. by Anita J. Glaze et al. (Illus.). 92p. (Orig.). (C). 1989. pap. 19.95 (*0-8122-1402-1*) U of Pa Pr.

***Discoveries: Expanding Your Child's Vocational Horizons.** Richard P. Olson & Helen E. Froyd. (Illus.). (Orig.). 1995. pap. 14.95 (*0-8298-1106-0*) Pilgrim OH.

Discoveries: Fifty Stories of the Quest. Harold Schechter & Jonna G. Semeiks. 608p. (Orig.). (C). 1983. pap. write for info. (*0-02-406980-9*) Macmillan.

Discoveries: Fifty Stories of the Quest. 2nd ed. Ed. by Harold Schechter & Jonna G. Semeiks. 672p. (Orig.). (C). 1992. pap. text ed. 22.00 (*0-19-506850-5*) OUP.

Discoveries & Inventions, 8 vols., Set. Ed. by Rodney Dale. (Discoveries & Inventions Ser.). (Illus.). 512p. (J). 1994. lib. bdg. 128.00 (*0-19-520973-7*) OUP.

Discoveries & Inventions, 8 vols., Set. Ed. by Rodney Dale. (Illus.). (J). 1995. reprint ed. pap. 79.60 (*0-19-520974-5*) OUP.

Discoveries & Opinions of Galileo. Galileo Galilei. LC 57-6305. 1957. mass mkt. 7.95 (*0-385-09239-3*, A94, Anchor NY) Doubleday.

Discoveries! French Masterpieces from St. Etienne: Essays. Philip Conisbee & William Kloss. LC 92-17435. 1992. write for info. (*0-89951-086-8*) Santa Barb Mus Art.

Discoveries from Kurdish Looms. Ed. by Robert D. Biggs. LC 83-19535. (Illus.). 116p. (Orig.). 1983. pap. 22.50 (*0-941680-02-9*) M&L Block.

Discoveries from the Time of Jesus. Alan Millard. 1990. 29.95 (*0-7459-1207-9*) Lion USA.

Discoveries in Antisense Nucleic Acids. Ed. by Christine L. Brakel. (Advances in Applied Biotechnology Ser.: Vol. 2). (Illus.). 208p. (C). 1989. 55.00 (*0-943255-04-X*) Portfolio Pub.

Discoveries in Asia Minor: Including a Description of the Ruins of Several Ancient Cities, Especially Antioch of Pisidia, 2 vols. in 1. Francis V. Arundell. (Illus.). xxx, 797p. 1975. reprint ed. lib. bdg. 109.20 (*3-487-05440-X*, Pub. by Georg Olms GW) Lubrecht & Cramer.

Discoveries in Biological Psychiatry, 1984. Ed. by Frank Ayd & Barry Blackwell. LC 78-124542. 254p. text ed. 28.50 (*0-685-19220-2*) Ayd Medical Comm.

Discoveries in Earth Science. Richard Osmun et al. (Upco's Science Ser.). (Illus.). (Orig.). 1987. teacher ed 9.95 (*0-937323-07-1*); student ed 5.95 (*0-937323-06-3*) United Pub Co.

Discoveries in Earth Science: Testing Program Master Sheets. Osmun et al. 56p. (Orig.). 1990. 49.95 (*0-937323-10-1*) United Pub Co.

***Discoveries in God's Family.** Anne Russell. (1992 50-Day Spiritual Adventure Ser.). (Illus.). 64p. (Orig.). (J). (gr. 3-6). 1991. student ed, pap. text ed. 4.95 (*1-879050-05-6*) Chapel of Air.

Discoveries in Martin's Hundred. rev. ed. Ivor Noel Hume. LC 83-1951. (Archaeological Ser.: No. 10). (Illus.). 64p. (Orig.). 1987. pap. 5.95 (*0-87935-069-5*) Colonial Williamsburg.

Discoveries in Plant Biology, 2 vols., Set. S. D. Kung. 800p. 1995. text ed. 217.00 (*981-02-1313-1*) World Scientific Pub.

Discoveries in the Judaean Desert: Qumran Grotte 4-11, Vol. 6. Roland De Vaux & Jozef T. Milik. (Illus.). 1977. text ed. 98.00 (*0-19-826317-1*) OUP.

Discoveries in the Wadi ed-Daliyeh. Ed. by Paul W. Lapp & Nancy L. Lapp. (Annual of the American Schools of Oriental Research Ser.: Vol. 41). (Illus.). 106p. 1974. text ed. 20.00 (*0-89757-041-3*) Am Sch Orient Res.

Discoveries of Ephesus Including the Site & Remains of the Great Temple of Diana. John T. Wood. (Illus.). xviii, 507p. 1975. reprint ed. lib. bdg. 115.70 (*3-487-05482-5*, Pub. by Georg Olms GW) Lubrecht & Cramer.

Discoveries of Epithermal Precious Metal Deposits, Vol. 1. Ed. by Victor F. Hollister. LC 85-71492. 185p. reprint ed. pap. 52.80 (*0-8357-3481-1*, 2039740) Bks Demand.

Discoveries of Mrs. Christopher Columbus. Paula Di Perna. LC 93-27525. 287p. 1994. 24.00 (*1-877946-48-6*) Permanent Pr.

Discoveries of the New World. LC 60-10300. 1988. 14.95 (*0-8167-1521-1*) Troll Assocs.

Discoveries of the Norsemen in America, with Special Relation to Their Early Cartographical Representation. Joseph Fischer. 1977. lib. bdg. 59.95 (*0-8490-1728-9*) Gordon Pr.

Discoveries of the Other: Alterity in the Work of Leonard Cohen, Hubert Aquin, Michael Ondaatje, & Nicole Brossard. Winfried Siemerling. (Theory - Culture Ser.). 240p. (C). 1994. 45.00 (*0-8020-0517-9*) U of Toronto Pr.

Discoveries of Waldron Phoenix Belknap, Jr. Concerning the Influence of the English Mezzotint on Colonial Painting. Ed. by John M. Phillips & Barbara N. Parker. LC 55-14827. (Illus.). 39p. reprint ed. pap. 25.00 (*0-7837-4177-4*, 2059026) Bks Demand.

Discoveries of Witchcraft. Reginald Scot. 589p. 1994. 35.00 (*1-885366-13-2*) Visionary CA.

Discoveries That Changed Science. Lois Markham. (Twenty Events Ser.). (Illus.). 48p. (J). (gr. 4-8). 1994. lib. bdg. 22.80 (*0-8114-4936-X*) Raintree Steck-V.

Discovering. Robert S. Root-Bernstein. LC 88-35768. (Illus.). 520p. 1989. text ed. 39.95 (*0-674-21175-8*) HUP.

Discovering: Inventing & Solving Problems at the Frontiers of Scientific Knowledge. Robert S. Root-Bernstein. 520p. (C). 1991. pap. text ed. 15.95 (*0-674-21176-6*) HUP.

Discovering a Personal Photographic Vision: A National Anthology of Photography Assignments. Ed. by Philip Krejcarek. 1985. sl., pap. 28.00 (*0-318-20459-2*); pap. 10.00 (*0-317-01266-5*) P Krejcarek.

Discovering Aberdeenshire. Robert Smith. 226p. (C). 1989. pap. text ed. 24.00 (*0-85976-229-7*, Pub. by J Donald) St Mut.

Discovering Acadia: A Guide for Young Naturalists. Margaret Scheid. LC 86-71350. (Illus.). 80p. (J). (ps-12). 1988. reprint ed. pap. 12.95 (*0-934745-04-8*) Acadia Pub Co.

Discovering Acadia National Park & Mount Desert Island, Maine *see* **Maine Itineraries: Discovering Acadia National Park & Mount Desert Island: 12 Places to Begin**

Discovering African-American St. Louis: A Guide to Historic Sites. John A. Wright. 210p. 1994. pap. 14.95 (*1-883982-00-6*) MO Hist Soc.

Discovering Alaska. Ed. by Tom Hughes. 144p. (Orig.). 1986. pap. 9.95 (*0-930571-01-0*) Alaska Heritage.

Discovering Alvarez: Selected Works of Luis W. Alvarez, with Commentary by His Students & Colleagues. Ed. by W. Peter Trower. (Illus.). 282p. (C). 1987. 37.50 (*0-226-81304-5*) U Ch Pr.

Discovering America: A Coin Collectors Connection. Russell Rulau. LC 89-85218. (Illus.). 328p. (Orig.). 1989. pap. 19.95 (*0-87341-129-3*) Krause Pubns.

Discovering America: Bicycle Adventures in All 50 States. Martha J. Retallick. LC 93-79530. 256p. (Orig.). 1993. pap. 15.95 (*0-9637803-0-1*) Lone Rider.

Discovering America: Essays on the Search for an Identity. Ed. by David Thelen & Frederick E. Hoxie. LC 93-33604. (Illus.). 280p. 1994. pap. 14.95 (*0-252-06384-8*) U of Ill Pr.

Discovering America: Stories. Liza Wieland. 1994. 20.00 (*0-679-42459-8*) Random.

Discovering American Folk Art. Cynthia V. Schaffner. 1991. 29.95 (*0-8109-3206-7*) Abrams.

Discovering American Folklife: Studies in Ethnic, Religious, & Regional Culture. Don Yoder. Ed. by Simon J. Bronner. LC 89-20236. (American Material Culture & Folklife Ser.). 326p. reprint ed. 93.00 (*0-8357-1973-1*, 2070679) Bks Demand.

Discovering American History. Dexter Akinsheye. Ed. by Dayo Akinsheye. (African American Inventors & Scientists Workbook & Coloring Book Ser.). 20p. (Orig.). (J). (gr. 2-3). 1992. pap. 4.99 (*1-877835-70-6*) TD Pub.

Discovering America's Fire Museums. Ed. by W. Fred Conway, Sr. (Illus.). 188p. (Orig.). 1993. pap. 9.95 (*0-925165-12-3*) Fire Buff Hse.

Discovering America's Past: Customs, Legends, History & Lore of Our Great Nation. Reader's Digest Editors. LC 93-3508. (Illus.). 400p. 1993. 32.95 (*0-89577-520-4*, Random) RD Assn.

Discovering America's Southeast: A Sixteenth Century View Based on the Mannerist Engravings of Theodore de Bry. Gloria Deak. (Illus.). 205p. (Orig.). 1992. pap. 15.00 (*0-942301-20-X*) Birm Pub Lib.

Discovering an Evangelical Heritage. Donald W. Dayton. 160p. 1988. pap. 9.95 (*0-943575-06-0*) Hendrickson MA.

Discovering Ancient Egypt. Rosalie David. LC 93-38601. (Illus.). 192p. 1994. 22.95 (*0-8160-3105-3*) Facts on File.

***Discovering & Exploring New Jersey's Fishing Streams & the Deleware River.** Ed. & Pref. by Steve Perrone. (Illus.). 152p. (Orig.). Date not set. pap. 10.95 (*1-887544-00-3*) NJ Sportsmens Guides.

Discovering & Using Your Spiritual Gifts. Kenneth C. Kinghorn & Gus Gustafson. 1987. Four lectures on tape by Kinghorn, search manual by Gustafson. 6.95 (*0-917851-05-6*); audio 11.90 (*0-917851-09-9*) Bristol Hse.

D

An Asterisk (*) at the beginning of an entry indicates that the title is appearing in BIP for the first time.

An Asterisk (*) at the beginning of an entry indicates that the title is appearing in BIP for the first time.

2027

D

Discovering Geometry Teacher's Resource Book. Michael Serra. 364p. (gr. 9-12). 1991. pap. text ed. 54.95 (0-913684-09-0); write for info. (0-318-68072-6) Key Curr Pr.

Discovering God. Philip Yancey. Orig. Title: A Devotional Journal Through the Bible. 208p. 1993. reprint ed. 14.99 (0-310-40240-9) Zondervan.

Discovering God: Life's Adventure. John M. Scott. LC 91-66662. 160p. (Orig.). 1992. pap. 6.95 (0-87973-429-9, 429) Our Sunday Visitor.

Discovering God Through the Daily Practice of His Presence. Anthony M. Coniaris. 1989. pap. 7.95 (0-937032-68-9) Light&Life Pub Co MN.

Discovering God's Power: Studies in Genesis 1-17. Doris W. Greig. Ed. by Earl Roe. LC 88-32494. (Joy of Living Bible Study Ser.). 154p. (Orig.). 1989. pap. 5.99 (0-8307-1344-1, 5419764) Regal.

Discovering God's Promises: Studies in Genesis 18-31. Doris W. Greig. Ed. by Earl Roe. LC 89-38119. (Joy of Living Bible Study Ser.). 140p. (Orig.). 1989. pap. 5.99 (0-8307-1361-1, 5419845) Regal.

Discovering God's Will. Sinclair B. Ferguson. 125p. (Orig.). 1981. pap. 6.50 (0-85151-334-4) Banner of Truth.

***Discovering God's Will.** Charles Stanley. (Guided Growth Ser.). 24p. (Orig.). 1995. pap. 1.99 (1-56476-439-7, Victor Books) SP Pubns.

Discovering Grace in Grief. James Mayfield. 112p. 1994. pap. 7.95 (0-8358-0696-0) Upper Room Bks.

Discovering Great Jazz: A New Listener's Guide to the Sounds & Styles of the Top Musicians & Their Recordings. Stephen Stroff. LC 91-20285. (Discovering Great Music Ser.). (Illus.). 192p. 1991. 18.95 (1-55704-103-2) Newmarket.

Discovering Great Jazz: A New Listener's Guide to the Sounds & Styles of the Top Musicians & Their Recordings. Stephen Stroff. 1993. pap. 10.95 (1-55704-169-5) Newmarket.

***Discovering Great Music: A New Listener's Guide to the Top Classical Composers & Their Masterworks.** 2nd ed. Roy Hemming. 336p. 1994. 15.00 (1-55704-210-1) Newmarket.

Discovering Great Music: A New Listener's Guide to the Top Classical Composers & Their Masterworks on CD's, LP's & Tapes. Roy Hemming. LC 88-25285. 336p. 1990. 21.95 (1-55704-027-3) Newmarket.

Discovering Great Music: A New Listener's Guide to the Top Classical Composers & Their Masterworks on CD's, LP's & Tapes. Roy Hemming. LC 88-25285. 336p. 1991. pap. 14.95 (1-55704-115-6) Newmarket.

Discovering Great Singers of Classic Pop: A New Listener's Guide to the Sounds & Lives of the Top Performers & Their Recordings, Movies, & Videos. Roy Hemming & David Hajdu. LC 90-27452. (Discovering Great Music Ser.). (Illus.). 320p. 1991. 22.95 (1-55704-072-9) Newmarket.

Discovering Great Singers of Classic Pop: A New Listener's Guide to the Sounds & Lives of the Top Performers & Their Recordings, Movies, & Videos. Roy Hemming & David Hajdu. LC 90-27452. (Discovering Great Music Ser.). (Illus.). 320p. 1992. pap. 14.95 (1-55704-148-2) Newmarket.

***Discovering H. P. Lovecraft: Essays on America's Master Writer of Horror.** Ed. by Darrell Schweitzer. LC 95-2759. (I. O. Evans Studies in the Philosophy & Criticism of Literature: No. 21). 1995. lib. bdg. write for info. (0-615-00497-0) Borgo Pr.

D

Discovering Hadrian's Wall. Dudley Green. 176p. (C). 1989. pap. text ed. 24.00 (0-85976-365-X, Pub. by J Donald) St Mut.

Discovering Hall Marks on English Silver. John Bly. 1989. pap. 25.00 (0-85263-796-9, Pub. by Shire UK) St Mut.

Discovering Happiness: Personal Conversations about Getting the Most Out of Life. Dennis Wholey. 1988. pap. 3.95 (0-380-70488-9) Avon.

Discovering Hardy's Wessex. Anne-Marie Edwards. 176p. 1987. 30.00 (0-317-61920-9) St Mut.

Discovering Heirloom Sewing. Diana Oakley. (Illus.). 72p. 1993. 14.95 (1-86351-093-1, Pub. by S Milner AT) Sterling.

Discovering Hemi-Syne: Whole-Brain Audio Technology As Developed at the Monroe Institute. Genia P. Haddon. 51p. 1994. spiral bd. 5.95 (1-881311-09-0) Plus Pubns CT.

Discovering Heraldry. Jacqueline Fearn. 1989. pap. 25.00 (0-85263-476-5, Pub. by Shire UK) St Mut.

Discovering Herbs. Kay N. Sanecki. 1989. pap. 25.00 (0-7478-0198-3, Pub. by Shire UK) St Mut.

Discovering Hill Figures. Kate Bergamar. 1989. pap. 25.00 (0-85263-798-5, Pub. by Shire UK) St Mut.

Discovering Hilton Head Island: A View of Nature's Wonders. Margaret Creer & William Cornelia. LC 87-60225. (Illus.). 72p. 1987. 16.95 (0-9610698-1-3) SouthArt Inc.

Discovering History in China: American Historical Writing on the Recent Chinese Past. Paul Cohen. LC 83-20868. 264p. 1985. text ed. 43.00 (0-231-05810-1); pap. text ed. 15.50 (0-231-05811-X) Col U Pr.

Discovering Homeopathy: Your Introduction to the Science & Art of Homeopathic Medicine. 2nd rev. ed. Dana Ullman. Orig. Title: Homeopathy: Medicine for the 21st Century. 277p. 1991. pap. 12.95 (1-55643-108-2) North Atlantic.

Discovering Ideas: An Anthology for Writers. 3rd ed. Jean Wyrick. 352p. (C). 1991. pap. text ed. 19.50 (0-03-052207-2) HB Coll Pubs.

Discovering Ideas: An Anthology for Writers. 4th ed. Ed. by Jean Wyrick. LC 93-38338. 1993. pap. text ed. 22.00 (0-15-501134-0) HB Coll Pubs.

Discovering Illinois. rev. ed. William Stepien et al. (Illus.). 184p. (J). (gr. 4). 1992. 16.95 (0-87905-197-3, Peregrine Smith) Gibbs Smith Pub.

Discovering Indian Sculpture. Charles Fabri. (Illus.). 84p. 1970. 10.00 (0-88253-798-9); pap. 5.00 (0-88253-037-2) Ind-US Inc.

Discovering Inland Lancashire. Ron Freethy & Marlene Freethy. 170p. (C). 1989. pap. text ed. 40.00 (0-85976-336-6, Pub. by J Donald) St Mut.

Discovering Inland Yorkshire. Ron Freethy & Marlene Freethy. 180p. (C). 1989. pap. 24.00 (0-85976-368-4, Pub. by J Donald) St Mut.

Discovering Islam: Making Sense of Muslim History. Akbar S. Ahmed. 272p. 1989. 57.50 (0-7102-1049-3, 10493, RKP); pap. 12.95 (0-415-03930-4, A3525, RKP) Routledge.

Discovering Israel: An Archeological Guide to the Holy Land. Jack Finegan. LC 80-26952. 155p. reprint ed. pap. 44.20 (0-317-19818-1, 2023211) Bks Demand.

Discovering Italian One. Anna M. Sabbionet & Colin McCormich. 1989. pap. text ed. 21.00 (0-582-68843-4, 74685) Longman.

Discovering Jazz Dance: America's Energy & Soul. Janice D. LaPointe-Crump & Kimberly T. Staley. 224p. (C). 1992. pap. text ed. write for info. (0-697-11392-2) Brown & Benchmark.

Discovering Joy. Marie Chapian. (Heart for God Ser.). 192p. (Orig.). 1990. 10.99 (1-55661-122-6) Bethany Hse.

Discovering Landscape in England & Wales. Andrew Gondie & Rita Gardner. (Illus.). 192p. 1988. 39.95 (0-04-551076-8) Routledge Chapman & Hall.

Discovering Landscape in England & Wales. Andrew Gondie & Rita Gardner. (Illus.). 192p. 1992. pap. 38.50 (0-412-47850-1, A9498) Routledge Chapman & Hall.

Discovering Language. William Vesterman. 400p. (C). 1991. pap. text ed. 23.00 (0-205-12829-7, 640506) Allyn.

***Discovering Latino Religion: A Comprehensive Social Science Bibliography.** (Paral Studies Ser.: Vol. IV). Date not set. write for info. (0-929972-13-9) CUNY Bildner Ctr.

***Discovering Latino Religion: A Comprehensive Social Science Bibliography.** (Paral Studies Ser.: Vol. IV). Date not set. pap. write for info. (0-929972-14-7) CUNY Bildner Ctr.

***Discovering Learning Preferences & Learning Differences in the Classroom.** Jamie Cano et al. Ed. by Jacqueline Stuts. (Illus.). 76p. (Orig.). 1995. teacher ed 15.95 (1-56502-007-3, 0312G) Ohio Agri Educ.

Discovering Lewis & Harris. James S. Grant. 250p. (C). 1989. pap. text ed. 26.00 (0-85976-185-1, Pub. by J Donald) St Mut.

***Discovering Life after Divorce.** Concordia Publishing Staff. (Master's Touch Ser.). 1994. pap. 3.99 (0-570-09438-0) Concordia.

Discovering Life in Christ. Joseph Miller. (Illus.). 62p. (C). 1989. teacher ed 2.95 (0-87227-137-4); student ed 2.95 (0-87227-136-6) Reg Baptist.

Discovering Life in the Church. Joseph Miller. 94p. 1990. student ed 2.95 (0-87227-141-2); teacher ed, pap. 2.95 (0-87227-142-0) Reg Baptist.

Discovering Life's Meaning. Samuel Chiel. 20.00 (0-88125-362-6) Ktav.

Discovering Life's Purpose. David M. Lindsey. 1990. pap. 8.95 (1-878040-01-4) Personal Growth.

Discovering Life's Trails: Adventures in Living. Tom Dennard. LC 93-2903. (Illus.). 330p. (Orig.). 1993. pap. 14.95 (0-935834-97-4) Rainbow Bks.

Discovering Lifetime Fitness: Concepts of Exercise & Weight Control. 2nd ed. George B. Dintiman et al. Ed. by Marshall. 312p. (C). 1989. pap. text ed. 41.75 (0-314-48120-6) West Pub.

Discovering Lincolnshire. Ron Freethy & Marlene Freethy. 170p. (C). 1993. pap. 27.00 (0-85976-394-3, Pub. by J Donald) St Mut.

Discovering Literature: Fiction, Poetry, & Drama. Hans P. Guth & Gabriele L. Rico. 1808p. 1992. text ed. write for info. (0-13-219734-0) P-H.

Discovering Logic. Mark Schoenfield & Jeanette Rosenblatt. (J). (gr. 4-6). 1985. pap. 8.99 (0-8224-1915-7) Fearon Teach Aids.

Discovering London Ceremonial & Traditions. Julian Paget. 1989. pap. 25.00 (0-85263-994-5, Pub. by Shire UK) St Mut.

Discovering London Curiosities. John Wittich. 1989. pap. 25.00 (0-7478-0074-X, Pub. by Shire UK) St Mut.

Discovering London Street Names. John Wittich. (Discovering Ser.). 96p. (Orig.). (J). (gr. 6 up). 1977. pap. 3.00 (0-913714-09-7) Legacy Books.

Discovering London Street Names. John Wittich. (Orig.). 1989. pap. 25.00 (0-7478-0075-8, Pub. by Shire UK) St Mut.

Discovering London's Canals. Derek Pratt. 1989. pap. 25.00 (0-85263-901-5, Pub. by Shire UK) St Mut.

Discovering London's Guilds & Liveries. J. K. Melling. 1989. pap. 25.00 (0-85263-971-6, Pub. by Shire UK) St Mut.

Discovering London's Inns & Taverns. John Wittich. 1989. pap. 25.00 (0-7478-0166-5, Pub. by Shire UK) St Mut.

Discovering Long Island. William Stevens. 17.50 (0-911660-14-3) Yankee Peddler.

Discovering Lost Railways. F. G. Cockman. 1989. pap. 25.00 (0-7478-0165-7, Pub. by Shire UK) St Mut.

Discovering Louisiana. Photos & Text by C. C. Lockwood. LC 83-25614. (Illus.). vii, 150p. 1986. 39.95 (0-8071-1335-2) La State U Pr.

Discovering Mah-Jong. R. C. Bell. 1989. pap. 25.00 (0-85263-444-7, Pub. by Shire UK) St Mut.

Discovering Maps: A Young Person's World Atlas. Hammond. (YA). 1993. 11.95 (0-8437-3414-0) Hammond Inc.

Discovering Marine Mammals. Nancy Field & Sally Machlis. (Illus.). 32p. (Orig.). (J). (gr. 1-6). 1987. pap. 3.95 (0-941042-06-5) Dog Eared Pubns.

Discovering Marketing: Building Knowledge, Skills & Values. Thomas Bertsch et al. Ed. by Jeanne Busemeyer & David Shaut. (Illus.). 121p. (C). 1993. pap. 13.95 (0-538-82647-9) S-W Pub.

Discovering Mars: The Amazing Story of the Red Planet. Melvin Berger. (J). (gr. 4-7). 1992. pap. 3.95 (0-590-45221-5) Scholastic Inc.

***Discovering Martha.** J. Rocklin. 1994. pap. 2.99 (0-517-13319-9) Random.

Discovering Maryland's First City. Henry M. Miller. (Archaeology Ser.: No. 2). (Illus.). 164p. 1986. pap. 16.00 (1-878399-32-2) Div Hist Cult Progs.

Discovering Mass Communication. 2nd ed. Samuel L. Becker. (C). 1987. pap. text ed. 16.75 (0-673-18390-4) HarpCollege.

Discovering Mass Communications. 3rd ed. Becker & Roberts. (C). 1992. text ed. 44.00 (0-673-46119-X) HarpCollege.

***Discovering Math, 6 vols., Set.** (J). (gr. 3-5). 1995. lib. bdg. write for info. (0-7614-0592-5, Benchmark NY) Marshall Cavendish.

Discovering Mathematics. Richard H. Lavoie. LC 92-30662. 640p. 1993. text ed. 55.95 (0-534-93340-8) PWS Pubs.

Discovering Mathematics: The Art of Investigation. Alan Gardiner. 220p. 1987. pap. 19.95 (0-19-853265-2) OUP.

Discovering Meanings in Elementary School Mathematics. 8th ed. Foster E. Grossnickle et al. 576p. (C). 1990. text ed. 42.75 (0-03-030987-5) HB Coll Pubs.

Discovering Men. David Morgan. 240p. 1992. 39.95 (0-04-445599-2, A8163); pap. 15.95 (0-04-445598-4, A8164) Routledge Chapman & Hall.

Discovering Microsoft Works for the IBM Personal Computer. David Sachs & Babette Kronstadt. 300p. 1989. Net. pap. text ed. write for info. (0-471-51767-4) Wiley.

***Discovering Microsoft Works for Windows 3.0.** Babette Kronstadt. LC 94-27270. 1994. pap. text ed. write for info. (0-471-07654-6) Wiley.

***Discovering Microsoft Works for Windows 3.0.** Babette Kronstadt et al. 1994. text ed. 48.00 (0-471-07656-2) Wiley.

Discovering Microsoft Works 2.0. Babette Kronstadt & David Sachs. 384p. (Orig.). 1993. pap. write for info. (0-471-58895-4); pap. write for info. (0-471-58894-6) Wiley.

Discovering Microsoft Works 3.0. Babette Kronstadt & David Sachs. LC 93-23147. 384p. 1993. Net. write for info. (0-471-30542-1) Wiley.

Discovering Modern Horror Fiction I. Ed. by Darrell Schweitzer. LC 84-2763. (Starmont Studies in Literary Criticism: No. 4). (Illus.). iv, 156p. (Orig.). 1985. lib. bdg. 29.00x (0-916732-94-0); pap. 19.00x (0-916732-93-2) Borgo Pr.

Discovering Modern Horror Fiction II. Ed. by Darrell Schweitzer. LC 84-2763. (Starmont Studies in Literary Criticism: No. 16). (Illus.). 174p. (Orig.). 1988. lib. bdg. 29.00 (0-930261-48-8); pap. 19.00x (0-930261-47-X) Borgo Pr.

Discovering Modernism: T. S. Eliot & His Context. Louis Menand. 224p. 1988. pap. 14.95 (0-19-505717-1) OUP.

Discovering More Science Secrets. Sandra Markle. (J). (ps-3). 1993. pap. 2.50 (0-590-44879-X) Scholastic Inc.

Discovering Moscow: The Complete Companion Guide. Helen B. Semler. 1990. pap. 19.95 (0-312-05076-3) St Martin.

Discovering Motherhood. Ed. by Heidi L. Brennan et al. (Illus.). 80p. (Orig.). 1991. pap. 9.95 (0-9631188-0-3) Mothers at Home.

Discovering Mount Rainier. rev. ed. Nancy Field & Sally Maehlis. (Illus.). 32p. (Orig.). (J). (gr. 1-6). 1992. pap. 3.95 (0-941042-13-8) Dog Eared Pubns.

Discovering My Biblical Dream Heritage. Lois L. Hendricks. 264p. (Orig.). (C). 1989. pap. 9.95 (0-89390-144-X) Resource Pubns.

Discovering My Experience of God: Awareness & Witness. Frank DeSiano & Kenneth Boyack. 80p. 1992. pap. 3.95 (0-8091-3300-8) Paulist Pr.

Discovering Myself: Who Am I Anyway? Dale Larsen & Sandy Larsen. (Bible Discovery Guide Ser.). (Illus.). 32p. (Orig.). (YA). (gr. 7-10). 1987. Camper Ed. 1.50 (0-87788-178-2); Counselor Ed. 3.50 (0-87788-179-0) Shaw Pubs.

Discovering Natural Foods. Roy Bruder. LC 82-2705. (Illus.). 288p. (Orig.). 1982. pap. 7.95 (0-912800-86-0) Woodbridge Pr.

Discovering Nature in New England's Mountains. Ed Frost. (Illus.). 128p. (Orig.). 1993. pap. 9.95 (0-9618806-4-3) Glove Compart Bks.

Discovering Nature with Young People: An Annotated Bibliography & Selection Guide. Comp. by Carolyn M. Johnson. LC 87-8694. 512p. 1987. text ed. 65.00 (0-313-23823-5, JOD/, Greenwood Pr) Greenwood.

Discovering New Medicines: Careers in Pharmaceutical Research & Development. Ed. by P. D. Stonier. LC 94-16151. 1995. pap. text ed. 29.95 (0-471-94194-8) Wiley.

Discovering North Carolina: A Tar Heel Reader. Ed. by Jack Claiborne & William Price. LC 90-50009. xviii, 372p. (C). 1991. 29.95 (0-8078-1931-X) U of NC Pr.

Discovering North Carolina: A Tar Heel Reader. Ed. by Jack Claiborne & William Price. LC 90-50009. xviii, 372p. 1993. reprint ed. pap. 12.95 (0-8078-4434-9) U of NC Pr.

Discovering Northumberland. Ron Freethy & Marlene Freethy. 192p. (C). 1989. pap. text ed. 24.00 (0-85976-359-5, Pub. by J Donald) St Mut.

Discovering Northwest Volcanoes. rev. ed. Nancy Field & Sally Machlis. 32p. (Orig.). (J). (gr. 2-6). 1980. reprint ed. pap. 3.95 (0-941042-03-0) Dog Eared Pubns.

Discovering Nutrition. Helen Kowtaluk. student ed 2.00 (0-02-667900-0); text ed. 17.00 (0-02-667810-1); student ed 7.00 (0-02-667890-X); teacher ed 10.60 (0-02-667910-8) Bennett IL.

Discovering Oceans, Lakes, Ponds & Puddles. Jeron A. Frame. (J). (gr. 4-7). 1994. pap. 8.99 (0-7459-2621-5) Lion USA.

Discovering Off-Beat Walks in London. John Wittich & Ron Phillips. 1989. pap. 25.00 (0-7478-0076-6, Pub. by Shire UK) St Mut.

Discovering Old Buttons. Primrose Peacock. 1989. pap. 25.00 (0-85263-445-5, Pub. by Shire UK) St Mut.

Discovering Old Cameras. Robert White. 1989. pap. 25.00 (0-85263-691-1, Pub. by Shire UK) St Mut.

Discovering Old Testament Origins: The Books of Genesis, Exodus, & Samuel. Margaret N. Ralph. LC 92-8494. (Discovering the Living Word Ser.). 1992. pap. 12.95 (0-8091-3322-9) Paulist Pr.

Discovering Omnipoint: A Common Approach to the Integrated Management of Networked Information. Network Management Forum. LC 92-82680. 224p. (C). 1993. pap. text ed. 32.00 (0-13-106121-6) P-H.

Discovering Ontario's Wine Country. Linda Bramble & Shari Darling. (Illus.). 96p. (Orig.). pap. 16.95 (1-55046-054-4, Pub. by Boston Mills Pr CN) Genl Dist Srvs.

Discovering ORFF: A Curriculum for Music Teachers. Jane Frazee & Kent Kreuter. 1987. pap. 39.95 (0-930448-99-5, STAP099) Eur-Am Music.

Discovering Our Gifts. Thomas D. DeVries. 1992. 2.50 (0-8091-9328-0) Paulist Pr.

Discovering Our Past. Peter Seymour. (Science Action Bk.). (Illus.). 10p. (J). (gr. 2-5). 1987. 8.95 (0-02-782200-1, Mac Bks Young Read) S&S Childrens.

Discovering Our Past: A Brief Introduction to Archaeology. Wendy Ashmore & Robert J. Sharer. LC 87-24796. 239p. (C). 1988. pap. text ed. 20.95 (0-87484-748-6) Mayfield Pub.

***Discovering Our Past: A Brief Introduction to Archaeology.** 2nd ed. Wendy Ashmore & Robert J. Sharer. LC 95-3683. 1995. write for info. (1-55934-521-7) Mayfield Pub.

Discovering Our Roots: Ancestry of the Churches of Christ. Leonard Allen. LC 87-72685. 200p. 1988. 15.95 (0-89112-008-4); pap. 10.95 (0-89112-006-8) Abilene Christ U.

Discovering Our World. Rosie Seaman. (J). (ps-00). 1987. pap. 7.99 (0-8224-1926-2) Fearon Teach Aids.

Discovering Ourselves. Rosie Seaman. (J). (ps-00). 1987. pap. 7.99 (0-8224-1927-0) Fearon Teach Aids.

Discovering Ourselves in Whitman: The Contemporary American Long Poem. Thomas Gardner. LC 88-39406. 224p. 1989. 24.95 (0-252-01630-0) U of Ill Pr.

Discovering Paris Bistros: A Personal Guide to over Sixty Affordable Restaurants. Gaston Wijnen. LC 91-20229. (Illus.). 185p. (Orig.). 1991. pap. 12.95 (0-940793-84-9) Interlink Pub.

Discovering Parish Boundaries. Angus Winchester. 1989. pap. 25.00 (0-7478-0060-X, Pub. by Shire UK) St Mut.

Discovering Past Behavior: Experiments in the Archaeology of the American Southwest. P. Grebinger. (Library of Anthropology). 296p. 1978. text ed. 77.00 (0-677-16080-1) Gordon & Breach.

Discovering Pathways to Prayer. David E. Rosage. 160p. (Orig.). 1975. pap. 6.95 (0-914544-08-X) Living Flame Pr.

Discovering Period Gardens. John Anthony. 1989. pap. 25.00 (0-7478-0168-1, Pub. by Shire UK) St Mut.

Discovering Philosophy. Nina E. Crosby & Elizabeth H. Marten. (Illus.). 72p. (Orig.). 1980. pap. 9.95 (0-914634-81-X, 8009) DOK Pubs.

Discovering Philosophy. Thomas I. White. 576p. (C). 1990. text ed. write for info. (0-13-497181-7) P-H.

Discovering Pittsburgh's Sculpture. Photos by Vernon Gay. LC 82-50225. (Illus.). 464p. 1982. pap. 19.95 (0-8229-5348-X) U of Pittsburgh Pr.

Discovering Place-Names: Their Origins & Meanings. 2nd ed. John Field. (Discovering Ser.). 55p. 1978. pap. 4.50 (0-913714-18-6) Legacy Books.

Discovering Plants & Animals. Rosie Seaman. (J). (ps-00). 1987. pap. 7.99 (0-8224-1928-9) Fearon Teach Aids.

Discovering Plato. Alexandre Koyre. Tr. by Leonara C. Rosenfield. 128p. reprint ed. pap. 36.50 (0-317-09006-2, 2012182) Bks Demand.

Discovering Poetry. Hans P. Guth & Gabriele L. Rico. 608p. (C). 1993. pap. text ed. write for info. (0-13-221987-5) P-H.

Discovering Prayer. Andrew Knowles. LC 92-44876. (Manuals Ser.). (Illus.). 128p. (Orig.). (YA). (gr. 10 up). 1993. 9.99 (0-7459-2644-4) Lion USA.

Discovering Prehistoric Animals. Janet Craig. LC 89-4973. (Illus.). 32p. (J). (gr. 2-4). 1990. lib. bdg. 11.59 (0-8167-1755-9); pap. text ed. 2.95 (0-8167-1756-7) Troll Assocs.

Discovering Prehistoric England. James Dyer. 1989. pap. 25.00 (0-7478-0197-5, Pub. by Shire UK) St Mut.

Discovering Prehistoric Rock Art: A Recording Manual. Kay K. Sanger & Clement W. Meighan. (Illus.). 237p. 1990. pap. text ed. 22.95 (0-937523-03-8) Wormwood Pr.

Discovering Preserved Railways. F. G. Cockman. 1989. pap. 25.00 (0-7478-0073-1, Pub. by Shire UK) St Mut.

Discovering Programming with Smalltalk. Wilf R. Lalonde. (C). 1994. pap. text ed. 40.95 (0-8053-2720-5) Benjamin-Cummings.

Discovering Prophecy & Wisdom: The Books of Isaiah, Job, Proverbs & Psalms. Margaret N. Ralph. LC 93-10245. (Discovering the Living Word Ser.: Vol. IV). 336p. 1993. pap. 12.95 (0-8091-3402-0) Paulist Pr.

An Asterisk (*) at the beginning of an entry indicates that the title is appearing in BIP for the first time.

An Asterisk (*) at the beginning of an entry indicates that the title is appearing in BIP for the first time.

2029

D

Discovering Whales & Dolphins. Janet Craig. LC 89-5004. (Illus.). 32p. (J). (gr. 2-4). 1990. lib. bdg. 11.59 (*0-8167-1759-1*); pap. text ed. 2.95 (*0-8167-1760-5*) Troll Assocs.

Discovering Wild Plants: Alaska, Western Canada, the Northwest. Janice J. Schofield. LC 89-6583. (Illus.). 368p. 1989. 34.95 (*0-88240-355-9*); pap. 26.95 (*0-88240-369-9*) Alaska Northwest.

Discovering Windmills. John Vince. 5.95 (*0-85263-888-4*) Legacy Books.

Discovering Windmills. John Vince. 1989. pap. 25.00 (*0-7478-0209-2*, Pub. by Shire UK) St Mut.

Discovering Wine: A Refreshingly Unfussy Beginner's Guide to Finding, Tasting, Judging, Storing, Serving, Cellaring, &, Most of All, Discovering Wine. Joanna Simon. LC 94-20751. 1995. pap. 15.00 (*0-671-50570-X*, Fireside) S&S Trade.

Discovering with God. Lois H. Dick. (Illus.). 22p. (J). (gr. k-6). 1984. pap. text ed. 4.25 (*1-55976-143-1*) CEF Press.

Discovering Wolves. Nancy Field & Corliss Karasov. (Illus.). 40p. (Orig.). (J). (gr. 3-6). 1991. pap. 5.95 (*0-941042-10-3*) Dog Eared Pubns.

Discovering Words: The Stories Behind English. Jean Fargo. Ed. by Literacy Volunteers of New York City Staff. (Illus.). 80p. (Orig.). 1992. pap. text ed. 3.50 (*0-929631-66-8*, Signal Hill) New Readers.

Discovering World Cultures Through Literature: Grades 3-6. Gerry Edwards. (Illus.). 208p. (Orig.). 1994. pap. 14.95 (*0-673-36130-6*) GdYrBks.

Discovering You Unlimited. Patricia Turner. LC 87-40265. 197p. 1987. 8.95 (*1-55523-105-5*) Winston-Derek.

Discovering Your Child's Design. Ralph Mattson & Thom Black. LC 89-32705. 256p. 1989. 14.99 (*1-55513-226-X*, LifeJourney) Chariot Family.

Discovering Your Divine Design: The Network Seminar. 2nd abr. ed. Bruce L. Bugby et al. 1994. Participant's Wkbk. student ed 14.99 (*0-310-41231-5*); Seminar Leader's Guide. 29.99 (*0-310-41241-2*); Consultant's Manual. 29.99 (*0-310-41221-8*) Zondervan.

Discovering Your Divine Design: The Network Seminar. 2nd abr. ed. Bruce L. Bugby et al. 1994. 119.99 (*0-310-41228-5*) Zondervan.

***Discovering Your Divine Friend.** D. Schultz. 96p. 1995. 4.95 (*0-9645707-0-X*) Schultz & Assocs.

Discovering Your Family Tree. David Iredale & John Barrett. 1989. pap. 25.00 (*0-85263-767-5*, Pub. by Shire UK) St Mut.

Discovering Your Heritage. Alice Eichholz. (Illus.). 32p. (Orig.). 1986. pap. 2.95 (*0-916489-10-8*) Ancestry.

***Discovering Your Hidden Wealth: Coopers & Lybrand's Guide to Finding & Growing Your Personal Assets.** George R. Auxier et al. 300p. 1995. 24.95 (*0-525-93923-7*, Dutton) NAL-Dutton.

Discovering Your Human Spirit. Kirk Eland. 12p. (Orig.). 1992. pap. 0.50 (*0-914271-36-9*) Mnstry Wrd.

Discovering Your Inner Power: A Workbook for the Warrior Within. Shale Paul & Candace Paul. (Illus.). 208p. (Orig.). 1992. pap. 12.95 (*0-913787-07-8*) Delta G Pr.

Discovering Your Iowa Civil War Ancestry: A Practical Little How to Book on Finding the What's & Where's of Your Iowa Civil War Ancestors. 2nd ed. Steve Meyer. 64p. 1993. pap. 8.00 (*0-9630284-1-3*) Meyer Pub.

D

Discovering Your Light: Common Journeys of Young Adults. Margaret O'Brien. Ed. by Emilie Teutschman. LC 90-66455. 64p. (Orig.). 1991. student ed 6.95 (*1-878718-09-6*) Resurrection.

Discovering Your Own Space. Sandra L. Smith. (Self-Esteem Library). (YA). (gr. 7-12). 1992. lib. bdg. 14.95 (*0-8239-1279-5*) Rosen Group.

Discovering Your Past Lives. Gloria Chadwick. 224p. (Orig.). 1988. pap. 10.95 (*0-8092-4546-9*) Contemp Bks.

Discovering Your Past Lives & Other Dimensions. Bettye B. Binder. 144p. 1994. pap. 10.00 (*1-879005-12-3*) Reincarnation Bks.

Discovering Your Self Through the Tarot: A Jungian Guide to Archetypes & Personality. Rose Gwain. (Illus.). 224p. (Orig.). 1993. pap. 12.95 (*0-89281-412-8*, Destiny Bks) Inner Tradit.

Discovering Your Soul's Purpose. Mark Thurston. 175p. 1984. pap. 9.95 (*0-87604-157-8*, 324) ARE Pr.

Discovering Your Spiritual Gifts: A Personal Inventory Method. Kenneth C. Kinghorn. 1984. pap. 3.99 (*0-310-75061-X*, 17029P) Zondervan.

Discovering Your Subpersonalities: Our Inner World & the People in It. John Rowan. LC 93-14812. (Illus.). 160p. 1994. pap. 17.95 (*0-415-07366-9*, A7634) Routledge.

Discovering Your Teaching Self: Humanistic Approaches to Effective Teaching. Richard Curwin & Barbara Fuhrmann. LC 74-11371. (Curriculum & Teaching Ser.). (Illus.). 256p. 1975. pap. text ed. 18.95 (*0-685-03837-8*) P-H.

Discovering Yourself: A Journey Through Psychotherapy & Counselling. Reinhard Kowalski. LC 92-45835. (Strategies for Mental Health Ser.). 272p. 1993. 49.95 (*0-415-07649-8*, B2206, Routledge NY); pap. 15.95 (*0-415-07650-1*, B2210, Routledge NY) Routledge.

Discovery. 1979. 8.00 (*0-939418-15-0*) Ferguson-Florissant.

***Discovery.** Steven D. Ayers. 64p. 1994. pap. 5.95 (*0-9642319-0-5*) S D Ayers.

Discovery. Judy Baer. (Cedar River Daydreams Ser.: No. 20). 144p. (Orig.). (J). 1993. pap. 3.99 (*1-55661-330-X*) Bethany Hse.

Discovery. James L. Branton & Jim D. Lovett. (Trial Lawyer's Ser.: Vol. 6). (Illus.). 319p. 1988. ring bd. 135.00 (*1-878337-09-2*) Knowles Law.

Discovery. Arthur I. Miltz. (Art of Advocacy Ser.). 1982. Looseleaf Updates Avail. write for info. (*0-8205-1044-0*) Bender.

Discovery. Monastery of Arkashea Staff & Susan Nier. 580p. 1993. pap. 24.95 (*0-9636142-0-7*) Gldn Scribe.

Discovery. large type ed. Steve Shagan. 498p. 1985. 23.95 (*0-7089-8291-3*, Trail West Pubs) Ulverscroft.

Discovery. John Drinkwater. 1988. reprint ed. lib. bdg. 75.00 (*0-685-55953-X*) Rprt Serv.

Discovery: An Inductive Approach to Writing. Thomas E. Tyner. LC 88-63053. 289p. (Orig.). (C). 1990. pap. text ed. 20.50 (*0-312-01720-0*) St Martin.

Discovery: An Inductive Approach to Writing. Thomas E. Tyner. LC 88-63053. 289p. (Orig.). (C). 1990. pap. text ed. 1.02 (*0-312-01721-9*) St Martin.

Discovery: Developing Views of the Earth from Ancient Times to Captain Cook. John Parker. (Illus.). 216p. 1990. 17.95 (*0-88029-460-4*) Dorset Pr.

Discovery: Finding the Buried Treasure. Jerry Moe. 1994. pap. 14.95 (*0-922641-93-5*) Stem Pubns.

Discovery: How to Win Your Case Without Trial. John A. DeMay. 199p. 1982. text ed. 49.95 (*0-13-215640-7*, Busn) P-H.

Discovery: Reading, Writing & Thinking in the Academic Disciplines. Linda R. Robertson. 576p. (C). 1989. text ed. 22.75 (*0-03-007313-8*) HB Coll Pubs.

Discovery: The Adventure of Shipboard Education. Paul W. Liebhardt. Ed. by Judy S. Rogers. LC 85-50383. (Illus.). 1985. 50.00 (*0-9614403-0-9*) William & Allen.

Discovery: The Common Sense Weight Solution. Jacklyn K. Brown. (Illus.). 160p. (Orig.). 1993. pap. 10.00 (*0-9632367-3-3*) Brown Ent.

Discovery: The Story of the Second Byrd Antarctic Expedition. Richard E. Byrd. LC 71-37874. (Select Bibliographies Reprint Ser.). 1977. reprint ed. 39.95 (*0-8369-6711-9*) Ayer.

Discovery: The Story of the Second Byrd Antarctic Expedition. Richard E. Byrd. (American Biography Ser.). 397p. 1991. reprint ed. lib. bdg. 79.00 (*0-7812-8055-9*) Rprt Serv.

Discovery: Theory, Practice & Problems. Roger S. Haydock & David F. Herr. 432p. (C). 1983. 28.00 (*0-316-35162-8*) Little.

Discovery: Writing about Your World. George Eppley & Anita D. Eppley. (C). 1990. teacher ed write for info. (*0-03-026393-X*); pap. text ed. 19.50 (*0-03-026392-1*) HB Coll Pubs.

Discovery: Writing to Learn. Bruce Leland. 304p. (C). 1992. per. 20.95 (*0-8403-8230-8*) Kendall-Hunt.

***Discovery - Interviewing & Investigation.** 2nd ed. Michael A. Pener. 1995. pap. 36.95 (*0-929563-17-4*) Pearson Pubns.

Discovery! A Guide to Entry-Level Adult Groups. 4th ed. LC 83-71852. (Illus.). 82p. 1983. pap. text ed. 9.95 (*0-934396-38-8*) Churches Alive.

Discovery, an Introduction: Alaska Sea Week Curriculum Series. Belle Mickelson. (Alaska Sea Grant Report: No. 83-06). (Illus.). 130p. (Orig.). 1993. reprint ed. teacher ed, pap. 6.50 (*1-56612-019-5*) AK Sea Grant CP.

***Discovery & Commitment: A Guide for College Writers.** Leonard J. Rosen. LC 94-39162. 1994. text ed. write for info. (*0-205-14249-4*) Allyn.

***Discovery & Commitment: A Guide for College Writers.** Leonard J. Rosen. LC 94-39163. 1994. pap. text ed. write for info. (*0-205-17126-5*) Allyn.

Discovery & Conquest of Mexico 1517-1521. Bernal Del Castillo. Tr. by A. P. Maudslay. 506p. 1986. reprint ed. lib. bdg. 38.95 (*0-89966-559-4*) Buccaneer Bks.

Discovery & Development of the Southern Colonial Landscape, Six Commentators. Thad W. Tate. 22p. 1984. pap. 3.25 (*0-912296-63-1*) Am Antiquarian.

Discovery & Explanation in Biology & Medicine. Kenneth F. Schaffner. LC 93-21826. (Science & Its Conceptual Foundations Ser.). (Illus.). 528p. (C). 1993. lib. bdg. 55.00 (*0-226-73591-5*); pap. text ed. 27.95 (*0-226-73592-3*) U Ch Pr.

Discovery & Exploitation of the Minnesota Iron Lands. Fremont P. Wirth. Ed. by Stuart Bruchey. LC 78-53544. (Development of Public Land Law in the U. S. Ser.). 1979. reprint ed. lib. bdg. 21.95 (*0-405-11393-5*) Ayer.

Discovery & Exploration, 17 vols., Set. LC 89-15723. (Illus.). 2866p. (YA). (gr. 7-12). 1990. lib. bdg. 399.95 (*1-85435-114-1*) Marshall Cavendish.

Discovery & Exploration: A Reference Handbook, Vol. 1: Old World. Alan E. Day. LC 80-119195. 295p. reprint ed. pap. 84.10 (*0-7837-5295-4*, 2045049) Bks Demand.

Discovery & Interrogatories. 2nd ed. S. D. Simpson et al. 1990. Australia. 98.00 (*0-409-49514-X*) Butterworth Legal Pubs.

Discovery & Invention: The Urban Plays of Lanford Wilson. Anne M. Dean. LC 94-3180. 1994. write for info. (*0-8386-3548-2*) Fairleigh Dickinson.

***Discovery & Other Poems.** Roberta Tinkham. 1995. 13.95 (*0-533-11167-6*) Vantage.

***Discovery & Proof in Police Misconduct Cases.** Stephen M. Royals. LC 95-1372. (Civil Rights Library). 1995. text ed. 125.00 (*0-471-01974-7*, Pub. by Wiley Law Pubns) Wiley.

Discovery & Recognition. Ed. by James Alinder. LC 81-65401. (Untitled Ser.: No. 25). (Illus.). 56p. (Orig.). 1981. pap. 12.00 (*0-933286-24-4*) Frnds Photography.

Discovery & Service of Process in International Litigation: An Annotated Bibliography. Ed. by William R. Slomanson. (Collection of Bibliographic & Research Resources). 58p. (Orig.). 1988. 50.00 (*0-379-20916-0*) Oceana.

Discovery & Settlement: Europe Meets the New World (1490-1700) Gene Brown. LC 93-8537. (First Person America Ser.). (Illus.). 64p. (J). (gr. 5-8). 1993. lib. bdg. 15.98 (*0-8050-2574-X*) TFC Bks NY.

Discovery & Settlement: How to Win Your Case Without Trial. John A. DeMay. LC 92-16404. 1992. write for info. (*0-13-224882-4*) P-H.

Discovery & the Capitalist Process. Israel M. Kirzner. LC 85-5799. 200p. 1985. lib. bdg. 22.50 (*0-226-43777-9*) U Ch Pr.

Discovery at Coyote Point. Ann Gabhart. 176p. (Orig.). 1989. pap. 2.95 (*0-380-75497-5*, Camelot) Avon.

Discovery at Walden. Roland W. Robbins. (Illus.). 1970. reprint ed. pap. 3.00 (*0-912130-02-4*) Thoreau Found.

Discovery Atlas of Animals. LC 93-7252. (J). 1993. 4.95 (*0-528-83579-3*) Rand McNally.

Discovery Atlas of Dinosaurs & Prehistoric Creatures. Francis Reddy. LC 93-43086. Orig. Title: Rand McNally Children's Atlas of Earth Through Time. (Illus.). (J). 1994. 4.95 (*0-528-83677-3*) Rand McNally.

Discovery Atlas of Native Americans. LC 93-39472. (J). 1994. pap. 4.95 (*0-528-83678-1*) Rand McNally.

Discovery Atlas of Planets & Stars. LC 93-16805. (J). 1993. 4.95 (*0-528-83580-7*) Rand McNally.

Discovery Atlas of the United States. LC 93-18713. (Illus.). (J). 1993. 4.95 (*0-528-83578-5*) Rand McNally.

Discovery Atlas of the World. LC 93-12560. (J). 1993. 4.95 (*0-528-83577-7*) Rand McNally.

Discovery, Being the Second Book of an Autobiography. John Drinkwater. LC 78-131691. 435p. 1983. reprint ed. lib. bdg. 13.00 (*0-403-00578-7*) Scholarly.

Discovery Bible: New Testament. Gary Hill. Ed. by Gleason L. Archer. 610p. 17.95 (*0-88469-202-7*) BMH Bks.

Discovery (Blu) S. Reid. (Famous Lives Ser.). (Illus.). 144p. (J). (gr. 4 up). 1994. pap. 14.95 (*0-7460-1872-X*, Usborne) EDC.

Discovery Book: A Helpful Guide for the World Written by Children with Disabilities. rev. ed. Ed. by Sky Chaney & Pam Fisher. (Illus.). 100p. (J). (gr. 3-10). 1989. pap. 7.95 (*0-9616891-1-0*) UCPANB.

Discovery Book for the Seattle Aquarium. abr. rev. ed. Nancy Field & Sally Machlis. (Illus.). 32p. (Orig.). (J). (gr. 1-6). 1987. pap. 3.95 (*0-941042-07-3*) Dog Eared Pubns.

Discovery Conquest, & Early History of the Philippine Islands. Edward G. Bourne. (Works of Edward Gaylord Bourne). 1989. reprint ed. lib. bdg. 79.00 (*0-7812-2013-0*) Rprt Serv.

Discovery, Creativity & Problem-Solving. David Lamb. 168p. 1991. text ed. 49.95 (*1-85628-043-8*, Pub. by Avebury Pub UK) Ashgate Pub Co.

Discovery for Playground & Sports: A Learning Guide. Carolyn Sumners. (Illus.). 52p. 1993. pap. text ed. 7.95 (*0-944584-34-9*) Sopris.

Discovery Guide to Syria. David Claymore. 224p. (C). 1990. 79.00 (*0-685-74646-1*, Pub. by IMMEL Pubng UK) St Mut.

Discovery Guide to Aegean & Mediterranean Turkey. Diana Darke. 320p. (C). 1990. 79.00 (*0-902743-70-8*, Pub. by IMMEL Pubng UK) St Mut.

Discovery Guide to Cairo Including the Pyramids & Saqqara. Michael Haag. 152p. (C). 1990. 79.00 (*0-902743-73-2*, Pub. by IMMEL Pubng UK) St Mut.

Discovery Guide to Central Africa. Pamela McKinstry. 224p. (C). 1990. 95.00 (*0-907151-96-5*, Pub. by IMMEL Pubng UK) St Mut.

Discovery Guide to Eastern Turkey & the Black Sea Coast. Diana Darke. 352p. (C). 1990. 79.00 (*0-902743-74-0*, Pub. by IMMEL Pubng UK) St Mut.

Discovery Guide to Egypt. Michael Haag. 448p. (C). 1990. 79.00 (*0-902743-75-9*, Pub. by IMMEL Pubng UK) St Mut.

Discovery Guide to Game Parks of Southern Africa. Pamela McKinstry. 232p. (C). 1990. 79.00 (*0-907151-97-3*, Pub. by IMMEL Pubng UK) St Mut.

Discovery Guide to Jordan & the Holy Land. Diana Darke. 224p. (C). 1990. 79.00 (*0-907151-70-1*, Pub. by IMMEL Pubng UK) St Mut.

Discovery Guide to Rajasthan with Delhi & Agra. Kim Naylor. 224p. (C). 1990. 90.00 (*0-902743-49-X*, Pub. by IMMEL Pubng UK) St Mut.

Discovery Guide to Southern Africa: Namibia, Botswana & South Africa. Ed. by Pamela McKinstry. 256p. (C). 1990. 79.00 (*0-907151-73-6*, Pub. by IMMEL Pubng UK) St Mut.

Discovery Guide to Vietnam. Kim Naylor. 224p. (C). 1990. 79.00 (*0-907151-71-X*, Pub. by IMMEL Pubng UK) St Mut.

Discovery Guide to West Africa: The Niger & Gambia River Route. Kim Naylor. 224p. (C). 1990. 79.00 (*0-902743-67-8*, Pub. by IMMEL Pubng UK) St Mut.

Discovery Guide to Yemen. Chris Bradley. 192p. (C). 1990. 79.00 (*0-685-74645-3*, Pub. by IMMEL Pubng UK) St Mut.

Discovery Guide to Zimbabwe. Melissa Shales. 232p. (C). 1990. 79.00 (*0-907151-72-8*, Pub. by IMMEL Pubng UK) St Mut.

Discovery in Construction Litigation: With 1991 Cumulative Supplement. 2nd ed. Michael T. Callahan et al. 685p. 1994. 95.00x (*0-87473-320-0*) Michie Butterworth.

Discovery in Mathematics: A Text for Teachers. Robert B. Davis. 274p. (J). (gr. 4-8). 1980. pap. text ed. 16.50 (*0-914040-86-3*) Cuisenaire.

Discovery in the Archives of Spain & Portugal: Quincentenary Essays, 1492-1992. Intro. by Lawrence J. McCrank. LC 93-50115. (Primary Sources & Original Works). (Illus.). 347p. 1994. 119.95 (*1-56024-643-X*) Haworth Pr.

Discovery, Innovation, & Risk: Case Studies in Science & Technology. Newton H. Copp & Andrew W. Zanella. (Illus.). 400p. 1992. 45.00 (*0-262-03199-X*); pap. 25.00 (*0-262-53111-9*) MIT Pr.

Discovery Method for Popular Piano, Vol. 1. Robert Benedict. 1993. 4.95 (*0-685-64680-7*, 94398) Mel Bay.

Discovery Method for Popular Piano, Vol. 2. Robert Benedict. 1993. 4.95 (*0-685-64681-5*, 94486) Mel Bay.

Discovery of a Dead Sea Scroll: Its Importance in the History of Jesus Research. James H. Charlesworth. 41p. 1985. pap. 6.00 (*0-318-18993-3*, 85-1) Intl Ctr Arid & Semi-Arid.

Discovery of a Fragment of the Printed Copy of the Work on the Millcayac Language of Chile. R. R. Schuller. (Harvard University Peabody Museum of Archaeology & Ethnology Papers). 1972. reprint ed. pap. 10.00 (*0-527-01196-7*) Periodicals Srv.

Discovery of a Human Fossil. Adrienne Wolfert. (Illus.). 64p. (Orig.). 1979. pap. 4.95 (*0-931642-06-X*) Lintel.

Discovery of a New World (Mundus Alter et Idem) Joseph Hall. Tr. by J. Healey. LC 72-6935. (English Experience Ser.: No. 119). 1969. reprint ed. 65.00 (*90-221-0119-3*) Walter J Johnson.

Discovery of a World in the Moone. John Wilkins. LC 70-38230. (English Experience Ser.: No. 494). 224p. 1972. reprint ed. 30.00 (*90-221-0494-X*) Walter J Johnson.

Discovery of a World in the Moone: 1638. John Wilkins. LC 73-14920. 1973. lib. bdg. 50.00 (*0-8201-1123-6*) Schol Facsimiles.

Discovery of a World in the Moone: or a Discourse Tending to Prove That 'Tis Probable There May Be Another Habitable World in That Planet. John Wilkins. (Anglistica & Americana Ser.: No. 95). 211p. 1981. reprint ed. 44.20 (*3-487-06445-6*, Pub. by Georg Olms GW) Lubrecht & Cramer.

***Discovery of America.** (Picture Books Ser.). 1975. pap. 4.00 (*0-934909-58-X*) Mass Hist Soc.

Discovery of America. Cesare Pascarella. Tr. by John Duval. 120p. 1991. 17.95 (*1-55728-229-3*); pap. 9.95 (*1-55728-230-7*) U of Ark Pr.

Discovery of America. Saul Steinberg. LC 92-52959. (Illus.). 228p. 1992. 50.00 (*0-679-40278-0*) Knopf.

Discovery of America. John Fiske. (Notable American Authors Ser.). 1992. reprint ed. lib. bdg. 75.00 (*0-7812-2853-0*) Rprt Serv.

Discovery of America: Opposing Viewpoints. Renardo Barden. LC 89-11709. (Great Mysteries Ser.). (Illus.). 112p. (J). (gr. 5-8). 1989. lib. bdg. 16.95 (*0-89908-071-5*) Greenhaven.

***Discovery of America & Other Tales of Terror & Self-Exploration: Stories.** fac. ed. Alvin Greenberg. LC 79-13068. 128p. 1980. reprint ed. pap. 36.50 (*0-7837-7735-3*, 2047491) Bks Demand.

***Discovery of Being.** Rollo May. 1995. 22.75 (*0-8446-6855-9*) Peter Smith.

Discovery of Being. May Rollo. 192p. 1994. pap. 11.00 (*0-393-31240-2*) Norton.

***Discovery of California.** O. Von Sadovszky. 200p. 1993. 108.00 (*963-05-6630-3*, Pub. by Akad Kiado HU) St Mut.

Discovery of Canada. Lawrence J. Burpee. LC 74-2412. (Essay Index Reprint Ser.). 1977. reprint ed. 22.95 (*0-518-10161-4*) Ayer.

Discovery of Childhood in Puritan England. C. John Sommerville. LC 90-23436. 208p. 1992. 35.00 (*0-8203-1353-X*) U of Ga Pr.

Discovery of Chocolate. William Van Wert. 52p. 1989. pap. 8.95 (*0-912527-07-2*) Word Beat.

Discovery of Competence: Teaching & Learning with Diverse Student Writers. Eleanor Kutz et al. LC 93-16574. 204p. (J). 1993. pap. text ed. 20.00 (*0-86709-323-4*, 0323) Boynton Cook Pubs.

Discovery of Discovery. Charles Tenney. Ed. by Harold M. Kaplan et al. 842p. (C). 1990. lib. bdg. 89.50 (*0-8191-7913-2*) U Pr of Amer.

Discovery of Dura-Europos. Clark Hopkins. Ed. by Bernard Goldman. LC 78-31193. 333p. reprint ed. pap. 95.00 (*0-7837-3298-8*, 2057700) Bks Demand.

Discovery of Egypt. Leslie Greener. (Dorset Reprints Ser.). (Illus.). 216p. 1990. reprint ed. 18.95 (*0-88029-396-9*) Marboro Bks.

Discovery of Egypt: Artists, Travellers & Scientists. Fernand Beaucour et al. (Illus.). 272p. 50.00 (*1-55859-506-6*, Pub. by Flammarion) Abbeville Pr.

Discovery of Egypt: Artists, Travellers & Scientists. Fernand Beaucour et al. Tr. by Bambi Ballard. (Illus.). 272p. 1993. 50.00 (*2-08-013506-6*, Pub. by Flammarion) Abbeville Pr.

Discovery of Evolution. David G. Young. 240p. (C). 1993. 79.95 (*0-521-43441-6*); pap. 24.95 (*0-521-43587-0*) Cambridge U Pr.

Discovery of Fire. David Shevin. (Ohio Writers Ser.: No. 12). 64p. (Orig.). 1988. pap. 6.00 (*0-933087-12-8*) Bottom Dog Pr.

Discovery of Francis Bacon's Cipher Signatures in James Anderson's Constitutions of the Free Masons. George V. Tudhope. 15p. 1993. spiral bd. 5.50 (*0-7873-0899-4*) Mokelumne.

Discovery of Freedom: Man's Struggle Against Authority. 3rd ed. R. Wilder Lane. 284p. 1984. pap. 12.95 (*0-930073-00-2*) Fox & Wilkes.

Discovery of Freedom: Man's Struggle Against Authority. Rose W. Lane. LC 73-172216. (Right Wing Individualist Tradition in America Ser.). 1979. reprint ed. 21.95 (*0-405-00425-7*) Ayer.

Discovery of Glacier Bay (1879) John Muir. Ed. by William R. Jones. (Illus.). 16p. 1978. reprint ed. pap. 3.95 (*0-89646-045-2*) Vistabooks.

Discovery of Glass: Experiments in the Smelting of Rich "Dry" Iron Ores, & the Reproduction of Bronze Age-Type Cobalt Blue As a Slag. John E. Dayton. (Peabody Museum of Archaeology & Ethnology American School of Prehistoric Research Ser.: Vol. 41). (Illus.). 72p. 1991. pap. 16.95 (*0-685-38743-7*, DAYDIS) HUP.

Discovery of Grounded Theory: Strategies for Qualitative Research. Barney G. Glaser & Anselm L. Strauss. LC 66-28314. 281p. 1967. pap. text ed. 24.95 (*0-202-30260-1*) Aldine de Gruyter.

Discovery of Hebrew in Tudor England: A Third Language. G. Lloyd Jones. LC 82-20875. 300p. 1988. text ed. 100.00 (0-7190-0875-1, Pub. by Manchester Univ Pr UK) St Martin.

Discovery of India. Jawaharlal Nehru. 1990. pap. 11.95 (0-19-562359-2) OUP.

Discovery of Indian Heritage. George Vallatt. 1993. 12.00 (81-202-0389-5, Pub. by Ajanta II) S Asia.

Discovery of Infinite Treasure, Hidden Since the Worlde's Beginning. Gabriel Plattes. LC 74-80202. (English Experience Ser.: No. 682). 96p. 1974. reprint ed. 13.00 (90-221-0682-9) Walter J Johnson.

Discovery of Insulin. Michael Bliss. LC 82-50911. (Illus.). 304p. (C). 1984. pap. text ed. 13.95 (0-226-05898-0) U Ch Pr.

Discovery of Intracranial Ossicles in a Carboniferous North American Paleoniscid: Pisces: Actinopterygii. Cecil M. Poplin. (Occasional Papers: No. 99). 17p. 1982. 1.00 (0-317-04811-2) U of KS Mus Nat Hist.

Discovery of Kepler's Laws: The Interaction of Science, Philosophy, & Religion. Job Kozhamthadam. LC 92-56863. (C). 1994. text ed. 39.95 (0-268-00868-X) U of Notre Dame Pr.

***Discovery of Kepler's Laws: The Interaction of Science, Philosophy, & Religion.** Job Kozhamthadam. LC 92-56863. (C). Date not set. reprint ed. pap. text ed. 19.95 (0-268-00880-9) U of Notre Dame Pr.

Discovery of King Arthur. Geoffrey Ashe & Debrett's Peerage. LC 86-9784. (Illus.). 256p. 1987. pap. 10.95 (0-8050-0115-8, Owl) H Holt & Co.

Discovery of Lakes Rudolf & Stefanie. L. Von Hohnel. Tr. by N. Bell. (Illus.). 1968. reprint ed. 85.00 (0-7146-1814-4, Pub. by F Cass Pubs UK) Intl Spec Bk.

Discovery of Life. Christopher A. Anderson. LC 93-74324. (Illus.). 154p. (Orig.). 1994. pap. text ed. 12.50 (0-931353-35-1) Andersons Pubns.

Discovery of Light. J. P. Smith. 224p. 1993. pap. 10.00 (0-14-015275-X, Penguin Bks) Viking Penguin.

***Discovery of Luminous Being.** Anthony Maulucci. LC 94-96880. 112p. 1995. pap. 7.95 (0-9645226-0-8) Lorenzo Pr.

Discovery of Magnetic Health. George J. Washnis & Richard Z. Hricak. 356p. 1993. pap. text ed. 21.95 (0-9639560-1-9) Nova Pubng.

Discovery of Music. Art Beck. (Chapbook Ser.: No. 9). 1977. pap. 3.00 (0-912824-18-2) Vagabond Pr.

Discovery of Natural Products with Therapeutic Potential. Ed. by Vincent P. Gullo. LC 93-23111. (Biotechnology: A Comprehensive Treatise in Eight Volumes: Vol. 26). 544p. (C). 1993. 115.00 (0-7506-9003-8) Buttrwrth-Heinemann.

Discovery of New Mexico by the Franciscan Monk Friar Marcos de Niza in 1539. Adolph F. Bandelier. Tr. by Madeleine T. Rodack. LC 80-25083. 135p. (C). 1981. 26.95 (0-8165-0717-1) U of Ariz Pr.

Discovery of New Spain in Fifteen Eighteen by Juan De Grijalva. Tr. by H. R. Wagner. (Cortes Society Ser.). 1972. reprint ed. 25.00 (0-527-19731-9) Periodicals Srv.

Discovery of North America: A Critical Documentary & Historic Investigation. H. Harrisse. (Illus.). 1969. reprint ed. 124.00 (90-6072-515-8) IBD Ltd.

Discovery of Nuclear Fission. Hans G. Graetzerk & David L. Anderson. Ed. by I. Bernard Cohen. LC 80-2123. (Development of Science Ser.). (Illus.). 1981. lib. bdg. 15.95 (0-405-13846-6) Ayer.

Discovery of Our Galaxy. Charles A. Whitney. LC 88-12791. (History of Science & Technology Reprint Ser.). 334p. 1988. reprint ed. pap. 13.95 (0-8138-0088-9) Iowa St U Pr.

Discovery of Painting: The Growth of Interest in the Arts in England, 1680-1768. Iain Pears. (Illus.). 301p. (C). 1991. reprint ed. pap. text ed. 22.50 (0-300-05147-6) Yale U Pr.

Discovery of Poetry. Frances Mayes. 583p. (C). 1987. pap. text ed. 22.75 (0-15-517678-1) HB Coll Pubs.

Discovery of Poetry. 2nd ed. Frances Mayes. 600p. (C). 1993. pap. text ed. write for info. (0-15-500162-0) HB Coll Pubs.

Discovery of Poverty in the United States. Robert H. Bremner. 399p. (C). 1992. pap. 21.95 (1-56000-582-3) Transaction Pubs.

Discovery of San Francisco Bay; The Portola Expedition of 1769-1770, The Diary of Miguel Costanso: El Descubrimiento de la Bahia de San Francisco; La Expedicion de Portola de 1769-1770, Miguel Costanso. Tr. by Maria L. Wait. LC 92-7885. 256p. (ENG & SPA.). (C). 1992. reprint ed. pap. 14.95 (0-944220-06-1) Great West Bks.

Discovery of Satyagraha, 1896-1902 see Mahatma Gandhi

Discovery of Secrets Attributed to Geber. Geber. Tr. by Robert R. Steele. reprint ed. pap. 2.95 (1-55818-108-3) Holmes Pub.

Discovery of Society. 5th ed. Randall Collins & Michael Makowsky. LC 92-9953. 1992. pap. text ed. write for info. (0-07-011841-8) McGraw.

Discovery of Specific & Latent Heats. Douglas McKie & Niels De Heathcote. LC 74-26274. (History, Philosophy & Sociology of Science Ser.). 1975. reprint ed. 21.95 (0-405-06602-3) Ayer.

Discovery of Subatomic Particles. Steven Weinberg. LC 89-24294. (Illus.). 206p. 1995. pap. text ed. write for info. (0-7167-1489-2) W H Freeman.

Discovery of Subatomic Particles. Steven Weinberg. LC 82-23157. (Scientific American Library). (Illus.). 206p. 1995. text ed. write for info. (0-7167-1488-4) W H Freeman.

Discovery of Subatomic Particles. Steven Weinberg. 1995. pap. text ed. write for info. (0-7167-2121-X) W H Freeman.

"Discovery" of Sudden Infant Death Syndrome: Lessons in the Practice of Political Medicine. Abraham B. Bergman. 257p. 1988. pap. 12.50 (0-295-96601-7) U of Wash Pr.

Discovery of Sudden Infant Death Syndrome: Lessons in the Practice of Political Medicine. Abraham B. Bergman. LC 85-30778. (Illus.). 254p. 1986. text ed. 75.00 (0-275-92059-3, C2059, Praeger Pubs) Greenwood.

Discovery of Talent: The Walter Van Dyke Bingham Lectures on the Development of Exceptional Abilities & Capacities. Ed. by Dael Wolfle. LC 69-18046. 338p. 1969. 38.50 (0-674-21235-5) HUP.

Discovery of the Amazon. 2nd ed. Ed. by Jose T. Medina. (Illus.). 480p. 1988. reprint ed. pap. 9.95 (0-486-25589-1) Dover.

Discovery of the Amazon According to the Accounts of Friar Gaspar De Carvajal & Other Documents. Gaspar de Carvajal. Ed. by H. C. Heaton & Bertram T. Lee. LC 77-120567. reprint ed. 31.50 (0-404-01404-6) AMS Pr.

Discovery of the Americas. Betsy Maestro. (J). (ps-3). 1991. lib. bdg. 15.93 (0-688-06838-3) Lothrop.

Discovery of the Americas. Betsy Maestro & Giulio Maestro. (J). (gr. 4-7). 1991. 16.00 (0-688-06837-5) Lothrop.

Discovery of the Americas. Betsy Maestro & Giulio Maestro. LC 89-32375. (Illus.). 48p. (J). (gr. k up). 1992. pap. 5.95 (0-688-11512-8, Mulberry) Morrow.

Discovery of the Americas Activities Book. Betsy Maestro. (Illus.). 92p. (J). (gr. 1-6). 1992. pap. 7.95 (0-688-08590-3) Lothrop.

Discovery of the Ancient World. Harry E. Burton. LC 75-102228. (Select Bibliographies Reprint Ser.). 1977. 27.95 (0-8369-5113-1) Ayer.

Discovery of the Art of the Insane. John M. MacGregor. (Illus.). 512p. (C). 1992. text ed. 80.00 (0-691-04071-0, Spir Rsch Edit); pap. text ed. 29.95 (0-691-00036-0, Spir Rsch Edit) Princeton U Pr.

Discovery of the Asylum: Social Order & Disorder in the New Republic, Vol. 1. David J. Rothman. 1990. pap. 15.95 (0-316-75745-4) Little.

Discovery of the Asylum: Social Order & Disorder in the New Republic, Vol. 1. David J. Rothman. 1994. 42.50 (0-316-75744-6) Little.

Discovery of the Chesapeake Bay: An Account of the Explorations of Captain John Smith in the year 1608. Francis d'A. Collings. LC 88-23703. (Illus.). (Orig.). 1988. pap. 10.95 (0-922249-00-8) Ches Bay Mus.

Discovery of the Child. 1990. write for info. (81-900106-2-X, Pub. by Kalakshetra Pubns II) N Montessori.

Discovery of the Child. Maria Montessori. 1986. mass mkt. 5.95 (0-345-33656-9) Ballantine.

Discovery of the Child. Maria Montessori. 1976. 23.95 (0-8488-0583-6) Amereon Ltd.

Discovery of the Electron. Ed. by David L. Anderson & I. Bernard Cohen. LC 80-2114. (Development of Science Ser.). (Illus.). 1981. lib. bdg. 18.95 (0-405-13834-2) Ayer.

Discovery of the Elements. 7th rev. ed. Mary E. Weeks. LC 68-15217. (Illus.). 906p. reprint ed. pap. 180.00 (0-317-09341-X, 2011897) Bks Demand.

Discovery of the Essene Gospel of Peace: The Essenes & the Vatican. Edmond B. Szekely. (Illus.). 96p. 1977. pap. 5.95 (0-89564-004-X) IBS Intl.

Discovery of the Great Subtiltie & Wonderful Wisdom of the Italians. LC 74-80221. (English Experience Ser.: No. 656). 1974. reprint ed. 10.50 (90-221-0656-X) Walter J Johnson.

Discovery of the Great West: La Salle. Francis Parkman, Jr. Ed. by William R. Taylor. LC 86-22763. 377p. 1986. reprint ed. text ed. 89.50 (0-313-24223-2, PDGW, Greenwood Pr) Greenwood.

Discovery of the Igorots: Spanish Contacts with the Pagans of Northern Luzon. rev. ed. William F. Scott. 1977. 15.00 (971-10-0087-3, Pub. by New Day Pub PH) Cellar.

Discovery of the Individual 1051-1200. Colin Morris. (Medieval Academy Reprints for Teaching Ser.). 188p. 1987. reprint ed. pap. text ed. 10.95 (0-8020-6665-8) U of Toronto Pr.

***Discovery of the Little Yodel People.** R. Keith Goodridge. (Illus.). 24p. (J). (gr. k-3). 1994. pap. 3.95 (1-885945-10-8) Goodreeder Pubns.

Discovery of the Mind in Early Greek Philosophy & Literature. Bruno Snell. (Illus.). 128p. (C). 1982. pap. 7.50 (0-486-24264-1) Dover.

Discovery of the Neutrino, Franklin Symposium Proceedings in Celebration. C. E. Lane & R. Steinberg. 232p. 1993. text ed. 91.00 (981-02-1567-3) World Scientific Pub.

Discovery of the North-West Passage by H.M.S. Investigator: 1850-54. Robert J. McClure. Ed. by Sherard Osborn. LC 74-5853. reprint ed. 26.50 (0-404-11660-4) AMS Pr.

***Discovery of the Oregon Trail: Robert Stuart's Narratives of His Overland Trip Eastward from Astoria in 1812-13.** Ed. by Philip A. Rollins. LC 95-2134. (Illus.). 535p. (J). 1995. pap. 18.95 (0-8032-9234-1, Bison Books) U of Nebr Pr.

Discovery of the Outer Planets. Joylyn Hill. LC 83-71863. 200p. 1985. 16.00 (0-86690-253-8, H2401-014) Am Fed Astrologers.

Discovery of the Pacific Islands. Andrew Sharp. LC 84-25237. (Illus.). xvi, 259p. 1985. reprint ed. text ed. 65.00 (0-313-24689-0, SHDP, Greenwood Pr) Greenwood.

Discovery of the Photon-Drag Effect: The Ioffe Institute in Leningrad. Anatoly Grinberg. Ed. by Ben Armfield. 130p. (Orig.). 1986. pap. text ed. 75.00 (1-55831-015-0) Delphic Associates.

Discovery of the Sea. J. H. Parry. LC 81-51174. 350p. 1981. pap. 14.00 (0-520-04237-9) U CA Pr.

Discovery of the Solomon Islands by Alvaro de Mendana in 1568, 2 vols. in 1. Ed. by William A. Amherst & Basil Thomson. (Hakluyt Society Works Ser.: No. 2, Vols. 7 & 8). (Illus.). 1972. reprint ed. 95.00 (0-8115-0330-5) Periodicals Srv.

Discovery of the Titanic. Robert Ballard. 230p. 1990. 17.99 (0-517-03574-X) Random Hse Value.

***Discovery of the Titanic.** Robert D. Ballard. 336p. 1995. pap. 12.99 (0-446-67174-6) Warner Bks.

Discovery of the Tomb of Tutankhamen. Howard Carter & A. C. Mace. (Illus.). 19.75 (0-8446-5562-7) Peter Smith.

Discovery of the Tomb of Tutankhamen. Howard Carter & A. C. Mace. LC 77-71042. (Illus.). 382p. 1977. reprint ed. pap. 7.95 (0-486-23500-9) Dover.

Discovery of the True Causes Why Ireland Was Never Entirely Subdued & Brought under Obedience of the Crown of England until the Beginning of His Majesty's Happy Reign (1612) John Davies. Ed. by James P. Myers, Jr. LC 87-25595. 1988. 35.95 (0-8132-0652-9) Cath U Pr.

***Discovery of the True Causes Why Ireland Was Never Entirely Subdued & Brought under Obedience of the Crown of England until the Beginning of His Majesty's Happy Reign (1612)** John Davies. Ed. by James P. Myers, Jr. LC 87-25595. reprint ed. pap. 73.00 (0-7837-9192-5, 2049893) Bks Demand.

Discovery of the Unconscious: The History & Evolution of Dynamic Psychiatry. Henri F. Ellenberger. LC 79-94287. (Illus.). 932p. 1981. pap. text ed. 35.00 (0-465-01673-1) Basic.

Discovery of the World: Maps of the Earth & the Cosmos. Elizabeth Hale. (Illus.). 88p. 1986. lib. bdg. 60.00 (0-226-31302-6, 31302-6); pap. 25.00 (0-226-31303-4, 31303-4) U Ch Pr.

Discovery of the Yosemite: And the Indian War of 1851 Which Led to That Event. Lafayette H. Bunnell. Ed. by Steven P. Medley. (High Sierra Classics Ser.). 315p. (C). 1990. reprint ed. pap. 9.95 (0-939666-58-8) Yosemite Assn.

Discovery of the Yosemite & the Indian War of 1851. Lafayette H. Bunnell. LC 72-146854. (Select Bibliographies Reprint Ser.). 1977. reprint ed. 23.95 (0-8369-5621-4) Ayer.

Discovery of the Yosemite in 1851. Lafayette H. Bunnell. Ed. by William R. Jones. (Illus.). 1977. reprint ed. pap. 7.95 (0-89646-021-5) Vistabooks.

Discovery of Time. Stephen E. Toulmin. LC 81-71398. 280p. 1982. pap. text ed. 11.95 (0-226-80842-4) U Ch Pr.

***Discovery of Weak Neutral Currents: The Weak Interaction Before & After.** Ed. by Alfred K. Mann & David B. Cline. LC 94-70515. (AIP Conference Proceeding Ser.: Vol. 300). 676p. 1994. 145.00 (1-56396-306-X) Am Inst Physics.

Discovery of Witches. Montague Summers. LC 79-8105. (Satanism Ser.). 64p. reprint ed. 18.50 (0-404-18416-2) AMS Pr.

Discovery of Witches: A Study of Master Matthew Hopkins. Montague Summers. 1993. reprint ed. 27.50 (1-55818-224-1, First Impress) Holmes Pub.

Discovery of Yellowstone Park: Journal of the Washburn Expedition to the Yellowstone & Firehole Rivers in the Year 1870. Nathaniel P. Langford. LC 78-93106. (Illus.). lxii, 147p. 1972. pap. 8.95 (0-8032-5705-8) U of Nebr Pr.

Discovery of Yellowstone Park, Journal of the Washburn Expedition to the Yellowstone & Firehole Rivers in the Year 1870. Nathaniel P. Langford. (American Biography Ser.). 125p. 1991. reprint ed. lib. bdg. 59.00 (0-7812-8238-1) Rprt Serv.

Discovery on Dusty Creek. Zeno Zeplin. (Illus.). 112p. (J). (gr. 3-6). 1994. 16.95 (1-877740-23-3); pap. 9.95 (1-877740-24-1) Nel-Mar Pub.

Discovery PAC Insects. (J). (gr. k-8). 1991. pap. 7.95 (0-945051-35-2, 75035) Natl Wildlife.

Discovery Passage. Marky Daniel. (Illus.). 148p. (C). 1988. text ed. 10.95 (0-910303-11-8) Writers Pub Serv.

Discovery Play: Loving & Learning with Your Baby. Art Ulene & Steven Shelov. LC 94-60059. (Illus.). 225p. 1994. pap. 9.95 (1-56975-012-2) Ulysses Pr.

Discovery Practice. Roger S. Haydock & David F. Herr. LC 81-81902. 704p. 1982. 80.00 (0-316-35159-8) Little.

Discovery Practice. 2nd ed. Roger S. Haydock & David F. Herr. 750p. 1988. 125.00 (0-316-35181-4) Little.

Discovery Proceedings in Federal Court. 2nd ed. Shepard's Citation, Inc. Staff. 1149p. 1991. text ed. 195.00 (0-07-172343-9) Shepards-McGraw.

Discovery Science. David Winnett. 1994. pap. text ed. 31.25 (0-201-29063-4) Addison-Wesley.

***Discovery Science, Preschool: Explorations for the Early Years.** D. A. Winnett et al. Ed. by Mali Apple. (Discovery Science Ser.). (Illus.). 304p. (Orig.). (J). (ps). 1995. teacher ed, pap. 31.25 (0-201-49364-0) Altrntv Pub Grp.

Discovery Strategies in the Psychology of Action, Vol. 35. Ed. by Gerry Ginsburg et al. (European Monographs in Social Psychology). 1985. text ed. 124.00 (0-12-284760-1) Acad Pr.

Discovery Techniques. Irving Younger. 1979. 5.00 (1-55917-118-9, 109); audio 60.00 (1-55917-116-2); vhs 195.00 (1-55917-117-0) Natl Prac Inst.

Discovery Trails see California

Discovery Two Thousand One. Ross Asher. LC 78-51727. 1978. 9.95 (0-931662-00-1) Photo-Go Pr.

Discovery Units for Young Children. Marj Hart. (J). (gr. k-3). 1991. pap. 12.99 (0-8224-2323-5) Fearon Teach Aids.

***Discovery Weekend Workbook Four.** 7th ed. Robert D. Noble. (Reach Out Ser.). (Illus.). 79p. (Orig.). 1994. pap. 20.00 (0-944687-16-4) Gather Family Inst.

Discovery with Cap'n Bob & Matey: Voyages of Courage & Adventure. (Cap'n Bob & Matey Ser.). (Illus.). 32p. (J). (gr. 1-4). 1991. 13.95 (0-931595-08-8); pap. 7.95 (0-931595-09-6) Seascape Enters.

Discovery with 1990 Cumulative Supplement. suppl. ed. Mark A. Dombroff. LC 86-20980. 687p. 1986. 30.00 (0-930273-73-7) Michie Butterworth.

Discovery with 1990 Cumulative Supplement. suppl. ed. Mark A. Dombroff. LC 86-20980. 687p. 1990. 80.00 (0-930273-44-3) Michie Butterworth.

Discovery Your Personality Type: The New Enneagram Questionnaire. Don R. Riso. 128p. 1994. pap. 6.95 (0-395-71092-8) HM.

Discredited Tax: The Capital Gains Tax Problem & Its Solution. Ed. by Barry Bracewell-Milnes. 90p. (C). 1992. text ed. 59.95 (0-255-36309-5, Pub. by Inst Economic Affairs UK) St Mut.

Discreet Affections. Wanda S. Dieckow. 40p. 1993. 7.50 (1-882560-00-0) W Dieckow.

Discreet Indiscretions: The Social Organization of Gossip. Jorg R. Bergmann. Tr. by John Bednarz, Jr. LC 93-4263. (Communication & Social Order Ser.). 224p. 1993. lib. bdg. 44.95 (0-202-30467-1); pap. text ed. 22.95 (0-202-30468-X) Aldine de Gruyter.

***Discrepant Dislocations: Feminism, Theory & Postcolonial Histories.** Mary E. John. LC 95-12580. 1996. pap. write for info. (0-520-20135-3) U CA Pr.

Discrepant Engagement: Dissonance, Cross-Culturality, & Experimental Writing. Nathaniel Mackey. LC 93-626. (Cambridge Studies in American Literature & Culture: No. 71). 336p. (C). 1993. 59.95 (0-521-44453-5) Cambridge U Pr.

***Discrepant Histories: Translocal Essays on Filipino Cultures.** Ed. by Vicente Rafael. (Asian American History & Culture Ser.). 240p. (Orig.). (C). 1995. lib. bdg. 39.95 (1-56639-355-8) Temple U Pr.

***Discrepant Histories: Translocal Essays on Filipino Cultures.** Ed. by Vicente Rafael. (Asian American History & Culture Ser.). 240p. (Orig.). (C). 1995. pap. text ed. 12.95 (1-56639-356-6) Temple U Pr.

Discrete - Group Methods: Integrating Equations of Nonlinear Mechanics. 1993. write for info. (0-8493-9916-5, QA) CRC Pr.

***Discrete Algorithmic Mathematics.** Stephen B. Maurer & A. Ralston. 720p. (C). 1991. text ed. 58.25 (0-201-15585-0) Addison-Wesley.

Discrete Algorithms & Complexity: Japan--U. S. Seminar. Ed. by David S. Johnson et al. (Perspectives in Computing Ser.: Vol. 15). 497p. 1987. text ed. 79.00 (0-12-386870-X) Acad Pr.

Discrete & Combinatorial Mathematics. Ralph P. Grimaldi & Rose-Hulman. LC 84-9359. (C). 1985. text ed. write for info. (0-201-12590-0); write for info. (0-201-12591-9) Addison-Wesley.

Discrete & Combinatorial Mathematics. 3rd ed. Ralph P. Grimaldi. (Illus.). 880p. (C). 1994. text ed. 59.25 (0-201-54983-2) Addison-Wesley.

Discrete & Combinatorial Mathematics: An Applied Introduction. 2nd ed. Ralph P. Grimaldi. (Illus.). 722p. (C). 1989. text ed. 55.95 (0-201-11954-4) Addison-Wesley.

Discrete & Computational Geometry: Papers from the DIMACS Special Year. J. Goodman et al. LC 91-36806. 378p. 1991. 66.00 (0-8218-6595-1, DIMACS-6) Am Math.

***Discrete & Fractional Programming Techniques for Location Models.** Anna I. De Barros. (Tinbergen Institute Research Ser.: No. 89). 148p. 1995. pap. 25.00 (90-5170-320-1) IBD Ltd.

Discrete & Integrated Circuit Electronics. Donald P. Leach. 790p. (C). 1992. text ed. 55.00 (0-03-020844-0) SCP.

Discrete & Numerical Control Systems with Variable Structure. Emel 'Yanov. 1993. write for info. (0-8493-7539-8, Q) CRC Pr.

Discrete Choice Analysis: Theory & Application to Travel Demand. Moshe Ben-Akiva & Steven Lerman. (Transportation Studies). 384p. (C). 1985. 52.50 (0-262-02217-6) MIT Pr.

Discrete Choice Theory of Product Differentiation. Simon P. Anderson & Andre De Palma. (Illus.). 398p. 1992. 50.00 (0-262-01128-X) MIT Pr.

Discrete Computational Structures. 2nd ed. Robert Korfhage. LC 83-2554. (Computer Science & Applied Mathematics Ser.). 1983. text ed. 73.00 (0-12-420860-6) Acad Pr.

Discrete Cosine Transform: Algorithms, Advantages, Applications. K. Ramamohan Rao & P. Yip. 490p. 1990. text ed. 59.95 (0-12-580203-X) Acad Pr.

Discrete Dynamical Modeling. James T. Sandefur. (Illus.). 448p. (C). 1993. text ed. 39.95 (0-19-508438-1) OUP.

Discrete Dynamical Systems. James T. Sandefur. (Illus.). 464p. (C). 1990. text ed. 39.95 (0-19-853384-5) OUP.

Discrete Dynamical Systems & Chaos. Mario Martelli. (Pitman Monographs & Surveys in Pure & Applied Mathematics). 282p. 1993. text ed. 197.00 (0-470-22066-X) Halsted Pr.

Discrete Electronic Components. F. F. Mazda. 200p. 1981. 59.95 (0-521-23470-0) Cambridge U Pr.

Discrete Event Dynamic Systems: Analyzing Complexity & Performance in the Modern World. Ed. by Yu-Chi Ho. LC 91-18049. (Illus.). 304p. (C). 1992. text ed. 59.95 (0-87942-281-5, PC0275-8) Inst Electrical.

Discrete Event Modelling on Simula. G. M. Birtwistle. 176p. 1987. pap. 33.00 (0-387-91301-7) Spr-Verlag.

Discrete Event Simulation: A Practical Approach. Udo W. Pooch. 1992. 59.95 (0-8493-7174-0, QA) CRC Pr.

Discrete Event Simulation & Operations Research (ESM 1987, Austria) 156p. 1987. 30.00 (0-911801-22-7, EMC87-1) Soc Computer Sim.

D

An Asterisk (*) at the beginning of an entry indicates that the title is appearing in BIP for the first time.

Discrete Event Simulation in C. Kevin Watkins. LC 93-17755. (International Series in Software Engineering). 1994. text ed. 40.00 (0-07-707733-4) McGraw.

Discrete Event System Simulation. Jerry Banks & John H. Carson. (Illus.). 560p. (C). 1983. text ed. 69.00 (0-13-215582-6) P-H.

Discrete Event Systems: Modeling & Control: Proceedings of a Joint Workshop Held in Prague, August 1992. Ed. by S. Balemi et al. LC 93-9970. (Progress in Systems & Control Theory Ser.: No. 13). vii, 230p. 1993. 69.00 (0-8176-2845-2) Birkhauser.

Discrete Event Systems: Modeling & Performance Analysis. Christos Cassandras. 450p. (C). 1993. text ed. 67.95 (0-256-11212-6, 19-3766-01) Irwin.

***Discrete Event Systems: Proceedings of the Eleventh International Conference on Analysis & Optimization of Systems, Sophia-Antipolis, June 15-17, 1994.** International Conference on Analysis & Optimization of Systems Staff. Ed. by A. Bensoussan et al. LC 94-29960. (Lecture Notes in Control & Information Sciences Ser.: Vol. 199). 1994. 99.00 (0-387-19896-2) Spr-Verlag.

Discrete Event Systems: Sensitivity Analysis & Stochastic Optimization by the Score Function Method. R. Rubinstein & A. Shapiro. LC 92-32372. (Probability & Mathematical Statistics Ser.). 334p. 1993. text ed. 69.95 (0-471-93419-4) Wiley.

***Discrete Event Systems, Manufacturing Systems, & Communication Networks.** Ed. by P. R. Kumar & P. Varaiya. (IMA Volumes in Mathematics & Its Applications Ser.: Vol. 73). (Illus.). 271p. 1995. 59.00 (0-387-97987-5) Spr-Verlag.

Discrete Fourier Transformation & Its Applications to Power Spectra Estimation. Ed. by N. C. Geckinli & D. Yavus. (Studies in Electrical & Electronic Engineering: No. 8). 340p. 1983. 78.75 (0-444-41713-3) Elsevier.

Discrete Fourier Transforms & Their Applications. V. Cizek. (Illus.). 141p. 1986. 49.00 (0-85274-800-0) IOP Pub.

Discrete Geometry & Topology: On the 100th Anniversary of the Birth of Boris Nikolaevich Delone: Collection of Papers. Ed. by S. P. Novikov et al. LC 92-37675. 193p. 1993. 129.00 (0-8218-3147-X, STEKLO 196) Am Math.

Discrete Groups & Geometry. Ed. by W. J. Harvey & C. Maclachlan. (London Mathematical Society Lecture Note Ser.: No. 173). (Illus.). 250p. (C). 1992. pap. 42.95 (0-521-42932-3) Cambridge U Pr.

***Discrete Groups, Expanding Graphs & Invariant Measures.** Alexander Lubotzky. Ed. by Jonathan D. Rogawski. LC 94-21726. (Progress in Mathematics Ser.: Vol. 125). 208p. 1994. 49.50 (0-8176-5075-X) Birkhauser.

Discrete Groups in Geometry & Analysis. Roger Howe. (Progress in Mathematics Ser.: Vol. 67). 230p. 1987. 47.50 (0-8176-3301-4) Birkhauser.

Discrete Images, Objects, & Functions in Zn. Klaus Voss. LC 92-45827. (Algorithms & Combinatorics Ser.: No. 11). 270p. 1993. 89.00 (0-387-55943-4) Spr-Verlag.

Discrete Iterated Function Systems. Mario Peruggia. LC 93-20664. (Illus.). 200p. (C). 1993. text ed. 39.95 (1-56881-015-6) AK Peters.

Discrete Iterations. F. Robert. Tr. by J. Rokne. (Computational Mathematics Ser.: Vol. 6). (Illus.). 195p. 1986. 64.00 (0-387-13623-1) Spr-Verlag.

Discrete Linear Control: The Polynomial Equation Approach. Vladimir Kucera. LC 78-12956. (Wiley-Interscience Publication Ser.). 206p. reprint ed. pap. 58.80 (0-317-26329-3, 2025201) Bks Demand.

Discrete Linear Control Systems. V. N. Fomin. (C). 1991. lib. bdg. 142.00 (0-7923-1248-1) Kluwer Ac.

Discrete Location Theory. Ed. by Pitu B. Mirchandani & Richard L. Francis. 576p. 1990. text ed. 105.00 (0-471-89233-5) Wiley.

Discrete Math. Gerstein. (C). 1995. pap. text ed. write for info. (0-7167-1906-1) W H Freeman.

Discrete Mathematical Structures. Mario Benedicty & Frank R. Sledge. 529p. (C). 1987. 1.50 (0-15-517684-6) SCP.

Discrete Mathematical Structures for Computer Science, No. 2/E. 2nd ed. Robert C. Busby & Bernard Kolman. (Illus.). 432p. 1987. text ed. write for info. (0-13-216003-X) P-H.

Discrete Mathematics. Kenneth R. Bogart. LC 87-80567. 658p. (C). 1988. text ed. 36.00 (0-669-08665-7); Instr.'s guide. teacher ed. 2.00 (0-669-08666-5); Introductory programming exercises. 8.50 (0-669-16975-7) Heath.

Discrete Mathematics. Paul Dierker & William L. Voxman. 589p. (C). 1986. text ed. 51.00 (0-15-517691-9); write for info. (0-318-60393-4) SCP.

Discrete Mathematics. John A. Dossey et al. (C). 1987. text ed. 39.50 (0-673-18191-X) HarpCollege.

Discrete Mathematics. Jerrold W. Grossman. (Illus.). 831p. (C). 1989. Incl. instr's. manual. teacher ed, text ed. write for info. (0-02-348331-8) Macmillan.

Discrete Mathematics. Melvin Hausner. 640p. (C). 1992. text ed. 60.00 (0-03-003278-4) SCP.

Discrete Mathematics. Kenneth H. Rosen. 600p. (C). 1988. text ed. 38.95 (0-685-13440-7) McGraw.

Discrete Mathematics. Kenneth Ross & Charles R. Wright. (Illus.). 672p. (C). 1985. pap. text ed. write for info. (0-13-215286-X) P-H.

Discrete Mathematics. rev. ed. Norman L. Biggs. (Illus.). 496p. (C). 1993. reprint ed. pap. text ed. 35.00 (0-19-853427-2) OUP.

Discrete Mathematics. 2nd ed. John A. Dossey et al. LC 92-19327. (C). 1992. text ed. 46.00 (0-673-46287-0) HarpCollege.

***Discrete Mathematics.** 2nd ed. Susanna S. Epp. LC 94-31184. 800p. 1995. text ed. 65.95 (0-534-94446-9) PWS Pubs.

Discrete Mathematics. 3rd ed. Richard Johnsonbaugh. LC 92-26014. 816p. (C). 1993. write for info. (0-02-360721-1) Macmillan.

Discrete Mathematics. 3rd ed. Kenneth A. Ross & Charles R. Wright. 752p. (C). 1992. text ed. write for info. (0-13-218157-6) P-H.

Discrete Mathematics: A Bridge to Computer Science & Advanced Mathematics. Olympia Nicodemi. LC 86-24616. (Illus.). 491p. (C). 1987. text ed. 57.50 (0-314-28503-2) West Pub.

Discrete Mathematics: An Introduction for Software Engineers. Mike Piff. (Illus.). 320p. (C). 1991. 64.95 (0-521-38475-3); pap. 19.95 (0-521-38622-5) Cambridge U Pr.

Discrete Mathematics: Applied Combinatorics & Graph Theory. Michael Townsend. 385p. (C). 1987. write for info. (0-318-61909-1); text ed. 47.50 (0-8053-9355-2) Addison-Wesley.

Discrete Mathematics Across the Curriculum, K-12: 1991 Yearbook. Ed. by Margaret J. Kenney. LC 90-26358. (Illus.). 248p. 1991. 20.00 (0-87353-305-4) NCTM.

Discrete Mathematics & Algebraic Structures. Larry Gerstein. LC 86-18417. (Mathematics Ser.). (Illus.). 413p. (C). 1987. 7.95 (0-685-17227-9) W H Freeman.

Discrete Mathematics & Its Applications. 2nd ed. Kenneth H. Rosen. 1991. text ed. write for info. (0-07-053744-5) McGraw.

Discrete Mathematics & Its Applications. 2nd ed. Kenneth H. Rosen. 1991. pap. text ed. write for info. (0-07-053746-1) McGraw.

***Discrete Mathematics & Its Applications.** 3rd ed. Kenneth H. Rosen. LC 95-942. 1995. text ed. write for info. (0-07-053965-0) McGraw.

Discrete Mathematics for Computer Science. Angela Shiflet. LC 86-19112. 450p. (C). 1987. text ed. 59.25 (0-314-28513-X) West Pub.

Discrete Mathematics for Computer Scientists. John K. Truss. (C). 1991. pap. text ed. 49.50 (0-201-17564-9) Addison-Wesley.

Discrete Mathematics for Computing. J. Munro. (Illus.). 306p. 1992. pap. 25.00 (0-412-45650-8, A9584) Chapman & Hall.

Discrete Mathematics for Engineers. O. P. Kuznetsov & G. M. Adelson-Velsky. (Computer Mathematics Ser.). 420p. 1985. text ed. 325.00 (2-88124-201-4) Gordon & Breach.

Discrete Mathematics for New Technology. R. Garnier & J. Taylor. (Illus.). 696p. 1992. 170.00 (0-7503-0136-8); pap. 39.00 (0-7503-0135-X) IOP Pub.

Discrete Mathematics in the First Two Years. Ed. by Anthony Ralston. 112p. 1989. 5.00 (0-88385-064-8, NTE-15) Math Assn.

Discrete Mathematics Students Solutions Manual. Jerrold W. Grossman. 214p. (C). 1990. pap. write for info. (0-02-348329-6) Macmillan.

***Discrete Mathematics Through Applications.** Nancy Crisler. LC 94-2597. 1994. 35.95 (0-7167-2427-8) W H Freeman.

Discrete Mathematics Through Applications. Nancy Crisler et al. LC 94-2597. (C). 1995. text ed. write for info. (0-7167-2577-0) W H Freeman.

Discrete Mathematics with Algorithms. Michael O. Albertson & Joan P. Hutchinson. 576p. 1988. Net. text ed. write for info. (0-471-84902-2) Wiley.

Discrete Mathematics with Applications to Computer Science. Harold F. Mattson. LC 92-33772. 672p. 1993. Net. text ed. write for info. (0-471-60672-3) Wiley.

Discrete Mathematics with Computer Science Applications. Romualdas Skvarcius & William B. Robinson. (Illus.). 448p. (C). 1986. text ed. 44.95 (0-8053-7044-7); 9.95 (0-8053-7045-5) Addison-Wesley.

Discrete Mechanics: A Unified Approach. Hayrettin Kardestuncer. (International Centre for Mechanical Sciences Ser.: No. 221). (Illus.). 1976. pap. 12.00 (0-387-81379-9) Spr-Verlag.

Discrete Models of Fluid Dynamics: Advances in Mathematics for Applied Science, Vol. 2. A. S. Alves. 272p. 1991. text ed. 89.00 (981-02-0521-X) World Scientific Pub.

Discrete Multivariate Analysis: Theory & Practice. Yvonne Bishop et al. 1974. pap. 32.50x (0-262-52040-0) MIT Pr.

Discrete Neural Computation: A Theoretical Foundation. Vwani Roychowdhury et al. 1995. text ed. 52.00 (0-13-300708-1) P-H.

Discrete Optimization. Ed. by R. Gary Parker & Ronald L. Rardin. (Computer Science & Scientific Computing Ser.). 472p. 1988. text ed. 99.00 (0-12-545075-3) Acad Pr.

Discrete Optimization: I & II. P. L. Hammer et al. (Annals of Discrete Mathematics Ser.: Vols. 4 & 5). 1979. I. 113.00 (0-444-85322-7, North Holland); II. 133.50 (0-444-85323-5, North Holland) Elsevier.

Discrete Probability. Hegarty & Schroeder. 189p. (C). 1993. 15.07 (1-56870-037-7) RonJon Pub.

Discrete Random Signals & Statistical Signal Processing. Charles W. Therrien. 784p. 1992. pap. text ed. 77.00 (0-13-852112-3) P-H.

Discrete Relaxation Techniques. Thomas C. Henderson. (International Series of Monographs on Computer Science: No. 5). (Illus.). 160p. 1989. 29.95 (0-19-504894-6) OUP.

***Discrete Semiconductor Products Handbook.** 200p. (Orig.). 1995. pap. 125.00 (0-7605-1835-1) Rector Pr.

Discrete Semiconductors & Opto-Electronics. Sy Levine. Ed. by Esther Levine & Jerry Worthing. (Library on Basic Electronics: Vol. 2). (Illus.). 356p. 1988. text ed. 35.00 (0-939527-01-4) Electro Horiz.

Discrete Series Representations of the General Linear Groups Over a Finite Field. George Lusztig. (Annals of Mathematics Studies: Vol. 1). 150p. 1974. 19.95 (0-691-08154-9) Princeton U Pr.

Discrete Simulation: Fundamentals & Microcomputer Support. Guy L. Curry et al. 312p. (C). 1989. 49.95 (0-8162-2060-3) Holden-Day.

Discrete Simulation & Related Fields. Ed. by A. Javor. 246p. 1982. 46.25 (0-444-86429-6, I-255-82, North Holland) Elsevier.

Discrete, Static, & Other Order Quantity Models Training Aid. Donald W. Fogarty. LC 83-73023. 26p. 1984. 30.00 (0-935406-37-9) Am Prod & Inventory.

Discrete Statistical Models with Social Science Applications. E. B. Andersen. 383p. 1980. 92.50 (0-444-85334-0, North Holland) Elsevier.

***Discrete Stochastic Processes.** Robert G. Gallager. LC 95-14891. (International Series in Engineering & Computer Science). 288p. (C). 1995. lib. bdg. 61.00 (0-7923-9583-2) Kluwer Ac.

Discrete Stochastics. K. Jacobs. (Basaler Lehrbucher Ser.: Vol. 3). 296p. 1991. text ed. 49.50 (0-8176-2591-7) Spr-Verlag.

Discrete Structural Optimization: IUTAM Symposium, Zakopane, Poland, August 31-September 3, 1993. Witold Gutkowski & Jacek Bauer. LC 94-21245. (IUTAM Symposia Ser.). 1994. 99.00 (0-387-57719-X) Spr-Verlag.

Discrete Structure Logic & Computability. James Hein. (Math Ser.). 600p. (C). 1994. pap. text ed. 31.25 (0-86720-467-2) Jones & Bartlett.

Discrete Structures & Combinatorics. K. D. Joshi. 550p. 1989. text ed. 74.95 (0-470-21152-0) Wiley.

Discrete Structures, Logic & Computability. James Hein. (Computer Science Ser.). 600p. 1994. boxed 49.95 (0-86720-477-X) Jones & Bartlett.

Discrete Subgroups of Lie Groups. M. S. Raghunathan. LC 71-189389. (Ergebnisse der Mathematik und Ihrer Grenzgebiete Ser.: Vol. 68). 240p. 1972. 42.00 (0-387-05749-8) Spr-Verlag.

Discrete Subgroups of Semisimple Lie Groups. G. A. Margulis. (Ergebnisse der Mathematik und Ihrer Grenzgebiete Ser.: Vol. 17). ix, 338p. 1991. 85.00 (0-387-12179-X) Spr-Verlag.

Discrete Systems: Analysis, Control & Optimization. M. S. Mahmoud et al. (Communications & Control Engineering Ser.). (Illus.). 690p. 1984. 109.00 (0-387-13645-2) Spr-Verlag.

Discrete Systems Simulation. Behrokh Khoshnevis. LC 93-48562. (McGraw-Hill Series in Industrial Engineering & Management Science). 1994. text ed. write for info. (0-07-833302-4) McGraw.

Discrete Techniques of Parameter Estimation: The Equation Error Formulation. Jerry M. Mendel. (Control & Systems Theory Ser.: Vol. 1). 408p. 1973. 150.00 (0-8247-1455-5) Dekker.

Discrete Thoughts: Essays on Mathematics, Science, & Philosophy. Mark Kac et al. 276p. 1986. 65.00 (0-8176-3285-9) Birkhauser.

Discrete Thoughts: Essays on Mathematics, Science & Philosophy. 2nd ed. Mark Kac et al. xii, 264p. 1994. pap. 29.50 (0-8176-3636-6) Birkhauser.

Discrete-Time & Continuous-Time Linear Systems. Robert J. Mayhan. LC 83-5999. (Electrical Engineering Ser.). (Illus.). 640p. 1984. write for info. (0-201-05597-X) Addison-Wesley.

Discrete-Time & Continuous-Time Linear Systems. Robert J. Mayhan. LC 83-5999. (Electrical Engineering Ser.). (Illus.). 640p. (C). 1984. text ed. 72.25 (0-201-05596-1) Addison-Wesley.

Discrete-Time Control Systems. Katsuhiko Ogata. (Illus.). 928p. 1986. text ed. 76.00 (0-13-216102-8) P-H.

Discrete Time-Control Systems. 2nd ed. Katsuhiko Ogata. LC 94-19896. 1994. text ed. 74.00 (0-13-034281-5) P-H.

Discrete-Time Models for Communication Systems Including ATM. Herwig Bruneel & Dyung G. Kim. LC 92-33773. (International Series in Engineering & Computer Science, VLSI, Computer Architecture, & Digital Screen Processing). 224p. (C). 1995. lib. bdg. 75.00 (0-7923-9292-2) Kluwer Ac.

Discrete Time Processing of Speech Signals. John R. Deller, Jr. et al. LC 92-38644. (Illus.). 800p. (C). 1993. write for info. (0-02-328301-7) Macmillan.

Discrete-Time Signal Processing. Alan V. Oppenheim & Ronald W. Schafer. 640p. 1988. text ed. 75.00 (0-13-216292-X) P-H.

Discrete-Time Stochastic Systems: Estimation & Control. Torsten Soderstrom. LC 94-20087. (International Series in Systems & Control Engineering). 1995. pap. text ed. 49.00 (0-13-309683-1) P-H.

Discrete-Time Systems. Herbert Freeman. LC 80-15357. 256p. 1980. reprint ed. lib. bdg. 25.50 (0-89874-228-5) Krieger.

Discrete Time Systems & Signals. Nasir Ahmed & T. Natarajan. (C). 1983. (0-8359-1376-7, Reston) P-H.

Discrete Transforms & Their Applications. Ed. by K. Ramamohan Rao. LC 89-48054. 350p. 1990. reprint ed. 54.50 (0-89464-442-4) Krieger.

Discretion: An Art of the Possible. Anders Lidstrom. 208p. (Orig.). 1991. pap. 58.50x (0-685-62398-X, Pub. by Almqv & Wiksell SW) Coronet Bks.

Discretion in Criminal Justice: The Tension Between Individualization & Uniformity. Ed. by Lloyd E. Ohlin & Frank J. Remington. LC 92-30233. (SUNY Series in New Directions in Crime & Justice Studies). 365p. (C). 1993. 64.50 (0-7914-1563-5); pap. 21.95 (0-7914-1564-3) State U NY Pr.

Discretion to Disobey: A Study of Lawful Departures from Legal Rules. Mortimer R. Kadish & Sanford H. Kadish. LC 72-97201. 256p. 1973. 32.50 (0-8047-0832-0); pap. 11.95 (0-8047-1010-4) Stanford U Pr.

Discretionary Authority of the Prosecutor see Roles & Functions of the Prosecutor

Discretionary Justice: A Preliminary Inquiry. Kenneth C. Davis. LC 80-16898. xii, 233p. 1980. reprint ed. text ed. 59.50 (0-313-22503-6, DADC, Greenwood Pr) Greenwood.

***Discretionary Land Use Controls.** Brian Blaessre. (Real Property - Zoning Ser.). 1995. pap. write for info. (0-614-06264-0) Clark Boardman Callaghan.

Discretionary Powers of the Member States in the Field of Economic Policies & Their Limits under the EEC Treaty. Ed. by Jurgen Schwarze. 189p. (ENG & FRE.). 1988. 54.00 (3-7890-1506-7, Pub. by Nomos Verlags GW) Intl Bk Import.

Discretionary Trusts. 2nd ed. I. J. Hardingham & R. Baxt. 1984. Australia. 55.00 (0-409-49383-X) Butterworth Legal Pubs.

Discretization Methods & Structural Optimization Procedures & Applications. Ed. by H. A. Eschenauer & G. Thierauf. (Lecture Notes in Engineering Ser.: Vol. 42). (Illus.). 360p. 1989. pap. 62.00 (0-387-50784-1) Spr-Verlag.

Discretization Methods for Stable Initial Value Problems. E. Gekeler. (Lecture Notes in Mathematics Ser.: Vol. 1044). viii, 201p. 1984. pap. 27.00 (0-387-12880-8) Spr-Verlag.

Discretization Methods in Structural Mechanics. G. Kuhn & H. Mang. (International Union of Theoretical & Applied Mechanics Symposia Ser.). (Illus.). 464p. 1990. 96.00 (0-387-52011-2) Spr-Verlag.

Discriminant Analysis. William R. Klecka. LC 80-50927. (Quantitative Applications in the Social Sciences Ser.: Vol. 19). (Illus.). 72p. 1980. pap. 9.95 (0-8039-1491-1) Sage.

Discriminant Analysis & Statistical Pattern Recognition. Geoffrey McLachlan. (Probability & Mathematical Statistics: Applied Probability & Statistics Section Ser.: No. 1346). 1992. text ed. 89.95 (0-471-61531-5) Wiley.

Discriminants, Resultants, & Multidimensional Determinants. I. M. Gelfand et al. LC 93-46733. (Mathematics: Theory & Applications Ser.). 523p. 1994. 74.50 (0-8176-3660-9) Birkhauser.

Discriminate Deterrence: Report of the Commission on Integrated Long-Term Strategy. Fred C. Ikle & Albert Wohlstetter. 78p. (Orig.). 1988. pap. 6.50 (0-16-001490-5, S/N 008-000-00489-7) USGPO.

Discriminating Against Discrimination: Preferential Admissions & the DeFunis Case. Robert M. O'Neil. LC 75-3888. 282p. reprint ed. pap. 80.40 (0-685-20431-6, 2056433) Bks Demand.

Discriminating Evidence. Mary Logue. (First Poetry Ser.). 70p. 1990. pap. 8.95 (0-922811-09-1) Mid-List.

Discrimination. Linda Clarke. 216p. 1993. 45.00 (0-85292-528-X, Pub. by IPM Hse UK) St Mut.

Discrimination. Lee. (Troubled Society Ser.: Set II). (J). 1991. 12.95 (0-86593-113-5) Rourke Corp.

Discrimination. Angela Phillips. LC 92-39446. (Past & Present Ser.). (Illus.). 48p. (YA). (gr. 6 up). 1993. text ed. 12.95 (0-02-786881-8, Mac Bks Young Read) S&S Childrens.

Discrimination. Ed. by Charles Russo. (Case Citation Ser.: No. 14). 53p. 1992. 40.00 (1-56534-078-7) NOLPE.

Discrimination. Gail Stewart. LC 89-31259. (Facts About Ser.). (Illus.). 48p. (J). (gr. 5-6). 1989. text ed. 4.95 (0-89686-445-6, Crstwood Hse) Silver Burdett Pr.

Discrimination, Vol. 2: No. 2. Betty Reardon. 111p. 1977. 5.00 (0-910365-03-2) Decade Media.

Discrimination: Its Economic Impact on Blacks, Women & Jews. Robert D. Cherry. 256p. 1989. pap. 19.95 (0-669-20419-6) Free Pr.

Discrimination: The Limits of Law. Ed. by Bob Hepple & Erika M. Szyszczak. (Studies in Labour & Social Law). 496p. 1992. text ed. 100.00 (0-7201-2126-4, Mansell Pub); pap. text ed. 50.00 (0-7201-2122-1, Mansell Pub) Cassell.

Discrimination Against Pregnant Professionals. (Special Report Series on Work & Family: No. 46). 32p. 1991. 35.00 (1-55871-261-5, BSP227) BNA.

Discrimination Against Women: A Global Survey of the Economic, Educational, Social & Political Status of Women. Eschel M. Rhoodie. LC 89-42748. 630p. 1989. lib. bdg. 49.95x (0-89950-448-5) McFarland & Co.

Discrimination American Style: Institutional Racism & Sexism. 2nd ed. Joe R. Feagin & Clairece B. Feagin. LC 85-24195. 204p. (C). 1986. reprint ed. pap. text ed. 12.50 (0-89874-915-8) Krieger.

Discrimination & Classification. D. J. Hand. LC 81-13045. (Probability & Mathematical Statistics Ser.). 218p. 1981. text ed. 205.00 (0-471-28048-8, Wiley-Interscience) Wiley.

Discrimination & Congressional Campaign Contributions. John Theilmann & Al Wilhite. LC 91-8298. 200p. 1991. text ed. 49.95 (0-275-93695-3, C3695, Praeger Pubs) Greenwood.

Discrimination & Prejudice: An Annotated Bibliography. Ed. by Luis Oritz-Franco et al. LC 92-11244. 312p. 1992. 89.95 (0-942259-03-3); pap. 59.95 (0-942259-02-5) Westerfield Enter.

Discrimination & Public Policy in Northern Ireland. Ed. by Robert J. Cormack & Robert D. Osborne. (Illus.). 304p. 1991. 63.00 (0-19-827519-6) OUP.

Discrimination & Retaliation in the Workplace. Charles Hinton. (Illus.). 80p. (Orig.). 1994. pap. text ed. write for info. (0-9639934-1-0) C Hinton.

Discrimination & the Law: Papers. Ed. by Vern Countryman. LC 65-24422. 184p. reprint ed. pap. 52.50 (0-317-26499-0, 2024039) Bks Demand.

Discrimination by Design: A Feminist Critique of the Man-Made Environment. Leslie K. Weisman. (Illus.). 200p. 1992. 24.95 (0-252-01849-4); 11.95 (0-252-06399-6) U of Ill Pr.

Discrimination in Employment. Barry Mordsley. 1993. U.K. pap. 51.00 (0-406-16480-0) Butterworth Legal Pubs.

Discrimination in Employment. 5th ed. James J. Jones, Jr. et al. (American Casebook Ser.). 1116p. 1991. reprint ed. text ed. 47.00 (0-314-26129-X) West Pub.

An Asterisk (*) at the beginning of an entry indicates that the title is appearing in BIP for the first time.

D

An Asterisk (*) at the beginning of an entry indicates that the title is appearing in BIP for the first time.

2033

Disease in the Popular American Press: The Case of Diphtheria, Typhoid Fever, & Syphilis, 1870-1920. Terra Ziporyn. LC 88-5585. (Contributions in Medical Studies: No. 24). 208p. 1988. text ed. 49.95 (0-313-26035-4, ZDE/, Greenwood Pr) Greenwood.

Disease, Life, & Man: Selected Essays by Rudolf Virchow. Rudolf Virchow. Tr. by Lelland J. Rather. ix, 273p. 1958. 37.50 (0-8047-0557-7) Stanford U Pr.

Disease Management in Cocoa: Comparative Epidemiology of Witches' Broom. Ed. by S. A. Rudgard & A. C. Maddison. LC 93-23543. 249p. 1993. 85.00 (0-412-58190-6) Chapman & Hall.

Disease Mechanisms in Small Animal Surgery. 2nd ed. M. Joseph Bojrab et al. (Illus.). 1000p. 1992. text ed. 105.00 (0-8121-1491-4) Williams & Wilkins.

Disease, Medicine & Empire. Ed. by Roy Macleod & Milton Lewis. 302p. (C). 1989. lib. bdg. 79.95 (0-415-00685-6) Routledge.

Disease, Metabolism & Reproduction in the Toxic Response to Drugs & Other Chemicals: Proceedings of the European Society of Toxicology Meeting Held in Rome, March 28-30, 1983. P. L. Chambers et al. (Archives of Toxicology Ser.: Suppl. 7). (Illus.). 400p. 1984. pap. 94.00 (0-387-12452-7) Spr-Verlag.

Disease Mongers: How Doctors, Drug Companies, & Insurers Are Making You Feel Sick. Lynn Payer. 304p. 1992. text ed. 22.95 (0-471-54385-3) Wiley.

Disease Mongers: How Doctors, Drug Companies & Insurers Are Making You Feel Sick. Lynn Payer. 1994. pap. text ed. 12.95 (0-471-00737-4) Wiley.

Disease, Mortality & Population in Transition. Alex Mercer. 1991. text ed. 69.00 (0-7185-1344-4, Pub. by Pinter Pubs UK) St Martin.

Disease of Aging. Hans Kugler. Ed. by Richard A. Passwater & Earl Mindell. (Good Health Guide Ser.). 32p. (Orig.). 1984. pap. 2.50 (0-87983-366-1) Keats.

***Disease of Alcoholism.** rev. ed. David L. Ohlms. Ed. & Intro. by GWC, Inc. Staff. (Illus.). 30p. (Orig.). 1994. pap. 2.50 (1-56168-025-7, B101) GWC Inc.

Disease of Inebriety from Alcohol, Opium & Other Narcotic Drugs: Its Etiology, Pathology Treatment & Medico-Legal Relations. American Association for the Study & Cure of Inebriates Staff. Ed. by Gerald N. Grob. LC 80-1210. (Addiction in America Ser.). 1981. reprint ed. lib. bdg. 38.95 (0-405-13566-1) Ayer.

Disease of Society: Cultural & Institutional Responses to AIDS. Ed. by Dorothy Nelkin et al. 240p. (C). 1991. 54.95 (0-521-40411-8); pap. 17.95 (0-521-40743-5) Cambridge U Pr.

Disease of the Tongue. Pindborg Van der Waal. (Illus.). 196p. 1988. text ed. 72.00 (0-86715-165-X, 165X) Quint Pub Co.

Disease Patterns. Ed. by G. Jasmin & M. Cantin. (Methods & Achievements in Experimental Pathology Ser.: Vol. 7). 1975. 103.25 (3-8055-2155-3) S Karger.

Disease Prevention: Health Facts. Lucas Stang & Kathleen R. Miner. LC 93-43465. 1994. 12.95 (1-56071-182-5, H302) ETR Assocs.

Disease Prevention & Health Promotion: A Handbook for Physicians. Ed. by John H. Holbrook. LC 85-25983. 268p. 1985. text ed. 69.50 (0-275-91303-1, C1303, Praeger Pubs) Greenwood.

***Disease Prevention Research.** 1995. lib. bdg. 255.95 (0-8490-7577-7) Gordon Pr.

Disease Prevention Through Immunization: The Beginning of Health Care Reform. (Illus.). 52p. (Orig.). (C). 1993. pap. text ed. 35.00 (0-7881-0034-3) Diane Pub.

Disease Processes in Marine Bivalve Molluscs. Ed. by W. S. Fisher. LC 88-83123. (AFS Special Publication Ser.: No. 18). 315p. 1988. text ed. 34.50 (0-913235-52-0) Am Fisheries Soc.

Disease Resistance in Plants. 2nd ed. J. E. Vanderplank. LC 83-21328. 1984. text ed. 59.00 (0-12-711442-4) Acad Pr.

Disease Staging Clinical Criteria. 4th ed. Ed. by Joseph S. Gonnella et al. 994p. 1994. write for info. (0-9641308-0-7) MEDSTAT Systs.

Disease Susceptibility: Medical Subject Analysis with Reference Bibliography. Shirley L. Mettler. LC 85-48180. 150p. 1987. 44.50 (0-88164-968-6); pap. 39.50 (0-88164-969-4) ABBE Pubs Assn.

Disease Susceptibility: Medical Subject Analysis with Reference Bibliography. rev. ed. Shirley L. Mettler. LC 92-31212. 150p. 1992. 49.50 (1-55914-896-9); pap. 39.50 (1-55914-897-7) ABBE Pubs Assn.

Disease, the Individual & Society. Gerald Gordon et al. 1968. pap. 25.95x (0-8084-0107-6) NCUP.

Disease Transmission by Insects: Its Discovery & 90 Years of Effort to Prevent It. James R. Busvine. LC 92-48241. 1993. 69.00 (0-387-55457-2); pap. write for info. (3-540-55457-2) Spr-Verlag.

Diseases. LC 92-2309. 1992. 34.95 (0-87434-490-5) Springhouse Pub.

Diseases Affecting the Eye & the Kidney. Ed. by L. S. Regenbogen & H. E. Eliahou. (Illus.). xviii, 458p. 1993. 358.50 (3-8055-5660-8) S Karger.

Diseases & Disorders Handbook. Ed. by Regina D. Ford. (Illus.). 864p. 1988. 23.95 (0-87434-087-X) Springhouse Pub.

Diseases & Disorders of Ornamental Palms. Ed. by A. R. Chase & T. K. Broschat. LC 91-70724. (Illus.). 56p. (Orig.). 1991. 30.00 (0-89054-119-1) Am Phytopathol Soc.

Diseases & Management of Breeding Stallions. Dickson D. Varner et al. LC 90-85393. (Illus.). 350p. 1990. 33.00 (0-939674-33-5) Am Vet Pubns.

Diseases & People Series, 6 bks., Set. Alvin Silverstein et al. (Illus.). (YA). (gr. 6 up). 1994. lib. bdg. 107.70 (0-89490-571-6) Enslow Pubs.

Diseases & Pests of Ornamental Plants. 5th ed. Pascal P. Pirone. LC 77-26893. 566p. 1978. text ed. 69.95 (0-471-07249-4) Wiley.

Diseases in Antiquity: A Survey of the Diseases, Injuries & Surgery of Early Populations. Don Brothwell & A. T. Sandison. (Illus.). 792p. 1967. 119.95 (0-398-00233-9) C C Thomas.

***Diseases in Antiquity: A Survey of the Diseases, Injuries & Surgery of Early Populations.** fac. ed. Don Brothwell & A. T. Sandison. (Illus.). 792p. 1967. pap. 59.95 (0-398-06034-7) C C Thomas.

Diseases in the Ancient Greek World. Mirko D. Grmek. Tr. by Mireille Muellner & Leonard Muellner. LC 88-45412. 470p. 1991. reprint ed. pap. text ed. 24.95 (0-8018-4225-5) Johns Hopkins.

Diseases in the Cranio-Cervical Junction: Anatomical & Pathological Aspects & Detailed Clinical Accounts. Ed. by D. Voth & P. Glees. xi, 412p. (Orig.). 1987. lib. bdg. 113.85 (0-89925-265-6) De Gruyter.

***Diseases in Wax: The History of the Medical Moulage.** Thomas Schnalke. Tr. by Kathy Spatschek. LC 95-3773. 1995. text ed. 210.00 (0-86715-306-7) Quint Pub Co.

Diseases of Amphibians & Reptiles. Ed. by Gerald L. Hoff et al. LC 84-8385. 794p. 1984. 135.00 (0-306-41711-1, Plenum Pr) Plenum.

Diseases of Annual Edible Oilseed Crops, Vol. I. S. J. Kolte. 160p. 1984. 132.00 (0-8493-5380-7, SB608, CRC Reprint) Franklin.

Diseases of Annual Edible Oilseed Crops, Vol. II. S. J. Kolte. 152p. 1985. 132.00 (0-8493-5381-5, SB608, CRC Reprint) Franklin.

Diseases of Annual Edible Oilseed Crops, Vol. III. S. J. Kolte. 168p. 1985. 132.00 (0-8493-5382-3, SB608, CRC Reprint) Franklin.

***Diseases of Annuals & Perennials: A Ball Guide: Identification & Control.** A. R. Chase et al. LC 95-11629. (Illus.). 208p. (Orig.). 1995. pap. 69.00 (1-883052-08-4) Ball Pub.

Diseases of Attention & Perception. M. Meldman & Hans J. Eysenck. LC 78-112614. (International Series of Monographs in Experimental Social Psychology: Vol. 10). 1970. 106.00 (0-08-006870-7, Pub. by Pergamon Repr UK) Franklin.

Diseases of Cage & Aviary Birds. 2nd ed. Ed. by Margaret L. Petrak. LC 81-3792. (Illus.). 720p. reprint ed. pap. 180.00 (0-8357-7653-0, 2056979) Bks Demand.

Diseases of Cage Birds. Elisha Burr. (Illus.). 200p. 1989. 29.95 (0-86622-945-0, H-1096) TFH Pubns.

Diseases of Cattle. D. C. Blood. 1990. pap. text ed. 24.95 (0-7020-1509-1) Saunders.

Diseases of Cattle in the Tropics. Miodrag Ristic. 1981. lib. bdg. 183.00 (90-247-2399-X) Kluwer Ac.

Diseases of Cattle in the Tropics. Miodrag Ristic. 1981. pap. text ed. 84.00 (90-247-2495-3) Kluwer Ac.

Diseases of Civilization: Why We Need a New Approach to Medical Treatment. Brian Inglis. 400p. 1983. pap. 9.00 (0-586-08443-6, Pub. by Granada UK) Academy Chi Pubs.

Diseases of Cultured Penaeid Shrimp in Asia & the United States: Proceedings of a Workshop in Honolulu, Hawaii, April 27-30, 1992. Ed. by Wendy Fulks & Kevan L. Main. (C). 1992. pap. write for info. (0-9617016-5-X) Oceanic Inst.

***Diseases of Dairy Cattle.** William C. Rebhun. LC 94-44191. 1995. write for info. (0-683-07193-9) Williams & Wilkins.

Diseases of Domestic Guinea Pigs. V. C. Richardson. (Library of Veterinary Practice). (Illus.). 144p. 1992. pap. 39.95 (0-632-03301-0) Blackwell Sci.

Diseases of Domestic Rabbits. 2nd ed. Lieve Okerman. Tr. by Richard Sundahl. LC 93-29982. (Library of Veterinary Practice). 1994. write for info. (0-632-03804-7, Pub. by Blckwell Sci Pubns UK) Blackwell Sci.

Diseases of Feedlot Cattle. 3rd ed. Rue Jensen & Donald R. Mackey. LC 78-18729. (Illus.). 308p. reprint ed. pap. 87.80 (0-318-39704-8, 2056741) Bks Demand.

Diseases of Fish. Lionel E. Mawdesley-Thomas et al. 277p. (C). 1974. text ed. 24.50 (0-8422-7178-3) Irvington.

Diseases of Floral Crops, 2 vols., 1. Ed. by David L. Strider. LC 84-24912. 1180p. 1985. text ed. 125.00 (0-275-90170-X, C01701, Praeger Pubs) Greenwood.

Diseases of Floral Crops, 2 vols., Vol. 2. Ed. by David L. Strider. LC 84-24912. 1180p. 1985. text ed. 125.00 (0-275-90169-6, C01692, Praeger Pubs) Greenwood.

Diseases of Forest Trees Widely Planted As Exotics in the Tropics & Southern Hemisphere, Pt. 1. J. A. Gibson. 1975. 45.00 (0-85074-036-3) St Mut.

Diseases of Forest Trees Widely Planted As Exotics in the Tropics & Southern Hemisphere, Pt. 2. J. A. Gibson. 1978. 60.00 (0-85074-028-2) St Mut.

Diseases of Goats. R. Robins. (Library of Veterinary Practice). 250p. 1994. pap. 39.95 (0-632-03362-2, Pub. by Blckwell Sci Pubns UK) Blackwell Sci.

Diseases of Gren Gram & Black Gram. S. C. Agarwal. 250p. (C). 1991. 60.00 (81-7089-161-2, Pub. by Intl Bk Distr II) St Mut.

Diseases of Hematopoietic System. Ed. by Philip H. Lieberman & Robert A. Good. LC 81-4946. (Anatomic Pathology Slide Seminar Ser.). (Illus.). 121p. 1981. pap. text ed. 35.00 (0-89189-085-8, 50-1-046-00) Am Soc Clinical.

Diseases of Infection: An Illustrated Textbook. 2nd ed. Norman R. Grist et al. LC 92-16185. (Illus.). 472p. 1993. 73.50 (0-19-262308-7); pap. 37.50 (0-19-262307-9) OUP.

Diseases of Livestock. 9th ed. Tom G. Hungerford. 1942p. 1991. text ed. 175.00 (0-07-031280-X) Hlth Prof Div.

Diseases of Marine Animals, Vol. 1: General Aspects, Protozoa to Gastropoda. Ed. by Otto Kinne. LC 79-40580. (Illus.). 482p. reprint ed. pap. 137.40 (0-685-20608-4, 2030542) Bks Demand.

Diseases of Memory. Theodule A. Ribot. Tr. by W. H. Smith & M. M. Snell. Bd. with Diseases of Personality. LC 77-72191.; Diseases of the Will. LC 77-72191. LC 77-72191. (Contributions to the History of Psychology Ser.: Vol. 1, Pt. C, Medical Psychology). 240p. 1977. reprint ed. Set text ed. 75.00 (0-313-26940-8, U6940, Greenwood Pr) Greenwood.

Diseases of Nematodes. Ed. by George O. Poinar, Jr. & Hans-Borje Jansson. 1988. write for info. (0-318-62929-1, SF997) CRC Pr.

Diseases of Nematodes. Ed. by George O. Poinar, Jr. & Hans-Borje Jansson. 160p. 1988. Vol. I, 160 pgs. 95.00 (0-8493-4317-8, SF997, CRC Reprint); Vol. II, 160 pgs. 96.00 (0-8493-4318-6, SF997, CRC Reprint) Franklin.

***Diseases of Ornamental Plants in India.** Madhu Meeta. (C). 1994. 42.50x (81-7035-129-4, Pub. by Daya Pub Hse II) S Asia.

Diseases of Personality see Diseases of Memory

Diseases of Plants. H. Marshall. 200p. 1991. 100.00 (81-7158-246-X, Pub. by Scientific Pubs II) St Mut.

Diseases of Pond Fishes. O. N. Bauer et al. 228p. 1973. text ed. 66.00 (0-7065-1309-6, Pub. by Keter Pub IS) Coronet Bks.

Diseases of Poultry. 9th ed. Ed. by Bruce W. Calnek et al. LC 90-33648. (Illus.). 944p. (C). 1991. text ed. 114.95 (0-8138-0429-9) Iowa St U Pr.

Diseases of Shade Trees. 2nd rev. ed. Terry A. Tattar. 391p. 1989. text ed. 49.95 (0-12-684351-1) Acad Pr.

Diseases of Sheep. 2nd ed. Rue Jensen & Brinton L. Swift. LC 81-20701. (Illus.). 340p. reprint ed. pap. 96.90 (0-8357-8685-4, 2056842) Bks Demand.

Diseases of Sheep. 2nd ed. W. Martin & I. Aitken. 1991. 160.00 (0-632-02957-9) Blackwell Sci.

Diseases of Sugarcane: Major Diseases. Ed. by B. C. Ricaud et al. 410p. 1989. 128.25 (0-444-42797-X) Elsevier.

Diseases of Swine. 7th ed. Ed. by A. D. Leman et al. LC 91-35402. (Illus.). 1038p. (C). 1992. text ed. 114.95 (0-8138-0442-6) Iowa St U Pr.

Diseases of Temperate Zone Tree Fruit & Nut Crops. Joseph M. Ogawa & Harley English. LC 91-65409. (Illus.). 464p. 1991. 55.00 (0-931876-97-4, 3345) ANR Pubns CA.

Diseases of the Anus & Rectum. Ed. by J. Alexander-Williams. LC 76-182437. (Clinics in Gastroenterology Ser.: Vol. 4, No. 3). 216p. reprint ed. pap. 61.60 (0-685-23513-0, 2014073) Bks Demand.

Diseases of the Aorta. Joseph Lindsay. (Illus.). 370p. 1993. 75.00 (0-8121-1694-1) Williams & Wilkins.

Diseases of the Aorta: Including an Atlas of Angiographic Pathology & Surgical Technique. John L. Crawford. Ed. by E. Stanley Crawford. (Illus.). 402p. 1984. lib. bdg. 180.00 (0-683-02235-0) Williams & Wilkins.

Diseases of the Arterial Wall. Ed. by J. P. Camilleri et al. (Illus.). 730p. 1989. 434.00 (0-387-17492-3) Spr-Verlag.

Diseases of the Breast. 3rd ed. Cushman D. Haagensen. (Illus.). 1050p. 1986. text ed. 142.00 (0-7216-4442-2) Saunders.

Diseases of the Breast Test & Syllabus, Vol. 24. Stephen A. Feig et al. (Professional Self-Evaluation & Continuing Education Program Ser.). (Illus.). 650p. 1988. 150.00 (1-55903-024-0) Am Coll Radiology.

Diseases of the Bronchioles. Ed. by Gary R. Epler. LC 93-36029. 464p. 1994. 105.00 (0-7817-0123-6) Raven.

Diseases of the Cat. G. Wilkinson & P. Scott. LC 66-18239. 1966. 160.00 (0-08-011723-6, Pub. by Pergamon Repr UK) Franklin.

Diseases of the Cat: Medicine & Surgery, Vol. 1. Jean Holzworth. (Illus.). 960p. 1987. text ed. 121.00 (0-7216-4763-4) Saunders.

Diseases of the Colon & Rectum. Him-che Yeung. 100p. 1993. pap. text ed. 10.00 (0-9639715-0-6) Inst Chinese Med.

Diseases of the Cultivated Plants of the Southwest. Robert B. Streets. LC 68-13545. 407p. reprint ed. pap. 116.00 (0-317-28656-0, 2055343) Bks Demand.

Diseases of the Endocrine Glands. 4th ed. Hermann Zondek. LC 45-1109. 504p. reprint ed. pap. 143.70 (0-685-15849-7, 2056182) Bks Demand.

Diseases of the Esophagus. Ed. by Sidney Cohen & Roger D. Soloway. LC 82-17681. (Contemporary Issues in Gastroenterology Ser.: No. 1). (Illus.). 317p. reprint ed. pap. 90.40 (0-7837-2569-8, 2042728) Bks Demand.

***Diseases of the Esophagus Vol. 1: Malignant Diseases.** Ed. by Mark K. Ferguson et al. 416p. 1990. 75.00 (0-87993-367-4) Futura Pub.

***Diseases of the Esophagus Vol. 2: Benign Diseases.** Ed. by Alex G. Little et al. (Illus.). 448p. 1990. 75.00 (0-87993-368-2) Futura Pub.

***Diseases of the External Ear.** 3rd ed. Frank E. Lucente et al. (Illus.). 352p. 1995. text ed. 89.00 (0-7216-5667-6) Saunders.

Diseases of the External Eye & Adnexa: A Text & Atlas. H. Bruce Ostler. (Illus.). 864p. 1993. 250.00 (0-683-06651-X) Williams & Wilkins.

Diseases of the Eye & Ear Consequent on Inherited Syphilis: A Clinical Memoir. deluxe ed. Jonathan Hutchinson. 272p. 1979. 47.50 (0-88275-945-0) Krieger.

Diseases of the Eye & Ear Consequent on Inherited Syphilis: A Clinical Memoir. Jonathan Hutchinson. LC 78-27655. 272p. 1979. reprint ed. lib. bdg. 32.50 (0-88275-838-1) Krieger.

Diseases of the Fetus & Newborn. Reed et al. 1989. 175.00 (0-8016-5800-4) Mosby Yr Bk.

Diseases of the Gallbladder & Biliary System. Leslie J. Schoenfield & Frank Moddy. LC 77-5695. (Clinical Gastroenterology Monograph Ser.). 375p. reprint ed. pap. 106.90 (0-7837-3467-0, 2057798) Bks Demand.

Diseases of the Gastrointestinal Tract: Proceedings of the Fifty Fifth Annual Anatomic Pathology Slide Seminar of the ASCP. Ed. by Roger C. Haggitt et al. LC 91-4560. 126p. 1991. 35.00 (0-89189-336-9, 50-1-056-00) Am Soc Clinical.

Diseases of the Gastrointestinal Tract & Liver. 2nd ed. David J. Shearman & Niall D. Finlayson. (Illus.). 1350p. 1989. text ed. 145.00 (0-443-03110-X) Churchill.

Diseases of the Gut & Pancreas. 2nd ed. J. J. Misiewicz. (Illus.). 1994. write for info. (0-632-02783-5, Pub. by Blckwell Sci Pubns UK) Blackwell Sci.

Diseases of the Hair & Nails. Ed. by Howard P. Baden. (Illus.). 350p. 1986. 59.95 (0-8151-0410-3, WKL-1, Yr Bk Med Pubs) Mosby Yr Bk.

Diseases of the Hair & Scalp. 2nd ed. A. Rook & R. Dawber. 1990. 165.00 (0-632-02719-3) Blackwell Sci.

Diseases of the Hair & the Scalp. Ludmila Bartosova et al. (Current Problems in Dermatology Ser.: Vol. 12). (Illus.). x, 252p. 1984. 65.75 (3-8055-3783-2) S Karger.

Diseases of the Head & Neck: An Atlas of Histopathology. Wolfgang Arnold et al. (Illus.). 344p. 1987. text ed. 199.00 (0-86577-225-8) Thieme Med Pubs.

Diseases of the Heart. Julian. (Illus.). 1728p. 1989. text ed. 138.00 (0-7020-1260-2, Bailliere-Tindall) Saunders.

Diseases of the Hip, Knee, & Ankle Joints. deluxe ed. Hugh O. Thomas. (Illus.). 283p. 1991. 375.00 (0-930405-52-8) Norman SF.

Diseases of the Hip, Knee, & Ankle Joints. Hugh O. Thomas. (Illus.). 283p. 1991. reprint ed. 125.00 (0-930405-31-5) Norman SF.

Diseases of the Human Body. 2nd ed. Carol Tamparo & Marcia A. Lewis. 500p. 1994. pap. 23.95 (0-8036-9056-8) Davis Co.

Diseases of the Human Carotid Body. D. Heath & P. Smith. (Illus.). xii, 205p. 1991. 179.00 (0-387-19687-0) Spr-Verlag.

Diseases of the Jaw. Isaac Van der Waal. 304p. 1991. 99.00 (87-16-10618-0) Mosby Yr Bk.

Diseases of the Kidney. 5th ed. Ed. by Robert W. Schrier & Carl W. Gottschalk. LC 92-15282. (Illus.). 3566p. 1992. 425.00 (0-316-77501-0) Little.

Diseases of the Lens & Vitreous see System of Ophthalmology Series

Diseases of the Liver. Eugene R. Schiff. 1516p. 1993. 195.00 (0-397-51127-2) Lippincott.

Diseases of the Liver. 6th ed. Ed. by Leon Schiff & Eugene R. Schiff. LC 65-9111. (Illus.). 1536p. 1987. text ed. 150.00 (0-397-50747-X, Lippincott Nursing) Lippincott.

Diseases of the Liver & Bile Ducts: Proceedings of the Fifty Fourth Annual Anatomic Pathology Slide Seminar of the ASCP. Ed. by Jurgen Ludwig & Kamal G. Ishak. LC 89-17874. 133p. 1989. 35.00 (0-89189-294-X, D50-1-055-00) Am Soc Clinical.

Diseases of the Liver & Biliary System. 9th ed. Sheila Sherlock. (Illus.). 640p. 1993. 135.00 (0-632-03345-2) Blackwell Sci.

Diseases of the Liver & Biliary Tract: Standardization of Nomenclature, Diagnostic Criteria, & Prognosis. Carroll M. Leevy et al. LC 94-2183. 224p. 1995. 40.00 (0-7817-0211-9) Raven.

Diseases of the Liver & Biliary Tract with Standardization of Nomenclature Diagnostic Criteria & Diagnostic Methodology: Proceedings of the International Association for the Study of the Liver Quadrennial Meeting, 5th, Acapulco, October 1974. International Association for the Study of the Liver Staff. Ed. by C. M. Leevy. (Illus.). 250p. 1976. 48.00 (3-8055-2276-2) S Karger.

Diseases of the Lymphatic System: Diagnosis & Therapy. Ed. by D. W. Molander. (Illus.). 500p. 1983. 152.00 (0-387-90850-1) Spr-Verlag.

Diseases of the Muscle see Handbook of Clinical Neurology

Diseases of the Nails & Their Management. 2nd ed. Ed. by R. Baran & R. P. R. Dawber. LC 93-41599. (Illus.). 576p. 1994. 150.00 (0-632-03754-7) Blackwell Sci.

Diseases of the Nerves see Handbook of Clinical Neurology

Diseases of the Nerves & Spinal Cord see Manual of Diseases of the Nervous System

Diseases of the Nervous System in Childhood. Jean Aicardi. (Clinics in Developmental Medicine Ser.: No. 115-118). (Illus.). 1000p. (C). 1992. 165.00 (0-521-41273-0) Cambridge U Pr.

Diseases of the Nose, Throat & Ear. 14th ed. Colman. (Illus.). 304p. (Orig.). 1992. pap. text ed. 29.95 (0-443-04563-1) Churchill.

Diseases of the Nose, Throat, Ear, Head & Neck. 14th ed. John J. Ballenger. LC 90-6143. (Illus.). 1376p. 1992. text ed. 199.50 (0-8121-1345-4) Williams & Wilkins.

Diseases of the Oral Mucosa. 2nd ed. Philip L. McCarthy & Gerald Shklar. LC 80-10335. (Illus.). 589p. reprint ed. pap. 167.90 (0-8357-8687-0, 2056844) Bks Demand.

Diseases of the Orbit. Jack Rootman. LC 65-8162. (Illus.). 704p. 1988. text ed. 130.00 (0-397-50651-1, Lippincott Medical) Lippincott.

Diseases of the Outer Eye: Conjunctiva, Cornea & Sclera see System of Ophthalmology Series

Diseases of the Patellofemoral Joint. 2nd ed. John Fulkerson. 320p. 1990. 69.00 (0-683-03382-4) Williams & Wilkins.

Diseases of the Placenta, Fetus & Neonate: Clinical Correlations & Medical - Diagnos. Naeye. (Illus.). 375p. 1991. 79.00 (0-8016-3352-4) Mosby Yr Bk.

Diseases of the Retina see System of Ophthalmology Series

Diseases of the Retina & Uvea. Ed. by S. Mishima. (Journal: Ophthalmologica: Vol. 185, No. 3). (Illus.). 72p. 1982. pap. 38.50 (3-8055-3563-5) S Karger.

D

An Asterisk (*) at the beginning of an entry indicates that the title is appearing in BIP for the first time.

An Asterisk (*) at the beginning of an entry indicates that the title is appearing in BIP for the first time.

2035

An Asterisk (*) at the beginning of an entry indicates that the title is appearing in BIP for the first time.

D

D

An Asterisk (*) at the beginning of an entry indicates that the title is appearing in BIP for the first time.

2037

Disorderly Knights. Dorothy Dunnett. 1976. 20.95 (0-8488-1297-2) Amereon Ltd.

Disorderly Knights. Dorothy Dunnett. 334p. 1981. reprint ed. lib. bdg. 36.95 (0-89966-295-1) Buccaneer Bks.

***Disorderly Women: Sexual Politics & Evangelicalism in Revolutionary New England.** Susan Juster. LC 94-191656. 224p. 1994. pap. write for info. (0-8014-3024-0) Cornell U Pr.

Disorderly Women: Sexual Politics & Evangelicalism in Revolutionary New England. Susan Juster. LC 94-191656. 240p. 1994. 32.95 (0-8014-2732-0) Cornell U Pr.

Disorderly Women & Female Power in the Street Literature of Early Modern England & Germany. Joy Wiltenburg. (Feminist Issues: Practice, Politics, Theory Ser.). (Illus.). 304p. (C). 1992. text ed. 39.50 (0-8139-1350-0); pap. 14.95 (0-8139-1351-9) U Pr of Va.

Disorders & Dysfunctions of the Self. Ed. by Dante Cicchetti & Sheree L. Toth. (Rochester Symposium on Developmental Psychopathology Ser.: Vol. 5). 272p. (C). 1994. text ed. 71.00 (1-878822-31-4) Univ Rochester Pr.

Disorders & Terrorism: Report of the Task Force on Disorders & Terrorism, 1976, 1 vol. National Advisory Committee on Criminal Justice Standards & Goals Staff. LC 77-601645. 1978. reprint ed. lib. bdg. 58.00 (0-89941-530-X, 200420) W S Hein.

***Disorders Fluency.** 2nd ed. Dalton. 1989. 61.50 (1-56593-564-0, 0022) Singular Publishing.

Disorders in Higher Education. American Assembly Staff. LC 79-9350. (Spectrum Book Ser.). 224p. reprint ed. pap. 63.90 (0-685-23514-9, 2027977) Bks Demand.

Disorders of Articulation: Aspects of Dysarthria & Verbal Dyspraxia. M. Edwards. (Disorders of Human Communication Ser.: Vol. 7). (Illus.). 130p. 1984. 49.00 (0-387-81787-5) Spr-Verlag.

Disorders of Bone & Mineral Metabolism. Murray J. Favus. Ed. by Fredric L. Coe. 1136p. 1992. 205.00 (0-88167-749-3) Raven.

Disorders of Carbohydrate Metabolism in Infancy & Childhood. 3rd ed. Cornblath & Schwartz. (Illus.). 416p. 1991. 65.00 (0-86542-137-4) Blackwell Sci.

Disorders of Cardiac Function. Ed. by Helmut Roskamm & Georg Csapo. LC 82-2406. (Basic & Clinical Cardiology Ser.: No. 2). (Illus.). 376p. reprint ed. pap. 107.20 (0-7837-0933-1, 2041238) Bks Demand.

***Disorders of Communication: The Science of Intervention.** 2nd ed. Ed. by Margaret Leahy. (Illus.). 346p. (C). 1995. pap. text ed. 37.50 (1-56593-515-2, 1188) Singular Publishing.

Disorders of Connective Tissue. Ed. by Daniel Bergsma. LC 75-17345. (March of Dimes Ser.: Vol. 11, No. 6). 1976. 16.95 (0-686-14574-7) March of Dimes.

Disorders of Desire: Sex & Gender in Modern American Sexology. Janice M. Irvine. 352p. 1990. 39.95 (0-87722-689-X); pap. 18.95 (0-87722-898-1) Temple U Pr.

***Disorders of Eating & Nutrients in Treatment of Brain Diseases.** Ed. by Richard J. Wurtman & Judith J. Wurtman. LC 79-2071. (Nutrition & the Brain Ser.). (Illus.). Date not set. reprint ed. pap. 91.00 (0-7837-9521-1, 2060270) Bks Demand.

Disorders of Eating Behaviour: A Psychoneuroendocrine Approach - Proceedings of the International Symposium, September 1985, Pavia, Italy. Ed. by E. Ferrari & F. G. Brambilla. (Advances in the Biosciences Ser.: No. 60). (Illus.). 400p. 1986. 120.00 (0-08-032024-4, Pergamon Pr) Elsevier.

Disorders of Executive Function: Civil & Criminal Law Applications. Ed. by Harold V. Hall & Robert J. Sbordone. LC 93-35852. (Illus.). 345p. (Orig.). 1993. 80.00 (1-878205-16-1) GR Press.

Disorders of Feeding & Swallowing in Infants & Children. Ed. by David N. Tuchman & Rhonda S. Walter. LC 93-19636. (Illus.). 448p. (Orig.). (C). 1993. pap. text ed. 75.00 (1-56593-092-4, 0396) Singular Publishing.

Disorders of Fluid & Electrolyte Balance: Diagnosis & Treatment. Jules B. Puschett. (Illus.). 259p. (Orig.). 1985. pap. text ed. 32.00 (0-443-08318-5) Churchill.

Disorders of Glucose Metabolism. Nelson B. Watts. LC 86-708234. 25p. 1987. Monograph, audio cassette & 49 35mm slides. 75.00 (0-89189-236-2, 21-2-006-00) Am Soc Clinical.

Disorders of Growth & Development, 2 vols. Ed. by D. W. Kaplan. (Journal: Pediatrician: Vol. 14, Nos. 3 & 4, 1987). (Illus.). 96p. 1988. Pt. I, 96 pgs. pap. 45.75 (3-8055-4799-4); Pt. II, iv, 84 pgs. pap. 40.00 (3-8055-4801-X) S Karger.

Disorders of Hair Growth: Diagnosis & Treatment. Elise A. Olsen. (Illus.). 448p. 1994. 115.00 (0-07-047934-8) Hlth Prof Div.

Disorders of Hemostasis. 2nd ed. Ratnoff & Forbes. 624p. 1990. text ed. 145.00 (0-7216-3432-X) Saunders.

Disorders of Hemostasis & Thrombosis: A Clinical Guide. William E. Hathaway & Scott H. Goodnight, Jr. (Illus.). 592p. 1993. pap. text ed. 45.00 (0-07-027015-5) Hlth Prof Div.

***Disorders of Hemotasis.** 3rd ed. Ed. by Oscar D. Ratnoff & Charles D. Forbes. LC 95-2349. 1996. write for info. (0-7216-5273-5) Saunders.

Disorders of Higher Nervous Activity see Handbook of Clinical Neurology

Disorders of Learning in Childhood. Archie A. Silver & Rose A. Hagin. 1990. text ed. 97.50 (0-471-50828-4) Wiley.

Disorders of Lipid Metabolism. G. V. Marinetti. LC 89-72205. (Illus.). 240p. 1990. 50.00 (0-306-43431-8, Plenum Pr) Plenum.

Disorders of Male Sexual Function. Ed. by Drogo K. Montague. (Illus.). 280p. 1987. 75.00 (0-8151-5939-0, MSF-1, Yr Bk Med Pubs) Mosby Yr Bk.

Disorders of Mood: Based on the Proceedings of the Sixtieth Annual Meeting of the American Psychopathological Association. Ed. by Joseph Zubin & Fritz A. Freyhan. LC 74-185972. 208p. reprint ed. pap. 59.30 (0-317-07816-X, 2020748) Bks Demand.

***Disorders of Motor Speech: Recent Advances in Assessment, Treatment, & Clinical Characterization.** Robin et al. 448p. 1995. boxed 45.00 (1-55766-223-1) P H Brookes.

Disorders of Movement: Clinical, Pharmacological & Physiological Aspects. Ed. by Niall Quinn & Peter Jenner. 567p. 1989. text ed. 157.00 (0-12-569685-X) Acad Pr.

Disorders of Movement in Neurology & Neurupsychiatry. A. B. Joseph & R. R. Young. (Illus.). 784p. 1992. 145.00 (0-86542-146-3) Blackwell Sci.

Disorders of Nutrition & Metabolism in Clinical Surgery. Graham L. Hill. (Illus.). 324p. 1992. text ed. 89.95 (0-443-04457-0) Churchill.

Disorders of Peripheral Nerves. 2nd ed. Herbert H. Schaumburg et al. LC 91-24890. (Contemporary Neurology Ser.: No. 36). (Illus.). 348p. (C). 1992. text ed. 70.00 (0-8036-7734-0) Davis Co.

Disorders of Personality: DSM-III: AXIS II. Theodore Millon. LC 80-28249. 458p. 1981. text ed. 64.95 (0-471-06403-3) Wiley.

Disorders of Porphyrin Metabolism. M. R. Moore et al. LC 87-14125. (Topics in Hematology Ser.). (Illus.). 396p. 1987. 89.50 (0-306-42625-0, Plenum Med Bk) Plenum.

Disorders of Sexual Desire & Other New Concepts & Techniques in Sex Therapy. Helen S. Kaplan. LC 79-18908. 257p. 1979. 39.95 (0-87630-212-6) Brunner-Mazel.

Disorders of Speech Perception & Symbolic Behavior see Handbook of Clinical Neurology

Disorders of Syntactic Comprehension. David N. Caplan & Nancy Hildebrandt. (Issues in the Biology of Language & Cognition Ser.). 288p. 1988. 42.50 (0-262-03132-9, Bradford Bks) MIT Pr.

Disorders of the Ankle. Hampar Kelikian & Armen S. Kelikian. (Illus.). 1200p. 1985. text ed. 185.00 (0-7216-1094-3) Saunders.

Disorders of the Cerebellum. Ed. by Sid Gilman et al. LC 80-23393. (Contemporary Neurology Ser.: No. 21). (Illus.). 415p. 1981. text ed. 45.00 (0-8036-4150-8) Davis Co.

Disorders of the Cervical Spine. Martin B. Camins & Patrick F. O'Leary. (Illus.). 656p. 1992. 155.00 (0-683-01401-3) Williams & Wilkins.

Disorders of the Cervical Spine. 2nd ed. T. E. Jeffreys. LC 92-48341. 240p. 1993. 110.00 (0-7506-1361-0) Buttrwrth-Heinemann.

Disorders of the Cervical Spine: Diagnosis & Medical Management. 2nd ed. John H. Bland. LC 93-33171. 1994. text ed. 89.50 (0-7216-5015-5) Saunders.

Disorders of the Developing Central Nervous System: Diagnosis & Treatment. Fred Epstein. Ed. by Harold J. Hoffman. (Illus.). 840p. 1986. text ed. 129.95 (0-86542-023-8) Blackwell Sci.

Disorders of the Endocrine System. Utiger. 1991. write for info. (0-8151-8941-9, Yr Bk Med Pubs) Mosby Yr Bk.

Disorders of the Facial Nerve: Anatomy, Diagnosis & Management. Ed. by Malcolm D. Graham & William F. House. (House Ear Institute Ser.). 576p. 1982. text ed. 159.50 (0-89004-624-7) Raven.

Disorders of the Foot & Ankle: Medical & Surgical Management, 3 vols., Set. 2nd ed. Melvin H. Jahss. (Illus.). 3392p. 1990. text ed. 465.00 (0-7216-1327-6) Saunders.

Disorders of the Horse & What to Do about Them. Elsie V. Hanauer. 1974. pap. 5.00 (0-87980-281-2) Wilshire.

***Disorders of the Lymph Nodes & Related Organs: Based on the Proceedings of the 58th Annual Anatomic Pathology Slide Seminar of the American Society of Clinical Pathologists.** Nancy L. Harris et al. LC 94-25191. 1994. write for info. (0-89189-365-2) Am Soc Clinical.

Disorders of the Musculoskeletal System. Scoles. 450p. 1991. 49.95 (0-8151-7817-4, Yr Bk Med Pubs) Mosby Yr Bk.

Disorders of the Nervous System: A Primer. Alexander G. Reeves. LC 80-24086. (Internal Medicine Ser.). 252p. reprint ed. pap. 71.90 (0-318-34997-3, 2030851) Bks Demand.

Disorders of the Pancreas: Controversies in Diagnosis & Management. Ed. by Gerard P. Burns & Simmy Bank. (Illus.). 450p. 1991. 68.01 (0-08-040317-4, Pub. by PPI UK) McGraw.

Disorders of the Pancreas: Current Issues in Diagnosis & Management. Gerard P. Burns & Simmy Bank. (Illus.). 506p. 1992. text ed. 82.00 (0-07-105402-2) Hlth Prof Div.

Disorders of the Pediatric Spine. Ed. by Dachling Pang. LC 94-9398. 694p. 1995. 185.00 (0-7817-0158-9) Raven.

Disorders of the Real. Alan Sondheim. Ed. by George Quasha. (Illus.). 128p. (C). 1988. pap. 8.95 (0-940170-14-0) Station Hill Pr.

Disorders of the Self: New Therapeutic Horizons - The Masterson Approach. Ed. by James Masterson & Klein. LC 83-3865. 400p. 1995. 48.95 (0-87630-334-3) Brunner-Mazel.

Disorders of the Spine: A Coding System for Diagnoses. Ed. by North American Spine Society Staff & David F. Fardon. LC 91-71142. 132p. (Orig.). 1991. pap. text ed. 27.00 (1-56053-014-6) Hanley & Belfus.

Disorders of the Spleen. A. Cuschieri. (Illus.). 608p. 1994. write for info. (0-632-03314-2) Blackwell Sci.

Disorders of the Spleen. Wolf & Neiman. 1989. text ed. 84.50 (0-7216-2503-7) Saunders.

Disorders of the Spleen: Pathophysiology & Management. Pochedly et al. (Hematology Ser.: Vol. 10). 488p. 1988. 170.00 (0-8247-7933-9) Dekker.

Disorders of the Vitreous, Retina & Choroid. Ed. by Jack J. Kanski & Peter H. Morse. (BIMR Ophthalmology Ser.: Vol. 1). 128p. 1983. text ed. 65.00 (0-407-02340-2) Buttrwrth-Heinemann.

***Disorders of Thrombosis.** Ed. by Russell Hull & Graham F. Pineo. LC 95-4086. 1995. text ed. write for info. (0-7216-5278-6) Saunders.

Disorders of Tubular Transport: Physiologic & Clinical Correlations. Ed. by J. A. Arruda & N. A. Kurtzman. (Journal: Mineral & Electrolyte Metabolism: Vol. 5, Nos. 2-4). (Illus.). 144p. 1981. pap. 84.00 (3-8055-2515-X) S Karger.

Disorders of Voice. Margaret Greene. LC 77-183113. (Studies in Communicative Disorders). (C). 1972. pap. write for info. (0-672-61279-8, Bobbs) Macmillan.

Disorders of Voice. Margaret C. Greene. Ed. by Harvey Halpern. LC 86-489. (PRO-ED Studies in Communicative Disorders). (Illus.). 76p. 1986. pap. text ed. 9.00 (0-89079-092-2, 1382) PRO-ED.

Disorders of Voluntary Muscle. Ed. by John Walton et al. LC 94-3177. 1994. 225.00 (0-443-04624-7) Churchill.

Disorders of Voluntary Muscle. 5th ed. Ed. by J. A. Walton. (Illus.). 1166p. 1988. text ed. 200.00 (0-443-03882-1) Churchill.

Disorders of War: The Revolution in South Carolina. Jerome J. Nadelhaft. 310p. 1981. reprint ed. 27.50 (0-89101-048-3); reprint ed. pap. 12.95 (0-89101-049-1) U Maine Pr.

Disorders with Defective Hearing. Ed. by V. Colletti & S. D. Stephens. (Advances in Audiology Ser.: Vol. 3). (Illus.). viii, 216p. 1985. 131.25 (3-8055-3965-7) S Karger.

Disorganized Baseball: History of Quebec Provincial League, 1890-1976. Merritt Clifton. 64p. 1991. pap. 6.00 (0-686-89393-X) Samisdat.

Disorganized Capitalism: Contemporary Transformations of Work & Politics. Claus Offe. Tr. by John B. Keane. (German Social Thought Ser.). 280p. 1985. 30.00 (0-262-15029-8) MIT Pr.

Disorganized Crime. Richard Hall. LC 86-973. (Illus.). 280p. (Orig.). 1987. pap. 12.95 (0-7022-1956-8, Pub. by Univ Queensland Pr AT) Intl Spec Bk.

Disorganized Crime: Illegal Markets & the Mafia. Peter Reuter. (Organization Studies: No. 3). 256p. 1985. pap. 10.95 (0-262-68048-3) MIT Pr.

Disorganized Crime: True Stories of Unlucky Thieves & Stupid Robbers. Ron Bell. LC 93-81147. (Illus.). 144p. 1994. pap. 7.95 (1-56352-126-1) Longstreet Pr Inc.

Disorientations: Kuwait in the 1950's, a Society in Flux. Ed. by Peter L. Al-Shahi. 108p. 1993. 39.95 (0-86372-166-4, Pub. by Ithaca UK) Paul & Co Pubs.

Disorienting Encounters: Travels of a Moroccan Scholar in France in 1845-1846, the Voyage of Muhammad As-Saffar. Muhammad As-Saffar. Tr. & Intro. by Susan G. Miller. (Comparative Studies on Muslim Societies: Vol. 14). (C). 1992. 38.00 (0-520-07461-0); pap. 13.00 (0-520-07462-9) U CA Pr.

Disowning Knowledge: In Six Plays of Shakespeare. Stanley Cavell. 250p. 1987. pap. 17.95 (0-521-33890-5) Cambridge U Pr.

***"Disparate Impact" & "Business Necessity" - an Assessment & Guidelines for the Civil Rights Debate.** Douglas S. McDowell. 68p. 1991. pap. 10.00 (0-614-06158-X, 2029-PP-4040) EPF.

Disparate Voices. Jimmie R. Rankin. 30p. 1993. pap. 4.95 (1-883938-08-2) Dry Bones Pr.

Disparates. Francisco Goya. LC 68-28063. 1969. pap. 9.95 (0-486-22319-1) Dover.

Disparities in the Forms of River Meanders & Oxbow Lakes: A Case Study. J. G. Weihaupt. 195p. (Orig.). 1989. disk, pap. text ed. 22.00 (0-918334-65-9) WRP.

Disparition. Georges Perec. (Imaginaire Ser.). (FRE.). pap. 15.95 (2-07-071523-X) Schoenhof.

Disparition. Georges Perec. (FRE.). 1989. pap. 19.95 (0-7859-3394-8) Fr & Eur.

***Disparo de Argon: The Eyes of San Lorenzo.** Villoro. 1995. pap. 16.95 (0-679-76093-8, Vin) Random.

Dispatch from Cadiz. Bruce Weiser. (Chenevix Ser.: No. 2). 1981. pap. 2.25 (0-8439-0826-2) Dorchester Pub Co.

Dispatcher. Jack Rudman. (Career Examination Ser.: C-213). 1994. pap. 23.95 (0-8373-0213-7) Nat Learn.

Dispatches. Michael Herr. (Vietnam Ser.). 288p. 1978. mass mkt. 4.50 (0-380-01976-0) Avon.

Dispatches. Michael Herr. LC 90-50771. 272p. 1991. pap. 11.00 (0-679-73525-9, Vin) Random.

Dispatches from Maine: Fifty Different Sharps & Flats. John Gould. LC 93-33215. 1994. 23.00 (0-393-03624-3) Norton.

***Dispatches from the Deep Woods.** John G. Mitchell. LC 90-36842. 318p. 1991. reprint ed. pap. 90.70 (0-7837-8906-8, 2049617) Bks Demand.

Dispatches from the Fields. Raymond Henri. LC 81-67496. (Living Poets' Library Ser.: Vol. 26). 1981. pap. 4.50 (0-686-81660-9) Dragons Teeth.

***Dispatches from the Front: News Accounts of American Wars, 1776-1991.** Nathaniel Lande. 336p. 1995. 35.00 (0-8050-3664-4) H Holt & Co.

Dispatches from the Front: Theological Engagements with the Secular. Stanley Hauerwas. LC 93-44504. 256p. 1994. 24.95 (0-8223-1475-4) Duke.

Dispatches from the Pacific Century. Frank Viviano. (Illus.). 399p. 1993. 21.11 (0-201-63290-X) Addison-Wesley.

Dispatches from the Pacific Century. Frank Viviano. (Illus.). 272p. 1994. pap. 12.50 (0-201-62699-3) Addison-Wesley.

Dispatches with Related Documents of Milanese Ambassadors in France & Burgundy, 1450-1483. Ed. by Paul M. Kendall & Vincent Ilardi. LC 68-20933. 390p. Vol. I, 1450-1460, 390p., 1970. 35.00 (0-8214-0067-3); Vol. II, 1460-1461, 486p., 1970. 35.00 (0-8214-0082-7) N Ill U Pr.

Dispeller of Delusion, Vol. 1. (C). 1990. 44.00 (0-86013-155-6, Pub. by Pali Text) Wisdom MA.

Dispeller of Delusion, Vol. II. 1991. write for info. (0-86013-291-9) Wisdom MA.

Dispelling Illusion: Guadapada's Alatasanti with an Introduction. Douglas A. Fox. LC 92-24051. (SUNY Series in Religious Studies). 146p. 1993. 49.50 (0-7914-1501-5); pap. 16.95 (0-7914-1502-3) State U NY Pr.

Dispelling the Manufacturing Myth: American Factories Can Compete in the Global Marketplace. Committee on Comparative Cost Factors & Structures in Global Manufacturing, National Research Council Staff. (Illus.). 128p. (C). 1992. pap. text ed. 24.95 (0-309-04676-9) Natl Acad Pr.

Dispelling the Megatrends Myths: A Leader's Guide to Managing Change. Sherry Schiller. Ed. by Sharon Block. LC 94-92143. (Illus.). 160p. 1994. text ed. 28.00 (0-9641259-0-0) Schiller Ctr.

Dispelling the Myth of Globalization: The Case for Regionalization. Hazel J. Johnson. LC 91-4281. 176p. 1991. text ed. 49.95 (0-275-93795-X, C3795, Praeger Pubs) Greenwood.

***Dispelling the Myths: An Analysis of American Attitudes & Prejudice.** Todd Rheingold. 1993. 19.95 (0-912526-75-0) Believe Dream.

Dispelling the Myths: An Analysis of American Attitudes & Prejudices. Todd Rheingold. 1993. write for info. (0-318-71676-3) Believe Dream.

Dispensacionalismo, Hoy. Charles C. Ryrie. Orig. Title: Dispensationalism Today. 208p. (SPA.). 1974. pap. 6.99 (0-8254-1627-2) Kregel.

Dispensaries, Their Management & Development: A Book for Administrators, Public Health Workers. Michael M. Davis, Jr. & Andrew R. Warner. Ed. by Barbara G. Rosenkrantz. LC 76-25658. (Public Health in America Ser.). (Illus.). 1977. reprint ed. lib. bdg. 36.95 (0-405-09813-8) Ayer.

Dispensary: With a Short Account of the Proceedings of the College of Physicians, London, in Relation to the Sick Poor (1697) & Claremont (1715) Samuel Garth. LC 74-23391. 160p. 1975. reprint ed. lib. bdg. 50.00 (0-8201-1145-7) Schol Facsimiles.

Dispensational Theology. Charles F. Baker. 688p. (C). 1971. text ed. 19.95 (0-912340-01-0); pap. text ed. 14.95 (0-912340-02-9) Grace Bible Coll.

***Dispensationalism: Rightly Dividing the People of God.** Keith A. Mathison. 176p. (Orig.). 1995. pap. 9.99 (0-87552-359-5) Presby & Reformed.

Dispensationalism, Israel & the Church: The Search for Definition. Ed. by Craig A. Blaising & Darrell L. Bock. LC 92-17751. 1992. pap. 21.99 (0-310-34611-8) Zondervan.

Dispensationalism Today. Charles C. Ryrie. LC 65-14611. 211p. (C). 1973. pap. 8.99 (0-8024-2256-X) Moody.

Dispensationalism Today see Dispensacionalismo, Hoy

Dispensationalism Today, Yesterday, & Tomorrow. Curtis I. Crensham & Grover E. Gunn, III. 350p. (Orig.). (YA). 1994. pap. 12.95 (1-877818-01-1) Footstool Pubns.

Dispensations. Lester Sumrall. 65p. (C). 1986. pap. text ed. 6.00 (0-937580-94-5) LeSEA Pub Co.

Dispensations: The Future of South Africa as South Africans See It. Richard J. Neuhaus. LC 86-2150. 333p. reprint ed. pap. 95.00 (0-8357-8562-9, 2034922) Bks Demand.

***Dispensing & Handling Motor Fuel License.** (Career Examination Ser.: Series 1). Date not set. pap. 23.95 (0-8373-3763-1) Nat Learn.

Dispensing of Medication. 9th ed. Robert F. King. LC 84-61218. 1984. 28.95 (0-912734-08-6) Mack Pub.

Dispensing Optician. Ronald R. Smith. Ed. by Diane Parker. LC 92-50924. (Smith's Career Notes Ser.). 24p. 1993. pap. 1.95 (1-56875-010-2) R & E Pubs.

Dispensing Optician Manual: An Introduction to Vision Care for the New Ophthalmic Technician. A. J. Zelada. (Illus.). 146p. (C). 1987. 39.95x (0-398-05359-6) C C Thomas.

Disperal Centres of Sphingidae (Lepidoptera) in the Neotropical Region. Harold Schreiber. (Biogeographica Ser.: No. 10). (Illus.). 1978. lib. bdg. 74.50 (90-6193-211-4) Kluwer Ac.

Dispersal of Living Organisms into Aquatic Ecosystems. Ed. by Aaron Rosenfield & Roger Mann. 1992. 35.00 (0-943676-56-8) MD Sea Grant Col.

Dispersal of Plants Throughout the World. Henry N. Ridley. (Illus.). 744p. 1990. reprint ed. 175.00 (0-685-61648-7, 043826) Koeltz Sci Bks.

Dispersants, Solvents, & Solubilizers. Ed. by Michael Ash & Irene Ash. (What Every Chemical Technologist Wants to Know About...Ser.: Vol. II). 478p. 1988. 60.00 (0-8206-0327-9) Chem Pub.

Disperse Systems, Interfaces, & Membranes. Ed. by K. Hummel & J. Schurz. (Progress in Colloid & Polymer Science Ser.: Vol. 77). 220p. 1989. 119.00 (0-387-91337-8) Spr-Verlag.

Dispersed City: The Case of Piedmont, North Carolina. Charles R. Hayes. (Research Papers Ser.: No. 173). (Illus.). 1976. pap. 12.00 (0-89065-080-2) U Chicago Comm Geo.

Dispersing Population: What America Can Learn from Europe. James L. Sundquist. LC 75-5942. 290p. 1975. 28.95 (0-8157-8214-4) Brookings.

Dispersing Powders in Liquids. R. D. Nelson, Jr. (Handbook of Powder Technology Ser.: No. 7). 244p. 1988. 82.00 (0-444-43004-0) Elsevier.

D

An Asterisk (*) at the beginning of an entry indicates that the title is appearing in BIP for the first time.

An Asterisk (*) at the beginning of an entry indicates that the title is appearing in BIP for the first time.

D

Dispute Resolution & Lawyers: 1993 Supplement to Hardcover Edition. Leonard L. Riskin & James E. Westbrook. (American Casebook Ser.). 276p. 1992. pap. text ed. 14.50 (*0-314-01920-0*) West Pub.

Dispute Resolution Devices in a Democratic Society: Final report of the 1985 Chief Justice Earl Warren Conference on Advocacy in the United States. Roscoe Pound-American Trial Lawyers Foundation Staff. 152p. 1985. pap. 25.00 (*0-941916-41-3*) Roscoe Pound Found.

***Dispute Resolution in Australia.** H. Astor. 388p. 1991. pap. 72.00 (*0-614-05476-1*, Austral) Butterworth Legal Pubs.

***Dispute Resolution in Australia.** Hilary Astor & Christine Chinkin. 338p. 1992. pap. 72.00 (*0-409-30316-X*, Austral) Butterworth Legal Pubs.

***Dispute Resolution Methods: Comparative Law Yearbook of International Business Special Issue.** 480p. (C). 1994. lib. bdg. 167.00 (*1-85966-180-7*, Pub. by Graham & Trotman UK) Kluwer Ac.

Dispute Resolution Processes: A Comparative State Study. Raymond L. Cox, III. (Public Employee Relations Library: No. 67). 68p. 1988. 14.00 (*0-685-33391-4*) Intl Personnel Mgmt.

Dispute Resolution, Processes of, The Role of Lawyers. John S. Murray et al. (University Casebook Ser.). 761p. 1988. text ed. 37.00 (*0-88277-688-6*) Foundation Pr.

Dispute Resolution Program Directory, 1993. 300p. 1993. pap. 50.00 (*0-89707-440-8*, 474-0049) Amer Bar Assn.

Dispute Resolution Today - The State of the Art. Ed. by Megan J. Walline & Lance Gould. LC 91-70256. 152p. 1991. 9.50 (*0-943001-26-9*) Am Arbitration.

Dispute Resolution Training - The State of the Art. Ed. by Charlotte Gold & Ruth Lyons. LC 78-51451. 116p. 1978. pap. 2.50 (*0-943001-14-5*) Am Arbitration.

Dispute Resolution under Fact-Finding & Arbitration: An Empirical Analysis. Thomas A. Kochan et al. LC 78-60233. 238p. 1979. 12.00 (*0-318-43198-X*) Am Arbitration.

Dispute Resolutions. Paul Pretorius. 1993. pap. write for info. (*0-7021-2833-3*, Pub. by Juta SA) W W Gaunt.

Dispute Settlement in Public International Law: Texts & Materials. Ed. by K. Oellers-Frahm et al. 930p. 1985. 179.00 (*0-387-13190-6*) Spr-Verlag.

Disputed Issues in Renal Failure Therapy. Ed. by M. J. Lysaght et al. (Contributions to Nephrology Ser.: Vol. 44). (Illus.). xii, 294p. 1984. 78.50 (*3-8055-3938-X*) S Karger.

Disputed Jurisdiction & Recognition of Judgments Between Tribal & State Courts: A Survey of Seven States. Carol Friesen. 49p. 1990. 3.00 (*0-685-38111-0*, ICM-002) Natl Ctr St Courts.

Disputed Passage. Lloyd Douglas. 27.95 (*0-88411-535-6*, Aeonian Pr) Amereon Ltd.

Disputed Paternity Proceedings, 2 vols. 4th ed. Sidney Schatkin. 1975. Looseleaf Updates Avail. write for info. (*0-8205-1607-4*) Bender.

Disputed Pleasures: Sport & Society in Preindustrial England. Thomas S. Henricks. LC 90-22619. (Contributions to the Study of World History Ser.: No. 28). 208p. 1991. text ed. 55.00 (*0-313-27453-3*, HSP, Greenwood Pr) Greenwood.

Disputed Questions. Thomas Merton. LC 79-14717. 310p. 1985. pap. 7.95 (*0-15-626105-7*, Harvest Bks) HarBrace.

Disputed Questions: On Being a Christian. Rosemary R. Ruether. 142p. 1989. pap. 13.95 (*0-88344-549-2*) Orbis Bks.

Disputed Questions in the Liturgy Today. John M. Huels. 125p. 1988. pap. 6.95 (*0-930467-95-7*) Liturgy Tr Pubns.

Disputed Questions in Theology & the Philosophy of Religion. John Hick. LC 92-19344. 216p. (C). 1993. text ed. 25.00 (*0-300-05354-1*) Yale U Pr.

Disputed Subjects: Essays on Psychoanalysis, Politics, & Philosophy. Jane Flax. LC 93-15321. 224p. 1993. 49.95 (*0-415-90789-6*, B0663, Routledge NY); pap. 15.95 (*0-415-90790-X*, B0667, Routledge NY) Routledge.

Disputed Waters: Native Americans & the Great Lake Fishery. Robert Doherty. LC 90-39198. 184p. 1990. 24.00 (*0-8131-1715-1*) U Pr of Ky.

Disputers of the Tao: Philosophical Argument in Ancient China. A. C. Graham. LC 89-32227. 480p. 1989. pap. 19.95 (*0-8126-9088-5*) Open Court.

Disputes & Negotiations: A Cross-Cultural Perspective. Philip H. Gulliver. LC 79-22735. (Studies on Law & Social Control). 1979. text ed. 59.00 (*0-12-305550-4*) Acad Pr.

Disputes & the Law: For the European Coordination Centre for Research & Documentation in Social Sciences. Maureen Cain & Kalman Kulcsar. 286p. 1983. 100.00 (*0-569-08757-0*, Pub. by Collets UK) Pro-Am Music.

Disputing Process in Ten Societies. Ed. by Laura Nader & Harry F. Todd, Jr. LC 78-8729. 372p. 1978. pap. text ed. 21.50 (*0-231-04537-9*) Col U Pr.

Disputing the Dead: U. S. Law on Aboriginal Remains & Grave Goods. H. Marcus Price, III. 152p. 1991. text ed. 37.50 (*0-8262-0779-0*) U of Mo Pr.

Disquectomia Cervical Anterior. Oliver D. Grin & Dorothy L. Bouwman. Ed. by Laura C. Kienbaum. Tr. by Hector BeltrandelRio & Marisa BeltrandelRio. (Patient Education Ser.). (Illus.). 18p. (Orig.). (SPA.). 1993. pap. text ed. 3.50 (*0-929689-58-5*) Ludann Co.

Disquisitiones Arithmeticae. rev. ed. C. F. Gauss. Tr. by A. A. Clarke. 1986. 96.00 (*0-387-96254-9*) Spr-Verlag.

Disquisitions Relating Matter & Spirit, 2 vols. in 1. Joseph Priestley. Ed. by Rene Wellek. Bd. with Doctrine of Philosophical Necessity Illustrated: Being an Appendix to the Disquestions Relating to Matter & Spirit. LC 75-11248. LC 75-11248. (British Philosophers & Theologians of the 17th & 18th Centuries Ser.: Vol. 47). 1976. reprint ed. Set lib. bdg. 51.00 (*0-8240-1799-4*) Garland.

Disquisitions Relating to Matter & Spirit. Joseph Priestly. 356p. 1993. pap. 21.00 (*1-56459-314-2*) Kessinger Pub.

Disquisitions Relating to Matter & Spirit. Joseph Priestley. LC 74-26285. (History, Philosophy & Sociology of Science Ser.). 1975. reprint ed. 29.95 (*0-405-06612-0*) Ayer.

Disraeli. Ian Machin. LC 94-11277. (Profiles in Power Ser.). 208p. (C). 1995. text ed. 36.95 (*0-582-09806-8*, 76875, Pub. by Longman UK); pap. text ed. 14.95 (*0-582-09805-X*, 76874, Pub. by Longman UK) Longman.

Disraeli. John Vincent. (Past Masters Ser.). 144p. 1990. pap. 7.95 (*0-19-287681-3*) OUP.

Disraeli; A Study in Personality & Ideas. Walter S. Sichel. 1977. text ed. 20.95 (*0-8369-8192-8*, 8330) Ayer.

Disraeli & Victorian Conservative Party. John Walton. 80p. 1990. pap. 7.95 (*0-415-00059-9*, A3847) Routledge.

Disraeli, Gladstone & Eastern Question. 2nd ed. R. W. Seton-Watson. 590p. 1962. 35.00 (*0-7146-1513-7*, Pub. by F Cass Pubs UK) Intl Spec Bk.

Disraeli's Fiction. Daniel R. Scharz. 167p. 1979. text ed. 44.00 (*0-06-496124-9*, N6663) B&N Imports.

Disraeli's Novels Reviewed, Eighteen Twenty-Six to Nineteen Sixty-Eight. R. W. Stewart. LC 74-28454. 291p. 1975. 20.00 (*0-8108-0759-9*) Scarecrow.

Disregard of a Legal Entity for Tax Purposes. International Fiscal Association Staff. (Cahiers de Droit Fiscal International Ser.). 538p. 1989. pap. 100.00 (*90-6544-413-0*) Kluwer Law Tax Pubs.

Disreputable Profession: The Actor in Society. Mendel Kohansky. LC 83-12807. (Contributions in American Studies: No. 72). x, 194p. 1984. text ed. 49.95 (*0-313-23824-3*, KOP, Greenwood Pr) Greenwood.

Disrobing: Sex & Satire. Royal Murdoch. 112p. (Orig.). 1982. pap. 5.95 (*0-917342-96-8*) Gay Sunshine.

Disrobing: Sex & Satire. limited ed. Royal Murdoch. 112p. (Orig.). 1982. 30.00 (*0-917342-95-X*) Gay Sunshine.

Disrupted Borders: An Intervention in Definitions of Boundaries. Ed. by Sunil Gupta. (Illus.). 224p. (Orig.). 1994. text ed. 49.50 (*1-85489-044-1*, Pub. by Rivers Oram Pr UK); pap. text ed. 21.95 (*1-85489-045-X*, Pub. by Rivers Oram Pr UK) Paul & Co Pubs.

Disrupted Decades: The Civil War & Reconstruction Years. Robert H. Jones. LC 78-27422. 560p. 1979. reprint ed. pap. 19.50 (*0-88275-714-8*) Krieger.

Disruption & Delight in the Nineteenth-Century Novel. Cathy Comstock. Ed. by Juliet McMaster. LC 87-30075. (Nineteenth-Century Studies). 104p. 1991. 39.95 (*0-8357-1812-3*) Univ Rochester Pr.

Disruption of American Democracy. Roy F. Nichols. LC 83-45826. 1983. reprint ed. 48.50 (*0-404-20190-3*) AMS Pr.

Disruption of American Democracy. Roy F. Nichols. LC 48-6344. 630p. reprint ed. pap. 179.60 (*0-317-42219-7*, 2052043) Bks Demand.

Disruption of the Feminine in Henry James. Priscilla L. Walton. 208p. 1992. 40.00 (*0-8020-5987-2*) U of Toronto Pr.

Disruption of the Pennsylvania Democracy, 1848-1860. John F. Coleman. LC 75-623874. (Illus.). 184p. 1975. 7.95 (*0-911124-82-9*) Pa Hist & Mus.

Disruptive Behavior: Three Techniques to Use in Your Classroom. Ennio Cipani. LC 93-28966. 1993. 8.90 (*0-86586-243-5*, P390) Coun Exc Child.

Disruptive Behavior Disorders in Childhood. Ed. by D. K. Routh. (Illus.). 219p. (C). 1994. 39.50 (*0-306-44695-2*, Plenum Pr) Plenum.

Disruptive Behavior Disorders in Children: Treatment-Focused Assessment. Michael J. Breen & Thomas S. Altepeter. LC 90-3817. 288p. 1990. lib. bdg. 32.00 (*0-89862-439-8*) Guilford Pr.

Disruptive Behavior in Schools. Ed. by Neil Frude & Hugh Gault. LC 84-7237. 234p. 1984. text ed. 143.00 (*0-471-90070-2*) Wiley.

Disruptive Child. C. Clarke. 1990. 35.00 (*0-7463-0576-1*, Pub. by Northcote UK) St Mut.

Disruptive Children: Disruptive Schools? Jean Lawrence et al. 288p. 1984. 35.95 (*0-89397-200-2*) Nichols Pub.

Disruptive Influence. Lass Small. (Silhouette Desire Ser.). 1993. pap. 2.89 (*0-373-05775-X*, 5-05775-7) Silhouette.

Disruptive Pupil Management. Delwyn Tattum. 280p. (Orig.). 1990. pap. 23.95 (*0-8464-1480-5*) Beekman Pubs.

Disruptive Pupils in School & Units. Delwyn P. Tattum. LC 81-19727. 341p. reprint ed. pap. 97.20 (*0-8357-6710-8*, 2035341) Bks Demand.

Disruptive School Behavior: Class, Race, & Culture. Judith L. Hanna. LC 87-11947. 288p. 1988. 39.50 (*0-8419-1134-7*); pap. 22.50 (*0-8419-1164-9*) Holmes & Meier.

Disruptive Terrorism. Victor Santoro. LC 84-81632. 135p. (Orig.). 1984. pap. 12.95 (*0-915179-17-2*) Loompanics.

Disruptive Voices: The Possibilities of Feminist Research. Michelle Fine. 200p. (C). 1992. text ed. 39.50 (*0-472-09465-3*); pap. text ed. 15.95 (*0-472-06465-7*) U of Mich Pr.

Dissecting DOS. Michael Podanoffsky. LC 93-42508. 1994. write for info. (*0-201-62687-X*) Addison-Wesley.

Dissection & Tissue Culture Manual of the Nervous System. Ed. by Abraham Shahar et al. 1989. text ed. 89.95 (*0-471-56237-8*) Wiley.

Dissection Guide to the Fetal Pig: A Photographic Guide. Jones & Kennedy. (Illus.). 64p. (C). 1991. 9.95 (*0-8403-6682-5*) Kendall-Hunt.

Dissection Manual: Companion to Rohen - Yokochi Color Atlas of Anatomy. 3rd ed. Jack L. Wilson. LC 92-49400. (Illus.). 288p. 1993. 36.00 (*0-89640-230-4*) Igaku-Shoin.

Dissection of the Dog & Cat. Michael J. Shively & Bonnie G. Beaver. LC 84-8969. (Illus.). 152p. 1985. pap. text ed. 31.95 (*0-8138-0826-X*) Iowa St U Pr.

Dissection of the Frog: Laboratory Studies in Biology, 770-776, 7 studies. 2nd ed. Warren F. Walker, Jr. (C). 1967. write for info. (*0-7167-0661-X*) W H Freeman.

Dissection of the Rat: Laboratory studies in Biology, 840-845, 6 studies. 2nd ed. Warren F. Walker, Jr. (C). 1970. write for info. (*0-7167-0679-2*) W H Freeman.

Disseminated Intravascular Coagulation. Ed. by T. Abe & M. Yamamaka. (Bibliotheca Haematologica Ser.: No. 49). (Illus.). xiv, 356p. 1983. 157.75 (*3-8055-3726-3*) S Karger.

Disseminated Intravascular Coagulation & Related Syndromes. Ed. by Roger L. Bick. 144p. 1983. 132.00 (*0-8493-6636-4*, RC647, CRC Reprint) Franklin.

Disseminating Community Social Work in Scotland: An Initial Appraisal. David Crosbie et al. (C). 1989. 50.00 (*0-7855-0091-X*, Pub. by Natl Inst Soc Work) St Mut.

Disseminating Community Social Work in Scotland: An Intial Appraisal. David Crosbie et al. (C). 1989. 49.00 (*0-902789-65-1*, Pub. by Natl Inst Soc Work) St Mut.

***Disseminating Lacan.** Ed. by David Pettigrew & Francois Raffoul. (SUNY Series in Contemporary Continental Philosophy). 330p. (C). 1996. text ed. 59.50x (*0-7914-2785-4*) State U NY Pr.

***Disseminating Lacan.** Ed. by David Pettigrew & Francois Raffoul. (SUNY Series in Contemporary Continental Philosophy). 330p. (C). 1996. pap. text ed. 19.95x (*0-7914-2786-2*) State U NY Pr.

Disseminating Research - Impacting Practice. Ed. by Earl V. Dunn et al. LC 94-10317. (Research Methods for Primary Care Ser.: Vol. 6). 1994. 49.95 (*0-8039-5705-X*); pap. 24.00 (*0-8039-5706-8*) Sage.

Disseminating Whitman: Revision & Corporeality in Leaves of Grass. Michael Moon. LC 90-35138. 249p. 1991. 40.00 (*0-674-21276-2*, MOODIS) HUP.

Disseminating Whitman: Revision & Corporeality in Leaves of Grass. Michael Moon. 249p. (C). 1993. pap. 18.95 (*0-674-21245-2*) HUP.

Dissemination. Jacques Derrida. 1994. 23.75 (*0-8446-6737-4*) Peter Smith.

Dissemination. Jacques Derrida. Tr. by Barbara Johnson. LC 81-3359. xxiv, 366p. (C). 1983. pap. text ed. 14.95 (*0-226-14334-1*) U Ch Pr.

Dissemination Division Two of the Organization Executive Course see Organization Executive Course

Dissemination of Health Information: A Case Study in Adult Learning. Jacob J. Feldman. LC 66-14570. (Monographs in Social Research: No. 11). 1966. 9.95 (*0-202-27001-7*) NORC.

Dissension in Arcady: Bear Flag Revolution. James L. Brown. 1978. 18.00 (*0-912314-15-X*) Academy Santa Clara.

Dissent: Explorations in the History of American Radicalism. Ed. by Alfred F. Young. LC 68-57389. 388p. 1968. pap. 10.00 (*0-87580-502-7*) N Ill U Pr.

Dissent: The Issue of Modern Art in Boston. Elizabeth Sussman. (Illus.). 1985. 12.00 (*0-910663-43-2*) ICA Inc.

Dissent & Consensus: Social Protest in Pre-Industrial Societies. Ed. by Basudeb Chattopadhyaya et al. (C). 1989. 31.50 (*81-7074-043-6*, Pub. by KP Bagchi IA) S Asia.

Dissent & Disruption: A University under Siege. Richard A. Siggelkow. (Illus.). 248p. 1991. 31.95 (*0-87975-681-0*) Prometheus Bks.

Dissent & Dogma see Complete Prose Works of Matthew Arnold

Dissent & Order in the Middle Ages. J. B. Russell. (Twayne's Studies in Intellectual & Cultural History). 200p. (Orig.). (C). 1992. text ed. 22.95 (*0-8057-8603-1*, Twayne); pap. 12.95 (*0-8057-8628-7*, Twayne) Macmillan.

Dissent & Reform in the Early Middle Ages. Jeffrey B. Russell. LC 78-63178. (Heresies of the Early Christian & Medieval Era Ser.: Second Ser.). 344p. reprint ed. 36.00 (*0-404-16196-0*) AMS Pr.

Dissent & the State. Ed. by C. E. Franks. 296p. 1989. pap. 14.95 (*0-19-540742-3*) OUP.

Dissent from Irish America. John P. McCarthy. LC 92-45195. 1993. 39.50 (*0-8191-9048-9*) U Pr of Amer.

Dissent in Eastern Europe. Ed. by Jane L. Curry. LC 83-2168. 240p. 1983. text ed. 38.50 (*0-275-90965-4*, C0965, Praeger Pubs) Greenwood.

Dissent in the U. S. S. R. Politics, Ideology & People. Ed. by Rudolf L. Tokes. LC 74-24391. 469p. reprint ed. pap. 133.70 (*0-8357-9267-6*, 2014850) Bks Demand.

Dissent on Keynes: A Critical Appraisal of Keynesian Economics. Ed. by Mark Skousen. LC 91-27161. 264p. 1992. text ed. 59.95 (*0-275-93778-X*, C3778, Praeger Pubs) Greenwood.

Dissent on Trial: The Story of a Political Life. William Schneiderman. LC 82-17940. 250p. 1983. 17.50 (*0-930656-25-3*) MEP Pubns.

Dissent, Symbolic Behavior & Rhetorical Strategies. Ed. by Haig A. Bosmajian. LC 79-25821. 328p. 1980. reprint ed. text ed. 35.00 (*0-313-22253-3*, BODI, Greenwood Pr) Greenwood.

Dissenter in the Baptist Southland: Fifty Years in the Career of William Wallace Finlator. G. McLeod Bryan. LC 85-13752. (Illus.). xi, 198p. 1985. 19.95 (*0-86554-176-0*, MUP-H166) Mercer Univ Pr.

Dissenter in Zion: From the Writings of Judah L. Magnes. Ed. by Arthur A. Goren. (Illus.). 576p. 1982. 50.00 (*0-674-21283-5*) HUP.

Dissenters: America's Voices of Opposition. Intro. by John G. Hunt. LC 93-15527. (Library of Freedom). 1993. 8.99 (*0-517-09346-4*, Pub. by Gramercy) Random Hse Value.

Dissenters: Charles Fourier, 1772-1837, Henri de St. Simon, 1760-1825, Pierre-Joseph Proudhon, 1809-1865, John Hobson. Ed. by Mark Blaug. (Pioneers in Economics Ser.). 1992. 84.95 (*1-85278-494-6*, Pub. by E Elgar Pub UK) Ashgate Pub Co.

Dissenters: From the Reformation to the French Revolution. Michael R. Watts. 568p. 1986. pap. 34.00 (*0-19-822956-9*) OUP.

***Dissenters Vol. II: The Evolution of Evangelical Nonconformity 1791-1859.** Michael R. Watts. (Illus.). 620p. 1995. 89.00 (*0-19-822968-2*) OUP.

Dissenting & Separate Opinions at the World Court. Ijaz Hussain. LC 83-25508. 1984. lib. bdg. 122.50 (*90-247-2920-3*) Kluwer Ac.

Dissenting Doctors in Medicine. 1991. lib. bdg. 77.75 (*0-8490-4667-X*) Gordon Pr.

Dissenting Feminist Academy: A History of the Barriers to Feminist Scholarship. Gisele M. Thibault. (American University Studies: Anthropology & Science: Ser. XI, Vol. 9). 228p. (C). 1987. text ed. 36.50 (*0-8204-0396-2*) P Lang Pubs.

Dissenting Feminist Academy: A History of the Barriers to Feminist Scholarship. rev. ed. Gisele M. Thibault. LC 93-9871. 1993. write for info. (*0-8204-2262-2*) P Lang Pubs.

Dissenting Judicial Opinions: Foreshadows of Constitutional Law. Donald E. Lively. LC 92-19827. 200p. 1992. text ed. 59.95 (*0-275-94382-8*, C4382, Praeger Pubs); pap. text ed. 17.95 (*0-275-94383-6*, B4386, Praeger Pubs) Greenwood.

Dissenting Opinions: Feminist Explorations in Law & Society. Ed. by Regina Graycar. 144p. 1991. pap. text ed. 17.95 (*0-04-442240-7*, Pub. by Allen Unwin AT) Paul & Co Pubs.

Dissenting Opinions of Mr. Justice Holmes. Ed. by Alfred Lief. xviii, 314p. 1981. reprint ed. lib. bdg. 27.50 (*0-8377-0811-7*) Rothman.

Dissenting Thought & the Life of the Church: Studies in an English Tradition. Alan P. Sell. LC 90-20790. 732p. 1991. lib. bdg. 139.95 (*0-7734-9931-8*) E Mellen.

Dissenting Voice: Protestant Democracy in Ulster from Plantation to Partition. Flann Campbell. 513p. (Orig.). 1991. pap. 29.00 (*0-85640-457-8*, Pub. by Blackstaff Pr IE) Dufour.

Dissenting Voice: The New Essay of Spanish America, 1960-1985. Martin S. Stabb. LC 93-44720. (The Texas Pan American Ser.). 176p. (C). 1995. text ed. 25.00x (*0-292-77684-5*) U of Tex Pr.

Dissertation Concerning Meteors of Stile, or False Sublimity (from "A Discourse of Logomachys, or Controversys about Words") Samuel Werenfels. LC 92-25462. (Augustan Reprints Ser.: No. 199 (1980)). reprint ed. 12.00 (*0-404-70199-X*, PN203) AMS Pr.

Dissertation Cookbook: From Soup to Nuts, A Practical Guide to Start & Complete Your Dissertation. Simon & Francis. 288p. (C). 1991. pap. text ed. 29.95 (*0-8403-7037-7*) Kendall-Hunt.

Dissertation Handbook: A Guide to Successful Dissertations. 2nd ed. Eileen T. Nickerson. 152p. (C). 1994. per. 22.95 (*0-8403-8300-2*) Kendall-Hunt.

Dissertation in European Economic History Series, 30 bks., Set. Ed. by Stuart Bruchey. (Illus.). 1977. lib. bdg. 581.00 (*0-405-10773-0*) Ayer.

Dissertation on Elective Attractions. T. Bergman. 400p. 1970. reprint ed. 37.50 (*0-7146-1592-7*, Pub. by F Cass Pubs UK) Intl Spec Bk.

Dissertation on Liberty, Necessity, Pleasure, & Pain. Benjamin Franklin. (Notable American Authors Ser.). 1992. reprint ed. lib. bdg. 75.00 (*0-7812-2884-0*) Rprt Serv.

Dissertation on Musical Taste. Thomas Hastings. LC 68-16237. (Music Ser.). 228p. 1974. reprint ed. lib. bdg. 35.00 (*0-306-71085-4*) Da Capo.

Dissertation on Servitude. Leicester A. Sawyer. LC 70-152930. (Black Heritage Library Collection). 1977. 17.95 (*0-8369-8775-6*) Ayer.

Dissertation on Speech. J. C. Amman. Tr. by C. Baker. 1966. 5.00 (*0-934454-29-9*) Lubrecht & Cramer.

Dissertation on the Cause of the Corruption & Smutting of the Kernels of Wheat in the Head. M. Tillet. Tr. by H. B. Humphrey. (Phytopathological Classics Ser.: No. 5). 191p. (FRE.). 1755. 15.00 (*0-89054-006-3*) Am Phytopathol Soc.

Dissertation on the Disorder of Death: That State of the Frame Under the Signs of Death Called Suspended Animation. Walter Whiter. Ed. by Robert Kastenbaum. LC 76-19598. (Death & Dying Ser.). 1977. reprint ed. lib. bdg. 42.95 (*0-405-09592-9*) Ayer.

Dissertation on the Functions of the Nervous System. Georg Prochaska. Tr. by T. Laycock. LC 78-72819. (Brainedness, Handedness, & Mental Abilities Ser.). reprint ed. 34.50 (*0-404-60888-4*) AMS Pr.

Dissertation on the Functions of the Nervous System. Georg Prochaska. Tr. by T. Laycock. Bd. with On the Study of Character. (Contributions to the History of Psychology Ser.: Vol. XIV, Pt. A). 1983. reprint ed. (*0-89093-316-2*) U Pubns Amer.

Dissertation on the Influence of Opinions on Language & of Language on Opinions. Johann D. Michaelis. LC 72-147981. reprint ed. pap. 25.00 (*0-404-08236-X*) AMS Pr.

Dissertation on the Law of Nature, the Law of Nations, & the Civil Law in General. Together with Some Observations on the Roman Civil Law in Particular: To Which Is Added, by Way of Appendix, a Curious Catalogue of Books, Very Useful to the Students of These Several Laws, Together with the Canon Law. iv, 132p. 1980. reprint ed. lib. bdg. 20.00 (*0-8377-0510-X*) Rothman.

Dissertation on the Nature & Extent of the Jurisdiction of the Court of the United States. Peter S. Du Ponceau. 296p. 1993. reprint ed. lib. bdg. 65.00 (*0-8377-2038-9*) Rothman.

D

An Asterisk (*) at the beginning of an entry indicates that the title is appearing in BIP for the first time.

Dissertation on the Nature & Extent of the Jurisdiction of the Courts of the U. S., Being a Valedictory Address Delivered... Peter S. Du Ponceau. LC 79-37971. (American Law Ser.: The Formative Years). 296p. 1972. reprint ed. 24.95 (*0-405-04007-5*) Ayer.

Dissertation on the Numbers of Mankind in Ancient & Modern Times. 2nd ed. Robert Wallace. LC 68-30549. (Reprints of Economic Classics Ser.). 1969. reprint ed. 45.00 (*0-678-00450-1*) Kelley.

Dissertation on the Origin of Springs; Silliman, Benjamin-Experiments on the Fusion of Various Refractory Bodies, etc. Sereno E. Dwight et al. (Connecticut Academy of Arts & Sciences Ser., Trans.: Vol. 1, Pt. 3). 1813. pap. 300.00 (*0-685-22875-4*) Elliots Bks.

Dissertation on the Platonic Doctrine of Ideas. Thomas Taylor. 1988. reprint ed. pap. 7.95 (*1-55818-117-2*) Holmes Pub.

Dissertation on the Poor Laws. rev. ed. Joseph Townsend. (Illus.). 64p. (C). 1991. pap. text ed. 2.25 (*1-877891-08-8*) Paperbook Pr Inc.

Dissertation on the Poor Laws: By a Well-Wisher to Mankind. Joseph Townsend. (C). 1971. pap. 11.00 (*0-520-05466-0*) U CA Pr.

Dissertation on the Sanskrit Language. A. S. Paulinus & S. Bartholomaeo. (Studies in History of Linguistics: No. 12). xxviii, 224p. 1977. 59.00x (*90-272-0953-7*) Benjamins North Am.

Dissertation on the Subject of a Congress of Nations, for the Adjustment of International Disputes Without Recourse to Arms. William Ladd. 156p. 1994. reprint ed. lib. bdg. 47.50 (*0-8377-2415-5*) Rothman.

Dissertation Proposal Guidebook: How to Prepare a Research Proposal & Get It Accepted. David C. Gardner & Grace J. Beatty. (Illus.). 112p. 1980. pap. 14.95x (*0-398-04087-7*) C C Thomas.

Dissertation, the Tinieblas Trilogy. R. M. Koster. 1989. pap. 9.95 (*0-393-30648-8*) Norton.

Dissertation upon Genius. William Sharpe. LC 72-13112. (History of Psychology Ser.). 168p. 1973. reprint ed. lib. bdg. 50.00 (*0-8201-1110-4*) Schol Facsimiles.

Dissertations: Being the Preliminary Part of a Course of Law Lectures. James Kent. 87p. 1991. reprint ed. lib. bdg. 65.00 (*0-8377-2340-X*) Rothman.

Dissertations & Discussions, 2 vols. John Stuart Mill. LC 72-94. (Studies in Philosophy: No. 40). 1972. reprint ed. lib. bdg. 150.00 (*0-8383-1400-7*) M S G Haskell Hse.

Dissertations & Theses from Start to Finish: Psychology & Related Fields. John D. Cone & Sharon L. Foster. 362p. (Orig.). 1993. pap. text ed. 24.95 (*1-55798-194-9*) Am Psychol.

Dissertations & Theses on Venezuelan Topics, 1900-1985. William M. Sullivan. LC 87-13111. 284p. 1988. 32.50 (*0-8108-2017-X*) Scarecrow.

Dissertations Concerning the Fundamental Principle & Immediate Criterion of Virtue see Essay on the Origin of Evil

Dissertations Historiques, Artistiques et Scientifiques sur la Photographie. Alexander Ken. Ed. by Peter C. Bunnell & Robert A. Sobieszek. LC 76-24663. (Sources of Modern Photography Ser.). (FRE.). 1979. reprint ed. lib. bdg. 16.95 (*0-405-09640-2*) Ayer.

Dissertations in American Biography Series, 38 bks. Ed. by Richard B. Morris et al. 1982. write for info. (*0-318-50808-7*) Ayer.

Dissertations in American Economic History, 29 vols. Ed. by Stuart Bruchey. 7894p. 1975. 2,914.00 (*0-405-07252-X*) Ayer.

Dissertations in American Economic History: 1977, 34 titles. Ed. by Stuart Bruchey. (Continuing Series for American Dissertations). (Illus.). 1977. reprint ed. lib. bdg. 734.00 (*0-405-11024-3*) Ayer.

Dissertations in American Literature, 1891-1966. Ed. by James Woodress. LC 68-18961. 197p. reprint ed. pap. 56.20 (*0-317-26803-1*, 2023474) Bks Demand.

Dissertations in Broadcasting Series, 26 books, Set. Ed. by Christopher H. Sterling. 1979. lib. bdg. 739.50 (*0-405-11754-X*) Ayer.

Dissertations in English & American Literature: Theses Accepted by American, British & German Universities, 1865-1964. Ed. by Lawrence McNamee. LC 68-27446. 1136p. reprint ed. pap. 180.00 (*0-8357-9041-X*, 2013297) Bks Demand.

Dissertations in European Economic History II Series, 39 vols., Set. Ed. by Stuart Bruchey. 1981. lib. bdg. 2,492.50 (*0-405-13975-6*) Ayer.

Dissertations in Hispanic Languages & Literatures: An Index of Dissertations Completed in the United States & Canada, 2 vols., Vol. 1: 1876-1966. James R. Chathan. LC 70-80093. 134p. reprint ed. pap. 36.20 (*0-685-72573-1*, 2045491) Bks Demand.

Dissertations in Hispanic Languages & Literatures: An Index of Dissertations Completed in the United States & Canada, 2 vols., Vol. 2: 1967-1977. James R. Chathan. LC 70-80093. 174p. reprint ed. pap. 47.00 (*0-685-72574-X*) Bks Demand.

Dissertations in History: An Index to Dissertations Completed in History Departments of United States & Canadian Universities, 1837-1960, 2 vols. Warren F. Kuehl. reprint ed. pap. write for info. (*0-318-71725-5*, 2045492); reprint ed. Vol. 1: 1873-1960, 263p. pap. 75.00 (*0-7837-5725-5*); reprint ed. Vol. 2: 1961-June 1970, 248p. pap. 70.70 (*0-7837-5726-3*) Bks Demand.

Dissertations in the History of Education 1970-1980. Edward R. Beauchamp. LC 84-14125. 267p. 1984. 27.50 (*0-8108-1742-X*) Scarecrow.

***Dissertations of Maximus Tyrius.** Tr. by Thomas Taylor. (Thomas Taylor Ser.: Vol. 6). Date not set. 34.00 (*1-898910-05-7*) Minerva CA.

Dissertations on Early Law & Custom Chiefly Selected from Lectures Delivered at Oxford. Henry S. Maine. LC 74-25768. (European Sociology Ser.). 414p. 1975. reprint ed. 30.95 (*0-405-06522-1*) Ayer.

Dissertations on Film, Nineteen Eighty Series, 23 bks., Set. Ed. by Garth S. Jowett. 1980. lib. bdg. 532.00 (*0-686-71580-2*) Ayer.

Dissertations on Iberian & Latin American History. Carl A. Hanson. LC 74-97478. 400p. 1975. 20.00 (*0-87875-073-8*) Whitston Pub.

Dissertations on Latin America by U. S. Historians, 1960-1970: A Bibliography. Wilber A. Chaffee & Honor M. Griffin. LC 72-96194. (Guides & Bibliographies Ser.: 7). 72p. reprint ed. pap. 25.00 (*0-685-16456-X*, 2027320) Bks Demand.

Dissertations on Sociology Series, 61 bks., Set. Ed. by Harriet Zuckerman & Robert K. Merton. 1980. lib. bdg. 1,760.00 (*0-405-12945-9*) Ayer.

Dissertations on the Progress of Knowledge, 2 vols. in one. Ed. by Stewart et al. LC 74-25149. (History, Philosophy & Sociology of Science Ser.). 1975. reprint ed. 40.95 (*0-405-06634-1*) Ayer.

Dissident M. L. A. Asif Currimbhoy. (Bluebird Ser.). 56p. 1975. pap. 4.80 (*0-88253-842-X*) Ind-US Inc.

Dissident Montaigne. Max Gauna. (American University Studies: Romance Languages & Literature: Ser. II, Vol. 118). 305p. (C). 1989. text ed. 46.95 (*0-8204-0922-7*) P Lang Pubs.

Dissident Postmodernists: Barthelme, Coover, Pynchon. Paul Maltby. LC 91-25115. (Pennsylvania Studies in Contemporary American Fiction). 232p. (C). 1992. text ed. 29.95 (*0-8122-3064-7*) U of Pa Pr.

Dissident Press. Lauren Kessler. (CommText Ser.: Vol. 13). 1984. 37.00 (*0-8039-2086-5*); pap. 16.95 (*0-8039-2087-3*) Sage.

Dissident Voice: Poetry. Mike Jenkins. (Illus.). 88p. 1990. pap. 13.95 (*1-85411-025-X*, Pub. by Bloodaxe Bks UK) Dufour.

Dissident Voice: The Poems of N.M. Rashed. M. A. Habib. (Oxford India Paperbacks). 138p. 1993. pap. 6.95 (*0-19-562741-5*) OUP.

Dissidents. Neal Shusterman. 224p. (YA). (gr. 7 up). 1989. 13.95 (*0-316-78904-6*) Little.

Dissidents. Neil Shusterman. 192p. (YA). 1994. mass mkt. 3.99 (*0-8125-3461-1*) Tor Bks.

Dissimulating Harmony: The Image of Interpretation in Nietzsche, Rilke, Artaud, & Benjamin. Carol Jacobs. LC 77-18392. 149p. reprint ed. pap. 42.50 (*0-317-28818-0*, 2020332) Bks Demand.

Dissipative Processes in Tribology: Proceedings of the 20th Leeds-Lyon Symposium on Tribology Held in the Laboratoire de Mecanique des Contacts, Institut National des Sciences Appliquees de Lyon, France, 7th-10th September 1993. Ed. by D. Dowson et al. LC 94-18428. (Tribology Ser.: Vol. 27). 1994. write for info. (*0-444-81764-6*) Elsevier.

Dissipative Structures & Weak Turbulence. Ed. by Paul Manneville. 485p. 1990. text ed. 69.95 (*0-12-469260-5*) Acad Pr.

Dissipative Structures in Transport Processes & Combustion: Interdisciplinary Seminar, Bielefeld, 17-21 July, 1989. Ed. by D. Meinkohn & H. Haken. (Synergetics Ser.: Vol. 48). (Illus.). 256p. 1990. 71.00 (*0-387-52751-6*) Spr-Verlag.

Dissipative Strukturen in Integrierten Systemen. Ali B. Cambel et al. 351p. (ENG & GER.). 1989. 73.50 (*3-7890-1711-6*, Pub. by Nomos Verlags GW) Intl Bk Import.

Dissociated Identities: Ethnicity, Religion, & Class in an Indonesian Society. Rita S. Kipp. LC 93-49776. 300p. (C). 1993. text ed. 57.50x (*0-472-10412-8*) U of Mich Pr.

***Dissociated States.** Simon. 1995. mass mkt. (*0-553-56952-X*) Bantam.

Dissociated States. Leonard Simon. LC 93-26679. 1994. 21.95 (*0-553-09586-2*) Bantam.

Dissociation: Clinical, Research & Theoretical Perspectives. Steven J. Lynn & Judith W. Rhue. 477p. 1994. lib. bdg. 40.00 (*0-89862-186-0*) Guilford Pr.

Dissociation: Culture, Mind & Body. Ed. by David Spiegel. LC 93-47478. 272p. 1994. text ed. 32.95 (*0-88048-557-4*) Am Psychiatric.

Dissociation & Wholeness in Patrick White's Fiction. Laurence Steven. 176p. (C). 1989. text ed. 35.00 (*0-88920-959-6*, Pub. by Wilfrid Laurier CN) Humanities.

Dissociation Constants of Organic Bases in Aqueous Solution, Vol. 12. D. D. Perrin. 524p. 1972. 480.00 (*0-08-020827-4*, Pub. by Pergamon Repr UK) Franklin.

Dissociation of a Personality: A Biographical Study in Abnormal Psychology. Morton Prince. LC 69-10148. 575p. 1969. reprint ed. text ed. 35.00 (*0-8371-1988-X*, PRAP, Greenwood Pr) Greenwood.

***Dissociative Children: Bridging the Inner & Outer Worlds.** Lynda Shirar. 176p. 1995. 23.00 (*0-393-70213-8*) Norton.

Dissociative Disorders: A Clinical Review. Ed. by David Spiegel. LC 92-82037. x, 134p. (Orig.). (C). 1993. pap. 14.95 (*0-9629164-1-2*) Sidran Pr.

***Dissociative Identity Disorder: Theoretical & Treatment Controversies.** Ed. by Lewis M. Cohen et al. LC 94-32539. 584p. 1995. text ed. 50.00 (*1-56821-380-8*) Aronson.

Dissociative Recombination: Theory, Experiment, & Applications. Ed. by B. R. Rowe et al. (NATO ASI Series B, Physics: Vol. 313). 286p. (C). 1993. 95.00 (*0-306-44568-9*, Plenum Pr) Plenum.

Dissolute Characters: Irish Literary History Through Balzac, Sheridan Le Fanu, Yeats, & Bowen. W. J. McCormack. LC 92-37200. 1993. text ed. 69.95 (*0-7190-3962-2*, Pub. by Manchester Univ Pr UK) St Martin.

Dissolution. Jill McArthur. (Illus.). 96p. (Orig.). 1991. pap. 15.95 (*0-9629518-0-3*) J McArthur.

Dissolution, Bioavailability & Bioequivalence. Hamed M. Abdou. LC 89-90760. 1989. 69.95 (*0-912734-20-5*) Mack Pub.

Dissolution of an Empire. Meriel Buchanan. LC 75-115512. (Russia Observed Ser.). (Illus.). 1971. reprint ed. 19.95 (*0-405-03078-9*) Ayer.

Dissolution of Austro-Hungarian Empire: Lessons for Currency Reform. Peter M. Garber & Michael G. Spencer. LC 94-4721. (Essays in International Finance Ser.: Vol. 191). 1994. 8.00 (*0-88165-098-6*) Princeton U Int Finan Econ.

Dissolution of Character: Changing Perspectives in La Bruyere's Caracteres. Michael S. Koppisch. LC 80-70808. (French Forum Monographs: No. 24). 127p. (Orig.). 1981. pap. 9.95 (*0-917058-23-2*) French Forum.

Dissolution of Colonial Empires. Franz Ansprenger. 336p. 1989. 45.00 (*0-415-00838-7*); pap. 16.95 (*0-415-03143-5*) Routledge.

Dissolution of Communist Power: The Case of Hungary. Arpad Szakolczai & Agnes Horvath. 272p. 1992. 49.95 (*0-415-06709-X*, A6894) Routledge.

Dissolution of Eastern European Jewry. Walter N. Sanning. 215p. (Orig.). 1983. pap. 8.00 (*0-939484-11-0*) Inst Hist Rev.

Dissolution of Marriage. J. Green et al. 544p. 1986. text ed. 75.00 (*0-07-172056-1*) Shepards-McGraw.

Dissolution of Marriage in Washington. Terrence V. Sawyer. LC 92-17746. 460p. 1992. ring bd. 85.00 (*0-88063-986-5*) Michie Butterworth.

Dissolution of Nicholas Dee. Matthew Stadler. (Robert Stewart Book Ser.). (Illus.). 325p. 1993. text ed. 20.00 (*0-684-19352-3*, Scribners) S&S Trade.

Dissolution of Nicholas Dee: A Novel. Matther Stadler. LC 94-12790. 1994. pap. 12.00 (*0-06-097627-6*, PL) HarpC.

***Dissolution of Society.** Jack R. Nageley. 112p. 1994. pap. text ed. 6.90 (*0-9642631-0-6*) J R Nageley.

Dissolution of the British Parliament 1832-1931. Wang Chi-Kao. LC 79-127433. (Columbia University. Studies in the Social Sciences: No. 396). reprint ed. 21.50 (*0-404-51396-4*) AMS Pr.

Dissolution of the Carolingian Fisc in the Ninth Century. James Thompson. LC 35-1937. (University of California Publications in Social Welfare: Vol. 23). 220p. reprint ed. pap. 62.70 (*0-317-29062-2*, 2021448) Bks Demand.

Dissolution of the Celestial Sphere. Ed. by William H. Donahue & I. Bernard Cohen. LC 80-2087. (Development of Science Ser.). (Illus.). 1981. lib. bdg. 30.95 (*0-405-13853-9*) Ayer.

***Dissolution of the Luftwaffe, 2 vols., Set.** 384p. 1995. 104.95 (*0-11-772822-5*, HM28225, Pub. by HMSO UK) UNIPUB.

Dissolution of Traditional Rural Culture in Nineteenth Century France: A Study of the Bethmale Costume. Roberta P. Seid. Ed. by William H. McNeill & David H. Pinkney. (Modern European History Ser.). 456p. 1987. lib. bdg. 20.00 (*0-8240-8042-4*) Garland.

Dissolved Organic Matter in Lacustrine Ecosystems: Energy Source & System Regulator. Ed. by K. Salonen. (Developments in Hydrobiology Ser.). 300p. (C). 1992. lib. bdg. 172.00 (*0-7923-1652-5*) Kluwer Ac.

Dissolved Oxygen in the Chesapeake Bay: Processes & Effects. Gail Mackerian. 6.95 (*0-943676-26-6*) MD Sea Grant Col.

Dissolves. deluxe ed. Debra Bruce. (Burning Deck Poetry Ser.). 1977. pap. 15.00 (*0-930900-14-6*) Burning Deck.

Dissolving Alliance: The U. S. & the Future of Europe. Ed. by Richard L. Rubenstein. LC 86-25191. 216p. 1987. 22.95 (*0-88702-216-2*); pap. 12.95 (*0-88702-217-0*) Washington Inst Pr.

***Dissolving Clouds: Writings of Peter Hutchinson, Vol. III.** Peter Hutchinson. Ed. & Intro. by Christopher Busa. LC 94-67734. (Provincetown Artists Ser.: III). (Illus.). 100p. (Orig.). 1994. 30.00 (*0-944854-16-8*); pap. text ed. 15.00 (*0-944854-15-X*) Provincetown Arts.

Dissolving Co-Dependency: Powerful Insights from the Core-Empowerment-Training. Paula Horan & Brigitte Ziegler. 99p. (Orig.). 1992. pap. 9.95 (*0-941524-86-8*) Lotus Light.

Dissolving Depression & Finding Peace. Richard J. Green. 1978. pap. 2.50 (*0-87516-278-9*) DeVorss.

Dissolving Image: The Spiritual-Esthetic Development of W. B. Yeats. Ed. by Levine Bernard. LC 70-86953. 181p. reprint ed. pap. 51.60 (*0-7837-3815-3*, 2043635) Bks Demand.

Dissolving the Colonial Bond: American Ambassadors to the Philippines, 1946-1984. Lewis E. Gleeck, Jr. (Illus.). x, 403p. (Orig.). (C). 1988. pap. 18.75 (*971-10-0269-8*, Pub. by New Day Pub PH) Cellar.

Dissolving the Reins of Mental Control & Physical Domination. Jerry Parker. 120p. Date not set. pap. 15.00 (*0-9637021-0-6*, 055795981) Gldn Obelisk.

Dissolving Wedlock. Colin Gibson. LC 93-7386. 1994. write for info. (*0-415-03225-3*) Routledge.

Dissonance: Feminism & the Arts 1970-90. Ed. by Catriona Moore. (Illus.). 240p. 1994. pap. 18.95 (*1-86373-325-6*, Pub. by Allen Unwin AT) Paul & Co Pubs.

Dissonance in Zion. Michael Jansen. (Illus.). 160p. (C). 1987. text ed. 39.95 (*0-86232-682-6*, Pub. by Zed Books UK); pap. 15.00 (*0-86232-683-4*, Pub. by Zed Books UK) Humanities.

***Dissonant Heritage.** Gregory Ashworth & John E. Tunbridge. Date not set. text ed. 59.95 (*0-470-22037-6*); text ed. 59.95 (*0-471-94887-X*) Wiley.

Dissonant Identities: The Rock 'n Roll Scene in Austin, Texas. Barry Shank. LC 93-41385. (Music - Culture Ser.). (Illus.). 312p. (C). 1994. text ed. 39.95 (*0-8195-5272-0*, Wesleyan Univ Pr); pap. 16.95 (*0-8195-6276-9*, Wesleyan Univ Pr) U Pr of New Eng.

Dissonant Legacy of Modernismo: Lugones, Herrera y Reissig, & the Voices of Modern Spanish American Poetry. Gwen Kirkpatrick. (Latin American Literature & Culture Ser.: No. 3). 240p. (C). 1989. 42.50 (*0-520-06233-7*) U CA Pr.

Dissonant Voices: Religious Pluralism & the Question of Truth. Harold A. Netland. xii, 324p. (Orig.). 1991. pap. 14.99 (*0-8028-0602-3*) Eerdmans.

***Dissonant Worlds: Rogier Vandersteene O.M.I. among the Cree.** Earle H. Waugh. (Illus.). 344p. (C). 1995. text ed. 45.00 (*0-88920-259-1*, Pub. by Wilfrid Laurier CN) Humanities.

Dissuasion Crowds the Slow Worker. Lori Lubeski. LC 88-90557. 56p. 1988. 6.50 (*0-929022-01-7*) O Bks.

Dist Law Set. Banks. 1990. 145.00 (*0-316-08027-6*) Little.

***Dist-O-Map.** Rand McNally Staff. 1995. 7.95 (*0-528-88369-0*) Rand McNally.

Distaff Factor. large type ed. John Wainwright. 352p. 1985. 22.95 (*0-7089-1319-9*) Ulverscroft.

Distaff Side. large type ed. Frances Paige. 1989. 23.95 (*0-7089-8531-9*, Trail West Pubs) Ulverscroft.

***Distaff Side: Representing the Female in Homer's Odyssey.** Ed. by Beth Cohen. (Illus.). 288p. 1995. text ed. 45.00 (*0-19-508682-1*) OUP.

***Distaff Side: Representing the Female in Homer's Odyssey.** Ed. by Beth Cohen. (Illus.). 288p. 1995. pap. 19.95 (*0-19-508683-X*) OUP.

Distaff Sketchbook. R. L. Klinger. 1974. 3.50 (*0-913150-25-8*) Pioneer Pr.

Distance. Stephen Ratcliffe. LC 86-71933. 112p. (Orig.). 1986. pap. 6.00 (*0-939691-00-0*) Avenue B.

Distance Anywhere. Kenneth O. Hanson. LC 67-13113. 1968. reprint ed. 15.00 (*0-295-73710-7*) U of Wash Pr.

Distance Education: A Practical Guide. Barry Willis. LC 92-32544. (Illus.). 150p. 1993. 29.95 (*0-87778-255-5*) Educ Tech Pubns.

Distance Education: A Selected Bibliography. Cleborne D. Maddux. Ed. by William D. Milheim. LC 92-24055. (Educational Technology Selected Bibliography Ser.: Vol. 7). 71p. (Orig.). 1992. 14.95 (*0-87778-249-0*) Educ Tech Pubns.

***Distance Education: An Annotated Bibliography.** Terry A. Mood. 200p. 1995. pap. text ed. 27.50 (*1-56308-160-1*) Libs Unl.

Distance Education: An Information Age Approach to Adult Education. James Zigerell. 69p. 1984. 7.25 (*0-318-22079-2*, IN283) Ctr Educ Trng Employ.

Distance Education: International Perspectives. David Sewart et al. 200p. 1988. 19.95 (*0-415-01051-9*) Routledge.

Distance Education: New Perspectives. Ed. by Keith Harry et al. (Studies in Distance Education). 320p. 1993. 59.95 (*0-415-08941-7*, B0163) Routledge.

Distance Education: Staff Handbook. Harold Markowitz, Jr. Ed. by Charles E. Kozoll. 59p. (Orig.). 1990. pap. 13.95 (*1-877847-06-2*) Univ IL UCOCE&PS.

Distance Education: Strategies & Tools. Ed. by Barry Willis. LC 93-23229. 350p. 1994. 39.95 (*0-87778-268-7*) Educ Tech Pubns.

Distance Education: The Foundations of Effective Practice. John R. Verduin, Jr. & Thomas A. Clark. LC 90-46107. (Higher & Adult Education Ser.). 295p. 1991. 32.95 (*1-55542-306-X*) Jossey-Bass.

Distance Education & Mainstream: Convergence in Education. Ed. by Peter J. Smith & Mavis Kelly. 224p. 1987. lib. bdg. 49.95 (*0-7099-4499-3*, Pub. by Croom Helm UK) Routledge Chapman & Hall.

Distance Education for Corporate & Military Training. Pref. by Michael G. Moore. 145p. (C). 1992. pap. text ed. 20.00 (*1-877780-08-1*) ACSDE.

***Distance Education for Language Teachers: A UK Perspective.** Ed. by Ron Howard & Ian McGrath. 220p. 1995. 79.00x (*1-85359-292-7*, Pub. by Multilingual Matters UK); pap. 29.95x (*1-85359-291-9*, Pub. by Multilingual Matters UK) Taylor & Francis.

Distance Education for Teacher Training. Ed. by Hilary Perraton. LC 93-541. 432p. 1993. 65.00 (*0-415-09465-8*, B0170) Routledge.

Distance Education Handbook: An Administrator's Guide for Rural & Remote Schools. Bruce O. Barker. LC 91-43540. 66p. 1992. pap. 10.00 (*1-880785-01-3*) ERIC-CRESS.

Distance Education in Anglophone Africa: Experience with Secondary Education & Teacher Training. Ed. by Abdelwahed Zhiri & Paud Murphy. (EDI Analytical Case Study Ser.: No. 9). 160p. 1992. 9.95 (*0-8213-1908-6*, 11908) World Bank.

Distance Education in Canada. Ed. by Ian Mugridge & David Kaufman. 336p. 1986. 39.95 (*0-7099-4619-8*, Pub. by Croom Helm UK) Routledge Chapman & Hall.

Distance Education in Rural Alaska. Barry Sponder. 137p. 1991. 5.00 (*1-877962-18-X*) Univ AK Ctr CCS.

Distance Education Symposium: Selected Papers, Pt. 2. D. Billings et al. (ACSDE Research Monograph: No. 8). 75p. (C). 1993. pap. text ed. 20.00 (*1-877780-10-3*) ACSDE.

Distance Education Symposium Papers. Michael Beaudoin et al. (C). 1991. pap. 20.00 (*1-877780-06-5*) ACSDE.

Distance Education Symposium Selected Papers, Pt. 3. Ed. by K. Atman et al. (ACSDE Research Monograph: No. 9). 65p. (C). 1993. pap. 20.00 (*1-877780-11-1*) ACSDE.

Distance Education Systems. Sergio Elliot. (Economic & Social Development Papers: No. 67). 80p. 1990. pap. 12.00 (*92-5-102448-0*, F4480) UNIPUB.

D

An Asterisk (*) at the beginning of an entry indicates that the title is appearing in BIP for the first time.

Distance Flights. Don Berliner. (Space & Aviation Ser.). (Illus.). 72p. (J). (gr. 5 up). 1990. 21.50 (*0-8225-1589-X*, Lerner Publctns) Lerner Group.

Distance from Loved Ones. James Tate. LC 89-70659. (Wesleyan Poetry Ser.). 64p. 1990. 22.50 (*0-8195-2189-2*, Wesleyan Univ Pr); pap. 10.95 (*0-8195-1191-9*, Wesleyan Univ Pr) U Pr of New Eng.

Distance Geometry & Molecular Conformation. G. M. Crippen & T. F. Havel. 541p. 1988. text ed. 275.00 (*0-471-92061-4*) Wiley.

Distance in Graphs. Fred Buckley & Frank Harary. (Illus.). 352p. (C). 1990. 44.95 (*0-201-09591-2*, Adv Bk Prog) Addison-Wesley.

Distance in the Theatre: The Aesthetics of Audience Response. Daphna Ben Chaim. LC 83-24231. (Theater & Dramatic Studies: No. 17). 124p. reprint ed. pap. 35.40 (*0-8357-1940-5*, 2070657) Bks Demand.

Distance Learning: New Technology & New Potential. Julie D. Bell. (State Legislative Reports: Vol. 16, No. 6). 6p. 1991. pap. text ed. 5.00 (*1-55516-305-X*, 7302-1606) Natl Conf State Legis.

Distance Learning: On the Design of an Open University. T. M. Chang et al. 1982. lib. bdg. 49.50 (*0-89838-096-0*) Kluwer Ac.

Distance off Tables. Daniel E. Nichols. LC 43-15657. 253p. reprint ed. pap. 72.20 (*0-7837-4377-7*, 2044117) Bks Demand.

Distance Points: Studies in Theory & Renaissance Art & Architecture. James S. Ackerman. (Illus.). 600p. 1991. 63.00 (*0-262-01122-0*) MIT Pr.

Distance Points: Studies in Theory & Renaissance Art & Architecture. James S. Ackerman. (Illus.). 561p. 1994. pap. 30.00x (*0-262-51077-4*) MIT Pr.

Distance Regular Graphs. A. E. Brouwer et al. (Ergebnisse der Mathematik und Ihrer Grenzgebiete Ser.: Vol. 18). xvii, 495p. 1989. 89.00 (*0-387-50619-5*) Spr-Verlag.

Distance Sampling: Estimating Abundance of Biological Populations. S. T. Buckland et al. 400p. 1993. 85.00 (*0-412-42660-9*, A9788); pap. 35.00 (*0-412-42670-6*, A6959) Chapman & Hall.

Distance Vision & Perceptual Training: A Concept for Use in the Mobility Training of Low Vision Clients. Loyal E. Apple & Marianne May. LC 70-155919. 23p. reprint ed. pap. 25.00 (*0-685-16062-9*, 2027346) Bks Demand.

Distance We Travel. W. D. Ehrhart. 46p. 1993. 30.00 (*0-938566-58-X*) Adastra Pr.

***Distance We Travel.** 2nd ed. W. D. Ehrhart. 46p. 1994. pap. 8.00 (*0-938566-65-2*) Adastra Pr.

Distance Without Distance. Barbara Einzig. Ed. by Rena Rosenwasser & Patricia Dienstfrey. LC 95-2637. 142p. (Orig.). 1994. pap. 10.00 (*0-932716-34-2*) Kelsey St Pr.

Distanced Land: The Photographs of John Pfahl. John Pfahl. LC 89-70882. (Illus.). 220p. 1990. 45.00 (*0-8263-1214-4*); pap. 25.00 (*0-8263-1215-2*) U of NM Pr.

Distances. Rupert Loydell. LC 93-13724. 1993. pap. 4.00 (*0-940895-12-9*) Cornerstone IL.

Distances. limited ed. Josephine Jacobson. Ed. by John Wheatcroft. (Bucknell University Fine Editions: Series in Contemporary Poetry). (Illus.). 48p. 1992. 150.00 (*0-916375-14-5*) Press Alley.

Distancia de un Espacio Prometido. Mary Calleiro. LC 84-73242. (Coleccion Espejo de Paciencia Ser.). (Illus.). 78p. (Orig.). (SPA.). 1985. pap. 6.95 (*0-89729-365-7*) Ediciones.

Distancias - Distances. Susana Thenon. Tr. by Renata Treitel. (Sun & Moon Classics Ser.: No. 40). 92p. (Orig.). 1993. pap. 10.95 (*1-55713-153-8*) Sun & Moon CA.

Distancing. Nathan Whiting. 1974. pap. 1.25 (*0-912284-53-6*) New Rivers Pr.

Distancing: A Guide to Avoidance & Avoidant Personality Disorder. Martin D. Kantor. LC 93-294. 200p. 1993. text ed. 55.00 (*0-275-94408-5*, C4408, Praeger Pubs) Greenwood.

Distant Challenge: The U. S. Infantryman in Vietnam, 1967-72. Ed. by Albert N. Garland. (Vietnam War Ser.: No. 3). (Illus.). 372p. 1984. reprint ed. 24.95 (*0-89839-071-0*) Battery Pr.

Distant City: Images of Urban Experience in the Medieval World. Chiara Frugoni. Tr. by William McCuaig. (Illus.). 250p. 1991. text ed. 42.50 (*0-691-04083-4*) Princeton U Pr.

Distant Companions: Servants & Employers in Zambia, 1900-1985. Karen T. Hansen. LC 88-47771. (Anthropology of Contemporary Issues Ser.). 368p. 1988. 47.50 (*0-8014-2217-5*); pap. 16.95 (*0-8014-9546-6*) Cornell U Pr.

Distant Cousins: The Caribbean-Latin American Relationship. Ed. by Anthony T. Bryan & Andres Serbin. 275p. (C). 1994. pap. 19.95 (*1-56000-750-8*, U Miami North-South Ctr) Transaction Pubs.

Distant Cycles: Schubert & the Conceiving of Song. Richard Kramer. LC 93-39891. (C). 1994. lib. bdg. 56.00 (*0-226-45234-4*); pap. text ed. 24.95 (*0-226-45235-2*) U Ch Pr.

***Distant Dawn.** Jane Peart. (Westward Dreams Ser.). 256p. 1995. pap. 9.99 (*0-310-41301-X*) Zondervan.

Distant Death. Jose E. Pacheco. Tr. by Linda Scheer. (Sun & Moon Classics Ser.: No. 41). 186p. (Orig.). 1995. text ed. 21.95 (*1-55713-155-4*) Sun & Moon CA.

Distant Democracy: Social Inequality, Political Resources & Political Influence in Norway. Willy Martinussen. LC 76-18748. 254p. reprint ed. pap. 72.40 (*0-317-28154-2*, 2024281) Bks Demand.

Distant Desire: Homoerotic Codes & the Subversion of the English Novel in E. M. F orster's Fiction. Parminder K. Bakshi. LC 94-19454. (Sexuality & Literature Ser.: Vol. 5). 1995. write for info. (*0-8204-2544-3*) P Lang Pubs.

***Distant Dream.** large type ed. Jean Musson. (Romance Ser.). 1994. pap. 14.95 (*0-7089-7620-4*, Linford) Ulverscroft.

***Distant Dreams.** large type ed. Anne Griffiths. (Dales Large Print Ser.). 1994. pap. 16.95 (*1-85389-502-4*) Ulverscroft.

Distant Drum. Mahohar Malgonkar. 270p. 1974. reprint ed. pap. write for info. (*0-88253-286-3*) Ind-US Inc.

Distant Drums. Miles Dungan. (Illus.). 184p. (Orig.). 1994. pap. 14.95 (*0-86281-384-0*, Pub. by Appletree Pr IE) Irish Bks Media.

Distant Echoes: Painted Reliefs & Drawings by Miguel Zapata. Marcus Burke. Ed. by Betsey McDougall. LC 86-62683. (Illus.). 43p. (Orig.). 1986. pap. 8.00 (*0-935937-02-1*) Meadows Mus.

Distant Episode. Paul Bowles. 300p. (Orig.). (C). 1989. pap. 14.95 (*0-88001-204-8*) Ecco Pr.

Distant Face: Poems. Martin King. 96p. (Orig.). 1994. pap. 8.95 (*1-56474-106-0*) Fithian Pr.

Distant Fever. Gisela P. Alonzo. 231p. 1984. 6.95 (*0-89697-172-4*) Intl Univ Pr.

Distant Field of Murder. Jan Critchett. 1990. 34.95 (*0-522-84389-1*) Intl Spec Bk.

Distant Fires. Scott Anderson. LC 90-61838. (Illus.). 176p. 1990. pap. 12.95 (*0-938586-33-5*) Pfeifer-Hamilton.

Distant Fires. Kevin Heelen. 1993. pap. 4.75 (*0-8222-1304-4*) Dramatists Play.

Distant Flame: The Inspiring Story of Jack VanBebber's Quest for a World Olympic Title. Jack VanBebber. (Oklahoma Legacies Ser.). 196p. (Orig.). 1992. pap. 12.95 (*0-913507-26-1*) New Forums.

Distant Friend. Claude Roy. Tr. by Hugh Harter. LC 90-30540. (French Expressions Ser.). 176p. 1990. 19.95 (*0-8419-1196-7*) Holmes & Meier.

Distant Friends. Greg Johnson. LC 90-7384. 201p. 1990. 17.95 (*0-86538-071-6*) Ontario Rev NJ.

Distant Friends. Timothy Zahn. 1992. mass mkt. 4.99 (*0-671-72131-3*) Baen Bks.

Distant Friends: The United States & Russia, 1763-1867. Norman E. Saul. LC 90-41807. (Illus.). xii, 448p. 1991. 40.00 (*0-7006-0438-3*) U Pr of KS.

Distant Heritage: The Growth of Free Speech in Early America. Larry D. Eldridge. 198p. (C). 1993. 40.00 (*0-8147-2192-3*) NYU Pr.

***Distant Heritage: The Growth of Free Speech in Early America.** Larry D. Eldridge. 198p. 1995. pap. 16.95 (*0-8147-2195-8*) NYU Pr.

Distant Hills. large type ed. Mason Macrae. (Linford Western Library). 352p. 1985. pap. 11.95 (*0-7089-6188-6*) Ulverscroft.

Distant Hope. large type ed. Sylvia E. Kirk. 1991. 21.95 (*0-7089-2369-0*) Ulverscroft.

Distant Hunger: Agriculture, Food, & Human Values. Heather J. Nicholson & Ralph L. Nicholson. LC 78-60761. (Science & Society: Series in Science, Technology, & Human Values: Vol. 3). (Illus.). 240p. 1979. pap. 6.95 (*0-931682-00-2*) Purdue U Pubns.

Distant Hybridization of Crop Plants. Ed. by G. Kalloo & J. B. Chowdhury. LC 92-9753. (Monographs on Theoretical & Applied Genetics: Vol. 16). (Illus.). 280p. 1992. 138.00 (*0-387-53173-4*) Spr-Verlag.

***Distant Isle: Studies & Translations of Japanese Literature in Honor of Robert H. Brower.** Ed. by Thomas Hare et al. (Michigan Monograph Series in Japanese Studies: No. 15). 1995. write for info. (*0-939512-72-6*) U MI Japan.

Distant Journeys. Rafael Castillo. LC 91-8477. 112p. 1991. pap. 10.00 (*0-927534-15-0*) Biling Rev-Pr.

Distant Justice: Policing the Alaskan Frontier. William R. Hunt. LC 86-40528. 1987. 26.95 (*0-8061-2050-9*) U of Okla Pr.

Distant Kingdom. large type ed. Daphne Wright. 541p. 1989. 17.95 (*0-7089-1938-3*) Ulverscroft.

Distant Land - Near. Leon Knight & Zhang Yun. 1988. 6.00 (*0-940248-33-6*) Guild Pr.

Distant Lands. Julian Green. Tr. by Barbara Beaumont. 902p. (FRE.). 1991. 24.95 (*0-7145-2909-5*) M Boyars Pubs.

***Distant Lands: The Genesis & Evolution of Romanian-American Relations.** Ion Stanciu & Paul Cernovodeanu. 384p. 1986. 59.00 (*0-88033-088-0*) East Eur Quarterly.

***Distant Lights: And Other Adventure Stories.** Highlights Staff. LC 94-72486. (Illus.). 96p. (J). (gr. 2-5). 1995. 2.95 (*1-56397-445-2*, Wordsong) Boyds Mills Pr.

Distant Love. A. L. Reine. (Orig.). 1992. pap. 4.95 (*1-56333-056-3*) Masquerade.

Distant Love, Lasting Love. large type ed. C. O. Lamp. 544p. 1984. 15.95 (*0-7089-1129-3*) Ulverscroft.

Distant Magnets: Expectations & Realities in the Immigrant Experience. Ed. by Dirk Hoerder & Horst Rossler. LC 91-33415. (Ellis Island Ser.). 312p. (C). 1993. 45.00 (*0-8419-1302-1*) Holmes & Meier.

Distant Melodies: North Carolina School of the Arts International Music Program, 25 Summers, 1967-1991. 1992. write for info. (*0-9615354-1-5*) Semans Pub.

Distant Mirror: The Calamitous Fourteenth Century. Barbara W. Tuchman. LC 78-5988. (Illus.). 1978. 50.00 (*0-394-40026-7*) Knopf.

Distant Mirror: The Calamitous 14th Century. Barbara W. Tuchman. (Illus.). 704p. 1987. pap. 16.00 (*0-345-34957-1*, Ballantine Trade) Ballantine.

Distant Mirrors: America As a Foreign Culture. Philip R. DeVita & James D. Armstrong. 145p. (C). 1993. pap. 13.95 (*0-534-17676-3*) Intl Thomson.

Distant Mountains: Chinese Painting of the Late Ming Dynasty, 1570-1644. James Cahill. (History of Later Chinese Painting Ser.: Vol. 3). (Illus.). 336p. (C). 1982. 49.95 (*0-8348-0174-4*) Weatherhill.

Distant Neighbors: A Comparative History of Seattle & Vancouver. Norbert MacDonald. LC 86-30892. (Illus.). xxii, 291p. 1987. 30.00 (*0-8032-3111-3*) U of Nebr Pr.

Distant Neighbors: A Portrait of the Mexicans. Alan Riding. 1985. pap. 4.95 (*0-394-74015-7*) Random.

Distant Neighbors: A Portrait of the Mexicans. Alan Riding. 352p. 1989. pap. 11.00 (*0-679-72441-9*, Vin) Random.

Distant Neighbors: The Political Economy of European-Middle Eastern Relations. Ed. by Nazih Ayubi. 240p. 1994. 65.00 (*0-86372-181-8*, Pub. by Ithaca UK) Paul & Co Pubs.

Distant Neighbors in the Caribbean: The Dominican Republic & Jamaica in Comparative Perspective. Richard S. Hillman & Thomas J. D'Agostino. LC 91-37746. 224p. 1992. text ed. 45.00 (*0-275-93927-8*, C3927, Praeger Pubs) Greenwood.

Distant Neighbours: China & Europe. Harish Kapur. 224p. 1992. 49.00 (*0-86187-122-7*, Pub. by Pinter Pubs UK) St Martin.

Distant Parents. Jacob Climo. LC 91-32605. 286p. (C). 1992. 40.00 (*0-8135-1796-6*); pap. 15.00 (*0-8135-1797-4*) Rutgers U Pr.

Distant Partners: Community Change Through Project Renewal. Ben W. Lappin & Morton I. Teicher. 298p. (Orig.). (C). 1990. lib. bdg. 49.00 (*0-8191-7760-1*); pap. text ed. 25.50 (*0-8191-7761-X*) U Pr of Amer.

Distant Planets. Donald K. Yeomans. (Planetary Exploration Ser.). 48p. 1989. 13.95 (*0-8160-2050-7*) Facts on File.

Distant Pleasures: Alexander Pushkin & the Writing of Exile. Stephanie Sandler. LC 88-39678. 280p. 1989. 35.00 (*0-8047-1542-4*) Stanford U Pr.

Distant Puzzle: The Planet Uranus. rev. ed. Isaac Asimov et al. (Library of the Universe). (Illus.). (J). (gr. 3 up). 1994. lib. bdg. 18.60 (*0-8368-1136-4*) Gareth Stevens Inc.

Distant Relations. Carlos Fuentes. Tr. by Margaret S. Peden. LC 81-9904. 225p. 1982. 11.95 (*0-374-14082-0*) FS&G.

Distant Relations. Carlos Fuentes. Tr. by Margaret S. Peden. LC 81-9904. 225p. 1987. pap. 8.95 (*0-374-51813-0*) FS&G.

Distant Secrets: Unravelling the Mysteries of Our Ancient Past. Ronald Schiller. Ed. by Hillel Black. (Illus.). 256p. 1989. 17.95 (*1-55972-004-2*, Birch Ln Pr) Carol Pub Group.

Distant Serenade. Michael McLean. LC 93-73186. (Illus.). 44p. 1993. 9.99 (*0-87579-777-6*) Deseret Bk.

Distant Shore. Jan De Hartog. 1976. 22.95 (*0-8488-0981-5*) Amereon Ltd.

Distant Shores: Music & Photographs from Lake Superior & Lake Michigan. Richard Olsenius. 112p. (Orig.). 1990. audio, pap. 19.95 (*0-9609064-4-4*); pap. 14.95 (*0-9609064-5-2*); audio 9.95 (*0-9609064-6-0*) Bluestem Prod.

***Distant Shores: Music & Photographs from Lake Superior & Lake Michigan.** Richard Olsenius. 112p. (Orig.). 1993. cd-rom, pap. 24.95 (*0-9609064-8-7*) Bluestem Prod.

***Distant Shores: Music & Photographs from Lake Superior & Lake Michigan.** Richard Olsenius. (Orig.). 1993. cd-rom 14.95 (*0-9609064-7-9*) Bluestem Prod.

Distant Shrine: The Islamic Centuries in Jerusalem. Francis E. Peters. LC 89-45876. (Studies in Modern Society: No. 22). 275p. 1993. 39.50 (*0-404-61629-1*) AMS Pr.

Distant Siren. James DePreist. 64p. (Orig.). 1989. pap. 8.00 (*0-685-28041-1*) Wllmtt U Pr.

Distant Soil: Knights of the Angel. Colleen Doran. Ed. by Kay Reynolds. (Illus.). 120p. (Orig.). 1988. pap. 12.95 (*0-89865-557-9*, Starblaze) Donning Co.

Distant Soil: The Immigrant Song. Colleen Doran. Ed. by Kay Reynolds. (Illus.). 64p. (Orig.). 1987. pap. 6.95 (*0-89865-514-5*, Starblaze) Donning Co.

Distant Star. Anne Avery. 400p. (Orig.). 1993. pap. 4.99 (*0-505-51905-4*, Love Spell) Dorchester Pub Co.

Distant Star. Barbara Bickmore. (Illus.). 544p. (Orig.). 1993. pap. 10.00 (*0-345-36109-1*, Ballantine Trade) Ballantine.

Distant Summer. large type ed. Sarah Patterson. 1978. 12.00 (*0-7089-0134-4*) Ulverscroft.

***Distant Talking Drum: Poems from Nigeria.** Isaac Olaleye. (Illus.). (J). (gr. 3-6). 1995. 14.95 (*1-56397-095-3*, Wordsong) Boyds Mills Pr.

***Distant Thunder.** Vera Bay. 175p. 1995. write for info. (*0-9643212-0-3*) Ragga Inshallah.

Distant Thunder. Nick Casto. 350p. (C). 1995. 24.95 (*0-942597-83-4*, Burd St Pr) White Mane Pub.

Distant Thunder. Teresa De Luca. 624p. 1991. mass mkt. 5.95 (*0-380-71086-2*) Avon.

Distant Thunder. Richard Parque. 352p. 1989. pap. 3.95 (*0-8217-2557-2*) Zebra.

Distant Thunder: A Sequel to the Christmas Surprise. Ruth N. Moore. LC 91-10845. 160p. (Orig.). (J). (gr. 4-8). 1991. pap. 5.95 (*0-8361-3557-1*) Herald Pr.

Distant Thunder: Intimate Recollections of the Kaiser's Court. Anne Topham. (Illus.). 324p. 1992. 22.95 (*0-942257-26-X*) New Chapter Pr.

Distant Thunder: Third World Conflict & the New International Order. Donald M. Snow. LC 92-50022. (Illus.). 226p. (C). 1992. text ed. 35.00 (*0-685-60786-0*); pap. text ed. 15.00 (*0-312-06666-X*) St Martin.

Distant Thunder: Third World Conflict & the New International Order. Donald M. Snow. LC 92-50022. 226p. 1993. 35.00 (*0-312-08684-9*) St Martin.

Distant Trumpet. Paul Horgan. 1991. pap. 16.95 (*0-87923-863-1*) Godine.

Distant Valleys: Poems of Chong Chi-Yong. Tr. by Daniel A. Kister. LC 93-51018. 160p. (Orig.). 1994. pap. 14.00 (*0-87573-032-9*, Asian Human Pr) Jain Pub Co.

Distant View of a Minaret. Alifa Rifaat. Tr. by Denys Johnson-Davis. 116p. 1993. 12.95 (*0-7043-2401-6*, Pub. by Quartet UK) Interlink Pub.

Distant View of a Minaret & Other Stories. Alifa Rifaat. (African Writers Ser.). x, 116p. (C). 1987. reprint ed. pap. 9.95 (*0-435-90912-6*) Heinemann.

Distant Vision: Romance & Discovery on an Invisible Frontier. Elma G. Farnsworth. 275p. 1989. 20.95 (*0-9623276-0-3*) Pemberly Kent.

Distant Voices: Discovering a Forgotten Past. C. Leonard Allen. 1993. 17.95 (*0-89112-155-2*); pap. 11.95 (*0-89112-154-4*) Abilene Christ U.

Distant Voices: Poetry of the Preliterate. Ed. by Denys Thompson. (Illus.). 143p. 1978. 23.00 (*0-8476-6102-4*) Rowman.

Distant Voices, Different Drums: An Anthology of True Stories Chosen from Annals of Northern California & the State of Nevada, Historically Dated from 1805 to 1915. Norman McLeod. (Illus.). 251p. (Orig.). 1990. pap. 10.95 (*0-9618678-1-7*) Goldridge Pr.

Distant Water Fisheries & the Two Hundred Mile Economic Zone. Vladimir Kaczynski. LC 83-24912. (Law of the Sea Occasional Papers: No. 34). 1983. 4.25 (*0-911189-09-2*) Law Sea Inst.

Distant Worlds: The Story of a Voyage to the Planets. Friedrich W. Mader. Tr. by Max Shachtman. LC 75-28859. (Classics of Science Fiction Ser.). (Illus.). vi, 343p. 1976. reprint ed. 15.40 (*0-88355-374-0*); reprint ed. pap. 10.00 (*0-88355-458-5*) Hyperion Conn.

Distant, Yet Familiar. I. E. Repin. 1982. 46.00 (*0-317-57247-4*, Pub. by Collets UK) St Mut.

Distaves & Dames: Renaissance Treatises for & About Women. LC 78-15069. 1978. 90.00 (*0-8201-1317-4*) Schol Facsimiles.

Distillate Fuel: Contamination, Storage & Handling, STP 1005. Ed. by Howard L. Chesneau & Michele M. Dorris. LC 88-23587. (Special Technical Publication (STP) Ser.). (Illus.). 200p. 1988. pap. text ed. 34.00 (*0-8031-1186-X*, 04-010050-12) ASTM.

Distillate Fuel Stability & Cleanliness - STP 751. Ed. by Stavinoha & Henry. 168p. 1981. 20.00 (*0-8031-0762-5*, 04-751000-12) ASTM.

***Distillation.** Multimedia Development Services Staff. (Plant Fundamentals Ser.: Vol. VII, Module IV). (Illus.). 1995. teacher ed 45.00 (*1-57431-064-X*); student ed 30.00 (*1-57431-024-0*) Tech Trng Systs.

Distillation & Absorption, 2 vols., 1. Ed. by G. G. Haselden et al. (European Federation of Chemical Engineering Ser.). 1184p. 1988. 136.00 (*0-89116-841-9*) Hemisp Pub.

Distillation & Absorption, 2 vols., 2. Ed. by G. G. Haselden et al. (European Federation of Chemical Engineering Ser.). 1184p. 1988. 136.00 (*0-89116-842-7*) Hemisp Pub.

Distillation & Absorption, 2 vols., Set. Ed. by G. G. Haselden et al. (European Federation of Chemical Engineering Ser.). 1184p. 1988. 275.00 (*0-89116-840-0*) Hemisp Pub.

Distillation & Absorption '92: A Three Day Symposium Organised by the Institution of Chemical Engineers on Behalf of the EFCE Working Party on Distillation & Absorption & Held at the International Conference Centre, Birmingham, 7-9 September, 1992, 2 vols., Set. Ed. by J. D. Jenkins & D. W. Reay. LC 92-34396. (Institution of Chemical Engineers Symposium Ser.: No. 128). 900p. 1992. 225.00 (*1-56032-257-8*) Hemisp Pub.

Distillation Columns. A. Eli Nisenfeld & Richard C. Seemann. LC 80-85271. (Instrument Society of America: Monograph: No. 2). (Illus.). 256p. reprint ed. pap. 73.00 (*0-7837-5155-9*, 2044884) Bks Demand.

Distillation Design. Henry Z. Kister. 1992. text ed. 75.00 (*0-07-034909-6*) McGraw.

Distillation Design in Practice. L. M. Rose. (Computer Aided Chemical Engineering Ser.: No. 1). 308p. 1985. 89.75 (*0-444-42477-6*); pap. 37.50 (*0-444-42481-4*) Elsevier.

***Distillation Dynamics & Control.** Pradeep B. Deshpande. LC 85-5110. (Illus.). reprint ed. pap. 150.80 (*0-7837-9047-3*, 2049798) Bks Demand.

Distillation Process Applications & Operations. Henry Z. Kister. (Illus.). 700p. 1990. text ed. 65.00 (*0-07-034910-X*) McGraw.

Distilled Beverage Flavour: Recent Developments. Ed. by J. R. Piggott & A. Paterson. LC 88-35234. (Ellis Horwood Series in Food Science & Technology). 352p. 1989. text ed. 155.00 (*0-89573-819-8*) VCH Pubs.

***Distilled Spirits Market.** 100p. (Orig.). 1995. pap. 1,295.00 (*0-7605-2167-0*) Rector Pr.

Distilled Wisdom. 10th ed. Alfred A. Montapert. LC 64-8181. 1977. 8.95 (*0-9603174-0-6*, 21618) Bks of Value.

***Distilling the Scene.** Ron Ranson. (Illus.). 128p. 1995. 24.95 (*0-7153-0067-9*, Pub. by D & C Pub UK) Sterling.

***Distinct & Separate Feeling.** Frances Jablway. 345p. (Orig.). Date not set. pap. 12.00 (*0-9645650-0-5*) Bearwrites.

Distinct People: A History of the Churches of Christ in the 20th Century. Robert E. Hooper. 391p. (C). 1993. text ed. 19.95 (*1-878990-26-8*) Howard Pub LA.

Distinction: A Social Critique of the Judgement of Taste. Pierre Bourdieu. Tr. by Richard Nice. LC 84-491. 640p. 1987. pap. text ed. 18.95 (*0-674-21277-0*) HUP.

Distinction of Stories: The Medieval Unity of Chaucer's Fair Chain of Narratives for Canterbury. Judson B. Allen & Theresa A. Moritz. LC 80-26629. 270p. 1981. 44.50 (*0-8142-0310-8*) Ohio St U Pr.

Distinctions. (Start Smart Ser.). (J). 1990. student ed 4.50 (*1-878396-01-3*) Start Smart Bks.

Distinctive Approach to Psychological Research: The Influence of Stanley Schachter. Ed. by Neil Grunberg et al. 248p. 1987. text ed. 49.95 (*0-89859-910-5*) L Erlbaum Assocs.

Distinctive Black College: Talladega, Tuskegee, & Morehouse. Addie J. Butler. LC 77-22756. 176p. 1977. 20.00 (*0-8108-1055-7*) Scarecrow.

D

An Asterisk (*) at the beginning of an entry indicates that the title is appearing in BIP for the first time.

Distinctive Characteristics of Re-Evaluation Counseling. Harvey Jackins. 1973. pap. 2.00 (*0-911214-26-7*) Rational Isl.

Distinctive Characteristics of Re-Evaluation Counseling: Chinese Translation. Sun Jian-Min. 1987. pap. 1.00 (*0-913937-31-2*) Rational Isl.

Distinctive College: Antioch, Reed & Swarthmore. Burton R. Clark. 292p. (C). 1992. pap. 19.95 (*1-56000-592-0*) Transaction Pubs.

***Distinctive Details: Great Embellishment Techniques for Clothing.** Threads Editors Staff. LC 94-37377. 1995. 15. 95 (*1-56158-095-3*) Taunton.

Distinctive Home Plans: Two Hundred Designs from 3,400 to 7,700 Square Feet. LC 93-74839. (Home Plans Ser.). 240p. 1994. pap. 9.95 (*1-880029-32-4*) Creative Homeowner.

Distinctive Homes. Hiawatha T. Estes. (Illus.). 1988. 2.95 (*0-318-35145-5*) Hiawatha Homes.

Distinctive Industrialization: Cotton in Barcelona, 1728-1832. J. K. Thomson. 320p. (C). 1992. 89.95 (*0-521-39482-1*) Cambridge U Pr.

Distinctive Inns of Colorado Presents a Boutique Collection of Breakfast & Brunch Recipes, Vol. 1. Ed. by Kerrelyn M. Trent. 36p. (Orig.). 1993. pap. 4.50 (*0-9616308-3-3*) Hearthstn Inn.

Distinctive Qualities of the Catholic School. Edwim J. McDermott. 78p. 1986. 6.60 (*0-318-20560-2*) Natl Cath Educ.

Distinctive Qualities of Third Sector Organizations. James E. Ruckle. LC 92-32113. (Non-profit Institutions in America Ser.). 168p. 1992. 49.00 (*0-8153-0905-8*) Garland.

Distinctive Serger Gifts & Crafts: An Idea Book for All Occasions. Naomi Baker & Tammy Young. LC 89-42852. (Illus.). 200p. 1989. pap. 14.95 (*0-8019-7985-4*) Chilton.

Distinctive Skiing. Bill W. West. LC 85-51249. (Illus.). 137p. 1985. 9.95 (*0-934189-00-5*) Unique Pub CA.

Distinctive Skiing. 2nd ed. Bill W. West. LC 86-50762. (Illus.). 160p. 1986. pap. 9.95 (*0-89709-151-5*) Liberty Pub.

***Distinctives of the Believer: A Series of Homilies on the Titles of Distinction.** R. Lloyd Wilson. 1994. pap. 7.95 (*0-533-10876-4*) Vantage.

Distinctly Narcissistic: Diary Fiction in Quebec. Valerie Raoul. (Theory - Culture Ser.). 336p. 1993. 55.00 (*0-8020-2882-9*) U of Toronto Pr.

Distinguer Pour Unir: Les Degres du Savoir. 8th ed. Jacques Maritain. 946p. (FRE.). 1959. 59.95 (*0-8288-9850-2*, F111720) Fr & Eur.

***Distinguished African American Scientists of the Twentieth Century.** Katherine A. Morin et al. Ed. by Tracy More. (Illus.). 384p. 1995. 49.95 (*0-89774-955-3*, 2309) Oryx Pr.

Distinguished American Jews. Ed. by Philip H. Lotz. LC 78-111842. (Essay Index Reprint Ser.). 1977. 17.95 (*0-8369-1671-9*) Ayer.

Distinguished American Lawyers, with Their Struggles & Triumphs in the Forum: Containing an Elegantly Engraved Portrait, Autograph & Biography of Each Subject, Embracing His Professional Work & the Public Career of Those Called to Serve Their Country. Henry W. Scott. (Illus.). 716p. 1989. reprint ed. lib. bdg. 85.00 (*0-8377-1157-6*) Rothman.

Distinguished Classics of Reference Publishing. James Rettig. 376p. 1992. 55.00 (*0-89774-640-6*) Oryx Pr.

Distinguished Company: Distinguished Program in Teacher Education Awards. Ed. by Sara D. Smith. 1991. 12.50 (*0-685-57419-9*) Assn Tchr Ed.

***Distinguished Dissenters & Opposition to the 1919-1920 Red Scare.** W. Anthony Gengarelli. LC 95-14453. 428p. 1996. 109.95 (*0-7734-8894-4*) E Mellen.

***Distinguished German-Americans.** Charles R. Haller. 303p. (Orig.). 1995. pap. text ed. 24.00 (*0-7884-0193-9*) Heritage Bk.

***Distinguished Guest.** large type ed. Sue Miller. 1995. 26.95 (*1-56895-229-5*) Wheeler Pub.

***Distinguished Guest: A Novel.** Sue Miller. 288p. 1995. 24. 00 (*0-06-017673-3*) HarpC.

Distinguished Home Plans, No. D02: One-Story Home Plans. (Illus.). 1990. pap. text ed. 4.95 (*0-945471-28-9*) HomeStyles Pub & Mkt.

Distinguished Home Plans, No. D03: Home for Sloping Or Hillside Lots. (Illus.). 1990. pap. text ed. 4.95 (*0-945471-34-3*) HomeStyles Pub & Mkt.

Distinguished Homes of Shaker Heights: An Architectural Overview. Richard N. Campen. LC 91-72012. (Illus.). 144p. 1992. (*0-9601356-7-7*) West Summit.

Distinguished Jurist's Primer, Vol. 1. Ibn Rushd. Tr. by Imran Nyazee. 640p. 1994. 95.00 (*1-873938-13-6*, Pub. by Garnet Pubng Ltd UK) Paul & Co Pubs.

Distinguished Jurist's Primer, Vol. 2. Ibn Rushd. Tr. by Imran Nyazee. 500p. 1994. 95.00 (*1-873938-93-4*, Pub. by Garnet Pubng Ltd UK) Paul & Co Pubs.

Distinguished Negroes Abroad. rev. ed. Beatrice J. Fleming & Marion J. Pryde. (Illus.). (J). (gr. 1-6). 1990. 21.95 (*0-87498-002-X*) Assoc Pubs DC.

Distinguished Outsider: Robert Musil & His Critics. Christian Rogowski. (Literary Criticism in Perspective Ser.). 230p. 1994. 55.95 (*1-879751-52-6*) Camden Hse.

Distinguished Service Cross. Donald E. Zlotnik. (Fields of Honor Ser.: No. 2). 320p. 1991. pap. 4.50 (*0-451-16873-9*, Sig) NAL-Dutton.

Distinguished Service Medal, 1914-1920. William H. Fevyer. 121p. (C). 1987. 133.00 (*0-317-90435-3*, Pub. by Picton UK) St Mut.

Distinguished Service Medal, 1939-46. William H. Fevyer. 164p. (C). 1987. 147.00 (*0-317-90433-7*, Pub. by Picton UK) St Mut.

Distinguished Shades: Americans Whose Lives Live On. Louis Filler. (Illus.). 279p. (C). 1992. text ed. 24.95 (*0-9631527-0-X*); pap. text ed. 12.95 (*0-9631527-1-8*) Belfry Pubns.

Distinguished Shades: Americans Whose Lives Live On. Louis Filler. LC 91-77228. (Illus.). 279p. 1992. 24.95 (*0-9615270-3-X*); pap. 12.95 (*0-9615271-8-8*) Wayne St U Pr.

Distinguished Teachers on Effective Teaching. Ed. by Peter G. Beidler. LC 85-81906. (New Directions for Teaching & Learning Ser.: No. 28). (Orig.). 1986. pap. 16.95x (*1-55542-995-5*) Jossey-Bass.

Distinguishing Between Fact & Opinion. Sheldon L. Tlkin & Judith Conoway. (Horizons E Ser.). (Illus.). 24p. (J). (gr. 3-4). 1980. student ed 3.50 (*0-89403-572-X*) EDC.

Distinguishing Features: Film Criticism & Comment. Stanley Kauffmann. LC 93-23112. (PAJ Bks.). 1994. text ed. 45.00 (*0-8018-4721-4*); pap. 14.95 (*0-8018-4722-2*) Johns Hopkins.

Distinguishing Jonson: Imitation, Rivalry, & the Direction of a Dramatic Career. George E. Rowe. LC 87-13198. xii, 220p. 1988. 25.00 (*0-8032-3883-5*) U of Nebr Pr.

Distinguishing Marks of a Work of the Spirit of God. Jonathan Edwards. (Notable American Authors Ser.). 1992. reprint ed. lib. bdg. 75.00 (*0-7812-2766-6*) Rprt Serv.

Distinguishing Psychological from Organic Disorders: Screening for Psychological Masquerade. Robert L. Taylor. LC 90-9477. 256p. 1990. 29.95 (*0-8261-6950-3*) Springer Pub.

Distinguishing Traits of Christian Character. Gardiner Spring. LC 66-30202. 1966. pap. 4.99 (*0-87552-441-9*) Presby & Reformed.

Distinguo: Reading Montaigne Differently. Steven Rendall. 180p. 1992. 39.95 (*0-19-815180-2*) OUP.

Distinquishing Between Fact & Opinion. Sheldon L. Tilkin & Judith Conoway. (Horizons F Ser.). (Illus.). 24p. (J). (gr. 4-5). 1980. student ed. 3.50 (*0-89403-582-7*) EDC.

Distintivos de la Iglesia de Dios. Ed. by Ray H. Hughes. 116p. (SPA.). 1970. pap. 5.95 (*0-87148-256-8*) Pathway Pr.

Distorsion de la Logica y la Polifonia en la Prosa de Quevedo. Mirta A. Gonzalez. LC 92-43637. (American University Studies: Romance Languages & Literature: Ser. II, Vol. 182). 152p. (C). 1994. text ed. 36.95 (*0-8204-1788-2*) P Lang Pubs.

Distorted Bamburak. Gary Bamburak. (Illus.). 96p. (Orig.). 1989. pap. 5.89 (*0-9622560-1-3*) Bamburak Designs.

Distorted Development: Mexico in the World Economy. David Barkin. (Political Economy & Economic Development in Latin America Ser.). 162p. (C). 1990. pap. text ed. 36.50 (*0-8133-7608-4*) Westview.

Distorted Images: Misunderstandings Between Men & Women. Anne Borrowdale. 160p. (Orig.). 1991. pap. 12. 99 (*0-664-25242-7*) Westminster John Knox.

Distorted Mirror of History see Distorted Past

***Distorted Past.** Josep Fontana. Tr. by Colin Smith. (The/ Making of Europe Ser.). Orig. Title: The Distorted Mirror of History. (Illus.). 256p. 1995. 24.95 (*0-631-17622-5*) Blackwell Pubs.

Distorted Probabilities & Choice under Risk. C. Puppe. Ed. by Martin J. Beckmann & W. Krelle. (Lecture Notes in Economics & Mathematical Systems Ser.: Vol. 363). (Illus.). viii, 100p. 1991. pap. 27.00 (*0-387-54247-7*) Spr-Verlag.

Distortion & Stress. Joseph E. Shigley & Charles R. Mischke. (Mechanical Designer's Workbook Ser.). 204p. 1990. pap. text ed. 31.95 (*0-07-056924-X*) McGraw.

Distortion by Compensation. Ralph E. Cowles. 39p. 1976. reprint ed. spiral bd. 5.50 (*0-7873-0227-9*) Mokelumne.

Distortion des Echanges en Europe Occidentale see Cooperation Financiere Internationale

Distortion Theory of Macro-Economic Forecasting: A Guide for Econimists & Investors. Steven Marquard. LC 93-42761. 224p. 1994. text ed. 59.95 (*0-89930-910-0*, Quorum Bks) Greenwood.

Distortions. Ann Beattie. LC 90-39020. (Vintage Contemporaries Ser.). 288p. 1990. pap. 12.00 (*0-679-73235-7*, Vin) Random.

Distortions of Agricultural Incentives: Papers Presented at a 1977 Three-Day Workshop Sponsored by the Midwest Center of the American Academy of Arts & Sciences. Ed. by Theodore W. Schultz. LC 78-3246. 351p. reprint ed. pap. 100.10 (*0-317-28580-7*, 2055201) Bks Demand.

***Distortions of Historical Facts.** Shannon Jolly. 224p. (Orig.). 1994. pap. 12.95 (*1-55523-722-3*) Winston-Derek.

Distortions of Reality: Let The Fool Be Fooled But Don't You Be The Fool. Glenn J. Epps. (Illus.). 192p. 1992. 19.95 (*0-9695730-0-6*) Sunrise Niagara.

Distracted. Jalal Toufic. 208p. 1992. pap. 12.95 (*0-88268-059-5*) Station Hill Pr.

Distracted Preacher & Other Tales. Thomas Hardy. (English Library). 1980. mass mkt. 6.95 (*0-14-043124-1*, Penguin Classics) Viking Penguin.

Distractions. Poems. Miller Williams. LC 80-39502. x, 67p. 1981. pap. 6.95 (*0-8071-0797-2*) La State U Pr.

Distrbution's Place in the American Economy Since 1869. Harold Barger. 1975. 20.95 (*0-405-07584-7*, 16412) Ayer.

Distress & Comfort. Judy Dunn. LC 76-30319. (Developing Child Ser.). 137p. reprint ed. pap. 39.10 (*0-7837-5933-9*, 2045732) Bks Demand.

Distress Identification Manual for the Long-Term Pavement Performance Project. SHRP Staff. 147p. (Orig.). (C). 1993. pap. text ed. 20.00 (*0-309-05271-8*, SHRP-P-338) SHRP.

Distress Property: How to Buy It in California. 356p. 1981. 55.00 (*0-934668-07-8*) J C Print.

Distress Signals. Louise Neaderland. 58p. 1985. 3.00 (*0-942561-07-4*) Bone Hollow.

Distress Signals. Isadore Rosenfeld. 1989. 18.95 (*0-318-37668-7*) S&S Trade.

Distress'd Orphan: or Love in a Mad-House. Eliza Haywood. (Augustan Reprints Ser.: Nos. 267-268 (1991)). reprint ed. 18.50 (*0-404-70267-8*) AMS Pr.

Distressed Workers in the Eighties. Daniel H. Saks. LC 83-63104. (Committee on New American Realities Ser.). 80p. 1983. pap. 7.00 (*0-89068-070-1*, NPA 202) Natl Planning.

Distributed ADA: Developments & Experiences: Proceedings of the Distributed ADA '89 Symposium, University of Southampton, 11-12 December, 1989. Ed. by Judy Bishop. (Ada Companion Ser.). (Illus.). 300p. (C). 1990. 54.95 (*0-521-39251-9*) Cambridge U Pr.

Distributed Algorithms. Ed. by J. C. Bermond & Michel Raynal. (Lecture Notes in Computer Science Ser.: Vol. 392). vi, 315p. 1989. pap. 40.00 (*0-387-51687-5*, 3543) Spr-Verlag.

***Distributed Algorithms.** Nancy Lynch. 1995. 54.95 (*1-55860-348-4*) Morgan Kaufmann.

Distributed Algorithms. Ed. by S. Toueg et al. (Lecture Notes in Computer Science Ser.: Vol. 579). 319p. 1992. pap. 48.00 (*0-387-55236-7*) Spr-Verlag.

Distributed Algorithms. Ed. by Jan Van Leeuwen. (Lecture Notes in Computer Science Ser.: Vol. 312). 430p. 1988. pap. 45.00 (*0-387-19366-9*) Spr-Verlag.

Distributed Algorithms: Fourth International Workshop, Bari, Italy September 24-26, 1990 Proceedings. Ed. by Jan Van Leeuwen & N. Santoro. (Lecture Notes in Computer Science Ser.: Vol. 486). vi, 433p. 1991. pap. 41.00 (*0-387-54099-7*) Spr-Verlag.

Distributed Algorithms: International Workshop, 7th, WDAG '93, Lausanne, Switzerland, September 27-29, 1993: Proceedings. Ed. by Andre Schiper. LC 93-23379. (Lecture Notes in Computer Science Ser.: Vol. 725). 1993. 50.00 (*0-387-57271-6*) Spr-Verlag.

Distributed Algorithms: Sixth International Workshop, WDAG '92, Haifa, Israel, November 2-4, 1992 Proceedings. Ed. by A. Segall et al. (Lecture Notes in Computer Science Ser.: Vol. 647). x, 380p. 1992. pap. 57.00 (*0-387-56188-9*) Spr-Verlag.

***Distributed Algorithms: 8th International Workshop.** Ed. by Gerard Tel & Paul Vitanyi. (Lecture Notes in Computer Science Ser.: Vol. 857). 1994. 52.00 (*3-540-58449-8*); 52.00 (*0-387-58449-8*) Spr-Verlag.

Distributed Algorithms & Protocols. Michel Raynal. LC 87-25409. (Computing Ser.). 163p. 1988. pap. text ed. 64.95 (*0-471-91754-0*) Wiley.

Distributed & Multiplexed Fiber Optic Sensors. J. P. Dakin & A. D. Kersey. 1992. 53.00 (*0-8194-0717-8*, 1586) SPIE.

***Distributed & Networked Environments: Proceedings of the First International Workshop on Services.** LC 94-75252. 187p. 1994. pap. text ed. 40.00 (*0-8186-5835-5*) IEEE Comp Soc.

Distributed & Parallel Database Object Management. Ed by Elisa Bertino. 132p. (C). 1994. lib. bdg. 80.00 (*0-7923-9440-2*) Kluwer Ac.

Distributed Application Services. Open Framework Staff. 195p. (C). 1993. pap. text ed. 22.00 (*0-13-630518-0*) P-H.

Distributed Artificial Intelligence. Michael N. Huhns. 400p. (C). 1987. pap. text ed. 210.00 (*0-273-08778-9*, Pub. by Pitman Pubng UK) St Mut.

Distributed Artificial Intelligence, Vol. 1. Ed. by Les Gasser & Michael Huhns. 520p. (C). 1989. pap. text ed. 250.00 (*0-273-08810-6*, Pub. by Pitman Pubng UK) St Mut.

Distributed Artificial Intelligence, Vol. 1. Michael N. Huhns. LC 86-33259. (Research Notes in Artificial Intelligence Ser.). (Illus.). 390p. 1987. pap. text ed. 34.95 (*0-934613-38-9*) Morgan Kaufmann.

Distributed Artificial Intelligence, Vol. 2. Les Gasser & Michael Huhns. (Research Notes in Artificial Intelligence Ser.). 1989. 34.95 (*1-55860-092-2*) Morgan Kaufmann.

Distributed Artificial Intelligence: Theory & Praxis. Ed. by Nicholas M. Avouris & Les Gasser. (C). 1992. lib. bdg. 95.50 (*0-7923-1585-5*) Kluwer Ac.

***Distributed Autonomous Robotic Systems.** H. Asami et al. LC 94-37490. 1995. 149.00 (*0-387-70147-8*) Spr-Verlag.

***Distributed CICS: An In-Depth Assessment for Downsizing Applications.** Richard Schreiber & William Ogden. 1994. pap. text ed. 39.95 (*0-471-06055-0*) Wiley.

Distributed Cognitions: Psychological & Educational Considerations. Ed. by Gavriel Salomon. LC 92-41220. (Learning in Doing: Social, Cognitive & Computational Perspectives Ser.). (Illus.). 288p. (C). 1993. 49.95 (*0-521-41406-7*) Cambridge U Pr.

Distributed Computer Control Systems: Proceedings of the IFAC Symposium, Tampa, Florida, Oct. 1979. IFAC Symposium Staff. Ed. by T. J. Harrison. (IFAC Proceedings Ser.). (Illus.). 240p. 1980. 103.00 (*0-08-024490-4*, Pub. by Pergamon Repr UK) Franklin.

Distributed Computer Control Systems in Industrial Automation. Popovic & Bhatkar. (Electrical Engineering & Electronics Ser.: Vol. 66). 712p. 1990. 160.00 (*0-8247-8118-X*) Dekker.

Distributed Computer Control Systems 1981: Proceedings of the IFAC Symposium, Beijing, China, Aug., 1981. IFAC Symposium Staff & W. E. Miller. (IFAC Proceedings Ser.). (Illus.). 176p. 1982. 79.00 (*0-08-028672-0*, Pub. by Pergamon Repr UK) Franklin.

Distributed Computer Control Systems, 1983: Proceedings of the IFAC Symposium, 5th, Johannesburg, South Africa, May, 1983. IFAC Symposium Staff & Mike G. Rodd. (IFAC Proceedings Ser.). 160p. 1984. 86.00 (*0-08-030546-6*, Pub. by Pergamon Repr UK) Franklin.

Distributed Computer Control Systems 1988: Proceedings of the 8th IFAC Workshop, Vitznau, Switzerland, 13-15 September, 1988. Ed. by Mike G. Rodd & Th. Lalive D'Epinay. (IFAC Publication Ser.: No. 84). (Illus.). 145p. 1989. 89.00 (*0-08-036938-3*, Pergamon Pr) Elsevier.

Distributed Computer Control Systems 1989. Ed. by L. Motus & S. Narita. (IFAC Workshop Ser.: No. 9005). 200p. 1990. 77.00 (*0-08-037870-6*, Pergamon Pr) Elsevier.

***Distributed Computer Control Systems, 1994: IFAC Workshop, Toledo, Spain, 28-30 September 1994.** IFAC Workshop on Distributed Computer Control Systems Staff. Ed. by J. A. De La Puente & M. G. Rodd. LC 94-47290. 1995. pap. 69.00 (*0-08-042237-3*, Pergamon Pr) Elsevier.

Distributed Computer Environments. Ed. by Dan Cerutti & Donna Pierson. LC 93-16402. (McGraw-Hill Series on Computer Communications). 1993. text ed. 50.00 (*0-07-010516-2*) McGraw.

Distributed Computer Systems. H. Zedan. 305p. 1990. text ed. 79.95 (*0-408-02938-2*) Buttrwrth-Heinemann.

Distributed Computing. Chambers D. Jones. 1984. text ed. 66.00 (*0-12-167350-2*) Acad Pr.

Distributed Computing: A Practical Synthesis. Amjad Umar. 960p. 1993. text ed. 76.00 (*0-13-036252-2*) P-H.

Distributed Computing: An Introduction to Heterogenous systems. Eric Wasiolek. 1992. text ed. 39.95 (*0-07-607036-0*) McGraw.

Distributed Computing: Concepts & Implementations. Ed. by P. L. McEntire et al. LC 84-6648. 460p. 1984. 59.95 (*0-87942-175-4*, PC01693) Inst Electrical.

Distributed Computing: Implementation & Management Strategies. Raman Khanna. 1993. text ed. 54.00 (*0-13-220138-0*) P-H.

Distributed Computing & Cryptography: Proceedings of the DIMACS Workshop. Feigenbaum et al. (DIMACS Ser.: Vol. 2). 262p. 1991. 53.00 (*0-8218-6590-0*, DIMACS-2) Am Math.

Distributed Computing & the Electronic Library: Micros to Superminis. Audrey N. Grosch. LC 85-7627. (Professional Librarian Ser.). 250p. 1985. text ed. 40.50 (*0-86729-145-1*, Hall Reference) Macmillan.

Distributed Computing & the Mainframe: Leveraging Your Investments. Kurt Ziegler. 387p. 1991. text ed. 79.95 (*0-471-51753-4*) Wiley.

Distributed Computing Network Reliability. Suresh Rai & Dharma P. Agrawal. LC 89-45995. 357p. 1990. 9.95 (*0-8186-8908-0*, 1908) IEEE Comp Soc.

Distributed Computing Systems. J. P. Verjus. Ed. by Yacup Paker. 1983. text ed. 66.00 (*0-12-543970-9*) Acad Pr.

Distributed Computing Systems: Concepts & Structures. A. Ananda & B. Srinivasan. LC 90-86252. 416p. 1991. 45. 00 (*0-8186-8975-7*, 1975) IEEE Comp Soc.

Distributed Computing Systems Programme. Ed. by D. Duce et al. (Digital Electronics, Computing & Software Engineering Ser.). 320p. 1984. boxed 68.00 (*0-86341-023-5*, CM004) Inst Elect Eng.

Distributed Computing Systems (Readings in) T. Casavant & M. Singhal. 450p. 1993. text ed. 88.00 (*0-8186-3032-9*, 3032) IEEE Comp Soc.

Distributed Computing Systems, 12th Conference, (ICDCS-12) LC 88-659565. 744p. 1992. pap. 120.00 (*0-8186-2865-0*, 2865) IEEE Comp Soc.

Distributed Computing Systems, 13th Conference (ICDCS-13) LC 88-659565. 592p. 1993. pap. text ed. 120.00 (*0-8186-3770-6*, 3770) IEEE Comp Soc.

Distributed Computing Systems, 14th Conference (ICDCS-14) 600p. 1994. pap. text ed. 120.00 (*0-8186-5840-1*, 5840) IEEE Comp Soc.

Distributed Constraint Logic Programming. H. F. Leung. 350p. 1993. text ed. 74.00 (*981-02-1456-1*) World Scientific Pub.

***Distributed Control Systems.** Multimedia Development Services Staff. (Plant Fundamentals Ser.: Vol. VIII, Module III). (Illus.). 1995. teacher ed 45.00 (*1-57431-067-4*); student ed 30.00 (*1-57431-027-5*) Tech Trng Systs.

Distributed Control Systems in Process Industries: End-Users Focus on Smaller, More Modular & Hybrid DCS's. Market Intelligence Staff. 361p. (Orig.). 1993. 1, 495.00 (*1-56753-657-3*) Frost & Sullivan.

Distributed Cooperative Computing. Abbas Birjandi & Pierre-Louis Neumann. 400p. 1993. text ed. 46.00 (*0-13-220377-4*) P-H.

Distributed Data Bases. Ed. by H. J. Schneider. 366p. 1982. 72.00 (*0-444-86474-1*, North Holland) Elsevier.

Distributed Data Processing in CICS: A Guide to Using MRO-ISC. Arlene Wipfler. (Illus.). 320p. 1989. text ed. 48.00 (*0-07-071136-4*) McGraw.

Distributed Data Sharing Systems. R. P. Van de Riet. 314p. 1982. 59.00 (*0-444-86374-5*, North Holland) Elsevier.

Distributed Data Sharing Systems: Proceedings of the Third International Seminar Held in Parma, Italy, 28-30 March, 1984. Ed. by F. A. Schreiber & Witold Litwin. 246p. 1985. 64.00 (*0-444-87637-5*, North Holland) Elsevier.

Distributed Database Systems. David Bell. (C). 1992. text ed. 39.75 (*0-201-54400-8*) Addison-Wesley.

Distributed Databases: Principles & Systems. S. Ceri & G. Pelagatti. 1984. text ed. write for info. (*0-07-010829-3*) McGraw.

Distributed Databases, Cooperative Processing, & Networking. Shaku Atre. 304p. 1992. 44.95 (*0-8306-2554-2*, TAB/TPR) TAB Bks.

Distributed Databases, Cooperative Processing & Networking. Shaku Atre. 1992. text ed. 55.00 (*0-07-157673-8*) McGraw.

D

An Asterisk (*) at the beginning of an entry indicates that the title is appearing in BIP for the first time.

Distributed Databases in Real-Time Control: Proceedings of the IFAC - IFIP Workshop, Budapest, Hungary, 16-18 October 1989. Ed. by Elod Knuth & Mike G. Rodd. LC 90-7277. (IFAC Publication Ser.: No. 9006). 80p. 1990. 77.00 (*0-08-040504-5*, Pergamon Pr) Elsevier.

Distributed Decision Making: Cognitive Models for Cooperative Work. Ed. by Jens Rasmussen et al. (New Technologies & Work Ser.). 397p. 1991. text ed. 142.95 (*0-471-92828-3*) Wiley.

Distributed Decision Making: Report of a Workshop. 74p. (C). 1990. pap. text ed. 15.00 (*0-309-04199-6*) Natl Acad Pr.

Distributed Development Environment: The Art of Using CASE. Ed. by S. Holloway. (Illus.). 314p. 1991. 97.95 (*0-442-31293-8*) Chapman & Hall.

Distributed Environments: Software Paradigms & Workstations. Ed. by Y. Ohno. (Illus.). xi, 322p. 1991. 117.00 (*0-387-70075-7*) Spr-Verlag.

Distributed Information Processing & IBM's Systems Application Architecture. Bradley B. Young. (Illus.). 320p. 1991. 39.95 (*0-8306-2556-9*) TAB Bks.

Distributed Information Systems & IBM's Systems Application Architecture. Bradley B. Young. 1992. text ed. 39.95 (*0-07-157745-9*) McGraw.

***Distributed Interactive Simulation Systems for Simulation & Training in the Aerospace Environment.** Ed. by Thomas L. Clarke. LC 95-10060. (Critical Reviews of Optical Science & Technology Ser.: Vol. CR58). 1995. write for info. (*0-8194-1850-1*) SPIE.

Distributed Memory Computing: 2nd European Conference, EDMCC2 Munich, FRG, April 22-24, 1991 Proceedings. Ed. by A. Bode. (Lecture Notes in Computer Science Ser.: Vol. 487). xv, 506p. 1991. pap. 51.00 (*0-387-53951-4*) Spr-Verlag.

Distributed Micro Minicomputer Systems: Structure, Implementation & Application. Cay Weitzman. (Illus.). 1980. text ed. 69.00 (*0-13-216481-7*) P-H.

Distributed Multimedia Through Broadband Communication Services. Daniel Minoli & Robert Keinath. LC 93-31143. 1993. 69.00 (*0-89006-689-2*) Artech Hse.

Distributed Mutual Exclusion Algorithm. S. Das & P. Srimani. 168p. 1993. pap. 35.00 (*0-8186-3380-8*, 3380) IEEE Comp Soc.

Distributed Object Management. M. Tamer Ozsu et al. LC 93-31654. 500p. 1993. pap. 49.95 (*1-55860-256-9*) Morgan Kaufmann.

Distributed Object Oriented Data-Systems Design. Prabhat K. Andleigh & Michael A. Gretzinger. 448p. 1992. text ed. 55.00 (*0-13-174913-7*) P-H.

Distributed Open Systems. F. M. Brazier & D. Johansen. LC 93-29386. 192p. 1993. text ed. 40.00 (*0-8186-4292-0*) IEEE Comp Soc.

***Distributed Operating Systems.** Andrew S. Tanenbaum. LC 94-27646. 1994. text ed. 57.00 (*0-13-219908-4*) P-H.

Distributed Parameter Control Systems: Trends & Applications. Ed. by Goong Chen et al. (Lecture Notes in Pure & Applied Mathematics Ser.: Vol. 128). 544p. 1991. 165.00 (*0-8247-8444-8*) Dekker.

Distributed Parameter Systems. Ed. by F. Kappel et al. (Lecture Notes in Control & Information Sciences Ser.: Vol. 102). vii, 343p. 1987. pap. 57.00 (*0-387-18468-6*) Spr-Verlag.

Distributed Parameter Systems: Identification, Estimation & Control. Ed. by Ray & Lainiotis. (Control & Systems Theory Ser.: Vol. 6). 616p. 1978. 195.00 (*0-8247-6601-6*) Dekker.

Distributed Parameter Systems: Theory & Applications. Sigeru Omatu & John H. Seinfeld. (Oxford Mathematical Monographs). (Illus.). 448p. 1989. 95.00 (*0-19-853295-4*) OUP.

Distributed Parameter Systems - Modelling & Simulation: Proceedings of the IMACS - IFAC International Symposium. Ed. by T. Futagami et al. 610p. 1989. 128.25 (*0-444-87278-7*, North Holland) Elsevier.

Distributed Processing: Proceedings of the IFIP WG10.3 Conference, Amsterdam, the Netherlands, 5-7 Oct., 1987. Ed. by M. H. Barton et al. 642p. 1988. 110.25 (*0-444-70419-1*) Elsevier.

Distributed Processing Systems. Robert J. Thierauf. (Illus.). 1978. pap. text ed. write for info. (*0-13-216507-4*) P-H.

Distributed Processing Systems: End of the Mainframe Era? Judson Breslin & Bradley C. Tashenberg. LC 77-16398. 240p. reprint ed. pap. 68.40 (*0-317-26022-7*, 2023892) Bks Demand.

***Distributed Programming Paradigma with Cryptography Applications.** J. S. Greenfield. (Lecture Notes in Computer Science: Vol. 870). xi, 182p. 1994. 33.00 (*3-540-58496-X*) Spr-Verlag.

***Distributed Programming Paradigms with Cryptography Applications.** Jonathan S. Greenfield. LC 94-36101. (Lecture Notes in Computer Science: Vol. 870). 1994. write for info. (*0-387-58496-X*) Spr-Verlag.

Distributed Simulation 1985--Multi '85, Vol. 15, No. 2. 112p. 1985. 40.00 (*0-685-43838-4*, SS15-2) Soc Computer Sim.

Distributed Simulation, 1988. Ed. by Brian Unger & David Jefferson. (Simulation Ser.: Vol. 19, No. 3). (Illus.). 194p. (C). 1988. 40.00 (*0-911801-25-1*, SS19-3) Soc Computer Sim.

Distributed Simulation, 1989. Ed. by Brian Unger & Richard Fujimoto. (Simulation Ser.: Vol. 21, No. 2). 204p. 1989. 48.00 (*0-911801-29-4*, SS21-2) Soc Computer Sim.

Distributed Simulation, 1990. Ed. by David Nicol & Richard Fujimoto. (Simulation Ser.: Vol. 22, No. 1). 230p. 1990. 50.00 (*0-911801-62-6*, SS22-1) Soc Computer Sim.

Distributed-Software Engineering. Sol M. Shatz. Ed. by Jai-Ping Wang. LC 88-45745. 279p. 1989. 9.95 (*0-8186-8856-4*, 856) IEEE Comp Soc.

Distributed Systems. Ed. by M. Paul & H. J. Siegert. (Lecture Notes in Computer Science Ser.: Vol. 190). vi, 573p. 1988. pap. 55.00 (*0-387-15216-4*) Spr-Verlag.

Distributed Systems. 2nd ed. Sape Mullender. (C). 1993. text ed. 49.50 (*0-201-62427-3*) Addison-Wesley.

***Distributed Systems: Application Development.** 442p. 1994. pap. 10.00 (*0-11-330623-7*, HM06237, Pub. by HMSO UK) UNIPUB.

Distributed Systems: Architecture & Implementation, An Advanced Course. Ed. by B. W. Lampson et al. (Springer Study Edition Ser.). 510p. 1988. pap. 41.00 (*0-387-12116-1*) Spr-Verlag.

Distributed Systems: Concepts & Design. George Coulouris & Jean Dollimore. (International Computer Science Ser.). (Illus.). 320p. (C). 1988. text ed. 43.25 (*0-201-18059-6*) Addison-Wesley.

Distributed Systems: Concepts & Design. 2nd ed. George Coulouris. (C). 1994. text ed. 49.50 (*0-201-62433-8*) Addison-Wesley.

Distributed Systems & Computer Networks. Joel Sloman & Kramer. (Illus.). 416p. (C). 1987. text ed. 87.00 (*0-13-215864-7*) P-H.

Distributed Systems Management. Alwyn Langsford. (C). 1993. text ed. 43.95 (*0-201-63176-8*) Addison-Wesley.

Distributed Systems, Vol. 2: Distributed Database Systems. Ed. by Wesley W. Chu. LC 86-70445. 527p. reprint ed. pap. 150.20 (*0-7837-1336-3*, 2041484) Bks Demand.

Distributed Training of Armor Officers. John D. Winkler et al. LC 93-4140. 1993. write for info. (*0-8330-1378-5*, MR-118-A) Rand Corp.

Distributed Window Systems: A Practical Guide to X11 & News. Allan Davison. (C). 1992. text ed. 37.75 (*0-201-41637-9*) Addison-Wesley.

Distributing Applications Across DCE & Windows NT. Ward Rosenberry & Jim Teague. 302p. 1993. pap. 24.95 (*1-56592-047-3*) OReilly & Assocs.

Distributing Georgia's General Purpose Local- Option Sales Tax Revenue. Dan W. Durning. 38p. (Orig.). 1992. pap. 5.00 (*0-89854-156-5*) U of GA Inst Govt.

Distributing Operating System. Ed. by Yacup Paker et al. (NATO Asi Series F: Vol. 28). x, 379p. 1987. 91.00 (*0-387-17699-3*) Spr-Verlag.

Distributing Risk: Insurance, Legal Theory, & Public Policy. Kenneth S. Abraham. LC 85-22459. 319p. 1986. 34.00 (*0-300-03460-1*) Yale U Pr.

Distribution Age: A Study of the Economy of Modern Distribution. Ralph Borsodi. LC 75-39235. (Getting & Spending: the Consumer's Dilemma Ser.). (Illus.). 1976. reprint ed. 29.95 (*0-405-08011-5*) Ayer.

Distribution, Allocation, Social Structure & Spatial Form: Elements of Planning Theory. Portugali. (Progress in Planning Ser.: Vol. 14, Part 3). (Illus.). 83p. 1980. pap. 16.25 (*0-08-026808-0*, Pergamon Pr) Elsevier.

Distribution & Abundance of Some Epibenthic Invertebrates of Cook Inlet, Alaska. Feder & Paul. (IMS Report Ser.: No. R80-3). 167p. 12.00 (*0-914500-11-2*) U of AK Inst Marine.

Distribution & Abundance of the Tsetse. J. Glasgow & G. A. Kerkut. LC 63-16861. (International Series of Monographs on Pure & Applied Mathematics: Vol. 20). 1963. 109.00 (*0-08-010074-0*, Pub. by Pergamon Repr UK) Franklin.

Distribution & Behavior of the Spadefoot Toad in Connecticut. Stanley C. Ball. (Connecticut Academy of Arts & Sciences Ser., Trans.: Vol. 32). 1936. pap. 39.50 (*0-685-44367-1*) Elliots Bks.

Distribution & Biogeography of Mammals of Iowa. John B. Bowles. (Special Publications: No. 9). (Illus.). 184p. (Orig.). 1975. pap. 12.00 (*0-89672-034-9*) Tex Tech Univ Pr.

***Distribution & Ecology of Stream Fishes of the Sacramento-San Joaquin Drainage System, California.** Peter B. Moyle et al. LC 81-13072. (University of California Publications in Zoology: No. 115). 266p. 1982. pap. 75.90 (*0-7837-7495-8*, 2049217) Bks Demand.

Distribution & Ecology of Vascular Plants in a Tropical Rain Forest. J. B. Hall & M. D. Swaine. (Geobotany Ser.: Vol. I). 392p. 1981. lib. bdg. 210.00 (*90-6193-681-0*) Kluwer Ac.

Distribution & Functions of Mental Imagery. George H. Betts. LC 76-176560. (Columbia University. Teachers College. Contributions to Education Ser.: No. 26). reprint ed. 37.50 (*0-404-55026-6*) AMS Pr.

Distribution & Marketing: Thirty-First Annual Advanced Antitrust Seminar. (Corporate Law & Practice Course Handbook, 1985-86 Ser.). 560p. 1992. pap. 70.00 (*0-685-69414-3*) PLI.

Distribution & Properties of Clinoptilolite-Bearing Tuffs in the Upper Jurassic Morrison Formation on the Ute Mountain Ute Reservation, Southwestern Colorado & Northwestern New Mexico. Paula L. Hansley & Richard A. Sheppard. 1994. write for info. (*0-318-70182-0*) US Geol Survey.

Distribution & Redistribution of Income: A Mathematical Analysis. 2nd ed. Peter J. Lambert. LC 93-17870. 1993. text ed. 24.95 (*0-7190-4059-0*, Pub. by Manchester Univ Pr UK) St Martin.

Distribution & Taxonomy of Birds of the World, 2 vols., Set. Charles G. Sibley & Bury L. Monroe, Jr. (Illus.). 1136p. (C). 1991. text ed. 125.00 (*0-300-04969-2*) Yale U Pr.

Distribution & Variability of Ceratium in the Northern & Western Pacific. A. Bohm. (BMB Ser.). 1931. pap. 15.00 (*0-527-02193-8*) Periodicals Srv.

Distribution, Biology & Management of Exotic Fishes. Ed. by Walter R. Courtenay, Jr. & Jay R. Stauffer, Jr. LC 83-18723. 448p. 1984. 65.00x (*0-8018-3037-0*) Johns Hopkins.

Distribution Channel Analysis of Desktops, Portables & Commercial Workstations: Understanding Distribution Patterns Is the Key to Survival. Market Intelligence Staff. 234p. 1993. 1,295.00 (*1-56753-428-7*) Frost & Sullivan.

Distribution Channel Strategy for Export Marketing: The Case of Hong Kong Firms. T. S. Chan. Ed. by Richard N. Farmer. LC 83-18158. (Research for Business Decisions Ser.: No. 67). 140p. reprint ed. 39.90 (*0-8357-1494-2*, 2070368) Bks Demand.

Distribution Channels & Institutions. Ed. by Louis P. Bucklin & James M. Carmen. (Research in Marketing Ser.: Vol. 8). 402p. 1986. 73.25 (*0-89232-549-6*) Jai Pr.

Distribution Clerk - Machine (U. S. P. S.) Jack Rudman. (Career Examination Ser.: C-2255). 1994. pap. 19.95 (*0-8373-2255-3*) Nat Learn.

Distribution Conference Proceedings. 90p. 50.00 (*0-318-14118-3*, P36) Food Marketing.

Distribution Consultant: A Managerial Guide to Their Identification, Selection & Use. Paul H. Zinszer & James R. Stock. 1983. 25.00 (*0-931880-03-3*) U OK Ctr Econ.

Distribution Cost Analysis. Donald R. Longman. Ed. by Henry Assael. LC 78-235. (Century of Marketing Ser.). 1979. reprint ed. lib. bdg. 25.95 (*0-405-11167-3*) Ayer.

Distribution Discs for ALT4.IBM: (Short Reference USR1.I), Vol. 1. Jerry Irvine. (C). 1990. pap. text ed. 2.00 (*0-912468-23-8*) CA Rocketry.

Distribution Discs for ALT4.IBM: (Short Reference USR2.I), Vol. 2. Jerry Irvine. (C). 1992. pap. text ed. 2.00 (*0-912468-24-6*) CA Rocketry.

Distribution Division Six of the Organization Executive Course see Organization Executive Course

Distribution-Free Statistics: An Applications-Oriented Approach. J. Krauth. (Techniques in the Behavioral & Neural Sciences Ser.: Vol. 2). 350p. 1988. 179.50 (*0-444-80934-1*) Elsevier.

Distribution Handbook. Ed. by James F. Robeson & Robert G. House. LC 83-49340. 978p. (C). 1984. 95.00 (*0-02-922700-3*) Free Pr.

Distribution Inventory Management for the 1990s! Gordon Graham. 350p. 1988. 59.00 (*0-317-01548-6*) Management Pr.

Distribution Inventory Management Training Aid. Donald W. Fogarty. LC 83-73025. 14p. 1984. 25.00 (*0-935406-39-5*) Am Prod & Inventory.

Distribution Law. Theodore L. Banks. 1989. 145.00 (*0-316-08023-3*) Little.

Distribution Law for the Practitioner. Theodore M. Banks. write for info. (*0-318-59310-6*) Little.

Distribution Management: Mathematical Modelling & Practical Analysis. S. Eilon et al. (Illus.). 240p. 1982. pap. text ed. 36.00 (*0-85264-191-5*) Lubrecht & Cramer.

Distribution Management Handbook. James A. Tompkins & Dale Harmelink. LC 93-2309. 1993. text ed. 79.50 (*0-07-065046-2*) McGraw.

Distribution Maps of Certain Plants in Ohio. E. N. Transeau & P. E. Williams. (Bulletin Ser.: No. 20). 1929. 2.00 (*0-86727-019-5*) Ohio Bio Survey.

Distribution Network Analysis for Water Utilities, No. M32. 112p. 1989. pap. 24.00 (*0-89867-457-3*, 30032) Am Water Wks Assn.

Distribution of Aboriginal Tribes & Languages in Northwestern Mexico. Carl O. Sauer. LC 76-43818. (Ibero-Americana Ser.: No. 5). reprint ed. 36.50 (*0-404-15671-1*) AMS Pr.

***Distribution of African Social Message Films & Videos: 1988 - April 1994.** Steve Smith & Christine Schlegel. (Illus.). 40p. 1995. write for info. (*0-614-05447-8*) Devel Self Rel.

Distribution of Air Quality in the New York Region. Jeffrey M. Zupan. LC 73-8141. (Illus.). 102p. reprint ed. pap. 29.10 (*0-317-10677-5*, 2020969) Bks Demand.

Distribution of Amphibians & Reptiles in Riverside County, California. H. S. Glaser. (Illus.). 40p. 1970. pap. 1.00 (*0-935661-03-4*) Riverside Mus Pr.

Distribution of Breeding Birds of Ohio. Lawrence E. Hicks. (Bulletin Ser.: No. 32). 1935. 2.00 (*0-86727-031-4*) Ohio Bio Survey.

Distribution of Cataracts in the Population & Influencing Factors. Ed. by K. Sasaki & O. Hockwin. (Developments in Ophthalmology Ser.: Vol. 21). (Illus.). viii, 182p. 1991. 148.00 (*3-8055-5335-8*) S Karger.

Distribution of Correlation Coefficients. H. Thomas. (Illus.). 115p. 1989. pap. 54.00 (*0-387-96863-6*) Spr-Verlag.

Distribution of Distances in Pregeographical Space. J. H. Kuiper. (Spatial Analysis Ser.). 300p. 1986. text ed. 75.00 (*0-566-05214-8*, Pub. by Avebury Pub UK) Ashgate Pub Co.

Distribution of Economic Well-Being. Conference on Economic Well-Being (1974: University of Michigan). Ed. by F. Thomas Juster. LC 76-58909. (Studies in Income & Wealth: No. 41). reprint ed. pap. 160.00 (*0-317-55568-5*, 2056363) Bks Demand.

Distribution of Farm Subsidies: Who Gets the Benefits? Charles L. Schultze. LC 75-156901. (Brookings Institution Staff Paper Ser.). 61p. reprint ed. pap. 25.00 (*0-317-26361-7*, 2025406) Bks Demand.

Distribution of Federal Funds for Vocational Education to Community, Technical, & Junior Colleges. Thomas H. McKinney & Dale A. Davis. LC 88-170893. (AACJC-ACCT Keeping America Working Task Force Ser.: No. 6). 70p. reprint ed. pap. 25.00 (*0-7837-2480-2*, 2042636) Bks Demand.

Distribution of Illinois Vascular Plants. Robert H. Mohlenbrock & Douglas M. Ladd. LC 77-15987. (Illus.). 289p. (Orig.). 1978. pap. 12.95 (*0-8093-0848-7*) S Ill U Pr.

Distribution of Income & Wealth in Korea. Danny M. Leipziger et al. LC 92-14468. (EDI Development Studies). 135p. 1992. 9.95 (*0-8213-2124-2*, 12124) World Bank.

Distribution of Income & Wealth in Ontario: Theory & Evidence. Charles M. Beach et al. (Ontario Economic Council Research Studies). 1981. pap. 10.95 (*0-8020-3369-5*) U of Toronto Pr.

Distribution of Income in China. Ed. by Keith Griffin & Zhao Renwei. LC 93-7939. 1993. text ed. 49.95 (*0-312-10022-1*) St Martin.

Distribution of Incomes in the United States. Frank H. Streightoff. LC 68-56688. (Columbia University. Studies in the Social Sciences: No. 129). reprint ed. 31.50 (*0-404-51129-5*) AMS Pr.

Distribution of Industrial Occupations in England, 1841-1861. Clive Day. (Connecticut Academy of Arts & Sciences Ser., Trans.: Vol. 28). 1927. pap. 75.00 (*0-685-44360-4*) Elliots Bks.

Distribution of Information: How to Select the Appropriate Technology. Claude Fleury & Yvon Bernatchez. (Orig.). 1993. pap. 38.95 (*0-660-14991-5*, Pub. by Canada Commun Grp CN) Accents Pubns.

Distribution of Land, Employment & Income in Rural Egypt. Iliya Harik & Susan Randolph. (Special Series on Landlessness & Near-Landlessness: No. 5). 166p. (Orig.). (C). 1979. pap. text ed. 9.55 (*0-86731-072-3*) Cornell CIS RDC.

Distribution of Living & Fossil Foraminifera & Their Use in the Interpretation of the Post-Pleistocene History of Little Lake, San Salvador Island, Bahamas. Patricia A. Bowman & James W. Teeter. (Occasional Papers - 1982: No. 2). 27p. 1982. pap. text ed. 2.25 (*0-935909-05-2*) Bahamian.

Distribution of Living & Fossil Ostracoda & Their Use in the Interpretation of the Post-Pleistocene History of Little Lake, San Slavador Island, Bahamas. Daniel B. Sanger & James W. Teeter. (Occasional Papers - 1982: No. 1). 26p. 1982. pap. text ed. 1.50 (*0-935909-04-4*) Bahamian.

Distribution of Matrimonial Assets on Divorce. 3rd ed. Michael L. Rakusen et al. 1989. boxed 122.00 (*0-406-51021-0*, UK) Butterworth Legal Pubs.

Distribution of Middle Woodland Sites Within the Environment of the Lower Sangamon River, Illinois. Donna C. Roper. (Reports of Investigations Ser.: No. 30). (Illus.). 22p. 1974. pap. 1.00 (*0-89792-054-6*) Ill St Museum.

Distribution of Native Grasses in California. Alan A. Beetle. (Illus.). 52p. 1987. reprint ed. pap. 4.50 (*0-933421-11-7*) Redwood Seed.

Distribution of Opportunity for Participation Among the Various Pupils in Classroom Recitations. Ernest Horn. LC 77-176878. (Columbia University. Teachers College. Contributions to Education Ser.: No. 67). reprint ed. 37.50 (*0-404-55067-3*) AMS Pr.

Distribution of Ownership. Joseph H. Underwood. LC 68-56691. (Columbia University. Studies in the Social Sciences: No. 77). 1968. reprint ed. 37.50 (*0-404-51077-9*) AMS Pr.

Distribution of Personal Wealth in Britain. Anthony B. Atkinson & A. J. Harrison. LC 77-2715. 344p. reprint ed. pap. 98.10 (*0-318-34757-1*, 2031617) Bks Demand.

Distribution of Positive Definite Quadratic Forms: Confidence Limits on the Correlation Coefficient. B. K. Shah & R. Odeh. LC 74-6283. (Selected Tables in Mathematical Statistics Ser.: Vol. 10). 347p. 1986. text ed. 50.00 (*0-8218-1910-0*, TABLES-10) Am Math.

Distribution of Power & Rewards: Proceedings of the International Conference on Democracy & Social Justice. Ed. by James C. Hsiung & Chung-Ying Cheng. 462p. (C). 1991. lib. bdg. 63.50 (*0-8191-7969-8*, Contemporary US Asia Rsch Inst) U Pr of Amer.

Distribution of Power to Regulate Interstate Carriers Between the Nation & the States. George G. Reynolds. LC 68-57578. (Columbia University. Studies in the Social Sciences: No. 295). reprint ed. 28.50 (*0-404-51295-X*) AMS Pr.

Distribution of Prime Numbers. A. E. Ingham. (Mathematical Library). (Illus.). 114p. (C). 1990. pap. 19.95 (*0-521-39789-8*) Cambridge U Pr.

Distribution of Productive Forces: Theory & Practice. V. Mozhin. 326p. (C). 1988. 70.00 (*0-685-31521-5*, Pub. by Collets UK) Pro-Am Music.

Distribution of Recent Benthic Foraminifera off the North American Pacific Coast from California to Baja. Stephen J. Culver. LC 86-600087. (Smithsonian Contributions to the Marine Sciences Ser.: No. 28). 638p. reprint ed. pap. 180.00 (*0-317-58132-5*, 2029683) Bks Demand.

Distribution of Recent Benthic Foraminifera off the North American Pacific Coast from Oregon to Alaska. Martin A. Buzas & Stephen Culver. LC 85-600001. (Smithsonian Contributions to the Marine Sciences Ser.: No. 26). 238p. reprint ed. pap. 67.90 (*0-317-41860-2*, 2026176) Bks Demand.

Distribution of Shallow-Water Marine Mollusca, Yucatan Peninsula, Mexico. Vokes & Vokes Staff. LC 83-62103. (Publication Ser.: No. 54). (Illus.). viii, 183p. 1983. pap. 25.00 (*0-939238-83-7*) Tulane MARI.

Distribution of Social Service Facilities Within the City of Philadelphia. Robert E. Coughlin et al. (Discussion Paper Ser.: No. 93). 1976. pap. 10.00 (*1-55869-027-1*) Regional Sci Res Inst.

Distribution of Subcutaneous Fat in Childhood & Adolescence. E. L. Reynolds. (SRCD Ser.: Vol. 15, No. 2). 1950. 16.00 (*0-527-01551-2*) Periodicals Srv.

D

An Asterisk (*) at the beginning of an entry indicates that the title is appearing in BIP for the first time.

An Asterisk (*) at the beginning of an entry indicates that the title is appearing in BIP for the first time.

2045

Disturbances in Lipid & Lipoprotein Metabolism. Ed. by John M. Dietschy et al. (Clinical Psychology Ser.). (Illus.). 303p. 1988. 45.00 (*0-19-520694-0*) OUP.

Disturbances in Neurogenic Control of the Circulation. Ed. by Francois M. Abboud et al. (Coping Ser.). (Illus.). 288p. 1988. 42.50 (*0-19-520691-6*) OUP.

Disturbances in the Field. Lynne S. Schwartz. 416p. 1985. pap. 10.95 (*0-553-34377-7*) Bantam.

Disturbances in the Linear Model: Estimation & Hypothesis Testing. C. Dubbelman. 1978. pap. 16.00 (*90-207-0772-8*) Kluwer Ac.

Disturbances of Lower & Higher Visual Capacities Caused by Occipital Damage: With Special Reference to the Psychopathological, Pedagogical, Industrial, & Social Implications. W. Poppelreuter. Tr. by J. Zihl. (History of Neuroscience Ser.: No. 2). (Illus.). 392p. 1991. 47.50 (*0-19-852190-1*) OUP.

Disturbances of Nervous Function see Handbook of Clinical Neurology

Disturbances of Water & Electrolyte Metabolism. Ed. by J. Bahlmann & J. Brod. (Contributions to Nephrology Ser.: Vol. 21). (Illus.). 1980. pap. 60.00 (*3-8055-0215-X*) S Karger.

Disturbed Children: Examination & Assessment Through Team Process. Menninger Foundation, Children's Division Staff. LC 68-54941. (Jossey-Bass Behavioral Science Ser.). 318p. reprint ed. pap. 90.70 (*0-317-41977-3*, 2025677) Bks Demand.

***Disturbed Ground.** Carla Norton. 440p. 1995. mass mkt. 5.50 (*0-380-71188-5*) Avon.

Disturbed Ground: The True Story of the Arsenic & Old Lace Case. Carla Norton. 1994. 23.00 (*0-688-09704-9*) Morrow.

Disturbed State of the Russian Realm. Conrad Bussow. Ed. & Tr. by G. Edward Orchard. (Illus.). 244p. 1994. 44.95 (*0-7735-1165-2*, Pub. by McGill CN) U of Toronto Pr.

Disturbed Subject: Epistemological & Ethical Implication of Reactivity in Videotape Research. Jeffrey Roth. (American University Studies: Psychology: Ser. VIII, Vol. 20). 144p. 1990. text ed. 30.50 (*0-8204-1150-7*) P Lang Pubs.

Disturbed Violent Offender. Hans Toch & Kenneth Adams. LC 89-5771. 176p. (C). 1989. text ed. 30.00 (*0-300-04533-6*) Yale U Pr.

***Disturbed Violent Offender.** rev. ed. Hans Toch & Kenneth Adams. 252p. 1994. pap. text ed. 19.95 (*1-55798-260-0*, 431-6470) Am Psychol.

Disturbed Violent Offender. Hans Toch & Kenneth Adams. 230p. (C). 1991. reprint ed. pap. text ed. 18.00 (*0-300-05148-4*) Yale U Pr.

Disturber of the Peace: The Life of H. L. Mencken. 2nd ed. William Manchester. LC 86-6999. (Illus.). 376p. 1986. pap. 18.95 (*0-87023-544-3*) U of Mass Pr.

Disturbing Pleasures: Learning Popular Culture. Henry A. Giroux. LC 93-36255. 1994. write for info. (*0-415-90900-7*, Routledge NY); pap. write for info. (*0-415-90901-5*, Routledge NY) Routledge.

Disturbing the Nest: Family Change & Decline in Modern Societies. David Popenoe. (Social Institutions & Social Change Ser.). 407p. (Orig.). 1988. lib. bdg. 56.95 (*0-202-30350-0*); pap. text ed. 29.95 (*0-202-30351-9*) Aldine de Gruyter.

Disturbing the Peace. Vaclav Havel. LC 90-55678. 256p. 1991. 11.00 (*0-679-73402-3*, Vin) Random.

Disturbing the Peace: A Conversation with Karel Hvizdala. Vaclav Havel. 1990. 19.95 (*0-685-46183-1*) Knopf.

Disturbing the Peace: The Way of Disciples. Eamonn Bredin. 290p. (Orig.). 1991. pap. 9.95 (*0-948183-00-4*, Pub. by Columba Pr IE) Twenty-Third.

Disturbing the Universe. Freeman J. Dyson. 304p. 1981. reprint ed. pap. text ed. 15.00 (*0-465-01677-4*) Basic.

Disturbing the Universe see Innenansichten: Erinnerungen in die Zukunft

Disulfiram & Its Metabolite, Dithiocarb: Pharmacology & Status in the Treatment of Alcoholism, Human Immunodeficiency Virus Infections & Heavy Metal Intoxication. P. K. Gessner & T. Gessner. 176p. 1991. 99.95 (*0-412-36010-1*, A4752) Chapman & Hall.

Disunion & Restoration in Tennessee. John R. Neal. LC 78-164390. (Black Heritage Library Collection). 1977. reprint ed. 15.95 (*0-8369-8849-3*) Ayer.

Disuniting of America. Arthur M. Schlesinger, Jr. 160p. 1992. 15.95 (*0-393-03380-5*) Norton.

Disuniting of America: Reflections on a Multicultural Society. Arthur M. Schlesinger, Jr. 160p. 1993. pap. 7.95 (*0-393-30987-8*) Norton.

Disuniting of America: Reflections on a Multicultural Society. Arthur M. Schlesinger, Jr. LC 91-65510. (Larger Agenda Ser.). (Illus.). 92p. 1991. 11.95 (*1-879736-00-4*) Whittle Comns.

***Disunity of Science: Boundaries, Contexts & Power.** Ed. by Peter Galison & David J. Stump. 508p. (C). 1995. 65.00 (*0-8047-2436-9*); pap. 24.95 (*0-8047-2562-4*) Stanford Univ Committee on Linguistics.

Dit. Mark Dunster. LC 78-100964. 1978. pap. 4.00 (*0-89642-004-3*) Linden Pubs.

Dita Saxova. Arnost Lustig. 320p. 1994. 49.95 (*0-8101-1131-4*); pap. 17.95 (*0-8101-1132-2*) Northwestern U Pr.

Ditado. Ildazio Tavares. (ENG & POR.). 1981. pap. 1.50 (*0-686-28966-8*) Ghost Dance.

Ditch Medicine: Advanced Field Procedures for Emergencies. Hugh L. Coffee. (Illus.). 224p. 1993. pap. 25.00 (*0-87364-717-3*) Paladin Pr.

***Ditchdigger's Daughters: A Black Family's Astonishing Success Story.** Yvonne S. Thornton. (Illus.). 288p. 1995. 19.95 (*1-55972-271-1*, Birch Ln Pr) Carol Pub Group.

***Ditched Blonde: A Carl Wilcox Mystery.** Harold Adams. LC 95-11743. 168p. 1995. 19.95 (*0-8027-3263-1*) Walker & Co.

Ditches of Edison County. Ronald R. Roberts. 1993. pap. 7.00 (*0-452-27256-4*, Plume) NAL-Dutton.

Ditches of Edison County. Ronald R. Roberts. LC 93-37206. 1993. write for info. (*0-525-27256-9*, Plume) NAL-Dutton.

Ditches, Stumps & Boulders. Albert E. Teller & John R. Dasef. (Blasting Techniques Ser.: No. 2). 61p. 1986. pap. 20.00 (*0-940427-02-8*) Explosive Servs.

***Ditching Your Debts.** G. B. Clark. LC 94-73082. 150p. (Orig.). (C). 1995. pap. text ed. 14.95 (*1-55950-112-X*, 76049) Loompanics.

Diterpense of Flowering Plants One. F. Seaman et al. (Illus.). vi, 638p. 1989. 149.00 (*0-387-97058-4*) Spr-Verlag.

Dither Farm. Sid Hite. LC 91-31323. 224p. (YA). (gr. 7 up). 1992. 15.95 (*0-8050-1871-9*, Bks Young Read) H Holt & Co.

Dithmarschen, A Medieval Peasant Republic. William L. Urban. LC 91-24906. (Mediaeval Studies: Vol. 7). (Illus.). 180p. 1991. lib. bdg. 79.95 (*0-7734-9783-8*) E Mellen.

Dithyrambographi Graeci. Ed. by Dana F. Sutton. 144p. 1989. write for info. (*3-615-00034-X*, Pub. by Georg Olms GW) Lubrecht & Cramer.

Dithyrambs of Dionysus. Friedrich Nietzsche. Ed. & Tr. by R. J. Hollingdale. (Austrian-German Culture Ser.). 96p. 1984. 25.00 (*0-933806-15-9*) Black Swan CT.

Ditka: An Autobiography. Mike Ditka & Don Pierson. LC 86-70706. 283p. 1986. 16.95 (*0-933893-07-8*); pap. 7.95 (*0-933893-38-8*); audio 7.95 (*0-933893-39-6*) Bonus Books.

Ditka: Monster of the Midway. Armen Keteyian. Ed. by Doug Grad. 456p. 1993. reprint ed. mass mkt. 5.99 (*0-671-75000-3*) PB.

Dittersdorfiana. Carl Krebs. LC 72-166092. (Music Ser.). 1972. reprint ed. lib. bdg. 29.50 (*0-306-70259-2*) Da Capo.

DIU Guide a l'Intention des Programmes de Planification Familiale. rev. ed. Ed. by Noel McIntosh et al. (Illus.). 160p. (FRE.). 1993. pap. text ed. 6.00 (*0-929817-03-6*) JHPIEGO.

Diuretic Drug Cessation in General Practice: Withdrawing Diuretic Drugs Prescribed for Ankle Oedema. Jan-Willem De Jonge. 183p. 1993. pap. 23.50 (*90-5170-221-3*, Pub. by Thesis Pubs NE) IBD Ltd.

Diuretica. Ed. by H. Herken. (Handbook of Experimental Pharmacology Ser.: Vol. 24). (Illus.). xix, 764p. 1969. 194.00 (*0-387-04520-1*) Spr-Verlag.

***Diuretics.** O. S. Better et al. Ed. by R. F. Gregor et al. LC 95-3116. (Handbook of Experimental Pharmacology Ser.: Vol. 117). 1995. write for info. (*0-387-58965-1*) Spr-Verlag.

Diuretics: Physiology, Pharmacology & Clinical Use. John H. Dirks & Roger A. Sutton. (Illus.). 396p. 1986. text ed. 90.50 (*0-7216-1243-1*) Saunders.

Diuretics IV: Chemistry, Pharmacology, & Clinical Applications, Proceedings of the Fourth International Conference on Diuretics, Boca Raton, Florida, 11-16 October 1992. Ed. by Jules B. Puschett & Arthur Greenberg. LC 93-10691. (International Congress Ser.: No. 1023). 1993. 248.50 (*0-444-89630-9*, Excerpta Medica) Elsevier.

Diuretics to Emulsions see Encyclopedia of Chemical Technology

***Diurnal Distribution in Cardiovascular Disease: Prognosis & Therapy.** Ed. by John E. Deanfield & Philippe Sellier. (Journal: Cardiology: Vol. 85, Suppl. 2, 1994). (Illus.). iv, 32p. 1994. pap. 9.75 (*3-8055-6092-3*) S Karger.

Diurnal of Remarkable Occurrents That Have Passed Within the Country of Scotland. Ed. by Thomas Thomson. LC 78-164839. 1833. 37.50 (*0-404-52753-1*) AMS Pr.

Div, Grad, Curl, & All That: An Informal Text on Vector Calculus. 2nd ed. Harry M. Schey. (C). 1992. pap. text ed. 14.95 (*0-393-96251-2*) Norton.

***Diva.** Jeffrey Bowman. 1994. pap. 4.99 (*0-06-100853-2*, Harp PBks) HarpC.

Diva. Stanley B. Clay. (Orig.). (J). (ps-12). 1988. pap. 3.50 (*0-87067-839-6*) Holloway.

Diva: A Novel. Carol Kane. 1991. mass mkt. 5.95 (*0-06-109926-0*, Harp PBks) HarpC.

Diva: Great Sopranos & Mezzos Discuss Their Art. Helena Matheopoulos. 352p. 1992. text ed. 29.95 (*1-55553-132-6*) NE U Pr.

Divan of Gada'i. Janos Eckmann. LC 76-630300. (Uralic & Altaic Ser.: Vol. 113). (Illus.). 538p. (Orig.). 1971. pap. text ed. 23.00 (*0-87750-053-3*) Res Inst Inner Asian Studies.

Divan of Manuchihri Damghani: A Critical Study. Jerome W. Clinton. LC 72-87873. (Studies in Middle Eastern Literatures: No. 1). 1972. pap. 15.00 (*0-88297-001-1*) Bibliotheca.

Divane Parvin E'tesami (The Divan of Parvin E'tesami) rev. ed. Parvin E'tesami. (Mazda Special Persian Langauge Publications). 350p. (PER.). (C). 1987. pap. text ed. 14.95 (*0-939214-38-5*) Mazda Pubs.

Divani Nurbakhsh: Sufi Poetry. Javad Nurbakhsh. Ed. by Jeffrey Rothschild & Paul Weber. Tr. by Alan Godlas et al. LC 80-84113. 265p. (ENG & PER.). 1980. 30.00 (*0-933546-04-1*) KNP.

Dive. Stacey Donovan. 175p. (YA). (gr. 7 up). 1994. 15.99 (*0-525-45154-4*) Dutton Child Bks.

Dive Boats of California: The H & H Guide. 2nd ed. Irene Hashimoto & John Hunt. (Illus.). 176p. (Orig.). 1994. pap. 12.95 (*0-9638682-0-9*) H&H Haliograph.

Dive Bomber: Learning to Fly the Navy's Fighting Planes. Robert A. Winston. LC 90-22874. (Illus.). 192p. 1991. 18.95 (*1-55750-901-8*) Naval Inst Pr.

Dive Computers: A Consumer's Guide to History, Theory & Performance. Ken Loyst et al. 191p. (Orig.). 1991. pap. text ed. 12.95 (*0-922769-09-5*) Watersport Pub.

Dive Control Specialist Instructor Manual. 71p. 1988. reprint ed. pap. text ed. 29.95 (*0-943717-62-0*) Concept Sys.

Dive-First Responder. Richard A. Clinchy. 1994. pap. 27.95 (*0-8016-7525-1*) Mosby Yr Bk.

Dive into History, Vol. 1: Warships. Henry C. Keatts & George Farr. 256p. 1990. 18.95 (*1-55992-039-4*, Pisces Bks) Gulf Pub.

Dive into History, Vol. 2: U. S. Submarines. Henry C. Keatts & George Farr. 256p. 1991. 18.95 (*1-55992-047-5*, Pisces Bks) Gulf Pub.

Dive into History, Vol. 3: U-Boats. Henry Keatts. 252p. 1994. 18.95 (*1-55992-064-5*) Gulf Pub.

Dive Miami: The Complete Divers Guide of Shipwrecks & Reefs off Miami, Florida. Joel Auerbach. LC 91-71064. (Illus.). 80p. (Orig.). 1991. pap. 19.95 (*0-9629330-0-7*) Scuba Pubns.

Dive Rescue Specialist Training Manual. Steve J. Linton et al. 81p. 1986. pap. text ed. 14.95 (*0-943717-42-6*) Concept Sys.

***Dive Right In-The Sharks Won't Bite: The Entrepreneurial Woman's Guide to Success.** Jane Wesman. 208p. 1995. 19.95 (*0-7931-1101-3*) Dearborn Finan.

Dive Supervisor: An Analytical & Practical Approach. Glenn R. Williams. Ed. by Doris Murphy. (Illus.). 100p. 1990. write for info. (*0-9626120-0-6*) PDI Intl.

Dive Through the Wave. Mary Towne. LC 93-40999. (Illus.). 128p. (J). (gr. 3-6). 1994. lib. bdg. 13.95 (*0-8167-3478-X*) BrdgeWater.

Dive to Oblivion. Richard P. Henrick. 352p. 1993. mass mkt. 4.99 (*0-8217-4026-1*) Zebra.

***Diver.** Warren Carrier. (QRL Poetry Book Ser.: Vol. XXVI). 20.00 (*0-614-06414-7*) Quarterly Rev.

Diver Stress & Rescue Instructor Manual. Laurie K. Clark & Dennis Pulley. 60p. 1990. pap. text ed. 19.95 (*0-943717-85-X*) Concept Sys.

Diver Stress & Rescue Manual. 134p. 1990. pap. text ed. 13.95 (*0-943717-84-1*) Concept Sys.

Divergence. Charles Sheffield. (Heritage Universe Ser.: Bk. 2). 288p. 1991. 16.45 (*0-345-36039-7*, Del Rey) Ballantine.

Divergence. Charles Sheffield. (Heritage Universe Ser.: Bk. 2). 1992. mass mkt. 4.99 (*0-345-36938-6*, Del Rey) Ballantine.

Divergent-Passive Margin Basins. Ed. by J. D. Edwards & P. A. Santogrossi. (AAPG Memoir Ser.: No. 48). (Illus.). 252p. 1990. 102.00 (*0-89181-326-8*) AAPG.

***Divergent Realities.** Larson. 1995. pap. 16.00 (*0-465-01663-4*) Basic.

Divergent Realities: The Emotional Lives of Mothers, Fathers, & Adolescents. Reed Larson & Maryse H. Richards. LC 93-46394. 256p. 1994. 26.00 (*0-465-01662-6*) Basic.

Divergent Series. 2nd ed. Godfrey H. Hardy. LC 91-75377. xvi, 396p. (C). 1991. lib. bdg. 28.50 (*0-8284-0334-1*, 334) Chelsea Pub.

Divergent Thinking. Mark A. Runco. (Creativity Research Ser.). 240p. (C). 1991. text ed. 42.50 (*0-89391-700-1*); pap. 24.50 (*0-89391-716-8*) Ablex Pub.

Diverging. Robin Cravey. (Illus.). 64p. (Orig.). 1983. pap. 5.00 (*0-912973-00-5*) Tilted Planet.

Diverging: Poems by Robin Cravey. Robin Cravey. LC 83-5029. (Illus.). 64p. (Orig.). 1984. 12.00 (*0-912973-03-X*); pap. 5.00 (*0-685-09609-2*) Tilted Planet.

Diverging Paths: Comparing a Century of Scandinavian & Latin American Economic Development. Ed. by Magnus Blomstrom & Patricio Meller. 286p. 1991. 21.00 (*0-940602-36-9*) IADB.

Diverging Pathways: Social Structure & Career Deflections. Alan C. Kerckhoff. (Illus.). 268p. (C). 1993. 49.95 (*0-521-43397-5*) Cambridge U Pr.

Diverless & Deepwater Technology, Vol. 19. Ed. by Society for Underwater Technology Staff. (C). 1990. lib. bdg. 110.00 (*1-85333-193-7*, Pub. by Graham & Trotman UK) Kluwer Ac.

Divers. Kendall McDonald. Ed. by Rebecca Stefoff. LC 91-46577. (Living Dangerously Ser.). (Illus.). 32p. (J). (gr. 5-9). 1992. lib. bdg. 17.26 (*1-56074-043-4*) Garrett Ed Corp.

Diver's Almanac: Guide to Florida & the Keys. Philip Z. Trupp. 1991. pap. 24.95 (*0-9628680-0-0*) Triton Pub.

Diver's Almanac: Guide to the West Coast Update. Sandy Frame. Ed. by Rick Baker. LC 84-649716. 204p. 1989. pap. text ed. 24.95 (*0-929887-03-4*) R H Comns.

Diver's & Snorkeler's Guide to the Fishes & Sea Life of the Caribbean, Florida, Bahamas & Bermuda. F. Joseph Stokes. (Illus.). 160p. 1984. reprint ed. 12.95 (*0-910006-46-6*) Acad Nat Sci Phila.

Divers' Guide to Coral Reefs. Elizabeth Wood. 240p. (C). 1990. 125.00 (*0-907151-61-2*, Pub. by IMMEL Pubng UK) St Mut.

Diver's Guide to Fishes of the Maldives. John E. Randall. 192p. (C). 1990. 125.00 (*0-907151-53-1*, Pub. by IMMEL Pubng UK) St Mut.

Diver's Guide to Florida & the Florida Keys. Jim Stachowicz. LC 76-12928. (Illus.). 64p. (Orig.). 1994. pap. 5.95 (*0-89317-007-0*) Windward Pub.

Divers Guide to Long Island Waters. Les Glick. LC 90-81580. (Illus.). 70p. (Orig.). 1990. pap. 14.95 (*0-9626492-0-1*) Amphilbian Enterprises.

Divers' Guide to Michigan. Steve E. Harrington. (Illus.). 300p. 1990. 19.95 (*0-9624629-9-3*) Beagle Pub.

Divers Guide to Shipwrecks: Cape Canaveral to Jupiter Light. Mark R. Mondano. (Illus.). 150p. (Orig.). 1992. pap. 19.00 (*0-9631346-1-2*) Sandman Prods.

Divers Guide to Wisconsin. Steve Harrington. (Illus.). 288p. (Orig.). 1991. pap. 19.95 (*0-685-49096-3*) Beagle Pub.

Divers Guide to Wisconsin Including Minnesota's North Shore. Steve Harrington & David J. Cooper. (Illus.). 275p. (Orig.). 1991. pap. text ed. 19.95 (*0-685-47871-8*) Beagle Pub.

Diver's Handbook of Underwater Calculations. Wayne C. Tucker. LC 79-27451. (Illus.). 191p. 1980. pap. text ed. 12.00 (*0-87033-254-6*) Cornell Maritime.

Divers Jeux Rustiques. Joachim Du Bellay & V. L. Saulnier. 232p. 1965. 35.00 (*0-8288-9915-0*, F28915) Fr & Eur.

Divers Log: The Professional Dive Log for the Serious Scuba Sport Diver. David R. Scott. 240p. 1993. 14.99 (*0-9637233-0-8*) Aqua Images.

Divers Log Book. Reg Vallintine. (C). 1990. pap. 90.00 (*0-907151-99-X*, Pub. by IMMEL Pubng UK) St Mut.

Diver's Reference Dictionary. S. E. Corbett. 1986. text ed. 22.50 (*0-941332-03-9*) Best Pub Co.

Diver's Shadow. Rochelle L. Holt. 115p. 1993. pap. 9.95 (*0-934536-55-4*) Rose Shell Pr.

Divers Travel Guide to the Caribbean & the Bahamas. John Dean. (Illus.). 268p. 1987. pap. 19.95 (*0-942427-00-9*) Travel & Sports SF.

Diverse Divers. Gerald L. Kooyman. (Zoophysiology Ser.: Vol. 23). (Illus.). 215p. 1989. 149.00 (*0-387-50274-2*) Spr-Verlag.

Diverse Paths of Economic Development. Richard Pomfret. 256p. 1992. text ed. 63.00 (*0-13-220351-0*) P-H.

Diverse Paths to Modernity in Southeastern Europe: Essays in National Development. Ed. by Gerasimos Augustinos. LC 90-38424. (Contributions to the Study of World History Ser.: No. 20). 192p. 1990. text ed. 49.95 (*0-313-26670-0*, ANF, Greenwood Pr) Greenwood.

Diverse People: Connecticut 1914 to the Present see Series in Connecticut History

Diverse Perspectives on Marxist Philosophy: East & West. Sara F. Luther et al. LC 94-25057. (Contributions in Philosophy Ser.: Vol. 53). 158p. 1995. text ed. 55.00 (*0-313-29396-1*, Greenwood Pr) Greenwood.

Diverse Representation, 1990. John Yau. 48p. (C). 1990. 4.50 (*0-9613046-5-0*) Morris Mus.

Diverse Society: Implications for Social Policy. Ed. by Pastora S. Cafferty & Leon Chestang. LC 76-43633. 176p. 1976. pap. 16.95 (*0-87101-072-0*) Natl Assn Soc Wkrs.

***Diverse Teams at Work: Capitalizing on the Power of Diversity.** Lee Gardenswartz & Anita Rowe. 175p. 1995. 25.00 (*0-7863-0425-1*) Irwin Prof Pubng.

***Diverse Techniques of Analysis by 27 Eminent Clinicians.** Ed. by Benjamin B. Wolman. LC 94-49232. 610p. 1995. pap. 49.50 (*1-56821-493-6*) Aronson.

Diverse Topics in Theoretical & Mathematical Physics. Roman Jackiw. (Advanced Series in Mathematical Physics). 550p. 1995. text ed. 106.00 (*981-02-1696-3*); pap. text ed. 61.00 (*981-02-1697-1*) World Scientific Pub.

Diverse Voices: Essays on Poets & Poetry. Mark Rudman. 282p. (C). 1993. 26.95 (*0-934257-67-1*); pap. 18.95 (*0-934257-68-X*) Story Line.

Diverse Voices: Essays on Twentieth-Century Women Writers in English. Ed. by Harriet D. Jump. LC 91-2001. 320p. 1991. text ed. 39.95 (*0-312-06189-7*) St Martin.

Diverse Voices of Women. Susan Frank Ballentine & Jessica Barksdale Inclan. LC 94-7137. 412p. (C). 1994. pap. 29.95 (*1-55934-194-7*) Mayfield Pub.

Diverse Voyages Touching on the Discouerie of America. Richard Hakluyt. 117p. 1981. 12.00 (*0-87770-242-X*) Ye Galleon.

Diverse World Views in an English Village. Nigel Rapport. 224p. 1993. 55.00 (*0-7486-0417-0*, Pub. by Edinburgh U Pr UK) Col U Pr.

Diversification. Marjorie Cherry. 72p. (Orig.). 1992. pap. 10.95 (*0-9637041-0-9*) Louis IX Pr.

Diversification & Conversion Strategies for Rural Hospitals. Scott Mason et al. 52p. (Orig.). 1989. pap. 35.00 (*0-87258-524-7*, 184207) Am Hospital.

***Diversification & Corporate-Level Strategy: Strategic Issues for Multibusiness Companies.** Ed. by Michael Goold & Kathleen Luchs. LC 95-13899. 1995. write for info. (*0-415-13268-1*); pap. write for info. (*0-415-13269-X*) Routledge.

Diversification & Integration in American Industry. Michael Gort. LC 84-10730. xxi, 238p. 1984. reprint ed. text ed. 65.00 (*0-313-24423-5*, GDIV, Greenwood Pr) Greenwood.

Diversification in Modern Language Teaching: Choice & the National Curriculum. David Phillips & Caroline Filmer-Sankey. LC 92-15265. 208p. 1992. 59.95 (*0-415-07200-X*, A9807, Routledge NY); pap. write for info. (*0-415-07201-8*, Routledge NY) Routledge.

Diversification of National Income Sources in ESCWA Gulf Countries. (Economic & Social Commission for Western Asia (ESCWA) Publications). 150p. (ARA & ENG.). 1991. 17.00 (*92-1-128076-1*, AE.88.II.L.1) UN.

Diversification Through Acquisition: Strategies for Maximizing Economic Value. Malcolm S. Salter & Wolf A. Weinhold. LC 79-7370. (Illus.). 1979. text ed. 45.00 (*0-02-928020-6*) Free Pr.

Diversified Company: An Endangered Species. Walter R. Mahler. 1992. 24.95 (*0-914431-03-X*) Mahler Pub Co.

Diversified Health Occupations. 2nd ed. Louise M. Simmers. LC 82-73084. (Illus.). 560p. (Orig.). 1988. teacher ed 15.00 (*0-8273-3045-6*); teacher ed 15.00 (*0-8273-2290-9*); text ed. 32.95 (*0-8273-3044-8*) Delmar.

Diversified Health Occupations. 3rd ed. Louise Simmers. LC 92-14881. 623p. (Orig.). 1993. text ed. 34.95 (*0-8273-4971-8*) Delmar.

Diversified Health Occupations. 3rd ed. Louise Simmers. 76p. (Orig.). 1993. teacher ed 15.00 (*0-8273-4972-6*); student ed 19.50 (*0-8273-4973-4*) Delmar.

An Asterisk (*) at the beginning of an entry indicates that the title is appearing in BIP for the first time.

Diversified Health Occupations Teacher's Resource Kit. 3rd ed. Louise Simmers. 1993. 89.95 (*0-8273-4974-2*) Delmar.

Diversified Mutual Fund Investment Strategies: How to Build a High-Return, Low-Risk Portfolio of Mutual Funds. Terry G. Maxwell. Ed. by Ilene Stankiewicz. LC 91-75315. (Illus.). 165p. 1991. 19.95 (*0-9630625-0-6*) Capital MI.

Diversify Your Way to Wealth: How to Customize Your Investment Portfolio to Protect & Build. Gerald Perritt & Alan Lavine. 1993. 22.95 (*1-55738-546-7*) Probus Pub Co.

Diversifying Historically Black Colleges & Universities: A New Higher Education Paradigm. Serbrenia J. Sims. LC 93-44503. (Contributions to the Study of Education Ser.: Vol. 62). 200p. 1994. text ed. 49.95 (*0-313-28785-6*, Greenwood Pr) Greenwood.

Diversifying Historically Black Colleges & Universities: The New Higher Education Paradigm. Serbrenia J. Sims. Vol. 62. 1994. write for info. (*0-318-72321-2*, Greenwood Pr) Greenwood.

Diversion of Land: Conservation in a Period of Farming Contraction. Clive Potter et al. (Natural Environment: Problems & Management Ser.). (Illus.). 260p. (C). 1991. text ed. 65.00 (*0-415-03627-5*, A5127) Routledge.

Diversions: Eight Original Solos for the Pianist. June Edison. (Illus.). 24p. (Orig.). (C). 1991. pap. 7.95 (*1-56516-056-8*) Houston IN.

***Diversions: Fifty Comic Short Stories.** Richard Markgraf. LC 95-90221. 128p. (Orig.). 1995. pap. 8.95 (*0-9646025-0-4*) WMKB Ent.

Diversions & Pastimes with Cards, Strings, Coins, Paper & Matches see Tricks & Amusements

Diversions by the Wayside. K. D. Katrak. 23p. 1975. 8.00 (*0-88253-528-5*); pap. text ed. 4.80 (*0-88253-527-7*) Ind-US Inc.

Diversions of a Naturalist. Edwin R. Lankester. LC 77-105024. (Essay Index Reprint Ser.). 1977. 29.95 (*0-8369-1471-6*) Ayer.

Diversions of Galway: Papers on the History of Linguistics from ICHoLS V. Ed. by Anders Ahlqvist. LC 92-24473. (Studies in the History of the Language Sciences: No. 68). xxvii, 384p. 1992. 100.00x (*1-55619-363-7*) Benjamins North Am.

Diversions of Keramos: American Clay Sculpture, 1925-1950. Ross Anderson & Barbara Perry. Ed. by Annis Grover-Rogoff. LC 83-82416. (Illus.). 118p. (Orig.). 1983. pap. text ed. 12.00 (*0-914407-00-7*) Everson Mus.

Diversions of Pleasure: Luis Bunuel & the Crises of Desire. Paul Sandro. LC 86-31192. (Illus.). 181p. 1987. pap. 20.00 (*0-8142-0439-2*) Ohio St U Pr.

Diversities of Gifts: Field Studies in Southern Religion. Ed. by Ruel W. Tyson, Jr. et al. LC 87-22576. (Folklore & Society Ser.). (Illus.). 232p. 1988. 24.95 (*0-252-01517-7*) U of Ill Pr.

***Diversity: ASTD Trainer's Sourcebook.** Rasmueen. 1995. pap. text ed. 39.95 (*0-07-053438-1*) McGraw.

Diversity: Challenges & Opportunities. B. Eugene Griessman. LC 93-13952. (C). 1993. 5.75 (*0-06-501845-1*) HarpCollege.

Diversity: New Approaches to Ethnic Minority Aging. Ed. by E. Percil Stanford & Fernando M. Torres-Gil. (Generations & Aging Ser.). 171p. 1992. pap. 14.95 (*0-89503-102-7*) Baywood Pub.

Diversity Activities & Training Designs. Julie O'Mara. LC 94-65469. (Illus.). 416p. 1994. ring bd. 149.00 (*0-88390-436-5*) Pfeiffer & Co.

Diversity Advantage: How American Business Can Out-Perform Japanese & European Companies in the Global Marketplace. John P. Fernandez & Mary Barr. 300p. 1993. 24.95 (*0-669-27978-1*) Heath.

***Diversity, Affirmative Action & Law Enforcement.** George T. Felkenes & Peter C. Unsinger. 224p. 1992. pap. 29.95 (*0-398-06117-3*) C C Thomas.

Diversity, Affirmative Action & Law Enforcement. George T. Felkenes & Peter C. Unsinger. 224p. (C). 1992. text ed. 44.95x (*0-398-05777-X*) C C Thomas.

Diversity & Change in American Society. William Bridgeland. 158p. (C). 1993. pap. text ed. 12.75 (*1-57074-064-X*) Greyden Pr.

***Diversity & Change in Families: Patterns, Prospects & Policies.** Ed. by Mark R. Rank & Edward L. Kain. LC 94-28524. 480p. 1994. pap. text ed. write for info. (*0-13-219668-9*) P-H.

***Diversity & Citizenship: New Challenges for American Statehood.** Ed. by Gary J. Jacobsohn & Susan Dunn. 156p. (C). 1995. text ed. 49.50 (*0-8476-8091-6*); pap. text ed. 18.95 (*0-8476-8092-4*) Rowman.

Diversity & Complexity in Feminist Therapy. Ed. by Laura S. Brown & Maria P. Root. LC 90-31689. (Women in Therapy Ser.: Vol. 9, Nos. 1-2). 355p. 1990. pap. text ed. 19.95 (*0-918393-74-4*) Harrington Pk.

Diversity & Complexity in Feminist Therapy: Women in Therapy, Vol. 9, Nos. 1-3. Ed. by Laura S. Brown & Maria P. Root. LC 90-31160. 355p. 1990. text ed. 44.95 (*0-86656-997-9*) Haworth Pr.

***Diversity & Complexity in Prehistoric Maritime Societies: A Gulf of Maine Perspective.** Bruce J. Bourque. LC 95-1085. (Interdisciplinary Contributions to Archaeology Ser.). 400p. (C). 1995. 59.50 (*0-306-44874-2*, Plenum Pr) Plenum.

Diversity & Development in Community Practice. Ed. by Maria Roberts-DeGennaro & Marie Weil. LC 93-39428. (Journal of Community Practice). (Illus.). 144p. 1994. lib. bdg. 29.95 (*1-56024-611-1*); pap. text ed. 12.95 (*1-56024-612-X*) Haworth Pr.

Diversity & Developmentally Appropriate Practice in Early Childhood Education: Challenges for Early Childhood Education. Bruce Mallory & Rebecca New. (Early Childhood Education Ser.). (C). 1993. text ed. 41.00 (*0-8077-3300-8*); pap. text ed. 17.95 (*0-8077-3299-0*) Tchrs Coll.

Diversity & Diachrony. Ed. by David Sankoff. LC 86-31707. (Current Issues in Linguistic Theory Ser.: Vol. 53). xiii, 430p. 1986. 84.00x (*90-272-3547-3*) Benjamins North Am.

Diversity & Differences in Organizations: An Agenda for Answers & Questions. Ed. by Ronald R. Sims & Robert P. Dennehy. LC 93-18524. 208p. 1993. text ed. 49.95 (*0-89930-798-1*, ZDD, Quorum Bks) Greenwood.

Diversity & Dominance in Indian Politics: Changing Bases of Congress Supports. Ed. by Richard Sisson. 312p. (C). 1990. text ed. 35.00 (*0-8039-9649-7*) Sage.

Diversity & Evolution of Land Plants. Martin J. Ingrouille. (Illus.). 344p. 1992. pap. 39.95 (*0-412-44230-2*, A9563) Chapman & Hall.

***Diversity & Evolution of Plants.** Lorentz C. Pearson. LC 94-37366. 624p. 1995. 59.95 (*0-8493-2483-1*, 2483) CRC Pr.

Diversity & Evolutionary Biology of Tropical Flowers. Peter K. Endress. (Cambridge Tropical Biology Ser.). (Illus.). 420p. (C). 1994. 84.95 (*0-521-42088-1*) Cambridge U Pr.

Diversity & Homogeneity in World Societies. Erika Bourguignon & Lenora Greenbaum. LC 73-86218. (Comparative Studies). (Illus.). 208p. 1973. 15.00 (*0-87536-329-6*); pap. 10.00 (*0-87536-330-X*) HRAFP.

***Diversity & Motivation: Culturally Responsive Teaching.** Raymond J. Wlodkowski & Margery B. Ginsberg. LC 95-15679. (Higher & Adult Education Ser.). 1995. 32.95 (*0-7879-0126-1*) Jossey-Bass.

***Diversity & Multiculturalism in Libraries.** Ed. by Katherine H. Hill. LC 94-28566. (Foundation in Library & Information Science: Vol. 32). (C). 1994. 73.25 (*1-55938-751-3*) Jai Pr.

***Diversity & Oppression.** Maurianne Adams. 46p. (C). 1994. 6.00 (*0-7872-0034-4*) Kendall-Hunt.

Diversity & Pattern in Plant Communities. Ed. by H. J. During et al. (Illus.). viii, 278p. 1988. pap. 65.00 (*90-5103-021-5*, Pub. by SPB Acad Pub NE) Koeltz Sci Bks.

Diversity & Presence: Women Faculty Artists of the University of California. Katherine Diage & Melinda Wortz. Ed. by Sue Henger. LC 87-50967. (Illus.). 72p. (Orig.). (C). 1987. pap. 15.00 (*0-932173-03-9*) J & M Sweeney.

Diversity & Teaching. Mary O'Hair & Sandra J. Odell. 320p. (C). 1993. pap. text ed. write for info. (*0-15-500498-0*) HB Coll Pubs.

Diversity & Teaching: Teacher Education Yearbook I. Ed. by Mary J. O'Hair & Sandra J. Odell. 1993. pap. 18.75 (*0-685-74809-X*) Assn Tchr Ed.

Diversity & the Tropical Rain Forest. John Terborgh. (Scientific American Library). 1995. text ed. write for info. (*0-7167-5030-9*) W H Freeman.

Diversity & Unity in Cross-Cultural Psychology. Ed. by R. Rath et al. vi, 374p. 1982. 32.75 (*90-265-0431-4*, Pub. by Swets Pub Serv NE) Taylor & Francis.

Diversity & Unity in Early North America. Ed. by Philip D. Morgan. LC 93-16763. (Re-writing Histories Ser.). 296p. 1993. 59.95 (*0-415-08798-8*, B2408); pap. 16.95 (*0-415-08799-6*, B2412) Routledge.

Diversity & Writing: Dialogue Within a Modern University: Proceedings First Annual Conference, April 1990. Ed. by Lillian Bridwell-Bowles & Susan Batchelder. (Monograph Ser.: Vol. 2). 41p. (Orig.). 1992. pap. 4.50 (*1-881221-01-6*) U Minn Ctr Interdis.

Diversity As Resource: Redefining Cultural Literacy. Ed. by Denise E. Murray. LC 92-61747. 326p. 1992. pap. 22.95 (*0-939791-42-0*) Tchrs Eng Spkrs.

Diversity-Based Hiring: An Introduction from Legal Ethnical & Psychological Perspectives. M. Singer. 206p. 1993. 54.95 (*1-85628-628-2*, Pub. by Avebury Pub UK) Ashgate Pub Co.

Diversity Bingo: An Experiential Learning Event. Pfeiffer & Co. Staff. 65p. 1992. ring bd. 99.95 (*0-88390-332-6*) Pfeiffer & Co.

Diversity by Design. Non-Traditional Study Commission. LC 73-3772. (Jossey-Bass Higher Education Ser.). 208p. reprint ed. pap. 59.30 (*0-317-27219-5*, 2023875) Bks Demand.

Diversity, Conflict, & State Politics: Regionalism in Illinois. Ed. by Peter F. Nardulli. LC 88-18719. 352p. 1989. 34.95 (*0-252-01576-2*); pap. 19.95 (*0-252-06036-9*) U of Ill Pr.

***Diversity Factor: Reading Book.** Ed. by Elsie Y. Cross et al. 150p. 1995. pap. 50.00 (*0-9646451-0-6*) Diversity Factor.

Diversity, Farmer Knowledge, & Sustainability. Ed. by Joyce L. Moock & Robert E. Rhoades. LC 92-52768. (Food Systems in Agrarian Change Ser.). (Illus.). 296p. 1992. 49.95 (*0-8014-2682-0*); pap. 18.95 (*0-8014-9968-2*) Cornell U Pr.

***Diversity, Globalization, & Ways of Nature.** Danilo Anton. 200p. 1994. pap. 19.50 (*0-88936-724-8*, IDRC7248, Pub. by IDRC CN) UNIPUB.

***Diversity Icebreaker: A Trainer's Guide.** Selma Myers & Jonamay Lambert. 60p. 1994. 55.00 (*1-883998-12-3*) Amherst Educ.

Diversity Icebreakers: A Guide for Diversity Training. Selma Myers & Joanna Lambert. 56p. 1994. pap. text ed. 55.00 (*1-883998-11-5*) Amherst Educ.

Diversity in American Families. 2nd ed. Maxine B. Zinn & D. Stanley Eitzen. 496p. (C). 1989. text ed. 33.50 (*0-06-047373-8*) HarpCollege.

Diversity in Corporate America: 1994-1995. Ed. by Tracy Steyer. 443p. (Orig.). 1994. pap. 195.00 (*0-9640975-0-8*) Inst Corp Diversity.

***Diversity in Corporate America, 1995-1996.** Date not set. write for info. (*0-614-04989-X*) Inst Corp Diversity.

Diversity in Day Care: Many Options for Many Families. Rebecca Wheat. LC 88-50949. 112p. 1988. pap. 19.50 (*0-87762-602-2*) Technomic.

Diversity in Faith-Unity in Christ. Shirley C. Gutherie, Jr. LC 86-9157. 144p. (Orig.). (C). 1986. pap. 12.99 (*0-664-24013-5*, Westminster) Westminster John Knox.

Diversity in Families. 3rd ed. Maxine B. Zinn & D. Stanley Eitzen. LC 92-31424. (C). 1992. 51.00 (*0-06-500718-2*) HarpCollege.

Diversity in Holiness. Robert H. Steuart. LC 67-28770. (Essay Index Reprint Ser.). 1977. 19.95 (*0-8369-0906-2*) Ayer.

***Diversity in Japanese Culture & Language.** Ed. by John C. Maher & Gaynor Macdonald. LC 94-44932. (Japanese Studies). 1995. write for info. (*0-7103-0477-3*, Pub. by Kegan Paul Intl UK) Routledge Chapman & Hall.

***Diversity in Oneness.** Mavis Aldridge. 256p. 1995. pap. text ed. 21.95 (*0-7872-0583-4*) Kendall-Hunt.

***Diversity in Organizations: New Perspectives for a Changing Workplace.** Ed. by Martin M. Chemers et al. LC 95-8231. (Claremont Symposium on Applied Social Psychology Ser.: Vol. 8). 252p. (C). 1995. 45.00 (*0-8039-5548-0*); pap. 22.50 (*0-8039-5549-9*) Sage.

***Diversity in Pre-Exilic Hebrew.** Ian Young. 256p. 1993. 117.50 (*3-16-146058-8*, Pub. by J C B Mohr GW) Coronet Bks.

Diversity in Psychotherapy: The Politics of Race, Gender, & Ethnicity. Jean L. Chin et al. LC 93-18240. 224p. 1993. text ed. 49.95 (*0-275-94180-9*, C4180, Praeger Pubs) Greenwood.

Diversity in Teacher Education: New Expectations. Ed. by Mary E. Dilworth. LC 92-20123. (Education-Higher Education Ser.). 306p. 1992. 32.95 (*1-55542-472-4*) Jossey-Bass.

Diversity in the Classroom: A Casebook for Teachers & Teacher Educators. Ed. by Judith H. Shulman & Amalia Mesa-Bains. 136p. 1993. text ed. 29.95 (*0-8058-1428-0*); pap. 16.95 (*0-8058-1429-9*) L Erlbaum Assocs.

Diversity in the Classroom: A Multicultural Approach to the Education of Young Children. Frances E. Kendall. LC 83-6704. (Early Childhood Education Ser.). (Orig.). (C). 1983. pap. text ed. 13.95 (*0-8077-2740-7*) Tchrs Coll.

Diversity in the Genus Apis. Ed. by Deborah R. Smith. (Studies in Insect Biology). 265p. (C). 1991. text ed. 77.50 (*0-8133-8057-X*) Westview.

Diversity in the Workplace: A Resource Manual. 120p. 1994. pap. 8.00 (*0-87125-214-7*, 220) Cath Health.

Diversity in the Workplace: Human Resources Inititiatives. Susan E. Jackson & Associates Staff. (Professional Practice Ser.). 356p. 1993. pap. text ed. 19.95 (*0-89862-477-0*) Guilford Pr.

Diversity in the Workplace: Human Resources Initiatives. Susan E. Jackson et al. LC 92-1422. (Professional Practice Ser.). 356p. 1992. lib. bdg. 42.00 (*0-89862-476-2*) Guilford Pr.

Diversity of Animal Reproduction. Ed. by Richard E. Blackwelder & Benjamin A. Shepherd. 152p. 1981. 144.00 (*0-8493-6355-1*, QP251) CRC Pr.

Diversity of Bacterial Respiratory Systems, 2 vols. Christopher J. Knowles. 272p. 1980. Vol. 1, 272p. 132.00 (*0-8493-5399-8*, QR89); Vol. 2, 256p. 113.95 (*0-8493-5400-5*, QR89) CRC Pr.

Diversity of Creatures. Rudyard Kipling. 368p. 1994. 10.95 (*0-14-018694-8*, Penguin Classics) Viking Penguin.

Diversity of Desert Life. J. L. Cloudsley-Thompson. (C). 1992. text ed. 75.00 (*81-7233-050-2*, Pub. by Scientific Pubs II) St Mut.

Diversity of Discipleship: Presbyterians & Twentieth-Century Christian Witness. Ed. by John Mulder et al. (Presbyterian Presene Ser.). 372p. (Orig.). 1991. pap. 16.99 (*0-664-25196-X*) Westminster John Knox.

Diversity of Environmental Biogeochemistry. Ed. by J. Berthelin. (Developments in Geochemistry Ser.: No. 6). 550p. 1991. 143.00 (*0-444-88900-0*) Elsevier.

***Diversity of Interacting Receptors.** Ed. by Leo G. Abood & Abel Lajtha. LC 95-11515. (Annals Ser.: Vol. 757). 1995. write for info. (*0-89766-923-1*); pap. write for info. (*0-89766-924-X*) NY Acad Sci.

Diversity of Life. Edward O. Wilson. (Questions of Science Ser.). (Illus.). 424p. 1992. text ed. 29.95 (*0-674-21298-3*) HUP.

Diversity of Life. Edward O. Wilson. (Illus.). 424p. (C). 1993. pap. text ed. 16.95 (*0-393-96457-4*) Norton.

Diversity of Life. Edward O. Wilson. 448p. 1993. pap. 14.95 (*0-393-31047-7*) Norton.

Diversity of Life. Edward O. Wilson. (Illus.). 424p. (C). 1993. pap. text ed. write for info. (*0-393-96469-8*) Norton.

Diversity of Life, Set. Edward O. Wilson. 464p. 1993. boxed 49.95 (*0-674-21299-1*) HUP.

Diversity of Marine Animals. Bobby N. Irby et al. LC 83-19721. (Man & the Gulf Ser.: Vol. 3). 88p. (gr. 10-12). 1984. pap. text ed. 7.50 (*0-87805-203-8*) U Pr of Miss.

Diversity of Marine Plants. Bobby N. Irby et al. LC 83-16994. (Man & the Gulf Ser.: Vol. 4). (Illus.). 88p. (gr. 10-12). 1984. pap. text ed. 7.50 (*0-87805-204-6*) U Pr of Miss.

Diversity of Moral Thinking. Neil Cooper. (CLLP Ser.). (Illus.). (C). 1981. text ed. 65.00 (*0-19-824423-1*) OUP.

Diversity of Oceanic Life: An Evaluative Review. Ed. by Melvin N. Peterson. LC 92-39818. (Significant Issues Ser.: Vol. 14, No. 12). 120p. (gr. 13). 1993. pap. text ed. 14.95 (*0-89206-206-1*) CSI Studies.

***Diversity of Old Malt Quatrains: or A Garland of Frothy Sentments.** Slow Tempo Press Staff. (Illus.). 84p. (Orig.). 1994. pap. 9.95 (*0-9635559-4-4*) Slow Tempo.

Diversity of Religions: A Christian Perspective. J. A. DiNoia. LC 91-33001. 199p. 1992. 29.95 (*0-8132-0763-0*); pap. 17.95 (*0-8132-0769-X*) Cath U Pr.

Diversity of Scripture: A Theological Interpretation. Paul D. Hanson. LC 81-43079. (Overtures to Biblical Theology Ser.: Vol. 11). 175p. reprint ed. pap. 49.90 (*0-685-24169-6*, 2033046) Bks Demand.

***Diversity of Women: Women in Ontario since 1945.** Ed. by Joy Parr. (Illus.). 392p. 1995. 65.00 (*0-8020-2615-X*) U of Toronto Pr.

***Diversity of Women: Women in Ontario since 1945.** Ed. by Joy Parr. (Illus.). 392p. 1995. pap. 24.95 (*0-8020-7695-5*) U of Toronto Pr.

Diversity of Worlds. Raymond Aron & August Heckscher. LC 72-12631. 178p. 1973. reprint ed. text ed. 59.75 (*0-8371-6686-1*, ARDW, Greenwood Pr) Greenwood.

Diversity on Campus. David Schuman & Dick Olufs. LC 94-8971. 320p. (C). 1994. pap. write for info. (*0-02-408142-6*) Macmillan.

Diversity Principle: Friend or Foe of the First Amendment? Ed. by Craig R. Smith. LC 89-63287. 75p. (Orig.). (C). 1989. Avail. through publisher only. 10.95 (*0-937790-40-0*, 4330) Media Institute.

***Diversity Simulation Games: Diversity Simulation Games.** Sivasailam Thiagarajan. (Games by Thiagi Ser.). 48p. (Orig.). 1995. pap. 25.00 (*0-87425-262-8*) Human Res Dev Pr.

Diversity Task Force Exercise: Managing a Diverse Work Force. John W. Work. 113p. (Orig.). 1991. pap. 24.95 (*0-925652-11-3*) Orgn Design & Dev.

Diversity Tool Kit. Lee Gardenswartz. 288p. 1994. 300.00 (*0-7863-0266-6*) Irwin Prof Pubng.

Diverted Dream: Community Colleges & the Promise of Educational Opportunity in America, 1900-1985. Steven Brint & Jerome Karabel. (Illus.). 336p. 1989. 30.00 (*0-19-504815-6*) OUP.

Diverted Dream: Community Colleges & the Promise of Educational Opportunity in America, 1900-1985. Steven Brint & Jerome Karabel. (Illus.). 336p. 1991. reprint ed. pap. 17.95 (*0-19-504816-4*) OUP.

Diverticular Disease of the Colon. Neil S. Painter. LC 76-58771. (Illus.). 320p. 1977. 12.95 (*0-87983-144-8*) Keats.

Divertimenti or Pleasure Abounding for the Idle Hour. S. Gorton Green. 197p. (C). 1989. 39.00 (*0-7212-0835-5*, Pub. by Regency Press) St Mut.

Dives & Pauper (1493) LC 73-17391. 1973. reprint ed. lib. bdg. 90.00 (*0-8201-1111-2*) Schol Facsimiles.

Divesting Business Units: Making the Decision & Making It Work. Marilyn L. Taylor. LC 88-45765. 288p. 1988. text ed. 45.00 (*0-669-14294-8*) Free Pr.

Divesting Nature's Capital: The Political Economy of Environmental Abuse in the Third World. Ed. by H. Jeffrey Leonard. LC 83-18534. 350p. 1985. 59.50 (*0-8419-0897-4*) Holmes & Meier.

***Divestiture-A.** Bruce Andrews. 56p. (Orig.). 1994. pap. 7.00 (*0-9628456-3-9*) Drogue Pr.

Divestiture in Developing Countries. Elliot Berg & Mary M. Shirley. (Discussion Paper Ser.: No. 11). 40p. 1987. pap. 6.95 (*0-8213-0917-X*, 20011) World Bank.

Divestiture of State Enterprises: An Overview of the Legal Framework. Pierre Guislain. LC 92-29526. (Technical Paper Ser.: No. 186). 109p. 1992. 7.95 (*0-8213-2251-6*, 12251) World Bank.

Divestiture Option: A Guide for Financial & Corporate Planning Executives. Richard J. Schmidt. LC 89-10879. 202p. 1990. text ed. 55.00 (*0-89930-397-8*, SDQ/, Greenwood Pr) Greenwood.

Divestment & Strategic Change. Ed. by John Coyne & Mike Wright. LC 84-24456. 224p. 1986. 53.00 (*0-389-20547-8*, 08111) B&N Imports.

Divestment on Campus: Issues & Implementation. Jennifer D. Kibbe. 86p. (Orig.). 1989. pap. 45.00 (*0-931035-37-6*) IRRC Inc DC.

Divestment on Campus Update: The Top 50 Schools. Jennifer Kibbe. 16p. (Orig.). 1992. pap. 20.00 (*0-931035-98-8*) IRRC Inc DC.

Divide & Conquer. L. L. Farrar, Jr. 1978. text ed. 42.00 (*0-914710-38-9*) East Eur Quarterly.

Divide & Conquer. Marcia L. Odell. Ed. by Stuart Bruchey. LC 78-56681. (Management of Public Lands in the United States Ser.). 1979. lib. bdg. 42.95 (*0-405-11347-1*) Ayer.

Divide & Dissent: Kentucky Politics, 1930-1963. John E. Pearce. LC 86-28978. (Illus.). 272p. 1987. 15.00 (*0-8131-0804-7*) U Pr of Ky.

***Divide & School: Gender & Class Dynamics in Comprehensive Education.** John Abraham. 210p. 1995. 79.00 (*0-7507-0390-3*, Falmer Pr); pap. 27.00 (*0-7507-0391-1*, Falmer Pr) Taylor & Francis.

Divided Allegiance. Elizabeth Moon. (Deed of Paksenarrion Ser.: Bk. 2). 528p. (Orig.). 1988. mass mkt. 5.99 (*0-671-69786-2*) Baen Bks.

Divided & Conquered: The French High Command & the Defeat of the West, 1940. Jeffrey A. Gunsburg. LC 78-22725. (Contributions in Military History Ser.: No. 18). (Illus.). 303p. 1979. text ed. 59.95 (*0-313-21092-6*, GDC/, Greenwood Pr) Greenwood.

Divided Apple: A Story about Teaching in Chicago. Alan Balter. 176p. (C). 1994. pap. text ed. 18.95 (*0-8403-9170-6*) Kendall-Hunt.

Divided Arrival: Narratives of the Puerto Rican Migration, 1920-50. Ed. by Juan Flores. 73p. (Orig.). Date not set. pap. 7.00 (*1-878483-03-X*) Hunter Coll CEP.

Divided Battle. G. L. Hill. 12.95 (*0-89190-063-2*, Am Repr) Amereon Ltd.

Divided Borders. Juan Flores. LC 91-37313. 252p. 1993. pap. 11.00 (*1-55885-046-5*) Arte Publico.

D

An Asterisk (*) at the beginning of an entry indicates that the title is appearing in BIP for the first time. 2047

***Divided Britain.** 2nd ed. Raymond Hudson & Allan W. Williams. LC 94-30675. 1995. pap. text ed. 20.95 (*0-471-95204-4*) Wiley.

Divided Children. Lynn Jay & Steve Jay. LC 81-71019. 128p. (Orig.). 1982. pap. 5.25 (*0-87516-474-9*) DeVorss.

Divided Cities: New York & London in the Contemporary World. Ed. by Susan Fainstein et al. 288p. (Orig.). 1991. pap. text ed. 19.95 (*0-631-18302-7*) Blackwell Pubs.

Divided Consciousness: Multiple Controls in Human Thought & Action. Ernest R. Hilgard. LC 86-1578. (Wiley Series in Behavior). 331p. reprint ed. pap. 94.40 (*0-7837-5202-4*, AU00440) Bks Demand.

Divided Counsel: The Anglo-American Response to Communist Victory in China. Edwin W. Martin. LC 86-1708. (Illus.). 288p. 1986. 31.00 (*0-8131-1591-4*) U Pr of Ky.

Divided Democracy: Presidents & Congress in Cooperation & Conflict. James Thurber. 323p. 1990. 21.95 (*0-87187-582-9*) Congr Quarterly.

Divided Elite: Economics, Politics, & Anglo Jewry, 1882-1917. Daniel Gutwein. LC 92-15366. (Brill's Series in Jewish Studies: Vol. 5). 501p. 1992. 125.75 (*90-04-09447-4*) E J Brill.

***Divided Empire: Milton's Political Imagery.** Robert T. Fallon. LC 94-41636. 216p. 1996. 40.00 (*0-271-01460-1*) Pa St U Pr.

Divided Families: What Happens to Children When Parents Part. Frank F. Furstenberg, Jr. & Andrew J. Cherlin. LC 90-48171. (Family & Public Policy Ser.: No. 1). 142p. 1991. text ed. 19.95 (*0-674-65576-1*, FURDIV) HUP.

Divided Families: What Happens to Children When Parents Part. Frank F. Furstenberg. 142p. 1994. pap. 11.95 (*0-674-65577-X*) HUP.

Divided Fictions: Fanny Burney & Feminine Strategy. Kristina Straub. LC 87-21600. 248p. 1988. text ed. 27.00 (*0-8131-1633-3*) U Pr of Ky.

Divided Future. William Klink. (Illus.). 160p. (Orig.). 1989. pap. 5.95 (*0-913811-03-3*) Northeast A S.

Divided Future. William J. Klink. (Illus.). 112p. (Orig.). 1994. pap. 7.95 (*0-8059-3443-X*) Dorrance.

Divided Government. Lloyd N. Cutler & James L. Sundquist. (C). 1929. text ed. 39.95 (*0-8133-0950-6*); pap. text ed. 12.95 (*0-8133-0951-4*) Westview.

Divided Heart. Marcy E. Rothman. 224p. (Orig.). 1994. pap. 3.99 (*0-451-17931-5*, Sig) NAL-Dutton.

***Divided Heart.** large type ed. Jean Davidson. (Romance Ser.). 1994. pap. 14.95 (*0-7089-7606-9*, Linford) Ulverscroft.

Divided Heart: Essays on Protestantism & the Enlightment in America. Henry F. May. 240p. 1991. 35.00 (*0-19-505899-2*) OUP.

Divided Heart: Letters of Sally Baxter Hampton, 1853-1862. Sally B. Hampton. LC 94-65837. (Illus.). xl, 150p. 1994. pap. 14.95 (*0-9640576-0-3*) Phantom Press.

Divided Heritage: Themes & Problems in German Modernism. Ed. by Irit Rogoff. (Illus.). 424p. (C). 1991. 74.95 (*0-521-34553-7*) Cambridge U Pr.

Divided Heroine: A Recurrent Pattern in Six English Novels. H. M. Daleski. LC 83-12897. 164p. 1984. 34.50 (*0-8419-0885-0*) Holmes & Meier.

Divided Home-Land: Contemporary German Women's Plays. Ed. by Sue-Ellen Case. (Illus.). 284p. (C). 1992. text ed. 42.50 (*0-472-09406-8*); pap. 18.95 (*0-472-06406-1*) U of Mich Pr.

Divided Houses: Gender & the Civil War. Catherine Clinton & Nina Silber. (Illus.). 320p. 1992. pap. 15.95 (*0-19-508034-3*) OUP.

Divided Image. Margaret E. Rudd. LC 73-118003. (Studies in Blake: No. 3). 1970. reprint ed. lib. bdg. 75.00 (*0-8383-1015-X*) M S G Haskell Hse.

Divided Island: Faction & Unity on Saint Pierre. William A. Christian. LC 69-12720. (Illus.). 228p. 1969. 29.00 (*0-674-21289-4*) HUP.

***Divided It Stands: Can the United Nations Work?** James Holtje. 256p. 1995. pap. 12.95 (*1-57036-226-2*) Turner Pub GA.

***Divided Kashmir.** Mushtaqur Rahman. 1995. lib. bdg. 40.00 (*1-55587-598-X*) Lynne Rienner.

Divided Kingdom: Work, Community, & the Mining Wars in the Central Illinois Coal Fields During the Great Depression. Carl D. Oblinger. (Illus.). 273p. (Orig.). 1991. pap. text ed. 12.50 (*0-912226-28-5*) Ill St Hist Soc.

Divided Knowledge: Across Disciplines, Across Cultures. Ed. by David Easton & Corrine S. Schelling. (Illus.). 288p. 1991. 46.00 (*0-8039-4038-6*); pap. 21.95 (*0-8039-4039-4*) Sage.

Divided Korea: The Politics of Development, 1945-1972. Joungwon A. Kim. LC 74-24936. (East Asian Monographs: No. 59). 330p. (C). 1975. 21.00 (*0-674-21287-8*) HUP.

Divided Legacy: A History of the Schism in Medical Thought, 4 vols. Harris L. Coulter. 1973. Vol. I, The Patterns Emerge: Hippocrates to Paracelsus, 1975. 35.00 (*0-916386-01-5*); Vol. II, Progress & Regress: J.B. Van Helmont to Claude Bernard, 1977. 35.00 (*0-916386-02-3*); Vol. III, Science & Ethics in American Medicine, 1800-1914. 35.00 (*0-685-05338-5*); Vol. IV, The Bacteriological Era, 1870-1990. 50.00 (*0-685-66658-1*) Ctr Emp Med.

Divided Legacy: A History of the Schism in Medical Thought, 4 vols., Set. Harris L. Coulter. 1973. 105.00 (*0-916386-00-7*) Ctr Emp Med.

Divided Legacy: The Conflict Between Homoeopathy & the American Medical Association: Science & Ethics in American Medicine 1800-1914, Vol. III. Harris L. Coulter. 546p. (Orig.). 1982. reprint ed. pap. 14.95 (*0-913028-96-7*) North Atlantic.

Divided Legacy: The Origins of Modern Western Medicine - J.B. Van Helmont to Claude Bernard. Harris L. Coulter. 816p. 1988. 35.00 (*1-55643-035-3*) Ctr Emp Med.

Divided Legacy - the Bacteriological Age: Twentieth Century Medicine - the Bacteriological Era, Vol. IV. Harris L. Coulter. 776p. 1994. text ed. 50.00 (*1-55643-170-8*) North Atlantic.
In this fourth & concluding volume of the author's history of Western medicine, the ideas of Pasteur, Koch, Ehrlich, Metchnikoff, & Von Behring are analyzed for their contributions to bacteriology, immunology & pharmacology. However, as in the earlier volumes, the author situates their thinking in the context of the conflict between the Rationalist & the Empirical therapeutic philosophies. Rather than visualizing conventional medicine since 1880 as emerging from "non-science" to "science," the author shows that the movement of medical ideas is strongly affected by social & economic factors which not only inhibit conventional medicine from achieving "scientific" status but generate dichotomy in the medicine of late twentieth-century industrialized societies between the analytical (allopathic) & holistic (homeopathic, osteopathic, naturopathic, chiropractic) approaches. This volume represents the first & only historically based analysis of the theory & method of "alternative medicine." It devotes equal space to the holistic therapeutic doctrines & shows them to be strong in precisely the area -- therapeutics -- where analytical medicine is weak. Since industrialized societies today are increasingly emphasizing holistic approaches to therapeutics, DIVIDED LEGACY is an indispensable tool of analysis. *Publisher Provided Annotation.*

Divided Light: Father & Son Poems. Ed. by Jason Shinder. LC 83-18449. 293p. (Orig.). 1983. pap. 12.95 (*0-935296-47-6*) Sheep Meadow.

Divided Lives: American Women in the Twentieth Century. Rosalind Rosenberg. Ed. by Eric Foner. (American Century Ser.). 288p. 1992. pap. 10.95 (*0-374-52347-9*) Hill & Wang.

***Divided Lives: The Public & Private Struggle of Three Accomplished Women.** Elsa Walsh. 288p. 1995. 23.00 (*0-684-80401-8*) S&S Trade.

Divided Loyalties. Lewis D. Einstein. LC 78-99690. (Essay Index Reprint Ser.). 1977. 30.95 (*0-8369-1349-3*) Ayer.

***Divided Loyalties.** Hurley. 1995. mass mkt. 4.99 (*0-7860-0163-1*, Pinnacle NY) Windsor NY.

Divided Loyalties: Canadian Concepts of Federalism. Edwin R. Black. LC 75-319658. 286p. reprint ed. pap. 81.60 (*0-7837-6896-6*, 2046726) Bks Demand.

Divided Loyalties: Diary of a Basketball Father. Bob Hurley, Sr. & Phil Pepe. 208p. 1993. 19.95 (*0-8217-4391-0*) Zebra.

Divided Loyalties: Tensions for Religious Americans Arising from U. S. Foreign Policy. 325p. 10.00 (*0-318-17396-4*) Minority Rights.

Divided Loyalties: The Public & Private Life of Labor Leader John Mitchell. Craig Phelan. LC 93-42774. (SUNY Series in American Labor History). 438p. (C). 1994. text ed. 64.50x (*0-7914-2087-6*); pap. text ed. 19.95 (*0-7914-2088-4*) State U NY Pr.

Divided Loyalties: Whistle-Blowing at Bart. Robert M. Anderson et al. LC 79-89588. (Science & Society: Series in Science, Technology, & Human Values: Vol. 4). (Illus.). 400p. 1980. pap. 7.95 (*0-931682-09-6*) Purdue U Pubns.

Divided Metropolis: Social & Spatial Dimensions of Philadelphia, 1800-1975. Ed. by William W. Cutler, 3rd & Howard Gillette, Jr. LC 79-7729. (Contributions in American History Ser.: No. 85). (Illus.). 308p. 1980. text ed. 59.95 (*0-313-21351-8*, GDM/) Greenwood.

Divided Mind: Ideology & Imagination in America, 1898-1917. Peter Conn. (Cambridge Studies in American Literature & Culture: No. 7). (Illus.). 358p. 1989. pap. 21.95 (*0-521-36868-5*) Cambridge U Pr.

***Divided Mind of Protestant America, 1880-1930.** Ferenc M. Szasz. LC 81-7597. 212p. 1982. pap. 60.50 (*0-7837-8411-2*, 2059222) Bks Demand.

Divided Nation: A History of Germany, 1918-1990. Mary Fulbrook. 416p. (C). 1992. 45.00 (*0-19-507570-6*); pap. text ed. 17.95 (*0-19-507571-4*) OUP.

***Divided Nations: Class, Politics, & Nationalism in the Basque Country & Catalonia.** Juan Diez Medrano. (Wilder House Ser.). 256p. 1995. 29.95x (*0-8014-3092-5*) Cornell U Pr.

Divided Neighborhoods: Changing Patterns of Racial Segregation. Ed. by Gary A. Tobin. (Urban Affairs Annual Reviews Ser.: Vol. 32). 284p. 1987. text ed. 54.00 (*0-8039-2670-7*); pap. text ed. 24.00 (*0-8039-2671-5*) Sage.

Divided Opportunities: Minorities, Poverty, & Social Policy. Ed. by G. D. Sandefur & Marta Tienda. (Environment, Development, & Public Policy: Public Policy & Social Services Ser.). (Illus.). 296p. 1988. 42.50 (*0-306-42876-8*, Plenum Pr) Plenum.

Divided Passions: Jewish Intellectuals & the Experience of Modernity. Paul Mendes-Flohr. LC 89-22557. 450p. 1991. 42.95 (*0-8143-2030-9*) Wayne St U Pr.

Divided Path: The German Influence on Social Reform in France after 1870. Allan Mitchell. LC 90-23845. xx, 410p. (C). 1991. 49.95 (*0-8078-1964-6*) U of NC Pr.

Divided People. Kenneth S. Lynn. LC 76-25779. (Contributions in American Studies: No. 30). 113p. 1977. text ed. 42.95 (*0-8371-9271-4*, LYD/, Greenwood Pr) Greenwood.

Divided People of God. Ogbu Kalu. LC 74-81853. 1978. 13.95 (*0-88357-048-3*); pap. 4.95 (*0-88357-070-X*) NOK Pubs.

***Divided Planet: The Ecology of Rich & Poor.** Tom Athanasiou. 1996. 23.95 (*0-316-05635-9*) Little.

Divided Self: A Biography of Arishma Takeo. Leith Morton. 288p. (Orig.). 1989. pap. text ed. 24.95 (*0-04-378006-7*, Pub. by Allen Unwin AT) Paul & Co Pubs.

Divided Skies: Establishing Segregated Flight Training at Tuskegee, Alabama, 1934-1942. Robert J. Jakeman. LC 91-11459. 432p. (C). 1992. 37.95 (*0-8173-0527-0*) U of Ala Pr.

Divided Societies: Class Struggle in Contemporary Capitalism. Ralph Miliband. 288p. 1990. 49.95 (*0-19-827535-8*) OUP.

Divided Societies: Class Struggle in Contemporary Capitalism. Ralph Miliband. 288p. 1991. reprint ed. pap. 16.95 (*0-19-285234-5*, 9048) OUP.

Divided Soul: The Life of Marvin Gaye. David Ritz. (Quality Paperbacks Ser.). (Illus.). 367p. 1991. reprint ed. pap. 13.95 (*0-306-80443-3*) Da Capo.

Divided Sphere. Joan Wolf. 96p. (Orig.). 1985. pap. 6.00 (*0-912449-14-4*) Floating Island.

Divided Staffs, Divided Selves: A Case Approach to Mental Health Ethics. Ed. by Stanley J. Reiser et al. LC 86-28416. (Illus.). 160p. 1987. pap. 14.95 (*0-521-31890-4*) Cambridge U Pr.

***Divided Sun: MITI & the Breakdown of Japanese High Tech Industrial Policy, 1975-1993.** Scott Callon. LC 95-11675. (Studies in International Policy). 296p. 1995. 29.50x (*0-8047-2505-5*) Stanford U Pr.

Divided Visual Field Studies of Cerebral Organization. Ed. by J. Graham Beaumont. 1982. text ed. 126.00 (*0-12-084080-4*) Acad Pr.

***Divided Waters.** Ivan Musicant. 496p. 1995. 30.00 (*0-06-016482-4*, HarpT) HarpC.

***Divided Waters: Bridging the U. S.-Mexico Border.** Helen Ingram et al. LC 95-13626. 1995. write for info. (*0-8165-1513-1*); pap. write for info. (*0-8165-1564-6*) U of Ariz Pr.

Divided We Fall: A History of Ethnic, Religious, & Racial Prejudice in America. Philip Perlmutter. LC 90-20153. 414p. 1992. text ed. 44.95 (*0-8138-0644-5*) Iowa St U Pr.

Divided We Fall: Essays on Confederate Nation-Building. Ed. by John M. Behlolavek et al. LC 91-60159. (Illus.). 264p. 1991. pap. 15.95 (*0-945759-03-7*) St Leo Col Pr.

***Divided We Fall: Gambling with History in the Nineties.** Haynes Johnson. 480p. 1995. pap. 12.95 (*0-393-31306-9*, Norton Paperbks) Norton.

Divided We Fall: Gambling with History in the Nineties. Haynes B. Johnson. LC 93-45713. 1994. 25.00 (*0-393-03629-4*) Norton.

Divided We Fall: Moving from Suspicion to Solidarity. T. Richard Snyder. 160p. (Orig.). 1992. pap. 11.99 (*0-664-25297-4*) Westminster John Knox.

Divided We Govern: Party Control, Lawmaking & Investigations, 1946-1990. David R. Mayhew. 192p. (Orig.). 1991. text ed. 27.50 (*0-300-04835-1*) Yale U Pr.

Divided We Govern: Party Control, Lawmaking & Investigations, 1946-1990. David R. Mayhew. 192p. (Orig.). 1993. pap. 14.00 (*0-300-04837-8*) Yale U Pr.

Divided We Stand. Ed. by Gary Geddes. 216p. 1977. 15.00 (*0-88778-174-8*, Pub. by Stoddart Pubng CN); pap. 7.95 (*0-88778-175-6*, Pub. by Stoddart Pubng CN) Genl Dist Srvs.

Divided We Stand: Class Structure in Israel from 1948 to the 1980s. Amir Ben-Porat. LC 89-7493. (Contributions in Sociology Ser.: No. 85). 157p. 1989. text ed. 45.00 (*0-313-26402-3*, BDD/, Greenwood Pr) Greenwood.

Divided We Stand: Re-defining Politics, Technology & Social Choice. Michiel Schwarz & Michael Thompson. LC 89-38205. (Illus.). 184p. (C). 1990. text ed. 33.95 (*0-8122-8233-7*); pap. text ed. 16.95 (*0-8122-1319-X*) U of Pa Pr.

Divided We Stand: The Crisis of a Frontierless Democracy. Walter P. Webb. LC 79-1598. 151p. 1985. reprint ed. 18.00 (*0-88355-903-X*) Hyperion Conn.

Divided We Stand: Working-Class Stratification in America. William Form. LC 85-16537. 328p. 1986. 29.95 (*0-252-01168-6*) U of Ill Pr.

Divided Weather. Adrianne Marcus. 64p. (Orig.). 1985. 25.00 (*0-931757-24-X*); pap. 15.00 (*0-931757-25-8*) Pterodactyl Pr.

Divided World: Apinaye Social Structure. Roberto Da Matta. (Harvard Studies in Cultural Anthropology: No. 6). (Illus.). 200p. 1982. 48.00 (*0-674-21288-6*) HUP.

Divided World of the Bolivian Andes: A Structural View of Domination & Resistance. Dwight R. Hahn. (International Political Economy Ser.). 224p. 1991. 52.00 (*0-8448-1695-7*, Crane Russak) Taylor & Francis.

***Dividend Achievers Guide.** 60p. (Orig.). 1994. pap. 125.00 (*0-7605-0555-1*) Rector Pr.

***Dividend Achievers Handbook: Moody's.** 200p. 1995. pap. 195.00 (*0-7605-1819-X*) Rector Pr.

Dividend & Interest Withholding Compliance. write for info. (*0-318-57373-3*) P-H.

Dividend Connection. Geraldine Weiss & Gregory Weiss. 1995. 24.95 (*0-7931-1022-X*, 568005-01) Dearborn Finan.

***Dividend Imputation: Practice & Procedure.** Craig Elliffe. 175p. 1989. pap. 45.00 (*0-409-78891-0*, NZ) Butterworth Legal Pubs.

***Dividend Investor: A Safe & Sure Way to Build Wealth with High-Yield Dividend Stocks.** Harvey C. Knowles, 3rd & Damon H. Petty. 250p. 1995. 19.95 (*1-55738-892-X*) Probus Pub Co.

Dividend Potentials: A Productive Determinant for Investment Decision, 1990 Edition. 2nd ed. Duncan L. Marshall. (Illus.). 68p. (Orig.). 1990. pap. text ed. 25.00 (*0-9626505-1-X*) D Marshall Pub.

***Dividend Record Handbook: Moody's.** 300p. (Orig.). 1995. pap. 825.00 (*0-7605-1810-6*) Rector Pr.

Dividend Reinvestment Catalog. P. Y. Feng. 330p. 1981. pap. 8.50 (*0-934036-05-5*) PMF Research.

Dividend Reinvestment Directory. P. Y. Feng. LC 79-87718. 1979. pap. 4.95 (*0-934036-01-2*) PMF Research.

Dividend Reinvestment Guide. P. Y. Feng. LC 79-87719. 1979. pap. 3.95 (*0-934036-02-0*) PMF Research.

Dividend Reinvestment Handbook. P. Y. Feng. LC 79-84219. 1979. pap. 18.50 (*0-934036-00-4*) PMF Research.

Dividend Reinvestment Handbook. 2nd ed. P. Y. Feng. LC 80-84630. 701p. 1981. pap. 25.00 (*0-934036-04-7*) PMF Research.

Dividend Reinvestment Plans: Guide Almanac, 1991. Ed. by Sumie Kinoshita. 230p. 1992. 75.00 (*0-933183-10-0*) Evergreen Ent.

Dividend Reinvestment Plans: Guide Almanac, 1992. Ed. by Sumie Kinoshita. 230p. 1993. 65.00x (*0-933183-11-9*) Evergreen Ent.

Dividend Reinvestment Plans: Guide Almanac, 1993. Ed. by Sumie Kinoshita. 230p. (Orig.). 1994. 65.00 (*0-933183-14-3*) Evergreen Ent.

***Dividend Reinvestment Plans: Guide Almanac, 1994.** Sumie Kinoshita. 1995. pap. 65.00x (*0-933183-16-X*) Evergreen Ent.

Dividend Reinvestment Plans: Guide Annual, 1989. Ed. by Sumie Kinoshita. 220p. 1990. 75.00x (*0-933183-05-4*) Evergreen Ent.

Dividend Reinvestment Plans: Guide Annual, 1990. Sumie Kinoshita. 228p. 1991. 75.00x (*0-933183-07-0*) Evergreen Ent.

Dividends Don't Lie: Finding Value in Blue Chip Stocks. Geraldine Weiss & Janet Lowe. (Illus.). 233p. 1990. 23.95 (*0-88462-115-4*, 5608-11); pap. 12.95 (*0-7931-0023-2*, 5608-30) Dearborn Finan.

Dividends to Pay. Edward D. Kennedy. LC 68-56239. (Reprints of Economic Classics Ser.). xvii, 288p. 1969. reprint ed. 37.50 (*0-678-00522-2*) Kelley.

Dividends under the Income Tax. Daniel M. Holland. (Fiscal Studies Ser.: No. 7). 207p. 1962. reprint ed. 53.90 (*0-87014-455-3*) Natl Bur Econ Res.

Dividing & Reuniting of America, 1848-1877. 2nd ed. George T. McJimsey. Ed. by Vincent P. DeSantis. (Forums American History Ser.). 1990. pap. text ed. write for info. (*0-88273-170-X*) Forum Pr IL.

Dividing Discipline: Hegemony & Diversity in International Theory. Kalevi J. Holsti. 176p. 1987. pap. text ed. 19.95 (*0-04-445000-1*) Routledge Chapman & Hall.

Dividing Head & Deluxe Accessories. David J. Gingery. LC 80-66142. (Build Your Own Metalworking Shop from Scrap Ser.). (Illus.). 160p. 1982. pap. 8.95 (*1-878087-05-3*) D J Gingery.

Dividing Line. Richard Parrish. 1994. 5.99 (*0-451-40430-0*, Onyx) NAL-Dutton.

Dividing Lines: Canals, Railroads & Urban Rivalry in Ohio's Hocking Valley, 1825-1875. David H. Mould. 318p. (C). 1992. lib. bdg. 51.00 (*1-882090-06-3*) Wright State Univ Pr.

Dividing Lines: Poetry, Class & Ideology in the 1930s. Adrian Caesar. Ed. by Jonathan Dollimore & Alan Sinfield. (Cultural Politics Ser.). 176p. 1991. text ed. 59.95 (*0-7190-3375-6*, Pub. by Manchester Univ Pr UK); text ed. 16.95 (*0-7190-3376-4*, Pub. by Manchester Univ Pr UK) St Martin.

Dividing Muse: Images of Sacred Disjunction in Milton's Poetry. Sanford Budick. LC 84-17270. 223p. reprint ed. pap. 63.60 (*0-7837-3286-4*, 2057688) Bks Demand.

Dividing of Soul & Spirit. Bill Freeman. (Illus.). 15p. (Orig.). 1984. pap. 0.50 (*0-914271-03-2*) Mnstry Wrd.

Dividing Paths: Cherokees & South Carolinians Through the Era of Revolution. Tom Hatley. (Illus.). 352p. 1993. 49.95 (*0-19-506989-7*) OUP.

***Dividing Paths: Cherokees & South Carolinians Through the Era of Revolution.** Tom Hatley. (Illus.). 352p. 1995. pap. 19.95 (*0-19-509638-X*) OUP.

Dividing Public & Private: Law, Politics, & Social Theory. Gerald Turkel. LC 91-12105. 272p. 1992. text ed. 49.95 (*0-275-94154-X*, C4154, Praeger Pubs) Greenwood.

Dividing Reality. Eli Hirsch. LC 92-36251. (Illus.). 264p. 1993. 45.00 (*0-19-505754-6*) OUP.

Dividing Rhine: Politics & Society in Contemporary France & Germany. Ed. by Jack Trumpbour. LC 89-6568. (International Perspectives on Europe - An Annual Ser.: Vol. 1). 216p. 1989. 49.95 (*0-85496-589-0*) Berg Pubs.

Dividing River - The Meeting Shore. David Kherdian. 80p. (Orig.). 1991. 12.95 (*0-936385-01-4*); pap. 8.95 (*0-685-56349-9*) J Friedlander.

Dividing the Child: Social & Legal Dilemmas of Custody. Eleanor E. Maccoby & Robert H. Mnookin. (Illus.). 369p. 1992. 45.00 (*0-674-21294-0*) HUP.

***Dividing the Child: Social & Legal Dilemmas of Custody.** Eleanor E. Maccoby & Robert H. Mnookin. (Illus.). 369p. 1994. pap. text ed. 18.95 (*0-674-21295-9*, MACDIX) HUP.

D

2048 An Asterisk (*) at the beginning of an entry indicates that the title is appearing in BIP for the first time.

D

An Asterisk (*) at the beginning of an entry indicates that the title is appearing in BIP for the first time.

2049

Divine Hiddenness & Human Reason. J. L. Schellenberg. LC 92-32633. (Cornell Studies in the Philosophy of Religion). 232p. (C). 1993. 34.50 (*0-8014-2792-4*) Cornell U Pr.

Divine Hierarchy: Popular Hinduism in Central India. Lawrence A. Babb. LC 75-61693. (Illus.). 266p. 1989. text ed. 43.00 (*0-231-03882-8*); pap. text ed. 17.50 (*0-231-08387-4*) Col U Pr.

Divine Horsemen: The Living Gods of Haiti. Maya Deren. LC 83-16228. (Illus.). 350p. (C). 1984. reprint ed. 24.00 (*0-914232-64-9*, Documentext); reprint ed. pap. 15.00 (*0-914232-63-0*, Documentext) McPherson & Co.

Divine-Human Encounter. Emil Brunner. LC 80-12399. 207p. 1980. reprint ed. text ed. 35.00 (*0-313-22398-X*, BRDH, Greenwood Pr) Greenwood.

Divine Humanity see Proofs for the Proclamations of Christ

Divine Humanness. Aarne Siirala. Tr. by T. A. Kantonen. LC 70-99460. 192p. reprint ed. pap. 54.80 (*0-685-16160-9*, 2026964) Bks Demand.

Divine Hunger: Cannibalism As a Cultural System. Peggy R. Sanday. (Illus.). 304p. 1986. pap. 18.95 (*0-521-31114-4*) Cambridge U Pr.

Divine Hymns & Ancient Thought, Vol. 1: Rgveda Hymns & Ancient Thought. Sadashiv A. Dange. 1992. 36.00 (*81-8364-2862-5*, Pub. by Navrang) S Asia.

Divine Iliad, 2 vols. Walter Russell. (Illus.). 286p. 1971. reprint ed. Vol. I, 286p. text ed. 15.00 (*1-879605-22-8*); reprint ed. Vol. II, 238p. text ed. 15.00 (*1-879605-23-6*) U Sci & Philos.

Divine Iliad, 2 vols., Set. Walter Russell. (Illus.). 524p. 1971. reprint ed. text ed. write for info. (*1-879605-24-4*) U Sci & Philos.

***Divine Image.** Jonathan Murro. (Illus.). 477p. 1990. 14.95 (*0-917189-08-6*) Colton Found.

Divine Image: A Study of Blake's Interpretation of Christianity. Margaret Bottrall. 119p. (C). 1950. reprint ed. pap. text ed. 75.00 (*0-8383-0005-7*) M S G Haskell Hse.

Divine Images: A History of Jesus on the Screen. Roy Kinnard & Tim Davis. (Illus.). 256p. 1992. pap. 17.95 (*0-8065-1284-9*, Citadel Pr) Carol Pub Group.

Divine Immutability: A Critical Reconsideration. Isaak A. Dorner. LC 94-17160. 1994. pap. 16.00 (*0-8006-3213-3*, 1-3213, Fortress Pr) Augsburg Fortress.

Divine Impartiality: Paul & a Theological Axiom. Jouette M. Bassler. Ed. by William Baird. LC 81-1367. (Society of Biblical Literature Dissertation Ser.). (C). 1982. pap. text ed. 20.95 (*0-89130-475-4*, 0-06-01-59) Scholars Pr GA.

Divine Impassibility: An Essay in Philosophical Theology. Richard E. Creel. 300p. 1985. 74.95 (*0-521-30317-6*) Cambridge U Pr.

Divine Infinity in Greek & Medieval Thought. Leo Sweeney. LC 91-30855. 350p. 1992. text ed. 48.95 (*0-8204-1178-7*) P Lang Pubs.

***Divine Initiative: Grace, World-Order, & Human Freedom in the Early Writings of Bernard Lonergan.** J. Michael Stebbins. (Lonergan Studies). 480p. 1994. 65.00 (*0-8020-0464-4*) U of Toronto Pr.

Divine Inspiration: A Homer Kelly Mystery. Jane Langton. (Illus.). 416p. 1994. reprint ed. mass mkt. 5.95 (*0-14-017376-5*, Penguin Bks) Viking Penguin.

Divine Inspiration: From Benin to Bahia. Photos by Phyllis Galembo. LC 92-2340. (Illus.). 1993. 60.00 (*0-8263-1377-9*) U of NM Pr.

Divine Inspiration of the Bible. Arthur W. Pink. pap. 3.99 (*0-87377-075-7*) GAM Pubns.

Divine Institutes, Bks. 1-7. Lactantius. LC 64-18669. (Fathers of the Church Ser.: Vol. 49). 495p. 1964. 29.95 (*0-8132-0049-0*) Cath U Pr.

***Divine Intervention, Set, 4 vols.** Tristan A. MacAvery. 156p. (Orig.). 1993. 6.95 (*1-883688-04-3*) Starwolf Pr.

***Divine Intervention: Dies Irae, Pt. 4.** Tristan A. MacAvery. 45p. (Orig.). 1993. 3.00 (*1-883688-03-5*) Starwolf Pr.

***Divine Intervention: Invocation, Pt. 1.** Tristan A. MacAvery. 24p. (Orig.). 1993. 1.00 (*1-883688-00-0*) Starwolf Pr.

***Divine Intervention: Liturgy, Pt. 3.** Tristan A. MacAvery. 50p. (Orig.). 1993. 3.00 (*1-883688-02-7*) Starwolf Pr.

***Divine Intervention: Procession, Pt. 2.** Tristan A. MacAvery. 37p. (Orig.). 1993. 3.00 (*1-883688-01-9*) Starwolf Pr.

***Divine Intervention & Miracles in Jewish Theology.** Ed. by Dan Cohn-Sherbok. LC 95-18806. (Studies in Jewish Theology: Vol. 3). 220p. 1996. text ed. 89.95 (*0-7734-9093-0*) E Mellen.

Divine Intimacy: A Celebration of Prayer & the Joy of Christian Life, 4 vols. 2nd ed. Gabriel of St. Mary Magdalen. LC 86-83132. (Orig.). 1987. reprint ed. pap. 13.95 (*0-685-73842-6*); reprint ed. Vol. 1, 284p. pap. 13.95 (*0-89870-142-2*); reprint ed. Vol. 2, 265p. pap. 13.95 (*0-89870-143-0*); reprint ed. Vol. 3, 279p. pap. 13.95 (*0-89870-144-9*); reprint ed. Vol. 4, 284p. pap. 13.95 (*0-89870-145-7*) Ignatius Pr.

Divine Invasion. Philip K. Dick. LC 90-55677. 240p. 1991. pap. 10.00 (*0-679-73445-7*, Vin) Random.

Divine Invasions: A Life of Philip K. Dick. Lawrence Sutin. 1991. pap. 12.95 (*0-8065-1228-8*, Citadel Pr) Carol Pub Group.

Divine Joy at Play. Gayatri Devi. 1985. 11.50 (*0-8364-1487-X*, KL Mukhopadhyay) S Asia.

Divine Justice. Gisella Zamboni. Tr. by Ingram. 244p. 1994. pap. 8.95 (*1-56901-345-4*) NW Pub.

Divine King of England: A Study in Anthropology. Margaret A. Murray. LC 79-8115. reprint ed. 29.50 (*0-404-18428-6*) AMS Pr.

***Divine Kingdom.** Shaykh M. An-Naqshbandi. 112p. (Orig.). 1995. pap. 9.95 (*0-934905-28-2*) Kazi Pubns.

Divine Landscapes. Ronald Blythe. LC 86-4821. (Illus.). 256p. 1987. pap. write for info. (*0-15-626110-3*, Harvest Bks) HarBrace.

Divine Language of Celestial Correspondences. Coulson Turnbull. 352p. 1981. pap. 30.00 (*0-89540-116-9*, SB-116, Sun Bks) Sun Pub.

Divine Language of Celestial Correspondences. enl. rev. ed. Coulson Turnbull. 349p. 1970. reprint ed. spiral bd. 8.80 (*0-7873-0901-X*) Mokelumne.

Divine Library. James A. Stewart. pap. 1.99 (*1-56632-040-2*) Revival Lit.

Divine Library: A Comprehensive Reference Guide to the Sacred Texts & Spiritual Literature of the World. Rufus C. Camphausen. (Illus.). 128p. (Orig.). 1992. pap. 12.95 (*0-89281-351-2*) Inner Tradit.

Divine Life. rev. ed. Hilton Hotema. 168p. 1963. spiral bd. 7.70 (*0-7873-0442-5*) Mokelumne.

Divine Life in a Divine Body. Navajata. 260p. 1991. pap. 11.95 (*0-685-54536-9*) Aurobindo Assn.

Divine Light & Fire: Experiencing Esoteric Christianity. Peter Roche de Coppens. 192p. 1994. reprint ed. pap. text ed. 12.95 (*0-8264-0765-X*) Continuum.

Divine Light & Love: Practicing Esoteric Christianity. Peter Roche de Coppens. 192p. 1994. reprint ed. pap. text ed. 14.95 (*0-8264-0766-8*) Continuum.

Divine Light Invocation. 2nd ed. Sivananda Radha. LC 90-31896. (Illus.). 104p. 1990. pap. 10.95 (*0-931454-17-4*) Timeless Bks.

Divine Liturgy. 185p. (Orig.). 1989. pap. write for info. (*0-9623598-0-7*) O Poloukhine.

Divine Liturgy. Ed. by David Drillock et al. 368p. 1982. text ed. 30.00 (*0-913836-95-8*) St Vladimirs.

Divine Liturgy. Monks of New Skete Staff. Tr. by Laurence Mancuso. 306p. 1988. 50.00 (*0-935129-11-1*) Monks of New Skete.

Divine Liturgy: Liturgical Music. Vladimir Soroka. 158p. 1991. 18.95 (*1-878997-13-0*) St Tikhons Pr.

Divine Liturgy According to St. John Chrysostom with Appendicies. 2nd ed. Tr. by Russian Orthodox Greek Catholic Church of America Staff. 1977. Black Cover. 10.00 (*1-878997-17-3*); White Cover. 10.00 (*1-878997-30-0*); Large Altar ed. 16.95 (*1-878997-18-1*) St Tikhons Pr.

Divine Liturgy According to St. John Chrysostom with Scripture References & Commentary. T. Bobosh. 1989. pap. 4.95 (*0-937032-70-0*) Light&Life Pub Co MN.

Divine Liturgy for Choir & Laity: Liturgy of St. John Chrysostom. Tr. by Laurence Campbell. 107p. 1993. write for info. (*0-912927-56-9*, D017) St John Kronstadt.

Divine Liturgy of Saint John Chrysostom: With Transliteration Equals He Theia Leitourgia Tou Hagiou Ioannou Tou Chrysostomou: a New Translation. Holy Cross Greek Orthodox School of Theology, Hellenic College Faculty. 1992. write for info. (*0-318-69247-3*) Holy Cross Orthodox.

Divine Liturgy of St. Basil the Great. Tr. by Ernest T. Abdel-Massih et al. 257p. 1982. pap. 7.00 (*0-932098-19-3*) St Mark Coptic Orthodox.

Divine Liturgy of St. Basil the Great: (Clergyman's Edition) Hellenic College-Holy Cross Greek Orthodox School of Theology, Faculty Staff. (ENG & GRE.). 1988. 19.95 (*0-318-35074-2*); spiral bd. 16.95 (*0-318-35075-0*) Holy Cross Orthodox.

Divine Liturgy of St. Gregory. Tr. by Rassophor-Monk Laurence. 52p. (Orig.). 1993. pap. 3.50 (*0-912927-22-4*, D001) St John Kronstadt.

Divine Liturgy of St. Iakoos. Holy Cross Faculty Staff. 60p. 1988. spiral bd. 15.95 (*0-917651-60-X*) Holy Cross Orthodox.

***Divine Liturgy of St. John Chrysostom.** Monks of New Skete Staff. Tr. by Laurence Mancuso. 190p. (Orig.). 1994. pap. 25.00 (*0-935129-24-3*) Monks of New Skete.

***Divine Liturgy of St. John Chrysostom.** large type ed. Orthodox Eastern Church Staff. 1994. pap. 10.00 (*0-89981-306-2*) Eastern Orthodox.

Divine Liturgy of St. John Chrysostom: (Clergyman's Edition) Hellenic College-Holy Cross Greek Orthodox School of Theology, Faculty Staff. 87p. (ENG & GRE.). 1986. 18.95 (*0-917651-15-4*); spiral bd. 17.95 (*0-917651-16-2*) Holy Cross Orthodox.

Divine Liturgy of St. John Chrysostom: Large Edition. Hellenic College-Holy Cross Greek Orthodox School of Theology, Faculty Staff. 224p. 1986. 5.95 (*0-917651-17-0*) Holy Cross Orthodox.

Divine Liturgy of the Great Church with Melodies for Congregational Sin. Paul N. Harrilchak. (Illus.). x, 221p. (Orig.). 1984. 15.00 (*0-930055-00-4*) Holy Trinity Ortho.

Divine Love & Wisdom. Emanuel Swedenborg. Tr. by George Dole. LC 85-50918. 302p. 1986. pap. 6.95 (*0-87785-129-8*) Swedenborg.

Divine Love & Wisdom. Emanuel Swedenborg. Tr. by J. C. Ager. LC 75-37094. 305p. 1908. reprint ed. 12.00 (*0-87785-056-9*) Swedenborg.

Divine Luminous Wisdom That Dispels the Darkness God-Man Man-God. rev. ed. M. R. Bawa Muhaiyaddeen. (Illus.). 288p. 1977. pap. 9.00 (*0-914390-11-2*) Fellowship Pr PA.

Divine Madness: Mohammed Abdulle Hassan, 1856-1920. Abdi Sheik-Abdi. LC 93-20058. 240p. (C). 1993. text ed. 55.00 (*0-86232-443-2*, Pub. by Zed Books UK); pap. 22.50 (*0-86232-444-0*, Pub. by Zed Books UK) Humanities.

Divine Madness & the Absurd Paradox: Ibsen's Peer Gynt & the Philosophy of Kierkegaard. Bruce G. Shapiro. LC 89-49239. (Contributions in Drama & Theatre Studies: No. 29). 272p. 1990. text ed. 59.95 (*0-313-27290-5*, SGJ/, Greenwood Pr) Greenwood.

Divine Master Life & Teachings of Guru Nanak Dev. Sewaram Singh. (C). 1989. 32.50 (*81-212-0249-3*, Pub. by Gian Publng Hse II) S Asia.

***Divine Matrix: Creativity As Link Between East & West.** Joseph A. Bracken. LC 95-3202. (Faith Meets Faith Ser.). 225p. (Orig.). 1995. pap. 19.95 (*1-57075-004-1*) Orbis Bks.

Divine Memories of Sathya Sai Baba. Diana Baskin. 296p. (Orig.). 1990. pap. 9.00 (*1-878599-00-3*) Birth Day.

Divine Mercy: Re-Translation & Outline of Pope John Paul II's Encyclical Rich in Mercy. Ed. by Marians of the Immaculate Conception Staff. LC 87-62983. 76p. 1988. pap. text ed. write for info. (*0-944203-07-8*) Marian Pr.

Divine Mercy in My Soul: The Diary of the Servant of God Sister M. Faustian Kowalska. Faustina Kowalska. Ed. by Congregation of Marians of the Immaculate Conception. Tr. by Seraphim Michalenko. LC 87-90691. (Illus.). 744p. 1988. write for info. (*0-944203-03-5*); pap. text ed. 17.95 (*0-944203-04-3*) Marian Pr.

Divine Mercy Message & Devotion. rev. ed. Vinny Flynn & Seraphim Michalenko. LC 93-77440. (Illus.). 92p. 1994. write for info. (*0-944203-17-5*) Marian Pr.

Divine Milieu. Pierre Teilhard De Chardin. 160p. 1991. reprint ed. lib. bdg. 27.00x (*0-8095-9089-1*) Borgo Pr.

Divine Milieu: An Essay on the Interior Life. Pierre Teilhard De Chardin. 1975. pap. 11.00 (*0-06-090487-9*, CN487, PL) HarpC.

Divine Moment. James L. Prior. (Salamander Ser.: No. 4). 19p. 1993. pap. 2.95 (*1-56640-594-7*) Pomegranate Calif.

Divine Mosaic: Women's Images of the Sacred Other. Ed. by Theresa King. LC 93-44760. 300p. (Orig.). 1994. pap. 15.95 (*0-936663-10-3*) Yes Intl.

Divine Mother Speaks. Hilda Charlton. Ed. by Golden Quest Staff. (Illus.). 48p. (Orig.). 1993. pap. 5.50 (*0-927383-18-7*) Golden Quest.

Divine Mysteries. William J. Salva. 210p. (Orig.). 1991. 13.95 (*0-9629416-2-X*); lib. bdg. write for info. (*0-9629416-1-1*); pap. 10.95 (*0-9629416-0-3*) Knights Christ.

Divine Mystery. J. Reader. 79p. pap. 4.95 (*0-88172-117-4*) Believers Bkshelf.

Divine Name & Presence: The Memra. Robert Hayward. LC 81-10928. (Publications of the Oxford Centre for Postgraduate Hebrew Study). 208p. 1981. 46.00 (*0-86598-067-5*) Rowman.

Divine Name Controversy, Vol. 1. Firpo W. Carr. 1991. pap. 9.95 (*0-9631293-1-7*) ScholarTech.

Divine Name in the India Tradition: A Comparative Study. S. G. Tulpule. (C). 1991. 28.50 (*81-85182-50-7*, Pub. by Indus Pub II) S Asia.

***Divine Nature: A Spiritual Perspective on the Environmental Crisis.** Drutakarma Dasa & Mukunda D. Goswami. LC 95-5867. (Orig.). 1995. write for info. (*0-89213-297-3*) Bhaktivedanta.

***Divine Nature: A Spiritual Perspective on the Environmental Crisis.** Drutakarma Dasa & Mukunda D. Goswami. LC 95-5867. (Illus.). 128p. (Orig.). 1995. pap. 9.95 (*0-89213-296-5*) Bhaktivedanta.

Divine Nature & Human Language: Essays in Philosophical Theology. William P. Alston. LC 89-898. 288p. 1989. 42.50 (*0-8014-2258-2*); pap. 15.95 (*0-8014-9545-8*) Cornell U Pr.

***Divine New Order.** Gabriel of Sedona. 245p. (Orig.). 1995. pap. 14.95 (*0-9647357-0-9*) Ext Schls Melchizedek.

Divine Office-Christian Prayer: The Liturgy of the Hours. large type ed. Tr. by International Commission on English in the Liturgy Staff. 1600p. 1986. 25.95 (*0-89942-407-4*) Catholic Bk Pub.

Divine Omniscience & Human Freedom: Thomas Aquinas & Charles Hartshorne. John C. Moskop. LC 84-1172. xviii, 105p. 1984. 14.95 (*0-86554-123-X*, MUP/H102) Mercer Univ Pr.

Divine Omniscience & Omnipotence in Medieval Philosophy. Ed. by Tamar Rudavsky. 1984. lib. bdg. 119.00 (*90-277-1750-8*) Kluwer Ac.

Divine Order of Faith: How to Get from the Problem to the Answer. Creflo A. Dollar, Jr. 80p. (Orig.). 1993. pap. 8.75 (*0-9634781-1-7*) Wrld Chang Minist.

Divine Origin of the Restoration. F. E. Butterworth. 1989. 12.00 (*0-941227-01-4*) Cosmic Pr Chico.

Divine Outline of History: Dispensations & the Church. R. B. Thieme, Jr. Ed. by Wayne F. Hill. (Orig.). (C). 1989. pap. (*1-55764-043-2*) R B Thieme.

Divine Partnership: The God-Mind Plan for Saving Both Planet & Man. Jean K. Foster. (Truth for the New Age Ser.: Bk. 3). 170p. (Orig.). 1991. pap. text ed. 9.95 (*0-9626366-1-4*) TeamUp.

Divine Passions: The Social Construction of Emotion in India. Ed. by Owen M. Lynch. 340p. 1990. 45.00 (*0-520-06647-2*) U CA Pr.

Divine Pastorale et la Naissance de l'Univers: Traduction Francais par l'Auteur de la Premiere Veillee d'une Epopee Ecrit en Langue Ruandais, 2 vols., Vols. 1-2. Abbe A. Kagame. (B. E. Ser.: No. 105). (FRE.). 1955. 21.00 (*0-8115-3037-X*) Periodicals Srv.

***Divine Peacock: Understanding Contemporary India.** Ed. by K. Satchidananda Murty & Amit DasGupta. (C). 1994. text ed. 24.00 (*81-224-0699-8*, Pub. by Wiley Eastern II) S Asia.

Divine Perceptions: Paramhansa Yogananda. LC 85-71376. 1993. pap. 18.95 (*0-937134-09-0*) Amrita Found.

Divine Personality & Human Life: Being the Gifford Lectures Delivered in the University of Aberdeen in the Years 1918 & 1919, Second Course. Clement C. Webb. LC 77-37917. (Select Bibliographies Reprint Ser.). 1977. reprint ed. 23.95 (*0-8369-6754-2*) Ayer.

Divine Plan. Gabriel. 100p. 1996. pap. 9.99 (*0-9641745-1-0*) Bell Rock.

Divine Plan: Commentary on the Secret Doctrine. 3rd ed. Geoffrey Barborka. 1972. 45.00 (*81-7059-184-8*) Theos Pub Hse.

Divine Plot: Astrology, Reincarnation, Cosmology & History. A. T. Mann. (Illus.). 288p. 1991. pap. 15.95 (*1-85230-232-1*) Element MA.

Divine Plumbline: A Study Guide. Bruce Thompson. (Illus.). 128p. (Orig.). 1983. student ed 7.95 (*0-935779-00-0*); audio 49.95 (*0-935779-01-9*); vhs 275.00 (*0-935779-02-7*) Crown Min.

Divine Poetry & Drama in Sixteenth-century England. Lily B. Campbell. LC 59-3609. 276p. reprint ed. pap. 78.70 (*0-317-26043-X*, 2024437) Bks Demand.

Divine Poetry & Drama in 16th Century England. Lily B. Campbell. LC 79-148614. 276p. (C). 1972. reprint ed. 60.00 (*0-87752-143-3*) Gordian.

Divine Politician: Samuel Cooper & the American Revolution in Boston. Charles W. Akers. LC 81-18917. (Illus.). 465p. 1982. text ed. 45.00 (*0-930350-19-7*) NE U Pr.

Divine Possibilities in Man. Gopi Krishna. (C). 1993. pap. 7.50 (*81-85944-06-7*, Pub. by UBS Pubs Dist II) S Asia.

Divine Power: A Study of Karl Barth & Charles Hartshorne. Sheila G. Davaney. LC 85-45502. (Harvard Dissertations in Religion Ser.). 224p. 1986. pap. 17.00 (*0-8006-7072-8*, 1-7072, Fortress Pr) Augsburg Fortress.

Divine Power: The Medieval Power Distinction up to Its Adoption by Albert, Bonaventure, & Aquinas. Lawrence Moonan. LC 93-30542. 400p. 1994. 59.00 (*0-19-826755-X*, Clarendon Pr) OUP.

Divine Power & Possibility in St. Peter Damian's De Divina Omnipotencia. Irven M. Resnick. LC 91-43923. (Studien und Texte zur Geistesgeschichte des Mittelalters Ser.: No. 31). 128p. 1992. 43.00 (*90-04-09572-1*) E J Brill.

Divine Power in Process Theism: A Philosophical Critique. David Basinger. LC 87-24080. (SUNY Series in Philosophy). 135p. 1988. 64.50 (*0-88706-708-5*); pap. 21.95 (*0-88706-709-3*) State U NY Pr.

Divine Principle. 2nd rev. ed. Sun M. Moon. 536p. 1973. 10.95 (*0-910621-05-5*); pap. 7.95 (*0-685-42755-2*) HSA Pubns.

Divine Principle. 2nd rev. ed. Sun M. Moon. 536p. (C). 1973. pap. 7.95 (*0-910621-04-7*) HSA Pubns.

Divine Principle. 5th rev. ed. Sun M. Moon. 536p. (C). 1977. pap. 5.95 (*0-910621-03-9*) HSA Pubns.

Divine Principles of Gathering. R. K. Campbell. 40p. pap. 0.45 (*0-88172-015-1*) Believers Bkshelf.

Divine Proportion. Luca Pacioli. (Janus Ser.). (C). Date not set. 25.00 (*0-89835-065-4*) Abaris Bks.

Divine Proportion: A Study in Mathematical Beauty. H. E. Huntley. LC 70-93195. (Orig.). 1970. pap. 5.95 (*0-486-22254-3*) Dover.

Divine Providence. Emanuel Swedenborg. Tr. by W. Wunch. LC 74-30441. 386p. 1963. 12.00 (*0-87785-059-3*); pap. 3.95 (*0-87785-061-5*) Swedenborg.

Divine Providence & Human Suffering. P. G. Walsh & James Walsh. LC 84-48852. (Message of the Fathers of the Church Ser.: Vol. 17). 272p. 1985. 15.95 (*0-8146-5357-X*); pap. 14.95 (*0-8146-5328-6*) Liturgical Pr.

***Divine Providence in the England of Shakespeare's Histories.** Henry A. Kelly. LC 75-111485. 354p. 1970. reprint ed. pap. 100.90 (*0-7837-8650-6*, 2059231) Bks Demand.

***Divine Purpose & Heroic Response in Homer & Virgil: The Political Plan of Zeus.** John Alvis. 320p. 1995. lib. bdg. 58.50 (*0-8476-8014-2*); pap. text ed. 21.95 (*0-8476-8015-0*) Rowman.

Divine Pymander. Hermes Trismegistus. Tr. by J. Randolph. 144p. 1972. reprint ed. 9.00 (*0-911662-48-0*) Yoga.

Divine Pymander of Hermes Mercurius Trismegistus. Tr. by John Everard & Hargrave & J. C. Jennings. LC 73-84044. (Secret Doctrine Reference Ser.). 140p. 1994. reprint ed. 13.00 (*0-913510-07-6*) Wizards.

Divine Pymander of Hermes Trismegistus. G. R. Mead. 1990. pap. 5.95 (*1-55818-152-0*, Pub. by Alexandrian Pr) Holmes Pub.

Divine Realm. John Avedon. Date not set. 23.00 (*0-06-016894-3*, HarpT) HarpC.

Divine Remedies: A Textbook on Christian Healing. Theodosia D. Schobert. 116p. 1981. pap. 11.00 (*0-89540-114-2*, SB-114) Sun Pub.

***Divine Representations: Postmodernism & Spirituality.** Ed. by Ann W. Astell. LC 94-32753. 176p. 1995. pap. 17.95 (*0-8091-3528-0*) Paulist Pr.

Divine Revelation: Our Moral Relation with God. Kern R. Trembath. 240p. 1991. 39.95 (*0-19-506937-4*) OUP.

***Divine Revelation in Pali Buddhism.** 2nd ed. Peter Masefield. 187p. 1995. pap. 14.00 (*955-9028-02-2*) Paul & Co Pubs.

Divine Revelation of Hell. Mark K. Baxter. 224p. 1993. pap. 8.99 (*0-88368-279-6*) Whitaker Hse.

Divine Revelation of Hell - Una Revelacion Divina del Infierno. Mary K. Baxter. 144p. (SPA.). 1993. pap. 8.99 (*0-88368-288-5*) Whitaker Hse.

Divine Right & Democracy: An Anthology of Political Writing of Stuart England. Ed. by David Wootton. 512p. 1987. pap. 10.95 (*0-14-043250-7*, Penguin Classics) Viking Penguin.

Divine Right of Kings. John N. Figgis. 14.00 (*0-8446-0621-9*) Peter Smith.

Divine Right's Trip: A Novel of the Counterculture. 2nd ed. Gurney Norman. LC 90-80306. 320p. 1990. reprint ed. pap. 14.50 (*0-917788-42-7*) Gnomon Pr.

Divine Romance. Gene Edwards. LC 92-33145. 1993. 8.99 (*0-8423-1092-4*) Tyndale.

Divine Romance. Paramahansa Yogananda. LC 86-63172. (Illus.). 496p. 1986. 12.00 (*0-87612-240-3*); pap. 6.50 (*0-87612-241-1*) Self Realization.

Divine Romance. Fulton J. Sheen. 142p. 1982. pap. 4.50 (*0-8189-0437-2*) Alba.

D

An Asterisk (*) at the beginning of an entry indicates that the title is appearing in BIP for the first time.

Divine Romance: Teresa of Avila's Narrative Theology. Joseph F. Chorpenning. LC 92-2619. (Values & Ethics Ser.: Vol. IV). (Orig.). 1992. 12.75 (0-8294-0732-4) Loyola Univ Pr.

Divine Runner. Earl Paulk. LC 78-71967. 142p. (Orig.). 1978. pap. 3.25 (0-917595-00-9) Kingdom Pubs.

Divine Sarah: A Life of Sarah Bernhardt. Arthur Gold & Robert Fizdale. LC 91-51192. 1992. pap. 17.00 (0-679-74185-2, Vin) Random.

Divine Science: Its Principle & Practice. Comp. by Fannie B. James. 1957. 9.95 (0-317-00039-X); pap. 7.95 (0-317-00040-3) Divine Sci Fed.

Divine Science & the Science of God: A Reformulation of Thomas Aquinas. Victor Preller. LC 66-21838. 291p. reprint ed. pap. 83.00 (0-317-08468-2, 2010543) Bks Demand.

Divine Science Way. Irwin Gregg. 1975. 6.95 (0-686-24352-8); pap. 4.95 (0-686-24353-6) Divine Sci Fed.

Divine Soap Opera. Eric Felderman. LC 92-40021. (Illus.). 1993. 49.95 (0-945942-35-4); pap. 36.95 (0-945942-36-2) Portmanteau Editions.

***Divine Song on the Northeast Frontier: Maine's Sacred Tunebooks, 1800-1830.** Linda G. Davenport. LC 95-9756. (Composers of North America Ser.: No. 18). 1995. write for info. (0-8108-3025-6) Scarecrow.

Divine Songs of Zarathushtra. Ed. by Irach J. Taraporewala. LC 74-21251. reprint ed. 125.00 (0-404-12802-5) AMS Pr.

***Divine Sources.** Shaykh M. An-Naqshbandi. (Mercy Oceans Ser.). 104p. (Orig.). 1995. pap. 7.95 (0-934905-43-6) Kazi Pubns.

Divine Sovereignty & Human Freedom. Samuel Fisk. LC 73-81550. 1973. pap. 7.99 (0-87213-166-1) Loizeaux.

Divine Sovereignty & Human Responsibility: Biblical Perspectives in Tension. D. A. Carson. LC 93-40945. 283p. 1994. reprint ed. pap. 19.99 (0-8010-2587-7) Baker Bk.

Divine Sovereignty, Human Freedom, & Responsibility in Prophetic Thought. Hobart E. Freeman. 210p. (Orig.). 1990. pap. 4.50 (1-878725-00-9) Faith Min & Pubns.

Divine Subjectivity: Understanding Hegel's Philosophy of Religion. Dale M. Schlitt. LC 90-33188. 368p. 1990. 39.50 (0-940866-11-0) U Scranton Pr.

Divine Succession: A Science of Gods Old & New. Alfred De Grazia. (Quantavolution Ser.). 204p. 1983. pap. 14.00 (0-940268-05-1) Metron Pubns.

Divine Symphony & Other Poems. Gabriel J. Karmeli. 40p. (Orig.). 1991. pap. 5.00 (971-10-0441-0, Pub. by New Day Pub PH) Cellar.

Divine Therapy: Pearls of Wisdom from the Baha'i Writings. Comp. by Annamarie Honnald. 1986. pap. 12.95 (0-85398-237-6) G Ronald Pub.

***Divine Treason: The Trial of Judas Iscariot.** Carlo Crozatti. LC 94-71913. 154p. (Orig.). 1994. pap. 14.95 (1-885455-00-3) DEC Unicorn.

Divine Trinity. David Brown. LC 85-18941. 328p. (C). 1984. 36.95 (0-87548-439-5) Open Court.

Divine Unity: A Universal Spirituality. John P. Patton. 303p. (Orig.). 1994. 24.95 (0-9639382-3-1); student ed 20.00 (0-9639382-1-5); lib. bdg. 29.95 (0-9639382-2-3); pap. 14.95 (0-9639382-0-7) Ctr Creat Power.

Divine Unity of Scripture. Adolph Saphir. LC 84-9642. 376p. 1984. reprint ed. pap. 10.99 (0-8254-3747-4) Kregel.

Divine Vengeance. M. Mroz. LC 77-120130. (Studies in Shakespeare: No. 24). 1970. reprint ed. lib. bdg. 48.95 (0-8383-1091-5) M S G Haskell Hse.

Divine Verdict: A Study of Divine Judgement in the Ancient Religions. John G. Griffiths. LC 90-48119. (Studies in the History of Religions (Suppl. to Numen): No. 52). xviii, 410p. 1990. 103.00 (90-04-09231-5) E J Brill.

Divine Victim. Mary Wings. 256p. 1994. pap. 9.95 (0-452-27210-6, Plume) NAL-Dutton.

Divine Violence: Spectacle, Psychosexuality, & Radical Christianity in the Argentine "Dirty War" Frank Graziano. 328p. (C). 1992. pap. text ed. 21.50 (0-8133-8232-7) Westview.

Divine Virginia: A Biography of Virginia Zucchi. Ivor F. Guest. LC 76-20006. (Dance Program Ser.: Vol. 1). 206p. reprint ed. pap. 58.80 (0-685-16054-8, 2027088) Bks Demand.

Divine Vision. Ed. by Vivian De Sola Pinto. LC 68-24905. (Studies in Blake: No. 3). 1973. reprint ed. lib. bdg. 75.00 (0-8383-0790-6) M S G Haskell Hse.

Divine War in the Old Testament & in the Arab Near East. Sa-Moon Kang. xv, 251p. (C). 1989. lib. bdg. 95.40 (0-89925-278-8) De Gruyter.

***Divine War in the Old Testament & in the Arab Near East.** Sa-Moon Kang. xv, 251p. (C). 1989. lib. bdg. 95.40 (3-11-011156-X) De Gruyter.

Divine Will & the Mechanical Philosophy: Gassendi & Descartes on Contingency & Necessity in the Created World. Margaret J. Osler. LC 93-37129. 256p. (C). 1994. 49.95 (0-521-46104-9) Cambridge U Pr.

Divine Wind: Japan's Kamikaze Force in World War II. Rikihei Inoguchi et al. LC 58-13974. (Bluejacket Paperback Ser.). (Illus.). 264p. 1994. pap. 14.95 (1-55750-394-X) Naval Inst Pr.

Divine Wind: Japan's Kamikaze Force in World War II. Rikihei Inoguchi et al. LC 76-45166. (Illus.). 224p. 1978. reprint ed. text ed. 35.00 (0-8371-9303-6, INDW, Greenwood Pr) Greenwood.

Divine Word: Milton & the Redemption of Language. Robert L. Entzminger. LC 84-28799. (Duquesne Studies; Language & Literature Ser.: Vol. 6). 188p. 1985. text ed. 22.50x (0-8207-0172-6) Duquesne.

Divine Word & Prophetic Word in Early Islam: A Reconsideration of the Sources, with Special Reference to the Divine Saying or Hadith Qudsi. William A. Graham. (Religion & Society Ser.). 1977. text ed. 56.00 (90-279-7612-0) Mouton.

Divine Yes. E. Stanley Jones. (Abingdon Classics Ser.). 160p. 1992. reprint ed. pap. 4.95 (0-687-10990-6) Abingdon.

Divinely Established Female: Because There Is No Record. Paula K. Thomas. 1994. pap. 7.00 (1-882821-05-X) DPK Pubns.

***Divinely Responding Classic: A Translation of the Shen Ying Jing from the Zhen Jin Da Cheng.** Yang Ji-zhou. Ed. by Bob Flaws. Tr. by Yang Ji-zhou et al. LC 93-74979. (Great Masters Ser.). 165p. (Orig.). 1994. pap. 18.95 (0-936185-55-4) Blue Poppy.

Diviners. Margaret Laurence. (Phoenix Fiction Ser.). 392p. (C). 1993. pap. 12.95 (0-226-46935-2) U Ch Pr.

***Diviners: A Book Length Poem.** Robert McDowell. 108p. 1995. 18.00 (1-885266-19-7, Pub. by Peterloo Poets UK); pap. 10.00 (1-885266-10-3, Pub. by Peterloo Poets UK) Story Line.

Diviner's Handbook: A Guide to the Timeless Art of Dowsing. Tom Graves. (Illus.). 192p. (Orig.). 1990. pap. 8.95 (0-89281-303-2) Inner Tradit.

Diviners, Notes. Margaret Laurence. pap. 4.50 (0-8220-0398-8) Cliffs.

Diving above Sea Level. Bruce Wienke. 66p. (C). 1993. 9.95 (0-941332-30-6) Best Pub Co.

Diving & Digging for Gold. rev. ed. Mary Hill. LC 73-22389. (Illus.). 48p. 1974. pap. 4.95 (0-87961-005-0) Naturegraph.

Diving & Dredging for Gold. Dick Anderson. (Illus.). 147p. (C). 1994. 12.95 (0-941332-31-4) Best Pub Co.

Diving & Equipment. 2nd rev. ed. Rusty Haggard. Ed. by Nancy Janicek. (Rotary Drilling Ser.: Unit V, Lesson 5). (Illus.). 47p. 1982. pap. text ed. 12.00 (0-88698-073-9, 2.50520) PETEX.

Diving & Snorkeling Guide to Australia: Coral Sea & Great Barrier Reef. Carl Roessler. 96p. 1991. 11.95 (1-55992-044-0, Pisces Bks) Gulf Pub.

Diving & Snorkeling Guide to Australia: Southeast Coast & Tasmania. Peter Stone. 96p. 1992. 11.95 (1-55992-059-9, Pisces Bks) Gulf Pub.

Diving & Snorkeling Guide to Belize. Franz O. Meyer. 96p. 1990. 11.95 (1-55992-033-5, Pisces Bks) Gulf Pub.

Diving & Snorkeling Guide to Bonaire. Jerry Schnabel & Susan L. Swygert. 96p. 1991. 11.95 (1-55992-043-2, Pisces Bks) Gulf Pub.

Diving & Snorkeling Guide to California's Central Coast: Including Southern Monterey County, San Luis Obispo County, Santa Barbara County, Ventura County. Darren Douglass. LC 94-20893. 80p. 1994. pap. 12.95 (1-55992-079-3, Pisces Bks) Gulf Pub.

Diving & Snorkeling Guide to Cozumel. 2nd ed. George S. Lewbel & Larry R. Martin. 96p. 1991. 11.95 (1-55992-034-3, Pisces Bks) Gulf Pub.

Diving & Snorkeling Guide to Florida's East Coast. 2nd ed. Stuart Cummings & Susanne Cummings. (Illus.). 96p. 1993. pap. 11.95 (1-55992-062-9, 2062, Pisces Bks) Gulf Pub.

Diving & Snorkeling Guide to Guam & Yap. Tim Rock. LC 93-30820. Date not set. write for info. (1-55992-076-9, Pisces Bks) Gulf Pub.

Diving & Snorkeling Guide to Northern California & the Monterey Peninsula. 2nd ed. Steve Rosenberg. 96p. 1992. pap. 11.95 (1-55992-052-1, Pisces Bks) Gulf Pub.

Diving & Snorkeling Guide to Palau. Tim Rock & Francis Toribiong. LC 93-27894. (Illus.). 96p. 1994. 11.95 (1-55992-068-8, Pisces Bks) Gulf Pub.

Diving & Snorkeling Guide to Roatan & Honduras' Bay Islands. Sharon Collins. LC 93-17943. 96p. 1993. 11.95 (1-55992-074-2, Pisces Bks) Gulf Pub.

Diving & Snorkeling Guide to Southern California. 2nd ed. Darren Douglass. LC 93-20673. 96p. 1994. 11.95 (1-55992-057-2, Pisces Bks) Gulf Pub.

Diving & Snorkeling Guide to St. Maarten, Saba & St. Eustatois. Jerry Schnabel & Susan L. Swygert. LC 94-8698. 96p. 1994. 11.95 (1-55992-066-1, Pisces Bks) Gulf Pub.

Diving & Snorkeling Guide to Texas. Barbara Dunn & Stephan Myers. 96p. 1990. 11.95 (1-55992-032-7, Pisces Bks) Gulf Pub.

Diving & Snorkeling Guide to the Bahamas: Family Islands & Grand Bahama. 2nd ed. Bob Keller & Charlotte Keller. LC 94-18171. 96p. 1994. 11.95 (1-55992-078-5) Gulf Pub.

Diving & Snorkeling Guide to the British Virgin Islands. Linda Sorensen. (Illus.). 96p. 1991. pap. 11.95 (1-55992-050-5, 2050, Pisces Bks) Gulf Pub.

Diving & Snorkeling Guide to the Cayman Islands. 2nd ed. Carl Roessler. 96p. 1993. 11.95 (1-55992-042-4, Pisces Bks) Gulf Pub.

Diving & Snorkeling Guide to the Fiji Islands. W. Gregory Brown. LC 92-45216. 96p. 1993. pap. 11.95 (1-55992-063-7, Pisces Bks) Gulf Pub.

Diving & Snorkeling Guide to the Florida Keys. 2nd ed. John Halas et al. 96p. 1993. 11.95 (1-55992-055-6, Pisces Bks) Gulf Pub.

Diving & Snorkeling Guide to the Great Lakes. Kathy Johnson & Greg Lashbrook. 96p. 1991. 11.95 (1-55992-046-7, Pisces Bks) Gulf Pub.

Diving & Snorkeling Guide to the Hawaiian Islands. 2nd ed. Doug Wallin. 112p. 1991. 11.95 (1-55992-038-6, Pisces Bks) Gulf Pub.

Diving & Snorkeling Guide to the Pacific Northwest: Includes Puget Sound, San Juan Islands, & Vancouver Islands. Edward Weber. LC 92-23549. 1993. 11.95 (1-55992-075-0, Pisces Bks) Gulf Pub.

Diving & Snorkeling Guide to the Red Sea. John Ratterree. 96p. 1994. 11.95 (1-55992-081-5, PISCES) Gulf Pub.

Diving & Snorkeling Guide to the Turks & Caicos Islands. Stuart Cummings & Susanne Cummings. LC 92-34115. 1993. 11.95 (1-55992-067-X, Pisces Bks) Gulf Pub.

Diving & Snorkeling Guide to the U. S. Virgin Islands. Susanne Cummings & Stuart Cummings. 96p. 1992. pap. 11.95 (1-55992-053-X, Pisces Bks) Gulf Pub.

Diving & Snorkeling Guide to Truk Lagoon. Tim Rock. LC 93-30789. 96p. 1994. 11.95 (1-55992-069-6, Pisces Bks) Gulf Pub.

***Diving & Snorkeling Guide to Vanuatu.** Brian Ansell et al. LC 94-23351. 96p. 1995. pap. 12.95 (1-55992-080-7, Pisces Bks) Gulf Pub.

***Diving Baja California.** Susan Speck. Ed. by Anthony A. Bliss, Jr. (Illus.). 128p. (Orig.). 1995. pap. 18.95 (1-881652-05-X) Aqua Quest.

Diving Bay Islands. Cindy Garoutte. Ed. by Anthony A. Bliss, Jr. (Illus.). 128p. (Orig.). 1995. pap. 18.95 (1-881652-02-5) Aqua Quest.

Diving Beetle. Hidetomo Oda. Ed. by Kathy Pohl. LC 85-28300. (Nature Close-Ups Ser.). (Illus.). 32p. (J). (gr. 3-7). 1986. lib. bdg. 10.95 (0-8172-2533-1) Raintree Steck-V.

Diving Belize. Ned Middleton. (Illus.). 128p. (Orig.). 1994. pap. 18.95 (1-881652-01-7) Aqua Quest.

Diving Bell. Todd Strasser. 192p. (J). 1992. 13.95 (0-590-44620-7, Scholastic Hardcover) Scholastic Inc.

***Diving Bell.** Todd Strasser. (YA). 1994. pap. 3.25 (0-590-43045-9) Scholastic Inc.

Diving Bermuda. Jesse Cancelmo & Michael Strohofer. LC 90-82636. (Illus.). 128p. (Orig.). 1990. pap. 18.95 (0-9623389-0-7) Aqua Quest.

***Diving Birds of North America.** Paul A. Johnsgard. LC 96-6896. (Illus.). 330p. 1987. reprint ed. pap. 94.10 (0-7837-8889-4, 2049600) Bks Demand.

Diving Boards: Jumpstarts for Stories or If You See a Man Alone on the Beach in Mexico, It Means His Wife Is Upstairs Throwing up in the Room. Ina Hillebrandt & Jill Hannum. (Illus.). 96p. (Orig.). 1992. pap. text ed. 6.36 (1-880882-00-0) Pawpress.

Diving Bonaire. George S. Lewbel & Larry R. Martin. (Illus.). 132p. (Orig.). 1991. pap. 18.95 (0-9623389-4-X) Aqua Quest.

Diving British Virgin Islands. Jim Scheiner & Odile Scheiner. (Illus.). 128p. (Orig.). 1994. pap. 18.95 (0-9623389-6-6) Aqua Quest.

Diving Club Med. Michel Verdure. (Illus.). 128p. (Orig.). 1993. pap. 18.95 (1-881652-00-9) Aqua Quest.

Diving Cozumel. Steve Rosenberg. (Illus.). 114p. (Orig.). 1992. pap. 18.95 (0-9623389-7-4) Aqua Quest.

Diving Death. large type ed. Charles Forsyte. (Linford Mystery Library). 1989. pap. 11.95 (0-7089-6751-5, Trailtree Bookshop) Ulverscroft.

***Diving Deep & Surfacing: Women Writers on Spiritual Quest.** Carol P. Christ. 208p. (C). 1995. pap. 12.95 (0-8070-6207-3) Beacon Pr.

Diving Deep & Surfacing: Women Writers on Spiritual Quest. 2nd rev. ed. Carol Christ. LC 86-70552. 157p. 1986. pap. 12.00 (0-8070-6351-7, BP 722) Beacon Pr.

Diving for Northwest Relics. James S. White. LC 79-1869. (Illus.). 192p. 1979. 9.95 (0-8323-0335-6); pap. 7.95 (0-8323-0336-4) Binford Mort.

***Diving for the Moon.** Lee F. Bantle. LC 94-35207. (J). 1995. 14.95 (0-689-80004-5, Aladdin Paperbacks) S&S Childrens.

Diving Guide to the Eastern Caribbean. Martha Gilkes. (Illus.). 88p. (Orig.). 1994. pap. 15.95 (0-333-55467-1) Hunter NJ.

Diving Guide to Underwater Florida. 8th ed. Ned Deloach. (Illus.). 312p. 1993. pap. 16.95 (1-878348-04-3) New World FL.

Diving Hawaii. Steve Rosenberg. LC 90-82635. (Illus.). 128p. (Orig.). 1990. pap. 18.95 (0-9623389-1-5) Aqua Quest.

Diving in Thailand. Collin Piprell & Ashley Boyd. (Illus.). 192p. 1994. 22.50 (0-7818-0315-2) Hippocrene Bks.

Diving Injuries: A Critical Insight & Recommendations. Council for National Cooperation in Aquatics Staff. Ed. by Robert D. Clayton. LC 84-198346. (Illus.). 204p. reprint ed. pap. 58.20 (0-7837-5567-8, 2045342) Bks Demand.

Diving Inspection Personnel Log Book. Ed. by Best Publishing Co. Staff. 210p. (C). 1989. text ed. 21.00 (0-941332-15-2) Best Pub Co.

Diving into Darkness: A Submersible Explores the Sea. Rebecca L. Johnson. (Discovery! Ser.). (Illus.). 64p. (J). (gr. 5 up). 1989. 22.95 (0-8225-1587-3, Lerner Publctns) Lerner Group.

Diving into Oceans. National Wildlife Federation Staff. (J). (gr. k-8). 1991. pap. 7.95 (0-945051-36-0, 75042) Natl Wildlife.

Diving into Science, Grades Two-Four. Peggy K. Perdue. 96p. 1989. pap. 7.95 (0-673-38965-0) GdYrBks.

Diving into the Wreck: Poems, 1971-1972. Adrienne Rich. 1994. pap. 8.95 (0-393-31163-5) Norton.

Diving Medicine. 2nd ed. Alfred A. Bove & Davis. (Illus.). 352p. 1989. text ed. 64.95 (0-7216-2934-2) Saunders.

Diving Medicine for Scuba Divers. Carl Edmonds et al. (Illus.). 316p. 1992. pap. 27.95 (0-9590306-6-2) Aqua Quest.

Diving off the Beaten Track: Best of the Caribbean & Bahamas. Bob Burgess. (Illus.). 128p. 1995. pap. 18.95 (1-881652-03-3) Aqua Quest.

Diving Offshore California. Darren Douglass & Stacey Douglass. (Illus.). 128p. (Orig.). 1992. pap. 18.95 (0-9623389-5-8) Aqua Quest.

Diving Opportunities for Fun & Profit: Over 100 Ways to Make Money Diving. Jim Meuninck. Ed. by Claude Gunter & Jill Meuninck. (Illus.). 216p. (Orig.). 1986. pap. 9.95 (0-939865-00-9) Media Methods.

***Diving Rock on the Hudson, 2 vols.** Henry Roth. 418p. Date not set. 23.95 (0-615-00586-1) St Martin.

***Diving Rock on the Hudson: Mercy of a Rude Stream, Vol. II.** Henry Roth. 1995. 23.95 (0-312-11777-9) St Martin.

***Diving Technical Manual.** U. S. Navy Staff. (Illus.). 802p. (C). 1989. 79.50 (0-614-00489-6) Best Pub Co.

Diving the Great Barrier Reef. Lucy Ferrier. LC 75-23411. (Illus.). 32p. (J). (gr. 5-10). 1976. lib. bdg. 10.79 (0-89375-005-0) Troll Assocs.

Diving the Rainbow Reefs: Adventures of an Underwater Photographer. Paul S. Auerbach. LC 90-40340. (Illus.). 236p. 1991. 45.00 (0-87850-072-3) Darwin Pr.

Diving the Rainbow Reefs: Adventures of an Underwater Photographer. Paul S. Auerbach. 236p. 1991. 47.00 (0-8016-0321-8) Mosby Yr Bk.

Diving the San Juans. Dareld Clark & Janine Clark. 1989. spiral bd. 10.95 (0-945265-18-2) Accord Comm.

Diving to a Flash of Gold. Martin Meylach & Charles Whited. LC 73-116234. (Florida Classics Ser.). (Illus.). 382p. (Orig.). 1987. reprint ed. pap. 15.95 (0-912451-16-5) Florida Classics.

Diving to Adventure. M. Timothy O'Keefe. LC 92-74327. (Diving Ser.). 160p. (Orig.). (C). 1992. pap. text ed. 9.95 (0-936513-30-6) Larsens Outdoor.

Diving to the Past: Recovering Ancient Wrecks. W. John Hackwell. LC 87-233529. (Illus.). 64p. (J). (gr. 3-7). 1988. text ed. 14.95 (0-684-18918-6, C Scribner Sons Young) S&S Childrens.

Diving with Undercurrent, Vol. II. Ed. by Ken Smith. (Illus.). 108p. (Orig.). 1987. pap. 14.98 (0-915260-37-9) Atcom.

Divinidad De Cristo Vindicada: The Divinity of Christ. Fernando Saravi. (SPA.). 3.95 (84-7645-352-3, 223456, Pub. by Edit Clie SP) TSELF.

Divining Heart: Dowsing & Spiritual Unfoldment. Patricia Wright & Richard Wright. 176p. (Orig.). 1994. pap. 10.95 (0-89281-423-3) Inner Tradit.

Divining Mind. Terry Ross & Richard D. Wright. (Illus.). 176p. 1990. pap. 10.95 (0-89281-263-X, Destiny Bks) Inner Tradit.

Divining Rod. William Barrett & Theodore Besterman. (Illus.). 1967. 7.50 (0-8216-0071-0, Univ Bks) Carol Pub Group.

Divining the Dow: One Hundred of the World's Most Widely Followed Stock Market Prediction Systems. Richard J. Maturi. 200p. 1993. 22.95 (1-55738-475-4) Probus Pub Co.

***Divining the Future: The Complete Reference from Astrology to Zoomancy.** Eva Shaw. LC 94-255886. 1995. write for info. (0-8160-2937-7) Facts on File.

Divinity of Krishna. S. J. Seth. 1984. text ed. 20.00 (0-685-13697-3) Coronet Bks.

Divinity of Our Lord & Savior Jesus Christ. H. P. Liddon. 630p. lib. bdg. 22.99 (0-8254-5158-2) Kregel.

Divinity of the Roman Emperor. Lily R. Taylor. LC 32-22470. (American Philological Association Philological Monographs). 312p. (C). 1981. pap. 23.50 (0-89130-702-8, 40-00-01) Scholars Pr GA.

Divinity of the Roman Emperor. Lily R. Taylor. LC 75-7348. (Roman History Ser.). (Illus.). 1978. reprint ed. 41.95 (0-405-07068-3) Ayer.

Divino Romance (The Divine Romance) Gene Edwards. (SPA.). 1991. 5.99 (1-56063-086-8, 490228) Editorial Unilit.

Divinyl Sulfide: Synthesis, Properties, & Applications. B. A. Trofimov & S. V. Amosova. 88p. 1984. pap. text ed. 95.00 (3-7186-0211-3) Gordon & Breach.

Divinyl Sulfoxide: Synthesis, Properties, & Applications (SR) N. K. Gusarova et al. 80p. 1989. pap. text ed. 85.00 (3-7186-4992-6) Gordon & Breach.

Divirtamonos Con el Abecedario. Leslie C. Stockham. (Illus.). 96p. (J). (gr. k-2). 1993. student ed 8.95 (0-9624096-2-6) Bilingual Lang Mat.

Divirtamonos Con Letras y Sonidos. Leslie C. Stockham. (Illus.). 56p. (Orig.). (J). (gr. k-2). 1993. pap. 5.98 (0-9624096-1-8) Bilingual Lang Mat.

Divisia Indices for Money: An Appraisal of Theory & Practice. Paul Fisher et al. (Working Paper Ser.: No. 9). 84p. 1993. reprint ed. pap. 25.00 (0-7837-5947-9, 2045746) Bks Demand.

Division. Karen Hilderbrand & Kim Thompson. (Rap with the Facts Ser.). (Illus.). 48p. (J). (gr. 3). 1991. student ed 6.99 (0-9632249-4-8) Twin Sisters.

***Division.** David L. Stienecker. (Discovering Math Ser.). 32p. (J). (gr. 3-5). 1995. lib. bdg. write for info. (0-7614-0596-8, Benchmark NY) Marshall Cavendish.

Division. Kim M. Thompson & Karen M. Hilderbrand. (Rap with the Facts Ser.). (Illus.). 24p. (J). (gr. 3-6). 1993. student ed, audio 9.98 (1-882331-22-2, TWIN 404) Twin Sisters.

***Division: Basic Facts.** Bob DeWeese. (Math at Home Ser.). (Illus.). 44p. 1994. teacher ed, pap. text ed. 2.95 (1-55799-316-5, EMC 609) Evan-Moor Corp.

Division Algebras: Octonions, Quartnions, Complex Numbers, & the Algebraic Design of Physics. Geoffrey M. Dixon. LC 94-13948. (Mathematics & Its Applications Ser.: Vol. 290). 1994. lib. bdg. 94.00 (0-7923-2890-6) Kluwer Ac.

Division & Cohesion in Democracy: A Study of Norway. Harry Eckstein. (Center of International Studies). 1966. 49.50 (0-691-05611-0) Princeton U Pr.

Division & Cohesion in Democracy: A Study of Norway. Harry Eckstein. LC 66-17700. 315p. reprint ed. pap. 89.80 (0-8357-3688-1, 2036412) Bks Demand.

Division & Detente: The Germanies & Their Alliances. Eric G. Frey. LC 86-20516. 224p. 1986. text ed. 49.95 (0-275-92222-7, C2222, Praeger Pubs) Greenwood.

Division & Hierarchy: An Overview of Caste in Gujarat. A. M. Shah & I. P. Desai. 1988. 20.00 (81-7075-008-3, Pub. by Hindustan IA) S Asia.

Division & Reunion 1829-1889. Woodrow Wilson. 12.00 (0-8446-3188-4) Peter Smith.

D

An Asterisk (*) at the beginning of an entry indicates that the title is appearing in BIP for the first time. 2051

Division & Segregation of Organelles. Ed. by S. A. Boffey & D. Lloyd. (Society for Experimental Biology Seminar Ser.: No. 35). 286p. 1989. 79.95 (0-521-33436-5) Cambridge U Pr.

Division & Square Root: Digit-Recurrence Algorithms & Implementations. Milos D. Ercegovac & Tomas Lang. LC 93-48627. 240p. (C). 1994. lib. bdg. 95.00 (0-7923-9438-0) Kluwer Ac.

Division Book. Becky Daniel & Charlie Daniel. 64p. (J). (gr. 3-6). 1980. 8.95 (0-916456-77-3, GA 190) Good Apple.

***Division Facts in Five Minutes a Day.** Susan C. Anthony. (Math Facts in Five Minutes a Day Ser.). 88p. (Orig.). (J). (gr. 4-6). 1995. teacher ed, spiral bd. 11.95 (1-879478-08-0, 080) Instr Res Co.

Division in British Medicine: The Separation of General Practice from Hospital Care, 1911-1968. Frank Honigsbaum. LC 79-14789. 1980. text ed. 39.95 (0-312-21431-6) St Martin.

Division of Berlin. J. Dudman. (Flashpoints Ser.). (Illus.). 80p. (J). (gr. 7 up). 1988. 13.95 (0-685-58321-X); lib. bdg. 18.60 (0-86592-037-0) Rourke Corp.

Division of Europe after World War II: 1946. W. W. Rostow. (Ideas & Action Ser.: No. 2). 224p. 1981. text ed. 19.95 (0-292-70358-9); pap. 10.95 (0-292-70359-7) U of Tex Pr.

***Division of Korea & the Alliance Making Process: Internationalization of Internal Conflict & Internalization of International Struggle, 1945-1948.** Hyung-Kook Kim. 292p. (Orig.). (C). 1995. lib. bdg. 48.00 (0-8191-9867-6); pap. text ed. 32.50 (0-8191-9868-4) U Pr of Amer.

Division of Labor: A Political Perspective. Elliott A. Krause. LC 81-6971. (Contributions in Labor History Ser.: No. 12). xii, 203p. 1982. text ed. 49.95 (0-313-23162-1, KDL/, Greenwood Pr) Greenwood.

Division of Labor & Welfare: An Introduction to Economic Systems. Louis Putterman. (Library of Political Economy). (Illus.). 264p. 1990. 59.00 (0-19-877299-8); pap. text ed. 19.95 (0-19-877298-X) OUP.

Division of Labor in Society. Emile Durkheim. Tr. by W. D. Hall. 350p. (C). 1984. pap. 14.95 (0-02-907960-8); pap. 10.95 (0-685-10064-2) Free Pr.

Division of Labor in Society: Some Notes on Occupational Groups. Emile Durkheim. (Reprint Series in Social Sciences). (C). 1993. reprint ed. pap. text ed. 2.30 (0-8290-3848-5, S-76) Irvington.

Division of Labour, Specialization, & Technical Change: Global, Regional, & Workplace Level. Ed. by G. Tornqvist et al. 278p. (Orig.). 1987. pap. 31.00x (91-22-00894-2, Pub. by Almqv & Wiksell SW) Coronet Bks.

Division of Labour, Technical Change & Economic Growth. Marcella Corsi. 175p. 1991. 68.95 (1-85628-231-7, Pub. by Avebury Pub UK) Ashgate Pub Co.

Division of Plymouth Proposed in 1855 & 1856. Fred L. Barnes. (Pilgrim Society Notes Ser.: No. 11). 1962. 2.00 (0-940628-12-0) Pilgrim Soc.

Division of the Kingdoms: Shakespeare's Two Versions of "King Lear" Ed. by Gary Taylor & Michael Warren. (Oxford Shakespeare Studies). (Illus.). 512p. 1987. pap. 29.95 (0-19-812950-5) OUP.

Division of the Spoils. Roland J. Green. (Starcruiser Shenandoah Ser.: No. 2). 320p. 1990. pap. 3.95 (0-451-45024-8, ROC) NAL-Dutton.

Division of the Spoils. Paul Scott. (Raj Quartet Ser.: Vol. IV). 640p. 1979. mass mkt. 4.95 (0-380-45054-2) Avon.

Division of the Spoils. Paul Scott. (Raj Quartet Ser.). 640p. 1992. pap. 11.00 (0-380-71811-1) Avon.

Division Officers Guide. 9th ed. John V. Noel. LC 88-29130. 344p. 1989. pap. 14.95 (0-87021-205-2) Naval Inst Pr.

***Division Officer's Guide.** 10th rev. ed. James Stavridis. LC 95-14860. (Illus.). 352p. 1995. 17.95 (1-55750-163-7) Naval Inst Pr.

***Division Rap.** Brad Caudle & Richard Caudle. (J). (gr. 3 up). 1992. audio, pap. 9.95 (1-878489-08-9) Rock & Learn Educ Prod.

***Division Rap.** Brad Caudle & Richard Caudle. (J). (gr. 3 up). 1994. audio, pap. 9.95 (1-878489-41-0) Rock & Learn Educ Prod.

Division Recorder, Bk. 1. Holman. 1990. 4.95 (0-685-32171-1, H1020) Hansen Ed Mus.

Division Recorder, Bk. 2. Holman. 1990. 4.95 (0-685-32172-X, H1021) Hansen Ed Mus.

Division Street: America. Studs Terkel. LC 92-50823. 416p. 1993. pap. 12.95 (1-56584-075-5) New Press NY.

Division Street: America. Studs Terkel. 1994. 22.00 (0-8446-6741-2) Peter Smith.

Division Wipe-Off Book. 24p. (J). (gr. 1 up). 1988. pap. 1.95 (0-590-42041-0) Scholastic Inc.

Division Wrap-ups: Individual Sets. Marion W. Stuart. Date not set. text ed. write for info. (0-943343-04-6) Lrn Wrap-Ups.

Divisional Harmonics. H. M. Ishikawa. LC 83-73609. 176p. 1984. 17.95 (0-86690-273-2, I2528-014) Am Fed Astrologers.

Divisions & Separate Brigades. John B. Wilson. 1995. write for info. (0-318-72958-X) USGPO.

Divisions & Solidarities: Gender, Class, & Employment in Latin America. Alison M. Scott. LC 94-8498. 256p. 1995. 59.95x (0-415-01849-8, B4105); pap. 18.95 (0-415-01850-1, B4122) Routledge.

Divisions Between Traditionalism & Liberalism in the American Jewish Community: Cleft or Chasm. Ed. by Michael Shapiro. LC 91-42113. 124p. 1992. lib. bdg. 59.95 (0-7734-9442-1) E Mellen.

Divisions of Labour. R. E. Pahl. 376p. 1984. pap. 21.95 (0-631-13274-0) Blackwell Pubs.

***Divisions of the Tetrachord: A Prolegomenon to the Construction of Musical Scales.** John Chalmers, Jr. 234p. (C). 1993. pap. 35.00 (0-945996-04-7) Frog Peak Music.

Divisions of Welfare: A Critical Introduction to Comparative Social Policy. Norman Ginsburg. 256p. (C). 1992. text ed. 55.00 (0-8039-8440-5); pap. text ed. 21.95 (0-8039-8441-3) Sage.

Divisions on a Ground. Edith A. Jenkins. 55p. 1986. pap. 9.50 (0-932499-18-X) Lapis Pr.

Divisions on a Ground: Essays on Canadian Culture. Northrop Frye. 199p. (Orig.). 1982. pap. 19.95 (0-88784-093-0, Pub. by Hse of Anansi Pr CN) Genl Dist Srvs.

Divisions-One. Martin J. Rosenblum. 4.00 (0-686-15300-6) Great Raven Pr.

Divisiveness & Social Conflict: An Anthropological Approach. Alan R. Beals & Bernard J. Siegel. x, 185p. 1966. 29.50 (0-8047-0302-7) Stanford U Pr.

Divisor Theory. Harold M. Edwards. 184p. 1989. 38.50 (0-8176-3448-7) Birkhauser.

Divisors. R. R. Hall & G. Tenenbaum. (Cambridge Tracts in Mathematics Ser.: No. 90). 192p. 1988. 59.95 (0-521-34056-X) Cambridge U Pr.

***Divorce.** (E-Z Legal Guide Ser.). 160p. (Orig.). 1995. pap. text ed. 12.95 (1-56382-402-7) E-Z Legal.

Divorce. Caroline E. Lazo. LC 89-2156. (Facts About Ser.). (Illus.). 48p. (J). (gr. 5-6). 1989. text ed. 12.95 (0-89686-436-7, Crstwood Hse) Silver Burdett Pr.

Divorce. John Murray. 1961. pap. 5.99 (0-87552-344-7) Presby & Reformed.

Divorce. Sharon J. Price & Patrick C. Mckenry. (Family Studies Text Ser.: Vol. 9). 160p. (C). 1988. text ed. 37.00 (0-8039-2356-2); pap. text ed. 16.95 (0-8039-2357-0) Sage.

Divorce. Horace Greeley. LC 78-72342. (Free Love in America Ser.). reprint ed. 12.50 (0-404-60952-X) AMS Pr.

Divorce: "You Can Do It Yourself" Carl Wand & Eric Lutker. (Law Kits Ser.). 200p. (Orig.). 1992. pap. 29.95 (1-879191-05-9) Forms Man.

Divorce: A Client's Guide, Illinois Edition. Sheila Simon. (Klear-E-Lex Ser.). 105p. (Orig.). 1993. pap. 14.95 (1-884177-01-8) Justice IL.

Divorce: A Four Letter Word. Peter L. Grieco, Jr. et al. LC 92-38163. 362p. 1993. 23.95 (0-945456-09-3) PT Pubns.

***Divorce: A Guide for Women: What Every Woman Needs to Know about Getting a Fair Divorce Even When She Thinks She Doesn't Need to Know It.** Patricia Phillips & George Mair. LC 95-5872. 1995. write for info. (0-671-50057-0) Macmillan.

Divorce: A Romance. Paula Rankin. 56p. (Orig.). 1991. pap. 9.95 (0-88748-111-6) Carnegie-Mellon.

Divorce: A Social Interpretation. J. P. Lichtenberger. LC 70-169392. (Family in America Ser.). 488p. 1979. reprint ed. 28.95 (0-405-03869-0) Ayer.

Divorce: A Study in Social Causation. James P. Lichtenberger. LC 72-76685. (Columbia University. Studies in the Social Sciences: No. 94). reprint ed. 18.50 (0-404-51094-9) AMS Pr.

Divorce: An American Tradition. Glenda Riley. (Illus.). 288p. 1991. 24.95 (0-19-506123-3) OUP.

Divorce: An American Tradition. Glenda Riley. (Illus.). 280p. 1992. pap. 11.95 (0-19-507912-4) OUP.

***Divorce: An Oral Portrait.** George Feifer. LC 94-46493. 336p. 1995. 25.00 (1-56584-272-3) New Press NY.

Divorce: Crisis, Challenge or Relief? David A. Chiriboga et al. 328p. 1991. text ed. 45.00x (0-8147-1450-1) NYU Pr.

Divorce: Crisis, Challenge, or Relief? David A. Chiriboga & Linda S. Catron. 328p. (C). 1992. pap. text ed. 22.50 (0-8147-1485-4) NYU Pr.

Divorce: Facing the Issues. M. O'Brien. 1993. 64.00 (1-85594-077-9, Pub. by Attic Pr IE) St Mut.

***Divorce: Facing the Issues.** Ed. by Maas O'Brien. 160p. (Orig.). 1995. pap. 11.99 (1-85594-195-3) InBook.

Divorce: How & When to Let Go. John Adam & Nancy Adam. pap. 4.95 (0-13-216408-6) Divorce Res.

Divorce: How You Can Survive & Thrive in Spite of It. G. D. Lundahl & Ruth C. Lundahl. Ed. by John Achziger. 156p. (Orig.). 1989. pap. write for info. (0-318-64644-7) How Pub CA.

Divorce: The Child's Point of View. Yvette Walczak & Sheila Burns. 168p. 1984. pap. 21.00 (0-335-09820-7, Open Univ Pr) Taylor & Francis.

***Divorce: Young People Caught in the Middle.** Beth Levine. LC 94-34430. (Issues in Focus Ser.). 128p. (YA). (gr. 6 up). 1995. lib. bdg. 17.95 (0-89490-633-X) Enslow Pubs.

Divorce - There Can Be Silver Linings. Donald E. Heathcote, Jr. 72p. (Orig.). 1988. 4.95 (0-9620452-1-7) D E Heathcote.

Divorce: Adjusting to Change: Looking at Life. Center for Learning Network. 12p. (YA). (gr. 7-12). 1992. pap. text ed. 0.80 (1-56077-223-9) Ctr Learning.

Divorce & Beyond. Harry J. Ashenhurst. 1984. pap. 10.00 (0-8309-0385-2) Herald Hse.

Divorce & Beyond: Facilitators Manual. J. Greteman & L. Haverkamp. LC 82-72048. 80p. 1984. pap. 4.95 (0-915388-17-0, 177, Buckley Pubns) ACTA Pubns.

Divorce & Beyond: Participants Book. James Greteman & Leon Haverkamp. LC 82-72048. 132p. 1984. pap. 4.95 (0-915388-16-2, 176, Buckley Pubns) ACTA Pubns.

Divorce & Child Custody. 2nd ed. Deanna Peters & Richard L. Strohm. (Layman's Law Guides Ser.). 128p. 1994. pap. 8.95 (1-56414-084-9) Career Pr Inc.

Divorce & Child Custody: Your Options & Legal Rights. Richard L. Strohm & Deanna Peters. 96p. 1992. pap. 9.95 (0-9630356-1-4) Makai.

Divorce & Divorce Factors: Subject Analysis & Research Index with Bibliography. Alice M. Gibbons. LC 87-47659. 150p. 1987. 39.50 (0-88164-682-2); pap. 34.50 (0-88164-683-0) ABBE Pubs Assn.

Divorce & Divorce Therapy Handbook. Ed. by Martin R. Textor. LC 89-30761. 392p. 1989. 50.00 (0-87668-846-6) Aronson.

Divorce & Divorce Therapy Handbook. Ed. by Martin R. Textor. LC 89-30761. 392p. 1994. reprint ed. pap. 40.00 (1-56821-207-0) Aronson.

Divorce & Family Law in California: A Guide for the General Public. Bob Pickus. 141p. (Orig.). 1991. pap. 8.95 (0-9630684-0-7) B Pickus.

Divorce & Family Mediation. American Bar Association, Family Law Staff. LC 86-80203. 46p. 1986. pap. 22.95 (0-318-36124-8, 513-0022) Amer Bar Assn.

Divorce & Fatherhood: The Struggle for Parental Identity. Ed. by John W. Jacobs. LC 85-30749. (Clinical Insights Ser.). 109p. reprint ed. pap. 31.10 (0-8357-7834-7, 2036208) Bks Demand.

Divorce & Money: How to Make the Best Financial Decisions During Divorce. 2nd rev. ed. Violet Woodhouse et al. 288p. 1993. pap. 21.95 (0-87337-215-8) Nolo Pr.

Divorce & New Beginnings: An Authoritative Guide to Recovery & Growth, Solo Parenting, & Stepfamilies. Genevieve Clapp. 417p. 1992. pap. text ed. 14.95 (0-471-52631-2) Wiley.

Divorce & Remarriage. Guy Duty. LC 96-2485. 160p. 1967. 13.99 (0-87123-097-6) Bethany Hse.

Divorce & Remarriage. Kenneth E. Jones. 1990. teacher ed 3.95 (0-87162-587-3, D3374); pap. text ed. 3.95 (0-87162-503-2, D3375) Warner Pr.

Divorce & Remarriage. Theodore Mackin. (Marriage in the Catholic Church Ser.: Vol. II). 688p. (Orig.). 1984. pap. 19.95 (0-8091-2585-4) Paulist Pr.

Divorce & Remarriage. K. Stewart. 144p. (Orig.). 1992. pap. 4.99 (0-88368-274-5) Whitaker Hse.

Divorce & Remarriage. J. D. Thomas. (Way of Life Ser.: No.159). 1977. pap. 6.95 (0-89112-159-5) Abilene Christ U.

Divorce & Remarriage. Jim Tracy. (Illus.). 80p. (Orig.). 1986. pap. 9.95 (1-55630-008-5) Brentwood Comm.

Divorce & Remarriage: A Perspective for Counseling. John R. Martin. LC 73-18038. 144p. 1974. pap. 6.95 (0-8361-1328-4) Herald Pr.

Divorce & Remarriage: Are Non-Christians Amenable to the Law of Christ? Thomas B. Warren & E. C. Fuqua. 1977. reprint ed. pap. 7.00 (0-934916-30-6) Natl Christian Pr.

Divorce & Remarriage: Biblical Principles & Pastoral Practice. Andrew Cornes. 504p. (Orig.). 1993. pap. 24.99 (0-8028-0577-9) Eerdmans.

Divorce & Remarriage: Four Christian Views. Ed. by H. Wayne House. LC 90-30839. 252p. (Orig.). 1990. pap. 11.99 (0-8308-1283-0, 1283) InterVarsity.

Divorce & Remarriage: Problems, Adaptations & Adjustments. Stan L. Albrecht et al. LC 82-24250. (Contributions in Women's Studies: No. 42). (Illus.). 256p. 1983. text ed. 49.95 (0-313-23616-X, ALD/, Greenwood Pr) Greenwood.

Divorce & Remarriage: Religious & Psychological Perspectives. Ed. by William P. Roberts. LC 89-63115. 224p. (Orig.). (C). 1990. pap. 13.95 (1-55612-231-4) Sheed & Ward MO.

***Divorce & Remarriage: The Unpardonable Sin?** Debra Stroud. 92p. (Orig.). 1995. pap. 5.95 (1-885858-19-1) KILN Bks.

Divorce & Remarriage: What Does the Bible Really Say? Ralph Woodrow. LC 82-99960. (Illus.). 1982. pap. 4.95 (0-916938-06-9) R Woodrow.

Divorce & Remarriage in the Catholic Church. Gerald D. Coleman. 1988. pap. 5.95 (0-8091-3016-5) Paulist Pr.

Divorce & Taxes. 64p. 1992. pap. 5.00 (0-685-66970-X, 4822) Commerce.

Divorce & the Bible. D. R. Norbie. 1971. pap. 3.25 (0-937396-12-5) Walterick Pubs.

Divorce & the Faithful Church. G. Edwin Bontrager. LC 78-4671. 192p. reprint ed. pap. 54.80 (0-7837-5111-7, 2044810) Bks Demand.

Divorce & the Jewish Child. Thomas J. Cottle. 28p. 1981. pap. 2.50 (0-87495-034-1) Am Jewish Comm.

***Divorce & the Military.** Frank Ault & Marsha Thole. 209p. 1994. pap. 17.45 (0-614-04602-5) Poor Richards.

***Divorce & the Military.** Frank W. Ault & Marsha L. Thole. Ed. by Ruth B. Haas. 228p. (Orig.). 1994. pap. 14.95 (0-9639850-0-0) Am Retirees.

Divorce & the Myth of Lawyers. Lenard Marlow. 160p. 1992. 19.95 (0-9632741-0-4); pap. 10.95 (0-9632741-1-2) Harlan Pr.

Divorce & the Next Generation: Effects on Young Adults' Patterns of Intimacy & Expectations for Marriage. Intro. by Craig A. Everett. LC 92-43097. (Journal of Divorce & Remarriage: Vol. 18, Nos. 3-4). 200p. 1993. lib. bdg. 39.95 (1-56024-444-5) Haworth Pr.

Divorce-Another Chance? Herbert L. Zobel. Ed. by Mary K. Reith. (Illus.). 82p. (Orig.). 1985. pap. 5.50 (0-9614271-0-8) EarthZ.

Divorce-Anyone? John Patrick. 1976. pap. 4.75 (0-8222-0316-2) Dramatists Play.

Divorce As a Developmental Process. Ed. by Judith H. Gold. LC 87-33685. (Clinical Practice Ser.). 200p. 1988. pap. 23.50 (0-88048-146-3) Am Psychiatric.

***Divorce Assistance Service: An Organization Manual.** R. F. Doyle. 20p. 1992. pap. 6.00 (0-614-04601-7) Poor Richards.

Divorce Book. Harriet N. Cohen & Ralph Gardner, Jr. 192p. (Orig.). 1994. pap. 10.00 (0-380-75829-6) Avon.

Divorce Book. Matthew McKay et al. 264p. 1984. 24.95 (0-934986-11-8); pap. 11.95 (0-934986-06-1) New Harbinger.

Divorce Busting. Michele Weiner-Davis. 256p. 1993. pap. 11.00 (0-671-79725-5, Fireside) S&S Trade.

Divorce Busting: A Revolutionary & Rapid Program for "Staying Together" Michele Weiner-Davis. 320p. 1992. 21.00 (0-671-72598-X) Summit Bks.

Divorce Can Be Fun. Sandy Owen & Dani McNeil. 128p. (Orig.). pap. 7.00 (0-317-57794-8) Triumph Pr.

Divorce Can Happen to Nice People. Mayle. 1980. 9.95 (0-02-582500-3) Macmillan.

Divorce, Child Custody & the Family. Group for the Advancement of Psychiatry, Committee on the Family Staff. LC 80-25935. (Jossey-Bass Social & Behavioral Science Ser.). 200p. reprint ed. pap. 57.00 (0-8357-4980-0, 2037913) Bks Demand.

Divorce, Confidence & Relaxation: A Guide for Kids. M. S. Prokop. 1986. 9.95 (0-933879-31-8) Alegra Hse Pubs.

***Divorce Conflicts.** David W. Felder. 102p. (Orig.). 1995. 19.95 (0-910959-18-8, B&G 18H); teacher ed 39.95 (0-910959-38-2, B&G 18T) Felder Bks.

Divorce Counseling: A Practical Guide. Marian H. Mowatt. 176p. 1987. text ed. 29.95 (0-669-14573-4); pap. 12.95 (0-685-17564-2) Free Pr.

***Divorce Court.** David W. Felder. 44p. 1995. pap. text ed. 5.00 (0-910959-98-6, B&G 19D) Felder Bks.

Divorce Decision. Gary Richmond. 215p. 1988. pap. write for info. (0-8499-3104-5) Word Inc.

Divorce Decisions Workbook: A Planning & Action Guide. Marjorie L. Engel. 1992. text ed. 24.95 (0-07-019572-2); pap. text ed. 24.95 (0-07-019571-4) McGraw.

Divorce Dirty Tricks. Joan Brovins & Thomas Oehmke. 1993. pap. 12.95 (0-8119-0766-X) LIFETIME.

Divorce Experience of Working & Middle Class Women. Toni L'Hommedieu. LC 83-17967. (Research in Clinical Psychology Ser.: No. 8). 178p. reprint ed. pap. 50.80 (0-8357-1478-0, 2070400) Bks Demand.

Divorce Express. Paula Danziger. LC 82-70318. 144p. (J). (gr. 7 up). 1982. pap. 14.95 (0-385-28217-6) Delacorte.

Divorce Express. Paula Danziger. 160p. (YA). (gr. 7 up). 1983. pap. 3.99 (0-440-92062-0, LFL) Dell.

***Divorce Express.** Gail Erwin. 23p. (Orig.). (YA). (gr. 6-12). 1993. pap. 3.00 (1-57514-111-6, 1126) Encore Perform Pub.

Divorce for the Unbroken Marriage. Nester C. Kohut. 1973. pap. 5.00 (0-910574-08-1) Am Family.

Divorce Group Counseling for Secondary School Students. Janice M. Hammond. (Illus.). 28p. (Orig.). 1981. pap. 8.95 (0-9604690-2-8) Cranbrook Pub.

Divorce Group Counseling Program. M. S. Prokop. 1987. 164.95 (0-933879-34-2) Alegra Hse Pubs.

Divorce Guide for Alberta: Canadian Edition. 8th ed. R. Gary Dickson. (Legal Ser.). 96p. 1993. 11.95 (0-88908-270-7); 12.95 (0-88908-267-7) Self-Counsel Pr.

Divorce Guide for British Columbia. 15th ed. Wayne Powell. (Legal Ser.). 112p. 1992. 14.95 (0-88908-444-0); 14.95 (0-88908-466-1) Self-Counsel Pr.

***Divorce Guide for British Columbia.** 16th ed. Wayne Powell. (Legal Ser.). 128p. 1994. pap. text ed. 11.95 (0-88908-473-4) Self-Counsel Pr.

Divorce Guide for Florida (Including Forms) Step-by-Step Guide for Obtaining Your Own Divorce. Robert C. Waters. (Legal Ser.). 240p. (Orig.). 1992. pap. 21.95 (0-88908-775-X) Self-Counsel Pr.

Divorce Guide for Manitoba: Step-by-Step Guide to Obtaining Your Own Divorce. 2nd ed. Dorothy Pedlar. (Legal Ser.). 120p. (Orig.). 1991. Canadian ed. pap. 14.95 (0-88908-516-1); 14.95 (0-88908-517-X) Self-Counsel Pr.

Divorce Guide for Ontario: A Step-by-Step Guide to Obtaining Your Own Divorce. 10th ed. Gloria Epstein. (Legal Ser.). 144p. 1993. 14.95 (0-88908-475-0); 14.95 (0-88908-478-5); 14.95 (0-88908-394-0) Self-Counsel Pr.

Divorce Guide for Oregon. 6th ed. Richard Baldwin. (Legal Ser.). 144p. 1993. 14.95 (0-88908-836-5); 15.95 (0-88908-837-3); 15.95 (0-88908-838-1) Self-Counsel Pr.

Divorce Guide for Washington: Step-by-Step Guide for Obtaining Your Own Divorce. 8th ed. M. Pattersen. (Legal Ser.). 1992. 21.95 (0-88908-751-2) Self-Counsel Pr.

Divorce Handbook. James T. Friedman. 1984. pap. 12.00 (0-394-72327-9) Random.

Divorce Hangover. Anne Walther. Ed. by Judith Regan. 256p. 1992. reprint ed. mass mkt. 5.50 (0-671-70332-3) PB.

***Divorce Happens: Divorce Activity Book.** Jim Boulden & Joan Boulden. Ed. by Evelyn M. Ward. (Illus.). 16p. (Orig.). (J). (gr. k-2). 1994. pap. 3.95 (1-878076-34-5) Boulden Pub.

Divorce Happens to the Nicest Kids: A Self-Help Book For Kids (3-15) & Adults. Michael S. Prokop. Ed. by Robert C. Peters. LC 85-72180. (Illus.). 224p. (Orig.). (J). (gr. k up). 1986. 18.95 (0-933879-25-3); 6.45 (0-933879-27-X); pap. 6.45 (0-933879-26-1) Alegra Hse Pubs.

Divorce Help Sourcebook. Margorie Engel. 350p. 1994. pap. 17.95 (0-8103-9480-4) Gale.

***Divorce Hits Home.** Beverly Bates. Ed. by Becky Nelson. 20p. (Orig.). (YA). (gr. 7-12). 1994. pap. text ed. 1.95 (1-56309-087-2, Wrld Changers Res) Womans Mission Union.

Divorce, Humor Me. Karla Minnick. 66p. 1993. pap. 6.50 (1-880365-16-2) Prof Pr NC.

Divorce I: Small-Group Counseling Programs for Students in Grades Two Through Four. JoAnn Cooper & Arden Martenz. (Changing Family Ser.). 36p. 1993. 5.95 (1-884063-11-X) Mar Co Prods.

Divorce II: Small-Group Counseling for Students in Grades Five Through Eight. JoAnn Cooper & Arden Martenz. (Changing Family Ser.). 36p. 1993. 5.95 (1-884063-12-8) Mar Co Prods.

Divorce Illustrated. Molly A. Minnick. (Illus.). 50p. (Orig.). (C). 1990. 15.00 (1-878526-02-2) Pineapple MI.

D

An Asterisk (*) at the beginning of an entry indicates that the title is appearing in BIP for the first time.

An Asterisk (*) at the beginning of an entry indicates that the title is appearing in BIP for the first time.

2053

D

Dixie Clockmakers. James W. Gibbs. (Illus.). 191p. 1979. 27.95 (*0-88289-059-X*) Pelican.
Dixie Convoy. Don Pendelton. (Executioner Ser.: No. 27). 1989. pap. 3.50 (*1-55817-294-7*, Pinnacle NY) Windsor NY.
Dixie Dateline: A Journalistic Portrait of the Contemporary South. Ed. by John B. Boles. LC 83-60523. (New Ser.: No. 1). 182p. (C). 1983. 12.95 (*0-89263-251-8*); pap. 7.95 (*0-89263-252-6*) Rice Univ.
Dixie Does Dinner. Virginia L. Thomas & Peggy L. Schuler. (Illus.). 100p. (Orig.). 1990. spiral bd., pap. 9.95 (*0-9627974-2-1*) Tabby Hse Bks.
***Dixie Dog.** Barbara S. Hazan. LC 95-1689. (I Can Read Bks.). (J). 1995. lib. bdg. 13.89 (*0-06-026254-0*) HarpC Child Bks.
***Dixie Dregs - Full Circle.** 86p. (Orig.). (YA). Date not set. pap. 19.95 (*0-89524-894-8*, 02501243) Cherry Lane.
Dixie Farewell: The Life & Death of Chucky Mullins. Larry Woody. Ed. by Richard Courtney et al. (Illus.). 125p. 1994. 14.95 (*0-9635026-6-2*) Eggman Pub.
Dixie Frontier: A Social History of the Southern Frontier from the First Transmontaine Beginnings to the Civil War. Everett Dick. LC 92-54144. 1993. pap. 14.95 (*0-8061-2385-0*) U of Okla Pr.
Dixie Ghosts. Ed. by Frank D. McSherry, Jr. et al. LC 88-1991. (American Ghost Ser.). 1990. pap. 9.95 (*0-934395-73-X*) Rutledge Hill Pr.
***Dixie Gun Works: Book of Southern Recipes.** DGW Staff. 1994. 14.95 (*1-877704-14-8*) Pioneer Pr.
Dixie Gun Works Antique Arms Catalog. 2.00 (*0-913150-40-1*) Pioneer Pr.
Dixie Highway: The Eye of the Beholder. Jeff Bollerman. (Illus.). 128p. 1992. pap. 19.95 (*1-880680-02-5*) Sand Dllr Fl.
Dixie in the Big Pasture. Belinda Hurmence. LC 93-9983. (J). (gr. 4 up). 1994. 13.95 (*0-395-52002-9*, Pub. by Clarion II) HM.
Dixie Mission: The United States Army Observer Group in Yenan, 1944. David D. Barrett. (China Research Monographs: No. 6). (Illus.). 92p. 1970. pap. 2.00 (*0-912966-07-6*) IEAS.
Dixie Riggs. Sarah Gilbert. 208p. 1991. 18.95 (*0-446-51527-2*) Warner Bks.
Dixie Riggs. Sarah Gilbert. 208p. 1992. mass mkt. 4.99 (*0-446-36268-9*) Warner Bks.
Dixie Storms. Barbara Hall. 197p. (YA). (gr. 7 up). 1990. 15.95 (*0-15-223825-5*) HarBrace.
Dixie Widow. Gilbert Morris. (House of Winslow Ser.: Bk. 9). 302p. (Orig.). (YA). (gr. 9-12). 1991. text ed. 8.99 (*1-55661-115-3*) Bethany Hse.
Dixiecrats & Democrats: Alabama Politics 1942-1950. William D. Barnard. LC 73-22711. 208p. 1985. pap. 16.50 (*0-8173-0255-7*) U of Ala Pr.
Dixieme Indice et Autres Enquetes du Continental Op. Dashiell Hammett. 281p. (FRE.). 1987. pap. 10.95 (*0-7859-2528-7*, 2070378020) Fr & Eur.
Dixie's Forgotten People: The South's Poor Whites. J. Wayne Flynt. LC 78-20613. (Minorities in Modern America Ser.). (Illus.). 224p. reprint ed. pap. 63.90 (*0-8357-6675-6*, 2056853) Bks Demand.
***Dixit Dominus: Psalm 110.** rev. ed. Baldassare Galuppi & David Larson. Ed. by Scott Foss. 40p. (Orig.). (C). 1995. pap. text ed. 4.95 (*0-89328-130-1*, HCMC108); pap. text ed. 10.00 (*0-89328-131-X*, 30-1123R); pap. text ed. 10.00 (*0-89328-132-8*, 30-1124R); pap. text ed. 10.00 (*0-89328-133-6*, 30-1125R); pap. text ed. 10.00 (*0-89328-134-4*, 30-1126R); pap. text ed. 15.00 (*0-89328-135-2*, 30-1127R); pap. text ed. 25.00 (*0-89328-136-0*, 30-1122R) Lorenz Corp.
Dixon: A Pictorial History. George Lamb. (Illus.). 200p. 1987. 30.00 (*0-685-20016-7*) G Bradley.
Dixon & His Copyists, a Criticism of the Accounts of the Oneida Community in "New America," "Spiritual Wives," & Kindred Publications see Male Continence
***Dixon Cornbelt League & Other Baseball Stories.** W. P. Kinsella. LC 94-24653. 1995. 18.00 (*0-06-017188-X*) HarpC.
Dixon Legend. Solon Dixon. LC 82-60023. 1982. 9.95 (*0-87397-208-2*) Strode.
Dixon Valley: Its First 250 Years. T. Triplett Russell & John K. Gott. (Illus.). 168p. (Orig.). 1991. pap. 17.50 (*1-55613-427-4*) Heritage Bk.
Dixon vs. Providential Life Insurance Company. 4th ed. James H. Seckinger & Kenneth S. Broun. 85p. 1990. write for info. (*1-55681-223-X*); teacher ed write for info. (*1-55681-224-8*) Natl Inst Trial Ad.
Dixon-Yates: A Study in Power Politics. Aaron B. Wildavsky. LC 74-6788. (Illus.). 351p. 1976. reprint ed. text ed. 65.00 (*0-8371-7562-3*, WIDY, Greenwood Pr) Greenwood.
Dixon's Bluff. Sally T. Hayes. (Silhouette Intimate Moments Ser.). 1993. mass mkt. 3.39 (*0-373-07485-9*, 5-07485-1) Silhouette.
***Dixon's Road Traffic Law, 2 vols., Set.** Andrew Becroft. Date not set. ring bd. write for info. (*0-409-79048-6*, NZ) Butterworth Legal Pubs.
DIY & Hardware Retailing. Euromonitor Staff. 74p. (C). 1987. 825.00 (*0-86338-257-6*, Pub. by Euromonitor Pubns UK) Gale.
DIY & Home Improvements Survey. Euromonitor Staff. 220p. (C). 1987. 1,350.00 (*0-86338-266-5*, Pub. by Euromonitor Pubns UK) Gale.
Dizionario Bio-Bibliografico dei Bibliotecari e Bibliofili Italiani: Biographical & Bibliographical Dictionary of Italian Book Collectors & Libraries, 4 vols in 2, Set. Carlo Frati & Marino Parenti. (Illus.). (ITA.). 1995. reprint ed. 395.00 (*1-55660-178-6*) A Wofsy Fine Arts.
Dizionario Commerciale Francese-Italiano: French-Italian Commercial Dictionary. V. Emolumento. 533p. (FRE & ITA.). 1978. pap. 75.00 (*0-8288-5205-7*, M9281) Fr & Eur.
Dizionario Completo Italiano-Portoghese (Brasiliano), Portoghese (Brasiliano)-Italiano: Con L'etimologia Delle Voci Italiane e Portoghesi (Brasiliane), la Loro Esatta Traduzione, Frasi e Modi Di Dire, 2 vols., Set. (ITA & POR.). (C). 1990. 135.00 (*0-913298-89-1*) S F Vanni.
Dizionario dei Sinonimi e dei Contrari. D. Cinti. (ITA.). 1990. lib. bdg. 49.95 (*0-8288-3330-3*, M14419) Fr & Eur.
Dizionario dei Sinonimi e dei Contrari. Ed. by Decio Cinti. 585p. (ITA.). 1984. 40.95 (*0-913298-75-1*) S F Vanni.
Dizionario dei Sinonimi e dei Contrari Analogico e Nomenclatore. Aldo Gabrielli. 867p. (ITA.). 1983. 94.00 (*0-913298-68-9*) S F Vanni.
Dizionario Dei Verbi Italiani Regolari e Irregolari. A. Gabrielli. 260p. 1984. 58.00 (*0-913298-65-4*) S F Vanni.
Dizionario della Lingua e della Civilta Italiana Contemporanea. Ed. by E. De Felice & A. Duro. 1985. 120.00 (*0-913298-87-5*) S F Vanni.
Dizionario della Lingua Italiano. Ed. by G. Devoto & G. C. Oli. 2712p. (ITA.). write for info. (*0-318-56661-3*, M-9196) Fr & Eur.
Dizionario Delle Attivita Sementiere E Vivais Tiche. D. Montanari. 270p. (DUT, ENG, FRE, GER & ITA.). 1981. 35.00 (*0-8288-0038-3*, M15642) Fr & Eur.
Dizionario di Elettronica Italiano-Inglese, Inglese-Italiano. S. Handel. 284p. (ENG & ITA.). 1966. 59.95 (*0-8288-6711-9*, M-9192) Fr & Eur.
Dizionario Di Mitologia Egizia, 3 vols. R. V. Lanzone. 1312p. (ITA.). 1974. reprint ed. 590.00x (*90-272-0931-6*, 0932-4) Benjamins North Am.
Dizionario Enciclopedico Italiano Melzi, Set. 1500p. 1994. 75.00x (*0-913298-53-0*) S F Vanni.
Dizionario Enciclopedico Marinaresco. Lega Navale Italiana. (ITA.). 1991. 195.00 (*0-8288-8457-9*) Fr & Eur.
***Dizionario Garzanti dei Sinonimi e dei Contrari.** (ITA.). Date not set. 125.00 (*0-7859-8878-5*); 59.95 (*0-7859-8879-3*) Fr & Eur.
Dizionario Garzanti Della Lingua Italiana: Garzanti Dictionary of the Italian Language. G. Cusatelli. 1008p. (ITA.). 1979. 45.00 (*0-8288-4729-0*, M9189) Fr & Eur.
Dizionario Hazon Garzanti: Inglese-Italiano, Italiano-Inglese. Ed. by M. Hazon. 1686p. (ENG & ITA.). 45.00 (*0-7859-0588-X*, M-9185) Fr & Eur.
Dizionario Inglese-Italiano dei Termini Relativi all'Elettronica: all'Elettrotecnica e Alle Applicazioni Connesse: English-Italian Dictionary of Terms Relative to Electronics, Electrical Engineering & Related Applications. Henri Piraux. 534p. (ENG & ITA.). 1977. pap. 59.95 (*0-8288-5463-7*, M9195) Fr & Eur.
Dizionario Italiano-Bulgaro: Italian-Bulgarian Dictionary. deluxe ed. M. Cavaletto et al. 967p. (BUL & ITA.). 1979. 95.00 (*0-8288-4730-4*, M9835) Fr & Eur.
Dizionario Italiano-Finlandes, Finlandes-Italiano. deluxe ed. Ed. by G. Colussi. (FIN & ITA.). 9.95 (*0-686-92443-6*, M-9170) Fr & Eur.
Dizionario Italiano-Francese, Francese-Italiano. deluxe ed. G. Laurent. 413p. (FRE & ITA.). 1979. 14.95 (*0-8288-4731-2*, M9173) Fr & Eur.
Dizionario Italiano-Inglese, Inglese-Italiano: Italian-English, English-Italian Dictionary. deluxe ed. R. Musu-Boy. 463p. (ENG & ITA.). 1979. 9.95 (*0-8288-4732-0*, M9177) Fr & Eur.
Dizionario Italiano-Latino, Latino-Italiano: Italian-Latin, Latin-Italian Dictionary. N. Sacerdoti. 391p. (ITA & LAT.). 1977. 9.95 (*0-8288-5464-5*, M9175) Fr & Eur.
Dizionario Italiano-Russo, Russo-Italiane. deluxe ed. R. Fadanelli. 286p. (ITA & RUS.). 9.95 (*0-7859-0813-7*, M9179) Fr & Eur.
Dizionario Italiano-Serbocroato-Italiano. P. Livadic. 554p. (ITA & SER.). 1980. 9.95 (*0-8288-1640-9*, M9180) Fr & Eur.
Dizionario Italiano-Spagnolo, Spagnolo-Italiano: Spanish-Italian, Italian-Spanish Dictionary. A. Garcia. 437p. (ITA & SPA.). 1980. 9.95 (*0-8288-0378-1*, S31237) Fr & Eur.
Dizionario Italiano-Svedese, Svedese-Italiano. G. Gareff & F. Bassoli. 442p. (ITA & SWE.). 1973. 9.95 (*0-8288-6273-7*, M-9174) Fr & Eur.
Dizionario Italiano-Tedesco, Tedesco-Italian: Italian-German, German-Italian Dictionary. deluxe ed. G. A. Altenberg & V. Ubaldi. 395p. (GER & ITA.). 1979. 9.95 (*0-8288-4733-9*, M9176) Fr & Eur.
Dizionario Italiano-Turco-Italiano. M. Celalettin Bugday. (ITA & TUR.). 1980. 14.95 (*0-8288-1646-8*, F58090) Fr & Eur.
Dizionario Italiano-Turco, Turco-Italiano. M. Celalettin Bugday. 410p. (ITA & TUR.). 1979. 9.95 (*0-8288-4734-7*, M9178) Fr & Eur.
Dizionario Medico Poliglotta. deluxe ed. E. Veillon & Albert Nobel. (ENG, FRE, GER, ITA & SPA.). 295.00 (*0-7859-0803-X*, M-9636) Fr & Eur.
Dizionario Medico Ragionato Inglese-Italiano: Regionato English-Italian Medical Dictionary. M. Lucchesi. 1489p. (ENG & ITA.). 1978. 150.00 (*0-8288-5206-5*, M9353) Fr & Eur.
Dizionario Moderno Slovene-Italian-Slovene: Modern Slovene-Italian, Italian-Slovene Dictionary. Anton Grad. 445p. (ITA & SLV.). 1979. 14.95 (*0-8288-4735-5*, M9704) Fr & Eur.
Dizionario Moderno Spagnuolo-Italiano, Italiano-Spagnuolo, 2 vols. Gaetano Frisoni. 1865p. (ITA & SPA.). (C). 1991. 82.00 (*0-913298-51-4*) S F Vanni.
Dizionario Portoghese-Italiano, Italiano-Portoghese: Portuguese-Italian, Italian-Portuguese Dictionary. C. Parlagreco. 1138p. (ITA & POR.). 1979. 49.95 (*0-8288-4736-3*, M9183) Fr & Eur.
Dizionario Portoghese-Italiano-Portoghese: Portuguese-Italian, Italian-Portuguese Dictionary. A. Biava. 318p. (ITA & POR.). 1980. 14.95 (*0-8288-1635-2*, M9172) Fr & Eur.
Dizionario Pseudonimico degli Enigmorgrafi Italiani. A. Santi. 1990. reprint ed. 23.00 (*3-262-00059-0*) Periodicals Srv.
Dizionario Sandron della Lingua Italiana. 2160p. 1986. 98.00 (*0-913298-85-9*) S F Vanni.
Dizionario Sandron della Lingua Italiana. Sandron. (ITA.). lib. bdg. 145.00 (*0-8288-3329-X*, M14418) Fr & Eur.
Dizionario Sansoni Inglese-Italiano Italiano-Inglese. 1820p. (ENG & ITA.). 1988. lib. bdg. write for info. (*0-8288-3374-5*) Fr & Eur.
Dizionario Tecnico Italiano-Inglese, Inglese-Italiano. G. Marolli. 2048p. (ENG & ITA.). 1978. 250.00 (*0-685-42439-1*, M-9197) Fr & Eur.
Dizionario Tecnico Italiano-Inglese, Inglese-Italiano. 11th rev. ed. Renzo Denti. 2010p. (ENG & ITA.). (C). 1991. 100.00 (*88-203-1052-X*) S F Vanni.
Dizionario Tecnico Nautico: Italiano-Inglese, Inglese-Italiano. V. Mastropasqua. 879p. (ENG & ITA.). 1967. pap. 75.00 (*0-8288-6683-X*, M-9297) Fr & Eur.
Dizionario Tecnico Tedesco-Italiano e Italiano-Tedesco. G. Marolli. 2038p. (ITA.). 1991. lib. bdg. 250.00 (*0-685-54279-3*) Fr & Eur.
Dizzie the Pony. Jane Burton. LC 89-11395. (Baby Animals Growing up Ser.). (Illus.). 32p. (J). (gr. 2-3). 1989. lib. bdg. 17.27 (*0-8368-0207-1*) Gareth Stevens Inc.
Dizziness: Etiologic Approach to Management. W. Rubin & K. Brookler. (Illus.). 256p. 1991. text ed. 53.00 (*0-86577-391-2*) Thieme Med Pubs.
Dizziness & Balance Disorders: An Interdisciplinary Approach to Diagnosis, Therapy Treatment & Rehabilitation. Ed. by I. Kaufman Arenberg. LC 93-38841. (Illus.). 1993. lib. bdg. 210.00 (*90-6299-100-9*, Pub. by Kugler NE) Kugler Pubns.
Dizziness, Hope Through Research. (DHHS Publication NIH Ser.: No. 86-76). (Illus.). 27p. 1986. pap. 1.00 (*0-16-002641-5*, S/N 017-049-00134-4) USGPO.
Dizzionario Di Mitologia Egizia, Vol. 4. R. V. Lanzone. xv, 205p. 1975. 105.00 (*90-272-0934-0*) Benjamins North Am.
Dizzy. Peter O'Donnell. (Illus.). (J). (ps up). 1992. 14.95 (*0-590-45475-7*, 021, Scholastic Hardcover) Scholastic Inc.
Dizzy: The Life & Nature of Benjamin Disraeli, Earl of Beaconsfield. Hesketh Pearson. LC 74-12579. (Illus.). 284p. 1974. reprint ed. text ed. 59.75 (*0-8371-7729-4*, PEDIZ, Greenwood Pr) Greenwood.
Dizzy Dean. Jack Kavanagh. (Baseball Legends Ser.). (Illus.). 64p. (J). (gr. 3 up). 1991. lib. bdg. 14.95 (*0-7910-1173-9*) Chelsea Hse.
Dizzy Dervish. Mantinband. (J). Date not set. 13.95 (*0-06-020226-2*, HarpT); lib. bdg. 13.89 (*0-06-020227-0*, HarpT) HarpC.
Dizzy Doctor Riddles. Joanne E. Bernstein & Paul Cohen. Ed. by Kathy Tucker. LC 89-35392. (Illus.). 32p. (J). (gr. 1-5). 1989. 8.95 (*0-8075-1648-1*) A Whitman.
Dizzy from Fools. M. L. Miller. LC 85-9390. (Illus.). 32p. (J). (gr. 1 up). 1991. pap. 13.95 (*0-88708-004-9*, Picture Book Studio) S&S Childrens.
Dizzy Gillespie. Tony Gentry. 1993. pap. 3.95 (*0-87067-778-0*, Melrose Sq) Holloway.
Dizzy Gillespie. Barry McRae. (Illus.). 136p. pap. 11.95 (*0-7119-1441-9*, OP44635) Omnibus NY.
Dizzy Gillespie: Musician. Tony Gentry. (Black Americans of Achievement Ser.). (Illus.). 112p. (J). (gr. 5 up). 1994. lib. bdg. 18.95 (*0-7910-1127-5*, Am Art Analog); pap. write for info. (*0-7910-1152-6*, Am Art Analog) Chelsea Hse.
Dizzy Gillespie - Life & Times. Spellmount Ltd. Publishers Staff. (C). 1986. 75.00 (*0-946771-34-0*, Pub. by Spellmount UK) St Mut.
Dizzy Gillespie & the Birth of Bebop. Leslie Gourse. LC 93-30222. (Illus.). 160p. (YA). (gr. 7 up). 1994. text ed. 14.95 (*0-689-31869-3*, Atheneum Bks Young) S&S Childrens.
Dizzy Pilots. Clyde Bruckman. LC 92-11180. 1992. lib. bdg. 12.94 (*1-56239-166-6*) Abdo & Dghtrs.
***D.J. & the Zulu Parade.** Denise W. McConduit. LC 94-12210. (Illus.). 32p. (J). (gr. 4-8). 1994. 14.95 (*1-56554-063-8*) Pelican.
Djamila Boupacha. Simone de Beauvoir. 292p. (FRE.). 1962. 49.95 (*0-8288-9678-X*, 207020524X) Fr & Eur.
Django. John Cech. LC 93-46782. (Illus.). 40p. (J). (ps-3). 1994. text ed. 15.95 (*0-02-765705-1*, Four Winds Pr) S&S Childrens.
Django Reinhardt. Charles Delaunay. 300p. 1993. pap. 29.50 (*0-9506224-5-1*, 00183208, Pub. by Ashley Mark Pub UK) H Leonard.
Django Reinhardt. Charles Delaunay. Tr. by Michael James. (Quality Paperbacks Ser.). (Illus.). 247p. 1982. reprint ed. pap. 10.95 (*0-306-80171-X*) Da Capo.
Django Reinhardt (Jazz) Charles Delaunay. LC 80-27575. (Roots of Jazz Ser.). 247p. 1981. 27.50 (*0-306-76057-6*) Da Capo.
Djawanisch-Deutsches Woerterbuch. Hans Herrfurth. 574p. 1980. 95.00 (*0-8288-1596-8*, F67080) Fr & Eur.
Djbot Baghostus's Run. Nathaniel Mackey. (New American Fiction Ser.: No. 29). 208p. (Orig.). 1993. pap. 12.95 (*1-55713-055-8*) Sun & Moon CA.
Djibouti. Peter J. Shraeder. (World Bibliographical Ser.). 1991. lib. bdg. 80.50 (*1-85109-084-3*) ABC-CLIO.
Djibouti: Pawn of the Horn of Africa. Robert Tholomier. Tr. by Virginia Thompson & Richard Adloff. LC 81-143. 177p. 1981. 22.50 (*0-8108-1415-3*) Scarecrow.
Djibouti & the Horn of Africa. Virginia Thompson & Richard Adloff. LC 68-21289. (Illus.). xiii, 246p. 1968. 35.00 (*0-8047-0650-6*) Stanford U Pr.
***D.J.'s Angel.** Lori Handeland. 400p. (Orig.). 1995. mass mkt. 4.99 (*0-505-52050-8*) Dorchester Pub Co.
DJs, Ratings, & Hook Tapes: Pop Music Broadcasting. David Hautzig. LC 91-33588. (Illus.). 48p. (J). (gr. 3-7). 1993. text ed. 15.95 (*0-02-743471-0*, Mac Bks Young Read) S&S Childrens.
Djuka, the Bush Negroes of Dutch Guiana. Morton C. Kahn. LC 76-44739. reprint ed. 36.00 (*0-404-15939-7*) AMS Pr.
Djuna: The Formidable Miss Barnes. Andrew Field. (Illus.). 303p. 1985. pap. 10.95 (*0-292-71546-5*) U of Tex Pr.
***Djuna: The Life & Work of Djuna Barnes.** Phillip Herring. LC 95-7630. 1995. 27.95 (*0-670-84969-3*, Viking) Viking Penguin.
***DK Action Pack: Human Body.** (J). 1995. 19.95 (*1-56458-894-7*, 5-70550) Dorling Kindersley.
***DK Action Pack: Light & Illusion.** Dorling Kindersley Staff. (J). (ps-3). 1995. 19.95 (*1-56458-897-1*, 5-70552) Dorling Kindersley.
***DK Action Pack: Rome.** (J). 1995. 19.95 (*1-56458-896-3*, 5-70551) Dorling Kindersley.
***DK Great Herbs: Growing Herbs.** 80p. 1995. 19.95 (*0-7894-0191-6*, 6-70505) Dorling Kindersley.
***DK Ultimate Visual Encyclopedia.** (Illus.). 456p. (J). 1995. 45.00 (*1-56458-985-4*, 5-70556) Dorling Kindersley.
***DK Visual Timeline of Transportation: A Visual History.** Anthony Wilson. LC 94-48714. 64p. (J). 1995. 16.95 (*1-56458-880-7*, 5-70598) Dorling Kindersley.
DL&W Classification of Freight Equipment, 1952. 113p. 1992. pap. 18.00 (*0-9632787-1-1*) E L Hist Soc.
DLB Documentary Series, Vol. 12. Mary Bruccoli et al. 1994. 128.00 (*0-8103-5561-2*, 006486) Gale.
***DLB 148: German Writers & Works of the Early Middle Ages.** Ed. by Will Hasty & James Hardin. 414p. 1994. 112.00 (*0-8103-5709-7*) Gale.
***DLB 147: South Slavic Writers Before World War II.** Ed. by Vasa D. Mihailovich. 368p. 1994. 112.00 (*0-8103-5708-9*) Gale.
DLB Yearbook: 1989 Yearbook. 1990. 128.00 (*0-8103-4569-2*, 006459-99584) Gale.
DLB Yearbook, 1993. Mary Bruccoli et al. 1994. 128.00 (*0-8103-5560-4*, 006463) Gale.
***DLB Yearbook, 1994.** 1995. 128.00 (*0-8103-5705-4*) Gale.
Dlx. Anth. of O'Carolan Music. Date not set. write for info. (*0-7866-0104-3*, 95266) Mel Bay.
Dlx. Anth. of O'Carolan Music. Date not set. audio write for info. (*0-7866-0105-1*, 95266C) Mel Bay.
***DLX Instruction Set Architecture Handbook.** David R. Kaeli & Philip M. Sailor. 200p. 1995. 17.95 (*1-55860-371-9*) Morgan Kaufmann.
DM Hand Surgery. Chase. 500p. 1993. 59.00 (*1-55664-132-X*) Mosby Yr Bk.
DM in Infertility 2. DeCherney. 59.00 (*1-55664-352-7*) Mosby Yr Bk.
DM Periodontology, No. 2. Hall. 288p. 1992. 52.00 (*0-685-61664-9*) Mosby Yr Bk.
Dmitri Shostakovich. Victor I. Seroff. LC 73-126255. (Select Bibliographies Reprint Ser.). 1977. 21.95 (*0-8369-5482-3*) Ayer.
Dmitri Shostakovich: The Life Background of a Soviet Composer. Victor I. Seroff. 1988. reprint ed. lib. bdg. 59.00 (*0-7812-0226-4*) Rprt Serv.
Dmitri Shostakovich - a Complete Catalog. Comp. by Malcolm MacDonald. 1977. pap. text ed. 17.00 (*0-913932-39-6*) Boosey & Hawkes.
Dmitri Shostakovich, the Man & His Work. Ivan I. Martynov. Tr. by T. Guralsky. LC 75-88903. 197p. 1969. reprint ed. text ed. 59.75 (*0-8371-2100-0*, MAS, Greenwood Pr) Greenwood.
Dmitrii Alekseevich Golytsin, 1734-1803. G. K. Tsverava. 184p. 1985. 29.00 (*0-317-42726-1*, Pub. by Collets UK) St Mut.
Dmitrii Kantemir. V. N. Erunatskii. 114p. 1983. 30.00 (*0-685-12145-3*, Pub. by Collets UK) St Mut.
Dmitrii Miliutin & the Reform Era in Russia. Forrest A. Miller. LC 68-20545. 1968. 17.95 (*0-8265-1112-0*) Vanderbilt U Pr.
DMSO: Nature's Healer. Morton Walker. LC 92-34981. 352p. 1993. pap. 12.95 (*0-89529-548-2*) Avery Pub.
DMSO: The Complete Up-to-Date Guidebook. David G. Williams. 82p. 1987. pap. 9.95 (*0-944649-01-7*) Mtn Home Pub.
DMSO: The Responsible User's Guide. Thomas Bristol. (Illus.). 128p. (Orig.). 1982. pap. 5.95 (*0-940530-00-7*) DMSO News Serv.
DMSO Handbook. Bruce W. Halsted & Sylvia A. Youngberg. 1981. 10.95 (*0-933904-08-8*); pap. 5.95 (*0-933904-07-X*) Gold Quill Pubs CA.
DMZ Diary: A Combat Marine's Vietnam Memoir. Jeff Kelly. LC 91-52746. 219p. 1991. pap. 19.95x (*0-89950-631-3*) McFarland & Co.
DNA: Recombination, Interactions & Repair, Vol. 63. FEBS Symposium on DNA, Liblice, 24-29 September, 1979. Ed. by S. Zadrazil & J. Sponar. (Illus.). 600p. 1980. 247.00 (*0-08-025494-2*, Pub. by Pergamon Repr UK) Franklin.
***DNA: Replication & Recombination, Pt. 1.** Cold Spring Harbor Symposia on Quantitative Biology Staff. LC 34-8174. (Cold Spring Harbor Symposia on Quantitative Biology Ser.: Vol. 43). (Illus.). 679p. 1979. pap. 180.00 (*0-7837-8982-3*, 2049763) Bks Demand.
***DNA: Replication & Recombination, Pt. 2.** Cold Spring Harbor Symposia on Quantitative Biology Staff. LC 34-8174. (Cold Spring Harbor Symposia on Quantitative Biology Ser.: Vol. 43). (Illus.). 748p. 1979. pap. 180.00 (*0-7837-8983-1*, 2049763) Bks Demand.
***DNA: The Double Helix: Perspective & Prospective at Forty Years.** Donald A. Chambers. LC 95-8848. (Annals Ser.: Vol. 758). 1995. pap. write for info. (*0-89766-906-1*) NY Acad Sci.

An Asterisk (*) at the beginning of an entry indicates that the title is appearing in BIP for the first time.

An Asterisk (*) at the beginning of an entry indicates that the title is appearing in BIP for the first time.

2055

Do Community Health Centers Save Money? A Review of the Literature. Anjean B. Carter. 40p. (Orig.). 1984. pap. 5.00 (0-88156-019-7) Comm Serv Soc NY.

Do Compensation Policies Matter? Ed. by Ronald G. Ehrenberg. LC 89-71733. (Frank W. Pierce Memorial Lectureship & Conference Ser.: No. 8). 296p. 1990. 26.00 (0-87546-166-2) ILR Pr.

Do Cook for One. Kay Osborne. LC 84-90503. (Illus.). 216p. 1985. pap. 10.95 (0-9613877-0-X) K-D Enter.

***Do Demons Rule Your Town?** Mike R. Taylor. 1993. pap. 8.99 (0-85234-529-1, Pub. by Evangel Pr UK) Presby & Reformed.

Do Dogs Need Shrinks? What to Do When Man's Best Friend Misbehaves. Peter Neville. 288p. 1992. pap. 12.95 (0-8065-1332-2, Citadel Pr) Carol Pub Group.

Do Dzherel: Istorychno-Literaturni Ta Krytychni Statti. Mykola Zerov. LC 68-53064. (UKR.). 1967. text ed. 30.00 (0-918884-15-2) Slavia Lib.

Do Elections Matter? 2nd ed. Ed. by Benjamin Ginsberg & Alan Stone. LC 90-34527. 288p. (Orig.). (C). 1991. 57.95 (0-87332-592-3); pap. text ed. 20.95 (0-87332-593-1) M E Sharpe.

***Do Elections Matter?** 3rd ed. Ed. by Benjamin Ginsberg & Alan Stone. 256p. 1995. 49.95 (1-56324-445-4) M E Sharpe.

***Do Elections Matter?** 3rd ed. Ed. by Benjamin Ginsberg & Alan Stone. 256p. 1995. pap. 17.95 (1-56324-446-2) M E Sharpe.

Do Everything Reform: The Reform Oratory of Frances E. Willard. Richard W. Leeman. LC 91-35714. (Great American Orators: Critical Studies, Speeches & Sources: No. 15). 232p. 1992. text ed. 55.00 (0-313-27487-8, LEE/, Greenwood Pr) Greenwood.

Do Family of Origin Problems Cause Chemical Addiction? Terence T. Gorski. 1989. pap. 5.50 (0-8309-0544-8) Herald Hse.

Do Fish Drink? First Questions & Answers about Water. Time-Life Inc. Editors. Ed. by Neil Kagan. LC 92-40301. (Library of First Questions & Answers). (Illus.). 48p. (J). (ps). 1993. write for info. (0-7835-0850-6); lib. bdg. write for info. (0-7835-0851-4) Time-Life.

Do Fishes Get Thirsty? Questions Answered by the New England Aquarium. New England Aquarium Staff & Les Kaufman. (Illus.). 40p. (YA). (gr. 5 up). 1991. lib. bdg. 15.82 (0-531-10992-5) Watts.

Do for Self: One Hundred of the Best Businesses for Africans in the 21st Century. Gabriel Bandele & L. Hooper. LC 92-75200. 130p. 1992. pap. 10.00 (1-882706-02-1) Bandele Pubns.

Do Four Things Now. Brown Landone. 528p. 1967. reprint ed. spiral bd. 16.50 (0-7873-1253-3) Mokelumne.

Do Four Things Now: The Way to a New Life Beyond Your Dreams. B. Landone. 1991. lib. bdg. 98.99 (0-8490-5132-0) Gordon Pr.

Do-Gooders. Aidel Stein. (Baker's Dozen Ser.: No. 11). 162p. (J). (gr. 6-8). 1994. pap. 7.95 (1-56871-049-6) Targum Pr.

Do Growth Controls Matter? A Review of Empirical Evidence on the Effectiveness & Efficiency of Local Government Land Use Regulations. William A. Fischel. 68p. (Orig.). 1989. pap. text ed. 7.00 (1-55844-087-9) Lincoln Inst Land.

Do Housing Allowances Work? Ed. by Katharine L. Bradbury & Anthony Downs. LC 81-6689. (Studies in Social Experimentation). 419p. 1981. 32.95 (0-8157-1052-6); pap. 12.95 (0-8157-1051-8) Brookings.

Do I Dare Disturb the Universe? A Memorial to W. R. Bion. Ed. by James S. Grotstein. 674p. 1981. reprint ed. pap. 47.95 (0-946439-01-X, Pub. by Karnac Bks UK) Brunner-Mazel.

Do I Dare Disturb the Universe? From Projects to Prep School. Charlise Lyles. LC 93-46456. 200p. 1994. 22.95 (0-571-19836-8) Faber & Faber.

Do I Dust or Vacuum First? (& 99 Other Nitty-Gritty Housecleaning Questions) Don Aslett. 240p. 1993. pap. 3.99 (0-451-17569-7, Sig) NAL-Dutton.

Do I Have a Daddy? A Story about a Single-Parent Child. 2nd ed. Jeanne W. Lindsay. LC 90-49676. (Illus.). 48p. (J). 1991. 12.95 (0-930934-45-8); pap. 5.95 (0-930934-44-X) Morning Glory.

Do I Have To? Stacy Quigley. LC 85-24350. (Life & Living from a Child's Point of View Ser.). (Illus.). 32p. (J). (gr. k-6). 1980. lib. bdg. 19.97 (0-8172-1352-X) Raintree Steck-V.

Do I Have To? Children Who Do Too Little Around the House. Patricia H. Sprinkle. 144p. 1993. pap. 8.99 (0-310-58721-2) Zondervan.

***Do I Have to Give up Me to Be Loved by My Kids?** Jordan Paul & Margaret Paul. Orig. Title: From Conflict to Caring. 1994. pap. 12.95 (1-56838-068-2) Hazelden.

***Do I Have to Give up Me to Be Loved by You?** Jordan Paul & Margaret Paul. 1995. 7.98 (1-56731-067-2, MJF Bks) Fine Comms.

***Do I Have to Give up Me to Be Loved by You Workbook.** Jordan Paul. 1992. pap. 13.95 (1-56838-051-8) Hazelden.

Do I have to Go to School Today? Squib Measures Up. Larry Shles. Ed. by Bradley L. Winch. (Creative Parenting & Adventures of Squib Ser.: Vol. V). (Illus.). 64p. (Orig.). (J). (gr. k up). 1989. pap. 7.95 (0-915190-62-1, JP9062-1) Jalmar Pr.

Do I Hear a Waltz? (Vocal Score Ser.). 1981. pap. 35.00 (0-88188-013-2, 00312116) H Leonard.

Do I Hear a Waltz? (Illus.). 1991. 8.95 (0-88188-071-X, 00312115) H Leonard.

Do I Like Myself? Janice M. Holt. LC 82-82332. (Illus.). 119p. (J). (gr. 3-9). 1983. pap. 39.95 (0-9608812-1-2) Greenlf Pubns.

Do I Miss My Uterus? Lewis J. Marola. (Illus.). 80p. 1994. pap. 9.95 (0-8059-3465-0) Dorrance.

***Do I Want to Be a Teenage Parent?** Ed. by Mardi Richmond. (Illus.). 16p. 1995. write for info. (1-56885-058-1) Journeyworks Pub.

Do Ideata see Aim Higher

Do Iguanas Dance, under the Moonlight. Laurel A. Bogen. 100p. (Orig.). 1984. pap. 9.95 (0-89807-033-3) Illuminati.

Do-in One, the Art of Rejuvenation. rev. ed. (Illus.). 1993. per. 8.00 (0-916508-33-1) Happiness Pr.

Do-In Two: A Most Complete Work on the Ancient Art of Self-Massage. 7th ed. 160p. 1990. 16.00 (0-685-40854-X) Happiness Pr.

Do Institutions Matter? Government Capabilities in the United States & Abroad. Ed. by R. Kent Weaver & Bert A. Rockman. 410p. 1993. 36.95 (0-8157-9256-5); pap. 16.95 (0-8157-9255-7) Brookings.

***Do It: An Irreverent Guide to Poetry.** John Timpane. 144p. 1995. pap. 9.95 (0-89815-777-3) Ten Speed Pr.

***Do It! Let's Get off Our Buts.** Peter McWilliams. 1995. audio 24.95 (0-931580-15-3) Prelude Press.

***Do It! Let's Get off Our Buts.** rev. ed. Peter McWilliams. 494p. 1994. pap. 5.95 (0-931580-79-X) Prelude Press.

Do It! Active Learning in Youth Ministry. Thom Schultz & Joani Schultz. 144p. (Orig.). 1989. pap. 12.99 (0-931529-94-8) Group Pub.

Do-It-at-Home Retreat: The Spiritual Exercises of St. Ignatius of Loyola. Andre Ravier. Tr. by Cornelius Buckley. LC 90-85500. 233p. (Orig.). 1991. pap. 12.95 (0-89870-363-8) Ignatius Pr.

Do It My Way: A Handbook for Building Creative Teaching Experiences. Grace C. Nash et al. 172p. (Orig.). 1977. pap. text ed. 19.95 (0-88284-055-X, 1442) Alfred Pub.

Do It Now. Fred L. Fifer & Cynthia E. Ledbetter. 155p. (J). 1989. student ed 15.95 (1-885568-07-X) SCE Assocs.

***Do It Now.** J. Donald Walters. 160p. 1995. pap. 4.95 (1-56589-731-5) Crystal Clarity.

Do It Now: How to Stop Procrastinating. William J. Knaus. (Illus.). 1979. text ed. 11.95 (0-13-216614-3, Spectrum Bks); pap. text ed. 5.95 (0-13-206660-2) P-H.

Do It Right the First Time: Guide to Computer Installation. Selma Lamkin. 1983. 15.00 (0-686-37906-3) Nikmal Pub.

Do It with Chalk: Black Light Artistry: How to Do It Using Chalk. Wanda C. Vincent. 63p. 1993. pap. text ed. 13.00 (0-923463-95-X) Noble Pub Assocs.

Do It with the Sun. Edith S. Shedd & Alan Shedd. LC 82-81309. (Illus.). 208p. (Orig.). (J). (gr. 6-9). 1982. pap. 12.95 (0-9608358-0-6) Integ Energy.

Do It with Your Shoes on & One Hundred Other Fun Ways to Spice up Your Sex Life. David Abels. LC 93-95051. 128p. 1994. pap. 8.95 (1-884477-25-9) Three Cat Pr.

Do-It Write: How to Prepare a Great College Application. 5th ed. G. Gary Ripple. 32p. 1993. 4.00 (0-945981-77-5) Octameron Assocs.

Do-It-Yourself. Meredith Books Staff. 1994. 21.95 (0-696-20001-5) Meredith Bks.

Do It Yourself. Robert P. Sikking. 44p. 1981. pap. 1.50 (0-87516-436-6) DeVorss.

Do-It-Yourself. Hannah Tofts. LC 93-21218. (Hands-on Ser.). (Illus.). 48p. (J). (gr. 5-9). 1994. 16.95 (1-56847-147-5) Thomson Lrning.

Do-It-Yourself Advertising. David F. Ramacitti. 250p. (Orig.). 1992. pap. 18.95 (0-8144-7743-7) AMACOM.

Do-It-Yourself Advertising: How to Produce Great Ads, Catalogs, Direct Mail, & Much More. Fred Hahn. (Small Business Ser.). 246p. 1993. text ed. 45.00 (0-471-55389-1); pap. text ed. 14.95 (0-471-55390-5) Wiley.

***Do-It-Yourself Advertising, Direct Mail, & Publicity: Ready-to-Use Templates, Worksheets, & Samples for Creating Ads, Direct Mail Pieces, Press Releases, & Other Promotional Items.** Sarah White & John Woods. (Business Advisor Ser.). 300p. (Orig.). 1995. pap. 15.95 (1-55850-488-5) Adams Pubng.

Do-It-Yourself Allergy Analysis Handbook. Kate Ludeman & Louise Henderson. 154p. 1990. reprint ed. pap. 10.95 (0-87983-542-7) Keats.

Do-It-Yourself & Home Improvement Markets. 1985. 250.00 (0-686-71951-4, Pub. by Euromonitor Pubns UK) St Mut.

Do-It-Yourself Aspect Book. Emylu L. Hughes. LC 82-73125. 64p. 1982. 9.00 (0-86690-038-1, H2647-014) Am Fed Astrologers.

Do-It-Yourself Astronomy. Sydney G. Brewer. 96p. 1988. 15.00 (0-85224-573-4, Pub. by Edinburgh U Pr UK) Col U Pr.

Do It Yourself (At Home) Sewing Machine Care & Repair. Ronald L. Enger. (Illus.). 33p. 1978. pap. 3.95 (0-685-59470-X) R L Enger.

Do-It-Yourself Automotive Maintenance & Repair. Walter E. Billiet. LC 78-15055. (Illus.). 1979. 17.95 (0-13-217190-2, Spectrum Bks); pap. 7.95 (0-13-217182-1) P-H.

***Do-It-Yourself Black Bear Baiting & Hunting.** Ken Nordberg. Ed. by M. C. O'Donnell et al. 160p. (Orig.). 1990. pap. 8.95 (1-886422-50-8) Shingle Creek.

Do It Yourself Business Book. Gustav Berle. 1989. text ed. 49.95 (0-471-50768-7); pap. text ed. 14.95 (0-471-50769-5) Wiley.

***Do-It-Yourself Business Promotions Kit.** Jack Griffin. LC 94-39938. 1995. text ed. 29.95 (0-13-106014-7); pap. text ed. 18.95 (0-13-106006-6) P-H.

Do-It-Yourself Car Care. Larry W. Carley. (Illus.). 224p. (Orig.). 1987. 12.95 (0-8306-0843-5, 2143) TAB Bks.

Do-It-Yourself Career Kit: A Career Planning Tool. Rogene Baxter & Marcelle Brashear. LC 90-82007. (Illus.). 150p. (Orig.). 1990. student ed 14.95 (0-9626638-0-8) Bridgewater Pr.

Do-It Yourself Decorating. Family Circle Editors. 1977. 12.95 (0-405-11396-X) Ayer.

Do-It-Yourself Decorating. John McGowan & Roger DuBern. LC 90-23100. (Home Handbooks Ser.). (Illus.). 240p. (Orig.). 1991. pap. 16.00 (0-89577-381-3, Random) RD Assn.

Do-It-Yourself Direct Mail Handbook. Murray Raphel & Ken Erdman. LC 86-63913. 1986. 19.95 (0-939951-01-0) Marketers Bookshelf.

Do-It-Yourself Direct Marketing: Secrets for Small Business. Mark S. Bacon. 288p. 1991. text ed. 24.95 (0-471-53241-X) Wiley.

Do It Yourself Direct Marketing: Secrets for Small Business. Mark S. Bacon. 1994. pap. text ed. 17.95 (0-471-00876-1) Wiley.

Do-it-Yourself Divorce: Cook County, Illinois. rev. ed. Nik-ki Whittingham. 80p. 1984. pap. 14.95 (0-915867-01-X) ENAAQ Pubns.

Do-It-Yourself Divorce: Cook County, Illinois. 3rd rev. ed. Nik-ki Whittingham. 125p. 1991. pap. 19.95 (0-915867-05-2) ENAAQ Pubns.

Do-It-Yourself Furniture Layout Kit. Muncie Hendler. (Illus.). 32p. (Orig.). 1981. pap. 3.95 (0-486-24213-7) Dover.

Do-It-Yourself Genius Kit, 4 bks., Set. Gyles Brandeth. (Illus.). (J). (ps-3). 1989. pap. 3.95 (0-14-095331-0, Puffin) Puffin Bks.

Do-It-Yourself Graphic Design. John Laing. (Illus.). 160p. 1985. pap. 15.00 (0-02-011550-4, Pub. by Gebrueder Borntraeger GW) Macmillan.

Do-It-Yourself Guide to Probate & Estate Planning. Rae Donna Jones & Ann Allen Fadel. LC 83-83179. (Illus.). 191p. 1984. 17.98 (0-88290-234-2) Horizon Utah.

Do-It-Yourself Guitar Repair. Pieter J. Fillet. (Illus.). 80p. 1984. pap. 4.95 (0-8256-2345-6, AM34539) Music Sales.

Do-It-Yourself Gunpowder Cookbook. Don McLean. (Illus.). 80p. 1992. pap. 12.00 (0-87364-675-4) Paladin Pr.

Do-it Yourself Handbook for Keyboard Playing. Ed. by Sheet Music Magazine & Keyboard Classics Magazine. 1983. 15.00 (0-943748-00-3) Ekay Music.

Do It Yourself Happiness. Lee Schnebly. 161p. 1984. pap. 9.95 (0-930831-01-2) Manzanas Press.

Do-It-Yourself Happiness: How to be your own Counselor. Lee Schnebly. LC 88-3692. 218p. 1988. reprint ed. pap. 7.95 (1-55561-012-9) Fisher Bks.

Do It Yourself Hebrew & Greek: Everybody's Guide to the Language Tools. Edward W. Goodrick. 256p. (Orig.). (C). 1980. pap. 18.99 (0-310-41741-4, 6245P) Zondervan.

Do-It-Yourself Home Sales. L. T. Kramer. LC 94-13971. 1994. pap. text ed. 14.95 (0-471-07665-1) Wiley.

***Do-It-Yourself House That Jack Built.** John Yeoman. (Illus.). (J). (gr. 1 up). 1995. 15.00 (0-689-80006-1, Atheneum Bks Young) S&S Childrens.

Do-It-Yourself Housebuilding: The Complete Handbook. George Nash. LC 94-2371. (Illus.). 640p. 1995. pap. 24.95 (0-8069-0424-0) Sterling.

Do It Yourself Investing with No-Load-Mutual Funds. J. Stanley Levitt. 112p. 1991. pap. text ed. 19.95 (0-9631039-0-3) J S Levitt.

***Do-It-Yourself Japanese Through Comics: An Introduction to Japanese in Twelve Lessons.** Martin Lan & Kaoru Shimizu. 360p. 1995. pap. 25.00 (4-7700-1936-X) Kodansha.

***Do-It-Yourself Japanese Through Comics: An Introduction to Japanese in Twelve Lessons.** Kazuhiko Nagatomo & Miho Steinburg. (Illus.). 156p. 1995. pap. 15.00 (4-7700-1935-1) Kodansha.

Do It Yourself Job Search Manual. Metro Resource Publications Staff. (Keep it Simple Ser.). (Illus.). 176p. (Orig.). 1994. pap. 11.95 (0-945376-00-6) Metro Resrc Pubns.

Do-It-Yourself Lettering Book. Anna Burgess. (Illus.). 64p. (J). (gr. 4-7). 1993. pap. 5.95 (0-8167-3036-9) Troll Assocs.

Do-It-Yourself Library. Sunset Magazine & Books Editors. Incl. 1987. (0-318-61436-7); 1987. (0-318-61437-5); 1987. (0-318-61438-3); 1987. (0-318-61437-5); 1987. (0-318-61436-7); 1987. (0-318-61438-3); (Illus.). 1987. 19.95 (0-376-01779-1) Sunset Menlo Pk.

Do-It-Yourself Living Trust Plan: For a Married Couple. Steven W. Allen. 58p. 1990. 395.00 (1-879033-00-3) Legal Awareness.

Do-It-Yourself Living Trust Plan: For a Single Person. Steven W. Allen. 45p. 1990. 395.00 (1-879033-01-1) Legal Awareness.

Do-It-Yourself Marketing. David Ramacitti. 192p. 1994. 18.95 (0-8144-7800-X) AMACOM.

Do-It-Yourself Marketing. F. Lee Reid. Ed. by Dorris Tennyson. 96p. 1994. write for info. (0-318-72823-0) Home Builder.

Do-it-Yourself Marketing for the Professional Practice. Laura Sachs. 222p. 1986. text ed. 44.95 (0-13-216201-6, Busn) P-H.

Do-It-Yourself Marketing Research. George Breen & Albert B. Blankenship. 272p. 1992. pap. text ed. 16.95 (0-07-007451-8) McGraw.

Do-It-Yourself Marketing Research. 3rd ed. George Breen & Albert B. Blankenship. 320p. 1989. text ed. 44.95 (0-07-007450-X) McGraw.

***Do-It-Yourself Math Stories.** Brumbaugh. 1988. pap. (0-590-49155-5) Scholastic Inc.

Do-It-Yourself Medical Testing: More Than 240 Tests You Can Do at Home. 3rd ed. Cathey Pinckney & Edward R. Pinckney. 1989. pap. 14.95 (0-8160-2085-X) Facts on File.

Do-It-Yourself Mutual Fund Book. 4th ed. Frank L. Bouquet. (Illus.). 105p. 1990. 55.00x (0-937041-92-0); pap. 25.00x (0-937041-93-9) Systems Co.

Do-It-Yourself Mutual Fund Book. 5th ed. Frank L. Bouquet. (Illus.). 100p. 1992. 57.00x (1-56216-070-2); pap. text ed. 27.00x (1-56216-057-5) Systems Co.

Do-It-Yourself Mutual Funds, 1994. 6th ed. Frank L. Bouquet. (Illus.). 100p. 1994. 59.00x (1-56216-114-8); pap. 29.00x (1-56216-115-6) Systems Co.

Do-It-Yourself Networking with Lantastic. Mark Gibbs. (Illus.). 400p. (Orig.). 1992. pap. 24.95 (0-672-30026-5) Sams.

Do-It-Yourself Networking with Netware Lite. Patrick Chen. 1992. pap. 24.95 (0-672-30016-8) Sams.

Do It Yourself Over the Hill Birthday Parties. Thomas Antion. (Illus.). 32p. (Orig.). 1990. pap. 6.95 (0-926395-05-X) Anchor Maryland.

Do-It-Yourself Plumbing. Max Alth. LC 87-42815. (Illus.). 302p. (Orig.). 1987. pap. 12.95 (0-8069-6514-2) Sterling.

Do-It-Yourself Plumbing. Max Alth. (Illus.). 316p. (Orig.). (C). 1989. reprint ed. lib. bdg. 27.00x (0-8095-7508-6) Borgo Pr.

***Do-It-Yourself Plumbing... It's Easy with Genova.** Richard Day. Ed. by Jeanette Kellogg & Robert M. Williams. (Illus.). 142p. (C). Date not set. pap. text ed. 9.95 (0-9616509-0-7) Genova Products.

***Do-it Yourself Power Tools.** Hallie Deering. 91p. (Orig.). 1995. pap. 25.00 (0-929385-63-2) Light Tech Comns Servs.

Do-It-Yourself Project Book. Anna Burgess. (J). (gr. 4-7). 1994. pap. 5.95 (0-8167-3343-0) Troll Assocs.

Do-It-Yourself Projects from Attic to Basement. Bernard L. Price. LC 85-29023. (Illus.). 328p. 1986. 24.95 (0-937558-15-X) Scharff Ltd.

Do It Yourself Psychotherapy. Martin Shepard. 194p. pap. 6.95 (0-932966-23-3) Permanent Pr.

Do It Yourself Psychotherapy Book. Martin Shepard. 15.95 (0-88411-978-5, Aeonian Pr); pap. 10.95 (0-88411-979-3, Aeonian Pr) Amereon Ltd.

***Do It Yourself Publicity.** Ramacitti. 1994. 5.99 (0-517-13619-8) Random Hse Value.

Do-It-Yourself Publicity. David F. Ramacitti. LC 89-81026. 200p. 1991. pap. 17.95 (0-8144-7773-9) AMACOM.

Do-It-Yourself Publicity Directory. Lynne Palmer. LC 84-70907. 184p. 1984. 17.00 (0-86690-274-0, P2532-014) Am Fed Astrologers.

Do it Yourself Rod Building. Bill Stinson. (Illus.). 80p. (Orig.). 1983. pap. 8.95 (0-936608-01-3) F Amato Pubns.

Do-It-Yourself Shiatsu. Watari Ohashi & Vicki Lindner. 1976. pap. 10.95 (0-525-48312-8, Dutton) NAL-Dutton.

Do-It-Yourself Shiatsu. Watari Ohashi. Ed. by Vicki Lindner. 1976. pap. 9.95 (0-525-47416-1, Dutton) NAL-Dutton.

Do It Yourself Shiatsu. Watari Ohashi. 1993. reprint ed. pap. 13.95 (0-14-019351-0, Arkana) Viking Penguin.

Do-It-Yourself-Stocks. Frank L. Bouquet. (Illus.). 101p. (Orig.). 1989. 55.00x (0-937041-42-4); pap. 25.00x (0-937041-43-2) Systems Co.

Do-It-Yourself Stocks. 4th ed. Frank L. Bouquet. (Illus.). 120p. 1994. 59.00x (1-56216-207-1); pap. 29.00x (1-56216-208-X) Systems Co.

Do-It-Yourself Stocks, 1992. 3rd ed. Frank L. Bouquet. (Illus.). 100p. 1992. 59.00 (1-56216-116-4); pap. 29.00 (1-56216-117-2) Systems Co.

Do-It-Yourself Story Puzzle Book. Mary Lasley. (Illus.). 2p. (J). (ps). 1988. 9.95 (0-9622406-0-5) MOL Bks.

Do It Yourself Turbo C Plus Plus. Paul J. Perry. (Illus.). (Orig.). 1992. pap. 24.95 (0-672-30107-5) Sams.

Do-It-Yourself Vinyl Siding. Nuke DeLoach. 40p. 1994. pap. 14.95 (0-9640586-0-X) Pick-Up Pubns.

Do-It-Yourself Visual Basic. William J. Orvis. (First Book Ser.). (Illus.). 500p. (Orig.). 1992. pap. 19.95 (0-672-27382-9) Sams.

Do It Yourself Visual Basic for Windows. 2nd ed. William Orvis. 1992. pap. 24.95 (0-672-30259-4) Sams.

***Do-It Yourself Yearbook: Money Saving Projects.** Gene L. Schnaser. 192p. 1995. 24.95 (0-9645007-0-1) N Coast Prods.

Do-It-Yourselfer's Guide to Furniture Repair & Refinishing. 2nd ed. Percy W. Blandford. (Furniture Woodshop Ser.). (Illus.). 192p. 1988. 21.95 (0-8306-0994-6, 2994H) TAB Bks.

Do Justice: Linking Christian Faith & Modern Economic Life. Rebecca M. Blank. LC 91-48104. 200p. (Orig.). (C). 1992. pap. 14.95 (0-8298-0929-5) Pilgrim OH.

Do Kamo: La Personne et le Mythe Dans le Monde Melanesien. Maurice Leenhardt. Ed. by Kees W. Bolle. LC 77-79137. (Mythology Ser.). (FRE.). 1978. reprint ed. lib. bdg. 26.95 (0-405-10547-9) Ayer.

Do Less...& Be Loved More: How to Really Relate to Others. Peg Tompkins. 80p. (Orig.). 1989. pap. 8.95 (0-931892-64-3) B Dolphin Pub.

Do Like Kyla. Angela Johnson. LC 89-16229. (Illus.). 32p. (J). (ps-2). 1990. 14.95 (0-531-05852-2); lib. bdg. 14.99 (0-531-08452-3) Orchard Bks Watts.

Do Like Kyla. Angela Johnson. LC 89-16229. (Illus.). 32p. (J). (ps-2). 1993. pap. 5.95 (0-531-07040-9) Orchard Bks Watts.

Do, Lord, Remember Me. George Garrett. LC 65-17253. (Voices of the South Ser.). 288p. 1994. pap. 11.95 (0-8071-1928-8) La State U Pr.

***Do Lord Remember Me.** Julius Lester. (Illus.). 224p. 1995. pap. text ed. 11.95 (1-55970-322-9) Arcade Pub Inc.

Do Me! Stories. Susan Pagnucci & Franco Pagnucci. (Illus.). 64p. (Orig.). (J). (ps-3). 1993. pap. 8.95 (0-929326-07-5) Bur Oak Pr Inc.

Do Mommies Have Mommies? First Questions & Answers about Families. Time-Life Inc. Editors. Ed. by Allan Fallow. (Library of First Questions & Answers). (Illus.). 48p. (J). (ps-00). 1994. write for info. (0-7835-0876-X); lib. bdg. write for info. (0-7835-0875-1) Time-Life.

An Asterisk (*) at the beginning of an entry indicates that the title is appearing in BIP for the first time.

An Asterisk (*) at the beginning of an entry indicates that the title is appearing in BIP for the first time.

2057

Do You Think We Could Have Made It & Other Love Poems for the Separated & Divorced. Patricia A. Bunin. LC 77-91010. 1977. pap. 3.95 (*0-930946-01-4*) Newaves Pub.

Do You Understand? Handbook. Ed. by Chip Carlin. 119p. 1989. teacher ed 4.00 (*0-930713-61-3*); pap. text ed. 10.00 (*0-318-41708-1*) Lit Vol Am.

Do You Understand, Huh! A POW's Lament, 1941-1945. Theodore A. Abraham. (Illus.). 237p. (Orig.). 1992. pap. 19.95 (*0-89745-143-0*) Sunflower U Pr.

Do You Wanna Bet? Your Chance to Find Out about Probability. Jean Cushman. (Illus.). 112p. (J). (gr. 3-7). 1991. 14.95 (*0-395-56516-2*, Clarion Bks) HM.

Do You Want to Be My Friend? Eric Carle. LC 70-140643. (Illus.). 32p. (J). (ps-2). 1971. 15.00 (*0-690-24276-X*, Crowell Jr Bks); lib. bdg. 14.89 (*0-690-01137-7*, Crowell Jr Bks) HarpC Child Bks.

***Do You Want to Be My Friend?** Eric Carle. (Illus.). 32p. (J). (ps). 1987. 6.95 (*0-694-00709-9*, Festival) HarpC Child Bks.

Do You Want to Be My Friend? Eric Carle. LC 70-140643. (Trophy Picture Bk.). (Illus.). 32p. (J). (ps-2). 1987. reprint ed. pap. 5.95 (*0-06-443127-4*, Trophy) HarpC Child Bks.

Do You Want to Go to Heaven? Becky Tilotta. 1967. 0.60 (*0-88027-106-X*) Firm Foun Pub.

Do You Want to Have a Baby: Conception & Natural Prenatal Care. Linda Rector-Page. (Healthy Healing Library Ser.). 32p. 1993. pap. 2.95 (*1-884334-02-4*) Hlthy Healing.

Do You Want to Know a Secret? Making Sense of the Beatles' Unreleased Recordings. L. R. King. (Illus.). 332p. (Orig.). 1988. pap. 15.00 (*0-944692-00-1*) Storyteller Prodns.

Do Your Own Divorce in Connecticut. Michael Avery et al. 1991. pap. 30.00 (*0-89166-014-3*) Cobblesmith.

Do Your Own Divorce in Maine. Pine Tree Legal Assistance, Inc. Staff. (Illus.). 216p. 1991. reprint ed. pap. 16.50 (*0-9610570-0-9*) Bks by Village.

Do Your Own Drywall: An Illustrated Guide. Arnold Kozloski. (Illus.). (Orig.). 1985. pap. 11.95 (*0-07-156236-2*) McGraw.

Do Your Own Drywall: An Illustrated Guide. Arnold Kozloski. (Illus.). 160p. (Orig.). 1985. pap. 11.95 (*0-8306-1838-4*) TAB Bks.

Do Your Own H.I.V. & A.I.D.S. Survey. Damon F. Dunaway. (Illus.). 64p. 1994. 5.95 (*0-318-72335-2*) Dorrance.

Do Your Own Wiring. K. E. Armpriester. LC 91-18970. (Illus.). 128p. 1991. pap. 12.95 (*0-8069-8472-4*) Sterling.

Do Your Own Wiring. K. E. Armpriester. (Illus.). 128p. 1991. reprint ed. lib. bdg. 33.00x (*0-8095-7608-2*) Borgo Pr.

Do Your Prayers Bounce off the Ceiling? Grant A. Worth. LC 81-17411. (Illus.). x, 68p. 1989. reprint ed. pap. 5.95 (*0-87579-230-8*) Deseret Bk.

Do Yourself a Favor: Love Your Wife. John D. Coleman. 59p. 1976. student ed, pap. 1.25 (*0-88270-162-2*) Bridge Pub.

Do Yourself a Favor: Love Your Wife. H. Page Williams. LC 73-85896. 131p. 1973. pap. 3.95 (*0-88270-204-1*) Bridge Pub.

D.O.A. Dave Pedneau. 320p. 1988. mass mkt. 4.99 (*0-345-34677-7*) Ballantine.

DOA Sector Travelogue. 96p. 15.00 (*0-87431-078-4*, 12004) West End Games.

Doability of Curricula. Ed. by Theo H. Joostens et al. LC 93-9656. 168p. 1993. pap. 30.00 (*90-265-1341-0*, Pub. by Swets Pub Serv NE) Taylor & Francis.

Doable Dozen: A Checklist of Practical Ideas for School-Business PartnerShips. Cynthia W. Shelton. (Illus.). 88p. 1987. pap. 7.95 (*0-932399-01-0*) Natl Comm Ed.

Doane Family, Vol. 2. Ed. by Gilbert H. Doane & Gilbert J. Doane. 587p. 1976. text ed. 30.00 (*0-686-32800-0*) Doane Fam Assn.

Doane Family: Deacon John Doane of Plymouth & Dr. John Done of Maryland & Their Descendants with Notes on English Families of the Name, 2 pts. A. Doane. (Illus.). 554p. 1989. reprint ed. lib. bdg. 80.00 (*0-8328-0480-0*); reprint ed. pap. 70.00 (*0-8328-0481-9*) Higginson Bk Co.

Doane-Thompson Catalog of U. S. County & Postmaster Postmarks. Ed. by Kenneth L. Gilman. LC 90-91727. (Illus.). 238p. (Orig.). 1990. text ed. 34.95 (*1-877998-06-0*); pap. text ed. 24.95 (*1-877998-07-9*) D G Phillips.

Doane's Facts & Figures for Farmers. 4th rev. ed. (Illus.). 360p. 1981. pap. 19.95 (*0-932250-15-7*) Red Wing Busn.

Doane's Farm Management Guide. 16th ed. LC 85-70724. (Illus.). 336p. (YA). (gr. 10-12). 1985. pap. 17.95 (*0-932250-23-8*) Red Wing Busn.

Doane's Tax Guide for Farmers. John C. O'Byrne & Charles Davenport. (Illus.). 333p. (Orig.). 1988. pap. 29.95 (*0-932250-28-9*) Red Wing Busn.

Doane's World-Wide Time Change Update, 1986-1990. Doris C. Doane. 80p. 1991. 7.00 (*0-86690-393-3*, D3167-014) Am Fed Astrologers.

Doba Iskusenja. Intro. by Jovan P. Nikolic. LC 83-137480. 63p. (SER.). 1983. pap. 2.00 (*0-931931-13-4*) Ravnogorski.

Dobama Movement in Burma, 1930-1938. Khin Yi. (Southeast Asia Program Ser.: No. 2). 160p. (Orig.). (C). 1988. pap. text ed. 9.00 (*0-87727-118-6*) Cornell SE Asia.

***Dobbie: Probate & Administration Practice.** 4th ed. Gordon Cain & J. B. Curran. 463p. 1986. boxed 108.00 (*0-409-70215-3*, NZ) Butterworth Legal Pubs.

***Dobbin.** Kaye Umansky. (Illus.). 32p. (J). (ps-1). 1995. 19.95 (*0-370-31910-9*, Pub. by Bodley Head UK) Trafalgar.

Dobe Ju-'hoansi. Richard B. Lee. (Case Studies in Cultural Anthropology). (Illus.). 224p. (C). Date not set. pap. text ed. write for info. (*0-03-032284-7*) HB Coll Pubs.

Dobe! Kung. Richard B. Lee. LC 83-12916. (Case Studies in Cultural Anthropology). 173p. (C). 1984. pap. text ed. 13.50 (*0-03-063803-8*) HB Coll Pubs.

Doberman Pinscher. Woodrow Kerfmann. (Illus.). 255p. 1985. text ed. 19.95 (*0-86622-030-5*, PS-808) TFH Pubns.

Doberman Pinscher. Bill Sanford & Carl Green. LC 89-31071. (Top Dog Ser.). (Illus.). 48p. (J). (gr. 4-5). 1989. lib. bdg. 12.95 (*0-89686-454-5*, Crstwood Hse) Silver Burdett Pr.

Doberman Pinscher Champions, 1952-1980. Jan L. Pata. (Illus.). 220p. 1981. pap. 36.95 (*0-940808-01-3*) Camino E E & Bk.

Doberman Pinscher Champions, 1981-1985. Camino E. E. & B. Co. Staff. (Illus.). 221p. 1986. pap. 28.95 (*0-940808-26-9*) Camino E E & Bk.

Doberman Pinscher Champions, 1986-1987. (Illus.). 90p. (Orig.). 1988. pap. 24.95 (*0-940808-83-8*) Camino E E & Bk.

Doberman Pinscher Champions, 1988-1991. Camino E. E. & Book Co. Staff. (Illus.). 150p. 1992. pap. 32.95 (*1-55893-026-4*) Camino E E & Bk.

***Doberman Pinscher in America.** deluxe ed. William S. Schmidt. 218p. 1995. 35.00 (*0-614-04533-9*) Donald R Hoflin.

Doberman Pinschers. Kerry Donnelly. (Illus.). 1989. 11.95 (*0-86622-863-2*, KW-009); 9.95 (*0-86622-806-3*); pap. 5.95 (*0-86622-249-9*, PB-107) TFH Pubns.

Doberman Pinschers. Raymond Gudas. (Pet Care Ser.). (Illus.). 80p. 1987. pap. 5.95 (*0-8120-2999-2*) Barron.

Dobie Paradox. Desmond Cory. 240p. 1994. 19.95 (*0-312-10969-5*, Pub. by Thomas Dunne Bks) St Martin.

DOBIS-LIBIS: A Guide for Librarians & Systems Managers. Peter Brophy et al. (Illus.). 210p. 1990. text ed. 58.95 (*0-566-05590-2*, Pub. by Gower UK) Ashgate Pub Co.

***Doble Historia del Doctor Valmy.** Antonio Buero Vallejo. Ed. & Intro. by Barry Jordan. LC 95-5468. (Hispanic Texts Ser.). 1995. text ed. write for info. (*0-7190-4549-5*, Pub. by Manchester Univ Pr UK) St Martin.

***Doble Pensar: Tres Niveles de Exitoso Pensar Para Inteligencia Mas Elevada.** I. Frank Saunders & Amy Schlessman. Tr. by Esther B. Cuesta. (Illus.). 186p. (SPA.). (C). 1995. pap. text ed. 24.95 (*1-887082-00-X*) Double Think.

Doble Vida Del Creyente: The Twofold Life. A. J. Gordon. (SPA.). 5.50 (*84-7228-862-5*, 222322, Pub. by Edit Clie SP) TSELF.

Dobro Book. Stacy Phillips. (Illus.). 96p. 1977. pap. 15.95 (*0-8256-0183-5*, OK63289, Oak) Music Sales.

Dobro Case Chord Book. Stacy Phillips. (Illus.). 40p. pap. 4.95 (*0-8256-1124-5*, AM67158) Music Sales.

Dobro Songbook. Ken Eidson & Tom Swatzell. 1993. 6.95 (*1-56222-198-1*, 94077) Mel Bay.

Dobro Techniques: For Bluegrass & Country Music. Stephen Toth. (Illus.). 64p. 1993. audio, pap. text ed. 15.95 (*0-931759-68-4*) Centerstream Pub.

Dobrotoljubije, Tom Five, Vol. 5. 343p. reprint ed. pap. 15.00 (*0-317-28891-1*) Holy Trinity.

Dobrotoljubije, Tom Five, Vol. 5. 343p. reprint ed. 20.00 (*0-317-28890-3*) Holy Trinity.

Dobrotoljubije, Tom Four. 451p. reprint ed. pap. 20.00 (*0-317-37275-0*) Holy Trinity.

Dobrotoljubije, Tom Four. 451p. reprint ed. 25.00 (*0-317-28889-X*) Holy Trinity.

Dobrotoljubije, Tom Pjatij: Philokalia, Vol. 5. Ed. by St. Nicodemos the Hagiorite. Tr. by Theophan Govoroff. 350p. (Orig.). (RUS.). 1966. 20.00 (*0-88465-030-8*); pap. 15.00 (*0-88465-029-4*) Holy Trinity.

Dobrotoljubije, Tom Tchetvjortij: Philokalia, Vol. 4. Ed. by St. Nicodemos the Hagiorite. Tr. by Theophan Govoroff. 495p. (Orig.). (RUS.). 1965. 25.00 (*0-88465-027-8*); pap. 20.00 (*0-88465-028-6*) Holy Trinity.

Dobrovolniye Priznaniya - Vinuzhdennaya Perepiska (Voluntary Confessions - Forced Correspondence) Mikhail Armalinsky. 312p. (Orig.). (RUS.). 1991. pap. 9.00 (*0-916201-09-0*) M I P Co.

Dobry. Monica Shannon. LC 92-31442. (Newbery Library). (Illus.). 176p. (J). (gr. 5 up). 1993. pap. 4.99 (*0-14-036334-3*) Puffin Bks.

Dobson's Encyclopedia: The Publisher, Text, & Publication of America's First Britannica, 1789-1803. Robert D. Arner. LC 91-17624. (Illus.). 320p. (C). 1991. text ed. 39.95 (*0-8122-3092-2*) U of Pa Pr.

Dobuzhinskii, Mstislav. Comp. by A. Gusarova. 204p. (C). 1982. 132.00 (*0-685-22612-3*, Pub. by Collets UK) Pro-Am Music.

Dobyns-Bennett Football: The Sprankle Years. Dave Hoover. (Illus.). 56p. 1987. 6.95 (*0-932807-26-7*) Overmountain Pr.

Dobzhansky's Genetics of Natural Populations: I-XLIII. Theodosius Dobzhansky. Ed. by Richard C. Lewontin et al. LC 81-2073. 1024p. 1981. text ed. 91.00 (*0-231-05132-8*) Col U Pr.

Doc. Jack Olsen. 1990. mass mkt. 5.95 (*0-440-20668-5*) Dell.

Doc. Howard W. Roberts. LC 86-90702. (Illus.). 176p. 1987. 11.95 (*0-9617971-0-X*) Circuit Writer.

Doc. Howard W. Roberts. 176p. 1987. 12.95 (*0-317-56840-X*) McClain.

DOC: Memoirs of a Rocky Mountain Physician. R. E. Losee. (Illus.). 240p. 1994. 22.95 (*1-55821-323-6*) Lyons & Burford.

Doc & Fluff. Pat Califia. 319p. (Orig.). 1990. pap. 8.95 (*1-55583-176-1*) Alyson Pubns.

***Doc Atlas: Arctic Terror & The Nemesis: Claws of the Falcon.** Mike Black & Gary Lovisi. (Gryphon Double Novel Ser.: No. 9). 100p. 1994. per. 9.95 (*0-936071-42-7*) Gryphon Pubns.

Doc Ben Speaks Out. E. Curtis Alexander. LC 89-81784. (Monograph Ser.: No. 1). 52p. 1982. pap. 5.95 (*0-938818-04-X*, Alkebulan Hist Res Soc) ECA Assoc.

Doc Blakeley's Handbook of Wit & Pungent Humor. James D. Blakely. LC 83-61029. 228p. 1983. 20.00 (*0-9607256-2-8*) Rich Pub Co.

Doc Blakely's Handbook of Wit & Pungent Humor. James D. Blakely. 1989. 20.00 (*0-318-41180-6*) Doc Blakely.

Doc Blakely's "Push Button Wit" James D. Blakely. 1989. 20.00 (*0-318-41181-4*) Doc Blakely.

Doc Blakely's "Push Button Wit" James D. Blakely. LC 85-61515. (Illus.). 272p. 1986. text ed. 20.00 (*0-9607256-3-6*) Rich Pub Co.

***Doc Hall's Journal: The Ramblings of a Sportsman.** James Hall, 4th. (Illus.). 1995. text ed. 29.00 (*1-885106-11-4*) Wild Adven Pr.

***Doc Hall's Journal: The Ramblings of a Sportsman.** limited ed. James Hall, 4th. (Illus.). 1995. 90.00 (*1-885106-12-2*) Wild Adven Pr.

Doc Hemlock C.S.A. Are You Hurt Bad. T. A. Utley. LC 90-81952. (Illus.). 1990. pap. 9.95 (*0-938991-59-0*) Colonial Pr AL.

***Doc Holiday.** Debra Dixon. (Loveswept Ser.: No. 723). 1995. pap. 3.50 (*0-553-44432-8*, Loveswept) Bantam.

***Doc Holliday.** Carl R. Green & William R. Sanford. LC 94-24845. (Outlaws & Lawmen of the Wild West Ser.). (Illus.). 48p. (J). (gr. 4-10). 1995. lib. bdg. 14.95 (*0-89490-589-9*) Enslow Pubs.

Doc Holliday. John M. Myers. LC 55-5528. 224p. 1973. reprint ed. pap. 8.95 (*0-8032-5781-3*, Bison Books) U of Nebr Pr.

Doc Holliday, Bat Masterson, Wyatt Earp: Their Colorado Careers. E. Richard Churchill. 1978. 2.95 (*0-913488-05-4*) Timberline Bks.

Doc Holliday's Woman. Jane C. Coleman. 336p. 1995. 19.95 (*0-446-51825-5*) Warner Bks.

***Doc Holliday's Woman.** Jane C. Coleman. 1996. mass mkt. write for info. (*0-446-60344-9*) Warner Bks.

***Doc Holliday's Woman.** large type ed. Jane C. Coleman. LC 95-12545. 1995. write for info. (*0-7838-1369-4*) Hall.

***Doc Hollywood.** Neil Shulman. 210p. (Orig.). (YA). Date not set. pap. 20.00 (*0-9639002-5-0*) N Shulman.

Doc Hollywood. Neil B. Shulman. 210p. (Orig.). reprint ed. pap. 4.99 (*0-9639002-1-8*) N Shulman.

Doc Horne: A Story of the Streets & Town. George Ade. LC 77-104402. reprint ed. lib. bdg. 22.75 (*0-8398-0052-5*); reprint ed. pap. text ed. 7.25 (*0-89197-734-1*) Irvington.

Doc-in-a-Box. Robert A. Burton. LC 90-10315. 214p. 1991. 18.95 (*0-939149-47-8*) Soho Press.

Doc Middleton: Life & Legends of the Notorious Plains Outlaw see Luckiest Outlaw: The Life & Legends of Doc Middleton

Doc Pizzo's Nutrition Handbook. Albert Pizzo. 102p. 1980. pap. 4.95 (*0-939126-14-1*) Back Bay.

Doc Poe Reader. W. S. Furie. LC 90-55243. 80p. (Orig.). 1990. pap. 7.00 (*1-56002-052-0*) Aegina Pr.

***Doc Sidhe.** Aaron Allston. 352p. 1995. mass mkt. 5.99 (*0-671-87662-7*) Baen Bks.

Doc Source International. James Lowry. 1991. 95.00 (*0-316-53404-8*) Little.

Doc Susie. Virginia Cornell. 1992. reprint ed. mass mkt. 5.99 (*0-8041-0956-7*) Ivy Books.

Doc Susie: The True Story of a Country Physician in the Colorado Rockies. Virginia Cornell. (Illus.). 240p. 1991. 23.95 (*0-9627896-4-X*); pap. 14.95 (*0-9627896-5-8*) Manifest Pubns.

Doc Wyoming: Women Who Dare. Sharon Brondos. (Superromance Ser.). 1993. mass mkt. 3.50 (*0-373-70574-3*, 1-70574-8) Harlequin Bks.

***Doc Yak.** John Thomas. 131p. 1995. pap. 7.95 (*1-56901-545-7*) NW Pub.

Doce Historias de la Artamila de Ana Maria Matute. Gloria Duran. Ed. by Manuel Duran. 172p. (SPA.). (C). 1965. pap. text ed. 20.00 (*0-15-517949-7*) HB Coll Pubs.

Doce Mil Minibiografias. 2nd ed. Ed. by Maria E. Alvarez del Real. LC 81-72104. (Illus.). 800p. (SPA.). pap. 6.00 (*0-944499-12-0*) Editorial Amer.

Doce Mil Minibiografias. 3rd ed. Editorial America, S. A. Staff. Ed. by Maria E. Del Real. (Illus.). 800p. (SPA.). 1990. pap. write for info. (*0-944499-76-7*) Editorial Amer.

Doce Pasos y Las Doce Tradiciones. Alcoholics Anonymous World Services, Inc. Staff. 196p. (Orig.). (ENG & SPA.). 1985. pap. 2.50 (*0-916856-16-X*) AAWS.

Doce Poderes del Hombre. Charles Fillmore. 1930. 6.95 (*0-87159-080-8*) Unity Bks.

Doce Sermones Sobre la Oracion. Charles Spurgeon. 198p. 1992. 5.50 (*0-939125-65-X*) Evangelical Lit.

***Docia's Stories: A Collection for Parents & Teachers.** Docia Zavitkovsky. (Illus.). 26p. (Orig.). (C). 1994. pap. 5.00 (*0-942702-15-8*) Child Care.

Dock Leaves. Hugo Williams. 64p. (Orig.). 1994. pap. 9.95 (*0-571-17175-3*) Faber & Faber.

Dock Strike: Conflict & Restructuring in Britains Ports. Peter Turnbull et al. (Business School Library). 280p. 1992. 68.95 (*1-85628-176-0*, Pub. by Avebury Pub UK) Ashgate Pub Co.

Dockbuilder. Jack Rudman. (Career Examination Ser.: C-1696). 1994. pap. 27.95 (*0-8373-1696-0*) Nat Learn.

Docker Noir. 2nd ed. Ousmane Sembene. (FRE.). 1981. pap. 12.95 (*0-7859-3457-X*) Fr & Eur.

Dockers' Union: A Study of the National Union of Dock Labourers, 1889-1922. Eric Taplin. LC 85-26078. 216p. 1986. text ed. 29.95 (*0-312-21475-8*) St Martin.

Dockland Life: A Pictorial History of London's Docks 1860-1970. Chris Ellmers & Alex Werner. (Illus.). 208p. 1992. 39.95 (*1-85158-364-5*, Pub. by Mnstream UK) Trafalgar.

Docklands. Stephanie Williams. (Modern Architecture Guide Ser.). (Illus.). 192p. 1991. pap. 27.95 (*0-442-30814-0*) Van Nos Reinhold.

Dockmanship. David O. Bell. LC 91-55483. (Illus.). 104p. 1992. pap. 6.95 (*0-87033-425-5*) Cornell Maritime.

Dockominium: Opportunities & Problems Proceedings of the National Dockominium Conference, 1987. Ed. by Neil W. Ross & Paul E. Dodson. 180p. (Orig.). 1988. pap. 25.00 (*0-929803-02-7*) Intl Marina Inst.

Docks Regulations Nineteen Thirty-Four Explained. rev. ed. Rev. by C. H. Cotter. (C). 1987. 30.00 (*0-85174-122-3*, Pub. by Brwn Son Ferg) St Mut.

Docteur Jivago. Boris Pasternak. (FRE.). 1972. pap. 17.95 (*0-7859-3984-9*) Fr & Eur.

Docteur Mysterieux. Jean Goguel. (Methodique Ser.). 2456p. (FRE.). 1973. 95.00 (*0-7859-1211-8*, 2070107647; 2070107809) Fr & Eur.

Docteur Pascal. Emile Zola. pap. 7.50 (*0-685-23959-4*) Fr & Eur.

Docteur Pascal. Emile Zola. 440p. (FRE.). 1990. pap. 11.95 (*0-7859-1431-5*, 2080702807) Fr & Eur.

Doctor. Edward E. Rosenbaum. 1991. mass mkt. 4.99 (*0-8041-0873-0*) Ivy Books.

Doctor. Helen Slater. (What Happens When Ser.). (Illus.). 24p. (J). 1992. 2.98 (*0-8317-9508-5*) Smithmark.

Doctor: A Tale of the Rockies. Ralph Connor. 1976. lib. bdg. 17.25 (*0-89968-015-1*, Lghtyr Pr) Buccaneer Bks.

Doctor: Why Am I So Tired? Richard N. Podell. 1989. mass mkt. 4.99 (*0-449-45320-0*) Fawcett.

Doctor: Why Am I So Tired? Richard N. Podell. 1989. mass mkt. 4.99 (*0-449-14578-6*) Fawcett.

Dr. Abravanel's Diet. Elliot D. Abravanel. 1984. mass mkt. 5.99 (*0-553-27575-5*) Bantam.

Dr. Adder. K. W. Jeter. 1989. pap. 2.95 (*0-451-15197-6*) NAL-Dutton.

Doctor Agustin Stahl, Hombre de Ciencia: Perspectiva humanistica. Isabel Gutierrez del Arroyo. (Publicaciones de la Facultad de Humanidades). 56p. (SPA.). 1978. pap. 1.50 (*0-8477-3400-5*) U of PR Pr.

Dr. Ambedkar & Punjab. D. C. Ahir. (C). 1992. 14.00 (*81-7018-736-2*, Pub. by BR Pub II) S Asia.

Dr. Ambedkar & the Dalit Future. V. R. Iyer. 1990. 21.00 (*81-7018-574-2*, Pub. by BR Pub II) S Asia.

Dr. Ambedkar Life & Mission. Dhananjay Keer. 1990. reprint ed. 21.50 (*0-86132-145-6*, Pub. by Popular Prakashan II) S Asia.

Dr. Ambedkar's Economic Thought & Philosophy. Narendra Jadhav. 1993. 12.00 (*81-7154-731-1*, Pub. by Popular Prakashan II) S Asia.

Dr. An Wang: Computer Pioneer. Jim Hargrove. LC 92-35061. (People of Distinction Ser.). (Illus.). 152p. (J). (gr. 4 up). 1993. lib. bdg. 14.40 (*0-516-03290-9*); pap. 5.95 (*0-516-43290-7*) Childrens.

Doctor & Christian Marriage. H. P. Dunn. LC 92-15244. 1992. pap. 9.95 (*0-8189-0642-1*) Alba.

Doctor & Medicine. Daumier. 1989. 14.98 (*0-914427-23-7*) W S Konecky Assocs.

Doctor & Patient. Silas W. Mitchell. LC 71-180584. (Medicine & Society in America Ser.). 182p. 1972. reprint ed. 18.95 (*0-405-03961-1*) Ayer.

Doctor & the Devils & Other Scripts. Dylan Thomas. LC 65-15668. 1970. pap. 12.95 (*0-8112-0206-2*, NDP297) New Directions.

Doctor & the Enterprise. Jean Airey. 1989. pap. 9.95 (*1-55698-218-6*, Pioneer Bks) Movie Pubs Servs.

Doctor & the Law: A Practical Guide for the Canadian Physician. 2nd ed. Emson. 256p. 1989. 66.00 (*0-409-88875-3*) Butterworth Legal Pubs.

Doctor & the Soul: From Psychotherapy to Logotherapy. Viktor E. Frankl. LC 85-40681. 336p. 1986. pap. 12.00 (*0-394-74317-2*, Vin) Random.

Dr. Anderson's High-Fiber Fitness Plan. James W. Anderson & Nancy J. Gustafson. LC 93-45451. 264p. 1994. 19.95 (*0-8131-1867-0*) U Pr of Ky.

***Dr. Andrew Turnbull & the New Smyrna Colony.** Carita Doggett. 219p. 1994. write for info. (*1-886953-01-5*); lib. bdg. write for info. (*1-886953-02-3*) Fnders Pub.

***Dr. Anne's Cancer Journal.** Robert L. Owen. LC 90-81824. 414p. 1990. pap. 14.00 (*1-882657-06-3*) Health Hope.

Doctor Antonio: A Tale. John Ruffini. LC 79-8193. reprint ed. 44.50 (*0-404-62109-0*) AMS Pr.

Doctor Arnold's Ambition. large type ed. Pauline Ash. 1990. 21.95 (*0-7089-2196-5*) Ulverscroft.

Doctor Assisted Suicide: And the Euthanasia Movement. Ed. by Gary E. McCuen. (Ideas in Conflict Ser.). (Illus.). 172p. 1994. lib. bdg. 12.95 (*0-86596-093-3*) G E M.

Doctor at Calvary: The Passion of Our Lord Jesus Christ As Described by a Surgeon. Pierre Barbet. Tr. by Earl of Wicklow. (Illus.). 192p. 1993. reprint ed. text ed. 15.75 (*0-912141-04-2*) Roman Cath Bks.

Doctor at Large. Morris Gibson. 240p. 1987. pap. 3.95 (*0-449-21516-4*, Crest) Fawcett.

Doctor at Nagasaki: My First Assignment Was Mercy Killing. Masao Shiotsuki. Tr. by Simul International Inc. Staff. 191p. 1987. pap. 5.95 (*4-333-01250-3*, Pub. by Kosei Pub Co JA) C E Tuttle.

Doctor at the Crossroads. Elizabeth Seifert. 1974. reprint ed. lib. bdg. 21.95 (*0-88411-030-3*, Aeonian Pr) Amereon Ltd.

Dr. Atkin's Diet Revolution. Robert C. Atkins. 336p. 1981. 6.50 (*0-553-27157-1*) Bantam.

Dr. Atkin's Health Revolution: How Complementary Medicine Can Extend Your Life. Robert C. Atkins. 1990. mass mkt. 6.50 (*0-553-28360-X*) Bantam.

Doctor Atkins' New Diet Cookbook. Robert C. Atkins. 1994. 21.95 (*0-87131-755-9*) M Evans.

D

An Asterisk (*) at the beginning of an entry indicates that the title is appearing in BIP for the first time.

D

Dr. Ed: The Story of General Edward Hand. Mary V. Shelley. LC 78-10331. (Illus.). 36p. (J). (gr. 4-7). 1978. 5.75 (*0-915010-24-0*) Sutter House.

Dr. Eden's Healthy Kids: The Essential Diet, Exercise & Nutrition Program. Alvin N. Eden & Andrea P. Boyar. 304p. 1989. pap. 4.99 (*0-451-16065-7*, Sig) NAL-Dutton.

Dr. Edith Irby Jones: A Story of Triumph. Lydia E. Brew & Annie S. Brew. (Our Learn Together Book Ser.). 58p. (J). (gr. k-2). 1992. pap. text ed. 3.50 (*0-9635351-0-2*) Lydias Educ.

Dr. Edward McGlynn. Sylvester L. Malone. 1978. 19.95 (*0-405-10841-9*, 11847) Ayer.

Doctor Ellison's Decision. Elizabeth Seifert. 1973. reprint ed. lib. bdg. 19.95 (*0-88411-011-7*, Aeonian Pr) Amereon Ltd.

Dr. Evelyn's York: Illustrations of Bygone York 1891-1935. Hugh Murray. (Illus.). (C). 1988. 110.00 (*0-900657-85-5*, Pub. by W Sessions UK) St Mut.

Dr. Excitement's Elixir of Longevity. William Ryan. LC 86-81475. 1986. 17.95 (*0-917657-99-3*) D I Fine.

Dr. F. J. Furnivall: A Victorian Scholar Adventurer. William Benzie. LC 83-12095. 320p. 1983. 29.95 (*0-937664-57-X*) Pilgrim Bks OK.

Doctor Faustus. Thomas Mann. 1992. 20.00 (*0-679-41328-6*, Everymans Lib) Knopf.

Doctor Faustus. Thomas Mann. 1992. 20.00 (*0-679-40996-3*, Everymans Lib) Knopf.

Dr. Faustus. Thomas Mann. 1992. pap. 14.00 (*0-679-73905-X*, Vin) Random.

Doctor Faustus. Christopher Marlowe. 1976. 3.00 (*0-8488-0765-0*) Amereon Ltd.

Doctor Faustus. Christopher Marlowe. Ed. by John D. Jump. LC 62-51712. 144p. 1982. pap. 9.50 (*0-8419-0826-5*) Holmes & Meier.

Doctor Faustus. Christopher Marlowe. Ed. by Nicholas Rudall. (Plays for Performance Ser.). 69p. 1991. text ed. 15.95 (*0-929587-60-X*); pap. 7.95 (*0-929587-56-1*) I R Dee.

Doctor Faustus. Christopher Marlowe. (Study Texts Ser.). 1984. pap. text ed. 4.29 (*0-582-35390-4*, 72213) Longman.

Doctor Faustus. Christopher Marlowe. Ed. by Sylvan Barnet. 1969. pap. 3.95 (*0-451-52378-4*, Sig Classics) NAL-Dutton.

Doctor Faustus. Christopher Marlowe. 1989. pap. 3.50 (*0-451-52228-1*) NAL-Dutton.

Doctor Faustus. Christopher Marlowe. Ed. by John D. Jump. (Methuen English Classics Ser.). 1965. pap. 8.95 (*0-415-03960-6*, NO.2311) Routledge.

Doctor Faustus. Guy Williams. LC 91-51101. 1992. pap. 6.00 (*0-88734-419-4*) Players Pr.

Dr. Faustus. unabridged ed. Christopher Marlowe. LC 94-7856. (Thrift Editions Ser.). 64p. 1994. pap. text ed. 1.00 (*0-486-28208-2*) Dover.

Doctor Faustus. 2nd ed. Christopher Marlowe. Ed. by Roma Gill. (New Mermaid Ser.). (C). 1990. pap. text ed. 6.95 (*0-393-90059-2*) Norton.

Doctor Faustus. Christopher Marlowe. LC 73-133704. (Tudor Facsimile Texts. Old English Plays Ser.: No. 102). reprint ed. 49.50 (*0-404-53402-3*) AMS Pr.

Doctor Faustus: A 1604-Version Edition. Christopher Marlowe. Ed. by Michael Keefer. 250p. 1991. 29.95 (*0-921149-56-5*); pap. 11.95 (*0-921149-59-X*) Broadview Pr.

Doctor Faustus: Divine in Show. Thomas McAlindon. (Twayne's Masterwork Studies Ser.: No. 134). 125p. 1994. text ed. 22.95x (*0-8057-4453-3*, Twayne); pap. 12.95 (*0-8057-8388-1*, Twayne) Macmillan.

Dr. Faustus: The A-Text. D. A. Ormerod & C. J. Wortham. 159p. (C). 1985. pap. 14.95 (*0-85564-232-7*, Pub. by Univ of West Aust Pr AT) Intl Spec Bk.

Doctor Faustus: The Historie of the Damnable Life, & Deserued Death of Doctor John Faustus. Tr. by P. F. Gent. (Deutsche Volksbucher in Faksimiledrucken, Reihe A Ser.: Vol. 20). 85p. 1985. reprint ed. 37.70 (*3-487-07558-X*, Pub. by Georg Olms GW) Lubrecht & Cramer.

Doctor Faustus: The Life of the German Composer Adrian Leverk Uhn As Told by a Friend. Thomas Mann. Tr. by Helen T. Lowe-Porter. LC 92-24703. 1992. 18.50 (*0-679-60042-6*, Modern Lib) Random.

Doctor Faustus: The Life of the German Composer, Adrian Leverkuhn As Told by a Friend. Thomas Mann. LC 48-8940. 1971. pap. 11.00 (*0-394-71297-8*, Vin) Random.

***Doctor Faustus & Other Plays.** Christopher Marlowe. Ed. by David Bevington & Eric Rasmussen. (World's Classics Ser.). 528p. 1995. 55.00 (*0-19-812159-8*); pap. 9.95 (*0-19-282737-5*) OUP.

Doctor Faustus Notes. Eva Fitzwater. 1967. pap. 3.75 (*0-8220-0406-2*) Cliffs.

Dr. File Finder's Guide to Shareware with Disk. Mike Callahan. 1990. pap. text ed. 39.95 (*0-07-881646-7*) Osborne-McGraw.

Doctor for Blue Jay Cove. Elizabeth Seifert. 1973. reprint ed. lib. bdg. 23.95 (*0-88411-016-8*, Aeonian Pr) Amereon Ltd.

Doctor for the People: Two Thousand Years of General Practice in Britain. John Cule. (Illus.). 1980. lib. bdg. 48.00 (*0-906141-29-X*) Kluwer Ac.

***Doctor from Bugtussle.** Wendell W. Wilson. (Orig.). 1995. pap. 14.95 (*0-9647202-1-3*) Hillbilly Bks.

***Doctor from Bugtussle, Vol. 1.** Wendell W. Wilson. 329p. (Orig.). 1995. 19.95 (*0-9647202-2-1*) Hillbilly Bks.

Doctor from Lhasa. T. Lobsang Rampa. 1991. 10.95 (*0-938294-95-4*) Glob Comm-Inner Lght.

Doctor from Wales. large type ed. Sarah Franklin. 253p. 1992. 21.95 (*0-7505-0445-5*) Ulverscroft.

Dr. Gabler's die Sprache der Chefs. 227p. (GER.). 1977. 35.00 (*0-8288-5401-7*, M7352) Fr & Eur.

Doctor George Sheehan's Medical Advice for Runners. George Sheehan. LC 78-55788. (Illus.). 303p. 1978. 11.95 (*0-89037-134-2*) Anderson World.

Doctor George William Bagby. Joseph L. King. LC 27-23953. reprint ed. 20.00 (*0-404-03693-7*) AMS Pr.

Doctor Golf. William P. Fox. LC 94-20452. (Illus.). 1994. pap. write for info. (*1-57003-029-4*) U of SC Pr.

***Dr. Gollup's Survival Guide for New Parents.** 3rd ed. Howard J. Gollup. LC 94-72909. (Illus.). 154p. (Orig.). 1995. pap. 9.95 (*0-9643482-0-9*) Iguana Med Bks.

***Doctor Goodmom: Helpful Hints for Healthy Living. John J. Connolly & Christine Williams. Ed. by Christine Williams. LC 95-701701. (Orig.). 1995. pap. 5.95 (*1-883769-73-6*) Castle Connolly Med.**
With quotations & adages from "every mother", your family doctor & celebrities from all walks, passed down from generation to generation, DOCTOR GOODMOM outlines advice on how to care for oneself, physically & emotionally. From folk cures to prevention, this collection gives the reader, with some humor & nostalgia, advice to follow for a healthier lifestyle. *Publisher Provided Annotation.*

Dr. Graesler. Arthur Schnitzler. Tr. by E. C. Slade. LC 70-175575. reprint ed. 37.50 (*0-404-05618-0*) AMS Pr.

Doctor Gravity. Dennis Haseley. LC 92-4689. 1992. 17.00 (*0-374-31842-5*) FS&G.

Doctor Heidenhoff's Process. Edward Bellamy. LC 72-84878. (BCL Ser. I). 1969. reprint ed. 29.50 (*0-404-00734-1*) AMS Pr.

Doctor Herriott's Daughter. large type ed. Louise Ellis. (Linford Romance Library). 288p. 1989. pap. 11.95 (*0-7089-6663-2*, Linford) Ulverscroft.

Doctor, His Patient & the Illness. 2nd ed. Michael Balint. 395p. (Orig.). 1963. text ed. 55.00x (*0-8236-1380-1*) Intl Univs Pr.

Doctor Hoo. Betty Marrapodi. (Illus.). 22p. (J). (gr. 1-6). 1973. pap. 7.50 (*0-88680-039-0*); pap. 2.00 (*0-88680-038-2*) I E Clark.

Doctor Hudson's Secret Journal. large type ed. Lloyd C. Douglas. LC 93-13716. 1993. Alk. paper. 19.95 (*1-56054-776-6*) Thorndike Pr.

Doctor Hudson's Secret Journal. Lloyd C. Douglas. 240p. 1992. reprint ed. lib. bdg. 21.95 (*0-89966-944-1*) Buccaneer Bks.

Doctor Huguet. Ignatius Donnelly. LC 75-92230. (American Negro: His History & Literature, Ser. No 3). 1970. reprint ed. 18.95 (*0-405-01920-3*) Ayer.

Doctor Huguet. Ignatius Donnelly. 309p. 1993. reprint ed. lib. bdg. 35.00 (*0-8328-3173-5*) Higginson Bk Co.

Doctor Illuminatus: A Ramon Llull Reader. Ed. & Tr. by Anthony Bonner. Tr. by Eve Bonner. LC 93-13696. (Mythos: The Princeton - Bollingen Series in World Mythology). (Illus.). 512p. 1993. text ed. 65.00 (*0-691-03406-0*); pap. text ed. 17.95 (*0-691-00091-3*) Princeton U Pr.

Doctor in Bataan, 1941-42. Manuel E. De Veyra. (Illus.). 102p. (Orig.). (C). 1992. pap. 8.25 (*971-10-0460-7*, Pub. by New Day Pub PH) Cellar.

Doctor in Belle Starr Country. Charles W. Mooney. LC 74-30947. (Illus.). 291p. 1975. write for info. (*0-685-53674-2*) Century Pr.

Doctor in Demand. large type ed. Frances Crowne. 295p. 1993. 21.95 (*0-7505-0556-7*) Ulverscroft.

Doctor in French Drama: 1700-1775. Christine E. Petersen. LC 39-2239. reprint ed. 20.00 (*0-404-04996-6*) AMS Pr.

Doctor in Gray - Hunter Holmes McGuire. John W. Schildt. (Illus.). 137p. 1987. text ed. 13.50 (*0-936772-05-0*) Antietam.

Doctor in History. Howard W. Haggard. LC 79-99342. (Essay Index Reprint Ser.). 1977. 30.95 (*0-8369-1654-9*) Ayer.

Doctor in History. Howard W. Haggard. (Illus.). 406p. 1990. 24.95 (*0-88029-440-X*) Dorset Pr.

Doctor in History, Literature, Folklore. William Andrews. 1972. 59.95 (*0-8490-0052-1*) Gordon Pr.

Doctor in Judgment. large type ed. Elizabeth Seifert. LC 90-10729. 264p. 1990. lib. bdg. 18.95 (*0-89621-973-9*) Thorndike Pr.

Doctor in Medicine & Other Papers on Professional Subjects. Stephen Smith. LC 74-180590. (Medicine & Society in America Ser.). 318p. 1972. reprint ed. 25.95 (*0-405-03972-7*) Ayer.

***Doctor-in-My-Pocket.** Russell Dollinger. 264p. (SPA.). 1995. spiral bd. 9.95 (*0-945585-05-5*) JDV Pub.

Doctor in Saudi Arabia. G. E. Moloney. (Arabia Past & Present Ser.: Vol. 23). (Illus.). 356p. 1985. 32.50 (*0-906672-81-3*) Oleander Pr.

Doctor in Spite of Himself. Aurand Harris. (J). 1968. 5.00 (*0-87602-120-8*) Anchorage.

Doctor in Spite of Himself: One-Act Translation. (Illus.). 41p. 1969. pap. 10.00 (*0-88680-041-2*); pap. 2.00 (*0-88680-040-4*) I E Clark.

Doctor in Spite of Himself & the Bourgeois Gentleman. Moliere. Tr. by Albert Bermel. (Actor's Moliere Ser.: Vol. 2). 128p. (Orig.). 1987. pap. 6.95 (*0-936839-77-5*) Applause Theatre Bk Pubs.

Doctor in the Family. Elizabeth Seifert. 1974. reprint ed. lib. bdg. 20.95 (*0-88411-032-X*, Aeonian Pr) Amereon Ltd.

Doctor in the House: Your Guide to the Best Medical Care. John C. Harbert. LC 93-33242. (Illus.). 528p. 1993. 24.50 (*0-89603-219-1*) Humana.

Doctor in Your House: Dr. Lieberman's Unique Guide to Preventive Medicine & Sensible Money Saving Self Care. Donald Lieberman. 80p. (Orig.). 1989. pap. 6.95 (*0-317-93298-5*) Jadon Pubns.

Doctor Is In. Charlotte Rose. (Orig.). 1994. pap. 4.95 (*1-56333-195-0*) Masquerade.

Doctor Is Sick. Anthony Burgess. 272p. 1979. reprint ed. pap. 8.95 (*0-393-00959-9*) Norton.

Doctor James Africanus Beale Horton: West African Medical Scientist of the Nineteenth Century. Adelola Adeloye. (Illus.). 64p. 1992. pap. 8.95 (*0-8059-3233-X*) Dorrance.

Dr. Jekyll & Mr. Hyde. Amarantha Knight. (Darker Passions Ser.). (Orig.). 1995. pap. text ed. 4.95 (*1-56333-227-2*) Masquerade.

***Doctor Jekyll & Mister Hyde.** Stevenson. 1995. mass mkt. (*0-671-53210-3*, WSP) PB.

Dr. Jekyll & Mr. Hyde. Robert Louis Stevenson. (Airmont Classics Ser.). (YA). (gr. 8 up). 1964. pap. 2.25 (*0-8049-0042-6*, CL-42) Airmont.

Dr. Jekyll & Mr. Hyde. Robert Louis Stevenson. (Illus.). 1976. lib. bdg. 18.95 (*0-88411-994-7*, Aeonian Pr) Amereon Ltd.

Dr. Jekyll & Mr. Hyde. Robert Louis Stevenson. 128p. 1982. pap. 2.95 (*0-553-21277-X*, Bantam Classics) Bantam.

Dr. Jekyll & Mr. Hyde. Robert Louis Stevenson. Ed. by Bernd Metz. Tr. by Stefano Gaudiano. (Illus.). 88p. 1990. pap. 11.95 (*0-87416-079-0*) Catalan Communs.

Dr. Jekyll & Mr. Hyde. Robert Louis Stevenson & John K. Snyder, III. (Classics Illustrated Ser.). (Illus.). 52p. (YA). Date not set. pap. 4.95 (*1-57209-008-1*) Classics Int Ent.

Dr. Jekyll & Mr. Hyde. Robert Louis Stevenson. (Illustrated Classics Collection 1). 64p. 1994. pap. 3.60 (*1-56103-420-7*) Lake Pub Co.

Dr. Jekyll & Mr. Hyde. Robert Louis Stevenson. 128p. 1987. pap. 3.95 (*0-451-52393-8*, Sig Classics) NAL-Dutton.

Dr. Jekyll & Mr. Hyde. Robert Louis Stevenson. Ed. by Kin Platt. LC 73-75457. (Now Age Illustrated Ser.). (Illus.). 64p. (J). (gr. 5-10). 1973. student ed 1.25 (*0-88301-176-X*); pap. 2.95 (*0-88301-096-8*) Pendulum Pr.

Dr. Jekyll & Mr. Hyde. Robert Louis Stevenson. (Regents Illustrated Classics Ser.). (Illus.). (YA). (gr. 7-12). 1987. pap. text ed. 4.00 (*0-13-216680-1*, 20432) Prentice ESL.

Dr. Jekyll & Mr. Hyde. Robert Louis Stevenson. LC 90-50600. 112p. 1991. pap. 7.00 (*0-679-73476-7*, Vin) Random.

Dr. Jekyll & Mr. Hyde. Robert Louis Stevenson. (J). 1990. pap. 2.50 (*0-8125-0448-8*) Tor Bks.

Dr. Jekyll & Mr. Hyde. Robert Louis Stevenson. 1990. reprint ed. lib. bdg. 16.95 (*0-89968-552-8*) Buccaneer Bks.

Dr. Jekyll & Mr. Hyde. Robert Louis Stevenson. LC 83-15972. (Step-up Adventures Ser.: No. 9). (Illus.). 96p. (J). (gr. 2-6). 1994. reprint ed. pap. 3.50 (*0-394-86365-8*) Random Bks Yng Read.

Dr. Jekyll & Mr. Hyde & Other Stories. Robert Louis Stevenson. (Courage Literary Classics Ser.). 176p. (YA). 1994. 5.98 (*1-56138-474-7*) Running Pr.

Doctor Jessie, the Odyssey of a Woman Physician. Jessie L. Brodie. (Illus.). 395p. (Orig.). (C). 1991. 22.50 (*0-945490-03-8*); pap. 12.50 (*0-945490-04-6*) Carolina Pacific.

Dr. Jim's Animal Clinic for Cats. Jim Humphries. 1994. pap. 15.00 (*0-87605-790-3*) P-H.

Dr. Jim's Animal Clinic for Dogs: What People Want to Know. Jim Humphries. LC 94-12281. 1994. 15.00 (*0-87605-756-3*) Howell Bk.

Doctor Jim's Odyssey. James W. Pleasant. LC 94-60592. 138p. 1994. pap. 8.00 (*0-912400-14-5*) Western Res Pr.
Ohio Veterinarian Jim Pleasant's Multiple Myeloma bone marrow transplant treatment required quiet time. Encouraged by friends to put his journal, of reactions, stories of family & hospitals, animal care at his office, sailing & model train hobbies, into book form, Jim has done so & gone on to becoming active in the Gilda's Club startups. Clinical concerns, his wry grin at life, the sidestepping of internal spins of despair are shared here. Winding through these narratives is his grip on the Myeloma experience as another of life's adventures. He uses Bilbo Baggins of Tolkien's book The Hobbit to gear into survivorship, calls on early interest in a rock band, talks of his wife & sons & their own journeys with his illness. He is a winning skipper on the Great Lakes today, rich in his family, & busy in practice. He sees his book as helping him to talk to others about similar cancer challenges & to using his medical training to track current research. To order contact - Western Reserve Press, Inc., 1046 Locust Drive, P.O. Box 2245, Ashtabula, OH 44005. 216-964-2728. *Publisher Provided Annotation.*

Doctor Johann Weyer: Ein Rheinischer Arzt der Erste Bekampfer Des Hexenwahns Beitrag Zur Geschicte der Aufklarung und der Heilkunde. 2nd rev. ed. Carl Binz. LC 75-16683. (Classics in Psychiatry Ser.). (GER.). 1976. reprint ed. 18.95 (*0-405-07415-8*) Ayer.

Doctor Johannes Fausy's Miracle & Magic Book: The Black Ravenor the Threefold Coercion of Hell. rev. ed. Robert Blanchard. Ed. by I. G. O. S. Staff. LC 93-79454. (Illus.). 120p. (Orig.). (C). 1993. text ed. 25.00 (*1-883147-21-2*) Intern Guild ASRS.

Doctor John: Crusading Doctor & Politician. John O'Connell. (Illus.). 175p. 1989. pap. 9.95 (*1-85371-025-3*, Pub. by Poolbeg Pr IE) Dufour.

Doctor John Bull 1562-1628. Leigh Henry. LC 68-15589. (Music Ser.). (Illus.). 1968. reprint ed. lib. bdg. 39.50 (*0-306-70982-1*) Da Capo.

Dr. John Raymond Christopher: An Herbal Legacy of Courage. David Christopher. 90p. 1994. pap. 5.00 (*0-685-72139-6*, 99112) Dr Chris Pubns.

Dr. Johnson & Mr. Savage. Richard Holmes. LC 94-6219. 1994. 23.00 (*0-679-43585-9*) Pantheon.

Doctor Johnson & the Fair Sex: A Study of Contrasts. W. Craig. 1972. 59.95 (*0-8490-0053-X*) Gordon Pr.

Doctor Judas: A Portrayal of the Opium Habit. William R. Cobbe. Ed. by Gerald N. Grob. LC 80-1218. (Addiction in America Ser.). 1981. reprint ed. lib. bdg. 31.95 (*0-405-13574-2*) Ayer.

Doctor Kadans' Herbal Weight Loss Diet. Joseph M. Kadans. LC 82-7944. 1982. 18.95 (*0-13-216523-6*, Parker Publishing Co) P-H.

Dr. Kaplan's Lifestyle of the Fit & Famous: A Wellness Approach to "Thinning & Winning" Eric Kaplan. 352p. 1995. 21.95 (*0-914984-56-X*) Starburst.

Doctor Kerkhoven. Jacob Wassermann. 1960. 6.95 (*0-87140-817-1*) Liveright.

Doctor Kirwan's Irish Catechism. Augustine Kirwan & Thomas Hughes. Tr. & Intro. by William J. Mahon. (Illus.). xxxvii, 227p. (C). 1991. 30.00 (*1-879095-06-8*); pap. 15.00 (*1-879095-05-X*) Pangur Pubns.

Doctor Knickerbocker & Other Rhymes. Illus. by Maryann Kovalski. LC 92-46266. 80p. (J). (gr. 3 up). 1993. 16.95 (*0-395-67168-X*) Ticknor & Flds Bks Yng Read.

Doctor Knock-Knock's Official Knock-Knock Dictionary. Joseph Rosenbloom. LC 76-19796. (Illus.). 128p. (J). (gr. 3 up). 1980. pap. 3.95 (*0-8069-8936-X*) Sterling.

***Doctor Knows Best.** large type ed. Ann Jennings. (Romance Ser.). 1994. pap. 14.95 (*0-7089-7607-7*, Linford) Ulverscroft.

Doctor Lavendar's People. Margaret W. Deland. LC 75-113656. (Short Story Index Reprint Ser.). 1977. 21.95 (*0-8369-3385-0*) Ayer.

Doctor Lavendar's People. Margaret W. Deland. LC 70-90102. (BCL Ser. II). (Illus.). 1969. reprint ed. 14.00 (*0-404-02074-7*) AMS Pr.

Doctor Lavendar's People. Margaret W. Deland. (Illus.). 1972. reprint ed. 11.00 (*0-8422-8036-7*) Irvington.

Doctor Lavendar's People. Margaret W. Deland. 1988. reprint ed. lib. bdg. 65.00 (*0-7812-0140-3*) Rprt Serv.

Doctor Lavendar's People. Margaret W. Deland. LC 77-129345. (Illus.). 1971. reprint ed. 69.00 (*0-403-00478-0*) Scholarly.

Doctor, Lawyer, Indian Chief: The Story of Fifteen Major Professions & Careers - From the Ancient Past to the Turbulent Present. Richard X. Donovan. 200p. (Orig.). 1989. pap. 14.95 (*0-89420-256-1*, 341220) Natl Book.

Doctor Lindner's Special Weight Control Method. Peter G. Lindner. 1979. pap. 2.00 (*0-87980-030-5*) Wilshire.

Doctor Luther. Gustav Freytag. Tr. by G. C. Reimer. LC 83-45642. reprint ed. 27.50 (*0-404-19851-1*) AMS Pr.

***Dr. Lynch's Holistic Self-Health Program: Three Months to Total Well-Being.** James P. Lynch & Anita W. Bell. 256p. 1995. pap. 11.95 (*0-452-27150-9*, Plume) NAL-Dutton.

Doctor M. W. Lewis. 4th ed. (Illus.). 94p. 1993. pap. 2.50 (*0-87612-191-1*) Self Realization.

Dr. Mac: The Man, His Land & His People. L. W. MacFarlane. LC 85-79991. (Illus.). 466p. Date not set. 29.95 (*0-935615-00-8*) S Utah St Coll.

Tooth Fairy Legend: How the Custom Came to Be. Dr. Mac. (Illus.). 40p. (J). (gr. k-5). 1994. 12.95 (*0-9638033-8-7*) Storybk Pub.

***Doctor Magdalena.** 1995. per., pap. 9.95 (*0-89229-031-5*) TQS Pubns.

Doctor Makes a Choice. Elizabeth Seifert. 1974. reprint ed. lib. bdg. 21.95 (*0-88411-044-3*, Aeonian Pr) Amereon Ltd.

***Dr. Mandell's Ultimate PC Desk Reference.** 2nd ed. Steven Mandell. 628p. 1995. 26.99 (*1-56761-533-3*) Alpha Bks IN.

Doctor Martino & Other Stories, 1934. William Faulkner. Ed. by Thomas McHaney. (William Faulkner Manuscripts). 176p. 1987. 50.00 (*0-8240-6815-7*) Garland.

Doctor Mary Courage. large type ed. Alex Stuart. 400p. 1984. 21.95 (*0-7089-1233-8*) Ulverscroft.

Doctor Mary in Arabia: Memoirs. Mary B. Allison. Ed. by Sandra Shaw. LC 93-31393. 1994. 42.50x (*0-292-70454-2*); pap. 17.95 (*0-292-70456-9*) U of Tex Pr.

Doctor, Matilda's in Labor. James A. Porter, Jr. LC 85-23875. 200p. 1986. 17.95 (*0-8138-0463-9*) Iowa St U Pr.

Doctor Medium's Sun Coast Camping Guide. Gregory E. Stearns. xx, 308p. (Orig.). 1991. pap. 11.95 (*0-9626780-0-7*) Medium Prodns.

Dr. Midnight's Blues Harp. Date not set. 9.95 (*0-7866-0025-X*, 95051) Mel Bay.

Dr. Midnight's Blues Harp. Date not set. audio 9.98 (*0-7866-0053-5*, 95051C) Mel Bay.

Doctor Minor-a Sketch of the Life of Dr. Thomas T. Minor, 1844-1889. T. M. Pelly. (Shorey Historical Ser.). 142p. reprint ed. pap. 8.95 (*0-8466-0204-0*, S204) Shorey.

An Asterisk (*) at the beginning of an entry indicates that the title is appearing in BIP for the first time.

An Asterisk (*) at the beginning of an entry indicates that the title is appearing in BIP for the first time.

D

Doctor Who: The Two Doctors. Robert Holmes. pap. 3.50 (*0-426-20201-5*) Carol Pub Group.

Doctor Who: Time & The Rani. 1992. pap. 4.95 (*0-426-20232-5*, Dr Who) Carol Pub Group.

Doctor Who: Time Lash. Glen McCoy. 12.00 (*0-491-03851-8*) Carol Pub Group.

Doctor Who: Timelord. 1993. pap. 5.95 (*0-426-20362-3*, Dr Who) Carol Pub Group.

Doctor Who: Timewyrm: Apocalypse. 1992. pap. 5.95 (*0-426-20359-3*, Dr Who) Carol Pub Group.

Doctor Who: Timewyrm: Exodus. 1992. pap. 5.95 (*0-426-20357-7*, Dr Who) Carol Pub Group.

Doctor Who: Timewyrm: Genesys. 1992. pap. 5.95 (*0-426-20355-0*, Dr Who) Carol Pub Group.

Doctor Who: Timewyrm: Revelation. 1993. pap. 5.95 (*0-426-20360-7*, Dr Who) Carol Pub Group.

Doctor Who: Twenty-Five Glorious Years. 1990. pap. 17.95 (*0-86369-324-5*) Carol Pub Group.

Doctor Who: Twenty-Five Glorious Years. Peter Haining. 1988. 24.95 (*0-318-37661-X*) Carol Pub Group.

Doctor Who: Ultimate Foe. Pip Baker & Jane Baker. 1988. pap. 3.95 (*0-426-20329-1*) Carol Pub Group.

Doctor Who: Visitation. 1992. pap. 4.95 (*0-426-20135-3*, Dr Who) Carol Pub Group.

Doctor Who: Voyager. Parkhouse & Ridgeway. (Illus.). 100p. 1989. 8.95 (*1-85400-045-4*) Marvel Entmnt.

Doctor Who: War Machine. Ian Stuart. 1989. pap. 3.95 (*0-426-20332-1*, Univ Books) Carol Pub Group.

Doctor Who: Wheel in Space. Terrance Dicks. 1988. pap. 3.95 (*0-426-20321-6*) Carol Pub Group.

Doctor Who & the Android Invasion. Terrance Dicks. 15.95 (*0-8488-0150-4*, Amereon Hse) Amereon Ltd.

Doctor Who & the Day of the Daleks. Terrance Dicks. 16.95 (*0-8488-0151-2*, Amereon Hse) Amereon Ltd.

Doctor Who & the Genesis of the Daleks. Terrance Dicks. 15.95 (*0-8488-0152-0*, Amereon Hse) Amereon Ltd.

Doctor Who & the Giant Robot. Terrance Dicks. 15.95 (*0-8488-0153-9*, Amereon Hse) Amereon Ltd.

Doctor Who & the Image of the Fendall. Terrance Dicks. 15.95 (*0-8488-0154-7*, Amereon Hse) Amereon Ltd.

Doctor Who & the Loch Ness Monster. Terrance Dicks. 15.95 (*0-8488-0155-5*, Amereon Hse) Amereon Ltd.

Doctor Who & the Revenge of the Cybermen. Terrance Dicks. 15.95 (*0-8488-0156-3*, Amereon Hse) Amereon Ltd.

Doctor Who Classics, No. 7. 1989. pap. 5.95 (*0-352-32417-1*, Univ Books) Carol Pub Group.

Doctor Who Classics: The Daemons; The Time Monster, No. 5. 1989. pap. 5.95 (*0-352-32382-5*, Univ Books) Carol Pub Group.

Doctor Who Classics: The Mind of Evil; The Claws of Axos, No. 4. 1989. pap. 5.95 (*0-352-32381-7*, Univ Books) Carol Pub Group.

Doctor Who Classics: The Seeds of Doom; The Deadly Assassin, No. 6. 1989. pap. 5.95 (*0-352-32416-3*, Univ Books) Carol Pub Group.

Doctor Who File. Peter Haining. 1989. pap. 12.95 (*0-86379-169-7*, Univ Books) Carol Pub Group.

***Dr. Who Handbook: The First Doctor.** Daniel Blythe. (Dr. Who Ser.). (Illus.). Date not set. pap. 5.95 (*0-426-20430-1*, London Bridge) Genl Dist Srvs.

Doctor Who Handbook: The Sixth Doctor. 1993. pap. 5.95 (*0-426-20400-X*, Dr Who) Carol Pub Group.

Doctor Who Technical Manual. Mark Harris. LC 83-42868. (Illus.). 64p. (J). (gr. 5 up). 1983. lib. bdg. 6.99 (*0-394-96214-1*) Random Bks Yng Read.

Doctor, Why Am I So Tired? A Guide for Overcoming Chronic Fatigue. Richard N. Podell. LC 87-60161. 256p. 1988. 17.95 (*0-88687-321-5*, Pharos) Wrld Almnc.

Doctor, Why Do I Hurt So Much? How to Combat Your Arthritis or Arthritis-Like Condition & Start Enjoying an Active Life. Mark H. Greenberg & Lucille Frank. 365p. (Orig.). 1992. pap. 14.95 (*0-937721-88-3*) Chronimed.

Doctor Will See You Now: Four One Act Plays. John Patrick. 1991. pap. 4.75 (*0-8222-0317-0*) Dramatists Play.

Doctor with a Mission. Elizabeth Seifert. reprint ed. lib. bdg. 21.95 (*0-88411-034-6*, Aeonian Pr) Amereon Ltd.

***Doctor with Big Shoes.** Henry S. Nelson. (Illus.). 288p. (Orig.). 1995. pap. 17.95 (*1-881576-45-0*) Providence Hse.

Doctor with Two Heads & Other Essays. Gerald Weissman. LC 90-50489. 256p. 1991. pap. 11.00 (*0-679-73391-4*, Vin) Random.

Dr. Wortle's School. Anthony Trollope. Ed. by John Halperin. (World's Classics Ser.). 1984. pap. 8.95 (*0-19-281673-X*) OUP.

Dr. Wortle's School. Anthony Trollope. 288p. 1994. 6.95 (*0-14-043844-0*, Penguin Classics) Viking Penguin.

Doctor Your Own Compound Bow. Emery J. Loiselle. (Illus.). 148p. 1976. pap. 9.95 (*0-9613281-0-X*) E J Loiselle.

Doctor Zay. Elizabeth S. Phelps. LC 87-48. 336p. 1987. reprint ed. pap. 8.95 (*0-935312-72-2*) Feminist Pr.

Doctor Zhivago. Boris Pasternak. 1986. mass mkt. 5.95 (*0-345-34100-7*) Ballantine.

Doctor Zhivago. Boris Pasternak. LC 90-53445. 592p. 1991. pap. 14.00 (*0-679-73123-7*) Pantheon.

Doctor Zhivago. Boris Pasternak. 550p. 1991. reprint ed. lib. bdg. 36.95 (*0-89966-839-9*) Buccaneer Bks.

Doctoral Dissertations & Masters Theses Regarding Polish Subjects, 1900-1985: An Annotated Bibliography. Bernard Wielewinski. (East European Monographs: No. 235). 256p. 1988. text ed. 42.00 (*0-88033-132-1*) East Eur Quarterly.

Doctoral Dissertations in American Music: A Classified Bibliography. Rita H. Mead. LC 74-18893. (I.S.A.M. Monographs: No. 3). 155p. (Orig.). 1974. pap. 8.00 (*0-914678-02-7*) Inst Am Music.

Doctoral Dissertations in History, Vol. 15-16: January 1990-December 1991. Ed. by Eve Weisberg. 60p. (Orig.). 1992. pap. 10.00 (*0-685-48050-X*) Am Hist Assn.

Doctoral Dissertations in Military Affairs. Allan R. Millett & B. F. Cooling. LC 72-186550. (Libraries Bibliography: No. 10). 1973. reprint ed. 7.50 (*0-686-20812-9*) KSU.

Doctoral Dissertations on Catholic Schools, K-12, 1976-1987. Mary P. Traviss. 20p. (Orig.). 1989. pap. 4.30 (*1-55833-029-1*) Natl Cath Educ.

Doctoral Dissertations on China, 1971-1975: A Bibliography of Studies in Western Languages. Comp. by Frank J. Shulman. LC 77-15188. 342p. 1978. 30.00 (*0-295-95592-9*); pap. 20.00 (*0-295-95593-7*) U of Wash Pr.

Doctoral Education in Nursing. Ed. by Sylvia E. Hart. 128p. 1989. 29.95 (*0-88737-420-4*) Natl League Nurse.

Doctoral Programs, Theses, & Graduates in Library & Information Science in the United States: An Analysis of the Published Literature, 1960-1980. Josefa B. Abrera. (Occasional Papers: No. 183). 1988. pap. 5.00 (*0-685-34546-7*) U of Ill Lib Info Sci.

Doctorate in Mental Health: An Experiment in Mental Health Professional Education. Ed. by Robert S. Wallerstein. 298p. (Orig.). (C). 1991. lib. bdg. 51.00 (*0-8191-8316-4*); pap. text ed. 30.00 (*0-8191-8317-2*) U Pr of Amer.

Doctorial Dissertations on Japan & on Korea, 1969-1979: An Annotated Bibliography of Studies in Western Languages. Comp. by Frank J. Shulman. LC 82-13563. 400p. 1982. 35.00 (*0-295-95895-2*); pap. 20.00 (*0-295-95961-4*) U of Wash Pr.

***Doctors.** Tyler Cortland. 320p. (Orig.). 1995. mass mkt. 4.99 (*0-451-18407-6*, Sig) NAL-Dutton.

Doctors. H. Kavet. 64p. 1993. 8.95 (*0-88032-363-9*) Ivory Tower Pub.

Doctors. Erich Segal. 1989. mass mkt. 6.99 (*0-553-27811-8*) Bantam.

Doctors: The Biography of Medicine. Sherwin B. Nuland. 1989. pap. 15.00 (*0-679-72215-7*, Vin) Random.

***Doctors: The Biography of Medicine.** Sherwin B. Nuland. 1995. pap. 15.00 (*0-679-76009-1*, Vin) Random.

Doctors' Affairs. Frances Rickett. 1990. mass mkt. 4.50 (*1-55817-413-3*, Pinnacle NY) Windsor NY.

Doctors & Diseases in the Roman Empire. Ralph Jackson. LC 88-40206. (Illus.). 224p. 1988. 35.00 (*0-8061-2167-X*) U of Okla Pr.

Doctors & Doctors' Wives. Francis Roe. 424p. 1991. pap. 5.99 (*0-451-16910-7*, Sig) NAL-Dutton.

Doctors & Hospitals: Legal Duties. Meagher et al. 464p. 1991. 79.00 (*0-409-89767-1*) Butterworth Legal Pubs.

Doctors & Lovers. Jane Toombs. 1989. pap. 3.95 (*1-55817-203-3*, Pinnacle NY) Windsor NY.

Doctors & Medicine in Early Renaissance Florence. Katharine Park. LC 84-42898. (Illus.). 1985. text ed. 49.50x (*0-691-08373-8*) Princeton U Pr.

Doctors & Medicine in Medieval England, 1340-1530. Robert S. Gottfried. LC 86-8135. (Illus.). 384p. reprint ed. pap. 109.50 (*0-8357-8862-8*, 2032649) Bks Demand.

Doctors & Patients: What We Feel about You. Peter H. Berczeller. LC 93-23991. 288p. 1994. text ed. 20.00 (*0-02-509265-0*, L Drew Bks) S&S Trade.

Doctors & Rules. Joseph M. Jacob. (Sociology of Professional Values Ser.). 250p. (C). 1988. lib. bdg. 65.00 (*0-415-00688-0*) Routledge.

Doctors & the Law: Defendants & Expert Witnesses. Hiller B. Zobel & Stephen N. Rous. 224p. 1993. 22.95 (*0-393-03450-X*) Norton.

Doctors & the Law: Medical Jurisprudence in Nineteenth-Century America. James C. Mohr. LC 92-12876. (Illus.). 336p. 1993. 30.00 (*0-19-505384-2*) OUP.

Doctors & the State: The British Medical Profession & Government Action in Public Health, 1870-1912. Jeanne L. Brand. LC 65-27326. 339p. reprint ed. pap. 96.70 (*0-317-19887-4*, 2023085) Bks Demand.

Doctors & the State: The Politics of Health Care in France & the United States. David Wilsford. LC 90-13995. 375p. 1991. lib. bdg. 52.95 (*0-8223-1082-1*); pap. text ed. 21.95 (*0-8223-1092-9*) Duke.

Doctors & the State in the Soviet Union. Michael Ryan. LC 89-24049. 224p. 1990. text ed. 49.95 (*0-312-04029-6*) St Martin.

Doctors & Their Feelings: A Pharmacology of Medical Caring. Benjamin Maoz et al. LC 91-29032. 168p. 1992. text ed. 55.00 (*0-275-93990-1*, C3990, Praeger Pubs) Greenwood.

Doctors & Their Patients: A Social History. Edward Shorter. 330p. (C). 1990. pap. 19.95 (*0-88738-871-X*) Transaction Pubs.

Doctors & Their Workshops: Economic Models of Physician Behavior. Mark V. Pauly. LC 80-16112. (National Bureau of Economic Research Ser.). (Illus.). 144p. 1980. lib. bdg. 17.00 (*0-226-65044-8*) U Ch Pr.

Doctors Are Gods: Corruption & Unethical Practices in the Medical Profession. David Jacobson & D. Eric. 320p. 1994. 22.95 (*1-56025-070-4*) Thunders Mouth.

Doctors As Managers of Health Teams: A Career Guide for Hospital-Based Physicians. Roman L. Yanda. LC 76-54735. 278p. reprint ed. pap. 79.30 (*0-317-19940-4*, 2023568) Bks Demand.

Doctors at War. Ed. by Morris Fishbein. LC 72-4477. (Essay Index Reprint Ser.). 1977. reprint ed. 44.95 (*0-8369-2943-8*) Ayer.

Doctor's Book of Home Remedies. Prevention Magazine Editors. 1991. pap. 6.99 (*0-553-29156-4*) Bantam.

Doctor's Book of Home Remedies. Prevention Magazine Health Books Editors. LC 89-38656. 688p. 1990. 27.95 (*0-87857-873-0*, 05-627-0) Rodale Pr Inc.

***Doctors Book of Home Remedies Vol. II.** Sid Kirchheimer. 1995. mass mkt. 6.99 (*0-553-56984-8*) Bantam.

***Doctors Book of Home Remedies for Children.** Prevention Magazine Editors. 1995. mass mkt. 6.99 (*0-553-56985-6*) Bantam.

***Doctors' Book of Home Remedies for Children.** Prevention Magazine Health Books Editors. (Illus.). 450p. (SPA.). 1995. 27.95 (*0-87596-266-1*) Rodale Pr Inc.

Doctors Book of Home Remedies for Children: From Allergies & Animal Bites to Toothache & TV Addiction: Hundreds of Doctor-Proven Techniques & Tips to Care for Your Kid. Prevention Magazine Health Books Editors et al. LC 93-5854. 1993. write for info. (*0-87596-183-5*) Rodale Pr Inc.

Doctors' Book of Home Remedies Two: Over 1,000 New Doctor-Tested Tops & Techniques Anyone Can Use to Heal Hundreds of Everyday Health Problems. Prevention Magazine Health Books Editors & Sid Kirchheimer. LC 93-7754. 640p. 1993. 27.95 (*0-87596-158-4*) Rodale Pr Inc.

Doctor's Borneo. Derwent Kell. 166p. (C). 1990. 39.00 (*0-908175-80-9*, Pub. by Boolarong Pubns AT) St Mut.

Doctor's Bride. Elizabeth Seifert. 1974. reprint ed. lib. bdg. 21.95 (*0-88411-043-5*, Aeonian Pr) Amereon Ltd.

Doctors, Bureaucrats, & Public Health in France, 1888-1902. Martha Hildreth. Ed. by William H. McNeill & David H. Pinkney. (Modern European History Ser.). 350p. 1987. lib. bdg. 15.00 (*0-8240-8037-8*) Garland.

Doctor's Cabin. large type ed. Stephen Kerry. 1975. 12.00 (*0-85456-363-6*) Ulverscroft.

Doctors' Careers: Aims & Experiences of Medical Graduates. James Parkhouse. 256p. (C). 1991. text ed. 65.00 (*0-415-04649-1*, A5069) Routledge.

Doctors, Carpenters, Builders, Chiefs: Women of Hyde Park. Nancy H. Hannan. (Illus.). 100p. (Orig.). 1987. pap. 12.00 (*0-913553-03-4*) Albert Hse Pub.

***Doctors' Case Against the Pill.** 25th anniversary ed. Barbara Seaman. 1995. 24.95 (*0-89793-182-3*); pap. 14.95 (*0-89793-181-5*) Hunter Hse.

Doctor's Cholesterol & Low Salt Diet Guide. Sylvan R. Lewis. 128p. (Orig.). 1980. pap. 2.00 (*0-936320-02-8*) Compact Books.

Doctors Christmas Eve. James L. Allen. (Principle Works of James Lane Allen). 1989. reprint ed. lib. bdg. 90.00 (*0-7812-1737-7*) Rprt Serv.

***Doctor's Communication Handbook.** Peter Tate. 1995. pap. 17.95 (*1-85775-011-X*) Scovill Paterson.

Doctor's Complete Guide to Vitamins & Minerals. Mar D. Eades. 1994. mass mkt. 5.99 (*0-440-21502-1*) Dell.

Doctor's Computer Handbook. Fell & William D. Skees. 34.95 (*0-685-19108-7*) Van Nos Reinhold.

Doctor's Confession. Elizabeth Seifert. 21.95 (*0-89190-334-8*, Am Repr) Amereon Ltd.

Doctors' Decisions & the Cost of Medical Care: The Reasons for Doctor's Practice Patterns & Ways to Change Them. John M. Eisenberg. LC 86-14312. 190p. 1986. pap. text ed. 28.00 (*0-910701-14-8*, 0814) Health Admin Pr.

Doctor's Destiny. large type ed. Elizabeth Seifert. LC 89-39527. 314p. 1990. lib. bdg. 18.95 (*0-89621-886-4*) Thorndike Pr.

Doctors, Devils & the Woman: Fort Scott, Kansas 1870-1890. James C. Malin. 122p. 1975. 8.50 (*0-87291-074-1*) Coronado Pr.

Doctor's Diagnosis. large type ed. Grace Read. 1990. 17.95 (*0-7451-9915-1*, C0631, Atlantic Lrg Print); pap. 15.95 (*0-7927-0363-4*, C0825, Atlantic Lrg Print) Chivers N Amer.

Doctor's Dilemma. George Bernard Shaw. Ed. by Margery M. Morgan. LC 79-56709. (Bernard Shaw Early Texts: Play Manuscripts in Facsimile). 1981. lib. bdg. 20.00 (*0-8240-4584-X*) Garland.

Doctor's Dilemma. George Bernard Shaw. (Plays Ser.). 1950. pap. 2.95 (*0-14-048001-3*, Penguin Bks) Viking Penguin.

Doctors' Dilemma: In Vitro Fertilization. Veritas Publications Staff. 1989. pap. 15.00x (*1-85390-051-6*, Pub. by Veritas IE) St Mut.

***Doctor's Dilemma: Stress & the Role of the Carer.** John W. Holland. 250p. 1995. 40.00 (*1-85343-313-6*); pap. 24.95 (*1-85343-306-3*) NYU Pr.

Doctor's Dilemmas. Louis S. Lasagne. LC 70-105025. (Essay Index Reprint Ser.). 1977. 23.95 (*0-8369-1669-7*) Ayer.

Doctors' Dilemmas. 1982. 14.95 (*0-02-544820-X*) Macmillan.

Doctors' Dilemmas: Medical Ethics & Contemporary Science. John Dawson & Melanie Phillips. 224p. (Orig.). 1985. pap. 12.95 (*0-416-01121-7*, 9342) Routledge Chapman & Hall.

Doctors' Dilemmas: Moral Conflict & Medical Care. Samuel Gorovitz. 240p. 1985. reprint ed. pap. 9.95 (*0-19-503695-6*) OUP.

Doctors, Dollars & Death: Bad Medicine in America. Oliver S. Owen. 115p. (Orig.). (C). 1994. pap. text ed. 17.50 (*0-87527-508-7*) Green.

Doctors Don't Lie. R. Winn Henderson. (Illus.). 85p. (Orig.). 1993. pap. 11.95 (*0-9634173-3-9*) Hugos Pr.

Doctor's Favorite Nurse. large type ed. Julia Davis. (Linford Romance Library). 256p. 1993. pap. 14.95 (*0-7089-7468-6*, Trailtree Bookshop) Ulverscroft.

Doctors from Hell. Fred Rosen. (Illus.). 320p. 1993. mass mkt. 4.99 (*1-55817-764-7*, Pinnacle NY) Windsor NY.

Doctor's Guide for Buying X-Ray Equipment & Accessories. Diana Hunt. (Illus.). 200p. 1981. text ed. 25.00 (*0-685-04734-2*) Springtime Inter.

Doctor's Guide to Chronic Fatigue Syndrome: Understanding, Treating, & Living with CFIDS. David S. Bell. (Illus.). 256p. 1993. 20.19 (*0-201-62616-0*) Addison-Wesley.

***Doctor's Guide to Chronic Fatigue Syndrome: Understanding, Treating & Living with CFIDS.** David S. Bell. 304p. 1995. pap. 11.54 (*0-201-40797-3*) Addison-Wesley.

Doctors' Guide to Feeding Your Child. Atwood. 1982. 12.95 (*0-02-504400-1*) Macmillan.

Doctor's Guide to Instant Stress Relief. Ronald G. Nathan. 288p. 1989. mass mkt. 4.95 (*0-345-35622-5*) Ballantine.

Doctor's Guide to Men's Private Parts. James H. Gilbaugh, Jr. (Illus.). 128p. 1989. pap. 9.95 (*0-517-57138-2*, Crown) Crown Pub Group.

Doctor's Guide to Partnership Accounts. E. J. Parker. 76p. 1984. 25.00 (*0-7212-0698-0*, Pub. by Regency Press) St Mut.

Doctor's Guide to the Best Medical Care: A Practical, No-Nonsense Evaluation of Your Treatment Options for over 100 Conditions & Diseases. Michael Oppenheim. LC 91-4973. 288p. 1991. 24.95 (*0-87857-982-6*, 05-995-0) Rodale Pr Inc.

Doctor's Guide to the Best Medical Care: A Practical, No-Nonsense Evaluation of Your Treatment Options for over 100 Conditions & Diseases. Michael Oppenheim. LC 91-4973. 336p. 1992. pap. 14.95 (*0-87596-108-8*, 05-995-1) Rodale Pr Inc.

Doctor's Guide to Vitamin B6 *see* **B-Six: The Natural Healer**

Doctor's Hospital. Marilyn Gilman. (Orig.). 1983. pap. 2.95 (*0-8217-1206-3*) Zebra.

Doctor's Husband. Elizabeth Seifert. 1974. reprint ed. lib. bdg. 22.95 (*0-88411-037-0*, Aeonian Pr) Amereon Ltd.

Doctors in Canada: The Changing World of Medical Practice. Bernard R. Blishen. 224p. 1991. 50.00 (*0-8020-5926-0*); pap. 19.95 (*0-8020-6866-9*) U of Toronto Pr.

Doctors in Elizabethan Drama. Percival M. Yearsley. LC 75-23772. reprint ed. 29.50 (*0-404-13398-3*) AMS Pr.

Doctors in Gray: The Confederate Medical Service. H. H. Cunningham. LC 57-11544. (Illus.). 339p. (C). 1993. pap. 14.95 (*0-8071-1856-7*) La State U Pr.

Doctors in Gray: The Confederate Medical Service. H. H. Cunningham. (Illus.). 14.75 (*0-8446-0566-2*) Peter Smith.

Doctor's Journey: The Chronos Directive. Robert Klein & Bill Bryant. 1993. pap. 14.95 (*0-533-10192-1*) Vantage.

Doctor's Letters: Interludes of War: 1944-45. Kathryn J. Plowman. 1983. pap. 8.50 (*0-9613217-0-9*) Augusta Pubs.

***Doctor's Little Book of Wisdom.** William W. Forgey. LC 95-8833. 1995. 5.95 (*1-57034-016-1*) ICS Bks.

Doctors' Marriages: A Look at the Problems & Their Solutions. Michael F. Myers. LC 87-36054. 254p. 1988. 32.50 (*0-306-42754-0*, Plenum Med Bk) Plenum.

Doctors' Marriages: A Look at the Problems & Their Solutions. 2nd ed. M. F. Meyers. (Illus.). 1994. 32.50 (*0-306-44618-9*, Plenum Med Bk) Plenum.

***Doctor's Mouse: A Read-with-Me Story for Grown-Ups & Others.** David P. Williams & Helen C. Williams. (Read-with-Me Ser.: Vol. 1). (Illus.). 27p. (J). 1991. pap. 5.00 (*1-886058-01-6*) D P Williams.

Doctors Must Invest! a Primer on Where! Herman I. Kantor. LC 72-94163. (Illus.). 144p. 1974. 8.50 (*0-87527-110-3*) Green.

***Doctors of Conscience: The Struggle to Provide Abortion Before & after Roe vs. Wade.** Carol Joffe. LC 95-11851. 288p. (C). 1995. 24.00 (*0-8070-2100-8*) Beacon Pr.

Doctors of Death. Wensley Clarkson. 1994. mass mkt. 4.99 (*0-312-95182-5*) St Martin.

Doctors of Death: Ten True Crime Stories of Doctors Who Kill. Wensley Clarkson. LC 92-18776. 1992. 18.95 (*0-942637-66-6*) Barricade Bks.

Doctors of Deceit. Gus Sermos. 123p. reprint ed. per., pap. write for info. (*0-318-70108-1*) Rockford Pr.

Doctors of Modernity: Darwin, Marx, & Freud. R. F. Baum. 200p. (Orig.). 1986. pap. 8.95 (*0-89385-215-5*) Sugden.

Doctor's Office Guide to Medicare. 59.95 (*0-685-48157-3*, OP380589) AMA.

Doctors on Eden Place. Elizabeth Sufert. 18.95 (*0-88411-058-3*, Aeonian Pr) Amereon Ltd.

Doctors on Horseback: Pioneers of American Medicine. James T. Flexner. LC 92-19615. (Illus.). xiv, 370p. (C). 1992. reprint ed. pap. 20.00 (*0-8232-1379-X*) Fordham.

Doctors Only: The Evolving Image of the American Physician. Richard Malmsheimer. LC 88-5685. (Contributions in Medical Studies: No. 25). 185p. 1988. text ed. 55.00 (*0-313-23465-5*, MAD/, Greenwood Pr) Greenwood.

Doctor's Orders. Diane Duane. (Star Trek Ser.: No. 50). 288p. (Orig.). 1990. mass mkt. 5.50 (*0-671-66189-2*, Pocket Star Bks) PB.

Doctor's Orders. Paula Hamilton. (Candlelight Ecstasy Ser.: No. 420). 1986. pap. write for info. (*0-440-12074-8*) P-H.

Doctor's Orders. Albert Kovetz. (Orig.). 1981. pap. 2.95 (*0-89083-877-1*) Zebra.

Doctor's Orders. large type ed. Ann Jennings. (Romance Ser.). 320p. 1994. pap. 14.95 (*0-7089-7554-2*, Trailtree Bookshop) Ulverscroft.

Doctors, Patients, & Health Insurance: The Organization & Financing of Medical Care. Herman Somers & Anne R. Somers. LC 61-13235. 596p. reprint ed. pap. 169.90 (*0-317-26363-3*, 2025407) Bks Demand.

Doctors, Patients, & Placebos. Howard M. Spiro. LC 86-5593. 271p. reprint ed. pap. 77.30 (*0-7837-3278-3*, 2080295) Bks Demand.

Doctors, Patients, & Society: Power & Authority in Medical Care. Ed. by M. Staum & Donald Larsen. 347p. (C). 1981. pap. 17.50 (*0-88920-111-0*, Pub. by Wilfrid Laurier CN) Humanities.

D

An Asterisk (*) at the beginning of an entry indicates that the title is appearing in BIP for the first time.

An Asterisk (*) at the beginning of an entry indicates that the title is appearing in BIP for the first time.

2063

D

***Doctrines from the Prophets.** Alma P. Burton. 240p. 1995. pap. 10.95 (*1-55517-158-3*) CFI Dist.

Doctrines of American Foreign Policy: Their Meaning, Role, & Future. Albert E. Cowdrey. LC 81-20846. xviii, 446p. (C). 1982. pap. text ed. 16.95 (*0-8071-1060-4*) La State U Pr.

***Doctrines of Development.** M. P. Cowen & R. W. Shenton. LC 95-5870. 1996. write for info. (*0-415-12515-4*); pap. write for info. (*0-415-12516-2*) Routledge.

Doctrines of God & Christ in the Early Church. Ed. by Everett Ferguson. LC 92-41865. (Studies in Early Christianity: Vol. 9). 336p. 1993. 55.00 (*0-8153-1069-2*) Garland.

Doctrines of Grace. Grover E. Gunn, III. 30p. 1987. pap. text ed. 3.00 (*1-877818-03-8*) Footstool Pubns.

Doctrines of Heathen Philosophy. Joseph Priestly. 1987. 50.00 (*0-8201-1426-X*) Schol Facsimiles.

Doctrines of Human Nature, Sin, & Salvation in the Early Church. Ed. by Everett Ferguson. LC 92-41462. (Studies in Early Christianity: Vol. 10). 360p. 1993. 58.00 (*0-8153-1070-6*) Garland.

Doctrines of Salvation, 1. Joseph F. Smith. 10.95 (*0-88494-036-5*) Bookcraft Inc.

Doctrines of Salvation, 2. Joseph F. Smith. 10.95 (*0-88494-041-1*) Bookcraft Inc.

Doctrines of Salvation, 3. Joseph F. Smith. 10.95 (*0-88494-045-4*) Bookcraft Inc.

***Doctrines of Suka Nadi.** R. Santhanam. (C). 1994. pap. 7.50 (*0-8364-2901-X*, Pub. by Ranjan Pubs II) S Asia.

Doctrines of the Bible. Ed. by J. L. Hall & David K. Bernard. LC 90-36711. 296p. (Orig.). 1993. pap. text ed. 8.99 (*0-932581-71-4*) Word Aflame.

Doctrines of the Bible: A Brief Discussion of the Teachings of God's Word. Ed. by Daniel Kauffman. LC 93-6634. 1993. pap. 15.95 (*0-8361-3645-4*) Herald Pr.

Doctrines of the Book of Mormon: The 1991 Sperry Symposium. Ed. by Bruce VanOrden. LC 92-8019. 262p. 1992. 14.95 (*0-87579-609-5*) Deseret Bk.

Doctrines of the Restoration: The Sermons & Writings of Bruce R. McConkie. Mark L. McConkie. 15.95 (*0-88494-644-4*) Bookcraft Inc.

Doctrines on Race, Economics & Sex. Vigdor Schreibman. LC 87-6206. (Essays on the Impact of the Constitution & Legal System on American Life & Government Ser.: No. 4). 79p. (Orig.). 1988. pap. 17.90 (*0-942539-03-6*); pap. 10.90 (*0-942539-09-5*) Amicas Pubns.

Doctrines Politiques et Structures Ecclesiastiques dans l'Occident Medieval. Marcel Pacaut. (Collected Studies: No. CS 223). 304p. (FRE.). (C). 1985. reprint ed. lib. bdg. 89.95 (*0-86078-171-2*, Pub. by Variorum UK) Ashgate Pub Co.

DocuMate. Dudley B. Pate. 60p. 1991. pap. 9.95 (*0-88415-006-2*) Gulf Pub.

Document Analysis & Recognition, 2nd International Conference (ICDAR '93) LC 93-79398. 984p. 1993. pap. text ed. 100.00 (*0-8186-4960-7*, 4960) IEEE Comp Soc.

***Document Analysis Systems.** A. Dengel & L. Spitz. (Machine Perception & Artificial Intelligence Ser.: Vol. 14). 484p. 1995. text ed. 109.00 (*981-02-2122-3*) World Scientific Pub.

Document & Reference Text: An Index to Minority Group Employment Information. Institute of Labor & Industrial Relations Staff. 1967. pap. 15.00 (*0-87736-303-X*) U of Mich Inst Labor.

Document & Reference Text: 1971 Supplement, Vol. 2. Institute of Labor & Industrial Relations Staff. Ed. by Joe A. Miller & Steven C. Gold. 447p. 1971. pap. 15.00 (*0-87736-316-1*) U of Mich Inst Labor.

Document Architecture in Open Systems: The ODA Standard. W. Appelt. (Illus.). x, 350p. 1991. 70.00 (*0-387-54539-5*) Spr-Verlag.

Document Capture for Document Imaging Systems. David B. Black. (Illus.). 1992. pap. 36.00 (*0-89258-239-1*, R055) Assn Inform & Image Mgmt.

Document Databases. G. James. 184p. 1985. text ed. 39.95 (*0-442-28185-4*) Van Nos Reinhold.

Document Delivery for Sci-Tech Libraries. Ed. by Ellis Mount. (Science & Technology Libraries: Vol. 2, No. 4). 127p. 1982. pap. text ed. 29.95 (*0-86656-200-1*) Haworth Pr.

Document Delivery Services: Issues & Answers. Eleanor Mitchell & Sheila Walters. 175p. 1994. lib. bdg. 42.50 (*0-88736-913-8*) Learned Info.

Document for Guidance on Fishermen's Training & Certification. IMO Staff. (ENG, FRE & SPA.). (C). 1988. English ed. 120.00 (*0-7855-0020-0*, IMO 948E, Pub. by Intl Maritime Org UK); French ed. 120.00 (*0-685-74502-3*, IMO 949F, Pub. by Intl Maritime Org UK); Spanish ed. 120.00 (*0-685-74503-1*, IMO 950S, Pub. by Intl Maritime Org UK) St Mut.

Document Formatting & Typesetting on the UNIX System. 2nd ed. Narain Gehani. 380p. 1986. text ed. 35.95 (*0-9615336-2-5*) Silicon Pr.

Document Formatting & Typesetting on the UNIX Sytem, Vol. 2. Narain Gehani & Steven Lally. 320p. 1987. text ed. 32.95 (*0-9615336-3-3*) Silicon Pr.

Document Forms for Orders of Official Appointment in the Mughal Empire: Translation Notes & Text. Ed. by Richards. (Gibb Memorial New Ser.: Vol. 29). 1986. 65.00 (*0-906094-14-3*, Pub. by Aris & Phillips UK) David Brown.

Document History of Communism in the World: From Revolution to Collapse. Ed. by Robert V. Daniels. LC 93-46972. 418p. (C). 1994. reprint ed. pap. 19.95 (*0-87451-678-1*) U Pr of New Eng.

***Document Image Analysis.** H. Bunke et al. (Series in Machine Perception & Artificial Intelligence). 208p. 1994. text ed. 61.00 (*981-02-2046-4*) World Scientific Pub.

***Document Image Analysis.** Ed. by Lawrence O'Gorman & Rangachar Kasturi. LC 94-32859. 536p. 1994. text ed. 48.00 (*0-8186-6547-5*, BP06547) IEEE Comp Soc.

Document Image Processing: A Management Briefing and Market Survey. 200p. 1993. 1,200.00 (*1-85617-188-4*, Pub. by Elsevier Applied Sci UK) Elsevier.

Document Imaging Standards Development: How, Why, & for Whom? Marilyn Courtot. 60p. 1992. pap. text ed. 30.00 (*0-89258-236-7*, L034) Assn Inform & Image Mgmt.

Document Imaging Technology: How Automated Solutions Are Revolutionizing the Way Organizations & People Work. Edwin D. McDonell. 300p. 1992. 47.50 (*1-55738-336-7*) Probus Pub Co.

Document Long-Term Experience of Sludge Land Application Programs: Final Report. Lee Jacobs et al. 236p. 1993. pap. 75.00 (*1-881369-53-6*) Water Environ.

***Document on Canadian External Relations: 1948, Vol. 14.** International Trade Staff. Ed. by Hector MacKenzie. 1907p. 1994. 129.95x (*0-660-59102-2*, Pub. by Canada Commun Grp CN) Accents Pubns.

Document Preparation: Or Form-Filing for Fun & Profit. CWL. LC 87-51188. (Illus.). 80p. (Orig.). 1987. pap. 30.00 (*0-939856-82-4*) Tech Group.

Document Processing: A Collegiate Typewriting Simulation. Mearl Guthrie & Charlene Bunnell. 180p. (C). 1989. pap. text ed. 16.75 (*0-939693-06-2*) Collegiate Pr.

Document Processing Systems: Proceedings of the Inaugural ACM Conference on Document Processing Systems. (Illus.). 204p. 1989. pap. text ed. 20.00 (*0-685-28136-1*, 429882) Assn Compu Machinery.

Document Production Skills. Diane Canwell. 224p. (Orig.). 1993. pap. 33.00 (*0-273-60132-6*, Pub. by Pitman Pub Ltd UK) Trans-Atl Phila.

Document Retrieval Systems: Factors Affecting Search Time. K. Leon Montgomery. LC 75-18692. (Books in Library & Information Science: No. 14). 156p. reprint ed. pap. 44.50 (*0-7837-0928-5*, 2041233) Bks Demand.

Document Sets for Texas & the Southwest in U. S. History. Ed. by J'Nell L. Pate. 171p. (C). 1991. write for info. (*0-669-27109-8*) Heath.

Document Sets for the South in U. S. History. Ed. by Richard Purday. 256p. (C). 1991. write for info. (*0-669-27108-X*) Heath.

Documenta IX, 3 vols., Set. Ed. by Pier-Luigi Tazzi et al. (Illus.). 1992. pap. 95.00 (*0-8109-2510-9*) Abrams.

Documental History of Law Cases Affecting Japanese in the United States, 1916-1924, 2 vols., Set. Japanese General-Consulate Staff. Ed. by Roger Daniels. LC 78-54818. (Asian Experience in North America Ser.). 1979. reprint ed. lib. bdg. 107.95 (*0-405-11274-2*) Ayer.

Documentary: A History of the Non-Fiction Film. 2nd rev. ed. Erik Barnouw. (Illus.). 416p. 1993. pap. 12.95 (*0-19-507898-5*) OUP.

Documentary Archaeology in the New World. Ed. by Mary C. Beaudry. (New Directions in Archaeology Ser.). (Illus.). 232p. (C). 1993. pap. 19.95 (*0-521-44999-5*) Cambridge U Pr.

Documentary Conscience: A Casebook in Film-Making. Alan Rosenthal. LC 79-64487. (Illus.). 1980. pap. 14.00 (*0-520-04022-8*) U CA Pr.

Documentary Credits. F. P. De Rooy. 1984. lib. bdg. 98.00 (*90-6544-075-5*) Kluwer Law Tax Pubs.

Documentary Credits. Raymond Jack. 1991. 130.00 (*0-406-16511-4*, U.K.) Butterworth Legal Pubs.

Documentary Credits: Uniform Customs & Practice. Bernard Wheble & Hon Fib. 1983. 75.00 (*0-85297-135-4*, Pub. by Inst Bankers UK) St Mut.

Documentary Credits 1983. F. P. De Rooy. 250p. 40.00 (*0-686-41012-2*) Kluwer Ac.

Documentary Culture: Florence & Rome from Grand-Duke Ferdinand I to Pope Alexander VII. Ed. by Elizabeth Cropper et al. (Villa Spelman Colloquium Ser.: No. 3). (Illus.). 380p. 1992. text ed. 45.00 (*88-7779-327-9*) Johns Hopkins.

Documentary Dilemmas: Frederick Wiseman's "Titicut Follies" Carolyn Anderson & Thomas W. Benson. LC 88-29834. 176p. (Orig.). (C). 1990. pap. 14.95 (*0-8093-1518-1*) S Ill U Pr.

Documentary Evidence. Ashley Lipson. (Art of Advocacy Ser.). 1986. Looseleaf updates available. write for info. (*0-8205-1028-9*) Bender.

Documentary Evidence for the Spanish Missions of Texas. Ed. by Arthur R. Gomez. LC 91-15054. (Spanish Borderlands Sourcebooks Ser.: Vol. 22). 504p. 1991. 86.00 (*0-8240-2987-9*) Garland.

Documentary Evidence for the Spanish Missions of Alta California. Ed. by Julia Costello. LC 91-45782. (Spanish Borderlands Sourcebooks Ser.: Vol. 14). 552p. 1992. 82.00 (*0-8240-1953-9*) Garland.

Documentary Evidence in Australia. R. A. Brown. lii, 373p. 1988. 57.00 (*0-455-20763-1*, Pub. by Law Bk Co) W W Gaunt.

Documentary Expression & Thirties America. William Stott. LC 85-31819. (Illus.). xvi, 362p. 1986. pap. text ed. 16.95 (*0-226-77559-3*) U Ch Pr.

***Documentary Foundation of Rabbinic Culture: Mopping Up After Debates with Gerald L. Bruns, S. J. D. Cohen, Arnold Maria Goldberg, Susan Handelman, Christine Hayes, James Kugel, Peter Schaefer, Eliezer Segal, E. P. Sanders & Lawrence H. Schiffman.** Jacob Neusner. LC 95-1939. (South Florida Studies in the History of Judaism: No. 113). 1995. write for info. (*0-7885-0092-9*) Scholars Pr GA.

Documentary Guide to Commercial Leasing. Bernard H. Goldstein. LC 85-71421. 295p. 1985. 111.00 (*0-8318-0488-2*, B488/B663) Am Law Inst.

Documentary Guide to Commercial Leasing: 1990 Supplement. Bernard H. Goldstein. LC 85-71421. 81p. 1990. pap. text ed. 28.00 (*0-8318-0663-X*, B663) Am Law Inst.

Documentary History of American Industrial Society, 10 vols. John R. Commons et al. Ed. by Ulrich B. Phillips. 1988. reprint ed. Vols. 1-2, Plantation & Frontier, 1649-1863. write for info. (*0-318-63257-8*); reprint ed. Vols. 3-4, Labor Conspiracy Cases, 1806-1842. write for info. (*0-318-63258-6*); reprint ed. Vols. 5-6, Labor Movement, 1820-1840. write for info. (*0-318-63259-4*); reprint ed. Vols. 7-8, Labor Movement, 1840-1860. write for info. (*0-318-63260-8*); reprint ed. Vols. 9-10, Labor Movement, 1860-1880. write for info. (*0-318-63261-6*) AMS Pr.

Documentary History of American Industrial Society, 10 vols., Set. John R. Commons et al. Ed. by Ulrich B. Phillips. LC 88-47770. 1988. reprint ed. 920.00 (*0-404-20330-2*) AMS Pr.

Documentary History of Arkansas. Ed. by C. Fred Williams et al. 342p. 1984. text ed. 4.00 (*0-938626-20-5*) U of Ark Pr.

Documentary History of Art: Michelangelo & the Mannerists--the Baroque & the Eighteenth Century, Vol. II. Ed. by Elizabeth G. Holt. LC 81-47281. (Illus.). 380p. (C). 1983. reprint ed. pap. 17.95 (*0-691-00344-0*) Princeton U Pr.

Documentary History of Art: The Middle Ages & the Renaissance, Vol. I. Elizabeth G. Holt. LC 81-47281. (Illus.). 424p. 1981. reprint ed. pap. 17.95 (*0-691-00333-5*) Princeton U Pr.

Documentary History of Biochemistry, 1770-1940. Mikulas Teich & Dorothy M. Needham. LC 91-36678. (Illus.). 756p. 1992. 85.00 (*0-8386-3487-7*) Fairleigh Dickinson.

Documentary History of Chelsea, Including the Boston Precincts of Wimmisimmet, Rumney Marsh & Pullen Point, 1624-1824, Vol. I. Mellen Chamberlain. (Illus.). 712p. 1989. reprint ed. lib. bdg. 74.00 (*0-8328-0816-4*, MA0193) Higginson Bk Co.

Documentary History of Chelsea, Including the Boston Precincts of Wimmisimmet, Rumney Marsh & Pullen Point, 1624-1824, Vol. II. Mellen Chamberlain. (Illus.). 793p. 1989. reprint ed. lib. bdg. 81.00 (*0-8328-0817-2*, MA0194) Higginson Bk Co.

Documentary History of Communism, 2 vols. rev. ed. Ed. by Robert V. Daniels. Incl. Vol. II. Communism & the World. 480p. 1984. pap. 19.95 (*0-87451-300-6*); 1988. Set. 45.00 (*0-87451-298-0*) U Pr of New Eng.

Documentary History of Communism in Russia: From Lenin to Gorbachev. Tr. & Intro. by Robert V. Daniels. LC 92-56902. 428p. (C). 1993. pap. 19.95 (*0-87451-616-1*) U Pr of New Eng.

Documentary History of Dunmore's War, 1774. Ed. by Gold Thwaites & Louise P. Kellogg. (Illus.). 500p. 1989. reprint ed. pap. 25.00 (*1-55613-226-3*) Heritage Bk.

Documentary History of Oyster Bay Dutch Reformed Church, Vol 1. Henry A. Stoutenburgh. 533p. 1993. reprint ed. lib. bdg. 55.00 (*0-8328-3077-1*) Higginson Bk Co.

Documentary History of Queensland. W. Ross Johnston. LC 86-19163. (Illus.). 507p. (Orig.). (C). 1988. text ed. 29.95 (*0-7022-2059-0*, Pub. by Univ Queensland Pr AT) Intl Spec Bk.

Documentary History of Reconstruction, 2 vols. in 1. Walter L. Fleming. (History - United States Ser.). 1993. reprint ed. lib. bdg. 99.00 (*0-7812-4817-5*) Rprt Serv.

Documentary History of Religion in America, 2 vols. rev. ed. Ed. by Edwin S. Gaustad. 632p. (C). 1993. Vol. 2: Since 1865, 632p. pap. 24.99 (*0-8028-0618-X*) Eerdmans.

Documentary History of Religion in America, 2 vols. 2nd rev. ed. Ed. by Edwin S. Gaustad. 556p. (C). 1993. Vol. 1: To the Civil War, 556p. pap. 24.99 (*0-8028-0617-1*) Eerdmans.

Documentary History of Religion in America, 2 vols., Set. Edwin S. Gaustad. 1993. pap. 45.00 (*0-8028-0619-8*) Eerdmans.

Documentary History of Rhinebeck in Dutchess County, NY: Embracing Biographical Sketches & Genealogical Records of Our First Families & First Settlers with a History of Its Churches & Other Public Institutions. Edward M. Smith. (Palatine Transcripts Ser.). (Illus.). 280p. 1974. reprint ed. lib. bdg. 19.00 (*1-56012-024-X*) Kinship Rhinebeck.

Documentary History of Suffield, Connecticut in the Colony of Province of Massachusetts Bay in N. E. 1660-1749. Hezekiah S. Sheldon. (Illus.). 342p. 1992. reprint ed. lib. bdg. 37.00 (*0-8328-2517-4*) Higginson Bk Co.

Documentary History of the American Revolution, Consisting of Letters & Papers Relating to the Contest for Liberty Chiefly in South Carolina. Ed. by Robert W. Gibbes. LC 78-140873. (Eyewitness Accounts of the American Revolution Ser., No. 1). 1971. reprint ed. 57.95 (*0-405-01192-X*) Ayer.

Documentary History of the Arab-Israeli Conflict. Ed. by Charles L. Geddes. LC 90-23949. 496p. 1991. text ed. 59.95 (*0-275-93858-1*, C3858, Praeger Pubs) Greenwood.

Documentary History of the Campaign Upon the Niagara Frontier, 1812-1814, 4 Vols. Ed. by Ernest A. Cruikshank. LC 74-146387. (First American Frontier Ser.). (Illus.). 1971. reprint ed. 209.95 (*0-405-02838-5*) Ayer.

Documentary History of the Canadian Criminal Code of 1892. Ed. by Desmond H. Brown. 1008p. 1993. 75.00 (*0-8020-3472-1*) U of Toronto Pr.

Documentary History of the Communist Party of the United States. Ed. by Bernard K. Johnpoll. LC 93-15712. 640p. 1994. Vol. I: Birth & Gestation, 1918-1928. text ed. 395.00 (*0-313-28504-7*, JAC01, Greenwood Pr) Greenwood.

Documentary History of the Communist Party of the United States, Vol. 2. Ed. by Bernard K. Johnpoll. LC 93-15712. 640p. 1994. Vol. II: Toil & Trouble, 1928-1933. text ed. 395.00 (*0-313-28505-5*, JAC02, Greenwood Pr) Greenwood.

Documentary History of the Communist Party of the United States, Vol. 3. Ed. by Bernard K. Johnpoll. LC 93-15712. 928p. 1994. Vol. III: United & Fight, 1934-1935. text ed. 395.00 (*0-313-28506-3*, JAC03, Greenwood Pr) Greenwood.

Documentary History of the Communist Party of the United States, Vol. 4. Ed. by Bernard K. Johnpoll. LC 93-15712. 1040p. 1994. Vol. IV: People's Front, 1934-1937. text ed. 395.00 (*0-313-28507-1*, JAC04, Greenwood Pr) Greenwood.

Documentary History of the Communist Party of the United States, Vols. I-VIII. Ed. by Bernard K. Johnpoll. 1994. text ed. 1,750.00 (*0-313-28816-X*, JAC/, Greenwood Pr) Greenwood.

Documentary History of the Communist Party of the United States, Vol. V: Twentieth Century Americanism, 1937-1939, Vol. 5. Ed. by Bernard K. Johnpoll. LC 93-15712. 664p. 1994. text ed. 395.00 (*0-313-28810-0*, JAC05, Greenwood Pr) Greenwood.

Documentary History of the Communist Party of the United States, Vol. VI: The Yanks Are Not Coming, 1939-1941, Vol. 6. Ed. by Bernard K. Johnpoll. LC 93-15712. 1144p. 1994. text ed. 395.00 (*0-313-28811-9*, JAC06, Greenwood Pr) Greenwood.

Documentary History of the Communist Party of the United States, Vol. VII: The Great Patriotic War, 1941-1945, Vol. 7. Ed. by Bernard K. Johnpoll. LC 93-15712. 688p. 1994. text ed. 395.00 (*0-313-28812-7*, JAC07, Greenwood Pr) Greenwood.

Documentary History of the Destruction of the Gaspee. William R. Staples. Ed. by Richard M. Deasy. (Rhode Island Revolutionary Heritage Ser.: Vol. 5). 1990. 14.95 (*0-917012-05-4*) RI Pubns Soc.

***Documentary History of the First Federal Congress: Debates in the House of Representatives: Third Session Vol. 14: December 1790-March 1791.** Ed. by William C. DiGiacomantonio et al. 1002p. 1995. text ed. 75.00x (*0-8018-5015-0*) Johns Hopkins.

Documentary History of the First Federal Congress of the United States of America, March 4, 1789-March 3, 1791 Vol. 4: Legislative Histories - Amendments to the Constitution Through Foreign Officers Bill (HR-116) Ed. by Charlene B. Bickford & Helen E. Veit. LC 84-15465. 736p. 1986. text ed. 65.00x (*0-8018-3163-6*) Johns Hopkins.

Documentary History of the First Federal Congress of the United States of America, March 4, 1789-March 3, 1791 Vol. 5: Legislative Histories - Funding Act (HR-63) Through Militia Bill (HR-112) Ed. by Charlene B. Bickford & Helen E. Veit. LC 84-15465. 864p. 1986. text ed. 65.00x (*0-8018-3167-9*) Johns Hopkins.

Documentary History of the First Federal Congress of the United States of America, March 4, 1789-March 3, 1791 Vol. 6: Legislative Histories - Mitigation of Fines Bill (HR-38) Through Resolution on Unclaimed Western Lands. Ed. by Charlene B. Bickford & Helen E. Veit. LC 84-15465. 720p. 1986. text ed. 65.00x (*0-8018-3169-5*) Johns Hopkins.

Documentary History of the First Federal Congress of the United States of America, March 4, 1789-March 3, 1791 Vol. 9: The Diary of William Maclay & Other Notes on Senate Debates. Ed. by Kenneth R. Bowling & Helen E. Veit. LC 87-22793. 576p. 1988. text ed. 65.00x (*0-8018-3535-6*); pap. 14.95 (*0-8018-3683-2*) Johns Hopkins.

Documentary History of the First Federal Congress of the United States of America, March 4, 1789-March 3, 1791 Vol. 10: Debates in the House of Representatives, First Session: April-May 1789. Ed. by Charlene B. Bickford et al. 736p. 1992. text ed. 65.00x (*0-8018-4177-1*) Johns Hopkins.

Documentary History of the First Federal Congress of the United States of America, March 4, 1789-March 3, 1791 Vol. 11: Debates in the House of Representatives, First Session, June-September 1789. Ed. by Charlene B. Bickford et al. 736p. 1992. text ed. 65.00x (*0-8018-4178-X*) Johns Hopkins.

Documentary History of the First Federal Congress of the United States of America, March 4, 1789-March 3, 1791 Vol. 12: Debates in the House of Representatives, Second Session, January-March 1790. Ed. by Helen E. Veit et al. 989p. 1994. text ed. 75.00x (*0-8018-4576-9*) Johns Hopkins.

Documentary History of the First Federal Congress of the United States of America, March 4, 1789-March 3, 1791 Vol. 13: Debates in the House of Representatives, Second Session, April-August 1790. Ed. by Helen E. Veit et al. 904p. 1994. text ed. 75.00x (*0-8018-4577-7*) Johns Hopkins.

Documentary History of the First Federal Congress of the United States of America, March 4, 1789-March 3, 1791. Incl. Senate Legislative Journal. Ed. by Linda G. De Pauw. 800p. 1972. 65.00x (*0-8018-1280-1*); Senate Executive Journal & Related Documents. Ed. by Linda G. De Pauw. 592p. 1974. 65.00x (*0-8018-1572-X*); House of Representatives Journal. Ed. by Linda Grant De Pauw. 466p. 1977. 65.00x (*0-8018-1819-2*); write for info. (*0-318-53777-X*) Johns Hopkins.

Documentary History of the First Federal Elections: 1788-1790, Vol. I. Ed. by Merrill Jensen & Robert A. Becker. LC 74-5903. 928p. 1976. 50.00 (*0-299-06690-8*) U of Wis Pr.

Documentary History of the First Federal Elections, 1788-1790, Vol. II. Gordon DenBoer et al. LC 74-5903. 544p. 1984. text ed. 50.00 (*0-299-09510-X*) U of Wis Pr.

D

An Asterisk (*) at the beginning of an entry indicates that the title is appearing in BIP for the first time.

Documentation Skills for Quality Patient Care. R. Fay Yocum. Ed. by Esther Silverman. LC 93-79567. 184p. (Orig.). (C). 1993. pap. 18.95 (0-9637649-7-7) Awareness Prods.
DOCUMENTATION SKILLS FOR QUALITY PATIENT CARE is written for students & professional nurses who want to develop or strengthen existing documentation skills. Documentation meets many needs & requirements. This book reviews those needs & outlines the regulations that nurses must adhere to. JCAHO & ANA standards of nursing practice that relate to documentation are featured. Nursing process & writing NANDA nursing diagnoses are reviewed. The book describes what needs to be documented as well as techniques, & pitfalls of documentation. Numerous examples of nursing notes, based on the author's long & varied clinical experiences, are included to guide the reader. Written in a clear & accessible style, the book is intended for use as a primer & refresher guide. A busy teacher or hospital educator could use the book as a guideline for instruction. Order from: Awareness Productions, P.O. Box 85, Tipp City, OH 45371-0085. 513-845-3617. *Publisher Provided Annotation.*

D

An Asterisk (*) at the beginning of an entry indicates that the title is appearing in BIP for the first time.

2065

Documenting Ambulatory Care. Eric Joseph et al. 31p. 1986. pap. text ed. 2.00 (*0-916499-36-7*) Care Educ Grp.

Documenting America: A Reader in United States History, Vol. I: Colonial Times to 1877. Leonard Pitt. 320p. 1989. per. 42.95 (*0-8403-5245-X*) Kendall-Hunt.

Documenting America, 1935-1943. Ed. by Carl Fleischhauer & Beverly W. Brannan. (Approaches to American Culture Ser.: No. 2). (Illus.). 300p. 1988. 65.00 (*0-520-06220-5*); pap. 30.00 (*0-520-06221-3*) U CA Pr.

Documenting Care: Communication - The Nursing Process & Documentation Standards. Frances T. Fischbach. LC 90-14140. 677p. (Orig.). (C). 1991. pap. 27.95 (*0-8036-3561-3*) Davis Co.

Documenting Computer Application Systems. Derek A. Kelly. (Illus.). 192p. 1983. 22.50 (*0-89433-206-6*) Petrocelli.

Documenting Design: Works on Paper in the European Collection of the Royal Ontario Museum. Howard C. Collinson. LC 93-93488. 120p. 1993. 65.00 (*0-8020-0557-8*); pap. 35.00 (*0-8020-7454-5*) U of Toronto Pr.

***Documenting Discipline.** Michael Deblieux. Ed. by Dave Kirchner. (AMI How-to Ser.). 100p. 1995. 9.95 (*1-884926-34-7*) Amer Media.

***Documenting Employee Discipline.** Lee T. Paterson. 170p. 1994. pap. 42.00 (*0-250-47241-4*) Michie Butterworth.

Documenting Employee Discipline. Lee T. Patterson & Michael R. Deblieux. LC 88-61702. 1988. pap. 39.50 (*0-911110-61-5*) Butterworth Legal Pubs.

***Documenting Hospital Meetings.** 127p. (Orig.). 1994. pap. text ed. write for info. (*0-916499-60-X*) Care Educ Grp.

***Documenting Maine: Salt & the Photography of Place.** Ed. by Hugh T. French. (Illus.). 144p. 1995. 39.95 (*0-87451-716-8*) U Pr of New Eng.

***Documenting Maine: Salt & the Photography of Place.** Ed. by Hugh T. French. (Illus.). 144p. 1995. pap. 19.95 (*0-87451-717-6*) U Pr of New Eng.

Documenting Maritime Folklife: An Introductory Guide. David A. Taylor. LC 91-36699. 81p. 1992. 7.50 (*0-8444-0721-6*, 030-000-00236-9) Lib Congress.

***Documenting Native History.** Jennifer Brown & Elizabeth Vibert. 472p. 1995. pap. 26.95 (*1-55111-070-9*) Broadview Pr.

Documenting Quality for ISO 9000 & Other Industry Standards. Gary E. MacLean. LC 93-27743. 231p. 1993. pap. 24.95 (*0-87389-212-7*) ASQC Qual Pr.

Documenting the Impending Economic - Political Storm, Vol. 3: Life & Pursuit of Successful Living. Homer Wells. LC 92-74592. 207p. 1992. pap. 14.95 (*0-942963-36-9*) Distinctive Pub.

Documenting the Past: Essays in Medieval History Presented to George Peddy Cuttino. Ed. by J. S. Hamilton & Patricia J. Bradley. 256p. 1989. 90.00 (*0-85115-515-4*) Boydell & Brewer.

Documenting the Software Development Process: A Handbook of Structured Techniques. Steve Ayer. 1992. text ed. 49.50 (*0-07-002604-1*) McGraw.

Documenting Your Possessions: Workbook. Cecila W. Clover. 32p. 1994. reprint ed. 3.5 hd 34.95 (*0-9639374-1-3*); reprint ed. 5.25 hd 34.95 (*0-9639374-2-1*) Art Restoration.

Documentos de la Real Hacienda de Puerto Rico: 1510-1519, Vol. 1. Comp. by Qurelio Tanodi. 467p. (C). 1971. pap. 5.00 (*0-8477-0838-1*) U of PR Pr.

Documentos Historicos Relacionados Con El Estado Libre Asociado: Special Edition. 410p. 1986. pap. 20.00 (*0-88063-677-7*, Equity Pub NH) Michie Butterworth.

Documentos Oficiales de la Organizacion de los Estados Americanos Lista General de Documentos, Volumen XX: OEA Ser.Z I. 1. Enero-Diciembre de 1979. OAS, General Secretariat for Management. 144p. (SPA.). (C). 1980. lib. bdg. 9.00 (*0-8270-1289-6*) OAS.

Documentos "Que Dicen" Reece B. Bothwell & Lidio Cruz Monclava. 602p. (C). 1975. pap. 5.50 (*0-8477-0820-9*) U of PR Pr.

Documents see Melanges

Documents see Enseignement Francais de la Revolution a Nos Jours: Publications De L'universite Des Sciences Sociales De Grenoble-Collection Du Centre De Recherche D'histoire Economique, Sociale et Instututionnelle

Documents see International Monetary Fund, 1966-1971: The System Under Stress

Documents see Vpered, Eighteen Seventy-Three to Eighteen Seventy-Seven

Documents & Biography Pertaining to the Settlement & Progress of Stark County, Containing an Authentic Summary of Records, Documents, Historical Works & Newspapers. M. A. Leeson. (Illus.). 708p. 1989. reprint ed. lib. bdg. write for info. (*0-8328-0559-9*) Higginson Bk Co.

Documents & Essays on Jewish Labour Policy in Palestine. General Federation of Jewish Labour in Israel, Executive Committee. LC 76-97280. 239p. 1975. reprint ed. text ed. 55.00 (*0-8371-2602-9*, JELP, Greenwood Pr) Greenwood.

Documents, Chiefly Unpublished, Relating to the Huguenot Emigration to Virginia & the Settlement at Manakin-Town. Comp. by Robert A. Brock. LC 72-14424. (Virginia Historical Society. Collections First Ser.: No. 5). reprint ed. 38.50 (*0-404-57655-9*) AMS Pr.

Documents De Sculpture Francaise. Ed. by Paul Vitry & Gaston Briere. LC 78-88822. (Art Histories Collection Ser.). (FRE.). 1979. reprint ed. 107.95 (*0-405-02223-9*) Ayer.

Documents d'Etudes Sociales sur l'Anarchie. Ed. by A. Berard. (History of Political Violence Ser.). (FRE.). 1985. reprint ed. lib. bdg. 28.00 (*0-527-41197-3*) Periodicals Srv.

***Documents Diplomatiques Francais sur l'Histoire du Bassin des Carpates 1918-1932 Vol. 1: Octobre 1918-Aout 1919.** Ed. by M. Adam et al. 864p. (FRE.). 1994. 95.00 (*963-05-6659-1*, Pub. by A K HU) Intl Spec Bk.

Documents for the History of Collecting; Part 1: Italian Inventories, 3 vols. Incl. Vol.1. Collections of Paintings in Naples, 1600-1780. Ed. by Gerard Labrot. 900p. 1994. 150.00 (*3-598-21692-0*); Vol. 2. Colonna Inventories. Ed. by Eduard Safarik. 900p. 1992. 150.00 (*3-598-21693-9*); Vol. 3. 900p. 1992. 150.00 (*3-598-21694-7*); 1992. write for info. (*0-318-69471-9*) U Pubns Amer.

Documents for the Study of the Gospels. Ed. by David R. Cartlidge & David L. Dungan. LC 93-42366. (Orig.). 1993. 16.00 (*0-8006-2809-8*) Augsburg Fortress.

Documents from Old Testament Times. Ed. by D. Winton Thomas. 1961. pap. text ed. 14.00 (*0-06-130085-3*, TB85, Torch) HarpC.

Documents from Tablet Collections in Rochester New York. Marcel Sigrist. (Illus.). 124p. 1991. 48.00 (*0-9620013-8-4*) CDL Pr.

Documents from the Temple Archives of Nippur Dated in the Reigns of Cassite Rulers. Albert T. Clay. LC 13-1106. (University of Pennsylvania, The Museum, Publications of the Babylonian Section: Vol. 2, No. 2). 108p. reprint ed. pap. 30.80 (*0-317-28572-6*, 2052022) Bks Demand.

Documents from the Temple Archives of Nippur Dated in the Reigns of Cassite Rulers (Complete Dates) Albert T. Clay. LC 08-33649. (University of Pennsylvania, Babylonian Expedition, Series A: Cuneiform Texts: Vol. 14). 188p. reprint ed. pap. 53.60 (*0-317-29792-9*, 2052017) Bks Demand.

Documents Graphiques see Traitement Graphique D'une Information Hydrometeorologique Relative a L'espace Maritime Du Nord Sovietique

Documents Illustrating Papal Authority, A.D. 96-454. Ed. by Edward Giles. LC 78-59023. 1992. reprint ed. 33.00 (*0-88355-696-0*) Hyperion Conn.

Documents Illustrative of English Church History. Comp. by Henry Gee & William J. Hardy. LC 83-45580. reprint ed. 62.50 (*0-404-19898-8*) AMS Pr.

Documents Illustrative of Sir William Wallace, His Life & Times. Ed. by Joseph Stevenson. LC 73-176440. (Maitland Club, Glasgow. Publications: No. 54). reprint ed. 27.50 (*0-404-53037-0*) AMS Pr.

Documents Illustrative of the Canadian Constitution. Ed. by William Houston. LC 77-130553. (Select Bibliographies Reprint Ser.). 1977. reprint ed. 23.95 (*0-8369-5526-9*) Ayer.

Documents Illustrative of the Continental Reformation. Ed. by Beresford J. Kidd. LC 83-45663. reprint ed. 64. 50 (*0-404-19813-9*) AMS Pr.

Documents Illustrative of the Formation of the Union of the American States, 2 vols. Ed. by Charles C. Tansill. 1991. lib. bdg. 199.95 (*0-8490-5054-5*) Gordon Pr.

Documents Illustrative of the Social & Economic History of the Danelaw. Ed. by F. M. Stenton. (British Academy, London, Records of the Social & Economic History of England & Wales Ser.). 1972. reprint ed. pap. 75.00 (*0-8115-1245-2*) Periodicals Srv.

Documents in American Telecommunications Policy. Ed. by John M. Kittross. LC 75-23904. (Historical Studies in Telecommunications). (Illus.). 1980. reprint ed. 118.95 (*0-405-07764-5*) Ayer.

Documents in British History, Vol. 2. 2nd rev. ed. Ed. by Jacquelin Collins. LC 92-31437. 1992. pap. text ed. write for info. (*0-07-005702-8*) McGraw.

Documents in Canadian Architecture. Geoffrey Simmins. (Illus.). 250p. (Orig.). 1992. pap. text ed. 19.95x (*0-921149-79-4*) Broadview Pr.

Documents in Canadian Art. Ed. by Doug Fetherling. 327p. 1987. pap. 19.95 (*0-921149-06-9*) Broadview Pr.

Documents in Canadian Film. Ed. by Doug Fetherling. 343p. 1988. pap. 19.95 (*0-921149-24-7*) Broadview Pr.

Documents in Communist Affairs, 1985. Ed. by Bogdan Szajkowski. 352p. 1987. text ed. 65.00 (*0-312-00428-1*) St Martin.

Documents in Early Christian Thought. Ed. by Maurice F. Wiles & M. Santer. LC 74-31807. 304p. 1977. pap. 18. 95 (*0-521-09915-3*) Cambridge U Pr.

Documents in International Environment Law. Ed. by Philippe Sands et al. LC 93-27217. (Studies in Environmental Law). 1995. text ed. 250.00 (*0-7190-3985-1*, Pub. by Manchester Univ Pr UK) St Martin.

Documents in the Case. Dorothy L. Sayers & Robert Eustace. 320p. 1987. mass mkt. 6.00 (*0-06-080836-5*, P836, PL) HarpC.

Documents in the Case. large type ed. Dorothy L. Sayers. LC 91-47011. 364p. 1992. reprint ed. lib. bdg. 19.95 (*1-56054-358-2*) Thorndike Pr.

Documents in World History, Vol. I: The Great Traditions--From Ancient Times to 1500. Ed. by Peter N. Stearns et al. 208p. (C). 1990. pap. text ed. 28.50 (*0-06-046382-1*) HarpCollege.

Documents in World History, Vol. II: The Modern Centuries--From 1500 to the Present. Ed. by Peter N. Stearns et al. 214p. (C). 1990. pap. text ed. 28.50 (*0-06-046432-1*) HarpCollege.

Documents Inedits pour Servir a l'Histoire du Christianisme en Orient, 2 vols. Antoine Rabbath. LC 72-174293. reprint ed. lib. bdg. 125.00 (*0-404-05202-9*) AMS Pr.

Documents, Nineteen Hundred to Nineteen Twenty-Nine. Arthur Marwick & Simpson. 1990. 80.00 (*0-335-09301-9*, Open Univ Pr); pap. 27.00 (*0-335-09300-0*, Open Univ Pr) Taylor & Francis.

Documents of American Broadcasting. 4th ed. Frank J. Kahn. LC 83-11025. 1984. pap. text ed. write for info. (*0-13-217133-3*) P-H.

Documents of American Constitutional & Legal History, 2 vols., II. Melvin I. Urofsky. 512p. (C). 1989. pap. text ed. 15.50 (*0-394-38580-2*) McGraw.

Documents of American Constitutional & Legal History, 2 vols., Vol. 2. Melvin I. Urofsky. 512p. (C). 1989. pap. text ed. write for info. (*0-07-557092-0*) McGraw.

Documents of American History Vol. 1: To 1898. 10th ed. Henry S. Commager & Milton Cantor. 640p. 1988. text ed. 62.67 (*0-13-217274-7*) P-H.

Documents of American Theater History, Vol. 1, Famous American Playhouses, 1716-1899. William C. Young. LC 72-9837. 351p. reprint ed. pap. 100.10 (*0-317-26584-9*, 2024194) Bks Demand.

Documents of American Theater History, Vol. 2, Famous American Playhouses, 1900-1971. William C. Young. LC 72-9837. 311p. reprint ed. pap. 88.70 (*0-317-26784-1*, 2024194) Bks Demand.

Documents of Christian Worship: Descriptive & Interpretive Sources. James F. White. 288p. (Orig.). 1992. pap. 22.99 (*0-664-25399-7*) Westminster John Knox.

Documents of Dissent: Chinese Political Thought Since Mao. Tr. by J. Chester Cheng. (Publication Ser.: No. 230). 120p. (Orig.). 1980. pap. 7.95 (*0-8179-7302-8*) Hoover Inst Pr.

Documents of English History: 1832-1950. Ed. by W. A. Barker et al. 1954. 49.50 (*0-317-07647-7*) Elliots Bks.

Documents of Interaction: Biography, Autobiography, & Life History in Social Science Perspective. Michael V. Angrosino. 128p. 1989. pap. text ed. 14.95 (*0-8130-0925-1*) U Press Fla.

Documents of Jewish Sectaries, 2 Vols. in 1. rev. ed. Solomon Schechter. (Library of Biblical Studies). (Illus.). 1970. 45.00 (*0-87068-016-1*) Ktav.

Documents of Korean Communism, Nineteen Eighteen to Nineteen Forty-Eight. Tr. by Dea Sook Suh. LC 79-120763. (Studies of the East Asian Institute, Columbia University). 700p. 1970. 75.00 (*0-691-08723-7*) Princeton U Pr.

Documents of Korean Communism, 1918-1948. Dae-Sook Suh. LC 79-120763. (Studies of the East Asian Institute, Columbia University). 592p. reprint ed. pap. 168.80 (*0-7837-0557-3*, 2040901) Bks Demand.

Documents of Modern Literary Realism. Ed. by George J. Becker. LC 63-7064. 621p. reprint ed. pap. 177.00 (*0-8357-8863-6*, 2033380) Bks Demand.

Documents of Muslim Politics: A Study of Khilafat Movement. S. R. Bakshi. (C). 1990. 135.00 (*0-89771-154-8*) St Mut.

Documents of Russian History, 1914-1917. Frank A. Golder. 1964. 13.25 (*0-8446-1201-4*) Peter Smith.

Documents of Soviet-American Relations (Sovamdocs), Vol. 1. Ed. by Harold J. Goldberg. 1993. 95.00 (*0-87569-162-5*) Academic Intl.

Documents of Soviet-American Relations (Sovamdocs), Vol. 2. Ed. by Harold J. Goldberg. 1993. 72.00 (*0-685-60851-4*) Academic Intl.

Documents of Soviet-American Relations (Sovamdocs), Vols. 1 & 2. Ed. by Harold J. Goldberg. 1995. 95.00 (*0-87569-133-1*) Academic Intl.

Documents of Soviet History. Ed. by Rex A. Wade. 1991. 75.00 (*0-685-24295-1*) Academic Intl.

Documents of Soviet History Vol. 1. Ed. by Rex A. Wade. 95.00 (*0-87569-151-X*) Academic Intl.

Documents of Soviet History Vol. 2: Triumph & Retreat. Ed. by Rex A. Wade. 1993. 75.00 (*0-87569-170-6*) Academic Intl.

Documents of Texas History (1528-1993) Ernest Wallace. 337p. 1994. 32.95 (*1-880510-08-1*); pap. 19.95 (*1-880510-09-X*) State House Pr.

***Documents of Texas History (1528-1993)** limited ed. Ernest Wallace. 337p. 1994. 75.00 (*1-880510-10-3*) State House Pr.

Documents of the American Revolution, 1770-1783, 21 vols., Set. Ed. by K. G. Davis. 7780p. 650.00 (*0-7165-2085-0*, Pub. by Irish Acad Pr IE) Intl Spec Bk.

Documents of the Christian Church. 2nd ed. Ed. by Henry Bettenson. 1970. pap. 11.95 (*0-19-501293-3*) OUP.

Documents of the Constitution of England & America: From Magna Charta to the Federal Constitution of 1789. Francis Bowen. vii, 142p. 1992. reprint ed. 25.00 (*0-8377-1954-2*) Rothman.

Documents of the First Council of the International Working Men's Association: 1864-1872, 5 vols. Ed. by Lawrence & Wishart Ltd. Staff. 705p. 1974. 115.00 (*0-8464-0340-4*) Beekman Pubs.

Documents of the Homosexual Rights Movement in Germany, 1836-1927. Ed. by Jonathan N. Katz. LC 75-12326. (Homosexuality Ser.). (FRE & GER.). 1975. 54. 95 (*0-405-07367-4*) Ayer.

Documents of the Lodz Ghetto: An Inventory of the Nachman Zonabend Collection. Marek Web. Ed. by Jeffrey Shandler. (Illus.). 163p. (Orig.). 1988. pap. text ed. 12.00 (*0-914512-42-0*) Yivo Inst.

Documents of the Marriage Liturgy. Mark Searle & Kenneth Stevenson. 288p. (Orig.). 1991. pap. text ed. 19.95 (*0-8146-6008-8*) Liturgical Pr.

Documents of the Organization of African Unity. Gino J. Naldi. 256p. 1992. text ed. 100.00 (*0-7201-2136-1*, Mansell Pub) Cassell.

Documents of the Second Congress of the Marxist-Leninist Party, U. S. A. Central Committee, MLP, U. S. A. (Illus.). 95p. (Orig.). 1984. pap. 1.00 (*0-86714-026-7*) Marxist-Leninist.

Documents of the Thirty-First & Thirty-Second General Congregations of the Society of Jesus: An English Translation of the Official Latin Texts of the General Congregations & of the Accompanying Papal Documents. Ed. by John W. Padberg. LC 77-70881. (Jesuit Primary Sources in English Translation Series I: No. 2). x, 598p. 1977. pap. 6.00 (*0-912422-26-2*) Inst Jesuit.

Documents of the Thirty-Third General Congregation of the Society of Jesus: An English Translation of the Official Latin Texts. Ed. by Donald R. Campion & Albert C. Louapre. LC 84-80080. (Jesuit Primary Sources in English Translation Series I: No. 5). 115p. 1984. pap. 3.00 (*0-912422-64-5*) Inst Jesuit.

Documents of Title Under the Uniform Commercial Code. 2nd ed. Ray D. Henson. LC 90-55160. 362p. 1990. text ed. 90.00 (*0-8318-0626-5*, B626) Am Law Inst.

Documents of United States Indian Policy. Ed. by Francis P. Prucha. LC 89-16408. (Illus.). xiv, 338p. 1990. pap. 15.00 (*0-8032-8726-7*) U of Nebr Pr.

Documents of United States Indian Policy. 2nd ed. Ed. by Francis P. Prucha. LC 89-16408. (Illus.). xiv, 338p. 1990. 40.00 (*0-8032-3688-3*) U of Nebr Pr.

Documents of Vatican II. Austin P. Flannery. 1975. pap. 15.99 (*0-8028-1623-1*) Eerdmans.

***Documents of Youth Ministry.** 176p. Date not set. write for info. (*0-89944-324-9*) Don Bosco Multimedia.

Documents on Art & Taste in Australia, 1770-1914. Ed. by Bernard Smith. 312p. 1991. pap. 32.50 (*0-19-550476-3*) OUP.

Documents on British Policy Overseas, Vol. IV. (Britain & America Atomic Energy, Bases & Food, December 1945-July 1946 Ser.: No. I). 460p. (Orig.). 1987. pap. 80. 00 (*0-11-591685-7*, HM1422, Pub. by HMSO UK) UNIPUB.

Documents on Canadian External Relations, Vol. 13: 1947. Ed. by Norman Hillmer & Donald Page. (Illus.). 1654p. 1993. 128.70 (*0-660-57963-4*, Pub. by Canada Commun Grp CN) Accents Pubns.

***Documents on Contemporary Dervish Communities.** Roy W. Davidson. 28p. 1990. pap. 9.00 (*0-86302-015-1*, Pub. by Octagon Pr UK) ISHK Bk Service.

Documents on Germany, Nineteen Forty-Four to Nineteen Eighty-Five. (Department of State Publication Ser.: No. 9446). (Illus.). 1450p. 1985. pap. 24.00 (*0-16-004408-1*, S/N 044-000-02062-9) USGPO.

Documents on Germany, 1944-1985, 3 vols. 1992. lib. bdg. 1,555.95 (*0-8490-5492-3*) Gordon Pr.

Documents on Instrumental Music. Tom Burgess. 145p. 1989. reprint ed. pap. 4.99 (*0-89900-355-9*) College Pr Pub.

Documents on International Administrative Tribunals. C. F. Amerasinghe. 224p. 1989. 85.00 (*0-19-825636-1*) OUP.

Documents on International Organization & Integration. Ed. by Louis B. Sohn. 1986. pap. text ed. 99.50 (*0-89838-915-1*) Kluwer Ac.

Documents on Modern Africa. T. W. Wallbank. (Anvil Ser.). 191p. 1964. pap. 10.50 (*0-442-00072-3*) Van Nos Reinhold.

Documents on Muslim States: Iran: Selected Political Documents. Shiv Lal. 224p. 1986. 150.00 (*0-317-61944-6*, Pub. by Archives Pubs II) St Mut.

Documents on Muslim States: Morocco & Other African Nations. Shiv Lal. 300p. 1986. 120.00 (*0-317-61945-4*, Pub. by Archives Pubs II) St Mut.

Documents on Muslim States: Politics in Iraq. Shiv Lal. 160p. 1986. 120.00 (*0-317-61947-0*, Pub. by Archives Pubs II) St Mut.

Documents on Muslim States: Select Constitutions. Shiv Lal. 248p. 1986. 120.00 (*0-317-61948-9*, Pub. by Archives Pubs II) St Mut.

Documents on Russian-American Relations: Washington to Eisenhower. Stanley S. Jados. LC 65-12569. 424p. reprint ed. pap. 120.90 (*0-317-55474-3*, 2029527) Bks Demand.

Documents on the History of European Integration: Vol. 2, Plans for European Union in Great Britain & in Exile, 1939-1945. Ed. by Walter Lipgens. (European University Institute, Series B (History): Vols. 1/2). xxiv, 852p. 1986. 216.00 (*0-89925-212-5*) De Gruyter.

Documents on the History of European Integration Vol. 1: Continental Plans for European Union 1939-1945. Ed. by Walter Lipgens. LC 84-19842. (European University Institute, Series B (History)). (Illus.). xxiv, 823p. 1984. 290.80 (*3-11-009724-9*); fiche 290.80 (*0-318-59211-8*) De Gruyter.

***Documents on the History of European Integration Vol. 2: Plans for European Union in Great Britain & in Exile, 1939-1945.** Ed. by Walter Lipgens. (European University Institute, Series B (History): Vols. 1/2). xxiv, 852p. 1986. 261.55 (*3-11-010338-9*) De Gruyter.

***Documents on the History of European Integration Vol. 3: The Struggle for the European Union by Political Parties & Pressure Groups in Western European Countries, 1945-1950.** Ed. by Walter Lipgens & Wilfried Loth. xliv, 824p. (C). 1988. lib. bdg. 284.65x (*3-11-011429-1*) De Gruyter.

Documents on the History of European Integration, Vol. 3: The Struggle for the European Union by Political Parties & Pressure Groups in Western European Countries, 1945-1950. Ed. by Walter Lipgens & Wilfried Loth. xliv, 824p. (C). 1988. lib. bdg. 284.65x (*0-89925-416-0*) De Gruyter.

Documents on the History of European Integration, Vol. 4: Transnational Organizations of the Political Parties & Pressure Groups in the Struggle for European Union, 1945-1950. Ed. by Lipgens Loth. (European University Institute Ser.: No. 1-4). xxv, 650p. (C). 1990. fiche, lib. bdg. 229.25 (*3-11-011965-X*) De Gruyter.

An Asterisk (*) at the beginning of an entry indicates that the title is appearing in BIP for the first time.

An Asterisk (*) at the beginning of an entry indicates that the title is appearing in BIP for the first time.

2067

***Does Death Really Exist?** Muktananda. LC 95-14439. 1995. write for info. (0-911307-36-2) SYDA Found.

Does Death Really Exist? Swami Muktananda. LC 81-50161. 64p. 1983. reprint ed. pap. 6.95 (0-914602-69-1) SYDA Found.

Does Debt Management Matter? Jonas Agell et al. (FIEF Studies in Labor Markets & Economic Policy). (Illus.). 128p. 1992. 45.00 (0-19-828361-X) OUP.

Does Deconstruction Make Any Difference? Poststructuralism & the Defense of Poetry in Modern Criticism. Michael Fischer. LC 84-48044. 160p. 1985. 25.00 (0-253-31810-6) Ind U Pr.

Does Defense Beggar Welfare: Myths vs. Realities. James L. Clayton. 71p. 1979. pap. text ed. 16.95 (0-87855-802-0) Transaction Pubs.

Does Distribution Cost Too Much? Paul W. Stewart & J. Frederic Dewhurst. LC 75-39276. (Getting & Spending: the Consumer's Dilemma Ser.). (Illus.). 1976. reprint ed. 34.95 (0-405-08049-2) Ayer.

Does Economic Space Matter? Essays in Honour of Melvin L. Greenhut. Ed. by Hiroshi Ohta & Jacques-Francois Thisse. LC 93-3. 1993. text ed. 75.00 (0-312-09640-2) St Martin.

Does Education Have a Future? A. B. Bengtsson. (Plan Europe 2000 Ser: No. 10). 1975. pap. text ed. 42.50 (90-247-1760-4) Kluwer Ac.

Does Education Pay in the Labor Market? The Labor Force Participation, Occupation, & Earnings of Peruvian Women. Elizabeth M. King. (Living Standards Measurement Study Working Paper Ser.: No. 67). 64p. 1990. 6.95 (0-8213-1394-0, 11394) World Bank.

Does Foreign-Exchange Intervention Work? Kathryn Dominguez & Jeffrey A. Frankel. LC 93-2923. 170p. 1993. pap. 18.00 (0-88132-104-4) Inst Intl Eco.

***Does France Still Count? The French Role in the New Europe.** Steven P. Kramer. LC 94-22127. (Washington Papers: Vol. 164). 128p. 1994. text ed. 45.00 (0-275-95060-3, Praeger Pubs); pap. text ed. 12.95 (0-275-95061-1, Praeger Pubs) Greenwood.

***Does Freddy Dance.** Dick Scanlan. 256p. 1995. 19.95 (1-55583-287-3) Alyson Pubns.

Does Freedom Work: Liberty & Justice in America. Donald J. Devine. LC 77-15914. (Illus.). 1978. pap. 5.95 (0-916054-56-X) Green Hill.

Does God Answer Prayer? Peter Baelz. (Illus.). 122p. (Orig.). 1983. pap. 9.95 (0-87243-117-7) Templegate.

Does God Belong in the Bedroom? Michael Gold. LC 92-11984. 236p. 1992. 22.95 (0-8276-0421-1) JPS Phila.

***Does God Care if I Can't Pay My Bills? Comfort & Encouragement for Tough Times.** Linda C. Taylor. LC 95-8009. 1995. write for info. (0-8423-1637-X) Tyndale.

Does God Change? The Word's Becoming in the Incarnation. Thomas Weinandy. LC 84-26241. (Studies in Historical Theology). 1985. pap. 15.95 (0-932506-42-9) St Bedes Pubns.

Does God Delight in Me? Betty N. Edwards. 1988. pap. 6.25 (0-89137-444-2) Quality Pubns.

Does God Eat Us? A Contemporary Response to Old Questions. Hilda Terry. (Illus.). 271p. (Orig.). (YA). 1991. pap. 8.88 (0-685-54234-3) Art Ltd.

Does God Exist? Sebastian Faure. 1972. lib. bdg. 59.95 (0-8490-0054-8) Gordon Pr.

Does God Exist? A Believer & an Atheist Debate. Terry Miethe & Antony G. Flew. LC 91-70040. 224p. (Orig.). 1991. pap. 12.95 (0-06-065579-8) Harper SF.

Does God Exist? An Answer for Today. Hans Kung. 864p. 1991. pap. 29.50 (0-8245-1119-0) Crossroad NY.

Does God Exist? The Debate Between Theists & Atheists. J. P. Moreland & Kai Nielsen. LC 92-41375. 320p. (C). 1993. reprint ed. pap. 16.95 (0-87975-823-6) Prometheus Bks.

Does God Have a Big Toe? Stories about Stories in the Bible. Marc Gellman. LC 89-1893. (Illus.). 96p. (J). (gr. 4 up). 1989. 16.00 (0-06-022432-0) HarpC Child Bks.

Does God Have a Big Toe? Stories about Stories in the Bible. Marc Gellman. LC 89-1893. (Trophy Bk.). (Illus.). 96p. (J). (gr. 4-6). 1993. pap. 7.95 (0-06-440453-6, Trophy) HarpC Child Bks.

Does God Have a Nature? Alvin Plantinga. LC 80-6585. (Aquinas Lectures). 1980. pap. 10.00 (0-87462-145-3) Marquette.

Does God Know How to Tie Shoes? Nancy W. Carlstrom. (Illus.). 40p. (J). (ps-3). 1993. 14.99 (0-8028-5074-X) Eerdmans.

Does God Live Here Anymore? Fran Sciacca & Jill Sciacca. (Lifelines Ser.). (YA). 1988. pap. 3.95 (0-89066-113-8) World Wide Pubs.

Does God Play Dice? The Mathematics of Chaos. Ian Stewart. (Illus.). 1990. pap. 14.95 (1-55786-106-4) Blackwell Pubs.

Does God Still Guide? J. Sidlow Baxter. 192p. 1991. pap. 9.99 (0-8254-2199-3) Kregel.

Does God Want Christians to Perform Miracles Today? John C. Whitcomb, Jr. 1979. pap. 1.50 (0-88469-016-4) BMH Bks.

***Does God Want to Spoil My Fun?** Edith Bajema. (In Spirit Ser.). 1994. pap. 12.00 (1-56212-080-8) CRC Pubns.

Does God's Existence Need Proof? Richard Messer. LC 92-45110. 180p. 1993. 35.00 (0-19-826747-9) OUP.

***Does "Independent" Mean "Free from Influence?" Escape Clause Decision-Making at the United States International Trade Commission.** David A. Butler. LC 94-45050. (Foreign Economic Policy of the United States Ser.). 193p. 1995. 55.00 (0-8153-1941-X) Garland.

Does It Belong? Barbara Gregorich. Ed. by Joan Hoffman. (Get Ready! Bks.). (Illus.). 32p. (J). (ps). 1983. student ed 1.99 (0-938256-59-9) Sch Zone Pub Co.

Does It Matter. Alan W. Watts. LC 72-89988. 1971. pap. 8.00 (0-394-71665-5, Vin) Random.

Does It Matter How I Live? Applying Biblical Beliefs to Your Daily Life. Millard J. Erickson. LC 94-5642. 192p. (Orig.). 1994. pap. 9.99 (0-8010-3223-7) Baker Bk.

Does It Matter What I Believe? What the Bible Teaches & Why We Should Believe It. Millard J. Erickson & Sandra McMaken. LC 92-5644. 192p. 1992. pap. 9.99 (0-8010-3214-8) Baker Bk.

Does It Pay to Advertise? Cases Illustrating Successful Brand Advertising. John P. Jones. LC 86-46382. 416p. 1989. text ed. 49.95 (0-669-15897-6) Free Pr.

Does It Pay to Die? How to Pick a Dead Man's Pocket! rev. ed. Michael A. Monji. 224p. 1994. reprint ed. student ed 9.99 (0-9627839-1-9) M Monji Assocs.

***Does Jacob's Trouble Wear a Cross? The Ancient Legacy of Christian Anti-Semitism.** Randall A. Weiss. 159p. (Orig.). (C). 1995. pap. 12.95 (1-57376-000-5) EICB.

Does Jesus Know Us? Do We Know Him? Hans Urs von Balthasar. Tr. by Graham Harrison. LC 82-84581. Orig. Title: Kennt Uns Jesus-Kennen wir Inn?. 99p. (Orig.). 1983. pap. 8.95 (0-89870-023-X) Ignatius Pr.

Does Jesus Make a Difference? Ed. by Thomas M. McFadden. 240p. reprint ed. pap. 22.50 (0-8191-4155-0) U Pr of Amer.

Does Khaki Become You? The Militarization of Women's Lives. Cynthia Enloe. 270p. 1988. pap. 12.95 (0-86358-301-6) Routledge Chapman & Hall.

Does Life Have a Meaning? Milton K. Munitz. 114p. 1993. 22.95x (0-87975-860-0) Prometheus Bks.

Does Macroeconomic Policy Matter? Evidence from Developing Countries. Stanley Fischer. (Occasional Papers: No. 27). 48p. (Orig.). 1993. pap. 9.95 (1-55815-223-7) ICS Pr.

Does Mass Communication Change Public Opinion After All? A New Approach to Effects Analysis. James B. Lemert. LC 80-23826. 260p. (C). 1981. text ed. 31.95 (0-88229-474-1) Nelson-Hall.

***Does Money Matter? The Link Between Schools, Student Achievement, & Adult Success.** Ed. by Gary Burtless. (Integrating National Economies: Promise & Pitfalls Ser.). 150p. (C). 1995. pap. 12.95x (0-8157-1275-8) Brookings.

Does Not Compute: The Computer Users Guide. Roy Massen & Dale Hodkinson. LC 84-50190. (Illus.). 96p. (Orig.). 1984. pap. 4.95 (0-916437-00-0) Sarcastic.

Does Ownership Matter? Japanese Multinationals in Europe. Ed. by Dennis Encarnation & Mark Mason. (Illus.). 488p. 1994. 49.95 (0-19-828827-1) OUP.

***Does Ownership Matter? Japanese Multinationals in Europe.** Ed. by Mark Mason & Dennis Encarnation. (Illus.). 488p. 1995. pap. 24.95 (0-19-829026-8) OUP.

Does Parole Make a Difference? Howard R. Sacks & Charles H. Logan. LC 78-68712. 120p. (Orig.). 1979. pap. 8.00 (0-939328-03-8) U CT Law Sch Found.

Does Pornography Matter? Ed. by Cecil R. Hewitt. LC 71-152175. (Essay Index Reprint Ser.). 1977. reprint ed. 18.95 (0-8369-2651-X) Ayer.

Does Privatization Deliver? Highlights from a World Bank Conference. Ed. by Ahmed Galal & Mary Shirley. LC 93-23358. (EDI Development Study Ser.). 140p. 1994. write for info. (0-8213-2589-2) World Bank.

Does Profit Sharing Pay? Bert Metzger & Jerome Colletti. LC 70-156486. 112p. 1971. 8.50 (0-911192-19-0, 1-006) Profit Sharing.

Does Psychiatry Need a Public Philosophy? Ed. by Don S. Browning & Ian S. Evison. 131p. (Orig.). 1991. 30.95 (0-8304-1244-1); pap. 19.95 (0-8304-1263-8) Nelson-Hall.

Does Redistricting Make a Difference? Partisan Representation & Electoral Behavior. Mark E. Rush. LC 93-6670. 232p. (C). 1993. text ed. 32.50 (0-8018-4579-3) Johns Hopkins.

***Does Religion Matter Morally?** Musschenga. 1993. pap. text ed. (0-8028-6177-6) Eerdmans.

Does Someone at Work Treat You Badly? Leonard Felder. 256p. (Orig.). 1993. mass mkt. 4.99 (0-425-13711-2) Berkley Pub.

Does Strategic Defense Breed Offense? Herbert York. LC 87-2107. 68p. 1987. lib. bdg. 29.00 (0-8191-6172-1, Ctr Intl Affairs Harvard); pap. text ed. 10.50 (0-8191-6173-X, Ctr Intl Affairs Harvard) U Pr of Amer.

***Does Stress Cause Psychiatric Illness?, 46.** Carolyn M. Mazure. LC 94-22178. (Progress in Psychiatry Ser.: Vol. 46). 1994. boxed write for info. (0-88048-482-9) Am Psychiatric.

Does Technology Drive History? The Dilemma of Technological Determinism. Ed. by Merritt R. Smith & Leo Marx. LC 93-21422. (Illus.). 410p. 1994. 37.50 (0-262-19347-7); pap. 17.95 (0-262-69167-1) MIT Pr.

Does the Bible Teach Millennialism. L. R. Thomas. pap. 3.99 (0-87377-084-6) GAM Pubns.

Does the Center Hold? An Introduction to Western Philosophy. Donald Palmer. 529p. 1991. pap. text ed. 22.95 (0-87484-911-X) Mayfield Pub.

Does the Church Really Want Religious Education? Ed. by Marlene Mayr. LC 87-35592. 267p. (C). 1988. pap. 17.95 (0-89135-062-4) Religious Educ.

Does the Floater Have a Future on the UKCS? Norman J. Smith. 1989. 160.00 (90-6314-510-1, Pub. by Lorne & MacLean Marine) St Mut.

Does the Floater Have a Future on the UKCS? Ed. by Norman J. Smith. (C). 1989. 95.00 (0-89771-721-X, Pub. by Lorne & MacLean Marine) St Mut.

Does the Moon Change Shape? Meish Goldish. (Real Readers Ser.: Level Blue). (Illus.). 32p. (J). (gr. 1-4). 1989. lib. bdg. 19.97 (0-8172-3518-3); pap. 3.95 (0-8114-6718-X) Raintree Steck-V.

Does the Wet Suit You? The Confessions of a Kayak Bum. Whit Deschner. LC 80-70510. (Illus.). 96p. 1981. pap. 6.45 (0-9605388-0-1) Tern Pr.

Does There Have to Be an Occasion? A Harvest of Pulpit Reflections. Maurice S. Cohen. LC 92-34025. 1992. 20.00 (0-88125-433-9) Ktav.

***Does Thinking Make It So?** John Chrisci. 71p. 1995. 8.95 (1-55630-079-4) Pison River Hse.

Does Third Grade Last Forever? Mindy Schanback. LC 89-20603. (Making the Grade Ser.). (Illus.). 96p. (J). (gr. 2-4). 1990. lib. bdg. 9.89 (0-8167-1700-1); pap. text ed. 2.95 (0-8167-1701-X) Troll Assocs.

Does Training Work for Displaced Workers? A Survey of Existing Evidence. Duane E. Leigh. LC 90-38433. 120p. 1990. text ed. 21.00 (0-88099-093-7); pap. text ed. 11.00 (0-88099-094-5) W E Upjohn.

Does Undernutrition Respond to Incomes & Prices? Dominance Tests for Indonesia. Martin Ravallion. (Living Standards Measurement Study Working Paper Ser.: No. 82). 44p. 1991. 6.95 (0-8213-1883-7, 11883) World Bank.

Does Who Governs Matter? Ed. by Moshe M. Czudnowski. LC 82-22495. (International Yearbook for Studies of Leaders & Leadership Ser.). 292p. 1982. pap. 12.50 (0-87580-529-9) N Ill U Pr.

Does Your Child Have Epilepsy? 2nd ed. James E. Jan et al. LC 90-27089. (For Interested Parents Ser.). (Illus.). 201p. 1991. pap. 22.00 (0-89079-456-1, 1948) PRO-ED.

Does Your Company Need Multimedia? How to Maximize the Commercial Benefits. Peter Chatterton. (Financial Times Management Ser.). 224p. 1993. 105.00x (0-273-60171-7, Pub. by Pitman Pub Ltd UK) Trans-Atl Phila.

Does Your Fiberglass Boat Need Repair? Virgil Strahm. LC 81-90093. (Illus.). 46p. (Orig.). pap. 5.00 (0-9606050-0-2) Strahm.

Does Your Marriage Suffer from TMS? (Traveling Mate Syndrome) Lois Marie. LC 92-93583. 105p. 1993. pap. 9.00 (0-9635410-0-5) Beginnings.

Does Your Resume Wear Apron Strings? C. Edward Good. 156p. (Orig.). 1989. pap. 7.95 (0-934961-04-2) Prima Pub.

Does Your Resume Wear Blue Jeans? C. Edward Good. 178p. (Orig.). 1985. pap. 8.95 (0-934961-00-X) Blue Jeans Pr.

Does Your Resume Wear Blue Jeans? High School Edition. C. Edward Good. 139p. (Orig.). (YA). (gr. 9-12). 1989. pap. 6.95 (0-934961-05-0) Prima Pub.

Does Your Resume Wear Blue Jeans? The Student's First Guide to Finding a Real Job. C. Edward Good & William G. Fitzpatrick. 225p. (Orig.). 1993. pap. 9.95 (1-55958-293-6) Prima Pub.

Does Your Resume Wear Combat Boots? William Fitzpatrick & C. Edward Good. 175p. (Orig.). 1990. pap. 7.95 (0-934961-07-7) Blue Jeans Pr.

Does Your Resume Wear Combat Boots? How to Turn Your Military Experience into a Good Civilian Job Offer. William G. Fitzpatrick & C. Edward Good. 225p. (Orig.). 1993. pap. 9.95 (1-55958-294-4) Prima Pub.

Does Your Tongue Need Healing. Derek Prince. 112p. 1992. pap. 3.99 (0-88368-239-7) Whitaker Hse.

***Doesn't Allah's Beautiful Names Changes Things (Sister to Sister)? When to Say the Right One of Allah's Attributes to Need in Prayer.** Yuhaayaa L. Kaahena. Ed. by Latifa Ismail. 86p. (Orig.). 1994. pap. 5.00 (1-883781-07-8) Yuhaaya.

Doesn't Anyone Care about the Children? Includes Excerpts from the 1994 Harry Singer Foundation Essay Contest. Harry Singer Foundation Staff. Ed. by M. Bohannon-Kaplan. LC 94-60872. 200p. (Orig.). 1994. pap. text ed. 8.00 (0-915915-29-4) Wellington Pubns.

Doesn't Everyone...? Suzanne Topper. (Orig.). 1976. pap. 1.75 (0-8439-0338-4, LB338DK) Dorchester Pub Co.

Doesn't Fall off His Horse. Virginia A. Stroud. (Illus.). (J). 1994. 14.99 (0-8037-1634-6); lib. bdg. 14.89 (0-8037-1635-4) Dial Bks Young.

Doesticks. Mortimer E. Thomson. LC 86-1882. 1986. reprint ed. 50.00 (0-8201-1411-1) Schol Facsimiles.

Dog. (Ultimate Sticker Ser.). (J). (ps-3). 1993. pap. 6.95 (1-56458-242-6) Dorling Kindersley.

Dog. Robert J. Blake. LC 92-39313. (Illus.). 32p. (J). (ps-3). 1994. 14.95 (0-399-22019-4, Philomel Bks) Putnam Pub Group.

***Dog.** John Burningham. LC 93-10344. (Illus.). (J). 1995. pap. 2.99 (1-56402-435-0) Candlewick Pr.

Dog. Juliet Clutton-Brock. LC 91-10135. (Eyewitness Bks.). (Illus.). 64p. (J). (gr. 5 up). 1991. 17.00 (0-679-81459-0) Knopf Bks Yng Read.

Dog. Juliet Clutton-Brock. LC 91-10135. (Eyewitness Bks.). (Illus.). 64p. (J). (gr. 5 up). 1991. lib. bdg. 16.99 (0-679-91459-5) Knopf Bks Yng Read.

Dog. Joan Korea & Gene Korea. Ed. & Illus. by Joan Abell. 50p. (J). Date not set. 25.00 (1-56611-048-3); pap. 15.00 (1-56611-049-1) Jonas.

Dog. Kwok Man-Ho. LC 93-48006. (Chinese Horoscopes Library). (Illus.). 48p. 1994. 8.95 (1-56458-601-4) Dorling Kindersley.

Dog. Giovanna Mantegazza. (J). (ps). 1993. 6.95 (1-56397-200-X) Boyds Mills Pr.

Dog. Juan Wijngaard. LC 90-81895. (Baby Animal Board Bks.). (Illus.). 12p. (J). (ps). 1991. bds. 3.95 (0-517-58203-1) Crown Bks Yng Read.

Dog. 2nd ed. John Burningham. LC 93-10344. 24p. (J). (ps). 1994. 6.95 (1-56402-326-5) Candlewick Pr.

Dog: Its Domestication & Behavior. Michael W. Fox. LC 86-27649. 304p. 1987. reprint ed. lib. bdg. 28.50 (0-89464-202-2) Krieger.

Dog about Town: Keeping a Dog in the City - Myths, Facts & Advice. Pat Farley. (Illus.). 240p. 1988. pap. 8.95 (0-671-63925-0, Fireside) S&S Trade.

Dog Ailments: Recognition & Treatment. 4th ed. Eddie Straiton. (Illus.). 216p. 1989. reprint ed. 27.95 (0-85236-194-7, Pub. by Farming Pr UK) Diamond Farm Bk.

Dog Anatomy. Robert F. Way. LC 74-75114. (Illus.). 1974. pap. 5.95 (0-88376-054-1) Dreenan Pr.

Dog, & a Frog. Mercer Mayer. (J). (ps-3). 1992. pap. 3.99 (0-14-054611-1) Viking Child Bks.

Dog & Cat. Paul Fehiner. LC 90-30164. (My First Reader Ser.). (Illus.). 28p. (J). (ps-2). 1990. lib. bdg. 11.25 (0-516-05353-1); pap. 3.95 (0-516-45353-X) Childrens.

Dog & Cat. Lynn Reiser. LC 90-3553. (Illus.). 24p. (J). (ps up). 1991. 13.95 (0-688-09892-4); lib. bdg. 13.88 (0-688-09893-2) Greenwillow.

Dog & Cat Nutrition: A Handbook for Students, Veterinarians, Breeders & Owners. Ed. by A. T. Edney. (Illus.). 124p. 1982. text ed. 35.00 (0-08-028891-X, Pergamon Pr); pap. text ed. 16.25 (0-08-028890-1, Pergamon Pr) Elsevier.

Dog & Gun: A Few Loose Chapters on Shooting. Johnson J. Hooper. (Library of Alabama Classics). 1992. pap. 9.95 (0-8173-0561-0) U of Ala Pr.

Dog & Man: The Story of a Friendship. Alfred P. Sloan, Jr. & A. Farquhar. LC 70-177510. (Illus.). 1972. reprint ed. 23.95 (0-405-08981-3) Ayer.

Dog & Pony Shows: How to Make Winning Presentations When the Stakes Are High. John Quick. 1992. pap. text ed. 16.95 (0-07-051077-6) McGraw.

Dog & Puppies. Hill. Ed. by Karen Goaman. (Pets Ser.). (Illus.). (J). (gr. 2-5). 1983. pap. 4.50 (0-86020-646-7) EDC.

Dog & the Bone. Alice H. Garside. (Garside Readers Ser.). (Illus.). 14p. (Orig.). (J). (gr. k-2). 1990. pap. 2.10 (1-882063-11-2) Cottage Pr MA.

Dog & the Fleas, by One of the Dogs. Frederic Scrimshaw. 1976. lib. bdg. 150.00 (0-8490-1729-7) Gordon Pr.

Dog & the Wolf. Alice H. Garside. (Garside Readers Ser.). (Illus.). 20p. (Orig.). (J). (gr. k-2). 1990. pap. 2.10 (1-882063-08-2) Cottage Pr MA.

Dog Anthem. Amnon Katz. (Illus.). 8p. (Orig.). 1985. pap. 1.00 (0-938245-00-7) Inverted-A.

***Dog Ate My Car Keys: And Other Great Excuses Not to Go to Work.** Sherrie Weaver. 366p. (Orig.). 1995. pap. 5.95 (1-56245-181-2) Great Quotations.

Dog Ate My Homework. Carmen Caserta & Marilyn Nowitz. LC 94-75987. (Illus.). 32p. 1994. 9.95 (1-880851-14-8) Greene Bark Pr.

Dog Ate My Homework. Sara Holbrook. 44p. (J). (gr. 4-8). 1990. pap. 6.95 (1-881786-00-5) Kid Poems.

Dog Bark. Gene Mullins. Tr. by Ingram. 212p. 1994. pap. 7.95 (1-56901-340-3) NW Pub.

Dog Behavior. Ian Dunbar. (Illus.). 224p. 1989. 14.95 (0-86622-800-4, H-1016) TFH Pubns.

Dog Bite. Irene Ledwith. 1988. pap. 10.00 (0-932526-20-9) Nexus Pr.

Dog Bites! Rick Reynolds & Martha Reynolds. 96p. (Orig.). 1992. pap. 8.95 (0-425-13511-X) Berkley Pub.

Dog Blue Day: An Anthology of Writing from the Penitentiary of New Mexico. Inmates of the New Mexico State Penitentiary Staff. Ed. by John Brandi. (Poetry Anthology Ser.). (Illus.). 40p. 1985. pap. 5.00 (0-940510-12-X) Tooth of Time.

***Dog Book.** Ariel Bks. Staff. (Illus.). 40p. 1995. 6.95 (0-8362-4736-1) Andrews & McMeel.

Dog Book, 2 vols., Set. James Watson. 1992. lib. bdg. 289.95 (0-8490-5243-2) Gordon Pr.

Dog Boy Cap Skate. Nicki Weiss. LC 88-16390. (Illus.). 32p. (J). (ps up). 1989. 11.95 (0-688-08275-0); lib. bdg. 11.88 (0-688-08276-9) Greenwillow.

Dog Breath! The Horrible Terrible Trouble with Hally Tosis. Dav Pilkey. LC 93-43405. (J). 1994. 12.95 (0-590-47466-9, Blue Sky Press) Scholastic Inc.

Dog Breeders' Organizer. Muriel P. Lee. LC 83-62667. (Illus.). 1984. pap. 5.95 (0-9612546-1-0) Plantin Pr.

***Dog Breeding: The Theory & the Practice.** Frank Jackson. (Illus.). 208p. 1995. 39.95 (1-85223-794-5, Pub. by Crowood Pr UK) Trafalgar.

Dog Breeding for Professionals. Herbert Richards. (Illus.). 1978. 17.95 (0-86622-655-9, H969) TFH Pubns.

***Dog Called Dad.** John Bianchi & Frank B. Edwards. (Illus.). 24p. 1994. pap. 4.95 (0-921285-34-5, Pub. by Bungalo Bks CN) Firefly Bks Ltd.

***Dog Called Dad.** John Bianchi & Frank B. Edwards. (Illus.). 24p. 1994. lib. bdg. 14.95 (0-921285-35-3, Pub. by Bungalo Bks CN) Firefly Bks Ltd.

Dog Called Kitty. Bill Wallace. LC 80-16293. 160p. (J). (gr. 3-7). 1980. 14.95 (0-8234-0376-9) Holiday.

Dog Called Kitty. Bill Wallace. (J). (gr. 4-7). 1991. pap. 3.50 (0-671-74389-9, Archway) PB.

Dog Called Kitty. Bill Wallace. (J). (gr. 4-7). 1992. pap. 3.50 (0-671-77081-0, Minstrel Bks) PB.

Dog Called Mischief. Leslie Wood. (Illus.). 16p. (J). 1987. pap. 3.50 (0-19-272155-0) OUP.

Dog Came, Too: A True Story. Ainslie Manson. LC 91-44891. (Illus.). 32p. (J). (gr. 1-5). 1993. text ed. 13.95 (0-689-50567-1, McElderry) S&S Childrens.

***Dog Care.** (DK 101 Ser.). (Illus.). 80p. 1995. pap. 6.95 (1-56458-989-7) Dorling Kindersley.

Dog Care. Boy Scouts of America. (Illus.). 48p. (J). (gr. 6-12). 1984. pap. 1.85 (0-8395-3289-X, 33289) BSA.

Dog Care Book. 2nd rev. ed. Sheldon L. Gerstenfeld. 1989. pap. 14.42 (0-201-09667-6) Addison-Wesley.

Dog Care Manual. David Alderton. (Illus.). 160p. 1986. 19.95 (0-8120-5764-3) Barron.

Dog City: The Big Squeak. Jim Henson. (J). (ps-3). 1994. pap. 2.25 (0-307-12845-8, Golden Pr) Western Pub.

***Dog Collar Crime.** Cleary. 1993. mass mkt. 4.50 (0-425-14857-2) Berkley Pub.

Dog Collar Crime. Melissa Cleary. 192p. (Orig.). 1993. pap. 3.99 (1-55773-896-3) Diamond.

Dog Collar Murders. Barbara Wilson. LC 88-27016. 203p. (Orig.). 1989. pap. 9.95 (1-878067-25-7) Seal Pr Feminist.

D

An Asterisk (*) at the beginning of an entry indicates that the title is appearing in BIP for the first time.

An Asterisk (*) at the beginning of an entry indicates that the title is appearing in BIP for the first time.

D

Dog Who Wouldn't Be Left Behind. Joan Finnigan. (Illus.). 32p. (J). (ps-2). 1991. 12.95 (*0-88899-057-X*, Pub. by Groundwood-Douglas & McIntyre CN) Firefly Bks Ltd.

Dog Wizard. Barbara Hambly. (Windrose Chronicles Ser.: Bk. 3). 1992. mass mkt. 4.99 (*0-345-37714-1*, Del Rey) Ballantine.

***Dog Years.** Denisoff. Date not set. per. 9.95 (*0-88978-234-2*, Pub. by Arsenal Pulp CN) InBook.

Dog Years. Gunter Grass. 1986. mass mkt. 4.95 (*0-449-21192-4*, Crest) Fawcett.

Dog Years. Gunter Grass. 1989. pap. 12.95 (*0-15-626112-X*) HarBrace.

***Dog Years.** Sally Warner. LC 94-25457. (J). 1995. 13.00 (*0-679-87147-0*) Knopf.

Dogansay: Walls. Frederick T. Castle & Necmi Sonmez. Tr. by Ipek A. Duben. (Illus.). 60p. (Orig.). 1993. pap. write for info. (*0-932169-25-2*) Tenth Ave Edit.

Dogbert's Clues for the Clueless: All-New Original Cartoons Featuring Dogbert from the Nationally Syndicated Dilbert Strip. Scott Adams. (Illus.). 112p. (Orig.). 1993. pap. 7.95 (*0-8362-1737-3*) Andrews & McMeel.

Doge of Venice: The Symbolism of State Power in the Renaissance. Asa Boholm. (University of Gothenburg Institute for Advanced Studies in Social Anthropology). (Illus.). 298p. (Orig.). 1990. pap. 79.00x (*91-630-0135-7*, Pub. by Almqv & Wiksell SW) Coronet Bks.

Dogeater: Stories. Jesse L. Kercheval. LC 86-25066. 104p. (Orig.). 1987. pap. 10.95 (*0-8262-0632-8*, 83-36380) U of Mo Pr.

Dogeaters. Jessica Hagedorn. (Contemporary American Fiction Ser.). 272p. 1991. pap. 10.95 (*0-14-014904-X*, Penguin Bks) Viking Penguin.

Dogen & the Koan Tradition: A Tale of Two Shobogenzo Texts. Steven Heine. LC 93-18446. (SUNY Series in Philosophy & Psychotherapy). 329p. 1993. 57.50 (*0-7914-1773-5*); pap. 18.95 (*0-7914-1774-3*) State U NY Pr.

Dogen Kigen: Mystical Realist. rev. ed. Hee-Jin Kim. LC 87-10928. 324p. 1987. pap. 21.95 (*0-8165-1025-3*) U of Ariz Pr.

***Dogen Kigen, Mystical Realist.** fac. ed. Hee-Jin Kim. LC 74-33725. (Association for Asian Studies, Monographs & Papers: No. 29). 398p. 1994. pap. 113.50 (*0-7837-7673-X*, 2047426) Bks Demand.

Dogen Studies. Ed. by William R. LaFleur. LC 85-16427. (Studies in East Asian Buddhism: No. 2). 288p. 1985. pap. text ed. 19.00 (*0-8248-1011-2*) UH Pr.

Dogen, the Zen Master: A Search & a Fulfillment. Osho Rajneesh. Ed. by Swami Anand Burt. (Zen Ser.). 204p. 1989. 14.95 (*3-89338-063-9*, Pub. by Rebel Hse GW) Osho Chidvilas.

Dogen's Manuals of Zen Meditation. Carl Bielefeldt. 267p. 1988. pap. 15.00 (*0-520-06835-1*) U CA Pr.

Dogen's Manuals of Zen Meditation. Carl Bielefeldt. 336p. (C). 1988. 45.00 (*0-520-06056-3*) U CA Pr.

***Dogen's Pure Standards for the Zen Community: A Translation of Eihei Shingi.** Ed. & Tr. by Taigen D. Leighton. Tr. by Shohaku Okumura. (Buddhist Studies Ser.). 258p. (C). 1995. text ed. 59.50x (*0-7914-2709-9*) State U NY Pr.

***Dogen's Pure Standards for the Zen Community: A Translation of Eihei Shingi.** Ed. & Tr. by Taigen D. Leighton. Tr. by Shohaku Okumura. (Buddhist Studies Ser.). 258p. (C). 1995. pap. text ed. 19.95x (*0-7914-2710-2*) State U NY Pr.

Dogfaces Who Smiled Through Tears. Homer R. Ankrum. LC 87-72129. 661p. 1987. text ed. 24.95 (*0-89279-080-6*) Graphic Pub.

Dogfaces Who Smiled Through Tears. 2nd rev. ed. Homer R. Ankrum. LC 88-81739. 676p. 1988. reprint ed. 27.50 (*0-89279-081-4*) Graphic Pub.

Dogfight: The Transatlantic Battle over Airbus. Ian McIntyre. LC 92-168. 336p. 1992. text ed. 45.00 (*0-275-94278-3*, C4278, Praeger Pubs) Greenwood.

Dogfish. Susan Geason. 208p. (Orig.). 1993. pap. 9.95 (*1-86373-088-5*, Pub. by Allen & Unwin Aust Pty AT) IPG Chicago.

Dogfish Dissection Manual. Bruce D. Wingerd. (Laboratory Dissection Ser.). (Illus.). 80p. (Orig.). (C). 1989. pap. text ed. 9.95x (*0-8018-3709-X*) Johns Hopkins.

Dogged Victims of Inexorable Fate. Dan Jenkins. (Classics of Golf Ser.). 298p. 1985. 28.00 (*0-940889-03-X*) Classics Golf.

Dogger. Shirley Hughes. LC 87-33787. (Illus.). 32p. (J). (ps-2). 1988. 15.00 (*0-688-07980-6*); lib. bdg. 14.93 (*0-688-07981-4*) Lothrop.

Dogger. Shirley Hughes. LC 92-24602. (Illus.). 32p. (J). (ps up). 1993. reprint ed. pap. 4.95 (*0-688-11704-X*, Mulberry) Morrow.

Doggerel. George M. Henzel. (DOG-1 Ser.). (Illus.). 124p. (Orig.). (C). 1987. pap. 7.95 (*0-942611-00-4*) By George Pubns.

Doggerel for the Underdog. Joseph A. Labadie. (Men & Movements in the History & Philosophy of Anarchism Ser.). 1979. lib. bdg. 250.00 (*0-87700-308-4*) Revisionist Pr.

Doggerel in the Night-Time. Deborah Sage. (Illus.). 91p. (Orig.). pap. 10.95 (*0-938501-13-5*) Gasogene Pr.

Doggerel Too. George M. Henzel. (Illus.). 125p. (Orig.). 1989. pap. 7.95 (*0-942611-01-2*) By George Pubns.

Doggies. Sandra Boynton. (J). 1984. 3.95 (*0-671-49318-3*, Litl Simon S&S) S&S Childrens.

Doggone Mystery. Mary B. Christian. Ed. by Ann Fay. LC 80-10448. (First Read-Alone Mysteries Ser.). (Illus.). (J). (gr. 1-3). 1980. lib. bdg. 8.95 (*0-8075-1656-2*) A Whitman.

Doggonest Puppy Love. Richard L. Stack. (J). 1992. pap. 14.95 (*0-9628262-1-9*) Windmill MD.

Doggonest Vacation. Richard L. Stack. (J). 1991. write for info. (*0-9628262-0-0*) Windmill MD.

Doggy Bag: A Collection of Stories. Ronald Sukenick. (Black Ice Books Ser.). (Illus.). 128p. 1994. pap. 7.00 (*0-932511-82-1*) Fiction Coll.

Dogheaded Death. Ray F. Nelson. (Centurion Books). 184p. (Orig.). 1989. pap. 9.95 (*0-89407-079-7*) Strawberry Hill.

Doghouse. Jim Dawson. 224p. (Orig.). 1992. pap. 3.95 (*0-87067-379-3*) Holloway.

Dogleg Madness. Mike Bryan. 228p. 1990. pap. 8.95 (*0-87113-330-X*) Grove-Atltic.

Dogma, 6 vols., Set. Michael Schmaus. Incl. Vol. 1. God in Revelation. 1984. pap. 19.95 (*0-87061-098-8*); Vol. 2. God & Creation. 1984. pap. 16.95 (*0-87061-099-6*); Vol. 3. God & His Christ. 1984. pap. 15.95 (*0-87061-100-3*); Vol. 5. Church As Sacrament. 1984. pap. 24.95 (*0-87061-102-X*); Vol. 6. Justification of the Last Things. 1984. pap. 19.95 (*0-87061-103-8*); (C). 1984. Set pap. 105.00 (*0-87061-095-3*) Chr Classics.

Dogma & Compulsion. Theodor Reik. LC 72-9369. 332p. 1973. reprint ed. text ed. 65.00 (*0-8371-6577-6*, REDC, Greenwood Pr) Greenwood.

Dogma & Mysticism in Early Christianity: Epiphanius of Cyprus & the Legacy of Origen. Jon Dechow. 608p. (C). 1988. 25.00 (*0-86554-311-9*, MUP/H250) Mercer Univ Pr.

Dogma & Preaching. Joseph C. Ratzinger. Tr. by Matthew J. O'Connell. 1983. 5.95 (*0-8199-0819-3*, Frncscn Herld) Franciscan Pr.

Dogma in Medieval Jewish Thought: From Maimonides to Abravanel. Menachem Kellner. (Littman Library of Jewish Civilization). 324p. 1986. 25.00 (*0-19-710044-9*, Pub. by Littman Lib Jew UK) Bnai Brith Bk.

Dogma of Christ: And Other Essays on Religion, Psychology, & Culture. Erich Fromm. 224p. 1992. pap. 11.95 (*0-8050-1606-6*, Owl) H Holt & Co.

Dogma of the Battles of Annihilation: The Theories of Clausewitz & Schlieffen & Their Impact on the German Conduct of the Two World Wars. Jehuda L. Wallach. LC 84-27942. (Contributions in Military Studies). 343p. 1986. text ed. 59.95 (*0-313-24438-3*, WDO/) Greenwood.

***Dogman of Boggy Bottoms: A Biographical Sketch.** H. Clint Davis. 191p. 1994. 19.95 (*0-9641802-0-0*) Iluztrafix.

Dogmas & Dreams: Political Ideologies in the Modern World. Nancy S. Love. LC 90-19909. (Chatham House Studies in Political Thinking). 576p. (C). 1991. pap. text ed. 29.95x (*0-934540-84-5*) Chatham Hse Pubs.

Dogmat o Svjatejshej Evkharistii. Stefan Yavorsky. Ed. by Metropolitan Staff. 32p. reprint ed. pap. 1.00 (*0-317-28973-X*) Holy Trinity.

Dogmat Tserkvi v Sovrjemjennom Mire. George Grabbe. 1975. pap. 1.50 (*0-317-30381-3*) Holy Trinity.

Dogmatic & Mystical Theology of Donne. I. Husain. LC 70-119088. (Studies in Philosophy: No. 40). 1970. reprint ed. lib. bdg. 39.95 (*0-8383-1084-2*) M S G Haskell Hse.

Dogmatic & Mystical Theology of John Donne. Itrat Husain. LC 76-109753. 149p. 1970. reprint ed. text ed. 49.75 (*0-8371-4243-1*, HUJD, Greenwood Pr) Greenwood.

Dogmatic & Polemical Works. Jerome. LC 65-20802. (Fathers of the Church Ser.: Vol. 53). 405p. 1965. 21.95 (*0-8132-0053-9*) Cath U Pr.

Dogmatic Canons & Decrees of the Council of Trent, Vatican Council I, Plus the Decree on the Immaculate Conception & the Syllabus of Errors. Devin-Adair Staff. LC 79-112469. 1977. reprint ed. pap. 8.00 (*0-89555-018-0*) TAN Bks Pubs.

Dogmatic Constitution on the Church (Lumen Gentium) Vatican Council II, Staff. 94p. 1964. pap. 4.95 (*1-55586-000-1*) US Catholic.

Dogmatic Theology for the Laity. Mattias Premm. 1977. pap. 18.00 (*0-89555-022-9*) TAN Bks Pubs.

***Dogmatic Wisdom: How the Culture Wars Divert Education & Distract America.** Jacoby. 1995. pap. (*0-385-42517-1*, Anchor NY) Doubleday.

Dogmatic Wisdom: How the Education & Cultural Wars Have Misled America. Russell Jacoby. LC 93-36382. 1994. 22.95 (*0-385-42516-3*) Doubleday.

Dogmatics in Outline. Karl Barth. 1959. pap. text ed. 12.00 (*0-06-130056-X*, TB56, Torch) HarpC.

***Dogmatik.** Wilfried Haerle. xxviii, 719p. (GER.). (C). 1995. lib. bdg. 90.75 (*3-11-012686-9*) De Gruyter.

***Dogmatik.** Wilfried Haerle. (C). 1995. pap. text ed. 60.00 (*3-11-014895-1*) De Gruyter.

Dogmatik. 4th ed. Wolfgang Trillhaas. 543p. (C). 1972. 52.35 (*3-11-008423-6*) De Gruyter.

Dogmatism & Visual Loss. Phyllis N. Hallenbeck. (American Foundation for the Blind Research Ser.: No. 17). 118p. reprint ed. pap. 33.70 (*0-7837-0131-4*, 2027347) Bks Demand.

DogMinder. Monique Maniet. 98p. 1991. 19.95 (*0-914783-53-X*) Charles.

***Dogon.** Chukwuma Azuonye. LC 94-45814. (Heritage Library of African Peoples). (J). 1995. write for info. (*0-8239-1976-5*) Rosen Group.

Dogon Masks: A Structural Study of Form & Meaning. Barbara DeMott. LC 81-16308. (Studies in the Fine Arts: Iconography: No. 4). (Illus.). 220p. reprint ed. pap. 62.70 (*0-685-20820-6*, 2070035) Bks Demand.

***DogPerfect.** Sarah Hodgson. LC 95-15656. 1995. write for info. (*0-87605-534-X*) Howell Bk.

Dogs. (Colorguide Ser.). 1982. pap. 6.95 (*0-940842-15-7*) South Group.

***Dogs.** (J). 1983. 1.59 (*0-307-03093-8*, Golden Pr) Western Pub.

Dogs. Gwendolyn Albert. Ed. by Edward Mycue. (Took Modern Poetry in English Ser.: No. 13). (Illus.). 28p. (Orig.). 1991. pap. 5.00 (*1-879457-11-3*) Norton Coker Pr.

Dogs. David Alderton. LC 92-53450. (Eyewitness Handbks.). (Illus.). 320p. 1993. 29.95 (*1-56458-179-9*); 17.95 (*1-56458-176-4*) Dorling Kindersley.

Dogs. Ariel Books Staff. (Illus.). 80p. 1992. 4.95 (*0-8362-3017-5*) Andrews & McMeel.

Dogs. Wendy Boorer. LC 88-17653. (All about Bks.). (Illus.). 24p. (Orig.). (J). (gr. 2-5). 1989. lib. bdg. 5.99 (*0-394-99988-6*) Random Bks Yng Read.

Dogs, 2 vols. Mark Dunster. (Animals Ser.: Pt. 1). (Orig.). 1979. pap. 8.00 (*0-89642-058-2*) Linden Pubs.

Dogs. Walter Foster. (How to Draw & Paint Ser.). (Illus.). 32p. (Orig.). 1989. pap. 5.95 (*0-929261-71-2*, HT10) W Foster Pub.

***Dogs.** H. Glover. (Spotter's Guide Ser.). (Illus.). 64p. (J). (gr. 4 up). 1995. pap. 4.95 (*0-86020-253-4*, Usborne) EDC.

Dogs. P. Jameson. (Responsible Pet Care Ser.). (Illus.). 32p. (J). (gr. 2-5). 1989. 11.95 (*0-685-58610-3*); lib. bdg. 15.94 (*0-86625-184-7*) Rourke Corp.

Dogs. Teri C. Jones. (Childrens' Nature Library). (Illus.). 64p. (J). (gr. k-4). 1992. lib. bdg. 13.75 (*1-878363-83-2*, HTS Bks) Forest Hse.

Dogs. Ulrich Klever. (Mini Fact Finders Ser.). 64p. 1990. pap. 4.95 (*0-8120-4457-6*) Barron.

Dogs. Claudia Long & Britt Strader. 192p. 1994. 19.95 (*0-934429-73-1*) Thunder Bay CA.

Dogs. Peter Murray. (Nature Books Ser.). (J). (gr. 2-6). 1992. lib. bdg. 22.79 (*0-89565-848-8*) Childs World.

Dogs. Anne T. Perkins. (Big Books - Mini Bks.). (Illus.). 8p. (J). (ps-00). 1994. 12.00 (*1-884204-07-4*) Teach Nxt Door.

Dogs. Kate Petty. (First Pets Ser.). (Illus.). 24p. (J). (ps-3). 1993. pap. 3.95 (*0-8120-1484-7*) Barron.

Dogs. Fiona Pitt-Kethley. 84p. 1994. pap. 16.95 (*1-85619-285-7*, Sinclair-Stevenson) Trafalgar.

Dogs. Elsa Posell. LC 81-7742. (New True Bks.). (Illus.). 48p. (J). (gr. k-4). 1981. lib. bdg. 12.90 (*0-516-01614-8*); pap. 4.95 (*0-516-41614-6*) Childrens.

Dogs. Yvonne Rees. (Nature Library). (Illus.). 64p. (J). 1991. 4.99 (*0-517-05152-4*) Random Hse Value.

Dogs. Peggy Roalf. LC 93-10585. (Looking at Paintings Ser.). (Illus.). (J). (gr. 3-7). 1993. lib. bdg. 14.89 (*1-56282-531-3*) Hyprn Child.

Dogs. Peggy Roalf. LC 93-20585. (Looking at Paintings Ser.). (Illus.). 48p. (J). (gr. 3-7). 1993. lib. bdg. 14.89 (*1-56282-530-5*); pap. 6.95 (*0-685-70878-0*) Hyprn Ppbks.

Dogs. David Squire. 1988. 7.98 (*1-55521-219-0*) Bk Sales Inc.

***Dogs.** Laura Thompson. Date not set. 6.99 (*0-09-944871-8*) Random.

Dogs, 3 Vols., I. Jeanne Eichling. (Illus.). 48p. 1982. write for info. (*0-88014-051-8*) Mosaic Pr OH.

Dogs, 3 Vols., II. Jeanne Eichling. (Illus.). 48p. 1982. write for info. (*0-88014-052-6*) Mosaic Pr OH.

Dogs, 3 Vols., III. Jeanne Eichling. (Illus.). 48p. 1982. write for info. (*0-88014-053-4*) Mosaic Pr OH.

Dogs, 3 Vols., Set. Jeanne Eichling. (Illus.). 48p. 1982. 65.00 (*0-88014-050-X*) Mosaic Pr OH.

Dogs: A Complete Guide to More Than 200 Breeds. LC 93-85521. (Illus.). 240p. (YA). 1994. pap. 5.95 (*1-56138-382-1*) Running Pr.

Dogs: A Manual for Amateurs. M. De Salis. 1992. lib. bdg. 79.00 (*0-8490-5271-8*) Gordon Pr.

Dogs: A Personal History of Greyhound Racing. Laura Thompson. (Illus.). 254p. 1994. pap. 22.95 (*0-7011-3872-6*, Pub. by Chatto & Windus UK) Trafalgar.

***Dogs: A Postcard Book.** Tony Mendoza. (Illus.). 32p. (Orig.). 1995. pap. 8.95 (*0-88496-397-7*) Capra Pr.

Dogs: All about Them. Alvin Silverstein & Virginia Silverstein. LC 84-29723. (Illus.). 256p. (J). (gr. 6 up). 1986. 16.00 (*0-688-04805-6*) Lothrop.

Dogs: An Educational Coloring Book. Spizzirri Publishing Co. Staff. Ed. by Linda Spizzirri. (Illus.). 32p. (J). (gr. 1-8). 1986. pap. 1.75 (*0-86545-076-5*) Spizzirri.

***Dogs: Homoeopathic Remedies.** MacLeod. 1995. pap. 13.95 (*0-85207-218-X*) Atrium Pubs.

Dogs: Homoeopathic Remedies. George Macleod. 156p. (Orig.). 1990. pap. 20.95 (*0-8464-1334-5*) Beekman Pubs.

Dogs: How to Take Care of Them & Understand Them. Monika Wegler. LC 92-5794. (Illus.). 1992. pap. 5.95 (*0-8120-4822-9*) Barron.

Dogs: Look & Learn. Herbert Richards. (Illus.). 64p. 1993. 7.95 (*0-7938-0066-8*, KD005) TFH Pubns.

***Dogs: Our Faithful Friends.** Intervisual Books Staff. (Illus.). 10p. 1995. 4.95 (*0-8362-0046-2*) Andrews & McMeel.

Dogs: The Wolf Within. Dorothy H. Patent. LC 92-12334. (Understanding Animal Behavior Ser.). (J). (gr. 4-6). 1992. 19.95 (*0-87614-691-4*, Carolrhoda) Lerner Group.

Dogs: The Wolf Within. Dorothy H. Patent. (J). (gr. 4-6). 1993. pap. 7.95 (*0-87614-604-3*, Carolrhoda) Lerner Group.

Dogs: Their Care & Training. C. R. Acton. 1992. lib. bdg. 79.95 (*0-8490-5218-1*) Gordon Pr.

Dogs: Their History & Development, 2 vols., 1. Edward C. Ash. LC 72-79945. 1972. 30.95 (*0-405-08219-3*, Pub. by Blom Pubns UK) Ayer.

Dogs: Their History & Development, 2 vols., 2. Edward C. Ash. LC 72-79945. 1972. 27.95 (*0-405-08220-7*, Pub. by Blom Pubns UK) Ayer.

Dogs: Their History & Development, 2 vols., Set. Edward C. Ash. LC 72-79945. 1972. 55.95 (*0-405-08218-5*, Pub. by Blom Pubns UK) Ayer.

Dogs & Dragons, Trees & Dreams: A Collection of Poems. Karla Kuskin. LC 79-2814. (Illus.). 96p. (J). (gr. 1-6). 1980. lib. bdg. 14.89 (*0-06-023544-6*) HarpC Child Bks.

Dogs & Dragons, Trees & Dreams: A Collection of Poems. Karla Kuskin. LC 79-2814. (Trophy Nonfiction Bk.). (Illus.). 96p. (J). (gr. k-3). 1992. pap. 4.95 (*0-06-446122-X*, Trophy) HarpC Child Bks.

Dogs & How to Know Them. Edward C. Ash. 1991. lib. bdg. 79.95 (*0-8490-5214-9*) Gordon Pr.

Dogs & Kids: A Guide for Parents. Bardi McLennan. (Illus.). 240p. 1993. 18.95 (*0-87605-535-8*) Howell Bk.

Dogs & Men. Mary Ansell. LC 70-142257. (Short Story Index Reprint Ser.). 1977. 17.95 (*0-8369-3741-4*) Ayer.

Dogs & Puppies. LC 90-80292. (Animal Photo Bks.). (Illus.). 24p. (Orig.). (J). (ps-2). 1991. pap. 1.95 (*1-56288-075-6*) Checkerboard.

Dogs & Puppies. (Color & Story Bks.). (Illus.). 32p. (Orig.). (J). (gr. 1-6). 1983. pap. 4.50 (*0-8431-1700-1*, Troubador) Price Stern.

Dogs & the Law. Anmarie Barrie. (Illus.). 160p. 1989. lib. bdg. 9.95 (*0-86622-088-7*, TS-130) TFH Pubns.

***Dogs & the People They Own.** Lillian Lidofsky, pseud. LC 94-31192. 144p. (Orig.). 1995. pap. 8.00 (*0-399-51944-0*, Perigree Bks) Berkley Pub.

Dogs & Their Women. Barbara Cohen & Louise Taylor. (Illus.). 128p. (Orig.). 1989. pap. 12.95 (*0-316-15036-3*) Little.

***Dog's Best Friend.** Massimo Mostacchi. LC 95-8434. (Illus.). (J). 1995. write for info. (*1-55858-497-8*) North-South Bks NYC.

***Dog's Best Friend.** Massimo Mostacchi. LC 95-8434. (Illus.). (J). 1995. lib. bdg. write for info. (*1-55858-498-6*) North-South Bks NYC.

Dog's Body. Joanna Cole. LC 85-25885. (Illus.). 48p. (J). (ps-3). 1986. lib. bdg. 14.93 (*0-688-04154-X*) Morrow Jr Bks.

Dog's Body. large type ed. Janet Edmonds. 1989. 17.95 (*0-7089-2182-5*) Ulverscroft.

Dogs Can Be Vegetarians Too Cookbook. Gentle World. Ed. by Melinda Patnoi. 1988. 4.00 (*0-9614248-6-9*) Gentle World.

Dogs, Cats, & Horses: A Resource Guide to the Literature for Young People. Charlene Strickland. (Data Book Ser.). 225p. 1990. lib. bdg. 26.50 (*0-87287-719-1*) Libs Unl.

Dogs, Dogs & More Dogs: A Teacher's Resource Book of Dogs. Patricia A. Welsh. 42p. 1989. pap. text ed. 7.95 (*1-884620-06-X*) PAW Prods.

Dogs Don't Tell Jokes. Louis Sachar. LC 91-2042. 176p. (J). (gr. 5-9). 1991. lib. bdg. 14.99 (*0-679-92017-X*) Knopf Bks Yng Read.

Dogs Don't Wear Sneakers. Laura J. Numeroff. LC 92-27007. (Illus.). (J). 1993. pap. 14.00 (*0-671-79525-2*, S&S Bks Young Read) S&S Childrens.

Dogs for Pathfinders: A Basic Youth Enrichment Skill Honor Packet. L. S. Gattis, III. (Illus.). 20p. (Orig.). (J). (gr. 5 up). 1987. teacher ed, pap. 5.00 (*0-936241-24-1*) Cheetah Pub.

Dogs for Police Service: Programming & Training. Sam D. Watson, Jr. (Illus.). 100p. 1972. 22.95 (*0-398-02025-6*) C C Thomas.

Dogs Found in the Writings of Charles Dickens. John A. Donovan. (Other Dog Bks.). (Illus.). 1989. 12.95 (*0-87714-141-X*) Denlingers.

Dogs from a Sufi Point of View. Javad Nurbakhsh. Tr. by Terry Graham et al. (Illus.). 100p. 1989. pap. 11.95 (*0-933546-39-4*) KNP.

***Dogs from Illusion.** Illus. by Hiram Alvarez. 199p. 1994. pap. 11.95 (*0-9624536-5-X*) Chusma Hse.

Dogs, Geese, & Grizzly Bears: A Lifetime of Talking to Critters. Charlie Elliot. 1992. 17.95 (*1-879034-10-7*) MS River Pub.

***Dogs' Guide to New York City with Jack, the City Dog: With over 200 Wonderful Walks, Outings, Activities, Getaways & Places You Never Thought You Could Take Your Pooch.** Jane M. Rohman. (Illus.). 200p. (Orig.). 1994. pap. 14.95 (*0-9641824-0-8*) Richmond Pr.

Dogs Have Paws. (Illus.). (J). (ps-2). 1991. lib. bdg. 6.95 (*0-8136-5122-0*); pap. 3.50 (*0-8136-5622-2*) Modern Curr.

Dogs in an Omnibus. Gladys B. Stern. LC 79-125238. (Short Story Index Reprint Ser.). (Illus.). 1977. 19.95 (*0-8369-3605-1*) Ayer.

Dogs in Art. (Illus.). mass mkt. 6.95 (*0-449-90419-9*, Columbine) Fawcett.

Dogs in Britain: A Description of All Native Breeds & Most Foreign Breeds in Britain, Breeding, Training & Management. Clifford Hubbard. 1991. lib. bdg. 88.95 (*0-8490-5224-6*) Gordon Pr.

Dogs in Dickens. Cumberland Clark. LC 73-9642. (Studies in Dickens: No. 52). 1973. reprint ed. lib. bdg. 40.95 (*0-8383-1713-8*) M S G Haskell Hse.

Dogs in Lingerie. Danielle Willis. (Illus.). 75p. (Orig.). 1990. pap. 5.95 (*0-929730-22-4*) Zeitgeist Pr.

***Dogs in Marin: A Reference Guide for Marin County Dog Owners.** Kristin Lund. 200p. 1994. pap. 9.95 (*0-9643445-0-5*) Lundehund Pr.

Dogs in My Home: Tips on Handling More Than One Dog. F. F. Kotes. LC 91-67327. 80p. (Orig.). 1991. pap. 13.95 (*0-9615541-9-3*, Valley Hse Bks) Martin Mgmt.

Dogs in Shakespeare. John A. Donovan. LC 79-55728. (Other Dog Bks.). (Illus.). 1980. 12.95 (*0-87714-074-X*) Denlingers.

Dogs in Space. Nancy Coffelt. (Illus.). 32p. (J). (ps-3). 1993. 14.95 (*0-15-200440-8*) HarBrace.

Dogs in the News. Ed. by Alan F. Pater & Jason R. Pater. 1984. 17.50 (*0-917734-11-4*) Monitor Bk.

Dog's Life. Hans Bayer. Ed. & Tr. by Ray Miller, Jr. LC 93-17843. (Illus.). 180p. (C). 1993. lib. bdg. 48.50 (*0-8191-9140-X*); pap. text ed. 26.50 (*0-8191-9141-8*) U Pr of Amer.

Dog's Life. Henry Horenstein. 1986. 12.95 (*0-02-554160-9*) Macmillan.

An Asterisk (*) at the beginning of an entry indicates that the title is appearing in BIP for the first time.

***Dog's Life.** Peter Mayle. 1995. 20.00 (*0-679-44122-0*) Knopf.

Dog's Life: The History, Culture, & Everyday Life of the Dog. Amy Shojai. LC 94-9540. 1994. write for info. (*1-56799-112-2*, Friedman-Fairfax) M Friedman Pub Grp Inc.

Dog's Life in the Dales. large type ed. Katy Cropper. (Large Print Ser.). (Illus.). 448p. 1994. 21.95 (*0-7089-3003-4*) Ulverscroft.

***Dogs Love to Please...We Teach Them How! The Safe & Gentle Guide to Dog Obedience Through Interspecies Communication.** 4th rev. ed. September B. Morn. (Illus.). 248p. 1994. per., pap. 15.95 (*0-9633884-1-X*) Pawprince Pr.

Dogs Love to Please...We Teach Them How! The Safe & Gentle Guide to Dog Obedience Training Through Interspecies Communication. 3rd rev. ed. September B. Morn. (Illus.). 144p. 1992. pap. text ed. 15.00 (*0-9633884-0-1*) Pawprince Pr.

Dog's Mind: Understanding Your Dog's Behavior. Bruce Fogle. (Illus.). 224p. 1992. pap. 15.00 (*0-87605-513-7*) Howell Bk.

Dogs Need Our Love. Jack L. Tuttle. LC 82-82567. 1983. 10.95 (*0-87212-163-1*) Libra.

Dogs of Capitalism: Origins, Bk. 1. Mitchell Jones. 336p. 1988. 19.95 (*1-882719-00-X*) Twnty-Frst Cent Logic.

Dogs of God. Pinckney Benedict. LC 93-12565. 1994. 21.00 (*0-385-42022-6*) Doubleday.

***Dogs of God.** Pinckney Benedict. LC 94-32008. 368p. 1995. pap. 10.95 (*0-452-27370-6*, Plume) NAL-Dutton.

Dogs of March. Ernest Hebert. LC 78-26869. 255p. 1979. 25.00 (*0-89366-144-9*) Ultramarine Pub.

***Dogs of Our Lives: Heartwarming Celebrity Reminiscences of Canine Companions.** Comp. by Louise G. Murray. (Illus.). 256p. 1995. 17.95 (*1-55972-289-4*, Birch Ln Pr) Carol Pub Group.

Dogs of Paradise. Abel Posse. Tr. by Margaret S. Peden. 196p. 1990. text ed. 9.95 (*0-689-12091-5*, Pub. by Ctrl Bur voor Schimmel NE) Macmillan.

Dogs of Rudyard Kipling. John A. Donovan. (Illus.). 1991. 12.95 (*0-87714-158-4*) Denlingers.

Dogs of the American Indians. William Pferd, III. Ed. by William W. Denlinger & R. Annabel Rathman. LC 87-432. (Other Dog Bks.). (Illus.). 192p. 1987. 19.95 (*0-87714-126-6*) Denlingers.

Dogs of the Conquest. John G. Varner & Jeannette J. Varner. LC 83-47840. (Illus.). 256p. 1983. 26.95 (*0-8061-1793-1*) U of Okla Pr.

Dogs of the North. Ed. by Alaska Geographic Staff. (Alaska Geographic Ser.: Vol. 14, No. 1). (Illus.). 120p. 1987. pap. 17.95 (*0-88240-180-7*) Alaska Geog Soc.

Dogs of the Northeastern Woodland Indians. Eva M. Butler & Wendell S. Hadlock. (Robert Abbe Museum Bulletin Ser.: No. XIII). 54p. 1994. reprint ed. pap. write for info. (*1-885410-02-6*) R Abbe Museum.

Dogs of the Wild: An Educational Coloring Book. pap. 1.75 (*0-86545-216-4*) Spizzirri.

Dogs of the World: An Illustrated Encyclopedia. M. Bongianni. (Illus.). 1988. 17.99 (*0-517-65495-4*) Random Hse Value.

Dogs of War. Frederick Forsyth. 448p. 1982. mass mkt. 6.99 (*0-553-26846-5*) Bantam.

Dogs of War. large type ed. Frederick Forsyth. 1984. 13.95 (*0-7089-8187-9*, Charnwood) Ulverscroft.

Dogs on Duty. Catherine O'Neill. LC 88-15933. (Books for World Explorers Series 9: No. 4). (Illus.). 104p. (J). (gr. 4 up). 1988. lib. bdg. 12.50 (*0-87044-664-9*) Natl Geog.

Dogs on the Frontier. John E. Baur. LC 82-12765. (Other Dog Bks.). (Illus.). 1982. 17.95 (*0-87714-101-0*); pap. 13.95 (*0-685-57979-4*) Denlingers.

Dogs Playing Cards: Powerbrokers of Prejudice in Education, Art, & Culture. Dennis E. Fehr. LC 93-31944. (Counterpoints Ser.: Vol. 5). 232p. (C). 1994. pap. text ed. 29.95 (*0-8204-2325-4*) P Lang Pubs.

***Dogs Sticker Book.** H. Glover. (Spotter's Guides Sticker Bk. Ser.). (Illus.). 32p. (J). (gr. 1 up). 1995. pap. 6.95 (*0-7460-2119-4*, Usborne) EDC.

***Dog's Tale.** Seymour Reit. LC 94-49332. (Bank Street Ready-to-Read Ser.). (Illus.). (J). 1996. text ed. write for info. (*0-553-09745-8*); pap. write for info. (*0-553-37577-6*) Bantam.

***Dogs That Point, Fish That Bite: Outdoor Essays.** Jim Dean. LC 95-13393. 1995. write for info. (*0-8078-2234-5*) U of NC Pr.

Dogs Through History. Maxwell Riddle. Ed. by William W. Denlinger & R. Annabel Rathman. LC 87-533. (Other Dog Bks.). (Illus.). 192p. 1987. 19.95 (*0-87714-124-X*) Denlingers.

***Dogs Who Came to Stay.** George Pitcher. LC 95-13629. (Illus.). 156p. 1995. 18.95 (*0-525-94050-2*, Dutton) NAL-Dutton.

Dogs Wild & Domestic. Markus Kappeler. LC 91-2682. (Animal Families Ser.). (Illus.). 32p. (J). (gr. 4-6). 1991. lib. bdg. 18.60 (*0-8368-0686-7*) Gareth Stevens Inc.

Dogs Working for People see Books for Young Explorers

Dogs You'd Like to Meet: True Stories of Dog Heroes & Friends. Rowland Johns. 1992. lib. bdg. 75.00 (*0-8490-5266-1*) Gordon Pr.

Dogsbody. Diana W. Jones. LC 76-28715. 256p. (J). (gr. 5-9). 1988. 11.95 (*0-688-08191-6*) Greenwillow.

Dogsbody. Diana W. Jones. LC 76-28714. 256p. (J). (gr. 4-9). 1990. reprint ed. pap. 3.50 (*0-394-82031-2*) Random Bks Yng Read.

Dogsled Apostles. Alma H. Savage. LC 68-55857. (Essay Index Reprint Ser.). 1977. 23.95 (*0-8369-0851-1*) Ayer.

Dogsled to Dread. Robert Quackenbush. LC 86-25394. (Miss Mallard Mystery Ser.). (Illus.). 48p. (J). (gr. 2-6). 1988. pap. 12.95 (*0-671-66518-9*, S&S Bks Young Read) S&S Childrens.

Dogsong. Gary Paulsen. (J). (gr. 5-9). 1987. pap. 4.99 (*0-14-032235-3*, Puffin) Puffin Bks.

Dogsong. Gary Paulsen. LC 84-20443. 192p. (YA). (gr. 7 up). 1985. text ed. 14.95 (*0-02-770180-8*, Bradbury S&S) S&S Childrens.

Dogteam. Gary Paulsen & Ruth Paulsen. (J). 1993. pap. 15.95 (*0-385-30550-8*) Delacorte.

Dogtown: A Whitney Logan Mystery. Mercedes Lambert. 272p. 1992. mass mkt. 4.95 (*0-14-013928-1*, Penguin Bks) Viking Penguin.

Dogtown & Ditches: Life on the Westside. Wayne Pimentel. LC 87-82867. 134p. 1987. pap. 18.95 (*0-944707-00-9*) Loose Change.

Doguicimi. Paul Hazoume. Tr. by Richard Bjornson. LC 86-51305. 500p. (C). 1990. 35.00 (*0-89410-405-5*); pap. 18.00 (*0-89410-406-3*) Three Continents.

Dogwatch & Liberty Days: Seafaring Life in the Nineteenth Century. Margaret S. Creighton. LC 73-1982. (Illus.). 85p. 1982. 25.00 (*0-87577-070-3*, Peabody Museum); pap. 14.95 (*0-685-06120-5*, Peabody Museum) Peabody Essex Mus.

Dogwatching. Desmond Morris. 1987. 13.00 (*0-517-56519-6*, Crown) Crown Pub Group.

Dogwatching. Desmond Morris. 1993. pap. 8.00 (*0-517-88055-5*, Crown) Crown Pub Group.

Dogwolf. Alden R. Carter. LC 93-43518. (J). 1994. 13.95 (*0-590-46741-7*) Scholastic Inc.

Dogwood Stew & Catnip Tea. Jean Stephenson. LC 92-40804. (Granny Green-Gloves Adventure Ser.). 160p. (Orig.). (J). (gr. 4-7). 1993. pap. 4.99 (*0-89107-717-0*) Crossway Bks.

Dogwood Tree. Jennifer Atkinson. (Alabama Poetry Ser.). 96p. 1990. pap. 9.95 (*0-8173-0488-6*) U of Ala Pr.

Dogwoods Are Blooming. Carolyn T. Feagans. 388p. 1990. pap. 7.95 (*0-9634627-0-9*) C T Feagans.

Dogzilla. Dav Pilkey. LC 92-37906. (YA). (gr. 4 up). 1993. 10.95 (*0-15-223944-8*); pap. 5.95 (*0-15-223945-6*) HarBrace.

Dohack (11-S-642) Site. Ann B. Stahl. (American Bottom Archaeology Ser.: Selected FAI-270 Site Reports: Vol. 12). 392p. 1986. pap. 22.50 (*0-252-01074-4*) U of Ill Pr.

Dohrmann Kaspar Pischel, M. D. American Links with Germanic Ophthalmology Retinal Detachment Surgery San Francisco. Dohrmann K. Pischel. (Ophthalmology Oral History Ser.). (Illus.). xxii, 120p. (Orig.). (C). 1988. pap. 35.00 (*0-926866-00-1*) FAAO.

Doigt De Dieu. Erskine Caldwell. (FRE.). 1984. pap. 11.95 (*0-7859-1989-9*, 2070375358) Fr & Eur.

Doigt Magique. Roald Dahl. (Folio - Cadet Bleu Ser.: No. 185). (Illus.). 63p. (FRE.). (J). (gr. 1-5). 1989. pap. 9.95 (*2-07-031185-6*) Schoenhof.

Doihara Kenji & the North China Autonomy Movement, 1935-1936. B. Winston Kahn. (Monograph Ser.). 50p. 1973. pap. 6.00 (*0-939252-02-3*) ASU Ctr Asian.

***Doin' California with Your Pooch! Eileen's Directory of Dog-Friendly Lodging & Outdoor Adventures in California.** Eileen Barish. (Illus.). 688p. (Orig.). 1995. pap. 19.95 (*1-884465-02-1*) Pet-Friendly.

Doin' Dutch Oven: Inside & Out. Robert L. Ririe. 130p. (Orig.). 1990. pap. 8.98 (*0-88290-368-3*) Horizon Utah.

***Doin' the Box Step.** 3.99 (*0-517-13731-3*) Random Hse Value.

Doin' the Minneapolis Mammy Jammy Sleaze. Al Blair. 4p. 1988. pap. 3.95 (*0-930366-16-6*) Northcountry Pub.

Doin' the Puyallup: An Illustrated History of the Western Washington Fair Since 1900. Val Dumond. (Illus.). 270p. (Orig.). 1991. 32.95 (*0-9613673-2-6*) V Dumond.

Doing. Phillip Evans. (Beginning to Learn about Ser.). (J). (ps). 1990. 9.95 (*0-8172-3651-1*) Raintree Steck-V.

Doing a Feasibility Study: Training Activities for Starting or Reviewing a Small Business. Ed. by Suzanne Kindervatter. LC 86-61951. (Appropriate Business Skills for Third World Women Ser.). 170p. (Orig.). write for info. (*0-912917-07-5*) UNIFEM.

Doing a Feasibility Study: Training Activities for Starting or Reviewing a Small Business, Set. Ed. by Suzanne Kindervatter. LC 86-61951. (Appropriate Business Skills for Third World Women Ser.). 170p. (Orig.). pap. text ed. 16.00 (*0-685-18179-0*) UNIFEM.

Doing & Being: Selected Readings in Moral Philosophy. Joram G. Haber. (Illus.). 528p. (Orig.). (C). 1993. pap. write for info. (*0-02-348585-X*) Macmillan.

Doing & Rewarding: Inside a High-Performance Organization. Carl G. Thor. (Management Master Ser.: Set 1, No. 6). 56p. (Orig.). 1994. 15.95 (*1-56327-061-7*) Prod Press.

Doing Away with Personal Injury Law: New Compensation Mechanisms for Victims, Consumers, & Business. Stephen D. Sugarman. LC 88-38311. 242p. 1989. text ed. 59.95 (*0-89930-395-1*, SDZ/, Quorum Bks) Greenwood.

Doing Better & Feeling Worse. Ed. by John H. Knowles. 1977. pap. 10.95 (*0-393-06423-9*) Norton.

***Doing Business.** Beadle. Date not set. per. 10.95 (*0-85449-110-4*, Pub. by Gay Mens Pr UK) InBook.

Doing Business & Investing Abroad: Fourteenth Annual Institute for Corporate Counsel. (Corporate Law & Practice Course Handbook, 1985-86 Ser.). 492p. 1991. pap. 70.00 (*0-685-69415-1*) PLI.

Doing Business & Professional Speech Communications. 3rd ed. Henry L. Roubicek. 208p. 1992. per. 16.00 (*0-8403-8204-9*) Kendall-Hunt.

Doing Business in African Myths & Realities. Ron Watkins. 200p. Date not set. pap. 15.95 (*0-9640480-0-0*) Herit Pubng.

Doing Business in & with Latin America: An Information Sourcebook. E. Willard Miller & Ruby M. Miller. (Sourcebook Series in Business & Management). 128p. 1987. 35.00 (*0-89774-308-3*) Oryx Pr.

Doing Business in Asia: A Small Business Guide to Success in the World's Most Dynamic Market. David L. James. (Illus.). 192p. (Orig.). 1993. pap. 18.95 (*1-55870-295-4*) Betterway Bks.

***Doing Business in Asia: The Complete Guide.** Sanjyot P. Dunung. 1995. 23.00 (*0-02-907761-3*) Free Pr.

***Doing Business in Asia's Booming "China Triangle"** Christopher Engholm. LC 94-21176. 1994. text ed. 23.95 (*0-13-125188-0*) P-H.

Doing Business in Australia. Ed. by Edward J. Wright. 1992. ring bd. 165.00 (*1-56425-010-5*) Transnatl Juris Pubns.

Doing Business in Brazil. Ed. by Pinhiero Neto-Advogados. 1982. ring bd. 360.00 (*1-56425-008-3*) Transnatl Juris Pubns.

Doing Business in California: An Employment Law Handbook. Arthur F. Silbergeld. 1989. pap. 39.95 (*1-55840-308-6*) Exec Ent Pubns.

Doing Business in Canada. 85p. 1994. pap. 20.00 (*92-826-6312-4*, CT-77-93-926ENC, Pub. by Europ Com) UNIPUB.

Doing Business in Canada, 3 vols. Stikeman & Elliot. 1984. Looseleaf Updates Avail. write for info. (*0-8205-1268-0*) Bender.

Doing Business in China. Ed. by William P. Streng & Allen D. Cox. 1990. ring bd. 225.00 (*1-56425-009-1*) Transnatl Juris Pubns.

Doing Business in China: The Last Great Market. Geoffrey Murray. 240p. 1994. text ed. 80.00 (*1-873410-28-X*, Pub. by Curzon Pr UK); pap. 29.95 (*1-873410-29-8*, Pub. by Curzon Pr UK) St Martin.

Doing Business in China: The Last Great Market. Geoffrey Murray. LC 94-13029. 1994. text ed. 20.00 (*0-312-11683-7*) St Martin.

Doing Business in China: The Last Great Market. Geoffrey Murray. LC 94-13029. 1994. write for info. (*0-312-11682-9*) St Martin.

Doing Business in Developing Countries: Entry & Negotiation Strategies. S. Tamer Cavusgil & Pervez N. Ghaur. 160p. 1990. 35.00 (*0-415-04343-3*, A4722) Routledge.

Doing Business in Egypt. Nicholas A. Abraham. Ed. by Karl E. Prinz. (Doing Business in the Middle East Ser.: Vol. 2). (Illus.). 280p. (Orig.). 1979. pap. text ed. 79.95 (*0-934592-00-4*) Tradeship Pub Co.

Doing Business in Europe: Before & After 1992. Christopher E. Manno & Steven J. Gartner. Ed. by Raymond W. Merritt & Clifford M. Ennico. (Corporate Counseling Monograph Ser.). 125p. (Orig.). 1991. pap. 35.00 (*0-942954-46-7*) NYS Bar.

Doing Business in France, 2 vols. Simon M. Borde et al. 1983. Updates. ring bd. write for info. (*0-8205-1445-4*) Bender.

Doing Business in Ireland. Charles McCarthy. 1987. Looseleaf. ring bd. write for info. (*0-8205-1111-0*) Bender.

Doing Business in Japan, 10 vols., Set. Zentaro Kitagawa. 1980. ring bd. write for info. (*0-8205-1368-7*) Bender.

Doing Business in Kuwait. Nicholas A. Abraham. Ed. by Karl E. Prinz. (Doing Business in the Middle East Ser.: Vol. 3). (Illus.). 280p. (Orig.). 1981. pap. text ed. 79.95 (*0-934592-02-0*) Tradeship Pub Co.

Doing Business in Latin America & the Caribbean: Including Mexico, the U. S. Virgin Islands & Puerto Rico, Central America, South America. Lawrence W. Tuller. 368p. 1993. 32.95 (*0-8144-5035-0*) AMACOM.

***Doing Business in Less Developed Countries: Financial Opportunities & Risks.** Mashaalah Rahnama-Moghadam et al. LC 94-24986. 224p. 1995. text ed. 59.95 (*0-89930-854-6*, Quorum Bks) Greenwood.

Doing Business in Mexico, 3 vols., Set. Ed. by Andrea Bonmo-Blanc. reprint ed. ring bd. 515.00 (*0-929179-78-1*) Transnatl Juris Pubns.

***Doing Business in Mexico: Your Guide to Exporting, Importing, Investing, & Manufacturing.** Jay Jessup. 1994. pap. 14.95 (*1-55958-570-6*) Prima Pub.

Doing Business in Mexico: Your Guide to Exporting, Importing, Investing, & Manufacturing in the World's Fastest Growing Economy. Jay Jessup & Maggie Jessup. LC 92-30484. 256p. 1992. 21.95 (*1-55958-277-4*) Prima Pub.

Doing Business in Nigeria: Africa's Largest Market Beckons You. Eton Phillip-Eteng. 197p. (Orig.). 1992. pap. 19.95 (*0-9629214-3-2*) Intl Spectrum.

Doing Business in Russia. Touche Ross & Co. Staff et al. LC 93-43079. 1994. 17.95 (*0-8442-3562-8*, NTC Busn Bks) NTC Pub Grp.

Doing Business in Russia: Basic Facts for the Pioneering Entrepreneur. Larissa Nezhinskaya. 1995. pap. 19.95 (*1-55571-168-5*) Oasis Pr OR.

***Doing Business in Russia & the Other Former Soviet Republics: Accounting & Financial Management Issues, an Updated Study.** Adolph J. Enthoven et al. Ed. by Claire Barth. 164p. 1994. pap. 25.00 (*0-86641-205-0*, 94296) Inst Mgmt Account.

Doing Business in Saudi: An American Perspective. Larry Hammons. (Illus.). 160p. (Orig.). 1992. pap. 12.95 (*1-879660-12-1*) Lawcon Pub.

Doing Business in Saudi Arabia. Nicholas A. Abraham. Ed. by Christine A. Hanna. (Doing Business in the Middle East Ser.: Vol. 1). (Illus.). 336p. (Orig.). 1980. pap. text ed. 79.95 (*0-934592-01-2*) Tradeship Pub Co.

Doing Business in Singapore see Doing Business with Singapore

***Doing Business in South Africa.** Ed. by Jonathan Reuvid. 330p. 1995. pap. 55.00 (*0-7494-1347-6*, Pub. by Kogan Pg UK) Cassell.

Doing Business in Spain. Fernando Pombo. 1987. write for info. (*0-8205-1107-2*) Bender.

***Doing Business in the Czech Republic.** 2nd rev. ed. KPMG Peat Marwick Staff et al. (CBI Initiative Eastern Europe Ser.). 256p. 1995. pap. 32.50 (*0-7494-1474-X*, Pub. by Kogan Pg UK) Cassell.

***Doing Business in the New Vietnam: The Prentice Hall Emerging World Market.** Christopher Engholm. 1995. text ed. 24.95 (*0-13-325853-X*) P-H.

Doing Business in the NIS. 450p. (C). 1993. pap. 825.00 (*0-934393-83-4*) Rector Pr.

Doing Business in the United Kingdom, 3 vols., Set. Clifford Chance. 1985. ring bd. write for info. (*0-8205-1134-X*) Bender.

Doing Business in the United States. Gordon E. Harvey & Edward L. Lee, III. 64p. (Orig.). 1992. pap. 45.00 (*1-881561-00-3*) Busn Trvl Bks.

***Doing Business in the United States.** Christian Reuter. 64p. (GER.). 1995. 30.00 (*0-86640-052-4*) German Am Chamber.

Doing Business in the United States, 6 vols. Jeremiah J. Spires & Bender's Editorial Staff. 1978. Updates. ring bd. write for info. (*0-8205-1264-8*) Bender.

Doing Business in Vietnam. James W. Robinson. LC 94-13044. 1994. write for info. (*1-55958-591-9*) Prima Pub.

Doing Business Internationally: The Guide to Cross Cultural Success. Terence Brake. 300p. 1994. text ed. 25.00 (*0-7863-0117-1*) Irwin Prof Pubng.

***Doing Business Internationally: The Resource Book for Cross-Cultural Success.** 2nd ed. Ed. by Danielle Walker & Louise K. Forman. (Illus.). 300p. (Orig.). 1995. pap. 40.00 (*1-882390-05-9*) Princeton Trng.

***Doing Business Internationally: The Workbook to Cross-Cultural Success.** rev. ed. Terence Brake & Danielle Walker. Ed. by Tuula Piispanen-Krabbe. (Illus.). 285p. 1994. pap. text ed. 49.50 (*1-882390-02-4*) Princeton Trng.

Doing Business on the Internet. Mary J. Cronin. (Illus.). 256p. 1994. pap. 29.95 (*0-442-01770-7*) Van Nos Reinhold.

Doing Business Tax-Free: Perfectly Legal Techniques to Reduce or Eliminate Your Federal Business Taxes. Robert A. Cooke. LC 94-11206. 1995. text ed. 39.95 (*0-471-03417-7*); pap. text ed. 15.95 (*0-471-03416-9*) Wiley.

Doing Business with Banks. Gibson Heath. 104p. (Orig.). 1991. pap. 8.95 (*0-685-39474-3*) Dba-USA Pr.

Doing Business with Banks: A Common Sense Guide for Small Business Borrowers. Gibson Heath. (Illus.). 95p. (Orig.). 1989. write for info. (*0-318-65555-1*) United Banks.

Doing Business with C. Ray Swartz. (Illus.). 496p. 1988. 28.95 (*0-13-217258-5*) P-H.

Doing Business with China. Paul Leppert. LC 94-9350. (Global Business Ser.). 128p. (Orig.). 1994. pap. 12.00 (*0-87573-045-0*) Jain Pub Co.

Doing Business with East Germany: A Guide for Corporate Executives & Attorneys. James A. Hart & Jerome Ottmar. 1990. write for info. (*0-89930-514-8*, HBG/, Greenwood Pr) Greenwood.

Doing Business with Integrity: One Man's Story. J. Perry Bell. 70p. (Orig.). pap. 7.95 (*0-9628542-1-2*) Bell Pr.

Doing Business with Japan. H. William Tanaka & Nobuyuki Takashima. (Illus.). 212p. (Orig.). 1986. pap. 12.50 (*0-916673-03-0*) Business Bks CT.

Doing Business with Japanese Men: A Woman's Handbook. Christalyn Brannen & Tracey Wilen. LC 92-36102. (Illus.). 176p. (Orig.). 1993. pap. 9.95 (*1-880656-04-3*) Stone Bridge Pr.

***Doing Business with Korea.** Paul Leppert. LC 95-14750. (Global Business Ser.). Orig. Title: Doing Business with the Koreans. 144p. (Orig.). 1995. pap. 12.00 (*0-87573-043-4*) Jain Pub Co.

***Doing Business with Mexico.** Paul Leppert. (Global Business Ser.). 144p. (Orig.). 1995. pap. 12.00 (*0-87573-046-9*) Jain Pub Co.

Doing Business with NASA. (Illus.). 55p. (Orig.). (C). 1993. pap. text ed. 45.00 (*0-7881-0128-5*) Diane Pub.

***Doing Business with North America.** Ed. by Jonathan Reuvid. 320p. 1995. pap. 120.00 (*0-7494-1240-2*, Pub. by Kogan Pg UK) Cassell.

Doing Business with Romania. Donald E. DeKieffer. (Illus.). 180p. (Orig.). 1985. pap. 8.50 (*0-916673-02-2*) Business Bks CT.

***Doing Business with Singapore.** Paul Leppert. LC 95-14751. (Global Business Ser.). Orig. Title: Doing Business in Singapore. 144p. (Orig.). 1995. pap. 12.00 (*0-87573-042-6*) Jain Pub Co.

Doing Business with South Africa. rev. ed. Les De Villiers et al. (Illus.). 240p. 1986. pap. 12.50 (*0-916673-04-9*) Business Bks CT.

Doing Business with South Korea: A Handbook for Executives in the Public & Private Sectors. Larry M. Hynson, Jr. LC 90-30015. 304p. 1990. text ed. 59.95 (*0-89930-509-1*, Quorum Bks) Greenwood.

Doing Business with Southern Africa. Les De Villiers. (Illus.). 240p. 1989. pap. 12.50 (*0-916673-05-7*) Business Bks CT.

Doing Business with Southern Africa. 2nd ed. Les De Villiers. (Illus.). 224p. 1991. pap. write for info. (*0-916673-06-5*) Business Bks CT.

***Doing Business with Taiwan.** Paul Leppert. LC 95-14753. (Global Business Ser.). Orig. Title: Doing Business with the Chinese. 144p. (Orig.). 1995. pap. 12.00 (*0-87573-041-8*) Jain Pub Co.

***Doing Business with Thailand.** Paul Leppert. LC 95-14752. (Global Business Ser.). Orig. Title: Doing Business with the Thais. 144p. (Orig.). 1995. pap. 12.00 (*0-87573-044-2*) Jain Pub Co.

Doing Business with the Chinese see Doing Business with Taiwan

Doing Business with the Dictators: A Political History of United Fruit in Guatemala, 1899-1944. Paul J. Dosal. LC 93-10118. (Latin American Silhouettes Ser.). 248p. 1993. 45.00 (*0-8420-2475-1*) Scholarly Res Inc.

D

An Asterisk (*) at the beginning of an entry indicates that the title is appearing in BIP for the first time. 2071

Doing Business with the Japanese. John A. Abecasis-Phillips. LC 93-421. 1993. 9.95 (*0-8442-8392-4*, NTC Busn Bks) NTC Pub Grp.

Doing Business with the Japanese. Mitchell F. Deutsch. 1985. pap. 4.99 (*0-451-62349-5*, Ment) NAL-Dutton.

Doing Business with the Japanese: A Guide to Successful Communication, Management, & Diplomacy. Alan Goldman. LC 93-26777. (SUNY Series in Speech Communication). 338p. (C). 1994. 59.50 (*0-7914-1945-2*); pap. 19.95 (*0-7914-1946-0*) State U NY Pr.

Doing Business with the Koreans see Doing Business with Korea

Doing Business with the People's Republic of China: Industries & Markets. Bohdan O. Szuprowicz & Maria R. Szuprowicz. LC 78-2539. (Illus.). 466p. reprint ed. pap. 132.90 (*0-317-09683-4*, 2055516) Bks Demand.

Doing Business with the Russians. Westshore, Inc. Staff. LC 79-1229. (Praeger Special Studies). 176p. 1979. text ed. 45.00 (*0-275-90435-0*, C0435, Praeger Pubs) Greenwood.

Doing Business with the Thais see Doing Business with Thailand

Doing Business with the U. S. A. Les De Villiers & Donald De Kieffer. (Illus.). 304p. 1984. pap. 12.95 (*0-916673-00-6*) Business Bks CT.

Doing Business with the U. S. Government: How to Sell Your Goods & Services to the 200 Billion Dollar Federal Market. Herman Holtz. 275p. 1993. 24.95 (*1-55958-320-7*) Prima Pub.

Doing Business with Troubled Companies, 1991. Robert J. Rosenberg. 732p. 1991. pap. text ed. 17.50 (*0-685-49892-1*, A4-4340) PLI.

Doing CAD on a PC: Technology & Applications, Software & Systems, Suppliers & Cost. 121p. 179.00 (*0-317-65588-4*) TBC Inc.

Doing Children's Museums: A Guide to 265 Hands-on-Museums. 2nd rev. ed. Joanne Cleaver. LC 92-8280. 272p. 1992. pap. 13.95 (*0-913589-63-2*) Williamson Pub Co.

Doing Church History - Your Own! Edwin S. Gaustad. 32p. 1991. pap. 4.00 (*0-685-51595-8*) Am Baptist.

Doing Comparable Worth: Gender, Class, & Pay Equity. Joan Acker. (Women in the Political Economy Ser.). 272p. 1991. pap. 18.95 (*0-87722-834-5*) Temple U Pr.

***Doing Contextual Therapy: An Intergrated Model for Working with Individuals, Couples & Families.** Peter Goldenthal. 180p. 1996. 23.00 (*0-393-70208-1*) Norton.

***Doing Counselling Research.** John McLeod. 224p. 1994. 45.00 (*0-8039-7803-0*); pap. 19.95 (*0-8039-7804-9*) Sage.

Doing Countertrade: A Practical Guide. International Executive Reports Staff. Ed. by William C. Hearn. 450p. 1989. pap. 295.00 (*0-915797-02-X*) Intl Exec Reports.

Doing Critical Ethnography. Jim Thomas. (Qualitative Research Methods Ser.: Vol. 26). 96p. (C). 1992. 21.50 (*0-8039-3922-1*); pap. 9.50 (*0-8039-3923-X*) Sage.

Doing Daily Battle: Interviews with Moroccan Women. Fatima Mernissi. Tr. by Jo Lakeland. LC 88-34211. 224p. (C). 1989. text ed. 35.00 (*0-8135-1417-7*); pap. text ed. 15.00 (*0-8135-1418-5*) Rutgers U Pr.

***Doing Deals: A Guide to Buying Land for Conservation.** Trust for Public Land Staff. LC 95-10136. 175p. 1995. pap. 25.00 (*0-943915-11-2*) Land Trust DC.

Doing Deals: Investment Banks at Work. Robert G. Eccles & Dwight B. Crane. 1989. text ed. 29.95 (*0-07-103232-0*) McGraw.

***Doing Economic Research: Essays on the Applied Methodology of Economics.** Thomas Mayer. (Economists of the Twentieth Century Ser.). 200p. 1995. 69.95 (*1-85278-939-5*, Pub. by E Elgar Pub UK) Ashgate Pub Co.

Doing Educational Research. Ed. by Geoffrey Walford. 288p. 1991. 69.95 (*0-415-05289-0*, A5883); pap. 17.95 (*0-415-05290-4*, A5879) Routledge.

Doing Educational Research in Developing Countries: Qualitative Strategies. Vulliamy et al. 1990. 70.00 (*1-85000-712-8*, Falmer Pr); pap. 32.50 (*1-85000-713-6*, Falmer Pr) Taylor & Francis.

Doing Ethics in Context, Vol. II: South African Perspectives. Ed. by John De Gruchy & Charles Villa-Vicencio. 225p. (Orig.). 1994. pap. 18.95 (*0-88344-990-0*) Orbis Bks.

Doing Evil to Achieve Good: Moral Choice in Conflict Situations. Ed. by Richard A. McCormick & Paul Ramsey. LC 78-11316. 1978. 10.35 (*0-8294-0285-3*) Loyola Univ Pr.

Doing Exemplary Research. Ed. by Peter J. Frost & Ralph E. Stablein. 324p. (C). 1992. text ed. 46.00 (*0-8039-3908-6*); pap. text ed. 22.95 (*0-8039-3909-4*) Sage.

Doing Faith Justice: An Introduction to Catholic Social Thought. Fred Kammer. 1991. pap. 12.95 (*0-8091-3244-3*) Paulist Pr.

Doing Family & Local History in Ethnic Studies. rev. ed. (Ethnic Studies Bulletins: No. 5). 19p. 1986. 2.00 (*0-685-42398-0*) I N Thut World Educ Ctr.

Doing Feminist Research. Ed. by Helen Roberts. 224p. (Orig.). 1981. pap. 13.95 (*0-7100-0772-8*, RKP) Routledge.

Doing Field Research. John M. Johnson. LC 74-27599. 1975. text ed. 22.95 (*0-02-916600-4*) Free Pr.

Doing Field Research. John M. Johnson. LC 74-27599. 1978. pap. 16.95 (*0-02-916610-1*) Free Pr.

Doing Fieldwork: Eight Personal Accounts of Social Research. Ed. by John Perry. 155p. (C). 1989. pap. 69.00x (*0-7300-0786-3*, Pub. by Deakin Univ AT) St Mut.

Doing Fieldwork: Warnings & Advice. Rosalie H. Wax. (Midway Reprint Ser.). x, 396p. 1986. pap. text ed. 20.00 (*0-226-86951-2*) U Ch Pr.

Doing Good Better! How to Be an Effective Board Member of a Non-Profit Organization. Edgar Stoesz & Chester Raber. LC 94-7314. 150p. (Orig.). 1993. pap. 9.95 (*1-56148-099-1*) Good Bks PA.

Doing Good or Doing Well? Japan's Foreign Aid Program. Margee Ensign. LC 92-31536. (Illus.). 224p. (C). 1993. 24.50 (*0-231-08144-8*) Col U Pr.

Doing Grammar. Max Morenberg. 192p. (C). 1991. pap. text ed. 14.95 (*0-19-506427-5*) OUP.

Doing Historical Archaeology: Exercises Using Documentary, Oral, & Material Evidence. Russell . Barber. LC 93-39035. 248p. 1994. pap. text ed. write for info. (*0-13-176033-5*) P-H.

Doing History. R. Beery & Robert J. Todd. (Illus.). 90p. (gr. 6-8). 1984. pap. text ed. 4.95 (*0-917009-00-2*) Independ Sch.

Doing It All Isn't Everything: A Woman's Guide for Living in Harmony. Stephanie Allen & Carolyn A. Ziegler. 1993. 19.95 (*0-9632788-1-9*); pap. 12.95 (*0-9632788-0-0*) New Perspect.

Doing It for Daddy: Short & Sexy Fiction about a Very Forbidden Fantasy. Ed. by Pat Califia. 240p. (Orig.). 1994. pap. 9.95 (*1-55583-227-X*) Alyson Pubns.

Doing It Now. Edwin C. Bliss. 1984. mass mkt. 4.99 (*0-553-27875-4*) Bantam.

Doing It Right: A Guide to Improving Exhibit Labels. Barbara Punt. (Illus.). 72p. 1989. pap. 15.95 (*0-685-29595-8*, Brooklyn Children s Museum) AST Ctrs.

Doing It Right: Improving College Learning Skills. Ben E. Johnson. 423p. (C). 1992. pap. text ed. write for info. (*0-669-21555-4*); Instr.'s ed. teacher ed write for info. (*0-669-28173-5*) Heath.

Doing It Right: Making the Most of Your Life. Dorothy Lapadula. 1990. 16.95 (*0-944007-57-0*) Sure Sellers.

Doing It Right: Quality Through Employee Involvement. Irving J. DeToro. 168p. (Orig.). 1990. pap. 12.95 (*0-943456-38-X*) Bearly Ltd.

Doing It Right: The Best Criticism on Sam Peckinpah's The Wild Bunch. Intro. by Michael Bliss. LC 93-14502. (Illus.). 240p. (C). 1994. pap. 16.95 (*0-8093-1863-6*) S Ill U Pr.

Doing It Right: The Steelers of Three Rivers & Four Super Bowls Share Their Secrets for Success. Jim O'Brian. (Illus.). 536p. (Orig.). 1991. pap. 14.95 (*0-685-57076-2*) Wolfson.

Doing It Right ... Now: Life Advice & More - for the Enterprising Woman. Dorothy Lapadula. 1992. pap. 8.99 (*1-56171-165-9*, S P I Bks) Sure Sellers.

Doing it Right & Passing it On: North Louisiana Crafts. H. F. Gregory. (Illus.). 52p. (Orig.). (C). 1984. reprint ed. pap. 15.00 (*0-944564-03-8*) Alex Mus.

Doing It Right in L. A. Self-Producing for the Performing Artist. Jacki Apple. Ed. by Steven Durland. LC 90-82053. (Illus.). 136p. (Orig.). 1990. student ed, pap. 12.00 (*0-937122-13-0*) Astro Artz.

Doing It the Hard Way: Investigations of Gender & Technology. Sally L. Hacker. Ed. by Dorothy E. Smith & Susan M. Turner. 272p. 1990. text ed. 49.95 (*0-04-445434-1*); pap. text ed. 15.95 (*0-04-445435-X*) Routledge Chapman & Hall.

Doing Justice: The Choice of Punishments. Andrew Von Hirsch. 220p. 1986. reprint ed. pap. 10.95 (*0-930350-83-9*) NE U Pr.

Doing Justice, Showing Mercy: Christian Action in Today's World. Vinita H. Wright. (Fisherman Bible Studyguide Ser.). 80p. 1993. 4.99 (*0-87788-180-4*) Shaw Pubs.

Doing Less Time: Penal Reform in Crisis. Janet Chan. (Institute of Criminology Monograph Ser.: No. 2). xiv, 222p. 1992. pap. 40.00 (*0-86758-566-8*) W W Gaunt.

Doing Literary Business: American Women Writers in the Nineteenth Century. Susan Coultrap-McQuin. LC 90-12006. (Gender & American Culture Ser.). (Illus.). xviii, 254p. (C). 1990. 32.50 (*0-8078-1914-X*); pap. 12.95 (*0-8078-4284-2*) U of NC Pr.

Doing Mathematics: An Introduction to Proofs & Problem-Solving. Steven Galovich. 144p. (C). 1993. pap. text ed. 19.00 (*0-03-092800-1*) SCP.

***Doing More Business on the Internet.** 2nd rev. ed. Mary J. Cronin. LC 95-7186. 1995. pap. 29.95 (*0-442-02047-3*) Van Nos Reinhold.

Doing More Good Than Harm: The Evaluation of Health Care Interventions. Ed. by Kenneth S. Warren & Frederick Mosteller. LC 94-2873. (Annals Ser.: Vol. 703). 1994. write for info. (*0-89766-833-2*); pap. 90.00 (*0-89766-834-0*) NY Acad Sci.

Doing More with Less: Cutback Management in New York City. Demetrios Caraley. 160p. (Orig.). pap. 7.00 (*0-910955-01-8*) Columbia U GPPPA.

Doing More with Less: Turning Public Management Around. Jacob B. Ukeles. LC 81-69352. 320p. reprint ed. pap. 91.20 (*0-317-27309-4*, 2023531) Bks Demand.

Doing More with SAS-ASSIST Software, Version 6. 100p. 1994. 19.95 (*1-55544-502-0*, 56089) SAS Inst.

Doing Myself a Favor, Loving My Wife. H. Page Williams. 144p. (Orig.). 1994. pap. 5.95 (*0-88270-664-0*) Bridge Pub.

***Doing Narrative Therapy.** Jill Freedman & Gene Combs. 224p. 1996. 27.00 (*0-393-70207-3*) Norton.

Doing Naturalistic Inquiry: A Guide to Methods. David A. Erlandson et al. (Illus.). 200p. 1993. 44.00 (*0-8039-4937-5*); pap. 19.95 (*0-8039-4938-3*) Sage.

***Doing Naval History: Essays Toward Improvement.** Ed. & Intro. by John B. Hattendorf. (Naval War College Historical Monographs Ser.: Monograph 13). ix, 160p. (Orig.). 1995. pap. 10.00 (*1-884733-06-9*) Naval War Coll.

Doing Oral Histories in Ethnic Studies. (Ethnic Studies Bulletins: No. 3). 16p. 1982. 2.00 (*0-685-05140-4*) I N Thut World Educ Ctr.

***Doing Oral History.** Donald A. Ritchie. (Twayne's Oral History Ser.). (Illus.). 288p. 1994. text ed. 26.95x (*0-8057-9124-8*, Twayne); pap. 14.95 (*0-8057-9128-0*, Twayne) Macmillan.

Doing Our Babbage. Ira Slobodien. LC 91-75597. 288p. (Orig.). 1992. write for info. (*0-9631062-0-1*); pap. write for info. (*0-9631062-1-X*) Ilex Pr.

Doing Our Homework: How Schools Can Engage Hispanic Communities. Andrea B. Bermudez. LC 94-21398. (Orig.). 1993. pap. 12.00 (*1-880785-11-0*) ERIC-CRESS.

Doing Participatory Research: A Feminist Approach. Patricia Maguire. 305p. (Orig.). 1987. pap. 8.00 (*0-932288-79-0*) Ctr Intl Ed U of MA.

Doing Phenomenology. Herbert Spiegelberg. (Phaenomenologica Ser.: No. 63). 1975. lib. bdg. 80.00 (*90-247-1725-6*) Kluwer Ac.

Doing Philosophy Historically. Ed. by Peter H. Hare. 352p. (C). 1989. text ed. 42.95 (*0-87975-475-3*) Prometheus Bks.

Doing Physics: Building Understanding Through Laboratory Investigations. Dewey I. Dykstra. 112p. 1992. spiral bd. 14.95 (*0-8403-7572-7*) Kendall-Hunt.

Doing Physics: How Physicists Take Hold of the World. Martin H. Krieger. LC 91-20305. (Illus.). 192p. 1992. text ed. 29.95 (*0-253-33123-4*); pap. text ed. 9.95 (*0-253-20701-0*) Ind U Pr.

Doing Political Science: An Introduction to Political Analysis. Alan S. Zuckerman. 197p. (C). 1991. text ed. 55.50 (*0-8133-1002-4*); pap. text ed. 19.95 (*0-8133-1003-2*) Westview.

***Doing Pragmatics.** Peter Grundy. 192p. 1995. 49.95 (*0-340-62514-7*, Pub. by E Arnld UK); pap. 17.95 (*0-340-58965-5*, Pub. by E Arnld UK) St Martin.

Doing Psychology Experiments. 3rd ed. Martin. (C). 1991. pap. 27.95 (*0-534-14490-X*) Brooks-Cole.

***Doing Psychology Experiments.** 4th ed. David W. Martin. LC 94-47424. 1996. pap. 27.95 (*0-534-33840-2*) Brooks-Cole.

Doing Psychotherapy. Michael F. Basch. LC 79-3084. 188p. 1980. text ed. 30.00 (*0-465-01684-7*) Basic.

Doing Public Administration: Exercises in Public Management. 3rd ed. Nicholas L. Henry. 352p. (C). 1991. pap. write for info. (*0-697-11132-6*) Brown & Benchmark.

Doing Qualitative Research: Circles Within Circles. Margot Ely et al. 180p. 1991. 65.00 (*1-85000-813-2*, Falmer Pr); pap. 26.00 (*1-85000-814-0*, Falmer Pr) Taylor & Francis.

Doing Qualitative Research: Multiple Strategies. Benjamin F. Crabtree & William L. Miller. (Research Methods for Primary Care Ser.: Vol. 3). 272p. (C). 1992. text ed. 49.95 (*0-8039-4311-3*); pap. text ed. 24.00 (*0-8039-4312-1*) Sage.

Doing Research in Organisations. Ed. by Alan Bryman. 268p. 1988. lib. bdg. 55.00 (*0-415-00257-5*); pap. text ed. 16.95 (*0-415-00258-3*) Routledge.

Doing Research on Sensitive Topics. Raymond M. Lee. (Illus.). 240p. 1993. 55.00 (*0-8039-8860-5*); pap. 18.95 (*0-8039-8861-3*) Sage.

Doing Research on Women's Communication. Brenda Dervin. Ed. by Kathryn Carter & Carole Spitzack. LC 89-14900. (Communication & Information Science Ser.). 304p. (C). 1989. text ed. 55.00 (*0-89391-483-5*); pap. text ed. 24.50 (*0-89391-616-1*) Ablex Pub.

Doing Research That Is Useful for Theory & Practice. Edward E. Lawler, III et al. LC 84-43092. (Management-Social & Behavioral Science Ser.). 394p. 1985. 40.95 (*0-87589-649-9*) Jossey-Bass.

Doing RET: Albert Ellis in Action. Ed. by Joseph Yankura & Windy Dryden. LC 90-9575. 208p. 1990. 32.95 (*0-8261-6650-4*) Springer Pub.

Doing Right: Everyday Medical Ethics. Solomon Papper. 148p. 1983. 30.95 (*0-316-69044-9*) Little.

***Doing Rude Things: History of the British Sex Film.** David McGillivray. (Illus.). 141p. Date not set. pap. 19.95 (*0-9517012-2-3*, Pub. by Sun Tavern Flds UK) AK Pr Dist.

Doing Science: Images of Science in Science Education. Ed. by Robin Millar. 250p. 1989. 65.00 (*1-85000-506-0*, Falmer Pr); pap. 32.50 (*1-85000-507-9*, Falmer Pr) Taylor & Francis.

Doing Sex Education: Gender Politics & Schooling. Bonnie N. Trudell. (Critical Social Thought Ser.). 256p. 1993. 45.00 (*0-415-90502-8*, A6436, Routledge NY) Routledge.

Doing Simple Math in Your Head. W. J. Howard. LC 91-74030. (Illus.). 144p. (Orig.). 1992. pap. 9.95 (*0-9627341-5-2*) Coast Pub OR.

Doing Social Psychology: Laboratory & Field Exercises. Ed. by Glynis M. Breakwell et al. (Illus.). 285p. 1988. 69.95 (*0-521-34015-2*); pap. 22.95 (*0-521-33563-9*) Cambridge U Pr.

Doing Social Research. Therese L. Baker. 512p. (C). 1988. text ed. write for info. (*0-07-003453-2*) McGraw.

Doing Social Research. Therese L. Baker. 1988. pap. text ed. write for info. (*0-07-003456-7*) McGraw.

Doing Social Research. 2nd ed. Therese L. Baker. LC 93-4267. 1993. text ed. write for info. (*0-07-003492-3*) McGraw.

Doing Social Research. 2nd ed. Therese L. Baker. LC 93-4267. 1993. text ed. write for info. (*0-07-003494-X*) McGraw.

Doing Sociology: An Introduction Through Microcase. Microcase Corporation Staff & Rodney Stark. 160p. 1993. Version 3.5". 3.5 hd 19.95 (*0-534-19525-3*); Version 5.25". 5.25 hd 19.95 (*0-534-19524-5*) Intl Thomson.

Doing Sociology of Education, Vol. 7. Ed. by Geoffrey Walford. (Social Research & Education Studies Series). 250p. 1987. 70.00 (*1-85000-145-6*, Falmer Pr); pap. 40.00 (*1-85000-146-4*, Falmer Pr) Taylor & Francis.

Doing Something by Doing Nothing. Thomas Peterson. 1985. 6.55 (*0-89536-747-5*, 5853) CSS OH.

***Doing Something for Someone Else: A History of the Wisconsin Lions.** Donald P. Rasmussen. Ed. by Michael J. Goc. 288p. Date not set. 25.00 (*0-938627-27-9*) New Past Pr.

Doing Supervision & Being Supervised: The Supervision of Psychotherapy in Light of the Evolution & Architecture of the Human Mind. Robert Langs. 262p. 1994. pap. 36.50 (*1-85575-060-0*, Pub. by Karnac Bks UK) Brunner-Mazel.

Doing the Best We Can. Fred Feldman. 1986. lib. bdg. 89.00 (*90-277-2164-5*) Kluwer Ac.

Doing the Business: Entrepreneurship, the Working Class, & Detectives in the East End of London. Dick Hobbs. (Illus.). 272p. 1988. 59.00 (*0-19-825598-5*) OUP.

Doing the Days: A Year's Worth of Creative Journaling, Drawing, Listening, Reading, Thinking, Arts & Crafts Activities for Children Ages 8-12. Lorraine M. Dahlstrom. Ed. by Rosemary Wallner. LC 93-38119. (Free Spirited Classroom Ser.). (Illus.). 240p. (Orig.). (J). (gr. 3-7). 1994. pap. 21.95 (*0-915793-62-8*) Free Spirit Pub.

Doing the Dissertation: The Nuts & Bolts of Psychological Research. Brian T. Yates. (Illus.). 232p. 1982. spiral bd., pap. 24.95 (*0-398-04650-6*) C C Thomas.

Doing the Ethnography of Schooling: Educational Anthropology in Action. Ed. by George Spindler. 504p. (C). 1988. reprint ed. pap. 21.95 (*0-88133-316-6*) Waveland Pr.

Doing the Garden. Sarah Garland. (Illus.). 32p. (J). (ps-1). 1993. 15.95 (*0-370-31635-5*, Pub. by Bodley Head UK) Trafalgar.

Doing the Gospel: Local Congregations in Ministry. Roy C. Nichols. LC 90-33916. 1990. pap. 9.95 (*0-687-11030-0*) Abingdon.

Doing the Needful: The Dilemma of India's Population Policy. G. Narayana & John F. Kantner. 187p. (C). 1992. pap. text ed. 37.00 (*0-8133-8432-X*) Westview.

***Doing the Right Thing: A Real Estate Practitioner's Guide to Ethical Decision Making.** Deborah H. Long. LC 94-41398. 144p. 1995. per. 15.00 (*0-89787-939-2*) Gorsuch Scarisbrick.

Doing the Right Thing: Eleven Exercises for Your Ethical Mind. Alice S. Lawhead. 192p. (Orig.). 1991. pap. 7.99 (*0-87788-183-9*) Shaw Pubs.

Doing the Right Thing: Making Quality Decisions. Tom Rusk. 60p. 1992. student ed 14.95 (*0-88390-334-2*); student ed, ring bd. 595.00 (*0-88390-333-4*) Pfeiffer & Co.

Doing the Right Thing: The Ultimate Profit. Robert D. Sherer. 192p. 1993. pap. 12.95 (*1-884162-02-9*) Criterion Hse.

***Doing the Right Things for the Right Reasons.** Richard L. Bednar & Scott R. Peterson. 1995. write for info. (*0-87579-870-5*) Deseret Bk.

Doing the Truth in Charity: Statements of Popes Paul VI, John Paul I, John Paul II & the Secretariat for Promoting Christian Unity. Ed. by Thomas F. Stransky & John B. Sheerin. LC 81-85384. 400p. (Orig.). 1982. pap. 12.95 (*0-8091-2398-3*) Paulist Pr.

***Doing the Truth in Love: Conversations about God, Relationships & Service.** Michael J. Himes et al. LC 95-8644. 176p. (Orig.). 1995. pap. 12.95 (*0-8091-3584-1*) Paulist Pr.

Doing the White Pass. Howard Clifford. LC 82-62466. (Illus.). 96p. (Orig.). 1994. pap. 6.75 (*0-911803-04-1*) Sourdough.

Doing Their Bit: Wartime American Animated Short Films, 1939-1945. Michael S. Shull & David E. Wilt. LC 85-43589. 208p. 1987. lib. bdg. 32.50x (*0-89950-218-0*) McFarland & Co.

***Doing Their Share to Save the Planet: Children & the Environmental Crisis.** Donna L. King. LC 94-41056. (Illus.). 160p. (C). 1995. text ed. 42.00 (*0-8135-2184-X*); pap. text ed. 15.00 (*0-8135-2185-8*) Rutgers U Pr.

Doing Theology in a Divided World: Papers from the Sixth International Conference of the Ecumenical Association of Third World Theologians, January 5-13, 1983, Geneva, Switzerland. Ecumenical Association of Third World Theologians Staff. Ed. by Virginia Fabella & Sergio Torres. LC 84-14712. 240p. reprint ed. pap. 68.40 (*0-7837-5530-9*, 2045300) Bks Demand.

Doing Theology in Context, Vol. I: South African Perspectives. Ed. by John De Gruchy & Charles Villa-Vicencio. 225p. (Orig.). 1994. pap. 18.95 (*0-88344-989-7*) Orbis Bks.

Doing Theology in Today's World: Essays in Honor of Kenneth S. Kantzer. Ed. by John D. Woodbridge & Thomas E. McComiskey. 268p. 1994. pap. 19.99 (*0-310-44731-3*) Zondervan.

Doing Theology with Huck & Jim: Parables for Understanding Doctrine. Mark Shaw. LC 93-36209. 201p. (Orig.). 1993. pap. 9.99 (*0-8308-1654-2*, 1654) InterVarsity.

Doing Things. Illus. by Eira Reeves. LC 91-76214. (Let's Read Bks.). 12p. (J). (ps). 1992. bds. 3.99 (*0-8066-2590-2*, 9-2590, Augsburg) Augsburg Fortress.

Doing Things: A Guide to Programming Activities for Persons with Alzheimer's Disease & Related Disorders. Jitka M. Zgola. LC 86-46280. 160p. 1987. text ed. 32.50 (*0-8018-3466-X*); pap. text ed. 12.95 (*0-8018-3467-8*) Johns Hopkins.

Doing Things & Happenings. Mary G. Kellogg. LC 80-80271. (Illus.). 90p. (J). (gr. 1-6). 1979. 6.95 (*0-9603972-0-5*); pap. 4.95 (*0-9603972-1-3*) Bks by Kellogg.

Doing Things Right. William E. Ruxton. 249p. 1985. text ed. 49.95 (*0-910399-33-6*) Natl Tool & Mach.

An Asterisk (*) at the beginning of an entry indicates that the title is appearing in BIP for the first time.

D

Dollars & Dreams: The National Youth Administration in Texas. Carol A. Weisenberger. LC 93-36536. (Recent American History Ser.: Vol. 6). 216p. (C). 1994. text ed. 46.95 (*0-8204-2280-0*) P Lang Pubs.

Dollars & Sense. Larry Burkett. 1993. pap. 4.95 (*1-55748-415-5*) Barbour & Co.

***Dollars & Sense: A Guide to Spending on Children & Families in Illinois.** Ami Nagle. (C). 1995. pap. 15.00 (*1-886008-01-9*) Voices IL Chdrn.

Dollars & Sense: A Handbook for Seasonal Grass Dairying. Larry F. Tranel. LC 93-80642. (Illus.). 112p. (C). 1994. pap. text ed. 17.95 (*0-9632460-2-X*) Green Park.

Dollars & Sense: An Introduction to Economics. 7th ed. Marilu H. McCarty. 372p. (C). 1993. pap. 34.25 (*0-673-46806-2*) HarpCollege.

Dollars & Sense: An Introduction to Economics. 7th ed. Marilu H. McCarty. 372p. (C). 1993. Study guide, student ed 15.00 (*0-673-46807-0*) HarpCollege.

Dollars & Sense: Catholic High Schools & Their Finances 1992. Michael J. Guerra. 62p. (Orig.). 1993. pap. 16.00 (*1-55833-095-X*) Natl Cath Educ.

Dollars & Sense: Financial Wisdom in 101 Doses. Gerald W. Perritt. 312p. 1986. pap. 18.95 (*0-685-14685-5*) Invest Info.

Dollars & Sense: Making the Most of What You Have. Wilson J. Humber. LC 93-4097. 240p. (Orig.). 1993. pap. 12.00 (*0-89109-741-4*) NavPress.

Dollars & Sense Guide to Divorce: The Financial Guide for Women. Judith Briles. 352p. 1991. mass mkt. 4.95 (*0-345-36098-2*) Ballantine.

Dollars & Sense in Irrigated Agriculture: The Need for a Consistent Tax Policy. Justin Ward et al. 1987. 2.50 (*0-318-23635-4*) NRDC Newsletter.

***Dollars & Sense of Battlefield Preservation: The Economic Benefits of Protecting Civil War Battlefields: A Handbook for Community Leaders.** Frances H. Kennedy & Conservation Fund Staff. LC 94-25733. 96p. 1994. pap. 14.95 (*0-89133-257-X*) Preservation Pr.

Dollars & Sense of Estate Planning. Forest Bowman. 1988. text ed. 68.00 (*0-13-217795-1*) P-H.

Dollars & "Sense" of Government Contracting: Fiscal Law, Incremental Funding & Conditional Contracts. 200p. 1988. pap. 35.00 (*0-89707-371-1*, 539-0072-01) Amer Bar Assn.

Dollars, Debts & Deficits. Rudiger Dornbusch. 200p. 1987. 30.00x (*0-262-04085-9*) MIT Pr.

Dollars, Deficits, & Trade. Ed. by James A. Dorn & William A. Niskanen. LC 89-37481. 442p. 1989. pap. 5.00 (*0-7923-9024-5*) Cato Inst.

Dollars, Diplomacy, & Dependency: Dilemmas of U. S. Economic Aid. Robert F. Zimmerman. LC 92-43597. 235p. 1993. lib. bdg. 45.00 (*1-55587-362-6*); pap. text ed. 17.95 (*1-55587-399-5*) Lynne Rienner.

Dollars for Bullets: The Story of American Rule in Nicaragua. Harold N. Denny. LC 79-25688. (Illus.). 411p. 1980. reprint ed. text ed. 65.00 (*0-313-22269-X*, DEDB, Greenwood Pr) Greenwood.

Dollars for Bullets: The Story of American Rule in Nicaragua. Harold N. Denny. (BCL1 - U. S. History Ser.). 411p. 1991. reprint ed. lib. bdg. 99.00 (*0-7812-6048-5*) Rprt Serv.

Dollars for College: A Handbook of Financial Aid Sources for Minority Students. Sandra K. Williams & Mezell L. Williams, Jr. 122p. 1991. pap. 10.50 (*0-9629707-9-4*) Educ Facilitators.

***Dollars for College: The Quick Guide to Financial Aid for Art, Music, & Drama.** Ed. by Cheryl S. Hecht. LC 95-1364. (Dollars for College Ser.). 94p. (Orig.). 1995. pap. 6.95 (*1-880774-19-4*) Garrett Pk.

***Dollars for College: The Quick Guide to Financial Aid for Business & Related Fields, Vol. 1.** Ed. by Elizabeth A. Olson. LC 95-1364. (Dollars for College Ser.). 76p. (Orig.). 1995. pap. 6.95 (*1-880774-10-0*) Garrett Pk.

***Dollars for College: The Quick Guide to Financial Aid for Education.** Ed. by Cheryl S. Hecht. LC 95-1364. (Dollars for College Ser.). 79p. (Orig.). 1995. pap. 6.95 (*1-880774-12-7*) Garrett Pk.

***Dollars for College: The Quick Guide to Financial Aid for Engineering.** Ed. by Cheryl S. Hecht. LC 95-1364. (Dollars for College Ser.). 72p. (Orig.). 1995. pap. 6.95 (*1-880774-13-5*) Garrett Pk.

***Dollars for College: The Quick Guide to Financial Aid for Journalism & Mass Communications.** Ed. by Elizabeth A. Olson. LC 95-1364. (Dollars for College Ser.). 76p. (Orig.). 1995. pap. 6.95 (*1-880774-11-9*) Garrett Pk.

***Dollars for College: The Quick Guide to Financial Aid for Liberal Arts: Humanities & Social Science.** Ed. by Elizabeth A. Olson. LC 95-1364. (Dollars for College Ser.). 84p. (Orig.). 1995. pap. 6.95 (*1-880774-18-6*) Garrett Pk.

***Dollars for College: The Quick Guide to Financial Aid for Medicine, Dentistry, & Related Fields.** Ed. by Cheryl S. Hecht. LC 95-1364. (Dollars for College Ser.). 76p. 1995. pap. 6.95 (*1-880774-15-1*) Garrett Pk.

***Dollars for College: The Quick Guide to Financial Aid for Nursing & Other Health Fields.** Ed. by Cheryl S. Hecht. LC 95-1364. (Dollars for College Ser.). 76p. (Orig.). 1995. pap. 6.95 (*1-880774-17-8*) Garrett Pk.

***Dollars for College: The Quick Guide to Financial Aid for Science.** Ed. by Elizabeth A. Olson. LC 95-1364. (Dollars for College Ser.). 80p. (Orig.). 1995. pap. 6.95 (*1-880774-14-3*) Garrett Pk.

***Dollars for College: The Quick Guide to Financial Aid for Women in All Fields.** Ed. by Elizabeth A. Olson. LC 95-1364. (Dollars for College Ser.). 80p. (Orig.). 1995. pap. 6.95 (*1-880774-20-8*) Garrett Pk.

Dollars for Excellence. Roy Bunce & Stanton Leggett. LC 87-51102. 312p. 1987. 40.00 (*0-931028-97-3*) Precept Pr.

Dollars for Scholars: The Autobiography of Dr. Irving a Fradkin. Irving A. Fradkin & Michael J. Vieira. (Illus.). 256p. (Orig.). 1993. pap. 14.95 (*0-8283-1974-X*) Branden Pub Co.

Dollars for the Reaper. large type ed. B. J. Holmes. (Linford Western Library). 256p. 1992. pap. 14.95 (*0-7089-7180-6*, Trailtree Bookshop) Ulverscroft.

Dollars from Design. 48p. 1982. 16.00 (*0-317-35155-9*, 5506); 8.00 (*0-317-35156-7*) Natl League Cities.

Dollars from Your Discards: The Complete Garage Sale Handbook. Carolyn I. Kilmer. LC 80-81565. (Illus.). 56p. (Orig.). 1980. pap. 4.95 (*0-937028-00-2*, 101) Henry John & Co.

Dollars Making It...&...Keeping It: The Common Sense Guide to Financial Wellbeing. Alexander Odishelidze. 208p. 1993. 22.95 (*0-9633405-0-6*) Employ Benefits.

Dollarville. Pete Davies. 1989. 17.95 (*0-394-57780-9*) Random.

Dollarwise Guide to New England. Thomas Brosnahan. 408p. 1986. pap. 11.95 (*0-317-37801-5*) S&S Trade.

Dollevoet Theory, Vol. 1: The All Universal Hyper Correlative Domain of Electromagnetic Correlative Principles & Laws. George D. Dollevoet. LC 87-73316. (Illus.). 100p. (Orig.). (C). 1988. pap. 6.50 (*0-9619823-0-6*) G D Dollevoet.

***Dolley: A Novel of Dolley Madison in Love & War.** Brown. 1995. mass mkt. (*0-553-56949-X*) Bantam.

Dolley: A Novel of Dolley Madison in Love & War. Rita M. Brown. LC 93-44429. 1994. 22.95 (*0-553-08890-4*) Bantam.

Dolley Madison. Patricia R. Quiri. LC 92-28300. (First Bks.). (J). 1993. 13.93 (*0-531-20097-3*) Watts.

Dollhouse. (Chubby Shape Bks.). (Illus.). 16p. (J). (ps). 1984. pap. 2.95 (*0-671-49718-9*, Litl Simon S&S) S&S Childrens.

Dollhouse. Jacqueline Karas. LC 92-32262. (Illus.). 32p. (J). (ps up). 1993. 15.00 (*0-688-12480-1*, Tambourine Bks); lib. bdg. 14.93 (*0-688-12481-X*, Tambourine Bks) Morrow.

Dollhouse Book: Color & Counting Concepts. Illus. by Kenneth Brown. (J). 1994. 12.95 (*1-56743-044-9*) Amistad Pr.

Dollhouse Crafting Tips from Nutshell News see Workshop Wisdom Dollhouse Crafting Tips from Nutshell News

Dollhouse Decorating: A Guide to Interior Design in Miniature, in Twelve Distinctive Styles. Nick Forder. (Illus.). 128p. 1994. 12.98 (*1-56138-439-9*) Running Pr.

Dollhouse Decorator. Vivienne Boulton. LC 92-16014. (Illus.). 96p. 1993. 21.95 (*1-56458-077-6*) Dorling Kindersley.

Dollhouse Fun! Furniture You Can Make. Judith Conaway. LC 86-16133. (Illus.). 48p. (J). (gr. 1-5). 1987. lib. bdg. 11.89 (*0-8167-0862-2*); pap. text ed. 3.50 (*0-8167-0863-0*) Troll Assocs.

Dollhouse Furniture. Margaret Towner. LC 93-70595. (Collector's Library). (Illus.). 80p. 1993. 12.98 (*1-56138-325-2*) Courage Bks.

Dollhouse Miniatures. Ed. by Sybil Harp. (Creative Crafts Library). (Illus.). 36p. 1977. pap. 3.00 (*0-911868-30-5*, C30) Carstens Pubns.

Dollhouse Murders. Betty R. Wright. LC 83-6147. 160p. (J). (gr. 3-7). 1983. 14.95 (*0-8234-0497-8*) Holiday.

Dollhouse Murders. Betty R. Wright. 160p. (J). (gr. 3-7). 1985. pap. 2.75 (*0-590-43461-6*) Scholastic Inc.

Dollhouse Sourcebook: Classic Miniature Period Interiors. Carroline Clifton-Mogg. 1993. 37.50 (*1-55859-613-5*) Abbeville Pr.

***Dollhouses - Collector's Guide.** Douet. 1995. (*0-7858-0220-7*) Bk Sales Inc.

Dollies. Pat Graversen. 1990. pap. 3.95 (*0-8217-3071-1*) Zebra.

Dolliver Romance. Nathaniel Hawthorne. Bd. with Fanshawe. LC 75-125216.; Septimius Felton. LC 75-125216. LC 75-125216. (Short Story Index Reprint Ser.). 1977. reprint ed. 24.95 (*0-8369-3583-7*) Ayer.

Dolliver Romance Fanshawe, Septimus Felton with an Appendix Containing the Ancestral Footstep. Nathaniel Hawthorne. (Illus.). 522p. 1976. reprint ed. 21.00 (*0-403-02465-X*) Scholarly.

Dollkeeper. Jack Scaparro. 384p. 1987. pap. 3.95 (*0-8217-1988-2*) Zebra.

Dollmaker. Harriette Arnow. 608p. 1976. mass mkt. 5.99 (*0-380-00947-1*) Avon.

Dollmaker's Ghost. 2nd ed. Larry Levis. 72p. 1992. reprint ed. pap. 10.95 (*0-88748-125-6*) Carnegie-Mellon.

Dollmaking. E. J. Taylor. LC 87-42745. (Illus.). 112p. 1988. pap. 9.95 (*0-89480-311-5*, 1311) Workman Pub.

Dollmaking - One Artist's Approach. Robert K. McKinley. Ed. by Linda Nelson. 166p. (Orig.). 1991. teacher ed write for info. (*0-9628821-0-0*) McKinley Bk.

***Dolls.** Ariel Books Staff. (Illus.). 80p. 1995. 4.95 (*0-8362-3127-9*) Andrews & McMeel.

Dolls. Max Boehn. 1972. pap. 6.95 (*0-486-22847-9*) Dover.

***Dolls.** Ed. by Creative Craft Series Staff. 1994. 10.95 (*0-681-40954-1*) Longmeadow Pr.

Dolls. Jerome McDonough. 28p. (Orig.). 1988. pap. 3.00 (*0-88680-298-9*) I E Clark.

Dolls. Vivian Werner. 144p. (J). 1991. pap. 2.95 (*0-380-76044-4*, Camelot) Avon.

Dolls. Sarah Wilkins & Roxanna Mennella. Ed. by Barbara Fisher. (Illus.). 27p. (Orig.). (J). (gr. 4-6). 1984. pap. 2.00 (*0-934830-34-7*) Ten Penny.

Dolls. Robert S. Young. LC 92-3498. (Collectibles Ser.). (Illus.). 72p. (J). (gr. 5 up). 1992. text ed. 13.95 (*0-87518-517-7*, Dillon Silver Burdett) Silver Burdett Pr.

Dolls: A Postcard Book. Ed. by Running Press Staff. (Postcard Book Ser.). (Illus.). 64p. (Orig.). 1991. pap. 7.95 (*1-56138-017-2*) Running Pr.

Dolls: An Educational Coloring Book. Spizzirri Publishing Co. Staff. Ed. by Linda Spizzirri. (Illus.). 32p. (J). (gr. 1-8). 1981. pap. 1.75 (*0-86545-034-X*) Spizzirri.

Dolls: From Kewpie to Barbie & Beyond. Judy Sparrow. 1994. 15.98 (*0-8317-2262-2*) Smithmark.

Dolls: Portraits from the Golden Age. Pamela Sherer & Tom Kelley. LC 92-53681. 128p. 1992. 12.98 (*1-56138-102-0*) Courage Bks.

Dolls & Dungarees. Tutchell. 1990. 27.00 (*0-335-09287-X*, Open Univ Pr) Taylor & Francis.

Dolls & Puppets. Max Von Boehn. Tr. by Josephine Nicoll. (Illus.). 1966. reprint ed. 83.00 (*0-8154-0026-8*) Cooper Sq.

Dolls & Toys at the Essex Institute. Madeline Merrill & Richard Merrill. LC 76-40405. (E.I. Museum Booklet Ser.). 1976. 5.95 (*0-88389-066-6*, Essx Institute) Peabody Essex Mus.

***Dolls & Toys of Native America: A Journey Through Childhood.** Don McQuiston & Debra McQuiston. LC 94-34678. 1995. 35.00 (*0-8118-0572-7*); 19.95 (*0-8118-0570-0*) Chronicle Bks.

Dolls at Our House. limited ed. Diana Glissman. (Be'be's & Bears Ser.: Vol. 1). (Illus.). 64p. 1986. lib. bdg. 14.95 (*0-9616342-0-0*) Glynn Pubns.

Dolls at Our House. 2nd ed. Diana Glissman. (Be'be's & Bears Ser.: Vol. 1). (Illus.). 64p. 1986. lib. bdg. 16.95 (*0-9616342-1-9*) Glynn Pubns.

Dolls' Christmas. Tasha Tudor. LC 59-12744. (Illus.). (J). (gr. k-3). 1979. 6.95 (*0-8098-1026-3*); pap. 4.95 (*0-8098-2912-6*) McKay.

Doll's Clothes Pattern Book. Roselyn Gadia-Smitley. LC 87-14369. (Illus.). 192p. (Orig.). 1987. 24.95 (*0-8069-6436-7*); pap. 12.95 (*0-8069-6438-3*) Sterling.

Doll's Dressmaker. 1969. pap. 3.95 (*0-87282-023-8*) Am Life Foun.

Doll's Dressmaker: The Complete Pattern Book. Venus A. Dodge. (Illus.). 192p. 1991. pap. 19.95 (*0-7153-9289-1*, Pub. by D & C Pub UK) Sterling.

Dolls Dressmaking. Marilyn Carter. (Illus.). 104p. 1993. pap. 12.95 (*1-86351-078-8*, Pub. by S Milner AT) Sterling.

***Doll's Eyes.** Bari Wood. 384p. 1994. mass mkt. 5.50 (*0-380-72097-3*) Avon.

Doll's Eyes. Bari Wood. LC 92-39304. 1993. 20.00 (*0-688-12440-2*) Morrow.

Doll's House. E. Anthony. 1993. mass mkt. 4.99 (*0-06-109107-3*, Harp PBks) HarpC.

***Doll's House.** Rumer Godden. 1995. 17.25 (*0-8446-6801-X*) Peter Smith.

Doll's House. Rumer Godden. LC 62-18693. (Storybooks Ser.). (J). (ps-3). 1976. pap. 4.50 (*0-14-030942-X*, Puffin) Puffin Bks.

Doll's House. Henrik Ibsen. Tr. by William Archer. LC 93-13396. 62p. 1993. pap. 6.00 (*0-88734-269-8*) Players Pr.

Doll's House. Katherine Mansfield. (Creative's Collection of Classic Short Stories Ser.). 32p. (J). (gr. 4 up). 1986. lib. bdg. 13.95 (*0-88682-056-1*) Creative Ed.

Doll's House. Albert Pia. 47p. 1972. pap. 2.50 (*0-87129-102-9*, D19) Dramatic Pub.

Doll's House. large type ed. Evelyn Anthony. LC 92-32140. 464p. 1993. reprint ed. lib. bdg. 20.95 (*1-56054-559-3*) Thorndike Pr.

Doll's House. Henrik Ibsen. (Thrift Editions Ser.). 80p. 1992. reprint ed. pap. 1.00 (*0-486-27062-9*) Dover.

Doll's House: Ibsen's Myth of Transformation. Errol Durbach. (Twayne's Masterwork Studies: No. 75). 168p. (C). 1991. text ed. 21.95 (*0-8057-9403-4*, Twayne); pap. 12.95 (*0-8057-8147-1*, Pub. by Royal Botanic Garden UK) Macmillan.

Doll's House & Hedda Gabler (Ibsen) Linnea. (Book Notes Ser.). (J). (gr. 9-12). 1985. pap. 2.95 (*0-8120-3511-9*) Barron.

Doll's House & Hedda Gabler Notes. Marianne Sturman. 1965. pap. 3.95 (*0-8220-0614-6*) Cliffs.

Doll's House & Other Plays. Henrik Ibsen. Tr. by Peter Watts. Incl. League of Youth. 1965. (*0-318-55028-8*); Lady from the Sea. 1965. (*0-318-55029-6*); (Classics Ser.). 1965. Set mass mkt. 8.95 (*0-14-044146-8*, Penguin Classics) Viking Penguin.

***Doll's House Board Books.** Andrew Bale. (Illus.). (J). (ps). 1994. 14.95 (*0-316-07972-3*) Little.

Doll's House Do-It-Yourself Book. Venus A. Dodge & Martin Dodge. (Illus.). 224p. 1991. pap. 14.95 (*0-7153-9858-X*, Pub. by D & C Pub UK) Sterling.

***Dolls' House Needlecrafts: Over 250 Projects in 1-12 Scale.** Venus A. Dodge. (Illus.). 192p. 1995. 29.95 (*0-7153-0169-1*, Pub. by D & C Pub UK) Sterling.

Doll's House, The Lady from the Sea, The Wild Duck. Henrik Ibsen. Ed. by F. Farquharson Sharp & Eleanor Marx-Aveline. 294p. 1993. pap. 4.95 (*0-460-87293-1*, Everyman's Classic Lib) C E Tuttle.

Doll's Houses. Halina Pasierbska. (Shire Album Ser.: No. 271). (Illus.). 32p. 1991. pap. text ed. 6.00 (*0-7478-0135-5*, Pub. by Shire Pubns UK) Lubrecht & Cramer.

Dolls' Houses: An Architectural Design Profile. (Academy Architecture Ser.). (Illus.). 128p. 1983. pap. 21.95 (*0-312-21625-4*) St Martin.

Doll's Houses in America: Historic Preservation in Miniature. Flora G. Jacobs. (Illus.). 395p. 1974. pap. 16.95 (*0-686-37145-3*) Wash Dolls Hse.

Dolls of Canada: A Reference Guide. Evelyn R. Strahlendorf. 430p. 1990. 75.00 (*0-8020-2747-4*) U of Toronto Pr.

Dolls of Poplar House. Thomas Hischak. 1979. pap. 2.50 (*0-87129-201-7*, D31) Dramatic Pub.

Doll's Tea Party. M. C. Leeka. (Storytime Bks.). (Illus.). 24p. (J). (ps-2). 1993. pap. text ed. 0.99 (*1-56293-343-4*) McClanahan Bk.

Dolls Tell the Story. Dee H. Gronhovd & Pearl Steinkuehler. (Illus.). 196p. (Orig.). (C). 1988. text ed. 21.95 (*0-318-37918-X*); pap. text ed. 15.95 (*0-318-37919-8*) Assoc Print.

Dolls, the Early Years, 1780-1880. Theriault. Ed. by Florence Theriault. (Illus.). 80p. (Orig.). 1989. pap. 35.00 (*0-912823-01-1*) Gold Horse.

Dolly. Anita Brookner. 1994. 22.00 (*0-679-42318-4*) Random.

Dolly. Anita Brookner. LC 93-14537. 1995. 11.00 (*0-679-74578-5*) Random.

Dolly. Claudia Sardin. (J). (ps-12). 1987. pap. 2.95 (*0-87067-723-3*, BH723) Holloway.

***Dolly: My Life & Other Unfinished Business.** Parton. 1995. mass mkt. 5.99 (*0-06-109236-3*, Harp PBks) HarpC.

***Dolly: My Life & Other Unfinished Business.** Dolly Parton. LC 94-18714. 1994. 25.00 (*0-06-017720-9*) HarpC.

***Dolly: My Life & Other Unfinished Business.** large type ed. Dolly Parton. LC 94-39240. 1995. write for info. (*0-7862-0363-3*); pap. write for info. (*0-7862-0364-1*) Thorndike Pr.

Dolly Dialogues. Anthony H. Hawkins. LC 72-106288. (Short Story Index Reprint Ser.). (Illus.). 1977. 19.95 (*0-8369-3325-7*) Ayer.

Dolly Dolphin & the Strange New Something. Dina Anastasio. (Shamu & His Crew Adventure Ser.). (Illus.). 32p. (J). (gr. k-3). 1994. 5.95 (*1-884506-07-0*) Third Story.

Dolly Dolphin's Play School. Pam Adams. (J). 1981. 6.95 (*0-85953-266-6*) Childs Play.

***Dolly Duck Plants Corn.** S. Bernadine Riske. (Illus.). (Orig.). (J). (gr. 2 up). 1995. pap. 7.95 (*1-885981-08-2*, Brisk Pubns) Brisk Pubng.

***Dolly Is Dead.** J. S. Borthwick. LC 95-8567. 1995. write for info. (*0-312-13052-X*) St Martin.

Dolly Madison. Ruth Waldrop. LC 89-61360. (First Ladies Ser.). (Illus.). 112p. (J). (gr. 3 up). 1989. lib. bdg. 10.95 (*0-318-50084-1*); pap. 6.95 (*0-9616894-3-9*) RuSK Inc.

Dolly Madison: Famous First Lady. Mary R. Davidson. (Discovery Biographies Ser.). (Illus.). 80p. (J). (gr. 2-6). 1992. reprint ed. lib. bdg. 12.95 (*0-7910-1446-0*) Chelsea Hse.

Dolly Morton. 224p. 1984. pap. 3.95 (*0-88184-041-6*) Carroll & Graf.

Dolmen Book of Irish Christmas Stories. Ed. by Dermot Bolger. 164p. 1986. pap. 13.95 (*0-85105-456-0*, Pub. by Colin Smythe Ltd UK) Dufour.

Dolmen Book of Irish Stamps. Liam Miller. 1986. 17.95 (*0-85105-453-6*, Pub. by Colin Smythe Ltd UK) Dufour.

Dolmens for the Dead: Megalith-Building Throughout the World. Roger Joussaume. Tr. by Anne Chippindale & Christopher Chippindale. (Illus.). 312p. 1988. 38.50 (*0-8014-2156-X*) Cornell U Pr.

Dolmens of Jersey. Kinnes. 1988. pap. 15.00 (*0-86120-021-7*, Pub. by Aris & Phillips UK) David Brown.

Dolomite & Siliciclastic Dikes & Sills in Marginal-Marine Cretaceous Coals of Central Utah. John K. Hardie. Date not set. write for info. (*0-318-72610-6*) USGPO.

Dolomite Reservoirs: Geochemical Techniques for Evaluating Origin & Distribution. J. R. Allan & W. D. Wiggins. (Continuing Education Course Note Ser.: No. 36). (Illus.). 170p. (Orig.). 1993. pap. 20.00 (*0-89181-185-0*) AAPG.

Dolomites. Reginald Farrer. (Plant Hunter Ser.). 224p. 1987. reprint ed. pap. 11.95 (*0-946313-17-2*) Timber.

Dolomites: A Volume in Honour of Dolomieu. Ed. by Bruce Purser et al. LC 93-31068. (International Association of Sedimentologists Special Publication Ser.: No. 21). 432p. 1994. pap. 100.00 (*0-632-03787-3*) Blackwell Sci.

Dolomites of the Monterey Formation & Other Organic-Rich Units. Ed. by Robert E. Garrison et al. (Illus.). 215p. (Orig.). 1984. pap. 6.00 (*1-878861-31-X*) Pac Section SEPM.

***Dolomitization.** Lyton S. Land. (Continuing Education Course Note Ser.: No. 24). (Illus.). 20p. 1983. pap. 9.00 (*0-89181-173-7*) AAPG.

Dolomitization & Limestone Diagenesis: A Symposium. Ed. by Lloyd C. Pray & Raymond C. Murray. LC 73-15328. (Society of Economic Paleontologists & Mineralogists, Special Publication Ser.: No. 13). 190p. reprint ed. pap. 54.20 (*0-317-27156-3*, 2024739) Bks Demand.

Dolopathos: Or, the King & the Seven Wise Men. Johannes De Alta Silva. Tr. by Brady B. Gilleland. (Medieval & Renaissance Texts & Studies: Vol. 2). 136p. (C). 1981. 16.00 (*0-86698-001-6*); pap. 9.00 (*0-86698-006-7*) MRTS.

Dolor y Alegria: Women & Social Change in Urban Mexico. Sarah LeVine & Clara S. Correa. LC 92-39037. (Life Course Studies). (Illus.). 254p. (Orig.). 1993. 37.50 (*0-299-13790-2*); pap. 12.95 (*0-299-13794-5*) U of Wis Pr.

Doloras - Cantares. 7th ed. Ramon De Campoamor Y Campoosorio. 160p. (SPA.). 1981. pap. 9.95 (*0-7859-5139-3*) Fr & Eur.

***Dolores Claiborne.** Stephen King. 384p. 1995. 6.99 (*0-451-18411-4*, Sig) NAL-Dutton.

***Dolores Claiborne.** Stephen King. Date not set. 6.98 (*0-8317-1186-8*) Smithmark.

Dolores Claiborne. Stephen King. LC 92-15467. 1993. 23.50 (*0-670-84452-7*, Viking) Viking Penguin.

Dolores Claiborne. large type ed. Stephen King. (General Ser.). 355p. 1992. lib. bdg. 25.00 (*0-8161-5640-9*) G K Hall.

Dolores Claiborne. large type ed. Stephen King. (General Ser.). 355p. 1993. pap. 16.95 (*0-8161-5641-7*, Large Print Bks) Hall.

Dolores Claiborne. Stephen King. 384p. 1993. reprint ed. pap. 6.99 (*0-451-17709-6*, Sig) NAL-Dutton.

Dolores of the Sierra & Other One Act Plays. Harriet Holmes Haslett. LC 77-70357. (One-Act Plays in Reprint Ser.). 1977. reprint ed. 15.00 (*0-8486-2018-6*) Roth Pub Inc.

D

An Asterisk (*) at the beginning of an entry indicates that the title is appearing in BIP for the first time.

Dolorous Passion of Our Lord Jesus Christ. Anne C. Emmerich. 1980. lib. bdg. 250.00 (*0-8490-3100-1*) Gordon Pr.

Dolorous Passion of Our Lord Jesus Christ. Anne C. Emmerich. LC 83-70406. 382p. 1983. reprint ed. pap. 15.00 (*0-89555-210-8*) TAN Bks Pubs.

Dolpa the Hidden Paradise - A Journey to the Endangered Sanctuary of the Himalayan Kingdom of Nepal. Karna Sakya. (C). 1991. text ed. 75.00 (*0-7855-0135-5*, Pub. by Ratna Pustak Bhandar) St Mut.

Dolphin. (Animal World Bks.). (Illus.). 28p. (J). (gr. 2-5). 1988. pap. 3.50 (*0-8167-1576-9*) Troll Assocs.

Dolphin. Sue Houghton. LC 91-44819. (Life Story Ser.). (Illus.). 32p. (J). (gr. 4-6). 1993. lib. bdg. 11.59 (*0-8167-2767-8*); pap. text ed. 3.95 (*0-8167-2768-6*) Troll Assocs.

Dolphin. Robert A. Morris. LC 75-6292. (Trophy I Can Read Bk.). (Illus.). 64p. (J). (gr. k-3). 1983. pap. 3.50 (*0-06-444043-5*, Trophy) Irwin Prof Pubng.

Dolphin, Reading Level 3-4. Propper. (World Animal Library). (Illus.). 28p. (J). (gr. 2-5). 1983. 12.50 (*0-685-58815-7*); lib. bdg. 16.67 (*0-86592-861-4*) Rourke Corp.

Dolphin Adventure: A True Story. Wayne Grover. LC 89-27226. (Illus.). 48p. (J). (gr. 3 up). 1990. 14.00 (*0-688-09442-2*) Greenwillow.

Dolphin Adventure: A True Story. Wayne Grover. LC 92-25545. (Illus.). 48p. (J). (gr. 4 up). 1993. reprint ed. pap. 3.95 (*0-688-12277-9*, Pub. by Beech Tree Bks) Morrow.

Dolphin Bay. large type ed. Bevan. 1991. 17.95 (*0-7451-8037-X*, AH088, Atlantic Lrg Print); pap. 15.95 (*0-7927-0502-5*, AS0124, Atlantic Lrg Print) Chivers N Amer.

Dolphin Chase. (Read with Me Key Words to Reading Ser.: No. 9010-14). (Illus.). (J). (ps-2). 1990. 3.50 (*0-7214-1327-7*) Ladybird Bks.

Dolphin Chase. (Read with Me Key Words to Reading Ser.: No. 9010-14). (Illus.). (J). (ps-2). 1990. teacher ed 3.95 (*0-317-04037-5*) Ladybird Bks.

Dolphin Cognition & Behavior: A Comparative Approach. Ronald J. Schusterman et al. (Comparative Cognitive & Neuroscience Ser.). 408p. (C). 1986. pap. 39.95 (*0-89859-594-0*) L Erlbaum Assocs.

Dolphin Connection: Interdimensional Ways of Living. Joan Ocean. LC 89-81370. (Illus.). 144p. (Orig.). 1989. pap. 11.95 (*0-9625058-9-7*) Dolphin Connection.

Dolphin Days: My Life & Times with the Spinners. Kenneth S. Norris. 1991. 21.95 (*0-393-02945-X*) Norton.

Dolphin Days: The Life & Times of the Spinner Dolphin. Kenneth S. Norris. (Illus.). 336p. 1993. reprint ed. pap. 10.00 (*0-380-71965-7*) Avon.

Dolphin Divination Cards. Nancy Clemens. (Illus.). 108p. (Orig.). 1994. pap. 11.00 (*0-931892-79-1*) B Dolphin Pub.

Dolphin Doctor. Sam H. Ridgway. 1988. pap. 3.95 (*0-449-21622-5*) Fawcett.

Dolphin Experience. Lisa Tenzin-Dolma. 128p. 1995. pap. 9.95 (*0-572-01685-9*, Pub. by Foulsham UK) Atrium Pubs.

Dolphin Goes to School: The Story of Squirt, a Trained Dolphin. Elizabeth S. Smith. LC 85-28407. (Illus.). 96p. (J). (gr. 2-5). 1986. 12.95 (*0-688-04815-3*); lib. bdg. 12.88 (*0-688-04816-1*) Morrow Jr Bks.

***Dolphin KidKit, Set.** Paula C. Lowe & Richard F. Ferraro. (Dolphin KidKit Ser.). 30p. (J). (ps-3). 1994. audio, pap. 16.00 (*1-886476-00-4*) BigEye.

***Dolphin KidKit: Discovery Edition, Set.** Paula C. Lowe & Richard F. Ferraro. (Dolphin KidKit Ser.). 50p. (J). (gr. 2-7). 1994. audio, pap. 16.00 (*1-886476-01-2*) BigEye.

Dolphin Leaping in the Milky Way. Jeff Poniewaz. (Illus.). 148p. 1986. reprint ed. pap. 12.95 (*0-685-44851-7*) Inland Ocean Bks.

Dolphin Magic: The First Encounter. Terrill M. Burke. LC 91-76870. (Dolphin Ser.: Bk. 1). 315p. (Orig.). 1992. pap. 12.25 (*1-880485-65-6*) Alpha-Dolphin.

Dolphin Magic: The First Encounter. Terrill M. Burke. (Dolphin Ser.: Bk. 2). 305p. (Orig.). (J). (gr. 6 up). 1993. pap. 12.25 (*1-880485-69-9*) Alpha-Dolphin.

Dolphin Magic: The First Encounter. Terrill M. Burke. (Dolphin Ser.: Bk. 3). 362p. (Orig.). (YA). (gr. 6 up). 1993. pap. 12.25 (*1-880485-51-6*) Alpha-Dolphin.

***Dolphin Magic: The Unexpected Stranger.** Terrill M. Burke. (Dolphin Ser.). 400p. (J). (gr. 5 up). 1995. pap. 12.25 (*1-880485-54-0*) Alpha-Dolphin.

***Dolphin Man: Exploring The World of Dolphins.** Laurence Pringle. LC 95-5290. 1995. write for info. (*0-689-80299-4*, Atheneum S&S) S&S Trade.

Dolphin Mind. Jean C. Genet. Ed. by M. J. Bradbury. 61p. (Orig.). 1990. pap. text ed. write for info. (*0-9626383-0-7*) J C Genet.

Dolphin Ones. Sananjaleen. (Illus.). 64p. 1991. pap. text ed. 7.95 (*1-880757-00-1*) Sananda Pubns.

***Dolphin Queen.** Edmund S. Graves. 1994. 16.95 (*0-533-10770-9*) Vantage.

Dolphin Societies: Discoveries & Puzzles. Ed. by Karen Pryor & Kenneth S. Norris. (Illus.). 400p. 1990. 35.00 (*0-520-06717-7*) U CA Pr.

***Dolphin Sponsorship Kit.** Merryl Lambert. (Friends of the Ocean Ser.). 1994. 19.95 (*0-9641742-5-1*) Pequot Pubng.

***Dolphin Story.** Twig C. George. LC 95-8362. (Illus.). (J). 1996. 14.00 (*0-06-025362-2*, Festival); lib. bdg. 13.89 (*0-06-025363-0*, Festival) HarpC Child Bks.

Dolphin Sunrise. Elizabeth Webster. 368p. 1993. 21.95 (*0-312-09276-8*) St Martin.

Dolphin Sunrise. large type ed. Elizabeth Webster. 704p. 1994. 23.95 (*0-7089-3123-5*) Ulverscroft.

***Dolphin Treasure.** Wayne Grover. LC 95-7084. (Illus.). (J). 1996. 14.00 (*0-688-14343-1*) Greenwillow.

Dolphin Tribe: Remembering the Human-Dolphin Connection. Ashleea Nielsen. Ed. by Sara Patton. 136p. (Orig.). 1993. pap. 12.95 (*0-9637429-3-0*) Dancing Dolphin.

Dolphins. (Zoobooks Ser.). (J). 1991. lib. bdg. 14.95 (*0-88682-339-0*) Creative Ed.

Dolphins. Donna Bailey. LC 90-22110. (Animal World Ser.). (Illus.). 32p. (J). (gr. 1-4). 1992. lib. bdg. 19.97 (*0-8114-2647-5*); pap. 3.95 (*0-8114-4616-6*) Raintree Steck-V.

Dolphins. Sharon Bakoske & Margaret Davidson. (Step into Reading Bks.: Step 2). (Illus.). 48p. (Orig.). (J). (gr. 1-3). 1993. pap. 3.50 (*0-679-84437-6*) Random Bks Yng Read.

Dolphins. Sharon Bakoske & Margaret Davidson. (Step into Reading Bks.: Step 2). (Illus.). 48p. (Orig.). (J). (gr. 1-3). 1993. lib. bdg. 9.99 (*0-679-94437-0*) Random Bks Yng Read.

Dolphins! June Behrens. LC 89-33846. (Sea Life Ser.). 48p. (J). (gr. 1-4). 1989. lib. bdg. 12.68 (*0-516-00517-0*); pap. 5.95 (*0-516-40517-9*) Childrens.

Dolphins. Jacques-Yves Cousteau. 1987. 16.98 (*0-88486-015-9*) Arrowood Pr.

Dolphins. Cousteau Society Staff. LC 91-30589. (Illus.). 24p. (J). (ps-1). 1992. pap. 3.95 (*0-671-77062-4*, Litl Simon S&S) S&S Childrens.

***Dolphins.** Casey Horton. (Endangered! Ser.). 32p. (J). (gr. 3-5). 1995. lib. bdg. write for info. (*0-7614-0216-0*, Benchmark NY) Marshall Cavendish.

***Dolphins.** Bobbie Kalman. (Crabapple Ser.). (Illus.). 32p. (J). (ps-3). 1995. lib. bdg. 15.95 (*0-86505-622-6*) Crabtree Pub Co.

***Dolphins.** Bobbie Kalman. (Crabapple Ser.). (Illus.). 32p. (J). (ps-3). 1995. pap. 5.95 (*0-86505-722-2*) Crabtree Pub Co.

Dolphins. S. Palmer. (Sea Mammal Discovery Library). (Illus.). (J). (gr. k-5). 1989. 8.95 (*0-685-58619-7*); lib. bdg. 11.94 (*0-86592-363-9*) Rourke Corp.

Dolphins. Raintree Publishers Inc. Staff. LC 87-28717. (Science & Its Secrets Ser.). (Illus.). 64p. (Orig.). (J). (gr. 5-9). 1988. lib. bdg. 11.95 (*0-8172-3085-8*) Raintree Steck-V.

Dolphins. Stephen Spender. 64p. 1994. 18.95 (*0-312-11264-5*) St Martin.

Dolphins. Dean Stahl. (Nature Books Ser.). 32p. (J). (gr. 2-6). 1991. lib. bdg. 22.79 (*0-89565-718-X*) Childs World.

Dolphins. Barbara J. Zitwer. (Magic of the Ocean Ser.). (Illus.). 60p. 1995. write for info. (*0-446-51881-6*) Warner Bks.

Dolphins: An Educational Coloring Book. Spizzirri Publishing Co. Staff. Ed. by Linda Spizzirri. (Illus.). 32p. (J). (gr. 1-8). 1986. pap. 1.75 (*0-86545-073-0*) Spizzirri.

Dolphins: Our Friends in the Sea. Ed. by Donald J. Crump. LC 86-18126. (Books for World Explorers Series 8: No. 1). (Illus.). 104p. (J). (gr. 4-5). 1986. 8.95 (*0-87044-609-6*) Natl Geog.

Dolphins - Porpoises. Wildlife Education, Ltd. Staff. (Zoobooks Ser.). (Illus.). 20p. (J). 1990. 2.75 (*0-937934-62-3*) Wildlife Educ.

Dolphins & Me. Don C. Reed. (J). 1990. pap. 2.95 (*0-590-43294-X*) Scholastic Inc.

Dolphins & Porpoises. Richard Ellis. 1989. pap. 24.95 (*0-679-72286-6*) Knopf.

Dolphins & Porpoises. Sharon Gordon. LC 84-8594. (Now I Know Ser.). (Illus.). 32p. (J). (gr. k-2). 1985. lib. bdg. 11.59 (*0-8167-0340-X*); pap. text ed. 2.95 (*0-8167-0443-0*) Troll Assocs.

Dolphins & Porpoises. Janelle Hatherly & Delia Nicholls. (Great Creatures of the World Ser.). 72p. (YA). 1990. 17.95 (*0-8160-2272-0*) Facts on File.

Dolphins & Porpoises. Dorothy H. Patent. LC 87-45332. (Illus.). 96p. (J). (gr. 4 up). 1987. lib. bdg. 15.95 (*0-8234-0663-6*) Holiday.

Dolphins & Porpoises: A Worldwide Guide. Jean P. Sylvestre. LC 93-24789. (Illus.). 160p. 1993. 21.95 (*0-8069-8791-X*) Sterling.

Dolphins & the Tuna Industry. LC 92-10603. 1992. pap. text ed. 22.95 (*0-309-04735-8*) Natl Acad Pr.

Dolphins & Their Power to Heal. Amanda Cochrane & Karena Callen. (Illus.). 192p. (Orig.). 1992. pap. 19.95 (*0-89281-476-4*, Heal Arts VT) Inner Tradit.

Dolphins & Whales. Stephen Savage. 1990. 9.98 (*1-55521-578-5*) Bk Sales Inc.

Dolphins & Whales Model Set. Malcolm Whyte. (Action Sets Ser.). (Illus.). 24p. (J). (gr. 1 up). 1994. pap. 5.95 (*0-8431-2993-X*, Troubador) Price Stern.

Dolphin's Arc: Poems on Endangered Creatures of the Sea. Ed. by Elisavietta Ritchre. LC 89-60251. (SCOP Ser.: No. 12). 166p. 1989. pap. 10.95 (*0-930526-11-2*) Signal Bks.

Dolphins at Grassy Key. Marcia Seligson. LC 88-27143. (Illus.). 48p. (J). (gr. 1 up). 1989. text ed. 15.95 (*0-02-781800-4*, Mac Bks Young Read) S&S Childrens.

Dolphin's Cave. (Amazing Mazes Story Ser.). (Illus.). 48p. (Orig.). (J). (gr. k-3). 1989. pap. 2.95 (*0-8431-2707-4*) Price Stern.

Dolphins, ETs & Angels: Adventures among Spiritual Intelligences. Timothy Wyllie. LC 92-33121. (Illus.). 240p. 1993. reprint ed. pap. 10.95 (*1-879181-09-6*) Bear & Co.

Dolphin's First Day: The Story of a Bottlenose Dolphin. Kathleen W. Zoehfeld. LC 93-27270. (Smithsonian Oceanic Collection). (Illus.). 32p. (J). (ps-2). 1994. audio 19.95 (*1-56899-035-9*); 26.95 (*1-56899-034-0*); 4.95 (*1-56899-025-1*); 9.95 (*1-56899-036-7*); audio write for info. (*1-56899-033-2*) Soundprints.

Dolphin's First Day: The Story of a Bottlenose Dolphin. Kathleen W. Zoehfeld. LC 93-27270. (Smithsonian Oceanic Collection). (Illus.). 32p. (J). (ps-2). 1994. 15.95 (*1-56899-024-3*) Soundprints.

***Dolphins for Kids.** Patricia Corrigan. (Wildlife for Kids Ser.). (Illus.). 48p. (Orig.). (J). (gr. 3-7). 1995. pap. write for info. (*1-55971-460-3*) NorthWord.

***Dolphins of Coral Cove.** K. S. Rogriquez. LC 94-70052. (Little Mermaid Novels Ser.: No. 11). (Illus.). 80p. (J). (gr. 1-4). 1994. pap. text ed. 3.50 (*0-7868-4001-3*) Disney Pr.

Dolphins of Pern. Anne McCaffrey. 416p. 1994. 22.00 (*0-345-36894-0*, Del Rey) Ballantine.

Dolphins, Porpoises, & Whales of the World: The IUCN Red Data Book. Margaret Klinowska. (International Union for the Conservation of Nature & Natural Resources: A Belhaven Press Book Ser.). 438p. 1991. 55.00 (*2-88032-936-1*, Pub. by IUCN SZ) Island Pr.

Dolphins Swim Free. Marianne Rogers. (Illus.). 48p. (Orig.). 1994. pap. 10.95 (*0-86417-573-6*, Pub. by Kangaroo Pr AT) Seven Hills Bk.

Dolphins, Telepathy & Underwater Birthing: Further Adventures among Spiritual Intelligences. Timothy Wyllie. LC 92-38008. (Illus.). 304p. (Orig.). 1993. pap. 10.95 (*0-939680-99-8*) Bear & Co.

DolphinThink: The Workbook: Mastering the Skills You Need to Get Tough, Get Free, Get Focused & Get Going As a New Kind of Winner. Dudley Lynch & Paul L. Kordis. (Illus.). 122p. (Orig.). 1989. pap. 24.95 (*0-945822-02-2*) Brain Technologies.

Dolpo: Hidden Land of the Himalayas. Diane Summers & Eric Valli. (Illus.). 112p. 1987. 39.50 (*0-89381-258-7*) Aperture.

Dom Casmurro. Machado De Assis. Tr. by Helen Caldwell. 269p. 1991. pap. 12.00 (*0-374-52303-7*, Noonday) FS&G.

***Dom Casmurro.** Machado De Assis. Tr. & Intro. by Robert Scott-Buccleuch. 224p. 1995. 10.95 (*0-14-044612-5*, Penguin Classics) Viking Penguin.

Dom Casmurro (Lord Taciturn) Machado De Assis. Tr. by R. L. Scott-Buccleuch. 160p. 1992. 30.00 (*0-7206-0845-7*, Pub. by P Owen Ltd UK) Dufour.

***Dom Columba Marmion: A Biography.** Mark Tierney. 288p. (Orig.). 1995. pap. 17.95 (*1-85607-115-4*, Pub. by Columba Pr IE) Twenty-Third.

Dom Juan. Moliere, pseud. (Class. Ill. Hachette Ser.). (FRE.). pap. 7.95 (*0-8288-9936-3*, F39936) Fr & Eur.

Dom Pedro: The Struggle for Liberty in Brazil & Portugal, 1798-1834. Neill Macaulay. LC 86-16711. xiv, 362p. 1986. 41.95 (*0-8223-0681-6*) Duke.

Dom Perignon: Man & Myth. Richard L. Fetter. (Illus.). 56p. (Orig.). 1989. pap. 7.99 (*0-317-94026-0*) Fetter Pubns.

Domack. Mark Dunster. 15p. 1988. pap. 4.00 (*0-89642-157-0*) Linden Pubs.

Domain. G. T. James & Paul Vangelisti. 1986. 7.50 (*0-88031-066-9*) Invisible-Red Hill.

Domain Analysis & Software Systems Modeling. R. Prieto-Diaz & G. Arango. LC 91-11714. 312p. 1991. 50.00 (*0-8186-8996-X*, 1996) IEEE Comp Soc.

***Domain-Based Parallelism & Problem Decomposition Methods in Computational Science & Engineering.** Ed. by David E. Keyes et al. LC 95-7318. 1995. write for info. (*0-89871-348-X*) Soc Indus-Appl Math.

***Domain Decomposition Methods in Science & Engineering: Proceedings of the Seventh International Conference on Domain Decomposition, October 27-30, 1993, the Pennsylvania State University.** Ed. by David E. Keyes & Jinchao Xu. LC 94-41503. (Contemporary Mathematics Ser.: Vol. 180). 1994. write for info. (*0-8218-5171-3*) Am Math.

Domain Decomposition Methods in Science & Engineering: The Sixth International Conference on Domain Decomposition, June 15-19, 1992, Como, Italy. Sixth International Conference on Domain Decomposition. Ed. by Alfio Quarteroni et al. LC 93-36691. (Contemporary Mathematics Ser.: No. 157). 197p. 1994. 75.00 (*0-8218-5158-6*) Am Math.

Domain of Evil. 64p. 1991. 10.00 (*0-87431-148-9*, 40034) West End Games.

***Domain of Heroes: An Airman's Life Behind Barbed Wire in Germany in World War Ii.** Carrol F. Dillon. 311p. Date not set. write for info. (*0-9646671-0-X*) C F Dillon.

Domain of Natural Science. Ernest W. Hobson. LC 77-27210. (Gifford Lectures: 1921-22). reprint ed. 24.50 (*0-404-60467-6*) AMS Pr.

Domain of Natural Science. Ernest W. Hobson. LC 68-24653. 1969. reprint ed. pap. 5.95 (*0-486-21966-6*) Dover.

Domain-Referenced Testing. Ed. by Wells Hively. LC 74-13378. 160p. 1974. pap. 18.95 (*0-87778-075-7*) Educ Tech Pubns.

Domain Structures in Ferroelectrics, Ferroelastics & Other Ferroic Materials, Pts. 1 & 2: Special Issues of the Journal Ferroelectrics, Vols. 97-98. Ed. by Y. Ishibashi. xxxviii, 668p. 1989. text ed. 964.00 (*2-88124-393-2*) Gordon & Breach.

Domaine des Dieux. Rene De Goscinny & M. Uderzo. (Illus.). (FRE.). (J). (gr. 7-9). 1990. 19.95 (*0-8288-5123-9*, FC886) Fr & Eur.

Domaine des Dieux. Rene De Goscinny & A. Uderzo. (FRE.). 1992. 19.95 (*0-7859-0990-7*, 2205005820) Fr & Eur.

Domaine Royal Sous les Premiers Capetiens (987-1180) William M. Newman. LC 80-2014. reprint ed. 41.50 (*0-404-18581-9*) AMS Pr.

Domains & Dynasties: The Radical Autonomy of Syntax. J. Koster. (Studies in Generative Grammar). x, 400p. 1987. pap. 88.50 (*90-6765-270-9*) Mouton.

Domains Denotational Semantics. A. W. Roscoe & G. M. Reed. 300p. 1994. text ed. 34.00 (*0-13-219023-0*) P-H.

Domains of Darkover. Marion Zimmer Bradley. (Darkover Ser.). 256p. (Orig.). 1990. mass mkt. 3.99 (*0-88677-407-1*) DAW Bks.

Dombey & Son. Charles Dickens. LC 94-4778. (Everyman's Library of Children's Classics). 1994. 23.00 (*0-679-43591-3*) Knopf.

Dombey & Son. Charles Dickens. Ed. by Alan Horsman. (World's Classics Paperback Ser.). (Illus.). 1982. pap. 5.95 (*0-19-281565-2*) OUP.

Dombey & Son. Charles Dickens. (English Library). 992p. 1970. mass mkt. 6.95 (*0-14-043048-2*, Penguin Classics) Viking Penguin.

Dombey & Son. Charles Dickens. (J). (ps-8). 1990. reprint ed. lib. bdg. 29.95 (*0-89966-678-7*) Buccaneer Bks.

Dombey et Fils: Temps Difficiles. Charles Dickens. (FRE.). 1956. 95.00 (*0-8288-3426-1*, F77002) Fr & Eur.

Dombroff on Unfair Tactics. 2nd ed. Mark A. Dombroff. 633p. 1988. text ed. 125.00 (*0-471-61147-6*) Wiley.

Dome & the Rock: Structure in the Poetry of Wallace Stevens. James Baird. LC 68-19701. 368p. reprint ed. pap. 104.90 (*0-317-30116-0*, 2025301) Bks Demand.

Dome of Many-Coloured Glass. Amy Lowell. LC 78-64044. (Des Imagistes: Literature of the Imagist Movement Ser.). 152p. reprint ed. 20.00 (*0-404-17127-3*) AMS Pr.

Dome of the Continent: Colorado in 1872. Ed. by William R. Jones. (Illus.). 24p. 1977. reprint ed. pap. 3.95 (*0-89646-012-6*) Vistabooks.

Dome Scrap Book: Dimensions. Geodesic Service Staff. 192p. 1986. per., pap. 16.95 (*0-8403-4010-9*) Kendall-Hunt.

Dome Scrap Book: Domes & Homes. Geodesic Service Staff. 192p. 1986. per., pap. 16.95 (*0-8403-4009-5*) Kendall-Hunt.

Domebo: A Paleo-Indian Mammoth Kill in the Prairie-Plains. Frank C. Leonhardy. LC 65-26284. (Contributions of the Museum of the Great Plains Ser.: No. 1). 1966. 6.95 (*0-685-85506-6*) Mus Great Plains.

***Domelands.** Greg Vernon et al. (Southern Sierra Rock Climbing Ser.). (Illus.). 200p. 1994. pap. 20.00 (*0-934641-48-X*) Chockstone Pr.

Domenico Bollani, Bishop of Brescia: Devotion to Church & State in the Republic of Venice in the 16th Century. Christopher Cairns. 306p. 1976. 87.50 (*90-6004-346-4*, Pub. by B De Graaf NE) Coronet Bks.

***Domenico Corri's a Select Collection of the Most Admired Songs, Duetts, &C., Volume 4, & the Singer's Preceptor, Vols. 1-2.** Ed. by Richard Maunder. LC 93-8550. (Domenico Corri's Treatises on Singing Ser.: Vol. 3). 328p. 1995. 115.00 (*0-8153-0681-4*) Garland.

Domenico Corri's, Vols. 1-3: A Select Collection of the Most Admired Songs, Duetts, & C. Ed. by Richard Maunder. LC 93-8550. (Domenico Corri's Treatises on Singing Ser.: No.1). 364p. 1993. 119.00 (*0-8153-0679-2*) Garland.

***Domenico Ferrabosco: Il primo libro de madrigali a quatro voci (Venice, 1542)** Ed. by Jessie A. Owens. LC 94-41447. (Sixteenth Century Madrigal Ser.: Vol. 11). 248p. 1995. 84.00 (*0-8240-5511-X*) Garland.

Domenico Ghirlandaio. Emma Micheletti. Tr. by Anthony Brierley. (Library of Great Masters). (Illus.). 80p. (Orig.). 1990. pap. 12.99 (*1-878351-08-7*) Riverside NY.

Domenico Gnoli. Luigi Carluccio. LC 74-82606. (Illus.). 168p. 1975. 85.00 (*0-87951-026-9*) Overlook Pr.

Domenico Scarlatti. rev. ed. Ralph Kirkpatrick. LC 53-6387. (Illus.). 486p. 1953. pap. 22.95 (*0-691-02708-0*) Princeton U Pr.

Domenico Scarlatti: Master of Music. Malcolm Boyd. (Illus.). 302p. 1987. text ed. 22.50 (*0-02-870291-3*) Schirmer Bks.

Domenico Scarlatti: Ten Sonatas. Ed. by Ruth Slenczynska. 1978. pap. text ed. 5.20 (*0-87563-151-7*) Stipes.

Domenico Tiepolo: The Punchinello Drawings. Ed. by Adelheid Gealt. (Illus.). 196p. 85.00 (*0-8076-1132-8*) Braziller.

Domers: A Year at Notre Dame. Kevin Coyne. 320p. 1995. 23.95 (*0-670-85005-5*, Viking) Viking Penguin.

Domes, Cliffs & Waterfalls: A Brief Geology of Yosemite Valley. rev. ed. William R. Jones. (Illus.). 18p. 1991. pap. 1.95 (*0-939666-05-7*) Yosemite Assn.

Domes of America. Photos by Eric Oxendorf. LC 94-7930. (Illus.). 108p. 1994. 22.95 (*0-87654-070-1*) Pomegranate Calif.

Domes of Fire. David Eddings. (Tamuli Ser.). 1993. mass mkt. 5.99 (*0-345-38327-3*, Del Rey) Ballantine.

Domesday Book & Beyond: Three Essays in the Early History of England. Frederic W. Maitland. 550p. 1988. pap. 32.95 (*0-521-34918-4*) Cambridge U Pr.

Domesday Book Studies. Ed. by Alecto Historical Editions Board Staff. (Illus.). x, 179p. 1987. lib. bdg. 150.00 (*0-948459-51-4*) Omnigraphics Inc.

Domesday Book to Magna Carta, 1087-1216. 2nd ed. Austin L. Poole. LC 92-32686. (Illus.). 560p. (C). 1993. pap. 17.95 (*0-19-285287-6*) OUP.

Domesday Geography of Midland England. 2nd ed. Ed. by H. C. Darby & I. B. Terrett. LC 78-134626. 508p. reprint ed. pap. 144.80 (*0-317-28397-9*, 2022445) Bks Demand.

Domesday Geography of Northern England. Ed. by H. C. Darby & L. S. Maxwell. (Illus.). 1978. 125.00 (*0-521-04773-0*) Cambridge U Pr.

Domesday Inquest & the Making of the Domesday Book. Rex W. Finn. LC 78-2923. 201p. 1978. reprint ed. text ed. 35.00 (*0-313-20344-X*, FIDI, Greenwood Pr) Greenwood.

Domesday of Crown Lands. S. J. Madge. (Illus.). 499p. 1968. 39.50 (*0-7146-1341-X*, Pub. by F Cass Pubs UK) Intl Spec Bk.

Domesday of Crown Lands. Sidney J. Madge. LC 67-31560. (Illus.). xvii, 499p. 1968. reprint ed. 49.50 (*0-678-05071-6*) Kelley.

D

An Asterisk (*) at the beginning of an entry indicates that the title is appearing in BIP for the first time.

Domesday of St. Paul's of the Year Twelve Twenty-Two. Ed. by William H. Hale. LC 70-164771. (Camden Society, London. Publications, First Ser.: No. 69). (Illus.). reprint ed. 75.00 (*0-404-50169-9*) AMS Pr.

Domesday Studies. Ed. by J. C. Holt. 256p. 1987. pap. text ed. 29.00 (*0-85115-263-5*) Boydell & Brewer.

Domesday Studies. Ed. by J. C. Holt. 256p. 1990. 90.00 (*0-85115-477-8*) Boydell & Brewer.

Domesday Studies: The Eastern Counties. Reginald A. Finn. LC 80-2231. (Illus.). 1981. reprint ed. 37.50 (*0-404-18759-5*) AMS Pr.

Domesday Studies: The Liber Exoniensis. Reginald A. Finn. LC 80-2239. 1981. reprint ed. 32.50 (*0-404-18760-9*) AMS Pr.

***Domestic Abusers: Terrorists in Our Homes!** Sara L. Johann. LC 93-47036. 152p. 1994. pap. 22.95 (*0-398-06183-1*) C C Thomas.

Domestic Abusers: Terrorists in Our Homes! Sara L. Johann. LC 93-47036. 152p. (C). 1994. text ed. 37.95x (*0-398-05904-7*) C C Thomas.

Domestic Accidents. E. Maurice Backett. (Public Health Papers: No. 26). 137p. (ENG, FRE, RUS & SPA.). 1965. pap. 2.80 (*92-4-130026-4*) World Health.

Domestic Affair. Martin Russell. 192p. 1985. 13.95 (*0-8027-5633-6*) Walker & Co.

Domestic Affairs: Enduring the Pleasures of Motherhood & Family. Joyce Maynard. 1987. 17.95 (*0-8129-1244-6*, Times Bks) Random.

***Domestic Affections, 1812.** Felicia Hemans. LC 94-44533. (Revolution & Romanticism, 1789-1834, Ser.). 1995. 48.00 (*1-85477-181-7*, Pub. by Woodstock Bks UK) Cassell.

Domestic Agenda for the Nineties. 94p. 1989. 30.00 (*0-685-38253-2*, C-145) Coun State Govts.

Domestic Air Fares. Chris Hoosen & Francis Dix. (Travel Agent Training Ser.). (Illus.). (Orig.). 1989. student ed, pap. 20.00 (*0-917063-10-4*) Travel Text.

Domestic Air Reservations. Chris Hoosen & Francis Dix. (Travel Agent Training Ser.). (Illus.). (Orig.). 1989. student ed, pap. 20.00 (*0-917063-09-0*) Travel Text.

Domestic Air Ticketing. Chris Hoosen & Francis Dix. (Travel Agent Training Ser.). (Illus.). (Orig.). 1989. student ed, pap. 20.00 (*0-917063-11-2*) Travel Text.

Domestic Air Transportation Network of the United States. Walter F. Wacht. LC 73-92651. (Research Papers Ser.: No. 154). (Illus.). 98p. 1974. pap. 12.00 (*0-89065-061-6*) U Chicago Comm Geo.

Domestic Airlines see Travel Agent Training Workbook, 1987-88

Domestic Allegories of Political Desire: The Black Heroine's Text at the Turn of the Century. Claudia Tate. (Illus.). 312p. 1993. 35.00 (*0-19-507389-4*) OUP.

Domestic Analogy & World Order Proposals. Hidemi Suganami. (Cambridge Studies in International Relations: No. 6). (C). 1989. 59.95 (*0-521-34341-0*) Cambridge U Pr.

Domestic & Artistic Life of John Singleton Copley. Martha B. Amory. LC 71-77698. (Library of American Art Ser.). 1969. reprint ed. lib. bdg. 59.50 (*0-306-71336-5*) Da Capo.

Domestic & Artistic Life of John Singleton Copley, R.A. Martha B. Amory. LC 70-119925. (Select Bibliographies Reprint Ser.). 1977. 30.95 (*0-8369-5368-1*) Ayer.

Domestic & Commercial Oil Burners. 3rd ed. Charles H. Burkhardt. LC 68-31659. (Illus.). (C). 1969. text ed. 39.95 (*0-07-009039-4*) McGraw.

Domestic & Divine: Roman Mosaics in the House of Dionysos. Christine Kondoleon. (Illus.). 392p. 1995. 65.00 (*0-8014-3058-5*) Cornell U Pr.

Domestic & Foreign Finance in Modern Peru, 1850-1950: Financing Visions of Development. Alfonso W. Quiroz. LC 92-36947. (Latin American Ser.). 312p. (C). 1993. text ed. 49.95 (*0-8229-1174-4*) U of Pittsburgh Pr.

***Domestic & Import Labor Guide, 1982-96.** Ed. by Chilton Staff. 1800p. 1995. text ed. 145.00 (*0-8019-8724-5*) Chilton.

Domestic & Multinational Banking: The Effect of Monetary Policy. Rae Weston. LC 80-80791. 400p. 1980. text ed. 69.00 (*0-231-05058-5*) Col U Pr.

Domestic Animal Behavior for Veterinarians & Animal Scientists. 2nd ed. Katherine A. Houpt. LC 91-7030. (Illus.). 416p. (C). 1991. text ed. 39.95 (*0-8138-1062-0*) Iowa St U Pr.

Domestic Animal Behavior for Veterinarians & Animal Scientists. Katherine A. Houpt & Thomas R. Wolski. LC 81-2811. 368p. reprint ed. pap. 104.90 (*0-685-15508-0*, 2026698) Bks Demand.

Domestic Animals. Clarinda H. Lott. (Fanfare Ser.). 1982. pap. 2.00 (*0-932616-10-0*) New Poets Chestnut Hills.

Domestic Animals of China. H. Epstein. LC 73-152339. (Illus.). 166p. 1971. 39.50 (*0-8419-0073-6*) Holmes & Meier.

Domestic Animals of Nepal. H. Epstein. LC 75-6685. (Illus.). 160p. 1977. 39.50 (*0-8419-0202-X*) Holmes & Meier.

Domestic Architecture & the Use of Space: An Interdisciplinary Cross-Cultural Study. Ed. by Susan Kent. (New Directions in Archaeology Ser.). (Illus.). 200p. (C). 1993. pap. 19.95 (*0-521-44577-9*) Cambridge U Pr.

Domestic Architecture, Ethnicity, & Complementarity in the South-Central Andes. Ed. by Mark S. Aldenderfer. LC 92-35091. (Illus.). 188p. 1993. text ed. 47.95 (*0-87745-400-0*) U of Iowa Pr.

Domestic Architecture in Rural France. Samuel Chamberlain. (Illus.). 96p. (Orig.). 1986. reprint ed. pap. 7.95 (*0-8038-1578-6*) Archit CT.

Domestic Architecture of Sir Edward Lutyens. A. S. Butler. (Illus.). 110p. 1992. 175.00 (*1-85149-100-7*) Antique Collect.

Domestic Architecture of the Early American Republic. Howard Major. 236p. 1993. reprint ed. lib. bdg. 79.00 (*0-7812-5299-7*) Rprt Serv.

Domestic Assault of Women: Psychological & Criminal Justice Perspectives. Donald G. Dutton. 320p. (C). 1988. pap. text ed. 29.00 (*0-205-11323-0*, H13238) Allyn.

***Domestic Assault of Women: Psychological & Criminal Justice Perspectives New & Updated.** Donald G. Dutton. 256p. 1995. pap. 22.95 (*0-7748-0462-9*) U of Wash Pr.

***Domestic Auto Service Manual, 1992-96.** Ed. by Chilton Staff. 2504p. 1995. text ed. 100.00 (*0-8019-8726-1*) Chilton.

Domestic Bases of Grand Strategy. Ed. by Richard Rosecrance & Arthur A. Stein. LC 93-15396. (Cornell Studies in Security Affairs). 256p. 1993. 36.50 (*0-8014-2880-7*); pap. 13.95 (*0-8014-8116-3*) Cornell U Pr.

Domestic Battleground: Canada & the Arab-Israeli Conflict. Ed. by David Taras & David Goldberg. 264p. 1989. 47.95 (*0-7735-0705-1*, Pub. by McGill CN) U of Toronto Pr.

Domestic Bliss: Family Life in American Painting, 1840-1910. Lee M. Edwards. LC 87-146749. (Illus.). 160p. (Orig.). 1986. pap. 10.00 (*0-943651-06-9*) Hudson Riv.

***Domestic Boiler Emissions.** A. Teekaram. 120p. (C). 1993. 310.00x (*0-86022-332-9*, Pub. by Build Servs Info Assn UK) St Mut.

Domestic Boiler Market. BSRIA Staff. (C). 1984. 350.00 (*0-685-33890-8*, Pub. by Build Servs Info Assn UK) St Mut.

Domestic Buffalo Production in Asia. 225p. 1990. pap. 90.00 (*92-0-111490-7*, STI/PUB/855) UNIPUB.

Domestic Building Surveys. Andrew R. Williams. LC 93-25249. (Builder's Bookshelf Ser.). 1993. write for info. (*0-419-17800-7*, E & FN Spon) Routledge Chapman & Hall.

Domestic Bygones. Jacqueline Fearn. 1990. 4.50 (*0-913714-08-9*) Legacy Books.

Domestic Bygones. Jacqueline Fearn. 1989. pap. 25.00 (*0-85263-349-1*, Pub. by Shire UK) St Mut.

Domestic Capital Formation in the United Kingdom, 1920-1938. C. H. Feinstein. LC 64-21572. (Studies in the National Income & Expenditure of the United Kingdom: No. 4). 282p. reprint ed. pap. 80.40 (*0-317-26397-8*, 2024454) Bks Demand.

Domestic Cat: The Biology of Its Behaviour. Ed. by Dennis C. Turner & Patrick Bateson. (Illus.). 250p. 1989. pap. 32.95 (*0-521-35727-6*) Cambridge U Pr.

Domestic Central Heating Market in Great Britain. P. Crampton & S. Whittome. 1992. 1,580.00 (*0-86022-351-5*, Pub. by Build Servs Info Assn UK) St Mut.

Domestic Ceramic Production & Spatial Organization: A Mexican Case Study in Ethnoarchaeology. Philip J. Arnold, III. (New Studies in Archaeology). (Illus.). 184p. (C). 1991. 64.95 (*0-521-39199-7*) Cambridge U Pr.

Domestic Choices, International Markets: Dismantling National Barriers & Liberalizing Securities Markets. Andrew C. Sobel. LC 94-17691. 250p. 1994. 39.50 (*0-472-10506-X*) U of Mich Pr.

Domestic Coal Distribution: An Interregional Programming Model for the U. S. Coal Industry. Ed. by Richard L. Bernknopf. LC 85-5792. (Contemporary Studies in Energy Analysis & Policy: Vol. 5). 230p. 1985. 73.25 (*0-89232-431-7*) Jai Pr.

Domestic Colonial Architecture of Tidewater Virginia. Thomas T. Waterman & John A. Barrows. LC 69-11290. (Architecture & Decorative Art Ser.). 1968. reprint ed. lib. bdg. 45.00 (*0-306-71190-7*) Da Capo.

Domestic Conflicts in South Asia, Vol. 1: Political Dimensions. Urmilla Phadnis. 1986. 18.50 (*0-317-68066-8*, Pub. by S Asia Pubs II) S Asia.

Domestic Conflicts in South Asia, Vol. 2. Urmila Phadnis. 1986. 18.50 (*81-7003-071-4*, Pub. by S Asia Pubs II) S Asia.

Domestic Correspondence of Dominique-Marie Varlet: Bishop of Babylon 1678-1742. B. Guy. (Studies in the History of Christian Thought: No. 36). ix, 150p. 1986. 31.00 (*90-04-07671-9*) E J Brill.

Domestic Creatures: Poems. Manohar Shetty. (India Paperbacks Ser.). 72p. 1994. pap. 5.95 (*0-19-563454-3*) OUP.

Domestic Crime in the Victorian Novel. Anthea Trodd. LC 88-18831. 208p. 1988. text ed. 39.95 (*0-312-02443-6*) St Martin.

Domestic Determinants of Soviet Foreign Policy Towards South Asia & the Middle East. Ed. by Hafeez Malik. LC 89-24078. 234p. 1990. text ed. 49.95 (*0-312-04022-9*) St Martin.

Domestic Disharmony & Industrialization in D.H. Lawrence's Early Fiction. Marko Modiano. (Studia Anglistica Upsaliensia Ser.: No. 62). 124p. (Orig.). 1987. pap. 34.00x (*91-554-2084-2*, Pub. by Uppsala Univ Acta Univ Uppsaliensis SW) Coronet Bks.

Domestic Dog: An Introduction to Its History. Brian Vesey-Fitzgerald. 1992. lib. bdg. 79.95 (*0-8490-5235-1*) Gordon Pr.

Domestic Dramas: (Drames De Famille) Paul C. Bourget. Tr. by William Marchant. LC 76-37259. (Short Story Index Reprint Ser.). 1977. reprint ed. 23.95 (*0-8369-4070-9*) Ayer.

Domestic Economic Policies in the Industrial Countries: A Tripartite Report by Fourteen Economists from Japan, Europe & North America. Brookings Institution Staff. LC 78-308154. 17p. reprint ed. pap. 25.00 (*0-317-20797-0*, 2025371) Bks Demand.

Domestic Economics & International Politics of U. S. Trade Policy, 1945-1980: Case Study: Japan. Susan B. Shearer. LC 90-20186. (Foreign Economic Policy of the United States Ser.). 344p. 1990. 20.00 (*0-8240-7435-1*) Garland.

Domestic Emergency Assistance Program. 110p. (Orig.). (C). 1993. pap. text ed. 40.00 (*1-56806-372-5*) Diane Pub.

Domestic Enemies. abr. ed. Joel Marcuse. 298p. 1994. pap. 9.95 (*1-56901-303-9*) NW Pub.

Domestic Enemies: Servants & Their Masters in Old Regime France. Cissie C. Fairchilds. LC 83-48059. (Illus.). 344p. reprint ed. pap. 98.10 (*0-7837-4782-9*, 2044538) Bks Demand.

Domestic Fables. Barriss Mills. 1971. 8.00 (*0-685-01006-6*) Elizabeth Pr.

Domestic Factors in Foreign Policy: A Cross-Natonal Statistical Analysis. Daniel S. Geller. 200p. (Orig.). 1985. 19.95 (*0-87047-014-0*); pap. 12.95 (*0-87047-015-9*) Schenkman Bks Inc.

Domestic Fuel. Erin Moure. 108p. (Orig.). 1985. pap. 8.95 (*0-88784-143-0*, Pub. by Hse of Anansi Pr CN) Genl Dist Srvs.

Domestic Furniture Purchase in 1982: An Analysis. 1983. 175.00 (*0-317-43742-9*) St Mut.

Domestic Furniture Purchasing Habits 1986. 1986. 175.00 (*0-317-43757-7*) St Mut.

Domestic Goals & Financial Interdependence: The Frankfurt Dialogue. Frankfurt International Monetary Conference Staff. Ed. by Randall Hinshaw. LC 80-16637. (Business Economics & Finance Ser.: No. 12). 183p. reprint ed. pap. 52.20 (*0-8357-6096-0*, 2034540) Bks Demand.

Domestic Goddess Planning Notebook. 1982. 15.00 (*0-911094-11-3*) Pacific Santa Barbara.

Domestic Goddess Planning Notebook. 1982. vinyl bd. 15.00 (*0-685-53880-X*) Pacific Santa Barbara.

***Domestic Government: Kinship, Community, & Polity in North Yemen.** Martha Mundy. (Society & Culture in the Modern Middle East Ser.). 256p. 1995. text ed. 59.50 (*1-85043-918-4*) St Martin.

Domestic Help Services: Suggestive Ideas for Services Plus Work Pages. rev. ed. Center for Self-Sufficiency Staff. 114p. 1992. student ed 21.95 (*0-910811-49-0*) Ctr Self Suff.

Domestic History of the Bank of England, 1930-1960. Elizabeth Hennessy. 448p. (C). 1992. 125.00 (*0-521-39140-7*) Cambridge U Pr.

Domestic Ideology & Domestic Work see History of Women in the United States: Topically Arranged Articles on the Evolution of Women's History in the United States

Domestic Ideology & Domestic Work, Vol.4, Pt. I see History of Women in the United States: Topically Arranged Articles on the Evolution of Women's History in the United States

Domestic Individualism: Imagining Self in Nineteenth-Century America. Gillian Brown. (New Historicism: Studies in Cultural Poetics: No. 14). (C). 1990. pap. 13.00 (*0-520-08099-8*) U CA Pr.

Domestic Intelligence: Monitoring Dissent in America. Richard E. Morgan. LC 80-13254. 204p. 1980. text ed. 14.95 (*0-292-76463-4*); pap. 6.95 (*0-292-71529-3*) U of Tex Pr.

Domestic Issues. Corinne Jacker. 1983. pap. 4.75 (*0-8222-0322-7*) Dramatists Play.

Domestic Labor Guide & Parts Manual, 1991-95. Ed. by Chilton Staff. 1696p. 1994. text ed. 95.00 (*0-8019-8570-6*) Chilton.

***Domestic Labor Guide & Parts Manual, 1992-96.** Ed. by Chilton Staff. 1632p. 1995. text ed. 95.00 (*0-8019-8727-X*) Chilton.

Domestic Law Reforms in Post-Mao China. Ed. by Pitman B. Potter. LC 93-23228. (Studies on Contemporary China). 326p. (C). 1994. 55.00 (*1-56324-107-2*, East Gate Bk) M E Sharpe.

Domestic Life. Hunt Hawkins. (Poetry Ser.). 112p. (C). 1993. text ed. 19.95 (*0-8229-3770-0*); pap. text ed. 10.95 (*0-8229-5515-6*) U of Pittsburgh Pr.

Domestic Life in New England in the Seventeenth Century. George F. Dow. LC 72-83087. (Illus.). 1972. reprint ed. 19.95 (*0-405-08462-5*, Pub. by Blom Pubns UK) Ayer.

Domestic Life in Palestine. Mary E. Rogers. 390p. 1988. pap. 19.95 (*0-7103-0290-8*) Routledge Chapman & Hall.

***Domestic Life in Virginia in the Seventeenth Century.** Annie L. Jester. (Illus.). 91p. 1994. pap. 12.00 (*0-614-00901-4*, 9165) Clearfield Co.

Domestic Life of a Medieval City: Women, Children, & the Family in Fourteenth Century Ghent. David Nicholas. LC 84-22011. (Illus.). x, 261p. 1985. 30.00 (*0-8032-3310-8*) U of Nebr Pr.

Domestic Life of Thomas Jefferson. Sarah N. Randolph. LC 78-14312. (Illus.). 452p. 1979. pap. 16.95 (*0-8139-0718-7*) U Pr of Va.

Domestic Manners of the Americans. Frances Trollope. 212p. (C). 1993. pap. text ed. 10.96 (*1-881089-13-4*) Brandywine Press.

Domestic Manners of the Americans. Frances Trollope. Ed. by Smalley. 28.50 (*0-8446-3090-X*) Peter Smith.

Domestic Manners of the Americans. Frances M. Trollope. 1993. reprint ed. lib. bdg. 89.00 (*0-7812-5408-6*) Rprt Serv.

Domestic Manners of the Americans, 2 vols., Set. F. M. Trollope. 1993. reprint ed. lib. bdg. 150.00 (*0-7812-5137-0*) Rprt Serv.

Domestic Marijuana: A Neglected Industry. Ralph A. Weisheit. LC 91-34695. (Contributions in Criminology & Penology Ser.: No. 35). 196p. 1992. text ed. 49.95 (*0-313-28040-1*, WDK/, Greenwood Pr) Greenwood.

Domestic Metalwork, 1640-1820. rev. ed. Rupert Gentle & Rachael Feild. Ed. by Belinda Gentle. 1994. 89.50 (*1-85149-187-2*) Antique Collect.

Domestic Misconduct in the Novels of Defoe, Richardson, & Fielding. Jacqueline E. Lawson. LC 93-26975. 200p. 1993. text ed. 79.95 (*0-7734-9978-4*) E Mellen.

Domestic Novelists in the Old South: Defenders of Southern Culture. Elizabeth Moss. LC 91-40827. (Southern Literary Studies). 272p. (C). 1992. text ed. 130.00 (*0-8071-1730-7*) La State U Pr.

Domestic Origins of the Monetary Approach to the Balance of Payments. Herbert G. Grubel. LC 76-21698. (Princeton University, International Finance Section, Essays in International Finance Ser.: No. 117). 25p. reprint ed. pap. 25.00 (*0-317-29051-7*, 2019247) Bks Demand.

Domestic Particulars: A Family Chronicle. Frederick Busch. LC 76-8904. 1976. 11.95 (*0-8112-0605-X*) New Directions.

Domestic Particulars: The Novels of Frederick Busch. Donald J. Greiner. 209p. 1988. text ed. 29.95 (*0-87249-573-6*) U of SC Pr.

***Domestic Partner Abuse.** Ed. by L. Kevin Hamberger & Claire Renzetti. (Illus.). 140p. 1995. write for info. (*0-8261-9090-1*) Springer Pub.

***Domestic Partner Benefits: A Case Study.** Barbara Fried. 100p. 1994. 20.00 (*1-878240-31-5*) Coll & U Personnel.

Domestic Plants & Animals: The Ancient Egyptian Origins. Brewer. 1994. 85.00 (*0-85668-584-4*, Pub. by Aris & Phillips UK); pap. 59.95 (*0-85668-585-2*, Pub. by Aris & Phillips UK) David Brown.

Domestic Pleasures. Beth Gutcheon. 1991. 19.50 (*0-394-54579-6*, Villard Bks) Random.

Domestic Pleasures. Beth Gutcheon. 1992. mass mkt. 5.99 (*0-312-92861-0*) St Martin.

Domestic Policy & Ideology: Presidents & the American State, 1964-1987. David McKay. (Illus.). (C). 1989. 54.95 (*0-521-32033-X*) Cambridge U Pr.

Domestic Policy Formation: Presidential-Congressional Partnership? Steven A. Shull. LC 82-24174. (Contributions in Political Science Ser.: No. 100). (Illus.). xvii, 218p. 1983. text ed. 49.95 (*0-313-23770-0*, SDP/, Greenwood Pr) Greenwood.

Domestic Political Factors. Ed. by Shahram Chubin. LC 81-572. (Security in the Persian Gulf Ser.: Vol. 1). 104p. 1981. pap. text ed. 19.50 (*0-86598-044-6*) Rowman.

Domestic Political Structures & Regional Economic Co-Operation. Harold Crouch. 101p. 1985. pap. text ed. 14.80 (*9971-902-80-X*, Pub. by Inst SE Asian Studies SI) Ashgate Pub Co.

Domestic Politics. Brian Daldorph. (Chapbook Ser.: No. 2). 24p. (Orig.). 1992. pap. 3.00 (*1-879259-01-X*) Dusty Dog.

Domestic Politics & Regional Security: Jordan, Syria & Israel: The End of an Era? Valerie Yorke. 1988. text ed. 69.95 (*0-566-05652-6*, Pub. by Dartmth Pub UK) Ashgate Pub Co.

Domestic Politics of Arms Control. Paul C. Warnke. (CISA Working Paper Ser.: No. 60). 17p. (Orig.). Date not set. pap. 10.00 (*0-86682-077-9*) Ctr Intl Relations.

Domestic Politics of German Unification. Ed. by Christopher Anderson et al. LC 93-10015. 254p. 1993. lib. bdg. 30.00 (*1-55587-409-6*) Lynne Rienner.

Domestic Pottery of the Northeastern United States, 1625-1850. Ed. by Sarah P. Turnbaugh. (Studies in Historical Archaeology). 1985. pap. text ed. 44.00 (*0-12-703871-X*) Acad Pr.

Domestic Problem: Work & Culture in the Household. see Liberating the Home

Domestic Public Debt of Externally Indebted Countries. Pablo E. Guidotti & Manmohan S. Kumar. (Occasional Paper Ser.: No. 80). v, 31p. 1991. pap. 10.00 (*1-55775-208-7*) Intl Monetary.

Domestic Pursuits: Historical Archaeology of American Households. Mary C. Beaudry. 1994. write for info. (*0-8493-8884-8*) CRC Pr.

Domestic Rabbit Biology & Production. L. R. Arrington & Kathleen C. Kelley. LC 76-10173. 1976. 19.95 (*0-8130-0537-X*) U Press Fla.

Domestic Realities & Imperial Fictions: Jane Austen's Novels in Eighteenth-Century Contexts. Maaja A. Stewart. LC 92-39954. 224p. (C). 1993. 35.00 (*0-8203-1540-0*) U of Ga Pr.

Domestic Relations: Adaptable to Courses Utilizing Materials by Wadlington. 2nd ed. Walter J. Wadlington. LC 87-115167. (Legalines Ser.). 226p. 10.95 (*0-685-18528-1*) HarBrace.

***Domestic Relations: Cases & Materials.** 3rd ed. Walter Wadlington. (University Casebook Ser.). 1240p. 1994. text ed. 47.50 (*1-56662-182-8*) Foundation Pr.

***Domestic Relations: Cases & Materials.** 3rd ed. Walter Wadlington. (University Casebook Ser.). 89p. (C). 1994. teacher ed, pap. text ed. write for info. (*1-56662-252-2*) Foundation Pr.

Domestic Relations: Cases & Materials On. 4th ed. Homer H. Clark, Jr. & Carol Glowinsky. (American Casebook Ser.). 900p. 1993. reprint ed. text ed. 51.00 (*0-314-73781-2*) West Pub.

Domestic Relations: Manual for Teachers to Accompany Cases & Other Materials. 2nd ed. Walter J. Wadlington. (University Casebook Ser.). 73p. 1990. pap. text ed. write for info. (*0-88277-845-5*) Foundation Pr.

Domestic Relations & Law, Vol. 3 see History of Women in the United States: Topically Arranged Articles on the Evolution of Women's History in the United States

***Domestic Relations, Cases & Problems On.** 5th ed. Homer H. Clark, Jr & Carol Glowinsky. (American Casebook Ser.). 1144p. (C). 1995. text ed. 53.00 (*0-314-05905-9*) West Pub.

An Asterisk (*) at the beginning of an entry indicates that the title is appearing in BIP for the first time.

An Asterisk (*) at the beginning of an entry indicates that the title is appearing in BIP for the first time.

***Dominguez-Escalante Journal: Their Expedition Through Colorado, Utah, Arizona, & New Mexico in 1776.** Silvestre Velez de Escalante, pseud. Ed. by Ted J. Warner. Tr. by Angelico Chavez. LC 94-34187. 1995. pap. 12.95 (0-87480-448-5) U of Utah Pr.

***Dominguez-Escalante Journal: Their Expedition Through Colorado, Utah, Arizona & New Mexico in 1776.** Ed. by Ted J. Warner. Tr. by Fray A. Chavez. (Illus.). 176p. (C). 1995. text ed. 25.00x (0-87480-447-7) U of Utah Pr.

Dominic. William Steig. LC 70-188272. (Illus.). 160p. (J). (gr. 2 up). 1984. pap. 3.95 (0-374-41826-8, Sunburst Bks) FS&G.

Dominica. Robert A. Myers. (World Bibliographical Ser.: No. 82). 190p. 1987. lib. bdg. 55.00 (1-85109-031-2) ABC-CLIO.

Dominica. Wilson Ltd. Staff & Imray L. Norie. (C). 1982. 100.00 (0-685-40395-5, Pub. by Imray Laurie Norie & Wilson UK) St Mut.

***Dominica: Commercial Law.** 300p. (Orig.). 1994. pap. 295.00 (0-7605-1244-2) Rector Pr.

***Dominica Commercial Law.** 150p. (C). 1994. pap. 295.00 (0-7605-0108-4) Rector Pr.

***Dominican Americans.** Alexandra Bandon. (Footsteps to America Ser.). (J). 1995. 14.95 (0-02-768152-1, Mac Bks Young Read) S&S Childrens.

Dominican Americans. Christopher Dwyer. (Peoples of North America Ser.). (Illus.). 112p. (J). (gr. 5 up). 1991. lib. bdg. 17.95 (0-87754-872-2) Chelsea Hse.

Dominican Cookbook (La Cocina Dominicana) Collectors Edition. 2nd ed. Maria R. De Carias. (Illus.). 240p. 1993. 23.95 (0-9635548-0-8) Pilon FL.

Dominican Crisis: The 1965 Constitutionalist Revolt & American Intervention. Piero Gleijeses. Tr. by Lawrence Lipson. LC 77-29253. 476p. reprint ed. pap. 135.70 (0-7837-2196-X, 2042534) Bks Demand.

Dominican Diaspora: From the Dominican Republic to New York City, Villagers in Transition. Glenn Hendricks. LC 74-4203. (Publications of the Center for Education in Africa). (Illus.). 183p. reprint ed. pap. 52.20 (0-685-20393-X, 2030163) Bks Demand.

Dominican Intervention. Abraham F Lowenthal. 246p. (C). 1994. reprint ed. pap. text ed. 14.95x (0-8018-4755-9) Johns Hopkins.

Dominican Painting: Masters & Novices. 2nd rev. ed. Eva Pataki. LC 89-91748. (Illus.). 102p. (C). 1989. pap. 15.00 (0-9615932-1-0) E Pataki.

Dominican Painting in East Anglia: The Thornham Parva Retable & the Musee De Cluny Frontal. Christopher Norton et al. 1987. 79.00 (0-85115-424-7) Boydell & Brewer.

Dominican People, Eighteen Fifty to Nineteen Hundred: Notes for an Historical Sociology. Harry Hoetink. Tr. by Stephen Ault. (Johns Hopkins Studies in Atlantic History & Culture Ser.). 256p. 1981. 38.00 (0-8018-2223-8) Johns Hopkins.

***Dominican Republic.** Erin L. Foley. (Cultures of the World Ser.). (Illus.). (J). 1994. 21.95 (1-85435-694-1) Marshall Cavendish.

Dominican Republic. Paul Lisicky. (Let's Visit Places & Peoples of the World Ser.). (Illus.). 96p. 1987. lib. bdg. 14.95 (1-55546-163-8) Chelsea Hse.

Dominican Republic. Kathleen T. Sellew. LC 87-11578. (World Education Ser.). (Illus.). 136p. (Orig.). (C). 1987. pap. text ed. 12.00 (0-910054-86-X) Am Assn Coll Registrars.

Dominican Republic. annot. ed. Ed. by Kai P. Schoenhals. (World Bibliographical Ser.: No. 111). 212p. 1990. lib. bdg. 62.50 (1-85109-110-6) ABC-CLIO.

Dominican Republic: A Caribbean Crucible, Vol. 2. Howard J. Wiarda & Michael J. Kryzanek. LC 92-14476. (Profiles - Nations of Contemporary Latin America Ser.). 167p. (C). 1992. pap. text ed. 17.95 (0-8133-8236-X) Westview.

Dominican Republic: A Caribbean Crucible, Vol. 2. 2nd ed. Howard J. Wiarda & Michael J. Kryzanek. LC 92-14476. (Profiles - Nations of Contemporary Latin America Ser.). 167p. 1992. text ed. 54.50 (0-8133-8235-1) Westview.

***Dominican Republic: A National History.** Frank M. Pons. 520p. 1994. 32.00 (1-885509-00-6); pap. 22.00 (1-885509-01-4) Hispaniola Bks.

Dominican Republic: Beyond the Lighthouse. James Ferguson. 150p. 1992. pap. 10.00 (0-85345-853-7, Pub. by Lat Am Bur UK) Monthly Rev.

***Dominican Republic: Commercial Law.** 300p. (Orig.). 1994. pap. 295.00 (0-7605-1245-0) Rector Pr.

Dominican Republic: Hippocrene Insider's Guide. Jack Tucker. 1992. pap. 14.95 (0-7818-0075-7) Hippocrene Bks.

Dominican Republic: Politics & Development in an Unsovereign State. Jan K. Black. (Illus.). 160p. (C). 1986. text ed. 39.95 (0-04-497000-5); pap. text ed. 13.95 (0-04-497001-3) Routledge Chapman & Hall.

Dominican Republic: Rebellion & Repression. Carlos M. Gutierrez. LC 72-81763. 172p. reprint ed. pap. 49.10 (0-318-34970-1, 2030769) Bks Demand.

Dominican Republic see American Nations Past & Present

Dominican Republic see Statements of the Laws of the OAS Member States in Matters Affecting Business

Dominican Republic "Adventure Guide" 2nd ed. Harry S. Pariser. (Illus.). 288p. 1994. pap. 14.95 (1-55650-629-5) Hunter NJ.

Dominican Republic & Haiti: A Country Study. Richard A. Haggerty. LC 91-9495. 456p. 1991. 20.00 (0-8444-0728-3) Lib Congress.

***Dominican Republic Business Risk Outlook.** 70p. (Orig.). 1994. pap. 495.00 (0-7605-1384-8) Rector Pr.

***Dominican Republic Commercial Law.** 150p. (C). 1994. pap. 295.00 (0-7605-0110-6) Rector Pr.

Dominican Republic Guidebook. Marta Lugo. 1989. pap. 15.95 (0-932030-29-7) Eurasia Pr NY.

Dominican Republic in Pictures. Nathan A. Haverstock. (Visual Geography Ser.). (Illus.). 64p. (YA). (gr. 5 up). 1988. lib. bdg. 18.95 (0-8225-1812-0, Lerner Publctns) Lerner Group.

Dominican Republic Investors Handbook: A Guide for Investing in Santo Domingo. W. A. Rood. 1978. lib. bdg. 69.95 (0-8490-1389-5) Gordon Pr.

***Dominican Republic Tax Law.** 150p. (C). 1994. pap. 295.00 (0-7605-0109-2) Rector Pr.

***Dominican Republic Today: Realities & Perspectives - Realidades y Perspectivas.** Emelio Betances & Hobart Spalding. 200p. (ENG & SPA.). (C). 1995. write for info. (0-929972-18-X); pap. write for info. (0-929972-17-1) CUNY Bildner Ctr.

Dominican Sugar Plantations: Production & Foreign Labor Integration. Martin F. Murphy. LC 90-44147. 200p. 1991. text ed. 55.00 (0-275-93113-7, C3113, Praeger Pubs) Greenwood.

Dominicanos en Puerto Rico: Migracion en la Semi-Periferia. Ed. by Jorge Duany. LC 90-81615. 132p. 1990. pap. 8.95 (0-929157-08-7) Ediciones Huracan.

Dominicans. Benedict Ashley. (Religious Orders Ser.). 280p. 1991. text ed. 21.95 (0-8146-5723-0) Liturgical Pr.

Dominico. William Steig. (J). (gr. 4-7). 1994. 15.00 (0-374-31823-9, Mirasol); pap. 4.95 (0-374-41927-2, Mirasol) FS&G.

Dominico. William Steig. (J). (gr. 4-7). 1994. pap. 5.95 (0-374-41827-6) FS&G.

Dominico Blanchi, No. 15. Ed. by Kyoichi Tsuzuki. (Art Random Ser.). (Illus.). 48p. 1990. 32.95 (4-7636-8505-8) Bks Nippan.

Dominio de la Ortografia Espanola. Caleb Gattegno & Patricia Iniguez. 65p. (SPA.). 1978. pap. text ed. 6.00 (0-87825-146-4) Ed Solutions.

Dominio Romano in Grecia Dalla Guerra Acaica Ad Augusto. Silvio Accame. LC 75-7302. (Roman History Ser.). (ITA.). 1975. reprint ed. 21.95 (0-405-07179-5) Ayer.

Dominio y Autoridad: Para Gobernar y Reinar. David T. Demola. 64p. 1990. pap. 3.95 (0-88144-144-9) Christian Pub.

***Dominion.** Niles Eldredge. LC 95-13644. 1995. 25.00 (0-8050-2982-6, J Macrae Bks) H Holt & Co.

Dominion. Andrew Forster. 1989. 20.00 (0-932526-27-6) Nexus Pr.

***Dominion.** Fred Saberhagen. 320p. 1992. mass mkt. 4.99 (0-8125-2386-5) Tor Bks.

Dominion & Authority. David Demola. 62p. 1987. pap. 3.25 (0-88144-098-1) Christian Pub.

Dominion & Common Grace. Gary North. 295p. 1987. pap. 8.95 (0-930464-09-5) Inst Christian.

Dominion & Liberty: Ideology in the Anglo-American World, 1660-1801. Robert M. Calhoon. (Illus.). 160p. (C). 1994. pap. text ed. write for info. (0-88295-913-1) Harlan Davidson.

Dominion & Wealth: A Critical Analysis of Karl Marx' Theory of Commercial Law. Donna C. Kline. LC 87-9555. 1987. lib. bdg. 95.00 (90-277-2499-7) Kluwer Ac.

Dominion Collection. Masamune Shirow. (Illus.). 214p. pap. 13.95 (1-878574-74-4) Dark Horse Comics.

Dominion Covenant: Genesis. Gary North. write for info. (0-930462-24-6) Am Bur Eco Res.

Dominion Covenant: Genesis. Gary North. 512p. 1987. reprint ed. 19.95 (0-930464-03-6) Inst Christian.

Dominion Lighting Company, Set. 5th ed. Brenda Hartman. 56p. (C). 1991. Manual practice set. pap. text ed. 21.95 (0-256-09252-4, 34-1345-05) Irwin.

Dominion Maximum. Vic N. Imperio. 1992. 13.95 (0-533-10077-1) Vantage.

Dominion of Canada. Suzanne LeVert. (Let's Discover Canada Ser.). (Illus.). (J). (gr. 3 up). 1992. lib. bdg. 16.95 (0-7910-1034-1) Chelsea Hse.

Dominion of Dreams under the Dark Star. William Sharp. 1977. 23.95 (0-8369-4227-2, 6038) Ayer.

Dominion of Women: The Personal & the Political in Canadian Women's Literature. Wayne Fraser. LC 90-38417. (Contributions in Women's Studies: No. 116). 216p. 1991. text ed. 49.95 (0-313-26749-9, FWU, Greenwood Pr) Greenwood.

Dominion over Demons. H. A. Whyte. 96p. pap. 3.99 (0-88368-020-3) Whitaker Hse.

Dominion Partnership in Imperial Defense, 1870-1914. Donald C. Gordon. LC 65-11661. 333p. reprint ed. pap. 95.00 (0-317-41657-X, 2025845) Bks Demand.

Dominions & India Since 1900: Select Documents on the Constitutional History of the British Empire & Commonwealth, Vol. 6. Ed. by Frederick Madden & John Darwin. LC 84-21213. 906p. 1993. text ed. 125.00 (0-313-27317-0, Greenwood Pr) Greenwood.

Dominions of the Gadiantons. Robert Marcum. 1991. pap. 9.95 (0-88494-813-7) Bookcraft Inc.

Dominique. Eugene Fromentin. 352p. (FRE.). 1987. pap. 10.95 (0-7859-2622-4, 2080704796) Fr & Eur.

Dominique. Eugene Fromentin. Tr. by Edward Marsh. 250p. 1986. reprint ed. pap. 11.95 (0-948166-06-1, Pub. by Soho Bk Co UK) Dufour.

Dominium Terrae: Studien Zur Genese Einer Alttestamentlichen Vorstellung. Udo Rueterswoerden. (Beiheft zur Zeitschrift fuer die Alttestamentliche Wissenschaft Ser.: No. 215). x, 205p. 1993. lib. bdg. 95.40 (3-11-013948-0) De Gruyter.

Domino. large type ed. Phyllis A. Whitney. LC 93-19792. 1993. 22.95 (0-7927-1668-X, Eagle Lrg Print); pap. 21.95 (0-7927-1667-1, Eagle Lrg Print) Chivers N Amer.

Domino: Traditional Children's Songs, Proverbs & Culture from the American Virgin Islands. Illus. by Alaria Arpino. 96p. (Orig.). (J). (gr. 1-6). 1990. pap. text ed. 14.50 (0-9625560-3-3); audio 10.00 (0-9625560-0-9) Guavaberry Bks.

Domino: Traditional Children's Songs, Proverbs & Culture from the American Virgin Islands, Set. Illus. by Alaria Arpino. 96p. (Orig.). (J). (gr. 1-6). 1990. pap. 21.50 (0-9625560-7-6) Guavaberry Bks.

Domino Azul. Manuel R. Mancebo. LC 80-66398. (Coleccion Caniqui Ser.). 146p. (Orig.). (SPA.). 1982. pap. 7.95 (0-89729-259-6) Ediciones.

***Domino Conspiracy.** J. Heywood. 1994. pap. 4.99 (0-517-13034-3) Random.

***Domino Del Creyente.** Victor Ricardo. 28p. 1992. pap. 1.00 (1-885630-13-1) HLM Producciones.

Domino Effect: How to Grow Sales, Profits, & Market Share Through Super Vision. Donald J. Vlcek, Jr. & Jeffrey P. Davidson. 225p. 1991. text ed. 27.00 (1-55623-602-6) Irwin Prof Pubng.

Domino Image. B. J. Hoff. LC 86-70648. 1987. pap. 6.99 (0-7814-0520-3, LifeJourney) Chariot Family.

Domino Math, 2 bks. Arthur Wiebe. (Illus.). 60p. (J). Bk. A, Grades 1-4, 1973. pap. text ed. 6.95 (1-878669-19-2, 4145); Bk. B, Grades 2-6, 1974. pap. text ed. 6.95 (0-685-74216-4, 4146) Crea Tea Assocs.

Domino Math, 2 bks., Set. Arthur Wiebe. (Illus.). 60p. (J). Bks. A & B. write for info. (1-878669-18-4, 4145) Crea Tea Assocs.

Domino Spill. William Story. 1981. pap. 2.25 (0-8439-0918-8) Dorchester Pub Co.

Domino Tattoo. (Red Stripe Ser.). 1991. pap. 4.50 (0-8216-5094-7) Carol Pub Group.

Dominoes. Laura Gordon. (Intrigue Ser.). 1994. mass mkt. 2.99 (0-373-22282-3, 1-22282-7) Harlequin Bks.

***Dominoes: Basic Rules & Variations.** Reiner F. Muller. (Illus.). 96p. 1995. pap. 5.95 (0-8069-3880-3) Sterling.

Dominoes: Five-up & Other Games. Dominic C. Armanino. LC 59-12264. 194p. 1980. pap. 4.95 (0-679-14009-3) McKay.

Dominoes & Bandwagons: Strategic Beliefs & Great Power Competition in the Eurasian Rimland. Ed. by Robert Jervis & Jack Snyder. (Illus.). 320p. 1991. 45.00 (0-19-506246-9) OUP.

Dominoes & Other Stories. Jack Agueros. LC 93-4849. 145p. 1993. 14.95 (1-880684-11-X) Curbstone.

Dominoes Texas Style. George A. McAlister & Lloyd McLeod. (Illus.). 164p. (Orig.). (YA). (gr. 9). 1977. pap. 5.95 (0-924307-02-1) Docutex Inc.

Domino's Mansion: Thomas Monaghan, Gunnar Birkerts, & the Spirit of Frank Lloyd Wright. Gordon Bugbee. Ed. by Paul Chu Lin. LC 88-62139. 184p. 1989. 40.00 (0-8093-9990-3) S Ill U Pr.

Domino's Mansion: Thomas Monaghan, Gunnar Birkerts & the Spirit of Frank Lloyd Wright. Gordon P. Bugbee. LC 88-62139. (Illus.). 184p. 1988. 40.00 (0-9621045-0-7) PROBE Troy.

Domitian & the Senatorial Order: A Prosopographical Study of Domitian's Relationship with the Senate, A.D. 81-96. Brian W. Jones. LC 78-73165. (American Philosophical Society, Memoirs Ser.: No. 132). 200p. reprint ed. pap. 57.00 (0-8357-7913-0, 2036342) Bks Demand.

Domitien: Avec Joseph a Dothan. Jean Giono. 296p. (FRE.). 1959. 10.95 (0-7859-1137-5, 2070228320) Fr & Eur.

Domitila: The Romance of an Emperor's Mistress. Paulo De Oliveira Setubal. Tr. by Margaret Richardson. 1977. lib. bdg. 59.95 (0-8490-1730-0) Gordon Pr.

Domke on Commercial Arbitration: The Law & Practice of Commercial Arbitration, 2 vols. rev. ed. Gabriel M. Wilner & Rudolphe DeSeife. LC 83-26207. 1992. 225.00 (0-685-08314-4) Clark Boardman Callaghan.

Domke on Commercial Arbitration: The Law & Practice of Commercial Arbitration. annuals rev. suppl. ed. Gabriel M. Wilner & Rudolphe DeSeife. 1992. write for info. (0-318-57720-8) Clark Boardman Callaghan.

***Domme: A Dominatrix Anthology.** Ed. by Claire Baeder. (Orig.). 1995. mass mkt., pap. 5.95 (1-56333-366-X) Masquerade.

Domnei. James B. Cabell. LC 75-133517. (Select Bibliographies Reprint Ser.). 1977. 18.95 (0-8369-5549-8) Ayer.

Domnitza de Snagov. Panait Istrati. 224p. (FRE.). 1983. pap. 10.95 (0-7859-2481-7, 2070374947) Fr & Eur.

Domoic Acid: Final Report of the Workshop. Ed. by A. Michelle Woods et al. 28p. 1994. pap. 4.00 (1-881826-02-3) OR Sea Grant.

Domostroi: Rules for Russian Households in the Time of Ivan the Terrible. Ed. & Tr. by Carolyn J. Pouncy. (Illus.). 280p. 1994. 29.95 (0-8014-2410-0) Cornell U Pr.

Dompim: The Spirituality of African Peoples. Guerin Montilus. LC 89-50459. 1990. pap. 9.95 (1-55523-227-2) Winston-Derek.

***Domus 1 & Dymaxion: Two Concept Designs for Lunar Habitats.** Janis Huebner-Moths et al. (Illus.). xiv, 77p. (C). 1995. 15.00 (0-938744-91-7, R95-1) U of Wis Ctr Arch-Urban.

Don: Story of a Lion Dog. Zane Grey. 140p. 1993. 40.95 (1-56723-115-2) Yestermorrow.

Don Alvaro. Duque De Rivas. 229p. (SPA.). 1975. 10.00 (0-8288-8561-3) Fr & Eur.

Don Alvaro O Fuerza Del Sino - Lanuza. Duque De Rivas. 229p. (SPA.). 1975. 6.95 (0-8288-7181-7) Fr & Eur.

Don Alvaro O la Fuerza del Sino. Duque de Rivas. Ed. by Carlos Ruiz Silva. (Nueva Austral Ser.: Vol. 162). (SPA.). 1991. pap. text ed. 17.95 (84-239-1962-5) Elliots Bks.

Don Aronow: The King of Thunderboat Row. Michael Aronow. Ed. by Jeffrey L. Rodengen. (Illus.). 144p. 1994. 39.95 (0-945903-22-7) Write Stuff Syndicate.

Don Aslett's Clean in a Minute. Don Aslett. (Illus.). 72p. (Orig.). 1992. pap. 5.00 (0-937750-01-8) Article One.

Don at War. 2nd ed. David Hunt. 200p. 1990. text ed. 30.00 (0-7146-3383-6, Pub. by F Cass Pubs UK) Intl Spec Bk.

Don Austin V. Zamorano: Statesman, Soldier, Craftsman & California's First Printer. George L. Harding. Ed. by Carlos E. Cortes. LC 76-1269. (Chicano Heritage Ser.). (Illus.). 1977. reprint ed. 28.95 (0-405-09505-8) Ayer.

Don Baum: Domus. Rene P. Barilleaux & Sue Taylor. (Illus.). 64p. (Orig.). 1988. pap. 15.95 (0-913883-17-4) Madison Art.

Don Berry. Glen A. Love. LC 78-52564. (Western Writers Ser.: No. 35). 46p. 1978. pap. 3.95 (0-88430-059-5) Boise St U W Writ Ser.

***Don Berry Short Stories.** Don Berry. 44p. (Orig.). 1994. pap. 4.95 (0-9636614-1-8) Alder Pr OR.

Don Bosco, Pt. 2. (Illus.). 1989. 1.50 (0-89944-114-9) Don Bosco Multimedia.

Don Bosco: Life & Work. Pietro Stella. Tr. by John Drury. (Don Bosco in the History of Catholic Religious Thought & Practice Ser.). 56p. (Orig.). 1985. pap. 24.95 (0-89944-080-0) Don Bosco Multimedia.

Don Bosco: Religious Outlook & Spirituality. Pietro Stella. Tr. by John Drury. LC 93-20644. (ENG.). 1993. pap. write for info. (0-89944-162-9, D Bosco Pubns) Don Bosco Multimedia.

Don Bosco & the Salesians. Morand Wirth. Tr. by David DeBurgh. LC 82-72675. Orig. Title: Don Bosco e i Salesiani. 432p. (Orig.). 1982. pap. 10.95 (0-89944-065-7) Don Bosco Multimedia.

Don Bosco & the Spiritual Life. Francis Desramaut. Tr. by Roger M. Luna. LC 79-52674. 361p. (Orig.). 1979. pap. 8.95 (0-89944-022-3) Don Bosco Multimedia.

Don Bosco e i Salesiani see Don Bosco & the Salesians

Don Bosco the Catechist. Gian Carlo Isoardi. Tr. by Wallace L. Cornell. 89p. 1981. pap. 3.50 (0-89944-053-3) Don Bosco Multimedia.

Don Bosco's Dreams: A Historico-Documentary Analysis of Selected Samples. Pietro Stella. Tr. by John Drury. LC 93-14172. (ENG.). 1993. pap. write for info. (0-89944-270-6, D Bosco Pubns) Don Bosco Multimedia.

Don C. Wallace W6AM: Amateur Radio's Pioneer. Jan D. Perkins. LC 91-8094. (Illus.). 296p. 1991. 29.95 (0-911572-99-6) Vestal.

Don Carlo. Giuseppe Verdi. Ed. by Nicholas John. (English National Opera Guide Series: Bilingual Libretto, Articles: No. 46). (Illus.). 160p. (Orig.). 1992. pap. 11.95 (0-7145-4208-3) Riverrun NY.

Don Carlo Gesualdo see Gesualdo: The Man & His Music

Don Chisciotti & Sanciu Panza. Giovanni Meli. Ed. by Leonard G. Sbrocchi. (Biblioteca di Quaderni d'Italianistica Ser.: Vol. 2). (Illus.). 324p. (Orig.). 1986. pap. 20.00 (0-317-04132-0, Pub. by Can Soc Ital Stu CN) Speedimpex.

***Don Coldsmith: Three Complete Novels.** Coldsmith. 1995. 12.99 (0-517-12333-9) Random Hse Value.

Don Coyote. Sylvia Ashby. (Illus.). 40p. (Orig.). (J). (ps up). 1986. pap. 3.00 (0-88680-260-1) I E Clark.

Don De la Libertad: Setting Men Free. Bruce Larson. (SPA.). 4.25 (84-7228-132-9, 220318, Pub. by Edit Clie SP) TSELF.

***Don de Lenguas y el Nuevo Testamento.** Merrill F. Unger. 170p. (SPA.). 1974. mass mkt., pap. 5.99 (0-8254-1776-7) Kregel.

Don del Espirita Santo - The Gift of the Holy Spirit. Horacio Alonso. 362p. (SPA.). 1992. text ed. 21.95 (84-7645-571-2) TSELF.

Don del Espiritu Santo. Ed. by T. L. Lowery. 80p. (SPA.). 1978. pap. 3.95 (0-87148-307-6) Pathway Pr.

Don DeLillo. Douglas Keesey. LC 93-29927. (Twayne's United States Authors Ser.: No. 629). 256p. 1993. text ed. 22.95 (0-8057-4009-0, Pub. by Royal Botanic Garden UK) Macmillan.

Don Fernando. Somerset W. Maugham. 1994. pap. 10.95 (1-56924-902-4) Marlowe & Co.

Don Fernando: Or Variations on Some Spanish Themes. W. Somerset Maugham. LC 75-25382. (Works of W. Somerset Maugham Ser.). 1977. reprint ed. 23.95 (0-405-07834-X) Ayer.

Don Francisco de Paula Marin; A Biography: The Letters & Journal of Francisco de Paula Marin. Ross H. Gast. Ed. by Agnes C. Conrad. LC 77-188980. (Illus.). 362p. reprint ed. pap. 103.20 (0-8357-8677-3, 2056834) Bks Demand.

Don Gil of the Green Breeches. Tirso De Molina. Ed. by Minter. 55.00 (0-85668-465-1, Pub. by Aris & Phillips UK); pap. 25.00 (0-85668-466-X, Pub. by Aris & Phillips UK) David Brown.

Don Gil y el Paraguas Magico: Sir Gil & the Magic Umbrella. Merce Company. Tr. by Aurora M. Serra. (Coleccion Barril Sin Fondo Ser.). (Illus.). 26p. (SPA.). (J). (gr. 1-4). 1990. 13.95 (968-6465-03-0) Hispanic Bk Dist.

Don Giovanni. Wolfgang Amadeus Mozart. 19.00 (0-8446-5069-2) Peter Smith.

Don Giovanni. Wolfgang Amadeus Mozart. Ed. by Nicholas John. Tr. by Norman Platt & L. Sarti. (English National Opera Guide Series: Bilingual Libretto, Articles: No. 18). (Illus.). 128p. 1982. pap. 9.95 (0-7145-3853-1) Riverrun NY.

Don Giovanni: Complete Orchestral & Vocal Score. Wolfgang Amadeus Mozart. Ed. by Georg Schunemann & Kurt Soldan. LC 73-91488. (Opera Libretto Ser.). 480p. 1974. reprint ed. pap. 16.95 (0-486-23026-0) Dover.

Don Giovanni: Myths of Seduction & Betrayal. Jonathan Miller. 1991. pap. 10.95 (0-8018-4332-4) Johns Hopkins.

Don Giovanni's Progress: A Rake Goes to the Opera. Nino Pirrotta. Tr. by Harris Saunders. (Illus.). 280p. 1994. 32.00 (0-685-66912-2); pap. 17.00 (0-941419-94-0) Marsilio Pubs.

An Asterisk (*) at the beginning of an entry indicates that the title is appearing in BIP for the first time.

An Asterisk (*) at the beginning of an entry indicates that the title is appearing in BIP for the first time.

2079

Donald Borthwick: Selected Paintings & Drawings 1958-1988. Donald Borthwick. (Illus.). 20p. (Orig.). 1988. pap. text ed. 25.00 (0-317-91181-3) D Borthwick.

Donald Cries "Wolf" Walt Disney Productions Staff. (Walt Disney's Fun-to-Read Library Ser.: Vol. 14). (Illus.). 44p. (J). (gr. 1-6). reprint ed. 2.99 (1-885222-26-2) Advance Pubs.

Donald Davidson. Simon Evnine. LC 90-70701. (Key Contemporary Thinkers Ser.). 222p. 1991. 35.00 (0-8047-1852-0); pap. 11.95 (0-8047-1853-9) Stanford U Pr.

Donald Davidson. T. D. Young. Ed. by Sylvia E. Bowman. LC 72-125815. (Twayne's United States Authors Ser.). 171p. (C). 1971. lib. bdg. 17.95 (0-8290-1716-X) Irvington.

Donald Davidson's Philosophy of Language: An Introduction. Bjorn T. Ramberg. 240p. 1989. pap. text ed. 24.95 (0-631-16786-2) Blackwell Pubs.

Donald Davie: A Checklist of His Writings, 1946-1988. Comp. by Stuart Wright. LC 90-47462. (Bibliographies & Indexes in World Literature Ser.: No. 28). 168p. 1991. text ed. 47.95 (0-313-27701-X, WDL/, Greenwood Pr) Greenwood.

Donald Davie & the Responsibilities of Literature. Ed. by George Dekker. LC 83-61320. 154p. 1984. 18.95 (0-915032-38-4) Natl Poet Foun.

Donald Duck. Intro. by Carl Barks. (Walt Disney's Best Comics Ser.). (Illus.). 195p. (J). 1991. 17.99 (0-517-69714-9) Random Hse Value.

***Donald Duck & Sailboat.** (J). Date not set. 1.59 (0-307-02145-9, Golden Pr) Western Pub.

Donald Duk. Frank Chin. LC 90-29994. 173p. (Orig.). (YA). 1991. pap. 11.95 (0-918273-83-8) Coffee Hse.

Donald Fagen: Kamakiriad. (Illus.). 64p. (Orig.). 1993. pap. 19.95 (0-89724-022-7, VF1992) Warner Brothers.

Donald Fagen: The Nightfly. Ed. by Milton Okun & Dan Fox. (Illus.). 64p. 1983. pap. 12.95 (0-89524-176-5) Cherry Lane.

Donald Francis Tovey: A Biography Based on Letters. Mary Grierson. LC 70-104237. (Illus.). xi, 337p. 1970. reprint ed. text ed. 59.75 (0-8371-3935-X, GRDT, Greenwood Pr) Greenwood.

Donald Judd: Architecture. Marianne Stockebrand et al. (Illus.). 216p. 1992. 45.00 (3-89322-495-5, Pub. by Edition Cantz GW) Dist Art Pubs.

***Donald Judd: Furniture.** Brigitte Huck & Donald Judd. 128p. 1995. pap. 29.95 (90-6918-139-8) Dist Art Pubs.

Donald Judd: Large Scale Works. Ed. by Donald Judd. LC 93-83853. (Illus.). 42p. (Orig.). 1993. pap. write for info. (1-878283-31-6) PaceWildenstein.

***Donald Judd: Sculpture.** Text by William C. Agee. 32p. (Orig.). 1994. pap. write for info. (1-878283-46-4) PaceWildenstein.

***Donald Judd: Spaces.** Donald Judd. 160p. 1995. 45.00 (3-89322-618-4) Dist Art Pubs.

Donald Justice Reader: Selected Poetry & Prose. Donald Justice. LC 91-50369. (Bread Loaf Series of Contemporary Writers). 185p. (C). 1991. text ed. 25.00 (0-87451-567-X); pap. 12.95 (0-87451-626-9) U Pr of New Eng.

Donald Kagin's Personal Guide to Rare Coin Investments. Donald Kagin. 280p. 1985. 24.95 (0-13-218512-1); pap. 9.95 (0-13-218504-0) P-H.

Donald Learns His Lesson. Walt Disney Productions Staff. (Walt Disney's Fun-to-Read Library Ser.: Vol. 17). (Illus.). 44p. (J). (gr. 1-6). reprint ed. 2.99 (1-885222-29-7) Advance Pubs.

Donald Lipski: Poetic Sculpture. David S. Rubin. LC 89-82748. (Illus.). 56p. (Orig.). 1990. pap. text ed. 12.00 (0-941972-10-0) Freedman.

Donald Lipski: Who's Afraid of Red, White & Blue? Marion B. Stroud et al. Ed. by Paula Marincola & Gerry Zeigerman. 150p. (Orig.). 1991. pap. 15.00 (0-9619760-2-0) Fabric Workshop Inc.

Donald S. Klopfer. Donald S. Klopfer. 1988. write for info. (0-394-20091-8) Random.

Donald Saff, Mixed Metaphors, 1956-1989. Ruth E. Fine et al. LC 89-50471. (Illus.). 112p. (Orig.). (C). 1989. pap. 21.00 (0-685-30697-6) Tampa Mus Art.

Donald Sultan. Ian Dunlop & Lynne Warren. Ed. by Terry Neff. (Illus.). 112p. (Orig.). 1987. pap. write for info. (0-933856-26-1) Mus Art Chicago.

Donald Sultan. Lynne Warren & Ian Dunlop. (Illus.). 112p. 1987. 39.95 (0-8109-1513-8) Abrams.

Donald Sultan, No. 17. Ed. by Kyoichi Tsuzuki. (Art Random Ser.). (Illus.). 48p. 1990. 32.95 (4-7636-8549-X) Bks Nippan.

Donald Sultan: A Print Retrospective. Barry Walker. LC 92-14630. (Illus.). 96p. 1992. pap. 19.95 (0-8478-1591-9) Rizzoli Intl.

Donald Sultan: Appoggiaturas. Philippe Sergeant. Tr. by Joachim Neugroschel. (Arts & Letters Ser.). (Illus.). (Orig.). (C). 1991. text ed. 29.95 (1-878552-00-7) Ptmanteau Pr.

Donald Teague: A Life in Color. Claudia Meyer. (Illus.). 144p. 1988. 75.00 (0-9620327-0-0); 300.00 (0-9620327-1-9) Nygard Pub.

Donald W. Douglas: A Heart with Wings. Wilbur H. Morrison. LC 90-48685. (Illus.). 280p. 1991. 29.95 (0-8138-1834-6) Iowa St U Pr.

Donald Windham: A Bio-Bibliography. Bruce Kellner. LC 91-10777. (Bio-Bibliographies in American Literature Ser.: No. 2). 144p. 1991. text ed. 49.95 (0-313-26857-6, KDB/, Greenwood Pr) Greenwood.

Donald Writes No More. Eddie Stone. (Orig.). (J). (ps-12). 1988. pap. 2.95 (0-87067-733-0, BH733) Holloway.

Donald's Big News. Walt Disney Productions Staff. (Mickey's Young Readers Library Ser.: Vol. 2). (Illus.). (J). (gr. 1-6). reprint ed. 2.99 (1-885222-35-1) Advance Pubs.

Donald's Big News, Vols. 2 & 9: Young Readers Guide. Walt Disney Productions Staff. (Mickey's Young Readers Library Ser.). (Illus.). (J). (gr. 1-6). reprint ed. 2.99 (1-885222-53-X) Advance Pubs.

Donald's Dream. Walt Disney Productions Staff. (Mickey's Young Readers Library Ser.: Vol. 7). (Illus.). (J). (gr. 1-6). reprint ed. 2.99 (1-885222-40-8) Advance Pubs.

Donald's Magic Stone. Walt Disney Productions Staff. (Mickey's Young Readers Library Ser.: Vol. 10). (Illus.). (J). (gr. 1-6). reprint ed. 2.99 (1-885222-43-2) Advance Pubs.

Donald's Wild Adventure. Stephanie Hill. (Disney's Adventures in Music Ser.). (Illus.). 24p. (Orig.). (J). (ps-7). 1992. audio, pap. 8.98 (0-943351-55-3, XD 1002) Astor Bks.

Donaldson Mansion. Freddie O. Durant. LC 80-53470. 415p. 1984. 13.95 (0-86632-000-8); pap. 3.95 (0-317-05215-2) Shane Pub.

Donatello. Giovanna G. Bertela. Tr. by Nancy Pearson & Anthony Brierley. (Library of Great Masters). (Illus.). 80p. (Orig.). 1991. pap. 12.99 (1-878351-19-2) Riverside NY.

Donatello. Maud Cruttwell. LC 71-37334. (Select Bibliographies Reprint Ser.). (Illus.). 1977. reprint ed. 39.95 (0-8369-6681-3) Ayer.

Donatello: An Introduction. Charles Avery. (Illus.). 160p. 1994. 26.00 (0-06-430311-X, Icon Edns) HarpC.

Donatello & His Sources. Michael Greenhalgh. (Illus.). 200p. 1982. 59.50 (0-8419-0827-3) Holmes & Meier.

Donatello & His World: Italian Renaissance Sculpture. Joachim Poeschke. Tr. by Russell Stockman. LC 92-38115. 1993. 95.00 (0-8109-3211-3) Abrams.

Donatello Sculptor. John Pope-Hennessy. 1993. 95.00 (1-55859-645-3) Abbeville Pr.

Donatello und Nanni di Banco. Manfred Wundram. (Beitraege zur Kunstgeschichte Ser.: No. 3). (C). 1969. 52.35 (3-11-002541-8) De Gruyter.

Donatien Francois, Marquis de Sade. Maurice Japrisot. LC 92-717130. 1993. 23.00 (0-374-28335-4) FS&G.

Donatist Church: A Movement of Protest in Roman North Africa. 2nd ed. William H. Frend. LC 82-45814. (Orthodoxies & Heresies in the Early Church Ser.). reprint ed. 49.50 (0-404-62383-2) AMS Pr.

***Donato & Daughter.** Sandra Scoppetone. 384p. 1995. mass mkt. 5.95 (0-7867-0284-2) Carroll & Graf.

***Donauland - Danubians.** Adam Wolfarth. 26p. 1994. pap. 6.95 (1-887420-01-0) A Wolfarth.

Donauschwabische Gedankenskizzen aus U. S. A. Reflections of Danube Swabians in America, Aufsatze - Articles 1968-1982. Jacob Steigerwald. LC 83-151340. (Illus.). 130p. (GER.). 1983. pap. 8.95 (0-9615505-0-3) Trans Inter Serv.

Doncella De Galilea (The Maiden of Galilee) D. L. Bruchez. (SPA.). Date not set. 4.50 (1-56063-542-8, 498585) Editorial Unilit.

Donde, Como y Porque Esta Escrito? Understanding & Interpreting. Conrado Grandville. (SPA.). 4.25 (84-7645-139-3, 223189, Pub. by Edit Clie SP) TSELF.

Donde Esta Dios Cuando Se Sufre? Where Is God When It Hurts? Philip Yancey. (SPA.). 5.95 (84-7228-539-1, 220320, Pub. by Edit Clie SP) TSELF.

Donde Esta el Pato? - Where's That Duck? Mary Blocksma. LC 85-15001. (Just One More Ser.). (Illus.). 24p. (SPA.). (J). (ps-2). 1990. pap. 4.50 (0-516-51587-X) Childrens.

Donde Esta Jake? (Where Is Jake?) (My First Reader Ser.). (Illus.). 28p. (SPA.). (J). (ps-2). 1991. pap. 3.95 (0-516-55361-5) Childrens.

Donde Esta Jake? (Where Is Jake?) (My First Reader Ser.). (Illus.). 28p. (SPA.). (J). (ps-2). 1991. lib. bdg. 11.93 (0-516-35361-6) Childrens.

***Donde Esta Mi Osito? Where's My Teddy?** Jez Alborough. 18p. (SPA.). (J). (gr. k-1). 1994. pap. 11.95 (1-56014-582-X) Santillana.

Donde Esta Pedro? Sneaky Pete. Rita Milios. LC 89-34666. (Rookie Reader Ser.). (Illus.). 32p. (SPA.). (J). (ps-2). 1991. lib. bdg. 10.35 (0-516-32092-0); pap. 2.95 (0-516-52092-X) Childrens.

Donde Esta Spot? (Where's Spot?) Eric Hill. (Illus.). 22p. (SPA.). (J). (ps-2). 1983. 12.95 (0-399-21018-0, Putnam) Putnam Pub Group.

Donde Esta Springer? Ivo De Wijs. (Illus.). 32p. (SPA.). (J). (ps-2). 1993. pap. 5.95 (0-8120-1747-1) Barron.

Donde Esta Waldo? Martin Handford. LC 92-54399. (Illus.). 32p. (J). (ps up). 1993. lib. bdg. 14.88 (1-56402-228-5) Candlewick Pr.

Donde Esta Waldo Ahora? Martin Handford. LC 92-54507. (Illus.). 32p. (J). (ps up). 1993. lib. bdg. 14.88 (1-56402-229-3) Candlewick Pr.

Donde Estaba la Iglesia Cuando: Where Was the Church When Youth. Stuart Briscoe. (SPA.). 4.95 (84-7228-203-1, 220321, Pub. by Edit Clie SP) TSELF.

Donde Estabas Tu Cuando Yo Estaba Herido (Where Were You When I Was Hurting) Nicky Cruz. (SPA.). 1990. 4.99 (0-8423-6520-6, 490243) Editorial Unilit.

Donde Estan los Muertos? Gavin Hamilton & David Fernandez. Orig. Title: Where Are the Dead?. 64p. (SPA.). 1983. pap. 2.99 (0-8254-1301-X) Kregel.

Donde Estan los Ninos? Mary Higgins Clark. 272p. (SPA.). 1992. pap. 3.95 (1-56780-055-6) La Costa Pr.

***Donde Hay Huomo (Where There's Smoke)** Janet Munsil. (Illus.). 24p. 1994. pap. 5.95 (1-55037-968-2, Pub. by Annick CN) Firefly Bks Ltd.

Donde Nace el Rio. Patricia St. John. Orig. Title: Where the River Begins. 128p. (SPA.). 1990. pap. 3.50 (0-8254-1682-5) Kregel.

Donde Nace la Corriente. Alexander Aznares. LC 88-81473. (Caniqui Ser.). 80p. (Orig.). (SPA.). 1989. pap. 7.95 (0-89729-486-6) Ediciones.

Donde No Hay Doctor: Una Guia Para los Campesinos Que Viven Lejos De los Centros Medicos. 4th rev. ed. David Werner. LC 79-28502. (Illus.). 414p. (SPA.). 1981. pap. 13.00 (0-942364-00-7) Hesperian Found.

Donde No Hay Doctor see Where There Is No Doctor: A Village Health Care Handbook

Donde Reinan las Arpias. Antonio G. Del Toro. (Biblioteca de Autores de Puerto Rico Ser.). 62p. (SPA.). 1992. pap. 5.00 (1-56328-020-5) Edit Plaza Mayor.

***Donde Renuncia una Madre?** Barbara Johnson. 160p. (SPA.). 1995. pap. 6.99 (0-8254-1359-1) Kregel.

Donde Termina la Noche. Olga Rosado. LC 78-74598. (Coleccion Caniqui Ser.). (Illus.). 1979. pap. 6.00 (0-89729-217-0) Ediciones.

Done Crabbin' Noah Leaves the River. Gilbert Byron. 1990. 16.95 (0-8018-3988-2) Johns Hopkins.

***Done Cryin'** Janis Flores. (Superromance Ser.). 1995. mass mkt. 3.75 (0-373-70658-8, 1-70658-9) Harlequin Bks.

***Done Deal.** Ed. by Randy Southern. (Main Thing Ser.). 1995. 9.95 (0-7814-5203-1, 29637) Cook.

***Done Deal.** Date not set. teacher ed (0-8317-5433-8) Smithmark.

***Done Deal.** Les Standford. 1994. pap. 5.50 (0-06-109143-X, Harp PBks) HarpC.

***Done Deal Journal.** Ed. by Randy Southern. (Main Thing Ser.). (YA). 1995. 9.95 (0-7814-5198-1, 29629) Cook.

***Done Driftin'** Janis Flores. (Superromance Ser.). 1995. mass mkt. 3.75 (0-373-70654-5, 1-70654-8) Harlequin Bks.

Done in Oil: An Autobiography. J. Howard Marshall, II. LC 94-10098. (Illus.). 1994. 29.95 (0-89096-533-1) Tex A&M Univ Pr.

Done in the Sun: Solar Projects for Children. Anne Hillerman. LC 83-638. (Illus.). 48p. (Orig.). (J). (gr. 3-5). 1983. pap. 6.95 (0-86534-018-8) Sunstone Pr.

***Done into Dance: Isadora Duncan in America.** Ann Daly. LC 95-11633. 1995. write for info. (0-253-32924-8); pap. write for info. (0-253-20989-7) Ind U Pr.

Done on Time. Barbara L. McCombs & Linda Brannan. (Skills for Job Success Ser.). (Illus.). 32p. (Orig.). 1990. student ed, pap. 4.95 (1-56119-047-0) Educ Pr MD.

Done on Time. Barbara L. McCombs & Linda Brannan. (Skills for Job Success Ser.). (Illus.). 32p. (Orig.). 1990. teacher ed 1.95 (1-56119-048-9); disk 39.95 (1-56119-124-8) Educ Pr MD.

Done on Time, Set. Barbara L. McCombs & Linda Brannan. (Skills for Job Success Ser.). (Illus.). 32p. (Orig.). 1990. 44.95 (1-56119-082-9) Educ Pr MD.

***Done with Mirrors.** (Spike Ser.: No. 5). 40p. (Orig.). 1994. pap. 5.00 (1-885089-02-3) Cityful Pr.

***Done Wrong.** Eleanor T. Bland. 224p. 1995. 20.95 (0-312-13053-8) St Martin.

Donegal Fairy Stories. Ed. by Seumas MacManus. (Illus.). xii, 256p. (J). (gr. 4-6). 1968. pap. 5.95 (0-486-21971-2) Dover.

Donegal Mafia: An Irish Political Machine. Paul M. Sacks. LC 75-43332. 253p. reprint ed. pap. 72.20 (0-7837-2795-X, 2043187) Bks Demand.

Donegal's Changing Traditions: An Ethnographic Study. Eugenia Shanklin. (Library of Anthropology: Vol. 8). 230p. 1985. text ed. 37.00 (2-88124-001-1) Gordon & Breach.

Donelan, Drawing on the Gay Experience. Gerard Donelan. (Illus.). 1987. pap. 5.95 (0-917076-07-9) Liberation Pubns.

Donelan's Back. Gerard Donelan. (Illus.). 1988. pap. 5.95 (0-917076-09-5) Liberation Pubns.

Dones del Espirito Santo. Pablo Wickham. 112p. (SPA.). 1993. pap. 3.99 (0-8254-1871-2) Kregel.

Dones del Espiritu. Ed. by Hiram Almirudus. 88p. (SPA.). 1978. pap. 3.50 (0-87148-520-6) Pathway Pr.

Dones Del Espiritu (Gifts of the Spirit) Yiye Avila. (SPA.). 1993. 3.50 (1-56063-434-0, 550036) Editorial Unilit.

Dones del Espiritu y el Don de Lenguas: (The Gift of the Spirit & the Gift of the Tongues) James D. Crane & Cecilio McConnell. 96p. (Orig.). (SPA.). 1991. pap. 3.60 (0-311-05766-7) Casa Bautista.

Dones Del Ministerio. Kenneth E. Hagin. 1983. spiral bd., pap. 10.00 (0-89276-192-X) Hagin Ministries.

Dones Espirituales - Spiritual Gifts. Kenneth S. Hemphill. Tr. by Juan P. Tamayo. 208p. (Orig.). (SPA.). 1991. pap. 5.95 (0-311-09134-2) Casa Bautista.

Donet. R. Pecock. (EETS, OS Ser.: No. 156). 1972. reprint ed. 43.00 (0-527-00153-8) Periodicals Srv.

Dong-A's Basic English Grammar for Korean Speakers. Dong-A. (ENG & KOR.). 1985. 24.95 (0-8288-3957-3, F52740) Fr & Eur.

Dong-A's Junior English Dictionary. Dong-A. (ENG & KOR.). 1981. 29.95 (0-8288-3959-X, F130750) Fr & Eur.

Dong-A's Korean Dictionary. Dong-A. (KOR.). 1991. 24.95 (0-8288-3951-4, F96270) Fr & Eur.

Dong-A's New Little English Dictionary. Dong-A. (ENG & KOR.). 1984. 29.95 (0-8288-3955-7, F99520) Fr & Eur.

Dong-A's Present Day English-Korean Dictionary. Dong-A. (ENG & KOR.). 1983. 24.95 (0-8288-3958-1, F139480) Fr & Eur.

Dong-A's Present Day Korean-English Dictionary. Dong-A. (ENG & KOR.). 1984. 24.95 (0-8288-3956-5, F81170) Fr & Eur.

Dong-A's Prime English - Korean Dictionary. Dong-A. (ENG & KOR.). 1989. 59.95 (0-8288-3952-2, F116290) Fr & Eur.

Dong-A's Prime Korean-English Dictionary. Dong-A. (ENG & KOR.). 1981. 49.95 (0-8288-3954-9, F92260) Fr & Eur.

Dong People of China: A Hidden Civilization. Gail Rossi. (Illus.). 96p. (Orig.). 1991. pap. 18.95 (981-00-1551-8, Pub. by Hagley & Hoyle SI) Seven Hills Bk.

Dong with a Luminous Nose. Edward Lear. LC 86-1143. (Illus.). 1986. 6.95 (0-915361-46-9) Modan-Adama Bks.

Dongan Papers, 1683-1688, Pt. I. Ed. by Peter R. Christoph. (New York Historical Manuscripts). 200p. (C). 1993. text ed. 45.00 (0-8156-2570-7) Syracuse U Pr.

***Dongan Papers, 1683-1688 Pt. 2: Files of the Provincial Secretary of New York During the Administration of Governor Thomas Dongan.** Ed. by Peter R. Christoph. 596p. 1995. 75.00 (0-8156-2624-X) Syracuse U Pr.

Doniphan's Expedition: Containing an Account of the Conquest of New Mexico. John T. Hughes. LC 72-9453. (Far Western Frontier Ser.). (Illus.). 156p. 1973. reprint ed. 20.95 (0-405-04981-1) Ayer.

Donizetti: In the Light of Romanticism & the Teaching of John Simon Mayr. John S. Allitt. (Illus.). 304p. 1991. 29.95 (1-85230-299-2) Element MA.

Donizetti Society Journal, Vol. 1. Ed. by John Watts. (Music Reprint Ser.). 152p. 1988. reprint ed. lib. bdg. 25.00 (0-306-76272-2) Da Capo.

Donizetti Society Journal, Vol. 2. (Music Reprint Ser.). 1988. 35.00 (0-318-35216-8) Da Capo.

Donkey Driving. Vivian Ellis et al. 128p. 1990. pap. 32.00 (0-85131-327-2, Pub. by J A Allen & Co UK) St Mut.

Donkey Ears. Robert D. San Souci. LC 93-36333. (J). 1994. 14.95 (0-399-22694-X, Philomel Bks) Putnam Pub Group.

Donkey Hide. John R. Rose. 261p. (Orig.). (J). 1993. pap. 10.00 (1-881170-04-7) Rose Pub OR.

***Donkey Kong Country Game Secrets: The Unauthorized Edition.** Bill Kunkel. 1994. pap. 12.95 (1-55958-760-1) Prima Pub.

***Donkey Kong Country Totally Unofficial Strategy Guide.** 1994. pap. 9.99 (1-56686-216-7) Brady Compu Bks.

Donkey on the Bridge. Manorama Jafa. (Illus.). 24p. (Orig.). (J). (gr. k-3). 1980. pap. 2.50 (0-89744-209-1, Pub. by Childrens Bk Trust II) Auromere.

***Donkey Trouble.** Ed Young. LC 95-2135. (J). 1995. 16.00 (0-689-31854-5, Atheneum S&S) S&S Trade.

Donkey Wrinkles & Tales. Marjorie Dunkels. 80p. 1990. pap. 21.00 (0-85131-274-8, Pub. by J A Allen & Co UK) St Mut.

Donkeys. Diana Noonan. LC 93-28998. (Voyages Ser.). (Illus.). (J). 1994. 4.25 (0-383-03741-7) SRA Schl Grp.

Donkeys. Tessa Potter. LC 89-26079. (Animal World Ser.). (Illus.). 32p. (J). (gr. 1-4). 1990. lib. bdg. 19.97 (0-8114-2631-9) Raintree Steck-V.

Donkeys. Alan Clark. (Illus.). 216p. 1993. reprint ed. pap. 17.95 (0-7126-5035-0, Pub. by Pimlico) Trafalgar.

Donkeys: Their Care & Management. M. R. De Wesselow. 1969. pap. 17.50x (0-87556-076-8) Saifer.

***Donkey's Christmas Story.** Hal. (J). 1993. pap. 7.95 (0-571-10098-8) Faber & Faber.

Donkey's Dream. Barbara H. Berger. LC 84-18905. (Illus.). 32p. (J). (ps-5). 1986. 14.95 (0-399-21233-7, Philomel Bks) Putnam Pub Group.

Donkey's Dream. Barbara H. Berger. LC 84-18905. (Illus.). 32p. (J). (ps-5). 1986. pap. 5.95 (0-399-22014-3, Sandcastle Bks) Putnam Pub Group.

Donkey's Gratitude. Tim Harris. 490p. (C). 1989. text ed. 75.00 (1-872795-28-5, Pub. by Pentland Pr UK) St Mut.

Donkey's Life: A Story for Children. J. A. Cheadle. LC 80-123421. iii, 88p. (Orig.). (J). (gr. 2-6). 1979. pap. 3.50 (0-9604244-0-7) Heahstan Pr.

Donkey's Story. Illus. by Susan J. Cohen. LC 85-27. 32p. (J). (gr. k-5). 1988. 12.95 (0-688-04104-3); lib. bdg. 12.88 (0-688-04105-1) Lothrop.

Donkey's Tale. Joanne Oppenhelm. (J). (ps-3). 1991. pap. 3.99 (0-553-35208-3) Bantam.

Donna: Women in Italian Culture. Ed. by Ada Testaferri. 320p. 1985. pap. 16.00 (0-919473-54-7, DH85, Pub. by Dovehouse CN) MRTS.

Donna De Varona's Hydro Aerobics. Donna De Varona. 1984. 17.95 (0-02-531250-2) Macmillan.

Donna del Lago: Melo-Dramma in Two Acts, 4 vols. Gioachino Rossini. Ed. by H. Colin Slim. (Works of Gioachino Rossini Critical Edition Ser.). 1992. 300.00 (0-226-72844-7) U Ch Pr.

***Donna Hamilton's Gracious Country Inns & Favorite Recipes.** Donna Hamilton. Ed. by David Paulson. LC 94-79475. (Illus.). 256p. 1994. 24.95 (0-9643337-0-8) Mockngbird MD.

Donna in Guerra see Woman at War

Donna Jean's Disaster. Barbara Williams. Ed. by Abby Levine. LC 86-15817. (Albert Whitman Concept Bks.). (Illus.). 32p. (J). (gr. 1-5). 1986. lib. bdg. 11.95 (0-8075-1682-1) A Whitman.

Donna Karan: Designing an American Dream. Sherill Tippins. Ed. by Richard G. Young. LC 91-32784. (Wizards of Business Ser.). (Illus.). 64p. (J). (gr. 4-8). 1992. lib. bdg. 17.26 (1-56074-019-1) Garrett Ed Corp.

Donna Kooler's Cross-Stitch Christmas. Donna Kooler. LC 94-4191. (Illus.). 128p. 1994. 24.95 (0-8069-0793-2, Chapelle) Sterling.

Donna O'Neeshuck Was Chased by Some Cows. Bill Grossman. LC 85-45823. (Illus.). 40p. (J). (gr. k-3). 1988. lib. bdg. 12.89 (0-06-022159-3) HarpC Child Bks.

Donna O'Neeshuck Was Chased by Some Cows. Bill Grossman. LC 85-45823. (Trophy Picture Bk.). (Illus.). 40p. (J). (ps-3). 1991. pap. 5.95 (0-06-443255-6, Trophy) HarpC Child Bks.

Donna Reed: A Bio-Bibliography. Brenda S. Royce. LC 90-44109. (Bio-Bibliographies in the Performing Arts Ser.). 160p. 1990. text ed. 39.95 (0-313-26806-1, RDB, Greenwood Pr) Greenwood.

Donna Summer: An Unauthorized Biography. James S. Haskins & J. M. Stifle. (Illus.). 144p. (J). (gr. 7 up). 1983. 14.95 (0-316-35003-6, Joy St Bks) Little.

Donna's Hell. Charles B. McLaughlin. 50p. 1971. pap. 2.00 (0-686-01900-8) Dnomro Pubns.

Donne: Complete Poems. John Donne. Ed. by Roger Bennett. 336p. 1992. pap. write for info. (0-87532-103-8) Hendricks House.

D

D

An Asterisk (*) at the beginning of an entry indicates that the title is appearing in BIP for the first time.

2081

*__Don't Count Me Out: A Different Perception of Fear.__ Joann Czyz. 272p. 1995. 16.95 (0-9645587-0-X); pap. 12.95 (0-9645587-1-8) LAF Pub.

*__Don't Count on Forever.__ Nancy P. Gilsenan. 1983. 5.00 (0-87129-391-9, D38) Dramatic Pub.

Don't Count on It. Thomas Donlan. 1994. 23.00 (0-671-87466-7) S&S Trade.

Don't Count Your Chickens until They Cry Wolf: Musical. Carol L. Pearson. (J). 1979. 5.00 (0-87602-122-4) Anchorage.

Don't Count Your Chicks. Ingri D'Aulaire. (J). (ps-3). 1993. mass mkt. 4.99 (0-440-40771-0) Dell.

Don't Count Yourself Out: Staying Fit after 35. Jimmy Connors & Neil Gordon. (Illus.). 256p. 1994. pap. 9.95 (1-56282-756-1) Hyperion.

Don't Crowd. Charles Dickens. 1972. 59.95 (0-8490-0058-0) Gordon Pr.

Don't Cry Alone. large type ed. Josephine Cox. 608p. 1994. 26.95 (0-7089-8768-0, Trail West Pubs) Ulverscroft.

Don't Cry, Baby Sam. Harriet Ziefert. (Lift-the-Flap Bks.). (Illus.). 20p. (J). (gr. 2-6). 1988. pap. 4.95 (0-14-050858-9, Puffin) Puffin Bks.

Don't Cry, Big Bird. Sarah Roberts. LC 81-4075. (Sesame Street Start-to-Read Bks.). (Illus.). 40p. (J). (gr. k-2). 1981. 4.95 (0-394-84868-3) Random Bks Yng Read.

Don't Cry, Big Bird. Sarah Roberts. LC 81-4075. (Sesame Street Start-to-Read Bks.). (Illus.). 40p. (J). (ps-3). 1993. pap. 2.99 (0-679-83950-X) Random Bks Yng Read.

Don't Cry for Me, Locust Valley! Ann Woodward Scrap Book. Comp. by Dick Frost. Orig. Title: The Two Mrs. Greenvilles Scrap Book. 200p. 1986. pap. 30.00 (0-933883-03-X) Aquarius Rising Pr.

Don't Cry, Little Girl. Janet Lambert. 18.95 (0-8488-0131-8, Amereon Hse) Amereon Ltd.

*__Don't Cry Now.__ Joy Fielding. LC 94-42095. 1995. 23.00 (0-688-12673-1) Morrow.

Don't Cry Past Tuesday: Hopeful Words for Difficult Days. Charles E. Poole. 106p. (Orig.). 1991. pap. 9.95 (0-9628455-7-4) Smyth & Helwys.

Don't Cry, Scream. Haki R. Madhubuti. 1992. pap. 8.00 (0-88378-016-X) Third World.

Don't Cry "Timber"! Genealogical Research Guide. 8th ed. Prudence G. Michael. LC 78-20129. 1987. pap. 6.95 (0-318-35186-2) P G Michael.

Don't Cut down This Tree. Honey Anderson & Bill Reinholdt. LC 92-21446. (Voyages Ser.). (Illus.). (J). 1993. 3.75 (0-383-03621-6) SRA Schl Grp.

Don't Cut the Apron Strings: An Early Childhood Resource Featuring Integrated Curriculum & Theme Aprons. Linda Martinson & Joanne O'Leary. (Illus.). 114p. (Orig.). 1993. pap. 10.95 (0-9637759-0-1) Apron Strings.

*__Don't Deliberate...Litigate!__ Les Ambromovitz. 168p. (Orig.). 1995. pap. 5.95 (1-56245-184-7) Great Quotations.

*__Don't Despair on Thursdays! The Children's Grief-Management Book.__ Adolph Moser. Ed. by Nancy R. Thatch. LC 95-8653. (Emotional Impact Ser.). (Illus.). 60p. (J). (gr. k-8). 1995. lib. bdg. 14.95 (0-933849-60-5) Vanderbilt U Pr.

Don't Die As a Fool Dies. Wayne C. Gwilliam. 34p. (Orig.). 1993. pap. 2.50 (0-9631477-5-7) Reach Out NY.

*__Don't Die in the Winter.__ Millicent Thompson. 126p. (Orig.). 1995. pap. 7.99 (1-56043-558-5) Destiny Image.

Don't Die, Marvin. Penny J. Mann. No. 3. 80p. Date not set. pap. write for info. (0-318-72211-9) Good News Express.

*__Don't Die, My Love.__ McDaniel. 1995. mass mkt. 3.99 (0-553-56715-2) Bantam.

Don't Do, Delegate! James M. Jenks & John M. Kelly. 208p. 1986. mass mkt. 5.99 (0-345-33462-0) Ballantine.

*__Don't Do That! A Child's Guide to Bad Manners, Ridiculous Rules & Inadequate Etiquette.__ Barry L. Polisar. (Illus.). 32p. (J). (gr. 2-6). 1995. reprint ed. write for info. (0-938663-20-8) Rainbow Morn.

Don't Drink Your Milk. Frank Oski. 312p. pap. 4.95 (0-671-22804-8) Park City Pr.

Don't Drink Your Milk. 9th rev. ed. Frank A. Oski. LC 77-8102. 96p. 1994. per. 7.95 (0-945383-34-7, 945-5807) Teach Servs.

Don't Drive Without It! Complete Car & Drivers Guidekit. William S. Carson. (Illus.). 192p. 1987. pap. 12.95 (0-940855-00-3) Preparepak Pub.

Don't Drown in the Mainstream. rev. ed. Jeannine G. Douglas. 66p. (YA). (gr. k-12). 1986. pap. text ed. 5.50 (0-9607872-1-6) Vail Pub.

Don't Dump Daddy in the Flower Bed. Debby Safranski. (Illus.). 192p. (Orig.). 1995. pap. 9.95 (0-89407-072-X) Strawberry Hill.

Don't Dump the Teacher. Reita Mills. 1987. 8.95 (0-533-07345-6) Vantage.

Don't Eat the Mystery Meat! Tom B. Stone. (Graveyard School Ser.: No. 1). (J). (gr. 4-7). 1994. pap. 3.50 (0-553-48223-8) Bantam.

Don't Eat This Book. Charleston Area Medical Center Foundation Staff. LC 92-31744. 1992. write for info. (0-87197-352-9) Favorite Recipes.

Don't Eat Too Much Turkey! Miriam Cohen. LC 86-25660. (Illus.). 32p. (J). (gr. k-3). 1987. 15.00 (0-688-07141-4); lib. bdg. 14.93 (0-688-07142-2) Greenwillow.

Don't Eat Too Much Turkey. Miriam Cohen. (J). (gr. k-6). 1988. pap. 3.25 (0-440-40106-2, YB) Dell.

Don't Eat Your Heart Out. Joseph C. Piscatella. 1989. pap. 15.95 (0-8161-4747-7) G K Hall.

Don't Eat Your Heart out Cookbook. Joseph Piscatella. LC 83-14830. 560p. 1983. pap. 15.95 (0-89480-488-X, 488) Workman Pub.

Don't Eat Your Heart Out Cookbook. rev. ed. Joseph C. Piscatella. Ed. by Sally Kovalchick. LC 94-32730. 664p. 1994. pap. 17.95 (1-56305-558-9) Workman Pub.

Don't Ever Forget Me. Rose Alan. LC 86-46441. 1988. 15.00 (0-87212-204-2) Libra.

Don't Ever Give Up Your Dreams. Ed. by Susan P. Schutz. LC 82-74095. (Illus.). 64p. (Orig.). 1983. pap. 7.95 (0-88396-183-0) Blue Mtn Pr CO.

Don't Ever Leave Me. Katharine Brush. 1993. reprint ed. lib. bdg. 89.00 (0-7812-5438-8) Rprt Serv.

Don't Ever Stop Dreaming Your Dreams. Ed. by Susan P. Schutz. (Illus.). 1991. mass mkt. 6.99 (0-446-39319-3) Warner Bks.

Don't Exaggerate (Desire & Abuse) Howard Barker. 72p. (Orig.). 1986. pap. 9.95 (0-7145-4076-5) Riverrun NY.

Don't Explain: A Song of Billie Holiday. Alexis De Veaux. 151p. (YA). (gr. 9 up). 1988. reprint ed. pap. 7.95 (0-86316-132-4) Writers & Readers.

Don't Fall off the Mountain. Shirley MacLaine. 1985. mass mkt. 5.99 (0-553-27438-4) Bantam.

Don't Feed the Monster on Tuesdays! The Children's Self-Esteem Book. Adolph Moser. Ed. by Nancy R. Thatch. LC 91-12941. (Emotional Impact Ser.). (Illus.). 55p. (J). (gr. k-12). 1991. lib. bdg. 14.95 (0-933849-38-9) Landmark Edns.

*__Don't Fence Me In.__ Douglas H. Young. LC 94-66500. 361p. 1995. 21.95 (0-9606510-2-0) Writers Pub Hse.

Don't Fence Me In: An American Teenager in the Holocaust. 12th ed. Barry Spanjaard. Ed. by Bunnie J. Spanjaard. LC 81-68713. (Illus.). 224p. (Orig.). 1981. reprint ed. pap. 9.95 (0-9607008-0-3) B & B Pub CA.

*__Don't Fence Me In: An Anecdotal Biography of Lewis Grizzard.__ (Illus.). 192p. 1995. 20.00 (1-56352-250-0) Longstreet Pr Inc.

Don't Fidget A Feather! Erica Silverman. LC 93-8707. (Illus.). 32p. (J). (ps-2). 1994. 15.00 (0-02-782685-6) Macmillan.

Don't Fire the Plant Engineer. Calvin W. Wilson. 145p. 1991. pap. 14.95 (0-9630880-0-9) Calson Pub.

Don't Fire Them, Fire Them Up. Frank Pacetta. 1994. 23.00 (0-671-86949-3) S&S Trade.

*__Don't Fire Them, Fire Them Up.__ Frank Pacetta. 1995. pap. 12.00 (0-684-80050-0, Fireside) S&S Trade.

Don't Fish under the Dingleberry Tree. Robert H. Neill. 1991. 19.95 (0-9617591-9-4) MS River Pub.

*__Don't Fool Yourself...That's My Business.__ Carolann Wright. 330p. Date not set. pap. 9.95 (0-7610-0210-3) NW Pub.

Don't Forget. Patricia Lakin. LC 93-20341. (Illus.). 32p. (J). 1994. 14.00 (0-688-12075-X, Tambourine Bks); lib. bdg. 13.93 (0-688-12076-8, Tambourine Bks) Morrow.

*__Don't Forget! Easy Exercises for a Better Memory.__ expanded ed. Danielle C. Lapp. LC 95-798. 288p. (C). 1995. pap. 9.62 (0-201-48336-X) Addison-Wesley.

Don't Forget, Dumbo! (Squeeze Me Ser.). 18p. (J). 1994. 6.98 (1-57082-099-6) Mouse Works.

Don't Forget Me, Mommy! Kay W. Anderson. (Orig.). Date not set. write for info. (0-318-70109-X) Marin Pub.

Don't Forget Me, Mommy! Kay W. Anderson. LC 81-85048. (Illus.). 118p. (Orig.). 1982. pap. 6.95 (0-685-05552-3) Marin Pub.

Dont' Forget Me Santa Claus. Virginia Mayo. (J). (ps). 1993. 12.95 (0-8120-6391-0) Barron.

Don't Forget the Bacon! Pat Hutchins. LC 75-17935. (Illus.). 32p. (J). (gr. k-3). 1976. 13.95 (0-688-06787-5); lib. bdg. 14.93 (0-688-06788-3) Greenwillow.

*__Don't Forget the Bacon.__ Pat Hutchins. (Illus.). (J). (gr. k-3). 1992. audio 22.95 (0-87499-253-2); audio, pap. 14.95 (0-87499-252-4) Live Oak Media.

Don't Forget the Bacon. Pat Hutchins. LC 75-17935. (J). (ps up). 1989. 4.95 (0-688-08743-4, Mulberry) Morrow.

*__Don't Forget the Bacon, 4 bks., Set.__ Pat Hutchins. (Illus.). (J). (gr. k-3). 1992. audio, pap. 31.95 (0-87499-254-0) Live Oak Media.

Don't Forget the Bacon: Big Book Edition. Pat Hutchins. (Illus.). 32p. (J). (ps up). 1994. reprint ed. pap. 18.95 (0-688-13102-6, Mulberry) Morrow.

*__Don't Forget the Rubber Ducky! The Ultimate Book of Lists for Parents of Young Children.__ Riverside. 1995. pap. 12.00 (0-671-51125-4) PB.

Don't Forget the Star. George D. Durrant. pap. 4.95 (0-88494-467-0) Bookcraft Inc.

Don't Forget to Call Your Mama - I Wish I Could Call Mine. Lewis Grizzard. LC 90-63904. 144p. (Orig.). 1991. pap. 8.95 (0-929264-93-2) Longstreet Pr Inc.

Don't Forget to Smile or How to Stay Sane & Fit over Ninety. Ruth Stout. Date not set. write for info. (0-912846-21-6) Bookstore Pr.

Don't Forget to Write. Chelsea Brooks. LC 94-14181. (California Dreams Ser.: Vol. 7). (YA). (gr. 5 up). 1994. pap. 2.95 (0-02-041651-2, Mac Bks Young Read) S&S Childrens.

Don't Forget to Write. Martina Selway. LC 91-28430. (Illus.). 32p. (J). (ps-2). 1992. 12.95 (0-8249-8543-5, Ideals Child) Hambleton-Hill.

Don't Forget to Write. Martina Selway. LC 91-28430. (Illus.). 32p. (J). (ps-2). 1994. reprint ed. pap. 4.95 (0-8249-8636-9, Ideals Child) Hambleton-Hill.

Don't Fuss, Mr. Ambrose. Spellmount Ltd. Publishers Staff. (C). 1986. 75.00 (0-946771-63-4, Pub. by Spellmount UK) St Mut.

Don't Get Burned: A Family Fire-Safety Guide. Gary A. Glenn & Peggy Glenn. LC 82-6872. (Illus.). 210p. (Orig.). 1982. 10.95 (0-936930-81-0); pap. 7.95 (0-936930-73-X) Aames-Allen.

Don't Get Burned! A Family Fire Safety Guide. Gary A. Glenn & Peggy Glenn. 1982. 10.95 (0-939930-81-1); pap. 7.95 (0-317-01032-8) Phoenix Soc.

*__Don't Get Mad, Get Even: The Fine Art of Revengemanship.__ Jane Inder & Hilary Eyre. (Illus.). 256p. 1994. 22.95 (0-87364-793-9) Paladin Pr.

Don't Get Married until You Read This: A Layman's Guide to Prenuptial Agreements. David Saltman. 1989. pap. 9.95 (0-8120-4123-2) Barron.

Don't Get Me Wrong! Mike Ditka's Insights, Outbursts, Kudos & Comebacks. Ed. by Jim Stamborski. LC 88-20238. 276p. 1988. pap. 9.95 (1-55652-040-9) Chicago Review.

Don't Get Stuck! The Case Against Vaccinations & Injections. 2nd ed. Hannah Allen. LC 84-62791. 1985. pap. 9.95 (0-914532-33-2) Natural Hygiene.

Don't Get Taken. rev. ed. Remar Sutton. 1986. mass mkt. 4.95 (0-14-009613-2, Penguin Bks) Viking Penguin.

Don't Get Taken: Bunco & Bunkum Exposed - How to Protect Yourself. Robert A. Steiner. xii, 218p. (Orig.). 1989. pap. 14.95 (0-9623473-0-2) Wide-Awake Bks.

Don't Get Taken: How to Avoid Everyday Consumer Rip-Offs. Consumer Reports Books Editors & Steven M. Sack. LC 92-34507. 1993. pap. 15.95 (0-89043-422-0) Consumer Reports.

Don't Get Taken Every Time: The Insider's Guide to Buying or Leasing Your Next Car or Truck. Remar Sutton. 256p. 1991. pap. 9.00 (0-14-015263-6, Penguin Bks) Viking Penguin.

Don't Get Taken Every Time: The Insider's Guide to Buying or Leasing Your Next Car or Truck. 3rd rev. ed. Remar Sutton. LC 94-2880. 384p. 1994. 9.95 (0-14-023632-5, Penguin Bks) Viking Penguin.

Don't Get Taken Every Time: The Insider's Guide to Buying Your Next Car or Truck. Remar Sutton. 400p. 1988. mass mkt. 4.95 (0-14-011133-6, Penguin Bks) Viking Penguin.

Don't Git Hit by a Coconut. Cahimite. 200p. reprint ed. pap. 57.00 (0-317-26232-7, 2055570) Bks Demand.

Don't-Give-up Kid & Learning Differences: Learning Differences. 2nd ed. Jeanne Gehret. (Illus.). 40p. (J). (gr. 1-5). 1992. 13.95 (0-9625136-3-6); pap. 8.95 (0-9625136-2-8) Verbal Images Pr.

Don't Give up On Me - I'm Not Finished: Putting the Finishing Touches on the Person You Want To Be. Ray S. Anderson. LC 94-7485. 256p. 1994. pap. text ed. 14.95 (1-56977-607-5) McCracken Pr.

Don't Give up the Ghost: The Delacorte Book of Original Ghost Stories. Ed. by David Gale. LC 92-47088. (J). 1993. 14.95 (0-385-31109-5) Delacorte.

Don't Go. Debra W. Alexander. 16p. (J). (gr. k-5). 1992. 3.95 (1-56688-057-2) Bur For At-Risk.

Don't Go Back to Sleep. Sarah Gorham. (Orig.). 1989. pap. text ed. 9.95 (0-913123-23-4) Galileo.

Don't Go Dancing Mother. Rose Safran. LC 79-66288. (Illus.). (C). 1979. pap. 6.95 (0-9602786-1-3) Tide Bk Pub Co.

Don't Go Europe! Chris Harris. (Illus.). 160p. 1994. pap. 7.95 (0-8092-3659-1) Contemp Bks.

Don't Go Home with John. Francine Pascal. (Sweet Valley High Ser.: No. 90). (YA). 1993. pap. 3.50 (0-553-29236-6) Bantam.

*__Don't Go into the Graveyard!__ R. A. Noonan. LC 95-1602. (Monsterville U. S. A. Ser.: No. 2). (J). 1995. pap. write for info. (0-689-71864-0, Aladdin Paperbacks) S&S Childrens.

*__Don't Go Near Mrs. Tallie.__ Peg Kehret. LC 94-42090. (Frightmares Ser.: Vol. 3). (J). 1995. 14.00 (0-671-89192-8) PB.

Don't Go Near the Water. William Brinkley. 1993. reprint ed. lib. bdg. 19.95 (1-56849-144-1) Buccaneer Bks.

*__Don't Go Shopping for Hair Care Products Without Me.__ Begoun. 1995. pap. text ed. 14.95 (1-877988-15-4) Beginning Pr.

*__Don't Go to Strangers.__ 1994. 3.50 (0-614-01261-9, AM75979) Omnibus NY.

Don't Go to the Cosmetics Counter Without Me: An Eye Opening Guide to Brand Name Cosmetics. 2nd ed. Paula Begoun. Ed. by Miriam Bulmer. 300p. 1994. pap. 13.95 (1-877988-09-X) Beginning Pr.

Don't Go to Work Unless It's Fun! State of the Hearttime Management. Frank Sanitate. Ed. by Ernest Weckbaugh. 244p. 1994. 14.95 (1-881474-03-8) Sta Barb Press.

Don't Go up Kettle Creek: Verbal Legacy of the Upper Cumberland. William L. Montell. LC 82-8566. (Illus.). 264p. 1983. text ed. 31.00x (0-87049-365-5) U of Tenn Pr.

Dont Grieve after Me: The Black Experience in Virginia 1619-1986. Michael Hucles et al. LC 86-81445. (Illus.). 101p. (Orig.). 1986. pap. text ed. 7.50 (0-9616982-0-9) Hampton Univ Muse.

*__Don't Grow up Too Soon.__ Marc Dabagian. (Illus.). 48p. (Orig.). 1995. pap. 6.95 (0-9646396-0-2) Ogden Pr.

Don't Hang Up. Ed. by Andrew Miller. LC 92-24845. (C). 1992. write for info. (0-929925-20-3) Univ SD Pr.

Don't Hassle Me with Your Sighs, Chuck. Charles M. Schulz. (J). (gr. 4-6). 1976. pap. 4.95 (0-03-018211-5, Bks Young Read) H Holt & Co.

Don't Hassle Me with Your Sighs, Chuck. Charles M. Schulz. (Peanuts Classics Ser.). 128p. 1993. pap. 6.95 (0-8050-1866-2) H Holt & Co.

*__Don't Hit Your Brother with Your Mouth Full.__ Cathy D. Better. LC 94-96250. (Illus.). (Orig.). 1995. pap. 10.00 (0-9629880-7-3) ACME Pr.

Don't Hold Your Breath. large type ed. William Newton. (Linford Mystery Library). 288p. 1992. pap. 14.95 (0-7089-7272-1, Trailtree Bookshop) Ulverscroft.

Don't Hug a Grudge. Donna Perugini. (Orig.). (J). (gr. k-3). 1987. 3.98 (0-89274-433-2) Harrison Hse.

Don't Hurt Laurie! Willo D. Roberts. LC 76-46569. (Illus.). 176p. (J). (gr. 4-6). 1977. text ed. 14.95 (0-689-30571-0, Atheneum Bks Young) S&S Childrens.

Don't Hurt Laurie! 2nd ed. Willo D. Roberts. LC 87-21742. (Illus.). 176p. (J). (gr. 3-7). 1988. reprint ed. pap. 3.95 (0-689-71206-5, Aladdin Paperbacks) S&S Childrens.

Don't Hurt Me, Mama. Muriel Stanek. Ed. by Ann Fay. LC 83-16771. (Albert Whitman Concept Bks.). (Illus.). 32p. (J). (gr. 1-3). 1983. lib. bdg. 11.95 (0-8075-1689-9) A Whitman.

*__Don't Just Applaud, Send Money! The Most Successful Strategies for Funding & Marketing the Arts.__ Alvin H. Reiss. (Illus.). 200p. (Orig.). 1995. pap. 15.95 (1-55936-105-0) Theatre Comm.

Don't Just Bake Cookies: A Handbook to Creative Volunteering in the Elementary School. Traci Maxted & Melinda S. Tomsic. (Illus.). 146p. 1990. pap. text ed. 18.00 (0-87287-791-4) Libs Unl.

Don't Just Say No! Safety Workbook for Children. 2nd ed. Judy A. Hall. Ed. by Juanita Edwards. (Illus.). 40p. (Orig.). (J). (gr. k-5). 1991. pap. text ed. write for info. (0-9629597-1-5) Personal Prods.

Don't Just Sit There! Fifty Ways to Have a Nickelodeon Day. Daniella Burr. LC 90-86411. (Nickelodeon Ser.). (Illus.). 96p. (Orig.). (J). (gr. 2-6). 1992. pap. 2.95 (0-448-40202-5, G&D) Putnam Pub Group.

Don't Kill the Messenger. Charles P. Arnot. 1994. 21.95 (0-533-10804-7) Vantage.

Don't Kiss Toads: Finding Your Prince or Princess. Sandra Humphrey. (Illus.). 83p. 1988. pap. 5.99 (0-89225-334-7) Gospel Advocate.

*__Don't Kiss Your Turtle Goodbye: True Tales of a Hill Country Vet.__ Jerry Orr. (Illus.). 180p. (Orig.). 1995. pap. 13.95 (1-878086-45-6) Down Home NC.

Don't Know Much about Geography. Kenneth C. Davis. (Illus.). 480p. 1992. 23.00 (0-688-10332-4) Morrow.

Don't Know Much about Geography: Everything You Need to Know about the World but Never Learned. Kenneth C. Davis. 384p. 1993. pap. 12.00 (0-380-71379-9) Avon.

Don't Know Much about History. Kenneth C. Davis. 1990. 24.95 (0-517-57706-2, Crown) Crown Pub Group.

Don't Know Much about History. braille ed. Kenneth C. Davis. 1050p. 1992. vinyl bd. 84.00 (1-56956-051-X, BR8627) W A T Braille.

Don't Know Much about History: Everything You Need to Know about American History but Never Learned. Kenneth C. Davis. 480p. 1991. reprint ed. pap. 12.00 (0-380-71252-0) Avon.

*__Don't Leave an Elephant to Go & Chase a Bird.__ James Berry. LC 94-24317. (Illus.). 1996. write for info. (0-671-89021-2, S&S Bks Young Read) S&S Childrens.

Don't Leave Me This Way. Joan Smith. 1991. mass mkt. 5.99 (0-449-21964-X) Fawcett.

*__Don't Leave Me This Way: Art in the Age of AIDS.__ LC 94-61764. (Australian National Gallery Ser.). (Illus.). 256p. 1995. pap. 19.95 (0-500-97420-9) Thames Hudson.

*__Don't Let AIDS Catch You: Straight Talk about AIDS.__ Duane Crumb. (Illus.). (YA). (gr. 6-12). Date not set. write for info. (1-885625-07-3) Am Inst Teen AIDS.

Don't Let It Get Around. Christine Devault. 1990. pap. 3.95 (0-941816-78-8) ETR Assocs.

Don't Let People Rip You Off. Harry S. Dahlstrom. (Illus.). 40p. (Orig.). 1984. pap. text ed. 3.99 (0-940712-26-1) Dahlstrom & Co.

Don't Let the Goats Eat the Loquat Trees. Thomas Hale, Jr. 304p. 1986. pap. 10.99 (0-310-21301-0, 18318P) Zondervan.

Don't Let the Messenger They Shoot Be You! A Survival Guide for Public Speaking. C. Mike Jousan. LC 91-78373. (Illus.). 128p. (Orig.). 1992. pap. 9.95 (1-881012-07-7) Clear Comm Bks.

Don't Let the Turkeys Get You Down. Sandra Boynton. LC 85-26308. (Illus.). 112p. 1986. pap. 5.95 (0-89480-013-2, 1013) Workman Pub.

Don't Let Them Psych You Out! George Zgourides. LC 93-77857. 198p. (Orig.). (C). 1993. pap. 14.95 (1-55950-097-2, 88173) Loompanics.

Don't Let Them Scare You. Roger Burlingame. LC 73-21284. (Illus.). 352p. 1974. reprint ed. text ed. 65.00 (0-8371-6146-0, BUSY, Greenwood Pr) Greenwood.

Don't Let Your Participles Dangle in Public! M. Kay DuPont. (Illus.). 152p. (Orig.). 1984. pap. 12.95 (0-9614927-0-8) Comm Connect.

Don't Let Your Participles Dangle in Public! 5th ed. M. Kay DuPont. (Illus.). 272p. (Orig.). 1990. reprint ed. pap. 14.95 (0-318-50082-5) Comm Connect.

Don't Let Yourself Be Upset by the Sutra: Rather Upset the Sutra Yourself. Osho Rajneesh. Ed. by Swami Krishna Prabhu. LC 85-43054. (Initiation Talks Ser.). 560p. (Orig.). 1985. pap. 5.95 (0-88050-584-2) Osho Chidvilas.

Don't Lick the Spoon Before You Put It in the Pot. 1982. 11.00 (0-939418-46-0) Ferguson-Florissant.

Don't Limit God. Charles Hunter & Frances Hunter. 1976. pap. 6.95 (0-917726-04-9) Hunter Bks.

Don't Look & It Won't Hurt. Richard Peck. (YA). 1992. pap. 3.50 (0-440-21213-8) Dell.

Don't Look at Me: A Child's Book about Feeling Different. Doris Sanford. LC 86-185484. (Hurts of Childhood Ser.). (Illus.). 24p. (J). (gr. k-6). 1986. 7.99 (0-88070-150-1, Gold & Honey) Questar Pubs.

Don't Look Back. Mary W. Baker. 225p. (Orig.). 1991. pap. write for info. (1-879019-01-9) Amer Edit Servs.

Don't Look Back. Eva Conover. Ed. by James B. Van Treese. Tr. by Ingram. 550p. 1993. text ed. 23.95 (1-880416-97-2) NW Pub.

Don't Look Back. Mary Engelbreit. 1994. 6.95 (0-8362-4626-8) Andrews & McMeel.

*__Don't Look Back.__ Carolyn Keene. (Nancy Drew on Campus Ser.: No. 3). (J). 1995. mass mkt. 3.99 (0-671-52744-4) PB.

Don't Look Back. Anita Posey. LC 90-71364. 175p. 1991. 12.95 (1-55523-389-9) Winston-Derek.

Don't Look Back. David Seemuth. LC 92-15194. (Groupbuilders Resources Ser.). (Illus.). (Orig.). 1992. pap. 5.99 (1-56476-032-4, Victor Books) SP Pubns.

D

An Asterisk (*) at the beginning of an entry indicates that the title is appearing in BIP for the first time.

Don't Resist Cigarettes: A Mathematician's System to Solve the Smoking Problem. Vern Benson. (Illus.). 100p. (Orig.). 1994. pap. 9.95 (*0-9635792-5-8*) First Data Pubs.
Ever since the Surgeon General's report some 35 years ago, smokers have been admonished to quit smoking & have been given dozens of "programs" on how to do it. Unfortunately, they all say basically the same thing--"resist the urge to smoke". Instead, author Vern Benson, a physical scientist, explains the brain functions & shows how that approach only makes the problem more difficult. DON'T RESIST CIGARETTES gives a clear, concise explanation of the learning system, how thinking becomes data in the memory bank of the brain, how this becomes "you". You can then "learn" to get what you want in life, in this case become a true non-smoker, not an ex- smoker resisting the urge to smoke. The author gives specific instructions on how to program the brain to get rid of the habit, get rid of the desire to smoke & become a happy, healthy, stress free non-smoker. This has been found to be the only way to quit smoking permanently without spending many years of agony resisting the desire to smoke. The author also uses the same basic system to stay young & healthy & at age 77 still spends his winters skiing in the Utah mountains! Price $9.95. Distributed by Baker & Taylor Books.
Publisher Provided Annotation.

An Asterisk (*) at the beginning of an entry indicates that the title is appearing in BIP for the first time.

2083

D

Don't Teach Let Me Learn: About Art, Poetry, Shakespeare & Music. Nina Crosby & Elizabeth H. Marten. (Illus.). 72p. 1979. teacher ed, pap. 8.95 (*0-914634-68-2*, 7911) DOK Pubs.

Don't Teach Let Me Learn: About Fantasy, Magic, Monkeys & Monsters. Nina E. Crosby & Elizabeth H. Marten. (Don't Teach! Let Me Learn Ser.). (Illus.). 72p. (Orig.). (J). (gr. 3-10). 1984. 8.95 (*0-88047-045-3*, 8410) DOK Pubs.

Don't Teach Let Me Learn: About Mysteries, Mythology, Fairy Tales, Fables, Legends, the Supernatural. Nina E. Crosby & Elizabeth H. Marten. (Don't Teach! Let Me Learn Ser.). (Illus.). 72p. (J). (gr. 3-6). 1978. 8.95 (*0-88047-006-2*, 8209) DOK Pubs.

Don't Teach Let Me Learn: About Nutrition, Chemistry, Medicine, Nursing. Nina E. Crosby & Elizabeth H. Marten. (Don't Teach! Let Me Learn Ser.). (Illus.). 72p. (J). (gr. 3-6). 1983. 8.95 (*0-88047-030-5*, 8313) DOK Pubs.

Don't Teach Let Me Learn: About Opera, Ballet, American Theatre, Cinema. Nina E. Crosby & Elizabeth H. Marten. (Don't Teach! Let Me Learn Ser.). (Illus.). 72p. (J). (gr. 3-6). 1983. 8.95 (*0-88047-008-9*, 8210) DOK Pubs.

Don't Teach Let Me Learn: About Pirates, Kings & Things, From Girls to Women, Famous Women. Nina E. Crobsy & Elizabeth H. Marten. (Don't Teach! Let Me Learn Ser.). (Illus.). 72p. (gr. 3-10). 1983. teacher ed, pap. 8.95 (*0-88047-031-3*, 8314) DOK Pubs.

Don't Teach Let Me Learn: About Presidents, of the U. S. People, Genealogy, Immigrants. Nina E. Crosby & Elizabeth H. Marten. (Illus.). 80p. (Orig.). (J). (gr. 3-9). 1979. teacher ed, pap. 8.95 (*0-914634-67-4*, 7912) DOK Pubs.

Don't Teach Let Me Learn: About the F.B.I., Firefighters, Felines, Futures. Nina E. Crosby & Elizabeth H. Marten. (Don't Teach! Let Me Learn Ser.). (Illus.). 72p. (J). (gr. 3-6). 1983. teacher ed 8.95 (*0-88047-029-1*, 8312) DOK Pubs.

Don't Teach Let Me Learn: About World War II, Adventure, Dreams & Superstition. Nina E. Crosby & Elizabeth H. Marten. (Don't Teach! Let Me Learn Ser.). (Illus.). 72p. (Orig.). (J). (gr. 3-10). 1984. 8.95 (*0-88047-044-5*, 8411) DOK Pubs.

Don't Teach Let Me Learn about Aerodynamics, Robots & Computers, Science Fiction & Astronomy. Nina E. Crosby & Elizabeth H. Marten. (Illus.). 80p. (Orig.). (J). (gr. 3-10). 1979. pap. 8.95 (*0-914634-60-7*, 7902) DOK Pubs.

Don't Teach Let Me Learn About Arachnids, Frogs, & Toads, the Animal Kingdom, Fish & Undersea Life. Nina E. Crosby & Elizabeth H. Marten. (Illus.). 88p. 1981. teacher ed, pap. 8.95 (*0-914634-97-6*, 8110) DOK Pubs.

Don't Tease the Guppies. Pat L. Collins. LC 92-25336. (Illus.). 32p. (J). (ps-1). 1994. 14.95 (*0-399-22530-7*) Putnam Pub Group.

Don't Tell a Soul. cruise Beth. (Saved by the Bell Ser.: No. 11). 144p. (Orig.). (YA). (gr. 5 up). 1994. pap. 2.95 (*0-02-042783-2*, Collier Bks Young) S&S Childrens.

Don't Tell a Soul. Barbara S. Cole. Ed. by R. Rosen. (Flipside Fiction Ser.). 175p. (YA). (gr. 7-12). 1987. lib. bdg. 12.95 (*0-8239-0701-5*) Rosen Group.

Don't Tell Alfred. Nancy Mitford. 223p. 1990. pap. 7.95 (*0-88184-597-3*) Carroll & Graf.

Don't Tell America! Michael R. Conroy. LC 92-72812. (Illus.). 500p. (Orig.). 1992. 29.95 (*1-879027-06-2*) Eagle Red Bluff.

Don't Tell the Grown-Ups: Why Kids Love the Books They Do. Alison Lurie. 256p. 1991. reprint ed. pap. 9.95 (*0-380-71402-7*) Avon.

Don't Tell the Whole World! Joanna Cole. LC 89-29283. (Trophy Picture Bk.). (Illus.). 32p. (J). (gr. k-3). 1992. pap. 4.95 (*0-06-443292-0*, Trophy) HarpC Child Bks.

Don't They Know the World Stopped Breathing? Reminiscences of a Child During the Holocaust Years. Renee Fersen-Osten. 280p. (J). (gr. 5-8). 1990. 16.95 (*1-56171-019-9*) Sure Sellers.

Don't Think: Look. William Corbett. LC 91-65385. 128p. (Orig.). 1991. pap. 9.95 (*0-944072-17-8*) Zoland Bks.

Don't Think about Monkeys: Extraordinary Stories by People with Tourette Syndrome. Ed. by Adam W. Seligman & John S. Hilkevich. LC 92-15489. 200p. (Orig.). 1992. pap. 12.95 (*1-878267-33-7*) Hope Pr CA.

Don't Think About Retiring Until... Martin Ragaway. (Illus.). 48p. (Orig.). 1982. pap. 2.95 (*0-8431-0413-9*) Putnam Pub Group.

***Don't Think of a Monkey: And Other Stories My Guru Told Me.** Swami Prakashananda. LC 94-92302. 224p. (Orig.). 1994. pap. 13.95 (*1-886140-10-3*) Sarasvati Prod.

Don't Throw Feathers at Chickens: A Collection of Texas Political Humor. Charles Herring, Jr. & Walter Richter. (Illus.). 191p. (Orig.). 1992. pap. 12.95 (*1-55622-311-0*) Wordware Pub.

***Don't Throw It Away! Fun Things to Make & Do with Recycled Materials.** Debra L. Kaiser. (Illus.). 103p. (Orig.). (J). (gr. k-9). 1991. pap. text ed. 9.95 (*0-9632368-0-6*) Cay Sea Pr.

Don't Throw it out--Sell It: Convert the Clutter in Your Closets into Cash in Your Pocket. J. Sutherland Gould. (Illus.). 138p. 1983. 14.95 (*0-685-06717-3*) P-H.

Don't Throw That Out! A Pennywise Parents Guide to Creative Uses for over 200 Household Items: A Pennywise Parents Guide for Creative Uses to over 200 Household Items. Vicki Lansky. (Illus.). 112p. (Orig.). 1994. pap. 6.95 (*0-916773-40-X*) Book Peddlers.

Don't Tie Yourself up in "Nots" How to Untie Yourself from the Can "Nots" & Should "Nots" of Life. David P. Schloss. 116p. (Orig.). 1991. pap. 6.95 (*0-9629230-0-1*) D P Schloss.

Don't Touch! Suzy Kline. Ed. by Kathleen Tucker. LC 85-612. (Albert Whitman Concept Bks.). (Illus.). 32p. (J). (ps-1). 1985. 13.95 (*0-8075-1707-0*) A Whitman.

Don't Touch My Heart: Helping Parents Deal with the Pain of an Unattached Child. Lynda Mansfield & Christopher H. Waldmann. LC 94-5508. (Illus.). 128p. (Orig.). 1994. pap. 10.00 (*0-89109-820-8*) Pinon Press.

Don't Touch My Tutu. Eddie Cope. (Illus.). 40p. (Orig.). (J). (gr. 4 up). 1985. pap. 4.00 (*0-88680-242-3*) I E Clark.

Don't Touch That Dial. Barbara Hattemer & Robert Showers. LC 92-71225. 240p. 1992. 19.99 (*1-56384-035-9*); pap. 9.99 (*1-56384-032-4*) Huntington Hse.

Don't Touch That Dial! J. Fred MacDonald. LC 79-87700. 408p. 1979. pap. 20.95 (*0-88229-673-6*); student ed write for info. (*0-8304-1178-X*) Nelson-Hall.

Don't Turn Away Series, 9 vols., Set. (Illus.). (J). (gr. 4 up). lib. bdg. 167.40 (*0-8368-1097-X*) Gareth Stevens Inc.

Don't Turn Your Back on Life's Important Lessons. David Tarrasch. 85p. 1992. pap. 11.95 (*0-9635325-0-2*) D L Tarrasch.

Don't Turn Your Back on the Ocean. Janet Dawson. LC 94-9781. 336p. 1994. 20.00 (*0-449-90766-X*) Fawcett.

Don't Use a Resume. Richard Lathrop. 64p. 1980. pap. 3.95 (*0-89815-027-2*) Ten Speed Pr.

Don't Wager on Love. Monette Cummings. (Orig.). 1981. pap. 1.95 (*0-8439-8041-9*) Dorchester Pub Co.

Don't Wait for Your Ship to Come in; Swim out & Meet It. John Mason. 1994. pap. 5.95 (*1-56292-058-8*) Honor Bks OK.

Don't Wait to Be Rescued: Transcending the Death Experience. Shirley Pratt. LC 91-90036. 179p. (Orig.). 1991. pap. 8.50 (*0-9628951-0-5*) S Pratt.

Don't Wait until You See Me. Healthworks Theatre Staff. 50p. (Orig.). 1993. pap. 5.95 (*1-56850-028-9*) Chicago Plays.

Don't Wait...Celebrate! Patty Sachs. (Illus.). 140p. (Orig.). 1994. pap. 7.95 (*0-9616680-5-9*) P Sachs Celebration.

Don't Wake the Animals. Annie Ingle. LC 91-67720. (Lift-&-Peek-a-Board Bks.). (Illus.). 14p. (J). (ps-00). 1992. bds. 3.99 (*0-679-83433-8*) Random Bks Yng Read.

Don't Wake the Baby. Jonathan Franklin. (Illus.). 32p. (J). (ps-1). 1991. bds. 13.95 (*0-374-31826-3*) FS&G.

Don't Wake up Mama! Another Five Little Monkeys Story. Eileen Christelow. (Illus.). 32p. (J). (ps-3). 1992. 13.95 (*0-395-60176-2*, Clarion Bks) HM.

Don't Walk Home Alone. Beverly Hastings. 240p. 1989. pap. text ed. 3.99 (*0-425-11764-2*) Berkley Pub.

Don't Walk on My Dreams. Annie G. Nelson. LC 76-18308. (Illus.). 121p. 1976. reprint ed. 10.00 (*0-87152-245-4*) Reprint.

Don't Waste the Miracle. Mary Engelbreit. (Illus.). 48p. 1993. 4.95 (*0-8362-4609-8*) Andrews & McMeel.

Don't Waste Your Sorrows. Paul E. Billheimer. LC 83-15821. 130p. 1983. pap. 6.99 (*0-87123-310-X*) Bethany Hse.

Don't Waste Your Sorrows. Paul E. Billheimer. 1992. pap. 5.95 (*0-87508-007-3*) Chr Lit.

Don't Waste Your Wastes - Compost 'em: The Homeowner's Guide to Recycling Yard Wastes. Bert Whitehead. LC 91-66324. (Illus.). 168p. (Orig.). 1991. pap. 10.95 (*0-9630612-0-8*) Sunnyvale. DON'T WASTE YOUR WASTES - COMPOST 'EM fully explains over a half dozen proven methods to make homemade compost & leaf mold, & it provides over fifty photographs, twenty-two of which are in color. (Ten of the colored pictures show compost in various stages of decomposition.) In addition to helping to save our landfills & improving our environment, by following the detailed instructions contained in this book, homeowners can easily learn how to make & use the best natural soil conditioner/fertilizer on earth. Dr. Sam Cotner, Associate Dept. Head & Extension Program Leader, Texas A&M University, says "It is extremely well-written (and it) contains much-needed information." The Master Gardeners International Corporation wrote, "This book should be useful to would-be composters everywhere." A review in NEIL SPERRY'S GARDENS magazine reported, "Beginning gardeners & students involved in projects about recycling or ecology would do well to use Whitehead's book as a resource." Libraries, schools, & universities get 50% discounts on single copies. To order: Send $5.50 plus $1.50 for shipping (or send $13.00 total for two books) to Sunnyvale Press, P.O. Box 851971, Mesquite, TX 75185-1971. Any who want larger discounts for larger quantities, write or call Sunnyvale Press at (214)226-4636.
Publisher Provided Annotation.

Don't Weep for Me. Claudette E. Sims. (Orig.). 1985. pap. text ed. 7.95 (*0-9616121-0-X*) Impressions TX.

Don't Whistle "Macbeth" large type ed. David Fletcher. 1979. 12.00 (*0-7089-0281-2*) Ulverscroft.

Don't Wipe Away My Tears. Bonnie Wright. 69p. (Orig.). pap. 5.95 (*0-9617778-0-X*) Vivs Pub Hse.

Don't Work for Anybody - Work for Yourself. (Self-Employment Ser.). 1993. lib. bdg. 225.95 (*0-8490-9005-9*) Gordon Pr.

***Don't Work Forever: Simple Steps Baby Boomers Must Take to Ever Retire.** Steve Vernon. 1994. pap. text ed. 14.95 (*0-471-04141-6*) Wiley.

***Don't Worry.** Geoff Hattersley. 112p. 1995. 17.95 (*0-614-07443-6*) Dufour.

Don't Worry, Be Crabby! Maxine's Guide to Life. Shoebox Greetings Book Staff. (Illus.). 96p. (Orig.). 1993. pap. 6.95 (*0-8362-1729-2*) Andrews & McMeel.

Don't Worry, Be Crabby! Maxine's Guide to Life. Shoebox Greetings Staff. (Illus.). 72p. (Orig.). 1990. pap. 5.95 (*0-87529-639-4*) Hallmark.

***Don't Worry Grandpa.** Nick Ward. LC 95-9970. (J). 1995. write for info. (*0-8120-9425-5*) Barron.

Don't Worry He Won't Get Far on Foot. John Callahan. LC 89-40488. 224p. 1990. pap. 10.00 (*0-679-72824-4*, Vin) Random.

Don't Worry Mom-I Can Take Care of Myself: A Little Person's Guide to a Big Person's World. Nabil Antoine. 60p. 1991. pap. 6.95 (*1-880979-00-4*) Alert Pubns.

***Don't Worry, They'll Grow Up: A Parent's Survival Guide.** 151p. 1992. spiral bd., pap. 19.95 (*1-881185-03-6*) Arcadia AZ.

***Don't Worry, They'll Grow Up: A Parent's Survival Guide.** 169p. (SPA.). 1994. spiral bd., pap. 19.95 (*1-881185-04-4*) Arcadia AZ.

***Don't Worry...Be Faithful: God Has a Plan for Mankind.** Collins Hamblen. 80p. 1994. 15.00 (*0-9643107-7-5*) Lion & Lamb.

Don't You Dare Shoot That Bear. Robert Quackenbush. LC 84-4693. (J). 1990. pap. 3.95 (*0-671-69440-5*) S&S Trade.

Don't You Hate It When. Timothy Crosby & Abigail Allen. (Illus.). 64p. (Orig.). (J). (gr. 7-8). 1994. pap. 5.00 (*0-9641796-4-4*) Rhed Harering.

Don't You Know There's a War On? James Stevenson. LC 91-31461. (Illus.). 32p. (J). (gr. k-8). 1992. 14.00 (*0-688-11383-4*); lib. bdg. 13.93 (*0-688-11384-2*) Greenwillow.

Don't You Want Somebody to Love: Reflections on The San Francisco Sound. Darby Slick. 144p. (Orig.). 1991. pap. 15.95 (*0-943389-08-9*) Snow Lion-SLG Bks.

Donum Estonicum. Aleksis Rannit. 1976. 16.00 (*0-685-79486-5*); pap. 8.00 (*0-685-79487-3*) Elizabeth Pr.

Donvier Ice Cream Dessert Book. Anna Creery. (Illus.). 112p. 1988. pap. 7.95 (*0-89865-627-3*) Donning Co.

Doo Wop: The Forgotten Third of Rock 'n Roll. Anthony Gribin & Matt Schiff. LC 91-77560. 616p. 1992. pap. 19.95 (*0-87341-197-8*) Krause Pubns.

Doo-Wop Sing-Along Songbook: The Classic Rock & Roll Songs You Always Wanted to Sing. John Javna. 128p. 1986. pap. 5.95 (*0-312-21784-6*) St Martin.

Doo-Wop Songbook. (Piano-Vocal-Guitar Ser.). 128p. 1989. pap. 10.95 (*0-88188-844-3*, HL 00490046) H Leonard.

Doodle Dandy. Lynda Graham-Barber. 160p. (J). (gr. 4-7). 1994. pap. 3.99 (*0-380-72100-7*, Camelot) Avon.

Doodle Dandy! The Complete Book of Independence Day Words. Lynda Graham-Barber. LC 91-19409. (Illus.). 128p. (J). (gr. 4-10). 1992. text ed. 13.95 (*0-02-736675-8*, Bradbury S&S) S&S Childrens.

Doodle Flute. Daniel Pinkwater. LC 90-6622. (Illus.). 32p. (J). (gr. k-3). 1991. text ed. 13.95 (*0-02-774635-6*, Mac Bks Young Read) S&S Childrens.

Doodle Soup. John Ciardi. (J). (gr. 4-7). 1992. pap. 3.95 (*0-395-61617-4*) HM.

Doodlebug Country: The Rail Motorcar on the Class One Railroads of the United States. Edmund Keilty. LC 82-10053. (Illus.). 184p. 1990. 39.95 (*0-916374-50-5*, SPECIAL 77) Interurban.

Doodlebugs & Rockets: The Battle of the Flying Bombs. Bob Ogley. (Illus.). 208p. 1993. pap. 24.95 (*1-872337-21-X*, Pub. by AMCD Pubs UK) Motorbooks Intl.

***Doodled Family Haggadah.** Reudor. (Illus.). 80p. (J). 1995. 24.95 (*1-886611-22-X*) Atara Publ.

***Doodles & Oodles of Art: Hands-On, Process-Oriented Art Experiences from Everyday Materials.** Iris Siegler & Kim Torgerson. 144p. 1994. teacher ed, pap. 11.95 (*1-57310-006-4*) Teachng & Lrning Co.

Doodles, Diddles, Puzzles, Quizzes & Fun Stuff for the Sports Fan, Vol. 3. George H. Brown. Ed. & Illus. by Judith E. Donaldson. 144p. (Orig.). 1982. pap. 2.50 (*0-939942-02-X*) Larkspur.

Doodles, Diddles, Puzzles, Quizzies & Fun Stuff, Vol. 2. Judith E. Donaldson. (Illus.). 144p. (Orig.). (J). (gr. 2 up). 1981. pap. 2.25 (*0-939942-00-3*) Larkspur.

Doodling My Way to Enlightenment. Sonia Wadsworth. (Illus.). 160p. (Orig.). 1993. pap. text ed. 9.95 (*0-9630463-3-0*) S & D.

Doody's Health Sciences Book Review Annual, 1993. Intro. by Daniel J. Doody. 712p. 1994. 295.00 (*1-885234-00-7*) Doody Pubng.

***Doody's Health Sciences Book Review Annual, 1994-1995.** (Doody's Health Sciences Book Review Annual Ser.). 1000p. 1995. 150.00 (*1-885234-02-3*) Doody Pubng.

Doody's Rating Service: A Buyer's Guide to the 250 Best Health Sciences Books, 1993. Intro. by Daniel J. Doody. 200p. 1994. 49.95 (*1-885234-01-5*) Doody Pubng.

***Doody's Rating Service: A Buyer's Guide to the 250 Best Health Sciences Books, 1994-1995.** (Doody's Rating Service Ser.). 200p. 1995. pap. 45.00 (*1-885234-03-1*) Doody Pubng.

***Dooger, the Grasshopper.** Lee Roddy. 132p. (J). 1996. pap. 4.99 (*1-56476-504-0*, 6-3504) SP Pubns.

Dooger, the Grasshopper Hound. Lee Roddy. (D. J. Dillon Ser.: No. 3). 144p. (J). (gr. 3-7). 1985. pap. 4.99 (*0-88207-497-0*, Victor Books) SP Pubns.

Dooky Chase Cookbook. Leah Chase. LC 89-48272. 224p. 1990. 17.95 (*0-88289-661-X*) Pelican.

Dooley Poems. John Gilgun. 25p. 1991. 90.00 (*0-924433-02-7*) R Price.

Dooley's Dawgs. Vince Dooley & Loran Smith. LC 89-84530. (Illus.). 192p. 1989. 24.95 (*0-929264-60-6*) Longstreet Pr Inc.

Doolin's Trouble Shooters Bible. Doolin. 1985. 35.00 (*0-914626-00-0*) Doolco Inc.

Doolin's Trouble Shooters Bible. 2nd ed. James H. Doolin & Bob Dixon. 287p. 1989. 50.00 (*0-914626-10-8*) Doolco Inc.

Doolitle Raid: America's Daring First Strike Against Japan. rev. ed. C. V. Clines. LC 88-1822. (Illus.). 272p. 1991. reprint ed. 19.95 (*0-88740-347-6*) Schiffer.

Doolittle: A Biography. Lowell Thomas & Edward Jablonski. (Quality Paperbacks Ser.). (Illus.). xvi, 368p. 1982. reprint ed. pap. 8.95 (*0-306-80158-2*) Da Capo.

Doolittle Family in America. W. F. Doolittle. (Illus.). 730p. 1989. reprint ed. lib. bdg. 102.00 (*0-8328-0484-3*); reprint ed. pap. 92.00 (*0-8328-0485-1*) Higginson Bk Co.

Doolittle's Tokyo Raiders. Carroll V. Glines, Jr. Ed. by James B. Gilbert. LC 79-7259. (Flight: Its First Seventy-Five Years Ser.). (Illus.). 1980. reprint ed. lib. bdg. 44.95 (*0-405-12170-9*) Ayer.

***Doom BattleBook the Authorized Strategy Guide Vol. 1.** Rick Barba. 1994. pap. 14.95 (*1-55958-651-6*) Prima Pub.

Doom Commander. John Sievert. (C.A.D.S. Ser.: No. 7). 224p. 1989. pap. 2.95 (*0-8217-2685-4*) Zebra.

***Doom Contraction Kit.** Joseph Bell. 350p. 1995. cd-rom, pap. 27.95 (*1-57169-003-4*) Waite Group Pr.

***Doom Game Editor.** Joe Pantuso. 1995. disk, pap. 24.95 (*0-471-12128-2*) Wiley.

***Doom Hacker's Guide.** Hank Leukart. 256p. 1995. cd-rom, pap. 21.95 (*1-55828-428-1*) MIS Press.

***Doom II: Official Strategy Guide.** Ed Dille. 1994. pap. 19.95 (*1-55958-711-3*) Prima Pub.

***Doom II: Totally Unauthorized Tips & Secrets.** Robert Waring & Brady Games Staff. (Illus.). 208p. (Orig.). 1994. pap. text ed. 14.99 (*1-56686-228-0*) Brady Compu Bks.

Doom Laden Years. Alida Harvie. 142p. (C). 1988. 35.00 (*0-7212-0755-3*, Pub. by Regency Press) St Mut.

Doom of Daggerdale. TSR, Inc. Staff. (Illus.). 1993. 6.95 (*1-56076-654-9*) TSR Inc.

Doom of Deville. George L. Aiken. (Works of George Aiken (1830-1876)). 1989. reprint ed. lib. bdg. 79.00 (*0-7812-1593-5*) Rprt Serv.

Doom of the Darksword, No. 2. Margaret Weis & Tracy Hickman. (Spectra Ser.). 368p. (Orig.). 1988. mass mkt. 5.50 (*0-553-27164-4*) Bantam.

Doom of the Dictators. Delber H. Elliot. LC 59-14581. 92p. reprint ed. pap. 26.30 (*0-317-07875-5*, 2012820) Bks Demand.

Doom of the Gods. Michael Harrison. (Oxford Myths & Legends Ser.). (Illus.). 80p. (J). (gr. 3 up). 1987. 20.00 (*0-19-274128-4*) OUP.

***Doom of the Haunted Opera.** John Bellairs & Brad Strickland. LC 94-45798. (J). 1995. 14.99 (*0-8037-1464-5*); lib. bdg. 14.89 (*0-8037-1465-3*) Dial Bks Young.

Doom of Youth. Wyndham Lewis. LC 72-2090. (English Literature Ser.: No. 33). 1972. reprint ed. lib. bdg. 75.00 (*0-8383-1475-9*) M S G Haskell Hse.

Doom Patrol: Crawling from the Wreckage. Grant Morrison. Ed. by Bob Kahan. 192p. 1992. pap. 19.95 (*1-56389-034-8*, Vertigo) DC Comics.

Doom Pussy II. 2nd ed. Elaine Shepard. LC 89-85621. (Illus.). 368p. 1992. lib. bdg. 29.50 (*0-9628388-0-2*) Rockoon Pr.

***Doom Stone.** Paul Zindel. (Illus.). 192p. (J). (gr. 6-10). 1995. 14.95 (*0-06-024726-6*); lib. bdg. 14.89 (*0-06-024727-4*) HarpC Child Bks.

Doom That Came to Sarnath. H. P. Lovecraft. 224p. 1991. mass mkt. 4.95 (*0-345-33105-2*, Del Rey) Ballantine.

Doome Warning All Men to the Judgement. Stephen Batman. LC 84-1441. 1984. reprint ed. 75.00 (*0-8201-1394-8*) Schol Facsimiles.

Doomed at the Start: American Pursuit Pilots in the Philippines, 1941-1942. William H. Bartsch. LC 91-34307. (Military History Ser.: No. 24). 528p. (Orig.). 1992. 35.00 (*0-89096-492-0*) Tex A&M Univ Pr.

***Doomed at the Start: American Pursuit Pilots in the Philippines, 1941-1942.** William H. Bartsch. LC 91-34307. (Texas A&M University Military History Ser.: No. 24). (Illus.). 528p. (Orig.). (C). 1995. pap. 16.95 (*0-89096-679-6*) Tex A&M Univ Pr.

Doomed Democracy: Czechoslovakia in a Disrupted Europe, 1914-38. Vera Olivova. Tr. by George Theiner. LC 78-189266. 294p. reprint ed. pap. 83.80 (*0-7837-1018-6*, 2041329) Bks Demand.

Doomed Expeditions. John Duggleby. LC 89-25459. (Incredible Histories Ser.). (Illus.). 48p. (J). (gr. 5-6). 1990. text ed. 11.95 (*0-89686-506-1*, Crstwood Hse) Silver Burdett Pr.

Doomed Oasis. Hammond Innes. 1978. pap. 2.25 (*0-345-27418-0*) Ballantine.

Doomed Planet. L. Ron Hubbard. (Mission Earth Ser.: No. 10). 1995. pap. 5.99 (*0-88404-291-X*) Bridge Pubns Inc.

Doomed Rabbit: Recipes from the Kitchens of Leather Folk & Friends. Illus. by Michael M. Youngs. LC 94-70799. 200p. 1994. 14.95 (*0-9640919-0-9*) EROS WA.

Doomed to Die. Dorothy Simpson. 1992. pap. 4.50 (*0-553-29694-9*) Bantam.

Doomed to Die. large type ed. Dorothy Simpson. 356p. 1992. reprint ed. lib. bdg. 20.95 (*1-56054-339-6*) Thorndike Pr.

An Asterisk (*) at the beginning of an entry indicates that the title is appearing in BIP for the first time.

Doomed to Die: A Lonely Walk. Kevin Dounuts. Ed. by Mignon Anderson. 70p. (Orig.). (YA). 1993. pap. 9.95 (0-9636006-3-X) Old Ctry Bks.

Doomed to Die: An Inspector Luke Thanet Novel. Dorothy Simpson. 288p. 1991. text ed. 19.95 (0-684-19381-7, Scribners) S&S Trade.

Doomed to Hate. large type ed. Jeanne Bowman. LC 93-49365. 1994. 18.95 (0-7927-1987-5, Curley Lrg Print); pap. 17.95 (0-7927-1986-7, Curley Lrg Print) Chivers N Amer.

Doomfarers of Coramonde. Brian Daley. (Orig.). 1986. pap. 3.50 (0-345-33953-3, Del Rey) Ballantine.

Dooming Eye. Peter Edler. LC 77-92991. (Illus.). 126p. 1978. pap. 5.00 (0-912292-48-2) The Smith.

Doomsayer. Jerry Ahern. (Survivalist Ser.: No. 4). (Orig.). 1981. pap. 2.50 (0-89083-893-3) Zebra.

Doomsday. Jack McKinney. (Robotech Ser.: No.6). 224p. (Orig.). 1987. mass mkt. 4.95 (0-345-34139-2, Del Rey) Ballantine.

Doomsday: The End of the World - a View Through Time. Russell Chandler. 332p. 1993. 16.99 (0-89283-731-4, Vine Bks) Servant.

***Doomsday: The End of the World: A View Through Time.** Russell Chandler. 330p. 1995. pap. 12.99 (0-89283-868-X, Vine Bks) Servant.

Doomsday Book. J. MacLaren-Ross. 1961. 11.95 (0-8392-1027-2) Astor-Honor.

Doomsday Book. Connie Willis. 1993. mass mkt. 5.99 (0-553-56273-8, Spectra) Bantam.

Doomsday Carrier. large type ed. Victor Canning. 365p. 1979. 12.00 (0-7089-0277-4) Ulverscroft.

Doomsday Conspiracy. Sidney Sheldon. 416p. 1992. mass mkt. 6.99 (0-446-36366-9) Warner Bks.

Doomsday Conspiracy. Sidney Sheldon. 1991. 22.00 (0-688-08489-3) Morrow.

***Doomsday Conspiracy.** Sidney Sheldon. (Sheldon Continuity Ser.). 320p. 1994. 12.95 (1-56865-095-7, GuildAmerica) Dblday Bk Music.

***Doomsday Conspiracy.** Sidney Sheldon. 1991. pap. 4.98 (0-8317-0937-5) Smithmark.

Doomsday Conspiracy. large type ed. Sidney Sheldon. 1991. 25.00 (0-688-10444-4) Morrow.

Doomsday Creek. large type ed. Clifton Adams. (Linford Western Library). 368p. 1992. pap. 14.95 (0-7089-7177-6, Trailtree Bookshop) Ulverscroft.

Doomsday Cult: A Study of Conversion, Proselytization, & Maintenance of Faith. enl. ed. John Lofland. LC 77-23028. 1981. 29.00 (0-8290-1111-0); pap. text ed. 14.95 (0-8290-0095-X) Irvington.

Doomsday Deposit. large type ed. Stanley Johnson. 416p. 1984. 15.95 (0-7089-1227-3) Ulverscroft.

Doomsday Factor. Glenn L. Anderson. LC 87-82113. 160p. 1987. 11.98 (0-88290-319-5) Horizon Utah.

***Doomsday Flight.** Ed Stewart. 475p. 1995. pap. 11.99 (1-56476-482-6, 6-3482, Victor Books) SP Pubns.

Doomsday Marshal & the Comancheros. large type ed. Ray Hogan. 227p. 1992. pap. 14.95 (0-8161-5356-6, Nightingale) Hall.

Doomsday Myth: Ten Thousand Years of Economic Crises. Charles Maurice & Charles W. Smithson. (Publication Ser.: No. 296). (Illus.). xx, 142p. (C). 1984. pap. 11.95 (0-8179-7962-X) Hoover Inst Pr.

***Doomsday Rock.** Ralph W. Luce. 200p. Date not set. pap. 8.95 (0-7610-0259-6) NW Pub.

Doomsday Ship. John-Allen Price. 1982. pap. 3.25 (0-8217-1107-5) Zebra.

Doomsday Speculation As a Strategy of Persuasion: A Study of Apocalypticism As Rhetoric. Frank L. Borchardt. LC 90-44688. (Studies in Comparative Religion: Vol. 4). 264p. 1990. lib. bdg. 89.95 (0-88946-506-1) E Mellen.

Doomsday Spiral. Jon Land. 1983. pap. 2.95 (0-8217-1175-X) Zebra.

Doomsday Warrior. Ryder Stacy. 288p. 1984. pap. 2.95 (0-8217-1356-6) Zebra.

Doomsday Weapon. Malcolm Hulke. (Dr. Who Ser.: No. 2). 1989. pap. 3.50 (1-55817-189-4, Pinnacle NY) Windsor NY.

Doomsday Weapons in the Hands of Many: The Arms Control Challenge of the '90s. Kathleen C. Bailey. 168p. 1991. 22.95 (0-252-01826-5) U of Ill Pr.

Doomsday World. Carmen Carter et al. Ed. by David Stern. (Star Trek: The Next Generation Ser.: No. 12). 288p. (Orig.). 1991. mass mkt. 5.50 (0-671-74144-6) PB.

Doomstalker. Gary Brandner. 240p. 1989. pap. 3.95 (0-449-14577-8, GM) Fawcett.

Doomswoman. Gertrude Atherton. 375p. 1977. reprint ed. lib. bdg. 15.50 (0-89966-281-1) Buccaneer Bks.

Doomswoman: An Historical Romance of Old California. Gertrude Atherton. LC 71-104406. reprint ed. lib. bdg. 14.00 (0-8398-0064-9) Irvington.

Doomswoman: An Historical Romance of Old California. Gertrude Atherton. 1987. reprint ed. pap. text ed. 7.95 (0-8290-2103-5) Irvington.

Doon the Watter. Fred Rendell & Arnold Bell. (C). 1989. 50.00 (1-85098-079-9, Pub. by Jordanhill College UK) St Mut.

Doone Walk. large type ed. Douglas Clark. (Linford Mystery Library). 368p. 1987. pap. 11.95 (0-7089-6394-3, Linford) Ulverscroft.

Doonesbury: The Original Yale Cartoons. G. B. Trudeau. LC 73-9100. (Alligator Bks.). (Illus.). 96p. (Orig.). 1973. pap. 4.95 (0-8362-0550-2) Andrews & McMeel.

Doonesbury Chronicles. Garry B. Trudeau. LC 75-5460. 224p. 1975. pap. 16.95 (0-8050-1062-9) H Holt & Co.

Doonesbury Chronicles. Garry B. Trudeau. 1975. pap. 12.95 (0-03-015256-9) HB Coll Pubs.

Doonesbury Deluxe: Selected Glances Askance. Garry B. Trudeau. LC 87-80724. (Illus.). 224p. 1987. pap. 16.95 (0-8050-0596-X, Owl) H Holt & Co.

Doonesbury Dossier: The Reagan Years. Garry B. Trudeau. LC 84-80587. 224p. 1984. pap. 12.95 (0-03-000072-6, Owl) H Holt & Co.

***Doonesbury Nation: A Doonesbury Book.** G. B. Trudeau. (Illus.). 96p. 1995. pap. 7.95 (0-8362-1784-5) Andrews & McMeel.

Doonesbury's Greatest Hits. Garry B. Trudeau. LC 78-53780. (Illus.). 224p. 1978. pap. 16.95 (0-8050-0883-7, Owl) H Holt & Co.

Doople: The Eternal Law of African Dance. Alphonse Tierou. Tr. by Dierdre McMahon. LC 92-19972. (Choreography & Dance Studies: Vol. 2). 1992. pap. text ed. 32.00 (3-7186-5306-0) Gordon & Breach.

Door. Mary R. Rhinehart. 352p. 1986. pap. 3.50 (0-8217-1895-9) Zebra.

Door. Georges Simenon. 1990. 18.95 (0-15-126370-1) HarBrace.

Door Ajar: The Record of a Spiritual Journey. Alix Taylor. 208p. (Orig.). 1994. pap. 11.95 (0-9641691-0-X) White Wolf CA.

Door Bell. Jan Pienkowski. (Pienkowski Pop-up Sound Ser.). (Illus.). 10p. (J). (ps up). 1992. 13.95 (0-8431-3452-6) Price Stern.

Door Between. Nancy Garden. LC 87-8778. 192p. (J). (gr. 5 up). 1987. 15.00 (0-374-31833-6) FS&G.

Door Country Family Fun & Adventure Guide. Barbara McCaig. Ed. by Rod Bussler. 120p. (Orig.). 1987. pap. text ed. 7.95 (0-935201-21-1) Affordable Adven.

***Door County: A Place to Remember.** (Illus.). 128p. 1996. 36.00 (1-886154-11-2) Phoenix IL.

Door County Almanac, No. 1. Ed. by Frederick Johnson & Pat McNamara. (Illus.). 144p. (Orig.). 1982. pap. 4.95 (0-943122-00-7) Future Arts.

Door County Almanak, Vol. 2. Ed. by Fred Johnson. (Illus.). 224p. (Orig.). 1985. pap. 5.95 (0-943120-01-2) Dragonsbreath.

Door County Almanak, Vol. 3. Ed. by Fred Johnson. (Illus.). 336p. (Orig.). 1986. pap. 7.95 (0-943120-02-0) Dragonsbreath.

Door County Almanak, Vol. 4. Ed. by Fred Johnson. (Illus.). 304p. (Orig.). 1987. pap. 7.95 (0-943120-03-9) Dragonsbreath.

***Door I Shut Behind Me.** Uma Paramesaran. 1990. pap. 13.00 (81-85336-34-2) Three Continents.

Door in the Air. Margaret Mahy. (J). (gr. 4-7). 1993. pap. 3.50 (0-440-40774-5) Dell.

Door in the Dragons Throat. Frank E. Peretti. (Cooper Kids Adventure Ser.: No. 1). (J). (gr. 4-7). 1990. pap. 4.99 (0-89107-591-7) Crossway Bks.

Door in the Hedge. Robin McKinley. 1984. mass mkt. 4.99 (0-441-15315-1) Ace Bks.

Door in the Hedge. Robin McKinley. LC 80-21903. 224p. (J). (gr. 7 up). 1981. 11.75 (0-688-00312-5) Greenwillow.

Door in the Hive. Denise Levertov. LC 89-8304. 96p. 1989. 16.95 (0-8112-1118-5); pap. 8.95 (0-8112-1119-3, NDP685) New Directions.

Door in the Wall. (J). 1986. mass mkt. 5.25 (0-440-80356-X) Dell.

***Door in the Wall.** Marguerite De Angeli. 1995. 17.25 (0-8446-6834-6) Peter Smith.

Door in the Wall. Benita K. Jaro. LC 93-36292. 220p. 1994. 24.00 (1-877946-38-9) Permanent Pr.

Door in the Wall. Benita K. Jaro. 1994. 24.00 (1-877946-39-7) Permanent Pr.

Door in the Wall. Charles Tomlinson. 72p. 1992. pap. 11.95 (0-19-282939-4) OUP.

Door in the Wall: A Study Guide. Stewart & Champanier. (Novel-Ties Ser.). (YA). (gr. 9-12). 1990. pap. text ed. 15.95 (0-88122-410-3) Lrn Links.

Door in the Wall: L-I-T Guide. Charlotte Jaffe & Barbara Roberts. (L-I-T Guides: Literature in Teaching Ser.). (J). (gr. 4-8). Date not set. Grades 4-8. teacher ed 8.95 (0-910857-83-0) Educ Impress.

Door in the Wall: Story of Medieval London. Marguerite De Angeli. 1990. reprint ed. mass mkt. 3.99 (0-440-40283-2, Yearling Classics) Dell.

Door into Ocean. Joan Slonczewski. 416p. 1987. mass mkt. 5.99 (0-380-70150-2) Avon.

Door into Ocean. Joan Slonczewski. LC 85-11141. 403p. 1986. 25.00 (0-89366-156-2) Ultramarine Pub.

Door into Summer. Robert A. Heinlein. (J). (gr. 7). pap. 2.50 (0-451-13777-9, AE2363, Sig) NAL-Dutton.

Door into Summer. Robert A. Heinlein. 1986. mass mkt. 5.99 (0-345-33012-9, Del Rey) Ballantine.

Door into Sunset. Diane E. Duane. (Tale of the Five Ser.: No. 3). 384p. 1994. mass mkt. 4.99 (0-8125-1431-9) Tor Bks.

Door into Sunset, No. 3: The Tale of the Five. Diane E. Duane. 384p. 1993. 21.95 (0-312-85184-7) Tor Bks.

Door into the Dark. Seamus Heaney. 56p. 1972. pap. 8.95 (0-571-10126-7) Faber & Faber.

Door Is Always Open. James Gettins. Ed. by Jude Berman. 168p. 1992. pap. 10.95 (0-9605022-3-8) Pathwys Pr CA.

Door Keeper in the House. Victor M. Depta. 96p. (Orig.). 1993. pap. 10.95 (0-938507-21-4) Ion Books.

Door Knob Five Two. Fredric Arnold. (Illus.). 274p. 1984. 14.95 (0-914961-00-4) Maxwell Pub Co.

Door Knocker's Delight! Room Mottos for Teens (Counted Cross-Stitch) Annette Bradshaw & Gwyn Franson. 1983. 5.98 (0-88290-229-6) Horizon Utah.

***Door Number Three.** Patrick O'Leary. 1995. 23.95 (0-312-85872-8) Tor Bks.

Door of Everything. Ruby Nelson. 1963. pap. 8.95 (0-87516-069-7) DeVorss.

***Door of Hope for the Wounded Black Family.** Alfredo R. Jones & Doris M. Jones. 1992. pap. 14.95 (0-9633378-1-5) Fam Outreach.

Door of Liberation: Essential Teachings of the Tibetan Buddhist Tradition. Tr. by Geshe Wangyal. 304p. 1994. reprint ed. pap. 15.00 (0-86171-032-0) Wisdom MA.

***Door of My Heart.** Tynes. 1994. per. 9.95 (0-919001-81-5, Pub. by Pottersfield Pr CN) InBook.

Door of No Return: The Legend of Goree Island. Steven Barboza. LC 93-21163. (Illus.). 48p. (J). (gr. 5 up). 1994. 14.99 (0-525-65188-8, Cobblehill Bks) Dutton Child Bks.

Door Opens: Writing in Fifth Grade. Jack Wilde. LC 92-30965. 144p. (C). 1993. pap. text ed. 16.00 (0-435-08761-4, 08761) Heinemann.

Door Slammers: The Chassis Book. Dave Morgan. (Illus.). 188p. (Orig.). reprint ed. pap. 30.00 (0-9631217-0-7) Lamplighter MI.

Door Steps: The Days, the Seasons. Norbert Blei. 288p. 1983. 14.95 (0-933180-44-6) Ellis Pr.

***Door Through Darkness: John of the Cross & Mysticism in Everyday Life.** Eileen Lyddon. 176p. (Orig.). 1995. pap. 9.95 (1-56548-037-6) New City.

Door to December. Dean Koontz. 512p. (Orig.). 1994. pap. 6.99 (0-451-18137-9, Sig) NAL-Dutton.

Door to December. Richard Paige. 408p. 1985. pap. 4.99 (0-451-13605-5, Sig) NAL-Dutton.

Door to December. Richard Paige. 1990. pap. 4.95 (0-451-16667-1) NAL-Dutton.

Door to Doom. John Dickson Carr. 352p. pap. 10.95 (1-55882-102-3) Intl Polygonics.

Door to Door. Norbert Blei. 242p. 1985. 14.95 (0-933180-73-X) Ellis Pr.

Door to Door. Bernard Lodge. LC 93-22203. (Illus.). 32p. (J). (ps-3). 1993. 14.95 (1-879085-80-1) Whsprng Coyote Pr.

Door to Joy. Ken L. Williams & Gaylyn W. Whalin. LC 92-35747. (Orig.). 1993. pap. 6.99 (0-8054-1083-X) Broadman.

Door to the Moon. Eric Torgersen. Ed. by Robert Bixby. 32p. 1993. pap. 6.00 (1-882983-05-X) March Street Pr.

Door under the Stairs. Keith Moseley & Andy Everitt-Stewart. (Illus.). 12p. (J). 1990. 8.95 (0-448-40044-8, G&D) Putnam Pub Group.

Door under the Stairs. Keith Moseley. (Spooky Pop-Ups Ser.). (Illus.). 12p. (J). (gr. 1-4). 1994. 4.95 (0-448-40834-1, G&D) Putnam Pub Group.

Door Way. Norbert Blei. 320p. 1992. 19.95 (0-933180-22-5) Ellis Pr.

Door Without a Lock. Maude F. Zimmer. LC 74-149634. 1972. 8.95 (0-8315-0004-2) Speller.

Door Yard. Donald Berg. 144p. (Orig.). 1987. pap. 7.95 (0-89815-231-3) Ten Speed Pr.

Doorbell Rang. Pat Hutchins. LC 85-12615. (Illus.). 24p. (J). (ps-3). 1986. 15.00 (0-688-05251-7); lib. bdg. 15.93 (0-688-05252-5) Greenwillow.

Doorbell Rang. Pat Hutchins. LC 85-12615. (Illus.). 24p. (J). (ps up). 1989. pap. 3.95 (0-688-09234-9, Mulberry) Morrow.

Doorbell Rang: Big Book Edition. Pat Hutchins. (Illus.). 24p. (J). (ps up). 1994. reprint ed. pap. 18.95 (0-688-13101-8, Mulberry) Morrow.

Doorkeeper of the Heart: Versions of Rabia. Tr. by Charles Upton. LC 87-51468. 64p. (Orig.). 1987. pap. 9.00 (0-939660-24-5) Threshold VT.

Doorknob Collection of Bedtime Rhymes, Vol. 1. Judith S. Hannant. (Illus.). (J). (ps). 1993. 13.95 (0-316-34366-8) Little.

Doorknob Collection of Nursery Rhymes. Judith S. Hannant. (J). (ps). 1991. 13.95 (0-316-34343-9) Little.

***Doorknob Collection of Pets & Pals.** Judith S. Hannant. (Illus.). (J). (ps). 1994. 12.95 (0-316-34387-0) Little.

Doormaking Patterns & Ideas. John Birchard. LC 90-9430. (Illus.). 200p. (Orig.). 1990. pap. 19.95 (0-8069-6996-2) Sterling.

Doorman. Reinaldo Arenas. 204p. 1995. pap. 10.00 (0-8021-3405-X) Grove-Atltic.

***Doornroosje.** Tr. by DigiPro Staff. (Comes to Life Bks.). 16p. (DUT.). (J). (ps-2). 1994. write for info. (1-883366-93-3) YES Ent.

Doorposts. Tim Botts. 128p. 1986. 25.00 (0-8423-0595-5) Tyndale.

Doors. Ed McBain. 256p. 1988. pap. 3.50 (0-380-70371-8) Avon.

***Doors.** Ed McBain. 288p. (Orig.). 1995. mass mkt. 5.99 (0-446-60148-9) Warner Bks.

Doors. John Tobler & Andrew Doe. (Illus.). 128p. 1987. pap. 14.95 (0-7119-1180-0, BO10070, Pub. by Bobcat UK) Music Sales.

Doors. Suzan Zeder. (Orig.). (J). (gr. 4 up). 1985. 5.00 (0-87602-261-1) Anchorage.

Doors: Dance on Fire. Ross Clarke. (Illus.). 224p. 1993. pap. 14.00 (0-685-72582-0, Pub. by Castle Communs UK) Viking Penguin.

***Doors: Dance on Fire.** Ross Clarke. 1993. pap. 14.00 (1-898141-05-3, Pub. by Castle Communs UK) Viking Penguin.

Doors: The Complete Lyrics. Danny Sugerman. 1992. pap. 16.95 (0-385-30840-X, Delta) Dell.

Doors: The Illustrated History. Danny Sugerman. LC 83-691. (Illus.). 1983. pap. 15.95 (0-688-01363-5, Quill) Morrow.

Doors & Gates of Charleston. Joseph F. Thompson. LC 90-40814. (Illus.). 95p. 1990. 35.00 (0-87249-745-3) U of SC Pr.

Doors & Windows. (Home Repair & Improvement Ser.). (Illus.). 136p. 1978. 14.60 (0-8094-2406-1); lib. bdg. 20.60 (0-8094-2407-X) Time-Life.

***Doors Complete.** Cpp Belwin Staff. 1993. pap. 18.95 (0-89898-180-8) CPP Belwin.

Doors Complete. Doors. 232p. (Orig.). (YA). 1983. pap. text ed. 18.95 (0-89898-637-0) CPP Belwin.

Doors into the Play: A Few Practical Keys for Theatricians. Sydney H. Spayde & Douglas A. Mackey. LC 93-9431. (Clipper Studies in the Theatre: No. 10). 160p. 1993. lib. bdg. 27.00x (0-89370-316-8); pap. 17.00x (0-89370-416-4) Borgo Pr.

Doors of His Face, the Lamps of His Mouth & Other Stories. Roger Zelazny. 1976. pap. 3.50 (0-380-01146-8) Avon.

Doors of Perception. Harry Duncan. 99p. 1987. reprint ed. pap. 16.50 (0-935072-12-8); reprint ed. pap. text ed. write for info. (0-318-62980-1) W T Taylor.

Doors of Perception. Aldous Huxley. Bd. with Heaven & Hell. LC 89-46101. LC 89-46101. 185p. 1963. reprint ed. Set pap. 11.00 (0-06-090007-5, CN7, PL) HarpC.

Doors of Perception: Icons & Their Spiritual Significance. John Baggley & Richard Temple. (Illus.). 155p. (Orig.). 1988. pap. 15.95 (0-88141-071-3) St Vladimirs.

Doors of Perception; & Heaven & Hell. Aldous Huxley. 185p. (C). 1990. reprint ed. lib. bdg. 27.00x (0-8095-9002-6) Borgo Pr.

Doors of San Miguel de Allende. Robert De Gast. LC 94-20415. (Illus.). 96p. 1994. 16.95 (1-56640-990-X) Pomegranate Calif.

***Doors of Truth...Unlocking Biblical Mysteries.** Frank E. Stranges. Ed. by Julie A. Corcoran. 121p. 1994. pap. text ed. 9.95 (0-933470-12-6) Intl Evang.

Doors Open. Michael Gilbert. 1989. pap. 3.95 (0-88184-544-2) Carroll & Graf.

Doors-Poems-1982. Zahl et al. Tr. by Stuart Hood. 112p. 1982. 8.95 (0-87376-037-9) Red Dust.

Doors to America's Past Series, 8 bks., Set. L. Wade. (J). 1991. 95.60 (0-86592-464-3) Rourke Enter.

Doors to Lock & Doors to Open: The Discerning People of God. Leland Harder. 200p. (Orig.). 1993. pap. 11.95 (0-8361-3628-4) Herald Pr.

Doors to Other Worlds: A Practical Guide to Communicating with Spirits. Raymond Buckland. LC 93-940. (Illus.). 272p. (Orig.). 1993. pap. 10.00 (0-87542-061-3) Llewellyn Pubns.

Doors to the Future: Steps to English Proficiency. rev. ed. T. Robert Purcell. (Illus.). 154p. (C). 1989. pap. text ed. write for info. (1-878251-00-7) English Tutors.

Doors to the Future, Vol. 2: Steps to English Proficiency. rev. ed. T. Robert Purcell. (Illus.). 120p. (C). 1990. text ed. write for info. (0-318-65773-2) English Tutors.

Doors to the Sacred: A Historical Introduction to Sacraments in the Catholic Church. Joseph Martos. LC 91-12298. 488p. 1991. reprint ed. pap. 15.95 (0-89243-493-7, Triumph Books) Liguori Pubns.

Doors, Windows & Skylights. 2nd ed. Dan Ramsey. (Illus.). 240p. 1990. 14.95 (0-8306-8248-1, 3248); pap. 14.95 (0-8306-3248-4) TAB Bks.

Doors, Windows & Skylights: Selecting & Installing. rev. ed. Roberto Lombardi. Ed. by Alan Ahlstrand. (Illus.). 112p. 1992. pap. text ed. 9.95 (0-89721-241-X) Ortho Info.

***Doors, Words & Silence.** R. A. Ford. 96p. 1995. lib. bdg. 27.00 (0-8095-4539-X) Borgo Pr.

Doorstops, Identification & Values. Jeanne Bertoia. (Illus.). 176p. 1989. pap. 9.95 (0-89145-298-2) Collector Bks.

Doorway. Karla Andersdatter. 275p. 1990. 17.95 (0-911051-50-3) Plain View.

***Doorway to the Soul: How to Have a Profound Spiritual Experience.** Ron Scolastico. LC 95-7499. 1995. write for info. (0-684-81352-1, Scribners); pap. write for info. (0-671-53510-2, Scribners) S&S Trade.

Doorways in the Sand. Roger Zelazny. 192p. 1977. pap. 2.95 (0-380-00949-8) Avon.

Doorways in the Sand. Roger Zelazny. 1991. mass mkt. 4.50 (0-06-100328-X, Harp PBks) HarpC.

Doorways Series, 2. Jacqueline McMakin & Rhoda Nary. LC 92-53917. 1993. pap. 7.00 (0-06-065377-9) Harper SF.

Doorways Series, Vol. 1: Encountering God in Others. Jacqueline McMakin & Rhoda Nary. LC 92-53917. 1993. 7.00 (0-685-61102-7) Harper SF.

Doorways Series, Vol. 3: Journeying with the Spirit. Jacqueline McMakin & Rhoda Nary. LC 92-53917. 1993. pap. 7.00 (0-06-065379-5) Harper SF.

Doorways Series, Vol. 4: Discovering Gifts Vision Call. Jacqueline McMakin & Rhoda Nary. LC 92-53917. 1993. pap. 7.00 (0-06-065380-9) Harper SF.

Doorways Through Time: The Romance of Archaeology. Stephen Bertman. (Illus.). 288p. 1991. pap. 10.95 (0-87477-622-8) J P Tarcher.

Doorways to Christian Growth. Jacqueline McMakin & Rhoda Nary. 300p. 1984. pap. 9.95 (0-86683-818-X) Harper SF.

Doorways to Discipleship. Winkie Pratney. LC 77-80008. 272p. 1977. pap. 7.99 (0-87123-106-9) Bethany Hse.

Doorways to Learning: A Model for Developing the Brain's Full Potential. Peter Majoy. LC 93-8573. 256p. 1993. 25.00 (0-913705-86-1) Zephyr Pr AZ.

***Doorways to Thinking: Decision-Making Episodes for the Study of History & the Humanities.** Robert J. Stahl et al. LC 94-49054. 1995. write for info. (1-56976-018-7) Zephyr Pr AZ.

Dooryard Full of Flowers. Isabel Miller. 192p. 1993. pap. 9.95 (1-56280-029-9) Naiad Pr.

Dooryard Herb Cookbook. Linda O. Rago. LC 88-60522. (Illus.). 128p. 1988. pap. 7.95 (0-933126-92-1) Pictorial Hist.

Dooryard Herbs. Linda Rago. Ed. by Susan Knott. LC 83-62799. (Illus.). 144p. (Orig.). 1984. pap. 12.95 (0-938634-04-6) Carabelle.

DOP: Dizionario d'Ortografia e di Pronunzia. Ed. by B. Migliorini et al. 755p. 1981. 95.00 (0-913298-62-X) S F Vanni.

Dopamine Aging & Diseases Endogenous Anorectics & Prostanoids, Sects. 5-7. J. Borsy & B. Knoll. LC 86-9349. (Advances in Pharmacological Research & Practice Ser.: Vol. 3). 1986. 234.00 (0-08-034192-6, Pub. by Pergamon Repr UK) Franklin.

An Asterisk (*) at the beginning of an entry indicates that the title is appearing in BIP for the first time. 2085

Dopamine & Mental Depression: Proceedings of the Biannual Capo Boi Conference on Neuroscience, June 1989, Villasimius, Italy. Ed. by G. L. Gessa & G. Serra. (Advances in the Biosciences Ser.: Vol. 77). (Illus.). 200p. 1990. 165.00 (*0-08-040762-5*, Pergamon Pr) Elsevier.

Dopamine & Neuroendocrine Active Substances. Emilio Del Pozo & Edward Fluckiger. 1985. text ed. 71.00 (*0-12-209045-4*) Acad Pr.

Dopamine Receptor Agonists. Ed. by George Poste & Stanley T. Crooke. LC 84-8290. (New Horizons in Therapeutics Ser.). 414p. 1984. 89.50 (*0-306-41654-9*, Plenum Pr) Plenum.

Dopamine Receptors. Carl Kaiser & John W. Kebabian. LC 83-6433. (ACS Symposium Ser.: No. 224). 289p. 1983. lib. bdg. 38.95 (*0-8412-0781-X*) Am Chemical.

Dopamine Receptors & Transporters, Pharmacology, Structure & Function: Pharmacology, Structure & Function. Niznik. LC 93-42705. 712p. 1994. 195.00 (*0-8247-9158-4*) Dekker.

Dopamine Receptors, Vol. 8: Receptor Biochemistry & Methodology. Ed. by Ian Creese & Claire Fraser. 264p. 1987. text ed. 129.95 (*0-471-63327-5*) Wiley.

Dopaminergic Ergot Derivatives & Motor Function: Proceedings of an International Symposium, Stockholm, 1978. Ed. by K. Fuxe & D. B. Calne. (Wenner-Gren Center International Symposium Ser.: Vol. 31). (Illus.). 1979. 271.00 (*0-08-024408-4*, Pub. by Pergamon Repr UK) Franklin.

Dopaminergic System. (Basic & Clinical Aspects of Neuroscience Ser.). (Illus.). 50p. 1985. pap. 22.50 (*0-387-13700-9*) Spr-Verlag.

Dopaminergic Systems & Their Regulation. G. N. Woodruff et al. LC 85-22608. (Satellite Symposium of the 9th IUPHAR Congress Ser.). 501p. 1986. lib. bdg. 200.00 (*0-89573-509-1*) VCH Pubs.

Dope & Trouble: Portraits of Delinquent Youth. Elliott Currie. LC 90-52577. 352p. 1991. 21.50 (*0-394-56151-1*) Pantheon.

Dope Girls: The Birth of the British Drug Underground. Marek Kohn. (Illus.). 200p. (C). 1992. pap. 19.95 (*0-85315-772-3*, Pub. by Lawrence & Wishart UK) Humanities.

***Dope, Inc. The Book That Drove Henry Kissinger Crazy.** Executive Intelligence Review Editors. 697p. 1992. pap. 16.00 (*0-614-04993-8*) Exec Intel Review.

Doped up, Knocked up, & ... Locked Up? The Criminal Prosecution of Women Who Use Drugs During Pregnancy. Valerie Green. LC 92-35296. (Children of Poverty Ser.). 128p. 1993. 37.00 (*0-8153-1125-7*) Garland.

Dopefiend. Donald Goines. (Orig.). 1971. pap. 3.50 (*0-87067-190-1*, BH190) Holloway.

Dopey Loses the Diamonds. (Shimmer Book Ser.). 24p. (J). 1994. 7.98 (*1-57082-150-X*) Mouse Works.

Dopie Dope Goes to the Fair. Joe Larke. (Illus.). 49p. (J). (gr. k-5). 1992. 13.95 (*0-9620112-7-4*) Grin A Bit.

Dopie Dope Grin A Bit Poetry Series. Joe Larke. (Illus.). (J). (gr. k-6). 1992. write for info. (*0-9620112-9-0*) Grin A Bit.

Doping: Proceedings, International Seminar Organ. University Ghent Brussels, May 1964. A. Schaepdryv & M. Hebbelinck. LC 65-12294. 1965. 84.00 (*0-08-011046-0*, Pub. by Pergamon Repr UK) Franklin.

Doping Game. Ken Donald. (C). 1990. pap. 33.00 (*0-908175-73-6*, Pub. by Boolarong Pubns AT) St Mut.

Doping in III-V Semiconductors. E. Fred Schubert. (Studies in Semiconductor Physics & Microelectronic Engineering: No. 1). (Illus.). 275p. (C). 1993. 84.95 (*0-521-41919-0*) Cambridge U Pr.

Dopp "We're from Iowa?" Revisited: A Family History Tracing Dopp, Marr, Sandvig & Omundson Ancestors. Roy Dopp. 370p. 1993. reprint ed. lib. bdg. 66.00 (*0-8328-3250-2*); reprint ed. pap. 56.00 (*0-8328-3251-0*) Higginson Bk Co.

***Doppelgangers.** Nick Baron & Michele Nicholas. 224p. 1995. pap. 3.99 (*0-8217-5060-7*) Zebra.

Doppler Color Flow Imaging. Joseph Kisslo et al. (Illus.). 184p. 1988. text ed. 84.95 (*0-443-08563-3*) Churchill.

Doppler Color Imaging. Ed. by Christopher R. Merritt. (Clinics in Diagnostic Ultrasound Ser.: Vol. 27). (Illus.). 282p. 1992. text ed. 134.95 (*0-443-08763-6*) Churchill.

Doppler Echocardiography. 2nd ed. Navin Nanda. (Illus.). 700p. 1992. text ed. 129.00 (*0-8121-1588-0*) Williams & Wilkins.

Doppler Echocardiography. Stanley J. Goldberg. LC 84-12245. (Illus.). 191p. reprint ed. pap. 54.80 (*0-8357-8684-6*, 2056841) Bks Demand.

Doppler Echocardiography: A Case Studies Approach. Julio E. Perez. (Illus.). 259p. 1987. text ed. 45.00 (*0-07-049322-7*) Hlth Prof Div.

Doppler Echocardiography: A Practical Manual. Pravin M. Shah et al. LC 84-21883. (Illus.). 155p. reprint ed. pap. 44.20 (*0-8357-4656-9*, 2037588) Bks Demand.

Doppler Echocardiography: The Quantitative Approach. 3rd ed. Arthur J. Labovitz & George A. Williams. 1992. text ed. 33.00 (*0-8121-1429-9*) Williams & Wilkins.

***Doppler Echocardiography in Heart Disease.** fac. ed. Marvin Berger. LC 86-32787. (Basic & Clinical Cardiology Ser.: No. 10). 383p. 1987. reprint ed. pap. 109.20 (*0-7837-8332-9*, 2049119) Bks Demand.

Doppler Radar & Weather Observations. 2nd ed. Richard J. Doviak & Dusan S. Zrnic. (Illus.). 562p. 1993. text ed. 69.95 (*0-12-221422-6*) Acad Pr.

Doppler Ultrasound. Frederick W. Kremkau. 1990. text ed. 42.00 (*0-7216-2864-8*) Saunders.

Doppler Ultrasound: Physics Instrumentation & Clinical Applications. D. H. Evans et al. 320p. 1989. text ed. 199.95 (*0-471-91489-4*) Wiley.

Doppler Ultrasound: Principles & Instruments. 2nd ed. Frederick W. Kremkau. LC 94-10940. (Illus.). 384p. 1994. text ed. 48.00 (*0-7216-4869-X*) Saunders.

Doppler Ultrasound & Its Use in Clinical Measurement. Peter Atkinson & John Woodcock. (Medical Physics Ser.: Vol. 5). 1982. text ed. 128.00 (*0-12-066260-4*) Acad Pr.

Doppler Ultrasound in Cardiology: Physical Principles & Clinical Applications. 3rd ed. Liv Hatle & Bjorn Angelsen. (Illus.). 1994. 55.00 (*0-8121-1267-9*) Williams & Wilkins.

Doppler Ultrasound in Obstetrics & Gynecology. Ed. by Joshua A. Copel & Kathryn L. Reed. LC 93-48969. 342p. 1995. 130.00 (*0-7817-0206-2*) Raven.

Doppler Ultrasound in Perinatal Medicine. Ed. by J. Malcolm Pearce. 362p. 1992. 98.00 (*0-19-262019-3*) OUP.

Doppler Ultrasound in the Diagnosis of Cerebrovascular Disease. Ed. by Robert S. Reneman & Arnold P. Hoeks. LC 81-19854. (Ultrasound in Biomedicine Ser.: No. 5). (Illus.). 312p. reprint ed. pap. 89.00 (*0-8357-6097-9*, 2034235) Bks Demand.

Doppler Ultrasound Measurement of Maternal-Fetal Hemodynamics. Ed. by D. Maulik & D. McNellis. LC 87-29083. (Reproductive & Perinatal Medicine Ser.: No. VIII). 1987. 77.50 (*0-916859-29-0*) Perinatology.

***Dor.** John Williams. LC 94-42340. (Illus.). 72p. 1995. pap. 12.95 (*0-7734-2742-2*, Mellen Poetry Pr) E Mellen.

Dora: An Analysis of a Case of Hysteria. Sigmund Freud. 160p. (C). 1993. pap. 10.00 (*0-02-050987-1*) Macmillan.

Dora: An Analysis of a Case of Hysteria. Sigmund Freud. 1963. pap. 5.95 (*0-02-076250-X*, Collier S&S) S&S Trade.

Dora Darling. Jane G. Austin. (Works of Jane (Goodin) Austin). 1989. reprint ed. lib. bdg. 79.00 (*0-7812-1838-1*) Rprt Serv.

Dora Deane. Mary J. Holmes. (Notable American Authors Ser.). 1992. reprint ed. lib. bdg. 75.00 (*0-7812-3154-X*) Rprt Serv.

Dora, Doralina. Rachel De Queiroz. Tr. by Dorothy S. Loos. 228p. (Orig.). 1984. mass mkt. 4.50 (*0-380-84822-8*, 84822, Bard) Avon.

Dora Stock, Portrait Painter of the Korner Circle in Dresden 1785-1815. Linda Siegel. LC 94-14163. (Studies in German Thought & History: Vol. 12). (Illus.). 208p. 1994. text ed. 89.95 (*0-7734-9551-7*) E Mellen.

***Dora Teitelboim: Selected Poems.** Dora Teitelboim. Ed. & Tr. by Aaron Kramer. LC 94-45688. 1995. write for info. (*0-88125-494-0*) Ktav.

***DORA '94-'96: Directory of Rare Analyses.** Ed. by Joycelyn M. Hicks & Donald S. Young. 440p. 1994. 80. 00 (*0-915274-72-8*, 629) Am Assn Clinical Chem.

***Dorado: Lament for the Gold Double Eagle.** William Oppenheimer. LC 94-77949. 152p. 1994. 23.00 (*0-913559-25-3*); pap. 14.00 (*0-913559-24-5*) Birch Brook Pr.

Dorados. Carlos Morton. Ed. by William A. Landes. LC 90-53688. 30p. (Orig.). 1991. pap. 5.00 (*0-88734-321-X*) Players Pr.

***Doraemon No A, I, U, E, O Asobi - Doraemon's Japanese Alphabet Study.** Tr. by Tomy Company Ltd. Staff. (Comes to Life Bks.). 20p. (ENG & JPN.). (J). (ps-2). 1995. write for info. (*1-57234-047-9*) YES Ent.

***Doraemon No Densha Zukan - Doraemon's Electronic Trains Illustrated Book.** Tr. by Tomy Company Ltd. Staff. (Comes to Life Bks.). 20p. (ENG & JPN.). (J). (ps-2). 1995. write for info. (*1-57234-048-7*) YES Ent.

***Doraemon No Hataraku Kuruma Zukan - Doraemon's Industrial Cars Illustrated Book.** Tr. by Tomy Company Ltd. Staff. (Comes to Life Bks.). 20p. (ENG & JPN.). (J). (ps-2). 1995. write for info. (*1-57234-046-0*) YES Ent.

Doran: Taxation of Corporation Joint Ventures. Nigel Doran. 193p. 1993. 150.00 (*0-406-01880-4*, U.K.) Butterworth Legal Pubs.

Dorando. James Boswell. Ed. by Robert S. Hunting. LC 73-78276. 1973. 3.50 (*0-913006-05-X*) Puckerbrush.

Dora's Book. Michelle Edwards. (Illus.). 32p. (J). (ps-3). 1990. lib. bdg. 19.95 (*0-87614-411-3*, Carolrhoda) Lerner Group.

Dora's Book. Michelle Edwards. (J). (ps-3). 1993. pap. 6.95 (*0-87614-535-7*, Carolrhoda) Lerner Group.

***Dora's Box.** Campbell. write for info. (*0-679-87642-1*) Random.

Dora's New Brother. Dee Shulman. (Illus.). 32p. (J). (ps-1). 1994. 19.95 (*0-370-31814-5*, Pub. by Bodley Head UK) Trafalgar.

Dora's Room. large type ed. Joanna Hines. 720p. 1994. 23. 95 (*0-7089-3113-8*) Ulverscroft.

Dorcas. Gordon Stowell. Tr. by S. D. de Lerin. (Libros Pescaditos Sobre Personajes Biblicos Ser.). (Illus.). 24p. (J). (gr. 1). 1978. reprint ed. pap. 0.75 (*0-311-38517-6*, Edit Mundo) Casa Bautista.

Dordogne. Simon Cobley. (Country Ser.). (Illus.). 160p. 1994. pap. 16.95 (*0-297-83283-2*) Trafalgar.

***Dordogne.** Neil Lands. (Visitors Guides Ser.). (Illus.). 256p. (Orig.). 1990. pap. 13.95 (*0-8169-0505-3*) Hunter NJ.

Dordogne. Michael Marriott. (Crowood Travel Guides Ser.). (Illus.). 320p. 1992. pap. 24.95 (*1-85223-461-X*, Pub. by Crowood Pr UK) Trafalgar.

Dordogne & Lot. 2nd ed. Arthur Eperon. 1992. pap. 16.95 (*0-8442-9946-4*, Passport Bks) NTC Pub Grp.

Dordogne Gastronomique. Vicky Jones. 1994. 27.50 (*1-55859-873-1*) Abbeville Pr.

***Dordogne Green Guide.** 3rd ed. Michelin Staff. (Orig.). Date not set. pap. 18.00 (*2-06-132303-0*, 1323) Michelin.

***Dordogne Green Guide English Edition.** Michelin Staff. Date not set. pap. 17.95 (*0-7859-7203-X*, 2067013238) Fr & Eur.

Dordogne on a Budget. Ed. by D. Delaforce. (C). 1989. text ed. 29.95 (*0-948032-83-9*, Pub. by Rosters Ltd) St Mut.

Dore. Jeanne Beckett. LC 92-25233. 404p. 1992. 14.95 (*0-916147-27-4*) Regent Pr.

Dore Bible Illustrations. Gustave Dore. (Illus.). 256p. 1974. pap. 9.95 (*0-486-23004-X*) Dover.

Dore Lectures on Mental Sciences. Thomas Troward. 1989. 10.95 (*0-396-02063-1*, Putnam) Putnam Pub Group.

Dore Spot Illustrations: A Treasury from His Masterworks. Gustave Dore. Ed. by Carol B. Grafton. (Pictorial Archive Ser.). (Illus.). iii, 123p. (Orig.). 1987. pap. 6.95 (*0-486-25495-X*) Dover.

Dorella. Mark Garland & Charles C. McGraw. 256p. 1992. mass mkt. 4.50 (*0-671-72136-4*) Baen Bks.

Dore's Illustrations for Ariosto's "Orlando Furioso" 208 Illustrations by Gustave Dore. Gustave Dore & S. Appelbaum. (Illus.). (Orig.). 1980. pap. 7.95 (*0-486-23973-X*) Dover.

Dore's Illustrations for Dante's Divine Comedy. Gustave Dore. LC 75-17176. (Illus.). (Orig.). 1976. reprint ed. pap. 6.95 (*0-486-23231-X*) Dover.

Dore's Illustrations for Don Quixote: A Selection of 190 Illustrations by Gustave Dore. Gustave Dore. (Illus.). 160p. (C). 1982. pap. 7.95 (*0-486-24300-1*) Dover.

***Dore's Illustrations for "Idylls of the King"** Gustave Dore. (Dover Pictorial Archives Ser.). (Illus.). 80p. 1995. pap. text ed. 6.95 (*0-486-28465-4*) Dover.

Dore's Illustrations for "Paradise Lost" Gustav Dore & John Milton. (Illus.). 64p. 1993. reprint ed. pap. text ed. 6.95 (*0-486-27719-4*) Dover.

Dore's Illustrations for Rabelais: A Selection of 252 Illustrations. Gustave Dore. (Illus.). 1978. pap. 9.95 (*0-486-23656-0*) Dover.

Doreset Downs Walk. Alan Proctor. (C). 1988. pap. text ed. 29.00 (*0-904110-96-6*, Pub. by Thornhill Pr UK) St Mut.

Dorevoliutsionnye Izdaniia Po Istorii SSSR v Inostrannom Fonde Gosudarstvennoi Publichnoi Biblioteki Im. M. E. Saltykova-Shchedrina - Pre-Revolutionary Publications on the History of the USSR in the Foreign Collection of the State Public Library M. E. Saltykov-Shchedrin: Sistematicheskii Ukazatel' - Systematic Index, 3 vols. 1993. reprint ed. Vol. 1, 281p. write for info. (*0-88354-111-4*); reprint ed. Vol. 2, 201p. write for info. (*0-88354-112-2*); reprint ed. Vol. 3, 377p. write for info. (*0-88354-113-0*) N Ross.

Dorfdeputierten: Weimar, Seventeen Seventy-Two, Vol. 2. Ernst W. Wolf. Ed. by Thomas Bauman. (German Opera Ser., 1770-1800). 400p. 1985. lib. bdg. 15.00 (*0-8240-8851-4*) Garland.

Dorflinger, America's Finest Glass, 1852-1921. John Q. Feller. (Illus.). 392p. 1988. text ed. 49.95 (*0-915410-55-9*) Antique Pubns.

Dorflinger Kalana Art Glass. John Q. Feller. (Illus.). 52p. 1988. pap. text ed. 6.00 (*0-915410-54-0*) Antique Pubns.

***Dori Sanders' Farmstand Cookbook.** Dori Sanders. 200p. Date not set. write for info. (*1-56512-117-1*) Algonquin Bks.

Dori the Mallard. Gordon Allred. (Illus.). (J). (gr. 5 up). 1968. 8.95 (*0-8392-3052-4*) Astor-Honor.

***Dorian Gray.** Amarantha Knight. (The Darker Passions Ser.). 1995. pap. text ed. 5.95 (*1-56333-342-2*) Masquerade.

***Dorian, Graying: Is Youth the Only Thing Worth Having?** Robert Kastenbaum. LC 94-24834. (Society & Aging Ser.). (C). 1995. text ed. 27.95 (*0-89503-169-8*); pap. text ed. 19.95 (*0-89503-172-8*) Baywood Pub.

Dorian's Dictionary of Science & Technology: English - French. A. F. Dorian. 1586p. (ENG & FRE.). 1979. 350.00 (*0-8288-9273-3*, M7892) Fr & Eur.

Dorian's Dictionary of Science & Technology: English - German. A. F. Dorian. 1402p. (ENG & GER.). 1989. reprint ed. 350.00 (*0-8288-9275-X*, M7894) Fr & Eur.

Dorian's Dictionary of Science & Technology: French - English. A. F. Dorian. 1086p. (ENG & FRE.). 1980. 350.00 (*0-8288-9274-1*, F98320) Fr & Eur.

Dorian's Dictionary of Science & Technology: German - English. A. F. Dorian. 1120p. (ENG & GER.). 1981. 350.00 (*0-8288-9276-8*, M7895) Fr & Eur.

Doric Hymns of Mesomedes. Bernhard Ziehn. 1979. pap. 3.00 (*0-911028-11-0*) Newberry.

Doricio. Mark Dunster. 11p. (Orig.). (J). 1989. pap. 4.00 (*0-89642-170-8*) Linden Pubs.

Dorie: The Girl Nobody Loved. Erwin W. Lutzer & Doris Van Stone. 1981. pap. 7.99 (*0-8024-2275-6*) Moody.

Dorie: Woman of the Mountains. Florence C. Bush. LC 91-12875. (Illus.). 254p. (Orig.). (YA). (gr. 6 up). 1992. reprint ed. text ed. 24.95 (*0-87049-725-1*); reprint ed. pap. 13.95 (*0-87049-726-X*) U of Tenn Pr.

Dorier, 2 vols., Set. Karl O. Muller. (Geschichten Hellenischer Stamme und Stadte Ser.: Bd. II und III). xxiii, 1110p. 1989. reprint ed. write for info. (*3-487-09261-1*, Pub. by Georg Olms GW) Lubrecht & Cramer.

Doris. Ivor Cutler. LC 92-5923. (Illus.). 32p. (J). (gr. k-3). 1992. lib. bdg. 14.00 (*0-688-11939-5*, Tambourine Bks) Morrow.

Doris: The Story of a Disfigured Deaf Child. Aron R. Bodenheimer. LC 72-11341. 139p. reprint ed. pap. 39.70 (*0-7837-3813-7*, 2043633) Bks Demand.

Doris Chase, Artist in Motion: From Painting & Sculpture to Video Art. Patricia Failing. LC 91-7629. (Samuel & Althea Stroum Book Ser.). (Illus.). 136p. 1991. 35.00 (*0-295-97112-6*) U of Wash Pr.

Doris Dingle's Crafty Cat Activity Book: Games, Toys & Hobbies to Keep Your Cat's Mind Active. Helen Levchuk. LC 91-2701. (Illus.). 96p. (Orig.). 1991. pap. 12.95 (*0-88240-415-6*) Alaska Northwest.

***Doris Duke Probate Proceeding: Will of Doris Duke.** 100p. (Orig.). 1995. pap. 24.95 (*0-7605-2275-8*) Rector Pr.

Doris Humphrey: The Collected Works, Vol. 1. Intro. by Selma J. Cohen. LC 78-67320. 320p. 1995. 125.00 (*0-932582-00-1*) Dance Notation.

Doris Humphrey: The Collected Works, Vol. 2, Set. Doris Humphrey. LC 78-67320. 230p. 1992. 125.00 (*0-932582-28-1*) Princeton Bk Co.

Doris Humphrey: The Collected Works, Vol. 2, Vol. 2. Doris Humphrey & Ernestine Stodelle. LC 78-67320. 230p. 1992. 125.00 (*0-932582-29-X*) Dance Notation.

***Doris Klein: Poems & Paintings.** Radio Poet. 1995. write for info. (*0-681-00784-2*) Longmeadow Pr.

Doris Lessing. Intro. by Harold Bloom. (Modern Critical Views Ser.). 224p. 1986. 29.95 (*0-87754-704-1*) Chelsea Hse.

Doris Lessing. Jeannette King. 128p. 1989. pap. 9.95 (*0-7131-6555-3*, A3850, Pub. by E Arnold UK) Routledge Chapman & Hall.

Doris Lessing. Elizabeth Maslen. 1990. 40.00 (*0-7463-0700-4*, Pub. by Northcote House UK) St Mut.

Doris Lessing. Elizabeth Maslen. (Writers & Their Work Ser.). 96p. 1994. pap. text ed. 11.50 (*0-7463-0705-5*, Pub. by Northcote House UK) Trans-Atl Phila.

Doris Lessing. Margaret M. Rowe. LC 94-16871. (Women Writers Ser.). 1994. text ed. 24.95 (*0-312-12192-X*) St Martin.

Doris Lessing. Ruth Whittaker. LC 88-4416. (Modern Novelists Ser.). 154p. 1991. pap. 12.95 (*0-333-40753-9*) St Martin.

Doris Lessing: A Checklist of Primary & Secondary Sources. Selma R. Burkom. LC 72-87109. iv, 88p. 1973. 7.50 (*0-87875-039-8*) Whitston Pub.

Doris Lessing: A Novelist with Organic Sensibility. Anita Myles. 1990. text ed. 22.50 (*81-7045-068-3*, Pub. by Associated Pub Hse II) Advent Bks Div.

Doris Lessing: An Annotated Bibliography of Criticism. Comp. by Dee Seligman. LC 80-24540. xv, 139p. 1981. text ed. 42.95 (*0-313-21270-8*, SDL/, Greenwood Pr) Greenwood.

Doris Lessing: Conversations. Intro. by Earl G. Ingersoll. LC 93-43760. (Critical Ser.). 248p. (Orig.). 1994. pap. 13.95 (*0-86538-080-5*) Ontario Rev NJ.

Doris Lessing: Critical Essays. Ed. by L. S. Dembo & Annis Pratt. LC 74-5909. 184p. reprint ed. pap. 52.50 (*0-8357-9774-0*, 2010188) Bks Demand.

Doris Lessing: Sufi Equilibrium & the Form of the Novel. Shadia S. Fahim. LC 93-25162. 1993. write for info. (*0-312-10293-3*) St Martin.

Doris Lessing: The Alchemy of Survival. Ed. by Carey Kaplan & Ellen C. Rose. LC 87-34777. 190p. 1988. 29. 95x (*0-8214-0891-7*) Ohio U Pr.

***Doris Lessing: The Poetics of Change.** Gayle Greene. 296p. (C). 1994. text ed. 39.50 (*0-472-10568-X*) U of Mich Pr.

Doris Lessing: The Problem of Alienation & the Form of the Novel. Rotraut Spiegel. (Neue Studien zur Anglistik und Amerikanistik: Vol. 19). 173p. 1980. pap. 28.40 (*3-8204-6021-7*) P Lang Pubs.

Doris Lessing Reader. Doris Lessing. 656p. 1989. 24.95 (*0-394-57307-2*) Knopf.

***Doris Wild Helmering's 100 Best Loved Columns.** Doris W. Helmering. 127p. Date not set. 14.95 (*0-9642381-0-1*) D Helmering.

Dorismus del Corpus Bucolicorum. Teresa M. Tejada. (Classical & Byzantine Monographs: No. 17). xxii, 474p. (Orig.). (SPA.). 1990. pap. 62.00 (*90-256-0979-1*, Pub. by A M Hakkert NE) Benjamins North Am.

Dorits Soft Sculpture Doll Techniques. Dorit Schendzielorz & Adalu Justus. Ed. by Gary H. Justus. (Illus.). (Orig.). 1990. reprint ed. pap. 12.50 (*0-937109-03-7*) Silo Pubs.

***Dork of Cork.** C. Raymo. Date not set. pap. 3.98 (*0-517-13158-7*) Random Hse Value.

Dork of Cork. Chet Raymo. (Fresh Voices Ser.). 368p. 1994. pap. 9.99 (*0-446-67000-6*) Warner Bks.

***Dorland Illustrated Medical Dictionary.** 28th ed. Newman W. Dorland. (Illus.). 1994. text ed. 39.95 (*0-7216-2859-1*) Saunders.

Dorland's Cardiology Speller. 287p. 1992. pap. text ed. 22. 50 (*0-7216-3748-5*) Saunders.

Dorland's Dentistry Speller. LC 92-13389. 192p. 1993. pap. text ed. 15.00 (*0-7216-4572-0*) Saunders.

Dorlands Gastroenterology Speller. LC 92-13353. 192p. 1993. pap. text ed. 22.50 (*0-7216-4568-2*) Saunders.

Dorland's Hematology - Oncology Speller. LC 92-13352. 255p. 1992. pap. text ed. 16.00 (*0-7216-3750-7*) Saunders.

Dorland's Medical Abbreviations. LC 92-11623. 1992. pap. text ed. 23.00 (*0-7216-3751-5*) Saunders.

Dorland's Orthopedics Speller. LC 92-13380. 320p. 1993. pap. text ed. 22.50 (*0-7216-3752-3*) Saunders.

Dorland's Pocket Medical Dictionary. 24th ed. 688p. 1989. pap. text ed. 22.00 (*0-7216-2202-X*) Saunders.

***Dorland's Pocket Medical Dictionary.** 25th ed. 816p. 1995. pap. text ed. 21.95 (*0-7216-5738-9*) Saunders.

Dorland's Psychiatry & Psychology Speller. 272p. 1992. pap. text ed. 19.00 (*0-7216-3749-3*) Saunders.

***Dorland's Spanish English Illustrated Medical Dictionary.** 27th ed. Dorland. (Illus.). (ENG & SPA.). 1992. 250.00 (*0-7859-7485-7*, 8476158920) Fr & Eur.

Dorlands Spanish-English Illustrated Medical Dictionary, 2 vols., Set, Vol. 1: A-L, Vol. 2: M-Z. 27th ed. (Illus.). 1992. 250.00 (*84-7615-892-0*) IBD Ltd.

Dorling Kindersley Big Book of Knowledge. LC 93-31723. (Illus.). 480p. (J). (gr. k-5). 1994. 29.95 (*1-56458-518-2*) Dorling Kindersley.

Dorling Kindersley Children's Illustrated Dictionary. John McIlwain. LC 94-9561. (Illus.). 256p. (J). (gr. 3-6). 1994. 19.95 (*1-56458-625-1*) Dorling Kindersley.

Dorling Kindersley Encyclopedia of Fishing. LC 93-28861. (Illus.). 288p. 1994. 39.95 (*1-56458-492-5*) Dorling Kindersley.

D

An Asterisk (*) at the beginning of an entry indicates that the title is appearing in BIP for the first time.

An Asterisk (*) at the beginning of an entry indicates that the title is appearing in BIP for the first time.

2087

DOS: Guia para Usarious Expertos. Kris Jamsa. 1991. pap. text ed. 22.95 (*0-07-104049-8*) McGraw.

DOS: Includes DOS 6.0. Jack Nimersheim. LC 93-60387. (In Plain English Ser.). (Illus.). 144p. (Orig.). 1993. pap. 9.95 (*1-56664-029-6*) WorldComm.

DOS: Inside & Out. Kris Jamsa. 1992. pap. text ed. 24.95 (*0-07-881780-3*) Osborne-McGraw.

D.O.'s: Osteopathic Medicine in America. Norman Gevitz. LC 82-47978. 200p. 1991. reprint ed. pap. text ed. 16.95 (*0-8018-4321-9*) Johns Hopkins.

D.O.'s: Osteopathic Medicine in the Mountains. Penny Ellis & Alayne R. Steiger. (Illus.). (Orig.). 1986. 12.00 (*0-9617546-0-5*); pap. 7.00 (*0-9617546-1-3*) WV Soc Osteo Med.

DOS: The Useable Portable Guide. Jon Haber & Herbert R. Haber. (Illus.). (C). 1990. spiral bd. write for info. (*0-945765-20-7*, 14-3440-01) Useable Portable Pubns.

DOS - VSE: An Introduction to the Operating System. Gary A. Stotts. 330p. 1993. text ed. 39.95 (*0-471-60294-9*) Wiley.

DOS - VSE: CICS Systems Programming. Gary A. Stotts. 1991. text ed. 39.95 (*0-89435-379-9*) Wiley.

DOS - VSE: CICS Systems Programming. Gary A. Stotts. 1993. text ed. 44.95 (*0-471-60223-X*, GB6516) Wiley.

DOS - VSE - SP Guide for Systems Programming: Concepts, Programs, Macros, Subroutines. Leo J. Langevin. 456p. 1993. pap. text ed. 39.95 (*0-471-56021-9*) Wiley.

DOS - VSE Assembler Language. Kevin McQuillen & Anne Prince. LC 86-60203. 242p. 1986. teacher ed, ring bd. 75.00 (*0-911625-32-1*) M Murach & Assoc.

Dos Amigos: Viajando por Hispanoamerica. Roselio A. Castro-Amaya & Jorge Kattan-Zablah. 1986. pap. 9.95 (*0-910286-66-3*) Boxwood.

Do's & Do Nots in Islam. A. R. Shad. 16.50 (*0-935782-77-X*) Kazi Pubns.

Do's & Don'ts for Ancestor-Hunters. Angus Baxter. 115p. 1988. 10.95 (*0-8063-1227-0*, 392) Genealog Pub.

Do's & Dont's for Family Members: How to Pull Your Life Together When You're Suffering. Terence Williams. 24p. 1982. pap. 3.50 (*0-89486-221-9*, 1235B) Hazelden.

Do's & Don'ts for Publications. Campbell. 1.75 (*0-318-19217-9*) Quill & Scroll.

Do's & Don't's for the Japanese Businessman Abroad. Barbara T. Okada & Nancy T. Okada. 130p. (C). (gr. 10 up). 1973. pap. text ed. 4.75 (*0-88345-208-1*, 18133) Prentice ESL.

Do's & Don't's of a Happy Marriage. Fatimatu Sister. 16p. (Orig.). (YA). 1987. pap. 0.50 (*0-916157-10-5*) African Islam Miss Pubns.

Do's & Don'ts of Delegation. Gary Fellows. 1988. 8.95 (*0-671-66254-6*) S&S Trade.

Do's & Don'ts of Drama. rev. ed. Comp. by Jean L. Latham. 1983. 5.95 (*0-87129-311-0*, D22) Dramatic Pub.

Do's & Dont's of Low Blood Sugar. Roberta Ruggiero. 1993. pap. 9.95 (*0-8119-0791-0*) LIFETIME.

Do's & Don'ts of Parent Involvement: How to Build a Positive School-Home Partnership. Catherine K. McLaughlin. Ed. by Dianne Schilling. 192p. 1993. teacher ed 16.95 (*1-56499-015-X*) Innerchoice Pub.

Do's & Don'ts of Puts & Calls. Milton Pauley. LC 76-2045. 79p. 1976. 9.95 (*0-678-09957-X*) Kelley.

Do's & Don'ts of Translation. Peter Whigham. 16p. (C). 1982. text ed. 12.00 (*0-918824-34-6*) Turkey Pr.

Do's & Dont's of Writing Your Management Plan. (Illus.). 64p. (Orig.). 1990. pap. text ed. 21.95 (*0-944298-67-2*) Inst Real Estate.

Do's & Don'ts of Writing Your Management Plan: A Must for Every Candidate. 60p. 1990. pap. 21.95 (*0-685-71679-1*, 756) Inst Real Estate.

Do's & Taboos Around the World. Roger Axtell. LC 93-7558. 1993. 12.95 (*0-87502-247-2*) Benjamin Co.

Do's & Taboos Around the World. 3rd ed. Roger E. Axtell. 208p. 1993. pap. text ed. 12.95 (*0-471-59528-4*) Wiley.

Do's & Taboos of Hosting International Visitors. Roger E. Axtell. 1990. pap. text ed. 17.95 (*0-471-51570-1*) Wiley.

Do's & Taboos of Hosting International Visitors. Roger E. Axtell. 1990. text ed. 34.95 (*0-471-51572-8*) Wiley.

Do's & Taboos of International Trade: A Small Business Primer. Roger E. Axtell. 1989. pap. 12.95 (*0-685-44611-5*) Wiley.

Do's & Taboos of International Trade: A Small Business Primer. Roger E. Axtell. LC 94-8586. 1994. pap. text ed. 17.95 (*0-471-00760-9*) Wiley.

Do's & Taboos of Preparing for Your Trip Abroad. Roger E. Axtell & John P. Healy. LC 94-8585. 1994. pap. text ed. 10.95 (*0-471-02567-4*) Wiley.

Do's & Taboos of Public Speaking: How to Get Those Butterflies Flying in Formation. Roger E. Axtell. 224p. 1992. text ed. 29.95 (*0-471-53671-7*); pap. text ed. 14.95 (*0-471-53670-9*) Wiley.

Do's & Taboos of Using English Around the World. Roger E. Axtell. LC 94-25738. (Illus.). 1995. pap. text ed. 12.95 (*0-471-30841-2*) Wiley.

DOS & Windows Protected Mode: Programming with DOS Extenders in C. Al Williams. 1992. pap. 39.95 (*0-201-63218-7*) Addison-Wesley.

Dos Anos Sin Dormir: Madres Que Trabajan Hablan Acerca de Tener un Bebe y un Trabajo. Ed. by Cathy Feldman. Tr. by Maria E. Marelli. (Illus.). 110p. (Orig.). (SPA.). 1994. pap. 9.95 (*1-880710-03-1*) Blue Pt Bks.

DOS Answers Certified Tech Support. Mary Campbell. 1994. pap. text ed. 16.05 (*0-07-882030-8*) Osborne-McGraw.

DOS Beyond 640K. 3rd ed. Jim Forney. 1993. disk, pap. text ed. 24.95 (*0-07-021610-X*) McGraw.

DOS Beyond 640K. 3rd ed. Jim Forney. LC 93-10184. (Illus.). 336p. 1993. text ed. 39.95 (*0-8306-4351-6*, Windcrest); pap. text ed. 29.95 (*0-8306-4350-8*, Windcrest) TAB Bks.

DOS Beyond 640K. 3rd ed. Jim S. Forney. 1993. text ed. 39.95 (*0-07-021609-6*) McGraw.

DOS Book. Electronic Learning Facilitators, Inc. Staff. 213p. (C). 1989. pap. text ed. 22.00 (*0-15-517921-7*) Dryden Pr.

DOS Book. Electronic Learning Facilitators, Inc. Staff. 213p. (C). 1989. disk 5.00 (*0-15-517922-5*) Dryden Pr.

Dos Californios. Harry Knill. (Illus.). 1978. pap. text ed. 3.95 (*0-88388-056-3*) Bellerophon Bks.

Dos Caras De la Escritura. Marithelma Costa. 238p. 1989. 12.00 (*0-8477-3634-2*) U of PR Pr.

Dos Caras Del Amor. Gary Smalley. (SPA.). Date not set. pap. 8.99 (*0-88113-101-6*) Edit Betania.

***DOS Cheat Sheet.** Jennifer Fulton. (Illus.). 400p. (Orig.). 1995. pap. 19.99 (*1-56761-626-7*) Alpha Bks IN.

DOS Coursebook. Forest Lin. 620p. (Orig.). 1991. pap. 25.00 (*0-9624230-3-3*) Scott Jones Inc.

Dos Decadas (Versos) Olga Rosado. LC 86-83334. (Coleccion Espejo de Paciencia Ser.). 41p. (Orig.). (SPA.). 1987. pap. 5.00 (*0-89729-424-6*) Ediciones.

Dos Elegias-Two Elegies. Alfredo C. Pena & Alvaro Cardona-Hine. 1977. per. 2.50 (*0-685-04493-9*) Invisible-Red Hill.

Dos Ensayos por Raya Dunayevskaya. 1989. pap. 2.00 (*0-914441-41-8*) News & Letters.

Dos Ensayos Sobre el Gobierno Civil. John Locke. Ed. by Joaquin Abellan. Tr. by Francisco Jimenez Gracia. (Nueva Austral Ser.: Vol. 240). (SPA.). 1991. pap. text ed. 29.50x (*84-239-7240-2*) Elliots Bks.

Dos Equals Uno: Two Be One. Ernest Steed. (SPA.). 3.95 (*84-7228-616-9*, 220326, Pub. by Edit Clie SP) TSELF.

DOS Essentials. Rod B. Southworth. 64p. 1991. 3.25 (*0-87835-690-8*) Boyd & Fraser.

***DOS Exposed! How to Get the Most from DOS!** Brian C. Elwood. (Illus.). (C). 1994. pap. text ed. 17.95 (*1-881432-12-2*) BCS Pub.

Dos Figuras Cubanas Y Una Sola Actitud: Felix Varela 1788-1853 - Jorge Manach 1898-1961. Rosario Rexach. LC 90-86072. 258p. 1991. pap. 19.00 (*0-89729-592-7*) Ediciones.

Dos Filmes de Mariel: El Exodo Cubano de 1980, en sus Propias Palabras; La Ciudad de las Carpas; Documentos. Jorge Ulloa et al. (Biblioteca Cubana Contemporanea Ser.). (Illus.). (Orig.). (SPA.). 1986. pap. 6.95 (*84-359-0440-7*) Ediciones.

DOS 5.0. Don Cassel. 1994. pap. text ed. write for info. (*0-13-045659-4*) P-H.

DOS Five Simplified. Rod B. Southworth. LC 92-32362. 240p. 1993. write for info. (*0-87835-943-5*) Boyd & Fraser.

DOS for Beginners. Udo Bretschneider. 1993. disk, pap. 22.95 (*1-55755-193-6*) Abacus MI.

DOS for Dummies. 2nd ed. Dan Gookin. 1993. pap. 16.95 (*1-878058-75-4*); pap. 16.95 (*1-878058-93-2*) IDG Bks.

DOS for Dummies Command Reference. Greg Harvey. 132p. 1993. pap. 8.95 (*1-878058-91-6*) IDG Bks.

DOS for WordPerfect Users. Pamela Mills. 1993. pap. 11.95 (*1-56052-216-X*) Crisp Pubns.

DOS Handbook. Jack Nimersheim. 1993. pap. 27.95 (*0-679-79151-5*) Random.

DOS in a Day. Jeff Weber & Jean Knox. (Illus.). 650p. (Orig.). 1994. pap. 29.95 (*0-929704-14-2*) Weber Systems.

DOS Inside & Out, Second Edition. 2nd ed. Kris Jamsa. 1993. pap. text ed. 27.95 (*0-07-881918-0*) Osborne-McGraw.

DOS Made Easy. Herbert Schildt. 385p. 1988. pap. text ed. 19.95 (*0-07-881295-X*) Osborne-McGraw.

DOS Made Easy, Fourth Edition. 4th ed. Herbert Schildt. 1993. pap. text ed. 19.95 (*0-07-881896-6*) Osborne-McGraw.

Dos Mil Doscientos Veinte y Dos (2222) Modismos Esenciales en Ingles. Ed. by Maria E. Alvarez del Real. (Illus.). 288p. (Orig.). (ENG & SPA.). 1987. pap. 4.00 (*0-944499-19-8*) Editorial Amer.

Dos Mil Doscientos Veinte y Dos (2222) Modismos Esenciales en Ingles. 2nd ed. Editorial America, S. A. Staff. Ed. by Maria E. Del Real. (Illus.). 288p. (SPA.). 1989. pap. 3.95 (*0-944499-64-3*) Editorial Amer.

Dos Mundos: A Communicative Approach. Tracy D. Terrell et al. (C). 1986. student ed 15.95 (*0-685-10330-7*) McGraw.

Dos Mundos: A Communicative Approach. Tracy D. Terrell et al. 1990. teacher ed write for info. (*0-318-67204-9*) McGraw.

Dos Mundos: A Communicative Approach. 2nd ed. Tracy D. Terrell et al. 1990. text ed. write for info. (*0-07-540810-4*) McGraw.

Dos Mundos: A Communicative Approach. 2nd ed. Tracy D. Terrell et al. 1990. teacher ed, audio 15.00 (*0-07-540821-X*); audio write for info. (*0-318-67205-7*) McGraw.

Dos Mundos: A Communicative Approach. 3rd ed. Tracy D. Terrell et al. LC 93-20783. 1994. text ed. write for info. (*0-07-063865-9*) McGraw.

***Dos Mundos: Rural Mexican Americans, Another America.** Richard Baker. LC 94-28073. 294p. 1994. pap. 24.95x (*0-87421-184-0*) Utah St U Pr.

Dos Naturalezas del Creyente. 2nd ed. Guillermo Collingwood. Ed. by Gordon H. Bennett. Tr. by Sara Bautista. (Serie Diamante). (Illus.). 52p. (SPA.). 1982. pap. 0.85 (*0-942504-03-8*) Overcomer Pr.

Dos Novelas Cortas. Miguel De Unamuno & Herbert E. Isar. Ed. by James R. Stamm. LC 61-14661. 127p. (C). 1975. Net. pap. text ed. write for info. (*0-471-00597-5*) Wiley.

DOS Operating System: With Coverage of 5.0. Leonard Lindenmeyer. 540p. (C). 1993. pap. 35.95 (*0-87835-752-1*, BF7521) S-W Pub.

Dos Palabras Sobre las Palabras: Apuntes sobre la traduccion y sus problemas. Angel J. Casares. LC 82-4938. 118p. (SPA.). 1982. pap. 5.00 (*0-8477-3503-6*) U of PR Pr.

DOS para Inexpertos - DOS for Dummies. Goodin. 390p. 1992. pap. text ed. 27.95 (*968-18-4295-2*, Pub. by Limusa MX) Computer & Tech.

Dos Pasos. Ed. by Barry Maine. (Critical Heritage Ser.). 320p. (C). 1988. text ed. 49.50 (*0-415-00229-X*) Routledge.

Dos Passos: A Collection of Critical Essays. Ed. by Andrew Hook. LC 73-21561. 192p. 1974. pap. 2.45 (*0-13-218859-7*, STC114, Spectrum Bks) P-H.

Dos Passos: Artist as American. Linda W. Wagner. LC 78-9922. 244p. 1979. 16.95 (*0-292-74011-5*) U of Tex Pr.

Dos Passos: Artist as American. Linda W. Wagner-Martin. LC 78-9922. 244p. reprint ed. pap. 69.60 (*0-8357-7767-7*, 2036126) Bks Demand.

Dos Passos: The Critics & the Writer's Intention. Allen Belkind. LC 70-156782. (Crosscurrents-Modern Critiques Ser.). 352p. reprint ed. pap. 100.40 (*0-317-58108-2*, AU00344) Bks Demand.

Dos Passos & "The Revolting Playwrights" G. A. Knox & H. M. Stahl. (Essays & Studies on American Language & Literature: Vol. 15). 1964. pap. 18.00 (*0-8115-0195-7*) Periodicals Srv.

Dos Passos Path to U. S. A. A Political Biography, 1912-1936. Melvin Landsberg. LC 72-75880. (Illus.). 304p. reprint ed. pap. 86.70 (*0-8357-9058-4*, 2012202) Bks Demand.

Dos Passos' U. S. A. A Critical Study. Donald Pizer. LC 87-27905. 222p. reprint ed. pap. 63.30 (*0-8357-2570-7*, 2040262) Bks Demand.

Dos Passos's Early Fiction, 1912-1938. Michael Clark. LC 85-63015. 172p. 1987. 32.50 (*0-941664-18-X*) Susquehanna U Pr.

Dos Pistoleros Earp - The Two Earp Pistoleers. Michael M. Hickey. LC 93-23038. (Illus.). 52p. (Orig.). 1993. pap. 18.95 (*0-9637172-1-4*) Talei Pubs.

DOS Power Tools Techniques. John Socha. 1993. pap. 39.95 (*0-679-79138-8*) Random.

DOS Primer. Dorthy Calvin. (Illus.). 390p. (Orig.). (C). 1993. pap. text ed. 17.00 (*0-9624230-4-1*) Scott Jones Inc.

Dos Primer for the IBM PC & XT. Waite Group Staff. 1984. pap. 16.95 (*0-452-26045-0*) NAL-Dutton.

DOS Programmer's Reference. 4th ed. Terry Dettmann, Sr. & Allen L. Wyatt. (Illus.). 1200p. 1993. pap. 34.95 (*1-56529-150-6*) Que.

DOS Quick. Carolyn Z. Gillay & Patricia L. Sullivan. LC 93-44649. (Illus.). 170p. 1994. pap. 15.95 (*0-938661-70-1*) Franklin Beedle.

DOS Quick & Easy Reference. Ron Mansfield. LC 93-85945. 149p. 1993. 6.99 (*0-7821-1379-6*) Sybex.

DOS Quick Reference Guide. Dennis P. Curtin. 64p. 1991. pap. text ed. 12.80 (*0-13-218074-X*, 220504) P-H.

Dos Reinos: The Kingdom of Self. Earl Jabay. (SPA.). 4.25 (*84-7228-466-2*, 220558, Pub. by Edit Clie SP) TSELF.

DOS Secrets Unleashed. Alan Simpson. 1993. disk, pap. 39.95 (*0-672-30288-8*) Sams.

DOS Shareware Utilities. PC-SIG, Inc. Staff. 1992. pap. 29.95 (*0-07-157859-5*) McGraw.

DOS Shareware Utilities. PC-SIG, Inc. Staff. 304p. 1991. pap. 29.95 (*0-8306-2488-0*, 3012, Windcrest) TAB Bks.

DOS Six. Alfred Glossbrenner. 1993. 3.5 hd, pap. 24.00 (*0-679-74470-3*) Random.

***DOS 6: Fundamentals.** Carolyn Z. Gillay. LC 94-29627. 1994. 29.95 (*0-938661-65-5*) Franklin Beedle.

***DOS 6 for Dummies 101.** Dan Gookin. 1995. pap. 24.99 (*1-56884-625-8*) IDG Bks.

DOS Subroutines for C & Assembler. Leo J. Scanlon & Mark R. Parker. 1992. text ed. 44.95 (*0-07-055021-2*); pap. text ed. 34.95 (*0-07-055022-0*) McGraw.

DOS Subroutines for C & Assembler. Leo J. Scanlon & Mark R. Parker. LC 92-12274. (Illus.). 360p. 1992. 44.95 (*0-8306-4159-9*, 4239, Windcrest); pap. 34.95 (*0-8306-4160-2*, 4239, Windcrest) TAB Bks.

DOS the Complete Reference: Fourth Edition. 4th ed. Kris Jamsa. 1993. pap. text ed. 29.95 (*0-07-881904-0*) Osborne-McGraw.

DOS the Easy Way: A Complete Guide to Microsoft's MS-DOS. Everett E. Murdock. 350p. (Orig.). (C). 1988. pap. text ed. 18.50 (*0-923178-00-7*) HOT Pr.

DOS the Pocket Reference. 3rd ed. Kris Jamsa. 1993. pap. text ed. 9.95 (*0-07-881906-7*) Osborne-McGraw.

DOS to OS-2: Conversion, Migration, Application Design, Set. Jay Ranade & Angelo R. Bobak. 640p. 1991. text ed. 50.00 (*0-07-051264-7*) McGraw.

DOS UNIX: Becoming a Super User. Martin D. Seyer & William J. Mills. (Illus.). 192p. 1986. 30.95 (*0-13-218645-4*, Busn) P-H.

DOS-UNIX: Networking & Internetworking. Michael J. Burgard & Kenneth D. Phillips. (Orig.). 1994. pap. text ed. 34.95 (*0-471-59516-0*) Wiley.

DOS User's Guide to the Internet. Jim Gardner. LC 93-38076. 1993. pap. 34.95 (*0-13-106873-3*) P-H.

DOS Utilities. Doug Lowe. LC 80-84103. (Illus.). 185p. 1981. pap. 17.50 (*0-911625-11-9*) M Murach & Assoc.

DOS Utilities Microsoft Forgot! Tim Stanley. (Illus.). 128p. (Orig.). 1993. pap. 19.95 (*1-56529-475-0*) Que.

DOS-VSE: Introduction to the Operating System. Gary A. Stotts. LC 90-38716. 358p. 1990. 34.95 (*0-89435-332-2*) Wiley.

DOS-VSE & VSE-Power Job Control Language & Concepts. Iva H. Lee. 175p. 1989. pap. text ed. 45.00 (*0-13-218629-2*) P-H.

DOS-VSE Assembler Language. rev. ed. Kevin McQuillen & Anne Prince. LC 85-63465. 492p. 1986. pap. 36.50 (*0-911625-31-3*) M Murach & Assoc.

DOS-VSE ICCF. Steve Eckols. LC 86-61650. 372p. 1986. pap. 31.00 (*0-911625-36-4*) M Murach & Assoc.

DOS-VSE JCL. 2nd ed. Steve Eckols & Michelle Milnes. LC 88-62699. (Illus.). 448p. 1989. pap. 34.50 (*0-911625-50-X*) M Murach & Assoc.

DOS-VSE-SP Guide for Systems Programming: Programs, Macros, Subroutines. Leo J. Langevin. LC 89-10368. 1989. 39.95 (*0-89435-299-7*) Wiley.

***DOS Windows Book.** George Markowski. 240p. (C). 1994. per., pap. text ed. 24.95 (*0-8403-9968-5*) Kendall-Hunt.

DOS, WordPerfect, & Lotus Essentials. Patrick Bultema & Joel Murach. LC 92-35689. (Illus.). 527p. 1992. pap. 20.00 (*0-911625-69-0*) M Murach & Assoc.

DOS, WordPerfect & Lotus Office Companion. 3rd ed. Robert W. Harris. 1993. pap. 21.95 (*1-56604-048-5*) Ventana Pr.

***DOS, WordPerfect, & Lotus Office Companion.** 4th ed. Robert Harris. 1994. pap. 21.95 (*1-56604-031-0*) Ventana Pr.

DOS, WordPerfect & Lotus Office Companion. 4th ed. Robert W. Harris. LC 94-9322. 1994. 21.95 (*1-56604-131-7*) Ventana Pr.

Dos y Dos Son Cinco y Otras 4 Comedias. Gonzalez W. Alfredo. LC 80-69553. (Coleccion Teatro). 255p. (Orig.). (SPA.). 1984. pap. 9.95 (*0-89729-276-6*) Ediciones.

Dos Yiddishe Vort. S. Yefroikin & H. Bass. 320p. 1983. pap. 7.50 (*0-318-22119-5*) Workmen's Circle.

DOS 4 Made Easy. Herbert Schildt. 350p. 1989. pap. text ed. 19.95 (*0-07-881448-0*) Osborne-McGraw.

DOS 4.0. Don Cassel. 1992. write for info. (*0-13-045642-X*) P-H.

DOS 4.0 a Su Alcance. Herbert Schildt. 1990. pap. text ed. 19.95 (*0-07-104051-X*) McGraw.

DOS 5: The Easy Way. Everett E. Murdock. 224p. (C). 1993. spiral bd. write for info. (*0-697-16800-X*) Bus & Educ Tech.

DOS 5 - Everything You Need to Know: A Clear, Simple, Easy-to-Use Guide - From Getting Started to Customizing Your System. Jonathan Kamin. (Illus.). 425p. (Orig.). 1991. pap. 22.95 (*1-55958-123-9*) Prima Pub.

DOS 5: A Developer's Guide: Advanced Programming Guide to DOS - with Disk. Al Williams. 1991. pap. 39.95 (*1-55851-179-2*) M&T Bks.

DOS 5 Commander: Complete MS-DOS version 5 in Plain English. Christopher Fara. LC 91-62773. 160p. 1991. 19.95 (*1-880099-11-X*) Microdex Bkshelf.

DOS 5 Concepts & Commands. Steven Forsythe. 448p. 1993. disk write for info. (*0-87709-060-2*); Incl. 5.25" disk. disk write for info. (*0-318-69729-7*); Incl. 3.5" disk. disk write for info. (*0-87709-061-0*) Boyd & Fraser.

DOS 5 Coursebook. Forest Lin. (Illus.). 664p. (Orig.). (C). 1992. pap. text ed. 33.95 (*0-9624230-9-2*) Scott Jones Inc.

DOS 5 Essentials. Rod B. Southworth. (C). 1994. pap. 4.95 (*0-87835-974-5*, BF9745) S-W Pub.

DOS 5 Quick Reference Guide. Karl Schwartz & Angelo Cassano. (DDC Quick Reference Guide Ser.). 1991. pap. 8.95 (*1-56243-012-2*, J-17) DDC Pub.

DOS 5 S. A. V. E. Edition. Dennis P. Curtin. 144p. (C). 1993. pap. text ed. write for info. (*0-13-045592-X*) P-H.

DOS 5.0. Vanderpool. (C). 1994. text ed. write for info. (*0-318-70366-1*, BF0517) S-W Pub.

DOS 5.0: A Developer's Guide. Al Williams. 1993. Incl. disk. disk 39.95 (*1-55851-309-4*) M&T Bks.

DOS 5.0: With Introduction to Labs. Timothy J. O'Leary et al. 1993. pap. text ed. write for info. (*0-07-048877-0*) McGraw.

DOS 5.0 at Work. Mary Campbell. 1991. pap. 22.95 (*0-201-57716-X*) Addison-Wesley.

DOS 5.0 Fundamentals. Carolyn Z. Gillay. LC 92-379. 208p. 1992. student ed, pap. 27.95 (*0-938661-23-X*) Franklin Beedle.

DOS 5.0 Power Tools. 2nd ed. Paul Somerson. 1991. digital audio, disk 49.95 (*0-679-79088-8*) Random.

DOS 5.0 Principles with Practice. Carolyn Z. Gillay. LC 92-13663. (Illus.). 95p. (C). 1992. student ed, pap. text ed. 34.95 (*0-938661-39-6*) Franklin Beedle.

DOS 6: A Tutorial Accompany Peter Norton's Introduction to Computers. Terrence P. O'Donnell. LC 93-44147. 1994. write for info. (*0-02-801328-X*) Glencoe.

DOS 6: Everything You Need to Know. Jonathan Kamin. 510p. (Orig.). 1993. pap. 19.95 (*1-55958-336-3*) Prima Pub.

DOS 6: Quick Reference Guide. 1993. pap. 8.95 (*1-56243-100-5*) DDC Pub.

DOS 6: Self-Teaching Guide. Ruth Ashley & Judi N. Fernandez. 400p. 1993. pap. text ed. 22.95 (*0-471-59074-6*) Wiley.

DOS 6: Visual QuickStart Guide. Webster & Associates Staff. (Illus.). 208p. (Orig.). 1993. pap. 12.00 (*1-56609-059-8*) Peachpit Pr.

DOS 6 Consulta Instantanea. Jaime Schlittler. 317p. 1993. pap. text ed. 14.95 (*968-6346-82-1*, Pub. by Ventura Ediciones MX) Computer & Tech.

DOS 6 Coursebook. Forest Lin. 700p. (Orig.). 1993. pap. 33.95 (*1-881991-28-8*) Scott Jones Inc.

DOS 6 Developer's Guide. Jim Kyle. 1993. disk, pap. 39.95 (*0-672-30291-8*) Sams.

Dos 6 Extension (Generic) Dennis Curtis. 1993. pap. text ed. 2.00 (*0-13-099862-1*) P-H.

DOS 6 for the Guru Wanna-Be. Paul McFedries. 384p. 1993. pap. 18.95 (*0-672-30349-3*) Sams.

DOS 6 Insider. Ron Pronk & Keith Weiskamp. 544p. 1993. pap. text ed. 26.95 (*0-471-59394-X*) Wiley.

***DOS 6 Principles with Practice.** Carolyn Z. Gillay. LC 94-29628. 1994. 36.95 (*0-938661-66-3*) Franklin Beedle.

DOS 6 Quick Reference Guide. 1993. pap. 14.95 (*1-56351-172-X*) Microref Educ Systs.

DOS 6 Secrets. Robert D. Ainsbury. 1993. pap. 39.95 (*1-878058-70-3*) IDG Bks.

DOS 6.0. Shelly Cashman. (C). 1994. text ed. write for info. (*0-318-70358-0*) S-W Pub.

An Asterisk (*) at the beginning of an entry indicates that the title is appearing in BIP for the first time.

DOS 6.0. Timothy J. O'Leary & Linda I. O'Leary. 1994. pap. text ed. write for info. (*0-07-048996-3*) McGraw.
DOS 6.0: Learn PC. Ed. by Robert Krumm. LC 93-6081. 1993. pap. text ed. 16.00 (*0-13-100587-1*) P-H Gen Ref & Trav.
DOS 6.0 Essentials. Rod B. Southworth. 1993. pap. 3.95 (*0-87709-419-5*) Boyd & Fraser.
DOS 6.0 Sure Steps. Que Development Group Staff & Yvonne Johnson. (Sure Steps Ser.). (Illus.). 300p. (Orig.). 1993. Incl. disk. disk 24.95 (*1-56529-262-6*) Que.
DOS 6.2 Complete: Special Edition. Michael Tornsdorf. 1993. pap. 39.95 (*1-55755-251-7*) Abacus MI.
***DOS 6.2 Concepts & Commands.** Steven Forsythe. (Illus.). 440p. 1995. disk, pap. 38.00 (*0-87709-817-4*) Boyd & Fraser.
***DOS 6.2 Concepts & Commands.** Steven G. Forsythe. LC 94-21590. 1994. Incl. 3.5" diskette. write for info. (*0-87709-838-7*); Incl. 5.25 diskette. write for info. (*0-87709-844-1*) Boyd & Fraser.
DOS 6.2 Everything You Need to Know. Jonathan Kamin. 1993. pap. 24.95 (*1-55958-509-9*) Prima Pub.
DOS 6.2 Instant Reference. 2nd ed. Robert M. Thomas. LC 93-86580. 346p. 1993. 9.99 (*0-7821-1445-8*) Sybex.
DOS 6.2 Quick & Easy. Ron Mansfield. LC 94-66292. 205p. 1994. pap. 19.99 (*0-7821-1582-9*) Sybex.
DOS 6.2 Simplified. Rod B. Southworth. LC 94-5952. (Illus.). 215p. 1994. 17.95 (*0-87709-628-7*) Boyd & Fraser.
DOS 6.2 Slick Tricks. Jack Nimershein. 1994. pap. 16.00 (*0-679-79177-9*) Random.
Dosadi Experiment. Frank Herbert. 352p. 1987. pap. 4.95 (*0-441-16027-1*) Ace Bks.
Dosadi Experiment see Worlds Beyond Dune: The Best of Frank Herbert
Dosage & Solutions Calculations: The Dimensional Analysis Way. Smith. (Illus.). 400p. 1989. pap. 19.95 (*0-8016-5146-8*) Mosby Yr Bk.
Dosage Calculation Manual. 2nd ed. Todd & Erickson. 1991. 19.95 (*0-87434-395-X*) Springhouse Pub.
Dosage Calculation Method & Workbook. 3rd ed. Ann Aurigemma. 282p. 1987. pap. 15.95 (*0-88737-382-8*, 20-2197) Natl League Nurse.
Dosage Calculations. Olsen & Murray. (Nursetest: A Review Ser.). 1991. 19.95 (*0-87434-301-1*) Springhouse Pub.
Dosage Calculations. 2nd ed. Gloria Pickar. 128p. (C). 1982. disk 149.95 (*0-8273-2693-9*) Delmar.
Dosage Calculations. 3rd ed. Gloria Pickar. 144p. 1989. pap. text ed 23.95 (*0-8273-3951-8*) Delmar.
Dosage Calculations. 4th ed. Gloria D. Pickar. LC 92-23154. 1992. pap. text ed. 23.95 (*0-8273-4982-3*) Delmar.
Dosage Calculations. Gloria D. Pickar. LC 82-71146. (Illus.). 128p. (C). 1982. reprint ed. pap. text ed. 16.95 (*0-8273-2090-6*); reprint ed. disk 149.95 (*0-8273-2778-1*) Delmar.
Dosage Calculations: Instructor's Guide. 4th ed. Gloria D. Pickar. 153p. 1993. 14.00 (*0-8273-5741-9*) Delmar.
Dosage Calculations in SI Units, No. 2. Osis. (Illus.). 192p. 1990. 15.95 (*0-8016-3753-8*) Mosby Yr Bk.
Dosage Calculations in SI Units, No. 2. Osis. 176p. 1990. spiral bd. 15.95 (*0-8016-3721-X*) Mosby Yr Bk.
Dosages & Calculations. Richard Wiederhold. 224p. 1991. pap. 24.00 (*0-89303-729-X*, 740804) P-H.
Dosages & Solutions: A Programmed Approach to Meds & Math. 5th ed. Emily F. Cornett & Dorothy M. Blume. LC 91-9455. (Illus.). 273p. (C). 1991. pap. 21.95 (*0-8036-1981-2*) Davis Co.
Doscientas Anecdotas e Ilustraciones. Dwight L. Moody. Orig. Title: Two Hundred Anecdotes & Illustrations. 128p. (SPA.). 1983. pap. 3.99 (*0-8254-1491-1*) Kregel.
Dose & Risk in Diagnostic Radiology: How Big? How Little? Edward W. Webster. LC 92-49772. (Taylor Lecture Ser.: No. 16). 40p. (Orig.). 1992. pap. text ed. 20.00 (*0-929600-26-6*) NCRP Pubns.
Dose & Volume Specification for Reporting Intracavitary Therapy in Gynecology, No. 38. International Commission on Radiation Units & Measurements. LC 84-28860. (ICRU Report Ser.). 30p. 1985. pap. text ed. 35.00 (*0-913394-32-7*) Intl Comm Rad Meas.
Dos'e Begletsa: Po Sledam Neizvestnogo Pushkina. Druzhnikov Yuri. LC 93-15791. 270p. (Orig.). (RUS.). 1993. pap. 15.00 (*1-55779-055-8*) Hermitage.
***Dose Control at Nuclear Power Plants: National Council on Radiation Protection and Measurements.** Intro. by Charles B. Meinhold. (Report Ser.: No. 120). 138p. (Orig.). 1994. pap. text ed. 20.00 (*0-929600-39-8*) NCRP Pubns.
***Dose Limits for Individuals Who Receive Exposure from Radionuclide Therapy Patients.** Pref. by Charles B. Meinhold. (NCRP Commentaries Ser.). 21p. (Orig.). Date not set. pap. text ed. 20.00 (*0-929600-42-8*) NCRP Pubns.
Dose Makes the Poison: A Plain Language Guide to Toxicology. 2nd enl. ed. Alice Ottoboni. 272p. 1991. text ed. 24.95 (*0-442-00660-8*) Van Nos Reinhold.
Dose of Emptiness: An Annotated Translation of the "Stong Thun Chen Mo" of MKhas Grub dGe Legs Dpal Bzang. Jose I. Cabezon. LC 90-45292. (SUNY Series in Buddhist Studies). 590p. (C). 1992. 89.50 (*0-7914-0729-2*); pap. 29.95 (*0-7914-0730-6*) State U NY Pr.
Dose of Frontier Soldiering: The Memoirs of Corporal E. A. Bode, U. S. Army Regular Infantry, 1877-1882. E. A. Bode. Ed. by Thomas T. Smith. LC 93-26155. x, 240p. (C). 1994. 29.95 (*0-8032-4232-8*) U of Nebr Pr.
Dose of My Own Medicine. Paul Compbell. (Illus.). 213p. (Orig.). 1992. pap. 12.95 (*0-9695852-0-9*) Grosvenor USA.
Dose-Response Relationship of Drugs. Ed. by J. Kuhlmann & W. Wingender. (Clinical Pharmacology Ser.: Vol. 3). (Illus.). 225p. 1990. text ed. 48.00 (*3-88603-366-X*, Pub. by W Zuckschwerdt GW) Scholium Intl.
Dose-Response Relationships in Clinical Pharmacology: Proceedings of Esteve Foundation Symposium III - Dose Response Relationships in Man, Son Vida, Mallorca, 12-15 Oct., 1988. Ed. by Louis S. Lasagne et al. (International Congress Ser.: No. 808). 348p. 1989. 102.75 (*0-444-81084-6*, Excerpta Medica) Elsevier.
Doses in Radiation Accidents Investigated by Chromosome Aberration Analysis: XVII: A Review of Cases Investigated, 1986. Edwards A. Lloyd et al. (National Radiological Protection Board R Ser.: No. 207). (Orig.). 1987. pap. text ed. 8.00 (*0-85951-284-3*, HM1123, Pub. by HMSO UK) UNIPUB.
Dosimetry for Radiation Processing. W. L. McLaufhlin et al. 260p. 1989. 90.00 (*0-85066-740-2*) Taylor & Francis.
Dosimetry in Radiotherapy, Vol. I. (Illus.). 385p. 1988. pap. 140.00 (*92-0-010088-0*, ISP760 1) UNIPUB.
Dosimetry in Radiotherapy, Vols. 1 & 2. (Illus.). 1988. write for info. (*0-318-62961-5*) UNIPUB.
Dosimetry of Ionizing Radiation. Ed. by Kenneth R. Kase et al. 1985. text ed. 125.00 (*0-12-400401-6*) Acad Pr.
Dosimetry of Ionizing Radiation, Vol. 2. Ed. by Kenneth R. Kase et al. 416p. 1987. text ed. 125.00 (*0-12-400402-4*) Acad Pr.
Dosimetry of Ionizing Radiation, Vol. 3. Ed. by Kenneth R. Kase & Bengt E. Bjorngard. 631p. 1990. text ed. 237.00 (*0-12-400403-2*) Acad Pr.
Dosimetry of Laser Radiation in Medicine & Biology (Institute) G. J. Mueller & D. H. Sliney. 253p. 1989. 81.00 (*0-8194-0070-X*, IS05/HC); pap. 66.00 (*0-685-52035-8*, IS05) SPIE.
Dosimetry of Pulsed Radiation, No. 34. International Commission on Radiation Units & Measurements. LC 82-82417. 1982. 40.00 (*0-913394-28-9*) Intl Comm Rad Meas.
Dosimetry of X-Ray & Gamma-Ray Beams for Radiation Therapy in the Energy Range 10 keV to 50 MeV. LC 81-81430. (Report Ser.: No. 69). 1981. 25.00 (*0-913392-55-3*) NCRP Pubns.
Dosimetry Yearbook. Ponnunni K. Kartha & Phyllis Thompson. LC 82-1846. 208p. reprint ed. pap. 59.30 (*0-317-58139-2*, 2029737) Bks Demand.
Dosparth Edeyrn Davod Aur. Davod A. Edeyrn. Ed. by John Williams ab Ithel. LC 78-72626. (Celtic Language & Literature Ser.: Goidelic & Brythonic). reprint ed. 37.50 (*0-404-17548-1*) AMS Pr.
Dossier H. Ismail Kadare. 217p. (FRE.). 1991. pap. 10.95 (*0-7859-2606-2*, 2070383377) Fr & Eur.
Dossier of Solar Pons. Basil Cooper. (Solar Pons Ser.). 278p. 1987. pap. 7.95 (*0-89733-252-0*) Academy Chi Pubs.
Dossier on the Ascension. Serapis Bey. 234p. 1979. pap. 5.95 (*0-916766-21-7*) Summit Univ.
Dossier Secreto: Argentina's Desaparecidos & the Myth of the "Dirty War" Martin E. Andersen. LC 92-33310. 412p. (C). 1993. pap. text ed. 19.95 (*0-8133-8213-0*) Westview.
Dossier Society: Value Choices in the Design of National Information Systems. Kenneth C. Laudon. LC 85-29154. (Illus.). 400p. 1986. text ed. 63.00 (*0-231-06188-9*) Col U Pr.
Dossiers Secrets. Snowdon Barnett. 64p. (C). 1986. pap. 38.00 (*0-947612-18-1*, Pub. by Rivelin Grapheme Pr) St Mut.
Dostoevski. Gerald Abraham. LC 74-6398. (Studies in Dostoyevsky: No. 86). 1974. lib. bdg. 49.95 (*0-8383-1869-X*) M S G Haskell Hse.
***Dostoevskii & Britain.** Ed. by W. J. Leatherbarrow. LC 94-32406. 1995. 54.95 (*0-85496-784-2*) Berg Pubs.
Dostoevskij & Schiller. Alexandra H. Lyngstad. 1975. pap. text ed. 32.35 (*3-10-800094-2*) Mouton.
Dostoevskijs Ideendialektik. Wolfgang Mueller-Lauter. 66p. (C). 1974. 11.55 (*3-11-005731-X*) De Gruyter.
Dostoevsky. J. A. Lloyd. LC 75-30857. (Studies in Russian Literature & Life: No. 100). 1975. lib. bdg. 42.95 (*0-8383-2099-6*) M S G Haskell Hse.
Dostoevsky. Andre Gide. LC 78-14443. 181p. 1979. reprint ed. text ed. 38.50 (*0-313-21178-7*, GIDO, Greenwood Pr) Greenwood.
Dostoevsky: A Self Portrait. Jessie Coulson. LC 75-26212. (Illus.). 279p. 1975. reprint ed. text ed. 49.50 (*0-8371-8405-3*, CODO, Greenwood Pr) Greenwood.
Dostoevsky: His Life & Work. Konstantin Mochulsky. Tr. by Michael A. Minihan. 1967. pap. 24.95 (*0-691-01299-7*) Princeton U Pr.
Dostoevsky: Letters & Reminiscences. Fyodor Dostoyevsky. Tr. by Samuel S. Koteliansky & J. Middleton Murray. (Select Bibliographies Reprint Ser.). 1977. reprint ed. 25.95 (*0-8369-5835-7*) Ayer.
Dostoevsky: Myths of Duality. Roger B. Anderson. LC 86-15650. (University of Florida Humanities Monographs: No. 58). 160p. (Orig.). 1986. pap. 22.95 (*0-8130-0803-4*) U Press Fla.
Dostoevsky: The Author as Psychoanalyst. Louis Breger. 320p. 1989. 50.00x (*0-8147-1112-X*); pap. 17.50 (*0-8147-1151-0*) NYU Pr.
***Dostoevsky: The Miraculos Years, 1865-1871.** Joseph Frank. Date not set. 35.00 (*0-615-00588-8*) Princeton U Pr.
***Dostoevsky: The Miraculous Years, 1865-1871.** Joseph Frank. 1995. 35.00 (*0-691-04364-7*) Princeton U Pr.
Dostoevsky: The Seeds of Revolt, 1821-1849. Joseph Frank. 1976. 65.00 (*0-691-06260-9*); pap. 15.95x (*0-691-01355-1*) Princeton U Pr.
Dostoevsky: The Stir of Liberation, 1860-1865. Joseph Frank. 1988. pap. 15.95 (*0-691-01452-3*) Princeton U Pr.
Dostoevsky: The Stir of Liberation, 1860-1865, Vol. 3. Joseph Frank. LC 85-43280. 350p. 1986. 65.00 (*0-691-06652-3*) Princeton U Pr.
Dostoevsky: The Years of Ordeal, 1850-1859. Joseph Frank. LC 76-3704. (Illus.). 338p. 1986. text ed. 55.00 (*0-691-06576-4*); pap. text ed. 14.95x (*0-691-01422-1*) Princeton U Pr.
Dostoevsky: A Screenplay see King Dog: A Screenplay
Dostoevsky: A Screenplay - King Dog: A Screenplay. Raymond Carver et al. (Capra Back-to-Back Ser.: No. 5). Ill, 125p. (C). 1988. reprint ed. lib. bdg. 33.00x (*0-8095-4104-1*) Borgo Pr.
Dostoevsky & Existentialism: With Reflections on the "Grand Inquisitor" Albert D. Menut. 100p. 1972. 7.50 (*0-87291-044-X*) Coronado Pr.
Dostoevsky & Soviet Film: Visions of Demonic Realism. N. M. Lary. LC 86-47645. (Illus.). 280p. 1986. 32.95 (*0-8014-1882-8*) Cornell U Pr.
***Dostoevsky & Suicide.** N. N. Shneidman. 128p. 1995. lib. bdg. 27.00 (*0-8095-4819-4*) Borgo Pr.
Dostoevsky & the Catholic Church. Denis Dirscherl. 179p. 1986. 3.95 (*0-8294-0502-X*) Loyola Univ Pr.
Dostoevsky & the Human Condition after a Century. Ed. by Alexej Ugrinsky et al. LC 86-362. (Contributions to Study of World Literature Ser.: No. 16). 244p. 1986. text ed. 55.00 (*0-313-25379-X*, UGD/, Greenwood Pr) Greenwood.
Dostoevsky & The Idiot: Author, Narrator & Reader. Robin F. Miller. LC 80-29496. 305p. 1981. 34.00 (*0-674-21490-0*) HUP.
Dostoevsky & the Novel. Michael Holquist. 202p. 1986. pap. 12.95 (*0-8101-0717-9*) Northwestern U Pr.
Dostoevsky & the Woman Question: Rereadings at the End of a Century. Nina P. Straus. LC 93-46929. 1994. text ed. 39.95 (*0-312-10749-8*) St Martin.
Dostoevsky, Kierkegaard, Nietzsche & Kafka. William Hubben. Orig. Title: Four Prophets of Our Destiny. 192p. 1962. pap. 6.00 (*0-02-065750-1*, Pub. by Gebrueder Borntraeger GW) Macmillan.
Dostoevsky on Evil & Atonement: The Ontology of Personalism in His Major Fiction. Linda Kraeger & Joe Barnhart. LC 92-37926. 212p. 1992. text ed. 89.95 (*0-7734-9189-9*) E Mellen.
Dostoevsky, the Man & His Work. J. Meier-Graefe. LC 77-38843. (Studies in European Literature: No. 56). 406p. 1972. reprint ed. lib. bdg. 75.00 (*0-8383-1390-6*) M S G Haskell Hse.
Dostoevsky's Concept of Spiritual Rebirth. Antony Khrapovitsky. Tr. by Ludmila Koehler. 58p. (Orig.). 1986. reprint ed. pap. 3.00 (*0-913026-96-4*) Synaxis Pr.
Dostoevsky's Grave: (New & Selected Poems) Leland Bardwell. 70p. (C). 1991. 25.00 (*0-948268-91-3*, Pub. by Dedalus Pr IE); pap. 15.00 (*0-685-60829-8*, Pub. by Dedalus Pr IE) St Mut.
***Dostoevsky's Last Night: A Novel.** Christina P. Rossi. 192p. 1995. 20.00 (*0-312-13054-6*) St Martin.
Dostoevsky's Secret Code: The Allegory of Elijah the Prophet. Yuri Marmeladov. Tr. by Jay MacPherson. 125p. (C). 1987. 12.50 (*0-87291-171-3*) Coronado Pr.
Dostoevsky's Underground Man in Russian Literature. Robert L. Jackson. Ed. by C. H. Van Schooneveld. LC 81-2010. 223p. 1981. reprint ed. text ed. 55.00 (*0-313-22932-5*, JADM, Greenwood Pr) Greenwood.
Dostoievski. S. Mackiewicz. LC 73-21635. (Studies in Dostoyevsky: No. 86). 1974. lib. bdg. 75.00 (*0-8383-1818-5*) M S G Haskell Hse.
Dostoievski. C. M. Woodhouse. LC 73-21563. (Studies in Dostoyevsky: No. 86). 1974. lib. bdg. 75.00 (*0-8383-1820-7*) M S G Haskell Hse.
Dostoievsky. Dimitri Merejkowski. LC 73-21712. (Studies in Dostoyevsky: No. 86). (C). 1974. lib. bdg. 49.95 (*0-8383-1816-9*) M S G Haskell Hse.
Dostoievsky. John C. Powys. LC 72-8975. (Studies in European Literature: No. 56). 1973. reprint ed. lib. bdg. 75.00 (*0-8383-1677-8*) M S G Haskell Hse.
Dostojino Jest', 8-mi glasov, znamennago rospjeva. Johann V. Gardner. 1967. pap. 3.00 (*0-317-30397-X*) Holy Trinity.
Dostoyevsky. L. A. Zander. LC 73-21713. (Studies in Dostoyevsky: No. 86). 1974. lib. bdg. 75.00 (*0-8383-1801-0*) M S G Haskell Hse.
Dostoyevsky: "The Brothers Karamazov" William J. Leatherbarrow. (Landmarks of World Literature Ser.). (Illus.). 128p. (C). 1992. 29.95 (*0-521-38424-9*); pap. 10.95 (*0-521-38601-2*) Cambridge U Pr.
Dostoyevsky after Bakhtin: Readings in Dostoyevsky's Fantastic Realism. Malcolm V. Jones. 240p. (C). 1990. 59.95 (*0-521-38423-0*) Cambridge U Pr.
Dostoyevsky & the Process of Literary Creation. Jacques Catteau. Tr. by Audrey Littlewood. (Cambridge Studies in Russian Literature). 544p. 1989. 94.95 (*0-521-32436-X*) Cambridge U Pr.
Dostoyevsky's Critique of the West: The Quest for the Earthly Paradise. Bruce K. Ward. 204p. (C). 1986. text ed. 32.50 (*0-88920-190-0*, Pub. by Wilfrid Laurier CN) Humanities.
Dot . . . Dot . . . Dot. Bill E. Burk. LC 87-28895. 232p. 1987. 14.95 (*0-942179-03-X*) Shelby Hse.
Dot & the Line. Norton Juster. 1977. pap. 7.95 (*0-394-73352-5*) Random.
***Dot & Tot of Merryland.** L. Frank Baum. (Illus.). 140p. (J). (gr. 2 up). 1995. 34.95 (*0-929605-38-1*); pap. 11.95 (*0-929605-37-3*) Books Wonder.
Dot for Short. Frieda Friedman. (Illus.). (J). (gr. 5-7). 1988. pap. 3.95 (*0-317-69653-X*, Puffin) Puffin Bks.
Dot for Short. Frieda Friedman. 173p. (J). 1981. reprint ed. lib. bdg. 14.95 (*0-686-73781-4*) Buccaneer Bks.
Dot for Short. Frieda Friedman. 168p. (J). 1981. reprint ed. lib. bdg. 10.95 (*0-89967-038-5*) Harmony Raine.
DOT Hazardous Materials Regulations: Generators. Ed. by John Wargo & Linda Wargo. 1174p. 650.00 (*1-880955-04-0*) Legi-Slate.
***DOT Hazardous Materials Shipping Guide.** Ed. by Gabrielle Fay. (Environmental Management Guides Ser.). 30p. 1994. pap. text ed. 25.00 (*0-86587-439-5*) Gov Insts.
***Dot Man: George Andrews of Madison, Georgia.** 1994. text ed. 14.95 (*0-9638753-3-7*) Morris Mus Art.
Dot on the Map: Selected Stories & Poems. Sait Faik. Ed. by Ilhan Basgoz & Talat S. Halman. (Turkish Studies Ser.: Vol. 4). 307p. (C). 1983. 12.95 (*0-685-29322-X*) IN Univ Turkish.
Dot Paper Geometry: With or Without a Geoboard. Charles Lund. (Illus.). 84p. (J). (gr. 4-8). 1980. pap. text ed. 9.95 (*0-914040-87-1*) Cuisenaire.
Dot to Dot Animals. (Dot to Dot Ser.). (Illus.). 24p. (J). (ps-2). 1991. pap. 3.50 (*0-7460-0616-0*, Usborne) EDC.
Dot-to-Dot at the Seaside. Karen Bryant-Mole. (Dot-to-Dot Ser.). (Illus.). 24p. (J). (gr. k-1). 1993. pap. 3.50 (*0-7460-1376-0*, Usborne) EDC.
Dot to Dot (B - U) K. Bryant-Mole & J. Tyler. (Illus.). 72p. (J). (ps-2). 1992. 7.95 (*0-7460-1448-1*) EDC.
Dot-to-Dot Dinos. Kathy Nevins. (Illus.). 48p. (Orig.). (J). (gr. 2 up). 1989. bds. 2.95 (*0-8431-2338-9*) Price Stern.
Dot-to-Dot Dinosaurs. Karen Bryant-Mole. (Dot-to-Dot Ser.). (Illus.). 24p. (J). (gr. k-1). 1993. pap. 3.50 (*0-7460-1374-4*, Usborne) EDC.
Dot-to-Dot Dinosaurs: An Educational Activity-Coloring Book. Spizzirri Publishing Co. Staff. Ed. by Linda Spizzirri. (Illus.). 32p. (J). (gr. 1-8). 1986. pap. 1.00 (*0-86545-078-1*) Spizzirri.
***Dot to Dot Hawaiian Style.** Wren. 24p. 1994. pap. 4.95 (*1-56647-081-1*) Mutual Pub HI.
Dot to Dot Machines. J. Tyler. (Dot to Dot Ser.). (Illus.). 24p. (J). (ps-2). 1991. pap. 3.50 (*0-7460-0606-3*, Usborne) EDC.
Dot to Dot Nature. K. Bryant-Mole. (Dot to Dot Ser.). (Illus.). 24p. (J). (ps-4). 1993. pap. 3.50 (*0-7460-1375-2*, Usborne) EDC.
Dot to Dot on the Farm. J. Tyler. (Dot to Dot Ser.). (Illus.). 24p. (J). (ps-2). 1991. pap. 3.50 (*0-7460-0595-4*, Usborne) EDC.
Dot-to-Dot Space. Karen Bryant-Mole. (Dot-to-Dot Ser.). (Illus.). 24p. (J). (gr. k-1). 1993. pap. 3.50 (*0-7460-1373-6*, Usborne) EDC.
Dot-to-Dot Whales: An Educational Activity-Coloring Book. Spizzirri Publishing Co. Staff. Ed. by Linda Spizzirri. (Illus.). 32p. (J). (gr. 1-8). 1986. pap. 1.00 (*0-86545-079-X*) Spizzirri.
Dot to Dot Zen: A Primer of Buddhist Psychology. Gerald L. Ericksen. LC 92-5665. 112p. 1993. 8.95 (*0-8048-1801-0*) C E Tuttle.
***Dotchka.** Helen V. Long. 290p. Date not set. pap. 8.95 (*0-7610-0301-0*) NW Pub.
Dothead Americans: The Silent Minority in the United States. Mahin Gosine. 204p. 1992. write for info. (*0-9639318-3-0*) M Gosine.
Doting. Henry Green. LC 70-122054. 248p. 1970. reprint ed. 25.00 (*0-678-03159-2*) Kelley.
Dots: Active Graphic Design. 80p. 1991. pap. 18.95 (*88-7070-161-1*) Belvedere USA.
Dots & Lines. Richard J. Trudeau. LC 78-16894. 213p. reprint ed. pap. 60.80 (*0-7837-1350-9*, 2041498) Bks Demand.
Dot's Pot. Patty Carratello. Ed. by Darlene Spivak. (Easy Rainbow Reader Ser.). (Illus.). 16p. (J). (gr. k-2). 1988. student ed 1.95 (*1-55734-389-6*) Tchr Create Mat.
Dots, Spots, Speckles, & Stripes. Tana Hoban. (J). (ps-3). 1987. 14.00 (*0-688-06862-6*); lib. bdg. 13.93 (*0-688-06863-4*) Greenwillow.
Dotsey's Diary: Her Days & Yours. Dotsey Welliver. (Orig.). 1979. pap. text ed. 3.95 (*0-89367-034-0*) Light & Life.
Dotted Swiss & Gingham. Gay G. Gunn. 87p. (Orig.). (C). 1986. pap. 6.95 (*0-9616587-0-3*) Tremar Prod.
Dottie. Peta Coplans. LC 92-41955. (Illus.). (J). 1994. 14.95 (*0-395-66788-7*) HM.
Dottie. Meg Wolitzer. 274p. 1992. pap. 8.00 (*0-14-016926-1*, Penguin Bks) Viking Penguin.
Dottie, the Unfoolish Mule. Jane B. Baily. LC 90-93258. (Illus.). 32p. (Orig.). (J). (gr. k-3). 1990. pap. 6.95 (*0-9626642-1-9*) J B Baily.
***Dottore...Internment in Italy 1940-1945.** Salim Diamand. (Illus.). 140p. 1995. lib. bdg. 33.00 (*0-8095-4936-0*) Borgo Pr.
Dottrina Degli "Status" Nella Retorica Greca e Romana. Lucia Calboli-Montefusco. viii, 218p. 1986. write for info. (*3-487-07783-3*, Pub. by Georg Olms GW) Lubrecht & Cramer.
Dotty the Ladybug Plays Hide-&-Seek. LC 93-85488. (Baby Bug Bks.). (Illus.). 20p. (J). (ps-1). 1994. 3.99 (*0-89577-568-9*) RD Assn.
Doty - Doten Family in America: Descendants of Edward Doty, an Emigrant by the Mayflower, 1620, 2 vols. E. A. Doty. 1035p. 1989. reprint ed. lib. bdg. 165.00 (*0-8328-0488-6*); reprint ed. pap. 155.00 (*0-8328-0489-4*) Higginson Bk Co.
Doty Dontcare. Mary F. Foster. LC 78-39082. (Black Heritage Library Collection). 1977. reprint ed. 20.95 (*0-8369-9020-X*) Ayer.
Douanier Rousseau en Son Temps: Biographie et Catalogue Raisonne, 2 vols., Set. Henry Certigny. (Illus.). 699p. (FRE.). 1984. 2,500.00 (*0-87817-305-6*) Hacker.
Douay-Rheims New Testament. Tr. by St. Jerome. LC 77-80634. 1977. reprint ed. pap. 13.00 (*0-89555-001-6*) TAN Bks Pubs.
Douay-Rheims Old Testament of the Holy Catholic Bible. 75.00 (*0-9620994-4-9*); pap. 69.95 (*0-685-66936-X*) Cath Treas.

D

An Asterisk (*) at the beginning of an entry indicates that the title is appearing in BIP for the first time. 2089

Double. Fyodor Dostoyevsky. Tr. by Evelyn Harden. 1985. pap. 10.95 (*0-88233-757-2*) Ardis Pubs.

Double. Fyodor Dostoyevsky. 288p. (FRE.). 1980. pap. 10.95 (*0-7859-1924-4*, 2070372278) Fr & Eur.

Double. Marcia Muller & Bill Prozini. 288p. 1995. mass mkt. 5.50 (*0-446-40413-6*, Mysterious Paperbk) Warner Bks.

*__Double.__ John H. Williams. 64p. 1995. 14.95 (*1-85224-273-6*) Dufour.

Double: A Psychoanalytic Study. Otto Rank. 120p. 1971. reprint ed. pap. 21.95 (*0-946439-58-3*, Pub. by Karnac Bks UK) Brunner-Mazel.

Double see Three Short Novels of Dostoyevsky

Double Action. Kit Dalton. (Buckskin Ser.: No. 27). 176p. 1989. pap. 2.95 (*0-8439-2845-X*) Dorchester Pub Co.

Double Agent: Essays in Craft & Elucidation. Richard Blackmur. (BCL1-PS American Literature Ser.). 302p. 1993. reprint ed. lib. bdg. 89.00 (*0-7812-6583-5*) Rprt Serv.

Double & the Other: Identity as Ideology in Post-Romantic Fiction. Paul Coates. LC 87-32217. 176p. 1988. text ed. 39.95 (*0-312-01874-6*) St Martin.

Double Armed Man. limited ed. William Neade. LC 68-59329. (Illus.). 51p. 1971. boxed 10.00 (*0-87387-022-0*) Shumway.

Double Auction Market: Institutions, Theories, & Evidence. Ed. by Daniel P. Friedman & John Rust. LC 92-34829. (C). 1993. 44.95 (*0-201-62263-7*) Addison-Wesley.

Double Auction Market: Institutions, Theories, & Evidence. Daniel P. Friedman. (C). 1993. pap. 24.95 (*0-201-62459-1*) Addison-Wesley.

Double-Barrel Carmody: Tough Bullet & The Killers. Peter McCurtin. 304p. 1989. pap. 3.95 (*0-8439-2847-6*) Dorchester Pub Co.

Double-Barrel Lassiter: Guerilla - Man from Lordsburg. Jack Slade. (Lassiter Ser.). 320p. 1988. pap. 3.50 (*0-8439-2637-6*) Dorchester Pub Co.

Double-Barrel Lassiter: Gunfight at Ringo Junction - Man from Tombstone. Jack Slade. 288p. 1988. pap. 3.50 (*0-8439-2677-5*) Dorchester Pub Co.

Double-Barrel Sundance: The Savage - Gold Strike. Peter McCurtin. 384p. 1988. pap. 3.95 (*0-8439-2651-1*) Dorchester Pub Co.

Double-Barrel Western: The Bushwackers - Ride the Wild Country. Lee Floren. 368p. 1988. pap. 3.95 (*0-8439-2610-4*) Dorchester Pub Co.

Double-Barrel Western: The Tough Texan & Bandit in Black. Paul E. Lehman. 272p. 1989. pap. 3.95 (*0-8439-2821-2*) Dorchester Pub Co.

Double-Barrel Western: Track of the Snake- Day of the Scorpion. Gene Shelton. 416p. 1988. pap. 3.95 (*0-8439-2665-1*) Dorchester Pub Co.

Double Barrel Western--Sundance: The Marauders & Day of the Halfbreed. Peter McCurtin. 368p. pap. 3.95 (*0-8439-2689-9*) Dorchester Pub Co.

*__Double-Barrelled.__ Mark Twain. 1994. audio, lib. bdg. 18.95 (*1-883049-30-X*) Commuters Lib.

*__Double-Barrelled Detective Story.__ Mark Twain. (Mark Twain Ser.). 1994. audio 16.95 (*1-883049-11-3*) Commuters Lib.

Double-Bed Machine Knitting: For All Double-Bed Machines or Single-Bed Machines with Ribber Attachment. Ruth Lee. (Illus.). 128p. 1994. pap. 34.95 (*0-7134-6817-3*, Pub. by Batsford UK) Trafalgar.

Double Belonging: Interchurch Families & Christian Unity. George Kilcourse. 176p. 1992. pap. 11.95 (*0-8091-3292-3*) Paulist Pr.

Double Bind: A Guide to Recovery & Relapse Prevention for the Chemically Dependent Sexual Abuse Survivor. Caryl Trotter. (Illus.). 135p. (Orig.). 1992. pap. text ed. 9.50 (*0-8309-0613-4*) Herald Hse.

*__Double Bind: Women Affected by Alcohol & Other Drugs.__ Ed. by Dorothy Broom. 235p. 1995. pap. 24.95 (*1-86373-724-3*, Pub. by Allen Unwin AT) Paul & Co Pubs.

Double Black Diamond. Laura Gordon. (Intrigue Ser.). 1993. pap. 2.89 (*0-373-22220-3*, 1-22220-7) Harlequin Bks.

Double Blessings. Contrib by Jolene Boyd. 1988. 8.95 (*0-8341-9096-6*, MB-601) Lillenas.

Double Blind. Phil Baxter. 1994. mass mkt. 4.50 (*0-06-100518-5*, Harp PBks) HarpC.

Double Blind Research in Psychotherapy. F. L. Wojciechowski. xvi, 188p. 1984. 18.50 (*90-265-0587-6*, Pub. by Swets Pub Serv NE) Taylor & Francis.

*__Double Bluff: A Carol Ashton Mystery.__ Claire McNab. 192p. 1995. pap. 10.95 (*1-56280-096-5*) Naiad Pr.

Double Bond: The Constitutional Documents of American Jewry. Ed. by Daniel J. Elazar et al. 492p. (C). 1992. lib. bdg. 62.50 (*0-8191-8586-8*) U Pr of Amer.

*__Double Canister at Ten Yards: The Federal Artillery at Gettysburg.__ Ed. by Richard Rollins. 1995. pap. write for info. (*0-9638993-5-X*) Rank & File.

Double Case: Agreement by Suffixaufnahme. Ed. by Frans Plank. (Illus.). 416p. 1995. 75.00 (*0-19-508775-5*) OUP.

Double Caution Totem, Bk. 1. Lewis Koch. 1993. 15.00 (*0-932526-43-8*) Nexus Pr.

Double Cipher: Encounter Between Word & Image in Bonnefoy, Tardieu & Michaux. Adelia V. Williams. Ed. by Ernest Gilman. (Literature & the Visual Arts: New Foundations Ser.: Vol. 6). (Illus.). 252p. 1990. 59.95 (*0-8204-1317-8*) P Lang Pubs.

Double Concerto. J. Peter Voute. 1990. pap. 13.95 (*0-932298-79-6*) Tri-State Pr Corp.

Double Consciousness - Double Bind: Theoretical Issues in Twentieth-Century Black Literature. Sandra Adell. LC 93-49578. (Illus.). 192p. 1994. 25.95 (*0-252-02109-6*) U of Ill Pr.

Double Contrast Imaging of the Small Intestine. G. Salerno & V. Alessi. 184p. 1988. text ed. 64.00 (*1-57235-036-9*) Piccin NY.

Double Contrast Radiology of the Aesophagus. G. Rossetti et al. 154p. 1985. text ed. 56.00 (*1-57235-035-0*) Piccin NY.

Double Counterpoint & Canon. J. F. Bridges. 1972. 59.95 (*0-8490-0059-9*) Gordon Pr.

Double Counterpoint & Canon. E. Prout. LC 68-25300. (Studies in Music: No. 42). 1969. reprint ed. lib. bdg. 75.00 (*0-8383-0312-9*) M S G Haskell Hse.

Double Counterpoint & Canon. Ebenezer Prout. 273p. 1990. reprint ed. lib. bdg. 69.00 (*0-7812-9142-9*) Rprt Serv.

*__Double Cousins: Stories & Photos of Early Day Life in the Cherokee Strip of Oklahoma with the Schuman & Waugh Families.__ Meredith Waugh. Ed. by Carolyn Leonard. (Illus.). 184p. (Orig.). 1995. per. 19.95 (*1-883852-04-8*) Sage Pr OK.

Double Cross. John Lutz. (BePuzzled Ser.). 4p. (Orig.). (J). 1989. pap. 19.95 (*0-922242-14-3*) Lombard Mktg.

Double Cross: Ordination, Abortion, & Catholic Feminism. Denise L. Carmody. 192p. (Orig.). 1986. pap. 10.95 (*0-8245-0736-3*) Crossroad NY.

Double Cross: The Explosive, Inside Story of the Mobster Who Controlled America. Sam Giancana & Chuck Giancana. (Illus.). 384p. 1992. 22.95 (*0-446-51624-4*) Warner Bks.

Double Cross: The Explosive, Inside Story of the Mobster Who Controlled America. Sam Giancana & Chuck Giancana. 528p. 1993. mass mkt. 6.99 (*0-446-36412-6*) Warner Bks.

Double Cross Ranch. large type ed. Lee Floren. (Linford Western Library). 256p. 1989. pap. 11.95 (*0-7089-6710-8*, Linford) Ulverscroft.

Double-Crossed. Francine Pascal. (Sweet Valley High Ser.: No. 109). (YA). 1994. 3.50 (*0-553-56231-2*) Bantam.

Double Crossed! The Case of the Missing Money. rev. ed. Hilda Stahl. LC 86-72124. 1993. reprint ed. pap. 4.99 (*0-7814-0524-6*, Chariot Bks) Chariot Family.

Double-Crossed in Gator Country. Ernest Herndon. (Eric Sterling, Secret Agent Ser.). 144p. (J). 1994. pap. 5.99 (*0-310-38261-0*) Zondervan.

Double Crossfire. Allen Conrad. 256p. 1988. pap. 2.95 (*0-8217-2363-4*) Zebra.

Double Crossing. Carolyn Keene. (Nancy Drew & Hardy Boys Supermystery Ser.). 224p. (Orig.). (YA). (gr. 7 up). 1991. mass mkt. 3.99 (*0-671-74616-2*, Archway) PB.

Double-Crostics, Vols. 5-18. Janet E. Cameron. Incl. Vol. 5. 1982. pap. 5.00 (*0-8317-2414-5*); Vol. 6. 1982. pap. 5.00 (*0-8317-2415-3*); Vol. 7. 1982. pap. 5.00 (*0-8317-2416-1*); Vol. 8. 1982. pap. 5.00 (*0-8317-2417-X*); Vol. 9. 1982. pap. 5.00 (*0-8317-2418-8*); Vol. 10. 1982. pap. 5.00 (*0-8317-2419-6*); Vol. 11. 1982. pap. 5.00 (*0-8317-2420-X*); Vol. 12. 1982. pap. 5.00 (*0-8317-2421-8*); Vol. 13. 1982. pap. 5.00 (*0-8317-2422-6*); Vol. 14. 1982. pap. 5.00 (*0-8317-2411-0*); Vol. 15. 1982. pap. 5.00 (*0-8317-2412-9*); Vol. 16. 1982. pap. 5.00 (*0-8317-2413-7*); Vol. 17. 1982. pap. 5.00 (*0-8317-2423-4*); Vol. 18. 1982. pap. 5.00 (*0-8317-2424-2*); 64p. 1982. write for info. (*0-318-56758-X*) Smithmark.

Double Crown Club: A History of Fifty Years. James Moran. (Illus.). 128p. (C). 1989. 400.00 (*0-903696-03-7*, Pub. by Hurtwood Pr Ltd) St Mut.

Double Cure, or Redemption Twofold. large type ed. D. O. Teasley. 160p. pap. 2.00 (*0-686-29147-6*) Faith Pub Hse.

*__Double Dabble Surprise.__ Beverly Lewis. (Cul-De-Sac Kids Ser.). 80p. 1995. mass mkt. 2.99 (*1-55661-625-2*) Bethany Hse.

Double Dabble Thanksgiving Surprise. Beverly Lewis. (J). (ps-3). 1993. pap. 3.95 (*1-56233-175-2*, Squeaky Sneaker) Star Song TN.

*__Double Danger.__ Judy Baer. (Live! From Brentwood High Ser.: Bk. 3). 160p. (YA). 1995. mass mkt. 3.99 (*1-55661-388-1*) Bethany Hse.

Double Dare Dog. Jamie Gilson. LC 87-37855. (Illus.). 126p. (J). (gr. 3-5). 1988. 15.00 (*0-688-07969-5*) Lothrop.

Double Date. R. L. Stine. (Fear Street Ser.). (YA). 1994. mass mkt. 3.99 (*0-671-78570-2*, Archway) PB.

Double Daughter. Vicki P. McConnell. 1994. pap. 9.95 (*0-9630822-5-6*) Madwoman Pr.

Double Dealing. Ann Smock. LC 85-16490. vi, 137p. 1985. 20.00 (*0-8032-4165-8*) U of Nebr Pr.

Double Death. large type ed. Charles Forsyte. 1989. 17.95 (*0-7089-2180-9*) Ulverscroft.

Double Deceit. large type ed. Palma Harcourt. 1991. 23.95 (*0-7089-8590-4*, Trail West Pubs) Ulverscroft.

Double Deception. Elizabeth Law. 224p. 1987. 16.95 (*0-8027-0950-8*) Walker & Co.

Double Deception. Elizabeth Law. 1989. pap. 2.95 (*0-8217-2825-3*) Zebra.

Double Deception. Joan Wolf. (Regency Romance Ser.). 1983. pap. 3.99 (*0-451-15808-3*, Sig) NAL-Dutton.

Double Deception. large type ed. Clive Egelton. 496p. 1994. 25.95 (*0-7089-8769-9*, Trailtree Bookshop) Ulverscroft.

Double Deception: Stalin, Hitler, & the Invasion of Russia. James Barros & James Gregor. LC 94-11771. (Illus.). 270p. 1995. lib. bdg. 32.00 (*0-87580-191-9*) N Ill U Pr.

Double-Decker Double-Decker Double-Decker Bus. Patty Wolcott. LC 91-14210. (Ten-Word Readers Ser.). (Illus.). 32p. (J). (ps-2). 1991. lib. bdg. 6.99 (*0-679-91930-9*) Random Bks Yng Read.

Double Descent in an African Society. Simon Ottenberg. LC 84-45540. (American Ethnological Society Monographs: No. 47). 1988. reprint ed. 36.00 (*0-404-62945-8*) AMS Pr.

Double Deuce. Robert B. Parker. 256p. 1993. mass mkt. 5.99 (*0-425-13793-7*) Berkley Pub.

Double Deuce. large type ed. Robert B. Parker, Jr. LC 92-38590. (General Ser.). 233p. 1993. 20.95 (*0-8161-5596-8*); pap. 16.95 (*0-8161-5597-6*) G K Hall.

Double Deuce: A Spenser Thriller. Robert B. Parker. 224p. 1992. 100.00 (*0-399-13754-8*, Putnam) Putnam Pub Group.

Double Dilemma: Minorities & Women in Science Education. Jane B. Kahle. LC 81-84383. (Illus.). 181p. (Orig.). 1982. pap. 5.95 (*0-931682-13-4*) Purdue U Pubns.

Double-Dip Feelings: A Book to Help Children Understand Emotions. Barbara S. Cain. LC 89-49382. (Illus.). 32p. (J). 1990. 16.95 (*0-945354-23-1*); pap. 8.95 (*0-945354-20-7*) Magination Pr.

Double-Dip Feelings: Stories to Help Children Understand Emotions. Barbara S. Cain. LC 92-56870. (Books to Help Children Ser.). (Illus.). (J). 1993. reprint ed. lib. bdg. 17.27 (*0-8368-0931-9*) Gareth Stevens Inc.

Double Disappearance of Walter Fozbek. Steve Senn. (Illus.). 128p. (J). (gr. 3-5). 1983. pap. 2.50 (*0-380-62737-X*, 60064-1, Camelot) Avon.

Double Dividends? U. S. Biotechnology & Third World Development. John Elkington. LC 86-51479. 60p. (Orig.). 1986. pap. text ed. 10.00 (*0-915825-16-3*) World Resources Inst.

Double Dog Dare. Jamie Gilson. (Illus.). (J). 1989. pap. 2.75 (*0-671-67898-1*, Minstrel Bks) PB.

Double Dose. Peter Nelson. (Mollie Fox Mystery Ser.: No. 2). (YA). 1992. mass mkt. 3.50 (*0-06-106101-8*, Harp PBks) HarpC.

Double-Dot - Duotone Guide. Harvey Sternbach. (Illus.). 226p. (C). 1993. 79.50 (*0-685-66943-2*) Perfect Graphic.

Double, Double. Michael J. Friedman. (Star Trek Ser.: No. 45). 1989. mass mkt. 4.99 (*0-671-66130-2*, Pocket Star Bks) PB.

Double Down. Tom Kakonis. 400p. 1992. pap. 5.99 (*0-451-40304-5*, Onyx) NAL-Dutton.

*__Double Dragon 5: The Shadow Falls Official Strategy Guide.__ Bradygames Staff. 1994. pap. 9.99 (*1-56686-211-6*) Brady Compu Bks.

Double Dribble. Vern McLellan. (Illus.). 78p. (Orig.). 1992. pap. 7.95 (*1-56245-008-5*) Great Quotations.

Double Dunk: The Inspiring Story of a Harlem Basketball Legend. Barry Beckham. 192p. 1995. pap. 9.95 (*0-931761-22-0*) Beckham House.

Double Dutch & the Voodoo Shoes: An Urban Folktale. Melodye Rosales. LC 91-13153. (Adventures in Storytelling Ser.). (Illus.). 32p. (J). (ps-3). 1991. lib. bdg. 13.85 (*0-516-05133-4*); pap. 5.95 (*0-516-45133-2*) Childrens.

Double Duty: Chemically Dependent. Claudia Black. (Orig.). 1992. mass mkt. 4.99 (*0-345-37630-7*) Ballantine.

Double Duty: Chemically Dependent. Claudia Black. 74p. (Orig.). 1990. pap. 7.95 (*0-910223-17-3*) MAC Pub.

Double Duty: Dual Dynamics Within the Chemically Dependent Home. Claudia Black. 1990. 25.00 (*0-345-36152-0*, Ballantine Trade) Ballantine.

Double Duty: Food Addicted. Claudia Black. 1991. mass mkt. 4.99 (*0-345-37629-3*) Ballantine.

Double Duty: Food Addiction. Claudia Black. 84p. (Orig.). 1990. pap. 7.95 (*0-910223-16-5*) MAC Pub.

Double Duty: Gay-Lesbian. Claudia Black. 75p. (Orig.). 1990. pap. 7.95 (*0-910223-14-9*) MAC Pub.

Double Duty: Sexual Abuse. Claudia Black. 81p. (Orig.). 1990. pap. 7.95 (*0-910223-15-7*) MAC Pub.

Double Duty: Sexually Abused. Claudia Black. (Orig.). 1992. mass mkt. 4.99 (*0-345-37632-3*) Ballantine.

Double Duty Nurse. large type ed. Arlene J. Fitzgerald. (Romance Ser.). 336p. 1994. pap. 14.95 (*0-7089-7532-1*, Trailtree Bookshop) Ulverscroft.

Double-Dyed. Raymond Chaplim. (C). 1989. pap. 30.00 (*0-7223-2356-5*, Pub. by A H S Ltd UK) St Mut.

Double Dying: Reflections on Holocaust Literature. Alvin H. Rosenfeld. LC 79-3006. 222p. 1980. 29.95 (*0-253-13337-8*); pap. 9.95 (*0-253-20492-5*, MB-492) Ind U Pr.

Double Eagle. large type ed. Charles McCarry. 441p. 1982. 15.95 (*0-7089-0812-8*) Ulverscroft.

Double Eagle. large type ed. Keith Miles. 355p. 1992. 21.95 (*0-7505-0337-8*) Ulverscroft.

Double Eagle & Crescent: Vienna's 2nd Turkish Siege & Its Historical Setting. Thomas M. Barker. LC 67-63760. (Illus.). 465p. reprint ed. pap. 132.60 (*0-8357-9592-6*, 2010104) Bks Demand.

Double Eagle & Rising Sun: The Russians & Japanese at Portsmouth in 1905. Raymond Esthus. LC 87-20183. x, 265p. (C). 1988. 39.50 (*0-8223-0778-2*) Duke.

*__Double Eagle Guide to Camping in Wesern Parks & Forests: Washington.__ large type ed. Thomas Preston & Elizabeth Preston. (Double Eagle Guides Ser.). (Illus.). 188p. 1995. 17.95 (*0-929760-41-7*) Discovery MT.

*__Double Eagle Guide to Camping in Western Parks & Forests: Arizona.__ large type ed. Thomas Preston & Elizabeth Preston. (Double Eagle Guides Ser.). (Illus.). 128p. 1995. 16.95 (*0-929760-49-2*) Discovery MT.

*__Double Eagle Guide to Camping in Western Parks & Forests: Colorado.__ large type ed. Thomas Preston & Elizabeth Preston. (Double Eagle Guides Ser.). 190p. 1995. 17.95 (*0-929760-44-1*) Discovery MT.

*__Double Eagle Guide to Camping in Western Parks & Forests: Idaho.__ large type ed. Thomas Preston & Elizabeth Preston. (Double Eagle Guides Ser.). (Illus.). 120p. 1995. 15.95 (*0-929760-43-3*) Discovery MT.

*__Double Eagle Guide to Camping in Western Parks & Forests: Montana.__ large type ed. Thomas Preston & Elizabeth Preston. (Double Eagle Guides Ser.). (Illus.). 128p. 1995. 16.95 (*0-929760-45-X*) Discovery MT.

*__Double Eagle Guide to Camping in Western Parks & Forests: Nebraska & Kansas.__ large type ed. Thomas Preston & Elizabeth Preston. (Double Eagle Guides Ser.). (Illus.). 162p. 1995. 17.95 (*0-929760-53-0*) Discovery MT.

*__Double Eagle Guide to Camping in Western Parks & Forests: Nevada-Utah.__ large type ed. Thomas Preston & Elizabeth Preston. (Double Eagle Guides Ser.). (Illus.). 188p. 1995. 17.95 (*0-929760-51-4*) Discovery MT.

*__Double Eagle Guide to Camping in Western Parks & Forests: New Mexico.__ large type ed. Thomas Preston & Elizabeth Preston. (Double Eagle Guides Ser.). (Illus.). 118p. 1995. 15.95 (*0-929760-50-6*) Discovery MT.

*__Double Eagle Guide to Camping in Western Parks & Forests: North Dakota-South Dakota.__ large type ed. Thomas Preston & Elizabeth Preston. (Double Eagle Guides Ser.). (Illus.). 138p. 1995. 16.95 (*0-929760-52-2*) Discovery MT.

*__Double Eagle Guide to Camping in Western Parks & Forests: Northern California.__ large type ed. Thomas Preston & Elizabeth Preston. (Double Eagle Guide Ser.). (Illus.). 230p. 1995. 18.95 (*0-929760-47-6*) Discovery MT.

*__Double Eagle Guide to Camping in Western Parks & Forests: Oklahoma.__ large type ed. Thomas Preston & Elizabeth Preston. (Double Eagle Guides Ser.). (Illus.). 150p. 1995. 16.95 (*0-929760-54-9*) Discovery MT.

*__Double Eagle Guide to Camping in Western Parks & Forests: Oregon.__ large type ed. Thomas Preston & Elizabeth Preston. (Double Eagle Guides Ser.). (Illus.). 168p. 1995. 16.95 (*0-929760-42-5*) Discovery MT.

*__Double Eagle Guide to Camping in Western Parks & Forests: Southern California.__ large type ed. Thomas Preston & Elizabeth Preston. (Double Eagle Guides Ser.). (Illus.). 220p. 1995. 18.95 (*0-929760-48-4*) Discovery MT.

*__Double Eagle Guide to Camping in Western Parks & Forests: Texas.__ large type ed. Thomas Preston & Elizabeth Preston. (Double Eagle Guides Ser.). (Illus.). 210p. 1995. 17.95 (*0-929760-55-7*) Discovery MT.

*__Double Eagle Guide to Camping in Western Parks & Forests: Wyoming.__ large type ed. Thomas Preston & Elizabeth Preston. (Double Eagle Guides Ser.). (Illus.). 116p. 1995. 15.95 (*0-929760-46-8*) Discovery MT.

*__Double Eagle Guide to Camping in Western Parks & Forests Vol. I: Pacific Northwest.__ Thomas Preston & Elizabeth Preston. (Double Eagle Guides). (Illus.). 448p. (Orig.). 1992. pap. 12.95 (*0-929760-21-2*) Discovery MT.

*__Double Eagle Guide to Camping in Western Parks & Forests Vol. I: Pacific Northwest.__ Thomas Preston & Elizabeth Preston. (Double Eagle Guides). (Illus.). 238p. 1994. 18.95 (*0-929760-27-1*) Discovery MT.

*__Double Eagle Guide to Camping in Western Parks & Forests Vol. II: Far West.__ Thomas Preston & Elizabeth Preston. (Double Eagle Guides). (Illus.). 240p. 1994. 18.95 (*0-929760-23-9*) Discovery MT.

*__Double Eagle Guide to Camping in Western Parks & Forests Vol. II: Rocky Mountains.__ Thomas Preston & Elizabeth Preston. (Double Eagle Guides). (Illus.). 214p. 1994. 17.95 (*0-929760-22-0*) Discovery MT.

*__Double Eagle Guide to Camping in Western Parks & Forests Vol. IV: Desert Southwest.__ Thomas Preston & Elizabeth Preston. (Double Eagle Guides). (Illus.). 384p. (Orig.). 1992. pap. 12.95 (*0-929760-24-7*) Discovery MT.

*__Double Eagle Guide to Camping in Western Parks & Forests Vol. IV: Desert Southwest.__ Thomas Preston & Elizabeth Preston. (Double Eagle Guides). (Illus.). 212p. 1994. 17.95 (*0-929760-29-8*) Discovery MT.

*__Double Eagle Guide to Camping in Western Parks & Forests Vol. V: Northern Plains.__ Thomas Preston & Elizabeth Preston. (Double Eagle Guides). (Illus.). 170p. 1994. 16.95 (*0-929760-25-5*) Discovery MT.

*__Double Eagle Guide to Camping in Western Parks & Forests Vol. VI: Southwest Plains.__ Thomas Preston & Elizabeth Preston. (Double Eagle Guides). (Illus.). 192p. 1994. 17.95 (*0-929760-26-3*) Discovery MT.

Double Eagle Guide to Western Public Campgrounds: Far West. Ed. by Elizabeth Preston. (Double Eagle Guides Ser.: Vol. III). (Illus.). 336p. (Orig.). 1988. pap. 8.95 (*0-929760-03-4*) Discovery MT.

Double Eagle Guide to Western Public Campgrounds: Northern Great Plains. Intro. by Thomas Preston & Elizabeth Preston. (Double Eagle Guides Ser.: Vol. V). (Illus.). 304p. (Orig.). 1989. pap. 8.95 (*0-929760-05-0*) Discovery MT.

Double Eagle Guide to Western Public Campgrounds: Pacific Northwest. Ed. by Elizabeth Preston. (Double Eagle Guides Ser.: Vol. I). (Illus.). 336p. (Orig.). 1988. pap. 8.95 (*0-929760-01-8*) Discovery MT.

Double Eagle Guide to Western Public Campgrounds: Rocky Mountains. Ed. by Elizabeth Preston. (Double Eagle Guides Ser.: Vol. II). (Illus.). 304p. (Orig.). 1988. pap. 8.95 (*0-929760-02-6*) Discovery MT.

Double Eagle Guide to Western Public Campgrounds: Southwest. Ed. by Elizabeth Preston. (Double Eagle Guides Ser.: Vol. IV). (Illus.). 304p. (Orig.). 1988. pap. 8.95 (*0-929760-04-2*) Discovery MT.

Double Eagle Guide to Western Public Campgrounds: Southwest Plains. Intro. by Thomas Preston & Elizabeth Preston. (Double Eagle Guides Ser.: Vol. VI). (Illus.). 336p. (Orig.). 1990. pap. 8.95 (*0-929760-06-9*) Discovery MT.

Double Eagle Guide to Western State Parks Vol. 1: Pacific Northwest. Intro. by Thomas Preston. (Double Eagle Guides Ser.). (Illus.). 304p. (Orig.). 1991. pap. 11.95 (*0-929760-11-5*) Discovery MT.

D

An Asterisk (*) at the beginning of an entry indicates that the title is appearing in BIP for the first time.

An Asterisk (*) at the beginning of an entry indicates that the title is appearing in BIP for the first time.

2091

D

Double Sin & Other Stories. large type ed. Agatha Christie. (Popular Author Ser.). (Orig.). 1991. pap. 11.95 (*0-8161-4542-3*) G K Hall.

Double Sin & Other Stories. large type ed. Agatha Christie. (Agatha Christie Ser.). 266p. (Orig.). 1990. 19.95 (*0-8161-4541-5*, Large Print Bks) Hall.

Double Singleness: Gender & the Writings of Charles & Mary Lamb. Jane Aaron. 232p. 1991. 55.00 (*0-19-812890-8*) OUP.

Double-Slot Antennas on Extended Hemispherical Silicon Lenses--General Treatment. George V. Eleftheriades & Gabriel M. Rebeiz. (University of Michigan Report Ser.: No. RL903). 34p. reprint ed. pap. 25.00 (*0-7837-6785-4*, 2046617) Bks Demand.

***Double Snaps: For Advanced Snappers & Those Who Like the Dozens Raw...an All New Book.** James Percelay et al. LC 94-24792. 1995. pap. 9.95 (*0-688-14011-4*, Quill) Morrow.

Double Solitaire. large type ed. Sara Chance. (Desire Ser.). 1992. pap. 13.95 (*0-373-58463-6*, C0465, Silhouette Lrg Print) Chivers N Amer.

Double-Speak: Rom Revenue Enhancement to Terminal Living How Government, Business, Advertisers & Others Use the Language to Deceive You. William D. Lutz. 1990. 8.95 (*0-00-003850-4*, PL) HarpC.

Double Spell. Janet Lunn. (Novels Ser.). 144p. (J). (gr. 3-7). 1986. pap. 3.95 (*0-14-031858-5*, Puffin) Puffin Bks.

Double Springs Scrapbook: Centennial Day, Double Springs, Alabama. Ed. by Dess Sangster & Tom Sangster. (Illus.). 86p. (Orig.). 1983. pap. 10.00 (*0-685-48820-9*) Coffeetable.

Double Squeeze. Henry B. Needham. LC 75-150557. (Short Story Index Reprint Ser.). (Illus.). 1977. reprint ed. 20.95 (*0-8369-3854-2*) Ayer.

Double Squeezes. Hugh Kelsey. 128p. 1988. 22.95 (*0-575-04115-3*, Pub. by V Gollancz UK) Trafalgar.

Double Standard. Linda Dubreuil. 1980. pap. 2.25 (*0-8439-0801-7*) Dorchester Pub Co.

Double Standard. Elizabeth Levy. 160p. (J). (gr. 7 up). 1984. pap. 2.25 (*0-380-87379-6*, 87379-6, Flare) Avon.

Double Standard in Shakespeare & Related Plays: Changing Status of Women in 16th & 17th Century England. Sarup Singh. 226p. 1989. text ed. 27.95 (*81-220-0080-0*, Pub. by Konark Pubs Pvt Ltd II) Advent Bks Div.

Double Standards. Judith McNaught. Ed. by Linda Marrow. 1991. pap. 6.50 (*0-671-73760-0*) PB.

Double Standards. large type ed. Judith McNaught. (General Ser.). 306p. 1992. text ed. 20.95 (*0-8161-5261-6*) G K Hall.

Double Star. Robert A. Heinlein. 1986. mass mkt. 4.95 (*0-345-33013-7*, Del Rey) Ballantine.

Double Stars. Wulff D. Heintz. (Geophysics & Astrophysics Monographs: No. 15). 1978. lib. bdg. 70.00 (*90-277-0885-1*) Kluwer Ac.

Double Stars, Physical Properties & Generic Relations. Ed. by Bambang Hidayat et al. 1984. lib. bdg. 195.00 (*90-277-1748-6*) Kluwer Ac.

Double Stitch: Black Women Write about Mothers & Daughters. Maya Angelou et al. LC 92-53416. 288p. 1993. pap. 13.00 (*0-06-097503-2*, PL) HarpC.

Double Stitch: Black Women Write about Mothers & Daughters. Ed. by Patricia Bell-Scott et al. LC 91-10284. 288p. 1991. 19.95 (*0-8070-0910-5*) Beacon Pr.

Double Strand: Five Contemporary Mexican Poets. Frank Dauster. LC 86-14653. 208p. 1987. 23.00 (*0-8131-1618-X*) U Pr of Ky.

Double Take. Liz Rideal. (Illus.). 48p. 1991. pap. 14.95 (*0-9515642-5-0*) Antique Collect.

Double Take. large type ed. Roger Ormerod. (Mystery Ser.). 320p. 1994. pap. 14.95 (*0-7089-7566-6*, Trailtree Bookshop) Ulverscroft.

Double Take: ("Unholy") Insights on the "Holy" Institutions of Formal Education, Religion, Marriage, Social Work, Etc.) Margarita Ventenilla-Hamada. 158p. (Orig.). (C). 1991. pap. 8.25 (*971-10-0432-1*, Pub. by New Day Pub PH) Cellar.

Double Take: A Mellingham Mystery. Susan P. Oleksiw. 256p. 1994. text ed. 20.00 (*0-684-19656-5*, Scribners) S&S Trade.

Double Talk: Bilingualism & the Politics of Ethnicity in Catalonia. Kathryn A. Woolard. LC 88-28616. 208p. 1989. 32.50 (*0-8047-1502-5*) Stanford U Pr.

Double Talk: The Erotics of Male Literary Collaboration. Wayne Koestenbaum. (Illus.). 256p. 1989. 39.50 (*0-415-90109-X*, Routledge NY); pap. 13.95 (*0-415-90110-3*, Routledge NY) Routledge.

Double Talking: Essays on Verbal & Visual Ironies in Canadian Contemporary Art & Literature. Linda Hutcheon. 160p. (C). 1992. pap. text ed. 25.00 (*1-55022-139-6*, Pub. by ECW Press CN) Genl Dist Srvs.

Double Talking Helix Blues. Joel Herskowitz & Ira Herskowitz. LC 93-36775. (Illus.). 32p. (J). (gr. k-8). 1994. 20.00 (*0-87969-431-9*) Cold Spring Harbor.

Double Taxation Agreements & Taxation of Foreign Investments in India. D. P. Mittal. (C). 1989. 350.00 (*0-685-27886-7*) St Mut.

Double Taxation in the United States. Francis Walker. (Columbia University. Studies in the Social Sciences: No. 13). reprint ed. 32.50 (*0-404-51013-2*) AMS Pr.

Double Taxation of Property & Income: A Study in the Judicial Delimitation of the Conflicting Claims of Taxing Jurisdiction Advanced by the American States. Arthur L. Harding. LC 33-36208. (Harvard Studies in the Conflict of Laws: Vol. 1). x, 326p. 1978. reprint ed. lib. bdg. 45.00 (*0-89941-126-6*, 300500) W S Hein.

Double Taxation Treaties Between Industrialised and Developing Countries: OECD and UN Models. International Fiscal Association Staff. (IFA Congress Ser.: Vol. 15). 100p. 1992. pap. 30.00 (*90-6544-610-9*) Kluwer Law Tax Pubs.

Double Tenth. George Brown. 544p. 1994. pap. 5.99 (*0-09-992760-8*, Pub. by Arrow Bks UK) Trafalgar.

Double the Power of Your Immune System. John Heinerman. 1991. pap. text ed. 10.95 (*0-13-218017-0*) P-H.

Double the Power of Your Immune System. John Heinerman. 1991. 24.95 (*0-13-218025-1*) P-H.

***Double the Trouble.** Ellen Javernick. LC 94-29254. (Gifted & Talented Reader Ser.). (Illus.). (J). 1994. write for info. (*1-56565-162-6*) Lowell Hse Juvenile.

***Double Think: Three Levels of Successful Thinking for Higher Intelligence.** 2nd ed. T. Frank Saunders & Amy Schlessman. (Illus.). 186p. (C). 1995. pap. text ed. 24.95 (*1-887082-01-8*) Double Think.

***Double Thread.** Walter J. Starcke. 160p. Date not set. 11.95 (*0-227-67738-2*) Attic Pr.

Double Thread. Walter Starcke. LC 88-72195. 160p. (C). 1988. reprint ed. pap. 7.95 (*0-929845-00-5*) Guadalupe Pr.

***Double Time.** Star Black. 64p. 1995. pap. write for info. (*1-877593-00-1*) GP Hudson NY.

***Double Tongue: A Draft of a Novel.** William Golding. LC 95-10101. 165p. 1995. 20.00 (*0-374-14329-3*) FS&G.

Double Tongues. Mary Hawley. 80p. (Orig.). 1993. pap. 7.95 (*1-882688-00-7*) Tia Chucha Pr.

Double Track. Don R. Ayres. (Illus.). 288p. (Orig.). 1991. pap. 8.95 (*0-943857-06-6*) D R Ayres.

Double Trouble. (Brookville Chese Committee Ser. - Tamar Bks.: Vol. III). 1992. pap. 7.95 (*0-89906-138-9*) Mesorah Pubns.

***Double Trouble.** Robert P. Gorrell, Jr. & Donald G. Brookins. (Illus.). 75p. (Orig.). 1994. pap. 9.95 (*0-9635288-1-5*) Richmnd-Times-Dispatch.

Double Trouble. Rose Greydanus. LC 81-2358. (Illus.). 32p. (J). (gr. k-2). 1981. lib. bdg. 11.59 (*0-89375-529-X*); pap. 2.95 (*0-89375-530-3*) Troll Assocs.

Double Trouble. Sally Horton. 160p. (Orig.). 1993. pap. 10.95 (*0-571-16859-0*) Faber & Faber.

Double Trouble. Marlene Matthew. (Road to Avonlea Ser.: No. 24). (J). (gr. 4-7). 1994. 3.99 (*0-553-48123-1*) Bantam.

Double Trouble. Michael J. Pellowski. 120p. (J). (gr. 3-5). 1994. pap. 2.99 (*0-87406-700-6*) Willowisp Pr.

Double Trouble: A Bibliographic Chronicle of Ace Mystery Doubles. Sheldon Jaffery. LC 89-11447. (Starmont Popular Culture Studies: No. 11). iv, 150p. 1992. lib. bdg. 29.00x (*1-55742-119-6*); pap. 19.00x (*1-55742-118-8*) Borgo Pr.

***Double Trouble for Jess McColl.** Elaine Schulte. (Twelve Candles Club Ser.: Bk. 7). 128p. (J). 1995. pap. 4.99 (*1-55661-535-3*) Bethany Hse.

Double Trouble Squared. Kathryn Lasky. (J). (gr. 3 up). 1991. 14.95 (*0-15-224126-4*, HB Juv Bks) HarBrace.

Double Trouble Squared. Kathryn Lasky. (J). (gr. 4-7). 1991. pap. 5.95 (*0-15-224127-2*) HarBrace.

Double Truth. John Sallis. LC 94-5768. (SUNY Series in Contemporary Continental Philosophy). 214p. 1994. text ed. 59.50 (*0-7914-2268-2*); pap. text ed. 19.95 (*0-7914-2267-4*) State U NY Pr.

Double V: The Civil Rights Struggle of the Tuskegee Airman. Lawrence P. Scott. 1994. 35.00 (*0-87013-347-0*) Mich St U Pr.

Double Valve Bass Trombone A Method. Alan Raph. (Illus.). 64p. 1949. pap. 10.95 (*0-8258-0190-7*, 0-4808) Fischer Inc NY.

Double View. W. R. Moses. (Inland Seas Ser.: No. 3). 1984. pap. 10.00 (*1-55780-083-9*) Juniper Pr WI.

Double Vision. Tamara Cohen & Judith Skutch. LC 84-45364. 300p. (Orig.). 1986. pap. 9.95 (*0-89087-411-5*) Celestial Arts.

Double Vision. Kathleen Dougherty. 336p. (Orig.). 1993. mass mkt. 4.99 (*1-55773-963-3*) Diamond.

Double Vision. Diana Hendry. LC 92-52996. 272p. (J). (gr. 7-11). 1993. 14.95 (*1-56402-125-4*) Candlewick Pr.

***Double Vision.** Diana Hendry. LC 92-52996. 1995. pap. 6.99 (*1-56402-436-9*) Candlewick Pr.

Double Vision. Fred Wilson & Kellie Jones. (Illus.). 31p. (Orig.). 1987. pap. write for info. (*0-318-64545-9*) Hallwalls Inc.

Double Vision: An East-West Collaboration for Coping with Cancer. Alexandra D. Todd. LC 94-8013. 224p. 1994. 22.50 (*0-8195-5279-8*, Wesleyan Univ Pr) U Pr of New Eng.

***Double Vision: An East-West Dialogue for Coping with Cancer.** Alexandra Todd. LC 94-8013. 208p. (C). 1995. pap. 12.95 (*0-8195-6289-0*, Wesleyan Univ Pr) U Pr of New Eng.

Double Vision: Anthropologists at Law. Ed. by Randy F. Kandel. LC 92-15054. (NAPA Bulletin Ser.: Vol. 11). 1992. pap. write for info. (*0-913167-50-9*) Am Anthro Assn.

Double Vision: Four Slovene Poets. Ed. by Richard Jackson. Tr. by Michael Biggins & Ales Debeljak. 110p. 1992. pap. 16.00 (*1-881489-04-3*) Poetry Miscellany.

Double Vision: Language & Meaning in Religion. Northrop Frye. 124p. 1991. 35.00 (*0-8020-5925-2*); pap. 12.95 (*0-8020-6865-0*) U of Toronto Pr.

Double Vision: Perspectives on Gender & the Visual Arts. Ed. by Natalie H. Bluestone. LC 92-55110. 1994. write for info. (*0-8386-3540-7*) Fairleigh Dickinson.

***Double Vision: Reflections on My Heritage, Life & Profession.** Ben H. Bagdikan. LC 94-40333. 288p. 1995. 24.00 (*0-8070-7066-1*) Beacon Pr.

Double Wager. Mary Balogh. 224p. 1990. pap. 3.50 (*0-451-16477-6*, Sig) NAL-Dutton.

Double Weave, Plain & Patterned. Harriet Tidball. LC 61-669. (Guild Monographs: No. 1). (Illus.). 34p. 1960. pap. 9.95 (*0-916658-01-5*) Shuttle Craft.

***Double Wedding Ring.** John F. Flynn. 1990. 13.95 (*0-9627889-0-2*) Flynn Quilt Frame.

***Double Wedding Ring.** Peg Sutherland. 1995. pap. 3.75 (*0-373-70673-1*, 1-70673-8) Harlequin Bks.

Double Wedding Ring: New Quilts from an Old Favorite. LC 94-10943. 1994. 14.95 (*0-89145-838-7*) Collector Bks.

Double Wedding Ring Design Variations. Betty Boyink. 68p. (Orig.). 1988. pap. 13.00 (*0-9612608-9-0*) B Boyink.

Double Wedding Ring Patchwork: With Plastic Templates. Mary C. Waldrep. (Illus.). 32p. (Orig.). 1992. pap. 3.95 (*0-486-27142-0*) Dover.

Double Whammy. Carl Hiaasen. 320p. 1989. mass mkt. 6.99 (*0-446-35276-4*) Warner Bks.

Double Win. Denis Waitley. 256p. 1986. mass mkt. 4.99 (*0-425-08530-9*) Berkley Pub.

Double-Wolf. Brian Castro. 224p. (Orig.). 1993. pap. 14.95 (*0-04-442347-0*, Pub. by Allen & Unwin Aust Pty AT) IPG Chicago.

Double Woven Treasures from Old Peru. Adele Cahlander. LC 85-70065. 1985. 30.00 (*0-932394-08-6*); pap. 28.00 (*0-932394-05-1*) Dos Tejedoras.

Double-Woven Treasures from Old Peru. Adele Cahlander & Suzanne Baizerman. LC 85-70065. (Illus.). 158p. 1990. pap. 29.95 (*0-295-97031-6*) U of Wash Pr.

Double Yoke. Buchi Emecheta. LC 83-7048. 167p. 1983. pap. 8.95 (*0-8076-1128-X*) Braziller.

Double You Double You Too. Ray Obermayr. (Illus.). 40p. (Orig.). 1991. pap. 15.00 (*0-931659-11-6*) Limberlost Pr.

Double Your Income in Real Estate Sales. Danielle Kennedy. 1993. text ed. 19.95 (*0-471-57973-4*) Wiley.

Double Your Income with Your Own Home Business. Laurence J. Pino. 1991. write for info. (*0-318-68778-X*) Open U FL.

Double Your Money in Antiques in Sixty Days. George Grotz. LC 85-10280. (Illus.). 192p. 1986. mass mkt. 9.95 (*0-385-19515-X*) Doubleday.

Double Your Pleasure: The Ace Science Fiction Double. 2nd ed. James A. Corrick & Gary Lovisi. (Illus.). 88p. 1991. pap. text ed. 6.95 (*0-936071-21-4*) Gryphon Pubns.

Double Your Pleasure: The Ace SF Double. James A. Corrick. Ed. by Gary Lovisi. (Illus.). 80p. 1989. 5.95 (*0-936071-13-3*) Gryphon Pubns.

***Double Your Profits.** Bob Fifer. 1995. pap. 12.00 (*0-88730-740-X*) Harper Busn.

Double Your Profits: Seventy-Eight Ways to Cut Costs, Increase Sales & Dramatically Improve Your Bottom Line in 6 Months or Less. Bob Fifer. 1994. 23.00 (*0-88730-705-1*) Harper Busn.

Double Your Profits: Seventy-Eight Ways to Cut Costs, Increase Sales & Dramatically Improve Your Bottom Line in 6 Months or Less. Bob Fifer. 225p. 1993. write for info. (*0-9636888-0-4*) Lincoln Hall.

Double Your Reading Speed. Reading Laboratory Staff. 1986. pap. write for info. (*0-449-44250-0*, Prem) Fawcett.

Double-Yuck Magic. Kathleen Duey. 144p. (Orig.). (YA). 1991. pap. 2.99 (*0-380-76116-5*, Camelot) Avon.

Doublebreasted Operations & Pre-Hire Agreements in Construction: The Facts & the Law: A Supplement to Open Shop Construction Revisited. Herbert R. Northrup et al. LC 87-81475. (Major Industrial Research Unit Ser.: No. 62a). (Illus.). 136p. reprint ed. pap. 38.80 (*0-7837-4334-3*, 2044045) Bks Demand.

Doubled & Venerable: Further Miracles of Card Play. Terence Reese & David Bird. (Illus.). 183p. 1993. pap. 15.95 (*0-575-05425-5*, Pub. by V Gollancz UK) Trafalgar.

Doubleday Children's Atlas. Ed. by Jane Olliver. LC 86-67523. (Illus.). 96p. (J). (gr. k-6). 1987. pap. 14.00 (*0-385-23760-X*) Doubleday.

Doubleday Cookbook. Jean Anderson & Elaine Hanna. LC 85-16844. (Illus.). 984p. 1990. pap. 35.00 (*0-385-19577-X*) Doubleday.

Doubleday Crime Club Compendium, 1928-1991. Ellen Nehr. 1992. lib. bdg. 75.00 (*0-9634420-0-7*) Offspring Pr.

Doubleday Illustrated Children's Bible. Sandol Stoddard. LC 82-45340. (Illus.). 384p. (J). (gr. 4-6). 1983. pap. 25.00 (*0-385-18521-9*) Doubleday.

Doubleday Roget's Thesaurus in Dictionary Form. rev. ed. Sidney I. Landau & Ronald Bogus. LC 86-24184. 816p. 1987. Thumb-indexed. pap. 14.00 (*0-385-23997-1*) Doubleday.

Doubleheader. Kenneth Patchen. Incl. Hurrah for Anything. LC 66-17822. 1966. (*0-318-54636-1*); Poemscapes. LC 66-17822. 1966. (*0-318-54637-X*); Letter to God. LC 66-17822. 1966. (*0-318-54638-8*); LC 66-17822. 1966. Set pap. 1.50 (*0-8112-0139-2*, NDP211) New Directions.

Doubleminded Men. Philip R. Craig. (Martha's Vineyard Mystery Ser.: No. 3). 256p. 1992. text ed. 20.00 (*0-684-19396-5*, Scribners) S&S Trade.

***Doubles.** Robert Polito. LC 95-2818. (Phoenix Poets Ser.). 1995. lib. bdg. 20.00 (*0-226-67337-5*); pap. 8.95 (*0-226-67338-3*) U Ch Pr.

Doubles, Demons & Dreamers: A Collection of International Symbolist Drama. Ed. by Daniel Gerould. 1985. pap. 12.95 (*0-933826-78-8*) PAJ Pubns.

Doublescape: An Illustrated Tutorial. Dan Gookin. 1994. pap. text ed. 15.95 (*0-07-024015-9*) McGraw.

Doublespace. Hank Lazer. LC 91-66723. 192p. (Orig.). 1992. pap. 12.00 (*0-937804-44-4*) Segue NYC.

DoubleSpace: An Illustrated Tutorial. Dan Gookin. 1993. pap. 15.95 (*0-8306-4629-9*, Windcrest) TAB Bks.

Doubletake: Collective Memory & Current Art. Lynne Cooke et al. 1992. pap. 39.95 (*3-907509-18-8*, Pub. by Parkett Pubs SZ) Dist Art Pubs.

Doubletalk: Codes, Signs & Symbols. Helene Hovanec. (Illus.). (J). (gr. 7-10). 1993. pap. 1.25 (*0-553-37218-1*) Bantam.

Doubletalk: Fifty Comedy Duets for Actors. Bill Majeski. Ed. by Arthur L. Zapel. LC 90-52981. 208p. (Orig.). 1990. pap. 9.95 (*0-916260-66-6*, B186) Meriwether Pub.

Doubletalk: The Story of SALT I. Gerard C. Smith. LC 85-6222. (Illus.). 582p. (Orig.). 1985. lib. bdg. 57.00 (*0-8191-4676-5*); pap. text ed. 26.00 (*0-8191-4677-3*) U Pr of Amer.

Doubling & Incest - Repetition & Revenge: A Speculative Reading of Faulkner. John T. Irwin. LC 75-11341. 192p. (C). 1981. pap. 12.95x (*0-8018-2564-4*) Johns Hopkins.

***Doubling & Incest - Repetition & Revenge: A Speculative Reading of Faulkner.** John T. Irwin. 184p. 1995. reprint ed. pap. text ed. 15.95x (*0-8018-5231-5*) Johns Hopkins.

Doubling Development Finance, Meeting a Global Challenge. 47p. 1987. pap. 5.00 (*0-685-19345-4*, E.86. II.A.10) UN.

Doubling the Brain: On the Evolution of Brain Lateralization & Its Implications for Language. Janet Dunaif-Hattis. LC 83-48765. (American University Studies: Anthropology & Science: Ser. XI, Vol. 3). (Illus.). 215p. (Orig.). (C). 1984. text ed. 27.00 (*0-8204-0056-4*) P Lang Pubs.

Doubling the Point: Essays & Interviews. J. M. Coetzee. Ed. by David Atwell. (Illus.). 348p. 1992. 49.95 (*0-674-21517-6*); pap. 19.95 (*0-674-21518-4*) HUP.

Doubloons & Other Buried Treasure. Thomas P. Terry. (Illus.). 139p. (Orig.). 1970. pap. 5.95 (*0-939850-02-8*) Spec Pub.

Doubly Delicious. large type ed. Emma Goldrick. 1991. reprint ed. lib. bdg. 18.95 (*0-263-12683-8*) Thorndike Pr.

Doubly Timelike Surfaces. J. K. Beem & P. Y. Woo. LC 52-42839. (Memoirs Ser.: No. 1/92). 116p. 1969. pap. 16.00 (*0-8218-1292-0*, MEMO 1/92) Am Math.

Doubt & Assurance. Ed. by R. C. Sproul. LC 92-37764. 80p. (Orig.). 1993. pap. 4.99 (*0-8010-8352-4*) Baker Bk.

Doubt & Certainty in Science: A Biologist's Reflections on the Brain. John Z. Young. LC 81-20226. (Illus.). vi, 168p. 1982. reprint ed. text ed. 49.75 (*0-313-23364-0*, YODC, Greenwood Pr) Greenwood.

Doubt & Dogma in Maria Edgeworth. Mark D. Hawthorne. LC 67-63755. (University of Florida Humanities Monographs: No. 25). 100p. reprint ed. pap. 28.50 (*0-7837-4939-2*, 2044605) Bks Demand.

Doubt & Dogmatism: Studies in Hellenistic Epistemology. Malcolm Schofield et al. Ed. by Myles F. Burnyeat & Jonathan Barnes. 360p. 1989. pap. 24.95 (*0-19-824872-5*) OUP.

Doubt & Identity in Romantic Poetry. Andrew M. Cooper. LC 87-10651. 244p. (C). 1988. text ed. 35.00x (*0-300-04004-0*) Yale U Pr.

Doubt & Religious Commitment: The Role of the Will in Newman's Thought. M. Jamie Ferreira. 1980. 39.95 (*0-19-826654-5*) OUP.

Doubt, Time, Violence. Piotr Hoffman. LC 86-16127. 176p. (C). 1987. 25.00 (*0-226-34791-5*) U Ch Pr.

Doubter's Companion. John R. Saul. 1994. 22.95 (*0-02-927722-1*) Free Pr.

Doubter's Prayer Book. William Cleary. LC 93-40800. 80p. (Orig.). 1994. pap. 3.95 (*0-8091-3454-3*) Paulist Pr.

***Doubters Welcome.** Charles E. Hummel. Tr. by David L. Chen. 33p. (CHI.). 1984. pap. 0.75 (*1-56582-076-2*) Christ Renew Min.

Doubtful Guest. Edward Gorey. LC 57-10200. (Illus.). 32p. 1986. reprint ed. 11.95 (*0-926637-02-9*) P Weed Bks.

***Doubtful Guests.** Marion Douglas. 196p. (Orig.). 1993. pap. 12.95 (*0-920501-92-3*) Orca Bk Pubs.

Doubtful Prospect. large type ed. Grace Driver. 1991. 21.95 (*0-7089-2406-9*) Ulverscroft.

Doubtful Strait. Ernesto Cardenal. Tr. by John Lyons & Tamara R. Williams. LC 94-633. Date not set. 29.95 (*0-253-31318-X*); pap. 12.95 (*0-253-20903-X*) Ind U Pr.

Doubtful Year. Harold B. Wright. 50.95 (*1-56723-113-6*) Yestermorrow.

Doubting: Contemporary Perspectives on Skepticism. Ed. by Michael D. Roth & Glenn Ross. (Philosophical Studies). 225p. (C). 1990. lib. bdg. 77.50 (*0-7923-0576-0*) Kluwer Ac.

Doubting Believer: A Treatise Containing the Nature, the Kinds the Springs, & the Remedies of Doubtings Incident to Weak Believers. Obadiah Sedgwick. Ed. by Don Kistler. 214p. 1993. reprint ed. 19.95 (*1-877611-65-4*) Soli Deo Gloria.

Doubting Conscience: Donne & the Poetry of Moral Argument. Dwight Cathcart. LC 74-78985. 1975. 37.50x (*0-472-08198-5*) U of Mich Pr.

***Doubting Disease: Help for Scrupulosity & Religious Compulsions.** Joseph W. Ciarrocchi. LC 94-25222. (Integration Bks.). 208p. (Orig.). 1995. pap. 14.95 (*0-8091-3553-1*) Paulist Pr.

Doubting Love. large type ed. Sylvia E. Kirk. (Linford Romance Library). 288p. 1992. pap. 14.95 (*0-7089-7292-6*, Trailtree Bookshop) Ulverscroft.

Doubting Thomas. Yvonne Patterson. (Arch Bks.). (J). (gr. k-4). 1981. pap. 1.99 (*0-570-06144-X*, 59-1261) Concordia.

Doubts about Dualism: Implications for Development Planning. Terry G. McGee. (Working Papers Ser.: No. 78-3). 25p. 1978. pap. 5.00 (*0-686-78219-4*, CRD013) UNIPUB.

Doubts & Certainties: Working Together to Restructure Schools. Peter A. Barrett. 208p. 1991. 18.95 (*0-8106-1843-5*) NEA.

An Asterisk (*) at the beginning of an entry indicates that the title is appearing in BIP for the first time.

An Asterisk (*) at the beginning of an entry indicates that the title is appearing in BIP for the first time.

2093

D

Down a Country Road. Roy G. Taylor. LC 86-90422. (Illus.). 246p. 1986. 15.95 (*0-9613485-1-8*) J Mark.

Down a Dark Hall. Lois Duncan. 192p. (YA). (gr. 5-9). 1990. mass mkt. 3.99 (*0-440-91805-7*, LFL) Dell.

Down a Dark Hall. Lois Duncan. 192p. (J). (gr. 7 up). 1974. 15.95 (*0-316-19547-2*) Little.

***Down a Dark Hall.** Kathleen Fischer. Ed. by J. Friedland & R. Kessler. (Novel-Ties Ser.). (YA). 1992. student ed, pap. text ed. 15.95 (*0-88122-718-8*) Lrn Links.

Down a Magic Stream. Fred Hanson. (Illus.). 65p. (Orig.). (J). (gr. 2-5). 1992. pap. 9.95 (*0-9624292-2-8*) Black Willow Pr.

Down a Spiral Staircase, Never Ending: Motion as Design in the Writing of Czeslaw Milosz. Judith A. Dompkowski. (American University Studies: Slavic Languages & Literature: Ser. XII, Vol. 6). 180p. 1990. 38.95 (*0-8204-0979-0*) P Lang Pubs.

Down a Winding Road. Betty Hockett. 1985. pap. 3.50 (*0-913342-51-3*) Barclay Pr.

Down a Winding Road. Betty M. Hockett. (Illus.). 80p. (J). (gr. 3-8). 1985. pap. 4.95 (*0-943701-11-2*) George Fox Pr.

Down All the Days. Christy Brown. 266p. (C). 1991. pap. 7.95 (*0-7493-9179-0*, A0570, Pub. by Mandarin UK) Heinemann.

Down along the Old Bel-Del: The History of the Belvidere Delaware Railroad Company. Warren F. Lee. LC 86-61285. (Illus.). 350p. 1987. 34.95 (*0-9616893-0-7*) Bel-Del Ent.

Down along the Old Bel Del: The Chronology. 1987. write for info. (*0-318-61815-X*) Bel-Del Ent.

Down among the Dead. Geraldine Evans. 192p. 1994. 18.95 (*0-312-11451-6*, Pub. by Thomas Dunne Bks) St Martin.

Down among the Dead Men. Simon R. Green. 288p. (Orig.). 1993. pap. 4.50 (*0-451-45301-8*, ROC) NAL-Dutton.

Down among the Dead Men. Patricia Moyes. (Black Dagger Crime Ser.). 16.50 (*0-86220-823-8*, BD022, Black Dagger) Chivers N Amer.

Down among the Dead Men. Patricia Moyes. LC 86-9834. 240p. 1986. pap. 5.95 (*0-8050-0117-4*, Owl) H Holt & Co.

Down among the Dead Men. large type ed. Evelyn Harris. 296p. 1979. 12.00 (*0-7089-0519-6*) Ulverscroft.

Down Among the Dead Men. large type ed. Michael Hartland. 528p. 1994. 23.95 (*0-7089-3092-1*) Ulverscroft.

***Down among the Dead Men.** large type ed. Patricia Moyes. 1994. 18.95 (*0-7451-6461-7*, Scarlet Dagger Lrg Print) Chivers N Amer.

Down among the Dead Men. large type ed. Ralph Stephenson. (Linford Mystery Library). 1991. pap. 13.95 (*0-7089-7088-5*) Ulverscroft.

Down among the Dead Men & Other Essays. Bernard Van Dieren. LC 67-26732. (Essay Index Reprint Ser.). 1977. 20.95 (*0-8369-0374-9*) Ayer.

Down among the Women. Fay Weldon. 222p. 1991. pap. 8.95 (*0-89733-116-8*) Academy Chi Pubs.

Down & Back. Kit Robinson. 1978. pap. 7.50 (*0-685-99355-8*); per. 10.00 (*0-935724-58-3*) Figures.

***Down & Back: Poems of a Nervous Breakdown & Beyond.** Jack Veasey. (Illus.). 32p. 1993. pap. 6.00 (*1-879294-05-2*) Warm Spring Pr.

Down & Country. Glenn Myles. LC 74-82249. (Bebop Drawing Club Book Ser.). (Illus.). 58p. 1974. pap. 4.95 (*0-9605468-0-4*) Artmans Pr.

Down & Dirty. Linda Warren. (Loveswept Ser.: No. 699). 1994. pap. 3.50 (*0-553-44403-4*, Loveswept) Bantam.

Down & Dirty: Hollywood's Exploitation Filmmakers & Their Movies. Mike Quarles. LC 92-56683. (Illus.). 208p. 1993. lib. bdg. 29.95 (*0-89950-877-4*) McFarland & Co.

Down & Dirty: The Life & Crimes of Oklahoma Football. Charles Thompson & Allan Sonnenschein. 288p. 1991. pap. 4.95 (*0-88184-785-2*) Carroll & Graf.

Down & In: Life in the Underground. Ronald Sukenick. 288p. 1991. 18.95 (*0-9626530-2-0*) In Pr CO.

Down & Out in America: The Origins of Homelessness. Peter H. Rossi. LC 89-31598. (Illus.). 264p. 1991. pap. 10.95 (*0-226-72829-3*) U Ch Pr.

Down & Out in New York City: Homelessness: a Dishonorable Poverty. T. Guzewicz. (Illus.). 89p. 1994. lib. bdg. 24.95 (*1-56072-159-6*) Nova Sci Pubs.

Down & Out in Paris & London. George Orwell. LC 65-67354. 213p. 1972. reprint ed. pap. 7.95 (*0-15-626224-X*, Harvest Bks) HarBrace.

Down & Out in the Great Depression: Letters from the Forgotten Man. Ed. by Robert S. McElvaine. LC 82-7022. (Illus.). xvii, 251p. 1983. pap. 10.95 (*0-8078-4099-8*) U of NC Pr.

Down at Angel's. Sharon Chmielarz. LC 93-11020. (Illus.). 32p. (J). (ps-2). 1994. 14.95 (*0-395-65993-0*) Ticknor & Flds Bks Yng Read.

Down at Dinsmore. Colin Blincoe. (Illus.). 60p. (Orig.). 1991. pap. write for info. (*0-9624673-4-0*) Picture This Bks.

Down at the Billabong. Wilma Culton. LC 92-31951. (Voyages Ser.). (Illus.). (J). 1993. 3.75 (*0-383-03565-1*) SRA Schl Grp.

Down at the Bottom of the Deep Dark Sea. Rebecca C. Jones. LC 90-33981. (Illus.). 40p. (J). (ps-k). 1991. text ed. 14.95 (*0-02-747901-3*, Bradbury S&S) S&S Childrens.

Down at the Doctor's: The Sick Book. Michael J. Rosen. (Illus.). 24p. (J). (gr. k-4). 1988. 10.95 (*0-13-218942-9*, Litl Simon S&S) S&S Childrens.

Down Beat: Sixty Years of Jazz. (Illus.). 272p. (Orig.). 1995. pap. 19.95 (*0-7935-3491-7*, HL00330114) H Leonard.

Down-Beat Kill. large type ed. Peter Chambers. (Linford Mystery Library). 368p. 1994. pap. 14.95 (*0-7089-7485-6*, Linford) Ulverscroft.

Down Beat's Yearbook of Swing. Paul E. Miller. LC 78-6152. 183p. 1978. reprint ed. text ed. 35.00 (*0-313-20476-4*, MIYS, Greenwood Pr) Greenwood.

Down Below. Leonora Carrington. (Illus.). 56p. 1982. pap. 14.00 (*0-941194-17-5*) Black Swan Pr.

Down Buttermilk Lane. Barbara Mitchell. LC 90-46876. 32p. (J). (ps-3). 1993. 15.00 (*0-688-10114-3*); lib. bdg. 14.93 (*0-688-10115-1*) Lothrop.

Down by the Bay. Raffi. (Raffi Songs to Read Ser.). (Illus.). 32p. (J). (ps-2). 1988. lib. bdg. 14.00 (*0-517-56644-3*) Crown Bks Yng Read.

Down by the Bay. Raffi. LC 87-750291. (Raffi Songs to Read Ser.). (Illus.). 32p. (J). (ps-2). 1988. pap. 4.99 (*0-517-56645-1*) Crown Bks Yng Read.

Down by the Bay. 2nd ed. Henrick Drescher. (Let Me Read Ser.). 16p. (J). (ps-2). 1994. text ed. 2.95 (*0-673-36201-9*) GdYrBks.

Down by the Bay Big Book. Illus. by Dale Champlin. (J). (ps-2). 1988. pap. text ed. 14.00 (*0-922053-02-2*) N Edge Res.

Down by the Christmas Stream. Sally Bowen. (Illus.). 38p. (J). 1992. pap. 10.95 (*0-9633546-0-4*) Bowen & Assocs.

Down by the Enchanted Stream. Sally Bowen. (Illus.). 38p. (J). 1992. pap. 10.95 (*0-9633546-1-2*) Bowen & Assocs.

Down by the Glenside. Sean O'Callaghan. 1992. pap. 14.95 (*1-85635-004-5*) Dufour.

***Down by the Pond.** Margrit Cruickshank. LC 94-45724. (Illus.). (J). 1995. 16.00 (*0-689-80205-6*, Mac Bks Young Read) S&S Childrens.

Down by the River. Monte Schulz. 416p. 1992. pap. 4.99 (*0-451-17253-1*, Sig) NAL-Dutton.

***Down by the River Where the Dead Men Go.** George P. Pelecanos. 240p. 1995. 20.95 (*0-312-13056-2*) St Martin.

Down by the Riverside. Ken Yeso. (Illus.). 105p. pap. 7.95 (*0-317-04930-5*, DB12) Hudson Clearwater.

Down by the Riverside: A South Carolina Slave Community. Charles Joyner. LC 83-10369. (Blacks in the New World Ser.). (Illus.). 372p. 1984. 29.95 (*0-252-01058-2*) U of Ill Pr.

Down by the Riverside: A South Carolina Slave Community. Charles Joyner. LC 83-10369. (Blacks in the New World Ser.). (Illus.). 372p. 1986. pap. 11.95 (*0-252-01305-0*) U of Ill Pr.

Down by the Station. Illus. by Karen L. Schmidt. (Sing-a-Story Ser.). (J). 1987. audio, pap. 6.99 (*0-553-45902-3*) Bantam.

Down Came a Blackbird. Nicholas Wilde. LC 92-20209. 192p. (YA). (gr. 5 up). 1992. 15.95 (*0-8050-2001-2*, Bks Young Read) H Holt & Co.

Down Channel. R. T. McMullen. 328p. 1984. reprint ed. 18.95 (*0-916025-01-2*) Armchair Sail Pub.

Down Dairy Farm Road. C. L. Martin. LC 92-42848. (Illus.). 32p. (J). (gr. k-3). 1994. text ed. 14.95 (*0-02-762450-1*, Mac Bks Young Read) S&S Childrens.

Down East Diary by Benjamin Browne Foster. Ed. by Charles H. Foster. 1975. 19.95 (*0-89101-030-0*) U Maine Pr.

Down East Guide to the Lakes & Ponds of Mt. Desert. William V. Newlin. LC 89-50792. (Illus.). 208p. (Orig.). 1989. pap. 12.95 (*0-89272-270-3*) Down East.

Down-East Murders. J. S. Borthwick. 304p. 1991. mass mkt. 4.50 (*0-312-92606-5*) St Martin.

Down East Netting: A History & How-To of Netmaking. Barbara M. Morton. (Illus.). 1988. pap. 9.95 (*0-89272-246-0*) Down East.

***Down East Netting: A History & How-to of Netmaking.** Barbara M. Morton. LC 88-51283. (Illus.). 1988. pap. 9.95 (*0-89272-231-2*) Down East.

Down East Puzzles & Word Games. Barbara Baker & Evelyn Boyington. (Illus.). 80p. (Orig.). (J). 1989. pap. 3.95 (*0-89272-272-X*) Down East.

Down-East Spirituals & Others: Three Hundred Songs Supplementary to the Author's "Spiritual Folk-Songs of Early America" Ed. by George P. Jackson. LC 74-34317. (Music Reprint Ser.). (Illus.). 296p. 1975. reprint ed. lib. bdg. 35.00 (*0-306-70666-0*) Da Capo.

Down Easters. Basil Lubbock. (C). 1987. 114.00 (*0-85174-112-6*, Pub. by Brwn Son Ferg) St Mut.

Down-Easters, 2 vols. John Neal. LC 78-64083. reprint ed. 75.00 (*0-404-17310-1*) AMS Pr.

Down Easters: American Deep-Water Sailing Ships, 1869-1929. Basil Lubbock. 384p. 1987. reprint ed. pap. 8.95 (*0-486-25338-4*) Dover.

Down Eats: The Essential Maine Restaurant Guide. Cynthia Hacinli. (Illus.). 240p. (Orig.). 1991. pap. 8.95 (*0-88448-090-9*) Tilbury Hse.

Down Fall. Per O. Enquist. Tr. by Anna Paterson. 112p. (Orig.). 1990. pap. 9.95 (*0-7043-0130-X*, Pub. by Quartet UK) Interlink Pub.

Down for Double: An Informative Novel. Raleigh Janes. 1983. 12.95 (*0-930628-01-2*) Patchwork Pubns.

***Down for the Count: A Prison Library Handbook.** Brenda Vogel. LC 94-41630. 206p. 1995. 29.50 (*0-8108-2927-4*) Scarecrow.

Down for the Count: The Shocking Truth Behind the Mike Tyson Rape Trial. Mark Shaw. LC 93-84245. (Illus.). 262p. 1993. 19.95 (*0-915611-78-3*) Sagamore Pub.

Down from Colonialism: Mexico's Nineteenth Century Crisis. Jaime E. Rodriguez. LC 83-14331. (Popular Ser.: No. 3). 84p. (Orig.). 1983. pap. 5.50 (*0-89551-064-2*, S161) UCLA Chicano Studies.

Down from the Hills. Orval E. Faubus. (Illus.). 528p. 1980. text ed. 25.00 (*0-686-29007-0*) Faubus.

Down from the Hills Two. Orval E. Faubus. (Illus.). 534p. 1986. 25.00 (*0-318-22301-5*) Faubus.

Down from the Ivory Tower: Eight Sessions on the Roles of Men & Women. John M. Dettoni. LC 93-50844. 1994. pap. 5.99 (*1-56476-323-4*, Victor Books) SP Pubns.

Down from the Ivory Tower: Graduates & Their Jobs. Peter Herriot. LC 83-16947. 221p. 1984. text ed. 54.95 (*0-471-90308-6*) Wiley.

***Down from the Ivory Tower: Graduates & Their Jobs.** fac. ed. Peter Herriot. LC 83-16947. 235p. 1984. reprint ed. pap. 67.00 (*0-7837-8288-8*, 2049070) Bks Demand.

Down from the Mountain: The Oral History of the Hemings Family, Are They the Black Descendants of Thomas Jefferson? rev. ed. Judith P. Justus. (Illus.). 180p. reprint ed. pap. 14.95 (*0-9630554-0-2*) Jeskurtara.

Down from the Mountaintop: Black Women's Novels in the Wake of the Civil Rights Movement, 1966-1989. Melissa Walker. 248p. (C). 1991. text ed. 30.00 (*0-300-04855-6*) Yale U Pr.

Down from the Mountaintop: Black Women's Novels in the Wake of the Civil Rights Movement, 1966-1989. Melissa Walker. 226p. (C). 1993. reprint ed. pap. text ed. 13.00 (*0-300-05432-7*) Yale U Pr.

Down from the Pedestal: Moving Beyond Idealized Images of Womanhood. Maxine Harris. LC 93-192. 1994. 22.50 (*0-385-46994-2*) Doubleday.

***Down from the Pedestal: Moving Beyond the Idealized Images of Womanhood.** Maxine Harris. 1995. pap. 12.95 (*0-385-46995-0*, Anchor NY) Doubleday.

Down from the Sky. Geraldine A. Snyder & Paul Lenzi. 49p. (Orig.). 1990. 3.75 (*0-87129-020-0*, D52) Dramatic Pub.

Down from Troy: A Doctor Comes of Age. Richard Selzer. 1993. pap. 10.95 (*0-316-78065-0*) Little.

Down from Troy: A Doctor Comes of Age. large type ed. Richard Selzer. LC 93-17747. 1993. 23.95 (*0-7927-1640-X*, Curley Lrg Print); pap. 21.95 (*0-7927-1639-6*, Curley Lrg Print) Chivers N Amer.

Down Garden Paths. William H. Gerdts. LC 83-16335. (Illus.). 144p. 1984. 35.00 (*0-8386-3214-9*) Fairleigh Dickinson.

Down Grade Controversy. C. H. Spurgeon. 1978. pap. 4.95 (*1-56186-211-8*) Pilgrim Pubns.

Down Highway One: Journeys Through Vietnam & Cambodia. Sue Downie. 1993. pap. 14.95 (*1-86373-322-1*, Pub. by Allen & Unwin Aust Pty AT) IPG Chicago.

Down-Home. Roger Karshner. 64p. (Orig.). 1987. pap. 7.95 (*0-940669-00-5*) Dramaline Pubns.

Down Home. George Mettler. 352p. (Orig.). 1981. pap. 2.95 (*0-449-14403-8*, GM) Fawcett.

Down Home: A History of Afro-American Short Fiction from Its Beginning to the End of the Harlem Renaissance. Robert Bone. (Morningside Bk.). 350p. 1988. text ed. 54.00 (*0-231-06858-1*); pap. text ed. 16.50 (*0-231-06859-X*) Col U Pr.

Down Home & Uptown. Sylvia W. Holton. LC 82-48270. 216p. 1984. 39.50 (*0-8386-3130-4*) Fairleigh Dickinson.

***Down Home Cooking the New, Healthier Way.** Ed. by Reader's Digest Editors. LC 94-13511. (Illus.). 384p. 1995. 28.00 (*0-89577-646-4*) RD Assn.

Down-Home Gallery of American Wildlife. Ralph J. McDonald. (Illus.). 101p. 1980. 39.95 (*0-9605428-1-7*) Countryside Studio.

Down-Home Gallery of American Wildlife. deluxe limited ed. Ralph J. McDonald. (Illus.). 101p. 1980. 95.00 (*0-9605428-0-9*) Countryside Studio.

Down Home Guide to the Blues: Over 3,000 Annotated Entries on Blues & Gospel Records, Cassettes, & Compact Discs. Frank Scott. LC 90-37638. (Illus.). 200p. (Orig.). 1991. pap. 14.95 (*1-55652-130-8*) A cappella Bks.

Down Home Gynecology. Marvin Jaffee & Mary S. Jaffee. LC 88-71122. (Illus.). 106p. (Orig.). 1989. pap. 9.00 (*0-916383-63-6*) Aegina Pr.

Down Home Heifer Heist. Eve K. Sandstrom. 1994. mass mkt. 3.99 (*0-373-26153-5*, 1-26153-6) Harlequin Bks.

Down Home Heifer Heist: A Sam & Nicky Titus Mystery. Eve K. Sandstrom. 256p. 1993. text ed. 20.00 (*0-684-19428-7*, Scribners) S&S Trade.

Down Home Murder. Toni L. Kelner. 304p. 1993. mass mkt. 3.99 (*0-8217-4196-9*) Zebra.

Down Home Southern Cooking. Lamont Burns. 1987. pap. 9.50 (*0-9627145-2-6*, Cyrus Pr) Waterside Prodns.

Down-Home Talk: An Outrageous Dictionary of Colorful Country Expressions. Diann S. Smith. 62p. (Orig.). 1986. pap. 3.95 (*0-932531-02-4*) Emerald City.

Down-Home Texas Cooking: Generations of Traditional Texas Recipes. James Stroman. LC 94-50665. 1994. reprint ed. write for info. (*0-88415-183-2*) Gulf Pub.

Down Home Ways: Old-Fangled Skills for Making Hundreds of Simple, Useful Things. Jerry M. Johnson. LC 78-58164. 1978. write for info. (*0-8129-0788-4*, Times Bks) Random.

***Down-Home Wholesome: 300 Low-Fat Recipes from a New Soul Kitchen.** Danella Carter. (Illus.). 372p. 1995. 24.95 (*0-525-93909-1*, Dutton) NAL-Dutton.

***Down Home Wisdom from a City Slicker.** Ken Vegotsky. (Love Living & Live Loving Ser.). 1996. pap. write for info. (*1-886508-18-6*, Ages Pubns); audio write for info. (*1-886508-19-4*, Ages Pubns) Adi Gaia Esalen.

***Down Home with the Chief & Miss Maggie.** Jimmy B. Taylor. (Illus.). 156p. (Orig.). 1995. pap. 14.95 (*0-9646898-0-4*) Ad Center.

Down Illinois Rivers. George W. May. (Illus.). 400p. 1981. 16.00 (*0-9605566-5-6*) G W May.

***Down in Africa.** Hajara E. Mdurvwa. (Illus.). 16p. (J). 1995. pap. 5.95 (*0-8059-3689-0*) Dorrance.

Down in My Heart. 2nd ed. William Stafford. 96p. 1985. reprint ed. pap. 9.95 (*0-930769-00-7*) Bench Pr SC.

Down in Puerto Rico. G. M. Fowles. 1976. lib. bdg. 250.00 (*0-8490-1380-1*) Gordon Pr.

Down in Tennessee & Back by Way of Richmond. James R. Gilmore. LC 76-157368. (Black Heritage Library Collection). 1977. 21.95 (*0-8369-8806-X*) Ayer.

Down in the Dumps: Administration of the Unfair Trade Laws. Ed. by Richard Boltuck & Robert E. Litan. 360p. 1991. 36.95 (*0-8157-1020-8*); pap. 16.95 (*0-8157-1019-4*) Brookings.

Down in the Holler: A Gallery of Ozark Folk Speech. Vance Randolph & George P. Wilson. 330p. 1979. pap. 15.95 (*0-8061-1535-1*) U of Okla Pr.

***Down in the Marvelous Deep: A Book of Sea Poems.** Comp. by Sophie Windham. 1996. write for info. (*0-615-00240-4*) Scholastic Inc.

Down in the Piney Woods. Ethel F. Smothers. LC 91-328. 144p. (J). (gr. 5-9). 1992. 14.00 (*0-679-80360-2*); lib. bdg. 14.99 (*0-679-90360-7*) Knopf Bks Yng Read.

Down in the Piney Woods. Ethel F. Smothers. 156p. (J). (gr. 3-7). 1994. pap. 3.99 (*0-679-84714-6*, Bullseye Bks) Random Bks Yng Read.

Down in the Sea: The Crab. Patricia Kite. LC 93-21494. (J). 1994. write for info. (*0-8075-1709-7*) A Whitman.

Down in the Sea: The Jellyfish. Patricia Kite. Ed. by Abby Levine. LC 92-12834. (Illus.). 24p. (J). (ps-3). 1993. 13.95 (*0-8075-1712-7*) A Whitman.

Down in the Sea: The Octopus. Patricia Kite. Ed. by Abby Levine. LC 92-12284. (Illus.). 24p. (J). 1993. 13.95 (*0-8075-1715-1*) A Whitman.

Down in the Sea: The Sea Slug. Patricia Kite. LC 93-3765. (J). 1994. write for info. (*0-8075-1717-8*) A Whitman.

Down in the Valley. Michael Snedeker. 190p. (Orig.). 1993. pap. 10.00 (*0-931425-23-9*) Clear Glass.

Down in the Valley: A Satirical Romance. William Schaffer. LC 94-90226. (Orig.). 1994. pap. 12.95 (*0-9641498-6-9*) Temblor Pr.

***Down in the Zero.** Vachss. pap. 11.00 (*0-679-76066-0*) Random.

Down in the Zero. Andrew Vachss. 1994. pap. 21.00 (*0-679-43328-7*) Knopf.

***Down in Zero.** Andrew Vachss. Date not set. pap. write for info. (*0-679-76087-3*) Random.

Down Is up for Aaron Eagle: A Mother's Spiritual Journey with Downs Syndrome. Vicki Nobel. LC 92-56118. 224p. 1993. 17.00 (*0-06-250737-0*) Harper SF.

Down-Island Caribbean Cookery. Virginie Elbert & George Elbert. (Illus.). 352p. 1991. 24.95 (*0-671-67203-7*) S&S Trade.

***Down Jacket Syndrome.** Sara Klepe. 140p. (Orig.). 1995. pap. 7.95 (*0-7610-0159-X*) NW Pub.

Down Ladybug Lane. LC 92-62555. (Little Look-Around Bks.). (Illus.). 10p. (J). (ps-k). 1992. 3.99 (*0-89577-481-X*) RD Assn.

Down Mailer's Way. Robert Soltaroff. LC 73-5406. 289p. 1974. 22.50 (*0-252-00398-5*) Lib Soc Sci.

Down Mailer's Way. Robert Solotaroff. LC 73-5406. 301p. reprint ed. pap. 85.80 (*0-317-28193-3*, 2022782) Bks Demand.

Down Mare Creek Road. Ernestine A. Collins. Ed. by Mark Sohn & Kathy Sohn. 148p. 1993. 7.95 (*0-9616911-9-0*) M F Sohn Pubns.

Down Melody Lane. G. N. Joshi. (Illus.). 187p. 1984. 20.00 (*0-86131-175-2*, Pub. by Orient Longman Ltd II) Apt Bks.

Down Memory Lane. Arthur Murray. (Ballroom Dance Ser.). 1986. lib. bdg. 79.95 (*0-8490-3370-5*) Gordon Pr.

Down Memory Lane. Arthur Murray. (Ballroom Dance Ser.). 1985. lib. bdg. 120.00 (*0-87700-697-0*) Revisionist Pr.

Down Memory Lane. Parthasarathi Rajagopalachari. 384p. 1993. 15.00 (*0-945242-23-9*) Shri Ram Chandra.

Down Memory Lane: A Pictorial History of Ballroom & Social Dancing. Arthur Murray et al. (Ballroom Dance Ser.). 1989. lib. bdg. 79.95 (*0-8490-3966-5*) Gordon Pr.

Down Memory Lane: From Patchogue to Upstate New York. Albert T. Skinner. (Illus.). 219p. (Orig.). 1990. pap. 10.00 (*1-55787-060-8*, Empire State Bks) Hrt of the Lakes.

Down Memory Lane: Reading Between the Wars. Roger Searing. 96p. 1987. 30.00 (*0-905392-56-6*) St Mut.

Down Memory Lane: Topics & Ideas for Reminiscence Groups. Beckie Karras. (Illus.). 138p. (Orig.). 1985. pap. 18.95 (*1-879633-00-0*) Eldersong.

Down North on the Labrador. Wilfred T. Grenfell. LC 70-122712. (Short Story Index Reprint Ser.). 1977. 19.95 (*0-8369-3545-4*) Ayer.

***Down on Grandpa's Farm Big Book.** Illus. by Bryce Kimberling. (J). (ps-2). 1994. pap. text ed. 14.00 (*0-922053-30-8*) N Edge Res.

Down on T Wharf: The Boston Fisheries As Seen Through The Photographs of Henry D. Fisher. Andrew W. German. (American Maritime Library: Vol. 10). (Illus.). xvi, 160p. 1982. 21.95 (*0-913372-26-9*) Mystic Seaport.

Down on the Corner. Kevin Fitzpatrick. LC 86-90561. 64p. (Orig.). 1987. pap. 4.95 (*0-935697-02-0*) Midwest Villages.

Down on the Farm. Karen T. Dauer. LC 93-60298. (Illus.). 150p. (Orig.). 1993. pap. 11.95 (*0-9630213-2-X*) Winsted Pubns.

***Down on the Farm.** Greg Scelsa. (Emergent Reader Bks.). 16p. 1994. 2.49 (*0-916119-65-3*) Creat Teach Pr.

Down on the Farm: A Story of Stanford Football. Fred Merrick. LC 75-12202. (College Sports Book Ser.). 1975. 12.95 (*0-87397-070-5*) Strode.

Down on the Funny Farm: A Step Two Book. P. E. King. LC 85-11893. (Step into Reading Bks.). (Illus.). 48p. (J). (gr. 1-3). 1986. pap. 3.99 (*0-394-87460-9*) Random Bks Yng Read.

Down on the Funny Farm: A Step Two Book. P. E. King. LC 85-11893. (Step into Reading Bks.). (Illus.). 48p. (J). (gr. 1-3). 1986. lib. bdg. 7.99 (*0-394-97460-3*) Random Bks Yng Read.

Down on the Slough: Poems by Ronald K. Webb. Ronald K. Webb. (Illus.). 20p. (Orig.). 1989. pap. 5.00 (*0-9620335-1-0*) R K Webb.

An Asterisk (*) at the beginning of an entry indicates that the title is appearing in BIP for the first time.

D

An Asterisk (*) at the beginning of an entry indicates that the title is appearing in BIP for the first time.

D

Downing Legends. John W. De Forest. (Collected Works of John W. De Forest). 1988. reprint ed. lib. bdg. 59.00 (0-7812-1167-0) Rprt Serv.

Downing Legends see Collected Works of John W. De Forest

Downing Legends-Stories in Rhyme. John W. DeForest. Incl. Witch of Shiloh. 1901. (0-318-51811-2); Last of the Wampanoags. 1901. (0-318-51812-0); Gentle Earl. 1901. (0-318-51813-9); Enchanted Voyage. 1901. (0-318-51814-7); 1901. 100.00 (0-685-91097-0) Elliots Bks.

Downing of Flight Six Heavy. Perry Lafferty. 1990. 18.95 (1-55611-213-0) D I Fine.

Downing of Flight Six Heavy. Perry Lafferty. 384p. 1992. mass mkt. 4.99 (1-55817-622-5, Pinnacle NY) Windsor NY.

Downing Street: The War Years. John Martin. (Illus.). 200p. 1992. 39.95 (0-7475-0838-0, Pub. by Bloomsbury Pub Ltd UK) Trafalgar.

***Downing Street Years.** Margaret Thatcher. 928p. 1995. pap. 16.00 (0-06-092563-9, PL) HarpC.

Downing Street Years. limited ed. Margaret Thatcher. (Illus.). 512p. 1993. 150.00 (0-06-017075-1, HarpT) HarpC.

Downland Shepherds. Gordon Beningfield et al. (Illus.). 192p. 1991. pap. text ed. 16.00 (0-7509-0021-0) A Sutton Pub.

Downlink Directory 1985-1986, Vol. 1. Ed. by Helen Lauck & Mary A. Roybal. 294p. (Orig.). 1985. pap. 125.00 (0-937007-01-3) V A Ostendorf.

Downlink Directory, 1987, Vol. 2. Ed. by Mary A. Roybal & Virginia A. Ostendorf. 555p. (Orig.). 1987. pap. 125.00 (0-317-56097-2) V A Ostendorf.

***Downloaders Companion for Windows.** Scott Meyers. 192p. 1994. disk, pap. 19.95 (0-13-342254-2) P-H.

Downloading-Uploading: Online Databases & Catalogs. Ed. by Bella H. Weinberg & James A. Benson. LC 85-9414. (Library Hi Tech Special Studies Ser.: No. 1). 1985. pap. 45.00 (0-87650-195-1) Pierian.

Downriver. Will Hobbs. (YA). (gr. 7 up). 1992. mass mkt. 3.99 (0-553-29717-1, Starfire) Bantam.

Downriver. Will Hobbs. LC 90-1044. 208p. (YA). (gr. 7 up). 1991. text ed. 14.95 (0-689-31690-9, Atheneum Bks Young) S&S Childrens.

Downriver: A Yellowstone Journey. Dean Krakel, II. LC 86-22087. (Illus.). 272p. 1987. 16.95 (0-87156-708-3) Sierra.

Downriver: A Yellowstone Journey. Dean Krakel, II. LC 86-22087. 228p. 1988. pap. 8.95 (0-87156-785-7) Sierra.

Downriver: Currents of Style in Louisiana Painting, 1800-1950. Estill C. Pennington. LC 90-6932. (Illus.). 208p. 1991. 49.95 (0-88289-800-0) Pelican.

Downriver: Orrin H. Ingram & the Empire Lumber Company. Charles E. Twining. LC 74-34404. (Illus.). 344p. 1975. 17.50 (0-87020-149-2) State Hist Soc Wis.

Downriver: or The Vessels of Wrath: A Narrative in Twelve Tales. Iain Sinclair. LC 92-36509. 448p. 1993. 23.00 (0-679-42062-2) Random.

Down's Syndrome: A Comprehensive Bibliography. Pueschel & Steinberg. 1980. 50.00 (0-685-42735-8) Acad Guild.

Down's Syndrome: Advances in Biomedicine & the Behavioral Sciences. Pueschel & Rynders. 1982. 65.00 (0-938552-50-3) Acad Guild.

Down's Syndrome: An Introduction for Parents. rev. ed. Cliff Cunningham. 251p. 1988. pap. 12.95 (0-914797-52-2) Brookline Bks.

***Down's Syndrome: Children Growing Up: a Longitudinal Perspective.** Janet Carr. (Illus.). 170p. (C). 1995. write for info. (0-521-46532-X); pap. write for info. (0-521-46933-3) Cambridge U Pr.

Down's Syndrome: The Psychology of Mongolism. D. Gibson. LC 77-87381. 1979. 79.95 (0-521-21914-0) Cambridge U Pr.

Down's Syndrome: Today's Health Care Issues. Ira Lott & Ernest McCoy. 212p. 1992. text ed. 69.95 (0-471-56181-9, Wiley-Liss); pap. text ed. 34.95 (0-471-56184-3, Wiley-Liss) Wiley.

Downscaling: Simplify & Enrich Your Lifestyle. Dave Babbitt & Kathy Babbitt. 192p. 1993. pap. 9.99 (0-8024-1784-1) Moody.

Downscoping: How to Tame the Diversified Firm. Robert E. Hoskisson & Michael A. Hitt. LC 93-21408. (Illus.). 224p. 1994. 24.95 (0-19-507843-8) OUP.

Downside of Drugs. Regina Avraham. (Encyclopedia of Psychoactive Drugs Ser.: No. 2). (Illus.). 112p. (YA). (gr. 5 up). 1988. lib. bdg. 19.95 (1-55546-232-4) Chelsea Hse.

Downsize Your Debt: How to Take Control of Your Personal Finances. Andrew Feinberg. 224p. (Orig.). 1993. pap. 10.95 (0-14-013428-X, Penguin Bks) Viking Penguin.

Downsized but Not Out: How to Get Your Next Computer Job. Alan Simon. 1994. text ed. 30.00 (0-07-057614-9); pap. text ed. 17.95 (0-07-057615-7) McGraw.

Downsizing: A Collection of Materials for Senior Executives & Managers. rev. ed. Dorri Jacobs. (Change: How to Live with, Manage, Create & Enjoy It Ser.). 1992. spiral bd. 75.50 (0-916471-26-8) Progs on Change.

Downsizing: A Collection of Materials for Senior Executives & Managers. 2nd rev. ed. Dorri Jacobs. (Change: How to Live with, Manage, Create & Enjoy It Ser.). 1992. spiral bd. 95.00 (0-916471-24-1) Progs on Change.

Downsizing: Creative Approaches to Corporate Change. Steven Teske. LC 91-25942. 1991. 40.00 (1-55871-225-9, BSP215) BNA.

Downsizing: How to Get Big Gains from Smaller Computer Systems. Richard H. Baker. 1992. text ed. 40.00 (0-07-004563-1); pap. text ed. 29.95 (0-07-004564-X) McGraw.

Downsizing: Reshaping the Corporation for the Future. Robert M. Tomasko. LC 87-47709. 336p. 1990. pap. 17.95 (0-8144-7734-8) AMACOM.

Downsizing: Strategies for Success in the Modern Computer World. Dan Trimmer. (C). 1993. pap. text ed. 30.25 (0-201-62409-5) Addison-Wesley.

Downsizing Computer Systems. Ken Mann & Gary Jones. (Illus.). 350p. 1995. pap. 29.95 (0-7506-0907-9) Buttrwrth-Heinemann.

Downsizing Defense. Ethan B Kapstein. LC 93-5636. 230p. 1993. 36.95 (0-87187-945-X) Congr Quarterly.

Downsizing Detroit: The Future of the U. S. Automobile Industry. Narisimhan P. Kannan. Ed. by Kathy ReBibo et al. LC 82-11271. 202p. 1982. text ed. 49.95 (0-275-90831-3, C0831, Praeger Pubs) Greenwood.

Downsizing for Client/Server Applications. Paul Kavanagh. (Illus.). 400p. 1994. pap. 39.95 (0-12-402680-X, AP Prof) Acad Pr.

Downsizing for Cost-Effective Enterprise Computing. Computer Technology Research Corp. Staff. (Illus.). 144p. (Orig.). 1993. pap. 210.00 (1-56607-006-6) Comput Tech Res.

***Downsizing Future USAF Fighter Forces: Living Within the Constraints of History.** Kevin N. Lewis. LC 94-48047. 130p. 1995. pap. text ed. 15.00 (0-8330-1621-0) Rand Corp.

Downsizing Information Systems. BSG Inc. Staff. (Illus.). 500p. (Orig.). 1992. pap. 39.95 (0-672-30153-9) Sams.

Downsizing the News: Network Cutbacks in the Nation's Capital. Penn Kimball. LC 93-49001. 200p. (C). 1994. text ed. 30.00 (0-943875-58-7); pap. 13.95 (0-943875-59-5) W Wilson Ctr Pr.

Downsizing the United States Government: A Simple, Straightforward, Proven Approach That Can Cut the Government Payroll by up to Fifty Percent. Albert G. Young. 136p. (Orig.). 1995. pap. 19.95 (0-9641397-0-7) Com Sense VA.

Downsizing Without Disaster. Lynn Tylczak. Ed. by Nancy Shotwell. LC 90-83483. (Fifty-Minute Ser.). (Illus.). 79p. (Orig.). 1991. pap. 9.95 (1-56052-081-7) Crisp Pubns.

Downstairs in the Royal Navy. W. B. Harvey. (C). 1987. 24.00 (0-85174-352-8, Pub. by Brwn Son Ferg) St Mut.

***Downstate Illinois Business Directory, 1994-95.** rev. ed. American Business Directories Staff. 1440p. 1994. 325.00 (1-56105-551-4) Am Busn Direct.

***Downstate Illinois Business Directory, 1995-96, Vol. 3 Downstate.** rev. ed. 1995. 325.00 (1-56105-781-9) Am Busn Direct.

Downstream Processing & Bioseparation: Recovery & Purification of Biological Products. Ed. by Jean-Francois P. Hamel et al. LC 89-49336. (ACS Symposium Ser.: No. 419). 303p. 1990. 69.95 (0-8412-1738-6) Am Chemical.

Downtiming the Night Side. Jack L. Chalker. 288p. (Orig.). 1993. reprint ed. mass mkt. 4.99 (0-671-72170-4) Baen Bks.

Downtonian & Devonian Vertebrates of Spitsbergen: Pt. 1, Family Cephalaspidea, Det Norske Videnskaps-Akademii Oslo, Skrifter M Svalbard G Nordishav et, Nr. 12, 2 vols. Erik A. Stensio. Ed. by Stephen J. Gould. LC 79-8553. (History of Paleontology Ser.). (Illus.). 1980. reprint ed. lib. bdg. 88.95 (0-405-12746-4) Ayer.

Downtonian & Devonian Vertebrates of Spitsbergen: Pt. 1, Family Cephalaspidea, Det Norske Videnskaps-Akademii Oslo, Skrifter M Svalbard G Nordishav et, Nr. 12, 2 vols., 1. Erik A. Stensio. Ed. by Stephen J. Gould. LC 79-8553. (History of Paleontology Ser.). (Illus.). 1980. reprint ed. lib. bdg. 44.95 (0-405-12747-2) Ayer.

Downtonian & Devonian Vertebrates of Spitsbergen: Pt. 1, Family Cephalaspidea, Det Norske Videnskaps-Akademii Oslo, Skrifter M Svalbard G Nordishav et, Nr. 12, 2 vols., 2. Erik A. Stensio. Ed. by Stephen J. Gould. LC 79-8553. (History of Paleontology Ser.). (Illus.). 1980. reprint ed. lib. bdg. 44.95 (0-405-12748-0) Ayer.

Downtown. Norma F. Mazer. 208p. 1984. pap. 3.50 (0-380-88534-4, Flare) Avon.

Downtown. Norma F. Mazer. LC 84-91105. 192p. (YA). (gr. 7 up). 1984. 15.00 (0-688-03859-X) Morrow Jr Bks.

Downtown. Ed McBain. 302p. 1991. 20.00 (0-688-08736-1) Morrow.

Downtown. Michael Musto. 1986. 10.95 (0-317-53541-2, Vin) Random.

Downtown. A. Siddons. 352p. 1994. 24.00 (0-06-017934-1, HarpT) HarpC.

***Downtown.** braille ed. Ed McBain. 495p. 1993. text ed. 39.60 (1-56956-500-7, BR8899) W A T Braille.

Downtown. large type ed. Ed McBain. 1992. 18.95 (0-7927-1112-2, E0032, Eagle Lrg Print) Chivers N Amer.

Downtown. large type ed. Ed McBain. 1992. pap. 17.95 (0-7927-1111-4, Paragon Lrg Print) Chivers N Amer.

Downtown. large type ed. Anne R. Siddons. LC 94-17134. 647p. 1994. 23.95 (0-8161-7410-5) Hall.

Downtown. large type ed. Anne R. Siddons. LC 94-17134. 1995. pap. 19.95 (0-8161-7411-3) Hall.

Downtown. Ed McBain. 352p. 1993. reprint ed. mass mkt. 5.99 (0-380-70761-6) Avon.

***Downtown Berlin - Building the Metropolitan Max.** A. Burg. Ed. by H. Stimmann. 218p. 1995. 89.00 (0-8176-5062-8); 69.00 (0-8176-5063-6) Spr-Verlag.

Downtown Birmingham: Architectural & Historical Walking Tour Guide. 2nd ed. Marjorie L. White. LC 77-608282. (Illus.). 142p. 1980. pap. 6.95 (0-943994-04-7) Birmingham Hist Soc.

Downtown Birmingham-Architectural & Historical Walking Tour Guide. Marjorie L. White. Ed. by Gray G. Plosser & Richard W. Sprague. LC 77-608282. (Illus.). 144p. 1980. pap. 6.95 (0-943994-03-9) Birmingham Hist Soc.

Downtown Boy. Laura Battanyi-Petose. (YA). 1993. mass mkt. 3.50 (0-06-106154-9, Harp PBks) HarpC.

Downtown Design Guidelines: A Handbook for Preservation, New Construction & Loft Re-Use. Illus. by Michael Klement. 119p. (Orig.). 1989. pap. 10.00 (1-882574-04-4) Ann Arbor Hist.

Downtown Desperadoes. Sigmund Brouwer. (Accidental Detective Ser.). 132p. (J). 1991. pap. 4.99 (0-89693-860-3) SP Pubns.

***Downtown Desperados.** Sigmund Brouwer. LC 94-24747. 132p. (YA). (gr. 8-12). 1995. pap. 4.99 (1-56476-377-3, 6-3377, Victor Books) SP Pubns.

***Downtown Development Handbook.** Ralph J. Basile et al. LC 80-50928. (Community Builders Handbook Ser.). (Illus.). 278p. 1980. reprint ed. pap. 79.30 (0-7837-8935-1, 2049645) Bks Demand.

Downtown Discovery Tour. rev. ed. Marjorie L. White. (Illus.). 44p. (Orig.). (J). (gr. 3-9). 1984. pap. 5.00 (0-943994-07-1) Birmingham Hist Soc.

Downtown Improvement Districts: Creating Money & Power for Downtown Action. 80p. 1986. 36.00 (0-317-05050-8) Natl Coun Econ Dev.

Downtown Inc. How America Rebuilds Cities. Bernard J. Frieden & Lynne B. Sagalyn. (Illus.). 345p. 1989. 35.00 (0-262-06128-7) MIT Pr.

Downtown, Inc. How America Rebuilds Cities. Bernard J. Frieden & Lynne B. Sagalyn. (Illus.). 440p. 1989. pap. 17.95 (0-262-56059-3) MIT Pr.

Downtown Jews: Portraits of an Immigrant Generation. Ronald Sanders. (Illus.). 416p. 1987. reprint ed. pap. 10.95 (0-486-25510-7) Dover.

Downtown Lady. Cissy Lacks. LC 76-41077. 1976. pap. 2.95 (0-933530-00-5) Beanie Bks.

Downtown Linkages. ULI Policy Education Program Staff. 71p. 1985. pap. 26.95 (0-87420-643-X) Urban Land.

Downtown Office Growth & the Role of Public Transit. James T. Black et al. LC 82-50921. (Illus.). 128p. (Orig.). reprint ed. pap. 36.50 (0-8357-8102-X, 2033946) Bks Demand.

Downtown Retail Development: Conditions for Success & Project Profiles. J. Thomas Black et al. LC 83-81784. 90p. (Orig.). 1983. pap. 32.95 (0-87420-650-2, D35) Urban Land.

Downtown Retail Revitalization: Strategies to Maximize Your Market. Carol Patrylick. Ed. by Jenny Murphy. 42p. (Orig.). 1989. pap. 21.50 (0-317-04898-8) Natl Coun Econ Dev.

Downtown Safety, Security & Economic Development. 148p. 1986. 48.50 (0-317-05047-8) Natl Coun Econ Dev.

Downtown Safety, Security, & Economic Development. Citizens Crime Commission of New York City Staff & Regional Plan Association Staff. (Regional Plan Technical Report Ser.: No. 3). 105p. 1986. pap. text ed. 45.00 (0-318-19016-8) Regional Plan Assn.

Downtown Safety, Security & Economic Development. Citizens Crime Commission of New York Staff & Regional Plan Association Staff. LC 86-50000. (Illus.). 148p. (Orig.). 1986. pap. 38.00 (0-915910-22-5) Downtown Res.

Downtown Street Views (c. 1990) of Early Tall Buildings from the Bayside Cities & Tidewater Towns of Northern California: A Main Street California (c. 1930) Sentimental Sketchbook Collection. Dickinson Weber. LC 91-66476. (Downtown (the California Region) Ser.: No. 4). (Illus.). 136p. (Orig.). 1992. pap. 15.00 (0-936721-03-0) Sandscape Pr.

Downturn & Economic Recovery in Ghana: Impacts on the Poor. Harold Alderman. (Monograph Ser.). (Illus.). 121p. (C). 1991. pap. text ed. 12.00 (1-56401-010-4) Cornell Food.

Downward Bound: A Mad Guide to Rockclimbing. rev. ed. Warren Harding. (Illus.). 198p. 1975. reprint ed. pap. 10.95 (0-89732-101-4) Menasha Ridge.

Downwardly Mobile for Conscience Sake: Ten Autobiographical Sketches: Each a Personal Search for Justice, Peace, & Eco-sanity. Anne Near et al. 206p. (Orig.). 1993. pap. 10.00 (0-931803-03-9) T Paine Inst.

***Downwardly Mobile for Conscience Sake: Ten Autobiographical Sketches: Each a Personal Search for Justice, Peace, & Eco-sanity.** rev. ed. Dorothy N. Andersen et al. (Illus.). 206p. 1995. pap. 10.00 (0-931803-04-7) T Paine Inst.

Downy Duckling. (Rhyming Stories Ser.: No. 401-5). (Illus.). (J). (ps-00). 3.50 (0-7214-0210-0) Ladybird Bks.

Downy Duckling. Demi. (Soft & Furry Board Bks.). (Illus.). 12p. (J). (ps). 1987. bds. 6.95 (0-448-19153-9, G&D) Putnam Pub Group.

Downy Mildews. Ed. by D. N. Spencer. LC 81-66686. 1981. text ed. 248.00 (0-12-656860-X) Acad Pr.

Downy, Pistachio & Fanny. Anne-Marie Chapouton. (I Love to Read Collection). (Illus.). 48p. (J). (gr. 3-8). 1990. lib. bdg. 12.79 (0-89565-808-9) Childs World.

Dowry. Ginger Whittaker. (Orig.). 1989. pap. 3.50 (0-87067-332-7, BH332-7) Holloway.

***Dowry.** rev. ed. Ginger Whittaker. Ed. by Edwina Walker. LC 95-75612. 166p. Date not set. 18.00 (1-886911-01-0) GHAAWG.

Dowry & Position of Women of India. Madan P. Chandra. 211p. 1986. 44.95 (81-210-0047-5) Asia Bk Corp.

Dowry & Proection to Married Women: With up-to-Date Amendments. Paras Diwan. (C). 1990. 138.00 (0-89771-153-X) St Mut.

Dowry & Protection to Married Women. Paras Diwan. 1987. 37.50 (0-8364-2086-1, Pub. by Deep) S Asia.

Dowry of Death. Melvin A. Casberg. (Illus.). 240p. (Orig.). 1984. pap. 6.95 (0-89407-062-2) Strawberry Hill.

Dowry of Uncommon Women: "She Married a Flying Officer & a Gentleman Which She Knew to Be an Enviable Thing." Jane Metcalf. (Orig.). 1988. pap. 12.95 (0-9619194-4-2) X-Press Pubns.

Dow's Chemical Exposure Index Guide. 38p. 1994. 30.00 (0-8169-0647-5) Am Inst Chem Eng.

***Dow's Fire & Explosion Index Hazard Classification Guide.** 7th ed. LC 80-29237. 74p. 1994. 40.00 (0-8169-0623-8, T80) Am Inst Chem Eng.

***Dowsing.** Naomi Ozaniec. (For Beginners Ser.). (Illus.). 112p. 1995. pap. 9.95 (0-340-60882-X, Pub. by Hodder & Stoughton Ltd UK) Trafalgar.

Dowsing for Everyone. Harvey Howells. LC 78-26713. (Illus.). 1979. 8.95 (0-8289-0341-7) Viking Penguin.

***Dowsing for Love.** Dick Croy. LC 94-62198. 320p. (Orig.). 1995. 21.95 (0-9645252-0-8); pap. 14.95 (0-9645252-1-6) Watrshed Bks.

Dowsing for Treasures. Russ Simmons. (Illus.). 84p. (Orig.). 1984. pap. text ed. write for info. (0-931740-01-0) Dowsing Inst.

***Dowsing Rod Kit.** Comp. by Sig Lonegren. (Illus.). 160p. 1995. boxed 27.95 (0-8048-3049-5) C E Tuttle.

Doxology: The Praise of God in Worship, Doctrine & Life: A Systematic Theology. Geoffrey Wainwright. 1984. pap. 16.95 (0-19-520433-6) OUP.

Doyayo Language: Selected Studies. Elisabeth Wiering & Marinus Wiering. LC 94-60051. (Publications in Linguistics: No. 121). 300p. 1994. pap. 28.00 (0-88312-620-6); fiche 24.00 (1-55671-991-4) Summer Instit Ling.

Doyen of Librarians: A Biography of William Warner Bishop. C. Glenn Sparks. LC 93-32335. (Illus.). 467p. 1993. 47.50 (0-8108-2772-7) Scarecrow.

Doyle & Hodge: Criminal Procedure in New Zealand. 3rd ed. W. C. Hodge. xxiv, 283p. 1991. pap. 48.00 (0-455-21028-4, Pub. by Law Bk Co) W W Gaunt.

Doyle, Massey, Maher & McCormick Families. Marian M. Doyle. (Illus.). 112p. (Orig.). 1989. pap. write for info. (0-318-65902-6) M M Doyle.

Doyle vs. NITA Power & Light Co. & Northern Electric Co. Personal Injury & Products Liability Case. 2nd ed. Joseph J. Kalo et al. 185p. 1982. 19.95 (1-55681-010-5); teacher ed 8.75 (1-55681-011-3) Natl Inst Trial Ad.

Doyle's Disciples. Bob Leuci. 272p. 1984. 14.95 (0-88191-006-6) Freundlich.

Doyle's Fish Cookbook. Alice Doyle. 218p. 1993. 20.00 (0-207-16022-8, Pub. by Angus & Robertson AT) HarpC.

Dozen & One. Jim Tully. LC 72-4513. (Essay Index Reprint Ser.). 1977. reprint ed. 19.95 (0-8369-2980-2) Ayer.

Dozen Dangers to Your Baby's Brain & How to Reduce Those Dangers. 12p. 1987. write for info. (1-55672-025-4) US HHS.

Dozen Delicious Doughnuts. Elaine Weimann & Rita Friedman. (Read to Me Bks.). (Illus.). 30p. (J). (ps-1). 1988. lib. bdg. 12.50 (0-89796-803-4) New Dimens Educ.

Dozen Doctors: Autobiographic Sketches. Ed. by Dwight J. Ingle. LC 63-20908. 295p. reprint ed. pap. 84.10 (0-317-42277-4, 2025796) Bks Demand.

Dozen Dogs: A Read-&-Count Story. Harriet Ziefert. LC 84-17797. (Step into Reading Bks.). (Illus.). 32p. (J). (ps-1). 1985. 3.50 (0-394-86935-4); lib. bdg. 6.99 (0-394-96935-9) Random Bks Yng Read.

Dozen Good Reasons. Sarah Shleimer. 1992. 11.95 (0-87306-600-6); pap. 9.95 (0-87306-601-4) Feldheim.

Dozen Lips. (LIP Pamphlets Ser.). 180p. 1994. pap. 33.99 (1-85594-060-4, Pub. by Attic IE) InBook.

Dozen Roses. Comp. by Esther L. Beilenson. (Gift Editions Ser.). (Illus.). 48p. 1993. 7.99 (0-88088-135-6) Peter Pauper.

Dozen Silk Diapers. Melissa Kajpust. LC 92-41937. (Illus.). 32p. (J). (ps-2). 1993. 13.95 (1-56282-456-2); lib. bdg. 13.89 (1-56282-457-0) Hyprn Child.

***Dozen Silk Diapers: A Christmas Story.** Melissa Kajpust. (Illus.). (J). (ps-2). Date not set. pap. 4.95 (0-7868-1074-2) Hyprn Child.

Dozen Variables. Marsha McCloskey. 1992. pap. 5.95 (0-486-27201-X) Dover.

Dozens. Laird Koenig. 1969. pap. 4.75 (0-8222-0325-1) Dramatists Play.

Dozens of Bible Quizzles, No. 2. Fannie L. Houck. 48p. 1992. pap. 3.99 (0-87403-677-1, 28-02787) Standard Pub.

Dozens of Dolls. Crafts Magazine Staff. 1992. pap. 19.95 (0-9621148-8-X) PJS Pubns.

Dozens of Uses for a Dead D. Linda S. Amstutz. (Illus.). 112p. (Orig.). 1994. pap. 6.95 (0-9640362-1-5) Off Color Pr.

DP & the Law. Data Processing Management Association. (MR.3) PAP. Data Process Mgmt. CDP. Jr T. J. Westermeir. 56p. 7.50 (0-318-17042-6); 10.50 (0-318-17043-4) Data Process Mgmt.

DP-Report see Future of the International Legal Order

DPG Student Atlas of World Politics. 2nd ed. John Allen. 112p. 1994. 9.95 (1-56134-229-7) Dushkin Pub.

DPK Inspirations: Little Hearts - Little Minds. Dorothy P. Koger. 50p. (J). 1994. pap. 5.00 (1-882821-04-1) DPK Pubns.

DPK Inspirations: Little Minds - Little Hearts. Dorothy P. Koger. 56p. (J). (gr. 6-8). 1995. pap. 5.00 (1-882821-03-3) DPK Pubns.

DPK Inspirations: This World. Dorothy P. Koger. 51p. 1993. pap. 25.00 (1-882821-06-8) DPK Pubns.

***DPL Decision Analysis Software for Microsft Windows: Advanced Version User Guide.** ADA Decision Systems Staff. 1995. student ed, pap. text ed. 87.95 (0-534-24816-0) Intl Thomson.

***DPL Decision Analysis Software for Microsoft Windows: Standard Version User Guide.** ADA Decision Systems Staff. 1994. disk write for info. (0-614-02486-2) Intl Thomson.

An Asterisk (*) at the beginning of an entry indicates that the title is appearing in BIP for the first time.

***DPL Decision Analysis Software for Microsoft Windows: Standard Version User Guide.** ADA Decision Systems Staff. 441p. 1995. pap. text ed. 43.95 (*0-534-24810-1*) Intl Thomson.

DPT Gastroenterology. Allison. 127p. 1991. pap. 14.95 (*0-8151-0117-1*) Mosby Yr Bk.

DR DOS 6 Quick Reference. Que Development Group Staff. (Quick Reference Ser.). (Illus.). 160p. (Orig.). 1992. pap. 9.95 (*0-88022-827-X*) Que.

Dr. Fischer of Geneva or the Bomb Party. Graham Greene. (Uniform Editions Ser.). 160p. 20.00 (*0-670-27522-0*) Viking Penguin.

Dr. Flatto's Weight & Blood Pressure & Cholesterol Reduction Program. Edwin Flatto. 1984. pap. 8.95 (*0-317-20245-6*) Plymouth Pr.

Dr. Frank: Life with Frank Porter Graham. John Ehle. 304p. 1993. lib. bdg. 19.95 (*0-9638915-0-2*) Franklin St.

Dr. Frankenstein's Mormon Monsters: Brigham Young's Body Shop. Darr Anderson. 1992. 12.95 (*0-9620810-2-7*) B Deviladog & Co.

Dr. Frau. Grace Kaiser. LC 86-81059. 168p. 1986. 14.95 (*0-934672-34-2*); pap. 8.95 (*0-934672-71-7*) Good Bks PA.

Dr. Fu Man Chu Meets the Lonesome Cowboy: Sorcery & the UFO Experience. 300p. 1991. 35.00 (*1-879980-02-9*) Magick Mirror.

Dr. Gabler's Business Lexicon: Dr. Gabler's Wirtschaftslexicon. 11th ed. R. Sellien. 2502p. (GER.). 1984. 175.00 (*0-8288-1280-2*, M7351) Fr & Eur.

Dr. Gardner's Fables for Our Times. Richard A. Gardner. LC 80-26098. (Illus.). 125p. (J). (gr. k-6). 1981. 14.95 (*0-933812-06-X*) Creative Therapeutics.

Dr. Gardner's Fairy Tales for Today's Children. Richard A. Gardner. LC 80-16187. (Illus.). 96p. (J). (gr. 1-6). 1978. reprint ed. lib. bdg. 14.95 (*0-933812-02-7*) Creative Therapeutics.

Dr. Gardner's Modern Fairy Tales. Richard A. Gardner. LC 83-40149. (Illus.). 106p. (J). (gr. 2-6). reprint ed. 14.95 (*0-933812-09-4*) Creative Therapeutics.

Dr. Gardner's Stories about the Real World, Vol. I. Richard A. Gardner. LC 80-16542. (Illus.). 127p. (J). (gr. k-6). 1980. pap. 4.99 (*0-933812-07-8*) Creative Therapeutics.

Dr. Gardner's Stories About the Real World, Vol. I. Richard A. Gardner. LC 80-16542. (Illus.). 127p. (J). (gr. k-6). 1980. reprint ed. lib. bdg. 14.95 (*0-933812-04-3*) Creative Therapeutics.

Dr. Gardner's Stories About the Real World, Vol. II. Richard A. Gardner. LC 80-16592. (Illus.). 95p. (J). (gr. k-6). 1983. 14.95 (*0-933812-05-1*) Creative Therapeutics.

Dr. Gary Gruber's Essential Guide to Test Taking for Kids. Gary R. Gruber. LC 86-8655. 120p. (Orig.). (J). (gr. 3-5). 1986. pap. text ed. 7.95 (*0-688-06350-0*, Quill) Morrow.

Dr. Gary Gruber's Essential Guide to Test-Taking for Kids. Gary R. Gruber. Ed. by Maria D. Guarnaschelli. LC 86-9392. 120p. (Orig.). (YA). (gr. 6-9). 1986. pap. text ed. 7.95 (*0-688-06351-9*, Quill) Morrow.

Dr. George: An Account of the Life of a Country Doctor. George T. Mitchell. LC 93-16589. (Illus.). 400p. 1994. 39.95 (*0-8093-1915-2*); pap. 19.95 (*0-8093-1916-0*) S Ill U Pr.

Dr. Grammar's Writes from Wrongs: A Supremely Authoritative Guide to the Common & Not-So-Common Rules of the English Language. Grammar. LC 91-50202. (Vintage Original Ser.). 256p. 1991. pap. 10.00 (*0-679-72715-9*, Vin) Random.

Dr. Green's Baby Book. Christopher Green. (Illus.). 1989. pap. 7.95 (*0-449-90332-X*, Columbine) Fawcett.

Dr. Grinshawe's Secret: A Romance. Nathaniel Hawthorne. 368p. 1992. reprint ed. lib. bdg. 41.00 (*0-8328-2435-6*) Higginson Bk Co.

Dr. Haggard's Disease. Patrick McGrath. 1994. pap. 10.00 (*0-679-75261-7*) Random.

Dr. Haggard's Disease. Patrick McGrath. 192p. 1993. 20.00 (*0-671-72733-8*) S&S Trade.

Dr. Hathern's Daughter. Mary J. Holmes. (Notable American Authors Ser.). 1992. reprint ed. lib. bdg. 75.00 (*0-7812-3150-7*) Rprt Serv.

Dr. Heidegger's Experiment. Nathaniel Hawthorne. (Classic Short Stories Ser.). (J). 1991. lib. bdg. 13.95 (*0-88682-465-6*) Creative Ed.

Dr. Hero. Israel Horovitz. 1973. pap. 4.75 (*0-8222-0329-4*) Dramatists Play.

Dr. History's Whiz Bang: Favorite Stories of California's Past. Jim Rawls. LC 91-27640. (Illus.). 118p. (Orig.). 1991. pap. 9.95 (*0-935382-77-1*) Tioga Pub Co.

Dr. Hugh Greer Carruthers: His Life & His Teachings. Ruth R. Carruthers. (Illus.). 325p. 1994. 29.50 (*0-9641194-0-4*) H G Carruthers.

Dr. Humor's Health Book: Old Cures - New Jokes. J. Edward Thornberg. (Illus.). 56p. (Orig.). 1986. pap. 3.00 (*0-929082-07-9*) Natl Hall Humor.

Dr. Inez Watercloud. Bonnie Seefeldt. 13p. 1988. pap. text ed. 4.00 (*1-884112-05-6*) See More Bks.

Dr. Jack's Adventure in Videoconferencing Land: A Guide to Communicating Effectively on Camera. Jan D'Arcy. (Illus.). 80p. 1990. 15.95 (*0-9627822-0-3*) J Darcy & Assocs.

Dr. Jekyll. Robert Louis Stevenson. 1992. pap. 15.00 (*0-679-40538-0*) McKay.

Dr. Jekyll & Mr. Hyde. Ed. by Richard J. Anobile. (Illus.). 1975. mass mkt. 6.45 (*0-380-00450-X*) Avon.

Dr. Jekyll & Mr. Hyde. Ed. by Jenni Calder. 1980. mass mkt. 4.95 (*0-14-043117-9*, Penguin Classics) Viking Penguin.

Dr. Jekyll & Mr. Hyde. Ret. by Samantha Lee. (Fleshcreepers Ser.). 160p. (J). (gr. 6 up). 1988. pap. 2.95 (*0-8120-4072-4*) Barron.

Dr. Jekyll & Mr. Hyde after One Hundred Years. Ed. by William Veeder & Gordon Hirsch. (Illus.). xx, 312p. 1988. pap. text ed. 16.95 (*0-226-85229-6*) U Ch Pr.

Dr. Jekyll & Mr. Hyde & Weir of Hermiston. Robert Louis Stevenson. (World's Classics Ser.). 272p. 1987. pap. 4.95 (*0-19-281740-X*) OUP.

Dr. Jekyll & Mr. Hyde Notes. James L. Roberts. 60p. (Orig.). (C). 1984. pap. 4.25 (*0-8220-0408-9*) Cliffs.

Dr. Jekyll & Mr. Hyde Readalong. Robert Louis Stevenson. (Illustrated Classics Collection 1). 64p. 1994. audio, pap. 13.50 (*1-56103-422-3*) Lake Pub Co.

Dr. Jekyll-Mr. Hyde Syndrome: Couples in Chaos. Andrew Casey. 1993. 16.95 (*0-533-10584-6*) Vantage.

Dr. Jensen's Favorite Exercises. Bernard Jensen. 1988. pap. 4.95 (*0-932615-15-5*) B Jensen.

Dr. Jensen's Real Soup & Salad Book. Bernard Jensen. LC 89-30557. (Illus.). 192p. 1989. pap. 11.95 (*0-89529-410-9*) Avery Pub.

Dr. Jeremy's Wife. Elizabeth Seifert. 1974. reprint ed. lib. bdg. 21.95 (*0-88411-045-1*, Aeonian Pr) Amereon Ltd.

Dr. Jimmy: Some Reminiscences by James Fowler Fraser 1893-1979. James F. Fraser. 150p. 1982. pap. text ed. 10.00 (*0-08-025737-2*, Pergamon Pr) Elsevier.

Dr. Joe Bell: Model for Sherlock Holmes. Ely Liebow. LC 81-85520. 286p. 1982. 16.95 (*0-87972-197-9*); pap. 11.95 (*0-87972-198-7*) Bowling Green Univ.

Dr. John: He Can Read Your Past Lives. Helen Hussey & Sandra Sherrod. Ed. by Franklin Loehr. LC 83-81110. 270p. (Orig.). (C). 1983. pap. 10.50 (*0-915151-01-4*) Religious Res Pr.

Dr. John Dee: Elizabethan Mystic & Astrologer. G. M. Hort. 72p. 1993. pap. 10.95 (*1-56459-377-0*) Kessinger Pub.

Dr. John McLoughlin, Master of Fort Vancouver, Father of Oregon. Nancy Wilson & Bert Webber. LC 94-8878. (Illus.). 208p. (Orig.). 1994. pap. 12.95 (*0-936738-76-6*) Webb Research.

Dr. John Mott-Smith: Hawaii's First Royal Dentist & Last Royal Ambassador. Robert M. Gibson & Terry Lawhead. LC 89-61907. (Illus.). 320p. 1989. 26.95 (*0-9623371-1-0*); pap. write for info. (*0-9623371-2-9*) Smilepower Inst.

***Dr. John Willard's Catalyst Altered Water.** Beth M. Ley. 64p. (Orig.). 1992. pap. 3.95 (*91-49-59100-2*) B L Pubns.

Dr. Johnson: Interviews & Recollections. Ed. by Norman Page. 256p. 1986. 53.00 (*0-389-20628-8*, N8186) B&N Imports.

Dr. Johnson & Company. Robert Lynd. LC 73-21749. (English Biography Ser.: No. 31). 1974. lib. bdg. 49.95 (*0-8383-1836-3*) M S G Haskell Hse.

Dr. Johnson & Fanny Burney. Frances B. D'Arblay. (BCL1-PR English Literature Ser.). 252p. 1992. reprint ed. lib. bdg. 79.00 (*0-7812-7366-8*) Rprt Serv.

Dr. Johnson Chronology. Norman Page. 140p. 1990. text ed. 38.50 (*0-8161-9091-7*, Hall Reference) Macmillan.

Dr. Johnson-Poetry & Prose. Ed. by Mona Wilson. 959p. 1969. 35.00 (*0-8464-1090-7*) Beekman Pubs.

Dr. Johnson's Prayers. Samuel Johnson. Ed. by Elton Trueblood. 88p. 1980. reprint ed. pap. 2.50 (*0-932970-17-6*) Prinit Pr.

Dr. Johnson's Printer: The Life of William Strahan. J. A. Cochrane. (Illus.). 225p. 1964. 20.00 (*0-910278-73-3*) Boulevard.

Dr. Johnson's Printer: The Life of William Strahan. J. A. Cochrane. (Illus.). xiii, 225p. 1964. text ed. 42.50x (*0-317-55856-0*, Pub. by B De Graaf NE) Coronet Bks.

Dr. Judd, Hawaii's Friend: A Biography of Gerrit Parmele Judd, 1803-1873. Gerrit P. Judd. LC 60-10394. 312p. reprint ed. pap. 89.00 (*0-317-28946-2*, 2020442) Bks Demand.

Dr. K. M. Nadkarni's Indian Materia Medica. Ed. by K. M. Nadkarni. (C). 1988. 70.00 (*0-8364-2337-2*, Pub. by Popular Prakashan II) S Asia.

Dr. Kellon's Guide to First Aid for Horses. Eleanor Kellon. (Illus.). 254p. (Orig.). 1989. pap. 22.50 (*0-914327-29-1*) Breakthrgh NY.

Dr. Kenneth H. Cooper's Preventive Medicine Program: Preventing Osteoporosis. Kenneth H. Cooper. 1989. 18.95 (*0-685-24550-0*) Bantam.

Dr. Kildare Takes Charge. Max Brand. 160p. reprint ed. lib. bdg. 16.95 (*0-88411-531-3*, Aeonian Pr) Amereon Ltd.

Dr. Kildare's Crisis. large type ed. Max Brand. LC 93-21148. 1994. write for info. (*0-8161-5873-8*) G K Hall.

Dr. Kildare's Search & Dr. Kildare's Hardest Case. large type ed. Max Brand. LC 93-34676. 1994. pap. 15.95 (*0-8161-5896-7*, Large Print Bks) Hall.

Dr. Kildare's Trial. Max Brand. 174p. reprint ed. lib. bdg. 17.95 (*0-88411-532-1*, Aeonian Pr) Amereon Ltd.

Dr. Kilgore's Feel Good Parenting Book. James E. Kilgore. LC 86-15585. 1989. pap. 5.99 (*0-8007-5297-X*) Revell.

Dr. Kinsey & the Institute for Sex Research. Wardell B. Pomeroy. LC 82-4924. 496p. 1982. text ed. 52.00 (*0-300-02916-0*) Yale U Pr.

Dr. Kiss Says Yes. Teddy Jam. (Illus.). 32p. (J). (ps-1). 1992. 12.95 (*0-88899-141-X*, Pub. by Groundwood-Douglas & McIntyre CN) Firefly Bks Ltd.

Dr. Kitchiner & the Cook's Oracle. Elspeth Davies. 91p. (C). 1989. text ed. 39.00 (*1-872795-83-8*, Pub. by Pentland Pr UK) St Mut.

Dr. Kugler's Seven Keys to a Longer Life. Hans J. Kugler. 1979. pap. 2.25 (*0-449-23811-3*, Crest) Fawcett.

Dr. Larry Silver's Advice to Parents on Attention-Deficit Hyperactivity. Larry B. Silver. LC 92-10778. 240p. 1992. 17.95 (*0-88048-561-2*) Am Psychiatric.

Dr. Lavendar's People. Margaret W. Deland. (BCL1-PS American Literature Ser.). 369p. 1992. reprint ed. lib. bdg. 89.00 (*0-7812-6703-X*) Rprt Serv.

Dr. Lawrence A. Nixon & the White Primary. 2nd ed. Conrey Bryson. (Southwestern Studies: No. 42). 92p. 1993. pap. 12.50 (*0-87404-100-7*) Tex Western.

Dr. LeBaron & His Daughters. Jane G. Austin. (Works of Jane (Goodin) Austin). 1989. reprint ed. lib. bdg. 79.00 (*0-7812-1832-2*) Rprt Serv.

Dr. Lee's Return. large type ed. Kathleen Treves. 1991. 21.95 (*0-7089-2489-1*) Ulverscroft.

Dr. Luke A. Port, Builder of Deepwood: An Urban Report - From England to Salem, Oregon & San Diego, California. David Duniway. LC 89-12608. (Illus.). 94p. (Orig.). 1989. pap. 9.95 (*0-943297-01-X*) Marion Coun Hist Soc.

Dr. Mac, Planner for Schools: Memoirs of My First 80 Years. James D. MacConnell. (Illus.). vi, 194p. 1988. 17.95 (*0-929558-00-6*) Johnson-Dole.

Dr. Macintosh. 2nd ed. Bob Levitus. 1992. pap. 26.95 (*0-201-57050-5*) Addison-Wesley.

Dr. Macintosh's Desktop Video: The Complete Quidktime & Animation Handbook. Bob Levitus. 1993. pap. 39.95 (*1-56686-025-3*) Brady Compu Bks.

Dr. Macintosh's Guide to the On-Line Universe. Bob Levitus. 1992. pap. 24.95 (*0-201-58125-6*) Addison-Wesley.

Dr. Malone, I Presume? large type ed. Holly North. 291p. 1994. 17.95 (*0-7505-0633-4*, Pub. by Magna Print Bks) Ulverscroft.

Dr. Mandell's Lifetime Arthritis Relief System. Marshall Mandell. 336p. 1986. mass mkt. 4.99 (*0-425-09355-7*) Berkley Pub.

Dr. Marcia Emery's Intuition Workbook: An Expert's Guide to Unlocking the Wisdom of Your... Marcia Emery. 1994. pap. text ed. 14.00 (*0-13-091670-6*) P-H.

Dr. Martin Luther King, Jr. Al-Imam Obaba. (Great Nubian Quiz Bks.). (Illus.). 43p. (Orig.). (YA). 1989. pap. 3.95 (*0-916157-14-8*) African Islam Miss Pubns.

Dr. Martin Luther King, Jr. Remembered. J. E. Grubbs. Ed. by Abell. (J). (gr. 1-4). 1994. 25.00 (*1-56611-091-2*); pap. 15.00 (*1-56611-092-0*) Jonas.

Dr. Mary Walker: The Little Little Lady in Pants. Charles M. Snyder. LC 74-2973. (Women in America Ser.). (Illus.). 178p. 1977. reprint ed. 22.95 (*0-405-06122-6*) Ayer.

Dr. Max Gerson's Cancer Therapy. 1992. lib. bdg. 79.95 (*0-8490-5416-8*) Gordon Pr.

Dr. Miriam Stoppard's Pregnancy & Birth Book. Miriam Stoppard. 240p. 1987. pap. 10.00 (*0-345-31908-7*, Ballantine Trade) Ballantine.

Dr. Mom. Marianne E. Neifert et al. 544p. 1987. pap. 5.99 (*0-451-16311-7*, Sig) NAL-Dutton.

Dr. Mom's Parenting Guide. Marianne E. Neifert. 336p. 1993. reprint ed. pap. 5.99 (*0-451-17363-5*, Sig) NAL-Dutton.

Dr. Montessori's Own Handbook. Maria Montessori. LC 65-14827. (Illus.). 192p. (C). 1988. pap. 11.00 (*0-8052-0921-2*) Schocken.

Dr. Montessori's Own Handbook. Maria Montessori. (Basic Montessori Library Ser.). (Illus.). 170p. reprint ed. pap. text ed. 8.50 (*0-916011-01-1*) Ed Sys Pub.

Dr. Morgan's Guide to North American Wild Life: 1992-1993 Edition. P. Roderick Maura. 258p. 1992. pap. 16.95 (*0-9630814-7-0*) Dr Morgans.

Dr. Morris Cranmer's the Final Report on Saccharin. Ed. by George H. Scherr. LC 78-71211. 588p. 65.00 (*0-930376-06-4*) Chem-Orbital.

Dr. Mouse, Bungle Jungle Doctor. Robert Kraus. (Golden Softcover Fast Start Readers Ser.: Level 2). (Illus.). 32p. (J). (ps-2). 1992. pap. write for info. (*0-307-15964-7*, 15964) Western Pub.

Dr. Mugford's Casebook: Understanding Dogs - Their Companions. Roger Mugford. (Illus.). 224p. 1993. pap. 19.95 (*0-09-177163-3*, Pub. by Jonathan Cape UK) Trafalgar.

Dr. Multree's Obsession. Proctor Jones. LC 89-91211. 124p. (Orig.). 1990. pap. 3.50 (*0-9608860-7-9*) Proctor Jones.

Dr. Newbold's Nutrition for Your Nerves. H. L. Newbold. 368p. (Orig.). 1993. pap. 14.95 (*0-87983-606-7*) Keats.

Dr. Newbold's Nutrition for Your Nerves see Dr. Newbold's Diet to Cure Incurable Diseases

Dr. Newbold's Revolutionary New. Newbold. 1977. 1.25 (*0-89256-014-2*, Rawson Assocs) Macmillan.

Dr. Nikola Tesla - Complete Patents, 2 vols. 2nd ed. Comp. by John T. Ratzlaff. LC 79-67722. (Illus.). 500p. lib. bdg. 43.50 (*0-9603536-8-2*); 35.00 (*0-914119-27-3*) Tesla Bk Co.

Dr. Nikola Tesla - Complete Patents, 2 vols., Vol. I. 2nd ed. Comp. by John T. Ratzlaff. LC 79-67722. (Illus.). 500p. write for info. (*0-914119-10-9*) Tesla Bk Co.

Dr. Nikola Tesla - Complete Patents, 2 vols., Vol. II. 2nd ed. Comp. by John T. Ratzlaff. LC 79-67722. (Illus.). 500p. write for info. (*0-914119-11-7*) Tesla Bk Co.

Dr. Ox's Experiment: Drama in the Air. Jules Verne. reprint ed. lib. bdg. 16.95 (*0-88411-915-7*, Aeonian Pr) Amereon Ltd.

Dr. Pak's Pre-School. deluxe limited ed. David Brin. (Illus.). 84p. 1989. Collector's Edition: signed, numbered, slipcased. boxed 95.00 (*0-941826-19-8*) Cheap St.

Dr. Panofsky & Mr. Tarkington: An Exchange of Letters, 1938-1946. Ed. by Richard M. Ludwig. LC 74-10252. (Illus.). 151p. 1974. 25.00 (*0-87811-019-4*) Princeton Lib.

Dr. Paul's Amazing Eyewear. Paul Koeleman. (J). (ps-3). 1993. 12.95 (*0-8478-5707-7*) Rizzoli Intl.

Dr. Pepper: King of Beverages. Harry E. Ellis. (Illus.). 268p. 1979. 24.95 (*0-9607448-0-0*) Dr Pepper.

Dr. Pilgrim's Progress. large type ed. Anne Vinton. 256p. 1992. 21.95 (*0-7505-0331-9*) Ulverscroft.

Dr. Pitcairn's Complete Guide To Natural Health for Dogs & Cats. Richard H. Pitcairn & Susan Hubble Pitcairn. LC 82-5336. (Illus.). 304p. 1982. pap. 12.95 (*0-87857-395-X*, 13-779-1) Rodale Pr Inc.

Dr. Quake. Warren Murphy. (Destroyer Ser.: No. 5). 1988. pap. 3.50 (*1-55817-040-5*, Pinnacle NY) Windsor NY.

Dr. Rajendra Prasad: Correspondence & Select Documents, Vol. I. Ed. by Valmiki Choudhary. 1984. 24.00 (*0-8364-1179-X*, Pub. by Allied II) S Asia.

Dr. Rajendra Prasad: Correspondence & Select Documents, Vol. II. Ed. by Valmiki Choudhary. 1985. 22.50 (*0-8364-1440-3*, Pub. by Allied II) S Asia.

Dr. Rajendra Prasad: Correspondence & Select Documents, Vol. III. Ed. by Valmiki Choudhary. 1985. 22.50 (*0-8364-1441-1*, Pub. by Allied II) S Asia.

Dr. Rajendra Prasad: Correspondence & Select Documents, Vol. IX. Ed. by Valmiki Choudhary. 1987. 27.00 (*81-7023-012-8*, Pub. by Allied II) S Asia.

Dr. Rajendra Prasad Correspondence & Select Documents, Vol. IV. 1985. 20.00 (*0-8364-2050-0*, Pub. by Allied II) S Asia.

Dr. Rajendra Prasad Correspondence & Select Documents, Vol. V. 1986. 20.00 (*0-8364-2051-9*, Pub. by Allied II) S Asia.

Dr. Rajendra Prasad Correspondence & Select Documents, Vol. VI. 1986. 20.00 (*0-8364-2052-7*, Pub. by Allied II) S Asia.

Dr. Rajendra Prasad Correspondence & Select Documents, Vol. VII. 1987. 27.00 (*0-8364-2053-5*, Pub. by Allied II) S Asia.

Dr. Rajendra Prasad Correspondence & Select Documents, Vol. VIII. 1987. 28.50 (*0-8364-2054-3*, Pub. by Allied II) S Asia.

Dr. Reuben Mental First Aid Manual. Reuben. 1982. 12.98 (*0-02-605730-1*) Macmillan.

Dr. Richard Furman's Save Your Life Cholesterol Plan. Richard Furman. 1991. pap. 4.50 (*0-425-12735-4*) Berkley Pub.

Dr. Rinse Formula: How to Prevent Hardening of the Arteries. Morton Walker. (Dr. Morton Walker Good Health Guides Ser.). (Illus.). 56p. (Orig.). 1984. pap. 2.95 (*0-8159-6721-7*) Devin.

Dr. Robert Anthony's Advanced Formula for Total Success. Robert Anthony. Ed. by Sallye Levanthal. 176p. (Orig.). 1988. pap. 4.99 (*0-425-10804-X*) Berkley Pub.

Dr. Robert Anthony's Magic Power of Super Persuasion. Robert Anthony. 1988. pap. 3.99 (*0-425-10981-X*) Berkley Pub.

Dr. Ruth Phenomenon. Barbara Multer. 240p. 1988. reprint ed. pap. 3.95 (*0-8439-2589-2*) Dorchester Pub Co.

Dr. Ruth Talks to Kids: Where You Came from, How Your Body Changes, & What Sex Is All About. Ruth Westheimer. LC 92-11387. (Illus.). 96p. (J). (gr. 4-9). 1993. text ed. 13.95 (*0-02-792532-3*, Mac Bks Young Read) S&S Childrens.

Dr. Ruth Westheimer. Margaret M. Scariano. LC 91-40923. (Contemporary Women Ser.). (Illus.). 128p. (J). (gr. 6 up). 1992. lib. bdg. 17.95 (*0-89490-333-0*) Enslow Pubs.

Dr. Ruth's Encyclopedia of Sex. Ruth Westheimer. (Illus.). 324p. 1994. 29.50 (*0-8264-0625-4*) Continuum.

Dr. Ruth's Guide for Married Lovers. Ruth Westheimer. 288p. 1987. mass mkt. 4.99 (*0-446-34562-8*) Warner Bks.

Dr. Ruth's Guide for Married Lovers. Ruth K. Westheimer. LC 87-59. 1992. 7.99 (*0-517-63174-1*) Random Hse Value.

Dr. Ruth's Guide to Erotic & Sensuous Pleasures. Ruth Westheimer & Louis Lieberman. 230p. 1992. 5.99 (*1-56171-099-7*, S P I Bks) Sure Sellers.

Dr. Ruth's Guide to Erotic & Sensuous Pleasures. Ruth K. Westheimer. 1991. 18.95 (*1-56171-035-0*) Sure Sellers.

Dr. Ruth's Guide to Good Sex. Ruth Westheimer. 1986. mass mkt. 5.99 (*0-446-34529-6*) Warner Bks.

Dr. Ruth's Guide to Safer Sex. Ruth Westheimer. (Illus.). 160p. 1992. mass mkt. 4.99 (*0-446-36399-5*) Warner Bks.

Dr. S. Radhakrishnan: His Life & Work. C. Nagaraja Rao. 1986. 12.50 (*0-8364-2566-9*, Pub. by Mittal II) S Asia.

Dr. S. S. Wesley 1810-1876: Portrait of a Victorian Musician. Paul Chappell. (Illus.). 220p. 1977. pap. text ed. 14.00 (*0-85597-198-3*) Attic Pr.

Dr. Sa'eed of Iran: Kurdish Physician to Princes & Peasants, Nobles & Nomads. Jay M. Rasooli & Cady H. Allen. LC 57-13245. (Illus.). 192p. 1983. reprint ed. pap. 6.95 (*0-87808-743-5*) William Carey Lib.

Dr. Sam Johnson, Detector. Lillian De La Torre. LC 83-82009. (Compleat Adventures of Dr. Sam Johnson, Detector Ser.). 257p. 1983. pap. 6.95 (*0-930330-08-0*) Intl Polygonics.

Dr. Samaritan. Elizabeth Seifert. 1974. reprint ed. lib. bdg. 21.95 (*0-88411-052-4*, Aeonian Pr) Amereon Ltd.

Dr. Samuel Guthrie, Discoverer of Chloroform. Jesse R. Pawling. (Illus.). 123p. 1994. reprint ed. lib. bdg. 22.00 (*0-8328-3628-1*) Higginson Bk Co.

Dr. Samuel Johnson & James Boswell. Intro. by Harold Bloom. (Modern Critical Views Ser.). 280p. 1986. 34.95 (*0-87754-678-9*) Chelsea Hse.

Dr. Sanders' Guide to Boosting Dairy Profits. Donald E. Sanders. LC 89-84351. (Illus.). 300p. 1990. 12.00 (*0-939674-26-2*) Am Vet Pubns.

Dr. Sax. Jack Kerouac. 256p. 1988. 10.95 (*0-8021-3049-6*) Grove-Atltic.

Dr. Schuessler's Biochemistry. J. B. Chapman. 300p. 1963. spiral bd. 11.00 (*0-7873-0163-9*) Mokelumne.

Dr. Science's Book of Shocking Domestic Revelations. Dr. Science, pseud. & Merle Kessler. LC 93-16375. 1993. 17.00 (*0-688-11444-X*) Morrow.

Dr. Scott: Surgeon on Call. Elizabeth Seifert. 1974. reprint ed. lib. bdg. 20.95 (*0-88411-049-4*, Aeonian Pr) Amereon Ltd.

***Dr. S.D. Sharman, President of India: The Elder Statesman, a Political Biography.** Rajendra Verma. (C). 1994. text ed. 20.00 (*81-224-0599-1*, Pub. by Wiley Eastern II) S Asia.

Dr. Seuss. Jill Wheeler. Ed. by Rosemary Wallner. LC 92-16569. (Young at Heart Ser.). (J). (gr. 4). 1992. lib. bdg. 13.99 (*1-56239-112-7*) Abdo & Dghtrs.

D

An Asterisk (*) at the beginning of an entry indicates that the title is appearing in BIP for the first time. 2097

***Dr. Seuss.** Jill Wheeler. Ed. by Rosemary Wallner. (Young at Heart Ser.). (J). (gr. 4). 1992. pap. 4.95 (1-56239-366-9) Abdo & Dghtrs.

Dr. Seuss: We Love You. Patricia S. Martin. (Reaching Your Goal Bks.). (Illus.). 24p. (J). (gr. 1-4). 1987. lib. bdg. 14.60 (0-86592-168-7) Rourke Corp.

Dr. Seuss: We Love You, Set. Patricia S. Martin. (Reaching Your Goal Bks.). (Illus.). 24p. (J). (gr. 1-4). 1987. 10.95 (0-685-67570-X) Rourke Corp.

Dr. Seuss Beginner Book Classics, 5 bks., Set. Dr. Seuss. (Illus.). (J). (ps-3). 1992. Boxed set incls. The Cat in the Hat, Dr. Seuss's ABC, Fox in Socks, Green Eggs & Ham & One Fish Two. boxed 50.00 (0-679-83846-5) Random Bks Yng Read.

Dr. Seuss (Theodore Seuss Geisel) Ruth K. MacDonald. 208p. 1988. text ed. 21.95 (0-8057-7524-2, TUSAS NO. 54, Twayne) Macmillan.

Dr. Seuss's ABC. Dr. Seuss. LC 63-9810. (Illus.). 72p. (J). (gr. k-3). 1960. 7.99 (0-394-80030-3) Random Bks Yng Read.

Dr. Seuss's ABC. Dr. Seuss. LC 63-9810. (Illus.). 72p. (J) (gr. k-3). 1963. lib. bdg. 9.99 (0-394-90030-8) Random Bks Yng Read.

Dr. Seuss's ABC. Dr. Seuss. (Beginner Book & Cassette Library). (Illus.). 64p. (J). (ps-1). 1988. audio, pap. 7.95 (0-394-89784-6) Random Bks Yng Read.

Dr. Seuss's Sleep Book. Dr. Seuss. (Illus.). (J). (gr. 3-7). 1962. 13.00 (0-394-80091-5) Random Bks Yng Read.

Dr. Seuss's Sleep Book. Dr. Seuss. (Illus.). (J). (gr. 3-7). 1962. lib. bdg. 13.99 (0-394-90091-X) Random Bks Yng Read.

Dr. Sevier. George W. Cable. (Works of George Washington Cable). 1990. reprint ed. lib. bdg. 79.00 (0-7812-1136-0) Rprt Serv.

Dr. Shaw's Secretary. large type ed. Kay Winchester. 1989. 17.95 (0-7089-2114-0) Ulverscroft.

Dr. Sheehan Get Fit & Feel Great. George A. Sheehan. LC 92-15351. 1992. 11.99 (0-517-08462-7, Pub. by Wings Bks) Random Hse Value.

Dr. Simplespread: Or, How I Learned to Quit Losing & Started Taking Money out of Wall Street. Thomas Mongle. 171p. 1986. pap. 21.95 (0-938063-05-7) Ivers St Lloyd.

Dr. Strange - Into Shamballa. DeMatteis & Greene. 64p. 1986. 5.95 (0-87135-166-8) Marvel Entmnt.

Dr. Strangegod: On the Symbolic Meaning of Nuclear Weapons. Ira Chernus. Ed. by Frederick M. Denny. (Studies in Comparative Religion). 280p. 1989. 14.95 (0-87249-631-7) U of SC Pr.

Dr. Sunshine: A Novel. Oscar London. LC 92-34863. 1993. pap. 9.95 (0-89815-526-6) Ten Speed Pr.

Dr. Sweet's Guide to Rude Health. Quentin Brown & Phil Gould. 160p. 1988. 40.00 (1-85283-213-4, Pub. by Boxtree Ltd UK); pap. 30.00 (1-85283-219-3, Pub. by Boxtree Ltd UK) St Mut.

Dr. Taymora. James W. Fraley. Ed. by James B. Van Treese. 296p. 1994. pap. 8.95 (1-56901-204-0) NW Pub.

Dr. Thomas Keith & John Forbe White: Sun Pictures Catalogue 6. Larry J. Schaaf. (Illus.). 80p. (Orig.). 1993. pap. 30.00 (0-9621096-4-9) H P Kraus Jr.

Dr. Thomas Sydenham, 1624-1689: His Life & Original Writings. Thomas Sydenham & Kenneth Dewhurst. LC 66-19348. (Illus.). 215p. reprint ed. pap. 61.30 (0-685-20501-0, 2029950) Bks Demand.

Dr. Thorne. Anthony Trollope. 592p. 1991. 8.95 (0-14-043326-0, Penguin Classics) Viking Penguin.

Dr. Valdez. Judith A. Green. (Adult Basic Learner Ser.). (Illus.). 215p. (Orig.). 1981. pap. text ed. 6.50 (0-89061-211-0, 203) Jamestown Pubs.

Dr. Walter Scott Beal Poetry & Prose: My Favorite Collection. Walter S. Beal et al. Ed. by Virginia Nichols. (Illus.). 100p. 1984. pap. 5.00 (0-940178-25-7) Sitare.

Dr. Watchstop. Ken Macklin. (Illus.). 1989. 7.95 (0-913035-85-8) Eclipse Bks.

Dr. Webb of Colorado Springs. Helen Clapesattle. LC 84-70852. (Illus.). 518p. reprint ed. pap. 147.70 (0-8357-5520-7, 2035136) Bks Demand.

Dr. Wechsler's New You Diet. Arnold Wechsler. 1978. 10.00 (0-8065-0630-X, Citadel Pr) Carol Pub Group.

Dr. Weisinger's Anger Work-out Book. Hendrie D. Weisinger. Ed. by Pat Golbitz. LC 85-6483. 204p. 1985. pap. 13.00 (0-688-04114-0, Quill) Morrow.

Dr. Whacko's Guide to Slow-Pitch Softball. Bruce C. Brown. 160p. (Orig.). 1991. pap. 8.95 (0-02-013096-1, Collier S&S) S&S Trade.

Dr. Who: Giftpack. Terrance Dicks. 1985. pap. 11.80 (0-8065-2700-5, Citadel Pr) Carol Pub Group.

Dr. Who: Season 3, Pt. 1. John Peel. Ed. by Hal Schuster. (Files Ser.). 60p. pap. 5.95 (1-55698-001-9) Movie Pubs Servs.

Dr. Who: Season 3, Pt. 2. John Peel. Ed. by Hal Schuster. (Files Ser.). 60p. pap. 5.95 (1-55698-002-7) Movie Pubs Servs.

Dr Who Quiz Book of Space. Holt. 1986. pap. 2.95 (0-416-20450-3) Routledge Chapman & Hall.

Dr. Who Yearbook. Abnett et al. 64p. 1991. 8.95 (1-85400-283-X) Marvel Entmnt.

Dr. William Beaumont: The Mackinac Years. Keith R. Widder. (Illus.). 40p. (Orig.). 1975. pap. 3.50 (0-911872-15-9) Mackinac Island.

Dr. William Goodell & Camp Paoli: The Goodell Collection at West Chester University Including Camp Paoli Documents (Camp Parole) W. Robert Penman & Emily J. Penman. (Illus.). 104p. 1987. pap. 19.95 (0-9619411-1-1) Serpentine Pr.

Dr. Willis in Japan, 1862-1877: A British Medical Pioneer. Hugh Cortazzi. LC 85-1334. (Illus.). 273p. (C). 1985. text ed. 29.50 (0-485-11264-7, Pub. by Athlone Pr UK) Humanities.

Dr. Wise Arithmetic Series, Vol. I. Francis H. Wise & Joyce M. Wise. (Illus.). 105p. (J). (ps-1). 1980. pap. text ed. 7.50 (0-915766-55-8) Wise Pub.

Dr. Wise Arithmetic Series, Vol. II. Francis H. Wise & Joyce M. Wise. (Illus.). 105p. (J). (gr. k-1). 1980. pap. text ed. 7.50 (0-915766-56-6) Wise Pub.

Dr. Wise Learn to Read, Vol. 4. Francis Wise. 1985. 7.50 (0-915766-44-2) Wise Pub.

Dr. Wise Learn to Read Series, Vols. 1-4. Francis H. Wise & Joyce M. Wise. Incl. Vol. 1. Readers 1-5 Phonetic Reader Ser. 1979. 7.50 (0-915766-42-6); Vol. 2. Readers 6-10 in Phonetic Reader Ser. 1979. 7.50 (0-915766-43-4); Vol. 3. Readers 11-15 in Phonetic Reader Ser. (Illus.). 104p. 1979. 7.50 (0-915766-64-7); Readers 16-20 in Phonetic Learn to Read Ser. (Illus.). 105p. 1979. 7.50 (0-685-73474-9); (Illus.). 105p. (J). (ps-1). 1979. write for info. (0-318-56467-X) Wise Pub.

Dr. Woodward's Ambition. Elizabeth Seifert. 1973. reprint ed. lib. bdg. 19.95 (0-88411-012-5, Aeonian Pr) Amereon Ltd.

Dr. Woodward's Shield: History, Science, & Satire in Augustan England. Joseph M. Levine. LC 75-27927. (Illus.). 376p. 1991. reprint ed. pap. 15.95 (0-8014-9935-6) Cornell U Pr.

Dr. Wren's Receptionist. large type ed. Kathleen Treves. (Linford Romance Library). 283p. 1984. pap. 11.95 (0-7089-6036-7, Trailtree Bookshop) Ulverscroft.

Dr. Wright's Guide to Healing with Nutrition. Jonathan V. Wright. 603p. 1990. pap. 17.95 (0-87983-530-3) Keats.

Dr. Xargle's Book of Earth Weather see Earth Weather As Explained by Professor Xargle

Dr. Y. C. James Yen: His Movement for Mass Education & Rural Reconstruction. John C. Kiang. (Illus.). 294p. 1976. 18.50 (0-942717-04-X) Intl Inst Rural.

Dr. Yocum Teaches the Epistles of Paul, Vol. I. Dale M. Yocum. 1992. pap. 14.99 (0-88019-295-X) Schmul Pub Co.

Dr. Yocum Teaches the Epistles of Paul, Vol. II. Dale M. Yocum. 1992. pap. 14.99 (0-88019-297-6) Schmul Pub Co.

Dr. Zed's Dazzling Book of Science Activities. Gordon Penrose. (Illus.). 48p. (J). 1993. pap. 7.95 (0-919872-78-6, Pub. by Greey dePencier CN) Firefly Bks Ltd.

Dr. Zed's Science Surprises. Gordon Penrose. (J). 1990. pap. 6.95 (0-671-70541-5) PB.

Dr. Zhivago. Boris Pasternak. 544p. 1991. 20.00 (0-679-40759-6, Everymans Lib) Knopf.

Dr. Z's Beat the Racetrack. rev. ed. William T. Ziemba & Donald B. Hausch. LC 87-15025. (Illus.). 420p. 1987. 24.95 (0-688-07221-6) Morrow.

Drabne of Dole. Bernard Evslin. (Monsters of Mythology Ser.). (Illus.). 86p. 1990. lib. bdg. 19.95 (1-55546-245-6) Chelsea Hse.

Drac & the Gremlin. Allan Baillie. LC 88-20275. (Illus.). 32p. (J). (ps-3). 1992. pap. 4.99 (0-14-054542-5, Puff Pied Piper) Puffin Bks.

Drachenkampfe: Untersuchungen Sagenkunde, Vol. 1-pt. 1. Ernst Siecke. Ed. by Kees W. Bolle. LC 77-79155. (Mythology Ser.). (GER.). 1978. reprint ed. lib. bdg. 17.95 (0-405-10564-9) Ayer.

Drackenberg Adventure. Lloyd Alexander. (J). (gr. k-6). 1990. reprint ed. pap. 3.50 (0-440-40296-4, Yearling Classics) Dell.

Drackenburg Adventure. Lloyd Alexander. LC 87-36881. 160p. (YA). (gr. 5-9). 1988. 12.95 (0-525-44389-4, 01258-370, DCB) Dutton Child Bks.

Drackett Company's Work with Soybeans & Soy Proteins. Ed. by Akiko Aoyagi. (Bibliographies & Sourcebooks on Soya Ser.). 59p. (Orig.). 1993. spiral bd. 39.95 (0-933332-80-7) Soyfoods Center.

***Draconian Measures: A History of F. B. I. Political Repression.** Ward Churchill. 1995. 29.95 (1-56751-059-0); pap. 16.95 (1-56751-058-2) Common Courage.

Draconian New York. Robert Sheckley. 1995. 20.95 (0-312-85130-8) Forge NYC.

Dracula. Keith Faulkner. (Illus.). 16p. (J). (ps-2). 1993. 10.95 (0-694-00559-2, Festival) HarpC Child Bks.

Dracula. Steven P. Jones. Ed. by Chris Ulm. (Illus.). 120p. 1990. pap. 9.95 (0-944735-47-9) Malibu Graphics.

Dracula. Russ Jones Production. (Illus.). 160p. (Orig.). 1975. pap. 1.25 (0-532-12356-5) Kearny Pub.

Dracula. Fred Saberhagen & James V. Hart. 1992. pap. 4.99 (0-451-17575-1, Sig) NAL-Dutton.

Dracula. Ian Thorne. LC 76-51145. (Monsters Ser.). (Illus.). 48p. (J). (gr. 3-5). 1977. text ed. 11.95 (0-913940-67-4, Crstwood Hse) Silver Burdett Pr.

Dracula. adapted ed. Crane Johnson. 1975. pap. 4.75 (0-8222-0326-X) Dramatists Play.

Dracula. rev. ed. Tom Clapp. LC 91-51165. 1985. pap. 6.00 (0-88734-202-7) Players Pr.

***Dracula.** 2nd ed. Amarantha Knight. (The Darker Passions Ser.). 1995. pap. text ed. 5.95 (1-56333-326-0) Masquerade.

Dracula: A Symphony in Moonlight & Nightmares. Jon J. Muth. (Illus.). 80p. 1986. 7.95 (0-87135-171-4) Marvel Entmnt.

Dracula: A Symphony in Moonlight & Nightmares. Jon J. Muth. 80p. 1993. 45.00 (1-56163-060-8); pap. 11.95 (1-56163-059-4) NBM.

Dracula: A Translation of the 1488 Nurnberg Edition with an Essay by Beverley Eddy. 16p. 1985. pap. 4.90 (0-939084-18-X) R Mus & Lib.

Dracula: Death of Nosferatu. Christopher Nichols. 40p. 1991. pap. 2.50 (0-87129-091-X, D54) Dramatic Pub.

Dracula: Essays on the Life & Times of Vlad Tepes. Ed. by Kurt W. Treptow. 320p. 1991. text ed. 36.00 (0-88033-220-4) Col U Pr.

Dracula: Prince of Darkness. Ed. by Martin H. Greenberg. 320p. (Orig.). 1992. mass mkt. 4.99 (0-88677-531-0) DAW Bks.

Dracula: The Original 1931 Shooting Script. Philip J. Riley & George Turner. LC 90-61035. (Universal Filmscript Series: Classic Horror Films). (Illus.). 256p. (Orig.). 1990. pap. 19.95 (1-882127-09-9) Magicimage Filmbooks.

Dracula: The Ultimate, Illustrated Edition of the World-Famous Vampire Play. Hamilton Deane & John L. Balderston. (Illus.). 176p. (Orig.). 1993. 24.95 (0-312-09278-4); pap. 14.95 (0-312-09279-2) St Martin.

Dracula: The Vampire & the Critics. Margaret L. Carter. Ed. by Robert Scholes. LC 88-17244. (Studies in Speculative Fiction: No. 19). 274p. reprint ed. 73.80 (0-8357-1889-1, 207667) Bks Demand.

Dracula: The Vampire Legend on Film. Robert Marrero. (Illus.). 128p. 1992. pap. 12.95 (0-9634982-0-7) Fantasma Bks.

Dracula: The Vampire Play. Tim Kelly. 56p. (J). (gr. 4 up). 1978. pap. 4.00 (0-88680-043-9) I E Clark.

Dracula & Other Vampire Stories. Eric Kudalis. (Monsters & Their Stories Ser.). 48p. (J). (gr. 3-10). 1994. lib. bdg. 17.27 (1-56065-212-8) Capstone Pr.

Dracula Book. Donald F. Glut. LC 75-4917. (Illus.). 410p. 1975. 35.00 (0-8108-0804-8) Scarecrow.

Dracula Book of Great Horror Stories. Ed. by Leslie Shepard. 288p. 1983. pap. 6.95 (0-8065-0859-0, Citadel Pr) Carol Pub Group.

Dracula Book of Great Horror Stories. Ed. by Leslie Shepard. 288p. 1991. pap. 4.50 (0-8216-2505-5, Carol Paperbacks) Carol Pub Group.

Dracula Book of Great Vampire Stories. Ed. by Leslie Shepard. 1977. 10.00 (0-8065-0565-6, Citadel Pr); pap. 6.95 (0-8065-0704-7, Citadel Pr) Carol Pub Group.

Dracula Cookbook of Blood. Ardin C. Price & Trishna Leszczyc. 160p. (Orig.). Date not set. pap. 14.95 (1-883281-42-3) Mugwort Soup.

Dracula, Frankenstein, Dr. Jekyll & Mr. Hyde. Bram Stoker et al. 672p. (J). (gr. 7). 1978. pap. 5.95 (0-451-52363-6, Sig Classics) NAL-Dutton.

Dracula in Love. John Shirley. 1990. pap. 3.95 (0-8217-3001-0) Zebra.

Dracula Is a Pain in the Neck. Elizabeth Levy. LC 82-47707. (Illus.). 80p. (J). (gr. 2-6). 1983. lib. bdg. 13.89 (0-06-023823-2) HarpC Child Bks.

Dracula Is a Pain in the Neck. Elizabeth Levy. LC 82-47707. (Trophy Bk.). (Illus.). 80p. (J). (gr. 2-5). 1984. pap. 3.95 (0-06-440146-4, Trophy) HarpC Child Bks.

Dracula Is a Pain in the Neck. Elizabeth Levy. (J). 1990. mass mkt. 3.50 (0-06-107014-9) HarpC.

Dracula Kidds: The House on Blood Pudding Lane. Tim Kelly. (Illus.). 60p. (Orig.). 1986. pap. 3.00 (0-88680-251-2) I E Clark.

Dracula Killer. Ray Biondi & Walt Hecox. Ed. by Eric Tobias. 232p. (Orig.). 1992. mass mkt. 4.99 (0-671-74003-2) PB.

Dracula Murders. large type ed. Philip Daniels. (Linford Mystery Library). 256p. 1988. pap. 11.95 (0-7089-6565-2, Trailtree Bookshop) Ulverscroft.

Dracula Notes. Samuel J. Umland. 77p. (Orig.). 1983. pap. text ed. 3.95 (0-8220-0417-8) Cliffs.

Dracula Ou le Jeu du Vampire. Tim Kelly. Tr. by Solly Levy. (Illus.). 67p. (Orig.). (FRE.). 1985. pap. 2.50 (0-88680-244-X) I E Clark.

Dracula Poems: A Poetic Encounter with the Lord of Vampires. Robin Spriggs & Brent L. Glenn. LC 92-90518. (Illus.). 1992. 10.00 (0-9634296-5-5) Circle Myth.

Dracula, Prince of Many Faces: His Life & His Times. Radu R. Florescu. 1990. pap. 14.95 (0-316-28656-7) Little.

Dracula Readalong. Bram Stoker. (Illustrated Classics Collection 1). 64p. 1994. audio, pap. 13.50 (1-56103-425-8) Lake Pub Co.

Dracula Syndrome. Richard Monaco & Bill Burt. 184p. (Orig.). 1993. mass mkt. 4.99 (0-380-77062-8) Avon.

Dracula Unbound: A Novel. Brian W. Aldiss. 1992. mass mkt. 4.50 (0-06-109946-5, Harp PBks) HarpC.

Dracula Unleashed: Official Strategy Guide & Novel. Rick Barba. 1994. pap. 19.95 (1-55958-539-0) Prima Pub.

Dracula's Cat. Jan Wahl. LC 77-27051. (Illus.). (J). (ps-3). 1981. 6.95 (0-685-03842-4); pap. 2.50 (0-685-03843-2) P-H.

Dracula's Cat & Frankenstein's Dog. Jan Wahl. (Illus.). (J). (ps-2). 1990. pap. 13.95 (0-671-70820-1) S&S Trade.

Dracula's Children. Richard Lortz. 208p. 1982. 22.00 (0-932966-15-2) Permanent Pr.

Dracula's Daughter. Mary Hoffman. (Banana Bks.). (Illus.). 42p. (J). (gr. 2-4). 1989. 3.95 (0-8120-6135-7) Barron.

Dracula's Daughter. William Sanford & Carl Green. LC 84-27462. (Movie Monsters Ser.). (Illus.). 48p. (J). (gr. 3-5). 1985. text ed. 10.95 (0-89686-260-7, Crstwood Hse) Silver Burdett Pr.

Dracula's Guest. Bram Stoker. 1978. pap. 1.95 (0-89083-401-6) Zebra.

Dracula's Guest. Bram Stoker. reprint ed. lib. bdg. 19.95 (0-88411-132-6, Aeonian Pr) Amereon Ltd.

Dracula's Guest: Nine Stories of Horror & Suspense. Bram Stoker. 160p. 1990. reprint ed. pap. 9.95 (0-86322-120-3, Pub. by Brandon Bk Pubs IE) Irish Bks Media.

Dracula's Treasure. Dudley Saunders. (J). 1975. 5.00 (0-87602-123-2) Anchorage.

Draft. Gruenwald et al. 48p. 1988. 3.50 (0-87135-395-4) Marvel Entmnt.

Draft: A Handbook of Facts & Alternatives. Sol Tax. LC 67-25517. 511p. reprint ed. pap. 145.70 (0-317-08173-X, 2020168) Bks Demand.

Draft & Final Environmental Impact Reports: Bay Trail Plan. 160p. 1989. 10.00 (0-317-05695-6, P90003PLN) Assn Bay Area.

Draft & Its Enemies: A Documentary History. Ed. by John O'Sullivan et al. LC 74-10979. 309p. reprint ed. pap. 88.10 (0-317-08169-1, 2022262) Bks Demand.

Draft Anthology of Prairie Poetry. Ed. by Dennis Cooley. 198p. (C). 1981. pap. text ed. 14.50 (0-920802-07-9, Pub. by ECW Press CN) Genl Dist Srvs.

***Draft Criminal Code for South Africa: With a Commentary.** C. R. Snyman. 126p. 1995. pap. 32.00 (0-7021-3334-5, Pub. by Juta SA) W W Gaunt.

Draft Dodger. Louis Caron. Tr. by David T. Homel. 150p. (Orig.). 1980. pap. 9.95 (0-88784-085-X, Pub. by Hse of Anansi Pr CN) Genl Dist Srvs.

Draft Environmental Impact Statement--Proposed Domestic Livestock Grazing Program for the Challis Planning Unit: Review. (Reports Ser.: No. 58). 68p. 1976. 4.00 (0-318-13834-4) CAST.

***Draft Horse Images.** Robert A. Mischka. (Illus.). 160p. 1995. pap. 24.00 (1-882199-03-0) Heart Prairie Pr.

Draft Horse Primer. Maurice Telleen. LC 77-898. (Illus.). 386p. 1993. reprint ed. pap. 13.00 (0-9629076-1-8) Draft Horse Jrnl.

Draft Horses Today: Work Horses & Mules Find Their Way into the 21st Century. Robert A. Mischka. (Illus.). 176p. 1992. 29.50 (0-9622663-6-1) Heart Prairie Pr.

Draft International Code of Conduct on the Transfer of Technology. Wolfgang Fikentscher. (IIC Studies: Vol. 4). 195p. (Orig.). 1980. pap. 45.00 (0-89573-030-8) VCH Pubs.

Draft International Criminal Code & Draft Statute for An International Criminal Tribunal. M. Cherif Bassiouni. 1987. lib. bdg. 202.50 (0-89838-918-6) Kluwer Ac.

Draft of Proposed Standard on APL. (APL Quote Quad Ser.: Vol. 14, No. 2). (Illus.). 308p. 1983. pap. text ed. 28.00 (0-89791-124-5, 826830) Assn Compu Machinery.

Draft of Shadows & Other Poems. Octavio Paz. Tr. by Eliot Weinberger. LC 79-15588. 1979. pap. 8.95 (0-8112-0738-2, NDP489) New Directions.

Draft of XXX Cantos. Ezra Pound. LC 74-6379. (Studies in Pound: No. 103). 1974. lib. bdg. 75.00 (0-8383-1997-1) M S G Haskell Hse.

Draft of XXX Cantos. Ezra Pound. LC 89-13432. 160p. 1990. reprint ed. pap. 9.95 (0-8112-1128-2, NDP690) New Directions.

Draft Program of the Communist International: A Criticism of Fundamentals. Lev Trotskii. LC 75-41275. reprint ed. 12.50 (0-685-70801-2) AMS Pr.

Draft Program of the Communist International: A Criticism of Fundamentals. Lev Trotskii. LC 75-41166. reprint ed. 20.00 (0-404-14618-X) AMS Pr.

Draft Proposal for a Comprehensive Program of Music Education for the City of Chicago. Herbert Zipper. 1969. 20.00 (0-318-21718-X) NGCSA.

Draft Registration & the Law. 2nd rev. ed. R. Charles Johnson. Ed. by Charles E. Sherman. LC 85-89693. (Illus.). 256p. 1991. pap. 9.95 (0-944508-07-3) Nolo Occidental.

Draft X: Letters. Rachel B. DuPlessis. 32p. (Orig.). 1991. pap. 6.00 (0-935162-10-0) Singing Horse.

Draft, 1940-1973. George Q. Flynn. LC 92-31081. (Modern War Studies). (Illus.). 360p. 1993. 45.00 (0-7006-0586-X) U Pr of KS.

Draftee Division: The Eighty-Eighth Infantry Division in World War II. John S. Brown. LC 86-18990. (Illus.). 256p. 1986. 28.00 (0-8131-1581-7) U Pr of Ky.

Drafting. Boy Scouts of America. (Illus.). 32p. (J). (gr. 6-12). 1965. pap. 1.85 (0-8395-3273-3, 33262) BSA.

Drafting. Los Angeles Unified School District Staff. LC 77-73291. 64p. (gr. 7-9). 1978. pap. text ed. 5.76 (0-02-820320-8) Glencoe.

Drafting: Metric. Charles Rohlmeier. LC 79-55761. 320p. reprint ed. pap. 91.20 (0-317-19778-9, 2023202) Bks Demand.

Drafting: Tips & Tricks on Drawing & Designing House Plans. 2nd ed. Bob Syvanen. LC 93-11223. (Home Builder's Library). (Illus.). 112p. 1993. pap. 12.95 (1-56440-250-9) Globe Pequot.

Drafting - Its Application to Conveyancing & Commercial Documents. S. Robinson. 1980. U.K. 115.00 (0-406-35890-7) Butterworth Legal Pubs.

Drafting a Constitution for a Nation Or Republic Emerging into Freedom. 2nd ed. Bernard H. Siegan. 126p. (C). 1994. lib. bdg. 29.50 (0-913969-70-2, G Mason Univ Pr) Univ Pub Assocs.

Drafting a Fair Office Lease. suppl. ed. Gary Goldman. 413p. 1989. text ed. 94.00 (0-8318-0586-2, B586/B656) Am Law Inst.

Drafting a Fair Office Lease, Suppl. 1991. Gary Goldman. LC 89-84770. 413p. 1989. Supplement 1991. 25.00 (0-8318-0656-7, B656) Am Law Inst.

Drafting Agreements for the Sale of Businesses. California Continuing Education of the Bar Staff. LC 88-62938. 350p. 1988. 110.00 (0-88124-015-X, BU-39670) Cont Ed Bar-CA.

Drafting Aide. Jack Rudman. (Career Examination Ser.: C-202). 1994. pap. 23.95 (0-8373-0202-1) Nat Learn.

Drafting & Design with Computer Graphics. 2nd ed. James H. Earle. 106p. 1985. 8.95 (0-932702-78-3); write for info. (0-318-66026-1) Creative Texas.

Drafting & Enforcing Contracts in Civil & Common Law Jurisdictions. Ed. by K. Yelpaala et al. 288p. 1986. pap. 63.00 (90-6544-279-0) Kluwer Law Tax Pubs.

Drafting & Negotiating Commercial Leases. 3rd ed. Murray J. Ross. 1989. 100.00 (0-406-35909-1, U.K.) Butterworth Legal Pubs.

***Drafting & Negotiating Commercial Leases in Australia.** T. Barnett. 256p. 1990. boxed 78.00 (0-409-49555-7, Austral) Butterworth Legal Pubs.

Drafting & Negotiating Commercial Leases in Scotland. Murray J. Ross et al. 1985. 90.00 (0-406-35906-7, U.K.) Butterworth Legal Pubs.

2098 An Asterisk (*) at the beginning of an entry indicates that the title is appearing in BIP for the first time.

Drafting & Negotiating Commercial Leases in Scotland. 2nd ed. Ross. 1993. 130.00 (*0-406-02006-X*, UK) Butterworth Legal Pubs.

***Drafting & Negotiating Commerical Leases.** 4th ed. Ralf Rogowski. 347p. 1994. pap. text ed. 143.00 (*0-406-01026-9*, UK) Butterworth Legal Pubs.

Drafting & Negotiating Computer Contracts. Paul Klinger & Rachel Burnett. 336p. 1993. U.K. 79.00 (*0-406-15605-0*) Butterworth Legal Pubs.

Drafting & Pattern Designing. Woman's Institute of Domestic Arts & Sciences. 160p. 1994. 22.00 (*0-916896-56-0*) Lacis Pubns.

Drafting & Revising Employment Contracts. Kurt H. Decker & H. Thomas Felix. (Employment Law Library). 358p. 1991. text ed. 128.00 (*0-471-54292-X*) Wiley.

Drafting & Revising Employment Handbooks. Kurt H. Decker & H. Thomas Felix. (Employment Law Library). 429p. 1991. text ed. 115.00 (*0-471-54293-8*) Wiley.

Drafting & Revising Employment Policies & Handbooks, 1. Kurt H. Decker. LC 94-10238. (Human Resources Library). 1994. write for info. (*0-471-04666-3*) Wiley.

Drafting & Revising Employment Policies & Handbooks, 2. Kurt H. Decker. LC 94-10238. (Human Resources Library). 1994. write for info. (*0-471-04667-1*) Wiley.

Drafting & Revising Employment Policies & Handbooks, Vol. 2. 2nd ed. Kurt H. Decker. LC 94-10238. (Human Resources Library). 1994. Set. text ed. 215.00 (*0-471-04663-9*) Wiley.

Drafting Association Rules: Drafting Association Rules, No. 7. rev. ed. Gordon H. Buck. (GAP Report Ser.: Vol. 7). 16p. (C). 1993. pap. 14.50 (*0-944715-25-7*) CAI.

Drafting Bankruptcy Reorganization Plans, 3 vols., Vol. 3. 2nd ed. John K. Pearson et al. LC 93-10016. (Bankruptcy Practice Library). 1616p. 1993. Acid-free paper. text ed. 315.00 (*0-471-59631-0*) Wiley.

Drafting California Irrevocable Living Trusts: February 1992 Update. 2nd ed. Edith M. Doyle. Ed. by Carol Gamble. LC 86-72863. 941p. 1992. ring bd. 55.00 (*0-88124-452-X*, ES-32343) Cont Ed Bar-CA.

Drafting California Revocable Living Trusts. 2nd ed. Ed. by John R. Cohan. 491p. 1984. 75.00 (*0-88124-136-9*, ES-38830) Cont Ed Bar-CA.

Drafting California Revocable Living Trusts: June 1993 Update. 2nd ed. Charles A. Larson. Ed. by Carine Archer. LC 84-71499. 179p. 1993. pap. text ed. 28.00 (*0-88124-650-6*, ES-38837) Cont Ed Bar-CA.

Drafting Careers. Mark Rowh. (Opportunities in...Ser.). (Illus.). 160p. 1991. 13.95 (*0-8442-6143-2*, Passport Bks); pap. 10.95 (*0-8442-6144-0*, Passport Bks) NTC Pub Grp.

Drafting Commercial Agreements. (Commercial Law & Practice Course Handbook Ser.). 272p. 1992. pap. 65.00 (*0-685-69416-X*) PLI.

Drafting Commercial Agreements. Alan Berg. 285p. 1991. pap. 50.00 (*0-406-00142-1*, U.K.) Butterworth Legal Pubs.

Drafting Construction Contracts: Strategy & Forms for Contractors. Samuel F. Schoninger. (Construction Law Library). 1990. text ed. 115.00 (*0-471-52946-X*) Wiley.

Drafting Construction Contracts: Strategy & Forms for Contractors. suppl. ed. Samuel F. Schoninger. (Construction Law Library). 1993. Cummulative Supplement, 1993. 55.00 (*0-471-59455-5*) Wiley.

Drafting Construction Contracts & Handling Construction Litigation 1993: Preparing for the New Public & Private Works. (Real Estate Law & Practice Course Handbook Ser.: Vol. 391). 468p. 1993. 70.00 (*0-685-69753-3*, N4-4573) PLI.

Drafting Effective Contracts: A Practitioner's Guide. R. A. Feldman. 958p. 1989. ring bd. 110.00 (*0-13-297590-4*) Aspen Law.

Drafting Employment & Termination Agreements. Lawrence Leader. LC 93-15610. 1993. write for info. (*0-8205-1274-5*) Bender.

Drafting, Enacting & Maintaining Local Ordinances. George B. Davis. 1991. 15.00 (*0-317-05701-4*) MI Municipal.

Drafting Engineering Contracts. H. Henkin. 240p. 1988. 72.00 (*1-85166-223-5*) Elsevier.

Drafting for Electronics. 2nd ed. Louis G. Lamit & Sandra J. Lloyd. 592p. (C). 1993. write for info. (*0-02-367342-7*, Merrill Pub Co) Macmillan.

***Drafting for Industry.** rev. ed. Walter C. Brown. (Illus.). 704p. 1995. text ed. 47.00 (*1-56637-048-5*) Goodheart.

Drafting for the Theatre. Dennis Dorn & Mark Shanda. LC 89-20915. (Illus.). 224p. (C). 1991. pap. 24.95 (*0-8093-1508-4*) S Ill U Pr.

Drafting for Trades & Industry. John Nelson. LC 77-91450. (Drafting Ser.). teacher ed 15.00 (*0-8273-1641-0*) Delmar.

Drafting for Trades & Industry - Architectural. John Nelson. LC 77-91450. (Drafting Ser.). 138p. (C). 1979. pap. text ed. 24.95 (*0-8273-1839-1*) Delmar.

Drafting for Trades & Industry - Basic Skills. John Nelson. LC 77-91450. (Drafting Ser.). 464p. (C). 1979. pap. text ed. 32.95 (*0-8273-1841-3*) Delmar.

Drafting for Trades & Industry - Civil. John Nelson. LC 77-91450. (Drafting Ser.). 942p. (C). 1979. pap. text ed. 24.95 (*0-8273-1844-8*) Delmar.

Drafting for Trades & Industry - Mechanical & Electronic. John Nelson. LC 77-91450. (Drafting Ser.). 328p. (C). 1979. pap. text ed. 24.95 (*0-8273-1846-4*) Delmar.

Drafting Fundamentals. 5th ed. Cecil H. Jensen & F. H. Mason. 333p. 1982. text ed. 40.95 (*0-07-548068-9*) McGraw.

Drafting Fundamentals 1. 2nd ed. James H. Earle et al. (gr. 8-12). 1988. reprint ed. 8.95 (*0-932702-54-6*) Creative Texas.

Drafting Fundamentals 1. 2nd ed. James H. Earle et al. (YA). (gr. 8-12). 1988. reprint ed. teacher ed 3.50 (*0-932702-84-8*) Creative Texas.

Drafting Fundamentals 2. James H. Earle et al. (gr. 8-12). 1969. 8.95 (*0-932702-55-4*) Creative Texas.

Drafting History of the Federal Rules of Criminal Procedure, 7 vols. in 5 bks., Set. Nicholas Triffin & Madeleine Wilken. LC 90-86245. 2050p. 1991. lib. bdg. 385.00 (*0-685-47989-7*, 307040) W S Hein.

***Drafting House Plans.** June N. Curran. (Illus.). 188p. 1995. pap. 27.50 (*0-932370-03-9*) Brooks Pub Co.

Drafting House Plans: A Simplified Drafting System for Planning & Design. June Curran. LC 90-81254. (Simplified Design Systems Ser.: Bk. 1). (Illus.). 200p. 1990. pap. 24.95 (*0-932370-04-7*) Brooks Pub Co.

***Drafting in a Computer Age.** Paul I. Wallach. 1989. 46.95 (*0-8273-2925-3*) Delmar.

Drafting Legal Documents: Materials & Problems. Barbara Child. (University Casebook Ser.). 422p. 1992. pap. text ed. 25.50 (*0-314-00325-8*) West Pub.

Drafting Legal Documents: Principles & Practices, Teacher's Manual to Accompany. 2nd ed. Barbara Child. (American Casebook Ser.). 333p. (C). 1992. pap. text ed. write for info. (*0-314-01085-8*) West Pub.

***Drafting Legal Opinion Letters, 3.** 2nd ed. Ed. by A. Sidney Holderness & Brooke Wunnicke. text ed. write for info. (*0-471-05972-2*) Wiley.

Drafting Legal Opinion Letters, 2 vols., Vol. 2. 2nd ed. Ed. by John M. Sterba. (Business Practice Library). 856p. 1992. Set. text ed. 225.00 (*0-471-57439-2*) Wiley.

***Drafting Legal Opinion Letters: Formbook, Vol. 3.** 2nd ed. Ed. by A. Sidney Holderness et al. (Business Practice Library: Vol. 3). 1994. text ed. 118.00 (*0-471-58622-6*) Wiley.

Drafting Legislation & Rules in Plain English. Robert J. Martineau. 155p. 1991. pap. text ed. 13.00 (*0-314-89023-8*) West Pub.

Drafting Legislation & Rules in Plain English, Instructor's Manual of Drafting Exercises. Robert J. Martineau. (American Casebook Ser.). 88p. (C). 1991. pap. text ed. write for info. (*0-314-90368-2*) West Pub.

***Drafting License Agreements.** 2nd ed. Ed. by Michael A. Epstein & Frank L. Politano. LC 94-32936. 1994. ring bd. 145.00 (*0-13-346578-0*) Aspen Law.

Drafting Manual Pocket Companion. Ed. by Gerald J. Cavanaugh. (Illus.). 73p. (Orig.). 1991. pap. text ed. 14.95 (*0-931690-36-6*) Genium Pub.

***Drafting Marriage Contracts in Florida.** 3rd ed. Florida Bar Staff. LC 94-70117. 276p. 1994. disk, ring bd. 75.00 (*0-945979-56-8*, 230) FL Bar Legal Ed.

Drafting Natural Gas Contracts after Order Four Hundred Thirty-Six: The Producer's Perspective. 1989. pap. 29.95 (*0-89707-484-X*, 535-0021) Amer Bar Assn.

Drafting New York Wills: Law & Forms, 2 vols. 3rd ed. Harold D. Klipstein. 1969. Updates available. ring bd. write for info. (*0-8205-1338-5*) Bender.

Drafting of Partnership Agreements. 7th ed. Marlin M. Volz et al. 251p. 1986. 76.00 (*0-8318-0514-5*, B514) Am Law Inst.

Drafting of Wills. H. Barker. 1993. write for info. (*0-7021-3012-5*, Pub. by Juta SA) W W Gaunt.

Drafting Patent License Agreements. 3rd ed. Harry R. Mayers & Brian G. Brunsvold. LC 90-48874. 292p. 1991. text ed. 68.00 (*0-87179-674-0*, 0674) BNA.

Drafting Plus: Five Simple Steps to Pattern Drafting & More! Sharyn S. Craig. Ed. by Pamela M. Watts & Patti L. Bachelder. LC 94-5637. (Illus.). 80p. (Orig.). 1994. pap. 14.95 (*0-9622565-4-4*) Chariot Pub PA.

***Drafting Prenuptial Agreements.** Gary N. Skoloff et al. 600p. 1994. 95.00 (*0-13-346586-1*, D0002) Aspen Law.

Drafting Scenery for Theater, Film, & Television. Rich Rose. LC 94-7095. (Illus.). 176p. 1994. pap. 18.99 (*1-55870-348-9*) Betterway Bks.

Drafting Settlements: A Guide for Litigators. Michael Arnbeim. 130p. 1993. 55.00 (*0-85459-756-5*, Pub. by Tolley Pubng UK) St Mut.

Drafting Standard Form Farmout Agreements. American Bar Association, Natural Resources Law Staff. LC 86-72566. 62p. 1986. pap. 29.95 (*0-89707-273-1*, 535-0007) Amer Bar Assn.

Drafting: Syllabus. David A. Madsen. 1974. pap. text ed. 8.95 (*0-89420-070-4*, 107015); audio 104.35 (*0-89420-140-9*, 107000) Natl Book.

Drafting Technician. Jack Rudman. (Career Examination Ser.: C-2678). 1994. pap. 23.95 (*0-8373-2678-8*) Nat Learn.

Drafting Technology. 2nd ed. James H. Earle. LC 85-7487. 700p. (C). 1986. text ed. write for info. (*0-201-10239-0*) Addison-Wesley.

Drafting Technology. 2nd ed. Joseph W. Giachino & Henry J. Beukema. LC 64-12817. (Illus.). 464p. reprint ed. pap. 132.30 (*0-317-10628-7*, 2011278) Bks Demand.

Drafting Technology. 2nd rev. ed. James H. Earle. (Illus.). (C). 1991. text ed. 46.25 (*0-201-53473-8*) Addison-Wesley.

Drafting Technology & Practice. rev. ed. William P. Spence. (gr. 9-12). 1981. text ed. 29.20 (*0-02-663440-6*); 16.60 (*0-02-663460-0*) Bennett IL.

Drafting Technology Problems. James H. Earle. 91p. 1982. teacher ed 3.50 (*0-932702-68-6*); disk (*0-932702-43-0*) Creative Texas.

Drafting Technology Problems with Computer Graphics. 2nd ed. James H. Earle. LC 89-23952. 120p. 1985. 11.95 (*0-932702-82-1*) Creative Texas.

Drafting the Durable Power of Attorney: A Systems Approach, 2 vols. 2nd ed. 1987. text ed. 170.00 (*0-07-172141-X*) Shepards-McGraw.

Drafting the Federal Constitution: A Rearrangement of Madison's Notes, Giving Consecutive Developments of Provisions in the Constitution of the United States. Ed. by Arthur T. Prescott. LC 68-54433. (Illus.). 838p. 1969. reprint ed. text ed. 105.00 (*0-8371-0196-4*, PRFC) Greenwood.

Drafting the Union Contract: A Handbook for the Management Negotiator. Peter N. Lareau. 1988. write for info. (*0-8205-1494-2*) Bender.

Drafting Torchon Lace Patterns. Alexandra Stillwell. 1987. pap. 18.50 (*0-7134-7197-2*) Robin & Russ.

Drafting Wills & Trusts Agreements: A Systems Approach. 2nd ed. Robert P. Wilkins. 1964p. 1989. text ed. 225.00 (*0-07-172191-6*) Shepards-McGraw.

Drafting Wills & Trusts in Massachusetts. Alette E. Reed et al. LC 89-64081. 500p. 1990. ring bd. 95.00 (*0-944490-17-4*) Mass CLE.

Drafting with AutoCAD. Peter Ingham. 208p. 1991. pap. text ed. 36.95 (*0-7506-0073-X*) Buttrwrth-Heinemann.

Drafting with AutoCAD. Paul Wallach. 1990. pap. write for info. (*0-07-909590-9*) McGraw.

Draftmen Go Free. Bob Scates. 109p. (C). 1990. 33.00 (*0-7316-6100-1*, Pub. by Pascoe Pub AT) St Mut.

Drafts. Rachel B. DuPlessis. 99p. (Orig.). 1991. pap. 9.50 (*0-937013-37-4*) Potes Poets.

Drafts Agenda 21, Rio Declaration Forest Principles. 600p. (Orig.). 1992. pap. 75.00 (*92-1-100482-9*) UN.

Drafts For: The Army Has Announced That Body Bags Will from Now on be Known As "Human Remains Pouches" Nathaniel Tarn. (Chaplets Ser.). 8p. (Orig.). (gr. 10 up). 1992. pap. 1.50 (*0-916155-19-6*) Trout Creek.

Drafts for Laon & Cythna: Facsimiles of Bodleian Mss. Shelley Adds. E. 14 & Adds. E. 19, Vol. XIII, No. E.19. Contrib by Tatsuo Tokoo. LC 91-43904. (Bodleian Shelley Manuscripts). 294p. 1992. 162.00 (*0-8240-5873-9*) Garland.

Drafts for Laon & Cythna, Cantos V-XII: Bodleian MS Shelley adds, E. 10. Percy Bysshe Shelley. Tr. & Intro. by Steven E. Jones. LC 94-721. (Bodleian Shelley Manuscripts: Vol. 17). 264p. 1994. 151.00 (*0-8153-1152-4*) Garland.

Drafts for the Essay Concerning Human Understanding, & Other Philosophical Writings, Vol. 1, Drafts A & B. John Locke. Ed. by Peter H. Nidditch & G. A. Rogers. (Clarendon Edition of the Works of John Locke Ser.). (Illus.). 330p. 1990. 98.00 (*0-19-824545-9*) OUP.

Draftsman. Jack Rudman. (Career Examination Ser.: C-203). 1994. pap. 23.95 (*0-8373-0203-X*) Nat Learn.

Draftsman Raphael. Francis Ames-Lewis. LC 86-1593. 174p. reprint ed. pap. 49.60 (*0-7837-4540-0*, 2080289) Bks Demand.

Draftsman's Mathematical Manual. 2nd ed. Erick V. Oberg. LC 41-20206. 271p. reprint ed. pap. 77.30 (*0-317-08775-4*, 2001911) Bks Demand.

***Drag: A History of Female Impersonation in the Performing Arts.** Roger Baker. LC 94-37485. (Illus.). 268p. 1995. 45.00 (*0-8147-1253-3*); pap. 15.95 (*0-8147-1254-1*) NYU Pr.

Drag Boat Racing: The National Championships. Al Jackson & Gene Tardy. (Sports Action Ser.). (Illus.). 48p. (J). (gr. 3-7). 1973. lib. bdg. 6.89 (*0-914844-05-9*); pap. 3.95 (*0-914844-06-7*) J Alden.

Drag Gags: Fun with Female Impersonation from the Movies. Ralph Judd. LC 91-90040. (Illus.). 68p. (Orig.). 1991. pap. 7.95 (*0-9628928-0-7*) R Judd Commun.

Drag Gags Return: Tongue-in-Cheek Fun with Female Impersonation from the Movies. Ralph Judd. LC 92-90020. (Illus.). 80p. (Orig.). 1992. pap. 8.95 (*0-9628928-1-5*) R Judd Commun.

Drag Harlan. Charles A. Seltzer. reprint ed. lib. bdg. 21.95 (*0-88411-104-0*, Aeonian Pr) Amereon Ltd.

Drag Hunting. Jane Kidd. 1990. pap. 40.00 (*0-85131-295-0*, Pub. by J A Allen & Co UK) St Mut.

Drag! Male & Female Impersonators on Stage, Screen & Television: An Illustrated World History. F. Michael Moore. 336p. 1994. lib. bdg. 45.00 (*0-89950-996-7*) McFarland & Co.

***Drag Queen.** Robert Rodi. 224p. 1995. 21.95 (*0-525-93925-3*, Dutton) NAL-Dutton.

***Drag Racing.** Smith. (J). 1995. pap. 5.95 (*0-516-40230-7*) Childrens.

***Drag Racing.** Jay H. Smith. LC 94-22625. (Motorsports Ser.). 48p. (J). (gr. 3-4). 1994. lib. bdg. 13.35 (*1-56065-230-6*) Capstone Pr.

Drag Racing: How to Get Started. Frank Hawley. LC 93-15680. 1993. pap. 14.95 (*0-87938-752-1*) Motorbooks Intl.

Drag Racing to Win: How to Drive Dragsters. Frank A. Hawley. (Illus.). 144p. 1989. pap. 15.95 (*0-87938-386-0*) Motorbooks Intl.

Drag Reduction in Two-Phase Gas-Liquid Flow. N. Sylvester et al. 182p. 1977. pap. 5.00 (*0-318-12598-6*, L11477) Am Gas Assn.

***Drag Reduction of Turbulent Flows by Additives.** A. Gyr & H. W. Bewersdorff. LC 95-12572. (Fluid Mechanics & Its Applications Ser.: Vol. 32). 1995. write for info. (*0-7923-3485-X*) Kluwer Ac.

***Draggerman's Haul: The Personal History of a Connecticut Fishing Captain.** 3rd ed. Ellery Thompson. 1994. pap. 20.00 (*0-910258-21-X*) Book & Tackle.

Draggin' S Ranch Cowpokes. 14th ed. Ace Reid. (Illus.). 65p. (J). (gr. 5 up). reprint ed. pap. 5.95 (*0-917207-04-1*) Reid Ent.

Dragging Sand Creek for Minnows. William Kloefkorn. 80p. 1992. pap. 5.95 (*0-944024-21-1*) Spoon Riv Poetry.

Dragmalogia de Elgibili Vite Genere, by Giovanni di Conversino da Ravenna. Giovanni Da Ravenna. Ed. by Helen L. Eaker & Benjamin G. Kohl. LC 79-2342. (Bucknell Renaissance Texts in Translation Ser.). 296p. (ENG & LAT.). 1980. 38.50 (*0-8387-1897-3*) Bucknell U Pr.

Dragmalogia de Eligibili Vitae Genere (1404) Giovanni Di Conversino da Ravenna. Ed. by Benjamin G. Kohl & Helen L. Eaker. (Renaissance Text Ser.: No. 7). 1980. 24.50 (*0-318-11900-5*) Renaiss Society Am.

Drago. (Illus.). (J). (ps). 1992. 7.00 (*1-56021-149-0*) W J Fantasy.

Drago Blu. Herge. (Illus.). 62p. (ITA.). (J). pap. 19.95 (*0-8288-5028-3*) Fr & Eur.

Dragolin. Stephen Cosgrove. LC 85-14400. (Serendipity Bks.). (Illus.). 32p. (Orig.). (J). (gr. 1-4). 1984. pap. 3.95 (*0-8431-1165-8*) Price Stern.

***Dragolin.** Stephen Cosgrove. LC 94-25729. (Serendipity Ser.). (Illus.). 32p. 1995. 3.95 (*0-8431-3825-4*) Price Stern.

Dragomir. Alfred Friendly. Ed. by Jane Weinberger & Albert Black. LC 88-50316. (Illus.). 46p. (J). (ps up). 1988. pap. 5.95 (*0-932433-44-8*) Windswept Hse.

Dragon. Wayne Anderson. LC 91-4790. (J). (ps-3). 1992. 15.00 (*0-671-78397-1*, Green Tiger S&S) S&S Childrens.

Dragon. Clive Cussler. 1990. write for info. (*0-671-94486-X*); pap. 21.95 (*0-685-34802-4*) S&S Trade.

Dragon. Francis Huxley. LC 87-51294. (Art & Imagination Ser.). (Illus.). 96p. 1988. pap. 14.95 (*0-500-81020-6*) Thames Hudson.

Dragon. Michael Jahn. (Orig.). 1993. pap. 4.50 (*0-515-11171-6*) Jove Pubns.

Dragon. Kwok Man-Ho. LC 93-48006. (Chinese Horoscopes Library). (Illus.). 48p. 1994. 8.95 (*1-56458-602-2*) Dorling Kindersley.

Dragon. William Schoell. 368p. pap. 3.95 (*0-8439-2758-5*) Dorchester Pub Co.

Dragon. Eugene Schwarz. Tr. by Elizabeth R. Hapgood. (Orig.). 1969. pap. 6.95 (*0-87830-512-2*, Theatre Arts Bks) Routledge Chapman & Hall.

Dragon. large type ed. Clive Cussler. (General Ser.). 654p. 1991. lib. bdg. 22.95 (*0-8161-5096-6*, Large Print Bks) Hall.

Dragon. Clive Cussler. Ed. by Paul McCarthy. 544p. 1991. reprint ed. pap. 6.99 (*0-671-74276-0*) PB.

Dragon! A Sicilian Counterattack. Ron Henley & Paul Hodges. (ChessBase University Power Play! Ser.). (Illus.). 64p. (Orig.). 1993. pap. 10.95 (*1-883358-06-X*) R&D Pub NJ.

Dragon ABC Hunt. Loreen Leedy. LC 85-21907. (Illus.). 36p. (J). (ps-1). 1986. lib. bdg. 14.95 (*0-8234-0596-6*) Holiday.

Dragon Acts to Dragon Ends. Kay Ryan. LC 82-51255. 64p. (Orig.). pap. 4.95 (*0-911407-00-6*) Taylor Street.

Dragon & Monster Tales. Corinne Denan. LC 79-66329. (Illus.). 48p. (J). (gr. 3-6). 1980. lib. bdg. 9.89 (*0-89375-326-2*); pap. 2.95 (*0-89375-325-4*) Troll Assocs.

***Dragon & Sleepy Owl.** Lucy Kincaid. (Read by Yourself Ser.). 32p. (J). 1994. 2.98 (*1-85854-132-8*) Brimax Bks.

Dragon & the Bat. Geary Gravel. (Batman: The Animated Ser.). 1994. mass mkt. 4.99 (*0-553-56608-3*) Bantam.

***Dragon & the Doctor.** rev. ed. Barbara Danish. (Illus.). 40p. (J). 1995. pap. 5.95 (*1-55861-117-7*) Feminist Pr.

Dragon & the Dove: The Protestant Plays of Thomas Dekker. Julia Gasper. (Oxford English Monographs). (Illus.). 256p. 1990. 59.00 (*0-19-811758-2*) OUP.

Dragon & the Eagle: The Presence of China in the American Enlightenment. A. Owen Aldridge. LC 93-1060. (Illus.). 288p. 1993. text ed. 39.95 (*0-8143-2455-X*) Wayne St U Pr.

Dragon & the George. Gordon R. Dickson. 1987. mass mkt. 4.95 (*0-345-35050-2*, Del Rey) Ballantine.

Dragon & the Iron Horse: The Economics of Railroads in China, 1876-1937. Ralph W. Huenemann. (Monographs: No. 129). (Illus.). 1983. 20.00 (*0-317-01567-2*) Harvard E Asian.

Dragon & the Iron Horse: The Economics of Railroads in China, 1876-1937. Ralph W. Huenemann. (East Asian Monographs: No. 109). 368p. (C). 1984. 28.00 (*0-674-21535-4*) HUP.

Dragon & the Jewel. Virginia Henley. 1991. mass mkt. 5.50 (*0-440-20624-3*) Dell.

Dragon & The Lemon Tree. Robert Walton. LC 89-92122. (Illus.). 86p. (J). (gr. 3-7). 1989. write for info. (*0-9623802-0-2*) Pisces Pr CA.

Dragon & the Mouse. Stephen A. Timm. (Illus.). 1981. pap. 4.95 (*0-939728-01-X*) Steppingstone Ent.

Dragon & the Mouse: The Dream. Stephen A. Timm. (Illus.). 45p. (J). 1982. 12.95 (*0-939728-05-2*); pap. 4.95 (*0-939728-06-0*) Steppingstone Ent.

Dragon & the Mouse: Together Again. Stephen A. Timm. LC 81-90230. (Illus.). 46p. (J). (ps-8). 1981. 12.95 (*0-939728-03-6*); pap. 4.95 (*0-939728-04-4*) Steppingstone Ent.

***Dragon & the Rabbits.** Lucy Kincaid. (Read by Yourself Ser.). 32p. (J). 1994. 2.98 (*1-85854-131-X*) Brimax Bks.

Dragon & the Snake: An American Account of the Turmoil in China, 1976-1977. Millicent A. Gates et al. LC 86-19218. (Illus.). 235p. 1986. 42.95 (*0-8122-8036-9*) U of Pa Pr.

Dragon & the Thief. Gillian Bradshaw. LC 90-48259. (Illus.). (J). (gr. 5 up). 1991. 13.95 (*0-688-10575-0*) Greenwillow.

Dragon & the Unicorn. Lynne Cherry. LC 92-30321. (Gulliver Green Book Ser.). (J). 1994. write for info. (*0-15-224193-0*) HarBrace.

Dragon & the Wild Goose: China & India. Jay Taylor. LC 87-7563. (Contributions to the Study of World History Ser.: No. 8). 288p. 1987. text ed. 55.00 (*0-313-25899-6*, TDG/, Greenwood Pr) Greenwood.

Dragon & Tiger: The Oakland Years. Greglon Lee & Sid Campbell. (Illus.). 300p. 1983. write for info. (*0-318-57559-0*) Gong Prods.

Dragon Apparent. Norman Lewis. (Eland Travel Classics Ser.). 317p. 1993. reprint ed. pap. 14.95 (*0-907871-00-3*) Hippocrene Bks.

Dragon Arises. Nat Yogachandra. 146p. 1992. pap. text ed. 9.50 (*0-9632559-3-2*) Ramega Pub Hse.

D

An Asterisk (*) at the beginning of an entry indicates that the title is appearing in BIP for the first time. 2099

***Dragon Ascending: Vietnam & the Vietnamese.** Henry Kamm. (Illus.). 288p. 1996. 24.95 (1-55970-306-7) Arcade Pub Inc.

Dragon at Noonday: The Brothers of Gwynedd II. Edith Pargeter. 342p. 1991. pap. 11.95 (0-7472-3017-X, Pub. by Headline UK) Trafalgar.

Dragon at War. Gordon Dickson. 1992. 18.95 (0-441-75698-0) Ace Bks.

Dragon at War. Gordon R. Dickson. 1993. mass mkt. 5.50 (0-441-16611-3) Ace Bks.

***Dragon Bones.** N. Evans & P. Hindman. (J). Date not set. write for info. (0-679-87435-6) Random.

Dragon Book. Jude Rodger. (J). 1993. pap. 15.95 (1-85756-042-6, Pub. by Janus Pub UK) Intl Spec Bk.

Dragon Cauldron. Laurence Yep. LC 90-39584. (Illus.). 320p. (YA). (gr. 7 up). 1991. lib. bdg. 16.89 (0-06-026754-2) HarpC Child Bks.

Dragon Cauldron. Laurence Yep. LC 90-39584. (Trophy Bk.). 320p. (YA). (gr. 7 up). 1994. pap. 4.95 (0-06-440398-X, Trophy) HarpC Child Bks.

Dragon Chiang. Truman & Bradstreet. (Illus.). 1991. 3.95 (1-56060-117-5) Eclipse Bks.

Dragon Christmas: Things to Make & Do. Loreen Leedy. LC 88-4635. (Illus.). 32p. (J). (ps-3). 1988. lib. bdg. 13.95 (0-8234-0716-0) Holiday.

Dragon Circle. Stephen Krensky. 128p. (YA). (gr. 7 up). 1990. reprint ed. pap. 3.95 (0-689-71365-7, Aladdin Paperbacks) S&S Childrens.

Dragon Circle: Dragon Sleeping. Craig S. Gardner. LC 93-8723. 368p. (Orig.). 1994. 19.95 (0-441-00049-5) Ace Bks.

***Dragon Circle: Dragon Sleeping.** Craig S. Gardner. 448p. (Orig.). 1995. pap. 5.99 (0-441-00260-9) Ace Bks.

***Dragon Companion.** Don Callander. 336p. (Orig.). 1994. pap. text ed. 5.50 (0-441-00115-7) Ace Bks.

Dragon Country: Eight Plays. Tennessee Williams. Ed. by A. J. Guerard. Incl. In the Bar of a Tokyo Hotel. LC 76-79724. (0-318-54639-6); Mutilated. LC 76-79724. (0-318-54640-X); Gnadiges Fraulein. LC 76-79724. (0-318-54641-8); I Rise in Flames, Cried the Phoenix. LC 76-79724. (0-318-54642-6); I Can't Imagine Tomorrow. LC 76-79724. (0-318-54643-4); Confessional. LC 76-79724. (0-318-54644-2); Frosted Glass Coffin. LC 76-79724. (0-318-54645-0); Perfect Analysis Given by a Parrot. LC 76-79724. (0-318-54646-9); LC 76-79724. 10.00 (0-8112-0406-5); Incl. (0-318-54639-6); (0-318-54640-X); (0-318-54641-8); (0-318-54642-6); (0-318-54643-4); (0-318-54644-2); (0-318-54645-0); (0-318-54646-9); Set pap. 10.95 (0-8112-0219-4, NDP287) New Directions.

Dragon Crown. Richard A. Knaak. 336p. (Orig.). 1994. mass mkt. 5.50 (0-446-36464-9, Aspect) Warner Bks.

Dragon Dance. John Christopher. LC 85-31149. 160p. (J). (gr. 5-9). 1986. 12.95 (0-525-44227-8, DCB) Dutton Child Bks.

Dragon Days. large type ed. Willis Hall. (Lythway Ser.). 200p. (J). (gr. 3-7). 1991. 16.95 (0-7451-1294-3, Galaxy Child Lrg Print) Chivers N Amer.

Dragon Death. Gael Baudino. (Dragonsword Ser.: No. 3). 384p. (Orig.). 1992. pap. 4.99 (0-451-45147-3, ROC) NAL-Dutton.

Dragon Den. (Series 9011-2: No. 2). (Illus.). (J). (ps-2). 1990. Series 9011-2, No. 2. 2.95 (0-7214-3221-2) Ladybird Bks.

Dragon Den. (Read with Me Key Words to Reading Ser.: No. 9010-2). (Illus.). (J). (ps-2). 1990. 3.50 (0-7214-1315-3); teacher ed 3.95 (0-317-04026-X) Ladybird Bks.

Dragon Doesn't Live Here Anymore: Living Fully, Loving Freely. Alan Cohen. 416p. 1993. pap. 12.50 (0-449-90840-2, Columbine) Fawcett.

Dragon Doesn't Live Here Anymore: Loving Fully Living Freely. Alan Cohen. (Illus.). 381p. (Orig.). (C). 1981. pap. 9.95 (0-910367-30-2) A Cohen.

Dragon Drinks Just One Drop. Vicki Armstrong. (Beginning Sounds Readers Ser.). (Illus.). 32p. (J). (gr. 1-6). 1990. student ed 5.99 (0-933367-01-5) See the Sounds.

Dragon Empress. Marina Warner. LC 86-7909. (Illus.). 256p. 1986. pap. 11.95 (0-689-70714-2, 344, Pub. by Ctrl Bur voor Schimmel NE) Macmillan.

Dragon Fall. Lee J. Hindle. 1984. pap. 2.95 (0-380-88468-2, Flare) Avon.

Dragon Fantastic. Ed. by Rosalind M. Greenberg & Martin H. Greenberg. 320p. (Orig.). 1992. mass mkt. 4.99 (0-88677-511-6) DAW Bks.

Dragon Feathers. Andrej Dugin & Olga Dugina. LC 93-8700. (Illus.). 24p. (J). 1993. 14.95 (1-56566-047-1) Thomasson-Grant.

Dragon Fire. Linda Ladd. 368p. (Orig.). 1992. mass mkt. 4.99 (0-380-75698-6) Avon.

Dragon Fire, No. 1. G. John Juray. Ed. by Don Lily. LC 92-90170. 432p. (Orig.). 1992. pap. 15.95 (0-9632497-1-1) Juray-Hse Gd Bks.

Dragon for Breakfast. Eunice McMullen & Nigel McMullen. (Illus.). 28p. (J). (ps-3). 1990. lib. bdg. 18.95 (0-87614-650-7, Carolrhoda) Lerner Group.

Dragon Gate. Date not set. 5.95 (1-56222-048-9, 94511) Mel Bay.

Dragon Gets By. Dav Pilkey. LC 90-46027. (Illus.). 48p. (J). (gr. 1-3). 1991. 13.95 (0-531-05935-9); lib. bdg. 13.99 (0-531-08535-X) Orchard Bks Watts.

Dragon Halloween Party. Loreen Leedy. LC 86-286. (Illus.). 32p. (J). (ps-3). 1986. lib. bdg. 14.95 (0-8234-0611-3); pap. 5.95 (0-8234-0765-9) Holiday.

Dragon Hammer & the Tale of Oniroku. Joanna Kraus. LC 77-83857. (Illus.). 64p. (J). (gr. 3-5). 1977. 7.95 (0-932720-18-8); pap. 4.95 (0-932720-17-X) New Plays Inc.

***Dragon Has Many Faces: Concept.** Richard-Michael Diedrich. (Interethnic Relations & Cultural Changes Ser.). (C). 1994. pap. text ed. 24.50 (3-89473-646-1) Westview.

Dragon in a Wagon. Lynley Dodd. Ed. by Rhoda Sherwood. LC 88-42925. (Gold Star First Readers Ser.). (Illus.). 32p. (J). (gr. 1-2). 1988. lib. bdg. 17.27 (1-55532-911-X) Gareth Stevens Inc.

***Dragon in a Wagon.** Jane B. Moncure. LC 87-11755. (Magic Castle Readers Ser.). (Illus.). 32p. (ENG & SPA.). (J). (ps-2). 1987. pap. text ed. 21.36 (0-89565-907-7) Childs World.

Dragon in a Wagon. Jane B. Moncure. LC 87-11755. (Magic Castle Readers Ser.). (Illus.). 32p. (ENG & SPA.). (J). (ps-2). 1987. lib. bdg. 21.36 (0-89565-400-8) Childs World.

Dragon in My Cup. Baumgart. (J). Date not set. 13.95 (0-06-021677-8, HarpT); lib. bdg. 13.89 (0-06-021678-6, HarpT) HarpC.

Dragon in the Cliff: A Novel Based on the Life of Mary Anning. Shelia Cole. LC 90-40455. (J). (gr. 4-7). 1991. 13.95 (0-688-10196-8) Lothrop.

Dragon in the Clouds: Poems & Translations. Sam Hamill. LC 89-61141. 128p. (Orig.). 1989. pap. 10.00 (0-913089-11-7) Broken Moon.

***Dragon in the Cupboard.** Karen Dolby. (Young Puzzle Adventure Ser.). (Illus.). 32p. (J). (ps-2). 1995. lib. bdg. 12.96 (0-88110-761-1, Usborne); pap. 4.95 (0-7460-1355-8, Usborne) EDC.

Dragon in the Family. Jackie F. Koller. LC 93-7028. (Springboard Bks.). (Illus.). (J). 1993. 12.95 (0-316-50151-4) Little.

Dragon in the Forest. Lina Johnson. (Illus.). 96p. (Orig.). (J). (gr. k-8). 1994. lib. bdg. 5.95 (1-885100-00-0) Read Me CA.

Dragon in the House. David Rosser. 235p. (C). 1987. 21.00x (0-86383-357-8, Pub. by Gomer Pr UK) St Mut.

Dragon in the Rocks: A Story Based on the Childhood of the Early Paleontologist, Mary Anning. Marie Day. (Illus.). 32p. (J). (ps up). 1992. 12.95 (0-920775-76-4, Pub. by Greey dePencier CN) Firefly Bks Ltd.

***Dragon in the Wood.** Lucy Kincaid. (Read by Yourself Ser.). 32p. (J). 1994. 2.98 (1-85854-130-1) Brimax Bks.

***Dragon King of Mystara.** Thorarinn Gunnarsson. (Dragonlord Chronicles Ser.). 400p. (Orig.). 1995. pap. 5.95 (0-7869-0153-5) TSR Inc.

***Dragon King of the Sea: Japanese Decorative Art from the Meiji Period from the John R. Young Collection.** Oliver Impey & Malcolm Fairley. (Illus.). 112p. 1995. 25.00 (1-85444-007-1, 0070, Pub. by Ashmolean Mus UK) A Schwartz & Co.

Dragon King Trilogy, Bk. 1: In the Hall of the Dragon King. Stephen R. Lawhead. 1992. mass mkt. 4.99 (0-380-71629-1, AvoNova) Avon.

Dragon King Trilogy, Bk. 2: The Warlords of Nin. Stephen R. Lawhead. 416p. 1992. mass mkt. 4.99 (0-380-71630-5, AvoNova) Avon.

Dragon King Trilogy, Bk. 3: The Sword & the Flame. Stephen R. Lawhead. 384p. 1992. mass mkt. 4.99 (0-380-71631-3, AvoNova) Avon.

Dragon Kingdom Journeys Through Bhutan. Eavas. 372p. 1986. 36.00 (81-7062-007-4, Pub. by Lancer II) S Asia.

Dragon Kings. Timothy B. Brown. (Advanced Dungeons & Dragons, Second Edition; Al-Qadim Ser.). (Illus.). 1992. 20.00 (1-56076-235-7) TSR Inc.

Dragon Kite. Nancy Luenn. LC 81-11709. (Illus.). 12p. (J). (ps-3). 1983. pap. 5.95 (0-15-224197-3, Voyager Bks) HarBrace.

Dragon Kite of the Autumn Moon. Valerie Reddix. LC 91-1506. (J). (ps-3). 1992. 14.00 (0-688-11030-4); lib. bdg. 14.93 (0-688-11031-2) Lothrop.

Dragon Kites & Dragonflies: A Collection of Chinese Nursery Rhymes. Demi. LC 86-7637. (Illus.). 32p. (J). (ps-3). 1986. 14.95 (0-15-224199-X, HB Juv Bks) HarBrace.

Dragon Knight. Gordon R. Dickson. 1991. mass mkt. 5.99 (0-8125-0943-9) Tor Bks.

Dragon Lady: The Life & Legend of the Last Empress of China. Sterling Seagrave & Peggy Seagrave. LC 92-50582. 1993. pap. 16.00 (0-679-73369-8, Vin) Random.

Dragon Lady: The Secret World of the Lockheed U-2. Chris Pocock. (Illus.). 224p. 1989. pap. 12.98 (0-87938-393-3) Motorbooks Intl.

Dragon Lives Forever. John R. Riggs. LC 92-17748. (Garth Ryland Mystery Ser.). 1992. pap. 17.95 (0-942637-78-X) Barricade Bks.

Dragon Lives Forever. large type ed. John Riggs. LC 92-40988. (Cloak & Dagger Ser.). 350p. 1993. reprint ed. lib. bdg. 19.95 (1-56054-605-0) Thorndike Pr.

Dragon Lives Forever. John R. Riggs. 224p. 1994. reprint ed. pap. text ed. 4.50 (0-425-14301-5, Prime Crime) Berkley Pub.

Dragon Lord. David Drake. 320p. 1989. pap. 4.99 (0-8125-3605-3) Tor Bks.

***Dragon Lore: Official Strategy Guide.** Rusel Demaria. 1994. pap. 19.95 (1-55958-672-9) Prima Pub.

Dragon-Lover's Treasury of the Fantastic. Ed. by Margaret Weis. 336p. (Orig.). 1994. pap. 12.99 (0-446-67063-4, Aspect) Warner Bks.

Dragon Master: The Kaiser's One-Man Air Force in Tsingtau, China 1914. Robert E. Whittaker. Tr. by Susanne Kawatsu. LC 94-70291. (Illus.). 272p. 1994. 25.00 (0-9639310-1-6); pap. 15.00 (0-9639310-0-8) COMPASS Bks.

Dragon Masters. Jack Vance. 1993. reprint ed. lib. bdg. 18.95 (0-89968-378-9, Lghtyr Pr) Buccaneer Bks.

Dragon Mobiles. Anne Wild. (Illus.). 32p. (Orig.). (J). (gr. 3-5). 1990. pap. 5.95 (0-906212-10-3, Pub. by Tarquin UK) Parkwest Pubns.

***Dragon Mom: Confessions of a Child Development Expert. Janet Gonzalez-Mena. (Illus.). 144p. 1995. pap. 9.95 (1-883965-29-2) Rattle Ok Pubns. Have you ever wondered what goes on in the homes of child-development experts? Do these child-rearing professionals follow their own advice? In DRAGON MOM: CONFESSIONS OF A CHILD DEVELOPMENT EXPERT, the truth is revealed. As the author of the weekly newspaper column, FROM A PARENT'S PERSPECTIVE, & six college textbooks on early childhood education, Janet Gonzalez-Mena has achieved worldwide recognition as a speaker & author. How does this expertise carry over into her day-to-day life as the mother of five? With the characteristic wit & frank honesty that make Ms. Gonzalez-Mena such a popular speaker, she shares the discrepancies between her expert self & the many-faceted, passionate "Dragon Mom" that is only known to those in her own household. Hot topics such as toilet training, anger, sex education, bedtime, messes & responsibility are discussed. "DRAGON MOM GIVES PARENTS TOOLS TO NURTURE THEMSELVES AS WELL AS THEIR CHILDREN. WARM, ENGAGING, & HOPEFUL..." Reverend Jane Vennard. "A WISE & FUNNY BOOK THAT MOVES A PARENT FROM DOUBT & GUILT TO SELF-ACCEPTANCE & HUMOR. I WISH THIS BOOK HAD COME MY WAY WHEN I WAS A YOUNG PARENT!" Elizabeth Prescott, co-author PLANNING ENVIRONMENTS FOR YOUNG CHILDREN.** *Publisher Provided Annotation.*

***Dragon Moon.** Chris Claremont. 1994. pap. 14.95 (0-553-37448-6) Bantam.

Dragon Murder Case. S. S. Van Dine. 336p. 1994. 35.00 (1-883402-21-2) S&S Trade.

Dragon Nanny. C. L. Martin. LC 90-39985. (Illus.). 32p. (J). (gr. k-3). 1991. reprint ed. pap. 3.95 (0-689-71451-3, Aladdin Paperbacks) S&S Childrens.

Dragon of an Ordinary Family. Margaret Mahy. LC 91-2513. (Illus.). 48p. (J). (ps-3). 1992. 14.00 (0-8037-1062-3) Dial Bks Young.

Dragon of Boeotia. Bernard Evslin. (Monsters of Mythology Ser.). (Illus.). 94p. 1987. lib. bdg. 19.95 (1-55546-246-4) Chelsea Hse.

Dragon of Mith. Kate Walker. (Illus.). 128p. (Orig.). (J). (gr. 1-5). 1993. pap. 7.95 (0-04-928064-3, Pub. by Allen & Unwin Aust Pty AT) IPG Chicago.

Dragon of Nitt. Phil Grecian. 65p. 1986. reprint ed. pap. 3.45 (0-87129-039-1, D50) Dramatic Pub.

Dragon of Ord. David McAdoo. LC 85-81417. (Books for Students by Students Ser.). 1985. lib. bdg. 14.95 (0-933849-23-0) Landmark Edns.

Dragon of the Island. Mary Gillgannon. 416p. 1994. mass mkt. 4.99 (0-7860-0067-8) Windsor NY.

Dragon of the Lost Sea. Laurence Yep. LC 81-48644. (Charlotte Zolotow Bk.). 224p. (J). (gr. 6 up). 1988. pap. 4.95 (0-06-440227-4, Trophy) HarpC Child Bks.

***Dragon of the Lost Sea.** Laurence Yep. 1995. 18.00 (0-8446-6816-8) Peter Smith.

Dragon of the Winds. Carson Wright. 62p. (Orig.). 1991. pap. 2.75 (0-87129-019-7, D53) Dramatic Pub.

Dragon on the Border. Gordon R. Dickson. 400p. 1993. mass mkt. 5.50 (0-441-16657-1) Ace Bks.

Dragon Operations: Hostage Rescues in the Congo, 1964-1965. Thomas P. Odom. LC 87-36503. (Leavenworth Papers: No. 14). (Illus.). 236p. 1988. per., pap. 9.50 (0-16-001695-9, S/N 008-020-011) USGPO.

Dragon Pack Snack Attack. Joel E. Tanis & Jeff Grooters. LC 92-18933. (Illus.). 32p. (J). (ps-2). 1993. text ed. 14.95 (0-02-788840-1, Four Winds Pr) S&S Childrens.

Dragon Parade: A Chinese New Year Story. Steven A. Chin. LC 92-18079. (Stories of America Ser.). (Illus.). 32p. (J). (gr. 2-5). 1992. lib. bdg. 19.97 (0-8114-7215-9) Raintree Steck-V.

Dragon Path: The Collected Tales of Kenneth Morris. Kenneth Morris. 384p. 1995. 23.95 (0-312-85309-2) Tor Bks.

Dragon Pilgrims: A Historical Study of a Chinese-American Church. Karl Fung. 200p. (Orig.). (C). 1989. pap. 9.95 (0-317-93977-7) Providence Pr.

Dragon Poems. Nancy C. Carter. LC 92-44223. 64p. 1993. pap. 12.95 (0-7734-2768-6, Mellen Poetry Pr) E Mellen.

Dragon Poems. Ed. by John Foster. (Pocket Poetry Ser.). (Illus.). 32p. (J). (gr. 1 up). 1992. bds. 14.00 (0-19-276096-3) OUP.

Dragon Poems. Ed. by John Foster. (Pocket Poetry Ser.). (Illus.). 32p. (J). (gr. 1 up). 1992. pap. 2.95 (0-19-916425-8) OUP.

Dragon Portfolio. Richard Hoyt. 352p. 1988. pap. 4.99 (0-8125-0496-8) Tor Bks.

Dragon Prince. Melanie Rawn. (Dragon Prince Ser.: No. 1). 576p. 1988. reprint ed. mass mkt. 6.99 (0-88677-450-0) DAW Bks.

Dragon Reborn. Robert Jordan. (Wheel of Time Ser.: Bk. 3). 624p. 1991. 22.95 (0-312-85248-7) Tor Bks.

Dragon Reborn. Robert Jordan. 704p. 1992. mass mkt. 5.99 (0-8125-1371-1) Tor Bks.

Dragon Reborn. Robert Jordan. 1991. 344.25 (0-312-85254-1) St Martin.

***Dragon Reforged.** Chrys Cymri. LC 94-68161. 320p. (Orig.). 1995. pap. 4.95 (0-7869-0177-2) TSR Inc.

***Dragon Rescue.** Don Callander. 240p. (Orig.). 1995. pap. 5.50 (0-441-00263-3) Ace Bks.

Dragon Revenant. Katharine Kerr. 1991. mass mkt. 5.99 (0-553-28909-8, Spectra) Bantam.

Dragon Rigger. Jeffrey A. Carver. LC 93-3868. 480p. 1993. 23.95 (0-312-85061-1) Tor Bks.

Dragon Rigger. Jeffrey A. Carver. 1994. mass mkt. 4.99 (0-8125-3323-2) Tor Bks.

Dragon Rises Red Bird Flies. Leon Hammer. 1991. pap. 19.95 (0-88268-133-8) Station Hill Pr.

Dragon Rises, Red Bird Flies: Psychology & Chinese Medicine. Leon Hammer. (Illus.). 400p. 1980. 24.95 (0-88268-062-5) Station Hill Pr.

Dragon Scales & Willow Leaves. Terryl Givens. LC 93-665. (J). Date not set. write for info. (0-399-22619-2, Putnam) Putnam Pub Group.

Dragon Seed. Pearl S. Buck. 1993. reprint ed. lib. bdg. 19.95 (1-56849-133-6) Buccaneer Bks.

Dragon Seed. Pearl S. Buck. (Oriental Novels of Pearl S. Buck Ser.). 378p. 1992. reprint ed. pap. 8.95 (1-55921-033-8) Moyer Bell.

Dragon Slayer. Richard E. Blaisdell. 110p. 1992. write for info. (1-882359-04-6); pap. write for info. (1-882359-03-8) At Ease Pubns.

Dragon Slayer. Rosemary Sutcliff. (J). (gr. 4-6). 1976. pap. 4.99 (0-14-030254-9, Puffin) Puffin Bks.

Dragon Slaying for Parents. Tom Prinz. 336p. 1992. pap. 9.95 (0-914984-35-7) Starburst.

***Dragon Sleep.** A. G. Pradissis. 1995. pap. 7.00 (0-533-11327-X) Vantage.

***Dragon Soup.** Arlene Williams. LC 94-23216. (Illus.). (J). 1996. 14.95 (0-915811-63-4) H J Kramer Inc.

Dragon Steel. Laurence Yep. LC 84-48338. 288p. (YA). (gr. 7 up). 1985. lib. bdg. 12.89 (0-06-026751-8) HarpC Child Bks.

Dragon Steel. Laurence Yep. LC 84-48338. (Trophy Bk.). 288p. (YA). (gr. 7 up). 1993. pap. 4.95 (0-06-440486-2, Trophy) HarpC Child Bks.

Dragon Story. Gayle Gerig. (Illus.). 41p. (gr. k-7). 1985. pap. 6.95 (0-936835-00-1) Hugworks.

Dragon Study. David A. Wilson. (Illus.). 100p. (Orig.). 1986. pap. 6.00 (0-934852-30-8) Lorien Hse.

Dragon Sword & Wind Child. Noriko Ogiwara. Tr. by Cathy Hirano. LC 92-7970. 1993. 17.00 (0-374-30466-1) FS&G.

Dragon Takes a Wife. Walter D. Myers. LC 93-26877. (Illus.). (J). 1995. 14.95 (0-590-46693-3) Scholastic Inc.

Dragon Tales. Isaac Asimov. 1982. pap. 2.95 (0-449-24523-3) Fawcett.

Dragon Tales. John Patience. (Happy Ending Stories Ser.). (Illus.). 32p. (J). (gr. k-6). 1991. 3.99 (0-517-02329-6) Random Hse Value.

Dragon Tattoo Design. Donald E. Hardy. (Illus.). 96p. (C). 1988. 50.00 (0-945367-01-5) Hardy Marks Pubns.

Dragon Tears. Dean Koontz. 416p. 1993. pap. text ed. 6.99 (0-425-14003-2) Berkley Pub.

***Dragon Tears.** Dean Koontz. Date not set. pap. 6.98 (0-8317-4384-0) Smithmark.

Dragon Tears. large type ed. Dean Koontz. LC 92-44775. (Basic Ser.). 627p. 1993. reprint ed. lib. bdg. 22.95 (1-56054-666-2); reprint ed. pap. 14.95 (1-56054-881-9) Thorndike Pr.

Dragon Thanksgiving Feast: Things to Make & Do. Loreen Leedy. LC 90-55110. (Illus.). 32p. (J). (ps-3). 1990. lib. bdg. 14.95 (0-8234-0828-0) Holiday.

Dragon That Ate Summer. Brenda Seabrooke. (J). (gr. 4-7). 1993. pap. 2.95 (0-590-46986-X) Scholastic Inc.

Dragon, the Earl & the Troll. Gordon R. Dickson. LC 94-7538. 448p. (Orig.). 1994. text ed. 21.95 (0-441-00098-3) Ace Bks.

Dragon, the Lion, & the Eagle: Chinese-British-American Relations, 1949-1958. Qiang Zhai. LC 93-36348. (American Diplomatic History Ser.: No. 7). 296p. (C). 1994. lib. bdg. 32.00 (0-87338-490-3) Kent St U Pr.

Dragon, the Winds & the Witches. Marjorie Waltz. LC 86-72867. 64p. (Orig.). (J). (gr. k-2). 1987. pap. 5.00 (0-916383-14-8) Aegina Pr.

Dragon Thread. Laura Beheler. LC 80-84202. 164p. 1981. 9.95 (0-937884-00-6) Hystry Mystry.

Dragon Threads: Court Costumes of the Celestial Kingdom. Iris B. Apfel. Ed. by Mary S. Price. LC 92-36266. (Illus.). 44p. (Orig.). 1992. pap. 12.95 (0-932828-28-0) Newark Mus.

Dragon Time: Magic & Mystery of Menstruation. Luisa Francia. Tr. by Sasha Daucus. (Best of Europe Ser.). (Illus.). 156p. (Orig.). (C). 1991. pap. text ed. 9.95 (0-9614620-3-5) Ash Tree.

Dragon Token. Melanie Rawn. (Dragon Star Ser.: Bk. 2). 656p. 1993. mass mkt. 5.99 (0-88677-542-6) DAW Bks.

Dragon Tree Spell Book. Ed. by Ben R. Ezzell et al. (Illus.). 80p. (Orig.). 1981. pap. text ed. 11.95 (0-940918-02-1, STK 81-003) Dragon Tree.

Dragon Trouble. Penelope Lively. (Banana Bks.). (Illus.). 42p. (J). (gr. 2-4). 1989. 3.95 (0-8120-6136-5) Barron.

Dragon Waiting. John M. Ford. 400p. 1985. pap. 3.95 (0-380-69887-0) Avon.

***Dragon Waking.** Craig S. Gardner. LC 95-7141. (Dragon Circle Ser.). 1995. write for info. (0-441-00248-X) Ace Bks.

Dragon War. Mark Acres. (Dark Divide Ser.: Bk. 2). 192p. (Orig.). 1994. mass mkt. 4.99 (0-380-77296-5, AvoNova) Avon.

An Asterisk (*) at the beginning of an entry indicates that the title is appearing in BIP for the first time.

Dragon War. Laurence Yep. LC 91-28921. 320p. (YA). (gr. 7 up). 1992. 15.00 (*0-06-020302-1*); lib. bdg. 14.89 (*0-06-020303-X*) HarpC Child Bks.

Dragon War. Laurence Yep. LC 91-28921. (Illus.). 320p. (YA). (gr. 8 up). 1994. pap. 4.95 (*0-06-440525-7*, Trophy) HarpC Child Bks.

Dragon Warrior IV: Hint Book. (R.P.G. Strategy Guide Ser.). pap. 9.95 (*4-19-086950-3*) Tokuma Pub.

Dragon Who Never Sleeps: Verses for Zen Buddhist Practice. Robert Aitken. LC 92-33717. 111p. 1992. pap. 9.50 (*0-938077-60-0*) Parallax Pr.

***Dragon Who Wanted to Fly.** Jeffrey Comanor. LC 94-40726. (J). 1995. 14.95 (*1-57036-202-5*) Turner Pub GA.

Dragon Will Survive. Marjorie T. Whittlesey. LC 89-17585. (YA). 1991. 13.95 (*0-87949-315-1*) Ashley Bks.

Dragon Wing, Vol. 1: Death Gate Cycle. Margaret Weis. 1990. mass mkt. 5.99 (*0-553-28639-0*, Spectra) Bantam.

Dragon Within the Gates: The Once & Future AIDS Epidemic. Stephen Joseph. 256p. 1992. 20.95 (*0-88184-905-7*) Carroll & Graf.

Dragon Within the Gates: The Once & Future AIDS Epidemic. Stephen C. Joseph. 272p. 1993. pap. 9.95 (*0-7867-0033-5*) Carroll & Graf.

***Dragon 209.** TSR Staff. 1994. 3.95 (*1-56076-967-X*) TSR Inc.

Dragonbone Chair. Tad Williams. (Memory, Sorrow & Thorn Ser.: Bk. 1). 800p. 1989. mass mkt. 6.99 (*0-88677-384-9*, 037) DAW Bks.

Dragonbone Chair: Memory, Sorrow & Thorn, Bk. 1. Tad Williams. 1988. 19.95 (*0-8099-0003-3*) DAW Bks.

Dragonbrood. Alex Jack. 1978. pap. 5.50 (*0-916926-04-4*) Kanthaka.

Dragondoom. Dennis Mckiernan. 1990. mass mkt. 5.99 (*0-553-28337-5*, Spectra) Bantam.

Dragondrums. Anne McCaffrey. 208p. 1980. mass mkt. 5.99 (*0-553-25855-9*, Spectra) Bantam.

Dragondrums. Anne McCaffrey. LC 78-11318. (Illus.). 256p. (YA). (gr. 6 up). 1979. text ed. 16.95 (*0-689-30685-7*, Atheneum Bks Young) S&S Childrens.

Dragones Bien Intencionados - Well-Intentioned Dragons: Como Ministrar a Gente Problematica en la Iglesia - Ministering to Problem People in the Church. Marshall Shelley. Tr. by Edgar O. Morales. 144p. (Orig.). (SPA.). 1992. pap. 4.85 (*0-311-42092-3*) Casa Bautista.

Dragonfire. G. John Juray. 1992. pap. 15.95 (*1-880937-03-4*) Taylor Desktop.

Dragonfire. Patricia Potter. (Historical Ser.: No. 48). 1990. mass mkt. 3.25 (*0-373-28648-1*) Harlequin Bks.

Dragonflame & Other Bedtime Nightmares. Don McGregor. LC 77-17761. (Illus.). 1978. pap. 7.00 (*0-934882-02-9*) Fictioneer Bks.

***Dragonflies.** James E. Gerholdt. LC 95-7391. (Incredible Insects Ser.). (J). 1995. write for info. (*1-56239-484-3*) Abdo & Dghtrs.

Dragonflies. Molly McLaughlin. (J). (gr. 1-5). 1989. 14.95 (*0-8027-6846-6*); lib. bdg. 15.85 (*0-8027-6847-4*) Walker & Co.

Dragonflies. Hidetomo Oda. Ed. by Kathy Pohl. LC 85-28197. (Nature Close-Ups Ser.). (Illus.). 32p. (J). (gr. 3-7). 1986. text ed. 10.95 (*0-8172-2534-X*) Raintree Steck-V.

Dragonflies & Damselflies of Cape Cod. Virginia Carpenter. (Natural History Ser.: No. 4). (Illus.). 96p. 1991. pap. 9.95 (*0-685-47873-4*) Cape Cod Mus Nat His.

Dragonflies Draw Flame. Monika Varma. 4.80 (*0-89253-745-0*); 4.00 (*0-89253-746-9*) Ind-US Inc.

Dragonflies of Britian, Europe. D'aguilar & Dommanger. 1987. 34.95 (*0-685-43767-1*) Viking Penguin.

Dragonflies of the Florida Peninsula, Bermuda, & the Bahamas. Sidney W. Dunkle. (Illus.). 154p. (Orig.). 1989. pap. 14.95 (*0-945417-23-3*) Sci Pubs.

Dragonflight. Anne McCaffrey. 1978. 8.95 (*0-345-27749-X*, Del Rey) Ballantine.

Dragonflight. Anne McCaffrey. 1986. mass mkt. 4.95 (*0-345-33546-5*, Del Rey) Ballantine.

Dragonflight, Bk. 1. Anne McCaffrey et al. (Illus.). 1991. 4.95 (*1-56060-074-8*) Eclipse Bks.

Dragonflight, Bk. 2. Anne McCaffrey et al. (Illus.). 1991. 4.95 (*1-56060-075-6*) Eclipse Bks.

Dragonflight, Bk. 3. Anne McCaffrey et al. (Illus.). 1991. 4.95 (*1-56060-076-4*) Eclipse Bks.

Dragonflight Graphic Novel. Anne McCaffrey. 1993. pap. 12.99 (*0-06-105003-2*, PL) HarpC.

Dragonfly. Emery Bernhard. LC 92-39930. (Illus.). 32p. (J). (ps-3). 1993. lib. bdg. 15.95 (*0-8234-1033-1*) Holiday.

Dragonfly. Everard Meade. 174p. 1987. 14.95 (*0-933905-00-9*) Claycomb Pr.

Dragonfly. Everard Meade. (YA). 1992. pap. 7.95 (*0-933905-20-3*) Claycomb Pr.

***Dragonfly.** Ami Offenbacher. LC 94-60832. (Illus.). 44p. (J). (gr. k-3). 1995. 6.95 (*1-55523-712-6*) Winston-Derek.

Dragonfly. Barrie Watts. LC 88-18412. (Stopwatch Ser.). (Illus.). 25p. (J). (gr. k-4). 1991. lib. bdg. 9.95 (*0-382-09799-8*) Silver Pr.

Dragonfly: Cycle of Fire. Rik Lewis. Ed. by Bill Black. (Illus.). 52p. (Orig.). 1991. pap. 9.95 (*1-56225-000-0*) A C Comics.

Dragonfly in Amber. Diana Gabaldon. 1992. 21.50 (*0-385-30231-2*) Delacorte.

Dragonfly in Amber. Diana Gabaldon. 1993. mass mkt. 5.99 (*0-440-21562-5*) Dell.

Dragonfly over the Water. Christopher O'Toole. LC 87-42613. (Animal Habitats Ser.). (Illus.). 32p. (J). (gr. 4-6). 1988. lib. bdg. 17.27 (*1-55532-306-5*) Gareth Stevens Inc.

Dragonfly's Tale. Ret. by Kristina Rodanas. (Illus.). 32p. (J). (gr. k-3). 1992. 14.95 (*0-395-57003-4*, Clarion Bks) HM.

***Dragonfly's Tale.** Kristina Rodanas. LC 90-28758. (J). (ps-3). 1995. pap. 5.95 (*0-395-72076-1*, Clarion Bks) HM.

Dragonlace Legends Gift Set. Margaret Weis. 1986. pap. 11.85 (*0-88038-303-8*) TSR Inc.

Dragonlance: The Legend Becomes Reality, Vol. 1. Margaret Weis & Tracy Hickman. (Illus.). 1986. write for info. (*0-318-61327-1*) Random.

Dragonlance Calendar 1995. (Illus.). (Orig.). 1994. pap. 10.95 (*1-56076-849-5*) TSR Inc.

Dragonlance Chronicles. Margaret Weis & TSR Hobbies, Inc. Staff. 1988. pap. 16.95 (*0-88038-543-X*) TSR Inc.

Dragonlance Classics Vol. 2. TSR Staff. (Advanced Dungeons & Dragons, Second Edition; Al-Qadim Ser.). (Illus.). 1993. 15.00 (*1-56076-570-4*) TSR Inc.

Dragonlance Legends. Margaret Weis & Tracy Hickman. LC 88-50058. (Dragonlance Collector's Edition Ser.). 912p. 1988. 16.95 (*0-88038-610-X*); pap. 12.95 (*0-88038-653-3*) TSR Inc.

DragonLance New Tales: The Land Reborn. (Advanced Dungeons & Dragons 2nd Ed. Accessory Ser.: DLT1). 1993. pap. 10.95 (*1-56076-607-7*) TSR Inc.

***DragonLance the Second Generation.** (Dragonlance Saga Ser.). (Illus.). 448p. (Orig.). 1995. pap. 5.95 (*0-7869-0260-4*) TSR Inc.

Dragonlance: The Second Generation. Margaret Weis & Tracy Hickman. (Dragonlance Saga Ser.). 320p. 1994. 19.95 (*1-56076-822-3*) TSR Inc.

Dragonlord of Mystara. Thorarinn Gunnarsson. 400p. (Orig.). 1994. pap. 5.95 (*1-56076-906-8*) TSR Inc.

Dragonlover's Guide to Pern. Jody L. Nye & Anne McCaffrey. LC 89-6715. (Illus.). 192p. 1989. 19.95 (*0-345-35424-9*, Del Rey) Ballantine.

Dragonlover's Guide to Pern. Jody L. Nye & Anne McCaffrey. (Illus.). 192p. 1992. pap. 12.95 (*0-345-37946-2*, Del Rey) Ballantine.

Dragonology. Justin Delaney. Ed. by James B. Van Treese. 270p. 1994. pap. 8.95 (*1-56901-091-9*) NW Pub.

Dragonquest, Vol. 2. Anne McCaffrey. 1979. 8.95 (*0-345-28030-X*, Del Rey) Ballantine.

Dragonquest, Vol. 2. Anne McCaffrey. 1986. mass mkt. 5.95 (*0-345-33508-2*, Del Rey) Ballantine.

Dragonriders of Pern, 3 vols., Set. Anne McCaffrey. 1986. Boxed set. boxed 23.80 (*0-345-34045-0*, Del Rey) Ballantine.

Dragonriders of Pern: Dragonflight, Dragonquest, The White Dragon. Anne McCaffrey. 832p. 1988. pap. 16.00 (*0-345-34024-8*, Del Rey) Ballantine.

Dragons. Jo E. Moore. (Illus.). 48p. (J). (gr. 2-5). 1990. pap. 5.95 (*1-55799-161-8*) Evan-Moor Corp.

Dragons. Bill Padgett. (Illus.). 174p. 1984. 17.95 (*0-934073-00-7*) Rountree Pub NC.

Dragons. Gilles Ragache. LC 90-25902. (Myths & Legends Ser.: Gp. 2). (Illus.). 48p. (J). (gr. 4-8). 1991. lib. bdg. 9.95 (*1-85435-265-2*) Marshall Cavendish.

***Dragons: A Natural History.** Karl Shuker. LC 95-12104. 1995. 22.50 (*0-684-81443-9*) S&S Trade.

Dragons: An Integrated Activity Unit. Bev McKay. (Illus.). 32p. (J). (gr. 4-7). 1992. pap. text ed. 4.95 (*0-86530-227-8*, IP NO. 140-2) Incentive Pubns.

Dragons: Truth, Myth & Legend. David Passes. LC 92-44745. (Illus.). 48p. (J). (gr. 7 up). 1993. 12.95 (*0-307-17500-6*, Artsts Writrs) Western Pub.

***Dragons & Bulls: Profitable Investment Strategies for Trading Stocks & Commodities.** Stanley Kroll. LC 94-29648. (C). 1994. text ed. write for info. (*0-201-42084-8*) Addison-Wesley.

***Dragons & Chariots.** Wes Bateman. 65p. (Orig.). 1991. pap. 9.95 (*0-929385-45-4*) Light Tech Comns Servs.

Dragons & Demons, Angels & Eagles: Morality Tales for Teens. Stephen Chappell. LC 89-63202. 128p. (Orig.). (YA). 1990. pap. 6.95 (*0-89243-314-0*) Liguori Pubns.

Dragons & Dinosaurs: A Thematic Unit. Kathy Hofer. (Thematic Units Ser.). (Illus.). 80p. (gr. 1-3). 1990. student ed 8.95 (*1-55734-271-7*) Tchr Create Mat.

Dragons & Dungeons Dingbats Book. Carole Marsh. (Carole Marsh Dingbats Book Ser.). (Illus.). (YA). (gr. 3-12). 1994. lib. bdg. 24.95 (*0-7933-5395-5*); pap. 14.95 (*0-7933-5396-3*); disk 29.95 (*0-7933-5397-1*) Gallopade Pub Group.

Dragons & Dynasties: An Introduction to Chinese Mythology. Yuan Ke. Ed. by Nie Zhixiong. Tr. by Kim Echlin & Nie Zhixiong. (Illus.). 208p. (Orig.). 1993. pap. 12.00 (*0-14-058653-9*, Penguin Bks) Viking Penguin.

***Dragons & Fabulous Beasts: A Book of Symbols.** LC 94-37304. (Prospero's Library). 1995. 7.95 (*0-8118-1018-6*) Chronicle Bks.

Dragons & Lizards. Norman S. Barrett. LC 90-43335. (Picture Library). (Illus.). 32p. (J). (gr. k-4). 1991. lib. bdg. 12.53 (*0-531-14111-X*) Watts.

Dragons & Martinis: The Skewed Realism of John Cheever. Michael D. Byrne. LC 93-337. (Milford Series: Popular Writers of Today: Popular Writers of Today: Vol. 55). 136p. 1993. lib. bdg. 27.00x (*0-8095-2000-1*); pap. 17.00x (*0-8095-3000-7*) Borgo Pr.

Dragons & Stuff. Lenore Morgan. LC 70-108725. (Illus.). 32p. (J). (gr. 2-4). 1970. lib. bdg. 9.95 (*0-87783-012-6*) Oddo.

Dragons & Stuff. deluxe ed. Lenore Morgan. LC 70-108725. (Illus.). 32p. (J). (gr. 2-4). 1970. pap. 3.94 (*0-87783-091-6*) Oddo.

Dragons & Tigers. James R. Badey. (Illus.). 178p. 1988. pap. 16.00 (*0-87729-05-1*) Palmer Pr.

Dragons & Unicorns. Johnsgard. 1993. pap. 3.99 (*0-517-11079-2*) Random Hse Value.

Dragons & Unicorns: A Natural History. Paul Johnsgard & Karin Johnsgard. (Illus.). 176p. 1992. pap. 6.95 (*0-312-08499-4*, Pub. by Thomas Dunne Bks) St Martin.

Dragons Are Lonely. John R. Lewis. LC 93-12977. (Illus.). 32p. (J). (gr. 1-3). 1993. 14.95 (*0-87797-239-7*) Cherokee.

Dragons Are Singing Tonight. Jack Prelutsky. LC 92-29013. (Illus.). 40p. (J). (ps up). 1993. 16.00 (*0-688-09645-X*); lib. bdg. 15.93 (*0-688-12511-5*) Greenwillow.

Dragons at the Party. large type ed. Jon Cleary. 464p. 1988. 23.95 (*0-7089-8474-6*, Charnwood) Ulverscroft.

Dragons at War: Land Battle in the Desert. Daniel P. Bolger. 1991. mass mkt. 5.95 (*0-8041-0899-4*) Ivy Books.

Dragons Backbone. William G. Sewell. (Illus.). 200p. (C). 1989. pap. 21.00 (*1-85072-006-1*, Pub. by W Sessions UK) St Mut.

Dragon's Bait. Vande Velde. (J). 1992. 16.95 (*0-15-200726-1*, J Yolen Bks) HarBrace.

Dragon's Blood: Feminist Intertextuality in Eudora Welty's 'The Golden Apples' Rebecca Mark. LC 93-29518. 320p. 1994. text ed. 35.00 (*0-87805-661-0*) U Pr of Miss.

Dragon's Boy. Jane Yolen. LC 89-24642. 128p. (J). (gr. 3-7). 1990. 14.95 (*0-06-026789-5*); lib. bdg. 14.89 (*0-06-026790-9*) HarpC Child Bks.

***Dragon's Breath: Hurricane at Sea.** Robert A. Dawes, Jr. LC 95-12441. (Illus.). 240p. 1995. 28.95 (*1-55750-153-X*) Naval Inst Pr.

***Dragons Can Only Rust.** Chrys Cymri. 320p. (Orig.). 1995. pap. 4.95 (*0-7869-0157-8*) TSR Inc.

Dragon's Crown. TSR Staff. (Advanced Dungeons & Dragons, Second Edition; Al-Qadim Ser.). (Illus.). 1993. pap. 24.95 (*1-56076-567-4*) TSR Inc.

Dragon's Dagger. R. A. Salvatore. 320p. (Orig.). 1994. pap. text ed. 4.99 (*0-441-00078-9*) Ace Bks.

Dragons, Delinquents & Destiny: An Essay on Positive Superego Functions. Wolfgang Lederer. LC 64-23955. (Psychological Issues Monograph: No. 15, Vol. 4, No. 3). 83p. (Orig.). 1964. text ed. 25.00 (*0-8236-1420-4*) Intl Univs Pr.

Dragons, Dolphins & Dinosaurs. Shirley Greenway & Michael Evans. LC 93-20397. (Illus.). 32p. (J). (ps-6). 1993. 13.95 (*1-879085-83-6*) Whsprng Coyote Pr.

Dragons Dragons & Other Creatures That Never Were. Eric Carle. (Illus.). 72p. (J). (ps up). 1991. 18.95 (*0-399-22105-0*, Philomel Bks) Putnam Pub Group.

***Dragon's Eden.** Glenna McReynolds. (Loveswept Ser.: No. 726). 1995. pap. 3.50 (*0-553-44487-5*, Loveswept) Bantam.

Dragon's Egg. Robert L. Forward. 352p. 1983. pap. 3.95 (*0-345-31666-5*, Del Rey) Ballantine.

Dragon's Egg - Starquake, 2 bks. in 1. Robert L. Forward. 1994. mass mkt. 5.50 (*0-345-38898-4*, Del Rey) Ballantine.

Dragons Entangled: Indo-China & the China-Vietnam War. Steven J. Hood. LC 91-10743. 200p. (C). 1992. 44.95 (*0-87332-862-0*) M E Sharpe.

Dragons Entangled: Indo-China & the China-Vietnam War. Steven J. Hood. LC 91-10743. 200p. (C). 1993. pap. text ed. 20.95 (*1-56324-270-2*) M E Sharpe.

Dragon's Eye. Norma Johnston. LC 90-34388. 176p. (YA). (gr. 7 up). 1990. text ed. 14.95 (*0-02-747701-0*, Four Winds Pr) S&S Childrens.

Dragon's Eye. Ed. by Christopher Stasheff. 400p. (Orig.). 1994. mass mkt. 5.99 (*0-671-87609-0*) Baen Bks.

Dragon's Eye: An Artist's View. Duncan Regehr. (Illus.). 208p. 1994. 45.00 (*1-885203-03-9*) Jrny Editions.

Dragons, Fairies & Monsters. (Letts Pattern Library). (Illus.). 48p. pap. 6.95 (*1-85238-442-5*, Pub. by New Holland Pubs UK) Sterling.

***Dragon's Familiar.** Lawrence J. Cohen. Tr. by Ingram. 250p. (YA). 1996. pap. 8.95 (*0-7610-0442-4*) NW Pub.

Dragon's Fat Cat. Dav Pilkey. LC 91-16369. (Illus.). 48p. (J). (gr. 1-3). 1992. 13.95 (*0-531-05982-0*); lib. bdg. 13.99 (*0-531-08582-1*) Orchard Bks Watts.

***Dragon's Fat Cat.** Dav Pilkey. LC 91-16369. (Illus.). 48p. (J). (gr. 1-3). 1995. pap. 4.95 (*0-531-07068-9*) Orchard Bks Watts.

Dragon's Fire. Ralph Hayes. 1979. pap. 1.95 (*0-8439-0630-8*) Dorchester Pub Co.

Dragons for Sale: Studies in Unreason. Robert E. Wheeler. 166p. (C). 1993. 22.95 (*0-87975-827-9*) Prometheus Bks.

Dragon's Gate. Laurence Yep. LC 92-43649. 288p. (YA). (gr. 7 up). 1993. 15.00 (*0-06-022971-3*); lib. bdg. 14.89 (*0-06-022972-1*) HarpC Child Bks.

***Dragon's Gate.** Laurence Yep. LC 92-43649. 288p. (YA). (gr. 5 up). 1995. pap. 3.95 (*0-06-440489-7*, Trophy) HarpC Child Bks.

***Dragons, Gods & Spirits from Chinese Mythology.** Tao T. Liu Sanders. LC 94-8354. (World Mythology Ser.). (Illus.). 132p. 1994. lib. bdg. 22.50 (*0-87226-922-1*) P Bedrick Bks.

Dragon's Gold. Piers Anthony. (Orig.). 1991. mass mkt. 4.99 (*0-8125-1384-3*) Tor Bks.

Dragon's Halloween. Dav Pilkey. LC 91-21107. (Illus.). 48p. (J). (gr. 1-3). 1993. 13.95 (*0-531-05990-1*); lib. bdg. 13.99 (*0-531-08590-2*) Orchard Bks Watts.

***Dragon's Halloween.** Dav Pilkey. LC 91-21107. (Illus.). 48p. (J). (gr. 1-3). 1995. pap. 4.95 (*0-531-07069-7*) Orchard Bks Watts.

Dragon's Head: A Planetary Guide. rev. ed. Linda W. Griffin. (Illus.). 1988. pap. 7.50 (*0-9620950-0-1*) Dragons Head Pr.

***Dragon's Hiding Place.** Lucy Kincaid. (Read by Yourself Ser.). 32p. (J). 1994. 2.98 (*1-85854-133-6*) Brimax Bks.

***Dragon's Honor.** Kij Johnson. Ed. by John Ordover. (Star Trek: Next Generation Ser.: No. 34). 288p. (Orig.). 1996. mass mkt. 5.50 (*0-671-50107-0*) PB.

Dragons in Distress: Asia's Miracle Economies in Crisis. Walden Bello & Stephanie Rosenfeld. 425p. (Orig.). (C). 1990. pap. 12.95 (*0-935028-55-2*) Inst Food & Develop.

Dragons in the Stars. Jeffrey A. Carver. 352p. 1992. mass mkt. 4.99 (*0-8125-3303-8*) Tor Bks.

Dragons in the Waters. Madeleine L'Engle. 288p. (J). (gr. 7 up). 1982. mass mkt. 4.50 (*0-440-91719-0*, LFL) Dell.

Dragons in the Waters. Madeleine L'Engle. LC 76-2477. 304p. (J). (gr. 7 up). 1976. 17.00 (*0-374-31868-9*) FS&G.

Dragons in the West: An Historical Profile of 20th Century Chinese American Pioneers. Wei Li Fang. (Illus.). 224p. Date not set. write for info. (*0-9639266-0-8*); lib. bdg. write for info. (*0-9639266-1-6*) Wei Li Fang.

***Dragons Live Forever.** June Bennett. (Illus.). 32p. (J). (gr. 1-6). 1990. 11.95 (*9971-4-9120-6*) Heian Intl.

Dragon's Merry Christmas. Dav Pilkey. LC 91-1996. (Illus.). 48p. (J). (gr. 1-3). 1991. 13.95 (*0-531-05957-X*); 13.99 (*0-531-08557-0*) Orchard Bks Watts.

Dragon's Merry Christmas. Dav Pilkey. LC 91-1996. (Illus.). 48p. (J). (gr. 1-3). 1994. pap. 4.95 (*0-531-07055-7*) Orchard Bks Watts.

Dragon's Milk. Susan Fletcher. LC 88-35059. 224p. (YA). (gr. 6 up). 1989. text ed. 15.95 (*0-689-31579-1*, Atheneum Bks Young) S&S Childrens.

Dragon's Milk. Susan Fletcher. LC 91-31358. 256p. (J). (gr. 3-7). 1992. reprint ed. pap. 3.95 (*0-689-71623-0*, Aladdin Paperbacks) S&S Childrens.

Dragons of Autumn Twilight, Vol. 1. Tracy Hickman et al. LC 84-51122. (Dragonlance Chronicles Ser.: Vol. 1). (Illus.). 448p. (Orig.). 1984. pap. 4.95 (*0-88038-173-6*) TSR Inc.

Dragons of Blueland. Ruth S. Gannett. LC 86-27480. (Borzoi Sprinters Ser.). (Illus.). 96p. (J). (gr. 2-5). 1987. 4.99 (*0-394-89050-7*) Knopf Bks Yng Read.

Dragons of Eden. Carl Sagan. 1986. mass mkt. 6.99 (*0-345-34629-7*) Ballantine.

Dragons of Eden. Carl Sagan. 1977. 10.95 (*0-394-41045-9*) Random.

Dragons of Krynn. Ed. by Margaret Weiss & Tracy Hickman. (Dragonlance Ser.). 320p. (Orig.). 1994. pap. 4.95 (*1-56076-830-4*) TSR Inc.

Dragons of North Chittendon. Susan F. Schaeffer. (Illus.). (J). (gr. 4-6). 1986. pap. 2.95 (*0-685-14462-3*) S&S Trade.

Dragons of Spring Dawning. Margaret Weis & Tracy Hickman. LC 85-90078. (Dragonlance Chronicles Ser.: Vol. 3). (Illus.). 384p. (Orig.). 1985. pap. 4.95 (*0-88038-175-2*) TSR Inc.

***Dragons of Summer Flame.** Margaret Weis & Tracy Hickman. (Dragonlance Saga Ser.). 560p. (Orig.). 1995. 22.95 (*0-7869-0189-6*) TSR Inc.

***Dragons of the Rhine.** Diana L. Paxson. LC 94-3198. (J). 1995. 23.00 (*0-688-13986-8*, AvoNova) Avon.

Dragons of Tiananmen: Beijing As a Sacred City. Jeffrey F. Meyer. Ed. by Frederick M. Denny. (Studies in Comparative Religion). (Illus.). 220p. 1991. text ed. 34.95 (*0-87249-739-9*) U of SC Pr.

Dragons of War. Christopher Rowley. 464p. (Orig.). 1994. pap. 5.99 (*0-451-45342-5*, ROC) NAL-Dutton.

Dragons of Winter Night, Vol. 2. Tracy Hickman & Margaret Weis. LC 84-91366. (Dragonlance Chronicles Ser.: Vol. 2). (Illus.). 400p. (Orig.). 1985. pap. 4.95 (*0-88038-174-4*) TSR Inc.

Dragons over London. 352p. 1992. per., pap. 4.95 (*0-87431-342-2*, 20605) West End Games.

Dragon's Pearl. Julie Lawson. (Illus.). 32p. (J). (gr. k-3). 1993. 15.95 (*0-395-63623-X*, Clarion Bks) HM.

Dragon's Pearl. Sirin Phathanothai. 1994. 23.00 (*0-671-79546-5*) S&S Trade.

Dragon's Pen. Bobi Jones & Gwyn Thomas. 100p. (C). 1986. text ed. 35.00 (*0-86383-208-3*, Pub. by Gomer Pr UK) St Mut.

Dragon's Play: A New Taoist Transmission of the Complete Experience of Human Life. Charles Belyea & Steven Tainer. LC 91-72597. (Illus.). 200p. (Orig.). 1991. pap. 14.95 (*0-9629308-1-4*) Grt Cir Life.

Dragon's Plunder. Brad Strickland. LC 91-45664. (Dragonflight Fantasy Ser.). (Illus.). 160p. (YA). (gr. 7 up). 1992. text ed. 14.95 (*0-689-31573-2*, Atheneum Bks Young) S&S Childrens.

Dragon's Progress: Development Administration in Korea. Ed. by Gerald E. Caiden & Bun Woong Kim. LC 90-21333. (Library of Management for Development). 274p. 1991. pap. 18.95 (*0-931816-89-0*) Kumarian Pr.

Dragon's Pupils: A China Odyssey. Kenneth Starck. LC 90-47593. (Illus.). 250p. 1991. 24.95 (*0-8138-1267-4*) Iowa St U Pr.

Dragon's Robe. Deborah N. Lattimore. LC 89-34512. (Illus.). 32p. (J). (gr. 1-5). 1990. lib. bdg. 14.89 (*0-06-023723-6*) HarpC Child Bks.

Dragon's Robe. Deborah N. Lattimore. LC 89-34512. (Illus.). 32p. (J). (gr. 1-5). 1990. 15.00 (*0-06-023719-8*) HarpC Child Bks.

Dragon's Robe. Deborah N. Lattimore. LC 89-34512. (Trophy Picture Bk.). (Illus.). 32p. (J). (gr. 1-5). 1993. pap. 4.95 (*0-06-443321-8*, Trophy) HarpC Child Bks.

Dragon's Sceptre. Pref. by Patricia Shelton. LC 85-51000. 80p. 1985. pap. 7.95 (*0-9615026-0-6*) Sarasvati.

Dragon's Sceptre: Hitting the Sixth Patriarch (the Way He Hit Shin Su) & Other Zen Poems & Koans. Patricia Shelton. 84p. 1985. pap. 7.95 (*0-9615026-1-4*) Sarasvati.

Dragons, Smoke-Holes, & Propwash. Howard Hood. 280p. 1989. pap. 12.95 (*0-9624079-0-9*, TXU 345-351) Sierra Co.

Dragon's Tail: Radiation Safety in the Manhattan Project, 1942-1946. Barton C. Hacker. 260p. (C). 1987. 38.00 (*0-520-05852-6*) U CA Pr.

Dragon's Tapestry. Martine Bates. 128p. 1995. pap. 7.95 (*0-88995-080-6*, Pub. by Red Deer CN) BookWorld Dist.

Dragon's Teeth. Ross Whitney. (Illus.). 1992. 40.00 (*1-880418-03-7*) D M Grant.

Dragon's Teeth. Upton Sinclair. 1992. reprint ed. lib. bdg. 18.95 (*0-89966-956-5*) Buccaneer Bks.

Dragon's Teeth? The Creation of United States Air Power for World War II. Benjamin S. Kelsey. LC 82-600279. (Illus.). 148p. 1983. 24.95 (*0-87474-574-8*, KEDT) Smithsonian.

D

An Asterisk (*) at the beginning of an entry indicates that the title is appearing in BIP for the first time. 2101

Dragon's Tomb. D. J. Heinrich. (Penhaligon Trilogy Ser.: Bk. 2). 320p. (Orig.). 1993. pap. write for info. (1-56076-592-5) TSR Inc.

Dragons Touch: Weaknesses of the Human Anatomy. Hei Long. (Illus.). 184p. 1983. pap. 12.00 (0-87364-271-6) Paladin Pr.

Dragon's Village. Yuan-Tsun Chen. 1981. pap. 11.95 (0-14-005811-7, Penguin Bks) Viking Penguin.

Dragons Yet to Slay. Vincent Lockhart. 288p. 1993. pap. 5.95 (0-9635610-0-6) A-L Pub.

Dragonsbane. Barbara Hambly. LC 85-90837. 352p. (Orig.). 1987. mass mkt. 4.95 (0-345-34939-3, Del Rey) Ballantine.

Dragonsdawn. Anne McCaffrey. (Dragonriders of Pern Ser.). 1989. mass mkt. 5.99 (0-345-36286-1, Del Rey) Ballantine.

Dragonsdawn. Anne McCaffrey. 431p. 1988. 25.00 (0-89366-213-5) Ultramarine Pub.

Dragonsdawn. braille ed. Anne McCaffrey. 804p. 1991. vinyl bd. 64.32 (1-56956-222-9, BR7601) W A T Braille.

Dragonship. large type ed. Robert MacLeod. 1978. 15.95 (0-7089-0182-4) Ulverscroft.

Dragonsinger. Anne McCaffrey. 256p. 1983. mass mkt. 5.99 (0-553-25854-0, Spectra) Bantam.

Dragonsinger. Anne McCaffrey. LC 76-40988. 276p. (J). (gr. 5-9). 1977. text ed. 16.95 (0-689-30570-2, Atheneum Bks Young) S&S Childrens.

Dragonslayer. Wayland Drew. (Orig.). 1985. pap. 2.95 (0-345-32306-8, Del Rey) Ballantine.

Dragonslayers. Bruce Coville. Ed. by Pat MacDonald. LC 93-40194. (Illus.). 128p. (YA). (gr. 7 up). 1994. 14.00 (0-671-89036-0, Minstrel Bks); pap. 3.50 (0-671-79832-4, Minstrel Bks) PB.

***Dragonslayer's Return.** R. A. Salvatore. 336p. (Orig.). 1995. pap. text ed. 5.50 (0-441-00228-5) Ace Bks.

Dragonsong. Irene Elliot. (Orig.). (J). 1991. Playscript. pap. 5.50 (0-87602-294-8) Anchorage.

Dragonsong. Anne McCaffrey. 176p. 1977. mass mkt. 5.99 (0-553-25852-4, Bantam Classics) Bantam.

Dragonsong. Anne McCaffrey. LC 75-30530. 224p. (J). (gr. 5-9). 1976. text ed. 16.95 (0-689-30507-9, Atheneum Bks Young) S&S Childrens.

Dragonspawn. Mark Acres. 224p. (Orig.). 1994. mass mkt. 4.99 (0-380-77295-7, AvoNova) Avon.

Dragonstrike: Dungeon of Fear. Michael Andrews. (Endless Quest Ser.: No. 1). 192p. (Orig.). 1994. pap. 3.95 (1-56076-835-5) TSR Inc.

Dragonsword. Gael Baudino. (Orig.). 1991. pap. 4.99 (0-451-45081-7, ROC) NAL-Dutton.

Dragonwall. Troy Denning. LC 89-51889. (Forgotten Realms Empires Trilogy Bks.: Bk. 2). (Illus.). 320p. (Orig.). 1990. pap. 4.95 (0-88038-919-2) TSR Inc.

***Dragonwings.** Estelle Kleinman. Ed. by J. Friedland & R. Kessler. (Novel-Ties Ser.). (J). (gr. 4-6). 1994. student ed, pap. text ed. 15.95 (1-56982-062-7) Lrn Links.

Dragonwings. Laurence Yep. 1993. 4.75 (0-8222-1326-5) Dramatists Play.

Dragonwings. Laurence Yep. LC 74-2625. 256p. (YA). (gr. 7 up). 1975. lib. bdg. 14.89 (0-06-026738-0) HarpC Child Bks.

Dragonwings. Laurence Yep. LC 74-2625. (Trophy Bk.). 256p. (J). (gr. 6 up). 1977. pap. 4.95 (0-06-440085-9, Trophy) HarpC Child Bks.

Dragonwings: A Literature Unit. Mari L. Robbins. (Literature Units Ser.). (Illus.). 48p. 1993. student ed 6.95 (1-55734-429-9) Tchr Create Mat.

***Dragonwyck.** Anya Seton. 1994. lib. bdg. 29.95x (1-56849-484-X) Buccaneer Bks.

Dragonzord. (Mighty Morphin Power Rangers Large Flip-Ups Ser.). (Illus.). 8p. (J). (gr. k-2). 1994. bds. write for info. (1-56144-475-8, Honey Bear Bks) Modern Pub NYC.

Dragoon Campaigns to the Rocky Mountains: Being a History of the Enlistment, Organization & First Campaigns of the Regiment of U. S. Dragoons. James Hildreth. (Far Western Frontier Ser.). 292p. 1973. reprint ed. 23.95 (0-405-04977-3) Ayer.

Dragsters. Maureen Connolly. (Cruisin' Ser.). (Illus.). 48p. (J). (gr. 3-6). 1992. lib. bdg. 12.95 (1-56065-074-5) Capstone Pr.

Dragsters. Maria Sosa. LC 87-15568. (Super-Charged Ser.). (Illus.). 48p. (J). (gr. 5-6). 1987. text ed. 11.95 (0-89686-350-6, Crstwood Hse) Silver Burdett Pr.

***Drainage.** 1995. lib. bdg. 250.99 (0-8490-6615-8) Gordon Pr.

Drainage & Sanitation. Rolf Payne. LC 82-1455. (Illus.). 192p. reprint ed. pap. 54.80 (0-685-20296-8, 2030330) Bks Demand.

Drainage & Water Table Control. LC 92-74577. 501p. 1993. pap. 59.00 (0-929355-34-2, P1392) Am Soc Ag Eng.

Drainage Design & Management: Proceedings of the Fifth National Drainage Symposium. American Society of Agricultural Engineers. LC 87-72844. 440p. 1987. pap. 47.00 (0-916150-88-7, P0787) Am Soc Ag Eng.

Drainage Engineering. rev. ed. James N. Luthin. LC 77-9299. (Illus.). 288p. 1978. 29.50 (0-88275-578-1) Krieger.

Drainage for Agriculture. Ed. by J. Van Schilfgaarde. (Illus.). 700p. 1974. 16.00 (0-89118-018-4) Am Soc Agron.

Drainage Geochemistry in Mineral Exploration. Ed. by M. Hale & J. A. Plant. LC 94-8945. (Handbook of Exploration Geochemistry Ser.: Vol. 6). 1994. write for info. (0-444-81854-5) Elsevier.

Drainage Guidelines. Walter J. Ochs & Bishay G. Bishay. LC 92-40966. (Technical Paper Ser.: No. 195). 193p. 1992. 11.95 (0-8213-2312-1, 12312) World Bank.

Drainage in Homoeopathy. E. A. Maury. (C). 1980. text ed. 8.95 (0-8464-1007-9) Beekman Pubs.

Drainage Manual: A Guide to Integrating Plant, Soil, & Water Relationships for Drainage of Irrigated Lands. 1994. lib. bdg. 263.95 (0-8490-9063-6) Gordon Pr.

Drainage of Agricultural Land. Soil Conservation Service Staff. 423p. (C). 1988. text ed. 250.00 (0-685-44235-7, Scientific) St Mut.

Drainage of Agricultural Land. U. S. Department of Agriculture, Soil Conservation Service Staff. LC 72-92351. (Illus.). 430p. 1973. pap. text ed. 35.00 (0-912394-06-4) Water Info.

Drainage of Asphalt Pavement Structures. (Illus.). 128p. 1984. 10.00 (0-318-13389-X, MS-15) Asphalt Inst.

Drainage of Highway & Airfield Pavements. Harry R. Cedergren. LC 86-21018. 306p. 1987. reprint ed. lib. bdg. 49.50 (0-89874-986-7) Krieger.

Drainage of Highway Pavements. (Hydraulic Engineering Circular 12, Technology Sharing Report Ser.: No. 84-202). (Illus.). 152p. 1984. pap. 5.50 (0-16-005028-6, S/N 050-001-00280-9) USGPO.

Draining of the Somerset Levels. Michael Williams. LC 73-75830. 304p. reprint ed. pap. 86.70 (0-685-16230-3, 2027268) Bks Demand.

Draining the Sea: An Americas Watch Report. Aryeh Neier. LC 86-113890. 77p. 1985. 8.00 (0-938579-03-7, Am Watch) Hum Rts Watch.

Drake. Ernle Bradford. (Dorset Classic Reprints Ser.). 252p. 1991. 19.95 (0-88029-668-2) Marboro Bks.

Drake. Fred Rendell & Arnold Bell. (C). 1989. 30.00 (1-85098-071-3, Pub. by Jordanhill College UK) St Mut.

***Drake: Captain of the South Seas.** Grover S. McLeod. (Illus.). 488p. 1994. 24.95 (1-884150-10-1) Manchester AL.

Drake: The Family of Nelson Drake Back to 1630: New York & MIchigan Pioneers, with Genealogy Supplement. F. N. Drake. (Illus.). 146p. 1993. reprint ed. lib. bdg. 32.50 (0-8328-3296-0); reprint ed. pap. 22.50 (0-8328-3297-9) Higginson Bk Co.

Drake, Arrington, White, Turner, Linn, Brown: And Two Dozen Related Southern Lines. Jo W. Linn. LC 84-81760. (Illus.). 1984. 35.00 (0-918470-17-X) J W Linn.

***Drake Beam Morin Guide to Getting Started with Your Career.** Drake. 126p. 1994. 10.95 (1-880030-23-3) DBM Pub.

***Drake Beam Morin Guide to Resumes & Marketing Letters.** Drake. 154p. 1994. 10.95 (1-880030-22-5) DBM Pub.

***Drake Beam Morin Guide to Retirement Planning.** Drake. 141p. 1994. 10.95 (1-880030-28-4) DBM Pub.

Drake Family in England & America, 1360-1895 & the Descendants of Thomas Drake of Weymouth, MA, 1635-1691. L. S. Drake. (Illus.). 347p. 1989. reprint ed. lib. bdg. 52.00 (0-8328-0492-4); reprint ed. pap. 42.00 (0-8328-0493-2) Higginson Bk Co.

***Drake Guide to Technical Certification.** Drake Prometric. LC 95-9204. 1995. pap. 24.95 (0-07-017949-2) McGraw.

***Drake Guide to Technical Certification.** Drake Prometric. LC 95-9204. 1995. write for info. (0-07-017948-4) McGraw.

Drake in Central California, Fifteen Seventy-Nine. Justin M. Ruhge. (Illus.). 92p. pap. 8.00 (0-685-63227-X) Quantum Imaging.

Drake in Central California, 1579: Unraveling One of California's Great Historical Mysteries. Justin M. Ruhge. (Illus.). 92p. (Orig.). 1992. pap. 8.00 (0-9614807-7-7) Quantum Imaging.

Drake Law Review: 1951-1991, 41 vols. mic. film write for info. (0-318-57431-4) Rothman.

Drake Law Review: 1951-1991, 41 vols., Set. 1,697.50 (0-8377-9054-9) Rothman.

Drake's of Van Buren County, Michigan. Toni J. Benson. (Illus.). 278p. 1991. 27.00 (0-9620998-2-1); pap. 22.00 (0-9620998-1-3) F-Ami-Lee.

Drake's Spanish Grants, with Johnson's Fraudulent California Land Grants. Eugene B. Drake & Clinton Johnson. (West Coast Studies: No. 9). 96p. Date not set. lib. bdg. write for info. (0-8095-2802-9); pap. write for info. (0-8095-3802-4) Borgo Pr.

Drakon & Early Athenian Homicide Law. Michael Gagarin. LC 81-2370. (Classical Monographs). 208p. (C). 1981. text ed. 37.00 (0-300-02627-7) Yale U Pr.

***Drak's Slumber Praty.** Gertrude Gruesome. (Monsterkids Ser.: No. 1). (J). (gr. 4-7). 1994. pap. 2.99 (0-06-106236-7) HarpC Child Bks.

Drakula's Brood. Richard Dalby. 1992. 19.95 (0-88029-676-3) Dorset Pr.

***Drakulya.** Earl Lee. Date not set. 21.95 (1-884365-01-9) See Sharp Pr.

***Drakulya: The Lost Journal of Mircea Drakulya, Lord of the Undead.** Earl Lee. 224p. (Orig.). 1994. pap. 10.95 (1-884365-02-7) See Sharp Pr.

***DRAM Management Guide.** 200p. (Orig.). 1995. pap. 125.00 (0-7605-1824-6) Rector Pr.

Dram of Poison. Charlotte Armstrong. LC 88-82344. 160p. 1989. pap. 4.95 (0-930330-98-6, Lib Crime Classics) Intl Polygonics.

Dram of Poison. Charlotte Armstrong. reprint ed. lib. bdg. 16.95 (0-88411-565-8, Aeonian Pr) Amereon Ltd.

Dram of Poison. Charlotte Armstrong. 1994. reprint ed. lib. bdg. 24.95 (1-56849-253-7) Buccaneer Bks.

Drama. Jeffrey D. Hoeper et al. (Illus.). 1392p. (Orig.). (C). 1993. teacher ed write for info. (0-318-69910-9) Macmillan.

Drama. Jeffrey D. Hoeper et al. (Illus.). 1392p. (Orig.). (C). 1994. pap. write for info. (0-02-355601-3) Macmillan.

***Drama: A Harper Collins Pocket Anthology.** Gwynn. 1994. pap. text ed. (0-8230-4954-X) Watsn-Guptill.

Drama: Addresses. Henry Irving. LC 70-91525. 1972. 17.95 (0-405-08660-1, Pub. by Blom Pubns UK) Ayer.

Drama Activities with Older Adults: A Handbook for Leaders. Anne H. Thurman & Carol Ann Piggins. LC 82-11861. (Activities, Adaptation & Aging Ser.: Vol. 2, Nos. 2-3). (Illus.). 182p. 1982. text ed. 39.95 (0-86656-167-6) Haworth Pr.

Drama Addresses. H. Irving. 176p. (C). 1988. 50.00 (1-85077-185-5, Darf Pubs Ltd) St Mut.

Drama & Commitment. Gerald Rabkin. LC 72-6866. (Studies in Drama: No. 39). (C). 1972. reprint ed. lib. bdg. 75.00 (0-8383-1659-X) M S G Haskell Hse.

Drama & Discussion. 2nd ed. Stanley A. Clayes. (Illus.). 1978. pap. text ed. write for info. (0-13-219030-3) P-H.

***Drama & Feeling: An Aesthetic Theory.** Richard Courtney. 256p. 1995. 55.00 (0-7735-1228-4, Pub. by McGill CN) U of Toronto Pr.

Drama & Healing: The Roots of Drama Therapy. Roger Grainger. 156p. 1990. 39.95 (1-85302-048-6, Pub. by J Kingsley Pubs UK) Taylor & Francis.

Drama & Intelligence: A Cognitive Theory. Richard Courtney. 192p. (C). 1990. text ed. 49.95 (0-7735-0766-3, Pub. by McGill CN) U of Toronto Pr.

***Drama & Learning: A Critical Review.** Jacqueline Hamilton. 1992. pap. 32.00 (0-7300-1478-9, ECT465, Pub. by Deakin Univ AT) St Mut.

Drama & Life. Arthur B. Walkley. LC 67-26791. (Essay Index Reprint Ser.). 1977. reprint ed. 20.95 (0-8369-0967-4) Ayer.

Drama & Liturgy. Oscar Cargill. (BCL1-PR English Literature Ser.). 151p. 1992. reprint ed. lib. bdg. 69.00 (0-7812-7256-4) Rprt Serv.

***Drama & Music: Creative Activities for Young Children.** Comp. by Margaret Merrion & Janet Rubin. LC 94-24087. 192p. 1995. 18.95 (0-89334-236-X) Humanics Ltd.

***Drama & Music: Creative Activities for Young Children.** Janet Rubin & Margaret Merrion. LC 94-24087. (Illus.). 196p. 1995. lib. bdg. 28.95 (0-89334-244-0, 2440X34) Humanics Lrning.

Drama & Nemesis. Ed. by James Redmond. LC 79-9054. (Themes in Drama Ser.: No. 2). (Illus.). 1980. write for info. (0-521-22179-X) Cambridge U Pr.

***Drama & Performance: An Anthology.** Gary Vena & Andrea J. Nouryeh. 1152p. (C). 1995. pap. write for info. (0-697-14566-2) Brown & Benchmark.

Drama & Power in a Hunting Society: The Selk'nam of Tierra del Fuego. Anne Chapman. LC 82-4286. (Illus.). 240p. 1982. 69.95 (0-521-23884-6) Cambridge U Pr.

Drama & Religion in the English Mystery Plays: A Re-evaluation. Eleanor Prosser. vi, 229p. 1961. 32.50 (0-8047-0060-5) Stanford U Pr.

***Drama & Ritual of Early Hinduism.** Natalia Lidova. (C). 1994. text ed. 14.00 (0-614-04134-1, Pub. by Motilal Banarsidass II) S Asia.

Drama & Symbolism. Ed. by James Redmond. LC 81-10250. (Themes in Drama Ser.: No. 4). (Illus.). 280p. 1982. write for info. (0-521-22181-1) Cambridge U Pr.

Drama & the Classical Heritage: Comparative & Critical Essays. Ed. by Clifford Davidson. LC 91-57957. (Ancient & Classical Studies: No. 1). 1993. 47.50 (0-404-64301-9) AMS Pr.

***Drama & the Curriculum.** E. Darvell. 1992. pap. 32.00 (0-7300-1477-0, ECT465, Pub. by Deakin Univ AT) St Mut.

Drama & the Market in the Age of Shakespeare. Douglas Bruster. (Cambridge Studies in Renaissance Literature & Culture: No. 1). 180p. (C). 1992. 49.95 (0-521-41664-7) Cambridge U Pr.

Drama & the South African State. Martin Orkin. Ed. by Jonathan Dollimore & Alan Sinfield. LC 90-6556. (Cultural Politics Ser.). 192p. 1991. text ed. 59.95 (0-7190-2576-1, Pub. by Manchester Univ Pr UK); text ed. 16.95 (0-7190-2577-X, Pub. by Manchester Univ Pr UK) St Martin.

Drama & the Stage. Ludwig Lewisohn. LC 71-84319. (Essay Index Reprint Ser.). 1977. 19.95 (0-8369-1089-3) Ayer.

Drama & the Teacher. Arthur Brittin. (C). 1989. 35.00 (1-85098-325-9, Pub. by Jordanhill College UK) St Mut.

Drama & Theatre. Jack Rudman. (Undergraduate Program Field Test Ser.: UPFT-5). 1994. pap. 23.95 (0-8373-6005-6) Nat Learn.

Drama & Theatre Arts Course Book. David Self. LC 93-30038. 1995. pap. 17.00 (0-88734-639-1) Players Pr.

Drama & Theatre in Education. Ed. by Nigel Dodd & Winifred Hickson. 1971. pap. text ed. 12.50 (0-435-18271-4) Heinemann.

Drama Anytime. Jill Charters & Anne Gately. vii, 88p. (Orig.). 1987. pap. text ed. 14.00 (0-909955-64-6, 00591, Pub. by PETA AT) Heinemann.

Drama As a Meaning Maker. Ed. by Judith Kase-Polisini. LC 88-27828. 262p. (Orig.). (C). 1989. lib. bdg. 42.00 (0-8191-7231-6); pap. text ed. 25.50 (0-8191-7232-4) U Pr of Amer.

Drama As Literature. Jiri Veltrusky. 95p. 1977. pap. 12.00 (90-316-0127-6, Pub. by Gruner NE) Benjamins North Am.

Drama as Mode of Religious Realization: The Vidaghamadhava of Rupa Gosvamin. Donna M. Wulff. (American Academy of Religion Academy Ser.: No. 43). 280p. (C). 1985. 22.95 (0-89130-608-0, 01 01 43) Scholars Pr GA.

***Drama As Therapy: Theatre As Living.** Philip Jones. 256p. 1995. 59.95x (0-415-09969-2, C0323); pap. 18.95 (0-415-09970-6, C0324) Routledge.

Drama Criticism, Vol. 1. Ed. by Lawrence J. Trudeau. 500p. 1991. 81.00 (0-8103-7911-2, 100938-M94800) Gale.

Drama Criticism, Vol. 2. Lawrence J. Trudeau. 1992. 81.00 (0-8103-7958-9) Gale.

Drama Criticism, Vol. 3. Lawrence J. Trudeau. 1993. 81.00 (0-8103-7959-7) Gale.

Drama Criticism, Vol. 4. Lawrence J. Trudeau. 1994. 81.00 (0-8103-8465-5) Gale.

Drama, Dance & Music. Ed. by James Redmond. (Themes in Drama Ser.: No. 3). (Illus.). 260p. 1981. write for info. (0-521-22180-3) Cambridge U Pr.

Drama del Siglo de Oro: A Study of Magic: Witchcraft & Occult Beliefs. Maria N. Pavia. 116p. 1959. 4.00 (0-318-22344-9) Hispanic Inst.

Drama Dictionary. Terry Hodgson. (Illus.). 400p. (C). 1988. text ed. 35.00 (0-941533-40-9) New Amsterdam Bks.

***Drama for All: Developing Drama in the Curriculum with Pupils with Special Educational Needs.** Melanie Peter. 96p. 1994. pap. 19.95x (1-85346-315-9, Pub. by D Fulton UK) Taylor & Francis.

Drama for Discussion. Arthur Brittin. (C). 1989. 40.00 (1-85098-032-2, Pub. by Jordanhill College UK) St Mut.

Drama for Learning: Dorothy Heathcote's "Mantle of the Expert" Approach to Education. Dorothy Heathcote & Gavin Bolton. LC 94-20582. 1995. pap. text ed. 20.00 (0-435-08643-X) Heinemann.

Drama for People with Special Needs. Ann Cattanach. (Illus.). 160p. 1992. pap. 15.00 (0-89676-123-1) Drama Bk.

Drama for the Church at Worship. Henry R. Rust. 1990. 5.95 (0-940754-92-4, 3556) Ed Ministries.

Drama Games. rev. ed. Bernie Warren & Tim Dunne. 60p. 1993. pap. 7.00 (0-921801-15-7, Pub. by Captus CN) Empire Pub Srvs.

Drama Games: Techniques for Self-Development. Tian Dayton. 104p. 1989. 7.95 (1-55874-021-X) Health Comm.

Drama Guidelines. Cecily O'Neill et al. 75p. (C). 1977. pap. text ed. 15.00 (0-435-18670-1) Heinemann.

Drama in Contemporary South Asia: Varieties & Settings. Lothar Lutze. (South Asian Digest of Regional Writing Ser.: No. 10). 86p. (Orig.). 1984. pap. 32.50x (3-515-04207-5) Coronet Bks.

***Drama in Early Tudor Britain, 1485-1558.** Howard B. Norland. 506p. 1995. text ed. 45.00 (0-8032-3337-X) U of Nebr Pr.

Drama in Europe in Theory & Practice. Eleanor Jourdain. LC 72-3216. (Studies in Drama: No. 39). 1972. reprint ed. lib. bdg. 49.95 (0-8383-1497-X) M S G Haskell Hse.

Drama in Hardwicke Street. William J. Feeney. LC 82-49315. (Illus.). 320p. 1984. 42.50 (0-8386-3188-6) Fairleigh Dickinson.

Drama in Muslin. George Moore. 330p. 1981. 30.00 (0-86140-055-0, Pub. by Colin Smythe Ltd UK); pap. 11.95 (0-86140-056-9, Pub. by Colin Smythe Ltd UK) Dufour.

Drama in Performance. Raymond Williams. 192p. 1991. pap. 27.00 (0-335-09658-1, Open Univ Pr) Taylor & Francis.

Drama in Pokerville. Joseph M. Field. LC 76-91078. (American Humorists Ser.). reprint ed. lib. bdg. 18.75 (0-8398-0556-X) Irvington.

Drama in Practice: A Handbook for Students. Peter Spalding. 150p. (Orig.). 1986. 19.95 (0-89341-535-9, Longwood Academic); pap. 8.95 (0-89341-536-7, Longwood Academic) Hollowbrook.

Drama in Society. Ed. by James Redmond. LC 77-54723. (Themes in Drama Ser.: No. 1). (Illus.). 1979. write for info. (0-521-22076-9) Cambridge U Pr.

Drama in the Air: Extraordinary True Stories of Daring. John Beattie. (Illus.). 223p. 1992. pap. 9.95 (0-86051-664-4, Robson-Parkwest) Parkwest Pubns.

Drama in the Curriculum. John Somers. Ed. by C. E. Wragg. (Education Matters Ser.). (Illus.). 128p. 1992. 75.00 (0-304-32594-5); pap. 30.00 (0-304-32589-9) Weidner & Sons.

Drama in the English Classroom. Ken Byron. (Teaching Secondary English Ser.). 220p. 1986. 35.00 (0-416-38030-1, 9895); pap. 14.95 (0-416-38040-9, 9911) Routledge Chapman & Hall.

Drama in the Garden: Extraordinary Stories of the Creators of Twelve Unique Old Gardens in Seven Countries of Europe. Dorothy L. McFadden. LC 92-97120. 128p. 1992. pap. 19.95 (0-9634140-0-3) Little Owl Pr.

Drama in the Middle Ages: Comparative & Critical Essays. Ed. by Clifford Davidson et al. LC 81-68995. (Studies in the Middle Ages: No. 4). 400p. 1982. reprint ed. 39.50 (0-404-61434-5) AMS Pr.

Drama in the Middle Ages: Comparative & Critical Essays, Second Series. Ed. by Clifford Davidson et al. LC 90-1191. (Studies in the Middle Ages: No. 18). 1991. 47.50 (0-404-61448-5) AMS Pr.

***Drama in the Ministry Tool Box, Vol. 1.** Mark Schaufler. 58p. 1992. 10.00 (1-886904-08-1) MST Minist.

***Drama in the Ministry Tool Box, Vol. 2.** Mark Schaufler. 50p. 1995. 10.00 (1-886904-09-X) MST Minist.

***Drama in the Ministry Tool Box: Workshop.** Mark Schaufler. 20p. 1993. 2.00 (1-886904-10-3) MST Minist.

Drama in the People's Republic of China. Constantine Tung & Colin Mackerras. LC 86-5932. 353p. (C). 1987. 64.50 (0-88706-389-6); pap. 21.95 (0-88706-390-X) State U NY Pr.

Drama in the Renaissance: Comparative & Critical Essays. Ed. by Clifford Davidson et al. LC 83-45277. (Studies in the Renaissance: No. 12). 1986. 39.50 (0-404-62282-8) AMS Pr.

Drama in the Text: Beckett's Late Fiction. Enoch Brater. LC 93-30405. 248p. 1994. reprint ed. pap. 39.95 (0-19-508892-1) OUP.

Drama in the Twentieth Century: Comparative & Critical Essays. Ed. by Clifford Davidson et al. LC 83-45289. (Studies in Modern Literature: No. 11). (Illus.). 1984. 39.50 (0-404-61581-3) AMS Pr.

Drama in Therapy. Ed. by Gertrud Schattner & Richard Courtney. Incl. Vol. 2: Adults. LC 80-15680. 392p. 1981. text ed. 19.95 (0-89676-014-6); LC 80-15680. write for info. (0-318-51777-9) Drama Bk.

An Asterisk (*) at the beginning of an entry indicates that the title is appearing in BIP for the first time.

An Asterisk (*) at the beginning of an entry indicates that the title is appearing in BIP for the first time.

D

Dramatic Records of Sir Henry Herbert. Henry Herbert. Ed. by Joseph Q. Adams. LC 63-23180. 1972. reprint ed. 20.95 (0-405-08180-4) Ayer.

***Dramatic Representations of British Soldiers & Sailors on the London Stage, 1660-1800: Britons, Strike Home.** Terence M. Freeman. LC 94-48864. (Studies in British History: Vol. 36). 364p. 1995. text ed. 99.95 (0-7734-8928-2) E Mellen.

Dramatic Strategies in the Plays of Edward Bond. Jenny S. Spencer. (Illus.). 280p. (C). 1993. 59.95 (0-521-39304-3) Cambridge U Pr.

Dramatic Structure: The Shaping of Experience. Jackson G. Barry. LC 78-100607. 1970. 50.00 (0-520-01624-6) U CA Pr.

Dramatic Structure & Meaning in Theatrical Productions. Thomas Price. LC 92-21128. 364p. 1992. pap. text ed. 34.95 (0-7734-9897-4) E Mellen.

Dramatic Suspense in Euripides' & Seneca's "Medea" Stephen Ohlander. (American University Studies: Classical Languages & Literature: Ser. XVII, Vol. 6). 345p. (C). 1989. text ed. 49.50 (0-8204-0873-5) P Lang Pubs.

Dramatic Technique. George P. Baker. LC 77-77706. (Theatre, Film & the Performing Arts Ser.). 532p. 1976. reprint ed. lib. bdg. 55.00 (0-306-71344-6); reprint ed. pap. 13.95 (0-306-80030-6) Da Capo.

Dramatic Technique. George P. Baker. LC 74-100220. 531p. 1970. reprint ed. text ed. 65.00 (0-8371-3005-0, BADT, Greenwood Pr) Greenwood.

Dramatic Texts & Records of Britain: A Chronological Topography to 1558. Ian Lancashire. (Studies in Early English Drama). 633p. 1984. 85.00 (0-8020-5592-3) U of Toronto Pr.

Dramatic Theory & Criticism. B. F. Dukore. LC 73-9778. (C). 1974. text ed. 35.25 (0-03-091152-4) HB Coll Pubs.

Dramatic Theory & Practice in France 1690-1808. Eleanor F. Jourdain. LC 68-20232. 1972. reprint ed. 23.95 (0-405-08675-X) Ayer.

Dramatic Tournaments in the Secondary Schools. Magdalene E. Kramer. LC 75-176943. (Columbia University. Teachers College. Contributions to Education Ser.: No. 685). reprint ed. 37.50 (0-404-55685-X) AMS Pr.

Dramatic Unity of "Huckleberry Finn" George C. Carrington, Jr. LC 76-939. (Illus.). 219p. 1976. 32.50 (0-8142-0238-1) Ohio St U Pr.

Dramatic Use of Bawdy in Shakespeare. Ernest A. Colman. LC 73-86132. 240p. reprint ed. pap. 68.40 (0-317-27691-3, 2025220) Bks Demand.

Dramatic Uses of Biblical Allusions in Marlowe & Shakespeare. James H. Sims. LC 66-64917. (University of Florida Humanities Monographs: No. 24). 94p. reprint ed. pap. 26.80 (0-7837-5836-7, 2045555) Bks Demand.

Dramatic Values. Charles E. Montague. (BCL1-PR English Literature Ser.). 274p. 1992. reprint ed. lib. bdg. 79.00 (0-7812-7095-2) Rprt Serv.

Dramatic Values. Charles E. Montague. reprint ed. 14.00 (0-403-01112-4) Scholarly.

Dramatic Verse, 1973-1985. Tony Harrison. 464p. 1985. 45.00 (0-906427-81-9, Pub. by Bloodaxe Bks UK) Dufour.

Dramatic Verses. Trumbull Stickney. LC 79-104570. reprint ed. lib. bdg. 27.00 (0-8398-1872-6) Irvington.

***Dramatic Vision on August Wilson.** 1995. 27.95 (0-614-06549-6, SHDV) Howard U Pr.

Dramatic Works. Jean De la Taille. Ed. by Kathleen M. Hall & C. N. Smith. (Renaissance Library). 212p. (FRE.). (C). 1972. text ed. 36.50 (0-485-13804-2, Pub. by Athlone Pr UK) Humanities.

Dramatic Works. Henry Carey. (Anglistica & Americana Ser.: No. 101). 256p. 1982. reprint ed. 63.70 (3-487-07183-5, Pub. by Georg Olms GW) Lubrecht & Cramer.

Dramatic Works, 5 vols. Colley Cibber. Ed. by D. E. Baker. reprint ed. write for info. (0-318-50560-6) AMS Pr.

Dramatic Works, 5 vols. William D'Avenant. (BCL1-PR English Literature Ser.). 1992. reprint ed. lib. bdg. 450.00 (0-7812-7239-4) Rprt Serv.

Dramatic Works, 6 vols. John Heywood. (BCL1-PR English Literature Ser.). 1992. reprint ed. lib. bdg. 540.00 (0-7812-7245-9) Rprt Serv.

Dramatic Works, 5 vols, 1. Colley Cibber. Ed. by D. E. Baker. reprint ed. 77.00 (0-404-01591-3) AMS Pr.

Dramatic Works, 5 vols, 2. Colley Cibber. Ed. by D. E. Baker. reprint ed. 77.00 (0-404-01592-1) AMS Pr.

Dramatic Works, 5 vols, 3. Colley Cibber. Ed. by D. E. Baker. reprint ed. 77.00 (0-404-01593-X) AMS Pr.

Dramatic Works, 5 vols, 4. Colley Cibber. Ed. by D. E. Baker. reprint ed. 77.00 (0-404-01594-8) AMS Pr.

Dramatic Works, 5 vols, 5. Colley Cibber. Ed. by D. E. Baker. reprint ed. 77.00 (0-404-01595-6) AMS Pr.

Dramatic Works, 5 vols, Set. Colley Cibber. Ed. by D. E. Baker. reprint ed. 385.00 (0-404-01590-5) AMS Pr.

Dramatic Works, 6 Vols, Set. John Dryden. Ed. by Montague Summers. LC 68-15208. 490p. 1968. reprint ed. 450.00 (0-87752-030-5) Gordian.

Dramatic Works, 2 vols., Set. George Etherege. (BCL1-PR English Literature Ser.). 1992. reprint ed. lib. bdg. 150.00 (0-7812-7348-X) Rprt Serv.

Dramatic Works & Poems, with Notes by William Gifford, 6 vols., Set. James Shirley. (BCL1-PR English Literature Ser.). 1992. reprint ed. lib. bdg. 540.00 (0-7812-7311-0) Rprt Serv.

Dramatic Works & Poetical Works, 2 Vols, 1. Bayard Taylor. LC 77-131498. 1969. reprint ed. write for info. (0-404-06353-5) AMS Pr.

Dramatic Works & Poetical Works, 2 Vols, 2. Bayard Taylor. LC 77-131498. 1969. reprint ed. write for info. (0-404-06354-3) AMS Pr.

Dramatic Works & Poetical Works, 2 Vols, Set. Bayard Taylor. LC 77-131498. 1969. reprint ed. 47.50 (0-404-06352-7) AMS Pr.

Dramatic Works from the Old English Quarto, Vol. 1. John Ford. Bd. with Forde's Contribution to the Decadence of the Drama & Reprint of Dekker' Penny-Wise, Pound-Foolish. (Material for the Study of the Old English Drama Ser.: No. 1, Vol. 23). 1972. reprint ed. Set pap. (0-8115-0272-4) Periodicals Srv.

Dramatic Works in the Beaumont & Fletcher Canon Vol. 6. Ed. by Fredson Bowers. 730p. 1985. 155.00 (0-521-25941-X) Cambridge U Pr.

Dramatic Works in the Beaumont & Fletcher Canon Vol. 8: The Queen of Corinth, the False One, Four Plays, or Moral Representations, in One, The Knight of Malta, The Tragedy of St. John Van Olden Barnavelt, The Custom of the Country. Ed. by Fredson Bowers. 766p. (C). 1992. 155.00 (0-521-36187-7) Cambridge U Pr.

Dramatic Works in the Beaumont & Fletcher Canon Vol. 9: The Sea Voyage, The Double Marriage, The Prophetess, The Little French Lawyer, The Elder Brother, The Maid in the Mill. Ed. by Fredson Bowers. 700p. (C). 1995. 130.00 (0-521-36188-5) Cambridge U Pr.

Dramatic Works of Bayard Taylor. Bayard Taylor. LC 79-145324. 1971. reprint ed. 39.00 (0-403-01235-X) Scholarly.

Dramatic Works of Bayard Taylor. Bayard Taylor. (BCL1-PS American Literature Ser.). 345p. 1992. reprint ed. lib. bdg. 89.00 (0-7812-6876-1) Rprt Serv.

Dramatic Works of Denis Johnston, Vol. 2. Denis Johnston. 1977. 50.00 (0-901072-53-2, Pub. by Colin Smythe Ltd UK) Dufour.

Dramatic Works of Denis Johnston, Vol.1. Denis Johnston. 1977. 50.00 (0-901072-52-4, Pub. by Colin Smythe Ltd UK) Dufour.

Dramatic Works of Denis Johnston, Vol. 3: The Radio & Television Plays. Frwd. by Joseph Ronsley. 516p. 1992. 70.00 (0-86140-080-1, Pub. by Colin Smythe Ltd UK) Dufour.

Dramatic Works of George Lillo. George Lillo & Richard Noble. Ed. by James L. Steffensen, Jr. (Oxford English Texts Ser.). (Illus.). 784p. 1993. 145.00 (0-19-812714-6) OUP.

Dramatic Works of George Peele, 3 vols. Ed. by R. Mark Benbow. Incl. Araygnement of Paris. 1970. 52.50 (0-300-01185-7); (Life & Works of George Peele, Ser.: 3). (Illus.). 1970. write for info. (0-318-56519-6) Yale U Pr.

Dramatic Works of John Crowne, 4 vols., 1. John Crowne. Ed. by James Maidment & W. H. Logan. LC 67-18423. 1972. reprint ed. 30.95 (0-405-08408-0, Pub. by Blom Pubns UK) Ayer.

Dramatic Works of John Crowne, 4 vols., 2. John Crowne. Ed. by James Maidment & W. H. Logan. LC 67-18423. 1972. reprint ed. 30.95 (0-405-08409-9, Pub. by Blom Pubns UK) Ayer.

Dramatic Works of John Crowne, 4 vols., 3. John Crowne. Ed. by James Maidment & W. H. Logan. LC 67-18423. 1972. reprint ed. 30.95 (0-405-08410-2, Pub. by Blom Pubns UK) Ayer.

Dramatic Works of John Crowne, 4 vols., 4. John Crowne. Ed. by James Maidment & W. H. Logan. LC 67-18423. 1972. reprint ed. 30.95 (0-405-08411-0, Pub. by Blom Pubns UK) Ayer.

Dramatic Works of John Crowne, 4 vols., Set. John Crowne. Ed. by James Maidment & W. H. Logan. LC 67-18423. 1972. reprint ed. 121.95 (0-405-08407-2, Pub. by Blom Pubns UK) Ayer.

Dramatic Works of John Lacy, Comedian. John Lacy. Ed. by James Maidment & W. H. Logan. LC 67-18423. 1972. reprint ed. 24.95 (0-405-08722-5) Ayer.

Dramatic Works of John Tatham. John Tatham. Ed. by James Maidment & W. H. Logan. LC 67-18423. 1972. reprint ed. 24.95 (0-405-09022-6) Ayer.

Dramatic Works of John Wilson. John Wilson. Ed. by James Maidment & W. H. Logan. LC 67-18423. 1972. reprint ed. 30.95 (0-405-09082-X) Ayer.

Dramatic Works of Richard Brome, 3 Vols. Richard Brome. Ed. by R. H. Shepherd. reprint ed. write for info. (0-318-50561-4) AMS Pr.

Dramatic Works of Richard Brome, 3 Vols, 1. Richard Brome. Ed. by R. H. Shepherd. reprint ed. 55.00 (0-404-01111-X) AMS Pr.

Dramatic Works of Richard Brome, 3 Vols, 2. Richard Brome. Ed. by R. H. Shepherd. reprint ed. 55.00 (0-404-01112-8) AMS Pr.

Dramatic Works of Richard Brome, 3 Vols, 3. Richard Brome. Ed. by R. H. Shepherd. reprint ed. 55.00 (0-404-01113-6) AMS Pr.

Dramatic Works of Richard Brome, 3 Vols, Set. Richard Brome. Ed. by R. H. Shepherd. reprint ed. 165.00 (0-404-01110-1) AMS Pr.

Dramatic Works of Samuel Foote, 2 Vols. Samuel Foote. LC 68-20223. 1972. 60.95 (0-405-08523-0, Pub. by Blom Pubns UK) Ayer.

Dramatic Works of Samuel Foote, 2 Vols, I. Samuel Foote. LC 68-20223. 1972. 30.95 (0-405-08524-9, Pub. by Blom Pubns UK) Ayer.

Dramatic Works of Shakerley Marmion. Shakerley Marmion. Ed. by James Maidment & W. H. Logan. LC 67-18423. 1972. reprint ed. 24.95 (0-405-08760-8, Pub. by Blom Pubns UK) Ayer.

Dramatic Works of Sir Aston Cokain. Aston Cokain. Ed. by James Maidment & W. H. Logan. LC 67-18423. 1972. reprint ed. 24.95 (0-405-08365-3, Pub. by Blom Pubns UK) Ayer.

Dramatic Works of Sir George Etherege, 2 vols., Set. George Etherege. Ed. by H. F. Brett-Smith. LC 76-145003. 1971. reprint ed. 39.00 (0-403-00956-1) Scholarly.

Dramatic Works of St. John Hankin: Three Volumes, Set. John Hankin. LC 77-70356. (One-Act Plays in Reprint Ser.). 1977. reprint ed. 74.50 (0-8486-2017-8) Roth Pub Inc.

Dramatic Works of the Celebrated Mrs. Centlivre, 3 Vols, Set. Susanna Centlivre. LC 69-20425. reprint ed. 230.00 (0-404-01480-1) AMS Pr.

Dramatic Works of the Right Hon. Lord Lytton: Comprising; the Duchess De la Valliere, Richelieu, the Lady of Lyons, Money, Not So Bad As We Seem. Edward G. Bulwer-Lytton. LC 71-39197. (Select Bibliographies Reprint Ser.). 1977. reprint ed. 29.95 (0-8369-6799-2) Ayer.

Dramatic works of Thomas Dekker, Vol. 1. Thomas Dekker. LC 53-13115. reprint ed. pap. 100.70 (0-318-34780-6, 2031641) Bks Demand.

Dramatic Works of William Shakespeare. William Shakespeare. Ed. by Thomas Campbell. LC 72-1024. reprint ed. lib. bdg. 85.00 (0-404-01376-7) AMS Pr.

Dramatic World of Harold Pinter: Its Basis in Ritual. Katherine H. Burkman. LC 70-125099. 189p. 1971. 32.50 (0-8142-0146-6) Ohio St U Pr.

Dramatic Writings. John Bale. (BCL1-PR English Literature Ser.). 347p. 1992. reprint ed. lib. bdg. 89.00 (0-7812-7234-3) Rprt Serv.

Dramatic Writings. John Heywood. (BCL1-PR English Literature Ser.). 280p. 1992. reprint ed. lib. bdg. 79.00 (0-7812-7244-0) Rprt Serv.

Dramatic Writings. John Heywood. Ed. by John S. Farmer. (Anglistica & Americana Ser.: No. 178). 280p. 1977. reprint ed. 44.20 (3-487-06357-3, Pub. by Georg Olms GW) Lubrecht & Cramer.

Dramatic Writings, Ed. by John S. Farmer. Nicholas Udall. (BCL1-PR English Literature Ser.). 160p. 1992. reprint ed. lib. bdg. 69.00 (0-7812-7312-9) Rprt Serv.

Dramatick Works, 4 vols. in 2, Set. George Colman. (Anglistica & Americana Ser.: No. 172). 1976. reprint ed. 193.70 (3-487-05961-4, Pub. by Georg Olms GW) Lubrecht & Cramer.

***Dramatics for Children.** enl. rev. ed. Eleanor Silverman. LC 94-9602. (Illus.). 175p. 1994. pap. 29.50 (0-8108-2637-2) Scarecrow.

Dramatics for Creative Teaching. Samuel J. Citron. (Illus.). 1961. 9.50 (0-8381-0212-3) United Syn Bk.

Dramaticules. Samuel Beckett. 80p. (Orig.). 1997. pap. 7.95 (0-7145-4214-8) Riverrun NY.

Dramatis Personae. Arthur Symons. LC 75-128318. (Essay Index Reprint Ser.). 1977. 23.95 (0-8369-2177-1) Ayer.

Dramatische Dichtungen see Saemtliche Werke

Dramatische Dichtungen: Irenaromachia, Perseus see Saemtliche Werke

***Dramatische Kommunikation: Modell und Reflexion bei Duerrenmatt, Handke, Weiss.** Thorsten Roelcke. (Quellen & Forschungen Zur Sprach- & Kulturgeschichte der Germanischen Voelker Ser.: No. 231). xii, 313p. (GER.). (C). 1994. lib. bdg. 113.85 (3-11-014646-0, 98-94) De Gruyter.

Dramatische Werke, 2-2: Rubezahl (Bruchstucke); Silvana, Vol. 2. Carl M. Weber. (Musikalische Werke Ser.). (Illus.). 1977. reprint ed. pap. 85.00 (0-89371-022-9) Broude Intl Edns.

Dramatische Werke, 2-3: Preciosa, Vol. 1. Carl M. Weber. (Musikalische Werke Ser.). (Illus.). 1977. reprint ed. pap. 95.00 (0-89371-021-0) Broude Intl Edns.

Dramatist & His Characters: Jose Cid Perez. Michele S. Davis. LC 83-60447. (Senda de Estudios y Ensayos Ser.). (Illus.). 184p. (Orig.). 1983. pap. 13.95 (0-918454-33-6) Senda Nueva.

Dramatist in America: Letters of Maxwell Anderson, 1912-1958. Maxwell Anderson. Ed. by Laurence G. Avery. LC 77-4491. 451p. reprint ed. pap. 128.60 (0-7837-5235-0, 2044969) Bks Demand.

Dramatists & the Received Idea. Wilbur Sanders. LC 79-8525. 390p. 1980. pap. 24.95 (0-521-29800-8) Cambridge U Pr.

Dramatists of To-Day. Edward E. Hale. LC 79-90639. (Essay Index Reprint Ser.). 1977. 21.95 (0-8369-1261-6) Ayer.

***Dramatists Sourcebook: 1995-96 Edition.** Ed. by Linda MacColl et al. 300p. (Orig.). 1995. pap. 15.95 (1-55936-111-5) Theatre Comm.

Dramatists Sourcebook, 1994-95. Ed. by Gillian Richards & Linda MacColl. 312p. (Orig.). 1994. pap. 15.95 (1-55936-093-3) Theatre Comm.

Dramatist's Tool Kit: The Craft of the Working Playwright. Jeff Sweet. LC 93-14476. 220p. (C). 1993. pap. 12.95 (0-435-08629-4, 08629) Heinemann.

Dramatizaciones Infantiles Para Dias Especiales. Norma H. C. De Deiros. 96p. 1988. reprint ed. pap. 3.25 (0-311-07606-8) Casa Bautista.

***Dramatizando la Gallinita Roja: (Un Cuento para Contar y Actuar)** Louise Thistle. (Illus.). 32p. (Orig.). (SPA.). (J). (ps-2). 1994. pap. 9.95 (0-9644186-4-9) Lit Dramatization.

Dramatization of Three Melville Novels: With an Introduction on Interpretation by Dramatization. Joyce S. Adler. LC 92-5625. 200p. 1992. lib. bdg. 79.95 (0-7734-9443-X) E Mellen.

Dramatizations of Social Change: Herman Heijermans' Plays As Compared with Selected Dramas by Ibsen, Hauptmann, & Chekhov. Hilda V. Yoder. 1979. pap. 13.00 (0-686-24547-4) Kluwer Ac.

Dramatize Your Paintings with Tonal Value. Carole Katchen. (Elements of Painting Ser.). (Illus.). 144p. 1993. 27.95 (0-89134-477-2, 30523) North Light Bks.

Dramatized New Testament. Michael Perry. LC 93-23807. 440p. 1993. reprint ed. kivar 22.99 (0-8010-7123-2) Baker Bk.

Dramatized Old Testament Vol. 1: Genesis to Esther. Michael Perry. 400p. 1994. pap. 22.99 (0-8010-7136-4) Baker Bk.

Dramatizing Literature in Whole Language Classrooms. 2nd ed. John Stewig & Carol Buege. (Language & Literacy Ser.). 224p. (C). 1994. pap. text ed. 18.95x (0-8077-3307-5) Tchrs Coll.

***Dramatizing Myths & Tales Creating Plays for Large Groups.** Louis Thistle. Ed. by Martha P. Siegel & Lois Fowkes. (Illus.). 200p. Date not set. student ed 14.95 (0-86651-832-0) Seymour Pubns.

***Dramatizing the Little Red Hen: (A Say & Act Story)** Louise Thistle. (Illus.). 32p. (Orig.). (J). (ps-2). 1994. pap. text ed. 9.95 (0-9644186-5-7) Lit Dramatization.

Dramatizing Your Church's History. Loulie L. Owens. Ed. by charles W. Deweese. (Resource Kit for Your Church's History Ser.). 8p. 1984. pap. 0.60 (0-939804-21-2) Hist Comm S Baptist.

Dramaturgical Analysis of Social Interaction. A. Paul Hare & Herbert H. Blumberg. LC 87-30534. 192p. 1988. text ed. 49.95 (0-275-92762-8, C2762, Praeger Pubs) Greenwood.

Dramaturgy of Style: Voice in Short Fiction. Michael Stephens. LC 85-14327. (Crosscurrents-Modern Critiques, Third Ser.). 298p. 1986. text ed. 23.95 (0-8093-1231-X) S Ill U Pr.

Dramaturgy of the Daemonic: Studies in Anti-Generic Theater from Ruzante to Grimaldi. Jackson I. Cope. LC 83-23886. 184p. 1984. text ed. 32.50x (0-8018-3120-2) Johns Hopkins.

Dramawise: An Introduction to the Elements of Drama. Brad Haseman & John O'Toole. (Illus.). 148p. (Orig.). 1989. pap. text ed. 17.00 (0-85859-411-0, 00633) Heinemann.

Drame. Phillipe Sollers. 140p. (FRE.). 1990. pap. 14.95 (0-7859-1384-X, 2070718530) Fr & Eur.

Drame de la Terre. Jean-Baptiste Cineas. (B. E. Ser.: No. 46). (FRE.). 1933. 20.00 (0-8115-2997-5) Periodicals Srv.

Drame en Livonie. Jules Verne. (Illus.). 192p. 1974. pap. 3.95 (0-686-55046-3) Fr & Eur.

Drame Haitien. rev. ed. Antoine A. Raphael. 200p. (FRE.). (C). 1992. 24.95 (0-9631764-2-0); pap. 19.95 (0-9631764-3-9) A A Raphael.

Drames De la Vie Courante. Pierre Cami. 110p. (FRE.). 1991. pap. 10.95 (0-7859-2171-0, 2070384128) Fr & Eur.

Drames liturgiques du moyen age, texte et musique. Ed. by Edmond De Coussemaker. (Illus.). 370p. (FRE & LAT.). 1964. reprint ed. lib. bdg. 85.00 (0-8450-1004-2) Broude.

Dramouss. Camara Laye. (FRE.). 1991. pap. 8.95 (0-7859-3236-4, 2266040243) Fr & Eur.

Drangonlance Classics Vol. 3: DragonLance Adventure. Lisa Smedman & TSR Staff. (Advanced Dungeons & Dragons 2nd Ed. Ser.). 1994. 15.00 (1-56076-885-1) TSR Inc.

Draper Manuscripts Guide. Ed. by Josephine L. Harper. 464p. 1983. 70.00 (0-87020-215-4) Chadwyck-Healey.

Drapers Book of Quotations. Edythe Draper. 1200p. 1992. 30.00 (0-8423-5109-4) Tyndale.

Drapers in America, Being a History & Genealogy of Those of That Name & Connection. Thomas Draper. (Illus.). 324p. 1989. reprint ed. lib. bdg. 55.00 (0-8328-0494-0); reprint ed. pap. 45.00 (0-8328-0495-9) Higginson Bk Co.

Drapery Cleaning: On Location. Roy Moore & F. T. Smith. Ed. by William R. Griffin. (Illus.). 36p. (C). 1987. pap. text ed. 25.00 (0-944352-02-2) Cleaning Cons.

Drapery Secrets Simplified. Nancy C. Tabor. (Illus.). 57p. (Orig.). 1986. pap. 7.95 (0-318-21407-5) N C Tabor.

Drapery Solar-Liner. Richard L. Field. (Solar Energy Ser.: No. 581). (Illus.). (Orig.). 1978. pap. 3.95 (0-931912-12-1) Solpub.

Drapes Come. Charles Dizenzo. 1966. pap. 2.75 (0-8222-0327-8) Dramatists Play.

Draping & Designing with Scissors & Cloth - 1920's. rev. ed. Ed. by Sandra Ericson. LC 92-73092. (Illus.). 55p. 1992. pap. 18.95 (0-9617110-1-9) Antiquity Pr.

Draping for Fashion Design. 2nd ed. Hilde Jaffe & Nurie Relis. LC 92-43411. 1993. text ed. 48.00 (0-13-105842-8) P-H.

Drastic: A Standardized System for Evaluating Ground Water Pollution Potential Using Hydrogeologic Settings. 455p. 1985. 69.00 (1-56034-008-8, T058) Natl Water Well.

Drastic Measures. Pat Nolan. 30p. 1981. pap. 2.00 (0-916382-25-7) Telephone Bks.

Drastic Measures: A History of Wage & Price Controls in the United States. Hugh Rockoff. LC 83-21019. (Studies in Economic History & Policy: The United States in the Twentieth Century). 1984. 49.95 (0-521-24496-X) Cambridge U Pr.

Drat! Mythed Again: Second Thoughts on Utah. Steve Warren. LC 86-81186. (Illus.). 183p. 1986. pap. 10.95 (0-938117-02-5) Altair Pub UT.

Drat! The Cat! (Illus.). 1982. 7.95 (0-88188-072-8, 00383425) H Leonard.

Drat These Brats! X. J. Kennedy. LC 92-33686. (Illus.). 48p. (J). (gr. 3 up). 1993. text ed. 12.95 (0-689-50589-2, McElderry) S&S Childrens.

Draught Animal Power. J. Copland. 170p. (C). 1985. text ed. 108.00 (0-685-63250-4, Pub. by ACIAR) St Mut.

Draughts of Remembrance. Ann R. Colton. 177p. 1959. 8.95 (0-917187-09-1) A R Colton Fnd.

Draupadi & Jayadratha & Other Poems. P. Lal. 18p. 1973. 6.00 (0-88253-271-5); 4.00 (0-89253-540-7) Ind-US Inc.

Dravidian Architecture. G. Jouveau Dubreuil. ii, 47p. (C). 1987. reprint ed. 11.50 (0-8364-2189-2, Pub. by Usha II) S Asia.

Dravidian Borrowings from Indo-Aryan. Murray B. Emeneau & T. Burrow. LC 62-63438. (University of California Publications in Social Welfare: Vol. 26). 131p. reprint ed. pap. 37.40 (0-317-10183-8, 2011684) Bks Demand.

An Asterisk (*) at the beginning of an entry indicates that the title is appearing in BIP for the first time.

Dravidian Developments. Edwin H. Tuttle. (Language Monographs: No. 5). 1930. pap. 16.00 (*0-527-00809-5*) Periodicals Srv.

Dravidian Element in Indian Culture. G. Slater. (Illus.). 192p. 1986. reprint ed. 14.00 (*0-8364-1706-2*, Pub. by Manohar II) S Asia.

Dravidian Gods of Modern Hinduism. W. T. Elmore. 164p. 1986. reprint ed. 18.50 (*0-8364-1708-9*, Pub. by Manohar II) S Asia.

Dravidian India. Sesha Iyengar. 272p. 1986. reprint ed. 14.00 (*0-8364-1707-0*, Pub. by Manohar II) S Asia.

Dravidian India & Aponymous Bharata: An Indo-Sociological Dimension. Chitta R. Bisistha. (C). 1992. 24.00 (*0-8364-2790-4*, Pub. by Firma KLM) S Asia.

Dravidian Kinship. Thomas R. Trautman. LC 80-24214. (Cambridge Studies in Social & Cultural Anthropology: No. 36). (Illus.). 704p. 1982. 54.50 (*0-521-23703-3*) Cambridge U Pr.

Dravidian Phonological Systems. Ed. by Harold F. Schiffman & Carol M. Eastman. LC 76-3520. 432p. 1976. pap. 30.00 (*0-295-95507-4*) U of Wash Pr.

Dravidian Theories. R. Swaminatha Aiyar. (C). 1987. 26.00 (*81-208-0331-0*, Pub. by Motilal Banarsidass II) S Asia.

Dravidians (On the Original Inhabitants of Bharatvarsha or India. Gustove. 1988. reprint ed. 15.00 (*81-206-0348-6*, Pub. by Asian Educ Servs II) S Asia.

Dravya Samagraha (The Sacred Books of the Jainas) Ed. by Sarat C. Ghoshal. 300p. 1990. reprint ed. 50.00 (*0-685-59953-1*, Messers Today & Tomorrow) Scholarly Pubns.

Dravya Samgraha of Menimchandra Siddhanta Chakravarti. Ed. by S. C. Ghoshal. (C). 1989. reprint ed. 47.50 (*81-208-0634-4*, Pub. by Motilal Banarsidass II) S Asia.

***Draw.** (Five-Minute Art Ideas Ser.). (Illus.). 24p. (Orig.). (J). (ps-4). 1995. pap. 6.95 (*1-57102-038-1*, Ideals Child) Hambleton-Hill.

Draw! Kim Solga. (Illus.). 48p. (J). (gr. 1-6). 1991. 11.99 (*0-89134-385-7*, 30337) North Light Bks.

Draw! A Visual Approach to Learning, Thinking & Communicating. Kurt Hanks & Larry Belliston. Ed. by Phil Gerould. LC 90-22704. (Illus.). 242p. (C). 1990. reprint ed. pap. 15.95 (*1-56052-054-X*) Crisp Pubns.

Draw: How to Master the Art. Jeffery Camp. LC 93-34251. (Illus.). 256p. 1994. reprint ed. pap. 14.95 (*1-56458-526-3*) Dorling Kindersley.

Draw! Political Cartoons from Left to Right. Ed. by Stacey Bredhoff. LC 91-2559. (Illus.). 144p. (Orig.). 1991. pap. 7.95 (*0-911333-85-1*, 200021) National Archives & Recs.

Draw - & - Tell. R. Thompson. (Illus.). 88p. (J). 1988. 19.95 (*1-55037-032-4*, Pub. by Annick CN) Firefly Bks Ltd.

Draw - Write - Now: A Drawing & Handwriting Course for Kids! Marie Hablitzel & Kim H. Stitzer. (Illus.). 64p. (J). (gr. k-5). 1994. pap. 8.95 (*0-9639307-1-0*) Barker Creek.

Draw-a-Person Catalogue for Interpretative Analysis. William H. Urban. 72p. 1963. pap. 39.50x (*0-87424-044-1*, W-44) Western Psych.

Draw a Story: Screening for Depression & Age or Gender Differences. 2nd rev. ed. Rawley A. Silver. LC 93-72384. (Illus.). 112p. (C). 1993. pap. text ed. 25.00 (*0-9621429-4-8*) Ablin Pr.

Draw Animals: Learn From Former Disney Artist Bud Shackelford. Bud Shackelford. LC 92-96937. (Illus.). 64p. (Orig.). (J). (gr. k-6). 1993. pap. 9.50 (*0-9634693-0-4*) B Shackelford.

Draw Animals Around the World. Joy Evans. (Illus.). 36p. (J). (gr. 2-6). 1992. pap. 7.95 (*1-55799-223-1*) Evan-Moor Corp.

Draw Batons. large type ed. Bill Knox. (Linford Mystery Library). 368p. 1993. pap. 14.95 (*0-7089-7380-9*, Trailtree Bookshop) Ulverscroft.

Draw! Cars. Doug DuBosque. (Illus.). 80p. (Orig.). (J). (gr. 3-9). 1993. pap. 8.95 (*0-939217-19-8*) Peel Prod.

Draw! Desert Animals. Doug DuBosque. (Illus.). 64p. (Orig.). (J). (gr. 2-8). 1995. pap. 7.95 (*0-939217-26-0*) Peel Prod.

Draw, Design & Paint. Jan Barry. (Illus.). 144p. (J). (gr. 2-6). 1990. 12.95 (*0-86653-536-5*, GA1142) Good Apple.

Draw! Dinosaurs. Doug DuBosque. (Illus.). 80p. (J). (ps-4). 1993. pap. 8.95 (*0-939217-20-1*) Peel Prod.

Draw Farm Animals. Joy Evans. (Illus.). 36p. 1994. pap. text ed. 7.95 (*1-55799-278-9*) Evan-Moor Corp.

Draw Fifty Airplanes, Aircraft & Spacecraft. Lee J. Ames. LC 76-51554. (Illus.). 64p. 1987. mass mkt. 8.00 (*0-385-23629-8*, Zephyr-BFYR) Doubleday.

Draw Fifty Animals. Lee J. Ames. LC 73-13083. (Illus.). 64p. 1985. mass mkt. 8.00 (*0-385-19519-2*, Zephyr-BFYR) Doubleday.

Draw Fifty Athletes. Lee J. Ames. (Illus.). 1989. mass mkt. 8.00 (*0-385-24638-2*) Doubleday.

Draw Fifty Beasties: And Yugglies & Turnover Uglies & Things That Go Bump in the Night. Lee J. Ames. 1988. mass mkt. 8.00 (*0-385-26767-3*) Doubleday.

Draw Fifty Boats, Ships, Trucks & Trains. Lee J. Ames. LC 75-19011. (Illus.). 64p. 1976. mass mkt. 8.00 (*0-385-23630-1*, Zephyr-BFYR) Doubleday.

Draw Fifty Buildings & Other Structures. Lee J. Ames. 1991. mass mkt. 8.00 (*0-385-41777-2*) Doubleday.

Draw Fifty Cars, Trucks & Motorcycles. Lee J. Ames. (Illus.). 1986. mass mkt. 8.00 (*0-385-24639-0*) Doubleday.

Draw Fifty Cats. Lee J. Ames. (Illus.). 1986. mass mkt. 8.00 (*0-385-24640-4*) Doubleday.

Draw Fifty Creepy Crawlies: The Step-by-Step Way to Draw Bugs, Slugs, Spiders, Scorpions. Lee J. Ames. (J). 1992. mass mkt. 8.00 (*0-385-42449-3*) Doubleday.

Draw Fifty Dinosaurs & Other Prehistoric Animals. Lee J. Ames. LC 76-7285. (Illus.). 64p. 1985. mass mkt. 8.00 (*0-385-19520-6*, Zephyr-BFYR) Doubleday.

Draw Fifty Dogs. Lee J. Ames. LC 85-16197. 64p. 1981. mass mkt. 8.00 (*0-385-23431-7*, Zephyr-BFYR) Doubleday.

Draw Fifty Endangered Animals! Lee J. Ames & Warren Budd. (Illus.). 1993. mass mkt. 8.00 (*0-385-46985-3*) Doubleday.

Draw Fifty Famous Caricatures. Lee J. Ames. 1990. 12.95 (*0-385-24629-3*) Doubleday.

Draw Fifty Famous Cartoons. Lee J. Ames. LC 78-1176. (Illus.). 64p. 1985. mass mkt. 8.00 (*0-385-19521-4*, Zephyr-BFYR) Doubleday.

Draw Fifty Famous Faces. Lee J. Ames. LC 77-15878. 64p. 1990. mass mkt. 8.00 (*0-385-23432-5*, Zephyr-BFYR) Doubleday.

Draw Fifty Holiday Decorations. Lee J. Ames. (Illus.). 1987. mass mkt. 8.00 (*0-385-26770-3*) Doubleday.

Draw Fifty Horses. Lee J. Ames. LC 81-43646. (Illus.). 64p. 1984. mass mkt. 8.00 (*0-385-17642-2*, Zephyr-BFYR) Doubleday.

Draw Fifty Monsters, Creeps, Superheroes, Demons, Dragons, Nerds, Dirts, Ghoulds, Giants, Vampires, Zombies, & Other Curiosa. Lee J. Ames. LC 80-3006. (Illus.). 64p. 1986. mass mkt. 8.00 (*0-385-17639-2*, Zephyr-BFYR) Doubleday.

Draw Fifty People: The Step-by-Step Way to Draw Cavemen, Queens, Aztecs, Knights, Minutemen... Lee J. Ames. 1994. mass mkt. 8.00 (*0-385-41194-4*) Doubleday.

Draw Fifty Sharks, Whales, & Other Sea Creatures. Lee J. Ames. 1989. mass mkt. 8.00 (*0-385-26768-1*) Doubleday.

Draw Fifty Trees, Flowers & Other Plants. Lee J. Ames. (Illus.). 1994. 13.00 (*0-385-47004-5*); mass mkt. 8.00 (*0-385-47150-5*) Doubleday.

Draw Fifty Vehicles. Lee J. Ames. LC 77-94862. 1978. mass mkt. 8.00 (*0-385-14154-8*, Zephyr-BFYR) Doubleday.

Draw from Within: A Workbook for Self-Expression & Self-Discovery. Barbara B. Prochelo. (Illus.). 66p. (Orig.). 1990. pap. 9.95 (*0-9626838-0-9*) Sun Dance Creat.

Draw from Your Head: A Step-by-Step System for Drawing the Human Figure without a Model. Doug Jamieson. (Illus.). 192p. 1991. 32.50 (*0-8230-1374-X*, Watsn-Guptill) Watsn-Guptill.

Draw! Grassland Animals. Doug DuBosque. (Illus.). 64p. (Orig.). (J). (gr. 2-8). 1995. pap. 7.95 (*0-939217-25-2*) Peel Prod.

Draw Horses with Sam Savitt. Sam Savitt. (Illus.). 96p. (J). 1991. reprint ed. 20.95 (*0-939481-23-5*) Half Halt Pr.

Draw Me: Prayers for Every Occasion in a Woman's Life. Carmen Rojas. 200p. (Orig.). 1990. pap. 7.99 (*0-89283-660-1*) Servant.

Draw Me a Star. Eric Carle. (Illus.). 40p. (J). (ps up). 1992. lib. bdg. 15.95 (*0-399-21877-7*, Philomel Bks) Putnam Pub Group.

Draw Near to God see Lift up Your Hearts: The Pope John Paul II Reader

Draw! Ocean Animals. Doug DuBosque. (Illus.). 64p. (Orig.). (J). (gr. 2-8). 1994. pap. 7.95 (*0-939217-24-4*) Peel Prod.

Draw or Drag. Wayne D. Overholser. 1994. lib. bdg. 15.95 (*0-7451-4606-6*, Gunsmoke) Chivers N Amer.

Draw! Rainforest Animals. Doug DuBosque. (Illus.). 64p. (Orig.). (J). (gr. 2-8). 1994. pap. 7.95 (*0-939217-23-6*) Peel Prod.

Draw Science: Horses & Ponies. Nina Kidd. 64p. (J). 1994. pap. 4.95 (*1-56565-174-X*) Lowell Hse Juvenile.

Draw Science: Sharks, Whales, & Other Sea Creatures. Nina Kidd. 64p. 1992. pap. 4.95 (*1-56565-013-1*) Lowell Hse.

Draw Science - Dinosaurs. Nina Kidd. 64p. (J). (ps-3). 1992. pap. 4.95 (*0-929923-89-8*) Lowell Hse.

Draw Science - Wild Animals. Nina Kidd. 64p. (J). (ps-3). 1992. pap. 4.95 (*0-929923-90-1*) Lowell Hse.

Draw the Line. Nicole Grey. (Girl Friends Ser.: No. 1). 224p. 1993. pap. 3.50 (*0-8217-4350-3*) Zebra.

***Draw the Line: A Sexual Harassment-Free Workplace.** Frances Lynch. Ed. by Kathleen Doyle. (Successful Business Library). 250p. (Orig.). 1995. pap. 17.95 (*1-55571-370-X*) Oasis Pr OR.

***Draw the Marvel Super Heroes: A Mighty Manual of Massively Amazing Step-by-Step Instruction.** Klutz Press Editors. 94p. 1995. ring bd. 12.95 (*1-57054-000-4*) Klutz Pr.

Draw Us Nearer to You, Lord. Linda J. Werman. Ed. by Michael L. Sherer. LC 86-28378. (Orig.). 1987. pap. 7.60 (*0-89536-858-7*, 7817) CSS OH.

***Draw Write Now Bk. 2: Drawing & Handwriting Course for Kids!** Marie Hablitzel & Kim H. Stitzer. (Illus.). 64p. (J). (gr. k-5). 1995. pap. 8.95 (*0-9639307-2-9*) Barker Creek.

Draw Your Own House Plans. Mike Wolverton & Ruth Wolverton. (Illus.). 336p. 1983. 19.95 (*0-8306-0381-6*, 1381); pap. 15.95 (*0-8306-1381-1*) TAB Bks.

Drawdown Survival Guide. P. J. Budahn. LC 93-1671. 193p. 1993. pap. 12.95 (*1-55750-090-8*) Naval Inst Pr.

Drawer in a Drawer. David Christiana. 32p. (J). (ps-3). 1990. 13.95 (*0-374-31874-3*) FS&G.

Drawer in a Drawer. David Christiana. 32p. (J). (ps-3). 1992. pap. 4.95 (*0-374-41881-0*, Sunburst Bks) FS&G.

Drawers of Ocracoke. Carole Marsh. (Carole Marsh Short Story Ser.). (Illus.). (Orig.). (J). (ps-7). 1994. 24.95 (*1-55609-163-X*); pap. 14.95 (*1-55609-236-9*) Gallopade Pub Group.

Drawing. (Illus.). Date not set. text ed. write for info. (*1-56290-064-1*) Crystal.

Drawing. Robin Capon. (Illus.). 96p. 1991. 34.95 (*0-7134-6421-6*, Pub. by Batsford UK) Trafalgar.

Drawing. Patience Foster. (Hobby Guides Ser.). (J). (gr. 2-5). 1981. lib. bdg. 13.96 (*0-88110-025-0*, Usborne); pap. 6.95 (*0-86020-540-1*, Usborne) EDC.

***Drawing.** Ann Mullin & Jan Clough. 175p. (C). 1995. per., pap. text ed. 32.95 (*0-7872-1049-8*) Kendall-Hunt.

Drawing. Ziya N. Sever. (Illus.). 171p. (Orig.). 1979. pap. text ed. 13.95x (*0-89641-032-3*) American Pr.

Drawing. Sue Stocks. LC 94-374. (First Arts & Crafts Ser.). (Illus.). 32p. (J). (gr. 1-4). 1994. 14.95 (*1-56847-211-0*) Thomson Lrning.

***Drawing.** 1995. 14.95 (*1-57145-015-7*) Thunder Bay CA.

Drawing. Ruth Thomson. LC 94-17329. (Get Set-- Go! Ser.). (Illus.). 24p. (J). (ps-3). 1994. lib. bdg. 10.80 (*0-516-07989-1*); pap. 4.95 (*0-516-47989-X*) Childrens.

Drawing. 2nd ed. Philip Rawson. LC 87-10929. (Illus.). 336p. 1987. reprint ed. pap. text ed. 20.95 (*0-8122-1251-7*) U of Pa Pr.

Drawing. Daniel M. Mendelowitz. LC 80-50905. (Illus.). xvi, 464p. 1980. reprint ed. 39.50 (*0-8047-1089-9*) Stanford U Pr.

Drawing: A Contemporary Approach. 2nd ed. Claudia W. Betti & Teel Sale. 280p. (Orig.). (C). 1986. pap. text ed. 38.00 (*0-03-070339-5*) HB Coll Pubs.

Drawing: A Contemporary Approach. 3rd ed. Claudia Betti & Teel Sale. (Illus.). 288p. (Orig.). (C). 1992. pap. text ed. 41.25 (*0-03-053147-0*) HB Coll Pubs.

Drawing: A Creative Process. Frank Ching. (Illus.). 210p. 1990. pap. 24.95 (*0-442-31818-9*) Van Nos Reinhold.

Drawing: A Studio Guide. Lu Bro. (Illus.). 1985. pap. 18.95 (*0-393-95018-2*) Norton.

Drawing: A Young Artist's Guide. Elizabeth Waters & Annie Harris. LC 94-13103. (Illus.). 48p. (J): (gr. 3-6). 1994. 14.95 (*1-56458-676-6*) Dorling Kindersley.

Drawing: At the Henry. Norman Lundin et al. LC 80-17746. (Illus.). 56p. 1980. 5.95 (*0-935558-06-3*) Henry Art.

Drawing: Face to Face with Tim Bowers. Tim Bowers. (Illus.). 24p. (J). (gr. 1-6). 1994. pap. write for info. (*0-9641192-0-X*) Bowers Studio.

Drawing: Space Form & Expression. Wayne Enstice & Melody Peters. 320p. 1990. pap. text ed. 46.00 (*0-13-219254-3*) P-H.

***Drawing: Space, Form, & Expression.** 2nd ed. Wayne Enstice & Melody Peters. LC 94-48306. 1995. write for info. (*0-13-304543-9*) P-H.

Drawing: The Complete Course. Stan Smith. LC 94-12077. (Illus.). 160p. 1994. 25.00 (*0-89577-620-0*) RD Assn.

Drawing: The Creative Process. Seymour Simmons. 1977. pap. 17.00 (*0-671-76266-4*) P-H.

Drawing: You Can Do It! Greg Albert. (Illus.). 144p. 1992. 24.95 (*0-89134-428-4*, 30416) North Light Bks.

Drawing - Building - Text: Essays in Architectural Theory. Ed. by Andrea Kahn. LC 91-23014. (Illus.). 176p. (Orig.). 1991. pap. 14.95 (*0-910413-71-1*) Princeton Arch.

Drawing a Circle in the Square: Street Performing in New York's Washington Square Park. Sally Harrison-Pepper. LC 90-49787. 1990. 35.00 (*0-87805-464-2*); pap. 15.95 (*0-87805-470-7*) U Pr of Miss.

Drawing a Likeness. Douglas R. Graves. (Illus.). 176p. 1984. pap. 15.95 (*0-8230-1358-8*, Watsn-Guptill) Watsn-Guptill.

Drawing America: The Story of the First Thanksgiving. Don Bolognese & Elaine Raphael. 32p. (J). 1991. 10.95 (*0-590-44373-9*, Scholastic Hardcover) Scholastic Inc.

Drawing an Interest on the Bank on China. Abell. (Illus.). 50p. (Orig.). (J). (gr. 5 up). 1993. lib. bdg. 25.00 (*1-56611-083-1*) Jonas.

Drawing an Interest on the Bank on China. Abell. (Illus.). 50p. (Orig.). (YA). (gr. 5 up). 1993. pap. 15.00 (*1-56611-084-X*) Jonas.

***Drawing & Cartooning Comics.** Tony Tallarico. 96p. (Orig.). 1995. pap. 9.95 (*0-399-51946-7*, Perigree Bks) Berkley Pub.

Drawing & Cartooning Dinosaurs: A Step-by-Step Guide for the Aspiring Prehistoric Artist. Tony Tallarico. LC 93-16278. (Illus.). 96p. (Orig.). (J). 1993. pap. 7.95 (*0-399-51814-2*, Perigree Bks) Berkley Pub.

Drawing & Cartooning for Laughs. Jack Hamm. (Illus.). 128p. 1990. pap. 8.95 (*0-399-51634-4*, Perigree Bks) Berkley Pub.

Drawing & Cartooning Monsters: A Step-by-Step Guide for the Aspiring Monster-Maker. Tony Tallarico. (Illus.). 128p. (Orig.). (J). 1992. pap. 7.95 (*0-399-51785-5*, Perigree Bks) Berkley Pub.

***Drawing & Cartooning Myths, Magic & Legends: A Step-by-Step Guide for the Aspiring Myth-Maker.** Tony Tallarico. LC 94-26292. 96p. (Orig.). 1994. pap. 8.95 (*0-399-52139-9*, Perigree Bks) Berkley Pub.

Drawing & Cartooning One Thousand and One Figures in Action. Dick Gautier. (Illus.). 128p. (Orig.). 1994. pap. 10.95 (*0-399-51859-2*, Perigree Bks) Berkley Pub.

Drawing & Cartooning One Thousand One Faces. Dick Gautier. (Illus.). 128p. (Orig.). 1993. pap. 10.95 (*0-399-51767-7*, Perigree Bks) Berkley Pub.

***Drawing & Cartooning 1001 Caricatures.** Dick Gautier. 128p. (Orig.). 1995. pap. 11.00 (*0-399-51911-4*, Perigree Bks) Berkley Pub.

Drawing & Cognition: Descriptive & Experimental Studies of Graphic Production Processes. Peter Van Sommers. LC 83-7799. 284p. 1984. 54.95 (*0-521-25095-1*) Cambridge U Pr.

Drawing & Designing with Confidence. Mike W. Lin. (Illus.). 224p. 1993. text ed. 54.95 (*0-442-00176-2*) Van Nos Reinhold.

Drawing & Painting Animals. Cecile Curtis. (Illus.). 160p. 1990. 26.95 (*0-89134-352-0*, 30241) North Light Bks.

Drawing & Painting from Imagination. Don Stacy. LC 79-27795. (Illus.). 224p. (YA). (gr. 9-12). 1980. 14.95 (*0-87396-083-1*) Stravon.

Drawing & Painting from Nature. Cathy Johnson. 1989. text ed. 27.95 (*0-07-157372-0*) McGraw.

Drawing & Painting from Nature. Cathy Johnson. (Illus.). 160p. 1989. 27.95 (*0-8306-5502-6*, Design Pr) TAB Bks.

Drawing & Painting with Colored Pencils. Stefan Birker. LC 92-41349. (Illus.). 128p. (YA). (gr. 9-12). 1993. pap. 16.95 (*0-8069-0312-0*) Sterling.

Drawing & Perceiving. 2nd ed. Douglas Cooper. (Illus.). 224p. 1992. pap. 29.95 (*0-442-00994-1*) Van Nos Reinhold.

***Drawing & Sketching.** John Palmer. (Ron Ranson's Painting School Ser.). (Illus.). 120p. 1995. 22.95 (*1-85470-061-8*, Pub. by Anaya Pubs UK) Trafalgar.

Drawing & the Blind: Pictures to Touch. John M. Kennedy. LC 92-10624. (Illus.). 392p. (C). 1993. text ed. 37.50 (*0-300-05490-4*) Yale U Pr.

Drawing Animals. Norman Adams & Joe Singer. (Illus.). 160p. 1989. pap. 18.95 (*0-8230-1366-9*, Watsn-Guptill) Watsn-Guptill.

Drawing Animals. Victor Perard et al. (Illus.). 96p. 1987. pap. 9.00 (*0-399-51390-6*, Perigee Bks) Berkley Pub.

Drawing Animals & Pets. (Understand How to Draw Ser.: No. 6). (Illus.). 32p. pap. 4.95 (*0-85532-574-7*, Pub. by Search Pr UK) A Schwartz & Co.

Drawing As a Means to Architecture. William K. Lockard. (Illus.). 112p. 1995. reprint ed. pap. 19.95 (*1-56052-223-2*) Crisp Pubns.

Drawing Back the Curtains. Dori A. Steele. (Illus.). 104p. (Orig.). 1990. pap. 7.95 (*0-934411-28-X*, Banned Bks) Edward-William Austin.

***Drawing Basic Subjects.** Ed. by Parramon Ediciones Staff. LC 95-2347. (Easy Painting & Drawing Ser.). Orig. Title: Temas Basicos de Dibujo. 1995. write for info. (*0-8120-9290-2*) Barron.

Drawing Blood. Poppy Z. Brite. 1993. 19.95 (*0-385-30895-7*, Delta) Dell.

***Drawing Blood.** Poppy Z. Brite. 1994. pap. 4.99 (*0-440-21492-0*) Delacorte.

Drawing Book. 1990. 17.99 (*0-517-05381-0*) Random Hse Value.

Drawing Book. Leon Baxter. LC 90-4476. (Illus.). 64p. (J). (ps-4). 1990. 13.95 (*0-8249-8475-7*) Hambleton-Hill.

Drawing Book. John Deacon. (Illus.). 64p. (J). (gr. 4 up). 1989. pap. 5.95 (*0-590-42142-5*) Scholastic Inc.

Drawing Book. rev. ed. Leon Baxter. (Illus.). 62p. (J). 1991. reprint ed. lib. bdg. 15.95 (*1-878363-38-7*) Forest Hse.

Drawing Book. Leon Baxter. LC 90-4476. (Illus.). 64p. (J). (ps-4). 1993. reprint ed. pap. 5.95 (*0-8249-8633-4*) Hambleton-Hill.

Drawing Buildings & Towns. (Understand How to Draw Ser.: No. 5). (Illus.). 32p. pap. 4.95 (*0-85532-573-9*, Pub. by Search Pr UK) A Schwartz & Co.

Drawing Cartoon Animals. Bruce Blitz. (Blitz Cartoon Ser.). (Illus.). 48p. 1991. pap. 5.95 (*1-56010-102-4*, HT249) W Foster Pub.

Drawing Cartoon Portraits. Bruce Blitz. (Blitz Cartoon Ser.). (Illus.). 48p. (Orig.). 1994. pap. 5.95 (*1-56010-104-0*, HT246) W Foster Pub.

Drawing Cartoons. Bruce Blitz. (Blitz Cartoon Ser.). (Illus.). 48p. 1991. pap. 5.95 (*1-56010-100-8*, HT247) W Foster Pub.

***Drawing Cartoons.** Judy Tatchell. (Hotshots Ser.). (Illus.). 32p. (J). (gr. 1 up). 1995. pap. 2.95 (*0-7460-2276-X*, Usborne) EDC.

Drawing Cats & Dogs. (J). 1989. pap. 1.95 (*0-8167-1667-6*) Troll Assocs.

Drawing Cats & Kittens. Paul Frame. (J). (ps-3). 1990. pap. 3.95 (*0-531-15198-0*) Watts.

***Drawing Closer: A Step by Step Guide to Intimacy with God.** Glen S. Martin & Dian Ginter. LC 94-24526. 1995. 16.99 (*0-8054-6182-5*) Broadman.

Drawing Comic Strips. Bruce Blitz. (Blitz Cartoon Ser.). (Illus.). 48p. 1991. pap. 5.95 (*1-56010-101-6*, HT248) W Foster Pub.

Drawing Conclusions. Sheldon L. Tilkin & Judith Conoway. (Horizons E Ser.). (Illus.). 24p. (J). (gr. 3-4). 1980. 3.50 (*0-89403-573-8*) EDC.

Drawing Conclusions. Sheldon L. Tilkin & Judith Conoway. (Horizons F Ser.). (Illus.). 24p. (J). (gr. 4-5). 1980. student ed 3.50 (*0-89403-583-5*) EDC.

Drawing Conclusions: Advanced Level. 2nd ed. Ed. by Kraft. (Comprehension Skills Ser.). 64p. 1993. pap. 5.95 (*0-89061-617-5*) Jamestown Pubs.

Drawing Conclusions: An Artist's Guide to Adobe Illustrator 5.0. Susan G. Wheeler & Gary Wheeler. 416p. 1993. pap. write for info. (*0-697-21146-0*) Bus & Educ Tech.

Drawing Conclusions: Introductory Level. Ed. by Kraft. (Comprehension Skills Ser.). 64p. 1993. pap. 5.50 (*0-89061-657-4*) Jamestown Pubs.

Drawing Conclusions: Middle Level. 2nd ed. Ed. by Kraft. (Comprehension Skills Ser.). 64p. 1993. pap. 5.75 (*0-89061-637-X*) Jamestown Pubs.

***Drawing Conclusions.** Bob Gorrell. (Illus.). 160p. 1995. pap. text ed. 8.95 (*1-56554-145-6*) Pelican.

Drawing Dead. Pete Hautman. LC 93-11206. 1993. 21.00 (*0-671-79374-8*) S&S Trade.

Drawing Detail. (Understand How to Draw Ser.: No. 7). (Illus.). 32p. pap. 4.95 (*0-85532-611-5*, Pub. by Search Pr UK) A Schwartz & Co.

Drawing Dinosaurs. Jerome Goyallon. LC 93-2809. (Illus.). 80p. (J). (gr. 3 up). 1993. 14.95 (*0-8069-8742-1*) Sterling.

Drawing Dinosaurs. Jerome Goyallon. (Illus.). 80p. 1994. pap. 5.95 (*0-8069-8743-X*) Sterling.

***Drawing Dinosaurs: Activities & Investigations in Paleontology.** Armand Morgan. LC 94-28175. (Museum of Science Book Ser.). (Illus.). 96p. (J). (gr. 5-8). 1995. lib. bdg. 18.90 (*1-56294-517-3*) Millbrook Pr.

***Drawing Down a Daughter.** Harris. 1993. per. 10.95 (*0-86492-135-7*, Pub. by Goose Ln Edits CN) InBook.

Drawing Down the Moon: Witches, Druids, Goddess-Worshippers, & Other Pagans in America Today. expanded rev. ed. Margot Adler. LC 86-70551. 608p. 1987. pap. 18.00 (*0-8070-3253-0*, BP 723) Beacon Pr.

An Asterisk (*) at the beginning of an entry indicates that the title is appearing in BIP for the first time. 2105

An Asterisk (*) at the beginning of an entry indicates that the title is appearing in BIP for the first time.

D

An Asterisk (*) at the beginning of an entry indicates that the title is appearing in BIP for the first time.

2107

D

Dread of Plenty: Agricultural Relief Activities of the Federal Government in the Middle West, 1933-1939. Michael W. Schuyler. (Illus.). 264p. (Orig.). 1989. pap. 26.95 (*0-89745-117-1*) Sunflower U Pr.

Dread Road. Meridel Le Sueur. (Illus.). 65p. (Orig.). 1991. pap. 11.95 (*0-931122-63-5*) West End.

Dreaded Comparison: Human & Animal Slavery. rev. ed. Marjorie Spiegel. (Illus.). 112p. (Orig.). 1989. pap. 10.95 (*0-9624493-0-X*) Mirror Bks.

Dreaded Comparison: Human & Animal Slavery. 2nd rev. ed. Marjorie Spiegel. (Illus.). 112p. (Orig.). 1989. lib. bdg. 29.95 (*0-9624493-1-8*) Mirror Bks.

Dreaded One. Rae Wilder. 250p. Date not set. write for info. (*0-318-69934-6*) Longitude & Lat.

***Dreadful Debutante.** Marion Chesney. (Regency Romance Ser.). 1994. pap. 3.99 (*0-449-22261-6*, Crest) Fawcett.

Dreadful Decade: Detailing Some Phases in the History of the United States from Reconstruction to Resumption, 1869-1879. Don C. Seitz. LC 68-28646. (Illus.). 311p. 1968. reprint ed. text ed. 35.00 (*0-8371-0216-2*, SEDD, Greenwood Pr) Greenwood.

Dreadful Decade - 1869-1879. Don C. Seitz. (History - United States Ser.). 311p. 1992. reprint ed. lib. bdg. 89.00 (*0-7812-6189-9*) Rprt Serv.

Dreadful Delicacies. Mary A. Clayton & Al Clayton. LC 93-79664. (Illus.). 64p. 1993. 15.95 (*1-56352-105-9*) Longstreet Pr Inc.

Dreadful Fire! Burning of the Houses of Parliament. Katherine Solender. LC 84-17616. (Illus.). 82p. (Orig.). 1985. pap. 7.95 (*0-910386-74-9*) Cleveland Mus Art.

Dreadful Fury: Advanced Military Technology and the Atlantic Alliance. Michael Moodie. LC 88-38059. (CSIS Washington Papers). 190p. 1989. text ed. 45.00 (*0-275-93236-2*, Praeger Pubs); pap. text ed. 10.95 (*0-275-93237-0*, Praeger Pubs) Greenwood.

Dreadful Fury: Advanced Military Technology & the Atlantic Alliance. Michael Moodie. (Washington Papers: No. 136). 155p. 1989. 34.95 (*0-685-47126-8*, C3236, Praeger Pubs); pap. 10.95 (*0-685-47127-6*, B3237, Praeger Pubs) Greenwood.

Dreadful Future of Blossom Culp. Richard Peck. (J). (gr. 7 up). 1983. 15.00 (*0-385-29300-3*) Delacorte.

Dreadful Future of Blossom Culp. Richard Peck. (J). (gr. k-6). 1994. mass mkt. 3.99 (*0-440-42154-3*, YB) Dell.

Dreadful Games: The Play of Desire in the Nineteenth-Century Novel. Nancy Morrow. LC 87-35902. 209p. 1988. 24.00 (*0-87338-358-3*) Kent St U Pr.

Dreadful Lemon Sky. John D. MacDonald. 1987. mass mkt. 5.99 (*0-449-13404-0*) Fawcett.

***Dreadful Monsters of Yellow Mountain.** Mercedes M. Reitz & Russell T. Reitz. (Yellow Mountain Ser.). (Illus.). 216p. (Orig.). (J). (gr. 5-7). 1991. text ed. 19.95 (*0-9625344-2-0*); pap. 9.95 (*0-9625344-3-9*) Creative Multi-Media.

Dreadful Month. Carlton Jackson. LC 82-72582. (Illus.). 161p. (C). 1982. 17.95 (*0-87972-205-3*); pap. 8.95 (*0-87972-206-1*) Bowling Green Univ.

Dreadful Pleasures: An Anatomy of Modern Horror. James B. Twitchell. 1987. pap. 12.95 (*0-19-505067-3*) OUP.

Dreadful Sorry. Kathryn Reiss. LC 92-38780. (J). (gr. 5-9). 1993. 16.95 (*0-15-224213-9*) HarBrace.

Dreadnought. Diane Carey. (Star Trek Ser.). 1990. mass mkt. 5.50 (*0-671-72567-X*) PB.

Dreadnought: Britain, Germany, & the Coming of the Great War. Robert K. Massie. (Illus.). 1040p. 1992. pap. 17.50 (*0-345-37556-4*, Ballantine Trade) Ballantine.

Dreadnought Battleships & Battle Cruisers. William E. McMahon. LC 78-50769. (Illus.). 1978. lib. bdg. 27.00 (*0-8191-0465-5*) U Pr of Amer.

Dreads & Drolls. Arthur Machen. LC 67-28757. (Essay Index Reprint Ser.). 1977. 28.95 (*0-8369-0648-9*) Ayer.

Dreadstar. Jim Starlin. 64p. 1982. 4.95 (*0-939766-15-9*) Marvel Entmnt.

Dream. (Series 9011-6: No. 6). (Illus.). (J). (ps-2). 1990. Series 9011-6, No. 6. 2.95 (*0-7214-3225-5*) Ladybird Bks.

Dream. (Read with Me Key Words to Reading Ser.: No. 9010-6). (Illus.). (J). (ps-2). 1990. 3.50 (*0-7214-1319-6*) Ladybird Bks.

Dream. (Read with Me Key Words to Reading Ser.: No. 9010-6). (Illus.). (J). (ps-2). 1990. teacher ed 3.95 (*0-317-04759-0*) Ladybird Bks.

Dream. Winston S. Churchill. (Churchill Ser.: No. 1). (Illus.). 36p. 1994. pap. 15.00 (*0-943879-00-0*) Intl Churchill Soc.

Dream. Barbara Delinsky. (Temptation Ser.: No. 417). 1990. pap. 2.65 (*0-373-25417-2*) Harlequin Bks.

Dream. Avner Gold. Ed. by Y. Y. Reinman. (Ruach Ami Ser.: No. 2). (Illus.). 112p. (J). (gr. 7-11). 1983. pap. 7.95 (*0-935063-01-3*) CIS Comm.

***Dream.** Roderick Hunt. (Oxford Reading Tree Ser.). (Illus.). 16p. (J). (gr. k-k). 1994. pap. 1.99 (*0-19-916037-6*) OUP.

***Dream.** Kasey Mars. 416p. 1995. pap. 4.99 (*0-7860-0203-4*) Windsor NY.

Dream: Analytical Ground Water Flow Programs. Bernadine A. Bonn & Stewart A. Rounds. (Illus.). 115p. 1989. disk 94.95 (*0-87371-271-4*, GB1197) Lewis Pubs.

Dream: Analytical Ground Water Flow Programs. 2nd ed. Bernadine A. Bonn & Stewart A. Rounds. (Illus.). 115p. 1995. write for info. (*0-87371-737-6*) Lewis Pubs.

Dream: Four Thousand Years of Theory & Practice - A Critical, Descriptive, & Encylopedic Bibliography, 2 vols., 1. Nancy Parsifal-Charles. LC 86-15335. 1986. lib. bdg. write for info. (*0-933951-05-1*) Locust Hill Pr.

Dream: Four Thousand Years of Theory & Practice - A Critical, Descriptive, & Encylopedic Bibliography, 2 vols., 2. Nancy Parsifal-Charles. LC 86-15335. 1986. lib. bdg. write for info. (*0-933951-06-X*) Locust Hill Pr.

Dream: Four Thousand Years of Theory & Practice - A Critical, Descriptive, & Encylopedic Bibliography, 2 vols., Set. Nancy Parsifal-Charles. LC 86-15335. 1986. lib. bdg. 69.95 (*0-933951-07-8*) Locust Hill Pr.

Dream: The Vision of the Night. Max Zeller. 252p. 1990. pap. 14.95 (*0-938434-37-3*) Sigo Pr.

Dream: The Vision of the Night. Max Zeller. 252p. 1991. reprint ed. 27.50 (*0-938434-36-5*) Sigo Pr.

Dream ... the Journey: Lorain Community Hospital. Margaret Finnerty. Ed. by Amy Phillips & Rodney Nelson. 96p. (C). 1993. write for info. (*0-929690-20-6*) Herit Pubs AZ.

Dream a Deadly Dream. Allie Harrison. (Shadows Ser.). 1993. mass mkt. 3.50 (*0-373-27020-8*, 5-27020-2) Silhouette.

Dream a New Dream see Rebuild Your Life: How to Survive a Crisis

Dream Alchemy: Shaping Our Dreams to Transform Our Lives. Ted Andrews. LC 91-19444. (Practical Guide to Personal Power Ser.). (Illus.). 278p. (Orig.). 1991. pap. 12.95 (*0-87542-017-6*) Llewellyn Pubns.

Dream Analysis. Ella F. Sharpe. 211p. 1978. pap. 29.95 (*1-85575-174-7*, Pub. by Karnac Bks UK) Brunner-Mazel.

Dream Analysis: C. G. Jung Seminars, Vol. 1. Carl G. Jung. Ed. by William McGuire. LC 82-42787. (Bollingen Ser.: No. XCIX-1). (Illus.). 780p. 1984. 65.00 (*0-691-09896-4*) Princeton U Pr.

Dream Analysis in Psychotherapy. Richard A. Gardner. Date not set. write for info. (*0-933812-36-1*) Creative Therapeutics.

Dream Analysis in Psychotherapy. Weiss. (Practitioner Guidebook Ser.). (C). 1986. pap. 25.95 (*0-205-14499-3*, H4499, Longwood Div) Allyn.

Dream & a Promise: From a Child to a Woman with a Mother's Help along the Way. Donna J. Setterlund. (Illus.). 240p. (J). (gr. 8 up). 1990. write for info. (*0-9624342-2-1*) Carriage Hse Studio Pubns.

Dream & Culture: An Anthropological Study of the Western Intellectual Tradition. Susan Parman. LC 90-7459. 144p. 1990. text ed. 39.95 (*0-275-93230-3*, C3230, Praeger Pubs) Greenwood.

Dream & Drink of Freedom. Johnny Dolphin. 84p. 1987. pap. 5.00 (*0-907791-15-8*) Synerg AZ.

Dream & Existence. Michel Foucault & Ludwig Binswanger. Ed. by Keith Hoeller. LC 92-41852. (Studies in Existential Psychology & Psychiatry). 112p. (Orig.). (C). 1992. pap. 12.50 (*0-391-03783-8*) Humanities.

Dream & Image. Bettina Knapp. LC 77-80668. 1977. 17.50 (*0-87875-121-1*) Whitston Pub.

Dream & Play with Us: Come Share Tim's & Lisa's Adventures & Learn How to Play Their Games. Ruby Aries. Ed. by Randi Loft. (Illus.). 115p. (Orig.). (J). (gr. k-4). 1990. pap. 14.95 (*0-9626570-5-0*) Perk-Lo Pk Prodns.

Dream & Reality: The Modern Black Struggle for Freedom & Equality. Jeannine Swift. LC 90-46701. (Contributions in Afro-American & African Studies: No. 142). 168p. 1991. text ed. 49.95 (*0-313-27758-3*, SYU/, Greenwood Pr) Greenwood.

***Dream & the Awakening.** Michael Mason. 300p. (Orig.). 1995. pap. 9.95 (*0-7610-0064-X*) NW Pub.

***Dream & the Dialogue: Adrienne Rich's Feminist Poetics.** Alice Templeton. 208p. (C). 1995. text ed. 24.00 (*0-87049-859-2*) U of Tenn Pr.

Dream & the Nightmare: The Sixties' Legacy to the Underclass. Myron Magnet. LC 92-23260. 256p. 1993. 20.00 (*0-688-11951-4*) Morrow.

Dream & the Nightmare: The Sixties' Legacy to the Underclass. Myron Magnet. 1994. pap. 12.00 (*0-688-13512-9*, Quill) Morrow.

Dream & the Play: Ionesco's Theatrical Quest. Ed. by Moshe Lazar. LC 81-71734. (Interplay Ser.: Vol. 1). 184p. (Orig.). 1982. pap. 20.50 (*0-89003-108-8*) Undena Pubns.

Dream & the Text: Essays on Literature & Language. Ed. by Carol S. Rupprecht. LC 92-4560. (SUNY Series in Dream Studies). 325p. 1993. 59.50 (*0-7914-1361-6*); pap. 19.95 (*0-7914-1362-4*) State U NY Pr.

Dream & the Tomb: A History of the Crusades. pap. 14.95 (*0-8128-6227-9*, Scrbrough Hse) Madison Bks UPA.

Dream & the Underworld. James Hillman. LC 78-4733. 1979. pap. 13.00 (*0-06-090682-0*, CN 682, PL) HarpC.

Dream & Thought in the Business Community, 1860-1900. Edward C. Kirkland. 192p. 1990. reprint ed. pap. 7.95 (*0-929587-23-5*, Elephant Paperbacks) I R Dee.

Dream Anonymously Dreamt. Ed. by Edward Gadd. (Orig.). 1983. pap. 12.50 (*0-911623-02-7*) I Klang.

***Dream Apart.** Donovan. 1995. mass mkt. 4.99 (*0-7860-0123-2*, Pinnacle NY) Windsor NY.

***Dream Apart.** Kate Donovan. 416p. 1995. pap. 4.99 (*0-8217-0123-1*) Zebra.

Dream Assembly. Zalman Schachter-Shalomi. Ed. by Howard Schwart. (Chrysalis Bks.). 184p. pap. 8.95 (*0-317-65959-6*) Amity Hse Inc.

Dream Assembly. Zalman Schachter-Shalomi & Howard Schwartz. LC 89-23500. (Illus.). 210p. 1989. reprint ed. 12.50 (*0-89556-059-3*) Gateways Bks & Tapes.

Dream Baby. Bruce McAllister. 448p. 1994. pap. 13.95 (*0-312-89025-7*) Orb NYC.

Dream Barker & Other Poems. Jean Valentine. LC 75-21621. (Yale Series of Younger Poets: No. 61). reprint ed. 18.00 (*0-404-53861-4*) AMS Pr.

Dream Beside Me: The Movies & the Children of the Forties. Carol T. Williams. LC 78-66858. 304p. 1970. 35.00 (*0-8386-2290-9*) Fairleigh Dickinson.

Dream Betrayed. abr. ed. Florence J. Paul. 300p. 1995. pap. 8.95 (*1-56901-515-5*) NW Pub.

Dream Big: The Henrietta Mears Story. Comp. by Earl Roe. LC 90-33489. (Illus.). 368p. 1990. 16.99 (*0-8307-1254-2*, 5111768) Regal.

Dream Bikes... Dream Machines. Alan Cathcart. 1989. 15.99 (*0-517-68375-X*) Random Hse Value.

Dream Book. Margaret W. Brown. (J). (ps-3). 1991. mass mkt. 4.99 (*0-440-40567-X*, YB) Dell.

Dream Book. Margaret W. Brown. (J). (ps). 1990. 9.95 (*0-929077-12-1*) WaterMark Inc.

Dream Book. Meg Wolitzer. 160p. (J). (gr. 3-7). 1987. pap. 2.50 (*0-380-70356-4*, Camelot) Avon.

Dream Book. Margaret Wise Brown. LC 90-81630. (Illus.). 32p. (J). (ps-00). 1992. reprint ed. 10.95 (*1-56282-211-X*) Hyprn Child.

Dream Book: An Anthology of Writings by Italian-American Women. Helen Barolini. 411p. 1989. 19.95 (*0-685-29570-2*) Ayer.

Dream Book: First Comes the Dream. Margaret Wise Brown. (Illus.). 32p. (J). (gr. 1-3). 1990. reprint ed. 9.95 (*0-685-45149-6*) WaterMark Inc.

***Dream Book: Symbols for Self-Understanding.** Betty Bethards. 1995. pap. text ed. 12.95 (*1-85230-623-8*) Element MA.

***Dream Boy.** Jim Grimsley. 208p. 1995. write for info. (*1-56512-106-6*) Algonquin Bks.

Dream Builder. Julie Myers. (Superromance Ser.). 1993. mass mkt. 3.39 (*0-373-70535-2*, 1-70535-9) Harlequin Bks.

Dream Came True. large type ed. Mary Munro. 336p. 1988. 16.95 (*0-7089-1839-5*) Ulverscroft.

Dream Cards: Analyze Your Dreams & Enrich Your Life. Strephon Kaplan-Williams. (Illus.). 160p. (Orig.). 1991. pap. 24.95 (*0-671-73797-X*, Fireside) S&S Trade.

Dream Cars. Thomas G. Gunning. LC 89-11738. (Illus.). 72p. (J). (gr. 3 up). 1989. text ed. 14.95 (*0-87518-419-7*, Dillon Silver Burdett) Silver Burdett Pr.

Dream Cars. Jack C. Harris. LC 88-1827. (Super-Charged Ser.). (Illus.). 48p. (J). (gr. 5-6). 1988. text ed. 11.95 (*0-89686-376-X*, Crstwood Hse) Silver Burdett Pr.

Dream Cars. I. Kuah. 1989. 15.99 (*0-517-64948-9*) Random Hse Value.

Dream Cars: Style for the Nineteen Nineties. Serge Bellu & Peter Vann. (Illus.). 196p. 1989. 19.98 (*0-87938-364-X*) Motorbooks Intl.

Dream Carver. Sonja Massie. 1989. mass mkt. 4.50 (*1-55817-227-0*, Pinnacle NY) Windsor NY.

Dream Castle. Andrea Kane. Ed. by Carolyn Tolley. 384p. (Orig.). 1992. mass mkt. 5.50 (*0-671-73585-3*) PB.

***Dream Catcher.** Robert English. 1995. 10.95 (*0-8062-5047-X*) Carlton.

***Dream Catcher.** Pat L. Hare. 225p. 1995. pap. 8.95 (*1-56901-554-6*) NW Pub.

Dream Catcher. Terry C. Johnston. LC 94-11547. 1994. 21.95 (*0-553-09669-9*) Bantam.

Dream Catcher: A Starlight Journey with Meg Splendor. Meg Splendor. LC 93-1015. 77p. (Orig.). (J). (ps up). 1993. audio, pap. 12.95 (*1-882979-17-6*) What the Heck.

***Dream Catcher: And Other Native American Crafts.** (J). (gr. 4-7). 1995. pap. 9.95 (*0-590-20249-9*) Scholastic Inc.

***Dream Catcher: The Legend, the Lady, the Woman.** Karen L. Hartman. LC 94-60140. 72p. (J). (ps-12). 1994. 19.95 (*0-9635204-1-5*) Weeping Heart.

Dream Catchers: Developing Career & Educational Awareness in the Intermediate Grades. Ed. by Sara Hall & Sara Adams. (Illus.). 80p. 1993. teacher ed 14.95 (*1-56370-086-7*, DCTG); student ed, pap. 2.50 (*1-56370-085-9*, DCP); 24.95 (*1-56370-087-5*, DCAS) JIST Works.

Dream Chaser. Kenneth L. Hardin. (Illus.). 24p. (Orig.). 1991. pap. 1.00 (*0-9619153-3-1*) K L Hardin.

Dream Child. David McPhail. LC 84-18755. (Unicorn Paperbacks Ser.). (Illus.). 32p. (J). (ps-3). 1988. pap. 4.95 (*0-525-44366-5*, 0383-120, DCB) Dutton Child Bks.

Dream Children. Gail Godwin. 256p. 1983. mass mkt. 4.50 (*0-380-62406-0*, Bard) Avon.

Dream Chipper. FASA Staff. (Shadowrun Ser.). (Illus.). 1990. pap. 8.00 (*1-55560-120-0*, 7303) FASA Corp.

Dream City. Harry Jaffe. 1994. 24.00 (*0-671-76846-8*) S&S Trade.

Dream Coast. John Steppling. 1987. pap. 4.75 (*0-8222-0330-8*) Dramatists Play.

Dream Come True. Eliezer Ben-Yehuda. (Modern Hebrew Classics Ser.). 112p. 1993. text ed. 31.50 (*0-8133-1672-3*) Westview.

Dream Come True. Zelma Foster. 140p. (Orig.). 1994. pap. 8.95 (*1-883928-06-0*) Longwood.

Dream Come True. Ann Major. (Men Made in American Ser.). 1994. mass mkt. 3.59 (*0-373-45159-8*, 1-45159-0) Silhouette.

***Dream Come True, "Miss America 1995"** Daphne Gray & Gregg Lewis. 1995. pap. 18.99 (*0-310-20373-2*) Zondervan.

Dream Come True; No Easy Way Out, 2 vols. in 1. Elaine R. Chase. 400p. (Orig.). 1992. pap. 4.50 (*0-8439-3357-7*) Dorchester Pub Co.

Dream Compass. Jeff Bredenberg. 192p. (Orig.). 1991. pap. 3.50 (*0-380-75647-1*) Avon.

Dream Compels Us: Voices of Salvadoran Women. Pref. by Grace Paley. LC 89-11598. (Illus.). 248p. 1989. 25.00 (*0-89608-369-1*); pap. 11.00 (*0-89608-368-3*) South End Pr.

Dream Cruise. (Orig.). 1992. pap. 4.95 (*1-56333-045-8*) Masquerade.

***Dream Cycle of H. P. Lovecraft: Dreams of Terror & Death.** Howard P. Lovecraft. LC 95-15061. 1995. 10.00 (*0-345-38421-0*) Ballantine.

Dream Dance of the Chippewa & Menominee Indians of Northern Wisconsin. Samuel A. Barrett. LC 76-43647. (Bulletin of the Public Museum of the City of Milwaukee Ser.: Vol. 1). reprint ed. 44.50 (*0-404-15482-4*) AMS Pr.

Dream Dancer. Eve Bunting. (Eve Bunting Signature Library). (Illus.). 64p. (J). 1992. lib. bdg. 12.79 (*0-89565-779-1*) Childs World.

Dream Date. Sinclair Smith. (J). 1993. pap. 3.25 (*0-590-46126-5*) Scholastic Inc.

Dream Days. Kenneth Grahame. LC 92-44589. (Illus.). (J). 1993. 18.95 (*0-89815-546-0*) Ten Speed Pr.

Dream Dealers & Other Shadows. Steve Troyanovich. 22p. 1978. pap. 1.50 (*0-686-24670-5*) S Troyanovich.

Dream Deferred: A Survey of Black America 1840-1896. Berman E. Johnson. 176p. (C). 1993. per., pap. text ed. 14.95 (*0-8403-8501-3*) Kendall-Hunt.

Dream Deferred: America's Discontent & the Search for a New Democratic Ideal. Philip Slater. 240p. 1992. pap. 13.00 (*0-8070-4305-2*) Beacon Pr.

Dream Demon. Clark R. Schmidt. LC 88-72335. 57p. (Orig.). 1989. pap. 5.50 (*0-916383-78-4*) Aegina Pr.

***Dream Desserts.** Linda Fraser. (CCL Ser.). 96p. 1995. 10.98 (*0-8317-1143-4*) Smithmark.

Dream Desserts: Low-Fat, Calorie-Wise Recipes. Nancy Baggett. LC 92-37781. (Illus.). 160p. 1993. 24.95 (*1-55670-273-6*) Stewart Tabori & Chang.

Dream Destinations: A Boater's Guide to the Best Marina Resorts & Restaurants (From Tampa Bay to Key West, Florida) Dawn Saunders & Bill Saunders. (Illus.). 92p. (Orig.). 1989. pap. 14.97 (*0-9624966-0-X*) Dream Destinations Pr.

Dream Detective. Sax Rohmer. 16.95 (*0-89190-810-2*, Am Repr) Amereon Ltd.

Dream Diary. Eric Felderman. (Illus.). 1994. 52.00 (*0-945942-42-7*); pap. 38.95 (*0-945942-43-5*) Portmanteau Editions.

Dream Diary: Whose Dream Is This Anyway? Vaughan Bean. (Illus.). 144p. (Orig.). Date not set. pap. 16.95 (*0-9631740-0-2*) Holographic Bks.

Dream Dictionary. Tony Crisp. 1991. mass mkt. 5.99 (*0-440-20861-0*) Dell.

Dream Dictionary. Tony Crisp. LC 93-7742. 1993. 7.99 (*0-517-09331-6*, Pub. by Wings Bks) Random Hse Value.

Dream Dictionary: One Thousand Dream Symbols from A to Z. Jo J. Boushahla & Virginia Reidel-Geubtner. 1992. pap. 9.00 (*0-425-13190-4*, Berkley Trade) Berkley Pub.

Dream Discourse Today. Ed. by Sara Flanders. LC 92-37649. (New Library of Psychoanalysis: No. 17). 256p. 1993. 59.95 (*0-415-09354-6*, B0711, Routledge NY); pap. 19.95 (*0-415-09355-4*, B0715, Routledge NY) Routledge.

Dream Divided. Nancy Baxter. (Heartland Chronicles Ser.: Bk. III). 700p. 1990. pap. 14.95 (*1-878208-00-4*) Guild Pr IN.

Dream Doctor. large type ed. Baker. 1991. 17.95 (*0-7451-9992-5*, AH025, Atlantic Lrg Print); pap. 15.95 (*0-7927-0454-1*, AS061, Atlantic Lrg Print) Chivers N Amer.

***Dream Doll: The Ruth Handler Story.** Ruth Handler & Jacqueline Shannon. LC 94-29437. 230p. 1994. 19.95 (*0-681-00763-X*) Longmeadow Pr.

Dream Dredger. Roberta Silman. 224p. 1986. 14.95 (*0-89255-111-9*) Persea Bks.

Dream Driftings. Judith Zinn. (Orig.). 1986. pap. 14.95 (*0-930161-03-3*) St of the Art Bk.

Dream Eater. Christian Garrison. LC 85-26671. (Illus.). 32p. (J). (ps-2). 1986. reprint ed. pap. 4.95 (*0-689-71058-5*, Aladdin Paperbacks) S&S Childrens.

***Dream Encyclopedia.** James R. Lewis. LC 95-10759. 1995. pap. 14.95 (*0-7876-0156-X*) Gale.

***Dream Encyclopedia.** James R. Lewis. 600p. 1995. 49.95 (*0-7876-0155-1*) Gale.

Dream Feather. Viento Stan-Padilla. LC 87-17823. (Illus.). 60p. (J). (gr. 2 up). 1987. reprint ed. pap. 11.95 (*0-913990-57-4*) Book Pub Co.

Dream Fever. Katherine Sutcliffe. 416p. (Orig.). 1991. mass mkt. 4.99 (*0-380-75942-X*) Avon.

***Dream Fishing.** Lacey Kellett. 17p. 1993. 19.95 (*0-9641222-0-0*) Steamboat ME.

Dream Flights. Poems. Dave Smith. LC 80-25029. 96p. 1981. 11.95 (*0-252-00862-6*); pap. 8.95 (*0-252-00863-4*) U of Ill Pr.

Dream for South Central: The Autobiography of an Afro-Americanized Korean Christian Minister. Warren W. Lee. LC 93-80837. 114p. (Orig.). 1993. pap. 6.95 (*0-9639920-0-7*) W W Lee.

Dream for Tomorrow. large type ed. Grace Goodwin. 1990. 21.95 (*0-7089-2320-8*) Ulverscroft.

***Dream Fragment 19.** Lawrence E. Keith. 48p. 1995. 14.95 (*0-932222-04-8*); pap. 8.95 (*0-932222-05-6*) Sunrise Tortoise.

Dream Game. Ann Faraday. 1990. mass mkt. 5.95 (*0-06-100026-4*, Harp PBks) HarpC.

Dream Girl. Elmer Rice. 1950. pap. 4.75 (*0-8222-0332-4*) Dramatists Play.

***Dream Girl at Mystery Lake: A Door County Adventure.** Pauline Wanderer. LC 94-47098. (J). 1995. 12.50 (*0-940473-28-3*) Wm Caxton.

Dream Givers. Margo LaGattuta & Carol Speltus. 88p. 1990. pap. 8.95x (*0-941363-12-0*) Lake Shore Pub.

***Dream Guitars Illustrated.** Charles Dellavalle & Tom Mulhern. Ed. by MC Productions Staff. (Illus.). 64p. (Orig.). (C). 1995. pap. 19.95 (*0-8256-1451-1*, AM 92730, Amsco Music) Music Sales.

Dream Homes: Sixty-Six Plans to Make Your Dreams Come True. Jerold L. Axelrod. 1987. 29.95 (*0-8306-2129-6*, 2829) TAB Bks.

Dream Horse. Mary Sharp. 164p. (C). 1990. pap. 21.00 (*0-85131-531-3*, Pub. by J A Allen & Co UK) St Mut.

Dream Horse: A Girl with No Roots, a Boy with a Bad Reputation, a Horse Nobody Wants. Virginia C. Scott. (YA). 1993. mass mkt. 3.50 (*0-06-106149-2*, Harp PBks) HarpC.

***Dream House.** Coomer. 1994. 3.99 (*0-517-13623-6*) Random Hse Value.

D

An Asterisk (*) at the beginning of an entry indicates that the title is appearing in BIP for the first time.

An Asterisk (*) at the beginning of an entry indicates that the title is appearing in BIP for the first time.

2109

D

Dream of the Rood: An Old English Poem Attributed to Cynewulf. Ed. by A. S. Cook. 1977. lib. bdg. 59.95 (*0-8490-1733-5*) Gordon Pr.

Dream of the Seventh-Day Ark for Sores & Burns, for Soul & Body. Joyce L. Smith. 1992. 10.95 (*0-533-09090-3*) Vantage.

Dream of the Stone. Christina Askounis. 272p. (YA). (gr. 7 up). 1993. 17.00 (*0-374-31877-8*) FS&G.

Dream of the Stone. large type ed. Christina Askounis. LC 93-42092. (YA). 1994. 15.95 (*0-7862-0147-9*) Thorndike Pr.

Dream of the Traveler. Richard McCann. LC 76-17642. 68p. 1976. 3.50 (*0-87886-070-3*, Greenfld Rev Pr) Greenfld Rev Lit.

Dream of the Wolf. Scott Bradfield. 1992. 11.00 (*0-679-73638-7*, Vin) Random.

Dream of Their Hearts. large type ed. Honor Vincent. (Linford Romance Library). 304p. 1986. pap. 11.95 (*0-7089-6167-3*, Linford) Ulverscroft.

Dream of Unicorns. J. B. Herman. 256p. (Orig.). 1984. pap. 2.75 (*0-8439-2123-4*) Dorchester Pub Co.

Dream of Water. Kyoko Mori. 288p. 1995. 22.50 (*0-8050-3260-6*) H Holt & Co.

Dream of Wings: Americans & the Airplane, 1875-1905. Tom D. Crouch. LC 80-18077. (Illus.). 360p. (C). 1989. pap. 19.95 (*0-87474-325-7*) Smithsonian.

Dream of X. William H. Hodgson. 1977. 15.00 (*0-937986-10-0*) D M Grant.

Dream of Yesterday. large type ed. Nancy John. (Romance Ser.). 464p. 1993. 21.95 (*0-7089-2968-0*) Ulverscroft.

***Dream of You.** 1994. 3.50 (*0-8256-1998-X*, AM42615) Omnibus NY.

Dream On. Chrystos. (NFS Canada Ser.). Date not set. pap. 11.95 (*0-88974-029-1*, Pub. by Press Gang CN) InBook.

Dream on the Hill. large type ed. Peake. 1991. 17.95 (*0-7451-8064-7*, AH099, Atlantic Lrg Print) Chivers N Amer.

Dream on the Hill. large type ed. Lilian Peake. 1991. pap. 15.95 (*0-7927-0522-X*, AS0135, Atlantic Lrg Print) Chivers N Amer.

Dream Palace. Amanda Moores. 288p. 1994. 20.00 (*0-7867-0125-0*) Carroll & Graf.

Dream Palace. Amanda Moores. 288p. 1993. 21.00 (*0-671-75919-1*) S&S Trade.

Dream Park. Larry Niven & Steven Barnes. 448p. 1982. mass mkt. 5.50 (*0-441-16730-6*) Ace Bks.

Dream Park II: The Barsoom Project. Larry Niven & Steve Barnes. 1989. mass mkt. 4.99 (*0-441-16712-8*) Ace Bks.

Dream Patch. Christopher Woods. LC 85-71201. (Illus.). 106p. (Orig.). 1985. write for info. (*0-931722-42-X*) Corona Pub.

Dream Peddler. Gail E. Haley. LC 92-42074. (Illus.). 32p. (J). (ps-3). 1993. 14.99 (*0-525-45153-6*, DCB) Dutton Child Bks.

Dream, Phantasy & Art. Hanna Segal. (New Library of Psychoanalysis). 133p. 1990. 59.95 (*0-415-01797-1*, A5062); pap. 16.95 (*0-415-01798-X*, A5066) Routledge.

Dream Pillow. Mitra Modarressi. LC 93-49400. (Illus.). 32p. (J). (ps-2). 1994. 14.95 (*0-531-06855-2*); lib. bdg. 14.99 (*0-531-08705-0*) Orchard Bks Watts.

Dream Planes. Thomas G. Gunning. LC 92-8397. (Illus.). 72p. (J). (gr. 3 up). 1992. text ed. 14.95 (*0-87518-556-8*, Dillon Silver Burdett) Silver Burdett Pr.

Dream Play & Four Chamber Plays. August Strindberg. Tr. by Walter Johnson. LC 73-7535. (Illus.). 288p. 1973. 30.00 (*0-295-95286-5*) U of Wash Pr.

***Dream Police: Selected Poems, 1969-1993.** Dennis Cooper. 192p. 1994. 16.00 (*0-8021-1569-1*, Grove) Grove-Atltic.

Dream Portrait: A Study of Nineteen Sequential Dreams As Indicators of Pretermination. Alma Bond et al. LC 91-35421. 200p. (C). 1992. text ed. 27.50 (*0-8236-1438-7*) Intl Univs Pr.

Dream Power. Ann Faraday. 320p. 1986. mass mkt. 5.99 (*0-425-09498-7*) Berkley Pub.

Dream Protocols. Lee Ballentine. (Illus.). 96p. (Orig.). 1992. 19.95 (*0-9626708-2-0*); pap. 9.95 (*0-9626708-1-2*) Talisman IN.

Dream Quest of H. P. Lovecraft. Darrell Schweitzer. LC 78-891. (Milford Series: Popular Writers of Today: Popular Writers of Today: Vol. 12). 63p. 1978. lib. bdg. 20.00 (*0-89370-117-3*); pap. 10.00 (*0-89370-217-X*) Borgo Pr.

Dream-Quest of Unknown Kadath. H. P. Lovecraft. 1986. mass mkt. 4.95 (*0-345-33779-4*, Del Rey) Ballantine.

***Dream Quilt.** Jessie Zerner. (Illus.). 96p. (J). (ps up). 1995. 19.95 (*0-8048-1999-8*) C E Tuttle.

***Dream Reader: Contemporary Approaches to the Understanding of Dreams.** Anthony Shafton. (SUNY Series in Dream Studies). 677p. 1995. text ed. 59.50 (*0-7914-2617-3*); pap. 19.95 (*0-7914-2618-1*) State U NY Pr.

Dream Reader: Psychoanalytic Articles on Dreams. Ed. by Toni M. Alston et al. LC 93-17645. xviii, 772p. 1993. text ed. 95.00 (*0-8236-1452-2*) Intl Univs Pr.

***Dream Reaper: A Story of Modern Agriculture.** Craig Canine. 1995. 27.50 (*0-679-41272-7*) Knopf.

***Dream Rebellion.** Anne L. Davidson. 370p. 1994. pap. 9.95 (*1-56901-803-0*) NW Pub.

***Dream Revisionaries: Gender & Genre in Women's Utopian Fiction, 1870-1920.** Darby Lewes. LC 94-40947. 1995. write for info. (*0-8173-0795-8*) U of Ala Pr.

Dream River. Dorothy Garlock. (Orig.). 1990. 18.95 (*0-7278-4058-4*) Severn Hse.

Dream River. Dorothy Garlock. 384p. (Orig.). 1989. mass mkt. 5.99 (*0-445-20676-4*) Warner Bks.

Dream Road: A Journey of Discovery. Percy Trezise. 1994. 19.95 (*1-86373-403-1*, Pub. by Allen & Unwin Aust Pty AT) IPG Chicago.

Dream Rooms, Decorating with Flair. Victoria Sherrow. LC 90-48241. (Smart Talk Ser.). (Illus.). 128p. (J). (gr. 5-9). 1991. lib. bdg. 10.89 (*0-8167-2293-5*); pap. text ed. 2.95 (*0-8167-2294-3*) Troll Assocs.

***Dream Ryder Cup: The Best All-Time Players from America & Europe at the Home of Golf.** Derek Lawrenson. (Illus.). 208p. 1995. 24.95 (*0-7137-2525-7*, Pub. by Blandford Pr UK) Sterling.

Dream Scene: How to Interpret Your Dreams. Alison Bell. 80p. (J). 1994. pap. 4.95 (*1-56565-160-X*) Lowell Hse Juvenile.

Dream-Seeds. Mike Murdock. 169p. (Orig.). 1986. pap. 4.95 (*1-56292-392-7*) Honor Bks OK.

Dream-Seeker. Joseph S. Salzburg. 162p. 1972. 5.00 (*0-682-47559-9*) Sovereign MD.

Dream Seekers: Native American Visionary Traditions of the Great Plains. Lee Irwin. LC 93-45863. (Civilization of the American Indian Ser.: Vol. 213). 320p. 1994. 26.95 (*0-8061-2643-4*) U of Okla Pr.

Dream Sellers: Perspectives on Drug Dealers. Richard H. Blum et al. LC 79-184960. (Jossey-Bass Science Ser.). 406p. reprint ed. pap. 115.80 (*0-8357-9316-8*, 2013789) Bks Demand.

Dream Sequence. Mukul Sharma. 100p. 1984. pap. 6.00 (*0-86578-236-9*) Ind-US Inc.

***Dream Sequence, No. 1.** Joyce Carbone. (Illus.). 44p. (Orig.). 1994. 5.95 (*1-878116-31-2*) JVC Bks.

***Dream Shadows.** Dimitri Mihalas. Ed. by Carmen M. Pursifull. 53p. (Orig.). 1994. pap. 5.00 (*1-881900-02-9*) Hawk Prods.

Dream Sharing: How to Enhance Your Understanding of Dreams by Group Sharing & Discussion. Robin Shohet. LC 87-36831. 176p. (C). 1987. reprint ed. lib. bdg. 33.00x (*0-8095-7044-0*) Borgo Pr.

Dream Sleepers. Patricia Grace. pap. 4.95 (*0-317-60984-X*, Penguin Bks) Viking Penguin.

Dream Song. Paul L. Mariani. 1994. pap. 16.95 (*1-56924-947-4*) Marlowe & Co.

Dream Song of Olaf Asteson. 2nd ed. Tr. & Illus. by Eleanor C. Merry. 48p. 1988. pap. 12.95 (*0-85440-706-5*, Steinerbks) Anthroposophic.

Dream Songs. John Berryman. 427p. 1982. pap. 15.00 (*0-374-51670-7*) FS&G.

Dream Spinner. Joanne Hoppe. LC 92-5258. 240p. (YA). (gr. 7 up). 1992. 14.00 (*0-688-08559-8*) Morrow Jr Bks.

***Dream State.** Moira Crone. 144p. 1995. 18.95 (*0-87805-813-3*) U Pr of Miss.

Dream Stealer. Stephen Cosgrove. LC 89-83843. (Dreammaker Ser.). (Illus.). 48p. (J). (gr. 1-4). 1990. 16.95 (*1-55868-009-8*); pap. 5.95 (*1-55868-021-7*); audio, pap. 12.95 (*1-55868-042-X*) Gr Arts Ctr Pub.

***Dream Story.** Broadribb. 1995. pap. 18.00 (*0-919123-45-7*) Atrium Pubs.

Dream Story. Arthur Schnitzler. Tr. by Otto P. Schinnerer. (Sun & Moon Classics Ser.: No. 6). 167p. 1989. pap. 10.95 (*1-55713-081-7*) Sun & Moon CA.

Dream Street: The American Movies & the Popular Imagination, 1889-1939, 2 vols. Edward Ifkovic. (Cinema Ser.). (Illus.). 800p. 1977. lib. bdg. 300.00 (*0-87700-258-4*) Revisionist Pr.

Dream Structure of Pinter's Plays: A Psychoanalytic Approach. Lucinda P. Gabbard. LC 75-26209. 296p. 1977. 34.50 (*0-8386-1848-0*) Fairleigh Dickinson.

Dream Studies & Telepathy. Montague Ullman & Stanley Krippner. LC 71-113639. (Parapsychological Monograph Ser.: No. 12). 1970. pap. 7.00 (*0-912328-16-9*) Parapsych Foun.

Dream Symbol Work. Patricia H. Berne. 1991. pap. 11.95 (*0-8091-3219-2*) Paulist Pr.

Dream Symbolism. Manly P. Hall. 1979. pap. 6.95 (*0-89314-392-8*) Philos Res.

Dream Takes Flight: Hartsfield Atlanta International Airport & Aviation in Atlanta. Betsy Braden & Paul Hagan. LC 88-37597. (Illus.). 256p. 1989. 34.95 (*0-8203-1140-5*) U of Ga Pr.

Dream Tales & Prose Poems. Ivan S. Turgenev. Tr. by Constance Garnett. LC 79-103530. (Short Story Index Reprint Ser.). 1977. 23.95 (*0-8369-3273-0*) Ayer.

Dream Team. Molly Albright. LC 87-13821. (Two of a Kind Ser.). (Illus.). 96p. (J). (gr. 3-6). 1988. lib. bdg. 9.89 (*0-8167-1153-4*); pap. text ed. 2.95 (*0-8167-1154-2*) Troll Assocs.

Dream Team. Chelsea Brooks. (California Dreams Ser.: No. 6). 144p. (Orig.). (YA). (gr. 5 up). 1994. pap. 2.95 (*0-02-041976-7*, Collier Bks Young) S&S Childrens.

Dream Team. Jim Rothaus. LC 92-37938. (Illus.). 32p. 1992. lib. bdg. 21.36 (*1-56766-050-9*) Childs World.

Dream Team: The Inside Story of the Nineteen Ninety-Two U. S. Olympic Basketball Team. Jack McCallum. 1992. 19.95 (*0-316-55370-0*) Little.

Dream Telepathy: Experiments in Nocturnal ESP. 2nd ed. Montague Ullman et al. LC 88-39083. (Illus.). 280p. 1989. lib. bdg. 32.50x (*0-89950-349-7*) McFarland & Co.

Dream That Failed: Reflections on the Soviet Union. Walter Laqueur. 272p. 1994. 25.00 (*0-19-508978-2*) OUP.

***Dream That Failed: Reflections on the Soviet Union.** Walter Laqueur. 248p. 1996. pap. 11.95 (*0-19-510282-7*) OUP.

Dream That Needs Abuildin' Russell Voorhees. Ed. by John Pritchard. 256p. 1994. 21.95 (*0-9638791-0-3*) Chayah Pr.

Dream That Never Dies: Boris de Zirkoff Speaks Out on Theosophy. Boris De Zirkoff. Ed. by W. Emmett Small. (Illus.). 242p. 1983. pap. 8.00 (*0-913004-45-6*) Point Loma Pub.

Dream That Would Not Die: The Birth & Growth of the World Evangelical Fellowship, 1846-1986. David M. Howard. 256p. (Orig.). 1988. pap. 12.99 (*0-8010-4320-4*) Baker Bk.

***Dream Theater: Awake.** Ed. by Colgan Bryan & Aaron Stang. 160p. (Orig.). (YA). 1995. pap. text ed. 24.95 (*0-89724-608-X*) Warner Brothers.

Dream Theatres of the Soul: Empowering the Feminine Through Jungian Dreamwork. Jean B. Raffa. Ed. by Lura J. Geiger. 224p. (Orig.). 1994. pap. 15.45 (*1-880913-10-0*) LuraMedia.

Dream Theophany of Samuel: Its Structure in Relation to Ancient Near Eastern Dreams & its Theological Significance. Robert K. Gnuse. 278p. (Orig.). 1984. pap. text ed. 29.00 (*0-8191-3717-0*) U Pr of Amer.

Dream Thief. Stephen R. Lawhead. LC 83-71241. 450p. (Orig.). 1983. pap. 10.99 (*0-89107-266-7*) Crossway Bks.

Dream Thief see Forever Is Easy

***Dream Thinking: The Logic, Magic, & Meaning of Your Dreams.** Alex T. Quenk & Naomi L. Quenk. LC 95-8816. 232p. (Orig.). 1995. pap. 15.95 (*0-89106-076-6*, 7114) Davies-Black.

Dream Time. Parris A. Bonds. 1993. mass mkt. 5.50 (*0-06-108026-8*, Harp PBks) HarpC.

Dream Time. Holly Simpson. (Perfect Ten Ser.: No. 4). 144p. 1989. pap. 2.95 (*0-449-14592-1*) Fawcett.

Dream Train: A Novel of the Orient Express. Charlotte V. Allen. 384p. 1989. mass mkt. 4.95 (*0-8041-0418-2*) Ivy Books.

Dream Trains. Thomas G. Gunning. LC 92-9802. (Illus.). 72p. (J). (gr. 3 up). 1992. text ed. 14.95 (*0-87518-558-4*, Dillon Silver Burdett) Silver Burdett Pr.

Dream Tree. Stephen Cosgrove. (Serendipity Bks.). (Illus.). 32p. (Orig.). (J). (gr. 1-4). 1978. pap. 2.95 (*0-8431-0553-4*) Price Stern.

Dream Unfolds. Barbara Delinsky. (Temptation Ser.: No. 321). 1990. pap. 2.75 (*0-373-25421-0*) Harlequin Bks.

Dream Vessel. Jeff Bredenberg. 240p. (Orig.). 1992. mass mkt. 4.50 (*0-380-76567-5*, AvoNova) Avon.

Dream Vibrations. Illus. by Donna Sharrow. LC 90-92054. 87p. (Orig.). 1990. pap. 8.50 (*1-878116-03-7*) JVC Bks.

***Dream Violin: And Other Stories of Families from Around the World.** Highlights Staff. LC 94-72488. (Illus.). 96p. (J). (gr. 2-5). 1995. 2.95 (*1-56397-447-9*, Wordsong) Boyds Mills Pr.

Dream Vision: The Work of Arthur B. Davies. Stephen Prokopoff et al. (Illus.). 1981. pap. 5.00 (*0-910663-30-0*) ICA Inc.

***Dream Voyager.** Thomas Locke. (Spectrum Chronicles Ser.: Bk. 2). 176p. (J). 1995. pap. 5.99 (*1-55661-433-0*) Bethany Hse.

Dream Voyages. rev. ed. John-Roger. 1992. pap. 12.50 (*0-914829-31-9*) Mandeville LA.

Dream Walker. Charlotte Armstrong. 320p. 1992. mass mkt. 3.99 (*0-8217-3908-5*) Zebra.

Dream Walker. Jacqueline Marten. 1987. pap. 3.95 (*0-317-56906-6*) PB.

Dream Warrior. Bobbi Smith. 480p. 1993. mass mkt. 4.99 (*0-8217-4360-0*) Zebra.

Dream Warriors. Wes Craven & Bruce Wagner. Ed. by New Line Cinema Staff. LC 92-502. (Nightmare on Elm Street Ser.). 1992. lib. bdg. 13.95 (*1-56239-158-5*) Abdo & Dghtrs.

***Dream Weaver.** Laurel Collins. 384p. 1995. mass mkt. 4.99 (*0-8217-4969-2*) Windsor NY.

Dream Weaver: Survive until Dawn, Vol. 1, Issue 1. Robert D. Lankford. (Illus.). 24p. (YA). (gr. 11 up). 1987. pap. 1.95 (*0-9621811-0-2*) Lankford Comics.

Dream Weaver Chronicles. James P. Davis. 167p. 1993. pap. 11.00 (*1-57043-052-7*) ECKANKAR.

Dream Weaver Chronicles. James P. Davis. LC 93-71507. 158p. 1993. pap. 11.00 (*0-88155-128-7*) Illum Way Pub.

Dream Weaver in the Face of Fear, Vol. 1, No. 3. Robert D. Lankford. (Illus.). 48p. (YA). (gr. 11 up). 1991. pap. 2.75 (*0-9621811-2-9*) Lankford Comics.

Dream Weavers: Short Stories by the Pre-Raphaelite Poet-Painters. Ed. by John Weeks. LC 79-26749. (Orig.). 1980. pap. 4.95 (*0-912800-73-9*) Woodbridge Pr.

***Dream Wedding: (Just Married)** Pamela Macaluso. (Desire Ser.). 1995. mass mkt. 3.25 (*0-373-05928-0*, 1-05928-6) Silhouette.

Dream Weddings Do Come True: How to Plan a Stress-Free Wedding. Cynthia M. Kreuger. LC 92-34155. 192p. (Orig.). 1993. pap. 9.95 (*0-918420-18-0*) Brighton Pubns.

Dream with Storms: Reading Level 3. Fran Reed. (Sundown Fiction Collection). 64p. 1993. 3.75 (*0-88336-207-4*); audio 13.50 (*0-88336-226-0*); audio 10.50 (*0-88336-264-3*) New Readers.

Dream Within a Dream: Studies in Japanese Thought. Steven Heine. LC 90-41216. (Asian Thought & Culture Ser.: Vol. 5). 247p. (C). 1991. text ed. 43.95 (*0-8204-1350-X*) P Lang Pubs.

Dream Wolf. 2nd ed. Paul Goble. LC 89-687. (Illus.). 32p. (J). (gr. 3 up). 1990. text ed. 14.95 (*0-02-736585-9*, Bradbury S&S) S&S Childrens.

Dream Work. Mary Oliver. LC 86-7656. 90p. 1986. pap. 10.95 (*0-87113-069-6*) Grove-Atltic.

Dream Work: Techniques for Discovering the Creative Power of Dreams. Jeremy Taylor. LC 82-62411. 288p. 1983. pap. 12.95 (*0-8091-2525-0*) Paulist Pr.

Dream Work in Psychotherapy & Self-Change. Alvin R. Mahrer. 1990. 34.95 (*0-393-70089-5*) Norton.

Dream Workbook. Jill Morris. 1986. mass mkt. 4.95 (*0-449-21041-3*, Crest) Fawcett.

Dream Workbook: Simple Exercises to Unravel the Secrets to Your Dreams. Robert Langs. 208p. (Orig.). 1994. pap. text ed. 14.00 (*0-9641509-1-3*) Allian Pubng.

Dream Works: Lovers & Families in Shakespeare's Plays. Kay Stockholder. 1987. 40.00 (*0-8020-5743-8*) U of Toronto Pr.

Dream World, the History & Myth of Dreams. R. L. Megroz. 1972. 59.95 (*0-8490-0061-0*) Gordon Pr.

Dream Worlds: Mass Consumption in Late Nineteenth-Century France. Rosalind H. Williams. (Illus.). 463p. 1991. pap. 15.00 (*0-520-07424-6*) U CA Pr.

Dream Worlds of Pregnancy: How Understanding Your Dreams Can Help You Bond with Your Baby & Become a Better Parent with Your Mate. Eileen Stukane. LC 93-48356. 1994. 11.95 (*0-88268-165-6*) Station Hill Pr.

Dream Yoga & the Practice of Natural Light. Namkhai Norbu. Ed. by Michael Katz. LC 92-16147. 128p. (Orig.). 1992. pap. 12.95 (*1-55939-007-7*) Snow Lion Pubns.

Dream Zone. Jay Del. LC 90-70664. 256p. (Orig.). 1991. pap. 10.00 (*1-56002-005-9*) Aegina Pr.

***Dreamboat.** Singleton. (Sweet Dreams Ser.: No. 227). 1995. mass mkt. 3.50 (*0-553-56681-4*) Bantam.

***Dreamboat.** Doug J. Swanson. 288p. 1995. 20.00 (*0-06-017748-9*) HarpC.

Dreamboats: Hollywood Hunks of the '50s. Maria Ciaccia. LC 92-19150. (Illus.). 160p. (Orig.). 1992. pap. 21.95 (*0-9627226-4-2*) Excalibur Pub.

Dreambody: The Body's Role in Revealing the Self. Arnold Mindell. LC 82-3239. 219p. (Orig.). 1982. 30.00 (*0-938434-05-5*); pap. 16.95 (*0-938434-06-3*) Sigo Pr.

Dreambody in Relationships. Mindell. 1987. pap. 9.95 (*0-7102-1072-8*, RKP) Routledge.

Dreambody in Relationships. Arnold Mindell. 1988. pap. 10.00 (*0-14-019281-6*, Arkana) Viking Penguin.

Dreambuilder. Tom Deitz. 432p. (Orig.). 1992. mass mkt. 4.99 (*0-380-76290-0*, AvoNova) Avon.

***Dreamcatcher.** Lori Byrd. 176p. 1995. pap. 9.99 (*1-883061-06-7*) Rising NY.

***Dreamcatcher.** Meredy Maynard. 160p. (Orig.). (J). 1995. pap. 7.50 (*1-896095-01-1*) Orca Bk Pubs.

Dreamcatcher. Audrey Osofsky. LC 91-20029. (Illus.). 32p. (J). (ps-2). 1992. 15.95 (*0-531-05988-X*); lib. bdg. 15.99 (*0-531-08588-0*) Orchard Bks Watts.

Dreamcatcher. Thomasina Ring. 368p. (Orig.). 1992. pap. 4.50 (*0-8439-3284-8*) Dorchester Pub Co.

Dreamer. Scott Amour. Ed. by James B. Van Treese. 171p. 1994. pap. 7.95 (*1-56901-051-X*) NW Pub.

Dreamer. Will Eisner. Ed. by David Schreiner & Denis Kitchen. (Illus.). 50p. 1988. pap. 6.95 (*0-87816-016-7*) Kitchen Sink.

***Dreamer.** Brian Evans. 14.95 (*1-882320-02-6*) Helion Pub.

***Dreamer.** Cynthia Rylant. LC 93-19915. (Illus.). 32p. (J). (ps-6). 1993. 14.95 (*0-590-47341-7*) Scholastic Inc.

Dreamer. Primus St. John. LC 89-61326. (Poetry Ser.). 1990. pap. 9.95 (*0-88748-097-7*) Carnegie-Mellon.

***Dreamer: The Story of a Hollywood Kid Out of Control.** Brian Evans. 300p. 1994. pap. 5.99 (*1-56171-368-6*, S P I Bks) Sure Sellers.

Dreamer & Other Stories. Krishan Chander. Tr. by Jai Ratan. 160p. 1970. pap. 3.00 (*0-88253-025-9*, 4027) Ind-US Inc.

Dreamer Awakes. Alice Kane. 300p. 1995. 34.95 (*1-55111-045-8*); pap. 17.95 (*1-55111-047-4*) Broadview Pr.

Dreamer Examines His Pillow. John P. Shanley. 1987. pap. 4.75 (*0-8222-0331-6*) Dramatists Play.

Dreamer in the Desert: A Profile of Nelson Glueck. Ellen N. Stern. 1979. 11.95 (*0-87068-656-9*) Ktav.

***Dreamer of Pictures: Neil Young: The Man & His Music.** David Downing. LC 94-29686. (Illus.). 272p. (Orig.). 1995. pap. 14.95 (*0-306-80611-8*) Da Capo.

Dreamer of the Ghetto: The Life & Works of Israel Zangwill. Joseph H. Udelson. LC 89-4781. (Judaic Studies). (Illus.). 336p. 1990. 49.95 (*0-8173-0456-8*) U of Ala Pr.

Dreamer-Prophets of the Columbia Plateau: Smohalla & Skolaskin. Robert H. Ruby & John A. Brown. LC 89-5292. (Illus.). 272p. 1989. 24.95 (*0-8061-2183-1*) U of Okla Pr.

Dreamers: And Other Stories. Gary Sturm. LC 91-70158. 104p. 1991. 12.95 (*1-879608-23-5*); pap. 6.95 (*1-879608-24-3*) Blue Light Bks.

Dreamers, a Club. John K. Bangs. LC 72-98559. (Short Story Index Reprint Ser.). (Illus.). 1977. 20.95 (*0-8369-3133-5*) Ayer.

Dreamers, Adventurers & Storytellers of the American West. Peter R. Odens. (Illus.). 1988. pap. 5.00 (*0-9609484-8-1*) P R Odens.

Dreamers & Defenders: American Conservationists. Douglas H. Strong. LC 87-30210. (Illus.). x, 295p. 1988. pap. 9.95 (*0-8032-9156-6*) U of Nebr Pr.

Dreamers & Desperadoes: Contemporary Short Fiction of the American West. Craig Lesley. Ed. by Katheryn Stavrakis. 1993. pap. 12.95 (*0-440-50517-8*, LE) Dell.

Dreamers & Doers: Inventors Who Changed the World. Norman Richards. LC 81-21029. (Illus.). 168p. (YA). (gr. 5 up). 1984. lib. bdg. 13.95 (*0-689-30914-7*, Atheneum Bks Young) S&S Childrens.

Dreamers & Other Stories. Patricia Grace. 1987. pap. 4.95 (*0-317-58078-7*, Penguin Bks) Viking Penguin.

Dreamer's Dictionary. Barbara Condron. 308p. 1994. pap. 15.00 (*0-944386-16-4*) SOM Pub.

Dreamer's Dictionary. Lady S. Robinson & Tom Corbett. 384p. 1986. mass mkt. 5.99 (*0-446-34296-3*) Warner Bks.

Dreamer's Dictionary. Lady S. Robinson. 1994. mass mkt. 5.99 (*0-446-77879-6*) Warner Bks.

Dreamers Dreaming Dreams: A Celebration of the Human Spirit & the Wisdom That Comes with Age. Philip J. Webster. Ed. by Hope Sinclair. LC 92-22156. 52p. 1992. pap. 7.95 (*0-916147-24-X*) Regent Pr.

Dreamer's Journey: The Autobiography of Morris Raphael Cohen. Morris R. Cohen. LC 74-27972. (Modern Jewish Experience Ser.). (Illus.). 1975. reprint ed. 33.95 (*0-405-06702-X*) Ayer.

Dreamer's Log Cabin: A Woman's Walden. Laurie Shepherd. LC 81-3215. (Illus.). 176p. (Orig.). 1981. pap. 8.95 (*0-934878-06-4*, Dembner NY) Barricade Bks.

An Asterisk (*) at the beginning of an entry indicates that the title is appearing in BIP for the first time.

An Asterisk (*) at the beginning of an entry indicates that the title is appearing in BIP for the first time.

2111

D

Dreams & Spiritual Growth: A Christian Approach to Dreamwork. Louis M. Savary et al. LC 84-60566. 241p. 1984. pap. 11.95 (*0-8091-2629-X*) Paulist Pr.

Dreams & Swords. Katherine V. Forrest. 224p. 1987. pap. 9.95 (*0-941483-03-7*) Naiad Pr.

Dreams & the Growth of Personality: Expanding Awareness in Psychotherapy. Ernest L. Rossi. 232p. (C). 1972. 101.00 (*0-08-016787-X*, Pub. by Pergamon Repr UK) Franklin.

Dreams & the Growth of Personality: Expanding Awareness in Psychotherapy. 2nd ed. Ernest L. Rossi. LC 85-9693. 264p. 1985. 35.95 (*0-87630-397-1*) Brunner-Mazel.

Dreams & the Search for Meaning. Peter O'Connor. 264p. 1987. pap. 8.95 (*0-8091-2870-5*) Paulist Pr.

Dreams & the Unconscious in Nineteenth-Century Russian Fiction. Michael R. Katz. LC 83-40052. 227p. reprint ed. pap. 64.70 (*0-8357-6518-0*, 2035889) Bks Demand.

Dreams & Their Meanings. Tony Hazzard. (Family Matters Ser.). (Illus.). 96p. (Orig.). 1990. pap. 4.95 (*0-7063-6802-9*, Pub. by Ward Lock UK) Sterling.

***Dreams & Their Meanings.** rev. ed. Tony Hazzard. (Family Matters Ser.). (Illus.). 96p. (Orig.). 1995. pap. 6.95 (*0-7063-7324-3*, Pub. by Ward Lock UK) Sterling.

Dreams & Visions. Lester Sumrall. 68p. (C). 1985. pap. text ed. 10.00 (*0-937580-78-3*) LeSEA Pub Co.

Dreams & Visions: A Study of American Utopias, 1865-1917. Charles J. Rooney, Jr. LC 84-8932. (Contributions in American Studies: No. 77). (Illus.). xi, 209p. 1985. text ed. 49.95 (*0-313-23727-1*, RUL/, Greenwood Pr) Greenwood.

Dreams & What They Mean to You. Migene Gonzalez-Wippler. LC 88-45183. (New Age Ser.). 240p. 1989. pap. 3.95 (*0-87542-288-8*) Llewellyn Pubns.

Dreams & Wishes. Karren Radko. 224p. (Orig.). 1993. pap. 2.95 (*1-56597-070-5*, Kismet) Meteor Pub.

Dreams & Wishes, 2 Vols., 1, Ed. by Carolyn E. Cardwell. (Illus.). 225p. (Orig.). 1986. pap. 8.45 (*0-916395-20-0*, DW-1) Hieroglyphics.

Dreams & Wishes, 2 Vols., 2, Ed. by Carolyn E. Cardwell. (Illus.). 225p. (Orig.). 1986. pap. 10.95 (*0-916395-22-7*) Hieroglyphics.

Dreams Anointed in Despair. Myronn E. Hardy. (Illus.). 64p. 1989. write for info. (*0-9621696-0-9*); pap. write for info. (*0-9621696-1-7*) Ezra Pub Inc.

Dreams Are Another Set of Muscles. David Shaddock. write for info. (*0-935430-01-6*) In Between.

Dreams Are Dying. Everett Whealdon. Ed. by Richard J. Danbury, III. 152p. (Orig.). 1994. pap. 8.95 (*0-89754-091-3*) Dan River Pr.

Dreams Are for Tomorrow. large type ed. Frances Crowne. 249p. 1994. 17.95 (*0-7505-0603-2*, Pub. by Magna Print Bks) Ulverscroft.

Dreams Are Not Enough. Jacqueline Briskin. 464p. 1987. mass mkt. 5.99 (*0-425-10179-7*) Berkley Pub.

Dreams Are Not Enough. 2nd ed. Barbara Whitener. LC 77-77226. 1977. pap. 2.95 (*0-915216-18-3*) Marathon Intl Bk.

Dreams Are Wiser Than Men. Ed. by Richard Russo. 320p. 1987. text ed. 30.00 (*0-938190-95-4*); pap. 14.95 (*0-938190-94-6*) North Atlantic.

Dreams Are Your Truest Friends. Joseph Katz. 160p. 1994. reprint ed. pap. 9.00 (*0-425-14142-X*, Berkley Trade) Berkley Pub.

D

Dreams As Metaphor: The Power of the Image. Ann S. Wiseman. (Dream Exploration Ser.). (Illus.). 176p. (Orig.). 1987. pap. 12.50 (*0-937369-01-2*) Ansayre Pr.

Dreams Before Sleep. T. Alan Broughton. LC 81-71589. 1982. 16.95 (*0-915604-68-X*); pap. 9.95 (*0-915604-69-8*) Carnegie-Mellon.

Dreams Betrayed: Working in the Technological Age. Carlton Rochell & Christina Spellman. 160p. 1987. text ed. 18.95 (*0-669-11105-8*) Free Pr.

Dreams Beyond Dreaming. Jean Campbell. LC 79-26131. 1980. pap. 6.95 (*0-89865-015-1*) Donning Co.

Dreams Beyond Tomorrow. June M. Bacher. (Pioneer Romance Ser.). 192p. (Orig.). 1985. pap. 6.99 (*0-89081-474-0*) Harvest Hse.

Dreams by No One's Daughter. Leslie Ullman. LC 87-40159. (Poetry Ser.). 56p. 1987. 19.95 (*0-8229-3568-6*); pap. 10.95 (*0-8229-5395-1*) U of Pittsburgh Pr.

Dreams Can Help: A Journal Guide to Understanding Your Dreams & Making Them Work for You. Jonni Kincher. Ed. by Mary Morse & Pamela Espeland. LC 88-7630. (Illus.). 96p. (Orig.). (J). (gr. 3-9). 1988. pap. 9.95 (*0-915793-15-6*) Free Spirit Pub.

Dreams Come along With... A Self Help Dream Manual for Youth. Robert Selby. 50p. (Orig.). 1994. pap. text ed. 7.95 (*1-878647-12-1*) Duncan & Duncan.

Dreams Come True. Betty L. Burris. Ed. by James B. Van Treese. 250p. 1994. pap. 8.95 (*1-56901-132-X*) NW Pub.

Dreams Come True. Elizabeth Kornfield. Ed. by Lee Kornfield. (Illus.). 32p. (J). (gr. 3-6). 1986. pap. 5.95 (*0-940611-00-7*) Rocky Mntn Child.

Dreams Come True for Cowboys, Too! J. G. Huckle. (Illus.). 1991. 27.95 (*0-87026-077-4*) Westernlore.

Dreams Desire. Gwen Cleary. 1990. mass mkt. 4.50 (*0-8217-3093-2*) Zebra.

Dreams Die First. Robbins. 1993. mass mkt. 5.99 (*0-671-87487-X*) PB.

Dreams Die Hard: Three Men's Journey Through the Sixties. rev. ed. David Harris. LC 92-42344. 352p. 1993. reprint ed. pap. 14.95 (*1-56279-034-X*) Mercury Hse Inc.

Dreams, Disaster, Demise: The Milwaukee Road in Minnesota. John Luecke. (Illus.). 230p. (C). 1988. 39.95 (*0-9621020-0-8*) Grenadier Pubns.

Dreams Don't Make Noise When They Die. John Berutti. (Illus.). 1978. 15.00 (*0-912950-39-0*); pap. 10.00 (*0-912950-40-4*) Blue Oak.

Dreams Don't Wait. Carole Dean. 224p. (Orig.). 1993. pap. 2.95 (*1-56597-093-4*, Kismet) Meteor Pub.

Dreams, Dreamers, & Dreaming. Ed. by Dolores E. Brien. (PAJA Papers Nineteen Eighty-Nine). 64p. 1992. pap. 8.00 (*1-882275-00-4*) Rnd Table Pr.

Dream's End: A Love Story on Mount St. Helens. Virginia Fowler. 144p. 1994. pap. 14.95 (*1-880222-20-5*) Red-Apple Pub.

Dreams for a Quiet Night. Ernest Pate. LC 83-73639. 80p. (Orig.). 1984. pap. 4.95 (*0-87516-535-4*) DeVorss.

Dreams from a Wintry Night, Poems. Niles Bond. LC 92-74261. 88p. (Orig.). 1993. pap. 15.00 (*0-912650-07-9*) Brookdale Pr.

Dreams from Bunker Hill. John Fante. LC 81-15533. 151p. (C). 1993. reprint ed. 20.00 (*0-87685-529-X*); reprint ed. pap. 10.00 (*0-87685-528-1*) Black Sparrow.

***Dreams from My Father: A Story of Race & Inheritance.** Barack Obama. 1995. 23.00 (*0-8129-2343-X*, Times Bks) Random.

Dreams from the Soul. Prince A. Stewart. LC 94-92098. (Illus.). 128p. 1994. pap. 19.97 (*0-9640738-1-1*) P A Stewart.

Dreams Fulfilled: Success Stories from Boys Town. Terry Hyland & Kevin Warneke. Ed. by Ron Herron. (Illus.). 159p. (Orig.). 1992. pap. 5.95 (*0-938510-27-4*, 19-005) Boys Town Pr.

Dreams, Hallucinations, Visions. Ernst Benz. 46p. 1968. pap. 0.50 (*0-87785-099-2*) Swedenborg.

Dreams, Illusion & Other Realities. Wendy D. O'Flaherty. LC 83-17944. (Illus.). xvi, 384p. 1984. 25.00 (*0-226-61854-4*) U Ch Pr.

Dreams, Illusion & Other Realities. Wendy D. O'Flaherty. LC 83-17944. (Illus.). xvi, 384p. 1986. pap. text ed. 17.95 (*0-226-61855-2*) U Ch Pr.

Dreams, Illusions & Other Realities. W. D. O'Flaherty. 382p. 1987. 39.95 (*0-318-37018-2*) Asia Bk Corp.

Dreams, Images, & Fantasy: A Semantic Differential Casebook. Claude S. Moss. LC 79-105543. 317p. reprint ed. pap. 90.40 (*0-317-07824-0*, 2022781) Bks Demand.

Dreams in Dry Places. Roger Bruhn. LC 89-14680. (Great Plains Photography Ser.). (Illus.). xx, 146p. 1990. 45.00 (*0-8032-1214-3*) U of Nebr Pr.

Dreams in Folklore. Sigmund Freud & D. E. Oppenheim. LC 57-14990. 1958. text ed. 30.00x (*0-8236-1440-9*) Intl Univs Pr.

Dreams in Harrison Railroad Park. 4th ed. Nellie Wong. 48p. 1983. reprint ed. pap. 6.00 (*0-932716-14-8*) Kelsey St Pr.

Dreams in Islam. Umar Azam. (Illus.). 152p. 1992. 14.95 (*0-8059-3252-6*) Dorrance.

Dreams in Late Antiquity: Studies in the Imagination of a Culture. Patricia C. Miller. LC 93-40363. 1994. 39.50 (*0-691-07422-4*) Princeton U Pr.

Dreams in Motion: The Art of Windsor McCay. John Canemaker. (Illus.). 16p. 1988. 5.00 (*0-915171-09-0*) Katonah Gal.

Dreams in New Perspective: The Royal Road Revisited. Myron L. Glucksmam & Silas L. Warner. LC 86-27829. 152p. (C). 1987. 29.95 (*0-89885-339-7*) Human Sci Pr.

Dreams in Seventeenth-Century English Literature. Manfred Weidhorn. (Studies in English Literature: Vol. 57). 1970. text ed. 24.00 (*90-279-0533-9*) Mouton.

Dreams in Solitude. Prem Kirpal. 96p. (C). 1989. pap. 50.00 (*81-209-0163-0*, Pub. by Pitambar Pub II) St Mut.

Dreams in Soy Sauce. Rohan Preston. 66p. (Orig.). 1991. pap. 6.95 (*0-9624287-7-9*) Tia Chucha Pr.

Dreams in the Mirror. Richard Kennedy. 1994. pap. 20.00 (*0-87140-155-X*) Liveright.

Dreams into Deeds: Nine Women Who Dared. Linda Peavy & Ursula Smith. LC 85-40295. 160p. (J). (gr. 6-9). 1985. text ed. 14.95 (*0-684-18484-2*, C Scribner Sons Young) S&S Childrens.

Dreams into Glass. Emile Galle. 32.00 (*0-8446-6139-2*) Peter Smith.

***Dreams Journal.** Rita Milios. 48p. 1995. ring bd. 9.95 (*0-9641657-2-4*) Tools for Transform.

Dreams, Language of the Unconscious. rev. ed. Hugh L. Cayce et al. 94p. 1971. pap. 6.95 (*0-87604-047-4*, 218) ARE Pr.

Dreams, Life, & Literature: A Study of Franz Kafka. Calvin S. Hall & Richard E. Lind. LC 73-97014. 144p. reprint ed. pap. 41.10 (*0-317-29794-5*, 2016920) Bks Demand.

Dreams Like Thunder. Diane Simmons. 192p. 1992. 22.95 (*0-934257-64-7*) Story Line.

***Dreams Like Thunder.** Diane Simmons. 190p. 1995. pap. text ed. 14.95 (*1-885266-03-0*) Story Line.

***Dreams, Madness, & Creativity in Nineteenth-Century France.** Tony James. 312p. 1995. 56.00 (*0-19-815188-8*) OUP.

Dreams, Myths & Other Realities. D. H. Lloyd. 32p. (Orig.). 1984. pap. 3.00 (*0-917554-24-8*) Maelstrom.

Dream's Navel. Edmund Pennant. 80p. (Orig.). 1982. pap. 4.95 (*0-931642-08-6*) Lintel.

Dreams of a Final Theory. Steven Weinberg. LC 92-50466. 352p. 1992. 25.00 (*0-679-41923-3*) Pantheon.

Dreams of a Final Theory: The Scientist's Search for the Ultimate Laws of Nature. Steven Weinberg. 1994. pap. 13.00 (*0-679-74408-8*, Vin) Random.

Dreams of a Food Scientist. Jasper G. Woodroof. LC 87-8502. (Illus.). 120p. 1987. text ed. 19.95 (*0-9618207-0-5*) HDS Pubns.

Dreams of a Longing Heart. Jane Peart. LC 90-38382. 192p. (Orig.). (YA). (gr. 10 up). 1990. pap. 7.99 (*0-8007-5373-9*) Revell.

Dreams of a Woman: An Analyst's Inner Journey. Sheila Moon. LC 83-10826. (Illus.). 207p. 1983. 27.50 (*0-938434-17-9*); pap. 13.95 (*0-938434-14-4*) Sigo Pr.

Dreams of a Work. L. S. Asekoff. 80p. 1994. 18.95 (*0-914061-47-X*) Orchises Pr.

Dreams of Ada: A True Story of Murder, Obsession, & a Small Town. Robert Mayer. (Illus.). 544p. 1991. pap. 5.99 (*0-451-16981-6*) NAL-Dutton.

Dreams of an English Eden: Ruskin & His Tradition in Social Criticism. Jeffrey L. Spear. LC 84-5879. 224p. 1984. text ed. 50.00 (*0-231-05536-6*); pap. text ed. 20.50 (*0-231-05537-4*) Col U Pr.

Dreams of an Insomniac: Jewish Feminist Essays, Speeches & Diatribes. Irena Klepfisz. LC 90-3694. 256p. (Orig.). 1990. 22.95 (*0-933377-08-8*); pap. 11.95 (*0-933377-06-1*) Eighth Mount Pr.

Dreams of Ancient Peoples. Douglas Fetherling. 48p. (C). 1991. pap. text ed. 12.00 (*1-55022-147-7*, Pub. by ECW Press CN) Genl Dist Srvs.

Dreams of Another Day. Margaret Wakim. 1992. 8.95 (*0-533-10161-1*) Vantage.

Dreams of Another Day. large type ed. Daphne Wright. 528p. 1994. 25.95 (*0-7089-8766-4*, Trail West Pubs) Ulverscroft.

Dreams of Authority: Freud & the Fictions of the Unconscious. Ronald R. Thomas. LC 90-33550. 320p. 1990. 38.50 (*0-8014-2424-0*) Cornell U Pr.

Dreams of Authority: Freud & the Fictions of the Unconscious. Ronald R. Thomas. LC 90-33550. 320p. 1992. pap. 14.95 (*0-8014-9694-2*) Cornell U Pr.

Dreams of Bill: A Curious Collection of Funny, Strange, & Downright Peculiar Dreams about Our President, Bill Clinton. Ed. by Julia Anderson-Miller & Bruce J. Miller. LC 93-45367. 1994. 8.95 (*0-8065-1495-7*, Citadel Pr) Carol Pub Group.

Dreams of Chaos, Visions of Order: Understanding the American Avant-Garde Cinema. James Peterson. LC 93-25672. (Contemporary Film & Television Ser.). (Illus.). 212p. 1993. text ed. 44.95 (*0-8143-2456-8*); pap. 19.95 (*0-8143-2457-6*) Wayne St U Pr.

***Dreams of Childhood.** Outlet Staff. 1994. pap. 12.99 (*0-517-11934-X*) Random Hse Value.

Dreams of Cycling. Maia Wojciechowska. (Dreams of... Ser.). (Illus.). 80p. (J). Date not set. pap. 6.50 (*1-883740-13-4*) Pebble Bch Pr Ltd.

Dreams of Dead Women's Handbags: Collected Stories. Shena Mackay. LC 94-15578. 480p. 1994. 24.95 (*1-55921-121-0*) Moyer Bell.

Dreams of Destiny. Jackie Casto. 368p. 1994. mass mkt., pap. text ed. 4.50 (*0-8439-3550-2*) Dorchester Pub Co.

Dreams of Difference: The Japan Romantic School & the Crisis of Modernity. Kevin M. Doak. LC 93-5626. 1994. 35.00 (*0-520-08377-6*) U CA Pr.

Dreams of Distant Lives. Lee K. Abbott. 208p. 1990. pap. 10.00 (*1-877727-14-8*) White Pine.

Dreams of Dragons: An Exploration & Celebration of the Mysteries of Nature. Lyall Watson. 178p. 1992. pap. 9.95 (*0-89281-372-5*) Inner Tradit.

Dreams of Dusty Roads: New Poems. Tijan M. Sallah. LC 92-21517. 1993. 16.00 (*0-89410-765-8*); pap. 9.00 (*0-89410-766-6*) Three Continents.

Dreams of Eagles. William W. Johnstone. 416p. 1994. mass mkt. 4.50 (*0-8217-4619-7*) Zebra.

Dreams of Empire: Napoleon & the First World War, 1792-1914. Paul Fregosi. 1990. 21.95 (*1-55972-036-0*, Birch Ln Pr) Carol Pub Group.

Dreams of Exile: Robert Louis Stevenson, a Biography. Ian Bell. LC 93-3792. 320p. 1993. 25.00 (*0-8050-2807-2*) H Holt & Co.

***Dreams of Exile: Robert Louis Stevenson: A Biography.** Iran Bell. 320p. 1995. pap. 12.95 (*0-8050-3938-4*, Owl) H Holt & Co.

Dreams of Exiles. Katherine H. Privett. LC 82-2886. (Kestrel Chapbks.). 24p. 1982. pap. 3.00 (*0-914974-34-3*) Holmgangers.

***Dreams of Fair Women.** large type ed. Alexander Cordell. 624p. 1995. 23.95 (*0-7089-3255-X*) Ulverscroft.

Dreams of Fashions. Maia Wojciechowska. (Dreams of... Ser.). (Illus.). 80p. (J). Date not set. pap. 6.50 (*1-883740-05-3*) Pebble Bch Pr Ltd.

Dreams of Flight. Brian R. Mori. 1984. pap. 2.75 (*0-8222-0333-2*) Dramatists Play.

Dreams of Glass. Brenna Todd. (Superromance Ser.). 1993. mass mkt. 3.50 (*0-373-70560-3*, 1-70560-7) Harlequin Bks.

Dreams of Glory: A Family Saga. Dorothy Miles. 300p. (Orig.). 1989. 15.00 (*0-9623631-0-3*); pap. 8.00 (*0-9623631-1-1*) D Miles.

***Dreams of Glory: Poems Starring Young Girls.** Isabel J. Glaser. LC 95-15302. (Illus.). (J). 1995. write for info. (*0-689-31891-X*, Atheneum Bks Young) S&S Childrens.

Dreams of Gods & Men. W. T. Quick. 304p. 1989. pap. 3.95 (*0-318-39985-7*, Sig) NAL-Dutton.

Dreams of Gold. Lewis Orde. 532p. 1993. 20.00 (*0-8217-4015-6*) Zebra.

Dreams of Gold. Lewis Orde. 576p. 1993. mass mkt. 4.99 (*0-8217-4395-3*) Zebra.

Dreams of Gold: Nancy Kerrigan. Wayne Coffey. 1994. mass mkt. 4.99 (*0-312-95399-2*) St Martin.

Dreams of Golf. Maia Wojciechowska. (Dreams of...Ser.). (Illus.). 52p. (J). 1993. 14.50 (*1-883740-01-0*) Pebble Bch Pr Ltd.

Dreams of Green Base. Terry Wilson. 196p. 1986. pap. 10.00 (*0-934301-06-9*) Inkblot Pubns.

Dreams of Happiness: Social Art & the French Left, 1830-1850. Neil McWilliam. LC 92-38222. (Illus.). 424p. 1993. text ed. 49.50 (*0-691-03155-X*) Princeton U Pr.

Dreams of History That Came True. Adrienne Quinn. 224p. (Orig.). 1987. pap. 8.95 (*0-9607172-3-4*) Dream Res.

Dreams of Hummingbirds: Poems from Nature. Mary A. Coleman. Ed. by Judith Mathews. LC 92-28169. (Illus.). 32p. (J). (gr. 3-7). 1993. lib. bdg. 14.95 (*0-8075-1720-8*) A Whitman.

Dreams of Ice Dancing. Maia Wojciechowska. (Dreams of... Ser.). (Illus.). 80p. (J). Date not set. pap. 6.50 (*1-883740-08-8*) Pebble Bch Pr Ltd.

***Dreams of Innocence.** Lisa Appignanesi. LC 94-41652. 1995. 23.95 (*0-525-93884-2*, Dutton) NAL-Dutton.

Dreams of Isis: A Woman's Spiritual Sojourn. Normandi Ellis. 415p. 1995. 22.00 (*0-8356-0706-2*, Quest) Theos Pub Hse.

Dreams of Life. Timothy T. Fortune. LC 72-168125. reprint ed. 24.50 (*0-404-00051-7*) AMS Pr.

Dreams of Life: Miscellaneous Poems. Timothy T. Fortune. LC 77-89433. (Black Heritage Library Collection). 1977. 24.95 (*0-8369-8573-7*) Ayer.

Dreams of Long Lasting. Mark Medoff. 560p. 1993. mass mkt. 5.99 (*0-446-36460-6*) Warner Bks.

Dreams of Love & Fateful Encounters: The Power of Romantic Passion. Ethel S. Person. 384p. 1989. pap. 12.00 (*0-14-012055-6*, Penguin Bks) Viking Penguin.

Dreams of Love & Power: On Shakespeare's Play. Joseph H. Summers. 1984. 34.50 (*0-19-812823-1*) OUP.

Dreams of Our Generation & Selections from Beijing's People. Zhang Xinxin. Ed. by Edward Gunn et al. Tr. by Donna Jung et al. (Cornell East Asia Ser.: No. 41). 96p. 1993. reprint ed. 9.00 (*0-939657-41-4*) Cornell East Asia Pgm.

Dreams of Power: Tibetan Buddhism, Western Imagination. Peter Bishop. LC 92-53943. (Illus.). 168p. (C). 1993. 29.50 (*0-8386-3510-5*) Fairleigh Dickinson.

Dreams of Power & the Power of Dreams: Inaugural Addresses of the Governors of Arkansas, 1836-1986. Ed. by Marvin E. De Boer. LC 87-27495. 1203p. 1988. 60.00 (*1-55728-002-9*) U of Ark Pr.

Dreams of Reason: Science & Utopias. Rene J. Dubos. LC 61-11753. (George B. Pegram Lectures). (Illus.). 183p. reprint ed. pap. 52.20 (*0-8357-4276-8*, 2037074) Bks Demand.

Dreams of Revenge. Kevin Casey. 1987. pap. 7.95 (*0-86327-112-X*, Pub. by Wolfhound Pr IE) Dufour.

***Dreams of Revenge: Dark Moon, Bk. II.** Moore. 1995. mass mkt. (*0-590-25510-X*) Scholastic Inc.

Dreams of Samarkand. C. A. De Lomellini. (C). 1988. 30.00 (*0-904524-30-2*, Pub. by Rivelin Grapheme Pr) St Mut.

Dreams of Sleep. Josephine Humphreys. 240p. 1985. pap. 10.95 (*0-14-007787-1*, Penguin Bks) Viking Penguin.

Dreams of Soccer. Maia Wojciechowska. (Dreams of...Ser.). (Illus.). 70p. (J). 1994. pap. 6.50 (*1-883740-06-1*) Pebble Bch Pr Ltd.

Dreams of Speech & Violence: The Art of the Short Story in Canada & New Zealand. W. H. New. 302p. 1987. text ed. 35.00 (*0-8020-5663-6*) U of Toronto Pr.

Dreams of Steel: The Fifth Chronicle of the Black Company. Glen Cook. 1990. pap. 3.95 (*0-8125-0210-8*) Tor Bks.

Dreams of Tamalpais: The Complete Mount Tamalpais Sourcebook. Sharon Skolnick. (Illus.). 224p. (Orig.). 1989. pap. 16.95 (*0-86719-357-3*) Last Gasp.

***Dreams of the Centaur: A Novel.** Montserrat Fontes. LC 95-5822. 1996. 23.00 (*0-393-03847-5*) Norton.

Dreams of the Deep. Maia Wojciechowska. (Dreams of... Ser.). (Illus.). 80p. (J). Date not set. pap. 6.50 (*1-883740-12-6*) Pebble Bch Pr Ltd.

Dreams of the Hoop. Maia Wojciechowska. (Dreams of... Ser.). (Illus.). 80p. (J). Date not set. pap. 6.50 (*1-883740-10-X*) Pebble Bch Pr Ltd.

Dreams of the Indy Five Hundred. Maia Wojciechowska. (Dreams of...Ser.). (Illus.). 80p. (J). Date not set. pap. 6.50 (*1-883740-11-8*) Pebble Bch Pr Ltd.

Dreams of the Kentucky Derby. Maia Wojciechowska. (Dreams of...Ser.). (Illus.). 80p. (J). Date not set. pap. 6.50 (*1-883740-07-X*) Pebble Bch Pr Ltd.

Dreams of the Peaceful Dragon. large type ed. Katie Hickman. 1990. 21.95 (*0-7089-2122-1*) Ulverscroft.

Dreams of the Rarebit Fiend. Winsor McCay. (Illus.). 80p. 1973. reprint ed. pap. 4.95 (*0-486-21347-1*) Dover.

Dreams of the Raven. Carmen Carter. (Star Trek Ser.: No. 34). 1991. mass mkt. 5.50 (*0-671-74356-2*) PB.

Dreams of the Soul: The Yogi Sutras of Patanjali. Daniel R. Condron. 208p. (C). 1991. pap. 9.95 (*0-944386-11-3*) SOM Pub.

Dreams of the Super Bowl. Maia Wojciechowska. (Dreams of...Ser.). (Illus.). 80p. (J). Date not set. 14.50 (*1-883740-20-7*) Pebble Bch Pr Ltd.

Dreams of the Super Bowl. Maia Wojciechowska. (Dreams of...Ser.). (Illus.). 52p. (J). 1994. pap. 5.50 (*1-883740-03-7*) Pebble Bch Pr Ltd.

Dreams of the Woman Who Loved Sex. Tee A. Corinne. LC 87-20216. 136p. (Orig.). 1987. pap. 7.95 (*0-934411-05-0*, Banned Bks) Edward-William Austin.

Dreams of the World Series. Maia Wojciechowska. (Dreams of...Ser.). (Illus.). 80p. (J). Date not set. pap. 6.50 (*1-883740-09-6*) Pebble Bch Pr Ltd.

Dreams of Trespass: Tales of a Harem Girlhood. Fatima Mernissi. LC 93-39523. (Illus.). 1994. 22.12 (*0-201-62649-7*) Addison-Wesley.

Dreams of Two Yi-Min. Margaret K. Pai. LC 88-29539. (Illus.). 216p. 1989. 22.95 (*0-8248-1179-8*, Kolowalu Bk) UH Pr.

Dreams of Vengeance. Artemis OakGrove. 197p. (Orig.). 1991. reprint ed. pap. 8.95 (*1-55583-306-3*, Lace MA) Alyson Pubns.

Dreams of Victory. Ellen Conford. (Illus.). 144p. (J). (gr. 4-6). 1973. 14.95 (*0-316-15294-3*) Little.

Dreams of Wimbledon. Maia Wojciechowska. (Dreams of... Ser.). (Illus.). 80p. (J). 1994. pap. 6.50 (*1-883740-02-9*) Pebble Bch Pr Ltd.

Dreams of Winter Gold. Maia Wojciechowska. (Dreams of.. .Ser.). (Illus.). 52p. (J). 1993. 14.50 (*1-883740-04-5*) Pebble Bch Pr Ltd.

An Asterisk (*) at the beginning of an entry indicates that the title is appearing in BIP for the first time.

An Asterisk (*) at the beginning of an entry indicates that the title is appearing in BIP for the first time.

2113

D

Dressed to Kill: Cartoonists & the Northern Ireland Conflict. John Darby. (Illus.). 132p. 1983. pap. 10.95 (*0-904651-91-6*, Pub. by Appletree Pr IE) Irish Bks Media.

Dressed to Kill: Sex, Power & Clothes. Colin McDowell. (Illus.). 192p. 1993. 29.95 (*0-09-174464-4*, Pub. by Hutchinson UK) Trafalgar.

***Dressed to Kill: The Link Between Breast Cancer & Bras.** Sidney R. Singer & Soma Grismaijer. 196p. 1995. pap. 11.95 (*0-89529-664-0*) Avery Pub.

Dressed up Book. K. Stinson. (Illus.). 32p. (J). (ps-8). 1990. lib. bdg. 14.95 (*1-55037-103-7*, Pub. by Annick CN); pap. 4.95 (*1-55037-104-5*, Pub. by Annick CN) Firefly Bks Ltd.

Dresser of Sycamore Trees: The Finding of a Ministry. Garret Keizer. LC 92-56133. 224p. 1993. pap. 10.00 (*0-06-064357-9*) Harper SF.

Dresses & Related Apparel: (Women's Misses & Juniors) Fairchild Market Research Staff. (Fact File Ser.). 50p. 1989. pap. 25.00 (*0-87005-644-1*) Fairchild.

Dresses & Washable Services Apparel. Fairchild Market Research Staff. (Fact File Ser.). 50p. 1992. pap. 37.50 (*0-87005-724-3*) Fairchild.

Dresses Cut-to-Fit. Ruth Oblander. Ed. by Mary Leppert. LC 76-53237. 1976. 4.95 (*0-933956-02-9*) Sew-Fit.

Dressing. Helen Oxenbury. (Oxenbury Board Bks.). (Illus.). 14p. (J). (ps-00). 1981. 3.95 (*0-671-42113-1*, Litl Simon S&S) S&S Childrens.

Dressing & Cooking Wild Game. Teresa Marrone et al. LC 87-15445. (Hunting & Fishing Library). (Illus.). 160p. 1987. 19.95 (*0-86573-020-2*) Cy De Cosse.

Dressing Our Wounds in Warm Clothes. Donna Henes. LC 81-65197. (Illus.). 72p. (Orig.). 1981. pap. 12.00 (*0-937122-02-5*) Astro Artz.

Dressing Successfully, Vol. 1, No. 1. rev. ed. S. Jill Miller-Lewis. (Illus.). 52p. (Orig.). 1987. pap. 10.00 (*0-934155-00-3*) Miller Des.

Dressing the Loom. Ida Grae. 1975. reprint ed. pap. 6.00 (*1-56659-009-4*) Robin & Russ.

Dressing the Part: Sternberg, Dietrich, & Costume. Sybil DelGaudio. LC 91-58953. (Illus.). 200p. 1993. 38.50 (*0-8386-3471-0*) Fairleigh Dickinson.

***Dressing Tips & Clothing Resources for Making Life Easier.** Shelley P. Schwarz. (Illus.). 93p. (Orig.). 1995. pap. text ed. 18.95 (*0-9638706-0-2*); audio 18.95 (*0-9638706-1-0*); 3.5 hd 18.95 (*0-9638706-2-9*); 5.25 hd 18.95 (*0-9638706-3-7*) S P Schwarz.

Dressing Up. R. Gibson et al. (How to Make Ser.). (Illus.). 96p. (J). (gr. 4-8). 1994. pap. 12.95 (*0-7460-1517-8*, Usborne) EDC.

Dressing-up Book. Wendy Baker. LC 93-36430. (Activities Ser.). (Illus.). 48p. (J). (gr. 3-5). 1994. 14.95 (*1-56847-136-X*) Thomson Lrning.

Dressing up Like Mommy. Susan M. French. (Storytime Bks.). (Illus.). 24p. (Orig.). (J). (gr. k-1). 1990. pap. 0.99 (*1-878624-35-0*) McClanahan Bk.

Dressing with Color: The Designer's Guide to over 1000 Color Combinations. Jeanne Allen. (Illus.). 134p. 1992. pap. text ed. 12.95 (*0-8118-0094-6*) Chronicle Bks.

Dressing with Style: A Woman's Guide to Organizing Your Wardrobe & Shopping in Houston. Tina Fondren. (Illus.). 150p. (Orig.). 1993. pap. 14.95 (*0-9636352-0-4*) Spectrum TX.

Dressmaker. large type ed. Freda M. Long. 1990. 21.95 (*0-7089-2125-6*) Ulverscroft.

Dressmaking. Jack Rudman. (Occupational Competency Examination Ser.: OCE-17). 1994. pap. 23.95 (*0-8373-5717-9*) Nat Learn.

Dressmaking: A Step-by-Step Course. Leila Aitken. LC 93-43378. (Illus.). 160p. 1994. 24.95 (*0-8069-0627-8*) Sterling.

***Dressmaking: A Step-by-Step Course.** Leila Aitken. (Illus.). 176p. 1995. pap. 14.95 (*0-8069-0628-6*) Sterling.

Dressmaking Simplified. 3rd ed. Valerie Cock. (Illus.). 240p. (C). 1984. pap. text ed. 22.50 (*0-632-02216-7*, Pub. by Granada UK) Sheridan.

Dressmaking with Basic Patterns. Ann Ladbury. (Illus.). 120p. 1983. pap. 19.95 (*0-7134-3850-9*, Pub. by Batsford UK) Trafalgar.

Dretske & His Critics. Brian McLaughlin. 356p. 1991. 47.95 (*1-55786-198-6*) Blackwell Pubs.

Dreuyfus the Dragon. Sarai. (Illus.). 36p. (Orig.). 1993. pap. 11.50 (*0-938837-14-1*) Behav Sci Ctr Pubs.

Dreuyfus the Dragon Coloring Book. Sarai. (Illus.). 36p. (Orig.). 1993. pap. 9.95 (*0-938837-15-X*) Behav Sci Ctr Pubs.

Drevnii Kiev. P. P. Tolochko. 328p. (RUS.). 1983. 79.00 (*0-317-40786-4*, Pub. by Collets UK) Pro-Am Music.

Drevo Shizni: Poems. Yevgeny Lubin. 1984. 3.95 (*0-685-22659-X*) RWCPH.

***Drew & Jimmy.** John P. Salisbury. 112p. 1995. 50.00 (*0-944092-31-4*) Twin Palms Pub.

Drexel College - Then & Now. Photos by Chris Usher. (Illus.). 112p. 1992. 39.00 (*1-56469-001-6*) Harmony Hse Pub LO.

Dreyer in Double Reflection: Carl Dreyer's Writings on Film. Carl T. Dreyer. Tr. by Donald Skoller. (Quality Paperbacks Ser.). (Illus.). 205p. 1991. reprint ed. pap. 12.95 (*0-306-80458-1*) Da Capo.

Dreyfus Affair: A Love Story. Peter Lefcourt. LC 92-54926. 304p. 1993. pap. 12.00 (*0-06-097559-8*, PL) HarpC.

Dreyfus in Rehearsal. Jean-Claude Grumberg. 1983. pap. 4.75 (*0-8222-0334-0*) Dramatists Play.

Dreyfus Saga. Shibaz Khan. 103p. (Orig.). 1991. pap. 11.81 (*0-685-48261-8*) Dayspring Pr.

Drg-Drsya-Viveka. Tr. by Swami Nikhilananda. 69p. Bilingual ed. pap. 1.95 (*0-87481-402-2*, Pub. by Advaita Ashrama II) Vedanta Pr.

DRG Handbook: Comparative Clinical & Financial Standards. 3rd ed. HCIA Staff & Ernst & Young Staff. 444p. 1993. disk 1,299.00 (*0-685-69256-6*) HCIA.

DRG Handbook: Comparative Clinical & Financial Standards. 3rd ed. HCIA Staff & Ernst & Young LLP Staff. 448p. 1995. pap. text ed. 399.00 (*1-880678-56-X*) HCIA.

DRG Optimization. Launa L. Graham. 1993. 49.00 (*0-317-05428-7*) Am Hlth Info.

DRG Survival Manual for the Clinical Lab. Ed. by Robert J. Fitzgibbon & Bernard E. Statland. 264p. 1985. pap. 32.95 (*0-87489-413-1*) Med Economics.

DRG 1993. Raymond Fish et al. Ed. by Melanie Karaffa. 600p. 1993. 44.95 (*1-878487-51-5*, ME048) Practice Mgmt Info.

DRGs: Their Design & Development. Ed. by Robert B. Fetter. LC 90-4872. 341p. 1991. text ed. 38.00 (*0-910701-60-1*, 0820) Health Admin Pr.

DRI-McGraw-Hill Readings in Macroeconomics. Ed. by Allen R. Sanderson. (Illus.). 480p. (C). 1981. text ed. write for info. (*0-07-054659-2*) McGraw.

Dribble Drabble: Art Experiences for Young Children. rev. ed. Deya Brashears. (Illus.). 120p. reprint ed. pap. 9.95 (*0-9614717-0-0*) Deya Brashears.

Dribbles. Connie Heckert. LC 92-24846. (J). 1993. 14.95 (*0-395-62336-7*, Clarion Bks) HM.

***Dribblesome Teapots & Other Incredible Stories.** large type ed. Norman Hunter. (J). 1995. 16.95 (*0-7451-2687-1*, Pub. by Chivers Lrg Print UK) Chivers N Amer.

Dried & Pressed Flowers. (Illus.). 64p. 1993. spiral bd. 5.98 (*1-56173-290-7*, 3611000) Pubns Intl Ltd.

Dried BCG Vaccine. Y. Obayashi. (Monograph Ser.: No. 28). 220p. (ENG & FRE.). 1955. 7.20 (*92-4-140028-5*) World Health.

Dried Flower Arranger. Alex MacCormick. (Illus.). 144p. (Orig.). 1994. pap. 17.95 (*1-895565-32-4*) Firefly Bks Ltd.

Dried Flower Arranger's Companion. Kym Hatala. 1994. 10.98 (*0-7858-0098-0*) Bk Sales Inc.

Dried Flower Book: Growing, Picking, Drying Arranging. Annette Mierhof. (Illus.). 96p. 1981. pap. 13.50 (*0-525-47700-4*, Dutton) NAL-Dutton.

Dried Flower Designs. Ed. by Barbara Laking. (Plants & Gardens Ser.). (Illus.). 1989. ring bd. 3.95 (*0-945352-34-4*, Sterling) Bklyn Botanic.

Dried Flower Garden. Ann L. Mitchell. (Illus.). 128p. 1992. 34.95 (*0-7134-6221-3*, Pub. by Batsford UK) Trafalgar.

Dried Flower Gardening. Joanna Sheen & Caroline Alexander. (Illus.). 128p. 1992. pap. 14.95 (*0-7063-7085-6*, Pub. by Ward Lock UK) Sterling.

***Dried Flower Gifts.** Stephanie Donaldson. (Illus.). 128p. 1995. 24.95 (*0-7892-0005-8*) Abbeville Pr.

Dried Flowers. (Miniature Books of Flowers Ser.). (Illus.). 48p. 1991. 4.99 (*0-517-03393-3*) Random Hse Value.

Dried Flowers. Susan Conder. LC 87-45830. (Illus.). 1988. 20.00 (*0-87923-719-8*) Godine.

***Dried Flowers.** Ed. by Creative Craft Series Staff. 1994. 10.95 (*0-681-40724-7*) Longmeadow Pr.

***Dried Flowers.** Martha E. Krasda & Burpee Staff. (Burpee American Gardening Ser.). 96p. 1995. pap. 9.00 (*0-02-860035-5*) Macmillan.

Dried Flowers. Jeannie Walker. 72p. (C). 1989. 80.00 (*1-85368-071-0*, Pub. by New Holland Pubs UK) St Mut.

Dried Flowers: How to Prepare Them. Sarah Whitlock & Martha Rankin. LC 75-17126. 32p. 1975. reprint ed. pap. 1.00 (*0-486-21802-3*) Dover.

***Dried Flowers & Herbs.** Lynn Bryan. 1994. 5.99 (*0-517-10253-6*) Random Hse Value.

***Dried Flowers: Colors for Every Room in the House: 100's of Ideas for the Creative Arranger.** Pamela Westland. (Illus.). 144p. 1995. 27.99 (*0-89134-671-6*) North Light Bks.

Dried Flowers for All Seasons: A Complete Guide to Selecting, Drying & Arranging Flowers Throughout the Year. Jenny Raworth. LC 93-5026. (Illus.). 128p. 1993. 23.00 (*0-89577-522-0*, Random) RD Assn.

Dried Flowers from Antiquity to the Present: A History & Practical Guide to Flower Drying. Leonard Karel. LC 72-10909. 192p. 1973. 20.00 (*0-8108-0512-X*) Scarecrow.

Dried Fruit: Its Care, Protection from Worms, Packing, Storing, Etc. Chas Phelan. (Shorey Lost Arts Ser.). 48p. reprint ed. pap. 1.95 (*0-8466-6049-0*, U49) Shorey.

Dried Guide. Don R. Crater. LC 81-52464. (Illus.). 56p. (Orig.). 1981. pap. 7.95 (*0-940654-01-6*) Tribune Pub.

Dried Millet Breaking: Time, Words & Song in the Woi Epic of the Kpelle. Ruth M. Stone. LC 86-46142. (Illus.). 170p. (C). 1988. 29.95 (*0-253-31818-1*) Ind U Pr.

***Driedger on the Construction of Statutes.** 3rd ed. Ruth Sullivan. 1994. boxed 72.00 (*0-614-05557-1*, UK) Butterworth Legal Pubs.

Drieu La Rochelle & the Picture Gallery Novel: French Modernism in the Interwar Years. Rima D. Reck. LC 89-48255. (Illus.). 272p. 1990. text ed. 34.95 (*0-8071-1584-3*) La State U Pr.

***Drift.** Paul Kidd. Ed. by Janice Sellers & Hilary Ayer. (Illus.). 64p. (Orig.). 1994. pap. 12.00 (*1-883240-13-1*) Chessex.

Drift. William Mayne. 1992. 16.00 (*0-8446-6547-9*) Peter Smith.

Drift. Anthony R. Norton. Ed. by David B. Axelrod. (Student Chapbook Ser.). (Illus.). 24p. 1987. 10.00 (*0-685-25229-9*); pap. 5.00 (*0-685-25230-2*) Writers Ink Pr.

Drift. Lloyd Kropp. 1979. reprint ed. pap. 1.95 (*0-8439-0658-8*) Dorchester Pub Co.

Drift & Mastery. Walter Lippmann. LC 85-40764. 192p. 1986. reprint ed. pap. 10.95 (*0-299-10604-7*) U of Wis Pr.

Drift & Rescue Towage of Disabled Gas Tankers (Appendix 111 of Guide to Contingency Planning. 1983. 75.00 (*0-317-61182-8*, Pub. by Witherby & Co UK) St Mut.

Drift Away: A Libby Kincaid Mystery. Kerry Tucker. LC 94-17113. 1994. 20.00 (*0-06-017999-6*) HarpC.

***Drift Boat Fly Fishing.** Neal Streeks. (Illus.). 116p. 1986. pap. 34.95 (*1-57188-016-X*) F Amato Pubns.

Drift Bottles in History & Folklore. Dorothy B. Francis. (Illus.). 56p. (Orig.). 1990. pap. 6.95 (*0-936335-02-5*) Ballyhoo Bks.

Drift Characteristics of Fifty Thousand to Seventy Thousand DWT Tankers. OCIMF Staff. 1982. 180.00 (*0-900886-67-6*) St Mut.

Drift Characteristics of Fifty Thousand to Seventy Thousand DWT Tankers. OCIMF Staff. (C). 1982. 175.00 (*0-685-31785-4*, Pub. by Witherby & Co UK) St Mut.

Drift-Diffusion Equation & Its Applications in MOSFET Modeling. W. Hansch. (Computational Microelectronics Ser.). (Illus.). 300p. 1991. 106.00 (*0-387-82222-4*) Spr-Verlag.

Drift Fence. Zane Grey. 1992. mass mkt. 3.99 (*0-06-100455-3*, Harp PBks) HarpC.

Drift from Two Shores. Bret Harte. LC 73-113669. (Short Story Index Reprint Ser.). 1977. 20.95 (*0-8369-3398-2*) Ayer.

Drift into Heresy. Agnes C. Lawless & John W. Lawless. 192p. 1995. pap. 10.99 (*0-8254-3163-8*) Kregel.

Drift on the River. Harold Rozelle. Ed. by Pauline Rozelle. LC 88-60412. 208p. (Orig.). 1989. pap. 9.95 (*0-941903-00-1*) Ransom Hill.

***Drift Toward Dissolution: The Virginia Slavery Debate of 1831-1832.** fac. ed. Alison G. Freehling. LC 82-6517. 328p. 1982. reprint ed. pap. 93.50 (*0-7837-7764-7*, 2047520) Bks Demand.

Driftboater's Guide to the Upper McKenzie. Doc Crawford. (Illus.). 86p. 1986. pap. 8.95 (*0-936608-55-2*) F Amato Pubns.

Drifter. Richie Tankersley-Cusick. Ed. by Lisa Clancy. 240p. (Orig.). (YA). 1994. mass mkt. 3.99 (*0-671-88741-6*, Archway) PB.

***Drifter.** Vicki L. Thompson. 1995. mass mkt. 3.25 (*0-373-25659-0*, 1-25659-3) Harlequin Bks.

Drifters. James A. Michener. 1986. mass mkt. 5.95 (*0-449-21353-6*) Fawcett.

Drifters. James A. Michener. 1971. 29.95 (*0-394-46200-9*) Random.

Drifter's Luck. Dan Parkinson. 288p. 1991. pap. 3.95 (*0-8217-3396-6*) Zebra.

***Drifter's Moon.** Lisa Hendrix. 304p. (Orig.). 1995. pap. 4.99 (*0-7865-0070-0*) Diamond.

Drifter's Story. Chuck Taylor. 190p. (Orig.). 1986. 15.95 (*0-941720-34-9*); pap. 7.95 (*0-941720-33-0*) Slough Pr TX.

Drifter's War. William C. Deitz. 240p. (Orig.). 1992. mass mkt. 4.99 (*0-441-16815-9*) Ace Bks.

Driftin on a Nightriff. Stanley Nelson. (Illus.). 24p. (Orig.). 1988. pap. 3.50 (*0-945085-04-4*) Sub Rosa.

Drifting. Charles W. Harvey. Ed. by Bobbie Wallace-Wright. (Orig.). 1989. pap. 5.95 (*1-878774-01-8*) WES Writing.

Drifting Apart? The Superpowers & Their European Allies. Ed. by Christopher Coker. 190p. 1989. 48.00 (*0-08-036711-9*, Pub. by Brasseys UK) Brasseys Inc.

Drifting Away. Leon Stokesbury. LC 85-1148. 64p. 1986. 16.95 (*0-938626-51-5*); pap. 8.95 (*0-938626-52-3*) U of Ark Pr.

Drifting Badge. Tabor Evans. (Longarm Ser.: No. 185). 192p. (Orig.). 1994. pap. 3.99 (*0-515-11375-1*) Jove Pubns.

Drifting Boat: An Anthology of Chinese Zen Poetry. Ed. by J. P. Seaton & Dennis Maloney. 1994. 15.00 (*1-877727-37-7*) White Pine.

Drifting Continents & Colliding Paradigms: Perspectives on the Geoscience Revolution. John A. Stewart. LC 89-45195. (Science, Technology, & Society Ser.). (Illus.). 302p. 1990. 35.00 (*0-253-35405-6*) Ind U Pr.

Drifting Continents & Shifting Theories: The Modern Revolution in Geology & Scientific Change. H. E. Le Grand. (Illus.). 250p. 1989. pap. 24.95 (*0-521-31105-5*) Cambridge U Pr.

Drifting Down Memory Lane. Ward Hays. LC 85-81970. (Illus.). 124p. 1985. pap. 14.95 (*0-934188-19-X*) Evans Pubns.

Drifting into a Law & Order Society. Stuart Hall. (C). 1988. 21.00 (*0-900137-15-0*, Pub. by NCCL UK) St Mut.

Drifting Marriage. Donald R. Harvey. LC 87-28460. 256p. 1988. 14.99 (*0-8007-1571-3*) Revell.

Drifting Sands. Elsie Lee. 272p. 1986. pap. 2.95 (*0-8217-1917-3*) Zebra.

Drifting Snow: An Arctic Search. James Houston. LC 91-42674. (Illus.). 160p. (YA). (gr. 5 up). 1992. text ed. 13.95 (*0-689-50563-9*, McElderry) S&S Childrens.

Drifting Snow: An Arctic Search. James R. Houston. 160p. (J). 1994. pap. 3.99 (*0-14-036530-3*) Puffin Bks.

Drifting Thoughts. Mary A. Bell. 1994. 14.95 (*0-533-10718-0*) Vantage.

Drifting Through Ancestor Dreams: New & Selected Poems. Ramson Lomatewama. LC 92-82838. (Illus.). 72p. (Orig.). 1993. pap. 9.95 (*0-87358-552-6*, Entrada Bks) Northland AZ.

Drifting Together or Apart? An European Relations in the Paul-Henri Spaak Lectures Harvard University 1981-1984. Ed. by Richard C. Eichenberg. 216p. 1986. lib. bdg. 38.50 (*0-8191-5467-9*) U Pr of Amer.

Driftwood. Michael Glaser. LC 85-50601. (Illus.). 32p. (J). (ps-3). 1985. pap. 3.95 (*0-911635-01-7*) Knickerbocker.

Driftwood: Being Papers on Old-Time American Towns & Some Old People. Walter G. Shotwell. LC 67-22118. (Essay Index Reprint Ser.). 1977. 19.95 (*0-8369-0877-5*) Ayer.

***Driftwood: Prayers for Beached Travelers.** Don Kimball. LC 95-2882. (Illus.). 128p. (Orig.). (YA). 1995. pap. 19.95 (*0-8091-3578-7*) Paulist Pr.

Driftwood & Stone. William H. Davis. (Illus.). 64p. 1988. 8.00 (*0-8233-0448-5*) Golden Quill.

Driftwood Captain. Paul B. Kenyon. 17.00 (*0-8446-6248-8*) Peter Smith.

Driftwood House: Poems. J. Bernlef. Tr. by Scott Rollins. 44p. 1992. 28.00 (*0-930126-40-8*) Typographeum.

***Driftwood in a Time of War.** Marie Christopherson. (The Prairie Plains Ser.). (Illus.). 400p. (Orig.). 1995. pap. 14.95 (*0-931170-60-5*) Ctr Western Studies.

Driftwood-The Bull. N. P. Mohamed. LC 76-902191. 1976. lib. bdg. 3.75 (*0-88386-810-5*) S Asia.

Driftwood Whimsy: The Sculptures of the Emeryville Mudflats. Douglas Keister. (Illus.). 50p. 1985. pap. 9.95 (*0-9615357-0-9*) Calif Photo.

***Drill.** Patricia Armentrout & David Armentrout. LC 94-47277. (Learning about Tools Ser.). (J). 1995. write for info. (*1-55916-117-5*) Rourke Bk Co.

Drill & Rifle Instructions - Pattern 1853 Rifle & Rifle Musket - 1859. Intro. by R. Stephen Dorsey. (Illus.). 68p. 1994. reprint ed. pap. 8.00 (*0-9631208-3-2*) Collect Lib.

Drill Press. David J. Gingery. LC 80-66142. (Build Your Own Metalworking Shop from Scrap Ser.). (Illus.). 144p. (Orig.). 1982. pap. 8.95 (*1-878087-04-5*) D J Gingery.

Drill Press Book. R. J. De Cristoforo. 1991. pap. text ed. 18.95 (*0-07-016318-9*) McGraw.

Drill Press Book. R. J. De Cristoforo. (Illus.). 288p. 1991. 25.95 (*0-8306-7609-0*, 3609); pap. 16.95 (*0-8306-3609-9*) TAB Bks.

Drill Press Explained. Leo Rizzo. LC 81-730687. 1982. student ed 7.00 (*0-8064-0249-0*, 516); audio 219.00 (*0-8064-0250-4*) Bergwall.

Drill Stem. 2nd ed. Ed. by Fernando Albornoz. Tr. by Roberto Quiroga. (Rotary Drilling Ser.: Unit I, Lesson 3). (Illus.). 52p. (SPA.). 1983. pap. text ed. 14.00 (*0-88698-031-3*, 2.10322) PETEX.

Drill Stem: Canadian Metric Edition. 2nd rev. ed. Ed. by Jodie Leecraft. (Rotary Drilling Ser.: Unit I, Lesson 3). (Illus.). 52p. 1981. pap. text ed. 14.00 (*0-88698-019-4*, 2.10321) PETEX.

Drill Stem see Drill String & Drill Collars

Drill Stem Design & Inspection Standard DS-1. Tom H. Hill & Randy C. Money. 167p. 1992. 250.00 (*0-318-72531-2*, P7492) PennWell Bks.

Drill String & Drill Collars. S. T. Horton. Ed. by Kathy Bork. (Rotary Drilling Ser.: Unit I). Orig. Title: The Drill Stem. (Illus.). 60p. (Orig.). 1994. pap. text ed. 15.00 (*0-88698-168-9*, 2.10330) PETEX.

Drilled Piers & Caissons. Ed. by Michael W. O'Neill. LC 81-69227. 159p. 1981. 19.00 (*0-87262-285-1*) Am Soc Civil Eng.

Drilled Piers & Caissons II. Ed. by Clyde N. Baker, Jr. 153p. 1985. 18.00 (*0-87262-447-1*) Am Soc Civil Eng.

Driller's Safety Manual. Scientific Publishers Staff. (C). 1985. 60.00 (*81-85046-37-9*, Scientific Pubs II) St Mut.

Drillers Safety Manual. USDI Staff. (C). 1986. text ed. 25.00 (*81-85036-37-3*, Pub. by Scientific Pubs II) St Mut.

Drilling. (SPE Reprint Ser.). 321p. 1973. 9.60 (*0-317-32913-8*, 30506) Soc Petrol Engineers.

Drilling. (SPE Reprint Ser.). 348p. 1987. reprint ed. 22.80 (*1-55563-009-X*, 30522) Soc Petrol Engineers.

Drilling: Tools & Programme Management. J. S. Hartley. (Illus.). 192p. (C). 1994. text ed. 45.00 (*90-5410-159-8*, Pub. by A A Balkema NE); pap. 25.00 (*90-5410-160-1*, Pub. by A A Balkema NE) Ashgate Pub Co.

Drilling a Straight Hole. 2nd rev. ed. Ed. by Nancy Janicek. (Rotary Drilling Ser.: Unit II, Lesson 3). (Illus.). 37p. 1982. pap. text ed. 14.00 (*0-88698-055-0*, 2.20320) PETEX.

Drilling an Irrigation Well. Hal Werner. Ed. by M. N. Staples. (C). 1987. 50.00 (*0-685-54217-3*, H M Gousha) P-H Gen Ref & Trav.

***Drilling & Blasting of Rocks.** Ayala Carcedo et al. Tr. by B. Visser de Ramiro. 400p. 1995. 99.00 (*90-5410-199-7*, Pub. by A A Balkema NE) Ashgate Pub Co.

Drilling & Casing Operations. J. A. Short. 426p. 1982. 74.95 (*0-87814-177-4*, P4255) PennWell Bks.

Drilling & Drilling Fluids. G. V. Chilingarian & P. Vorabutr. (Developments in Petroleum Science Ser.: Vol. 11). xx, 802p. 1983. pap. 66.75 (*0-444-42177-7*) Elsevier.

Drilling & Excavation Technologies for the Future. National Research Council, Commission on PHysical Sciences, Mathematics, & Applications Staff. 176p. (Orig.). (C). 1994. pap. text ed. 27.00 (*0-309-05076-6*) Natl Acad Pr.

Drilling & Irrigation Well. W. Warner. (C). 1987. text ed. 25.00 (*81-85046-68-9*, Pub. by Scientific Pubs II) St Mut.

Drilling Data Handbook. 6th ed. 542p. 1991. 65.00 (*0-87201-206-9*) Gulf Pub.

Drilling Engineering: A Complete Well Planning Approach. Neal J. Adams. LC 84-1110. 976p. 1985. 114.95 (*0-87814-265-7*, P4366) PennWell Bks.

Drilling Engineering Handbook. Ellis H. Austin. (Short Course Handbks.). (Illus.). 288p. 1983. pap. text ed. 36.00 (*0-685-06336-4*); pap. text ed. 30.00 (*0-934634-54-8*) Intl Human Res.

Drilling Engineering Mechanics. J. J. Azar & James L. Lummus. 540p. 1993. boxed write for info. (*0-13-220369-3*) P-H.

Drilling Fluid Materials: Barytes. EEMUA Staff. 1978. 85.00 (*0-85931-107-4*, Pub. by EEMUA UK) St Mut.

Drilling Fluid Materials: Bentonite. EEMUA Staff. 1977. 75.00 (*0-85931-112-0*, Pub. by EEMUA UK) St Mut.

Drilling Fluid Materials: High Viscosity Carboxymethycellulose. 1973. 75.00 (*0-85931-122-8*, Pub. by EEMUA UK) St Mut.

An Asterisk (*) at the beginning of an entry indicates that the title is appearing in BIP for the first time.

An Asterisk (*) at the beginning of an entry indicates that the title is appearing in BIP for the first time.

D

2115

Drinking Water Treatment Technologies: Comparative Health Effects Assessment. EPA Staff. 206p. 1990. pap. text ed. 58.00 (*0-86587-217-1*) Gov Insts.

Drinking Water 1991. HMSO Staff. 272p. 1992. pap. 60.00 (*0-11-752676-2*, HM26762, Pub. by HMSO UK) UNIPUB.

Drinking with Dickens. Cedric Dickens. (Illus.). 127p. (C). 1988. pap. 11.95 (*0-941533-34-4*) New Amsterdam Bks.

Drinks, Drinkers & Drinking or the Law & History of Intoxicating Liquors. R. Vashon Rogers, Jr. iv, 241p. 1985. reprint ed. lib. bdg. 24.00 (*0-8377-1043-X*) Rothman.

Drinks Without Liquor. Jane Brandt. LC 82-40504. (Illus.). 144p. 1983. pap. 6.95 (*0-89480-358-1*, 358) Workman Pub.

***Drip & Microirrigation: For Trees, Vines, & Row Crops.** Charles M. Burt & Stuart W. Styles. LC 94-79774. (Illus.). 261p. (Orig.). 1994. pap. text ed. 34.95 (*0-9643634-0-2*) Irrigat Trning.

Drip Drop. Sharon Gordon. LC 81-5112. (Illus.). 32p. (J). (gr. k-2). 1981. lib. bdg. 11.59 (*0-89375-507-9*); pap. 2.95 (*0-89375-508-7*) Troll Assocs.

Drip Drop Waters Journey. Eve Stwertka. (J). (gr. 4-7). 1990. lib. bdg. 5.95 (*0-671-69462-6*, Julian Messner) Silver Burdett Pr.

Drip Irrigation for Every Landscape & All Climates. Robert Kourik. (Illus.). 128p. (Orig.). 1992. pap. 12.00 (*0-9615848-2-3*) Metamorphic Pr.

Drip-Trickle Irrigation in Puerto Rico. Tr. & Intro. by Megh R. Goyal. (Illus.). 425p. (Orig.). (C). 1989. pap. 10.00 (*0-685-24943-3*) UPR Agr Exper Sta.

Dripping Faucet As a Model Chaotic System. Robert Shaw. (Science Frontier Express Ser.). (Illus.). 122p. 1984. pap. 25.00 (*0-942344-05-7*) Aerial Pr.

Driss. Mark Dunster. 62p. (Orig.). 1982. pap. 4.00 (*0-89642-088-4*) Linden Pubs.

Drive: The Story of My Life. Larry Bird & Bob Ryan. 1990. reprint ed. mass mkt. 5.99 (*0-553-28758-3*) Bantam.

Drive & Determination: Developing Your Inner Motivation. Marie Dalloway. 80p. 1993. pap. text ed. 14.95 (*0-9634933-2-9*) Optimal Perf.

Drive & Survive. Gordon Cole. 180p. (Orig.). 1990. pap. 15.95 (*0-8464-1372-8*) Beekman Pubs.

Drive-By. Gary Rivlin. 1995. 25.00 (*0-8050-2921-4*) H Holt & Co.

***Drive-By: A Nebraska Mystery. William J. Reynolds. Ed. by Gayle Emmel. 330p. 1995. pap. 15.95 (*0-944287-14-X*) Ex Machina.**
Juvenile gangs have invaded the heartland. Cities like Minneapolis, Omaha & Des Moines are feeling the agony of children killing children. William J. Reynolds' writer-P.I. Nebraska, based in Omaha, takes on the gangs in DRIVE-BY. Reynolds brings his unique wit & sensitivity to the telling of this story. His sardonic sleuth has been appointed unofficial guardian angel of Darius LeClerc, a young man new to Omaha. When Darius is gunned down, Nebraska joins the boy's Uncle, Elmo Lammers, to find the killers. The backstreets through which the detective & his army buddy prowl for clues could be in a foreign country, teeming with fascinating, richly drawn people. The sense of the familiar suddenly grown alien should strike a chord with a public whose values have been challenged by the ruthlessness of young people with guns & an attitude. "In this sixth 'Nebraska' adventure, Reynolds once again reveals his delightful sense of humor as well as his ability to keep readers turning pages," writes William X. Kienzle, author of THE ROSARY MURDERS. For fans of Nebraska, DRIVE-BY is a landmark in the evolution of this intriguing character. For readers new to the series, it is a glorious introduction. ***Publisher Provided Annotation.***

Drive by Shootings: My Proverbial Mom. Ricardo Scott. 75p. (Orig.). (YA). 1994. write for info. (*1-883427-22-3*) Crnerstone GA.

DRIVE (Distribution & Repair in Variable Environments) Design & Operation of the Ogden Prototype. Louis W. Miller & John B. Abell. LC 92-13079. 1992. write for info. (*0-8330-1243-6*, R-4158-AF) Rand Corp.

Drive, Ego, Object, & Self: A Synthesis for Clinical Work. Fred Pine. LC 89-43168. 288p. 1990. text ed. 35.00 (*0-465-01722-3*) Basic.

Drive for Clean Air: Natural Gas & Methanol Vehicles. James S. Cannon. LC 89-20007. 252p. reprint ed. pap. 71.90 (*0-7837-6409-X*, 2046389) Bks Demand.

Drive for Self: Alfred Adler & the Founding of Individual Psychology. Edward Hoffman. (Illus.). 356p. 1994. 26.00 (*0-201-63280-2*) Addison-Wesley.

***Drive Free.** Ivan Knotts. 1994. pap. text ed. write for info. (*0-9642824-0-2*) I Knotts.

Drive Him Wild: The Ultimate Guide to Pleasing Your Man in Bed. Graham Masterton. 224p. (Orig.). 1993. pap. 5.99 (*0-451-17591-3*, Sig) NAL-Dutton.

Drive-in Madness: The Jiggle Movies. Bill George. 1990. pap. 14.95 (*0-911137-04-1*) Imagine.

Drive in the Country. Illus. by Mark Barry. 12p. (J). (ps). 1992. 3.95 (*1-56828-006-8*) Red Jacket Pr.

Drive-in Theaters: A History from Their Inception in 1933. Kerry Segrave. LC 92-50319. 296p. 1992. lib. bdg. 35.00x (*0-89950-752-2*) McFarland & Co.

Drive It Forever: Your Key to Long Automobile Life. 2nd ed. Robert B. Sikorsky. (Illus.). 1989. pap. text ed. 10.95 (*0-07-057522-3*) McGraw.

Drive North in Your Career. Brenda Avadian. 166p. 1992. pap. 14.95 (*0-9632752-0-8*) N Star Bks.

Drive On. Doris Ganton. 1982. pap. 7.00 (*0-87980-393-2*) Wilshire.

Drive, They Said: Poems about Americans & Their Cars. Ed. by Kurt Brown. LC 93-33856. 328p. 1994. 14.95 (*0-915943-90-5*) Milkweed Ed.

***Drive Thru Reflections.** Gregory S. Halmay. 46p. (Orig.). 1994. pap. 6.00 (*0-9643305-0-4*) G S Halmay.

Drive to Desegregate Places of Public Accommodation. Ed. by Michal R. Belknap. LC 91-3619. (Civil Rights, White House & Justice Dept. Ser.: Vol. 9). 176p. 1991. 55.00 (*0-8240-3378-7*) Garland.

Drive to Hegemony: The United States in the Caribbean, 1898-1917. David Healy. LC 88-40190. (Illus.). 384p. (C). 1988. text ed. 29.50 (*0-299-11720-0*) U of Wis Pr.

Drive to Industrial Maturity: The U. S. Economy, 1860-1914. Harold G. Vatter. LC 75-16970. (Contributions in Economics & Economic History Ser.: No. 13). (Illus.). 368p. 1976. text ed. 69.50 (*0-8371-8180-1*, VIM/, Greenwood Pr) Greenwood.

Drive with Less Stress: A Motorist's Survival Guide for the 90's. Andrew J. Lesser. Ed. by Jane W. Brown. LC 90-91498. (Illus.). 176p. (Orig.). 1990. pap. 5.95 (*0-945375-01-8*) Less Stress Pr.

Drive Your Woman Wild in Bed: A Lover's Guide to Sex & Romance. Staci Keith. 208p. (Orig.). 1994. pap. 10.99 (*0-446-67047-2*) Warner Bks.

Drive Yourself Sane! Using the Uncommon Sense of General Semantics. Susan P. Kodish & Bruce I. Kodish. 194p. 1994. pap. 11.95 (*0-685-72324-0*) Inst Gen Seman.

Driveability Manual Asian A. M., 1992-94, Vol. A-M. Ed. by Chilton Staff. 2304p. 1995. text ed. 110.00 (*0-8019-8551-X*) Chilton.

Driveability Manual Asian, 1992-94, European. Ed. by Chilton Staff. 2304p. 1995. text ed. 110.00 (*0-8019-8553-6*) Chilton.

Driveability Manual Asian, 1992-94, Vol. N-Z. Ed. by Chilton Staff. 2304p. 1995. text ed. 110.00 (*0-8019-8552-8*) Chilton.

Driveability Manual Chrysler 1992-94. Ed. by Chilton Staff. 1856p. 1994. text ed. 110.00 (*0-8019-8543-9*) Chilton.

Driveability Manual Ford 1992-94. Ed. by Chilton Staff. 1984p. 1994. text ed. 110.00 (*0-8019-8542-0*) Chilton.

Driven by Growth: Political Change in the Asia-Pacific Region. Ed. by James W. Morley. LC 91-28995. 382p. 1992. 62.95 (*1-56324-013-0*); pap. text ed. 23.95 (*1-56324-014-9*) M E Sharpe.

Driven by Nissan? A Critical Guide to New Management Techniques. David Beale. 200p. (C). 1994. pap. 19.95 (*0-85315-799-5*, Pub. by Lawrence & Wishart UK) Humanities.

Driven Clouds. large type ed. Christine Wilson. 1991. 21.95 (*0-7089-2563-4*) Ulverscroft.

Driven from Home. Horatio Alger, Jr. (Works of Horatio Alger Jr.). 1989. reprint ed. lib. bdg. 79.00 (*0-7812-3564-2*) Rprt Serv.

Driven Magnetic Fusion Reactors: Proceedings. B. Brunelli. (Commission of the European Communities Ser.: EUR 6146). (Illus.). 1979. pap. 203.00 (*0-08-024459-9*, Pub. by Pergamon Repr UK) Franklin.

Driven, Notes of a Neurotic Entrepreneur: His Trials, Failures & Victories. Max Barnet, pseud. Ed. by Barbara Feller-Roth. LC 93-85983. 465p. (Orig.). 1995. pap. text ed. 15.00 (*1-882521-01-3*) Stones Pt Pr.

Driven Patriot: The Life & Times of James Forrestal. Townsend Hoopes. 1992. 29.50 (*0-394-57761-2*) Knopf.

Driven Patriot: The Life & Times of James Forrestal. Townsend Hoopes & Douglas Brinkley. LC 93-7860. 1993. reprint ed. pap. 17.00 (*0-679-72721-3*, Vin) Random.

Driven to Create: The Anthony Petullo Collection of Self-Taught & Outsider Art. Roger Cardinal & Russell Bowman. LC 93-33028. (Illus.). 112p. (Orig.). 1993. pap. 24.95 (*0-944110-36-3*) Milwauk Art Mus.

Driven to Distraction: Attention Deficit Disorder in Children & Adults. Edward M. Hallowell & John Ratey. LC 93-29536. 1994. 23.00 (*0-679-42177-7*) Pantheon.

***Driven to Distraction: Recognizing & Coping with Attention Deficit Disorder from Childhood through Adulthood.** Edward Hallowell. 1995. pap. 12.00 (*0-684-80128-0*, Touchstone Bks) S&S Trade.

Driven to Kill. G. G. Garth. (YA). 1994. pap. 3.50 (*0-553-56651-2*) Bantam.

Driven to Kill. Gary C. King. 384p. 1993. mass mkt. 4.99 (*1-55817-729-9*, Pinnacle NY) Windsor NY.

Driver & Traffic Safety Education. 174p. 1984. reprint ed. pap. 7.00 (*0-87013-202-4*) Mich St U Pr.

Driver Education & Traffic Safety. 2nd ed. J. Glassman. 1976. 13.28 (*0-13-220590-4*); pap. text ed. 12.24 (*0-13-220582-3*); student ed. 10.48 (*0-13-220566-1*) P-H.

Driver Family: A Genealogical Memoir of the Descendants of Robert & Phebe Driver of Lynn, Mass. with Appendix Containing 83 Allied Families. H. R. Cooke. 556p. 1989. reprint ed. lib. bdg. 95.00 (*0-8328-0496-7*); reprint ed. pap. 85.00 (*0-8328-0497-5*) Higginson Bk Co.

Driver Handbook for Private Motor Carriers. 1.50 (*0-686-31448-4*) Private Carrier.

Driver License Written Examination. Jack Rudman. (Career Examination Ser.: C-1635). 1994. pap. 23.95 (*0-8373-1635-9*) Nat Learn.

Driver Performance: Measurement & Modeling, IVHS, Information Systems, & Simulation (TRR 1403) Ed. by Susan Brown. (Transportation Research Record Ser.). (Illus.). 106p. 1993. pap. text ed. 25.00 (*0-309-05551-2*) Transport Res Bd.

Driver Performance, Pedestrian Planning, & Bicycle Facilities. (Transportation Research Record Ser.: No. 1168). 91p. 1988. 13.00 (*0-309-04704-8*) Transport Res Bd.

Driver Training. Nick L. Nips. 1976. 2.00 (*0-686-75954-0*) Luna Bisonte.

Driver Visual Needs in Night Driving. (Special Report Ser.: No. 156). 120p. 1975. 5.00 (*0-309-02397-1*) Transport Res Bd.

***Driver's Dead.** Peter Lerangis. (YA). 1994. pap. 3.50 (*0-590-46677-1*) Scholastic Inc.

Driver's Ed. Caroline B. Cooney. LC 94-445. (YA). (gr. 6 up). 1994. 15.95 (*0-385-32087-6*) Delacorte.

Drivers Guide to Hazardous Materials. rev. ed. John V. Currie. 345p. 1994. 2.25 (*0-88711-177-7*) Am Trucking Assns.

Driver's Pocket Guide to Hazardous Materials, ORS-2. rev. ed. Keller, J. J., & Associates, Inc. Staff. LC 77-90372. (Orig.). 1991. pap. 2.25 (*0-934674-26-4*) J J Keller.

Driver's Seat. Muriel Spark. (Bibelot Ser.). 112p. (Orig.). 1994. pap. 6.00 (*0-8112-1271-8*, NDP786) New Directions.

Drives. Center for Occupational Research & Development Staff. (Mechanical Technology Ser.). (Illus.). 267p. (C). 1983. pap. text ed. 28.00 (*1-55502-152-2*) CORD Commns.

Drives, Affects, Behavior, 2 vols., Vol. 1. Ed. by Rudolph M. Loewenstein. LC 53-11056. 399p. 1960. text ed. 55.00x (*0-8236-1480-8*) Intl Univs Pr.

Drives, Affects, Behavior, 2 vols., Vol. 2. Ed. by Rudolph M. Loewenstein. LC 53-11056. 502p. 1960. text ed. 65.00 (*0-8236-1500-6*) Intl Univs Pr.

Drives & Reinforcements: Behavioral Studies of Hypothalamic Functions. James Olds. LC 75-31480. 148p. 1977. pap. 27.00 (*0-89004-087-7*) Raven.

Drives & Seals. Michael J. Neale. LC 93-20740. (Tribology Handbooks Ser.). (Illus.). 152p. 1994. write for info. (*0-7506-0981-8*) Buttrwrth-Heinemann.

Drives & Seals: A Tribology Handbook. M. J. Neale. 180p. 1993. 39.00 (*1-56091-452-1*, R-138) Soc Auto Engineers.

***Drivin' Steady: Coming Home a Stranger.** Ray Heick. 1995. 18.95 (*0-8062-5212-X*) Carlton.

***Drivin' Woman.** Elizabeth Chevalier. 1994. lib. bdg. 24.95x (*1-56849-427-0*) Buccaneer Bks.

Driving. Anne Norris & Caroline Douglas. (Illus.). 1990. pap. 21.00 (*0-85131-368-X*, Pub. by J A Allen & Co UK) St Mut.

Driving: An Instructional Guide to Driving Singles & Pairs. Clive Richardson. Date not set. 27.50 (*0-7134-6946-3*, Pub. by Batsford UK) Trafalgar.

Driving a Bargain: Automobile Industrialization & Japanese Firms in Southeast Asia. Richard F. Doner. 350p. 1990. 42.00 (*0-520-06938-2*) U CA Pr.

Driving a Harness Horse. Sallie Walrond. 200p. 1990. 60.00 (*0-85131-551-8*, Pub. by J A Allen & Co UK) St Mut.

Driving Ambitions: A Complete Guide to Amateur Auto Racing for Drivers, Spectators, Racing Fans. Lauren J. Fix. LC 93-72931. (Illus.). 136p. (Orig.). 1993. pap. 9.95 (*0-9624908-7-3*) CA Mustang Sales.

***Driving Amongst Idiots.** B. Witte & H. Kavet. 96p. 1994. pap. 5.95 (*0-88032-452-X*) Ivory Tower Pub.

Driving & Discovering Oahu. Richard Sullivan. LC 93-78114. (Illus.). 112p. (Orig.). 1993. pap. 16.95 (*0-9636828-8-1*) Montgmry Ewing.

Driving & Surviving. Jon C. Prothero. LC 80-82627. (Illus.). 73p. (Orig.). (gr. 10-12). 1980. pap. 5.00 (*0-938026-01-1*) Instruct Res.

Driving at Night. Samuel Kashner. 1976. pap. 5.00 (*0-914610-07-4*) Hanging Loose.

Driving Circuits & Interfaces for PIN Diode & Ferrite Phase Shifters. (Tech Edge Ser.). (Illus.). 125p. 1990. write for info. (*0-944916-18-X*) Inter Con Tech.

Driving Down Health Care Costs. Custer. 420p. 1992. 89.00 (*1-56706-002-1*, 60021) Panel Pubs.

Driving Down Health Care Costs: Strategies & Solutions. Ed. by JoAnne S. Haffeman. 1991. pap. 79.00 (*1-878375-52-0*) Panel Pubs.

Driving Down Health Care Costs: Strategies & Solutions, 1994. 560p. 1993. pap. 89.00 (*1-56706-015-3*) Panel Pubs.

Driving Down Worker's Compensation Costs. 1994. 69.00 (*1-56706-064-1*) Panel Pubs.

Driving Emergencies: What to Do When the Brakes Fail, the Car Skids, & Other Driving Emergencies. Consumer Reports Books Editors & James Joseph. LC 93-48002. (Illus.). 300p. (Orig.). 1994. pap. 16.95 (*0-89043-681-9*) Consumer Reports.

Driving Fear Out of the Workplace: How to Overcome the Invisible Barriers to Quality, Productivity, & Innovation. Kathleen D. Ryan & Daniel K. Oestreich. LC 90-47648. (Management Ser.). 283p. 1993. pap. 19.00 (*1-55542-509-7*) Jossey-Bass.

Driving Force. Dick Francis. 1993. mass mkt. 5.99 (*0-449-22139-3*, Crest) Fawcett.

Driving Force. Dick Francis. 320p. 1992. 21.95 (*0-399-13776-9*, Putnam) Putnam Pub Group.

Driving Force. large type ed. Dick Francis. LC 92-44637. (Basic Ser.). 494p. 1993. reprint ed. lib. bdg. 22.95 (*1-56054-655-7*); reprint ed. pap. 14.95 (*1-56054-883-5*) Thorndike Pr.

Driving Force of Spiritual Powers in World History. Rudolf Steiner. Tr. by Dorothy Osmond et al. 92p. 1983. reprint ed. pap. 8.95 (*0-919924-03-4*, Pub. by Steiner Book Centre CN) Anthroposophic.

Driving Forces: Motor Vehicle Trends & Their Implications for Global Warming, Energy Strategies, & Transportation Planning. large type ed. James J. MacKenzie & Michael P. Walsh. 50p. 1990. Large format. pap. 14.95 (*0-915825-61-9*, MADFP) World Resources Inst.

Driving Forces in History. Halvdan Koht. Tr. by Einar Haugen. LC 64-16065. 227p. reprint ed. pap. 64.70 (*0-7837-6076-0*, 2059122) Bks Demand.

Driving from Columbus: Poems. Peter Desy. LC 91-34457. (Lewiston Poetry Ser.: Vol. 19). 68p. 1992. pap. 12.95 (*0-7734-9617-3*) E Mellen.

Driving Future Vehicles. Ed. by Andrew M. Parkes. 386p. 1993. 85.00 (*0-7484-0042-7*) Taylor & Francis.

Driving Horse-Drawn Carriages for Pleasure. Francis T. Underhill. 304p. 1990. pap. 10.95 (*0-486-26102-6*) Dover.

Driving Horses. Sallie Walrond. 1979. pap. 7.00 (*0-87980-242-1*) Wilshire.

Driving Immediately Past Something Green. Philip Whalen. 1991. 45.00 (*0-685-57000-2*) Poltroon Pr.

Driving in Britain: What the Guide Books Don't Tell You. Charlene F. Palm. LC 83-72089. (Illus.). 168p. (Orig.). 1984. pap. 10.00 (*0-9611962-0-3*) Bittersweet Evanston.

Driving in Competition. Alan Johnson. (Illus.). 1979. pap. 11.95 (*0-393-60011-4*) Norton.

***Driving Lessons: Christian Meditations about Life from the Not-So-Fast Lane.** Sharon Elwell. Ed. by Arthur L. Zapel & Rhonda Wray. LC 94-47507. (Illus.). 144p. (Orig.). (YA). (gr. 9 up). 1995. pap. 10.95 (*1-56608-009-6*) Meriwether Pub.

Driving Like the Sun. Kent Taylor. (Chapbook Ser.: No. 6). 40p. 1976. pap. 3.00 (*0-912824-14-X*) Vagabond Pr.

Driving Manual. 320p. 1992. pap. 19.00 (*0-11-551054-0*, HM10540, Pub. by HMSO UK) UNIPUB.

Driving Me Crazy: Fun on Wheels Jokes. Illus. by Lee Lorenz. 40p. (J). (gr. 2-5). 1989. 13.95 (*0-945912-05-6*) Pippin Pr.

Driving Miss Daisy. Alfred Uhry. 1987. pap. 4.75 (*0-8222-0335-9*) Dramatists Play.

Driving North. Richard Aldridge. LC 89-9252. (Illus.). 64p. (Orig.). 1989. pap. 9.95 (*0-945980-09-4*) Nrth Country Pr.

***Driving over a Cliff? Strategy & Analysis of the World's Car Industry.** Graeme Maxton. (C). 1994. pap. text ed. 29.25 (*0-201-59392-0*) Addison-Wesley.

Driving Passion. Marco Vassi. LC 91-40181. 160p. 1992. 22.00 (*1-877946-19-2*) Permanent Pr.

Driving Passion. Marco Vassi. 1993. reprint ed. pap. 12.95 (*1-56333-134-9*) Masquerade.

Driving Stresses in Concrete Piles. (PCI Journal Reprints Ser.). 20p. 1985. pap. 6.00 (*0-318-19754-5*, JR172) P-PCI.

***Driving Techniques: For the Professional & Non-Professional.** Anthony J. Scotti. (Illus.). 208p. (Orig.). 1995. per., pap. 18.95 (*0-9643844-0-X*) Photograph Pub.

Driving the Body Back. Mary Swander. LC 85-45603. (Poetry Ser.: No. 23). 81p. 1986. 14.95 (*0-394-55008-0*) Knopf.

Driving the Drunk off the Road: A Handbook for Action. Sandy Golden. LC 83-8982. 192p. 1983. pap. 7.95 (*0-914757-01-6*) Quince Mill Bks.

Driving the Horse in Harness: Training & Technique for Pleasure & Performance. Charles W. Kellogg. LC 77-92777. (Illus.). 1979. pap. 7.95 (*0-8289-0333-6*) Viking Penguin.

Driving the Milford Blacktop. Robert A. Tremmel. LC 91-17689. 64p. (Orig.). 1991. pap. 7.25 (*0-933532-80-6*) BkMk.

Driving the Pacific Coast: California: Scenic Driving Tours along the Pacific Coast Highway. 2nd ed. Kenn Oberrecht. LC 94-854. (Illus.). 272p. (Orig.). 1994. pap. 12.95 (*1-56440-400-5*) Globe Pequot.

Driving the Pacific Coast: Oregon & Washington: Scenic Driving Tours along Pacific Coastal Highways. 2nd ed. Kenn Oberrecht. LC 93-31814. (Voyager Book Ser.). (Illus.). 256p. 1993. pap. 12.95 (*1-56440-271-1*) Globe Pequot.

Driving the Productivity Machine: Producton Planning & Control in Japan. APICS Repetitive Manufacturing Group. Ed. by Robert W. Hall. LC 81-68513. 62p. 1981. pap. 12.00 (*0-935406-02-6*) Am Prod & Inventory.

Driving Through Fidelity. Gerry Sloan. (Paper Moon Bks.). 30p. (Orig.). 1992. pap. 5.00 (*1-884438-00-8*) Epiphany AR.

Driving Through Nebraska. Marcia G. Kester. Ed. by Michael Hall et al. (Chapbook Ser.: Vol. 1). (Illus.). 24p. (Orig.). 1991. pap. 8.00 (*0-939121-00-X*) Cooper Hse.

Driving to Biloxi. Poems. Edgar Simmons. LC 68-8943. viii, 56p. 1968. text ed. 13.95 (*0-8071-0742-5*) La State U Pr.

Driving to Greenland. Peter Stark. 256p. 1994. 22.95 (*1-55821-320-1*) Lyons & Burford.

Driving to Here. David James. (Orig.). 1979. pap. 4.95 (*0-930090-10-1*) Applezaba.

Driving to Vegas: New & Selected Poems 1969-87. Kirk Robertson. (Sun Lizard, Desert Southwest Bk.). 296p. (Orig.). 1989. 25.00 (*0-933313-09-8*); pap. 14.95 (*0-933313-10-1*) SUN Gemini Pr.

Driving Too Fast. Dorothy Porter. 1989. pap. 11.95 (*0-7022-2222-4*, Pub. by Univ Queensland Pr AT) Intl Spec Bk.

An Asterisk (*) at the beginning of an entry indicates that the title is appearing in BIP for the first time.

Driving Tour of the Palos Verdes Peninsula. Barbara L. Dye. (Illus.). 136p. (Orig.). 1989. pap. 7.95 (*0-9620050-0-2*) Point Vicente.

***Driving Tour of the Palos Verdes Peninsula.** 2nd ed. (Illus.). 152p. Date not set. pap. 9.95 (*0-9634861-0-1*) Blikidy Pr.

Driving Tours Florida. (Driving Tours Ser.). (Illus.). 120p. 1992. pap. 19.00 (*0-13-220435-5*, P-H Travel) P-H Gen Ref & Trav.

Driving Tours Germany. (Driving Tours Ser.). (Illus.). 120p. 1992. pap. 19.00 (*0-13-220427-4*, P-H Travel) P-H Gen Ref & Trav.

Driving Tours Ireland. (Driving Tours Ser.). (Illus.). 120p. 1992. pap. 19.00 (*0-13-220443-6*, P-H Travel) P-H Gen Ref & Trav.

Driving Tours Scotland. (Driving Tours Ser.). (Illus.). 120p. 1992. pap. 19.00 (*0-13-220401-0*, P-H Travel) P-H Gen Ref & Trav.

Driving Tours Spain. (Driving Tours Ser.). (Illus.). 120p. 1992. pap. 19.00 (*0-13-220419-3*, P-H Travel) P-H Gen Ref & Trav.

***Driving under the Affluence.** Julia Phillips. Date not set. 24.00 (*0-06-017304-1*) HarpC.

Driving under the Cardboard Pines: And Other Stories. Colleen J. McElroy. 224p. (Orig.). 1989. pap. 10.95 (*0-88739-073-0*) Creat Arts Bk.

Driving Your Own Karma: Swami Beyondananda's Tour Guide to Enlightenment. Swami Beyondananda. 128p. (Orig.). 1989. pap. 7.95 (*0-89281-253-2*, Destiny Bks) Inner Tradit.

Drizzle & Other Korean Short Stories. Hwang Sun-Won & Yi Pom-son. Tr. by Kim Chong-un et al. (Modern Korean Short Stories Ser.: No. 2). viii, 191p. 1983. 20.00 (*0-89209-203-3*) Pace Intl Res.

Drizzle of Words. Kidship Associates Staff. (Illus.). 109p. 1993. pap. text ed. 2.50 (*1-878742-04-3*) Kidship Assoc.

Drogas y la Juventud: Drugs & Youth. Thelma Hollowaty. (SPA.). 8.95 (*84-7645-340-X*, 223452, Pub. by Edit Clie SP) TSELF.

Drogas y Nuestro Mundo (Drugs & Our World) (Drug-Free Kids Ser.). (Illus.). 48p. (SPA.). (J). (ps-3). 1991. lib. bdg. 16.88 (*0-516-37371-4*) Childrens.

Drogen & Alkohol. Ed. by D. Ladewig. (Illus.). xii, 220p. 1980. pap. 26.50 (*3-8055-1624-X*) S Karger.

Drogen & Alkohol Series, Vol. 3: Folgestudien und Therapieabbruch. Ed. by D. Ladewig. (Illus.). vi, 174p. (GER.). 1984. pap. 46.50 (*3-8055-3874-X*) S Karger.

Drogen und Drogenhandel Im Altertum. Alfred Schmidt. Ed. by Moses Finley. LC 79-5005. (Ancient Economic History Ser.). (Illus.). (GER.). 1979. reprint ed. lib. bdg. 17.95 (*0-405-12394-9*) Ayer.

Drogengefaehrdung als Zeiterscheinung. Ed. by K. Heymann. (Psychologische Praxis Ser.: No. 47). 64p. 1973. pap. 14.50 (*3-8055-1556-1*) S Karger.

Drogenkunde, 1. 8th ed. Heinz A. Hoppe. (C). 1975. 250.00 (*3-11-003849-8*) De Gruyter.

Drogenkunde, Vol. 2. 8th ed. Heinz A. Hoppe. (C). 1977. 100.00 (*3-11-006660-2*) De Gruyter.

Drogenpraevention: der Strafrechtliche Beitrag. H. U. Stoos. (Sozialmedizinische und Paedagogische Jugendkunde Ser.: Vol. 15). (Illus.). (GER.). 1978. 19.25 (*3-8055-2874-4*) S Karger.

Drohende Untergang: "Schopfung" In Mythos und Ritual Im Alten Orient und In Griechenland Am Beispiel der Odysee und Des Ezechielbuches. Christoph Auffarth. (Religionsgeschichtliche Versuche und Vorarbeiten Ser.: Vol. 39). xviii, 655p. (GER.). 1991. lib. bdg. 175.40 (*3-11-012640-0*) De Gruyter.

Drohung und Verheissung: Exegetische Untersuchungen zur Eschatologie bei den Apostolischen Vaetern. Hans Lohmann. (Beiheft zur Zeitschrift fuer die Neuetestamentliche Wissenschaft Ser.: No. 55). ix, 266p. (GER.). (C). 1989. lib. bdg. 79.25x (*3-11-012018-6*) De Gruyter.

Droit & Criminologie: Law & Criminology, Lectures & Vocabulary. Conrad J. Schmitt. (FRE.). 1994. pap. text ed. 11.95 (*0-07-056808-1*) McGraw.

Droit de l'Eglise et Vie Sociale au Moyen Age. Jean Gaudemet. (Collected Studies: No. CS300). 348p. (FRE & ITA.). (C). 1989. reprint ed. text ed. 99.50 (*0-86078-248-4*, Pub. by Variorum UK) Ashgate Pub Co.

Droit des Assurances de Personnes au Canada. Harriett E. Jones. (FLMI Insurance Education Program Ser.). 500p. (FRE.). (C). 1993. text ed. 110.00 (*0-939921-45-6*) LOMA.

***Droit des Femmes: Dictionnaire Juridique.** Francoise Dekeuwer-Defossez. 458p. (FRE.). 1985. pap. 65.00 (*0-7859-7842-9*, 2247005683) Fr & Eur.

Droit Des Fiefs Dans la Coutume De Hainaut Au Moyen Age. Noel Didier. LC 80-2032. reprint ed. 29.50 (*0-404-18561-4*) AMS Pr.

Droit et Coutume en France aux XIIe et XIIIe Siecles. Andre Gouron. (Collected Studies: No. CS 222). 352p. 1993. 99.50 (*0-86078-356-1*, Pub. by Variorum UK) Ashgate Pub Co.

Droit et Societe dans la Grece Ancienne. Louis Garnet. Ed. by Gregory Vlastos. LC 78-19346. (Morals & Law in Ancient Greece Ser.). (FRE & GRE.). 1979. reprint ed. lib. bdg. 27.95 (*0-405-11543-1*) Ayer.

Droit Imperial et Traditions Locales dans l'Egypte Romaine. Joseph M. Modrezejewsci. (Collected Studies: No. 321). 336p. 1990. text ed. 95.00 (*0-86078-270-0*, Pub. by Variorum UK) Ashgate Pub Co.

Droit Romain en Dacie. Valeriu Sotropa. (Studia Amstelodamensia ad Epigraphicam, Ius Antiquum et Papyrologicam Pertinentia: Vol. 30). 294p. 1990. 102.00 (*90-5063-040-5*, Pub. by Gieben NE) Benjamins North Am.

Droit Savant au Moyen Age et sa Vulgarisation. Robert Feenstra. (Collected Studies: No. CS236). 330p. (ENG, FRE & GER.). (C). 1986. reprint ed. text ed. 95.00 (*0-86078-184-4*, Pub. by Variorum UK) Ashgate Pub Co.

Droles De Journal. Carl Rakosi. LC 80-28307. 20p. (Orig.). 1981. 30.00 (*0-915124-43-2*); pap. 5.00 (*0-915124-44-0*) Coffee Hse.

Droll Science: Being a Treasury of Whimsical Characters, Laboratory Levity, & Scholarly Follies. Robert L. Weber. LC 87-22642. (Illus.). 352p. 1987. 24.50 (*0-89603-112-8*) Humana.

Droll Troll: A View from under the Bridge. Tom McCann. (Illus.). 112p. 1994. pap. 10.00 (*0-943389-15-1*) Snow Lion-SLG Bks.

Droning Shaman: Poems. Nora M. Dauenhauer. LC 88-21079. (Orig.). 1988. pap. 8.95 (*0-938975-18-8*) Black Current.

Dronitz. James A. Taylor. (Illus.). 51p. (Orig.). 1985. pap. 4.95 (*0-9615675-0-3*) J A Taylor.

Drood Review's Mystery Yearbook, 1990. Ed. by Jim Huang. 144p. (Orig.). 1990. pap. 14.00 (*0-9625804-1-4*) Crum Creek Pr.

Drood Review's Mystery Yearbook, 1991. Ed. by Jim Huang. 160p. (Orig.). 1991. pap. 15.00 (*0-9625804-2-2*) Crum Creek Pr.

Drood Review's Mystery Yearbook, 1992. Ed. by Jim Huang. 176p. (Orig.). 1992. pap. 15.00 (*0-9625804-4-9*) Crum Creek Pr.

Drop a Dime on Your Kid: A Parent's Guide to Drug Abuse. Alfred E. Goehringer, Jr. 1977. pap. 1.50 (*0-9601704-1-3*) Goehringer & Sons.

***Drop Dead Gorgeous: (Dangerous Man)** Patricia Rosemoor. (Intrigue Ser.). 1995. mass mkt. 3.50 (*0-373-22317-X*, 1-22317-1) Harlequin Bks.

Drop Everything, It's D. E. A. R. Time! Ann McGovern. (J). (ps-3). 1993. pap. 3.95 (*0-590-45802-7*) Scholastic Inc.

Drop Forging Die Sinking. Joseph V. Woodworth. 1986. reprint ed. pap. 13.95 (*0-917914-41-4*) Lindsay Pubns.

Drop Hammer. Emanuel Fried. 128p. (C). 1977. pap. 4.50 (*0-9603888-1-8*) Labor Arts.

Drop Him Till He Dies: The Twisted Tragedy of Immigrant Homesteader Thomas Egan. C. John Egan, Jr. Ed. by Gayle Emmel & Ronald Robinson. LC 94-71243. (Illus.). 160p. 1994. pap. 12.95 (*0-944287-12-3*) Ex Machina.

Drop-in Bride. Margaret St. George. (American Romance Ser.). 1994. mass mkt. 3.50 (*0-373-16545-5*, 1-16545-5) Harlequin Bks.

Drop of Blood. Paul Showers. LC 67-23672. (Let's-Read-&-Find-Out Science Bk.). (Illus.). (J). (gr. k-3). 1967. lib. bdg. 12.89 (*0-690-24526-2*, Crowell Jr Bks) HarpC Child Bks.

Drop of Blood. rev. ed. Paul Showers. LC 85-43021. (Trophy Let's-Read-&-Find-Out Bk.). (Illus.). 32p. (J). (gr. k-4). 1989. pap. 4.95 (*0-06-445090-2*, Trophy) HarpC Child Bks.

Drop of Blood. rev. ed. Paul Showers. LC 88-3623. (Let's-Read-&-Find-Out Science Bk.). (Illus.). 32p. (J). (gr. k-4). 1989. lib. bdg. 14.89 (*0-690-04717-7*, Crowell Jr Bks) HarpC Child Bks.

Drop of Honey. Djemma Bider. (Illus.). (J). (ps-4). 1989. pap. 14.95 (*0-671-66265-1*, S&S Bks Young Read) S&S Childrens.

Drop of Murder. Benjamin Joshua. 352p. (Orig.). 1990. pap. 3.50 (*0-380-75794-X*) Avon.

***Drop of Rain.** Wong H. Yee. LC 94-28676. (J). 1995. 13.95 (*0-395-71549-0*) HM.

Drop-Off: A John Rodrigue Novel. Ken Grissom. 1989. pap. 3.95 (*0-312-91616-7*) St Martin.

Drop-Out of Students after the Second Year see Language Classroom

Drop Shipping As a Marketing Function: A Handbook of Methods & Policies. Nicholas T. Scheel. LC 89-24324. 200p. 1990. text ed. 55.00 (*0-89930-532-6*, SLY/, Quorum Bks) Greenwood.

Drop That Became the Sea: Selected Lyric Poetry of Yunus Emre. Tr. by Edmund Helminski. 80p. 1989. pap. 8.00 (*0-939660-30-X*) Threshold VT.

Drop the Rock! Removing Character Defects. Bill Pittman & Todd Weber. LC 92-4263. 128p. (Orig.). 1993. pap. 7.95 (*0-934125-27-9*) Hazelden.

Drop Too Many: Airborne Operations in World War II, a Memoir. John Frost. (Illus.). 288p. 1994. reprint ed. 39.50 (*0-85052-391-5*, Pub. by L Cooper Bks UK) Trans-Atl Phila.

***Drop Us a Line...Sucker! The Prank Letters of James & Stuart Wade.** James Wade, 3rd & Stuart Wade. 160p. 1995. pap. 8.95 (*0-7867-0205-2*) Carroll & Graf.

Drop-Weight Test for Determination of Nil-Ductility Transition Temperature: User's Experience with ASTM Method E 208. Ed. by John M. Holt & P. P. Puzak. LC 86-25913. (Special Technical Publication Ser.: No. 919). (Illus.). 182p. 1986. text ed. 37.00 (*0-8031-0487-1*, 04-919000-23) ASTM.

***Drop Zone.** Robert Tine. 192p. (Orig.). 1995. pap. text ed. 4.99 (*0-515-11645-9*) Jove Pubns.

Drop Zone Flashes of the British Airborne Forces. Charles A. Edwards et al. (Illus.). 56p. (Orig.). 1993. pap. 7.95 (*0-943349-02-8*) Pass in Review.

Droplet Separation. Ed. by Armin Burkholz. LC 89-37417. 246p. 1989. text ed. 120.00 (*0-89573-879-1*) VCH Pubs.

Dropout Kid. Alexander Cowie. 250p. 1992. 25.00 (*0-89733-381-0*) Academy Chi Pubs.

***Dropout Prevention Education: A Guidebook for Administrators.** Hester. 1990. 15.00 (*0-614-04727-7*) Royal Fireworks.

Dropout Prevention Handbook: A Guide for Administrators, Counselors & Teachers. Nancy Myll. 224p. 1988. text ed. 29.95 (*0-13-220799-0*) P-H.

Dropout Prevention Handbook: Apprenticeships & Other Solutions. William Callison. LC 93-61848. 420p. 1993. pap. text ed. 29.00 (*1-56676-063-1*) Technomic.

Dropout Rates in the U. S. 1994. lib. bdg. 250.00 (*0-8490-5775-2*) Gordon Pr.

***Dropout Rates in the U. S., 1992.** Marilyn M. McMilen et al. (Illus.). 168p. (Orig.). (C). 1994. pap. text ed. 45.00x (*0-7881-0892-1*) Diane Pub.

Dropout Rates in the United States, 1988. (National Center for Education Statistics Ser.: No. 89-609). (Illus.). 105p. (Orig.). 1989. per., pap. 5.00 (*0-16-006767-7*, S/N 065-000-003) USGPO.

Dropout Rates in the United States, 1989. Phillip Kaufman & Mary J. Frase. (Illus.). 80p. 1990. pap. 4.25 (*0-16-025968-1*, S/N 065-000-00424-1) USGPO.

Dropouts: Who Drops Out & Why - & the Recommended Action. Robert F. Kronick & Charles H. Hargis. (Illus.). 162p. 1990. pap. 29.95 (*0-398-05658-7*) C C Thomas.

Dropouts from Schools: Issues, Dilemmas & Solutions. Ed. by Lois Weis et al. LC 88-34932. (SUNY Series, Frontiers in Education). 238p. 1989. 59.50 (*0-7914-0108-1*); pap. 19.95 (*0-7914-0109-X*) State U NY Pr.

Dropouts in America: Enough Is Known for Action. 69p. 1987. 8.00 (*0-937846-87-2*) Inst Educ Lead.

Dropouts in the U. S. (Illus.). 101p. (Orig.). (C). 1994. pap. text ed. 40.00 (*0-7881-0289-3*) Diane Pub.

Dropped Stitches in Tennessee History: Little Known Facts in the Earliest History of Tennessee. John Allison. (Illus.). 208p. 1991. reprint ed. 17.95 (*0-932807-52-6*) Overmountain Pr.

***Droppin' Science: Critical Essays on Rap Music & Hip Hop Culture.** Ed. by William E. Perkins. LC 95-1532. (Critical Perspectives on the Past Ser.). (Illus.). 352p. (C). 1995. lib. bdg. 49.95 (*1-56639-361-2*); pap. text ed. 18.95 (*1-56639-362-0*) Temple U Pr.

Dropping Ashes on the Buddha: The Teachings of Zen Master Seung Sahn. Ed. & Tr. by Stephen Mitchell. 256p. (Orig.). 1987. pap. 12.00 (*0-8021-3052-6*) Grove-Atltic.

Dropping in on Egypt. Lewis K. Parker. LC 93-47098. (Dropping in On Ser.). (J). 1994. write for info. (*1-55916-004-7*) Rourke Bk Co.

Dropping in on Gravity: An Integrated Activity Unit. Bev McKay. (Illus.). 32p. 1993. pap. text ed. 4.95 (*0-86530-228-6*) Incentive Pubns.

Dropping in on Mexico. Lewis Parker. LC 93-42777. (J). 1994. write for info. (*1-55916-001-2*) Rourke Bk Co.

***Dropping Out.** Victoria Sherrow. (Life Issues Ser.). 96p. (J). (gr. 3-5). 1995. lib. bdg. write for info. (*0-7614-0018-4*, Benchmark NY) Marshall Cavendish.

Dropping Out: Issues & Answers. James A. Farmer & Yolanda Payne. 104p. (C). 1992. text ed. 28.95x (*0-398-05812-1*) C C Thomas.

Dropping Out: Problem or Symptom? Jerald G. Bachman et al. LC 72-179807. (Youth in Transition Ser.: No. 3). (Illus.). 264p. reprint ed. pap. 75.30 (*0-685-23940-3*, 2031492) Bks Demand.

Dropping Out of School. Debra Goldentyer. LC 93-14251. (Teen Hotline Ser.). (Illus.). 80p. (J). (gr. 6-9). 1993. lib. bdg. 22.80 (*0-8114-3526-1*) Raintree Steck-V.

Dropping out or Hanging in. Duane Brown. 1990. pap. 7.95 (*0-8442-8687-7*, Natl Textbk) NTC Pub Grp.

Dropping the Bow: Poems from Ancient India. Tr. by Andrew Schelling. LC 90-86378. (International Ser.). 96p. (Orig.). 1991. pap. 10.00 (*0-913089-18-4*) Broken Moon.

Dropping Your Guard. Swindoll. 197p. 1990. pap. write for info. (*0-8499-3213-0*) Word Inc.

***Dropping Your Guard.** Swindoll. 1986. pap. 4.99 (*0-8499-8210-3*) Word Inc.

Dropping Your Guard. Charles Swindoll. 197p. 1987. 8.99 (*0-8499-4178-4*) Word Inc.

Drops & Bubbles. Ed. by Taylor Wang. LC 89-46360. (AIP Conference Proceedings Ser.: No. 197). 560p. 1989. lib. bdg. 85.00 (*0-88318-392-7*) Am Inst Physics.

Drops from the Honeycomb. James A. Stewart. 1964. 6.99 (*1-56632-050-X*); pap. 4.99 (*1-56632-051-8*) Revival Lit.

Drops from the Living Water: Orthodox Homilies on the Sunday Gospel Readings. Augoustinos N. Kantiotes. Tr. by Asterios Gerostergios. LC 91-76722. 210p. 1991. 17.50 (*0-914744-91-7*) Inst Byzantine.

Dropshot. Jack M. Bickham. 1991. mass mkt. 4.50 (*0-8125-0052-0*) Tor Bks.

***Dropsie Avenue: The Neighborhood.** Will Eisner. LC 95-13159. 1995. write for info. (*0-87816-349-2*); pap. write for info. (*0-87816-348-4*) Kitchen Sink.

***Dropsie Avenue: The Neighborhood.** deluxe ed. Will Eisner. LC 95-13159. 1995. write for info. (*0-87816-350-6*) Kitchen Sink.

Drosophila: A Laboratory Handbook & a Laboratory Manual. Michael Ashburner. (Illus.). 1989. 180.00 (*0-87969-321-5*); 60.00 (*0-87969-322-3*) Cold Spring Harbor.

Drosophila Ananassae: Genetical & Biological Aspects. Ed. by Y. N. Tobari. (Illus.). xvi, 290p. 1993. 158.50 (*3-8055-5774-4*) S Karger.

Drosophila Genetics: A Practical Course. U. Graf et al. (Illus.). x, 239p. 1992. pap. 40.00 (*0-387-54327-9*) Spr-Verlag.

Drosophila Genome Map: A Practical Guide. Daniel L. Hartl & Elena R. Lozovskaya. (Medical Intelligence Unit Ser.). 242p. 1995. 59.00 (*1-57059-101-6*) R G Landes.

Drosophila Guide: Introduction to the Genetics & Cytology of Drosophila Melanogaster. 9th ed. M. Demerc & B. P. Kaufmann. (Illus.). 50p. 1986. pap. 2.50 (*0-87279-950-6*) Carnegie Inst.

Drosophila Inversion Polymorphism. Krimbas. 1992. 173.00 (*0-8493-6547-3*, QL537) CRC Pr.

***Drosophila Retrotransposons.** Ed. by Irina R. Arkhipova et al. LC 94-44104. (Molecular Biology Intelligence Unit Ser.). 136p. 1995. 59.00 (*1-57059-192-X*) R G Landes.

Drought! Ralph Hayes. 1981. pap. 2.95 (*0-89083-774-0*) Zebra.

Drought. Brian Knapp. LC 89-19730. (World Disasters Ser.). (Illus.). 48p. (J). (gr. 5-9). 1990. lib. bdg. 22.80 (*0-8114-2376-X*) Raintree Steck-V.

Drought. Christopher Lampton. LC 91-18053. (Disaster! Ser.). (Illus.). 64p. (J). (gr. 4-6). 1992. lib. bdg. 13.90 (*1-56294-125-9*) Millbrook Pr.

Drought. Christopher Lampton. LC 91-18053. 1992. pap. 5.95 (*1-878841-91-2*) Millbrook Pr.

Drought. Gail B. Stewart. LC 90-36293. (Earth Alert Ser.). (Illus.). 48p. (J). (gr. 6). 1990. text ed. 12.95 (*0-89686-544-4*, Crstwood Hse) Silver Burdett Pr.

Drought: A Disaster Book. Christopher Lampton. (J). (gr. 4-7). 1992. pap. 5.92 (*0-395-62465-7*) HM.

Drought: The Past, Present, & Future Enemy. Edward F. Dolan. LC 89-25016. (YA). (gr. 9-12). 1990. lib. bdg. 14.77 (*0-531-10900-3*) Watts.

Drought & Natural Resource Management in the United States: Impacts & Implications of the 1987-1989 Drought. William E. Riebsame et al. 174p. (C). 1990. pap. text ed. 51.00 (*0-8133-8026-X*) Westview.

Drought & Water Supply: Implications of the Massachusetts Experience for Municipal Planning. Clifford S. Russell et al. LC 72-123861. 232p. 1970. 21.00 (*0-8018-1183-X*) Resources Future.

Drought Assessment, Management, & Planning: Theory & Case Studies. Ed. by Donald A. Wilhite. LC 93-22111. (Natural Resource Management & Policy Ser.). 320p. 1993. lib. bdg. 99.95 (*0-7923-9337-6*) Kluwer Ac.

Drought Busters: Thirty Easy Ways to Save Water...& Money. William Slater & Peter Orzechowski. (Illus.). 96p. (Orig.). 1991. pap. 5.95 (*1-879326-14-0*) Living Planet Pr.

Drought Follows the Plow: Cultivating Marginal Areas. Michael H. Glantz. LC 94-4148. (Illus.). 240p. (C). 1994. 39.95 (*0-521-44252-4*); pap. 19.95 (*0-521-47721-2*) Cambridge U Pr.

Drought in Africa Two - Secheresse en Afrique. rev. ed. Ed. by David Dalby et al. LC 78-310180. (African Environment: Special Report Ser.: No. 6). 208p. reprint ed. pap. 59.30 (*0-8357-6950-X*, 2039009) Bks Demand.

Drought in the Great Plains: Research on Impacts & Strategies. Ed. by Norman J. Rosenberg. LC 80-51532. 1980. 25.00 (*0-918334-34-9*) WRP.

Drought, Its Causes & Effects. Ivan R. Tannehill. LC 47-2193. 277p. reprint ed. pap. 79.00 (*0-317-07873-9*, 2000594) Bks Demand.

Drought Management & Its Impact on Public Water Systems: Report on a Colloquium Sponsored by the Water Science & Technology Board, September 5, 1985. Colloquium on Drought Management & Its Impact on Public Water Systems Staff. 135p. reprint ed. pap. 38.50 (*0-7837-1266-9*, 2041405) Bks Demand.

Drought or Deluge: Man in the Cooper's Creek Region. Helen M. Tolcher. 280p. 1986. 27.95 (*0-522-84305-0*) Intl Spec Bk.

Drought Planning & Water Efficiency Implications in Water Resources Management. Harald D. Frederiksen. LC 92-29531. (Technical Paper Ser.: No. 185). 45p. 1992. 6.95 (*0-8213-2220-6*, 12220) World Bank.

Drought, Policy & Politics in India: The Need for a Long-Term Perspective. Kuldeep Mathur & Niraja G. Jayal. (Illus.). 140p. (C). 1993. text ed. 26.00 (*0-8039-9122-3*) Sage.

Drought Research Needs. Ed. by V. Yevjevich et al. LC 78-64652. 1978. 25.00 (*0-918334-26-8*) WRP.

Drought Resistance in Cereals. Ed. by F. W. Baker. 240p. 1989. text ed. 55.50 (*0-85198-641-2*) CAB Intl.

Drought Resistance in Crops with Emphasis on Rice. International Rice Research Institute Staff. (Illus.). 420p. 1982. pap. 27.00 (*0-8138-0056-0*) Iowa St U Pr.

Drought Strategy. M. A. Quraishi. (C). 1989. 21.50 (*81-7018-562-9*, Pub. by BR Pub II) S Asia.

Drought Tolerance in Winter Cereals: Proceedings of an International Workshop, 27-31, October 1985, Capri, Italy. Ed. by J. P. Srivastava et al. LC 87-16139. 300p. 1988. text ed. 175.00 (*0-471-91650-1*) Wiley.

Drought-Tolerant Plants. Jane Taylor. LC 92-40097. 1993. 30.00 (*0-671-86500-5*, P-H Gardening) P-H Gen Ref & Trav.

Drove Rider. Orlando Rigoni. 1992. 13.95 (*0-7451-4543-4*, Gunsmoke) Chivers N Amer.

Drover. Bill Granger. 272p. 1992. mass mkt. 4.99 (*0-380-71210-5*) Avon.

Drover: A Novel. Bill Granger. 288p. 1991. 20.00 (*0-688-09856-8*) Morrow.

***Drover & the Designated Hitter.** Bill Granger. 240p. 1995. mass mkt. 4.99 (*0-380-71909-6*) Avon.

Drover & the Designated Hitter: The Third Drover Novel. Bill Granger. LC 93-43217. 1994. 20.00 (*0-688-11884-4*) Morrow.

Drover & the Zebras. Bill Granger. 240p. 1993. mass mkt. 4.99 (*0-380-71211-3*) Avon.

Drover & the Zebras. large type ed. Bill Granger. LC 92-36980. 461p. 1993. reprint ed. lib. bdg. 17.95 (*1-56054-590-9*) Thorndike Pr.

Drover & the Zebras: A Novel. Bill Granger. 1992. 20.00 (*0-688-09857-6*) Morrow.

Drover's Wife & Other Stories. Murray Bail. (Paperbacks Ser.). Orig. Title: Contemporary Portraits. 183p. 1985. pap. 14.95 (*0-7022-1818-9*, Pub. by Univ Queensland Pr AT) Intl Spec Bk.

Drow of Underdark. Ed Greenwood. (Advanced Dungeons & Dragons Ser.). (Illus.). 1991. FOR2. pap. 15.00 (*1-56076-132-6*) TSR Inc.

D

An Asterisk (*) at the beginning of an entry indicates that the title is appearing in BIP for the first time.

*__Drown All the Dogs.__ Thomas Adcock. Ed. by Jane Chelius. 368p. 1995. mass mkt. 5.99 (*0-671-88329-1*) PB.

Drown Radio-Vision & Homo-Vibra Ray Instruments & Their Use. Ruth B. Drown. 96p. 1994. reprint ed. spiral bd. 24.75 (*0-7873-1015-8*) Mokelumne.

*__Drowned.__ Elizabeth Levy. 208p. (J). (gr. 5-9). 1995. 16.95 (*0-7868-0135-2*) Hyprn Child.

Drowned Ammet. Diana W. Jones. LC 94-1513. (Dalemark Quartet Ser.: Bk. II). 320p. (YA). (gr. 7 up). 1995. 15.00 (*0-688-13361-4*) Greenwillow.

Drowned Ammet. Diana W. Jones. Ed. by Amy Cohn. LC 94-1513. (Dalemark Quartet Ser.). (J). 1995. pap. 4.95 (*0-688-13400-9*) Morrow.

Drowned & Saved. Primo Levi. Tr. by Raymond Rosenthal. (International Ser.). 1989. pap. 10.00 (*0-679-72186-X*, Vin) Random.

Drowned Hopes. Donald E. Westlake. 1990. 18.95 (*0-89296-178-3*) Mysterious Pr.

Drowned Hopes. Donald E. Westlake. 464p. 1991. mass mkt. 5.99 (*0-446-40006-8*, Mysterious Paperbk) Warner Bks.

Drowned Man to the Fish. Robert Peters. (Illus.). (Orig.). 1978. pap. 3.00 (*0-89823-002-0*) New Rivers Pr.

Drowned Rat. large type ed. Elizabeth X. Ferrars. 1977. 12.00 (*0-7089-0053-4*) Ulverscroft.

Drowned River. Thomas Lux. 68p. (C). 1993. reprint ed. pap. 7.00 (*0-938566-60-1*) Adastra Pr.

Drowned River: New Poems. Thomas Lux. 80p. 1990. pap. 8.95 (*0-685-29459-5*) HM.

Drowned Valley: The Piscataqua River Basin. John Adams. LC 75-40868. (Illus.). 294p. 1976. 35.00 (*0-87451-123-2*) U Pr of New Eng.

Drowned World. J. G. Ballard. 175p. 1987. pap. 3.95 (*0-88184-324-5*) Carroll & Graf.

Drowning: Growing up in the Third Reich. Gerhard Durlacher. 1994. pap. 12.99 (*1-85242-282-3*) Serpents Tail.

*__Drowning in the Sea of Love: Essays on Music.__ Al Young. LC 94-33861. 1995. 22.00 (*0-88001-388-5*) Ecco Pr.

Drowning Man is Never Tall Enough. Patrick Lawler. LC 89-4823. (Contemporary Poetry Ser.). 104p. 1990. pap. 7.95 (*0-8203-1158-8*) U of Ga Pr.

Drowning Nets. large type ed. Bill Knox. 392p. 1993. 21.95 (*0-7505-0427-7*) Ulverscroft.

Drowning of a Goldfish. Lidmila Sovakova. LC 89-62633. 152p. 1990. 22.00 (*0-932966-95-0*) Permanent Pr.

Drowning of Stephan Jones. Bette Greene. (YA). 1992. mass mkt. 3.99 (*0-553-29793-7*) Bantam.

Drowning Season. Alice Hoffman. 400p. 1993. pap. 4.99 (*0-451-17815-7*, Sig) NAL-Dutton.

Drowning Season. Alice Hoffman. 1989. pap. 9.95 (*0-452-26302-6*, Plume) NAL-Dutton.

*__Drowning the Hullaballoo Blues.__ Michael O'Dwyer. 256p. (Orig.). 1995. pap. 11.99 (*1-85594-151-1*) InBook.

Drowning the National Heritage: Climate Change & Coastal Biodiversity in the United States. large type ed. Walter V. Reid & Mark C. Trexler. 48p. 1991. Large format. pap. 14.95 (*0-915825-62-7*, REDNP) World Resources Inst.

Drownproofing: A New Technique for Water Safety. F. Lanoue. 1978. pap. 3.95 (*0-685-03844-0*) P-H.

Drownt Boy: An Ozark Tale. Art Homer. 168p. 1994. 19.95 (*0-8262-0981-5*) U of Mo Pr.

Drowsy. John A. Mitchell. LC 74-16512. (Science Fiction Ser.). (Illus.). 316p. 1975. reprint ed. 25.95 (*0-405-06306-7*) Ayer.

Droysen & Prussian School of History. Robert Southard. LC 94-16878. 272p. 1995. lib. bdg. 39.95x (*0-8131-1884-0*) U Pr of Ky.

Drozdovtsy V Ogne (Drozdovsky's Man under Fire) Kartiny Grazhdanskoi Voiny, 1918. A. V. Turkul. LC 90-61583. 277p. (Orig.). (RUS.). 1990. pap. 15.00 (*0-911971-53-X*) Effect Pub.

Druce. Mark Dunster. (Rin Ser.: Part 2). 1976. pap. 4.00 (*0-89642-015-9*) Linden Pubs.

Drucker Foundation Self-Assessment Tool for Nonprofit Management. Peter Drucker. 1993. pap. 79.95 (*1-55542-646-8*) Jossey-Bass.

Drucker in the Harvard Business Review, 1963-1989. Harvard Business Review Staff. (Help for the General Manager Ser.). 83p. 1991. pap. 19.95 (*0-87584-289-5*) Harvard Busn.

Drucker in the Harvard Business Review, 1963-1989. Harvard Business School Press Staff. 1991. pap. text ed. 19.95 (*0-07-103349-1*) McGraw.

Drudgery Divine: On the Comparison of Early Christianity's & the Religions of Late Antiquity. Jonathan Z. Smith. LC 90-38519. (Chicago Studies in the History of Judaism). 175p. 1990. 24.95 (*0-226-76362-5*) U Ch Pr.

Drudgery Divine: On the Comparison of Early Christianity's & the Religions of Late Antiquity. Jonathan Z. Smith. (Chicago Studies in the History of Judaism). xiv, 146p. 1994. pap. text ed. 11.95 (*0-226-76363-3*) U Ch Pr.

Drug Absorption Enhancement: Concepts, Possibilities, Limitations, & Trends. Ed. by A. G. De Boer. LC 93-38330. (Drug Targeting & Delivery Ser.: Vol. 3). 1994. text ed. 120.00 (*3-7186-5492-X*) Gordon & Breach.

Drug Abuse. Dennis B. Fradin. LC 87-33789. (New True Bks.). (Illus.). 48p. (J). (gr. k-4). 1988. lib. bdg. 12.90 (*0-516-01212-6*); pap. 4.95 (*0-516-41212-4*) Childrens.

Drug Abuse. Lynn Phillips. LC 93-44346. (Life Issues Ser.: Vol. 8). (J). 1994. 14.95 (*1-85435-617-8*) Marshall Cavendish.

Drug Abuse: An Introduction. 2nd ed. Howard Abadinsky. (Illus.). 400p. 1993. text ed. 37.95 (*0-8304-1344-8*); write for info. (*0-8304-1346-4*) Nelson-Hall.

Drug Abuse: Foundation for a Psychosocial Approach. George J. Hubba. Ed. by Seymour Eiseman & John Wingard. 290p. (Orig.). (C). 1984. pap. text ed. 24.95 (*0-89503-039-X*) Baywood Pub.

Drug Abuse: Guide for Pharmacists. Maddock. 1987. pap. 12.00 (*0-85369-190-8*, Pub. by Pharmaceutical Pr UK) Rittenhouse.

Drug Abuse: Investigation & Control. Paul Fuqua. LC 77-5809. (Illus.). 1977. text ed. 40.95 (*0-07-022665-2*) McGraw.

Drug Abuse: Its Natural History & the Effectiveness of Current Treatments. Marvin R. Burt. 362p. 1979. text ed. 39.95 (*0-87073-995-6*) Transaction Pubs.

Drug Abuse: Opposing Viewpoints. Ed. by Karin L. Swisher & Katie DeKoster. LC 93-12375. (YA). 1994. lib. bdg. 19.95 (*1-56510-060-3*); pap. 11.55 (*1-56510-059-X*) Greenhaven.

Drug Abuse: Proceedings of the International Conference. Ed. by Chris J. Zarafonetis. LC 72-154243. (Illus.). 629p. reprint ed. pap. 179.30 (*0-8357-9401-6*, 2014591) Bks Demand.

Drug Abuse: Why It Happens & How to Prevent It. Russel R. Allinson. LC 84-7369. 130p. (Orig.). 1984. pap. 9.95 (*0-9612990-1-0*) Valley Publishing.

Drug Abuse A-Z. Gilda Berger & Melvin Berger. LC 89-1512. 144p. (J). (gr. 6 up). 1990. lib. bdg. 18.95 (*0-89490-193-1*) Enslow Pubs.

Drug Abuse among Ethnic Minorities. 1991. lib. bdg. 74.00 (*0-8490-4366-2*) Gordon Pr.

*__Drug Abuse Among Minority Youth: Advances in Research & Methodology.__ 1995. lib. bdg. 299.99 (*0-8490-6526-7*) Gordon Pr.

*__Drug Abuse & Alcohol Misuse.__ AMS Distributors Staff & CTTS - Safety Products Staff. 48p. 1994. 2.95 (*0-7872-0234-7*) Kendall-Hunt.

Drug Abuse & Alcoholism: Current Critical Issues. Ed. by Sidney Cohen. LC 79-25648. 62p. 1981. pap. text ed. 9.95 (*0-917724-10-0*) Haworth Pr.

Drug Abuse & Drug Abuse Research. 1991. lib. bdg. 75.00 (*0-8490-4345-X*) Gordon Pr.

Drug Abuse & Drug Addiction. Ed. by Max Rosenbaum. 102p. (Orig.). 1973. text ed. 79.00 (*0-677-15710-X*) Gordon & Breach.

Drug Abuse & Misuse: Developing Educational Strategies in Partnership. Ed. by Roy Evans & Louis O'Connor. 96p. 1992. pap. 15.95 (*1-85346-231-4*, Pub. by D Fulton UK) Taylor & Francis.

Drug Abuse & Society: The Indian Scenario. Saroj Prashant. (Illus.). xii, 219p. 1993. 17.95 (*1-881338-34-7*) Nataraj Bks.

Drug Abuse & the American Adolescent. 1986. lib. bdg. 79.95 (*0-8490-3520-1*) Gordon Pr.

Drug Abuse & the Elderly: An Annotated Bibliography. Douglas H. Ruben. LC 83-20463. 269p. 1984. 25.00 (*0-8108-1677-6*) Scarecrow.

Drug Abuse & the Law Sourcebook, 2 vols., Set. Gerald F. Uelmen & Victor G. Haddox. LC 81-21711. (Criminal Law Ser.). 1983. ring bd. 240.00 (*0-87632-370-0*) Clark Boardman Callaghan.

Drug Abuse & Your Company. Susan Halpern. LC 79-184053. 160p. reprint ed. pap. 45.60 (*0-317-42077-1*, 2056086) Bks Demand.

Drug Abuse Bibliography for 1970. LC 79-116588. 1971. 10.00 (*0-87875-016-9*) Whitston Pub.

Drug Abuse Bibliography for 1971. LC 79-116588. 400p. 1972. 15.00 (*0-87875-025-8*) Whitston Pub.

Drug Abuse Bibliography for 1972. LC 79-116588. xii, 472p. 1974. 18.00 (*0-87875-046-0*) Whitston Pub.

Drug Abuse Bibliography for 1973. LC 79-116588. xli, 410p. 1975. 18.00 (*0-87875-057-6*) Whitston Pub.

Drug Abuse Bibliography for 1974. LC 79-116588. 450p. 1976. 18.00 (*0-87875-077-0*) Whitston Pub.

Drug Abuse Bibliography for 1976. LC 79-116588. (Annual Bibliography Ser.: No. 7). 383p. 1979. 22.50 (*0-87875-127-0*) Whitston Pub.

Drug Abuse Bibliography for 1977. LC 79-116588. 730p. 1980. 42.50 (*0-87875-176-9*) Whitston Pub.

Drug Abuse Bibliography for 1978-1979, Pt. I. 1863p. 1983. Part I. 50.00 (*0-87875-269-2*) Whitston Pub.

Drug Abuse Bibliography for 1978-1979, Pt. II. 1863p. 1983. Part II. 50.00 (*0-87875-270-6*) Whitston Pub.

Drug Abuse Bibliography for 1978-1979, Set. 1863p. 1983. 100.00 (*0-87875-222-6*) Whitston Pub.

Drug Abuse Bibliography for 1980, No. 10. LC 79-116588. xxxii, 689p. 1984. 48.50 (*0-87875-285-4*) Whitston Pub.

Drug Abuse Bibliography for 1981, 2 vols., Pt. I. LC 79-116588. 1600p. 1985. Part I. 50.00 (*0-87875-297-8*) Whitston Pub.

Drug Abuse Bibliography for 1981, 2 vols., Pt. II. LC 79-116588. 1600p. 1985. Part II. 50.00 (*0-87875-298-6*) Whitston Pub.

Drug Abuse Bibliography for 1981, 2 vols., Set. LC 79-116588. 1600p. 1985. 100.00 (*0-87875-283-8*) Whitston Pub.

Drug Abuse Bibliography for 1983, Vol. 14. LC 79-116588. xxiii, 478p. 1986. 45.00 (*0-87875-321-4*) Whitston Pub.

Drug Abuse Bibliography for 1984. LC 79-116588. 725p. 1987. 63.50 (*0-87875-322-2*) Whitston Pub.

Drug Abuse Bibliography for 1985. LC 79-116588. 700p. 1989. 68.50 (*0-87875-366-4*) Whitston Pub.

Drug Abuse Bibliography for 1986. LC 79-116588. 1200p. 1989. 120.00 (*0-87875-372-9*) Whitston Pub.

Drug Abuse Bibliography for 1987. LC 79-116588. 695p. 1991. 75.00 (*0-87875-406-7*) Whitston Pub.

Drug Abuse Bibliography for 1988. LC 79-116588. 790p. 1992. 85.00 (*0-87875-412-1*) Whitston Pub.

Drug Abuse Bibliography for 1989. xxxiv, 593p. 1992. 65.00 (*0-87875-434-2*) Whitston Pub.

Drug Abuse Bibliography for 1990. LC 79-116588. xxviii, 556p. 1993. 65.00 (*0-87875-439-3*) Whitston Pub.

Drug Abuse Bibliography for 1991. LC 79-116588. 600p. 1993. 65.00 (*0-87875-445-8*) Whitston Pub.

Drug Abuse Counselor. Jack Rudman. (Career Examination Ser.: C-2725). 1994. pap. 29.95 (*0-8373-2725-3*) Nat Learn.

Drug Abuse Education Group Leader. Jack Rudman. (Career Examination Ser.: C-1259). 1994. pap. 29.95 (*0-8373-1259-0*) Nat Learn.

Drug Abuse Educator. Jack Rudman. (Career Examination Ser.: C-1597). 1994. pap. 29.95 (*0-8373-1597-2*) Nat Learn.

Drug Abuse from the Family Perspective. 1986. lib. bdg. 79.95 (*0-8490-3511-2*) Gordon Pr.

Drug Abuse Group Worker. Jack Rudman. (Career Examination Ser.: C-1260). 1994. pap. 27.95 (*0-8373-1260-4*) Nat Learn.

*__Drug Abuse in America: An Historical Perspective.__ John Rippey. 36p. 1994. pap. 39.50 (*1-884937-12-8*) Manisses Communs.

Drug Abuse in Marin County. Eugene Lesser. 136p. (Orig.). 1985. pap. 8.95 (*0-912449-09-8*) Floating Island.

Drug Abuse in Society: A Reference Handbook. Geraldine Woods. (Contemporary World Issues Ser.). 269p. 1993. lib. bdg. 39.50 (*0-87436-720-4*) ABC-CLIO.

*__Drug Abuse in Sports: A Student Course Manual.__ 2nd ed. Mark J. Minelli. 99p. (C). 1995. pap. text ed. 9.80 (*0-87563-554-7*) Stipes.

Drug Abuse in Sports: An Annotated Bibliography. Betty Weiner. (CompuBibs Ser.: No. 10). 34p. 1985. pap. 10.00 (*0-914791-09-5*, 997) Vantage Info.

Drug Abuse in the Workplace: Prevention & Control, Proceedings of the Tenth Annual Arnold O. Beckman Conference in Clinical Chemistry. Ed. by Kura M. Dubowski. (Special Issue of Clinical Chemistry Ser.: Vol. 33, No. 11(B)). 112p. 1987. 10.00 (*0-915274-39-6*) Am Assn Clinical Chem.

Drug Abuse, Mental Health & Delinquency. 1986. lib. bdg. 79.95 (*0-8490-3499-X*) Gordon Pr.

Drug Abuse: Modern Trends, Issues, & Perspectives: Proceedings of the Second National Drug Abuse Conference, Inc., New Orleans, Louisiana, 1975. National Drug Abuse Conference, 2nd, 1975, New Orleans. Ed. by Arnold Schecter et al. LC 78-4091. 1254p. reprint ed. pap. 180.00 (*0-685-16089-0*, 2027089) Bks Demand.

Drug Abuse Prevention Program Leader Guide. Leah G. Davies. 56p. (J). 1993. pap. write for info. (*0-9621054-5-7*) Kelly Bear Pr.

*__Drug Abuse Prevention with Multiethnic Youth.__ Ed. by Gilbert J. Botvin et al. LC 95-13489. 368p. (C). 1995. 54.00 (*0-8039-5711-4*); pap. 25.95 (*0-8039-5712-2*) Sage.

Drug Abuse Rehabilitation Counselor. Jack Rudman. (Career Examination Ser.: C-2929). 1994. pap. 29.95 (*0-8373-2929-9*) Nat Learn.

Drug Abuse Secretarial Aide. Jack Rudman. (Career Examination Ser.: C-1261). 1994. pap. 23.95 (*0-8373-1261-2*) Nat Learn.

Drug Abuse Technician. Jack Rudman. (Career Examination Ser.: C-1405). 1994. pap. 27.95 (*0-8373-1405-4*) Nat Learn.

Drug Abuse Technician Trainee. Jack Rudman. (Career Examination Ser.: C-1406). 1994. pap. 23.95 (*0-8373-1406-2*) Nat Learn.

Drug Abuse Testing Business. BCC Staff. 151p. 1988. 1,950.00 (*0-89336-521-1*, C104) BCC.

Drug Abuse Treatment. Ed. by Ronald R. Watson. LC 92-1691. (Drug & Alcohol Abuse Reviews Ser.). (Illus.). 224p. 1992. 59.50 (*0-89603-233-7*) Humana.

Drug Abuse Treatment: A National Study of Effectiveness. Robert L. Hubbard et al. LC 89-4937. xix, 213p. 1991. reprint ed. 37.50 (*0-8078-1864-X*); reprint ed. pap. 14.95 (*0-8078-4313-X*) U of NC Pr.

Drug Abuse Treatment: The Implementation of Innovative Approaches. Ed. by Frank M. Tims et al. LC 94-11221. (Contributions in Criminology & Penology Ser.: No. 45). 280p. 1994. text ed. 65.00 (*0-313-28906-9*, Greenwood Pr) Greenwood.

Drug Abuse Treatment Client Characteristics. (Illus.). 105p. (Orig.). (C). 1994. pap. text ed. 30.00 (*0-7881-0433-0*) Diane Pub.

Drug Abuse Treatment Evaluation: Strategies, Progress, & Prospects. 1986. lib. bdg. 250.00 (*0-8490-3504-X*) Gordon Pr.

*__Drug Abuse Treatment in Prisons & Jails.__ 1995. lib. bdg. 253.95 (*0-8490-6812-6*) Gordon Pr.

Drug Abuse Treatment System: Prospects for Reform. John G. Haaga & Elizabeth A. McGlynn. LC 93-1445. 1993. write for info. (*0-8330-1377-7*, MR-226-DPRC) Rand Corp.

Drug Action Modifications in Comparative Pharmacology: Proceedings of the 7th International Congress of Pharmacology, Paris 1978. G. Olive & J. Boissier. LC 78-41031. (Advances in Pharmacology & Therapeutics Ser.: Vol. 8). 1979. 150.00 (*0-08-023198-5*, Pub. by Pergamon Repr UK) Franklin.

Drug Addiction & AIDS. Ed. by N. Loimer et al. (Illus.). x, 431p. 1991. pap. 69.00 (*0-387-82298-4*) Spr-Verlag.

*__Drug Addiction & Related Clinical Problems.__ Ed. by Alessandro Tagliamonte & Icro Maremmani. LC 95-5162. 1995. write for info. (*3-211-82674-2*) Spr-Verlag.

Drug Addiction in Youth. E. Harms. LC 64-13628. (International Series Mono on Child Psychiatry: Vol. 3). 1971. 94.00 (*0-08-010576-9*, Pub. by Pergamon Repr UK) Franklin.

Drug Addiction, Substance Abuse & Narcotic Dependence: A Medical Subject Analysis & Research Index With Bibliography. John C. Bartone. LC 83-71653. 150p. 1983. 37.50 (*0-88164-006-9*); pap. 29.50 (*0-88164-007-7*) ABBE Pubs Assn.

Drug Addiction Treatment Research: German & American Perspectives. Ed. by Gerhard Buhringer & Jerome J. Platt. 550p. (C). 1992. lib. bdg. 88.50 (*0-89464-628-1*) Krieger.

Drug Addiction with Special Reference to India. R. N. Chopra. 264p. 1965. 12.95 (*0-318-36932-X*) Asia Bk Corp.

Drug Addicts: Are They out of Control? John C. Brady, II. Ed. by Nancy McFall. LC 90-71961. 240p. (Orig.). (C). 1991. 14.95 (*0-936029-24-2*); pap. text ed. 10.95 (*0-936029-25-0*) Western Bk Journ.

Drug Adulteration: Detection & Control in Nineteenth-Century Britain. Ed. by Ernst W. Stieb. LC 66-22859. (Illus.). 359p. reprint ed. pap. 102.40 (*0-8357-6775-2*, 2035451) Bks Demand.

Drug Agent U. S. A. Richard R. Radford. 1991. pap. 3.95 (*0-312-92326-0*) St Martin.

Drug-Alert Dictionary & Resource Guide. Jeffrey Shulman. (Drug-Alert Ser.). (Illus.). 91p. (J). (gr. 2-4). 1991. lib. bdg. 14.98 (*0-941477-85-1*) TFC Bks NY.

*__Drug-Alert Series, 9 vols., Set.__ Illus. by David Neuhaus. 64p. (J). (gr. 2-4). 1991. lib. bdg. 134.82 (*0-8050-3448-X*) TFC Bks NY.

*__Drug Allergy & Protocols for Management of Drug Allergies.__ 2nd ed. Roy Patterson et al. LC 94-69157. 55p. (C). 1995. pap. 33.50 (*0-936587-06-7*) Oceanside Pubns.

Drug Analysis: Keynote & Plenary Papers from the First International Symposium, June 1983, Brussels, Belgium. Ed. by A. F. Fell. 200p. 1984. pap. 22.00 (*0-08-031441-4*, Pergamon Pr) Elsevier.

Drug Analysis by Gas Chromatography. David B. Jack. 1984. text ed. 99.00 (*0-12-378250-3*) Acad Pr.

Drug & Alcohol Abuse: A Clinical Guide to Diagnosis & Treatment. 3rd ed. M. A. Schuckit. LC 88-39817. (Critical Issues in Psychiatry Ser.). (Illus.). 330p. 1989. 29.50 (*0-306-43041-X*, Plenum Med Bk) Plenum.

*__Drug & Alcohol Abuse: A Clinical Guide to Diagnosis & Treatment.__ 4th ed. Marc A. Schuckit. LC 94-48434. (Critical Issues in Psychiatry Ser.). 350p. 1995. 34.50 (*0-306-44864-5*, Plenum Med Bk) Plenum.

Drug & Alcohol Abuse: The Authoritative Guide for Parents, Teachers, & Counselors. H. T. Milhorn, Jr. (Illus.). 325p. 1994. 27.95 (*0-306-44640-5*, Plenum Pr) Plenum.

*__Drug & Alcohol Abuse During Pregnancy & Childhood.__ Ed. & Intro. by Ronald R. Watson. LC 94-4482. (Drug & Alcohol Abuse Reviews Ser.: Vol. 8). 144p. 1995. text ed. 59.50 (*0-89603-295-7*) Humana.

Drug & Alcohol Abuse in Children & Adolescence. Ed. by D. W. Kaplan. (Journal: Pediatrician: Vol. 14, No. 1-2, 1987). (Illus.). 92p. 1987. pap. 44.00 (*3-8055-4631-9*) S Karger.

*__Drug & Alcohol Abuse in Older Americans: A Prevention Resource Guide.__ 1995. lib. bdg. 251.95 (*0-8490-6801-0*) Gordon Pr.

Drug & Alcohol Abuse in Schools: A Practical Guide for Administrators & Educators for Combatting Drug & Alcohol Abuse. 2nd ed. John F. Lewis et al. 40p. 1992. pap. 12.95 (*1-56534-050-7*) NOLPE.

Drug & Alcohol Abuse in the Workplace: A Guide to the Issues. J. Michael Walsh & Stephen C. Yohay. LC 87-60167. (Monograph Ser.). (Orig.). 1987. pap. 25.00 (*0-916559-08-4*) EPF.

Drug & Alcohol Abuse in the Workplace: An Assessment of Economic & Productivity Losses. Joseph H. Lodge. LC 87-627. 107p. reprint ed. pap. 30.50 (*0-7837-0683-9*, 2041016) Bks Demand.

Drug & Alcohol Abuse Prevention. Ed. by Ronald Watson. LC 90-28904. (Drug & Alcohol Abuse Reviews Ser.). 416p. 1991. 64.95 (*0-89603-179-9*) Humana.

Drug & Alcohol Community Coordinator. Jack Rudman. (Career Examination Ser.: C-2776). 1994. pap. 34.95 (*0-8373-2776-8*) Nat Learn.

Drug & Alcohol Counselor. Jack Rudman. (Career Examination Ser.: C-2741). 1994. pap. 29.95 (*0-8373-2741-5*) Nat Learn.

Drug & Alcohol Dependency Nursing. James Kennedy & Jean Faugier. 188p. 1990. pap. text ed. 34.95 (*0-433-00016-3*) Buttrwrth-Heinemann.

Drug & Alcohol Education Across the Curriculum. Scott H. Decker. Ed. by Diane Parker. LC 92-50863. 150p. 1993. pap. 14.95 (*0-88247-962-8*) R & E Pubs.

Drug & Alcohol Issues in the Workplace. Arthur Chinski. Ed. by Kathleen Vinson. 530p. 1992. pap. text ed. 49.95 (*1-880940-01-9*) Inst Busn Law.

Drug & Alcohol Program Coordinator. Jack Rudman. (Career Examination Ser.: C-2775). 1994. pap. 34.95 (*0-8373-2775-X*) Nat Learn.

*__Drug & Alcohol Testing: Advising the Employer.__ William D. Turkula. 510p. 1994. ring bd. 110.00 (*0-614-05812-0*) Michie Butterworth.

Drug & Alcohol Testing: Advising the Employer 1990. William D. Turkula. 500p. 1991. ring bd. 110.00 (*0-88063-369-7*) Butterworth Legal Pubs.

Drug & Alcohol Testing: Advising the Employer 1990. suppl. ed. William D. Turkula. 500p. 1993. 32.00 (*0-685-70851-9*) Butterworth Legal Pubs.

*__Drug & Alcohol Testing for Local Government Transportation Employees: The Public Employer's Guide.__ Katharine Gustafson. (Special Report Ser.). 390p. (Orig.). 1994. pap. text ed. 49.95 (*0-87326-096-1*, 40942) Intl City-Cnty Mgt.

Drug & Alcohol Use: Issues & Factors. Ed. by Stanley Einstein. LC 83-19098. 396p. 1989. 95.00 (*0-306-41378-7*, Plenum Pr) Plenum.

Drug & Chemical Action in Pregnancy. Fabro & Scialli. (Reproductive Medicine Ser.: Vol. 8). 544p. 1986. 165.00 (*0-8247-7507-4*) Dekker.

An Asterisk (*) at the beginning of an entry indicates that the title is appearing in BIP for the first time.

An Asterisk (*) at the beginning of an entry indicates that the title is appearing in BIP for the first time.

2119

Drug Interaction & Lethality Analysis. Ed. by Marshall N. Brunden et al. 192p. 1988. 168.00 (*0-8493-5743-8*, RM302) CRC Pr.

Drug Interaction Compendium. Weiner. (Clinical Pharmacology Ser.: Vol. 12). 34p. 1988. 29.75 (*0-8247-7982-7*) Dekker.

Drug Interaction Facts, 1992. 3rd ed. Tatro & Bernie R. Olin. 953p. 1992. 44.95 (*0-932686-39-7*) Facts & Comparisons.

Drug Interaction Facts, 1993. Tatro & Bernie R. Olin. 1993. pap. text ed. 82.50 (*0-932686-41-9*); ring bd. 44.95 (*0-932686-47-8*) Facts & Comparisons.

Drug Interactions. 2nd ed. Stockley. 1991. 99.95 (*0-632-02713-4*) Blackwell Sci.

Drug Interactions: The Effects of Alcohol & Meprobamate Applied Singly & Jointly in Human Subjects. Ed. by J. A. Carpenter. (Journal of Studies on Alcohol: Suppl. No. 7). 1975. 10.00 (*0-911290-02-8*) Rutgers Ctr Alcohol.

Drug Interactions & Updates. 7th ed. Philip D. Hansten & John R. Horn. xi, 500p. 1991. text ed. 75.00 (*0-8121-1381-0*) Williams & Wilkins.

Drug Interactions Guide Book. Richard Harkness. 300p. 1991. pap. 12.95 (*0-13-219619-0*) P-H.

Drug Interactions Guide Book. Richard Harkness. 300p. 1991. text ed. 24.95 (*0-13-219601-8*) P-H.

Drug Interactions in Anesthesia. Norman T. Smith & Aldo N. Corbascio. LC 85-18236. 500p. reprint ed. pap. 142.50 (*0-7837-2750-X*, 2043130) Bks Demand.

Drug Interactions in Psychiatry. 2nd ed. Domenic A. Ciraulo. 1994. pap. write for info. (*0-683-01944-9*) Williams & Wilkins.

Drug Interactions Index. 2nd ed. Robert T. Weibert et al. 304p. (Orig.). 1988. pap. 35.95 (*0-87489-435-2*) Med Economics.

Drug Interference & Drug Management in Clinical Chemistry: Proceedings of the 3rd International Colloquium on Prospective Biology, Pont-a-Mousson, Oct. 1975. International Colloquium on Prospective Biology Staff. Ed. by G. Siest & D. Young. 250p. 1976. 78.50 (*3-8055-2360-2*) S Karger.

Drug Issues Affecting State Judicial Systems: Briefing Papers. CCJ-COSCA Staff. 220p. 1991. 13.50 (*0-685-55350-7*, NCSC129) Natl Ctr St Courts.

***Drug Labeling in Developing Countries.** (Illus.). 193p. (C). 1993. pap. text ed. 95.00 (*0-7881-0109-9*) Diane Pub.

Drug Labeling in Developing Countries. 1994. lib. bdg. 250.00 (*0-8490-9064-4*) Gordon Pr.

Drug Law: Strategies & Tactics. Kevin B. Zeese & Eve E. Zeese. LC 93-23185. (Criminal Law Ser.). 1993. ring bd. 125.00 (*0-87632-019-1*) Clark Boardman Callaghan.

Drug Law Enforcement Bibliography. 200p. (Orig.). (C). 1993. pap. text ed. 35.00 (*1-56806-873-5*) Diane Pub.

Drug Law in New South Wales. Peter Zahra & Robert Arden. 300p. 1991. pap. 58.00 (*1-86287-051-9*, Pub. by Federation Pr AU) W W Gaunt.

Drug Law in the Code States. Peter Alcorn et al. 235p. 1993. 64.00 (*1-86287-112-4*, Pub. by Federation Pr AU) W W Gaunt.

Drug Laws of Ohio: 1993 Official Edition. Ed. by Ohio State Board of Pharmacy Staff. 1142p. 1993. ring bd. 64.00 (*0-8322-0380-7*) Banks-Baldwin.

Drug Legalization: For & Against. Ed. by Rod L. Evans & Irwin M. Berent. LC 92-1626. 355p. (C). 1992. 32.95 (*0-8126-9183-0*); pap. 15.95 (*0-8126-9184-9*) Open Court.

***Drug Lessons & Education Programs in Developing Countries.** Ed. by Henry Kirsch. LC 95-818. 1995. write for info. (*1-56000-220-4*); pap. write for info. (*1-56000-824-5*) Transaction Pubs.

Drug Level Monitoring, Vol. 2. Ed. by Emil T. Lin & Wolfgang Sadee. LC 85-17833. 375p. reprint ed. pap. 106.90 (*0-7837-2814-X*, 2057658) Bks Demand.

Drug Library Series, 6 bks., Set. (Illus.). (YA). (gr. 6 up). 1994. lib. bdg. 107.70 (*0-89490-580-5*) Enslow Pubs.

***Drug Literature Evaluation, Module 2.** Gary H. Smith et al. (Clinical Skills Program Drug Information Ser.). (Illus.). (C). 1994. 70.00 (*1-879907-52-6*) Am Soc Hlth-Syst.

Drug Lord. Peter A. Neissa. 210p. 1990. 23.00 (*0-685-38358-X*) Floricanto Pr.

Drug Maintenance Strategies in Schizophrenia. Ed. by John M. Kane. LC 84-14628. (Clinical Insights Ser.). 106p. reprint ed. pap. 30.30 (*0-8357-7814-2*, 2036186) Bks Demand.

Drug Measurement & Drug Effect in Laboratory Health Science: Proceedings of the 4th International Colloquium on Prospective Biology, Pont-a-Mousson, October 1978. International Colloquium on Prospective Biology Staff. Ed. by G. Siest & D. S. Young. (Illus.). 1979. 106.50 (*3-8055-3045-5*) S Karger.

Drug Mechanisms. Ed. by M. E. Caplis et al. (Journal: Clinical Physiology & Biochemistry: Vol. 3, No. 2-3). (Illus.). 96p. 1985. pap. 67.25 (*3-8055-4051-5*) S Karger.

Drug Metabolism: Chemical & Biochemical Aspects. Bernard Testa & Peter Jenner. LC 75-26114. (Drugs & Pharmaceutical Sciences Ser.: No. 4). 518p. reprint ed. pap. 147.70 (*0-7837-2206-0*, 2052456) Bks Demand.

Drug Metabolism Concepts. Ed. by Donald M. Jerina. LC 77-2279. (ACS Symposium Ser.: No. 44). 1977. 27.95 (*0-8412-0370-9*) Am Chemical.

Drug Metabolism from Molecules to Man. Ed. by D. Benford et al. 750p. 1987. 155.00 (*0-85066-373-3*) Taylor & Francis.

***Drug Metabolism in the Immature Human.** fac. ed. Ed. by Lester F. Soyka & Geoffrey P. Redmond. LC 81-15852. (Illus.). 301p. Date not set. pap. 85.80 (*0-7837-7161-4*, 2047136) Bks Demand.

Drug Metabolism: Molecular Approaches & Pharmacological Implications: Proceedings of the 9th European Workshop on Drug Metabolism Held at Pont-a-Mousson, France June 11-15 1984. Ed. by G. Siest. (Illus.). 242p. 1985. 50.00 (*0-08-031995-5*, Pub. by PPL UK) Elsevier.

Drug Metabolism Reviews, Vol. 3: 1975. Ed. by Frederick J. Di Carlo. LC 72-76719. (Illus.). 367p. reprint ed. pap. 104.60 (*0-7837-0784-3*, 2041098) Bks Demand.

Drug Misuse & Dependence. Ed. by A. H. Ghodse et al. (Illus.). 230p. (C). 1990. 68.00 (*1-85070-239-X*) Prthnon Pub.

Drug Misuse, Human Abuse. Helen I. Green & Michael H. Levy. LC 76-1580. (Illus.). 584p. reprint ed. pap. 166.50 (*0-7837-4322-X*, 2044008) Bks Demand.

Drug Money Laundering Law Enforcement, Recent Trends & Issues (1992) 63p. 1992. pap. text ed. 15.00 (*1-56986-061-0*) Federal Bar.

Drug Monitoring & Pharmacokinetic Data. Hugo C. Pribor et al. LC 79-90657. 190p. 29.50 (*0-930376-10-2*) Chem-Orbital.

***Drug Monitoring Data Pocket Guide II.** Ed. by AACC TDM-TOX Staff. 143p. 1994. 15.00 (*0-915274-70-1*, 625) Am Assn Clinical Chem.

Drug-Nutrient Interactions. T. K. Basu. 180p. 1988. lib. bdg. 55.00 (*0-7099-3203-0*) Routledge Chapman & Hall.

Drug Offences in Australia: Sentencing. Fiori Rinaldi. xxv, 247p. 1986. pap. 48.50 (*0-455-20649-X*, Pub. by Law Bk Co) W W Gaunt.

Drug Packaging. Business Communications Co., Inc. Staff. 82p. 1984. 975.00 (*0-89336-421-5*, GB-082) BCC.

***Drug Packaging Market.** 400p. (Orig.). 1994. pap. 2,295.00 (*1-57205-989-3*) Rector Pr.

Drug Permeation Enhancement: Theory & Applications. Hseih. (Drugs & the Pharmaceutical Sciences Ser.: Vol. 62). 448p. 1994. 165.00 (*0-8247-9015-4*) Dekker.

Drug Phenomenon: Social Aspects of Drug Taking. Erich Goode. LC 73-920. (Studies in Sociology). 66p. 1973. pap. text ed. 3.50 (*0-672-61326-3*, Bobbs) Macmillan.

Drug Plant Resources of Central India - An Inventory. R. C. Srivastava. 250p. 1988. 50.00 (*1-55528-152-4*, Messers Today & Tomorrow) Scholarly Pubns.

Drug Plants of Africa. Thomas S. Githens. (African Handbooks Ser.: Vol. 8). 125p. 1949. 10.00 (*0-686-24086-3*) U PA Mus Pubns.

Drug Policy & the Decline of the American City. Sam Staley. 272p. (C). 1993. 35.95 (*1-56000-039-2*); pap. 19.95 (*1-56000-718-4*) Transaction Pubs.

Drug Policy in the Americas. Ed. by Peter H. Smith. LC 92-15740. 366p. (C). 1992. text ed. 67.00 (*0-8133-8239-4*); pap. text ed. 21.50 (*0-8133-8240-8*) Westview.

Drug Policy in the U. S. Elaine B. Sharp. LC 93-44564. 186p. (C). 1994. pap. 20.50 (*0-06-500973-8*) HarpCollege.

Drug Prescribing for the Elderly. Harrison G. Bloom & Elizabeth A. Shlom. 320p. 1993. 34.00 (*0-88167-989-5*) Raven.

Drug Prescribing in Renal Failure: Dosing Guidelines for Adults. William M. Bennett et al. 150p. 1991. pap. 19.00 (*0-943126-16-9*, DRF90) Amer Coll Phys.

Drug Prescribing in Renal Failure: Dosing Guidelines for Adults. 3rd ed. William M. Bennett et al. LC 93-49372. 1994. 23.00 (*0-943126-29-0*) Amer Coll Phys.

Drug Prevention - Just Say Now. Peter Stoker. 176p. 1992. pap. 23.00 (*1-85346-235-7*, Pub. by D Fulton UK) Taylor & Francis.

Drug Prevention Curricula: A Guide to Selection & Implementation. 1991. lib. bdg. 75.00 (*0-8490-5048-0*) Gordon Pr.

Drug Prevention Materials Catalog for Counselors Working with Parents with Sections for Minority Groups. Bonnie Walker. 1993. 12.95 (*1-55691-083-5*, 835) Learning Pubns.

Drug Product Liability, 3 vols. Marden G. Dixon & Frank Woodside. 1974. Updates. ring bd. write for info. (*0-8205-1257-5*) Bender.

Drug Product R&D (Seminar Notes - Dec. 1993) ring bd. 150.00 (*1-56676-109-3*) Technomic.

Drug Prohibition & the Conscience of Nations. Arnold S. Trebach & Kevin B. Zeese. (Orig.). (C). 1990. pap. text ed. 9.95 (*1-879189-00-3*) Drug Policy.

Drug-Protein Binding: Esteve Foundation Symposium I. Ed. by Marcus S. Reidenberg & Sergio Erill. LC 85-12479. (Clinical Pharmacology & Therapeutics Ser.: Vol. 6). 380p. 1985. 49.95 (*0-275-90010-X*, C0010, Praeger Pubs) Greenwood.

Drug Questions & Answers. L. Schwartz. (Health Ser.). (J). (gr. 6-9). 1989. 5.95 (*0-88160-171-3*, LW 282) Learning Wks.

Drug Reactions & the Liver. Ed. by M. Davis et al. 300p. (C). 1981. text ed. 69.00 (*0-8464-1220-9*) Beekman Pubs.

Drug Regimen Review: A Process Guide for Pharmacists, 1992. 2nd ed. Ed. by Gary Ermn. 372p. 1992. ring bd. 83.00 (*0-934322-11-2*) Am Soc Consult Phar.

Drug Regulation in African Countries. Evans C. Chidomere. 151p. 1991. 49.00 (*0-935184-26-0*) Interpharm.

Drug Related Arrests & Client Admissions in South Carolina. (Illus.). 48p. (Orig.). (C). 1993. pap. text ed. 20.00 (*1-56806-804-2*) Diane Pub.

Drug-Related Problems in Geriatric Nursing Home Patients. James W. Cooper. (Pharmaceutical Sciences Ser.). 101p. 1991. text ed. 29.95 (*1-56024-085-7*); pap. text ed. 14.95 (*1-56024-086-5*) Haworth Pr.

Drug Research on Human Subjects: A Source Guide. 1991. lib. bdg. 76.00 (*0-8490-4842-7*) Gordon Pr.

Drug Research Related to Neuroactive Amino Acids. Schousboe. (ABS Ser.: No. 32). 500p. 1992. 89.50 (*87-16-10808-6*) Mosby Yr Bk.

Drug Residues in Animals. Andre G. Rico. (Veterinary Science & Comparative Medicine Ser.). 1986. text ed. 99.00 (*0-12-587970-9*) Acad Pr.

Drug Residues in Food-Producing Animals. Ed. by Jerry Brunton & M. A. Mehlman. LC 79-91220. 150p. pap. 22.00 (*0-930376-11-0*) Chem-Orbital.

Drug Resistance As a Biochemical Target in Cancer Chemotherapy. Ed. by Takashi Tsuruo & Makoto Ogawa. (Bristol-Myers Squibb Cancer Symposia Ser.: Vol. 13). (Illus.). 342p. 1991. text ed. 66.00 (*0-12-702295-3*) Acad Pr.

Drug Resistance in Cancer Therapy. Ed. by Robert F. Ozols. (C). 1989. lib. bdg. 112.50 (*0-7923-0244-3*) Kluwer Ac.

Drug Resistance in Mammalian Cells, 2 vols., Vol. I. Ed. by Radhey S. Gupta. 304p. 1989. Vol I, 304p. 216.00 (*0-8493-6921-5*, RC271) CRC Pr.

Drug Resistance in Mammalian Cells, 2 vols., Vol. II. Ed. by Radhey S. Gupta. 320p. 1989. 173.00 (*0-8493-6922-3*, RC271, CRC Reprint) Franklin.

Drug Resistance in Mycobacteria. Pattisapu R. Gangadharam. 176p. 1984. 144.00 (*0-8493-6574-0*, QR82) CRC Pr.

Drug Resistance in Oncology. Teicher. 672p. 1993. 215.00 (*0-8247-8804-4*) Dekker.

Drug Resistance in Viruses, Other Microbes & Eukaryotes. Ed. by John S. Oxford et al. 232p. 1987. pap. text ed. 64.00 (*0-12-531765-4*) Acad Pr.

Drug Resistance on Leukemia & Lymphoma: The Clinical Value of Laboratory Studies. Ed. by G. J. Kaspers et al. LC 93-20039. 1993. text ed. 150.00 (*3-7186-5387-7*) Gordon & Breach.

Drug Safety: A Shared Responsibility. Ed. by International Drug Surveillance Dept. Staff. 126p. 1991. text ed. 24.95 (*0-443-04655-7*) Churchill.

Drug Safety Assessment in Clinical Trials. Gilbert. (Statistics: Vol. 138). 456p. 1993. 150.00 (*0-8247-8893-1*) Dekker.

Drug Safety in Pregnancy. P. I. Folb. 1991. 243.00 (*0-685-40472-2*) Elsevier.

Drug Scenes: A Report Published by the Royal College of Psychiatrists. Ed. by U. K. Royal College of Psychiatrists Staff. 238p. 1980. pap. 25.00 (*0-88048-306-7*, Pub. by Royal Coll Psych UK) Am Psychiatric.

Drug, Set, & Setting: The Basis for Controlled Intoxicant Use. Norman Zinberg. LC 83-16803. 296p. 1984. 37.00 (*0-300-03110-6*) Yale U Pr.

Drug Side Effects, Drug-Drug Interactions, Drug Resistance, & Patient Compliance in the Management of Hypertension. Ed. by Michael J. Horan & Lot B. Page. LC 73-2002. (Hypertension Monographs: No. 5). 106p. 1988. 12.00 (*0-87493-654-3*) Am Heart.

Drug Smuggling: The Forbidden Book. K. Hawkeye Gross. 152p. 1992. pap. 16.00 (*0-87364-685-1*) Paladin Pr.

Drug Solution: How We Can Solve Every Major Problem Faced by Our Society Today. Mark Greer. LC 94-65041. 240p. 1994. 27.95 (*0-9640123-8-3*); pap. 19.95 (*0-9640123-7-5*) RFTI Pubng.

Drug Stability: Principles & Practices. Carstensen. (Drugs & the Pharmaceutical Sciences Ser.: Vol. 43). 504p. 1990. 140.00 (*0-8247-8285-2*) Dekker.

Drug Stereochemistry: Analytical Methods & Pharmacology. 2nd expanded rev. ed. Wainer. (Clinical Pharmacology Ser.: Vol. 18). 432p. 1993. 175.00 (*0-8247-8819-2*) Dekker.

Drug Store Market Guide, 1991. Ed. by Melanie R. Buse. 674p. 1990. pap. 239.00 (*1-879463-00-8*) Melnor Pub.

Drug Store Market Guide, 1992. Ed. by Melanie R. Buse. (Orig.). 1991. pap. 249.00 (*1-879463-01-6*) Melnor Pub.

***Drug Store Market Guide, 1995.** Ed. by Melanie R. Buse. 1995. pap. 285.00 (*1-879463-04-0*) Melnor Pub.

Drug Store Tins & Their Prices. Al Bergevin. LC 90-70545. (Illus.). 288p. 1990. pap. 17.95 (*0-87069-568-1*, Wallace-Hmestead) Chilton.

Drug Studies in the Elderly: Methodological Concerns. Ed. by Neal R. Cutler & Prem K. Narang. LC 86-18738. 464p. 1986. 95.00 (*0-306-42311-1*, Plenum Pr) Plenum.

Drug Susceptibility in the Chemotherapy of Mycobacterial Infections. Leonid Heifets. 1991. 121.00 (*0-8493-6716-6*, QR201) CRC Pr.

Drug-Taking Behavior among School-Aged Youth: The Alaska Experience & Comparisons with Lower-48 States. Intro. by Bernard Segal. LC 89-29119. (Drugs & Society Ser.: Vol. 4, Nos. 1-2). (Illus.). 168p. 1990. text ed. 29.95 (*0-86656-966-9*) Haworth Pr.

Drug Targeting: Proceedings of the Symposium on Drug Targeting Held in Nyon, Switzerland, 3-5 October 1984. Ed. by P. Buri & A. Gumma. 198p. 1985. 75.00 (*0-444-80687-3*) Elsevier.

Drug Targeting & Delivery: Concepts in Dosage Form Design. Junginger. 300p. 1993. text ed. 97.00 (*0-13-220468-1*) P-H.

Drug-Test Interactions Handbook. Jack G. Salway. 1104p. 1990. 370.00 (*0-88167-602-0*) Raven.

Drug Testing. John Fay. 432p. 1990. text ed. 49.95 (*0-409-90239-X*) Buttrwrth-Heinemann.

Drug Testing. Judy Monroe. LC 89-25425. (Facts About Ser.). (Illus.). 48p. (J). (gr. 5-6). 1990. text ed. 12.95 (*0-89686-492-8*, Crstwood Hse) Silver Burdett Pr.

Drug Testing: A Workplace Guide to Designing Practical Policies & Winning Arbitrations. LC 90-15136. 1990. 95.00 (*1-55871-186-4*, BSP 176) BNA.

Drug Testing: Issues & Options. Ed. by Robert H. Coombs & Louis J. West. 277p. 1991. 42.50 (*0-19-505414-8*) OUP.

Drug Testing: Protection for Society or a Violation of Civil Rights? Council of State Governments Staff. LC 88-143569. (Publication Ser.: No. C86). 95p. reprint ed. pap. 27.10 (*0-7837-2659-7*, 2043019) Bks Demand.

***Drug Testing & Privacy in Canada.** 169p. (Orig.). (C). 1993. pap. text ed. 40.00x (*0-7881-0115-3*) Diane Pub.

Drug Testing at Work. Beverly A. Potter & J. Sebastian Orfali. (Guide for Employers & Employees Working in the New Age Ser.). (Illus.). 252p. (Orig.). 1990. pap. 17.95 (*0-914171-32-1*) Ronin Pub.

Drug Testing at Work: A Guide for Employers & Employees. 2nd ed. Beverly Potter. 1995. pap. 14.95 (*0-914171-70-4*) Ronin Pub.

Drug Testing Compliance Manual. Keller, J. J. & Assoc., Inc. Staff. LC 89-85158. 300p. 1992. 95.00 (*0-934674-78-7*, 35M) J J Keller.

Drug Testing Guidelines & Practices for Juvenile Probation & Parole Agencies. 142p. (Orig.). (C). 1994. pap. text ed. 40.00 (*0-7881-0275-3*) Diane Pub.

Drug Testing in the Workplace. (National Benchmarking Report Ser.: No. 0300). 1988. ring bd. 295.00 (*0-317-91042-6*) Exec Knowledge.

Drug Testing in the Workplace. (Monograph Ser.). 1990. 10.00 (*0-685-61708-4*) Intl Personnel Mgmt.

Drug Testing in the Workplace. Ed. by Scott Macdonald & Paul M. Roman. (Research Advances in Alcohol & Drug Problems: Vol. 11). (Illus.). 315p. (C). 1994. 85.00 (*0-306-44557-3*, Plenum Pr) Plenum.

Drug Testing in the Workplace: A Resource Manual & Benchmarking Report on Nationwide Practices & Trends. Executive KnowledgeWorks Staff. (Illus.). 300p. 1987. ring bd. 550.00 (*0-943353-02-5*) Exec Knowledge.

Drug Testing in the Workplace: An Update. Neil Reichenberg. (Monograph Ser.). 1991. 10.00 (*0-685-41301-2*) Intl Personnel Mgmt.

Drug Testing Law, Technology & Practice. David G. Evans. (Criminal Law Ser.). 1992. 140.00 (*0-685-46257-9*) Clark Boardman Callaghan.

Drug Testing Legal Manual, 2 vols. Kevin B. Zeese. LC 87-37516. (Criminal Law Ser.). 1988. Three-ring binder. ring bd. 210.00 (*0-87632-586-X*) Clark Boardman Callaghan.

Drug Testing Programs by Public Employers: Suggested Guidelines. 12p. 1988. pap. 3.95 (*0-89707-380-0*, 533-0035-01) Amer Bar Assn.

Drug Tests & Polygraphs: Essential Tools or Violations of Privacy? Daniel Jussim. LC 87-11192. (Illus.). 128p. (YA). (gr. 7 up). 1987. lib. bdg. 12.98 (*0-671-64438-6*, Julian Messner); pap. 5.95 (*0-671-65977-4*, Julian Messner) Silver Burdett Pr.

Drug Therapy. 2nd ed. Bertram G. Katzung. (Illus.). 543p. (C). 1991. spiral bd. 26.00 (*0-8385-1312-3*, A1312-6) Appleton & Lange.

Drug Therapy: Supplement to Pharmacology & Therapeutics. H. Vapaatalo & J. Tuomisto. LC 75-33070. (Proceedings Sixth International Congress of Pharmacology Ser.: Vol. 4). 1976. 104.00 (*0-08-020542-9*, Pub. by Pergamon Repr UK) Franklin.

***Drug Therapy Decision Making Guide.** James McCormack et al. 992p. 1995. pap. text ed. write for info. (*0-7216-4215-2*) Saunders.

Drug Therapy Factors & Adverse Effects: Medical Analysis Index with Research Bibliography. Kathleen U. Langstrom. LC 88-47785. 173p. 1988. 39.50 (*0-88164-708-X*); pap. 34.50 (*0-88164-709-8*) ABBE Pubs Assn.

Drug Therapy for Asthma: Research & Clinical Practice. Jenne & Murphy. (Lung Biology in Health & Disease Ser.: Vol. 31). 1152p. 1987. 275.00 (*0-8247-7633-X*) Dekker.

Drug Therapy for Behavior Disorders. Alan Poling et al. (Practitioner Guidebook Ser.). (C). 1991. pap. 20.95 (*0-205-14453-5*, H4453, Longwood Div) Allyn.

Drug Therapy for Headache. Ed. by Michael Gallagher. (Inflammatory Disease & Therapy Ser.: Vol. 6). 296p. 1991. 110.00 (*0-8247-8179-1*) Dekker.

Drug Therapy in Dialysis Patients. Ed. by E. Ritz & K. Schaefer. (Journal: Blood Purification: Vol. 3, Nos. 1-3, 1985). (Illus.). 168p. 1986. pap. 89.75 (*3-8055-4288-7*) S Karger.

Drug Therapy in Dilated Cardiomyopathy & Myocarditis. Engelmeier & O'Connell. (Basic & Clinical Cardiology Ser.: Vol. 11). 312p. 1988. 125.00 (*0-8247-7834-0*) Dekker.

Drug Therapy in Emergency Medicine. Ed. by Joseph P. Ornato & Edgar R. Gonzalez. (Illus.). 607p. 1990. pap. text ed. 63.00 (*0-443-08599-4*) Churchill.

Drug Therapy in Health, Medicine & Disease: Subject Analysis Index with Reference Bibliography. American Health Research Institute Staff. LC 85-47872. 150p. 1987. 39.50 (*0-88164-416-1*); pap. 34.50 (*0-88164-417-X*) ABBE Pubs Assn.

Drug Therapy in Hypertension. Drayer et al. (Clinical Pharmacology Ser.: Vol. 6). 416p. 1987. 140.00 (*0-8247-7505-8*) Dekker.

Drug Therapy in Infants & Children with Cardiovascular Diseases. Adam Schneeweiss. LC 85-10384. 406p. reprint ed. pap. 115.80 (*0-7837-2745-3*, 2043125) Bks Demand.

Drug Therapy in Neurology. Ed. by Mervyn J. Eadie. (Illus.). 595p. 1992. text ed. 139.95 (*0-443-04407-4*) Churchill.

Drug Therapy in Obstetrics & Gynecology. 3rd ed. William F. Rayburn & Zuspan. 661p. 1991. 55.00 (*0-8016-4052-0*) Mosby Yr Bk.

Drug Therapy of Cancer. G. Brule et al. 1973. 8.00 (*0-686-16780-5*) World Health.

Drug Therapy of Skin Disease. D. R. Bickers & H. F. Merk. (Illus.). 1993. write for info. (*0-86542-224-9*) Blackwell Sci.

***Drug Therapy of the Rheumatic Diseases.** Ed. by Michael H. Weisman & Michael E. Weinblatt. LC 94-28994. 1994. text ed. 50.00 (*0-7216-5382-0*) Saunders.

An Asterisk (*) at the beginning of an entry indicates that the title is appearing in BIP for the first time.

An Asterisk (*) at the beginning of an entry indicates that the title is appearing in BIP for the first time.

2121

D

Drugs & Drinking. (Active Bible Curriculum Ser.). 48p. 1990. pap. 9.99 (*1-55945-118-1*) Group Pub.

Drugs & Drinks--Painful Questions: How Substance Abusers & Their Loved Ones Ask for Help. Frank N. Shiromoto & Edgar F. Soren. LC 88-70397. (Orig.). 1988. pap. 8.95 (*0-9620157-0-9*) Choices Pr.

Drugs & Driving. Ed. by J. J. De Gier & J. F. O'Hanlon. 300p. 1986. 125.00 (*0-85066-290-7*) Taylor & Francis.

Drugs & Driving. rev. ed. Janet Grosshandler. Ed. by Ruth Rosen. (Drug Abuse Prevention Library). (YA). (gr. 7-12). 1994. 15.95 (*0-8239-2039-9*) Rosen Group.

Drugs & Driving: A Survey of the Relationship of Adverse Drug Reactions, & Drug-Alcohol Interaction to Driving Safety. G. Milner. Ed. by G. S. Avery. (Monographs on Drugs: Vol. 1). (Illus.). xi, 124p. 1972. 24.00 (*3-8055-1242-2*) S Karger.

Drugs & Eating Disorders. Clifford J. Shery. LC 93-35719. (Drug Abuse Prevention Library). (J). 1994. 15.95 (*0-8239-1540-9*) Rosen Group.

***Drugs & Emotions.** Arthur Myers. LC 95-13902. (Drug Abuse Prevention Library). (J). 1995. write for info. (*0-8239-2143-3*) Rosen Group.

Drugs & Enzymes: Proceedings of Second International Pharmacological Meeting, Prague, August 1963, Vol. 4. Bernard B. Brodie & J. Gillette. LC 64-15320. 1965. 214.00 (*0-08-010806-7*, Pub. by Pergamon Repr UK) Franklin.

Drugs & Foods from Little Known Plants: Notes in Harvard University Herbaria. Siri V. Altschul. LC 72-85145. 518p. 1973. 47.50 (*0-674-21676-8*) HUP.

Drugs & Foreign Policy: A Critical Review. Ed. by Raphael Perl. 256p. (C). 1994. text ed. 58.00 (*0-8133-8786-8*) Westview.

***Drugs & Gun Violence.** Maryann Miller. LC 95-5910. (Drug Abuse Prevention Library). (J). 1995. write for info. (*0-8239-2060-7*) Rosen Group.

Drugs & Handwriting. Patricia Wellingham-Jones. (Illus.). 92p. (C). 1991. pap. 16.00 (*0-939221-08-X*) Wellingham-Jones.

Drugs & Health: Economic Issues & Policy Objectives. Ed. by Robert B. Helms. LC 80-28825. (AEI Symposia Ser.: No. 81B). 372p. reprint ed. pap. 106.10 (*0-8357-4466-3*, 2037310) Bks Demand.

Drugs & Hormones in Brain Development. Ed. by M. Schlumpf & W. Lichtensteiger. (Monographs in Neural Sciences: Vol. 9). (Illus.). viii, 244p. 1983. 132.00 (*3-8055-3514-7*) S Karger.

Drugs & Human Behavior. David M. Grilly. 384p. 1989. write for info. (*0-318-63851-7*, H20670) Allyn.

Drugs & Human Behavior. Tibor Palfai & Henry Jankiewicz. 544p. (C). 1991. pap. write for info. (*0-697-06431-X*) Brown & Benchmark.

Drugs & Human Behavior. 2nd ed. David M. Grilly. LC 93-17310. 1993. pap. text ed. write for info. (*0-205-15361-5*) Allyn.

Drugs & Information Control: The Role of Men & Manipulation in the Control of Drug Trafficking. Jerald W. Cloyd. LC 81-6675. (Contributions in Legal Studies: No. 23). xi, 195p. 1982. text ed. 49.95 (*0-313-22178-2*, CDS/, Greenwood Pr) Greenwood.

***Drugs & Life.** Harry H. Avis. 480p. (C). 1995. pap. write for info. (*0-697-22290-X*) Brown & Benchmark.

Drugs & Life. 2nd ed. Harry H. Avis. 528p. (C). 1993. pap. text ed. write for info. (*0-697-12598-X*) Brown & Benchmark.

Drugs & Medicines: A Consumers' Guide. Roderick Cawson & Roy Spector. 288p. 1990. pap. 14.95 (*0-19-261655-2*) OUP.

Drugs & Music. Carlienne Frisch. LC 94-1026. (Drug Abuse Prevention Library). (J). 1994. 15.95 (*0-8239-1707-X*) Rosen Group.

***Drugs & Narcotics in History.** Ed. by Roy Porter & Mikulas Teich. (Illus.). 240p. (C). 1995. 49.95 (*0-521-43163-8*) Cambridge U Pr.

***Drugs & Nursing Implications.** 8th ed. Margaret T. Shannon et al. LC 94-38407. (C). 1994. pap. text ed. 34.95 (*0-8385-1780-3*, Medical Exam) Appleton & Lange.

Drugs & Nutrients: The Interactive Effects. Roe & Campbell. (Drugs & the Pharmaceutical Sciences Ser.: Vol. 21). 624p. 1984. 210.00 (*0-8247-7054-4*) Dekker.

Drugs & Nutrients to Improve Your Brain Power, Increase Productivity & Job Performance. 1992. lib. bdg. 88.95 (*0-8490-5529-6*) Gordon Pr.

Drugs & Our World. Gretchen Super. 48p. (J). (ps-3). 1990. pap. 3.95 (*0-8167-2365-6*) Troll Assocs.

Drugs & Our World. Gretchen Super. (Drug-Free Kids Ser.). (Illus.). 48p. (J). (gr. k-3). 1991. lib. bdg. 14.98 (*0-8050-2888-9*) TFC Bks NY.

Drugs & Pain. Joann Rodgers. (Encyclopedia of Psychoactive Drugs Ser.: No. 2). (Illus.). 144p. 1987. lib. bdg. 19.95 (*1-55546-212-X*) Chelsea Hse.

***Drugs & Peer Pressure.** Arthur Myers. LC 94-37885. (Drug Abuse Prevention Library). 1995. 15.95 (*0-8239-2066-6*) Rosen Group.

***Drugs & People: Medications, Their History & Origins, & the Way They Act.** rev. ed. Alfred Burger. LC 88-12218. 186p. 1988. pap. 53.10 (*0-7837-8438-4*, 2049242) Bks Demand.

Drugs & Perception. William A. Check. (Encyclopedia of Psychoactive Drugs Ser.: No. 2). (Illus.). 112p. (YA). (gr. 5 up). 1988. lib. bdg. 19.95 (*1-55546-214-6*) Chelsea Hse.

Drugs & Performance in Sports. Richard H. Strauss. (Illus.). 220p. 1987. pap. text ed. 30.50 (*0-7216-1865-0*) Saunders.

Drugs & Pharmacology for Nurses. 11th ed. S. J. Hopkins. (Illus.). 612p. (Orig.). 1992. pap. text ed. 23.00 (*0-443-04389-2*) Churchill.

***Drugs & Pharmacology for Nurses.** 12th rev. ed. S. J. Hopkins. LC 95-7245. 1995. write for info. (*0-443-05249-2*) Churchill.

Drugs & Politics. Ed. by Paul Rock. LC 76-1766. (Society Bks.). 333p. 1977. 34.95 (*0-87855-076-3*); pap. text ed. 21.95 (*0-87855-572-2*) Transaction Pubs.

Drugs & Politics. Peggy Santamaria. LC 94-1024. (Drug Abuse Prevention Library). (J). 1994. 15.95 (*0-8239-1703-7*) Rosen Group.

Drugs & Pregnancy. Ed. by Larry C. Gilstrap, III & Bertis B. Little. LC 92-14733. 1992. write for info. (*0-444-01655-4*) Elsevier.

Drugs & Pregnancy. Ed. by Franz Krauer. 1984. text ed. 69.00 (*0-12-425960-X*) Acad Pr.

Drugs & Pregnancy. Patrick Young. (Encyclopedia of Psychoactive Drugs Ser.: No. 2). (Illus.). 112p. 1987. lib. bdg. 19.95 (*1-55546-203-0*) Chelsea Hse.

Drugs & Pregnancy. Patrick Young. (Encyclopedia of Psychoactive Drugs - Compact Paperback Library). (Illus.). 32p. (YA). (gr. 5 up). 1991. pap. 4.49 (*0-7910-0001-X*) Chelsea Hse.

Drugs & Pregnancy: It's Not Worth the Risk. rev. ed. Paddy Cook. LC 86-70944. 36p. 1991. pap. 3.00 (*0-942348-17-6*) Am Council Drug Ed.

Drugs & Prison. Victor Adint. LC 94-1025. (Drug Abuse Prevention Library). (J). 1994. 15.95 (*0-8239-1705-3*) Rosen Group.

Drugs & Punishment: An Up-to-Date Interregional Survey on Drug Related Offences. 146p. 1988. 15.00 (*92-9078-004-5*, E. 88. III.N.1) UN.

Drugs & Renal Disease. 2nd ed. Ed. by William M. Bennett. (Monographs in Clinical Pharmacology: Vol. 2). (Illus.). 205p. 1986. text ed. 38.00 (*0-443-08403-3*) Churchill.

Drugs & Respiration. D. M. Aviado & F. Palecek. LC 64-15320. (Proceedings of the Second International Pharmacological Meeting Ser.: No. 11). 1964. 109.00 (*0-08-010813-X*, Pub. by Pergamon Repr UK) Franklin.

Drugs & Rights. Douglas N. Husak. (Studies in Philosophy & Public Policy). 352p. (C). 1992. 59.95 (*0-521-41739-2*); pap. 19.95 (*0-521-42727-4*) Cambridge U Pr.

Drugs & Sex. George A. Boyd. LC 93-5873. (Drug Abuse Prevention Library). (J). 1994. 15.95 (*0-8239-1538-7*) Rosen Group.

Drugs & Sex: A Bibliography. Comp. by Ernest L. Abel. LC 83-5656. xvii, 129p. 1983. text ed. 42.95 (*0-313-23941-X*, ADS/, Greenwood Pr) Greenwood.

Drugs & Sexual Behavior. Joann Rodgers. (Encyclopedia of Psychoactive Drugs Ser.: No. 2). (Illus.). 96p. (YA). (gr. 5 up). 1988. lib. bdg. 19.95 (*1-55546-215-4*) Chelsea Hse.

Drugs & Ships. Kenneth Luck. 60p. 1992. 75.00 (*1-85609-005-1*, Pub. by Witherby & Co UK) St Mut.

Drugs & Sleep. Lynn Lamberg. (Encyclopedia of Psychoactive Drugs Ser.: No. 2). (Illus.). 128p. 1988. lib. bdg. 19.95 (*1-55546-213-8*) Chelsea Hse.

***Drugs & Sleeping Disorders.** Gina Strzzabosco-Hayn. LC 95-13023. (Drug Abuse Prevention Library). (J). 1995. write for info. (*0-8239-2144-1*) Rosen Pub.

Drugs & Society. rev. ed. Richard Hawley. (Think Ser.). 160p. (YA). (gr. 7 up). 1993. lib. bdg. 15.85 (*0-8027-8114-4*); pap. 9.95 (*0-8027-7366-4*) Walker & Co.

Drugs & Society. 2nd ed. Witters & Venturelli. 448p. (C). 1988. teacher ed 10.00 (*0-86720-413-3*); pap. text ed. 36.25 (*0-86720-410-9*) Jones & Bartlett.

Drugs & Society. 3rd ed. Witters et al. (Health Science Ser.). 512p. (C). 1992. teacher ed 10.00 (*0-86720-766-3*); pap. text ed. 40.00 (*0-86720-317-X*); disk 195.00 (*0-86720-765-5*) Jones & Bartlett.

***Drugs & Society.** 4th ed. Glen Hanson & Peter Venturelli. LC 94-46298. (Health Science Ser.). 462p. 1995. pap. 40.00 (*0-86720-830-9*) Jones & Bartlett.

Drugs & Society: Behavioral Medicines & Abusable Drugs. Arthur P. Leccese. 1990. text ed. 30.00 (*0-13-221623-X*, 670111) P-H.

Drugs & Society: Contemporary Social Issues. Ed. by Louis Miller & Stanley Einstein. 317p. 1976. 34.95 (*0-87855-273-1*) Transaction Pubs.

Drugs & Society see Innovations in Alcoholism Treatment: State of the Art Reviews & Their Implications for Clinical Practice

Drugs & Solutions: A Programed Introduction. 4th ed. Claire B. Keane & Sybil M. Fletcher. (Illus.). 166p. 1980. pap. text ed. 23.50 (*0-7216-5343-X*) Saunders.

Drugs & Sports. Jeff Meer. (Encyclopedia of Psychoactive Drugs Ser.: No. 2). (Illus.). 136p. (YA). (gr. 5 up). 1988. lib. bdg. 19.95 (*1-55546-226-X*); pap. 9.95 (*0-7910-0794-4*) Chelsea Hse.

Drugs & Sports. Jeff Meer. (Encyclopedia of Psychoactive Drugs - Compact Paperback Library). (Illus.). 32p. (YA). (gr. 5 up). 1991. pap. 4.49 (*1-55546-996-5*) Chelsea Hse.

Drugs & Sports. Don Nardo. LC 90-6686. (Overview Ser.). (Illus.). 112p. (J). (gr. 5-8). 1990. lib. bdg. 16.95 (*1-56006-112-X*) Lucent Bks.

Drugs & Sports. Rodney Peck. Ed. by Ruth Rosen. LC 92-12359. (Drug Abuse Prevention Library). (YA). (gr. 7-12). 1992. 15.95 (*0-8239-1420-8*) Rosen Group.

Drugs & Sports. Katherine S. Talmadge. (Social Impact Ser.). (Illus.). 88p. (J). (gr. 5-8). 1991. lib. bdg. 14.98 (*0-941477-59-2*) TFC Bks NY.

Drugs & Sports: Locating the Author's Main Idea. Carol O'Sullivan. LC 89-36322. (Opposing Viewpoints Juniors Ser.). (Illus.). 32p. (J). (gr. 3-6). 1990. lib. bdg. 11.95 (*0-89908-637-3*) Greenhaven.

Drugs & Stress. M. Walker Buckalew. Ed. by Ruth Rosen. (Drug Abuse Prevention Library). (YA). (gr. 7-12). 1993. 15.95 (*0-8239-1418-6*) Rosen Group.

Drugs & Suicide. Judie Smith. Ed. by Ruth Rosen. (Drug Abuse Prevention Library). (YA). (gr. 7-12). 1992. 15.95 (*0-8239-1421-6*) Rosen Group.

Drugs & Suicide: When Other Coping Strategies Fail. Ed. by Dan J. Lettieri. LC 78-50826. (Sage Annual Reviews of Drug & Alcohol Abuse Ser.: No. 2). (Illus.). 303p. reprint ed. pap. 86.40 (*0-8357-8448-7*, 2034712) Bks Demand.

Drugs & the Athlete. Gary I. Wadler & Brian Hainline. LC 88-33612. (Contemporary Exercise & Sports Medicine Ser.: Vol. 2). (Illus.). 353p. (C). 1989. text ed. 49.00 (*0-8036-9008-8*); pap. 35.00 (*0-8036-9009-6*) Davis Co.

Drugs & the Brain. Edward Edelson. (Encyclopedia of Psychoactive Drugs Ser.: No. 2). (Illus.). 112p. 1987. lib. bdg. 19.95 (*1-55546-209-X*) Chelsea Hse.

Drugs & the Brain: A Scientific American Book. S. H. Snyder. 228p. 1995. text ed. 32.95 (*0-7167-5015-5*) W H Freeman.

Drugs & The Brain: Papers on the Action, Use, & Abuse of Psychotropic Agents. Ed. by Perry Black. LC 68-31642. 416p. reprint ed. pap. 118.60 (*0-317-07918-2*, 2001191) Bks Demand.

Drugs & the Community: Involving Community Residents in Combatting the Sale of Illegal Drugs. Ed. by Robert C. Davis et al. LC 92-33880. (Illus.). 328p. (C). 1993. 66.95 (*0-398-05835-0*) C C Thomas.

***Drugs & the Community: Involving Community Residents in Combatting the Sale of Illegal Drugs.** Ed. by Robert C. Davis et al. LC 93-33880. (Illus.). 328p. 1993. pap. 36.95 (*0-398-06086-X*) C C Thomas.

Drugs & the Criminal Justice System. Ed. by James A. Inciardi & Carl D. Chambers. LC 72-98036. (Sage Criminal Justice System Annuals Ser.: Vol. 2). (Illus.). 250p. reprint ed. pap. 71.30 (*0-317-08937-4*, 2021913) Bks Demand.

Drugs & the Delivery of Oxygen to Tissues. 1989. 191.00 (*0-8493-6656-9*, RC700) CRC Pr.

***Drugs & the Elderly: A Complete Guide for Healthcare Professionals to Optimizing Drug Therapy for Elderly Clients.** Alvin K. Swonger & Patricia M. Burbank. LC 94-29758. 1995. 34.95 (*0-86720-716-7*) Jones & Bartlett.

Drugs & the Elderly: Clinical, Social, & Policy Perspectives. Helene L. Lipton & Philip R. Lee. LC 87-33574. 280p. 1988. 37.50 (*0-8047-1295-6*) Stanford U Pr.

Drugs & the Eye. 3rd ed. Janet Vale & Barry Cox. 132p. 1992. pap. 115.00 (*0-7506-1041-7*) Buttrwrth-Heinemann.

Drugs & the Family. Susan DeStefano. (Social Impact Ser.). (Illus.). 88p. (J). (gr. 5-8). 1991. lib. bdg. 14.98 (*0-941477-61-4*) TFC Bks NY.

Drugs & the Family. Jo Martin. (Encyclopedia of Psychoactive Drugs Ser.: No. 2). (Illus.). 104p. (YA). (gr. 5 up). 1988. lib. bdg. 19.95 (*1-55546-220-0*); pap. 9.95 (*0-7910-0797-9*) Chelsea Hse.

Drugs & the Higher Consciousness: A New Model for Solving the Drug Problem. 1991. lib. bdg. 78.95 (*0-8490-4653-X*) Gordon Pr.

Drugs & the Human Body: With Implications for Society. 4th ed. Ken Liska. (Illus.). 464p. (C). 1993. pap. write for info. (*0-02-371091-8*) Macmillan.

Drugs & the Kidney. Graeme R. Catto. 176p. 1990. lib. bdg. 71.00 (*0-7923-8918-2*) Kluwer Ac.

Drugs & the Kidney. Ed. by K. D. Edwards. (Progress in Biochemical Pharmacology Ser.: Vol. 9). 300p. 1974. 88.00 (*3-8055-1693-2*) S Karger.

Drugs & the Law. Neil Grauer. (Encyclopedia of Psychoactive Drugs Ser.: No. 2). (Illus.). 120p. (J). (gr. 5 up). 1988. lib. bdg. 19.95 (*1-55546-230-8*) Chelsea Hse.

Drugs & the Law. Janet Grosshandler. Ed. by Ruth Rosen. (Drug Abuse Prevention Library). (YA). (gr. 7-12). 1993. 15.95 (*0-8239-1463-1*) Rosen Group.

DRUGS & the LAW: Detection, Recognition & Investigation. G. Miller. 1994. pap. 34.95 (*0-87526-398-4*) Gould.

Drugs & the Liver: High Risk Patients & Transplantation. Ed. by D. Galmarini et al. LC 93-1383. (Medical Science Symposia Ser.: Vol. 4). 204p. (C). 1993. lib. bdg. 76.50 (*0-7923-2307-6*) Kluwer Ac.

Drugs & the Lung. Ed. by Clive P. Page & W. James Metzger. (Advances in Clinical Pharmacology Ser.: Vol. 1). 624p. 1994. 125.00 (*0-7817-0135-X*) Raven.

Drugs & the Media. Richard S. Lee & Mary P. Lee. LC 93-21099. (Drug Abuse Prevention Library). (J). 1994. 15.95 (*0-8239-1537-9*) Rosen Group.

Drugs & the Peptic Ulcer, Vol. 1. C. J. Pfeiffer. 224p. 1982. 144.00 (*0-8493-6211-3*, RC821, CRC Reprint) Franklin.

Drugs & the Peptic Ulcer, Vol. 2. C. J. Pfeiffer. 280p. 1982. 144.00 (*0-8493-6212-1*, CRC Reprint) Franklin.

Drugs & the Performance Horse. Thomas Tobin. (Illus.). 488p. 1981. 67.95 (*0-398-04446-5*) C C Thomas.

Drugs & the Special Child. Michael J. Cohen. LC 77-10151. 1979. 29.95 (*0-89876-070-4*) Gardner Pr.

Drugs & the Youth Culture. Ed. by Frank R. Scarpitti & Susan K. Datesman. LC 80-11613. (Sage Annual Reviews of Drug & Alcohol Abuse Ser.: No. 4). (Illus.). 320p. reprint ed. pap. 91.20 (*0-8357-8508-4*, 2034798) Bks Demand.

Drugs & Therapy. Alvin K. Swonger & Larry Constantine. 431p. 1983. pap. text ed. 20.00 (*0-318-37137-5*) Little.

Drugs & Violence. 1992. lib. bdg. 75.00 (*0-8490-8821-6*) Gordon Pr.

Drugs & Violence: Causes, Correlates & Consequences in Crack Distribution Networks. 1992. lib. bdg. 250.00 (*0-8490-5465-6*) Gordon Pr.

Drugs & Where to Turn. Bea O. Rawls & Gwen Johnson. Ed. by Ruth Rosen. (Drug Abuse Prevention Library). (YA). (gr. 7-12). 1993. 15.95 (*0-8239-1466-6*) Rosen Group.

Drugs & Women. Paul August. (Encyclopedia of Psychoactive Drugs Ser.: No. 2). (Illus.). 128p. 1987. lib. bdg. 19.95 (*1-55546-227-8*) Chelsea Hse.

Drugs & Women. Paul N. August. (Encyclopedia of Psychoactive Drugs - Compact Paperback Library). (Illus.). 32p. (YA). (gr. 5 up). 1991. pap. 4.49 (*0-7910-0002-8*) Chelsea Hse.

Drugs & You. rev. ed. Arnold Madison. LC 82-3450. (Illus.). 80p. (J). (gr. 4 up). 1982. lib. bdg. 9.79 (*0-671-43986-3*, Julian Messner); pap. 4.95 (*0-671-49477-5*, Julian Messner) Silver Burdett Pr.

Drugs & You. rev. ed. Arnold Madison. Ed. by Jane Steltenpohl. (Illus.). 128p. (J). (gr. 4-6). 1990. lib. bdg. 13.98 (*0-671-69147-3*, Julian Messner); pap. 5.95 (*0-671-69148-1*, Julian Messner) Silver Burdett Pr.

Drugs & Your Brothers & Sisters. rev. ed. Rhoda McFarland. (Drug Abuse Prevention Library). (YA). (gr. 7-12). 1993. lib. bdg. 15.95 (*0-8239-1754-1*) Rosen Group.

Drugs & Your Child: What Can a Parent Do? Bobby A. La Loge. 32p. (Orig.). 1987. pap. 8.95 (*0-938147-03-X*) Flying Eagle.

Drugs & Your Friends. rev. ed. Sandra L. Smith. (Drug Abuse Prevention Library). (Illus.). 64p. (YA). (gr. 7-12). 1993. lib. bdg. 15.95 (*0-8239-1657-X*) Rosen Group.

Drugs & Your Parents. rev. ed. Sandra L. Smith. (Drug Abuse Prevention Library). (Illus.). 64p. (YA). (gr. 7-12). 1993. lib. bdg. 15.95 (*0-8239-1684-7*) Rosen Group.

Drugs & Youth: The Challenge of Today. Ed. by E. Harms. (C). 1973. 114.00 (*0-08-017063-3*, Pub. by Pergamon Repr UK) Franklin.

Drugs As a Social Problem. Wright & Devine. (C). 1994. 5.50 (*0-673-99399-X*) HarpCollege.

Drugs, Athletes, & Physical Performance. Ed. by J. A. Thomas. LC 88-22381. (Illus.). 254p. 1988. 47.50 (*0-306-42888-1*, Plenum Med Bk) Plenum.

Drugs Available Abroad. 2nd ed. Backus. 1994. 89.95 (*0-8103-7529-X*) Gale.

Drugs, Banks & Money Laundering: The Sordid Side of the Story the News Media Isn't Telling You. 1992. lib. bdg. 75.00 (*0-8490-5259-9*) Gordon Pr.

Drugs Between Research & Regulations. Ed. by C. Steichele et al. 300p. 1986. 55.00 (*0-387-91265-7*) Spr-Verlag.

Drugs, Biogenic Amines & Body Temperature: Proceedings of the Pharmacology of Thermoregulation Symposium, 3rd, Banff, Alberta, Sept. 1976. Pharmacology of Thermoregulation Symposium Staff et al. Ed. by K. E. Cooper. (Illus.). 1977. 93.00 (*3-8055-2395-5*) S Karger.

Drugs, Chemicals & Blood Dyscrasias. Margo Swanson & Ray Cook. LC 76-10190. 1133p. 1977. 68.50 (*0-914768-01-8*) Drug Intell Pubns.

***Drugs, Crime, & Corruption: Thinking the Unthinkable.** Richard Clutterbuck. LC 95-13890. 256p. 1995. 42.50 (*0-8147-1524-9*); pap. 17.50 (*0-8147-1529-X*) NYU Pr.

***Drugs, Crime & Criminal Justice, Set: Vols. I & II.** Ed. by Nigel South. LC 94-39196. (International Library of Criminology, Criminal Justice & Penology). (Illus.). 1000p. 1995. text ed. 224.95 (*1-85521-352-4*, Pub. by Dartmth Pub UK) Ashgate Pub Co.

***Drugs, Crime, & Other Deviant Adaptations: Longitudinal Studies.** Ed. by Howard B. Kaplan. (Longitudinal Research in the Social & Behavioral Sciences). 250p. 1995. 39.50 (*0-306-44876-9*, Plenum Pr) Plenum.

Drugs, Crime, & Social Isolation: Barriers to Urban Opportunity. Ed. by Adele V. Harrell & George E. Peterson. LC 92-15121. (Urban Opportunity Ser.). (Illus.). 318p. (Orig.). 1992. lib. bdg. 58.00 (*0-87766-570-2*); pap. text ed. 26.50 (*0-87766-571-0*) Urban Inst.

Drugs, Crime, & Social Policy. Thomas M. Mieczkowski. 416p. (C). 1991. pap. text ed. 48.00 (*0-205-13205-7*) Allyn.

Drugs, Crime & the Criminal Justice System. Ralph A. Weisheit. LC 90-80231. 405p. (C). 1990. pap. 21.95 (*0-87084-225-0*) Anderson Pub Co.

Drugs, Crime, & the Justice System. (Illus.). 224p. (Orig.). (C). 1993. pap. text ed. 40.00 (*1-56806-417-9*) Diane Pub.

Drugs, Crime & the Justice System. 1994. lib. bdg. 255.75 (*0-8490-9054-7*) Gordon Pr.

Drugs, Daydreaming, & Personality: A Study of College Youth. Bernard Segal et al. LC 80-10094. 254p. 1980. 49.95 (*0-89859-042-6*) L Erlbaum Assocs.

Drugs, Disease & the Periodontium. Robin A. Seymour & Peter A. Heasman. (Illus.). 384p. 1992. 98.00 (*0-19-261992-6*) OUP.

***Drugs, Divorce & a Slipping Image: The Unauthorized Story of the Beatles' "Get Back" Sessions.** Doug Sulpy & Ray Schweighardt. LC 94-69318. 320p. (Orig.). 1994. pap. 29.95 (*0-9643869-0-9*) The NineTen.

Drugs, Doctors, Demons & Disease. Perry A. Sperber. LC 70-111808. 294p. 1973. 13.10 (*0-87527-127-8*) Green.

Drugs Don't Take People, People Take Drugs. Eugene H. Kaplan & Herbert Wieder. 1974. 8.00 (*0-8184-0154-0*) Carol Pub Group.

Drugs, Drinking & Adolescence. 2nd ed. MacDonald. 264p. 1989. pap. 23.95 (*0-8151-5993-5*, Yr Bk Med Pubs) Mosby Yr Bk.

Drugs, Drug Addiction, & Drug Dealing: The Origin & Nature of, & the Solution to, the American Drug Problem. R. D. Rucker. 1991. 11.95 (*0-533-09334-1*) Vantage.

***Drugs, Family & My Life.** Bernice Hudson. 1995. 10.95 (*0-8062-5349-5*) Carlton.

Drugs for Control of Epilepsy: Actions on Neuronal Networks Involved in Seizure Disorders. Carl L. Faingold. 224p. 1991. 115.00 (*0-8493-5059-X*, RC374) CRC Pr.

Drugs for Mental Illness see Medicine & Mental Illness

Drugs for Rheumatic Disease: Vol. 8, MCP. Harold Paulus et al. (Illus.). 488p. 1987. 85.00 (*0-443-08011-9*) Churchill.

An Asterisk (*) at the beginning of an entry indicates that the title is appearing in BIP for the first time.

An Asterisk (*) at the beginning of an entry indicates that the title is appearing in BIP for the first time.

2123

Drumbeats, Masks, & Metaphor: Contemporary Afro-American Theatre. Genevieve Fabre. Tr. by Melvin Dixon. (Illus.). 304p. (C). 1983. 34.50 (*0-674-21678-4*) HUP.

Drumfire. Peter McCurtin. (Sundance Ser.: No. 38). 192p. 1982. pap. 1.95 (*0-8439-0976-5*) Dorchester Pub Co.

Drumfire - Buffalo War. Peter McCurtin. (Double Barrel Sundance Ser.). 384p. 1989. reprint ed. pap. 3.95 (*0-8439-2742-9*) Dorchester Pub Co.

Drumlin Symposium: Proceedings of the Drumlin Symposium-First International Conference on Geomorphology, Manchester, 16-18 September 1985. Ed. by J. Menzies & J. Rose. 362p. 1987. text ed. 105.00 (*90-6191-792-1*, Pub. by A A Balkema NE) Ashgate Pub Co.

Drummer Boy. Ed. by Mary W. De Young. 1990. 45.00 (*0-936128-40-2*) De Young Pr.

***Drummer Boy.** Ed. by Newell Chester. 160p. 1995. reprint ed. pap. 9.95 (*0-87839-095-2*) North Star.

***Drummer Boy: Comprising Four Years of Service with the Second Regiment, Minnesota Veteran Volunteers, 1861-1865.** William Bircher. Ed. by Newell L. Chester. (Illus.). 160p. 1995. reprint ed. 24.95 (*0-87839-094-4*) North Star.

***Drummer Boy at Bull Run.** Morris. (Bonnets & Bugles Ser.: No. 1). 1995. pap. 5.99 (*0-8024-0911-3*) Moody.

Drummer Girl Girl Talk, No. 12. L. E. Blair. 1991. pap. 2.95 (*0-307-22012-5*, Golden Pr) Western Pub.

Drummer Hoff. Barbara Emberley. LC 74-8201. (Illus.). 32p. (J). (gr. k-4). 1985. pap. 12.95 (*0-671-66682-7*, S&S Bks Young Read); pap. 5.95 (*0-671-66745-9*, S&S Bks Young Read) S&S Childrens.

Drummer in Our Time. A. W. Kayper-Mensah. (African Writers Ser.). 103p. 1975. pap. 8.95 (*0-435-90157-5*) Heinemann.

Drummer in the Woods. Burton L. Spiller. LC 79-19424. (Illus.). 256p. 1990. pap. 16.95 (*0-8117-2320-8*) Stackpole.

Drummers & Dreamers. Click Relander. (Illus.). 345p. (Orig.). 1986. reprint ed. pap. text ed. 9.95 (*0-914019-09-0*) NW Interpretive.

Drummer's Cook Book. John Pickering. 1993. 6.95 (*0-87166-826-2*, 93301) Mel Bay.

Drummer's Fitness Guide. Michael Johnson. (Illus.). 120p. (Orig.). 1988. pap. 14.95 (*0-317-91087-6*) Fit-to-Be Pub.

***Drummers of Jericho.** Carolyn Meyer. (J). 1995. 11.00 (*0-15-200441-6*); pap. 5.00 (*0-15-200190-5*) HarBrace.

Drummer's Path: Moving the Spirit with Traditional Drumming in Performance & Invocation. Sule G. Wilson. 128p. (Orig.). 1992. pap. 10.95 (*0-89281-359-8*) Inner Tradit.

Drummin' Men: The Swing Years. Burt Korall. 400p. 1990. text ed. 25.95 (*0-02-872000-8*) Schirmer Bks.

Drummin' Men, the Heartbeat of Jazz: The Be-Bop Years. Burt Korall. (Illus.). 1996. text ed. 27.95 (*0-02-870711-7*) Schirmer Bks.

Drumming at the Edge of Magic: A Journey into the Spirit of Percussion. Mickey Hart & Jay Stevens. LC 89-45985. (Illus.). 240p. (Orig.). 1990. pap. 19.95 (*0-06-250374-X*) Harper SF.

Drumming Patterns: The Components of Rhythm & Technique. Chuck P. Braman. (Illus.). 176p. (Orig.). 1988. pap. text ed. 20.00 (*0-9622293-0-X*) Drumstroke Pubns.

Drumming Rock & Roll Style. 1990. 5.95 (*0-685-32226-2*, K630) Hansen Ed Mus.

Drummond of Hawthornden: The Story of His Life & Writings. D. Masson. LC 68-24912. (English Biography Ser.: No. 31). 1969. reprint ed. lib. bdg. 59.95 (*0-8383-0282-3*) M S G Haskell Hse.

Drummond of Hawthornden: The Story of His Life & Writings. David Masson. (BCL1-PR English Literature Ser.). 490p. 1992. reprint ed. lib. bdg. 99.00 (*0-7812-7207-6*) Rprt Serv.

Drumm's War. William F. Bragg & R. C. House. LC 92-28138. (Novel of the West Ser.). 1992. 16.95 (*0-87131-695-1*) M Evans.

Drumright II (& Shamrock, Pemeta, Oilton & Olive) A Thousand Memories. D. Earl Newsom. (Illus.). 288p. 1987. 19.95 (*0-934188-25-4*) Evans Pubns.

Drumright, the Glory Days of a Boom Town. D. Earl Newson. LC 85-70033. (Illus.). 200p. 1985. 19.95 (*0-934188-17-3*) Evans Pubns.

***Drums.** James Boyd. LC 95-14812. (Illustrated Classics Ser.). (Illus.). (J). 1995. write for info. (*0-689-80176-9*, Atheneum Bks Young) S&S Childrens.

Drums. Joseph D. Ossorio et al. (Under Twenty Writing Society Ser.). (Illus.). 48p. (J). (gr. 3-5). 1994. pap. 6.95 (*1-56721-078-3*) Twenty-Fifth Cent Pr.

***Drums.** deluxe ed. James Boyd. LC 95-14812. (Illustrated Classics Ser.). (Illus.). (J). 1995. write for info. (*0-689-80177-7*, Atheneum Bks Young) S&S Childrens.

***Drums Bk. 1.** (Breeze Easy Method Ser.). 32p. (Orig.). 1994. pap. 6.50 (*0-89724-367-6*) Warner Brothers.

Drums A'Beating, Trumpets Sounding: Artistically Carved Powder Horns in the Provincial Manner, 1746-1781. William H. Guthman. (Illus.). 232p. 1993. 75.00 (*1-881264-05-X*) Conn Hist Soc.

Drums along the Amazon. large type ed. Victor G. Norwood. (Non-Fiction Ser.). 1974. 15.95 (*0-85456-269-9*) Ulverscroft.

Drums along the Mohawk. Walter D. Edmonds. 1992. 5.50 (*0-553-27412-0*, Starfire) Bantam.

Drums along the Mohawk. Walter Edmonds. 320p. 1981. reprint ed. lib. bdg. 27.95 (*0-89966-291-9*) Buccaneer Bks.

Drums & Shadows: Survival Studies among the Georgia Coastal Negroes. Georgia Writers' Program Staff. LC 73-3018. (Illus.). 274p. 1973. reprint ed. text ed. 55.00 (*0-8371-6832-5*, WRDS, Greenwood Pr) Greenwood.

Drums & Shadows: Survival Studies among the Georgia Coastal Negroes. Georgia Writers' Project Staff. LC 86-3370. (Brown Thrasher Bks.). (Illus.). 312p. 1986. reprint ed. 30.00 (*0-8203-0850-1*); reprint ed. pap. 14.95 (*0-8203-0851-X*) U of Ga Pr.

Drums Around the Fire. Nigel Findley et al. Ed. by Bill Bridges. (Orig.). 1993. per., pap. 8.00 (*1-56504-058-9*) White Wolf.

Drums at Saratoga. Lisa Banim. LC 93-16460. (Stories of the States Ser.). 64p. (Orig.). (J). (gr. 4-6). 1993. lib. bdg. 12.95 (*1-881889-20-3*) Silver Moon.

***Drums at Saratoga.** Lisa Banim. (Stories of the States Ser.). 108p. (Orig.). (J). (gr. 4-6). 1995. pap. 4.95 (*1-881889-70-X*) Silver Moon.

Drums at Sunset. Elsie W. Strother. LC 89-64494. (Historical Novel Ser.). 224p. (Orig.). 1990. pap. 5.00 (*0-88100-068-X*) Natl Writ Pr.

Drums in the Night see Jungle of Cities & Other Plays

Drums of a Different War. Joseph Polselli. LC 83-6443. 261p. 1984. 22.95 (*0-87949-241-4*) Ashley Bks.

Drums of ECK. Paul Twitchell. 242p. 1987. pap. 9.00 (*1-57043-040-3*) ECKANKAR.

Drums of ECK. rev. ed. Paul Twitchell. 242p. 1988. 9.00 (*0-88155-064-7*) Illum Way Pub.

Drums of Fu Manchu. Sax Rohmer. 18.95 (*0-8488-0619-0*) Amereon Ltd.

Drums of Moloch. Herbert C. Casteel. LC 90-55602. 164p. (Orig.). 1990. pap. 6.95 (*0-89900-384-2*) College Pr Pub.

Drums of Redemption: An Introduction to African Christianity. Harvey J. Sindima. LC 93-31637. (Contributions to the Study of Religion Ser.: Vol. 35). 232p. 1994. text ed. 55.00 (*0-313-29088-1*, Greenwood Pr) Greenwood.

Drums of the Head Hunters. Hap Gilliland. LC 87-40264. 207p. 1987. 7.95 (*1-55523-104-7*) Winston-Derek.

Drums of Vodou. Lois Wilcken. LC 92-368. (Performance in World Music Ser.: No. 8). 1992. 39.95 (*0-941677-26-5*); pap. 19.95 (*0-941677-16-8*); spiral bd. 29.95 (*0-941677-45-1*); audio 12.95 (*0-941677-01-X*) White Cliffs Media.

Drums of War. Ed. by George M. Daniels. LC 73-92611. 1974. 25.95 (*0-89388-126-0*) Okpaku Communications.

Drums of War. large type ed. Roy Clews. 560p. 1982. 15.95 (*0-7089-0866-7*) Ulverscroft.

Drums, Tomtoms & Rattles: Primitive Percussion Instruments for Modern Use. Bernard S. Mason. (Illus.). (YA). (gr. 5 up). 18.75 (*0-8446-5063-3*) Peter Smith.

Drums under the Windows. adapted ed. Sean O'Casey. 1961. pap. 4.75 (*0-8222-0336-7*) Dramatists Play.

Drunk Driving. 3rd ed. Lawrence E. Taylor. 1991. 110.00 (*0-316-83394-0*) Little.

Drunk Driving: An American Dilemma. James B. Jacobs. LC 88-17383. (Studies in Crime & Justice). (Illus.). xxii, 260p. 1989. pap. text ed. 13.95 (*0-226-38979-0*) U Ch Pr.

Drunk Driving: The Effects of Enforcement. HMSO Staff. (Home Office Research Study Ser.: No. 121). 86p. 1991. pap. 14.00 (*0-11-340999-0*, HM9099) UNIPUB.

Drunk Driving Defense. 2nd ed. Lawrence E. Taylor. LC 85-82121. (Illus.). 735p. 1986. 75.00 (*0-316-83383-5*) Little.

Drunk Driving in America: Strategies & Approaches to Treatment. Ed. by Stephen K. Valle. LC 86-18449. (Alcoholism Treatment Quarterly Ser.: Vol. 3, No. 2). 176p. 1986. text ed. 39.95 (*0-86656-603-1*) Haworth Pr.

Drunk Driving Laws in Foreign Countries. 56p. (Orig.). (C). 1993. pap. text ed. 20.00 (*1-56806-837-9*) Diane Pub.

Drunk on a Glacier, Talking to Flies. Janine P. Vega. 80p. 1988. pap. 6.00 (*0-940510-18-9*) Tooth of Time.

Drunk with Love. Ellen Gilchrist. 1987. pap. 10.95 (*0-316-31314-9*) Little.

Drunkard: Or, the Fallen Saved. William Smith. LC 70-104568. reprint ed. lib. bdg. 22.00 (*0-8398-1869-6*) Irvington.

Drunkard: or, the Fallen Saved. William Smith. LC 70-104568. 1987. reprint ed. pap. text ed. 4.95 (*0-8290-2104-3*) Irvington.

Drunkard: or The Fallen Saved! William H. Smith. (BCL1-PS American Literature Ser.). 50p. 1992. reprint ed. lib. bdg. 59.00 (*0-7812-6862-1*) Rprt Serv.

Drunkard's Children. 1983. 6.70 (*0-686-37693-5*) Rod & Staff.

Drunkard's Path Quilts: With Plastic Templates. Mary C. Waldrep. LC 93-2830. (Needlework Ser.). (Illus.). 32p. (Orig.). 1993. spiral bd. 3.95 (*0-486-27595-7*) Dover.

***Drunken Boat: Art, Rebellion, Anarchy.** Ed. by Max Blechman. (Illus.). 288p. 1994. pap. 12.00 (*1-57027-002-3*) Left Bank.

Drunken Boat see Season in Hell

Drunken King, or, The Origin of the State. Luc De Heusch. Tr. by Roy Willis. LC 81-47569. (African Systems of Thought Ser.). (Illus.). 288p. 1982. 35.00 (*0-253-31832-7*) Ind U Pr.

Drunken Sailor. Contrib by Herbert Rothgarber. 1975. 4.50 (*0-913334-28-6*, CM1035) Consort Music.

Drunken Universe: An Anthology of Persian Sufi Poetry. Tr. by Peter L. Wilson & Nasrollah Pourjavady. LC 87-32698. 155p. (Orig.). (PER.). 1988. pap. 10.95 (*0-933999-65-8*) Phanes Pr.

Drunkenness Offence: Proceedings of the International Symposium on Drunkenness Offence London, May, 1968. T. Cook & D. Gath. LC 75-80073. 1969. 88.00 (*0-08-006420-5*, Pub. by Pergamon Repr UK) Franklin.

Drunks, Whores & Idle Apprentices: Criminal Biographies of the Eighteenth Century. Philip Rawlings. LC 91-46370. 272p. 1992. 79.95 (*0-415-05056-1*, A7964) Routledge.

Drury Lane's Last Case. Ellery Queen. LC 87-82441. 232p. 1987. reprint ed. pap. 4.95 (*0-930330-70-6*) Intl Polygonics.

Drury Robertson, Sr. (1770-1797) Betty R. Kaufman. Ed. by Cheryl D. Robertson. (Illus.). 880p. 1990. lib. bdg. 70.00 (*0-9626602-0-5*) B Kaufman.

Drury's Guide to Best Plays. 4th ed. James M. Salem. LC 87-380. 488p. 1987. 39.50 (*0-8108-1980-5*) Scarecrow.

Druuna: Carnivora. Paolo E. Serpieri. LC 94-70743. (Illus.). 64p. 1994. reprint ed. 14.95 (*0-87816-224-0*) Kitchen Sink.

Druze. Robert B. Betts. LC 87-22696. (C). 1988. text ed. 27.00 (*0-300-04100-4*) Yale U Pr.

Druze. Abdallah M. Najjar. Ed. by Abdallah E. Najjar. Tr. & Intro. by Fred I. Massey. 215p. 1973. write for info. (*0-9600800-1-5*) A E Najjar.

Druze. Robert B. Betts. 192p. (C). 1990. reprint ed. pap. 11.00 (*0-300-04810-6*) Yale U Pr.

Druze Document. Gregory Fitzgerald & John Dillon. Ed. by John Magill. LC 88-23714. 256p. 1989. 14.95 (*0-912761-14-8*) Cliffhanger Pr.

Druze Faith. Sami N. Makarim. LC 73-19819. 1974. 25.00 (*0-88206-003-1*) Caravan Bks.

Druzes: A New Study of Their History, Faith, & Society. Nejla M. Abu-Izzeddin. LC 92-31449. (Illus.). xii, 259p. 1993. 74.50 (*90-04-09705-8*) E J Brill.

Druzes & the Maronites under the Turkish Rule from 1840 to 1860. Charles H. Churchill. LC 73-6273. (Middle East Ser.). 1977. reprint ed. 23.95 (*0-405-05329-0*) Ayer.

Dry All Night: The Picture Book Technique That Stops Bedwetting. Alison Mack. (Illus.). 1990. pap. 14.95 (*0-316-54225-3*) Little.

Dry & Wet-Dry Cooling Towers for Power Plants: Presented at the Winter Annual Meeting of the ASME, Detroit, MI, November 11-15, 1973 (Sponsored by the Heat Division, ASME) Ed. by Ralph L. Webb & Robert E. Barry. LC 73-89077. (American Society of Mechanical Engineers Handbook: Vol. 6). 159p. reprint ed. pap. 45.40 (*0-317-11240-6*, 2016895) Bks Demand.

***Dry Bones.** Illus. by Bob Barner. LC 95-29. (J). 1995. 13.95 (*0-8118-0827-0*) Chronicle Bks.

Dry Bones & Other Fossils. Gary Parker. LC 79-51174. (Illus.). (J). (gr. 2-4). 1979. pap. 5.95 (*0-89051-118-7*) Master Bks.

Dry Bones Live: Helping Congregations Discover New Life. Robert H. Craig & Robert C. Worley. LC 92-28535. 128p. (Orig.). 1993. pap. 9.99 (*0-664-25316-4*) Westminster John Knox.

***Dry Cell Battery Market.** 90p. (Orig.). 1995. pap. 2,195.00 (*0-7605-2084-4*) Rector Pr.

Dry Chemical Extinguishing Systems. National Fire Protection Association Staff. 1994. 20.25 (*0-317-63055-5*, 17-94) Natl Fire Prot.

Dry Chemistry: Analysis with Carrier-Bound Regents. O. Sonntag. LC 93-17796. (Laboratory Techniques in Biochemistry & Molecular Biology Ser.: Vol. 25). (ENG & GER.). 1993. lib. bdg. write for info. (*0-444-81458-2*); pap. write for info. (*0-444-81459-0*) Elsevier.

Dry Cleaning Plants. National Fire Protection Association Staff. 1990. 16.75 (*0-317-63066-0*, 32-90) Natl Fire Prot.

Dry Climate Gardening. LC 88-63839. (Illus.). 112p. 1989. pap. 9.95 (*0-89721-195-2*) Ortho Info.

***Dry Climate Gardening with Succulents.** James Folsom & Deborah Folsom. LC 94-29986. (American Garden Guides Ser.). 1995. pap. 25.00 (*0-679-75829-1*) Pantheon.

Dry Coastal Ecosystems. Ed. by E. Van der Maarel. 664p. 1994. 268.50 (*0-444-87349-X*) Elsevier.

Dry Collection of Subversive Literature. (Illus.). 143p. (Orig.). 1985. pap. 10.00 (*0-938245-01-5*) Inverted-A.

Dry Days, Wet Nights. Maribeth Boelts. LC 93-28674. (Illus.). (J). 1994. write for info. (*0-8075-1723-2*) A Whitman.

Dry Diplomacy: The United States, Great Britain, & Prohibition. Lawrence Spinelli. LC 88-11610. 181p. 1989. 40.00 (*0-8420-2298-8*) Scholarly Res Inc.

Dry Divide. Ralph Moody. Ed. by Jean S. Moody & Edna M. Morales. LC 94-14522. (Illus.). 230p. 1994. pap. 8.95 (*0-8032-8216-8*, Bison Books) U of Nebr Pr.

Dry Dock Planning Manual. (C). 1989. 495.00 (*0-89771-716-3*, Pub. by Lorne & MacLean Marine) St Mut.

Dry Dock Planning Manual. Lorne & MacLean Marine & Offshore Publications Staff. (C). 1987. 495.00 (*0-685-33852-5*, Pub. by Lorne & MacLean Marine) St Mut.

Dry Dock Planning Manual. OCS Marine Staff. (C). 1989. text ed. 720.00 (*0-906314-16-X*, Pub. by Lorne & MacLean Marine) St Mut.

Dry Drunk Revisited. R. J. Solberg. 10p. (Orig.). 1980. pap. 1.30 (*0-89486-091-7*, 1252B) Hazelden.

Dry Drunk Syndrome. rev. ed. R. J. Solberg. 20p. (Orig.). 1983. pap. 1.95 (*0-89486-172-7*, 1251B) Hazelden.

Dry Etch Technology. 1992. 53.00 (*0-8194-0724-0*, 1593) SPIE.

Dry Etching for Microelectronics. Ed. by R. A. Powell. (Materials Processing Theory & Practice Ser.: Vol. 4). 298p. 1985. 105.25 (*0-444-86905-0*, North Holland) Elsevier.

Dry Etching for VLSI. A. J. Van Roosmalen et al. (Updates in Applied Physics & Electrical Technology Ser.). (Illus.). 252p. 1991. 69.50 (*0-306-43835-6*, Plenum Pr) Plenum.

Dry Eye: A Comprehensive Guide. Ed. by M. A. Lemp & R. Marquardt. (Illus.). 256p. 1992. 98.00 (*0-387-53308-7*) Spr-Verlag.

Dry-Farming: A System of Agriculture for Countries Under a Low Rainfall. John A. Widtsoe. 1980. lib. bdg. 79.95 (*0-8490-3161-3*) Gordon Pr.

Dry Farming in the Northern Great Plains: Years of Readjustment, 1920-1990. Mary W. Hargreaves. LC 92-8558. (Development of Western Resources Ser.). 448p. 1992. 45.00 (*0-7006-0553-3*) U Pr of KS.

***Dry Fire: A Novel.** Catherine Lewis. 288p. 1996. 21.00 (*0-393-03835-1*) Norton.

Dry Fly: New Angles. Gary LaFontaine. (Illus.). 308p. 1990. 39.95 (*0-9626663-0-0*) Greycliff Pub.

Dry Fly Fishing. Dave Hughes. (Illus.). 56p. 1994. pap. 15.95 (*1-878175-68-8*) F Amato Pubns.

***Dry Fly-Fishing for Trout.** Tony Ritchie. (Illus.). 80p. 1994. 25.95 (*0-86417-622-8*) Seven Hills Bk.

***Dry Garden: A Practical Guide to Planning & Planting.** Mark Rumary. LC 95-18312. (Illus.). 128p. 1995. 19.95 (*0-8069-3831-5*) Sterling.

Dry Gulch Trail. large type ed. William M. Raine. 337p. 1992. reprint ed. lib. bdg. 17.95 (*1-56054-569-0*) Thorndike Pr.

Dry Humor: Tales of Arizona Weather. James E. Cook. Ed. by Robin Shepherd. LC 92-52500. (Illus.). 103p. (Orig.). 1992. pap. 6.95 (*0-935182-54-3*) Gem Guides Bk.

Dry It-You'll Like It. 3rd ed. Gen MacManiman. (Illus.). 80p. 1983. reprint ed. pap. 6.95 (*0-9611998-0-6*) MacManiman.

Dry Land Agriculture in India: The State of Art. L. L. Somani. (C). 1991. 300.00 (*0-685-74449-3*, Pub. by Scientific Pubs II) St Mut.

Dry Land Agriculture in India: The State of Art, Set. L. L. Somani. (C). 1991. write for info. (*81-7233-031-6*, Pub. by Scientific Pubs II) St Mut.

***Dry Land Tourist.** Maguire. Date not set. per. 12.95 (*0-920813-67-4*, Pub. by Sister Vision CN) InBook.

Dry Leaf in the Wind: A Saga of Pre-War Russia. Wolf Goodman. 1992. pap. 4.95 (*1-56171-070-9*) Sure Sellers.

Dry Mock, a Study of Irony in Drama. Alan R. Thompson. LC 80-20927. (Studies in Comparative Literature: No. 4). ix, 278p. 1981. reprint ed. lib. bdg. 37.50 (*0-87991-507-2*) Porcupine Pr.

Dry or Wet? Bruce McMillan. LC 86-27345. (Illus.). 32p. (J). (ps-2). 1988. 12.95 (*0-688-07100-7*); lib. bdg. 12.88 (*0-688-07101-5*) Lothrop.

Dry Peas & Lentils: Cooking with the "Protein Twins" Betty L. Janson. 224p. 1991. pap. 14.98 (*0-88290-370-5*) Horizon Utah.

Dry Pipeline: Increasing the Flow of Minority Faculty. Dorothy S. Linthicum. 62p. reprint ed. pap. 25.00 (*0-7837-5163-X*, 2044892) Bks Demand.

Dry Processing for Submicrometer Lithography. Ed. by James Bondur & Alan R. Reinberg. 307p. 1990. 53.00 (*0-8194-0221-4*, VOL. 1185) SPIE.

Dry Roof & a Cow: Dreams & Portraits of Our Neighbours. Henri Nouwen et al. LC 94-77014. (Illus.). 152p. (Orig.). 1994. pap. 19.95 (*0-9642003-2-5*) Mennonite Central.

***Dry Rot & Daffodils.** Mary Mackie. (Illus.). 192p. 1995. pap. 13.95 (*0-575-05934-6*, Pub. by V Gollancz UK) Trafalgar.

***Dry Rot & Daffodils: Life in a National Trust House.** Mary Mackie. (Illus.). 185p. 1995. 34.95 (*0-575-05754-8*, Pub. by V Gollancz UK) Trafalgar.

Dry Skin & Common Sense. Dale Alexander. LC 78-50125. 1978. 14.95 (*0-911638-05-9*) Witkower.

Dry Skull Dreams. Michael Greene. Ed. by Rebecca Todd. 256p. (Orig.). 1995. mass mkt. 5.50 (*0-671-89739-X*) PB.

Dry Stone Walls. Lawrence Garner. 1989. pap. 30.00 (*0-85263-666-0*, Pub. by Shire UK) St Mut.

Dry Strength Additives. Walter F. Reynolds. LC 79-67261. (Press Bks.). 188p. 1980. 28.00 (*0-89852-044-4*, 01-02-B044) TAPPI.

Dry Strength Additives. Technical Association of the Pulp & Paper Industry Staff. Ed. by Walter F. Reynolds. LC 79-67261. 200p. reprint ed. pap. 57.00 (*0-317-20573-0*, 2022792) Bks Demand.

Dry Suit Diving. Steven Barsky. (Specialty Diver Ser.). 93p. 1990. pap. text ed. 10.95 (*0-943717-87-6*) Concept Sys.

Dry Suit Diving: A Guide to Diving Dry. Steve Barsky et al. 1992. pap. 12.95 (*0-922769-36-2*) Watersport Pub.

Dry Suit Techniques Instructor Outline. (Specialty Diver Ser.). 26p. 1991. pap. text ed. 6.95 (*0-943717-95-7*) Concept Sys.

Dry Tears: The Story of a Lost Childhood. Nechama Tec. 1984. reprint ed. pap. 10.95 (*0-19-503500-3*) OUP.

Dry Those Tears. Robert A. Russell. 133p. 1975. reprint ed. pap. 6.95 (*0-87516-203-7*) DeVorss.

Dry Valley Drilling Project. Ed. by L. McGinnis. (Antarctic Research Ser.: Vol. 33). (Illus.). 480p. 1981. 39.00 (*0-87590-152-2*) Am Geophysical.

Dry Wall Contractors, 1995. American Business Directories Staff. 1995. spiral bd., pap. 665.00 (*1-56105-615-4*) Am Busn Direct.

Dry Washing for Gold. James Klein. LC 94-77565. (Illus.). 92p. (Orig.). 1994. pap. 7.95 (*0-935182-70-5*) Gem Guides Bk.

Dry White Season. Andre Brink. 320p. 1984. pap. 11.00 (*0-14-006890-2*, Penguin Bks) Viking Penguin.

Dry Years. rev. ed. Norman H. Clark. (Illus.). 352p. 1987. pap. 14.95 (*0-295-96466-9*) U of Wash Pr.

Drybrushing Soft Sculpture. Dona Snipes. LC 86-60508. (Illus.). 52p. 1986. pap. text ed. 8.95 (*0-916809-13-7*) Scott Pubns MI.

Dryclean-Laundry Managers Manual: Hazardous Materials Program. Mike Rager. (Illus.). (Orig.). (C). 1989. pap. write for info. (*0-318-65929-8*) Amer Hazmat.

Dryden. C. Hollis. LC 74-6383. (Studies in Dryden: No. 10). 1974. lib. bdg. 75.00 (*0-8383-1753-7*) M S G Haskell Hse.

Dryden. Ed. by Keith Walker. (Oxford Authors Ser.). 800p. 1987. pap. 19.95 (*0-19-281402-8*) OUP.

Dryden. George E. Saintsbury. Ed. by John Morley. LC 68-58394. (English Men of Letters Ser.). reprint ed. lib. bdg. 27.50 (*0-404-51726-9*) AMS Pr.

D

An Asterisk (*) at the beginning of an entry indicates that the title is appearing in BIP for the first time.

D

An Asterisk (*) at the beginning of an entry indicates that the title is appearing in BIP for the first time.

2125

Du Pont De Nemours on the Dangers of Inflation: An Address by Pierre Sanvel DuPont, 1790. Tr. by Edmond E. Lincoln. (Kress Library of Business & Economics Publication: No. 7). 58p. 1949. pap. 9.95 (*0-678-09902-2*, Kress Lib Business) Kelley.

Du Pont Dynasty: Behind the Nylon Curtain. Gerald Colby. 960p. 1954. 30.00 (*0-8184-0352-7*) Carol Pub Group.

Du Quesne: Washington's First Campaign. Richard C. Ashton. LC 93-93949. 232p. 1994. pap. 10.00 (*1-56002-355-4*, Univ Edtns) Aegina Pr.

Du Regime Des Fiefs En Normandie Au Moyen Age. Maurice Rabasse. LC 80-2006. reprint ed. 29.50 (*0-404-18588-6*) AMS Pr.

Du Roman, Sur Stendahl, Flaubert, et les Goncourt. Emile Zola. (FRE.). 1989. pap. 24.95 (*0-7859-3317-4*, 2870273045) Fr & Eur.

Du Style a la Pensee: Trois Etudes Sur les Caracteres de la Bruyere. Jules Brody. LC 80-66328. (French Forum Monographs: No. 20). 88p. (Orig.). (FRE.). 1980. pap. 9.95 (*0-917058-19-4*) French Forum.

Du Tac au Tac: Managing Conversations in French. 2nd ed. Jeannette Bragger & Donald Rice. 1991. audio, text ed. 33.95 (*0-8384-2221-7*) Heinle & Heinle.

Du Theatre. Louis-Sebastien Mercier. xvi, 372p. 1973. reprint ed. write for info. (*3-487-04908-2*, Pub. by Georg Olms GW) Lubrecht & Cramer.

Du Vall Method for Acquiring Great Self-Publishing Wealth. 7th ed. Dean F. Du Vall. 88p. 1980. pap. 25.00 (*0-931232-10-4*) Du Vall Financial.

Du Vouloir Dire: Traite d'Epistemologie des Sciences Humaines. J. Gagnepain. 1982. 123.00 (*0-08-027083-2*, Pub. by Pergamon Repr UK) Franklin.

DU-WOP. Johnny Keyes. LC 91-90853. (Illus.). 208p. (Orig.). 1991. pap. 9.95 (*0-9629061-0-7*) Vesti Pr.

Du'A, on Wings of Prayer. rev. ed. Ruth Moffet. Ed. by Keven Brown. 96p. 1984. 14.95 (*0-87961-142-1*); pap. 6.95 (*0-87961-143-X*) Naturegraph.

Dual Addiction: Pharmacological Issues in the Treatment of Concomitant Alcoholism & Drug Abuse. Ed. by Mary J. Kreek & Barry Stimmel. LC 84-6592. (Advances in Alcohol & Substance Abuse Ser.: Vol. 3, No. 4). 120p. 1984. text ed. 39.95 (*0-86656-318-0*) Haworth Pr.

Dual Algebras with Applications to Invariant Subspaces & Dilation Theory. H. Bercovici et al. LC 84-24528. (CBMS Regional Conference Series in Mathematics: No. 56). 108p. 1985. pap. text ed. 24.00 (*0-8218-0706-4*, CBMS56) Am Math.

Dual Allegiance: Freud As a Modern Jew. Moshe Gresser. LC 93-11648. 304p. (C). 1994. 59.50 (*0-7914-1811-1*); pap. 19.95 (*0-7914-1812-X*) State U NY Pr.

Dual Attraction: Understanding Bisexuality. Martin S. Weinberg et al. 400p. 1993. text ed. 27.95 (*0-02-934285-6*) Free Pr.

Dual Attraction: Understanding Bisexuality. Martin S. Weinberg et al. (Illus.). 448p. 1994. 27.50 (*0-19-508482-9*) OUP.

***Dual Attraction: Understanding Bisexuality.** Martin S. Weinberg et al. 448p. 1995. pap. 15.95 (*0-19-509841-2*) OUP.

Dual Boundary Element Analysis of Crack Growth. A. Portela. LC 92-75028. (Topics in Engineering Ser.: Vol. 14). 192p. 1993. 108.00 (*1-56252-116-0*) Computational Mech MA.

Dual Brain: Hemispheric Specialization in Humans. Ed. by D. Frank Benson & Eran Zaidel. LC 85-24955. 430p. 1985. lib. bdg. 49.95 (*0-89862-643-9*) Guilford Pr.

Dual Brain, Religion, & the Unconscious. Sim C. Liddon. 265p. 1989. lib. bdg. 27.95 (*0-87975-523-7*) Prometheus Bks.

Dual Career Couples: New Perspectives in Counseling. Marion Stoltz-Loike. 275p. 1992. 28.95 (*1-55620-093-5*, 72034) Am Coun Assn.

Dual Career Couples in the Public Sector: A Management Guide for Human Resource Professionals. Willa M. Bruce & Christine M. Reed. LC 90-22121. 184p. 1991. text ed. 55.00 (*0-89930-552-0*, BDB, Quorum Bks) Greenwood.

Dual-Career Families: Contemporary Organizational & Counseling Issues. Uma Sekaran. LC 86-15206. (Social & Behavioral Science Ser.). 272p. 1986. 34.95x (*1-55542-005-2*) Jossey-Bass.

Dual Career Marriage: A System in Transition. Lisa Silberstein. 216p. 1992. text ed. 39.95 (*0-8058-0712-8*); pap. 22.50 (*0-8058-1213-X*) L Erlbaum Assocs.

Dual-Career Marriage: Conflict & Treatment. David G. Rice. LC 79-7179. 1979. text ed. 22.95 (*0-02-926380-8*) Free Pr.

***Dual Citizenship.** Patrick Matriscrana & Dorothy Miller. 76p. (Orig.). Date not set. pap. 2.95 (*1-878993-66-6*) Jeremiah Pubs.

Dual City: The Restructuring of New York. John H. Mollenkopf & Manuel Castells. LC 90-45448. 256p. 1991. 45.00 (*0-87154-606-X*) Russell Sage.

Dual City: The Restructuring of New York. Ed. by John H. Mollenkopf & Manuel Castells. (Illus.). 496p. 1992. pap. 16.95 (*0-87154-608-6*) Russell Sage.

Dual Concordance to Leibniz's Philosophische Schriften. Leibniz & Lexicon. Ed. by Graeme Hunter et al. vii, 419p. 1988. write for info. (*3-487-09094-5*, Pub. by Georg Olms GW); fiche write for info. (*0-318-71367-5*, Pub. by Georg Olms GW) Lubrecht & Cramer.

Dual Destinies: The Jewish Encounter with Protestant America. Egal Feldman. 352p. 1990. 34.95 (*0-252-01726-9*) U of Ill Pr.

Dual Diagnosis: Counseling the Mentally Ill Substance Abuser. Katie Evans & J. Michael Sullivan. LC 90-3036. 191p. 1990. lib. bdg. 45.00 (*0-89862-436-3*); pap. text ed. 17.95 (*0-89862-450-9*) Guilford Pr.

Dual Diagnosis: Double Trouble in Chemical Dependency. J. Stephen Clifford. 16p. (Orig.). 1990. pap. 2.95 (*0-926028-03-0*) Edgehill Pubns.

Dual Diagnosis: Evaluation, Treatment, Training, & Program Development. Ed. by J. Solomon et al. 1994. 49.50 (*0-306-44543-3*, Plenum Med Bk) Plenum.

Dual Diagnosis Bibliography: 1993 Edition. Caroline Mohr & Kathryn Bays. 88p. 1993. pap. 15.00 (*1-884442-09-9*) Vida Pubng.

***Dual Diagnosis Bibliography: 1995 Edition.** Ed. by Caroline Mohn & Kathryn Bays. 101p. (C). 1995. pap. 18.00 (*1-884442-13-7*) Vida Pubng.

Dual Diagnosis in Substance Abuse. Ed. by Mark Gold & Andrew E. Slaby. 352p. 1991. 110.00 (*0-8247-8457-X*) Dekker.

Dual Diagnosis of Major Mental Illness & Substance Disorder. Ed. by Kenneth Minkoff & Robert Drake. LC 87-646993. (New Directions for Mental Health Services Ser.: No. MHS 50). 1991. 17.95 (*1-55542-794-4*) Jossey-Bass.

***Dual Diagnosis Workbook.** Dennis C. Daley. 163p. 1994. pap. 15.95 (*0-8309-0666-5*) Ind Pr MO.

Dual Disadvantage of Displaced Homemakers: Findings from the Study, Low-Wage Jobs & Workers: Trends & Options for Change. Roberta M. Spalter-Roth. 14p. 1989. pap. 5.00 (*0-685-29928-7*) Inst Womens Policy Rsch.

Dual Disorders: Counseling Clients with Chemical Dependency & Mental Illness. Dennis C. Daley & Frances Campbell. 23p. 1989. pap. 3.00 (*0-89486-586-2*, 5218B) Hazelden.

Dual Disorders: Counseling Clients with Chemical Dependency & Mental Illness. 2nd ed. Dennis C. Daley et al. LC 92-48321. 250p. 1993. pap. 16.95 (*0-89486-449-1*, 5023A) Hazelden.

Dual Disorders Recovery Book: A Twelve Step Program of Recovery for Those of Us with Addiction & an Emotional or Psychiatric Illness. LC 92-34149. 250p. (Orig.). 1993. pap. 10.00 (*0-89486-849-7*, 1500) Hazelden.

***Dual Disorders Recovery Counseling.** Dennis C. Daley & Michael E. Thase. 170p. 1994. pap. 15.95 (*0-8309-0694-0*) Ind Pr MO.

Dual-Earner Families: International Perspectives. Ed. by Suzan Lewis et al. 256p. 1991. 55.00 (*0-8039-8382-4*); pap. 22.50 (*0-8039-8383-2*) Sage.

***Dual-Earner Marriage: The Elaborate Balancing Act.** Jack Balswick & Judith Balswick. LC 94-48423. 192p. (Orig.). 1995. pap. 9.99 (*0-8007-5530-8*) Revell.

Dual Economy. Robert T. Averitt. (C). 1968. pap. text ed. 6.95 (*0-393-09781-1*) Norton.

Dual Enigma. large type ed. Michael Underwood. 1990. 21.95 (*0-7089-2263-5*) Ulverscroft.

Dual Frequency Induction Gear Hardening. John M. Storm & Michael R. Chaplin. (Fall Technical Meeting Papers). (Illus.). 8p. 1986. pap. 30.00 (*1-55589-472-0*, 86FTM8) AGMA.

Dual Heritage: Immigrants from the Atlas Mountains in an Israeli Village. Moshe Shokeid. 270p. 1985. text ed. 34.95x (*0-88738-028-X*) Transaction Pubs.

Dual Identities: Counseling Chemically Dependent Gay Men & Lesbians. Dana Finnegan & Emily McNally. 128p. (Orig.). 1989. pap. 11.00 (*0-89486-418-1*, 5011A) Hazelden.

Dual Image. Nora Roberts. (Language of Love Ser.: No. 29). 1993. mass mkt. 3.59 (*0-373-51029-2*, 1-51029-6) Silhouette.

Dual Legacies in the Contemporary Caribbean: Continuing Aspects of British & French Dominion. Ed. by Paul Sutton. 278p. 1986. 35.00 (*0-7146-3262-7*, Pub. by F Cass Pubs UK) Intl Spec Bk.

Dual Levels of Meaning of Satiric Devices in A Tale of a Tub. Hwal Kim. LC 89-85602. 117p. 1989. pap. 12.95 (*0-87921-081-8*) Attic Pr.

Dual Mode Cellular. Lawrence Harte. (Illus.). 280p. (C). 1992. 95.00 (*0-9631965-0-2*) P T Steiner.

Dual Models. Magnus J. Wenninger. LC 82-14767. (Illus.). 208p. 1983. 39.95 (*0-521-24524-9*) Cambridge U Pr.

Dual Perspective: Inclusion of Ethnic Minority Content in the Social Work Curriculum. Delores G. Norton. 1978. 3.85 (*0-685-21303-X*, 78-380-06) Coun Soc Wk Ed.

Dual Process Model of Impression Formation, Vol. 1. Ed. by Robert Wyer, Jr. & Thomas Srull, Jr. 208p. 1988. 39.95 (*0-89859-888-5*) L Erlbaum Assocs.

Dual Process Model of Impression Formation, Vol. 1. Ed. by Robert S. Wyer, Jr. & Thomas Srull, Jr. (Advances in Social Cognition Ser.). 208p. 1988. pap. 19.95 (*0-89859-673-4*) L Erlbaum Assocs.

Dual Reciprocity Boundary Element Method. P. W. Partridge et al. LC 91-70442. (Computational Engineering Ser.). 300p. 1991. 145.00 (*0-945824-82-3*) Computational Mech MA.

Dual Relationships in Counseling. Barbara Herlihy & Gerald Corey. 1992. 25.95 (*1-55620-090-0*) Am Coun Assn.

Dual Resonance Models & Superstrings. P. H. Frampton. 560p. 1986. text ed. 90.00 (*9971-5-0080-9*); pap. text ed. 47.00 (*9971-5-0081-7*) World Scientific Pub.

Dual Ring Dog. Jacqueline Fraser & Amy Ammen. (Illus.). 256p. 1991. 25.95 (*0-87605-539-0*) Howell Bk.

Dual Selection Criteria with Multiple Alternatives: Migration, Work Status, & Wages. Wim P. Vijverberg. (Living Standards Measurement Study Working Paper Ser.: No. 78). 46p. 1991. 6.95 (*0-8213-1766-0*, 11766) World Bank.

Dual Theory. Ed. by M. Jacob. LC 74-83266. (Physics Reports Reprint Bk.: Vol. 1). 399p. 1975. 36.00 (*0-444-10743-6*, North Holland) Elsevier.

Dual Theory. Ed. by M. Jacob. (Physics Reports Reprint Bk.: Vol. 1). 1986. reprint ed. pap. 32.50 (*0-444-87028-8*, North Holland) Elsevier.

Dual-Use Technologies & Export Administration in the Post-Cold War Era. National Research Council, Office of International Affairs Staff. 232p. (Orig.). (C). 1994. pap. text ed. 33.00 (*0-309-05031-6*) Natl Acad Pr.

Dual Water Systems, No. M24. 64p. 1983. pap. 17.50 (*0-89867-290-2*, 30024) Am Water Wks Assn.

Dual World Economy: Forty Years of Development Experience. Ed. by Willem L. Adriaansen & J. G. Waardenburg. 304p. 1992. 29.95 (*0-19-562732-6*) OUP.

Dualism. Herbert L. Beierle. 1979. 10.00 (*0-940480-06-9*) UNI Press.

Dualism & Discontinuity in Industrial Societies. Suzanne Berger & Michael J. Piore. LC 79-25172. (Illus.). 176p. 1980. 54.95 (*0-521-23134-5*) Cambridge U Pr.

Dualism & Hierarchy in Lowland South America: Trajectories of Indigenous Social Organization. Alf Hornborg. (Uppsala Studies in Cultural Anthropology: No. 9). 304p. (Orig.). 1988. pap. 53.00x (*91-554-2166-0*, Pub. by Uppsala Univ Acta Univ Uppsaliensis SW) Coronet Bks.

Dualism, Dependency, & Continuing Underdevelopment: Experience in Indian Ocean Countries. (Working Papers Ser.: No. 79-10). 62p. 1979. pap. 5.00 (*0-686-78220-8*, CRD014) UNIPUB.

Dualistic Unionism & Industrial Relations. Elias T. Ramos. 250p. (Orig.). (C). 1990. pap. 13.75 (*971-10-0415-1*, Pub. by New Day Pub PH) Cellar.

Dualists. Stephen Bowkett. (YA). (gr. 5-8). 1990. pap. 17.95 (*0-575-04106-4*, Pub. by V Gollancz UK) Trafalgar.

Dualities & Dichotomies: The Works of John Briggs. Katherine Duncan. (Illus.). 27p. (Orig.). (C). 1990. pap. 10.00 (*0-9619219-3-5*) Polk Mus Art.

Duality & Definability in First Order Logic. Michael Makkai. LC 93-4868. (Memoirs Ser.: No. 503). 106p. 1993. pap. 30.00 (*0-8218-2565-8*) Am Math.

Duality & Modern Economics. Richard Cornes. (Illus.). 304p. (C). 1992. 69.95 (*0-521-33291-5*); pap. 29.95 (*0-521-33601-5*) Cambridge U Pr.

Duality & Perturbation Methods in Critical Point Theory. N. Ghoussoub. (Cambridge Tracts in Mathematics Ser.: No. 107). 256p. (C). 1993. 54.95 (*0-521-44025-4*) Cambridge U Pr.

Duality & Unity of the Brain: Unified Functioning & Specialisation of the Hemispheres. Ed. by D. Ottoson. LC 87-42720. (Wenner-Gren International Symposia Ser.: Vol. 47). 516p. 1987. 125.00 (*0-306-42720-6*, Plenum Pr) Plenum.

Duality for Actions & Coactions of Measures Groupoids on Von Neumann Algebras. Yamanouchi. (MEMO Ser.). 109p. 1993. 26.00 (*0-8218-2545-3*) Am Math.

Duality of the Mind. A. L. Wigan. LC 85-50042. 368p. 1985. 35.00 (*0-934710-11-2*) J Simon.

Duality of the Mind. limited ed. A. L. Wigan. LC 85-50042. 368p. 1985. 48.00 (*0-934710-12-0*) J Simon.

Duality of Truth. Henry Wagner. 1968. 7.50 (*0-685-42486-3*) Green Dolphin.

Duality, Separability & Functional Structure: Theory & Economic Applications. C. Blackorby et al. (Dynamic Economics Ser.: Vol. 2). 396p. 1978. 85.50 (*0-444-00235-9*, North Holland) Elsevier.

Duality Theories in Linear, Quadratic & Convex Programming: A Survey. Nazir G. Dossani. (Discussion Paper Ser.: No. 44). 1971. pap. 10.00 (*1-55869-028-X*) Regional Sci Res Inst.

Duane Hanson. (Illus.). 112p. 1990. 45.00 (*3-89322-205-7*, Pub. by Edition Cantz GW) Dist Art Pubs.

Duane Hanson: Sculptures. Duane Hanson. (Illus.). 80p. 1992. 45.00 (*3-89322-394-0*, Pub. by Edition Cantz GW) Dist Art Pubs.

Duane's Clinical Ophthalmology, 5 vols. & index. Loose Leaf Reference Services Staff. Ed. by William Tasman et al. (Illus.). 80.00 (*0-685-71848-4*) Lippincott.

Duane's Clinical Ophthalmology, 5 vols. & index, Set. Loose Leaf Reference Services Staff. Ed. by William Tasman et al. (Illus.). ring bd. 495.00 (*0-06-148007-X*) Lippincott.

DUAT & Weather Interpretation Handbook. William B. Sanders & John P. Davis. LC 90-91561. (General Aviation Ser.). (Illus.). 96p. 1990. pap. 14.95 (*0-931145-13-9*) Sandlight Pubns.

Duayne Hatchett: Recent Paintings & Sculpture. Douglas G. Schultz. (Orig.). 1974. 2.50 (*0-914782-10-X*) Buffalo Acad.

Dub. Thom Jurek. (Illus.). 36p. (Orig.). 1986. pap. 4.95 (*0-932597-03-3*) In Camera.

Dubai Tales. Muhammed A. Murr. Tr. by Peter Clark. 160p. (Orig.). 1990. pap. 26.00 (*0-948259-86-8*, Pub. by Forest Bks UK) Dufour.

DuBellay's Les Antiquitez de Rome; Songe ou vision sur le mesme subject: Ruines of Rome, Visions of Bellay; Edmund Spenser's English translation on facing pages. Ed. by Malcolm C. Smith. 144p. 1994. pap. 8.00 (*0-86698-126-8*, P22) MRTS.

***Dubester's U. S. Census Bibliography with SuDocs Class Numbers & Indexes.** Kevin L. Cook. 450p. 1995. lib. bdg. 85.00 (*1-56308-295-0*) Libs Unl.

Dubhe. Tom Claffe. Ed. by James B. Van Treese. 200p. 1994. pap. 7.95 (*1-56901-078-1*) NW Pub.

Dubin's Lives. Bernard Malamud. 400p. 1994. 10.95 (*0-14-018760-X*, Penguin Classics) Viking Penguin.

Dubious Battles: Aggression, Defeat, & the International System. John Arquilla. 256p. 1992. 49.50 (*0-8448-1734-1*, Crane Russak); pap. 22.95 (*0-8448-1736-8*, Crane Russak) Taylor & Francis.

Dubious Hills. Pamela Dean. 320p. 1994. 21.95 (*0-312-85442-0*) Tor Bks.

Dubious Hills. Pamela Dean. 320p. 1995. mass mkt. 4.99 (*0-8125-2362-8*) Tor Bks.

Dubious Honors: A Book of Prefaces. M. F. Fisher. LC 87-82587. 224p. 1990. pap. 9.95 (*0-86547-414-1*, North Pt Pr) FS&G.

Dubious Journey: From Class to Class. Anne Near. LC 92-76050. (Illus.). (Orig.). 1993. pap. 10.00 (*0-9635674-0-3*) Hereford Pub.

Dubious Legacy. large type ed. Mary Wesley. LC 92-12650. 1992. 19.95 (*0-7927-1357-5*, Eagle Lrg Print) Chivers N Amer.

Dubious Legacy. large type ed. Mary Wesley. 1992. pap. 17.95 (*0-7927-1356-7*, Paragon Lrg Print) Chivers N Amer.

Dubious Legacy. Mary Wesley. 272p. 1993. reprint ed. pap. 10.00 (*0-14-017327-7*, Penguin Bks) Viking Penguin.

Dubious Miss Dalrymple. Kasey Michaels. 192p. 1990. pap. 2.95 (*0-380-89908-6*) Avon.

Dubious Persuasions: Short Stories by Jack Matthews. Jack Matthews. LC 81-47591. (Poetry & Fiction Ser.). 168p. 1981. 16.50 (*0-8018-2692-6*) Johns Hopkins.

Dubious Specter: A Skeptical Look at the Soviet Nuclear Threat. rev. ed. Fred Kaplan. LC 80-50894. 93p. 1980. pap. 4.95 (*0-89758-023-0*) Inst Policy Stud.

Dubious Victory: The Reconstruction Debate in Ohio. Robert D. Sawrey. LC 91-40414. (Illus.). 216p. 1992. lib. bdg. 30.00 (*0-8131-1776-3*) U Pr of Ky.

Dublin. (Insight Guides Ser.). (Orig.). 1993. pap. 21.95 (*0-395-66304-0*) HM.

Dublin. John Harvey. (Illus.). 1977. reprint ed. 11.50 (*0-85409-749-X*) Charles River Bks.

Dublin: A Grand Tour. Jacqueline O'Brien & Desmond Guinness. LC 94-262. 1994. write for info. (*0-8109-3216-4*) Abrams.

Dublin: A Traveller's Companion. Thomas Pakenham & Valerie Pakenham. 1988. write for info. (*0-318-62730-2*) Macmillan.

Dublin: City Guide. Tony Wheeler. (Illus.). 308p. (Orig.). 1993. pap. 9.95 (*0-86442-184-2*) Lonely Planet.

Dublin: One Thousand Years. Stephen Conlin. 1988. 19.95 (*0-86278-174-4*, Pub. by OBrien Pr IE); pap. 12.95 (*0-86278-171-X*, Pub. by OBrien Pr IE) Dufour.

Dublin: The Shaping of a Capital. Andrew Maclaran. LC 92-43255. (World Cities Ser.). 242p. 1993. text ed. 49.95 (*0-470-22009-0*, Belhaven) Halsted Pr.

***Dublin: The Shaping of a Capital.** Andrew Maclaran. (World Cities Ser.). 1993. text ed. 59.95 (*0-471-94711-3*) Wiley.

Dublin Affair. P. S. Donoghue. LC 87-46355. 352p. 1988. 18.95 (*1-55611-092-8*) D I Fine.

Dublin Affair. P. S. Donoghue. 1989. mass mkt. 4.95 (*1-55817-288-2*, Pinnacle NY) Windsor NY.

Dublin & Cork. (American Express Travel Guides Ser.). (Illus.). 192p. 1993. pap. 13.00 (*0-671-84932-8*, P-H Travel) P-H Gen Ref & Trav.

***Dublin Anthology.** Douglas Bennett. 288p. (Orig.). 1994. pap. 19.95 (*0-7171-2122-4*, Pub. by Gill & MacMill IE) Irish Bks Media.

Dublin As a Work of Art. Colm Lincoln. (Illus.). 224p. 1993. 45.00 (*0-86278-313-5*, Pub. by OBrien Pr IE) Dufour.

Dublin Bay: From Killiney to Howth. Brian Lalor. LC 89-82063. (Illus.). 160p. 1990. 45.00 (*0-86278-203-1*, Pub. by OBrien Pr IE) Dufour.

Dublin Book of Irish Verse, Seventeen Twenty-Eight - Nineteen Hundred Nine. Ed. by John E. Cooke. LC 70-152148. (Granger Index Reprint Ser.). 1977. reprint ed. 42.95 (*0-8369-6251-6*) Ayer.

Dublin Crossing: Romance & Adventure in the Viking Era. Sandy Dengler. (Misty Isle Ser.). 348p. 1993. pap. 9.99 (*0-8024-2293-4*) Moody.

Dublin Decorative Plasterwork. C. P. Durran. 1967. 35.00 (*0-693-01112-2*) Transatl Arts.

Dublin Diary. Joseph A. Schufle. (Illus.). 240p. 1993. 48.00 (*0-945407-09-2*) Meadow Pr NM.

Dublin Drawn & Quartered. Brian Lalor. (Illus.). 64p. 1991. 10.95 (*0-86278-251-1*, Pub. by OBrien Pr IE) Dufour.

Dublin Gate Theatre 1928-1978. Richard Pine & Richard Cave. (Theatre in Focus Ser.). (Illus.). 124p. 1984. sl., pap. 105.00 (*0-85964-156-2*) Chadwyck-Healey.

Dublin Hanged: Crime, Law Enforcement, & Punishment in Dublin, 1780-95. Brian Henry. 224p. 1994. text ed. 39.50 (*0-7165-2512-7*, Pub. by Irish Acad Pr IE) Intl Spec Bk.

Dublin in the Age of William Butler Yeats & James Joyce. Richard M. Kain. LC 62-16474. (Centers of Civilization Ser.: Vol. 7). (Illus.). 232p. (C). 1990. pap. 9.95 (*0-8061-2263-3*) U of Okla Pr.

Dublin Musical Calendar 1700-1760. Brian Boydell. 320p. 1988. 45.00 (*0-7165-2430-9*, Pub. by Irish Acad Pr IE) Intl Spec Bk.

Dublin, Nineteen Thirteen. Ed. by Gary Granville. 112p. 1989. pap. 9.95 (*0-86278-023-3*, Pub. by OBrien Pr IE) Dufour.

Dublin Paper War of 1786-88. W. J. McCormack. 176p. 1993. text ed. 39.50 (*0-7165-2505-4*, Pub. by Irish Acad Pr IE) Intl Spec Bk.

Dublin Pocket Guide. Berlitz Editors. (Pocket Guides Ser.). 144p. 1994. pap. 7.95 (*2-8315-2675-2*) Berlitz.

Dublin School, a New Beginning, 1970-1985. Charles Latham, Jr. (Illus.). 1987. pap. 10.00 (*0-87233-089-3*) Bauhan.

Dublin Stage, 1720-1745: A Calendar of Plays, Entertainments, & Afterpieces. John C. Greene & Gladys L. Clark. LC 91-58886. 480p. 1993. 65.00 (*0-934223-22-X*) Lehigh Univ Pr.

Dublin Street Life & Lore: An Oral History. Kevin C. Kearns. (Illus.). 256p. 1991. 34.95 (*0-907606-97-0*, Pub. by Lilliput Pr Ltd IE) Irish Bks Media.

***Dublin Tenement Life: An Oral History.** Kevin C. Kearns. (Illus.). 320p. Date not set. 33.95 (*0-7171-2178-X*, Pub. by Gill & MacMill IE) Irish Bks Media.

Dublin Theatres & Theatre Customs, 1637-1820. L. T. Stockwell. LC 67-29560. 1972. 24.95 (*0-405-09002-1*) Ayer.

Dublin Wit. Paul Ryan. 1986. pap. 6.95 (*0-86278-103-5*, Pub. by OBrien Pr IE) Dufour.

An Asterisk (*) at the beginning of an entry indicates that the title is appearing in BIP for the first time.

An Asterisk (*) at the beginning of an entry indicates that the title is appearing in BIP for the first time.

D

***Dude in Distress.** Haynes. (J). 1995. 3.99 (*0-679-86023-1*) Random.
***Dude of My Dreams.** Lisa Simon. (Full House: Stephanie Ser.). (J). (gr. 3-6). 1995. mass mkt. 3.99 (*0-671-52274-4*, Minstrel Bks) PB.
Dude on Arrival: A Christmas Mystery. J. S. Borthwick. 1992. mass mkt. 4.50 (*0-312-92955-2*) St Martin.
***Dude Ranch.** large type ed. Bonnie Bryant. LC 94-36414. (Saddle Club Ser.: Vol. 6). 144p. (J). (gr. 3 up). 1995. lib. bdg. 15.93 (*0-8368-1285-9*) Gareth Stevens Inc.
Dude Ranches & Vacation Guest Ranches: A How to Find or Locate References & Planning Guides, U. S. A. Ed. rev. ed. Alpha Pyramis Research Division Staff. 126p. 1992. 17.95 (*0-317-05494-5*) Prosperity & Profits.
Dude Ranches, Vacation Guest Ranches: A How to Find or Locate Reference & Planning Guide. rev. ed. Lamplight Press Staff. (Illus.). 70p. 1995. ring bd. 19.95 (*0-917593-13-8*, Lamp Light Pr) Prosperity & Profits.
Dude Ranger. Zane Grey. 1990. mass mkt. 3.99 (*0-06-100055-8*, Harp PBks) HarpC.
Dude Ranger. large type ed. Zane Grey. LC 94-8814. (Western Ser.). 375p. 1994. 18.95 (*0-7862-0209-2*) Thorndike Pr.
Dude Woman. Peter B. Kyne. reprint ed. lib. bdg. 21.95 (*0-88411-694-8*, Aeonian Pr) Amereon Ltd.
Duden-Bildworterb. F. Kinder. 72p. 1991. 17.95 (*3-411-04581-7*, Pub. by Bibliogr Inst Brockhaus GW) Langenscheidt.
Duden Dictionary of Borrowed Words: Duden Fremdwoerterbuch. Duden. 813p. (GER.). 1982. 49.95 (*0-8288-1958-0*, M14171) Fr & Eur.
Duden Grammar of Modern Spoken German: Duden Grammatik der Deutschen Gegenwartssprache. Duden. 804p. (GER.). 1984. 49.95 (*0-8288-1959-9*, M14170) Fr & Eur.
***Duden Grosse Woerterbuch Vol. 1: A-Bim.** Drosdowksi. (GER.). 1993. 125.00 (*0-7859-7555-1*, 3411047429) Fr & Eur.
***Duden Grosse Woerterbuch Vol. 2: Bl-Fe.** Drosdowksi. (GER.). 1993. 125.00 (*0-7859-7556-X*, 3411047526) Fr & Eur.
***Duden Grosse Woerterbuch Vol. 3: Fe-Hi.** Drosdowksi. (GER.). 1993. 125.00 (*0-7859-7557-8*, 3411047623) Fr & Eur.
***Duden Grosse Woerterbuch Vol. 4.** Drosdowksi. (GER.). 1994. 125.00 (*0-7859-7558-6*, 3411047720) Fr & Eur.
***Duden Grosse Woerterbuch Vol. 5.** Drosdowksi. (GER.). 1994. 125.00 (*0-7859-7559-4*, 3411047828) Fr & Eur.
***Duden Grosse Woerterbuch Deutsch: Sp - Z, No. 6.** Drosdowksi. 559p. (GER.). 1981. write for info. (*0-7859-7554-3*) Fr & Eur.
***Duden Grosse Woerterbuch Deutsch Vol. 1: A-Ci.** Drosdowksi. 464p. (GER.). 1976. 95.00 (*0-7859-7549-7*, 3411013559) Fr & Eur.
***Duden Grosse Woerterbuch Deutsch Vol. 2: Ci-F.** Drosdowksi. 463p. (GER.). 1976. write for info. (*0-7859-7550-0*, 3411013567) Fr & Eur.
***Duden Grosse Woerterbuch Deutsch Vol. 3: G-Kal.** Drosdowksi. 479p. (GER.). 1977. write for info. (*0-7859-7551-9*, 3411013575) Fr & Eur.
***Duden Grosse Woerterbuch Deutsch Vol. 4: Kam-N.** Drosdowksi. 495p. (GER.). 1978. 95.00 (*0-7859-7552-7*, 3411013583) Fr & Eur.
***Duden Grosse Woerterbuch Deutsch Vol. 5: O-So.** Drosdowksi. 527p. (GER.). 1980. 95.00 (*0-7859-7553-5*, 3411013605) Fr & Eur.
Duden-Langenscheidt Deutsches Lernworterbuch. 461p. 1986. 19.95 (*3-468-96101-4*) Langenscheidt.
***Duden Mein Erstes Woerterbuch.** Wilkes. 64p. (GER.). 1992. 49.95 (*0-7859-7242-0*, 3411051310) Fr & Eur.
Duden-Mein Erstes Worterbuch. 64p. 1992. 21.95 (*3-411-05131-0*, Pub. by Bibliogr Inst Brockhaus GW) Langenscheidt.
Duden Rechtschreibung der Deutschen Sprache und der Fremdwoerter. Duden. 792p. (GER.). 1980. 49.95 (*0-8288-1960-2*, M14167) Fr & Eur.
Duden Scholar's Dictionary of Chemistry: Schulerduden-Die Chemie. Duden. 424p. (GER.). 1984. 35.00 (*0-8288-1310-8*, M15295) Fr & Eur.
Duden-Stilwoerterbuch. (Duden: Vol. 2). (GER.). 29.95 (*3-411-20902-X*) Langenscheidt.
***Duden Taschenbucher: Fremdworter Woerterbuch.** Karl-Heinz Ahlheim. 368p. (GER.). 1970. 29.95 (*0-7859-8347-3*, 3411011394) Fr & Eur.
***Duden Taschenbucher: Jiddisches Woerterbuch.** 2nd ed. Ronald Lotzsch. 204p. (GER & YID.). 1992. 29.95 (*0-7859-8676-6*, 341106241x) Fr & Eur.
***Duden Taschenbucher: Woerterbuch der Abkuerzungen.** 3rd ed. Josef Werlin. 300p. (GER.). 1987. 19.95 (*0-7859-8675-8*, 341102741x) Fr & Eur.
***Duden Taschenbucher: Woerterbuch der Osterreich.** 2nd ed. Jakob Ebner. 252p. (GER.). 1980. 29.95 (*0-7859-8348-1*, 3411017945) Fr & Eur.
***Duden Taschenbucher: Woerterbuch der Schweizerischen.** Kurt Meyer. 380p. (GER.). 1989. 29.95 (*0-7859-8350-3*, 3411041315) Fr & Eur.
Duden-Universalworterbuch. 1800p. 1989. 43.95 (*3-411-02176-4*, Pub. by Bibliogr Inst Brockhaus GW) Langenscheidt.
***Duden Woertbuch Vol. 9: Richtiges.** 3rd ed. Duden. 803p. (GER.). 1985. 49.95 (*0-614-00348-2*, M14175) Fr & Eur.
***Duden Woerterbuch Vol. 6: Aussptache.** Mangold. 794p. (GER.). 1990. 49.95 (*0-614-00369-5*, 341120916X) Fr & Eur.
***Duden Woerterbuch Vol. 8: Sinnverwandte.** 2nd ed. Muller. 800p. (GER.). 1986. 59.95 (*0-7859-7224-2*, 3411209089) Fr & Eur.
***Duden Woerterbuch Vol. 11: Idiomatik.** Drosdowski. 864p. (GER.). 1992. text ed. 49.95 (*0-614-00347-4*, 3411041110) Fr & Eur.
Duden-Woerterbuch Geographischer Namen: Europa. Duden. 65.00 (*0-8288-7720-3*, M7345) Fr & Eur.
Duden Worterbuch, 6 vols., Set. 350.00 (*3-411-01354-0*, Pub. by Bibliogr Inst Brockhaus GW) Langenscheidt.
Duden Worterbuch, Vol. 1, A-Ci. 464p. 1976. 60.00 (*3-411-01355-9*, Pub. by Bibliogr Inst Brockhaus GW) Langenscheidt.
Duden Worterbuch, Vol. 2, Cl-F. 928p. 1976. 60.00 (*3-411-01356-7*, Pub. by Bibliogr Inst Brockhaus GW) Langenscheidt.
Duden Worterbuch, Vol. 3, G-Kal. 1408p. 1977. 60.00 (*3-411-01357-5*, Pub. by Bibliogr Inst Brockhaus GW) Langenscheidt.
Duden Worterbuch, Vol. 4, Kam-N. 1904p. 1978. 60.00 (*3-411-01358-3*, Pub. by Bibliogr Inst Brockhaus GW) Langenscheidt.
Duden Worterbuch, Vol. 5, O-So. 2432p. 1980. 60.00 (*3-411-01359-1*, Pub. by Bibliogr Inst Brockhaus GW) Langenscheidt.
Duden Worterbuch, Vol. 6, Sp-Z. 2992p. 1981. 60.00 (*3-411-01360-5*, Pub. by Bibliogr Inst Brockhaus GW) Langenscheidt.
Dudick on Manufacturing Cost Controls. Thomas S. Dudick. LC 84-15090. 331p. 1985. text ed. 64.95 (*0-13-220971-3*, Busn) P-H.
Dudick on Manufacturing Cost Controls. 2nd ed. Thomas S. Dudick. 1992. 69.95 (*0-13-220245-X*) P-H.
D.U.D.LEY. Angela D. Seals. (J). 1992. 7.95 (*0-533-09734-7*) Vantage.
***Dudley.** Ellsworth Zahn. (Illus.). 32p. (J). (gr. k-5). 1995. 17.95 (*1-885340-20-6*) Coming Age Pr.
Dudley. Ellsworth E. Zahn. (Illus.). 40p. (Orig.). (J). Date not set. pap. text ed. 14.95 (*0-9637308-0-0*) L E Zahn.
Dudley: History of the Dudley Family, 2 vols., Set. D. Dudley. 1993. reprint ed. lib. bdg. 168.00 (*0-8328-3298-7*); reprint ed. pap. 158.00 (*0-8328-3299-5*) Higginson Bk Co.
Dudley: Yearbook of Governor Thomas Dudley Family Associates. 252p. 1994. reprint ed. lib. bdg. 48.00 (*0-8328-4171-4*) Higginson Bk Co.
Dudley: Yearbook of Governor Thomas Dudley Family Associates. 252p. 1994. reprint ed. pap. 38.00 (*0-8328-4172-2*) Higginson Bk Co.
Dudley Allen Sargent: An Autobiography. Dudley A. Sargent. (Physical Education Reprint Ser.). (Illus.). reprint ed. lib. bdg. 29.00 (*0-697-00105-9*) Irvington.
Dudley Docker: The Life & Times of a Trade Warrior. R. P. Davenport-Hines. (Illus.). 280p. 1985. 74.95 (*0-521-26557-6*) Cambridge U Pr.
***Dudley Finds a Home: Picture Book.** Alex Galatis. (Adventures of Dudley the Dragon Ser.: No. 1). (Illus.). (J). (gr. 2-4). 1995. pap. 2.50 (*0-590-47493-6*) Scholastic Inc.
Dudley Genealogies. James H. Mason. LC 82-62705. 216p. 1987. 35.00 (*0-9609032-1-6*) J H Mason.
Dudleya & Hasseanthus Handbook: (Crassulaceae) Paul H. Thomson. (Horticultural Handbook Ser.). (Illus.). 256p. 1993. 50.00 (*0-9602066-5-5*) Bonsall Pub.
Dudley's Gear Handbook: Design, Manufacture, & Application of Gears. 2nd ed. Dennis Townsend. (Illus.). 1992. text ed. 82.50 (*0-07-017903-4*) McGraw.
***Dudley's Tea Party.** Galatis. (Adventures of Dudley the Dragon Ser.: No. 02). 1995. pap. (*0-590-47494-4*) Scholastic Inc.
Due Canzoni for Four Viols. Giovanni Salvatore. Ed. by Peter Ballinger. (Viol Consort Ser.: No. 2). i, 32p. 1989. 10.00 (*1-56571-023-1*) PRB Prods.
Due Canzoni, for Four Viols. Giovanni Salvatore. Ed. by Peter Ballinger. (Viol Consort Ser.: No. 2). 27p. 1993. 10.00 (*1-56571-063-0*, VC002) PRB Prods.
Due Diligence, Disclosure, & Warranties in the Corporate Acquisitions Practice. International Bar Association Staff. (C). 1988. lib. bdg. 101.50 (*1-85333-086-8*, Pub. by Graham & Trotman UK) Kluwer Ac.
Due Diligence, Disclosures & Warranties in the Corporate Acquisitions Practice. 2nd ed. Ed. by David Baker. 288p. 1992. lib. bdg. 115.00 (*1-85333-633-5*, Pub. by Graham & Trotman UK) Kluwer Ac.
Due Diligence Handbook. William M. Crilly. LC 93-92762. 790p. 1993. ring bd. 249.00 (*0-9637605-0-5*) Newport Pacific.
***Due Diligence in Business Transactions.** Gary M. Lawrence. LC 94-43241. 1994. write for info. (*0-615-00435-0*) Law Journal.
***Due Diligence Manual.** 94p. 1993. pap. 42.00 (*0-614-06615-8*, DUE) Rocky Mtn Mineral Law Found.
***Due Dilligence: A Rachel Gold Mystery.** Michael A. Kahn. LC 95-9853. 1995. 20.95 (*0-525-93743-9*, Dutton) NAL-Dutton.
Due Epistole Di Giovanni Conversini Da Ravenna. Diego Rossi. (Romanistische Texte und Studien Ser.: Vol. 3). vi, 64p. 1988. write for info. (*3-487-07965-8*, Pub. by Georg Olms GW) Lubrecht & Cramer.
Due Mondi. Nat Scammacca. (Orig.). 1979. 20.00 (*0-89304-562-4*, CCC123); pap. 10.00 (*0-89304-561-6*) Cross-Cultrl NY.
***Due North.** braille ed. Mitchell Smith. 716p. 1994. text ed. 57.28 (*1-56956-451-5*, BR9330) W A T Braille.
Due Preparations for the Plague, As Well for Soul As Body. Daniel Defoe. LC 74-13434. (Illus.). reprint ed. 32.50 (*0-404-07925-3*) AMS Pr.
Due Process. Dan Juster. 182p. (Orig.). 1992. pap. 8.99 (*1-56043-077-X*) Destiny Image.
Due Process. Ed. by J. Roland Pennock & John W. Chapman. LC 76-40511. (Nomos Ser.: Vol. 18). 1977. 45.00 (*0-8147-6569-6*) NYU Pr.
***Due Process: Americans of Japanese Ancestry & the United States Constitution.** 2nd rev. ed. Ed. by Clifford I. Uyeda. 1995. pap. 22.00 (*1-881506-04-5*) Natl Japnse Am HS.
Due Process & Participation at the FASB: A Study of the Comment Period. Stephen J. Mezias & Seungwha Chung. 50p. 1989. pap. 12.00 (*0-910586-77-2*, 085-89) Finan Exec.
Due Process for School Officials: A Guide to the Conduct of Administrative Proceedings. Edgar H. Bittle. 1986. 9.95 (*1-56534-012-4*) NOLPE.
Due Process in Disciplinary Hearings: Decisions of the National Railroad Adjustment Board. Joseph Lazar. (Monograph & Research Ser.: No. 25). 459p. 1980. 10.50 (*0-89215-108-0*) U Cal LA Indus Rel.
Due Process in the Administrative State. Jerry L. Mashaw. LC 84-20948. 280p. 1985. text ed. 37.00 (*0-300-03258-7*) Yale U Pr.
Due Process of Law. Lord Denning. 1980. 26.00 (*0-406-17608-6*, U.K.) Butterworth Legal Pubs.
Due Process of Law. J. M. Gora. Ed. by Franklyn S. Haiman. (To Protect These Rights Ser.). 278p. 1983. pap. 12.95 (*0-8442-6003-7*, Passport Bks) NTC Pub Grp.
Due Process of Law. Rodney L. Mott. LC 72-165604. (American Constitutional & Legal History Ser). 702p. 1973. reprint ed. lib. bdg. 85.00 (*0-306-70225-8*) Da Capo.
Due Process of Law - Fifth & Fourteenth Amendments of the U. S. Constitution. Vadakeparambil M. Mathew. 49p. (Orig.). (C). 1980. lib. bdg. 5.00 (*0-9614320-0-4*) Mathew.
Due Process of Law, Nineteen Thirty-Two to Nineteen Forty-Nine: The Supreme Court's Use of a Constitutional Tool. Virginia L. Wood. LC 51-13877. 448p. reprint ed. pap. 127.70 (*0-317-29851-8*, 2019595) Bks Demand.
Due Process of Law Under the Federal Constitution. Lucius P. McGehee. (Studies in Constitutional Law). x, 452p. 1981. reprint ed. lib. bdg. 37.50 (*0-8377-0837-0*) Rothman.
Due Regole Della Prospettiva Practica: Danti. Jiacomo B. Da Vignola. Ed. by I. Danti. (Perspective Ser.). (Illus.). 176p. (ITA.). (C). 1989. reprint ed. 495.00 (*1-85297-025-1*, Pub. by Archival Facs UK) St Mut.
Due Reverence: Antiques in the Possession of the American Philosophical Society. Murphy D. Smith. LC 92-71644. (Memoirs Ser.: Vol. 203). (Illus.). 150p. (C). 1993. 30.00 (*0-87169-203-1*, M203-SMM) Am Philos.
Due Season. rev. ed. Pat Dugas-Bonds. Ed. by Sarah Mitchell. 110p. (Orig.). (YA). 1988. 15.00 (*0-317-93048-6*) BDB Unlimited.
Due South. large type ed. Jan Webster. 576p. 1983. 21.95 (*0-7089-1022-X*) Ulverscroft.
Due South, Cuba, Past & Present. Maturin M. Ballou. LC 72-91661. 316p. 1969. reprint ed. text ed. 52.50 (*0-8371-2071-3*, BAD&, Negro U Pr) Greenwood.
Due Trattati. Benvenuto Cellini. (Documents of Art & Architectural History Ser.: Vol. 3). (Illus.). 148p. (ITA.). 1981. reprint ed. lib. bdg. 35.00 (*0-89371-203-5*) Broude Intl Edns.
Due West. Hillerman. 1994. 23.00 (*0-06-017785-3*, HarpT) HarpC.
Duel. Mark Dunster. 10p. (Orig.). 1989. pap. 4.00 (*0-89642-173-2*) Linden Pubs.
Duel. Giles Tippette. Ed. by Doug Grad. 256p. (Orig.). 1994. mass mkt. 4.99 (*0-671-87159-5*) PB.
Duel. Aleksandr I. Kuprin. LC 76-23881. (Classics of Russian Literature Ser.). 1987. reprint ed. 25.00 (*0-88355-491-7*) Hyperion Conn.
Duel: Its Rise & Fall in Early Modern France. Francois Billacois. 288p. (C). 1990. text ed. 35.00 (*0-300-04028-8*) Yale U Pr.
Duel: May 10-July 31, 1940: The Eighty-Day Struggle Between Churchill & Hitler. John Lukacs. 1992. pap. 10.95 (*0-395-61863-0*) HM.
Duel & Other Stories. Anton P. Chekhov. Tr. by Ronald Wilks. 256p. 1984. mass mkt. 8.95 (*0-14-044415-7*, Penguin Classics) Viking Penguin.
Duel at Gold Buttes. William Jeffrey. (Gunsmoke Western Ser.). 176p. (Orig.). 1990. reprint ed. text ed. 12.95 (*0-86220-941-2*, Gunsmoke) Chivers N Amer.
Duel Between the First Ironclads. William C. Davis. LC 75-11071. (Illus.). xii, 220p. 1981. pap. 11.95 (*0-8071-0868-5*) La State U Pr.
Duel Between the First Ironclads. 2nd ed. William C. Davis. LC 93-26867. (Illus.). 240p. 1994. 18.95 (*0-8117-0536-6*) Stackpole.
Duel for Kilemanjaro. Leonard Mosley. 19.95 (*0-89190-158-2*, Am Repr) Amereon Ltd.
Duel for the Doctor. large type ed. Lynne Collins. 1994. 18.95 (*0-7927-1926-3*, Curley Lrg Print); pap. 16.95 (*0-7927-1925-5*, Curley Lrg Print) Chivers N Amer.
Duel for the Dunes: Land Use Conflict on the Shores of Lake Michigan. Kay Franklin & Norma Schaeffer. LC 82-25601. (Illus.). 302p. 1983. 29.95 (*0-252-01034-5*) U of Ill Pr.
Duel in Purgatory. Jory Sherman. (Gunn Ser.: No. 6). 1981. pap. 1.95 (*0-89083-739-2*) Zebra.
Duel in the Sun. Niven Busch. 20.95 (*0-8488-0934-3*) Amereon Ltd.
***Duel in the Sun.** large type ed. Sally Wentworth. Date not set. 18.95 (*0-263-14042-3*) Thorndike Pr.
Duel in the Sun. Niven Busch. 1993. reprint ed. lib. bdg. 18.95 (*1-56849-192-1*) Buccaneer Bks.
Duel of Angels. Jean Giraudoux. Tr. & Adapt. by Christopher Fry. 1961. pap. 4.75 (*0-8222-0339-1*) Dramatists Play.
Duel of Assassins. Daniel Pollock. Ed. by Bill Grose. 352p. 1992. reprint ed. mass mkt. 5.50 (*0-671-70577-6*) PB.
Duel of Dragons. Gael Baudino. (Dragonsword Ser.: No. 2). 384p. (Orig.). 1991. pap. 4.99 (*0-451-45097-3*, ROC) NAL-Dutton.
Duel of Eagles: The Mexican & U. S. Fight for the Alamo. Jeff Long. (Illus.). 432p. 1991. pap. 12.00 (*0-688-10967-5*, Quill) Morrow.
***Duel of Hearts.** Helen Archery. 1994. pap. 3.99 (*0-06-108271-6*, Harp PBks) HarpC.
Duel of Hearts. Anita Mills. 240p. 1988. pap. 3.99 (*0-451-15713-3*, Sig) NAL-Dutton.
Duel of Jewels. Barbara Cartland. 176p. 1993. lib. bdg. 19.00 (*0-7278-4474-1*) Severn Hse.
Duel of the Heart. Sara Blayne. (Zebra Regency Romance Ser.). 320p. 1989. pap. 2.95 (*0-8217-2851-2*) Zebra.
Duel on the Diamond. Tommy Hallowell. 128p. (J). (gr. 3 up). 1990. pap. 3.50 (*0-14-032910-2*, Puffin) Puffin Bks.
Duel on the Mesa. Bill Dugan. 1990. mass mkt. 3.50 (*0-06-100033-7*, Harp PBks) HarpC.

Duel with Destiny: Reflections of a Twenty-First Century Catholic & Heretic. Remy Theberge. Ed. by Ed Moisan. LC 94-75846. 215p. (Orig.). 1995. pap. 10.50x (*0-918862-05-1*) Golden Gambit.
Cured as a child, nearly 60 years ago, a nonconformist recalls his life & faith - Catholic Church praised, assailed - major world religion queried. RELUCTANT REBEL IN AIR FORCE BLUES, hardcover, 270 pgs. (Illus). $22.50 postpaid. A unique military biography - how the full-force establishment cheated to crush a "man alone" - "Best book I ever read on military (in)justice."--LT. COL., USAF, JUDGE ADVOCATE, GERMANY. THROUGH TWISTED THORNS. American historical; fiction oversize softcover ed., 355 pgs. (Illus). $16.50 postpaid. Literary entertainment of the 1st order with characters of Dickensian proportions - old time prizefighting celebrated - American Indian history expounded, expounded in all its glory & misery - the "real" General Custer exposed - A reader's delight. ATTN. BOOKSTORES/BOOK CLUBS GREAT SALES POTENTIAL 35% DISCOUNT. ***Publisher Provided Annotation.***

Duel with the Wind: The Story of Emperor Charles V. Griffith A. Hamlin. 84p. 1991. pap. 12.95 (*0-9631511-0-X*) G A Hamlin.
Dueling: The Cult of Honor in Fin-de-siecle Germany. Kevin McAleer. LC 94-4401. 1994. 24.95 (*0-691-03462-1*) Princeton U Pr.
Dueling in the Old South: Vignettes of Social History. Jack K. Williams. LC 79-7414. 128p. 1980. 9.95 (*0-89096-098-4*) Tex A&M Univ Pr.
Dueling Pistols. Omar Fletcher. (Orig.). 1991. pap. 3.95 (*0-87067-368-8*) Holloway.
Dueling Voices. Donald H. Carpenter. 427p. 1993. 24.95 (*0-914339-42-7*) P E Randall Pub.
Duelling in America. Ben C. Truman. Ed. by Steven R. Wood. (Classical Library of the Obscure & Remote). (Illus.). 256p. 1992. reprint ed. pap. 9.95 (*0-9610330-5-3*) J Tabler-Bks.
Duelling Languages: Grammatical Structure in Codeswitching. Carol Myers-Scotton. LC 92-39655. 1993. 49.95 (*0-19-824059-7*, Clarendon Pr) OUP.
Duelo de la Virgen, Los Himnos, Los Loores de Nuestra Senora, Los Signos del Juicio Final (Vol. III of the Oras Completas) Gonzalo De Berceo. Ed. by Brian Dutton. (Serie A: Monagrafias, XVIII). 163p. (Orig.). (SPA.). (C). 1975. pap. 36.00 (*0-900411-96-1*, Pub. by Tamesis Bks Ltd UK) Boydell & Brewer.
Duels in the Sky: WWII Naval Aircraft in Combat. Eric M. Brown. LC 88-15258. (Illus.). 288p. 1988. 24.95 (*0-87021-063-7*) Naval Inst Pr.
Duels of the Mind: The Twelve Greatest Games of Chess. Raymond Keene. 1991. pap. 19.95 (*0-02-028701-1*) Macmillan.
***Duende: Poems.** Donald Rawley. LC 94-22714. 1994. pap. 13.95 (*0-941749-32-0*) Black Tie Pr.
Duendes y el Zapatero. (Spanish Well Loved Tales Ser.: No. 700-4). (SPA.). (J). (gr. 1). 1990. boxed 3.50 (*0-7214-1411-7*) Ladybird Bks.
***Duerme.** Carmen Boullosa. 1995. pap. 12.50 (*0-679-76323-6*, Vin) Random.
Dues: A Novel of War & After. Michael H. Cooper. (Orig.). 1994. pap. 11.95 (*1-880684-19-5*) Curbstone.
Duesenberg Model J Owners Companion. Ed. by Dan R. Post. 192p. 1974. 18.95 (*0-911160-53-1*) Post Group.
Duet. Patricia Collinge. 224p. (Orig.). 1991. pap. 2.75 (*1-878702-42-4*) Meteor Pub.
Duet. Kitty B. Florey. 512p. 1988. pap. 3.95 (*1-55817-130-4*, Pinnacle NY) Windsor NY.
Duet. Wendy Susans. 384p. 1985. pap. 3.75 (*0-8439-2188-9*) Dorchester Pub Co.
Duet, 3 bks, No. 2. Benjamin Benedict. (Eggs Benedict Ser.). (Illus.). (Orig.). 1982. pap. 2.95 (*0-942764-02-1*) Falcon Pub Venice.
***Duet: Gertrude Katz.** 64p. 1995. lib. bdg. 25.00 (*0-8095-4540-3*) Borgo Pr.
Duet & Dialogue in the Age of Monteverdi, 2 vols., 1. John Whenham. LC 82-1837. (Studies in British Musicology: No. 7). 299p. reprint ed. pap. 85.30 (*0-8357-1355-5*, 2070258) Bks Demand.

An Asterisk (*) at the beginning of an entry indicates that the title is appearing in BIP for the first time.

D

An Asterisk (*) at the beginning of an entry indicates that the title is appearing in BIP for the first time.

2129

Dukesborough Tales. Richard M. Johnston. LC 68-20015. (Americans in Fiction Ser.). reprint ed. lib. bdg. 19.00 (*0-8398-0956-5*); reprint ed. pap. text ed. 4.95 (*0-89197-738-4*) Irvington.

***Dukhbhanjanee Sahib: A Part of Sikh Scriptures.** S. Bawa. (Books on Sikhism). 107p. (PAN.). (YA). (gr. 8-12). 1993. 7.50 (*0-942245-07-5*) Wash Sikh Ctr.

Dukhovnija Posjevi. Gregory Diachenko. (Illus.). 475p. 1977. reprint ed. 20.00 (*0-317-30414-3*); reprint ed. pap. 15.00 (*0-317-30415-1*) Holy Trinity.

Dukhovnye Osnovy Obschestva: Vvedenie V Sotsial'niui Filosofiiu. S. L. Frank. LC 88-62274. 320p. (RUS.). 1988. reprint ed. 18.00 (*0-911971-37-8*) Effect Pub.

Dulac, Dat Cajun Cat: Dulac, Dat Cajun Party Animal. Patsy K. Powell. LC 87-91307. (Illus.). 32p. (J). (gr. k up). 1988. pap. 6.95 (*0-944512-00-3*) Radiant LA.

***Dulanys of Welbourne: A Family in Mosby's Confederacy.** Margaret A. Vogtsberger. (Illus.). 325p. 1995. write for info. (*1-883522-03-X*) Rockbridge Pub.

Dulcamara. Ninoska Perez Castellon. LC 82-82596. (Coleccion Espejo de Paciencia Ser.). 77p. (Orig.). (ENG & SPA.). 1982. pap. 5.00 (*0-89729-317-7*) Ediciones.

Dulce. Patricia Williams-Lein. Ed. by James C. Smith, Jr. LC 93-23522. 128p. (Orig.). 1994. pap. 10.95 (*0-86534-207-5*) Sunstone Pr.

Dulcehombre Prohibido. Olga Nolla. 150p. 1994. pap. write for info. (*1-56758-052-1*) Edit Cultl.

Dulces Suenos: Sweet Dreams. Barbara J. Neasi. LC 87-15083. (Rookie Reader Ser.). (Illus.). 32p. (SPA.). (J). (ps-2). 1991. lib. bdg. 10.35 (*0-516-32084-X*); pap. 2.95 (*0-516-52084-9*) Childrens.

***Dulcie Domum's Bad Housekeeping.** Sue Limb. 224p. 1995. pap. 13.95 (*1-85702-066-9*, Pub. by Fourth Estate UK) Trafalgar.

Dulcimer. Date not set. pap. 0.95 (*0-87166-540-9*, 93711) Mel Bay.

Dulcimer Book. Jean Ritchie. (Illus.). 1963. pap. 9.95 (*0-8256-0016-2*, 000016, Oak) Music Sales.

Dulcimer Chord Book. Neal Hellman. 1993. 5.95 (*1-56222-248-1*, 94662) Mel Bay.

Dulcimer Chord Encyclopedia. James Major. 1993. 9.95 (*0-87166-613-8*, 93858) Mel Bay.

Dulcimer Christmas. Bud Ford & Donna Ford. 1993. 3.95 (*0-87166-721-5*, 93816) Mel Bay.

Dulcimer Duets, Rounds & Ensembles. Lois Hornbostel. 1993. 9.95 (*0-87166-971-4*, 94041); audio 10.98 (*1-56222-829-3*, 94041) Mel Bay.

Dulcimer Fiddle Tunes. Lois Hornbostel. 1993. 7.95 (*0-87166-561-1*, 93713); audio 10.98 (*0-87166-562-X*, 93713) Mel Bay.

Dulcimer-Friendly Worship, Vol. I: The Season of Advent: The Coming of the Lord. Steven B. Eulberg. xi, 47p. 1993. pap. text ed. 9.95 (*0-9639663-0-8*) Owl Mtn Music.

Dulcimer Hymn Book. Bud Ford & Donna Ford. 72p. 1979. student ed 4.95 (*0-89228-054-9*) Impact Christian.

Dulcimer Hymn Book. Bud Ford & Donna Ford. 1993. 5.95 (*0-87166-727-4*, 93622) Mel Bay.

Dulcimer Song Book. Bud Ford & Donna Ford. 1993. 7.95 (*0-87166-644-8*, 93682) Mel Bay.

Dulcimer Songbook. Neal Hellman. (Illus.). 96p. 1977. pap. 14.95 (*0-8256-0191-6*, OK63404, Oak) Music Sales.

Dulcimers. Nina Dulabaum. (Illus.). 48p. 1982. 20.00 (*0-88014-036-4*) Mosaic Pr OH.

Dull Knife Battle. Fred H. Werner. 1981. pap. 8.95 (*0-933147-02-3*) Werner Pubn.

***Dull Knifes of Pine Ridge: A Lakota Odyssey.** Joe Starita. LC 94-42883. 1995. write for info. (*0-399-14010-7*) Putnam Pub Group.

Dull Moments, Never. Norm Ross. 24p. 1993. pap. 3.00 (*1-884226-02-7*) Dark River.

Dulled Feelings. Igort. Ed. by Bernd Metz. Tr. by Elizabeth Bell. (Illus.). 49p. (Orig.). 1991. pap. 10.95 (*0-87416-090-1*) Catalan Communs.

Dulles Era: America Enters West Asia. Gulshan Dietl. 260p. 1986. 34.00 (*0-8364-1639-2*, Pub. by Lancer II) S Asia.

Dullmage System of Pelvic Adjustment. Frederick W. Collins. 6p. 1993. reprint ed. spiral bd. 5.50 (*0-7873-0192-2*) Mokelumne.

Duluth. Gore Vidal. 272p. 1984. mass mkt. 5.99 (*0-345-31220-1*) Ballantine.

Duluth: An Illustrated History of the Zenith City. Glenn N. Sandvik. LC 82-50190. (Illus.). 128p. 1983. 24.95 (*0-89781-059-7*) Preferred Mktg.

Duluth: The City & Its People. Chuck Frederick. (Illus.). 112p. (Orig.). 1994. pap. 14.95 (*1-56037-068-8*) Am Wrld Geog.

Duluth Area Fishing Map Guide. rev. ed. James F. Billig & Thomas C. Billig. 1992. pap. 12.95 (*1-885010-00-1*) Sptsmans Connect.

Duluth Complex & Associated Rocks of the Midcontinent Rift System. Ed. by Weiblen. (IGC Field Trip Guidebooks Ser.). 1989. 21.00 (*0-87590-671-0*, T345) Am Geophysical.

Dumas on Food: Selections from Le Grand Dictionnaire de Cuisine. Alexandre Dumas. Tr. by Alan Davidson & Jane Davidson. LC 79-321517. 327p. reprint ed. pap. 93.20 (*0-7837-2020-3*, 2042293) Bks Demand.

***Dumb & Dumber.** Troll Staff. (J). (gr. 4-7). 1994. pap. 3.95 (*0-8167-3695-2*) Troll Assocs.

Dumb Angel Gazette, No. 3: Potpourri. Ed. by Domenic Priore. 145p. (Orig.). 1989. pap. 6.00 (*0-9621744-1-6*) Surfin Colours.

Dumb-Bell of Brookfield, Pocono Shot, & Other Great Dog Stories. John T. Foote. 192p. 1993. 20.00 (*1-55821-262-0*) Lyons & Burford.

Dumb Bunnies. Sue Denim. LC 93-2255. (Illus.). 32p. (J). (ps-3). 1994. 12.95 (*0-590-47708-0*, Blue Sky Press) Scholastic Inc.

***Dumb Bunnies' Easter.** Sue Denim. LC 94-15050. (Illus.). (J). 1995. 12.95 (*0-590-20241-3*, Blue Sky Press) Scholastic Inc.

Dumb Cane & Daffodils: Poisonous Plants in the House & Garden. Carol Lerner. LC 89-33622. (Illus.). 32p. (J). 1990. lib. bdg. 13.88 (*0-688-08796-5*) Morrow Jr Bks.

Dumb Clucks! Jokes about Chickens. Rick Walton & Ann Walton. (Make Me Laugh! Joke Bks.). (Illus.). 32p. (J). (gr. 1-4). 1987. lib. bdg. 11.96 (*0-8225-0991-1*, Lerner Publctns) Lerner Group.

Dumb Clucks: Jokes about Chickens. braille ed. Rick Walton & Ann Walton. 12p. (J). 1992. vinyl bd. 0.92 (*1-56956-110-9*, BR8259) W A T Braille.

Dumb Foxglove, & Other Stories. Annie T. Slosson. LC 79-142278. (Short Story Index Reprint Ser.). 1977. 18.95 (*0-8369-3762-7*) Ayer.

Dumb Men Joke Book. Nan Tucket. 1992. mass mkt. 4.99 (*0-446-36074-0*) Warner Bks.

Dumb Men Joke Book, Vol. 2. Nan Tucket. 112p. 1994. mass mkt. 4.99 (*0-446-60118-7*) Warner Bks.

Dumb Show. Susan Hartman. LC 79-440. (Contemporary Poetry Ser.). 64p. reprint ed. pap. 25.00 (*0-7837-5026-9*, 2044694) Bks Demand.

Dumb Witness. Agatha Christie. 256p. 1986. pap. text ed. 4.99 (*0-425-09854-0*) Berkley Pub.

Dumba Nengue: Run for Your Life: Peasant Tales of Tragedy in Mozambique. Lina Magaia. Tr. by Michael Wolfers. LC 87-72780. (Illus.). 115p. (C). 1988. 14.95 (*0-86543-073-X*); pap. 6.95 (*0-86543-074-8*) Africa World.

Dumbarton Oaks: The History of a Georgetown House & Garden, 1800-1966. Walter M. Whitehill. LC 67-20887. (Illus.). 157p. 1967. 16.00 (*0-674-21850-7*) Belknap Pr.

Dumbarton Oaks: The History of a Georgetown House & Garden, 1800-1966. Walter M. Whitehill. LC 67-20887. (Illus.). 148p. 1967. pap. 8.00 (*0-88402-125-4*) Dumbarton Oaks.

Dumbarton Oaks: The Origins of the United Nations & the Search for Postwar Security. Robert C. Hilderbrand. LC 89-28392. xii, 320p. (C). 1990. 49.95 (*0-8078-1894-1*) U of NC Pr.

Dumbarton Oaks Conference on Chavin, October 26 & 27, 1968. Ed. by Elizabeth P. Benson. LC 73-153502. (Illus.). 124p. 1971. 15.00 (*0-88402-037-1*) Dumbarton Oaks.

***Dumbarton Oaks Conversations, 1944-1994: A Look Behind the Scenes.** Joachim Wolschke-Bulmahn. (Illus.). 84p. 1994. pap. 18.00x (*0-88402-231-5*) Dumbarton Oaks.

Dumbarton Oaks Papers, 27. LC 42-6499. 1973. 50.00 (*0-88402-046-0*) Dumbarton Oaks.

Dumbarton Oaks Papers, 28. LC 42-6499. 1973. 50.00 (*0-88402-051-7*) Dumbarton Oaks.

Dumbarton Oaks Papers, 29. LC 42-6499. 1983. 50.00 (*0-88402-057-6*) Dumbarton Oaks.

Dumbarton Oaks Papers, 30. LC 42-6499. 1983. 50.00 (*0-88402-067-3*) Dumbarton Oaks.

Dumbarton Oaks Papers, 31. LC 42-6499. 1983. 50.00 (*0-88402-072-X*) Dumbarton Oaks.

Dumbarton Oaks Papers, 32. LC 42-6499. 1983. 50.00 (*0-88402-081-9*) Dumbarton Oaks.

Dumbarton Oaks Papers, 33. LC 42-6499. 1983. 50.00 (*0-88402-087-8*) Dumbarton Oaks.

Dumbarton Oaks Papers, 34-35. LC 42-6499. 1983. 65.00 (*0-88402-096-7*) Dumbarton Oaks.

Dumbarton Oaks Papers, 36. LC 42-6499. 1983. 55.00 (*0-88402-114-9*) Dumbarton Oaks.

Dumbarton Oaks Papers, 37. LC 42-6499. 1983. 55.00 (*0-88402-121-1*) Dumbarton Oaks.

Dumbarton Oaks Papers, No. 39. (Dumbarton Oaks Papers). (Illus.). 266p. 1985. 50.00 (*0-88402-143-2*) Dumbarton Oaks.

Dumbarton Oaks Papers, No. 40. Ed. by Robert W. Thomson. LC 42-6499. (Illus.). 276p. 1986. 50.00 (*0-88402-151-3*, DP40) Dumbarton Oaks.

Dumbarton Oaks Papers, No. 42. Ed. by Robert W. Thomson. LC 42-6499. (Illus.). 306p. 1988. 60.00 (*0-88402-174-2*) Dumbarton Oaks.

Dumbarton Oaks Papers, No. 43. Ed. by Robert W. Thomson. LC 42-6499. (Illus.). 328p. 1990. 65.00 (*0-88402-181-5*, DP43) Dumbarton Oaks.

Dumbarton Oaks Papers, No. 44. Ed. by Angeliki E. Laiou. LC 42-6499. (Illus.). 396p. 1991. 85.00 (*0-88402-189-0*, DP44) Dumbarton Oaks.

Dumbarton Oaks Papers, No. 45. Ed. by Angeliki E. Laiou. LC 42-6499. (Illus.). 272p. 1992. 60.00 (*0-88402-196-3*, DP45) Dumbarton Oaks.

Dumbarton Oaks Papers, No. 47. Ed. by Henry Maguire. LC 42-6499. 1993. 78.00 (*0-88402-199-8*) Dumbarton Oaks.

***Dumbarton Oaks Papers No. 48, No. 48.** Ed. by Henry Maguire. LC 42-6499. (Illus.). 448p. 1995. 100.00x (*0-88402-236-6*) Dumbarton Oaks.

Dumbarton, 1815-1851. (C). 1989. 35.00 (*0-903915-24-3*, Pub. by Jordanhill College UK) St Mut.

Dumbbell Book: Fitness Without a Gym. Mark Miele. 112p. 1992. pap. 11.95 (*1-880680-01-7*) Sand Dllr Fl.

Dumbest Dumb Blonde Joke Book. Joey West. 160p. 1994. mass mkt. 4.50 (*1-55817-889-9*, Pinnacle NY) Windsor NY.

***Dumbing Down: Essays on the Strip-Mining of American Culture.** Ed. by Katharine Washburn & John Thornton. 320p. 1996. 22.50 (*0-393-03829-7*) Norton.

Dumbing Us Down: The Hidden Curriculum of Compulsory Schooling. John T. Gatto. 120p. (Orig.). 1992. lib. bdg. 34.95 (*0-86571-230-1*); pap. 9.95 (*0-86571-231-X*) New Soc Pubs.

Dumbo. (Classics Ser.). 96p. (J). 1986. 6.98 (*1-57082-037-6*) Mouse Works.

Dumbo. Walt Disney. (Disney Animated Ser.). (J). 1988. 5.99 (*0-517-66197-7*) Random Hse Value.

***Dumbo.** Little Golden Books Staff. (J). Date not set. 1.59 (*0-307-01040-6*, Golden Pr) Western Pub.

***Dumbo.** Walt Disney Company Staff. (FRE.). Date not set. pap. 9.95 (*0-7859-8849-1*) Fr & Eur.

Dumbo. Walt Disney Staff. (Penguin-Disney Ser.). (J). 1987. 6.98 (*0-8317-2463-3*) Viking Child Bks.

Dumbo at Bat. Walt Disney Productions Staff. (Walt Disney's Fun-to-Read Library Ser.: Vol. 8). (Illus.). 44p. (J). (gr. 1-6). reprint ed. 2.99 (*1-885222-20-3*) Advance Pubs.

Dumbo Dilemma: Learning to Fly in Spite of Life's Worries. Dianne D. Pita. LC 93-21662. 178p. (Orig.). 1993. pap. 11.95 (*0-8245-1367-3*) Crossroad NY.

Dumbocracy in America: Studies in the Theatre of Guilt, 1987-1994. Robert Brustein. LC 94-17515. 288p. 1994. 26.00 (*1-56663-060-6*) I R Dee.

***Dumbocracy in America: Studies in the Theatre of Guilt, 1987-1994.** Robert Brustein. 288p. 1995. pap. 12.95 (*1-56663-098-3*) I R Dee.

***Dumbo's Circus Train.** (Rolling Wheels Book Ser.). 14p. (J). 1995. 6.98 (*1-57082-107-0*) Mouse Works.

Dumbstruck. Sara Pennypacker. (Illus.). 112p. (J). (gr. 4-7). 1994. 14.95 (*0-8234-1123-0*) Holiday.

Dumbth: And Eighty-One Ways to Make Americans Smarter. Steve Allen. 359p. 1989. 22.95 (*0-87975-539-3*) Prometheus Bks.

Dumbth: And Eighty-One Ways to Make Americans Smarter. Steve Allen. 359p. (C). 1991. reprint ed. pap. 15.95 (*0-87975-650-0*) Prometheus Bks.

Dumferling Castle & Other Plays. Jim O'Neal. 235p. 1993. pap. 11.95 (*1-883457-03-3*) Mouseion Pub.

Dummy Boards & Chimney Boards. Clare Graham. 1989. pap. 25.00 (*0-85263-921-X*, Pub. by Shire UK) St Mut.

Dummy Stockton. Stockton. (C). 1995. text ed. write for info. (*0-7167-7045-8*) W H Freeman.

Dummy's Soliloquy. Eric Felderman. LC 92-39303. (Illus.). 197p. (Orig.). 1993. pap. 98.95 (*0-945942-28-1*) Portmanteau Editions.

Dump Cake, Twenty-Five & More Ways to Make a Dump Cake. Cookbook Consortium Staff. 1984. pap. text ed. 12.95 (*0-318-04310-6*, Cookbk Consort) Prosperity & Profits.

Dump-Silence of the Lamb. Thomas Harris. 1989. pap. 214.20 (*0-312-91566-7*) St Martin.

Dump the Diet. Susan Barrie. 1994. pap. 7.95 (*0-533-10963-9*) Vantage.

***Dump Truck.** Arlene Blanchard. LC 94-25704. (Illus.). (J). 1995. write for info. (*1-56402-506-3*) Candlewick Pr.

Dump Truck. Norman Gorbaty. (Baby Fast Rolling Ser.). (Illus.). 12p. (J). (ps). 1993. bds. 6.95 (*0-448-40594-6*, G&D) Putnam Pub Group.

Dump Truck Cover Legislative File. 83p. 1987. 30.00 (*0-318-01562-5*, 24010) Indus Fabrics.

Dump Your Hang-ups ... Without Dumping Them on Others: Twelve Steps for Life-Changing Power. Robert A. Schuller. LC 93-15175. 228p. 1993. 14.99 (*0-8007-1682-5*) Revell.

***Dump Your Hang-Ups...Without Dumping Them on Others: 12 Steps for Life-Changing Power.** Robert A. Schuller & Beth Funk. 288p. 1995. pap. 14.99 (*0-8007-5560-X*) Revell.

Dump Your Stress in the Compost Pile. Douglas Schar. (Illus.). 144p. (Orig.). 1994. pap. 12.95 (*1-880216-21-3*) Elliott & Clark.

Dumped! The Broken Relationship Survival Manual. Rick D. Potter. (Illus.). 112p. 1983. pap. 6.95 (*0-317-01200-2*) Laylah Pubns.

Dumping: A Problem in International Trade. Jacob Viner. LC 90-35119. (Reprints of Economic Classics Ser.). xiii, 343p. 1991. reprint ed. lib. bdg. 39.50 (*0-678-01398-5*) Kelley.

Dumping Ground. Elizabeth Diggs. 1982. pap. 2.75 (*0-8222-0340-5*) Dramatists Play.

Dumping in Dixie: Race, Class, & Environmental Quality. 2nd ed. Robert D. Bullard. LC 93-41558. 1994. text ed. 58.00 (*0-8133-1962-5*) Westview.

Dumping in Dixie: Race, Class, & Environmental Quality. 2nd ed. Robert D. Bullard. LC 93-41558. (C). 1994. pap. text ed. 21.50 (*0-8133-1963-3*) Westview.

***Dumplin Creek.** Sydney Greybern. 150p. 1995. pap. 9.95 (*1-880308-01-0*) Suntop.

Dumpling Cookbook. Maria Polushkin. LC 76-25437. (Illus.). 200p. 1976. pap. 7.95 (*0-911104-85-2*, 119) Workman Pub.

Dumpling Field: Haiku of Issa. Kobayashi Issa. Tr. by Lucien Stryk & Noboru Fujiwara. LC 91-17639. 144p. 1991. 24.95 (*0-8040-0952-X*); pap. 14.95 (*0-8040-0953-8*) Ohio U Pr.

Dumpling Soup. Jama K. Rattigan. 32p. (J). (gr. 4-8). 1993. 15.95 (*0-316-73445-4*) Little.

***Dumplings: A Collection of Poems.** James W. Lancaster. (Orig.). Date not set. write for info. (*0-614-03057-9*) Sewalls Pt.

Dumpy the Dump Truck. Cathy E. Dubowski. (Storytime Bks.). (Illus.). 24p. (Orig.). (J). (gr. k-1). 1990. pap. 0.99 (*1-878624-32-6*) McClanahan Bk.

DUMU-E2-DUB-BA-A: Studies in Honor of Ake W. Sjoberg. Ed. by Hermann Behrens et al. (Occasional Publications of the Samuel Noah Kramer Fund: No. 11). xxiii, 599p. 1989. 108.00 (*0-934718-98-9*) U PA Mus Pubns.

Dun & Bradstreet Guide to Your Investments 1990. Nancy Dunnan. 1990. pap. 12.95 (*0-685-30576-7*, HarpT) HarpC.

***Dun & Bradstreet Guide to Your Investments, 1995.** Nancy Dunnan. 1995. pap. 18.00 (*0-06-273287-0*, HarpT) HarpC.

D'un Chateau a l'Autre. Louis-Ferdinand D. Celine. (Folio Ser.: No. 776). (FRE.). 1973. pap. 10.95 (*2-07-036776-2*) Schoenhof.

D'un Chateau l'Autre. Louis-Ferdinand D. Celine. (FRE.). 1976. pap. 13.95 (*0-7859-0645-2*, M3189) Fr & Eur.

D'un Complot contre les Industriels. Stendhal, pseud. (Nouv. Bibliotheque Romantique Ser.). 192p. (FRE.). pap. 19.95 (*0-7859-1414-5*, 2080610031) Fr & Eur.

Dun Lady's Jess. Doranna Durgin. (Orig.). 1994. mass mkt. 4.99 (*0-671-87617-1*) Baen Bks.

Dun Laoghaire - Kingstown. Peter Pearson. (Illus.). 176p. (Orig.). 1991. pap. 19.95 (*0-86278-256-2*, Pub. by OBrien Pr IE) Dufour.

Dun Laoghaire-Kingstown. Peter Pearson. 176p. 1981. 28.00 (*0-905140-83-4*, Pub. by OBrien Pr IE) Dufour.

D'un Nouveau Complot Contre les Industriels. Stendhal. 192p. 15.95 (*0-686-55058-7*) Fr & Eur.

Dunaliella: Physiology, Biochemistry & Biotechnology. Ben-Amotz. 1992. 173.00 (*0-8493-6647-X*) CRC Pr.

Dunarea Noastra: Romania, the Great Powers, & the Danube Question, 1914-1921. Richard C. Frucht. (East European Monographs: No. 113). 216p. 1983. text ed. 47.50 (*0-88033-007-4*) East Eur Quarterly.

Dunaway: The Dunaways of Virginia. A. E. Clendening. (Illus.). 156p. 1991. reprint ed. lib. bdg. 35.00 (*0-8328-2060-1*); reprint ed. pap. 25.00 (*0-8328-2061-X*) Higginson Bk Co.

Dunbar: The Poet & His Period. Rachel A. Taylor. LC 74-124261. (Select Bibliographies Reprint Ser.). 1977. 15.95 (*0-8369-5449-1*) Ayer.

Dunbar the Makar. Priscilla Bawcutt. 416p. 1992. 95.00 (*0-19-812963-7*) OUP.

Dunbier Art Companion: American Picture Prices. Roger Dunbier. (Illus.). 310p. 1989. 35.00 (*0-685-30118-4*) Genus.

Dunc & Amos & the Red Tatoos, No. 12. Gary Paulsen. (J). (gr. 4-7). 1993. pap. 3.50 (*0-440-40790-7*) Dell.

***Dunc & Amos Go to the Dogs.** Paulsen. (Culpepper Adventures Ser.: No. 25). (J). 1995. pap. 3.50 (*0-440-41040-1*) Dell.

Dunc & Amos Hit the Big Top. Gary Paulsen. (Culpepper Adventures Ser.: No. 9). (J). (gr. 4-7). 1993. pap. 3.25 (*0-440-40756-7*) Dell.

Dunc & the Flaming Ghost. Gary Paulsen. (Culpepper Adventures Ser.: No. 7). 96p. (J). (gr. 3-7). 1992. pap. 3.50 (*0-440-40686-2*, YB) Dell.

Dunc & the Haunted House. Gary Paulsen. (Culpepper Adventures Ser.: No. 15). (J). 1993. pap. 3.50 (*0-440-40893-8*) Dell.

Dunc Breaks the Record. Gary Paulsen. (Culpepper Adventures Ser.: No. 6). 96p. (Orig.). (J). (gr. 3-7). 1992. pap. 3.25 (*0-440-40678-1*, YB) Dell.

Dunc Gets Tweaked. Gary Paulsen. (Culpepper Adventures Ser.: No. 4). 96p. (Orig.). (J). (gr. 3-5). 1992. pap. 3.25 (*0-440-40642-0*, YB) Dell.

Duncan: Descendants of William Duncan the Elder. Nancy R. Roy. 276p. 1992. reprint ed. lib. bdg. 52.50 (*0-8328-2466-6*); reprint ed. pap. 42.50 (*0-8328-2467-4*) Higginson Bk Co.

Duncan & Dolores. Barbara Samuels. LC 85-17119. (Illus.). 32p. (J). (ps-3). 1986. text ed. 13.95 (*0-02-778210-7*, Bradbury S&S) S&S Childrens.

Duncan & Dolores. Barbara Samuels. LC 85-17119. (Illus.). 32p. (J). (ps-3). 1989. reprint ed. pap. 3.95 (*0-689-71294-4*, Mac Bks Young Read) S&S Childrens.

Duncan & Mallory, No. 1. Robert Asprin & Mel White. LC 86-4488. (Duncan & Mallory Ser.). (Illus.). 64p. (Orig.). 1986. pap. 6.95 (*0-89865-456-4*, Starblaze) Donning Co.

Duncan & Mallory: The Bar-None Ranch. Robert Asprin & Mel White. Ed. by Laurie Sutton & Mary Gray. (Duncan & Mallory Ser.: No. 2). (Illus.). 64p. (Orig.). 1987. pap. 6.95 (*0-89865-506-4*, Starblaze) Donning Co.

Duncan & Mallory & the Raiders. Robert Asprin et al. (Duncan & Mallory Ser.: No. 3). (Illus.). 64p. (Orig.). 1987. pap. 7.95 (*0-89865-558-7*, Starblaze) Donning Co.

Duncan & Neill: Defamation. 3rd ed. Richard Rampton & Victoria Sharp. Ed. by Brian Neill. 1992. 169.00 (*0-406-17831-3*, U.K.) Butterworth Legal Pubs.

Duncan & Scully - Marriage Breakdown in Ireland: Law & Practice. William R. Duncan & Paula E. Scully. 1990. 122.00 (*1-85475-046-1*) Butterworth Legal Pubs.

Duncan & the Bird. Amanda Vesey. LC 92-37335. (J). (ps-3). 1993. 18.95 (*0-87614-785-6*, Carolrhoda) Lerner Group.

Duncan Dance: A Guide for Young People Ages Six to Sixteen. Julia Levien. (Illus.). 112p. (Orig.). (J). (gr. 1-11). 1994. pap. 12.95 (*0-87127-198-2*) Princeton Bk Co.

Duncan Dancer. Irma Duncan. LC 79-7759. (Dance Ser.). 1980. reprint ed. lib. bdg. 41.95 (*0-8369-9288-1*) Ayer.

Duncan Grant & the Bloomsbury Group. Douglas B. Turnbaugh. (Illus.). 192p. 1987. 18.95 (*0-8184-0442-6*, Citadel Pr) Carol Pub Group.

Duncan Hannah: Mythic Times. Contrib by Laurie Dahlberg. (Illus.). 56p. 1990. per. 18.00 (*0-945558-08-2*) ISU Univ Galls.

Duncan Hines Baking for Special Occasions. (Favorite All Time Recipes Ser.). (Illus.). 96p. 1993. 7.98 (*0-7853-0126-7*, 2014301) Pubns Intl Ltd.

Duncan Hines Deliciously Simple Desserts. (Favorite All Time Recipes Ser.). (Illus.). 96p. 1993. spiral bd. 3.50 (*0-7853-0111-9*, 2021501) Pubns Intl Ltd.

Duncan Hines Treasury of Baking. (Illus.). 224p. 1993. 19.98 (*1-56173-260-5*, 2013602) Pubns Intl Ltd.

Duncan Hines Treasury of Baking. Consumer Guide Staff. 1992. 14.99 (*0-517-05896-0*) Random Hse Value.

Duncan Masonic Ritual & Monito. Malcolm C. Duncan. 1976. 7.00 (*0-679-50626-8*) Random.

Duncan Phillips & His Collection. Marjorie Phillips. (Illus.). 1982. 35.00 (*0-393-01608-0*) Norton.

Duncan Phillips & His Collection. Marjorie Phillips. (Illus.). 1982. pap. 18.95 (*0-393-30041-2*) Norton.

Duncan Phillips Collects: Paris Between the Wars. Elizabeth H. Turner. LC 91-30904. 64p. 1991. pap. 12.00 (*0-943044-16-2*) Phillips Coll.

An Asterisk (*) at the beginning of an entry indicates that the title is appearing in BIP for the first time.

Duncan the Dancing Duck. Bernard Hoff. LC 93-13058. (Illus.). 32p. (J). (ps-3). 1994. 13.95 (*0-395-67400-X*, Clarion Bks) HM.

Duncan Upshaw Fletcher: Dixie's Reluctant Progressive. J. Wayne Flynt. LC 73-149954. 223p. reprint ed. pap. 63. 60 (*0-7837-4941-4*, 2044607) Bks Demand.

***Duncan's Bride.** Linda Howard. (Mira Bks.). 1995. mass mkt. 4.99 (*1-55166-051-2*, 1-66051-3, Mira Bks) Harlequin Bks.

Duncan's Bride. large type ed. Linda Howard. (Silhouette Sensation Ser.). 1993. 17.95 (*0-373-58838-0*, Silhouette Lrg Print); pap. 16.95 (*0-373-58930-1*, Silhouette Lrg Print) Chivers N Amer.

Duncan's Colony. Natalie L. M. Petesch. LC 81-14188. 220p. 1982. 21.95 (*0-8040-0401-3*); pap. 9.95 (*0-8040-0402-1*) Swallow.

Duncan's Dictionary for Nurses. 2nd ed. Helen Duncan. 816p. 1989. 53.95 (*0-8261-6201-0*); pap. 24.95 (*0-8261-6200-2*) Springer Pub.

***Duncan's Lady: (Heartbreakers, the Men of Midnight)** Emilie Richards. (Intimate Moments Ser.). 1995. pap. 3.75 (*0-373-07625-8*, 1-07625-6) Silhouette.

Duncan's Masonic Ritual & Monitor. Malcolm C. Duncan. 288p. 1976. 10.95 (*0-679-50979-8*); pap. 5.95 (*0-685-03267-1*) McKay.

***Duncan's Masonic Ritual & Monitor: Or a Guide to the Three Symbolic Degrees of the Ancient York Rite & to the Degrees of Mark Master, Past Master, Most Excellent Master & the Royal Arch. Explained & Interpreted by Copious Notes & Numerous Engravings.** Malcolm C. Duncan. 281p. 1995. pap. 16.95 (*1-56459-488-2*) Kessinger Pub.

Duncan's Tree House. Amanda Vesey. LC 92-37334. (J). (ps-3). 1993. 18.95 (*0-87614-784-8*, Carolrhoda) Lerner Group.

Dunchad: Glossae in Martianum. Cora E. Lutz. (American Philological Association Philological Monographs). 1982. 15.95 (*0-89130-705-2*, 40-00-12) Scholars Pr GA.

Dunciad see Popeiana

Dunciad & Other Matters see Popeiana

Dunciad, One see Popeiana

Dunciad, Three see Popeiana

Dunciad, Two see Popeiana

Duncklee: Sketch of the Duncklee Family & a History of the Descendants of David Duncklee of Amherst, NH, & His Sister Hannah Duncklee Howe of Milford. A. M. Duncklee. 260p. 1993. reprint ed. lib. bdg. 49.50 (*0-8328-3665-6*); reprint ed. pap. 39.50 (*0-8328-3666-4*) Higginson Bk Co.

Duncombe's Free Banking: An Essay on Banking, Currency, Finance, Exchanges & Political Economy. Charles Duncombe. LC 68-27852. (Library of Money & Banking History). 356p. 1969. reprint ed. 39.50 (*0-678-00530-3*) Kelley.

Dunc's Doll. Gary Paulsen. (Culpepper Adventures Ser.: No. 2). 80p. (J). (gr. 4-7). 1992. pap. 3.50 (*0-440-40601-3*, YB) Dell.

Dunc's Dump. Gary Paulsen. (Culpepper Adventures Ser.: No. 10). (J). (gr. 4-7). 1993. pap. 3.25 (*0-440-40762-1*) Dell.

Dunc's Halloween. Gary Paulsen. (Culpepper Adventures Ser.: No. 5). 96p. (J). (gr. 3-7). 1992. pap. 3.50 (*0-440-40659-5*, YB) Dell.

Dunc's Undercover. Gary Paulsen. (J). 1993. pap. 3.50 (*0-440-40874-1*) Dell.

Dundas Despotism. Michael Fry. 480p. 1992. text ed. 79.00 (*0-7486-0352-2*, Pub. by Edinburgh U Pr UK) Col U Pr.

***Dundee: An Illustrated Architectural Guide.** Charles McKean & David Walker. (Illus.). 184p. (C). 1993. pap. 35.00x (*1-873190-09-3*, Pub. by Rutland Pr UK) St Mut.

Dundee College of Education. Ed. by William Shearer & Anne McIntyre. (C). 1989. 40.00 (*1-85098-146-9*, Pub. by Jordanhill College UK) St Mut.

Dundee Greats. Jim Hendry. 190p. (C). 1989. pap. 24.00 (*0-85976-347-1*, Pub. by J Donald) St Mut.

Dundee on Record. HMSO Staff. 96p. 1992. pap. 25.00 (*0-11-494208-0*, HM42080, Pub. by HMSO UK) UNIPUB.

Dundee Textiles Industry 1960-1977: Decline & Diversification. W. S. Howe. 1982. text ed. 28.00 (*0-08-028454-X*, Pergamon Pr) Elsevier.

Dundurn Castle. Donalda Badone. (Illus.). 48p. (Orig.). pap. 4.95 (*1-55046-001-3*, Pub. by Boston Mills Pr CN) Genl Dist Srvs.

Dundy County, Nebraska. Lucille Edwards. (Illus.). 660p. 1988. 62.50 (*0-88107-116-1*) Curtis Media.

***Dundy, Nebraska War Book.** Lucille Edwards. (Illus.). 128p. 1992. 25.00 (*0-88107-219-2*) Curtis Media.

Dune. Frank Herbert. LC 83-16030. 528p. 1984. 24.95 (*0-399-12896-4*, Putnam) Putnam Pub Group.

Dune. 25th anniversary ed. Frank Herbert. 1990. mass mkt. 5.99 (*0-441-17271-7*) Ace Bks.

Dune Boy: The Early Years of a Naturalist. Edwin W. Teale. LC 86-45957. (Library of Indiana Classics). (Illus.). 288p. 1986. 20.00 (*0-253-11860-3*); pap. 7.95 (*0-253-20421-6*, MB-421) Ind U Pr.

Dune Country. Earl H. Reed. (Illus.). 1979. reprint ed. 10. 50 (*0-915056-09-7*) Hardscrabble Bks.

Dune Country: A Hiker's Guide to the Indiana Dunes. rev. ed. Glenda Daniel. LC 84-10366. (Illus.). vii, 176p. 1984. pap. 12.95 (*0-8040-0854-X*, Swallow) Ohio U Pr.

Dune Master: A Frank Herbert Bibliography. Daniel J. Levack. 300p. 1988. text ed. 59.95 (*0-313-27679-X*) Greenwood.

Dune Messiah. Frank Herbert. 1987. mass mkt. 5.99 (*0-441-17269-5*) Ace Bks.

D'une Rive a l'Autre: Herman Hess et Romain Rolland, Correspondance et Fragments du Journal. Romain Rolland. (Illus.). 192p. (FRE.). 1972. pap. 9.95 (*0-7859-5448-1*) Fr & Eur.

Dune to Death. Mary R. Daheim. 240p. (Orig.). 1993. mass mkt. 4.99 (*0-380-76933-6*) Avon.

Dunedin. Shena MacKay. 1994. pap. 5.95 (*1-55921-119-9*) Moyer Bell.

Dunedin. Sheena Mackay. LC 93-15236. 296p. 1993. reprint ed. 21.95 (*1-55921-093-1*) Moyer Bell.

Dunes: Continental & Coastal. Ed. by Joe Jennings & H. Hagedorn. (Annals of Geomorphology Ser.: Suppl. 45). (Illus.). 319p. 1983. pap. text ed. 105.00 (*3-443-21045-7*, Pub. by Gebruder Borntraeger GW) Lubrecht & Cramer.

Duneshadows: Poetry, Prose & Drama. Michael Stevens. 1991. pap. 8.95 (*0-9627336-0-1*) Red Arrow Pr.

Dunfermline College of Physical Education. Philip O'Neill. (C). 1989. 45.00 (*1-85098-148-5*, Pub. by Jordanhill College UK) St Mut.

Dunfords Travels Every Wheres. William M. Kelley. LC 70-118849. 1970. 25.00 (*0-89366-101-5*) Ultramarine Pub.

***Dung Annual: Collector's Issue.** Christopher L. Clutter et al. (Illus.). 62p. 1994. pap. 15.85 (*0-9644321-0-2*, CDWC) Camel Dung Writ.

***Dung Annual 1995: The Year of the Newet.** Legro Bennett. Ed. by Christopher L. Clutter. 90p. 1995. pap. text ed. 13.30 (*0-9644321-1-0*) Camel Dung Writ.

Dung Beetle Ecology. Ed. by Ikka Hanski & Yves Cambefort. (Illus.). 516p. 1991. text ed. 69.50 (*0-691-08739-3*) Princeton U Pr.

Dung Fungi: Illustrated Guide to Coprophilous Fungi in New Zealand. Ann Bell. (Illus.). 88p. 1983. pap. text ed., spiral bd. 19.95 (*0-86473-001-2*, Pub. by Victoria Univ Pr NZ) Lubrecht & Cramer.

Dungeness Crabs & Blackberry Cobblers: The Northwest Heritage Cookbook. Janie Hibler. LC 91-52733. (Illus.). 352p. 1991. 25.00 (*0-394-57745-0*) Knopf.

Dungeon, Fire & Sword: The Knights Templar in the Crusades. John J. Robinson. LC 91-27495. 494p. 1992. 24.95 (*0-87131-657-9*) M Evans.

Dungeon Master: The Disappearance of James Dallas Egbert III. William C. Dear. 352p. 1985. mass mkt. 4.95 (*0-345-32695-4*) Ballantine.

***Dungeon Master II: Official Adventurer's Guide.** John Withers. 1994. pap. 19.95 (*1-55958-712-1*) Prima Pub.

***Dungeon Master II: Skullkeep: The Official Strategy Guide.** 1995. 12.95 (*1-884364-03-9*) Sandwich Islands.

Dungeon of the Bear Set. Jim B. Peters. 1982. 6.95 (*0-940244-58-6*) Flying Buffalo.

Dungeons & Dragons, No. D1: Dragonlance Chronicles. Margaret Weis. 1988. pap. 12.95 (*0-88038-652-5*) TSR Inc.

Dungeons & Dragons: Art of D&D Game-Osi. Margaret Weis. 1985. pap. 14.95 (*0-394-74179-X*) Random.

Dunham-Singletary Genealogy. Kenneth R. Dunham. (Illus.). 207p. 1987. text ed. 23.50 (*0-9616641-1-8*) Royal Pr.

Dunham's Green Book: Service for the Funeral Directors of New England. 23th ed. Neil F. Weathers. 976p. 1986. 135.00 (*0-317-67320-3*) Dunham Serv.

Dunio Elegies. Rainer M. Rilke. Tr. by Young David. 104p. 1992. pap. 8.95 (*0-393-30931-2*) Norton.

Dunkard-Dutch Cook Book. (Pennsylvania Dutch Bks.). (Illus.). 1965. 3.00 (*0-911410-10-4*) Applied Arts.

Dunkel Draft from the GATT Secretariat: Multilateral Trade Negotiations - The Uruguay Round Track Negotiations Committee Draft Final Act Embodying the Results of the Uruguay Round of Multilateral Trade Negotiations. Multilateral Trade Negotiations, the Uruguay Trade Negotiations Committee. Ed. by Institute for International Legal Information Staff. LC 92-17248. 547p. 1992. 75.00 (*0-89941-799-X*, 307560) W S Hein.

Dunkerleys. large type ed. Howard Spring. 384p. 1986. 23. 95 (*0-7089-8329-4*, Charnwood) Ulverscroft.

Dunkirk: Anatomy of Disaster. Patrick Turnbull. LC 78-8146. (Illus.). 262p. 1978. 35.00 (*0-8419-0396-4*) Holmes & Meier.

Dunkirk: The Complete Story of the First Step in the Defeat of Hitler. Norman Gelb. LC 89-32357. (Illus.). 352p. 1991. reprint ed. pap. 12.00 (*0-688-10737-0*, Quill) Morrow.

Dunkirk: The Storms of War. John Harris. LC 89-574. (Battle Standards Ser.). (Illus.). 144p. (Orig.). (C). 1989. reprint ed. lib. bdg. 25.00x (*0-8095-7509-4*) Borgo Pr.

Dunlap: The House of Dunlap. James A. Hanna. (Illus.). 412p. 1993. reprint ed. lib. bdg. 72.00 (*0-8328-3300-2*); reprint ed. pap. 62.00 (*0-8328-3301-0*) Higginson Bk Co.

Dunlap Cabinetmakers: A Tradition in Craftmanship. Philip Zea & Donald Dunlap. (Illus.). 224p. 1994. 49.95 (*0-8117-0990-6*) Stackpole.

Dunlap-Hanna: Pennsylvania Forms, 13 vols. Obermayer et al. 1985. Updates. ring bd. write for info. (*0-8205-1260-5*) Bender.

Dunlap-Hanna Pennsylvania Forms, 12 vols. rev. ed. Paul C. Heintz. LC 49-13527. 1995. ring bd. 1,250.00 (*0-318-02644-9*) Bisel Co.

Dunlins & Sanderlings: Under the Winds of Yaquina see Under the Winds of Yaquina

Dunn-Crostics, Vol. 1. Robert H. Dunn. 48p. (Orig.). 1993. student ed, pap. 7.95 (*1-884202-00-4*) Systs Qual Sftware.

Dunnage Melange & Subduction of the Protacadic Ocean, Northeast Newfoundland. George M. Kay. LC 76-11901. (Geological Society of America, Special Paper Ser.: No. 175). 65p. reprint ed. pap. 25.00 (*0-317-29098-3*, 2023741) Bks Demand.

Dunnell Minnesota Digest, 1978, 49 vols. 4th ed. Butterworths Staff. 1991. 72.50 (*0-685-74051-X*) Butterworth Legal Pubs.

Dunnell Minnesota Digest, 1978, 54 vols., Set. 4th ed. Butterworths Staff. 1978. Replacement vols. boxed 1, 350.00 (*0-86678-002-5*) Michie Butterworth.

Dunninger's Complete Encyclopedia of Magic. Joseph Dunninger. (Illus.). 1967. 20.00 (*0-8184-0029-3*) Carol Pub Group.

Dunninger's Complete Encyclopedia of Magic. Joseph Dunninger. 1989. pap. 12.95 (*0-8216-0182-2*, Univ Books) Carol Pub Group.

Dunninger's Secrets. Walter Gibson. LC 73-76823. 220p. 1974. 7.95 (*0-8184-0166-4*) Carol Pub Group.

Dunnock Behaviour & Social Evolution. N. B. Davies. (Oxford Series in Ecology & Evolution). (Illus.). 288p. 1992. 70.00 (*0-19-854674-2*); pap. 28.00 (*0-19-854675-0*) OUP.

Dunny & the Duck. Baxter Black. (Illus.). 64p. (J). 1994. pap. 12.95 (*0-939343-14-2*) R Stockman & Coyote.

***Dunoon & Cowal - a Guide.** Julian Hill. 112p. (C). 1992. pap. 32.00x (*1-874640-00-9*, Pub. by Argyll Pubng UK) St Mut.

***Dunoon & Cowal Business Directory 1994.** Argyll & the Islands Enterprise Staff. 112p. (C). 1993. pap. 32.00x (*1-874640-60-2*, Pub. by Argyll Pubng UK) St Mut.

***Dunroamin' The Suburban Semi & Its Enemies.** Paul Oliver et al. (Illus.). 224p. 1995. pap. 22.95 (*0-7126-6029-1*, Pub. by Pimlico) Trafalgar.

Dun's Business Rankings, 1993. Dun & Bradstreet Information Services Staff. 1993. 465.00 (*1-56203-270-4*, 01223537) Dun & Bradstreet.

Dun's Census of American Business, 1993. Dun & Bradstreet Information Services Staff. 1993. 395.00 (*1-56203-262-3*, 01389598) Dun & Bradstreet.

Dun's Consultants Directory, 1994. Dun & Bradstreet Information Services Staff. 1993. 395.00 (*1-56203-272-0*, 01361810) Dun & Bradstreet.

Dun's Directory of Service Companies, 1994. Dun & Bradstreet Information Services Staff. 1993. 525.00 (*1-56203-273-9*, 02074876) Dun & Bradstreet.

Dun's Employment Opportunities Directory, 1983-1984: The Career Guide. Dun & Bradstreet Staff. 4256p. 1983. 295.00 (*0-318-00213-2*) Dun.

Dun's Healthcare Reference Book, 1993-94. Dun & Bradstreet Information Services Staff. 1993. 410.00 (*1-56203-274-7*) Dun & Bradstreet.

Dun's Industrial Guide: The Metalworking Directory, 1993-94, 3 vols., Set. Dun & Bradstreet Information Services Staff. 1993. 795.00 (*1-56203-225-9*) Dun & Bradstreet.

Dun's Regional Business Directories: Houston Area, 1994. Dun & Bradstreet Information Services Staff. 1993. 475. 00 (*1-56203-244-5*) Dun & Bradstreet.

Dun's Regional Business Directories: Iowa Metros, 1994. Dun & Bradstreet Information Services Staff. 1993. 475. 00 (*1-56203-245-3*) Dun & Bradstreet.

Dun's Regional Business Directories: Kansas City Area, 1994. Dun & Bradstreet Information Services Staff. 1993. 475.00 (*1-56203-246-1*) Dun & Bradstreet.

Dun's Regional Business Directories: Kentucky Metros Area, 1994. Dun & Bradstreet Information Services Staff. 1993. 475.00 (*1-56203-247-X*) Dun & Bradstreet.

Dun's Regional Business Directories: Long Island Area, 1994. Dun & Bradstreet Information Services Staff. 1993. 475.00 (*1-56203-248-8*) Dun & Bradstreet.

Dun's Regional Business Directories: Los Angeles Metropolitan Area, 1994. Dun & Bradstreet Information Services Staff. 1993. 475.00 (*1-56203-249-6*) Dun & Bradstreet.

Dun's Regional Business Directories: Los Angeles Suburban Area, 1994. Dun & Bradstreet Information Services Staff. 1993. 475.00 (*1-56203-275-5*) Dun & Bradstreet.

Dun's Regional Business Directories: Memphis Area, 1994. Dun & Bradstreet Information Services Staff. 1993. 475. 00 (*1-56203-276-3*) Dun & Bradstreet.

Dun's Regional Business Directories: Miami - Ft. Lauderdale - West Palm Beach Area, 1994. Dun & Bradstreet Information Services Staff. 1993. 475.00 (*1-56203-277-1*) Dun & Bradstreet.

Dun's Regional Business Directories: Michigan Metros Area, 1994. Dun & Bradstreet Information Services Staff. 1993. 475.00 (*1-56203-278-X*) Dun & Bradstreet.

Dun's Regional Business Directories: Milwaukee - Madison Area, 1994. Dun & Bradstreet Information Services Staff. 1993. 475.00 (*1-56203-279-8*) Dun & Bradstreet.

Dun's Regional Business Directories: Minneapolis - St. Paul Area, 1994. Dun & Bradstreet Information Services Staff. 1993. 475.00 (*1-56203-280-1*) Dun & Bradstreet.

Dun's Regional Business Directories: New England Area, 1994. Dun & Bradstreet Information Services Staff. 1993. 475.00 (*1-56203-281-X*) Dun & Bradstreet.

Dun's Regional Business Directories: New Orleans Area, 1994. Dun & Bradstreet Information Services Staff. 1993. 475.00 (*1-56203-282-8*) Dun & Bradstreet.

Dun's Regional Business Directories: New York Metropolitan Area, 1994. Dun & Bradstreet Information Services Staff. 1993. 475.00 (*1-56203-283-6*) Dun & Bradstreet.

Dun's Regional Business Directories: New York Suburban Area, 1994. Dun & Bradstreet Information Services Staff. 1993. 475.00 (*1-56203-284-4*) Dun & Bradstreet.

Dun's Regional Business Directories: Norfolk - Richmond Area, 1994. Dun & Bradstreet Information Services Staff. 1993. 475.00 (*1-56203-285-2*) Dun & Bradstreet.

Dun's Regional Business Directories: Northern California Area, 1994. Dun & Bradstreet Information Services Staff. 1993. 475.00 (*1-56203-286-0*) Dun & Bradstreet.

Dun's Regional Business Directories: Northern New Jersey Area, 1994. Dun & Bradstreet Information Services Staff. 1993. 475.00 (*1-56203-287-9*) Dun & Bradstreet.

Dun's Regional Business Directories: Northern New York State Area, 1994. Dun & Bradstreet Information Services Staff. 1993. 475.00 (*1-56203-288-7*) Dun & Bradstreet.

Dun's Regional Business Directories: Oklahoma City Area, 1994. Dun & Bradstreet Information Services Staff. 1993. 475.00 (*1-56203-289-5*) Dun & Bradstreet.

Dun's Regional Business Directories: Orlando - Jacksonville Area, 1994. Dun & Bradstreet Information Services Staff. 1993. 475.00 (*1-56203-290-9*) Dun & Bradstreet.

Dun's Regional Business Directories: Philadelphia Area, 1994. Dun & Bradstreet Information Services Staff. 1993. 475.00 (*1-56203-291-7*) Dun & Bradstreet.

Dun's Regional Business Directories: Phoenix - Tucson Area, 1994. Dun & Bradstreet Information Services Staff. 1993. 475.00 (*1-56203-292-5*) Dun & Bradstreet.

Dun's Regional Business Directories: Pittsburgh Area, 1994. Dun & Bradstreet Information Services Staff. 1993. 475. 00 (*1-56203-293-3*) Dun & Bradstreet.

Dun's Regional Business Directories: Portland Area, 1994. Dun & Bradstreet Information Services Staff. 1993. 475. 00 (*1-56203-294-1*) Dun & Bradstreet.

Dun's Regional Business Directories: Raleigh - Durham - Fayetteville Area, 1994. Dun & Bradstreet Information Services Staff. 1993. 475.00 (*1-56203-295-X*) Dun & Bradstreet.

Dun's Regional Business Directories: San Antonio Area, 1994. Dun & Bradstreet Information Services Staff. 1993. 475.00 (*1-56203-296-8*) Dun & Bradstreet.

Dun's Regional Business Directories: San Diego Area. Dun & Bradstreet Information Services Staff. 1993. 475.00 (*1-56203-297-6*) Dun & Bradstreet.

Dun's Regional Business Directories: San Francisco Bay Area, 1994. Dun & Bradstreet Information Services Staff. 1993. 475.00 (*1-56203-298-4*) Dun & Bradstreet.

Dun's Regional Business Directories: Savannah - Augusta Area, 1994. Dun & Bradstreet Information Services Staff. 1993. 475.00 (*1-56203-299-2*) Dun & Bradstreet.

Dun's Regional Business Directories: Seattle Area, 1994. Dun & Bradstreet Information Services Staff. 1993. 475. 00 (*1-56203-300-X*) Dun & Bradstreet.

Dun's Regional Business Directories: South Carolina, 1994. Dun & Bradstreet Information Services Staff. 1993. 475. 00 (*1-56203-301-8*) Dun & Bradstreet.

Dun's Regional Business Directories: St. Louis Area, 1994. Dun & Bradstreet Information Services Staff. 1993. 475. 00 (*1-56203-302-6*) Dun & Bradstreet.

Dun's Regional Business Directories: Tampa - St. Petersburg Area, 1994. Dun & Bradstreet Information Services Staff. 1993. 475.00 (*1-56203-303-4*) Dun & Bradstreet.

Dun's Regional Business Directories: Washington, DC - Baltimore Area, 1994. Dun & Bradstreet Information Services Staff. 1993. 475.00 (*1-56203-304-2*) Dun & Bradstreet.

Dun's Regional Business Directories & Their Product Codes: Atlanta Area, 1994. Dun & Bradstreet Information Services Staff. 1993. 475.00 (*1-56203-228-3*) Dun & Bradstreet.

Dun's Regional Business Directories & Their Product Codes: Birmingham - Montgomery Area, 1994. Dun & Bradstreet Information Services Staff. 1993. 475.00 (*1-56203-229-1*) Dun & Bradstreet.

Dun's Regional Business Directories & Their Product Codes: Boston Area, 1994. Dun & Bradstreet Information Services Staff. 1993. 475.00 (*1-56203-230-5*) Dun & Bradstreet.

Dun's Regional Business Directories & Their Product Codes: Central Indiana Area, 1994. Dun & Bradstreet Information Services Staff. 1993. 475.00 (*1-56203-231-3*) Dun & Bradstreet.

Dun's Regional Business Directories & Their Product Codes: Central Pennsylvania Area, 1994. Dun & Bradstreet Information Services Staff. 1993. 475.00 (*1-56203-232-1*) Dun & Bradstreet.

Dun's Regional Business Directories & Their Product Codes: Charlotte - Greensboro Area, 1994. Dun & Bradstreet Information Services Staff. 1993. 475.00 (*1-56203-233-X*) Dun & Bradstreet.

Dun's Regional Business Directories & Their Product Codes: Chattanooga - Nashville - Knoxville Area, 1994. Dun & Bradstreet Information Services Staff. 1993. 475. 00 (*1-56203-234-8*) Dun & Bradstreet.

Dun's Regional Business Directories & Their Product Codes: Chicago Metropolitan Area, 1994. Dun & Bradstreet Information Services Staff. 1993. 475.00 (*1-56203-235-6*) Dun & Bradstreet.

Dun's Regional Business Directories & Their Product Codes: Chicago Suburban Area, 1994. Dun & Bradstreet Information Services Staff. 1993. 475.00 (*1-56203-236-4*) Dun & Bradstreet.

Dun's Regional Business Directories & Their Product Codes: Cincinnati Area, 1994. Dun & Bradstreet Information Services Staff. 1993. 475.00 (*1-56203-237-2*) Dun & Bradstreet.

Dun's Regional Business Directories & Their Product Codes: Cleveland Area, 1994. Dun & Bradstreet Information Services Staff. 1993. 475.00 (*1-56203-238-0*) Dun & Bradstreet.

Dun's Regional Business Directories & Their Product Codes: Columbus - Dayton - Toledo Area, 1994. Dun & Bradstreet Information Services Staff. 1993. 475.00 (*1-56203-239-9*) Dun & Bradstreet.

Dun's Regional Business Directories & Their Product Codes: Dallas - Ft. Worth Area, 1994. Dun & Bradstreet Information Services Staff. 1993. 475.00 (*1-56203-240-2*) Dun & Bradstreet.

Dun's Regional Business Directories & Their Product Codes: Denver Area, 1994. Dun & Bradstreet Information Services Staff. 1993. 475.00 (*1-56203-241-0*) Dun & Bradstreet.

Dun's Regional Business Directories & Their Product Codes: Detroit Area, 1994. Dun & Bradstreet Information Services Staff. 1993. 475.00 (*1-56203-242-9*) Dun & Bradstreet.

D

An Asterisk (*) at the beginning of an entry indicates that the title is appearing in BIP for the first time. 2131

Dun's Regional Business Directories & Their Product Codes: Hartford - New Haven - Springfield Area, 1994. Dun & Bradstreet Information Services Staff. 1993. 475.00 (*1-56203-243-7*) Dun & Bradstreet.

Duns Scotus: The Basic Principles of His Philosophy. Efrem Bettoni. Ed. by Berbardine Bonansea. LC 78-14031. 220p. 1979. reprint ed. text ed. 67.50 (*0-313-21142-6*, BEDS, Greenwood Pr) Greenwood.

***Duns Scotus, Metaphysician.** William A. Frank & Allan B. Wolter. LC 95-6138. (Series in the History of Philosophy). 220p. (C). 1995. 28.95x (*1-55753-071-8*); pap. 14.95x (*1-55753-072-6*) Purdue U Pr.

Duns Scotus on the Will & Morality. Ed. & Tr. by Allan B. Wolter. LC 85-14907. 554p. 1986. 54.95 (*0-8132-0622-7*) Cath U Pr.

***Duns Scotus on the Will & Morality.** John Duns Scotus. Tr. & Sel. by Allan B. Wolter. LC 85-14907. reprint ed. pap. 157.70 (*0-7837-9193-3*, 2049894) Bks Demand.

Dunsmuir Centennial Book. Ed. by Reva P. Coon & Grace M. Harris. LC 85-50084. (Illus.). (Orig.). 1985. 39.95 (*0-9614838-0-6*) Dunsmuir Centennial.

Dunsmuir House. limited ed. Lois Rather. (Illus.). 1982. 25.00 (*0-686-37970-5*) Rather Pr.

Dunster. John Mortimer. 304p. 1994. pap. 10.95 (*0-14-023270-2*, Penguin Bks) Viking Penguin.

***Dunster.** large type ed. John C. Mortimer. LC 94-26347. 407p. 1994. pap. 18.95 (*0-8161-7476-8*) Hall.

Dunwich Horror & Others. rev. ed. H. P. Lovecraft. Ed. by S. T. Joshi. LC 84-14478. (Collected Lovecraft Fiction Ser.: Vol. 1). (Illus.). 433p. 1985. reprint ed. 19.95 (*0-87054-037-8*) Arkham.

Dunwoody Pond: Reflections on the High Plains Wetlands & Cultivations of Naturalists. John Janovy, Jr. 304p. 1994. 22.95 (*0-312-11456-7*, Pub. by Thomas Dunne Bks) St Martin.

Duo. Sidonie-Gabrielle Colette. Incl. Toutounier. (*0-318-51987-9*); (FRE.). Set pap. 10.95 (*0-8288-9158-3*, F97100) Fr & Eur.

Duo. Herb Ritts. 64p. 1991. 45.00 (*0-944092-17-9*) Twin Palms Pub.

Duo. limited ed. Herb Ritts. 64p. 1991. 150.00 (*0-944092-18-7*) Twin Palms Pub.

Duo! The Best Scenes for the 90s. Ed. by John Horvath & Lavonne Mueller. (Acting Ser.). 532p. (Orig.). 1995. pap. 12.95 (*1-55783-030-4*) Applause Theatre Bk Pubs.

Duo & le Toutounier. Sidonie-Gabrielle Colette. 1974. 25.00 (*0-7206-0273-4*, Pub. by P Owen Ltd UK) Dufour.

Duo-Art Aeolian Pipe-Organ. George A. Audsley. (Illus.). 1921. pap. 10.00 (*0-913746-15-0*) Organ Lit.

Duo-Art Roll Catalog, 1915. 82p. 1977. reprint ed. pap. 14.95 (*1-56642-172-1*, R-49) AMR Pub Co.

Duo-Art Technical Manual: A Compilation of Service Manuals, Technical Charts, Photos. Ed. by Frank Adams. (Illus.). 72p. 1984. reprint ed. spiral bd. 25.00 (*0-913599-45-X*, R-36B) AMR Pub Co.

***Duo Romantique.** Leigh Michaels. (Horizon Ser.). (FRE.). 1994. pap. 3.50 (*0-373-39289-3*, 1-39289-3) Harlequin Bks.

Duodenal Ulcer. Ed. by H. Weiner. (Advances in Psychosomatic Medicine Ser.: Vol. 6). 1971. 59.75 (*3-8055-1159-0*) S Karger.

Duodenary System of Astrology. Frances J. Littlejohn. 1967. 11.00 (*0-86690-371-2*, L2241-074) Am Fed Astrologers.

Duoist from Del Remo. Artemis Quint & Sherman Storr. 183p. (Orig.). 1991. pap. 8.00 (*1-56002-123-3*) Aegina Pr.

***Duong Tinh Doinga.** Lieu Quoc Nhi. 314p. (Orig.). (YA). 1994. pap. 14.00 (*1-886535-02-7*) Dong Van.

Duos see Florilege du Concert Vocal de la Renaissance

***Dupage & Kane Counties Atlas.** (Illus.). 1995. per. 8.95 (*0-933162-87-1*) Creative Sales.

Duplamente Perdoado. Harold Morris. 240p. (POR.). 1990. pap. 9.95 (*0-8297-1629-7*) Life Pubs Intl.

Duplechin Descendants: Genealogical Research of Over 600 Duplechin's. Maxine Duplechain Duhon. Ed. by Linda Fuqua. (Illus.). 166p. 1986. per., pap. 22.00 (*0-9617489-0-7*, TXU 237-556) Duplechain Pub.

Dupleix & Clive: Beginning of Empire. Henry Dodwell. 277p. 1967. 32.00 (*0-7146-1125-5*, Pub. by F Cass Pubs UK) Intl Spec Bk.

Duplex Doppler Ultrasound. Ed. by Kenneth J. Taylor & D. Eugene Strandness, Jr. (Clinics in Diagnostic Ultrasound Ser.: Vol. 26). (Illus.). 182p. 1990. text ed. 69.00 (*0-443-08646-X*) Churchill.

Duplex Plan Book: Professional Builder & Remodeler. (Illus.). Date not set. pap. 29.95 (*1-56056-003-7*) Cahners Pub.

Duplex Planet: Everybody's Asking Who I Was. Ed. by David Greenberger. (Illus.). 224p. (Orig.). 1994. pap. 14.95 (*0-571-19814-7*) Faber & Faber.

Duplex Scanning in Vascular Disorders. 2nd ed. D. Eugene Strandness, Jr. LC 93-12955. 352p. 1993. 105.00 (*0-7817-0014-0*) Raven.

Duplex Sonography. E. G. Grant & E. M. White. (Illus.). 290p. 1991. 120.00 (*0-387-96564-5*) Spr-Verlag.

Duplex Stainless Steels. American Society for Metals Staff. Ed. by R. A. Lula. LC 83-71074. (Conference Proceedings - American Society for Metals Ser.). (Illus.). 811p. reprint ed. pap. 180.00 (*0-8357-6098-7*, 2034311) Bks Demand.

Duplex Systems: Hot Dip Galvanizing Plus Painting. J. F. Van Eijnsbergen. LC 94-5804. 1994. 168.50 (*0-444-81799-9*) Elsevier.

Duplex-Townhouse Plans. rev. ed. Ed. by National Plan Service, Inc. Staff. (Illus.). 32p. (Orig.). reprint ed. pap. 3.95 (*0-934039-08-9*, A51) Natl Plan Serv.

Duplexsonographie der Pfortader. W. G. Zoller. (Illus.). xii, 142p. 1991. pap. 32.00 (*3-8055-5476-1*) S Karger.

Duplicate. William Sleator. (J). (gr. 5 up). 1990. mass mkt. 3.99 (*0-553-28634-X*, Starfire) Bantam.

Duplicate. William Sleator. LC 87-30562. 160p. (YA). (gr. 5-11). 1988. 13.95 (*0-525-44390-8*, 01258-370, DCB) Dutton Child Bks.

Duplicate Bridge. Alfred Sheinwold. pap. 3.95 (*0-486-22741-3*) Dover.

Duplicate Bridge Direction: A Complete Handbook. rev. ed. Alex Groner. LC 67-29818. 1973. pap. 11.95 (*0-87643-012-4*) Barclay Bridge.

***Duplicate Bridge Flipper.** Ron Klinger & Hugh Kelsey. 32p. 1995. pap. 5.95 (*0-575-05942-7*, Pub. by V Gollancz UK) Trafalgar.

Duplicate Copy of the Souvenir from the Afro-American League of Tennessee to Hon. James M Ashley, of Ohio. James M. Ashley & Benjamin H. Arnett. 1977. 45.95 (*0-8369-9218-0*, 9073) Ayer.

Duplicate Death. Georgette Heyer. reprint ed. lib. bdg. 20.95 (*0-89190-643-6*) Amereon Ltd.

Duplicate Keys. Jane Smiley. 320p. 1993. pap. 12.00 (*0-449-90879-8*, Columbine) Fawcett.

Duplicate Pairs for You. Andrew Kambites. 144p. 1992. 22.95 (*0-575-05108-6*, Pub. by V Gollancz UK) Trafalgar.

***Duplicates.** Andrew Neiderman. 272p. (Orig.). 1994. pap. text ed. 4.99 (*0-425-14395-3*) Berkley Pub.

Duplicating Equipment Operator. Jack Rudman. (Career Examination Ser.: C-208). 1994. pap. 19.95 (*0-8373-0208-0*) Nat Learn.

Duplicating Imagination: Twain & the Twain Papers. Maria O. Marotti. LC 88-19560. 1990. lib. bdg. 30.00 (*0-271-00650-1*) Pa St U Pr.

Duplicating Machine Operator. Jack Rudman. (Career Examination Ser.: C-1407). 1994. pap. 19.95 (*0-8373-1407-0*) Nat Learn.

Duplicating Machine Supervisor. Jack Rudman. (Career Examination Ser.: C-1408). 1994. pap. 27.95 (*0-8373-1408-9*) Nat Learn.

Duplications: And Other Stories. Enrique J. Levi. Ed. by Yvette E. Miller. Tr. by Leland H. Chambers. LC 94-19375. (Discoveries Ser.). 192p. 1994. pap. 15.95 (*0-935480-65-X*) Lat Am Lit Rev Pr.

***Duplicities: New & Selected Poems.** Christopher Levenson. 128p. 1995. lib. bdg. 37.00 (*0-8095-4802-X*) Borgo Pr.

Duplicity. Stephen Milanowski & Bob Tarte. LC 91-65127. (Illus.). 42p. 1992. 22.95 (*0-942159-11-X*) U of Wash Pr.

***Duplin County, North Carolina Marriage Bonds & Certificates, 1755-1868.** Francis T. Ingmire. 62p. 1994. lib. bdg. 27.00 (*0-8095-8045-4*); pap. 9.50 (*0-8095-8558-8*) Borgo Pr.

Duplin County Wills, Genealogical Abstracts Of, 1730-1860. William L. Murphy. 280p. 1986. reprint ed. 27.50 (*0-89308-597-9*, NC 32) Southern Hist Pr.

Dupolytheisme Romain: Considere dans ses rapports avec la philosophie grecque et la religion chertienne. Constant De Rebecque & Henri Benjamin. Ed. by Kees W. Bolle. LC 77-79118. (Mythology Ser.). (FRE.). 1978. reprint ed. lib. bdg. 65.95 (*0-405-10530-4*) Ayer.

***DuPont Guerry III, M. D. Ophthalmologist, Richmond, Virginia & the Medical College of Virginia.** DuPont Guerry, 3rd. (Ophthalmology Oral History Ser.). (Illus.). xxiv, 240p. 1993. pap. 35.00 (*1-56055-067-8*) FAAO.

Duppy Talk: West Indian Tales of Mystery & Magic. Told by Gerald Hausman. LC 93-40586. (J). 1994. 14.00 (*0-671-89000-X*, S&S Bks Young Read) S&S Childrens.

Dupuyer Centennial: By Gone Days & Modern Ways. Ed. by James K. Griggs. 1977. pap. 8.50 (*0-918292-01-8*) Griggs Print.

Dupuytren's Disease: Biology & Treatment. Ed. by R. M. McFarlane et al. (Hand & Upper Limb Ser.: Vol. 5). (Illus.). 451p. 1990. text ed. 110.00 (*0-443-03818-X*) Churchill.

Dupuytren's Disease: Pathobiochemistry & Clinical Management. Ed. by A. Berger. LC 93-34322. 1994. 98.00 (*0-387-57239-2*) Spr-Verlag.

Duquesne Studies in Phenomenological Psychology, Vol. 3. Ed. by A. Giorgi et al. LC 71-172383. 281p. 1980. pap. text ed. 15.00x (*0-8207-0137-8*) Duquesne.

Dura-Europos: The Ancient City & the Yale Collection. Susan B. Matheson. LC 82-50113. (Illus.). 42p. (Orig.). 1983. pap. 6.50 (*0-8143-1752-9*) Wayne St U Pr.

Dura-Europos: The Ancient City & the Yale Collection. Susan B. Matheson. (Illus.). 48p. (Orig.). 1982. pap. 3.75 (*0-89467-022-0*) Yale Art Gallery.

Dura-Europos & Its Art. Mikhail I. Rostovtsev. LC 75-41237. reprint ed. 34.50 (*0-404-14594-9*) AMS Pr.

Durability & Aging of Geosynthetics: Represents Papers Presented at a Seminar, Geosynthetic Research Institute, Drexel University, Philadelphia, 8-9 December, 1988. Ed. by Robert M. Koerner. 334p. 1989. 112.00 (*1-85166-363-0*) Elsevier.

Durability & Change - the Science, Responsibility & Cost of Sustaining Cultural Heritage. Ed. by W. E. Krumbein et al. LC 94-18011. (Dahlem Workshop Reports). 1994. text ed. 99.95 (*0-471-95221-4*) Wiley.

***Durability & Damage Tolerance: 1994 International Mechanical Engineering Congress & Exposition, Chicago, Illinois - November 6-11, 1994.** Ed. by A. K. Noor & K. L. Reifsnider. (AD Ser.: Vol. 43). 352p. 1994. 96.00 (*0-7918-1445-9*, G00940) ASME.

Durability & Fracture. Ed. by E. M. Cashell. 200p. 1988. text ed. 56.00 (*0-87849-573-8*, Pub. by Trans Tech GW) LPS Dist Ctr.

Durability by Design: Integrated Approaches to Mechanical Durability Assurance of Ground Vehicles. 1987. 19.00 (*0-89883-657-3*, SP730) Soc Auto Engineers.

Durability of Building Materials & Components: Proceedings of the International Conference, 4-6 November 1987, 2 vols., Set. Ed. by S. L. Lee. 1048p. 1987. pap. 436.00 (*0-08-035914-0*, Pub. by Pergamon Repr UK) Franklin.

Durability of Building Materials & Components - STP 691. Ed. by P. J. Sereda & G. G. Litvan. 1034p. 1980. 74.95 (*0-8031-0325-5*, 04-691000-10) ASTM.

***Durability of Composite Materials: 1994 International Mechanical Engineering Congress & Exposition, Chicago, Illinois - November 6-11, 1994.** (MD Ser.: Vol. 51). 276p. 1994. 90.00 (*0-7918-1401-7*, G00896) ASME.

Durability of Concrete. 1370p. 1991. 128.95 (*0-685-60173-0*, SP-126) ACI.

Durability of Concrete. American Concrete Institute Staff. LC 74-33723. (ACI Publication Ser.: No. SP-47). (Illus.). 391p. reprint ed. pap. 111.50 (*0-685-23516-5*, 2027960) Bks Demand.

Durability of Concrete - G. M. Idorn International Symposium. 430p. 1992. 99.95 (*0-685-60178-1*, SP-131) ACI.

***Durability of Concrete - Third International Conference.** 1224p. 1994. pap. 84.95 (*0-614-02517-6*, SP145) ACI.

Durability of Concrete Construction. Hubert Woods. LC 67-11868. (ACI Monograph Ser.: No. 4). (Illus.). 203p. reprint ed. pap. 57.90 (*0-7837-5214-8*, 2044945) Bks Demand.

Durability of Concrete Road Bridges. OECD Staff. (Road Transport Research Ser.). 136p. (Orig.). 1989. pap. 23.50 (*92-64-13199-X*) OECD.

Durability of Concrete Structures: Investigation, Repair, Protection. Ed. by G. C. Mays. 264p. 1991. 59.95 (*0-419-15620-8*, E & FN Spon) Routledge Chapman & Hall.

Durability of Disease Resistance. Ed. by Thomas Jacobs & J. E. Parlevliet. LC 93-13342. (Current Plant Science & Biotechnology in Agriculture Ser.: Vol. 18). 388p. (C). 1993. Acid-free paper. lib. bdg. 119.50 (*0-7923-2314-9*) Kluwer Ac.

***Durability of Geosynthetics (TRR 1439)** Ed. by Susan Brown. (Transportation Research Record Ser.). (Illus.). 64p. 1994. pap. text ed. 17.00 (*0-309-05520-2*) Transport Res Bd.

Durability of Geotextiles. (RILEM Report Ser.). 250p. 1988. lib. bdg. 69.50 (*0-412-30660-3*) Chapman & Hall.

Durability of Glass Fiber Reinforced Concrete Symposium: Proceedings. 1985. 100.00 (*0-318-35228-1*, GFRC-2) P-PCI.

Durability of In-Place Concrete Containing High-Range Water-Reducing Admixtures. (National Cooperative Highway Research Program Report Ser.: No. 296). 63p. 1987. 10.40 (*0-309-04565-7*) Transport Res Bd.

Durability of Macromolecular Materials. Ed. by Ronald K. Eby. LC 78-31777. (Symposium Ser.: No. 95). 1979. 54.95 (*0-8412-0485-3*) Am Chemical.

Durability of Polymer Based Composite Systems for Structural Applications: Proceedings of the International Colloquium Held in Brussels, Belgium, 27-31 August 1990. Ed. by A. H. Cardon & G. Verchery. 536p. 1991. 150.00 (*1-85166-586-2*) Elsevier.

Durability of Prestressed Concrete Highway Structures. (National Cooperative Highway Research Program Report Ser.: No. 140). 65p. 1988. 9.00 (*0-309-04550-9*) Transport Res Bd.

Durability of Reinforced Concrete in Aggressive Media. S. N. Alkeseev et al. (Russian Translation Ser.: No. 96). (Illus.). 388p. (ENG.). 1993. 85.00 (*90-5410-202-0*, Pub. by A A Balkema NE) Ashgate Pub Co.

Durability of Stone for Rubble Mound Breakwaters. Ed. by Orville T. Magoon & W. F. Baird. LC 91-39609. 277p. 1992. pap. text ed. 29.00 (*0-87262-863-9*) Am Soc Civil Eng.

Durability of Structural Adhesives. Ed. by A. J. Kinloch. (Illus.). 352p. 1983. 106.25 (*0-85334-214-8*, Pub. by Elsevier Applied Sci UK) Elsevier.

***Durability Testing of Concrete & Aggregates - Users Manual.** David Whiting et al. (SHRP Ser.: C-413). (Illus.). 103p. (Orig.). (C). 1994. pap. text ed. 35.00 (*0-309-05817-1*) Natl Res Coun.

Durable Breath: Contemporary Native American Poetry. Ed. by D. L. Birchfield & John E. Smelcer. (Illus.). 190p. (Orig.). (C). 1994. pap. 14.00 (*0-9634000-7-X*) Salmon Run.

Durable Concrete. 71p. 1993. 29.75 (*0-685-72304-6*, C-24) ACI.

Durable Concrete in Hot Climates. 194p. 1993. 50.75 (*0-685-72303-8*, SP-139) ACI.

Durable Fire. Virginia Bernhard. 528p. 1991. mass mkt. 4.95 (*0-380-70873-6*) Avon.

Durable Fire. large type ed. Sheila Bishop. (Romance Ser.). 592p. 1992. 21.95 (*0-7089-2745-9*) Ulverscroft.

Durable Goods. Elizabeth Berg. 208p. 1994. pap. 9.00 (*0-380-72308-5*) Avon.

Durable Goods. Elizabeth Berg. LC 92-28203. 208p. 1993. 17.00 (*0-679-42208-0*) Random.

Durable Goods. Suzanne Matson. LC 93-14958. 72p. (Orig.). 1993. pap. 9.95 (*1-882295-00-5*) Alicejamesbooks.

Durable Powers of Attorney. Shale D. Stiller & Sandra P. Gohn. 1986. write for info. (*0-318-61818-4*) Am Coll Trust & Est.

Durable Resistance in Crops. Ed. by F. Lamberti et al. LC 82-18980. (NATO ASI Series A, Life Sciences: Vol. 55). 464p. 1983. 115.00 (*0-306-41183-0*, Plenum Pr) Plenum.

Durable Satisfaction of Life. Charles W. Eliot. LC 71-99691. (Essay Index Reprint Ser.). 1977. 20.95 (*0-8369-1348-5*) Ayer.

Durable Stability in Southeast Asia. Ed. by Kusuma Snitwongse & Sukhumbhand Paribatra. 237p. 1987. pap. 18.00 (*9971-988-68-2*, Pub. by Inst SE Asian Studies SI) Ashgate Pub Co.

Durable Stability in Southeast Asia. Ed. by Kusuma Snitwongse & Sukhumbhand Paribatra. 237p. 1987. text ed. 38.50 (*9971-988-69-0*, Pub. by Inst SE Asian Studies SI) Ashgate Pub Co.

***Duracell Corporate Report.** 60p. (Orig.). 1995. pap. 295.00 (*0-7605-2104-2*) Rector Pr.

Dural Arteriovenous Malformations. Ed. by Issam Awad & Daniel Barrow. (Illus.). 200p. 1993. 90.00 (*1-879284-06-5*) Am Assn Neuro.

Duran Duran. (Piano-Vocal-Guitar Ser.). (Illus.). 88p. (Orig.). 1993. pap. 14.95 (*0-7935-2387-7*, 00308183) H Leonard.

Duran Duran. Susan Martin. (J). 1984. 8.29 (*0-685-09673-4*) S&S Trade.

Durandal. Harold Lamb. (Illus.). 1981. 15.00 (*0-937986-45-3*); 35.00 (*0-937986-64-X*) D M Grant.

Durandrium Find. Leo LaDell. Ed. by Terry K. Amthor. (Space Master Ser.). (Illus.). 32p. (Orig.). (YA). (gr. 12). 1989. pap. 6.00 (*1-55806-021-9*, 9105) Iron Crown Ent Inc.

***Durang, Durang.** Christopher Durang. 1995. pap. 4.75 (*0-8222-1460-1*) Dramatists Play.

Durango. John B. Keane. 329p. (Orig.). 1992. pap. 12.95 (*1-85635-001-0*, Pub. by Mercier Pr IE) Dufour.

Durango. Terry Kennedy. LC 78-59768. 72p. (Orig.). 1979. pap. 6.00 (*0-912292-54-7*) The Smith.

Durango Area Mountain Bike, CO. rev. ed. Ed. by Trails Illustrated Staff. (Illus.). 1994. 6.99 (*0-925873-93-4*) Trails Illustrated.

Durango Gunfight. Jack Ballas. 208p. (Orig.). 1992. pap. 3.99 (*0-515-10979-7*) Jove Pubns.

Durango South Project: Archaeological Salvage of Two Basketmaker III Sites in the Durango District. John D. Gooding. LC 80-16361. (Anthropological Papers: No. 34). 200p. 1980. pap. 21.95 (*0-8165-0705-8*) U of Ariz Pr.

Durant: The Fortunes & Woodland Camps of a Family in the Adirondacks. Craig Gilborn. LC 81-81438. (Illus.). 170p. 1981. pap. 19.95 (*0-932052-24-X*) Cornell U Pr.

Duras: A Biography. Alain Vircondelet. Tr. by Thomas Buckley. LC 94-8745. (Illus.). xii, 378p. 1994. 24.95 (*1-56478-065-1*) Dalkey Arch.

Duration. Jan Clausen. 1983. pap. 7.00 (*0-914610-36-8*) Hanging Loose.

***Duration & Change: Fifty Years at Oberwolfach.** Ed. by Michael Artin et al. LC 94-28935. 1994. write for info. (*0-387-57214-7*); write for info. (*3-540-57214-7*) Spr-Verlag.

Duration in English: A Basic Choice, Illustrated in Comparison with Dutch. Lia Korrel. LC 91-36113. (Topics in English Linguistics Ser.: No. 5). x, 146p. (C). 1992. lib. bdg. 60.00 (*3-11-012921-3*) Mouton.

Duration of Care Proceedings - Replication Study. C. Thomas et al. 90p. 1993. pap. 25.00 (*0-11-321570-3*, HM15703, Pub. by HMSO UK) UNIPUB.

Duration Tables for Bond & Mortgage Portfolio Management. Financial Publishing Co. Staff. 224p. 1985. pap. 42.00 (*0-87600-561-X*) Finan Pub.

Durations. Poems. Herbert Scott. LC 83-14947. 61p. 1984. pap. 6.95 (*0-8071-1150-3*) La State U Pr.

Durative & Aoristic Tenses in Thucydides. J. L. Rose. (LD Ser.: No. 35). 1942. pap. 16.00 (*0-527-00781-1*) Periodicals Srv.

Durban, 1942: A British Troopship Revolt. Gerry R. Rubin. LC 92-3361. 158p. 1992. boxed 40.00 (*1-85285-080-9*) Hambledon Press.

Durbin & Logsdon Genealogy: With Related Families, 1626-1991. Comp. by Betty J. Carson. (Illus.). 631p. (Orig.). 1991. pap. 36.50 (*1-55613-491-6*) Heritage Bk.

Durbin & Logsdon Genealogy with Related Families, 1626-1991, Vol. 2. Betty J. Carson. (Illus.). x, 253p. (Orig.). 1993. pap. text ed. 21.00 (*1-55613-729-X*) Heritage Bk.

***Durbin & Logsdon Genealogy with Related Families, 1626-1994, 2 vols., Set.** rev. ed. Betty J. Carson. (Illus.). 771p. (Orig.). 1995. pap. text ed. 47.00 (*0-7884-0142-4*) Heritage Bk.

Durbin-Logsdon Genealogy & Related Families from Maryland to Kentucky, 2 vols., Set. Betty J. Carson. xix, 581p. (Orig.). 1993. pap. 37.50 (*1-55613-817-2*) Heritage Bk.

Duree et Simultaneite. Henri L. Bergson. (FRE.). 1968. pap. 35.95 (*0-8288-9072-2*) Fr & Eur.

Duree et Simultaneite see Melanges

***Durer.** Martin Bailey. (Color Library). (Illus.). (C). 1995. pap. 14.95 (*0-7148-3334-7*, Pub. by Phaidon Press UK) Chronicle Bks.

***Durer.** Martin Bailey. (Color Library). (Illus.). 128p. (C). 1995. 19.95 (*0-7148-3335-5*, Pub. by Phaidon Press UK) Chronicle Bks.

Durer-Katalog. J. Meder & Ein Handbuck. LC 75-87642. (Graphic Art Ser.: Vol. 12). (Illus.). 358p. 1971. reprint ed. lib. bdg. 85.00 (*0-306-71788-3*) Da Capo.

Durer to Delacroix: Great Master Drawings from Stockholm. Per Bjurstrom et al. LC 85-80676. (Illus.). 197p. (Orig.). 1985. pap. 24.95 (*0-912804-21-1*) Kimbell Art.

Durer to Diebenkorn: Recent Acquisitions of Art on Paper. Andrew Robison et al. LC 92-12706. (Illus.). 100p. (Orig.). 1992. pap. 24.00 (*0-89468-182-6*) Natl Gallery Art.

Durer's Angel. Tr. by Blais & Lobdell. (NFS Canada Ser.). 1993. pap. 10.95 (*0-88922-111-1*, Pub. by Talonbooks CN) InBook.

Durer's Animals. Colin Eisler. LC 90-21006. (Illus.). 386p. (C). 1991. 90.00 (*0-87474-408-3*) Smithsonian.

Durer's Engravings, Etchings & Drypoints. Walter Strauss. (Illus.). 352p. 1977. 95.00 (*1-55660-155-7*) A Wofsy Fine Arts.

***Durer's Record of Journeys to Venice & the Low Countries.** enl. unabridged ed. Albrecht Durer. (Illus.). 160p. 1995. pap. 6.95 (*0-486-28348-8*) Dover.

Duress in a Cul De Sac: Ghetto Truth & Rights. Ricardo A. Scott. (Illus.). 94p. (Orig.). 1994. write for info. (*1-883427-09-6*) Crnerstone GA.

An Asterisk (*) at the beginning of an entry indicates that the title is appearing in BIP for the first time.

An Asterisk (*) at the beginning of an entry indicates that the title is appearing in BIP for the first time.

2133

D

Dusty Universe. Field & Cameron. 1975. text ed. 15.00 (*0-07-020685-6*) McGraw.

Dusty Universe. 3rd ed. Aneurin Evans. 150p. 1993. text ed. 55.00 (*0-13-221649-3*) P-H.

***Dusty Wagons.** large type ed. Matt Stuart. LC 95-6688. 299p. 1995. pap. 16.95 (*0-7838-1149-7*, Large Print Bks) Hall.

Dusty Wants to Borrow Everything. Inger Sandberg. Tr. by Judy A. Maurer. (Illus.). 32p. (J). (ps up). 1988. 6.95 (*91-29-58782-4*, Pub. by R & S Bks) FS&G.

Dusty Wants to Help. Inger Sandberg. Tr. by Judy A. Mauver. (Illus.). 32p. (J). (ps up). 1988. 6.95 (*91-29-58336-5*, Pub. by R & S Bks) FS&G.

Dusty Was My Friend. Andrea F. Clardy. (Illus.). 32p. (J). (gr. 5 up). 1984. 16.95 (*0-89885-141-6*) Human Sci Pr.

Dusty Wheels. large type ed. Lew Smith. (Linford Western Library). 288p. 1993. pap. 14.95 (*0-7089-7360-4*, Trailtree Bookshop) Ulverscroft.

Dutch. (Handy Dictionaries Ser.). 120p. (Orig.). 1991. pap. 6.95 (*0-87052-049-0*) Hippocrene Bks.

Dutch. (Hugo's Language Ser.). 128p. (Orig.). 1988. pap. 4.95 (*0-85285-093-X*) Hunter NJ.

Dutch: A Linguistic History of Holland & Belgium. B. C. Donaldson. lib. bdg. 14.50 (*0-318-00842-4*) Kluwer Ac.

Dutch: A Linguistic History of Holland & Belgium. B. C. Donaldson. 212p. (C). 1983. text ed. 150.00 (*90-247-9166-9*, Pub. by S Thornes Pubs UK) St Mut.

Dutch: An Essential Grammar. William Z. Shetter. LC 94-11342. 1994. write for info. (*0-415-11277-X*) Routledge.

Dutch: The Language of Twenty Million Dutch & Flemish People. 1994. lib. bdg. 250.75 (*0-8490-5675-6*) Gordon Pr.

Dutch see Dei Gloria Intacta: The Christian Mystery of Initiation of the Holy Rosycross for the New Era

Dutch-Afrikaans, Afrikaans-Dutch Dictionary: Woordeboek Duits-Afrikaans-Duits. 3rd ed. G. P. Trumpelmann & E. Erbe. 879p. (AFR & DUT.). 1983. 125.00 (*0-8288-1704-9*, F75442) Fr & Eur.

Dutch-American Farm. David S. Cohen. (American Social Experience Ser.: No. 15). (Illus.). 256p. 1992. text ed. 50.00x (*0-8147-1454-4*); pap. text ed. 16.50 (*0-8147-1500-1*) NYU Pr.

***Dutch American Voices: Letters from the United States, 1850-1930.** Ed. by Herbert J. Brinks. (Documents in American Social History Ser.). (Illus.). 520p. 1995. 35.00 (*0-8014-3063-1*) Cornell U Pr.

Dutch Anabaptism: Origin, Spread Life, & Thought (1450-1600) Cornelius Krahn. LC 81-583. 320p. (Orig.). 1981. pap. 19.95 (*0-8361-1243-1*) Herald Pr.

Dutch Anabaptists: Stone Lectures Delivered at Princeton Theological Seminary, 1918-1919. Ed. by Henry E. Dosker. LC 83-45610. reprint ed. 36.50 (*0-404-19828-7*) AMS Pr.

Dutch Ancestors: The Glerums - Jan, Jacob, John; Plus "The Norwegian Connection" Maryellen G. Thompson. (Illus.). 200p. (Orig.). 1988. 30.00 (*0-9619909-0-2*); pap. 26.00 (*0-9619909-1-0*) Pac Family Hist Pub.

Dutch & English on the Hudson: A Chronicle of Colonial New York. Maud W. Goodwin. (BCL1 - United States Local History Ser.). 243p. 1991. reprint ed. lib. bdg. 79.00 (*0-7812-6272-0*) Rprt Serv.

Dutch & Flemish Drawings & Watercolors. (Illus.). 295p. 1988. pap. 18.95 (*0-89558-124-8*) Det Inst Arts.

Dutch & Flemish Drawings at Windsor Castle. Christopher White & Charlotte Crawley. LC 93-31550. (Pictures in the Collection of Her Majesty the Queen). (Illus.). 500p. (C). 1995. 250.00 (*0-521-37355-7*) Cambridge U Pr.

Dutch & Flemish Etchings Engravings & Woodcuts, Vol. 35. Ed. by C. Schuckman & D. De Hoop Scheffer. (Illus.). 258p. 1990. 310.00 (*90-72658-09-4*) IBD Ltd.

Dutch & Flemish Etchings Engravings & Woodcuts, Vol. 36. Ed. by C. Schuckman & D. De Hoop Scheffer. (Illus.). 260p. 1990. 310.00 (*90-72658-10-8*) IBD Ltd.

Dutch & Flemish Flower & Fruit Painters of the 17th & 18th Centuries. Ralph Warner. (Illus.). 252p. reprint ed. lib. bdg. 297.50 (*90-6078-072-8*, Pub. by B M Israel NE) Coronet Bks.

Dutch & Flemish Painters. Carel Van Mander. LC 71-88823. (Art Histories Collection Ser.). 1978. reprint ed. 29.95 (*0-405-02224-7*) Ayer.

Dutch & Flemish Painting, Vol. 1: 1400-1600. Gorel Cavalli-Bjorkman. (Illus.). 128p. 1986. 79.00x (*91-7100-304-5*) Coronet Bks.

Dutch & Flemish Woodcuts of the Fifteenth Century. M. J. Schretlen. LC 68-9013. (Illus.). 1969. reprint ed. 30.00 (*0-87817-022-7*) Hacker.

Dutch & Flemish Writers. Ed. by Stanley H. Barkan & Hans Van De Waarsenburg. 1991. 50.00 (*0-89304-910-7*); boxed 75.00 (*0-89304-911-5*) Cross-Cultrl NY.

Dutch & German Dictionary of the Automotive Industry: Worterbuch Automobil-Industrie. Hans Schnellman. 120p. (DUT & GER.). 1987. 95.00 (*0-8288-1187-3*, F25750) Fr & Eur.

Dutch & Quaker Colonies. John Fiske. (Notable American Authors Ser.). 1992. reprint ed. lib. bdg. 75.00 (*0-7812-2856-5*) Rprt Serv.

Dutch & Spanish Dictionary of Electronics & Waveguides: Worterbuch der Elektonik & Wellenleiter. Hans Schnellman. 120p. (DUT & SPA.). 1990. 95.00 (*0-8288-0911-9*, M1360) Fr & Eur.

Dutch & Swedish Place-Names in Delaware. A. R. Dunlap. LC 57-62613. 66p. pap. 2.50 (*0-87413-110-3*) U Delaware Pr.

Dutch Annual of Psychoanalysis, 1993. Han Groen-Prakken & A. Ladan. 300p. 1993. 51.00 (*90-265-1368-2*, Pub. by Swets Pub Serv NE) Taylor & Francis.

Dutch Art & Architecture: 1600-1800. 3rd ed. Jakob Rosenberg et al. (Pelican History of Art Ser.). (Illus.). 502p. (C). 1987. reprint ed. pap. text ed. 26.50 (*0-300-05312-6*) Yale U Pr.

Dutch Art & Character: Psychoanalytical Perspectives on Bosch, Brueghel, Rembrandt, Van Gogh, Mondrian, Willink, Queen Wilhelmina. Joost Baneke et al. 224p. 1993. 52.50 (*90-265-1369-0*, Pub. by Swets Pub Serv NE); pap. 37.50 (*90-265-1373-9*, Pub. by Swets Pub Serv NE) Taylor & Francis.

Dutch at Your Fingertips. Ed Lexus. 1987. pap. 8.95 (*0-7102-0953-3*, RKP) Routledge.

Dutch Barns of New York: An Introduction. Vincent J. Schaefer. LC 94-12435. 1994. pap. 15.00 (*0-935796-50-9*) Purple Mnt Pr.

Dutch-Belgian Troops of the Napoleonic Wars. Otto Von Pivka. (Men-at-Arms Ser.: No. 98). (Illus.). 48p. pap. 11.95 (*0-85045-347-X*, 9215, Pub. by Osprey UK) Stackpole.

Dutch Blue Error. William G. Tapply. 224p. 1985. pap. 2.95 (*0-345-32341-6*) Ballantine.

Dutch Business Law. Jan M. V. D. Beek. Ed. by Steven R. Schuit et al. ring bd. 265.00 (*90-6544-974-4*) Kluwer Law Tax Pubs.

Dutch Calvinism in Modern America: A History of a Conservative Subculture. James D. Bratt. LC 84-13717. 366p. (Orig.). reprint ed. pap. 104.40 (*0-8357-4356-X*, 2037184) Bks Demand.

Dutch Calvinists in Early Stuart London: The Dutch Church in Austin Friars, 1603-1642. Ole P. Grell. LC 88-36552. (Publications of the Sir Thomas Browne Institute, Leiden, New Ser.: No. 2). 331p. 1989. text ed. 81.25 (*90-04-08955-1*) E J Brill.

Dutch Caribbean: Old & New Connections. Ed. by B. Sedoc-Dahlberg. 360p. 1990. text ed. 70.00 (*2-88124-385-1*) Gordon & Breach.

Dutch Cassette Pack. Berlitz Editors. (Cassettepaks Ser.). 1993. audio 15.95 (*2-8315-1096-1*) Berlitz.

Dutch Catholic Immigrant Settlement in Wisconsin, 1850-1905. Yda Schreuder. (Studies in Historical Demography). 300p. 1990. reprint ed. 20.00 (*0-8240-4669-2*) Garland.

Dutch Classicist Architecture: A Survey of Dutch Architecture, Gardens, & Anglo-Dutch Architectural Relations from 1625-1700. W. Kuyper. (Illus.). 648p. (Orig.). 1989. pap. text ed. 87.50 (*90-6275-501-1*, Pub. by Delft U Pr NE) Coronet Bks.

Dutch Colonial System In the East Indies. Jacob Van Klaveren. 1976. lib. bdg. 59.95 (*0-8490-1735-1*) Gordon Pr.

Dutch Connection in South Cook County since 1847. Ross K. Ettema. Ed. by Peggy Ettema. 350p. (C). 1984. text ed. 25.00 (*0-318-18368-4*, TX1-410-036) R K Ettema.

Dutch Continuous Survey, 1972. University of Amsterdam, Institute for Political Science Staff & Baschwitz Institute for Public Opinion & Mass Psychology Staff. 1974. write for info. (*0-89138-074-4*) ICPSR.

Dutch Contributions to the Eighth International Congress of Slavists. Ed. by Jan M. Meijer. iv, 425p. 1979. pap. 82.00x (*90-272-2010-7*) Benjamins North Am.

Dutch Courtesan. John Marston. Ed. by M. L. Wine. LC 65-11519. (Regents Renaissance Drama Ser.). 156p. reprint ed. pap. 44.50 (*0-8357-7933-5*, 2057006) Bks Demand.

Dutch Dissenters: A Critical Companion to Their History & Ideas with a Bibliographical Survey of Recent Research Pertaining to the Early Reformation in the Netherlands. I. B. Horst. (Kerkhistorische Bijdragen Ser.: No. 13). vii, 233p. 1986. 55.00 (*90-04-07454-6*) E J Brill.

Dutch Drawings from the Age of Van Gogh: From the Collection of the Haags Gemeentemuseum. John J. Sillevis. LC 92-85466. (Illus.). 88p. (Orig.). 1992. pap. text ed. 21.95 (*0-915577-24-0*, U of Pa Pr) Taft Museum.

Dutch Eagle: An Illustrated B iography. Maggie Peters & Madelyn K. Peters. Ed. & Illus. by C. D. Peters. 300p. 1992. per. 25.00 (*0-922484-04-X*) Poligion Pub.

Dutch East India Company & the Economy of Bengal, 1630-1720. Om Prakash. LC 84-26484. 320p. 1985. text ed. 49.50x (*0-691-05447-9*) Princeton U Pr.

***Dutch East India Company & the Economy of Bengal, 1630-1720.** Om Prakash. LC 84-26484. (Illus.). Date not set. reprint ed. pap. 86.70 (*0-7837-9426-6*, 2060167) Bks Demand.

Dutch Election Study, 1970-1973. Felix Heunks. LC 75-41583. 1976. write for info. (*0-89138-124-4*) ICPSR.

Dutch Elm Disease: Cellular & Molecular Approaches. Ed. by Mariam B. Sticklen & James L. Sherald. LC 93-17484. 1993. 59.00 (*0-387-94061-8*) Spr-Verlag.

Dutch Elm Disease - The Early Papers: Selected Works of Seven Dutch Women Phytopathologists. Francis W. Holmes & Hans M. Heybroek. LC 90-82571. (Illus.). 154p. 1990. 15.00 (*0-89054-110-8*) Am Phytopathol Soc.

Dutch Emigrants to the United States, South Africa, South America, & Southeast Asia, 1835-1880: An Alphabetical Listing by Household Heads & Independent Persons. Comp. by Robert P. Swierenga & P. William Filby. LC 82-23056. 346p. 1983. lib. bdg. 65.00 (*0-8420-2207-4*) Scholarly Res Inc.

Dutch Emigration to North America, 1624-1860. Bertus H. Wabeke. LC 78-119946. (Select Bibliographies Reprint Ser.). 1977. 19.95 (*0-8369-5389-4*) Ayer.

Dutch Emigration to North America, 1624-1860, a Short History. Bertus H. Wabeke. (History - United States Ser.). 160p. 1993. reprint ed. lib. bdg. 69.00 (*0-7812-4835-3*) Rprt Serv.

Dutch-English: Van Dale. 2nd ed. M. W. Tops. 1560p. 1991. 138.00 (*90-6648-127-7*) IBD Ltd.

Dutch-English - English-Dutch Dictionary. Fernand G. Renier. 1985. pap. 13.95 (*0-415-04610-6*) Routledge.

Dutch-English - English-Dutch Dictionary of Information Technology. Bakker. 366p. (DUT & ENG.). 1985. 47.50 (*90-201-1823-4*, Pub. by Kluwer NE) IBD Ltd.

Dutch-English & English-Dutch Dictionary. Ed. by Fernand G. Renier. (DUT & ENG.). 1949. pap. 13.95 (*0-7100-9352-7*, RKP) Routledge.

Dutch-English Book on Business Terminology. H. J. Van Moll. 326p. (DUT & ENG.). 1986. 49.95 (*0-8288-7904-4*) Fr & Eur.

***Dutch-English Concise Dictionary of Engineering.** S. Stekhoven. (DUT & ENG.). 1991. 68.00 (*0-7859-8929-3*) Fr & Eur.

***Dutch-English Concise Dictionary of Engineering.** S. Stekhoven. (DUT & ENG.). 1991. 50.00 (*0-7859-8930-7*) Fr & Eur.

Dutch-English Concise Dictionary of Engineering. Schuurmans Stekhoven. 315p. 1991. 68.00 (*90-201-2526-5*, Pub. by Kluwer NE); pap. 50.00 (*90-201-2468-4*, Pub. by Kluwer NE) IBD Ltd.

Dutch-English Dictionary. Berlitz Editors. LC 78-78084. (Bilingual Pocket Dictionary Ser.). 360p. (DUT & ENG.). 1994. pap. 7.95 (*2-8315-0988-2*) Berlitz.

***Dutch-English Dictionary.** 19th ed. Ten K. Bruggencate. (DUT & ENG.). 1990. 58.00 (*0-7859-8950-1*) Fr & Eur.

Dutch-English Dictionary: Nederlands-Engels Woordenboek. A. Broers & J. Smith. 725p. (DUT & ENG.). 1981. pap. 29.95 (*0-8288-0449-4*, M10060) Fr & Eur.

Dutch-English Dictionary (New Prisma) 612p. 1991. pap. 21.00 (*90-274-2497-7*) IBD Ltd.

Dutch-English Dictionary of Business & Commerce. J. G. Sanders. 244p. 1980. 75.00 (*0-8288-0074-X*, M 8347) Fr & Eur.

Dutch-English Dictionary of Financial Management. 4th ed. F. Van Amerongen. 348p. 1992. 109.00 (*90-14-04687-1*, Pub. by Samsom NE) IBD Ltd.

***Dutch-English Dictionary of Financial Management.** 4th ed. F. Van Amerongen. (DUT & ENG.). 1992. 109.00 (*0-7859-8836-X*) Fr & Eur.

Dutch-English Dictionary of Informatics: With Eng-Dutch Vocabulary Plus Eng. Acronyms. 2nd ed. C. Van Uitert & A. M. Kaspers. 1063p. 1989. 99.00 (*90-14-03828-3*) IBD Ltd.

Dutch-English, English-Dutch Concise Dictionary: With a Brief Introduction to Dutch Grammar. (Hippocrene Concise Dictionaries Ser.). 418p. (Orig.). 1990. pap. 7.95 (*0-87052-910-2*) Marboro Bks.

Dutch-English, English-Dutch Dictionary. Fernand G. Renier. (DUT & ENG.). 39.50 (*0-87557-014-3*, 014-3) Saphrograph.

Dutch-English, English-Dutch Dictionary of Information Science. Bakker. 366p. (DUT & ENG.). 1985. 45.00 (*0-8288-4024-5*, F116490) Fr & Eur.

***Dutch-English, English-Dutch Medical Dictionary.** 3rd ed. Mostert. 206p. (DUT & ENG.). 1990. 75.00 (*0-7859-7519-5*, 9031310786) Fr & Eur.

Dutch-English, English-Dutch Medical Dictionary. 3rd rev. ed. F. J. Mostert. 206p. 1990. 73.00 (*90-313-1078-6*, Pub. by Bohn Scheltema) IBD Ltd.

***Dutch-English, English-Dutch Technical Dictionary.** Jansonius. 555p. (DUT & ENG.). 1976. 150.00 (*0-7859-7504-7*, 9061100291) Fr & Eur.

Dutch-English, English-Dutch Technical Dictionary. H. Jansonius. 555p. (DUT & ENG.). 1976. 120.00 (*90-6110-029-1*) IBD Ltd.

Dutch-English Financial Management Terms. 2nd rev. ed. F. Van Amerongen. 323p. (DUT & ENG.). 1989. 75.00 (*0-8288-4018-0*, F113290) Fr & Eur.

***Dutch-English Great Polytechnic Dictionary.** S. Stekhoven. 850p. (DUT & ENG.). 1993. write for info. (*0-7859-8767-3*) Fr & Eur.

Dutch-English Great Polytechnic Dictionary. Schuurmans Stekhoven. 850p. 1993. 110.00 (*90-201-2328-9*, Pub. by Kluwer NE) IBD Ltd.

Dutch-English, Kramer's. G. Van Kooten. 520p. 1987. pap. 28.00 (*90-10-05955-3*) IBD Ltd.

Dutch-English Laboratory Vocabulary. H. Bokx. 143p. (DUT & ENG.). 1993. 38.00 (*90-201-2768-3*, Pub. by Kluwer NE) IBD Ltd.

***Dutch-English Laboratory Vocabulary.** H. Bokx. 143p. (DUT & ENG.). 1993. write for info. (*0-7859-8768-1*) Fr & Eur.

Dutch-English (New Great) Dictionary, 3 vols., Set. 2nd ed. H. Jansonius. (DUT & ENG.). 1973. 345.00 (*90-6110-032-1*) IBD Ltd.

Dutch-English, Ten K. Bruggencate. 19th ed. 1004p. 1990. reprint ed. 58.00 (*90-01-96819-8*) IBD Ltd.

***Dutch-English Vocabulary of the Laboratory.** K. Bokx. 143p. (DUT & ENG.). 1993. 39.95 (*0-7859-7466-0*, 9020127683) Fr & Eur.

Dutch Family in the Middle Colonies, 1660-1800. Firth H. Fabend. LC 90-37644. (Illus.). 304p. (C). 1991. text ed. 50.00 (*0-8135-1627-7*) Rutgers U Pr.

***Dutch Farmer in the Missouri Valley: The Life & Letters of Ulbe Eringa, 1866-1950.** Brian W. Beltman. LC 95-13565. (Statue of Liberty-Ellis Island Centennial Ser.). 1996. write for info. (*0-252-02195-9*) U of Ill Pr.

Dutch, Fast-Track. Peter Leimbigler. 344p. 1993. 16.95 (*0-88432-686-1*, FTDU91); audio 125.00 (*0-88432-685-3*, FTDU20) Audio-Forum.

Dutch, Flemish & German Paintings in the Cincinnati Art Museum: 15th-18th Centuries. Mary A. Scott. Ed. by Carol Schoellkopf. (Illus.). 188p. 1988. pap. text ed. 29.95 (*0-931537-06-1*) Cincinnati Mus.

***Dutch Flower Painting, 1600-1720.** Paul Taylor. LC 94-40131. 1995. write for info. (*0-300-05390-8*) Yale U Pr.

***Dutch Foreign Direct Investment in the United States 1974-1994.** Francis M. Jeffries. 300p. (Orig.). 1995. pap. 125.00 (*1-878974-16-5*) Jeffries & Assocs.

Dutch Foreign Policy Since Eighteen Fifteen: A Study in Small Power Politics. Amry Vandenbosch. LC 79-2292. 1981. reprint ed. 25.85 (*0-88355-968-4*) Hyperion Conn.

Dutch Fork. O. B. Mayer et al. Ed. by Brent Holcomb. (Illus.). 155p. (C). 1982. 20.00 (*0-9611610-0-0*) Dutch Fork Pr.

Dutch Fork Cookery: A Treasury of Traditional Recipes from the German Kitchens of Central South Carolina. Juanita C. Kibler. (Illus.). 150p. 1989. 17.00 (*0-9611610-3-5*) Dutch Fork Pr.

Dutch Founding of New York. Thomas A. Janvier. 217p. 1993. reprint ed. lib. bdg. 79.00 (*0-7812-5186-9*) Rprt Serv.

Dutch Founding of New York. Thomas A. Janvier. (Illus.). 250p. 1989. reprint ed. pap. 15.00 (*1-55613-164-X*) Heritage Bk.

Dutch-French Dictionary: Dictionnaire Neerlandais-Francais. C. Herckenrath & A. Dory. 1020p. (DUT & FRE.). 1981. 49.95 (*0-8288-0453-2*, M9742) Fr & Eur.

Dutch Garden in the Seventeenth Century. Ed. by John D. Hunt. LC 89-23831. (Dumbarton Oaks Colloquium on the History of Landscape Architecture Ser.: No. 12). (Illus.). 220p. 1990. 50.00 (*0-88402-187-4*, HUDG) Dumbarton Oaks.

Dutch Genre Art of the Seventeenth Century. (Shorewood Art Programs for Education Ser.). 12p. 1974. 143.00 (*0-685-07230-4*) Shorewood Fine Art.

Dutch Genre Art of the Seventeenth Century. (Shorewood Art Programs for Education Ser.). 12p. 1974. teacher ed 107.00 (*0-88185-055-1*) Shorewood Fine Art.

Dutch Gentry, Fifteen Hundred to Sixteen-Fifty: Family, Faith, & Fortune. Sherrin D. Marshall. LC 86-7647. (Contributions in Family Studies: No. 11). 252p. 1987. text ed. 59.95 (*0-313-25021-9*, WYD/, Greenwood Pr) Greenwood.

Dutch Grammar & Reader. Jacob Smit. Ed. by Reinder P. Meijer. 216p. (C). 1984. text ed. 100.00 (*0-85950-022-5*, Pub. by S Thornes Pubs UK) St Mut.

Dutch Graphic Design: A Century. Kees Broos & Paul Hefting. (Illus.). 216p. 1993. 80.00x (*0-262-02358-X*) MIT Pr.

Dutch Graphic Design: 1918-1945. Alston W. Purvis. (Illus.). 228p. 1992. text ed. 39.95 (*0-442-00444-3*) Van Nos Reinhold.

Dutch Homesteader on the Prairies: Letters of Willem de Gelder 1910-13. Willem De Gelder. LC 73-85658. 109p. reprint ed. pap. 31.10 (*0-685-15880-2*, 2026382) Bks Demand.

Dutch Households in U. S. Population Censuses, 1850, 1860, 1870: An Alphabetical Listing by Heads of Family, 3 vols. Ed. by Robert P. Swierenga. LC 86-26123. 1987. 180.00 (*0-8420-2237-6*) Scholarly Res Inc.

Dutch Houses & Castles. Jorge Guillermo. (Illus.). 207p. Date not set. 55.00 (*0-935748-94-6*) M T Train.

Dutch Houses in the Hudson Valley Before 1776. H. W. Reynolds. 467p. 1993. reprint ed. lib. bdg. 99.00 (*0-7812-5303-9*) Rprt Serv.

Dutch Hunebedden: Megalithic Tombs of the Funnel Beaker Culture. Jan A. Bakker. (Archaeological Ser.: No. 2). (Illus.). xiv, 214p. (Orig.). 1992. pap. 34.00 (*1-879621-02-9*) Intl Mono Prehstry.

***Dutch-Hungarian Pocket Dictionary.** I. Zugor. 860p. (C). 1993. 21.00x (*963-05-6499-8*, Pub. by Akad Kiado HU) St Mut.

Dutch Immigrants in U. S. Ship Passenger Manifests, 1820-1880: An Alphabetical Listing by Household Heads & Independent Persons, 2 vols., Set. Comp. by Robert P. Swierenga. LC 82-23078. 1223p. 1983. lib. bdg. 150.00 (*0-8420-2206-6*) Scholarly Res Inc.

Dutch in America: Immigration, Settlement & Cultural Change. Ed. by Robert P. Swierenga. 219p. (C). 1985. text ed. 45.00 (*0-8135-1063-5*) Rutgers U Pr.

Dutch in America Orange Pages, 1992: A Guide A-Z Ein Gids. Ed. by Miriam Jacobs. 192p. 1991. pap. 14.95 (*0-9631013-0-7*) Dutch Netwk.

Dutch in Malabar. Ed. & Tr. by A. Galletti. 1985. reprint ed. 50.00 (*0-8364-1340-7*, Pub. by Usha Il) S Asia.

Dutch in the Atlantic Slave Trade. Johannes M. Postma. (Illus.). (C). 1990. 74.95 (*0-521-36585-6*) Cambridge U Pr.

Dutch in the Caribbean & on the Wild Coast 1580-1680. Cornelis C. Goslinga. LC 72-93193. 704p. reprint ed. pap. 180.00 (*0-8357-6920-8*, 2037979) Bks Demand.

Dutch in Three Months. (Hugo's Language Bks.: No. 522). 192p. 1986. pap. 7.95 (*0-85285-060-3*) Littlefield.

Dutch in Three Months. (Hugo's Language Bks.). 192p. 1986. audio 39.95 (*0-85285-073-5*); audio (*0-318-61461-8*) Hunter NJ.

Dutch Influence on English Vocabulary see Persian Words in English

Dutch Influences on English Culture, 1558-1625. D. W. Davies. LC 64-18226. (Folger Guides to the Age of Shakespeare Ser.). 1964. pap. 4.95 (*0-918016-13-4*) Folger Bks.

Dutch Interior: Post-War Poetry of the Netherlands & Flanders. Ed. by William J. Smith & James S. Holmes. LC 83-27332. 288p. 1984. text ed. 38.00 (*0-231-05746-6*) Col U Pr.

Dutch-Italian, Italian-Dutch Dictionary: Dizionario Olandese-Italiano-Olandese. J. Van Kampen. 486p. (DUT & ITA.). 1980. 14.95 (*0-8288-0458-3*, M9171) Fr & Eur.

Dutch Landscape Painting of the Seventeenth Century. Wolfgang Stechow. LC 81-66148. (Cornell-Phaidon Bks.; Landmarks in Art History). (Illus.). 494p. (C). 1981. reprint ed. pap. 19.95 (*0-8014-9228-9*) Cornell U Pr.

Dutch Landscape Painting of the Seventeenth Century. Wolfgang Stechow. LC 79-91824. (Illus.). 494p. 1980. reprint ed. lib. bdg. 60.00 (*0-87817-268-8*) Hacker.

Dutch Language: A Survey. Pierre Brachin. Tr. & Adapt. by Paul Vincent. 160p. (Orig.). (C). 1985. 90.00 (*0-85950-246-5*, Pub. by S Thornes Pubs UK) St Mut.

An Asterisk (*) at the beginning of an entry indicates that the title is appearing in BIP for the first time.

An Asterisk (*) at the beginning of an entry indicates that the title is appearing in BIP for the first time.

D

Dvorak in America, 1892-1895. Ed. by John C. Tibbetts. LC 92-19768. (Illus.). 458p. 1993. 32.95 (0-931340-56-X, Amadeus Pr) Timber.

Dvorak in Love. Josef Skvorecky. 1987. 18.95 (0-317-58073-6) Knopf.

Dvorak in Love. Josef Skvorecky. 1988. pap. 10.00 (0-393-30548-1) Norton.

Dvorak Keyboard: The Ergonomically Designed Typewriter Keyboard. R. C. Cassingham. (Illus.). 96p. (C). 1986. pap. 12.95 (0-935309-10-1) Freelance Comm.

Dvorak Predicts: An Insider's Look at the Computer Industry. John C. Dvorak. 1994. pap. text ed. 16.95 (0-07-881981-4) McGraw.

Dvorak's Guide to OS-2, Version 2.0: Learn to Navigate the Operating System of the Future. John C. Dvorak. 1993. pap. 45.00 (0-679-74648-X) Random.

Dvorak's Guide to PC Connectivity. John C. Dvorak. 1992. pap. 49.95 (0-679-79065-9) Random.

Dvorak's Guide to PC Games. John C. Dvorak. 1991. disk, pap. 29.95 (0-553-35144-3) Bantam.

Dvorak's Guide to PC Telecommunications: Second Edition. 2nd ed. John C. Dvorak. 912p. 1992. 3.5 hd, pap. text ed. 39.95 (0-07-881787-0) Osborne-McGraw.

Dvorak's Guide to Windows 3.1 Basics. John C. Dvorak & Nick Anis. 1992. 3.5 hd, pap. 50.00 (0-679-73935-1) Random.

Dvoraks of Minnetonka Township Minnesota. Helen M. Vavra & Albert J. Kranz. Ed. by Leo F. Dvorak. LC 88-82028. (Illus.). 275p. 1988. 36.00 (0-9620312-0-8) A Kranz.

***D.W. Thinks Big.** Marc Brown. (Illus.). (J). (ps-3). 1995. pap. 4.95 (0-316-10922-3) Little.

Dwadashamsas: Degree Analyses & Deeper Meanings. rev. ed. John Sandbach. (Illus.). 190p. 1983. reprint ed. per., pap. 6.95 (0-930706-03-X) Seek-It Pubns.

Dwanscie Krokow I Dwanascie Tradycji: Twelve Steps & Twelve Traditions. 154p. (POL.). 1986. pap. 3.65 (0-916856-24-0) AAWS.

Dwarf. Par Lagerkvist. Tr. by Alexandra Dick. 228p. (Orig.). 1958. pap. 9.95 (0-374-52135-2, Noonday) FS&G.

***Dwarf & Slow-Growing Conifers.** John Bond & Lyn Randall. (Illus.). 64p. 1995. pap. 5.95 (0-304-32065-X, Pub. by Cassell UK) Sterling.

Dwarf & Slow-Growing Conifers. Murray Hornibrook. LC 75-174547. (Illus.). 1973. reprint ed. 8.50 (0-913728-01-2) Theophrastus.

Dwarf Bamboo. Marilyn Chin. LC 87-80181. (Illus.). 84p. (Orig.). 1987. pap. 8.95 (0-912678-71-2, Greenfld Rev Pr) Greenfld Rev Lit.

Dwarf Cichlids. Jorg Vierke. (Illus.). 158p. 1988. lib. bdg. 19.95 (0-86622-982-5, TS-118) TFH Pubns.

***Dwarf Dinosaur.** Esther A. Barnes. 1994. 6.95 (0-533-11103-X) Vantage.

***Dwarf Giant.** Anita Lobel. LC 95-6790. (Illus.). 32p. (J). 1996. 15.00 (0-688-14407-1) Greenwillow.

***Dwarf Nose.** Wilhelm Hauff. Tr. by Anthea Bell. LC 94-9374. (Illus.). 56p. (J). 1994. 17.95 (1-55858-261-4) North-South Bks NYC.

***Dwarf Nose.** Wilhelm Hauff. Tr. by Anthea Bell. LC 94-9374. (Illus.). 56p. (J). (ps-2). 1994. lib. bdg. 17.88 (1-55858-262-2) North-South Bks NYC.

Dwarf Rabbits: A Complete Pet Owner's Manual. Monika Wegler. 1992. pap. 5.95 (0-8120-1352-2) Barron.

Dwarf Rabbits: Selection, Care & Breeding. Gunter Flauhaus. Tr. by Christa Ahrens. (Illus.). 128p. 1985. reprint ed. 11.95 (0-86622-671-0, H-1073) TFH Pubns.

Dwarf Rabbits As a New Pet. Andrea Dieker & Jutta Steinkamp. (Illus.). 64p. 1992. pap. 5.95 (0-86622-537-4, TU-026) TFH Pubns.

***Dwarf Rabbits...As a Hobby.** Kelsey Wood. 1995. pap. text ed. 7.95 (0-86622-713-X) TFH Pubns.

Dwarf Rhododenrons. Cox. 1985. 17.95 (0-02-528560-2) Macmillan.

Dwarf, the Giant, & the Unicorn: A Tale of King Arthur. Illus. by Claire Ewart. LC 92-34031. (J). 1994. write for info. (0-395-60520-2, Clarion Bks) HM.

Dwarf-Wizard of Uxmal. Susan H. Shetterly. LC 89-32864. (Illus.). 32p. (J). (gr. k-3). 1990. text ed. 13.95 (0-689-31455-8, Atheneum Bks Young) S&S Childrens.

Dwarfed Fruit Trees. Harold B. Tukey. LC 77-12289. (Comstock Book Ser.). (Illus.). 576p. 1978. 49.50 (0-8014-1126-2) Cornell U Pr.

Dwarfed Potted Trees: The Bonsai of Japan. Ed. by Kan Yashiroda. (Plants & Gardens Ser.). (Illus.). 96p. 1992. per., pap. 6.95 (0-945352-17-4) Bklyn Botanic.

Dwarfs. Harold Pinter. 224p. (Orig.). 1991. pap. 11.95 (0-8021-3266-9) Grove-Atltic.

Dwarfs see Three Plays

Dwarfs & Eight Review Sketches. Harold Pinter. 1965. pap. 4.75 (0-8222-0344-8) Dramatists Play.

Dwarfs Don't Live in Doll Houses. Angela M. Van Etten. LC 88-70331. 255p. (Orig.). 1988. pap. 15.95 (0-945727-80-1) Adaptive Living.

Dwarfs in Ancient Egypt & Greece. Veronique Dasen. LC 92-35446. (Oxford Monographs on Classical Archaeology). 464p. 1994. 89.00 (0-19-814699-X) OUP.

Dwarf's Legacy. Tolly Kizilos. Ed. by Sylvia Ashton. LC 76-2302. 1977. 22.95 (0-87949-065-9) Ashley Bks.

Dwarfs Tailor, & Other Fairy Tales. Ed. by Zoe D. Underhill. LC 78-74521. (Children's Literature Reprint Ser.). (J). (gr. 4-5). 1979. reprint ed. 21.75 (0-8486-0224-2) Roth Pub Inc.

Dwasuparna: A Novel in Two Parts, 2 vols. Nishi Khanolkar. (Greenbird Ser.). 1976. 12.00 (0-89253-136-3) Ind-US Inc.

Dwasuparna: A Novel in Two Parts, 2 vols., Set. Nishi Khanolkar. (Greenbird Ser.). 1976. text ed. 20.00 (0-89253-120-7) Ind-US Inc.

Dwell. Jeff Derksen. 80p. 1994. pap. 9.95 (0-88922-328-9, Pub. by Talonbooks CN) InBook.

Dwell in the Wilderness. Bienvenido N. Santos. 129p. (Orig.). 1985. pap. 7.50 (971-10-0182-9) Cellar.

Dwell Within These Distances, Vol. 10. Hugh Burgess. 50p. 1982. pap. 3.95 (0-932616-08-9) New Poets Chestnut Hills.

Dweller in the Gulf. Clark A. Smith. (Unexpurgated Clark Ashton Smith Ser.). (Orig.). 1987. pap. 2.50 (0-940884-07-0) Necronomicon.

Dweller on Two Planets. Phylos. 1952. pap. 13.50 (0-87505-088-3) Borden.

Dweller on Two Planets: The Dividing of the Way. Phylos the Thibetan. 423p. 1964. reprint ed. spiral bd. 13.20 (0-7873-0670-3) Mokelumne.

Dweller on Two Planets, or the Dividing of the Way. 2nd ed. Phylos the Thibetan. (Illus.). 432p. 1991. pap. 15.00 (0-8334-0022-3, Spir Lit Lib) Garber Comm.

Dwellers. Roger Elwood. LC 90-81608. 1990. pap. 9.99 (0-88419-273-3, Creation Hse) Strang Comms Co.

Dwellers at the Source: Southwestern Indian Photographs of A.C. Vroman, 1895-1904. William Webb & Robert A. Weinstein. (Illus.). 223p. 1987. reprint ed. pap. 35.00 (0-8263-1009-5) U of NM Pr.

Dwellers in Arcady: Essays in Folk-Lore. Richard L. Gales. LC 68-8463. (Essay Index Reprint Ser.). 1977. reprint ed. 19.95 (0-8369-0467-2) Ayer.

***Dwellers in Darkness.** Brandon Blackmoor & Susan Blackmoor. 150p. (J). (gr. 1). 1995. pap. text ed. 15.00 (0-9641722-5-9) Black Gate.

Dwellers in the Crucible. Margaret W. Bonanno. (Star Trek Ser.: No. 25). 320p. 1991. mass mkt. 4.95 (0-671-74147-0) PB.

Dwellers in the Land: The Bioregional Vision. 2nd ed. Kirkpatrick Sale. 238p. 1991. lib. bdg. 39.95 (0-86571-224-7); pap. 12.95 (0-86571-225-5) New Soc Pubs.

Dwellers in the Mirage. A. Merritt. 288p. 1991. pap. 5.95 (0-02-022872-4, Pub. by Gebrueder Borntraeger GW) Macmillan.

Dwellers in the Mirage. A. Merrit. 1993. reprint ed. lib. bdg. 18.95 (0-89968-407-6, Lghtyr Pr) Buccaneer Bks.

Dwellers on the Nile. E. Wallis Budge. LC 72-80141. (Illus.). 1972. reprint ed. 19.95 (0-405-08316-5, Pub. by Blom Pubns UK) Ayer.

Dwellers on the Nile: The Life, History, Religion, & Literature of the Ancient Egyptians. Wallis E. Budge. (Illus.). 326p. 1977. reprint ed. pap. 7.95 (0-486-23501-7) Dover.

***Dwelling & Mobile Home Monetary Losses Due to the 1989 Loma Prieta Earthquake: With an Emphasis on Loss Estimation.** Karl V. Steinbrugge & Richard J. Roth, Jr. LC 94-33201. (Bulletin: Estimation of Earthquake Losses to Housing in California Ser.: Vol. 1939-B). 1994. write for info. (0-615-00183-1) US Geol Survey.

Dwelling Construction under the Uniform Building Code. 1994. pap. text ed. 15.60 (1-884590-06-3, 107S94) Intl Conf Bldg Off.

Dwelling House Construction. 5th ed. Albert G. Dietz. (Illus.). 456p. 1990. 47.50 (0-262-04108-1) MIT Pr.

Dwelling House Construction. 5th ed. Albert G. Dietz. (Illus.). 454p. 1992. reprint ed. pap. 19.95 (0-262-54069-X) MIT Pr.

Dwelling in the Text: Houses in American Fiction. Marilyn R. Chandler. (Illus.). 326p. 1991. 33.00 (0-520-07363-0) U CA Pr.

Dwelling of God: The Tabernacle in the Old Testament, Intertestamental Jewish Literature, & the New Testament. Craig R. Koester. Ed. by Robert Karris. LC 89-9853. (Catholic Biblical Quarterly Monographs: No. 22). x, 228p. 1989. pap. 9.00 (0-915170-21-3) Catholic Bibl Assn.

Dwelling, Place & Environment: Towards a Phenomenology of Person & World. David Seamon & Robert Mugerauer. (Illus.). 320p. 1989. pap. text ed. 15.50 (0-231-07113-2) Col U Pr.

Dwelling Place for Wisdom. Raimon Panikkar. Tr. by Annemarie S. Kidder. LC 92-19450. 176p. (Orig.). 1993. pap. 12.99 (0-664-25362-8) Westminster John Knox.

Dwelling Places: Poems & Translations. David K. Ferry. LC 92-31605. (Phoenix Poets Ser.). 72p. (C). 1993. lib. bdg. 20.00 (0-226-24478-4); pap. 7.95 (0-226-24479-2) U Ch Pr.

Dwelling, Seeing, & Designing: Toward a Phenomenological Ecology. Ed. by David Seamon. LC 91-43854. (SUNY Series in Environmental & Architectural Phenomenology). (Illus.). 363p. (C). 1993. 59.50 (0-7914-1277-6); pap. 21.95 (0-7914-1278-4) State U NY Pr.

***Dwellings: Reflections on the Natural World.** Linda Hogan. 224p. 1995. 22.00 (0-393-03784-3) Norton.

Dwellings: The House across the World. Paul Oliver. (Illus.). 256p. 1987. 40.00 (0-292-71554-4); pap. 27.50 (0-292-71555-2) U of Tex Pr.

Dwellings, Settlements & Tradition: Cross-Cultural Perspectives. Ed. by Jean-Paul Bourdier & Nezar Alsayyad. LC 89-34496. 548p. 1989. pap. 53.50 (0-8191-7524-2) U Pr of Amer.

DWI - Texas Cases & Forms Annotated. David Chapman. 676p. 1993. ring bd. 150.00 (1-878337-34-3) Knowles Law.

DWI-DUI Sentencing Evaluation, Maryland District Court. Don Hardenbergh et al. 127p. 1990. 8.00 (0-685-34852-0, SERO-056) Natl Ctr St Courts.

Dwiggins Marionettes: A Complete Experimental Theatre in Miniature. Dorothy Abbe. (Puppet Library). 1970. 45.00 (0-8238-0146-2) Plays.

Dwight A. Nelson: Recollections of My Life & Work in Nevada Education, 1932-1945; & Juvenile Probation & Detention in Washoe County, 1949-1969; a Term As Washoe County Commissioner. Ed. by Mary E. Glass. 384p. 1972. lib. bdg. 52.00 (1-56475-117-1); fiche write for info. (1-56475-118-X) U NV Oral Hist.

Dwight & Lucille Beeson Wedgwood Collection. Elizabeth B. Adams. (Illus.). 401p. Date not set. 70.00 (0-931394-33-3, Antique Collect); pap. 45.00 (0-931394-32-5, Antique Collect) Birmingham Mus.

Dwight & Lucille Beeson Wedgwood Collection at the Birmingham Museum. (Illus.). Date not set. 70.00 (0-685-67982-9) Birmingham Mus.

Dwight & Lucille Beeson Wedgwood Collection at the Birmingham Museum of Art. Elizabeth B. Adams. (Illus.). 400p. 1993. 70.00 (0-295-97257-2); pap. 45.00 (0-295-97258-0) U of Wash Pr.

Dwight & the Trilobite. Gina C. Erickson & Kelli C. Foster. (Get Ready...Get Set...Read! Ser.). (Illus.). 24p. (J). (ps-3). 1994. pap. 3.50 (0-8120-1839-7) Barron.

Dwight D. Eisenhower. Jean Darby. (Lerner Biography Ser.). (Illus.). 112p. (J). (gr. 5 up). 1989. 21.50 (0-8225-4900-X, Lerner Publctns) Lerner Group.

***Dwight D. Eisenhower.** Ed. by Henry J. Gwiazda & McCarthy Janel. (Presidential Perspectives from the National Archives Ser.). (Illus.). 32p. 1995. pap. 3.50 (1-880875-05-5) National Archives & Recs.

Dwight D. Eisenhower. Jim Hargrove. LC 86-29918. (Encyclopedia of Presidents Ser.). (Illus.). 100p. (J). (gr. 3 up). 1987. lib. bdg. 14.40 (0-516-01389-0) Childrens.

Dwight D. Eisenhower. Peter L. Sandberg. (World Leaders - Past & Present Ser.). (Illus.). 112p. (YA). (gr. 5 up). 1986. lib. bdg. 16.95 (0-87754-521-9); pap. 9.95 (0-7910-0566-6) Chelsea Hse.

Dwight D. Eisenhower: Hero & Politician. Robert F. Burk. (Twayne's Twentieth Century American Biography Ser.: No. 2). 232p. (C). 1986. text ed. 26.95 (0-8057-7752-0, Pub. by Royal Botanic Garden UK) Macmillan.

Dwight D. Eisenhower: Hero & Politician. Robert F. Burk. (Twayne's Twentieth Century American Biography Ser.: No. 2). 232p. (C). 1987. pap. 14.95 (0-8057-7773-3, Pub. by Royal Botanic Garden UK) Macmillan.

Dwight D. Eisenhower: Man of Many Hats; With a Message from John S. D. Eisenhower. Kenneth M. Deitch & JoAnne B. Weisman. LC 90-82588. (Picture-Book Biography Ser.). (Illus.). 48p. (J). (gr. 5-12). 1990. lib. bdg. 14.95 (1-878668-02-1) Disc Enter Ltd.

Dwight D. Eisenhower: Soldier & Statesman. Alton R. Lee. LC 81-519. (Illus.). 384p. (C). 1981. text ed. 29.95 (0-88229-626-4) Nelson-Hall.

Dwight D. Eisenhower: Soldier, President, & Statesman. Ed. by Joann P. Krieg. LC 87-7511. (Contributions in Political Science Ser.: No. 183). 382p. 1987. text ed. 65.00 (0-313-25955-0, KGW/, Greenwood Pr) Greenwood.

Dwight D. Eisenhower: Strategic Communicator. Martin J. Medhurst. LC 92-36608. (Great American Orators Ser.: No. 19). 280p. 1993. text ed. 59.95 (0-313-26140-7, MDW, Greenwood Pr) Greenwood.

Dwight D. Eisenhower: Thirty-Fourth President of the United States. Rafaela Ellis. Ed. by Richard G. Young. LC 88-24538. (Presidents of the United States Ser.). (Illus.). (J). (gr. 5-9). 1989. lib. bdg. 17.26 (0-944483-13-5) Garrett Ed Corp.

Dwight D. Eisenhower: Young Military Leader. Wilma J. Hudson. LC 92-8377. (Childhood of Famous Americans Ser.). (Illus.). 192p. (J). (gr. 3-7). 1992. pap. 3.95 (0-689-71656-7, Aladdin Paperbacks) S&S Childrens.

Dwight David Eisenhower: A Bibliography of His Times & Presidency. Comp. by Alton Lee. LC 90-23694. (Twentieth-Century Presidential Bibliography Ser.). 240p. 1991. 70.00 (0-8420-2288-0) Scholarly Res Inc.

Dwight David Eisenhower: President. 128p. (J). (gr. 5 up). 1987. 12.95 (0-8027-6670-6); lib. bdg. 13.85 (0-8027-6671-4) Walker & Co.

Dwight David Eisenhower: War Hero & President. Marian G. Cannon. LC 89-24791. (J). (gr. 4-7). 1990. lib. bdg. 15.47 (0-531-10915-1) Watts.

Dwight David Eisenhower, An American Power. William Pickett. Ed. by Alan M. Kraut & Jon L. Wakelyn. (American Biographical History Ser.). (Illus.). 144p. (C). 1995. pap. text ed. 11.95 (0-88295-918-2) Harlan Davidson.

Dwight Gooden. Matthew Newman. LC 86-16527. (Sports Close-Ups 2 Ser.). (Illus.). 48p. (J). (gr. 5-6). 1986. text ed. 11.95 (0-89686-317-4, Crstwood Hse) Silver Burdett Pr.

Dwight Gooden: King of the Ks. Bert Rosenthal. LC 85-11687. (Sports Stars Ser.). (Illus.). 48p. (J). (gr. 2-8). 1985. pap. 3.95 (0-516-44348-8) Childrens.

Dwight Gooden: Strikeout King. Nathan Aaseng. (Sports Achievers Ser.). (Illus.). 56p. (J). (gr. 4-9). 1988. lib. bdg. 13.50 (0-8225-0478-2, Lerner Publctns); pap. 4.95 (0-8225-9549-4, Lerner Publctns) Lerner Group.

Dwight L. Moody: A Biography. Arboleda. (SPA.). 3.95 (84-7645-439-2, 223430, Pub. by Edit Clie SP) TSELF.

***Dwight L. Moody: Danger on the Flying Trapeze.** Dave Jackson & Neta Jackson. (Trailblazer Ser.). 144p. (J). 1995. pap. text ed. 4.99 (1-55661-469-1) Bethany Hse.

Dwight L. Moody, American Evangelist, 1837-1899. James F. Findley. LC 69-13200. 450p. reprint ed. pap. 128.30 (0-317-20698-2, 2024113) Bks Demand.

Dwight Morrow. Harold G. Nicolson. LC 75-2657. (Wall Street & the Security Market Ser.). (Illus.). 1975. reprint ed. 39.95 (0-405-06982-0) Ayer.

Dwight Morrow. Harold G. Nicolson. (History - United States Ser.). 409p. 1993. reprint ed. lib. bdg. 99.00 (0-7812-4922-8) Rprt Serv.

Dwight W. Morrow. H. H. Rowland. 1972. 59.95 (0-8490-0063-7) Gordon Pr.

Dwight W. Tryon: A Retrospective Exhibition. Intro. by Paul Rovetti. 48p. 1971. 3.00 (0-918386-05-5) W Benton Mus.

***Dwight Yoakam-This Time.** 48p. (Orig.). 1994. pap. 18.95 (0-89724-422-2) Warner Brothers.

Dwight's Journal of Music 1852-1881, 6 vols., Set. Ed. by H. Robert Cohen. (Repertoire International de la Presse Musicale Ser.). 1991. lib. bdg. 720.00 (0-8357-2084-5) Univ Microfilms.

Dworkin-Culatta Oral Mechanism Examination. James P. Dworkin & Richard Culatta. (Illus.). 76p. (Orig.). (C). 1980. 13.00 (0-938820-00-1) Edgewood KY.

DX Brings Danger. Tompkins. 1985. pap. 5.00 (0-87259-502-1) Am Radio.

***DX Centers: Donors in AlGaAs & Related Compounds.** Ed. by Elias M. Merino. (Defect & Diffusion Forum Ser.: Vol. 108). (Illus.). 186p. (C). 1994. text ed. 96.00 (3-908450-03-9, Pub. by Trans Tech SZ) LPS Dist Ctr.

DXCC Companion. 1990. pap. 8.00 (0-87259-339-8) Am Radio.

DXCC Countries List. 1995. pap. 2.00 (0-87259-029-1) Am Radio.

DXers Technical Guide. 2nd ed. International Radio Club of America Staff. 118p. 1983. 6.50 (0-318-22251-5) Intl Radio Club Am.

DXF Translator: PowerDraw. Hoyle Fulbright & Bill Stanley. (Powercadd Ser.). (Illus.). 15p. 1988. 195.00 (1-878250-01-9) Eng Soft NC.

Dyad. Michael Brodsky. LC 89-36339. 300p. 1989. 23.95 (0-941423-30-1); pap. 11.95 (0-941423-31-X) FWEW.

Dyadic Communication. 3rd ed. William W. Wilmot. 266p. (C). 1987. pap. text ed. write for info. (0-07-553965-9) McGraw.

Dyadic Decision Making. Ed. by D. Brinberg & J. Jaccard. (Illus.). xii, 351p. 1988. 116.00 (0-387-96749-4) Spr-Verlag.

Dyadic Disputes, 1920-1968. 2nd ed. William D. Coplin & J. Martin Rochester. 1976. write for info. (0-89138-021-3) ICPSR.

Dyadic Green Functions in Electromagnetic Theory. 2nd ed. Chen-To Tai. LC 93-24201. (Illus.). 360p. 1994. text ed. 59.95 (0-7803-0449-7, PC0348-3) Inst Electrical.

Dyadic Interaction: Choice & Change in Conversations & Relationships. Theodore G. Grove. 368p. (C). 1991. pap. write for info. (0-697-11291-8) Brown & Benchmark.

Dyadic Transaction: An Investigation into the Nature of the Psychotherapeutic Process. Samuel Eisenstein et al. LC 93-23866. 180p. (C). 1994. text ed. 32.95 (1-56000-136-4) Transaction Pubs.

Dyakout 1, 2, 3, 4. Felix Morisseau-Leroy. 177p. (CRP.). 1992. pap. text ed. 11.95 (0-944987-69-9) Haitiana Pubns.

Dyaloge Called Funus, Trans. of Erasmus's Colloquy, 1534 & a Very Pleasaunt & Fruitful Diologe Called the Epicure. Ed. by Robert R. Allen. Tr. by Gerrard. (Renaissance English Text Society Ser.: Vol. 3). 114p. 1969. 7.50 (0-911028-10-2) Newberry.

Dyaloge Descrybyng the Orygynall Ground of These Lutheran Saccyons, That Is, Faccyons. William Barlow. LC 74-80161. (English Experience Ser.: No. 641). 200p. 1974. reprint ed. 13.00 (90-221-0641-1) Walter J Johnson.

Dyaloge of Syr T. More...Wherein Be Treatyd Dyvers Maters, As of the Veneration & Worshyp of Ymagys. Thomas More. LC 74-28873. (English Experience Ser.: No. 752). 1975. reprint ed. 26.50 (90-221-0752-3) Walter J Johnson.

Dyarchy in Punjab. Virinder Singh. 1991. 33.00 (81-85135-56-8, Pub. by National Bk Organ) S Asia.

Dybbuk. S. Ansky. Tr. by S. Morris Engel. LC 74-82063. (Illus.). 160p. 1974. 15.95 (0-8402-1356-5) Boulevard.

Dybbuk. Bruce Myer. 48p. (Orig.). 1990. 7.95 (0-317-91356-5) Playsmith.

Dybbuk. S. Ansky. Tr. by S. Morris Engel. LC 79-63047. (Illus.). 1979. reprint ed. pap. 8.95 (0-89526-904-X) Regnery Pub.

Dybbuk & Other Writings. S. Ansky. LC 91-52619. (Library of Yiddish Classics). 256p. 1992. 25.00 (0-8052-4111-6) Schocken.

Dyddiau Olaf Stem Yng Ngwynedd: The Last Days of Steam in Gwynedd. Mike Hitches. (Illus.). 160p. 1991. 24.00 (0-86299-924-3) A Sutton Pub.

Dye Curves: The Theory & Practice of Indicator Dilution. Ed. by Dennis A. Bloomfield. LC 77-356568. 466p. reprint ed. pap. 132.90 (0-317-26199-1, 2052067) Bks Demand.

Dye It Wild! Dye It Mild! A Design & Idea Book for Fabric Dyes. Nancy C. Strutt. (Illus.). 32p. (Orig.). 1989. pap. write for info. (0-318-65753-8) Simply Elgnt.

Dye Laser Principles: With Applications. Ed. by Frank J. Duarte & L. W. Hillman. (Quantum Electronics - Principles & Applications Ser.). 456p. 1990. text ed. 82.50 (0-12-222700-X) Acad Pr.

Dye Lasers. 3rd enl. rev. ed. Ed. by F. P. Schafer. (Topics in Applied Physics Ser.: Vol. 1). (Illus.). 256p. 1990. pap. 56.00 (0-387-51558-5, 3459) Spr-Verlag.

Dye-Painting! Ann Johnston. LC 92-23444. 1992. pap. 19.95 (0-89145-803-4) Collector Bks.

Dye Plants & Dyeing. John Cannon & Margaret Cannon. (Illus.). 112p. 1994. reprint ed. pap. 19.95 (0-88192-302-8) Timber.

Dye Pot. 3rd rev. ed. Mary F. Davidson. 1981. pap. text ed. 4.00 (0-686-10137-5) M F Davidson.

Dye Pot. 4th rev. ed. Mary F. Davidson. 1990. pap. text ed. 6.00 (0-317-99817-X) M F Davidson.

Dyed for Death. Rick Ryder. 240p. 1984. pap. 2.50 (0-8439-2119-6) Dorchester Pub Co.

Dyeing & Bleaching Natural Fly-Tying Materials. A. K. Best. 140p. 1993. 24.95 (1-55821-214-0) Lyons & Burford.

D

An Asterisk (*) at the beginning of an entry indicates that the title is appearing in BIP for the first time.

An Asterisk (*) at the beginning of an entry indicates that the title is appearing in BIP for the first time.

2137

Dynamic Accounting. Eugen Schmalenbach. Ed. by Richard P. Brief. Tr. by G. W. Murphy & Kenneth S. Most. LC 80-1577. (Dimensions of Accounting Theory & Practice Ser.). 1980. reprint ed. lib. bdg. 24.95 (*0-405-13543-2*) Ayer.

Dynamic Agricultural Systems: Economic Prediction & Control. Gordon Rausser & Eleanor Hochman. (Dynamic Economics Ser.: Vol. 3). 364p. 1980. 56.75 (*0-444-00274-X*, North Holland) Elsevier.

Dynamic Aikido. G. Shioda. 14.00 (*0-685-63751-4*) Wehman.

Dynamic Aikido. Gozo Shioda. Tr. by Geoffrey Hamilton. LC 68-31356. (Illus.). 1977. pap. 15.00 (*0-87011-301-1*) Kodansha.

Dynamic Airbrush. David Miller & James M. Effler. (Illus.). 168p. 1987. 29.95 (*0-89134-190-0*, 7492) North Light Bks.

Dynamic Analysis & Design Considerations for High-Level Nuclear Waste Repositories: Proceedings of the Symposium Sponsored by the Nuclear Dynamic Analysis Committee of the Structural Division of the American Society of Civil Engineers & Co-Sponsored by the U. S. Department of Energy, Office of Civilian Radioactive Waste Management, Holiday Inn Golden Gateway, San Francisco, California, August 19-20, 1992. Ed. by Quazi A. Hossain. LC 93-18314. 448p. 1993. 37.00 (*0-87262-945-7*) Am Soc Civil Eng.

Dynamic Analysis & Failure Modes of Simple Structures. Daniel Schiff. 1990. text ed. 99.95 (*0-471-63505-7*) Wiley.

Dynamic Analysis of Innovation & Diffusion. Hagedoorn. (C). 1992. text ed. 59.00 (*0-86187-739-X*, Pub. by Pinter Pubs UK) St Martin.

Dynamic Analysis of Open Economies. Masanao Aoki. LC 80-2763. 1981. text ed. 91.00 (*0-12-058940-0*) Acad Pr.

Dynamic Analysis of Pressure Vessel & Piping Components: Presented at the Energy Technology Conference, Houston, Texas, September 18-23, 1977. Energy Technology Conference Staff. Ed. by C. Sundararajan. LC 77-82209. (Illus.). 113p. reprint ed. pap. 32.30 (*0-317-09157-3*, 2017309) Bks Demand.

Dynamic Analysis of Robot Manipulators: A Cartesian Tensor Approach. Constantinos A. Balafoutis & Rajnikant V. Patel. (C). 1991. lib. bdg. 76.50 (*0-7923-9145-4*) Kluwer Ac.

Dynamic Analysis of Suspended Roof Systems. V. A. Ivovich & L. N. Pokrovskii. Ed. by R. S. Ayyar. (Russian Translation Ser.: No. 88). (Illus.). 286p. (C). 1991. text ed. 90.00 (*90-6191-114-1*, Pub. by A A Balkema NE) Ashgate Pub Co.

Dynamic Anatomy. Burne Hogarth. (Illus.). 232p. 1990. pap. 18.95 (*0-8230-1551-3*, Watsn-Guptill) Watsn-Guptill.

Dynamic Anatomy & Physiology. 5th ed. L. L. Langley et al. (Illus.). 1980. text ed. 43.95 (*0-07-036275-0*) McGraw.

Dynamic & Immobilist Politics in Japan. J. A. Stockwin et al. 1989. text ed. 36.00 (*0-8248-1230-1*) UH Pr.

Dynamic & Static Sounding of Soils in Engineering Geology. G. K. Bondarik. 144p. 1967. text ed. 40.50 (*0-7065-0470-4*, Pub. by Keter Pub IS) Coronet Bks.

Dynamic Approaches to the Understanding & Treatment of Alcoholism. Ed. by Margaret H. Bean & Norman E. Zinberg. LC 81-65033. 256p. 1981. 29.95 (*0-02-902110-3*) Free Pr.

Dynamic Aquaria: Building Living Ecosystems. Ed. by Walter H. Adey & Karen Loveland. 643p. 1991. text ed. 49.95 (*0-12-043790-2*) Acad Pr.

Dynamic Aspects of Cell Surface Organization. Ed. by George Poste & G. Nicolson. (Cell Surface Reviews Ser.: Vol. 3). 1977. 236.50 (*0-7204-0623-4*) Elsevier.

Dynamic Aspects of Conformation Changes in Biological Macromolecules: Proceedings of the Societe de Chimie Physique, 23rd. Societe de Chimie Physique Staff. Ed. by C. Sadron. LC 72-97962. 400p. 1973. lib. bdg. 158.00 (*90-277-0334-5*) Kluwer Ac.

Dynamic Aspects of Dental Pulp: Molecular Biology, Pharmacology & Pathophysiology. Ed. by R. Inoki et al. 250p. 1990. 175.00 (*0-412-35860-3*, A4930) Chapman & Hall.

Dynamic Aspects of Detonations. Kuhl et al. (PAAS Ser.: Vol. 153). 473p. 1993. 99.95 (*1-56347-057-8*) AIAA.

Dynamic Aspects of Explosion Phenomena. Kuhl et al. (PAAS Ser.: Vol. 154). 563p. 1993. 99.95 (*1-56347-059-4*) AIAA.

Dynamic Aspects of Language Processing: Focus & Presupposition. J. Engelkamp & H. D. Zimmer. (Language & Communication Ser.: Vol. 16). (Illus.). 145p. 1983. 44.00 (*0-387-12433-0*) Spr-Verlag.

Dynamic Aspects of Microtubule Biology, Vol. 466. Ed. by David Soifer. 245.00 (*0-89766-327-6*); pap. 245.00 (*0-89766-328-4*) NY Acad Sci.

Dynamic Aspects of Neocortical Function. Ed. by Gerald M. Edelman et al. LC 84-11825. (Neuroscience Institute Monograph Ser.). 718p. 1984. text ed. 165.00 (*0-471-80559-9*) Wiley.

Dynamic Aspects of Speech Production: Current Results, Emerging Problems, & New Instrumentation. Ed. by Masayuki Sawashima & Franklin S. Cooper. 417p. 1977. pap. 22.50 (*0-86008-192-3*, Pub. by U of Tokyo JA) Col U Pr.

Dynamic Assessment: An Interactional Approach to Evaluating Learning Potential. Ed. by Carol S. Lidz. LC 86-19375. 511p. 1987. lib. bdg. 47.50 (*0-89862-695-1*) Guilford Pr.

Dynamic Assessment in Couple Therapy. William J. Hiebert et al. LC 93-11168. 132p. 1993. pap. 15.95 (*0-669-24863-0*) Free Pr.

Dynamic Asset Allocation: Strategies for the Stock, Bond, & Money Markets. David A. Hammer. (Finance Editions Ser.). 336p. 1991. text ed. 59.50 (*0-471-53028-X*) Wiley.

Dynamic Asset Pricing Theory. Darrell Duffie. 224p. 1992. text ed. 45.00 (*0-691-04302-7*) Princeton U Pr.

Dynamic Astrology. Sven Frederick & Fischer Svensson. 176p. Date not set. 19.95 (*0-8464-4190-X*) Beekman Pubs.

***Dynamic Astrology: Using Planetary Cycles to Make Personal & Career Choices.** John Townley. (Illus.). 176p. 1996. pap. 12.95 (*0-89281-568-X*, Destiny Bks) Inner Tradit.

Dynamic Astronomy. 6th ed. Robert T. Dixon. 528p. (C). 1992. pap. text ed. write for info. (*0-13-221870-4*) P-H.

Dynamic Balance Sheet: A German Theory of Accounting. Catherine De Motte Green. Ed. by Richard P. Brief. LC 80-1497. (Dimensions of Accounting Theory & Practice Ser.). 1980. lib. bdg. 42.95 (*0-405-13491-6*) Ayer.

Dynamic Behavior of Concrete Structures. Y. L. Mo. LC 94-17073. (Developments in Civil Engineering Ser.: Vol. 44). 1994. write for info. (*0-444-81885-5*) Elsevier.

Dynamic Behavior of Materials. Marc A. Meyers. LC 93-33109. 1994. text ed. 79.95 (*0-471-58262-X*) Wiley.

Dynamic Behaviour of Concrete Structures: Report of the RILEM 65 MDB Committee. Ed. by G. P. Tilly. (Developments in Civil Engineering Ser.: No. 13). 1986. 115.50 (*0-444-42624-8*) Elsevier.

Dynamic Behaviour of Foundations & Buried Structures. Ed. by P. K. Banerjee & R. Butterfield. (Developments in Soil Mechanic & Foundation Engineering Ser.: Vol. 3). 278p. 1988. 88.25 (*1-85166-097-6*, Pub. by Elsevier Applied Sci UK) Elsevier.

Dynamic Behaviour of the Mooring System of a Deepwater Turret Floating Production Vessel, Etc. Pasquala Brando. 1989. 150.00 (*90-6314-564-0*, Pub. by Lorne & MacLean Marine) St Mut.

Dynamic Bible Study Methods. rev. ed. Rick Warren. 252p. 1989. pap. 10.99 (*0-89693-761-5*) SP Pubns.

Dynamic Bifurcations: Proceedings of a Conference Held in Luminy, France, March 5-10, 1990. Ed. by E. Benoit. (Lecture Notes in Mathematics Ser.: Vol. 1493). vii, 219p. 1991. pap. 33.00 (*0-387-54900-5*) Spr-Verlag.

Dynamic Biochemistry of Animal Production. P. M. Riis. (World Animal Science Ser.: Vol. 3A). 502p. 1983. 161.75 (*0-444-42052-5*, I-311-83) Elsevier.

Dynamic Biogeography. R. Hangeveld. (Cambridge Studies in Ecology). (Illus.). 250p. (C). 1992. pap. 32.95 (*0-521-43756-3*) Cambridge U Pr.

Dynamic Biological Networks: The Stomatogastric Nervous System. Ed. by Ronald M. Harris-Warrick et al. (Bradford-Computational Neuroscience Ser.). (Illus.). 352p. 1992. 65.00 (*0-262-08214-4*, Bradford Bks) MIT Pr.

Dynamic Black Americans. Flossie E. Thompson-Peters. (Illus.). 32p. (J). (gr. 1-8). 1988. pap. 4.70 (*1-880784-07-6*) Atlas Pr.

Dynamic Black & White Illustrations. Leslie Cabarga. LC 93-71343. (Illus.). 192p. 1993. text ed. 19.50 (*0-88108-113-2*); pap. text ed. 14.95 (*0-88108-114-0*) Art Dir.

Dynamic Capitalism: The Economics of Business Firm Formation & Growth. Bruce A. Kirchhoff. LC 93-24833. 240p. 1993. text ed. 55.00 (*0-275-93757-7*, C3757, Praeger Pubs) Greenwood.

Dynamic Caro-Kann: The Brownstein Larsen & the Original Caro System. Jeremy Silman. (Illus.). 190p. 1989. pap. 14.95 (*0-945806-03-5*) Summit CA.

Dynamic Character of Christian Culture: Essays on Dawsonian Themes. Ed. by Peter J. Cataldo. 242p. (Orig.). (C). 1984. lib. bdg. 49.50 (*0-8191-3959-9*); pap. text ed. 20.50 (*0-8191-3960-2*) U Pr of Amer.

Dynamic Characteristics of Ion-Selective Electrodes. Ed. by Erno Pungor et al. 192p. 1988. 89.00 (*0-8493-6493-0*, QD571, CRC Reprint) Franklin.

Dynamic Characteristics of Today's Passenger Car Transmissions. 1990. 45.00 (*1-56091-077-1*, SP-837) Soc Auto Engineers.

Dynamic Characterization of Advanced Materials. Ed. by P. K. Raju & R. F. Gibson. LC 93-73264. 215p. Date not set. pap. 60.00 (*0-7918-1028-3*) ASME.

Dynamic Chess: The Modern Style of Aggressive Play. enl. rev. ed. Richard N. Coles. (Illus.). 1966. pap. 4.95 (*0-486-21676-4*) Dover.

Dynamic Chess Strategy. Mihai Suba. (Chess Library). 150p. 1991. pap. 15.95 (*0-08-037141-8*, Pub. by CHES UK) Macmillan.

Dynamic Chiropractic: The Complete & Authoritative Guide to This Major Therapy. Michael Copland-Griffiths. 1991. 34.95 (*0-7225-1595-2*) Thorsons SF.

Dynamic Choice & Asset Markets. Sumru Altug & Pamela Labadie. (Illus.). 374p. 1994. text ed. 49.95 (*0-12-055455-0*) Acad Pr.

Dynamic Choral Conductor. Royal Stanton. LC 79-143878. 1971. 15.95 (*0-9603394-1-8*) Shawnee Pr.

***Dynamic Church.** O. J. Gibson. Date not set. pap. text ed. 9.50 (*0-937396-84-2*) Walterick Pubs.

Dynamic Circuit Theory, Chapters 1-5. H. Messerle. LC 63-22598. 1965. 160.00 (*0-08-010469-X*, Pub. by Pergamon Repr UK) Franklin.

Dynamic Classroom. Billie C. Davis. LC 86-83084. (Sunday School Staff Training Ser.). 144p. (Orig.). 1987. teacher ed, pap. 2.95 (*0-88243-798-4*, 02-0798) Gospel Pub.

***Dynamic Classroom.** Bruce Mitchell et al. 256p. (C). 1995. per., pap. text ed. 25.95 (*0-7872-0587-7*) Kendall-Hunt.

Dynamic Classroom. Bruce M. Mitchell et al. 256p. 1990. per. 19.95 (*0-8403-6261-7*) Kendall-Hunt.

Dynamic Clinical Studies with Radioisotopes: Proceedings. Ed. by Ralph M. Kniseley et al. (AEC Symposium Ser.). 634p. 1964. pap. 6.25 (*0-87079-181-8*, TID-7678); fiche 6.50 (*0-87079-182-6*, TID-7678) DOE.

Dynamic Communication for Engineers. Richard H. McCuen et al. LC 93-9395. 192p. 1993. 29.00 (*0-87262-856-6*) Am Soc Civil Eng.

Dynamic Community Library: Creative, Practical & Inexpensive Ideas for the Library Director. Beth W. Fox. LC 88-10057. 154p. (C). 1988. pap. text ed. 25.00 (*0-8389-0496-3*, 0496-3) ALA.

Dynamic Computer Design. Jake Widman. (Illus.). 144p. 1994. pap. 26.95 (*0-89134-495-0*) North Light Bks.

Dynamic Computing for Critical Applications. Ed. by A. Avizienis & J. C. Laprie. (Dependable Computing & Fault-Tolerant Systems Ser.: Vol. 4). xiii, 431p. 1991. 105.00 (*0-387-82249-6*) Spr-Verlag.

Dynamic Constitution: A Historical Bibliography. Ed. by Suzanne R. Ontiveros. (ABC-Clio Research Guides Ser.: No. 19). 343p. 1986. lib. bdg. 49.50 (*0-87436-470-1*) ABC-CLIO.

Dynamic Costing. R. L. Martino. 162p. 1968. text ed. 158.00 (*0-677-61060-2*) Gordon & Breach.

***Dynamic Counseling.** 3rd ed. James L. Lee et al. LC 94-72559. 288p. (C). 1994. pap. text ed. 21.95x (*0-932796-66-4*) Ed Media Corp.

Dynamic Cover Letters. Katharine Hansen. 96p. (Orig.). 1990. pap. 7.95 (*0-89815-356-5*) Ten Speed Pr.

***Dynamic Cover Letters.** rev. ed. Katharine Hansen. 144p. 1995. pap. 7.95 (*0-89815-675-0*) Ten Speed Pr.

Dynamic Credit Granting System. Credit Research Foundation Staff. 1989. 40.00 (*0-939050-59-5*) Credit Res NYS.

Dynamic Cube Strategy. Gabriel Monet & Bruce W. Roman. (Illus.). 134p. (Orig.). 1980. pap. text ed. 50.00 (*0-9608566-0-9*) Advanced Back.

Dynamic Data Structures: Theory & Application. Todd King. (Illus.). 299p. 1992. text ed. 49.95 (*0-12-407530-4*) Acad Pr.

Dynamic Decision Maker: Five Decision Styles for Executives. Michael Driver et al. 1993. pap. 25.95 (*1-55542-593-3*) Jossey-Bass.

Dynamic Decision Theory: Applications to Urban & Regional Topics. G. Haag. (C). 1989. lib. bdg. 94.50 (*0-7923-0194-3*) Kluwer Ac.

Dynamic Defense. Mike Lawrence. 228p. 1991. pap. 11.95 (*0-910791-01-5*) Devyn Pr.

Dynamic Delegation! A Manager's Guide for Active Empowerment. Mark Towers. Ed. by Kelly Scanlon. 81p. (Orig.). 1993. pap. 10.95 (*1-878542-33-8*) SkillPath Pubns.

Dynamic Demand for Energy Stocks: An Analysis of Tax Policy Options for Solar Processes. G. T. Sav. LC 83-4892. (Contemporary Studies in Energy Analysis & Policy: Vol. 2). 1983. 73.25 (*0-89232-316-7*) Jai Pr.

Dynamic Devotions for Teens. Marvin Osborn. Ed. by Cindy G. Spear. 108p. (Orig.). (YA). (gr. 7-12). 1993. spiral bd., pap. 9.95 (*0-941005-90-9*) Chrch Grwth VA.

Dynamic Dinosaur of Faith's History, Vol. I: From Christ to 1000 AD. David Bertch & Barbara A. Bertch. Ed. by Terry Martin & Dyna Martin. (Roots of the Past Ser.: Bk. 1). (Illus.). 150p. (J). (gr. 6). Date not set. student ed 9.95 (*0-9634472-4-6*) Good Works Pr.

Dynamic Dominion: Realignment & the Rise of Virginia's Republican Party since 1945. Frank B. Atkinson. 1992. 29.95 (*0-913969-39-7*, G Mason Univ Pr) Univ Pub Assocs.

Dynamic Duo: The Holy Spirit & You. Rick Renner. 1994. pap. 9.99 (*0-88419-362-4*, Creation Hse) Strang Comms Co.

Dynamic Earth: An Introduction to Physical Geology. 2nd ed. Brian J. Skinner & Stephen C. Porter. 592p. (C). 1991. Net. pap. text ed. write for info. (*0-471-53131-6*); Net. write for info. (*0-471-55065-5*) Wiley.

***Dynamic Earth: An Introduction to Physical Geology.** 3rd ed. B. J. Skinner & S. C. Porter. LC 94-34422. 1995. pap. text ed. write for info. (*0-471-59549-7*) Wiley.

***Dynamic Earth: An Introduction to Physical Geology with Study Guide.** 2nd ed. Brian J. Skinner & Stephen C. Porter. 1994. pap. text ed. write for info. (*0-471-11133-3*) Wiley.

Dynamic Earth: Textbook in Geosciences. Peter J. Wyllie. LC 73-155909. (Illus.). 432p. 1971. reprint ed. pap. 123.20 (*0-7837-3483-2*, 2057816) Bks Demand.

Dynamic East Central. (All about the U. S. A. Ser.). (J). (gr. 5-9). 1987. text ed. write for info. (*0-8347-3387-0*) Ency Brit Ed.

Dynamic Econometric Modeling: Proceedings of the 3rd International Symposium. Ed. by William A. Barnett et al. (International Symposia in Economic Theory & Econometrics Ser.: No. 3). 385p. 1988. 74.95 (*0-521-33395-4*) Cambridge U Pr.

***Dynamic Econometrics.** David Hendry. (Advanced Texts in Econometrics Ser.). (Illus.). 800p. 1995. text ed. 79.00 (*0-19-828317-2*); pap. text ed. 39.95 (*0-19-828316-4*) OUP.

Dynamic Economic Analysis. Milton Harris. (Illus.). 152p. 1987. 26.00 (*0-19-504406-1*); Solutions manual. teacher ed write for info. (*0-318-62231-9*) OUP.

Dynamic Economic Models & Optimal Control: Fourth Viennese Workshop on Dynamic Economic Models & Optimal Control, Held in Vienna, June 12-14, 1991. Ed. by Gustav Feichtinger. LC 92-30069. 1992. write for info. (*0-444-88491-2*, North Holland) Elsevier.

Dynamic Economic Systems: A Post-Keynesian Approach. John M. Blatt. LC 82-24013. 370p. 1983. 51.95 (*0-87332-215-0*); pap. text ed. 25.95 (*0-87332-306-8*) M E Sharpe.

Dynamic Economics. Burton H. Klein. LC 76-58550. 303p. reprint ed. pap. 86.40 (*0-7837-4481-1*, 2044189) Bks Demand.

Dynamic Elastic Modulus Measurements. Ed. by Alan Wolfenden. LC 90-31702. (Special Technical Publication Ser.: No. 1045). (Illus.). 230p. 1990. text ed. 56.00 (*0-8031-1291-2*, 04-010450-23) ASTM.

Dynamic Energy Budgets in Biological Systems: Theory & Applications in Ecotoxicology. S. A. Kooijman. (Illus.). 330p. (C). 1994. 64.95 (*0-521-45223-6*) Cambridge U Pr.

***Dynamic Environment: Computer Models to Accompany Consider a Spherical Cow, Macintosh.** Leonard J. Soltzberg. (Illus.). 170p. (C). Date not set. pap. text ed. 57.00 (*0-935702-38-5*) Univ Sci Bks.

***Dynamic Environment: Computer Models to Accompany Consider a Spherical Cow, Windows.** Leonard J. Soltzberg. (Illus.). 170p. (C). Date not set. pap. text ed. 57.00 (*0-935702-37-7*) Univ Sci Bks.

Dynamic Environment: Water, Transportation, & Energy. Edwin H. Marston. LC 74-82346. 432p. reprint ed. pap. 123.20 (*0-317-10809-3*, 2012461) Bks Demand.

Dynamic Evangelism. Luisa J. Walker. 276p. 1989. pap. 9.95 (*0-8297-0737-9*) Life Pubs Intl.

Dynamic Evolution of Globular Clusters. Lyman Spitzer, Jr. (Astrophysics Ser.). (Illus.). 275p. 1987. text ed. 45.00 (*0-691-08309-6*); pap. text ed. 19.95 (*0-691-08460-2*) Princeton U Pr.

Dynamic Experiments in the Electron Microscope. Butler. 458p. 1981. 83.00 (*0-685-01554-8*); pap. 46.50 (*0-444-80286-X*) Elsevier.

Dynamic Facets of Indian Thought: Six Vedic Systems & Other Currents, Vol. 3. Anil K. Sarkar. 1987. 21.00 (*81-7003-086-2*, Pub. by S Asia Pubs II) S Asia.

Dynamic Facets of Indian Thought: Three Non-Vedic Systems Corvaka, Jains & Buddha. Anil Sarkar. (C). 1987. 20.00 (*81-7003-078-1*, Pub. by S Asia Pubs II) S Asia.

Dynamic Facets of Indian Thought, Vol. 4: Western Impact on Indian Thought. Anil K. Sarkar. 1988. 23.00 (*81-7003-091-9*) South Asia Pubns.

Dynamic Factor Demand in a Rationing Context: Theory & Estimation of a Macroeconomic Disequilibrium Model for the Federal Republic of Germany. W. Smolny. (Studies in Contemporary Economics). (Illus.). viii, 241p. 1993. pap. 58.00 (*0-387-91458-7*) Spr-Verlag.

Dynamic Factory Automation: Creating Flexible Systems for Competitive Manufacturing. Alastair Ross. (IBM Ser.). 1992. text ed. 47.00i (*0-07-707440-8*) McGraw.

Dynamic Failure of Materials: Theory, Experiments & Numerics. H. P. Rossmanith & A. J. Roskis. 398p. 1991. 102.00 (*1-85166-665-6*) Elsevier.

Dynamic Feature Space Modelling, Filtering & Self-Tuning Control of Stochastic Systems. P. W. Otter. (Lecture Notes in Economics & Mathematical Systems Ser.: Vol. 246). xiv, 177p. 1985. pap. 31.00 (*0-387-15654-2*) Spr-Verlag.

Dynamic Figure Drawing. Burne Hogarth. LC 73-87324. (Illus.). 176p. 1970. 22.95 (*0-8230-1575-0*, Watsn-Guptill) Watsn-Guptill.

***Dynamic Financial Condition Analysis.** 1995. pap. write for info. (*0-938959-36-0*) Soc Actuaries.

Dynamic Fingertip Devotions. Amy Bolding. LC 73-78081. (Paperback Program Ser.). 1977. pap. 5.99 (*0-8010-0708-9*) Baker Bk.

Dynamic Firm & Investor Behaviour under Progressive Personal Taxation. G. J. Van Schijndel. (Lecture Notes in Economics & Mathematical Systems Ser.: Vol. 305). xii, 215p. 1988. pap. 28.70 (*0-387-19230-1*) Spr-Verlag.

Dynamic Fiscal Policy. Alan J. Auerbach & Laurence J. Kotlikoff. (Illus.). 224p. 1987. 49.95 (*0-521-30041-X*) Cambridge U Pr.

Dynamic Forces in Capitalist Development. Angus Maddison. (Illus.). 352p. 1991. pap. 24.95 (*0-19-828398-9*) OUP.

Dynamic Fracture. Ed. by M. L. Williams & W. G. Knauss. LC 85-10582. 1985. lib. bdg. 113.00 (*90-247-3179-8*) Kluwer Ac.

Dynamic Fracture Mechanics. Ed. by M. H. Aliabadi. LC 94-69711. (Computational Engineering Ser.). 311p. 1995. 136.00 (*1-56252-267-1*) Computational Mech MA.

Dynamic Fracture Mechanics. L. B. Freund. (Cambridge Monographs on Mechanics & Applied Mathematics). (Illus.). 450p. (C). 1990. 74.95 (*0-521-30330-3*) Cambridge U Pr.

Dynamic Fracture Mechanics, Vol. 1: Stationary Cracks. V. Z. Parton & V. G. Boriskovsky. Ed. by Richard B. Hetnarski. Tr. by Ram S. Wadwha. 260p. 1989. 131.00 (*0-89116-550-9*) Hemisp Pub.

Dynamic Fracture Mechanics, Vol. 2: Propagating Cracks. V. Z. Parton & V. G. Boriskovsky. Ed. by Richard B. Hetnarski. LC 66-55120. 1989. 152.00 (*0-89116-605-X*) Hemisp Pub.

Dynamic Games & Applications in Economics. Ed. by Tamer S. Basar. (Lecture Notes in Economics & Mathematical Systems Ser.: Vol. 265). ix, 288p. 1986. pap. 41.70 (*0-387-16435-9*) Spr-Verlag.

Dynamic Games in Economic Analysis: Proceedings of the 4th International Symposium on Differential Games & Applications August 9-10, 1990, Helsinki, Finland. Ed. by R. P. Hamalainen et al. (Lecture Notes in Control & Information Sciences Ser.: Vol. 157). (Illus.). xiii, 311p. 1991. pap. 51.00 (*0-387-53785-6*) Spr-Verlag.

Dynamic, Genetic & Chaotic Programming: The Sixth Generation. Iris Group Staff & Branko Soucek. (Sixth Generation Computer Technologies Ser.: No. 1880). 1992. text ed. 95.00 (*0-471-55717-X*) Wiley.

Dynamic Genome: Barbara McClintock's Ideas in the Century of Genetics. Ed. by Nina Fedoroff & David Botstein. LC 92-10074. 422p. 1992. pap. 40.00 (*0-87969-396-7*) Cold Spring Harbor.

Dynamic Geography of Marine Fish Populations. Alec D. MacCall. 200p. 1990. text ed. 25.00 (*0-295-96911-3*); pap. 15.00 (*0-295-96912-1*) U of Wash Pr.

Dynamic Geometry. Paul H. Fejer. Ed. by Leonard G. Johnson. (Illus.). 520p. (C). 1995. text ed. 125.00x (*0-685-45824-5*) P H Fejer.

D

An Asterisk (*) at the beginning of an entry indicates that the title is appearing in BIP for the first time.

D

Dynamic Programming: Applications to Agriculture & Natural Resources. J. O. Kennedy. 312p. 1986. 102.75 (0-85334-424-8) Elsevier.

Dynamic Programming: Deterministic & Stochastic Models. Dimitri P. Bertsekas. (Illus.). 416p. 1987. text ed. 74.00 (0-13-221581-0) P-H.

Dynamic Programming & Modern Control. Richard E. Bellman & Robert Kalaba. 1966. text ed. 73.00 (0-12-084856-2) Acad Pr.

***Dynamic Programming & Optimal Control.** Dimitri P. Bertsekas. 300p. (C). 1995. text ed. 55.50 (1-886529-13-2) Athena Scientific.

***Dynamic Programming & Optimal Control, Vol. I.** Dimitri P. Bertsekas. 400p. (C). 1995. text ed. 64.00 (1-886529-12-4) Athena Scientific.

***Dynamic Programming & Optimal Control, Vols. I-II.** Dimitri P. Bertsekas. 700p. (C). 1995. text ed. 119.50 (1-886529-11-6) Athena Scientific.

Dynamic Programming & Stochastic Control. Dimitri P. Bertsekas. (Mathematics in Science & Engineering Ser.). 1976. text ed. 84.00 (0-12-093250-4) Acad Pr.

Dynamic Programming & the Calculus of Variations. Stuart E. Dreyfus. (Mathematics in Science & Engineering Ser.: Vol. 21). 1965. text ed. 106.00 (0-12-221850-7) Acad Pr.

Dynamic Programming for Optimal Water Resource Systems Analysis. Augustine O. Esogbue. 448p. 1989. text ed. 59.00 (0-13-221516-0) P-H.

Dynamic Project Management: A Practical Guide for Managers & Engineers. Kezsbom et al. 1989. text ed. 79.95 (0-471-85248-1) Wiley.

Dynamic Properties of Forest Ecosystems. D. E. Reichle. (C). 1991. text ed. 910.00 (0-89771-648-5, Pub. by Intl Bk Distr II) St Mut.

Dynamic Properties of Gila Cells II - Cellular & Molecular Aspects: Proceedings of an International Symposium Held in Liege, Belgium, from 12-15 May, 1985. Ed. by T. Grisar et al. (Advances in the Biosciences Ser.: No. 61). (Illus.). 442p. 1986. 94.00 (0-08-032023-6, Pergamon Pr) Elsevier.

Dynamic Psychiatry: Explorations in Psychotherapy, Psychoanalysis, & Psychosomatic Medicine. Pietro Castelnuovo-Tedesco. LC 90-4927. (Emotions & Behavior Monographs: No. 10). 450p. 1991. 50.00 (0-8236-1515-4) Intl Univs Pr.

Dynamic Psychiatry & the Sense of Justice. Warren H. Gorman. LC 70-96982. (Illus.). 320p. 1974. 19.10 (0-87527-106-5) Green.

Dynamic Psychology. Robert S. Woodworth. LC 73-2998. (Classics in Psychology Ser.). 1980. reprint ed. 21.95 (0-405-05172-7) Ayer.

Dynamic Psychotherapy: An Introductory Approach. Marc Hollender & Charles Ford. LC 90-77. 200p. 1990. text ed. 32.50 (0-88048-319-9) Am Psychiatric.

Dynamic Pulse Buckling: Theory & Experiment. H. E. Lindberg & A. L. Florence. (C). 1987. lib. bdg. 144.00 (90-247-3566-1) Kluwer Ac.

Dynamic Radiology of the Abdomen. M. A. Meyers. (Illus.). 592p. 1988. 134.00 (0-387-96624-2) Spr-Verlag.

Dynamic Radiology of the Abdomen: Normal & Pathologic Anatomy. 4th ed. M. A. Meyers. (Illus.). 680p. 1993. write for info. (3-540-94022-7) Spr-Verlag.

Dynamic Radiology of the Abdomen: Normal & Pathologic Anatomy. 4th ed. Morton A. Meyers. LC 93-16236. (Illus.). 680p. 1995. 149.00 (0-387-94022-7) Spr-Verlag.

Dynamic Reading Skill. Venkata Iyer. 184p. 1986. text ed. 22.50 (81-207-0113-5, Pub. by Sterling Pubs II) Apt Bks.

Dynamic Reality: God's Supernatural Power Within. Hazel M. Salmon. 252p. (Orig.). 1990. pap. 7.99 (1-56043-050-8) Destiny Image.

Dynamic Response & Progressive Failure of Special Structures: Proceedings of the Technical Sessions on Response of Truss & Truss-Type Structures During Progressive Failure & Dynamic Loading & Analysis of Structures. Ed. by Ramesh B. Malla. LC 93-40323. 1993. write for info. (0-87262-946-5) Am Soc Civil Eng.

Dynamic Response of Biomechanical Systems: Papers Presented at the Winter Annual Meeting of the ASME, N.Y, N.Y., Dec. 2, 1970. Nicholas Perrone. LC 78-143213. 156p. reprint ed. pap. 44.50 (0-317-08321-X, 2016913) Bks Demand.

Dynamic Response of Pile Foundations: Analytical Aspects. Ed. by Michael W. O'Neill & Ricardo Dobry. LC 80-69151. 118p. 1980. pap. 13.00 (0-87262-257-6) Am Soc Civil Eng.

Dynamic Response of Pile Foundations: Experiment, Analysis & Observation. Ed. by Toyoaki Nogami. 192p. 1987. 21.00 (0-87262-591-5) Am Soc Civil Eng.

Dynamic Response of Structures. Ed. by Gary C. Hart & Richard B. Nelson. (Conference Proceedings Ser.). 877p. 1986. 78.00 (0-87262-526-5) Am Soc Civil Eng.

Dynamic Response of Structures. Ed. by G. Herrmann & N. Perrone. 1972. 154.00 (0-08-016850-7, Pub. by Pergamon Repr UK) Franklin.

Dynamic Response of Structures: Experimentation, Observation, Prediction & Control. Gary Hart. LC 80-70135. 960p. 1980. pap. 71.00 (0-87262-261-4) Am Soc Civil Eng.

Dynamic Response Testing of Process Control Instrumentation Standard. Instrument Society of America Staff. (ANSI-ISA MC4.1-1975, ISA Standard S26 Ser.). 1975. pap. text ed. 30.00 (0-87664-349-7, 1349-7) Instru Soc.

Dynamic Retirement: How to Retire & Love It. Mark J. Staley & Ralph H. Singleton. 173p. (C). 17.95 (0-912904-02-X) Uniline Div.

***Dynamic Safety of Earth & Rockfill Dams: Proceedings of a Course, New Delhi, August 1993.** Ed. by T. Ohmachi & J. Kuwano. (Illus.). 160p. (C). 1994. text ed. 55.00 (90-5410-265-9) Ashgate Pub Co.

Dynamic Sealing of Rotating & Reciprocating Shafts. EEMUA Staff. 1971. 125.00 (0-85931-067-1, Pub. by EEMUA UK) St Mut.

Dynamic Sealing Systems for Commercial Vehicles. 56p. 1984. 20.00 (0-89883-334-5, SP563) Soc Auto Engineers.

***Dynamic Secretary.** Frieda Porat & Mimi Will. 1978. pap. text ed. write for info. (0-13-221846-1) NewLife Bks.

Dynamic Secretary: A Practical Guide to Achieving Success as an Executive Assistant. Freida Porat & Mimi Will. (Illus.). 196p. 1983. pap. 7.95 (0-685-06199-X) P-H.

Dynamic Self see Dynamic Infant: Activities to Enhance Infant & Toddler Development

Dynamic Semiconductor RAM Structures. A. Cardon & L. Fransen. (European Patent Office Ser.: Vol. 1). (Illus.). 488p. 1984. 194.00 (0-08-030578-4, Pub. by Pergamon Repr UK) Franklin.

Dynamic Sermon Outlines. Russell E. Spray. (Pulpit Library). 80p. (Orig.). 1989. pap. 3.99 (0-8010-8297-8) Baker Bk.

Dynamic Small Groups: How to Make Them Happen. W. Clarence Schilt. LC 92-13027. 1992. pap. 7.95 (0-8280-0676-8) Review & Herald.

Dynamic Soil-Structure Interaction: Proceedings of the International Symposium, Minneapolis, 4-5 Sept. 1984. Ed. by D. E. Beskos et al. 184p. (C). 1984. text ed. 95.00 (90-6191-558-9, Pub. by A A Balkema NE) Ashgate Pub Co.

Dynamic Stability of Structures: Proceedings of the International Conference, Evanston, Oct. 1965. G. Herrmann. LC 66-25863. 1967. 138.00 (0-08-012087-3, Pub. by Pergamon Repr UK) Franklin.

Dynamic Stability of Suddenly Loaded Structures. G. J. Simitses. (Illus.). 264p. 1989. 69.00 (0-387-97010-X, 2879) Spr-Verlag.

Dynamic State of Muscle Fibers: Proceedings of the Int'l Symposium Oct. 1-6, 1989, Konstanz, Fed. Rep. of Germany. Ed. by Dirk Pette. (Illus.). xxiv, 729p. (C). 1990. lib. bdg. 288.50 (3-11-012168-9) De Gruyter.

Dynamic Statutory Interpretation. William N. Eskridge, Jr. LC 94-14151. (Illus.). 448p. 1994. text ed. 49.95 (0-674-21878-7, ESKDYN) HUP.

Dynamic Stiffness & Substructures. A. Y. Leung. LC 93-15461. 1993. 169.00 (0-387-19807-5) Spr-Verlag.

Dynamic Stillness: The Practice of Trika Yoga, Pt. I. Swami Chetanananda. Ed. by Linda L. Barnes. 263p. (Orig.). 1990. 26.95 (0-915801-29-9); pap. 15.95 (0-915801-19-1) Rudra Pr.

Dynamic Stillness, Pt. Two: The Fulfillment of Trika Yoga. Swami Chetanananda. LC 90-62101. 358p. (Orig.). 1991. 29.95 (0-915801-28-0); pap. 18.95 (0-915801-27-2) Rudra Pr.

Dynamic Stochastic Model for Current Asset & Liability Management of a Multinational Corporation. Solmaz D. Ayarslan. Ed. by Stuart Bruchey. LC 80-565. (Multinational Corporations Ser.). (Illus.). 1981. lib. bdg. 31.95 (0-405-13362-6) Ayer.

Dynamic Stratigraphy & Depositional Environments of the Hamilton Group (Middle Devonian) in New York State, Pt. I. Ed. by Carlton E. Brett. (Bulletin Ser.: No. 457). (Illus.). 156p. (Orig.). 1986. pap. 12.00 (1-55557-003-8) NYS Museum.

Dynamic Stratigraphy & Depositional Environments of the Hamilton Group (Middle Devonian) in New York State, Pt. II. Ed. by Ed Landing. (Bulletin Ser.: No. 469). (Illus.). 177p. (Orig.). (C). 1991. pap. text ed. 20.00 (1-55557-183-2) NYS Museum.

Dynamic Stretching & Kicking. Bill Wallace. LC 81-69809. (Illus.). 150p. (Orig.). 1981. pap. 14.95 (0-86568-018-3, 405) Unique Pubns.

Dynamic Structure of Detonation in Gaseous & Dispersed Media. Ed. by A. A. Borissov. (C). 1991. lib. bdg. 135.00 (0-7923-1340-2) Kluwer Ac.

Dynamic Structure of Household Expenditures in the Federal Republic of Germany. Gollnick. LC 74-84207. 1975. 36.00 (0-444-10796-7, North Holland) Elsevier.

Dynamic Structure of Nuclear States: Proceedings of 1971 Mont Tremblant International Summer School. Ed. by D. J. Rowe. LC 75-186282. 599p. reprint ed. pap. 170.80 (0-317-08960-9, 2014391) Bks Demand.

Dynamic Structures in Biology. Brian C. Goodwin et al. 400p. 1989. 68.50 (0-85224-599-8, Pub. by Edinburgh U Pr UK) Col U Pr.

Dynamic Sumo. Clyde Newton. Ed. by Pockell et al. (Illus.). 112p. 1994. 30.00 (4-7700-1802-9) Kodansha.

Dynamic Symmetry: Proportional System Is Found in Some Byzantine & Russian Icons of the 14th to 16th Century. Karyl Knee. LC 88-90738. (Illus.). 90p. 1988. spiral bd. 10.00 (0-9618545-2-9) Oakwood Pubns.

***Dynamic Symmetry & Holistic Asymmetry in Navajo & Western Art & Cosmology.** Gary Witherspoon & Glen Peterson. LC 94-32200. (American Indian Studies: Vol. 5). 208p. (C). 1995. pap. text ed. 27.95 (0-8204-1860-9) P Lang Pubs.

***Dynamic Systems & Control: 1994 International Mechanical Engineering Congress & Exposition, Chicago, Illinois - November 6-11, 1994, 2 vols., Set.** (DSC Ser.: Vols. 55-1 & 55-2). 1208p. 1994. 240.00 (0-614-05616-0, GX0909) ASME.

***Dynamic Systems & Control Vol. 1: 1994 International Mechanical Engineering Congress & Exposition, Chicago, Illinois - November 6-11, 1994.** (DSC Ser.: Vol. 55-1). 584p. 1994. 150.00 (0-7918-1414-9, G0909A) ASME.

***Dynamic Systems & Control Vol. 2: 1994 International Mechanical Engineering Congress & Exposition, Chicago, Illinois - November 6-11, 1994.** (DSC Ser.: Vol. 55-2). 624p. 1994. 150.00 (0-614-05615-2, G0909B) ASME.

Dynamic Systems Approach to Development: Applications. Ed. by Linda B. Smith & Esther Thelen. LC 92-46558. (Cognitive Psychology Ser.). (Illus.). 660p. (C). 1993. 52.50 (0-262-19333-7, Bradford Bks) MIT Pr.

Dynamic Systems Approach to the Development of Cognition & Action. Esther Thelen & Linda B. Smith. LC 93-6037. (Cognitive Psychology Ser.). (Illus.). 368p. 1994. 52.00 (0-262-20095-3, Bradford Bks) MIT Pr.

Dynamic Systems Control: UCLA Symposia on Molecular & Cellular Biology, Vol. 107. Robert E. Skelton. LC 87-27944. 504p. 1988. Net. text ed. write for info. (0-471-83779-2) Wiley.

***Dynamic Systems of Basic Economic Growth Models.** Bjarne S. Jensen. LC 94-23069. (Mathematics & Its Applications Ser.: 302). 368p. (C). 1994. lib. bdg. 166.00 (0-7923-3091-9) Kluwer Ac.

Dynamic Systems, Simulation & Control. Vol. 6. 216p. 1994. write for info. (0-318-72842-7, H0912F) ASME.

***Dynamic Teachers: Leaders of Change.** Sharon F. Rallis et al. (Illus.). 176p. 1995. 39.95 (0-8039-6235-5); pap. 18.95 (0-8039-6236-3) Corwin Pr.

Dynamic Telephone Related - Hardware Business. Business Communications Co., Inc. Staff. 172p. 1984. 1,250.00 (0-89336-338-3, G-071) BCC.

Dynamic Tension. Harry Wong. LC 80-53545. (Illus.). 144p. 1980. pap. 6.95 (0-86568-013-2, 209) Unique Pubns.

Dynamic Testing of Aggregates & Soils & Lateral Stress Measurements, 1990. (Transportation Research Record Ser.: No. 1278). 224p. 1990. 34.00 (0-309-05055-3) Transport Res Bd.

Dynamic Theory of Inflation & Stagflation. Carolyn J. Siino. LC 83-90353. 71p. 1983. pap. 13.75 (0-9611860-0-3, A001) Lucky Lit.

***Dynamic Therapies for Psychiatric Disorders: Axis I.** Ed. by Jacques P. Barber & Paul Crits-Christoph. LC 94-42944. 1995. text ed. 55.00 (0-465-01742-8) Basic.

Dynamic Therapy in Brief Hospitalization. John M. Oldham & L. Mark Russakoff. LC 87-12629. 235p. 1987. 30.00x (0-87668-965-9) Aronson.

Dynamic Therapy of the Older Patient. Wayne A. Myers. LC 83-25772. 270p. 1984. 30.00 (0-87668-623-4) Aronson.

Dynamic Thermal Modelling. Ed. by J. Wix. (C). 1987. 300.00 (0-9510862-1-9, Pub. by Build Servs Info Assn UK) St Mut.

Dynamic Thinking. Melvin Powers. 1980. pap. 5.00 (0-87980-031-3) Wilshire.

Dynamic Thought. limited ed. Henry T. Hamblin. 12.00 (0-911662-22-7) Yoga.

Dynamic Thought: The Law of Vibrant Energy. William W. Atkinson. 281p. 1976. spiral bd. 7.70 (0-7873-0047-0) Mokelumne.

Dynamic Timing Decisions under Uncertainty: Essays on Invention, Innovation & Exploration in Resource Economics. Nguyen M. Hung & Nguyen Van Quyen. LC 93-46881. (Lecture Notes in Economics & Mathematical Systems Ser.: Vol. 406). (Illus.). x, 194p. 1994. pap. 46.00 (0-387-57649-5) Spr-Verlag.

Dynamic Tradition: The History of Alabama Academic Libraries from Their Establishment Through 1988. Ed. by Vicki L. Gregory. LC 91-8371. (Illus.). 396p. 1991. lib. bdg. 45.00 (0-942301-16-1) Birm Pub Lib.

Dynamic Transcendence: The Correlation of Confessional Heritage & Contemporary Experience in a Biblical Model of Divine Activity. Paul D. Hanson. LC 78-54552. 109p. reprint ed. pap. 31.10 (0-685-16023-8, 2026940) Bks Demand.

***Dynamic Trial Practice.** Ronald Carlson & Edward Imwinkelreid. 1995. 39.95 (0-614-06012-5, 3327) Natl Prac Inst.

Dynamic Truths for the Spirit-Filled Life. C. S. Lovett. 1973. pap. 7.95 (0-938148-13-3) Prsnl Christianity.

Dynamic Universe: An Introduction to Astronomy. 4th ed. Theodore P. Snow. Ed. by Simon. 716p. (C). 1991. text ed. 56.00 (0-314-77104-2) West Pub.

***Dynamic Urban Transportation Network Models: Theory & Implications for Intelligent Vehicle-Highway Systems.** Bin Ran & David E. Boyce. LC 94-22844. 1994. write for info. (0-387-58360-2) Spr-Verlag.

Dynamic Uses of Imagery. Leslie Dale. (Orig.). 1994. pap. 9.95 (0-913412-75-9) Brandon Hse.

Dynamic Vibration Absorbers: Theory & Technical Applications. Boris G. Korenev & L. M. Reznikov. LC 93-9750. 296p. 1993. text ed. 99.95 (0-471-92850-X) Wiley.

Dynamic Vocabulary, 2 vols., Set. Peter Funk & Mary Funk. 1993. 29.95 (1-56015-211-7) Penton Overseas.

Dynamic Vocabulary! Series 1. Peter Funk & Mary Funk. Date not set. 15.95 (1-56015-204-4) Penton Overseas.

Dynamic Vocabulary Series Two. Peter Funk & Mary Funk. 1993. 15.95 (1-56015-210-9) Penton Overseas.

Dynamic West: A Region in Transition. 58p. 1989. 15.00 (0-87292-086-0, C-129) Coun State Govts.

Dynamic Word: New Testament Insights for Contemporary Christians. Karl P. Donfried. LC 80-8905. 244p. 1981. 12.95 (0-06-061945-7) Harper SF.

Dynamic World of Physics. Robert T. Dixon. 512p. (C). 1984. write for info. (0-675-20093-8, Merrill Pub Co) Macmillan.

Dynamic Worship: Mission, Grace, Praise, & Power. Kennon L. Callahan. LC 94-1873. 160p. 1994. 16.00 (0-06-061281-9) Harper SF.

Dynamic Wrinkles & Drapery: Solutions for Drawing the Clothed Figure. Burne Hogarth. (Illus.). 144p. 1992. 29.95 (0-8230-1586-6, Watsn-Guptill) Watsn-Guptill.

Dynamical & Chemical Coupling of the Neutral & Ionized Atmosphere. Ed. by Bjorn Grandal & Jan A. Holtet. (Nato Advanced Study Institute Ser. C: No. 35). 1977. lib. bdg. 103.00 (90-277-0840-1) Kluwer Ac.

Dynamical Aspects of Critical Phenomena. J. I. Budnick & M. P. Kawatra. LC 77-183846. 638p. 1972. text ed. 432.00 (0-677-12350-7) Gordon & Breach.

***Dynamical Aspects of Nuclear Fission: Proceeding of II International Conference.** Ed. by J. Kristiak & B. I. Pustylnik. (Illus.). 320p. (Orig.). (C). 1994. pap. 45.00 (0-911767-89-4) Hadronic Pr Inc.

Dynamical Aspects of Nuclear Fission: Proceedings of the International Workshop Held in the Smolenice Castle in Czechoslovakia on June 17-21, 1991. Ed. by J. Kristiak & B. I. Pustylnik. 363p. 1992. pap. text ed. 35.00 (0-911767-58-4) Hadronic Pr Inc.

Dynamical Astronomy: Proceedings of the Second U.S.-Hungary Workshop. Ed. by Victor G. Szebehely & Bela Balazs. (Illus.). 195p. (C). 1986. text ed. 25.00 (0-292-71507-2) U of Tex Pr.

Dynamical Behaviour of Structures. 2nd ed. Ed. by Geoffrey B. Warburton. 1976. 153.00 (0-08-020364-7, Pub. by Pergamon Repr UK) Franklin.

Dynamical Chaos. Ed. by M. V. Berry et al. 200p. 1989. pap. text ed. 19.95 (0-691-08519-6) Princeton U Pr.

***Dynamical Chaos: Models & Experiments: Appearance Routes & Structure of Chaos in Simple Dynamical Systems.** Vadim S. Anishchenko. LC 94-48586. (Nonlinear Science, Series A, Monographs & Treatises: Vol. 8). 400p. 1995. text ed. 74.00 (981-02-2142-8) World Scientific Pub.

Dynamical Chaos of Solitons: An Introduction to Perturbed Soliton Systems. K. H. Spatschek. 350p. 1995. text ed. 67.00 (981-02-1160-0) World Scientific Pub.

Dynamical Collision Theory & Its Applications. Sadhan K. Adhikari & Kenneth L. Kowalski. 494p. 1991. text ed. 99.00 (0-12-044273-6) Acad Pr.

Dynamical Critical Phenomena & Related Topics: Proceedings of the International Conference, 1979. International Conference, Geneva Staff. Ed. by C. P. Enz. (Lecture Notes in Physics Ser.: Vol. 104). 1979. pap. 24.00 (3-540-09523-3) Spr-Verlag.

***Dynamical Disease: Mathematical Analysis of Human Illness.** Ed. by L. Glass et al. 1995. pap. 40.00 (1-56396-370-1, AIP Pr) Am Inst Physics.

Dynamical Features of Nuclei & Finite Fermi Systems: Proceedings of the Conference. X. Vinas et al. 520p. 1994. text ed. 137.00 (981-02-1556-8) World Scientific Pub.

Dynamical Gauge Symmetry Breaking. Ed. by E. Farhi & R. Jackiw. vi, 404p. 1982. text ed. 67.00 (9971-950-24-3); pap. text ed. 33.00 (9971-950-25-1) World Scientific Pub.

Dynamical Geology of Salt & Related Structures. Ed. by Ian Lerche & J. J. O'Brien. 856p. 1987. text ed. 81.00 (0-12-444170-X) Acad Pr.

Dynamical Groups & Spectrum Generating Algebra, 2 vols. Asim O. Barut et al. 1168p. (C). 1988. pap. text ed. 106.00 (9971-5-0147-3) World Scientific Pub.

Dynamical Groups & Spectrum Generating Algebra, 2 vols., Vol. I. Asim O. Barut et al. 1168p. (C). 1988. text ed. 240.00 (9971-5-0146-5) World Scientific Pub.

Dynamical Issues in Combustion Theory. Ed. by P. C. Fife et al. (IMA Volumes in Mathematics & Its Applications Ser.: Vol. 35). (Illus.). 272p. 1991. 43.00 (0-387-97583-7) Spr-Verlag.

Dynamical Meteorology: An Introductory Selection. Ed. by B. W. Atkinson. LC 80-41675. 250p. 1981. pap. 16.95 (0-416-73840-0, NO.3462) Routledge Chapman & Hall.

Dynamical Phenomena at Interfaces: Surfaces & Membranes. Ed. by D. Beysens et al. 610p. (C). 1993. lib. bdg. 145.00 (1-56072-089-1) Nova Sci Pubs.

Dynamical Phenomena at Surfaces, Intersurfaces & Superlattices, Vol. 3. Ed. by F Nizzoli et al. (Surface Sciences Ser.: Vol. 3). (Illus.). 350p. 1985. 71.00 (0-387-15505-8) Spr-Verlag.

Dynamical Prediction of Wind Tides on Lake Erie. (Meteorological Monograph Ser.: No. 26). 1963. 17.00 (0-933876-15-7) Am Meteorological.

Dynamical Problems in Continuum Physics. Ed. by J. L. Bona et al. (IMA Volumes in Mathematics & Its Applications Ser.: Vol. 4). (Illus.). 325p. 1986. 39.00 (0-387-96463-0) Spr-Verlag.

Dynamical Problems in Soliton Systems. Ed. by S Takeno. (Synergetics Ser.: Vol. 30). (Illus.). 310p. 1985. 67.00 (0-387-15372-1) Spr-Verlag.

Dynamical Problems of Rigid-Elastic Systems & Structures: IUTAM Symposium, Moscow, USSR, May 23-27, 1990. Ed. by N. V. Banichuk et al. (Illus.). xvi, 236p. 1991. 75.00 (0-387-53788-0) Spr-Verlag.

Dynamical Processes & Ordering on Solid Surfaces. Ed. by A. Yoshimori & M. Tsukada. (Solid-State Sciences Ser.: Vol. 59). (Illus.). xii, 195p. 1985. 55.00 (0-387-15108-7) Spr-Verlag.

Dynamical Processes in Disordered Systems. Ed. by Wm. M. Yen. (Materials Science Forum Ser.: Vol. 51). 252p. 1990. text ed. 76.00 (0-87849-591-6, Pub. by Trans Tech GW) LPS Dist Ctr.

Dynamical Processes in Molecular Physics: Lectures from the First EPS Southern European School of Physics, Avila, September 1991. Ed. by G. Delgado-Barrio. (Illus.). 328p. 1993. 79.00 (0-7503-0205-4) IOP Pub.

Dynamical Properties of Solids: The Modern Physics of Phonons: Transport, Surfaces & Simulations, Vol. 6. Ed. by G. K. Horton & A. A. Maradudin. 500p. 1990. 197.50 (0-444-88561-7, North Holland) Elsevier.

Dynamical Properties of Solids, Vol. 3: Metals, Superconductors, Magnetic Materials & Liquids. Ed. by G. K. Horton & A. A. Maradudin. 334p. 1980. 113.00 (0-444-85314-6, North Holland) Elsevier.

Dynamical Properties of Solids, Vol. 4: Disordered Solids, Optical Properties. Ed. by G. K. Horton & A. A. Maradudin. 478p. 1980. 138.50 (0-444-85315-4, North Holland) Elsevier.

An Asterisk (*) at the beginning of an entry indicates that the title is appearing in BIP for the first time.

***Dynamics of Arthropod Predator-Prey Systems.** Michael P. Hassell. LC 78-51169. (Monographs in Population Biology: No. 13). (Illus.). 246p. 1978. reprint ed. pap. 70.20 (0-7837-8591-7, 2049406) Bks Demand.

Dynamics of Aspect Analysis: New Perceptions in Astrology. 2nd rev. ed. Bil Tierney. 288p. 1993. pap. 13.95 (0-916360-56-3) CRCS Pubns CA.

Dynamics of Astrophysical Discs. Ed. by J. A. Sellwood. (Illus.). 260p. (C). 1990. 59.95 (0-521-37485-5) Cambridge U Pr.

Dynamics of Atmospheric Flight. Bernard Etkin. LC 73-165946. (Illus.). 579p. 1972. Net. text ed. write for info. (0-471-24620-4) Wiley.

***Dynamics of Atmospheric Motion.** John A. Dutton. LC 94-25265. (Illus.). 640p. 1995. pap. text ed. 18.95 (0-486-68486-5) Dover.

Dynamics of Atmospheric Re-Entry. Frank J. Regan & Satya M. Anandakrishnan. LC 92-33727. (Educ Ser.). 604p. 1993. 99.95 (1-56347-048-9) AIAA.

Dynamics of Automatic Controls. Rudolf C. Oldenbourg & Hans Sartorius. Ed. by H. L. Mason. LC 49-2386. 276p. reprint ed. pap. 78.70 (0-317-08004-0, 2051945) Bks Demand.

Dynamics of Banking. Robert Schweitzer & John T. Boorman. Ed. by Thomas M. Havrilesky et al. LC 84-251570. (Illus.). 460p. (C). 1985. text ed. write for info. (0-88295-411-3) Harlan Davidson.

Dynamics of Bargaining Games. J. Keith Murnighan. 240p. 1991. pap. text ed. 25.40 (0-13-222118-7, 140107) P-H.

Dynamics of Biblical Parallelism. Adele Berlin. LC 84-48250. 192p. 1985. 29.95 (0-253-31850-5); pap. 10.95 (0-253-20765-7, MB 765) Ind U Pr.

Dynamics of Biochemical Systems: Lectures Presented at the FEBS Advanced Course & Round Table Discussion of the IUB Interest Group on Kinetics & Mechanics of Enzymes & Metabolic Networks, Debrecchen, Hungary, 18-24 August 1985. Ed. by S. Damjanovich et al. 550p. 1986. 172.00 (0-444-99503-X) Elsevier.

Dynamics of Biological Invasions. R. Hengeveld. 176p. 1990. 55.00 (0-412-31470-3, A3814) Chapman & Hall.

Dynamics of Biological Membranes: Influence on Synthesis Structure & Function. Miles D. Houslay & Keith K. Stanley. 330p. 1982. pap. text ed. 57.50 (0-471-10095-1, Wiley-Interscience) Wiley.

***Dynamics of Business Cycles: Contributions to Economics.** Ed. by M. Reiter. 215p. 1995. pap. 54.00 (3-7908-0823-7) Spr-Verlag.

Dynamics of Business-Government Relations: Industry, & Exports, 1893 to 1921. William H. Becker. LC 81-10318. (Chicago Original Paperback Ser.). 1982. pap. text ed. 20.00 (0-226-04121-2) U Ch Pr.

Dynamics of Canine Gait. 2nd ed. Leon Hollenbeck. LC 81-12643. (Other Dog Bks.). (Illus.). 240p. 1981. 24.95 (0-87714-081-2) Denlingers.

Dynamics of Caste Relations in Rural India. L. S. Ainapur. 1986. 26.00 (81-7033-024-6, Pub. by Rawat II) S Asia.

Dynamics of Catholic Identity in Healthcare: A Working Document. 64p. 1987. pap. 5.00 (0-87125-134-5, 233) Cath Health.

Dynamics of Cellular Motility. Masatoshi Murase. (Nonlinear Science: Theory & Applications Ser.). 376p. 1992. text ed. 229.00 (0-471-93576-X) Wiley.

Dynamics of Change: The Crisis of the 1750s & English Party Systems. J. C. Clark. LC 81-9999. (Cambridge Studies in the History & Theory of Politics). 600p. 1982. 89.95 (0-521-23830-7) Cambridge U Pr.

Dynamics of Change in a Slave Society: A Sociopolitical History of the Free Colored's of Jamaica, 1800-1865. Mavis C. Campbell. LC 74-4968. 393p. (C). 1976. 38.50 (0-8386-1584-8) Fairleigh Dickinson.

Dynamics of Change in NATO: A Burden Sharing Perspective. James R. Golden. LC 83-19185. (Washington Papers: No. 96). 256p. 1983. text ed. 55.00 (0-275-90991-3, C0991, Praeger Pubs) Greenwood.

Dynamics of Change in Southern Africa. Ed. by Paul B. Rich. LC 93-45832. 1994. text ed. 59.95 (0-312-12120-2) St Martin.

Dynamics of Change in the Modern Hindu Family. Raghuvir Sinha. 1993. 30.00 (81-7022-448-9, Pub. by Concept II) S Asia.

Dynamics of Channel Flow. V. N. Goncharov. 328p. 1964. text ed. 82.00 (0-7065-0320-1, Pub. by Keter Pub IS) Coronet Bks.

Dynamics of China's Foreign Relations. Ed. by Jerome A. Cohen. LC 78-133219. (East Asian Monographs: No. 39). 939p. 1970. 14.00 (0-674-21875-2) HUP.

Dynamics of Cholinergic Function. Ed. by Israel Hanin. LC 86-18732. (Advances in Behavioral Biology Ser.: Vol. 30). 1292p. 1986. 175.00 (0-306-42384-7, Plenum Pr) Plenum.

Dynamics of Cities: Ecological Determinism, Dualism & Chaos. Demetrios Dendrinos. (Illus.). 240p. 1992. 59.95 (0-415-07721-4, A7410) Routledge.

Dynamics of Climate: Proceedings Conference Application Num Integration Tech Gen Circ, 10-55. Institute Advanced Study Geophysics Staff & R. Pfeffer. LC 59-10526. 1960. 67.00 (0-08-013590-0, Pub. by Pergamon Repr UK) Franklin.

Dynamics of Clinical Dietetics. Marion Mason et al. LC 81-16160. 354p. 1982. text ed. 30.95 (0-8273-4298-5) Delmar.

Dynamics of Clinical Rehabilitative Exercise: Dynamics of Clinical Rehabilitative Exercise. Stephen M. Ordet & Leonard S. Grand. (Illus.). 304p. 1992. 55.00 (0-683-06654-4) Williams & Wilkins.

Dynamics of Clipper. Arthur Fuller. 560p. 1988. pap. 28.00 (1-55623-131-8) Irwin Prof Pubng.

Dynamics of Clipper: Featuring Version 5.0. Arthur Fuller & Peter Brawley. Ed. by Susan Glinert. 500p. 1991. 28.00 (1-55623-374-4) Irwin Prof Pubng.

Dynamics of Close Binary Systems. Zdenek Kopal. (Astrophysics & Space Science Library: No. 68). 1978. lib. bdg. 169.00 (90-277-0820-7) Kluwer Ac.

Dynamics of Cohort & Generations Research: Proceedings. H. A. Becker. (Tinbergen Institute Ser.). 656p. 1993. pap. 53.00 (90-5170-192-6, Pub. by Thesis Pubs NE) IBD Ltd.

Dynamics of Collective Conflict: Riots at the Bathurst 'Bike Races. C. Cunneen et al. (Illus.). xxviii, 207p. 1989. 57.00 (0-455-20816-6, Pub. by Law Bk Co); pap. 30.50 (0-455-20817-4, Pub. by Law Bk Co) W W Gaunt.

Dynamics of Collodial Systems: 1984 Olaf A. Hougen Lectures. William B. Russel. LC 86-40060. (Illus.). 136p. 1986. text ed. 22.50 (0-299-10530-X) U of Wis Pr.

Dynamics of Comets: Their Origin & Evolution. Ed. by Andrea Carusi & Giovanni B. Valsecchi. (Astrophysics & Space Science Library). 1985. lib. bdg. 134.50 (90-277-2047-9) Kluwer Ac.

Dynamics of Commodity Production Cycles. Dennis L. Meadows. LC 70-125415. (Illus.). 104p. (C). 1970. text ed. 35.00 (0-262-13141-2) Prod Press.

Dynamics of Communicating. Robert G. Davidson. 20p. (Orig.). 1987. pap. 5.50 (0-940754-46-0) Ed Ministries.

Dynamics of Communicative Development. Vera W. Lane & Dorothy Molyneaux. 432p. (C). 1992. text ed. write for info. (0-13-222019-9) P-H.

Dynamics of Company Profits. Dennis C. Mueller. (Illus.). 250p. (C). 1990. 64.95 (0-521-38372-2) Cambridge U Pr.

Dynamics of Competitive Strategy. Ken G. Smith & Curtis M. Grimm. Ed. by Martin J. Gannon. 224p. (C). 1992. text ed. 45.00 (0-8039-4370-9); pap. text ed. 19.95 (0-8039-4371-7) Sage.

Dynamics of Complex & Irregular Systems - Biefefeld Encounters in Mathematics & Physics VIII. Blanchard et al. 372p. 1993. text ed. 106.00 (981-02-1570-3) World Scientific Pub.

Dynamics of Complex Interconnected Biological Systems. Thomas L. Vincent et al. (Mathematical Modelling Ser.: Vol. 6). 332p. 1990. 47.50 (0-8176-3504-1) Birkhauser.

Dynamics of Composite Materials: Proceedings of the Joint National & Western Applied Mechanics Conference, La Jolla, CA, 1972. Joint National & Western Applied Mechanics Conference Staff. Ed. by E. H. Lee. LC 72-78966. reprint ed. pap. 39.00 (0-317-08029-6, 20-16328) Bks Demand.

Dynamics of Computing. John L. King. LC 84-15528. 280p. 1985. text ed. 62.00 (0-231-05432-7) Col U Pr.

Dynamics of Concepts: A Connectionist Model. Philip R. Van Loocke. LC 93-46746. 1994. 49.00 (0-387-57647-9) Spr-Verlag.

Dynamics of Conduction Electrons. A. B. Pippard. 158p. 1965. text ed. 114.00 (0-677-00720-5) Gordon & Breach.

Dynamics of Conflict Between Bureaucrats & Legislators. Cathy M. Johnson. LC 91-28375. (Bureaucracies, Public Administration & Public Policy Ser.). 195p. 1992. 49.95 (1-56324-015-7) M E Sharpe.

***Dynamics of Conflict Between Bureaucrats & Legislators.** Cathy M. Johnson. (Bureaucracies, Public Administration & Public Policy Ser.). 195p. 1994. pap. 22.50 (1-56324-510-8) M E Sharpe.

Dynamics of Congress: A Guide to the People & Process in the U. S. Congress. Patricia D. Woods. (Illus.). 192p. (Orig.). 1991. pap. text ed. 15.00 (1-879319-00-4) Woods Inst.

Dynamics of Contraceptive Use. Ed. by Amy O. Tsui & M. A. Herbertson. (Journal of Biosocial Science, Supplement Ser.: No. 11). 148p. 1989. lib. bdg. 48.00 (0-907232-07-8) Portland NC.

Dynamics of Controlled Mechanical Systems. Ed. by G. E. Schweitzer & M. Mansour. (Illus.). xiv, 378p. 1988. 91.00 (0-387-50201-7) Spr-Verlag.

Dynamics of Corporate Gathering. Frank Damazio. 116p. 1986. 7.95 (0-914936-83-2) Bible Temple.

Dynamics of Couples Therapy. Jurg Willi. Tr. by Jan Van Heurck. LC 83-21350. Orig. Title: Therapie der Zweierbeziehung. 288p. (Orig.). 1990. reprint ed. 40.00x (0-87668-649-8) Aronson.

Dynamics of Creation. Anthony Storr. 368p. 1993. pap. 10.00 (0-345-37673-0, Ballantine Trade) Ballantine.

Dynamics of Creativity. Robert R. Leichtman. (From Heaven to Earth Ser.). 256p. 1995. pap. 11.95 (0-89804-085-X) Ariel GA.

Dynamics of Criminal Corrections. Poulos. 1976. pap. text ed. 16.95 (0-88277-422-0) Foundation Pr.

Dynamics of Culture Change. Bronislaw Malinowski. Ed. by Phyllis M. Kaberry. LC 75-14599. 171p. 1976. reprint ed. text ed. 35.00 (0-8371-8216-6, MADCC, Greenwood Pr) Greenwood.

Dynamics of Current Developments in Fire Safety of Polymers: New Products, Compounding, Research Test Developments, Hazard Assessment: Joint Meeting - SPE, Polymer Modifiers & Additives Division, & the Fire Retardant Chemicals Association, March 20-23, 1988, Grenelefe Conference Center, Grenelefe, Florida. Society of Plastics Engineers Staff. (Illus.). 221p. reprint ed. pap. 63.00 (0-8357-6099-5, 2034188) Bks Demand.

Dynamics of Current Developments in Fire Safety of Polymers: Proceedings of Joint Conference of SPE & FRCA. 215p. 1988. pap. 45.00 (0-87762-628-6) Technomic.

Dynamics of Curved Fronts. Ed. by Pierre Pelce. (Perspectives in Physics Ser.). 450p. 1988. text ed. 118.00 (0-12-550355-5) Acad Pr.

***Dynamics of Data Envelopment Analysis: Theory of Systems Efficiency.** Jati K. Sengupta. (Diverse Ser.). 300p. (C). 1995. lib. bdg. 98.00 (0-7923-3581-3) Kluwer Ac.

Dynamics of Decision Support Systems & Expert Systems. Jay Liebowitz. 288p. (C). 1990. pap. text ed. 43.00 (0-03-026383-2) Dryden Pr.

Dynamics of Defeat: The Vietnam War in Hau Nghia Province. Eric M. Bergerud. 383p. 1990. text ed. 47.50 (0-8133-7807-9) Westview.

Dynamics of Defeat: The Vietnam War in Hau Nghia Province. Eric M. Bergerud. 383p. (C). 1993. pap. text ed. 21.50 (0-8133-1874-2) Westview.

Dynamics of Deflagrations & Reactive Systems: Flames. Ed. by A. L. Kuhl et al. (PAAS Ser.: Vol. 131). (Illus.). 418p. 1991. 74.95 (0-930403-95-9) AIAA.

Dynamics of Deflagrations & Reactive Systems: Heterogeneous Combustion. (PAAS Ser.: Vol. 132). (Illus.). 386p. 1991. 74.95 (0-930403-96-7) AIAA.

Dynamics of Degeneration & Growth in Neurons. Ed. by K. Fuxe et al. 1974. 256.00 (0-08-017917-7, Pub. by Pergamon Repr UK) Franklin.

Dynamics of Dense Stellar Systems. Ed. by David Merritt. (Illus.). (C). 1989. 64.95 (0-521-36432-9) Cambridge U Pr.

Dynamics of Deprivation. S. M. Miller & Zsuzsa Ferge. (Studies in Social Policy & Welfare). 330p. 1986. text ed. 68.95 (0-566-05137-0, Pub. by Avebury Pub UK) Ashgate Pub Co.

Dynamics of Deterrence. Frank C. Zagare. LC 86-7037. (Illus.). 208p. 1987. 22.00 (0-226-97763-3) U Ch Pr.

Dynamics of Detonations & Explosions: Detonations. (PAAS Ser.: Vol. 133). (Illus.). 383p. 1991. 74.95 (0-930403-97-5) AIAA.

Dynamics of Detonations & Explosions: Explosion Phenomena. (PAAS Ser.: Vol. 134). (Illus.). 408p. 1991. 74.95 (0-930403-98-3) AIAA.

Dynamics of Development & Development Administration. Kempe R. Hope. LC 83-16623. (Contributions in Economics & Economic History Ser.: No. 56). (Illus.). xi, 128p. 1984. text ed. 47.95 (0-313-24269-0, HDY/, Greenwood Pr) Greenwood.

Dynamics of Development & the Therapeutic Process. Richard Lasky. LC 92-17808. 488p. 1993. 50.00x (0-87668-565-3) Aronson.

Dynamics of Development in the European Human Rights Convention System. Clovis C. Morrisson. 192p. 1981. lib. bdg. 94.00 (90-247-2546-1) Kluwer Ac.

Dynamics of Dialogue. Ed. by I. Markova & K. Foppa. 200p. 1990. 54.00 (0-387-91388-2) Spr-Verlag.

Dynamics of Dinosaurs & Other Extinct Giants. R. McNeill Alexander. (Illus.). 224p. 1989. text ed. 52.50 (0-231-06666-X) Col U Pr.

Dynamics of Dinosaurs & Other Extinct Giants. R. McNeill Alexander. 1991. pap. 12.95 (0-231-06667-8) Col U Pr.

Dynamics of Discrimination: Systemic Discrimination, Generic Racism, Administrative Lynching. Garry DeYoung. 20.95 (0-936128-38-0) De Young Pr.

Dynamics of Disordered Materials. Ed. by D. Richter et al. (Proceedings in Physics Ser.: Vol. 37). (Illus.). 320p. 1989. 64.00 (0-387-50942-9, 2789) Spr-Verlag.

Dynamics of Dispensing see Opticianry: The Practice & the Art

Dynamics of Dispute: Machlokess in Talmudic Times. Zvi Lampel. 270p. 1991. 17.95 (0-910818-96-7); pap. 13.95 (0-910818-99-1) Judaica Pr.

Dynamics of Dissent in Indonesia: Sawito & the Phantom Coup. David Bourchier. LC 84-227917. (Interim Reports Ser.). 140p. reprint ed. pap. 39.90 (0-7837-2427-6, 2042574) Bks Demand.

Dynamics of Diversity. Odette Pollar. Ed. by W. Philip Gerould. LC 93-73147. (Fifty-Minute Ser.). (Illus.). 100p. (Orig.). 1994. pap. 9.95 (1-56052-247-X) Crisp Pubns.

Dynamics of Divorce: A Life Cycle Perspective. Florence W. Kaslow & Lita L. Schwartz. LC 87-693. (Frontiers in Couples & Family Therapy Ser.: No. 1). 346p. 1987. 41.95 (0-87630-455-2) Brunner-Mazel.

Dynamics of Domestic Politics & Arms Control: The Salt II Treaty Ratification Debate. Dan Caldwell. (Illus.). 245p. (C). 1991. text ed. 34.95 (0-87249-747-X) U of SC Pr.

Dynamics of Domination: State, Class, & Social Reform in Mexico, 1910-1990. Vivian Brachet-Marquez. LC 93-30949. (Latin American Ser.). 264p. (C). 1994. 59.95 (0-8229-3780-8) U of Pittsburgh Pr.

Dynamics of Earth's Deep Interior & Earth Rotation. Ed. by J. L. Le Mouel et al. LC 93-7784. (Geophysical Monograph Ser.: No. 72). 1993. 30.00 (0-87590-463-7) Am Geophysical.

Dynamics of East European Ethnicity Outside of Eastern Europe: With Special Emphasis on the American Case. Ed. by Irene P. Winner & Rudolph M. Susel. 242p. 1983. 24.95 (0-87073-234-X); pap. 15.95 (0-87073-235-8) Schenkman Bks Inc.

Dynamics of Economic Life in Rural India: A Case Study. L. N. Dahiya. (C). 1991. 20.00 (81-212-0391-0, Pub. by Gian Publng Hse II) S Asia.

Dynamics of Economic Policymaking in Egypt. Paul Rivlin. LC 85-12190. 220p. 1985. text ed. 49.95 (0-275-90156-4, C0156, Praeger Pubs) Greenwood.

Dynamics of Education Policymaking: Case Studies of Burkina Faso, Jordan, Peru, & Thailand. Wadi D. Haddad & Terri Demsky. LC 93-34335. (EDI Development Policy Series: Analytical Case Studies: No. 10). 280p. 1994. write for info. (0-8213-2660-0) World Bank.

Dynamics of Effective Negotiation. 2nd ed. Donald B. Sparks. LC 93-23839. 150p. 1993. 12.95 (0-88415-102-6) Gulf Pub.

Dynamics of Effective Teaching. 2nd ed. Richard Kindsvatter et al. 384p. (C). 1992. pap. text ed. 37.95 (0-8013-0485-7, 78318) Longman.

Dynamics of Electrophoresis. W. Thormann et al. (Electrophoresis Library). (Illus.). 236p. 1992. text ed. 140.00 (1-56081-192-7) VCH Pubs.

Dynamics of Elementary Atomic Molecular Processes in Gases & Plasma. Ed. by V. A. Shcheglov. (Proceedings of the Lebedev Physics Institute Ser.: Vol. 212). (Illus.). 282p. (C). 1994. lib. bdg. 97.00 (1-56072-153-7) Nova Sci Pubs.

***Dynamics of Environmental Bioprocesses: Modelling & Simulation.** Jonathan B. Snape et al. LC 95-7132. 1995. write for info. (3-527-28705-1, Pub. by Vlg Chemie) VCH Pubs.

Dynamics of Ethnic Competition & Conflict. Susan Olzak. 288p. (C). 1992. 32.50 (0-8047-2028-2) Stanford U Pr.

Dynamics of Ethnic Competition & Conflict. Susan Olzak. 1994. pap. 14.95 (0-8047-2337-0) Stanford U Pr.

Dynamics of Ethnicity. Marshall Hyatt & Franz Boas. LC 89-25910. (Contributions to the Study of Anthropology Ser.: No. 6). 192p. 1990. text ed. 49.95 (0-313-27320-0, HFY/, Greenwood Pr) Greenwood.

Dynamics of Euro-African Co-Operation. Djamson. 1977. lib. bdg. 107.50 (90-247-1841-4) Kluwer Ac.

Dynamics of European Integration. Ed. by William Wallace. 308p. 1992. pap. text ed. 19.75 (1-85567-087-9, Pub. by Pinter Pubs UK) St Martin.

Dynamics of European Nuclear Disarmament. Alva Myrdal et al. 1982. 35.00 (0-85124-320-7, Pub. by Spkesman UK); pap. 13.95 (0-85124-321-5, Pub. by Spkesman UK) Dufour.

Dynamics of European Union. Ed. by Roy Pryce. LC 87-592. 288p. 1986. 55.00 (0-7099-4327-X, Pub. by Croom Helm UK) Routledge Chapman & Hall.

Dynamics of Evolution: The Punctuated Equilibrium Debate in the Natural & Social Sciences. Ed. by Albert Somit & Steven A. Peterson. LC 91-55569. (Illus.). 328p. 1992. 49.95 (0-8014-2531-X); pap. 17.95 (0-8014-9763-9) Cornell U Pr.

Dynamics of Excited Molecules. Ed. by K. Kuchitsu. LC 93-45534. (Studies in Physical & Theoretical Chemistry: No. 82). 1994. 282.75 (0-444-81796-4) Elsevier.

***Dynamics of Existence.** Concept by L. Ron Hubbard. 40p. 1994. pap. 4.00 (0-88404-909-4) Bridge Pubns Inc.

***Dynamics of Expendability: A Study of the Abbreviation of Man.** Benjamin Braginsky. 124p. (C). 1995. lib. bdg. 26.50 (0-8191-9804-8) U Pr of Amer.

Dynamics of Explosion & Its Use. J. Henrych. LC 76-29648. (Developments in Civil Engineering Ser.: Vol. 1). 1979. 164.00 (0-444-99819-5) Elsevier.

Dynamics of Explosions. Ed. by J. R. Bowen et al. LC 86-22170. (PAAS Ser.: Vol. 106). (Illus.). 664p. 1986. 92.95 (0-930403-15-0) AIAA.

Dynamics of Extinction. Ed. by David K. Elliot. LC 85-17974. 294p. 1986. text ed. 77.95 (0-471-81034-7) Wiley.

***Dynamics of Faith.** Paul Tillich. 145p. 1994. lib. bdg. 29.00 (0-8095-9158-8) Borgo Pr.

Dynamics of Faith. Paul Tillich. 1958. pap. text ed. 12.00 (0-06-130042-X, TB42, Torch) HarpC.

Dynamics of Faith & Confession. Charles Capps. 315p. (Orig.). 1987. pap. 8.95 (0-89274-444-8) Harrison Hse.

Dynamics of Family Development: A Theoretical Perspective. James M. White. LC 91-9053. (Perspectives on Marriage & the Family Ser.). 254p. 1991. lib. bdg. 32.50 (0-89862-080-5) Guilford Pr.

Dynamics of Feedback Systems. A. I. Mees. LC 80-40501. (Illus.). 224p. reprint ed. pap. 63.90 (0-8357-6651-9, 2035320) Bks Demand.

Dynamics of Feminist Therapy. Ed. by Doris Howard. LC 86-26937. (Women & Therapy Ser.: Vol. 5, Nos. 2-3). 341p. 1987. text ed. 49.95 (0-86656-629-5) Haworth Pr.

Dynamics of Field Instruction: Learning Through Doing. 1975. 3.85 (0-685-21306-4, 75-650-03) Coun Soc Wk Ed.

Dynamics of Fine Powders. K. Rietema. (Handling & Processing of Solids Ser.). 1991. 98.75 (1-85166-594-3) Elsevier.

Dynamics of First Order Phase Transitions: Proceedings of the Workshop. H. J. Herrmann et al. 404p. 1992. text ed. 121.00 (981-02-1260-7) World Scientific Pub.

Dynamics of First-Order Phase Transitions in Equilibrium & Nonequilibrium Systems. Stephan W. Koch. (Lecture Notes in Physics Ser.: Vol. 207). iii, 148p. 1984. pap. 17.00 (0-387-13379-8) Spr-Verlag.

Dynamics of Fitness: A Practical Approach. 2nd ed. George McGlynn. 304p. 1990. pap. write for info. (0-697-07637-7) Brown & Benchmark.

Dynamics of Fitness: A Practical Approach. 3rd ed. George McGlynn. 336p. (C). 1993. pap. text ed. write for info. (0-697-12647-1) Brown & Benchmark.

Dynamics of Fitness & Health. 6th ed. F. Compton Jenkins. 240p. 1993. spiral bd. 14.95 (0-8403-7920-X) Kendall-Hunt.

Dynamics of Fixed Marine Structures. 3rd ed. A. J. Adams & N. D. Barltrop. (Illus.). 740p. 1991. 195.00 (0-7506-1046-8) Buttrwrth-Heinemann.

Dynamics of Flames & Reactive Systems. Ed. by J. R. Bowen et al. LC 84-21560. (PAAS Ser.). (Illus.). 766p. 1985. 92.95 (0-915928-92-2, VOL. 95) AIAA.

***Dynamics of Flexible Multibody Systems.** (Illus.). 300p. (C). 1994. 195.00 (1-57205-837-4) Rector Pr.

Dynamics of Flexible Multibody Systems: Theory & Experiment. Ed. by S. C. Sinha et al. (AMD Series, Vol. 141: DSC: Vol. 37). 240p. 1992. 57.50 (0-7918-1076-3, G00720) ASME.

Dynamics of Flexible Structures in Space. Ed. by C. L. Kirk & J. L. Junkins. LC 90-81264. 672p. 1990. 112.00 (0-945824-46-7) Computational Mech MA.

Dynamics of Flexible Structures in Space: Proceedings of the First International Conference, Cranfield, UK, 15-18 May 1990. Ed. by C. Kirk & J. L. Junkins. ix, 661p. 1990. 128.00 (0-387-52644-7) Spr-Verlag.

Dynamics of Flight. Robin L. Stratton. 206p. 1991. pap. 9.95 (0-9626541-2-4) Mockngbrd Square.

An Asterisk (*) at the beginning of an entry indicates that the title is appearing in BIP for the first time.

An Asterisk (*) at the beginning of an entry indicates that the title is appearing in BIP for the first time.

2143

D

Dynamics of Physiologically Structured Populations. Ed. by J. A. Metz & O. Diekmann. (Lecture Notes in Biomathematics Ser.: Vol. 68). xii, 511p. 1986. pap. 70.00 (*0-387-16786-2*) Spr-Verlag.

Dynamics of Placement: How to Develop a Successful Career Planning & Placement Program. John D. Shingleton & Edwin B. Fitzpatrick. 1985. 19.95 (*0-914885-09-X*) Coll Placement.

Dynamics of Planets & Satellites & Theories of Their Motion. Ed. by Victor G. Szebehely. (Astrophysics & Space Science Library: No. 72). 1978. lib. bdg. 99.00 (*90-277-0869-X*) Kluwer Ac.

Dynamics of Plate Interiors. Ed. by A. W. Bally et al. LC 80-28968. (Geodynamics Ser.: Vol. 1). 168p. 1980. 20.00 (*0-87590-508-0*, G00100) Am Geophysical.

Dynamics of Pluralism & Education That Is Multicultural. Carl A. Grant. (Keynote Address: 8th Annual Vivian O. Windley Weekend Institute of the Department of Elementary Education, City College of New York Ser.). 1988. pap. text ed. 3.00 (*0-918374-25-1*) City Coll Wk.

Dynamics of Police Administration: Cases & Problems. 2nd ed. John O. Truitt. 125p. 1988. pap. text ed. 15.95 (*0-87084-855-0*) Anderson Pub Co.

Dynamics of Polyandry: Kinship, Domesticity, & Population on the Tibetan Border. Nancy E. Levine. (Illus.). 344p. 1988. lib. bdg. 47.50 (*0-226-47568-9*); pap. text ed. 17.95 (*0-226-47569-7*) U Ch Pr.

Dynamics of Polyatomic Van Der Waals Complexes. Ed. by N. Halberstadt & K. C. Janda. (NATO ASI Series B, Physics: Vol. 227). (Illus.). 536p. 1990. 125.00 (*0-306-43612-4*, Plenum Pr) Plenum.

Dynamics of Polymer Liquids, 2 vols., Set. 2nd ed. R. Byron Bird et al. LC 86-13230. 1987. 190.00 (*0-471-51844-1*) Wiley.

Dynamics of Polymer Liquids, 2 vols., Vol. 1: Fluid Mechanics. 2nd ed. R. Byron Bird et al. LC 86-13230. 649p. 1987. text ed. 127.00 (*0-471-80245-X*) Wiley.

Dynamics of Polymer Liquids, 2 vols., Vol. 2. 2nd ed. R. Byron Bird et al. LC 86-13230. 437p. 1987. text ed. 124.00 (*0-471-80244-1*) Wiley.

Dynamics of Polymeric Liquids, 2 vols. Incl. Vol. 1. Fluid Mechanics. R. Byron Bird et al. LC 76-15408. 576p. 74.50 (*0-471-07375-X*); Vol. 2. Kinetic Theory. R. Byron Bird et al. LC 76-15408. 304p. 1977. 74.95 (*0-471-01596-2*); LC 76-15408. 1977. write for info. (*0-318-56424-6*) Wiley.

Dynamics of Power: Fighting Shame & Building Self-Esteem. rev. ed. Gershen Kaufman & Lev Raphael. 147p. 1991. pap. 10.95 (*0-87047-051-5*) Schenkman Bks Inc.

Dynamics of Power: Fighting Shame & Building Self-Esteem. 2nd rev. ed. Gershen Kaufman & Lev Raphael. 147p. 1991. 19.95 (*0-87047-050-7*) Schenkman Bks Inc.

Dynamics of Presentation Graphics. 2nd ed. Dona Z. Meilach. 326p. 1990. pap. 30.00 (*1-55623-229-2*) Irwin Prof Pubng.

Dynamics of Progress: Time, Method, & Measure. Samuel L. Macey. LC 89-31886. (Illus.). 272p. 1989. 35.00 (*0-8203-1159-6*) U of Ga Pr.

Dynamics of Proteins & Nucleic Acids. J. A. McCammon & S. C. Harvey. (Illus.). 220p. 1988. pap. 32.95 (*0-521-35652-0*) Cambridge U Pr.

Dynamics of Quiescent Prominences: Proceedings of IAU Colloquium No. 117 Held in Hvar, SR Croatia, Yugoslavia, 25-29 September 1989. Ed. by V. Ruzdjak et al. (Lecture Notes in Physics Ser.: Vol. 363). xii, 304p. 1990. 42.00 (*0-387-52973-X*) Spr-Verlag.

Dynamics of Race & Gender: Some Feminist Interventions. Ed. by Haleh Afshar & Mary Maynard. LC 93-45986. 224p. 1994. 75.00 (*0-7484-0211-X*, Pub. by Tay Francis Ltd UK); pap. 27.00 (*0-7484-0212-8*, Pub. by Tay Francis Ltd UK) Taylor & Francis.

Dynamics of Racism in Social Work Practice. Ed. by James A. Goodman. LC 73-88446. 389p. reprint ed. pap. 110.90 (*0-317-55738-6*, 2029272) Bks Demand.

Dynamics of Railway Bridges. Ladislav Fryba. 300p. 1993. 69.00 (*0-13-221656-6*) P-H.

Dynamics of Railway Vehicle Systems. Vijay K. Garg et al. LC 83-21475. (Monograph). 1984. text ed. 143.00 (*0-12-275950-8*) Acad Pr.

Dynamics of Rational Deliberation. Brian Skyrms. (Illus.). 216p. 1990. 39.95x (*0-674-21885-X*) HUP.

Dynamics of Reactive Systems, Pts. I & II. Ed. by J. R. Bowen et al. LC 86-22171. (PAAS Ser.: Vol. 105). (Illus.). 900p. 1986. 135.00 (*0-930403-14-2*) AIAA.

Dynamics of Reactive Systems, Pt. 1: Flames. Ed. by A. L. Kuhl et al. (PAAS Ser.: Vol. 114). 540p. 1988. 92.95 (*0-930403-47-9*) AIAA.

Dynamics of Regional Politics: Four Systems on the Indian Ocean Rim. W. Howard Wriggins, III et al. LC 92-9119. 350p. 1992. text ed. 40.00 (*0-231-07860-9*) Col U Pr.

Dynamics of Relationships. Ed. by Steve Duck. LC 93-48820. (Understanding Relationship Processes Ser.: Vol. 4). 1994. 36.00 (*0-8039-5413-1*); pap. 16.95 (*0-8039-5414-X*) Sage.

Dynamics of Relationships. rev. ed. Patricia Kramer. (Illus.). 430p. (YA). (gr. 8-12). 1990. teacher ed, pap. text ed. 34.95 (*0-317-90984-3*) Equal Partners.

Dynamics of Relationships. rev. ed. Patricia Kramer & Linda Frazer. (Illus.). 125p. (J). (gr. 4-7). 1990. student ed, pap. text ed. 13.95 (*0-317-90982-7*) Equal Partners.

Dynamics of Relationships: A Guide for Developing Self-Esteem & Social Skills for Preteens & Young Children. rev. ed. Patricia Kramer & Linda Frazer. (Illus.). (YA). (gr. 9 up). 1990. teacher ed, pap. text ed. 17.95 (*0-929577-03-5*) Equal Partners.

Dynamics of Relationships: A Guide to Developing Self-Esteem & Social Skills for Teens & Young Adults, Bk. 1. rev. ed. Patricia Kramer. (Illus.). 331p. (YA). (gr. 8-12). 1990. student ed, pap. text ed. 16.95 (*0-317-90983-5*) Equal Partners.

Dynamics of Relationships: A Guide to Developing Self-Esteem & Social Skills for Teens & Young Adults, Bk. 2. rev. ed. Patricia Kramer. (Illus.). 49p. (YA). (gr. 8-12). 1990. student ed, pap. text ed. 8.95 (*0-317-90981-9*) Equal Partners.

Dynamics of Religious Conversion: Identity & Transformation. V. Bailey Gillespie. 261p. (Orig.). 1991. pap. 16.95 (*0-89135-084-5*) Religious Educ.

Dynamics of Rental Housing in New York City. Michael A. Stegman. LC 82-4248. 271p. 1982. pap. 1.00x (*0-88285-088-1*) Ctr Urban Pol Res.

Dynamics of Reservation Policy. Ed. by Haroobhai Mehta & H. Patel. 315p. 1986. 31.00 (*0-8364-1818-2*, Pub. by Minerva II) S Asia.

Dynamics of Role-Playing in Jacobean Tragedy. Joan L. Hall. LC 91-15057. 223p. 1992. text ed. 45.00 (*0-312-06610-4*) St Martin.

Dynamics of Rotating Machinery: Proceedings of the International Symposia on Transport Phenomena, Pt. 2. Ed. by Jong H. Kim & Wen-Jei Yang. 1989. 172.00 (*1-56032-014-1*) Hemisp Pub.

Dynamics of Rotating Machinery: Proceedings of the Third International Symposium, Vol. 2. Ed. by Jong H. Kim & W. J. Yang. (Proceedings of the International Symposium on Transport Phenomena, Dynamics & Design of Rotating Machinery Ser.). 350p. 1991. 110.00 (*0-685-47888-2*) Hemisp Pub.

Dynamics of Rotor Bearing Systems. M. J. Goodwin. 320p. 1989. text ed. 65.00 (*0-04-621032-6*) Routledge Chapman & Hall.

Dynamics of Rotors: Proceedings of the International Union of Theoretical & Applied Mechanics, Lyngby, Denmark, Aug. 1974. Symposium of International Union of Theoretical & Applied Mechanics, Lyngby, Denmark, Aug. 1974. Ed. by F. I. Niordson. (Illus.). xii, 564p. 1975. 64.00 (*0-387-07384-1*) Spr-Verlag.

Dynamics of Rotors: Selected Papers. Indian Society of Theoretical & Applied Mechanics, 20th Congress, India, 1975. Ed. by J. S. Rao. 1977. pap. 29.00 (*0-08-022124-6*, Pergamon Pr) Elsevier.

Dynamics of Rotors & Foundations. E. Kramer. LC 93-18580. 1993. Alk. paper. 98.00 (*0-387-55725-3*) Spr-Verlag.

Dynamics of Russian Politics: A Short History. Barbara B. Green. LC 93-28042. 248p. 1994. pap. text ed. 18.95 (*0-275-94828-5*, Praeger Pubs) Greenwood.

Dynamics of Russian Politics: A Short History. Barbara B. Green. LC 93-28042. (Contributions in Political Science Ser.: No. 337). 248p. 1994. text ed. 59.95 (*0-313-28886-0*, Greenwood Pr) Greenwood.

Dynamics of Salvation: A Study in Gregory of Nazianzus. Donald F. Winslow. LC 79-89897. (Patristic Monograph: No. 7). 1979. pap. 8.50 (*0-915646-06-4*) N Amer Patristic Soc.

Dynamics of Santal Traditions in a Peasant Society. George E. Somers. 1985. 14.50 (*0-8364-1516-7*, Pub. by Abhinav II) S Asia.

Dynamics of Saturated Electric Machines. V. Ostovic. (Illus.). xiii, 445p. 1989. 73.00 (*0-387-97079-7*, 3103) Spr-Verlag.

Dynamics of School Integration: Problems & Approaches in a Northern City. Donald H. Bouma. LC 68-20582. 158p. reprint ed. pap. 45.10 (*0-317-07888-7*, 2012959) Bks Demand.

Dynamics of Science & Technology. Ed. by E. T. Layton et al. (Sociology of the Sciences Yearbook Ser.: No. 2). 1978. lib. bdg. 80.00 (*90-277-0880-0*); pap. text ed. 44.50 (*90-277-0881-9*) Kluwer Ac.

Dynamics of Science-Based Innovation. Ed. by H. Grupp. (Illus.). xii, 371p. 1992. 109.00 (*0-387-55062-3*) Spr-Verlag.

Dynamics of Secondary Programs Assisted under the Carl D. Perkins Act. James M. Weber & Nancy F. Puleo. 1988. 4.75 (*0-318-40012-X*, RD 269) Ctr Educ Trng Employ.

Dynamics of Self-Determination in Palestine: Protection of Peoples as a Human Right. Paul J. de Waart. LC 94-16581. (Social, Economic, & Political Studies of the Middle East: Vol. 49). 1994. 80.00 (*90-04-09825-9*) E J Brill.

Dynamics of Sensory & Cognitive Processing by the Brain. Ed. by E Baser. (Brain Dynamics Ser.). (Illus.). 420p. 1988. 99.00 (*0-387-16994-6*) Spr-Verlag.

***Dynamics of Service: Reflections on the Changing Nature of Customer-Provider Interactions.** Barbara A. Gutek. LC 95-12631. (Management, Health, Social & Behavioral Studies). 1995. 29.95 (*0-7879-0101-6*) Jossey-Bass.

Dynamics of Sex & Gender: A Sociological Perspective. 3rd ed. Laurel Richardson. 294p. (C). 1989. pap. text ed. 27.50 (*0-06-045407-5*) HarpCollege.

Dynamics of Shock Waves, Explosions, & Detonations. Ed. by J. R. Bowen et al. LC 84-21564. (PAAS Ser.: Vol. 94). (Illus.). 595p. 1984. 86.95 (*0-915928-91-4*) AIAA.

Dynamics of Snow & Ice Masses. Samuel C. Colbeck. LC 79-17949. 1980. text ed. 118.00 (*0-12-179450-4*) Acad Pr.

Dynamics of Social Change. Ed. by Howard Selsam et al. LC 77-120820. 416p. (C). 1970. pap. 4.95 (*0-7178-0264-7*) Intl Pubs Co.

Dynamics of Social Change in Bengal. Dilip K. Chattopadhyay. (C). 1990. text ed. 62.50 (*81-85094-32-2*, Pub. by Punthi Pus II) S Asia.

Dynamics of Social Systems. Paul Colomy. (International Sociology Ser.: Vol. 42). (Illus.). 272p. (C). 1992. 69.95 (*0-8039-8759-5*); pap. 25.95 (*0-8039-8760-9*) Sage.

***Dynamics of Software Development.** Jim McCarthy. 1995. 24.95 (*1-55615-823-8*) Microsoft.

Dynamics of Soil Organic Matter in Tropical Ecosystems. Ed. by David C. Coleman et al. 352p. 1989. text ed. 30.00 (*0-8248-1251-4*) UH Pr.

***Dynamics of Solutions & Fluid Mixtures by NMR.** Ed. by J. J. Delpuech. LC 94-24759. 1995. text ed. 79.95 (*0-471-95411-X*) Wiley.

Dynamics of Southwest Prehistory. Ed. by Linda S. Cordell & George J. Gumerman. LC 89-5954. (Archaeological Inquiry Ser.). (Illus.). 389p. (C). 1989. 42.00 (*0-87474-334-6*) Smithsonian.

Dynamics of Southwest Prehistory. Ed. by Linda S. Cordell & George J. Gumerman. LC 89-5954. (Archaeological Inquiry Ser.). (Illus.). 389p. (C). 1993. reprint ed. pap. text ed. 19.95 (*1-56098-307-8*) Smithsonian.

Dynamics of Soviet Defense Policy. Ed. by Bruce Parrott. 400p. 1990. text ed. 25.25 (*0-943875-25-0*, Johns Hopkins) W Wilson Ctr Pr.

Dynamics of Soviet Foreign Policy. Jonathan R. Adelman & Deborah A. Palmieri. 384p. (C). 1990. pap. text ed. 22.00 (*0-06-040167-2*) HarpCollege.

***Dynamics of Soviet Foreign Policy.** fac. ed. Jonathan R. Adelman & Deborah A. Palmieri. LC 88-24690. (Illus.). 367p. 1989. reprint ed. pap. 104.60 (*0-7837-8110-5*, 2047913) Bks Demand.

Dynamics of Soviet Policy in Sub-Saharan Africa. Michael Radu & Arthur J. Klinghoffer. LC 89-34604. x, 160p. 1991. 22.50 (*0-8419-1226-2*) Holmes & Meier.

Dynamics of Soviet Policy in the Middle East: Between Old Thinking & New. Mark A. Heller. LC 92-27567. (JCSS Study Ser.: No. 18). 130p. (C). 1992. pap. text ed. 32.50 (*0-8133-1415-1*) Westview.

Dynamics of Soviet Politics. Paul Cocks et al. (Russian Research Center Studies: Vol. No. 76). 351p. 1976. 37.50 (*0-674-21881-7*) HUP.

Dynamics of Space: Mallarme's Un Coup De Des Jamais N' abolira le Hasard. Virginia A. La Charite. LC 86-82794. (French Forum Monographs: No. 67). 192p. (Orig.). 1987. pap. 13.95 (*0-917058-68-2*) French Forum.

Dynamics of Space Tether Systems. Vladimir V. Beletsky & Evgenii M. Levin. LC 57-54769. (Advances in the Astronautical Sciences Ser.: Vol. 83). (Illus.). 508p. 1993. lib. bdg. 120.00 (*0-87703-370-6*, Pub. by Am Astro Soc); pap. text ed. 90.00 (*0-87703-371-4*, Pub. by Am Astro Soc) Univelt Inc.

Dynamics of Spectroscopic Transitions: Illustrated by Magnetic Resonance & Laser Effects. James D. Macomber. LC 75-25852. (Wiley-Interscience Monographs in Chemical Physics). (Illus.). 358p. reprint ed. pap. 102.10 (*0-317-09275-8*, 2013078) Bks Demand.

Dynamics of Spiritual Deception. Dan Juster. 144p. (Orig.). 1993. pap. 5.99 (*1-56043-120-2*) Destiny Image.

Dynamics of Spiritual Gifts. William J. McRae. 144p. 1983. reprint ed. pap. 8.99 (*0-310-29091-0*, 9976P) Zondervan.

Dynamics of Spiritual Life. Richard F. Lovelace. LC 78-24757. 1979. pap. 19.99 (*0-87784-626-X*, 626) InterVarsity.

***Dynamics of Sports: Why That's the Way the Ball Bounces.** 4th ed. David F. Griffing. (Illus.). 242p. 1995. pap. text ed. 21.25 (*0-9618365-2-0*) Dalog Co.

Dynamics of Star Clusters. Ed. by Jeremy Goodman & Piet Hut. 1985. lib. bdg. 154.00 (*90-277-1963-2*); pap. text ed. 69.00 (*90-277-1965-9*) Kluwer Ac.

Dynamics of State Politics: Kerala. N. Jose Chander. 1987. text ed. 27.50 (*81-207-0604-8*, Pub. by Sterling Pubs II) Apt Bks.

Dynamics of Stellar Systems: Proceedings of the I.A.U. Symposium, No. 69, Besancon, France, September 9-13 1974. International Astronomical Union Staff. LC 75-12976. 470p. 1975. lib. bdg. 158.00 (*90-277-0589-5*); pap. text ed. 117.00 (*90-277-0590-9*) Kluwer Ac.

Dynamics of Strength Training. Gary T. Moran & George McGlynn. 176p. (C). 1990. pap. write for info. (*0-697-07638-5*) Brown & Benchmark.

Dynamics of Stress: Physiological, Psychological & Social Perspectives. Ed. by Mortimer H. Appley & Richard A. Trumbull. LC 86-25175. (Stress & Coping Ser.). 360p. 1986. 52.50 (*0-306-42252-2*, Plenum Pr) Plenum.

Dynamics of Structured Solids. American Society of Mechanical Engineers Staff. Ed. by George Hermann. LC 68-58743. 114p. reprint ed. pap. 32.50 (*0-317-08722-3*, 2016807) Bks Demand.

Dynamics of Structures. J. L. Humar. 672p. 1989. text ed. 76.00 (*0-13-222068-7*) P-H.

Dynamics of Structures. Walter C. Hurty & Moshe F. Rubinstein. (Illus.). 1964. 41.95 (*0-685-03847-5*) P-H.

Dynamics of Structures. Ed. by Jose M. Roesset. 892p. 1987. 77.00 (*0-87262-615-6*) Am Soc Civil Eng.

Dynamics of Structures. 2nd ed. Ray W. Clough & Joseph Penzien. LC 92-44039. 1993. text ed. write for info. (*0-07-011394-7*) McGraw.

Dynamics of Structures: Proceedings of the 2nd World Conference, Stuttgart, Germany, 27-31 Aug., 1990. Ed. by J. H. Argyris & H. P. Mlejnek. (Texts on Computational Mechanics Ser.: Vol. 5). 606p. 1991. 160.00 (*0-444-89045-9*, North Holland); pap. 60.00 (*0-444-89112-9*, North Holland) Elsevier.

***Dynamics of Structures: Theory & Applications to Earthquake Engineering.** Anil K. Chopra. LC 94-46527. 1995. write for info. (*0-615-00521-7*) P-H.

Dynamics of Subversion & Violence in Contemporary Italy. Vittorfranco S. Pisano. 224p. (C). 1987. pap. text ed. 14.95 (*0-8179-8552-2*) Hoover Inst Pr.

Dynamics of Success. Torkom Saraydarian. LC 91-91402. 136p. 1992. pap. 8.95 (*0-929874-26-9*) TSG Pub Found.

Dynamics of Successful International Business Negotiations. Robert T. Moran & William G. Stripp. 256p. 1991. 27.50 (*0-87201-196-8*) Gulf Pub.

Dynamics of Symbols: Fundamentals of Jungian Psychotherapy. Verena Kast. Tr. by Susan A. Schwarz. (Psychology Ser.). (Illus.). 240p. 1992. 24.95 (*0-88064-200-9*); pap. 14.95 (*0-88064-201-7*) Fromm Intl Pub.

Dynamics of Synergetics Systems: Proceedings. Ed. by H. Haken. (Synergetics Ser.: Vol. 6). (Illus.). 271p. 1980. 60.00 (*0-387-09918-2*) Spr-Verlag.

Dynamics of Systems of Rigid Bodies. V. Wittenburg. 1977. 88.00 (*3-519-02337-7*) Adlers Foreign Bks.

Dynamics of Taking Charge. John J. Gabarro. 1987. text ed. 22.95 (*0-07-103236-3*) McGraw.

Dynamics of Tamil Nadu Politics in Sri Lankan Ethnicity. G. Palanithurai. 1993. 14.00 (*81-7211-040-5*, National Bk Ctr) S Asia.

Dynamics of Teaching Secondary School Mathematics. Thomas J. Cooney et al. 448p. (C). 1983. text ed. 32.95x (*0-88133-061-2*) Waveland Pr.

Dynamics of Technological Change. Louis A. Girifalco. LC 90-45717. (Illus.). 576p. 1991. text ed. 72.95 (*0-442-00563-6*) Chapman & Hall.

***Dynamics of Technology, Trade & Growth.** Ed. by Jan Fagerberg et al. LC 94-22218. 1995. 67.95 (*1-85278-922-0*, Pub. by E Elgar Pub UK) Ashgate Pub Co.

Dynamics of the Absurd in the Existentialist Novel. Richard E. Baker. LC 92-38883. (American University Studies: General Literature: Ser. XIX, Vol. 31). 150p. (C). 1994. text ed. 34.95 (*0-8204-2079-4*) P Lang Pubs.

Dynamics of the African-Afro-American Connection: From Dependency to Self-Reliance. Ed. by Adelaide Cromwell. 160p. 1987. 21.95 (*0-88258-172-4*) Howard U Pr.

Dynamics of the Breakthrough in Eastern Europe: The Polish Experience. Jadwiga Staniszkis. Tr. by Chester A. Kisiel. LC 90-23848. 250p. 1991. 35.00 (*0-520-07218-9*) U CA Pr.

Dynamics of the Computer Industry: Modeling the Supply of Workstations & Their Components. Walid R. Touma. LC 93-9419. 240p. (C). 1993. lib. bdg. 69.95 (*0-7923-9331-7*) Kluwer Ac.

Dynamics of the Cuban Revolution: The Trotskyist View. Joseph Hansen. LC 78-59357. 1978. lib. bdg. 55.00 (*0-87348-558-0*); pap. 19.95 (*0-87348-559-9*) Pathfinder NY.

Dynamics of the Earth's Evolution. Ed. by L. Czechowski et al. LC 92-21413. (Physics & Evolution of the Earth's Interior Ser.: Vol. 6). 1993. 218.75 (*0-444-98662-6*) Elsevier.

Dynamics of the Empowered School: Getting to the Core. Joseph W. Hoff. Ed. by John H. Lounsbury. (Illus.). 232p. 1993. pap. 23.95 (*0-9636285-0-X*) E-Factor.

Dynamics of the English Phonological Systems. V. Y. Plotkin. (Janua Linguarum, Ser. Practica: No. 155). 98p. 1972. pap. text ed. 20.00 (*90-279-2324-8*) Mouton.

Dynamics of the Excited State. Ed. by K. P. Lawley. (Advances in Chemical Physics Ser.: No. 50). (Illus.). 675p. reprint ed. pap. 180.00 (*0-8357-3078-6*, 2039335) Bks Demand.

Dynamics of the Film. Joseph Feldman & Harry Feldman. LC 73-169342. (Arno Press Cinema Program Ser.). (Illus.). 1977. reprint ed. 20.95 (*0-405-03917-4*) Ayer.

Dynamics of the Firm: Strategies of Pricing & Organisation. Ed. by John Groenewegen. 1994. 59.95 (*1-85278-934-4*, Pub. by E Elgar Pub UK) Ashgate Pub Co.

Dynamics of the Iranian Revolution: The Pahlavis' Triumph & Tragedy. Jahangir Amuzegar. LC 90-44904. 367p. (C). 1991. 74.50 (*0-7914-0731-4*); pap. 24.95 (*0-7914-0732-2*) State U NY Pr.

Dynamics of the Javelin Throw. Robert F. Sing. (Illus.). 168p. (Orig.). 1984. pap. 14.95 (*0-914715-03-8*) Spectracolor-Reynolds.

***Dynamics of the Liquid State.** Umberto Balucani & Marco Zoppi. (Illus.). 384p. 1995. text ed. 95.00 (*0-19-851739-4*) OUP.

Dynamics of the Lower Self. John-Roger. LC 77-70406. 1976. pap. 5.00 (*0-914829-10-6*) Mandeville LA.

Dynamics of the Magnetosphere. Ed. by Syun-Ichi Akasofu. (Astrophysics & Space Science Library: No. 78). 1979. lib. bdg. 140.00 (*90-277-1052-X*) Kluwer Ac.

Dynamics of the Marxian System see Economics & Marxism

Dynamics of the Metaphoric Field: A Cognitive View of Literature. Nicolae Babuts. LC 90-50931. 184p. 1992. 35.00 (*0-87413-424-2*) U Delaware Pr.

Dynamics of the Middle Atmosphere. T. Matsuno. Ed. by James S. Holton. LC 84-8291. 550p. 1984. lib. bdg. 182.00 (*90-277-1758-3*) Kluwer Ac.

Dynamics of the Party System: Alignment & Realignment of Political Parties in the United States. rev. ed. James L. Sundquist. LC 83-6354. 466p. 1983. 39.95 (*0-8157-8226-8*); pap. 18.95 (*0-8157-8225-X*) Brookings.

***Dynamics of the Protection of Human Rights in Europe: Essays in Honour of Henry G. Schermers, Vol. III.** Ed. by Rick Lawson. 440p. (C). 1994. lib. bdg. 169.50 (*0-7923-3161-3*, Pub. by M Nijhoff) Kluwer Ac.

Dynamics of the Self. Gerhard Adler. 1991. 27.50 (*0-904575-45-4*, Coventure Ltd); pap. 13.95 (*0-904576-92-2*, Coventure Ltd) Sigo Pr.

Dynamics of the Singing Voice. 2nd rev. ed. M. Bunch. (Illus.). 208p. 1993. pap. 39.00 (*0-387-82394-8*) Spr-Verlag.

***Dynamics of the Singing Voice.** 3rd ed. Meribeth Bunch. LC 94-35638. 196p. 1995. pap. 39.00 (*0-387-82623-8*) Spr-Verlag.

Dynamics of the Social, Vol. 2: Selected Essays. Isabel M. Lyth. 279p. 1989. 60.00 (*1-85343-051-X*); pap. 19.50 (*1-85343-052-8*) Col U Pr.

An Asterisk (*) at the beginning of an entry indicates that the title is appearing in BIP for the first time.

Dyslexia: A Global Issue. Ed. by Rattihalli N. Malatesha & Harry A. Whitaker. (NATO Advanced Study Institutes Series D: Behavioural & Social Sciences). 1983. lib. bdg. 202.00 (*90-247-2909-2*) Kluwer Ac.

Dyslexia: A Hundred Years On. T. R. Miles & Elaine Miles. 176p. 1990. 80.00 (*0-335-09541-0*, Open Univ Pr); pap. 25.00 (*0-335-09540-2*, Open Univ Pr) Taylor & Francis.

Dyslexia: A Neuroscientific Approach. Frank H. Duffy & Norman Geschwind. 223p. 1985. 57.00 (*0-316-19454-9*, Little Med Div) Little.

Dyslexia: An Annotated Bibliography. Ed. by Martha M. Evans. LC 81-20319. (Contemporary Problems of Childhood Ser.: No. 5.). (Illus.). xxvi, 644p. 1982. text ed. 79.50 (*0-313-21344-5*, EVD/, Greenwood Pr) Greenwood.

Dyslexia: How Do We Learn? John O'Shea et al. 108p. (Orig.). 1994. pap. 10.95 (*0-85572-236-3*, Pub. by Hill Content Pubng AT) Seven Hills Bk.

Dyslexia: How Would I Cope? 2nd ed. Michael Ryden. 64p. 1992. pap. 13.95 (*1-85302-154-7*, Pub. by J Kingsley Pubs UK) Taylor & Francis.

*****Dyslexia: Integrating Theory & Practice.** Ed. by Margaret Snowling & Michael Thomson. 325p. 1993. 34.95 (*0-614-00861-1*, 0214) Singular Publishing.

Dyslexia: Its Neuropsychology & Treatment. Ed. by George T. Pavlidis & Dennis F. Fisher. LC 85-16780. 316p. 1986. text ed. 82.95 (*0-471-90875-4*) Wiley.

Dyslexia: Neuronal, Cognitive & Linguistic Aspects - Proceedings. Wenner-Gren Center, International Symposium Staff. Ed. by Y. Zotterman. (Wenner-Gren Center International Symposium Ser.: Vol. 35). (Illus.). 180p. 1982. 80.00 (*0-08-026863-3*, Pub. by Pergamon Repr UK) Franklin.

Dyslexia: Neuropsychological Theory, Research, & Clinical Differentiation. George Hynd & Morris Cohen. 1983. text ed. 50.95 (*0-205-10117-8*) Allyn.

*****Dyslexia: Research & Resource Guide.** Carol S. Spafford & George S. Grosser. LC 95-13738. 1995. write for info. (*0-205-15907-9*) Allyn.

Dyslexia: Subject, Reference & Research Guidebook. Leo I. Powills. LC 87-47651. 160p. 1987. 39.50 (*0-88164-602-4*); pap. 34.50 (*0-88164-603-2*) ABBE Pubs Assn.

*****Dyslexia: The Pattern of Difficulties.** 2nd ed. T. R. Miles. 315p. 1993. text ed. 34.95 (*0-614-00860-3*, 0548) Singular Publishing.

Dyslexia: The Pattern of Difficulties. 2nd ed. T. R. Miles. 315p. 1993. pap. 34.95 (*1-56593-249-8*, 0548) Singular Publishing.

Dyslexia: Theory & Practice of Remedial Instruction. Diana B. Clark. LC 88-51242. 240p. 1988. text ed. 36.50 (*0-912752-17-3*) York Pr.

Dyslexia: Understanding Reading Problems. John F. Savage. LC 85-8925. (Illus.). 96p. (J). (gr. 4-9). 1985. lib. bdg. 10.98 (*0-671-54289-3*, Julian Messner) Silver Burdett Pr.

Dyslexia & Development: Neurobiological Aspects of Extra-Ordinary Brains. Ed. by Albert M. Galaburda. LC 92-49952. (Illus.). 400p. 1993. 47.50 (*0-674-21940-6*) HUP.

Dyslexia & Hyperlexia. P. G. Aaron. (C). 1989. lib. bdg. 102.00 (*1-55608-079-4*) Kluwer Ac.

*****Dyslexia & Hyperlexia: Diagnosis & Management of Developmental Reading Disabilities.** P. G. Aaron. (Neuropsychology & Cognition Ser.). 319p. (C). 1994. pap. text ed. 54.00 (*0-7923-3155-9*) Kluwer Ac.

Dyslexia & Mathematics. Ed. by T. R. Miles & E. Miles. 128p. 1991. 59.95 (*0-415-06480-5*, A6178); pap. 13.95 (*0-415-04987-3*, A5962) Routledge.

Dyslexia & Other Learning Difficulties: The Facts. Mark Selikowitz. LC 92-29862. (Facts Ser.). (Illus.). 144p. 1993. 19.95 (*0-19-262299-4*) OUP.

Dyslexia & Other Learning Difficulties: The Facts. Mark Selikowitz. LC 92-29862. (Facts Ser.). (Illus.). 144p. 1995. reprint ed. pap. 15.95 (*0-19-262300-1*) OUP.

Dyslexia & Reading Disabilities. Richmond Paine et al. 224p. 1972. text ed. 29.50 (*0-8422-7005-1*) Irvington.

*****Dyslexia & Stress.** Ed. by T. R. Miles & V. Varma. 200p. 1995. pap. 49.95 (*1-56593-593-4*, 1214) Singular Publishing.

Dyslexia at College. Tim R. Miles. 160p. 1987. 12.95 (*0-416-39670-4*) Routledge Chapman & Hall.

*****Dyslexia at College.** 2nd ed. Dorothy E. Gilroy & Thomas R. Miles. LC 95-9181. 1996. write for info. (*0-415-12778-5*) Routledge.

*****Dyslexia in Children.** Angela Fawcett. 1995. pap. 39.00 (*0-13-342858-3*) P-H.

Dyslexia Matters. Gerald Hales. (Illus.). 236p. (Orig.). (C). 1994. pap. text ed. 39.99 (*1-56593-367-2*, 0740) Singular Publishing.

Dyslexia Reconsidered: A Cognitive-Developmental Perspective. Margaret Snowling. 250p. (Orig.). 1987. pap. text ed. 21.95 (*0-631-14433-1*) Blackwell Pubs.

Dyslexia Research & Its Applications to Education. George T. Pavlidis & Timothy R. Miles. LC 80-49975. 307p. 1981. text ed. 114.95 (*0-471-27841-6*, Wiley-Interscience) Wiley.

*****Dyslexia Teaching Handbook.** Thomson. 1990. 62.25 (*1-56593-549-7*, 0070) Singular Publishing.

*****Dyslexic Scholar: Helping Your Child Achieve Academic Success.** Kathleen Nosek. LC 94-45423. 1995. 11.95 (*0-87833-882-9*) Taylor Pub.

Dyslexic Spel-Wel Dictionary: A Phonetic-English Translation for Learning Disabilities. Suzanne H. Green. LC 90-35942. 340p. 1990. pap. text ed. 9.95 (*0-9622259-0-8*) GIES.

Dyslipoproteinaemias & Diabetes. Ed. by R. W. James & D. Pometta. (Monographs on Atherosclerosis: Vol. 13). (Illus.). viii, 180p. 1985. 119.25 (*3-8055-4139-2*) S Karger.

Dysmorphic Child: An Orthopedic Perspective. Michael J. Goldberg. (Illus.). 444p. 1987. text ed. 101.00 (*0-88167-238-6*) Raven.

Dysphagia: Diagnosis & Management. 2nd ed. Ed. by Michael E. Groher & James A. Haley. (Illus.). 368p. 1992. 49.95 (*0-7506-9078-X*) Buttrwrth-Heinemann.

Dysphagia: Diagnosis & Treatment. David Gelfand & Joel Richter. (Illus.). 400p. 1989. 95.00 (*0-89640-158-8*) Igaku-Shoin.

*****Dysphagia & the Child with Developmental Disabilities: Medical, Clinical & Family Interventions.** Ed. by Susan R. Rosenthal et al. (Illus.). 432p. (Orig.). (C). 1994. pap. text ed. 65.00 (*1-56593-089-4*, 0394) Singular Publishing.

Dysphagia Care: Team Approach. Nadine O'Sullivan. (Team Approach with Acute & Long Term Patients). (Illus.). 112p. (Orig.). (C). 1990. pap. 29.95 (*0-9633234-0-7*) Cottage Sq Pr.

*****Dysphagia Care Team Approach with Acute & Long Term Patients.** 2nd ed. Nadine O'Sullivan. Ed. by Arthur C. Turner. (Illus.). 212p. (C). 1995. pap. 20.97 (*0-9633234-1-5*) Cottage Sq Pr.

Dysplasia & Cancer in Colitis: Proceedings of the Symposium Held June 1-4, 1989, Baltimore, MD. Ed. by R. H. Riddell. 296p. 1991. 155.00 (*0-444-01570-1*) P-H.

Dyspnea. Ed. by Donald A. Mahler. (Illus.). 288p. 1990. 40.00 (*0-87993-361-5*) Futura Pub.

Dysrhythmia Recognition & Management. 2nd ed. Karen Fenstermacher. LC 93-9835. (Illus.). 176p. 1993. pap. text ed. 23.00 (*0-7216-3790-6*) Saunders.

Dysthymic Disorder. Ed. by S. W. Burton & H. S. Akiskal. 144p. 1990. pap. text ed. 21.00 (*0-88048-600-7*, 8600, Pub. by Royal Coll Psych UK) Am Psychiatric.

Dystopian Impulse in Modern Literature: Fiction as Social Criticism. M. Keith Booker. LC 93-40174. (Contributions to the Study of Science Fiction & Fantasy Ser.: Vol. 58). 208p. 1994. text ed. 49.95 (*0-313-29092-X*, Greenwood Pr) Greenwood.

Dystopian Literature: A Theory & Research Guide. M. Keith Booker. LC 93-40173. 424p. 1994. text ed. 75.00 (*0-313-29115-2*, Greenwood Pr) Greenwood.

Dzien Jak Co Dzien (Day As Any Other) Halina Bonikowska. 72p. (Orig.). (POL.). 1989. pap. 7.00 (*0-930401-21-2*) Artex Pub.

Dziennik Pisany Na Wyspie. Halina Bonikowska. 76p. (Orig.). 1987. pap. write for info. (*0-318-61881-8*) Artex Pub.

Dziennik Pisany na Wyspie: Diary Written on an Island. Halina Bonikowska. LC 87-70340. 72p. (Orig.). (POL.). 1987. pap. 7.95 (*0-930401-08-5*) Artex Pub.

Dzog Chen & Zen. Namkhai Norbu. Ed. by Kennard Lipman. Tr. by Namkhai Norbu. (Illus.). 48p. (Orig.). 1987. pap. 5.00 (*0-931892-08-2*) B Dolphin Pub.

*****Dzog Chen Meditation.** Khamtul Rinpoche. Tr. by Gareth Sparham. (C). 1994. text ed. 14.00 (*81-7030-407-5*, Pub. by Sri Satguru Pubns II) S Asia.

Dzovn Arhamarhets Jri Mi Katile. Abraham Anpart. (One Thousand Ser.). 198p. (Orig.). 1993. pap. 10.00 (*0-9639662-4-3*) A M Karabajakyan.

Dzurlord. Adventure Architects Staff. 256p. 1987. pap. 3.50 (*0-8125-6410-3*) Tor Bks.

D1: D2 Dopamine Receptors: Neuroscience & Psychopharmacology. Ed. by John L. Waddington. (Neuroscience Perspectives Ser.). (Illus.). 304p. 1993. text ed. 69.95 (*0-12-729045-1*) Acad Pr.

D

An Asterisk (*) at the beginning of an entry indicates that the title is appearing in BIP for the first time.